M000287562

THE INTERNATIONAL INDUCTIVE STUDY BIBLE

IISB

NEW INTERNATIONAL VERSION

HARVEST HOUSE PUBLISHERS
EUGENE, OREGON

DEDICATED
to the church of the
living God…to those
whose passion is to be
*"the pillar and foundation
of the truth."*
1 TIMOTHY 3:15

Precept Ministries
P.O. Box 182218
Chattanooga, TN 37422

Inductive study material in *The International Inductive Study Bible* compiled by
K. Arthur and the staff of Precept Ministries.

Precept Ministries exists to serve the body of Jesus Christ by providing inductive Bible studies
for individuals, churches, home study groups, and mission organizations.

Cover, interior design, and typesetting by Koechel Peterson and Associates, Inc.
Tabernacle and Temple illustrations by Stanley C. Stein

The Holy Bible, New International Version®.
Copyright © 1973, 1978, 1984 by International Bible Society. Used by permission of Zondervan Publishing House. All rights reserved.

The "NIV" and "New International Version" are trademarks registered in the United States Patent and Trademark Office by International Bible Society. Use of either trademark requires the permission of the International Bible Society.

The NIV Concordance
Copyright© 1982 by the Zondervan Corporation.
Used by permission. All rights reserved.

THE INTERNATIONAL INDUCTIVE STUDY BIBLE
© 1995 Precept Ministries
Published by Harvest House Publishers
1075 Arrowsmith
Eugene, Oregon 97402

All rights reserved. No part of this publication may be reproduced, stored in a retrieval system, or transmitted, in any form or by any means, electronic, mechanical, photocopying, recording, or otherwise, without the prior written permission of the Publisher as to the study helps, book introductions, illustrations, maps, charts, and other study materials.

Library of Congress Cataloging-in-Publication Data
Bible. English. New International. 1995.
        The international inductive study bible : IISB, New International Version
                p. cm.
        ISBN 1-56507-298-7 (hardcover).
        ISBN 1-56507-350-9 (leather : alk. paper).
        ISBN 1-56507-349-5 (bonded)
        ISBN 1-56507-359-2 (hardcover indexed).
        ISBN 1-56507-360-6 (bonded indexed).
        ISBN 1-56507-361-4 (leather indexed)
        I. Title.
BS195.N37 1995   95-1098
220.5'208—dc20   CIP

1   2   3   4   5   6   7   8   9   /   01   00   99   98   97   96   95

Printed in the United States of America.

PREFACE

~~~~~~~

*T*HE NEW INTERNATIONAL VERSION is a completely new translation of the Holy Bible made by over a hundred scholars working directly from the best available Hebrew, Aramaic and Greek texts. It had its beginning in 1965 when, after several years of exploratory study by committees from the Christian Reformed Church and the National Association of Evangelicals, a group of scholars met at Palos Heights, Illinois, and concurred in the need for a new translation of the Bible in contemporary English. This group, though not made up of official church representatives, was transdenominational. Its conclusion was endorsed by a large number of leaders from many denominations who met in Chicago in 1966.

Responsibility for the new version was delegated by the Palos Heights group to a self-governing body of fifteen, the Committee on Bible Translation, composed for the most part of biblical scholars from colleges, universities and seminaries. In 1967 the New York Bible Society (now the International Bible Society) generously undertook the financial sponsorship of the project—a sponsorship that made it possible to enlist the help of many distinguished scholars. The fact that participants from the United States, Great Britain, Canada, Australia and New Zealand worked together gave the project its international scope. That they were from many denominations— including Anglican, Assemblies of God, Baptist, Brethren, Christian Reformed, Church of Christ, Evangelical Free, Lutheran, Mennonite, Methodist, Nazarene, Presbyterian, Wesleyan and other churches—helped to safeguard the translation from sectarian bias.

How it was made helps to give the New International Version its distinctiveness. The translation of each book was assigned to a team of scholars. Next, one of the Intermediate Editorial Committees revised the initial translation, with constant reference to the Hebrew, Aramaic or Greek. Their work then went to one of the General Editorial Committees, which checked it in detail and made another thorough revision. This revision in turn was carefully reviewed by the Committee on Bible Translation, which made further changes and then released the final version for publication. In this way the entire Bible underwent three revisions, during each of which the translation was examined for its faithfulness to the original languages and for its English style. All this involved many thousands of hours of research and discussion regarding the meaning of the texts and the precise way of putting them into English. It may well be that no other translation has been made by a more thorough process of review and revision from committee to committee than this one.

From the beginning of the project, the Committee on Bible Translation held to certain goals for the New International Version: that it would be an accurate translation and one that would have clarity and literary quality and so prove suitable for public and private reading, teaching, preaching, memorizing and liturgical use. The Committee also sought to preserve some measure of continuity with the long tradition of translating the Scriptures into English.

In working toward these goals, the translators were united in their commitment to the authority and infallibility of the Bible as God's Word in written form. They believe that it contains the divine answer to the deepest needs of humanity, that it sheds unique light on our path in a dark world, and that it sets forth the way to our eternal well-being.

The first concern of the translators has been the accuracy of the translation and its fidelity to the thought of the biblical writers. They have weighed the significance of the lexical and grammatical details of the Hebrew, Aramaic and Greek texts. At the same time, they have striven for more than a word-for-word translation. Because thought patterns and syntax differ from language to language, faithful communication of the meaning of the writers of the Bible demands frequent modifications in sentence structure and constant regard for the contextual meanings of words.

A sensitive feeling for style does not always accompany scholarship. Accordingly the Committee on Bible Translation submitted the developing version to a number of stylistic consultants. Two of them read every book of both Old and New Testaments twice—once before and once after the last major revision—and made invaluable suggestions. Samples of the translation were tested for clarity and ease of reading by various kinds of people—young and old, highly educated and less well educated, ministers and laymen.

Concern for clear and natural English—that the New International Version should be idiomatic but not idiosyncratic, contemporary but not dated— motivated the translators and consultants. At the same time, they tried to reflect the differing styles of the biblical writers. In view of the international use of English, the translators sought to avoid obvious Americanisms on the one hand and obvious Anglicisms on the other. A British edition reflects the comparatively few differences of significant idiom and of spelling.

As for the traditional pronouns "thou," "thee" and "thine" in reference to the Deity, the translators judged that to use these archaisms (along with the old verb forms such as "doest," "wouldest" and "hadst") would violate accuracy in translation. Neither Hebrew, Aramaic nor Greek uses special pronouns for the persons of the Godhead. A present-day translation is not enhanced by forms that in the time of the King James Version were used in everyday speech, whether referring to God or man.

For the Old Testament the standard Hebrew text, the Masoretic Text as published in the latest editions of *Biblia Hebraica*, was used throughout. The Dead Sea Scrolls contain material bearing on an earlier stage of the Hebrew text. They were consulted, as were the Samaritan Pentateuch and the ancient scribal traditions relating to textual changes. Sometimes a variant Hebrew reading in the margin of the Masoretic Text was followed instead of the text itself. Such instances, being variants within the Masoretic tradition, are not specified by footnotes. In rare cases, words in the consonantal text were divided differently from the way they appear in the Masoretic Text. Footnotes indicate this. The translators also consulted the more important early versions—the Septuagint; Aquila, Symmachus and Theodotion; the Vulgate; the Syriac Peshitta; the Targums; and for the Psalms the *Juxta Hebraica* of Jerome. Readings from these versions were occasionally followed where the Masoretic Text seemed doubtful and where accepted principles of textual criticism showed that one or more of these textual witnesses appeared to provide the correct reading. Such instances are footnoted. Sometimes vowel letters and vowel signs did not, in the judgment of the translators, represent the correct vowels for the original consonantal text. Accordingly some words were read with a different set of vowels. These instances are usually not indicated by footnotes.

The Greek text used in translating the New Testament was an eclectic one. No other piece of ancient literature has such an abundance of manuscript witnesses as does the New Testament. Where existing manuscripts differ, the translators made their choice of readings according to accepted principles of New Testament textual criticism. Footnotes call attention to places where there was uncertainty about what the original text was. The best current printed texts of the Greek New Testament were used.

There is a sense in which the work of translation is never wholly finished. This applies to all great literature and uniquely so to the Bible. In 1973 the New Testament in the New International Version was published. Since then, suggestions for corrections and revisions have been received from various sources. The Committee on Bible Translation carefully considered the suggestions and adopted a number of them. These were incorporated in the first printing of the entire Bible in 1978. Additional revisions were made by the Committee on Bible Translation in 1983 and appear in printings after that date.

As in other ancient documents, the precise meaning of the biblical texts is sometimes uncertain. This is more often the case with the Hebrew and Aramaic texts than with the Greek text. Although archaeological and linguistic discoveries in this century aid in understanding difficult passages, some uncertainties remain. The more significant of these have been called to the reader's attention in the footnotes.

In regard to the divine name *YHWH*, commonly referred to as the *Tetragrammaton*, the translators adopted the device used in most English versions of rendering that name as "LORD" in capital letters to distinguish it from *Adonai*, another Hebrew word rendered "Lord," for which small letters are used. Wherever the two names stand together in the Old Testament as a compound name of God, they are rendered "Sovereign LORD."

Because for most readers today the phrases "the LORD of hosts" and "God of hosts" have little meaning, this version renders them "the LORD Almighty" and "God Almighty." These renderings convey the sense of the Hebrew, namely, "he who is sovereign over all the 'hosts' (powers) in heaven and on earth, especially over the 'hosts' (armies) of Israel." For readers unacquainted with Hebrew this does not make clear the distinction between *Sabaoth* ("hosts" or "Almighty") and *Shaddai* (which can also be translated "Almighty"), but the latter occurs infrequently and is always footnoted. When *Adonai* and *YHWH Sabaoth* occur together, they are rendered "the Lord, the LORD Almighty."

As for other proper nouns, the familiar spellings of the King James Version are generally retained. Names traditionally spelled with "ch," except where it is final, are usually spelled in this translation with "k" or "c," since the biblical languages do not have the sound that "ch" frequently indicates in English—for example, in *chant*. For well-known names such as Zechariah, however, the traditional spelling has been retained. Variation in the spelling of names in the original languages has usually not been indicated. Where a person or place has two or more different names in the Hebrew, Aramaic or Greek texts, the more familiar one has generally been used, with footnotes where needed.

To achieve clarity the translators sometimes supplied words not in the original texts but required by the context. If there was uncertainty about such material, it is enclosed in brackets. Also for the sake of clarity or style, nouns, including some proper nouns, are sometimes substituted for pronouns, and vice versa. And though the Hebrew writers often shifted back and forth between first, second and third personal pronouns without change of antecedent, this translation often makes them uniform, in accordance with English style and without the use of footnotes.

Poetical passages are printed as poetry, that is, with indentation of lines and with separate stanzas. These are generally designed to reflect the structure of Hebrew poetry. This poetry is normally characterized by parallelism in balanced lines. Most of the poetry in the Bible is in the Old Testament, and scholars differ regarding the scansion of Hebrew lines. The translators determined the stanza divisions for the most part by analysis of the subject matter. The stanzas therefore serve as poetic paragraphs.

As an aid to the reader, italicized sectional headings are inserted in most of the books. They are not to be regarded as part of the NIV text, are not for oral reading, and are not intended to dictate the interpretation of the sections they head.

The footnotes in this version are of several kinds, most of which need no explanation. Those giving alternative translations begin with "Or" and generally introduce the alternative with the last word preceding it in the text, except when it is a single-word alternative; in poetry quoted in a footnote a slant mark indicates a line division. Footnotes introduced by "Or" do not have uniform significance. In some cases two possible translations were considered to have about equal validity. In other cases, though the translators were convinced that the translation in the text was correct, they judged that another interpretation was possible and of sufficient importance to be represented in a footnote.

In the New Testament, footnotes that refer to uncertainty regarding the original text are introduced by "Some manuscripts" or similar expressions. In the Old Testament, evidence for the reading chosen is given first and evidence for the alternative is added after a semicolon (for example: Septuagint; Hebrew *father*). In such notes the term "Hebrew" refers to the Masoretic Text.

It should be noted that minerals, flora and fauna, architectural details, articles of clothing and jewelry, musical instruments and other articles cannot always be identified with precision. Also measures of capacity in the biblical period are particularly uncertain (see the table of weights and measures following the text).

Like all translations of the Bible, made as they are by imperfect man, this one undoubtedly falls short of its goals. Yet we are grateful to God for the extent to which he has enabled us to realize these goals and for the strength he has given us and our colleagues to complete our task. We offer this version of the Bible to him in whose name and for whose glory it has been made. We pray that it will lead many into a better understanding of the Holy Scriptures and a fuller knowledge of Jesus Christ the incarnate Word, of whom the Scriptures so faithfully testify.

The Committee on Bible Translation
June 1978
(Revised August 1983)

Names of the translators and editors may be secured from the International Bible Society, translation sponsors of the New International Version, P.O. Box 62970, Colorado Springs, Colorado, 80962-2970 U.S.A.

WELCOME TO THE INTERNATIONAL INDUCTIVE STUDY BIBLE

Do you long to know God? Do you yearn for a deep and abiding relationship with him? Do you want to live the Christian life faithfully—and to know what He requires of you? If so, *The International Inductive Study Bible* is designed for you.

God reveals himself through his Word. Through it, he shows us how to live. Jesus made it clear: "Man does not live on bread alone, but on every word that comes from the mouth of God" (Matthew 4:4). And where do we find this divine bread? In the Scriptures.

As you study this Bible with the help of the Holy Spirit, and live out the truths that God reveals to you, you will discover new stability, strength, and confidence. You will be able to say with the prophet Jeremiah: "When your words came I ate them; they were my joy and heart's delight" (Jeremiah 15:16).

Today, many people are convinced they cannot know truth for themselves. A babble of voices surrounds us claiming to know and interpret God's truth for us. Which voices are right? Which are wrong? How can you discern the true from the counterfeit unless you spend time with God and his Word?

Most Christians have been encouraged to study the Word of God, yet many have never been shown how. Others even feel inadequate to do so because they are not ministers or seminary students or scholars. Nothing could be further from the truth.

In fact, if you want to satisfy your hunger and thirst to know God and his Word in a deeper way, you must do more than merely read Scripture and study what someone else has said about it. Just as no one else can eat and digest your food for you, so no one else can feed on God's Word for you. You must interact with the text yourself, absorbing its truths and letting God engrave his truth on your heart and mind and life.

That is the very heart of inductive study: seeing truth for yourself, discerning what it means, and applying that truth to your life. In his inspired Word, God has given us everything we need to know about life and godliness. But he doesn't stop there. He gives every believer a resident teacher—the Holy Spirit—who guides us into his truth.

The Bible is unlike any other book. It is supernatural. It is complete in itself. The Bible needs no other books or truths to supplement it. In inductive study the Bible becomes its own commentary, and it can be understood by any believer.

Anyone who will take the time can see and understand what God has given us in his Word and how it applies to us today.

CONTENTS

The Old Testament

The New Testament

Bible Study Helps

HOW TO USE
THE INTERNATIONAL
INDUCTIVE
STUDY BIBLE

IISB

HOW TO USE THE INDUCTIVE STUDY APPROACH

*I*f you know there is more to the Word of God than you have discovered so far...

~ If you sense there must be concrete answers to the complexities of life...

~ If you want a bedrock faith that keeps you from being tossed around by conflicting philosophies in the world and the church...

~ If you want to be able to face the uncertainties of the future without fear...

...then *The International Inductive Study Bible* is designed for you.

God's eternal, infallible Word is your guidebook for all of life, and inductive study gives you the key to understanding that guide.

Inductive study, a method anyone can use, involves three skills: *observation, interpretation,* and *application.*

OBSERVATION
Discover What It Says! **Observation** teaches you to see precisely what the passage says. It is the basis for accurate interpretation and correct application. Observation answers the question: What does the passage say?

INTERPRETATION
Discover What It Means! **Interpretation** answers the question: What does the passage mean?

APPLICATION
Discover How It Works! **Application** answers the question: What does it mean to me personally? What truths can I put into practice? What changes should I make in my life?

When you know what God says, what he means, and how to put his truths into practice, you will be equipped for every circumstance of life. Ultimately, the goal of personal Bible study is a transformed life and a deep and abiding relationship with Jesus Christ.

The following ten steps provide the basis for inductive study. As you take these steps, observation, interpretation, and application will sometimes happen simultaneously. God can give you insight at any point in your study, so be sensitive to his leading. When words or passages make an impression on you, stop for a moment and meditate on what God has shown you. Record your personal notes and insights in the margin so that you can remember what you've learned.

One of the most valuable aspects of the *IISB* is its wide-margin format, which has been specifically designed to enable you to easily keep a record of what God personally reveals to you from his Word. Some people are hesitant to mark in their Bibles, but this interactive Bible has been designed with marking in mind.

As you study the Bible chapter by chapter and book by book, you will grow in your ability to comprehend the whole counsel of God. In the future, you will be able to refer to your notes again and again as you study portions of Scripture and grow in your knowledge of him.

OBSERVATION

Discover What It Says!

STEP ONE

BEGIN WITH PRAYER

Prayer is often the missing element in Bible study. You are about to learn the most effective method of Bible study there is. Yet apart from the work of the Holy Spirit, that's all it will be—a method. It is the indwelling Holy Spirit who guides us into all truth, who takes the things of God and reveals them to us. Always ask God to teach you as you open the Scriptures.

STEP TWO

ASK THE "5 W'S AND AN H"

As you study any passage of Scripture, any book of the Bible, train yourself to constantly ask: *Who? What? When? Where? Why? How?* These questions are the building blocks of precise observation, which is essential for accurate interpretation. Many times Scripture is misinterpreted because the context isn't carefully observed.

When we rush into interpretation without laying the vital foundation of observation, our understanding becomes colored by our presuppositions—what we think, what we feel, or what other people have said. We must be careful not to distort the Scriptures to our own destruction (2 Peter 3:16).

Accurate answers to the following questions will help assure correct interpretation.

Who is speaking? Who is this about? Who are the main characters? For example, look at the sample passage from 1 Peter 5 (see page IISB-19). In this chapter, "I" is speaking. Verse 1 tells us that "I" is a fellow elder, a witness of the sufferings of Christ, and one who will share in the glory to follow. From reading this and previous chapters (the context), you recognize that the "I" is Peter, the author of this epistle.

And, *to whom* is he speaking? Verse 1 refers to "the elders," verse 5 to "young men," and verse 6 to "yourselves" (the recipients of the epistle).

What is the subject or event covered in the chapter? What do you learn about the people, the event, or the teaching from the text? What instructions are given? In 1 Peter 5:2, Peter instructs the elders to be shepherds of God's flock and serve as overseers.

When do or will the events occur? When did or will something happen to a particular person, people, or nation? When is a key question in determining the progression of events. In 1 Peter 5:4, we learn that "when the Chief Shepherd appears," the elders will receive their "crown of glory that will never fade away."

Where did or will this happen? Where was it said? In 1 Peter 5, the only reference to a place is in verse 13, where there is a greeting from "she who is in Babylon."

Why is something being said or mentioned? Why would or will this happen? Why at this time? Why this person? First Peter 5:12 explains why and how Peter wrote this epistle, establishing the book's purpose: to encourage and testify that this is the true grace of God, that they may stand fast (or firm) in it.

How will it happen? How is it to be done? How is it illustrated? In 1 Peter 5:2, note *how* the elders are to exercise oversight: voluntarily and eagerly, according to the will of God.

Every time you study a passage of the Bible, you should keep the "5 W's and an H" in mind. Don't be concerned if you can't find the answer to each question every time. Remember, there are many types of literature in the Bible and not all the questions will apply. As you ask *what, when, who, where, why,* and *how,* make notes in the margin of your Bible. Meditate on the truths God reveals to you. Think how they apply to you. This will keep your study from becoming an intellectual pursuit of knowledge for its own sake.

STEP *Three*

MARK KEY WORDS AND PHRASES

A key word is one that is essential to the text. It might be a noun, a descriptive word, or an action that plays a part in conveying the author's message. A key word or phrase is one which, when removed, leaves the passage devoid of meaning. Often key words and phrases are repeated in order to convey the author's point or purpose for writing. They may be repeated throughout a chapter, a segment of a book, or the book as a whole. For example, notice that some form of the word *suffering* is used three times in 1 Peter 5.

As you mark key words, ask the same *who, what, when, where, why,* and *how* questions of them as you did of the passage as a whole. For example, *who* suffers?, *what* caused the suffering?, etc.

Key words can be marked in several ways:

↶ *Through the use of symbols.*

↶ *Through the use of colors.* Colored pencils and multicolored ballpoint pens with fine tips work best.

FAITH   HUMILITY   GRACE

↶ *Through a combination of colors and symbols.*

GLORY   CHRIST   SUFFERING

The value of a distinctive marking system cannot be overestimated. Whichever system you choose, mark each key word the same way every time you observe it. Then, in future study, the visual impact of your marks will help you track key subjects and quickly identify significant truths throughout Scripture. To be sure that you are consistent, list key words, symbols, and color codes on an index card and use it as a bookmark in your Bible.

Be sure to mark pronouns (*I, you, he, she, it, we, our,* and so on) and synonyms (words that have the same meaning in the context) the same way you mark the words to which they refer. For example, a synonym for the devil in 1 Peter 5:8 is "adversary." The pronoun "him" in verse 9 also refers to the devil. Notice how marking the synonym "adversary" for the devil gives additional insight into his nature.

STEP *Four*

LOOK FOR LISTS

Making lists can be one of the most enlightening things you do as you study a section of Scripture. Lists reveal truths and highlight

THE IISB MARKING APPROACH

1 PETER 5 ~ SAMPLE A

DEVELOP CHAPTER THEMES

IDENTIFY SIMPLE LISTS

MARK KEY WORDS AND PHRASES

MAKE TOPICAL LISTS FROM KEY WORDS — COMPILE IN THE MARGIN

Chapter 5 Theme *Be Humble & Self-Controlled; Resist & Stand Fast*

5 To the elders among you, I appeal as a fellow elder,[j] a witness[k] of Christ's sufferings and one who also will share in the glory to be revealed:[l] [2]Be shepherds of God's flock[m] that is under your care, serving as overseers—not because you must, but because you are willing, as God wants you to be; not greedy for money, but eager to serve; [3]not lording it over[o] those entrusted to you, but being examples[p] to the flock. [4]And when the Chief Shepherd appears, you will receive the crown of glory[q] that will never fade away.

[5]Young men, in the same way be submissive[r] to those who are older. All of you, clothe yourselves with humility toward one another, because,

> "God opposes the proud
>   but gives grace to the humble."[bs]

[6]Humble yourselves, therefore, under God's mighty hand, that he may lift you up in due time.[t] [7]Cast all your anxiety on him[u] because he cares for you.[v]

[8]Be self-controlled and alert. Your enemy the devil prowls around[w] like a roaring lion looking for someone to devour. [9]Resist him,[x] standing firm in the faith,[y] because you know that your brothers throughout the world are undergoing the same kind of sufferings.[a]

[10]And the God of all grace, who called you to his eternal glory[b] in Christ, after you have suffered a little while, will himself restore you and make you strong,[c] firm and steadfast. [11]To him be the power for ever and ever. Amen.[d]

[12]With the help of Silas,[ae] whom I regard as a faithful brother, I have written to you briefly,[f] encouraging you and testifying that this is the true grace of God. Stand fast in it.
[13]She who is in Babylon, chosen together with you, sends you her greetings, and so does my son Mark.[g] [14]Greet one another with a kiss of love.[h]
Peace[i] to all of you who are in Christ.

Suffering:
1. *Christ suffered.*
2. *Brothers are suffering.*
3. *You will suffer.*
4. *But God will restore, make you strong, firm, and steadfast after you have suffered!*

important concepts. The best way to discover lists in the text is to observe how a key word is described, note what is said about someone or something, or group related thoughts or instructions together. (You may want to develop your lists on a worksheet before transferring them to your Bible.)

1 Peter 5:2, 3, for example, contains a *simple list* instructing the elders how to shepherd their flock. You can number simple lists within the text for easy reference.

Topical lists capture a truth, quality, or characteristic of a specific subject throughout a passage. One way to discover a topical list is to follow a key word through a chapter and note what the text says about the word each time it is used. (You may want to develop your lists on a worksheet before transferring them to the margin of your *IISB*.) See sample A for how a list could be made for the key word "suffering."

As you write your observations on suffering, you will begin to have a better and broader understanding of God's thoughts on this subject. You will learn that:

- Christ suffered
- the brothers in the world are suffering
- the recipients of the letter may also endure suffering

You will also discover that God:

- restores
- makes strong
- makes firm
- makes steadfast those who suffer

The application value of lists such as these is immeasurable. The next time you endure suffering, you will be able to recall more quickly that:

- Christ suffered
- others are suffering
- ultimately God will use suffering to strengthen your own life

Discovering truths that apply to your daily life is what makes lists such an important part of the inductive method.

STEP *FIVE*

WATCH FOR CONTRASTS AND COMPARISONS

Contrasts and comparisons use highly descriptive language to drive home significant truths and vital lessons. The word pictures they paint make it easier to remember what you've learned.

A *contrast* is a comparison of things that are different or opposite, such as light/darkness or proud/humble. The word "but" often signifies that a contrast is being made. Note contrasts in the text or in the margin of your Bible.

A *comparison* points out similarities and is often indicated by the use of words such as "like," "as," and "as it were." For example, Peter says in 1 Peter 5:8: "Your enemy the devil prowls around *like* a roaring lion." Highlight comparisons in a distinctive way in the text so that you will recognize them immediately when you return to the passage in the future.

STEP *SIX*

NOTE EXPRESSIONS OF TIME

The relationship of events in time often sheds light on the true meaning of the text. The timing of something can be observed in exact statements such as "on the tenth day of the eleventh month" or "at the feast of Booths." These phrases can be indicated in the margin by drawing a simple clock face 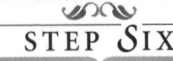 or a similar symbol.

Time is also indicated by words such as *until, then, when,* and *after.* These words show the relationship of one statement or event to another. Marking them will help you see the

THE *IISB* MARKING APPROACH

1 PETER 5 ∾ SAMPLE B

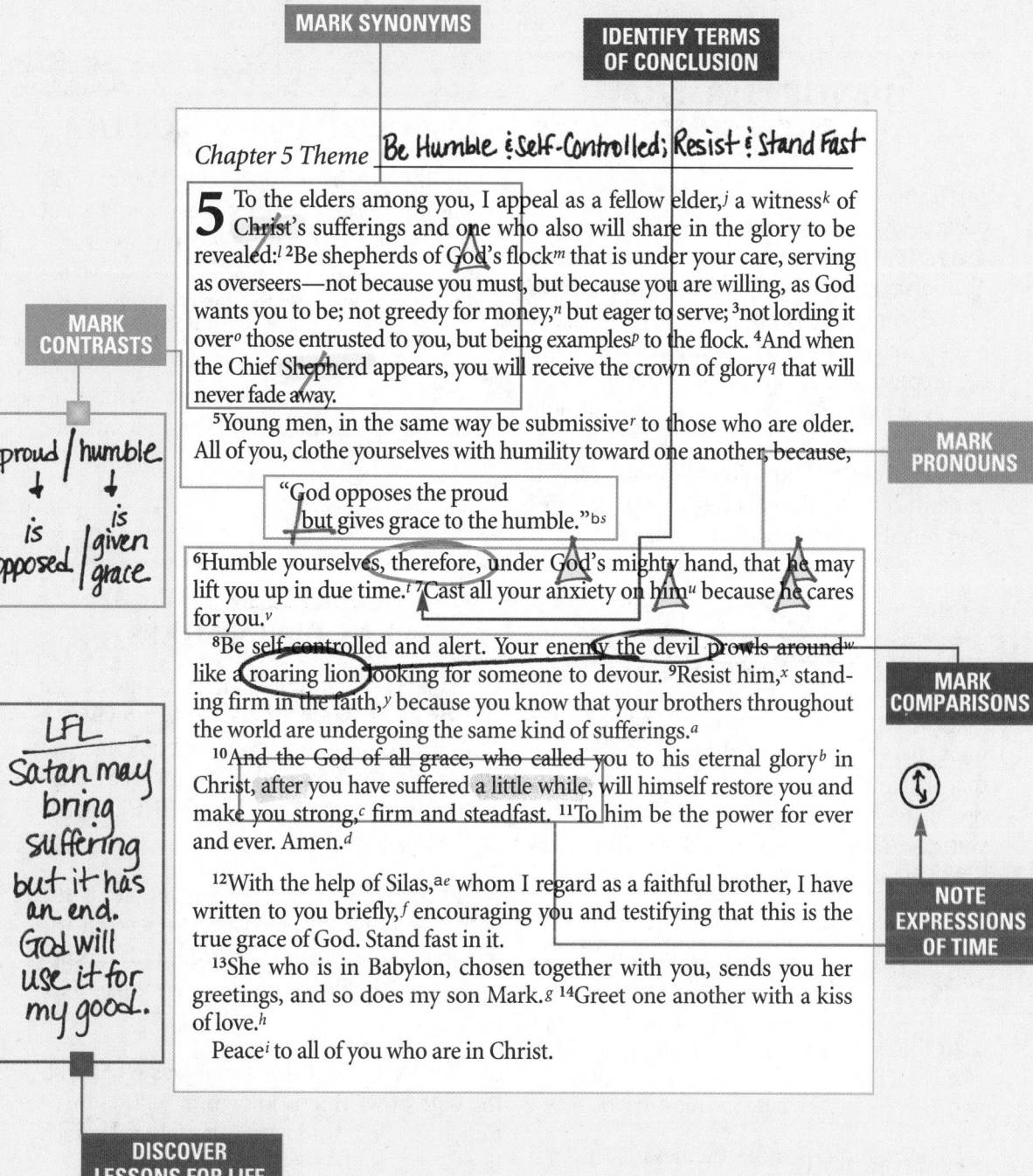

MARK SYNONYMS

IDENTIFY TERMS OF CONCLUSION

MARK CONTRASTS

proud / humble
↓ ↓
is / is
opposed / given grace

MARK PRONOUNS

MARK COMPARISONS

NOTE EXPRESSIONS OF TIME

LFL
Satan may bring suffering but it has an end. God will use it for my good.

DISCOVER LESSONS FOR LIFE

Chapter 5 Theme Be Humble & Self-Controlled; Resist & Stand Fast

5 To the elders among you, I appeal as a fellow elder,[j] a witness[k] of Christ's sufferings and one who also will share in the glory to be revealed:[l] [2]Be shepherds of God's flock[m] that is under your care, serving as overseers—not because you must, but because you are willing, as God wants you to be; not greedy for money,[n] but eager to serve; [3]not lording it over[o] those entrusted to you, but being examples[p] to the flock. [4]And when the Chief Shepherd appears, you will receive the crown of glory[q] that will never fade away.

[5]Young men, in the same way be submissive[r] to those who are older. All of you, clothe yourselves with humility toward one another, because,

"God opposes the proud
but gives grace to the humble."[bs]

[6]Humble yourselves, therefore, under God's mighty hand, that he may lift you up in due time.[t] [7]Cast all your anxiety on him[u] because he cares for you.[v]

[8]Be self-controlled and alert. Your enemy the devil prowls around[w] like a roaring lion looking for someone to devour. [9]Resist him,[x] standing firm in the faith,[y] because you know that your brothers throughout the world are undergoing the same kind of sufferings.[a]

[10]And the God of all grace, who called you to his eternal glory[b] in Christ, after you have suffered a little while, will himself restore you and make you strong,[c] firm and steadfast. [11]To him be the power for ever and ever. Amen.[d]

[12]With the help of Silas,[ae] whom I regard as a faithful brother, I have written to you briefly,[f] encouraging you and testifying that this is the true grace of God. Stand fast in it.

[13]She who is in Babylon, chosen together with you, sends you her greetings, and so does my son Mark.[g] [14]Greet one another with a kiss of love.[h]

Peace[i] to all of you who are in Christ.

sequence of events and lead to accurate interpretation of Scripture.

STEP SEVEN

IDENTIFY TERMS OF CONCLUSION

Terms of conclusion usually follow an important sequence of thought and include words such as *therefore, for this reason,* and *finally.* As the saying goes, when you see a "therefore" (or any term of conclusion), note what it is there for. You should be able to look through the preceding verses and summarize the message. For example, 1 Peter 5:6 says, "Humble yourselves, *therefore....*" If you will look, you will discover that you should humble yourself under the hand of God because God "opposes the proud but gives grace to the humble."

STEP EIGHT

DEVELOP CHAPTER THEMES

The theme of a chapter will center on the main person, event, teaching, or subject of that section of Scripture. Themes are often revealed by reviewing the key words and lists you developed. Try to express the theme as briefly as possible, using words found in the text.

Chapter 5 Theme ___Be Humble & Self-Controlle___

5 To the elders among you, I appeal as a fello Christ's sufferings and one who also will sh revealed:*ˡ* ²Be shepherds of God's flock*ᵐ* that is u as overseers—not because you must, but because

---

For example, possible themes for 1 Peter 5 might be *Appeals to Elders, Young Men, and the Suffering,* or *God Gives Grace to the Humble.* The point of observation is to answer the question: What does the passage say? The theme summarizes the answer. If needed, you can adjust your themes as your study deepens.

STEP NINE

DISCOVER LESSONS FOR LIFE

In the process of observing the text and seeing how God instructed people and dealt with various individuals, the Holy Spirit will bring to your attention truths that God wants you to be aware of and live by in your own life. These "Lessons for Life" can be noted in the margin under the abbreviation "LFL," or you may wish to create a distinctive symbol to mark your Lessons for Life throughout your *IISB.*

STEP TEN

COMPLETE THE AT A GLANCE CHART

The AT A GLANCE chart, found at the end of every book in the *IISB,* provides a compact visual summary of the book that you can return to again and again for easy reference. See the sample AT A GLANCE charts on the following pages.

☙ **Record the author of the book.** If the author is not mentioned by name, read the introduction for that book. If the author is not mentioned in either place, leave this space blank.

☙ **Record the date the book was written.** If the date of writing is known, it will be mentioned in the introduction that precedes each book.

☙ **Record the key words.** If the key words are not already listed on the AT A GLANCE

THE *IISB* AT A GLANCE CHARTS
1 PETER ∾ SAMPLE C

---

1 PETER AT A GLANCE

Theme of 1 Peter: Suffering and Glory

SEGMENT
DIVISIONS

	CHAPTER THEMES	
1	Trials Prove Your Faith – Be Holy	**Author:** Peter
2	You're Chosen: Follow Christ's Example – Submit	**Date:** 63 or 64 A.D.
3		**Purpose:** To encourage them to stand firm in true grace
4		**Key Words:** suffering (and all its synonyms) grace, gracious gift glory, glorious, glorify salvation Jesus Christ God Holy Spirit called chosen, elect holy
5		

Complete the AT A GLANCE charts throughout the Bible as you discover book and chapter themes chart, you will find them listed in the THINGS TO DO section at the beginning of each book.

In order to notice subjects which run throughout the entire Bible, there are some key words or phrases you will want to consistently mark in a distinctive manner. Write these on a card, color code them in the way you intend to mark them throughout your Bible, and use the card as a bookmark.

Some of the key words you will want to mark are listed below:

  sin (wickedness, evil, iniquity)
  covenant
  death (die)
  life (live)
  repent
  love
  law
  grace
  believe (faith)
  righteousness (righteous)
  holy (holiness)
  cry (cries, cried)
  Babylon
  nations
  day of the Lord (that day)
  Satan (any reference to the devil,
    spirits, demons, mediums)
  any reference to:
    Jesus' first coming
    Jesus' second coming

∾ **Copy the chapter themes** that you recorded at the beginning of each chapter. Because chapter divisions were added much later than the Bible was originally written, they do not always fall naturally in the text. Occasionally you will find a chapter with more than one theme. If this is true, record both themes.

∾ **Look for and record segment divisions.** See if any of the chapters can be grouped under a common theme or a common event. This is called a *segment division*. Segment divisions help you see the framework of a book.

The number and types of segment divisions will vary. A book might be divided according to dates, geographical locations, reigns of kings, major characters or events, topics, or doctrines.

When you gain a broad view of a book through its segment divisions, it is easier to understand its content and purpose. The AT A GLANCE chart for the book of John (sample D) shows a number of ways this book could be divided. For example, on the last line under "Segment Divisions," you will notice "Structure of Book." This shows you how John presents his material to achieve his purpose for writing this gospel.

∾ **Record the purpose of the book.** Discerning the author's purpose for writing and then keeping this purpose in mind while you study the text will help you handle the Word of God accurately. Unless the author specifically states his purpose for writing, as in 1 Peter 5:12 and John 20:31, you will have to discover it by other means:

1. Look for the main subjects covered in the book. These can often be recognized as you study the key repeated words.
2. Watch for any problems that are addressed. It may be that the author's purpose in writing was to deal with these problems.
3. Note exhortations and warnings that are given. These may be the reason for the book.
4. Observe what the author did *not* cover in his writing. When you know what the author covered and what was left unsaid, you are better able to narrow down the real purpose of the book.

Generally the instructions at the beginning of each book in your *IISB* will help you understand how that book might be divided.

THE IISB AT A GLANCE CHARTS
GOSPEL OF JOHN ❧ SAMPLE D

JOHN AT A GLANCE

Theme of John: Eternal life through Jesus Christ, Son of God

Author: John

Date: about A.D. 85

Purpose: that his readers would believe that Jesus is the Christ, God's Son, and thus have eternal life

Key Words:
signs/miracles
believe (believed, faith, trust)
life, live
judge, judging judgment
condemn, verdict, condemned, decision
witness, testify testifying, testimony
true, truth, truthful, real, valid, right, reliable, truly, surely
king
kingdom
love, loved
works, work
command
fruit, fruitful
remain
ask, pray
prayer, praying

Structure of Book	Portrayals of Jesus Christ	Signs and Miracles	Ministry		Chapter Themes
Introduces Jesus as Christ, Son of God	That you may believe that Jesus is the Christ, Son of God	Water to wine	To Israel	1	Prologue—The Word / John the Baptist / calling disciples
				2	wedding Cana / cleansing temple
Gives signs that prove Jesus is Christ, Son of God		Heals official's son		3	born again
				4	woman at well / royal official
		Heals lame man		5	father / son
		Feeds 5,000		6	bread / feeding 5,000
		walks on water		7	feast of tabernacles / thirst-drink
		Heals blind man		8	adulterous woman / truth sets free
				9	blind man
		Raises Lazarus from dead		10	sheep / shepherd
				11	raising Lazarus
		Hour has come		12	dinner at Bethany / King on donkey
Life that belongs to those who believe God	That you may have life		To Disciples	13	last supper / washing-disciples
				14	Father's house / hearts be troubled
				15	remain / vine and branches
				16	Holy Spirit / another helper
				17	Lord's prayer / high-priestly prayer
Obtaining of that life—by death and resurrection			To All Mankind	18	arrest and trial
				19	crucifixion
		Resurrection appearances		20	resurrection
Purpose of life: love and follow			To Disciples	21	do you love me?

∾ **Record the main theme of the book.** Once you have listed the theme for each chapter, evaluated the author's purpose for writing, and observed the content of the book chapter by chapter and segment by segment, you will be prepared to determine the theme of the book. What one statement best describes the book as a whole?

∾∾∾∾∾

Once you have completed the ten steps of observation, you are ready to move into interpretation and application.

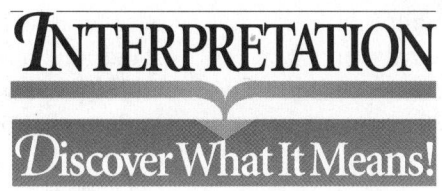

INTERPRETATION

Discover What It Means!

While observation leads to an accurate understanding of what the Word of God *says*, interpretation goes a step further and helps you understand what it *means*. When you accurately interpret the Word of God, you will be able to confidently put its truths into practice in your daily life.

Like many other people, you may have been taught a system of belief before you ever studied God's Word for yourself. Or you may have formed opinions of what the Bible teaches before you carefully examined the Scriptures. As you learn to handle God's Word accurately, you will be able to discern if what you believe is in agreement with Scripture. If this is your desire and you come to the Word of God with a teachable spirit, God will lead you and guide you into all truth.

As you seek to interpret the Bible accurately, the following guidelines will be helpful.

1. Remember that context rules.

The word *context* means "that which goes with the text." To understand the context you must be familiar with the Word of God. If you lay the solid foundation of observation, you will be prepared to consider each verse in the light of:

- ∾ the surrounding verses
- ∾ the book in which it is found
- ∾ the entire Word of God

As you study, ask yourself: Is my interpretation of a particular section of Scripture consistent with the theme, purpose, and structure of the book in which it is found? Is it consistent with other Scripture about the same subject, or is there a glaring difference? Am I considering the historic and cultural context of what is being said? Never take a Scripture out of its context to make it say what you want it to say. Discover what the author is saying; don't add to his meaning.

2. Always seek the full counsel of the Word of God.

When you know God's Word thoroughly, you will not accept a teaching simply because someone has used one or two isolated verses to support it. Those verses may have been taken out of context, or other important passages might have been overlooked or ignored that would have led to a different understanding. As you read the Bible regularly and extensively, and as you become more familiar with the whole counsel of God's Word, you will be able to discern whether a teaching is biblical or not.

Saturate yourself in the Word of God; it is your safeguard against wrong doctrine.

3. Remember that Scripture will never contradict Scripture.

The best interpretation of Scripture is Scripture. Remember, all Scripture is inspired by God; it is God-breathed. Therefore, Scripture will never contradict itself.

The Bible contains all the truth you

will ever need for any situation in life. Sometimes, however, you may find it difficult to reconcile two seemingly contradictory truths taught in Scripture. An example of this would be the sovereignty of God and the responsibility of man. When two or more truths that are clearly taught in the Word seem to be in conflict, remember that we as humans have finite minds. Don't take a teaching to an extreme that God doesn't. Simply humble your heart in faith and believe what God says, even if you can't fully understand or reconcile it at the moment.

4. Don't base your convictions on an obscure passage of Scripture.

An obscure passage is one in which the meaning is not easily understood. Because these passages are difficult to understand even when proper principles of interpretation are used, they should not be used as a basis for establishing doctrine.

5. Interpret Scripture literally.

The Bible is not a book of mysticism. God spoke to us that we might know truth. Therefore, take the Word of God at face value—in its natural, normal sense. Look for the clear teaching of Scripture, not a hidden meaning. Understand and recognize figures of speech and interpret them accordingly (see Bible Study Helps, page. 2205).

Consider what is being said in the light of its literary style. For example, you will find more similes and metaphors in poetical and prophetic literature than in historical or biographical books. Interpret portions of Scripture according to their literary style.

Some literary styles in the Bible are:

- ⚭ Historical—Acts
- ⚭ Prophetic—Revelation
- ⚭ Biographical—Luke
- ⚭ Didactic (teaching)—Romans
- ⚭ Poetic—Psalms
- ⚭ Epistle (letter)—2 Timothy
- ⚭ Proverbial—Proverbs

6. Look for the single meaning of the passage.

Always try to understand what the author had in mind when you interpret a portion of the Bible. Don't twist verses to support a meaning that is not clearly taught. Unless the author of a particular book indicates that there is another meaning to what he says, let the passage speak for itself.

APPLICATION

Discover How It Works!

No matter how much you know *about* God's Word, if you don't apply what you learn, Scripture will never benefit your life. To be a hearer of the Word and not a doer is to deceive yourself (James 1:22-25). This is why application is so vital. Observation and interpretation are the "hearing" of God's Word. With *application*, you will be transformed into Christ's image. Application is the embracing of the truth, the "doing" of God's Word. It is this process which allows God to work in your life.

Second Timothy 3:16, 17 says: "All Scripture is God-breathed and is useful for teaching, rebuking, correcting and training in righteousness, so that the man of God may be thoroughly equipped for every good work." Here is the key to application: Apply Scripture in the light of its teaching, rebuking, correcting, and instructions on life.

Teaching (doctrine) is what the Word of God says on any particular subject. That teaching, whatever the subject, is always true. Therefore, everything that God says in his Bible about any given subject is absolute truth.

The first step in application is to find out what the Word of God says on any particular subject through accurate observation and correct interpretation of the text. Once you understand what the Word of God teaches, you are then obligated before God to accept that truth and to live by it. When you have adjusted any false concepts or teaching you may have believed, and embraced the truth revealed in God's Word, then you have *applied* what you have learned.

Rebuking exposes areas in your thinking and behavior that do not align with God's Word.

Rebuking is finding out where you have thought wrongly or have not been doing what God says is right. The application of rebuking is to accept it and agree with God, acknowledging where you are wrong in thought or in behavior. This is how you are set free from unbelief, from sin.

Correcting is the next step in application, and often the most difficult. Many times we can see what is wrong, but we are reluctant to take the necessary steps to correct it. God has not left you without help or without answers in this step of correcting what is wrong. Sometimes the answers are difficult to find, but they are always there, and any child of God who wants to please his or her Father will be shown by the Spirit of God how to do so.

Many times correction comes by simply confessing and forsaking what is wrong. Other times, God gives very definite steps to take. An example of this is in Matthew 18:15-17, in which God tells us how to approach a brother when he sins. When you apply correction to your actions and attitudes, God will work in you to do his good purpose (Philippians 2:13). Joy will follow obedience.

Training in righteousness: Although God's Word is profitable for rebuking and correcting, the Bible was also given to us as a handbook for living. As we spend time studying his Word, God equips us through:

- teachings
- commands
- promises
- encouragements
- warnings
- and the lives of biblical characters and God's dealings with man

Scripture has everything you need to meet any and all situations of life, so that you "may be thoroughly equipped for every good work." The most effective application takes place as you go before the Lord and talk with him about those things that you have read, studied, seen, and heard.

INSIGHTS ON
APPLYING SCRIPTURE

In applying Scripture to your life, the following questions may be helpful:

1. **What does the passage teach?** Is it general or specific? Does it apply only to specific people? To a cultural problem of the day? To a certain time in history? Has it been superseded by a broader teaching? For example, in the Old Testament, Jews were not allowed to eat certain foods or to wear a certain combination of materials. Are those prohibitions applicable to Christians today?

2. **Does this section of Scripture expose any error in my beliefs or in my behavior?** Are there any commandments that I have not obeyed? Are there any wrong attitudes or motives in my life that the Scriptures bring to light?

3. **What is God's instruction to me as his child?** Are there any new truths to be believed?

Are there any new commandments to be acted upon? Are there any new insights I am to pursue? Are there any promises I am to embrace?

4. **When applying Scripture, beware of the following:**

∾ Applying cultural standards rather than biblical standards

∾ Attempting to strengthen a legitimate truth by using a Scripture incorrectly

∾ Applying Scripture out of prejudice from past training or teaching

One of the apostle Paul's concerns for Timothy, his son in the faith, was that Timothy learn to handle God's Word in a way that would please the Lord (2 Timothy 2:15). Someday we too will want to give a good account of our stewardship of God's Word. Did we handle it accurately? Were we gentle and reasonable about our faith, giving honor to those whom God has called to lead us, while at the same time searching Scripture ourselves to understand its truths? Did we allow God's living and active Word to change our lives?

Observation, interpretation, and application lead to *transformation*. This is the goal of our study of the Word of God. Through it we are changed from glory to glory into the image of Jesus.

GETTING STARTED

With this basic understanding of the inductive process, you are ready to begin a lifetime of personal Bible study. Prayerfully choose one of the Bible's 66 books, and then begin your study.

As you begin, quickly read through the THINGS TO DO section for an overview, but don't let the instructions overwhelm you. Taken one by one, chapter by chapter, and book by book, they become very manageable.

The THINGS TO THINK ABOUT section encourages you to get alone with God to consider how the truths of the book apply to you.

Old Testament historical and prophetic books have a HISTORICAL CHART usually located just before the first chapter to help you see where the book fits historically and chronologically. And many of the books in the New Testament contain an OBSERVATIONS CHART on which to record information you are instructed to look for in the THINGS TO DO section.

Finally, each book of the Bible ends with an AT A GLANCE chart, as discussed earlier.

For added insights on particular topics relevant to your personal Bible study, you will find a BIBLE STUDY HELPS section at the end of the Bible. This section also includes an overview of major events in Israel's history, a concordance, and color maps to provide a geographical frame of reference for your study of God's Word.

As you study the Bible inductively, you will get to know God in a deep, exciting, and enlightening way.

The
SPIRITUAL
LIFE OF ISRAEL

COMPARATIVE
TIMETABLE
OF HISTORY

THE TABERNACLE
and the High Priest in his priestly garments

∽ The tabernacle was a sanctuary, built for God according to the pattern of his throne in heaven, where he chose to dwell among his people. It was the focal point of Israel's national life from the time God brought them out of the land of Egypt under Moses until they settled in the land of Canaan. For more than four centuries this elect nation would worship God in the tabernacle—yet from a distance, separated by the curtain from the presence of his glory, which hovered over the atonement cover on the ark of the covenant. Only the high priest in his priestly garments could enter, and that only once a year on the Day of Atonement.

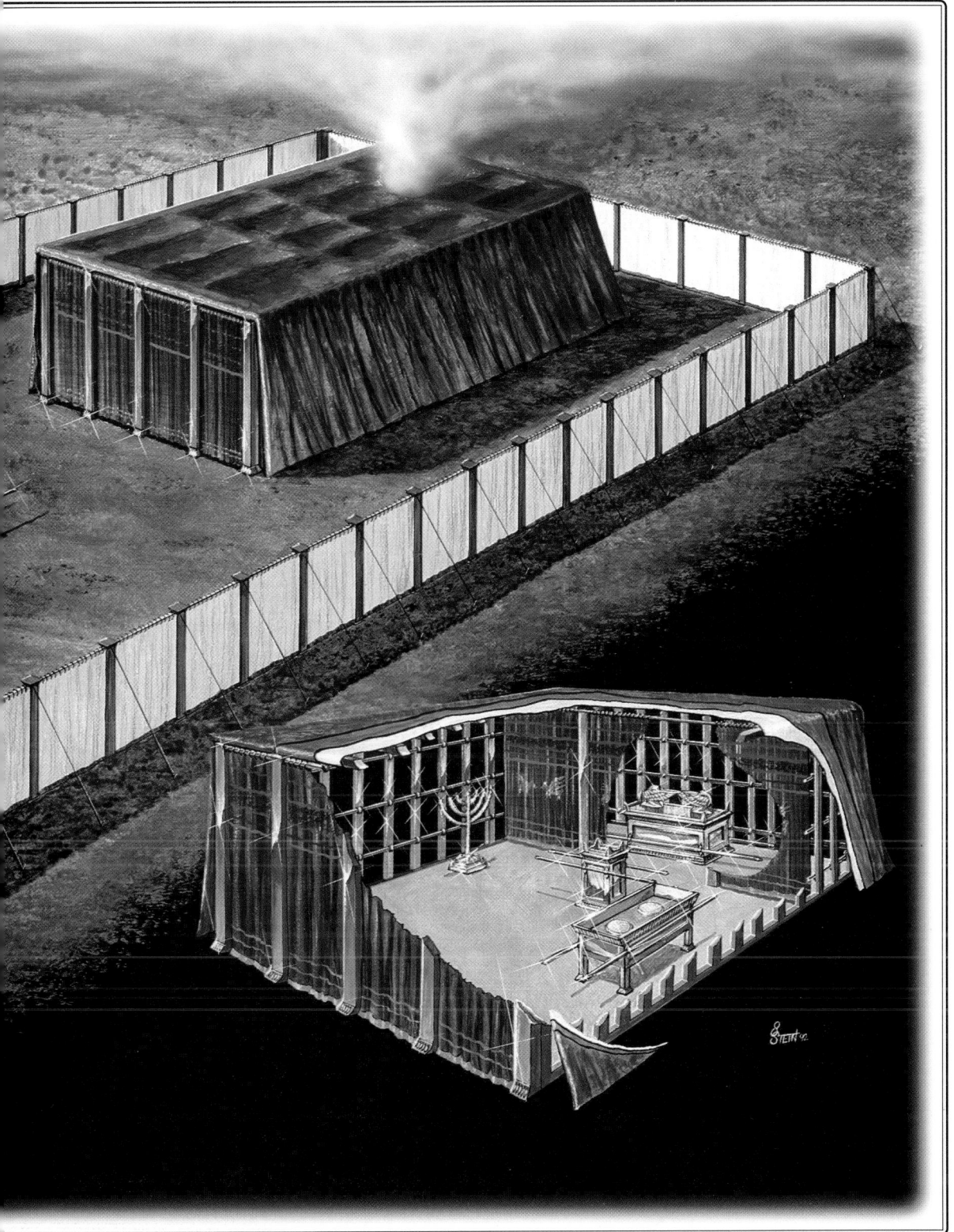

SOLOMON'S TEMPLE

∽ King David was grieved because he lived in Jerusalem in a house of cedar while the ark of the Lord was covered by curtains in the tabernacle. However, because David was a man of war, God gave the privilege of building the temple to David's son Solomon, who was a man of peace. ∽ Solomon's magnificent work was overshadowed only when God's glory itself filled his temple. God's presence remained there for more than 350 years, until the days of Ezekiel the prophet. Then because of Judah's sin and God's impending judgment, the glory of the Lord departed. ∽ In 586 B.C. the temple lay in ruins, destroyed by the Babylonians.

HEROD'S TEMPLE
at the Time of Jesus During the Feast of Tabernacles

When the remnant of Israel returned after the Babylonian captivity, the task of rebuilding the temple was overwhelming. The work began in 536 B.C. but stopped two years later. The people found it easier to rebuild their own houses rather than the house of God. Then the Lord spoke through the prophet Haggai. Convicted, the people completed the temple. Although this temple, built under Zerubbabel's leadership, could not compare with Solomon's temple, and although God did not fill this temple with his glory, he honored the people's obedience. When Herod became king of Judea, he aspired to make this second temple more glorious than Solomon's. Magnificent as it was, the temple remained void of God's glory until Joseph and his wife, Mary, took their son, Jesus, there to present him to the Lord. The glory of God in the person of Jesus Christ (John 1:14) would frequent Herod's Temple until the day he walked out for the last time, leaving the temple desolate. The day they crucified him, the curtain in the temple was torn in two, for a new covenant had begun. In A.D. 70 Herod's Temple was destroyed, as Jesus prophesied it would be, by the Roman general Titus.

THE TEMPLE MOUNT
During the Second Temple Period

1. Second Temple (Herod's)
2. Western Wall
3. Wilson's Arch*
4. Barclay's Gate*
5. Small Shops
6. Main N-S Street
7. Robinson's Arch*
8. Upper City
9. Royal Porch
10. Pilasters
11. Double Gate
12. Triple Gate
13. Plaza
14. Ritual Bathhouse
15. Council House
16. Herodian Tower
17. Largest Ashlars
18. Antonia Fortress
19. Warren's Gate*
20. Court of the Gentiles
21. Eastern Gate

*Named after nineteenth-century explorers
Note: See page 1723 for a floor plan of Herod's Temple

THE HISTORY OF ISRAEL—ADAM TO SOLOMON

| 00 | 4000 | 3000 | 2000 | 1800 | 1600 | 1400 | 1200 | 1150 | 1100 | 1050 | 1000 | 95 |

*T*o truly appreciate and fully comprehend the totality of God's revelation to man in the Word of God, one needs a clear understanding of the whole counsel of God. Keeping events, revelations, truths, and peoples in perspective is essential. This easy-to-understand guide to Israel's history from the beginning to modern times is designed to help you place Scripture in its proper historical and chronological context. It is a tool which will make your inductive study even more rewarding and enlightening.

(For a written history of this timeline, see pages 2189-2201.)

PHARAOHS OF EGYPT

Thutmose III
Pharaoh of the oppression
1483-1450

Amenhotep II
Pharaoh of the Exodus
1450-1423

Father
▼ Abraham

Exodus
1445

Saul
1051 (or 1043)-1011 ▼

Solomon
971 ▼

Adam	Joseph	Israel in Egypt	Moses 1525		Judges		David

1875

1804   276 years between

Aaron

1373   1020   1011 971 ...

▲ Joshua and elders
1405-1381

Israel	Prophets: Southern Kingdom	Babylon
Northern Kingdom (Israel)	Egypt	Medes and Persians
Prophets: Northern Kingdom	Aram/Damascus/Syria	Greece
Southern Kingdom (Judah)	Assyria	Rome

| 5000 | 4000 | 3000 | 2000 | 1800 | 1600 | 1400 | 1200 | 1150 | 1100 | 1050 | 1000 | 9 |

Scholars vary in the dating systems they use. The IISB generally follows John Whitcomb's system throughout for the sake of consistency.

THE HISTORY OF ISRAEL—THE DIVIDED KINGDOM

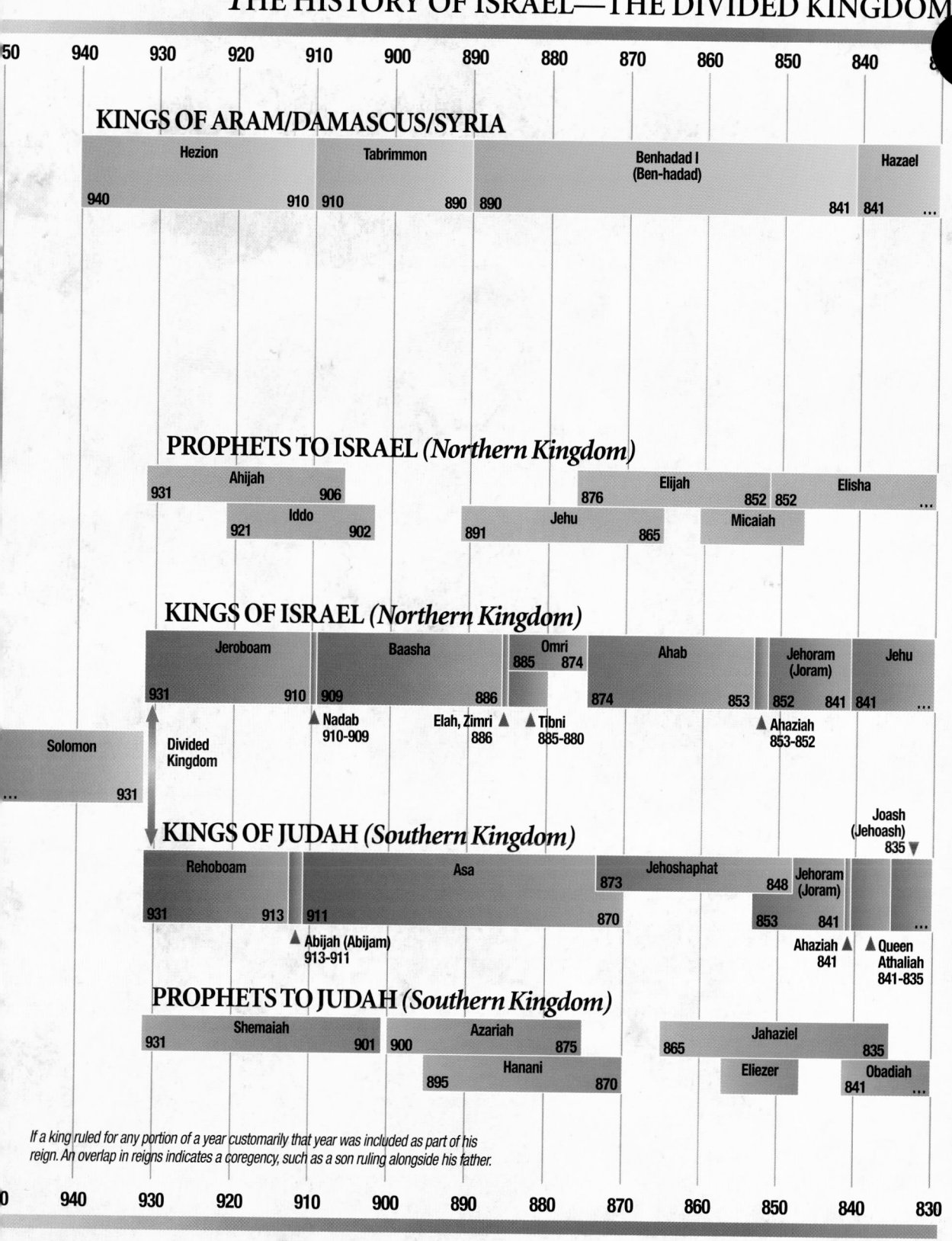

| | 940 | 930 | 920 | 910 | 900 | 890 | 880 | 870 | 860 | 850 | 840 | |

KINGS OF ARAM/DAMASCUS/SYRIA

- Hezion — 940–910
- Tabrimmon — 910–890
- Benhadad I (Ben-hadad) — 890–841
- Hazael — 841–…

PROPHETS TO ISRAEL (Northern Kingdom)

- Ahijah — 931–906
- Iddo — 921–902
- Elijah — 876–852
- Elisha — 852–…
- Jehu — 891–865
- Micaiah

KINGS OF ISRAEL (Northern Kingdom)

- Jeroboam — 931–910
- Baasha — 909–886
- Omri — 885–874
- Ahab — 874–853
- Jehoram (Joram) — 852–841
- Jehu — 841–…
- ▲ Nadab 910–909
- ▲ Elah, Zimri 886
- ▲ Tibni 885–880
- ▲ Ahaziah 853–852

Solomon — …–931

Divided Kingdom

KINGS OF JUDAH (Southern Kingdom)

- Rehoboam — 931–913
- Asa — 911–870
- Jehoshaphat — 873–848
- Jehoram (Joram) — 853–841
- Joash (Jehoash) 835 ▼
- Ahaziah ▲ 841
- ▲ Queen Athaliah 841–835
- ▲ Abijah (Abijam) 913–911

PROPHETS TO JUDAH (Southern Kingdom)

- Shemaiah — 931–901
- Azariah — 900–875
- Hanani — 895–870
- Jahaziel — 865–835
- Eliezer
- Obadiah — 841–…

If a king ruled for any portion of a year customarily that year was included as part of his reign. An overlap in reigns indicates a coregency, such as a son ruling alongside his father.

| 940 | 930 | 920 | 910 | 900 | 890 | 880 | 870 | 860 | 850 | 840 | 830 |

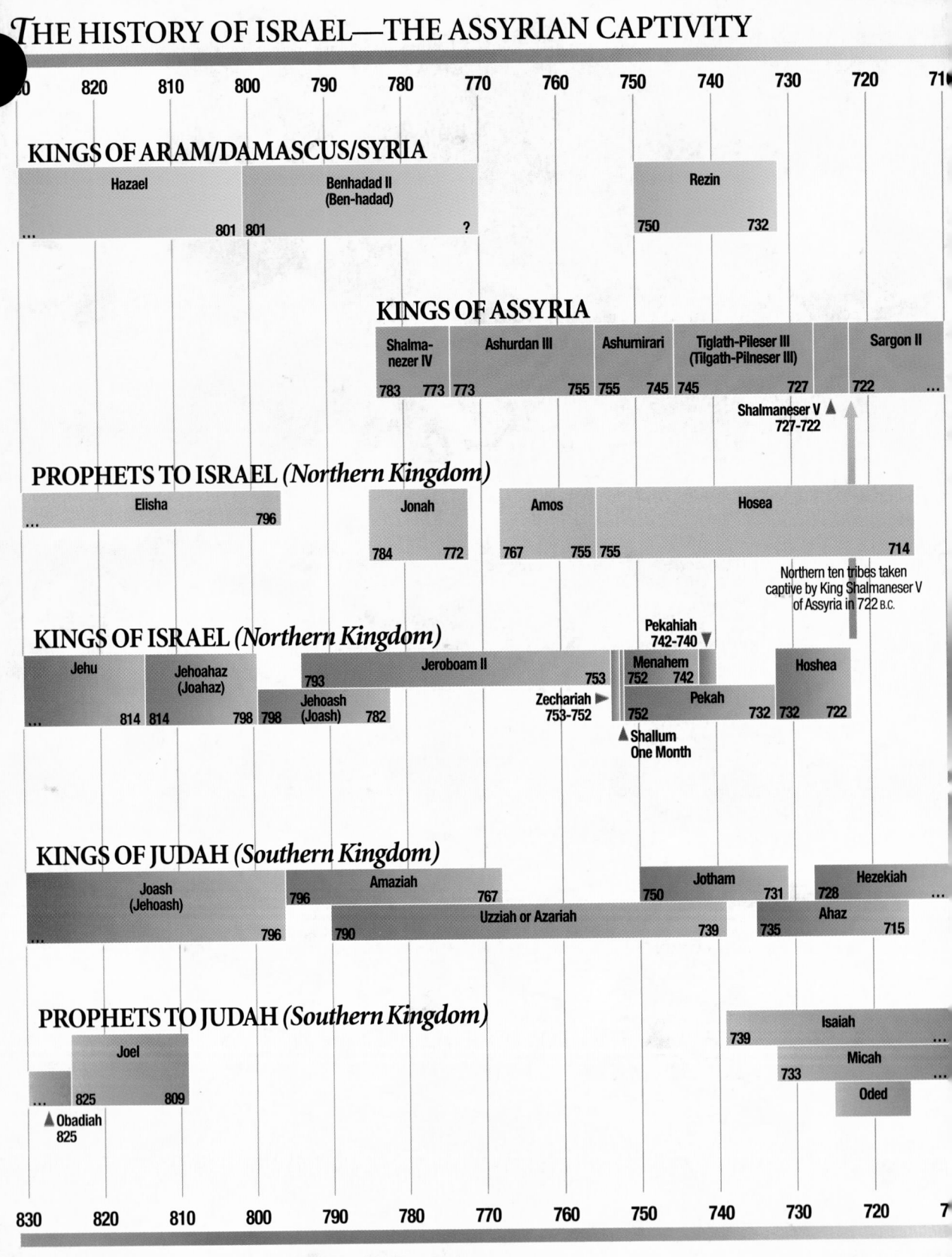

THE HISTORY OF ISRAEL—THE BABYLONIAN CAPTIVITY

| 700 | 690 | 680 | 670 | 660 | 650 | 640 | 630 | 620 | 610 | 600 | 590 |

KINGS OF BABYLON

Neo-Babylonian Empire

Nabopolassar	Nebuchadnezzar
626 — 605	605 ...

Sennacherib · Esarhaddon · Ashurbanipal · Sinsharishkun

705 — 681 | 681 — 669 | 669 — 633 | 629 — 612

▲ Sargon II
722-705

Ashuretililani ▲
633-629

605 B.C.
Battle of
Carchemish
between Babylon
and Egypt

**Pharaoh Neco
of Egypt**

609 — 594

1 Daniel
and friends
taken captive
605 B.C.

2 Ezekiel
and ten
thousand
captive
597 B.C.

**Babylonian
captivity**

**Judah's
3 stages
of captivity**
605 ...

Pharaoh
Neco
kills
Josiah
in battle

Hezekiah	Manasseh	Josiah	Jehoiakim (Eliakim)	Zedekiah (Mattaniah)
697 — 686	— 642	640 — 609	609 — 597	597 ...

Amon ▲
2 years

Jehoahaz ▲
(Joahaz/Shallum)
3 months

Jehoiachin ▲
(Coniah/
Jeconiah)
3 months

Isaiah
681

Micah
701

Huldah

Nahum
650 — 620

Ezekiel
593 ►

Zephaniah
636 — 623

Habakkuk
621 — 609

Daniel
605 ...

Jeremiah
627 ...

| 700 | 690 | 680 | 670 | 660 | 650 | 640 | 630 | 620 | 610 | 600 | 590 |

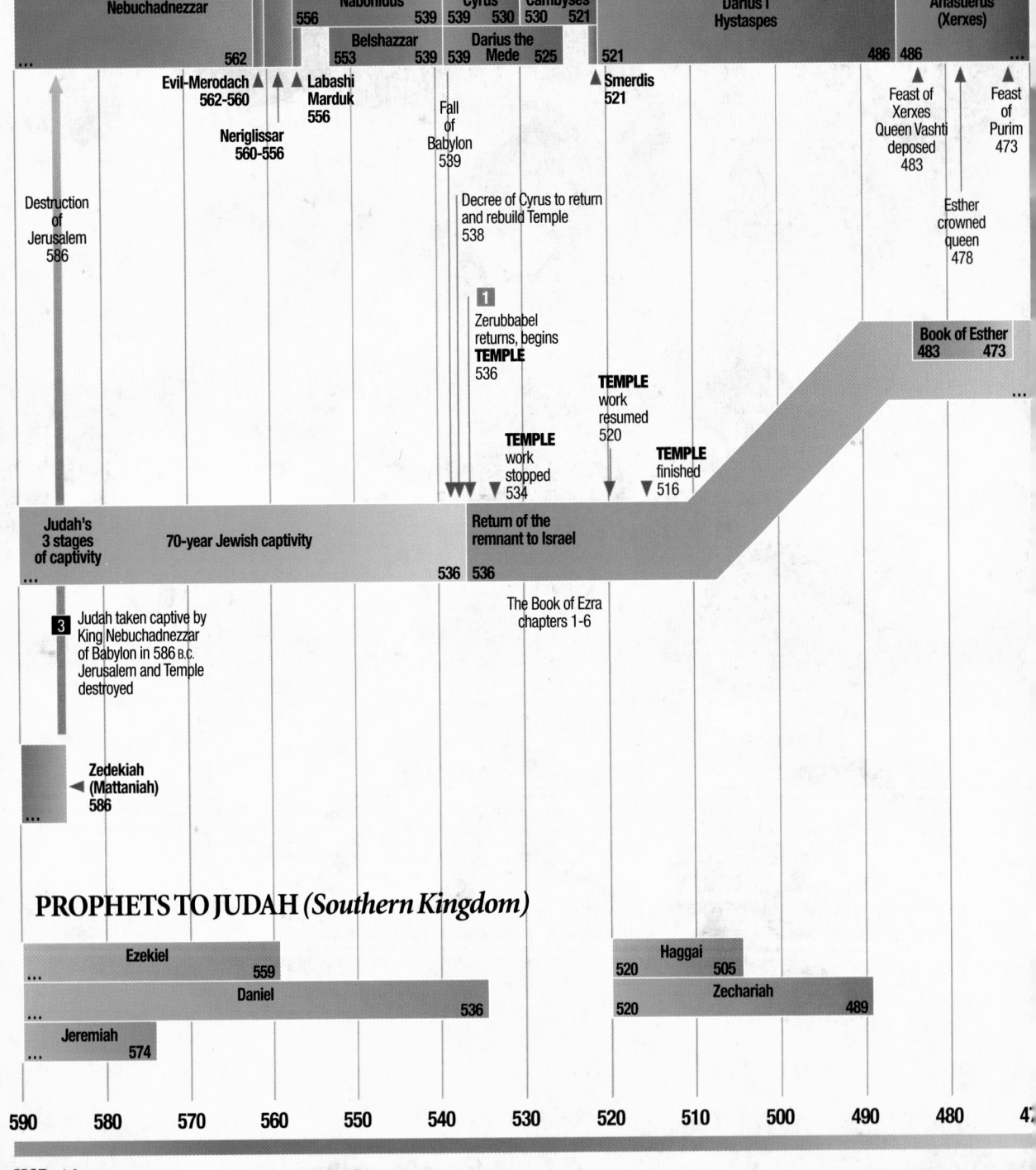

THE HISTORY OF ISRAEL—THE GREEK AND ROMAN PERIODS

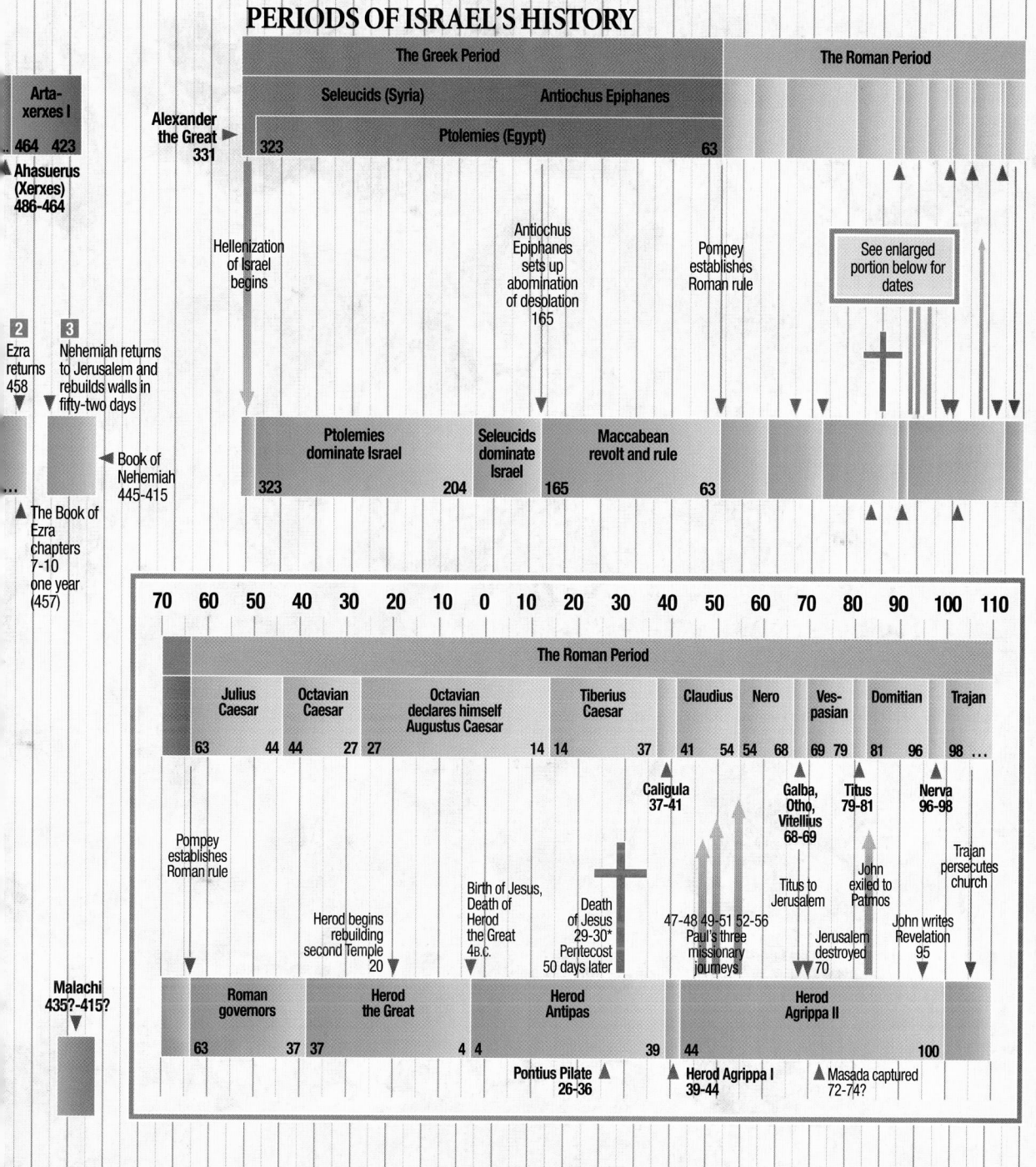

PERIODS OF ISRAEL'S HISTORY

The Greek Period

The Roman Period

Seleucids (Syria) — Antiochus Epiphanes

Ptolemies (Egypt)

323 — 63

Arta-xerxes I
464 423

Alexander the Great 331

Ahasuerus (Xerxes) 486-464

Hellenization of Israel begins

Antiochus Epiphanes sets up abomination of desolation 165

Pompey establishes Roman rule

See enlarged portion below for dates

2 Ezra returns 458

3 Nehemiah returns to Jerusalem and rebuilds walls in fifty-two days

Book of Nehemiah 445-415

The Book of Ezra chapters 7-10 one year (457)

Ptolemies dominate Israel 323 — 204

Seleucids dominate Israel 165

Maccabean revolt and rule 165 — 63

The Roman Period

70 60 50 40 30 20 10 0 10 20 30 40 50 60 70 80 90 100 110

Julius Caesar	Octavian Caesar	Octavian declares himself Augustus Caesar	Tiberius Caesar	Claudius	Nero	Ves-pasian	Domitian	Trajan
63 44	44 27	27 14	14 37	41 54	54 68	69 79	81 96	98 ...

Caligula 37-41

Galba, Otho, Vitellius 68-69

Titus 79-81

Nerva 96-98

Pompey establishes Roman rule

Herod begins rebuilding second Temple 20

Birth of Jesus, Death of Herod the Great 4 B.C.

Death of Jesus 29-30* Pentecost 50 days later

47-48 49-51 52-56 Paul's three missionary journeys

Titus to Jerusalem

Jerusalem destroyed 70

John exiled to Patmos

John writes Revelation 95

Trajan persecutes church

Malachi 435?-415?

Roman governors	Herod the Great	Herod Antipas	Herod Agrippa II
63 37	37 4	4 39	44 100

Pontius Pilate 26-36

Herod Agrippa I 39-44

Masada captured 72-74?

450 430 410 390 370 350 330 310 290 270 250 230 210 190 170 150 130 110 90 70 50 30 10 10 30 50 70 90 110

THE HISTORY OF ISRAEL—110 A.D. TO MODERN TIMES

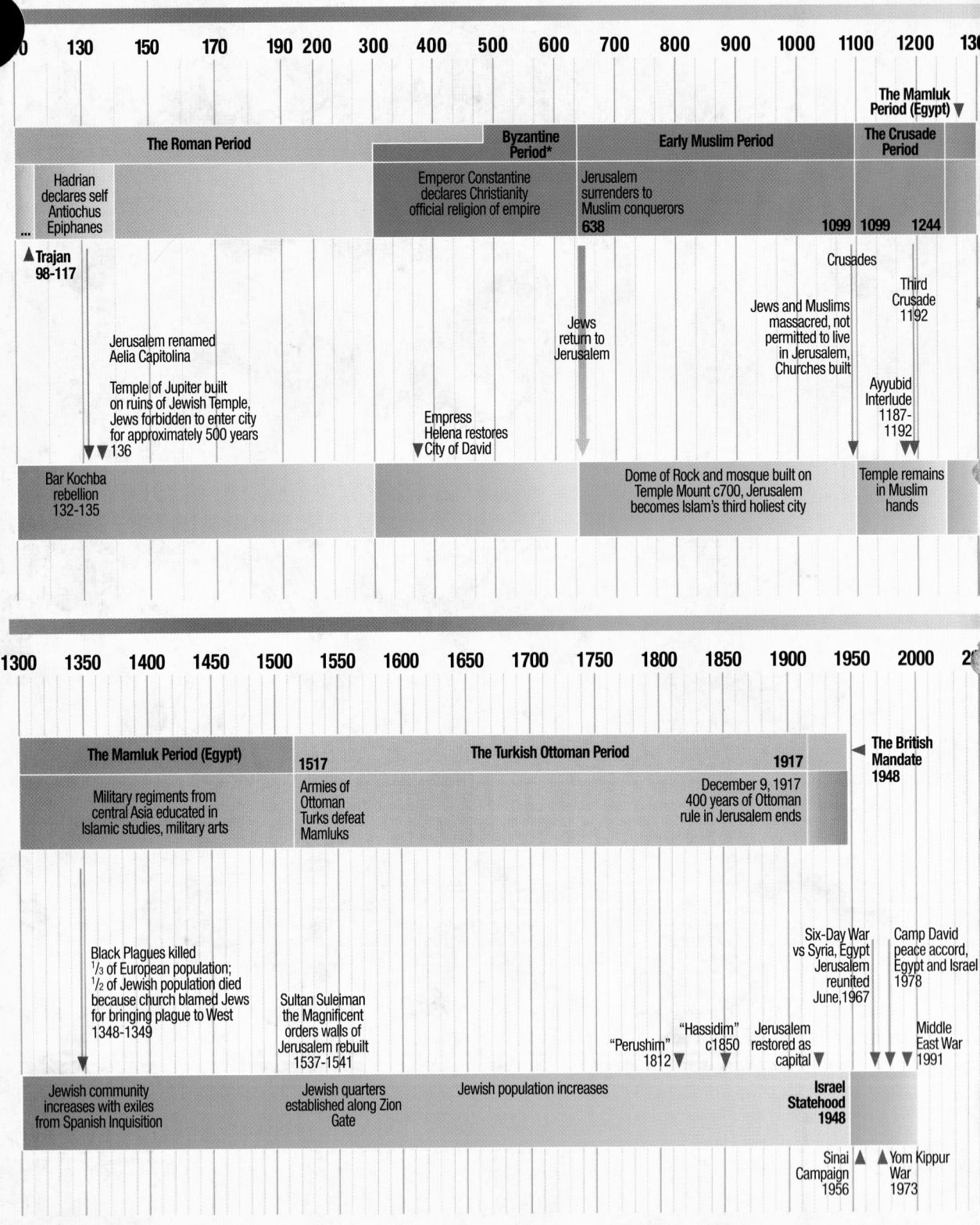

Top timeline (110 to 1300):

130 | 150 | 170 | 190 | 200 | 300 | 400 | 500 | 600 | 700 | 800 | 900 | 1000 | 1100 | 1200 | 130

The Mamluk Period (Egypt) ▼

The Roman Period | Byzantine Period* | Early Muslim Period | The Crusade Period

Hadrian declares self Antiochus Epiphanes ...

Emperor Constantine declares Christianity official religion of empire

Jerusalem surrenders to Muslim conquerors **638**

1099 | 1099 | 1244

▲ Trajan 98-117

Crusades

Jews and Muslims massacred, not permitted to live in Jerusalem, Churches built

Third Crusade 1192

Jews return to Jerusalem

Jerusalem renamed Aelia Capitolina

Temple of Jupiter built on ruins of Jewish Temple, Jews forbidden to enter city for approximately 500 years
▼▼ 136

Empress Helena restores ▼ City of David

Ayyubid Interlude 1187-1192

Bar Kochba rebellion 132-135

Dome of Rock and mosque built on Temple Mount c700, Jerusalem becomes Islam's third holiest city

Temple remains in Muslim hands

Bottom timeline (1300 to 2000):

1300 | 1350 | 1400 | 1450 | 1500 | 1550 | 1600 | 1650 | 1700 | 1750 | 1800 | 1850 | 1900 | 1950 | 2000 | 2

The Mamluk Period (Egypt) | **1517** | The Turkish Ottoman Period | **1917** | ◄ The British Mandate 1948

Military regiments from central Asia educated in Islamic studies, military arts

Armies of Ottoman Turks defeat Mamluks

December 9, 1917 400 years of Ottoman rule in Jerusalem ends

Black Plagues killed 1/3 of European population; 1/2 of Jewish population died because church blamed Jews for bringing plague to West 1348-1349

Sultan Suleiman the Magnificent orders walls of Jerusalem rebuilt 1537-1541

"Perushim" 1812 ▼

"Hassidim" c1850 ▼

Jerusalem restored as capital ▼

Six-Day War vs Syria, Egypt Jerusalem reunited June,1967

Camp David peace accord, Egypt and Israel 1978

Middle East War 1991

Jewish community increases with exiles from Spanish Inquisition

Jewish quarters established along Zion Gate

Jewish population increases

Israel Statehood 1948

Sinai Campaign 1956 ▲

▲ Yom Kippur War 1973

IISB-48   *The dates from the Byzantine Period are taken from **The Tower of David**, Museum of the History of Jerusalem.

THE OLD
TESTAMENT

LSB

GENESIS

When there was nothing, there was God. Then God spoke.

∾ THINGS TO DO

General Instructions

Genesis falls into two segments. The first, chapters 1 through 11, covers four major events. The second segment, chapters 12 through 50, covers the lives of four major characters. The instructions on how to study this book will be divided according to these two segments.

1. As you read chapter by chapter train yourself to ask the five W's and an H about the text: Who? What? When? Where? Why? and How? Ask questions such as: Who is speaking? What is happening? When is it happening? Where will it happen? Why was this said or done and what were the consequences? How did it happen? How was it to be done? etc.

2. Mark in a distinctive way any repeated words or phrases which are key to understanding the content of the chapter. There are several key words you should look for throughout the book of Genesis. These are listed on the GENESIS AT A GLANCE chart on page 90. Write these on an index card and use it as a bookmark while you study Genesis. (Instructions on how to mark key words and observe the text are in the introduction of this Bible. If you haven't read them, do so before you proceed any further.)

3. The timing of events can be very important. When you see a time phrase, draw in the margin an appropriate symbol in a color of your choice so you will be able to see it immediately.

4. In the margin, summarize the main things which occur in the chapter. List them in the order in which they occur. You may want to number them. For example, in Genesis 1 you could summarize what happens on each of the six days of creation.

5. As you study you will gain insights into God's character and ways. As you read each chapter, in the margin note what you learn about God. You may want to put a distinguishing mark such as this △ in the margin and then color it yellow so you can easily recognize it. Then list your insights under this symbol for God.

6. Look for the theme (subject) of each chapter. Record it on GENESIS AT A GLANCE. Also record the theme on the line next to the chapter number in the text.

7. Genesis is often referred to as the book of beginnings; it is the seedbed of truth. This is because the Word of God is a progressive revelation. *Progressive revelation* means that truth is unveiled over a period of time throughout various books of the Bible. God doesn't say everything he has to say about a particular subject at one time or in one place. Rather he will introduce a truth and then progressively reveal more and more about it.

Since Genesis is the book of beginnings, when you come to the "first" of anything, record it in the chapter margin in a special way or color so you can spot it easily. For example, next to Genesis 1:26, 27 you could write: "First man and woman."

Chapters 1-11

1. Genesis 1, 2

    a. In the margin note what is created on each day.

    b. Notice when a day begins and ends.

GENESIS

    c. Chapter 2 gives a more detailed explanation of the creation of man: male and female. Note the order of events and the man's relationship and responsibilities to God and to the woman.

  2. Genesis 3-5

    a. In the margin of chapter 3 list all you learn about the serpent and his tactics: how he tempts Eve, what he says. Then note what happens to Satan because he deceives Eve.

    b. Note Eve's progression into sin. List what happens before and after she sins.

    c. Watch what happens to Adam and Eve's relationship with God. Note the consequence of Adam's disobedience.

    d. In chapters 3 through 5 note the consequences of sin's entrance into the world. Record your insights in the chapter margins.

  3. Genesis 6-9

    a. As you study these chapters observe the reasons for the flood, how and when it came, who was affected and how.

    b. Watch the timing of events. Mark time phrases with an appropriate symbol or record these in the margin; e.g., "Rains forty days and nights."

    c. Mark the word *covenant* and list all you learn from the text about covenant.

  4. Genesis 10, 11

    a. Observe who was separated and why, how they were separated, when and where this occurred, and what happened as a result. Look at THE SETTLEMENT OF THE DESCENDANTS OF SHEM, HAM, AND JAPHETH on page 2306.

    b. Babylon plays an intermittently prominent role throughout the Bible, and of course its roots are in Genesis. Therefore whenever you come to any mention of Babel or Babylon you need to record what you learn on WHAT THE BIBLE TEACHES ABOUT BABYLON, a chart beginning on page 2176. When you record your observations on Babylon note the book, chapter, and verse for future reference.

  5. When you finish reading Genesis 11, look at GENESIS AT A GLANCE. Next to "Chapter Themes" you will find a place for segment divisions. Fill in the four main events covered in Genesis 1 through 11. The chapter divisions are noted on the chart.

Chapters 12-50

  1. Genesis 12 through 50 covers the biographical segment of Genesis, which focuses on the lives of four main characters: Abraham, Isaac, Jacob (also called Israel), and Joseph. When you read:

    a. Follow the "General Instructions" for studying each chapter (see page 1).

    b. Watch for and mark every reference to time in the life of each of the major characters (including their wives and children) in these chapters. God will often tell how old the person was when certain events occurred in his or her life.

    c. The word *covenant (treaty)* is more prominent in this last segment. Mark each occurrence of the word and then in the margin list everything you learn about covenant (treaty) from observing the text.

    d. In the chapter margins note any insights or lessons you learned from the way these people lived. Note how and why God deals with these men, their families, and their associates, and what happens as a result.

  2. Watch when the focus of a chapter moves from Abraham to Isaac, then to Jacob, and then to Joseph. Then on GENESIS AT A GLANCE, on the line where you recorded the four major events

of Genesis 1 through 11, divide the chapters into segments that cover the lives of Abraham, Isaac, Jacob, and Joseph. Look at the chapter themes to see where the focus moves from one of these men to the other.

3. When you finish reading Genesis 50, record on GENESIS AT A GLANCE the theme of Genesis. Under Segment Divisions, record the "firsts" that you marked throughout Genesis. (There is a blank line for any other segment divisions you might want to note.)

∾ THINGS TO THINK ABOUT

1. What have you learned from the lives of those mentioned in Genesis—from Adam and Eve through Joseph? Remember that the things which were written in the Old Testament were written to teach us, that through endurance and the encouragement of Scripture we might have hope (Romans 15:4). What are the blessings of obedience and the consequences of disobedience?

2. What have you learned about God—his character, his attributes, and the ways he moves in the lives of men and nations? Since God never changes, can you trust him? Can you rely on what the Word of God reveals about him even though you may not fully understand his ways?

3. Jesus took the book of Genesis at face value. As you study the Gospels you will see that Jesus referred to the creation of Adam and Eve, to the flood, and to the destruction of Sodom and Gomorrah. He even referred to Satan as a murderer from the beginning. Jesus never contradicted the teachings of Genesis; he only affirmed them. Are you going to take God's Word at face value and believe as Jesus did, or are you going to listen to the philosophies of men? Are you going to follow men with finite minds who critique God and his Word, or are you going to accept the Bible as the Word of God and then think and live accordingly?

ᔕᔕᔕᔕ

Chapter 1 Theme _____

1:1
a Jn 1:1-2
b Ps 90:2;
Isa 42:5;
Ac 17:24;
Heb 11:3;
Rev 4:11

1:2
c Jer 4:23
d Ps 104:30

1:3
e Ps 33:6,9
f 2Co 4:6*

1:5
g Ps 74:16

1:6
h Jer 10:12

1:7
i Job 38:8-11,16;
Ps 148:4

1:9
j Job 38:8-11;
Ps 104:6-9;
Pr 8:29;
Jer 5:22;
2Pe 3:5

1 In the beginning*a* God created the heavens and the earth.*b* ²Now the earth was*a* formless and empty,*c* darkness was over the surface of the deep, and the Spirit of God*d* was hovering over the waters.

³And God said,*e* "Let there be light," and there was light.*f* ⁴God saw that the light was good, and he separated the light from the darkness. ⁵God called the light "day," and the darkness he called "night."*g* And there was evening, and there was morning—the first day.

⁶And God said, "Let there be an expanse*h* between the waters to separate water from water." ⁷So God made the expanse and separated the water under the expanse from the water above it.*i* And it was so. ⁸God called the expanse "sky." And there was evening, and there was morning—the second day.

⁹And God said, "Let the water under the sky be gathered to one place,*j* and let dry ground appear." And it was so. ¹⁰God called the dry ground "land," and the gathered waters he called "seas." And God saw that it was good.

a 2 Or possibly *became*

INSIGHT

The first five books of the Bible—Genesis, Exodus, Leviticus, Numbers, and Deuteronomy—are referred to as the *Torah* or the *Pentateuch*. *Torah*, a term used by the Jews, refers to the law or the teaching. *Pentateuch*, a word coined about A.D. 200, means "the five scrolls" or the "five-volume book."

¹¹Then God said, "Let the land produce vegetation:ᵃ seed-bearing plants and trees on the land that bear fruit with seed in it, according to their various kinds." And it was so. ¹²The land produced vegetation: plants bearing seed according to their kinds and trees bearing fruit with seed in it according to their kinds. And God saw that it was good. ¹³And there was evening, and there was morning—the third day.

¹⁴And God said, "Let there be lightsᵇ in the expanse of the sky to separate the day from the night, and let them serve as signsᶜ to mark seasonsᵈ and days and years, ¹⁵and let them be lights in the expanse of the sky to give light on the earth." And it was so. ¹⁶God made two great lights—the greater light to governᵉ the day and the lesser light to governᶠ the night. He also made the stars.ᵍ ¹⁷God set them in the expanse of the sky to give light on the earth, ¹⁸to govern the day and the night,ʰ and to separate light from darkness. And God saw that it was good. ¹⁹And there was evening, and there was morning—the fourth day.

²⁰And God said, "Let the water teem with living creatures, and let birds fly above the earth across the expanse of the sky." ²¹So God created the great creatures of the sea and every living and moving thing with which the water teems,ⁱ according to their kinds, and every winged bird according to its kind. And God saw that it was good. ²²God blessed them and said, "Be fruitful and increase in number and fill the water in the seas, and let the birds increase on the earth."ʲ ²³And there was evening, and there was morning—the fifth day.

²⁴And God said, "Let the land produce living creatures according to their kinds: livestock, creatures that move along the ground, and wild animals, each according to its kind." And it was so. ²⁵God made the wild animalsᵏ according to their kinds, the livestock according to their kinds, and all the creatures that move along the ground according to their kinds. And God saw that it was good.

²⁶Then God said, "Let usˡ make man in our image,ᵐ in our likeness, and let them ruleⁿ over the fish of the sea and the birds of the air, over the livestock, over all the earth,ᵃ and over all the creatures that move along the ground."

²⁷So God created man in his own image,ᵒ
  in the image of God he created him;
  male and female ᵖ he created them.

²⁸God blessed them and said to them, "Be fruitful and increase in number; fill the earth�q and subdue it. Rule over

ᵃ 26 Hebrew; Syriac *all the wild animals*

1:11 ᵃPs 65:9-13; 104:14

1:14 ᵇPs 74:16; ᶜJer 10:2; ᵈPs 104:19

1:16 ᵉPs 136:8; ᶠPs 136:9; ᵍJob 38:7, 31-32; Ps 8:3; Isa 40:26

1:18 ʰJer 33:20,25

1:21 ⁱPs 104:25-26

1:22 ʲver 28; Ge 8:17

1:25 ᵏJer 27:5

1:26 ˡPs 100:3; ᵐGe 9:6; Jas 3:9; ⁿPs 8:6-8

1:27 ᵒ1Co 11:7; ᵖGe 5:2; Mt 19:4*; Mk 10:6*

1:28 qGe 9:1,7; Lev 26:9

the fish of the sea and the birds of the air and over every living creature that moves on the ground."

²⁹Then God said, "I give you every seed-bearing plant on the face of the whole earth and every tree that has fruit with seed in it. They will be yours for food.^a ³⁰And to all the beasts of the earth and all the birds of the air and all the creatures that move on the ground—everything that has the breath of life in it—I give every green plant for food.^b" And it was so.

³¹God saw all that he had made,^c and it was very good.^d And there was evening, and there was morning—the sixth day.

Chapter 2 Theme

2 Thus the heavens and the earth were completed in all their vast array.

²By the seventh day God had finished the work he had been doing; so on the seventh day he rested^a from all his work.^e ³And God blessed the seventh day and made it holy,^f because on it he rested from all the work of creating that he had done.

The Garden of Eden

⁴This is the account of the heavens and the earth when they were created.

When the LORD God made the earth and the heavens— ⁵and no shrub of the field had yet appeared on the earth^b and no plant of the field had yet sprung up,^g for the LORD God had not sent rain on the earth^{b h} and there was no man to work the ground, ⁶but streams^c came up from the earth and watered the

1:29
^aPs 104:14

1:30
^bPs 104:14,27;
145:15

1:31
^cPs 104:24
^d1Ti 4:4

2:2
^eEx 20:11;
31:17;
Heb 4:4*

2:3
^fLev 23:3;
Isa 58:13

2:5
^gGe 1:11
^hPs 65:9-10

^a2 Or *ceased*; also in verse 3   ^b5 Or *land*; also in verse 6   ^c6 Or *mist*

whole surface of the ground— [7]the LORD God formed the man[a] from the dust[a] of the ground[b] and breathed into his nostrils the breath[c] of life,[d] and the man became a living being.[e]

[8]Now the LORD God had planted a garden in the east, in Eden;[f] and there he put the man he had formed. [9]And the LORD God made all kinds of trees grow out of the ground—trees that were pleasing to the eye and good for food. In the middle of the garden were the tree of life[g] and the tree of the knowledge of good and evil.[h]

[10]A river watering the garden flowed from Eden; from there it was separated into four headwaters. [11]The name of the first is the Pishon; it winds through the entire land of Havilah, where there is gold. [12](The gold of that land is good; aromatic resin[b] and onyx are also there.) [13]The name of the second river is the Gihon; it winds through the entire land of Cush.[c] [14]The name of the third river is the Tigris;[i] it runs along the east side of Asshur. And the fourth river is the Euphrates.

[15]The LORD God took the man and put him in the Garden of Eden to work it and take care of it. [16]And the LORD God commanded the man, "You are free to eat from any tree in the garden; [17]but you must not eat from the tree of the knowledge of good and evil, for when you eat of it you will surely die."[j]

[18]The LORD God said, "It is not good for the man to be alone. I will make a helper suitable for him."[k]

[19]Now the LORD God had formed out of the ground all the beasts of the field[l] and all the birds of the air. He brought them to the man to see what he would name them; and whatever the man called each living creature,[m] that was its name. [20]So the man gave names to all the livestock, the birds of the air and all the beasts of the field.

But for Adam[d] no suitable helper was found. [21]So the LORD God caused the man to fall into a deep sleep; and while he was sleeping, he took one of the man's ribs[e] and closed up the place with flesh. [22]Then the LORD God made a woman from the rib[f][n] he had taken out of the man, and he brought her to the man.

[23]The man said,

> "This is now bone of my bones
>   and flesh of my flesh;[o]
> she shall be called 'woman,[g]'
>   for she was taken out of man."

[24]For this reason a man will leave his father and mother and be united[p] to his wife, and they will become one flesh.[q]

---

[a]7 The Hebrew for *man* (adam) sounds like and may be related to the Hebrew for *ground* (adamah); it is also the name *Adam* (see Gen. 2:20). [b]12 Or *good; pearls* [c]13 Possibly southeast Mesopotamia [d]20 Or *the man* [e]21 Or *took part of the man's side* [f]22 Or *part* [g]23 The Hebrew for *woman* sounds like the Hebrew for *man*.

2:7
[a]Ge 3:19
[b]Ps 103:14
[c]Job 33:4
[d]Ac 17:25
[e]1Co 15:45*

2:8
[f]Ge 3:23,24;
Isa 51:3

2:9
[g]Ge 3:22,24;
Rev 2:7;
22:2,14,19
[h]Eze 47:12

2:14
[i]Da 10:4

2:17
[j]Dt 30:15,19;
Ro 5:12; 6:23;
Jas 1:15

2:18
[k]1Co 11:9

2:19
[l]Ps 8:7
[m]Ge 1:24

2:22
[n]1Co 11:8,9,12

2:23
[o]Ge 29:14;
Eph 5:28-30

2:24
[p]Mal 2:15
[q]Mt 19:5*;
Mk 10:7-8*;
1Co 6:16*;
Eph 5:31*

he will crush[a] your head,[a]
and you will strike his heel."

3:15
[a] Ro 16:20;
Heb 2:14

¹⁶To the woman he said,

"I will greatly increase your pains in childbearing;
with pain you will give birth to children.
Your desire will be for your husband,
and he will rule over you.[b]"

3:16
[b] 1Co 11:3;
Eph 5:22

¹⁷To Adam he said, "Because you listened to your wife and ate from the tree about which I commanded you, 'You must not eat of it,'

3:17
[c] Ge 5:29;
Ro 8:20-22
[d] Job 5:7; 14:1;
Ecc 2:23

"Cursed[c] is the ground because of you;
through painful toil you will eat of it
all the days of your life.[d]
¹⁸It will produce thorns and thistles for you,
and you will eat the plants of the field.[e]

3:18
[e] Ps 104:14

¹⁹By the sweat of your brow
you will eat your food[f]
until you return to the ground,
since from it you were taken;
for dust you are
and to dust you will return."[g]

3:19
[f] 2Th 3:10
[g] Ge 2:7;
Ps 90:3;
104:29;
Ecc 12:7

²⁰Adam[b] named his wife Eve,[c] because she would become the mother of all the living. ²¹The LORD God made garments of skin for Adam and his wife and clothed them. ²²And the LORD God said, "The man has now become like one of us, knowing good and evil. He must not be allowed to reach out his hand and take also from the tree of life[h] and eat, and live forever." ²³So the LORD God banished him from the Garden of Eden[i] to work the ground[j] from which he had been taken. ²⁴After he drove the man out, he placed on the east side[d] of the Garden of Eden cherubim[k] and a flaming sword[l] flashing back and forth to guard the way to the tree of life.[m]

3:22
[h] Rev 22:14

3:23
[i] Ge 2:8
[j] Ge 4:2

3:24
[k] Ex 25:18-22
[l] Ps 104:4
[m] Ge 2:9

Chapter 4 Theme _____

4 Adam[b] lay with his wife Eve, and she became pregnant and gave birth to Cain.[e] She said, "With the help of the LORD I have brought forth[f] a man." ²Later she gave birth to his brother Abel.[n]

Now Abel kept flocks, and Cain worked the soil. ³In the course of time Cain brought some of the fruits of the soil as an offering to the LORD.[o] ⁴But Abel brought fat portions[p] from some of the

4:2
[n] Lk 11:51

4:3
[o] Nu 18:12

[a] 15 Or *strike*   [b] 20, 1 Or *The man*   [c] 20 *Eve* probably means *living.*   [d] 24 Or *placed in front*   [e] 1 *Cain* sounds like the Hebrew for *brought forth* or *acquired.*   [f] 1 Or *have acquired*

4:4
[p] Lev 3:16

4:4
*a*Ex 13:2,12
*b*Heb 11:4
firstborn of his flock.*a* The LORD looked with favor on Abel and his offering,*b* 5but on Cain and his offering he did not look with favor. So Cain was very angry, and his face was downcast.

4:7
*c*Nu 32:23
*d*Ro 6:16
6Then the LORD said to Cain, "Why are you angry? Why is your face downcast? 7If you do what is right, will you not be accepted? But if you do not do what is right, sin is crouching at your door;*c* it desires to have you, but you must master it.*d*"

8Now Cain said to his brother Abel, "Let's go out to the field."*a* And while they were in the field, Cain attacked his brother Abel and killed him.*e*

9Then the LORD said to Cain, "Where is your brother Abel?"

"I don't know," he replied. "Am I my brother's keeper?"

4:8
*e*Mt 23:35;
1Jn 3:12
10The LORD said, "What have you done? Listen! Your brother's blood cries out to me from the ground.*f* 11Now you are under a curse and driven from the ground, which opened its mouth to receive your brother's blood from your hand. 12When you work the ground, it will no longer yield its crops for you. You will be a restless wanderer on the earth."

4:10
*f*Ge 9:5;
Nu 35:33;
Heb 12:24;
Rev 6:9-10
13Cain said to the LORD, "My punishment is more than I can bear. 14Today you are driving me from the land, and I will be hidden from your presence;*g* I will be a restless wanderer on the earth, and whoever finds me will kill me."*h*

15But the LORD said to him, "Not so*b*; if anyone kills Cain,*i* he will suffer vengeance seven times over.*j*" Then the LORD put a mark on Cain so that no one who found him would kill him. 16So Cain went out from the LORD's presence and lived in the land of Nod,*c* east of Eden.*k*

4:14
*g*2Ki 17:18;
Ps 51:11;
139:7-12;
Jer 7:15; 52:3
*h*Ge 9:6;
Nu 35:19,
21,27,33
17Cain lay with his wife, and she became pregnant and gave birth to Enoch. Cain was then building a city, and he named it after his son*l* Enoch. 18To Enoch was born Irad, and Irad was the father of Mehujael, and Mehujael was the father of Methushael, and Methushael was the father of Lamech.

4:15
*i*Eze 9:4,6
*j*ver 24;
Ps 79:12
19Lamech married two women, one named Adah and the other Zillah. 20Adah gave birth to Jabal; he was the father of those who live in tents and raise livestock. 21His brother's name was Jubal; he was the father of all who play the harp and flute. 22Zillah also had a son, Tubal-Cain, who forged all kinds of tools out of*d* bronze and iron. Tubal-Cain's sister was Naamah.

4:16
*k*Ge 2:8
23Lamech said to his wives,

"Adah and Zillah, listen to me;
wives of Lamech, hear my words.

4:17
*l*Ps 49:11
a 8 Samaritan Pentateuch, Septuagint, Vulgate and Syriac; Masoretic Text does not have *"Let's go out to the field."* *b 15* Septuagint, Vulgate and Syriac; Hebrew *Very well* *c 16* Nod *means* wandering *(see verses 12 and 14).* *d 22* Or *who instructed all who work in*

I have killed[aa] a man for wounding me,
    a young man for injuring me.
[24]If Cain is avenged[b] seven times,[c]
    then Lamech seventy-seven times."

[25]Adam lay with his wife again, and she gave birth to a son and named him Seth,[bd] saying, "God has granted me another child in place of Abel, since Cain killed him."[e] [26]Seth also had a son, and he named him Enosh.

At that time men began to call on[c] the name of the LORD.[f]

Chapter 5 Theme

5
This is the written account of Adam's line.

When God created man, he made him in the likeness of God.[g] [2]He created them male and female[h] and blessed them. And when they were created, he called them "man.[d]"

[3]When Adam had lived 130 years, he had a son in his own likeness, in his own image;[i] and he named him Seth. [4]After Seth was born, Adam lived 800 years and had other sons and daughters. [5]Altogether, Adam lived 930 years, and then he died.[j]

[6]When Seth had lived 105 years, he became the father[e] of Enosh. [7]And after he became the father of Enosh, Seth lived 807 years and had other sons and daughters. [8]Altogether, Seth lived 912 years, and then he died.

[9]When Enosh had lived 90 years, he became the father of Kenan. [10]And after he became the father of Kenan, Enosh lived 815 years and had other sons and daughters. [11]Altogether, Enosh lived 905 years, and then he died.

[12]When Kenan had lived 70 years, he became the father of Mahalalel. [13]And after he became the father of Mahalalel, Kenan lived 840 years and had other sons and daughters. [14]Altogether, Kenan lived 910 years, and then he died.

[15]When Mahalalel had lived 65 years, he became the father of Jared. [16]And after he became the father of Jared, Mahalalel lived 830 years and had other sons and daughters. [17]Altogether, Mahalalel lived 895 years, and then he died.

[18]When Jared had lived 162 years, he became the father of Enoch.[k] [19]And after he became the father of Enoch, Jared lived 800 years and had other sons and daughters. [20]Altogether, Jared lived 962 years, and then he died.

[21]When Enoch had lived 65 years, he became the father of Methuselah. [22]And after he became the father of Methuselah, Enoch walked with God[l] 300 years and had other sons and

### Cross references (margin)

4:23 [a]Ex 20:13; Lev 19:18

4:24 [b]Dt 32:35 [c]ver 15

4:25 [d]Ge 5:3 [e]ver 8

4:26 [f]Ge 12:8; 1Ki 18:24; Ps 116:17; Joel 2:32; Zep 3:9; Ac 2:21; 1Co 1:2

5:1 [g]Ge 1:27; Eph 4:24; Col 3:10

5:2 [h]Ge 1:27; Mt 19:4; Mk 10:6; Gal 3:28

5:3 [i]Ge 1:26; 1Co 15:49

5:5 [j]Ge 3:19

5:18 [k]Jude 14

5:22 [l]ver 24; Ge 6:9; 17:1; 48:15; Mic 6:8; Mal 2:6

---

[a]23 Or *I will kill*   [b]25 *Seth* probably means *granted.*   [c]26 Or *to proclaim*   [d]2 Hebrew *adam*   [e]6 *Father* may mean *ancestor*; also in verses 7-26.

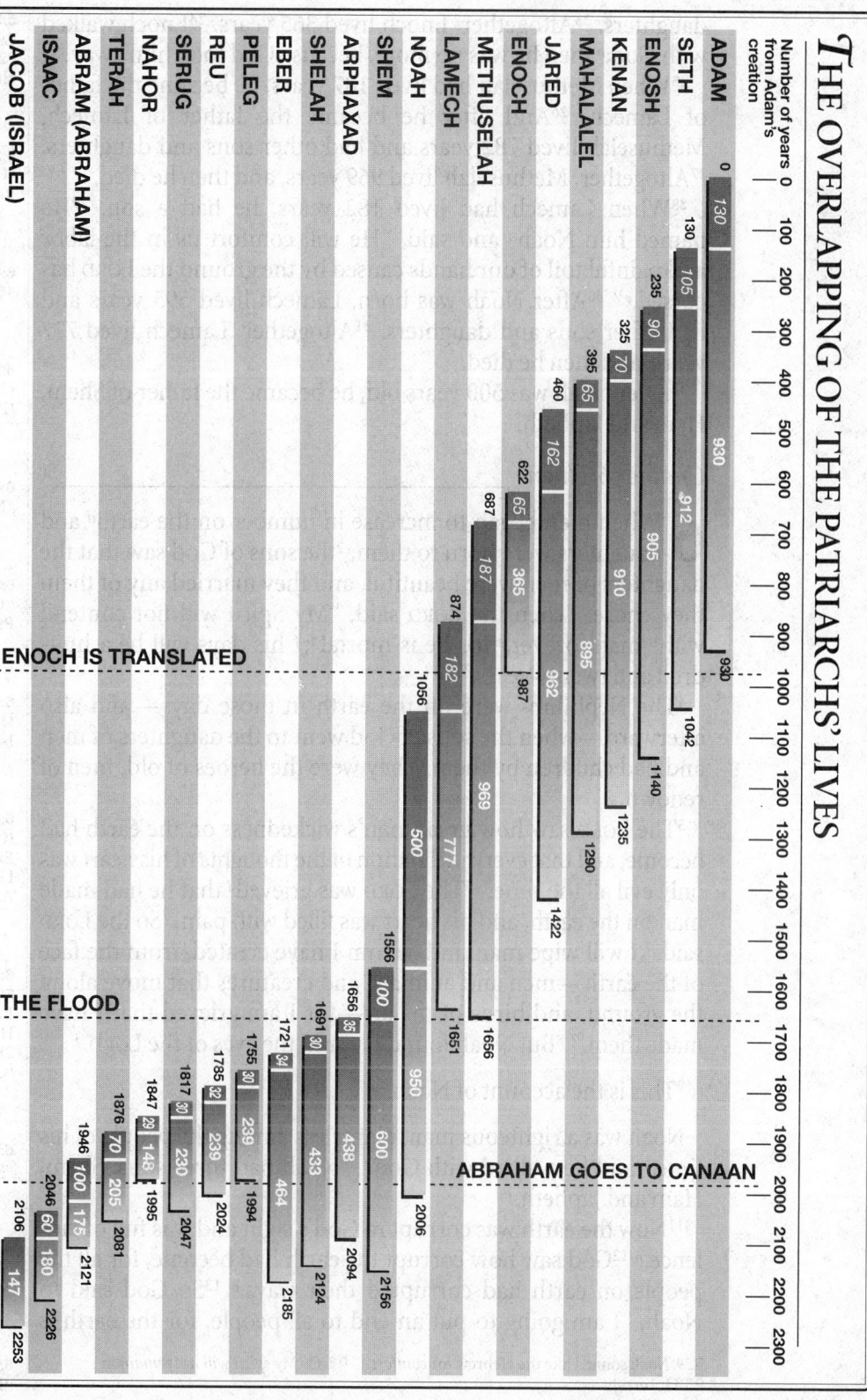

THE OVERLAPPING OF THE PATRIARCHS' LIVES

Number of years from Adam's creation

| 0 | 100 | 200 | 300 | 400 | 500 | 600 | 700 | 800 | 900 | 1000 | 1100 | 1200 | 1300 | 1400 | 1500 | 1600 | 1700 | 1800 | 1900 | 2000 | 2100 | 2200 | 2300 |

ADAM 0 930 930
SETH 130 105 912 1042
ENOSH 235 90 905 1140
KENAN 325 70 910 1235
MAHALALEL 395 65 895 1290
JARED 460 162 962 1422

ENOCH IS TRANSLATED

ENOCH 622 65 365 987
METHUSELAH 687 187 969 1656
LAMECH 874 182 777 1651
NOAH 1056 500 950 2006

THE FLOOD

SHEM 1556 100 600 2156
ARPHAXAD 1656 35 438 2094
SHELAH 1691 30 433 2124
EBER 1721 34 464 2185
PELEG 1755 30 239 1994
REU 1785 32 239 2024
SERUG 1817 30 230 2047
NAHOR 1847 29 148 1995
TERAH 1876 70 205 2081

ABRAHAM GOES TO CANAAN

ABRAM (ABRAHAM) 1946 100 175 2121
ISAAC 2046 60 180 2226
JACOB (ISRAEL) 2106 147 2253

KEY: The first number inside the block is the man's age when his son (whose name is in the next line below) was born. The second number in the block is the number of years the man lived. The numbers preceding and following each block are the number of years from Adam's creation. The years on this chart begin with Adam's creation and are *not* calendar years.

daughters. ²³Altogether, Enoch lived 365 years. ²⁴Enoch walked with God;ᵃ then he was no more, because God took him away.ᵇ

²⁵When Methuselah had lived 187 years, he became the father of Lamech. ²⁶And after he became the father of Lamech, Methuselah lived 782 years and had other sons and daughters. ²⁷Altogether, Methuselah lived 969 years, and then he died.

²⁸When Lamech had lived 182 years, he had a son. ²⁹He named him Noahᵃ and said, "He will comfort us in the labor and painful toil of our hands caused by the ground the LORD has cursed.ᶜ" ³⁰After Noah was born, Lamech lived 595 years and had other sons and daughters. ³¹Altogether, Lamech lived 777 years, and then he died.

³²After Noah was 500 years old, he became the father of Shem, Ham and Japheth.

Chapter 6 Theme

6 When men began to increase in number on the earthᵈ and daughters were born to them, ²the sons of God saw that the daughters of men were beautiful, and they married any of them they chose. ³Then the LORD said, "My Spirit will not contend withᵇ man forever,ᵉ for he is mortalᶜ;ᶠ his days will be a hundred and twenty years."

⁴The Nephilimᵍ were on the earth in those days—and also afterward—when the sons of God went to the daughters of men and had children by them. They were the heroes of old, men of renown.

⁵The LORD saw how great man's wickedness on the earth had become, and that every inclination of the thoughts of his heart was only evil all the time.ʰ ⁶The LORD was grievedⁱ that he had made man on the earth, and his heart was filled with pain. ⁷So the LORD said, "I will wipe mankind, whom I have created, from the face of the earth—men and animals, and creatures that move along the ground, and birds of the air—for I am grieved that I have made them." ⁸But Noah found favor in the eyes of the LORD.ʲ

⁹This is the account of Noah.

Noah was a righteous man, blameless among the people of his time,ᵏ and he walked with God.ˡ ¹⁰Noah had three sons: Shem, Ham and Japheth.ᵐ

¹¹Now the earth was corrupt in God's sight and was full of violence.ⁿ ¹²God saw how corrupt the earth had become, for all the people on earth had corrupted their ways.ᵒ ¹³So God said to Noah, "I am going to put an end to all people, for the earth is

---

ᵃ29 *Noah* sounds like the Hebrew for *comfort.* ᵇ3 Or *My spirit will not remain in*
ᶜ3 Or *corrupt*

5:24
ᵃver 22
ᵇ2Ki 2:1,11;
Heb 11:5

5:29
ᶜGe 3:17;
Ro 8:20

6:1
ᵈGe 1:28

6:3
ᵉIsa 57:16
ᶠPs 78:39

6:4
ᵍNu 13:33

6:5
ʰGe 8:21;
Ps 14:1-3

6:6
ⁱ1Sa 15:11,35;
Isa 63:10

6:8
ʲGe 19:19;
Ex 33:12,13,17;
Lk 1:30;
Ac 7:46

6:9
ᵏGe 7:1;
Eze 14:14,20;
Heb 11:7;
2Pe 2:5
ˡGe 5:22

6:10
ᵐGe 5:32

6:11
ⁿEze 7:23;
8:17

6:12
ᵒPs 14:1-3

filled with violence because of them. I am surely going to destroy both them and the earth.[a] [14]So make yourself an ark of cypress[a] wood;[b] make rooms in it and coat it with pitch[c] inside and out. [15]This is how you are to build it: The ark is to be 450 feet long, 75 feet wide and 45 feet high.[b] [16]Make a roof for it and finish[c] the ark to within 18 inches[d] of the top. Put a door in the side of the ark and make lower, middle and upper decks. [17]I am going to bring floodwaters on the earth to destroy all life under the heavens, every creature that has the breath of life in it. Everything on earth will perish.[d] [18]But I will establish my covenant with you,[e] and you will enter the ark[f]—you and your sons and your wife and your sons' wives with you. [19]You are to bring into the ark two of all living creatures, male and female, to keep them alive with you. [20]Two[g] of every kind of bird, of every kind of animal and of every kind of creature that moves along the ground will come to you to be kept alive. [21]You are to take every kind of food that is to be eaten and store it away as food for you and for them."

[22]Noah did everything just as God commanded him.[h]

Chapter 7 Theme

7 The Lord then said to Noah, "Go into the ark, you and your whole family,[i] because I have found you righteous[j] in this generation. [2]Take with you seven[k] of every kind of clean[e] animal, a male and its mate, and two of every kind of unclean animal, a male and its mate, [3]and also seven of every kind of bird, male and female, to keep their various kinds alive throughout the earth. [4]Seven days from now I will send rain on the earth for forty days and forty nights, and I will wipe from the face of the earth every living creature I have made."

[5]And Noah did all that the LORD commanded him.[l]

[6]Noah was six hundred years old when the floodwaters came on the earth. [7]And Noah and his sons and his wife and his sons' wives entered the ark to escape the waters of the flood. [8]Pairs of clean and unclean animals, of birds and of all creatures that move along the ground, [9]male and female, came to Noah and entered the ark, as God had commanded Noah. [10]And after the seven days the floodwaters came on the earth.

[11]In the six hundredth year of Noah's life, on the seventeenth day of the second month—on that day all the springs of the great deep[m] burst forth, and the floodgates of the heavens[n] were opened. [12]And rain fell on the earth forty days and forty nights.[o]

6:13
[a] ver 17;
Eze 7:2-3

6:14
[b] Heb 11:7;
1Pe 3:20
[c] Ex 2:3

6:17
[d] Ge 7:4,21-23;
2Pe 2:5

6:18
[e] Ge 9:9-16
[f] Ge 7:1,7,13

6:20
[g] Ge 7:15

6:22
[h] Ge 7:5,9,16

7:1
[i] Mt 24:38
[j] Ge 6:9;
Eze 14:14

7:2
[k] ver 8;
Ge 8:20;
Lev 10:10;
11:1-47

7:5
[l] Ge 6:22

7:11
[m] Eze 26:19
[n] Ge 8:2

7:12
[o] ver 4

a 14 The meaning of the Hebrew for this word is uncertain.   b 15 Hebrew *300 cubits long, 50 cubits wide and 30 cubits high* (about 140 meters long, 23 meters wide and 13.5 meters high)   c 16 Or *Make an opening for light by finishing*   d 16 Hebrew *a cubit* (about 0.5 meter)   e 2 Or *seven pairs*; also in verse 3

13

¹³On that very day Noah and his sons, Shem, Ham and Japheth, together with his wife and the wives of his three sons, entered the ark. ¹⁴They had with them every wild animal according to its kind, all livestock according to their kinds, every creature that moves along the ground according to its kind and every bird according to its kind, everything with wings. ¹⁵Pairs of all creatures that have the breath of life in them came to Noah and entered the ark.^a ¹⁶The animals going in were male and female of every living thing, as God had commanded Noah. Then the LORD shut him in.

¹⁷For forty days^b the flood kept coming on the earth, and as the waters increased they lifted the ark high above the earth. ¹⁸The waters rose and increased greatly on the earth, and the ark floated on the surface of the water. ¹⁹They rose greatly on the earth, and all the high mountains under the entire heavens were covered.^c ²⁰The waters rose and covered the mountains to a depth of more than twenty feet.^{a,b} ²¹Every living thing that moved on the earth perished—birds, livestock, wild animals, all the creatures that swarm over the earth, and all mankind.^d ²²Everything on dry land that had the breath of life^e in its nostrils died. ²³Every living thing on the face of the earth was wiped out; men and animals and the creatures that move along the ground and the birds of the air were wiped from the earth.^f Only Noah was left, and those with him in the ark.^g

²⁴The waters flooded the earth for a hundred and fifty days.^h

Chapter 8 Theme

8 But God rememberedⁱ Noah and all the wild animals and the livestock that were with him in the ark, and he sent a wind over the earth,^j and the waters receded. ²Now the springs of the deep and the floodgates of the heavens^k had been closed, and the rain had stopped falling from the sky. ³The water receded steadily from the earth. At the end of the hundred and fifty days the water had gone down, ⁴and on the seventeenth day of the seventh month the ark came to rest on the mountains of Ararat. ⁵The waters continued to recede until the tenth month, and on the first day of the tenth month the tops of the mountains became visible.

⁶After forty days Noah opened the window he had made in the ark ⁷and sent out a raven, and it kept flying back and forth until the water had dried up from the earth. ⁸Then he sent out a dove to see if the water had receded from the surface of the ground. ⁹But the dove could find no place to set its feet because there was water over all the surface of the earth; so it returned to

---

7:15
^aGe 6:19

7:17
^bver 4

7:19
^cPs 104:6

7:21
^dGe 6:7,13

7:22
^eGe 1:30

7:23
^fMt 24:39;
Lk 17:27;
1Pe 3:20;
2Pe 2:5
^gHeb 11:7

7:24
^hGe 8:3

8:1
ⁱGe 9:15;
19:29;
Ex 2:24;
1Sa 1:11,19
^jEx 14:21

8:2
^kGe 7:11

---

^a20 Hebrew *fifteen cubits* (about 6.9 meters)   ^b20 Or *rose more than twenty feet, and the mountains were covered*

8:16
a Ge 7:13

8:17
b Ge 1:22

8:20
c Ge 12:7-8;
13:18; 22:9
d Ge 7:8;
Lev 11:1-47
e Ge 22:2,13;
Ex 10:25

8:21
f Lev 1:9,13;
2Co 2:15
g Ge 3:17
h Ge 6:5;
Ps 51:5;
Jer 17:9
i Ge 9:11,15;
Isa 54:9

8:22
j Ge 1:14;
Jer 33:20,25

9:1
k Ge 1:22

9:3
l Ge 1:29

Noah in the ark. He reached out his hand and took the dove and brought it back to himself in the ark. ¹⁰He waited seven more days and again sent out the dove from the ark. ¹¹When the dove returned to him in the evening, there in its beak was a freshly plucked olive leaf! Then Noah knew that the water had receded from the earth. ¹²He waited seven more days and sent the dove out again, but this time it did not return to him.

¹³By the first day of the first month of Noah's six hundred and first year, the water had dried up from the earth. Noah then removed the covering from the ark and saw that the surface of the ground was dry. ¹⁴By the twenty-seventh day of the second month the earth was completely dry.

¹⁵Then God said to Noah, ¹⁶"Come out of the ark, you and your wife and your sons and their wives.*a* ¹⁷Bring out every kind of living creature that is with you—the birds, the animals, and all the creatures that move along the ground—so they can multiply on the earth and be fruitful and increase in number upon it."*b*

¹⁸So Noah came out, together with his sons and his wife and his sons' wives. ¹⁹All the animals and all the creatures that move along the ground and all the birds—everything that moves on the earth—came out of the ark, one kind after another.

²⁰Then Noah built an altar to the LORD*c* and, taking some of all the clean animals and clean*d* birds, he sacrificed burnt offerings*e* on it. ²¹The LORD smelled the pleasing aroma*f* and said in his heart: "Never again will I curse the ground*g* because of man, even though*a* every inclination of his heart is evil from childhood.*h* And never again will I destroy all living creatures,*i* as I have done.

²²"As long as the earth endures,
seedtime and harvest,
cold and heat,
summer and winter,
day and night
will never cease."*j*

Chapter 9 Theme _____

9 Then God blessed Noah and his sons, saying to them, "Be fruitful and increase in number and fill the earth.*k* ²The fear and dread of you will fall upon all the beasts of the earth and all the birds of the air, upon every creature that moves along the ground, and upon all the fish of the sea; they are given into your hands. ³Everything that lives and moves will be food for you.*l* Just as I gave you the green plants, I now give you everything.

a 21 Or *man, for*

4"But you must not eat meat that has its lifeblood still in it.*a*
5And for your lifeblood I will surely demand an accounting. I will
demand an accounting from every animal.*b* And from each man,
too, I will demand an accounting for the life of his fellow man.*c*

6"Whoever sheds the blood of man,
　　by man shall his blood be shed;*d*
　for in the image of God*e*
　　has God made man.

7As for you, be fruitful and increase in number; multiply on the
earth and increase upon it."*f*

8Then God said to Noah and to his sons with him: 9"I now
establish my covenant with you*g* and with your descendants
after you 10and with every living creature that was with you—
the birds, the livestock and all the wild animals, all those that
came out of the ark with you—every living creature on earth.
11I establish my covenant*h* with you: Never again will all life be
cut off by the waters of a flood; never again will there be a flood
to destroy the earth.*i*"

12And God said, "This is the sign of the covenant*j* I am making between me and you and every living creature with you, a
covenant for all generations to come: 13I have set my rainbow in
the clouds, and it will be the sign of the covenant between me
and the earth. 14Whenever I bring clouds over the earth and the
rainbow appears in the clouds, 15I will remember my covenant *k*
between me and you and all living creatures of every kind. Never again will the waters become a flood to destroy all life.
16Whenever the rainbow appears in the clouds, I will see it and
remember the everlasting covenant*l* between God and all living
creatures of every kind on the earth."

17So God said to Noah, "This is the sign of the covenant*m* I have
established between me and all life on the earth."

18The sons of Noah who came out of the ark were Shem, Ham
and Japheth. (Ham was the father of Canaan.)*n* 19These were
the three sons of Noah, and from them came the people who
were scattered over the earth.*o*

20Noah, a man of the soil, proceeded*a* to plant a vineyard.
21When he drank some of its wine, he became drunk and lay
uncovered inside his tent. 22Ham, the father of Canaan, saw his
father's nakedness and told his two brothers outside. 23But Shem
and Japheth took a garment and laid it across their shoulders;
then they walked in backward and covered their father's nakedness. Their faces were turned the other way so that they would
not see their father's nakedness.

a 20 Or soil, was the first

9:4
*a*Lev 3:17;
17:10-14;
Dt 12:16,
23-25;
1Sa 14:33

9:5
*b*Ex 21:28-32
*c*Ge 4:10

9:6
*d*Ge 4:14;
Ex 21:12,14;
Lev 24:17;
Mt 26:52
*e*Ge 1:26

9:7
*f*Ge 1:22

9:9
*g*Ge 6:18

9:11
*h*ver 16;
Isa 24:5
*i*Ge 8:21;
Isa 54:9

9:12
*j*ver 17;
Ge 17:11

9:15
*k*Ex 2:24;
Lev 26:42,45;
Dt 7:9;
Eze 16:60

9:16
*l*ver 11;
Ge 17:7,13,19;
2Sa 7:13; 23:5

9:17
*m*ver 12;
Ge 17:11

9:18
*n*ver 25-27;
Ge 10:6,15

9:19
*o*Ge 10:32

9:25
a ver 18
b Ge 25:23;
Jos 9:23

[24]When Noah awoke from his wine and found out what his youngest son had done to him, [25]he said,

"Cursed be Canaan!*a*
The lowest of slaves
will he be to his brothers.*b*"

[26]He also said,

10:1
c Ge 2:4

"Blessed be the LORD, the God of Shem!
May Canaan be the slave of Shem.ª
[27]May God extend the territory of Japheth*b*;
may Japheth live in the tents of Shem,
and may Canaan be his*c* slave."

10:2
d Eze 38:6
e Eze 38:2;
Rev 20:8
f Isa 66:19

[28]After the flood Noah lived 350 years. [29]Altogether, Noah lived 950 years, and then he died.

Chapter 10 Theme

10 This is the account*c* of Shem, Ham and Japheth, Noah's sons, who themselves had sons after the flood.
[2]The sons*d* of Japheth:
Gomer,*d* Magog,*e* Madai, Javan, Tubal,*f* Meshech and Tiras.

10:3
g Jer 51:27
h Eze 27:14;
38:6

[3]The sons of Gomer:
Ashkenaz,*g* Riphath and Togarmah.*h*
[4]The sons of Javan:
Elishah, Tarshish,*i* the Kittim and the Rodanim.*e* [5](From these the maritime peoples spread out into their territories by their clans within their nations, each with its own language.)

10:4
i Eze 27:12,25;
Jnh 1:3

[6]The sons of Ham:
Cush, Mizraim,*f* Put and Canaan.*j*
[7]The sons of Cush:
Seba, Havilah, Sabtah, Raamah and Sabteca.
The sons of Raamah:
Sheba and Dedan.

10:6
j ver 15;
Ge 9:18

[8]Cush was the father*g* of Nimrod, who grew to be a mighty warrior on the earth. [9]He was a mighty hunter before the LORD; that is why it is said, "Like Nimrod, a mighty hunter before the LORD." [10]The first centers of his kingdom were Babylon,*k* Erech,

INSIGHT

In order to see where the sons of Shem, Ham, and Japheth settled, refer to the map **The Settlement of the Descendants of Shem, Ham, and Japheth** on page 2306.

10:10
k Ge 11:9

ª 26 Or *be his slave*   *b* 27 *Japheth* sounds like the Hebrew for *extend.*   *c* 27 Or *their*
d 2 *Sons* may mean *descendants* or *successors* or *nations*; also in verses 3, 4, 6, 7, 20-23, 29 and 31.   *e* 4 Some manuscripts of the Masoretic Text and Samaritan Pentateuch (see also Septuagint and 1 Chron. 1:7); most manuscripts of the Masoretic Text *Dodanim*   *f* 6 That is, Egypt; also in verse 13   *g* 8 *Father* may mean *ancestor* or *predecessor* or *founder*; also in verses 13, 15, 24 and 26.

Akkad and Calneh, in[a] Shinar.[b][a] [11]From that land he went to Assyria,[b] where he built Nineveh,[c] Rehoboth Ir,[c] Calah [12]and Resen, which is between Nineveh and Calah; that is the great city.

[13]Mizraim was the father of
the Ludites, Anamites, Lehabites, Naphtuhites, [14]Pathrusites, Casluhites (from whom the Philistines [d] came) and Caphtorites.
[15]Canaan[e] was the father of
Sidon[f] his firstborn,[d] and of the Hittites,[g] [16]Jebusites,[h] Amorites, Girgashites, [17]Hivites, Arkites, Sinites, [18]Arvadites, Zemarites and Hamathites.

Later the Canaanite[i] clans scattered [19]and the borders of Canaan[j] reached from Sidon[k] toward Gerar as far as Gaza, and then toward Sodom, Gomorrah, Admah and Zeboiim, as far as Lasha. [20]These are the sons of Ham by their clans and languages, in their territories and nations.

[21]Sons were also born to Shem, whose older brother was[e] Japheth; Shem was the ancestor of all the sons of Eber.[l]

[22]The sons of Shem:
Elam,[m] Asshur, Arphaxad,[n] Lud and Aram.
[23]The sons of Aram:
Uz,[o] Hul, Gether and Meshech.[f]
[24]Arphaxad was the father of[g] Shelah,
and Shelah the father of Eber.[p]
[25]Two sons were born to Eber:
One was named Peleg,[h] because in his time the earth was divided; his brother was named Joktan.
[26]Joktan was the father of
Almodad, Sheleph, Hazarmaveth, Jerah, [27]Hadoram, Uzal, Diklah, [28]Obal, Abimael, Sheba, [29]Ophir, Havilah and Jobab. All these were sons of Joktan.

[30]The region where they lived stretched from Mesha toward Sephar, in the eastern hill country.
[31]These are the sons of Shem by their clans and languages, in their territories and nations.

[32]These are the clans of Noah's sons,[q] according to their lines of descent, within their nations. From these the nations spread out over the earth[r] after the flood.

a 10 Or Erech and Akkad—all of them in   b 10 That is, Babylonia   c 11 Or Nineveh with its city squares   d 15 Or of the Sidonians, the foremost   e 21 Or Shem, the older brother of   f 23 See Septuagint and 1 Chron. 1:17; Hebrew Mash   g 24 Hebrew; Septuagint father of Cainan, and Cainan was the father of   h 25 Peleg means division.

10:10 aGe 11:2
10:11 bPs 83:8; Mic 5:6 cJnh 1:2; 4:11; Na 1:1
10:14 dGe 21:32,34; 26:1,8
10:15 ever 6; Ge 9:18 fEze 28:21 gGe 23:3,20
10:16 h1Ch 11:4
10:18 iGe 12:6; Ex 13:11
10:19 jGe 11:31; 13:12; 17:8 kver 15
10:21 lver 24; Nu 24:24
10:22 mJer 49:34 nLk 3:36
10:23 oJob 1:1
10:24 pver 21
10:32 qver 1 rGe 9:19

11:2
a Ge 10:10

Chapter 11 Theme _____

11 Now the whole world had one language and a common speech. ²As men moved eastward,*a* they found a plain in Shinar*ᵇᵃ* and settled there.

11:3
b Ex 1:14
c Ge 14:10

³They said to each other, "Come, let's make bricks*ᵇ* and bake them thoroughly." They used brick instead of stone, and tar*ᶜ* for mortar. ⁴Then they said, "Come, let us build ourselves a city, with a tower that reaches to the heavens,*ᵈ* so that we may make a name*ᵉ* for ourselves and not be scattered over the face of the whole earth."*ᶠ*

11:4
d Dt 1:28; 9:1
e Ge 6:4
f Dt 4:27

⁵But the LORD came down*ᵍ* to see the city and the tower that the men were building. ⁶The LORD said, "If as one people speaking the same language they have begun to do this, then nothing they plan to do will be impossible for them. ⁷Come, let us*ʰ* go down and confuse their language so they will not understand each other."*ⁱ*

11:5
g ver 7;
Ge 18:21;
Ex 3:8;
19:11,18,20

⁸So the LORD scattered them from there over all the earth,*ʲ* and they stopped building the city. ⁹That is why it was called Babel*ᶜᵏ*—because there the LORD confused the language of the whole world. From there the LORD scattered them over the face of the whole earth.

¹⁰This is the account of Shem.

11:7
h Ge 1:26
i Ge 42:23

Two years after the flood, when Shem was 100 years old, he became the father*ᵈ* of Arphaxad. ¹¹And after he became the father of Arphaxad, Shem lived 500 years and had other sons and daughters.

¹²When Arphaxad had lived 35 years, he became the father of Shelah.*ˡ* ¹³And after he became the father of Shelah, Arphaxad lived 403 years and had other sons and daughters.*ᵉ*

¹⁴When Shelah had lived 30 years, he became the father of Eber. ¹⁵And after he became the father of Eber, Shelah lived 403 years and had other sons and daughters.

11:8
j Ge 9:19;
Lk 1:51

¹⁶When Eber had lived 34 years, he became the father of Peleg. ¹⁷And after he became the father of Peleg, Eber lived 430 years and had other sons and daughters.

¹⁸When Peleg had lived 30 years, he became the father of Reu. ¹⁹And after he became the father of Reu, Peleg lived 209 years and had other sons and daughters.

11:9
k Ge 10:10

a 2 Or *from the east;* or *in the east*   *b 2* That is, Babylonia   *c 9* That is, Babylon; *Babel* sounds like the Hebrew for *confused.*   *d 10* Father may mean *ancestor;* also in verses 11-25. *e 12,13* Hebrew; Septuagint (see also Luke 3:35, 36 and note at Gen. 10:24) *35 years, he became the father of Cainan.* ¹³*And after he became the father of Cainan, Arphaxad lived 430 years and had other sons and daughters, and then he died. When Cainan had lived 130 years, he became the father of Shelah. And after he became the father of Shelah, Cainan lived 330 years and had other sons and daughters*

11:12
l Lk 3:35

²⁰When Reu had lived 32 years, he became the father of Serug.ᵃ ²¹And after he became the father of Serug, Reu lived 207 years and had other sons and daughters.

²²When Serug had lived 30 years, he became the father of Nahor. ²³And after he became the father of Nahor, Serug lived 200 years and had other sons and daughters.

²⁴When Nahor had lived 29 years, he became the father of Terah.ᵇ ²⁵And after he became the father of Terah, Nahor lived 119 years and had other sons and daughters.

²⁶After Terah had lived 70 years, he became the father of Abram,ᶜ Nahorᵈ and Haran.

²⁷This is the account of Terah.

Terah became the father of Abram, Nahor and Haran. And Haran became the father of Lot.ᵉ ²⁸While his father Terah was still alive, Haran died in Ur of the Chaldeans,ᶠ in the land of his birth. ²⁹Abram and Nahor both married. The name of Abram's wife was Sarai,ᵍ and the name of Nahor's wife was Milcah;ʰ she was the daughter of Haran, the father of both Milcah and Iscah. ³⁰Now Sarai was barren; she had no children.ⁱ

³¹Terah took his son Abram, his grandson Lot son of Haran, and his daughter-in-law Sarai, the wife of his son Abram, and together they set out from Ur of the Chaldeansʲ to go to Canaan.ᵏ But when they came to Haran, they settled there.

³²Terah lived 205 years, and he died in Haran.

Journeys of Abraham

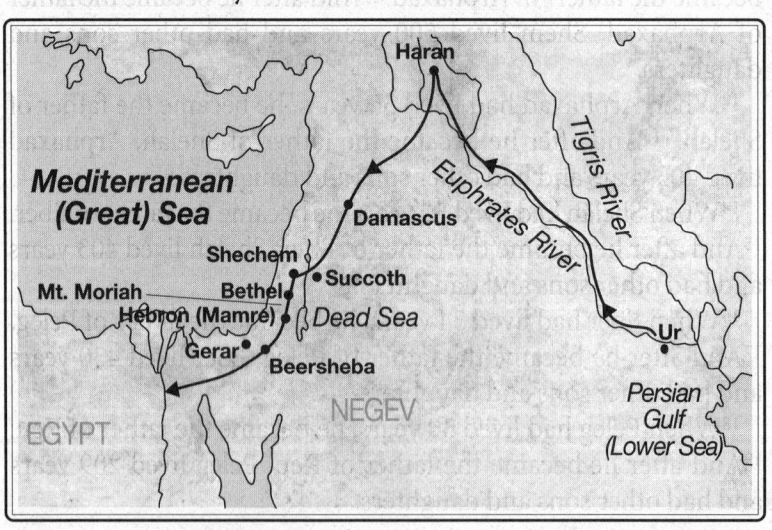

Chapter 12 Theme _____

12 The LORD had said to Abram, "Leave your country, your people and your father's household and go to the land I will show you.ˡ

11:20
ᵃLk 3:35

11:24
ᵇLk 3:34

11:26
ᶜLk 3:34
ᵈJos 24:2

11:27
ᵉver 31;
Ge 12:4;
14:12; 19:1;
2Pe 2:7

11:28
ᶠver 31;
Ge 15:7

11:29
ᵍGe 17:15
ʰGe 22:20

11:30
ⁱGe 16:1;
18:11

11:31
ʲGe 15:7;
Ne 9:7;
Ac 7:4
ᵏGe 10:19

12:1
ˡAc 7:3*;
Heb 11:8

12:2
a Ge 15:5;
17:2,4; 18:18;
22:17;
Dt 26:5
b Ge 24:1,35

12:3
c Ge 27:29;
Ex 23:22;
Nu 24:9
d Ge 18:18;
22:18; 26:4;
Ac 3:25;
Gal 3:8*

12:4
e Ge 11:31

12:5
f Ge 14:14;
17:23

12:6
g Heb 11:9
h Ge 35:4;
Dt 11:30
i Ge 10:18

12:7
j Ge 17:1;
18:1; Ex 6:3
k Ge 13:15,17;
15:18; 17:8;
Ps 105:9-11
l Ge 13:4

12:8
m Ge 13:3

12:9
n Ge 13:1,3

12:13
o Ge 20:2;
26:7

12:17
p 1Ch 16:21

12:18
q Ge 20:9;
26:10

²"I will make you into a great nation*a*
and I will bless you;*b*
I will make your name great,
and you will be a blessing.
³I will bless those who bless you,
and whoever curses you I will curse;*c*
and all peoples on earth
will be blessed through you.*d*"

⁴So Abram left, as the LORD had told him; and Lot went with him. Abram was seventy-five years old when he set out from Haran.*e* ⁵He took his wife Sarai, his nephew Lot, all the possessions they had accumulated and the people*f* they had acquired in Haran, and they set out for the land of Canaan, and they arrived there.

⁶Abram traveled through the land*g* as far as the site of the great tree of Moreh*h* at Shechem. At that time the Canaanites*i* were in the land. ⁷The LORD appeared to Abram*j* and said, "To your offspring*a* I will give this land."*k* So he built an altar there to the LORD,*l* who had appeared to him.

⁸From there he went on toward the hills east of Bethel*m* and pitched his tent, with Bethel on the west and Ai on the east. There he built an altar to the LORD and called on the name of the LORD. ⁹Then Abram set out and continued toward the Negev.*n*

¹⁰Now there was a famine in the land, and Abram went down to Egypt to live there for a while because the famine was severe. ¹¹As he was about to enter Egypt, he said to his wife Sarai, "I know what a beautiful woman you are. ¹²When the Egyptians see you, they will say, 'This is his wife.' Then they will kill me but will let you live. ¹³Say you are my sister,*o* so that I will be treated well for your sake and my life will be spared because of you."

¹⁴When Abram came to Egypt, the Egyptians saw that she was a very beautiful woman. ¹⁵And when Pharaoh's officials saw her, they praised her to Pharaoh, and she was taken into his palace. ¹⁶He treated Abram well for her sake, and Abram acquired sheep and cattle, male and female donkeys, menservants and maidservants, and camels.

¹⁷But the LORD inflicted serious diseases on Pharaoh and his household*p* because of Abram's wife Sarai. ¹⁸So Pharaoh summoned Abram. "What have you done to me?"*q* he said. "Why didn't you tell me she was your wife? ¹⁹Why did you say, 'She is my sister,' so that I took her to be my wife? Now then, here is your wife. Take her and go!" ²⁰Then Pharaoh gave orders about Abram to his men, and they sent him on his way, with his wife and everything he had.

a 7 Or *seed*

Chapter 13 Theme

13 So Abram went up from Egypt to the Negev,[a] with his wife and everything he had, and Lot went with him. [2]Abram had become very wealthy in livestock and in silver and gold.

[3]From the Negev he went from place to place until he came to Bethel,[b] to the place between Bethel and Ai where his tent had been earlier [4]and where he had first built an altar.[c] There Abram called on the name of the LORD.

[5]Now Lot, who was moving about with Abram, also had flocks and herds and tents. [6]But the land could not support them while they stayed together, for their possessions were so great that they were not able to stay together.[d] [7]And quarreling[e] arose between Abram's herdsmen and the herdsmen of Lot. The Canaanites and Perizzites were also living in the land[f] at that time.

[8]So Abram said to Lot, "Let's not have any quarreling between you and me,[g] or between your herdsmen and mine, for we are brothers.[h] [9]Is not the whole land before you? Let's part company. If you go to the left, I'll go to the right; if you go to the right, I'll go to the left."

[10]Lot looked up and saw that the whole plain of the Jordan was well watered, like the garden of the LORD,[i] like the land of Egypt, toward Zoar.[j] (This was before the LORD destroyed Sodom and Gomorrah.)[k] [11]So Lot chose for himself the whole plain of the Jordan and set out toward the east. The two men parted company: [12]Abram lived in the land of Canaan, while Lot lived among the cities of the plain[l] and pitched his tents near Sodom.[m] [13]Now the men of Sodom were wicked and were sinning greatly against the LORD.[n]

[14]The LORD said to Abram after Lot had parted from him, "Lift up your eyes from where you are and look north and south, east and west.[o] [15]All the land that you see I will give to you and your offspring[a] forever.[p] [16]I will make your offspring like the dust of the earth, so that if anyone could count the dust, then your offspring could be counted. [17]Go, walk through the length and breadth of the land,[q] for I am giving it to you."

[18]So Abram moved his tents and went to live near the great trees of Mamre[r] at Hebron,[s] where he built an altar to the LORD.[t]

Chapter 14 Theme

14 At this time Amraphel king of Shinar,[b][u] Arioch king of Ellasar, Kedorlaomer king of Elam and Tidal king of Goiim [2]went to war against Bera king of Sodom, Birsha king of Gomorrah, Shinab king of Admah, Shemeber king of Zeboiim,[v] and the king of Bela (that is, Zoar).[w] [3]All these latter kings joined

---

a15 Or *seed*; also in verse 16   b1 That is, Babylonia; also in verse 9

13:1
[a]Ge 12:9

13:3
[b]Ge 12:8

13:4
[c]Ge 12:7

13:6
[d]Ge 36:7

13:7
[e]Ge 26:20,21
[f]Ge 12:6

13:8
[g]Pr 15:18;
20:3
[h]Ps 133:1

13:10
[i]Ge 2:8-10;
Isa 51:3
[j]Ge 19:22,30
[k]Ge 14:8;
19:17-29

13:12
[l]Ge 19:17,25,29
[m]Ge 14:12

13:13
[n]Ge 18:20;
Eze 16:49-50;
2Pe 2:8

13:14
[o]Ge 28:14;
Dt 3:27

13:15
[p]Ge 12:7;
Gal 3:16*

13:17
[q]ver 15;
Nu 13:17-25

13:18
[r]Ge 14:13,24;
18:1
[s]Ge 35:27
[t]Ge 8:20

14:1
[u]Ge 10:10

14:2
[v]Ge 10:19
[w]Ge 13:10

14:3
a Nu 34:3,12;
Dt 3:17;
Jos 3:16;
15:2,5

14:5
b Ge 15:20;
Dt 2:11,20
c Dt 2:10

14:6
d Dt 2:12,22
e Dt 2:1,5,22
f Ge 21:21;
Nu 10:12

14:7
g 2Ch 20:2

14:8
h Ge 13:10;
19:17-29
i Dt 29:23

14:10
j Ge 19:17,30

14:13
k ver 24;
Ge 13:18

14:14
l Ge 15:3
m Dt 34:1;
Jdg 18:29

14:17
n 2Sa 18:18

14:18
o Ps 110:4;
Heb 5:6
p Ps 76:2;
Heb 7:2

14:19
q Heb 7:6
r ver 22

14:20
s Ge 24:27
t Ge 28:22;
Dt 26:12;
Heb 7:4

forces in the Valley of Siddim (the Salt Sea ᵃᵃ). ⁴For twelve years they had been subject to Kedorlaomer, but in the thirteenth year they rebelled.

⁵In the fourteenth year, Kedorlaomer and the kings allied with him went out and defeated the Rephaites[b] in Ashteroth Karnaim, the Zuzites in Ham, the Emites[c] in Shaveh Kiriathaim ⁶and the Horites[d] in the hill country of Seir,[e] as far as El Paran[f] near the desert. ⁷Then they turned back and went to En Mishpat (that is, Kadesh), and they conquered the whole territory of the Amalekites, as well as the Amorites who were living in Hazazon Tamar.[g]

⁸Then the king of Sodom, the king of Gomorrah,[h] the king of Admah, the king of Zeboiim[i] and the king of Bela (that is, Zoar) marched out and drew up their battle lines in the Valley of Siddim ⁹against Kedorlaomer king of Elam, Tidal king of Goiim, Amraphel king of Shinar and Arioch king of Ellasar—four kings against five. ¹⁰Now the Valley of Siddim was full of tar pits, and when the kings of Sodom and Gomorrah fled, some of the men fell into them and the rest fled to the hills.[j] ¹¹The four kings seized all the goods of Sodom and Gomorrah and all their food; then they went away. ¹²They also carried off Abram's nephew Lot and his possessions, since he was living in Sodom.

¹³One who had escaped came and reported this to Abram the Hebrew. Now Abram was living near the great trees of Mamre[k] the Amorite, a brother[b] of Eshcol and Aner, all of whom were allied with Abram. ¹⁴When Abram heard that his relative had been taken captive, he called out the 318 trained men born in his household[l] and went in pursuit as far as Dan.[m] ¹⁵During the night Abram divided his men to attack them and he routed them, pursuing them as far as Hobah, north of Damascus. ¹⁶He recovered all the goods and brought back his relative Lot and his possessions, together with the women and the other people.

¹⁷After Abram returned from defeating Kedorlaomer and the kings allied with him, the king of Sodom came out to meet him in the Valley of Shaveh (that is, the King's Valley).[n]

¹⁸Then Melchizedek[o] king of Salem[cp] brought out bread and wine. He was priest of God Most High, ¹⁹and he blessed Abram,[q] saying,

> "Blessed be Abram by God Most High,
> Creator[d] of heaven and earth.[r]
> ²⁰And blessed be[e] God Most High,[s]
> who delivered your enemies into your hand."

Then Abram gave him a tenth of everything.[t]

a 3 That is, the Dead Sea   b 13 Or *a relative*; or *an ally*   c 18 That is, Jerusalem   d 19 Or *Possessor*; also in verse 22   e 20 Or *And praise be to*

23

²¹The king of Sodom said to Abram, "Give me the people and keep the goods for yourself."

²²But Abram said to the king of Sodom, "I have raised my hand*a* to the LORD, God Most High, Creator of heaven and earth,*b* and have taken an oath ²³that I will accept nothing belonging to you,*c* not even a thread or the thong of a sandal, so that you will never be able to say, 'I made Abram rich.' ²⁴I will accept nothing but what my men have eaten and the share that belongs to the men who went with me—to Aner, Eshcol and Mamre. Let them have their share."

Chapter 15 Theme

15 After this, the word of the LORD came to Abram*d* in a vision:

> "Do not be afraid,*e* Abram.
>   I am your shield,*af*
>   your very great reward.*b*"

²But Abram said, "O Sovereign LORD, what can you give me since I remain childless*g* and the one who will inherit*c* my estate is Eliezer of Damascus?" ³And Abram said, "You have given me no children; so a servant*h* in my household will be my heir."

⁴Then the word of the LORD came to him: "This man will not be your heir, but a son coming from your own body will be your heir.*i*" ⁵He took him outside and said, "Look up at the heavens and count the stars*j*—if indeed you can count them." Then he said to him, "So shall your offspring be."*k*

⁶Abram believed the LORD, and he credited it to him as righteousness.*l*

⁷He also said to him, "I am the LORD, who brought you out of Ur of the Chaldeans to give you this land to take possession of it."

⁸But Abram said, "O Sovereign LORD, how can I know*m* that I will gain possession of it?"

⁹So the LORD said to him, "Bring me a heifer, a goat and a ram, each three years old, along with a dove and a young pigeon."

¹⁰Abram brought all these to him, cut them in two and arranged the halves opposite each other;*n* the birds, however, he did not cut in half.*o* ¹¹Then birds of prey came down on the carcasses, but Abram drove them away.

¹²As the sun was setting, Abram fell into a deep sleep,*p* and a thick and dreadful darkness came over him. ¹³Then the LORD said to him, "Know for certain that your descendants will be strangers in a country not their own, and they will be enslaved*q*

INSIGHT

Beriyt, the Hebrew word for covenant, is a solemn binding agreement made by passing through pieces of flesh. The Greek word for covenant, *diatheke*, means a testament or an agreement. The Bible is divided into the Old and New Testaments—or covenants. Everything God does is based on covenant.

---

a 1 Or *sovereign*   *b 1* Or *shield; I your reward will be very great*   *c 2* The meaning of the Hebrew for this phrase is uncertain.

14:22 *a*Ex 6:8; Da 12:7; Rev 10:5-6 *b*ver 19

14:23 *c*2Ki 5:16

15:1 *d*Da 10:1 *e*Ge 21:17; 26:24; 46:3; 2Ki 6:16; Ps 27:1; Isa 41:10,13-14 *f*Dt 33:29; 2Sa 22:3,31; Ps 3:3

15:2 *g*Ac 7:5

15:3 *h*Ge 24:2,34

15:4 *i*Gal 4:28

15:5 *j*Ps 147:4; Jer 33:22 *k*Ge 12:2; 22:17; Ex 32:13; Ro 4:18*; Heb 11:12

15:6 *l*Ps 106:31; Ro 4:3*, 20-24*; Gal 3:6*; Jas 2:23*

15:8 *m*Lk 1:18

15:10 *n*ver 17; Jer 34:18 *o*Lev 1:17

15:12 *p*Ge 2:21

15:13 *q*Ex 1:11

and mistreated four hundred years.*a* [14]But I will punish the nation they serve as slaves, and afterward they will come out*b* with great possessions.*c* [15]You, however, will go to your fathers in peace and be buried at a good old age.*d* [16]In the fourth generation your descendants will come back here, for the sin of the Amorites*e* has not yet reached its full measure."

[17]When the sun had set and darkness had fallen, a smoking firepot with a blazing torch appeared and passed between the pieces.*f* [18]On that day the LORD made a covenant with Abram and said, "To your descendants I give this land,*g* from the river*a* of Egypt*h* to the great river, the Euphrates— [19]the land of the Kenites, Kenizzites, Kadmonites, [20]Hittites, Perizzites, Rephaites, [21]Amorites, Canaanites, Girgashites and Jebusites."

Chapter 16 Theme

16 Now Sarai, Abram's wife, had borne him no children.*i* But she had an Egyptian maidservant*j* named Hagar; [2]so she said to Abram, "The LORD has kept me from having children. Go, sleep with my maidservant; perhaps I can build a family through her."*k*

Abram agreed to what Sarai said. [3]So after Abram had been living in Canaan*l* ten years, Sarai his wife took her Egyptian maidservant Hagar and gave her to her husband to be his wife. [4]He slept with Hagar, and she conceived.

When she knew she was pregnant, she began to despise her mistress. [5]Then Sarai said to Abram, "You are responsible for the wrong I am suffering. I put my servant in your arms, and now that she knows she is pregnant, she despises me. May the LORD judge between you and me."*m*

[6]"Your servant is in your hands," Abram said. "Do with her whatever you think best." Then Sarai mistreated Hagar; so she fled from her.

[7]The angel of the LORD*n* found Hagar near a spring in the desert; it was the spring that is beside the road to Shur.*o* [8]And he said, "Hagar, servant of Sarai, where have you come from, and where are you going?"

"I'm running away from my mistress Sarai," she answered.

[9]Then the angel of the LORD told her, "Go back to your mistress and submit to her." [10]The angel added, "I will so increase your descendants that they will be too numerous to count."*p*

[11]The angel of the LORD also said to her:

> "You are now with child
> and you will have a son.

a18 Or Wadi

15:13
*a*ver 16;
Ex 12:40;
Ac 7:6,17

15:14
*b*Ac 7:7*
*c*Ex 12:32-38

15:15
*d*Ge 25:8

15:16
*e*1Ki 21:26

15:17
*f*ver 10

15:18
*g*Ge 12:7
*h*Nu 34:5

16:1
*i*Ge 11:30;
Gal 4:24-25
*j*Ge 21:9

16:2
*k*Ge 30:3-4,
9-10

16:3
*l*Ge 12:5

16:5
*m*Ge 31:53

16:7
*n*Ge 21:17;
22:11,15;
31:11
*o*Ge 20:1

16:10
*p*Ge 13:16;
17:20

You shall name him Ishmael,^a
  for the LORD has heard of your misery.^a
¹²He will be a wild donkey of a man;
  his hand will be against everyone
  and everyone's hand against him,
  and he will live in hostility
  toward^b all his brothers.^b"

¹³She gave this name to the LORD who spoke to her: "You are the God who sees me," for she said, "I have now seen^c the One who sees me."^c ¹⁴That is why the well was called Beer Lahai Roi^d; it is still there, between Kadesh and Bered.

¹⁵So Hagar bore Abram a son,^d and Abram gave the name Ishmael to the son she had borne. ¹⁶Abram was eighty-six years old when Hagar bore him Ishmael.

Chapter 17 Theme

17 When Abram was ninety-nine years old, the LORD appeared to him and said, "I am God Almighty^e;^e walk before me and be blameless.^f ²I will confirm my covenant between me and you^g and will greatly increase your numbers."

³Abram fell facedown, and God said to him, ⁴"As for me, this is my covenant with you:^h You will be the father of many nations.ⁱ ⁵No longer will you be called Abram^f; your name will be Abraham,^{gj} for I have made you a father of many nations.^k ⁶I will make you very fruitful;^l I will make nations of you, and kings will come from you.^m ⁷I will establish my covenant as an everlasting covenant between me and you and your descendants after you for the generations to come, to be your Godⁿ and the God of your descendants after you. ^o ⁸The whole land of Canaan,^p where you are now an alien,^q I will give as an everlasting possession to you and your descendants after you;^r and I will be their God."

⁹Then God said to Abraham, "As for you, you must keep my covenant, you and your descendants after you for the generations to come. ¹⁰This is my covenant with you and your descendants after you, the covenant you are to keep: Every male among you shall be circumcised.^s ¹¹You are to undergo circumcision,^t and it will be the sign of the covenant^u between me and you. ¹²For the generations to come every male among you who is eight days old must be circumcised,^v including those born in your household or bought with money from a foreigner—those who are not your offspring. ¹³Whether born

---

^a11 Ishmael means *God hears*.   ^b12 Or *live to the east / of*   ^c13 Or *seen the back of*
^d14 *Beer Lahai Roi* means *well of the Living One who sees me.*   ^e1 Hebrew *El-Shaddai*
^f5 *Abram* means *exalted father.*   ^g5 *Abraham* means *father of many.*

16:11
^aEx 2:24;
3:7,9

16:12
^bGe 25:18

16:13
^cGe 32:30

16:15
^dGal 4:22

17:1
^eGe 28:3;
Ex 6:3
^fDt 18:13

17:2
^gGe 15:18

17:4
^hGe 15:18
ⁱver 16;
Ge 12:2;
35:11; 48:19

17:5
^jver 15;
Ne 9:7
^kRo 4:17*

17:6
^lGe 35:11
^mMt 1:6

17:7
ⁿEx 29:45,46
^oRo 9:8;
Gal 3:16

17:8
^pPs 105:9,11
^qGe 23:4;
28:4; Ex 6:4
^rGe 12:7

17:10
^sver 23;
Ge 21:4;
Jn 7:22;
Ac 7:8;
Ro 4:11

17:11
^tEx 12:48;
Dt 10:16
^uRo 4:11

17:12
^vLev 12:3;
Lk 2:21

17:14
a Ex 4:24-26

17:16
b Ge 18:10
c Ge 35:11;
Gal 4:31

17:17
d Ge 18:12; 21:6

17:19
e Ge 18:14; 21:2
f Ge 26:3

17:20
g Ge 16:10
h Ge 25:12-16
i Ge 21:18

17:21
j Ge 21:2

17:24
k Ro 4:11

18:1
l Ge 13:18;
14:13

18:2
m ver 16,22;
Ge 32:24;
Jos 5:13;
Jdg 13:6-11;
Heb 13:2

18:4
n Ge 19:2;
43:24

18:5
o Jdg 13:15

in your household or bought with your money, they must be circumcised. My covenant in your flesh is to be an everlasting covenant. ¹⁴Any uncircumcised male, who has not been circumcised in the flesh, will be cut off from his people;*ᵃ* he has broken my covenant."

¹⁵God also said to Abraham, "As for Sarai your wife, you are no longer to call her Sarai; her name will be Sarah. ¹⁶I will bless her and will surely give you a son by her.*ᵇ* I will bless her so that she will be the mother of nations;*ᶜ* kings of peoples will come from her."

¹⁷Abraham fell facedown; he laughed*ᵈ* and said to himself, "Will a son be born to a man a hundred years old? Will Sarah bear a child at the age of ninety?" ¹⁸And Abraham said to God, "If only Ishmael might live under your blessing!"

¹⁹Then God said, "Yes, but your wife Sarah will bear you a son,*ᵉ* and you will call him Isaac.*ᵃ* I will establish my covenant with him *f* as an everlasting covenant for his descendants after him. ²⁰And as for Ishmael, I have heard you: I will surely bless him; I will make him fruitful and will greatly increase his numbers.*ᵍ* He will be the father of twelve rulers,*ʰ* and I will make him into a great nation.*ⁱ* ²¹But my covenant I will establish with Isaac, whom Sarah will bear to you by this time next year."*ʲ* ²²When he had finished speaking with Abraham, God went up from him.

²³On that very day Abraham took his son Ishmael and all those born in his household or bought with his money, every male in his household, and circumcised them, as God told him. ²⁴Abraham was ninety-nine years old when he was circumcised,*ᵏ* ²⁵and his son Ishmael was thirteen; ²⁶Abraham and his son Ishmael were both circumcised on that same day. ²⁷And every male in Abraham's household, including those born in his household or bought from a foreigner, was circumcised with him.

Chapter 18 Theme

18 The LORD appeared to Abraham near the great trees of Mamre*ˡ* while he was sitting at the entrance to his tent in the heat of the day. ²Abraham looked up and saw three men*ᵐ* standing nearby. When he saw them, he hurried from the entrance of his tent to meet them and bowed low to the ground.

³He said, "If I have found favor in your eyes, my lord,*ᵇ* do not pass your servant by. ⁴Let a little water be brought, and then you may all wash your feet*ⁿ* and rest under this tree. ⁵Let me get you something to eat,*ᵒ* so you can be refreshed and then go on your way—now that you have come to your servant."

a 19 Isaac means *he laughs.* *b 3 Or O Lord*

"Very well," they answered, "do as you say."

⁶So Abraham hurried into the tent to Sarah. "Quick," he said, "get three seahsª of fine flour and knead it and bake some bread."

⁷Then he ran to the herd and selected a choice, tender calf and gave it to a servant, who hurried to prepare it. ⁸He then brought some curds and milk and the calf that had been prepared, and set these before them.ª While they ate, he stood near them under a tree.

⁹"Where is your wife Sarah?" they asked him.

"There, in the tent," he said.

¹⁰Then the LORDᵇ said, "I will surely return to you about this time next year, and Sarah your wife will have a son."ᵇ

Now Sarah was listening at the entrance to the tent, which was behind him. ¹¹Abraham and Sarah were already old and well advanced in years,ᶜ and Sarah was past the age of childbearing.ᵈ ¹²So Sarah laughedᵉ to herself as she thought, "After I am worn out and my masterᶜᶠ is old, will I now have this pleasure?"

¹³Then the LORD said to Abraham, "Why did Sarah laugh and say, 'Will I really have a child, now that I am old?' ¹⁴Is anything too hard for the LORD?ᵍ I will return to you at the appointed time next year and Sarah will have a son."

¹⁵Sarah was afraid, so she lied and said, "I did not laugh."

But he said, "Yes, you did laugh."

¹⁶When the men got up to leave, they looked down toward Sodom, and Abraham walked along with them to see them on their way. ¹⁷Then the LORD said, "Shall I hide from Abrahamʰ what I am about to do?ⁱ ¹⁸Abraham will surely become a great and powerful nation,ʲ and all nations on earth will be blessed through him. ¹⁹For I have chosen him, so that he will direct his childrenᵏ and his household after him to keep the way of the LORDˡ by doing what is right and just, so that the LORD will bring about for Abraham what he has promised him."

²⁰Then the LORD said, "The outcry against Sodom and Gomorrah is so great and their sin so grievous ²¹that I will go downᵐ and see if what they have done is as bad as the outcry that has reached me. If not, I will know."

²²The men turned away and went toward Sodom,ⁿ but Abraham remained standing before the LORD.ᵈ ²³Then Abraham approached him and said: "Will you sweep away the righteous with the wicked?ᵒ ²⁴What if there are fifty righteous people in the city? Will you really sweep it away and not spareᵉ the place for the sake of the fifty righteous people in it?ᵖ ²⁵Far be it from you to do such a thing—to kill the righteous with the wicked,

---

ª6 That is, probably about 20 quarts (about 22 liters)   ᵇ10 Hebrew *Then he*   ᶜ12 Or *husband*   ᵈ22 Masoretic Text; an ancient Hebrew scribal tradition *but the LORD remained standing before Abraham*   ᵉ24 Or *forgive*; also in verse 26

18:8
ªGe 19:3

18:10
ᵇRo 9:9*

18:11
ᶜGe 17:17
ᵈRo 4:19

18:12
ᵉGe 17:17; 21:6
ᶠ1Pe 3:6

18:14
ᵍJer 32:17,27;
Zec 8:6;
Mt 19:26;
Lk 1:37;
Ro 4:21

18:17
ʰAm 3:7
ⁱGe 19:24

18:18
ʲGal 3:8*

18:19
ᵏDt 4:9-10; 6:7
ˡJos 24:15;
Eph 6:4

18:21
ᵐGe 11:5

18:22
ⁿGe 19:1

18:23
ᵒNu 16:22

18:24
ᵖJer 5:1

18:25
a Job 8:3,20;
Ps 58:11; 94:2;
Isa 3:10-11;
Ro 3:6

treating the righteous and the wicked alike. Far be it from you! Will not the Judge[a] of all the earth do right?"[a]

²⁶The LORD said, "If I find fifty righteous people in the city of Sodom, I will spare the whole place for their sake.[b]"

²⁷Then Abraham spoke up again: "Now that I have been so bold as to speak to the Lord, though I am nothing but dust and ashes,[c] ²⁸what if the number of the righteous is five less than fifty? Will you destroy the whole city because of five people?"

"If I find forty-five there," he said, "I will not destroy it."

²⁹Once again he spoke to him, "What if only forty are found there?"

He said, "For the sake of forty, I will not do it."

³⁰Then he said, "May the Lord not be angry, but let me speak. What if only thirty can be found there?"

He answered, "I will not do it if I find thirty there."

³¹Abraham said, "Now that I have been so bold as to speak to the Lord, what if only twenty can be found there?"

He said, "For the sake of twenty, I will not destroy it."

³²Then he said, "May the Lord not be angry, but let me speak just once more.[d] What if only ten can be found there?"

He answered, "For the sake of ten,[e] I will not destroy it."

³³When the LORD had finished speaking with Abraham, he left, and Abraham returned home.

18:26
b Jer 5:1

18:27
c Ge 2:7; 3:19;
Job 30:19; 42:6

18:32
d Jdg 6:39
e Jer 5:1

19:1
f Ge 18:22
g Ge 18:1

Chapter 19 Theme _____

19 The two angels arrived at Sodom[f] in the evening, and Lot was sitting in the gateway of the city.[g] When he saw them, he got up to meet them and bowed down with his face to the ground. ²"My lords," he said, "please turn aside to your servant's house. You can wash your feet[h] and spend the night and then go on your way early in the morning."

"No," they answered, "we will spend the night in the square."

³But he insisted so strongly that they did go with him and entered his house. He prepared a meal for them, baking bread without yeast, and they ate. [i] ⁴Before they had gone to bed, all the men from every part of the city of Sodom—both young and old—surrounded the house. ⁵They called to Lot, "Where are the men who came to you tonight? Bring them out to us so that we can have sex with them."[j]

⁶Lot went outside to meet them[k] and shut the door behind him ⁷and said, "No, my friends. Don't do this wicked thing. ⁸Look, I have two daughters who have never slept with a man. Let me bring them out to you, and you can do what you like

19:2
h Ge 18:4;
Lk 7:44

19:3
i Ge 18:6

19:5
j Jdg 19:22;
Isa 3:9;
Ro 1:24-27

19:6
k Jdg 19:23

a 25 Or *Ruler*

with them. But don't do anything to these men, for they have come under the protection of my roof."*a*

9"Get out of our way," they replied. And they said, "This fellow came here as an alien, and now he wants to play the judge!*b* We'll treat you worse than them." They kept bringing pressure on Lot and moved forward to break down the door.

10But the men inside reached out and pulled Lot back into the house and shut the door. 11Then they struck the men who were at the door of the house, young and old, with blindness*c* so that they could not find the door.

12The two men said to Lot, "Do you have anyone else here— sons-in-law, sons or daughters, or anyone else in the city who belongs to you?*d* Get them out of here, 13because we are going to destroy this place. The outcry to the LORD against its people is so great that he has sent us to destroy it."*e*

14So Lot went out and spoke to his sons-in-law, who were pledged to marry*a* his daughters. He said, "Hurry and get out of this place, because the LORD is about to destroy the city!*f*" But his sons-in-law thought he was joking.*g*

15With the coming of dawn, the angels urged Lot, saying, "Hurry! Take your wife and your two daughters who are here, or you will be swept away*h* when the city is punished.*i*"

16When he hesitated, the men grasped his hand and the hands of his wife and of his two daughters and led them safely out of the city, for the LORD was merciful to them. 17As soon as they had brought them out, one of them said, "Flee for your lives!*j* Don't look back,*k* and don't stop anywhere in the plain! Flee to the mountains or you will be swept away!"

18But Lot said to them, "No, my lords,*b* please! 19Your*c* servant has found favor in your*c* eyes, and you*c* have shown great kindness to me in sparing my life. But I can't flee to the mountains; this disaster will overtake me, and I'll die. 20Look, here is a town near enough to run to, and it is small. Let me flee to it—it is very small, isn't it? Then my life will be spared."

21He said to him, "Very well, I will grant this request too; I will not overthrow the town you speak of. 22But flee there quickly, because I cannot do anything until you reach it." (That is why the town was called Zoar.*d*)

23By the time Lot reached Zoar, the sun had risen over the land. 24Then the LORD rained down burning sulfur on Sodom and Gomorrah*l*—from the LORD out of the heavens.*m* 25Thus he overthrew those cities and the entire plain, including all those living in the cities—and also the vegetation in the land.*n* 26But Lot's wife looked back,*o* and she became a pillar of salt.*p*

a *14* Or *were married to* b *18* Or *No, Lord;* or *No, my lord* c *19* The Hebrew is singular.
d *22* Zoar means *small.*

30

19:8
a Jdg 19:24

19:9
b Ex 2:14;
Ac 7:27

19:11
c Dt 28:28-29;
2Ki 6:18;
Ac 13:11

19:12
d Ge 7:1

19:13
e 1Ch 21:15

19:14
f Nu 16:21
g Ex 9:21;
Lk 17:28

19:15
h Nu 16:26
i Rev 18:4

19:17
j Jer 48:6
k ver 26

19:24
l Dt 29:23;
Isa 1:9; 13:19
m Lk 17:29;
2Pe 2:6;
Jude 7

19:25
n Ps 107:34;
Eze 16:48

19:26
o ver 17
p Lk 17:32

19:27
a Ge 18:22

²⁷Early the next morning Abraham got up and returned to the place where he had stood before the LORD.*a* ²⁸He looked down toward Sodom and Gomorrah, toward all the land of the plain, and he saw dense smoke rising from the land, like smoke from a furnace.*b*

19:28
b Rev 9:2; 18:9

²⁹So when God destroyed the cities of the plain, he remembered Abraham, and he brought Lot out of the catastrophe*c* that overthrew the cities where Lot had lived.

19:29
c 2Pe 2:7

³⁰Lot and his two daughters left Zoar and settled in the mountains,*d* for he was afraid to stay in Zoar. He and his two daughters lived in a cave. ³¹One day the older daughter said to the younger, "Our father is old, and there is no man around here to lie with us, as is the custom all over the earth. ³²Let's get our father to drink wine and then lie with him and preserve our family line through our father."

19:30
d ver 19

³³That night they got their father to drink wine, and the older daughter went in and lay with him. He was not aware of it when she lay down or when she got up.

³⁴The next day the older daughter said to the younger, "Last night I lay with my father. Let's get him to drink wine again tonight, and you go in and lie with him so we can preserve our family line through our father." ³⁵So they got their father to drink wine that night also, and the younger daughter went and lay with him. Again he was not aware of it when she lay down or when she got up.

19:37
e Dt 2:9

19:38
f Dt 2:19

³⁶So both of Lot's daughters became pregnant by their father. ³⁷The older daughter had a son, and she named him Moab*a*; he is the father of the Moabites*e* of today. ³⁸The younger daughter also had a son, and she named him Ben-Ammi*b*; he is the father of the Ammonites*f* of today.

20:1
g Ge 18:1
h Ge 26:1,6,17

Chapter 20 Theme _____

20

Now Abraham moved on from there*g* into the region of the Negev and lived between Kadesh and Shur. For a while he stayed in Gerar,*h* ²and there Abraham said of his wife Sarah, "She is my sister.*i*" Then Abimelech king of Gerar sent for Sarah and took her.*j*

20:2
i ver 12;
Ge 12:13; 26:7
j Ge 12:15

³But God came to Abimelech in a dream*k* one night and said to him, "You are as good as dead because of the woman you have taken; she is a married woman."*l*

20:3
k Job 33:15;
Mt 27:19
l Ps 105:14

⁴Now Abimelech had not gone near her, so he said, "Lord, will you destroy an innocent nation?*m* ⁵Did he not say to me, 'She is my sister,' and didn't she also say, 'He is my brother'? I have done this with a clear conscience and clean hands."

20:4
m Ge 18:25

a 37 *Moab* sounds like the Hebrew for *from father.* *b* 38 *Ben-Ammi* means *son of my people.*

⁶Then God said to him in the dream, "Yes, I know you did this with a clear conscience, and so I have kept*ᵃ* you from sinning against me. That is why I did not let you touch her. ⁷Now return the man's wife, for he is a prophet, and he will pray for you*ᵇ* and you will live. But if you do not return her, you may be sure that you and all yours will die."

⁸Early the next morning Abimelech summoned all his officials, and when he told them all that had happened, they were very much afraid. ⁹Then Abimelech called Abraham in and said, "What have you done to us? How have I wronged you that you have brought such great guilt upon me and my kingdom? You have done things to me that should not be done.*ᶜ*" ¹⁰And Abimelech asked Abraham, "What was your reason for doing this?"

¹¹Abraham replied, "I said to myself, 'There is surely no fear of God*ᵈ* in this place, and they will kill me because of my wife.'*ᵉ* ¹²Besides, she really is my sister, the daughter of my father though not of my mother; and she became my wife. ¹³And when God had me wander from my father's household, I said to her, 'This is how you can show your love to me: Everywhere we go, say of me, "He is my brother."'"

¹⁴Then Abimelech brought sheep and cattle and male and female slaves and gave them to Abraham,*ᶠ* and he returned Sarah his wife to him. ¹⁵And Abimelech said, "My land is before you; live wherever you like."*ᵍ*

¹⁶To Sarah he said, "I am giving your brother a thousand shekels*ᵃ* of silver. This is to cover the offense against you before all who are with you; you are completely vindicated."

¹⁷Then Abraham prayed to God,*ʰ* and God healed Abimelech, his wife and his slave girls so they could have children again, ¹⁸for the LORD had closed up every womb in Abimelech's household because of Abraham's wife Sarah.*ⁱ*

Chapter 21 Theme

21 Now the LORD was gracious to Sarah*ʲ* as he had said, and the LORD did for Sarah what he had promised.*ᵏ* ²Sarah became pregnant and bore a son*ˡ* to Abraham in his old age,*ᵐ* at the very time God had promised him. ³Abraham gave the name Isaac*ᵇⁿ* to the son Sarah bore him. ⁴When his son Isaac was eight days old, Abraham circumcised him,*ᵒ* as God commanded him. ⁵Abraham was a hundred years old when his son Isaac was born to him.

⁶Sarah said, "God has brought me laughter,*ᵖ* and everyone who hears about this will laugh with me." ⁷And she added, "Who

Cross references
20:6 *ᵃ*1Sa 25:26,34

20:7 *ᵇ*ver 17; 1Sa 7:5; Job 42:8

20:9 *ᶜ*Ge 12:18; 26:10; 34:7

20:11 *ᵈ*Ge 42:18; Ps 36:1 *ᵉ*Ge 12:12; 26:7

20:14 *ᶠ*Ge 12:16

20:15 *ᵍ*Ge 13:9

20:17 *ʰ*Job 42:9

20:18 *ⁱ*Ge 12:17

21:1 *ʲ*1Sa 2:21 *ᵏ*Ge 8:1; 17:16,21; Gal 4:23

21:2 *ˡ*Ge 17:19 *ᵐ*Gal 4:22; Heb 11:11

21:3 *ⁿ*Ge 17:19

21:4 *ᵒ*Ge 17:10,12; Ac 7:8

21:6 *ᵖ*Ge 17:17; Isa 54:1

ᵃ 16 That is, about 25 pounds (about 11.5 kilograms)   *ᵇ 3 Isaac* means *he laughs.*

21:9
a Ge 16:15
b Gal 4:29

21:10
c Gal 4:30*

21:11
d Ge 17:18

21:12
e Ro 9:7*;
Heb 11:18*

21:13
f ver 18

21:14
g ver 31,32

21:17
h Ex 3:7

21:18
i ver 13

21:19
j Nu 22:31

21:20
k Ge 26:3,24;
28:15;
39:2,21,23

21:21
l Ge 24:4,38

21:23
m ver 31;
Jos 2:12

21:25
n Ge 26:15,18,
20-22

would have said to Abraham that Sarah would nurse children? Yet I have borne him a son in his old age."

⁸The child grew and was weaned, and on the day Isaac was weaned Abraham held a great feast. ⁹But Sarah saw that the son whom Hagar the Egyptian had borne to Abraham*a* was mocking,*b* ¹⁰and she said to Abraham, "Get rid of that slave woman and her son, for that slave woman's son will never share in the inheritance with my son Isaac."*c*

¹¹The matter distressed Abraham greatly because it concerned his son.*d* ¹²But God said to him, "Do not be so distressed about the boy and your maidservant. Listen to whatever Sarah tells you, because it is through Isaac that your offspring*a* will be reckoned.*e* ¹³I will make the son of the maidservant into a nation*f* also, because he is your offspring."

¹⁴Early the next morning Abraham took some food and a skin of water and gave them to Hagar. He set them on her shoulders and then sent her off with the boy. She went on her way and wandered in the desert of Beersheba.*g*

¹⁵When the water in the skin was gone, she put the boy under one of the bushes. ¹⁶Then she went off and sat down nearby, about a bowshot away, for she thought, "I cannot watch the boy die." And as she sat there nearby, she*b* began to sob.

¹⁷God heard the boy crying,*h* and the angel of God called to Hagar from heaven and said to her, "What is the matter, Hagar? Do not be afraid; God has heard the boy crying as he lies there. ¹⁸Lift the boy up and take him by the hand, for I will make him into a great nation."*i*

¹⁹Then God opened her eyes*j* and she saw a well of water. So she went and filled the skin with water and gave the boy a drink.

²⁰God was with the boy*k* as he grew up. He lived in the desert and became an archer. ²¹While he was living in the Desert of Paran, his mother got a wife for him*l* from Egypt.

²²At that time Abimelech and Phicol the commander of his forces said to Abraham, "God is with you in everything you do. ²³Now swear*m* to me here before God that you will not deal falsely with me or my children or my descendants. Show to me and the country where you are living as an alien the same kindness I have shown to you."

²⁴Abraham said, "I swear it."

²⁵Then Abraham complained to Abimelech about a well of water that Abimelech's servants had seized.*n* ²⁶But Abimelech said, "I don't know who has done this. You did not tell me, and I heard about it only today."

a 12 Or seed   b 16 Hebrew; Septuagint the child

²⁷So Abraham brought sheep and cattle and gave them to Abimelech, and the two men made a treaty.ᵃ ²⁸Abraham set apart seven ewe lambs from the flock, ²⁹and Abimelech asked Abraham, "What is the meaning of these seven ewe lambs you have set apart by themselves?"

³⁰He replied, "Accept these seven lambs from my hand as a witnessᵇ that I dug this well."

³¹So that place was called Beersheba,ᵃᶜ because the two men swore an oath there.

³²After the treaty had been made at Beersheba, Abimelech and Phicol the commander of his forces returned to the land of the Philistines. ³³Abraham planted a tamarisk tree in Beersheba, and there he called upon the name of the LORD,ᵈ the Eternal God.ᵉ ³⁴And Abraham stayed in the land of the Philistines for a long time.

Chapter 22 Theme _____

INSIGHT

The first references to *love*, *obedience*, and *worship* are found in Genesis 22. Note the context.

22 Some time later God testedᶠ Abraham. He said to him, "Abraham!"

"Here I am," he replied.

²Then God said, "Take your son,ᵍ your only son, Isaac, whom you love, and go to the region of Moriah.ʰ Sacrifice him there as a burnt offering on one of the mountains I will tell you about."

³Early the next morning Abraham got up and saddled his donkey. He took with him two of his servants and his son Isaac. When he had cut enough wood for the burnt offering, he set out for the place God had told him about. ⁴On the third day Abraham looked up and saw the place in the distance. ⁵He said to his servants, "Stay here with the donkey while I and the boy go over there. We will worship and then we will come back to you."

⁶Abraham took the wood for the burnt offering and placed it on his son Isaac,ⁱ and he himself carried the fire and the knife. As the two of them went on together, ⁷Isaac spoke up and said to his father Abraham, "Father?"

"Yes, my son?" Abraham replied.

"The fire and wood are here," Isaac said, "but where is the lambʲ for the burnt offering?"

⁸Abraham answered, "God himself will provide the lamb for the burnt offering, my son." And the two of them went on together.

⁹When they reached the place God had told him about, Abraham built an altar there and arranged the wood on it. He bound his son Isaac and laid him on the altar,ᵏ on top of the wood. ¹⁰Then he reached out his hand and took the knife to slay his

21:27
ᵃGe 26:28,31

21:30
ᵇGe 31:44,47, 48,50,52

21:31
ᶜGe 26:33

21:33
ᵈGe 4:26
ᵉDt 33:27

22:1
ᶠDt 8:2,16;
Heb 11:17;
Jas 1:12-13

22:2
ᵍver 12,16;
Jn 3:16;
Heb 11:17;
1Jn 4:9
ʰ2Ch 3:1

22:6
ⁱJn 19:17

22:7
ʲLev 1:10

22:9
ᵏHeb 11:17-19;
Jas 2:21

ᵃ31 *Beersheba* can mean *well of seven* or *well of the oath.*

22:12
a 1Sa 15:22;
Jas 2:21-22
b ver 2;
Jn 3:16

22:13
c Ro 8:32

22:14
d ver 8

22:16
e Lk 1:73;
Heb 6:13

22:17
f Heb 6:14*
g Ge 15:5
h Ge 26:24;
32:12
i Ge 24:60

22:18
j Ge 12:2,3;
Ac 3:25*;
Gal 3:8*
k ver 10

22:20
l Ge 11:29

22:23
m Ge 24:15

23:2
n Jos 14:15
o ver 19;
Ge 13:18

23:4
p Ge 17:8;
1Ch 29:15;
Ps 105:12;
Heb 11:9,13

23:6
q Ge 14:14-16;
24:35

son. [11]But the angel of the Lord called out to him from heaven, "Abraham! Abraham!"

"Here I am," he replied.

[12]"Do not lay a hand on the boy," he said. "Do not do anything to him. Now I know that you fear God,[a] because you have not withheld from me your son, your only son.[b]"

[13]Abraham looked up and there in a thicket he saw a ram[a] caught by its horns. He went over and took the ram and sacrificed it as a burnt offering instead of his son.[c] [14]So Abraham called that place The Lord Will Provide. And to this day it is said, "On the mountain of the Lord it will be provided.[d]"

[15]The angel of the Lord called to Abraham from heaven a second time [16]and said, "I swear by myself,[e] declares the Lord, that because you have done this and have not withheld your son, your only son, [17]I will surely bless you and make your descendants[f] as numerous as the stars in the sky[g] and as the sand on the seashore.[h] Your descendants will take possession of the cities of their enemies,[i] [18]and through your offspring[b] all nations on earth will be blessed,[j] because you have obeyed me."[k]

[19]Then Abraham returned to his servants, and they set off together for Beersheba. And Abraham stayed in Beersheba.

[20]Some time later Abraham was told, "Milcah is also a mother; she has borne sons to your brother Nahor:[l] [21]Uz the firstborn, Buz his brother, Kemuel (the father of Aram), [22]Kesed, Hazo, Pildash, Jidlaph and Bethuel." [23]Bethuel became the father of Rebekah.[m] Milcah bore these eight sons to Abraham's brother Nahor. [24]His concubine, whose name was Reumah, also had sons: Tebah, Gaham, Tahash and Maacah.

Chapter 23 Theme

23 Sarah lived to be a hundred and twenty-seven years old. [2]She died at Kiriath Arba[n] (that is, Hebron)[o] in the land of Canaan, and Abraham went to mourn for Sarah and to weep over her.

[3]Then Abraham rose from beside his dead wife and spoke to the Hittites.[c] He said, [4]"I am an alien and a stranger[p] among you. Sell me some property for a burial site here so I can bury my dead."

[5]The Hittites replied to Abraham, [6]"Sir, listen to us. You are a mighty prince[q] among us. Bury your dead in the choicest of our tombs. None of us will refuse you his tomb for burying your dead."

a 13 Many manuscripts of the Masoretic Text, Samaritan Pentateuch, Septuagint and Syriac; most manuscripts of the Masoretic Text *a ram behind* ⌊*him*⌋   *b* 18 Or *seed*   *c* 3 Or *the sons of Heth*; also in verses 5, 7, 10, 16, 18 and 20

[7]Then Abraham rose and bowed down before the people of the land, the Hittites. [8]He said to them, "If you are willing to let me bury my dead, then listen to me and intercede with Ephron son of Zohar[a] on my behalf [9]so he will sell me the cave of Machpelah, which belongs to him and is at the end of his field. Ask him to sell it to me for the full price as a burial site among you."

[10]Ephron the Hittite was sitting among his people and he replied to Abraham in the hearing of all the Hittites who had come to the gate[b] of his city. [11]"No, my lord," he said. "Listen to me; I give[ac] you the field, and I give[a] you the cave that is in it. I give[a] it to you in the presence of my people. Bury your dead."

[12]Again Abraham bowed down before the people of the land [13]and he said to Ephron in their hearing, "Listen to me, if you will. I will pay the price of the field. Accept it from me so I can bury my dead there."

[14]Ephron answered Abraham, [15]"Listen to me, my lord; the land is worth four hundred shekels[b] of silver,[d] but what is that between me and you? Bury your dead."

[16]Abraham agreed to Ephron's terms and weighed out for him the price he had named in the hearing of the Hittites: four hundred shekels of silver,[e] according to the weight current among the merchants.

[17]So Ephron's field in Machpelah near Mamre[f]—both the field and the cave in it, and all the trees within the borders of the field—was deeded [18]to Abraham as his property in the presence of all the Hittites who had come to the gate of the city. [19]Afterward Abraham buried his wife Sarah in the cave in the field of Machpelah near Mamre (which is at Hebron) in the land of Canaan. [20]So the field and the cave in it were deeded[g] to Abraham by the Hittites as a burial site.

Chapter 24 Theme

24 Abraham was now old and well advanced in years, and the LORD had blessed him in every way.[h] [2]He said to the chief[c] servant in his household, the one in charge of all that he had,[i] "Put your hand under my thigh.[j] [3]I want you to swear by the LORD, the God of heaven and the God of earth,[k] that you will not get a wife for my son[l] from the daughters of the Canaanites,[m] among whom I am living, [4]but will go to my country and my own relatives[n] and get a wife for my son Isaac."

[5]The servant asked him, "What if the woman is unwilling to come back with me to this land? Shall I then take your son back to the country you came from?"

---

[a]11 Or *sell*   [b]15 That is, about 10 pounds (about 4.5 kilograms)   [c]2 Or *oldest*

23:8
[a]Ge 25:9

23:10
[b]Ge 34:20-24;
Ru 4:4

23:11
[c]2Sa 24:23

23:15
[d]Eze 45:12

23:16
[e]Jer 32:9;
Zec 11:12

23:17
[f]Ge 25:9;
49:30-32;
50:13;
Ac 7:16

23:20
[g]Jer 32:10

24:1
[h]ver 35

24:2
[i]Ge 39:4-6
[j]ver 9;
Ge 47:29

24:3
[k]Ge 14:19
[l]Ge 28:1;
Dt 7:3
[m]Ge 10:15-19

24:4
[n]Ge 12:1; 28:2

24:7
a Gal 3:16*
b Ge 12:7; 13:15
c Ex 23:20,23

24:9
d ver 2

24:11
e Ex 2:15
f ver 13;
1Sa 9:11

24:12
g ver 27,42,48;
Ge 26:24;
Ex 3:6,15,16

24:14
h Jdg 6:17,37

24:15
i ver 45
j Ge 22:23
k Ge 22:20
l Ge 11:29

24:16
m Ge 26:7

24:18
n ver 14

24:19
o ver 14

24:21
p ver 12

24:22
q ver 47

⁶"Make sure that you do not take my son back there," Abraham said. ⁷"The LORD, the God of heaven, who brought me out of my father's household and my native land and who spoke to me and promised me on oath, saying, 'To your offspring[a][a] I will give this land'[b]—he will send his angel before you[c] so that you can get a wife for my son from there. ⁸If the woman is unwilling to come back with you, then you will be released from this oath of mine. Only do not take my son back there." ⁹So the servant put his hand under the thigh[d] of his master Abraham and swore an oath to him concerning this matter.

¹⁰Then the servant took ten of his master's camels and left, taking with him all kinds of good things from his master. He set out for Aram Naharaim[b] and made his way to the town of Nahor. ¹¹He had the camels kneel down near the well[e] outside the town; it was toward evening, the time the women go out to draw water.[f]

¹²Then he prayed, "O LORD, God of my master Abraham,[g] give me success today, and show kindness to my master Abraham. ¹³See, I am standing beside this spring, and the daughters of the townspeople are coming out to draw water. ¹⁴May it be that when I say to a girl, 'Please let down your jar that I may have a drink,' and she says, 'Drink, and I'll water your camels too'—let her be the one you have chosen for your servant Isaac. By this I will know[h] that you have shown kindness to my master."

¹⁵Before he had finished praying,[i] Rebekah[j] came out with her jar on her shoulder. She was the daughter of Bethuel son of Milcah,[k] who was the wife of Abraham's brother Nahor.[l] ¹⁶The girl was very beautiful,[m] a virgin; no man had ever lain with her. She went down to the spring, filled her jar and came up again.

¹⁷The servant hurried to meet her and said, "Please give me a little water from your jar."

¹⁸"Drink,[n] my lord," she said, and quickly lowered the jar to her hands and gave him a drink.

¹⁹After she had given him a drink, she said, "I'll draw water for your camels too,[o] until they have finished drinking." ²⁰So she quickly emptied her jar into the trough, ran back to the well to draw more water, and drew enough for all his camels. ²¹Without saying a word, the man watched her closely to learn whether or not the LORD had made his journey successful.[p]

²²When the camels had finished drinking, the man took out a gold nose ring[q] weighing a beka[c] and two gold bracelets weighing ten shekels.[d] ²³Then he asked, "Whose daughter are you? Please tell me, is there room in your father's house for us to spend the night?"

a 7 Or seed   b 10 That is, Northwest Mesopotamia   c 22 That is, about 1/5 ounce (about 5.5 grams)   d 22 That is, about 4 ounces (about 110 grams)

²⁴She answered him, "I am the daughter of Bethuel, the son that Milcah bore to Nahor.ᵃ" ²⁵And she added, "We have plenty of straw and fodder, as well as room for you to spend the night."

²⁶Then the man bowed down and worshiped the LORD,ᵇ ²⁷saying, "Praise be to the LORD,ᶜ the God of my master Abraham, who has not abandoned his kindness and faithfulnessᵈ to my master. As for me, the LORD has led me on the journeyᵉ to the house of my master's relatives."ᶠ

²⁸The girl ran and told her mother's household about these things. ²⁹Now Rebekah had a brother named Laban,ᵍ and he hurried out to the man at the spring. ³⁰As soon as he had seen the nose ring, and the bracelets on his sister's arms, and had heard Rebekah tell what the man said to her, he went out to the man and found him standing by the camels near the spring. ³¹"Come, you who are blessed by the LORD,"ʰ he said. "Why are you standing out here? I have prepared the house and a place for the camels."

³²So the man went to the house, and the camels were unloaded. Straw and fodder were brought for the camels, and water for him and his men to wash their feet.ⁱ ³³Then food was set before him, but he said, "I will not eat until I have told you what I have to say."

"Then tell us," ₎Laban₎ said.

³⁴So he said, "I am Abraham's servant. ³⁵The LORD has blessed my master abundantly,ʲ and he has become wealthy. He has given him sheep and cattle, silver and gold, menservants and maidservants, and camels and donkeys.ᵏ ³⁶My master's wife Sarah has borne him a son in herᵃ old age,ˡ and he has given him everything he owns.ᵐ ³⁷And my master made me swear an oath, and said, 'You must not get a wife for my son from the daughters of the Canaanites, in whose land I live,ⁿ ³⁸but go to my father's family and to my own clan, and get a wife for my son.'ᵒ

³⁹"Then I asked my master, 'What if the woman will not come back with me?'ᵖ

⁴⁰"He replied, 'The LORD, before whom I have walked, will send his angel with you�q and make your journey a success, so that you can get a wife for my son from my own clan and from my father's family. ⁴¹Then, when you go to my clan, you will be released from my oath even if they refuse to give her to you—you will be released from my oath.'ʳ

⁴²"When I came to the spring today, I said, 'O LORD, God of my master Abraham, if you will, please grant successˢ to the journey on which I have come. ⁴³See, I am standing beside this

ᵃ36 Or *his*

24:24
ᵃver 15

24:26
ᵇver 48,52;
Ex 4:31

24:27
ᶜEx 18:10;
Ru 4:14;
1Sa 25:32
ᵈver 49;
Ge 32:10;
Ps 98:3
ᵉver 21
ᶠver 12,48

24:29
ᵍver 4;
Ge 29:5,12,13

24:31
ʰGe 26:29;
Ru 3:10;
Ps 115:15

24:32
ⁱGe 43:24;
Jdg 19:21

24:35
ʲver 1
ᵏGe 13:2

24:36
ˡGe 21:2,10
ᵐGe 25:5

24:37
ⁿver 3

24:38
ᵒver 4

24:39
ᵖver 5

24:40
qver 7

24:41
ʳver 8

24:42
ˢver 12

24:43
a ver 13
b ver 14

24:45
c 1Sa 1:13
d ver 15
e ver 17

24:46
f ver 18-19

24:47
g ver 23
h ver 24
i Eze 16:11-12

24:48
j ver 26
k ver 27

24:49
l Ge 47:29;
Jos 2:14

24:50
m Ps 118:23
n Ge 31:7,24,
29,42

24:52
o ver 26

24:53
p ver 10,22

24:54
q ver 56,59

24:59
r Ge 35:8

spring;[a] if a maiden comes out to draw water and I say to her, "Please let me drink a little water from your jar,"[b] [44]and if she says to me, "Drink, and I'll draw water for your camels too," let her be the one the LORD has chosen for my master's son.'

[45]"Before I finished praying in my heart,[c] Rebekah came out, with her jar on her shoulder.[d] She went down to the spring and drew water, and I said to her, 'Please give me a drink.'[e]

[46]"She quickly lowered her jar from her shoulder and said, 'Drink, and I'll water your camels too.'[f] So I drank, and she watered the camels also.

[47]"I asked her, 'Whose daughter are you?'[g]

"She said, 'The daughter of Bethuel son of Nahor, whom Milcah bore to him.'[h]

"Then I put the ring in her nose and the bracelets on her arms,[i] [48]and I bowed down and worshiped the LORD.[j] I praised the LORD, the God of my master Abraham, who had led me on the right road to get the granddaughter of my master's brother for his son.[k] [49]Now if you will show kindness and faithfulness[l] to my master, tell me; and if not, tell me, so I may know which way to turn."

[50]Laban and Bethuel answered, "This is from the LORD;[m] we can say nothing to you one way or the other.[n] [51]Here is Rebekah; take her and go, and let her become the wife of your master's son, as the LORD has directed."

[52]When Abraham's servant heard what they said, he bowed down to the ground before the LORD.[o] [53]Then the servant brought out gold and silver jewelry and articles of clothing and gave them to Rebekah; he also gave costly gifts[p] to her brother and to her mother. [54]Then he and the men who were with him ate and drank and spent the night there.

When they got up the next morning, he said, "Send me on my way[q] to my master."

[55]But her brother and her mother replied, "Let the girl remain with us ten days or so; then you[a] may go."

[56]But he said to them, "Do not detain me, now that the LORD has granted success to my journey. Send me on my way so I may go to my master."

[57]Then they said, "Let's call the girl and ask her about it." [58]So they called Rebekah and asked her, "Will you go with this man?"

"I will go," she said.

[59]So they sent their sister Rebekah on her way, along with her nurse[r] and Abraham's servant and his men. [60]And they blessed Rebekah and said to her,

"Our sister, may you increase
    to thousands upon thousands;[a]
may your offspring possess
    the gates of their enemies."[b]

[61]Then Rebekah and her maids got ready and mounted their camels and went back with the man. So the servant took Rebekah and left.

[62]Now Isaac had come from Beer Lahai Roi,[c] for he was living in the Negev.[d] [63]He went out to the field one evening to meditate,[a][e] and as he looked up, he saw camels approaching. [64]Rebekah also looked up and saw Isaac. She got down from her camel [65]and asked the servant, "Who is that man in the field coming to meet us?"

"He is my master," the servant answered. So she took her veil and covered herself.

[66]Then the servant told Isaac all he had done. [67]Isaac brought her into the tent of his mother Sarah, and he married Rebekah.[f] So she became his wife, and he loved her;[g] and Isaac was comforted after his mother's death.[h]

Chapter 25 Theme _____

25 Abraham took[b] another wife, whose name was Keturah. [2]She bore him Zimran, Jokshan, Medan, Midian, Ishbak and Shuah.[i] [3]Jokshan was the father of Sheba and Dedan; the descendants of Dedan were the Asshurites, the Letushites and the Leummites. [4]The sons of Midian were Ephah, Epher, Hanoch, Abida and Eldaah. All these were descendants of Keturah.

[5]Abraham left everything he owned to Isaac.[j] [6]But while he was still living, he gave gifts to the sons of his concubines[k] and sent them away from his son Isaac[l] to the land of the east.

[7]Altogether, Abraham lived a hundred and seventy-five years. [8]Then Abraham breathed his last and died at a good old age,[m] an old man and full of years; and he was gathered to his people.[n] [9]His sons Isaac and Ishmael buried him[o] in the cave of Machpelah near Mamre, in the field of Ephron son of Zohar the Hittite,[p] [10]the field Abraham had bought from the Hittites.[c][q] There Abraham was buried with his wife Sarah. [11]After Abraham's death, God blessed his son Isaac, who then lived near Beer Lahai Roi.[r]

[12]This is the account of Abraham's son Ishmael, whom Sarah's maidservant, Hagar[s] the Egyptian, bore to Abraham.[t]

24:60
[a] Ge 17:16
[b] Ge 22:17

24:62
[c] Ge 16:14; 25:11
[d] Ge 20:1

24:63
[e] Ps 1:2; 77:12;
119:15,27,48,
97,148; 143:5;
145:5

24:67
[f] Ge 25:20
[g] Ge 29:18,20
[h] Ge 23:1-2

25:2
[i] 1Ch 1:32,33

25:5
[j] Ge 24:36

25:6
[k] Ge 22:24
[l] Ge 21:10,14

25:8
[m] Ge 15:15
[n] ver 17;
Ge 35:29;
49:29,33

25:9
[o] Ge 35:29
[p] Ge 50:13

25:10
[q] Ge 23:16

25:11
[r] Ge 16:14

25:12
[s] Ge 16:1
[t] Ge 16:15

---

[a] 63 The meaning of the Hebrew for this word is uncertain. [b] 1 Or *had taken* [c] 10 Or *the sons of Heth*

25:16
ᵃGe 17:20

25:17
ᵇver 8

25:18
ᶜGe 16:12

25:20
ᵈver 26;
Ge 26:34
ᵉGe 24:67
ᶠGe 24:29

25:21
ᵍ1Ch 5:20;
2Ch 33:13;
Ezr 8:23;
Ps 127:3;
Ro 9:10

25:22
ʰ1Sa 9:9;
10:22

25:23
ⁱGe 17:4
ʲGe 27:29,40;
Mal 1:3;
Ro 9:11-12*

25:25
ᵏGe 27:11

25:26
ˡHos 12:3
ᵐGe 27:36

25:27
ⁿGe 27:3,5

25:28
ᵒGe 27:19
ᵖGe 27:6

¹³These are the names of the sons of Ishmael, listed in the order of their birth: Nebaioth the firstborn of Ishmael, Kedar, Adbeel, Mibsam, ¹⁴Mishma, Dumah, Massa, ¹⁵Hadad, Tema, Jetur, Naphish and Kedemah. ¹⁶These were the sons of Ishmael, and these are the names of the twelve tribal rulers[a] according to their settlements and camps. ¹⁷Altogether, Ishmael lived a hundred and thirty-seven years. He breathed his last and died, and he was gathered to his people.[b] ¹⁸His descendants settled in the area from Havilah to Shur, near the border of Egypt, as you go toward Asshur. And they lived in hostility toward[a] all their brothers.[c]

¹⁹This is the account of Abraham's son Isaac.

Abraham became the father of Isaac, ²⁰and Isaac was forty years old[d] when he married Rebekah[e] daughter of Bethuel the Aramean from Paddan Aram[b] and sister of Laban[f] the Aramean.

²¹Isaac prayed to the LORD on behalf of his wife, because she was barren. The LORD answered his prayer,[g] and his wife Rebekah became pregnant. ²²The babies jostled each other within her, and she said, "Why is this happening to me?" So she went to inquire of the LORD.[h]

²³The LORD said to her,

"Two nations[i] are in your womb,
    and two peoples from within you will be separated;
one people will be stronger than the other,
    and the older will serve the younger.[j]"

²⁴When the time came for her to give birth, there were twin boys in her womb. ²⁵The first to come out was red, and his whole body was like a hairy garment;[k] so they named him Esau.[c] ²⁶After this, his brother came out, with his hand grasping Esau's heel;[l] so he was named Jacob.[d][m] Isaac was sixty years old when Rebekah gave birth to them.

²⁷The boys grew up, and Esau became a skillful hunter, a man of the open country,[n] while Jacob was a quiet man, staying among the tents. ²⁸Isaac, who had a taste for wild game,[o] loved Esau, but Rebekah loved Jacob.[p]

²⁹Once when Jacob was cooking some stew, Esau came in from the open country, famished. ³⁰He said to Jacob, "Quick, let me have some of that red stew! I'm famished!" (That is why he was also called Edom.[e])

³¹Jacob replied, "First sell me your birthright."

ᵃ18 Or *lived to the east of*   ᵇ20 That is, Northwest Mesopotamia   ᶜ25 *Esau* may mean *hairy*; he was also called Edom, which means *red*.   ᵈ26 *Jacob* means *he grasps the heel* (figuratively, *he deceives*).   ᵉ30 *Edom* means *red*.

41

³²"Look, I am about to die," Esau said. "What good is the birthright to me?"

³³But Jacob said, "Swear to me first." So he swore an oath to him, selling his birthright[a] to Jacob.

³⁴Then Jacob gave Esau some bread and some lentil stew. He ate and drank, and then got up and left.

So Esau despised his birthright.

Chapter 26 Theme _____

26 Now there was a famine in the land[b]—besides the earlier famine of Abraham's time—and Isaac went to Abimelech king of the Philistines in Gerar.[c] ²The LORD appeared[d] to Isaac and said, "Do not go down to Egypt; live in the land where I tell you to live.[e] ³Stay in this land for a while,[f] and I will be with you and will bless you.[g] For to you and your descendants I will give all these lands[h] and will confirm the oath I swore to your father Abraham. ⁴I will make your descendants as numerous as the stars in the sky[i] and will give them all these lands, and through your offspring[a] all nations on earth will be blessed,[j] ⁵because Abraham obeyed me[k] and kept my requirements, my commands, my decrees and my laws." ⁶So Isaac stayed in Gerar.

⁷When the men of that place asked him about his wife, he said, "She is my sister,[l]" because he was afraid to say, "She is my wife." He thought, "The men of this place might kill me on account of Rebekah, because she is beautiful."

⁸When Isaac had been there a long time, Abimelech king of the Philistines looked down from a window and saw Isaac caressing his wife Rebekah. ⁹So Abimelech summoned Isaac and said, "She is really your wife! Why did you say, 'She is my sister'?"

Isaac answered him, "Because I thought I might lose my life on account of her."

¹⁰Then Abimelech said, "What is this you have done to us?[m] One of the men might well have slept with your wife, and you would have brought guilt upon us."

¹¹So Abimelech gave orders to all the people: "Anyone who molests[n] this man or his wife shall surely be put to death."

¹²Isaac planted crops in that land and the same year reaped a hundredfold, because the LORD blessed him.[o] ¹³The man became rich, and his wealth continued to grow until he became very wealthy.[p] ¹⁴He had so many flocks and herds and servants[q] that the Philistines envied him.[r] ¹⁵So all the wells[s] that his father's servants had dug in the time of his father Abraham, the Philistines stopped up,[t] filling them with earth.

a 4 Or *seed*

25:33
a Ge 27:36;
Heb 12:16

26:1
b Ge 12:10
c Ge 20:1

26:2
d Ge 12:7;
17:1; 18:1
e Ge 12:1

26:3
f Ge 20:1; 28:15
g Ge 12:2;
22:16-18
h Ge 12:7; 13:15;
15:18

26:4
i Ge 15:5;
22:17;
Ex 32:13
j Ge 12:3; 22:18;
Gal 3:8

26:5
k Ge 22:16

26:7
l Ge 12:13;
20:2,12;
Pr 29:25

26:10
m Ge 20:9

26:11
n Ps 105:15

26:12
o ver 3;
Job 42:12

26:13
p Pr 10:22

26:14
q Ge 24:36
r Ge 37:11

26:15
s Ge 21:30
t Ge 21:25

26:16
a Ex 1:9

26:18
b Ge 21:30

26:20
c Ge 21:25

26:22
d Ge 17:6;
Ex 1:7

26:24
e Ge 24:12;
Ex 3:6
f Ge 15:1
g ver 4
h Ge 17:7

26:25
i Ge 12:7,8;
13:4,18;
Ps 116:17

26:26
j Ge 21:22

26:27
k ver 16

26:28
l Ge 21:22

26:29
m Ge 24:31;
Ps 115:15

26:30
n Ge 19:3

26:31
o Ge 21:31

26:33
p Ge 21:14

26:34
q Ge 25:20
r Ge 28:9; 36:2

26:35
s Ge 27:46

¹⁶Then Abimelech said to Isaac, "Move away from us; you have become too powerful for us.*a*"

¹⁷So Isaac moved away from there and encamped in the Valley of Gerar and settled there. ¹⁸Isaac reopened the wells*b* that had been dug in the time of his father Abraham, which the Philistines had stopped up after Abraham died, and he gave them the same names his father had given them.

¹⁹Isaac's servants dug in the valley and discovered a well of fresh water there. ²⁰But the herdsmen of Gerar quarreled with Isaac's herdsmen and said, "The water is ours!"*c* So he named the well Esek,ᵃ because they disputed with him. ²¹Then they dug another well, but they quarreled over that one also; so he named it Sitnah.ᵇ ²²He moved on from there and dug another well, and no one quarreled over it. He named it Rehoboth,ᶜ saying, "Now the LORD has given us room and we will flourishᵈ in the land."

²³From there he went up to Beersheba. ²⁴That night the LORD appeared to him and said, "I am the God of your father Abraham.*e* Do not be afraid,*f* for I am with you; I will bless you and will increase the number of your descendants*g* for the sake of my servant Abraham."*h*

²⁵Isaac built an altar*i* there and called on the name of the LORD. There he pitched his tent, and there his servants dug a well.

²⁶Meanwhile, Abimelech had come to him from Gerar, with Ahuzzath his personal adviser and Phicol the commander of his forces.*j* ²⁷Isaac asked them, "Why have you come to me, since you were hostile to me and sent me away?*k*"

²⁸They answered, "We saw clearly that the LORD was with you;*l* so we said, 'There ought to be a sworn agreement between us'— between us and you. Let us make a treaty with you ²⁹that you will do us no harm, just as we did not molest you but always treated you well and sent you away in peace. And now you are blessed by the LORD."*m*

³⁰Isaac then made a feast*n* for them, and they ate and drank. ³¹Early the next morning the men swore an oath*o* to each other. Then Isaac sent them on their way, and they left him in peace.

³²That day Isaac's servants came and told him about the well they had dug. They said, "We've found water!" ³³He called it Shibah,ᵈ and to this day the name of the town has been Beersheba.ᵉ*p*

³⁴When Esau was forty years old,*q* he married Judith daughter of Beeri the Hittite, and also Basemath daughter of Elon the Hittite.*r* ³⁵They were a source of grief to Isaac and Rebekah.*s*

ᵃ*20* *Esek* means *dispute.*   ᵇ*21* *Sitnah* means *opposition.*   ᶜ*22* *Rehoboth* means *room.*
ᵈ*33* *Shibah* can mean *oath* or *seven.*   ᵉ*33* *Beersheba* can mean *well of the oath* or *well of seven.*

Chapter 27 Theme _____

27 When Isaac was old and his eyes were so weak that he could no longer see,[a] he called for Esau his older son[b] and said to him, "My son."

"Here I am," he answered.

[2]Isaac said, "I am now an old man and don't know the day of my death.[c] [3]Now then, get your weapons—your quiver and bow—and go out to the open country[d] to hunt some wild game for me. [4]Prepare me the kind of tasty food I like and bring it to me to eat, so that I may give you my blessing[e] before I die."

[5]Now Rebekah was listening as Isaac spoke to his son Esau. When Esau left for the open country to hunt game and bring it back, [6]Rebekah said to her son Jacob,[f] "Look, I overheard your father say to your brother Esau, [7]'Bring me some game and prepare me some tasty food to eat, so that I may give you my blessing in the presence of the LORD before I die.' [8]Now, my son, listen carefully and do what I tell you:[g] [9]Go out to the flock and bring me two choice young goats, so I can prepare some tasty food for your father, just the way he likes it. [10]Then take it to your father to eat, so that he may give you his blessing before he dies."

[11]Jacob said to Rebekah his mother, "But my brother Esau is a hairy man,[h] and I'm a man with smooth skin. [12]What if my father touches me?[i] I would appear to be tricking him and would bring down a curse on myself rather than a blessing."

[13]His mother said to him, "My son, let the curse fall on me.[j] Just do what I say;[k] go and get them for me."

[14]So he went and got them and brought them to his mother, and she prepared some tasty food, just the way his father liked it. [15]Then Rebekah took the best clothes[l] of Esau her older son, which she had in the house, and put them on her younger son Jacob. [16]She also covered his hands and the smooth part of his neck with the goatskins. [17]Then she handed to her son Jacob the tasty food and the bread she had made.

[18]He went to his father and said, "My father."

"Yes, my son," he answered. "Who is it?"

[19]Jacob said to his father, "I am Esau your firstborn. I have done as you told me. Please sit up and eat some of my game so that you may give me your blessing."[m]

[20]Isaac asked his son, "How did you find it so quickly, my son?"

"The LORD your God gave me success,[n]" he replied.

[21]Then Isaac said to Jacob, "Come near so I can touch you,[o] my son, to know whether you really are my son Esau or not."

[22]Jacob went close to his father Isaac, who touched him and said, "The voice is the voice of Jacob, but the hands are the hands

27:1
[a] Ge 48:10;
1Sa 3:2
[b] Ge 25:25

27:2
[c] Ge 47:29

27:3
[d] Ge 25:27

27:4
[e] ver 10,25,31;
Ge 49:28;
Dt 33:1;
Heb 11:20

27:6
[f] Ge 25:28

27:8
[g] ver 13,43

27:11
[h] Ge 25:25

27:12
[i] ver 22

27:13
[j] Mt 27:25
[k] ver 8

27:15
[l] ver 27

27:19
[m] ver 4

27:20
[n] Ge 24:12

27:21
[o] ver 12

27:23
a ver 16

of Esau." ²³He did not recognize him, for his hands were hairy like those of his brother Esau;*a* so he blessed him. ²⁴"Are you really my son Esau?" he asked.

"I am," he replied.

27:25
b ver 4

²⁵Then he said, "My son, bring me some of your game to eat, so that I may give you my blessing."*b*

Jacob brought it to him and he ate; and he brought some wine and he drank. ²⁶Then his father Isaac said to him, "Come here, my son, and kiss me."

27:27
c Heb 11:20
d SS 4:11
e Ps 65:9-13

²⁷So he went to him and kissed him*c*. When Isaac caught the smell of his clothes,*d* he blessed him and said,

27:28
f Dt 33:13
g ver 39
h Ge 45:18;
Nu 18:12;
Dt 33:28

"Ah, the smell of my son
is like the smell of a field
that the LORD has blessed.*e*
²⁸May God give you of heaven's dew *f*
and of earth's richness*g*—
an abundance of grain and new wine.*h*
²⁹May nations serve you
and peoples bow down to you.*i*
Be lord over your brothers,
and may the sons of your mother bow down to you.*j*
May those who curse you be cursed
and those who bless you be blessed.*k*"

27:29
i Isa 45:14,23;
49:7,23
j Ge 9:25;
25:23; 37:7
k Ge 12:3;
Nu 24:9;
Zep 2:8

27:31
l ver 4

³⁰After Isaac finished blessing him and Jacob had scarcely left his father's presence, his brother Esau came in from hunting. ³¹He too prepared some tasty food and brought it to his father. Then he said to him, "My father, sit up and eat some of my game, so that you may give me your blessing."*l*

27:32
m ver 18

³²His father Isaac asked him, "Who are you?"*m*

"I am your son," he answered, "your firstborn, Esau."

27:33
n ver 29;
Ge 28:3,4;
Ro 11:29

³³Isaac trembled violently and said, "Who was it, then, that hunted game and brought it to me? I ate it just before you came and I blessed him—and indeed he will be blessed!*n*"

³⁴When Esau heard his father's words, he burst out with a loud and bitter cry*o* and said to his father, "Bless me—me too, my father!"

27:34
o Heb 12:17

³⁵But he said, "Your brother came deceitfully*p* and took your blessing."

27:35
p Jer 9:4; 12:6

³⁶Esau said, "Isn't he rightly named Jacob*a*?*q* He has deceived me these two times: He took my birthright,*r* and now he's taken my blessing!" Then he asked, "Haven't you reserved any blessing for me?"

27:36
q Ge 25:26
r Ge 25:33

a36 Jacob means *he grasps the heel* (figuratively, *he deceives*).

GENESIS 27

³⁷Isaac answered Esau, "I have made him lord over you and have made all his relatives his servants, and I have sustained him with grain and new wine.ᵃ So what can I possibly do for you, my son?"

³⁸Esau said to his father, "Do you have only one blessing, my father? Bless me too, my father!" Then Esau wept aloud.ᵇ

³⁹His father Isaac answered him,

"Your dwelling will be
    away from the earth's richness,
    away from the dewᶜ of heaven above.
⁴⁰You will live by the sword
    and you will serveᵈ your brother.ᵉ
But when you grow restless,
    you will throw his yoke
    from off your neck.ᶠ"

⁴¹Esau held a grudgeᵍ against Jacobʰ because of the blessing his father had given him. He said to himself, "The days of mourningⁱ for my father are near; then I will kill my brother Jacob."ʲ

⁴²When Rebekah was told what her older son Esau had said, she sent for her younger son Jacob and said to him, "Your brother Esau is consoling himself with the thought of killing you. ⁴³Now then, my son, do what I say:ᵏ Flee at once to my brother Labanˡ in Haran.ᵐ ⁴⁴Stay with him for a whileⁿ until your brother's fury subsides. ⁴⁵When your brother is no longer angry with you and forgets what you did to him,ᵒ I'll send word for you to come back from there. Why should I lose both of you in one day?"

⁴⁶Then Rebekah said to Isaac, "I'm disgusted with living because of these Hittite women. If Jacob takes a wife from among the women of this land, from Hittite women like these, my life will not be worth living."ᵖ

Chapter 28 Theme

28 So Isaac called for Jacob and blessedᵃ him and commanded him: "Do not marry a Canaanite woman.�q ²Go at once to Paddan Aram,ᵇ to the house of your mother's father Bethuel.ʳ Take a wife for yourself there, from among the daughters of Laban, your mother's brother. ³May God Almightyᶜˢ bless you and make you fruitfulᵗ and increase your numbers until you become a community of peoples. ⁴May he give you and your descendants the blessing given to Abraham,ᵘ so that you may take possession of the land where you now live as an

---

ᵃ1 Or *greeted*   ᵇ2 That is, Northwest Mesopotamia; also in verses 5, 6 and 7
ᶜ3 Hebrew *El-Shaddai*

46

27:37 ᵃver 28
27:38 ᵇHeb 12:17
27:39 ᶜver 28
27:40 ᵈ2Sa 8:14 ᵉGe 25:23 ᶠ2Ki 8:20-22
27:41 ᵍGe 37:4 ʰGe 32:11 ⁱGe 50:4,10 ʲOb 1:10
27:43 ᵏver 8 ˡGe 24:29 ᵐGe 11:31
27:44 ⁿGe 31:38,41
27:45 ᵒver 35
27:46 ᵖGe 26:35
28:1 qGe 24:3
28:2 ʳGe 25:20
28:3 ˢGe 17:1 ᵗGe 17:6
28:4 ᵘGe 12:2,3

28:4
aGe 17:8

28:5
bHos 12:12
cGe 24:29

28:6
dver 1

28:8
eGe 24:3
fGe 26:35

28:9
gGe 25:13
hGe 26:34

28:10
iGe 11:31

28:12
jGe 20:3
kJn 1:51

28:13
lGe 12:7;
35:7,9; 48:3
mGe 26:24
nGe 13:15;
35:12

28:14
oGe 26:4
pGe 13:14
qGe 12:3;
18:18; 22:18;
Gal 3:8

28:15
rGe 26:3; 48:21
sNu 6:24;
Ps 121:5,7-8
tDt 31:6,8
uNu 23:19

28:17
vEx 3:5;
Jos 5:15

28:18
wGe 35:14
xLev 8:11

28:19
yJdg 1:23,26

28:20
zGe 31:13;
Jdg 11:30;
2Sa 15:8
aver 15

28:21
bJdg 11:31
cDt 26:17

28:22
dGe 35:7,14
eGe 14:20;
Lev 27:30

alien,a the land God gave to Abraham." 5Then Isaac sent Jacob on his way, and he went to Paddan Aram,b to Laban son of Bethuel the Aramean, the brother of Rebekah,c who was the mother of Jacob and Esau.

6Now Esau learned that Isaac had blessed Jacob and had sent him to Paddan Aram to take a wife from there, and that when he blessed him he commanded him, "Do not marry a Canaanite woman,"d 7and that Jacob had obeyed his father and mother and had gone to Paddan Aram. 8Esau then realized how displeasing the Canaanite womene were to his father Isaac;f 9so he went to Ishmael and married Mahalath, the sister of Nebaiothg and daughter of Ishmael son of Abraham, in addition to the wives he already had.h

10Jacob left Beersheba and set out for Haran.i 11When he reached a certain place, he stopped for the night because the sun had set. Taking one of the stones there, he put it under his head and lay down to sleep. 12He had a dreamj in which he saw a stairwaya resting on the earth, with its top reaching to heaven, and the angels of God were ascending and descending on it.k 13There above itb stood the LORD,l and he said: "I am the LORD, the God of your father Abraham and the God of Isaac.m I will give you and your descendants the landn on which you are lying. 14Your descendants will be like the dust of the earth, and youo will spread out to the west and to the east, to the north and to the south.p All peoples on earth will be blessed through you and your offspring.q 15I am with your and will watch over yous wherever you go, and I will bring you back to this land. I will not leave yout until I have done what I have promised you."u

16When Jacob awoke from his sleep, he thought, "Surely the LORD is in this place, and I was not aware of it." 17He was afraid and said, "How awesome is this place!v This is none other than the house of God; this is the gate of heaven."

18Early the next morning Jacob took the stone he had placed under his head and set it up as a pillarw and poured oil on top of it.x 19He called that place Bethel,c though the city used to be called Luz.y

20Then Jacob made a vow,z saying, "If God will be with me and will watch over mea on this journey I am taking and will give me food to eat and clothes to wear 21so that I return safelyb to my father's house, then the LORDd will be my Godc 22ande this stone that I have set up as a pillar will be God's house,d and of all that you give me I will give you a tenth.e "

a12 Or ladder   b13 Or There beside him   c19 Bethel means house of God.   d20,21 Or Since God...father's house, the LORD   e21,22 Or house, and the LORD will be my God, 22then

Chapter 29 Theme _____

29 Then Jacob continued on his journey and came to the land of the eastern peoples.ᵃ ²There he saw a well in the field, with three flocks of sheep lying near it because the flocks were watered from that well. The stone over the mouth of the well was large. ³When all the flocks were gathered there, the shepherds would roll the stone away from the well's mouth and water the sheep. Then they would return the stone to its place over the mouth of the well.

⁴Jacob asked the shepherds, "My brothers, where are you from?"

"We're from Haran,ᵇ" they replied.

⁵He said to them, "Do you know Laban, Nahor's grandson?"

"Yes, we know him," they answered.

⁶Then Jacob asked them, "Is he well?"

"Yes, he is," they said, "and here comes his daughter Rachel with the sheep."

⁷"Look," he said, "the sun is still high; it is not time for the flocks to be gathered. Water the sheep and take them back to pasture."

⁸"We can't," they replied, "until all the flocks are gathered and the stone has been rolled away from the mouth of the well. Then we will water the sheep."

⁹While he was still talking with them, Rachel came with her father's sheep,ᶜ for she was a shepherdess. ¹⁰When Jacob saw Rachel daughter of Laban, his mother's brother, and Laban's sheep, he went over and rolled the stone away from the mouth of the well and watered his uncle's sheep.ᵈ ¹¹Then Jacob kissed Rachel and began to weep aloud.ᵉ ¹²He had told Rachel that he was a relativeᶠ of her father and a son of Rebekah. So she ran and told her father.ᵍ

¹³As soon as Labanʰ heard the news about Jacob, his sister's son, he hurried to meet him. He embraced him and kissed him and brought him to his home, and there Jacob told him all these things. ¹⁴Then Laban said to him, "You are my own flesh and blood."ⁱ

After Jacob had stayed with him for a whole month, ¹⁵Laban said to him, "Just because you are a relative of mine, should you work for me for nothing? Tell me what your wages should be."

¹⁶Now Laban had two daughters; the name of the older was Leah, and the name of the younger was Rachel. ¹⁷Leah had weakᵃ eyes, but Rachel was lovely in form, and beautiful. ¹⁸Jacob was in love with Rachel and said, "I'll work for you seven years in return for your younger daughter Rachel."ʲ

ᵃ17 Or *delicate*

29:1
ᵃJdg 6:3,33

29:4
ᵇGe 28:10

29:9
ᶜEx 2:16

29:10
ᵈEx 2:17

29:11
ᵉGe 33:4

29:12
ᶠGe 13:8;
14:14,16
ᵍGe 24:28

29:13
ʰGe 24:29

29:14
ⁱGe 2:23;
Jdg 9:2;
2Sa 19:12-13

29:18
ʲHos 12:12

29:20
a SS 8:7;
Hos 12:12

29:21
b Jdg 15:1

29:22
c Jdg 14:10;
Jn 2:1-2

29:25
d Ge 12:18
e Ge 27:36

29:27
f Jdg 14:12

29:29
g Ge 30:3
h Ge 16:1

29:30
i ver 16
j Ge 31:41

29:31
k Dt 21:15-17
l Ge 11:30; 30:1;
Ps 127:3

29:32
m Ge 16:11;
31:42;
Ex 4:31;
Dt 26:7;
Ps 25:18

29:33
n Ge 34:25;
49:5

29:34
o Ge 30:20;
1Sa 1:2-4
p Ge 49:5-7

29:35
q Ge 49:8;
Mt 1:2-3

30:1
r Ge 29:31;
1Sa 1:5-6
s Lev 18:18

¹⁹Laban said, "It's better that I give her to you than to some other man. Stay here with me." ²⁰So Jacob served seven years to get Rachel, but they seemed like only a few days to him because of his love for her.*ᵃ*

²¹Then Jacob said to Laban, "Give me my wife. My time is completed, and I want to lie with her.*ᵇ*"

²²So Laban brought together all the people of the place and gave a feast.*ᶜ* ²³But when evening came, he took his daughter Leah and gave her to Jacob, and Jacob lay with her. ²⁴And Laban gave his servant girl Zilpah to his daughter as her maidservant.

²⁵When morning came, there was Leah! So Jacob said to Laban, "What is this you have done to me?*ᵈ* I served you for Rachel, didn't I? Why have you deceived me?*ᵉ*"

²⁶Laban replied, "It is not our custom here to give the younger daughter in marriage before the older one. ²⁷Finish this daughter's bridal week;*ᶠ* then we will give you the younger one also, in return for another seven years of work."

²⁸And Jacob did so. He finished the week with Leah, and then Laban gave him his daughter Rachel to be his wife. ²⁹Laban gave his servant girl Bilhah*ᵍ* to his daughter Rachel as her maidservant.*ʰ* ³⁰Jacob lay with Rachel also, and he loved Rachel more than Leah.*ⁱ* And he worked for Laban another seven years.*ʲ*

³¹When the LORD saw that Leah was not loved,*ᵏ* he opened her womb,*ˡ* but Rachel was barren. ³²Leah became pregnant and gave birth to a son. She named him Reuben,*ᵃ* for she said, "It is because the LORD has seen my misery.*ᵐ* Surely my husband will love me now."

³³She conceived again, and when she gave birth to a son she said, "Because the LORD heard that I am not loved, he gave me this one too." So she named him Simeon.*ᵇⁿ*

³⁴Again she conceived, and when she gave birth to a son she said, "Now at last my husband will become attached to me,*ᵒ* because I have borne him three sons." So he was named Levi.*ᶜᵖ*

³⁵She conceived again, and when she gave birth to a son she said, "This time I will praise the LORD." So she named him Judah.*ᵈᵠ* Then she stopped having children.

Chapter 30 Theme

30 When Rachel saw that she was not bearing Jacob any children,*ʳ* she became jealous of her sister.*ˢ* So she said to Jacob, "Give me children, or I'll die!"

a 32 Reuben sounds like the Hebrew for *he has seen my misery*; the name means *see, a son.* *b 33 Simeon* probably means *one who hears.* *c 34 Levi* sounds like and may be derived from the Hebrew for *attached.* *d 35 Judah* sounds like and may be derived from the Hebrew for *praise.*

²Jacob became angry with her and said, "Am I in the place of God, who has kept you from having children?"ᵃ

³Then she said, "Here is Bilhah, my maidservant. Sleep with her so that she can bear children for me and that through her I too can build a family."ᵇ

⁴So she gave him her servant Bilhah as a wife.ᶜ Jacob slept with her,ᵈ ⁵and she became pregnant and bore him a son. ⁶Then Rachel said, "God has vindicated me;ᵉ he has listened to my plea and given me a son." Because of this she named him Dan.ᵃᶠ

⁷Rachel's servant Bilhah conceived again and bore Jacob a second son. ⁸Then Rachel said, "I have had a great struggle with my sister, and I have won."ᵍ So she named him Naphtali.ᵇʰ

⁹When Leah saw that she had stopped having children, she took her maidservant Zilpah and gave her to Jacob as a wife.ⁱ ¹⁰Leah's servant Zilpah bore Jacob a son. ¹¹Then Leah said, "What good fortune!"ᶜ So she named him Gad.ᵈʲ

¹²Leah's servant Zilpah bore Jacob a second son. ¹³Then Leah said, "How happy I am! The women will call meᵏ happy."ˡ So she named him Asher.ᵉᵐ

¹⁴During wheat harvest, Reuben went out into the fields and found some mandrake plants,ⁿ which he brought to his mother Leah. Rachel said to Leah, "Please give me some of your son's mandrakes."

¹⁵But she said to her, "Wasn't it enoughᵒ that you took away my husband? Will you take my son's mandrakes too?"

"Very well," Rachel said, "he can sleep with you tonight in return for your son's mandrakes."

¹⁶So when Jacob came in from the fields that evening, Leah went out to meet him. "You must sleep with me," she said. "I have hired you with my son's mandrakes." So he slept with her that night.

¹⁷God listened to Leah,ᵖ and she became pregnant and bore Jacob a fifth son. ¹⁸Then Leah said, "God has rewarded me for giving my maidservant to my husband." So she named him Issachar.ᶠ�q

¹⁹Leah conceived again and bore Jacob a sixth son. ²⁰Then Leah said, "God has presented me with a precious gift. This time my husband will treat me with honor, because I have borne him six sons." So she named him Zebulun.ᵍʳ

²¹Some time later she gave birth to a daughter and named her Dinah.

²²Then God remembered Rachel;ˢ he listened to her and opened her womb.ᵗ ²³She became pregnant and gave birth to a

ᵃ6 *Dan* here means *he has vindicated.*   ᵇ8 *Naphtali* means *my struggle.*   ᶜ11 Or "A troop is coming!"   ᵈ11 *Gad* can mean *good fortune* or *a troop.*   ᵉ13 *Asher* means *happy.*   ᶠ18 *Issachar* sounds like the Hebrew for *reward.*   ᵍ20 *Zebulun* probably means *honor.*

50

30:2 ᵃGe 16:2; 20:18; 29:31
30:3 ᵇGe 16:2
30:4 ᶜver 9,18 ᵈGe 16:3-4
30:6 ᵉPs 35:24; 43:1; La 3:59 ᶠGe 49:16-17
30:8 ᵍHos 12:3-4 ʰGe 49:21
30:9 ⁱver 4
30:11 ʲGe 49:19
30:13 ᵏPs 127:3 ˡPr 31:28; Lk 1:48 ᵐGe 49:20
30:14 ⁿSS 7:13
30:15 ᵒNu 16:9,13
30:17 ᵖGe 25:21
30:18 qGe 49:14
30:20 ʳGe 35:23; 49:13; Mt 4:13
30:22 ˢGe 8:1; 1Sa 1:19-20 ᵗGe 29:31

30:23
a ver 6
b Isa 4:1;
Lk 1:25

30:24
c Ge 35:24;
37:2; 39:1;
49:22-26
d Ge 35:17

30:25
e Ge 24:54

30:26
f Ge 29:20,30;
Hos 12:12

30:27
g Ge 26:24;
39:3,5

30:28
h Ge 29:15

30:29
i Ge 31:6
j Ge 31:38-40

30:30
k 1Ti 5:8

30:32
l Ge 31:8,12

30:35
m Ge 31:1

son*a* and said, "God has taken away my disgrace."*b* ²⁴She named him Joseph,*a c* and said, "May the LORD add to me another son."*d*

²⁵After Rachel gave birth to Joseph, Jacob said to Laban, "Send me on my way*e* so I can go back to my own homeland. ²⁶Give me my wives and children, for whom I have served you,*f* and I will be on my way. You know how much work I've done for you."

²⁷But Laban said to him, "If I have found favor in your eyes, please stay. I have learned by divination that*b* the LORD has blessed me because of you."*g* ²⁸He added, "Name your wages,*h* and I will pay them."

²⁹Jacob said to him, "You know how I have worked for you*i* and how your livestock has fared under my care.*j* ³⁰The little you had before I came has increased greatly, and the LORD has blessed you wherever I have been. But now, when may I do something for my own household?*k*"

³¹"What shall I give you?" he asked.

"Don't give me anything," Jacob replied. "But if you will do this one thing for me, I will go on tending your flocks and watching over them: ³²Let me go through all your flocks today and remove from them every speckled or spotted sheep, every dark-colored lamb and every spotted or speckled goat.*l* They will be my wages. ³³And my honesty will testify for me in the future, whenever you check on the wages you have paid me. Any goat in my possession that is not speckled or spotted, or any lamb that is not dark-colored, will be considered stolen."

³⁴"Agreed," said Laban. "Let it be as you have said." ³⁵That same day he removed all the male goats that were streaked or spotted, and all the speckled or spotted female goats (all that had white on them) and all the dark-colored lambs, and he placed them in the care of his sons.*m* ³⁶Then he put a three-day journey between himself and Jacob, while Jacob continued to tend the rest of Laban's flocks.

³⁷Jacob, however, took fresh-cut branches from poplar, almond and plane trees and made white stripes on them by peeling the bark and exposing the white inner wood of the branches. ³⁸Then he placed the peeled branches in all the watering troughs, so that they would be directly in front of the flocks when they came to drink. When the flocks were in heat and came to drink, ³⁹they mated in front of the branches. And they bore young that were streaked or speckled or spotted. ⁴⁰Jacob set apart the young of the flock by themselves, but made the rest face the streaked and dark-colored animals that belonged to Laban. Thus he made separate flocks for himself and did not

a 24 *Joseph* means *may he add.*   *b 27* Or possibly *have become rich and* put them with Laban's animals. ⁴¹Whenever the stronger females were in heat, Jacob would place the branches in the troughs in front of the animals so they would mate near the branches, ⁴²but if the animals were weak, he would not place them there. So the weak animals went to Laban and the strong ones to Jacob. ⁴³In this way the man grew exceedingly prosperous and came to own large flocks, and maidservants and menservants, and camels and donkeys.ᵃ

Chapter 31 Theme _____

31 Jacob heard that Laban's sons were saying, "Jacob has taken everything our father owned and has gained all this wealth from what belonged to our father." ²And Jacob noticed that Laban's attitude toward him was not what it had been.

³Then the LORD said to Jacob, "Go backᵇ to the land of your fathers and to your relatives, and I will be with you."ᶜ

⁴So Jacob sent word to Rachel and Leah to come out to the fields where his flocks were. ⁵He said to them, "I see that your father's attitude toward me is not what it was before, but the God of my father has been with me.ᵈ ⁶You know that I've worked for your father with all my strength,ᵉ ⁷yet your father has cheated me by changing my wages ten times.ᶠ However, God has not allowed him to harm me.ᵍ ⁸If he said, 'The speckled ones will be your wages,' then all the flocks gave birth to speckled young; and if he said, 'The streaked ones will be your wages,'ʰ then all the flocks bore streaked young. ⁹So God has taken away your father's livestock and has given them to me.ⁱ

¹⁰"In breeding season I once had a dream in which I looked up and saw that the male goats mating with the flock were streaked, speckled or spotted. ¹¹The angel of Godʲ said to me in the dream, 'Jacob.' I answered, 'Here I am.' ¹²And he said, 'Look up and see that all the male goats mating with the flock are streaked, speckled or spotted, for I have seen all that Laban has been doing to you.ᵏ ¹³I am the God of Bethel,ˡ where you anointed a pillar and where you made a vow to me. Now leave this land at once and go back to your native land.ᵐ'"

¹⁴Then Rachel and Leah replied, "Do we still have any share in the inheritance of our father's estate? ¹⁵Does he not regard us as foreigners? Not only has he sold us, but he has used up what was paid for us.ⁿ ¹⁶Surely all the wealth that God took away from our father belongs to us and our children. So do whatever God has told you."

¹⁷Then Jacob put his children and his wives on camels, ¹⁸and he drove all his livestock ahead of him, along with all the goods

30:43 ᵃver 30; Ge 12:16; 13:2; 24:35; 26:13-14

31:3 ᵇver 13; Ge 32:9 ᶜGe 21:22; 26:3; 28:15

31:5 ᵈGe 21:22; 26:3

31:6 ᵉGe 30:29

31:7 ᶠver 41; Job 19:3 ᵍver 52; Ps 37:28; 105:14

31:8 ʰGe 30:32

31:9 ⁱver 1,16; Ge 30:42

31:11 ʲGe 16:7; 48:16

31:12 ᵏEx 3:7

31:13 ˡGe 28:10-22 ᵐver 3; Ge 32:9

31:15 ⁿGe 29:20

31:18
a Ge 35:27
b Ge 10:19

31:19
c ver 30,32,
34-35;
Ge 35:2;
Jdg 17:5;
1Sa 19:13;
Hos 3:4

31:20
d Ge 27:36
e ver 27

31:24
g Ge 20:3;
Job 33:15
h Ge 24:50

31:26
i Ge 27:36
j 1Sa 30:2-3

31:27
k Ex 15:20
l Ge 4:21

31:28
m ver 55

31:29
n ver 7
o ver 53

31:30
p ver 19;
Jdg 18:24

31:32
q Ge 44:9

31:34
r ver 37;
Ge 44:12

31:35
s Ex 20:12;
Lev 19:3,32

he had accumulated in Paddan Aram,ª to go to his father Isaacᵃ in the land of Canaan.ᵇ

¹⁹When Laban had gone to shear his sheep, Rachel stole her father's household gods.ᶜ ²⁰Moreover, Jacob deceivedᵈ Laban the Aramean by not telling him he was running away.ᵉ ²¹So he fled with all he had, and crossing the River,ᵇ he headed for the hill country of Gilead.ᶠ

²²On the third day Laban was told that Jacob had fled. ²³Taking his relatives with him, he pursued Jacob for seven days and caught up with him in the hill country of Gilead. ²⁴Then God came to Laban the Aramean in a dream at night and said to him,ᵍ "Be careful not to say anything to Jacob, either good or bad."ʰ

²⁵Jacob had pitched his tent in the hill country of Gilead when Laban overtook him, and Laban and his relatives camped there too. ²⁶Then Laban said to Jacob, "What have you done? You've deceived me,ⁱ and you've carried off my daughters like captives in war.ʲ ²⁷Why did you run off secretly and deceive me? Why didn't you tell me, so I could send you away with joy and singing to the music of tambourinesᵏ and harps?ˡ ²⁸You didn't even let me kiss my grandchildren and my daughters good-by.ᵐ You have done a foolish thing. ²⁹I have the power to harm you;ⁿ but last night the God of your fatherᵒ said to me, 'Be careful not to say anything to Jacob, either good or bad.' ³⁰Now you have gone off because you longed to return to your father's house. But why did you steal my gods?ᵖ"

³¹Jacob answered Laban, "I was afraid, because I thought you would take your daughters away from me by force. ³²But if you find anyone who has your gods, he shall not live.�q In the presence of our relatives, see for yourself whether there is anything of yours here with me; and if so, take it." Now Jacob did not know that Rachel had stolen the gods.

³³So Laban went into Jacob's tent and into Leah's tent and into the tent of the two maidservants, but he found nothing. After he came out of Leah's tent, he entered Rachel's tent. ³⁴Now Rachel had taken the household gods and put them inside her camel's saddle and was sitting on them. Laban searchedʳ through everything in the tent but found nothing.

³⁵Rachel said to her father, "Don't be angry, my lord, that I cannot stand up in your presence;ˢ I'm having my period." So he searched but could not find the household gods.

³⁶Jacob was angry and took Laban to task. "What is my crime?" he asked Laban. "What sin have I committed that you hunt me down? ³⁷Now that you have searched through all my goods,

a 18 That is, Northwest Mesopotamia   b 21 That is, the Euphrates what have you found that belongs to your household? Put it here in front of your relatives[a] and mine, and let them judge between the two of us.

[38]"I have been with you for twenty years now. Your sheep and goats have not miscarried, nor have I eaten rams from your flocks. [39]I did not bring you animals torn by wild beasts; I bore the loss myself. And you demanded payment from me for whatever was stolen by day or night.[b] [40]This was my situation: The heat consumed me in the daytime and the cold at night, and sleep fled from my eyes. [41]It was like this for the twenty years I was in your household. I worked for you fourteen years for your two daughters[c] and six years for your flocks, and you changed my wages ten times.[d] [42]If the God of my father,[e] the God of Abraham and the Fear of Isaac,[f] had not been with me,[g] you would surely have sent me away empty-handed. But God has seen my hardship and the toil of my hands,[h] and last night he rebuked you."

[43]Laban answered Jacob, "The women are my daughters, the children are my children, and the flocks are my flocks. All you see is mine. Yet what can I do today about these daughters of mine, or about the children they have borne? [44]Come now, let's make a covenant,[i] you and I, and let it serve as a witness between us."[j]

[45]So Jacob took a stone and set it up as a pillar.[k] [46]He said to his relatives, "Gather some stones." So they took stones and piled them in a heap, and they ate there by the heap. [47]Laban called it Jegar Sahadutha,[a] and Jacob called it Galeed.[b]

[48]Laban said, "This heap is a witness between you and me today." That is why it was called Galeed. [49]It was also called Mizpah,[c][l] because he said, "May the LORD keep watch between you and me when we are away from each other. [50]If you mistreat my daughters or if you take any wives besides my daughters, even though no one is with us, remember that God is a witness[m] between you and me."

[51]Laban also said to Jacob, "Here is this heap, and here is this pillar[n] I have set up between you and me. [52]This heap is a witness, and this pillar is a witness,[o] that I will not go past this heap to your side to harm you and that you will not go past this heap and pillar to my side to harm me.[p] [53]May the God of Abraham[q] and the God of Nahor, the God of their father, judge between us."[r]

So Jacob took an oath[s] in the name of the Fear of his father Isaac.[t] [54]He offered a sacrifice there in the hill country and

---

31:37
[a] ver 23

31:39
[b] Ex 22:13

31:41
[c] Ge 29:30
[d] ver 7

31:42
[e] ver 5;
Ex 3:15;
1Ch 12:17
[f] ver 53;
Isa 8:13
[g] Ps 124:1-2
[h] Ge 29:32

31:44
[i] Ge 21:27;
26:28
[j] Jos 24:27

31:45
[k] Ge 28:18

31:49
[l] Jdg 11:29;
1Sa 7:5-6

31:50
[m] Jer 29:23;
42:5

31:51
[n] Ge 28:18

31:52
[o] Ge 21:30
[p] ver 7;
Ge 26:29

31:53
[q] Ge 28:13
[r] Ge 16:5
[s] Ge 21:23,27
[t] ver 42

---

[a] 47 The Aramaic *Jegar Sahadutha* means *witness heap.*   [b] 47 The Hebrew *Galeed* means *witness heap.*   [c] 49 *Mizpah* means *watchtower.*

31:55
a ver 28
b Ge 18:33;
30:25

32:1
c Ge 16:11;
2Ki 6:16-17;
Ps 34:7; 91:11;
Heb 1:14

32:2
d Ge 28:17
e 2Sa 2:8,29

32:3
f Ge 27:41-42
g Ge 25:30;
36:8,9

32:5
h Ge 12:16;
30:43
i Ge 33:8,10,15

32:6
j Ge 33:1

32:7
k ver 11

32:9
l Ge 28:13;
31:42
m Ge 31:13

32:10
n Ge 24:27

32:11
o Ps 59:2
p Ge 27:41

32:12
q Ge 22:17
r Ge 28:13-15;
Hos 1:10;
Ro 9:27

32:13
s Ge 43:11,
15,25,26;
Pr 18:16

invited his relatives to a meal. After they had eaten, they spent the night there.

⁵⁵Early the next morning Laban kissed his grandchildren and his daughters*a* and blessed them. Then he left and returned home.*b*

Chapter 32 Theme

32 Jacob also went on his way, and the angels of God*c* met him. ²When Jacob saw them, he said, "This is the camp of God!"*d* So he named that place Mahanaim.*ae*

³Jacob sent messengers ahead of him to his brother Esau*f* in the land of Seir, the country of Edom.*g* ⁴He instructed them: "This is what you are to say to my master Esau: 'Your servant Jacob says, I have been staying with Laban and have remained there till now. ⁵I have cattle and donkeys, sheep and goats, menservants and maidservants.*h* Now I am sending this message to my lord, that I may find favor in your eyes.*i*'"

⁶When the messengers returned to Jacob, they said, "We went to your brother Esau, and now he is coming to meet you, and four hundred men are with him."*j*

⁷In great fear*k* and distress Jacob divided the people who were with him into two groups,*b* and the flocks and herds and camels as well. ⁸He thought, "If Esau comes and attacks one group,*c* the group*c* that is left may escape."

⁹Then Jacob prayed, "O God of my father Abraham, God of my father Isaac,*l* O LORD, who said to me, 'Go back to your country and your relatives, and I will make you prosper,'*m* ¹⁰I am unworthy of all the kindness and faithfulness*n* you have shown your servant. I had only my staff when I crossed this Jordan, but now I have become two groups. ¹¹Save me, I pray, from the hand of my brother Esau, for I am afraid he will come and attack me,*o* and also the mothers with their children.*p* ¹²But you have said, 'I will surely make you prosper and will make your descendants like the sand*q* of the sea, which cannot be counted.*r*'"

¹³He spent the night there, and from what he had with him he selected a gift*s* for his brother Esau: ¹⁴two hundred female goats and twenty male goats, two hundred ewes and twenty rams, ¹⁵thirty female camels with their young, forty cows and ten bulls, and twenty female donkeys and ten male donkeys. ¹⁶He put them in the care of his servants, each herd by itself, and said to his servants, "Go ahead of me, and keep some space between the herds."

¹⁷He instructed the one in the lead: "When my brother Esau meets you and asks, 'To whom do you belong, and where are

*a*2 *Mahanaim* means *two camps.*   *b*7 Or *camps;* also in verse 10   *c*8 Or *camp* you going, and who owns all these animals in front of you?' [18]then you are to say, 'They belong to your servant[a] Jacob. They are a gift sent to my lord Esau, and he is coming behind us.'"

[19]He also instructed the second, the third and all the others who followed the herds: "You are to say the same thing to Esau when you meet him. [20]And be sure to say, 'Your servant Jacob is coming behind us.'" For he thought, "I will pacify him with these gifts I am sending on ahead; later, when I see him, perhaps he will receive me."[b] [21]So Jacob's gifts went on ahead of him, but he himself spent the night in the camp.

[22]That night Jacob got up and took his two wives, his two maidservants and his eleven sons and crossed the ford of the Jabbok.[c] [23]After he had sent them across the stream, he sent over all his possessions. [24]So Jacob was left alone, and a man[d] wrestled with him till daybreak. [25]When the man saw that he could not overpower him, he touched the socket of Jacob's hip[e] so that his hip was wrenched as he wrestled with the man. [26]Then the man said, "Let me go, for it is daybreak."

But Jacob replied, "I will not let you go unless you bless me."[f]

[27]The man asked him, "What is your name?"

"Jacob," he answered.

[28]Then the man said, "Your name will no longer be Jacob, but Israel,[a][g] because you have struggled with God and with men and have overcome."

[29]Jacob said, "Please tell me your name."[h]

But he replied, "Why do you ask my name?"[i] Then he blessed[j] him there.

[30]So Jacob called the place Peniel,[b] saying, "It is because I saw God face to face,[k] and yet my life was spared."

[31]The sun rose above him as he passed Peniel,[c] and he was limping because of his hip. [32]Therefore to this day the Israelites do not eat the tendon attached to the socket of the hip, because the socket of Jacob's hip was touched near the tendon.

Chapter 33 Theme

33 Jacob looked up and there was Esau, coming with his four hundred men;[l] so he divided the children among Leah, Rachel and the two maidservants. [2]He put the maidservants and their children in front, Leah and her children next, and Rachel and Joseph in the rear. [3]He himself went on ahead and bowed down to the ground[m] seven times as he approached his brother.

[4]But Esau ran to meet him and embraced him; he threw his arms around his neck and kissed him. And they wept.[n] [5]Then

---

a 28 Israel means he struggles with God.   b 30 Peniel means face of God.   c 31 Hebrew Penuel, a variant of Peniel

---

32:18
a Ge 18:3

32:20
b Ge 33:10;
Pr 21:14

32:22
c Dt 2:37; 3:16;
Jos 12:2

32:24
d Ge 18:2

32:25
e ver 32

32:26
f Hos 12:4

32:28
g Ge 17:5;
35:10;
1Ki 18:31

32:29
h Jdg 13:17
i Jdg 13:18
j Ge 35:9

32:30
k Ge 16:13;
Ex 24:11;
Nu 12:8;
Jdg 6:22; 13:22

33:1
l Ge 32:6

33:3
m Ge 18:2; 42:6

33:4
n Ge 45:14-15

Esau looked up and saw the women and children. "Who are these with you?" he asked.

Jacob answered, "They are the children God has graciously given your servant.*a*"

6Then the maidservants and their children approached and bowed down. **7**Next, Leah and her children came and bowed down. Last of all came Joseph and Rachel, and they too bowed down.

8Esau asked, "What do you mean by all these droves I met?"*b*

"To find favor in your eyes, my lord,"*c* he said.

9But Esau said, "I already have plenty, my brother. Keep what you have for yourself."

10"No, please!" said Jacob. "If I have found favor in your eyes, accept this gift from me. For to see your face is like seeing the face of God,*d* now that you have received me favorably.*e* **11**Please accept the present*f* that was brought to you, for God has been gracious to me*g* and I have all I need." And because Jacob insisted, Esau accepted it.

12Then Esau said, "Let us be on our way; I'll accompany you."

13But Jacob said to him, "My lord knows that the children are tender and that I must care for the ewes and cows that are nursing their young. If they are driven hard just one day, all the animals will die. **14**So let my lord go on ahead of his servant, while I move along slowly at the pace of the droves before me and that of the children, until I come to my lord in Seir.*h*"

15Esau said, "Then let me leave some of my men with you."

"But why do that?" Jacob asked. "Just let me find favor in the eyes of my lord."*i*

16So that day Esau started on his way back to Seir. **17**Jacob, however, went to Succoth,*j* where he built a place for himself and made shelters for his livestock. That is why the place is called Succoth.*a*

18After Jacob came from Paddan Aram,*b k* he arrived safely at the*c* city of Shechem*l* in Canaan and camped within sight of the city. **19**For a hundred pieces of silver,*d* he bought from the sons of Hamor, the father of Shechem,*m* the plot of ground*n* where he pitched his tent. **20**There he set up an altar and called it El Elohe Israel.*e*

Chapter 34 Theme

34 Now Dinah,*o* the daughter Leah had borne to Jacob, went out to visit the women of the land. **2**When Shechem son of Hamor the Hivite, the ruler of that area, saw her, he took her

---

a17 Succoth means *shelters*. *b18* That is, Northwest Mesopotamia *c18* Or *arrived at Shalem, a* *d19* Hebrew *hundred kesitahs*; a kesitah was a unit of money of unknown weight and value. *e20* El Elohe Israel can mean *God, the God of Israel* or *mighty is the God of Israel.*

Cross-references (margin):

33:5 *a*Ge 48:9; Ps 127:3; Isa 8:18

33:8 *b*Ge 32:14-16 *c*Ge 24:9; 32:5

33:10 *d*Ge 16:13 *e*Ge 32:20

33:11 *f*1Sa 25:27 *g*Ge 30:43

33:14 *h*Ge 32:3

33:15 *i*Ge 34:11; 47:25; Ru 2:13

33:17 *j*Jos 13:27; Jdg 8:5,6,8, 14-16; Ps 60:6

33:18 *k*Ge 25:20; 28:2 *l*Jos 24:1; Jdg 9:1

33:19 *m*Jos 24:32 *n*Jn 4:5

34:1 *o*Ge 30:21

and violated her. ³His heart was drawn to Dinah daughter of Jacob, and he loved the girl and spoke tenderly to her. ⁴And Shechem said to his father Hamor, "Get me this girl as my wife."

⁵When Jacob heard that his daughter Dinah had been defiled, his sons were in the fields with his livestock; so he kept quiet about it until they came home.

⁶Then Shechem's father Hamor went out to talk with Jacob. *a* ⁷Now Jacob's sons had come in from the fields as soon as they heard what had happened. They were filled with grief and fury, because Shechem had done a disgraceful thing in*a* Israel*b* by lying with Jacob's daughter—a thing that should not be done.*c*

⁸But Hamor said to them, "My son Shechem has his heart set on your daughter. Please give her to him as his wife. ⁹Intermarry with us; give us your daughters and take our daughters for yourselves. ¹⁰You can settle among us;*d* the land is open to you. *e* Live in it, trade*b* in it,*f* and acquire property in it."

¹¹Then Shechem said to Dinah's father and brothers, "Let me find favor in your eyes, and I will give you whatever you ask. ¹²Make the price for the bride*g* and the gift I am to bring as great as you like, and I'll pay whatever you ask me. Only give me the girl as my wife."

¹³Because their sister Dinah had been defiled, Jacob's sons replied deceitfully as they spoke to Shechem and his father Hamor. ¹⁴They said to them, "We can't do such a thing; we can't give our sister to a man who is not circumcised.*h* That would be a disgrace to us. ¹⁵We will give our consent to you on one condition only: that you become like us by circumcising all your males.*i* ¹⁶Then we will give you our daughters and take your daughters for ourselves. We'll settle among you and become one people with you. ¹⁷But if you will not agree to be circumcised, we'll take our sister*c* and go."

¹⁸Their proposal seemed good to Hamor and his son Shechem. ¹⁹The young man, who was the most honored of all his father's household, lost no time in doing what they said, because he was delighted with Jacob's daughter.*j* ²⁰So Hamor and his son Shechem went to the gate of their city*k* to speak to their fellow townsmen. ²¹"These men are friendly toward us," they said. "Let them live in our land and trade in it; the land has plenty of room for them. We can marry their daughters and they can marry ours. ²²But the men will consent to live with us as one people only on the condition that our males be circumcised, as they themselves are. ²³Won't their livestock, their property and all their other animals become ours? So let us give our consent to them, and they will settle among us."

---

a 7 Or against   *b 10 Or move about freely; also in verse 21*   *c 17 Hebrew daughter*

34:6
a Jdg 14:2-5

34:7
b Dt 22:21;
Jdg 20:6;
2Sa 13:12
c Jos 7:15

34:10
d Ge 47:6,27
e Ge 13:9; 20:15
f Ge 42:34

34:12
g Ex 22:16;
Dt 22:29;
1Sa 18:25

34:14
h Ge 17:14;
Jdg 14:3

34:15
i Ex 12:48

34:19
j ver 3

34:20
k Ru 4:1;
2Sa 15:2

34:24
a Ge 23:10

34:25
b Ge 49:5
c Ge 49:7

34:30
d Ex 5:21;
1Sa 13:4
e Ge 13:7
f Ge 46:27;
1Ch 16:19;
Ps 105:12

35:1
g Ge 28:19
h Ge 27:43

35:2
i Ge 18:19;
Jos 24:15
j Ge 31:19
k Ex 19:10,14

35:3
l Ge 32:7
m Ge 28:15,
20-22;
31:3,42

35:4
n Jos 24:25-26

35:5
o Ex 15:16;
23:27;
Jos 2:9

35:6
p Ge 28:19;
48:3

35:7
q Ge 28:13

35:8
r Ge 24:59

35:9
s Ge 32:29

35:10
t Ge 17:5

²⁴All the men who went out of the city gate*a* agreed with Hamor and his son Shechem, and every male in the city was circumcised.

²⁵Three days later, while all of them were still in pain, two of Jacob's sons, Simeon and Levi, Dinah's brothers, took their swords*b* and attacked the unsuspecting city, killing every male.*c* ²⁶They put Hamor and his son Shechem to the sword and took Dinah from Shechem's house and left. ²⁷The sons of Jacob came upon the dead bodies and looted the city where*a* their sister had been defiled. ²⁸They seized their flocks and herds and donkeys and everything else of theirs in the city and out in the fields. ²⁹They carried off all their wealth and all their women and children, taking as plunder everything in the houses.

³⁰Then Jacob said to Simeon and Levi, "You have brought trouble on me by making me a stench*d* to the Canaanites and Perizzites, the people living in this land.*e* We are few in number,*f* and if they join forces against me and attack me, I and my household will be destroyed."

³¹But they replied, "Should he have treated our sister like a prostitute?"

Chapter 35 Theme

35 Then God said to Jacob, "Go up to Bethel*g* and settle there, and build an altar there to God, who appeared to you when you were fleeing from your brother Esau."*h*

²So Jacob said to his household*i* and to all who were with him, "Get rid of the foreign gods*j* you have with you, and purify yourselves and change your clothes. *k* ³Then come, let us go up to Bethel, where I will build an altar to God, who answered me in the day of my distress*l* and who has been with me wherever I have gone.*m*" ⁴So they gave Jacob all the foreign gods they had and the rings in their ears, and Jacob buried them under the oak at Shechem.*n* ⁵Then they set out, and the terror of God*o* fell upon the towns all around them so that no one pursued them.

⁶Jacob and all the people with him came to Luz*p* (that is, Bethel) in the land of Canaan. ⁷There he built an altar, and he called the place El Bethel,*b* because it was there that God revealed himself to him*q* when he was fleeing from his brother.

⁸Now Deborah, Rebekah's nurse,*r* died and was buried under the oak below Bethel. So it was named Allon Bacuth.*c*

⁹After Jacob returned from Paddan Aram,*d* God appeared to him again and blessed him.*s* ¹⁰God said to him, "Your name is Jacob,*e* but you will no longer be called Jacob; your name will be Israel.*f*"*t* So he named him Israel.

---

a 27 Or *because*   *b 7* *El Bethel* means *God of Bethel.*   *c 8* *Allon Bacuth* means *oak of weeping.*   *d 9* That is, Northwest Mesopotamia; also in verse 26   *e 10* *Jacob* means *he grasps the heel* (figuratively, *he deceives*).   *f 10* *Israel* means *he struggles with God.*

¹¹And God said to him, "I am God Almighty[a];[a] be fruitful and increase in number. A nation[b] and a community of nations will come from you, and kings will come from your body.[c] ¹²The land I gave to Abraham and Isaac I also give to you, and I will give this land to your descendants after you.[d]"[e] ¹³Then God went up from him[f] at the place where he had talked with him.

¹⁴Jacob set up a stone pillar at the place where God had talked with him, and he poured out a drink offering on it; he also poured oil on it.[g] ¹⁵Jacob called the place where God had talked with him Bethel.[b][h]

¹⁶Then they moved on from Bethel. While they were still some distance from Ephrath, Rachel began to give birth and had great difficulty. ¹⁷And as she was having great difficulty in childbirth, the midwife said to her, "Don't be afraid, for you have another son."[i] ¹⁸As she breathed her last—for she was dying—she named her son Ben-Oni.[c] But his father named him Benjamin.[d]

¹⁹So Rachel died and was buried on the way to Ephrath (that is, Bethlehem[j]). ²⁰Over her tomb Jacob set up a pillar, and to this day that pillar marks Rachel's tomb.[k]

²¹Israel moved on again and pitched his tent beyond Migdal Eder. ²²While Israel was living in that region, Reuben went in and slept with his father's concubine[l] Bilhah,[m] and Israel heard of it.

Jacob had twelve sons:

²³The sons of Leah:
  Reuben the firstborn[n] of Jacob,
  Simeon, Levi, Judah,[o] Issachar and Zebulun.[p]
²⁴The sons of Rachel:
  Joseph[q] and Benjamin.[r]
²⁵The sons of Rachel's maidservant Bilhah:
  Dan and Naphtali.[s]
²⁶The sons of Leah's maidservant Zilpah:
  Gad[t] and Asher.[u]

These were the sons of Jacob, who were born to him in Paddan Aram.

²⁷Jacob came home to his father Isaac in Mamre,[v] near Kiriath Arba[w] (that is, Hebron), where Abraham and Isaac had stayed. ²⁸Isaac lived a hundred and eighty years.[x] ²⁹Then he breathed his last and died and was gathered to his people,[y] old and full of years.[z] And his sons Esau and Jacob buried him.[a]

INSIGHT

The Birth Order of Jacob's (Israel's) Sons

Mother	Son
Leah	Reuben (born 1921 B.C.) Simeon Levi Judah
Bilhah (Rachel's maidservant)	Dan Naphtali
Zilpah (Leah's maidservant)	Gad Asher
Leah	Issachar Zebulun
Rachel	Joseph (born 1914 B.C.) Benjamin

---

a11 Hebrew *El-Shaddai*   b15 *Bethel* means *house of God.*   c18 *Ben-Oni* means *son of my trouble.*   d18 *Benjamin* means *son of my right hand.*

Cross-references:

35:11 a Ge 17:1; Ex 6:3 b Ge 28:3; 48:4 c Ge 17:6
35:12 d Ge 13:15; 28:13 e Ge 12:7; 26:3
35:13 f Ge 17:22
35:14 g Ge 28:18
35:15 h Ge 28:19
35:17 i Ge 30:24
35:19 j Ge 48:7; Ru 1:1,19; Mic 5:2; Mt 2:16
35:20 k 1Sa 10:2
35:22 l Ge 49:4; 1Ch 5:1 m Ge 29:29; Lev 18:8
35:23 n Ge 46:8 o Ge 29:35 p Ge 30:20
35:24 q Ge 30:24 r ver 18
35:25 s Ge 30:8
35:26 t Ge 30:11 u Ge 30:13
35:27 v Ge 13:18; 18:1 w Jos 14:15
35:28 x Ge 25:7,20
35:29 y Ge 25:8; 49:33 z Ge 15:15 a Ge 25:9

36:1
a Ge 25:30

Chapter 36 Theme _____

36 This is the account of Esau (that is, Edom).[a]

36:2
b Ge 28:8-9
c Ge 26:34
d ver 25

[2]Esau took his wives from the women of Canaan:[b] Adah daughter of Elon the Hittite,[c] and Oholibamah daughter of Anah[d] and granddaughter of Zibeon the Hivite— [3]also Basemath daughter of Ishmael and sister of Nebaioth.

36:4
e 1Ch 1:35

[4]Adah bore Eliphaz to Esau, Basemath bore Reuel,[e] [5]and Oholibamah bore Jeush, Jalam and Korah. These were the sons of Esau, who were born to him in Canaan.

[6]Esau took his wives and sons and daughters and all the members of his household, as well as his livestock and all his other animals and all the goods he had acquired in Canaan,[f] and moved to a land some distance from his brother Jacob.

36:6
f Ge 12:5

[7]Their possessions were too great for them to remain together; the land where they were staying could not support them both because of their livestock.[g] [8]So Esau[h] (that is, Edom) settled in the hill country of Seir.[i]

36:7
g Ge 13:6;
17:8; 28:4

[9]This is the account of Esau the father of the Edomites in the hill country of Seir.

36:8
h Dt 2:4
i Ge 32:3

[10]These are the names of Esau's sons:

Eliphaz, the son of Esau's wife Adah, and Reuel, the son of Esau's wife Basemath.

[11]The sons of Eliphaz:[j]

Teman,[k] Omar, Zepho, Gatam and Kenaz.

36:11
j ver 15-16;
Job 2:11
k Am 1:12;
Hab 3:3

[12]Esau's son Eliphaz also had a concubine named Timna, who bore him Amalek.[l] These were grandsons of Esau's wife Adah.[m]

[13]The sons of Reuel:

Nahath, Zerah, Shammah and Mizzah. These were grandsons of Esau's wife Basemath.

36:12
l Ex 17:8,16;
Nu 24:20;
1Sa 15:2
m ver 16

[14]The sons of Esau's wife Oholibamah daughter of Anah and granddaughter of Zibeon, whom she bore to Esau:

Jeush, Jalam and Korah.

[15]These were the chiefs[n] among Esau's descendants:

The sons of Eliphaz the firstborn of Esau:

36:15
n Ex 15:15
o Job 2:11

Chiefs Teman,[o] Omar, Zepho, Kenaz, [16]Korah,[a] Gatam and Amalek. These were the chiefs descended from Eliphaz in Edom; they were grandsons of Adah.[p]

36:16
P ver 12

a 16 Masoretic Text; Samaritan Pentateuch (see also Gen. 36:11 and 1 Chron. 1:36) does not have *Korah*.

¹⁷The sons of Esau's son Reuel:^a

Chiefs Nahath, Zerah, Shammah and Mizzah. These were the chiefs descended from Reuel in Edom; they were grandsons of Esau's wife Basemath.

¹⁸The sons of Esau's wife Oholibamah:

Chiefs Jeush, Jalam and Korah. These were the chiefs descended from Esau's wife Oholibamah daughter of Anah.

¹⁹These were the sons of Esau (that is, Edom),^b and these were their chiefs.

²⁰These were the sons of Seir the Horite,^c who were living in the region:

Lotan, Shobal, Zibeon, Anah, ²¹Dishon, Ezer and Dishan. These sons of Seir in Edom were Horite chiefs.

²²The sons of Lotan:

Hori and Homam.^a Timna was Lotan's sister.

²³The sons of Shobal:

Alvan, Manahath, Ebal, Shepho and Onam.

²⁴The sons of Zibeon:

Aiah and Anah. This is the Anah who discovered the hot springs^b in the desert while he was grazing the donkeys of his father Zibeon.

²⁵The children of Anah:

Dishon and Oholibamah daughter of Anah.

²⁶The sons of Dishon^c:

Hemdan, Eshban, Ithran and Keran.

²⁷The sons of Ezer:

Bilhan, Zaavan and Akan.

²⁸The sons of Dishan:

Uz and Aran.

²⁹These were the Horite chiefs:

Lotan, Shobal, Zibeon, Anah, ³⁰Dishon, Ezer and Dishan. These were the Horite chiefs, according to their divisions, in the land of Seir.

³¹These were the kings who reigned in Edom before any Israelite king^d reigned^d:

³²Bela son of Beor became king of Edom. His city was named Dinhabah.

³³When Bela died, Jobab son of Zerah from Bozrah^e succeeded him as king.

³⁴When Jobab died, Husham from the land of the Temanites^f succeeded him as king.

a 22 Hebrew *Hemam,* a variant of *Homam* (see 1 Chron. 1:39)   b 24 Vulgate; Syriac *discovered water;* the meaning of the Hebrew for this word is uncertain.   c 26 Hebrew *Dishan,* a variant of *Dishon*   d 31 Or *before an Israelite king reigned over them*

36:17
a 1Ch 1:37

36:19
b Ge 25:30

36:20
c Ge 14:6;
Dt 2:12,22;
1Ch 1:38

36:31
d Ge 17:6;
1Ch 1:43

36:33
e Jer 49:13,22

36:34
f Eze 25:13

36:35
a Ge 19:37;
Nu 22:1;
Dt 1:5;
Ru 1:1,6

35When Husham died, Hadad son of Bedad, who defeated Midian in the country of Moab,a succeeded him as king. His city was named Avith.

36When Hadad died, Samlah from Masrekah succeeded him as king.

37When Samlah died, Shaul from Rehoboth on the rivera succeeded him as king.

37:1
b Ge 17:8
c Ge 10:19

38When Shaul died, Baal-Hanan son of Acbor succeeded him as king.

39When Baal-Hanan son of Acbor died, Hadadb succeeded him as king. His city was named Pau, and his wife's name was Mehetabel daughter of Matred, the daughter of Me-Zahab.

37:2
d Ps 78:71
e Ge 35:25
f Ge 35:26
g 1Sa 2:24

40These were the chiefs descended from Esau, by name, according to their clans and regions:

Timna, Alvah, Jetheth, 41Oholibamah, Elah, Pinon, 42Kenaz, Teman, Mibzar, 43Magdiel and Iram. These were the chiefs of Edom, according to their settlements in the land they occupied.

This was Esau the father of the Edomites.

Chapter 37 Theme

37:3
h Ge 25:28
i Ge 44:20
j 2Sa 13:18-19

37

Jacob lived in the land where his father had stayed,b the land of Canaan.c

2This is the account of Jacob.

Joseph, a young man of seventeen, was tending the flocksd with his brothers, the sons of Bilhahe and the sons of Zilpah,f his father's wives, and he brought their father a bad reportg about them.

37:4
k Ge 27:41;
49:22-23;
Ac 7:9

3Now Israel loved Joseph more than any of his other sons,h because he had been born to him in his old age;i and he made a richly ornamentedc robej for him. 4When his brothers saw that their father loved him more than any of them, they hated himk and could not speak a kind word to him.

37:5
l Ge 20:3;
28:12

5Joseph had a dream,l and when he told it to his brothers, they hated him all the more. 6He said to them, "Listen to this dream I had: 7We were binding sheaves of grain out in the field when suddenly my sheaf rose and stood upright, while your sheaves gathered around mine and bowed down to it."m

37:7
m Ge 42:6,9;
43:26,28;
44:14; 50:18

a 37 Possibly the Euphrates   b 39 Many manuscripts of the Masoretic Text, Samaritan Pentateuch and Syriac (see also 1Chron. 1:50); most manuscripts of the Masoretic Text *Hadar*   c 3 The meaning of the Hebrew for *richly ornamented* is uncertain; also in verses 23 and 32.

⁸His brothers said to him, "Do you intend to reign over us? Will you actually rule us?"ᵃ And they hated him all the more because of his dream and what he had said.

⁹Then he had another dream, and he told it to his brothers. "Listen," he said, "I had another dream, and this time the sun and moon and eleven stars were bowing down to me."

¹⁰When he told his father as well as his brothers,ᵇ his father rebuked him and said, "What is this dream you had? Will your mother and I and your brothers actually come and bow down to the ground before you?"ᶜ ¹¹His brothers were jealous of him,ᵈ but his father kept the matter in mind.ᵉ

¹²Now his brothers had gone to graze their father's flocks near Shechem, ¹³and Israel said to Joseph, "As you know, your brothers are grazing the flocks near Shechem. Come, I am going to send you to them."

"Very well," he replied.

¹⁴So he said to him, "Go and see if all is well with your brothers and with the flocks, and bring word back to me." Then he sent him off from the Valley of Hebron.ᶠ

When Joseph arrived at Shechem, ¹⁵a man found him wandering around in the fields and asked him, "What are you looking for?"

¹⁶He replied, "I'm looking for my brothers. Can you tell me where they are grazing their flocks?"

¹⁷"They have moved on from here," the man answered. "I heard them say, 'Let's go to Dothan.'ᵍ"

So Joseph went after his brothers and found them near Dothan. ¹⁸But they saw him in the distance, and before he reached them, they plotted to kill him.ʰ

¹⁹"Here comes that dreamer!" they said to each other. ²⁰"Come now, let's kill him and throw him into one of these cisternsⁱ and say that a ferocious animal devoured him. Then we'll see what comes of his dreams."ʲ

²¹When Reuben heard this, he tried to rescue him from their hands. "Let's not take his life," he said.ᵏ ²²"Don't shed any blood. Throw him into this cistern here in the desert, but don't lay a hand on him." Reuben said this to rescue him from them and take him back to his father.

²³So when Joseph came to his brothers, they stripped him of his robe—the richly ornamented robe he was wearing— ²⁴and they took him and threw him into the cistern.ˡ Now the cistern was empty; there was no water in it.

²⁵As they sat down to eat their meal, they looked up and saw a caravan of Ishmaelites coming from Gilead. Their camels were loaded with spices, balm and myrrh,ᵐ and they were on their way to take them down to Egypt.ⁿ

37:8
ᵃGe 49:26

37:10
ᵇver 5
ᶜver 7;
Ge 27:29

37:11
ᵈAc 7:9
ᵉLk 2:19,51

37:14
ᶠGe 13:18;
35:27

37:17
ᵍ2Ki 6:13

37:18
ʰ1Sa 19:1;
Mk 14:1;
Ac 23:12

37:20
ⁱJer 38:6,9
ʲGe 50:20

37:21
ᵏGe 42:22

37:24
ˡJer 41:7

37:25
ᵐGe 43:11
ⁿver 28

37:26
a ver 20;
Ge 4:10

37:27
b Ge 42:21

37:28
c Ge 25:2;
Jdg 6:1-3
d Ge 45:4-5;
Ps 105:17;
Ac 7:9

37:29
e ver 34;
Ge 44:13;
Job 1:20

37:30
f ver 22;
Ge 42:13,36

37:31
g ver 3,23

37:33
h ver 20
i Ge 44:20,28

37:34
j ver 29
k 2Sa 3:31
l Ge 50:3,10,11

37:35
m Ge 42:38;
44:22,29,31

37:36
n Ge 39:1

38:2
o 1Ch 2:3

38:3
p ver 6;
Ge 46:12;
Nu 26:19

38:7
q ver 10;
Ge 46:12;
1Ch 2:3

38:8
r Dt 25:5-6;
Mt 22:24-28

38:10
s Ge 46:12;
Dt 25:7-10

26Judah said to his brothers, "What will we gain if we kill our brother and cover up his blood?a 27Come, let's sell him to the Ishmaelites and not lay our hands on him; after all, he is our brother,b our own flesh and blood." His brothers agreed.

28So when the Midianitec merchants came by, his brothers pulled Joseph up out of the cistern and sold him for twenty shekelsa of silver to the Ishmaelites, who took him to Egypt.d

29When Reuben returned to the cistern and saw that Joseph was not there, he tore his clothes.e 30He went back to his brothers and said, "The boy isn't there! Where can I turn now?"f

31Then they got Joseph's robe,g slaughtered a goat and dipped the robe in the blood. 32They took the ornamented robe back to their father and said, "We found this. Examine it to see whether it is your son's robe."

33He recognized it and said, "It is my son's robe! Some ferocious animalh has devoured him. Joseph has surely been torn to pieces."i

34Then Jacob tore his clothes,j put on sacklothk and mourned for his son many days.l 35All his sons and daughters came to comfort him, but he refused to be comforted. "No," he said, "in mourning will I go down to the gravebm to my son." So his father wept for him.

36Meanwhile, the Midianitesc sold Joseph in Egypt to Potiphar, one of Pharaoh's officials, the captain of the guard.n

Chapter 38 Theme

38 At that time, Judah left his brothers and went down to stay with a man of Adullam named Hirah. 2There Judah met the daughter of a Canaanite man named Shua.o He married her and lay with her; 3she became pregnant and gave birth to a son, who was named Er.p 4She conceived again and gave birth to a son and named him Onan. 5She gave birth to still another son and named him Shelah. It was at Kezib that she gave birth to him.

6Judah got a wife for Er, his firstborn, and her name was Tamar. 7But Er, Judah's firstborn, was wicked in the LORD's sight; so the LORD put him to death.q

8Then Judah said to Onan, "Lie with your brother's wife and fulfill your duty to her as a brother-in-law to produce offspring for your brother."r 9But Onan knew that the offspring would not be his; so whenever he lay with his brother's wife, he spilled his semen on the ground to keep from producing offspring for his brother. 10What he did was wicked in the LORD's sight; so he put him to death also.s

a 28 That is, about 8 ounces (about 0.2 kilogram)   b 35 Hebrew *Sheol*   c 36 Samaritan Pentateuch, Septuagint, Vulgate and Syriac (see also verse 28); Masoretic Text *Medanites*

¹¹Judah then said to his daughter-in-law Tamar, "Live as a widow in your father's house until my son Shelah grows up."ᵃ For he thought, "He may die too, just like his brothers." So Tamar went to live in her father's house.

¹²After a long time Judah's wife, the daughter of Shua, died. When Judah had recovered from his grief, he went up to Timnah,ᵇ to the men who were shearing his sheep, and his friend Hirah the Adullamite went with him.

¹³When Tamar was told, "Your father-in-law is on his way to Timnah to shear his sheep," ¹⁴she took off her widow's clothes, covered herself with a veil to disguise herself, and then sat down at the entrance to Enaim, which is on the road to Timnah. For she saw that, though Shelahᶜ had now grown up, she had not been given to him as his wife.

¹⁵When Judah saw her, he thought she was a prostitute, for she had covered her face. ¹⁶Not realizing that she was his daughter-in-law,ᵈ he went over to her by the roadside and said, "Come now, let me sleep with you."

"And what will you give me to sleep with you?" she asked.

¹⁷"I'll send you a young goatᵉ from my flock," he said.

"Will you give me something as a pledgeᶠ until you send it?" she asked.

¹⁸He said, "What pledge should I give you?"

"Your sealᵍ and its cord, and the staff in your hand," she answered. So he gave them to her and slept with her, and she became pregnant by him. ¹⁹After she left, she took off her veil and put on her widow's clothesʰ again.

²⁰Meanwhile Judah sent the young goat by his friend the Adullamite in order to get his pledge back from the woman, but he did not find her. ²¹He asked the men who lived there, "Where is the shrine prostituteⁱ who was beside the road at Enaim?"

"There hasn't been any shrine prostitute here," they said.

²²So he went back to Judah and said, "I didn't find her. Besides, the men who lived there said, 'There hasn't been any shrine prostitute here.'"

²³Then Judah said, "Let her keep what she has, or we will become a laughingstock. After all, I did send her this young goat, but you didn't find her."

²⁴About three months later Judah was told, "Your daughter-in-law Tamar is guilty of prostitution, and as a result she is now pregnant."

Judah said, "Bring her out and have her burned to death!"ʲ

²⁵As she was being brought out, she sent a message to her father-in-law. "I am pregnant by the man who owns these," she said. And she added, "See if you recognize whose seal and cord and staff these are."ᵏ

38:11
ᵃRu 1:13

38:12
ᵇver 14;
Jos 15:10,57

38:14
ᶜver 11

38:16
ᵈLev 18:15;
20:12

38:17
ᵉEze 16:33
ᶠver 20

38:18
ᵍver 25

38:19
ʰver 14

38:21
ⁱLev 19:29;
Hos 4:14

38:24
ʲLev 21:9;
Dt 22:21,22

38:25
ᵏver 18

38:26
a 1Sa 24:17
b ver 11

38:27
c Ge 25:24

38:29
d Ge 46:12;
Nu 26:20,21;
Ru 4:12,18;
1Ch 2:4;
Mt 1:3

38:30
e 1Ch 2:4

39:1
f Ge 37:36
g Ge 37:25;
Ps 105:17

39:2
h Ge 21:20,22;
Ac 7:9

39:3
i Ge 21:22;
26:28
j Ps 1:3

39:4
k ver 8,22;
Ge 24:2

39:5
l Ge 26:24;
30:27

39:6
m 1Sa 16:12

39:7
n 2Sa 13:11;
Pr 7:15-18

39:8
o Pr 6:23-24

39:9
p Ge 41:33,40
q Ge 20:6;
42:18;
2Sa 12:13

39:12
r Pr 7:13

²⁶Judah recognized them and said, "She is more righteous than I,*a* since I wouldn't give her to my son Shelah.*b*" And he did not sleep with her again.

²⁷When the time came for her to give birth, there were twin boys in her womb.*c* ²⁸As she was giving birth, one of them put out his hand; so the midwife took a scarlet thread and tied it on his wrist and said, "This one came out first." ²⁹But when he drew back his hand, his brother came out, and she said, "So this is how you have broken out!" And he was named Perez.*a d* ³⁰Then his brother, who had the scarlet thread on his wrist, came out and he was given the name Zerah.*b e*

Chapter 39 Theme _____

39 Now Joseph had been taken down to Egypt. Potiphar, an Egyptian who was one of Pharaoh's officials, the captain of the guard,*f* bought him from the Ishmaelites who had taken him there.*g*

²The LORD was with Joseph*h* and he prospered, and he lived in the house of his Egyptian master. ³When his master saw that the LORD was with him*i* and that the LORD gave him success in everything he did,*j* ⁴Joseph found favor in his eyes and became his attendant. Potiphar put him in charge of his household, and he entrusted to his care everything he owned.*k* ⁵From the time he put him in charge of his household and of all that he owned, the LORD blessed the household of the Egyptian because of Joseph.*l* The blessing of the LORD was on everything Potiphar had, both in the house and in the field. ⁶So he left in Joseph's care everything he had; with Joseph in charge, he did not concern himself with anything except the food he ate.

Now Joseph was well-built and handsome,*m* ⁷and after a while his master's wife took notice of Joseph and said, "Come to bed with me!"*n*

⁸But he refused.*o* "With me in charge," he told her, "my master does not concern himself with anything in the house; everything he owns he has entrusted to my care. ⁹No one is greater in this house than I am.*p* My master has withheld nothing from me except you, because you are his wife. How then could I do such a wicked thing and sin against God?"*q* ¹⁰And though she spoke to Joseph day after day, he refused to go to bed with her or even be with her.

¹¹One day he went into the house to attend to his duties, and none of the household servants was inside. ¹²She caught him by his cloak*r* and said, "Come to bed with me!" But he left his cloak in her hand and ran out of the house.

a 29 Perez means *breaking out.*   *b 30 Zerah* can mean *scarlet* or *brightness.*

¹³When she saw that he had left his cloak in her hand and had run out of the house, ¹⁴she called her household servants. "Look," she said to them, "this Hebrew has been brought to us to make sport of us! He came in here to sleep with me, but I screamed.ᵃ ¹⁵When he heard me scream for help, he left his cloak beside me and ran out of the house."

¹⁶She kept his cloak beside her until his master came home. ¹⁷Then she told him this story:ᵇ "That Hebrew slave you brought us came to me to make sport of me. ¹⁸But as soon as I screamed for help, he left his cloak beside me and ran out of the house."

¹⁹When his master heard the story his wife told him, saying, "This is how your slave treated me," he burned with anger.ᶜ ²⁰Joseph's master took him and put him in prison,ᵈ the place where the king's prisoners were confined.

But while Joseph was there in the prison, ²¹the Lᴏʀᴅ was with him; he showed him kindness and granted him favor in the eyes of the prison warden.ᵉ ²²So the warden put Joseph in charge of all those held in the prison, and he was made responsible for all that was done there.ᶠ ²³The warden paid no attention to anything under Joseph's care, because the Lᴏʀᴅ was with Joseph and gave him success in whatever he did.ᵍ

Chapter 40 Theme _____

40 Some time later, the cupbearerʰ and the baker of the king of Egypt offended their master, the king of Egypt. ²Pharaoh was angryⁱ with his two officials, the chief cupbearer and the chief baker, ³and put them in custody in the house of the captain of the guard,ʲ in the same prison where Joseph was confined. ⁴The captain of the guard assigned them to Joseph,ᵏ and he attended them.

After they had been in custody for some time, ⁵each of the two men—the cupbearer and the baker of the king of Egypt, who were being held in prison—had a dream the same night, and each dream had a meaning of its own.ˡ

⁶When Joseph came to them the next morning, he saw that they were dejected. ⁷So he asked Pharaoh's officials who were in custody with him in his master's house, "Why are your faces so sad today?"ᵐ

⁸"We both had dreams," they answered, "but there is no one to interpret them."ⁿ

Then Joseph said to them, "Do not interpretations belong to God?ᵒ Tell me your dreams."

⁹So the chief cupbearer told Joseph his dream. He said to him, "In my dream I saw a vine in front of me, ¹⁰and on the vine were

39:14
ᵃ Dt 22:24,27

39:17
ᵇ Ex 23:1,7;
Ps 101:5

39:19
ᶜ Pr 6:34

39:20
ᵈ Ge 40:3;
Ps 105:18

39:21
ᵉ Ex 3:21

39:22
ᶠ ver 4

39:23
ᵍ ver 3

40:1
ʰ Ne 1:11

40:2
ⁱ Pr 16:14,15

40:3
ʲ Ge 39:20

40:4
ᵏ Ge 39:4

40:5
ˡ Ge 41:11

40:7
ᵐ Ne 2:2

40:8
ⁿ Ge 41:8,15
ᵒ Ge 41:16;
Da 2:22,28,47

40:12
a Ge 41:12,
15,25;
Da 2:36; 4:19

40:14
b Lk 23:42
c Jos 2:12;
1Sa 20:14,42;
1Ki 2:7

40:15
d Ge 37:26-28

40:18
e ver 12

40:19
f ver 13

40:20
g Mt 14:6-10
h Mk 6:21

40:21
i ver 13

40:22
j ver 19
k Ps 105:19

40:23
l Job 19:14;
Ecc 9:15

41:1
m Ge 20:3

41:2
n ver 26
o Isa 19:6

three branches. As soon as it budded, it blossomed, and its clusters ripened into grapes. ¹¹Pharaoh's cup was in my hand, and I took the grapes, squeezed them into Pharaoh's cup and put the cup in his hand."

¹²"This is what it means,*a*" Joseph said to him. "The three branches are three days. ¹³Within three days Pharaoh will lift up your head and restore you to your position, and you will put Pharaoh's cup in his hand, just as you used to do when you were his cupbearer. ¹⁴But when all goes well with you, remember me*b* and show me kindness;*c* mention me to Pharaoh and get me out of this prison. ¹⁵For I was forcibly carried off from the land of the Hebrews,*d* and even here I have done nothing to deserve being put in a dungeon."

¹⁶When the chief baker saw that Joseph had given a favorable interpretation, he said to Joseph, "I too had a dream: On my head were three baskets of bread.*a* ¹⁷In the top basket were all kinds of baked goods for Pharaoh, but the birds were eating them out of the basket on my head."

¹⁸"This is what it means," Joseph said. "The three baskets are three days. *e* ¹⁹Within three days Pharaoh will lift off your head *f* and hang you on a tree.*b* And the birds will eat away your flesh."

²⁰Now the third day was Pharaoh's birthday,*g* and he gave a feast for all his officials.*h* He lifted up the heads of the chief cupbearer and the chief baker in the presence of his officials: ²¹He restored the chief cupbearer to his position, so that he once again put the cup into Pharaoh's hand,*i* ²²but he hanged*c* the chief baker,*j* just as Joseph had said to them in his interpretation.*k*

²³The chief cupbearer, however, did not remember Joseph; he forgot him.*l*

Chapter 41 Theme

41 When two full years had passed, Pharaoh had a dream:*m* He was standing by the Nile, ²when out of the river there came up seven cows, sleek and fat,*n* and they grazed among the reeds.*o* ³After them, seven other cows, ugly and gaunt, came up out of the Nile and stood beside those on the riverbank. ⁴And the cows that were ugly and gaunt ate up the seven sleek, fat cows. Then Pharaoh woke up.

⁵He fell asleep again and had a second dream: Seven heads of grain, healthy and good, were growing on a single stalk. ⁶After them, seven other heads of grain sprouted—thin and scorched by the east wind. ⁷The thin heads of grain swallowed up the seven healthy, full heads. Then Pharaoh woke up; it had been a dream.

a 16 Or *three wicker baskets*   *b 19* Or *and impale you on a pole*   *c 22* Or *impaled*

[8] In the morning his mind was troubled,[a] so he sent for all the magicians[b] and wise men of Egypt. Pharaoh told them his dreams, but no one could interpret them for him.

[9] Then the chief cupbearer said to Pharaoh, "Today I am reminded of my shortcomings. [10] Pharaoh was once angry with his servants,[c] and he imprisoned me and the chief baker in the house of the captain of the guard.[d] [11] Each of us had a dream the same night, and each dream had a meaning of its own.[e] [12] Now a young Hebrew was there with us, a servant of the captain of the guard. We told him our dreams, and he interpreted them for us, giving each man the interpretation of his dream.[f] [13] And things turned out exactly as he interpreted them to us: I was restored to my position, and the other man was hanged.[a][g]"

[14] So Pharaoh sent for Joseph, and he was quickly brought from the dungeon.[h] When he had shaved and changed his clothes, he came before Pharaoh.

[15] Pharaoh said to Joseph, "I had a dream, and no one can interpret it. But I have heard it said of you that when you hear a dream you can interpret it."[i]

[16] "I cannot do it," Joseph replied to Pharaoh, "but God will give Pharaoh the answer he desires."[j]

[17] Then Pharaoh said to Joseph, "In my dream I was standing on the bank of the Nile, [18] when out of the river there came up seven cows, fat and sleek, and they grazed among the reeds. [19] After them, seven other cows came up— scrawny and very ugly and lean. I had never seen such ugly cows in all the land of Egypt. [20] The lean, ugly cows ate up the seven fat cows that came up first. [21] But even after they ate them, no one could tell that they had done so; they looked just as ugly as before. Then I woke up.

[22] "In my dreams I also saw seven heads of grain, full and good, growing on a single stalk. [23] After them, seven other heads sprouted—withered and thin and scorched by the east wind. [24] The thin heads of grain swallowed up the seven good heads. I told this to the magicians, but none could explain it to me.[k]"

[25] Then Joseph said to Pharaoh, "The dreams of Pharaoh are one and the same. God has revealed to Pharaoh what he is about to do.[l] [26] The seven good cows[m] are seven years, and the seven good heads of grain are seven years; it is one and the same dream. [27] The seven lean, ugly cows that came up afterward are seven years, and so are the seven worthless heads of grain scorched by the east wind: They are seven years of famine.[n]

[28] "It is just as I said to Pharaoh: God has shown Pharaoh what he is about to do. [29] Seven years of great abundance[o] are coming

---

41:8
[a] Da 2:1,3; 4:5,19
[b] Ex 7:11,22; Da 1:20; 2:2,27; 4:7

41:10
[c] Ge 40:2
[d] Ge 39:20

41:11
[e] Ge 40:5

41:12
[f] Ge 40:12

41:13
[g] Ge 40:22

41:14
[h] Ps 105:20; Da 2:25

41:15
[i] Da 5:16

41:16
[j] Ge 40:8; Da 2:30; Ac 3:12; 2Co 3:5

41:24
[k] ver 8

41:25
[l] Da 2:45

41:26
[m] ver 2

41:27
[n] Ge 12:10; 2Ki 8:1

41:29
[o] ver 47

---

[a] 13 Or *impaled*

41:30
a ver 54;
Ge 47:13
b ver 56

41:32
c Nu 23:19;
Isa 46:10-11

41:33
d ver 39

41:34
e 1Sa 8:15
f ver 48

41:35
g ver 48

41:36
h ver 56

41:37
i Ge 45:16

41:38
j Nu 27:18;
Job 32:8;
Da 4:8,8-9,18;
5:11,14

41:40
k Ps 105:21-22;
Ac 7:10

41:41
l Ge 42:6;
Da 6:3

41:42
m Est 3:10
n Da 5:7,16,29

41:43
o Est 6:9

41:44
p Ps 105:22

41:45
q ver 50;
Ge 46:20,27

41:46
r Ge 37:2
s 1Sa 16:21;
Da 1:19

throughout the land of Egypt, 30but seven years of famine*a* will follow them. Then all the abundance in Egypt will be forgotten, and the famine will ravage the land.*b* 31The abundance in the land will not be remembered, because the famine that follows it will be so severe. 32The reason the dream was given to Pharaoh in two forms is that the matter has been firmly decided*c* by God, and God will do it soon.

33"And now let Pharaoh look for a discerning and wise man*d* and put him in charge of the land of Egypt. 34Let Pharaoh appoint commissioners over the land to take a fifth*e* of the harvest of Egypt during the seven years of abundance.*f* 35They should collect all the food of these good years that are coming and store up the grain under the authority of Pharaoh, to be kept in the cities for food.*g* 36This food should be held in reserve for the country, to be used during the seven years of famine that will come upon Egypt,*h* so that the country may not be ruined by the famine."

37The plan seemed good to Pharaoh and to all his officials.*i* 38So Pharaoh asked them, "Can we find anyone like this man, one in whom is the spirit of God*a*?"*j*

39Then Pharaoh said to Joseph, "Since God has made all this known to you, there is no one so discerning and wise as you. 40You shall be in charge of my palace, and all my people are to submit to your orders.*k* Only with respect to the throne will I be greater than you."

41So Pharaoh said to Joseph, "I hereby put you in charge of the whole land of Egypt."*l* 42Then Pharaoh took his signet ring*m* from his finger and put it on Joseph's finger. He dressed him in robes of fine linen and put a gold chain around his neck.*n* 43He had him ride in a chariot as his second-in-command,*b* and men shouted before him, "Make way*c*!"*o* Thus he put him in charge of the whole land of Egypt.

44Then Pharaoh said to Joseph, "I am Pharaoh, but without your word no one will lift hand or foot in all Egypt."*p* 45Pharaoh gave Joseph the name Zaphenath-Paneah and gave him Asenath daughter of Potiphera, priest of On,*d* to be his wife.*q* And Joseph went throughout the land of Egypt.

46Joseph was thirty years old*r* when he entered the service*s* of Pharaoh king of Egypt. And Joseph went out from Pharaoh's presence and traveled throughout Egypt. 47During the seven years of abundance the land produced plentifully. 48Joseph collected all the food produced in those seven years of abundance in Egypt and stored it in the cities. In each city he put the food grown in the fields surrounding it. 49Joseph stored up huge

a 38 Or *of the gods*   *b* 43 Or *in the chariot of his second-in-command*; or *in his second chariot*   *c* 43 Or *Bow down*   *d* 45 That is, Heliopolis; also in verse 50 quantities of grain, like the sand of the sea; it was so much that he stopped keeping records because it was beyond measure.

⁵⁰Before the years of famine came, two sons were born to Joseph by Asenath daughter of Potiphera, priest of On.ᵃ ⁵¹Joseph named his firstbornᵇ Manassehᵃ and said, "It is because God has made me forget all my trouble and all my father's household." ⁵²The second son he named Ephraimᵇᶜ and said, "It is because God has made me fruitfulᵈ in the land of my suffering."

⁵³The seven years of abundance in Egypt came to an end, ⁵⁴and the seven years of famine began,ᵉ just as Joseph had said. There was famine in all the other lands, but in the whole land of Egypt there was food. ⁵⁵When all Egypt began to feel the famine,ᶠ the people cried to Pharaoh for food. Then Pharaoh told all the Egyptians, "Go to Joseph and do what he tells you."ᵍ

⁵⁶When the famine had spread over the whole country, Joseph opened the storehouses and sold grain to the Egyptians, for the famineʰ was severe throughout Egypt. ⁵⁷And all the countries came to Egypt to buy grain from Joseph,ⁱ because the famine was severe in all the world.

Chapter 42 Theme

42 When Jacob learned that there was grain in Egypt,ʲ he said to his sons, "Why do you just keep looking at each other?" ²He continued, "I have heard that there is grain in Egypt. Go down there and buy some for us, so that we may live and not die."ᵏ

³Then ten of Joseph's brothers went down to buy grain from Egypt. ⁴But Jacob did not send Benjamin, Joseph's brother, with the others, because he was afraid that harm might come to him.ˡ ⁵So Israel's sons were among those who went to buy grain,ᵐ for the famine was in the land of Canaan also.ⁿ

⁶Now Joseph was the governor of the land,ᵒ the one who sold grain to all its people. So when Joseph's brothers arrived, they bowed down to him with their faces to the ground.ᵖ ⁷As soon as Joseph saw his brothers, he recognized them, but he pretended to be a stranger and spoke harshly to them.�q "Where do you come from?" he asked.

"From the land of Canaan," they replied, "to buy food."

⁸Although Joseph recognized his brothers, they did not recognize him.ʳ ⁹Then he remembered his dreamsˢ about them and said to them, "You are spies! You have come to see where our land is unprotected."

ᵃ51 *Manasseh* sounds like and may be derived from the Hebrew for *forget*. ᵇ52 *Ephraim* sounds like the Hebrew for *twice fruitful*.

41:50
ᵃGe 46:20; 48:5

41:51
ᵇGe 48:14, 18,20

41:52
ᶜGe 48:1,5; 50:23
ᵈGe 17:6; 28:3; 49:22

41:54
ᵉver 30; Ps 105:11; Ac 7:11

41:55
ᶠDt 32:24
ᵍver 41

41:56
ʰGe 12:10

41:57
ⁱGe 42:5; 47:15

42:1
ʲAc 7:12

42:2
ᵏGe 43:8

42:4
ˡver 38

42:5
ᵐGe 41:57
ⁿGe 12:10; Ac 7:11

42:6
ᵒGe 41:41
ᵖGe 37:7-10

42:7
qver 30

42:8
ʳGe 37:2

42:9
ˢGe 37:7

42:13
a Ge 37:30,33;
44:20

42:15
b 1Sa 17:55

42:16
c ver 11

42:17
d Ge 40:4

42:18
e Ge 20:11;
Lev 25:43

42:20
f ver 15,34;
Ge 43:5; 44:23

42:21
g Ge 37:26-28
h Hos 5:15

42:22
i Ge 37:21-22
j Ge 9:5
k 1Ki 2:32;
2Ch 24:22;
Ps 9:12

42:24
l ver 13;
Ge 43:14,23;
45:14-15

42:25
m Ge 43:2
n Ge 44:1,8
o Ro 12:17,
20-21

42:27
p Ge 43:21-22

42:28
q Ge 43:23

¹⁰"No, my lord," they answered. "Your servants have come to buy food. ¹¹We are all the sons of one man. Your servants are honest men, not spies."

¹²"No!" he said to them. "You have come to see where our land is unprotected."

¹³But they replied, "Your servants were twelve brothers, the sons of one man, who lives in the land of Canaan. The youngest is now with our father, and one is no more."*a*

¹⁴Joseph said to them, "It is just as I told you: You are spies! ¹⁵And this is how you will be tested: As surely as Pharaoh lives,*b* you will not leave this place unless your youngest brother comes here. ¹⁶Send one of your number to get your brother; the rest of you will be kept in prison, so that your words may be tested to see if you are telling the truth.*c* If you are not, then as surely as Pharaoh lives, you are spies!" ¹⁷And he put them all in custody*d* for three days.

¹⁸On the third day, Joseph said to them, "Do this and you will live, for I fear God:*e* ¹⁹If you are honest men, let one of your brothers stay here in prison, while the rest of you go and take grain back for your starving households. ²⁰But you must bring your youngest brother to me,*f* so that your words may be verified and that you may not die." This they proceeded to do.

²¹They said to one another, "Surely we are being punished because of our brother.*g* We saw how distressed he was when he pleaded with us for his life, but we would not listen; that's why this distress*h* has come upon us."

²²Reuben replied, "Didn't I tell you not to sin against the boy?*i* But you wouldn't listen! Now we must give an accounting*j* for his blood."*k* ²³They did not realize that Joseph could understand them, since he was using an interpreter.

²⁴He turned away from them and began to weep, but then turned back and spoke to them again. He had Simeon taken from them and bound before their eyes.*l*

²⁵Joseph gave orders to fill their bags with grain,*m* to put each man's silver back in his sack,*n* and to give them provisions for their journey.*o* After this was done for them, ²⁶they loaded their grain on their donkeys and left.

²⁷At the place where they stopped for the night one of them opened his sack to get feed for his donkey, and he saw his silver in the mouth of his sack.*p* ²⁸"My silver has been returned," he said to his brothers. "Here it is in my sack."

Their hearts sank and they turned to each other trembling and said, "What is this that God has done to us?"*q*

²⁹When they came to their father Jacob in the land of Canaan, they told him all that had happened to them. They said, ³⁰"The

man who is lord over the land spoke harshly to us[a] and treated us as though we were spying on the land. [31]But we said to him, 'We are honest men; we are not spies.[b] [32]We were twelve brothers, sons of one father. One is no more, and the youngest is now with our father in Canaan.'

[33]"Then the man who is lord over the land said to us, 'This is how I will know whether you are honest men: Leave one of your brothers here with me, and take food for your starving households and go.[c] [34]But bring your youngest brother to me so I will know that you are not spies but honest men. Then I will give your brother back to you, and you can trade[a] in the land.[d]'"

[35]As they were emptying their sacks, there in each man's sack was his pouch of silver! When they and their father saw the money pouches, they were frightened.[e] [36]Their father Jacob said to them, "You have deprived me of my children. Joseph is no more and Simeon is no more, and now you want to take Benjamin.[f] Everything is against me!"

[37]Then Reuben said to his father, "You may put both of my sons to death if I do not bring him back to you. Entrust him to my care, and I will bring him back."

[38]But Jacob said, "My son will not go down there with you; his brother is dead[g] and he is the only one left. If harm comes to him[h] on the journey you are taking, you will bring my gray head down to the grave[b][i] in sorrow.[j]"

Chapter 43 Theme _____

43 Now the famine was still severe in the land.[k] [2]So when they had eaten all the grain they had brought from Egypt, their father said to them, "Go back and buy us a little more food."

[3]But Judah said to him, "The man warned us solemnly, 'You will not see my face again unless your brother is with you.'[l] [4]If you will send our brother along with us, we will go down and buy food for you. [5]But if you will not send him, we will not go down, because the man said to us, 'You will not see my face again unless your brother is with you.[m]'"

[6]Israel asked, "Why did you bring this trouble on me by telling the man you had another brother?"

[7]They replied, "The man questioned us closely about ourselves and our family. 'Is your father still living?'[n] he asked us. 'Do you have another brother?'[o] We simply answered his questions. How were we to know he would say, 'Bring your brother down here'?"

[8]Then Judah said to Israel his father, "Send the boy along with me and we will go at once, so that we and you and our children

42:30
[a] ver 7

42:31
[b] ver 11

42:33
[c] ver 19,20

42:34
[d] Ge 34:10

42:35
[e] Ge 43:12,15,18

42:36
[f] Ge 43:14

42:38
[g] Ge 37:33
[h] ver 4
[i] Ge 37:35
[j] Ge 44:29,34

43:1
[k] Ge 12:10;
41:56-57

43:3
[l] Ge 42:15; 44:23

43:5
[m] Ge 42:15;
2Sa 3:13

43:7
[n] ver 27
[o] Ge 42:13

[a]34 Or *move about freely* [b]38 Hebrew *Sheol*

43:8
a Ge 42:2;
Ps 33:18-19

43:9
b Ge 42:37;
44:32;
Phm 1:18-19

43:11
c Ge 32:20;
Pr 18:16
d Ge 37:25;
Jer 8:22
e 1Ki 10:2

43:12
f Ge 42:25

43:14
g Ge 17:1;
28:3; 35:11
h Ge 42:24
i Est 4:16

43:15
j Ge 45:9,13
k Ge 47:2,7

43:16
l Ge 44:1,4,12
m ver 31;
Lk 15:23

43:18
n Ge 42:35

43:20
o Ge 42:3

43:21
p ver 15;
Ge 42:27,35

43:23
q Ge 42:28
r Ge 42:24

43:24
s ver 16
t Ge 18:4; 24:32

may live and not die.*a* ⁹I myself will guarantee his safety; you can hold me personally responsible for him. If I do not bring him back to you and set him here before you, I will bear the blame before you all my life.*b* ¹⁰As it is, if we had not delayed, we could have gone and returned twice."

¹¹Then their father Israel said to them, "If it must be, then do this: Put some of the best products of the land in your bags and take them down to the man as a gift*c*—a little balm*d* and a little honey, some spices*e* and myrrh, some pistachio nuts and almonds. ¹²Take double the amount of silver with you, for you must return the silver that was put back into the mouths of your sacks.*f* Perhaps it was a mistake. ¹³Take your brother also and go back to the man at once. ¹⁴And may God Almighty*a* *g* grant you mercy before the man so that he will let your other brother and Benjamin come back with you.*h* As for me, if I am bereaved, I am bereaved."*i*

¹⁵So the men took the gifts and double the amount of silver, and Benjamin also. They hurried*j* down to Egypt and presented themselves*k* to Joseph. ¹⁶When Joseph saw Benjamin with them, he said to the steward of his house,*l* "Take these men to my house, slaughter an animal and prepare dinner;*m* they are to eat with me at noon."

¹⁷The man did as Joseph told him and took the men to Joseph's house. ¹⁸Now the men were frightened*n* when they were taken to his house. They thought, "We were brought here because of the silver that was put back into our sacks the first time. He wants to attack us and overpower us and seize us as slaves and take our donkeys."

¹⁹So they went up to Joseph's steward and spoke to him at the entrance to the house. ²⁰"Please, sir," they said, "we came down here the first time to buy food.*o* ²¹But at the place where we stopped for the night we opened our sacks and each of us found his silver—the exact weight—in the mouth of his sack. So we have brought it back with us.*p* ²²We have also brought additional silver with us to buy food. We don't know who put our silver in our sacks."

²³"It's all right," he said. "Don't be afraid. Your God, the God of your father, has given you treasure in your sacks;*q* I received your silver." Then he brought Simeon out to them.*r*

²⁴The steward took the men into Joseph's house,*s* gave them water to wash their feet*t* and provided fodder for their donkeys. ²⁵They prepared their gifts for Joseph's arrival at noon, because they had heard that they were to eat there.

a 14 Hebrew *El-Shaddai*

²⁶When Joseph came home, they presented to him the gifts^a they had brought into the house, and they bowed down before him to the ground.^b ²⁷He asked them how they were, and then he said, "How is your aged father you told me about? Is he still living?"^c

²⁸They replied, "Your servant our father is still alive and well." And they bowed low to pay him honor.^d

²⁹As he looked about and saw his brother Benjamin, his own mother's son, he asked, "Is this your youngest brother, the one you told me about?"^e And he said, "God be gracious to you,^f my son." ³⁰Deeply moved^g at the sight of his brother, Joseph hurried out and looked for a place to weep. He went into his private room and wept^h there.

³¹After he had washed his face, he came out and, controlling himself,ⁱ said, "Serve the food."

³²They served him by himself, the brothers by themselves, and the Egyptians who ate with him by themselves, because Egyptians could not eat with Hebrews,^j for that is detestable to Egyptians.^k ³³The men had been seated before him in the order of their ages, from the firstborn to the youngest; and they looked at each other in astonishment. ³⁴When portions were served to them from Joseph's table, Benjamin's portion was five times as much as anyone else's.^l So they feasted and drank freely with him.

Chapter 44 Theme

44 Now Joseph gave these instructions to the steward of his house: "Fill the men's sacks with as much food as they can carry, and put each man's silver in the mouth of his sack.^m ²Then put my cup, the silver one, in the mouth of the youngest one's sack, along with the silver for his grain." And he did as Joseph said.

³As morning dawned, the men were sent on their way with their donkeys. ⁴They had not gone far from the city when Joseph said to his steward, "Go after those men at once, and when you catch up with them, say to them, 'Why have you repaid good with evil?ⁿ ⁵Isn't this the cup my master drinks from and also uses for divination?^o This is a wicked thing you have done.'"

⁶When he caught up with them, he repeated these words to them. ⁷But they said to him, "Why does my lord say such things? Far be it from your servants to do anything like that! ⁸We even brought back to you from the land of Canaan the silver we found inside the mouths of our sacks.^p So why would we steal silver or gold from your master's house? ⁹If any of your servants is found to have it, he will die;^q and the rest of us will become my lord's slaves."

43:26
^aMt 2:11
^bGe 37:7,10

43:27
^cver 7

43:28
^dGe 37:7

43:29
^eGe 42:13
^fNu 6:25;
Ps 67:1

43:30
^gJn 11:33,38
^hGe 42:24;
45:2,14,15;
46:29

43:31
ⁱGe 45:1

43:32
^jGal 2:12
^kGe 46:34;
Ex 8:26

43:34
^lGe 37:3; 45:22

44:1
^mGe 42:25

44:4
ⁿPs 35:12

44:5
^oGe 30:27;
Dt 18:10-14

44:8
^pGe 42:25; 43:21

44:9
^qGe 31:32

44:12
a ver 2

44:13
b Ge 37:29;
Nu 14:6;
2Sa 1:11

44:14
c Ge 37:7,10

44:15
d ver 5;
Ge 30:27

44:16
e ver 9;
Ge 43:18
f ver 2

44:18
g Ge 18:30;
Ex 32:22

44:19
h Ge 43:7

44:20
i Ge 37:3
j Ge 37:33
k Ge 42:13

44:21
l Ge 42:15

44:22
m Ge 37:35

44:23
n Ge 43:5

44:25
o Ge 43:2

44:27
p Ge 46:19

44:28
q Ge 37:33

44:29
r Ge 42:38

44:30
s 1Sa 18:1

10"Very well, then," he said, "let it be as you say. Whoever is found to have it will become my slave; the rest of you will be free from blame."

11Each of them quickly lowered his sack to the ground and opened it. 12Then the steward proceeded to search, beginning with the oldest and ending with the youngest. And the cup was found in Benjamin's sack.a 13At this, they tore their clothes.b Then they all loaded their donkeys and returned to the city.

14Joseph was still in the house when Judah and his brothers came in, and they threw themselves to the ground before him.c 15Joseph said to them, "What is this you have done? Don't you know that a man like me can find things out by divination?d"

16"What can we say to my lord?" Judah replied. "What can we say? How can we prove our innocence? God has uncovered your servants' guilt. We are now my lord's slavese—we ourselves and the one who was found to have the cup.f"

17But Joseph said, "Far be it from me to do such a thing! Only the man who was found to have the cup will become my slave. The rest of you, go back to your father in peace."

18Then Judah went up to him and said: "Please, my lord, let your servant speak a word to my lord. Do not be angryg with your servant, though you are equal to Pharaoh himself. 19My lord asked his servants, 'Do you have a father or a brother?'h 20And we answered, 'We have an aged father, and there is a young son born to him in his old age.i His brother is dead,j and he is the only one of his mother's sons left, and his father loves him.'k

21"Then you said to your servants, 'Bring him down to me so I can see him for myself.'l 22And we said to my lord, 'The boy cannot leave his father; if he leaves him, his father will die.'m 23But you told your servants, 'Unless your youngest brother comes down with you, you will not see my face again.'n 24When we went back to your servant my father, we told him what my lord had said.

25"Then our father said, 'Go back and buy a little more food.'o 26But we said, 'We cannot go down. Only if our youngest brother is with us will we go. We cannot see the man's face unless our youngest brother is with us.'

27"Your servant my father said to us, 'You know that my wife bore me two sons.p 28One of them went away from me, and I said, "He has surely been torn to pieces."q And I have not seen him since. 29If you take this one from me too and harm comes to him, you will bring my gray head down to the gravea in misery.'r

30"So now, if the boy is not with us when I go back to your servant my father and if my father, whose life is closely bound up with the boy's life,s 31sees that the boy isn't there, he will die. Your

a 29 Hebrew Sheol; also in verse 31

servants will bring the gray head of our father down to the grave in sorrow. [32]Your servant guaranteed the boy's safety to my father. I said, 'If I do not bring him back to you, I will bear the blame before you, my father, all my life!'[a]

[33]"Now then, please let your servant remain here as my lord's slave[b] in place of the boy,[c] and let the boy return with his brothers. [34]How can I go back to my father if the boy is not with me? No! Do not let me see the misery that would come upon my father."[d]

Chapter 45 Theme _____

45 Then Joseph could no longer control himself[e] before all his attendants, and he cried out, "Have everyone leave my presence!" So there was no one with Joseph when he made himself known to his brothers. [2]And he wept[f] so loudly that the Egyptians heard him, and Pharaoh's household heard about it.[g]

[3]Joseph said to his brothers, "I am Joseph! Is my father still living?"[h] But his brothers were not able to answer him,[i] because they were terrified at his presence.

[4]Then Joseph said to his brothers, "Come close to me." When they had done so, he said, "I am your brother Joseph, the one you sold into Egypt![j] [5]And now, do not be distressed[k] and do not be angry with yourselves for selling me here,[l] because it was to save lives that God sent me ahead of you.[m] [6]For two years now there has been famine in the land, and for the next five years there will not be plowing and reaping. [7]But God sent me ahead of you to preserve for you a remnant[n] on earth and to save your lives by a great deliverance.[a][o]

[8]"So then, it was not you who sent me here, but God. He made me father[p] to Pharaoh, lord of his entire household and ruler of all Egypt.[q] [9]Now hurry back to my father and say to him, 'This is what your son Joseph says: God has made me lord of all Egypt. Come down to me; don't delay.[r] [10]You shall live in the region of Goshen[s] and be near me—you, your children and grandchildren, your flocks and herds, and all you have. [11]I will provide for you there,[t] because five years of famine are still to come. Otherwise you and your household and all who belong to you will become destitute.'

[12]"You can see for yourselves, and so can my brother Benjamin, that it is really I who am speaking to you. [13]Tell my father about all the honor accorded me in Egypt and about everything you have seen. And bring my father down here quickly.[u]"

[14]Then he threw his arms around his brother Benjamin and wept, and Benjamin embraced him, weeping. [15]And he kissed[v]

---

a 7 Or *save you as a great band of survivors*

44:32
a Ge 43:9

44:33
b Ge 43:18
c Jn 15:13

44:34
d Est 8:6

45:1
e Ge 43:31

45:2
f Ge 29:11
g ver 16; Ge 46:29

45:3
h Ac 7:13
i ver 15

45:4
j Ge 37:28

45:5
k Ge 42:21
l Ge 42:22
m ver 7-8; Ge 50:20; Ps 105:17

45:7
n 2Ki 19:4, 30,31; Isa 10:20,21; Mic 4:7; Zep 2:7
o Ex 15:2; Est 4:14; Isa 25:9

45:8
p Jdg 17:10
q Ge 41:41

45:9
r Ge 43:10

45:10
s Ge 46:28,34; 47:1

45:11
t Ge 47:12

45:13
u Ac 7:14

45:15
v Lk 15:20

45:15
a ver 3

45:16
b Ac 7:13

45:18
c Ge 27:28;
46:34;
47:6,11,27;
Nu 18:12,29
d Ps 37:19

45:19
e Ge 46:5

45:21
f Ge 42:25

45:22
g Ge 37:3;
43:34

45:24
h Ge 42:21-22

45:26
i Ge 44:28

45:27
j ver 19

46:1
k Ge 21:14;
28:10
l Ge 26:24;
28:13; 31:42

46:2
m Ge 15:1;
Job 33:14-15
n Ge 22:1;
31:11

46:3
o Ge 28:13
p Ge 12:2;
Dt 26:5
q Ex 1:7

46:4
r Ge 28:15;
48:21;
Ex 3:8
s Ge 50:1,24

46:5
t Ge 45:19

all his brothers and wept over them. Afterward his brothers talked with him.*a*

¹⁶When the news reached Pharaoh's palace that Joseph's brothers had come,*b* Pharaoh and all his officials were pleased. ¹⁷Pharaoh said to Joseph, "Tell your brothers, 'Do this: Load your animals and return to the land of Canaan, ¹⁸and bring your father and your families back to me. I will give you the best of the land of Egypt*c* and you can enjoy the fat of the land.'*d*

¹⁹"You are also directed to tell them, 'Do this: Take some carts*e* from Egypt for your children and your wives, and get your father and come. ²⁰Never mind about your belongings, because the best of all Egypt will be yours.'"

²¹So the sons of Israel did this. Joseph gave them carts, as Pharaoh had commanded, and he also gave them provisions for their journey.*f* ²²To each of them he gave new clothing, but to Benjamin he gave three hundred shekels*a* of silver and five sets of clothes.*g* ²³And this is what he sent to his father: ten donkeys loaded with the best things of Egypt, and ten female donkeys loaded with grain and bread and other provisions for his journey. ²⁴Then he sent his brothers away, and as they were leaving he said to them, "Don't quarrel on the way!"*h*

²⁵So they went up out of Egypt and came to their father Jacob in the land of Canaan. ²⁶They told him, "Joseph is still alive! In fact, he is ruler of all Egypt." Jacob was stunned; he did not believe them.*i* ²⁷But when they told him everything Joseph had said to them, and when he saw the carts*j* Joseph had sent to carry him back, the spirit of their father Jacob revived. ²⁸And Israel said, "I'm convinced! My son Joseph is still alive. I will go and see him before I die."

Chapter 46 Theme

46 So Israel set out with all that was his, and when he reached Beersheba,*k* he offered sacrifices to the God of his father Isaac.*l*

²And God spoke to Israel in a vision at night*m* and said, "Jacob! Jacob!"

"Here I am,"*n* he replied.

³"I am God, the God of your father,"*o* he said. "Do not be afraid to go down to Egypt, for I will make you into a great nation*p* there.*q* ⁴I will go down to Egypt with you, and I will surely bring you back again.*r* And Joseph's own hand will close your eyes.*s*"

⁵Then Jacob left Beersheba, and Israel's sons took their father Jacob and their children and their wives in the carts*t* that Pharaoh

a 22 That is, about 7 1/2 pounds (about 3.5 kilograms)

had sent to transport him. ⁶They also took with them their livestock and the possessions they had acquired in Canaan, and Jacob and all his offspring went to Egypt.ᵃ ⁷He took with him to Egypt his sons and grandsons and his daughters and granddaughters—all his offspring.ᵇ

⁸These are the names of the sons of Israelᶜ (Jacob and his descendants) who went to Egypt:

Reuben the firstborn of Jacob.
⁹The sons of Reuben:ᵈ
Hanoch, Pallu, Hezron and Carmi.
¹⁰The sons of Simeon:ᵉ
Jemuel,ᶠ Jamin, Ohad, Jakin, Zohar and Shaul the son of a Canaanite woman.
¹¹The sons of Levi:ᵍ
Gershon, Kohath and Merari.
¹²The sons of Judah:ʰ
Er, Onan, Shelah, Perez and Zerah (but Er and Onan had died in the land of Canaan).
The sons of Perez:ⁱ
Hezron and Hamul.
¹³The sons of Issachar:ʲ
Tola, Puah,ᵃᵏ Jashubᵇ and Shimron.
¹⁴The sons of Zebulun:ˡ
Sered, Elon and Jahleel.

¹⁵These were the sons Leah bore to Jacob in Paddan Aram,ᶜ besides his daughter Dinah. These sons and daughters of his were thirty-three in all.

¹⁶The sons of Gad:ᵐ
Zephon,ᵈⁿ Haggi, Shuni, Ezbon, Eri, Arodi and Areli.
¹⁷The sons of Asher:ᵒ
Imnah, Ishvah, Ishvi and Beriah.
Their sister was Serah.
The sons of Beriah:
Heber and Malkiel.
¹⁸These were the children born to Jacob by Zilpah,ᵖ whom Laban had given to his daughter Leah�q—sixteen in all.

¹⁹The sons of Jacob's wife Rachel:
Joseph and Benjamin.ʳ ²⁰In Egypt, Manassehˢ and Ephraimᵗ were born to Joseph by Asenath daughter of Potiphera, priest of On.ᵉ

ᵃ 13 Samaritan Pentateuch and Syriac (see also 1 Chron. 7:1); Masoretic Text *Puvah*
ᵇ 13 Samaritan Pentateuch and some Septuagint manuscripts (see also Num. 26:24 and 1 Chron. 7:1); Masoretic Text *Iob*   ᶜ 15 That is, Northwest Mesopotamia   ᵈ 16 Samaritan Pentateuch and Septuagint (see also Num. 26:15); Masoretic Text *Ziphion*   ᵉ 20 That is, Heliopolis

---

46:6
ᵃ Dt 26:5;
Jos 24:4;
Ps 105:23;
Isa 52:4;
Ac 7:15

46:7
ᵇ Ge 45:10

46:8
ᶜ Ex 1:1;
Nu 26:4

46:9
ᵈ 1Ch 5:3

46:10
ᵉ Ge 29:33;
Nu 26:14
ᶠ Ex 6:15

46:11
ᵍ Ge 29:34;
Nu 3:17

46:12
ʰ Ge 29:35
ⁱ 1Ch 2:5
Mt 1:3

46:13
ʲ Ge 30:18
ᵏ 1Ch 7:1

46:14
ˡ Ge 30:20

46:16
ᵐ Ge 30:11
ⁿ Nu 26:15

46:17
ᵒ Ge 30:13;
1Ch 7:30-31

46:18
ᵖ Ge 30:10
q Ge 29:24

46:19
ʳ Ge 44:27

46:20
ˢ Ge 41:51
ᵗ Ge 41:52

46:21
*a*Nu 26:38-41;
1Ch 7:6-12; 8:1

46:25
*b*Ge 30:8
*c*Ge 29:29

46:26
*d*ver 5-7;
Ex 1:5;
Dt 10:22

46:27
*e*Ac 7:14

46:28
*f*Ge 45:10

46:29
*g*Ge 45:14-15;
Lk 15:20

46:31
*h*Ge 47:1

46:33
*i*Ge 47:3

46:34
*j*Ge 45:10
*k*Ge 43:32;
Ex 8:26

47:1
*l*Ge 46:31

47:3
*m*Ge 46:33

²¹The sons of Benjamin:*a*

Bela, Beker, Ashbel, Gera, Naaman, Ehi, Rosh, Muppim, Huppim and Ard.

²²These were the sons of Rachel who were born to Jacob—fourteen in all.

²³The son of Dan:

Hushim.

²⁴The sons of Naphtali:

Jahziel, Guni, Jezer and Shillem.

²⁵These were the sons born to Jacob by Bilhah,*b* whom Laban had given to his daughter Rachel*c*—seven in all.

²⁶All those who went to Egypt with Jacob—those who were his direct descendants, not counting his sons' wives—numbered sixty-six persons.*d* ²⁷With the two sons*a* who had been born to Joseph in Egypt, the members of Jacob's family, which went to Egypt, were seventy*b* in all.*e*

²⁸Now Jacob sent Judah ahead of him to Joseph to get directions to Goshen.*f* When they arrived in the region of Goshen, ²⁹Joseph had his chariot made ready and went to Goshen to meet his father Israel. As soon as Joseph appeared before him, he threw his arms around his father*c* and wept for a long time.*g*

³⁰Israel said to Joseph, "Now I am ready to die, since I have seen for myself that you are still alive."

³¹Then Joseph said to his brothers and to his father's household, "I will go up and speak to Pharaoh and will say to him, 'My brothers and my father's household, who were living in the land of Canaan, have come to me.*h* ³²The men are shepherds; they tend livestock, and they have brought along their flocks and herds and everything they own.' ³³When Pharaoh calls you in and asks, 'What is your occupation?'*i* ³⁴you should answer, 'Your servants have tended livestock from our boyhood on, just as our fathers did.' Then you will be allowed to settle in the region of Goshen,*j* for all shepherds are detestable to the Egyptians.*k*"

Chapter 47 Theme

47 Joseph went and told Pharaoh, "My father and brothers, with their flocks and herds and everything they own, have come from the land of Canaan and are now in Goshen."*l* ²He chose five of his brothers and presented them before Pharaoh.

³Pharaoh asked the brothers, "What is your occupation?"*m*

"Your servants are shepherds," they replied to Pharaoh, "just as our fathers were." ⁴They also said to him, "We have come to

a 27 Hebrew; Septuagint *the nine children*   *b* 27 Hebrew (see also Exodus 1:5 and footnote); Septuagint (see also Acts 7:14) *seventy-five*   *c* 29 Hebrew *around him* live here awhile,^{a} because the famine is severe in Canaan^b and your servants' flocks have no pasture. So now, please let your servants settle in Goshen."^{c}

^{5}Pharaoh said to Joseph, "Your father and your brothers have come to you, ^{6}and the land of Egypt is before you; settle your father and your brothers in the best part of the land.^{d} Let them live in Goshen. And if you know of any among them with special ability,^{e} put them in charge of my own livestock."

^{7}Then Joseph brought his father Jacob in and presented him before Pharaoh. After Jacob blessed^a Pharaoh,^{f} ^{8}Pharaoh asked him, "How old are you?"

^{9}And Jacob said to Pharaoh, "The years of my pilgrimage are a hundred and thirty.^{g} My years have been few and difficult,^{h} and they do not equal the years of the pilgrimage of my fathers.^{i}"
^{10}Then Jacob blessed^b Pharaoh^j and went out from his presence.

^{11}So Joseph settled his father and his brothers in Egypt and gave them property in the best part of the land, the district of Rameses,^{k} as Pharaoh directed. ^{12}Joseph also provided his father and his brothers and all his father's household with food, according to the number of their children.^{l}

^{13}There was no food, however, in the whole region because the famine was severe; both Egypt and Canaan wasted away because of the famine.^{m} ^{14}Joseph collected all the money that was to be found in Egypt and Canaan in payment for the grain they were buying, and he brought it to Pharaoh's palace.^{n} ^{15}When the money of the people of Egypt and Canaan was gone, all Egypt came to Joseph and said, "Give us food. Why should we die before your eyes?^{o} Our money is used up."

^{16}"Then bring your livestock," said Joseph. "I will sell you food in exchange for your livestock, since your money is gone."
^{17}So they brought their livestock to Joseph, and he gave them food in exchange for their horses,^{p} their sheep and goats, their cattle and donkeys. And he brought them through that year with food in exchange for all their livestock.

^{18}When that year was over, they came to him the following year and said, "We cannot hide from our lord the fact that since our money is gone and our livestock belongs to you, there is nothing left for our lord except our bodies and our land. ^{19}Why should we perish before your eyes—we and our land as well? Buy us and our land in exchange for food, and we with our land will be in bondage to Pharaoh. Give us seed so that we may live and not die, and that the land may not become desolate."

^{20}So Joseph bought all the land in Egypt for Pharaoh. The Egyptians, one and all, sold their fields, because the famine was

a 7 Or *greeted*   b 10 Or *said farewell to*

47:4
^{a}Ge 15:13;
Dt 26:5
^{b}Ge 43:1
^{c}Ge 46:34

47:6
^{d}Ge 45:18
^{e}Ex 18:21,25

47:7
^{f}ver 10;
2Sa 14:22

47:9
^{g}Ge 25:7
^{h}Heb 11:9,13
^{i}Ge 35:28

47:10
^{j}ver 7

47:11
^{k}Ex 1:11;
12:37

47:12
^{l}Ge 45:11

47:13
^{m}Ge 41:30;
Ac 7:11

47:14
^{n}Ge 41:56

47:15
^{o}ver 19;
Ex 16:3

47:17
^{p}Ex 14:9

47:22
aDt 14:28-29;
Ezr 7:24

47:24
bGe 41:34

47:25
cGe 32:5

47:26
dver 22

47:27
eGe 17:6; 46:3;
Ex 1:7

47:28
fPs 105:23

47:29
gDt 31:14
hGe 24:2
iGe 24:49

47:30
jGe 49:29-32;
50:5,13;
Ac 7:15-16

47:31
kGe 21:23
lGe 24:3
mHeb 11:21 fn;
1Ki 1:47

48:1
nGe 41:52

48:3
oGe 28:19
pGe 28:13;
35:9-12

48:4
qGe 17:6

too severe for them. The land became Pharaoh's, [21]and Joseph reduced the people to servitude,[a] from one end of Egypt to the other. [22]However, he did not buy the land of the priests, because they received a regular allotment from Pharaoh and had food enough from the allotment[a] Pharaoh gave them. That is why they did not sell their land.

[23]Joseph said to the people, "Now that I have bought you and your land today for Pharaoh, here is seed for you so you can plant the ground. [24]But when the crop comes in, give a fifth[b] of it to Pharaoh. The other four-fifths you may keep as seed for the fields and as food for yourselves and your households and your children."

[25]"You have saved our lives," they said. "May we find favor in the eyes of our lord;[c] we will be in bondage to Pharaoh."

[26]So Joseph established it as a law concerning land in Egypt—still in force today—that a fifth of the produce belongs to Pharaoh. It was only the land of the priests that did not become Pharaoh's.[d]

[27]Now the Israelites settled in Egypt in the region of Goshen. They acquired property there and were fruitful and increased greatly in number.[e]

[28]Jacob lived in Egypt [f] seventeen years, and the years of his life were a hundred and forty-seven. [29]When the time drew near for Israel to die,[g] he called for his son Joseph and said to him, "If I have found favor in your eyes, put your hand under my thigh[h] and promise that you will show me kindness and faithfulness.[i] Do not bury me in Egypt, [30]but when I rest with my fathers, carry me out of Egypt and bury me where they are buried."[j]

"I will do as you say," he said.

[31]"Swear to me,"[k] he said. Then Joseph swore to him,[l] and Israel worshiped as he leaned on the top of his staff.[b m]

Chapter 48 Theme

48 Some time later Joseph was told, "Your father is ill." So he took his two sons Manasseh and Ephraim[n] along with him. [2]When Jacob was told, "Your son Joseph has come to you," Israel rallied his strength and sat up on the bed.

[3]Jacob said to Joseph, "God Almighty[c] appeared to me at Luz[o] in the land of Canaan, and there he blessed me [p] [4]and said to me, 'I am going to make you fruitful and will increase your numbers.[q] I will make you a community of peoples, and I will give this land as an everlasting possession to your descendants after you.'

a21 Samaritan Pentateuch and Septuagint (see also Vulgate); Masoretic Text *and he moved the people into the cities*   b31 Or *Israel bowed down at the head of his bed*   c3 Hebrew *El-Shaddai*

83

5"Now then, your two sons born to you in Egypt[a] before I came to you here will be reckoned as mine; Ephraim and Manasseh will be mine,[b] just as Reuben and Simeon are mine. 6Any children born to you after them will be yours; in the territory they inherit they will be reckoned under the names of their brothers. 7As I was returning from Paddan,[a] to my sorrow Rachel died in the land of Canaan while we were still on the way, a little distance from Ephrath. So I buried her there beside the road to Ephrath" (that is, Bethlehem).[c]

8When Israel saw the sons of Joseph, he asked, "Who are these?"

9"They are the sons God has given me here,"[d] Joseph said to his father.

Then Israel said, "Bring them to me so I may bless[e] them."

10Now Israel's eyes were failing because of old age, and he could hardly see.[f] So Joseph brought his sons close to him, and his father kissed them[g] and embraced them.

11Israel said to Joseph, "I never expected to see your face again, and now God has allowed me to see your children too."[h]

12Then Joseph removed them from Israel's knees and bowed down with his face to the ground. 13And Joseph took both of them, Ephraim on his right toward Israel's left hand and Manasseh on his left toward Israel's right hand,[i] and brought them close to him. 14But Israel reached out his right hand and put it on Ephraim's head, though he was the younger, and crossing his arms, he put his left hand on Manasseh's head, even though Manasseh was the firstborn.[j]

15Then he blessed[k] Joseph and said,

"May the God before whom my fathers
    Abraham and Isaac walked,
the God who has been my shepherd[l]
    all my life to this day,
16the Angel who has delivered me from all harm
    —may he bless these boys.[m]
May they be called by my name
    and the names of my fathers Abraham and Isaac,[n]
and may they increase greatly
    upon the earth."

17When Joseph saw his father placing his right hand on Ephraim's head[o] he was displeased; so he took hold of his father's hand to move it from Ephraim's head to Manasseh's head. 18Joseph said to him, "No, my father, this one is the firstborn; put your right hand on his head."

a 7 That is, Northwest Mesopotamia

48:5
[a] Ge 41:50-52; 46:20
[b] 1Ch 5:1; Jos 14:4

48:7
[c] Ge 35:19

48:9
[d] Ge 33:5
[e] Ge 27:4

48:10
[f] Ge 27:1
[g] Ge 27:27

48:11
[h] Ge 50:23; Ps 128:6

48:13
[i] Ps 110:1

48:14
[j] Ge 41:51

48:15
[k] Ge 17:1
[l] Ge 49:24

48:16
[m] Heb 11:21
[n] Ge 28:13

48:17
[o] ver 14

48:19
a Ge 17:20
b Ge 25:23

48:20
c Nu 2:18
d Nu 2:20;
Ru 4:11

48:21
e Ge 26:3; 46:4
f Ge 28:13;
50:24

48:22
g Ge 37:8
h Jos 24:32;
Jn 4:5

49:1
i Nu 24:14;
Jer 23:20

49:2
j Ps 34:11

49:3
k Ge 29:32
l Dt 21:17;
Ps 78:51

49:4
m Isa 57:20
n Ge 35:22;
Dt 27:20

49:5
o Ge 34:25;
Pr 4:17

49:6
p Pr 1:15;
Eph 5:11
q Ge 34:26

49:7
r Jos 19:1,9;
21:1-42

49:8
s Dt 33:7;
1Ch 5:2

49:9
t Nu 24:9;
Eze 19:5;
Mic 5:8
u Rev 5:5

¹⁹But his father refused and said, "I know, my son, I know. He too will become a people, and he too will become great.*ᵃ* Nevertheless, his younger brother will be greater than he,*ᵇ* and his descendants will become a group of nations." ²⁰He blessed them that day and said,

> "In your*ᵃ* name will Israel pronounce this blessing:
> 'May God make you like Ephraim*ᶜ* and Manasseh.*ᵈ*'"

So he put Ephraim ahead of Manasseh.

²¹Then Israel said to Joseph, "I am about to die, but God will be with you*ᵇᵉ* and take you*ᵇ* back to the land of your*ᵇ* fathers.*ᶠ* ²²And to you, as one who is over your brothers,*ᵍ* I give the ridge of land*ᶜ ʰ* I took from the Amorites with my sword and my bow."

Chapter 49 Theme

49 Then Jacob called for his sons and said: "Gather around so I can tell you what will happen to you in days to come.*ᶦ*

²"Assemble and listen, sons of Jacob;
  listen to your father Israel.*ʲ*

³"Reuben, you are my firstborn,*ᵏ*
  my might, the first sign of my strength,*ˡ*
  excelling in honor, excelling in power.
⁴Turbulent as the waters,*ᵐ* you will no longer excel,
  for you went up onto your father's bed,
  onto my couch and defiled it.*ⁿ*

⁵"Simeon and Levi are brothers—
  their swords*ᵈ* are weapons of violence.*ᵒ*
⁶Let me not enter their council,
  let me not join their assembly,*ᵖ*
 for they have killed men in their anger*�q*
  and hamstrung oxen as they pleased.
⁷Cursed be their anger, so fierce,
  and their fury, so cruel!
 I will scatter them in Jacob
  and disperse them in Israel.*ʳ*

⁸"Judah,*ᵉ* your brothers will praise you;
  your hand will be on the neck of your enemies;
  your father's sons will bow down to you.*ˢ*
⁹You are a lion*ᵗ*'s cub, O Judah;*ᵘ*
  you return from the prey, my son.

ᵃ 20 The Hebrew is singular.   *ᵇ 21* The Hebrew is plural.   *ᶜ 22* Or *And to you I give one portion more than to your brothers—the portion*   *ᵈ 5* The meaning of the Hebrew for this word is uncertain.   *ᵉ 8 Judah* sounds like and may be derived from the Hebrew for *praise.*

Like a lion he crouches and lies down,
    like a lioness—who dares to rouse him?
¹⁰The scepter will not depart from Judah,ᵃ
    nor the ruler's staff from between his feet,
until he comes to whom it belongsᵃ
    and the obedience of the nations is his.ᵇ
¹¹He will tether his donkey to a vine,
    his colt to the choicest branch;
he will wash his garments in wine,
    his robes in the blood of grapes.
¹²His eyes will be darker than wine,
    his teeth whiter than milk.ᵇ

¹³"Zebulunᶜ will live by the seashore
    and become a haven for ships;
    his border will extend toward Sidon.

¹⁴"Issacharᵈ is a rawbonedᶜ donkey
    lying down between two saddlebags.ᵈ
¹⁵When he sees how good is his resting place
    and how pleasant is his land,
he will bend his shoulder to the burden
    and submit to forced labor.

¹⁶"Danᵉ ᵉ will provide justice for his people
    as one of the tribes of Israel.
¹⁷Danᶠ will be a serpent by the roadside,
    a viper along the path,
that bites the horse's heels
    so that its rider tumbles backward.

¹⁸"I look for your deliverance, O LORD.ᵍ

¹⁹"Gadᶠʰ will be attacked by a band of raiders,
    but he will attack them at their heels.

²⁰"Asher'sⁱ food will be rich;
    he will provide delicacies fit for a king.

²¹"Naphtaliʲ is a doe set free
    that bears beautiful fawns.ᵍ

²²"Josephᵏ is a fruitful vine,
    a fruitful vine near a spring,
    whose branches climb over a wall.ʰ

ᵃ 10 Or *until Shiloh comes*; or *until he comes to whom tribute belongs*   ᵇ 12 Or *will be dull from wine, / his teeth white from milk*   ᶜ 14 Or *strong*   ᵈ 14 Or *campfires*   ᵉ 16 *Dan* here means *he provides justice.*   ᶠ 19 *Gad* can mean *attack* and *band of raiders.*   ᵍ 21 Or *free; / he utters beautiful words*   ʰ 22 Or *Joseph is a wild colt, / a wild colt near a spring, / a wild donkey on a terraced hill*

**Cross-references (right margin):**

49:10
ᵃ Nu 24:17,19;
Ps 60:7
ᵇ Ps 2:9;
Isa 42:1,4

49:13
ᶜ Ge 30:20;
Dt 33:18-19;
Jos 19:10-11

49:14
ᵈ Ge 30:18

49:16
ᵉ Ge 30:6;
Dt 33:22;
Jdg 18:26-27

49:17
ᶠ Jdg 18:27

49:18
ᵍ Ps 119:166,174

49:19
ʰ Ge 30:11;
Dt 33:20;
1Ch 5:18

49:20
ⁱ Ge 30:13;
Dt 33:24

49:21
ʲ Ge 30:8;
Dt 33:23

49:22
ᵏ Ge 30:24;
Dt 33:13-17

49:23
a Ge 37:24

49:24
b Ps 18:34
c Ps 132:2,5;
Isa 1:24; 41:10
d Isa 28:16

49:25
e Ge 28:13
f Ge 27:28

49:26
g Dt 33:15-16

49:27
h Ge 35:18;
Jdg 20:12-13

49:29
i Ge 50:16
j Ge 25:8
k Ge 15:15;
47:30; 50:13

49:30
l Ge 23:9
m Ge 23:20

49:31
n Ge 25:9
o Ge 23:19
p Ge 35:29

49:33
q ver 29;
Ge 25:8;
Ac 7:15

50:1
r Ge 46:4

50:2
s ver 26;
2Ch 16:14

50:3
t Ge 37:34;
Nu 20:29;
Dt 34:8

²³With bitterness archers attacked him;
 they shot at him with hostility.*a*

²⁴But his bow remained steady,
 his strong arms*b* stayed*a* limber,
because of the hand of the Mighty One of Jacob,*c*
 because of the Shepherd, the Rock of Israel,*d*
²⁵because of your father's God,*e* who helps you,
 because of the Almighty,*b* who blesses you
with blessings of the heavens above,
 blessings of the deep that lies below,*f*
 blessings of the breast and womb.
²⁶Your father's blessings are greater
 than the blessings of the ancient mountains,
 than*c* the bounty of the age-old hills.
Let all these rest on the head of Joseph,
 on the brow of the prince among*d* his brothers.*g*

²⁷"Benjamin*h* is a ravenous wolf;
 in the morning he devours the prey,
 in the evening he divides the plunder."

²⁸All these are the twelve tribes of Israel, and this is what their father said to them when he blessed them, giving each the blessing appropriate to him.

²⁹Then he gave them these instructions:*i* "I am about to be gathered to my people.*j* Bury me with my fathers*k* in the cave in the field of Ephron the Hittite, ³⁰the cave in the field of Machpelah,*l* near Mamre in Canaan, which Abraham bought as a burial place from Ephron the Hittite, along with the field.*m* ³¹There Abraham*n* and his wife Sarah*o* were buried, there Isaac and his wife Rebekah*p* were buried, and there I buried Leah. ³²The field and the cave in it were bought from the Hittites.*e*"

³³When Jacob had finished giving instructions to his sons, he drew his feet up into the bed, breathed his last and was gathered to his people.*q*

Chapter 50 Theme

50 Joseph threw himself upon his father and wept over him and kissed him.*r* ²Then Joseph directed the physicians in his service to embalm his father Israel. So the physicians embalmed him,*s* ³taking a full forty days, for that was the time required for embalming. And the Egyptians mourned for him seventy days.*t*

a 23,24 Or *archers will attack . . . will shoot . . . will remain . . . will stay* *b 25* Hebrew *Shaddai* *c 26* Or *of my progenitors, / as great as* *d 26* Or *the one separated from* *e 32* Or *the sons of Heth*

⁴When the days of mourning had passed, Joseph said to Pharaoh's court, "If I have found favor in your eyes, speak to Pharaoh for me. Tell him, ⁵'My father made me swear an oath^a and said, "I am about to die; bury me in the tomb I dug for myself^b in the land of Canaan."^c Now let me go up and bury my father; then I will return.'"

⁶Pharaoh said, "Go up and bury your father, as he made you swear to do."

⁷So Joseph went up to bury his father. All Pharaoh's officials accompanied him—the dignitaries of his court and all the dignitaries of Egypt— ⁸besides all the members of Joseph's household and his brothers and those belonging to his father's household. Only their children and their flocks and herds were left in Goshen. ⁹Chariots and horsemen^a also went up with him. It was a very large company.

¹⁰When they reached the threshing floor of Atad, near the Jordan, they lamented loudly and bitterly;^d and there Joseph observed a seven-day period^e of mourning for his father. ¹¹When the Canaanites who lived there saw the mourning at the threshing floor of Atad, they said, "The Egyptians are holding a solemn ceremony of mourning." That is why that place near the Jordan is called Abel Mizraim.^b

¹²So Jacob's sons did as he had commanded them: ¹³They carried him to the land of Canaan and buried him in the cave in the field of Machpelah, near Mamre, which Abraham had bought as a burial place from Ephron the Hittite, along with the field.^f ¹⁴After burying his father, Joseph returned to Egypt, together with his brothers and all the others who had gone with him to bury his father.

¹⁵When Joseph's brothers saw that their father was dead, they said, "What if Joseph holds a grudge against us and pays us back for all the wrongs we did to him?"^g ¹⁶So they sent word to Joseph, saying, "Your father left these instructions before he died: ¹⁷'This is what you are to say to Joseph: I ask you to forgive your brothers the sins and the wrongs they committed in treating you so badly.' Now please forgive the sins of the servants of the God of your father." When their message came to him, Joseph wept.

¹⁸His brothers then came and threw themselves down before him.^h "We are your slaves,"ⁱ they said.

¹⁹But Joseph said to them, "Don't be afraid. Am I in the place of God?^j ²⁰You intended to harm me,^k but God intended^l it for good^m to accomplish what is now being done, the saving of many lives.ⁿ ²¹So then, don't be afraid. I will provide for you and your children.^o" And he reassured them and spoke kindly to them.

^a9 Or *charioteers*   ^b11 *Abel Mizraim* means *mourning of the Egyptians.*

50:5 ^aGe 47:31; ^b2Ch 16:14; Isa 22:16; ^cGe 47:31

50:10 ^d2Sa 1:17; Ac 8:2; ^e1Sa 31:13; Job 2:13

50:13 ^fGe 23:20; Ac 7:16

50:15 ^gGe 37:28; 42:21-22

50:18 ^hGe 37:7; ⁱGe 43:18

50:19 ^jRo 12:19; Heb 10:30

50:20 ^kGe 37:20; ^lMic 4:11-12; ^mRo 8:28; ⁿGe 45:5

50:21 ^oGe 45:11; 47:12

50:22
a Ge 25:7;
Jos 24:29

50:23
b Job 42:16
c Nu 32:39,40

50:24
d Ge 48:21
e Ex 3:16-17
f Ge 15:14
g Ge 12:7;
26:3; 28:13;
35:12

50:25
h Ge 47:29-30;
Ex 13:19;
Jos 24:32;
Heb 11:22

50:26
i ver 2

²²Joseph stayed in Egypt, along with all his father's family. He lived a hundred and ten years^a ²³and saw the third generation^b of Ephraim's children. Also the children of Makir^c son of Manasseh were placed at birth on Joseph's knees.^a

²⁴Then Joseph said to his brothers, "I am about to die.^d But God will surely come to your aid^e and take you up out of this land to the land^f he promised on oath to Abraham, Isaac and Jacob."^g ²⁵And Joseph made the sons of Israel swear an oath and said, "God will surely come to your aid, and then you must carry my bones up from this place."^h

²⁶So Joseph died at the age of a hundred and ten. And after they embalmed him,^i he was placed in a coffin in Egypt.

a 23 That is, were counted as his

Theme of Genesis:

SEGMENT DIVISIONS

THE FIRSTS		4 MAIN EVENTS/4 CHARACTERS	TIME SPANS	CHAPTER THEMES
MAN			1	
MARRIAGE			2	
	BEGINNINGS OF MAN		3	
			4	
			5	
			6	
		APPROXIMATELY 2080 YEARS	7	
			8	
			9	
			10	
			11	
	BEGINNINGS OF ISRAEL (CONTINUED NEXT PAGE)		12	
			13	
			14	
			15	
		APPROXIMATELY 300 YEARS (CONTINUED NEXT PAGE)	16	
			17	
			18	
			19	
			20	
			21	
			22	
			23	
			24	
			25	

Author:
Moses
(Luke 24:27)

Date:

Purpose:

Key Words:
God said
(or commanded)

the account of

covenant, treaty

altar

circumcised,
circumcision,
circumcising

Abram
(or Abraham)

Segment Divisions

The Firsts	4 Main Events/4 Characters	Time Spans	Chapter Themes
		26	
		27	
		28	
		29	
		30	
		31	
		32	
		33	
		34	
		35	
	Beginnings of Israel	36	
		37	
	Approximately 300 Years	38	
		39	
		40	
		41	
		42	
		43	
		44	
		45	
		46	
		47	
		48	
		49	
		50	

EXODUS

When Jacob and his family, a relatively small group, went into Egypt, they were welcomed and honored because they were relatives of Joseph. Four hundred and thirty years later the children of Israel were Egypt's slaves, a people so numerous it frightened the Egyptians.

The Israelites were God's covenant people, different from all the nations, a people of his own choosing. And because God is a covenant-keeping God he could not leave Jacob's people in Egypt—they had to be redeemed by the blood of a lamb, a Passover lamb.

❧ THINGS TO DO

General Instructions

1. As Genesis comes to a close, the children of Israel are living in Egypt rather than in Canaan, the land of promise. The book that began with the creation of man in Eden ends with the children of Israel looking into a coffin in Egypt—but not without a promise that someday they would leave Egypt. Read Genesis 50:22-26 and Exodus 1:1-7 and notice how the book of Exodus relates chronologically to the book of Genesis.

2. Exodus can be divided into three segments according to the location of the children of Israel. In Exodus 1 through 12 they are in Egypt. In Exodus 13 through 18 they journey to Sinai and then in Exodus 19 through 40 they camp at Sinai. Record this information on the EXODUS AT A GLANCE chart on pages 159, 160 on the first line for segment divisions. This division will be the basis of some of your instructions.

3. Read through Exodus one chapter at a time. As you read do the following:

   a. Remember that you are reading a historical account. As you read, ask the five W's and an H: Who? What? When? Where? Why? and How? Ask questions such as: Who are the main characters in this chapter? What is happening? When and where is it happening? What were the consequences of their actions? How and why did this occur?

   b. Mark key repeated words. Although a list of the key words for Exodus is recorded on EXODUS AT A GLANCE, remember that there will be other words which are predominant in specific chapters. Don't miss these. You will find it helpful to write the key words on an index card and use it as a bookmark while you study Exodus.

   c. If you glean insights from the repeated use of a key word, list them in the margin of the chapter.

   d. Mark all references to time in a distinctive way so you can immediately notice them.

   e. List in the margin the main points or events covered in a particular chapter or group of chapters. This will give you a concise analysis of the content of the chapter.

   For example, Exodus 2 gives an account of Moses from his birth to the birth of his first son. In the margin you could list the major events in this chapter: Moses' birth, Moses' adoption by Pharaoh's daughter, Moses kills Egyptian, Moses flees to Midian, etc.

4. When you finish reading a chapter, record the main theme or subject of the chapter on EXODUS AT A GLANCE under "Chapter Themes." Also record it in the text next to the chapter number.

Chapters 1-12

1. As you study these chapters, add *Pharaoh* and *staff* to your list of key words. Mark these words and their synonyms in a distinctive way. Then in the margin list everything you observe from marking them.

2. You can gain insights into God's character, power, and dealings with mankind from these chapters. As

you read each chapter, in the margin note what you learn about God. You may want to put a distinguishing mark such as this △ in the margin and then color it yellow so you can easily recognize it. Then list your insights under the symbol for God.

3. There are lessons to be learned from Moses' life in these chapters. Although you will probably want to note these lessons in the margins, you will also find it profitable to record what you learn on LESSONS FROM THE LIFE OF MOSES, a chart on pages 346, 347. When you record an insight, make sure you note the book, chapter, and verse from which it came.

4. As you read chapters 7 through 12, in the margin of the chapter list the plagues as they appear in the text, numbering each one in the order in which they appear.

5. When you come to Exodus 12, in the margin list everything you learn about the Passover. Ask the five W's and an H: Who? What? When? Where? Why? and How?

Chapters 13-18

1. As you read:

    a. Watch for the key words, including those you marked in the first segment. Add *test* and *grumble* (*grumbled, grumbling*), along with their synonyms. In the margin note what the tests were and why the people grumbled. Also continue your list of insights on Pharaoh and on Moses' staff.

    b. Mark references to time with a symbol and note where events occur. Locate these places on the map in the text on page 97.

2. Add to your list of insights on Moses and also note in the margin new insights on God. Note what he is called in 15:26 and 17:15 and the circumstances in which these names are revealed.

3. In chapter 16 note in the margin all you learn from the text about manna and why it was given. When you finish you might compare this with Deuteronomy 8:1-3.

4. In chapter 17 note the conditions under which Moses strikes the rock. Compare this with 1 Corinthians 10:1-4 and John 7:37-39. Also note what happens after the rock is smitten and the battle is fought in the valley.

Chapters 19-40

1. In chapters 19 through 24 God gives Moses the law. As you read these important chapters, ask the five W's and an H.

    a. Chapter 20 presents the ten commandments. Number these within the text or list them in the margin.

    b. Chapter 24 is very important because it deals with the inauguration of the law, the old covenant. In the margin note the circumstances and procedure connected with its inauguration and how the people respond.

2. In chapters 25 through 31 God gives the pattern for the tabernacle and all that is necessary for the priests.

    a. Note in the margin the main points of these chapters.

    b. Watch for other key words which are predominant in specific chapters. Mark them.

    c. In chapter 31 notice what is said about the Sabbath. List in the margin everything you learn about it from the text.

3. Chapters 32 through 34 are significant in light of what happens.

    a. Note how Moses deals with this situation. Record your insights in the margin and on the chart LESSONS FROM THE LIFE OF MOSES on pages 346, 347.

    b. Read 2 Corinthians 3:12-18 for additional insights regarding the veil over Moses' face.

4. Chapters 35 through 40 are an account of the construction of the tabernacle and the making of the priests' garments. As you read, highlight or mark in a distinguishable way the specific instructions which are given in regard to each piece of furniture.

5. After you have recorded all the chapter themes on EXODUS AT A GLANCE, see if any of the chapters can be grouped according to main events. Record these segment divisions on the appropriate line next to the chapter themes. Then record the theme of Exodus on the chart.

∾ THINGS TO THINK ABOUT

1. What have you learned about God, his character, and his ways? What have you seen of his power and sovereignty? When we speak of God as being sovereign, we mean he rules over all. How do you see God's sovereignty and power manifested in Exodus? Meditate on what you have learned and then make it a matter of prayer and application.

2. Since the Bible is a progressive revelation of truth, keep in mind what you have observed about redemption and the Passover. These are Old Testament pictures of the salvation to be offered through the Lord Jesus Christ; therefore, they are pictures of truths to be applied to your life (1 Corinthians 5:6-8). Are you a slave to sin? Jesus Christ has provided for your redemption from sin through his blood. Have you been redeemed?

3. What have you learned from Moses' life? How did he deal with difficult situations and people? What was his overriding passion? What did you learn about Moses' relationship with God that you can apply to your own life today?

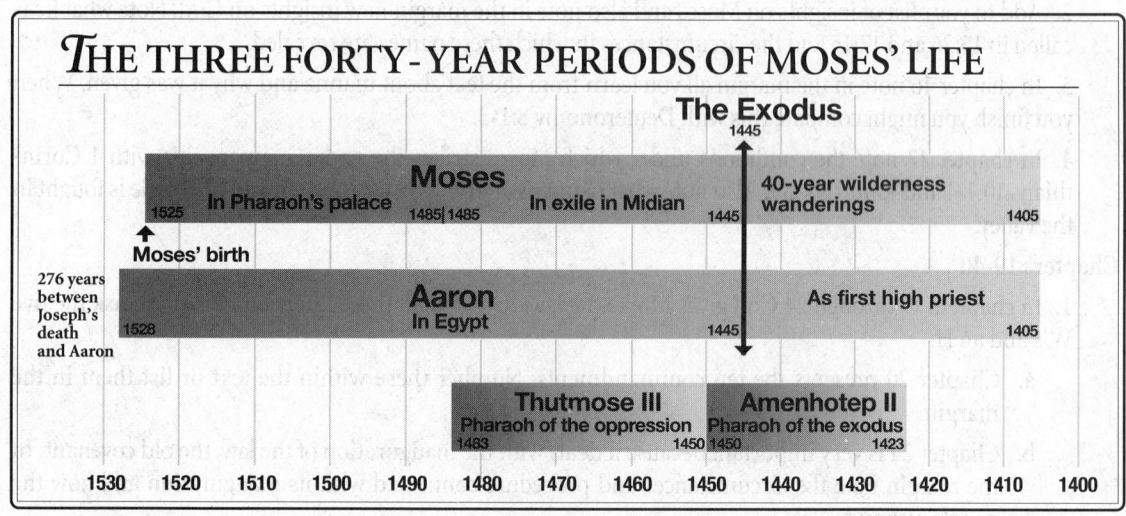

THE THREE FORTY-YEAR PERIODS OF MOSES' LIFE

The Exodus
1445

Moses
In Pharaoh's palace 1485 | 1485 In exile in Midian 1445   40-year wilderness wanderings 1405
1525

↑ Moses' birth

276 years between Joseph's death and Aaron

Aaron
In Egypt 1528 1445   As first high priest 1405

Thutmose III
Pharaoh of the oppression
1483   1450

Amenhotep II
Pharaoh of the exodus
1450   1423

1530 1520 1510 1500 1490 1480 1470 1460 1450 1440 1430 1420 1410 1400

∾∾∾∾∾∾

Chapter 1 Theme _____   1:1
                                                 a Ge 46:8

1 These are the names of the sons of Israel[a] who went to Egypt with Jacob, each with his family: ²Reuben, Simeon, Levi and Judah; ³Issachar, Zebulun and Benjamin; ⁴Dan and Naphtali; Gad and Asher. ⁵The descendants of Jacob numbered seventy[a] in all;[b] Joseph was already in Egypt.

a5 Masoretic Text (see also Gen. 46:27); Dead Sea Scrolls and Septuagint (see also Acts 7:14 and note at Gen. 46:27) *seventy-five*   1:5
                                                                                                                                        b Ge 46:26

1:6
a Ge 50:26

1:7
b Ge 46:3;
Dt 26:5; Ac 7:17

1:9
c Ps 105:24-25

1:10
d Ps 83:3
e Ac 7:17-19

1:11
f Ex 3:7
g Ge 15:13;
Ex 2:11; 5:4;
6:6-7
h Ge 47:11
i 1Ki 9:19;
2Ch 8:4

1:13
j Dt 4:20

1:14
k Ex 2:23; 6:9;
Nu 20:15;
Ps 81:6; Ac 7:19

1:17
l ver 21; Pr 16:6
m Da 3:16-18;
Ac 4:18-20; 5:29

1:19
n Jos 2:4-6;
2Sa 17:20

1:20
o ver 12;
Pr 11:18;
Isa 3:10

1:21
p 1Sa 2:35;
2Sa 7:11,27-29;
1Ki 11:38

1:22
q Ac 7:19

2:1
r Ex 6:20;
Nu 26:59

2:2
s Ac 7:20;
Heb 11:23

2:4
t Ex 15:20;
Nu 26:59

[6]Now Joseph and all his brothers and all that generation died,[a] [7]but the Israelites were fruitful and multiplied greatly and became exceedingly numerous,[b] so that the land was filled with them.

[8]Then a new king, who did not know about Joseph, came to power in Egypt. [9]"Look," he said to his people, "the Israelites have become much too numerous[c] for us. [10]Come, we must deal shrewdly[d] with them or they will become even more numerous and, if war breaks out, will join our enemies, fight against us and leave the country."[e]

[11]So they put slave masters[f] over them to oppress them with forced labor,[g] and they built Pithom and Rameses[h] as store cities[i] for Pharaoh. [12]But the more they were oppressed, the more they multiplied and spread; so the Egyptians came to dread the Israelites [13]and worked them ruthlessly.[j] [14]They made their lives bitter with hard labor in brick and mortar and with all kinds of work in the fields; in all their hard labor the Egyptians used them ruthlessly.[k]

[15]The king of Egypt said to the Hebrew midwives, whose names were Shiphrah and Puah, [16]"When you help the Hebrew women in childbirth and observe them on the delivery stool, if it is a boy, kill him; but if it is a girl, let her live." [17]The midwives, however, feared[l] God and did not do what the king of Egypt had told them to do;[m] they let the boys live. [18]Then the king of Egypt summoned the midwives and asked them, "Why have you done this? Why have you let the boys live?"

[19]The midwives answered Pharaoh, "Hebrew women are not like Egyptian women; they are vigorous and give birth before the midwives arrive."[n]

[20]So God was kind to the midwives[o] and the people increased and became even more numerous. [21]And because the midwives feared God, he gave them families[p] of their own.

[22]Then Pharaoh gave this order to all his people: "Every boy that is born[a] you must throw into the Nile, but let every girl live."[q]

Chapter 2 Theme

2 Now a man of the house of Levi married a Levite woman,[r] [2]and she became pregnant and gave birth to a son. When she saw that he was a fine child, she hid him for three months.[s] [3]But when she could hide him no longer, she got a papyrus basket for him and coated it with tar and pitch. Then she placed the child in it and put it among the reeds along the bank of the Nile. [4]His sister[t] stood at a distance to see what would happen to him.

a22 Masoretic Text; Samaritan Pentateuch, Septuagint and Targums *born to the Hebrews*

⁵Then Pharaoh's daughter went down to the Nile to bathe, and her attendants were walking along the river bank.ᵃ She saw the basket among the reeds and sent her slave girl to get it. ⁶She opened it and saw the baby. He was crying, and she felt sorry for him. "This is one of the Hebrew babies," she said.

⁷Then his sister asked Pharaoh's daughter, "Shall I go and get one of the Hebrew women to nurse the baby for you?"

⁸"Yes, go," she answered. And the girl went and got the baby's mother. ⁹Pharaoh's daughter said to her, "Take this baby and nurse him for me, and I will pay you." So the woman took the baby and nursed him. ¹⁰When the child grew older, she took him to Pharaoh's daughter and he became her son. She named him Moses,ᵃ saying, "I drew him out of the water."

¹¹One day, after Moses had grown up, he went out to where his own peopleᵇ were and watched them at their hard labor. He saw an Egyptian beating a Hebrew, one of his own people. ¹²Glancing this way and that and seeing no one, he killed the Egyptian and hid him in the sand. ¹³The next day he went out and saw two Hebrews fighting. He asked the one in the wrong, "Why are you hitting your fellow Hebrew?"ᶜ

¹⁴The man said, "Who made you ruler and judge over us?ᵈ Are you thinking of killing me as you killed the Egyptian?" Then Moses was afraid and thought, "What I did must have become known."

¹⁵When Pharaoh heard of this, he tried to kill Moses, but Moses fled from Pharaoh and went to live in Midian,ᵉ where he sat down by a well. ¹⁶Now a priest of Midianᶠ had seven daughters, and they came to draw waterᵍ and fill the troughs to water their father's flock. ¹⁷Some shepherds came along and drove them away, but Moses got up and came to their rescue and watered their flock.ʰ

¹⁸When the girls returned to Reuelⁱ their father, he asked them, "Why have you returned so early today?"

¹⁹They answered, "An Egyptian rescued us from the shepherds. He even drew water for us and watered the flock."

²⁰"And where is he?" he asked his daughters. "Why did you leave him? Invite him to have something to eat."ʲ

²¹Moses agreed to stay with the man, who gave his daughter Zipporahᵏ to Moses in marriage. ²²Zipporah gave birth to a son, and Moses named him Gershom,ᵇ saying, "I have become an alienˡ in a foreign land."

²³During that long period,ᵐ the king of Egypt died. The Israelites groaned in their slavery and cried out, and their cryⁿ for

ᵃ10 Moses sounds like the Hebrew for draw out.   ᵇ22 Gershom sounds like the Hebrew for an alien there.

2:5
ᵃ Ex 7:15; 8:20

2:11
ᵇ Ac 7:23;
Heb 11:24-26

2:13
ᶜ Ac 7:26

2:14
ᵈ Ac 7:27*

2:15
ᵉ Ac 7:29;
Heb 11:27

2:16
ᶠ Ex 3:1
ᵍ Ge 24:11

2:17
ʰ Ge 29:10

2:18
ⁱ Nu 10:29

2:20
ʲ Ge 31:54

2:21
ᵏ Ex 18:2

2:22
ˡ Ex 18:3-4;
Heb 11:13

2:23
ᵐ Ac 7:30
ⁿ Ex 3:7,9;
Dt 26:7;
Jas 5:4

2:24
a Ex 6:5;
Ps 105:10,42

help because of their slavery went up to God. [24]God heard their groaning and he remembered his covenant*a* with Abraham, with Isaac and with Jacob. [25]So God looked on the Israelites and was concerned*b* about them.

2:25
b Ex 3:7; 4:31

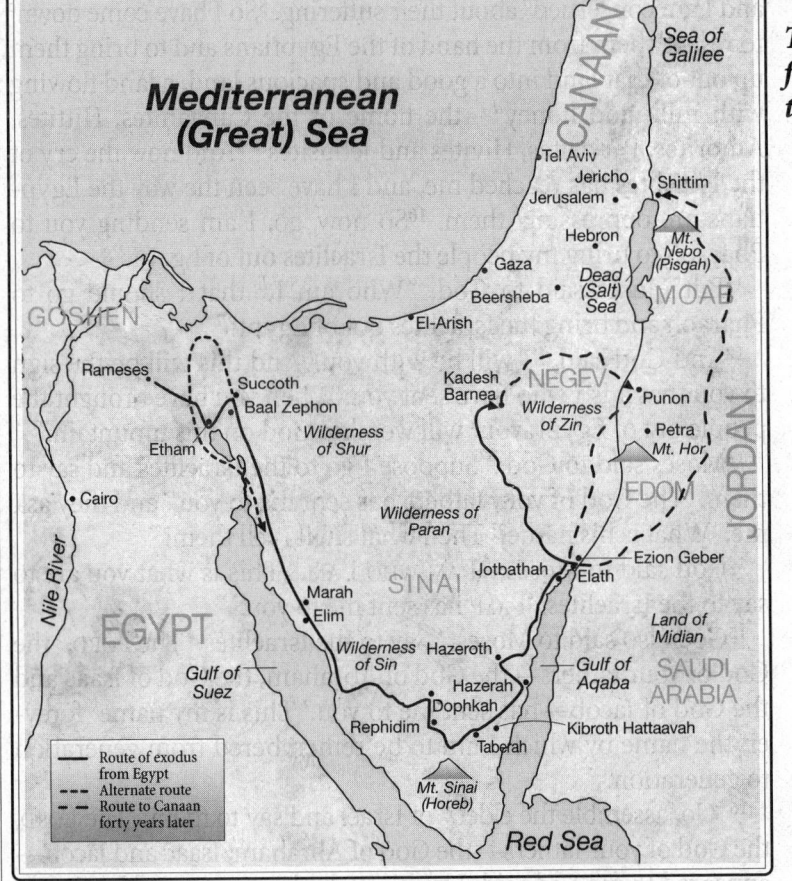

The Exodus from Egypt to Canaan

3:1
c Ex 2:18
d 1Ki 19:8
e Ex 18:5

3:2
f Ge 16:7
g Dt 33:16;
Mk 12:26;
Ac 7:30

Chapter 3 Theme _____

3 Now Moses was tending the flock of Jethro*c* his father-in-law, the priest of Midian, and he led the flock to the far side of the desert and came to Horeb,*d* the mountain*e* of God. [2]There the angel of the LORD*f* appeared to him in flames of fire from within a bush.*g* Moses saw that though the bush was on fire it did not burn up. [3]So Moses thought, "I will go over and see this strange sight—why the bush does not burn up."

[4]When the LORD saw that he had gone over to look, God called to him from within the bush, "Moses! Moses!"

And Moses said, "Here I am."

3:5
h Ge 28:17;
Jos 5:15;
Ac 7:33*

[5]"Do not come any closer," God said. "Take off your sandals, for the place where you are standing is holy ground."*h* [6]Then he said,

"I am the God of your father, the God of Abraham, the God of Isaac and the God of Jacob."[a] At this, Moses hid his face, because he was afraid to look at God.

[7]The LORD said, "I have indeed seen the misery of my people in Egypt. I have heard them crying out because of their slave drivers, and I am concerned[b] about their suffering. [8]So I have come down[c] to rescue them from the hand of the Egyptians and to bring them up out of that land into a good and spacious land, a land flowing with milk and honey[d]—the home of the Canaanites, Hittites, Amorites, Perizzites, Hivites and Jebusites.[e] [9]And now the cry of the Israelites has reached me, and I have seen the way the Egyptians are oppressing[f] them. [10]So now, go. I am sending you to Pharaoh to bring my people the Israelites out of Egypt."[g]

[11]But Moses said to God, "Who am I,[h] that I should go to Pharaoh and bring the Israelites out of Egypt?"

[12]And God said, "I will be with you.[i] And this will be the sign to you that it is I who have sent you: When you have brought the people out of Egypt, you[a] will worship God on this mountain."

[13]Moses said to God, "Suppose I go to the Israelites and say to them, 'The God of your fathers has sent me to you,' and they ask me, 'What is his name?' Then what shall I tell them?"

[14]God said to Moses, "I AM WHO I AM.[b] This is what you are to say to the Israelites: 'I AM[j] has sent me to you.'"

[15]God also said to Moses, "Say to the Israelites, 'The LORD,[c] the God of your fathers—the God of Abraham, the God of Isaac and the God of Jacob—has sent me to you.' This is my name[k] forever, the name by which I am to be remembered from generation to generation.

[16]"Go, assemble the elders[l] of Israel and say to them, 'The LORD, the God of your fathers—the God of Abraham, Isaac and Jacob—appeared to me and said: I have watched over you and have seen what has been done to you in Egypt. [17]And I have promised to bring you up out of your misery in Egypt[m] into the land of the Canaanites, Hittites, Amorites, Perizzites, Hivites and Jebusites—a land flowing with milk and honey.'

[18]"The elders of Israel will listen[n] to you. Then you and the elders are to go to the king of Egypt and say to him, 'The LORD, the God of the Hebrews, has met with us. Let us take a three-day journey into the desert to offer sacrifices[o] to the LORD our God.' [19]But I know that the king of Egypt will not let you go unless a mighty hand[p] compels him. [20]So I will stretch out my hand[q] and strike the Egyptians with all the wonders[r] that I will perform among them. After that, he will let you go.[s]

a12 The Hebrew is plural.   b14 Or I WILL BE WHAT I WILL BE   c15 The Hebrew for LORD sounds like and may be derived from the Hebrew for I AM in verse 14.

3:6 a Ex 4:5; Mt 22:32*; Mk 12:26*; Lk 20:37*; Ac 7:32*
3:7 b Ex 2:25
3:8 c Ge 50:24 d ver 17; Ex 13:5; Dt 1:25 e Ge 15:18-21
3:9 f Ex 1:14; 2:23
3:10 g Mic 6:4
3:11 h Ex 6:12,30; 1Sa 18:18
3:12 i Ge 31:3; Jos 1:5; Ro 8:31
3:14 j Ex 6:2-3; Jn 8:58; Heb 13:8
3:15 k Ps 135:13; Hos 12:5
3:16 l Ex 4:29
3:17 m Ge 15:16; Jos 24:11
3:18 n Ex 4:1,8,31 o Ex 5:1,3
3:19 p Ex 4:21; 5:2
3:20 q Ex 6:1,6; 9:15 r Dt 6:22; Ne 9:10; Ac 7:36 s Ex 12:31-33

3:21
a Ex 12:36
b Ps 105:37

3:22
c Ex 11:2
d Eze 39:10

4:1
e Ex 3:18; 6:30

4:2
f ver 17,20

4:5
g Ex 19:9

4:6
h Nu 12:10;
2Ki 5:1,27

4:7
i Nu 12:13-15;
Dt 32:39;
2Ki 5:14;
Mt 8:3

4:9
j Ex 7:17-21

4:10
k Ex 6:12;
Jer 1:6

4:11
l Ps 94:9;
Mt 11:5

4:12
m Isa 50:4;
Jer 1:9;
Mt 10:19-20;
Mk 13:11;
Lk 12:12;
21:14-15

4:14
n ver 27

21"And I will make the Egyptians favorably disposed[a] toward this people, so that when you leave you will not go empty-handed.[b] 22Every woman is to ask her neighbor and any woman living in her house for articles of silver and gold[c] and for clothing, which you will put on your sons and daughters. And so you will plunder[d] the Egyptians."

Chapter 4 Theme _____

4 Moses answered, "What if they do not believe me or listen[e] to me and say, 'The LORD did not appear to you'?"

2Then the LORD said to him, "What is that in your hand?"

"A staff,"[f] he replied.

3The LORD said, "Throw it on the ground."

Moses threw it on the ground and it became a snake, and he ran from it. 4Then the LORD said to him, "Reach out your hand and take it by the tail." So Moses reached out and took hold of the snake and it turned back into a staff in his hand. 5"This," said the LORD, "is so that they may believe[g] that the LORD, the God of their fathers—the God of Abraham, the God of Isaac and the God of Jacob—has appeared to you."

6Then the LORD said, "Put your hand inside your cloak." So Moses put his hand into his cloak, and when he took it out, it was leprous,[a] like snow.[h]

7"Now put it back into your cloak," he said. So Moses put his hand back into his cloak, and when he took it out, it was restored,[i] like the rest of his flesh.

8Then the LORD said, "If they do not believe you or pay attention to the first miraculous sign, they may believe the second. 9But if they do not believe these two signs or listen to you, take some water from the Nile and pour it on the dry ground. The water you take from the river will become blood[j] on the ground."

10Moses said to the LORD, "O Lord, I have never been eloquent, neither in the past nor since you have spoken to your servant. I am slow of speech and tongue."[k]

11The LORD said to him, "Who gave man his mouth? Who makes him deaf or mute? Who gives him sight or makes him blind?[l] Is it not I, the LORD? 12Now go; I will help you speak and will teach you what to say."[m]

13But Moses said, "O Lord, please send someone else to do it."

14Then the LORD's anger burned against Moses and he said, "What about your brother, Aaron the Levite? I know he can speak well. He is already on his way to meet[n] you, and his heart

a 6 The Hebrew word was used for various diseases affecting the skin—not necessarily leprosy.

will be glad when he sees you. ¹⁵You shall speak to him and put words in his mouth;^a I will help both of you speak and will teach you what to do. ¹⁶He will speak to the people for you, and it will be as if he were your mouth^b and as if you were God to him. ¹⁷But take this staff^c in your hand so you can perform miraculous signs^d with it."

¹⁸Then Moses went back to Jethro his father-in-law and said to him, "Let me go back to my own people in Egypt to see if any of them are still alive."

Jethro said, "Go, and I wish you well."

¹⁹Now the LORD had said to Moses in Midian, "Go back to Egypt, for all the men who wanted to kill^e you are dead.^f" ²⁰So Moses took his wife and sons, put them on a donkey and started back to Egypt. And he took the staff^g of God in his hand.

²¹The LORD said to Moses, "When you return to Egypt, see that you perform before Pharaoh all the wonders^h I have given you the power to do. But I will harden his heartⁱ so that he will not let the people go. ²²Then say to Pharaoh, 'This is what the LORD says: Israel is my firstborn son,^j ²³and I told you, "Let my son go,^k so he may worship me." But you refused to let him go; so I will kill your firstborn son.'"^l

²⁴At a lodging place on the way, the LORD met ⌊Moses⌋^a and was about to kill^m him. ²⁵But Zipporah took a flint knife, cut off her son's foreskinⁿ and touched ⌊Moses'⌋ feet with it.^b "Surely you are a bridegroom of blood to me," she said. ²⁶So the LORD let him alone. (At that time she said "bridegroom of blood," referring to circumcision.)

²⁷The LORD said to Aaron, "Go into the desert to meet Moses." So he met Moses at the mountain^o of God and kissed^p him. ²⁸Then Moses told Aaron everything the LORD had sent him to say,^q and also about all the miraculous signs he had commanded him to perform.

²⁹Moses and Aaron brought together all the elders^r of the Israelites, ³⁰and Aaron told them everything the LORD had said to Moses. He also performed the signs before the people, ³¹and they believed.^s And when they heard that the LORD was concerned^t about them and had seen their misery, they bowed down and worshiped.

Chapter 5 Theme

5 Afterward Moses and Aaron went to Pharaoh and said, "This is what the LORD, the God of Israel, says: 'Let my people go, so that they may hold a festival^u to me in the desert.'"

^a24 Or ⌊Moses' son⌋; Hebrew *him*   ^b25 Or *and drew near* ⌊Moses'⌋ *feet*

100

4:15 ^a Nu 23:5,12,16

4:16 ^b Ex 7:1-2

4:17 ^c ver 2 ^d Ex 7:9-21

4:19 ^e Ex 2:15 ^f Ex 2:23

4:20 ^g Ex 17:9; Nu 20:8-9,11

4:21 ^h Ex 3:19,20 ⁱ Ex 7:3,13; 9:12,35; 14:4, 8; Dt 2:30; Isa 63:17; Jn 12:40; Ro 9:18

4:22 ^j Isa 63:16; 64:8; Jer 31:9; Hos 11:1; Ro 9:4

4:23 ^k Ex 5:1; 7:16 ^l Ex 11:5; 12:12,29

4:24 ^m Nu 22:22

4:25 ⁿ Ge 17:14; Jos 5:2,3

4:27 ^o Ex 3:1 ^p ver 14

4:28 ^q ver 8-9,16

4:29 ^r Ex 3:16

4:31 ^s ver 8; Ex 3:18 ^t Ex 2:25

5:1 ^u Ex 3:18

5:2
a 2Ki 18:35;
Job 21:15
b Ex 3:19

²Pharaoh said, "Who is the Lord,ᵃ that I should obey him and let Israel go? I do not know the Lord and I will not let Israel go."ᵇ

³Then they said, "The God of the Hebrews has met with us. Now let us take a three-day journey into the desert to offer sacrifices to the Lord our God, or he may strike us with plaguesᶜ or with the sword."

5:3
c Ex 3:18

⁴But the king of Egypt said, "Moses and Aaron, why are you taking the people away from their labor?ᵈ Get back to your work!" ⁵Then Pharaoh said, "Look, the people of the land are now numerous,ᵉ and you are stopping them from working."

5:4
d Ex 1:11

⁶That same day Pharaoh gave this order to the slave drivers and foremen in charge of the people: ⁷"You are no longer to supply the people with straw for making bricks; let them go and gather their own straw. ⁸But require them to make the same number of bricks as before; don't reduce the quota. They are lazy; that is why they are crying out, 'Let us go and sacrifice to our God.' ⁹Make the work harder for the men so that they keep working and pay no attention to lies."

⁰Then the slave drivers and the foremen went out and said to the people, "This is what Pharaoh says: 'I will not give you any more straw. ¹¹Go and get your own straw wherever you can find it, but your work will not be reduced at all.'" ¹²So the people scattered all over Egypt to gather stubble to use for straw. ¹³The slave drivers kept pressing them, saying, "Complete the work required of you for each day, just as when you had straw." ¹⁴The Israelite foremen appointed by Pharaoh's slave drivers were beatenᶠ and were asked, "Why didn't you meet your quota of bricks yesterday or today, as before?"

5:5
e Ex 1:7,9

5:14
f Isa 10:24

¹⁵Then the Israelite foremen went and appealed to Pharaoh: "Why have you treated your servants this way? ¹⁶Your servants are given no straw, yet we are told, 'Make bricks!' Your servants are being beaten, but the fault is with your own people."

5:17
g ver 8

¹⁷Pharaoh said, "Lazy, that's what you are—lazy!ᵍ That is why you keep saying, 'Let us go and sacrifice to the Lord.' ¹⁸Now get to work. You will not be given any straw, yet you must produce your full quota of bricks."

¹⁹The Israelite foremen realized they were in trouble when they were told, "You are not to reduce the number of bricks required of you for each day." ²⁰When they left Pharaoh, they found Moses and Aaron waiting to meet them, ²¹and they said, "May the Lord look upon you and judge you! You have made us a stenchʰ to Pharaoh and his officials and have put a sword in their hand to kill us."ⁱ

5:21
h Ge 34:30
i Ex 14:11

²²Moses returned to the Lord and said, "O Lord, why have you brought trouble upon this people?ʲ Is this why you sent me?

5:22
j Nu 11:11

INSIGHT

Pharaoh is a title that was given to the kings of Egypt. An ancient Pharaoh had absolute power; and during his reign, he was considered a god who owned the lands and the people. He was also the high priest of all religions in Egypt. The Pharaoh mentioned in Exodus chapters 5-12 is believed to have been Amenhotep II.

²³Ever since I went to Pharaoh to speak in your name, he has brought trouble upon this people, and you have not rescued*ᵃ* your people at all."

Chapter 6 Theme

6 Then the LORD said to Moses, "Now you will see what I will do to Pharaoh: Because of my mighty hand*ᵇ* he will let them go;*ᶜ* because of my mighty hand he will drive them out of his country."*ᵈ*

²God also said to Moses, "I am the LORD. ³I appeared to Abraham, to Isaac and to Jacob as God Almighty,*ᵃᵉ* but by my name*ᶠ* the LORD*ᵇᵍ* I did not make myself known to them.*ᶜ* ⁴I also established my covenant*ʰ* with them to give them the land of Canaan, where they lived as aliens.*ⁱ* ⁵Moreover, I have heard the groaning*ʲ* of the Israelites, whom the Egyptians are enslaving, and I have remembered my covenant.

⁶"Therefore, say to the Israelites: 'I am the LORD, and I will bring you out from under the yoke of the Egyptians. I will free you from being slaves to them, and I will redeem*ᵏ* you with an outstretched arm*ˡ* and with mighty acts of judgment. ⁷I will take you as my own people, and I will be your God.*ᵐ* Then you will know*ⁿ* that I am the LORD your God, who brought you out from under the yoke of the Egyptians. ⁸And I will bring you to the land*ᵒ* I swore with uplifted hand*ᵖ* to give to Abraham, to Isaac and to Jacob.*�q* I will give it to you as a possession. I am the LORD.'"

⁹Moses reported this to the Israelites, but they did not listen to him because of their discouragement and cruel bondage.

¹⁰Then the LORD said to Moses, ¹¹"Go, tell Pharaoh king of Egypt to let the Israelites go out of his country."

¹²But Moses said to the LORD, "If the Israelites will not listen to me, why would Pharaoh listen to me, since I speak with faltering lips*ᵈ?"ʳ*

¹³Now the LORD spoke to Moses and Aaron about the Israelites and Pharaoh king of Egypt, and he commanded them to bring the Israelites out of Egypt.

¹⁴These were the heads of their families*ᵉ:ˢ*

The sons of Reuben the firstborn son of Israel were Hanoch and Pallu, Hezron and Carmi. These were the clans of Reuben.

ᵃ3 Hebrew El-Shaddai ᵇ3 See note at Exodus 3:15. ᶜ3 Or Almighty, and by my name the LORD did I not let myself be known to them? ᵈ12 Hebrew I am uncircumcised of lips; also in verse 30 ᵉ14 The Hebrew for families here and in verse 25 refers to units larger than clans.

5:23 *a* Jer 4:10

6:1 *b* Ex 3:19 *c* Ex 3:20 *d* Ex 12:31, 33,39

6:3 *e* Ge 17:1 *f* Ps 68:4; 83:18; Isa 52:6 *g* Ex 3:14

6:4 *h* Ge 15:18 *i* Ge 28:4,13

6:5 *j* Ex 2:23

6:6 *k* Dt 7:8; 1Ch 17:21 *l* Dt 26:8

6:7 *m* Dt 4:20; 2Sa 7:24 *n* Ex 16:12; Isa 41:20

6:8 *o* Ge 15:18; 26:3 *p* Ge 14:22 *q* Ps 136:21-22

6:12 *r* ver 30; Ex 4:10; Jer 1:6

6:14 *s* Ge 46:9

6:15
a Ge 46:10;
1Ch 4:24

6:16
b Ge 46:11
c Nu 3:17

6:17
d 1Ch 6:17

6:18
e 1Ch 6:2,18

6:19
f 1Ch 6:19;
23:21

6:20
g Ex 2:1-2;
Nu 26:59

6:21
h 1Ch 6:38

6:22
i Lev 10:4;
Nu 3:30

6:23
j Ru 4:19,20
k Lev 10:1
l Nu 3:2,32
m Nu 26:60

6:24
n Nu 26:11

6:25
o Nu 25:7,11;
Jos 24:33;
Ps 106:30

6:26
p Ex 7:4;
12:17,41,51

6:29
q ver 11;
Ex 7:2

6:30
r ver 12;
Ex 4:10

7:1
s Ex 4:16

7:3
t Ex 4:21; 11:9

7:4
u Ex 11:9
v Ex 3:20; 6:6

7:5
w ver 17;
Ex 8:19,22
x Ex 3:20

¹⁵The sons of Simeon^a were Jemuel, Jamin, Ohad, Jakin, Zohar and Shaul the son of a Canaanite woman. These were the clans of Simeon.

¹⁶These were the names of the sons of Levi according to their records: Gershon,^b Kohath and Merari.^c Levi lived 137 years.

¹⁷The sons of Gershon, by clans, were Libni and Shimei.^d

¹⁸The sons of Kohath were Amram, Izhar, Hebron and Uzziel.^e Kohath lived 133 years.

¹⁹The sons of Merari were Mahli and Mushi.^f

These were the clans of Levi according to their records.

²⁰Amram married his father's sister Jochebed, who bore him Aaron and Moses.^g Amram lived 137 years.

²¹The sons of Izhar^h were Korah, Nepheg and Zicri.

²²The sons of Uzziel were Mishael, Elzaphan^i and Sithri.

²³Aaron married Elisheba, daughter of Amminadab^j and sister of Nahshon, and she bore him Nadab and Abihu,^k Eleazar^l and Ithamar.^m

²⁴The sons of Korah^n were Assir, Elkanah and Abiasaph. These were the Korahite clans.

²⁵Eleazar son of Aaron married one of the daughters of Putiel, and she bore him Phinehas.^o

These were the heads of the Levite families, clan by clan.

²⁶It was this same Aaron and Moses to whom the Lord said, "Bring the Israelites out of Egypt by their divisions."^p ²⁷They were the ones who spoke to Pharaoh king of Egypt about bringing the Israelites out of Egypt. It was the same Moses and Aaron.

²⁸Now when the Lord spoke to Moses in Egypt, ²⁹he said to him, "I am the Lord.^q Tell Pharaoh king of Egypt everything I tell you."

³⁰But Moses said to the Lord, "Since I speak with faltering lips,^r why would Pharaoh listen to me?"

Chapter 7 Theme

7 Then the Lord said to Moses, "See, I have made you like God^s to Pharaoh, and your brother Aaron will be your prophet. ²You are to say everything I command you, and your brother Aaron is to tell Pharaoh to let the Israelites go out of his country. ³But I will harden Pharaoh's heart,^t and though I multiply my miraculous signs and wonders in Egypt, ⁴he will not listen^u to you. Then I will lay my hand on Egypt and with mighty acts of judgment^v I will bring out my divisions, my people the Israelites. ⁵And the Egyptians will know that I am the Lord^w when I stretch out my hand^x against Egypt and bring the Israelites out of it."

⁶Moses and Aaron did just as the LORD commanded^a them. ⁷Moses was eighty years old^b and Aaron eighty-three when they spoke to Pharaoh.

Some of the Gods of Egypt		
The god:	**Ruled over:**	**How symbolized:**
Aker	Earth-god • Helper of the dead	*Two lion heads*
Aton	Sun-god	
Bes	Protection at birth • Dispenser of virility	*Group of demons*
Heket	Primordial goddess	*Frog*
Isis	Goddess of life and healing	*Human*
Khepri	Primordial god • Rising sun	*Scarabaeus (beetle)*
Khnum	Giver of the Nile • Creator of mankind	*Human with ram's head*
Mut	"Eye of the sun"	*Vulture or human*
Nut	Sky goddess • Mother of heavenly bodies	
Osiris	Dead Pharaohs • Ruler of dead, life, vegetation	
Ra	God of sun, earth, and sky • National god	*Human with falcon head*
Selket	Guardian of life • Protector of dead	*Scorpion*
Seth	God of chaos, desert and storm, crops	
Sothis	God of Nile floodwaters	
Thermuthis	Goddess of fertility and harvest; fate	*Serpent*

⁸The LORD said to Moses and Aaron, ⁹"When Pharaoh says to you, 'Perform a miracle,'^c then say to Aaron, 'Take your staff and throw it down before Pharaoh,' and it will become a snake."^d

¹⁰So Moses and Aaron went to Pharaoh and did just as the LORD commanded. Aaron threw his staff down in front of Pharaoh and his officials, and it became a snake. ¹¹Pharaoh then summoned wise men and sorcerers, and the Egyptian magicians^e also did the same things by their secret arts:^f ¹²Each one threw down his staff and it became a snake. But Aaron's staff swallowed up their staffs. ¹³Yet Pharaoh's heart^g became hard and he would not listen to them, just as the LORD had said.

¹⁴Then the LORD said to Moses, "Pharaoh's heart is unyielding;^h he refuses to let the people go. ¹⁵Go to Pharaoh in the morning as he goes out to the water. Wait on the bank of the Nile to meet him, and take in your hand the staff that was changed into a snake. ¹⁶Then say to him, 'The LORD, the God of the Hebrews, has sent me to say to you: Let my people go, so that they may worshipⁱ me in the desert. But until now you have not listened. ¹⁷This is what the LORD says: By this you will know that I am the LORD:^j With the staff that is in my hand I will strike the water of the Nile, and it will be changed into blood.^k ¹⁸The fish in the Nile will die, and the river will stink; the Egyptians will not be able to drink its water.'"^l

7:6 *a* ver 2

7:7 *b* Dt 31:2; 34:7; Ac 7:23,30

7:9 *c* Isa 7:11; Jn 2:18 *d* Ex 4:2-5

7:11 *e* Ge 41:8; 2Ti 3:8 *f* ver 22; Ex 8:7,18

7:13 *g* Ex 4:21

7:14 *h* Ex 8:15,32; 10:1,20,27

7:16 *i* Ex 3:18; 5:1,3

7:17 *j* Ex 5:2 *k* Ex 4:9; Rev 11:6; 16:4

7:18 *l* ver 21,24

7:19
a Ex 8:5-6,16;
9:22; 10:12,21;
14:21

¹⁹The LORD said to Moses, "Tell Aaron, 'Take your staff and stretch out your hand*a* over the waters of Egypt—over the streams and canals, over the ponds and all the reservoirs'—and they will turn to blood. Blood will be everywhere in Egypt, even in the wooden buckets and stone jars."

7:20
b Ex 17:5
c Ps 78:44;
105:29

²⁰Moses and Aaron did just as the LORD had commanded. He raised his staff in the presence of Pharaoh and his officials and struck the water of the Nile,*b* and all the water was changed into blood.*c* ²¹The fish in the Nile died, and the river smelled so bad that the Egyptians could not drink its water. Blood was everywhere in Egypt.

7:22
d ver 11

²²But the Egyptian magicians did the same things by their secret arts,*d* and Pharaoh's heart became hard; he would not listen to Moses and Aaron, just as the LORD had said. ²³Instead, he turned and went into his palace, and did not take even this to heart.

8:1
e Ex 3:12,18;
4:23

²⁴And all the Egyptians dug along the Nile to get drinking water, because they could not drink the water of the river.

Chapter 8 Theme

8:3
f Ex 10:6

8 ²⁵Seven days passed after the LORD struck the Nile. ¹Then the LORD said to Moses, "Go to Pharaoh and say to him, 'This is what the LORD says: Let my people go, so that they may worship*e* me. ²If you refuse to let them go, I will plague your whole country with frogs. ³The Nile will teem with frogs. They will come up into your palace and your bedroom and onto your bed, into the houses of your officials and on your people,*f* and into your ovens and kneading troughs. ⁴The frogs will go up on you and your people and all your officials.'"

8:5
g Ex 7:19

⁵Then the LORD said to Moses, "Tell Aaron, 'Stretch out your hand with your staff*g* over the streams and canals and ponds, and make frogs come up on the land of Egypt.'"

8:6
h Ps 78:45;
105:30

⁶So Aaron stretched out his hand over the waters of Egypt, and the frogs*h* came up and covered the land. ⁷But the magicians did the same things by their secret arts;*i* they also made frogs come up on the land of Egypt.

8:7
i Ex 7:11

⁸Pharaoh summoned Moses and Aaron and said, "Pray*j* to the LORD to take the frogs away from me and my people, and I will let your people go to offer sacrifices*k* to the LORD."

8:8
j ver 28;
Ex 9:28; 10:17
k ver 25

⁹Moses said to Pharaoh, "I leave to you the honor of setting the time for me to pray for you and your officials and your people that you and your houses may be rid of the frogs, except for those that remain in the Nile."

8:10
l Ex 9:14;
Dt 4:35; 33:26;
2Sa 7:22;
1Ch 17:20;
Ps 86:8;
Isa 46:9;
Jer 10:6

¹⁰"Tomorrow," Pharaoh said.

Moses replied, "It will be as you say, so that you may know there is no one like the LORD our God.*l* ¹¹The frogs will leave you and your houses, your officials and your people; they will remain only in the Nile."

¹²After Moses and Aaron left Pharaoh, Moses cried out to the LORD about the frogs he had brought on Pharaoh. ¹³And the LORD did what Moses asked. The frogs died in the houses, in the courtyards and in the fields. ¹⁴They were piled into heaps, and the land reeked of them. ¹⁵But when Pharaoh saw that there was relief, he hardened his heart[a] and would not listen to Moses and Aaron, just as the LORD had said.

¹⁶Then the LORD said to Moses, "Tell Aaron, 'Stretch out your staff and strike the dust of the ground,' and throughout the land of Egypt the dust will become gnats." ¹⁷They did this, and when Aaron stretched out his hand with the staff and struck the dust of the ground, gnats[b] came upon men and animals. All the dust throughout the land of Egypt became gnats. ¹⁸But when the magicians[c] tried to produce gnats by their secret arts,[d] they could not. And the gnats were on men and animals.

¹⁹The magicians said to Pharaoh, "This is the finger[e] of God." But Pharaoh's heart was hard and he would not listen, just as the LORD had said.

²⁰Then the LORD said to Moses, "Get up early in the morning[f] and confront Pharaoh as he goes to the water and say to him, 'This is what the LORD says: Let my people go, so that they may worship[g] me. ²¹If you do not let my people go, I will send swarms of flies on you and your officials, on your people and into your houses. The houses of the Egyptians will be full of flies, and even the ground where they are.

²²"'But on that day I will deal differently with the land of Goshen, where my people live;[h] no swarms of flies will be there, so that you will know[i] that I, the LORD, am in this land. ²³I will make a distinction[a] between my people and your people. This miraculous sign will occur tomorrow.'"

²⁴And the LORD did this. Dense swarms of flies poured into Pharaoh's palace and into the houses of his officials, and throughout Egypt the land was ruined by the flies.[j]

²⁵Then Pharaoh summoned[k] Moses and Aaron and said, "Go, sacrifice to your God here in the land."

²⁶But Moses said, "That would not be right. The sacrifices we offer the LORD our God would be detestable to the Egyptians.[l] And if we offer sacrifices that are detestable in their eyes, will they not stone us? ²⁷We must take a three-day journey into the desert to offer sacrifices[m] to the LORD our God, as he commands us."

²⁸Pharaoh said, "I will let you go to offer sacrifices to the LORD your God in the desert, but you must not go very far. Now pray[n] for me."

---

a23 Septuagint and Vulgate; Hebrew *will put a deliverance*

8:15
a Ex 7:14

8:17
b Ps 105:31

8:18
c Ex 9:11;
Da 5:8
d Ex 7:11

8:19
e Ex 7:5; 10:7;
Ps 8:3;
Lk 11:20

8:20
f Ex 7:15; 9:13
g ver 1;
Ex 3:18

8:22
h Ex 9:4,6,26;
10:23; 11:7
i Ex 7:5; 9:29

8:24
j Ps 78:45;
105:31

8:25
k ver 8; Ex 9:27

8:26
l Ge 43:32; 46:34

8:27
m Ex 3:18

8:28
n ver 8; Ex 9:28;
1Ki 13:6

8:29
a ver 15

8:30
b ver 12

8:32
c ver 8,15;
Ex 4:21

9:1
d Ex 8:1

9:3
e Ex 7:4

9:4
f ver 26;
Ex 8:22

9:6
g ver 19-21;
Ex 11:5
h Ps 78:48-50

9:7
i Ex 7:14; 8:32

9:9
j Dt 28:27,35;
Rev 16:2

9:11
k Ex 8:18

9:12
l Ex 4:21

9:13
m Ex 8:20

9:14
n Ex 8:10
o 2Sa 7:22;
1Ch 17:20;
Ps 86:8;
Isa 46:9;
Jer 10:6

9:15
p Ex 3:20

9:16
q Pr 16:4

²⁹Moses answered, "As soon as I leave you, I will pray to the LORD, and tomorrow the flies will leave Pharaoh and his officials and his people. Only be sure that Pharaoh does not act deceitfully^a again by not letting the people go to offer sacrifices to the LORD."

³⁰Then Moses left Pharaoh and prayed to the LORD,^b ³¹and the LORD did what Moses asked: The flies left Pharaoh and his officials and his people; not a fly remained. ³²But this time also Pharaoh hardened his heart^c and would not let the people go.

Chapter 9 Theme

9 Then the LORD said to Moses, "Go to Pharaoh and say to him, 'This is what the LORD, the God of the Hebrews, says: "Let my people go, so that they may worship^d me." ²If you refuse to let them go and continue to hold them back, ³the hand^e of the LORD will bring a terrible plague on your livestock in the field— on your horses and donkeys and camels and on your cattle and sheep and goats. ⁴But the LORD will make a distinction between the livestock of Israel and that of Egypt,^f so that no animal belonging to the Israelites will die.'"

⁵The LORD set a time and said, "Tomorrow the LORD will do this in the land." ⁶And the next day the LORD did it: All the livestock^g of the Egyptians died,^h but not one animal belonging to the Israelites died. ⁷Pharaoh sent men to investigate and found that not even one of the animals of the Israelites had died. Yet his heart was unyielding and he would not let the people go.ⁱ

⁸Then the LORD said to Moses and Aaron, "Take handfuls of soot from a furnace and have Moses toss it into the air in the presence of Pharaoh. ⁹It will become fine dust over the whole land of Egypt, and festering boils^j will break out on men and animals throughout the land."

¹⁰So they took soot from a furnace and stood before Pharaoh. Moses tossed it into the air, and festering boils broke out on men and animals. ¹¹The magicians^k could not stand before Moses because of the boils that were on them and on all the Egyptians. ¹²But the LORD hardened Pharaoh's heart^l and he would not listen to Moses and Aaron, just as the LORD had said to Moses.

¹³Then the LORD said to Moses, "Get up early in the morning, confront Pharaoh and say to him, 'This is what the LORD, the God of the Hebrews, says: Let my people go, so that they may worship^m me, ¹⁴or this time I will send the full force of my plagues against you and against your officials and your people, so you may knowⁿ that there is no one like^o me in all the earth. ¹⁵For by now I could have stretched out my hand and struck you and your people^p with a plague that would have wiped you off the earth. ¹⁶But I have raised you up^a for this very purpose,^q that

^a16 Or *have spared you*

I might show you my power[a] and that my name might be proclaimed in all the earth. [17]You still set yourself against my people and will not let them go. [18]Therefore, at this time tomorrow I will send the worst hailstorm[b] that has ever fallen on Egypt, from the day it was founded till now.[c] [19]Give an order now to bring your livestock and everything you have in the field to a place of shelter, because the hail will fall on every man and animal that has not been brought in and is still out in the field, and they will die.'"

[20]Those officials of Pharaoh who feared[d] the word of the LORD hurried to bring their slaves and their livestock inside. [21]But those who ignored the word of the LORD left their slaves and livestock in the field.

[22]Then the LORD said to Moses, "Stretch out your hand toward the sky so that hail will fall all over Egypt—on men and animals and on everything growing in the fields of Egypt." [23]When Moses stretched out his staff toward the sky, the LORD sent thunder[e] and hail,[f] and lightning flashed down to the ground. So the LORD rained hail on the land of Egypt; [24]hail fell and lightning flashed back and forth. It was the worst storm in all the land of Egypt since it had become a nation. [25]Throughout Egypt hail struck everything in the fields—both men and animals; it beat down everything growing in the fields and stripped every tree.[g] [26]The only place it did not hail was the land of Goshen,[h] where the Israelites were.[i]

[27]Then Pharaoh summoned Moses and Aaron. "This time I have sinned,"[j] he said to them. "The LORD is in the right,[k] and I and my people are in the wrong. [28]Pray[l] to the LORD, for we have had enough thunder and hail. I will let you go;[m] you don't have to stay any longer."

[29]Moses replied, "When I have gone out of the city, I will spread out my hands[n] in prayer to the LORD. The thunder will stop and there will be no more hail, so you may know that the earth[o] is the LORD's. [30]But I know that you and your officials still do not fear the LORD God."

[31](The flax and barley[p] were destroyed, since the barley had headed and the flax was in bloom. [32]The wheat and spelt, however, were not destroyed, because they ripen later.)

[33]Then Moses left Pharaoh and went out of the city. He spread out his hands toward the LORD; the thunder and hail stopped, and the rain no longer poured down on the land. [34]When Pharaoh saw that the rain and hail and thunder had stopped, he sinned again: He and his officials hardened their hearts. [35]So Pharaoh's heart[q] was hard and he would not let the Israelites go, just as the LORD had said through Moses.

9:16
a Ro 9:17*

9:18
b ver 23
c ver 24

9:20
d Pr 13:13

9:23
e Ps 18:13
f Jos 10:11;
Ps 78:47;
105:32;
Isa 30:30;
Eze 38:22;
Rev 8:7; 16:21

9:25
g Ps 105:32-33

9:26
h ver 4
i Ex 8:22; 10:23;
11:7; 12:13

9:27
j Ex 10:16
k 2Ch 12:6;
Ps 129:4;
La 1:18

9:28
l Ex 10:17
m Ex 8:8

9:29
n 1Ki 8:22,38;
Ps 143:6;
Isa 1:15
o Ex 19:5;
Ps 24:1;
1Co 10:26

9:31
p Ru 1:22; 2:23

9:35
q Ex 4:21

10:1
a Ex 4:21
b Ex 7:3

10:2
c Ex 12:26-27;
13:8,14;
Dt 4:9;
Ps 44:1; 78:4,5;
Joel 1:3

10:3
d 1Ki 21:29;
Jas 4:10;
1Pe 5:6

10:4
e Rev 9:3

10:5
f Ex 9:32;
Joel 1:4

10:7
g Ex 23:33;
Jos 23:7-13;
1Sa 18:21;
Ecc 7:26
h Ex 8:19

10:8
i Ex 8:8

10:12
j Ex 7:19

10:13
k Ps 105:34

10:14
l Ps 78:46;
Joel 2:1-11,25

10:15
m ver 5;
Ps 105:34-35

Chapter 10 Theme

10 Then the LORD said to Moses, "Go to Pharaoh, for I have hardened his heart[a] and the hearts of his officials so that I may perform these miraculous signs[b] of mine among them [2]that you may tell your children[c] and grandchildren how I dealt harshly with the Egyptians and how I performed my signs among them, and that you may know that I am the LORD."

[3]So Moses and Aaron went to Pharaoh and said to him, "This is what the LORD, the God of the Hebrews, says: 'How long will you refuse to humble[d] yourself before me? Let my people go, so that they may worship me. [4]If you refuse to let them go, I will bring locusts[e] into your country tomorrow. [5]They will cover the face of the ground so that it cannot be seen. They will devour what little you have left[f] after the hail, including every tree that is growing in your fields. [6]They will fill your houses and those of all your officials and all the Egyptians—something neither your fathers nor your forefathers have ever seen from the day they settled in this land till now.'" Then Moses turned and left Pharaoh.

[7]Pharaoh's officials said to him, "How long will this man be a snare[g] to us? Let the people go, so that they may worship the LORD their God. Do you not yet realize that Egypt is ruined?"[h]

[8]Then Moses and Aaron were brought back to Pharaoh. "Go, worship[i] the LORD your God," he said. "But just who will be going?"

[9]Moses answered, "We will go with our young and old, with our sons and daughters, and with our flocks and herds, because we are to celebrate a festival to the LORD."

[10]Pharaoh said, "The LORD be with you—if I let you go, along with your women and children! Clearly you are bent on evil.[a] [11]No! Have only the men go; and worship the LORD, since that's what you have been asking for." Then Moses and Aaron were driven out of Pharaoh's presence.

[12]And the LORD said to Moses, "Stretch out your hand[j] over Egypt so that locusts will swarm over the land and devour everything growing in the fields, everything left by the hail."

[13]So Moses stretched out his staff over Egypt, and the LORD made an east wind blow across the land all that day and all that night. By morning the wind had brought the locusts;[k] [14]they invaded all Egypt and settled down in every area of the country in great numbers. Never before had there been such a plague of locusts,[l] nor will there ever be again. [15]They covered all the ground until it was black. They devoured[m] all that was left after the hail—

a10 Or *Be careful, trouble is in store for you!*

109

everything growing in the fields and the fruit on the trees. Nothing green remained on tree or plant in all the land of Egypt.

[16]Pharaoh quickly summoned Moses and Aaron and said, "I have sinned[a] against the LORD your God and against you. [17]Now forgive my sin once more and pray[b] to the LORD your God to take this deadly plague away from me."

[18]Moses then left Pharaoh and prayed to the LORD.[c] [19]And the LORD changed the wind to a very strong west wind, which caught up the locusts and carried them into the Red Sea.[a] Not a locust was left anywhere in Egypt. [20]But the LORD hardened Pharaoh's heart,[d] and he would not let the Israelites go.

[21]Then the LORD said to Moses, "Stretch out your hand toward the sky so that darkness[e] will spread over Egypt—darkness that can be felt." [22]So Moses stretched out his hand toward the sky, and total darkness[f] covered all Egypt for three days. [23]No one could see anyone else or leave his place for three days. Yet all the Israelites had light in the places where they lived.[g]

[24]Then Pharaoh summoned Moses and said, "Go, worship the LORD. Even your women and children[h] may go with you; only leave your flocks and herds behind."

[25]But Moses said, "You must allow us to have sacrifices and burnt offerings to present to the LORD our God. [26]Our livestock too must go with us; not a hoof is to be left behind. We have to use some of them in worshiping the LORD our God, and until we get there we will not know what we are to use to worship the LORD."

[27]But the LORD hardened Pharaoh's heart,[i] and he was not willing to let them go. [28]Pharaoh said to Moses, "Get out of my sight! Make sure you do not appear before me again! The day you see my face you will die."

[29]"Just as you say," Moses replied, "I will never appear[j] before you again."

Chapter 11 Theme

11 Now the LORD had said to Moses, "I will bring one more plague on Pharaoh and on Egypt. After that, he will let you go from here, and when he does, he will drive you out completely. [2]Tell the people that men and women alike are to ask their neighbors for articles of silver and gold."[k] [3](The LORD made the Egyptians favorably disposed toward the people, and Moses himself was highly regarded[l] in Egypt by Pharaoh's officials and by the people.)

[4]So Moses said, "This is what the LORD says: 'About midnight[m] I will go throughout Egypt. [5]Every firstborn[n] son in Egypt will

10:16
a Ex 9:27

10:17
b Ex 8:8

10:18
c Ex 8:30

10:20
d Ex 4:21; 11:10

10:21
e Dt 28:29

10:22
f Ps 105:28; Rev 16:10

10:23
g Ex 8:22

10:24
h ver 8-10

10:27
i ver 20; Ex 4:21

10:29
j Heb 11:27

11:2
k Ex 3:21,22

11:3
l Dt 34:11

11:4
m Ex 12:29

11:5
n Ex 4:23; Ps 78:51

a19 Hebrew Yam Suph; that is, Sea of Reeds

11:6
a Ex 12:30

11:7
b Ex 8:22

11:8
c Ex 12:31-33

11:9
d Ex 7:4

11:10
e Ex 4:21;
10:20,27

12:2
f Ex 13:4;
Dt 16:1

12:5
g Lev 22:18-21;
Heb 9:14

12:6
h Lev 23:5;
Nu 9:1-3,5,11
i Ex 16:12;
Dt 16:4,6

12:8
j Ex 34:25;
Nu 9:12
k Dt 16:7
l Nu 9:11
m Dt 16:3-4;
1Co 5:8

12:10
n Ex 23:18;
34:25

12:11
o Dt 16:3
p ver 13,21,27,
43; Dt 16:1

12:12
q Ex 11:4;
Am 5:17
r Nu 33:4
s Ex 6:2

die, from the firstborn son of Pharaoh, who sits on the throne, to the firstborn son of the slave girl, who is at her hand mill, and all the firstborn of the cattle as well. ⁶There will be loud wailing*a* throughout Egypt—worse than there has ever been or ever will be again. ⁷But among the Israelites not a dog will bark at any man or animal.' Then you will know that the LORD makes a distinction*b* between Egypt and Israel. ⁸All these officials of yours will come to me, bowing down before me and saying, 'Go,*c* you and all the people who follow you!' After that I will leave." Then Moses, hot with anger, left Pharaoh.

⁹The LORD had said to Moses, "Pharaoh will refuse to listen*d* to you—so that my wonders may be multiplied in Egypt." ¹⁰Moses and Aaron performed all these wonders before Pharaoh, but the LORD hardened Pharaoh's heart,*e* and he would not let the Israelites go out of his country.

Chapter 12 Theme

12 The LORD said to Moses and Aaron in Egypt, ²"This month is to be for you the first month,*f* the first month of your year. ³Tell the whole community of Israel that on the tenth day of this month each man is to take a lamb*a* for his family, one for each household. ⁴If any household is too small for a whole lamb, they must share one with their nearest neighbor, having taken into account the number of people there are. You are to determine the amount of lamb needed in accordance with what each person will eat. ⁵The animals you choose must be year-old males without defect,*g* and you may take them from the sheep or the goats. ⁶Take care of them until the fourteenth day of the month,*h* when all the people of the community of Israel must slaughter them at twilight.*i* ⁷Then they are to take some of the blood and put it on the sides and tops of the doorframes of the houses where they eat the lambs. ⁸That same night*j* they are to eat the meat roasted*k* over the fire, along with bitter herbs,*l* and bread made without yeast.*m* ⁹Do not eat the meat raw or cooked in water, but roast it over the fire—head, legs and inner parts. ¹⁰Do not leave any of it till morning;*n* if some is left till morning, you must burn it. ¹¹This is how you are to eat it: with your cloak tucked into your belt, your sandals on your feet and your staff in your hand. Eat it in haste;*o* it is the LORD's Passover.*p*

¹²"On that same night I will pass through*q* Egypt and strike down every firstborn—both men and animals—and I will bring judgment on all the gods*r* of Egypt. I am the LORD.*s* ¹³The blood

a3 The Hebrew word can mean *lamb* or *kid*; also in verse 4.

will be a sign for you on the houses where you are; and when I see the blood, I will pass over you. No destructive plague will touch you when I strike Egypt.

¹⁴"This is a day you are to commemorate;[a] for the generations to come you shall celebrate it as a festival to the LORD—a lasting ordinance.[b] ¹⁵For seven days you are to eat bread made without yeast.[c] On the first day remove the yeast from your houses, for whoever eats anything with yeast in it from the first day through the seventh must be cut off[d] from Israel. ¹⁶On the first day hold a sacred assembly, and another one on the seventh day. Do no work at all on these days, except to prepare food for everyone to eat—that is all you may do.

¹⁷"Celebrate the Feast of Unleavened Bread, because it was on this very day that I brought your divisions out of Egypt.[e] Celebrate this day as a lasting ordinance for the generations to come. ¹⁸In the first month[f] you are to eat bread made without yeast, from the evening of the fourteenth day until the evening of the twenty-first day. ¹⁹For seven days no yeast is to be found in your houses. And whoever eats anything with yeast in it must be cut off from the community of Israel, whether he is an alien or native-born. ²⁰Eat nothing made with yeast. Wherever you live, you must eat unleavened bread."

²¹Then Moses summoned all the elders of Israel and said to them, "Go at once and select the animals for your families and slaughter the Passover[g] lamb. ²²Take a bunch of hyssop, dip it into the blood in the basin and put some of the blood[h] on the top and on both sides of the doorframe. Not one of you shall go out the door of his house until morning. ²³When the LORD goes through the land to strike down the Egyptians, he will see the blood[i] on the top and sides of the doorframe and will pass over[j] that doorway, and he will not permit the destroyer[k] to enter your houses and strike you down.

²⁴"Obey these instructions as a lasting ordinance for you and your descendants. ²⁵When you enter the land that the LORD will give you as he promised, observe this ceremony. ²⁶And when your children[l] ask you, 'What does this ceremony mean to you?' ²⁷then tell them, 'It is the Passover[m] sacrifice to the LORD, who passed over the houses of the Israelites in Egypt and spared our homes when he struck down the Egyptians.'" Then the people bowed down and worshiped.[n] ²⁸The Israelites did just what the LORD commanded Moses and Aaron.

²⁹At midnight[o] the LORD struck down all the firstborn[p] in Egypt, from the firstborn of Pharaoh, who sat on the throne, to the firstborn of the prisoner, who was in the dungeon, and the firstborn of all the livestock[q] as well. ³⁰Pharaoh and all his officials and all

12:14
[a] Ex 13:9
[b] ver 17,24;
Ex 13:5,10;
2Ki 23:21

12:15
[c] Ex 13:6-7;
23:15; 34:18;
Lev 23:6;
Dt 16:3
[d] Ge 17:14;
Nu 9:13

12:17
[e] ver 41;
Ex 13:3

12:18
[f] ver 2; Lev 23:5-8; Nu 28:16-25

12:21
[g] ver 11;
Mk 14:12-16

12:22
[h] ver 7;
Heb 11:28

12:23
[i] Rev 7:3
[j] ver 13
[k] 1Co 10:10;
Heb 11:28

12:26
[l] Ex 10:2;
13:8,14-15;
Jos 4:6

12:27
[m] ver 11
[n] Ex 4:31

12:29
[o] Ex 11:4
[p] Ex 4:23;
Ps 78:51
[q] Ex 9:6

12:30
a Ex 11:6

12:31
b Ex 8:8

12:32
c Ex 10:9,26

12:33
d Ps 105:38

12:35
e Ex 3:22

12:36
f Ex 3:22

12:37
g Nu 33:3-5
h Ex 38:26;
Nu 1:46;
11:13,21

12:38
i Nu 11:4

12:39
j ver 31-33;
Ex 6:1; 11:1

12:40
k Ge 15:13;
Ac 7:6;
Gal 3:17

12:41
l ver 17;
Ex 6:26
m Ex 3:10

12:42
n Ex 13:10;
Dt 16:1,6

12:43
o ver 11
p ver 48;
Nu 9:14

12:44
q Ge 17:12-13

12:45
r Lev 22:10

12:46
s Nu 9:12;
Jn 19:36*

12:48
t Nu 9:14

12:49
u Nu 15:15-16,
29; Gal 3:28

12:51
v ver 41; Ex 6:26

the Egyptians got up during the night, and there was loud wailing[a] in Egypt, for there was not a house without someone dead.

[31]During the night Pharaoh summoned Moses and Aaron and said, "Up! Leave my people, you and the Israelites! Go, worship[b] the LORD as you have requested. [32]Take your flocks and herds,[c] as you have said, and go. And also bless me."

[33]The Egyptians urged the people to hurry and leave[d] the country. "For otherwise," they said, "we will all die!" [34]So the people took their dough before the yeast was added, and carried it on their shoulders in kneading troughs wrapped in clothing. [35]The Israelites did as Moses instructed and asked the Egyptians for articles of silver and gold[e] and for clothing. [36]The LORD had made the Egyptians favorably disposed toward the people, and they gave them what they asked for; so they plundered[f] the Egyptians.

[37]The Israelites journeyed from Rameses to Succoth.[g] There were about six hundred thousand men[h] on foot, besides women and children. [38]Many other people[i] went up with them, as well as large droves of livestock, both flocks and herds. [39]With the dough they had brought from Egypt, they baked cakes of unleavened bread. The dough was without yeast because they had been driven out[j] of Egypt and did not have time to prepare food for themselves.

[40]Now the length of time the Israelite people lived in Egypt[a] was 430 years.[k] [41]At the end of the 430 years, to the very day, all the LORD's divisions[l] left Egypt.[m] [42]Because the LORD kept vigil that night to bring them out of Egypt, on this night all the Israelites are to keep vigil to honor the LORD for the generations to come.[n]

[43]The LORD said to Moses and Aaron, "These are the regulations for the Passover:[o]

"No foreigner[p] is to eat of it. [44]Any slave you have bought may eat of it after you have circumcised[q] him, [45]but a temporary resident and a hired worker[r] may not eat of it.

[46]"It must be eaten inside one house; take none of the meat outside the house. Do not break any of the bones.[s] [47]The whole community of Israel must celebrate it.

[48]"An alien living among you who wants to celebrate the LORD's Passover must have all the males in his household circumcised; then he may take part like one born in the land.[t] No uncircumcised male may eat of it. [49]The same law applies to the native-born and to the alien[u] living among you."

[50]All the Israelites did just what the LORD had commanded Moses and Aaron. [51]And on that very day the LORD brought the Israelites out of Egypt by their divisions.[v]

a 40 Masoretic Text; Samaritan Pentateuch and Septuagint *Egypt and Canaan*

Chapter 13 Theme

13 The LORD said to Moses, [2]"Consecrate to me every first-born male.[a] The first offspring of every womb among the Israelites belongs to me, whether man or animal."

[3]Then Moses said to the people, "Commemorate this day, the day you came out of Egypt, out of the land of slavery, because the LORD brought you out of it with a mighty hand.[b] Eat nothing containing yeast.[c] [4]Today, in the month of Abib,[d] you are leaving. [5]When the LORD brings you into the land of the Canaanites, Hittites, Amorites, Hivites and Jebusites[e]—the land he swore to your forefathers to give you, a land flowing with milk and honey—you are to observe this ceremony[f] in this month: [6]For seven days eat bread made without yeast and on the seventh day hold a festival[g] to the LORD. [7]Eat unleavened bread during those seven days; nothing with yeast in it is to be seen among you, nor shall any yeast be seen anywhere within your borders. [8]On that day tell your son,[h] 'I do this because of what the LORD did for me when I came out of Egypt.' [9]This observance will be for you like a sign on your hand and a reminder on your forehead[i] that the law of the LORD is to be on your lips. For the LORD brought you out of Egypt with his mighty hand. [10]You must keep this ordinance[j] at the appointed time year after year.

[11]"After the LORD brings you into the land of the Canaanites and gives it to you, as he promised on oath to you and your forefathers, [12]you are to give over to the LORD the first offspring of every womb. All the firstborn males of your livestock belong to the LORD.[k] [13]Redeem with a lamb every firstborn donkey, but if you do not redeem it, break its neck.[l] Redeem every firstborn among your sons.[m]

[14]"In days to come, when your son[n] asks you, 'What does this mean?' say to him, 'With a mighty hand the LORD brought us out of Egypt, out of the land of slavery.[o] [15]When Pharaoh stubbornly refused to let us go, the LORD killed every firstborn in Egypt, both man and animal. This is why I sacrifice to the LORD the first male offspring of every womb and redeem each of my firstborn sons.'[p] [16]And it will be like a sign on your hand and a symbol on your forehead[q] that the LORD brought us out of Egypt with his mighty hand."

[17]When Pharaoh let the people go, God did not lead them on the road through the Philistine country, though that was shorter. For God said, "If they face war, they might change their minds and return to Egypt."[r] [18]So God led[s] the people around by the desert road toward the Red Sea.[a] The Israelites went up out of Egypt armed for battle.[t]

[a]18 Hebrew *Yam Suph*; that is, Sea of Reeds

13:2 [a] ver 12,13,15; Ex 22:29; Nu 3:13; Dt 15:19; Lk 2:23*

13:3 [b] Ex 3:20; 6:1 [c] Ex 12:19

13:4 [d] Ex 12:2

13:5 [e] Ex 3:8 [f] Ex 12:25-26

13:6 [g] Ex 12:15-20

13:8 [h] ver 14; Ex 10:2; Ps 78:5-6

13:9 [i] ver 16; Dt 6:8; 11:18

13:10 [j] Ex 12:24-25

13:12 [k] Lev 27:26; Lk 2:23*

13:13 [l] Ex 34:20 [m] Nu 18:15

13:14 [n] Ex 10:2; 12:26-27; Dt 6:20 [o] ver 3,9

13:15 [p] Ex 12:29

13:16 [q] ver 9

13:17 [r] Ex 14:11; Nu 14:1-4; Dt 17:16

13:18 [s] Ps 136:16 [t] Jos 1:14

13:19
a Jos 24:32;
Ac 7:16
b Ge 50:24-25

13:20
c Nu 33:6

13:21
d Ex 14:19,24;
33:9-10;
Nu 9:16;
Dt 1:33;
Ne 9:12,19;
Ps 78:14; 99:7;
105:39;
Isa 4:5;
1Co 10:1

14:2
e Nu 33:7;
Jer 44:1

14:4
f Ex 4:21
g Ro 9:17, 22-23
h Ex 7:5

14:8
i ver 4;
Ex 11:10
j Nu 33:3;
Ac 13:17

14:9
k Ex 15:9

14:10
l Jos 24:7;
Ne 9:9;
Ps 34:17

14:11
m Ps 106:7-8

14:13
n Ge 15:1
o 2Ch 20:17;
Isa 41:10, 13-14
p ver 30

14:14
q ver 25;
Ex 15:3;
Dt 1:30; 3:22;
2Ch 20:29
r Ps 37:7; 46:10;
Isa 30:15

[19]Moses took the bones of Joseph[a] with him because Joseph had made the sons of Israel swear an oath. He had said, "God will surely come to your aid, and then you must carry my bones up with you from this place."[ab]

[20]After leaving Succoth they camped at Etham on the edge of the desert.[c] [21]By day the LORD went ahead of them in a pillar of cloud[d] to guide them on their way and by night in a pillar of fire to give them light, so that they could travel by day or night. [22]Neither the pillar of cloud by day nor the pillar of fire by night left its place in front of the people.

Chapter 14 Theme

14 Then the LORD said to Moses, [2]"Tell the Israelites to turn back and encamp near Pi Hahiroth, between Migdol[e] and the sea. They are to encamp by the sea, directly opposite Baal Zephon. [3]Pharaoh will think, 'The Israelites are wandering around the land in confusion, hemmed in by the desert.' [4]And I will harden Pharaoh's heart,[f] and he will pursue them. But I will gain glory[g] for myself through Pharaoh and all his army, and the Egyptians will know that I am the LORD."[h] So the Israelites did this.

[5]When the king of Egypt was told that the people had fled, Pharaoh and his officials changed their minds about them and said, "What have we done? We have let the Israelites go and have lost their services!" [6]So he had his chariot made ready and took his army with him. [7]He took six hundred of the best chariots, along with all the other chariots of Egypt, with officers over all of them. [8]The LORD hardened the heart[i] of Pharaoh king of Egypt, so that he pursued the Israelites, who were marching out boldly.[j] [9]The Egyptians—all Pharaoh's horses and chariots, horsemen[b] and troops—pursued the Isrelites and overtook[k] them as they camped by the sea near Pi Hahiroth, opposite Baal Zephon.

[10]As Pharaoh approached, the Israelites looked up, and there were the Egyptians, marching after them. They were terrified and cried[l] out to the LORD. [11]They said to Moses, "Was it because there were no graves in Egypt that you brought us to the desert to die?[m] What have you done to us by bringing us out of Egypt? [12]Didn't we say to you in Egypt, 'Leave us alone; let us serve the Egyptians'? It would have been better for us to serve the Egyptians than to die in the desert!"

[13]Moses answered the people, "Do not be afraid.[n] Stand firm and you will see[o] the deliverance the LORD will bring you today. The Egyptians you see today you will never see[p] again. [14]The LORD will fight[q] for you; you need only to be still."[r]

a19 See Gen. 50:25.   b9 Or *charioteers*; also in verses 17, 18, 23, 26 and 28

[15]Then the LORD said to Moses, "Why are you crying out to me? Tell the Israelites to move on. [16]Raise your staff[a] and stretch out your hand over the sea to divide the water[b] so that the Israelites can go through the sea on dry ground. [17]I will harden the hearts of the Egyptians so that they will go in after them.[c] And I will gain glory through Pharaoh and all his army, through his chariots and his horsemen. [18]The Egyptians will know that I am the LORD when I gain glory through Pharaoh, his chariots and his horsemen."

[19]Then the angel of God, who had been traveling in front of Israel's army, withdrew and went behind them. The pillar of cloud[d] also moved from in front and stood behind them, [20]coming between the armies of Egypt and Israel. Throughout the night the cloud brought darkness to the one side and light to the other side; so neither went near the other all night long.

[21]Then Moses stretched out his hand over the sea, and all that night the LORD drove the sea back with a strong east wind[e] and turned it into dry land. The waters were divided,[f] [22]and the Israelites went through the sea on dry ground,[g] with a wall of water on their right and on their left.

[23]The Egyptians pursued them, and all Pharaoh's horses and chariots and horsemen followed them into the sea. [24]During the last watch of the night the LORD looked down from the pillar of fire and cloud[h] at the Egyptian army and threw it into confusion. [25]He made the wheels of their chariots come off[a] so that they had difficulty driving. And the Egyptians said, "Let's get away from the Israelites! The LORD is fighting[i] for them against Egypt."

[26]Then the LORD said to Moses, "Stretch out your hand over the sea so that the waters may flow back over the Egyptians and their chariots and horsemen." [27]Moses stretched out his hand over the sea, and at daybreak the sea went back to its place.[j] The Egyptians were fleeing toward[b] it, and the LORD swept them into the sea.[k] [28]The water flowed back and covered the chariots and horsemen—the entire army of Pharaoh that had followed the Israelites into the sea. Not one of them survived.

[29]But the Israelites went through the sea on dry ground,[l] with a wall of water on their right and on their left. [30]That day the LORD saved[m] Israel from the hands of the Egyptians, and Israel saw the Egyptians lying dead on the shore. [31]And when the Israelites saw the great power the LORD displayed against the Egyptians, the people feared the LORD and put their trust[n] in him and in Moses his servant.

---

a25 Or *He jammed the wheels of their chariots* (see Samaritan Pentateuch, Septuagint and Syriac)   b27 Or *from*

14:16
a Ex 4:17;
Nu 20:8-9,11
b Isa 10:26

14:17
c ver 4

14:19
d Ex 13:21

14:21
e Ex 15:8
f Ps 74:13;
114:5;
Isa 63:12

14:22
g Ex 15:19;
Ne 9:11;
Ps 66:6;
Heb 11:29

14:24
h Ex 13:21

14:25
i ver 14

14:27
j Jos 4:18
k Ex 15:1,21;
Ps 78:53; 106:11

14:29
l ver 22

14:30
m Ps 106:8,
10,21

14:31
n Ps 106:12;
Jn 2:11

Chapter 15 Theme _____

15:1
a Rev 15:3
b Ps 106:12

15 Then Moses and the Israelites sang this song*a* to the
LORD:

"I will sing*b* to the LORD,
for he is highly exalted.
The horse and its rider
he has hurled into the sea.
²The LORD is my strength*c* and my song;
he has become my salvation.*d*
He is my God,*e* and I will praise him,
my father's God, and I will exalt*f* him.
³The LORD is a warrior;*g*
the LORD is his name.*h*
⁴Pharaoh's chariots and his army*i*
he has hurled into the sea.
The best of Pharaoh's officers
are drowned in the Red Sea.*a*
⁵The deep waters have covered them;
they sank to the depths like a stone.*j*

⁶"Your right hand,*k* O LORD,
was majestic in power.
Your right hand, O LORD,
shattered the enemy.
⁷In the greatness of your majesty
you threw down those who opposed you.
You unleashed your burning anger;*l*
it consumed them like stubble.
⁸By the blast of your nostrils*m*
the waters piled up.*n*
The surging waters stood firm like a wall;*o*
the deep waters congealed in the heart
of the sea.

⁹"The enemy boasted,
'I will pursue,*p* I will overtake them.
I will divide the spoils;*q*
I will gorge myself on them.
I will draw my sword
and my hand will destroy them.'
¹⁰But you blew with your breath,
and the sea covered them.
They sank like lead
in the mighty waters.*r*

*Cross-references (left margin):*

15:1
a Rev 15:3
b Ps 106:12

15:2
c Ps 59:17
d Ps 18:2,46;
Isa 12:2;
Hab 3:18
e Ge 28:21
f Ex 3:6,15-16;
Isa 25:1

15:3
g Ex 14:14;
Ps 24:8;
Rev 19:11
h Ex 6:2-3,7-8;
Ps 83:18

15:4
i Ex 14:6-7

15:5
j ver 10;
Ne 9:11

15:6
k Ps 118:15

15:7
l Ps 78:49-50

15:8
m Ex 14:21
n Ps 78:13
o Ex 14:22

15:9
p Ex 14:5-9
q Jdg 5:30;
Isa 53:12

15:10
r ver 5;
Ex 14:27-28

a 4 Hebrew *Yam Suph*; that is, Sea of Reeds; also in verse 22

11"Who among the gods is like you,[a] O LORD?
  Who is like you—
    majestic in holiness,[b]
    awesome in glory,[c]
    working wonders?
12You stretched out your right hand
  and the earth swallowed them.

13"In your unfailing love you will lead[d]
  the people you have redeemed.
In your strength you will guide them
  to your holy dwelling.[e]
14The nations will hear and tremble;[f]
  anguish will grip the people of Philistia.
15The chiefs[g] of Edom will be terrified,
  the leaders of Moab will be seized with trembling,[h]
the people[a] of Canaan will melt[i] away;
16   terror[j] and dread will fall upon them.
By the power of your arm
  they will be as still as a stone[k]—
until your people pass by, O LORD,
  until the people you bought[b][l] pass by.
17You will bring them in and plant[m] them
  on the mountain[n] of your inheritance—
the place, O LORD, you made for your dwelling,
  the sanctuary, O Lord, your hands established.
18The LORD will reign
  for ever and ever."

19When Pharaoh's horses, chariots and horsemen[c] went into the sea,[o] the LORD brought the waters of the sea back over them, but the Israelites walked through the sea on dry ground.[p] 20Then Miriam[q] the prophetess,[r] Aaron's sister, took a tambourine in her hand, and all the women followed her, with tambourines and dancing.[s] 21Miriam sang to them:

"Sing to the LORD,
  for he is highly exalted.
The horse and its rider
  he has hurled into the sea."[t]

22Then Moses led Israel from the Red Sea and they went into the Desert of Shur. For three days they traveled in the desert without finding water. 23When they came to Marah, they could not drink its water because it was bitter. (That is why the place is

a15 Or rulers   b16 Or created   c19 Or charioteers

15:11
a Ex 8:10;
Dt 3:24;
Ps 77:13
b Isa 6:3;
Rev 4:8
c Ps 8:1

15:13
d Ne 9:12;
Ps 77:20
e Ps 78:54

15:14
f Dt 2:25

15:15
g Ge 36:15
h Nu 22:3
i Jos 5:1

15:16
j Ex 23:27
Jos 2:9
k 1Sa 25:37
l Ps 74:2

15:17
m Ps 44:2
n Ps 78:54,68

15:19
o Ex 14:28
p Ex 14:22

15:20
q Nu 26:59
r Jdg 4:4
s Jdg 11:34;
1Sa 18:6;
Ps 30:11; 150:4

15:21
t ver 1;
Ex 14:27

15:23
a Nu 33:8

15:24
b Ex 14:12;
16:2

15:25
c Ex 14:10
d Jdg 3:4

15:26
e Dt 7:12
f Dt 28:27,
58-60
g Ex 23:25-26

15:27
h Nu 33:9

16:1
i Nu 33:11,12

16:2
j Ex 14:11;
15:24;
1Co 10:10

16:3
k Ex 17:3
l Nu 11:4,34

16:4
m Dt 8:3;
Jn 6:31*

16:5
n ver 22

16:6
o Ex 6:6

16:7
p ver 10;
Isa 35:2; 40:5
q ver 12;
Nu 14:2,27,28
r Nu 16:11

16:8
s 1Sa 8:7;
Ro 13:2

16:10
t ver 7;
Nu 16:19
u Ex 13:21;
1Ki 8:10

called Marah.ᵃ*ᵃ*) ²⁴So the people grumbledᵇ against Moses, saying, "What are we to drink?"

²⁵Then Moses cried outᶜ to the LORD, and the LORD showed him a piece of wood. He threw it into the water, and the water became sweet.

There the LORD made a decree and a law for them, and there he testedᵈ them. ²⁶He said, "If you listen carefully to the voice of the LORD your God and do what is right in his eyes, if you pay attention to his commands and keep all his decrees,ᵉ I will not bring on you any of the diseasesᶠ I brought on the Egyptians, for I am the LORD, who healsᵍ you."

²⁷Then they came to Elim, where there were twelve springs and seventy palm trees, and they campedʰ there near the water.

Chapter 16 Theme

16 The whole Israelite community set out from Elim and came to the Desert of Sin,ⁱ which is between Elim and Sinai, on the fifteenth day of the second month after they had come out of Egypt. ²In the desert the whole community grumbledʲ against Moses and Aaron. ³The Israelites said to them, "If only we had died by the LORD's hand in Egypt!ᵏ There we sat around pots of meat and ate all the foodˡ we wanted, but you have brought us out into this desert to starve this entire assembly to death."

⁴Then the LORD said to Moses, "I will rain down bread from heavenᵐ for you. The people are to go out each day and gather enough for that day. In this way I will test them and see whether they will follow my instructions. ⁵On the sixth day they are to prepare what they bring in, and that is to be twiceⁿ as much as they gather on the other days."

⁶So Moses and Aaron said to all the Israelites, "In the evening you will know that it was the LORD who brought you out of Egypt,ᵒ ⁷and in the morning you will see the gloryᵖ of the LORD, because he has heard your grumbling�q against him. Who are we, that you should grumble against us?"ʳ ⁸Moses also said, "You will know that it was the LORD when he gives you meat to eat in the evening and all the bread you want in the morning, because he has heard your grumbling against him. Who are we? You are not grumbling against us, but against the LORD."ˢ

⁹Then Moses told Aaron, "Say to the entire Israelite community, 'Come before the LORD, for he has heard your grumbling.'"

¹⁰While Aaron was speaking to the whole Israelite community, they looked toward the desert, and there was the gloryᵗ of the LORD appearing in the cloud.ᵘ

ᵃ23 *Marah* means *bitter.*

¹¹The L<small>ORD</small> said to Moses, ¹²"I have heard the grumbling^a of the Israelites. Tell them, 'At twilight you will eat meat, and in the morning you will be filled with bread. Then you will know that I am the L<small>ORD</small> your God.'"

¹³That evening quail^b came and covered the camp, and in the morning there was a layer of dew^c around the camp. ¹⁴When the dew was gone, thin flakes like frost^d on the ground appeared on the desert floor. ¹⁵When the Israelites saw it, they said to each other, "What is it?" For they did not know what it was.

Moses said to them, "It is the bread^e the L<small>ORD</small> has given you to eat. ¹⁶This is what the L<small>ORD</small> has commanded: 'Each one is to gather as much as he needs. Take an omer^{af} for each person you have in your tent.'"

¹⁷The Israelites did as they were told; some gathered much, some little. ¹⁸And when they measured it by the omer, he who gathered much did not have too much, and he who gathered little did not have too little.^g Each one gathered as much as he needed.

¹⁹Then Moses said to them, "No one is to keep any of it until morning."^h

²⁰However, some of them paid no attention to Moses; they kept part of it until morning, but it was full of maggots and began to smell. So Moses was angry with them.

²¹Each morning everyone gathered as much as he needed, and when the sun grew hot, it melted away. ²²On the sixth day, they gathered twiceⁱ as much—two omers^b for each person—and the leaders of the community^j came and reported this to Moses. ²³He said to them, "This is what the L<small>ORD</small> commanded: 'Tomorrow is to be a day of rest, a holy Sabbath^k to the L<small>ORD</small>. So bake what you want to bake and boil what you want to boil. Save whatever is left and keep it until morning.'"

²⁴So they saved it until morning, as Moses commanded, and it did not stink or get maggots in it. ²⁵"Eat it today," Moses said, "because today is a Sabbath to the L<small>ORD</small>. You will not find any of it on the ground today. ²⁶Six days you are to gather it, but on the seventh day, the Sabbath,^l there will not be any."

²⁷Nevertheless, some of the people went out on the seventh day to gather it, but they found none. ²⁸Then the L<small>ORD</small> said to Moses, "How long will you^c refuse to keep my commands^m and my instructions? ²⁹Bear in mind that the L<small>ORD</small> has given you the Sabbath; that is why on the sixth day he gives you bread for two days. Everyone is to stay where he is on the seventh day; no one is to go out." ³⁰So the people rested on the seventh day.

---

^a16 That is, probably about 2 quarts (about 2 liters); also in verses 18, 32, 33 and 36
^b22 That is, probably about 4 quarts (about 4.5 liters)   ^c28 The Hebrew is plural.

16:12
^a ver 7

16:13
^b Nu 11:31;
Ps 78:27-28;
105:40
^c Nu 11:9

16:14
^d ver 31;
Nu 11:7-9;
Ps 105:40

16:15
^e ver 4;
Jn 6:31

16:16
^f ver 32,36

16:18
^g 2Co 8:15*

16:19
^h ver 23;
Ex 12:10; 23:18

16:22
ⁱ ver 5
^j Ex 34:31

16:23
^k Ge 2:3;
Ex 20:8; 23:12;
Lev 23:3

16:26
^l Ex 20:9-10

16:28
^m 2Ki 17:14;
Ps 78:10; 106:13

³¹The people of Israel called the bread manna.^{aa} It was white like coriander seed and tasted like wafers made with honey. ³²Moses said, "This is what the LORD has commanded: 'Take an omer of manna and keep it for the generations to come, so they can see the bread I gave you to eat in the desert when I brought you out of Egypt.'"

³³So Moses said to Aaron, "Take a jar and put an omer of manna^b in it. Then place it before the LORD to be kept for the generations to come."

³⁴As the LORD commanded Moses, Aaron put the manna in front of the Testimony,^c that it might be kept. ³⁵The Israelites ate manna^d forty years,^e until they came to a land that was settled; they ate manna until they reached the border of Canaan.^f

³⁶(An omer is one tenth of an ephah.)

Chapter 17 Theme

17 The whole Israelite community set out from the Desert of Sin,^g traveling from place to place as the LORD commanded. They camped at Rephidim, but there was no water^h for the people to drink. ²So they quarreled with Moses and said, "Give us waterⁱ to drink."

Moses replied, "Why do you quarrel with me? Why do you put the LORD to the test?"^j

³But the people were thirsty for water there, and they grumbled^k against Moses. They said, "Why did you bring us up out of Egypt to make us and our children and livestock die of thirst?"

⁴Then Moses cried out to the LORD, "What am I to do with these people? They are almost ready to stone^l me."

⁵The LORD answered Moses, "Walk on ahead of the people. Take with you some of the elders of Israel and take in your hand the staff with which you struck the Nile,^m and go. ⁶I will stand there before you by the rock at Horeb. Strike the rock, and waterⁿ will come out of it for the people to drink." So Moses did this in the sight of the elders of Israel. ⁷And he called the place Massah^b and Meribah^{co} because the Israelites quarreled and because they tested the LORD saying, "Is the LORD among us or not?"

⁸The Amalekites^p came and attacked the Israelites at Rephidim. ⁹Moses said to Joshua, "Choose some of our men and go out to fight the Amalekites. Tomorrow I will stand on top of the hill with the staff^q of God in my hands."

¹⁰So Joshua fought the Amalekites as Moses had ordered, and Moses, Aaron and Hur^r went to the top of the hill. ¹¹As long as

a31 *Manna* means *What is it?* (see verse 15).   b7 *Massah* means *testing.*   c7 *Meribah* means *quarreling.*

Moses held up his hands, the Israelites were winning,ᵃ but whenever he lowered his hands, the Amalekites were winning. ¹²When Moses' hands grew tired, they took a stone and put it under him and he sat on it. Aaron and Hur held his hands up—one on one side, one on the other—so that his hands remained steady till sunset. ¹³So Joshua overcame the Amalekite army with the sword.

¹⁴Then the LORD said to Moses, "Writeᵇ this on a scroll as something to be remembered and make sure that Joshua hears it, because I will completely blot out the memory of Amalekᶜ from under heaven."

¹⁵Moses built an altar and called it The LORD is my Banner. ¹⁶He said, "For hands were lifted up to the throne of the LORD. Theᵃ LORD will be at war against the Amalekites from generation to generation."

Chapter 18 Theme _____

18 Now Jethro, the priest of Midianᵈ and father-in-law of Moses, heard of everything God had done for Moses and for his people Israel, and how the LORD had brought Israel out of Egypt.

²After Moses had sent away his wife Zipporah,ᵉ his father-in-law Jethro received her ³and her two sons.ᶠ One son was named Gershom,ᵇ for Moses said, "I have become an alien in a foreign land";ᵍ ⁴and the other was named Eliezer,ᶜʰ for he said, "My father's God was my helper; he saved me from the sword of Pharaoh."

⁵Jethro, Moses' father-in-law, together with Moses' sons and wife, came to him in the desert, where he was camped near the mountainⁱ of God. ⁶Jethro had sent word to him, "I, your father-in-law Jethro, am coming to you with your wife and her two sons."

⁷So Moses went out to meet his father-in-law and bowed downʲ and kissedᵏ him. They greeted each other and then went into the tent. ⁸Moses told his father-in-law about everything the LORD had done to Pharaoh and the Egyptians for Israel's sake and about all the hardships they had met along the way and how the LORD had savedˡ them.

⁹Jethro was delighted to hear about all the good things the LORD had done for Israel in rescuing them from the hand of the Egyptians. ¹⁰He said, "Praise be to the LORD,ᵐ who rescued you from the hand of the Egyptians and of Pharaoh, and who rescued the people from the hand of the Egyptians. ¹¹Now I know that the LORD is greater than all other gods,ⁿ for he did this to

ᵃ16 Or "Because a hand was against the throne of the LORD, the   ᵇ3 Gershom sounds like the Hebrew for an alien there.   ᶜ4 Eliezer means my God is helper.

17:11
ᵃ Jas 5:16

17:14
ᵇ Ex 24:4; 34:27; Nu 33:2
ᶜ 1Sa 15:3; 30:17-18

18:1
ᵈ Ex 2:16; 3:1

18:2
ᵉ Ex 2:21; 4:25

18:3
ᶠ Ex 4:20; Ac 7:29
ᵍ Ex 2:22

18:4
ʰ 1Ch 23:15

18:5
ⁱ Ex 3:1

18:7
ʲ Ge 43:28
ᵏ Ge 29:13

18:8
ˡ Ex 15:6,16; Ps 81:7

18:10
ᵐ Ge 14:20; Ps 68:19-20

18:11
ⁿ Ex 12:12; 15:11; 2Ch 2:5

18:11
a Lk 1:51

18:12
b Dt 12:7

18:15
c Nu 9:6,8;
Dt 17:8-13

18:16
d Lev 24:12

18:18
e Nu 11:11,
14,17

18:19
f Ex 3:12
g Nu 27:5

18:20
h Dt 5:1
i Ps 143:8
j Dt 1:18

18:21
k Ac 6:3
l Dt 16:19;
Ps 15:5;
Eze 18:8
m Dt 1:13,15;
2Ch 19:5-10

18:22
n Dt 1:17-18
o Nu 11:17

18:25
p Dt 1:13-15

18:26
q ver 22

18:27
r Nu 10:29-30

19:2
s Ex 17:1
t Ex 3:1

those who had treated Israel arrogantly."[a] [12]Then Jethro, Moses' father-in-law, brought a burnt offering and other sacrifices to God, and Aaron came with all the elders of Israel to eat bread with Moses' father-in-law in the presence[b] of God.

[13]The next day Moses took his seat to serve as judge for the people, and they stood around him from morning till evening. [14]When his father-in-law saw all that Moses was doing for the people, he said, "What is this you are doing for the people? Why do you alone sit as judge, while all these people stand around you from morning till evening?"

[15]Moses answered him, "Because the people come to me to seek God's will.[c] [16]Whenever they have a dispute, it is brought to me, and I decide between the parties and inform them of God's decrees and laws."[d]

[17]Moses' father-in-law replied, "What you are doing is not good. [18]You and these people who come to you will only wear yourselves out. The work is too heavy for you; you cannot handle it alone.[e] [19]Listen now to me and I will give you some advice, and may God be with you.[f] You must be the people's representative before God and bring their disputes[g] to him. [20]Teach them the decrees and laws,[h] and show them the way to live[i] and the duties they are to perform.[j] [21]But select capable men[k] from all the people—men who fear God, trustworthy men who hate dishonest gain[l]—and appoint them as officials[m] over thousands, hundreds, fifties and tens. [22]Have them serve as judges for the people at all times, but have them bring every difficult case[n] to you; the simple cases they can decide themselves. That will make your load lighter, because they will share[o] it with you. [23]If you do this and God so commands, you will be able to stand the strain, and all these people will go home satisfied."

[24]Moses listened to his father-in-law and did everything he said. [25]He chose capable men from all Israel and made them leaders of the people, officials over thousands, hundreds, fifties and tens.[p] [26]They served as judges for the people at all times. The difficult cases they brought to Moses, but the simple ones they decided themselves.[q]

[27]Then Moses sent his father-in-law on his way, and Jethro returned to his own country.[r]

Chapter 19 Theme

19 In the third month after the Israelites left Egypt—on the very day—they came to the Desert of Sinai. [2]After they set out from Rephidim,[s] they entered the Desert of Sinai, and Israel camped there in the desert in front of the mountain.[t]

³Then Moses went up to God, and the LORD called[a] to him from the mountain and said, "This is what you are to say to the house of Jacob and what you are to tell the people of Israel: ⁴'You yourselves have seen what I did to Egypt,[b] and how I carried you on eagles' wings[c] and brought you to myself. ⁵Now if you obey me fully[d] and keep my covenant,[e] then out of all nations you will be my treasured possession.[f] Although the whole earth[g] is mine, ⁶you[a] will be for me a kingdom of priests[h] and a holy nation.'[i] These are the words you are to speak to the Israelites."

⁷So Moses went back and summoned the elders of the people and set before them all the words the LORD had commanded him to speak. ⁸The people all responded together, "We will do everything the LORD has said."[j] So Moses brought their answer back to the LORD.

⁹The LORD said to Moses, "I am going to come to you in a dense cloud,[k] so that the people will hear me speaking[l] with you and will always put their trust in you." Then Moses told the LORD what the people had said.

¹⁰And the LORD said to Moses, "Go to the people and consecrate[m] them today and tomorrow. Have them wash their clothes[n] ¹¹and be ready by the third day,[o] because on that day the LORD will come down on Mount Sinai in the sight of all the people. ¹²Put limits for the people around the mountain and tell them, 'Be careful that you do not go up the mountain or touch the foot of it. Whoever touches the mountain shall surely be put to death. ¹³He shall surely be stoned[p] or shot with arrows; not a hand is to be laid on him. Whether man or animal, he shall not be permitted to live.' Only when the ram's horn sounds a long blast may they go up to the mountain."

¹⁴After Moses had gone down the mountain to the people, he consecrated them, and they washed their clothes. ¹⁵Then he said to the people, "Prepare yourselves for the third day. Abstain from sexual relations."

¹⁶On the morning of the third day there was thunder and lightning, with a thick cloud over the mountain, and a very loud trumpet blast.[q] Everyone in the camp trembled.[r] ¹⁷Then Moses led the people out of the camp to meet with God, and they stood at the foot of the mountain. ¹⁸Mount Sinai was covered with smoke,[s] because the LORD descended on it in fire.[t] The smoke billowed up from it like smoke from a furnace,[u] the whole mountain[b] trembled[v] violently, ¹⁹and the sound of the trumpet grew louder and louder. Then Moses spoke and the voice[w] of God answered[x] him.[c]

---

[a]5,6 Or possession, for the whole earth is mine. ⁶You   [b]18 Most Hebrew manuscripts; a few Hebrew manuscripts and Septuagint all the people   [c]19 Or and God answered him with thunder

---

19:3
[a] Ex 3:4;
Ac 7:38

19:4
[b] Dt 29:2
[c] Isa 63:9

19:5
[d] Ex 15:26
[e] Dt 5:2
[f] Dt 14:2;
Ps 135:4
[g] Ex 9:29;
Dt 10:14

19:6
[h] 1Pe 2:5
[i] Dt 7:6; 26:19;
Isa 62:12

19:8
[j] Ex 24:3,7;
Dt 5:27

19:9
[k] ver 16;
Ex 24:15-16
[l] Dt 4:12,36

19:10
[m] Lev 11:44;
Heb 10:22
[n] Ge 35:2

19:11
[o] ver 16

19:13
[p] Heb 12:20*

19:16
[q] Heb 12:18-19;
Rev 4:1
[r] Heb 12:21

19:18
[s] Ps 104:32
[t] Ex 3:2; 24:17;
Dt 4:11;
2Ch 7:1;
Ps 18:8;
Heb 12:18
[u] Ge 19:28
[v] Jdg 5:5;
Ps 68:8; Jer 4:24

19:19
[w] Ne 9:13
[x] Ps 81:7

19:21
a Ex 3:5;
1Sa 6:19

19:22
b Lev 10:3
c 2Sa 6:7

19:23
d ver 12

19:24
e Ex 24:1,9

20:2
f Ex 13:3

20:3
g Dt 6:14;
Jer 35:15

20:4
h Lev 26:1;
Dt 4:15-19,23;
27:15

20:5
i Isa 44:15,
17,19
j Ex 34:14;
Dt 4:24
k Nu 14:18;
Jer 32:18

20:6
l Dt 7:9

20:7
m Lev 19:12;
Mt 5:33

20:8
n Ex 31:13-16;
Lev 26:2

20:9
o Ex 34:21;
Lk 13:14

20:11
p Ge 2:2

20:12
q Mt 15:4*;
Mk 7:10*;
Eph 6:2

²⁰The LORD descended to the top of Mount Sinai and called Moses to the top of the mountain. So Moses went up ²¹and the LORD said to him, "Go down and warn the people so they do not force their way through to see*a* the LORD and many of them perish. ²²Even the priests, who approach*b* the LORD, must consecrate themselves, or the LORD will break out against them."*c*

²³Moses said to the LORD, "The people cannot come up Mount Sinai, because you yourself warned us, 'Put limits*d* around the mountain and set it apart as holy.'"

²⁴The LORD replied, "Go down and bring Aaron*e* up with you. But the priests and the people must not force their way through to come up to the LORD, or he will break out against them."

²⁵So Moses went down to the people and told them.

Chapter 20 Theme _____

20 And God spoke all these words:

²"I am the LORD your God, who brought you out of Egypt, out of the land of slavery.*f*

³"You shall have no other gods before*a* me.*g*

⁴"You shall not make for yourself an idol*h* in the form of anything in heaven above or on the earth beneath or in the waters below. ⁵You shall not bow down to them or worship*i* them; for I, the LORD your God, am a jealous God,*j* punishing the children for the sin of the fathers to the third and fourth generation*k* of those who hate me, ⁶but showing love to a thousand*l* ⌊generations⌋ of those who love me and keep my commandments.

⁷"You shall not misuse the name of the LORD your God, for the LORD will not hold anyone guiltless who misuses his name.*m*

⁸"Remember the Sabbath*n* day by keeping it holy. ⁹Six days you shall labor and do all your work,*o* ¹⁰but the seventh day is a Sabbath to the LORD your God. On it you shall not do any work, neither you, nor your son or daughter, nor your manservant or maidservant, nor your animals, nor the alien within your gates. ¹¹For in six days the LORD made the heavens and the earth, the sea, and all that is in them, but he rested*p* on the seventh day. Therefore the LORD blessed the Sabbath day and made it holy.

¹²"Honor your father and your mother,*q* so that you may live long in the land the LORD your God is giving you.

a3 Or *besides*

¹³"You shall not murder.^a

¹⁴"You shall not commit adultery.^b

¹⁵"You shall not steal.^c

¹⁶"You shall not give false testimony against your neighbor.^d

¹⁷"You shall not covet^e your neighbor's house. You shall not covet your neighbor's wife, or his manservant or maidservant, his ox or donkey, or anything that belongs to your neighbor."

¹⁸When the people saw the thunder and lightning and heard the trumpet^f and saw the mountain in smoke, they trembled with fear. They stayed at a distance ¹⁹and said to Moses, "Speak to us yourself and we will listen. But do not have God speak to us or we will die."^g

²⁰Moses said to the people, "Do not be afraid. God has come to test you, so that the fear^h of God will be with you to keep you from sinning."ⁱ

²¹The people remained at a distance, while Moses approached the thick darkness^j where God was.

²²Then the LORD said to Moses, "Tell the Israelites this: 'You have seen for yourselves that I have spoken to you from heaven:^k ²³Do not make any gods to be alongside me;^l do not make for yourselves gods of silver or gods of gold.^m

²⁴"'Make an altar of earth for me and sacrifice on it your burnt offerings and fellowship offerings,^a your sheep and goats and your cattle. Wherever I cause my nameⁿ to be honored, I will come to you and bless^o you. ²⁵If you make an altar of stones for me, do not build it with dressed stones, for you will defile it if you use a tool^p on it. ²⁶And do not go up to my altar on steps, lest your nakedness be exposed on it.'

Chapter 21 Theme

21 "These are the laws^q you are to set before them:

²"If you buy a Hebrew servant, he is to serve you for six years. But in the seventh year, he shall go free,^r without paying anything. ³If he comes alone, he is to go free alone; but if he has a wife when he comes, she is to go with him. ⁴If his master gives him a wife and she bears him sons or daughters, the woman and her children shall belong to her master, and only the man shall go free.

⁵"But if the servant declares, 'I love my master and my wife and children and do not want to go free,'^s ⁶then his master must take him before the judges.^{b t} He shall take him to the door or

---

^a24 Traditionally *peace offerings*   ^b6 Or *before God*

20:13
^a Mt 5:21*;
Ro 13:9*

20:14
^b Mt 19:18*

20:15
^c Lev 19:11,13;
Mt 19:18*

20:16
^d Ex 23:1,7;
Mt 19:18*

20:17
^e Ro 7:7*; 13:9*;
Eph 5:3

20:18
^f Ex 19:16-19;
Heb 12:18-19

20:19
^g Dt 5:5,23-27;
Gal 3:19

20:20
^h Dt 4:10;
Isa 8:13
ⁱ Pr 16:6

20:21
^j Dt 5:22

20:22
^k Ne 9:13

20:23
^l ver 3
^m Ex 32:4, 8, 31

20:24
ⁿ Dt 12:5;
16:6,11;
2Ch 6:6
^o Ge 12:2

20:25
^p Dt 27:5-6

21:1
^q Dt 4:14

21:2
^r Jer 34:8,14

21:5
^s Dt 15:16

21:6
^t Ex 22:8-9

21:6
a Ne 5:5

21:10
b 1Co 7:3-5

21:12
c Ge 9:6;
Mt 26:52

21:13
d Nu 35:10-34;
Dt 19:2-13;
Jos 20:9;
1Sa 24:4, 10,18

21:14
e Heb 10:26
f Dt 19:11-12;
1Ki 2:28-34

21:16
g Ge 37:28
h Ex 22:4;
Dt 24:7

21:17
i Lev 20:9-10;
Mt 15:4*;
Mk 7:10*

21:21
j Lev 25:44-46

21:22
k ver 30;
Dt 22:18-19

21:23
l Lev 24:19;
Dt 19:21

21:24
m Mt 5:38*

21:28
n ver 32;
Ge 9:5

the doorpost and pierce his ear with an awl. Then he will be his servant for life.*a*

[7]"If a man sells his daughter as a servant, she is not to go free as menservants do. [8]If she does not please the master who has selected her for himself,*a* he must let her be redeemed. He has no right to sell her to foreigners, because he has broken faith with her. [9]If he selects her for his son, he must grant her the rights of a daughter. [10]If he marries another woman, he must not deprive the first one of her food, clothing and marital rights.*b* [11]If he does not provide her with these three things, she is to go free, without any payment of money.

[12]"Anyone who strikes a man and kills him shall surely be put to death.*c* [13]However, if he does not do it intentionally, but God lets it happen, he is to flee to a place*d* I will designate. [14]But if a man schemes and kills another man deliberately,*e* take him away from my altar and put him to death.*f*

[15]"Anyone who attacks*b* his father or his mother must be put to death.

[16]"Anyone who kidnaps another and either sells*g* him or still has him when he is caught must be put to death.*h*

[17]"Anyone who curses his father or mother must be put to death.*i*

[18]"If men quarrel and one hits the other with a stone or with his fist*c* and he does not die but is confined to bed, [19]the one who struck the blow will not be held responsible if the other gets up and walks around outside with his staff; however, he must pay the injured man for the loss of his time and see that he is completely healed.

[20]"If a man beats his male or female slave with a rod and the slave dies as a direct result, he must be punished, [21]but he is not to be punished if the slave gets up after a day or two, since the slave is his property.*j*

[22]"If men who are fighting hit a pregnant woman and she gives birth prematurely*d* but there is no serious injury, the offender must be fined whatever the woman's husband demands*k* and the court allows. [23]But if there is serious injury, you are to take life for life,*l* [24]eye for eye, tooth for tooth,*m* hand for hand, foot for foot, [25]burn for burn, wound for wound, bruise for bruise.

[26]"If a man hits a manservant or maidservant in the eye and destroys it, he must let the servant go free to compensate for the eye. [27]And if he knocks out the tooth of a manservant or maidservant, he must let the servant go free to compensate for the tooth.

[28]"If a bull gores a man or a woman to death, the bull must be stoned to death,*n* and its meat must not be eaten. But the owner

*a*8 Or *master so that he does not choose her*   *b*15 Or *kills*   *c*18 Or *with a tool*   *d*22 Or *she has a miscarriage* of the bull will not be held responsible. ²⁹If, however, the bull has had the habit of goring and the owner has been warned but has not kept it penned up and it kills a man or woman, the bull must be stoned and the owner also must be put to death. ³⁰However, if payment is demanded of him, he may redeem his life by paying whatever is demanded.ᵃ ³¹This law also applies if the bull gores a son or daughter. ³²If the bull gores a male or female slave, the owner must pay thirty shekelsᵃᵇ of silver to the master of the slave, and the bull must be stoned.

³³"If a man uncovers a pit or digs one and fails to cover it and an ox or a donkey falls into it, ³⁴the owner of the pit must pay for the loss; he must pay its owner, and the dead animal will be his.

³⁵"If a man's bull injures the bull of another and it dies, they are to sell the live one and divide both the money and the dead animal equally. ³⁶However, if it was known that the bull had the habit of goring, yet the owner did not keep it penned up, the owner must pay, animal for animal, and the dead animal will be his.

Chapter 22 Theme _____

22 "If a man steals an ox or a sheep and slaughters it or sells it, he must pay backᶜ five head of cattle for the ox and four sheep for the sheep.

²"If a thief is caught breaking inᵈ and is struck so that he dies, the defender is not guilty of bloodshed;ᵉ ³but if it happensᵇ after sunrise, he is guilty of bloodshed.

"A thief must certainly make restitution, but if he has nothing, he must be soldᶠ to pay for his theft.

⁴"If the stolen animal is found alive in his possession— whether ox or donkey or sheep—he must pay back double.ᵍ

⁵"If a man grazes his livestock in a field or vineyard and lets them stray and they graze in another man's field, he must make restitution from the best of his own field or vineyard.

⁶"If a fire breaks out and spreads into thornbushes so that it burns shocks of grain or standing grain or the whole field, the one who started the fire must make restitution.

⁷"If a man gives his neighbor silver or goods for safekeeping and they are stolen from the neighbor's house, the thief, if he is caught, must pay back double.ʰ ⁸But if the thief is not found, the owner of the house must appear before the judgesᶜ ⁱ to determine whether he has laid his hands on the other man's property. ⁹In all cases of illegal possession of an ox, a donkey, a sheep, a garment, or any other lost property about which somebody says, 'This is mine,' both parties are to bring their cases before the

21:30
ᵃ ver 22;
Nu 35:31

21:32
ᵇ Zec 11:12-13;
Mt 26:15; 27:3,9

22:1
ᶜ 2Sa 12:6;
Pr 6:31;
Lk 19:8

22:2
ᵈ Mt 6:19-20;
24:43
ᵉ Nu 35:27

22:3
ᶠ Ex 21:2;
Mt 18:25

22:4
ᵍ Ge 43:12

22:7
ʰ ver 4

22:8
ⁱ Ex 21:6;
Dt 17:8-9; 19:17

ᵃ32 That is, about 12 ounces (about 0.3 kilogram)   ᵇ3 Or *if he strikes him*   ᶜ8 Or *before God*; also in verse 9

22:9
a ver 28;
Dt 25:1

22:11
b Heb 6:16

22:13
c Ge 31:39

22:16
d Dt 22:28

22:18
e Lev 20:27;
Dt 18:11;
1Sa 28:3

22:19
f Lev 18:23;
Dt 27:21

22:20
g Dt 17:2-5

22:21
h Lev 19:33
i Dt 10:19

22:22
j Dt 24:6,
10,12,17

22:23
k Lk 18:7
l Dt 15:9;
Ps 18:6

22:24
m Ps 69:24;
109:9

22:25
n Lev 25:35-37;
Dt 23:20;
Ps 15:5

22:26
o Dt 24:6

22:27
p Ex 34:6

22:28
q Lev 24:11,16
r Ecc 10:20;
Ac 23:5*

22:29
s Ex 23:15,16,19
t Ex 13:2

22:30
u Ex 13:12;
Dt 15:19
v Lev 22:27

judges.[a] The one whom the judges declare[a] guilty must pay back double to his neighbor.

10 "If a man gives a donkey, an ox, a sheep or any other animal to his neighbor for safekeeping and it dies or is injured or is taken away while no one is looking, 11 the issue between them will be settled by the taking of an oath[b] before the LORD that the neighbor did not lay hands on the other person's property. The owner is to accept this, and no restitution is required. 12 But if the animal was stolen from the neighbor, he must make restitution to the owner. 13 If it was torn to pieces by a wild animal, he shall bring in the remains as evidence and he will not be required to pay for the torn animal.[c]

14 "If a man borrows an animal from his neighbor and it is injured or dies while the owner is not present, he must make restitution. 15 But if the owner is with the animal, the borrower will not have to pay. If the animal was hired, the money paid for the hire covers the loss.

16 "If a man seduces a virgin[d] who is not pledged to be married and sleeps with her, he must pay the bride-price, and she shall be his wife. 17 If her father absolutely refuses to give her to him, he must still pay the bride-price for virgins.

18 "Do not allow a sorceress[e] to live.

19 "Anyone who has sexual relations with an animal[f] must be put to death.

20 "Whoever sacrifices to any god other than the LORD must be destroyed.[b][g]

21 "Do not mistreat an alien[h] or oppress him, for you were aliens[i] in Egypt.

22 "Do not take advantage of a widow or an orphan.[j] 23 If you do and they cry out[k] to me, I will certainly hear their cry.[l] 24 My anger will be aroused, and I will kill you with the sword; your wives will become widows and your children fatherless.[m]

25 "If you lend money to one of my people among you who is needy, do not be like a moneylender; charge him no interest.[c][n] 26 If you take your neighbor's cloak as a pledge,[o] return it to him by sunset, 27 because his cloak is the only covering he has for his body. What else will he sleep in? When he cries out to me, I will hear, for I am compassionate.[p]

28 "Do not blaspheme God[d][q] or curse the ruler of your people.[r]

29 "Do not hold back offerings[s] from your granaries or your vats.[e]

"You must give me the firstborn of your sons.[t] 30 Do the same with your cattle and your sheep.[u] Let them stay with their mothers for seven days, but give them to me on the eighth day.[v]

---

a9 Or whom God declares   b20 The Hebrew term refers to the irrevocable giving over of things or persons to the LORD, often by totally destroying them.   c25 Or excessive interest   d28 Or Do not revile the judges   e29 The meaning of the Hebrew for this phrase is uncertain.

³¹"You are to be my holy people.^a So do not eat the meat of an animal torn by wild beasts;^b throw it to the dogs.

Chapter 23 Theme

23 "Do not spread false reports.^c Do not help a wicked man by being a malicious witness.^d

²"Do not follow the crowd in doing wrong. When you give testimony in a lawsuit, do not pervert justice^e by siding with the crowd, ³and do not show favoritism to a poor man in his lawsuit.

⁴"If you come across your enemy's ox or donkey wandering off, be sure to take it back to him.^f ⁵If you see the donkey^g of someone who hates you fallen down under its load, do not leave it there; be sure you help him with it.

⁶"Do not deny justice^h to your poor people in their lawsuits. ⁷Have nothing to do with a false chargeⁱ and do not put an innocent or honest person to death, for I will not acquit the guilty.

⁸"Do not accept a bribe,^j for a bribe blinds those who see and twists the words of the righteous.

⁹"Do not oppress an alien;^k you yourselves know how it feels to be aliens, because you were aliens in Egypt.

¹⁰"For six years you are to sow your fields and harvest the crops, ¹¹but during the seventh year let the land lie unplowed and unused. Then the poor among your people may get food from it, and the wild animals may eat what they leave. Do the same with your vineyard and your olive grove.

¹²"Six days do your work,^l but on the seventh day do not work, so that your ox and your donkey may rest and the slave born in your household, and the alien as well, may be refreshed.

¹³"Be careful^m to do everything I have said to you. Do not invoke the names of other gods; do not let them be heard on your lips.

¹⁴"Three timesⁿ a year you are to celebrate a festival to me.

¹⁵"Celebrate the Feast of Unleavened Bread;^o for seven days eat bread made without yeast, as I commanded you. Do this at the appointed time in the month of Abib, for in that month you came out of Egypt.

"No one is to appear before me empty-handed.^p

¹⁶"Celebrate the Feast of Harvest with the firstfruits^q of the crops you sow in your field.

"Celebrate the Feast of Ingathering at the end of the year, when you gather in your crops from the field.^r

¹⁷"Three times^s a year all the men are to appear before the Sovereign LORD.

¹⁸"Do not offer the blood of a sacrifice to me along with anything containing yeast.^t

22:31
a Lev 19:2
b Eze 4:14

23:1
c Ex 20:16;
Ps 101:5
d Ps 35:11;
Ac 6:11

23:2
e Dt 16:19

23:4
f Dt 22:1-3

23:5
g Dt 22:4

23:6
h ver 2

23:7
i Eph 4:25

23:8
j Dt 10:17;
16:19;
Pr 15:27

23:9
k Ex 22:21

23:12
l Ex 20:9

23:13
m 1Ti 4:16

23:14
n Ex 34:23,24

23:15
o Ex 12:17

23:15
p Ex 34:20

23:16
q Ex 34:22
r Dt 16:13

23:17
s Dt 16:16

23:18
t Ex 34:25

23:18
a Dt 16:4

23:19
b Ex 22:29;
Dt 26:2,10
c Dt 14:21

23:20
d Ex 14:19;
32:34
e Ex 15:17

23:21
f Nu 14:11;
Dt 18:19
g Ps 78:8,40,56

23:22
h Ge 12:3;
Dt 30:7

23:23
i ver 20;
Jos 24:8,11

23:24
j Ex 20:5
k Dt 12:30-31
l Ex 34:13;
Nu 33:52

23:25
m Dt 6:13;
Mt 4:10
n Dt 7:12-15;
28:1-14
o Ex 15:26

23:26
p Dt 7:14;
Mal 3:11
q Job 5:26

23:27
r Ex 15:14;
Dt 2:25
s Dt 7:23

23:28
t Dt 7:20;
Jos 24:12

23:29
u Dt 7:22

23:31
v Ge 15:18
w Jos 21:44;
24:12,18

23:32
x Ex 34:12;
Dt 7:2

23:33
y Dt 7:16;
Ps 106:36

24:1
z Ex 6:23;
Lev 10:1-2
a Nu 11:16

"The fat of my festival offerings must not be kept until morning.*a*

¹⁹"Bring the best of the firstfruits*b* of your soil to the house of the LORD your God.

"Do not cook a young goat in its mother's milk.*c*

²⁰"See, I am sending an angel*d* ahead of you to guard you along the way and to bring you to the place I have prepared.*e* ²¹Pay attention to him and listen*f* to what he says. Do not rebel against him; he will not forgive your rebellion,*g* since my Name is in him. ²²If you listen carefully to what he says and do all that I say, I will be an enemy*h* to your enemies and will oppose those who oppose you. ²³My angel will go ahead of you and bring you into the land of the Amorites, Hittites, Perizzites, Canaanites, Hivites and Jebusites,*i* and I will wipe them out. ²⁴Do not bow down before their gods or worship*j* them or follow their practices.*k* You must demolish*l* them and break their sacred stones to pieces. ²⁵Worship the LORD your God,*m* and his blessing*n* will be on your food and water. I will take away sickness*o* from among you, ²⁶and none will miscarry or be barren*p* in your land. I will give you a full life span.*q*

²⁷"I will send my terror*r* ahead of you and throw into confusion*s* every nation you encounter. I will make all your enemies turn their backs and run. ²⁸I will send the hornet*t* ahead of you to drive the Hivites, Canaanites and Hittites out of your way. ²⁹But I will not drive them out in a single year, because the land would become desolate and the wild animals*u* too numerous for you. ³⁰Little by little I will drive them out before you, until you have increased enough to take possession of the land.

³¹"I will establish your borders from the Red Sea*a* to the Sea of the Philistines,*b* and from the desert to the River.*cv* I will hand over to you the people who live in the land and you will drive them out*w* before you. ³²Do not make a covenant*x* with them or with their gods. ³³Do not let them live in your land, or they will cause you to sin against me, because the worship of their gods will certainly be a snare*y* to you."

Chapter 24 Theme _____

24 Then he said to Moses, "Come up to the LORD, you and Aaron, Nadab and Abihu,*z* and seventy of the elders*a* of Israel. You are to worship at a distance, ²but Moses alone is to approach the LORD; the others must not come near. And the people may not come up with him."

³When Moses went and told the people all the LORD's words and laws, they responded with one voice, "Everything the LORD

a31 Hebrew *Yam Suph*; that is, Sea of Reeds   *b31* That is, the Mediterranean   *c31* That is, the Euphrates has said we will do."[a] [4]Moses then wrote[b] down everything the LORD had said.

He got up early the next morning and built an altar at the foot of the mountain and set up twelve stone pillars[c] representing the twelve tribes of Israel. [5]Then he sent young Israelite men, and they offered burnt offerings and sacrificed young bulls as fellowship offerings[a] to the LORD. [6]Moses took half of the blood[d] and put it in bowls, and the other half he sprinkled on the altar. [7]Then he took the Book of the Covenant[e] and read it to the people. They responded, "We will do everything the LORD has said; we will obey."

[8]Moses then took the blood, sprinkled it on the people and said, "This is the blood of the covenant[f] that the LORD has made with you in accordance with all these words."

[9]Moses and Aaron, Nadab and Abihu, and the seventy elders[g] of Israel went up [10]and saw[h] the God of Israel. Under his feet was something like a pavement made of sapphire,[b][i] clear as the sky[j] itself. [11]But God did not raise his hand against these leaders of the Israelites; they saw[k] God, and they ate and drank.

[12]The LORD said to Moses, "Come up to me on the mountain and stay here, and I will give you the tablets of stone,[l] with the law and commands I have written for their instruction."

[13]Then Moses set out with Joshua[m] his aide, and Moses went up on the mountain[n] of God. [14]He said to the elders, "Wait here for us until we come back to you. Aaron and Hur are with you, and anyone involved in a dispute can go to them."

[15]When Moses went up on the mountain, the cloud[o] covered it, [16]and the glory[p] of the LORD settled on Mount Sinai. For six days the cloud covered the mountain, and on the seventh day the LORD called to Moses from within the cloud.[q] [17]To the Israelites the glory of the LORD looked like a consuming fire[r] on top of the mountain. [18]Then Moses entered the cloud as he went on up the mountain. And he stayed on the mountain forty[s] days and forty nights.[t]

Chapter 25 Theme

25 The Lord said to Moses, [2]"Tell the Israelites to bring me an offering. You are to receive the offering for me from each man whose heart prompts[u] him to give. [3]These are the offerings you are to receive from them: gold, silver and bronze; [4]blue, purple and scarlet yarn and fine linen; goat hair; [5]ram skins dyed red and hides of sea cows[c]; acacia wood; [6]olive oil[v] for the light; spices for the anointing oil and for the fragrant

INSIGHT

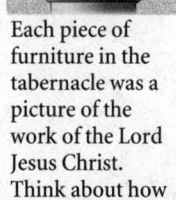

Each piece of furniture in the tabernacle was a picture of the work of the Lord Jesus Christ. Think about how each portrays this.

24:3
[a] Ex 19:8;
Dt 5:27

24:4
[b] Dt 31:9
[c] Ge 28:18

24:6
[d] Heb 9:18

24:7
[e] Heb 9:19

24:8
[f] Heb 9:20*;
1Pe 1:2

24:9
[g] ver 1

24:10
[h] Mt 17:2;
Jn 1:18; 6:46
[i] Eze 1:26
[j] Rev 4:3

24:11
[k] Ge 32:30;
Ex 19:21

24:12
[l] Ex 32:15-16

24:13
[m] Ex 17:9
[n] Ex 3:1

24:15
[o] Ex 19:9

24:16
[p] Ex 16:10
[q] Ps 99:7

24:17
[r] Ex 3:2;
Dt 4:36;
Heb 12:18,29

24:18
[s] Dt 9:9
[t] Ex 34:28

25:2
[u] Ex 35:21;
1Ch 29:5,7,9;
Ezr 2:68;
2Co 8:11-12; 9:7

25:6
[v] Ex 27:20;
30:22-32

[a]5 Traditionally *peace offerings*   [b]10 Or *lapis lazuli*   [c]5 That is, dugongs

25:7
a Ex 28:4,6-14
b Ex 28:15-30

25:8
c Ex 36:1-5;
Heb 9:1-2
d Ex 29:45;
1Ki 6:13;
2Co 6:16;
Rev 21:3

25:9
e ver 40;
Ac 7:44;
Heb 8:5

25:10
f Dt 10:1-5;
Heb 9:4

25:15
g 1Ki 8:8

25:16
h Dt 31:26;
Heb 9:4

25:17
i Ro 3:25

25:20
j 1Ki 8:7;
1Ch 28:18;
Heb 9:5

25:21
k Ex 26:34
l ver 16

25:22
m Nu 7:89;
1Sa 4:4;
2Sa 6:2;
2Ki 19:15;
Ps 80:1;
Isa 37:16
n Ex 29:42-43

25:23
o Heb 9:2

25:29
p Nu 4:7

25:30
q Lev 24:5-9

25:31
r 1Ki 7:49;
Zec 4:2;
Heb 9:2;
Rev 1:12

incense; ⁷and onyx stones and other gems to be mounted on the ephod*a* and breastpiece.*b*

⁸"Then have them make a sanctuary*c* for me, and I will dwell*d* among them. ⁹Make this tabernacle and all its furnishings exactly like the pattern*e* I will show you.

¹⁰"Have them make a chest*f* of acacia wood—two and a half cubits long, a cubit and a half wide, and a cubit and a half high.*a* ¹¹Overlay it with pure gold, both inside and out, and make a gold molding around it. ¹²Cast four gold rings for it and fasten them to its four feet, with two rings on one side and two rings on the other. ¹³Then make poles of acacia wood and overlay them with gold. ¹⁴Insert the poles into the rings on the sides of the chest to carry it. ¹⁵The poles are to remain in the rings of this ark; they are not to be removed.*g* ¹⁶Then put in the ark the Testimony,*h* which I will give you.

¹⁷"Make an atonement cover*bi* of pure gold—two and a half cubits long and a cubit and a half wide.*c* ¹⁸And make two cherubim out of hammered gold at the ends of the cover. ¹⁹Make one cherub on one end and the second cherub on the other; make the cherubim of one piece with the cover, at the two ends. ²⁰The cherubim are to have their wings spread upward, overshadowing*j* the cover with them. The cherubim are to face each other, looking toward the cover. ²¹Place the cover on top of the ark*k* and put in the ark the Testimony,*l* which I will give you. ²²There, above the cover between the two cherubim*m* that are over the ark of the Testimony, I will meet*n* with you and give you all my commands for the Israelites.

Ark of the Covenant (or Testimony)

²³"Make a table*o* of acacia wood—two cubits long, a cubit wide and a cubit and a half high.*d* ²⁴Overlay it with pure gold and make a gold molding around it. ²⁵Also make around it a rim a handbreadth*e* wide and put a gold molding on the rim. ²⁶Make four gold rings for the table and fasten them to the four corners, where the four legs are. ²⁷The rings are to be close to the rim to hold the poles used in carrying the table. ²⁸Make the poles of acacia wood, overlay them with gold and carry the table with them. ²⁹And make its plates and dishes of pure gold, as well as its pitchers and bowls for the pouring out of offerings.*p* ³⁰Put the bread of the Presence*q* on this table to be before me at all times.

³¹"Make a lampstand*r* of pure gold and hammer it out, base and shaft; its flowerlike cups, buds and blossoms shall be of one piece with it. ³²Six branches are to extend from the sides of the

Table for Consecrated Bread

a10 That is, about 3 3/4 feet (about 1.1 meters) long and 2 1/4 feet (about 0.7 meter) wide and high   *b17* Traditionally *a mercy seat*   *c17* That is, about 3 3/4 feet (about 1.1 meters) long and 2 1/4 feet (about 0.7 meter) wide   *d23* That is, about 3 feet (about 0.9 meter) long and 1 1/2 feet (about 0.5 meter) wide and 2 1/4 feet (about 0.7 meter) high   *e25* That is, about 3 inches (about 8 centimeters)

Lampstand

lampstand—three on one side and three on the other. ³³Three cups shaped like almond flowers with buds and blossoms are to be on one branch, three on the next branch, and the same for all six branches extending from the lampstand. ³⁴And on the lampstand there are to be four cups shaped like almond flowers with buds and blossoms. ³⁵One bud shall be under the first pair of branches extending from the lampstand, a second bud under the second pair, and a third bud under the third pair—six branches in all. ³⁶The buds and branches shall all be of one piece with the lampstand, hammered out of pure gold.

³⁷"Then make its seven lamps*a* and set them up on it so that they light the space in front of it. ³⁸Its wick trimmers and trays are to be of pure gold. ³⁹A talent*a* of pure gold is to be used for the lampstand and all these accessories. ⁴⁰See that you make them according to the pattern*b* shown you on the mountain.

Chapter 26 Theme

26 "Make the tabernacle with ten curtains of finely twisted linen and blue, purple and scarlet yarn, with cherubim worked into them by a skilled craftsman. ²All the curtains are to be the same size—twenty-eight cubits long and four cubits wide.*b* ³Join five of the curtains together, and do the same with the other five. ⁴Make loops of blue material along the edge of the end curtain in one set, and do the same with the end curtain in the other set. ⁵Make fifty loops on one curtain and fifty loops on the end curtain of the other set, with the loops opposite each other. ⁶Then make fifty gold clasps and use them to fasten the curtains together so that the tabernacle is a unit.

⁷"Make curtains of goat hair for the tent over the tabernacle—eleven altogether. ⁸All eleven curtains are to be the same size—thirty cubits long and four cubits wide.*c* ⁹Join five of the curtains together into one set and the other six into another set. Fold the sixth curtain double at the front of the tent. ¹⁰Make fifty loops along the edge of the end curtain in one set and also along the edge of the end curtain in the other set. ¹¹Then make fifty bronze clasps and put them in the loops to fasten the tent together as a unit. ¹²As for the additional length of the tent curtains, the half curtain that is left over is to hang down at the rear of the tabernacle. ¹³The tent curtains will be a cubit*d* longer on both sides; what is left will hang over the sides of the tabernacle so as to cover it. ¹⁴Make for the tent a covering of ram skins dyed red, and over that a covering of hides of sea cows.*ec*

a39 That is, about 75 pounds (about 34 kilograms)   b2 That is, about 42 feet (about 12.5 meters) long and 6 feet (about 1.8 meters) wide   c8 That is, about 45 feet (about 13.5 meters) long and 6 feet (about 1.8 meters) wide   d13 That is, about 1 1/2 feet (about 0.5 meter)   e14 That is, dugongs

25:37
a Ex 27:21; Lev 24:3-4; Nu 8:2

25:40
b Ex 26:30; Nu 8:4; Ac 7:44; Heb 8:5*

26:14
c Ex 36:19; Nu 4:25

26:30
a Ex 25:9,40;
Ac 7:44;
Heb 8:5

¹⁵"Make upright frames of acacia wood for the tabernacle. ¹⁶Each frame is to be ten cubits long and a cubit and a half wide,ᵃ ¹⁷with two projections set parallel to each other. Make all the frames of the tabernacle in this way. ¹⁸Make twenty frames for the south side of the tabernacle ¹⁹and make forty silver bases to go under them—two bases for each frame, one under each projection. ²⁰For the other side, the north side of the tabernacle, make twenty frames ²¹and forty silver bases—two under each frame.

26:31
b 2Ch 3:14;
Mt 27:51;
Heb 9:3
c Ex 36:35

²²Make six frames for the far end, that is, the west end of the tabernacle, ²³and make two frames for the corners at the far end. ²⁴At these two corners they must be double from the bottom all the way to the top, and fitted into a single ring; both shall be like that. ²⁵So there will be eight frames and sixteen silver bases—two under each frame.

²⁶"Also make crossbars of acacia wood: five for the frames on one side of the tabernacle, ²⁷five for those on the other side, and five for the frames on the west, at the far end of the tabernacle.

26:33
d Ex 40:3,21;
Lev 16:2
e Heb 9:2-3

²⁸The center crossbar is to extend from end to end at the middle of the frames. ²⁹Overlay the frames with gold and make gold rings to hold the crossbars. Also overlay the crossbars with gold.

³⁰"Set up the tabernacle according to the planᵃ shown you on the mountain.

³¹"Make a curtainᵇ of blue, purple and scarlet yarn and finely twisted linen, with cherubimᶜ worked into it by a skilled craftsman. ³²Hang it with gold hooks on four posts of acacia wood

26:34
f Ex 25:21;
40:20;
Heb 9:5

overlaid with gold and standing on four silver bases. ³³Hang the curtain from the clasps and place the ark of the Testimony behind the curtain.ᵈ The curtain will separate the Holy Place from the Most Holy Place.ᵉ ³⁴Put the atonement coverᶠ on the ark of the Testimony in the Most Holy Place. ³⁵Place the tableᵍ outside the curtain on the north side of the tabernacle and put the lampstandʰ

26:35
g Heb 9:2
h Ex 40:22,24

opposite it on the south side.

³⁶"For the entrance to the tent make a curtain of blue, purple and scarlet yarn and finely twisted linen—the work of an embroiderer. ³⁷Make gold hooks for this curtain and five posts of acacia wood overlaid with gold. And cast five bronze bases for them.

Chapter 27 Theme _____

27:1
i Eze 43:13

27 "Build an altarⁱ of acacia wood, three cubitsᵇ high; it is to be square, five cubits long and five cubits wide.ᶜ ²Make a hornʲ at each of the four corners, so that the horns and the altar are of one piece, and overlay the altar with bronze. ³Make all its utensils of bronze—its pots to remove the ashes, and its shovels,

*Bronze
Altar*

27:2
j Ps 118:27

ᵃ16 That is, about 15 feet (about 4.5 meters) long and 2 1/4 feet (about 0.7 meter) wide
ᵇ1 That is, about 4 1/2 feet (about 1.3 meters) ᶜ1 That is, about 7 1/2 feet (about 2.3 meters) long and wide

sprinkling bowls, meat forks and firepans. ⁴Make a grating for it, a bronze network, and make a bronze ring at each of the four corners of the network. ⁵Put it under the ledge of the altar so that it is halfway up the altar. ⁶Make poles of acacia wood for the altar and overlay them with bronze. ⁷The poles are to be inserted into the rings so they will be on two sides of the altar when it is carried. ⁸Make the altar hollow, out of boards. It is to be made just as you were shown*a* on the mountain.

⁹"Make a courtyard for the tabernacle. The south side shall be a hundred cubits*a* long and is to have curtains of finely twisted linen, ¹⁰with twenty posts and twenty bronze bases and with silver hooks and bands on the posts. ¹¹The north side shall also be a hundred cubits long and is to have curtains, with twenty posts and twenty bronze bases and with silver hooks and bands on the posts.

¹²"The west end of the courtyard shall be fifty cubits*b* wide and have curtains, with ten posts and ten bases. ¹³On the east end, toward the sunrise, the courtyard shall also be fifty cubits wide. ¹⁴Curtains fifteen cubits*c* long are to be on one side of the entrance, with three posts and three bases, ¹⁵and curtains fifteen cubits long are to be on the other side, with three posts and three bases.

¹⁶"For the entrance to the courtyard, provide a curtain twenty cubits*d* long, of blue, purple and scarlet yarn and finely twisted linen—the work of an embroiderer—with four posts and four bases. ¹⁷All the posts around the courtyard are to have silver bands and hooks, and bronze bases. ¹⁸The courtyard shall be a hundred cubits long and fifty cubits wide,*e* with curtains of finely twisted linen five cubits*f* high, and with bronze bases. ¹⁹All the other articles used in the service of the tabernacle, whatever their function, including all the tent pegs for it and those for the courtyard, are to be of bronze.

²⁰"Command the Israelites to bring you clear oil of pressed olives for the light so that the lamps may be kept burning. ²¹In the Tent of Meeting,*b* outside the curtain that is in front of the Testimony,*c* Aaron and his sons are to keep the lamps*d* burning before the LORD from evening till morning. This is to be a lasting ordinance*e* among the Israelites for the generations to come.

Chapter 28 Theme _____

28 "Have Aaron*f* your brother brought to you from among the Israelites, along with his sons Nadab and Abihu, Eleazar and Ithamar, so they may serve me as priests.*g* ²Make sacred garments*h* for your brother Aaron, to give him dignity and honor.

---

a9 That is, about 150 feet (about 46 meters); also in verse 11   b12 That is, about 75 feet (about 23 meters); also in verse 13   c14 That is, about 22 1/2 feet (about 6.9 meters); also in verse 15   d16 That is, about 30 feet (about 9 meters)   e18 That is, about 150 feet (about 46 meters) long and 75 feet (about 23 meters) wide   f18 That is, about 7 1/2 feet (about 2.3 meters)

27:8
a Ex 25:9,40

27:21
b Ex 28:43
c Ex 26:31,33
d Ex 25:37; 30:8;
1Sa 3:3;
2Ch 13:11
e Ex 29:9;
Lev 3:17; 16:34;
Nu 18:23; 19:21

28:1
f Heb 5:4
g Nu 18:1-7;
Heb 5:1

28:2
h Ex 29:5,29;
31:10; 39:1;
Lev 8:7-9,30

³Tell all the skilled men*ᵃ* to whom I have given wisdom*ᵇ* in such matters that they are to make garments for Aaron, for his consecration, so he may serve me as priest. ⁴These are the garments they are to make: a breastpiece,*ᶜ* an ephod, a robe,*ᵈ* a woven tunic,*ᵉ* a turban and a sash. They are to make these sacred garments for your brother Aaron and his sons, so they may serve me as priests. ⁵Have them use gold, and blue, purple and scarlet yarn, and fine linen.

⁶"Make the ephod of gold, and of blue, purple and scarlet yarn, and of finely twisted linen—the work of a skilled craftsman. ⁷It is to have two shoulder pieces attached to two of its corners, so it can be fastened. ⁸Its skillfully woven waistband is to be like it—of one piece with the ephod and made with gold, and with blue, purple and scarlet yarn, and with finely twisted linen.

⁹"Take two onyx stones and engrave on them the names of the sons of Israel ¹⁰in the order of their birth—six names on one stone and the remaining six on the other. ¹¹Engrave the names of the sons of Israel on the two stones the way a gem cutter engraves a seal. Then mount the stones in gold filigree settings ¹²and fasten them on the shoulder pieces of the ephod as memorial stones for the sons of Israel. Aaron is to bear the names on his shoulders as a memorial before the LORD. ¹³Make gold filigree settings ¹⁴and two braided chains of pure gold, like a rope, and attach the chains to the settings.

¹⁵"Fashion a breastpiece for making decisions—the work of a skilled craftsman. Make it like the ephod: of gold, and of blue, purple and scarlet yarn, and of finely twisted linen. ¹⁶It is to be square—a span*ᵃ* long and a span wide—and folded double. ¹⁷Then mount four rows of precious stones on it. In the first row there shall be a ruby, a topaz and a beryl; ¹⁸in the second row a turquoise, a sapphire*ᵇ* and an emerald; ¹⁹in the third row a jacinth, an agate and an amethyst; ²⁰in the fourth row a chrysolite, an onyx and a jasper.*ᶜ* Mount them in gold filigree settings. ²¹There are to be twelve stones, one for each of the names of the sons of Israel, each engraved like a seal with the name of one of the twelve tribes.

²²"For the breastpiece make braided chains of pure gold, like a rope. ²³Make two gold rings for it and fasten them to two corners of the breastpiece. ²⁴Fasten the two gold chains to the rings at the corners of the breastpiece, ²⁵and the other ends of the chains to the two settings, attaching them to the shoulder pieces of the ephod at the front. ²⁶Make two gold rings and attach them to the other two corners of the breastpiece on the inside edge next to the ephod. ²⁷Make two more gold rings and attach them to the

INSIGHT

The *ephod* was used to seek guidance from God. Described in Exodus 28, it was a linen garment worn by the priest and also by David when he was king (2 Samuel 6:14). The ephod was fastened on each shoulder by onyx clasps which had the names of six tribes engraved on one clasp and six tribes engraved on the other. The **breastpiece**, which was fastened to the ephod, had a linen pouch which held the **Urim** and **Thummim**, which may have been used as sacred lots to reveal God's will (1 Samuel 28:6).

Ephod

ᵃ16 That is, about 9 inches (about 22 centimeters)   *ᵇ18* Or *lapis lazuli*   *ᶜ20* The precise identification of some of these precious stones is uncertain.

*High Priest's
Garments*

*Robe of
the Ephod*

*Turban with
Plate of Gold*

bottom of the shoulder pieces on the front of the ephod, close to the seam just above the waistband of the ephod. ²⁸The rings of the breastpiece are to be tied to the rings of the ephod with blue cord, connecting it to the waistband, so that the breastpiece will not swing out from the ephod.

²⁹"Whenever Aaron enters the Holy Place,ᵃ he will bear the names of the sons of Israel over his heart on the breastpiece of decision as a continuing memorial before the LORD. ³⁰Also put the Urim and the Thummimᵇ in the breastpiece, so they may be over Aaron's heart whenever he enters the presence of the LORD. Thus Aaron will always bear the means of making decisions for the Israelites over his heart before the LORD.

³¹"Make the robe of the ephod entirely of blue cloth, ³²with an opening for the head in its center. There shall be a woven edge like a collarᵃ around this opening, so that it will not tear. ³³Make pomegranates of blue, purple and scarlet yarn around the hem of the robe, with gold bells between them. ³⁴The gold bells and the pomegranates are to alternate around the hem of the robe. ³⁵Aaron must wear it when he ministers. The sound of the bells will be heard when he enters the Holy Place before the LORD and when he comes out, so that he will not die.

³⁶"Make a plate of pure gold and engrave on it as on a seal: HOLY TO THE LORD.ᶜ ³⁷Fasten a blue cord to it to attach it to the turban; it is to be on the front of the turban. ³⁸It will be on Aaron's forehead, and he will bear the guiltᵈ involved in the sacred gifts the Israelites consecrate, whatever their gifts may be. It will be on Aaron's forehead continually so that they will be acceptable to the LORD.

³⁹"Weave the tunic of fine linen and make the turban of fine linen. The sash is to be the work of an embroiderer. ⁴⁰Make tunics, sashes and headbands for Aaron's sons,ᵉ to give them dignity and honor. ⁴¹After you put these clothes on your brother Aaron and his sons, anointᶠ and ordain them. Consecrate them so they may serve me as priests.ᵍ

⁴²"Make linen undergarmentsʰ as a covering for the body, reaching from the waist to the thigh. ⁴³Aaron and his sons must wear them whenever they enter the Tent of Meetingⁱ or approach the altar to minister in the Holy Place, so that they will not incur guilt and die.ʲ

"This is to be a lasting ordinanceᵏ for Aaron and his descendants.

Chapter 29 Theme

29 "This is what you are to do to consecrate them, so they may serve me as priests: Take a young bull and two rams without defect. ²And from fine wheat flour, without yeast, make

ᵃ32 The meaning of the Hebrew for this word is uncertain.

28:29
ᵃ ver 12

28:30
ᵇ Lev 8:8;
Nu 27:21;
Dt 33:8;
Ezr 2:63;
Ne 7:65

28:36
ᶜ Zec 14:20

28:38
ᵈ Lev 10:17;
22:9,16;
Nu 18:1;
Heb 9:28;
1Pe 2:24

28:40
ᵉ ver 4;
Ex 39:41

28:41
ᶠ Ex 29:7;
Lev 10:7
ᵍ Ex 29:7-9;
30:30; 40:15;
Lev 8:1-36;
Heb 7:28

28:42
ʰ Lev 6:10;
16:4,23;
Eze 44:18

28:43
ⁱ Ex 27:21
ʲ Ex 20:26
ᵏ Lev 17:7

29:2
a Lev 2:1,4;
6:19-23

29:4
b Ex 40:12;
Heb 10:22

29:5
c Ex 28:2;
Lev 8:7
d Ex 28:8

29:6
e Lev 8:9

29:7
f Ex 30:25,
30,31;
Lev 8:12; 21:10;
Nu 35:25;
Ps 133:2

29:9
g Ex 28:40
h Ex 40:15;
Nu 3:10;
18:7; 25:13;
Dt 18:5

29:10
i Lev 1:4

29:12
j Ex 27:2

29:13
k Lev 3:3,5,9

29:14
l Lev 4:11-12, 21;
Heb 13:11

29:18
m Ge 8:21

29:19
n ver 3

29:21
o Heb 9:22
p Ex 30:25,31
q ver 1

29:24
r Lev 7:30

bread, and cakes mixed with oil, and wafers spread with oil.*a* ³Put them in a basket and present them in it—along with the bull and the two rams. ⁴Then bring Aaron and his sons to the entrance to the Tent of Meeting and wash them with water.*b* ⁵Take the garments*c* and dress Aaron with the tunic, the robe of the ephod, the ephod itself and the breastpiece. Fasten the ephod on him by its skillfully woven waistband.*d* ⁶Put the turban on his head and attach the sacred diadem*e* to the turban. ⁷Take the anointing oil*f* and anoint him by pouring it on his head. ⁸Bring his sons and dress them in tunics ⁹and put headbands on them. Then tie sashes on Aaron and his sons.*ag* The priesthood is theirs by a lasting ordinance.*h* In this way you shall ordain Aaron and his sons.

¹⁰"Bring the bull to the front of the Tent of Meeting, and Aaron and his sons shall lay their hands on its head.*i* ¹¹Slaughter it in the LORD's presence at the entrance to the Tent of Meeting. ¹²Take some of the bull's blood and put it on the horns*j* of the altar with your finger, and pour out the rest of it at the base of the altar. ¹³Then take all the fat*k* around the inner parts, the covering of the liver, and both kidneys with the fat on them, and burn them on the altar. ¹⁴But burn the bull's flesh and its hide and its offal outside the camp.*l* It is a sin offering.

¹⁵"Take one of the rams, and Aaron and his sons shall lay their hands on its head. ¹⁶Slaughter it and take the blood and sprinkle it against the altar on all sides. ¹⁷Cut the ram into pieces and wash the inner parts and the legs, putting them with the head and the other pieces. ¹⁸Then burn the entire ram on the altar. It is a burnt offering to the LORD, a pleasing aroma,*m* an offering made to the LORD by fire.

¹⁹"Take the other ram,*n* and Aaron and his sons shall lay their hands on its head. ²⁰Slaughter it, take some of its blood and put it on the lobes of the right ears of Aaron and his sons, on the thumbs of their right hands, and on the big toes of their right feet. Then sprinkle blood against the altar on all sides. ²¹And take some of the blood*o* on the altar and some of the anointing oil*p* and sprinkle it on Aaron and his garments and on his sons and their garments. Then he and his sons and their garments will be consecrated.*q*

²²"Take from this ram the fat, the fat tail, the fat around the inner parts, the covering of the liver, both kidneys with the fat on them, and the right thigh. (This is the ram for the ordination.) ²³From the basket of bread made without yeast, which is before the LORD, take a loaf, and a cake made with oil, and a wafer. ²⁴Put all these in the hands of Aaron and his sons and wave them before the LORD as a wave offering.*r* ²⁵Then take them from their hands

a9 Hebrew; Septuagint *on them*

and burn them on the altar along with the burnt offering for a pleasing aroma to the LORD, an offering made to the LORD by fire. ²⁶After you take the breast of the ram for Aaron's ordination, wave it before the LORD as a wave offering, and it will be your share.ᵃ

²⁷"Consecrate those parts of the ordination ram that belong to Aaron and his sons:ᵇ the breast that was waved and the thigh that was presented. ²⁸This is always to be the regular share from the Israelites for Aaron and his sons. It is the contribution the Israelites are to make to the LORD from their fellowship offerings.ᵃᶜ

²⁹"Aaron's sacred garments will belong to his descendants so that they can be anointed and ordained in them.ᵈ ³⁰The sonᵉ who succeeds him as priest and comes to the Tent of Meeting to minister in the Holy Place is to wear them seven days.

³¹"Take the ram for the ordination and cook the meat in a sacred place. ³²At the entrance to the Tent of Meeting, Aaron and his sons are to eat the meat of the ram and the breadᶠ that is in the basket. ³³They are to eat these offerings by which atonement was made for their ordination and consecration. But no one else may eatᵍ them, because they are sacred. ³⁴And if any of the meat of the ordination ram or any bread is left over till morning,ʰ burn it up. It must not be eaten, because it is sacred.

³⁵"Do for Aaron and his sons everything I have commanded you, taking seven days to ordain them. ³⁶Sacrifice a bull each dayⁱ as a sin offering to make atonement. Purify the altar by making atonement for it, and anoint it to consecrateʲ it. ³⁷For seven days make atonement for the altar and consecrate it. Then the altar will be most holy, and whatever touches it will be holy.ᵏ

³⁸"This is what you are to offer on the altar regularly each day:ˡ two lambs a year old. ³⁹Offer one in the morning and the other at twilight.ᵐ ⁴⁰With the first lamb offer a tenth of an ephahᵇ of fine flour mixed with a quarter of a hinᶜ of oil from pressed olives, and a quarter of a hin of wine as a drink offering. ⁴¹Sacrifice the other lamb at twilight with the same grain offering and its drink offering as in the morning—a pleasing aroma, an offering made to the LORD by fire.

⁴²"For the generations to comeⁿ this burnt offering is to be made regularly at the entrance to the Tent of Meeting before the LORD. There I will meet you and speak to you;ᵒ ⁴³there also I will meet with the Israelites, and the place will be consecrated by my glory.ᵖ

⁴⁴"So I will consecrate the Tent of Meeting and the altar and will consecrate Aaron and his sons to serve me as priests.�q ⁴⁵Then I will dwellʳ among the Israelites and be their God.ˢ ⁴⁶They will

29:26
ᵃ Lev 7:31-34

29:27
ᵇ Lev 7:31,34; Dt 18:3

29:28
ᶜ Lev 10:15

29:29
ᵈ Nu 20:26,28

29:30
ᵉ Nu 20:28

29:32
ᶠ Mt 12:4

29:33
ᵍ Lev 10:14; 22:10,13

29:34
ʰ Ex 12:10

29:36
ⁱ Heb 10:11
ʲ Ex 40:10

29:37
ᵏ Ex 30:28-29; 40:10; Mt 23:19

29:38
ˡ Nu 28:3-8; 1Ch 16:40; Da 12:11

29:39
ᵐ Eze 46:13-15

29:42
ⁿ Ex 30:8
ᵒ Ex 25:22

29:43
ᵖ 1Ki 8:11

29:44
q Lev 21:15

29:45
ʳ Ex 25:8; Lev 26:12; Zec 2:10; Jn 14:17
ˢ 2Co 6:16; Rev 21:3

ᵃ28 Traditionally *peace offerings* ᵇ40 That is, probably about 2 quarts (about 2 liters) ᶜ40 That is, probably about 1 quart (about 1 liter)

29:46
a Ex 20:2

30:1
b Ex 37:25
c Rev 8:3

30:2
d Ex 27:2

30:6
e Ex 25:22;
26:34

30:7
f ver 34-35;
Ex 27:21;
1Sa 2:28

30:9
g Lev 10:1

30:10
h Lev 16:18-19,
30

30:12
i Ex 38:25;
Nu 1:2,49;
2Sa 24:1
j Nu 31:50;
Mt 20:28
k 2Sa 24:13

30:13
l Nu 3:47;
Mt 17:24

30:15
m Pr 22:2;
Eph 6:9

30:16
n Ex 38:25-28

30:18
o Ex 38:8;
40:7,30

30:19
p Ex 40:31-32;
Isa 52:11
q Ps 26:6

know that I am the LORD their God, who brought them out of Egypt so that I might dwell among them. I am the LORD their God.[a]

Chapter 30 Theme

30 "Make an altar[b] of acacia wood for burning incense.[c] [2]It is to be square, a cubit long and a cubit wide, and two cubits high[a]—its horns[d] of one piece with it. [3]Overlay the top and all the sides and the horns with pure gold, and make a gold molding around it. [4]Make two gold rings for the altar below the molding—two on opposite sides—to hold the poles used to carry it. [5]Make the poles of acacia wood and overlay them with gold. [6]Put the altar in front of the curtain that is before the ark of the Testimony—before the atonement cover[e] that is over the Testimony—where I will meet with you.

[7]"Aaron must burn fragrant incense[f] on the altar every morning when he tends the lamps. [8]He must burn incense again when he lights the lamps at twilight so incense will burn regularly before the LORD for the generations to come. [9]Do not offer on this altar any other incense[g] or any burnt offering or grain offering, and do not pour a drink offering on it. [10]Once a year Aaron shall make atonement[h] on its horns. This annual atonement must be made with the blood of the atoning sin offering for the generations to come. It is most holy to the LORD."

[11]Then the LORD said to Moses, [12]"When you take a census[i] of the Israelites to count them, each one must pay the LORD a ransom[j] for his life at the time he is counted. Then no plague[k] will come on them when you number them. [13]Each one who crosses over to those already counted is to give a half shekel,[b] according to the sanctuary shekel,[l] which weighs twenty gerahs. This half shekel is an offering to the LORD. [14]All who cross over, those twenty years old or more, are to give an offering to the LORD. [15]The rich are not to give more than a half shekel and the poor are not to give less[m] when you make the offering to the LORD to atone for your lives. [16]Receive the atonement money from the Israelites and use it for the service of the Tent of Meeting.[n] It will be a memorial for the Israelites before the LORD, making atonement for your lives."

[17]Then the LORD said to Moses, [18]"Make a bronze basin,[o] with its bronze stand, for washing. Place it between the Tent of Meeting and the altar, and put water in it. [19]Aaron and his sons are to wash their hands and feet[p] with water[q] from it. [20]Whenever they enter the Tent of Meeting, they shall wash with water so that they will

Altar of Incense (Gold or Golden Altar)

Bronze Basin

a2 That is, about 1 1/2 feet (about 0.5 meter) long and wide and about 3 feet (about 0.9 meter) high   b13 That is, about 1/5 ounce (about 6 grams); also in verse 15 not die. Also, when they approach the altar to minister by presenting an offering made to the LORD by fire, [21]they shall wash their hands and feet so that they will not die. This is to be a lasting ordinance[a] for Aaron and his descendants for the generations to come."

[22]Then the LORD said to Moses, [23]"Take the following fine spices: 500 shekels[a] of liquid myrrh,[b] half as much (that is, 250 shekels) of fragrant cinnamon, 250 shekels of fragrant cane, [24]500 shekels of cassia[c]—all according to the sanctuary shekel—and a hin[b] of olive oil. [25]Make these into a sacred anointing oil, a fragrant blend, the work of a perfumer.[d] It will be the sacred anointing oil.[e] [26]Then use it to anoint[f] the Tent of Meeting, the ark of the Testimony, [27]the table and all its articles, the lampstand and its accessories, the altar of incense, [28]the altar of burnt offering and all its utensils, and the basin with its stand. [29]You shall consecrate them so they will be most holy, and whatever touches them will be holy.[g]

[30]"Anoint Aaron and his sons and consecrate[h] them so they may serve me as priests. [31]Say to the Israelites, 'This is to be my sacred anointing oil for the generations to come. [32]Do not pour it on men's bodies and do not make any oil with the same formula. It is sacred, and you are to consider it sacred.[i] [33]Whoever makes perfume like it and whoever puts it on anyone other than a priest must be cut off[j] from his people.'"

[34]Then the LORD said to Moses, "Take fragrant spices—gum resin, onycha and galbanum—and pure frankincense, all in equal amounts, [35]and make a fragrant blend of incense, the work of a perfumer.[k] It is to be salted and pure and sacred. [36]Grind some of it to powder and place it in front of the Testimony in the Tent of Meeting, where I will meet with you. It shall be most holy[l] to you. [37]Do not make any incense with this formula for yourselves; consider it holy[m] to the LORD. [38]Whoever makes any like it to enjoy its fragrance must be cut off[n] from his people."

Chapter 31 Theme _____

31 Then the LORD said to Moses, [2]"See, I have chosen Bezalel[o] son of Uri, the son of Hur, of the tribe of Judah, [3]and I have filled him with the Spirit of God, with skill, ability and knowledge in all kinds of crafts[p]— [4]to make artistic designs for work in gold, silver and bronze, [5]to cut and set stones, to work in wood, and to engage in all kinds of craftsmanship. [6]Moreover, I have appointed Oholiab son of Ahisamach, of the tribe of Dan, to help him. Also I have given skill to all the craftsmen to make

30:21
a Ex 27:21;
28:43

30:23
b Ge 37:25

30:24
c Ps 45:8

30:25
d Ex 37:29
e Ex 40:9

30:26
f Ex 40:9;
Lev 8:10;
Nu 7:1

30:29
g Ex 29:37

30:30
h Ex 29:7;
Lev 8:2,12,30

30:32
i ver 25,37

30:33
j ver 38;
Ge 17:14

30:35
k ver 25

30:36
l ver 32;
Ex 29:37;
Lev 2:3

30:37
m ver 32

30:38
n ver 33

31:2
o Ex 36:1,2;
1Ch 2:20

31:3
p 1Ki 7:14

a23 That is, about 12 1/2 pounds (about 6 kilograms)   b24 That is, probably about 4 quarts (about 4 liters) everything I have commanded you: ⁷the Tent of Meeting,ᵃ the ark of the Testimonyᵇ with the atonement coverᶜ on it, and all the other furnishings of the tent— ⁸the tableᵈ and its articles, the pure gold lampstandᵉ and all its accessories, the altar of incense, ⁹the altar of burnt offering and all its utensils, the basin with its stand— ¹⁰and also the woven garments,ᶠ both the sacred garments for Aaron the priest and the garments for his sons when they serve as priests, ¹¹and the anointing oilᵍ and fragrant incense for the Holy Place. They are to make them just as I commanded you."

¹²Then the LORD said to Moses, ¹³"Say to the Israelites, 'You must observe my Sabbaths.ʰ This will be a signⁱ between me and you for the generations to come, so you may know that I am the LORD, who makes you holy.ᵃʲ

¹⁴"'Observe the Sabbath, because it is holy to you. Anyone who desecrates it must be put to death;ᵏ whoever does any work on that day must be cut off from his people. ¹⁵For six days, workˡ is to be done, but the seventh day is a Sabbath of rest,ᵐ holy to the LORD. Whoever does any work on the Sabbath day must be put to death. ¹⁶The Israelites are to observe the Sabbath, celebrating it for the generations to come as a lasting covenant. ¹⁷It will be a signⁿ between me and the Israelites forever, for in six days the LORD made the heavens and the earth, and on the seventh day he abstained from work and rested.ᵒ'"

¹⁸When the LORD finished speaking to Moses on Mount Sinai, he gave him the two tablets of the Testimony, the tablets of stoneᵖ inscribed by the finger of God.�q

Chapter 32 Theme

32 When the people saw that Moses was so long in coming down from the mountain,ʳ they gathered around Aaron and said, "Come, make us godsᵇ who will go before us. As for this fellow Moses who brought us up out of Egypt, we don't know what has happened to him."ˢ

²Aaron answered them, "Take off the gold earringsᵗ that your wives, your sons and your daughters are wearing, and bring them to me." ³So all the people took off their earrings and brought them to Aaron. ⁴He took what they handed him and made it into an idol cast in the shape of a calf,ᵘ fashioning it with a tool. Then they said, "These are your gods,ᶜ O Israel, who brought you up out of Egypt."

⁵When Aaron saw this, he built an altar in front of the calf and announced, "Tomorrow there will be a festivalᵛ to the LORD." ⁶So

ᵃ13 Or *who sanctifies you*; or *who sets you apart as holy*   ᵇ1 Or *a god*; also in verses 23 and 31   ᶜ4 Or *This is your god*; also in verse 8 the next day the people rose early and sacrificed burnt offerings and presented fellowship offerings.[aa] Afterward they sat down to eat and drink and got up to indulge in revelry.[b]

[7]Then the LORD said to Moses, "Go down, because your people, whom you brought up out of Egypt,[c] have become corrupt.[d] [8]They have been quick to turn away from what I commanded them and have made themselves an idol[e] cast in the shape of a calf. They have bowed down to it and sacrificed[f] to it and have said, 'These are your gods, O Israel, who brought you up out of Egypt.'[g]

[9]"I have seen these people," the LORD said to Moses, "and they are a stiff-necked[h] people. [10]Now leave me alone so that my anger may burn against them and that I may destroy them. Then I will make you into a great nation."[i]

[11]But Moses sought the favor[j] of the LORD his God. "O LORD," he said, "why should your anger burn against your people, whom you brought out of Egypt with great power and a mighty hand?[k] [12]Why should the Egyptians say, 'It was with evil intent that he brought them out, to kill them in the mountains and to wipe them off the face of the earth'?[l] Turn from your fierce anger; relent and do not bring disaster on your people. [13]Remember[m] your servants Abraham, Isaac and Israel, to whom you swore by your own self:[n] 'I will make your descendants as numerous as the stars[o] in the sky and I will give your descendants all this land[p] I promised them, and it will be their inheritance forever.'" [14]Then the LORD relented[q] and did not bring on his people the disaster he had threatened.

[15]Moses turned and went down the mountain with the two tablets of the Testimony[r] in his hands.[s] They were inscribed on both sides, front and back. [16]The tablets were the work of God; the writing was the writing of God, engraved on the tablets.[t]

[17]When Joshua heard the noise of the people shouting, he said to Moses, "There is the sound of war in the camp."

[18]Moses replied:

> "It is not the sound of victory,
>   it is not the sound of defeat;
>   it is the sound of singing that I hear."

[19]When Moses approached the camp and saw the calf[u] and the dancing, his anger burned and he threw the tablets out of his hands, breaking them to pieces[v] at the foot of the mountain. [20]And he took the calf they had made and burned it in the fire; then he ground it to powder, scattered it on the water[w] and made the Israelites drink it.

aa6 Traditionally *peace offerings*

Cross references

32:6
a Nu 25:2; Ac 7:41
b ver 17-19; 1Co 10:7*

32:7
c ver 4,11
d Ge 6:11-12; Dt 9:12

32:8
e Ex 20:4
f Ex 22:20
g 1Ki 12:28

32:9
h Ex 33:3,5; 34:9; Isa 48:4; Ac 7:51

32:10
i Nu 14:12; Dt 9:14

32:11
j Dt 9:18
k Dt 9:26

32:12
l Nu 14:13-16; Dt 9:28

32:13
m Ex 2:24
n Ge 22:16; Heb 6:13
o Ge 15:5; 26:4
p Ge 12:7

32:14
q 2Sa 24:16; Ps 106:45

32:15
r Ex 31:18
s Dt 9:15

32:16
t Ex 31:18

32:19
u Dt 9:16
v Dt 9:17

32:20
w Dt 9:21

32:22
a Dt 9:24

32:23
b ver 1

32:24
c ver 4

32:27
d Nu 25:3,5;
Dt 33:9

32:30
e 1Sa 12:20
f Lev 1:4;
Nu 25:13

32:31
g Dt 9:18
h Ex 20:23

32:32
i Ro 9:3
j Ps 69:28;
Da 12:1;
Php 4:3;
Rev 3:5; 21:27

32:33
k Dt 29:20;
Ps 9:5

32:34
l Ex 3:17
m Ex 23:20
n Dt 32:35;
Ps 99:8;
Ro 2:5-6

32:35
o ver 4

33:1
p Ge 12:7

33:2
q Ex 32:34
r Ex 23:27-31;
Jos 24:11

33:3
s Ex 3:8
t Ex 32:9
u Ex 32:10

²¹He said to Aaron, "What did these people do to you, that you led them into such great sin?"

²²"Do not be angry, my lord," Aaron answered. "You know how prone these people are to evil.*a* ²³They said to me, 'Make us gods who will go before us. As for this fellow Moses who brought us up out of Egypt, we don't know what has happened to him.'*b* ²⁴So I told them, 'Whoever has any gold jewelry, take it off.' Then they gave me the gold, and I threw it into the fire, and out came this calf!"*c*

²⁵Moses saw that the people were running wild and that Aaron had let them get out of control and so become a laughingstock to their enemies. ²⁶So he stood at the entrance to the camp and said, "Whoever is for the LORD, come to me." And all the Levites rallied to him.

²⁷Then he said to them, "This is what the LORD, the God of Israel, says: 'Each man strap a sword to his side. Go back and forth through the camp from one end to the other, each killing his brother and friend and neighbor.'"*d* ²⁸The Levites did as Moses commanded, and that day about three thousand of the people died. ²⁹Then Moses said, "You have been set apart to the LORD today, for you were against your own sons and brothers, and he has blessed you this day."

³⁰The next day Moses said to the people, "You have committed a great sin.*e* But now I will go up to the LORD; perhaps I can make atonement*f* for your sin."

³¹So Moses went back to the LORD and said, "Oh, what a great sin these people have committed!*g* They have made themselves gods of gold.*h* ³²But now, please forgive their sin—but if not, then blot me*i* out of the book*j* you have written."

³³The LORD replied to Moses, "Whoever has sinned against me I will blot out*k* of my book. ³⁴Now go, lead the people to the place*l* I spoke of, and my angel*m* will go before you. However, when the time comes for me to punish,*n* I will punish them for their sin."

³⁵And the LORD struck the people with a plague because of what they did with the calf*o* Aaron had made.

Chapter 33 Theme _____

33 Then the LORD said to Moses, "Leave this place, you and the people you brought up out of Egypt, and go up to the land I promised on oath to Abraham, Isaac and Jacob, saying, 'I will give it to your descendants.'*p* ²I will send an angel*q* before you and drive out the Canaanites, Amorites, Hittites, Perizzites, Hivites and Jebusites.*r* ³Go up to the land flowing with milk and honey.*s* But I will not go with you, because you are a stiff-necked*t* people and I might destroy*u* you on the way."

[4]When the people heard these distressing words, they began to mourn[a] and no one put on any ornaments. [5]For the LORD had said to Moses, "Tell the Israelites, 'You are a stiff-necked people. If I were to go with you even for a moment, I might destroy you. Now take off your ornaments and I will decide what to do with you.'" [6]So the Israelites stripped off their ornaments at Mount Horeb.

[7]Now Moses used to take a tent and pitch it outside the camp some distance away, calling it the "tent of meeting."[b] Anyone inquiring of the LORD would go to the tent of meeting outside the camp. [8]And whenever Moses went out to the tent, all the people rose and stood at the entrances to their tents,[c] watching Moses until he entered the tent. [9]As Moses went into the tent, the pillar of cloud[d] would come down and stay at the entrance, while the LORD spoke[e] with Moses. [10]Whenever the people saw the pillar of cloud standing at the entrance to the tent, they all stood and worshiped, each at the entrance to his tent. [11]The LORD would speak to Moses face to face,[f] as a man speaks with his friend. Then Moses would return to the camp, but his young aide Joshua son of Nun did not leave the tent.

[12]Moses said to the LORD, "You have been telling me, 'Lead these people,'[g] but you have not let me know whom you will send with me. You have said, 'I know you by name[h] and you have found favor with me.' [13]If you are pleased with me, teach me your ways[i] so I may know you and continue to find favor with you. Remember that this nation is your people."[j]

[14]The LORD replied, "My Presence[k] will go with you, and I will give you rest."[l]

[15]Then Moses said to him, "If your Presence does not go with us, do not send us up from here. [16]How will anyone know that you are pleased with me and with your people unless you go with us?[m] What else will distinguish me and your people from all the other people on the face of the earth?"[n]

[17]And the LORD said to Moses, "I will do the very thing you have asked, because I am pleased with you and I know you by name."

[18]Then Moses said, "Now show me your glory."

[19]And the LORD said, "I will cause all my goodness to pass in front of you, and I will proclaim my name, the LORD, in your presence. I will have mercy on whom I will have mercy, and I will have compassion on whom I will have compassion.[o] [20]But," he said, "you cannot see my face, for no one may see[p] me and live."

[21]Then the LORD said, "There is a place near me where you may stand on a rock. [22]When my glory passes by, I will put you in a cleft in the rock and cover you with my hand[q] until I have passed by. [23]Then I will remove my hand and you will see my back; but my face must not be seen."

33:4
a Nu 14:39

33:7
b Ex 29:42-43

33:8
c Nu 16:27

33:9
d Ex 13:21
e Ex 31:18;
Ps 99:7

33:11
f Nu 12:8;
Dt 34:10

33:12
g Ex 3:10
h ver 17;
Jn 10:14-15;
2Ti 2:19

33:13
i Ps 25:4; 86:11;
119:33
j Ex 34:9;
Dt 9:26,29

33:14
k Isa 63:9
l Jos 21:44; 22:4

33:16
m Nu 14:14
n Ex 34:10

33:19
o Ro 9:15*

33:20
p Ge 32:30;
Isa 6:5

33:22
q Ps 91:4

34:1
a Dt 10:2,4
b Ex 32:19

34:2
c Ex 19:11

34:3
d Ex 19:12-13, 21

34:5
e Ex 33:19

34:6
f Ps 86:15
g Nu 14:18;
Ro 2:4
h Ne 9:17;
Ps 103:8;
Joel 2:13
i Ps 108:4

34:7
j Ex 20:6
k Ps 103:3;
130:4,8;
Da 9:9;
1Jn 1:9
l Job 10:14;
Na 1:3

34:9
m Ex 33:15
n Ps 33:12

34:10
o Dt 5:2-3
p Ex 33:16;
Dt 4:32

34:11
q Ex 33:2

34:12
r Ex 23:32-33

34:13
s Ex 23:24;
Dt 12:3;
2Ki 18:4

34:14
t Ex 20:3
u Ex 20:5;
Dt 4:24

34:15
v Jdg 2:17
w Nu 25:2;
1Co 8:4

34:16
x Dt 7:3
y 1Ki 11:4

34:17
z Ex 32:8

34:18
a Ex 12:17
b Ex 12:15

Chapter 34 Theme _____

34 The LORD said to Moses, "Chisel out two stone tablets like the first ones, and I will write on them the words that were on the first tablets,*a* which you broke.*b* 2Be ready in the morning, and then come up on Mount Sinai.*c* Present yourself to me there on top of the mountain. 3No one is to come with you or be seen anywhere on the mountain;*d* not even the flocks and herds may graze in front of the mountain."

4So Moses chiseled out two stone tablets like the first ones and went up Mount Sinai early in the morning, as the LORD had commanded him; and he carried the two stone tablets in his hands. 5Then the LORD came down in the cloud and stood there with him and proclaimed his name, the LORD.*e* 6And he passed in front of Moses, proclaiming, "The LORD, the LORD, the compassionate*f* and gracious God, slow to anger,*g* abounding in love*h* and faithfulness,*i* 7maintaining love to thousands,*j* and forgiving wickedness, rebellion and sin.*k* Yet he does not leave the guilty unpunished;*l* he punishes the children and their children for the sin of the fathers to the third and fourth generation."

8Moses bowed to the ground at once and worshiped. 9"O Lord, if I have found favor in your eyes," he said, "then let the Lord go with us.*m* Although this is a stiff-necked people, forgive our wickedness and our sin, and take us as your inheritance."*n*

10Then the LORD said: "I am making a covenant*o* with you. Before all your people I will do wonders never before done in any nation in all the world.*p* The people you live among will see how awesome is the work that I, the LORD, will do for you. 11Obey what I command you today. I will drive out before you the Amorites, Canaanites, Hittites, Perizzites, Hivites and Jebusites.*q* 12Be careful not to make a treaty with those who live in the land where you are going, or they will be a snare*r* among you. 13Break down their altars, smash their sacred stones and cut down their Asherah poles.*a s* 14Do not worship any other god,*t* for the LORD, whose name is Jealous, is a jealous God.*u*

15"Be careful not to make a treaty with those who live in the land; for when they prostitute*v* themselves to their gods and sacrifice to them, they will invite you and you will eat their sacrifices.*w* 16And when you choose some of their daughters as wives*x* for your sons and those daughters prostitute themselves to their gods,*y* they will lead your sons to do the same.

17"Do not make cast idols.*z*

18"Celebrate the Feast of Unleavened Bread.*a* For seven days eat bread made without yeast,*b* as I commanded you. Do this at

a13 That is, symbols of the goddess Asherah

the appointed time in the month of Abib,[a] for in that month you came out of Egypt.

19"The first offspring[b] of every womb belongs to me, including all the firstborn males of your livestock, whether from herd or flock. 20Redeem the firstborn donkey with a lamb, but if you do not redeem it, break its neck.[c] Redeem all your firstborn sons.

"No one is to appear before me empty-handed.[d]

21"Six days you shall labor, but on the seventh day you shall rest;[e] even during the plowing season and harvest you must rest.

22"Celebrate the Feast of Weeks with the firstfruits of the wheat harvest, and the Feast of Ingathering[f] at the turn of the year.[a] 23Three times[g] a year all your men are to appear before the Sovereign LORD, the God of Israel. 24I will drive out nations[h] before you and enlarge your territory, and no one will covet your land when you go up three times each year to appear before the LORD your God.

25"Do not offer the blood of a sacrifice to me along with anything containing yeast,[i] and do not let any of the sacrifice from the Passover Feast remain until morning.[j]

26"Bring the best of the firstfruits of your soil to the house of the LORD your God.

"Do not cook a young goat in its mother's milk."[k]

27Then the LORD said to Moses, "Write[l] down these words, for in accordance with these words I have made a covenant with you and with Israel." 28Moses was there with the LORD forty days and forty nights[m] without eating bread or drinking water. And he wrote on the tablets[n] the words of the covenant—the Ten Commandments.[o]

29When Moses came down from Mount Sinai with the two tablets of the Testimony in his hands,[p] he was not aware that his face was radiant[q] because he had spoken with the LORD. 30When Aaron and all the Israelites saw Moses, his face was radiant, and they were afraid to come near him. 31But Moses called to them; so Aaron and all the leaders of the community came back to him, and he spoke to them. 32Afterward all the Israelites came near him, and he gave them all the commands[r] the LORD had given him on Mount Sinai.

33When Moses finished speaking to them, he put a veil[s] over his face. 34But whenever he entered the LORD's presence to speak with him, he removed the veil until he came out. And when he came out and told the Israelites what he had been commanded, 35they saw that his face was radiant. Then Moses would put the veil back over his face until he went in to speak with the LORD.

a22 That is, in the fall

34:18
a Ex 12:2

34:19
b Ex 13:2

34:20
c Ex 13:13,15
d Ex 23:15;
Dt 16:16

34:21
e Ex 20:9;
Lk 13:14

34:22
f Ex 23:16

34:23
g Ex 23:14

34:24
h Ex 23:28;
33:2;
Ps 78:55

34:25
i Ex 23:18
j Ex 12:8,10

34:26
k Ex 23:19

34:27
l Ex 17:14;
24:4

34:28
m Ge 7:4;
Ex 24:18;
Mt 4:2
n ver 1;
Ex 31:18
o Dt 4:13;
10:4

34:29
p Ex 32:15
q Ps 34:5;
Mt 17:2;
2Co 3:7,13

34:32
r Ex 24:3

34:33
s 2Co 3:13

Chapter 35 Theme

35 Moses assembled the whole Israelite community and said to them, "These are the things the LORD has commanded[a] you to do: ²For six days, work is to be done, but the seventh day shall be your holy day, a Sabbath[b] of rest to the LORD. Whoever does any work on it must be put to death. ³Do not light a fire in any of your dwellings on the Sabbath day.[c]"

⁴Moses said to the whole Israelite community, "This is what the LORD has commanded: ⁵From what you have, take an offering for the LORD. Everyone who is willing is to bring to the LORD an offering of gold, silver and bronze; ⁶blue, purple and scarlet yarn and fine linen; goat hair; ⁷ram skins dyed red and hides of sea cows[a]; acacia wood; ⁸olive oil for the light; spices for the anointing oil and for the fragrant incense; ⁹and onyx stones and other gems to be mounted on the ephod and breastpiece.

¹⁰"All who are skilled among you are to come and make everything the LORD has commanded:[d] ¹¹the tabernacle[e] with its tent and its covering, clasps, frames, crossbars, posts and bases; ¹²the ark[f] with its poles and the atonement cover and the curtain that shields it; ¹³the table[g] with its poles and all its articles and the bread of the Presence; ¹⁴the lampstand[h] that is for light with its accessories, lamps and oil for the light; ¹⁵the altar[i] of incense with its poles, the anointing oil[j] and the fragrant incense;[k] the curtain for the doorway at the entrance to the tabernacle; ¹⁶the altar[l] of burnt offering with its bronze grating, its poles and all its utensils; the bronze basin with its stand; ¹⁷the curtains of the courtyard with its posts and bases, and the curtain for the entrance to the courtyard;[m] ¹⁸the tent pegs for the tabernacle and for the courtyard, and their ropes; ¹⁹the woven garments worn for ministering in the sanctuary—both the sacred garments[n] for Aaron the priest and the garments for his sons when they serve as priests."

²⁰Then the whole Israelite community withdrew from Moses' presence, ²¹and everyone who was willing and whose heart moved him came and brought an offering to the LORD for the work on the Tent of Meeting, for all its service, and for the sacred garments. ²²All who were willing, men and women alike, came and brought gold jewelry of all kinds: brooches, earrings, rings and ornaments. They all presented their gold as a wave offering to the LORD. ²³Everyone who had blue, purple or scarlet yarn[o] or fine linen, or goat hair, ram skins dyed red or hides of sea cows brought them. ²⁴Those presenting an offering of silver or bronze brought it as an offering to the LORD, and everyone who had acacia wood for any part of the work brought it. ²⁵Every skilled

35:1
a Ex 34:32

35:2
b Ex 20:9-10;
34:21;
Lev 23:3

35:3
c Ex 16:23

35:10
d Ex 31:6

35:11
e Ex 26:1-37

35:12
f Ex 25:10-22

35:13
g Ex 25:23-30;
Lev 24:5-6

35:14
h Ex 25:31

35:15
i Ex 30:1-6
j Ex 30:25
k Ex 30:34-38

35:16
l Ex 27:1-8

35:17
m Ex 27:9

35:19
n Ex 28:2; 31:10;
39:1

35:23
o 1Ch 29:8

a 7 That is, dugongs; also in verse 23

woman[a] spun with her hands and brought what she had spun—blue, purple or scarlet yarn or fine linen. 26And all the women who were willing and had the skill spun the goat hair. 27The leaders[b] brought onyx stones and other gems to be mounted on the ephod and breastpiece. 28They also brought spices and olive oil for the light and for the anointing oil and for the fragrant incense.[c] 29All the Israelite men and women who were willing[d] brought to the LORD freewill offerings[e] for all the work the LORD through Moses had commanded them to do.

30Then Moses said to the Israelites, "See, the LORD has chosen Bezalel son of Uri, the son of Hur, of the tribe of Judah, 31and he has filled him with the Spirit of God, with skill, ability and knowledge in all kinds of crafts[f]— 32to make artistic designs for work in gold, silver and bronze, 33to cut and set stones, to work in wood and to engage in all kinds of artistic craftsmanship. 34And he has given both him and Oholiab[g] son of Ahisamach, of the tribe of Dan, the ability to teach[h] others. 35He has filled them with skill to do all kinds of work[i] as craftsmen, designers, embroiderers in blue, purple and scarlet yarn and fine linen, and weavers—all of them master craftsmen and designers.

Chapter 36 Theme

36 So Bezalel, Oholiab and every skilled person[j] to whom the LORD has given skill and ability to know how to carry out all the work of constructing the sanctuary[k] are to do the work just as the Lord has commanded."

2Then Moses summoned Bezalel[l] and Oholiab[m] and every skilled person to whom the LORD had given ability and who was willing[n] to come and do the work. 3They received from Moses all the offerings[o] the Israelites had brought to carry out the work of constructing the sanctuary. And the people continued to bring freewill offerings morning after morning. 4So all the skilled craftsmen who were doing all the work on the sanctuary left their work 5and said to Moses, "The people are bringing more than enough[p] for doing the work the LORD commanded to be done."

6Then Moses gave an order and they sent this word throughout the camp: "No man or woman is to make anything else as an offering for the sanctuary." And so the people were restrained from bringing more, 7because what they already had was more[q] than enough to do all the work.

8All the skilled men among the workmen made the tabernacle with ten curtains of finely twisted linen and blue, purple and scarlet yarn, with cherubim worked into them by a skilled craftsman. 9All the curtains were the same size—twenty-eight cubits long and

35:25
a Ex 28:3

35:27
b 1Ch 29:6;
Ezr 2:68

35:28
c Ex 25:6

35:29
d ver 21;
1Ch 29:9
e ver 4-9;
Ex 25:1-7; 36:3;
2Ki 12:4

35:31
f ver 35;
2Ch 2:7,14

35:34
g Ex 31:6
h 2Ch 2:14

35:35
i ver 31;
Ex 31:3,6;
1Ki 7:14

36:1
j Ex 28:3
k Ex 25:8

36:2
l Ex 31:2
m Ex 31:6
n Ex 25:2;
35:21,26;
1Ch 29:5

36:3
o Ex 35:29

36:5
p 2Ch 24:14;
31:10;
2 Co 8:2-3

36:7
q 1Ki 7:47

36:13
a ver 18

four cubits wide.ᵃ ¹⁰They joined five of the curtains together and did the same with the other five. ¹¹Then they made loops of blue material along the edge of the end curtain in one set, and the same was done with the end curtain in the other set. ¹²They also made fifty loops on one curtain and fifty loops on the end curtain of the other set, with the loops opposite each other. ¹³Then they made fifty gold clasps and used them to fasten the two sets of curtains together so that the tabernacle was a unit.ᵃ

¹⁴They made curtains of goat hair for the tent over the tabernacle—eleven altogether. ¹⁵All eleven curtains were the same size—thirty cubits long and four cubits wide.ᵇ ¹⁶They joined five of the curtains into one set and the other six into another set. ¹⁷Then they made fifty loops along the edge of the end curtain in one set and also along the edge of the end curtain in the other set. ¹⁸They made fifty bronze clasps to fasten the tent together as a unit.ᵇ ¹⁹Then they made for the tent a covering of ram skins dyed red, and over that a covering of hides of sea cows.ᶜ

²⁰They made upright frames of acacia wood for the tabernacle. ²¹Each frame was ten cubits long and a cubit and a half wide,ᵈ ²²with two projections set parallel to each other. They made all the frames of the tabernacle in this way. ²³They made twenty frames for the south side of the tabernacle ²⁴and made forty silver bases to go under them—two bases for each frame, one under each projection. ²⁵For the other side, the north side of the tabernacle, they made twenty frames ²⁶and forty silver bases—two under each frame. ²⁷They made six frames for the far end, that is, the west end of the tabernacle, ²⁸and two frames were made for the corners of the tabernacle at the far end. ²⁹At these two corners the frames were double from the bottom all the way to the top and fitted into a single ring; both were made alike. ³⁰So there were eight frames and sixteen silver bases—two under each frame.

36:18
b ver 13

³¹They also made crossbars of acacia wood: five for the frames on one side of the tabernacle, ³²five for those on the other side, and five for the frames on the west, at the far end of the tabernacle. ³³They made the center crossbar so that it extended from end to end at the middle of the frames. ³⁴They overlaid the frames with gold and made gold rings to hold the crossbars. They also overlaid the crossbars with gold.

³⁵They made the curtainᶜ of blue, purple and scarlet yarn and finely twisted linen, with cherubim worked into it by a skilled craftsman. ³⁶They made four posts of acacia wood for it and overlaid them with gold. They made gold hooks for them and cast

36:35
c Ex 39:38;
Mt 27:51;
Lk 23:45;
Heb 9:3

ᵃ9 That is, about 42 feet (about 12.5 meters) long and 6 feet (about 1.8 meters) wide ᵇ15 That is, about 45 feet (about 13.5 meters) long and 6 feet (about 1.8 meters) wide ᶜ19 That is, dugongs ᵈ21 That is, about 15 feet (about 4.5 meters) long and 2 1/4 feet (about 0.7 meter) wide their four silver bases. ³⁷For the entrance to the tent they made a curtain of blue, purple and scarlet yarn and finely twisted linen—the work of an embroiderer;*a* ³⁸and they made five posts with hooks for them. They overlaid the tops of the posts and their bands with gold and made their five bases of bronze.

Chapter 37 Theme

37 Bezalel*b* made the ark*c* of acacia wood—two and a half cubits long, a cubit and a half wide, and a cubit and a half high.*a* ²He overlaid it with pure gold,*d* both inside and out, and made a gold molding around it. ³He cast four gold rings for it and fastened them to its four feet, with two rings on one side and two rings on the other. ⁴Then he made poles of acacia wood and overlaid them with gold. ⁵And he inserted the poles into the rings on the sides of the ark to carry it.

⁶He made the atonement cover*e* of pure gold—two and a half cubits long and a cubit and a half wide.*b* ⁷Then he made two cherubim*f* out of hammered gold at the ends of the cover. ⁸He made one cherub on one end and the second cherub on the other; at the two ends he made them of one piece with the cover. ⁹The cherubim had their wings spread upward, overshadowing*g* the cover with them. The cherubim faced each other, looking toward the cover.*h*

¹⁰They*c* made the table*i* of acacia wood—two cubits long, a cubit wide, and a cubit and a half high.*d* ¹¹Then they overlaid it with pure gold*j* and made a gold molding around it. ¹²They also made around it a rim a handbreadth*e* wide and put a gold molding on the rim. ¹³They cast four gold rings for the table and fastened them to the four corners, where the four legs were. ¹⁴The rings*k* were put close to the rim to hold the poles used in carrying the table. ¹⁵The poles for carrying the table were made of acacia wood and were overlaid with gold. ¹⁶And they made from pure gold the articles for the table—its plates and dishes and bowls and its pitchers for the pouring out of drink offerings.

¹⁷They made the lampstand*l* of pure gold and hammered it out, base and shaft; its flowerlike cups, buds and blossoms were of one piece with it. ¹⁸Six branches extended from the sides of the lampstand—three on one side and three on the other. ¹⁹Three cups shaped like almond flowers with buds and blossoms were on one branch, three on the next branch and the same for all six branches extending from the lampstand. ²⁰And on the lampstand

Ark of the Covenant (or Testimony)

Table for Consecrated Bread

Lampstand

Cross references

36:37
a Ex 27:16

37:1
b Ex 31:2
c Ex 30:6; 39:35; Dt 10:3

37:2
d ver 11,26

37:6
e Ex 26:34; 31:7; Heb 9:5

37:7
f Eze 41:18

37:9
g Heb 9:5
h Dt 10:3

37:10
i Heb 9:2

37:11
j ver 2

37:14
k ver 27

37:17
l Heb 9:2; Rev 1:12

---

a1 That is, about 3 3/4 feet (about 1.1 meters) long and 2 1/4 feet (about 0.7 meter) wide and high   *b6* That is, about 3 3/4 feet (about 1.1 meters) long and 2 1/4 feet (about 0.7 meter) wide   *c10* Or *He*; also in verses 11-29   *d10* That is, about 3 feet (about 0.9 meter) long, 1 1/2 feet (about 0.5 meter) wide, and 2 1/4 feet (about 0.7 meter) high   *e12* That is, about 3 inches (about 8 centimeters)

37:22
a ver 17;
Nu 8:4

were four cups shaped like almond flowers with buds and blossoms. ²¹One bud was under the first pair of branches extending from the lampstand, a second bud under the second pair, and a third bud under the third pair—six branches in all. ²²The buds and the branches were all of one piece with the lampstand, hammered out of pure gold.ᵃ

37:23
b Ex 40:4,25

²³They made its seven lamps,ᵇ as well as its wick trimmers and trays, of pure gold. ²⁴They made the lampstand and all its accessories from one talentᵃ of pure gold.

37:25
c Ex 30:34-36;
Lk 1:11;
Heb 9:4;
Rev 8:3
d Ex 27:2;
Rev 9:13

²⁵They made the altar of incenseᶜ out of acacia wood. It was square, a cubit long and a cubit wide, and two cubits highᵇ—its hornsᵈ of one piece with it. ²⁶They overlaid the top and all the sides and the horns with pure gold, and made a gold molding around it. ²⁷They made two gold ringsᵉ below the molding—two on opposite sides—to hold the poles used to carry it. ²⁸They made the poles of acacia wood and overlaid them with gold.ᶠ

Altar of Incense (Gold or Golden Altar)

²⁹They also made the sacred anointing oilᵍ and the pure, fragrant incenseʰ—the work of a perfumer.

37:27
e ver 14

Chapter 38 Theme

38 Theyᶜ built the altar of burnt offering of acacia wood, three cubitsᵈ high; it was square, five cubits long and five cubits wide.ᵉ ²They made a horn at each of the four corners, so that the horns and the altar were of one piece, and they overlaid the altar with bronze.ⁱ ³They made all its utensilsʲ of bronze—its pots, shovels, sprinkling bowls, meat forks and firepans. ⁴They made a grating for the altar, a bronze network, to be under its ledge, halfway up the altar. ⁵They cast bronze rings to hold the poles for the four corners of the bronze grating. ⁶They made the poles of acacia wood and overlaid them with bronze. ⁷They inserted the poles into the rings so they would be on the sides of the altar for carrying it. They made it hollow, out of boards.

37:28
f Ex 25:13

Bronze Altar

37:29
g Ex 31:11
h Ex 30:1,25;
39:38

⁸They made the bronze basinᵏ and its bronze stand from the mirrors of the womenˡ who served at the entrance to the Tent of Meeting.

38:2
i 2Ch 1:5

⁹Next they made the courtyard. The south side was a hundred cubitsᶠ long and had curtains of finely twisted linen, ¹⁰with twenty posts and twenty bronze bases, and with silver hooks and bands on the posts. ¹¹The north side was also a hundred cubits long and had twenty posts and twenty bronze bases, with silver hooks and bands on the posts.

38:3
j Ex 31:9

Bronze Basin

38:8
k Ex 30:18; 40:7
l Dt 23:17;
1Sa 2:22;
1Ki 14:24

ᵃ24 That is, about 75 pounds (about 34 kilograms)   ᵇ25 That is, about 1 1/2 feet (about 0.5 meter) long and wide, and about 3 feet (about 0.9 meter) high   ᶜ1 Or *He*; also in verses 2-9   ᵈ1 That is, about 4 1/2 feet (about 1.3 meters)   ᵉ1 That is, about 7 1/2 feet (about 2.3 meters) long and wide   ᶠ9 That is, about 150 feet (about 46 meters)

¹²The west end was fifty cubits^a wide and had curtains, with ten posts and ten bases, with silver hooks and bands on the posts. ¹³The east end, toward the sunrise, was also fifty cubits wide. ¹⁴Curtains fifteen cubits^b long were on one side of the entrance, with three posts and three bases, ¹⁵and curtains fifteen cubits long were on the other side of the entrance to the courtyard, with three posts and three bases. ¹⁶All the curtains around the courtyard were of finely twisted linen. ¹⁷The bases for the posts were bronze. The hooks and bands on the posts were silver, and their tops were overlaid with silver; so all the posts of the courtyard had silver bands.

¹⁸The curtain for the entrance to the courtyard was of blue, purple and scarlet yarn and finely twisted linen—the work of an embroiderer. It was twenty cubits^c long and, like the curtains of the courtyard, five cubits^d high, ¹⁹with four posts and four bronze bases. Their hooks and bands were silver, and their tops were overlaid with silver. ²⁰All the tent pegs^a of the tabernacle and of the surrounding courtyard were bronze.

²¹These are the amounts of the materials used for the tabernacle, the tabernacle of the Testimony,^b which were recorded at Moses' command by the Levites under the direction of Ithamar^c son of Aaron, the priest. ²²(Bezalel^d son of Uri, the son of Hur, of the tribe of Judah, made everything the LORD commanded Moses; ²³with him was Oholiab^e son of Ahisamach, of the tribe of Dan—a craftsman and designer, and an embroiderer in blue, purple and scarlet yarn and fine linen.) ²⁴The total amount of the gold from the wave offering used for all the work on the sanctuary^f was 29 talents and 730 shekels,^e according to the sanctuary shekel.^g

²⁵The silver obtained from those of the community who were counted in the census^h was 100 talents and 1,775 shekels,^f according to the sanctuary shekel— ²⁶one beka per person,ⁱ that is, half a shekel,^g according to the sanctuary shekel,^j from everyone who had crossed over to those counted, twenty years old or more,^k a total of 603,550 men.^l ²⁷The 100 talents^h of silver were used to cast the bases^m for the sanctuary and for the curtain—100 bases from the 100 talents, one talent for each base. ²⁸They used the 1,775 shekelsⁱ to make the hooks for the posts, to overlay the tops of the posts, and to make their bands.

²⁹The bronze from the wave offering was 70 talents and 2,400 shekels.^j ³⁰They used it to make the bases for the entrance to the

INSIGHT

See the illustration of the tabernacle on page IISB-34.

38:20
^a Ex 35:18

38:21
^b Nu 1:50,53;
8:24; 9:15;
10:11; 17:7;
1Ch 23:32;
2Ch 24:6;
Ac 7:44;
Rev 15:5
^c Nu 4:28,33

38:22
^d Ex 31:2

38:23
^e Ex 31:6

38:24
^f Ex 30:16
^g Ex 30:13;
Lev 27:25;
Nu 3:47; 18:16

38:25
^h Ex 30:12

38:26
ⁱ Ex 30:12
^j Ex 30:13
^k Ex 30:14
^l Ex 12:37;
Nu 1:46

38:27
^m Ex 26:19

^a12 That is, about 75 feet (about 23 meters)   ^b14 That is, about 22 1/2 feet (about 6.9 meters)   ^c18 That is, about 30 feet (about 9 meters)   ^d18 That is, about 7 1/2 feet (about 2.3 meters)   ^e24 The weight of the gold was a little over one ton (about 1 metric ton).   ^f25 The weight of the silver was a little over 3 3/4 tons (about 3.4 metric tons).   ^g26 That is, about 1/5 ounce (about 5.5 grams)   ^h27 That is, about 3 3/4 tons (about 3.4 metric tons)   ⁱ28 That is, about 45 pounds (about 20 kilograms)   ^j29 The weight of the bronze was about 2 1/2 tons (about 2.4 metric tons).

Tent of Meeting, the bronze altar with its bronze grating and all its utensils, ³¹the bases for the surrounding courtyard and those for its entrance and all the tent pegs for the tabernacle and those for the surrounding courtyard.

Chapter 39 Theme _____

39

From the blue, purple and scarlet yarn*ᵃ* they made woven garments for ministering in the sanctuary.*ᵇ* They also made sacred garments*ᶜ* for Aaron, as the LORD commanded Moses.

²They*ᵃ* made the ephod of gold, and of blue, purple and scarlet yarn, and of finely twisted linen. ³They hammered out thin sheets of gold and cut strands to be worked into the blue, purple and scarlet yarn and fine linen—the work of a skilled craftsman. ⁴They made shoulder pieces for the ephod, which were attached to two of its corners, so it could be fastened. ⁵Its skillfully woven waistband was like it—of one piece with the ephod and made with gold, and with blue, purple and scarlet yarn, and with finely twisted linen, as the LORD commanded Moses.

⁶They mounted the onyx stones in gold filigree settings and engraved them like a seal with the names of the sons of Israel. ⁷Then they fastened them on the shoulder pieces of the ephod as memorial*ᵈ* stones for the sons of Israel, as the LORD commanded Moses.

⁸They fashioned the breastpiece*ᵉ*—the work of a skilled craftsman. They made it like the ephod: of gold, and of blue, purple and scarlet yarn, and of finely twisted linen. ⁹It was square—a span*ᵇ* long and a span wide—and folded double. ¹⁰Then they mounted four rows of precious stones on it. In the first row there was a ruby, a topaz and a beryl; ¹¹in the second row a turquoise, a sapphire*ᶜ* and an emerald; ¹²in the third row a jacinth, an agate and an amethyst; ¹³in the fourth row a chrysolite, an onyx and a jasper.*ᵈ* They were mounted in gold filigree settings. ¹⁴There were twelve stones, one for each of the names of the sons of Israel, each engraved like a seal with the name of one of the twelve tribes.*ᶠ*

¹⁵For the breastpiece they made braided chains of pure gold, like a rope. ¹⁶They made two gold filigree settings and two gold rings, and fastened the rings to two of the corners of the breastpiece. ¹⁷They fastened the two gold chains to the rings at the corners of the breastpiece, ¹⁸and the other ends of the chains to the two settings, attaching them to the shoulder pieces of the ephod at the front. ¹⁹They made two gold rings and attached them to the other two corners of the breastpiece on the inside edge next

Ephod

High Priest's Garments

39:1
a Ex 35:23
b Ex 35:19
c ver 41;
Ex 28:2

39:7
d Lev 24:7;
Jos 4:7

39:8
e Lev 8:8

39:14
f Rev 21:12

*a*2 Or *He*; also in verses 7, 8 and 22   *b*9 That is, about 9 inches (about 22 centimeters)   *c*11 Or *lapis lazuli*   *d*13 The precise identification of some of these precious stones is uncertain.

*Robe of
the Ephod*

*Turban with
Plate of Gold*

to the ephod. [20]Then they made two more gold rings and attached them to the bottom of the shoulder pieces on the front of the ephod, close to the seam just above the waistband of the ephod. [21]They tied the rings of the breastpiece to the rings of the ephod with blue cord, connecting it to the waistband so that the breastpiece would not swing out from the ephod—as the LORD commanded Moses.

[22]They made the robe of the ephod entirely of blue cloth—the work of a weaver— [23]with an opening in the center of the robe like the opening of a collar,[a] and a band around this opening, so that it would not tear. [24]They made pomegranates of blue, purple and scarlet yarn and finely twisted linen around the hem of the robe. [25]And they made bells of pure gold and attached them around the hem between the pomegranates. [26]The bells and pomegranates alternated around the hem of the robe to be worn for ministering, as the LORD commanded Moses.

[27]For Aaron and his sons, they made tunics of fine linen[a]—the work of a weaver— [28]and the turban[b] of fine linen, the linen headbands and the undergarments of finely twisted linen. [29]The sash was of finely twisted linen and blue, purple and scarlet yarn— the work of an embroiderer—as the LORD commanded Moses.

[30]They made the plate, the sacred diadem, out of pure gold and engraved on it, like an inscription on a seal: HOLY TO THE LORD. [31]Then they fastened a blue cord to it to attach it to the turban, as the LORD commanded Moses.

[32]So all the work on the tabernacle, the Tent of Meeting, was completed. The Israelites did everything just as the LORD commanded Moses.[c] [33]Then they brought the tabernacle to Moses: the tent and all its furnishings, its clasps, frames, crossbars, posts and bases; [34]the covering of ram skins dyed red, the covering of hides of sea cows[b] and the shielding curtain; [35]the ark of the Testimony[d] with its poles and the atonement cover; [36]the table with all its articles and the bread of the Presence; [37]the pure gold lampstand[e] with its row of lamps and all its accessories, and the oil for the light; [38]the gold altar,[f] the anointing oil, the fragrant incense, and the curtain[g] for the entrance to the tent; [39]the bronze altar with its bronze grating, its poles and all its utensils; the basin with its stand; [40]the curtains of the courtyard with its posts and bases, and the curtain for the entrance to the courtyard;[h] the ropes and tent pegs for the courtyard; all the furnishings for the tabernacle, the Tent of Meeting; [41]and the woven garments worn for ministering in the sanctuary, both the sacred garments for Aaron the priest and the garments for his sons when serving as priests.

39:27
a Lev 6:10

39:28
b Ex 28:4

39:32
c ver 42-43;
Ex 25:9

39:35
d Ex 30:6

39:37
e Ex 25:31

39:38
f Ex 30:1-10
g Ex 36:35

39:40
h Ex 27:9-19

a23 The meaning of the Hebrew for this word is uncertain.   b34 That is, dugongs

39:42
a Ex 25:9

39:43
b Lev 9:22,23;
Nu 6:23-27;
2Sa 6:18;
1Ki 8:14,55;
2Ch 30:27

40:2
c Nu 1:1
d ver 17;
Ex 12:2

40:3
e ver 21;
Nu 4:5;
Ex 26:33

40:4
f Ex 25:30
g ver 22-25;
Ex 26:35

40:5
h ver 26;
Ex 30:1

40:7
i ver 30;
Ex 30:18

40:9
j Ex 30:26;
Lev 8:10

40:10
k Ex 29:36

40:12
l Lev 8:1-13

40:13
m Ex 28:41
n Lev 8:12

40:15
o Ex 29:9;
Nu 25:13

⁴²The Israelites had done all the work just as the LORD had commanded Moses.*ᵃ* ⁴³Moses inspected the work and saw that they had done it just as the LORD had commanded. So Moses blessed*ᵇ* them.

Chapter 40 Theme

40 Then the LORD said to Moses: ²"Set up the tabernacle, the Tent of Meeting,*ᶜ* on the first day of the first month.*ᵈ* ³Place the ark*ᵉ* of the Testimony in it and shield the ark with the curtain. ⁴Bring in the table and set out what belongs on it.*ᶠ* Then bring in the lampstand*ᵍ* and set up its lamps. ⁵Place the gold altar*ʰ* of incense in front of the ark of the Testimony and put the curtain at the entrance to the tabernacle.

GOLD *or* GOLDEN ALTAR *or* ALTAR OF INCENSE

LAMPSTAND CURTAIN

THE CLOUD OF GOD'S GLORY

DOOR

BRONZE ALTAR

BRONZE BASIN

HOLY PLACE

MOST HOLY PLACE

TABLE FOR CONSECRATED BREAD

ATONEMENT COVER ON ARK OF COVENANT

Inside the Tabernacle

⁶"Place the altar of burnt offering in front of the entrance to the tabernacle, the Tent of Meeting; ⁷place the basin*ⁱ* between the Tent of Meeting and the altar and put water in it. ⁸Set up the courtyard around it and put the curtain at the entrance to the courtyard.

⁹"Take the anointing oil and anoint*ʲ* the tabernacle and everything in it; consecrate it and all its furnishings, and it will be holy. ¹⁰Then anoint the altar of burnt offering and all its utensils; consecrate*ᵏ* the altar, and it will be most holy. ¹¹Anoint the basin and its stand and consecrate them.

¹²"Bring Aaron and his sons to the entrance to the Tent of Meeting and wash them with water.*ˡ* ¹³Then dress Aaron in the sacred garments,*ᵐ* anoint him and consecrate*ⁿ* him so he may serve me as priest. ¹⁴Bring his sons and dress them in tunics. ¹⁵Anoint them just as you anointed their father, so they may serve me as priests. Their anointing will be to a priesthood that will continue for all generations to come.*ᵒ*" ¹⁶Moses did everything just as the LORD commanded him.

¹⁷So the tabernacle[a] was set up on the first day of the first month[b] in the second year. ¹⁸When Moses set up the tabernacle, he put the bases in place, erected the frames, inserted the crossbars and set up the posts. ¹⁹Then he spread the tent over the tabernacle and put the covering over the tent, as the LORD commanded him.

²⁰He took the Testimony[c] and placed it in the ark, attached the poles to the ark and put the atonement cover over it. ²¹Then he brought the ark into the tabernacle and hung the shielding curtain[d] and shielded the ark of the Testimony, as the LORD commanded him.

²²Moses placed the table[e] in the Tent of Meeting on the north side of the tabernacle outside the curtain ²³and set out the bread[f] on it before the LORD, as the LORD commanded him.

²⁴He placed the lampstand[g] in the Tent of Meeting opposite the table on the south side of the tabernacle ²⁵and set up the lamps[h] before the LORD, as the LORD commanded him.

²⁶Moses placed the gold altar[i] in the Tent of Meeting in front of the curtain ²⁷and burned fragrant incense on it, as the LORD commanded[j] him. ²⁸Then he put up the curtain[k] at the entrance to the tabernacle.

²⁹He set the altar of burnt offering near the entrance to the tabernacle, the Tent of Meeting, and offered on it burnt offerings and grain offerings,[l] as the LORD commanded him.

³⁰He placed the basin[m] between the Tent of Meeting and the altar and put water in it for washing, ³¹and Moses and Aaron and his sons used it to wash their hands and feet. ³²They washed whenever they entered the Tent of Meeting or approached the altar,[n] as the LORD commanded Moses.

³³Then Moses set up the courtyard[o] around the tabernacle and altar and put up the curtain[p] at the entrance to the courtyard. And so Moses finished the work.

³⁴Then the cloud[q] covered the Tent of Meeting, and the glory of the LORD filled the tabernacle. ³⁵Moses could not enter the Tent of Meeting because the cloud had settled upon it, and the glory of the LORD filled the tabernacle.[r]

³⁶In all the travels of the Israelites, whenever the cloud lifted from above the tabernacle, they would set out;[s] ³⁷but if the cloud did not lift, they did not set out—until the day it lifted. ³⁸So the cloud[t] of the LORD was over the tabernacle by day, and fire was in the cloud by night, in the sight of all the house of Israel during all their travels.

40:17
a Nu 7:1
b ver 2

40:20
c Ex 16:34;
25:16;
Dt 10:5;
1Ki 8:9;
Heb 9:4

40:21
d Ex 26:33

40:22
e Ex 26:35

40:23
f ver 4

40:24
g Ex 26:35

40:25
h ver 4;
Ex 25:37

40:26
i ver 5;
Ex 30:6

40:27
j Ex 30:7

40:28
k Ex 26:36

40:29
l ver 6;
Ex 29:38-42

40:30
m ver 7

40:32
n Ex 30:20

40:33
o Ex 27:9
p ver 8

40:34
q Nu 9:15-23;
1Ki 8:12

40:35
r 1Ki 8:11;
2Ch 5:13-14

40:36
s Nu 9:17-23;
10:13;
Ne 9:19

40:38
t Ex 13:21;
Nu 9:15;
1Co 10:1

Theme of Exodus:

Author:

			Chapter Themes
Date:			1
			2
Purpose:			3
			4
Key Words:			5
slaves (servant[s]) slavery			6
			7
rescue, free, hand over (rescued, saved)			8
holy (sacred)			9
the Lord commanded (I commanded)			10
			11
covenant (treaty)			12
cloud (darkness)			13
test(ed)			14
law			15
tabernacle (tent, Tent of Meeting)			16
			17
			18
			19
			20

SEGMENT DIVISIONS

				CHAPTER THEMES
			21	
			22	
			23	
			24	
			25	
			26	
			27	
			28	
			29	
			30	
			31	
			32	
			33	
			34	
			35	
			36	
			37	
			38	
			39	
			40	

LEVITICUS

*I*n Genesis we see the ruin of man as he listens to the serpent rather than to God. The human race is condemned to sin's awful wage—death. Yet in the mercy and grace of God comes the promise of redemption through the seed of the woman, through the seed of Abraham, as God calls out a people for himself. God makes a covenant with Abraham which he confirms to Isaac and then to Jacob, later to be named Israel.

However, as the book of Genesis comes to a close, the children of Israel are living in Egypt rather than in Canaan, the land of promise. The book that began with the creation of man in Eden ends with the children of Israel looking into a coffin in Egypt, yet not without a promise that someday they would leave Egypt.

Exodus plays out the drama of redemption as the nation of Israel is redeemed from slavery through the blood of the Passover lamb. After the descendants of Abraham were enslaved and oppressed for 400 years, just as God promised, they left Egypt with great possessions as God went before them in his cloud of glory.

And what follows the redemption of ruined man? That is what the book of Leviticus is all about. Study it well, for in picture form Leviticus shows us what God expects from those who have been redeemed.

∾ THINGS TO DO

General Instructions

1. As you read Leviticus watch for the verses which attribute the authorship of this book to Moses. When you come across those references, record them under "Author" on the LEVITICUS AT A GLANCE chart on page 212.

2. Read Exodus 40:17, 32-38 and Leviticus 1:1, 2 and note the uninterrupted transition from one book to the other. Then compare Numbers 1:1 with these verses. As you do this you will see that the book of Leviticus covers a period of one month.

3. As you read through Leviticus one chapter at a time, do the following:

   a. Ask the five W's and an H: Who? What? When? Where? Why? and How? For example: Who is to do what? When are they to do it? How are they to do it? Why? What if they didn't know why? Questions which interrogate the text help you see what is being said.

   b. Mark the key repeated words listed on LEVITICUS AT A GLANCE. You will find it helpful to list these key words on an index card that you can use as a bookmark while you study Leviticus. Also watch for any other key words which might be used in that particular chapter. If you gain insights from marking these words, list what you learn in the margin.

   c. Record the main theme or subject of the chapter on the line next to the chapter number in the text. Then record it on LEVITICUS AT A GLANCE.

   d. You may want to summarize the main points or the order of events covered in the chapter. Record them in the margin.

   e. Record any new insights about the character and ways of God. You could identify your insights on God with this symbol △ and then color it yellow, which would make it easy to recognize.

Chapters 1-7

1. As you read chapters 1 through 7, which give instructions regarding the various sacrifices or offerings, mark the text as instructed under "General Instructions" and then record what you learn about each of the offerings on the chart THE OFFERINGS AND THEIR PURPOSES. This chart is on page 209.

2. Watch what God says about unintentional sin, guilt, and restitution. Note what is to be done when a leader sins and when the congregation sins. Write it in the margin or mark it in the text.

Chapters 8-10

This segment covers the consecration of Aaron and his sons. There is an event in chapter 10 which occurs in conjunction with this. As you read these chapters, list in the margin of each chapter what was to be done and why. In chapter 10 note what happened, why it happened, and who was involved.

Chapters 11-15

This segment deals with laws of cleanliness.

1. In addition to the other key words, also mark *clean* and *unclean*.

2. In the margin record what the law covers. For example: food, women, infections, etc.

Chapters 16, 17

These chapters cover the Day of Atonement and regulations regarding the blood.

1. In the margin of chapter 16 carefully outline what is to be done on the Day of Atonement. As you do, you might want to consult the chart INSIDE THE TABERNACLE on page 187.

2. Note the regulations in chapter 17 regarding sacrifices and blood.

Chapters 18-27

This segment lays out statutes on issues regarding moral laws, the priests, the celebration of annual feasts, the land, etc.

1. As you read each chapter, in the margin list the main topics or situations.

2. If moral laws are given, note the consequences of breaking the laws and the reason for the consequences.

3. In chapter 23 note the feasts, when they are to be celebrated, and how. When you finish studying the chapter, consult the chart THE FEASTS OF ISRAEL on pages 210, 211.

4. Give special attention to any mention of the land—its Sabbath rest, principles of redemption, etc. Mark the words *redeem, redeems, redemption,* and any other synonyms. Record your insights in the margin.

5. When you finish reading through Leviticus, complete LEVITICUS AT A GLANCE.

   a. See if any of the chapters can be grouped categorically. If so, record this under "Segment Divisions" on the chart. Record any other possible segment divisions. For instance, you could do a segment division titled "Laws Regarding."

   b. Record the theme of Leviticus.

❧ THINGS TO THINK ABOUT

1. What have you learned about God and his attitude toward sin? What happens when sin goes unpunished?

2. What have you learned about the occult and about the types of sexual sin? How severely were these sins to be dealt with? What does this tell you about how God feels regarding these sins and their consequences? What do you think would happen in your country if these sins were dealt with according to God's law? Read 1 Timothy 1:8-11.

3. Jesus told the Jews that the Scriptures—the Old Testament—testified of him. Think about how Jesus Christ and his work are foreshadowed in Leviticus.

4. What have you learned about holiness from Leviticus? If you want to be holy, how will you live your life? Are there any changes you need to make? Are you willing? If not, why not?

Chapter 1 Theme

1 The LORD called to Moses[a] and spoke to him from the Tent of Meeting.[b] He said, 2"Speak to the Israelites and say to them: 'When any of you brings an offering to the LORD, bring as your offering an animal from either the herd or the flock.[c]

3"'If the offering is a burnt offering from the herd, he is to offer a male without defect.[d] He must present it at the entrance to the Tent[e] of Meeting so that it[a] will be acceptable to the LORD. 4He is to lay his hand on the head[f] of the burnt offering, and it will be accepted on his behalf to make atonement[g] for him. 5He is to slaughter[h] the young bull before the LORD, and then Aaron's sons the priests shall bring the blood and sprinkle it against the altar on all sides[i] at the entrance to the Tent of Meeting. 6He is to skin[j] the burnt offering and cut it into pieces. 7The sons of Aaron the priest are to put fire on the altar and arrange wood[k] on the fire. 8Then Aaron's sons the priests shall arrange the pieces, including the head and the fat,[l] on the burning wood that is on the altar. 9He is to wash the inner parts and the legs with water, and the priest is to burn all of it on the altar.[m] It is a burnt offering, an offering made by fire, an aroma pleasing to the LORD.[n]

10"'If the offering is a burnt offering from the flock, from either the sheep or the goats,[o] he is to offer a male without defect. 11He is to slaughter it at the north side of the altar before the LORD, and Aaron's sons the priests shall sprinkle its blood against the altar on all sides.[p] 12He is to cut it into pieces, and the priest shall arrange them, including the head and the fat, on the burning wood that is on the altar. 13He is to wash the inner parts and the legs with water, and the priest is to bring all of it and burn it on the altar. It is a burnt offering, an offering made by fire, an aroma pleasing to the LORD.

14"'If the offering to the LORD is a burnt offering of birds, he is to offer a dove or a young pigeon.[q] 15The priest shall bring it to the altar, wring off the head and burn it on the altar; its blood shall be drained out on the side of the altar.[r] 16He is to remove the crop with its contents[b] and throw it to the east side of the altar, where the ashes[s] are. 17He shall tear it open by the wings, not severing it completely,[t] and then the priest shall burn it on the wood[u] that is on the fire on the altar. It is a burnt offering, an offering made by fire, an aroma pleasing to the LORD.

Chapter 2 Theme

2 "'When someone brings a grain offering[v] to the LORD, his offering is to be of fine flour. He is to pour oil[w] on it, put incense on it 2and take it to Aaron's sons the priests. The priest

---

1:1
a Ex 19:3; 25:22
b Nu 7:89

1:2
c Lev 22:18-19

1:3
d Ex 12:5; Dt 15:21; Heb 9:14; 1Pe 1:19
e Lev 17:9

1:4
f Ex 29:10,15; Lev 3:2
g 2Ch 29:23-24

1:5
h Lev 3:2,8
i Heb 12:24; 1Pe 1:2

1:6
j Lev 7:8

1:7
k Lev 6:12

1:8
l ver 12

1:9
m Ex 29:18
n ver 13; Ge 8:21; Nu 15:8-10; Eph 5:2

1:10
o ver 3; Ex 12:5

1:11
p ver 5

1:14
q Ge 15:9; Lev 5:7; Lk 2:24

1:15
r Lev 5:9

1:16
s Lev 6:10

1:17
t Ge 15:10
u Lev 5:8

2:1
v Lev 6:14-18
w Nu 15:4

---

a 3 Or he   b 16 Or *crop and the feathers*; the meaning of the Hebrew for this word is uncertain.

shall take a handful of the fine flour*a* and oil, together with all the incense,*b* and burn this as a memorial portion*c* on the altar, an offering made by fire, an aroma pleasing to the Lord. ³The rest of the grain offering belongs to Aaron and his sons;*d* it is a most holy part of the offerings made to the LORD by fire.

⁴"'If you bring a grain offering baked in an oven, it is to consist of fine flour: cakes made without yeast and mixed with oil, or*a* wafers made without yeast and spread with oil.*e* ⁵If your grain offering is prepared on a griddle, it is to be made of fine flour mixed with oil, and without yeast. ⁶Crumble it and pour oil on it; it is a grain offering. ⁷If your grain offering is cooked in a pan,*f* it is to be made of fine flour and oil. ⁸Bring the grain offering made of these things to the LORD; present it to the priest, who shall take it to the altar. ⁹He shall take out the memorial portion*g* from the grain offering and burn it on the altar as an offering made by fire, an aroma pleasing to the LORD.*h* ¹⁰The rest of the grain offering belongs to Aaron and his sons;*i* it is a most holy part of the offerings made to the LORD by fire.

¹¹"'Every grain offering you bring to the LORD must be made without yeast,*j* for you are not to burn any yeast or honey in an offering made to the LORD by fire. ¹²You may bring them to the LORD as an offering of the firstfruits,*k* but they are not to be offered on the altar as a pleasing aroma. ¹³Season all your grain offerings with salt. Do not leave the salt of the covenant*l* of your God out of your grain offerings; add salt to all your offerings.

¹⁴"'If you bring a grain offering of firstfruits*m* to the LORD, offer crushed heads of new grain roasted in the fire. ¹⁵Put oil and incense on it; it is a grain offering. ¹⁶The priest shall burn the memorial portion*n* of the crushed grain and the oil, together with all the incense, as an offering made to the LORD by fire.

Chapter 3 Theme

3 "'If someone's offering is a fellowship offering,*b o* and he offers an animal from the herd, whether male or female, he is to present before the LORD an animal without defect.*p* ²He is to lay his hand on the head*q* of his offering and slaughter it*r* at the entrance to the Tent of Meeting. Then Aaron's sons the priests shall sprinkle the blood against the altar on all sides. ³From the fellowship offering he is to bring a sacrifice made to the LORD by fire: all the fat*s* that covers the inner parts or is connected to them, ⁴both kidneys with the fat on them near the loins, and the covering of the liver, which he will remove with the kidneys. ⁵Then Aaron's sons*t* are to burn it on the altar on top of the burnt

---

a4 Or and   *b1 Traditionally peace offering; also in verses 3, 6 and 9*

2:2
a Lev 5:11
b Lev 6:15;
Isa 66:3
c ver 9,16;
Lev 5:12;
6:15; 24:7;
Ac 10:4

2:3
d ver 10;
Lev 6:16;
10:12,13

2:4
e Ex 29:2

2:7
f Lev 7:9

2:9
g ver 2
h Ex 29:18;
Lev 6:15

2:10
i ver 3

2:11
j Ex 23:18;
34:25;
Lev 6:16

2:12
k Lev 7:13;
23:10

2:13
l Nu 18:19;
Eze 43:24

2:14
m Lev 23:10

2:16
n ver 2

3:1
o Lev 7:11-34
p Lev 1:3;
22:21

3:2
q Ex 29:10,15
r Lev 1:5

3:3
s Ex 29:13

3:5
t Lev 7:29-34

offering*a* that is on the burning wood, as an offering made by fire, an aroma pleasing to the LORD.

6"'If he offers an animal from the flock as a fellowship offering*b* to the LORD, he is to offer a male or female without defect. 7If he offers a lamb, he is to present it before the LORD.*c* 8He is to lay his hand on the head of his offering and slaughter it*d* in front of the Tent of Meeting. Then Aaron's sons shall sprinkle its blood against the altar on all sides. 9From the fellowship offering he is to bring a sacrifice made to the LORD by fire: its fat, the entire fat tail cut off close to the backbone, all the fat that covers the inner parts or is connected to them, 10both kidneys with the fat on them near the loins, and the covering of the liver, which he will remove with the kidneys. 11The priest shall burn them on the altar*e* as food,*f* an offering made to the LORD by fire.

12"'If his offering is a goat, he is to present it before the LORD. 13He is to lay his hand on its head and slaughter it in front of the Tent of Meeting. Then Aaron's sons shall sprinkle*g* its blood against the altar on all sides. 14From what he offers he is to make this offering to the LORD by fire: all the fat that covers the inner parts or is connected to them, 15both kidneys with the fat on them near the loins, and the covering of the liver, which he will remove with the kidneys. 16The priest shall burn them on the altar as food, an offering made by fire, a pleasing aroma. All the fat is the LORD's.*h*

17"'This is a lasting ordinance for the generations to come,*i* wherever you live: You must not eat any fat or any blood.*j*'"

Chapter 4 Theme

4 The LORD said to Moses, 2"Say to the Israelites: 'When anyone sins unintentionally*k* and does what is forbidden in any of the LORD's commands—

3"'If the anointed priest sins, bringing guilt on the people, he must bring to the LORD a young bull*l* without defect as a sin offering*m* for the sin he has committed. 4He is to present the bull at the entrance to the Tent of Meeting before the LORD.*n* He is to lay his hand on its head and slaughter it before the LORD. 5Then the anointed priest shall take some of the bull's blood*o* and carry it into the Tent of Meeting. 6He is to dip his finger into the blood and sprinkle some of it seven times before the LORD, in front of the curtain of the sanctuary. 7The priest shall then put some of the blood on the horns of the altar of fragrant incense that is before the LORD in the Tent of Meeting. The rest of the bull's blood he shall pour out at the base of the altar*p* of burnt offering*q* at the entrance to the Tent of Meeting. 8He shall remove all the

3:5
a Ex 29:13, 38-42

3:6
b ver 1

3:7
c Lev 17:8-9

3:8
d ver 2; Lev 1:5

3:11
e ver 5
f ver 16; Lev 21:6,17

3:13
g Ex 24:6

3:16
h 1Sa 2:16

3:17
i Lev 6:18; 17:7
j Ge 9:4; Lev 7:25-26; 17:10-16; Dt 12:16; Ac 15:20

4:2
k Lev 5:15-18; Ps 19:12; Heb 9:7

4:3
l ver 14; Ps 66:15
m Lev 9:2-22; Heb 9:13-14

4:4
n Lev 1:3

4:5
o Lev 16:14

4:7
p ver 34; Lev 8:15
q ver 18,30; Lev 5:9; 9:9; 16:18

fat^a from the bull of the sin offering—the fat that covers the inner parts or is connected to them, ⁹both kidneys with the fat on them near the loins, and the covering of the liver, which he will remove with the kidneys^b— ¹⁰just as the fat is removed from the ox^a sacrificed as a fellowship offering.^b Then the priest shall burn them on the altar of burnt offering. ¹¹But the hide of the bull and all its flesh, as well as the head and legs, the inner parts and offal^c— ¹²that is, all the rest of the bull—he must take outside the camp^d to a place ceremonially clean,^e where the ashes are thrown, and burn it in a wood fire on the ash heap.

¹³"'If the whole Israelite community sins unintentionally^f and does what is forbidden in any of the Lord's commands, even though the community is unaware of the matter, they are guilty. ¹⁴When they become aware of the sin they committed, the assembly must bring a young bull^g as a sin offering^h and present it before the Tent of Meeting. ¹⁵The elders of the community are to lay their hands on the bull's headⁱ before the Lord, and the bull shall be slaughtered before the Lord. ¹⁶Then the anointed priest is to take some of the bull's blood^j into the Tent of Meeting. ¹⁷He shall dip his finger into the blood and sprinkle it before the Lord^k seven times in front of the curtain. ¹⁸He is to put some of the blood on the horns of the altar that is before the Lord^l in the Tent of Meeting. The rest of the blood he shall pour out at the base of the altar of burnt offering at the entrance to the Tent of Meeting. ¹⁹He shall remove all the fat^m from it and burn it on the altar, ²⁰and do with this bull just as he did with the bull for the sin offering. In this way the priest will make atonementⁿ for them, and they will be forgiven.^o ²¹Then he shall take the bull outside the camp and burn it as he burned the first bull. This is the sin offering for the community.^p

²²"'When a leader^q sins unintentionally^r and does what is forbidden in any of the commands of the Lord his God, he is guilty. ²³When he is made aware of the sin he committed, he must bring as his offering a male goat without defect. ²⁴He is to lay his hand on the goat's head and slaughter it at the place where the burnt offering is slaughtered before the Lord. It is a sin offering. ²⁵Then the priest shall take some of the blood of the sin offering with his finger and put it on the horns of the altar of burnt offering and pour out the rest of the blood at the base of the altar.^s ²⁶He shall burn all the fat on the altar as he burned the fat of the fellowship offering. In this way the priest will make atonement for the man's sin, and he will be forgiven.^t

a10 The Hebrew word can include both male and female.　b10 Traditionally *peace offering*; also in verses 26, 31 and 35

4:8 aLev 3:3-5
4:9 bLev 3:4
4:11 cEx 29:14; Lev 9:11; Nu 19:5
4:12 dHeb 13:11 eLev 6:11
4:13 fver 2; Lev 5:2-4,17; Nu 15:24-26
4:14 gver 3 hver 23,28
4:15 iLev 1:4; 8:14,22; Nu 8:10
4:16 jver 5
4:17 kver 6
4:18 lver 7
4:19 mver 8
4:20 nHeb 10:10-12 oNu 15:25
4:21 pLev 16:5,15
4:22 qNu 31:13 rver 2
4:25 sver 7,18,30,34; Lev 9:9
4:26 tLev 5:10

4:27
a ver 2;
Nu 15:27

4:28
b ver 23
c ver 3

4:29
d ver 4,24
e Lev 1:4

4:30
f ver 7

4:31
g Ge 8:21

4:32
h ver 28

4:33
i ver 29

4:34
j ver 7

4:35
k ver 26,31

5:1
l Pr 29:24
m ver 17

5:2
n Lev 11:11,
24-40;
Dt 14:8

5:3
o Nu 19:11-16

5:4
p Nu 30:6,8

5:5
q Lev 16:21;
26:40;
Nu 5:7;
Pr 28:13

5:6
r Lev 4:28

27"'If a member of the community sins unintentionally*a* and does what is forbidden in any of the LORD's commands, he is guilty. 28When he is made aware of the sin he committed, he must bring as his offering*b* for the sin he committed a female goat*c* without defect. 29He is to lay his hand on the head*d* of the sin offering*e* and slaughter it at the place of the burnt offering. 30Then the priest is to take some of the blood with his finger and put it on the horns of the altar of burnt offering*f* and pour out the rest of the blood at the base of the altar. 31He shall remove all the fat, just as the fat is removed from the fellowship offering, and the priest shall burn it on the altar as an aroma pleasing to the LORD.*g* In this way the priest will make atonement for him, and he will be forgiven.

32"'If he brings a lamb as his sin offering, he is to bring a female without defect.*h* 33He is to lay his hand on its head and slaughter it for a sin offering at the place where the burnt offering is slaughtered.*i* 34Then the priest shall take some of the blood of the sin offering with his finger and put it on the horns of the altar of burnt offering and pour out the rest of the blood at the base of the altar.*j* 35He shall remove all the fat, just as the fat is removed from the lamb of the fellowship offering, and the priest shall burn it on the altar*k* on top of the offerings made to the LORD by fire. In this way the priest will make atonement for him for the sin he has committed, and he will be forgiven.

Chapter 5 Theme

5 "'If a person sins because he does not speak up when he hears a public charge to testify*l* regarding something he has seen or learned about, he will be held responsible.*m*

2"'Or if a person touches anything ceremonially unclean— whether the carcasses of unclean wild animals or of unclean livestock or of unclean creatures that move along the ground*n*—even though he is unaware of it, he has become unclean and is guilty.

3"'Or if he touches human uncleanness*o*—anything that would make him unclean—even though he is unaware of it, when he learns of it he will be guilty.

4"'Or if a person thoughtlessly takes an oath*p* to do anything, whether good or evil—in any matter one might carelessly swear about—even though he is unaware of it, in any case when he learns of it he will be guilty.

5"'When anyone is guilty in any of these ways, he must confess*q* in what way he has sinned 6and, as a penalty for the sin he has committed, he must bring to the LORD a female lamb or goat from the flock as a sin offering;*r* and the priest shall make atonement for him for his sin.

⁷"'If he cannot afford[a] a lamb, he is to bring two doves or two young pigeons to the LORD as a penalty for his sin—one for a sin offering and the other for a burnt offering. ⁸He is to bring them to the priest, who shall first offer the one for the sin offering. He is to wring its head from its neck,[b] not severing it completely,[c] ⁹and is to sprinkle some of the blood of the sin offering against the side of the altar; the rest of the blood must be drained out at the base of the altar.[d] It is a sin offering. ¹⁰The priest shall then offer the other as a burnt offering in the prescribed way[e] and make atonement for him for the sin he has committed, and he will be forgiven.[f]

¹¹"'If, however, he cannot afford two doves or two young pigeons, he is to bring as an offering for his sin a tenth of an ephah[a] of fine flour[g] for a sin offering. He must not put oil or incense on it, because it is a sin offering. ¹²He is to bring it to the priest, who shall take a handful of it as a memorial portion and burn it on the altar on top of the offerings made to the LORD by fire. It is a sin offering. ¹³In this way the priest will make atonement[h] for him for any of these sins he has committed, and he will be forgiven. The rest of the offering will belong to the priest,[i] as in the case of the grain offering.'"

¹⁴The LORD said to Moses: ¹⁵"When a person commits a violation and sins unintentionally in regard to any of the LORD's holy things, he is to bring to the LORD as a penalty[j] a ram[k] from the flock, one without defect and of the proper value in silver, according to the sanctuary shekel.[b][l] It is a guilt offering. ¹⁶He must make restitution[m] for what he has failed to do in regard to the holy things, add a fifth of the value[n] to that and give it all to the priest, who will make atonement for him with the ram as a guilt offering, and he will be forgiven.

¹⁷"If a person sins and does what is forbidden in any of the LORD's commands, even though he does not know it,[o] he is guilty and will be held responsible. ¹⁸He is to bring to the priest as a guilt offering a ram from the flock, one without defect and of the proper value. In this way the priest will make atonement for him for the wrong he has committed unintentionally, and he will be forgiven.[p] ¹⁹It is a guilt offering; he has been guilty of[c] wrongdoing against the LORD."

Chapter 6 Theme

6 The LORD said to Moses: ²"If anyone sins and is unfaithful to the LORD[q] by deceiving his neighbor[r] about something

---

[a]11 That is, probably about 2 quarts (about 2 liters)   [b]15 That is, about 2/5 ounce (about 11.5 grams)   [c]19 Or *has made full expiation for his*

5:7
[a]Lev 12:8; 14:21

5:8
[b]Lev 1:15
[c]Lev 1:17

5:9
[d]Lev 4:7,18

5:10
[e]Lev 1:14-17
[f]Lev 4:26

5:11
[g]Lev 2:1

5:13
[h]Lev 4:26
[i]Lev 2:3

5:15
[j]Lev 22:14
[k]Nu 5:8
[l]Ex 30:13

5:16
[m]Lev 6:4
[n]Lev 22:14; Nu 5:7

5:17
[o]ver 15; Lev 4:2

5:18
[p]ver 15

6:2
[q]Nu 5:6; Ac 5:4; Col 3:9
[r]Pr 24:28

6:2
*a*Ex 22:7

6:3
*b*Dt 22:1-3

6:4
*c*Lk 19:8

6:5
*d*Nu 5:7
*e*Lev 5:15

6:6
*f*Lev 5:15

6:7
*g*Lev 4:26

6:10
*h*Ex 28:39-42,
43; 39:28

6:11
*i*Lev 4:12

6:14
*j*Lev 2:1;
15:4

6:15
*k*Lev 2:9
*l*Lev 2:2

6:16
*m*Lev 2:3
*n*Eze 44:29
*o*Lev 2:11
*p*Lev 10:13

6:17
*q*ver 29;
Ex 40:10;
Nu 18:9,10

6:18
*r*ver 29;
Nu 18:9-10
*s*ver 27

6:20
*t*Ex 16:36
*u*Ex 29:2

entrusted to him or left in his care*ª* or stolen, or if he cheats him, *3*or if he finds lost property and lies about it,*b* or if he swears falsely, or if he commits any such sin that people may do— *4*when he thus sins and becomes guilty, he must return*c* what he has stolen or taken by extortion, or what was entrusted to him, or the lost property he found, *5*or whatever it was he swore falsely about. He must make restitution*d* in full, add a fifth of the value to it and give it all to the owner on the day he presents his guilt offering.*e* *6*And as a penalty he must bring to the priest, that is, to the LORD, his guilt offering,*f* a ram from the flock, one without defect and of the proper value. *7*In this way the priest will make atonement*g* for him before the LORD, and he will be forgiven for any of these things he did that made him guilty."

*8*The LORD said to Moses: *9*"Give Aaron and his sons this command: 'These are the regulations for the burnt offering: The burnt offering is to remain on the altar hearth throughout the night, till morning, and the fire must be kept burning on the altar. *10*The priest shall then put on his linen clothes, with linen undergarments next to his body,*h* and shall remove the ashes of the burnt offering that the fire has consumed on the altar and place them beside the altar. *11*Then he is to take off these clothes and put on others, and carry the ashes outside the camp to a place that is ceremonially clean.*i* *12*The fire on the altar must be kept burning; it must not go out. Every morning the priest is to add firewood and arrange the burnt offering on the fire and burn the fat of the fellowship offerings*ª* on it. *13*The fire must be kept burning on the altar continuously; it must not go out.

14"'These are the regulations for the grain offering:*j* Aaron's sons are to bring it before the LORD, in front of the altar. *15*The priest is to take a handful of fine flour and oil, together with all the incense on the grain offering,*k* and burn the memorial portion*l* on the altar as an aroma pleasing to the LORD. *16*Aaron and his sons*m* shall eat the rest*n* of it, but it is to be eaten without yeast*o* in a holy place;*p* they are to eat it in the courtyard of the Tent of Meeting. *17*It must not be baked with yeast; I have given it as their share of the offerings made to me by fire. Like the sin offering and the guilt offering, it is most holy.*q* *18*Any male descendant of Aaron may eat it.*r* It is his regular share of the offerings made to the LORD by fire for the generations to come. Whatever touches them will become holy.*bs*'"

*19*The LORD also said to Moses, *20*"This is the offering Aaron and his sons are to bring to the LORD on the day he*c* is anointed: a tenth of an ephah*dt* of fine flour as a regular grain offering,*u*

*a*12 Traditionally *peace offerings*   *b*18 Or *Whoever touches them must be holy*; similarly in verse 27   *c*20 Or *each*   *d*20 That is, probably about 2 quarts (about 2 liters) half of it in the morning and half in the evening. ²¹Prepare it with oil on a griddle;ᵃ bring it well-mixed and present the grain offering brokenᵃ in pieces as an aroma pleasing to the LORD. ²²The son who is to succeed him as anointed priest shall prepare it. It is the LORD's regular share and is to be burned completely. ²³Every grain offering of a priest shall be burned completely; it must not be eaten."

²⁴The LORD said to Moses, ²⁵"Say to Aaron and his sons: 'These are the regulations for the sin offering: The sin offering is to be slaughtered before the LORDᵇ in the placeᶜ the burnt offering is slaughtered; it is most holy. ²⁶The priest who offers it shall eat it; it is to be eaten in a holy place,ᵈ in the courtyardᵉ of the Tent of Meeting. ²⁷Whatever touches any of the flesh will become holy,ᶠ and if any of the blood is spattered on a garment, you must wash it in a holy place. ²⁸The clay potᵍ the meat is cooked in must be broken; but if it is cooked in a bronze pot, the pot is to be scoured and rinsed with water. ²⁹Any male in a priest's family may eat it;ʰ it is most holy.ⁱ ³⁰But any sin offering whose blood is brought into the Tent of Meeting to make atonement in the Holy Placeʲ must not be eaten; it must be burned.ᵏ

Chapter 7 Theme

7 "'These are the regulations for the guilt offering,ˡ which is most holy: ²The guilt offering is to be slaughtered in the place where the burnt offering is slaughtered, and its blood is to be sprinkled against the altar on all sides. ³All its fatᵐ shall be offered: the fat tail and the fat that covers the inner parts, ⁴both kidneys with the fat on them near the loins, and the covering of the liver, which is to be removed with the kidneys. ⁵The priest shall burn them on the altar as an offering made to the LORD by fire. It is a guilt offering. ⁶Any male in a priest's family may eat it,ⁿ but it must be eaten in a holy place; it is most holy.ᵒ

⁷"'The same law applies to both the sin offering and the guilt offering: They belong to the priestᵖ who makes atonement with them. ⁸The priest who offers a burnt offering for anyone may keep its hide for himself. ⁹Every grain offering baked in an oven or cooked in a pan or on a griddle�q belongs to the priest who offers it, ¹⁰and every grain offering, whether mixed with oil or dry, belongs equally to all the sons of Aaron.

¹¹"'These are the regulations for the fellowship offeringᵇ a person may present to the LORD:

¹²"'If he offers it as an expression of thankfulness, then along with this thank offeringʳ he is to offer cakes of bread made without

---

ᵃ21 The meaning of the Hebrew for this word is uncertain.   ᵇ11 Traditionally *peace offering*; also in verses 13-37

6:21
ᵃLev 2:5

6:25
ᵇLev 1:3
ᶜLev 1:5,11

6:26
ᵈver 16
ᵉLev 10:17-18

6:27
ᶠEx 29:37

6:28
ᵍLev 11:33;
15:12

6:29
ʰver 18
ⁱver 17

6:30
ʲLev 4:18
ᵏLev 4:12

7:1
ˡLev 5:14-6:7

7:3
ᵐEx 29:13;
Lev 3:4,9

7:6
ⁿLev 6:18;
Nu 18:9-10
ᵒLev 2:3

7:7
ᵖLev 6:17,26;
1Co 9:13

7:9
qLev 2:5

7:12
ʳver 13,15

7:12
aLev 2:4;
Nu 6:15

7:13
bLev 23:17;
Am 4:5

7:15
cLev 22:30

7:16
dLev 19:5-8

7:18
eLev 19:7
fNu 18:27

7:20
gLev 22:3-7

7:21
hLev 5:2;
11:24,28

7:23
iLev 3:17;
17:13-14

7:24
jEx 22:31

7:26
kGe 9:4

7:27
lLev 17:10-24;
Ac 15:20,29

7:30
mEx 29:24;
Nu 6:20

7:31
nver 34

7:32
over 34;
Lev 9:21;
Nu 6:20

yeast and mixed with oil, wafers[a] made without yeast and spread with oil, and cakes of fine flour well-kneaded and mixed with oil. ¹³Along with his fellowship offering of thanksgiving he is to present an offering with cakes of bread made with yeast.[b] ¹⁴He is to bring one of each kind as an offering, a contribution to the LORD; it belongs to the priest who sprinkles the blood of the fellowship offerings. ¹⁵The meat of his fellowship offering of thanksgiving must be eaten on the day it is offered; he must leave none of it till morning.[c]

¹⁶"If, however, his offering is the result of a vow or is a freewill offering, the sacrifice shall be eaten on the day he offers it, but anything left over may be eaten on the next day.[d] ¹⁷Any meat of the sacrifice left over till the third day must be burned up. ¹⁸If any meat of the fellowship offering is eaten on the third day, it will not be accepted.[e] It will not be credited[f] to the one who offered it, for it is impure; the person who eats any of it will be held responsible.

¹⁹"Meat that touches anything ceremonially unclean must not be eaten; it must be burned up. As for other meat, anyone ceremonially clean may eat it. ²⁰But if anyone who is unclean eats any meat of the fellowship offering belonging to the LORD, that person must be cut off from his people.[g] ²¹If anyone touches something unclean[h]—whether human uncleanness or an unclean animal or any unclean, detestable thing—and then eats any of the meat of the fellowship offering belonging to the LORD, that person must be cut off from his people.'"

²²The LORD said to Moses, ²³"Say to the Israelites: 'Do not eat any of the fat of cattle, sheep or goats.[i] ²⁴The fat of an animal found dead or torn by wild animals[j] may be used for any other purpose, but you must not eat it. ²⁵Anyone who eats the fat of an animal from which an offering by fire may be[a] made to the LORD must be cut off from his people. ²⁶And wherever you live, you must not eat the blood[k] of any bird or animal. ²⁷If anyone eats blood,[l] that person must be cut off from his people.'"

²⁸The LORD said to Moses, ²⁹"Say to the Israelites: 'Anyone who brings a fellowship offering to the LORD is to bring part of it as his sacrifice to the LORD. ³⁰With his own hands he is to bring the offering made to the LORD by fire; he is to bring the fat, together with the breast, and wave the breast before the LORD as a wave offering.[m] ³¹The priest shall burn the fat on the altar, but the breast belongs to Aaron and his sons.[n] ³²You are to give the right thigh of your fellowship offerings to the priest as a contribution.[o] ³³The son of Aaron who offers the blood and the fat of the fellowship offering shall have the right thigh as his share.

a25 Or *fire is*

³⁴From the fellowship offerings of the Israelites, I have taken the breast that is waved and the thigh*ᵃ* that is presented and have given them to Aaron the priest and his sons*ᵇ* as their regular share from the Israelites.'"

³⁵This is the portion of the offerings made to the LORD by fire that were allotted to Aaron and his sons on the day they were presented to serve the LORD as priests. ³⁶On the day they were anointed,*ᶜ* the LORD commanded that the Israelites give this to them as their regular share for the generations to come.

³⁷These, then, are the regulations for the burnt offering,*ᵈ* the grain offering,*ᵉ* the sin offering, the guilt offering, the ordination offering*ᶠ* and the fellowship offering, ³⁸which the LORD gave Moses on Mount Sinai on the day he commanded the Israelites to bring their offerings to the LORD,*ᵍ* in the Desert of Sinai.

Chapter 8 Theme

8 The LORD said to Moses, ²"Bring Aaron and his sons, their garments, the anointing oil,*ʰ* the bull for the sin offering, the two rams and the basket containing bread made without yeast,*ⁱ* ³and gather the entire assembly*ʲ* at the entrance to the Tent of Meeting." ⁴Moses did as the LORD commanded him, and the assembly gathered at the entrance to the Tent of Meeting.

⁵Moses said to the assembly, "This is what the LORD has commanded to be done." ⁶Then Moses brought Aaron and his sons forward and washed them with water.*ᵏ* ⁷He put the tunic on Aaron, tied the sash around him, clothed him with the robe and put the ephod on him. He also tied the ephod to him by its skillfully woven waistband; so it was fastened on him.*ˡ* ⁸He placed the breastpiece on him and put the Urim and Thummim*ᵐ* in the breastpiece. ⁹Then he placed the turban on Aaron's head and set the gold plate, the sacred diadem,*ⁿ* on the front of it, as the LORD commanded Moses.

¹⁰Then Moses took the anointing oil*ᵒ* and anointed*ᵖ* the tabernacle and everything in it, and so consecrated them. ¹¹He sprinkled some of the oil on the altar seven times, anointing the altar and all its utensils and the basin with its stand, to consecrate them.*�q* ¹²He poured some of the anointing oil on Aaron's head and anointed*ʳ* him to consecrate him.*ˢ* ¹³Then he brought Aaron's sons forward, put tunics on them, tied sashes around them and put headbands on them, as the LORD commanded Moses.

¹⁴He then presented the bull*ᵗ* for the sin offering,*ᵘ* and Aaron and his sons laid their hands on its head. ¹⁵Moses slaughtered the bull and took some of the blood, and with his finger he put it on all the horns of the altar*ᵛ* to purify the altar.*ʷ* He poured out the

7:34
ᵃ Lev 10:15
ᵇ Ex 29:27;
Nu 18:18-19

7:36
ᶜ Ex 40:13,15;
Lev 8:12,30

7:37
ᵈ Lev 6:9
ᵉ Lev 6:14
ᶠ ver 1,11

7:38
ᵍ Lev 1:2

8:2
ʰ Ex 30:23-25, 30
ⁱ Ex 29:2-3

8:3
ʲ Nu 8:9

8:6
ᵏ Ex 29:4;
30:19;
Ps 26:6;
Ac 22:16;
1Co 6:11;
Eph 5:26

8:7
ˡ Ex 28:4

8:8
ᵐ Ex 28:30

8:9
ⁿ Ex 28:36

8:10
ᵒ ver 2
ᵖ Ex 30:26

8:11
q Ex 30:29

8:12
ʳ Lev 21:10,12
ˢ Ex 30:30

8:14
ᵗ Lev 4:3
ᵘ Ps 66:15;
Eze 43:19

8:15
ᵛ Lev 4:7
ʷ Heb 9:22

8:15
a Eze 43:20
rest of the blood at the base of the altar. So he consecrated it to make atonement for it.ᵃ ¹⁶Moses also took all the fat around the inner parts, the covering of the liver, and both kidneys and their fat, and burned it on the altar. ¹⁷But the bull with its hide and its flesh and its offalᵇ he burned up outside the camp,ᶜ as the LORD commanded Moses.

¹⁸He then presented the ramᵈ for the burnt offering, and Aaron and his sons laid their hands on its head. ¹⁹Then Moses slaughtered the ram and sprinkled the blood against the altar on all sides. ²⁰He cut the ram into pieces and burned the head, the pieces and the fat. ²¹He washed the inner parts and the legs with water and burned the whole ram on the altar as a burnt offering, a pleasing aroma, an offering made to the LORD by fire, as the LORD commanded Moses.

8:17
b Lev 4:11
c Lev 4:12

8:18
d ver 2

²²He then presented the other ram, the ram for the ordination,ᵉ and Aaron and his sons laid their hands on its head. ²³Moses slaughtered the ram and took some of its blood and put it on the lobe of Aaron's right ear, on the thumb of his right hand and on the big toe of his right foot. ²⁴Moses also brought Aaron's sons forward and put some of the blood on the lobes of their right ears, on the thumbs of their right hands and on the big toes of their right feet. Then he sprinkled blood against the altar on all sides.ᶠ ²⁵He took the fat, the fat tail, all the fat around the inner parts, the covering of the liver, both kidneys and their fat and the right thigh. ²⁶Then from the basket of bread made without yeast, which was before the LORD, he took a cake of bread, and one made with oil, and a wafer; he put these on the fat portions and on the right thigh. ²⁷He put all these in the hands of Aaron and his sons and waved them before the LORD as a wave offering. ²⁸Then Moses took them from their hands and burned them on the altar on top of the burnt offering as an ordination offering, a pleasing aroma, an offering made to the LORD by fire. ²⁹He also took the breast—Moses' share of the ordination ramᵍ—and waved it before the LORD as a wave offering, as the LORD commanded Moses.

8:22
e ver 2

8:24
f Heb 9:18-22

8:29
g Lev 7:31-34

³⁰Then Moses took some of the anointing oil and some of the blood from the altar and sprinkled them on Aaron and his garmentsʰ and on his sons and their garments. So he consecratedⁱ Aaron and his garments and his sons and their garments.

³¹Moses then said to Aaron and his sons, "Cook the meat at the entrance to the Tent of Meeting and eat it there with the bread from the basket of ordination offerings, as I commanded, saying,ᵃ 'Aaron and his sons are to eat it.' ³²Then burn up the rest of the

8:30
h Ex 28:2
i Nu 3:3

a31 Or I was commanded:

meat and the bread. ³³Do not leave the entrance to the Tent of Meeting for seven days, until the days of your ordination are completed, for your ordination will last seven days. ³⁴What has been done today was commanded by the LORD^a to make atonement for you. ³⁵You must stay at the entrance to the Tent of Meeting day and night for seven days and do what the LORD requires,^b so you will not die; for that is what I have been commanded." ³⁶So Aaron and his sons did everything the LORD commanded through Moses.

Chapter 9 Theme _____

9 On the eighth day^c Moses summoned Aaron and his sons and the elders of Israel. ²He said to Aaron, "Take a bull calf for your sin offering and a ram for your burnt offering, both without defect, and present them before the LORD. ³Then say to the Israelites: 'Take a male goat for a sin offering, a calf and a lamb—both a year old and without defect—for a burnt offering, ⁴and an ox^a and a ram for a fellowship offering^b to sacrifice before the LORD, together with a grain offering mixed with oil. For today the LORD will appear to you.^d'"

⁵They took the things Moses commanded to the front of the Tent of Meeting, and the entire assembly came near and stood before the LORD. ⁶Then Moses said, "This is what the LORD has commanded you to do, so that the glory of the LORD^e may appear to you."

⁷Moses said to Aaron, "Come to the altar and sacrifice your sin offering and your burnt offering and make atonement for yourself and the people; sacrifice the offering that is for the people and make atonement for them, as the LORD has commanded.^f"

⁸So Aaron came to the altar and slaughtered the calf as a sin offering^g for himself. ⁹His sons brought the blood to him,^h and he dipped his finger into the blood and put it on the horns of the altar; the rest of the blood he poured out at the base of the altar.ⁱ ¹⁰On the altar he burned the fat, the kidneys and the covering of the liver from the sin offering, as the LORD commanded Moses; ¹¹the flesh and the hide^j he burned up outside the camp.^k

¹²Then he slaughtered the burnt offering. His sons handed him the blood, and he sprinkled it against the altar on all sides. ¹³They handed him the burnt offering piece by piece, including the head, and he burned them on the altar.^l ¹⁴He washed the inner parts and the legs and burned them on top of the burnt offering on the altar.

¹⁵Aaron then brought the offering that was for the people.^m He took the goat for the people's sin offering and slaughtered it and offered it for a sin offering as he did with the first one.

a4 The Hebrew word can include both male and female; also in verses 18 and 19.
b4 Traditionally *peace offering*; also in verses 18 and 22

### Cross references (margin)

8:34
^aHeb 7:16

8:35
^bNu 3:7; 9:19;
Dt 11:1;
1Ki 2:3;
Eze 48:11

9:1
^cEze 43:27

9:4
^dEx 29:43

9:6
^ever 23;
Ex 24:16

9:7
^fHeb 5:1,3;
7:27

9:8
^gLev 4:1-12

9:9
^hver 12,18
ⁱLev 4:7

9:11
^jLev 4:11
^kLev 4:12;
8:17

9:13
^lLev 1:8

9:15
^mLev 4:27-31

9:16
a Lev 1:1-13

9:17
b Lev 2:1-2;
3:5

9:18
c Lev 3:1-11

9:21
d Ex 29:24,26;
Lev 7:30-34

9:22
e Nu 6:23;
Dt 21:5;
Lk 24:50

9:23
f ver 6

9:24
g Jdg 6:21;
2Ch 7:1
h 1Ki 18:39

10:1
i Ex 24:1;
Nu 3:2-4;
26:61
j Lev 16:12
k Ex 30:9

10:2
l Nu 3:4;
16:35; 26:61

10:3
m Ex 19:22
n Ex 30:29;
Lev 21:6;
Eze 28:22
o Isa 49:3

10:4
p Ex 6:22
q Ex 6:18
r Ac 5:6,9,10

10:5
s Lev 8:13

10:6
t Lev 21:10

[16]He brought the burnt offering and offered it in the prescribed way.*a* [17]He also brought the grain offering, took a handful of it and burned it on the altar in addition to the morning's burnt offering.*b* [18]He slaughtered the ox and the ram as the fellowship offering for the people.*c* His sons handed him the blood, and he sprinkled it against the altar on all sides. [19]But the fat portions of the ox and the ram—the fat tail, the layer of fat, the kidneys and the covering of the liver— [20]these they laid on the breasts, and then Aaron burned the fat on the altar. [21]Aaron waved the breasts and the right thigh before the LORD as a wave offering,*d* as Moses commanded.

[22]Then Aaron lifted his hands toward the people and blessed them.*e* And having sacrificed the sin offering, the burnt offering and the fellowship offering, he stepped down.

[23]Moses and Aaron then went into the Tent of Meeting. When they came out, they blessed the people; and the glory of the LORD*f* appeared to all the people. [24]Fire*g* came out from the presence of the LORD and consumed the burnt offering and the fat portions on the altar. And when all the people saw it, they shouted for joy and fell facedown.*h*

Chapter 10 Theme

10 Aaron's sons Nadab and Abihu*i* took their censers, put fire in them*j* and added incense; and they offered unauthorized fire before the LORD, contrary to his command.*k* [2]So fire came out from the presence of the LORD and consumed them,*l* and they died before the LORD. [3]Moses then said to Aaron, "This is what the LORD spoke of when he said:

> "'Among those who approach me*m*
> I will show myself holy;*n*
> in the sight of all the people
> I will be honored.*o*'"

Aaron remained silent.

[4]Moses summoned Mishael and Elzaphan,*p* sons of Aaron's uncle Uzziel,*q* and said to them, "Come here; carry your cousins outside the camp,*r* away from the front of the sanctuary." [5]So they came and carried them, still in their tunics,*s* outside the camp, as Moses ordered.

[6]Then Moses said to Aaron and his sons Eleazar and Ithamar, "Do not let your hair become unkempt,*a t* and do not tear your clothes, or you will die and the LORD will be angry with the whole

a6 Or *Do not uncover your heads*

community.*a* But your relatives, all the house of Israel, may mourn for those the LORD has destroyed by fire. ⁷Do not leave the entrance to the Tent of Meeting or you will die, because the LORD's anointing oil*b* is on you." So they did as Moses said.

⁸Then the LORD said to Aaron, ⁹"You and your sons are not to drink wine*c* or other fermented drink*d* whenever you go into the Tent of Meeting, or you will die. This is a lasting ordinance for the generations to come. ¹⁰You must distinguish between the holy and the common, between the unclean and the clean,*e* ¹¹and you must teach*f* the Israelites all the decrees the LORD has given them through Moses.*g*"

¹²Moses said to Aaron and his remaining sons, Eleazar and Ithamar, "Take the grain offering left over from the offerings made to the LORD by fire and eat it prepared without yeast beside the altar,*h* for it is most holy. ¹³Eat it in a holy place, because it is your share and your sons' share of the offerings made to the LORD by fire; for so I have been commanded. ¹⁴But you and your sons and your daughters may eat the breast that was waved and the thigh that was presented. Eat them in a ceremonially clean place;*i* they have been given to you and your children as your share of the Israelites' fellowship offerings.*a* ¹⁵The thigh*j* that was presented and the breast that was waved must be brought with the fat portions of the offerings made by fire, to be waved before the LORD as a wave offering. This will be the regular share for you and your children, as the LORD has commanded."

¹⁶When Moses inquired about the goat of the sin offering*k* and found that it had been burned up, he was angry with Eleazar and Ithamar, Aaron's remaining sons, and asked, ¹⁷"Why didn't you eat the sin offering*l* in the sanctuary area? It is most holy; it was given to you to take away the guilt of the community by making atonement for them before the LORD. ¹⁸Since its blood was not taken into the Holy Place,*m* you should have eaten the goat in the sanctuary area, as I commanded."

¹⁹Aaron replied to Moses, "Today they sacrificed their sin offering and their burnt offering*n* before the LORD, but such things as this have happened to me. Would the LORD have been pleased if I had eaten the sin offering today?" ²⁰When Moses heard this, he was satisfied.

Chapter 11 Theme _____

11 The LORD said to Moses and Aaron, ²"Say to the Israelites: 'Of all the animals that live on land, these are the ones you

a14 Traditionally peace offerings

10:6
*a*Nu 1:53;
16:22;
Jos 7:1;
22:18;
2Sa 24:1

10:7
*b*Ex 28:41;
Lev 21:12

10:9
*c*Hos 4:11
*d*Pr 20:1;
Isa 28:7;
Eze 44:21;
Lk 1:15;
Eph 5:18;
1Ti 3:3;
Tit 1:7

10:10
*e*Lev 11:47;
20:25;
Eze 22:26

10:11
*f*Mal 2:7
*g*Dt 24:8

10:12
*h*Lev 6:14-18;
21:22

10:14
*i*Ex 29:24, 26-27;
Lev 7:31,34;
Nu 18:11

10:15
*j*Lev 7:34

10:16
*k*Lev 9:3

10:17
*l*Lev 6:24-30

10:18
*m*Lev 6:26,30

10:19
*n*Lev 9:12

11:2
a Ac 10:12-14

11:7
b Isa 65:4;
66:3,17

11:8
c Isa 52:11;
Heb 9:10

11:10
d Lev 7:18

11:20
e Ac 10:14

11:22
f Mt 3:4;
Mk 1:6

11:25
g Lev 14:8,47;
15:5

h ver 40;
Nu 31:24

may eat:*a* ³You may eat any animal that has a split hoof completely divided and that chews the cud.

⁴ "There are some that only chew the cud or only have a split hoof, but you must not eat them. The camel, though it chews the cud, does not have a split hoof; it is ceremonially unclean for you. ⁵The coney,*a* though it chews the cud, does not have a split hoof; it is unclean for you. ⁶The rabbit, though it chews the cud, does not have a split hoof; it is unclean for you. ⁷And the pig,*b* though it has a split hoof completely divided, does not chew the cud; it is unclean for you. ⁸You must not eat their meat or touch their carcasses; they are unclean for you.*c*

⁹ "Of all the creatures living in the water of the seas and the streams, you may eat any that have fins and scales. ¹⁰But all creatures in the seas or streams that do not have fins and scales—whether among all the swarming things or among all the other living creatures in the water—you are to detest.*d* ¹¹And since you are to detest them, you must not eat their meat and you must detest their carcasses. ¹²Anything living in the water that does not have fins and scales is to be detestable to you.

¹³ "These are the birds you are to detest and not eat because they are detestable: the eagle, the vulture, the black vulture, ¹⁴the red kite, any kind of black kite, ¹⁵any kind of raven, ¹⁶the horned owl, the screech owl, the gull, any kind of hawk, ¹⁷the little owl, the cormorant, the great owl, ¹⁸the white owl, the desert owl, the osprey, ¹⁹the stork, any kind of heron, the hoopoe and the bat.*b*

²⁰ "All flying insects that walk on all fours are to be detestable to you.*e* ²¹There are, however, some winged creatures that walk on all fours that you may eat: those that have jointed legs for hopping on the ground. ²²Of these you may eat any kind of locust,*f* katydid, cricket or grasshopper. ²³But all other winged creatures that have four legs you are to detest.

²⁴ "You will make yourselves unclean by these; whoever touches their carcasses will be unclean till evening. ²⁵Whoever picks up one of their carcasses must wash his clothes,*g* and he will be unclean till evening.*h*

²⁶ "Every animal that has a split hoof not completely divided or that does not chew the cud is unclean for you; whoever touches ₍the carcass of₎ any of them will be unclean. ²⁷Of all the animals that walk on all fours, those that walk on their paws are unclean for you; whoever touches their carcasses will be unclean till evening. ²⁸Anyone who picks up their carcasses must wash his clothes, and he will be unclean till evening. They are unclean for you.

a 5 That is, the hyrax or rock badger   *b* 19 The precise identification of some of the birds, insects and animals in this chapter is uncertain.

²⁹"'Of the animals that move about on the ground, these are unclean for you: the weasel, the rat,^a any kind of great lizard, ³⁰the gecko, the monitor lizard, the wall lizard, the skink and the chameleon. ³¹Of all those that move along the ground, these are unclean for you. Whoever touches them when they are dead will be unclean till evening. ³²When one of them dies and falls on something, that article, whatever its use, will be unclean, whether it is made of wood, cloth, hide or sackcloth.^b Put it in water; it will be unclean till evening, and then it will be clean. ³³If one of them falls into a clay pot, everything in it will be unclean, and you must break the pot.^c ³⁴Any food that could be eaten but has water on it from such a pot is unclean, and any liquid that could be drunk from it is unclean. ³⁵Anything that one of their carcasses falls on becomes unclean; an oven or cooking pot must be broken up. They are unclean, and you are to regard them as unclean. ³⁶A spring, however, or a cistern for collecting water remains clean, but anyone who touches one of these carcasses is unclean. ³⁷If a carcass falls on any seeds that are to be planted, they remain clean. ³⁸But if water has been put on the seed and a carcass falls on it, it is unclean for you.

³⁹"'If an animal that you are allowed to eat dies, anyone who touches the carcass will be unclean till evening. ⁴⁰Anyone who eats some of the carcass must wash his clothes, and he will be unclean till evening.^d Anyone who picks up the carcass must wash his clothes, and he will be unclean till evening.

⁴¹"'Every creature that moves about on the ground is detestable; it is not to be eaten. ⁴²You are not to eat any creature that moves about on the ground, whether it moves on its belly or walks on all fours or on many feet; it is detestable. ⁴³Do not defile yourselves by any of these creatures.^e Do not make yourselves unclean by means of them or be made unclean by them. ⁴⁴I am the LORD your God;^f consecrate yourselves^g and be holy,^h because I am holy.ⁱ Do not make yourselves unclean by any creature that moves about on the ground. ⁴⁵I am the LORD who brought you up out of Egypt^j to be your God;^k therefore be holy, because I am holy.^l

⁴⁶"'These are the regulations concerning animals, birds, every living thing that moves in the water and every creature that moves about on the ground. ⁴⁷You must distinguish between the unclean and the clean, between living creatures that may be eaten and those that may not be eaten.^m'"

Chapter 12 Theme

12 The LORD said to Moses, ²"Say to the Israelites: 'A woman who becomes pregnant and gives birth to a son will be

---

11:29
^aIsa 66:17

11:32
^bLev 15:12

11:33
^cLev 6:28;
15:12

11:40
^dLev 17:15;
22:8;
Eze 44:31

11:43
^eLev 20:25

11:44
^fEx 6:2,7;
Isa 43:3; 51:15
^gLev 20:7
^hEx 19:6
ⁱLev 19:2;
Ps 99:3;
Eph 1:4;
1Th 4:7;
1Pe 1:15,16*

11:45
^jLev 25:38,55;
Ex 6:7; 20:2
^kGe 17:7
^lEx 19:6;
1Pe 1:16*

11:47
^mLev 10:10

12:2
a Lev 15:19;
18:19

12:3
b Ge 17:12;
Lk 1:59; 2:21

12:6
c Lk 2:22
d Ex 29:38;
Lev 23:12;
Nu 6:12,14;
7:15
e Lev 5:7

12:8
f Ge 15:9;
Lev 14:22
g Lev 5:7;
Lk 2:22-24*
h Lev 4:26

13:2
i ver 10,19,
28,43
j ver 4,38,39;
Lev 14:56
k ver 3,9,15;
Ex 4:6;
Lev 14:3,32;
Nu 5:2;
Dt 24:8
l Dt 24:8

13:3
m ver 8,11,20,30;
Lev 21:1;
Nu 9:6

13:4
n ver 2
o ver 5,21,
26,33,46;
Lev 14:38;
Nu 12:14,15;
Dt 24:9

13:5
p Lev 14:9
q ver 27,32,
34,51

13:6
r ver 13,17,
23,28,34;
Mt 8:3;
Lk 5:12-14
s Lev 11:25
t Lev 11:25;
14:8,9,
20,48;
15:8;
Nu 8:7

13:7
u Lk 5:14

ceremonially unclean for seven days, just as she is unclean during her monthly period.ᵃ ³On the eighth day the boy is to be circumcised.ᵇ ⁴Then the woman must wait thirty-three days to be purified from her bleeding. She must not touch anything sacred or go to the sanctuary until the days of her purification are over. ⁵If she gives birth to a daughter, for two weeks the woman will be unclean, as during her period. Then she must wait sixty-six days to be purified from her bleeding.

⁶"'When the days of her purification for a son or daughter are over,ᶜ she is to bring to the priest at the entrance to the Tent of Meeting a year-old lambᵈ for a burnt offering and a young pigeon or a dove for a sin offering.ᵉ ⁷He shall offer them before the LORD to make atonement for her, and then she will be ceremonially clean from her flow of blood.

"'These are the regulations for the woman who gives birth to a boy or a girl. ⁸If she cannot afford a lamb, she is to bring two doves or two young pigeons,ᶠ one for a burnt offering and the other for a sin offering.ᵍ In this way the priest will make atonement for her, and she will be clean.ʰ'"

Chapter 13 Theme _____

13 The LORD said to Moses and Aaron, ²"When anyone has a swellingⁱ or a rash or a bright spotʲ on his skin that may become an infectious skin disease,ᵃᵏ he must be brought to Aaron the priestˡ or to one of his sonsᵇ who is a priest. ³The priest is to examine the sore on his skin, and if the hair in the sore has turned white and the sore appears to be more than skin deep,ᶜ it is an infectious skin disease. When the priest examines him, he shall pronounce him ceremonially unclean.ᵐ ⁴If the spotⁿ on his skin is white but does not appear to be more than skin deep and the hair in it has not turned white, the priest is to put the infected person in isolation for seven days.ᵒ ⁵On the seventh dayᵖ the priest is to examine him,�q and if he sees that the sore is unchanged and has not spread in the skin, he is to keep him in isolation another seven days. ⁶On the seventh day the priest is to examine him again, and if the sore has faded and has not spread in the skin, the priest shall pronounce him clean;ʳ it is only a rash. The man must wash his clothes,ˢ and he will be clean.ᵗ ⁷But if the rash does spread in his skin after he has shown himself to the priest to be pronounced clean, he must appear before the priest again.ᵘ ⁸The priest is to examine him, and if the rash has spread in the skin, he shall pronounce him unclean; it is an infectious disease.

ᵃ2 Traditionally *leprosy*; the Hebrew word was used for various diseases affecting the skin—not necessarily leprosy; also elsewhere in this chapter.   ᵇ2 Or *descendants*   ᶜ3 Or *be lower than the rest of the skin*; also elsewhere in this chapter

⁹"When anyone has an infectious skin disease, he must be brought to the priest. ¹⁰The priest is to examine him, and if there is a white swelling in the skin that has turned the hair white and if there is raw flesh in the swelling, ¹¹it is a chronic skin disease^a and the priest shall pronounce him unclean. He is not to put him in isolation, because he is already unclean.

¹²"If the disease breaks out all over his skin and, so far as the priest can see, it covers all the skin of the infected person from head to foot, ¹³the priest is to examine him, and if the disease has covered his whole body, he shall pronounce that person clean. Since it has all turned white, he is clean. ¹⁴But whenever raw flesh appears on him, he will be unclean. ¹⁵When the priest sees the raw flesh, he shall pronounce him unclean. The raw flesh is unclean; he has an infectious disease.^b ¹⁶Should the raw flesh change and turn white, he must go to the priest. ¹⁷The priest is to examine him, and if the sores have turned white, the priest shall pronounce the infected person clean;^c then he will be clean.

¹⁸"When someone has a boil^d on his skin and it heals, ¹⁹and in the place where the boil was, a white swelling or reddish-white^e spot^f appears, he must present himself to the priest. ²⁰The priest is to examine it, and if it appears to be more than skin deep and the hair in it has turned white, the priest shall pronounce him unclean. It is an infectious skin disease^g that has broken out where the boil was. ²¹But if, when the priest examines it, there is no white hair in it and it is not more than skin deep and has faded, then the priest is to put him in isolation for seven days. ²²If it is spreading in the skin, the priest shall pronounce him unclean; it is infectious. ²³But if the spot is unchanged and has not spread, it is only a scar from the boil, and the priest shall pronounce him clean.^h

²⁴"When someone has a burn on his skin and a reddish-white or white spot appears in the raw flesh of the burn, ²⁵the priest is to examine the spot, and if the hair in it has turned white, and it appears to be more than skin deep, it is an infectious disease that has broken out in the burn. The priest shall pronounce him unclean; it is an infectious skin disease.ⁱ ²⁶But if the priest examines it and there is no white hair in the spot and if it is not more than skin deep and has faded, then the priest is to put him in isolation for seven days.^j ²⁷On the seventh day the priest is to examine him,^k and if it is spreading in the skin, the priest shall pronounce him unclean; it is an infectious skin disease. ²⁸If, however, the spot is unchanged and has not spread in the skin but has faded, it is a swelling from the burn, and the priest shall pronounce him clean; it is only a scar from the burn.^l

13:11
^aEx 4:6;
Lev 14:8;
Nu 12:10;
Mt 8:2

13:15
^bver 2

13:17
^cver 6

13:18
^dEx 9:9

13:19
^ever 24,42;
Lev 14:37
^fver 2

13:20
^gver 2

13:23
^hver 6

13:25
ⁱver 11

13:26
^jver 4

13:27
^kver 5

13:28
^lver 2

13:29
a ver 43,44

²⁹"If a man or woman has a sore on the head[a] or on the chin, ³⁰the priest is to examine the sore, and if it appears to be more than skin deep and the hair in it is yellow and thin, the priest shall pronounce that person unclean; it is an itch, an infectious disease of the head or chin. ³¹But if, when the priest examines

13:31
b ver 4

this kind of sore, it does not seem to be more than skin deep and there is no black hair in it, then the priest is to put the infected person in isolation for seven days.[b] ³²On the seventh day the priest is to examine the sore,[c] and if the itch has not spread and there is no yellow hair in it and it does not appear to be more

13:32
c ver 5

than skin deep, ³³he must be shaved except for the diseased area, and the priest is to keep him in isolation another seven days. ³⁴On the seventh day the priest is to examine the itch,[d] and if it has not spread in the skin and appears to be no more than skin

13:34
d ver 5
e Lev 11:25

deep, the priest shall pronounce him clean. He must wash his clothes, and he will be clean.[e] ³⁵But if the itch does spread in the skin after he is pronounced clean, ³⁶the priest is to examine him, and if the itch has spread in the skin, the priest does not need to look for yellow hair; the person is unclean.[f] ³⁷If, however, in his judgment it is unchanged and black hair has grown in it, the itch

13:36
f ver 30

is healed. He is clean, and the priest shall pronounce him clean.

³⁸"When a man or woman has white spots on the skin, ³⁹the priest is to examine them, and if the spots are dull white, it is a harmless rash that has broken out on the skin; that person is clean.

13:40
g Lev 21:5;
2Ki 2:23;
Isa 3:24;
15:2; 22:12;
Eze 27:31;
29:18;
Am 8:10;
Mic 1:16

⁴⁰"When a man has lost his hair and is bald,[g] he is clean. ⁴¹If he has lost his hair from the front of his scalp and has a bald forehead, he is clean. ⁴²But if he has a reddish-white sore on his bald head or forehead, it is an infectious disease breaking out on his head or forehead. ⁴³The priest is to examine him, and if the swollen sore on his head or forehead is reddish-white like an infectious skin disease, ⁴⁴the man is diseased and is unclean. The priest shall pronounce him unclean because of the sore on his head.

13:45
h Lev 10:6
i Eze 24:17,22;
Mic 3:7
j Lev 5:2;
La 4:15;
Lk 17:12

⁴⁵"The person with such an infectious disease must wear torn clothes,[h] let his hair be unkempt,[a] cover the lower part of his face[i] and cry out, 'Unclean! Unclean!'[j] ⁴⁶As long as he has the infection he remains unclean. He must live alone; he must live outside the camp.[k]

⁴⁷"If any clothing is contaminated with mildew—any woolen or linen clothing, ⁴⁸any woven or knitted material of linen or wool, any leather or anything made of leather— ⁴⁹and if the contamination in the clothing, or leather, or woven or knitted material, or any leather article, is greenish or reddish, it is a spreading mildew

13:46
k Nu 5:1-4;
12:14;
2Ki 7:3; 15:5;
Lk 17:12

a45 Or clothes, uncover his head

and must be shown to the priest.*a* ⁵⁰The priest is to examine the mildew*b* and isolate the affected article for seven days. ⁵¹On the seventh day he is to examine it,*c* and if the mildew has spread in the clothing, or the woven or knitted material, or the leather, whatever its use, it is a destructive mildew; the article is unclean.*d* ⁵²He must burn up the clothing, or the woven or knitted material of wool or linen, or any leather article that has the contamination in it, because the mildew is destructive; the article must be burned up.*e*

⁵³"But if, when the priest examines it, the mildew has not spread in the clothing, or the woven or knitted material, or the leather article, ⁵⁴he shall order that the contaminated article be washed. Then he is to isolate it for another seven days. ⁵⁵After the affected article has been washed, the priest is to examine it, and if the mildew has not changed its appearance, even though it has not spread, it is unclean. Burn it with fire, whether the mildew has affected one side or the other. ⁵⁶If, when the priest examines it, the mildew has faded after the article has been washed, he is to tear the contaminated part out of the clothing, or the leather, or the woven or knitted material. ⁵⁷But if it reappears in the clothing, or in the woven or knitted material, or in the leather article, it is spreading, and whatever has the mildew must be burned with fire. ⁵⁸The clothing, or the woven or knitted material, or any leather article that has been washed and is rid of the mildew, must be washed again, and it will be clean."

⁵⁹These are the regulations concerning contamination by mildew in woolen or linen clothing, woven or knitted material, or any leather article, for pronouncing them clean or unclean.

Chapter 14 Theme

14 The LORD said to Moses, ²"These are the regulations for the diseased person at the time of his ceremonial cleansing, when he is brought to the priest:*f* ³The priest is to go outside the camp and examine him.*g* If the person has been healed of his infectious skin disease,*a* ⁴the priest shall order that two live clean birds and some cedar wood, scarlet yarn and hyssop be brought for the one to be cleansed.*h* ⁵Then the priest shall order that one of the birds be killed over fresh water in a clay pot. ⁶He is then to take the live bird and dip it, together with the cedar wood, the scarlet yarn and the hyssop, into the blood of the bird that was killed over the fresh water.*i* ⁷Seven times he shall sprinkle*j* the one to be cleansed of the infectious disease and pronounce him clean. Then he is to release the live bird in the open fields.

---

a3 Traditionally *leprosy*; the Hebrew word was used for various diseases affecting the skin—not necessarily leprosy; also elsewhere in this chapter.

13:49
a Mk 1:44

13:50
b Eze 44:23

13:51
c ver 5
d Lev 14:44

13:52
e ver 55,57

14:2
f Mt 8:2-4;
Mk 1:40-44;
Lk 5:12-14;
17:14

14:3
g Lev 13:46

14:4
h ver 6,49,51,52;
Nu 19:6;
Ps 51:7

14:6
i ver 4

14:7
j 2Ki 5:10,14;
Isa 52:15;
Eze 36:25

14:8
aLev 11:25;
13:6
bver 9
cver 20
dNu 5:2,3;
12:14,15;
2Ch 26:21

8"The person to be cleansed must wash his clothes,a shave off all his hair and bathe with water;b then he will be ceremonially clean.c After this he may come into the camp,d but he must stay outside his tent for seven days. 9On the seventh day he must shave off all his hair; he must shave his head, his beard, his eyebrows and the rest of his hair. He must wash his clothes and bathe himself with water, and he will be clean.

14:10
eMt 8:4;
Mk 1:44;
Lk 5:14
fLev 2:1
gver 12,15,
21,24

10"On the eighth daye he must bring two male lambs and one ewe lamb a year old, each without defect, along with three-tenths of an ephaha of fine flour mixed with oil for a grain offering,f and one logb of oil.g 11The priest who pronounces him clean shall present both the one to be cleansed and his offerings before the LORD at the entrance to the Tent of Meeting.

12"Then the priest is to take one of the male lambs and offer it as a guilt offering,h along with the log of oil; he shall wave them before the LORD as a wave offering.i 13He is to slaughter the lamb in the holy placej where the sin offering and the burnt offering are slaughtered. Like the sin offering, the guilt offering belongs to the priest;k it is most holy. 14The priest is to take some of the blood of the guilt offering and put it on the lobe of the right ear of the one to be cleansed, on the thumb of his right hand and on the big toe of his right foot.l 15The priest shall then take some of the log of oil, pour it in the palm of his own left hand, 16dip his right forefinger into the oil in his palm, and with his finger sprinkle some of it before the LORD seven times. 17The priest is to put some of the oil remaining in his palm on the lobe of the right ear of the one to be cleansed, on the thumb of his right hand and on the big toe of his right foot, on top of the blood of the guilt offering. 18The rest of the oil in his palm the priest shall put on the head of the one to be cleansed and make atonement for him before the LORD.

14:12
hLev 5:18;
6:6-7
iEx 29:24

14:13
jEx 29:11
kLev 6:24-30;
7:7

14:14
lEx 29:20;
Lev 8:23

19"Then the priest is to sacrifice the sin offering and make atonement for the one to be cleansed from his uncleanness. After that, the priest shall slaughter the burnt offering 20and offer it on the altar, together with the grain offering, and make atonement for him, and he will be clean.m

14:20
mver 8

21"If, however, he is poorn and cannot afford these,o he must take one male lamb as a guilt offering to be waved to make atonement for him, together with a tenth of an ephahc of fine flour mixed with oil for a grain offering, a log of oil, 22and two doves or two young pigeons,p which he can afford, one for a sin offering and the other for a burnt offering.

14:21
nLev 5:7; 12:8
over 22,32

a10 That is, probably about 6 quarts (about 6.5 liters)   b10 That is, probably about 2/3 pint (about 0.3 liter); also in verses 12, 15, 21 and 24   c21 That is, probably about 2 quarts (about 2 liters)

14:22
pLev 5:7

²³"On the eighth day he must bring them for his cleansing to the priest at the entrance to the Tent of Meeting, before the LORD.^a ²⁴The priest is to take the lamb for the guilt offering,^b together with the log of oil,^c and wave them before the LORD as a wave offering.^d ²⁵He shall slaughter the lamb for the guilt offering and take some of its blood and put it on the lobe of the right ear of the one to be cleansed, on the thumb of his right hand and on the big toe of his right foot.^e ²⁶The priest is to pour some of the oil into the palm of his own left hand,^f ²⁷and with his right forefinger sprinkle some of the oil from his palm seven times before the LORD. ²⁸Some of the oil in his palm he is to put on the same places he put the blood of the guilt offering—on the lobe of the right ear of the one to be cleansed, on the thumb of his right hand and on the big toe of his right foot. ²⁹The rest of the oil in his palm the priest shall put on the head of the one to be cleansed, to make atonement for him before the LORD.^g ³⁰Then he shall sacrifice the doves or the young pigeons, which the person can afford,^h ³¹one^a as a sin offering and the other as a burnt offering,ⁱ together with the grain offering. In this way the priest will make atonement before the LORD on behalf of the one to be cleansed.^j"

³²These are the regulations for anyone who has an infectious skin disease^k and who cannot afford the regular offerings^l for his cleansing.

³³The LORD said to Moses and Aaron, ³⁴"When you enter the land of Canaan,^m which I am giving you as your possession,ⁿ and I put a spreading mildew in a house in that land, ³⁵the owner of the house must go and tell the priest, 'I have seen something that looks like mildew in my house.' ³⁶The priest is to order the house to be emptied before he goes in to examine the mildew, so that nothing in the house will be pronounced unclean. After this the priest is to go in and inspect the house. ³⁷He is to examine the mildew on the walls, and if it has greenish or reddish^o depressions that appear to be deeper than the surface of the wall, ³⁸the priest shall go out the doorway of the house and close it up for seven days.^p ³⁹On the seventh day^q the priest shall return to inspect the house. If the mildew has spread on the walls, ⁴⁰he is to order that the contaminated stones be torn out and thrown into an unclean place outside the town.^r ⁴¹He must have all the inside walls of the house scraped and the material that is scraped off dumped into an unclean place outside the town. ⁴²Then they are to take other stones to replace these and take new clay and plaster the house.

⁴³"If the mildew reappears in the house after the stones have been torn out and the house scraped and plastered, ⁴⁴the priest

---

^a31 Septuagint and Syriac; Hebrew ³¹such as the person can afford, one

14:23
^aver 10,11

14:24
^bNu 6:14
^cver 10
^dver 12

14:25
^ever 14;
Ex 29:20

14:26
^fver 15

14:29
^gver 18

14:30
^hLev 5:7

14:31
ⁱver 22;
Lev 5:7;
15:15,30
^jver 18,19

14:32
^kLev 13:2
^lver 21

14:34
^mGe 12:5;
Ex 6:4;
Nu 13:2
ⁿGe 17:8;
48:4;
Nu 27:12;
32:22;
Dt 3:27; 7:1;
32:49

14:37
^oLev 13:19

14:38
^pLev 13:4

14:39
^qLev 13:5

14:40
^rver 45

14:44
a Lev 13:51

14:46
b Lev 11:24

14:47
c Lev 11:25

14:48
d Lev 13:6

14:49
e ver 4;
1Ki 4:33

14:50
f ver 5

14:51
g ver 6;
Ps 51:7
h ver 4,7

14:53
i ver 7
j ver 20

14:54
k Lev 13:2,30

14:55
l Lev 13:47-52

14:56
m Lev 13:2

14:57
n Lev 10:10

15:2
o ver 16,32;
Lev 22:4;
Nu 5:2;
2Sa 3:29;
Mt 9:20

15:5
p Lev 11:25
q Lev 14:8
r Lev 11:24

15:7
s ver 19;
Lev 22:5
t ver 16;
Lev 22:4

15:8
u Nu 12:14

is to go and examine it and, if the mildew has spread in the house, it is a destructive mildew; the house is unclean.*a* ⁴⁵It must be torn down—its stones, timbers and all the plaster—and taken out of the town to an unclean place.

⁴⁶"Anyone who goes into the house while it is closed up will be unclean till evening.*b* ⁴⁷Anyone who sleeps or eats in the house must wash his clothes.*c*

⁴⁸"But if the priest comes to examine it and the mildew has not spread after the house has been plastered, he shall pronounce the house clean,*d* because the mildew is gone. ⁴⁹To purify the house he is to take two birds and some cedar wood, scarlet yarn and hyssop.*e* ⁵⁰He shall kill one of the birds over fresh water in a clay pot.*f* ⁵¹Then he is to take the cedar wood, the hyssop,*g* the scarlet yarn and the live bird, dip them into the blood of the dead bird and the fresh water, and sprinkle the house seven times.*h* ⁵²He shall purify the house with the bird's blood, the fresh water, the live bird, the cedar wood, the hyssop and the scarlet yarn. ⁵³Then he is to release the live bird in the open fields*i* outside the town. In this way he will make atonement for the house, and it will be clean.*j*"

⁵⁴These are the regulations for any infectious skin disease,*k* for an itch, ⁵⁵for mildew*l* in clothing or in a house, ⁵⁶and for a swelling, a rash or a bright spot,*m* ⁵⁷to determine when something is clean or unclean.

These are the regulations for infectious skin diseases and mildew.*n*

Chapter 15 Theme _____

15 The LORD said to Moses and Aaron, ²"Speak to the Israelites and say to them: 'When any man has a bodily discharge,*o* the discharge is unclean. ³Whether it continues flowing from his body or is blocked, it will make him unclean. This is how his discharge will bring about uncleanness:

⁴"'Any bed the man with a discharge lies on will be unclean, and anything he sits on will be unclean. ⁵Anyone who touches his bed must wash his clothes*p* and bathe with water,*q* and he will be unclean till evening.*r* ⁶Whoever sits on anything that the man with a discharge sat on must wash his clothes and bathe with water, and he will be unclean till evening.

⁷"'Whoever touches the man*s* who has a discharge*t* must wash his clothes and bathe with water, and he will be unclean till evening.

⁸"'If the man with the discharge spits*u* on someone who is clean, that person must wash his clothes and bathe with water, and he will be unclean till evening.

⁹"'Everything the man sits on when riding will be unclean, ¹⁰and whoever touches any of the things that were under him will be unclean till evening; whoever picks up those things*ᵃ* must wash his clothes and bathe with water, and he will be unclean till evening.

¹¹"'Anyone the man with a discharge touches without rinsing his hands with water must wash his clothes and bathe with water, and he will be unclean till evening.

¹²"'A clay pot*ᵇ* that the man touches must be broken, and any wooden article*ᶜ* is to be rinsed with water.

¹³"'When a man is cleansed from his discharge, he is to count off seven days*ᵈ* for his ceremonial cleansing; he must wash his clothes and bathe himself with fresh water, and he will be clean.*ᵉ* ¹⁴On the eighth day he must take two doves or two young pigeons*ᶠ* and come before the LORD to the entrance to the Tent of Meeting and give them to the priest. ¹⁵The priest is to sacrifice them, the one for a sin offering*ᵍ* and the other for a burnt offering.*ʰ* In this way he will make atonement before the LORD for the man because of his discharge.*ⁱ*

¹⁶"'When a man has an emission of semen,*ʲ* he must bathe his whole body with water, and he will be unclean till evening.*ᵏ* ¹⁷Any clothing or leather that has semen on it must be washed with water, and it will be unclean till evening. ¹⁸When a man lies with a woman and there is an emission of semen,*ˡ* both must bathe with water, and they will be unclean till evening.

¹⁹"'When a woman has her regular flow of blood, the impurity of her monthly period*ᵐ* will last seven days, and anyone who touches her will be unclean till evening.

²⁰"'Anything she lies on during her period will be unclean, and anything she sits on will be unclean. ²¹Whoever touches her bed must wash his clothes and bathe with water, and he will be unclean till evening.*ⁿ* ²²Whoever touches anything she sits on must wash his clothes and bathe with water, and he will be unclean till evening. ²³Whether it is the bed or anything she was sitting on, when anyone touches it, he will be unclean till evening.

²⁴"'If a man lies with her and her monthly flow*ᵒ* touches him, he will be unclean for seven days; any bed he lies on will be unclean.

²⁵"'When a woman has a discharge of blood for many days at a time other than her monthly period*ᵖ* or has a discharge that continues beyond her period, she will be unclean as long as she has the discharge, just as in the days of her period. ²⁶Any bed she lies on while her discharge continues will be unclean, as is her bed during her monthly period, and anything she sits on will be unclean, as during her period. ²⁷Whoever touches them will be unclean; he must wash his clothes and bathe with water, and he will be unclean till evening.

15:10
*ᵃ*Nu 19:10

15:12
*ᵇ*Lev 6:28
*ᶜ*Lev 11:32

15:13
*ᵈ*Lev 8:33
*ᵉ*ver 5

15:14
*ᶠ*Lev 14:22

15:15
*ᵍ*Lev 5:7
*ʰ*Lev 14:31
*ⁱ*Lev 14:18,19

15:16
*ʲ*ver 2;
Lev 22:4;
Dt 23:10
*ᵏ*ver 5;
Dt 23:11

15:18
*ˡ*1Sa 21:4

15:19
*ᵐ*ver 24;
Lev 12:2

15:21
*ⁿ*ver 27

15:24
*ᵒ*ver 19;
Lev 12:2;
18:19; 20:18;
Eze 18:6

15:25
*ᵖ*Mt 9:20;
Mk 5:25;
Lk 8:43

15:29
aLev 14:22

15:30
bLev 5:10;
14:20,31;
18:19;
2Sa 11:4;
Mk 5:25;
Lk 8:43

15:31
cLev 20:3;
Nu 5:3;
19:13,20;
2Sa 15:25;
2Ki 21:7;
Ps 33:14;
74:7; 76:2;
Eze 5:11;
23:38

15:32
dver 2

15:33
ever 19,24,25

16:1
fLev 10:1

16:2
gEx 30:10;
Heb 9:7
hHeb 9:25;
10:19
iEx 25:22
jEx 40:34

16:3
kHeb 9:24,25

16:4
lEx 28:39
mEx 28:42
nver 24;
Heb 10:22

16:5
oLev 4:13-21
p2Ch 29:23

28"'When she is cleansed from her discharge, she must count off seven days, and after that she will be ceremonially clean. 29On the eighth day she must take two doves or two young pigeons*a* and bring them to the priest at the entrance to the Tent of Meeting. 30The priest is to sacrifice one for a sin offering and the other for a burnt offering. In this way he will make atonement for her before the LORD for the uncleanness of her discharge.*b*

31"'You must keep the Israelites separate from things that make them unclean, so they will not die in their uncleanness for defiling my dwelling place,*ac* which is among them.'"

32These are the regulations for a man with a discharge, for anyone made unclean by an emission of semen,*d* 33for a woman in her monthly period, for a man or a woman with a discharge, and for a man who lies with a woman who is ceremonially unclean.*e*

GOLD *or* GOLDEN ALTAR *or* ALTAR OF INCENSE
LAMPSTAND
CURTAIN
THE CLOUD OF GOD'S GLORY
DOOR
HOLY PLACE
MOST HOLY PLACE
BRONZE ALTAR
BRONZE BASIN
TABLE FOR CONSECRATED BREAD
ATONEMENT COVER ON ARK OF COVENANT

Inside the Tabernacle

Chapter 16 Theme

16 The LORD spoke to Moses after the death of the two sons of Aaron who died when they approached the LORD.*f* 2The LORD said to Moses: "Tell your brother Aaron not to come whenever he chooses*g* into the Most Holy Place*h* behind the curtain in front of the atonement cover on the ark, or else he will die, because I appear*i* in the cloud*j* over the atonement cover.

3"This is how Aaron is to enter the sanctuary area:*k* with a young bull for a sin offering and a ram for a burnt offering. 4He is to put on the sacred linen tunic, with linen undergarments next to his body; he is to tie the linen sash around him and put on the linen turban.*l* These are sacred garments;*m* so he must bathe himself with water*n* before he puts them on. 5From the Israelite community*o* he is to take two male goats*p* for a sin offering and a ram for a burnt offering.

INSIGHT

As you study the Day of Atonement in Leviticus, consult the chart **The Feasts of Israel** on pages 210, 211.

a31 Or *my tabernacle*

⁶"Aaron is to offer the bull for his own sin offering to make atonement for himself and his household.*a* ⁷Then he is to take the two goats and present them before the LORD at the entrance to the Tent of Meeting. ⁸He is to cast lots for the two goats—one lot for the LORD and the other for the scapegoat.*a* ⁹Aaron shall bring the goat whose lot falls to the LORD and sacrifice it for a sin offering. ¹⁰But the goat chosen by lot as the scapegoat shall be presented alive before the LORD to be used for making atonement*b* by sending it into the desert as a scapegoat.

¹¹"Aaron shall bring the bull for his own sin offering to make atonement for himself and his household,*c* and he is to slaughter the bull for his own sin offering. ¹²He is to take a censer full of burning coals*d* from the altar before the LORD and two handfuls of finely ground fragrant incense*e* and take them behind the curtain. ¹³He is to put the incense on the fire before the LORD, and the smoke of the incense will conceal the atonement cover above the Testimony, so that he will not die.*f* ¹⁴He is to take some of the bull's blood*g* and with his finger sprinkle it on the front of the atonement cover; then he shall sprinkle some of it with his finger seven times before the atonement cover.*h*

¹⁵"He shall then slaughter the goat for the sin offering for the people*i* and take its blood behind the curtain*j* and do with it as he did with the bull's blood: He shall sprinkle it on the atonement cover and in front of it. ¹⁶In this way he will make atonement*k* for the Most Holy Place because of the uncleanness and rebellion of the Israelites, whatever their sins have been. He is to do the same for the Tent of Meeting, which is among them in the midst of their uncleanness. ¹⁷No one is to be in the Tent of Meeting from the time Aaron goes in to make atonement in the Most Holy Place until he comes out, having made atonement for himself, his household and the whole community of Israel.

¹⁸"Then he shall come out to the altar*l* that is before the LORD and make atonement for it. He shall take some of the bull's blood and some of the goat's blood and put it on all the horns of the altar.*m* ¹⁹He shall sprinkle some of the blood on it with his finger seven times to cleanse it and to consecrate it from the uncleanness of the Israelites.*n*

²⁰"When Aaron has finished making atonement for the Most Holy Place, the Tent of Meeting and the altar, he shall bring forward the live goat. ²¹He is to lay both hands on the head of the live goat and confess*o* over it all the wickedness and rebellion of the Israelites—all their sins—and put them on the goat's head. He shall send the goat away into the desert in the care of a man appointed for the task. ²²The goat will carry on itself all their sins*p* to a solitary place; and the man shall release it in the desert.

---

a8 That is, the goat of removal; Hebrew *azazel*; also in verses 10 and 26

16:6
a Lev 9:7;
Heb 5:3; 7:27;
9:7,12

16:10
b Isa 53:4-10;
Ro 3:25;
1Jn 2:2

16:11
c Heb 7:27; 9:7

16:12
d Lev 10:1
e Ex 30:34-38

16:13
f Ex 28:43;
Lev 22:9

16:14
g Lev 4:5;
Heb 9:7,13,25
h Lev 4:6

16:15
i Heb 9:7,12
j Heb 9:3

16:16
k Ex 29:36

16:18
l Lev 4:7
m Lev 4:25

16:19
n Eze 43:20

16:21
o Lev 5:5

16:22
p Isa 53:12

16:23
a Eze 42:14;
44:19

²³"Then Aaron is to go into the Tent of Meeting and take off the linen garments he put on before he entered the Most Holy Place, and he is to leave them there.*a* ²⁴He shall bathe himself with water in a holy place and put on his regular garments.*b* Then he shall come out and sacrifice the burnt offering for himself and the burnt offering for the people, to make atonement for himself and for the people. ²⁵He shall also burn the fat of the sin offering on the altar.

16:24
b ver 3-5

16:26
c Lev 11:25

²⁶"The man who releases the goat as a scapegoat must wash his clothes*c* and bathe himself with water; afterward he may come into the camp. ²⁷The bull and the goat for the sin offerings, whose blood was brought into the Most Holy Place to make atonement, must be taken outside the camp;*d* their hides, flesh and offal are to be burned up. ²⁸The man who burns them must wash his clothes and bathe himself with water; afterward he may come into the camp.

16:27
d Lev 4:12,21;
Heb 13:11

16:29
e Lev 23:27,32;
Nu 29:7;
Isa 58:3

²⁹"This is to be a lasting ordinance for you: On the tenth day of the seventh month you must deny yourselves*ae* and not do any work—whether native-born or an alien living among you— ³⁰because on this day atonement will be made for you, to cleanse you. Then, before the LORD, you will be clean from all your sins.*f* ³¹It is a sabbath of rest, and you must deny yourselves;*g* it is a lasting ordinance. ³²The priest who is anointed and ordained to succeed his father as high priest is to make atonement. He is to put on the sacred linen garments*h* ³³and make atonement for the Most Holy Place, for the Tent of Meeting and the altar, and for the priests and all the people of the community.*i*

16:30
f Jer 33:8;
Eph 5:26

16:31
g Isa 58:3,5

³⁴"This is to be a lasting ordinance for you: Atonement is to be made once a year*j* for all the sins of the Israelites."

And it was done, as the LORD commanded Moses.

16:32
h ver 4;
Nu 20:26,28

Chapter 17 Theme

17 The LORD said to Moses, ²"Speak to Aaron and his sons and to all the Israelites and say to them: 'This is what the LORD has commanded: ³Any Israelite who sacrifices an ox,*b* a lamb or a goat in the camp or outside of it ⁴instead of bringing it to the entrance to the Tent of Meeting to present it as an offering to the LORD in front of the tabernacle of the LORD*k*—that man shall be considered guilty of bloodshed; he has shed blood and must be cut off from his people.*l* ⁵This is so the Israelites will bring to the LORD the sacrifices they are now making in the open fields. They must bring them to the priest, that is, to the LORD, at the entrance to the Tent of Meeting and sacrifice them as fellowship offerings.*c*

16:33
i ver 11,16-18

16:34
j Heb 9:7,25

17:4
k Dt 12:5-21
l Ge 17:14

a29 Or *must fast*; also in verse 31   **b**3 The Hebrew word can include both male and female.   **c**5 Traditionally *peace offerings*

⁶The priest is to sprinkle the blood against the altar of the Lord*a* at the entrance to the Tent of Meeting and burn the fat as an aroma pleasing to the Lord.*b* ⁷They must no longer offer any of their sacrifices to the goat idols*ac* to whom they prostitute themselves.*d* This is to be a lasting ordinance for them and for the generations to come.'

⁸"Say to them: 'Any Israelite or any alien living among them who offers a burnt offering or sacrifice ⁹and does not bring it to the entrance to the Tent of Meeting*e* to sacrifice it to the Lord—that man must be cut off from his people.

¹⁰"'Any Israelite or any alien living among them who eats any blood—I will set my face against that person who eats blood*f* and will cut him off from his people. ¹¹For the life of a creature is in the blood,*g* and I have given it to you to make atonement for yourselves on the altar; it is the blood that makes atonement for one's life.*h* ¹²Therefore I say to the Israelites, "None of you may eat blood, nor may an alien living among you eat blood."

¹³"'Any Israelite or any alien living among you who hunts any animal or bird that may be eaten must drain out the blood and cover it with earth,*i* ¹⁴because the life of every creature is its blood. That is why I have said to the Israelites, "You must not eat the blood of any creature, because the life of every creature is its blood; anyone who eats it must be cut off."*j*

¹⁵"'Anyone, whether native-born or alien, who eats anything found dead or torn by wild animals*k* must wash his clothes and bathe with water, and he will be ceremonially unclean till evening; then he will be clean. ¹⁶But if he does not wash his clothes and bathe himself, he will be held responsible.'"

Chapter 18 Theme

18 The Lord said to Moses, ²"Speak to the Israelites and say to them: 'I am the Lord your God.*l* ³You must not do as they do in Egypt, where you used to live, and you must not do as they do in the land of Canaan, where I am bringing you. Do not follow their practices.*m* ⁴You must obey my laws and be careful to follow my decrees. I am the Lord your God.*n* ⁵Keep my decrees and laws, for the man who obeys them will live by them.*o* I am the Lord.

⁶"'No one is to approach any close relative to have sexual relations. I am the Lord.

⁷"'Do not dishonor your father*p* by having sexual relations with your mother.*q* She is your mother; do not have relations with her.

⁸"'Do not have sexual relations with your father's wife;*r* that would dishonor your father.*s*

---

a7 Or demons

17:6
a Lev 3:2
b Nu 18:17

17:7
c Ex 22:20;
2Ch 11:15
d Ex 32:8; 34:15;
Dt 32:17;
1Co 10:20

17:9
e ver 4

17:10
f Ge 9:4;
Lev 3:17;
Dt 12:16,23;
1Sa 14:33

17:11
g ver 14;
Ge 9:4
h Heb 9:22

17:13
i Lev 7:26;
Dt 12:16

17:14
j ver 11;
Ge 9:4

17:15
k Ex 22:31;
Dt 14:21

18:2
l Ex 6:7;
Lev 11:44;
Eze 20:5

18:3
m ver 24-30;
Ex 23:24;
Lev 20:23

18:4
n ver 2

18:5
o Eze 20:11;
Ro 10:5*;
Gal 3:12*

18:7
p Lev 20:11
q Eze 22:10

18:8
r 1Co 5:1
s Lev 20:11

18:9
a Lev 20:17

18:12
b Lev 20:19

18:14
c Lev 20:20

18:15
d Lev 20:12

18:16
e Lev 20:21

18:17
f Lev 20:14

18:19
g Lev 15:24;
20:18

18:20
h Ex 20:14;
Lev 20:10;
Mt 5:27,28;
1Co 6:9;
Heb 13:4

18:21
i Dt 12:31
j Lev 20:2-5
k Lev 19:12;
21:6;
Eze 36:20

18:22
l Lev 20:13;
Dt 23:18;
Ro 1:27

18:23
m Ex 22:19;
Lev 20:15;
Dt 27:21

18:24
n ver 3,27,30
o Dt 18:12

18:25
p Lev 20:23;
Dt 9:5; 18:12
q ver 28;
Lev 20:22

9 " 'Do not have sexual relations with your sister,[a] either your father's daughter or your mother's daughter, whether she was born in the same home or elsewhere.

10 " 'Do not have sexual relations with your son's daughter or your daughter's daughter; that would dishonor you.

11 " 'Do not have sexual relations with the daughter of your father's wife, born to your father; she is your sister.

12 " 'Do not have sexual relations with your father's sister;[b] she is your father's close relative.

13 " 'Do not have sexual relations with your mother's sister, because she is your mother's close relative.

14 " 'Do not dishonor your father's brother by approaching his wife to have sexual relations; she is your aunt.[c]

15 " 'Do not have sexual relations with your daughter-in-law.[d] She is your son's wife; do not have relations with her.

16 " 'Do not have sexual relations with your brother's wife;[e] that would dishonor your brother.

17 " 'Do not have sexual relations with both a woman and her daughter.[f] Do not have sexual relations with either her son's daughter or her daughter's daughter; they are her close relatives. That is wickedness.

18 " 'Do not take your wife's sister as a rival wife and have sexual relations with her while your wife is living.

19 " 'Do not approach a woman to have sexual relations during the uncleanness of her monthly period.[g]

20 " 'Do not have sexual relations with your neighbor's wife[h] and defile yourself with her.

21 " 'Do not give any of your children[i] to be sacrificed[a] to Molech,[j] for you must not profane the name of your God.[k] I am the LORD.

22 " 'Do not lie with a man as one lies with a woman;[l] that is detestable.

23 " 'Do not have sexual relations with an animal and defile yourself with it. A woman must not present herself to an animal to have sexual relations with it; that is a perversion.[m]

24 " 'Do not defile yourselves in any of these ways, because this is how the nations that I am going to drive out before you[n] became defiled.[o] 25 Even the land was defiled; so I punished it for its sin,[p] and the land vomited out its inhabitants.[q] 26 But you must keep my decrees and my laws. The native-born and the aliens living among you must not do any of these detestable things, 27 for all these things were done by the people who lived in the land before you, and the land became defiled. 28 And if you

a21 Or to be passed through ⌞the fire⌟

defile the land, it will vomit you out as it vomited out the nations that were before you.

²⁹"'Everyone who does any of these detestable things—such persons must be cut off from their people. ³⁰Keep my requirements^a and do not follow any of the detestable customs that were practiced before you came and do not defile yourselves with them. I am the LORD your God.^b'"

Chapter 19 Theme

19 The LORD said to Moses, ²"Speak to the entire assembly of Israel and say to them: 'Be holy because I, the LORD your God, am holy.^c

³"'Each of you must respect his mother and father,^d and you must observe my Sabbaths. I am the LORD your God.^e

⁴"'Do not turn to idols or make gods of cast metal for yourselves.^f I am the LORD your God.

⁵"'When you sacrifice a fellowship offering^a to the LORD, sacrifice it in such a way that it will be accepted on your behalf. ⁶It shall be eaten on the day you sacrifice it or on the next day; anything left over until the third day must be burned up. ⁷If any of it is eaten on the third day, it is impure and will not be accepted. ⁸Whoever eats it will be held responsible because he has desecrated what is holy to the LORD; that person must be cut off from his people.

⁹"'When you reap the harvest of your land, do not reap to the very edges of your field or gather the gleanings of your harvest.^g ¹⁰Do not go over your vineyard a second time or pick up the grapes that have fallen. Leave them for the poor and the alien. I am the LORD your God.

¹¹"'Do not steal.^h

"'Do not lie.ⁱ

"'Do not deceive one another.

¹²"'Do not swear falsely by my name^j and so profane the name of your God. I am the LORD.

¹³"'Do not defraud your neighbor or rob him.^k

"'Do not hold back the wages of a hired man overnight.^l

¹⁴"'Do not curse the deaf or put a stumbling block in front of the blind,^m but fear your God. I am the LORD.

¹⁵"'Do not pervert justice;ⁿ do not show partiality^o to the poor or favoritism to the great, but judge your neighbor fairly.

¹⁶"'Do not go about spreading slander^p among your people.

"'Do not do anything that endangers your neighbor's life.^q I am the LORD.

^a5 Traditionally *peace offering*

18:30
^aDt 11:1
^bver 2

19:2
^c1Pe 1:16*;
Lev 11:44

19:3
^dEx 20:12
^eLev 11:44

19:4
^fEx 20:4,23;
34:17;
Lev 26:1;
Ps 96:5;
115:4-7

19:9
^gLev 23:10,22;
Dt 24:19-22

19:11
^hEx 20:15
ⁱEph 4:25

19:12
^jEx 20:7;
Mt 5:33

19:13
^kEx 22:15, 25-27
^lDt 24:15;
Jas 5:4

19:14
^mDt 27:18

19:15
ⁿEx 23:2,6
^oDt 1:17

19:16
^pPs 15:3;
Eze 22:9
^qEx 23:7

19:17
a 1Jn 2:9; 3:15
b Mt 18:15;
Lk 17:3

17 " 'Do not hate your brother in your heart.ᵃ Rebuke your neighbor franklyᵇ so you will not share in his guilt.

18 " 'Do not seek revengeᶜ or bear a grudgeᵈ against one of your people, but love your neighbor as yourself.ᵉ I am the LORD.

19 " 'Keep my decrees.

19:18
c Ro 12:19
d Ps 103:9
e Mt 5:43*;
19:16*;
22:39*;
Mk 12:31*;
Lk 10:27*;
Jn 13:34;
Ro 13:9*;
Gal 5:14*;
Jas 2:8*

" 'Do not mate different kinds of animals.

" 'Do not plant your field with two kinds of seed.ᶠ

" 'Do not wear clothing woven of two kinds of material.ᵍ

20 " 'If a man sleeps with a woman who is a slave girl promised to another man but who has not been ransomed or given her freedom, there must be due punishment. Yet they are not to be put to death, because she had not been freed. 21 The man, however, must bring a ram to the entrance to the Tent of Meeting for a guilt offering to the LORD.ʰ 22 With the ram of the guilt offering the priest is to make atonement for him before the LORD for the sin he has committed, and his sin will be forgiven.

19:19
f Dt 22:9
g Dt 22:11

19:21
h Lev 5:15

23 " 'When you enter the land and plant any kind of fruit tree, regard its fruit as forbidden.ᵃ For three years you are to consider it forbiddenᵃ; it must not be eaten. 24 In the fourth year all its fruit will be holy,ⁱ an offering of praise to the LORD. 25 But in the fifth year you may eat its fruit. In this way your harvest will be increased. I am the LORD your God.

19:24
i Pr 3:9

26 " 'Do not eat any meat with the blood still in it.ʲ

" 'Do not practice divination or sorcery.ᵏ

27 " 'Do not cut the hair at the sides of your head or clip off the edges of your beard.ˡ

19:26
j Lev 17:10
k Dt 18:10

28 " 'Do not cut your bodies for the dead or put tattoo marks on yourselves. I am the LORD.

19:27
l Lev 21:5

29 " 'Do not degrade your daughter by making her a prostitute,ᵐ or the land will turn to prostitution and be filled with wickedness.

19:29
m Dt 23:18

30 " 'Observe my Sabbaths and have reverence for my sanctuary. I am the LORD.ⁿ

19:30
n Lev 26:2

31 " 'Do not turn to mediums or seek out spiritists,ᵒ for you will be defiled by them. I am the LORD your God.

19:31
o Lev 20:6;
Isa 8:19

32 " 'Rise in the presence of the aged, show respect for the elderlyᵖ and revere your God. I am the LORD.

33 " 'When an alien lives with you in your land, do not mistreat him. 34 The alien living with you must be treated as one of your native-born.�q Love him as yourself, for you were aliens in Egypt.ʳ I am the LORD your God.

19:32
p 1Ti 5:1

35 " 'Do not use dishonest standards when measuring length, weight or quantity. 36 Use honest scales and honest weights, an honest ephahᵇ and an honest hin.ᶜ ˢ I am the LORD your God, who brought you out of Egypt.

19:34
q Ex 12:48
r Dt 10:19

19:36
s Dt 25:13-15

ᵃ23 Hebrew *uncircumcised* ᵇ36 An ephah was a dry measure. ᶜ36 A hin was a liquid measure.

37"'Keep all my decrees and all my laws and follow them. I am the LORD.'"

Chapter 20 Theme _____

20 The LORD said to Moses, 2"Say to the Israelites: 'Any Israelite or any alien living in Israel who gives*a* any of his children to Molech must be put to death. The people of the community are to stone him. 3I will set my face against that man and I will cut him off from his people; for by giving his children to Molech, he has defiled my sanctuary*a* and profaned my holy name.*b* 4If the people of the community close their eyes when that man gives one of his children to Molech and they fail to put him to death,*c* 5I will set my face against that man and his family and will cut off from their people both him and all who follow him in prostituting themselves to Molech.

6"'I will set my face against the person who turns to mediums and spiritists to prostitute himself by following them, and I will cut him off from his people.*d*

7"'Consecrate yourselves and be holy,*e* because I am the LORD your God. 8Keep my decrees and follow them. I am the LORD, who makes you holy.*bf*

9"'If anyone curses his father or mother,*g* he must be put to death.*h* He has cursed his father or his mother, and his blood will be on his own head.*i*

10"'If a man commits adultery with another man's wife*j*—with the wife of his neighbor—both the adulterer and the adulteress must be put to death.

11"'If a man sleeps with his father's wife, he has dishonored his father.*k* Both the man and the woman must be put to death; their blood will be on their own heads.

12"'If a man sleeps with his daughter-in-law,*l* both of them must be put to death. What they have done is a perversion; their blood will be on their own heads.

13"'If a man lies with a man as one lies with a woman, both of them have done what is detestable.*m* They must be put to death; their blood will be on their own heads.

14"'If a man marries both a woman and her mother,*n* it is wicked. Both he and they must be burned in the fire, so that no wickedness will be among you.*o*

15"'If a man has sexual relations with an animal,*p* he must be put to death, and you must kill the animal.

16"'If a woman approaches an animal to have sexual relations with it, kill both the woman and the animal. They must be put to death; their blood will be on their own heads.

a2 Or *sacrifices*; also in verses 3 and 4   b8 Or *who sanctifies you*; or *who sets you apart as holy*

20:3
a Lev 15:31
b Lev 18:21

20:4
c Dt 17:2-5

20:6
d Lev 19:31

20:7
e Eph 1:4;
1Pe 1:16*

20:8
f Ex 31:13

20:9
g Dt 27:16
h Ex 21:17;
Mt 15:4*;
Mk 7:10*
i ver 11;
2Sa 1:16

20:10
j Ex 20:14;
Dt 5:18;
22:22

20:11
k Lev 18:7;
Dt 27:23

20:12
l Lev 18:15

20:13
m Lev 18:22

20:14
n Lev 18:17
o Dt 27:23

20:15
p Lev 18:23

20:17
*a*Lev 18:9

20:18
*b*Lev 15:24;
18:19

20:19
*c*Lev 18:12-13

20:20
*d*Lev 18:14

20:21
*e*Lev 18:16

20:22
*f*Lev 18:25-28

20:23
*g*Lev 18:3
*h*Lev 18:24,
27,30

20:24
*i*Ex 3:8;
13:5; 33:3
*j*Ex 33:16

20:25
*k*Lev 11:1-47;
Dt 14:3-21

20:26
*l*Lev 19:2

20:27
*m*Lev 19:31

21:1
*n*Eze 44:25

¹⁷ "'If a man marries his sister*ᵃ*, the daughter of either his father or his mother, and they have sexual relations, it is a disgrace. They must be cut off before the eyes of their people. He has dishonored his sister and will be held responsible.

¹⁸ "'If a man lies with a woman during her monthly period*ᵇ* and has sexual relations with her, he has exposed the source of her flow, and she has also uncovered it. Both of them must be cut off from their people.

¹⁹ "'Do not have sexual relations with the sister of either your mother or your father,*ᶜ* for that would dishonor a close relative; both of you would be held responsible.

²⁰ "'If a man sleeps with his aunt,*ᵈ* he has dishonored his uncle. They will be held responsible; they will die childless.

²¹ "'If a man marries his brother's wife,*ᵉ* it is an act of impurity; he has dishonored his brother. They will be childless.

²² "'Keep all my decrees and laws and follow them, so that the land*ᶠ* where I am bringing you to live may not vomit you out. ²³You must not live according to the customs of the nations*ᵍ* I am going to drive out before you.*ʰ* Because they did all these things, I abhorred them. ²⁴But I said to you, "You will possess their land; I will give it to you as an inheritance, a land flowing with milk and honey."*ⁱ* I am the LORD your God, who has set you apart from the nations.*ʲ*

²⁵ "'You must therefore make a distinction between clean and unclean animals and between unclean and clean birds.*ᵏ* Do not defile yourselves by any animal or bird or anything that moves along the ground—those which I have set apart as unclean for you. ²⁶You are to be holy to me*ᵃ* because I, the LORD, am holy,*ˡ* and I have set you apart from the nations to be my own.

²⁷ "'A man or woman who is a medium or spiritist among you must be put to death.*ᵐ* You are to stone them; their blood will be on their own heads.'"

Chapter 21 Theme _____

21 The LORD said to Moses, "Speak to the priests, the sons of Aaron, and say to them: 'A priest must not make himself ceremonially unclean for any of his people who die,*ⁿ* ²except for a close relative, such as his mother or father, his son or daughter, his brother, ³or an unmarried sister who is dependent on him since she has no husband—for her he may make himself unclean. ⁴He must not make himself unclean for people related to him by marriage,*ᵇ* and so defile himself.

*ᵃ*26 Or *be my holy ones*   *ᵇ*4 Or *unclean as a leader among his people*

195

⁵"'Priests must not shave their heads or shave off the edges of their beards[a] or cut their bodies.[b] ⁶They must be holy to their God and must not profane the name of their God.[c] Because they present the offerings made to the LORD by fire,[d] the food of their God, they are to be holy.

⁷"'They must not marry women defiled by prostitution or divorced from their husbands,[e] because priests are holy to their God.[f] ⁸Regard them as holy,[g] because they offer up the food of your God. Consider them holy, because I the LORD am holy—I who make you holy.[a]

⁹"'If a priest's daughter defiles herself by becoming a prostitute, she disgraces her father; she must be burned in the fire.[h]

¹⁰"'The high priest, the one among his brothers who has had the anointing oil poured on his head and who has been ordained to wear the priestly garments,[i] must not let his hair become unkempt[b] or tear his clothes.[j] ¹¹He must not enter a place where there is a dead body.[k] He must not make himself unclean,[l] even for his father or mother, ¹²nor leave the sanctuary of his God or desecrate it, because he has been dedicated by the anointing oil[m] of his God. I am the LORD.

¹³"'The woman he marries must be a virgin.[n] ¹⁴He must not marry a widow, a divorced woman, or a woman defiled by prostitution, but only a virgin from his own people, ¹⁵so he will not defile his offspring among his people. I am the LORD, who makes him holy.[c]'"

¹⁶The LORD said to Moses, ¹⁷"Say to Aaron: 'For the generations to come none of your descendants who has a defect may come near to offer the food of his God.[o] ¹⁸No man who has any defect[p] may come near: no man who is blind or lame, disfigured or deformed; ¹⁹no man with a crippled foot or hand, ²⁰or who is hunchbacked or dwarfed, or who has any eye defect, or who has festering or running sores or damaged testicles.[q] ²¹No descendant of Aaron the priest who has any defect is to come near to present the offerings made to the LORD by fire. He has a defect; he must not come near to offer the food of his God. ²²He may eat the most holy food of his God,[r] as well as the holy food; ²³yet because of his defect, he must not go near the curtain or approach the altar, and so desecrate my sanctuary. I am the LORD, who makes them holy.[d]'"

²⁴So Moses told this to Aaron and his sons and to all the Israelites.

---

a8 Or who sanctify you; or who set you apart as holy   b10 Or not uncover his head
c15 Or who sanctifies him; or who sets him apart as holy   d23 Or who sanctifies them; or who sets them apart as holy

21:5
a Eze 44:20
b Lev 19:28;
Dt 14:1

21:6
c Lev 18:21
d Lev 3:11

21:7
e ver 13,14
f Eze 44:22

21:8
g ver 6

21:9
h Ge 38:24;
Lev 19:29

21:10
i Lev 16:32
j Lev 10:6

21:11
k Nu 19:11,13,14
l Lev 19:28

21:12
m Ex 29:6-7;
Lev 10:7

21:13
n Eze 44:22

21:17
o ver 6

21:18
p Lev 22:19-25

21:20
q Dt 23:1;
Isa 56:3

21:22
r 1Co 9:13

22:3
*a*Lev 7:20,21;
Nu 19:13

22:4
*b*Lev 14:1-32;
15:2-15
*c*Lev 11:24-28,39

22:5
*d*Lev
11:24-28,43
*e*Lev 15:7

22:7
*f*Nu 18:11

22:8
*g*Lev 11:39
*h*Ex 22:31;
Lev 17:15
*i*Lev 11:40

22:9
*j*ver 16;
Ex 28:43

22:11
*k*Ge 17:13;
Ex 12:44

22:14
*l*Lev 5:15

22:15
*m*Nu 18:32

22:16
*n*ver 9

22:18
*o*Lev 1:2

Chapter 22 Theme

22 The LORD said to Moses, [2]"Tell Aaron and his sons to treat with respect the sacred offerings the Israelites consecrate to me, so they will not profane my holy name. I am the LORD.

[3]"Say to them: 'For the generations to come, if any of your descendants is ceremonially unclean and yet comes near the sacred offerings that the Israelites consecrate to the LORD, that person must be cut off from my presence.[a] I am the LORD.

[4]"'If a descendant of Aaron has an infectious skin disease[a] or a bodily discharge,[b] he may not eat the sacred offerings until he is cleansed. He will also be unclean if he touches something defiled by a corpse[c] or by anyone who has an emission of semen, [5]or if he touches any crawling thing[d] that makes him unclean, or any person[e] who makes him unclean, whatever the uncleanness may be. [6]The one who touches any such thing will be unclean till evening. He must not eat any of the sacred offerings unless he has bathed himself with water. [7]When the sun goes down, he will be clean, and after that he may eat the sacred offerings, for they are his food.[f] [8]He must not eat anything found dead[g] or torn by wild animals,[h] and so become unclean[i] through it. I am the LORD.

[9]"'The priests are to keep my requirements so that they do not become guilty and die[j] for treating them with contempt. I am the LORD, who makes them holy.[b]

[10]"'No one outside a priest's family may eat the sacred offering, nor may the guest of a priest or his hired worker eat it. [11]But if a priest buys a slave with money, or if a slave is born in his household, that slave may eat his food.[k] [12]If a priest's daughter marries anyone other than a priest, she may not eat any of the sacred contributions. [13]But if a priest's daughter becomes a widow or is divorced, yet has no children, and she returns to live in her father's house as in her youth, she may eat of her father's food. No unauthorized person, however, may eat any of it.

[14]"'If anyone eats a sacred offering by mistake, he must make restitution to the priest for the offering and add a fifth of the value[l] to it. [15]The priests must not desecrate the sacred offerings the Israelites present to the LORD[m] [16]by allowing them to eat the sacred offerings and so bring upon them guilt requiring payment.[n] I am the LORD, who makes them holy.'"

[17]The LORD said to Moses, [18]"Speak to Aaron and his sons and to all the Israelites and say to them: 'If any of you—either an Israelite or an alien living in Israel—presents a gift[o] for a burnt offering to the LORD, either to fulfill a vow or as a freewill offering,

---

a4 Traditionally *leprosy*; the Hebrew word was used for various diseases affecting the skin—not necessarily leprosy.   *b9* Or *who sanctifies them*; or *who sets them apart as holy*; also in verse 16

¹⁹you must present a male without defect*ᵃ* from the cattle, sheep or goats in order that it may be accepted on your behalf. ²⁰Do not bring anything with a defect,*ᵇ* because it will not be accepted on your behalf. ²¹When anyone brings from the herd or flock a fellowship offering*ᵃᶜ* to the Lord to fulfill a special vow or as a freewill offering, it must be without defect or blemish to be acceptable. ²²Do not offer to the Lord the blind, the injured or the maimed, or anything with warts or festering or running sores. Do not place any of these on the altar as an offering made to the Lord by fire. ²³You may, however, present as a freewill offering an ox*ᵇ* or a sheep that is deformed or stunted, but it will not be accepted in fulfillment of a vow. ²⁴You must not offer to the Lord an animal whose testicles are bruised, crushed, torn or cut.*ᵈ* You must not do this in your own land, ²⁵and you must not accept such animals from the hand of a foreigner and offer them as the food of your God.*ᵉ* They will not be accepted on your behalf, because they are deformed and have defects.'"

²⁶The Lord said to Moses, ²⁷"When a calf, a lamb or a goat is born, it is to remain with its mother for seven days.*ᶠ* From the eighth day on, it will be acceptable as an offering made to the Lord by fire. ²⁸Do not slaughter a cow or a sheep and its young on the same day.*ᵍ*

²⁹"When you sacrifice a thank offering*ʰ* to the Lord, sacrifice it in such a way that it will be accepted on your behalf. ³⁰It must be eaten that same day; leave none of it till morning.*ⁱ* I am the Lord.

³¹"Keep*ʲ* my commands and follow them. I am the Lord. ³²Do not profane my holy name.*ᵏ* I must be acknowledged as holy by the Israelites.*ˡ* I am the Lord, who makes*ᶜ* you holy*ᵈ* ³³and who brought you out of Egypt to be your God.*ᵐ* I am the Lord."

Chapter 23 Theme

23

The Lord said to Moses, ²"Speak to the Israelites and say to them: 'These are my appointed feasts,*ⁿ* the appointed feasts of the Lord, which you are to proclaim as sacred assemblies.*ᵒ*

³"'There are six days when you may work,*ᵖ* but the seventh day is a Sabbath of rest,*�q* a day of sacred assembly. You are not to do any work; wherever you live, it is a Sabbath to the Lord.

⁴"'These are the Lord's appointed feasts, the sacred assemblies you are to proclaim at their appointed times: ⁵The Lord's Passover begins at twilight on the fourteenth day of the first month.*ʳ* ⁶On the fifteenth day of that month the Lord's Feast of Unleavened Bread begins; for seven days you must eat bread

INSIGHT

See the chart **The Feasts of Israel** on pages 210, 211.

22:19
*ᵃ*Lev 1:3

22:20
*ᵇ*Dt 15:21;
17:1;
Mal 1:8,14;
Heb 9:14;
1Pe 1:19

22:21
*ᶜ*Lev 3:6;
Nu 15:3,8

22:24
*ᵈ*Lev 21:20

22:25
*ᵉ*Lev 21:6

22:27
*ᶠ*Ex 22:30

22:28
*ᵍ*Dt 22:6,7

22:29
*ʰ*Lev 7:12;
Ps 107:22

22:30
*ⁱ*Lev 7:15

22:31
*ʲ*Dt 4:2,40;
Ps 105:45

22:32
*ᵏ*Lev 18:21
*ˡ*Lev 10:3

22:33
*ᵐ*Lev 11:45

23:2
*ⁿ*ver 4,37,44;
Nu 29:39
*ᵒ*ver 21,27

23:3
*ᵖ*Ex 20:9
*q*Ex 20:10;
31:13-17;
Lev 19:3;
Dt 5:13;
Heb 4:9,10

23:5
*ʳ*Ex 12:18-19;
Nu 28:16-17;
Dt 16:1-8

ᵃ21 Traditionally peace offering   *ᵇ23 The Hebrew word can include both male and female.*   *ᶜ32 Or* made   *ᵈ32 Or* who sanctifies you; *or* who sets you apart as holy

The Jewish Calendar

Babylonian names (B) for the months are still used today for the Jewish calendar. Canaanite names (C) were used prior to the Babylonian captivity in 586 B.C. Four are mentioned in the Old Testament. **Adar-Sheni** is an intercalary month used every two to three years or seven times in 19 years.

1st month	2nd month	3rd month	4th month
Nisan (B) Abib (C) March-April	Iyyar (B) Ziv (C) April-May	Sivan (B) May-June	Tammuz (B) June-July
7th month	*8th month*	*9th month*	*10th month*
5th month	**6th month**	**7th month**	**8th month**
Ab (B) July-August	Elul (B) August-September	Tishri (B) Ethanim (C) September-October	Marcheshvan (B) Bul (C) October-November
11th month	*12th month*	*1st month*	*2nd month*
9th month	**10th month**	**11th month**	**12th month**
Chislev (B) November-December	Tebeth (B) December-January	Shebat (B) January-February	Adar (B) February-March
3rd month	*4th month*	*5th month*	*6th month*

Sacred calendar appears in black • Civil calendar appears in gray

made without yeast. ⁷On the first day hold a sacred assembly[a] and do no regular work. ⁸For seven days present an offering made to the LORD by fire. And on the seventh day hold a sacred assembly and do no regular work.'"

⁹The LORD said to Moses, ¹⁰"Speak to the Israelites and say to them: 'When you enter the land I am going to give you and you reap its harvest, bring to the priest a sheaf[b] of the first grain you harvest. ¹¹He is to wave the sheaf before the LORD[c] so it will be accepted on your behalf; the priest is to wave it on the day after the Sabbath. ¹²On the day you wave the sheaf, you must sacrifice as a burnt offering to the LORD a lamb a year old without defect, ¹³together with its grain offering[d] of two-tenths of an ephah[a] of fine flour mixed with oil—an offering made to the LORD by fire, a pleasing aroma—and its drink offering of a quarter of a hin[b] of wine. ¹⁴You must not eat any bread, or roasted or new grain, until the very day you bring this offering to your God.[e] This is to be a lasting ordinance for the generations to come,[f] wherever you live.

¹⁵"'From the day after the Sabbath, the day you brought the sheaf of the wave offering, count off seven full weeks. ¹⁶Count off fifty days up to the day after the seventh Sabbath,[g] and then present an offering of new grain to the LORD. ¹⁷From wherever you live, bring two loaves made of two-tenths of an ephah of fine flour, baked with yeast, as a wave offering of firstfruits[h] to the LORD. ¹⁸Present with this bread seven male lambs, each a year old and without defect, one young bull and two rams. They will be a burnt offering to the LORD, together with their grain offerings

23:7
a ver 3,8

23:10
b Ex 23:16,19; 34:26

23:11
c Ex 29:24

23:13
d Lev 2:14-16; 6:20

23:14
e Ex 34:26
f Nu 15:21

23:16
g Nu 28:26; Ac 2:1

23:17
h Ex 34:22; Lev 2:12

a13 That is, probably about 4 quarts (about 4.5 liters); also in verse 17   b13 That is, probably about 1quart (about 1liter) and drink offerings—an offering made by fire, an aroma pleasing to the LORD. ¹⁹Then sacrifice one male goat for a sin offering and two lambs, each a year old, for a fellowship offering.ᵃ ²⁰The priest is to wave the two lambs before the LORD as a wave offering, together with the bread of the firstfruits. They are a sacred offering to the LORD for the priest. ²¹On that same day you are to proclaim a sacred assemblyᵃ and do no regular work.ᵇ This is to be a lasting ordinance for the generations to come, wherever you live.

²²"When you reap the harvestᶜ of your land, do not reap to the very edges of your field or gather the gleanings of your harvest.ᵈ Leave them for the poor and the alien. I am the LORD your God.'"

²³The LORD said to Moses, ²⁴"Say to the Israelites: 'On the first day of the seventh month you are to have a day of rest, a sacred assembly commemorated with trumpet blasts.ᵉ ²⁵Do no regular work,ᶠ but present an offering made to the LORD by fire.'"

²⁶The LORD said to Moses, ²⁷"The tenth day of this seventh monthᵍ is the Day of Atonement.ʰ Hold a sacred assemblyⁱ and deny yourselves,ᵇ and present an offering made to the LORD by fire. ²⁸Do no work on that day, because it is the Day of Atonement, when atonement is made for you before the LORD your God. ²⁹Anyone who does not deny himself on that day must be cut off from his people.ʲ ³⁰I will destroy from among his peopleᵏ anyone who does any work on that day. ³¹You shall do no work at all. This is to be a lasting ordinance for the generations to come, wherever you live. ³²It is a sabbath of rest for you, and you must deny yourselves. From the evening of the ninth day of the month until the following evening you are to observe your sabbath."

³³The LORD said to Moses, ³⁴"Say to the Israelites: 'On the fifteenth day of the seventh month the LORD's Feast of Tabernaclesˡ begins, and it lasts for seven days. ³⁵The first day is a sacred assembly; do no regular work. ³⁶For seven days present offerings made to the LORD by fire, and on the eighth day hold a sacred assemblyᵐ and present an offering made to the LORD by fire. It is the closing assembly; do no regular work.

³⁷("'These are the LORD's appointed feasts, which you are to proclaim as sacred assemblies for bringing offerings made to the LORD by fire—the burnt offerings and grain offerings, sacrifices and drink offeringsⁿ required for each day. ³⁸These offerings are in addition to those for the LORD's Sabbathsᵒ andᶜ in addition to your gifts and whatever you have vowed and all the freewill offerings you give to the LORD.)

³⁹"'So beginning with the fifteenth day of the seventh month, after you have gathered the crops of the land, celebrate the festival to the LORD for seven days;ᵖ the first day is a day of rest, and the

---

23:21
ᵃver 2
ᵇver 3

23:22
ᶜLev 19:9
ᵈLev 19:10;
Dt 24:19-21;
Ru 2:15

23:24
ᵉLev 25:9;
Nu 10:9,10;
29:1

23:25
ᶠver 21

23:27
ᵍLev 16:29
ʰEx 30:10
ⁱNu 29:7

23:29
ʲGe 17:14;
Nu 5:2

23:30
ᵏLev 20:3

23:34
ˡEx 23:16;
Dt 16:13;
Ezr 3:4;
Ne 8:14;
Zec 14:16;
Jn 7:2

23:36
ᵐ2Ch 7:9;
Ne 8:18;
Jn 7:37

23:37
ⁿver 2,4

23:38
ᵒEze 45:17

23:39
ᵖEx 23:16;
Dt 16:13

ᵃ19 Traditionally *peace offering*   ᵇ27 Or *and fast*; also in verses 29 and 32
ᶜ38 Or *These feasts are in addition to the Lord's Sabbaths, and these offerings are*

eighth day also is a day of rest. ⁴⁰On the first day you are to take choice fruit from the trees, and palm fronds, leafy branches and poplars,^a and rejoice before the LORD your God for seven days. ⁴¹Celebrate this as a festival to the LORD for seven days each year. This is to be a lasting ordinance for the generations to come; celebrate it in the seventh month. ⁴²Live in booths^b for seven days: All native-born Israelites are to live in booths ⁴³so your descendants will know^c that I had the Israelites live in booths when I brought them out of Egypt. I am the LORD your God.'"

⁴⁴So Moses announced to the Israelites the appointed feasts of the LORD.

Chapter 24 Theme _____

24 The LORD said to Moses, ²"Command the Israelites to bring you clear oil of pressed olives for the light so that the lamps may be kept burning continually. ³Outside the curtain of the Testimony in the Tent of Meeting, Aaron is to tend the lamps before the LORD from evening till morning, continually. This is to be a lasting ordinance for the generations to come. ⁴The lamps on the pure gold lampstand^d before the LORD must be tended continually.

⁵"Take fine flour and bake twelve loaves of bread,^e using two-tenths of an ephah^a for each loaf. ⁶Set them in two rows, six in each row, on the table of pure gold ^f before the LORD. ⁷Along each row put some pure incense as a memorial portion^g to represent the bread and to be an offering made to the LORD by fire. ⁸This bread is to be set out before the LORD regularly,^h Sabbath after Sabbath,ⁱ on behalf of the Israelites, as a lasting covenant. ⁹It belongs to Aaron and his sons,^j who are to eat it in a holy place, because it is a most holy part of their regular share of the offerings made to the LORD by fire."

¹⁰Now the son of an Israelite mother and an Egyptian father went out among the Israelites, and a fight broke out in the camp between him and an Israelite. ¹¹The son of the Israelite woman blasphemed the Name^k with a curse; so they brought him to Moses. (His mother's name was Shelomith, the daughter of Dibri the Danite.) ¹²They put him in custody until the will of the LORD should be made clear to them.^l

¹³Then the LORD said to Moses: ¹⁴"Take the blasphemer outside the camp. All those who heard him are to lay their hands on his head, and the entire assembly is to stone him.^m ¹⁵Say to the Israelites: 'If anyone curses his God,ⁿ he will be held responsible; ¹⁶anyone who blasphemes the name of the LORD must be put to death.^o The entire assembly must stone him. Whether an alien or

Lampstand

23:40
a Ne 8:14-17

23:42
b Ne 8:14-16

23:43
c Dt 31:13; Ps 78:5

24:4
d Ex 25:31; 31:8

24:5
e Ex 25:30

24:6
f Ex 25:23-30; 1Ki 7:48

24:7
g Lev 2:2

24:8
h Nu 4:7; 1Ch 9:32; 2Ch 2:4
i Mt 12:5

24:9
j Lev 8:31; Mt 12:4; Mk 2:26; Lk 6:4

24:11
k Ex 3:15

24:12
l Ex 18:16; Nu 15:34

24:14
m Lev 20:27; Dt 13:9; 17:5,7; 21:21

24:15
n Ex 22:28

24:16
o 1Ki 21:10,13; Mt 26:66

a5 That is, probably about 4 quarts (about 4.5 liters)

native-born, when he blasphemes the Name, he must be put to death.

17"'If anyone takes the life of a human being, he must be put to death.*a* 18Anyone who takes the life of someone's animal must make restitution*b*—life for life. 19If anyone injures his neighbor, whatever he has done must be done to him: 20fracture for fracture, eye for eye, tooth for tooth.*c* As he has injured the other, so he is to be injured. 21Whoever kills an animal must make restitution, but whoever kills a man must be put to death.*d* 22You are to have the same law for the alien*e* and the native-born.*f* I am the LORD your God.'"

23Then Moses spoke to the Israelites, and they took the blasphemer outside the camp and stoned him. The Israelites did as the LORD commanded Moses.

Chapter 25 Theme _____

25 The LORD said to Moses on Mount Sinai, 2"Speak to the Israelites and say to them: 'When you enter the land I am going to give you, the land itself must observe a sabbath to the LORD. 3For six years sow your fields, and for six years prune your vineyards and gather their crops.*g* 4But in the seventh year the land is to have a sabbath of rest, a sabbath to the LORD. Do not sow your fields or prune your vineyards. 5Do not reap what grows of itself or harvest the grapes of your untended vines. The land is to have a year of rest. 6Whatever the land yields during the sabbath year*h* will be food for you—for yourself, your manservant and maidservant, and the hired worker and temporary resident who live among you, 7as well as for your livestock and the wild animals in your land. Whatever the land produces may be eaten.

8"'Count off seven sabbaths of years—seven times seven years—so that the seven sabbaths of years amount to a period of forty-nine years. 9Then have the trumpet*i* sounded everywhere on the tenth day of the seventh month; on the Day of Atonement sound the trumpet throughout your land. 10Consecrate the fiftieth year and proclaim liberty*j* throughout the land to all its inhabitants. It shall be a jubilee*k* for you; each one of you is to return to his family property and each to his own clan. 11The fiftieth year shall be a jubilee for you; do not sow and do not reap what grows of itself or harvest the untended vines. 12For it is a jubilee and is to be holy for you; eat only what is taken directly from the fields.

13"'In this Year of Jubilee*l* everyone is to return to his own property.

14"'If you sell land to one of your countrymen or buy any from him, do not take advantage of each other.*m* 15You are to buy from your countryman on the basis of the number of years*n* since the

24:17
*a*Ge 9:6;
Ex 21:12;
Nu 35:30-31;
Dt 27:24

24:18
*b*ver 21

24:20
*c*Ex 21:24;
Mt 5:38*

24:21
*d*ver 17

24:22
*e*Ex 12:49
*f*Nu 9:14;
15:16

25:3
*g*Ex 23:10

25:6
*h*ver 20

25:9
*i*Lev 23:24

25:10
*j*Isa 61:1;
Jer 34:8,15,17;
Lk 4:19
*k*Nu 36:4

25:13
*l*ver 10

25:14
*m*Lev 19:13;
1Sa 12:3,4

25:15
*n*Lev 27:18,23

25:16
a ver 27,51,52

25:17
b Pr 22:22;
Jer 7:5,6;
1Th 4:6
c Lev 19:14
d Lev 19:32

25:18
e Lev 26:4,5;
Dt 12:10;
Ps 4:8;
Jer 23:6

25:19
f Lev 26:4

25:20
g ver 4

25:21
h Dt 28:8,12;
Hag 2:19;
Mal 3:10

25:22
i Lev 26:10

25:23
j Ex 19:5
k Ge 23:4;
1Ch 29:15;
Ps 39:12;
Heb 11:13;
1Pe 2:11

25:24
l ver 29,48;
Ru 4:7

25:25
m Ru 2:20;
Jer 32:7
n Lev 27:13,
19,31;
Ru 4:4

25:28
o ver 10

25:32
p Nu 35:1-8;
Jos 21:2

25:34
q Nu 35:2-5

25:35
r Dt 24:14,15
s Dt 15:8;
Ps 37:21,26;
Lk 6:35

Jubilee. And he is to sell to you on the basis of the number of years left for harvesting crops. [16]When the years are many, you are to increase the price, and when the years are few, you are to decrease the price,*a* because what he is really selling you is the number of crops. [17]Do not take advantage of each other,*b* but fear your God.*c* I am the LORD your God.*d*

[18]"'Follow my decrees and be careful to obey my laws, and you will live safely in the land.*e* [19]Then the land will yield its fruit,*f* and you will eat your fill and live there in safety. [20]You may ask, "What will we eat in the seventh year*g* if we do not plant or harvest our crops?" [21]I will send you such a blessing*h* in the sixth year that the land will yield enough for three years. [22]While you plant during the eighth year, you will eat from the old crop and will continue to eat from it until the harvest of the ninth year comes in.*i*

[23]"'The land must not be sold permanently, because the land is mine*j* and you are but aliens*k* and my tenants. [24]Throughout the country that you hold as a possession, you must provide for the redemption*l* of the land.

[25]"'If one of your countrymen becomes poor and sells some of his property, his nearest relative*m* is to come and redeem*n* what his countryman has sold. [26]If, however, a man has no one to redeem it for him but he himself prospers and acquires sufficient means to redeem it, [27]he is to determine the value for the years since he sold it and refund the balance to the man to whom he sold it; he can then go back to his own property. [28]But if he does not acquire the means to repay him, what he sold will remain in the possession of the buyer until the Year of Jubilee. It will be returned in the Jubilee, and he can then go back to his property.*o*

[29]"'If a man sells a house in a walled city, he retains the right of redemption a full year after its sale. During that time he may redeem it. [30]If it is not redeemed before a full year has passed, the house in the walled city shall belong permanently to the buyer and his descendants. It is not to be returned in the Jubilee. [31]But houses in villages without walls around them are to be considered as open country. They can be redeemed, and they are to be returned in the Jubilee.

[32]"'The Levites always have the right to redeem their houses in the Levitical towns,*p* which they possess. [33]So the property of the Levites is redeemable—that is, a house sold in any town they hold—and is to be returned in the Jubilee, because the houses in the towns of the Levites are their property among the Israelites. [34]But the pastureland belonging to their towns must not be sold; it is their permanent possession.*q*

[35]"'If one of your countrymen becomes poor*r* and is unable to support himself among you, help him*s* as you would an alien or a temporary resident, so he can continue to live among you.

³⁶Do not take interest^a of any kind^a from him, but fear your God, so that your countryman may continue to live among you. ³⁷You must not lend him money at interest or sell him food at a profit. ³⁸I am the LORD your God, who brought you out of Egypt to give you the land of Canaan and to be your God.^b

³⁹"'If one of your countrymen becomes poor among you and sells himself to you, do not make him work as a slave.^c ⁴⁰He is to be treated as a hired worker or a temporary resident among you; he is to work for you until the Year of Jubilee. ⁴¹Then he and his children are to be released, and he will go back to his own clan and to the property^d of his forefathers. ⁴²Because the Israelites are my servants, whom I brought out of Egypt, they must not be sold as slaves. ⁴³Do not rule over them ruthlessly,^e but fear your God.

⁴⁴"'Your male and female slaves are to come from the nations around you; from them you may buy slaves. ⁴⁵You may also buy some of the temporary residents living among you and members of their clans born in your country, and they will become your property. ⁴⁶You can will them to your children as inherited property and can make them slaves for life, but you must not rule over your fellow Israelites ruthlessly.

⁴⁷"'If an alien or a temporary resident among you becomes rich and one of your countrymen becomes poor and sells himself to the alien living among you or to a member of the alien's clan, ⁴⁸he retains the right of redemption after he has sold himself. One of his relatives^f may redeem him: ⁴⁹An uncle or a cousin or any blood relative in his clan may redeem him. Or if he prospers,^g he may redeem himself. ⁵⁰He and his buyer are to count the time from the year he sold himself up to the Year of Jubilee. The price for his release is to be based on the rate paid to a hired man^h for that number of years. ⁵¹If many years remain, he must pay for his redemption a larger share of the price paid for him. ⁵²If only a few years remain until the Year of Jubilee, he is to compute that and pay for his redemption accordingly. ⁵³He is to be treated as a man hired from year to year; you must see to it that his owner does not rule over him ruthlessly.

⁵⁴"'Even if he is not redeemed in any of these ways, he and his children are to be released in the Year of Jubilee, ⁵⁵for the Israelites belong to me as servants. They are my servants, whom I brought out of Egypt. I am the LORD your God.

Chapter 26 Theme _____

26 "'Do not make idolsⁱ or set up an image or a sacred stone^j for yourselves, and do not place a carved stone^k in your land to bow down before it. I am the LORD your God.

---

^a36 Or *take excessive interest*; similarly in verse 37

25:36
^aEx 22:25;
Dt 23:19-20

25:38
^bGe 17:7;
Lev 11:45

25:39
^cEx 21:2;
Dt 15:12;
1Ki 9:22

25:41
^dver 28

25:43
^eEx 1:13;
Eze 34:4;
Col 4:1

25:48
^fNe 5:5

25:49
^gver 26

25:50
^hJob 7:1;
Isa 16:14;
21:16

26:1
ⁱEx 20:4;
Lev 19:4;
Dt 5:8
^jEx 23:24
^kNu 33:52

26:2
a Lev 19:30

26:3
b Dt 7:12;
11:13,22;
28:1,9

26:4
c Dt 11:14
d Ps 67:6

26:5
e Dt 11:15;
Joel 2:19,26;
Am 9:13
f Lev 25:18

26:6
g Ps 29:11;
85:8; 147:14
h Ps 4:8
i Zep 3:13
j ver 22

26:8
k Dt 32:30;
Jos 23:10

26:9
l Ge 17:6;
Ne 9:23
m Ge 17:7

26:10
n Lev 25:22

26:11
o Ex 25:8;
Ps 76:2;
Eze 37:27

26:12
p Ge 3:8
q 2Co 6:16*

26:13
r Eze 34:27

26:14
s Dt 28:15-68;
Mal 2:2

26:16
t Dt 28:22,35
u 1Sa 2:33
v Job 31:8

26:17
w Lev 17:10
x Ps 106:41
y ver 36,37;
Dt 28:7,25;
Ps 53:5

26:18
z ver 21

26:19
a Isa 25:11
b Dt 28:23

26:20
c Ps 127:1;
Isa 17:11
d Dt 11:17

26:21
e ver 18

26:22
f Dt 32:24

²"'Observe my Sabbaths and have reverence for my sanctuary.*a* I am the LORD.

³"'If you follow my decrees and are careful to obey*b* my commands, ⁴I will send you rain*c* in its season, and the ground will yield its crops and the trees of the field their fruit.*d* ⁵Your threshing will continue until grape harvest and the grape harvest will continue until planting, and you will eat all the food you want*e* and live in safety in your land.*f*

⁶"'I will grant peace in the land,*g* and you will lie down*h* and no one will make you afraid.*i* I will remove savage beasts*j* from the land, and the sword will not pass through your country. ⁷You will pursue your enemies, and they will fall by the sword before you. ⁸Five of you will chase a hundred, and a hundred of you will chase ten thousand, and your enemies will fall by the sword before you.*k*

⁹"'I will look on you with favor and make you fruitful and increase your numbers,*l* and I will keep my covenant*m* with you. ¹⁰You will still be eating last year's harvest when you will have to move it out to make room for the new.*n* ¹¹I will put my dwelling place*ao* among you, and I will not abhor you. ¹²I will walk*p* among you and be your God, and you will be my people.*q* ¹³I am the LORD your God, who brought you out of Egypt so that you would no longer be slaves to the Egyptians; I broke the bars of your yoke*r* and enabled you to walk with heads held high.

¹⁴"'But if you will not listen to me and carry out all these commands,*s* ¹⁵and if you reject my decrees and abhor my laws and fail to carry out all my commands and so violate my covenant, ¹⁶then I will do this to you: I will bring upon you sudden terror, wasting diseases and fever*t* that will destroy your sight and drain away your life.*u* You will plant seed in vain, because your enemies will eat it.*v* ¹⁷I will set my face*w* against you so that you will be defeated by your enemies; those who hate you will rule over you,*x* and you will flee even when no one is pursuing you.*y*

¹⁸"'If after all this you will not listen to me, I will punish you for your sins seven times over.*z* ¹⁹I will break down your stubborn pride*a* and make the sky above you like iron and the ground beneath you like bronze.*b* ²⁰Your strength will be spent in vain,*c* because your soil will not yield its crops, nor will the trees of the land yield their fruit.*d*

²¹"'If you remain hostile toward me and refuse to listen to me, I will multiply your afflictions seven times over,*e* as your sins deserve. ²²I will send wild animals*f* against you, and they will rob you of your children, destroy your cattle and make you so few in number that your roads will be deserted.

a 11 Or *my tabernacle*

23 " 'If in spite of these things you do not accept my correction[a] but continue to be hostile toward me, 24 I myself will be hostile toward you and will afflict you for your sins seven times over. 25 And I will bring the sword upon you to avenge the breaking of the covenant. When you withdraw into your cities, I will send a plague[b] among you, and you will be given into enemy hands. 26 When I cut off your supply of bread,[c] ten women will be able to bake your bread in one oven, and they will dole out the bread by weight. You will eat, but you will not be satisfied.

27 " 'If in spite of this you still do not listen to me but continue to be hostile toward me, 28 then in my anger I will be hostile toward you, and I myself will punish you for your sins seven times over. 29 You will eat the flesh of your sons and the flesh of your daughters.[d] 30 I will destroy your high places,[e] cut down your incense altars[f] and pile your dead bodies on the lifeless forms of your idols,[g] and I will abhor you. 31 I will turn your cities into ruins and lay waste your sanctuaries,[h] and I will take no delight in the pleasing aroma of your offerings. 32 I will lay waste the land,[i] so that your enemies who live there will be appalled. 33 I will scatter you among the nations[j] and will draw out my sword and pursue you. Your land will be laid waste, and your cities will lie in ruins. 34 Then the land will enjoy its sabbath years all the time that it lies desolate and you are in the country of your enemies;[k] then the land will rest and enjoy its sabbaths. 35 All the time that it lies desolate, the land will have the rest it did not have during the sabbaths you lived in it.

36 " 'As for those of you who are left, I will make their hearts so fearful in the lands of their enemies that the sound of a wind-blown leaf will put them to flight.[l] They will run as though fleeing from the sword, and they will fall, even though no one is pursuing them. 37 They will stumble over one another as though fleeing from the sword, even though no one is pursuing them. So you will not be able to stand before your enemies.[m] 38 You will perish among the nations; the land of your enemies will devour you.[n] 39 Those of you who are left will waste away in the lands of their enemies because of their sins; also because of their fathers' sins they will waste away.[o]

40 " 'But if they will confess their sins and the sins of their fathers[p]—their treachery against me and their hostility toward me, 41 which made me hostile toward them so that I sent them into the land of their enemies—then when their uncircumcised hearts[q] are humbled and they pay for their sin, 42 I will remember my covenant with Jacob[r] and my covenant with Isaac[s] and my covenant with Abraham, and I will remember the land. 43 For the land will be deserted by them and will enjoy its sabbaths

26:23
[a] Jer 2:30; 5:3

26:25
[b] Nu 14:12;
Eze 5:17

26:26
[c] Ps 105:16;
Isa 3:1;
Mic 6:14

26:29
[d] Dt 28:53

26:30
[e] 2Ch 34:3;
Eze 6:3
[f] Eze 6:6
[g] Eze 6:13

26:31
[h] Ps 74:3-7

26:32
[i] Jer 9:11

26:33
[j] Dt 4:27;
Eze 12:15;
20:23;
Zec 7:14

26:34
[k] ver 43;
2Ch 36:21

26:36
[l] Eze 21:7

26:37
[m] Jos 7:12

26:38
[n] Dt 4:26

26:39
[o] Eze 4:17

26:40
[p] Jer 3:12-15;
Lk 15:18;
1Jn 1:9

26:41
[q] Eze 44:7,9;
Ac 7:51

26:42
[r] Ge 22:15-18;
28:15;
[s] Ge 26:5

26:44
aRo 11:2
bDt 4:31;
Jer 30:11
cJer 33:26

while it lies desolate without them. They will pay for their sins because they rejected my laws and abhorred my decrees. ⁴⁴Yet in spite of this, when they are in the land of their enemies, I will not reject them or abhor*ᵃ* them so as to destroy them completely,*ᵇ* breaking my covenant*ᶜ* with them. I am the LORD their God. ⁴⁵But for their sake I will remember*ᵈ* the covenant with their ancestors whom I brought out of Egypt*ᵉ* in the sight of the nations to be their God. I am the LORD.'"

26:45
dGe 17:7
eEx 6:8;
Lev 25:38

⁴⁶These are the decrees, the laws and the regulations that the LORD established on Mount Sinai between himself and the Israelites through Moses.*ᶠ*

Chapter 27 Theme _____

26:46
fLev 7:38;
27:34

27 The LORD said to Moses, ²"Speak to the Israelites and say to them: 'If anyone makes a special vow*ᵍ* to dedicate persons to the LORD by giving equivalent values, ³set the value of a male between the ages of twenty and sixty at fifty shekels*ᵃ* of silver, according to the sanctuary shekel*ᵇ;ʰ* ⁴and if it is a female, set her value at thirty shekels.*ᶜ* ⁵If it is a person between the ages of five and twenty, set the value of a male at twenty shekels*ᵈ* and of a female at ten shekels.*ᵉ* ⁶If it is a person between one month and five years, set the value of a male at five shekels*ᶠⁱ* of silver and that of a female at three shekels*ᵍ* of silver. ⁷If it is a person sixty years old or more, set the value of a male at fifteen shekels*ʰ* and of a female at ten shekels. ⁸If anyone making the vow is too poor to pay*ʲ* the specified amount, he is to present the person to the priest, who will set the value*ᵏ* for him according to what the man making the vow can afford.

27:2
gNu 6:2

27:3
hEx 30:13;
Nu 3:47;
18:16

⁹"'If what he vowed is an animal that is acceptable as an offering to the LORD, such an animal given to the LORD becomes holy. ¹⁰He must not exchange it or substitute a good one for a bad one, or a bad one for a good one;*ˡ* if he should substitute one animal for another, both it and the substitute become holy. ¹¹If what he vowed is a ceremonially unclean animal—one that is not acceptable as an offering to the LORD—the animal must be presented to the priest, ¹²who will judge its quality as good or bad. Whatever value the priest then sets, that is what it will be. ¹³If the owner wishes to redeem*ᵐ* the animal, he must add a fifth to its value.

27:6
iNu 18:16

27:8
jLev 5:11
kver 12,14

¹⁴"'If a man dedicates his house as something holy to the LORD, the priest will judge its quality as good or bad. Whatever value the priest then sets, so it will remain. ¹⁵If the man who dedicates

27:10
lver 33

27:13
mver 15,19;
Lev 25:25

a3 That is, about 1 1/4 pounds (about 0.6 kilogram); also in verse 16   b3 That is, about 2/5 ounce (about 11.5 grams); also in verse 25   c4 That is, about 12 ounces (about 0.3 kilogram)   d5 That is, about 8 ounces (about 0.2 kilogram)   e5 That is, about 4 ounces (about 110 grams); also in verse 7   f6 That is, about 2 ounces (about 55 grams)   g6 That is, about 1 1/4 ounces (about 35 grams)   h7 That is, about 6 ounces (about 170 grams) his house redeems it,[a] he must add a fifth to its value, and the house will again become his.

16"'If a man dedicates to the LORD part of his family land, its value is to be set according to the amount of seed required for it—fifty shekels of silver to a homer[a] of barley seed. 17If he dedicates his field during the Year of Jubilee, the value that has been set remains. 18But if he dedicates his field after the Jubilee, the priest will determine the value according to the number of years that remain[b] until the next Year of Jubilee, and its set value will be reduced. 19If the man who dedicates the field wishes to redeem it, he must add a fifth to its value, and the field will again become his. 20If, however, he does not redeem the field, or if he has sold it to someone else, it can never be redeemed. 21When the field is released in the Jubilee,[c] it will become holy, like a field devoted to the LORD;[d] it will become the property of the priests.[b]

22"'If a man dedicates to the LORD a field he has bought, which is not part of his family land, 23the priest will determine its value up to the Year of Jubilee, and the man must pay its value on that day as something holy to the LORD. 24In the Year of Jubilee the field will revert to the person from whom he bought it,[e] the one whose land it was. 25Every value is to be set according to the sanctuary shekel,[f] twenty gerahs[g] to the shekel.

26"'No one, however, may dedicate the firstborn of an animal, since the firstborn already belongs to the LORD;[h] whether an ox[c] or a sheep, it is the LORD's. 27If it is one of the unclean animals,[i] he may buy it back at its set value, adding a fifth of the value to it. If he does not redeem it, it is to be sold at its set value.

28"'But nothing that a man owns and devotes[d][j] to the LORD— whether man or animal or family land—may be sold or redeemed; everything so devoted is most holy to the LORD.

29"'No person devoted to destruction[e] may be ransomed; he must be put to death.

30"'A tithe[k] of everything from the land, whether grain from the soil or fruit from the trees, belongs to the LORD; it is holy to the LORD. 31If a man redeems any of his tithe, he must add a fifth of the value to it. 32The entire tithe of the herd and flock—every tenth animal that passes under the shepherd's rod[l]—will be holy to the LORD. 33He must not pick out the good from the bad or make any substitution.[m] If he does make a substitution, both the animal and its substitute become holy and cannot be redeemed.'"

34These are the commands the LORD gave Moses on Mount Sinai for the Israelites.[n]

---

a16 That is, probably about 6 bushels (about 220 liters)   b21 Or *priest*   c26 The Hebrew word can include both male and female.   d28 The Hebrew term refers to the irrevocable giving over of things or persons to the LORD.   e29 The Hebrew term refers to the irrevocable giving over of things or persons to the LORD, often by totally destroying them.

27:15
[a]ver 13,20

27:18
[b]Lev 25:15

27:21
[c]Lev 25:10
[d]ver 28;
Nu 18:14;
Eze 44:29

27:24
[e]Lev 25:28

27:25
[f]Ex 30:13;
Nu 18:16
[g]Nu 3:47;
Eze 45:12

27:26
[h]Ex 13:2,12

27:27
[i]ver 11

27:28
[j]Nu 18:14;
Jos 6:17-19

27:30
[k]Ge 28:22;
2Ch 31:6;
Mal 3:8

27:32
[l]Jer 33:13;
Eze 20:37

27:33
[m]ver 10

27:34
[n]Lev 26:46;
Dt 4:5

The Offerings and Their Purposes

The Offering	Chapter/ Verse	Voluntary/ Involuntary	Reason/Purpose

THE FEASTS OF ISRAEL

Slaves in Egypt	1st Month (Nisan) Festival of Passover				3rd Month (Sivan) Festival of Pentecost
	Passover	Yeast Bread	Firstfruits		Pentecost or Feast of Weeks
	Slaughter lamb & put blood on doorframe Exodus 12:6, 7	*Purging of all yeast* (symbol of sin)	*Wave offering of sheaf* (promise of harvest to come)		*Wave offering of two loaves of yeast bread*
	1st month, 14th day Leviticus 23:5	1st month, 15th day for 7 days Leviticus 23:6-8	Day after Sabbath Leviticus 23:9-14		50 days after firstfruits Leviticus 23:15-21
Everyone who sins is a slave to sin	Christ our Passover Lamb, has been sacrificed	Get rid of old yeast that you may be a new batch without yeast	Christ has been raised...the firstfruits	Going away so Counselor can come	Promise of the Spirit, mystery of church: Jews-Gentiles in one body
				Mount of Olives	
John 8:34	1 Corinthians 5:7	1 Corinthians 5:7, 8	1 Corinthians 15:20-23	John 16:7 Acts 1:9-12	Acts 2:1-47 1 Corinthians 12:13 Ephesians 2:11-22

Months: Nisan—*March, April* • **Sivan**—*May, June* • **Tishri**—*September, October*

7th Month (Tishri) Festival of Tabernacles			
Feast of Trumpets	**Day of Atonement**	**Feast of Booths or Tabernacles**	
Trumpet blown — a sacred assembly	*Atonement will be made to cleanse you* Leviticus 16:30	*Harvest celebration memorial of tabernacles in wilderness*	
7th month, 1st day Leviticus 23:23-25	7th month, 10th day Leviticus 23:26-32	7th month, 15th day, for 7 days; 8th day, sacred assembly Leviticus 23:33-44	
Regathering of Israel in preparation for final day of atonement Jeremiah 32:37-41	**Israel will repent and look to Messiah in one day** Zechariah 3:9,10; 12:10; 13:1; 14:9	**Peoples of the earth will come to Jerusalem to celebrate the Feast of Tabernacles** Zechariah 14:16-19	**New heaven and new earth** **God dwells with men** Revelation 21:1-3
	Coming of Christ		
Ezekiel 36:24	Ezekiel 36:25-27 Hebrews 9, 10 Romans 11:25-29	Ezekiel 36:28	

Israel had two harvests each year—spring and autumn

Theme of Leviticus:

SEGMENT DIVISIONS

Laws Regarding	Main Division		Chapter Themes	Author:
	WORSHIPING A HOLY GOD	1		
		2		
		3		Date:
		4		
		5		Purpose:
		6		
		7		
		8		Key Words:
		9		
		10		the Lord said to Moses
		11		
		12		tabernacle (dwelling place, Tent of Meeting)
		13		
		14		law (regulations)
		15		
		16		sacrifice(s), do this (offering[s])
		17		
	LIVING A HOLY LIFE	18		sin(s), held responsible (guilt, guilty)
		19		
		20		blood (bleeding)
		21		
		22		atonement
		23		holy (sacred)
		24		
		25		covenant
		26		
		27		

NUMBERS

*T*he Israelites cried out to God. And God heard and raised up Moses to deliver the children of Israel out of the land of Egypt, the house of bondage. The children of Israel had lived in Egypt for 430 years, most of those years as slaves. After camping at Sinai, they were to go to Canaan, the land promised to Abraham, Isaac, and Jacob. At last they would see the land with their own eyes. And God would go with them in a pillar of cloud by day and a pillar of fire by night.

Soon the journey would begin, but first there must be a numbering of all the sons of Israel from 20 years of age on up.

∾ THINGS TO DO

General Information

The book of Numbers can be divided into three segments according to the journeys and encampments of the children of Israel. In Numbers 1 through 10:10 they are encamped at Sinai. In Numbers 10:11 the cloud lifts and their journeying begins and does not end for about 39 years. In Numbers 22 Israel camps on the plains of Moab, opposite Jericho, as they prepare to enter the land of promise.

Chapters 1–10:10

1. The first five books of the Bible, Genesis through Deuteronomy, are closely related. They follow each other chronologically. To put Numbers into context:
   a. Read Exodus 40:1, 2, 17, 33-38, which gives an account of the building of the tabernacle at Mount Sinai.
   b. Read Leviticus 1:1 and then 27:34. All of the book of Leviticus takes place at Mount Sinai.
   c. Compare where Leviticus ends and Numbers begins. Read Numbers 1:1, 2.
   d. Look at Exodus 40:17 again and Numbers 1:1, and you will see one month elapsed between the close of Exodus and the beginning of Numbers. Leviticus covers a period of only one month.

2. Read through this first segment chapter by chapter. As you do, do not become discouraged and quit; Numbers becomes more interesting and practical after this segment. As you read:
   a. Mark the following key words in a distinctive way: *number, listing, listed, count(ed)* or *census (have counted)* (and their synonyms), *the Lord spoke to (the Lord said to, the Lord talked with, the Lord also said to, the Lord spoke with), of the sons of (of the people of, from the sons of, from the descendants of)* (then underline whose sons, descendants, or people they were), *service (serve, serving, work, ministering), cloud, desert (tent, Tent of Meeting, Tent of the Testimony, tabernacle),* and *war* (or any reference to being in the army or going to battle or fighting). Write them on an index card and use it as a bookmark as you study Numbers.
   b. Note every reference to time with a symbol.
   c. In the margin of each chapter make lists of key truths you want to be able to find with ease. For instance next to 9:15 you might write: "Instructions re: Cloud" or simply "The Cloud."
   d. Note the theme of each chapter and record it on the NUMBERS AT A GLANCE chart on page 285 and on the line next to the chapter number in the text.

Chapters 10:11–21:35

1. This segment covers about 39 years. As you study you will discover why it takes so long to cover such a relatively short distance. Do the following as you study chapter by chapter:
   a. Since much of what you will read in this segment is historical, you can learn a lot simply by

asking the five W's and an H. Ask: Who are the main characters in this chapter? What is happening? Why is it happening? When and where is it happening? Why are they told to do something? What were the consequences of their actions? How and why did this occur?

  1) You might want to note in the margin when and where events occur.

  2) Follow the movements of the Israelites on the map at Numbers 11 on page 236.

b. Mark key repeated words. Use the list you used in the first segment. Watch for key words which are not on the list but will be significant in a particular chapter.

c. Write on a piece of paper what you learn about the land the Israelites are to possess and what you learn about Korah and Balaam. (Balaam appears in Numbers 22.) These two men will be mentioned again, even in the New Testament, so it will be helpful to summarize all you learn about them. Record your insights on the chart INSIGHTS FROM NUMBERS on page 284.

d. There are lessons to be learned from Moses' life about leadership and about our relationship to God. Although you will probably want to note these lessons in the chapter margins, you will also find it profitable to summarize what you learn on LESSONS FROM THE LIFE OF MOSES, a chart on pages 346, 347. When you record your insights, make sure you note the book, chapter, and verse from which you took your insight.

2. As you did before, record each chapter theme on NUMBERS AT A GLANCE and in the text.

Chapters 22-36

1. This final segment of Numbers is a mixture of historical events, instructions, and numberings. As you read each chapter, remember to ask the five W's and an H and to record any pertinent insights in the margin.

2. To your list of key words add the following: *Balaam, Moab (Moabite)* (Moab is first mentioned in Numbers 21, so go back and mark Moab in that chapter also), *Midian (Midianite), covenant, burnt offering(s), (offering),* and *sin offering.*

3. Balaam plays a major role in this last segment. Note all you learn about him on INSIGHTS FROM NUMBERS on page 284.

4. Record the main points or events of these chapters in the margin. As you near the end of Numbers you will read more about Balaam, so note in the margin where these final verses on Balaam can be found.

5. Record what you learn about Moses. Give special attention to Numbers 27:12-23 in the light of Numbers 20. Next to Numbers 20:1-13 you might want to write Numbers 27:12-23 as a cross-reference.

6. Record your chapter themes as you did before.

7. Record the predominant theme or event in each of the three segments of Numbers on NUMBERS AT A GLANCE. See if any of the chapters can be grouped according to the types of commands, ordinances, and/or events. In other words, do several chapters cover similar topics or events? For example, chapters 1 and 2 cover the census. Note these in the first column under "Segment Divisions" and complete the NUMBERS AT A GLANCE chart.

❧ THINGS TO THINK ABOUT

1. Review all you learned from Moses' life and then pray about how it applies to your own life.

2. Remember, God is the same yesterday, today, and forever. His character did not change between the Old Testament and the New Testament. Think about what you have learned about God from the book of Numbers. Are you living accordingly?

3. Are you jealous because the children of Israel had a cloud to guide them? Have you realized that God's presence in the form of the indwelling Spirit is there to guide you? Do you seek and ask for his Spirit to lead and guide you just as surely as he led the children of Israel? What can you learn from the children of Israel so you won't make the same mistakes?

Chapter 1 Theme

1 The LORD spoke to Moses in the Tent of Meeting*a* in the Desert of Sinai*b* on the first day of the second month*c* of the second year after the Israelites came out of Egypt. He said: ²"Take a census*d* of the whole Israelite community by their clans and families, listing every man by name, one by one. ³You and Aaron are to number by their divisions all the men in Israel twenty years old or more*e* who are able to serve in the army. ⁴One man from each tribe, each the head of his family,*f* is to help you.*g* ⁵These are the names of the men who are to assist you:

from Reuben,*h* Elizur son of Shedeur;
⁶from Simeon, Shelumiel son of Zurishaddai;
⁷from Judah,*i* Nahshon son of Amminadab;*j*
⁸from Issachar,*k* Nethanel son of Zuar;
⁹from Zebulun,*l* Eliab son of Helon;
¹⁰from the sons of Joseph:
from Ephraim,*m* Elishama son of Ammihud;
from Manasseh, Gamaliel son of Pedahzur;
¹¹from Benjamin, Abidan son of Gideoni;
¹²from Dan,*n* Ahiezer son of Ammishaddai;
¹³from Asher,*o* Pagiel son of Ocran;
¹⁴from Gad, Eliasaph son of Deuel;*p*
¹⁵from Naphtali,*q* Ahira son of Enan."

¹⁶These were the men appointed from the community, the leaders*r* of their ancestral tribes. They were the heads of the clans of Israel.*s*

¹⁷Moses and Aaron took these men whose names had been given, ¹⁸and they called the whole community together on the first day of the second month.*t* The people indicated their ancestry*u* by their clans and families, and the men twenty years old or more were listed by name, one by one, ¹⁹as the LORD commanded Moses. And so he counted them in the Desert of Sinai:

²⁰From the descendants of Reuben*v* the firstborn son of Israel:
All the men twenty years old or more who were able to serve in the army were listed by name, one by one, according to the records of their clans and families. ²¹The number from the tribe of Reuben was 46,500.

²²From the descendants of Simeon:*w*
All the men twenty years old or more who were able to serve in the army were counted and listed by name, one by one, according to the records of their clans and families. ²³The number from the tribe of Simeon was 59,300.

1:1
a Ex 40:2
b Ex 19:1
c Ex 40:17

1:2
d Ex 30:11-16;
Nu 26:2

1:3
e Ex 30:14

1:4
f ver 16
g Ex 18:21;
Dt 1:15

1:5
h Ge 29:32;
Dt 33:6;
Rev 7:5

1:7
i Ge 29:35;
Ps 78:68
j Ru 4:20;
1Ch 2:10;
Lk 3:32

1:8
k Ge 30:18

1:9
l ver 30

1:10
m ver 32

1:12
n ver 38

1:13
o ver 40

1:14
p Nu 2:14

1:15
q ver 42

1:16
r Ex 18:25
s ver 4;
Ex 18:21;
Nu 7:2

1:18
t ver 1
u Ezr 2:59;
Heb 7:3

1:20
v Nu 26:5-11;
Rev 7:5

1:22
w Nu 26:12-14;
Rev 7:7

²⁴From the descendants of Gad:*ᵃ*

All the men twenty years old or more who were able to serve in the army were listed by name, according to the records of their clans and families. ²⁵The number from the tribe of Gad was 45,650.

²⁶From the descendants of Judah:*ᵇ*

All the men twenty years old or more who were able to serve in the army were listed by name, according to the records of their clans and families. ²⁷The number from the tribe of Judah was 74,600.

²⁸From the descendants of Issachar:*ᶜ*

All the men twenty years old or more who were able to serve in the army were listed by name, according to the records of their clans and families. ²⁹The number from the tribe of Issachar was 54,400.

³⁰From the descendants of Zebulun:*ᵈ*

All the men twenty years old or more who were able to serve in the army were listed by name, according to the records of their clans and families. ³¹The number from the tribe of Zebulun was 57,400.

³²From the sons of Joseph:

From the descendants of Ephraim:*ᵉ*

All the men twenty years old or more who were able to serve in the army were listed by name, according to the records of their clans and families. ³³The number from the tribe of Ephraim was 40,500.

³⁴From the descendants of Manasseh:*ᶠ*

All the men twenty years old or more who were able to serve in the army were listed by name, according to the records of their clans and families. ³⁵The number from the tribe of Manasseh was 32,200.

³⁶From the descendants of Benjamin:*ᵍ*

All the men twenty years old or more who were able to serve in the army were listed by name, according to the records of their clans and families. ³⁷The number from the tribe of Benjamin was 35,400.

³⁸From the descendants of Dan:*ʰ*

All the men twenty years old or more who were able to serve in the army were listed by name, according to the records of their clans and families. ³⁹The number from the tribe of Dan was 62,700.

1:24
*ᵃ*Ge 30:11;
Nu 26:15-18;
Rev 7:5

1:26
*ᵇ*Ge 29:35;
Nu 26:19-22;
Mt 1:2; Rev 7:5

1:28
*ᶜ*Nu 26:23-25;
Rev 7:7

1:30
*ᵈ*Nu 26:26-27;
Rev 7:8

1:32
*ᵉ*Nu 26:35-37

1:34
*ᶠ*Nu 26:28-34;
Rev 7:6

1:36
*ᵍ*Nu 26:38-41;
2Ch 17:17;
Rev 7:8

1:38
*ʰ*Ge 30:6;
Nu 26:42-43

1:40
a Nu 26:44-47;
Rev 7:6

1:42
b Nu 26:48-50;
Rev 7:6

1:44
c Nu 26:64

1:46
d Ex 12:37;
38:26;
Nu 2:32;
26:51

1:47
e Nu 2:33; 26:57
f Nu 4:3,49

1:50
g Ex 38:21;
Ac 7:44

1:51
h Nu 3:38;
4:1-33

1:52
i Nu 2:2;
Ps 20:5

1:53
j Lev 10:6;
Nu 16:46; 18:5
k Nu 18:2-4

2:2
l Nu 1:52;
Ps 74:4;
Isa 31:9

2:3
m Nu 10:14;
Ru 4:20;
1Ch 2:10

2:5
n Nu 1:8

[40] From the descendants of Asher:[a]

All the men twenty years old or more who were able to serve in the army were listed by name, according to the records of their clans and families. [41] The number from the tribe of Asher was 41,500.

[42] From the descendants of Naphtali:[b]

All the men twenty years old or more who were able to serve in the army were listed by name, according to the records of their clans and families. [43] The number from the tribe of Naphtali was 53,400.

[44] These were the men counted by Moses and Aaron[c] and the twelve leaders of Israel, each one representing his family. [45] All the Israelites twenty years old or more who were able to serve in Israel's army were counted according to their families. [46] The total number was 603,550.[d]

[47] The families of the tribe of Levi,[e] however, were not counted[f] along with the others. [48] The LORD had said to Moses: [49] "You must not count the tribe of Levi or include them in the census of the other Israelites. [50] Instead, appoint the Levites to be in charge of the tabernacle of the Testimony[g]—over all its furnishings and everything belonging to it. They are to carry the tabernacle and all its furnishings; they are to take care of it and encamp around it. [51] Whenever the tabernacle is to move, the Levites are to take it down, and whenever the tabernacle is to be set up, the Levites shall do it.[h] Anyone else who goes near it shall be put to death. [52] The Israelites are to set up their tents by divisions, each man in his own camp under his own standard.[i] [53] The Levites, however, are to set up their tents around the tabernacle of the Testimony so that wrath will not fall[j] on the Israelite community. The Levites are to be responsible for the care of the tabernacle of the Testimony.[k]"

[54] The Israelites did all this just as the LORD commanded Moses.

Chapter 2 Theme

2 The LORD said to Moses and Aaron: [2] "The Israelites are to camp around the Tent of Meeting some distance from it, each man under his standard[l] with the banners of his family."

[3] On the east, toward the sunrise, the divisions of the camp of Judah are to encamp under their standard. The leader of the people of Judah is Nahshon son of Amminadab.[m] [4] His division numbers 74,600.

[5] The tribe of Issachar will camp next to them. The leader of the people of Issachar is Nethanel son of Zuar.[n] [6] His division numbers 54,400.

Camp Arrangement of Israel's Tribes

[Diagram — Camp Arrangement of Israel's Tribes]

DAN · ASHER · NAPHTALI

BENJAMIN · MERARITES · EAST · JUDAH

MANASSEH · GERSHONITES · MOSES & AARON & SONS · TABERNACLE · ISSACHAR

EPHRAIM · KOHATHITES · ZEBULUN

GAD · SIMEON · REUBEN

Key:
▲ Denotes the leaders of each group
● Families of the tribe of Levi

⁷The tribe of Zebulun will be next. The leader of the people of Zebulun is Eliab son of Helon.ᵃ ⁸His division numbers 57,400.

⁹All the men assigned to the camp of Judah, according to their divisions, number 186,400. They will set out first.ᵇ

¹⁰On the south will be the divisions of the camp of Reuben under their standard. The leader of the people of Reuben is Elizur son of Shedeur.ᶜ ¹¹His division numbers 46,500.

¹²The tribe of Simeon will camp next to them. The leader of the people of Simeon is Shelumiel son of Zurishaddai.ᵈ ¹³His division numbers 59,300.

¹⁴The tribe of Gad will be next. The leader of the people of Gad is Eliasaph son of Deuel.ᵉᵃ ¹⁵His division numbers 45,650.

¹⁶All the men assigned to the camp of Reuben,ᶠ according to their divisions, number 151,450. They will set out second.

¹⁷Then the Tent of Meeting and the camp of the Levitesᵍ will set out in the middle of the camps. They will set out in the same order as they encamp, each in his own place under his standard.

¹⁸On the west will be the divisions of the camp of Ephraimʰ under their standard. The leader of the people of Ephraim is Elishama son of Ammihud.ⁱ ¹⁹His division numbers 40,500.

²⁰The tribe of Manasseh will be next to them. The leader of the people of Manasseh is Gamaliel son of Pedahzur.ʲ ²¹His division numbers 32,200.

²²The tribe of Benjamin will be next. The leader of the people of Benjamin is Abidan son of Gideoni.ᵏ ²³His division numbers 35,400.

²⁴All the men assigned to the camp of Ephraim,ˡ according to their divisions, number 108,100. They will set out third.ᵐ

ᵃ14 Many manuscripts of the Masoretic Text, Samaritan Pentateuch and Vulgate (see also Num. 1:14); most manuscripts of the Masoretic Text *Reuel*

2:7
ᵃNu 1:9

2:9
ᵇNu 10:14

2:10
ᶜNu 1:5

2:12
ᵈNu 1:6

2:14
ᵉNu 1:14

2:16
ᶠNu 10:18

2:17
ᵍNu 1:53; 10:21

2:18
ʰGe 48:20; Jer 31:18-20
ⁱNu 1:10

2:20
ʲNu 1:10

2:22
ᵏNu 1:11; Ps 68:27

2:24
ˡNu 10:22
ᵐPs 80:2

2:25
a Nu 1:12

2:27
b Nu 1:13

2:29
c Nu 1:15

2:31
d Nu 10:25

2:32
e Ex 38:26;
Nu 1:46

2:33
f Nu 1:47;
26:57-62

3:1
g Ex 6:27

3:2
h Ex 6:23;
Nu 26:60

3:3
i Ex 28:41

3:4
j Lev 10:2
k Lev 10:1
l 1Ch 24:1

3:6
m Dt 10:8; 31:9;
1Ch 15:2
n Nu 8:6-22;
18:1-7;
2Ch 29:11

3:7
o Lev 8:35;
Nu 1:50

3:9
p Nu 8:19; 18:6

3:10
q Ex 29:9
r Nu 1:51

3:12
s Mal 2:4
t ver 41;
Nu 8:16,18
u Ex 13:2

²⁵On the north will be the divisions of the camp of Dan, under their standard. The leader of the people of Dan is Ahiezer son of Ammishaddai.ᵃ ²⁶His division numbers 62,700.

²⁷The tribe of Asher will camp next to them. The leader of the people of Asher is Pagiel son of Ocran.ᵇ ²⁸His division numbers 41,500.

²⁹The tribe of Naphtali will be next. The leader of the people of Naphtali is Ahira son of Enan.ᶜ ³⁰His division numbers 53,400.

³¹All the men assigned to the camp of Dan number 157,600. They will set out last,ᵈ under their standards.

³²These are the Israelites, counted according to their families. All those in the camps, by their divisions, number 603,550.ᵉ ³³The Levites, however, were not countedᶠ along with the other Israelites, as the LORD commanded Moses.

³⁴So the Israelites did everything the LORD commanded Moses; that is the way they encamped under their standards, and that is the way they set out, each with his clan and family.

Chapter 3 Theme

3 This is the account of the family of Aaron and Mosesᵍ at the time the LORD talked with Moses on Mount Sinai.

²The names of the sons of Aaron were Nadab the firstborn and Abihu, Eleazar and Ithamar.ʰ ³Those were the names of Aaron's sons, the anointed priests,ⁱ who were ordained to serve as priests. ⁴Nadab and Abihu, however, fell dead before the LORDʲ when they made an offering with unauthorized fire before him in the Desert of Sinai.ᵏ They had no sons; so only Eleazar and Ithamar served as priests during the lifetime of their father Aaron.ˡ

⁵The LORD said to Moses, ⁶"Bring the tribe of Leviᵐ and present them to Aaron the priest to assist him.ⁿ ⁷They are to perform duties for him and for the whole community at the Tent of Meeting by doing the workᵒ of the tabernacle. ⁸They are to take care of all the furnishings of the Tent of Meeting, fulfilling the obligations of the Israelites by doing the work of the tabernacle. ⁹Give the Levites to Aaron and his sons;ᵖ they are the Israelites who are to be given wholly to him.ᵃ ¹⁰Appoint Aaron and his sons to serve as priests;�q anyone else who approaches the sanctuary must be put to death."ʳ

¹¹The LORD also said to Moses, ¹²"I have taken the Levitesˢ from among the Israelites in place of the first male offspringᵗ of every Israelite woman. The Levites are mine,ᵘ ¹³for all the firstborn are

ᵃ9 Most manuscripts of the Masoretic Text; some manuscripts of the Masoretic Text, Samaritan Pentateuch and Septuagint (see also Num. 8:16) *to me* mine.*a* When I struck down all the firstborn in Egypt, I set apart for myself every firstborn in Israel, whether man or animal. They are to be mine. I am the LORD."

14The LORD said to Moses in the Desert of Sinai, 15"Count*b* the Levites by their families and clans. Count every male a month old or more."*c* 16So Moses counted them, as he was commanded by the word of the LORD.

17These were the names of the sons of Levi:*d*
Gershon, Kohath and Merari.*e*
18These were the names of the Gershonite clans:
Libni and Shimei.*f*
19The Kohathite clans:
Amram, Izhar, Hebron and Uzziel.*g*
20The Merarite clans:*h*
Mahli and Mushi.*i*
These were the Levite clans, according to their families.

21To Gershon belonged the clans of the Libnites and Shimeites;*j* these were the Gershonite clans. 22The number of all the males a month old or more who were counted was 7,500. 23The Gershonite clans were to camp on the west, behind the tabernacle. 24The leader of the families of the Gershonites was Eliasaph son of Lael. 25At the Tent of Meeting the Gershonites were responsible for the care of the tabernacle*k* and tent, its coverings,*l* the curtain at the entrance*m* to the Tent of Meeting, 26the curtains of the courtyard*n*, the curtain at the entrance to the courtyard surrounding the tabernacle and altar, and the ropes*o*—and everything related to their use.

27To Kohath belonged the clans of the Amramites, Izharites, Hebronites and Uzzielites;*p* these were the Kohathite clans. 28The number of all the males a month old or more was 8,600.*a* The Kohathites were responsible for the care of the sanctuary. 29The Kohathite clans were to camp on the south side*q* of the tabernacle. 30The leader of the families of the Kohathite clans was Elizaphan son of Uzziel. 31They were responsible for the care of the ark,*r* the table,*s* the lampstand,*t* the altars,*u* the articles of the sanctuary used in ministering, the curtain,*v* and everything related to their use.*w* 32The chief leader of the Levites was Eleazar son of Aaron, the priest. He was appointed over those who were responsible for the care of the sanctuary.

33To Merari belonged the clans of the Mahlites and the Mushites;*x* these were the Merarite clans. 34The number of all the males a month old or more who were counted was 6,200. 35The

---

3:13
a Ex 13:12

3:15
b ver 39
c Nu 26:62

3:17
d Ge 46:11
e Ex 6:16

3:18
f Ex 6:17

3:19
g Ex 6:18

3:20
h Ge 46:11
i Ex 6:19

3:21
j Ex 6:17

3:25
k Ex 25:9
l Ex 26:14
m Ex 26:36; Nu 4:25

3:26
n Ex 27:9
o Ex 35:18

3:27
p 1Ch 26:23

3:29
q Nu 1:53

3:31
r Ex 25:10-22
s Ex 25:23
t Ex 25:31
u Ex 27:1; 30:1
v Ex 26:33
w Nu 4:15

3:33
x Ex 6:19

---

a 28 Hebrew; some Septuagint manuscripts *8,300*

3:35
a Nu 1:53;
2:25

3:36
b Nu 4:32

3:38
c Nu 2:3
d Nu 1:53
e ver 7;
Nu 18:5
f ver 10;
Nu 1:51

3:39
g Nu 26:62

3:40
h ver 15

3:41
i ver 12

3:43
j ver 39

3:46
k Ex 13:13;
Nu 18:15

3:47
l Lev 27:6
m Ex 30:13
n Lev 27:25

3:50
o ver 46-48

4:2
p Ex 30:12

4:3
q ver 23;
Nu 8:25;
1Ch 23:3,24,27;
Ezr 3:8

leader of the families of the Merarite clans was Zuriel son of Abihail; they were to camp on the north side of the tabernacle.*a* ³⁶The Merarites were appointed*b* to take care of the frames of the tabernacle, its crossbars, posts, bases, all its equipment, and everything related to their use, ³⁷as well as the posts of the surrounding courtyard with their bases, tent pegs and ropes.

³⁸Moses and Aaron and his sons were to camp to the east*c* of the tabernacle, toward the sunrise, in front of the Tent of Meeting.*d* They were responsible for the care of the sanctuary*e* on behalf of the Israelites. Anyone else who approached the sanctuary was to be put to death.*f*

³⁹The total number of Levites counted at the LORD's command by Moses and Aaron according to their clans, including every male a month old or more, was 22,000.*g*

⁴⁰The LORD said to Moses, "Count all the firstborn Israelite males who are a month old or more*h* and make a list of their names. ⁴¹Take the Levites for me in place of all the firstborn of the Israelites,*i* and the livestock of the Levites in place of all the firstborn of the livestock of the Israelites. I am the LORD."

⁴²So Moses counted all the firstborn of the Israelites, as the LORD commanded him. ⁴³The total number of firstborn males a month old or more, listed by name, was 22,273.*j*

⁴⁴The LORD also said to Moses, ⁴⁵"Take the Levites in place of all the firstborn of Israel, and the livestock of the Levites in place of their livestock. The Levites are to be mine. I am the LORD. ⁴⁶To redeem*k* the 273 firstborn Israelites who exceed the number of the Levites, ⁴⁷collect five shekels*a l* for each one, according to the sanctuary shekel,*m* which weighs twenty gerahs.*n* ⁴⁸Give the money for the redemption of the additional Israelites to Aaron and his sons."

⁴⁹So Moses collected the redemption money from those who exceeded the number redeemed by the Levites. ⁵⁰From the firstborn of the Israelites he collected silver weighing 1,365 shekels,*b o* according to the sanctuary shekel. ⁵¹Moses gave the redemption money to Aaron and his sons, as he was commanded by the word of the LORD.

Chapter 4 Theme

4 The LORD said to Moses and Aaron: ²"Take a census*p* of the Kohathite branch of the Levites by their clans and families. ³Count all the men from thirty to fifty years of age*q* who come to serve in the work in the Tent of Meeting.

a 47 That is, about 2 ounces (about 55 grams)   *b 50* That is, about 35 pounds (about 15.5 kilograms)

221

4"This is the work of the Kohathites in the Tent of Meeting: the care of the most holy things.ᵃ ⁵When the camp is to move, Aaron and his sons are to go in and take down the shielding curtainᵇ and cover the ark of the Testimony with it.ᶜ ⁶Then they are to cover this with hides of sea cows,ᵃ spread a cloth of solid blue over that and put the polesᵈ in place.

⁷"Over the table of the Presenceᵉ they are to spread a blue cloth and put on it the plates, dishes and bowls, and the jars for drink offerings; the bread that is continually thereᶠ is to remain on it. ⁸Over these they are to spread a scarlet cloth, cover that with hides of sea cows and put its poles in place.

⁹"They are to take a blue cloth and cover the lampstand that is for light, together with its lamps, its wick trimmers and trays,ᵍ and all its jars for the oil used to supply it. ¹⁰Then they are to wrap it and all its accessories in a covering of hides of sea cows and put it on a carrying frame.

¹¹"Over the gold altarʰ they are to spread a blue cloth and cover that with hides of sea cows and put its poles in place.

¹²"They are to take all the articles used for ministering in the sanctuary, wrap them in a blue cloth, cover that with hides of sea cows and put them on a carrying frame.

¹³"They are to remove the ashes from the bronze altarⁱ and spread a purple cloth over it. ¹⁴Then they are to place on it all the utensils used for ministering at the altar, including the firepans, meat forks,ʲ shovels and sprinkling bowls.ᵏ Over it they are to spread a covering of hides of sea cows and put its polesˡ in place.

¹⁵"After Aaron and his sons have finished covering the holy furnishings and all the holy articles, and when the camp is ready to move, the Kohathites are to come to do the carrying.ᵐ But they must not touch the holy things or they will die.ⁿ The Kohathites are to carry those things that are in the Tent of Meeting.

¹⁶"Eleazarᵒ son of Aaron, the priest, is to have charge of the oil for the light,ᵖ the fragrant incense, the regular grain offering�q and the anointing oil. He is to be in charge of the entire tabernacle and everything in it, including its holy furnishings and articles."

¹⁷The Lᴏʀᴅ said to Moses and Aaron, ¹⁸"See that the Kohathite tribal clans are not cut off from the Levites. ¹⁹So that they may live and not die when they come near the most holy things,ʳ do this for them: Aaron and his sons are to go into the sanctuary and assign to each man his work and what he is to carry. ²⁰But the Kohathites must not go in to lookˢ at the holy things, even for a moment, or they will die."

²¹The Lᴏʀᴅ said to Moses, ²²"Take a census also of the Gershonites by their families and clans. ²³Count all the men from

a 6 That is, dugongs; also in verses 8, 10, 11, 12, 14 and 25

4:4
ᵃver 19

4:5
ᵇEx 26:31,33
ᶜEx 25:10,16

4:6
ᵈEx 25:13-15;
1Ki 8:7;
2Ch 5:8

4:7
ᵉEx 25:23,29;
Lev 24:6
ᶠEx 25:30

4:9
ᵍEx 25:31,37,38

4:11
ʰEx 30:1

4:13
ⁱEx 27:1-8

4:14
ʲ2Ch 4:16
ᵏJer 52:18
ˡEx 27:6

4:15
ᵐNu 7:9
ⁿNu 1:51;
2Sa 6:6,7

4:16
ᵒLev 10:6
ᵖEx 25:6
qEx 29:41;
Lev 6:14-23

4:19
ʳver 15

4:20
ˢEx 19:21;
1Sa 6:19

4:23
a ver 3;
1Ch 23:3,24,27

thirty to fifty years of age*a* who come to serve in the work at the Tent of Meeting.

²⁴"This is the service of the Gershonite clans as they work and carry burdens: ²⁵They are to carry the curtains of the tabernacle,*b* the Tent of Meeting,*c* its covering*d* and the outer covering of hides of sea cows, the curtains for the entrance to the Tent of Meeting,

4:25
b Ex 27:10-18;
Nu 3:26
c Nu 3:25
d Ex 26:14

²⁶the curtains of the courtyard surrounding the tabernacle and altar, the curtain for the entrance, the ropes and all the equipment used in its service. The Gershonites are to do all that needs to be done with these things. ²⁷All their service, whether carrying or doing other work, is to be done under the direction of Aaron and his sons. You shall assign to them as their responsibility all they are to carry. ²⁸This is the service of the Gershonite clans*e* at the Tent of Meeting. Their duties are to be under the direction of Ithamar son of Aaron, the priest.

4:28
e Nu 7:7

²⁹"Count the Merarites by their clans and families.*f* ³⁰Count all the men from thirty to fifty years of age who come to serve in the work at the Tent of Meeting. ³¹This is their duty as they perform service at the Tent of Meeting: to carry the frames of the tabernacle, its crossbars, posts and bases,*g* ³²as well as the posts of the surrounding courtyard with their bases, tent pegs, ropes, all their equipment and everything related to their use. Assign to each man the specific things he is to carry. ³³This is the service of the Merarite clans as they work at the Tent of Meeting under the direction of Ithamar son of Aaron, the priest."

4:29
f Ge 46:11

4:31
g Nu 3:36

³⁴Moses, Aaron and the leaders of the community counted the Kohathites*h* by their clans and families. ³⁵All the men from thirty to fifty years of age who came to serve in the work in the Tent of Meeting, ³⁶counted by clans, were 2,750. ³⁷This was the total of all those in the Kohathite clans*i* who served in the Tent of Meeting. Moses and Aaron counted them according to the LORD's command through Moses.

4:34
h ver 2

³⁸The Gershonites*j* were counted by their clans and families. ³⁹All the men from thirty to fifty years of age who came to serve in the work at the Tent of Meeting, ⁴⁰counted by their clans and families, were 2,630. ⁴¹This was the total of those in the Gershonite clans who served at the Tent of Meeting. Moses and Aaron counted them according to the LORD's command.

4:37
i Nu 3:27

⁴²The Merarites were counted by their clans and families. ⁴³All the men from thirty to fifty years of age who came to serve in the work at the Tent of Meeting, ⁴⁴counted by their clans, were 3,200. ⁴⁵This was the total of those in the Merarite clans.*k* Moses and Aaron counted them according to the LORD's command through Moses.

4:38
j Ge 46:11

⁴⁶So Moses, Aaron and the leaders of Israel counted all the Levites by their clans and families. ⁴⁷All the men from thirty to

4:45
k ver 29

fifty years of age[a] who came to do the work of serving and carrying the Tent of Meeting [48]numbered 8,580.[b] [49]At the LORD's command through Moses, each was assigned his work and told what to carry.

Thus they were counted,[c] as the LORD commanded Moses.

Chapter 5 Theme _____

5 The LORD said to Moses, [2]"Command the Israelites to send away from the camp anyone who has an infectious skin disease[ad] or a discharge[e] of any kind, or who is ceremonially unclean[f] because of a dead body. [3]Send away male and female alike; send them outside the camp so they will not defile their camp, where I dwell among them.[g]" [4]The Israelites did this; they sent them outside the camp. They did just as the LORD had instructed Moses.

[5]The LORD said to Moses, [6]"Say to the Israelites: 'When a man or woman wrongs another in any way[b] and so is unfaithful[h] to the LORD, that person is guilty[i] [7]and must confess[j] the sin he has committed. He must make full restitution[k] for his wrong, add one fifth to it and give it all to the person he has wronged. [8]But if that person has no close relative to whom restitution can be made for the wrong, the restitution belongs to the LORD and must be given to the priest, along with the ram with which atonement is made for him.[l] [9]All the sacred contributions the Israelites bring to a priest will belong to him.[m] [10]Each man's sacred gifts are his own, but what he gives to the priest will belong to the priest.[n] '"

[11]Then the LORD said to Moses, [12]"Speak to the Israelites and say to them: 'If a man's wife goes astray[o] and is unfaithful to him [13]by sleeping with another man,[p] and this is hidden from her husband and her impurity is undetected (since there is no witness against her and she has not been caught in the act), [14]and if feelings of jealousy[q] come over her husband and he suspects his wife and she is impure—or if he is jealous and suspects her even though she is not impure— [15]then he is to take his wife to the priest. He must also take an offering of a tenth of an ephah[cr] of barley flour[s] on her behalf. He must not pour oil on it or put incense on it, because it is a grain offering for jealousy, a reminder[t] offering to draw attention to guilt.

[16]"'The priest shall bring her and have her stand before the LORD. [17]Then he shall take some holy water in a clay jar and put some dust from the tabernacle floor into the water. [18]After the priest has had the woman stand before the LORD, he shall loosen

---

a 2 Traditionally *leprosy*; the Hebrew word was used for various diseases affecting the skin—not necessarily leprosy. b 6 Or *woman commits any wrong common to mankind* c 15 That is, probably about 2 quarts (about 2 liters)

4:47
[a] ver 3

4:48
[b] Nu 3:39

4:49
[c] Nu 1:47

5:2
[d] Lev 13:46
[e] Lev 15:2;
Mt 9:20
[f] Lev 13:3;
Nu 9:6-10

5:3
[g] Lev 26:12;
Nu 35:34;
2Co 6:16

5:6
[h] Lev 6:2
[i] Lev 5:14–6:7

5:7
[j] Lev 5:5; 26:40;
Jos 7:19;
Lk 19:8
[k] Lev 6:5

5:8
[l] Lev 6:6,7; 7:7

5:9
[m] Lev 6:17;
7:6-14

5:10
[n] Lev 10:13

5:12
[o] Ex 20:14

5:13
[p] Lev 18:20;
20:10

5:14
[q] Pr 6:34;
SS 8:6

5:15
[r] Ex 16:36
[s] Lev 6:20
[t] Eze 29:16

5:18
*a*Lev 10:6;
1Co 11:6

her hair*a* and place in her hands the reminder offering, the grain offering for jealousy, while he himself holds the bitter water that brings a curse. ¹⁹Then the priest shall put the woman under oath

5:19
*b*ver 12,29

and say to her, "If no other man has slept with you and you have not gone astray*b* and become impure while married to your husband, may this bitter water that brings a curse not harm you.

5:20
*c*ver 12

²⁰But if you have gone astray*c* while married to your husband and you have defiled yourself by sleeping with a man other than your husband"— ²¹here the priest is to put the woman under this

5:21
*d*Jos 6:26;
1Sa 14:24;
Ne 10:29

curse of the oath*d*—"may the LORD cause your people to curse and denounce you when he causes your thigh to waste away and your abdomen to swell.*a* ²²May this water*e* that brings a curse*f* enter your body so that your abdomen swells and your thigh

5:22
*e*Ps 109:18
*f*ver 18
*g*Dt 27:15

wastes away.*b*"

""Then the woman is to say, "Amen. So be it.*g*"

²³"'The priest is to write these curses on a scroll*h* and then wash them off into the bitter water. ²⁴He shall have the woman drink the

5:23
*h*Jer 45:1

bitter water that brings a curse, and this water will enter her and cause bitter suffering. ²⁵The priest is to take from her hands the grain offering for jealousy, wave it before the LORD*i* and bring it to

5:25
*i*Lev 8:27

the altar. ²⁶The priest is then to take a handful of the grain offering as a memorial offering and burn it on the altar; after that, he is to have the woman drink the water. ²⁷If she has defiled herself and

5:27
*j*Isa 43:28;
65:15;
Jer 26:6;
29:18;
42:18;
44:12,22;
Zec 8:13

been unfaithful to her husband, then when she is made to drink the water that brings a curse, it will go into her and cause bitter suffering; her abdomen will swell and her thigh waste away,*c* and she will become accursed*j* among her people. ²⁸If, however, the woman has not defiled herself and is free from impurity, she will be cleared of guilt and will be able to have children.

5:29
*k*ver 19

²⁹"'This, then, is the law of jealousy when a woman goes astray*k* and defiles herself while married to her husband, ³⁰or when feelings of jealousy come over a man because he suspects his wife. The priest is to have her stand before the LORD and is to apply this

5:31
*l*Lev 5:1;
20:17

entire law to her. ³¹The husband will be innocent of any wrongdoing, but the woman will bear the consequences*l* of her sin.'"

Chapter 6 Theme

6:2
*m*Ge 28:20;
Ac 21:23
*n*Jdg 13:5;
16:17;
Am 2:11,12

6 The LORD said to Moses, ²"Speak to the Israelites and say to them: 'If a man or woman wants to make a special vow*m*, a vow of separation to the LORD as a Nazirite,*n* ³he must abstain from wine*o* and other fermented drink and must not drink vinegar*p* made from wine or from other fermented drink. He must not

6:3
*o*Lk 1:15
*p*Ru 2:14;
Ps 69:21;
Pr 10:26

a 21 Or causes you to have a miscarrying womb and barrenness *b 22 Or body and cause you to be barren and have a miscarrying womb* *c 27 Or suffering; she will have barrenness and a miscarrying womb* drink grape juice or eat grapes or raisins. ⁴As long as he is a Nazirite, he must not eat anything that comes from the grapevine, not even the seeds or skins.

⁵"'During the entire period of his vow of separation no razor*a* may be used on his head.*b* He must be holy until the period of his separation to the LORD is over; he must let the hair of his head grow long. ⁶Throughout the period of his separation to the LORD he must not go near a dead body.*c* ⁷Even if his own father or mother or brother or sister dies, he must not make himself ceremonially unclean*d* on account of them, because the symbol of his separation to God is on his head. ⁸Throughout the period of his separation he is consecrated to the LORD.

⁹"'If someone dies suddenly in his presence, thus defiling the hair he has dedicated,*e* he must shave his head on the day of his cleansing*f*—the seventh day. ¹⁰Then on the eighth day he must bring two doves or two young pigeons*g* to the priest at the entrance to the Tent of Meeting. ¹¹The priest is to offer one as a sin offering and the other as a burnt offering*h* to make atonement*i* for him because he sinned by being in the presence of the dead body. That same day he is to consecrate his head. ¹²He must dedicate himself to the LORD for the period of his separation and must bring a year-old male lamb as a guilt offering. The previous days do not count, because he became defiled during his separation.

¹³"'Now this is the law for the Nazirite when the period of his separation is over.*j* He is to be brought to the entrance to the Tent of Meeting. ¹⁴There he is to present his offerings to the LORD: a year-old male lamb without defect for a burnt offering, a year-old ewe lamb without defect for a sin offering,*k* a ram without defect for a fellowship offering,*a* ¹⁵together with their grain offerings and drink offerings,*l* and a basket of bread made without yeast—cakes made of fine flour mixed with oil, and wafers spread with oil.*m*

¹⁶"'The priest is to present them before the LORD and make the sin offering and the burnt offering. ¹⁷He is to present the basket of unleavened bread and is to sacrifice the ram as a fellowship offering to the LORD, together with its grain offering and drink offering.

¹⁸"'Then at the entrance to the Tent of Meeting, the Nazirite must shave off the hair that he dedicated.*n* He is to take the hair and put it in the fire that is under the sacrifice of the fellowship offering.

¹⁹"'After the Nazirite has shaved off the hair of his dedication, the priest is to place in his hands a boiled shoulder of the ram, and a cake and a wafer from the basket, both made without

---

a 14 Traditionally *peace offering*; also in verses 17 and 18

6:5
a Ps 52:2;
57:4; 59:7;
Isa 7:20;
Eze 5:1
b 1Sa 1:11

6:6
c Lev 21:1-3;
Nu 19:11-22

6:7
d Nu 9:6

6:9
e ver 18
f Lev 14:9

6:10
g Lev 5:7;
14:22

6:11
h Ge 8:20
i Ex 29:36

6:13
j Ac 21:26

6:14
k Lev 14:10;
Nu 15:27

6:15
l Nu 15:1-7
m Ex 29:2;
Lev 2:4

6:18
n ver 9;
Ac 21:24

6:20
a Ecc 9:7

6:23
b Dt 21:5;
1Ch 23:13

6:24
c Dt 28:3-6;
Ps 28:9
d 1Sa 2:9;
Ps 17:8

6:25
e Job 29:24;
Ps 31:16; 80:3;
119:135
f Ge 43:29;
Ps 25:16; 86:16

6:26
g Ps 4:6; 44:3
h Ps 29:11;
37:11,37;
Jn 14:27

6:27
i Dt 28:10;
2Sa 7:23;
2Ch 7:14;
Ne 9:10;
Jer 25:29

7:1
j Ex 40:17
k Ex 40:9
l ver 84,88;
Ex 40:10

7:2
m Nu 1:5-16

7:7
n Nu 4:24-26,28

7:8
o Nu 4:31-33

7:9
p Nu 4:15

7:10
q ver 1
r 2Ch 7:9

yeast. [20]The priest shall then wave them before the LORD as a wave offering; they are holy and belong to the priest, together with the breast that was waved and the thigh that was presented. After that, the Nazirite may drink wine.*a*

[21]"'This is the law of the Nazirite who vows his offering to the LORD in accordance with his separation, in addition to whatever else he can afford. He must fulfill the vow he has made, according to the law of the Nazirite.'"

[22]The LORD said to Moses, [23]"Tell Aaron and his sons, 'This is how you are to bless*b* the Israelites. Say to them:

[24]"'"The LORD bless you*c*
  and keep you;*d*
[25]the LORD make his face shine upon you*e*
  and be gracious to you;*f*
[26]the LORD turn his face*g* toward you
  and give you peace."'"

[27]"So they will put my name*i* on the Israelites, and I will bless them."

Chapter 7 Theme

7 When Moses finished setting up the tabernacle,*j* he anointed it and consecrated it and all its furnishings.*k* He also anointed and consecrated the altar and all its utensils.*l* [2]Then the leaders of Israel,*m* the heads of families who were the tribal leaders in charge of those who were counted, made offerings. [3]They brought as their gifts before the LORD six covered carts and twelve oxen— an ox from each leader and a cart from every two. These they presented before the tabernacle.

[4]The LORD said to Moses, [5]"Accept these from them, that they may be used in the work at the Tent of Meeting. Give them to the Levites as each man's work requires."

[6]So Moses took the carts and oxen and gave them to the Levites. [7]He gave two carts and four oxen to the Gershonites,*n* as their work required, [8]and he gave four carts and eight oxen to the Merarites,*o* as their work required. They were all under the direction of Ithamar son of Aaron, the priest. [9]But Moses did not give any to the Kohathites, because they were to carry on their shoulders*p* the holy things, for which they were responsible.

[10]When the altar was anointed,*q* the leaders brought their offerings for its dedication*r* and presented them before the altar. [11]For the LORD had said to Moses, "Each day one leader is to bring his offering for the dedication of the altar."

[12]The one who brought his offering on the first day was Nahshon son of Amminadab of the tribe of Judah.

¹³His offering was one silver plate weighing a hundred and thirty shekels,ᵃ and one silver sprinkling bowl weighing seventy shekels,ᵇ both according to the sanctuary shekel,ᵃ each filled with fine flour mixed with oil as a grain offering;ᵇ ¹⁴one gold dish weighing ten shekels,ᶜ filled with incense;ᶜ ¹⁵one young bull,ᵈ one ram and one male lamb a year old, for a burnt offering;ᵉ ¹⁶one male goat for a sin offering;ᶠ ¹⁷and two oxen, five rams, five male goats and five male lambs a year old, to be sacrificed as a fellowship offering.ᵈᵍ This was the offering of Nahshon son of Amminadab.ʰ

¹⁸On the second day Nethanel son of Zuar,ⁱ the leader of Issachar, brought his offering.

¹⁹The offering he brought was one silver plate weighing a hundred and thirty shekels, and one silver sprinkling bowl weighing seventy shekels, both according to the sanctuary shekel, each filled with fine flour mixed with oil as a grain offering; ²⁰one gold dishʲ weighing ten shekels, filled with incense; ²¹one young bull, one ram and one male lamb a year old, for a burnt offering; ²²one male goat for a sin offering; ²³and two oxen, five rams, five male goats and five male lambs a year old, to be sacrificed as a fellowship offering. This was the offering of Nethanel son of Zuar.

²⁴On the third day, Eliab son of Helon,ᵏ the leader of the people of Zebulun, brought his offering.

²⁵His offering was one silver plate weighing a hundred and thirty shekels, and one silver sprinkling bowl weighing seventy shekels, both according to the sanctuary shekel, each filled with fine flour mixed with oil as a grain offering; ²⁶one gold dish weighing ten shekels, filled with incense; ²⁷one young bull, one ram and one male lamb a year old, for a burnt offering; ²⁸one male goat for a sin offering; ²⁹and two oxen, five rams, five male goats and five male lambs a year old, to be sacrificed as a fellowship offering. This was the offering of Eliab son of Helon.

³⁰On the fourth day Elizur son of Shedeur,ˡ the leader of the people of Reuben, brought his offering.

³¹His offering was one silver plate weighing a hundred and thirty shekels, and one silver sprinkling bowl weighing seventy shekels, both according to the sanctuary shekel, each filled with fine flour mixed with oil as a grain offering; ³²one gold dish weighing ten shekels, filled with incense; ³³one

7:13
ᵃ Ex 30:13;
Nu 3:47
ᵇ Lev 2:1

7:14
ᶜ Ex 30:34

7:15
ᵈ Ex 24:5; 29:3;
Nu 28:11
ᵉ Lev 1:3

7:16
ᶠ Lev 4:3,23

7:17
ᵍ Lev 3:1
ʰ Nu 1:7

7:18
ⁱ Nu 1:8

7:20
ʲ ver 14

7:24
ᵏ Nu 1:9

7:30
ˡ Nu 1:5

ᵃ 13 That is, about 3 1/4 pounds (about 1.5 kilograms); also elsewhere in this chapter
ᵇ 13 That is, about 1 3/4 pounds (about 0.8 kilogram); also elsewhere in this chapter
ᶜ 14 That is, about 4 ounces (about 110 grams); also elsewhere in this chapter
ᵈ 17 Traditionally *peace offering*; also elsewhere in this chapter

7:36
a Nu 1:6

young bull, one ram and one male lamb a year old, for a burnt offering; ³⁴one male goat for a sin offering; ³⁵and two oxen, five rams, five male goats and five male lambs a year old, to be sacrificed as a fellowship offering. This was the offering of Elizur son of Shedeur.

³⁶On the fifth day Shelumiel son of Zurishaddai,ᵃ the leader of the people of Simeon, brought his offering.

³⁷His offering was one silver plate weighing a hundred and thirty shekels, and one silver sprinkling bowl weighing seventy shekels, both according to the sanctuary shekel, each filled with fine flour mixed with oil as a grain offering; ³⁸one gold dish weighing ten shekels, filled with incense; ³⁹one young bull, one ram and one male lamb a year old, for a burnt offering; ⁴⁰one male goat for a sin offering; ⁴¹and two oxen, five rams, five male goats and five male lambs a year old, to be sacrificed as a fellowship offering. This was the offering of Shelumiel son of Zurishaddai.

7:42
b Nu 1:14

⁴²On the sixth day Eliasaph son of Deuel,ᵇ the leader of the people of Gad, brought his offering.

⁴³His offering was one silver plate weighing a hundred and thirty shekels, and one silver sprinkling bowl weighing seventy shekels, both according to the sanctuary shekel, each filled with fine flour mixed with oil as a grain offering; ⁴⁴one gold dish weighing ten shekels, filled with incense; ⁴⁵one young bull, one ram and one male lamb a year old, for a burnt offering; ⁴⁶one male goat for a sin offering; ⁴⁷and two oxen, five rams, five male goats and five male lambs a year old, to be sacrificed as a fellowship offering. This was the offering of Eliasaph son of Deuel.

7:48
c Nu 1:10

⁴⁸On the seventh day Elishama son of Ammihud,ᶜ the leader of the people of Ephraim, brought his offering.

⁴⁹His offering was one silver plate weighing a hundred and thirty shekels, and one silver sprinkling bowl weighing seventy shekels, both according to the sanctuary shekel, each filled with fine flour mixed with oil as a grain offering; ⁵⁰one gold dish weighing ten shekels, filled with incense; ⁵¹one young bull, one ram and one male lamb a year old, for a burnt offering; ⁵²one male goat for a sin offering; ⁵³and two oxen, five rams, five male goats and five male lambs a year old, to be sacrificed as a fellowship offering. This was the offering of Elishama son of Ammihud.ᵈ

7:53
d Nu 1:10

7:54
e Nu 1:10; 2:20

⁵⁴On the eighth day Gamaliel son of Pedahzur,ᵉ the leader of the people of Manasseh, brought his offering.

⁵⁵His offering was one silver plate weighing a hundred and thirty shekels, and one silver sprinkling bowl weighing seventy shekels, both according to the sanctuary shekel, each filled with fine flour mixed with oil as a grain offering; ⁵⁶one gold dish weighing ten shekels, filled with incense; ⁵⁷one young bull, one ram and one male lamb a year old, for a burnt offering; ⁵⁸one male goat for a sin offering; ⁵⁹and two oxen, five rams, five male goats and five male lambs a year old, to be sacrificed as a fellowship offering. This was the offering of Gamaliel son of Pedahzur.

⁶⁰On the ninth day Abidan son of Gideoni,ᵃ the leader of the people of Benjamin, brought his offering.

⁶¹His offering was one silver plate weighing a hundred and thirty shekels, and one silver sprinkling bowl weighing seventy shekels, both according to the sanctuary shekel, each filled with fine flour mixed with oil as a grain offering; ⁶²one gold dish weighing ten shekels, filled with incense; ⁶³one young bull, one ram and one male lamb a year old, for a burnt offering; ⁶⁴one male goat for a sin offering; ⁶⁵and two oxen, five rams, five male goats and five male lambs a year old, to be sacrificed as a fellowship offering. This was the offering of Abidan son of Gideoni.

⁶⁶On the tenth day Ahiezer son of Ammishaddai,ᵇ the leader of the people of Dan, brought his offering.

⁶⁷His offering was one silver plate weighing a hundred and thirty shekels, and one silver sprinkling bowl weighing seventy shekels, both according to the sanctuary shekel, each filled with fine flour mixed with oil as a grain offering; ⁶⁸one gold dish weighing ten shekels, filled with incense; ⁶⁹one young bull, one ram and one male lamb a year old, for a burnt offering; ⁷⁰one male goat for a sin offering; ⁷¹and two oxen, five rams, five male goats and five male lambs a year old, to be sacrificed as a fellowship offering. This was the offering of Ahiezer son of Ammishaddai.

⁷²On the eleventh day Pagiel son of Ocran,ᶜ the leader of the people of Asher, brought his offering.

⁷³His offering was one silver plate weighing a hundred and thirty shekels, and one silver sprinkling bowl weighing seventy shekels, both according to the sanctuary shekel, each filled with fine flour mixed with oil as a grain offering; ⁷⁴one gold dish weighing ten shekels, filled with incense; ⁷⁵one young bull, one ram and one male lamb a year old, for a burnt offering; ⁷⁶one male goat for a sin offering; ⁷⁷and two oxen,

7:60
ᵃ Nu 1:11

7:66
ᵇ Nu 1:12; 2:25

7:72
ᶜ Nu 1:13

7:78
a Nu 1:15;
2:29

five rams, five male goats and five male lambs a year old, to be sacrificed as a fellowship offering. This was the offering of Pagiel son of Ocran.

⁷⁸On the twelfth day Ahira son of Enan,ᵃ the leader of the people of Naphtali, brought his offering.

⁷⁹His offering was one silver plate weighing a hundred and thirty shekels, and one silver sprinkling bowl weighing seventy shekels, both according to the sanctuary shekel, each filled with fine flour mixed with oil as a grain offering; ⁸⁰one gold dish weighing ten shekels, filled with incense; ⁸¹one young bull, one ram and one male lamb a year old, for a burnt offering; ⁸²one male goat for a sin offering; ⁸³and two oxen, five rams, five male goats and five male lambs a year old, to be sacrificed as a fellowship offering. This was the offering of Ahira son of Enan.

7:84
b ver 1,10
c Nu 4:14
d ver 14

⁸⁴These were the offerings of the Israelite leaders for the dedication of the altar when it was anointed:ᵇ twelve silver plates, twelve silver sprinkling bowlsᶜ and twelve gold dishes.ᵈ ⁸⁵Each silver plate weighed a hundred and thirty shekels, and each sprinkling bowl seventy shekels. Altogether, the silver dishes weighed two thousand four hundred shekels,ᵃ according to the sanctuary shekel. ⁸⁶The twelve gold dishes filled with incense weighed ten shekels each, according to the sanctuary shekel. Altogether, the gold dishes weighed a hundred and twenty shekels.ᵇ ⁸⁷The total number of animals for the burnt offering came to twelve young bulls, twelve rams and twelve male lambs a year old, together with their grain offering. Twelve male goats were used for the sin offering. ⁸⁸The total number of animals for the sacrifice of the fellowship offering came to twenty-four oxen, sixty rams, sixty male goats and sixty male lambs a year old. These were the offerings for the dedication of the altar after it was anointed.ᵉ

7:88
e ver 1,10

7:89
f Ex 25:21,22;
33:9,11
g Ps 80:1;
99:1

⁸⁹When Moses entered the Tent of Meeting to speak with the LORD,ᶠ he heard the voice speaking to him from between the two cherubim above the atonement coverᵍ on the ark of the Testimony. And he spoke with him.

Chapter 8 Theme

8 The LORD said to Moses, ²"Speak to Aaron and say to him, 'When you set up the seven lamps, they are to light the area in front of the lampstand.ʰ' "

³Aaron did so; he set up the lamps so that they faced forward on the lampstand, just as the LORD commanded Moses. ⁴This is

Lampstand

8:2
h Ex 25:37;
Lev 24:2,4

ᵃ 85 That is, about 60 pounds (about 28 kilograms)   ᵇ 86 That is, about 3 pounds (about 1.4 kilograms) how the lampstand was made: It was made of hammered gold *a*— from its base to its blossoms. The lampstand was made exactly like the pattern*b* the LORD had shown Moses.

[5]The LORD said to Moses: [6]"Take the Levites from among the other Israelites and make them ceremonially clean.*c* [7]To purify them, do this: Sprinkle the water of cleansing*d* on them; then have them shave their whole bodies*e* and wash their clothes,*f* and so purify themselves. [8]Have them take a young bull with its grain offering of fine flour mixed with oil;*g* then you are to take a second young bull for a sin offering. [9]Bring the Levites to the front of the Tent of Meeting*h* and assemble the whole Israelite community.*i* [10]You are to bring the Levites before the LORD, and the Israelites are to lay their hands on them.*j* [11]Aaron is to present the Levites before the LORD as a wave offering*k* from the Israelites, so that they may be ready to do the work of the LORD.

[12]"After the Levites lay their hands on the heads of the bulls,*l* use the one for a sin offering to the LORD and the other for a burnt offering, to make atonement*m* for the Levites. [13]Have the Levites stand in front of Aaron and his sons and then present them as a wave offering to the LORD. [14]In this way you are to set the Levites apart from the other Israelites, and the Levites will be mine.*n*

[15]"After you have purified the Levites and presented them as a wave offering,*o* they are to come to do their work at the Tent of Meeting. [16]They are the Israelites who are to be given wholly to me. I have taken them as my own in place of the firstborn, the first male offspring*p* from every Israelite woman. [17]Every firstborn male in Israel, whether man or animal,*q* is mine. When I struck down all the firstborn in Egypt, I set them apart for myself.*r* [18]And I have taken the Levites in place of all the firstborn sons in Israel.*s* [19]Of all the Israelites, I have given the Levites as gifts to Aaron and his sons*t* to do the work at the Tent of Meeting on behalf of the Israelites*u* and to make atonement for them*v* so that no plague will strike the Israelites when they go near the sanctuary."

[20]Moses, Aaron and the whole Israelite community did with the Levites just as the LORD commanded Moses. [21]The Levites purified themselves and washed their clothes.*w* Then Aaron presented them as a wave offering before the LORD and made atonement for them to purify them.*x* [22]After that, the Levites came to do their work at the Tent of Meeting under the supervision of Aaron and his sons. They did with the Levites just as the LORD commanded Moses.

[23]The LORD said to Moses, [24]"This applies to the Levites: Men twenty-five years old or more*y* shall come to take part in the work at the Tent of Meeting,*z* [25]but at the age of fifty, they must retire from their regular service and work no longer. [26]They may assist their brothers in performing their duties at the Tent of Meeting,

---

8:4
a Ex 25:18,36
b Ex 25:9

8:6
c Lev 22:2;
Isa 1:16; 52:11

8:7
d Nu 19:9,17
e Lev 14:9;
Dt 21:12
f Lev 14:8

8:8
g Lev 2:1;
Nu 15:8-10

8:9
h Ex 40:12
i Lev 8:3

8:10
j Ac 6:6

8:11
k Lev 7:30

8:12
l Ex 29:10
m Ex 29:36

8:14
n Nu 3:12

8:15
o Ex 29:24

8:16
p Nu 3:12

8:17
q Ex 4:23
r Ex 13:2;
Lk 2:23

8:18
s Nu 3:12

8:19
t Nu 3:9
u Nu 1:53
v Nu 16:46

8:21
w ver 7
x ver 12

8:24
y 1Ch 23:3
z Ex 38:21;
Nu 4:3

but they themselves must not do the work. This, then, is how you are to assign the responsibilities of the Levites."

Chapter 9 Theme _____

9 The LORD spoke to Moses in the Desert of Sinai in the first month[a] of the second year after they came out of Egypt.[b] He said, 2"Have the Israelites celebrate the Passover at the appointed time. 3Celebrate it at the appointed time, at twilight on the fourteenth day of this month, in accordance with all its rules and regulations.[c]"

4So Moses told the Israelites to celebrate the Passover, 5and they did so in the Desert of Sinai at twilight on the fourteenth day of the first month.[d] The Israelites did everything just as the LORD commanded Moses.

6But some of them could not celebrate the Passover on that day because they were ceremonially unclean[e] on account of a dead body. So they came to Moses and Aaron[f] that same day 7and said to Moses, "We have become unclean because of a dead body, but why should we be kept from presenting the LORD's offering with the other Israelites at the appointed time?"

8Moses answered them, "Wait until I find out what the LORD commands concerning you."[g]

9Then the LORD said to Moses, 10"Tell the Israelites: 'When any of you or your descendants are unclean because of a dead body or are away on a journey, they may still celebrate[h] the LORD's Passover. 11They are to celebrate it on the fourteenth day of the second month at twilight. They are to eat the lamb, together with unleavened bread and bitter herbs.[i] 12They must not leave any of it till morning[j] or break any of its bones.[k] When they celebrate the Passover, they must follow all the regulations. 13But if a man who is ceremonially clean and not on a journey fails to celebrate the Passover, that person must be cut off from his people[l] because he did not present the LORD's offering at the appointed time. That man will bear the consequences of his sin.

14"'An alien[m] living among you who wants to celebrate the LORD's Passover must do so in accordance with its rules and regulations. You must have the same regulations for the alien and the native-born.'"

15On the day the tabernacle, the Tent of the Testimony, was set up, the cloud[n] covered it. From evening till morning the cloud above the tabernacle looked like fire.[o] 16That is how it continued to be; the cloud covered it, and at night it looked like fire. 17Whenever the cloud lifted from above the Tent, the Israelites set out; wherever the cloud settled, the Israelites encamped.[p] 18At the LORD's command the Israelites set out, and at his command they

9:1
a Ex 40:2
b Nu 1:1

9:3
c Ex 12:2-11, 43-49; Lev 23:5-8; Dt 16:1-8

9:5
d Ex 12:1-13; Jos 5:10

9:6
e Lev 5:3
f Ex 18:15; Nu 27:2

9:8
g Ex 18:15; Nu 27:5,21; Ps 85:8

9:10
h 2Ch 30:2

9:11
i Ex 12:8

9:12
j Ex 12:10,43
k Ex 12:46; Jn 19:36*

9:13
l Ge 17:14; Ex 12:15

9:14
m Ex 12:48,49

9:15
n Ex 40:34
o Ex 13:21

9:17
p Ex 40:36-38; Nu 10:11,12; 1Co 10:1

encamped. As long as the cloud stayed over the tabernacle, they remained in camp. ¹⁹When the cloud remained over the tabernacle a long time, the Israelites obeyed the LORD's order and did not set out. ²⁰Sometimes the cloud was over the tabernacle only a few days; at the LORD's command they would encamp, and then at his command they would set out. ²¹Sometimes the cloud stayed only from evening till morning, and when it lifted in the morning, they set out. Whether by day or by night, whenever the cloud lifted, they set out. ²²Whether the cloud stayed over the tabernacle for two days or a month or a year, the Israelites would remain in camp and not set out; but when it lifted, they would set out. ²³At the LORD's command they encamped, and at the LORD's command they set out. They obeyed the LORD's order, in accordance with his command through Moses.

Chapter 10 Theme

10 The LORD said to Moses: ²"Make two trumpets*a* of hammered silver, and use them for calling the community*b* together and for having the camps set out. ³When both are sounded, the whole community is to assemble before you at the entrance to the Tent of Meeting. ⁴If only one is sounded, the leaders*c*—the heads of the clans of Israel—are to assemble before you. ⁵When a trumpet blast is sounded, the tribes camping on the east are to set out.*d* ⁶At the sounding of a second blast, the camps on the south are to set out.*e* The blast will be the signal for setting out. ⁷To gather the assembly, blow the trumpets,*f* but not with the same signal.*g*

⁸"The sons of Aaron, the priests, are to blow the trumpets. This is to be a lasting ordinance for you and the generations to come.*h* ⁹When you go into battle in your own land against an enemy who is oppressing you,*i* sound a blast on the trumpets. Then you will be remembered*j* by the LORD your God and rescued from your enemies.*k* ¹⁰Also at your times of rejoicing—your appointed feasts and New Moon festivals*l*—you are to sound the trumpets*m* over your burnt offerings and fellowship offerings,*a* and they will be a memorial for you before your God. I am the LORD your God."

¹¹On the twentieth day of the second month of the second year,*n* the cloud lifted*o* from above the tabernacle of the Testimony. ¹²Then the Israelites set out from the Desert of Sinai and traveled from place to place until the cloud came to rest in the Desert of Paran. ¹³They set out, this first time, at the LORD's command through Moses.*p*

¹⁴The divisions of the camp of Judah went first, under their standard.*q* Nahshon son of Amminadab*r* was in command.

a 10 Traditionally peace offerings

10:2
a Ne 12:35;
Ps 47:5
b Jer 4:5,19; 6:1;
Hos 5:8;
Joel 2:1,15;
Am 3:6

10:4
c Ex 18:21;
Nu 1:16; 7:2

10:5
d ver 14

10:6
e ver 18

10:7
f Eze 33:3;
Joel 2:1
g 1Co 14:8

10:8
h Nu 31:6

10:9
i Jdg 2:18; 6:9;
1Sa 10:18;
Ps 106:42
j Ge 8:1
k Ps 106:4

10:10
l Ps 81:3
m Lev 23:24

10:11
n Ex 40:17
o Nu 9:17

10:13
p Dt 1:6

10:14
q Nu 2:3-9
r Nu 1:7

10:17
a Nu 4:21-32

10:18
b Nu 2:10-16

10:21
c Nu 4:20
d ver 17

10:22
e Nu 2:24

10:25
f Nu 2:31;
Jos 6:9

10:29
g Jdg 4:11
h Ex 2:18
i Ex 3:1
j Ge 12:7

10:30
k Mt 21:29

10:31
l Job 29:15

10:32
m Dt 10:18
n Ps 22:27-31;
67:5-7

10:33
o ver 12;
Dt 1:33
p Jos 3:3

10:34
q Nu 9:15-23

10:35
r Ps 68:1
s Dt 7:10; 32:41;
Ps 68:2;
Isa 17:12-14

10:36
t Isa 63:17
u Dt 1:10

¹⁵Nethanel son of Zuar was over the division of the tribe of Issachar, ¹⁶and Eliab son of Helon was over the division of the tribe of Zebulun. ¹⁷Then the tabernacle was taken down, and the Gershonites and Merarites, who carried it, set out.ᵃ

¹⁸The divisions of the camp of Reuben went next, under their standard.ᵇ Elizur son of Shedeur was in command. ¹⁹Shelumiel son of Zurishaddai was over the division of the tribe of Simeon, ²⁰and Eliasaph son of Deuel was over the division of the tribe of Gad. ²¹Then the Kohathites set out, carrying the holy things.ᶜ The tabernacle was to be set up before they arrived.ᵈ

²²The divisions of the camp of Ephraimᵉ went next, under their standard. Elishama son of Ammihud was in command. ²³Gamaliel son of Pedahzur was over the division of the tribe of Manasseh, ²⁴and Abidan son of Gideoni was over the division of the tribe of Benjamin.

²⁵Finally, as the rear guardᶠ for all the units, the divisions of the camp of Dan set out, under their standard. Ahiezer son of Ammishaddai was in command. ²⁶Pagiel son of Ocran was over the division of the tribe of Asher, ²⁷and Ahira son of Enan was over the division of the tribe of Naphtali. ²⁸This was the order of march for the Israelite divisions as they set out.

²⁹Now Moses said to Hobabᵍ son of Reuelʰ the Midianite, Moses' father-in-law,ⁱ "We are setting out for the place about which the LORD said, 'I will give it to you.'ʲ Come with us and we will treat you well, for the LORD has promised good things to Israel."

³⁰He answered, "No, I will not go;ᵏ I am going back to my own land and my own people."

³¹But Moses said, "Please do not leave us. You know where we should camp in the desert, and you can be our eyes.ˡ ³²If you come with us, we will share with youᵐ whatever good things the LORD gives us.ⁿ"

³³So they set outᵒ from the mountain of the LORD and traveled for three days. The ark of the covenant of the LORDᵖ went before them during those three days to find them a place to rest. ³⁴The cloud of the LORD was over them by day when they set out from the camp.ᑫ

³⁵Whenever the ark set out, Moses said,

"Rise up, O LORD!
    May your enemies be scattered;ʳ
    may your foes flee before you.ˢ"

³⁶Whenever it came to rest, he said,

"Return,ᵗ O LORD,
    to the countless thousands of Israel.ᵘ"

The Exodus from Egypt to Canaan

Map labels:
Mediterranean (Great) Sea
CANAAN
Sea of Galilee
Tel Aviv
Jericho
Jerusalem
Shittim
Hebron
Mt. Nebo (Pisgah)
Gaza
Dead (Salt) Sea
MOAB
Beersheba
El-Arish
GOSHEN
Rameses
Succoth
Baal Zephon
Kadesh Barnea
NEGEV
Punon
Etham
Wilderness of Shur
Wilderness of Zin
Petra
Mt. Hor
Cairo
Wilderness of Paran
EDOM
JORDAN
Jotbathah
Ezion Geber
SINAI
Elath
Marah
Elim
Land of Midian
Nile River
EGYPT
Wilderness of Sin
Hazeroth
Gulf of Aqaba
SAUDI ARABIA
Gulf of Suez
Dophkah
Hazerah
Rephidim
Taberah
Kibroth Hattaavah
Mt. Sinai (Horeb)
Red Sea

Legend:
— Route of exodus from Egypt
- - - Alternate route
– – Route to Canaan forty years later

Chapter 11 Theme _____

11 Now the people complained about their hardships in the hearing of the LORD, and when he heard them his anger was aroused. Then fire from the LORD burned among them[a] and consumed some of the outskirts of the camp. [2]When the people cried out to Moses, he prayed to the LORD[b] and the fire died down. [3]So that place was called Taberah,[ac] because fire from the LORD had burned among them.

[4]The rabble with them began to crave other food,[d] and again the Israelites started wailing[e] and said, "If only we had meat to eat! [5]We remember the fish we ate in Egypt at no cost—also the cucumbers, melons, leeks, onions and garlic.[f] [6]But now we have lost our appetite; we never see anything but this manna!"

[7]The manna was like coriander seeds[g] and looked like resin.[h] [8]The people went around gathering it, and then ground it in a handmill or crushed it in a mortar. They cooked it in a pot or made it into cakes. And it tasted like something made with olive oil. [9]When the dew[i] settled on the camp at night, the manna also came down.

a 3 *Taberah* means *burning*.

Side references:
11:1 [a] Lev 10:2
11:2 [b] Nu 21:7
11:3 [c] Dt 9:22
11:4 [d] Ex 12:38; [e] Ps 78:18; 1Co 10:6
11:5 [f] Ex 16:3
11:7 [g] Ex 16:31; [h] Ge 2:12
11:9 [i] Ex 16:13

11:11
a Ex 5:22

11:12
b Isa 40:11;
49:23
c Ex 13:5

11:13
d Jn 6:5-9

11:14
e Ex 18:18

11:15
f Ex 32:32
g 1Ki 19:4;
Jnh 4:3

11:17
h ver 25,29;
1Sa 10:6;
2Ki 2:9,15;
Joel 2:28
i Ex 18:18

11:18
j Ex 19:10
k Ex 16:7
l ver 5; Ac 7:39

11:20
m Ps 78:29;
106:14,15
n Jos 24:27;
1Sa 10:19

11:21
o Ex 12:37

11:22
p Mt 15:33

11:23
q Isa 50:2; 59:1
r Nu 23:19;
Eze 12:25; 24:14

11:25
s Nu 12:5
t ver 17
u 1Sa 10:6
v Ac 2:17
w 1Sa 10:10

¹⁰Moses heard the people of every family wailing, each at the entrance to his tent. The LORD became exceedingly angry, and Moses was troubled. ¹¹He asked the LORD, "Why have you brought this trouble on your servant? What have I done to displease you that you put the burden of all these people on me?*a* ¹²Did I conceive all these people? Did I give them birth? Why do you tell me to carry them in my arms, as a nurse carries an infant,*b* to the land you promised on oath to their forefathers?*c* ¹³Where can I get meat for all these people?*d* They keep wailing to me, 'Give us meat to eat!' ¹⁴I cannot carry all these people by myself; the burden is too heavy for me.*e* ¹⁵If this is how you are going to treat me, put me to death*f* right now*g*—if I have found favor in your eyes—and do not let me face my own ruin."

¹⁶The LORD said to Moses: "Bring me seventy of Israel's elders who are known to you as leaders and officials among the people. Have them come to the Tent of Meeting, that they may stand there with you. ¹⁷I will come down and speak with you there, and I will take of the Spirit that is on you and put the Spirit on them.*h* They will help you carry the burden of the people so that you will not have to carry it alone.*i*

¹⁸"Tell the people: 'Consecrate yourselves*j* in preparation for tomorrow, when you will eat meat. The LORD heard you when you wailed,*k* "If only we had meat to eat! We were better off in Egypt!"*l* Now the LORD will give you meat, and you will eat it. ¹⁹You will not eat it for just one day, or two days, or five, ten or twenty days, ²⁰but for a whole month—until it comes out of your nostrils and you loathe it*m*—because you have rejected the LORD,*n* who is among you, and have wailed before him, saying, "Why did we ever leave Egypt?"'"

²¹But Moses said, "Here I am among six hundred thousand men*o* on foot, and you say, 'I will give them meat to eat for a whole month!' ²²Would they have enough if flocks and herds were slaughtered for them? Would they have enough if all the fish in the sea were caught for them?"*p*

²³The LORD answered Moses, "Is the LORD's arm too short?*q* You will now see whether or not what I say will come true for you.*r*"

²⁴So Moses went out and told the people what the LORD had said. He brought together seventy of their elders and had them stand around the Tent. ²⁵Then the LORD came down in the cloud*s* and spoke with him,*t* and he took of the Spirit*u* that was on him and put the Spirit on the seventy elders.*v* When the Spirit rested on them, they prophesied,*w* but they did not do so again.^a

²⁶However, two men, whose names were Eldad and Medad, had remained in the camp. They were listed among the elders,

a 25 Or prophesied and continued to do so

but did not go out to the Tent. Yet the Spirit also rested on them, and they prophesied in the camp. [27]A young man ran and told Moses, "Eldad and Medad are prophesying in the camp."

[28]Joshua son of Nun, who had been Moses' aide[a] since youth, spoke up and said, "Moses, my lord, stop them!"[b]

[29]But Moses replied, "Are you jealous for my sake? I wish that all the LORD's people were prophets[c] and that the LORD would put his Spirit on them!" [30]Then Moses and the elders of Israel returned to the camp.

[31]Now a wind went out from the LORD and drove quail[d] in from the sea. It brought them[a] down all around the camp to about three feet[b] above the ground, as far as a day's walk in any direction. [32]All that day and night and all the next day the people went out and gathered quail. No one gathered less than ten homers.[c] Then they spread them out all around the camp. [33]But while the meat was still between their teeth[e] and before it could be consumed, the anger of the LORD burned against the people, and he struck them with a severe plague.[f] [34]Therefore the place was named Kibroth Hattaavah,[d][g] because there they buried the people who had craved other food.

[35]From Kibroth Hattaavah the people traveled to Hazeroth[h] and stayed there.

Chapter 12 Theme _____

12 Miriam and Aaron began to talk against Moses because of his Cushite wife,[i] for he had married a Cushite. [2]"Has the LORD spoken only through Moses?" they asked. "Hasn't he also spoken through us?"[j] And the LORD heard this.[k]

[3](Now Moses was a very humble man,[l] more humble than anyone else on the face of the earth.)

[4]At once the LORD said to Moses, Aaron and Miriam, "Come out to the Tent of Meeting, all three of you." So the three of them came out. [5]Then the LORD came down in a pillar of cloud;[m] he stood at the entrance to the Tent and summoned Aaron and Miriam. When both of them stepped forward, [6]he said, "Listen to my words:

> "When a prophet of the LORD is among you,
> I reveal myself to him in visions,[n]
> I speak to him in dreams.[o]
> [7]But this is not true of my servant Moses;[p]
> he is faithful in all my house.[q]

a31 Or *They flew*   b31 Hebrew *two cubits* (about 1 meter)   c32 That is, probably about 60 bushels (about 2.2 kiloliters)   d34 *Kibroth Hattaavah* means *graves of craving.*

11:28
a Ex 33:11;
Jos 1:1
b Mk 9:38-40

11:29
c 1Co 14:5

11:31
d Ex 16:13;
Ps 78:26-28

11:33
e Ps 78:30
f Ps 106:15

11:34
g Dt 9:22

11:35
h Nu 33:17

12:1
i Ex 2:21

12:2
j Nu 16:3
k Nu 11:1

12:3
l Mt 11:29

12:5
m Nu 11:25

12:6
n Ge 15:1; 46:2
o Ge 31:10;
1Ki 3:5; Heb 1:1

12:7
p Jos 1:1-2;
Ps 105:26
q Heb 3:2,5

⁸With him I speak face to face,
  clearly and not in riddles;*a*
he sees the form of the Lord.*b*
Why then were you not afraid
  to speak against my servant Moses?"

⁹The anger of the Lord burned against them, and he left them.*c*

¹⁰When the cloud lifted from above the Tent, there stood Miriam—leprous,*a* like snow.*d* Aaron turned toward her and saw that she had leprosy;*e* ¹¹and he said to Moses, "Please, my lord, do not hold against us the sin we have so foolishly committed.*f* ¹²Do not let her be like a stillborn infant coming from its mother's womb with its flesh half eaten away."

¹³So Moses cried out to the Lord, "O God, please heal her!*g*"

¹⁴The Lord replied to Moses, "If her father had spit in her face,*h* would she not have been in disgrace for seven days? Confine her outside the camp*i* for seven days; after that she can be brought back." ¹⁵So Miriam was confined outside the camp for seven days, and the people did not move on till she was brought back.

¹⁶After that, the people left Hazeroth*j* and encamped in the Desert of Paran.

Chapter 13 Theme

13 The Lord said to Moses, ²"Send some men to explore*k* the land of Canaan, which I am giving to the Israelites. From each ancestral tribe send one of its leaders."

³So at the Lord's command Moses sent them out from the Desert of Paran. All of them were leaders of the Israelites. ⁴These are their names:

from the tribe of Reuben, Shammua son of Zaccur;
⁵from the tribe of Simeon, Shaphat son of Hori;
⁶from the tribe of Judah, Caleb son of Jephunneh;*l*
⁷from the tribe of Issachar, Igal son of Joseph;
⁸from the tribe of Ephraim, Hoshea son of Nun;
⁹from the tribe of Benjamin, Palti son of Raphu;
¹⁰from the tribe of Zebulun, Gaddiel son of Sodi;
¹¹from the tribe of Manasseh (a tribe of Joseph), Gaddi son of Susi;
¹²from the tribe of Dan, Ammiel son of Gemalli;
¹³from the tribe of Asher, Sethur son of Michael;
¹⁴from the tribe of Naphtali, Nahbi son of Vophsi;
¹⁵from the tribe of Gad, Geuel son of Maki.

12:9
c Ge 17:22

12:10
d Ex 4:6;
Dt 24:9
e 2Ki 5:1,27

12:11
f 2Sa 19:19;
24:10

12:13
g Isa 30:26;
Jer 17:14

12:14
h Dt 25:9;
Job 17:6;
30:9-10;
Isa 50:6
i Lev 13:46;
Nu 5:2-3

12:16
j Nu 11:35

13:2
k Dt 1:22

13:6
l ver 30;
Nu 14:6,24;
34:19;
Jdg 1:12-15

a 10 The Hebrew word was used for various diseases affecting the skin—not necessarily leprosy.

[16]These are the names of the men Moses sent to explore the land. (Moses gave Hoshea son of Nun[a] the name Joshua.)[b]

[17]When Moses sent them to explore Canaan, he said, "Go up through the Negev[c] and on into the hill country.[d] [18]See what the land is like and whether the people who live there are strong or weak, few or many. [19]What kind of land do they live in? Is it good or bad? What kind of towns do they live in? Are they unwalled or fortified? [20]How is the soil? Is it fertile or poor? Are there trees on it or not? Do your best to bring back some of the fruit of the land.[e]" (It was the season for the first ripe grapes.)

[21]So they went up and explored the land from the Desert of Zin[f] as far as Rehob,[g] toward Lebo[a] Hamath.[h] [22]They went up through the Negev and came to Hebron, where Ahiman, Sheshai and Talmai,[i] the descendants of Anak,[j] lived. (Hebron had been built seven years before Zoan in Egypt.)[k] [23]When they reached the Valley of Eshcol,[b] they cut off a branch bearing a single cluster of grapes. Two of them carried it on a pole between them, along with some pomegranates and figs. [24]That place was called the Valley of Eshcol because of the cluster of grapes the Israelites cut off there. [25]At the end of forty days they returned from exploring the land.

[26]They came back to Moses and Aaron and the whole Israelite community at Kadesh in the Desert of Paran. There they reported to them[l] and to the whole assembly and showed them the fruit of the land. [27]They gave Moses this account: "We went into the land to which you sent us, and it does flow with milk and honey![m] Here is its fruit.[n] [28]But the people who live there are powerful, and the cities are fortified and very large.[o] We even saw descendants of Anak there. [29]The Amalekites live in the Negev; the Hittites, Jebusites and Amorites live in the hill country; and the Canaanites live near the sea and along the Jordan."

[30]Then Caleb silenced the people before Moses and said, "We should go up and take possession of the land, for we can certainly do it."

[31]But the men who had gone up with him said, "We can't attack those people; they are stronger than we are."[p] [32]And they spread among the Israelites a bad report[q] about the land they had explored. They said, "The land we explored devours[r] those living in it. All the people we saw there are of great size.[s] [33]We saw the Nephilim[t] there (the descendants of Anak[u] come from the Nephilim). We seemed like grasshoppers in our own eyes, and we looked the same to them."

a 21 Or *toward the entrance to*   b 23 *Eshcol* means *cluster*; also in verse 24.

240

13:16
a ver 8
b Dt 32:44

13:17
c Ge 12:9
d Jdg 1:9

13:20
e Dt 1:25

13:21
f Nu 20:1; 27:14;
33:36;
Jos 15:1
g Jos 19:28
h Jos 13:5

13:22
i Jos 15:14
j Jos 15:13
k Ps 78:12,43;
Isa 19:11,13

13:26
l Nu 32:8

13:27
m Ex 3:8
n Dt 1:25

13:28
o Dt 1:28; 9:1,2

13:31
p Dt 1:28; 9:1;
Jos 14:8

13:32
q Nu 14:36,37
r Eze 36:13,14
s Am 2:9

13:33
t Ge 6:4
u Dt 1:28

14:2
a Nu 11:1

14:4
b Ne 9:17

14:5
c Nu 16:4,22,45

14:7
d Nu 13:27;
Dt 1:25

14:8
e Dt 10:15
f Nu 13:27

14:9
g Dt 1:26;
9:7,23,24
h Dt 1:21;
7:18; 20:1

14:10
i Ex 17:4
j Lev 9:23

14:11
k Ps 78:22;
106:24

14:12
l Ex 32:10

14:13
m Ex 32:11-14;
Ps 106:23

14:14
n Ex 15:14
o Ex 13:21

14:16
p Jos 7:7

14:18
q Ex 34:6;
Ps 145:8;
Jnh 4:2
r Ex 20:5

14:19
s Ex 34:9
t Ps 106:45
u Ps 78:38

14:20
v Ps 106:23;
Mic 7:18-20

14:21
w Dt 32:40;
Isa 49:18

Chapter 14 Theme _____

14 That night all the people of the community raised their voices and wept aloud. ²All the Israelites grumbled against Moses and Aaron, and the whole assembly said to them, "If only we had died in Egypt! Or in this desert!ᵃ ³Why is the LORD bringing us to this land only to let us fall by the sword? Our wives and children will be taken as plunder. Wouldn't it be better for us to go back to Egypt?" ⁴And they said to each other, "We should choose a leader and go back to Egypt.ᵇ"

⁵Then Moses and Aaron fell facedownᶜ in front of the whole Israelite assembly gathered there. ⁶Joshua son of Nun and Caleb son of Jephunneh, who were among those who had explored the land, tore their clothes ⁷and said to the entire Israelite assembly, "The land we passed through and explored is exceedingly good.ᵈ ⁸If the LORD is pleased with us,ᵉ he will lead us into that land, a land flowing with milk and honey,ᶠ and will give it to us. ⁹Only do not rebelᵍ against the LORD. And do not be afraid of the people of the land,ʰ because we will swallow them up. Their protection is gone, but the LORD is with us. Do not be afraid of them."

¹⁰But the whole assembly talked about stoningⁱ them. Then the glory of the LORDʲ appeared at the Tent of Meeting to all the Israelites. ¹¹The LORD said to Moses, "How long will these people treat me with contempt? How long will they refuse to believe in me,ᵏ in spite of all the miraculous signs I have performed among them? ¹²I will strike them down with a plague and destroy them, but I will make you into a nationˡ greater and stronger than they."

¹³Moses said to the LORD, "Then the Egyptians will hear about it! By your power you brought these people up from among them.ᵐ ¹⁴And they will tell the inhabitants of this land about it. They have already heardⁿ that you, O LORD, are with these people and that you, O LORD, have been seen face to face, that your cloud stays over them, and that you go before them in a pillar of cloud by day and a pillar of fire by night.ᵒ ¹⁵If you put these people to death all at one time, the nations who have heard this report about you will say, ¹⁶'The LORD was not able to bring these people into the land he promised them on oath; so he slaughtered them in the desert.'ᵖ

¹⁷"Now may the Lord's strength be displayed, just as you have declared: ¹⁸'The LORD is slow to anger, abounding in love and forgiving sin and rebellion.�q Yet he does not leave the guilty unpunished; he punishes the children for the sin of the fathers to the third and fourth generation.'ʳ ¹⁹In accordance with your great love, forgiveˢ the sin of these people,ᵗ just as you have pardoned them from the time they left Egypt until now."ᵘ

²⁰The LORD replied, "I have forgiven them,ᵛ as you asked. ²¹Nevertheless, as surely as I liveʷ and as surely as the glory of the LORD

fills the whole earth,^a ²²not one of the men who saw my glory and the miraculous signs I performed in Egypt and in the desert but who disobeyed me and tested me ten times^b— ²³not one of them will ever see the land I promised on oath^c to their forefathers. No one who has treated me with contempt will ever see it.^d ²⁴But because my servant Caleb has a different spirit and follows me wholeheartedly,^e I will bring him into the land he went to, and his descendants will inherit it.^f ²⁵Since the Amalekites and Canaanites are living in the valleys, turn^g back tomorrow and set out toward the desert along the route to the Red Sea.^a"

²⁶The LORD said to Moses and Aaron: ²⁷"How long will this wicked community grumble against me? I have heard the complaints of these grumbling Israelites.^h ²⁸So tell them, 'As surely as I live,ⁱ declares the LORD, I will do to you the very things I heard you say: ²⁹In this desert your bodies will fall^j—every one of you twenty years old or more^k who was counted in the census and who has grumbled against me. ³⁰Not one of you will enter the land I swore with uplifted hand to make your home, except Caleb son of Jephunneh and Joshua son of Nun. ³¹As for your children that you said would be taken as plunder, I will bring them in to enjoy the land you have rejected.^l ³²But you—your bodies will fall^m in this desert. ³³Your children will be shepherds here for forty years, suffering for your unfaithfulness, until the last of your bodies lies in the desert. ³⁴For forty years—one year for each of the forty days you explored the landⁿ—you will suffer for your sins and know what it is like to have me against you.' ³⁵I, the LORD, have spoken, and I will surely do these things^o to this whole wicked community, which has banded together against me. They will meet their end in this desert; here they will die."

³⁶So the men Moses had sent^p to explore the land, who returned and made the whole community grumble against him by spreading a bad report^q about it— ³⁷these men responsible for spreading the bad report^r about the land were struck down and died of a plague^s before the LORD. ³⁸Of the men who went to explore the land, only Joshua son of Nun and Caleb son of Jephunneh survived.^t

³⁹When Moses reported this to all the Israelites, they mourned^u bitterly. ⁴⁰Early the next morning they went up toward the high hill country. "We have sinned^v," they said. "We will go up to the place the LORD promised."

⁴¹But Moses said, "Why are you disobeying the LORD's command? This will not succeed!^w ⁴²Do not go up, because the LORD is not with you. You will be defeated by your enemies,^x ⁴³for the

a 25 Hebrew *Yam Suph*; that is, Sea of Reeds

14:21
^aPs 72:19;
Isa 6:3;
Hab 2:14

14:22
^bEx 14:11; 32:1;
1Co 10:5

14:23
^cNu 32:11
^dHeb 3:18

14:24
^ever 6-9;
Jos 14:8,14
^fNu 32:12

14:25
^gDt 1:40

14:27
^hEx 16:12

14:28
ⁱver 21

14:29
^jNu 26:65
^kNu 1:45

14:31
^lPs 106:24

14:32
^m1Co 10:5

14:34
ⁿNu 13:25

14:35
^oNu 23:19

14:36
^pNu 13:4-16
^qNu 13:32

14:37
^r1Co 10:10
^sNu 16:49

14:38
^tJos 14:6

14:39
^uEx 33:4

14:40
^vDt 1:41

14:41
^w2Ch 24:20

14:42
^xDt 1:42

14:44
a Dt 1:43
b Nu 31:6

14:45
c Nu 21:3;
Dt 1:44;
Jdg 1:17

15:2
d Lev 23:10

15:3
e Lev 1:2
f ver 24;
Ge 8:21;
Ex 29:18
g Nu 28:19,27
h Lev 22:18,21;
Ezr 1:4
i Lev 23:1-44

15:4
j Lev 2:1; 6:14

15:5
k Nu 28:7,14

15:6
l Lev 5:15
m Nu 28:12
n Eze 46:14

15:8
o Lev 1:3; 3:1

15:9
p Lev 14:10

15:13
q Lev 16:29

15:15
r ver 29;
Nu 9:14

15:16
s Nu 9:14

Amalekites and Canaanites will face you there. Because you have turned away from the LORD, he will not be with you and you will fall by the sword."

⁴⁴Nevertheless, in their presumption they went up*a* toward the high hill country, though neither Moses nor the ark of the LORD's covenant moved from the camp.*b* ⁴⁵Then the Amalekites and Canaanites who lived in that hill country came down and attacked them and beat them down all the way to Hormah.*c*

Chapter 15 Theme _____

15 The LORD said to Moses, ²"Speak to the Israelites and say to them: 'After you enter the land I am giving you*d* as a home ³and you present to the LORD offerings made by fire, from the herd or the flock,*e* as an aroma pleasing to the LORD*f*—whether burnt offerings*g* or sacrifices, for special vows or freewill offerings*h* or festival offerings*i*— ⁴then the one who brings his offering shall present to the LORD a grain offering*j* of a tenth of an ephah*a* of fine flour mixed with a quarter of a hin*b* of oil. ⁵With each lamb for the burnt offering or the sacrifice, prepare a quarter of a hin of wine*k* as a drink offering.

⁶"'With a ram*l* prepare a grain offering*m* of two-tenths of an ephah*c* of fine flour mixed with a third of a hin*d* of oil,*n* ⁷and a third of a hin of wine as a drink offering. Offer it as an aroma pleasing to the LORD.

⁸"'When you prepare a young bull as a burnt offering or sacrifice, for a special vow or a fellowship offering*eo* to the LORD, ⁹bring with the bull a grain offering of three-tenths of an ephah*fp* of fine flour mixed with half a hin*g* of oil. ¹⁰Also bring half a hin of wine as a drink offering. It will be an offering made by fire, an aroma pleasing to the LORD. ¹¹Each bull or ram, each lamb or young goat, is to be prepared in this manner. ¹²Do this for each one, for as many as you prepare.

¹³"'Everyone who is native-born*q* must do these things in this way when he brings an offering made by fire as an aroma pleasing to the LORD. ¹⁴For the generations to come, whenever an alien or anyone else living among you presents an offering made by fire as an aroma pleasing to the LORD, he must do exactly as you do. ¹⁵The community is to have the same rules for you and for the alien living among you; this is a lasting ordinance for the generations to come.*r* You and the alien shall be the same before the LORD: ¹⁶The same laws and regulations will apply both to you and to the alien living among you.*s*'"

a 4 That is, probably about 2 quarts (about 2 liters)   *b* 4 That is, probably about 1 quart (about 1 liter); also in verse 5   *c* 6 That is, probably about 4 quarts (about 4.5 liters)   *d* 6 That is, probably about 1 1/4 quarts (about 1.2 liters); also in verse 7   *e* 8 Traditionally *peace offering*   *f* 9 That is, probably about 6 quarts (about 6.5 liters)   *g* 9 That is, probably about 2 quarts (about 2 liters); also in verse 10

¹⁷The LORD said to Moses, ¹⁸"Speak to the Israelites and say to them: 'When you enter the land to which I am taking you ¹⁹and you eat the food of the land,ᵃ present a portion as an offering to the LORD. ²⁰Present a cake from the first of your ground mealᵇ and present it as an offering from the threshing floor.ᶜ ²¹Throughout the generations to come you are to give this offering to the LORD from the first of your ground meal.ᵈ

²²"'Now if you unintentionally fail to keep any of these commands the LORD gave Mosesᵉ— ²³any of the LORD's commands to you through him, from the day the LORD gave them and continuing through the generations to come— ²⁴and if this is done unintentionally without the community being aware of it,ᶠ then the whole community is to offer a young bull for a burnt offeringᵍ as an aroma pleasing to the LORD, along with its prescribed grain offering and drink offering, and a male goat for a sin offering.ʰ ²⁵The priest is to make atonement for the whole Israelite community, and they will be forgiven,ⁱ for it was not intentional and they have brought to the LORD for their wrong an offering made by fire and a sin offering. ²⁶The whole Israelite community and the aliens living among them will be forgiven, because all the people were involved in the unintentional wrong.ʲ

²⁷"'But if just one person sins unintentionally,ᵏ he must bring a year-old female goat for a sin offering. ²⁸The priest is to make atonement before the LORD for the one who erred by sinning unintentionally, and when atonement has been made for him, he will be forgiven.ˡ ²⁹One and the same law applies to everyone who sins unintentionally, whether he is a native-born Israelite or an alien.

³⁰"'But anyone who sins defiantly,ᵐ whether native-born or alien,ⁿ blasphemes the LORD, and that person must be cut off from his people. ³¹Because he has despised the LORD's word and broken his commands,ᵒ that person must surely be cut off; his guilt remains on him.ᵖ'"

³²While the Israelites were in the desert, a man was found gathering wood on the Sabbath day.�q ³³Those who found him gathering wood brought him to Moses and Aaron and the whole assembly, ³⁴and they kept him in custody, because it was not clear what should be done to him.ʳ ³⁵Then the LORD said to Moses, "The man must die.ˢ The whole assembly must stone him outside the camp.ᵗ" ³⁶So the assembly took him outside the camp and stoned him to death, as the LORD commanded Moses.

³⁷The LORD said to Moses, ³⁸"Speak to the Israelites and say to them: 'Throughout the generations to come you are to make tassels on the corners of your garments,ᵘ with a blue cord on each tassel. ³⁹You will have these tassels to look at and so you will

15:19
a Jos 5:11,12

15:20
b Ex 34:26;
Lev 23:14;
Dt 26:2,10
c Lev 2:14

15:21
d Ro 11:16

15:22
e Lev 4:2

15:24
f Lev 5:15
g Lev 4:14
h Lev 4:3

15:25
i Lev 4:20;
Ro 3:25;
Heb 2:17

15:26
j ver 24

15:27
k Lev 4:27

15:28
l Lev 4:35

15:30
m Nu 14:40-44;
Dt 1:43; 17:13;
Ps 19:13
n ver 14

15:31
o 2Sa 12:9;
Ps 119:126;
Pr 13:13
p Lev 5:1;
Eze 18:20

15:32
q Ex 31:14,15;
35:2,3

15:34
r Nu 9:8

15:35
s Ex 31:14,15;
Dt 21:21
t Lev 20:2;
24:14;
Ac 7:58

15:38
u Dt 22:12;
Mt 23:5

15:39
a Dt 4:23; 6:12;
Ps 73:27

15:40
b Lev 11:44;
Ro 12:1;
Col 1:22;
1Pe 1:15

16:1
c Jude 1:11
d Nu 26:8;
Dt 11:6

16:2
e Nu 1:16; 26:9

16:3
f ver 7;
Ps 106:16
g Ex 19:6
h Nu 14:14
i Nu 12:2

16:4
j Nu 14:5

16:5
k Lev 10:3;
2Ti 2:19*
l Nu 17:5;
Ps 65:4

16:9
m Nu 3:6;
Dt 10:8

16:10
n Nu 3:10; 18:7

16:11
o 1Co 10:10
p Ex 16:7

16:13
q Nu 14:2
r Ac 7:27,35

16:14
s Lev 20:24
t Ex 22:5; 23:11;
Nu 20:5
u Jdg 16:21;
1Sa 11:2

16:15
v 1Sa 12:3

remember^a all the commands of the Lord, that you may obey them and not prostitute yourselves by going after the lusts of your own hearts and eyes. ⁴⁰Then you will remember to obey all my commands and will be consecrated to your God.^b ⁴¹I am the Lord your God, who brought you out of Egypt to be your God. I am the Lord your God.'"

Chapter 16 Theme

16 Korah^c son of Izhar, the son of Kohath, the son of Levi, and certain Reubenites—Dathan and Abiram, sons of Eliab,^d and On son of Peleth—became insolent^a ²and rose up against Moses. With them were 250 Israelite men, well-known community leaders who had been appointed members of the council.^e ³They came as a group to oppose Moses and Aaron^f and said to them, "You have gone too far! The whole community is holy,^g every one of them, and the Lord is with them.^h Why then do you set yourselves above the Lord's assembly?"ⁱ

⁴When Moses heard this, he fell facedown.^j ⁵Then he said to Korah and all his followers: "In the morning the Lord will show who belongs to him and who is holy,^k and he will have that person come near him. The man he chooses^l he will cause to come near him. ⁶You, Korah, and all your followers are to do this: Take censers ⁷and tomorrow put fire and incense in them before the Lord. The man the Lord chooses will be the one who is holy. You Levites have gone too far!"

⁸Moses also said to Korah, "Now listen, you Levites! ⁹Isn't it enough for you that the God of Israel has separated you from the rest of the Israelite community and brought you near himself to do the work at the Lord's tabernacle and to stand before the community and minister to them?^m ¹⁰He has brought you and all your fellow Levites near himself, but now you are trying to get the priesthood too.ⁿ ¹¹It is against the Lord that you and all your followers have banded together. Who is Aaron that you should grumble^o against him?^p"

¹²Then Moses summoned Dathan and Abiram, the sons of Eliab. But they said, "We will not come! ¹³Isn't it enough that you have brought us up out of a land flowing with milk and honey to kill us in the desert?^q And now you also want to lord it over us?^r ¹⁴Moreover, you haven't brought us into a land flowing with milk and honey^s or given us an inheritance of fields and vineyards.^t Will you gouge out the eyes of^b these men?^u No, we will not come!"

¹⁵Then Moses became very angry and said to the Lord, "Do not accept their offering. I have not taken so much as a donkey^v from them, nor have I wronged any of them."

a 1 Or *Peleth—took ⌊men⌋*   b 14 Or *you make slaves of*; or *you deceive*

16Moses said to Korah, "You and all your followers are to appear before the Lord tomorrow—you and they and Aaron.*ᵃ* 17Each man is to take his censer and put incense in it—250 censers in all—and present it before the Lord. You and Aaron are to present your censers also." 18So each man took his censer, put fire and incense in it, and stood with Moses and Aaron at the entrance to the Tent of Meeting. 19When Korah had gathered all his followers in opposition to them*ᵇ* at the entrance to the Tent of Meeting, the glory of the Lord*ᶜ* appeared to the entire assembly. 20The Lord said to Moses and Aaron, 21"Separate yourselves from this assembly so I can put an end to them at once."*ᵈ*

22But Moses and Aaron fell facedown*ᵉ* and cried out, "O God, God of the spirits of all mankind,*ᶠ* will you be angry with the entire assembly when only one man sins?"*ᵍ*

23Then the Lord said to Moses, 24"Say to the assembly, 'Move away from the tents of Korah, Dathan and Abiram.'"

25Moses got up and went to Dathan and Abiram, and the elders of Israel followed him. 26He warned the assembly, "Move back from the tents of these wicked men!*ʰ* Do not touch anything belonging to them, or you will be swept away*ⁱ* because of all their sins." 27So they moved away from the tents of Korah, Dathan and Abiram. Dathan and Abiram had come out and were standing with their wives, children and little ones at the entrances to their tents.

28Then Moses said, "This is how you will know that the Lord has sent me*ʲ* to do all these things and that it was not my idea: 29If these men die a natural death and experience only what usually happens to men, then the Lord has not sent me.*ᵏ* 30But if the Lord brings about something totally new, and the earth opens its mouth and swallows them, with everything that belongs to them, and they go down alive into the grave,*ᵃˡ* then you will know that these men have treated the Lord with contempt."

31As soon as he finished saying all this, the ground under them split apart*ᵐ* 32and the earth opened its mouth and swallowed them,*ⁿ* with their households and all Korah's men and all their possessions. 33They went down alive into the grave, with everything they owned; the earth closed over them, and they perished and were gone from the community. 34At their cries, all the Israelites around them fled, shouting, "The earth is going to swallow us too!"

35And fire came out from the Lord*ᵒ* and consumed*ᵖ* the 250 men who were offering the incense.

36The Lord said to Moses, 37"Tell Eleazar son of Aaron, the priest, to take the censers out of the smoldering remains and

a 30 Hebrew Sheol; also in verse 33

16:16
ᵃ ver 6

16:19
ᵇ ver 42
ᶜ Ex 16:7;
Nu 14:10; 20:6

16:21
ᵈ Ex 32:10

16:22
ᵉ Nu 14:5
ᶠ Nu 27:16;
Job 12:10;
Heb 12:9
ᵍ Ge 18:23

16:26
ʰ Isa 52:11
ⁱ Ge 19:15

16:28
ʲ Ex 3:12;
Jn 5:36; 6:38

16:29
ᵏ Ecc 3:19

16:30
ˡ ver 33;
Ps 55:15

16:31
ᵐ Mic 1:3-4

16:32
ⁿ Nu 26:11;
Dt 11:6;
Ps 106:17

16:35
ᵒ Nu 11:1-3;
26:10
ᵖ Lev 10:2

scatter the coals some distance away, for the censers are holy—
[38]the censers of the men who sinned at the cost of their lives.[a] Hammer the censers into sheets to overlay the altar, for they were presented before the LORD and have become holy. Let them be a sign[b] to the Israelites."

[39]So Eleazar the priest collected the bronze censers brought by those who had been burned up, and he had them hammered out to overlay the altar, [40]as the LORD directed him through Moses. This was to remind the Israelites that no one except a descendant of Aaron should come to burn incense[c] before the LORD,[d] or he would become like Korah and his followers.[e]

[41]The next day the whole Israelite community grumbled against Moses and Aaron. "You have killed the LORD's people," they said.

[42]But when the assembly gathered in opposition[f] to Moses and Aaron and turned toward the Tent of Meeting, suddenly the cloud covered it and the glory of the LORD appeared. [43]Then Moses and Aaron went to the front of the Tent of Meeting, [44]and the LORD said to Moses, [45]"Get away from this assembly so I can put an end to them at once." And they fell facedown.

[46]Then Moses said to Aaron, "Take your censer and put incense in it, along with fire from the altar, and hurry to the assembly[g] to make atonement[h] for them. Wrath has come out from the LORD; the plague[i] has started." [47]So Aaron did as Moses said, and ran into the midst of the assembly. The plague had already started among the people,[j] but Aaron offered the incense and made atonement for them. [48]He stood between the living and the dead, and the plague stopped.[k] [49]But 14,700 people died from the plague, in addition to those who had died because of Korah.[l] [50]Then Aaron returned to Moses at the entrance to the Tent of Meeting, for the plague had stopped.

Chapter 17 Theme

17 The LORD said to Moses, [2]"Speak to the Israelites and get twelve staffs from them, one from the leader of each of their ancestral tribes. Write the name of each man on his staff. [3]On the staff of Levi write Aaron's name,[m] for there must be one staff for the head of each ancestral tribe. [4]Place them in the Tent of Meeting in front of the Testimony,[n] where I meet with you.[o] [5]The staff belonging to the man I choose[p] will sprout, and I will rid myself of this constant grumbling against you by the Israelites."

[6]So Moses spoke to the Israelites, and their leaders gave him twelve staffs, one for the leader of each of their ancestral tribes, and Aaron's staff was among them. [7]Moses placed the staffs before the LORD in the Tent of the Testimony.[q]

[8]The next day Moses entered the Tent of the Testimony and saw that Aaron's staff, which represented the house of Levi, had

---

16:38
a Pr 20:2
b Nu 26:10;
Eze 14:8;
2Pe 2:6

16:40
c Ex 30:7-10;
Nu 1:51
d 2Ch 26:18
e Nu 3:10

16:42
f ver 19;
Nu 20:6

16:46
g Lev 10:6
h Nu 18:5; 25:13;
Dt 9:22
i Nu 8:19;
Ps 106:29

16:47
j Nu 25:6-8

16:48
k Nu 25:8;
Ps 106:30

16:49
l ver 32

17:3
m Nu 1:3

17:4
n ver 7
o Ex 25:22

17:5
p Nu 16:5

17:7
q Ex 38:21;
Ac 7:44

not only sprouted but had budded, blossomed and produced almonds.[a] [9]Then Moses brought out all the staffs from the LORD's presence to all the Israelites. They looked at them, and each man took his own staff.

[10]The LORD said to Moses, "Put back Aaron's staff in front of the Testimony, to be kept as a sign to the rebellious.[b] This will put an end to their grumbling against me, so that they will not die." [11]Moses did just as the LORD commanded him.

[12]The Israelites said to Moses, "We will die! We are lost, we are all lost![c] [13]Anyone who even comes near the tabernacle of the LORD will die.[d] Are we all going to die?"

Chapter 18 Theme

18 The LORD said to Aaron, "You, your sons and your father's family are to bear the responsibility for offenses against the sanctuary,[e] and you and your sons alone are to bear the responsibility for offenses against the priesthood. [2]Bring your fellow Levites from your ancestral tribe to join you and assist you when you and your sons minister[f] before the Tent of the Testimony. [3]They are to be responsible to you and are to perform all the duties of the Tent,[g] but they must not go near the furnishings of the sanctuary or the altar, or both they and you will die.[h] [4]They are to join you and be responsible for the care of the Tent of Meeting—all the work at the Tent—and no one else may come near where you are.

[5]"You are to be responsible for the care of the sanctuary and the altar,[i] so that wrath will not fall on the Israelites again. [6]I myself have selected your fellow Levites from among the Israelites as a gift to you,[j] dedicated to the LORD to do the work at the Tent of Meeting. [7]But only you and your sons may serve as priests in connection with everything at the altar and inside the curtain.[k] I am giving you the service of the priesthood as a gift.[l] Anyone else who comes near the sanctuary must be put to death.[m]"

[8]Then the LORD said to Aaron, "I myself have put you in charge of the offerings presented to me; all the holy offerings the Israelites give me I give to you and your sons as your portion and regular share.[n] [9]You are to have the part of the most holy offerings that is kept from the fire. From all the gifts they bring me as most holy offerings, whether grain[o] or sin[p] or guilt offerings,[q] that part belongs to you and your sons. [10]Eat it as something most holy; every male shall eat it.[r] You must regard it as holy.

[11]"This also is yours: whatever is set aside from the gifts of all the wave offerings[s] of the Israelites. I give this to you and your sons and daughters as your regular share. Everyone in your household who is ceremonially clean[t] may eat it.

17:8
[a] Eze 17:24;
Heb 9:4

17:10
[b] Dt 9:24

17:12
[c] Isa 6:5

17:13
[d] Nu 1:51

18:1
[e] Ex 28:38

18:2
[f] Nu 3:10

18:3
[g] Nu 1:51
[h] ver 7;
Nu 4:15

18:5
[i] Nu 16:46

18:6
[j] Nu 3:9

18:7
[k] Heb 9:3,6
[l] ver 20;
Ex 29:9
[m] Nu 3:10

18:8
[n] Lev 6:16;
7:6,31-34,36

18:9
[o] Lev 2:1
[p] Lev 6:25
[q] Lev 5:15; 7:7

18:10
[r] Lev 6:16

18:11
[s] Ex 29:26
[t] Lev 22:1-16

18:12
a Ex 23:19;
Ne 10:35

18:13
b Ex 22:29;
23:19

18:14
c Lev 27:28

18:15
d Ex 13:2
e Nu 3:46
f Ex 13:13

18:16
g Lev 27:6
h Ex 30:13

18:17
i Dt 15:19
j Lev 3:2

18:18
k Lev 7:30

18:19
l Lev 2:13;
2Ch 13:5

18:20
m Dt 12:12
n Dt 10:9; 14:27;
18:1-2;
Jos 13:33;
Eze 44:28

18:21
o Dt 14:22;
Mal 3:8
p Lev 27:30-33;
Heb 7:5

18:22
q Lev 22:9;
Nu 1:51

18:23
r ver 20

18:26
s ver 21
t Ne 10:38

18:28
u Mal 3:8

¹²"I give you all the finest olive oil and all the finest new wine and grain they give the LORD as the firstfruits of their harvest.^a ¹³All the land's firstfruits that they bring to the LORD will be yours.^b Everyone in your household who is ceremonially clean may eat it.

¹⁴"Everything in Israel that is devoted^a to the LORD^c is yours. ¹⁵The first offspring of every womb, both man and animal, that is offered to the LORD is yours.^d But you must redeem^e every firstborn son and every firstborn male of unclean animals.^f ¹⁶When they are a month old, you must redeem them at the redemption price set at five shekels^{b g} of silver, according to the sanctuary shekel,^h which weighs twenty gerahs.

¹⁷"But you must not redeem the firstborn of an ox, a sheep or a goat; they are holy.ⁱ Sprinkle their blood^j on the altar and burn their fat as an offering made by fire, an aroma pleasing to the LORD. ¹⁸Their meat is to be yours, just as the breast of the wave offering^k and the right thigh are yours. ¹⁹Whatever is set aside from the holy offerings the Israelites present to the LORD I give to you and your sons and daughters as your regular share. It is an everlasting covenant of salt^l before the LORD for both you and your offspring."

²⁰The LORD said to Aaron, "You will have no inheritance in their land, nor will you have any share among them;^m I am your share and your inheritanceⁿ among the Israelites.

²¹"I give to the Levites all the tithes^o in Israel as their inheritance^p in return for the work they do while serving at the Tent of Meeting. ²²From now on the Israelites must not go near the Tent of Meeting, or they will bear the consequences of their sin and will die.^q ²³It is the Levites who are to do the work at the Tent of Meeting and bear the responsibility for offenses against it. This is a lasting ordinance for the generations to come. They will receive no inheritance^r among the Israelites. ²⁴Instead, I give to the Levites as their inheritance the tithes that the Israelites present as an offering to the LORD. That is why I said concerning them: 'They will have no inheritance among the Israelites.'"

²⁵The LORD said to Moses, ²⁶"Speak to the Levites and say to them: 'When you receive from the Israelites the tithe I give you^s as your inheritance, you must present a tenth of that tithe as the LORD's offering.^t ²⁷Your offering will be reckoned to you as grain from the threshing floor or juice from the winepress. ²⁸In this way you also will present an offering to the LORD from all the tithes^u you receive from the Israelites. From these tithes you must give the LORD's portion to Aaron the priest. ²⁹You must present as

a *14* The Hebrew term refers to the irrevocable giving over of things or persons to the LORD.
b *16* That is, about 2 ounces (about 55 grams)

the LORD's portion the best and holiest part of everything given to you.'

30"Say to the Levites: 'When you present the best part, it will be reckoned to you as the product of the threshing floor or the winepress.[a] 31You and your households may eat the rest of it anywhere, for it is your wages for your work at the Tent of Meeting. 32By presenting the best part[b] of it you will not be guilty in this matter; then you will not defile the holy offerings[c] of the Israelites, and you will not die.'"

Chapter 19 Theme _____

19 The LORD said to Moses and Aaron: 2"This is a requirement of the law that the LORD has commanded: Tell the Israelites to bring you a red heifer[d] without defect or blemish[e] and that has never been under a yoke.[f] 3Give it to Eleazar[g] the priest; it is to be taken outside the camp[h] and slaughtered in his presence. 4Then Eleazar the priest is to take some of its blood on his finger and sprinkle[i] it seven times toward the front of the Tent of Meeting. 5While he watches, the heifer is to be burned—its hide, flesh, blood and offal.[j] 6The priest is to take some cedar wood, hyssop[k] and scarlet wool[l] and throw them onto the burning heifer. 7After that, the priest must wash his clothes and bathe himself with water.[m] He may then come into the camp, but he will be ceremonially unclean till evening. 8The man who burns it must also wash his clothes and bathe with water, and he too will be unclean till evening.

9"A man who is clean shall gather up the ashes of the heifer[n] and put them in a ceremonially clean place outside the camp. They shall be kept by the Israelite community for use in the water of cleansing;[o] it is for purification from sin. 10The man who gathers up the ashes of the heifer must also wash his clothes, and he too will be unclean till evening. This will be a lasting ordinance both for the Israelites and for the aliens living among them.

11"Whoever touches the dead body[p] of anyone will be unclean for seven days.[q] 12He must purify himself with the water on the third day and on the seventh day;[r] then he will be clean. But if he does not purify himself on the third and seventh days, he will not be clean. 13Whoever touches the dead body[s] of anyone and fails to purify himself defiles the LORD's tabernacle.[t] That person must be cut off from Israel.[u] Because the water of cleansing has not been sprinkled on him, he is unclean;[v] his uncleanness remains on him.

14"This is the law that applies when a person dies in a tent: Anyone who enters the tent and anyone who is in it will be unclean for seven days, 15and every open container without a lid fastened on it will be unclean.

18:30
[a] ver 27

18:32
[b] Lev 22:15
[c] Lev 19:8

19:2
[d] Ge 15:9;
Heb 9:13
[e] Lev 22:19-25
[f] Dt 21:3;
1Sa 6:7

19:3
[g] Nu 3:4
[h] Lev 4:12,21;
Heb 13:11

19:4
[i] Lev 4:17

19:5
[j] Ex 29:14

19:6
[k] ver 18;
Ps 51:7
[l] Lev 14:4

19:7
[m] Lev 11:25;
16:26,28; 22:6

19:9
[n] Heb 9:13
[o] ver 13;
Nu 8:7

19:11
[p] Lev 21:1;
Nu 5:2
[q] Nu 31:19

19:12
[r] ver 19;
Nu 31:19

19:13
[s] Lev 20:3
[t] Lev 15:31;
2Ch 36:14
[u] Lev 7:20; 22:3
[v] Hag 2:13

19:16
a Nu 31:19
b Mt 23:27

¹⁶"Anyone out in the open who touches someone who has been killed with a sword or someone who has died a natural death,*a* or anyone who touches a human bone or a grave,*b* will be unclean for seven days.

19:17
c ver 9

¹⁷"For the unclean person, put some ashes*c* from the burned purification offering into a jar and pour fresh water over them.

19:18
d ver 6

¹⁸Then a man who is ceremonially clean is to take some hyssop,*d* dip it in the water and sprinkle the tent and all the furnishings and the people who were there. He must also sprinkle anyone who has touched a human bone or a grave or someone who has been killed or someone who has died a natural death. ¹⁹The man

19:19
e Eze 36:25;
Heb 10:22

who is clean is to sprinkle the unclean person on the third and seventh days, and on the seventh day he is to purify him.*e* The person being cleansed must wash his clothes and bathe with

19:22
f Lev 5:2;
Hag 2:13,14

water, and that evening he will be clean. ²⁰But if a person who is unclean does not purify himself, he must be cut off from the community, because he has defiled the sanctuary of the LORD. The water of cleansing has not been sprinkled on him, and he is

20:1
g Nu 13:21
h Nu 33:36
i Ex 15:20

unclean. ²¹This is a lasting ordinance for them.

"The man who sprinkles the water of cleansing must also wash his clothes, and anyone who touches the water of cleansing will be unclean till evening. ²²Anything that an unclean*f* person touches

20:2
j Ex 17:1
k Nu 16:19

becomes unclean, and anyone who touches it becomes unclean till evening."

Chapter 20 Theme

20:3
l Ex 17:2
m Nu 14:2;
16:31-35

20 In the first month the whole Israelite community arrived at the Desert of Zin,*g* and they stayed at Kadesh.*h* There Miriam*i* died and was buried.

20:4
n Ex 14:11; 17:3;
Nu 14:3; 16:13

²Now there was no water for the community,*j* and the people gathered in opposition*k* to Moses and Aaron. ³They quarreled*l* with Moses and said, "If only we had died when our brothers fell dead before the LORD!*m* ⁴Why did you bring the LORD's community into this desert, that we and our livestock should die here?*n*

20:5
o Nu 16:14

⁵Why did you bring us up out of Egypt to this terrible place? It has no grain or figs, grapevines or pomegranates.*o* And there is no water to drink!"

20:6
p Nu 14:5
q Nu 16:19

⁶Moses and Aaron went from the assembly to the entrance to the Tent of Meeting and fell facedown,*p* and the glory of the LORD*q* appeared to them. ⁷The LORD said to Moses, ⁸"Take the staff,*r* and

20:8
r Ex 4:17,20
s Ex 17:6;
Isa 43:20

you and your brother Aaron gather the assembly together. Speak to that rock before their eyes and it will pour out its water.*s* You will bring water out of the rock for the community so they and their livestock can drink."

20:9
t Nu 17:10

⁹So Moses took the staff from the LORD's presence,*t* just as he commanded him. ¹⁰He and Aaron gathered the assembly together

in front of the rock and Moses said to them, "Listen, you rebels, must we bring you water out of this rock?"*a* **11**Then Moses raised his arm and struck the rock twice with his staff. Water*b* gushed out, and the community and their livestock drank.

12But the LORD said to Moses and Aaron, "Because you did not trust in me enough to honor me as holy*c* in the sight of the Israelites, you will not bring this community into the land I give them."*d*

13These were the waters of Meribah,*ae* where the Israelites quarreled*f* with the LORD and where he showed himself holy among them.

14Moses sent messengers from Kadesh*g* to the king of Edom,*h* saying:

"This is what your brother Israel says: You know*i* about all the hardships that have come upon us. **15**Our forefathers went down into Egypt,*j* and we lived there many years.*k* The Egyptians mistreated*l* us and our fathers, **16**but when we cried out to the LORD, he heard our cry*m* and sent an angel*n* and brought us out of Egypt.

"Now we are here at Kadesh, a town on the edge of your territory. **17**Please let us pass through your country. We will not go through any field or vineyard, or drink water from any well. We will travel along the king's highway and not turn to the right or to the left until we have passed through your territory.*o*"

18But Edom answered:

"You may not pass through here; if you try, we will march out and attack you with the sword."

19The Israelites replied:

"We will go along the main road, and if we or our livestock*p* drink any of your water, we will pay for it.*q* We only want to pass through on foot—nothing else."

20Again they answered:

"You may not pass through."

Then Edom came out against them with a large and powerful army. **21**Since Edom refused to let them go through their territory, Israel turned away from them.*r*

22The whole Israelite community set out from Kadesh and came to Mount Hor.*s* **23**At Mount Hor, near the border of Edom,*t* the LORD said to Moses and Aaron, **24**"Aaron will be gathered to his

a 13 Meribah means quarreling.

20:10
a Ps 106:32,33

20:11
b Ex 17:6;
Dt 8:15;
Ps 78:16;
Isa 48:2;
1Co 10:4

20:12
c Nu 27:14
d ver 24;
Dt 1:37; 3:27

20:13
e Ex 17:7
f Dt 33:8;
Ps 95:8; 106:32

20:14
g Jdg 11:16-17
h Dt 2:4
i Jos 2:11; 9:9

20:15
j Ge 46:6
k Ge 15:13;
Ex 12:40
l Ex 1:11;
Dt 26:6

20:16
m Ex 2:23; 3:7
n Ex 14:19

20:17
o Nu 21:22

20:19
p Ex 12:38
q Dt 2:6,28

20:21
r Dt 2:8;
Jdg 11:18

20:22
s Nu 33:37

20:23
t Nu 33:37

20:24
a Ge 25:8
b ver 10

20:25
c Nu 33:38

20:26
d ver 24

20:28
e Ex 29:29
f Nu 33:38;
Dt 10:6; 32:50

20:29
g Dt 34:8

21:1
h Nu 33:40;
Jos 12:14
i Jdg 1:9,16

21:4
j Nu 20:22
k Dt 2:8;
Jdg 11:18

21:5
l Ps 78:19
m Nu 14:2,3
n Nu 11:6

21:6
o Dt 8:15;
Jer 8:17
p 1Co 10:9

21:7
q Ps 78:34;
Hos 5:15
r Ex 8:8;
Ac 8:24
s Nu 11:2

21:8
t Jn 3:14

21:9
u 2Ki 18:4
v Jn 3:14-15

21:10
w Nu 33:43

21:11
x Nu 33:44

21:12
y Dt 2:13,14

21:13
z Nu 22:36;
Jdg 11:13,18

people.*a* He will not enter the land I give the Israelites, because both of you rebelled against my command*b* at the waters of Meribah. ²⁵Get Aaron and his son Eleazar and take them up Mount Hor.*c* ²⁶Remove Aaron's garments and put them on his son Eleazar, for Aaron will be gathered to his people;*d* he will die there."

²⁷Moses did as the Lᴏʀᴅ commanded: They went up Mount Hor in the sight of the whole community. ²⁸Moses removed Aaron's garments and put them on his son Eleazar.*e* And Aaron died there*f* on top of the mountain. Then Moses and Eleazar came down from the mountain, ²⁹and when the whole community learned that Aaron had died, the entire house of Israel mourned for him*g* thirty days.

Chapter 21 Theme _____

21 When the Canaanite king of Arad,*h* who lived in the Negev,*i* heard that Israel was coming along the road to Atharim, he attacked the Israelites and captured some of them. ²Then Israel made this vow to the Lᴏʀᴅ: "If you will deliver these people into our hands, we will totally destroy*a* their cities." ³The Lᴏʀᴅ listened to Israel's plea and gave the Canaanites over to them. They completely destroyed them and their towns; so the place was named Hormah.*b*

⁴They traveled from Mount Hor*j* along the route to the Red Sea,*c* to go around Edom. But the people grew impatient on the way;*k* ⁵they spoke against God*l* and against Moses, and said, "Why have you brought us up out of Egypt to die in the desert?*m* There is no bread! There is no water! And we detest this miserable food!"*n*

⁶Then the Lᴏʀᴅ sent venomous snakes*o* among them; they bit the people and many Israelites died.*p* ⁷The people came to Moses*q* and said, "We sinned when we spoke against the Lᴏʀᴅ and against you. Pray that the Lᴏʀᴅ*r* will take the snakes away from us." So Moses prayed*s* for the people.

⁸The Lᴏʀᴅ said to Moses, "Make a snake and put it up on a pole;*t* anyone who is bitten can look at it and live." ⁹So Moses made a bronze snake*u* and put it up on a pole. Then when anyone was bitten by a snake and looked at the bronze snake, he lived.*v*

¹⁰The Israelites moved on and camped at Oboth.*w* ¹¹Then they set out from Oboth and camped in Iye Abarim, in the desert that faces Moab*x* toward the sunrise. ¹²From there they moved on and camped in the Zered Valley.*y* ¹³They set out from there and camped alongside the Arnon*z*, which is in the desert extending

a2 The Hebrew term refers to the irrevocable giving over of things or persons to the Lᴏʀᴅ, often by totally destroying them; also in verse 3.   *b3* *Hormah* means *destruction*.   *c4* Hebrew *Yam Suph*; that is, Sea of Reeds into Amorite territory. The Arnon is the border of Moab, between Moab and the Amorites. ¹⁴That is why the Book of the Wars of the LORD says:

> "...Waheb in Suphah^a and the ravines,
>> the Arnon ¹⁵and^b the slopes of the ravines
>>> that lead to the site of Ar^a
>>> and lie along the border of Moab."

¹⁶From there they continued on to Beer,^b the well where the LORD said to Moses, "Gather the people together and I will give them water."

¹⁷Then Israel sang this song:^c

> "Spring up, O well!
>> Sing about it,
> ¹⁸about the well that the princes dug,
>> that the nobles of the people sank—
>>> the nobles with scepters and staffs."

Then they went from the desert to Mattanah, ¹⁹from Mattanah to Nahaliel, from Nahaliel to Bamoth, ²⁰and from Bamoth to the valley in Moab where the top of Pisgah overlooks the wasteland.

²¹Israel sent messengers to say to Sihon^d king of the Amorites:

²²"Let us pass through your country. We will not turn aside into any field or vineyard, or drink water from any well. We will travel along the king's highway until we have passed through your territory.^e"

²³But Sihon would not let Israel pass through his territory.^f He mustered his entire army and marched out into the desert against Israel. When he reached Jahaz,^g he fought with Israel. ²⁴Israel, however, put him to the sword^h and took over his land from the Arnon to the Jabbok, but only as far as the Ammonites,ⁱ because their border was fortified. ²⁵Israel captured all the cities of the Amorites^j and occupied them, including Heshbon and all its surrounding settlements. ²⁶Heshbon was the city of Sihon^k king of the Amorites, who had fought against the former king of Moab and had taken from him all his land as far as the Arnon.

²⁷That is why the poets say:

> "Come to Heshbon and let it be rebuilt;
>> let Sihon's city be restored.

> ²⁸"Fire went out from Heshbon,
>> a blaze from the city of Sihon.^l

---

a 14 The meaning of the Hebrew for this phrase is uncertain.   b 14,15 Or "I have been given from Suphah and the ravines / of the Arnon ¹⁵to

---

**Margin references:**

21:15 ^aver 28; Dt 2:9,18

21:16 ^bJdg 9:21

21:17 ^cEx 15:1

21:21 ^dDt 1:4; 2:26-27; Jdg 11:19-21

21:22 ^eNu 20:17

21:23 ^fNu 20:21 ^gDt 2:32; Jdg 11:20

21:24 ^hDt 2:33; Ps 135:10-11; Am 2:9 ⁱDt 2:37

21:25 ^jNu 13:29; Jdg 10:11; Am 2:10

21:26 ^kDt 29:7; Ps 135:11

21:28 ^lJer 48:45

It consumed Ar[a] of Moab,
> the citizens of Arnon's heights.[b]
29Woe to you, O Moab![c]
> You are destroyed, O people of Chemosh![d]
> He has given up his sons as fugitives[e]
> and his daughters as captives[f]
> to Sihon king of the Amorites.

30"But we have overthrown them;
> Heshbon is destroyed all the way to Dibon.[g]
> We have demolished them as far as Nophah,
> which extends to Medeba."

31So Israel settled in the land of the Amorites.

32After Moses had sent spies to Jazer,[h] the Israelites captured its surrounding settlements and drove out the Amorites who were there. 33Then they turned and went up along the road toward Bashan[i,j] and Og king of Bashan and his whole army marched out to meet them in battle at Edrei.[k]

34The LORD said to Moses, "Do not be afraid of him, for I have handed him over to you, with his whole army and his land. Do to him what you did to Sihon king of the Amorites, who reigned in Heshbon.[l]"

35So they struck him down, together with his sons and his whole army, leaving them no survivors. And they took possession of his land.

Chapter 22 Theme _____

22 Then the Israelites traveled to the plains of Moab and camped along the Jordan across from Jericho.[a][m]

2Now Balak son of Zippor[n] saw all that Israel had done to the Amorites, 3and Moab was terrified because there were so many people. Indeed, Moab was filled with dread[o] because of the Israelites.

4The Moabites said to the elders of Midian, "This horde is going to lick up everything around us, as an ox licks up the grass of the field."

So Balak son of Zippor, who was king of Moab at that time, 5sent messengers to summon Balaam son of Beor,[p] who was at Pethor, near the River,[b] in his native land. Balak said:

> "A people has come out of Egypt; they cover the face of the land and have settled next to me. 6Now come and put a curse[q] on these people, because they are too powerful for me. Perhaps

### Cross references (left margin)

21:28
[a] ver 15
[b] Nu 22:41;
Isa 15:2

21:29
[c] Isa 25:10;
Jer 48:46;
[d] Jdg 11:24;
1Ki 11:7,33;
2Ki 23:13;
Jer 48:7,46
[e] Isa 15:5
[f] Isa 16:2

21:30
[g] Nu 32:3;
Isa 15:2;
Jer 48:18,22

21:32
[h] Nu 32:1,3,35;
Jer 48:32

21:33
[i] Dt 3:3
[j] Dt 3:4
[k] Dt 1:4;
3:1,10;
Jos 13:12,31

21:34
[l] Dt 3:2

22:1
[m] Nu 33:48

22:2
[n] Jdg 11:25

22:3
[o] Ex 15:15

22:5
[p] Dt 23:4;
Jos 13:22;
24:9;
Ne 13:2;
Mic 6:5;
2Pe 2:15

22:6
[q] ver 12,17;
Nu 23:7,11,13

Footnotes

[a] 1 Hebrew *Jordan of Jericho*; possibly an ancient name for the Jordan River   [b] 5 That is, the Euphrates

then I will be able to defeat them and drive them out of the country. For I know that those you bless are blessed, and those you curse are cursed."

[7]The elders of Moab and Midian left, taking with them the fee for divination.[a] When they came to Balaam, they told him what Balak had said.

[8]"Spend the night here," Balaam said to them, "and I will bring you back the answer the LORD gives me.[b]" So the Moabite princes stayed with him.

[9]God came to Balaam[c] and asked,[d] "Who are these men with you?"

[10]Balaam said to God, "Balak son of Zippor, king of Moab, sent me this message: [11]'A people that has come out of Egypt covers the face of the land. Now come and put a curse on them for me. Perhaps then I will be able to fight them and drive them away.'"

[12]But God said to Balaam, "Do not go with them. You must not put a curse on those people, because they are blessed.[e]"

[13]The next morning Balaam got up and said to Balak's princes, "Go back to your own country, for the LORD has refused to let me go with you."

INSIGHT

Midian was the son of Abraham by his wife Keturah (Genesis 25:2). Midian's descendants, the Midianites, took Joseph to Egypt (Genesis 37:28,36). After killing the Egyptian, Moses fled to Midian and there married the daughter of a priest.

The Lands of Israel's Journey from Mt. Hor to Moab

[14]So the Moabite princes returned to Balak and said, "Balaam refused to come with us."

[15]Then Balak sent other princes, more numerous and more distinguished than the first. [16]They came to Balaam and said:

"This is what Balak son of Zippor says: Do not let anything keep you from coming to me, [17]because I will reward you handsomely[f] and do whatever you say. Come and put a curse[g] on these people for me."

22:7 [a]Nu 23:23; 24:1

22:8 [b]ver 19

22:9 [c]Ge 20:3 [d]ver 20

22:12 [e]Ge 12:2; 22:17; Nu 23:20

22:17 [f]ver 37; Nu 24:11 [g]ver 6

22:18
a ver 38;
Nu 23:12,26;
24:13;
1Ki 22:14;
2Ch 18:13;
Jer 42:4

¹⁸But Balaam answered them, "Even if Balak gave me his palace filled with silver and gold, I could not do anything great or small to go beyond the command of the LORD my God.*a* ¹⁹Now stay here tonight as the others did, and I will find out what else the LORD will tell me.*b*"

22:19
b ver 8

²⁰That night God came to Balaam*c* and said, "Since these men have come to summon you, go with them, but do only what I tell you."*d*

22:20
c Ge 20:3
d ver 35,38;
Nu 23:5,12,
16,26; 24:13;
2Ch 18:13

²¹Balaam got up in the morning, saddled his donkey and went with the princes of Moab. ²²But God was very angry*e* when he went, and the angel of the LORD*f* stood in the road to oppose him. Balaam was riding on his donkey, and his two servants were with him. ²³When the donkey saw the angel of the LORD standing in the road with a drawn sword*g* in his hand, she turned off the road into a field. Balaam beat her*h* to get her back on the road.

22:22
e Ex 4:14
f Ge 16:7;
Ex 23:20;
Jdg 13:3,6,13

²⁴Then the angel of the LORD stood in a narrow path between two vineyards, with walls on both sides. ²⁵When the donkey saw the angel of the LORD, she pressed close to the wall, crushing Balaam's foot against it. So he beat her again.

22:23
g Jos 5:13
h ver 25,27

²⁶Then the angel of the LORD moved on ahead and stood in a narrow place where there was no room to turn, either to the right or to the left. ²⁷When the donkey saw the angel of the LORD, she lay down under Balaam, and he was angry*i* and beat her with his staff. ²⁸Then the LORD opened the donkey's mouth,*j* and she said to Balaam, "What have I done to you to make you beat me these three times?*k*"

22:27
i Nu 11:1;
Jas 1:19

²⁹Balaam answered the donkey, "You have made a fool of me! If I had a sword in my hand, I would kill you right now.*l*"

22:28
j 2Pe 2:16
k ver 32

³⁰The donkey said to Balaam, "Am I not your own donkey, which you have always ridden, to this day? Have I been in the habit of doing this to you?"

"No," he said.

22:29
l Dt 25:4;
Pr 12:10;
27:23-27;
Mt 15:19

³¹Then the LORD opened Balaam's eyes,*m* and he saw the angel of the LORD standing in the road with his sword drawn. So he bowed low and fell facedown.

22:31
m Ge 21:19

³²The angel of the LORD asked him, "Why have you beaten your donkey these three times? I have come here to oppose you because your path is a reckless one before me.*a* ³³The donkey saw me and turned away from me these three times. If she had not turned away, I would certainly have killed you by now,*n* but I would have spared her."

22:33
n ver 29

³⁴Balaam said to the angel of the LORD, "I have sinned.*o* I did not realize you were standing in the road to oppose me. Now if you are displeased, I will go back."

22:34
o Ge 39:9;
Nu 14:40;
1Sa 15:24,30;
2Sa 12:13;
24:10;
Job 33:27;
Ps 51:4

a 32 The meaning of the Hebrew for this clause is uncertain.

[35] The angel of the LORD said to Balaam, "Go with the men, but speak only what I tell you." So Balaam went with the princes of Balak.

[36] When Balak heard that Balaam was coming, he went out to meet him at the Moabite town on the Arnon[a] border, at the edge of his territory. [37] Balak said to Balaam, "Did I not send you an urgent summons? Why didn't you come to me? Am I really not able to reward you?"

[38] "Well, I have come to you now," Balaam replied. "But can I say just anything? I must speak only what God puts in my mouth."[b]

[39] Then Balaam went with Balak to Kiriath Huzoth. [40] Balak sacrificed cattle and sheep,[c] and gave some to Balaam and the princes who were with him. [41] The next morning Balak took Balaam up to Bamoth Baal,[d] and from there he saw part of the people.[e]

Chapter 23 Theme

23 Balaam said, "Build me seven altars here, and prepare seven bulls and seven rams[f] for me." [2] Balak did as Balaam said, and the two of them offered a bull and a ram on each altar.[g]

[3] Then Balaam said to Balak, "Stay here beside your offering while I go aside. Perhaps the LORD will come to meet with me.[h] Whatever he reveals to me I will tell you." Then he went off to a barren height.

[4] God met with him,[i] and Balaam said, "I have prepared seven altars, and on each altar I have offered a bull and a ram."

[5] The LORD put a message in Balaam's mouth[j] and said, "Go back to Balak and give him this message."[k]

[6] So he went back to him and found him standing beside his offering, with all the princes of Moab.[l] [7] Then Balaam[m] uttered his oracle:[n]

> "Balak brought me from Aram,
>   the king of Moab from the eastern mountains.
> 'Come,' he said, 'curse Jacob for me;
>   come, denounce Israel.'[o]
> [8] How can I curse
>   those whom God has not cursed?[p]
> How can I denounce
>   those whom the LORD has not denounced?
> [9] From the rocky peaks I see them,
>   from the heights I view them.
> I see a people who live apart
>   and do not consider themselves one of the nations.[q]
> [10] Who can count the dust of Jacob[r]
>   or number the fourth part of Israel?

22:36
[a] Nu 21:13

22:38
[b] Nu 23:5,16, 26

22:40
[c] Nu 23:1,14, 29;
Eze 45:23

22:41
[d] Nu 21:28
[e] Nu 23:13

23:1
[f] Nu 22:40

23:2
[g] ver 14,30

23:3
[h] ver 15

23:4
[i] ver 16

23:5
[j] Dt 18:18;
Jer 1:9
[k] Nu 22:20

23:6
[l] ver 17

23:7
[m] Nu 22:5
[n] ver 18;
Nu 24:3,21
[o] Nu 22:6;
Dt 23:4

23:8
[p] Nu 22:12

23:9
[q] Ex 33:16;
Dt 32:8; 33:28

23:10
[r] Ge 13:16

> Let me die the death of the righteous,*a*
>   and may my end be like theirs!*b*"

[11] Balak said to Balaam, "What have you done to me? I brought you to curse my enemies, but you have done nothing but bless them!"*c*

[12] He answered, "Must I not speak what the LORD puts in my mouth?"*d*

[13] Then Balak said to him, "Come with me to another place where you can see them; you will see only a part but not all of them. And from there, curse them for me." [14] So he took him to the field of Zophim on the top of Pisgah, and there he built seven altars and offered a bull and a ram on each altar.*e*

[15] Balaam said to Balak, "Stay here beside your offering while I meet with him over there."

[16] The LORD met with Balaam and put a message in his mouth*f* and said, "Go back to Balak and give him this message."

[17] So he went to him and found him standing beside his offering, with the princes of Moab. Balak asked him, "What did the LORD say?"

[18] Then he uttered his oracle:

> "Arise, Balak, and listen;
>   hear me, son of Zippor.

23:19
g Isa 55:9;
Hos 11:9
h 1Sa 15:29;
Mal 3:6;
Tit 1:2;
Jas 1:17

> [19] God is not a man,*g* that he should lie,
>   nor a son of man, that he should change his mind.*h*
> Does he speak and then not act?
>   Does he promise and not fulfill?

> [20] I have received a command to bless;
>   he has blessed,*i* and I cannot change it.*j*

23:21
k Ps 32:2,5;
Ro 4:7-8
l Isa 40:2;
Jer 50:20
m Ex 29:45,46;
Ps 145:18
n Dt 33:5;
Ps 89:15-18

> [21] "No misfortune is seen in Jacob,*k*
>   no misery observed in Israel.*a l*
> The LORD their God is with them;*m*
>   the shout of the King*n* is among them.

> [22] God brought them out of Egypt;*o*
>   they have the strength of a wild ox.*p*
> [23] There is no sorcery against Jacob,
>   no divination*q* against Israel.
> It will now be said of Jacob
>   and of Israel, 'See what God has done!'

> [24] The people rise like a lioness;*r*
>   they rouse themselves like a lion*s*
> that does not rest till he devours his prey
>   and drinks the blood of his victims."

a 21 Or *He has not looked on Jacob's offenses / or on the wrongs found in Israel.*

²⁵Then Balak said to Balaam, "Neither curse them at all nor bless them at all!"

²⁶Balaam answered, "Did I not tell you I must do whatever the LORD says?"

²⁷Then Balak said to Balaam, "Come, let me take you to another place.*ᵃ* Perhaps it will please God to let you curse them for me from there." ²⁸And Balak took Balaam to the top of Peor,*ᵇ* overlooking the wasteland.

²⁹Balaam said, "Build me seven altars here, and prepare seven bulls and seven rams for me." ³⁰Balak did as Balaam had said, and offered a bull and a ram on each altar.

Chapter 24 Theme

24 Now when Balaam saw that it pleased the LORD to bless Israel, he did not resort to sorcery*ᶜ* as at other times, but turned his face toward the desert.*ᵈ* ²When Balaam looked out and saw Israel encamped tribe by tribe, the Spirit of God came upon him*ᵉ* ³and he uttered his oracle:

"The oracle of Balaam son of Beor,
    the oracle of one whose eye sees clearly,
⁴the oracle of one who hears the words of God,*ᶠ*
    who sees a vision from the Almighty,*ᵃᵍ*
    who falls prostrate, and whose eyes are opened:

⁵"How beautiful are your tents, O Jacob,
    your dwelling places, O Israel!

⁶"Like valleys they spread out,
    like gardens beside a river,
like aloes*ʰ* planted by the LORD,
    like cedars beside the waters.*ⁱ*

⁷Water will flow from their buckets;
    their seed will have abundant water.

"Their king will be greater than Agag;*ʲ*
    their kingdom will be exalted.*ᵏ*

⁸"God brought them out of Egypt;
    they have the strength of a wild ox.
They devour hostile nations
    and break their bones in pieces;*ˡ*
with their arrows they pierce them.*ᵐ*
⁹Like a lion they crouch and lie down,
    like a lioness*ⁿ*—who dares to rouse them?

"May those who bless you be blessed
    and those who curse you be cursed!"*ᵒ*

ᵃ4 Hebrew *Shaddai*; also in verse 16

23:27
ᵃ ver 13

23:28
ᵇ Ps 106:28

24:1
ᶜ Nu 23:23
ᵈ Nu 23:28

24:2
ᵉ Nu 11:25,26;
1Sa 10:10;
19:20;
2Ch 15:1

24:4
ᶠ Nu 22:20
ᵍ Ge 15:1

24:6
ʰ Ps 45:8
ⁱ Ps 1:3;
104:16

24:7
ʲ 1Sa 15:8
ᵏ 2Sa 5:12;
1Ch 14:2;
Ps 145:11-13

24:8
ˡ Ps 2:9;
Jer 50:17
ᵐ Ps 45:5

24:9
ⁿ Ge 49:9;
Nu 23:24
ᵒ Ge 12:3

24:10
a Eze 21:14
b Nu 23:11
c Ne 13:2

24:11
d Nu 22:17

24:12
e Nu 22:18

24:13
f Nu 22:18
g Nu 22:20

24:14
h Ge 49:1;
Nu 31:8,16;
Da 2:28;
Mic 6:5

24:17
i Rev 1:7
j Mt 2:2
k Ge 49:10
l Nu 21:29;
Isa 15:1–16:14

24:18
m Am 9:12

24:19
n Ge 49:10;
Mic 5:2

24:20
o Ex 17:14

24:21
p Ge 15:19

24:22
q Ge 10:22

¹⁰Then Balak's anger burned against Balaam. He struck his hands together[a] and said to him, "I summoned you to curse my enemies, but you have blessed them[b] these three times.[c] ¹¹Now leave at once and go home! I said I would reward you handsomely,[d] but the LORD has kept you from being rewarded."

¹²Balaam answered Balak, "Did I not tell the messengers you sent me,[e] ¹³'Even if Balak gave me his palace filled with silver and gold, I could not do anything of my own accord, good or bad, to go beyond the command of the LORD[f]—and I must say only what the LORD says'?[g] ¹⁴Now I am going back to my people, but come, let me warn you of what this people will do to your people in days to come."[h]

¹⁵Then he uttered his oracle:

"The oracle of Balaam son of Beor,
    the oracle of one whose eye sees clearly,
¹⁶the oracle of one who hears the words of God,
    who has knowledge from the Most High,
who sees a vision from the Almighty,
    who falls prostrate, and whose eyes
        are opened:

¹⁷"I see him, but not now;
    I behold him, but not near.[i]
A star will come out of Jacob;[j]
    a scepter will rise out of Israel.[k]
He will crush the foreheads of Moab,[l]
    the skulls[a] of[b] all the sons of Sheth.[c]
¹⁸Edom[m] will be conquered;
    Seir, his enemy, will be conquered,
    but Israel will grow strong.
¹⁹A ruler will come out of Jacob[n]
    and destroy the survivors of the city."

²⁰Then Balaam saw Amalek[o] and uttered his oracle:

"Amalek was first among the nations,
    but he will come to ruin at last."

²¹Then he saw the Kenites[p] and uttered his oracle:

"Your dwelling place is secure,
    your nest is set in a rock;
²²yet you Kenites will be destroyed
    when Asshur[q] takes you captive."

a 17 Samaritan Pentateuch (see also Jer. 48:45); the meaning of the word in the Masoretic Text is uncertain.　b 17 Or possibly *Moab, / batter*　c 17 Or *all the noisy boasters*

²³Then he uttered his oracle:

"Ah, who can live when God does this?ᵃ
²⁴   Ships will come from the shores of Kittim;ᵃ
they will subdue Asshur and Eber,ᵇ
but they too will come to ruin.ᶜ"

²⁵Then Balaamᵈ got up and returned home and Balak went his own way.

Chapter 25 Theme

25 While Israel was staying in Shittim,ᵉ the men began to indulge in sexual immoralityᶠ with Moabite women,ᵍ ²who invited them to the sacrificesʰ to their gods.ⁱ The people ate and bowed down before these gods. ³So Israel joined in worshiping the Baal of Peor.ʲ And the LORD's anger burned against them.

⁴The LORD said to Moses, "Take all the leaders of these people, kill them and expose them in broad daylight before the LORD,ᵏ so that the LORD's fierce angerˡ may turn away from Israel."

⁵So Moses said to Israel's judges, "Each of you must put to deathᵐ those of your men who have joined in worshiping the Baal of Peor."

⁶Then an Israelite man brought to his family a Midianite woman right before the eyes of Moses and the whole assembly of Israel while they were weeping at the entrance to the Tent of Meeting. ⁷When Phinehas son of Eleazar, the son of Aaron, the priest, saw this, he left the assembly, took a spear in his hand ⁸and followed the Israelite into the tent. He drove the spear through both of them—through the Israelite and into the woman's body. Then the plague against the Israelites was stopped;ⁿ ⁹but those who died in the plagueᵒ numbered 24,000.ᵖ

¹⁰The LORD said to Moses, ¹¹"Phinehas son of Eleazar, the son of Aaron, the priest, has turned my anger away from the Israelites;�q for he was as zealous as I am for my honorʳ among them, so that in my zeal I did not put an end to them. ¹²Therefore tell him I am making my covenant of peaceˢ with him. ¹³He and his descendants will have a covenant of a lasting priesthood,ᵗ because he was zealous for the honor of his God and made atonementᵘ for the Israelites."

¹⁴The name of the Israelite who was killed with the Midianite woman was Zimri son of Salu, the leader of a Simeonite family. ¹⁵And the name of the Midianite woman who was put to death was Cozbiᵛ daughter of Zur, a tribal chief of a Midianite family.ʷ

ᵃ23 Masoretic Text; with a different word division of the Hebrew *A people will gather from the north.*

Cross references

24:24
ᵃ Ge 10:4
ᵇ Ge 10:21
ᶜ ver 20

24:25
ᵈ Nu 31:8

25:1
ᵉ Jos 2:1; Mic 6:5
ᶠ 1Co 10:8; Rev 2:14
ᵍ Nu 31:16

25:2
ʰ Ex 34:15
ⁱ Ex 20:5; Dt 32:38; 1Co 10:20

25:3
ʲ Ps 106:28; Hos 9:10

25:4
ᵏ Dt 4:3
ˡ Dt 13:17

25:5
ᵐ Ex 32:27

25:8
ⁿ Nu 16:46-48; Ps 106:30

25:9
ᵒ Nu 14:37; 1Co 10:8
ᵖ Nu 31:16

25:11
q Ps 106:30
ʳ Ex 20:5; Dt 32:16,21; Ps 78:58

25:12
ˢ Isa 54:10; Eze 34:25; Mal 2:4,5

25:13
ᵗ Ex 29:9
ᵘ Nu 16:46

25:15
ᵛ ver 18
ʷ Nu 31:8; Jos 13:21

25:17
a Nu 31:1-3

25:18
b Nu 31:16

26:2
c Ex 30:11-16;
38:25-26;
Nu 1:2
d Nu 1:3

26:3
e Nu 33:48
f Nu 22:1

26:5
g Ge 46:9
h 1Ch 5:3

26:9
i Nu 16:1
j Nu 1:16
k Nu 16:2

26:10
l Nu 16:35,38

26:11
m Ex 6:24
n Nu 16:33;
Dt 24:16

26:12
o 1Ch 4:24

26:13
p Ge 46:10

26:14
q Nu 1:23

26:15
r Ge 46:16

¹⁶The Lord said to Moses, ¹⁷"Treat the Midianites*a* as enemies and kill them, ¹⁸because they treated you as enemies when they deceived you in the affair of Peor*b* and their sister Cozbi, the daughter of a Midianite leader, the woman who was killed when the plague came as a result of Peor."

Chapter 26 Theme

26 After the plague the Lord said to Moses and Eleazar son of Aaron, the priest, ²"Take a census*c* of the whole Israelite community by families—all those twenty years old or more who are able to serve in the army*d* of Israel." ³So on the plains of Moab*e* by the Jordan across from Jericho,*a f* Moses and Eleazar the priest spoke with them and said, ⁴"Take a census of the men twenty years old or more, as the Lord commanded Moses."

These were the Israelites who came out of Egypt:

⁵The descendants of Reuben, the firstborn son of Israel, were:

through Hanoch,*g* the Hanochite clan;
through Pallu,*h* the Palluite clan;
⁶through Hezron, the Hezronite clan;
through Carmi, the Carmite clan.

⁷These were the clans of Reuben; those numbered were 43,730.

⁸The son of Pallu was Eliab, ⁹and the sons of Eliab*i* were Nemuel, Dathan and Abiram. The same Dathan and Abiram were the community*j* officials who rebelled against Moses and Aaron and were among Korah's followers when they rebelled against the Lord.*k* ¹⁰The earth opened its mouth and swallowed them along with Korah, whose followers died when the fire devoured the 250 men. And they served as a warning sign.*l* ¹¹The line of Korah,*m* however, did not die out.*n*

¹²The descendants of Simeon by their clans were:

through Nemuel, the Nemuelite clan;
through Jamin,*o* the Jaminite clan;
through Jakin, the Jakinite clan;
¹³through Zerah,*p* the Zerahite clan;
through Shaul, the Shaulite clan.

¹⁴These were the clans of Simeon; there were 22,200 men.*q*

¹⁵The descendants of Gad by their clans were:

through Zephon,*r* the Zephonite clan;
through Haggi, the Haggite clan;
through Shuni, the Shunite clan;
¹⁶through Ozni, the Oznite clan;
through Eri, the Erite clan;

---

a 3 Hebrew *Jordan of Jericho*; possibly an ancient name for the Jordan River; also in verse 63

¹⁷through Arodi,[a] the Arodite clan;
through Areli, the Arelite clan.
¹⁸These were the clans of Gad;[a] those numbered were 40,500.

¹⁹Er and Onan were sons of Judah, but they died[b] in Canaan.
²⁰The descendants of Judah by their clans were:
through Shelah,[c] the Shelanite clan;
through Perez, the Perezite clan;
through Zerah, the Zerahite clan.[d]
²¹The descendants of Perez were:
through Hezron,[e] the Hezronite clan;
through Hamul, the Hamulite clan.
²²These were the clans of Judah;[f] those numbered were 76,500.

²³The descendants of Issachar by their clans were:
through Tola,[g] the Tolaite clan;
through Puah, the Puite[b] clan;
²⁴through Jashub,[h] the Jashubite clan;
through Shimron, the Shimronite clan.
²⁵These were the clans of Issachar;[i] those numbered were 64,300.

²⁶The descendants of Zebulun by their clans were:
through Sered, the Seredite clan;
through Elon, the Elonite clan;
through Jahleel, the Jahleelite clan.
²⁷These were the clans of Zebulun;[j] those numbered were 60,500.

²⁸The descendants of Joseph by their clans through Manasseh and Ephraim were:
²⁹The descendants of Manasseh:
through Makir,[k] the Makirite clan (Makir was the father of Gilead[l]);
through Gilead, the Gileadite clan.
³⁰These were the descendants of Gilead:
through Iezer,[m] the Iezerite clan;
through Helek, the Helekite clan;
³¹through Asriel, the Asrielite clan;
through Shechem, the Shechemite clan;
³²through Shemida, the Shemidaite clan;
through Hepher, the Hepherite clan.
³³(Zelophehad[n] son of Hepher had no sons; he had only daughters, whose names were Mahlah, Noah, Hoglah, Milcah and Tirzah.)[o]

a 17 Samaritan Pentateuch and Syriac (see also Gen. 46:16); Masoretic Text *Arod*
b 23 Samaritan Pentateuch, Septuagint, Vulgate and Syriac (see also 1 Chron. 7:1); Masoretic Text *through Puvah, the Punite*

26:18
a Nu 1:25;
Jos 13:24-28

26:19
b Ge 38:2-10;
46:12

26:20
c 1Ch 2:3
d Jos 7:17

26:21
e Ru 4:19;
1Ch 2:9

26:22
f Nu 1:27

26:23
g Ge 46:13;
1Ch 7:1

26:24
h Ge 46:13

26:25
i Nu 1:29

26:27
j Nu 1:31

26:29
k Jos 17:1
l Jdg 11:1

26:30
m Jos 17:2;
Jdg 6:11

26:33
n Nu 27:1
o Nu 36:11

26:34
a Nu 1:35

³⁴These were the clans of Manasseh; those numbered were 52,700.^a

³⁵These were the descendants of Ephraim by their clans:

through Shuthelah, the Shuthelahite clan;

through Beker, the Bekerite clan;

through Tahan, the Tahanite clan.

26:37
b Nu 1:33

³⁶These were the descendants of Shuthelah:

through Eran, the Eranite clan.

³⁷These were the clans of Ephraim;^b those numbered were 32,500.

These were the descendants of Joseph by their clans.

26:38
c Ge 46:21;
1Ch 7:6

³⁸The descendants of Benjamin^c by their clans were:

through Bela, the Belaite clan;

through Ashbel, the Ashbelite clan;

through Ahiram, the Ahiramite clan;

³⁹through Shupham,^a the Shuphamite clan;

through Hupham, the Huphamite clan.

26:40
d Ge 46:21;
1Ch 8:3

⁴⁰The descendants of Bela through Ard^d and Naaman were:

through Ard,^b the Ardite clan;

through Naaman, the Naamite clan.

⁴¹These were the clans of Benjamin;^e those numbered were 45,600.

26:41
e Nu 1:37

⁴²These were the descendants of Dan by their clans:

through Shuham,^f the Shuhamite clan.

These were the clans of Dan: ⁴³All of them were Shuhamite clans; and those numbered were 64,400.

26:42
f Ge 46:23

⁴⁴The descendants of Asher by their clans were:

through Imnah, the Imnite clan;

through Ishvi, the Ishvite clan;

through Beriah, the Beriite clan;

⁴⁵and through the descendants of Beriah:

through Heber, the Heberite clan;

through Malkiel, the Malkielite clan.

26:47
g Nu 1:41

⁴⁶(Asher had a daughter named Serah.)

⁴⁷These were the clans of Asher;^g those numbered were 53,400.

⁴⁸The descendants of Naphtali^h by their clans were:

through Jahzeel, the Jahzeelite clan;

through Guni, the Gunite clan;

26:48
h Ge 46:24;
1Ch 7:13

⁴⁹through Jezer, the Jezerite clan;

through Shillem, the Shillemite clan.

⁵⁰These were the clans of Naphtali;ⁱ those numbered were 45,400.

26:50
i Nu 1:43

a 39 A few manuscripts of the Masoretic Text, Samaritan Pentateuch, Vulgate and Syriac (see also Septuagint); most manuscripts of the Masoretic Text *Shephupham*
b 40 Samaritan Pentateuch and Vulgate (see also Septuagint); Masoretic Text does not have *through Ard.*

⁵¹The total number of the men of Israel was 601,730.ᵃ

⁵²The LORD said to Moses, ⁵³"The land is to be allotted to them as an inheritance based on the number of names.ᵇ ⁵⁴To a larger group give a larger inheritance, and to a smaller group a smaller one; each is to receive its inheritance according to the numberᶜ of those listed. ⁵⁵Be sure that the land is distributed by lot.ᵈ What each group inherits will be according to the names for its ancestral tribe. ⁵⁶Each inheritance is to be distributed by lot among the larger and smaller groups."

⁵⁷These were the Levitesᵉ who were counted by their clans:

through Gershon, the Gershonite clan;
through Kohath, the Kohathite clan;
through Merari, the Merarite clan.

⁵⁸These also were Levite clans:

the Libnite clan,
the Hebronite clan,
the Mahlite clan,
the Mushite clan,
the Korahite clan.

(Kohath was the forefather of Amram;ᶠ ⁵⁹the name of Amram's wife was Jochebed,ᵍ a descendant of Levi, who was born to the Levitesᵃ in Egypt. To Amram she bore Aaron, Mosesʰ and their sister Miriam. ⁶⁰Aaron was the father of Nadab and Abihu, Eleazar and Ithamar.ⁱ ⁶¹But Nadab and Abihuʲ died when they made an offering before the LORD with unauthorized fire.)ᵏ

⁶²All the male Levites a month old or more numbered 23,000.ˡ They were not countedᵐ along with the other Israelites because they received no inheritanceⁿ among them.ᵒ

⁶³These are the ones counted by Moses and Eleazar the priest when they counted the Israelites on the plains of Moabᵖ by the Jordan across from Jericho. ⁶⁴Not one of them was among those counted�q by Moses and Aaron the priest when they counted the Israelites in the Desert of Sinai. ⁶⁵For the LORD had told those Israelites they would surely die in the desert,ʳ and not one of them was left except Caleb son of Jephunneh and Joshua son of Nun.ˢ

Chapter 27 Theme

27 The daughters of Zelophehadᵗ son of Hepher,ᵘ the son of Gilead, the son of Makir,ᵛ the son of Manasseh, belonged to the clans of Manasseh son of Joseph. The names of the daughters were Mahlah, Noah, Hoglah, Milcah and Tirzah. They approached ²the entrance to the Tent of Meeting and stood before

ᵃ59 Or *Jochebed, a daughter of Levi, who was born to Levi*

26:51
ᵃ Ex 12:37;
38:26;
Nu 1:46;
11:21

26:53
ᵇ Jos 11:23; 14:1;
Eze 45:8

26:54
ᶜ Nu 33:54

26:55
ᵈ Nu 34:14

26:57
ᵉ Ge 46:11;
Ex 6:16-19

26:58
ᶠ Ex 6:20

26:59
ᵍ Ex 2:1
ʰ Ex 6:20

26:60
ⁱ Nu 3:2

26:61
ʲ Lev 10:1-2
ᵏ Nu 3:4

26:62
ˡ Nu 3:39
ᵐ Nu 1:47
ⁿ Nu 18:23
ᵒ Nu 2:33;
Dt 10:9

26:63
ᵖ ver 3

26:64
q Nu 14:29;
Dt 2:14-15;
Heb 3:17

26:65
ʳ Nu 14:28;
1Co 10:5
ˢ Jos 14:6-10

27:1
ᵗ Nu 26:33
ᵘ Jos 17:2,3
ᵛ Nu 36:1

27:3
a Nu 26:65
b Nu 16:2
c Nu 26:33

27:5
d Ex 18:19
e Nu 9:8

27:7
f Job 42:15
g Jos 17:4

27:11
h Nu 35:29

27:12
i Nu 33:47;
Jer 22:20
j Dt 3:23-27;
32:48-52

27:13
k Nu 31:2
l Nu 20:28

27:14
m Nu 20:12
n Ex 17:7;
Dt 32:51;
Ps 106:32

27:16
o Nu 16:22

27:17
p Dt 31:2;
1Ki 22:17;
Eze 34:5;
Zec 10:2;
Mt 9:36;
Mk 6:34

27:18
q Ge 41:38;
Nu 11:25-29
r ver 23;
Dt 34:9

27:19
s Dt 3:28;
31:14,23
t Dt 31:7

27:20
u Jos 1:16,17

27:21
v Jos 9:14
w Ex 28:30

Moses, Eleazar the priest, the leaders and the whole assembly, and said, ³"Our father died in the desert.ᵃ He was not among Korah's followers, who banded together against the LORD,ᵇ but he died for his own sin and left no sons.ᶜ ⁴Why should our father's name disappear from his clan because he had no son? Give us property among our father's relatives."

⁵So Moses brought their caseᵈ before the LORDᵉ ⁶and the LORD said to him, ⁷"What Zelophehad's daughters are saying is right. You must certainly give them property as an inheritanceᶠ among their father's relatives and turn their father's inheritance over to them.ᵍ

⁸"Say to the Israelites, 'If a man dies and leaves no son, turn his inheritance over to his daughter. ⁹If he has no daughter, give his inheritance to his brothers. ¹⁰If he has no brothers, give his inheritance to his father's brothers. ¹¹If his father had no brothers, give his inheritance to the nearest relative in his clan, that he may possess it. This is to be a legal requirementʰ for the Israelites, as the LORD commanded Moses.'"

¹²Then the LORD said to Moses, "Go up this mountain in the Abarim rangeⁱ and see the landʲ I have given the Israelites. ¹³After you have seen it, you too will be gathered to your people,ᵏ as your brother Aaronˡ was, ¹⁴for when the community rebelled at the waters in the Desert of Zin, both of you disobeyed my command to honor me as holyᵐ before their eyes." (These were the waters of Meribahⁿ Kadesh, in the Desert of Zin.)

¹⁵Moses said to the LORD, ¹⁶"May the LORD, the God of the spirits of all mankind,ᵒ appoint a man over this community ¹⁷to go out and come in before them, one who will lead them out and bring them in, so the LORD's people will not be like sheep without a shepherd."ᵖ

¹⁸So the LORD said to Moses, "Take Joshua son of Nun, a man in whom is the spirit,ᵃᵠ and lay your hand on him.ʳ ¹⁹Have him stand before Eleazar the priest and the entire assembly and commission himˢ in their presence.ᵗ ²⁰Give him some of your authority so the whole Israelite community will obey him.ᵘ ²¹He is to stand before Eleazar the priest, who will obtain decisions for him by inquiringᵛ of the Urimʷ before the LORD. At his command he and the entire community of the Israelites will go out, and at his command they will come in."

²²Moses did as the LORD commanded him. He took Joshua and had him stand before Eleazar the priest and the whole assembly. ²³Then he laid his hands on him and commissioned him, as the LORD instructed through Moses.

a 18 Or Spirit

267

Chapter 28 Theme _____

28 The LORD said to Moses, [2]"Give this command to the Israelites and say to them: 'See that you present to me at the appointed time the food*a* for my offerings made by fire, as an aroma pleasing to me.' [3]Say to them: 'This is the offering made by fire that you are to present to the LORD: two lambs a year old without defect, as a regular burnt offering each day.*b* [4]Prepare one lamb in the morning and the other at twilight, [5]together with a grain offering of a tenth of an ephah*a* of fine flour mixed with a quarter of a hin*b* of oil*c* from pressed olives. [6]This is the regular burnt offering instituted at Mount Sinai*d* as a pleasing aroma, an offering made to the LORD by fire. [7]The accompanying drink offering*e* is to be a quarter of a hin of fermented drink with each lamb. Pour out the drink offering to the LORD at the sanctuary.*f* [8]Prepare the second lamb at twilight, along with the same kind of grain offering and drink offering that you prepare in the morning. This is an offering made by fire, an aroma pleasing to the LORD.*g*

[9]"'On the Sabbath*h* day, make an offering of two lambs a year old without defect, together with its drink offering and a grain offering of two-tenths of an ephah*c i* of fine flour mixed with oil. [10]This is the burnt offering for every Sabbath, in addition to the regular burnt offering*j* and its drink offering.

[11]"'On the first of every month,*k* present to the LORD a burnt offering of two young bulls, one ram and seven male lambs a year old, all without defect.*l* [12]With each bull there is to be a grain offering*m* of three-tenths of an ephah*d n* of fine flour mixed with oil; with the ram, a grain offering of two-tenths of an ephah of fine flour mixed with oil; [13]and with each lamb, a grain offering*o* of a tenth of an ephah of fine flour mixed with oil. This is for a burnt offering, a pleasing aroma, an offering made to the LORD by fire. [14]With each bull there is to be a drink offering*p* of half a hin*e* of wine; with the ram, a third of a hin*f*; and with each lamb, a quarter of a hin. This is the monthly burnt offering to be made at each new moon*q* during the year. [15]Besides the regular burnt offering*r* with its drink offering, one male goat is to be presented to the LORD as a sin offering.*s*

[16]"'On the fourteenth day of the first month the LORD's Passover*t* is to be held. [17]On the fifteenth day of this month there is to be a festival; for seven days*u* eat bread made without yeast.*v* [18]On

---

a5 That is, probably about 2 quarts (about 2 liters); also in verses 13, 21 and 29   *b5* That is, probably about 1 quart (about 1 liter); also in verses 7 and 14   *c9* That is, probably about 4 quarts (about 4.5 liters); also in verses 12, 20 and 28   *d12* That is, probably about 6 quarts (about 6.5 liters); also in verses 20 and 28   *e14* That is, probably about 2 quarts (about 2 liters)   *f14* That is, probably about 1 1/4 quarts (about 1.2 liters)

28:2
a Lev 3:11

28:3
b Ex 29:38

28:5
c Lev 2:1;
Nu 15:4

28:6
d Ex 19:3

28:7
e Ex 29:41
f Lev 3:7

28:8
g Lev 1:9

28:9
h Ex 20:10
i Lev 23:13

28:10
j ver 3

28:11
k Nu 10:10
l Lev 1:3

28:12
m Nu 15:6
n Nu 15:9

28:13
o Lev 6:14

28:14
p Nu 15:7
q Ezr 3:5

28:15
r ver 3,23,24
s Lev 4:3

28:16
t Ex 12:6,18;
Lev 23:5;
Dt 16:1

28:17
u Ex 12:19
v Ex 23:15;
34:18;
Lev 23:6;
Dt 16:3-8

28:18
a Ex 12:16;
Lev 23:7

28:20
b Lev 14:10

28:22
c Ro 8:3
d Nu 15:28

28:26
e Ex 34:22
f Ex 23:16
g ver 18;
Dt 16:10

28:29
h ver 13

28:31
i ver 3,19

29:1
j Lev 23:24

29:2
k Nu 28:2
l Nu 28:3

29:5
m Nu 28:15

29:6
n Nu 28:11
o Nu 28:3

29:7
p Ac 27:9
q Ex 31:15;
Lev 16:29;
23:26-32

the first day hold a sacred assembly and do no regular work.[a] [19]Present to the LORD an offering made by fire, a burnt offering of two young bulls, one ram and seven male lambs a year old, all without defect. [20]With each bull prepare a grain offering of three-tenths of an ephah[b] of fine flour mixed with oil; with the ram, two-tenths; [21]and with each of the seven lambs, one-tenth. [22]Include one male goat as a sin offering[c] to make atonement for you.[d] [23]Prepare these in addition to the regular morning burnt offering. [24]In this way prepare the food for the offering made by fire every day for seven days as an aroma pleasing to the LORD; it is to be prepared in addition to the regular burnt offering and its drink offering. [25]On the seventh day hold a sacred assembly and do no regular work.

[26]"'On the day of firstfruits,[e] when you present to the LORD an offering of new grain during the Feast of Weeks,[f] hold a sacred assembly and do no regular work.[g] [27]Present a burnt offering of two young bulls, one ram and seven male lambs a year old as an aroma pleasing to the LORD. [28]With each bull there is to be a grain offering of three-tenths of an ephah of fine flour mixed with oil; with the ram, two-tenths; [29]and with each of the seven lambs, one-tenth.[h] [30]Include one male goat to make atonement for you. [31]Prepare these together with their drink offerings, in addition to the regular burnt offering[i] and its grain offering. Be sure the animals are without defect.

Chapter 29 Theme

29 "'On the first day of the seventh month hold a sacred assembly and do no regular work.[j] It is a day for you to sound the trumpets. [2]As an aroma pleasing to the LORD,[k] prepare a burnt offering of one young bull, one ram and seven male lambs a year old, all without defect.[l] [3]With the bull prepare a grain offering of three-tenths of an ephah[a] of fine flour mixed with oil; with the ram, two-tenths[b]; [4]and with each of the seven lambs, one-tenth.[c] [5]Include one male goat[m] as a sin offering to make atonement for you. [6]These are in addition to the monthly[n] and daily burnt offerings[o] with their grain offerings and drink offerings as specified. They are offerings made to the LORD by fire—a pleasing aroma.

[7]"'On the tenth day of this seventh month hold a sacred assembly. You must deny yourselves[d][p] and do no work.[q] [8]Present as an aroma pleasing to the LORD a burnt offering of one young bull, one ram and seven male lambs a year old, all without defect.

a3 That is, probably about 6 quarts (about 6.5 liters); also in verses 9 and 14   b3 That is, probably about 4 quarts (about 4.5 liters); also in verses 9 and 14   c4 That is, probably about 2 quarts (about 2 liters); also in verses 10 and 15   d7 Or *must fast*

⁹With the bull prepare a grain offering*a* of three-tenths of an ephah of fine flour mixed with oil; with the ram, two-tenths; ¹⁰and with each of the seven lambs, one-tenth.*b* ¹¹Include one male goat as a sin offering, in addition to the sin offering for atonement and the regular burnt offering*c* with its grain offering, and their drink offerings.

¹²"'On the fifteenth day of the seventh*d* month,*e* hold a sacred assembly and do no regular work. Celebrate a festival to the LORD for seven days. ¹³Present an offering made by fire as an aroma pleasing to the LORD, a burnt offering of thirteen young bulls, two rams and fourteen male lambs a year old, all without defect. ¹⁴With each of the thirteen bulls prepare a grain offering*f* of three-tenths of an ephah of fine flour mixed with oil; with each of the two rams, two-tenths; ¹⁵and with each of the fourteen lambs, one-tenth. ¹⁶Include one male goat as a sin offering, in addition to the regular burnt offering with its grain offering and drink offering.*g*

¹⁷"'On the second day*h* prepare twelve young bulls, two rams and fourteen male lambs a year old, all without defect.*i* ¹⁸With the bulls, rams and lambs, prepare their grain offerings*j* and drink offerings*k* according to the number specified.*l* ¹⁹Include one male goat as a sin offering,*m* in addition to the regular burnt offering with its grain offering, and their drink offerings.

²⁰"'On the third day prepare eleven bulls, two rams and fourteen male lambs a year old, all without defect.*n* ²¹With the bulls, rams and lambs, prepare their grain offerings and drink offerings according to the number specified.*o* ²²Include one male goat as a sin offering, in addition to the regular burnt offering with its grain offering and drink offering.

²³"'On the fourth day prepare ten bulls, two rams and fourteen male lambs a year old, all without defect. ²⁴With the bulls, rams and lambs, prepare their grain offerings and drink offerings according to the number specified. ²⁵Include one male goat as a sin offering, in addition to the regular burnt offering with its grain offering and drink offering.

²⁶"'On the fifth day prepare nine bulls, two rams and fourteen male lambs a year old, all without defect. ²⁷With the bulls, rams and lambs, prepare their grain offerings and drink offerings according to the number specified. ²⁸Include one male goat as a sin offering, in addition to the regular burnt offering with its grain offering and drink offering.

²⁹"'On the sixth day prepare eight bulls, two rams and fourteen male lambs a year old, all without defect. ³⁰With the bulls, rams and lambs, prepare their grain offerings and drink offerings according to the number specified. ³¹Include one male goat as a sin

---

29:9
a ver 3,18

29:10
b Nu 28:13

29:11
c Lev 16:3;
Nu 28:3

29:12
d 1Ki 8:2
e Lev 23:24

29:14
f ver 3

29:16
g ver 6

29:17
h Lev 23:36
i Nu 28:3

29:18
j ver 9
k Nu 28:7
l Nu 15:4-12

29:19
m Nu 28:15

29:20
n ver 17

29:21
o ver 18

offering, in addition to the regular burnt offering with its grain offering and drink offering.

32 " 'On the seventh day prepare seven bulls, two rams and fourteen male lambs a year old, all without defect. 33With the bulls, rams and lambs, prepare their grain offerings and drink offerings according to the number specified. 34Include one male goat as a sin offering, in addition to the regular burnt offering with its grain offering and drink offering.

35 " 'On the eighth day hold an assembly[a] and do no regular work. 36Present an offering made by fire as an aroma pleasing to the LORD,[b] a burnt offering of one bull, one ram and seven male lambs a year old,[c] all without defect. 37With the bull, the ram and the lambs, prepare their grain offerings and drink offerings according to the number specified. 38Include one male goat as a sin offering, in addition to the regular burnt offering with its grain offering and drink offering.

39 " 'In addition to what you vow[d] and your freewill offerings, prepare these for the LORD at your appointed feasts:[e] your burnt offerings,[f] grain offerings, drink offerings and fellowship offerings.[a] ' "

40Moses told the Israelites all that the LORD commanded him.

Chapter 30 Theme _____

30 Moses said to the heads of the tribes of Israel:[g] "This is what the LORD commands: 2When a man makes a vow to the LORD or takes an oath to obligate himself by a pledge, he must not break his word but must do everything he said.[h]

3 "When a young woman still living in her father's house makes a vow to the LORD or obligates herself by a pledge 4and her father hears about her vow or pledge but says nothing to her, then all her vows and every pledge by which she obligated herself will stand.[i] 5But if her father forbids her when he hears about it, none of her vows or the pledges by which she obligated herself will stand; the LORD will release her because her father has forbidden her.

6 "If she marries after she makes a vow[j] or after her lips utter a rash promise by which she obligates herself 7and her husband hears about it but says nothing to her, then her vows or the pledges by which she obligated herself will stand. 8But if her husband[k] forbids her when he hears about it, he nullifies the vow that obligates her or the rash promise by which she obligates herself, and the LORD will release her.

9 "Any vow or obligation taken by a widow or divorced woman will be binding on her.

29:35
a Lev 23:36

29:36
b Lev 1:9
c ver 2

29:39
d Nu 6:2
e Lev 23:2
f Lev 1:3;
1Ch 23:31;
2Ch 31:3

30:1
g Nu 1:4

30:2
h Dt 23:21-23;
Jdg 11:35;
Job 22:27;
Ps 22:25; 50:14;
116:14;
Pr 20:25;
Ecc 5:4,5;
Jnh 1:16

30:4
i ver 7

30:6
j Lev 5:4

30:8
k Ge 3:16

a 39 Traditionally *peace offerings*

¹⁰"If a woman living with her husband makes a vow or obligates herself by a pledge under oath ¹¹and her husband hears about it but says nothing to her and does not forbid her, then all her vows or the pledges by which she obligated herself will stand. ¹²But if her husband nullifies them when he hears about them, then none of the vows or pledges that came from her lips will stand.^a Her husband has nullified them, and the LORD will release her. ¹³Her husband may confirm or nullify any vow she makes or any sworn pledge to deny herself. ¹⁴But if her husband says nothing to her about it from day to day, then he confirms all her vows or the pledges binding on her. He confirms them by saying nothing to her when he hears about them. ¹⁵If, however, he nullifies them some time after he hears about them, then he is responsible for her guilt."

¹⁶These are the regulations the LORD gave Moses concerning relationships between a man and his wife, and between a father and his young daughter still living in his house.

Chapter 31 Theme

31 The LORD said to Moses, ²"Take vengeance on the Midianites^b for the Israelites. After that, you will be gathered to your people.^c"

³So Moses said to the people, "Arm some of your men to go to war against the Midianites and to carry out the LORD's vengeance^d on them. ⁴Send into battle a thousand men from each of the tribes of Israel." ⁵So twelve thousand men armed for battle, a thousand from each tribe, were supplied from the clans of Israel. ⁶Moses sent them into battle, a thousand from each tribe, along with Phinehas son of Eleazar, the priest, who took with him articles from the sanctuary^e and the trumpets^f for signaling.

⁷They fought against Midian, as the LORD commanded Moses, and killed every man.^g ⁸Among their victims were Evi, Rekem, Zur, Hur and Reba^h—the five kings of Midian.ⁱ They also killed Balaam son of Beor with the sword.^j ⁹The Israelites captured the Midianite women and children and took all the Midianite herds, flocks and goods as plunder. ¹⁰They burned all the towns where the Midianites had settled, as well as all their camps.^k ¹¹They took all the plunder and spoils, including the people and animals,^l ¹²and brought the captives, spoils and plunder to Moses and Eleazar the priest and the Israelite assembly^m at their camp on the plains of Moab, by the Jordan across from Jericho.^a

¹³Moses, Eleazar the priest and all the leaders of the community went to meet them outside the camp. ¹⁴Moses was angry with the

---

30:12
^aEph 5:22;
Col 3:18

31:2
^bGe 25:2
^cNu 20:26;
27:13

31:3
^dJdg 11:36;
1Sa 24:12;
2Sa 4:8; 22:48;
Ps 94:1; 149:7

31:6
^eNu 14:44
^fNu 10:9

31:7
^gDt 20:13;
Jdg 21:11;
1Ki 11:15,16

31:8
^hJos 13:21
ⁱNu 25:15
^jJos 13:22

31:10
^kGe 25:16;
1Ch 6:54;
Ps 69:25;
Eze 25:4

31:11
^lDt 20:14

31:12
^mNu 27:2

---

^a12 Hebrew *Jordan of Jericho*; possibly an ancient name for the Jordan River

officers of the army[a]—the commanders of thousands and commanders of hundreds—who returned from the battle.

[15]"Have you allowed all the women to live?" he asked them. [16]"They were the ones who followed Balaam's advice[b] and were the means of turning the Israelites away from the LORD in what happened at Peor,[c] so that a plague struck the LORD's people. [17]Now kill all the boys. And kill every woman who has slept with a man,[d] [18]but save for yourselves every girl who has never slept with a man.

[19]"All of you who have killed anyone or touched anyone who was killed[e] must stay outside the camp seven days. On the third and seventh days you must purify yourselves[f] and your captives. [20]Purify every garment[g] as well as everything made of leather, goat hair or wood."

[21]Then Eleazar the priest said to the soldiers who had gone into battle, "This is the requirement of the law that the LORD gave Moses: [22]Gold, silver, bronze, iron,[h] tin, lead [23]and anything else that can withstand fire must be put through the fire,[i] and then it will be clean. But it must also be purified with the water of cleansing.[j] And whatever cannot withstand fire must be put through that water. [24]On the seventh day wash your clothes and you will be clean.[k] Then you may come into the camp."

[25]The LORD said to Moses, [26]"You and Eleazar the priest and the family heads of the community are to count all the people[l] and animals that were captured. [27]Divide[m] the spoils between the soldiers who took part in the battle and the rest of the community. [28]From the soldiers who fought in the battle, set apart as tribute for the LORD[n] one out of every five hundred, whether persons, cattle, donkeys, sheep or goats. [29]Take this tribute from their half share and give it to Eleazar the priest as the LORD's part. [30]From the Israelites' half, select one out of every fifty, whether persons, cattle, donkeys, sheep, goats or other animals. Give them to the Levites, who are responsible for the care of the LORD's tabernacle.[o]" [31]So Moses and Eleazar the priest did as the LORD commanded Moses.

[32]The plunder remaining from the spoils that the soldiers took was 675,000 sheep, [33]72,000 cattle, [34]61,000 donkeys [35]and 32,000 women who had never slept with a man.

[36]The half share of those who fought in the battle was:

337,500 sheep, [37]of which the tribute for the LORD[p] was 675;
[38]36,000 cattle, of which the tribute for the LORD was 72;
[39]30,500 donkeys, of which the tribute for the LORD was 61;
[40]16,000 people, of which the tribute for the LORD was 32.

31:14
[a] ver 48;
Ex 18:21;
Dt 1:15

31:16
[b] 2Pe 2:15;
Rev 2:14
[c] Nu 25:1-9

31:17
[d] Dt 7:2;
20:16-18;
Jdg 21:11

31:19
[e] Nu 19:16
[f] Nu 19:12

31:20
[g] Nu 19:19

31:22
[h] Jos 6:19; 22:8

31:23
[i] 1Co 3:13
[j] Nu 19:9,17

31:24
[k] Lev 11:25

31:26
[l] Nu 1:19

31:27
[m] Jos 22:8;
1Sa 30:24

31:28
[n] Nu 18:21

31:30
[o] Nu 3:7; 18:3

31:37
[p] ver 38-41

⁴¹Moses gave the tribute to Eleazar the priest as the LORD's part,ᵃ as the LORD commanded Moses.

⁴²The half belonging to the Israelites, which Moses set apart from that of the fighting men— ⁴³the community's half—was 337,500 sheep, ⁴⁴36,000 cattle, ⁴⁵30,500 donkeys ⁴⁶and 16,000 people. ⁴⁷From the Israelites' half, Moses selected one out of every fifty persons and animals, as the LORD commanded him, and gave them to the Levites, who were responsible for the care of the LORD's tabernacle.

⁴⁸Then the officers who were over the units of the army—the commanders of thousands and commanders of hundreds— went to Moses ⁴⁹and said to him, "Your servants have counted the soldiers under our command, and not one is missing.ᵇ ⁵⁰So we have brought as an offering to the LORD the gold articles each of us acquired—armlets, bracelets, signet rings, earrings and necklaces—to make atonement for ourselvesᶜ before the LORD."

⁵¹Moses and Eleazar the priest accepted from them the gold— all the crafted articles. ⁵²All the gold from the commanders of thousands and commanders of hundreds that Moses and Eleazar presented as a gift to the LORD weighed 16,750 shekels.ᵃ ⁵³Each soldier had taken plunderᵈ for himself. ⁵⁴Moses and Eleazar the priest accepted the gold from the commanders of thousands and commanders of hundreds and brought it into the Tent of Meeting as a memorialᵉ for the Israelites before the LORD.

Chapter 32 Theme

32 The Reubenites and Gadites, who had very large herds and flocks, saw that the lands of Jazerᶠ and Gilead were suitable for livestock.ᵍ ²So they came to Moses and Eleazar the priest and to the leaders of the community, and said, ³"Ataroth,ʰ Dibon, Jazer, Nimrah,ⁱ Heshbon, Elealeh,ʲ Sebam, Nebo and Beonᵏ— ⁴the land the LORD subduedˡ before the people of Israel—are suitable for livestock,ᵐ and your servants have livestock. ⁵If we have found favor in your eyes," they said, "let this land be given to your servants as our possession. Do not make us cross the Jordan."

⁶Moses said to the Gadites and Reubenites, "Shall your countrymen go to war while you sit here? ⁷Why do you discourage the Israelites from going over into the land the LORD has given them?ⁿ ⁸This is what your fathers did when I sent them from Kadesh Barnea to look over the land.ᵒ ⁹After they went up to the Valley of Eshcolᵖ and viewed the land, they discouraged the Israelites from entering the land the LORD had given them. ¹⁰The LORD's anger was arousedᵠ that day and he swore this oath: ¹¹"Because they

ᵃ 52 That is, about 420 pounds (about 190 kilograms)

31:41
ᵃ Nu 5:9; 18:8

31:49
ᵇ Jer 23:4

31:50
ᶜ Ex 30:16

31:53
ᵈ Dt 20:14

31:54
ᵉ Ex 28:12

32:1
ᶠ Nu 21:32
ᵍ Ex 12:38

32:3
ʰ ver 34
ⁱ ver 36
ʲ ver 37;
Isa 15:4; 16:9;
Jer 48:34
ᵏ ver 38;
Jos 13:17;
Eze 25:9

32:4
ˡ Nu 21:34
ᵐ Ex 12:38

32:7
ⁿ Nu 13:27–14:4

32:8
ᵒ Nu 13:3,26;
Dt 1:19-25

32:9
ᵖ Nu 13:23;
Dt 1:24

32:10
ᵠ Nu 11:1

32:11
aEx 30:14
bNu 14:23
cNu 14:28-30

32:12
dNu 14:24,30;
Dt 1:36;
Ps 63:8

32:13
eEx 4:14
fNu 14:28-35;
26:64,65

32:14
gver 10;
Dt 1:34;
Ps 78:59

32:15
hDt 30:17-18;
2Ch 7:20

32:16
iEx 12:38;
Dt 3:19

32:17
jJos 4:12,13
kNu 22:4;
Dt 3:20

32:18
lJos 22:1-4

32:19
mJos 12:1

32:20
nDt 3:18

32:22
oJos 22:4
pDt 3:18-20

32:23
qGe 4:7; 44:16;
Isa 59:12

32:24
rver 1,16
sNu 30:2

32:26
tJos 1:14

32:28
uDt 3:18-20;
Jos 1:13

have not followed me wholeheartedly, not one of the men twenty years old or more^a who came up out of Egypt will see the land I promised on oath^b to Abraham, Isaac and Jacob^c— ¹²not one except Caleb son of Jephunneh the Kenizzite and Joshua son of Nun, for they followed the LORD wholeheartedly.'^d ¹³The LORD's anger burned against Israel^e and he made them wander in the desert forty years, until the whole generation of those who had done evil in his sight was gone.^f

¹⁴"And here you are, a brood of sinners, standing in the place of your fathers and making the LORD even more angry with Israel.^g ¹⁵If you turn away from following him, he will again leave all this people in the desert, and you will be the cause of their destruction.^h"

¹⁶Then they came up to him and said, "We would like to build pens here for our livestockⁱ and cities for our women and children. ¹⁷But we are ready to arm ourselves and go ahead of the Israelites ^j until we have brought them to their place.^k Meanwhile our women and children will live in fortified cities, for protection from the inhabitants of the land. ¹⁸We will not return to our homes until every Israelite has received his inheritance.^l ¹⁹We will not receive any inheritance with them on the other side of the Jordan, because our inheritance has come to us on the east side of the Jordan."^m

²⁰Then Moses said to them, "If you will do this—if you will arm yourselves before the LORD for battle,ⁿ ²¹and if all of you will go armed over the Jordan before the LORD until he has driven his enemies out before him— ²²then when the land is subdued before the LORD, you may return^o and be free from your obligation to the LORD and to Israel. And this land will be your possession before the LORD.^p

²³"But if you fail to do this, you will be sinning against the LORD; and you may be sure that your sin will find you out.^q ²⁴Build cities for your women and children, and pens for your flocks,^r but do what you have promised.^s"

²⁵The Gadites and Reubenites said to Moses, "We your servants will do as our lord commands. ²⁶Our children and wives, our flocks and herds will remain here in the cities of Gilead.^t ²⁷But your servants, every man armed for battle, will cross over to fight before the LORD, just as our lord says."

²⁸Then Moses gave orders about them^u to Eleazar the priest and Joshua son of Nun and to the family heads of the Israelite tribes. ²⁹He said to them, "If the Gadites and Reubenites, every man armed for battle, cross over the Jordan with you before the LORD, then when the land is subdued before you, give them the land of Gilead as their possession. ³⁰But if they do not cross over with you armed, they must accept their possession with you in Canaan."

³¹The Gadites and Reubenites answered, "Your servants will do what the LORD has said.ᵃ ³²We will cross over before the LORD into Canaan armed, but the property we inherit will be on this side of the Jordan."

³³Then Moses gave to the Gadites,ᵇ the Reubenites and the half-tribe of Manasseh son of Joseph the kingdom of Sihon king of the Amoritesᶜ and the kingdom of Og king of Bashan—the whole land with its cities and the territory around them.ᵈ

³⁴The Gadites built up Dibon, Ataroth, Aroer,ᵉ ³⁵Atroth Shophan, Jazer,ᶠ Jogbehah, ³⁶Beth Nimrahᵍ and Beth Haran as fortified cities, and built pens for their flocks. ³⁷And the Reubenites rebuilt Heshbon, Elealeh and Kiriathaim, ³⁸as well as Neboʰ and Baal Meon (these names were changed) and Sibmah. They gave names to the cities they rebuilt.

³⁹The descendants of Makirⁱ son of Manasseh went to Gilead, captured it and drove out the Amorites who were there. ⁴⁰So Moses gave Gilead to the Makirites,ʲ the descendants of Manasseh, and they settled there. ⁴¹Jair, a descendant of Manasseh, captured their settlements and called them Havvoth Jair.ᵃᵏ ⁴²And Nobah captured Kenath and its surrounding settlements and called it Nobah after himself.ˡ

Chapter 33 Theme _____

33 Here are the stages in the journey of the Israelites when they came out of Egyptᵐ by divisions under the leadership of Moses and Aaron.ⁿ ²At the LORD's command Moses recorded the stages in their journey. This is their journey by stages:

³The Israelites set out from Rameses on the fifteenth day of the first month, the day after the Passover.ᵒ They marched out boldlyᵖ in full view of all the Egyptians, ⁴who were burying all their firstborn, whom the LORD had struck down among them; for the LORD had brought judgment on their gods.�q

⁵The Israelites left Rameses and camped at Succoth.ʳ ⁶They left Succoth and camped at Etham, on the edge of the desert.ˢ ⁷They left Etham, turned back to Pi Hahiroth, to the east of Baal Zephon,ᵗ and camped near Migdol.ᵘ ⁸They left Pi Hahirothᵇ and passed through the seaᵛ into the desert, and when they had traveled for three days in the Desert of Etham, they camped at Marah.ʷ ⁹They left Marah and went to Elim, where there were twelve springs and seventy palm trees, and they campedˣ there.

ᵃ41 Or *them the settlements of Jair* ᵇ8 Many manuscripts of the Masoretic Text, Samaritan Pentateuch and Vulgate; most manuscripts of the Masoretic Text *left from before Hahiroth*

32:31
ᵃver 29

32:33
ᵇJos 13:24-28;
1Sa 13:7
ᶜDt 2:26
ᵈNu 21:24;
Jos 12:6

32:34
ᵉDt 2:36;
Jdg 11:26

32:35
ᶠver 3

32:36
ᵍver 3

32:38
ʰver 3;
Isa 15:2;
Jer 48:1,22

32:39
ⁱGe 50:23

32:40
ʲDt 3:15;
Jos 17:1

32:41
ᵏDt 3:14;
Jos 13:30;
Jdg 10:4;
1Ch 2:23

32:42
ˡ2Sa 18:18;
Ps 49:11

33:1
ᵐMic 6:4
ⁿPs 77:20

33:3
ᵒEx 13:4
ᵖEx 14:8

33:4
qEx 12:12

33:5
ʳEx 12:37

33:6
ˢEx 13:20

33:7
ᵗEx 14:9
ᵘEx 14:2

33:8
ᵛEx 14:22
ʷEx 15:23

33:9
ˣEx 15:27

33:11
a Ex 16:1

33:15
b Ex 17:1
c Ex 19:1

33:16
d Nu 11:34

33:17
e Nu 11:35

33:20
f Jos 10:29

33:30
g Dt 10:6

33:33
h Dt 10:7

33:35
i Dt 2:8;
1Ki 9:26; 22:48

33:36
j Nu 20:1

33:37
k Nu 20:22
l Nu 20:16; 21:4

33:38
m Dt 10:6
n Nu 20:25-28

33:40
o Nu 21:1

33:43
p Nu 21:10

33:44
q Nu 21:11

[10]They left Elim and camped by the Red Sea.[a]

[11]They left the Red Sea and camped in the Desert of Sin.[a]

[12]They left the Desert of Sin and camped at Dophkah.

[13]They left Dophkah and camped at Alush.

[14]They left Alush and camped at Rephidim, where there was no water for the people to drink.

[15]They left Rephidim[b] and camped in the Desert of Sinai.[c]

[16]They left the Desert of Sinai and camped at Kibroth Hattaavah.[d]

[17]They left Kibroth Hattaavah and camped at Hazeroth.[e]

[18]They left Hazeroth and camped at Rithmah.

[19]They left Rithmah and camped at Rimmon Perez.

[20]They left Rimmon Perez and camped at Libnah.[f]

[21]They left Libnah and camped at Rissah.

[22]They left Rissah and camped at Kehelathah.

[23]They left Kehelathah and camped at Mount Shepher.

[24]They left Mount Shepher and camped at Haradah.

[25]They left Haradah and camped at Makheloth.

[26]They left Makheloth and camped at Tahath.

[27]They left Tahath and camped at Terah.

[28]They left Terah and camped at Mithcah.

[29]They left Mithcah and camped at Hashmonah.

[30]They left Hashmonah and camped at Moseroth.[g]

[31]They left Moseroth and camped at Bene Jaakan.

[32]They left Bene Jaakan and camped at Hor Haggidgad.

[33]They left Hor Haggidgad and camped at Jotbathah.[h]

[34]They left Jotbathah and camped at Abronah.

[35]They left Abronah and camped at Ezion Geber.[i]

[36]They left Ezion Geber and camped at Kadesh, in the Desert of Zin.[j]

[37]They left Kadesh and camped at Mount Hor,[k] on the border of Edom.[l] [38]At the LORD's command Aaron the priest went up Mount Hor, where he died[m] on the first day of the fifth month of the fortieth year after the Israelites came out of Egypt.[n] [39]Aaron was a hundred and twenty-three years old when he died on Mount Hor.

[40]The Canaanite king of Arad,[o] who lived in the Negev of Canaan, heard that the Israelites were coming.

[41]They left Mount Hor and camped at Zalmonah.

[42]They left Zalmonah and camped at Punon.

[43]They left Punon and camped at Oboth.[p]

[44]They left Oboth and camped at Iye Abarim, on the border of Moab.[q]

[45]They left Iyim[b] and camped at Dibon Gad.

a 10 Hebrew *Yam Suph*; that is, Sea of Reeds; also in verse 11   b 45 That is, Iye Abarim

⁴⁶They left Dibon Gad and camped at Almon Diblathaim.

⁴⁷They left Almon Diblathaim and camped in the mountains of Abarim,ᵃ near Nebo.

⁴⁸They left the mountains of Abarim and camped on the plains of Moab by the Jordan across from Jericho.ᵃᵇ ⁴⁹There on the plains of Moab they camped along the Jordan from Beth Jeshimoth to Abel Shittim.ᶜ

⁵⁰On the plains of Moab by the Jordan across from Jericho the LORD said to Moses, ⁵¹"Speak to the Israelites and say to them: 'When you cross the Jordan into Canaan,ᵈ ⁵²drive out all the inhabitants of the land before you. Destroy all their carved images and their cast idols, and demolish all their high places.ᵉ ⁵³Take possession of the land and settle in it, for I have given you the land to possess.ᶠ ⁵⁴Distribute the land by lot, according to your clans.ᵍ To a larger group give a larger inheritance, and to a smaller group a smaller one. Whatever falls to them by lot will be theirs. Distribute it according to your ancestral tribes.

⁵⁵"But if you do not drive out the inhabitants of the land, those you allow to remain will become barbs in your eyes and thornsʰ in your sides. They will give you trouble in the land where you will live. ⁵⁶And then I will do to you what I plan to do to them.'"

Chapter 34 Theme

34 The LORD said to Moses, ²"Command the Israelites and say to them: 'When you enter Canaan, the land that will be allotted to you as an inheritanceⁱ will have these boundaries:ʲ

³"'Your southern side will include some of the Desert of Zinᵏ along the border of Edom. On the east, your southern boundary will start from the end of the Salt Sea,ᵇˡ ⁴cross south of Scorpionᶜ Pass,ᵐ continue on to Zin and go south of Kadesh Barnea.ⁿ Then it will go to Hazar Addar and over to Azmon, ⁵where it will turn, join the Wadi of Egyptᵒ and end at the Sea.ᵈ

⁶"'Your western boundary will be the coast of the Great Sea. This will be your boundary on the west.

⁷"'For your northern boundary,ᵖ run a line from the Great Sea to Mount Hor ⁸and from Mount Hor to Leboᵉ Hamath.�q Then the boundary will go to Zedad, ⁹continue to Ziphron and end at Hazar Enan. This will be your boundary on the north.

¹⁰"'For your eastern boundary, run a line from Hazar Enan to Shepham. ¹¹The boundary will go down from Shepham to Riblahʳ

33:47
ᵃNu 27:12

33:48
ᵇNu 22:1

33:49
ᶜNu 25:1

33:51
ᵈJos 3:17

33:52
ᵉEx 23:24;
34:13;
Lev 26:1;
Dt 7:2,5; 12:3;
Jos 11:12;
Ps 106:34-36

33:53
ᶠDt 11:31;
Jos 21:43

33:54
ᵍNu 26:54

33:55
ʰJos 23:13;
Jdg 2:3;
Ps 106:36

34:2
ⁱGe 17:8;
Dt 1:7-8;
Ps 78:54-55
ʲEze 47:15

34:3
ᵏJos 15:1-3
ˡGe 14:3

34:4
ᵐJos 15:3
ⁿNu 32:8

34:5
ᵒGe 15:18;
Jos 15:4

34:7
ᵖEze 47:15-17

34:8
qNu 13:21;
Jos 13:5

34:11
ʳ2Ki 23:33;
Jer 39:5

ᵃ48 Hebrew *Jordan of Jericho*; possibly an ancient name for the Jordan River; also in verse 50   ᵇ3 That is, the Dead Sea; also in verse 12   ᶜ4 Hebrew *Akrabbim*   ᵈ5 That is, the Mediterranean; also in verses 6 and 7   ᵉ8 Or *to the entrance to*

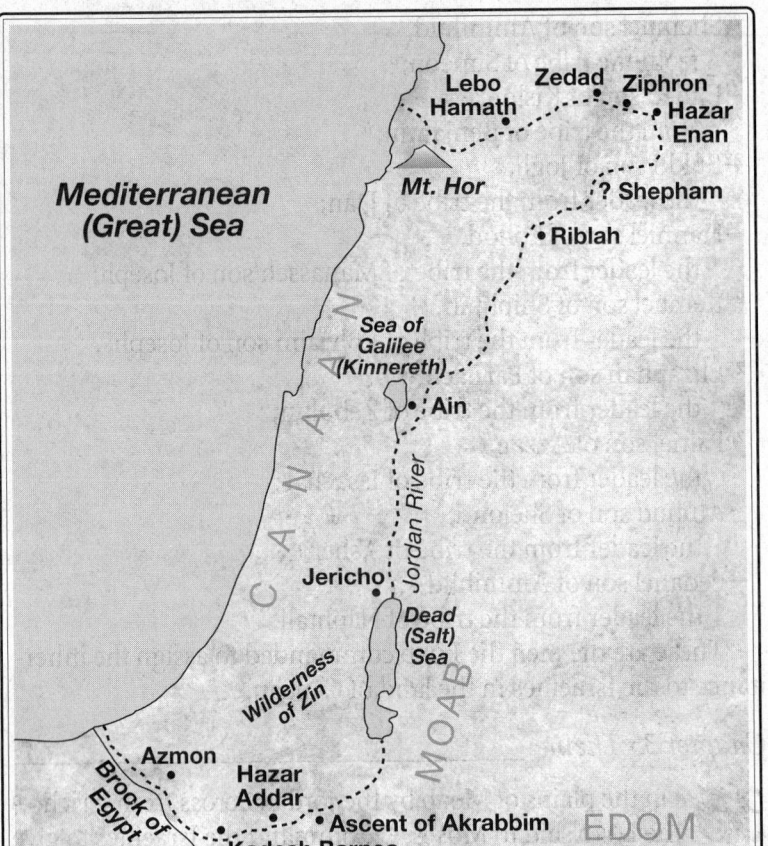

Border of Canaan

Mediterranean (Great) Sea

Lebo Hamath · Zedad · Ziphron · Hazar Enan

Mt. Hor · ? Shepham

· Riblah

Sea of Galilee (Kinnereth) · Ain

Jordan River

Jericho ·

Dead (Salt) Sea

CANAAN

Wilderness of Zin

MOAB

Azmon · Hazar Addar · Ascent of Akrabbim

Brook of Egypt

Kadesh Barnea

EDOM

34:11
a Dt 3:17;
Jos 11:2;
13:27

34:13
b Jos 14:1-5

34:14
c Nu 32:33;
Jos 14:3

34:17
d Jos 14:1

34:18
e Nu 1:4,16

34:19
f Nu 26:65
g Ge 29:35;
Dt 33:7

on the east side of Ain and continue along the slopes east of the Sea of Kinnereth.ᵃᵃ ¹²Then the boundary will go down along the Jordan and end at the Salt Sea.

" 'This will be your land, with its boundaries on every side.' "

¹³Moses commanded the Israelites: "Assign this land by lot as an inheritance.ᵇ The LORD has ordered that it be given to the nine and a half tribes, ¹⁴because the families of the tribe of Reuben, the tribe of Gad and the half-tribe of Manasseh have received their inheritance.ᶜ ¹⁵These two and a half tribes have received their inheritance on the east side of the Jordan of Jericho,ᵇ toward the sunrise."

¹⁶The LORD said to Moses, ¹⁷"These are the names of the men who are to assign the land for you as an inheritance: Eleazar the priest and Joshuaᵈ son of Nun. ¹⁸And appoint one leader from each tribe to helpᵉ assign the land. ¹⁹These are their names:

Calebᶠ son of Jephunneh,
from the tribe of Judah;ᵍ

a 11 That is, Galilee   b 15 *Jordan of Jericho* was possibly an ancient name for the Jordan River.

279

²⁰Shemuel son of Ammihud,
from the tribe of Simeon;ᵃ
²¹Elidad son of Kislon,
from the tribe of Benjamin;ᵇ
²²Bukki son of Jogli,
the leader from the tribe of Dan;
²³Hanniel son of Ephod,
the leader from the tribe of Manasseh son of Joseph;
²⁴Kemuel son of Shiphtan,
the leader from the tribe of Ephraim son of Joseph;
²⁵Elizaphan son of Parnach,
the leader from the tribe of Zebulun;
²⁶Paltiel son of Azzan,
the leader from the tribe of Issachar;
²⁷Ahihud son of Shelomi,
the leader from the tribe of Asher;ᶜ
²⁸Pedahel son of Ammihud,
the leader from the tribe of Naphtali."

²⁹These are the men the LORD commanded to assign the inheritance to the Israelites in the land of Canaan.

Chapter 35 Theme

35 On the plains of Moab by the Jordan across from Jericho,ᵃ the LORD said to Moses, ²"Command the Israelites to give the Levites towns to live inᵈ from the inheritance the Israelites will possess. And give them pasturelands around the towns. ³Then they will have towns to live in and pasturelands for their cattle, flocks and all their other livestock.

⁴"The pasturelands around the towns that you give the Levites will extend out fifteen hundred feetᵇ from the town wall. ⁵Outside the town, measure three thousand feetᶜ on the east side, three thousand on the south side, three thousand on the west and three thousand on the north, with the town in the center. They will have this area as pastureland for the towns.

⁶"Six of the towns you give the Levites will be cities of refuge, to which a person who has killed someone may flee.ᵉ In addition, give them forty-two other towns. ⁷In all you must give the Levites forty-eight towns, together with their pasturelands. ⁸The towns you give the Levites from the land the Israelites possess are to be given in proportion to the inheritance of each tribe: Take many towns from a tribe that has many, but few from one that has few."ᶠ

⁹Then the LORD said to Moses: ¹⁰"Speak to the Israelites and say to them: 'When you cross the Jordan into Canaan,ᵍ ¹¹select some

34:20 ᵃGe 49:5

34:21 ᵇGe 49:27; Ps 68:27

34:27 ᶜNu 1:40

35:2 ᵈLev 25:32-34; Jos 14:3,4

35:6 ᵉJos 20:7-9; 21:3,13

35:8 ᶠNu 26:54; 33:54; Jos 21:1-42

35:10 ᵍJos 20:2

ᵃ1 Hebrew *Jordan of Jericho*; possibly an ancient name for the Jordan River   ᵇ4 Hebrew *a thousand cubits* (about 450 meters)   ᶜ5 Hebrew *two thousand cubits* (about 900 meters)

Cities of Refuge

Mediterranean (Great) Sea

• **Kedesh**

•Acco

• **Golan**

•Dor

Beth Shan•

• **Ramoth**

Jordan River

Shechem •

•Peniel

Gezer•

Gibeon

• • **Bezer**

Heshbon

Hebron •

Dead (Salt) Sea

The six cities of refuge appear in bold type

Beersheba•

35:11
aver 22-25
bEx 21:13;
Dt 19:1-13

35:12
cDt 19:6;
Jos 20:3

35:16
dEx 21:12;
Lev 24:17

35:19
ever 21

35:20
fGe 4:8;
Ex 21:14;
Dt 19:11;
2Sa 3:27;
20:10

35:22
gver 11;
Ex 21:13

35:24
hver 12;
Jos 20:6

towns to be your cities of refuge, to which a person who has killed someone^a accidentally^b may flee. ¹²They will be places of refuge from the avenger,^c so that a person accused of murder may not die before he stands trial before the assembly. ¹³These six towns you give will be your cities of refuge. ¹⁴Give three on this side of the Jordan and three in Canaan as cities of refuge. ¹⁵These six towns will be a place of refuge for Israelites, aliens and any other people living among them, so that anyone who has killed another accidentally can flee there.

¹⁶" 'If a man strikes someone with an iron object so that he dies, he is a murderer; the murderer shall be put to death.^d ¹⁷Or if anyone has a stone in his hand that could kill, and he strikes someone so that he dies, he is a murderer; the murderer shall be put to death. ¹⁸Or if anyone has a wooden object in his hand that could kill, and he hits someone so that he dies, he is a murderer; the murderer shall be put to death. ¹⁹The avenger of blood shall put the murderer to death; when he meets him, he shall put him to death.^e ²⁰If anyone with malice aforethought shoves another or throws something at him intentionally^f so that he dies ²¹or if in hostility he hits him with his fist so that he dies, that person shall be put to death; he is a murderer. The avenger of blood shall put the murderer to death when he meets him.

²²" 'But if without hostility someone suddenly shoves another or throws something at him unintentionally^g ²³or, without seeing him, drops a stone on him that could kill him, and he dies, then since he was not his enemy and he did not intend to harm him, ²⁴the assembly^h must judge between him and the avenger of blood

according to these regulations. [25]The assembly must protect the one accused of murder from the avenger of blood and send him back to the city of refuge to which he fled. He must stay there until the death of the high priest, who was anointed with the holy oil.[a]

[26]"'But if the accused ever goes outside the limits of the city of refuge to which he has fled [27]and the avenger of blood finds him outside the city, the avenger of blood may kill the accused without being guilty of murder. [28]The accused must stay in his city of refuge until the death of the high priest; only after the death of the high priest may he return to his own property.

[29]"'These are to be legal requirements[b] for you throughout the generations to come, wherever you live.

[30]"'Anyone who kills a person is to be put to death as a murderer only on the testimony of witnesses. But no one is to be put to death on the testimony of only one witness.[c]

[31]"'Do not accept a ransom for the life of a murderer, who deserves to die. He must surely be put to death.

[32]"'Do not accept a ransom for anyone who has fled to a city of refuge and so allow him to go back and live on his own land before the death of the high priest.

[33]"'Do not pollute the land where you are. Bloodshed pollutes the land,[d] and atonement cannot be made for the land on which blood has been shed, except by the blood of the one who shed it. [34]Do not defile the land[e] where you live and where I dwell,[f] for I, the LORD, dwell among the Israelites.'"

Chapter 36 Theme

36 The family heads of the clan of Gilead[g] son of Makir, the son of Manasseh, who were from the clans of the descendants of Joseph, came and spoke before Moses and the leaders,[h] the heads of the Israelite families. [2]They said, "When the LORD commanded my lord to give the land as an inheritance to the Israelites by lot, he ordered you to give the inheritance of our brother Zelophehad[i] to his daughters. [3]Now suppose they marry men from other Israelite tribes; then their inheritance will be taken from our ancestral inheritance and added to that of the tribe they marry into. And so part of the inheritance allotted to us will be taken away. [4]When the Year of Jubilee[j] for the Israelites comes, their inheritance will be added to that of the tribe into which they marry, and their property will be taken from the tribal inheritance of our forefathers."

[5]Then at the LORD's command Moses gave this order to the Israelites: "What the tribe of the descendants of Joseph is saying is right. [6]This is what the LORD commands for Zelophehad's daughters: They may marry anyone they please as long as they

---

35:25
[a]Ex 29:7

35:29
[b]Nu 27:11

35:30
[c]ver 16;
Dt 17:6; 19:15;
Mt 18:16;
Jn 7:51;
2Co 13:1;
Heb 10:28

35:33
[d]Ge 9:6;
Ps 106:38;
Mic 4:11

35:34
[e]Lev 18:24,25
[f]Ex 29:45

36:1
[g]Nu 26:29
[h]Nu 27:2

36:2
[i]Nu 26:33;
27:1,7

36:4
[j]Lev 25:10

36:7
*a*1Ki 21:3

marry within the tribal clan of their father. ⁷No inheritance*ᵃ* in Israel is to pass from tribe to tribe, for every Israelite shall keep the tribal land inherited from his forefathers. ⁸Every daughter who inherits land in any Israelite tribe must marry someone in her father's tribal clan,*ᵇ* so that every Israelite will possess the inheritance of his fathers. ⁹No inheritance may pass from tribe to tribe, for each Israelite tribe is to keep the land it inherits."

36:8
*b*1Ch 23:22

¹⁰So Zelophehad's daughters did as the LORD commanded Moses. ¹¹Zelophehad's daughters—Mahlah, Tirzah, Hoglah, Milcah and Noah*ᶜ*—married their cousins on their father's side.

36:11
*c*Nu 26:33; 27:1

¹²They married within the clans of the descendants of Manasseh son of Joseph, and their inheritance remained in their father's clan and tribe.

¹³These are the commands and regulations the LORD gave through Moses*ᵈ* to the Israelites on the plains of Moab by the Jordan across from Jericho.*ᵃᵉ*

36:13
*d*Lev 26:46;
27:34
*e*Nu 22:1

a13 Hebrew *Jordan of Jericho*; possibly an ancient name for the Jordan River

INSIGHTS FROM NUMBERS

LAND OF CANAAN	BALAAM	KORAH

Theme of Numbers:

	SEGMENT DIVISIONS		
Author:		JOURNEYS/ ENCAMP- MENTS	**CHAPTER THEMES**
			1
Date:			2
			3
			4
Purpose:			5
			6
			7
			8
Key Words:			9
			10
			11
			12
			13
			14
			15
			16
			17
			18
			19
			20
			21
			22
			23
			24
			25
			26
			27
			28
			29
			30
			31
			32
			33
			34
			35
			36

DEUTERONOMY

euteronomy is the crown jewel of the Pentateuch. It lays before us clearly what God expects from those who have been redeemed: a life of uncompromising obedience.

God raised up Moses to deliver his people from the land of Egypt, the land of bondage. That Moses had done. Now he stood at Pisgah near the land of promise. He was 120 years old.

When Moses struck the rock a second time, he failed to treat God as holy. Because of this he could not enter the land of promise. But the people he had led so faithfully for the last 40 years would go in and possess it.

Moses had to do one more thing before God took him home: tell God's children how to live in the land which the God of their fathers was giving them.

✎ THINGS TO DO

General Instructions

1. For the book's historical context, read Numbers 21:21–22:1; 36:13; Deuteronomy 1:1-5.

   a. Record the author, date, and geographical setting of the book on the DEUTERONOMY AT A GLANCE chart on page 345.

   b. When you study Deuteronomy watch for any verses which confirm Moses' authorship. Although the last chapter tells of Moses' death, this doesn't negate the fact that Moses wrote the rest of the book. The last chapter would be an appropriate postscript after his death.

2. Read Romans 15:4 and 1 Corinthians 10:1-14 and keep these verses in mind as you study.

   a. As you study each chapter, note in the margin insights you glean in respect to the character of God and the ways he deals with his children and with unbelievers.

   b. Also note in the margin any specific instructions or admonitions that are to be followed in respect to God—for example, "Fear him."

   c. Record in the margin any "Lessons for Life" you learn from the text under the heading "LFL." Mark or color them in a distinctive way so you can recognize them immediately.

3. There are insightful lessons to be learned from Moses' life about leadership and about our relationship to God. As you study Deuteronomy note these lessons in the chapter margins. Also record all you learn about Moses on the chart LESSONS FROM THE LIFE OF MOSES on pages 346, 347. When you record your insights, make sure you note the book, chapter, and verse from which they came.

Chapters 1-3

Moses rehearses what happened from the time they left Horeb (Mount Sinai) until they camped in the valley opposite Beth Peor at the foot of Mount Nebo (Pisgah).

1. As you read these three chapters:

   a. Ask the five W's and an H: Who? What? When? Where? Why? and How? Watch what happens in each chapter, where it happens and to whom, why it happens, and what the consequences or results are. Also note how things are accomplished.

   b. Mark every use of *then* (*and, when, next, after that,* or *until*) so you can see the sequence of events.

   c. Look at the map in chapter 1 on page 289 to see where the events took place.

2. In a distinctive way mark these key words and their synonyms: *fear (be afraid, revere, revering), heart(s) (yourselves, yourself, integrity, hardhearted, disheartened, mind,* or *way), command(s) (orders,*

commanding, commanded), give(n), gave, giving, send, told, directed, or forbidden), and listen (pay attention, hear, obey, or obeying). Write these on an index card to use as a bookmark while studying Deuteronomy.

3. Choose the theme of each chapter and record it in the text on the line next to the chapter number and on DEUTERONOMY AT A GLANCE.

Chapters 4-11

Moses instructs the children of Israel regarding what they are to do when they enter the land.

1. Read this segment chapter by chapter, keeping in mind the five W's and an H. Words such as *when, after, since, how, in the future, then, but now, watch, be careful, hear, listen, proclaim, pay attention, obey, therefore* will come to your attention. When you see the word "when," look and see if "then" eventually follows it. If so, circle each word and connect them with a line.

2. Add the following key words to your list and mark them when you come to them in the text: *observe (follow, obey, be careful, keep, pay attention to, keeping, do, doing, go well, done), love (affection, loved, loves), remember,* and *commandment (commands, law(s), statutes, decrees).*

3. Record the main points of each chapter in the margin, or underline and note them in the text with a number 1, 2, 3, etc.

4. Record the chapter themes as you did previously.

Chapters 12-26

Moses gives the people the statutes and the judgments they are to observe.

1. Add the following phrase to your list of key words and make sure you mark every occurrence of it in these chapters: *you must purge* [remove] *the evil.* Also add the words *life (live, livelihood, kill him), death (die), curse,* and *blessing(s) (blessed).*

2. As you read these chapters note in the margin of the text what the people are to do and why.

3. Go back and read number 2 under "General Instructions." Don't forget this important process.

4. Record the theme of the chapters on DEUTERONOMY AT A GLANCE and in the text.

Chapters 27-30

Moses tells the people about the necessity of obedience and that if they obey they will be blessed, but if they disobey they will be cursed.

1. Add to your list of key words the following words along with their synonyms and pronouns: *curse(s) (oath), blessing(s), the Lord will (it will please him), nation (nations, enemies, people, countries), captivity,* and *covenant.* List in the margin what you observe from marking these words.

2. As you read these chapters keep asking the five W's and an H. Note who and/or what will be affected by their obedience or disobedience. Also note everything that will happen if they obey or disobey.

3. Don't forget to note what you learn about God from these chapters and to record the theme of each chapter.

Chapters 31-34

This segment contains Moses' parting words, song, and blessing, as well as the account of his death.

1. Mark the key repeated words listed on your index card.

2. As Moses sings his song in chapter 32 he recounts Israel's relationship to God and God's dealings with them. *Jeshurun* in 32:15 is a reference to Israel.

   a. Pay attention to what you learn about Israel. Observe what leads to Israel's downfall and what the consequences are.

   b. Remember that although Moses begged God to change his mind and allow him to enter the promised land, God said no. Keep this in mind as you read these chapters and see Moses' heart and hear his words in respect to God. Take note of all you learn about God from these significant chapters. Make a list in the margin of what you learn about "the Rock."

3. Observe what Moses says will happen after his death and note this in the margin.

4. When you study chapter 33, mark the name of each of the tribes of Israel and carefully observe how they are described and what is said about each one of them. Underline every occurrence of *they will*.

5. Record what you learn about Moses from chapter 34 on the chart LESSONS FROM THE LIFE OF MOSES on pages 346, 347. Then complete DEUTERONOMY AT A GLANCE.

THINGS TO THINK ABOUT

1. Since we are under the new covenant of grace, what is our relationship to the commands of God? Do you think grace allows us to continue in sin and disobedience without any consequences or chastening from the Father?

2. What kind of allegiance does God call for from Israel? Do you think he expects anything less from the church, the body of the Lord Jesus Christ?

3. What have you learned regarding the slowness of God's anger and his gracious ways with his covenant people?

4. How does a child of God demonstrate his love for the Lord?

Chapter 1 Theme _____

1 These are the words Moses spoke to all Israel in the desert east of the Jordan—that is, in the Arabah—opposite Suph, between Paran and Tophel, Laban, Hazeroth and Dizahab. ²(It takes eleven days to go from Horeb*ᵃ* to Kadesh Barnea*ᵇ* by the Mount Seir road.)

³In the fortieth year,*ᶜ* on the first day of the eleventh month, Moses proclaimed*ᵈ* to the Israelites all that the LORD had commanded him concerning them. ⁴This was after he had defeated Sihon*ᵉ* king of the Amorites, who reigned in Heshbon,*ᶠ* and at Edrei had defeated Og*ᵍ* king of Bashan, who reigned in Ashtaroth. ⁵East of the Jordan in the territory of Moab, Moses began to expound this law, saying:

⁶The LORD our God said to us*ʰ* at Horeb,*ⁱ* "You have stayed long enough at this mountain. ⁷Break camp and advance into the hill country of the Amorites; go to all the neighboring peoples in the Arabah, in the mountains, in the western foothills, in the Negev*ʲ* and along the coast, to the land of the Canaanites and to Lebanon,*ᵏ* as far as the great river, the Euphrates. ⁸See, I have given you this land. Go in and take possession of the land that the LORD swore*ˡ* he would give to your fathers—to Abraham, Isaac and Jacob—and to their descendants after them."

⁹At that time I said to you, "You are too heavy a burden for me to carry alone.*ᵐ* ¹⁰The LORD your God has increased your numbers

1:2
ᵃ Ex 3:1
ᵇ Nu 13:26;
Dt 9:23

1:3
ᶜ Nu 33:38
ᵈ Dt 4:1-2

1:4
ᵉ Nu 21:21-26
ᶠ Nu 21:25
ᵍ Nu 21:33-35;
Jos 13:12

1:6
ʰ Nu 10:13
ⁱ Ex 3:1

1:7
ʲ Jos 10:40
ᵏ Dt 11:24

1:8
ˡ Ge 12:7;
15:18;
17:7-8;
26:4;
28:13

1:9
ᵐ Ex 18:18

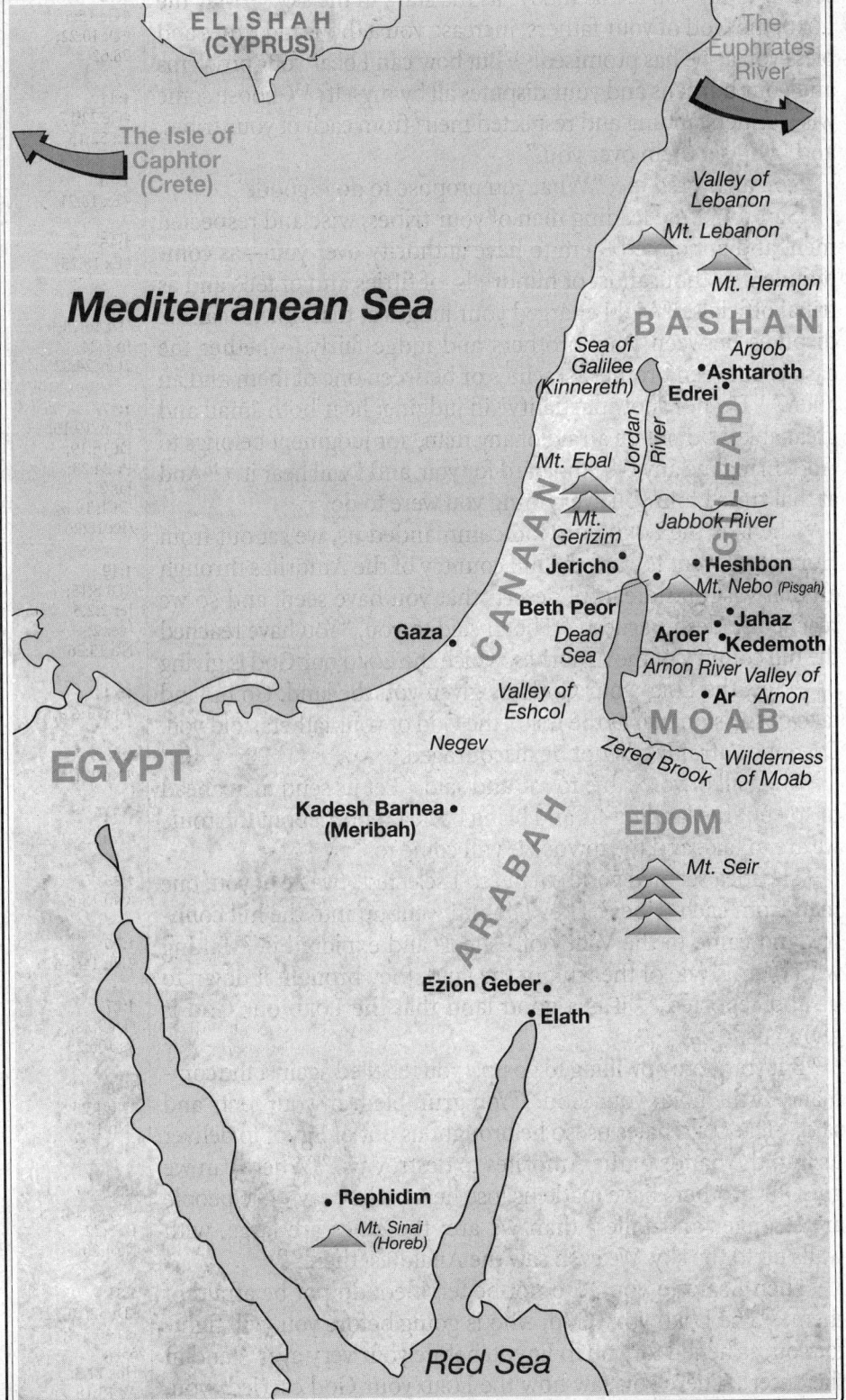

ELISHAH
(CYPRUS)

The Euphrates River

The Isle of Caphtor
(Crete)

Valley of Lebanon

Mt. Lebanon

Mediterranean Sea

Mt. Hermon

BASHAN

Argob

Sea of
Galilee
(Kinnereth)

•Ashtaroth

Edrei•

G
I
L
E
A
D

Jordan River

Mt. Ebal

Jabbok River

Mt.
Gerizim

CANAAN

Jericho•

•Heshbon
Mt. Nebo (Pisgah)

Beth Peor

Gaza •

Dead
Sea

•Jahaz
Aroer• •Kedemoth

Valley of
Eshcol

Arnon River Valley of
• Ar Arnon

Negev

MOAB

Zered Brook

Wilderness
of Moab

EGYPT

A
R
A
B
A
H

Kadesh Barnea •
(Meribah)

EDOM

Mt. Seir

Ezion Geber•

•Elath

•Rephidim

Mt. Sinai
(Horeb)

Red Sea

289

so that today you are as many[a] as the stars in the sky.[b] [11]May the LORD, the God of your fathers, increase you a thousand times and bless you as he has promised![c] [12]But how can I bear your problems and your burdens and your disputes all by myself? [13]Choose some wise, understanding and respected men[d] from each of your tribes, and I will set them over you."

[14]You answered me, "What you propose to do is good."

[15]So I took[e] the leading men of your tribes, wise and respected men, and appointed them to have authority over you—as commanders of thousands, of hundreds, of fifties and of tens and as tribal officials. [16]And I charged your judges at that time: Hear the disputes between your brothers and judge fairly,[f] whether the case is between brother Israelites or between one of them and an alien.[g] [17]Do not show partiality[h] in judging; hear both small and great alike. Do not be afraid of any man,[i] for judgment belongs to God. Bring me any case too hard for you, and I will hear it.[j] [18]And at that time I told you everything you were to do.

[19]Then, as the LORD our God commanded us, we set out from Horeb and went toward the hill country of the Amorites through all that vast and dreadful desert[k] that you have seen, and so we reached Kadesh Barnea.[l] [20]Then I said to you, "You have reached the hill country of the Amorites, which the LORD our God is giving us. [21]See, the LORD your God has given you the land. Go up and take possession of it as the LORD, the God of your fathers, told you. Do not be afraid;[m] do not be discouraged."

[22]Then all of you came to me and said, "Let us send men ahead to spy out the land for us and bring back a report about the route we are to take and the towns we will come to."

[23]The idea seemed good to me; so I selected[n] twelve of you, one man from each tribe. [24]They left and went up into the hill country, and came to the Valley of Eshcol[o] and explored it. [25]Taking with them some of the fruit of the land, they brought it down to us and reported,[p] "It is a good land that the LORD our God is giving us."

[26]But you were unwilling to go up;[q] you rebelled against the command of the LORD your God. [27]You grumbled[r] in your tents and said, "The LORD hates us; so he brought us out of Egypt to deliver us into the hands of the Amorites to destroy us. [28]Where can we go? Our brothers have made us lose heart. They say, 'The people are stronger and taller[s] than we are; the cities are large, with walls up to the sky. We even saw the Anakites[t] there.'"

[29]Then I said to you, "Do not be terrified; do not be afraid of them. [30]The LORD your God, who is going before you, will fight[u] for you, as he did for you in Egypt, before your very eyes, [31]and in the desert. There you saw how the LORD your God carried[v] you,

1:10
[a] Ge 15:5
[b] Dt 10:22;
28:62

1:11
[c] Ge 22:17;
Ex 32:13

1:13
[d] Ex 18:21

1:15
[e] Ex 18:25

1:16
[f] Dt 16:18;
Jn 7:24
[g] Lev 24:22

1:17
[h] Lev 19:15;
Dt 16:19;
Pr 24:23;
Jas 2:1
[i] 2Ch 19:6
[j] Ex 18:26

1:19
[k] Dt 8:15;
Jer 2:2,6
[l] ver 2;
Nu 13:26

1:21
[m] Jos 1:6,9,18

1:23
[n] Nu 13:1-3

1:24
[o] Nu 13:21-25

1:25
[p] Nu 13:27

1:26
[q] Nu 14:1-4

1:27
[r] Dt 9:28;
Ps 106:25

1:28
[s] Nu 13:32
[t] Nu 13:33;
Dt 9:1-3

1:30
[u] Ex 14:14;
Dt 3:22;
Ne 4:20

1:31
[v] Dt 32:10-12;
Isa 46:3-4;
63:9;
Hos 11:3;
Ac 13:18

1:32
a Ps 106:24;
Jude 1:5

1:33
b Ex 13:21;
Ps 78:14
c Nu 10:33

1:34
d Nu 14:23,
28-30

1:35
e Ps 95:11

1:36
f Nu 14:24;
Jos 14:9

1:37
g Dt 3:26;
4:21
h Nu 20:12

1:38
i Nu 14:30
j Dt 31:7
k Dt 3:28

1:39
l Nu 14:3
m Isa 7:15-16

1:40
n Nu 14:25

1:42
o Nu 14:41-43

1:44
p Ps 118:12

1:46
q Nu 20:1;
Jdg 11:17

2:1
r Nu 21:4

2:4
s Nu 20:14-21

as a father carries his son, all the way you went until you reached this place."

³²In spite of this, you did not trust^a in the LORD your God, ³³who went ahead of you on your journey, in fire by night and in a cloud by day,^{b} to search^c out places for you to camp and to show you the way you should go.

³⁴When the LORD heard what you said, he was angry and solemnly swore:^{d} ³⁵"Not a man of this evil generation shall see the good land^e I swore to give your forefathers, ³⁶except Caleb son of Jephunneh. He will see it, and I will give him and his descendants the land he set his feet on, because he followed the LORD wholeheartedly.^{f}"

³⁷Because of you the LORD became angry^g with me also and said, "You shall not enter^h it, either. ³⁸But your assistant, Joshua^i son of Nun, will enter it. Encourage^j him, because he will lead^k Israel to inherit it. ³⁹And the little ones that you said would be taken captive,^{l} your children who do not yet know^m good from bad—they will enter the land. I will give it to them and they will take possession of it. ⁴⁰But as for you, turn around and set out toward the desert along the route to the Red Sea.^{an}"

⁴¹Then you replied, "We have sinned against the LORD. We will go up and fight, as the LORD our God commanded us." So every one of you put on his weapons, thinking it easy to go up into the hill country.

⁴²But the LORD said to me, "Tell them, 'Do not go up and fight, because I will not be with you. You will be defeated by your enemies.'"^{o}

⁴³So I told you, but you would not listen. You rebelled against the LORD's command and in your arrogance you marched up into the hill country. ⁴⁴The Amorites who lived in those hills came out against you; they chased you like a swarm of bees^p and beat you down from Seir all the way to Hormah. ⁴⁵You came back and wept before the LORD, but he paid no attention to your weeping and turned a deaf ear to you. ⁴⁶And so you stayed in Kadesh^q many days—all the time you spent there.

Chapter 2 Theme

2 Then we turned back and set out toward the desert along the route to the Red Sea,^{ar} as the LORD had directed me. For a long time we made our way around the hill country of Seir.

²Then the LORD said to me, ³"You have made your way around this hill country long enough; now turn north. ⁴Give the people these orders:^{s} 'You are about to pass through the territory of your brothers the descendants of Esau, who live in Seir. They will be

a 40, 1 Hebrew *Yam Suph*; that is, Sea of Reeds

afraid of you, but be very careful. ⁵Do not provoke them to war, for I will not give you any of their land, not even enough to put your foot on. I have given Esau the hill country of Seir as his own.ᵃ ⁶You are to pay them in silver for the food you eat and the water you drink.'"

⁷The LORD your God has blessed you in all the work of your hands. He has watchedᵇ over your journey through this vast desert. These forty years the LORD your God has been with you, and you have not lacked anything.

⁸So we went on past our brothers the descendants of Esau, who live in Seir. We turned from the Arabah road, which comes up from Elath and Ezion Geber,ᶜ and traveled along the desert road of Moab.ᵈ

⁹Then the LORD said to me, "Do not harass the Moabites or provoke them to war, for I will not give you any part of their land. I have given Arᵉ to the descendants of Lotᶠ as a possession."

¹⁰(The Emitesᵍ used to live there—a people strong and numerous, and as tall as the Anakites.ʰ ¹¹Like the Anakites, they too were considered Rephaites, but the Moabites called them Emites. ¹²Horites used to live in Seir, but the descendants of Esau drove them out. They destroyed the Horites from before them and settled in their place, just as Israel didⁱ in the land the LORD gave them as their possession.)

¹³And the LORD said, "Now get up and cross the Zered Valley." So we crossed the valley.

¹⁴Thirty-eight years passed from the time we left Kadesh Barneaʲ until we crossed the Zered Valley. By then, that entire generationᵏ of fighting men had perished from the camp, as the LORD had sworn to them.ˡ ¹⁵The LORD's hand was against them until he had completely eliminatedᵐ them from the camp.

¹⁶Now when the last of these fighting men among the people had died, ¹⁷the LORD said to me, ¹⁸"Today you are to pass by the region of Moab at Ar. ¹⁹When you come to the Ammonites,ⁿ do not harass them or provoke them to war, for I will not give you possession of any land belonging to the Ammonites. I have given it as a possession to the descendants of Lot.ᵒ"

²⁰(That too was considered a land of the Rephaites, who used to live there; but the Ammonites called them Zamzummites. ²¹They were a people strong and numerous, and as tall as the Anakites.ᵖ The LORD destroyed them from before the Ammonites, who drove them out and settled in their place. ²²The LORD had done the same for the descendants of Esau, who lived in Seir,ᵠ when he destroyed the Horites from before them. They drove them out and have lived in their place to this day. ²³And as for the Avvitesʳ who lived in villages as far as Gaza, the Caphtoritesˢ

2:5 ᵃGe 36:8; Jos 24:4
2:7 ᵇDt 8:2-4
2:8 ᶜ1Ki 9:26 ᵈJdg 11:18
2:9 ᵉNu 21:15 ᶠGe 19:36-38
2:10 ᵍGe 14:5 ʰNu 13:22,33
2:12 ⁱver 22
2:14 ʲNu 13:26 ᵏNu 14:29-35 ˡDt 1:34-35
2:15 ᵐPs 106:26
2:19 ⁿGe 19:38 ᵒver 9
2:21 ᵖver 10
2:22 ᵠGe 36:8
2:23 ʳJos 13:3 ˢGe 10:14

2:23
aAm 9:7

2:24
bNu 21:13-14;
Jdg 11:13,18

2:25
cDt 11:25
dJos 2:9,11
eEx 15:14-16

2:27
fNu 21:21-22

2:28
gNu 20:19

2:30
hJos 11:20
iEx 4:21;
Nu 21:23;
Ro 9:18

2:31
jDt 1:8

2:32
kNu 21:23

2:33
lDt 29:7

2:34
mDt 3:6; 7:2

2:36
nDt 3:12;
4:48;
Jos 13:9
oPs 44:3

2:37
pver 18-19
qNu 21:24
rGe 32:22;
Dt 3:16

3:1
sNu 21:33

3:2
tNu 21:34

coming out from Caphtor[aa] destroyed them and settled in their place.)

²⁴"Set out now and cross the Arnon Gorge.[b] See, I have given into your hand Sihon the Amorite, king of Heshbon, and his country. Begin to take possession of it and engage him in battle. ²⁵This very day I will begin to put the terror[c] and fear[d] of you on all the nations under heaven. They will hear reports of you and will tremble[e] and be in anguish because of you."

²⁶From the desert of Kedemoth I sent messengers to Sihon king of Heshbon offering peace and saying, ²⁷"Let us pass through your country. We will stay on the main road; we will not turn aside to the right or to the left.[f] ²⁸Sell us food to eat and water to drink for their price in silver. Only let us pass through on foot[g]— ²⁹as the descendants of Esau, who live in Seir, and the Moabites, who live in Ar, did for us—until we cross the Jordan into the land the LORD our God is giving us." ³⁰But Sihon king of Heshbon refused to let us pass through. For the LORD[h] your God had made his spirit stubborn[i] and his heart obstinate in order to give him into your hands, as he has now done.

³¹The LORD said to me, "See, I have begun to deliver Sihon and his country over to you. Now begin to conquer and possess his land."[j]

³²When Sihon and all his army came out to meet us in battle[k] at Jahaz, ³³the LORD our God delivered him over to us and we struck him down,[l] together with his sons and his whole army. ³⁴At that time we took all his towns and completely destroyed[bm] them—men, women and children. We left no survivors. ³⁵But the livestock and the plunder from the towns we had captured we carried off for ourselves. ³⁶From Aroer[n] on the rim of the Arnon Gorge, and from the town in the gorge, even as far as Gilead, not one town was too strong for us. The LORD our God gave[o] us all of them. ³⁷But in accordance with the command of the LORD our God,[p] you did not encroach on any of the land of the Ammonites,[q] neither the land along the course of the Jabbok[r] nor that around the towns in the hills.

Chapter 3 Theme

3 Next we turned and went up along the road toward Bashan, and Og king of Bashan with his whole army marched out to meet us in battle at Edrei.[s] ²The LORD said to me, "Do not be afraid[t] of him, for I have handed him over to you with his whole army and his land. Do to him what you did to Sihon king of the Amorites, who reigned in Heshbon."

a 23 That is, Crete   b 34 The Hebrew term refers to the irrevocable giving over of things or persons to the LORD, often by totally destroying them.

³So the Lord our God also gave into our hands Og king of Bashan and all his army. We struck them down, leaving no survivors.^a ⁴At that time we took all his cities. There was not one of the sixty cities that we did not take from them—the whole region of Argob, Og's kingdom in Bashan.^b ⁵All these cities were fortified with high walls and with gates and bars, and there were also a great many unwalled villages. ⁶We completely destroyed^a them, as we had done with Sihon king of Heshbon, destroying^{ac} every city—men, women and children. ⁷But all the livestock and the plunder from their cities we carried off for ourselves.

⁸So at that time we took from these two kings of the Amorites the territory east of the Jordan, from the Arnon Gorge as far as Mount Hermon. ⁹(Hermon is called Sirion^d by the Sidonians; the Amorites call it Senir.)^e ¹⁰We took all the towns on the plateau, and all Gilead, and all Bashan as far as Salecah^f and Edrei, towns of Og's kingdom in Bashan. ¹¹(Only Og king of Bashan was left of the remnant of the Rephaites.^g His bed^b was made of iron and was more than thirteen feet long and six feet wide.^c It is still in Rabbah^h of the Ammonites.)

¹²Of the land that we took over at that time, I gave the Reubenites and the Gadites the territory north of Aroerⁱ by the Arnon Gorge, including half the hill country of Gilead, together with its towns. ¹³The rest of Gilead and also all of Bashan, the kingdom of Og, I gave to the half tribe of Manasseh. (The whole region of Argob in Bashan used to be known as a land of the Rephaites. ¹⁴Jair,^j a descendant of Manasseh, took the whole region of Argob as far as the border of the Geshurites and the Maacathites; it was named after him, so that to this day Bashan is called Havvoth Jair.^d) ¹⁵And I gave Gilead to Makir.^k ¹⁶But to the Reubenites and the Gadites I gave the territory extending from Gilead down to the Arnon Gorge (the middle of the gorge being the border) and out to the Jabbok River,^l which is the border of the Ammonites. ¹⁷Its western border was the Jordan in the Arabah, from Kinnereth^m to the Sea of the Arabah (the Salt Sea^{en}), below the slopes of Pisgah.

¹⁸I commanded you at that time: "The Lord your God has given you this land to take possession of it. But all your able-bodied men, armed for battle, must cross over ahead of your brother Israelites.^o ¹⁹However, your wives, your children and your livestock (I know you have much livestock) may stay in the towns I have given you, ²⁰until the Lord gives rest to your brothers as he has to you, and they too have taken over the land that the Lord your

---

3:3
^aNu 21:35

3:4
^b1Ki 4:13

3:6
^cDt 2:24,34

3:9
^dDt 4:48;
Ps 29:6
^e1Ch 5:23

3:10
^fJos 13:11

3:11
^gGe 14:5
^h2Sa 12:26;
Jer 49:2

3:12
ⁱNu 32:32-38;
Dt 2:36;
Jos 13:8-13

3:14
^jNu 32:41;
1Ch 2:22

3:15
^kNu 32:39-40

3:16
^lNu 21:24

3:17
^mNu 34:11;
Jos 13:27
ⁿGe 14:3;
Jos 12:3

3:18
^oNu 32:17

---

^a6 The Hebrew term refers to the irrevocable giving over of things or persons to the Lord, often by totally destroying them. ^b11 Or *sarcophagus* ^c11 Hebrew *nine cubits long and four cubits wide* (about 4 meters long and 1.8 meters wide) ^d14 Or *called the settlements of Jair* ^e17 That is, the Dead Sea

3:22
aDt 1:29
bEx 14:14;
Dt 20:4

3:24
cDt 11:2
dEx 15:11;
Ps 86:8
ePs 71:16,19
f2Sa 7:22

3:25
gDt 4:22

3:26
hDt 1:37;
31:2

3:27
iNu 27:12

3:28
jNu 27:18-23
kDt 31:3,23

3:29
lDt 4:46; 34:6

4:1
mDt 5:33;
8:1; 16:20;
30:15-20;
Eze 20:11;
Ro 10:5

4:2
nDt 12:32;
Jos 1:7;
Rev 22:18-19

4:3
oNu 25:1-9;
Ps 106:28

4:6
pDt 30:19-20;
Ps 19:7;
Pr 1:7
qJob 28:28

4:7
r2Sa 7:23
sPs 46:1;
Isa 55:6

4:9
tPr 4:23

God is giving them, across the Jordan. After that, each of you may go back to the possession I have given you."

²¹At that time I commanded Joshua: "You have seen with your own eyes all that the LORD your God has done to these two kings. The LORD will do the same to all the kingdoms over there where you are going. ²²Do not be afraid[a] of them; the LORD your God himself will fight[b] for you."

²³At that time I pleaded with the LORD: ²⁴"O Sovereign LORD, you have begun to show to your servant your greatness[c] and your strong hand. For what god[d] is there in heaven or on earth who can do the deeds and mighty works[e] you do?[f] ²⁵Let me go over and see the good land[g] beyond the Jordan—that fine hill country and Lebanon."

²⁶But because of you the LORD was angry[h] with me and would not listen to me. "That is enough," the LORD said. "Do not speak to me anymore about this matter. ²⁷Go up to the top of Pisgah and look west and north and south and east. Look at the land with your own eyes, since you are not going to cross this Jordan.[i] ²⁸But commission[j] Joshua, and encourage and strengthen him, for he will lead this people across[k] and will cause them to inherit the land that you will see." ²⁹So we stayed in the valley near Beth Peor.[l]

Chapter 4 Theme

4 Hear now, O Israel, the decrees and laws I am about to teach you. Follow them so that you may live[m] and may go in and take possession of the land that the LORD, the God of your fathers, is giving you. ²Do not add[n] to what I command you and do not subtract from it, but keep the commands of the LORD your God that I give you.

³You saw with your own eyes what the LORD did at Baal Peor.[o] The LORD your God destroyed from among you everyone who followed the Baal of Peor, ⁴but all of you who held fast to the LORD your God are still alive today.

⁵See, I have taught you decrees and laws as the LORD my God commanded me, so that you may follow them in the land you are entering to take possession of it. ⁶Observe them carefully, for this will show your wisdom[p] and understanding to the nations, who will hear about all these decrees and say, "Surely this great nation is a wise and understanding people."[q] ⁷What other nation is so great[r] as to have their gods near[s] them the way the LORD our God is near us whenever we pray to him? ⁸And what other nation is so great as to have such righteous decrees and laws as this body of laws I am setting before you today?

⁹Only be careful,[t] and watch yourselves closely so that you do not forget the things your eyes have seen or let them slip from

your heart as long as you live. Teach[a] them to your children[b] and to their children after them. [10]Remember the day you stood before the LORD your God at Horeb,[c] when he said to me, "Assemble the people before me to hear my words so that they may learn to revere me as long as they live in the land and may teach them to their children." [11]You came near and stood at the foot of the mountain while it blazed with fire[d] to the very heavens, with black clouds and deep darkness. [12]Then the LORD spoke[e] to you out of the fire. You heard the sound of words but saw no form; there was only a voice. [13]He declared to you his covenant,[f] the Ten Commandments,[g] which he commanded you to follow and then wrote them on two stone tablets. [14]And the LORD directed me at that time to teach you the decrees and laws you are to follow in the land that you are crossing the Jordan to possess.

[15]You saw no form[h] of any kind the day the LORD spoke to you at Horeb out of the fire. Therefore watch yourselves very carefully,[i] [16]so that you do not become corrupt and make for yourselves an idol,[j] an image of any shape, whether formed like a man or a woman, [17]or like any animal on earth or any bird that flies in the air, [18]or like any creature that moves along the ground or any fish in the waters below. [19]And when you look up to the sky and see the sun,[k] the moon and the stars—all the heavenly array[l]—do not be enticed into bowing down to them and worshiping things the LORD your God has apportioned to all the nations under heaven. [20]But as for you, the LORD took you and brought you out of the iron-smelting furnace,[m] out of Egypt, to be the people of his inheritance,[n] as you now are.

[21]The LORD was angry with me[o] because of you, and he solemnly swore that I would not cross the Jordan and enter the good land the LORD your God is giving you as your inheritance. [22]I will die in this land; I will not cross the Jordan; but you are about to cross over and take possession of that good land.[p] [23]Be careful not to forget the covenant[q] of the LORD your God that he made with you; do not make for yourselves an idol[r] in the form of anything the LORD your God has forbidden. [24]For the LORD your God is a consuming fire,[s] a jealous God.

[25]After you have had children and grandchildren and have lived in the land a long time—if you then become corrupt and make any kind of idol, doing evil[t] in the eyes of the LORD your God and provoking him to anger, [26]I call heaven and earth as witnesses against you[u] this day that you will quickly perish from the land that you are crossing the Jordan to possess. You will not live there long but will certainly be destroyed. [27]The LORD will scatter[v] you among the peoples, and only a few of you will survive among the nations to which the LORD will drive you. [28]There you will worship

4:9
[a] Ge 18:19;
Eph 6:4
[b] Ps 78:5-6

4:10
[c] Ex 19:9,16

4:11
[d] Ex 19:18;
Heb 12:18-19

4:12
[e] Ex 20:22;
Dt 5:4,22

4:13
[f] Dt 9:9,11
[g] Ex 24:12;
31:18; 34:28

4:15
[h] Isa 40:18
[i] Jos 23:11

4:16
[j] Ex 20:4-5;
32:7;
Dt 5:8;
Ro 1:23

4:19
[k] Dt 17:3;
Job 31:26
[l] 2Ki 17:16;
21:3;
Ro 1:25

4:20
[m] 1Ki 8:51;
Jer 11:4
[n] Ex 19:5;
Dt 9:29

4:21
[o] Nu 20:12;
Dt 1:37

4:22
[p] Dt 3:25

4:23
[q] ver 9,16
[r] Ex 20:4

4:24
[s] Ex 24:17;
Dt 9:3;
Heb 12:29

4:25
[t] 2Ki 17:2,17

4:26
[u] Dt 30:18-19;
Isa 1:2;
Mic 6:2

4:27
[v] Lev 26:33;
Dt 28:36,64;
Ne 1:8

4:28
*a*Dt 28:36,64;
1Sa 26:19;
Jer 16:13
*b*Ps 115:4-8;
135:15-18

4:29
*c*2Ch 15:4;
Isa 55:6
*d*Jer 29:13
*e*Dt 30:1-3,10

4:30
*f*Dt 31:29;
Jer 23:20;
Hos 3:5

4:31
*g*2Ch 30:9;
Ne 9:31;
Ps 116:5;
Jnh 4:2

4:32
*h*Dt 32:7;
Job 8:8
*i*Ge 1:27
*j*Mt 24:31

4:33
*k*Ex 20:22;
Dt 5:24-26

4:34
*l*Ex 6:6
*m*Ex 7:3
*n*Dt 7:19;
26:8
*o*Ex 13:3
*p*Dt 34:12

4:35
*q*Dt 32:39;
1Sa 2:2;
Isa 45:5,18

4:36
*r*Ex 19:9,19

4:37
*s*Dt 10:15
*t*Ex 13:3,9,14

4:38
*u*Dt 7:1; 9:5

4:39
*v*ver 35;
Jos 2:11

4:40
*w*Lev 22:31;
Dt 5:33
*x*Dt 5:16
*y*Dt 6:3,18;
Eph 6:2-3

4:46
*z*Nu 21:26;
Dt 3:29

man-made gods*a* of wood and stone, which cannot see or hear or eat or smell.*b* ²⁹But if from there you seek*c* the LORD your God, you will find him if you look for him with all your heart*d* and with all your soul.*e* ³⁰When you are in distress and all these things have happened to you, then in later days*f* you will return to the LORD your God and obey him. ³¹For the LORD your God is a merciful*g* God; he will not abandon or destroy you or forget the covenant with your forefathers, which he confirmed to them by oath.

³²Ask*h* now about the former days, long before your time, from the day God created man on the earth;*i* ask from one end of the heavens to the other.*j* Has anything so great as this ever happened, or has anything like it ever been heard of? ³³Has any other people heard the voice of God*a* speaking out of fire, as you have, and lived?*k* ³⁴Has any god ever tried to take for himself one nation out of another nation,*l* by testings, by miraculous signs*m* and wonders,*n* by war, by a mighty hand and an outstretched arm,*o* or by great and awesome deeds,*p* like all the things the LORD your God did for you in Egypt before your very eyes?

³⁵You were shown these things so that you might know that the LORD is God; besides him there is no other.*q* ³⁶From heaven he made you hear his voice*r* to discipline you. On earth he showed you his great fire, and you heard his words from out of the fire. ³⁷Because he loved*s* your forefathers and chose their descendants after them, he brought you out of Egypt by his Presence and his great strength,*t* ³⁸to drive out before you nations greater and stronger than you and to bring you into their land to give it to you for your inheritance,*u* as it is today.

³⁹Acknowledge and take to heart this day that the LORD is God in heaven above and on the earth below. There is no other.*v* ⁴⁰Keep*w* his decrees and commands, which I am giving you today, so that it may go well*x* with you and your children after you and that you may live long*y* in the land the LORD your God gives you for all time.

⁴¹Then Moses set aside three cities east of the Jordan, ⁴²to which anyone who had killed a person could flee if he had unintentionally killed his neighbor without malice aforethought. He could flee into one of these cities and save his life. ⁴³The cities were these: Bezer in the desert plateau, for the Reubenites; Ramoth in Gilead, for the Gadites; and Golan in Bashan, for the Manassites.

⁴⁴This is the law Moses set before the Israelites. ⁴⁵These are the stipulations, decrees and laws Moses gave them when they came out of Egypt ⁴⁶and were in the valley near Beth Peor east of the Jordan, in the land of Sihon*z* king of the Amorites, who reigned

*a*33 Or *of a god*

in Heshbon and was defeated by Moses and the Israelites as they came out of Egypt. [47]They took possession of his land and the land of Og king of Bashan, the two Amorite kings east of the Jordan. [48]This land extended from Aroer[a] on the rim of the Arnon Gorge to Mount Siyon[ab] (that is, Hermon), [49]and included all the Arabah east of the Jordan, as far as the Sea of the Arabah,[b] below the slopes of Pisgah.

Chapter 5 Theme _____

5 Moses summoned all Israel and said:
Hear, O Israel, the decrees and laws I declare in your hearing today. Learn them and be sure to follow them. [2]The LORD our God made a covenant[c] with us at Horeb. [3]It was not with our fathers that the LORD made this covenant, but with us, with all of us who are alive here today.[d] [4]The LORD spoke[e] to you face to face out of the fire on the mountain. [5](At that time I stood between[f] the LORD and you to declare to you the word of the LORD, because you were afraid[g] of the fire and did not go up the mountain.) And he said:

[6]"I am the LORD your God, who brought you out of Egypt, out of the land of slavery.
[7]"You shall have no other gods before[c] me.
[8]"You shall not make for yourself an idol in the form of anything in heaven above or on the earth beneath or in the waters below. [9]You shall not bow down to them or worship them; for I, the LORD your God, am a jealous God, punishing the children for the sin of the fathers to the third and fourth generation of those who hate me,[h] [10]but showing love to a thousand ₍generations₎ of those who love me and keep my commandments.[i]
[11]"You shall not misuse the name of the LORD your God, for the LORD will not hold anyone guiltless who misuses his name.[j]
[12]"Observe the Sabbath day by keeping it holy,[k] as the LORD your God has commanded you. [13]Six days you shall labor and do all your work, [14]but the seventh day[l] is a Sabbath to the LORD your God. On it you shall not do any work, neither you, nor your son or daughter, nor your manservant or maidservant, nor your ox, your donkey or any of your animals, nor the alien within your gates, so that your manservant and maidservant may rest, as you do. [15]Remember that you were slaves in Egypt and that the LORD your God brought you out of there with a

4:48
[a]Dt 2:36
[b]Dt 3:9

5:2
[c]Ex 19:5

5:3
[d]Heb 8:9

5:4
[e]Dt 4:12,33,36

5:5
[f]Gal 3:19
[g]Ex 20:18,21

5:9
[h]Ex 34:7

5:10
[i]Jer 32:18

5:11
[j]Lev 19:12;
Mt 5:33-37

5:12
[k]Ex 20:8

5:14
[l]Ge 2:2;
Heb 4:4

---

[a] 48 Hebrew; Syriac (see also Deut. 3:9) *Sirion*   [b] 49 That is, the Dead Sea   [c] 7 Or *besides*

5:15
a Dt 4:34

mighty hand and an outstretched arm.ᵃ Therefore the LORD your God has commanded you to observe the Sabbath day.

5:16
b Ex 20:12;
Lev 19:3;
Dt 27:16;
Eph 6:2-3*;
Col 3:20
c Dt 4:40

16"Honor your father and your mother,ᵇ as the LORD your God has commanded you, so that you may live longᶜ and that it may go well with you in the land the LORD your God is giving you.

17"You shall not murder.ᵈ

5:17
d Mt 5:21-22*

18"You shall not commit adultery.ᵉ

19"You shall not steal.

20"You shall not give false testimony against your neighbor.

5:18
e Mt 5:27-30;
Lk 18:20*;
Jas 2:11*

21"You shall not covet your neighbor's wife. You shall not set your desire on your neighbor's house or land, his manservant or maidservant, his ox or donkey, or anything that belongs to your neighbor."ᶠ

5:21
f Ro 7:7*;
13:9*

22These are the commandments the LORD proclaimed in a loud voice to your whole assembly there on the mountain from out of the fire, the cloud and the deep darkness; and he added nothing more. Then he wrote them on two stone tabletsᵍ and gave them to me.

5:22
g Ex 24:12;
31:18;
Dt 4:13

23When you heard the voice out of the darkness, while the mountain was ablaze with fire, all the leading men of your tribes and your elders came to me. 24And you said, "The LORD our God has shown us his glory and his majesty, and we have heard his voice from the fire. Today we have seen that a man can live even if God speaks with him.ʰ 25But now, why should we die? This great fire will consume us, and we will die if we hear the voice of the LORD our God any longer.ⁱ 26For what mortal man has ever heard the voice of the living God speaking out of fire, as we have, and survived?ʲ 27Go near and listen to all that the LORD our God says. Then tell us whatever the LORD our God tells you. We will listen and obey."

5:24
h Ex 19:19

5:25
i Dt 18:16

5:26
j Dt 4:33

5:28
k Dt 18:17

28The LORD heard you when you spoke to me and the LORD said to me, "I have heard what this people said to you. Everything they said was good.ᵏ 29Oh, that their hearts would be inclined to fear meˡ and keep all my commandsᵐ always, so that it might go well with them and their children forever!ⁿ

5:29
l Ps 81:8,13
m Dt 11:1;
Isa 48:18
n Dt 4:1,40

30"Go, tell them to return to their tents. 31But you stay hereᵒ with me so that I may give you all the commands, decrees and laws you are to teach them to follow in the land I am giving them to possess."

5:31
o Ex 24:12

32So be careful to do what the LORD your God has commanded you; do not turn aside to the right or to the left.ᵖ 33Walk in all the way that the LORD your God has commanded you,ᵠ so that you

5:32
p Dt 17:11,20;
28:14;
Jos 1:7;
23:6;
Pr 4:27

5:33
q Jer 7:23

may live and prosper and prolong your days[a] in the land that you will possess.

Chapter 6 Theme

6 These are the commands, decrees and laws the LORD your God directed me to teach you to observe in the land that you are crossing the Jordan to possess, [2]so that you, your children and their children after them may fear[b] the LORD your God as long as you live by keeping all his decrees and commands that I give you, and so that you may enjoy long life. [3]Hear, O Israel, and be careful to obey so that it may go well with you and that you may increase greatly[c] in a land flowing with milk and honey,[d] just as the LORD, the God of your fathers, promised you.

[4]Hear, O Israel: The LORD our God, the LORD is one.[a][e] [5]Love[f] the LORD your God with all your heart and with all your soul and with all your strength.[g] [6]These commandments that I give you today are to be upon your hearts.[h] [7]Impress them on your children. Talk about them when you sit at home and when you walk along the road, when you lie down and when you get up.[i] [8]Tie them as symbols on your hands and bind them on your foreheads.[j] [9]Write them on the doorframes of your houses and on your gates.[k]

[10]When the LORD your God brings you into the land he swore to your fathers, to Abraham, Isaac and Jacob, to give you—a land with large, flourishing cities you did not build,[l] [11]houses filled with all kinds of good things you did not provide, wells you did not dig, and vineyards and olive groves you did not plant—then when you eat and are satisfied,[m] [12]be careful that you do not forget the LORD, who brought you out of Egypt, out of the land of slavery.

[13]Fear the LORD[n] your God, serve him only[o] and take your oaths in his name. [14]Do not follow other gods, the gods of the peoples around you; [15]for the LORD your God[p], who is among you, is a jealous God and his anger will burn against you, and he will destroy you from the face of the land. [16]Do not test the LORD your God[q] as you did at Massah. [17]Be sure to keep the commands of the LORD your God and the stipulations and decrees he has given you.[r] [18]Do what is right and good in the LORD's sight, so that it may go well[s] with you and you may go in and take over the good land that the LORD promised on oath to your forefathers, [19]thrusting out all your enemies before you, as the LORD said.

[20]In the future, when your son asks you,[t] "What is the meaning of the stipulations, decrees and laws the LORD our God has commanded you?" [21]tell him: "We were slaves of Pharaoh in Egypt, but the LORD brought us out of Egypt with a mighty hand. [22]Before

a 4 Or *The LORD our God is one LORD*; or *The LORD is our God, the LORD is one*; or *The LORD is our God, the LORD alone*

5:33
[a] Dt 4:40

6:2
[b] Ex 20:20;
Dt 10:12-13

6:3
[c] Dt 5:33
[d] Ex 3:8

6:4
[e] Mk 12:29*;
1Co 8:4

6:5
[f] Mt 22:37*;
Mk 12:30*;
Lk 10:27*
[g] Dt 10:12

6:6
[h] Dt 11:18

6:7
[i] Dt 4:9;
11:19;
Eph 6:4

6:8
[j] Ex 13:9,16;
Dt 11:18

6:9
[k] Dt 11:20

6:10
[l] Jos 24:13

6:11
[m] Dt 8:10

6:13
[n] Dt 10:20
[o] Mt 4:10*;
Lk 4:8*

6:15
[p] Dt 4:24

6:16
[q] Ex 17:7;
Mt 4:7*;
Lk 4:12*

6:17
[r] Dt 11:22;
Ps 119:4

6:18
[s] Dt 4:40

6:20
[t] Ex 13:14

6:24
a Dt 10:12;
Jer 32:39
b Ps 41:2

6:25
c Dt 24:13;
Ro 10:3,5

7:1
d Dt 31:3;
Ac 13:19

7:2
e Ex 23:32
f Dt 13:8

7:3
g Ex 34:15-16;
Ezr 9:2

7:4
h Dt 6:15

7:5
i Ex 23:24;
Dt 12:2-3

7:6
j Ex 19:5-6;
1Pe 2:9
k Ps 50:5;
Jer 2:3
l Dt 14:2

7:7
m Dt 10:22

7:8
n Dt 10:15
o Ex 32:13
p Ex 13:14

7:9
q Dt 4:35
r 1Co 1:9;
2Ti 2:13
s Ne 1:5;
Da 9:4

our eyes the LORD sent miraculous signs and wonders—great and terrible—upon Egypt and Pharaoh and his whole household. ²³But he brought us out from there to bring us in and give us the land that he promised on oath to our forefathers. ²⁴The LORD commanded us to obey all these decrees and to fear the LORD our God,ᵃ so that we might always prosper and be kept alive, as is the case today.ᵇ ²⁵And if we are careful to obey all this law before the LORD our God, as he has commanded us, that will be our righteousness.ᶜ"

Chapter 7 Theme

7 When the LORD your God brings you into the land you are entering to possess and drives out before you many nationsᵈ—the Hittites, Girgashites, Amorites, Canaanites, Perizzites, Hivites and Jebusites, seven nations larger and stronger than you—²and when the LORD your God has delivered them over to you and you have defeated them, then you must destroy them totally.ᵃ Make no treatyᵉ with them, and show them no mercy.ᶠ ³Do not intermarry with them.ᵍ Do not give your daughters to their sons or take their daughters for your sons, ⁴for they will turn your sons away from following me to serve other gods, and the LORD's anger will burn against you and will quickly destroyʰ you. ⁵This is what you are to do to them: Break down their altars, smash their sacred stones, cut down their Asherah polesᵇ and burn their idols in the fire.ⁱ ⁶For you are a people holyʲ to the LORD your God.ᵏ The LORD your God has chosenˡ you out of all the peoples on the face of the earth to be his people, his treasured possession.

⁷The LORD did not set his affection on you and choose you because you were more numerous than other peoples, for you were the fewest of all peoples.ᵐ ⁸But it was because the LORD lovedⁿ you and kept the oath he sworeᵒ to your forefathers that he brought you out with a mighty hand and redeemed you from the land of slavery,ᵖ from the power of Pharaoh king of Egypt. ⁹Know therefore that the LORD your God is God;�q he is the faithful God,ʳ keeping his covenant of loveˢ to a thousand generations of those who love him and keep his commands. ¹⁰But

> those who hate him he will repay to their face by
>   destruction;
> he will not be slow to repay to their face those
>   who hate him.

¹¹Therefore, take care to follow the commands, decrees and laws I give you today.

ᵃ2 The Hebrew term refers to the irrevocable giving over of things or persons to the LORD, often by totally destroying them; also in verse 26.   ᵇ5 That is, symbols of the goddess Asherah; here and elsewhere in Deuteronomy

¹²If you pay attention to these laws and are careful to follow them, then the LORD your God will keep his covenant of love with you, as he swore to your forefathers.^a ¹³He will love you and bless you^b and increase your numbers. He will bless the fruit of your womb, the crops of your land—your grain, new wine and oil—the calves of your herds and the lambs of your flocks in the land that he swore to your forefathers to give you.^c ¹⁴You will be blessed more than any other people; none of your men or women will be childless, nor any of your livestock without young.^d ¹⁵The LORD will keep you free from every disease.^e He will not inflict on you the horrible diseases you knew in Egypt, but he will inflict them on all who hate you. ¹⁶You must destroy all the peoples the LORD your God gives over to you. Do not look on them with pity^f and do not serve their gods, for that will be a snare^g to you.

¹⁷You may say to yourselves, "These nations are stronger than we are. How can we drive them out?^h" ¹⁸But do not be afraidⁱ of them; remember well what the LORD your God did to Pharaoh and to all Egypt.^j ¹⁹You saw with your own eyes the great trials, the miraculous signs and wonders, the mighty hand and outstretched arm, with which the LORD your God brought you out. The LORD your God will do the same to all the peoples you now fear.^k ²⁰Moreover, the LORD your God will send the hornet^l among them until even the survivors who hide from you have perished. ²¹Do not be terrified by them, for the LORD your God, who is among you,^m is a great and awesome God.ⁿ ²²The LORD your God will drive out those nations before you, little by little.^o You will not be allowed to eliminate them all at once, or the wild animals will multiply around you. ²³But the LORD your God will deliver them over to you, throwing them into great confusion until they are destroyed. ²⁴He will give their kings into your hand, and you will wipe out their names from under heaven. No one will be able to stand up against you;^p you will destroy them. ²⁵The images of their gods you are to burn^q in the fire. Do not covet^r the silver and gold on them, and do not take it for yourselves, or you will be ensnared^s by it, for it is detestable^t to the LORD your God. ²⁶Do not bring a detestable thing into your house or you, like it, will be set apart for destruction.^u Utterly abhor and detest it, for it is set apart for destruction.

Chapter 8 Theme

8 Be careful to follow every command I am giving you today, so that you may live^v and increase and may enter and possess the land that the LORD promised on oath to your forefathers. ²Remember how the LORD your God led^w you all the way in the desert these forty years, to humble you and to test you in order to

---

7:12
^aLev 26:3-13;
Dt 28:1-14;
Ps 105:8-9

7:13
^bJn 14:21
^cDt 28:4

7:14
^dEx 23:26

7:15
^eEx 15:26

7:16
^fver 2;
Ex 23:33
^gJdg 8:27

7:17
^hNu 33:53

7:18
ⁱDt 31:6
^jPs 105:5

7:19
^kDt 4:34

7:20
^lEx 23:28;
Jos 24:12

7:21
^mJos 3:10
ⁿDt 10:17;
Ne 9:32

7:22
^oEx 23:28-30

7:24
^pJos 23:9

7:25
^qEx 32:20;
1Ch 14:12
^rJos 7:21
^sJdg 8:27
^tDt 17:1

7:26
^uLev 27:28-29

8:1
^vDt 4:1

8:2
^wAm 2:10

8:3
a Ex 16:12,14,35
b Ex 16:2-3;
Mt 4:4*;
Lk 4:4*

8:4
c Dt 29:5;
Ne 9:21

8:5
d 2Sa 7:14;
Pr 3:11-12;
Heb 12:5-11;
Rev 3:19

8:6
e Dt 5:33

8:7
f Dt 11:9-12

8:10
g Dt 6:10-12

8:12
h Hos 13:6

8:14
i Ps 106:21

8:15
j Jer 2:6
k Nu 21:6
l Nu 20:11;
Ps 78:15;
114:8

8:16
m Ex 16:15

8:17
n Dt 9:4,7,24

8:18
o Pr 10:22;
Hos 2:8

8:19
p Dt 4:26;
30:18

9:1
q Dt 4:38;
11:23,31
r Dt 1:28

know what was in your heart, whether or not you would keep his commands. ³He humbled you, causing you to hunger and then feeding you with manna,*a* which neither you nor your fathers had known, to teach you that man does not live on bread alone but on every word that comes from the mouth of the LORD.*b* ⁴Your clothes did not wear out and your feet did not swell during these forty years.*c* ⁵Know then in your heart that as a man disciplines his son, so the LORD your God disciplines you.*d*

⁶Observe the commands of the LORD your God, walking in his ways and revering him.*e* ⁷For the LORD your God is bringing you into a good land—a land with streams and pools of water, with springs flowing in the valleys and hills;*f* ⁸a land with wheat and barley, vines and fig trees, pomegranates, olive oil and honey; ⁹a land where bread will not be scarce and you will lack nothing; a land where the rocks are iron and you can dig copper out of the hills.

¹⁰When you have eaten and are satisfied,*g* praise the LORD your God for the good land he has given you. ¹¹Be careful that you do not forget the LORD your God, failing to observe his commands, his laws and his decrees that I am giving you this day. ¹²Otherwise, when you eat and are satisfied, when you build fine houses and settle down,*h* ¹³and when your herds and flocks grow large and your silver and gold increase and all you have is multiplied, ¹⁴then your heart will become proud and you will forget*i* the LORD your God, who brought you out of Egypt, out of the land of slavery. ¹⁵He led you through the vast and dreadful desert,*j* that thirsty and waterless land, with its venomous snakes*k* and scorpions. He brought you water out of hard rock.*l* ¹⁶He gave you manna to eat in the desert, something your fathers had never known,*m* to humble and to test you so that in the end it might go well with you. ¹⁷You may say to yourself,*n* "My power and the strength of my hands have produced this wealth for me." ¹⁸But remember the LORD your God, for it is he who gives you the ability to produce wealth,*o* and so confirms his covenant, which he swore to your forefathers, as it is today.

¹⁹If you ever forget the LORD your God and follow other gods and worship and bow down to them, I testify against you today that you will surely be destroyed.*p* ²⁰Like the nations the LORD destroyed before you, so you will be destroyed for not obeying the LORD your God.

Chapter 9 Theme _____

9 Hear, O Israel. You are now about to cross the Jordan to go in and dispossess nations greater and stronger than you,*q* with large cities that have walls up to the sky.*r* ²The people are strong and tall—Anakites! You know about them and have heard it said:

"Who can stand up against the Anakites?"*a* ³But be assured today that the LORD your God is the one who goes across ahead of you*b* like a devouring fire.*c* He will destroy them; he will subdue them before you. And you will drive them out and annihilate them quickly,*d* as the LORD has promised you.

⁴After the LORD your God has driven them out before you, do not say to yourself,*e* "The LORD has brought me here to take possession of this land because of my righteousness." No, it is on account of the wickedness of these nations*f* that the LORD is going to drive them out before you. ⁵It is not because of your righteousness or your integrity*g* that you are going in to take possession of their land; but on account of the wickedness of these nations, the LORD your God will drive them out before you, to accomplish what he swore*h* to your fathers, to Abraham, Isaac and Jacob. ⁶Understand, then, that it is not because of your righteousness that the LORD your God is giving you this good land to possess, for you are a stiff-necked people.*i*

⁷Remember this and never forget how you provoked the LORD your God to anger in the desert. From the day you left Egypt until you arrived here, you have been rebellious against the LORD. ⁸At Horeb you aroused the LORD's wrath so that he was angry enough to destroy you.*j* ⁹When I went up on the mountain to receive the tablets of stone, the tablets of the covenant that the LORD had made with you, I stayed on the mountain forty days and forty nights; I ate no bread and drank no water.*k* ¹⁰The LORD gave me two stone tablets inscribed by the finger of God.*l* On them were all the commandments the LORD proclaimed to you on the mountain out of the fire, on the day of the assembly.

¹¹At the end of the forty days and forty nights, the LORD gave me the two stone tablets, the tablets of the covenant. ¹²Then the LORD told me, "Go down from here at once, because your people whom you brought out of Egypt have become corrupt.*m* They have turned away quickly*n* from what I commanded them and have made a cast idol for themselves."

¹³And the LORD said to me, "I have seen this people*o*, and they are a stiff-necked people indeed! ¹⁴Let me alone,*p* so that I may destroy them and blot out*q* their name from under heaven. And I will make you into a nation stronger and more numerous than they."

¹⁵So I turned and went down from the mountain while it was ablaze with fire. And the two tablets of the covenant were in my hands.*a r* ¹⁶When I looked, I saw that you had sinned against the LORD your God; you had made for yourselves an idol cast in the shape of a calf.*s* You had turned aside quickly from the way that the LORD had commanded you. ¹⁷So I took the two tablets and

a 15 Or *And I had the two tablets of the covenant with me, one in each hand*

9:2
a Nu 13:22,28, 32-33

9:3
b Dt 31:3;
Jos 3:11
c Dt 4:24;
Heb 12:29
d Ex 23:31;
Dt 7:23-24

9:4
e Dt 8:17
f Lev 18:21, 24-30;
Dt 18:9-14

9:5
g Tit 3:5
h Ge 12:7;
13:15; 15:7;
17:8; 26:4

9:6
i ver 13;
Ex 32:9;
Dt 31:27

9:8
j Ex 32:7-10;
Ps 106:19

9:9
k Ex 24:12, 15,18;
34:28

9:10
l Ex 31:18;
Dt 4:13

9:12
m Ex 32:7-8;
Dt 31:29
n Jdg 2:17

9:13
o ver 6;
Ex 32:9;
Dt 10:16

9:14
p Ex 32:10
q Nu 14:12;
Dt 29:20

9:15
r Ex 19:18;
32:15

9:16
s Ex 32:19

9:18
a Ex 34:28

9:19
b Ex 32:10-11,14
c Dt 10:10

9:21
d Ex 32:20

9:22
e Nu 11:3
f Ex 17:7
g Nu 11:34

9:23
h Ps 106:24

9:24
i ver 7;
Dt 31:27

9:25
j ver 18

9:26
k Ex 32:11

9:28
l Ex 32:12;
Nu 14:16

9:29
m Dt 4:20;
1Ki 8:51
n Dt 4:34;
Ne 1:10

10:1
o Ex 25:10;
34:1-2

10:2
p Ex 25:16,21;
Dt 4:13

10:3
q Ex 25:5,10;
37:1-9
r Ex 34:4

threw them out of my hands, breaking them to pieces before your eyes.

[18] Then once again I fell[a] prostrate before the LORD for forty days and forty nights; I ate no bread and drank no water, because of all the sin you had committed, doing what was evil in the LORD's sight and so provoking him to anger. [19] I feared the anger and wrath of the LORD, for he was angry enough with you to destroy you.[b] But again the LORD listened to me.[c] [20] And the LORD was angry enough with Aaron to destroy him, but at that time I prayed for Aaron too. [21] Also I took that sinful thing of yours, the calf you had made, and burned it in the fire. Then I crushed it and ground it to powder as fine as dust and threw the dust into a stream that flowed down the mountain.[d]

[22] You also made the LORD angry at Taberah,[e] at Massah[f] and at Kibroth Hattaavah.[g]

[23] And when the LORD sent you out from Kadesh Barnea, he said, "Go up and take possession of the land I have given you." But you rebelled against the command of the LORD your God. You did not trust[h] him or obey him. [24] You have been rebellious against the LORD ever since I have known you.[i]

[25] I lay prostrate before the LORD those forty days and forty nights because the LORD had said he would destroy you.[j] [26] I prayed to the LORD and said, "O Sovereign LORD, do not destroy your people, your own inheritance that you redeemed by your great power and brought out of Egypt with a mighty hand.[k] [27] Remember your servants Abraham, Isaac and Jacob. Overlook the stubbornness of this people, their wickedness and their sin. [28] Otherwise, the country from which you brought us will say, 'Because the LORD was not able to take them into the land he had promised them, and because he hated them, he brought them out to put them to death in the desert.'[l] [29] But they are your people, your inheritance[m] that you brought out by your great power and your outstretched arm.[n]"

Chapter 10 Theme

10 At that time the LORD said to me, "Chisel out two stone tablets[o] like the first ones and come up to me on the mountain. Also make a wooden chest.[a] [2] I will write on the tablets the words that were on the first tablets, which you broke. Then you are to put them in the chest."[p]

[3] So I made the ark out of acacia wood[q] and chiseled[r] out two stone tablets like the first ones, and I went up on the mountain with the two tablets in my hands. [4] The LORD wrote on these tablets what he had written before, the Ten Commandments he

a 1 That is, an ark

had proclaimed*a* to you on the mountain, out of the fire, on the day of the assembly. And the LORD gave them to me. ⁵Then I came back down the mountain *b* and put the tablets in the ark*c* I had made, as the LORD commanded me, and they are there now.*d*

⁶(The Israelites traveled from the wells of the Jaakanites to Moserah.*e* There Aaron died and was buried, and Eleazar his son succeeded him as priest.*f* ⁷From there they traveled to Gudgodah and on to Jotbathah, a land with streams of water.*g* ⁸At that time the LORD set apart the tribe of Levi*h* to carry the ark of the covenant of the LORD, to stand before the LORD to minister*i* and to pronounce blessings*j* in his name, as they still do today. ⁹That is why the Levites have no share or inheritance among their brothers; the LORD is their inheritance,*k* as the LORD your God told them.)

¹⁰Now I had stayed on the mountain forty days and nights, as I did the first time, and the LORD listened to me at this time also. It was not his will to destroy you.*l* ¹¹"Go," the LORD said to me, "and lead the people on their way, so that they may enter and possess the land that I swore to their fathers to give them."

¹²And now, O Israel, what does the LORD your God ask of you*m* but to fear the LORD your God, to walk in all his ways, to love him,*n* to serve the LORD your God with all your heart*o* and with all your soul, ¹³and to observe the LORD's commands and decrees that I am giving you today for your own good?

¹⁴To the LORD your God belong the heavens, even the highest heavens,*p* the earth and everything in it.*q* ¹⁵Yet the LORD set his affection on your forefathers and loved*r* them, and he chose you, their descendants, above all the nations, as it is today. ¹⁶Circumcise*s* your hearts, therefore, and do not be stiff-necked*t* any longer. ¹⁷For the LORD your God is God of gods*u* and Lord of lords, the great God, mighty and awesome, who shows no partiality*v* and accepts no bribes. ¹⁸He defends the cause of the fatherless and the widow,*w* and loves the alien, giving him food and clothing. ¹⁹And you are to love those who are aliens, for you yourselves were aliens in Egypt.*x* ²⁰Fear the LORD your God and serve him.*y* Hold fast*z* to him and take your oaths in his name.*a* ²¹He is your praise;*b* he is your God, who performed for you those great and awesome wonders*c* you saw with your own eyes. ²²Your forefathers who went down into Egypt were seventy in all,*d* and now the LORD your God has made you as numerous as the stars in the sky.*e*

Chapter 11 Theme

11 Love*f* the LORD your God and keep his requirements, his decrees, his laws and his commands always.*g* ²Remember today that your children were not the ones who saw and experienced the discipline of the LORD your God:*h* his majesty, his mighty

10:4
a Ex 20:1

10:5
b Ex 34:29
c Ex 40:20
d 1Ki 8:9

10:6
e Nu 33:30-31,38
f Nu 20:25-28

10:7
g Nu 33:32-34

10:8
h Nu 3:6
i Dt 18:5
j Dt 21:5

10:9
k Nu 18:20;
Dt 18:1-2;
Eze 44:28

10:10
l Ex 33:17;
34:28;
Dt 9:18-19,25

10:12
m Mic 6:8
n Dt 5:33;
6:13;
Mt 22:37
o Dt 6:5

10:14
p 1Ki 8:27
q Ex 19:5

10:15
r Dt 4:37

10:16
s Jer 4:4
t Dt 9:6

10:17
u Jos 22:22;
Da 2:47
v Ac 10:34;
Ro 2:11;
Eph 6:9

10:18
w Ps 68:5

10:19
x Lev 19:34

10:20
y Mt 4:10
z Dt 11:22
a Ps 63:11

10:21
b Ex 15:2;
Jer 17:14
c Ps 106:21-22

10:22
d Ge 46:26-27
e Ge 15:5;
Dt 1:10

11:1
f Dt 10:12
g Zec 3:7

11:2
h Dt 5:24; 8:5

11:4
a Ex 14:27

11:6
b Nu 16:1-35

11:8
c Jos 1:7

11:9
d Dt 4:40;
Pr 10:27
e Dt 9:5
f Ex 3:8

11:11
g Dt 8:7

11:12
h 1Ki 9:3

11:13
i Dt 6:17
j Dt 10:12

11:14
k Lev 26:4;
Dt 28:12
l Joel 2:23;
Jas 5:7

11:15
m Ps 104:14
n Dt 6:11

11:16
o Dt 8:19;
29:18;
Job 31:9,27

11:17
p Dt 6:15
q 1Ki 8:35;
2Ch 6:26
r Dt 4:26

11:18
s Dt 6:6-8

11:19
t Dt 6:7
u Dt 4:9-10

11:20
v Dt 6:9

11:21
w Pr 3:2;
4:10
x Ps 72:5

hand, his outstretched arm; ³the signs he performed and the things he did in the heart of Egypt, both to Pharaoh king of Egypt and to his whole country; ⁴what he did to the Egyptian army, to its horses and chariots, how he overwhelmed them with the waters of the Red Sea*ᵃ* as they were pursuing you, and how the LORD brought lasting ruin on them. ⁵It was not your children who saw what he did for you in the desert until you arrived at this place, ⁶and what he did*ᵇ* to Dathan and Abiram, sons of Eliab the Reubenite, when the earth opened its mouth right in the middle of all Israel and swallowed them up with their households, their tents and every living thing that belonged to them. ⁷But it was your own eyes that saw all these great things the LORD has done.

⁸Observe therefore all the commands I am giving you today, so that you may have the strength to go in and take over the land that you are crossing the Jordan to possess,*ᶜ* ⁹and so that you may live long*ᵈ* in the land that the LORD swore*ᵉ* to your forefathers to give to them and their descendants, a land flowing with milk and honey.*ᶠ* ¹⁰The land you are entering to take over is not like the land of Egypt, from which you have come, where you planted your seed and irrigated it by foot as in a vegetable garden. ¹¹But the land you are crossing the Jordan to take possession of is a land of mountains and valleys that drinks rain from heaven.*ᵍ* ¹²It is a land the LORD your God cares for; the eyes*ʰ* of the LORD your God are continually on it from the beginning of the year to its end.

¹³So if you faithfully obey*ⁱ* the commands I am giving you today—to love*ʲ* the LORD your God and to serve him with all your heart and with all your soul— ¹⁴then I will send rain*ᵏ* on your land in its season, both autumn and spring rains,*ˡ* so that you may gather in your grain, new wine and oil. ¹⁵I will provide grass*ᵐ* in the fields for your cattle, and you will eat and be satisfied.*ⁿ*

¹⁶Be careful, or you will be enticed to turn away and worship other gods and bow down to them.*ᵒ* ¹⁷Then the LORD's anger*ᵖ* will burn against you, and he will shut*�q* the heavens so that it will not rain and the ground will yield no produce, and you will soon perish*ʳ* from the good land the LORD is giving you. ¹⁸Fix these words of mine in your hearts and minds; tie them as symbols on your hands and bind them on your foreheads.*ˢ* ¹⁹Teach them to your children,*ᵗ* talking about them when you sit at home and when you walk along the road, when you lie down and when you get up.*ᵘ* ²⁰Write them on the doorframes of your houses and on your gates,*ᵛ* ²¹so that your days and the days of your children may be many*ʷ* in the land that the LORD swore to give your forefathers, as many as the days that the heavens are above the earth.*ˣ*

a 4 Hebrew *Yam Suph*; that is, Sea of Reeds

²²If you carefully observe[a] all these commands I am giving you to follow—to love the LORD your God, to walk in all his ways and to hold fast[b] to him— ²³then the LORD will drive out all these nations before you, and you will dispossess nations larger and stronger than you.[c] ²⁴Every place where you set your foot will be yours:[d] Your territory will extend from the desert to Lebanon, and from the Euphrates River to the western sea.[a] ²⁵No man will be able to stand against you. The LORD your God, as he promised you, will put the terror and fear of you on the whole land, wherever you go.[e]

²⁶See, I am setting before you today a blessing and a curse[f]— ²⁷the blessing[g] if you obey the commands of the LORD your God that I am giving you today; ²⁸the curse if you disobey[h] the commands of the LORD your God and turn from the way that I command you today by following other gods, which you have not known. ²⁹When the LORD your God has brought you into the land you are entering to possess, you are to proclaim on Mount Gerizim the blessings, and on Mount Ebal the curses.[i] ³⁰As you know, these mountains are across the Jordan, west of the road,[b] toward the setting sun, near the great trees of Moreh,[j] in the territory of those Canaanites living in the Arabah in the vicinity of Gilgal.[k] ³¹You are about to cross the Jordan to enter and take possession[l] of the land the LORD your God is giving you. When you have taken it over and are living there, ³²be sure that you obey all the decrees and laws I am setting before you today.

Chapter 12 Theme

12 These are the decrees and laws you must be careful to follow in the land that the LORD, the God of your fathers, has given you to possess—as long as you live in the land.[m] ²Destroy completely all the places on the high mountains and on the hills and under every spreading tree[n] where the nations you are dispossessing worship their gods. ³Break down their altars, smash[o] their sacred stones and burn their Asherah poles in the fire; cut down the idols of their gods and wipe out their names from those places.

⁴You must not worship the LORD your God in their way. ⁵But you are to seek the place the LORD your God will choose from among all your tribes to put his Name there for his dwelling.[p] To that place you must go; ⁶there bring your burnt offerings and sacrifices, your tithes[q] and special gifts, what you have vowed to give and your freewill offerings, and the firstborn of your herds and

---

a 24 That is, the Mediterranean   b 30 Or *Jordan, westward*

11:22
a Dt 6:17
b Dt 10:20

11:23
c Dt 4:38;
9:1

11:24
d Ge 15:18;
Ex 23:31;
Jos 1:3;
14:9

11:25
e Ex 23:27;
Dt 7:24

11:26
f Dt 30:1,15,19

11:27
g Dt 28:1-14

11:28
h Dt 28:15

11:29
i Dt 27:12-13;
Jos 8:33

11:30
j Ge 12:6
k Jos 4:19

11:31
l Dt 9:1;
Jos 1:11

12:1
m Dt 4:9-10;
1Ki 8:40

12:2
n 2Ki 16:4;
17:10

12:3
o Nu 33:52;
Dt 7:5;
Jdg 2:2

12:5
p ver 11,13;
2Ch 7:12,16

12:6
q Dt 14:22-23

12:7
a ver 12,18;
Lev 23:40;
Dt 14:26

12:10
b Dt 11:31

12:11
c ver 5; Dt 15:20;
16:2

12:12
d ver 7
e Dt 10:9;
14:29

12:14
f ver 11

12:15
g ver 20-23;
Dt 14:5;
15:22

12:16
h Ge 9:4;
Lev 7:26;
17:10-12
i Dt 15:23

12:18
j Dt 14:23
k ver 5
l ver 7,12

12:19
m Dt 14:27

12:20
n Dt 19:8
o Ge 15:18;
Dt 11:24

12:22
p ver 15

12:23
q ver 16;
Ge 9:4;
Lev 17:11,14

flocks. ⁷There, in the presence of the LORD your God, you and your families shall eat and shall rejoice*a* in everything you have put your hand to, because the LORD your God has blessed you.

⁸You are not to do as we do here today, everyone as he sees fit, ⁹since you have not yet reached the resting place and the inheritance the LORD your God is giving you. ¹⁰But you will cross the Jordan and settle in the land the LORD your God is giving*b* you as an inheritance, and he will give you rest from all your enemies around you so that you will live in safety. ¹¹Then to the place the LORD your God will choose as a dwelling for his Name*c*—there you are to bring everything I command you: your burnt offerings and sacrifices, your tithes and special gifts, and all the choice possessions you have vowed to the LORD. ¹²And there rejoice*d* before the LORD your God, you, your sons and daughters, your menservants and maidservants, and the Levites from your towns, who have no allotment or inheritance*e* of their own. ¹³Be careful not to sacrifice your burnt offerings anywhere you please. ¹⁴Offer them only at the place the LORD will choose*f* in one of your tribes, and there observe everything I command you.

¹⁵Nevertheless, you may slaughter your animals in any of your towns and eat as much of the meat as you want, as if it were gazelle or deer,*g* according to the blessing the LORD your God gives you. Both the ceremonially unclean and the clean may eat it. ¹⁶But you must not eat the blood;*h* pour it out on the ground like water.*i* ¹⁷You must not eat in your own towns the tithe of your grain and new wine and oil, or the firstborn of your herds and flocks, or whatever you have vowed to give, or your freewill offerings or special gifts. ¹⁸Instead, you are to eat*j* them in the presence of the LORD your God at the place the LORD your God will choose*k*—you, your sons and daughters, your menservants and maidservants, and the Levites from your towns—and you are to rejoice*l* before the LORD your God in everything you put your hand to. ¹⁹Be careful not to neglect the Levites*m* as long as you live in your land.

²⁰When the LORD your God has enlarged your territory*n* as he promised*o* you, and you crave meat and say, "I would like some meat," then you may eat as much of it as you want. ²¹If the place where the LORD your God chooses to put his Name is too far away from you, you may slaughter animals from the herds and flocks the LORD has given you, as I have commanded you, and in your own towns you may eat as much of them as you want. ²²Eat them as you would gazelle or deer.*p* Both the ceremonially unclean and the clean may eat. ²³But be sure you do not eat the blood,*q* because the blood is the life, and you must not eat the life with the meat. ²⁴You must not eat the blood; pour it out on the ground

like water. 25Do not eat it, so that it may go well[a] with you and your children after you, because you will be doing what is right[b] in the eyes of the LORD.

26But take your consecrated things and whatever you have vowed to give,[c] and go to the place the LORD will choose. 27Present your burnt offerings[d] on the altar of the LORD your God, both the meat and the blood. The blood of your sacrifices must be poured beside the altar of the LORD your God, but you may eat the meat. 28Be careful to obey all these regulations I am giving you, so that it may always go well[e] with you and your children after you, because you will be doing what is good and right in the eyes of the LORD your God.

29The LORD your God will cut off[f] before you the nations you are about to invade and dispossess. But when you have driven them out and settled in their land, 30and after they have been destroyed before you, be careful not to be ensnared by inquiring about their gods, saying, "How do these nations serve their gods? We will do the same." 31You must not worship the LORD your God in their way, because in worshiping their gods, they do all kinds of detestable things the LORD hates.[g] They even burn their sons[h] and daughters in the fire as sacrifices to their gods.

32See that you do all I command you; do not add[i] to it or take away from it.

Chapter 13 Theme

13 If a prophet,[j] or one who foretells by dreams, appears among you and announces to you a miraculous sign or wonder, 2and if the sign or wonder of which he has spoken takes place, and he says, "Let us follow other gods"[k] (gods you have not known) "and let us worship them," 3you must not listen to the words of that prophet or dreamer. The LORD your God is testing[l] you to find out whether you love him with all your heart and with all your soul. 4It is the LORD your God you must follow,[m] and him you must revere. Keep his commands and obey him; serve him and hold fast[n] to him. 5That prophet or dreamer must be put to death, because he preached rebellion against the LORD your God, who brought you out of Egypt and redeemed you from the land of slavery; he has tried to turn you from the way the LORD your God commanded you to follow. You must purge the evil[o] from among you.

6If your very own brother, or your son or daughter, or the wife you love, or your closest friend secretly entices[p] you, saying, "Let us go and worship other gods" (gods that neither you nor your fathers have known, 7gods of the peoples around you, whether near or far, from one end of the land to the other), 8do not yield[q]

12:25 [a] Dt 4:40; Isa 3:10; [b] Ex 15:26; Dt 13:18; 1Ki 11:38

12:26 [c] ver 17; Nu 5:9-10

12:27 [d] Lev 1:5,9,13

12:28 [e] ver 25; Dt 4:40

12:29 [f] Jos 23:4

12:31 [g] Dt 9:5; [h] Dt 18:10; Jer 32:35

12:32 [i] Dt 4:2; Jos 1:7; Rev 22:18-19

13:1 [j] Mt 24:24; Mk 13:22; 2Th 2:9

13:2 [k] ver 6,13

13:3 [l] Dt 8:2,16

13:4 [m] 2Ki 23:3; 2Ch 34:31; [n] Dt 10:20

13:5 [o] Dt 17:7,12; 1Co 5:13

13:6 [p] Dt 17:2-7; 29:18

13:8 [q] Pr 1:10

13:9
a Dt 17:5,7

13:11
b Dt 19:20

13:13
c ver 2,6;
1Jn 2:19

13:16
d Jos 6:24
e Jos 8:28;
Jer 49:2

13:17
f Nu 25:4
g Dt 30:3
h Dt 7:13
i Ge 22:17;
26:4,24;
28:14

13:18
j Dt 12:25,28

14:1
k Lev 19:28;
21:5;
Jer 16:6;
41:5;
Ro 8:14;
9:8;
Gal 3:26

14:2
l Lev 20:26
m Dt 7:6;
26:18-19

14:3
n Eze 4:14

14:4
o Lev 11:2-45;
Ac 10:14

14:8
p Lev 11:26-27

to him or listen to him. Show him no pity. Do not spare him or shield him. ⁹You must certainly put him to death.ᵃ Your hand must be the first in putting him to death, and then the hands of all the people. ¹⁰Stone him to death, because he tried to turn you away from the LORD your God, who brought you out of Egypt, out of the land of slavery. ¹¹Then all Israel will hear and be afraid,ᵇ and no one among you will do such an evil thing again.

¹²If you hear it said about one of the towns the LORD your God is giving you to live in ¹³that wicked menᶜ have arisen among you and have led the people of their town astray, saying, "Let us go and worship other gods" (gods you have not known), ¹⁴then you must inquire, probe and investigate it thoroughly. And if it is true and it has been proved that this detestable thing has been done among you, ¹⁵you must certainly put to the sword all who live in that town. Destroy it completely,ᵃ both its people and its livestock. ¹⁶Gather all the plunder of the town into the middle of the public square and completely burn the town and all its plunder as a whole burnt offering to the LORD your God.ᵈ It is to remain a ruinᵉ forever, never to be rebuilt. ¹⁷None of those condemned thingsᵃ shall be found in your hands, so that the LORD will turn from his fierce anger;ᶠ he will show you mercy, have compassionᵍ on you, and increase your numbers,ʰ as he promisedⁱ on oath to your forefathers, ¹⁸because you obey the LORD your God, keeping all his commands that I am giving you today and doing what is rightʲ in his eyes.

Chapter 14 Theme

14 You are the childrenᵏ of the LORD your God. Do not cut yourselves or shave the front of your heads for the dead, ²for you are a people holy to the LORD your God.ˡ Out of all the peoples on the face of the earth, the LORD has chosen you to be his treasured possession.ᵐ

³Do not eat any detestable thing.ⁿ ⁴These are the animals you may eat:ᵒ the ox, the sheep, the goat, ⁵the deer, the gazelle, the roe deer, the wild goat, the ibex, the antelope and the mountain sheep.ᵇ ⁶You may eat any animal that has a split hoof divided in two and that chews the cud. ⁷However, of those that chew the cud or that have a split hoof completely divided you may not eat the camel, the rabbit or the coney.ᶜ Although they chew the cud, they do not have a split hoof; they are ceremonially unclean for you. ⁸The pig is also unclean; although it has a split hoof, it does not chew the cud. You are not to eat their meat or touch their carcasses.ᵖ

ᵃ *15, 17* The Hebrew term refers to the irrevocable giving over of things or persons to the LORD, often by totally destroying them.   ᵇ *5* The precise identification of some of the birds and animals in this chapter is uncertain.   ᶜ *7* That is, the hyrax or rock badger

⁹Of all the creatures living in the water, you may eat any that has fins and scales. ¹⁰But anything that does not have fins and scales you may not eat; for you it is unclean.

¹¹You may eat any clean bird. ¹²But these you may not eat: the eagle, the vulture, the black vulture, ¹³the red kite, the black kite, any kind of falcon, ¹⁴any kind of raven, ¹⁵the horned owl, the screech owl, the gull, any kind of hawk, ¹⁶the little owl, the great owl, the white owl, ¹⁷the desert owl, the osprey, the cormorant, ¹⁸the stork, any kind of heron, the hoopoe and the bat.

¹⁹All flying insects that swarm are unclean to you; do not eat them. ²⁰But any winged creature that is clean you may eat.

²¹Do not eat anything you find already dead.ᵃ You may give it to an alien living in any of your towns, and he may eat it, or you may sell it to a foreigner. But you are a people holy to the Lord your God.ᵇ

Do not cook a young goat in its mother's milk.ᶜ

²²Be sure to set aside a tenthᵈ of all that your fields produce each year. ²³Eat the tithe of your grain, new wine and oil, and the firstborn of your herds and flocks in the presence of the Lord your God at the place he will choose as a dwelling for his Name,ᵉ so that you may learnᶠ to revere the Lord your God always. ²⁴But if that place is too distant and you have been blessed by the Lord your God and cannot carry your tithe (because the place where the Lord will choose to put his Name is so far away), ²⁵then exchange your tithe for silver, and take the silver with you and go to the place the Lord your God will choose. ²⁶Use the silver to buy whatever you like: cattle, sheep, wine or other fermented drink, or anything you wish. Then you and your household shall eat there in the presence of the Lord your God and rejoice.ᵍ ²⁷And do not neglect the Levitesʰ living in your towns, for they have no allotment or inheritance of their own.ⁱ

²⁸At the end of every three years, bring all the tithes of that year's produce and store it in your towns,ʲ ²⁹so that the Levites (who have no allotmentᵏ or inheritance of their own) and the aliens,ˡ the fatherless and the widows who live in your towns may come and eat and be satisfied, and so that the Lord your God may blessᵐ you in all the work of your hands.

Chapter 15 Theme

15 At the end of every seven years you must cancel debts.ⁿ ²This is how it is to be done: Every creditor shall cancel the loan he has made to his fellow Israelite. He shall not require payment from his fellow Israelite or brother, because the Lord's time for canceling debts has been proclaimed. ³You may require payment from a foreigner,ᵒ but you must cancel any debt your

14:21 ᵃLev 17:15; 22:8 ᵇver 2 ᶜEx 23:19; 34:26

14:22 ᵈLev 27:30; Dt 12:6,17; Ne 10:37

14:23 ᵉDt 12:5 ᶠDt 4:10

14:26 ᵍDt 12:7-8

14:27 ʰDt 12:19 ⁱNu 18:20

14:28 ʲDt 26:12

14:29 ᵏver 27 ˡDt 26:12 ᵐDt 15:10; Mal 3:10

15:1 ⁿDt 31:10

15:3 ᵒDt 23:20

brother owes you. ⁴However, there should be no poor among you, for in the land the Lᴏʀᴅ your God is giving you to possess as your inheritance, he will richly bless^a you, ⁵if only you fully obey the Lᴏʀᴅ your God and are careful to follow^b all these commands I am giving you today. ⁶For the Lᴏʀᴅ your God will bless you as he has promised, and you will lend to many nations but will borrow from none. You will rule over many nations but none will rule over you.^c

⁷If there is a poor man among your brothers in any of the towns of the land that the Lᴏʀᴅ your God is giving you, do not be hardhearted or tightfisted^d toward your poor brother. ⁸Rather be openhanded^e and freely lend him whatever he needs. ⁹Be careful not to harbor this wicked thought: "The seventh year, the year for canceling debts,^f is near," so that you do not show ill will^g toward your needy brother and give him nothing. He may then appeal to the Lᴏʀᴅ against you, and you will be found guilty of sin.^h ¹⁰Give generously to him and do so without a grudging heart;ⁱ then because of this the Lᴏʀᴅ your God will bless^j you in all your work and in everything you put your hand to. ¹¹There will always be poor people in the land. Therefore I command you to be openhanded toward your brothers and toward the poor and needy in your land.^k

¹²If a fellow Hebrew, a man or a woman, sells himself to you and serves you six years, in the seventh year you must let him go free.^l ¹³And when you release him, do not send him away empty-handed. ¹⁴Supply him liberally from your flock, your threshing floor and your winepress. Give to him as the Lᴏʀᴅ your God has blessed you. ¹⁵Remember that you were slaves^m in Egypt and the Lᴏʀᴅ your God redeemed you.ⁿ That is why I give you this command today.

¹⁶But if your servant says to you, "I do not want to leave you," because he loves you and your family and is well off with you, ¹⁷then take an awl and push it through his ear lobe into the door, and he will become your servant for life. Do the same for your maidservant.

¹⁸Do not consider it a hardship to set your servant free, because his service to you these six years has been worth twice as much as that of a hired hand. And the Lᴏʀᴅ your God will bless you in everything you do.

¹⁹Set apart for the Lᴏʀᴅ your God every firstborn male^o of your herds and flocks. Do not put the firstborn of your oxen to work, and do not shear the firstborn of your sheep. ²⁰Each year you and your family are to eat them in the presence of the Lᴏʀᴅ your God at the place he will choose.^p ²¹If an animal has a defect, is lame or blind, or has any serious flaw, you must not sacrifice it to the

LORD your God.[a] [22]You are to eat it in your own towns. Both the ceremonially unclean and the clean may eat it, as if it were gazelle or deer.[b] [23]But you must not eat the blood; pour it out on the ground like water.[c]

Chapter 16 Theme

16 Observe the month of Abib[d] and celebrate the Passover of the LORD your God, because in the month of Abib he brought you out of Egypt by night. [2]Sacrifice as the Passover to the LORD your God an animal from your flock or herd at the place the LORD will choose as a dwelling for his Name.[e] [3]Do not eat it with bread made with yeast, but for seven days eat unleavened bread, the bread of affliction,[f] because you left Egypt in haste[g]—so that all the days of your life you may remember the time of your departure from Egypt.[h] [4]Let no yeast be found in your possession in all your land for seven days. Do not let any of the meat you sacrifice on the evening of the first day remain until morning.[i]

[5]You must not sacrifice the Passover in any town the LORD your God gives you [6]except in the place he will choose as a dwelling for his Name. There you must sacrifice the Passover in the evening, when the sun goes down, on the anniversary[a][j] of your departure from Egypt. [7]Roast[k] it and eat it at the place the LORD your God will choose. Then in the morning return to your tents. [8]For six days eat unleavened bread and on the seventh day hold an assembly[l] to the LORD your God and do no work.

[9]Count off seven weeks[m] from the time you begin to put the sickle to the standing grain.[n] [10]Then celebrate the Feast of Weeks to the LORD your God by giving a freewill offering in proportion to the blessings the LORD your God has given you. [11]And rejoice[o] before the LORD your God at the place he will choose as a dwelling for his Name—you, your sons and daughters, your menservants and maidservants, the Levites[p] in your towns, and the aliens, the fatherless and the widows living among you. [12]Remember that you were slaves in Egypt,[q] and follow carefully these decrees.

[13]Celebrate the Feast of Tabernacles for seven days after you have gathered the produce of your threshing floor[r] and your winepress.[s] [14]Be joyful[t] at your Feast—you, your sons and daughters, your menservants and maidservants, and the Levites, the aliens, the fatherless and the widows who live in your towns. [15]For seven days celebrate the Feast to the LORD your God at the place the LORD will choose. For the LORD your God will bless you in all your harvest and in all the work of your hands, and your joy[u] will be complete.

[a] 6 Or *down, at the time of day*

Cross-references

15:21
[a] Lev 22:19-25

15:22
[b] Dt 12:15,22

15:23
[c] Dt 12:16

16:1
[d] Ex 12:2; 13:4

16:2
[e] Dt 12:5,26

16:3
[f] Ex 12:8,39; 34:18
[g] Ex 12:11, 15,19
[h] Ex 13:3,6-7

16:4
[i] Ex 12:10; 34:25

16:6
[j] Ex 12:6; Dt 12:5

16:7
[k] Ex 12:8; 2Ch 35:13

16:8
[l] Ex 12:16; 13:6; Lev 23:8

16:9
[m] Ex 34:22; Lev 23:15
[n] Ex 23:16; Nu 28:26

16:11
[o] Dt 12:7
[p] Dt 12:12

16:12
[q] Dt 15:15

16:13
[r] Lev 23:34
[s] Ex 23:16

16:14
[t] ver 11

16:15
[u] Lev 23:39

16:16
a Ex 23:14,16
b Ex 34:20

16:18
c Dt 1:16

16:19
d Ex 23:2,8
e Lev 19:15;
Dt 1:17
f Ecc 7:7

16:21
g Dt 7:5
h Ex 34:13;
2Ki 17:16;
21:3;
2Ch 33:3

16:22
i Lev 26:1

17:1
j Mal 1:8,13
k Dt 15:21

17:2
l Dt 13:6-11

17:3
m Jer 7:22-23
n Job 31:26

17:4
o Dt 13:12-14

17:5
p Lev 24:14

17:6
q Nu 35:30;
Dt 19:15;
Jos 7:25;
Mt 18:16;
Jn 8:17;
2Co 13:1;
1Ti 5:19;
Heb 10:28

17:7
r Dt 13:5,9

17:8
s 2Ch 19:10
t Dt 12:5;
Hag 2:11

17:9
u Dt 19:17;
Eze 44:24

¹⁶Three times a year all your men must appear before the LORD your God at the place he will choose: at the Feast of Unleavened Bread, the Feast of Weeks and the Feast of Tabernacles.ᵃ No man should appear before the LORD empty-handed:ᵇ ¹⁷Each of you must bring a gift in proportion to the way the LORD your God has blessed you.

¹⁸Appoint judgesᶜ and officials for each of your tribes in every town the LORD your God is giving you, and they shall judge the people fairly. ¹⁹Do not pervert justiceᵈ or show partiality.ᵉ Do not accept a bribe,ᶠ for a bribe blinds the eyes of the wise and twists the words of the righteous. ²⁰Follow justice and justice alone, so that you may live and possess the land the LORD your God is giving you.

²¹Do not set up any wooden Asherah poleᵃᵍ beside the altar you build to the LORD your God,ʰ ²²and do not erect a sacred stone,ⁱ for these the LORD your God hates.

Chapter 17 Theme

17 Do not sacrifice to the LORD your God an ox or a sheep that has any defectʲ or flaw in it, for that would be detestable to him.ᵏ

²If a man or woman living among you in one of the towns the LORD gives you is found doing evil in the eyes of the LORD your God in violation of his covenant,ˡ ³and contrary to my commandᵐ has worshiped other gods, bowing down to them or to the sunⁿ or the moon or the stars of the sky, ⁴and this has been brought to your attention, then you must investigate it thoroughly. If it is true and it has been proved that this detestable thing has been done in Israel,ᵒ ⁵take the man or woman who has done this evil deed to your city gate and stone that person to death.ᵖ ⁶On the testimony of two or three witnesses a man shall be put to death, but no one shall be put to death on the testimony of only one witness.ᵠ ⁷The hands of the witnesses must be the first in putting him to death, and then the hands of all the people. You must purge the evilʳ from among you.

⁸If cases come before your courts that are too difficult for you to judge—whether bloodshed, lawsuits or assaultsˢ—take them to the place the LORD your God will choose.ᵗ ⁹Go to the priests, who are Levites, and to the judge who is in office at that time. Inquire of them and they will give you the verdict.ᵘ ¹⁰You must act according to the decisions they give you at the place the LORD will choose. Be careful to do everything they direct you to do. ¹¹Act according to the law they teach you and the decisions they give

a 21 Or *Do not plant any tree dedicated to Asherah*

you. Do not turn aside from what they tell you, to the right or to the left.*ᵃ* ¹²The man who shows contempt *ᵇ* for the judge or for the priest who stands ministering there to the Lord your God must be put to death. You must purge the evil from Israel. ¹³All the people will hear and be afraid, and will not be contemptuous again.*ᶜ*

¹⁴When you enter the land the Lord your God is giving you and have taken possession of it and settled in it, and you say, "Let us set a king over us like all the nations around us,"*ᵈ* ¹⁵be sure to appoint over you the king the Lord your God chooses. He must be from among your own brothers.*ᵉ* Do not place a foreigner over you, one who is not a brother Israelite. ¹⁶The king, moreover, must not acquire great numbers of horses for himself*ᶠ* or make the people return to Egypt*ᵍ* to get more of them,*ʰ* for the Lord has told you, "You are not to go back that way again."*ⁱ* ¹⁷He must not take many wives,*ʲ* or his heart will be led astray. He must not accumulate large amounts of silver and gold.

¹⁸When he takes the throne of his kingdom, he is to write*ᵏ* for himself on a scroll a copy of this law, taken from that of the priests, who are Levites. ¹⁹It is to be with him, and he is to read it all the days of his life*ˡ* so that he may learn to revere the Lord his God and follow carefully all the words of this law and these decrees ²⁰and not consider himself better than his brothers and turn from the law*ᵐ* to the right or to the left.*ⁿ* Then he and his descendants will reign a long time over his kingdom in Israel.

Chapter 18 Theme

18 The priests, who are Levites—indeed the whole tribe of Levi—are to have no allotment or inheritance with Israel. They shall live on the offerings made to the Lord by fire, for that is their inheritance.*ᵒ* ²They shall have no inheritance among their brothers; the Lord is their inheritance, as he promised them.

³This is the share due the priests from the people who sacrifice a bull or a sheep: the shoulder, the jowls and the inner parts.*ᵖ* ⁴You are to give them the firstfruits of your grain, new wine and oil, and the first wool from the shearing of your sheep,*�q* ⁵for the Lord your God has chosen them*ʳ* and their descendants out of all your tribes to stand and minister*ˢ* in the Lord's name always.

⁶If a Levite moves from one of your towns anywhere in Israel where he is living, and comes in all earnestness to the place the Lord will choose,*ᵗ* ⁷he may minister in the name of the Lord his God like all his fellow Levites who serve there in the presence of the Lord. ⁸He is to share equally in their benefits, even though he has received money from the sale of family possessions.*ᵘ*

⁹When you enter the land the Lord your God is giving you, do not learn to imitate*ᵛ* the detestable ways of the nations there. ¹⁰Let

17:11
ᵃ Dt 25:1

17:12
ᵇ Nu 15:30

17:13
ᶜ Dt 13:11;
19:20

17:14
ᵈ Dt 11:31;
1Sa 8:5,19-20

17:15
ᵉ Jer 30:21

17:16
ᶠ 1Ki 4:26;
10:26
ᵍ Isa 31:1;
Hos 11:5
ʰ 1Ki 10:28;
Eze 17:15
ⁱ Ex 13:17

17:17
ʲ 1Ki 11:3

17:18
ᵏ Dt 31:22,24

17:19
ˡ Jos 1:8

17:20
ᵐ 1Ki 15:5
ⁿ Dt 5:32

18:1
ᵒ Dt 10:9;
1Co 9:13

18:3
ᵖ Lev 7:28-34

18:4
q Ex 22:29;
Nu 18:12

18:5
ʳ Ex 28:1
ˢ Dt 10:8

18:6
ᵗ Nu 35:2-3

18:8
ᵘ 2Ch 31:4;
Ne 12:44,47

18:9
ᵛ Dt 12:29-31

18:10
a Dt 12:31
b Lev 19:31

18:12
c Lev 18:24;
Dt 9:4

18:15
d Jn 1:21;
Ac 3:22*;
7:37*

18:16
e Ex 20:19;
Dt 5:23-27

18:18
f Isa 51:16;
Jn 17:8
g Jn 4:25-26;
8:28;
12:49-50

18:19
h Ac 3:23*

18:20
i Jer 14:14
j Dt 13:1-5

18:22
k Jer 28:9
l ver 20

19:1
m Dt 12:29

no one be found among you who sacrifices his son or daughter in*a* the fire, who practices divination*a* or sorcery, interprets omens, engages in witchcraft,*b* 11or casts spells, or who is a medium or spiritist or who consults the dead. 12Anyone who does these things is detestable to the LORD, and because of these detestable practices the LORD your God will drive out those nations before you.*c* 13You must be blameless before the LORD your God.

14The nations you will dispossess listen to those who practice sorcery or divination. But as for you, the LORD your God has not permitted you to do so. 15The LORD your God will raise up for you a prophet like me from among your own brothers.*d* You must listen to him. 16For this is what you asked of the LORD your God at Horeb on the day of the assembly when you said, "Let us not hear the voice of the LORD our God nor see this great fire anymore, or we will die."*e*

17The LORD said to me: "What they say is good. 18I will raise up for them a prophet like you from among their brothers; I will put my words*f* in his mouth, and he will tell them everything I command him.*g* 19If anyone does not listen to my words that the prophet speaks in my name, I myself will call him to account.*h* 20But a prophet who presumes to speak in my name anything I have not commanded him to say, or a prophet who speaks in the name of other gods,*i* must be put to death."*j*

21You may say to yourselves, "How can we know when a message has not been spoken by the LORD?" 22If what a prophet proclaims in the name of the LORD does not take place or come true, that is a message the LORD has not spoken.*k* That prophet has spoken presumptuously.*l* Do not be afraid of him.

Chapter 19 Theme

19 When the LORD your God has destroyed the nations whose land he is giving you, and when you have driven them out and settled in their towns and houses,*m* 2then set aside for yourselves three cities centrally located in the land the LORD your God is giving you to possess. 3Build roads to them and divide into three parts the land the LORD your God is giving you as an inheritance, so that anyone who kills a man may flee there.

4This is the rule concerning the man who kills another and flees there to save his life—one who kills his neighbor unintentionally, without malice aforethought. 5For instance, a man may go into the forest with his neighbor to cut wood, and as he swings his ax to fell a tree, the head may fly off and hit his neighbor and kill him. That man may flee to one of these cities and save his life.

a 10 Or *who makes his son or daughter pass through*

⁶Otherwise, the avenger of blood*ᵃ* might pursue him in a rage, overtake him if the distance is too great, and kill him even though he is not deserving of death, since he did it to his neighbor without malice aforethought. ⁷This is why I command you to set aside for yourselves three cities.

⁸If the LORD your God enlarges your territory, as he promised on oath to your forefathers, and gives you the whole land he promised them, ⁹because you carefully follow all these laws I command you today—to love the LORD your God and to walk always in his ways*ᵇ*—then you are to set aside three more cities. ¹⁰Do this so that innocent blood will not be shed in your land, which the LORD your God is giving you as your inheritance, and so that you will not be guilty of bloodshed.*ᶜ*

¹¹But if a man hates his neighbor and lies in wait for him, assaults and kills him,*ᵈ* and then flees to one of these cities, ¹²the elders of his town shall send for him, bring him back from the city, and hand him over to the avenger of blood to die. ¹³Show him no pity.*ᵉ* You must purge from Israel the guilt of shedding innocent blood,*ᶠ* so that it may go well with you.

¹⁴Do not move your neighbor's boundary stone set up by your predecessors in the inheritance you receive in the land the LORD your God is giving you to possess.*ᵍ*

¹⁵One witness is not enough to convict a man accused of any crime or offense he may have committed. A matter must be established by the testimony of two or three witnesses.*ʰ*

¹⁶If a malicious witness*ⁱ* takes the stand to accuse a man of a crime, ¹⁷the two men involved in the dispute must stand in the presence of the LORD before the priests and the judges*ʲ* who are in office at the time. ¹⁸The judges must make a thorough investigation, and if the witness proves to be a liar, giving false testimony against his brother, ¹⁹then do to him as he intended to do to his brother.*ᵏ* You must purge the evil from among you. ²⁰The rest of the people will hear of this and be afraid,*ˡ* and never again will such an evil thing be done among you. ²¹Show no pity:*ᵐ* life for life, eye for eye, tooth for tooth, hand for hand, foot for foot.*ⁿ*

Chapter 20 Theme

20 When you go to war against your enemies and see horses and chariots and an army greater than yours,*ᵒ* do not be afraid*ᵖ* of them,* q* because the LORD your God, who brought you up out of Egypt, will be with you. ²When you are about to go into battle, the priest shall come forward and address the army. ³He shall say: "Hear, O Israel, today you are going into battle against your enemies. Do not be fainthearted*ʳ* or afraid; do not be terrified or give way to panic before them. ⁴For the LORD your God is

19:6
*ᵃ*Nu 35:12

19:9
*ᵇ*Jos 20:7-8

19:10
*ᶜ*Nu 35:33;
Dt 21:1-9

19:11
*ᵈ*Nu 35:16

19:13
*ᵉ*Dt 7:2
*ᶠ*1Ki 2:31

19:14
*ᵍ*Dt 27:17;
Pr 22:28;
Hos 5:10

19:15
*ʰ*Nu 35:30;
Dt 17:6;
Mt 18:16*;
Jn 8:17;
2Co 13:1*;
1Ti 5:19;
Heb 10:28

19:16
*ⁱ*Ex 23:1;
Ps 27:12

19:17
*ʲ*Dt 17:9

19:19
*ᵏ*Pr 19:5,9

19:20
*ˡ*Dt 17:13;
21:21

19:21
*ᵐ*ver 13
*ⁿ*Ex 21:24;
Lev 24:20;
Mt 5:38*

20:1
*ᵒ*Ps 20:7;
Isa 31:1
*ᵖ*Dt 31:6,8
*q*2Ch 32:7-8

20:3
*ʳ*Jos 23:10

20:4
a Dt 1:30;
3:22;
Jos 23:10

20:5
b Ne 12:27

20:7
c Dt 24:5

20:8
d Jdg 7:3

20:10
e Lk 14:31-32

20:11
f 1Ki 9:21

20:13
g Nu 31:7

20:14
h Jos 8:2;
22:8

20:16
i Ex 23:31-33;
Nu 21:2-3;
Dt 7:2;
Jos 11:14

20:18
j Ex 34:16;
Dt 7:4;
12:30-31
k Ex 23:33

the one who goes with you to fight*a* for you against your enemies to give you victory. ”

⁵The officers shall say to the army: "Has anyone built a new house and not dedicated*b* it? Let him go home, or he may die in battle and someone else may dedicate it. ⁶Has anyone planted a vineyard and not begun to enjoy it? Let him go home, or he may die in battle and someone else enjoy it. ⁷Has anyone become pledged to a woman and not married her? Let him go home, or he may die in battle and someone else marry her.*c*" ⁸Then the officers shall add, "Is any man afraid or fainthearted? Let him go home so that his brothers will not become disheartened too."*d* ⁹When the officers have finished speaking to the army, they shall appoint commanders over it.

¹⁰When you march up to attack a city, make its people an offer of peace.*e* ¹¹If they accept and open their gates, all the people in it shall be subject to forced labor*f* and shall work for you. ¹²If they refuse to make peace and they engage you in battle, lay siege to that city. ¹³When the LORD your God delivers it into your hand, put to the sword all the men in it.*g* ¹⁴As for the women, the children, the livestock*h* and everything else in the city, you may take these as plunder for yourselves. And you may use the plunder the LORD your God gives you from your enemies. ¹⁵This is how you are to treat all the cities that are at a distance from you and do not belong to the nations nearby.

¹⁶However, in the cities of the nations the LORD your God is giving you as an inheritance, do not leave alive anything that breathes.*i* ¹⁷Completely destroy*a* them—the Hittites, Amorites, Canaanites, Perizzites, Hivites and Jebusites—as the LORD your God has commanded you. ¹⁸Otherwise, they will teach you to follow all the detestable things they do in worshiping their gods,*j* and you will sin*k* against the LORD your God.

¹⁹When you lay siege to a city for a long time, fighting against it to capture it, do not destroy its trees by putting an ax to them, because you can eat their fruit. Do not cut them down. Are the trees of the field people, that you should besiege them?*b* ²⁰However, you may cut down trees that you know are not fruit trees and use them to build siege works until the city at war with you falls.

Chapter 21 Theme _____

21 If a man is found slain, lying in a field in the land the LORD your God is giving you to possess, and it is not known who killed him, ²your elders and judges shall go out and measure the

a 17 The Hebrew term refers to the irrevocable giving over of things or persons to the LORD, often by totally destroying them.   *b 19* Or *down to use in the siege, for the fruit trees are for the benefit of man.*

distance from the body to the neighboring towns. ³Then the elders of the town nearest the body shall take a heifer that has never been worked and has never worn a yoke ⁴and lead her down to a valley that has not been plowed or planted and where there is a flowing stream. There in the valley they are to break the heifer's neck. ⁵The priests, the sons of Levi, shall step forward, for the LORD your God has chosen them to minister and to pronounce blessings*a* in the name of the LORD and to decide all cases of dispute and assault.*b* ⁶Then all the elders of the town nearest the body shall wash their hands*c* over the heifer whose neck was broken in the valley, ⁷and they shall declare: "Our hands did not shed this blood, nor did our eyes see it done. ⁸Accept this atonement for your people Israel, whom you have redeemed, O LORD, and do not hold your people guilty of the blood of an innocent man." And the bloodshed will be atoned for.*d* ⁹So you will purge*e* from yourselves the guilt of shedding innocent blood, since you have done what is right in the eyes of the LORD.

¹⁰When you go to war against your enemies and the LORD your God delivers them into your hands*f* and you take captives, ¹¹if you notice among the captives a beautiful woman and are attracted to her, you may take her as your wife. ¹²Bring her into your home and have her shave her head,*g* trim her nails ¹³and put aside the clothes she was wearing when captured. After she has lived in your house and mourned her father and mother for a full month,*h* then you may go to her and be her husband and she shall be your wife. ¹⁴If you are not pleased with her, let her go wherever she wishes. You must not sell her or treat her as a slave, since you have dishonored her.*i*

¹⁵If a man has two wives, and he loves one but not the other, and both bear him sons but the firstborn is the son of the wife he does not love,*j* ¹⁶when he wills his property to his sons, he must not give the rights of the firstborn to the son of the wife he loves in preference to his actual firstborn, the son of the wife he does not love.*k* ¹⁷He must acknowledge the son of his unloved wife as the firstborn by giving him a double share of all he has. That son is the first sign of his father's strength.*l* The right of the firstborn belongs to him.*m*

¹⁸If a man has a stubborn and rebellious son who does not obey his father and mother*n* and will not listen to them when they discipline him, ¹⁹his father and mother shall take hold of him and bring him to the elders at the gate of his town. ²⁰They shall say to the elders, "This son of ours is stubborn and rebellious. He will not obey us. He is a profligate and a drunkard." ²¹Then all the men of his town shall stone him to death. You must purge the evil*o* from among you. All Israel will hear of it and be afraid.*p*

21:5
a 1Ch 23:13
b Dt 17:8-11

21:6
c Mt 27:24

21:8
d Nu 35:33-34

21:9
e Dt 19:13

21:10
f Jos 21:44

21:12
g Lev 14:9;
Nu 6:9

21:13
h Ps 45:10

21:14
i Ge 34:2

21:15
j Ge 29:33

21:16
k 1Ch 26:10

21:17
l Ge 49:3
m Ge 25:31

21:18
n Pr 1:8;
Isa 30:1;
Eph 6:1-3

21:21
o Dt 19:19
p Dt 13:11

21:22
a Dt 22:26;
Mk 14:64;
Ac 23:29

21:23
b Jos 8:29; 10:27;
Jn 19:31
c Gal 3:13*
d Lev 18:25;
Nu 35:34

22:1
e Ex 23:4-5

22:4
f Ex 23:5

22:6
g Lev 22:28

22:7
h Dt 4:40

22:9
i Lev 19:19

22:10
j 2Co 6:14

22:11
k Lev 19:19

22:12
l Nu 15:37-41;
Mt 23:5

22:13
m Dt 24:1

22:18
n Ex 18:21

22If a man guilty of a capital offense*a* is put to death and his body is hung on a tree, 23you must not leave his body on the tree overnight.*b* Be sure to bury him that same day, because anyone who is hung on a tree is under God's curse.*c* You must not desecrate*d* the land the LORD your God is giving you as an inheritance.

Chapter 22 Theme

22 If you see your brother's ox or sheep straying, do not ignore it but be sure to take it back to him.*e* 2If the brother does not live near you or if you do not know who he is, take it home with you and keep it until he comes looking for it. Then give it back to him. 3Do the same if you find your brother's donkey or his cloak or anything he loses. Do not ignore it.

4If you see your brother's donkey*f* or his ox fallen on the road, do not ignore it. Help him get it to its feet.

5A woman must not wear men's clothing, nor a man wear women's clothing, for the LORD your God detests anyone who does this.

6If you come across a bird's nest beside the road, either in a tree or on the ground, and the mother is sitting on the young or on the eggs, do not take the mother with the young.*g* 7You may take the young, but be sure to let the mother go, so that it may go well with you and you may have a long life.*h*

8When you build a new house, make a parapet around your roof so that you may not bring the guilt of bloodshed on your house if someone falls from the roof.

9Do not plant two kinds of seed in your vineyard;*i* if you do, not only the crops you plant but also the fruit of the vineyard will be defiled.*a*

10Do not plow with an ox and a donkey yoked together.*j*

11Do not wear clothes of wool and linen woven together.*k*

12Make tassels on the four corners of the cloak you wear.*l*

13If a man takes a wife and, after lying with her*m*, dislikes her 14and slanders her and gives her a bad name, saying, "I married this woman, but when I approached her, I did not find proof of her virginity," 15then the girl's father and mother shall bring proof that she was a virgin to the town elders at the gate. 16The girl's father will say to the elders, "I gave my daughter in marriage to this man, but he dislikes her. 17Now he has slandered her and said, 'I did not find your daughter to be a virgin.' But here is the proof of my daughter's virginity." Then her parents shall display the cloth before the elders of the town, 18and the elders*n* shall take the man and punish him. 19They shall fine him a hundred shekels of

a9 Or *be forfeited to the sanctuary*

silver[a] and give them to the girl's father, because this man has given an Israelite virgin a bad name. She shall continue to be his wife; he must not divorce her as long as he lives.

²⁰If, however, the charge is true and no proof of the girl's virginity can be found, ²¹she shall be brought to the door of her father's house and there the men of her town shall stone her to death. She has done a disgraceful thing[a] in Israel by being promiscuous while still in her father's house. You must purge the evil from among you.

²²If a man is found sleeping with another man's wife, both the man who slept with her and the woman must die.[b] You must purge the evil from Israel.

²³If a man happens to meet in a town a virgin pledged to be married and he sleeps with her, ²⁴you shall take both of them to the gate of that town and stone them to death—the girl because she was in a town and did not scream for help, and the man because he violated another man's wife. You must purge the evil from among you.[c]

²⁵But if out in the country a man happens to meet a girl pledged to be married and rapes her, only the man who has done this shall die. ²⁶Do nothing to the girl; she has committed no sin deserving death. This case is like that of someone who attacks and murders his neighbor, ²⁷for the man found the girl out in the country, and though the betrothed girl screamed, there was no one to rescue her.

²⁸If a man happens to meet a virgin who is not pledged to be married and rapes her and they are discovered,[d] ²⁹he shall pay the girl's father fifty shekels of silver.[b] He must marry the girl, for he has violated her. He can never divorce her as long as he lives.

³⁰A man is not to marry his father's wife; he must not dishonor his father's bed.[e]

Chapter 23 Theme

23

No one who has been emasculated by crushing or cutting may enter the assembly of the LORD.

²No one born of a forbidden marriage[c] nor any of his descendants may enter the assembly of the LORD, even down to the tenth generation.

³No Ammonite or Moabite or any of his descendants may enter the assembly of the LORD, even down to the tenth generation.[f] ⁴For they did not come to meet you with bread and water on your way when you came out of Egypt, and they hired Balaam[g] son of Beor from Pethor in Aram Naharai[d] to pronounce a curse

22:21
[a]Ge 34:7;
Dt 13:5;
23:17-18;
Jdg 20:6;
2Sa 13:12

22:22
[b]Lev 20:10;
Jn 8:5

22:24
[c]ver 21-22;
1Co 5:13*

22:28
[d]Ex 22:16

22:30
[e]Lev 18:8;
20:11;
Dt 27:20;
1Co 5:1

23:3
[f]Ne 13:2

23:4
[g]Nu 22:5-6;
23:7;
2Pe 2:15

---

[a]19 That is, about 2 1/2 pounds (about 1 kilogram)   [b]29 That is, about 1 1/4 pounds (about 0.6 kilogram)   [c]2 Or *one of illegitimate birth*   [d]4 That is, Northwest Mesopotamia

23:5
a Pr 26:2

23:6
b Ezr 9:12

23:7
c Ge 25:26;
Ob 1:10,12
d Ex 22:21;
23:9;
Lev 19:34;
Dt 10:19

23:10
e Lev 15:16

23:14
f Lev 26:12
g Ex 3:5

23:15
h 1Sa 30:15

23:16
i Ex 22:21

23:17
j Ge 19:25;
2Ki 23:7
k Lev 19:29;
Dt 22:21

23:19
l Ex 22:25;
Lev 25:35-37

23:20
m Dt 15:10;
28:12

23:21
n Nu 30:1-2;
Ecc 5:4-5;
Mt 5:33

23:25
o Mt 12:1;
Mk 2:23;
Lk 6:1

on you. [5]However, the LORD your God would not listen to Balaam but turned the curse[a] into a blessing for you, because the LORD your God loves you. [6]Do not seek a treaty of friendship with them as long as you live.[b]

[7]Do not abhor an Edomite, for he is your brother.[c] Do not abhor an Egyptian, because you lived as an alien in his country.[d] [8]The third generation of children born to them may enter the assembly of the LORD.

[9]When you are encamped against your enemies, keep away from everything impure. [10]If one of your men is unclean because of a nocturnal emission, he is to go outside the camp and stay there.[e] [11]But as evening approaches he is to wash himself, and at sunset he may return to the camp.

[12]Designate a place outside the camp where you can go to relieve yourself. [13]As part of your equipment have something to dig with, and when you relieve yourself, dig a hole and cover up your excrement. [14]For the LORD your God moves[f] about in your camp to protect you and to deliver your enemies to you. Your camp must be holy,[g] so that he will not see among you anything indecent and turn away from you.

[15]If a slave has taken refuge with you, do not hand him over to his master.[h] [16]Let him live among you wherever he likes and in whatever town he chooses. Do not oppress[i] him.

[17]No Israelite man[j] or woman is to become a shrine prostitute.[k] [18]You must not bring the earnings of a female prostitute or of a male prostitute[a] into the house of the LORD your God to pay any vow, because the LORD your God detests them both.

[19]Do not charge your brother interest, whether on money or food or anything else that may earn interest.[l] [20]You may charge a foreigner interest, but not a brother Israelite, so that the LORD your God may bless[m] you in everything you put your hand to in the land you are entering to possess.

[21]If you make a vow to the LORD your God, do not be slow to pay it, for the LORD your God will certainly demand it of you and you will be guilty of sin.[n] [22]But if you refrain from making a vow, you will not be guilty. [23]Whatever your lips utter you must be sure to do, because you made your vow freely to the LORD your God with your own mouth.

[24]If you enter your neighbor's vineyard, you may eat all the grapes you want, but do not put any in your basket. [25]If you enter your neighbor's grainfield, you may pick kernels with your hands, but you must not put a sickle to his standing grain.[o]

[a] 18 Hebrew *of a dog*

Chapter 24 Theme _____

24 If a man marries a woman who becomes displeasing to him[a] because he finds something indecent about her, and he writes her a certificate of divorce,[b] gives it to her and sends her from his house, ²and if after she leaves his house she becomes the wife of another man, ³and her second husband dislikes her and writes her a certificate of divorce, gives it to her and sends her from his house, or if he dies, ⁴then her first husband, who divorced her, is not allowed to marry her again after she has been defiled. That would be detestable in the eyes of the LORD. Do not bring sin upon the land the LORD[c] your God is giving you as an inheritance.

⁵If a man has recently married, he must not be sent to war or have any other duty laid on him. For one year he is to be free to stay at home and bring happiness to the wife he has married.[d]

⁶Do not take a pair of millstones—not even the upper one—as security for a debt, because that would be taking a man's livelihood as security.

⁷If a man is caught kidnapping one of his brother Israelites and treats him as a slave or sells him, the kidnapper must die.[e] You must purge the evil from among you.

⁸In cases of leprous[a] diseases be very careful to do exactly as the priests, who are Levites, instruct you. You must follow carefully what I have commanded them.[f] ⁹Remember what the LORD your God did to Miriam along the way after you came out of Egypt.[g]

¹⁰When you make a loan of any kind to your neighbor, do not go into his house to get what he is offering as a pledge. ¹¹Stay outside and let the man to whom you are making the loan bring the pledge out to you. ¹²If the man is poor, do not go to sleep with his pledge in your possession. ¹³Return his cloak to him by sunset[h] so that he may sleep in it. Then he will thank you, and it will be regarded as a righteous act in the sight of the LORD your God.[i]

¹⁴Do not take advantage of a hired man who is poor and needy, whether he is a brother Israelite or an alien living in one of your towns.[j] ¹⁵Pay him his wages each day before sunset, because he is poor[k] and is counting on it.[l] Otherwise he may cry to the LORD against you, and you will be guilty of sin.[m]

¹⁶Fathers shall not be put to death for their children, nor children put to death for their fathers; each is to die for his own sin.[n]

¹⁷Do not deprive the alien or the fatherless of justice,[o] or take the cloak of the widow as a pledge. ¹⁸Remember that you were slaves in Egypt and the LORD your God redeemed you from there. That is why I command you to do this.

a8 The Hebrew word was used for various diseases affecting the skin—not necessarily leprosy.

24:1
[a] Dt 22:13
[b] Mt 5:31*;
19:7-9;
Mk 10:4-5

24:4
[c] Jer 3:1

24:5
[d] Dt 20:7

24:7
[e] Ex 21:16

24:8
[f] Lev 13:1-46;
14:2

24:9
[g] Nu 12:10

24:13
[h] Ex 22:26
[i] Dt 6:25;
Da 4:27

24:14
[j] Lev 25:35-43;
Dt 15:12-18

24:15
[k] Jer 22:13
[l] Lev 19:13
[m] Dt 15:9;
Jas 5:4

24:16
[n] 2Ki 14:6;
2Ch 25:4;
Jer 31:29-30;
Eze 18:20

24:17
[o] Dt 1:17;
10:17-18;
16:19

24:19
a Lev 19:9; 23:22
b Pr 19:17

24:20
c Lev 19:10

24:22
d ver 18

25:1
e Dt 19:17
f Dt 1:16-17

25:2
g Lk 12:47-48

25:3
h 2Co 11:24
i Job 18:3

25:4
j Pr 12:10;
1Co 9:9*;
1Ti 5:18*

25:5
k Mt 22:24;
Mk 12:19;
Lk 20:28

25:6
l Ge 38:9;
Ru 4:5,10

25:7
m Ru 4:1-2,5-6

25:9
n Ru 4:7-8,11

25:12
o Dt 19:13

25:13
p Lev 19:35-37;
Pr 11:1;
Eze 45:10;
Mic 6:11

25:15
q Ex 20:12

25:16
r Pr 11:1

¹⁹When you are harvesting in your field and you overlook a sheaf, do not go back to get it.*ᵃ* Leave it for the alien, the fatherless and the widow, so that the Lᴏʀᴅ your God may bless*ᵇ* you in all the work of your hands. ²⁰When you beat the olives from your trees, do not go over the branches a second 'time.*ᶜ* Leave what remains for the alien, the fatherless and the widow. ²¹When you harvest the grapes in your vineyard, do not go over the vines again. Leave what remains for the alien, the fatherless and the widow. ²²Remember that you were slaves in Egypt. That is why I command you to do this.*ᵈ*

Chapter 25 Theme _____

25 When men have a dispute, they are to take it to court and the judges will decide the case,*ᵉ* acquitting the innocent and condemning the guilty.*ᶠ* ²If the guilty man deserves to be beaten,*ᵍ* the judge shall make him lie down and have him flogged in his presence with the number of lashes his crime deserves, ³but he must not give him more than forty lashes.*ʰ* If he is flogged more than that, your brother will be degraded in your eyes.*ⁱ*

⁴Do not muzzle an ox while it is treading out the grain.*ʲ*

⁵If brothers are living together and one of them dies without a son, his widow must not marry outside the family. Her husband's brother shall take her and marry her and fulfill the duty of a brother-in-law to her.*ᵏ* ⁶The first son she bears shall carry on the name of the dead brother so that his name will not be blotted out from Israel.*ˡ*

⁷However, if a man does not want to marry his brother's wife, she shall go to the elders at the town gate and say, "My husband's brother refuses to carry on his brother's name in Israel. He will not fulfill the duty of a brother-in-law to me."*ᵐ* ⁸Then the elders of his town shall summon him and talk to him. If he persists in saying, "I do not want to marry her," ⁹his brother's widow shall go up to him in the presence of the elders, take off one of his sandals,*ⁿ* spit in his face and say, "This is what is done to the man who will not build up his brother's family line." ¹⁰That man's line shall be known in Israel as The Family of the Unsandaled.

¹¹If two men are fighting and the wife of one of them comes to rescue her husband from his assailant, and she reaches out and seizes him by his private parts, ¹²you shall cut off her hand. Show her no pity.*ᵒ*

¹³Do not have two differing weights in your bag—one heavy, one light.*ᵖ* ¹⁴Do not have two differing measures in your house— one large, one small. ¹⁵You must have accurate and honest weights and measures, so that you may live long*�q* in the land the Lᴏʀᴅ your God is giving you. ¹⁶For the Lᴏʀᴅ your God detests anyone who does these things, anyone who deals dishonestly.*ʳ*

¹⁷Remember what the Amalekites[a] did to you along the way when you came out of Egypt. ¹⁸When you were weary and worn out, they met you on your journey and cut off all who were lagging behind; they had no fear of God.[b] ¹⁹When the LORD your God gives you rest from all the enemies around you in the land he is giving you to possess as an inheritance, you shall blot out the memory of Amalek[c] from under heaven. Do not forget!

Chapter 26 Theme

26 When you have entered the land the LORD your God is giving you as an inheritance and have taken possession of it and settled in it, ²take some of the firstfruits[d] of all that you produce from the soil of the land the LORD your God is giving you and put them in a basket. Then go to the place the LORD your God will choose as a dwelling for his Name[e] ³and say to the priest in office at the time, "I declare today to the LORD your God that I have come to the land the LORD swore to our forefathers to give us." ⁴The priest shall take the basket from your hands and set it down in front of the altar of the LORD your God. ⁵Then you shall declare before the LORD your God: "My father was a wandering Aramean,[f] and he went down into Egypt with a few people[g] and lived there and became a great nation, powerful and numerous. ⁶But the Egyptians mistreated us and made us suffer,[h] putting us to hard labor. ⁷Then we cried out to the LORD, the God of our fathers, and the LORD heard our voice[i] and saw[j] our misery, toil and oppression. ⁸So the LORD brought us out of Egypt with a mighty hand and an outstretched arm, with great terror and with miraculous signs and wonders.[k] ⁹He brought us to this place and gave us this land, a land flowing with milk and honey;[l] ¹⁰and now I bring the firstfruits of the soil that you, O LORD, have given me." Place the basket before the LORD your God and bow down before him. ¹¹And you and the Levites[m] and the aliens among you shall rejoice[n] in all the good things the LORD your God has given to you and your household.

¹²When you have finished setting aside a tenth[o] of all your produce in the third year, the year of the tithe,[p] you shall give it to the Levite, the alien, the fatherless and the widow, so that they may eat in your towns and be satisfied. ¹³Then say to the LORD your God: "I have removed from my house the sacred portion and have given it to the Levite, the alien, the fatherless and the widow, according to all you commanded. I have not turned aside from your commands nor have I forgotten any of them.[q] ¹⁴I have not eaten any of the sacred portion while I was in mourning, nor have I removed any of it while I was unclean,[r] nor have I offered any of it to the dead. I have obeyed the LORD my God; I have done

25:17
a Ex 17:8

25:18
b Ps 36:1;
Ro 3:18

25:19
c 1Sa 15:2-3

26:2
d Ex 22:29;
23:16,19;
Nu 18:13;
Pr 3:9
e Dt 12:5

26:5
f Hos 12:12
g Ge 43:1-2;
45:7,11;
46:27;
Dt 10:22

26:6
h Ex 1:11,14

26:7
i Ex 2:23-25
j Ex 3:9

26:8
k Dt 4:34

26:9
l Ex 3:8

26:11
m Dt 12:7
n Dt 16:11

26:12
o Lev 27:30
p Nu 18:24;
Dt 14:28-29;
Heb 7:5,9

26:13
q Ps 119:141,
153,176

26:14
r Lev 7:20;
Hos 9:4

26:15
a Isa 63:15;
Zec 2:13

26:16
b Dt 4:29

26:18
c Ex 6:7;
19:5;
Dt 7:6;
14:2;
28:9

26:19
d Dt 4:7-8;
28:1,13,44
e Ex 19:6; Dt 7:6;
1Pe 2:9

27:2
f Jos 8:31

27:3
g Dt 26:9

27:4
h Dt 11:29

27:5
i Jos 8:31
j Ex 20:25

27:9
k Dt 26:18

27:12
l Dt 11:29
m Jos 8:35

everything you commanded me. ¹⁵Look down from heaven,ᵃ your holy dwelling place, and bless your people Israel and the land you have given us as you promised on oath to our forefathers, a land flowing with milk and honey."

¹⁶The LORD your God commands you this day to follow these decrees and laws; carefully observe them with all your heart and with all your soul.ᵇ ¹⁷You have declared this day that the LORD is your God and that you will walk in his ways, that you will keep his decrees, commands and laws, and that you will obey him. ¹⁸And the LORD has declared this day that you are his people, his treasured possessionᶜ as he promised, and that you are to keep all his commands. ¹⁹He has declared that he will set you in praise, fame and honor high above all the nationsᵈ he has made and that you will be a people holyᵉ to the LORD your God, as he promised.

Chapter 27 Theme

27 Moses and the elders of Israel commanded the people: "Keep all these commands that I give you today. ²When you have crossed the Jordan into the land the LORD your God is giving you, set up some large stones and coat them with plaster.ᶠ ³Write on them all the words of this law when you have crossed over to enter the land the LORD your God is giving you, a land flowing with milk and honey,ᵍ just as the LORD, the God of your fathers, promised you. ⁴And when you have crossed the Jordan, set up these stones on Mount Ebal,ʰ as I command you today, and coat them with plaster. ⁵Build there an altarⁱ to the LORD your God, an altar of stones. Do not use any iron toolʲ upon them. ⁶Build the altar of the LORD your God with fieldstones and offer burnt offerings on it to the LORD your God. ⁷Sacrifice fellowship offeringsᵃ there, eating them and rejoicing in the presence of the LORD your God. ⁸And you shall write very clearly all the words of this law on these stones you have set up."

⁹Then Moses and the priests, who are Levites, said to all Israel, "Be silent, O Israel, and listen! You have now become the people of the LORD your God.ᵏ ¹⁰Obey the LORD your God and follow his commands and decrees that I give you today."

¹¹On the same day Moses commanded the people:

¹²When you have crossed the Jordan, these tribes shall stand on Mount Gerizimˡ to bless the people: Simeon, Levi, Judah, Issachar, Joseph and Benjamin.ᵐ ¹³And these tribes shall stand on Mount Ebal to pronounce curses: Reuben, Gad, Asher, Zebulun, Dan and Naphtali.

¹⁴The Levites shall recite to all the people of Israel in a loud voice:

a7 Traditionally *peace offerings*

¹⁵"Cursed is the man who carves an image or casts an idol*a*—a thing detestable to the LORD, the work of the craftsman's hands—and sets it up in secret."

Then all the people shall say, "Amen!"

¹⁶"Cursed is the man who dishonors his father or his mother."*b*

Then all the people shall say, "Amen!"

¹⁷"Cursed is the man who moves his neighbor's boundary stone."*c*

Then all the people shall say, "Amen!"

¹⁸"Cursed is the man who leads the blind astray on the road."*d*

Then all the people shall say, "Amen!"

¹⁹"Cursed is the man who withholds justice from the alien,*e* the fatherless or the widow."*f*

Then all the people shall say, "Amen!"

²⁰"Cursed is the man who sleeps with his father's wife, for he dishonors his father's bed."*g*

Then all the people shall say, "Amen!"

²¹"Cursed is the man who has sexual relations with any animal."*h*

Then all the people shall say, "Amen!"

²²"Cursed is the man who sleeps with his sister, the daughter of his father or the daughter of his mother."*i*

Then all the people shall say, "Amen!"

²³"Cursed is the man who sleeps with his mother-in-law."*j*

Then all the people shall say, "Amen!"

²⁴"Cursed is the man who kills*k* his neighbor secretly."

Then all the people shall say, "Amen!"

²⁵"Cursed is the man who accepts a bribe to kill an innocent person."*l*

Then all the people shall say, "Amen!"

²⁶"Cursed is the man who does not uphold the words of this law by carrying them out."*m*

Then all the people shall say, "Amen!"

Chapter 28 Theme

28 If you fully obey the LORD your God and carefully follow all his commands*n* I give you today, the LORD your God will set you high above all the nations on earth.*o* ²All these blessings will come upon you*p* and accompany you if you obey the LORD your God:

³You will be blessed*q* in the city and blessed in the country.*r*

27:15
a Ex 20:4;
34:17;
Lev 19:4;
26:1;
Dt 4:16,23;
5:8;
Isa 44:9

27:16
b Ex 20:12;
21:17;
Lev 19:3;
20:9

27:17
c Dt 19:14;
Pr 22:28

27:18
d Lev 19:14

27:19
e Ex 22:21;
Dt 24:19
f Dt 10:18

27:20
g Lev 18:7;
Dt 22:30

27:21
h Lev 18:23

27:22
i Lev 18:9;
20:17

27:23
j Lev 20:14

27:24
k Lev 24:17;
Nu 35:31

27:25
l Ex 23:7-8;
Dt 10:17;
Eze 22:12

27:26
m Jer 11:3;
Gal 3:10*

28:1
n Ex 15:26;
Lev 26:3;
Dt 7:12-26
o Dt 26:19

28:2
p Zec 1:6

28:3
q Ps 128:1,4
r Ge 39:5

28:4
a Ge 49:25;
Pr 10:22

28:6
b Ps 121:8

28:7
c Lev 26:8,17

28:9
d Ex 19:6;
Dt 7:6

28:10
e 2Ch 7:14

28:11
f Dt 30:9;
Pr 10:22

28:12
g Lev 26:4
h Dt 15:3,6

28:14
i Dt 5:32

28:15
j Lev 26:14
k Jos 23:15;
Da 9:11;
Mal 2:2

28:20
l Mal 2:2
m Isa 51:20;
66:15
n Dt 4:26

[4]The fruit of your womb will be blessed, and the crops of your land and the young of your livestock—the calves of your herds and the lambs of your flocks.[a]

[5]Your basket and your kneading trough will be blessed.

[6]You will be blessed when you come in and blessed when you go out.[b]

[7]The LORD will grant that the enemies who rise up against you will be defeated before you. They will come at you from one direction but flee from you in seven.[c]

[8]The LORD will send a blessing on your barns and on everything you put your hand to. The LORD your God will bless you in the land he is giving you.

[9]The LORD will establish you as his holy people,[d] as he promised you on oath, if you keep the commands of the LORD your God and walk in his ways. [10]Then all the peoples on earth will see that you are called by the name[e] of the LORD, and they will fear you. [11]The LORD will grant you abundant prosperity—in the fruit of your womb, the young of your livestock and the crops of your ground—in the land he swore to your forefathers to give you.[f]

[12]The LORD will open the heavens, the storehouse of his bounty, to send rain[g] on your land in season and to bless all the work of your hands. You will lend to many nations but will borrow from none.[h] [13]The LORD will make you the head, not the tail. If you pay attention to the commands of the LORD your God that I give you this day and carefully follow them, you will always be at the top, never at the bottom. [14]Do not turn aside from any of the commands I give you today, to the right or to the left,[i] following other gods and serving them.

[15]However, if you do not obey[j] the LORD your God and do not carefully follow all his commands and decrees I am giving you today, all these curses will come upon you and overtake you:[k]

[16]You will be cursed in the city and cursed in the country.

[17]Your basket and your kneading trough will be cursed.

[18]The fruit of your womb will be cursed, and the crops of your land, and the calves of your herds and the lambs of your flocks.

[19]You will be cursed when you come in and cursed when you go out.

[20]The LORD will send on you curses,[l] confusion and rebuke[m] in everything you put your hand to, until you are destroyed and come to sudden ruin[n] because of the evil you have done in forsaking him.[a] [21]The LORD will plague you with diseases until he

a20 Hebrew me

has destroyed you from the land you are entering to possess.ᵃ ²²The LORD will strike you with wasting disease, with fever and inflammation, with scorching heat and drought,ᵇ with blight and mildew, which will plague you until you perish.ᶜ ²³The sky over your head will be bronze, the ground beneath you iron.ᵈ ²⁴The LORD will turn the rain of your country into dust and powder; it will come down from the skies until you are destroyed.

²⁵The LORD will cause you to be defeated before your enemies. You will come at them from one direction but flee from them in seven,ᵉ and you will become a thing of horror to all the kingdoms on earth.ᶠ ²⁶Your carcasses will be food for all the birds of the air and the beasts of the earth, and there will be no one to frighten them away.ᵍ ²⁷The LORD will afflict you with the boils of Egyptʰ and with tumors, festering sores and the itch, from which you cannot be cured. ²⁸The LORD will afflict you with madness, blindness and confusion of mind. ²⁹At midday you will gropeⁱ about like a blind man in the dark. You will be unsuccessful in everything you do; day after day you will be oppressed and robbed, with no one to rescue you.

³⁰You will be pledged to be married to a woman, but another will take her and ravish her.ʲ You will build a house, but you will not live in it.ᵏ You will plant a vineyard, but you will not even begin to enjoy its fruit.ˡ ³¹Your ox will be slaughtered before your eyes, but you will eat none of it. Your donkey will be forcibly taken from you and will not be returned. Your sheep will be given to your enemies, and no one will rescue them. ³²Your sons and daughters will be given to another nation,ᵐ and you will wear out your eyes watching for them day after day, powerless to lift a hand. ³³A people that you do not know will eat what your land and labor produce, and you will have nothing but cruel oppression all your days.ⁿ ³⁴The sights you see will drive you mad. ³⁵The LORD will afflict your knees and legs with painful boilsᵒ that cannot be cured, spreading from the soles of your feet to the top of your head.

³⁶The LORD will drive you and the kingᵖ you set over you to a nation unknown to you or your fathers.�q There you will worship other gods, gods of wood and stone.ʳ ³⁷You will become a thing of horror and an object of scorn and ridicule to all the nations where the LORD will drive you.ˢ

³⁸You will sow much seed in the field but you will harvest little,ᵗ because locusts will devourᵘ it. ³⁹You will plant vineyards and cultivate them but you will not drink the wine or gather the grapes, because worms will eat them.ᵛ ⁴⁰You will have olive trees throughout your country but you will not use the oil, because the olives will drop off.ʷ ⁴¹You will have sons and daughters but you

28:21
ᵃLev 26:25; Jer 24:10

28:22
ᵇLev 26:16
ᶜAm 4:9

28:23
ᵈLev 26:19

28:25
ᵉIsa 30:17
ᶠJer 15:4; 24:9; Eze 23:46

28:26
ᵍJer 7:33; 16:4; 34:20

28:27
ʰver 60-61; 1Sa 5:6

28:29
ⁱJob 5:14; Isa 59:10

28:30
ʲJob 31:10; Jer 8:10
ᵏAm 5:11
ˡJer 12:13

28:32
ᵐver 41

28:33
ⁿJer 5:15-17

28:35
ᵒver 27

28:36
ᵖ2Ki 17:4,6; 24:12,14; 25:7,11
qJer 16:13
ʳDt 4:28

28:37
ˢJer 24:9

28:38
ᵗMic 6:15; Hag 1:6,9
ᵘJoel 1:4

28:39
ᵛIsa 5:10; 17:10-11

28:40
ʷMic 6:15

28:41
a ver 32

28:43
b ver 13

28:44
c ver 12
d ver 13

28:45
e ver 15

28:46
f Isa 8:18;
Eze 14:8

28:47
g Dt 32:15
h Ne 9:35

28:48
i Jer 28:13-14

28:49
j Jer 5:15;
6:22
k La 4:19;
Hos 8:1

28:50
l Isa 47:6

28:51
m ver 33

28:52
n Jer 10:18;
Zep 1:14-16,17

28:53
o Lev 26:29;
2Ki 6:28-29;
Jer 19:9;
La 2:20;
4:10

28:56
p ver 54

28:58
q Mal 1:14
r Ex 6:3

will not keep them, because they will go into captivity.*a* [42]Swarms of locusts will take over all your trees and the crops of your land.

[43]The alien who lives among you will rise above you higher and higher, but you will sink lower and lower.*b* [44]He will lend to you, but you will not lend to him.*c* He will be the head, but you will be the tail.*d*

[45]All these curses will come upon you. They will pursue you and overtake you until you are destroyed,*e* because you did not obey the LORD your God and observe the commands and decrees he gave you. [46]They will be a sign and a wonder to you and your descendants forever.*f* [47]Because you did not serve*g* the LORD your God joyfully and gladly*h* in the time of prosperity, [48]therefore in hunger and thirst, in nakedness and dire poverty, you will serve the enemies the LORD sends against you. He will put an iron yoke*i* on your neck until he has destroyed you.

[49]The LORD will bring a nation against you from far away, from the ends of the earth,*j* like an eagle*k* swooping down, a nation whose language you will not understand, [50]a fierce-looking nation without respect for the old*l* or pity for the young. [51]They will devour the young of your livestock and the crops of your land until you are destroyed. They will leave you no grain, new wine or oil, nor any calves of your herds or lambs of your flocks until you are ruined.*m* [52]They will lay siege to all the cities throughout your land until the high fortified walls in which you trust fall down. They will besiege all the cities throughout the land the LORD your God is giving you.*n*

[53]Because of the suffering that your enemy will inflict on you during the siege, you will eat the fruit of the womb, the flesh of the sons and daughters the LORD your God has given you.*o* [54]Even the most gentle and sensitive man among you will have no compassion on his own brother or the wife he loves or his surviving children, [55]and he will not give to one of them any of the flesh of his children that he is eating. It will be all he has left because of the suffering your enemy will inflict on you during the siege of all your cities. [56]The most gentle and sensitive*p* woman among you— so sensitive and gentle that she would not venture to touch the ground with the sole of her foot—will begrudge the husband she loves and her own son or daughter [57]the afterbirth from her womb and the children she bears. For she intends to eat them secretly during the siege and in the distress that your enemy will inflict on you in your cities.

[58]If you do not carefully follow all the words of this law, which are written in this book, and do not revere*q* this glorious and awesome name*r*—the LORD your God— [59]the LORD will send fearful plagues on you and your descendants, harsh and prolonged

disasters, and severe and lingering illnesses. ⁶⁰He will bring upon you all the diseases of Egypt[a] that you dreaded, and they will cling to you. ⁶¹The LORD will also bring on you every kind of sickness and disaster not recorded in this Book of the Law, until you are destroyed.[b] ⁶²You who were as numerous as the stars in the sky[c] will be left but few in number, because you did not obey the LORD your God. ⁶³Just as it pleased[d] the LORD to make you prosper and increase in number, so it will please[e] him to ruin and destroy you. You will be uprooted[f] from the land you are entering to possess.

⁶⁴Then the LORD will scatter[g] you among all nations,[h] from one end of the earth to the other. There you will worship other gods—gods of wood and stone, which neither you nor your fathers have known. ⁶⁵Among those nations you will find no repose, no resting place for the sole of your foot. There the LORD will give you an anxious mind, eyes weary with longing, and a despairing heart.[i] ⁶⁶You will live in constant suspense, filled with dread both night and day, never sure of your life. ⁶⁷In the morning you will say, "If only it were evening!" and in the evening, "If only it were morning!"—because of the terror that will fill your hearts and the sights that your eyes will see.[j] ⁶⁸The LORD will send you back in ships to Egypt on a journey I said you should never make again. There you will offer yourselves for sale to your enemies as male and female slaves, but no one will buy you.

Chapter 29 Theme

29 These are the terms of the covenant the LORD commanded Moses to make with the Israelites in Moab, in addition to the covenant he had made with them at Horeb.[k]

²Moses summoned all the Israelites and said to them:

Your eyes have seen all that the LORD did in Egypt to Pharaoh, to all his officials and to all his land.[l] ³With your own eyes you saw those great trials, those miraculous signs and great wonders.[m] ⁴But to this day the LORD has not given you a mind that understands or eyes that see or ears that hear.[n] ⁵During the forty years that I led you through the desert, your clothes did not wear out, nor did the sandals on your feet.[o] ⁶You ate no bread and drank no wine or other fermented drink. I did this so that you might know that I am the LORD your God.[p]

⁷When you reached this place, Sihon[q] king of Heshbon and Og king of Bashan came out to fight against us, but we defeated them.[r] ⁸We took their land and gave it as an inheritance to the Reubenites, the Gadites and the half-tribe of Manasseh.[s]

⁹Carefully follow[t] the terms of this covenant, so that you may prosper in everything you do.[u] ¹⁰All of you are standing today in

28:60
[a] ver 27

28:61
[b] Dt 4:25-26

28:62
[c] Dt 4:27; 10:22; Ne 9:23

28:63
[d] Jer 32:41
[e] Pr 1:26
[f] Jer 12:14; 45:4

28:64
[g] Lev 26:33; Dt 4:27
[h] Ne 1:8

28:65
[i] Lev 26:16,36

28:67
[j] ver 34; Job 7:4

29:1
[k] Dt 5:2-3

29:2
[l] Ex 19:4

29:3
[m] Dt 4:34; 7:19

29:4
[n] Isa 6:10; Ac 28:26-27; Ro 11:8*; Eph 4:18

29:5
[o] Dt 8:4

29:6
[p] Dt 8:3

29:7
[q] Dt 2:32; 3:1
[r] Nu 21:21-24, 33-35

29:8
[s] Nu 32:33; Dt 3:12-13

29:9
[t] Dt 4:6; Jos 1:7
[u] 1Ki 2:3

the presence of the LORD your God—your leaders and chief men, your elders and officials, and all the other men of Israel, [11]together with your children and your wives, and the aliens living in your camps who chop your wood and carry your water.[a] [12]You are standing here in order to enter into a covenant with the LORD your God, a covenant the LORD is making with you this day and sealing with an oath, [13]to confirm you this day as his people,[b] that he may be your God[c] as he promised you and as he swore to your fathers, Abraham, Isaac and Jacob. [14]I am making this covenant,[d] with its oath, not only with you [15]who are standing here with us today in the presence of the LORD our God but also with those who are not here today.[e]

[16]You yourselves know how we lived in Egypt and how we passed through the countries on the way here. [17]You saw among them their detestable images and idols of wood and stone, of silver and gold.[f] [18]Make sure there is no man or woman, clan or tribe among you today whose heart turns away from the LORD our God to go and worship the gods of those nations; make sure there is no root among you that produces such bitter poison.[g]

[19]When such a person hears the words of this oath, he invokes a blessing on himself and therefore thinks, "I will be safe, even though I persist in going my own way." This will bring disaster on the watered land as well as the dry.[a] [20]The LORD will never be willing to forgive him; his wrath and zeal[h] will burn[i] against that man. All the curses written in this book will fall upon him, and the LORD will blot[j] out his name from under heaven. [21]The LORD will single him out from all the tribes of Israel for disaster, according to all the curses of the covenant written in this Book of the Law.

[22]Your children who follow you in later generations and foreigners who come from distant lands will see the calamities that have fallen on the land and the diseases with which the LORD has afflicted it.[k] [23]The whole land will be a burning waste[l] of salt[m] and sulfur—nothing planted, nothing sprouting, no vegetation growing on it. It will be like the destruction of Sodom and Gomorrah,[n] Admah and Zeboiim, which the LORD overthrew in fierce anger. [24]All the nations will ask: "Why has the LORD done this to this land?[o] Why this fierce, burning anger?"

[25]And the answer will be: "It is because this people abandoned the covenant of the LORD, the God of their fathers, the covenant he made with them when he brought them out of Egypt. [26]They went off and worshiped other gods and bowed down to them, gods they did not know, gods he had not given them. [27]Therefore the LORD's anger burned against this land, so that he brought on

29:11
[a] Jos 9:21,23,27

29:13
[b] Dt 28:9
[c] Ge 17:7;
Ex 6:7

29:14
[d] Jer 31:31

29:15
[e] Ac 2:39

29:17
[f] Dt 28:36

29:18
[g] Dt 11:16;
Heb 12:15

29:20
[h] Eze 23:25
[i] Ps 74:1;
79:5
[j] Ex 32:33;
Dt 9:14

29:22
[k] Jer 19:8

29:23
[l] Isa 34:9
[m] Jer 17:6
[n] Ge 19:24,25;
Zep 2:9

29:24
[o] 1Ki 9:8;
Jer 22:8-9

[a] 19 Or way, in order to add drunkenness to thirst."

it all the curses written in this book.*a* ²⁸In furious anger and in great wrath the LORD uprooted*b* them from their land and thrust them into another land, as it is now.'"

²⁹The secret things belong to the LORD our God, but the things revealed belong to us and to our children forever, that we may follow all the words of this law.

Chapter 30 Theme

30 When all these blessings and curses*c* I have set before you come upon you and you take them to heart wherever the LORD your God disperses you among the nations,*d* ²and when you and your children return*e* to the LORD your God and obey him with all your heart and with all your soul according to everything I command you today, ³then the LORD your God will restore your fortunes*af* and have compassion on you and gather*g* you again from all the nations where he scattered you.*h* ⁴Even if you have been banished to the most distant land under the heavens, from there the LORD your God will gather you and bring you back.*i* ⁵He will bring*j* you to the land that belonged to your fathers, and you will take possession of it. He will make you more prosperous and numerous than your fathers. ⁶The LORD your God will circumcise your hearts and the hearts of your descendants,*k* so that you may love him with all your heart and with all your soul, and live. ⁷The LORD your God will put all these curses on your enemies who hate and persecute you.*l* ⁸You will again obey the LORD and follow all his commands I am giving you today. ⁹Then the LORD your God will make you most prosperous in all the work of your hands and in the fruit of your womb, the young of your livestock and the crops of your land.*m* The LORD will again delight in you and make you prosperous, just as he delighted in your fathers, ¹⁰if you obey the LORD your God and keep his commands and decrees that are written in this Book of the Law and turn to the LORD your God with all your heart and with all your soul.*n*

¹¹Now what I am commanding you today is not too difficult for you or beyond your reach.*o* ¹²It is not up in heaven, so that you have to ask, "Who will ascend into heaven to get it and proclaim it to us so we may obey it?"*p* ¹³Nor is it beyond the sea, so that you have to ask, "Who will cross the sea to get it and proclaim it to us so we may obey it?" ¹⁴No, the word is very near you; it is in your mouth and in your heart so you may obey it.

¹⁵See, I set before you today life and prosperity, death and destruction.*q* ¹⁶For I command you today to love the LORD your

a 3 Or will bring you back from captivity

29:27
a Da 9:11,13,14

29:28
b 1Ki 14:15;
2Ch 7:20;
Ps 52:5;
Pr 2:22

30:1
c ver 15,19;
Dt 11:26
d Lev 26:40-45;
Dt 28:64;
29:28;
1Ki 8:47

30:2
e Dt 4:30;
Ne 1:9

30:3
f Ps 126:4
g Ps 147:2;
Jer 32:37;
Eze 34:13
h Jer 29:14

30:4
i Ne 1:8-9;
Isa 43:6

30:5
j Jer 29:14

30:6
k Dt 10:16;
Jer 32:39

30:7
l Dt 7:15

30:9
m Dt 28:11;
Jer 31:28;
32:41

30:10
n Dt 4:29

30:11
o Isa 45:19,23

30:12
p Ro 10:6*

30:15
q Dt 11:26

God, to walk in his ways, and to keep his commands, decrees and laws; then you will live and increase, and the LORD your God will bless you in the land you are entering to possess.

¹⁷But if your heart turns away and you are not obedient, and if you are drawn away to bow down to other gods and worship them, ¹⁸I declare to you this day that you will certainly be destroyed.ᵃ You will not live long in the land you are crossing the Jordan to enter and possess.

¹⁹This day I call heaven and earth as witnesses against youᵇ that I have set before you life and death, blessings and curses.ᶜ Now choose life, so that you and your children may live ²⁰and that you may loveᵈ the LORD your God, listen to his voice, and hold fast to him. For the LORD is your life,ᵉ and he will give you many years in the land he swore to give to your fathers, Abraham, Isaac and Jacob.

Chapter 31 Theme

31 Then Moses went out and spoke these words to all Israel: ²"I am now a hundred and twenty years oldᶠ and I am no longer able to lead you.ᵍ The LORD has said to me, 'You shall not cross the Jordan.'ʰ ³The LORD your God himself will crossⁱ over ahead of you.ʲ He will destroy these nations before you, and you will take possession of their land. Joshua also will crossᵏ over ahead of you, as the LORD said. ⁴And the LORD will do to them what he did to Sihon and Og, the kings of the Amorites, whom he destroyed along with their land. ⁵The LORD will deliverˡ them to you, and you must do to them all that I have commanded you. ⁶Be strong and courageous.ᵐ Do not be afraid or terrifiedⁿ because of them, for the LORD your God goes with you;ᵒ he will never leave youᵖ nor forsake�q you."

⁷Then Moses summoned Joshua and saidʳ to him in the presence of all Israel, "Be strong and courageous, for you must go with this people into the land that the LORD swore to their forefathers to give them, and you must divide it among them as their inheritance. ⁸The LORD himself goes before you and will be with you;ˢ he will never leave you nor forsake you. Do not be afraid; do not be discouraged."

⁹So Moses wrote down this law and gave it to the priests, the sons of Levi, who carriedᵗ the ark of the covenant of the LORD, and to all the elders of Israel. ¹⁰Then Moses commanded them: "At the end of every seven years, in the year for canceling debts,ᵘ during the Feast of Tabernacles,ᵛ ¹¹when all Israel comes to appearʷ before the LORD your God at the place he will choose, you shall read this lawˣ before them in their hearing. ¹²Assemble the people—men, women and children, and the aliens living in

30:18
ᵃDt 8:19

30:19
ᵇDt 4:26
ᶜver 1

30:20
ᵈDt 6:5;
10:20
ᵉPs 27:1;
Jn 11:25

31:2
ᶠDt 34:7
ᵍNu 27:17;
1Ki 3:7
ʰDt 3:23,26

31:3
ⁱNu 27:18
ʲDt 9:3 ᵏDt 3:28

31:5
ˡDt 7:2

31:6
ᵐJos 10:25;
1Ch 22:13
ⁿDt 7:18
ᵒDt 1:29;
20:4
ᵖJos 1:5
qHeb 13:5*

31:7
ʳDt 1:38; 3:28

31:8
ˢEx 13:21;
33:14

31:9
ᵗver 25;
Nu 4:15;
Jos 3:3

31:10
ᵘDt 15:1
ᵛLev 23:34

31:11
ʷDt 16:16
ˣJos 8:34-35;
2Ki 23:2

your towns—so they can listen and learn[a] to fear the LORD your God and follow carefully all the words of this law. [13]Their children,[b] who do not know this law, must hear it and learn to fear the LORD your God as long as you live in the land you are crossing the Jordan to possess."

[14]The LORD said to Moses, "Now the day of your death[c] is near. Call Joshua and present yourselves at the Tent of Meeting, where I will commission him." So Moses and Joshua came and presented themselves at the Tent of Meeting.

[15]Then the LORD appeared at the Tent in a pillar of cloud, and the cloud stood over the entrance to the Tent.[d] [16]And the LORD said to Moses: "You are going to rest with your fathers, and these people will soon prostitute[e] themselves to the foreign gods of the land they are entering. They will forsake[f] me and break the covenant I made with them. [17]On that day I will become angry[g] with them and forsake[h] them; I will hide[i] my face from them, and they will be destroyed. Many disasters and difficulties will come upon them, and on that day they will ask, 'Have not these disasters come upon us because our God is not with us?'[j] [18]And I will certainly hide my face on that day because of all their wickedness in turning to other gods.

[19]"Now write down for yourselves this song and teach it to the Israelites and have them sing it, so that it may be a witness for me against them. [20]When I have brought them into the land flowing with milk and honey, the land I promised on oath to their forefathers,[k] and when they eat their fill and thrive, they will turn to other gods[l] and worship them, rejecting me and breaking my covenant.[m] [21]And when many disasters and difficulties come upon them,[n] this song will testify against them, because it will not be forgotten by their descendants. I know what they are disposed to do,[o] even before I bring them into the land I promised them on oath." [22]So Moses wrote[p] down this song that day and taught it to the Israelites.

[23]The LORD gave this command[q] to Joshua son of Nun: "Be strong and courageous,[r] for you will bring the Israelites into the land I promised them on oath, and I myself will be with you."

[24]After Moses finished writing in a book the words of this law from beginning to end, [25]he gave this command to the Levites who carried the ark of the covenant of the LORD: [26]"Take this Book of the Law and place it beside the ark of the covenant of the LORD your God. There it will remain as a witness against you.[s] [27]For I know how rebellious and stiff-necked[t] you are. If you have been rebellious against the LORD while I am still alive and with you, how much more will you rebel after I die! [28]Assemble before me all the elders of your tribes and all your officials, so that I can

31:12
[a] Dt 4:10

31:13
[b] Dt 11:2;
Ps 78:6-7

31:14
[c] Nu 27:13;
Dt 32:49-50

31:15
[d] Ex 33:9

31:16
[e] Jdg 2:12
[f] Jdg 10:6,13

31:17
[g] Jdg 2:14,20
[h] Jdg 6:13;
2Ch 15:2
[i] Dt 32:20;
Isa 1:15;
8:17
[j] Nu 14:42

31:20
[k] Dt 6:10-12
[l] Dt 32:15-17
[m] ver 16

31:21
[n] ver 17
[o] Hos 5:3

31:22
[p] ver 19

31:23
[q] ver 7
[r] Jos 1:6

31:26
[s] ver 19

31:27
[t] Ex 32:9;
Dt 9:6,24

speak these words in their hearing and call heaven and earth to testify against them.*a* ²⁹For I know that after my death you are sure to become utterly corrupt*b* and to turn from the way I have commanded you. In days to come, disaster*c* will fall upon you because you will do evil in the sight of the LORD and provoke him to anger by what your hands have made."

Chapter 32 Theme

³⁰And Moses recited the words of this song from beginning to end in the hearing of the whole assembly of Israel:

32 Listen, O heavens,*d* and I will speak;
  hear, O earth, the words of my mouth.
²Let my teaching fall like rain
  and my words descend like dew,*e*
like showers*f* on new grass,
  like abundant rain on tender plants.

³I will proclaim the name of the LORD.*g*
  Oh, praise the greatness*h* of our God!
⁴He is the Rock,*i* his works are perfect,*j*
  and all his ways are just.
A faithful God*k* who does no wrong,
  upright and just is he.

⁵They have acted corruptly toward him;
  to their shame they are no longer his children,
  but a warped and crooked generation.*al*
⁶Is this the way you repay*m* the LORD,
  O foolish and unwise people?*n*
Is he not your Father,*o* your Creator,*b*
  who made you and formed you?*p*

⁷Remember the days of old;
  consider the generations long past.
Ask your father and he will tell you,
  your elders, and they will explain to you.*q*
⁸When the Most High gave the nations their inheritance,
  when he divided all mankind,*r*
he set up boundaries for the peoples
  according to the number of the sons of Israel.*c*
⁹For the LORD's portion*s* is his people,
  Jacob his allotted inheritance.*t*

Cross references:
31:28 *a* Dt 4:26; 30:19; 32:1
31:29 *b* Dt 32:5; Jdg 2:19 *c* Dt 28:15
32:1 *d* Isa 1:2
32:2 *e* Isa 55:11 *f* Ps 72:6
32:3 *g* Ex 33:19 *h* Dt 3:24
32:4 *i* ver 15,18,30 *j* 2Sa 22:31 *k* Dt 7:9
32:5 *l* Dt 31:29
32:6 *m* Ps 116:12 *n* Ps 74:2 *o* Dt 1:31; Isa 63:16 *p* ver 15
32:7 *q* Ex 13:14
32:8 *r* Ge 11:8; Ac 17:26
32:9 *s* Jer 10:16 *t* 1Ki 8:51,53

*a*5 Or *Corrupt are they and not his children, / a generation warped and twisted to their shame*   *b*6 Or *Father, who bought you*   *c*8 Masoretic Text; Dead Sea Scrolls (see also Septuagint) *sons of God*

¹⁰In a desert^a land he found him,
 in a barren and howling waste.
He shielded him and cared for him;
 he guarded him as the apple of his eye,^b
¹¹like an eagle that stirs up its nest
 and hovers over its young,^c
that spreads its wings to catch them
 and carries them on its pinions.
¹²The Lord alone led him;
 no foreign god was with him.^d

¹³He made him ride on the heights^e of the land
 and fed him with the fruit of the fields.
He nourished him with honey from the rock,
 and with oil^f from the flinty crag,
¹⁴with curds and milk from herd and flock
 and with fattened lambs and goats,
with choice rams of Bashan
 and the finest kernels of wheat.^g
You drank the foaming blood of the grape.^h

¹⁵Jeshurun^a grew fatⁱ and kicked;
 filled with food, he became heavy and sleek.
He abandoned^j the God who made him
 and rejected the Rock^k his Savior.
¹⁶They made him jealous^l with their foreign gods
 and angered^m him with their detestable idols.
¹⁷They sacrificed to demons, which are not God—
 gods they had not known,ⁿ
 gods that recently appeared,^o
 gods your fathers did not fear.
¹⁸You deserted the Rock, who fathered you;
 you forgot^p the God who gave you birth.

¹⁹The Lord saw this and rejected them^q
 because he was angered by his sons and daughters.^r
²⁰"I will hide my face^s from them," he said,
 "and see what their end will be;
for they are a perverse generation,^t
 children who are unfaithful.
²¹They made me jealous^u by what is no god
 and angered me with their worthless idols.^v
I will make them envious by those who are not a people;
 I will make them angry by a nation that has no
  understanding.^w

a 15 *Jeshurun* means *the upright one*, that is, Israel.

32:10
a Jer 2:6
b Ps 17:8;
Zec 2:8

32:11
c Ex 19:4

32:12
d ver 39

32:13
e Isa 58:14
f Job 29:6

32:14
g Ps 81:16;
147:14
h Ge 49:11

32:15
i Dt 31:20
j ver 6; Isa 1:4,28
k ver 4

32:16
l 1Co 10:22
m Ps 78:58

32:17
n Dt 28:64
o Jdg 5:8

32:18
p Isa 17:10

32:19
q Jer 44:21-23
r Ps 106:40

32:20
s Dt 31:17,29
t ver 5

32:21
u 1Co 10:22
v 1Ki 16:13,26
w Ro 10:19*

32:22
a Ps 18:7-8;
Jer 15:14;
La 4:11

²²For a fire has been kindled by my wrath,
    one that burns to the realm of death[a] below.[a]
It will devour the earth and its harvests
    and set afire the foundations of the mountains.

32:23
b Dt 29:21
c Ps 7:13;
Eze 5:16

²³"I will heap calamities[b] upon them
    and spend my arrows[c] against them.
²⁴I will send wasting famine against them,
    consuming pestilence[d] and deadly plague;[e]
I will send against them the fangs of wild beasts, [f]
    the venom of vipers[g] that glide in the dust.

32:24
d Dt 28:22
e Ps 91:6
f Lev 26:22
g Am 5:18-19

²⁵In the street the sword will make them childless;
    in their homes terror will reign.[h]
Young men and young women will perish,
    infants and gray-haired men.[i]

32:25
h Eze 7:15
i 2Ch 36:17;
La 2:21

²⁶I said I would scatter[j] them
    and blot out their memory from mankind,[k]
²⁷but I dreaded the taunt of the enemy,
    lest the adversary misunderstand
and say, 'Our hand has triumphed;
    the LORD has not done all this.'"[l]

32:26
j Dt 4:27
k Ps 34:16

²⁸They are a nation without sense,
    there is no discernment in them.
²⁹If only they were wise and would understand this[m]
    and discern what their end will be!

32:27
l Isa 10:13

³⁰How could one man chase a thousand,
    or two put ten thousand to flight,[n]
unless their Rock had sold them,
    unless the LORD had given them up?[o]

32:29
m Dt 5:29;
Ps 81:13

³¹For their rock is not like our Rock,
    as even our enemies concede.
³²Their vine comes from the vine of Sodom
    and from the fields of Gomorrah.
Their grapes are filled with poison,
    and their clusters with bitterness.

32:30
n Lev 26:8
o Ps 44:12

³³Their wine is the venom of serpents,
    the deadly poison of cobras.[p]

32:33
p Ps 58:4

³⁴"Have I not kept this in reserve
    and sealed it in my vaults?[q]
³⁵It is mine to avenge; I will repay.[r]
    In due time their foot will slip;[s]
their day of disaster is near
    and their doom rushes upon them.[t]"

32:34
q Jer 2:22;
Hos 13:12

32:35
r Ro 12:19*;
Heb 10:30*
s Jer 23:12
t Eze 7:8-9

a 22 Hebrew *to Sheol*

³⁶The Lᴏʀᴅ will judge his people
    and have compassion on his servants ᵃ
when he sees their strength is gone
    and no one is left, slave or free.
³⁷He will say: "Now where are their gods,
    the rock they took refuge in,ᵇ
³⁸the gods who ate the fat of their sacrifices
    and drank the wine of their drink offerings?
Let them rise up to help you!
    Let them give you shelter!

³⁹"See now that I myself am He!ᶜ
    There is no god besides me.ᵈ
I put to death and I bring to life,ᵉ
    I have wounded and I will heal,ᶠ
    and no one can deliver out of my hand.ᵍ
⁴⁰I lift my hand to heaven and declare:
    As surely as I live forever,
⁴¹when I sharpen my flashing swordʰ
    and my hand grasps it in judgment,
I will take vengeance on my adversaries
    and repay those who hate me.ⁱ
⁴²I will make my arrows drunk with blood,ʲ
    while my sword devours flesh:ᵏ
the blood of the slain and the captives,
    the heads of the enemy leaders."

⁴³Rejoice,ˡ O nations, with his people, ᵃ,ᵇ
    for he will avenge the blood of his servants;ᵐ
he will take vengeance on his enemies
    and make atonement for his land and people.ⁿ

⁴⁴Moses came with Joshuaᶜᵒ son of Nun and spoke all the words of this song in the hearing of the people. ⁴⁵When Moses finished reciting all these words to all Israel, ⁴⁶he said to them, "Take to heart all the words I have solemnly declared to you this day,ᵖ so that you may command your children to obey carefully all the words of this law. ⁴⁷They are not just idle words for you— they are your life.�q By them you will live long in the land you are crossing the Jordan to possess."

⁴⁸On that same day the Lᴏʀᴅ told Moses, ⁴⁹"Go up into the Abarimʳ Range to Mount Nebo in Moab, across from Jericho, and view Canaan, the land I am giving the Israelites as their own possession. ⁵⁰There on the mountain that you have climbed you

---

a 43 Or *Make his people rejoice, O nations*   b 43 Masoretic Text; Dead Sea Scrolls (see also Septuagint) *people, / and let all the angels worship him /*   c 44 Hebrew *Hoshea,* a variant of *Joshua*

Cross-references (right margin):

32:36
a Dt 30:1-3;
Ps 135:14;
Joel 2:14

32:37
b Jdg 10:14;
Jer 2:28

32:39
c Isa 41:4
d Isa 45:5
e 1Sa 2:6;
Ps 68:20
f Hos 6:1
g Ps 50:22

32:41
h Isa 34:6; 66:16;
Eze 21:9-10
i Jer 50:29

32:42
j ver 23
k Jer 46:10,14

32:43
l Ro 15:10*
m 2Ki 9:7
n Ps 65:3;
85:1;
Rev 19:2

32:44
o Nu 13:8,16

32:46
p Eze 40:4

32:47
q Dt 30:20

32:49
r Nu 27:12

32:50
a Ge 25:8

will die*a* and be gathered to your people, just as your brother Aaron died on Mount Hor and was gathered to his people. ⁵¹This is because both of you broke faith with me in the presence of the Israelites at the waters of Meribah Kadesh in the Desert of Zin*b* and because you did not uphold my holiness among the Israelites.*c* ⁵²Therefore, you will see the land only from a distance;*d* you will not enter*e* the land I am giving to the people of Israel."

32:51
b Nu 20:11-13
c Nu 27:14

Chapter 33 Theme

32:52
d Dt 34:1-3
e Dt 1:37

33 This is the blessing that Moses the man of God *f* pronounced on the Israelites before his death. ²He said:

"The LORD came from Sinai*g*
  and dawned over them from Seir;*h*
  he shone forth from Mount Paran.*i*
He came with*a* myriads of holy ones*j*
  from the south, from his mountain slopes.*b*

33:1
f Jos 14:6

³Surely it is you who love*k* the people;
  all the holy ones are in your hand.*l*
At your feet they all bow down,*m*
  and from you receive instruction,
⁴the law that Moses gave us,*n*
  the possession of the assembly of Jacob.*o*
⁵He was king over Jeshurun*c*
  when the leaders of the people assembled,
  along with the tribes of Israel.

33:2
g Ex 19:18;
  Ps 68:8
h Jdg 5:4
i Hab 3:3
j Da 7:10;
  Ac 7:53;
  Rev 5:11

⁶"Let Reuben live and not die,
  nor*d* his men be few."

33:3
k Hos 11:1
l Dt 14:2
m Lk 10:39

⁷And this he said about Judah:*p*

"Hear, O LORD, the cry of Judah;
  bring him to his people.
With his own hands he defends his cause.
  Oh, be his help against his foes!"

33:4
n Jn 1:17
o Ps 119:111

⁸About Levi he said:

"Your Thummim and Urim*q* belong
  to the man you favored.
You tested him at Massah;
  you contended with him at the waters of Meribah.*r*
⁹He said of his father and mother,*s*
  'I have no regard for them.'

33:7
p Ge 49:10

33:8
q Ex 28:30
r Ex 17:7

33:9
s Ex 32:26-29

a 2 Or *from*   *b* 2 The meaning of the Hebrew for this phrase is uncertain.   *c* 5 *Jeshurun* means *the upright one,* that is, Israel; also in verse 26.   *d* 6 Or *but let*

He did not recognize his brothers
    or acknowledge his own children,
but he watched over your word
    and guarded your covenant.*a*
¹⁰He teaches your precepts to Jacob
    and your law to Israel.*b*
He offers incense before you
    and whole burnt offerings on your altar.*c*
¹¹Bless all his skills, O LORD,
    and be pleased with the work of his hands.*d*
Smite the loins of those who rise up against him;
    strike his foes till they rise no more."

¹²About Benjamin he said:

"Let the beloved of the LORD rest secure in him,*e*
    for he shields him all day long,
and the one the LORD loves rests between his
    shoulders.*f*"

¹³About Joseph*g* he said:

"May the LORD bless his land
    with the precious dew from heaven above
    and with the deep waters that lie below;*h*
¹⁴with the best the sun brings forth
    and the finest the moon can yield;
¹⁵with the choicest gifts of the ancient mountains*i*
    and the fruitfulness of the everlasting hills;
¹⁶with the best gifts of the earth and its fullness
    and the favor of him who dwelt in the burning bush.*j*
Let all these rest on the head of Joseph,
    on the brow of the prince among*a* his brothers.
¹⁷In majesty he is like a firstborn bull;
    his horns are the horns of a wild ox.*k*
With them he will gore*l* the nations,
    even those at the ends of the earth.
Such are the ten thousands of Ephraim;
    such are the thousands of Manasseh."

¹⁸About Zebulun*m* he said:

"Rejoice, Zebulun, in your going out,
    and you, Issachar, in your tents.
¹⁹They will summon peoples to the mountain*n*
    and there offer sacrifices of righteousness;*o*

a 16 Or *of the one separated from*

33:9
a Mal 2:5

33:10
b Lev 10:11;
Dt 31:9-13
c Ps 51:19

33:11
d 2Sa 24:23

33:12
e Dt 12:10
f Ex 28:12

33:13
g Ge 49:25
h Ge 27:28

33:15
i Hab 3:6

33:16
j Ex 3:2

33:17
k Nu 23:22
l 1Ki 22:11;
Ps 44:5

33:18
m Ge 49:13-15

33:19
n Ex 15:17;
Isa 2:3
o Ps 4:5

33:19
a Isa 60:5,11

they will feast on the abundance of the seas,*a*
on the treasures hidden in the sand."

20 About Gad*b* he said:

33:20
b Ge 49:19

"Blessed is he who enlarges Gad's domain!
Gad lives there like a lion,
tearing at arm or head.
21 He chose the best land for himself;*c*
the leader's portion was kept for him.
When the heads of the people assembled,
he carried out the LORD's righteous will,*d*
and his judgments concerning Israel."

33:21
c Nu 32:1-5,
31-32
d Jos 4:12;
22:1-3

22 About Dan*e* he said:

33:22
e Ge 49:16

"Dan is a lion's cub,
springing out of Bashan."

23 About Naphtali he said:

33:24
f Ge 49:21
g Ge 49:20;
Job 29:6

"Naphtali is abounding with the favor of the LORD
and is full of his blessing;
he will inherit southward to the lake."

24 About Asher*f* he said:

33:25
h Dt 4:40;
32:47

"Most blessed of sons is Asher;
let him be favored by his brothers,
and let him bathe his feet in oil.*g*
25 The bolts of your gates will be iron and bronze,
and your strength will equal your days.*h*

33:26
i Ex 15:11
j Ps 104:3

26 "There is no one like the God of Jeshurun,*i*
who rides on the heavens to help you*j*
and on the clouds in his majesty.

33:27
k Ps 90:1
l Jos 24:18
m Dt 7:2

27 The eternal God is your refuge,*k*
and underneath are the everlasting arms.
He will drive out your enemy before you,*l*
saying, 'Destroy him!'*m*
28 So Israel will live in safety alone;*n*
Jacob's spring is secure
in a land of grain and new wine,
where the heavens drop dew.*o*

33:28
n Nu 23:9;
Jer 23:6
o Ge 27:28

29 Blessed are you, O Israel!*p*
Who is like you,*q*
a people saved by the LORD?*r*
He is your shield and helper*s*
and your glorious sword.

33:29
p Ps 144:15
q Ps 18:44
r 2Sa 7:23
s Ps 115:9-11

Your enemies will cower before you,
and you will trample down their high places.ᵃ ᵃ"

Chapter 34 Theme _____

34 Then Moses climbed Mount Nebo from the plains of Moab to the top of Pisgah, across from Jericho.ᵇ There the LORD showedᶜ him the whole land—from Gilead to Dan, ²all of Naphtali, the territory of Ephraim and Manasseh, all the land of Judah as far as the western sea,ᵇ ᵈ ³the Negev and the whole region from the Valley of Jericho, the City of Palms,ᵉ as far as Zoar. ⁴Then the LORD said to him, "This is the land I promised on oathᶠ to Abraham, Isaac and Jacob when I said, 'I will itᵍ to your descendants.' I have let you see it with your eyes, but you will not crossʰ over into it."

⁵And Moses the servant of the LORDⁱ diedʲ there in Moab, as the LORD had said. ⁶He buried himᶜ in Moab, in the valley opposite Beth Peor,ᵏ but to this day no one knows where his grave is.ˡ ⁷Moses was a hundred and twenty years oldᵐ when he died, yet his eyes were not weakⁿ nor his strength gone. ⁸The Israelites grieved for Moses in the plains of Moab thirty days, until the time of weeping and mourningᵒ was over.

⁹Now Joshua son of Nun was filled with the spiritᵈ of wisdomᵖ because Moses had laid his hands on him.�q So the Israelites listened to him and did what the LORD had commanded Moses.

¹⁰Since then, no prophet has risen in Israel like Moses,ʳ whom the LORD knew face to face,ˢ ¹¹who did all those miraculous signs and wondersᵗ the LORD sent him to do in Egypt—to Pharaoh and to all his officialsᵘ and to his whole land. ¹²For no one has ever shown the mighty power or performed the awesome deeds that Moses did in the sight of all Israel.

ᵃ 29 Or *will tread upon their bodies*   ᵇ 2 That is, the Mediterranean   ᶜ 6 Or *He was buried*
ᵈ 9 Or *Spirit*

33:29
ᵃ Dt 32:13

34:1
ᵇ Dt 32:49
ᶜ Dt 32:52

34:2
ᵈ Dt 11:24

34:3
ᵉ Jdg 1:16;
3:13;
2Ch 28:15

34:4
ᶠ Ge 28:13
ᵍ Ge 12:7
ʰ Dt 3:27

34:5
ⁱ Nu 12:7
ʲ Dt 32:50;
Jos 1:1-2

34:6
ᵏ Dt 3:29
ˡ Jude 1:9

34:7
ᵐ Dt 31:2
ⁿ Ge 27:1

34:8
ᵒ Ge 50:3,10;
2Sa 11:27

34:9
ᵖ Ge 41:38;
Isa 11:2;
Da 6:3
q Nu 27:18,23

34:10
ʳ Dt 18:15,18
ˢ Ex 33:11;
Nu 12:6,8;
Dt 5:4

34:11
ᵗ Dt 4:34
ᵘ Dt 7:19

Theme of Deuteronomy:

Author:

SEGMENT DIVISIONS

Date:

Geographical Location:

Purpose:

Key Words:

		CHAPTER THEMES
		1
		2
		3
		4
		5
		6
		7
		8
		9
		10
		11
		12
		13
		14
		15
		16
		17
		18
		19
		20
		21
		22
		23
		24
		25
		26
		27
		28
		29
		30
		31
		32
		33
		34

LESSONS FROM THE LIFE OF MOSES

BOOK/ CHAPTER/ VERSE	LESSONS FOR MY LIFE

(continued)

BOOK/ CHAPTER/ VERSE	LESSONS FOR MY LIFE

JOSHUA

$\mathcal{F}$or years Joshua had faithfully served Moses—and God. How well Joshua understood the meaning of his name, "The Lord is salvation." All his contemporaries, except Caleb, had died in the wilderness because they had not believed God. But God had spared Joshua and Caleb because they had followed him fully.

Now Moses was dead and God had appointed Joshua to lead the children of Israel into the land of promise. Their salvation from their enemies would not come from the east nor from the west but from the one who made the heaven and the earth!

God's words rang in Joshua's heart: "Be strong and courageous."

✎ THINGS TO DO

General Instructions

1. If you are not familiar with who Joshua is, before you begin studying the book, read Numbers 13; 14; 27:18-23; Deuteronomy 34:9.

2. As you study Joshua one chapter at a time, it will help you keep everything in context if you will remember that Joshua falls into four segments. In chapters 1 through 5 the children of Israel prepare to enter the land. Chapters 6 through 12 describe the conquest of the land. Chapters 13 through 21 tell of the allocation of the land. In chapters 22 through 24 Joshua calls Israel to serve the Lord, who gave them the land.

3. As you read each chapter, ask the five W's and an H: Who? What? When? Where? Why? and How? For example, in a historical book such as Joshua ask: What is this chapter about? Who are the main characters? What is taking place? Where is it happening and when? Who is involved? Why is this occurring, being said, or to be done? What are the consequences? How is it going to happen? How should it be done? Record the main points or events of the chapter in the margin.

4. On the map on page 351 you will find many of the various cities and places mentioned throughout this book. Look them up so you can keep the book in its geographical context.

5. Mark every reference to time with a symbol. This will help you see when events occurred and the chronological relationship of one event to another.

6. After you finish studying each chapter, write the theme or event covered in that chapter on the line next to the chapter number. Then record it on the JOSHUA AT A GLANCE chart on page 391.

Chapters 1-5

1. As you read these chapters, mark the following key words and their synonyms: *Joshua, land (country), strong, courageous, firm, command (tell, word, commanded, directed, ordered, giving orders), occupy (for your own, take possession), covenant, ark of the Lord (ark of the covenant),* and *Israel (Israelites)*. Write these on an index card that you can use as a bookmark while studying this segment.

2. Watch how the events or the instructions prepare the Israelites to enter the land. Also note the procedure for entering the land and the requirements placed on them as they arrive in the land. You might list these in the margin under the heading "Occupying the Land."

3. If while reading chapter 5 you need a review of circumcision, read Genesis 17 and Exodus 4:24-26.

4. Don't forget to record the theme of each chapter in the text and on JOSHUA AT A GLANCE.

Chapters 6-12

1. As you study this section keep in mind the general instructions above.

2. Although you will mark many of the same key words, make a new bookmark of the following key words: *God, Lord, Joshua, covenant (treaty), strong, courageous, land (region, country, territory), be afraid, commanded (ordered, instructed, gave the order), fight (make war, fought, attacked, was fighting), captured (taken, took), ark of the covenant,* and *Israel (Israelites).*

3. Carefully observe what God tells the people to do when they conquer a city. Read Genesis 15:7-21 and note that God told Abraham he would bring his descendants into Canaan when "the sin of the Amorites has not yet reached its full measure." Also recall the covenant God made with Abraham on that day. You might write "Genesis 15:7-21" in the margin of this section as a cross-reference.

4. As you read, watch what happens when the people fail to consult God or to obey his commands in respect to the inhabitants of the land. Note this in the margin.

5. When you come to chapter 8, note where Mount Ebal and Mount Gerizim are located and what takes place there. Refer back to Deuteronomy 11:29 and Deuteronomy 27:11-14. Use the map on page 351 to locate these places. Also mark all clues to time with a symbol in the margin or above the verses where they occur.

6. Record the theme of each chapter.

Chapters 13-21

1. Once again make a new bookmark of the following key words, although some words will remain the same: *Israel (Israelites), land (area, country, region, plain), Joshua, Caleb, strong (stronger), fear, command (commanded, instructed), attacked, captured (took), inheritance(s), possession (occupy, territory), taken over* (also mark *possession (inheritance)* in chapter 12), and *promised.*

2. Continue to consult the map on page 351 so you are aware of the geographical location of the places mentioned in this segment. Also mark in the text the name of each tribe as it is allotted its portion of the land.

3. As you read, watch for any mention of Caleb. Remember what you read about Joshua and Caleb in Numbers 13 and 14. There are important lessons to be learned from their example.

4. Pay careful attention to chapter 20 and what you learn about the cities of refuge.

5. Also note the inheritance given to the Levites in Joshua 21.

6. Don't forget to record the chapter themes.

Chapters 22-24

1. Make this final bookmark of key words and mark them in the text: *land (border, country), possess, possession (acquired), covenant, powerful, strong, fear, command (commandment, commanded, gave), serve (serving, served, worshiped), Israel (Israelite(s)), Joshua, promised, fought (fight),* and *inheritance.*

2. In the margin also list God's instructions and what the people are to do in order to keep them. Also note in the margin the consequences of disobedience.

3. As you read Joshua 23, mark the words *hold fast* and *ally* and think of the illustration God uses in Jeremiah 13:1-11 of a belt and how Israel and Judah used to hold fast to him—to be bound to him. Then read Jeremiah 13:1-11.

4. Complete JOSHUA AT A GLANCE. Fill in the four main segment divisions and any others you see.

5. Compare what Joshua tells the children of Israel in chapter 23 with God's word to Joshua in chapter 1. You might write "Joshua 1:7-9" in the margin of Joshua 23.

∞ **THINGS TO THINK ABOUT**

1. Do you consult the Lord and his Word and then walk in obedience to what he says?

2. Joshua was admonished to be strong and courageous. What do you think this means? Read Revelation 21:8 and note what is said about the cowardly.

3. Have you decided whom you are going to follow? Have you counted the cost? What would cause you to compromise? Could you get away with compromise? What would it cost you? Would it be worth it?

---

*F*ROM THE PROMISE OF THE LAND TO THE OCCUPATION

The Exodus
1445

Elders
↓

| Moses | | | 40-year wilderness wanderings | Joshua | | | Othniel (Judge) |

Moses

In Pharaoh's palace   In exile in Midian   40-year wilderness wanderings   Joshua   Othniel (Judge)
1525   1485 | 1485   1445   1405   1405 1390? 1390? 1381   1371

↑
Moses' birth

430 years since Jacob came to Egypt and 480 years before Solomon begins the temple in Jerusalem (1 Kings 6:1)

1530 1520 1510 1500 1490 1480 1470 1460 1450 1440 1430 1420 1410 1400 1390 1380 1370 1360

Chapter 1 Theme

1 After the death of Moses the servant of the LORD,ᵃ the LORD said to Joshuaᵇ son of Nun, Moses' aide: ²"Moses my servant is dead. Now then, you and all these people, get ready to cross the Jordan Riverᶜ into the land I am about to give to them—to the Israelites. ³I will give you every place where you set your foot,ᵈ as I promised Moses. ⁴Your territory will extend from the desert to Lebanon, and from the great river, the Euphratesᵉ—all the Hittite country—to the Great Seaᵃ on the west.ᶠ ⁵No one will be able to stand up against youᵍ all the days of your life. As I was withʰ Moses, so I will be with you; I will never leave you nor forsakeⁱ you.

⁶"Be strong and courageous, because you will lead these people to inherit the land I swore to their forefathersʲ to give them. ⁷Be strong and very courageous. Be careful to obey all the law my servant Moses gave you; do not turn from it to the right or to

ᵃ4 That is, the Mediterranean

1:1
ᵃNu 12:7;
Dt 34:5
ᵇEx 24:13;
Dt 1:38

1:2
ᶜver 11

1:3
ᵈDt 11:24

1:4
ᵉGe 15:18
ᶠNu 34:2-12

1:5
ᵍDt 7:24
ʰJos 3:7; 6:27
ⁱDt 31:6-8

1:6
ʲDt 31:23

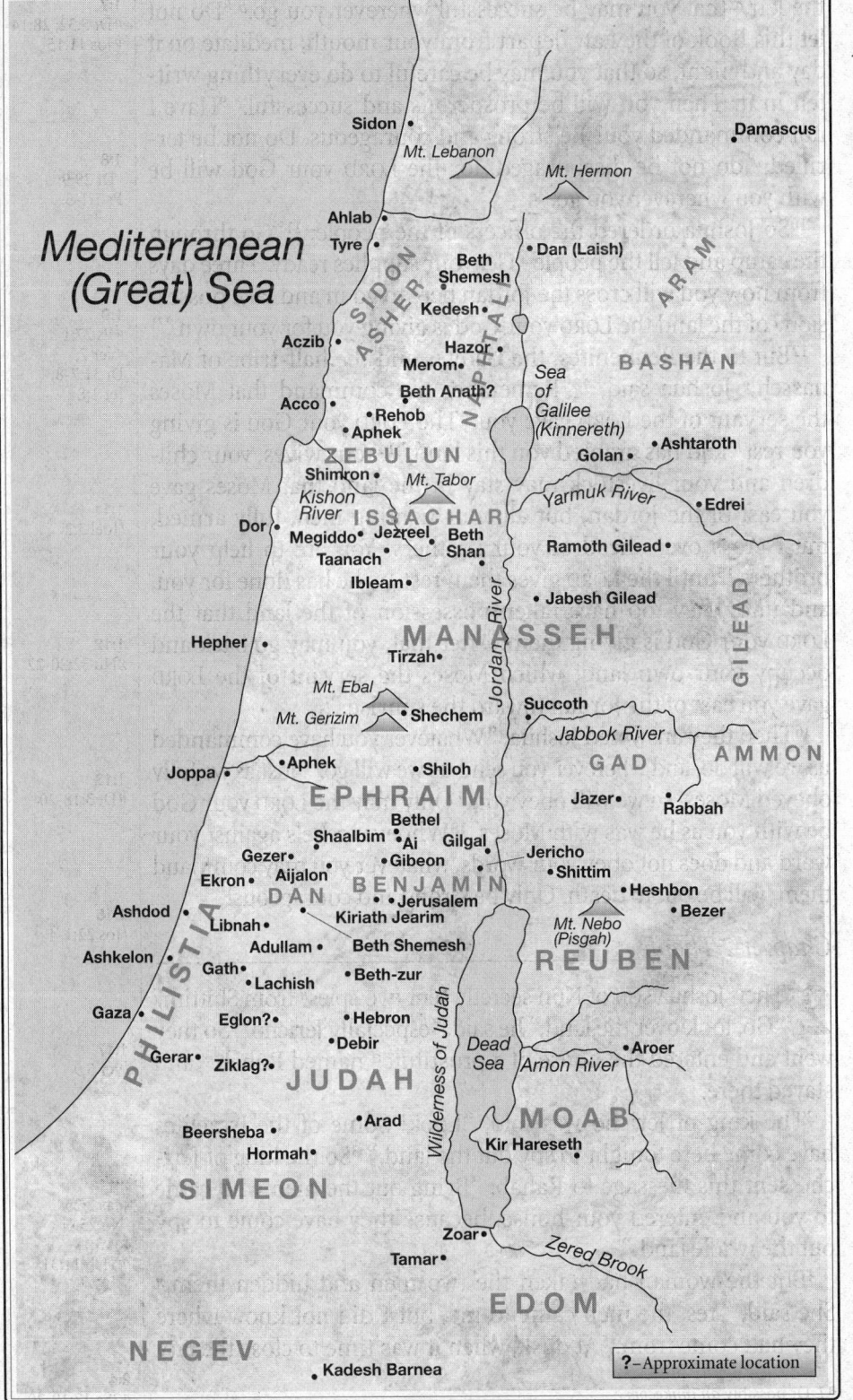

Damascus

Sidon

Mt. Lebanon

Mt. Hermon

Ahlab

Tyre

**Mediterranean
(Great) Sea**

Beth
Shemesh

Dan (Laish)

SIDON

ASHER

Kedesh

ARAM

BASHAN

Aczib

Hazor

Merom

Beth Anath?

NAPHTALI

Acco

Rehob

Aphek

*Sea
of
Galilee
(Kinnereth)*

ZEBULUN

Shimron

Mt. Tabor

Golan

Ashtaroth

*Kishon
River*

ISSACHAR

Yarmuk River

Edrei

Dor

Megiddo

Jezreel

Beth
Shan

Ramoth Gilead

Taanach

Ibleam

Jabesh Gilead

GILEAD

Hepher

MANASSEH

Tirzah

Jordan River

Mt. Ebal

Mt. Gerizim

Shechem

Succoth

Jabbok River

GAD

AMMON

Joppa

Aphek

Shiloh

EPHRAIM

Jazer

Rabbah

Bethel

Shaalbim

Ai

Gilgal

Gezer

Gibeon

Jericho

Ekron

Aijalon

Shittim

Heshbon

DAN

BENJAMIN

Ashdod

Jerusalem

Bezer

Libnah

Kiriath Jearim

*Mt. Nebo
(Pisgah)*

Ashkelon

Adullam

Beth Shemesh

Gath

Beth-zur

REUBEN

Lachish

Gaza

Eglon?

Hebron

Debir

*Dead
Sea*

Aroer

Gerar

Ziklag?

Wilderness of Judah

Arnon River

PHILISTIA

JUDAH

Arad

MOAB

Beersheba

Kir Hareseth

Hormah

SIMEON

Zoar

Tamar

Zered Brook

EDOM

NEGEV

Kadesh Barnea

? – Approximate location

the left,[a] that you may be successful wherever you go.[b] [8]Do not let this Book of the Law depart from your mouth; meditate on it day and night, so that you may be careful to do everything written in it. Then you will be prosperous and successful.[c] [9]Have I not commanded you? Be strong and courageous. Do not be terrified;[d] do not be discouraged, for the LORD your God will be with you wherever you go."[e]

[10]So Joshua ordered the officers of the people: [11]"Go through the camp and tell the people, 'Get your supplies ready. Three days from now you will cross the Jordan here to go in and take possession[f] of the land the LORD your God is giving you for your own.'"

[12]But to the Reubenites, the Gadites and the half-tribe of Manasseh,[g] Joshua said, [13]"Remember the command that Moses the servant of the LORD gave you: 'The LORD your God is giving you rest[h] and has granted you this land.' [14]Your wives, your children and your livestock may stay in the land that Moses gave you east of the Jordan, but all your fighting men, fully armed, must cross over ahead of your brothers. You are to help your brothers [15]until the LORD gives them rest, as he has done for you, and until they too have taken possession of the land that the LORD your God is giving them. After that, you may go back and occupy your own land, which Moses the servant of the LORD gave you east of the Jordan toward the sunrise."[i]

[16]Then they answered Joshua, "Whatever you have commanded us we will do, and wherever you send us we will go. [17]Just as we fully obeyed Moses, so we will obey you.[j] Only may the LORD your God be with you as he was with Moses. [18]Whoever rebels against your word and does not obey your words, whatever you may command them, will be put to death. Only be strong and courageous!"

Chapter 2 Theme

2 Then Joshua son of Nun secretly sent two spies[k] from Shittim.[l] "Go, look over the land," he said, "especially Jericho." So they went and entered the house of a prostitute[a] named Rahab[m] and stayed there.

[2]The king of Jericho was told, "Look! Some of the Israelites have come here tonight to spy out the land." [3]So the king of Jericho sent this message to Rahab: "Bring out the men who came to you and entered your house, because they have come to spy out the whole land."

[4]But the woman had taken the two men and hidden them.[n] She said, "Yes, the men came to me, but I did not know where they had come from. [5]At dusk, when it was time to close the city

---

1:7
[a]Dt 5:32; 28:14
[b]Jos 11:15

1:8
[c]Dt 29:9;
Ps 1:1-3

1:9
[d]Ps 27:1
[e]ver 7;
Dt 31:7-8;
Jer 1:8

1:11
[f]Joel 3:2

1:12
[g]Nu 32:20-22

1:13
[h]Dt 3:18-20

1:15
[i]Jos 22:1-4

1:17
[j]ver 5,9

2:1
[k]Jas 2:25
[l]Nu 25:1;
Jos 3:1
[m]Heb 11:31

2:4
[n]2Sa 17:19-20

---

[a]1 Or possibly *an innkeeper*

2:6
a Jas 2:25
b Ex 1:17,19;
2Sa 17:19

2:9
c Ge 35:5;
Ex 23:27;
Dt 2:25

2:10
d Ex 14:21
e Nu 23:22
f Nu 21:21,24,
34-35

2:11
g Ex 15:14;
Jos 5:1; 7:5;
Ps 22:14;
Isa 13:7
h Dt 4:39

2:12
i ver 18

2:14
j Jdg 1:24;
Mt 5:7

2:15
k Ac 9:25

2:16
l Jas 2:25
m Heb 11:31

2:17
n Ge 24:8

2:18
o ver 12;
Jos 6:23

2:19
p Eze 33:4
q Mt 27:25

gate, the men left. I don't know which way they went. Go after them quickly. You may catch up with them." 6(But she had taken them up to the roof and hidden them under the stalks of flax*a* she had laid out on the roof.)*b* 7So the men set out in pursuit of the spies on the road that leads to the fords of the Jordan, and as soon as the pursuers had gone out, the gate was shut.

8Before the spies lay down for the night, she went up on the roof 9and said to them, "I know that the LORD has given this land to you and that a great fear*c* of you has fallen on us, so that all who live in this country are melting in fear because of you. 10We have heard how the LORD dried up*d* the water of the Red Sea*a* for you when you came out of Egypt,*e* and what you did to Sihon and Og,*f* the two kings of the Amorites east of the Jordan, whom you completely destroyed.*b* 11When we heard of it, our hearts melted and everyone's courage failed because of you,*g* for the LORD your God is God in heaven above and on the earth*h* below. 12Now then, please swear to me by the LORD that you will show kindness to my family, because I have shown kindness to you. Give me a sure sign*i* 13that you will spare the lives of my father and mother, my brothers and sisters, and all who belong to them, and that you will save us from death."

14"Our lives for your lives!" the men assured her. "If you don't tell what we are doing, we will treat you kindly and faithfully*j* when the LORD gives us the land."

15So she let them down by a rope through the window,*k* for the house she lived in was part of the city wall. 16Now she had said to them, "Go to the hills so the pursuers will not find you. Hide yourselves there three days*l* until they return, and then go on your way."*m*

17The men said to her, "This oath*n* you made us swear will not be binding on us 18unless, when we enter the land, you have tied this scarlet cord in the window through which you let us down, and unless you have brought your father and mother, your brothers and all your family*o* into your house. 19If anyone goes outside your house into the street, his blood will be on his own head;*p* we will not be responsible. As for anyone who is in the house with you, his blood will be on our head*q* if a hand is laid on him. 20But if you tell what we are doing, we will be released from the oath you made us swear."

21"Agreed," she replied. "Let it be as you say." So she sent them away and they departed. And she tied the scarlet cord in the window.

a 10 Hebrew *Yam Suph*; that is, Sea of Reeds   *b* 10 The Hebrew term refers to the irrevocable giving over of things or persons to the LORD, often by totally destroying them.

²²When they left, they went into the hills and stayed there three days, until the pursuers had searched all along the road and returned without finding them. ²³Then the two men started back. They went down out of the hills, forded the river and came to Joshua son of Nun and told him everything that had happened to them. ²⁴They said to Joshua, "The LORD has surely given the whole land into our hands;ᵃ all the people are melting in fear because of us."

Chapter 3 Theme

3 Early in the morning Joshua and all the Israelites set out from Shittimᵇ and went to the Jordan, where they camped before crossing over. ²After three days the officers went throughout the camp,ᶜ ³giving orders to the people: "When you see the ark of the covenantᵈ of the LORD your God, and the priests,ᵉ who are Levites, carrying it, you are to move out from your positions and follow it. ⁴Then you will know which way to go, since you have never been this way before. But keep a distance of about a thousand yardsᵃ between you and the ark; do not go near it."

⁵Joshua told the people, "Consecrate yourselves,ᶠ for tomorrow the LORD will do amazing things among you."

⁶Joshua said to the priests, "Take up the ark of the covenant and pass on ahead of the people." So they took it up and went ahead of them.

⁷And the LORD said to Joshua, "Today I will begin to exalt youᵍ in the eyes of all Israel, so they may know that I am with you as I was with Moses.ʰ ⁸Tell the priestsⁱ who carry the ark of the covenant: 'When you reach the edge of the Jordan's waters, go and stand in the river.'"

⁹Joshua said to the Israelites, "Come here and listen to the words of the LORD your God. ¹⁰This is how you will know that the living Godʲ is among you and that he will certainly drive out before you the Canaanites, Hittites, Hivites, Perizzites, Girgashites, Amorites and Jebusites.ᵏ ¹¹See, the ark of the covenant of the Lord of all the earth ˡ will go into the Jordan ahead of you. ¹²Now then, choose twelve menᵐ from the tribes of Israel, one from each tribe. ¹³And as soon as the priests who carry the ark of the LORD—the Lord of all the earthⁿ—set foot in the Jordan, its waters flowing downstreamᵒ will be cut off and stand up in a heap.ᵖ"

¹⁴So when the people broke camp to cross the Jordan, the priests carrying the ark of the covenant�vᵖ went aheadʳ of them. ¹⁵Now the Jordan is at flood stageˢ all during harvest. Yet as soon as the priests who carried the ark reached the Jordan and their feet touched the water's edge, ¹⁶the water from upstream stopped flowing.ᵗ It piled up in a heap a great distance away, at a town

ᵃ4 Hebrew *about two thousand cubits* (about 900 meters)

Cross references

2:24 ᵃver 9; Jos 6:2

3:1 ᵇJos 2:1

3:2 ᶜJos 1:11

3:3 ᵈNu 10:33 ᵉDt 31:9

3:5 ᶠEx 19:10,14; Lev 20:7; Jos 7:13; 1Sa 16:5; Joel 2:16

3:7 ᵍJos 4:14; 1Ch 29:25 ʰJos 1:5

3:8 ⁱver 3

3:10 ʲDt 5:26; 1Sa 17:26,36; 2Ki 19:4,16; Hos 1:10; Mt 16:16; 1Th 1:9 ᵏEx 33:2; Dt 7:1

3:11 ˡver 13; Job 41:11; Zec 6:5

3:12 ᵐJos 4:2,4

3:13 ⁿver 11 ᵒver 16 ᵖEx 15:8; Ps 78:13

3:14 ᵠPs 132:8 ʳAc 7:44-45

3:15 ˢJos 4:18; 1Ch 12:15

3:16 ᵗPs 66:6; 74:15

3:16
a 1Ki 4:12;
7:46
b ver 13
c Dt 1:1
d Ge 14:3

called Adam in the vicinity of Zarethan,*a* while the water flowing down*b* to the Sea of the Arabah*c* (the Salt Sea*a d*) was completely cut off. So the people crossed over opposite Jericho. ¹⁷The priests who carried the ark of the covenant of the LORD stood firm on dry ground in the middle of the Jordan, while all Israel passed by until the whole nation had completed the crossing on dry ground.*e*

3:17
e Ex 14:22,29

Chapter 4 Theme

4:1
f Dt 27:2

4 When the whole nation had finished crossing the Jordan,*f* the LORD said to Joshua, ²"Choose twelve men*g* from among the people, one from each tribe, ³and tell them to take up twelve stones*h* from the middle of the Jordan from right where the priests stood and to carry them over with you and put them down at the place where you stay tonight.*i*"

4:2
g Jos 3:12

⁴So Joshua called together the twelve men he had appointed from the Israelites, one from each tribe, ⁵and said to them, "Go over before the ark of the LORD your God into the middle of the Jordan. Each of you is to take up a stone on his shoulder, according to the number of the tribes of the Israelites, ⁶to serve as a sign among you. In the future, when your children ask you, 'What do these stones mean?'*j* ⁷tell them that the flow of the Jordan was cut off*k* before the ark of the covenant of the LORD. When it crossed the Jordan, the waters of the Jordan were cut off. These stones are to be a memorial*l* to the people of Israel forever."

4:3
h ver 20
i ver 19

4:6
j ver 21;
Ex 12:26;
13:14

⁸So the Israelites did as Joshua commanded them. They took twelve stones from the middle of the Jordan, according to the number of the tribes of the Israelites, as the LORD had told Joshua;*m* and they carried them over with them to their camp, where they put them down. ⁹Joshua set up the twelve stones*n* that had been*b* in the middle of the Jordan at the spot where the priests who carried the ark of the covenant had stood. And they are there to this day.

4:7
k Jos 3:13
l Ex 12:14

¹⁰Now the priests who carried the ark remained standing in the middle of the Jordan until everything the LORD had commanded Joshua was done by the people, just as Moses had directed Joshua. The people hurried over, ¹¹and as soon as all of them had crossed, the ark of the LORD and the priests came to the other side while the people watched. ¹²The men of Reuben, Gad and the half-tribe of Manasseh crossed over, armed, in front of the Israelites,*o* as Moses had directed them. ¹³About forty thousand armed for battle crossed over before the LORD to the plains of Jericho for war.

4:8
m ver 20

4:9
n Ge 28:18;
Jos 24:26;
1Sa 7:12

4:12
o Nu 32:27

a 16 That is, the Dead Sea   *b 9* Or *Joshua also set up twelve stones*

¹⁴That day the LORD exalted^a Joshua in the sight of all Israel; and they revered him all the days of his life, just as they had revered Moses.

¹⁵Then the LORD said to Joshua, ¹⁶"Command the priests carrying the ark of the Testimony^b to come up out of the Jordan."

¹⁷So Joshua commanded the priests, "Come up out of the Jordan."

¹⁸And the priests came up out of the river carrying the ark of the covenant of the LORD. No sooner had they set their feet on the dry ground than the waters of the Jordan returned to their place and ran at flood stage^c as before.

¹⁹On the tenth day of the first month the people went up from the Jordan and camped at Gilgal^d on the eastern border of Jericho. ²⁰And Joshua set up at Gilgal the twelve stones^e they had taken out of the Jordan. ²¹He said to the Israelites, "In the future when your descendants ask their fathers, 'What do these stones mean?'^f ²²tell them, 'Israel crossed the Jordan on dry ground.'^g ²³For the LORD your God dried up the Jordan before you until you had crossed over. The LORD your God did to the Jordan just what he had done to the Red Sea^a when he dried it up before us until we had crossed over.^h ²⁴He did this so that all the peoples of the earth might knowⁱ that the hand of the LORD is powerful^j and so that you might always fear the LORD your God.^k"

Chapter 5 Theme

5 Now when all the Amorite kings west of the Jordan and all the Canaanite kings along the coast^l heard how the LORD had dried up the Jordan before the Israelites until we had crossed over, their hearts melted^m and they no longer had the courage to face the Israelites.

²At that time the LORD said to Joshua, "Make flint knivesⁿ and circumcise the Israelites again." ³So Joshua made flint knives and circumcised the Israelites at Gibeath Haaraloth.^b

⁴Now this is why he did so: All those who came out of Egypt— all the men of military age—died in the desert on the way after leaving Egypt.^o ⁵All the people that came out had been circumcised, but all the people born in the desert during the journey from Egypt had not. ⁶The Israelites had moved about in the desert forty years^p until all the men who were of military age when they left Egypt had died, since they had not obeyed the LORD. For the LORD had sworn to them that they would not see the land that he had solemnly promised their fathers to give us,^q a land flowing with milk and honey.^r ⁷So he raised up their sons

4:14
^aJos 3:7

4:16
^bEx 25:22

4:18
^cJos 3:15

4:19
^dJos 5:9

4:20
^ever 3,8

4:21
^fver 6

4:22
^gJos 3:17

4:23
^hEx 14:21

4:24
ⁱ1Ki 8:42-43;
2Ki 19:19;
Ps 106:8;
Jer 10:7
^jEx 15:16;
1Ch 29:12;
Ps 89:13
^kEx 14:31

5:1
^lNu 13:29
^mJos 2:9-11

5:2
ⁿEx 4:25

5:4
^oDt 2:14

5:6
^pDt 2:7
^qNu 14:23,
29-35;
Dt 2:14
^rEx 3:8

---

^a23 Hebrew *Yam Suph*; that is, Sea of Reeds   ^b3 *Gibeath Haaraloth* means *hill of foreskins.*

5:8
a Ge 34:25

5:10
b Ex 12:6

5:11
c Nu 15:19
d Lev 23:14

5:12
e Ex 16:35

5:13
f Ge 18:2; 32:24
g Nu 22:23

5:14
h Ge 17:3

5:15
i Ex 3:5; Ac 7:33

6:1
j Jos 24:11

6:2
k Dt 7:24;
Jos 2:9,24; 8:1

6:4
l Lev 25:9;
Nu 10:8

6:5
m Ex 19:13
n ver 20;
1Sa 4:5;
Ps 42:4;
Isa 42:13

6:7
o Ex 14:15

in their place, and these were the ones Joshua circumcised. They were still uncircumcised because they had not been circumcised on the way. ⁸And after the whole nation had been circumcised, they remained where they were in camp until they were healed.*a*

⁹Then the LORD said to Joshua, "Today I have rolled away the reproach of Egypt from you." So the place has been called Gilgal*a* to this day.

¹⁰On the evening of the fourteenth day of the month,*b* while camped at Gilgal on the plains of Jericho, the Israelites celebrated the Passover. ¹¹The day after the Passover, that very day, they ate some of the produce of the land:*c* unleavened bread and roasted grain.*d* ¹²The manna stopped the day after*b* they ate this food from the land; there was no longer any manna for the Israelites, but that year they ate of the produce of Canaan.*e*

¹³Now when Joshua was near Jericho, he looked up and saw a man*f* standing in front of him with a drawn sword*g* in his hand. Joshua went up to him and asked, "Are you for us or for our enemies?"

¹⁴"Neither," he replied, "but as commander of the army of the LORD I have now come." Then Joshua fell facedown*h* to the ground in reverence, and asked him, "What message does my Lord*c* have for his servant?"

¹⁵The commander of the LORD's army replied, "Take off your sandals, for the place where you are standing is holy."*i* And Joshua did so.

Chapter 6 Theme _____

6 Now Jericho*j* was tightly shut up because of the Israelites. No one went out and no one came in.

²Then the LORD said to Joshua, "See, I have delivered*k* Jericho into your hands, along with its king and its fighting men. ³March around the city once with all the armed men. Do this for six days. ⁴Have seven priests carry trumpets of rams' horns in front of the ark. On the seventh day, march around the city seven times, with the priests blowing the trumpets.*l* ⁵When you hear them sound a long blast*m* on the trumpets, have all the people give a loud shout;*n* then the wall of the city will collapse and the people will go up, every man straight in."

⁶So Joshua son of Nun called the priests and said to them, "Take up the ark of the covenant of the LORD and have seven priests carry trumpets in front of it." ⁷And he ordered the people, "Advance*o*! March around the city, with the armed guard going ahead of the ark of the LORD."

a 9 Gilgal sounds like the Hebrew for *roll.*   *b 12* Or *the day*   *c 14* Or *lord*

⁸When Joshua had spoken to the people, the seven priests carrying the seven trumpets before the LORD went forward, blowing their trumpets, and the ark of the LORD's covenant followed them. ⁹The armed guard marched ahead of the priests who blew the trumpets, and the rear guard*a* followed the ark. All this time the trumpets were sounding. ¹⁰But Joshua had commanded the people, "Do not give a war cry, do not raise your voices, do not say a word until the day I tell you to shout. Then shout!*b*" ¹¹So he had the ark of the LORD carried around the city, circling it once. Then the people returned to camp and spent the night there.

¹²Joshua got up early the next morning and the priests took up the ark of the LORD. ¹³The seven priests carrying the seven trumpets went forward, marching before the ark of the LORD and blowing the trumpets. The armed men went ahead of them and the rear guard followed the ark of the LORD, while the trumpets kept sounding. ¹⁴So on the second day they marched around the city once and returned to the camp. They did this for six days.

¹⁵On the seventh day, they got up at daybreak and marched around the city seven times in the same manner, except that on that day they circled the city seven times.*c* ¹⁶The seventh time around, when the priests sounded the trumpet blast, Joshua commanded the people, "Shout! For the LORD has given you the city! ¹⁷The city and all that is in it are to be devoted*a*d to the LORD. Only Rahab the prostitute*b* and all who are with her in her house shall be spared, because she hid*e* the spies we sent. ¹⁸But keep away from the devoted things,*f* so that you will not bring about your own destruction by taking any of them. Otherwise you will make the camp of Israel liable to destruction*g* and bring trouble*h* on it. ¹⁹All the silver and gold and the articles of bronze and iron*i* are sacred to the LORD and must go into his treasury."

²⁰When the trumpets sounded,*j* the people shouted, and at the sound of the trumpet, when the people gave a loud shout,*k* the wall collapsed; so every man charged straight in, and they took the city.*l* ²¹They devoted the city to the LORD and destroyed*m* with the sword every living thing in it—men and women, young and old, cattle, sheep and donkeys.

²²Joshua said to the two men who had spied out the land, "Go into the prostitute's house and bring her out and all who belong to her, in accordance with your oath to her.*n*" ²³So the young men who had done the spying went in and brought out Rahab, her father and mother and brothers and all who belonged to her.*o* They brought out her entire family and put them in a place outside the camp of Israel.

a 17 The Hebrew term refers to the irrevocable giving over of things or persons to the LORD, often by totally destroying them; also in verses 18 and 21.   b 17 Or possibly *innkeeper*; also in verses 22 and 25

6:9
a ver 13;
Isa 52:12

6:10
b ver 20

6:15
c 1Ki 18:44

6:17
d Lev 27:28;
Dt 20:17
e Jos 2:4

6:18
f Jos 7:1
g Jos 7:12
h Jos 7:25,26

6:19
i ver 24;
Nu 31:22

6:20
j Jdg 6:34;
Jer 4:21;
Am 2:2
k ver 5
l Heb 11:30

6:21
m Dt 20:16

6:22
n Jos 2:14;
Heb 11:31

6:23
o Jos 2:13

²⁴Then they burned the whole city and everything in it, but they put the silver and gold and the articles of bronze and iron*a* into the treasury of the LORD's house. ²⁵But Joshua spared Rahab the prostitute,*b* with her family and all who belonged to her, because she hid the men Joshua had sent as spies to Jericho*c*— and she lives among the Israelites to this day.

²⁶At that time Joshua pronounced this solemn oath: "Cursed before the LORD is the man who undertakes to rebuild this city, Jericho:

"At the cost of his firstborn son
     will he lay its foundations;
  at the cost of his youngest
     will he set up its gates."*d*

²⁷So the LORD was with Joshua,*e* and his fame spread*f* throughout the land.

Chapter 7 Theme

7 But the Israelites acted unfaithfully in regard to the devoted things*a*;*g* Achan son of Carmi, the son of Zimri,*b* the son of Zerah,*h* of the tribe of Judah, took some of them. So the LORD's anger burned against Israel.

²Now Joshua sent men from Jericho to Ai, which is near Beth Aven*i* to the east of Bethel, and told them, "Go up and spy out the region." So the men went up and spied out Ai.

³When they returned to Joshua, they said, "Not all the people will have to go up against Ai. Send two or three thousand men to take it and do not weary all the people, for only a few men are there." ⁴So about three thousand men went up; but they were routed by the men of Ai,*j* ⁵who killed about thirty-six of them. They chased the Israelites from the city gate as far as the stone quarries*c* and struck them down on the slopes. At this the hearts of the people melted*k* and became like water.

⁶Then Joshua tore his clothes*l* and fell facedown to the ground before the ark of the LORD, remaining there till evening. The elders of Israel did the same, and sprinkled dust*m* on their heads. ⁷And Joshua said, "Ah, Sovereign LORD, why did you ever bring this people across the Jordan to deliver us into the hands of the Amorites to destroy us?*n* If only we had been content to stay on the other side of the Jordan! ⁸O Lord, what can I say, now that Israel has been routed by its enemies? ⁹The Canaanites and the other people of the country will hear about this and they will

6:24 *a* ver 19
6:25 *b* Heb 11:31 *c* Jos 2:6
6:26 *d* 1Ki 16:34
6:27 *e* Ge 39:2; Jos 1:5 *f* Jos 9:1
7:1 *g* Jos 6:18 *h* Jos 22:20
7:2 *i* Jos 18:12; 1Sa 13:5; 14:23
7:4 *j* Lev 26:17; Dt 28:25
7:5 *k* Lev 26:36; Jos 2:9,11; Eze 21:7; Na 2:10
7:6 *l* Ge 37:29 *m* 1Sa 4:12; 2Sa 13:19; Ne 9:1; Job 2:12; La 2:10; Rev 18:19
7:7 *n* Ex 5:22

a 1 The Hebrew term refers to the irrevocable giving over of things or persons to the LORD, often by totally destroying them; also in verses 11, 12, 13 and 15.   *b 1* See Septuagint and 1Chron. 2:6; Hebrew *Zabdi*; also in verses 17 and 18.   *c 5* Or *as far as Shebarim* surround us and wipe out our name from the earth. *a* What then will you do for your own great name?"

¹⁰The LORD said to Joshua, "Stand up! What are you doing down on your face? ¹¹Israel has sinned; they have violated my covenant, *b* which I commanded them to keep. They have taken some of the devoted things; they have stolen, they have lied, *c* they have put them with their own possessions. ¹²That is why the Israelites cannot stand against their enemies; *d* they turn their backs and run because they have been made liable to destruction. *e* I will not be with you anymore unless you destroy whatever among you is devoted to destruction.

¹³"Go, consecrate the people. Tell them, 'Consecrate yourselves *f* in preparation for tomorrow; for this is what the LORD, the God of Israel, says: That which is devoted is among you, O Israel. You cannot stand against your enemies until you remove it.

¹⁴"'In the morning, present yourselves tribe by tribe. The tribe that the LORD takes *g* shall come forward clan by clan; the clan that the LORD takes shall come forward family by family; and the family that the LORD takes shall come forward man by man. ¹⁵He who is caught with the devoted things shall be destroyed by fire, along with all that belongs to him. *h* He has violated the covenant *i* of the LORD and has done a disgraceful thing in Israel!'"*j*

¹⁶Early the next morning Joshua had Israel come forward by tribes, and Judah was taken. ¹⁷The clans of Judah came forward, and he took the Zerahites. *k* He had the clan of the Zerahites come forward by families, and Zimri was taken. ¹⁸Joshua had his family come forward man by man, and Achan son of Carmi, the son of Zimri, the son of Zerah, of the tribe of Judah, was taken.

¹⁹Then Joshua said to Achan, "My son, give glory *l* to the LORD, *a* the God of Israel, and give him the praise. *b* Tell *m* me what you have done; do not hide it from me."

²⁰Achan replied, "It is true! I have sinned against the LORD, the God of Israel. This is what I have done: ²¹When I saw in the plunder a beautiful robe from Babylonia, *c* two hundred shekels *d* of silver and a wedge of gold weighing fifty shekels, *e* I coveted *n* them and took them. They are hidden in the ground inside my tent, with the silver underneath."

²²So Joshua sent messengers, and they ran to the tent, and there it was, hidden in his tent, with the silver underneath. ²³They took the things from the tent, brought them to Joshua and all the Israelites and spread them out before the LORD.

---

a 19 A solemn charge to tell the truth   *b 19* Or *and confess to him*   *c 21* Hebrew *Shinar*   *d 21* That is, about 5 pounds (about 2.3 kilograms)   *e 21* That is, about 1 1/4 pounds (about 0.6 kilogram)

7:9
a Ex 32:12;
Dt 9:28

7:11
b Jos 6:17-19
c Ac 5:1-2

7:12
d Nu 14:45;
Jdg 2:14
e Jos 6:18

7:13
f Jos 3:5; 6:18

7:14
g Pr 16:33

7:15
h 1Sa 14:39
i ver 11
j Ge 34:7

7:17
k Nu 26:20

7:19
l 1Sa 6:5;
Jer 13:16;
Jn 9:24*
m 1Sa 14:43

7:21
n Dt 7:25;
Eph 5:5;
1Ti 6:10

7:24
a ver 26;
Jos 15:7

24Then Joshua, together with all Israel, took Achan son of Ze-rah, the silver, the robe, the gold wedge, his sons and daughters, his cattle, donkeys and sheep, his tent and all that he had, to the Valley of Achor.*a* **25**Joshua said, "Why have you brought this trouble*b* on us? The Lord will bring trouble on you today."

Then all Israel stoned him,*c* and after they had stoned the rest, they burned them. **26**Over Achan they heaped up a large pile of rocks, which remains to this day. Then the Lord turned from his fierce anger.*d* Therefore that place has been called the Valley of Achor*ae* ever since.

7:25
b Jos 6:18
c Dt 17:5

Chapter 8 Theme

8 Then the Lord said to Joshua, "Do not be afraid;*f* do not be discouraged.*g* Take the whole army*h* with you, and go up and attack Ai. For I have delivered*i* into your hands the king of Ai, his people, his city and his land. **2**You shall do to Ai and its king as you did to Jericho and its king, except that you may carry off their plunder and livestock for yourselves.*j* Set an ambush behind the city."

7:26
d Nu 25:4;
Dt 13:17
e ver 24;
Isa 65:10;
Hos 2:15

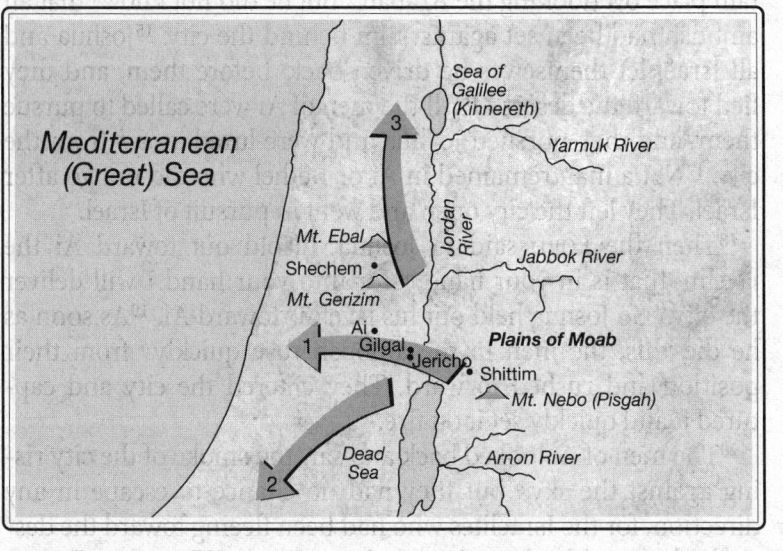

Joshua's 3-Pronged Invasion

8:1
f Dt 31:6
g Dt 1:21; 7:18;
Jos 1:9
h Jos 10:7
i Jos 6:2

3So Joshua and the whole army moved out to attack Ai. He chose thirty thousand of his best fighting men and sent them out at night **4**with these orders: "Listen carefully. You are to set an ambush behind the city. Don't go very far from it. All of you be on the alert. **5**I and all those with me will advance on the city, and when the men come out against us, as they did before, we will flee from them. **6**They will pursue us until we have lured them away from the city, for they will say, 'They are running away

8:2
j ver 27;
Dt 20:14

a 26 *Achor* means *trouble.*

from us as they did before.' So when we flee from them, ⁷you are to rise up from ambush and take the city. The LORD your God will give it into your hand.^a ⁸When you have taken the city, set it on fire.^b Do what the LORD has commanded.^c See to it; you have my orders."

⁹Then Joshua sent them off, and they went to the place of ambush^d and lay in wait between Bethel and Ai, to the west of Ai—but Joshua spent that night with the people.

¹⁰Early the next morning^e Joshua mustered his men, and he and the leaders of Israel^f marched before them to Ai. ¹¹The entire force that was with him marched up and approached the city and arrived in front of it. They set up camp north of Ai, with the valley between them and the city. ¹²Joshua had taken about five thousand men and set them in ambush between Bethel and Ai, to the west of the city. ¹³They had the soldiers take up their positions—all those in the camp to the north of the city and the ambush to the west of it. That night Joshua went into the valley.

¹⁴When the king of Ai saw this, he and all the men of the city hurried out early in the morning to meet Israel in battle at a certain place overlooking the Arabah.^g But he did not know^h that an ambush had been set against him behind the city. ¹⁵Joshua and all Israel let themselves be driven backⁱ before them, and they fled toward the desert.^j ¹⁶All the men of Ai were called to pursue them, and they pursued Joshua and were lured away^k from the city. ¹⁷Not a man remained in Ai or Bethel who did not go after Israel. They left the city open and went in pursuit of Israel.

¹⁸Then the LORD said to Joshua, "Hold out toward Ai the javelin^l that is in your hand,^m for into your hand I will deliver the city." So Joshua held out his javelinⁿ toward Ai. ¹⁹As soon as he did this, the men in the ambush rose quickly^o from their position and rushed forward. They entered the city and captured it and quickly set it on fire.^p

²⁰The men of Ai looked back and saw the smoke of the city rising against the sky,^q but they had no chance to escape in any direction, for the Israelites who had been fleeing toward the desert had turned back against their pursuers. ²¹For when Joshua and all Israel saw that the ambush had taken the city and that smoke was going up from the city, they turned around and attacked the men of Ai. ²²The men of the ambush also came out of the city against them, so that they were caught in the middle, with Israelites on both sides. Israel cut them down, leaving them neither survivors nor fugitives.^r ²³But they took the king of Ai alive^s and brought him to Joshua.

²⁴When Israel had finished killing all the men of Ai in the fields and in the desert where they had chased them, and when

8:7 ^aJdg 7:7; 1Sa 23:4

8:8 ^bJdg 20:29-38 ^cver 19

8:9 ^d2Ch 13:13

8:10 ^eGe 22:3 ^fJos 7:6

8:14 ^gDt 1:1 ^hJdg 20:34

8:15 ⁱJdg 20:36 ^jJos 15:61; 16:1; 18:12

8:16 ^kJdg 20:31

8:18 ^lJob 41:26; Ps 35:3 ^mEx 4:2; 14:16; 17:9-12 ⁿver 26

8:19 ^oJdg 20:33 ^pver 8

8:20 ^qJdg 20:40

8:22 ^rDt 7:2; Jos 10:1

8:23 ^s1Sa 15:8

8:25
a Dt 20:16-18

8:26
b Nu 21:2
c Ex 17:12

8:27
d ver 2

8:28
e Nu 31:10
f Jos 7:2;
Jer 49:3
g Dt 13:16;
Jos 10:1
h Ge 35:20

8:29
i Dt 21:23;
Jn 19:31
j 2Sa 18:17

8:30
k Dt 11:29
l Ex 20:24

8:31
m Ex 20:25
n Dt 27:6-7

8:32
o Dt 27:8

8:33
p Lev 16:29
q Dt 31:12
r Dt 11:29;
27:11-14

8:34
s Dt 28:61;
31:11;
Jos 1:8

8:35
t Ex 12:38;
Dt 31:12

9:1
u Nu 34:6
v Ex 3:17;
Jos 3:10

every one of them had been put to the sword, all the Israelites returned to Ai and killed those who were in it. ²⁵Twelve thousand men and women fell that day—all the people of Ai.ᵃ ²⁶For Joshua did not draw back the hand that held out his javelin until he had destroyedᵃᵇ all who lived in Ai.ᶜ ²⁷But Israel did carry off for themselves the livestock and plunder of this city, as the LORD had instructed Joshua.ᵈ

²⁸So Joshua burnedᵉ Aiᶠ and made it a permanent heap of ruins,ᵍ a desolate place to this day.ʰ ²⁹He hung the king of Ai on a tree and left him there until evening. At sunset,ⁱ Joshua ordered them to take his body from the tree and throw it down at the entrance of the city gate. And they raised a large pile of rocksʲ over it, which remains to this day.

³⁰Then Joshua built on Mount Ebalᵏ an altarˡ to the LORD, the God of Israel, ³¹as Moses the servant of the LORD had commanded the Israelites. He built it according to what is written in the Book of the Law of Moses—an altar of uncut stones, on which no iron toolᵐ had been used. On it they offered to the LORD burnt offerings and sacrificed fellowship offerings.ᵇⁿ ³²There, in the presence of the Israelites, Joshua copied on stones the law of Moses, which he had written.ᵒ ³³All Israel, aliens and citizensᵖ alike, with their elders, officials and judges, were standing on both sides of the ark of the covenant of the LORD, facing those who carried it—the priests, who were Levites.�q Half of the people stood in front of Mount Gerizim and half of them in front of Mount Ebal,ʳ as Moses the servant of the LORD had formerly commanded when he gave instructions to bless the people of Israel.

³⁴Afterward, Joshua read all the words of the law—the blessings and the curses—just as it is written in the Book of the Law.ˢ ³⁵There was not a word of all that Moses had commanded that Joshua did not read to the whole assembly of Israel, including the women and children, and the aliens who lived among them.ᵗ

Chapter 9 Theme

9 Now when all the kings west of the Jordan heard about these things—those in the hill country, in the western foothills, and along the entire coast of the Great Seaᶜᵘ as far as Lebanon (the kings of the Hittites, Amorites, Canaanites, Perizzites, Hivites and Jebusites)ᵛ— ²they came together to make war against Joshua and Israel.

---

a 26 The Hebrew term refers to the irrevocable giving over of things or persons to the LORD, often by totally destroying them.   b 31 Traditionally *peace offerings*   c 1 That is, the Mediterranean

³However, when the people of Gibeon*ᵃ* heard what Joshua had done to Jericho and Ai, ⁴they resorted to a ruse: They went as a delegation whose donkeys were loadedᵃ with worn-out sacks and old wineskins, cracked and mended. ⁵The men put worn and patched sandals on their feet and wore old clothes. All the bread of their food supply was dry and moldy. ⁶Then they went to Joshua in the camp at Gilgal*ᵇ* and said to him and the men of Israel, "We have come from a distant country; make a treaty with us."

⁷The men of Israel said to the Hivites,*ᶜ* "But perhaps you live near us. How then can we make a treatyᵈ with you?"

⁸"We are your servants,*ᵉ*" they said to Joshua.

But Joshua asked, "Who are you and where do you come from?"

⁹They answered: "Your servants have come from a very distant countryᶠ because of the fame of the LORD your God. For we have heard reportsᵍ of him: all that he did in Egypt, ¹⁰and all that he did to the two kings of the Amorites east of the Jordan—Sihon king of Heshbon, and Og king of Bashan,ʰ who reigned in Ashtaroth.ⁱ ¹¹And our elders and all those living in our country said to us, 'Take provisions for your journey; go and meet them and say to them, "We are your servants; make a treaty with us."' ¹²This bread of ours was warm when we packed it at home on the day we left to come to you. But now see how dry and moldy it is. ¹³And these wineskins that we filled were new, but see how cracked they are. And our clothes and sandals are worn out by the very long journey."

¹⁴The men of Israel sampled their provisions but did not inquireʲ of the LORD. ¹⁵Then Joshua made a treaty of peaceᵏ with them to let them live, and the leaders of the assembly ratified it by oath.

¹⁶Three days after they made the treaty with the Gibeonites, the Israelites heard that they were neighbors, living near them. ¹⁷So the Israelites set out and on the third day came to their cities: Gibeon, Kephirah, Beerothˡ and Kiriath Jearim.ᵐ ¹⁸But the Israelites did not attack them, because the leaders of the assembly had sworn an oathⁿ to them by the LORD, the God of Israel.

The whole assembly grumbledᵒ against the leaders, ¹⁹but all the leaders answered, "We have given them our oath by the LORD, the God of Israel, and we cannot touch them now. ²⁰This is what we will do to them: We will let them live, so that wrath will not fall on us for breaking the oath we swore to them." ²¹They continued, "Let them live,ᵖ but let them be woodcutters and water carriersᵠ for the entire community." So the leaders' promise to them was kept.

a 4 Most Hebrew manuscripts; some Hebrew manuscripts, Vulgate and Syriac (see also Septuagint) *They prepared provisions and loaded their donkeys*

9:3
a ver 17;
Jos 10:2;
2Sa 2:12;
2Ch 1:3;
Isa 28:21

9:6
b Jos 5:10

9:7
c ver 1;
Jos 11:19
d Ex 23:32;
Dt 7:2

9:8
e Dt 20:11;
2Ki 10:5

9:9
f Dt 20:15
g ver 24;
Jos 2:9

9:10
h Nu 21:33
i Nu 21:24,35

9:14
j Nu 27:21

9:15
k Ex 23:32;
Jos 11:19;
2Sa 21:2

9:17
l Jos 18:25
m 1Sa 7:1-2

9:18
n Ps 15:4
o Ex 15:24

9:21
p ver 15
q Dt 29:11

9:22
a ver 6
b ver 16

9:23
c Ge 9:25

9:24
d ver 9

9:25
e Ge 16:6

9:27
f Dt 12:5

10:1
g Jdg 1:7
h Jos 8:1
i Dt 20:16;
Jos 8:22
j Jos 9:15

10:3
k Ge 13:18
l 2Ch 11:9;
25:27;
Ne 11:30;
Isa 36:2; 37:8;
Jer 34:7;
Mic 1:13

10:4
m Jos 9:15

10:5
n Nu 13:29

10:7
o Jos 8:1

10:8
p Dt 3:2;
Jos 1:9

10:10
q Dt 7:23

²²Then Joshua summoned the Gibeonites and said, "Why did you deceive us by saying, 'We live a long way *a* from you,' while actually you live near *b* us? ²³You are now under a curse:*c* You will never cease to serve as woodcutters and water carriers for the house of my God."

²⁴They answered Joshua, "Your servants were clearly told*d* how the LORD your God had commanded his servant Moses to give you the whole land and to wipe out all its inhabitants from before you. So we feared for our lives because of you, and that is why we did this. ²⁵We are now in your hands.*e* Do to us whatever seems good and right to you."

²⁶So Joshua saved them from the Israelites, and they did not kill them. ²⁷That day he made the Gibeonites woodcutters and water carriers for the community and for the altar of the LORD at the place the LORD would choose.*f* And that is what they are to this day.

Chapter 10 Theme

10 Now Adoni-Zedek king of Jerusalem*g* heard that Joshua had taken Ai*h* and totally destroyed*a* *i* it, doing to Ai and its king as he had done to Jericho and its king, and that the people of Gibeon had made a treaty of peace*j* with Israel and were living near them. ²He and his people were very much alarmed at this, because Gibeon was an important city, like one of the royal cities; it was larger than Ai, and all its men were good fighters. ³So Adoni-Zedek king of Jerusalem appealed to Hoham king of Hebron,*k* Piram king of Jarmuth, Japhia king of Lachish*l* and Debir king of Eglon. ⁴"Come up and help me attack Gibeon," he said, "because it has made peace*m* with Joshua and the Israelites."

⁵Then the five kings of the Amorites*n*—the kings of Jerusalem, Hebron, Jarmuth, Lachish and Eglon—joined forces. They moved up with all their troops and took up positions against Gibeon and attacked it.

⁶The Gibeonites then sent word to Joshua in the camp at Gilgal: "Do not abandon your servants. Come up to us quickly and save us! Help us, because all the Amorite kings from the hill country have joined forces against us."

⁷So Joshua marched up from Gilgal with his entire army,*o* including all the best fighting men. ⁸The LORD said to Joshua, "Do not be afraid*p* of them; I have given them into your hand. Not one of them will be able to withstand you."

⁹After an all-night march from Gilgal, Joshua took them by surprise. ¹⁰The LORD threw them into confusion before Israel,*q* who defeated them in a great victory at Gibeon. Israel pursued

---

a 1 The Hebrew term refers to the irrevocable giving over of things or persons to the LORD, often by totally destroying them; also in verses 28, 35, 37, 39 and 40.

them along the road going up to Beth Horon*a* and cut them down all the way to Azekah*b* and Makkedah. ¹¹As they fled before Israel on the road down from Beth Horon to Azekah, the LORD hurled large hailstones*c* down on them from the sky, and more of them died from the hailstones than were killed by the swords of the Israelites.

¹²On the day the LORD gave the Amorites*d* over to Israel, Joshua said to the LORD in the presence of Israel:

> "O sun, stand still over Gibeon,
>> O moon, over the Valley of Aijalon.*e*"
> ¹³So the sun stood still,*f*
>> and the moon stopped,
>> till the nation avenged itself on*a* its enemies,

as it is written in the Book of Jashar.*g*

The sun stopped*h* in the middle of the sky and delayed going down about a full day. ¹⁴There has never been a day like it before or since, a day when the LORD listened to a man. Surely the LORD was fighting*i* for Israel!

¹⁵Then Joshua returned with all Israel to the camp at Gilgal.*j*

¹⁶Now the five kings had fled and hidden in the cave at Makkedah. ¹⁷When Joshua was told that the five kings had been found hiding in the cave at Makkedah, ¹⁸he said, "Roll large rocks up to the mouth of the cave, and post some men there to guard it. ¹⁹But don't stop! Pursue your enemies, attack them from the rear and don't let them reach their cities, for the LORD your God has given them into your hand."

²⁰So Joshua and the Israelites destroyed them completely*k*— almost to a man—but the few who were left reached their fortified cities. ²¹The whole army then returned safely to Joshua in the camp at Makkedah, and no one uttered a word against the Israelites.

²²Joshua said, "Open the mouth of the cave and bring those five kings out to me." ²³So they brought the five kings out of the cave—the kings of Jerusalem, Hebron, Jarmuth, Lachish and Eglon. ²⁴When they had brought these kings to Joshua, he summoned all the men of Israel and said to the army commanders who had come with him, "Come here and put your feet*l* on the necks of these kings." So they came forward and placed their feet*m* on their necks.

²⁵Joshua said to them, "Do not be afraid; do not be discouraged. Be strong and courageous.*n* This is what the LORD will do to all the enemies you are going to fight." ²⁶Then Joshua struck

INSIGHT

The *Book of Jashar* was a collection of poetical writings of important events in Israel's history which was gathered in the time of David or Solomon. It is often compared to "The Book of Wars of the Lord." Bible authors are believed to have quoted from this book.

10:10
a Jos 16:3,5
b Jos 15:35

10:11
c Ps 18:12;
Isa 28:2,17

10:12
d Am 2:9
e Jdg 1:35; 12:12

10:13
f Hab 3:11
g 2Sa 1:18
h Isa 38:8

10:14
i ver 42;
Ex 14:14;
Dt 1:30;
Ps 106:43;
136:24

10:15
j ver 43

10:20
k Dt 20:16

10:24
l Mal 4:3
m Ps 110:1

10:25
n Dt 31:6

a 13 Or *nation triumphed over*

and killed the kings and hung them on five trees, and they were left hanging on the trees until evening.

10:27
*a*Dt 21:23;
Jos 8:9,29

²⁷At sunset*a* Joshua gave the order and they took them down from the trees and threw them into the cave where they had been hiding. At the mouth of the cave they placed large rocks, which are there to this day.

10:28
*b*Dt 20:16
*c*Jos 6:21

²⁸That day Joshua took Makkedah. He put the city and its king to the sword and totally destroyed everyone in it. He left no survivors.*b* And he did to the king of Makkedah as he had done to the king of Jericho.*c*

10:33
*d*Jos 16:3,10;
Jdg 1:29;
1Ki 9:15

²⁹Then Joshua and all Israel with him moved on from Makkedah to Libnah and attacked it. ³⁰The Lord also gave that city and its king into Israel's hand. The city and everyone in it Joshua put to the sword. He left no survivors there. And he did to its king as he had done to the king of Jericho.

10:36
*e*Jos 14:13;
15:13;
Jdg 1:10

³¹Then Joshua and all Israel with him moved on from Libnah to Lachish; he took up positions against it and attacked it. ³²The Lord handed Lachish over to Israel, and Joshua took it on the second day. The city and everyone in it he put to the sword, just as he had done to Libnah. ³³Meanwhile, Horam king of Gezer*d* had come up to help Lachish, but Joshua defeated him and his army—until no survivors were left.

10:38
*f*Jos 15:15;
Jdg 1:11

³⁴Then Joshua and all Israel with him moved on from Lachish to Eglon; they took up positions against it and attacked it. ³⁵They captured it that same day and put it to the sword and totally destroyed everyone in it, just as they had done to Lachish.

10:40
*g*Ge 12:9;
Jos 12:8
*h*Dt 1:7
*i*Dt 7:24
*j*Dt 20:16-17

³⁶Then Joshua and all Israel with him went up from Eglon to Hebron*e* and attacked it. ³⁷They took the city and put it to the sword, together with its king, its villages and everyone in it. They left no survivors. Just as at Eglon, they totally destroyed it and everyone in it.

³⁸Then Joshua and all Israel with him turned around and attacked Debir.*f* ³⁹They took the city, its king and its villages, and put them to the sword. Everyone in it they totally destroyed. They left no survivors. They did to Debir and its king as they had done to Libnah and its king and to Hebron.

10:41
*k*Ge 14:7
*l*Ge 10:19
*m*Jos 11:16;
15:51

⁴⁰So Joshua subdued the whole region, including the hill country, the Negev,*g* the western foothills and the mountain slopes,*h* together with all their kings.*i* He left no survivors. He totally destroyed all who breathed, just as the Lord, the God of Israel, had

10:42
*n*ver 14

commanded.*j* ⁴¹Joshua subdued them from Kadesh Barnea*k* to Gaza*l* and from the whole region of Goshen*m* to Gibeon. ⁴²All these kings and their lands Joshua conquered in one campaign, because the Lord, the God of Israel, fought*n* for Israel.

10:43
*o*ver 15;
Jos 5:9

⁴³Then Joshua returned with all Israel to the camp at Gilgal.*o*

Chapter 11 Theme

11 When Jabin[a] king of Hazor[b] heard of this, he sent word to Jobab king of Madon, to the kings of Shimron[c] and Acshaph, ²and to the northern kings who were in the mountains, in the Arabah[d] south of Kinnereth,[e] in the western foothills and in Naphoth Dor[af] on the west; ³to the Canaanites in the east and west; to the Amorites, Hittites, Perizzites and Jebusites in the hill country; and to the Hivites[g] below Hermon in the region of Mizpah.[h] ⁴They came out with all their troops and a large number of horses and chariots—a huge army, as numerous as the sand on the seashore.[i] ⁵All these kings joined forces[j] and made camp together at the Waters of Merom, to fight against Israel.

⁶The LORD said to Joshua, "Do not be afraid of them, because by this time tomorrow I will hand all of them over[k] to Israel, slain. You are to hamstring[l] their horses and burn their chariots."

⁷So Joshua and his whole army came against them suddenly at the Waters of Merom and attacked them, ⁸and the LORD gave them into the hand of Israel. They defeated them and pursued them all the way to Greater Sidon, to Misrephoth Maim,[m] and to the Valley of Mizpah on the east, until no survivors were left. ⁹Joshua did to them as the LORD had directed: He hamstrung their horses and burned their chariots.

¹⁰At that time Joshua turned back and captured Hazor and put its king to the sword. (Hazor had been the head of all these kingdoms.) ¹¹Everyone in it they put to the sword. They totally destroyed[b] them, not sparing anything that breathed,[n] and he burned up Hazor itself.

¹²Joshua took all these royal cities and their kings and put them to the sword. He totally destroyed them, as Moses the servant of the LORD had commanded.[o] ¹³Yet Israel did not burn any of the cities built on their mounds—except Hazor, which Joshua burned. ¹⁴The Israelites carried off for themselves all the plunder and livestock of these cities, but all the people they put to the sword until they completely destroyed them, not sparing anyone that breathed.[p] ¹⁵As the LORD commanded his servant Moses, so Moses commanded Joshua, and Joshua did it; he left nothing undone of all that the LORD commanded Moses.[q]

¹⁶So Joshua took this entire land: the hill country, all the Negev, the whole region of Goshen, the western foothills,[r] the Arabah and the mountains of Israel with their foothills, ¹⁷from Mount Halak, which rises toward Seir, to Baal Gad in the Valley

---

11:1
a Jdg 4:2,7,23
b ver 10;
1Sa 12:9
c Jos 19:15

11:2
d Jos 12:3
e Nu 34:11
f Jos 17:11;
Jdg 1:27;
1Ki 4:11

11:3
g Dt 7:1;
Jdg 3:3,5;
1Ki 9:20
h Ge 31:49;
Jos 15:38; 18:26

11:4
i Jdg 7:12;
1Sa 13:5

11:5
j Jdg 5:19

11:6
k Jos 10:8
l 2Sa 8:4

11:8
m Jos 13:6

11:11
n Dt 20:16-17

11:12
o Nu 33:50-52;
Dt 7:2

11:14
p Nu 31:11-12

11:15
q Ex 34:11;
Jos 1:7

11:16
r Jos 10:41

---

a 2 Or *in the heights of Dor*   b 11 The Hebrew term refers to the irrevocable giving over of things or persons to the LORD, often by totally destroying them; also in verses 12, 20 and 21.

11:17
a Jos 12:7
b Dt 7:24

11:19
c Jos 9:3

11:20
d Ex 14:17;
Ro 9:18
e Dt 7:16;
Jdg 14:4

11:21
f Nu 13:22,33;
Dt 9:2

11:22
g 1Sa 17:4;
1Ki 2:39;
1Ch 8:13
h 1Sa 5:1;
Isa 20:1

11:23
i Jos 21:43-45
j Dt 1:38;
12:9-10; 25:19
k Nu 26:53
l Jos 14:15

12:1
m Dt 3:8

12:2
n Dt 2:36

12:3
o Jos 11:2
p Jos 13:20

12:4
q Nu 21:21,33;
Dt 3:11
r Dt 1:4

12:5
s Dt 3:10
t 1Sa 27:8
u Dt 3:14

12:6
v Nu 32:29,33;
Jos 13:8

of Lebanon*a* below Mount Hermon. He captured all their kings and struck them down, putting them to death.*b* 18Joshua waged war against all these kings for a long time. 19Except for the Hivites living in Gibeon,*c* not one city made a treaty of peace with the Israelites, who took them all in battle. 20For it was the LORD himself who hardened their hearts*d* to wage war against Israel, so that he might destroy them totally, exterminating them without mercy, as the LORD had commanded Moses.*e*

21At that time Joshua went and destroyed the Anakites*f* from the hill country: from Hebron, Debir and Anab, from all the hill country of Judah, and from all the hill country of Israel. Joshua totally destroyed them and their towns. 22No Anakites were left in Israelite territory; only in Gaza, Gath*g* and Ashdod*h* did any survive. 23So Joshua took the entire land,*i* just as the LORD had directed Moses, and he gave it as an inheritance*j* to Israel according to their tribal divisions.*k*

Then the land had rest from war.*l*

Chapter 12 Theme

12 These are the kings of the land whom the Israelites had defeated and whose territory they took over east of the Jordan, from the Arnon Gorge to Mount Hermon,*m* including all the eastern side of the Arabah:

2Sihon king of the Amorites,
who reigned in Heshbon. He ruled from Aroer on the rim of the Arnon Gorge—from the middle of the gorge—to the Jabbok River, which is the border of the Ammonites. This included half of Gilead.*n* 3He also ruled over the eastern Arabah from the Sea of Kinnereth*a o* to the Sea of the Arabah (the Salt Sea*b*), to Beth Jeshimoth,*p* and then southward below the slopes of Pisgah.

4And the territory of Og king of Bashan,*q*
one of the last of the Rephaites, who reigned in Ashtaroth*r* and Edrei. 5He ruled over Mount Hermon, Salecah,*s* all of Bashan to the border of the people of Geshur*t* and Maacah,*u* and half of Gilead to the border of Sihon king of Heshbon.

6Moses, the servant of the LORD, and the Israelites conquered them. And Moses the servant of the LORD gave their land to the Reubenites, the Gadites and the half-tribe of Manasseh to be their possession.*v*

7These are the kings of the land that Joshua and the Israelites conquered on the west side of the Jordan, from Baal Gad in the

*a*3 That is, Galilee   *b*3 That is, the Dead Sea

Valley of Lebanon*a* to Mount Halak, which rises toward Seir (their lands Joshua gave as an inheritance to the tribes of Israel according to their tribal divisions— ⁸the hill country, the western foothills, the Arabah, the mountain slopes, the desert and the Negev*b*—the lands of the Hittites, Amorites, Canaanites, Perizzites, Hivites and Jebusites):

⁹the king of Jericho*c*	one
the king of Ai*d* (near Bethel)	one
¹⁰the king of Jerusalem*e*	one
the king of Hebron	one
¹¹the king of Jarmuth	one
the king of Lachish	one
¹²the king of Eglon	one
the king of Gezer*f*	one
¹³the king of Debir	one
the king of Geder	one
¹⁴the king of Hormah	one
the king of Arad*g*	one
¹⁵the king of Libnah	one
the king of Adullam	one
¹⁶the king of Makkedah	one
the king of Bethel*h*	one
¹⁷the king of Tappuah	one
the king of Hepher*i*	one
¹⁸the king of Aphek *j*	one
the king of Lasharon	one
¹⁹the king of Madon	one
the king of Hazor	one
²⁰the king of Shimron Meron	one
the king of Acshaph*k*	one
²¹the king of Taanach	one
the king of Megiddo	one
²²the king of Kedesh*l*	one
the king of Jokneam in Carmel*m*	one
²³the king of Dor (in Naphoth Dor*a n*)	one
the king of Goyim in Gilgal	one
²⁴the king of Tirzah	one

thirty-one kings in all.*o*

Chapter 13 Theme

13 When Joshua was old and well advanced in years,*p* the LORD said to him, "You are very old, and there are still very large areas of land to be taken over.

a 23 Or in the heights of Dor

370

Cross references

12:7
a Jos 11:17

12:8
b Jos 11:16

12:9
c Jos 6:2
d Jos 8:29

12:10
e Jos 10:23

12:12
f Jos 10:33

12:14
g Nu 21:1

12:16
h Jos 7:2

12:17
i 1Ki 4:10

12:18
j Jos 13:4

12:20
k Jos 11:1

12:22
l Jos 19:37; 20:7; 21:32
m 1Sa 15:12

12:23
n Jos 11:2

12:24
o Ps 135:11; Dt 7:24

13:1
p Ge 24:1; Jos 14:10

13:3
a Jer 2:18
b Jdg 1:18
c Jdg 3:3
d Dt 2:23

13:4
e Jos 12:18;
19:30
f Am 2:10

13:5
g 1Ki 5:18;
Ps 83:7;
Eze 27:9
h Jos 12:7

13:6
i Jos 11:8
j Nu 33:54

13:7
k Jos 11:23;
Ps 78:55

13:8
l Jos 12:6

13:9
m ver 16;
Jdg 11:26
n Jer 48:8,21
o Nu 21:30

13:10
p Nu 21:24

13:11
q Jos 12:5

13:12
r Dt 3:11
s Jos 12:4
t Ge 14:5

13:13
u Jos 12:5
v Dt 3:14

13:14
w ver 33;
Dt 18:1-2

13:16
x ver 9;
Jos 12:2

2"This is the land that remains: all the regions of the Philistines and Geshurites: 3from the Shihor River a on the east of Egypt to the territory of Ekron b on the north, all of it counted as Canaanite (the territory of the five Philistine rulers c in Gaza, Ashdod, Ashkelon, Gath and Ekron—that of the Avvites); d 4from the south, all the land of the Canaanites, from Arah of the Sidonians as far as Aphek, e the region of the Amorites, f 5the area of the Gebalites a; g and all Lebanon h to the east, from Baal Gad below Mount Hermon to Lebo b Hamath.

6"As for all the inhabitants of the mountain regions from Lebanon to Misrephoth Maim, i that is, all the Sidonians, I myself will drive them out before the Israelites. Be sure to allocate this land to Israel for an inheritance, as I have instructed you, j 7and divide it as an inheritance k among the nine tribes and half of the tribe of Manasseh."

8The other half of Manasseh, c the Reubenites and the Gadites had received the inheritance that Moses had given them east of the Jordan, as he, the servant of the Lord, had assigned l it to them.

9It extended from Aroer m on the rim of the Arnon Gorge, and from the town in the middle of the gorge, and included the whole plateau n of Medeba as far as Dibon, o 10and all the towns of Sihon king of the Amorites, who ruled in Heshbon, out to the border of the Ammonites. p 11It also included Gilead, the territory of the people of Geshur and Maacah, all of Mount Hermon and all Bashan as far as Salecah q— 12that is, the whole kingdom of Og in Bashan, r who had reigned in Ashtaroth s and Edrei and had survived as one of the last of the Rephaites. t Moses had defeated them and taken over their land. 13But the Israelites did not drive out the people of Geshur u and Maacah, v so they continue to live among the Israelites to this day.

14But to the tribe of Levi he gave no inheritance, since the offerings made by fire to the Lord, the God of Israel, are their inheritance, as he promised them. w

15This is what Moses had given to the tribe of Reuben, clan by clan:

16The territory from Aroer x on the rim of the Arnon Gorge, and from the town in the middle of the gorge, and the whole

a 5 That is, the area of Byblos   b 5 Or to the entrance to   c 8 Hebrew With it (that is, with the other half of Manasseh) plateau past Medeba[a] [17]to Heshbon and all its towns on the plateau, including Dibon,[b] Bamoth Baal, Beth Baal Meon,[c] [18]Jahaz,[d] Kedemoth, Mephaath,[e] [19]Kiriathaim,[f] Sibmah, Zereth Shahar on the hill in the valley, [20]Beth Peor,[g] the slopes of Pisgah, and Beth Jeshimoth [21]—all the towns on the plateau and the entire realm of Sihon king of the Amorites, who ruled at Heshbon. Moses had defeated him and the Midianite chiefs,[h] Evi, Rekem, Zur, Hur and Reba[i]—princes allied with Sihon—who lived in that country. [22]In addition to those slain in battle, the Israelites had put to the sword Balaam son of Beor,[j] who practiced divination. [23]The boundary of the Reubenites was the bank of the Jordan. These towns and their villages were the inheritance of the Reubenites, clan by clan.

[24]This is what Moses had given to the tribe of Gad, clan by clan:

[25]The territory of Jazer,[k] all the towns of Gilead and half the Ammonite country as far as Aroer, near Rabbah; [26]and from Heshbon[l] to Ramath Mizpah and Betonim, and from Mahanaim to the territory of Debir;[m] [27]and in the valley, Beth Haram, Beth Nimrah, Succoth[n] and Zaphon with the rest of the realm of Sihon king of Heshbon (the east side of the Jordan, the territory up to the end of the Sea of Kinnereth[a][o]). [28]These towns and their villages were the inheritance of the Gadites,[p] clan by clan.

[29]This is what Moses had given to the half-tribe of Manasseh, that is, to half the family of the descendants of Manasseh, clan by clan:

[30]The territory extending from Mahanaim[q] and including all of Bashan, the entire realm of Og king of Bashan—all the settlements of Jair[r] in Bashan, sixty towns, [31]half of Gilead, and Ashtaroth and Edrei (the royal cities of Og in Bashan). This was for the descendants of Makir[s] son of Manasseh— for half of the sons of Makir, clan by clan.

[32]This is the inheritance Moses had given when he was in the plains of Moab across the Jordan east of Jericho. [33]But to the tribe of Levi, Moses had given no inheritance; the LORD, the God of Israel, is their inheritance,[t] as he promised them.[u]

Chapter 14 Theme

14 Now these are the areas the Israelites received as an inheritance in the land of Canaan, which Eleazar the priest, Joshua son of Nun and the heads of the tribal clans of Israel allotted

[a] 27 That is, Galilee

13:16
[a]Nu 21:30

13:17
[b]Nu 32:3
[c]1Ch 5:8

13:18
[d]Nu 21:23
[e]Jer 48:21

13:19
[f]Nu 32:37

13:20
[g]Dt 3:29

13:21
[h]Nu 25:15
[i]Nu 31:8

13:22
[j]Nu 22:5; 31:8

13:25
[k]Nu 21:32;
Jos 21:39

13:26
[l]Nu 21:25;
Jer 49:3
[m]Jos 10:3

13:27
[n]Ge 33:17
[o]Nu 34:11

13:28
[p]Nu 32:33

13:30
[q]Ge 32:2
[r]Nu 32:41

13:31
[s]Ge 50:23

13:33
[t]Nu 18:20
[u]ver 14;
Jos 18:7

14:1
a Nu 34:17-18

14:2
b Nu 26:55

14:3
c Nu 32:33
d Jos 13:14

14:4
e Ge 41:52; 48:5

14:5
f Nu 34:13; 35:2;
Jos 21:2

14:6
g Nu 13:6; 14:30
h Nu 13:26

14:7
i Nu 13:17
j Nu 13:30;
14:6-9

14:8
k Nu 13:31
l Nu 14:24

14:9
m Nu 14:24;
Dt 1:36

14:10
n Nu 14:30

14:11
o Dt 34:7

14:12
p Nu 13:33
q Nu 13:28

14:13
r Jos 22:6,7
s Jos 10:36
t Jdg 1:20;
1Ch 6:56

14:15
u Ge 23:2
v Jos 15:13
w Jos 11:23

15:1
x Nu 34:3
y Nu 33:36

to them.*a* ²Their inheritances were assigned by lot*b* to the nine-and-a-half tribes, as the LORD had commanded through Moses. ³Moses had granted the two-and-a-half tribes their inheritance east of the Jordan*c* but had not granted the Levites an inheritance among the rest,*d* ⁴for the sons of Joseph had become two tribes—Manasseh and Ephraim.*e* The Levites received no share of the land but only towns to live in, with pasturelands for their flocks and herds. ⁵So the Israelites divided the land, just as the LORD had commanded Moses.*f*

⁶Now the men of Judah approached Joshua at Gilgal, and Caleb son of Jephunneh*g* the Kenizzite said to him, "You know what the LORD said to Moses the man of God at Kadesh Barnea*h* about you and me. ⁷I was forty years old when Moses the servant of the LORD sent me from Kadesh Barnea to explore the land.*i* And I brought him back a report according to my convictions,*j* ⁸but my brothers who went up with me made the hearts of the people melt with fear.*k* I, however, followed the LORD my God wholeheartedly.*l* ⁹So on that day Moses swore to me, 'The land on which your feet have walked will be your inheritance and that of your children*m* forever, because you have followed the LORD my God wholeheartedly.'*a*

¹⁰"Now then, just as the LORD promised,*n* he has kept me alive for forty-five years since the time he said this to Moses, while Israel moved about in the desert. So here I am today, eighty-five years old! ¹¹I am still as strong*o* today as the day Moses sent me out; I'm just as vigorous to go out to battle now as I was then. ¹²Now give me this hill country that the LORD promised me that day. You yourself heard then that the Anakites*p* were there and their cities were large and fortified,*q* but, the LORD helping me, I will drive them out just as he said."

¹³Then Joshua blessed*r* Caleb son of Jephunneh and gave him Hebron*s* as his inheritance.*t* ¹⁴So Hebron has belonged to Caleb son of Jephunneh the Kenizzite ever since, because he followed the LORD, the God of Israel, wholeheartedly. ¹⁵(Hebron used to be called Kiriath Arba*u* after Arba,*v* who was the greatest man among the Anakites.)

Then the land had rest*w* from war.

Chapter 15 Theme

15 The allotment for the tribe of Judah, clan by clan, extended down to the territory of Edom,*x* to the Desert of Zin*y* in the extreme south.

*a*9 Deut. 1:36

²Their southern boundary started from the bay at the southern end of the Salt Sea,^a ³crossed south of Scorpion^b Pass,^a continued on to Zin and went over to the south of Kadesh Barnea. Then it ran past Hezron up to Addar and curved around to Karka. ⁴It then passed along to Azmon^b and joined the Wadi of Egypt,^c ending at the sea. This is their^c southern boundary.

⁵The eastern boundary^d is the Salt Sea as far as the mouth of the Jordan.

The northern boundary^e started from the bay of the sea at the mouth of the Jordan, ⁶went up to Beth Hoglah^f and continued north of Beth Arabah to the Stone of Bohan^g son of Reuben. ⁷The boundary then went up to Debir from the Valley of Achor^h and turned north to Gilgal, which faces the Pass of Adummim south of the gorge. It continued along to the waters of En Shemesh and came out at En Rogel.ⁱ ⁸Then it ran up the Valley of Ben Hinnom along the southern slope of the Jebusite^j city (that is, Jerusalem). From there it climbed to the top of the hill west of the Hinnom Valley at the northern end of the Valley of Rephaim. ⁹From the hilltop the boundary headed toward the spring of the waters of Nephtoah,^k came out at the towns of Mount Ephron and went down toward Baalah^l (that is, Kiriath Jearim). ¹⁰Then it curved westward from Baalah to Mount Seir, ran along the northern slope of Mount Jearim (that is, Kesalon), continued down to Beth Shemesh and crossed to Timnah.^m ¹¹It went to the northern slope of Ekron, turned toward Shikkeron, passed along to Mount Baalah and reached Jabneel.ⁿ The boundary ended at the sea.

¹²The western boundary is the coastline of the Great Sea.^{do} These are the boundaries around the people of Judah by their clans.

¹³In accordance with the LORD's command to him, Joshua gave to Caleb son of Jephunneh a portion in Judah—Kiriath Arba, that is, Hebron. (Arba was the forefather of Anak.)^p ¹⁴From Hebron Caleb drove out the three Anakites^q—Sheshai, Ahiman and Talmai^r—descendants of Anak.^s ¹⁵From there he marched against the people living in Debir (formerly called Kiriath Sepher). ¹⁶And Caleb said, "I will give my daughter Acsah^t in marriage to the man who attacks and captures Kiriath Sepher." ¹⁷Othniel^u son of Kenaz, Caleb's brother, took it; so Caleb gave his daughter Acsah to him in marriage.

15:3
^aNu 34:4

15:4
^bNu 34:5
^cGe 15:18

15:5
^dNu 34:10
^eJos 18:15-19

15:6
^fJos 18:19,21
^gJos 18:17

15:7
^hJos 7:24
ⁱ2Sa 17:17;
1Ki 1:9

15:8
^jver 63;
Jos 18:16,28;
Jdg 1:21; 19:10

15:9
^kJos 18:15
^l1Ch 13:6

15:10
^mGe 38:12;
Jdg 14:1

15:11
ⁿJos 19:33

15:12
^oNu 34:6

15:13
^pJos 14:13-15

15:14
^qNu 13:33
^rNu 13:22
^sJdg 1:10,20

15:16
^tJdg 1:12

15:17
^uJdg 3:9,11

---

^a2 That is, the Dead Sea; also in verse 5   ^b3 Hebrew *Akrabbim*   ^c4 Hebrew *your*   ^d12 That is, the Mediterranean; also in verse 47

15:21
ᵃGe 35:21

15:24
ᵇ1Sa 23:14

15:26
ᶜ1Ch 4:28

15:28
ᵈGe 21:31

15:29
ᵉver 9

15:30
ᶠJos 19:4

15:31
ᵍ1Sa 27:6

15:32
ʰJdg 20:45

15:33
ⁱJdg 13:25;
16:31

15:34
ʲ1Ch 4:18;
Ne 3:13

15:35
ᵏJos 10:3
ˡ1Sa 22:1

15:36
ᵐ1Ch 12:4

15:38
ⁿ2Ki 14:7

15:39
ᵒJos 10:3;
2Ki 14:19
ᵖ2Ki 22:1

15:41
�q Jos 10:10

15:42
ʳ1Sa 30:30

15:44
ˢJdg 1:31
ᵗMic 1:15

15:47
ᵘJos 11:22
ᵛver 4
ʷNu 34:6

15:48
ˣ1Sa 30:27

15:49
ʸJos 10:3

15:50
ᶻJos 21:14

15:51
ᵃJos 10:41;
11:16

15:52
ᵇGe 25:14

¹⁸One day when she came to Othniel, she urged himᵃ to ask her father for a field. When she got off her donkey, Caleb asked her, "What can I do for you?"

¹⁹She replied, "Do me a special favor. Since you have given me land in the Negev, give me also springs of water." So Caleb gave her the upper and lower springs.

²⁰This is the inheritance of the tribe of Judah, clan by clan:

²¹The southernmost towns of the tribe of Judah in the Negev toward the boundary of Edom were:

Kabzeel, Eder,ᵃ Jagur, ²²Kinah, Dimonah, Adadah, ²³Kedesh, Hazor, Ithnan, ²⁴Ziph,ᵇ Telem, Bealoth, ²⁵Hazor Hadattah, Kerioth Hezron (that is, Hazor), ²⁶Amam, Shema, Moladah,ᶜ ²⁷Hazar Gaddah, Heshmon, Beth Pelet, ²⁸Hazar Shual, Beersheba,ᵈ Biziothiah, ²⁹Baalah,ᵉ Iim, Ezem, ³⁰Eltolad,ᶠ Kesil, Hormah, ³¹Ziklag,ᵍ Madmannah, Sansannah, ³²Lebaoth, Shilhim, Ain and Rimmonʰ—a total of twenty-nine towns and their villages.

³³In the western foothills:

Eshtaol,ⁱ Zorah, Ashnah, ³⁴Zanoah,ʲ En Gannim, Tappuah, Enam, ³⁵Jarmuth,ᵏ Adullam,ˡ Socoh, Azekah, ³⁶Shaaraim, Adithaim and Gederahᵐ (or Gederothaim)ᵇ—fourteen towns and their villages.

³⁷Zenan, Hadashah, Migdal Gad, ³⁸Dilean, Mizpah, Joktheel,ⁿ ³⁹Lachish,ᵒ Bozkath,ᵖ Eglon, ⁴⁰Cabbon, Lahmas, Kitlish, ⁴¹Gederoth, Beth Dagon, Naamah and Makkedahq—sixteen towns and their villages.

⁴²Libnah, Ether, Ashan,ʳ ⁴³Iphtah, Ashnah, Nezib, ⁴⁴Keilah, Azibˢ and Mareshahᵗ—nine towns and their villages.

⁴⁵Ekron, with its surrounding settlements and villages; ⁴⁶west of Ekron, all that were in the vicinity of Ashdod, together with their villages; ⁴⁷Ashdod,ᵘ its surrounding settlements and villages; and Gaza, its settlements and villages, as far as the Wadi of Egypt ᵛ and the coastline of the Great Sea.ʷ

⁴⁸In the hill country:

Shamir, Jattir,ˣ Socoh, ⁴⁹Dannah, Kiriath Sannah (that is, Debirʸ), ⁵⁰Anab, Eshtemoh,ᶻ Anim, ⁵¹Goshen,ᵃ Holon and Giloh—eleven towns and their villages.

⁵²Arab, Dumah,ᵇ Eshan, ⁵³Janim, Beth Tappuah, Aphekah, ⁵⁴Humtah, Kiriath Arba (that is, Hebron) and Zior—nine towns and their villages.

ᵃ18 Hebrew and some Septuagint manuscripts; other Septuagint manuscripts (see also note at Judges 1:14) *Othniel, he urged her* ᵇ36 Or *Gederah and Gederothaim*

⁵⁵Maon, Carmel,ᵃ Ziph, Juttah, ⁵⁶Jezreel,ᵇ Jokdeam, Zanoah, ⁵⁷Kain, Gibeahᶜ and Timnah—ten towns and their villages.

⁵⁸Halhul, Beth Zur,ᵈ Gedor, ⁵⁹Maarath, Beth Anoth and Eltekon—six towns and their villages.

⁶⁰Kiriath Baal (that is, Kiriath Jearimᵉ) and Rabbahᶠ—two towns and their villages.

⁶¹In the desert:

Beth Arabah, Middin, Secacah, ⁶²Nibshan, the City of Salt and En Gediᵍ—six towns and their villages.

⁶³Judah could notʰ dislodge the Jebusitesⁱ, who were living in Jerusalem; to this day the Jebusites live there with the people of Judah.

Chapter 16 Theme _____

16 The allotment for Joseph began at the Jordan of Jericho,ᵃ east of the waters of Jericho, and went up from there through the desertʲ into the hill country of Bethel. ²It went on from Bethel (that is, Luzᵏ),ᵇ crossed over to the territory of the Arkites in Ataroth, ³descended westward to the territory of the Japhletites as far as the region of Lower Beth Horonˡ and on to Gezer,ᵐ ending at the sea.

⁴So Manasseh and Ephraim, the descendants of Joseph, received their inheritance.ⁿ

⁵This was the territory of Ephraim, clan by clan:

The boundary of their inheritance went from Ataroth Addarᵒ in the east to Upper Beth Horon ⁶and continued to the sea. From Micmethathᵖ on the north it curved eastward to Taanath Shiloh, passing by it to Janoah on the east. ⁷Then it went down from Janoah to Atarothᵠ and Naarah, touched Jericho and came out at the Jordan. ⁸From Tappuah the border went west to the Kanah Ravineʳ and ended at the sea. This was the inheritance of the tribe of the Ephraimites, clan by clan. ⁹It also included all the towns and their villages that were set aside for the Ephraimites within the inheritance of the Manassites.

¹⁰They did not dislodge the Canaanites living in Gezer; to this day the Canaanites live among the people of Ephraim but are required to do forced labor.ˢ

Chapter 17 Theme _____

17 This was the allotment for the tribe of Manasseh as Joseph's firstborn,ᵗ that is, for Makir,ᵘ Manasseh's firstborn.

ᵃ1 *Jordan of Jericho* was possibly an ancient name for the Jordan River.   ᵇ2 Septuagint; Hebrew *Bethel to Luz*

### Cross-references (margin)

15:55 ᵃJos 12:22

15:56 ᵇJos 17:16

15:57 ᶜJos 18:28; Jdg 19:12

15:58 ᵈ1Ch 2:45

15:60 ᵉJos 18:14; ᶠDt 3:11

15:62 ᵍ1Sa 23:29

15:63 ʰJdg 1:21; ⁱ2Sa 5:6

16:1 ʲJos 8:15; 18:12

16:2 ᵏJos 18:13

16:3 ˡ2Ch 8:5; ᵐJos 10:33; 1Ki 9:15

16:4 ⁿJos 17:14

16:5 ᵒJos 18:13

16:6 ᵖJos 17:7

16:7 ᵠ1Ch 7:28

16:8 ʳJos 17:9

16:10 ˢJos 17:13; Jdg 1:28-29; 1Ki 9:16

17:1 ᵗGe 41:51; ᵘGe 50:23

17:2
a Nu 26:30;
1Ch 7:18

17:3
b Nu 27:1
c Nu 26:33

17:4
d Nu 27:5-7

17:7
e Jos 16:6
f Ge 12:6;
Jos 21:21

17:8
g Jos 16:8

17:9
h Jos 16:8

17:10
i Ge 30:18

17:11
j 1Sa 31:10;
1Ki 4:12;
1Ch 7:29
k Jos 11:2
l 1Sa 28:7;
Ps 83:10
m 1Ki 9:15

17:12
n Jdg 1:27

17:13
o Jos 16:10

17:14
p Nu 26:28-37

Makir was the ancestor of the Gileadites, who had received Gilead and Bashan because the Makirites were great soldiers. ²So this allotment was for the rest of the people of Manasseh— the clans of Abiezer,*a* Helek, Asriel, Shechem, Hepher and Shemida. These are the other male descendants of Manasseh son of Joseph by their clans.

³Now Zelophehad son of Hepher,*b* the son of Gilead, the son of Makir, the son of Manasseh, had no sons but only daughters,*c* whose names were Mahlah, Noah, Hoglah, Milcah and Tirzah. ⁴They went to Eleazar the priest, Joshua son of Nun, and the leaders and said, "The LORD commanded Moses to give us an inheritance among our brothers." So Joshua gave them an inheritance along with the brothers of their father, according to the LORD's command.*d* ⁵Manasseh's share consisted of ten tracts of land besides Gilead and Bashan east of the Jordan, ⁶because the daughters of the tribe of Manasseh received an inheritance among the sons. The land of Gilead belonged to the rest of the descendants of Manasseh.

⁷The territory of Manasseh extended from Asher to Micmethath*e* east of Shechem.*f* The boundary ran southward from there to include the people living at En Tappuah. ⁸(Manasseh had the land of Tappuah, but Tappuah*g* itself, on the boundary of Manasseh, belonged to the Ephraimites.) ⁹Then the boundary continued south to the Kanah Ravine.*h* There were towns belonging to Ephraim lying among the towns of Manasseh, but the boundary of Manasseh was the northern side of the ravine and ended at the sea. ¹⁰On the south the land belonged to Ephraim, on the north to Manasseh. The territory of Manasseh reached the sea and bordered Asher on the north and Issachar*i* on the east. ¹¹Within Issachar and Asher, Manasseh also had Beth Shan,*j* Ibleam and the people of Dor,*k* Endor,*l* Taanach and Megiddo,*m* together with their surrounding settlements (the third in the list is Naphoth*a*).

¹²Yet the Manassites were not able*n* to occupy these towns, for the Canaanites were determined to live in that region. ¹³However, when the Israelites grew stronger, they subjected the Canaanites to forced labor but did not drive them out completely.*o*

¹⁴The people of Joseph said to Joshua, "Why have you given us only one allotment and one portion for an inheritance? We are a numerous people and the LORD has blessed us abundantly."*p*

¹⁵"If you are so numerous," Joshua answered, "and if the hill country of Ephraim is too small for you, go up into the forest

a 11 That is, Naphoth Dor

and clear land for yourselves there in the land of the Perizzites and Rephaites.*a*"

[16]The people of Joseph replied, "The hill country is not enough for us, and all the Canaanites who live in the plain have iron chariots,*b* both those in Beth Shan and its settlements and those in the Valley of Jezreel."

[17]But Joshua said to the house of Joseph—to Ephraim and Manasseh—"You are numerous and very powerful. You will have not only one allotment [18]but the forested hill country as well. Clear it, and its farthest limits will be yours; though the Canaanites have iron chariots*c* and though they are strong, you can drive them out."

Chapter 18 Theme

18 The whole assembly of the Israelites gathered at Shiloh*d* and set up the Tent of Meeting*e* there. The country was brought under their control, [2]but there were still seven Israelite tribes who had not yet received their inheritance.

[3]So Joshua said to the Israelites: "How long will you wait before you begin to take possession of the land that the LORD, the God of your fathers, has given you? [4]Appoint three men from each tribe. I will send them out to make a survey of the land and to write a description of it, according to the inheritance of each.*f* Then they will return to me. [5]You are to divide the land into seven parts. Judah is to remain in its territory on the south*g* and the house of Joseph in its territory on the north.*h* [6]After you have written descriptions of the seven parts of the land, bring them here to me and I will cast lots*i* for you in the presence of the LORD our God. [7]The Levites, however, do not get a portion among you, because the priestly service of the LORD is their inheritance.*j* And Gad, Reuben and the half-tribe of Manasseh have already received their inheritance on the east side of the Jordan. Moses the servant of the LORD gave it to them.*k*"

[8]As the men started on their way to map out the land, Joshua instructed them, "Go and make a survey of the land and write a description of it. Then return to me, and I will cast lots for you here at Shiloh*l* in the presence of the LORD." [9]So the men left and went through the land. They wrote its description on a scroll, town by town, in seven parts, and returned to Joshua in the camp at Shiloh. [10]Joshua then cast lots*m* for them in Shiloh in the presence*n* of the LORD, and there he distributed the land to the Israelites according to their tribal divisions.*o*

[11]The lot came up for the tribe of Benjamin, clan by clan. Their allotted territory lay between the tribes of Judah and Joseph:

17:15
a Ge 14:5

17:16
b Jdg 1:19; 4:3,13

17:18
c ver 16

18:1
d Jos 19:51; 21:2; Jdg 18:31; 21:12,19; 1Sa 1:3; 4:3; Jer 7:12; 26:6
e Ex 27:21

18:4
f Mic 2:5

18:5
g Jos 15:1
h Jos 16:1-4

18:6
i Jos 14:2

18:7
j Jos 13:33
k Jos 13:8

18:8
l ver 1

18:10
m Nu 34:13
n ver 1; Jer 7:12
o Nu 33:54; Jos 19:51

18:12
a Jos 16:1
b Jos 7:2

¹²On the north side their boundary began at the Jordan, passed the northern slope of Jericho and headed west into the hill country, coming out at the desert^a of Beth Aven.^b

18:13
c Ge 28:19
d Jdg 1:23
e Jos 16:5

¹³From there it crossed to the south slope of Luz^c (that is, Bethel^d) and went down to Ataroth Addar^e on the hill south of Lower Beth Horon.

18:14
f Jos 10:10

¹⁴From the hill facing Beth Horon^f on the south the boundary turned south along the western side and came out at Kiriath Baal (that is, Kiriath Jearim), a town of the people of Judah. This was the western side.

18:15
g Jos 15:9

¹⁵The southern side began at the outskirts of Kiriath Jearim on the west, and the boundary came out at the spring of the waters of Nephtoah.^g ¹⁶The boundary went down to the foot of the hill facing the Valley of Ben Hinnom, north of the Valley of Rephaim. It continued down the Hinnom Valley^h along the southern slope of the Jebusite city and so to En Rogel.ⁱ ¹⁷It then curved north, went to En Shemesh, continued to Geliloth, which faces the Pass of Adummim, and ran down to the Stone of Bohan^j son of Reuben. ¹⁸It continued to the northern slope of Beth Arabah^{ak} and on down into the Arabah. ¹⁹It then went to the northern slope of Beth Hoglah and came out at the northern bay of the Salt Sea,^{bl} at the mouth of the Jordan in the south. This was the southern boundary.

18:16
h Jos 15:8;
2Ki 23:10
i Jos 15:7

18:17
j Jos 15:6

18:18
k Jos 15:6

18:19
l Ge 14:3

²⁰The Jordan formed the boundary on the eastern side. These were the boundaries that marked out the inheritance of the clans of Benjamin on all sides.^m

18:20
m Jos 21:4,17;
1Sa 9:1

²¹The tribe of Benjamin, clan by clan, had the following cities:

Jericho, Beth Hoglah, Emek Keziz, ²²Beth Arabah, Zemaraim, Bethel,ⁿ ²³Avvim, Parah, Ophrah, ²⁴Kephar Ammoni, Ophni and Geba^o—twelve towns and their villages.

18:22
n Jos 16:1

18:24
o Isa 10:29

²⁵Gibeon,^p Ramah,^q Beeroth,^r ²⁶Mizpah,^s Kephirah, Mozah, ²⁷Rekem, Irpeel, Taralah, ²⁸Zelah,^t Haeleph, the Jebusite city^u (that is, Jerusalem^v), Gibeah^w and Kiriath—fourteen towns and their villages.

This was the inheritance of Benjamin for its clans.

18:25
p Jos 9:3
q Jdg 4:5
r Jos 9:17

18:26
s Jos 11:3

18:28
t 2Sa 21:14
u Jos 15:8
v Jos 10:1
w Jos 15:57

Chapter 19 Theme

19 The second lot came out for the tribe of Simeon, clan by clan. Their inheritance lay within the territory of Judah.^x ²It included:

Beersheba^y (or Sheba),^c Moladah, ³Hazar Shual, Balah, Ezem, ⁴Eltolad, Bethul, Hormah, ⁵Ziklag, Beth Marcaboth,

19:1
x ver 9;
Ge 49:7

19:2
y Ge 21:14;
1Ki 19:3

a 18 Septuagint; Hebrew *slope facing the Arabah*   b 19 That is, the Dead Sea   c 2 Or *Beersheba, Sheba*; 1 Chron. 4:28 does not have *Sheba*.

Hazar Susah, [6]Beth Lebaoth and Sharuhen—thirteen towns and their villages;

[7]Ain, Rimmon, Ether and Ashan[a]—four towns and their villages— [8]and all the villages around these towns as far as Baalath Beer (Ramah in the Negev).[b]

This was the inheritance of the tribe of the Simeonites, clan by clan. [9]The inheritance of the Simeonites was taken from the share of Judah,[c] because Judah's portion was more than they needed. So the Simeonites received their inheritance within the territory of Judah.[d]

[10]The third lot came up for Zebulun,[e] clan by clan:

The boundary of their inheritance went as far as Sarid. [11]Going west it ran to Maralah, touched Dabbesheth, and extended to the ravine near Jokneam.[f] [12]It turned east from Sarid toward the sunrise to the territory of Kisloth Tabor and went on to Daberath and up to Japhia. [13]Then it continued eastward to Gath Hepher and Eth Kazin; it came out at Rimmon[g] and turned toward Neah. [14]There the boundary went around on the north to Hannathon and ended at the Valley of Iphtah El. [15]Included were Kattath, Nahalal, Shimron, Idalah and Bethlehem.[h] There were twelve towns and their villages.
[16]These towns and their villages were the inheritance of Zebulun,[i] clan by clan.[j]

[17]The fourth lot came out for Issachar,[k] clan by clan. [18]Their territory included:

Jezreel,[l] Kesulloth, Shunem,[m] [19]Hapharaim, Shion, Anaharath, [20]Rabbith, Kishion, Ebez, [21]Remeth, En Gannim, En Haddah and Beth Pazzez. [22]The boundary touched Tabor,[n] Shahazumah and Beth Shemesh,[o] and ended at the Jordan. There were sixteen towns and their villages.
[23]These towns and their villages were the inheritance of the tribe of Issachar,[p] clan by clan.[q]

[24]The fifth lot came out for the tribe of Asher,[r] clan by clan. [25]Their territory included:

Helkath, Hali, Beten, Acshaph, [26]Allammelech, Amad and Mishal. On the west the boundary touched Carmel[s] and Shihor Libnath. [27]It then turned east toward Beth Dagon, touched Zebulun[t] and the Valley of Iphtah El, and went north to Beth Emek and Neiel, passing Cabul[u] on the left. [28]It went to Abdon,[a] Rehob,[v] Hammon[w] and Kanah, as far as Greater Sidon.[x] [29]The boundary then turned back toward Ramah[y] and went to the fortified city of Tyre,[z] turned toward Hosah

a 28 Some Hebrew manuscripts (see also Joshua 21:30); most Hebrew manuscripts *Ebron*

19:7
a Jos 15:42

19:8
b Jos 10:40

19:9
c Ge 49:7
d Eze 48:24

19:10
e Jos 21:7,34

19:11
f Jos 12:22

19:13
g Jos 15:32

19:15
h Ge 35:19

19:16
i ver 10;
Jos 21:7
j Eze 48:26

19:17
k Ge 30:18

19:18
l Jos 15:56
m 1Sa 28:4;
2Ki 4:8

19:22
n Jdg 4:6,12;
Ps 89:12
o Jos 15:10

19:23
p Jos 17:10
q Ge 49:15;
Eze 48:25

19:24
r Jos 17:7

19:26
s Jos 12:22

19:27
t ver 10
u 1Ki 9:13

19:28
v Jdg 1:31
w 1Ch 6:76
x Ge 10:19;
Jos 11:8

19:29
y Jos 18:25
z 2Sa 5:11; 24:7;
Isa 23:1;
Jer 25:22;
Eze 26:2

Moses, ³so that anyone who kills a person accidentally and unintentionally*a* may flee there and find protection from the avenger of blood.*b*

⁴"When he flees to one of these cities, he is to stand in the entrance of the city gate*c* and state his case before the elders*d* of that city. Then they are to admit him into their city and give him a place to live with them. ⁵If the avenger of blood pursues him, they must not surrender the one accused, because he killed his neighbor unintentionally and without malice aforethought. ⁶He is to stay in that city until he has stood trial before the assembly*e* and until the death of the high priest who is serving at that time. Then he may go back to his own home in the town from which he fled."

⁷So they set apart Kedesh*f* in Galilee in the hill country of Naphtali, Shechem*g* in the hill country of Ephraim, and Kiriath Arba (that is, Hebron*h*) in the hill country of Judah.*i* ⁸On the east side of the Jordan of Jericho*a* they designated Bezer*j* in the desert on the plateau in the tribe of Reuben, Ramoth in Gilead*k* in the tribe of Gad, and Golan in Bashan in the tribe of Manasseh. ⁹Any of the Israelites or any alien living among them who killed someone accidentally could flee to these designated cities and not be killed by the avenger of blood prior to standing trial before the assembly.*l*

Chapter 21 Theme

21 Now the family heads of the Levites approached Eleazar the priest, Joshua son of Nun, and the heads of the other tribal families of Israel*m* ²at Shiloh*n* in Canaan and said to them, "The LORD commanded through Moses that you give us towns to live in, with pasturelands for our livestock."*o* ³So, as the LORD had commanded, the Israelites gave the Levites the following towns and pasturelands out of their own inheritance:

⁴The first lot came out for the Kohathites, clan by clan. The Levites who were descendants of Aaron the priest were allotted thirteen towns from the tribes of Judah, Simeon and Benjamin.*p* ⁵The rest of Kohath's descendants were allotted ten towns from the clans of the tribes of Ephraim, Dan and half of Manasseh.*q*

⁶The descendants of Gershon were allotted thirteen towns from the clans of the tribes of Issachar,*r* Asher, Naphtali and the half-tribe of Manasseh in Bashan.

⁷The descendants of Merari,*s* clan by clan, received twelve towns from the tribes of Reuben, Gad and Zebulun.*t*

⁸So the Israelites allotted to the Levites these towns and their pasturelands, as the LORD had commanded through Moses.

---

a 8 Jordan of Jericho was possibly an ancient name for the Jordan River.

20:3
a Lev 4:2
b Nu 35:12

20:4
c Ru 4:1;
Jer 38:7
d Jos 7:6

20:6
e Nu 35:12

20:7
f Jos 21:32;
1Ch 6:76
g Ge 12:6
h Jos 10:36;
21:11
i Lk 1:39

20:8
j Jos 21:36;
1Ch 6:78
k Jos 12:2

20:9
l Ex 21:13;
Nu 35:15

21:1
m Jos 14:1

21:2
n Jos 18:1
o Nu 35:2-3

21:4
p ver 19

21:5
q ver 26

21:6
r Ge 30:18

21:7
s Ex 6:16
t Jos 19:10

19:29
a Jdg 1:31

19:31
b Ge 30:13;
Eze 48:2

19:35
c Jos 11:2

19:36
d Jos 18:25
e Jos 11:1

19:37
f Nu 21:33

19:39
g Dt 33:23;
Eze 48:3

19:42
h Jdg 1:35

19:43
i Ge 38:12

19:45
j Jos 21:24;
1Ch 6:69

19:46
k 2Ch 2:16;
Jnh 1:3

19:47
l Jdg 18:1
m Jdg 18:7,14
n Jdg 18:27,29

19:48
o Ge 30:6

19:50
p Jos 24:30

19:51
q Jos 14:1; 18:10;
Ac 13:19

and came out at the sea in the region of Aczib,*a* ³⁰Ummah, Aphek and Rehob. There were twenty-two towns and their villages.

³¹These towns and their villages were the inheritance of the tribe of Asher,*b* clan by clan.

³²The sixth lot came out for Naphtali, clan by clan:

³³Their boundary went from Heleph and the large tree in Zaanannim, passing Adami Nekeb and Jabneel to Lakkum and ending at the Jordan. ³⁴The boundary ran west through Aznoth Tabor and came out at Hukkok. It touched Zebulun on the south, Asher on the west and the Jordan*a* on the east. ³⁵The fortified cities were Ziddim, Zer, Hammath, Rakkath, Kinnereth,*c* ³⁶Adamah, Ramah,*d* Hazor,*e* ³⁷Kedesh, Edrei,*f* En Hazor, ³⁸Iron, Migdal El, Horem, Beth Anath and Beth She-mesh. There were nineteen towns and their villages.

³⁹These towns and their villages were the inheritance of the tribe of Naphtali, clan by clan.*g*

⁴⁰The seventh lot came out for the tribe of Dan, clan by clan. ⁴¹The territory of their inheritance included:

Zorah, Eshtaol, Ir Shemesh, ⁴²Shaalabbin, Aijalon,*h* Ithlah, ⁴³Elon, Timnah,*i* Ekron, ⁴⁴Eltekeh, Gibbethon, Baalath, ⁴⁵Je-hud, Bene Berak, Gath Rimmon,*j* ⁴⁶Me Jarkon and Rakkon, with the area facing Joppa.*k*

⁴⁷(But the Danites had difficulty taking possession of their ter-ritory,*l* so they went up and attacked Leshem*m*, took it, put it to the sword and occupied it. They settled in Leshem and named it Dan after their forefather.)*n*

⁴⁸These towns and their villages were the inheritance of the tribe of Dan,*o* clan by clan.

⁴⁹When they had finished dividing the land into its allotted portions, the Israelites gave Joshua son of Nun an inheritance among them, ⁵⁰as the LORD had commanded. They gave him the town he asked for—Timnath Serah*b* *p* in the hill country of Ephra-im. And he built up the town and settled there.

⁵¹These are the territories that Eleazar the priest, Joshua son of Nun and the heads of the tribal clans of Israel assigned by lot at Shiloh in the presence of the LORD at the entrance to the Tent of Meeting. And so they finished dividing the land.*q*

Chapter 20 Theme

20 Then the LORD said to Joshua: ²"Tell the Israelites to des-ignate the cities of refuge, as I instructed you through

a 34 Septuagint; Hebrew *west, and Judah, the Jordan,*   *b 50* Also known as *Timnath Heres* (see Judges 2:9)

21:11
a Jos 15:13;
1Ch 6:55

21:13
b Jos 15:42;
1Ch 6:57

21:14
c Jos 15:48
d Jos 15:50

21:15
e Jos 15:51

21:16
f Jos 15:55
g Jos 15:10

21:17
h Jos 18:24

21:21
i Jos 17:7; 20:7

21:22
j Jos 10:10
k 1Sa 1:1

21:24
l Jos 19:45

21:27
m Jos 12:5
n Nu 35:6

21:28
o Ge 30:18

21:30
p Jos 17:7

⁹From the tribes of Judah and Simeon they allotted the following towns by name ¹⁰(these towns were assigned to the descendants of Aaron who were from the Kohathite clans of the Levites, because the first lot fell to them):

¹¹They gave them Kiriath Arba (that is, Hebron*ᵃ*), with its surrounding pastureland, in the hill country of Judah. (Arba was the forefather of Anak.) ¹²But the fields and villages around the city they had given to Caleb son of Jephunneh as his possession.

¹³So to the descendants of Aaron the priest they gave Hebron (a city of refuge for one accused of murder), Libnah,*ᵇ* ¹⁴Jattir,*ᶜ* Eshtemoa,*ᵈ* ¹⁵Holon,*ᵉ* Debir, ¹⁶Ain, Juttah*ᶠ* and Beth Shemesh,*ᵍ* together with their pasturelands—nine towns from these two tribes.

¹⁷And from the tribe of Benjamin they gave them Gibeon, Geba,*ʰ* ¹⁸Anathoth and Almon, together with their pasturelands—four towns.

¹⁹All the towns for the priests, the descendants of Aaron, were thirteen, together with their pasturelands.

²⁰The rest of the Kohathite clans of the Levites were allotted towns from the tribe of Ephraim:

²¹In the hill country of Ephraim they were given Shechem*ⁱ* (a city of refuge for one accused of murder) and Gezer, ²²Kibzaim and Beth Horon,*ʲ* together with their pasturelands—four towns.*ᵏ*

²³Also from the tribe of Dan they received Eltekeh, Gibbethon, ²⁴Aijalon and Gath Rimmon,*ˡ* together with their pasturelands—four towns.

²⁵From half the tribe of Manasseh they received Taanach and Gath Rimmon, together with their pasturelands—two towns.

²⁶All these ten towns and their pasturelands were given to the rest of the Kohathite clans.

²⁷The Levite clans of the Gershonites were given:
from the half-tribe of Manasseh,
Golan in Bashan*ᵐ* (a city of refuge for one accused of murder*ⁿ*) and Be Eshtarah, together with their pasturelands—two towns;
²⁸from the tribe of Issachar,*ᵒ*
Kishion, Daberath, ²⁹Jarmuth and En Gannim, together with their pasturelands—four towns;
³⁰from the tribe of Asher,*ᵖ*
Mishal, Abdon, ³¹Helkath and Rehob, together with their pasturelands—four towns;
³²from the tribe of Naphtali,

Kedesh*a* in Galilee (a city of refuge for one accused of murder*b*), Hammoth Dor and Kartan, together with their pasturelands—three towns.

33All the towns of the Gershonite*c* clans were thirteen, together with their pasturelands.

34The Merarite clans (the rest of the Levites) were given:

from the tribe of Zebulun,*d*

Jokneam, Kartah, 35Dimnah and Nahalal, together with their pasturelands—four towns;

36from the tribe of Reuben,

Bezer,*e* Jahaz, 37Kedemoth and Mephaath, together with their pasturelands—four towns;

38from the tribe of Gad,

Ramoth*f* in Gilead (a city of refuge for one accused of murder), Mahanaim,*g* 39Heshbon and Jazer, together with their pasturelands—four towns in all.

40All the towns allotted to the Merarite clans, who were the rest of the Levites, were twelve.

41The towns of the Levites in the territory held by the Israelites were forty-eight in all, together with their pasturelands.*h* 42Each of these towns had pasturelands surrounding it; this was true for all these towns.

43So the LORD gave Israel all the land he had sworn to give their forefathers,*i* and they took possession*j* of it and settled there.*k* 44The LORD gave them rest*l* on every side, just as he had sworn to their forefathers. Not one of their enemies*m* withstood them; the LORD handed all their enemies*n* over to them.*o* 45Not one of all the LORD's good promises*p* to the house of Israel failed; every one was fulfilled.

Chapter 22 Theme

22 Then Joshua summoned the Reubenites, the Gadites and the half-tribe of Manasseh 2and said to them, "You have done all that Moses the servant of the LORD commanded,*q* and you have obeyed me in everything I commanded. 3For a long time now—to this very day—you have not deserted your brothers but have carried out the mission the LORD your God gave you. 4Now that the LORD your God has given your brothers rest as he promised, return to your homes*r* in the land that Moses the servant of the LORD gave you on the other side of the Jordan.*s* 5But be very careful to keep the commandment*t* and the law that Moses the servant of the LORD gave you: to love the LORD your God, to walk in all his ways, to obey his commands,*u* to hold fast to him and to serve him with all your heart and all your soul.*v*"

21:32
a Jos 12:22
b Nu 35:6;
Jos 20:7

21:33
c ver 6

21:34
d Jos 19:10;
1Ch 6:77

21:36
e Jos 20:8

21:38
f Dt 4:43
g Ge 32:2

21:41
h Nu 35:7

21:43
i Dt 34:4
j Dt 11:31
k Dt 17:14

21:44
l Ex 33:14;
Jos 1:13
m Dt 6:19
n Ex 23:31
o Dt 7:24; 21:10

21:45
p Jos 23:14;
Ne 9:8

22:2
q Nu 32:25

22:4
r Nu 32:22;
Dt 3:20
s Nu 32:18;
Jos 1:13-15

22:5
t Isa 43:22
u Dt 5:29
v Dt 6:6,17

²¹Then Reuben, Gad and the half-tribe of Manasseh replied to the heads of the clans of Israel: ²²"The Mighty One, God, the LORD! The Mighty One, God,ᵃ the LORD!ᵇ He knows!ᶜ And let Israel know! If this has been in rebellion or disobedience to the LORD, do not spare us this day. ²³If we have built our own altar to turn away from the LORD and to offer burnt offerings and grain offerings,ᵈ or to sacrifice fellowship offeringsᵃ on it, may the LORD himself call us to account.ᵉ

²⁴"No! We did it for fear that some day your descendants might say to ours, 'What do you have to do with the LORD, the God of Israel? ²⁵The LORD has made the Jordan a boundary between us and you—you Reubenites and Gadites! You have no share in the LORD.' So your descendants might cause ours to stop fearing the LORD.

²⁶"That is why we said, 'Let us get ready and build an altar—but not for burnt offerings or sacrifices.' ²⁷On the contrary, it is to be a witnessᶠ between us and you and the generations that follow, that we will worship the LORD at his sanctuary with our burnt offerings, sacrifices and fellowship offerings.ᵍ Then in the future your descendants will not be able to say to ours, 'You have no share in the LORD.'

²⁸"And we said, 'If they ever say this to us, or to our descendants, we will answer: Look at the replica of the LORD's altar, which our fathers built, not for burnt offerings and sacrifices, but as a witness between us and you.'

²⁹"Far be it from us to rebelʰ against the LORD and turn away from him today by building an altar for burnt offerings, grain offerings and sacrifices, other than the altar of the LORD our God that stands before his tabernacle.ⁱ"

³⁰When Phinehas the priest and the leaders of the community—the heads of the clans of the Israelites—heard what Reuben, Gad and Manasseh had to say, they were pleased. ³¹And Phinehas son of Eleazar, the priest, said to Reuben, Gad and Manasseh, "Today we know that the LORD is with us,ʲ because you have not acted unfaithfully toward the LORD in this matter. Now you have rescued the Israelites from the LORD's hand."

³²Then Phinehas son of Eleazar, the priest, and the leaders returned to Canaan from their meeting with the Reubenites and Gadites in Gilead and reported to the Israelites. ³³They were glad to hear the report and praised God.ᵏ And they talked no more about going to war against them to devastate the country where the Reubenites and the Gadites lived.

³⁴And the Reubenites and the Gadites gave the altar this name: A Witnessˡ Between Us that the LORD is God.

22:22 ᵃDt 10:17; ᵇPs 50:1; ᶜ1Ki 8:39; Job 10:7; Ps 44:21; Jer 17:10

22:23 ᵈJer 41:5; ᵉDt 12:11; 18:19; 1Sa 20:16

22:27 ᶠGe 21:30; Jos 24:27; ᵍDt 12:6

22:29 ʰJos 24:16; ⁱDt 12:13-14

22:31 ʲLev 26:11-12; 2Ch 15:2

22:33 ᵏ1Ch 29:20; Da 2:19; Lk 2:28

22:34 ˡGe 21:30

ᵃ 23 Traditionally *peace offerings*; also in verse 27

22:6
a Ex 39:43

22:7
b Nu 32:33;
Jos 12:5
c Jos 17:2,5

22:8
d Dt 20:14
e Nu 31:27
f Ge 49:27;
1Sa 30:16;
Isa 9:3

22:9
g Nu 32:26,29

22:12
h Jos 18:1

22:13
i Nu 25:7
j Nu 3:32;
Jos 24:33

22:14
k Nu 1:4

22:16
l Dt 13:14
m Dt 12:13-14

22:17
n Nu 25:1-9

22:18
o Lev 10:6;
Nu 16:22

22:20
p Jos 7:1
q Ps 7:11
r Jos 7:5

6Then Joshua blessed*a* them and sent them away, and they went to their homes. **7**(To the half-tribe of Manasseh Moses had given land in Bashan,*b* and to the other half of the tribe Joshua gave land on the west side*c* of the Jordan with their brothers.) When Joshua sent them home, he blessed them, **8**saying, "Return to your homes with your great wealth—with large herds of livestock,*d* with silver, gold, bronze and iron, and a great quantity of clothing—and divide*e* with your brothers the plunder*f* from your enemies."

9So the Reubenites, the Gadites and the half-tribe of Manasseh left the Israelites at Shiloh in Canaan to return to Gilead,*g* their own land, which they had acquired in accordance with the command of the LORD through Moses.

10When they came to Geliloth near the Jordan in the land of Canaan, the Reubenites, the Gadites and the half-tribe of Manasseh built an imposing altar there by the Jordan. **11**And when the Israelites heard that they had built the altar on the border of Canaan at Geliloth near the Jordan on the Israelite side, **12**the whole assembly of Israel gathered at Shiloh*h* to go to war against them.

13So the Israelites sent Phinehas*i* son of Eleazar,*j* the priest, to the land of Gilead—to Reuben, Gad and the half-tribe of Manasseh. **14**With him they sent ten of the chief men, one for each of the tribes of Israel, each the head of a family division among the Israelite clans.*k*

15When they went to Gilead—to Reuben, Gad and the half-tribe of Manasseh—they said to them: **16**"The whole assembly of the LORD says: 'How could you break faith*l* with the God of Israel like this? How could you turn away from the LORD and build yourselves an altar in rebellion*m* against him now? **17**Was not the sin of Peor*n* enough for us? Up to this very day we have not cleansed ourselves from that sin, even though a plague fell on the community of the LORD! **18**And are you now turning away from the LORD?

"'If you rebel against the LORD today, tomorrow he will be angry with the whole community*o* of Israel. **19**If the land you possess is defiled, come over to the LORD's land, where the LORD's tabernacle stands, and share the land with us. But do not rebel against the LORD or against us by building an altar for yourselves, other than the altar of the LORD our God. **20**When Achan son of Zerah acted unfaithfully regarding the devoted things,*a p* did not wrath*q* come upon the whole community of Israel? He was not the only one who died for his sin.'"*r*

a 20 The Hebrew term refers to the irrevocable giving over of things or persons to the LORD, often by totally destroying them.

23:1
a Dt 12:9;
Jos 21:44
b Jos 13:1

23:2
c Jos 7:6
d Jos 24:1

23:3
e Ex 14:14

23:4
f Jos 19:51
g Nu 34:6

23:5
h Ex 23:30;
Nu 33:53

23:6
i Dt 5:32;
Jos 1:7

23:7
j Ex 23:13;
Ps 16:4; Jer 5:7
k Ex 20:5

23:8
l Dt 10:20

23:9
m Dt 11:23
n Dt 7:24

23:10
o Lev 26:8
p Ex 14:14;
Dt 3:22

23:11
q Jos 22:5

23:12
r Dt 7:3
s Ex 34:16;
Ps 106:34-35

23:13
t Ex 23:33
u Nu 33:55

23:14
v 1Ki 2:2
w Jos 21:45

23:15
x Lev 26:17;
Dt 28:15

23:16
y Dt 4:25-26

Chapter 23 Theme _____

23 After a long time had passed and the LORD had given Israel rest[a] from all their enemies around them, Joshua, by then old and well advanced in years,[b] ²summoned all Israel— their elders,[c] leaders, judges and officials[d]—and said to them: "I am old and well advanced in years. ³You yourselves have seen everything the LORD your God has done to all these nations for your sake; it was the LORD your God who fought for you.[e] ⁴Remember how I have allotted[f] as an inheritance for your tribes all the land of the nations that remain—the nations I conquered—between the Jordan and the Great Sea[a][g] in the west. ⁵The LORD your God himself will drive them out of your way. He will push them out before you, and you will take possession of their land, as the LORD your God promised you.[h]

⁶"Be very strong; be careful to obey all that is written in the Book of the Law of Moses, without turning aside to the right or to the left.[i] ⁷Do not associate with these nations that remain among you; do not invoke the names of their gods or swear[j] by them. You must not serve them or bow down[k] to them. ⁸But you are to hold fast to the LORD[l] your God, as you have until now.

⁹"The LORD has driven out before you great and powerful nations;[m] to this day no one has been able to withstand you.[n] ¹⁰One of you routs a thousand,[o] because the LORD your God fights for you,[p] just as he promised. ¹¹So be very careful to love the LORD[q] your God.

¹²"But if you turn away and ally yourselves with the survivors of these nations that remain among you and if you intermarry with them[r] and associate with them,[s] ¹³then you may be sure that the LORD your God will no longer drive out these nations before you. Instead, they will become snares[t] and traps for you, whips on your backs and thorns in your eyes,[u] until you perish from this good land, which the LORD your God has given you.

¹⁴"Now I am about to go the way of all the earth.[v] You know with all your heart and soul that not one of all the good promises the LORD your God gave you has failed. Every promise has been fulfilled; not one has failed.[w] ¹⁵But just as every good promise of the LORD your God has come true, so the LORD will bring on you all the evil he has threatened, until he has destroyed you from this good land he has given you.[x] ¹⁶If you violate the covenant of the LORD your God, which he commanded you, and go and serve other gods and bow down to them, the LORD's anger will burn against you, and you will quickly perish from the good land he has given you.[y]"

a4 That is, the Mediterranean

Chapter 24 Theme _____

24 Then Joshua assembled all the tribes of Israel at Shechem. He summoned the elders, leaders, judges and officials of Israel,^a and they presented themselves before God.

²Joshua said to all the people, "This is what the LORD, the God of Israel, says: 'Long ago your forefathers, including Terah the father of Abraham and Nahor, lived beyond the River^a and worshiped other gods.^b ³But I took your father Abraham from the land beyond the River and led him throughout Canaan^c and gave him many descendants.^d I gave him Isaac,^e ⁴and to Isaac I gave Jacob and Esau.^f I assigned the hill country of Seir^g to Esau, but Jacob and his sons went down to Egypt.^h

⁵"'Then I sent Moses and Aaron,ⁱ and I afflicted the Egyptians by what I did there, and I brought you out. ⁶When I brought your fathers out of Egypt, you came to the sea, and the Egyptians pursued them with chariots and horsemen^{bj} as far as the Red Sea.^c ⁷But they cried to the LORD for help, and he put darkness^k between you and the Egyptians; he brought the sea over them and covered them.^l You saw with your own eyes what I did to the Egyptians. Then you lived in the desert for a long time.^m

⁸"'I brought you to the land of the Amorites who lived east of the Jordan. They fought against you, but I gave them into your hands. I destroyed them from before you, and you took possession of their land.ⁿ ⁹When Balak son of Zippor,^o the king of Moab, prepared to fight against Israel, he sent for Balaam son of Beor to put a curse on you.^p ¹⁰But I would not listen to Balaam, so he blessed you^q again and again, and I delivered you out of his hand.

¹¹"'Then you crossed the Jordan^r and came to Jericho.^s The citizens of Jericho fought against you, as did also the Amorites, Perizzites, Canaanites, Hittites, Girgashites, Hivites and Jebusites, but I gave them into your hands.^t ¹²I sent the hornet^u ahead of you, which drove them out before you—also the two Amorite kings. You did not do it with your own sword and bow. ¹³So I gave you a land on which you did not toil and cities you did not build; and you live in them and eat from vineyards and olive groves that you did not plant.'^v

¹⁴"Now fear the LORD and serve him with all faithfulness.^w Throw away the gods^x your forefathers worshiped beyond the River and in Egypt,^y and serve the LORD. ¹⁵But if serving the LORD seems undesirable to you, then choose for yourselves this day whom you will serve, whether the gods your forefathers served

---

^a2 That is, the Euphrates; also in verses 3, 14 and 15   ^b6 Or *charioteers*   ^c6 Hebrew *Yam Suph*; that is, Sea of Reeds

---

24:1
^aJos 23:2

24:2
^bGe 11:32

24:3
^cGe 12:1
^dGe 15:5
^eGe 21:3

24:4
^fGe 25:26
^gDt 2:5
^hGe 46:5-6

24:5
ⁱEx 3:10

24:6
^jEx 14:9

24:7
^kEx 14:20
^lEx 14:28
^mDt 1:46

24:8
ⁿNu 21:31

24:9
^oNu 22:2
^pNu 22:6

24:10
^qNu 23:11;
Dt 23:5

24:11
^rJos 3:16-17
^sJos 6:1
^tEx 23:23;
Dt 7:1

24:12
^uEx 23:28;
Dt 7:20;
Ps 44:3,6-7

24:13
^vDt 6:10-11

24:14
^wDt 10:12;
18:13;
1Sa 12:24;
2Co 1:12
^xver 23
^yEze 23:3

24:15
a Jdg 6:10;
Ru 1:15
b Ru 1:16;
1Ki 18:21

beyond the River, or the gods of the Amorites,*a* in whose land you are living. But as for me and my household, we will serve the LORD."*b*

16Then the people answered, "Far be it from us to forsake the LORD to serve other gods! ¹⁷It was the LORD our God himself who brought us and our fathers up out of Egypt, from that land of slavery, and performed those great signs before our eyes. He protected us on our entire journey and among all the nations through which we traveled. ¹⁸And the LORD drove out before us all the nations, including the Amorites, who lived in the land. We too will serve the LORD, because he is our God."

24:19
c Lev 19:2; 20:26
d Ex 20:5
e Ex 23:21

¹⁹Joshua said to the people, "You are not able to serve the LORD. He is a holy God;*c* he is a jealous God.*d* He will not forgive your rebellion*e* and your sins. ²⁰If you forsake the LORD*f* and serve foreign gods, he will turn*g* and bring disaster on you and make an end of you,*h* after he has been good to you."

24:20
f 1Ch 28:9,20
g Ac 7:42
h Jos 23:15

²¹But the people said to Joshua, "No! We will serve the LORD."

²²Then Joshua said, "You are witnesses against yourselves that you have chosen*i* to serve the LORD."

"Yes, we are witnesses," they replied.

24:22
i Ps 119:30,173

²³"Now then," said Joshua, "throw away the foreign gods*j* that are among you and yield your hearts*k* to the LORD, the God of Israel."

24:23
j ver 14
k 1Ki 8:58;
Ps 119:36; 141:4

²⁴And the people said to Joshua, "We will serve the LORD our God and obey him."*l*

24:24
l Ex 19:8; 24:3,7;
Dt 5:27

²⁵On that day Joshua made a covenant*m* for the people, and there at Shechem he drew up for them decrees and laws.*n* ²⁶And Joshua recorded these things in the Book of the Law of God.*o* Then he took a large stone*p* and set it up there under the oak near the holy place of the LORD.

24:25
m Ex 24:8
n Ex 15:25

24:26
o Dt 31:24
p Ge 28:18

²⁷"See!" he said to all the people. "This stone will be a witness*q* against us. It has heard all the words the LORD has said to us. It will be a witness against you if you are untrue to your God."

24:27
q Jos 22:27

²⁸Then Joshua sent the people away, each to his own inheritance.

²⁹After these things, Joshua son of Nun, the servant of the LORD, died at the age of a hundred and ten.*r* ³⁰And they buried him in the land of his inheritance, at Timnath Serah*as* in the hill country of Ephraim, north of Mount Gaash.

24:29
r Jdg 2:8

24:30
s Jos 19:50

³¹Israel served the LORD throughout the lifetime of Joshua and of the elders*t* who outlived him and who had experienced everything the LORD had done for Israel.

24:31
t Jdg 2:7

³²And Joseph's bones, which the Israelites had brought up from Egypt,*u* were buried at Shechem in the tract of land*v* that Jacob bought for a hundred pieces of silver*b* from the sons of Hamor,

24:32
u Ge 50:25;
Ex 13:19
v Ge 33:19;
Jn 4:5;
Ac 7:16

a 30 Also known as *Timnath Heres* (see Judges 2:9)　*b* 32 Hebrew *hundred kesitahs*; a kesitah was a unit of money of unknown weight and value.

the father of Shechem. This became the inheritance of Joseph's descendants.

³³And Eleazar son of Aaron^a died and was buried at Gibeah, which had been allotted to his son Phinehas^b in the hill country of Ephraim.

24:33
^aJos 22:13
^bEx 6:25

Theme of Joshua:

SEGMENT DIVISIONS

Author:

Date:

Purpose:

Key Words:

	CHAPTER THEMES
1	
2	
3	
4	
5	
6	
7	
8	
9	
10	
11	
12	
13	
14	
15	
16	
17	
18	
19	
20	
21	
22	
23	
24	

JUDGES

During Joshua's leadership Israel finally entered the land promised to Abraham. There were giants in the land, but none who were greater than God. The commander of the Lord's army was able to subdue all Israel's enemies. In one battle the sun even stood still and the moon stopped until the people of Israel avenged themselves on their enemies.

Then there arose a generation which did not know war, nor did they know the Lord or the work he had done for Israel. Israel went from victory to defeat and plunged into more than 300 years of darkness. These were the days of the judges, days from which we can learn valuable lessons.

∾ THINGS TO DO

Chapters 1, 2

1. Because the book of Judges is not strictly chronological, it is helpful to understand the setting of the book. Read chapters 1 and 2. Then go to the end of Judges and read Judges 17:6; 18:1; 19:1; 21:25 and look for the key repeated phrase. Mark this phrase in a distinctive way and record it on the JUDGES AT A GLANCE chart on page 433 under "Key Words."

2. Now read chapters 1 and 2 again and do the following:

   a. Mark in the text the key words and phrases listed on JUDGES AT A GLANCE. Put these on an index card that you can use as a bookmark while you study Judges.

   b. Chapter 1 also contains an important key phrase which is not on this list because it is not used after this chapter. Look for that phrase and mark its repeated use in a distinctive way. Then look up Exodus 23:20-33, Deuteronomy 7:1-11, 16, and Joshua 23:5-13. Record these references in the margin of chapter 1 for cross-references.

   c. As you read each chapter, question the text with the five W's and an H: Who? What? When? Where? Why? and How? You will not always find the answer to every question. As you read make sure you note who does what and why. Watch for where events take place and when. Always ask how something was accomplished, happened, or is to be done.

   d. Write in the chapter margin the names of key persons or groups of people (such as "the sons of Israel" and "judges"). Then list everything you learn about them from that chapter. Do this with the references to the Lord also.

3. When you finish your observations of chapter 2, review all you have learned, especially from verses 11 through 23. Notice the cycle of events. Make sure you record this in the margin; it sets the pattern for chapters 3 through 16.

4. Discern the themes of these chapters and record them on JUDGES AT A GLANCE and in the text on the line next to the chapter number.

Chapters 3-16

1. Study chapters 3 through 16 the same way you did chapters 1 and 2: Mark key words, ask the five W's and an H, list your insights in the margin, and record the theme of each chapter in the appropriate places.

2. As you read Judges 3 through 16, note the names of the judges and record them in the chapter margin where they appear. List everything you learn about them from the text. Then record this information on the chart THE JUDGES OF ISRAEL on page 432. To understand when these judges ruled and what their relationship was to one another, carefully study the historical chart before Judges chapter 1.

3. On page 394 is a map showing many locations mentioned in Judges. As you study each judge, note where the judge is from and write his or her name on the map next to the proper location.

Chapters 17-21

1. There is no indication that chapters 17 through 21 chronologically follow chapters 3 through 16. Rather, they give an overview of the moral setting of the time. Examine each chapter carefully as you have done the other chapters of Judges and note your insights. Watch the progression of events.

2. As you read these chapters, keep in mind the key phrase you marked when you began your study. Note how the result of this phrase is manifested in the way the people live.

3. Record the chapter themes as you have done previously on JUDGES AT A GLANCE. Also record the main theme of each segment division and any other segment division you may see. Finally, record the main theme of Judges.

∾ THINGS TO THINK ABOUT

1. What have you learned from Judges about carefully listening to and obeying the commands of the Lord? What have you seen about the consequences of doing as you see fit with your life? What parallels do you see between the sins committed in Judges 17 through 21 and today? What does it tell you?

2. Why wasn't the cycle of sin broken in the days of the judges? Are you caught in a cycle of sin in your own life? What will it take to break it?

3. What have you learned by studying the lives of the judges? Carefully review your chart on the judges on page 432 and meditate on the lessons you can apply to your own life.

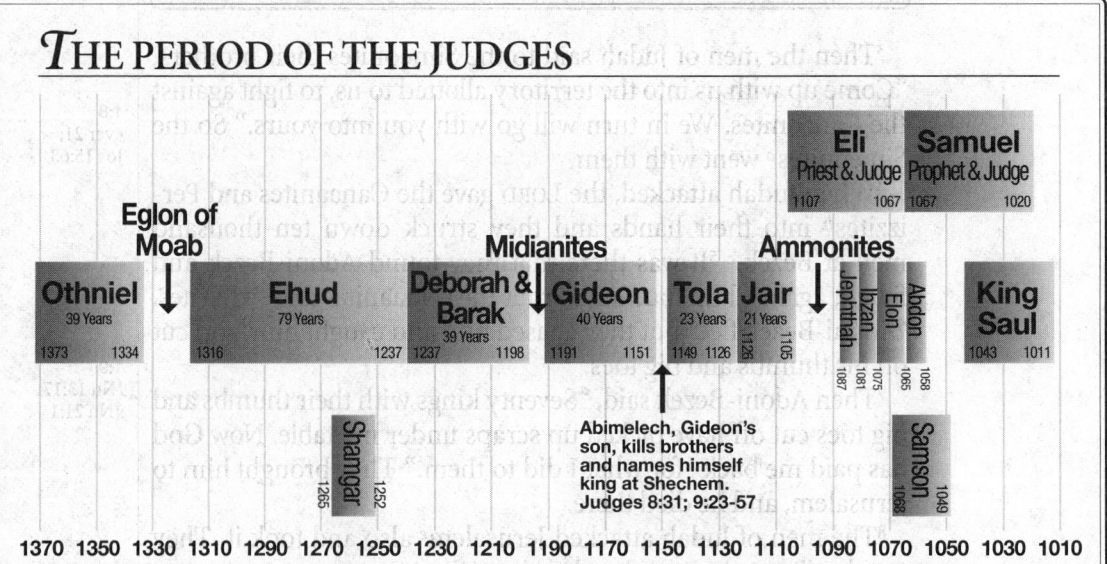

THE PERIOD OF THE JUDGES

∾∾∾∾∾∾

1:1
a Jos 24:29
b Nu 27:21
c ver 27;
Jdg 3:1-6

Chapter 1 Theme _____

1 After the death*a* of Joshua, the Israelites asked the LORD, "Who will be the first*b* to go up and fight for us against the Canaanites?*c*"

1:2
d Ge 49:8
e ver 4;
Jdg 3:28

²The LORD answered, "Judah*d* is to go; I have given the land into their hands.*e*"

Israelite Cities and Settlements in the Time of the Judges

1:3
a ver 17

1:4
b Ge 13:7;
Jos 3:10
c 1Sa 11:8

1:7
d Lev 24:19

1:8
e ver 21;
Jos 15:63

1:9
f Nu 13:17
g Nu 21:1

1:10
h Ge 13:18
i Ge 35:27
j Jos 15:14

1:11
k Jos 15:15

³Then the men of Judah said to the Simeonites their brothers, "Come up with us into the territory allotted to us, to fight against the Canaanites. We in turn will go with you into yours." So the Simeonites*a* went with them.

⁴When Judah attacked, the LORD gave the Canaanites and Perizzites*b* into their hands and they struck down ten thousand men at Bezek.*c* ⁵It was there that they found Adoni-Bezek and fought against him, putting to rout the Canaanites and Perizzites. ⁶Adoni-Bezek fled, but they chased him and caught him, and cut off his thumbs and big toes.

⁷Then Adoni-Bezek said, "Seventy kings with their thumbs and big toes cut off have picked up scraps under my table. Now God has paid me back*d* for what I did to them." They brought him to Jerusalem, and he died there.

⁸The men of Judah attacked Jerusalem*e* also and took it. They put the city to the sword and set it on fire.

⁹After that, the men of Judah went down to fight against the Canaanites living in the hill country,*f* the Negev*g* and the western foothills. ¹⁰They advanced against the Canaanites living in Hebron*h* (formerly called Kiriath Arba*i*) and defeated Sheshai, Ahiman and Talmai.*j*

¹¹From there they advanced against the people living in Debir*k* (formerly called Kiriath Sepher). ¹²And Caleb said, "I will give my daughter Acsah in marriage to the man who attacks and captures Kiriath Sepher." ¹³Othniel son of Kenaz, Caleb's younger brother, took it; so Caleb gave his daughter Acsah to him in marriage.

1:16
a Nu 10:29
b Ge 15:19;
Jdg 4:11
c Dt 34:3;
Jdg 3:13
d Nu 21:1

¹⁴One day when she came to Othniel, she urged him^a to ask her father for a field. When she got off her donkey, Caleb asked her, "What can I do for you?"

¹⁵She replied, "Do me a special favor. Since you have given me land in the Negev, give me also springs of water." Then Caleb gave her the upper and lower springs.

1:17
e ver 3
f Nu 21:3

¹⁶The descendants of Moses' father-in-law,^a the Kenite,^b went up from the City of Palms^{bc} with the men of Judah to live among the people of the Desert of Judah in the Negev near Arad.^d

¹⁷Then the men of Judah went with the Simeonites^e their brothers and attacked the Canaanites living in Zephath, and they totally destroyed^c the city. Therefore it was called Hormah.^{df}

1:18
g Jos 11:22

¹⁸The men of Judah also took^e Gaza,^g Ashkelon and Ekron—each city with its territory.

1:19
h ver 2
i Jos 17:16

¹⁹The LORD was with^h the men of Judah. They took possession of the hill country, but they were unable to drive the people from the plains, because they had iron chariots.ⁱ ²⁰As Moses had promised, Hebron^j was given to Caleb, who drove from it the three sons of Anak.^k ²¹The Benjamites, however, failed^l to dislodge the Jebusites, who were living in Jerusalem;^m to this day the Jebusites live there with the Benjamites.

1:20
j Jos 14:9;
15:13-14
k ver 10;
Jos 14:13

²²Now the house of Joseph attacked Bethel, and the LORD was with them. ²³When they sent men to spy out Bethel (formerly called Luz),ⁿ ²⁴the spies saw a man coming out of the city and they said to him, "Show us how to get into the city and we will see that you are treated well.^o" ²⁵So he showed them, and they put the city to the sword but spared^p the man and his whole family. ²⁶He then went to the land of the Hittites, where he built a city and called it Luz, which is its name to this day.

1:21
l Jos 15:63
m ver 8

1:23
n Ge 28:19

1:24
o Jos 2:12,14

²⁷But Manasseh did not drive out the people of Beth Shan or Taanach or Dor or Ibleam^q or Megiddo and their surrounding settlements, for the Canaanites^r were determined to live in that land. ²⁸When Israel became strong, they pressed the Canaanites into forced labor but never drove them out completely. ²⁹Nor did Ephraim drive out the Canaanites living in Gezer,^s but the Canaanites continued to live there among them.^t ³⁰Neither did Zebulun drive out the Canaanites living in Kitron or Nahalol, who remained among them; but they did subject them to forced labor. ³¹Nor did Asher drive out those living in Acco or Sidon or Ahlab or Aczib^u or Helbah or Aphek or Rehob, ³²and because of this the people of Asher lived among the Canaanite inhabitants of the land.

1:25
p Jos 6:25

1:27
q Jos 17:11
r ver 1

1:29
s 1Ki 9:16
t Jos 16:10

1:31
u Jdg 10:6

---

^a14 Hebrew; Septuagint and Vulgate *Othniel, he urged her*   ^b16 That is, Jericho   ^c17 The Hebrew term refers to the irrevocable giving over of things or persons to the LORD, often by totally destroying them.   ^d17 *Hormah* means *destruction.*   ^e18 Hebrew; Septuagint *Judah did not take*

³³Neither did Naphtali drive out those living in Beth Shemesh or Beth Anath^a; but the Naphtalites too lived among the Canaanite inhabitants of the land, and those living in Beth Shemesh and Beth Anath became forced laborers for them. ³⁴The Amorites^b confined the Danites to the hill country, not allowing them to come down into the plain. ³⁵And the Amorites were determined also to hold out in Mount Heres, Aijalon^c and Shaalbim, but when the power of the house of Joseph increased, they too were pressed into forced labor. ³⁶The boundary of the Amorites was from Scorpion^a Pass^d to Sela and beyond.

Chapter 2 Theme

2 The angel of the LORD^e went up from Gilgal to Bokim^f and said, "I brought you up out of Egypt^g and led you into the land that I swore to give to your forefathers.^h I said, 'I will never break my covenant with you,ⁱ ²and you shall not make a covenant with the people of this land,^j but you shall break down their altars.^k' Yet you have disobeyed me. Why have you done this? ³Now therefore I tell you that I will not drive them out before you;^l they will be ⌊thorns⌋^m in your sides and their gods will be a snareⁿ to you."

⁴When the angel of the LORD had spoken these things to all the Israelites, the people wept aloud, ⁵and they called that place Bokim.^b There they offered sacrifices to the LORD.

⁶After Joshua had dismissed the Israelites, they went to take possession of the land, each to his own inheritance. ⁷The people served the LORD throughout the lifetime of Joshua and of the elders who outlived him and who had seen all the great things the LORD had done for Israel.

⁸Joshua son of Nun, the servant of the LORD, died at the age of a hundred and ten. ⁹And they buried him in the land of his inheritance, at Timnath Heres^{c o} in the hill country of Ephraim, north of Mount Gaash.

¹⁰After that whole generation had been gathered to their fathers, another generation grew up, who knew neither the LORD nor what he had done for Israel.^p ¹¹Then the Israelites did evil in the eyes of the LORD^q and served the Baals.^r ¹²They forsook the LORD, the God of their fathers, who had brought them out of Egypt. They followed and worshiped various gods^s of the peoples around them.^t They provoked the LORD to anger ¹³because they forsook him and served Baal and the Ashtoreths.^u ¹⁴In his anger^v against Israel the LORD handed them over^w to raiders who plundered them. He sold them^x to their enemies all around, whom

INSIGHT

Baal, which meant "lord, owner, possessor, or husband," was the Canaanite god of fertility. **Baal** was part of several compound names for locations where Canaanite deities were worshiped, such as Baal Peor.

Ashtoreth is the Canaanite goddess of fertility, love, and war. According to Greek mythology she was the wife of Baal.

1:33
^aJos 19:38

1:34
^bEx 3:17

1:35
^cJos 19:42

1:36
^dJos 15:3

2:1
^eJdg 6:11
^fver 5
^gEx 20:2
^hGe 17:8
ⁱLev 26:42-44;
Dt 7:9

2:2
^jEx 23:32;
34:12;
Dt 7:2
^kEx 34:13

2:3
^lJos 23:13
^mNu 33:55
ⁿDt 7:16;
Jdg 3:6;
Ps 106:36

2:9
^oJos 19:50

2:10
^pEx 5:2;
1Sa 2:12;
1Ch 28:9;
Gal 4:8

2:11
^qJdg 3:12; 4:1;
6:1; 10:6
^rJdg 3:7; 8:33

2:12
^sPs 106:36
^tDt 31:16;
Jdg 10:6

2:13
^uJdg 10:6

2:14
^vDt 31:17
^wPs 106:41
^xDt 32:30;
Jdg 3:8

---

^a36 Hebrew *Akrabbim*   ^b5 *Bokim* means *weepers.*   ^c9 Also known as *Timnath Serah* (see Joshua 19:50 and 24:30)

2:14
a Dt 28:25

2:16
b Ac 13:20
c Ps 106:43

2:17
d Ex 34:15
e ver 7

2:18
f Dt 32:36;
Jos 1:5
g Ps 106:44

2:19
h Jdg 3:12
i Jdg 4:1;
8:33

2:20
j ver 14;
Jos 23:16

2:21
k Jos 23:13

2:22
l Dt 8:2,16;
Jdg 3:1,14

3:1
m Jdg 2:21-22

3:3
n Jos 13:3

3:4
o Dt 8:2;
Jdg 2:22

3:5
p Ps 106:35

3:6
q Ex 34:16;
Dt 7:3-4

3:7
r Dt 4:9
s Ex 34:13;
Jdg 2:11,13

3:8
t Jdg 2:14

they were no longer able to resist.*a* [15]Whenever Israel went out to fight, the hand of the LORD was against them to defeat them, just as he had sworn to them. They were in great distress.

[16]Then the LORD raised up judges,*a b* who saved*c* them out of the hands of these raiders. [17]Yet they would not listen to their judges but prostituted*d* themselves to other gods and worshiped them. Unlike their fathers, they quickly turned from the way in which their fathers had walked, the way of obedience to the LORD's commands.*e* [18]Whenever the LORD raised up a judge for them, he was with the judge and saved them out of the hands of their enemies as long as the judge lived; for the LORD had compassion*f* on them as they groaned*g* under those who oppressed and afflicted them. [19]But when the judge died, the people returned to ways even more corrupt*h* than those of their fathers, following other gods and serving and worshiping them.*i* They refused to give up their evil practices and stubborn ways.

[20]Therefore the LORD was very angry*j* with Israel and said, "Because this nation has violated the covenant that I laid down for their forefathers and has not listened to me, [21]I will no longer drive out*k* before them any of the nations Joshua left when he died. [22]I will use them to test*l* Israel and see whether they will keep the way of the LORD and walk in it as their forefathers did." [23]The LORD had allowed those nations to remain; he did not drive them out at once by giving them into the hands of Joshua.

Chapter 3 Theme

3 These are the nations the LORD left to test*m* all those Israelites who had not experienced any of the wars in Canaan [2](he did this only to teach warfare to the descendants of the Israelites who had not had previous battle experience): [3]the five*n* rulers of the Philistines, all the Canaanites, the Sidonians, and the Hivites living in the Lebanon mountains from Mount Baal Hermon to Lebo*b* Hamath. [4]They were left to test*o* the Israelites to see whether they would obey the LORD's commands, which he had given their forefathers through Moses.

[5]The Israelites lived*p* among the Canaanites, Hittites, Amorites, Perizzites, Hivites and Jebusites. [6]They took their daughters in marriage and gave their own daughters to their sons, and served their gods.*q*

[7]The Israelites did evil in the eyes of the LORD; they forgot the LORD*r* their God and served the Baals and the Asherahs.*s* [8]The anger of the LORD burned against Israel so that he sold*t* them into the hands of Cushan-Rishathaim king of Aram Naharaim,*c*

*a*16 Or *leaders*; similarly in verses 17-19   *b*3 Or *to the entrance to*   *c*8 That is, Northwest Mesopotamia to whom the Israelites were subject for eight years. [9]But when they cried out[a] to the LORD, he raised up for them a deliverer, Othniel[b] son of Kenaz, Caleb's younger brother, who saved them. [10]The Spirit of the LORD came upon him,[c] so that he became Israel's judge[a] and went to war. The LORD gave Cushan-Rishathaim king of Aram into the hands of Othniel, who overpowered him. [11]So the land had peace for forty years, until Othniel son of Kenaz died.

[12]Once again the Israelites did evil in the eyes of the LORD,[d] and because they did this evil the LORD gave Eglon king of Moab[e] power over Israel. [13]Getting the Ammonites and Amalekites to join him, Eglon came and attacked Israel, and they took possession of the City of Palms.[b][f] [14]The Israelites were subject to Eglon king of Moab for eighteen years.

[15]Again the Israelites cried out to the LORD, and he gave them a deliverer[g]—Ehud, a left-handed man, the son of Gera the Benjamite. The Israelites sent him with tribute to Eglon king of Moab. [16]Now Ehud had made a double-edged sword about a foot and a half[c] long, which he strapped to his right thigh under his clothing. [17]He presented the tribute to Eglon king of Moab, who was a very fat man.[h] [18]After Ehud had presented the tribute, he sent on their way the men who had carried it. [19]At the idols[d] near Gilgal he himself turned back and said, "I have a secret message for you, O king."

The king said, "Quiet!" And all his attendants left him.

[20]Ehud then approached him while he was sitting alone in the upper room of his summer palace[e] and said, "I have a message from God for you." As the king rose from his seat, [21]Ehud reached with his left hand, drew the sword from his right thigh and plunged it into the king's belly. [22]Even the handle sank in after the blade, which came out his back. Ehud did not pull the sword out, and the fat closed in over it. [23]Then Ehud went out to the porch[f]; he shut the doors of the upper room behind him and locked them.

[24]After he had gone, the servants came and found the doors of the upper room locked. They said, "He must be relieving himself[i] in the inner room of the house." [25]They waited to the point of embarrassment,[j] but when he did not open the doors of the room, they took a key and unlocked them. There they saw their lord fallen to the floor, dead.

[26]While they waited, Ehud got away. He passed by the idols and escaped to Seirah. [27]When he arrived there, he blew a trumpet[k]

---

a10 Or *leader* b13 That is, Jericho c16 Hebrew *a cubit* (about 0.5 meter) d19 Or *the stone quarries*; also in verse 26 e20 The meaning of the Hebrew for this phrase is uncertain. f23 The meaning of the Hebrew for this word is uncertain.

3:9
a ver 15;
Jdg 6:6,7;
10:10;
Ps 106:44
b Jdg 1:13

3:10
c Nu 11:25,29;
24:2;
Jdg 6:34;
11:29;
13:25;
14:6,19;
1Sa 11:6

3:12
d Jdg 2:11,14
e 1Sa 12:9

3:13
f Jdg 1:16

3:15
g ver 9;
Ps 78:34;
107:13

3:17
h ver 12

3:24
i 1Sa 24:3

3:25
j 2Ki 2:17;
8:11

3:27
k Jdg 6:34;
1Sa 13:3

in the hill country of Ephraim, and the Israelites went down with him from the hills, with him leading them.

28"Follow me," he ordered, "for the LORD has given Moab, your enemy, into your hands.[a]" So they followed him down and, taking possession of the fords of the Jordan[b] that led to Moab, they allowed no one to cross over. 29At that time they struck down about ten thousand Moabites, all vigorous and strong; not a man escaped. 30That day Moab was made subject to Israel, and the land had peace[c] for eighty years.

31After Ehud came Shamgar son of Anath,[d] who struck down six hundred[e] Philistines with an oxgoad. He too saved Israel.

Chapter 4 Theme

4 After Ehud died, the Israelites once again did evil[f] in the eyes of the LORD. 2So the LORD sold them into the hands of Jabin, a king of Canaan, who reigned in Hazor.[g] The commander of his army was Sisera,[h] who lived in Harosheth Haggoyim. 3Because he had nine hundred iron chariots[i] and had cruelly oppressed[j] the Israelites for twenty years, they cried to the LORD for help.

4Deborah, a prophetess, the wife of Lappidoth, was leading[a] Israel at that time. 5She held court under the Palm of Deborah between Ramah and Bethel[k] in the hill country of Ephraim, and the Israelites came to her to have their disputes decided. 6She sent for Barak son of Abinoam[l] from Kedesh in Naphtali and said to him, "The LORD, the God of Israel, commands you: 'Go, take with you ten thousand men of Naphtali and Zebulun and lead the way to Mount Tabor. 7I will lure Sisera, the commander of Jabin's army, with his chariots and his troops to the Kishon River[m] and give him into your hands.'"

8Barak said to her, "If you go with me, I will go; but if you don't go with me, I won't go."

9"Very well," Deborah said, "I will go with you. But because of the way you are going about this,[b] the honor will not be yours, for the LORD will hand Sisera over to a woman." So Deborah went with Barak to Kedesh,[n] 10where he summoned[o] Zebulun and Naphtali. Ten thousand men followed him, and Deborah also went with him.

11Now Heber the Kenite had left the other Kenites,[p] the descendants of Hobab,[q] Moses' brother-in-law,[c] and pitched his tent by the great tree in Zaanannim[r] near Kedesh.

12When they told Sisera that Barak son of Abinoam had gone up to Mount Tabor, 13Sisera gathered together his nine hundred

---

3:28
a Jdg 7:9,15
b Jos 2:7;
Jdg 7:24; 12:5

3:30
c ver 11

3:31
d Jdg 5:6
e Jos 23:10

4:1
f Jdg 2:19

4:2
g Jos 11:1
h ver 13,16;
1Sa 12:9;
Ps 83:9

4:3
i Jdg 1:19
j Ps 106:42

4:5
k Ge 35:8

4:6
l Heb 11:32

4:7
m Ps 83:9

4:9
n ver 21;
Jdg 2:14

4:10
o ver 14;
Jdg 5:15,18

4:11
p Jdg 1:16
q Nu 10:29
r Jos 19:33

---

a 4 Traditionally *judging*   b 9 Or *But on the expedition you are undertaking*   c 11 Or *father-in-law* iron chariots[a] and all the men with him, from Harosheth Hag-goyim to the Kishon River.

[14]Then Deborah said to Barak, "Go! This is the day the LORD has given Sisera into your hands. Has not the LORD gone ahead[b] of you?" So Barak went down Mount Tabor, followed by ten thousand men. [15]At Barak's advance, the LORD routed[c] Sisera and all his chariots and army by the sword, and Sisera abandoned his chariot and fled on foot. [16]But Barak pursued the chariots and army as far as Harosheth Haggoyim. All the troops of Sisera fell by the sword; not a man was left.[d]

[17]Sisera, however, fled on foot to the tent of Jael, the wife of Heber the Kenite, because there were friendly relations between Jabin king of Hazor and the clan of Heber the Kenite.

[18]Jael went out to meet Sisera and said to him, "Come, my lord, come right in. Don't be afraid." So he entered her tent, and she put a covering over him.

[19]"I'm thirsty," he said. "Please give me some water." She opened a skin of milk,[e] gave him a drink, and covered him up.

[20]"Stand in the doorway of the tent," he told her. "If someone comes by and asks you, 'Is anyone here?' say 'No.'"

[21]But Jael, Heber's wife, picked up a tent peg and a hammer and went quietly to him while he lay fast asleep, exhausted. She drove the peg through his temple into the ground, and he died.[f]

[22]Barak came by in pursuit of Sisera, and Jael went out to meet him. "Come," she said, "I will show you the man you're looking for." So he went in with her, and there lay Sisera with the tent peg through his temple—dead.

[23]On that day God subdued[g] Jabin, the Canaanite king, before the Israelites. [24]And the hand of the Israelites grew stronger and stronger against Jabin, the Canaanite king, until they destroyed him.

Chapter 5 Theme

5 On that day Deborah and Barak son of Abinoam sang this song:[h]

[2]"When the princes in Israel take the lead,
when the people willingly offer[i] themselves—
praise the LORD![j]

[3]"Hear this, you kings! Listen, you rulers!
I will sing to[a] the LORD, I will sing;
I will make music to[b] the LORD, the God of Israel.[k]

[4]"O LORD, when you went out from Seir,[l]
when you marched from the land of Edom,

---

a3 Or of   b3 Or / with song I will praise

### Cross references (margin)

4:13 [a]ver 3

4:14 [b]Dt 9:3;
2Sa 5:24;
Ps 68:7

4:15 [c]Jos 10:10;
Ps 83:9-10

4:16 [d]Ex 14:28;
Ps 83:9

4:19 [e]Jdg 5:25

4:21 [f]Jdg 5:26

4:23 [g]Ne 9:24;
Ps 18:47

5:1 [h]Ex 15:1

5:2 [i]2Ch 17:16;
Ps 110:3
[j]ver 9

5:3 [k]Ps 27:6

5:4 [l]Dt 33:2

5:4
a Ps 68:8

5:5
b Ex 19:18;
Ps 68:8; 97:5;
Isa 64:3

5:6
c Jdg 3:31
d Jdg 4:17
e Isa 33:8

5:8
f Dt 32:17

5:9
g ver 2

5:10
h Jdg 10:4;
12:14

5:11
i 1Sa 12:7;
Mic 6:5
j ver 8

5:12
k Ps 57:8
l Ps 68:18;
Eph 4:8

5:14
m Jdg 3:13

5:15
n Jdg 4:10

the earth shook, the heavens poured,
    the clouds poured down water.*a*
⁵The mountains quaked*b* before the LORD, the One
        of Sinai,
    before the LORD, the God of Israel.

⁶"In the days of Shamgar son of Anath,*c*
    in the days of Jael,*d* the roads*e* were abandoned;
    travelers took to winding paths.
⁷Village life*a* in Israel ceased,
    ceased until I,*b* Deborah, arose,
    arose a mother in Israel.
⁸When they chose new gods,*f*
    war came to the city gates,
and not a shield or spear was seen
    among forty thousand in Israel.
⁹My heart is with Israel's princes,
    with the willing volunteers*g* among the people.
    Praise the LORD!

¹⁰"You who ride on white donkeys,*h*
    sitting on your saddle blankets,
    and you who walk along the road,
consider ¹¹the voice of the singers*c* at the watering places.
    They recite the righteous acts*i* of the LORD,
    the righteous acts of his warriors*d* in Israel.

"Then the people of the LORD
    went down to the city gates.*j*
¹²"Wake up,*k* wake up, Deborah!
    Wake up, wake up, break out in song!
Arise, O Barak!
    Take captive your captives,*l* O son of Abinoam.'

¹³"Then the men who were left
    came down to the nobles;
the people of the LORD
    came to me with the mighty.
¹⁴Some came from Ephraim, whose roots were in Amalek;*m*
    Benjamin was with the people who followed you.
From Makir captains came down,
    from Zebulun those who bear a commander's staff.
¹⁵The princes of Issachar were with Deborah;*n*
    yes, Issachar was with Barak,
    rushing after him into the valley.

a 7 Or *Warriors*   b 7 Or *you*   c 11 Or *archers*; the meaning of the Hebrew for this word is uncertain.   d 11 Or *villagers*

In the districts of Reuben
　　there was much searching of heart.
¹⁶Why did you stay among the campfires^a
　　to hear the whistling for the flocks?^a
In the districts of Reuben
　　there was much searching of heart.
¹⁷Gilead stayed beyond the Jordan.
　　And Dan, why did he linger by the ships?
Asher remained on the coast^b
　　and stayed in his coves.
¹⁸The people of Zebulun risked their very lives;
　　so did Naphtali on the heights of the field.^c

¹⁹"Kings came^d, they fought;
　　the kings of Canaan fought
at Taanach by the waters of Megiddo,^e
　　but they carried off no silver, no plunder.^f
²⁰From the heavens^g the stars fought,
　　from their courses they fought against Sisera.
²¹The river Kishon^h swept them away,
　　the age-old river, the river Kishon.
　　March on, my soul; be strong!
²²Then thundered the horses' hoofs—
　　galloping, galloping go his mighty steeds.
²³'Curse Meroz,' said the angel of the LORD.
　　'Curse its people bitterly,
because they did not come to help the LORD,
　　to help the LORD against the mighty.'

²⁴"Most blessed of women be Jael,ⁱ
　　the wife of Heber the Kenite,
　　most blessed of tent-dwelling women.
²⁵He asked for water, and she gave him milk;^j
　　in a bowl fit for nobles she brought him curdled milk.
²⁶Her hand reached for the tent peg,
　　her right hand for the workman's hammer.
She struck Sisera, she crushed his head,
　　she shattered and pierced his temple.^k
²⁷At her feet he sank,
　　he fell; there he lay.
At her feet he sank, he fell;
　　where he sank, there he fell—dead.

²⁸"Through the window peered Sisera's mother;
　　behind the lattice she cried out,^l

5:16
^aNu 32:1

5:17
^bJos 19:29

5:18
^cJdg 4:6,10

5:19
^dJos 11:5;
Jdg 4:13
^eJdg 1:27
^fver 30

5:20
^gJos 10:11

5:21
^hJdg 4:7

5:24
ⁱJdg 4:17

5:25
^jJdg 4:19

5:26
^kJdg 4:21

5:28
^lPr 7:6

5:30
a Ex 15:9;
1Sa 30:24

5:31
b 2Sa 23:4;
Ps 19:4; 89:36
c Jdg 3:11

6:1
d Jdg 2:11
e Nu 25:15-18;
31:1-3

6:2
f 1Sa 13:6;
Isa 8:21
g Heb 11:38

6:3
h Jdg 3:13

6:4
i Lev 26:16;
Dt 28:30,51

6:5
j Jdg 7:12
k Jdg 8:10

6:6
l Jdg 3:9

6:8
m Jdg 2:1

6:9
n Ps 44:2

6:10
o 2Ki 17:35
p Jer 10:2

6:11
q Ge 16:7
r Jos 17:2
s Heb 11:32

6:12
t Jos 1:5;
Jdg 13:3;
Lk 1:11,28

'Why is his chariot so long in coming?
Why is the clatter of his chariots delayed?'
[29]The wisest of her ladies answer her;
indeed, she keeps saying to herself,
[30]'Are they not finding and dividing the spoils:[a]
a girl or two for each man,
colorful garments as plunder for Sisera,
colorful garments embroidered,
highly embroidered garments for my neck—
all this as plunder?'

[31]"So may all your enemies perish, O LORD!
But may they who love you be like the sun[b]
when it rises in its strength."

Then the land had peace[c] forty years.

Chapter 6 Theme _____

6 Again the Israelites did evil in the eyes of the LORD,[d] and for seven years he gave them into the hands of the Midianites.[e] [2]Because the power of Midian was so oppressive,[f] the Israelites prepared shelters for themselves in mountain clefts, caves and strongholds.[g] [3]Whenever the Israelites planted their crops, the Midianites, Amalekites[h] and other eastern peoples invaded the country. [4]They camped on the land and ruined the crops[i] all the way to Gaza and did not spare a living thing for Israel, neither sheep nor cattle nor donkeys. [5]They came up with their livestock and their tents like swarms of locusts.[j] It was impossible to count the men and their camels;[k] they invaded the land to ravage it. [6]Midian so impoverished the Israelites that they cried out[l] to the LORD for help.

[7]When the Israelites cried to the LORD because of Midian, [8]he sent them a prophet, who said, "This is what the LORD, the God of Israel, says: I brought you up out of Egypt,[m] out of the land of slavery. [9]I snatched you from the power of Egypt and from the hand of all your oppressors. I drove them from before you and gave you their land.[n] [10]I said to you, 'I am the LORD your God; do not worship[o] the gods of the Amorites,[p] in whose land you live.' But you have not listened to me."

[11]The angel of the LORD[q] came and sat down under the oak in Ophrah that belonged to Joash the Abiezrite,[r] where his son Gideon[s] was threshing wheat in a winepress to keep it from the Midianites. [12]When the angel of the LORD appeared to Gideon, he said, "The LORD is with you,[t] mighty warrior."

[13]"But sir," Gideon replied, "if the LORD is with us, why has all this happened to us? Where are all his wonders that our fathers

told[a] us about when they said, 'Did not the LORD bring us up out of Egypt?' But now the LORD has abandoned[b] us and put us into the hand of Midian."

[14]The LORD turned to him and said, "Go in the strength you have[c] and save Israel out of Midian's hand. Am I not sending you?"

[15]"But Lord,[a]" Gideon asked, "how can I save Israel? My clan is the weakest in Manasseh, and I am the least in my family.[d]"

[16]The LORD answered, "I will be with you[e], and you will strike down all the Midianites together."

[17]Gideon replied, "If now I have found favor in your eyes, give me a sign[f] that it is really you talking to me. [18]Please do not go away until I come back and bring my offering and set it before you."

And the LORD said, "I will wait until you return."

[19]Gideon went in, prepared a young goat, and from an ephah[b] of flour he made bread without yeast. Putting the meat in a basket and its broth in a pot, he brought them out and offered them to him under the oak.[g]

[20]The angel of God said to him, "Take the meat and the unleavened bread, place them on this rock,[h] and pour out the broth." And Gideon did so. [21]With the tip of the staff that was in his hand, the angel of the LORD touched the meat and the unleavened bread.[i] Fire flared from the rock, consuming the meat and the bread. And the angel of the LORD disappeared. [22]When Gideon realized[j] that it was the angel of the LORD, he exclaimed, "Ah, Sovereign LORD! I have seen the angel of the LORD face to face!"[k]

[23]But the LORD said to him, "Peace! Do not be afraid.[l] You are not going to die."

[24]So Gideon built an altar to the LORD there and called[m] it The LORD is Peace. To this day it stands in Ophrah[n] of the Abiezrites.

[25]That same night the LORD said to him, "Take the second bull from your father's herd, the one seven years old.[c] Tear down your father's altar to Baal and cut down the Asherah pole[d][o] beside it. [26]Then build a proper kind of[e] altar to the LORD your God on the top of this height. Using the wood of the Asherah pole that you cut down, offer the second[f] bull as a burnt offering."

[27]So Gideon took ten of his servants and did as the LORD told him. But because he was afraid of his family and the men of the town, he did it at night rather than in the daytime.

[28]In the morning when the men of the town got up, there was Baal's altar,[p] demolished, with the Asherah pole beside it cut down and the second bull sacrificed on the newly built altar!

6:13
[a]Ps 44:1
[b]2Ch 15:2

6:14
[c]Heb 11:34

6:15
[d]Ex 3:11;
1Sa 9:21

6:16
[e]Ex 3:12; Jos 1:5

6:17
[f]ver 36-37;
Ge 24:14;
Isa 38:7-8

6:19
[g]Ge 18:7-8

6:20
[h]Jdg 13:19

6:21
[i]Lev 9:24

6:22
[j]Jdg 13:16,21
[k]Ge 32:30;
Ex 33:20;
Jdg 13:22

6:23
[l]Da 10:19

6:24
[m]Ge 22:14
[n]Jdg 8:32

6:25
[o]Ex 34:13;
Dt 7:5

6:28
[p]1Ki 16:32

[a]15 Or sir   [b]19 That is, probably about 3/5 bushel (about 22 liters)   [c]25 Or Take a full-grown, mature bull from your father's herd   [d]25 That is, a symbol of the goddess Asherah; here and elsewhere in Judges   [e]26 Or build with layers of stone an   [f]26 Or full-grown; also in verse 28

6:32
a Jdg 7:1;
8:29,35;
1Sa 12:11

²⁹They asked each other, "Who did this?"

When they carefully investigated, they were told, "Gideon son of Joash did it."

³⁰The men of the town demanded of Joash, "Bring out your son. He must die, because he has broken down Baal's altar and cut down the Asherah pole beside it."

6:33
b ver 3
c Jos 17:16

³¹But Joash replied to the hostile crowd around him, "Are you going to plead Baal's cause? Are you trying to save him? Whoever fights for him shall be put to death by morning! If Baal really is a god, he can defend himself when someone breaks down his altar." ³²So that day they called Gideon "Jerub-Baal,ᵃ ᵃ" saying, "Let Baal contend with him," because he broke down Baal's altar.

6:34
d Jdg 3:10;
1Ch 12:18;
2Ch 24:20
e Jdg 3:27

³³Now all the Midianites, Amalekites and other eastern peoplesᵇ joined forces and crossed over the Jordan and camped in the Valley of Jezreel.ᶜ ³⁴Then the Spirit of the LORD came uponᵈ Gideon, and he blew a trumpet,ᵉ summoning the Abiezrites to follow him. ³⁵He sent messengers throughout Manasseh, calling them to arms, and also into Asher, Zebulun and Naphtali,ᶠ so that they too went up to meet them.

6:35
f Jdg 4:6

6:36
g ver 14

³⁶Gideon said to God, "If you will saveᵍ Israel by my hand as you have promised— ³⁷look, I will place a wool fleece on the threshing floor.ʰ If there is dew only on the fleece and all the ground is dry, then I will knowⁱ that you will save Israel by my hand, as you said." ³⁸And that is what happened. Gideon rose early the next day; he squeezed the fleece and wrung out the dew—a bowlful of water.

6:37
h Ex 4:3-7
i Ge 24:14

³⁹Then Gideon said to God, "Do not be angry with me. Let me make just one more request.ʲ Allow me one more test with the fleece. This time make the fleece dry and the ground covered with dew." ⁴⁰That night God did so. Only the fleece was dry; all the ground was covered with dew.

6:39
j Ge 18:32

Chapter 7 Theme

7:1
k Jdg 6:32
l Ge 12:6

7 Early in the morning, Jerub-Baalᵏ (that is, Gideon) and all his men camped at the spring of Harod. The camp of Midian was north of them in the valley near the hill of Moreh.ˡ ²The LORD said to Gideon, "You have too many men for me to deliver Midian into their hands. In order that Israel may not boast against me that her own strengthᵐ has saved her, ³announce now to the people, 'Anyone who trembles with fear may turn back and leave Mount Gilead.ⁿ'" So twenty-two thousand men left, while ten thousand remained.

7:2
m Dt 8:17;
2Co 4:7

7:3
n Dt 20:8

⁴But the LORD said to Gideon, "There are still too manyᵒ men. Take them down to the water, and I will sift them for you there. If

7:4
o 1Sa 14:6

ᵃ32 *Jerub-Baal* means *let Baal contend.*

I say, 'This one shall go with you,' he shall go; but if I say, 'This one shall not go with you,' he shall not go."

⁵So Gideon took the men down to the water. There the Lord told him, "Separate those who lap the water with their tongues like a dog from those who kneel down to drink." ⁶Three hundred men lapped with their hands to their mouths. All the rest got down on their knees to drink.

⁷The Lord said to Gideon, "With the three hundred men that lapped I will save you and give the Midianites into your hands. Let all the other men go, each to his own place."^a ⁸So Gideon sent the rest of the Israelites to their tents but kept the three hundred, who took over the provisions and trumpets of the others.

Now the camp of Midian lay below him in the valley. ⁹During that night the Lord said to Gideon, "Get up, go down against the camp, because I am going to give it into your hands.^b ¹⁰If you are afraid to attack, go down to the camp with your servant Purah ¹¹and listen to what they are saying. Afterward, you will be encouraged to attack the camp." So he and Purah his servant went down to the outposts of the camp. ¹²The Midianites, the Amalekites^c and all the other eastern peoples had settled in the valley, thick as locusts.^d Their camels^e could no more be counted than the sand on the seashore.^f

¹³Gideon arrived just as a man was telling a friend his dream. "I had a dream," he was saying. "A round loaf of barley bread came tumbling into the Midianite camp. It struck the tent with such force that the tent overturned and collapsed."

¹⁴His friend responded, "This can be nothing other than the sword of Gideon son of Joash, the Israelite. God has given the Midianites and the whole camp into his hands."

¹⁵When Gideon heard the dream and its interpretation, he worshiped God.^g He returned to the camp of Israel and called out, "Get up! The Lord has given the Midianite camp into your hands." ¹⁶Dividing the three hundred men^h into three companies,ⁱ he placed trumpets and empty jars in the hands of all of them, with torches inside.

¹⁷"Watch me," he told them. "Follow my lead. When I get to the edge of the camp, do exactly as I do. ¹⁸When I and all who are with me blow our trumpets,^j then from all around the camp blow yours and shout, 'For the Lord and for Gideon.'"

¹⁹Gideon and the hundred men with him reached the edge of the camp at the beginning of the middle watch, just after they had changed the guard. They blew their trumpets and broke the jars that were in their hands. ²⁰The three companies blew the trumpets and smashed the jars. Grasping the torches in their left hands and holding in their right hands the trumpets they were to

7:7
^a1Sa 14:6

7:9
^bJos 2:24; 10:8; 11:6

7:12
^cJdg 8:10
^dJdg 6:5
^eJer 49:29
^fJos 11:4

7:15
^g1Sa 15:31

7:16
^hGe 14:15
ⁱ2Sa 18:2

7:18
^jJdg 3:27

7:20
a ver 14

7:21
b 2Ki 7:7

7:22
c Jos 6:20
d 1Sa 14:20;
2Ch 20:23
e 1Ki 4:12;
19:16

7:23
f Jdg 6:35

7:24
g Jdg 3:28

7:25
h Jdg 8:3;
Ps 83:11
i Isa 10:26
j Jdg 8:4

8:1
k Jdg 12:1
l 2Sa 19:41

8:3
m Jdg 7:25;
Pr 15:1

8:4
n Jdg 7:25

8:5
o Ge 33:17
p Ps 83:11

8:6
q 1Sa 25:11
r ver 15

8:7
s Jdg 7:15

8:8
t Ge 32:30;
1Ki 12:25

8:9
u ver 17

blow, they shouted, "A sword[a] for the LORD and for Gideon!" ²¹While each man held his position around the camp, all the Midianites ran, crying out as they fled.[b]

²²When the three hundred trumpets sounded,[c] the LORD caused the men throughout the camp to turn on each other[d] with their swords. The army fled to Beth Shittah toward Zererah as far as the border of Abel Meholah[e] near Tabbath. ²³Israelites from Naphtali, Asher and all Manasseh were called out,[f] and they pursued the Midianites. ²⁴Gideon sent messengers throughout the hill country of Ephraim, saying, "Come down against the Midianites and seize the waters of the Jordan[g] ahead of them as far as Beth Barah."

So all the men of Ephraim were called out and they took the waters of the Jordan as far as Beth Barah. ²⁵They also captured two of the Midianite leaders, Oreb and Zeeb[h]. They killed Oreb at the rock of Oreb,[i] and Zeeb at the winepress of Zeeb. They pursued the Midianites and brought the heads of Oreb and Zeeb to Gideon, who was by the Jordan.[j]

Chapter 8 Theme

8 Now the Ephraimites asked Gideon, "Why have you treated us like this? Why didn't you call us when you went to fight Midian?"[k] And they criticized him sharply.[l]

²But he answered them, "What have I accomplished compared to you? Aren't the gleanings of Ephraim's grapes better than the full grape harvest of Abiezer? ³God gave Oreb and Zeeb,[m] the Midianite leaders, into your hands. What was I able to do compared to you?" At this, their resentment against him subsided.

⁴Gideon and his three hundred men, exhausted yet keeping up the pursuit, came to the Jordan[n] and crossed it. ⁵He said to the men of Succoth,[o] "Give my troops some bread; they are worn out, and I am still pursuing Zebah and Zalmunna,[p] the kings of Midian."

⁶But the officials of Succoth said, "Do you already have the hands of Zebah and Zalmunna in your possession? Why should we give bread[q] to your troops?"[r]

⁷Then Gideon replied, "Just for that, when the LORD has given Zebah and Zalmunna[s] into my hand, I will tear your flesh with desert thorns and briers."

⁸From there he went up to Peniel[a][t] and made the same request of them, but they answered as the men of Succoth had. ⁹So he said to the men of Peniel, "When I return in triumph, I will tear down this tower."[u]

¹⁰Now Zebah and Zalmunna were in Karkor with a force of about fifteen thousand men, all that were left of the armies of the eastern peoples; a hundred and twenty thousand swordsmen had

a 8 Hebrew *Penuel*, a variant of *Peniel*; also in verses 9 and 17 fallen.*a* ¹¹Gideon went up by the route of the nomads east of Nobah*b* and Jogbehah*c* and fell upon the unsuspecting army. ¹²Zebah and Zalmunna, the two kings of Midian, fled, but he pursued them and captured them, routing their entire army.

¹³Gideon son of Joash then returned from the battle by the Pass of Heres. ¹⁴He caught a young man of Succoth and questioned him, and the young man wrote down for him the names of the seventy-seven officials of Succoth, the elders of the town. ¹⁵Then Gideon came and said to the men of Succoth, "Here are Zebah and Zalmunna, about whom you taunted me by saying, 'Do you already have the hands of Zebah and Zalmunna in your possession? Why should we give bread to your exhausted men?*d*'" ¹⁶He took the elders of the town and taught the men of Succoth a lesson*e* by punishing them with desert thorns and briers. ¹⁷He also pulled down the tower of Peniel and killed the men of the town.*f*

¹⁸Then he asked Zebah and Zalmunna, "What kind of men did you kill at Tabor?*g*"

"Men like you," they answered, "each one with the bearing of a prince."

¹⁹Gideon replied, "Those were my brothers, the sons of my own mother. As surely as the LORD lives, if you had spared their lives, I would not kill you." ²⁰Turning to Jether, his oldest son, he said, "Kill them!" But Jether did not draw his sword, because he was only a boy and was afraid.

²¹Zebah and Zalmunna said, "Come, do it yourself. 'As is the man, so is his strength.'" So Gideon stepped forward and killed them, and took the ornaments*h* off their camels' necks.

²²The Israelites said to Gideon, "Rule over us—you, your son and your grandson—because you have saved us out of the hand of Midian."

²³But Gideon told them, "I will not rule over you, nor will my son rule over you. The LORD will rule*i* over you." ²⁴And he said, "I do have one request, that each of you give me an earring from your share of the plunder." (It was the custom of the Ishmaelites*j* to wear gold earrings.)

²⁵They answered, "We'll be glad to give them." So they spread out a garment, and each man threw a ring from his plunder onto it. ²⁶The weight of the gold rings he asked for came to seventeen hundred shekels,*a* not counting the ornaments, the pendants and the purple garments worn by the kings of Midian or the chains that were on their camels' necks. ²⁷Gideon made the gold into an ephod,*k* which he placed in Ophrah, his town. All Israel prostituted

---

a 26 That is, about 43 pounds (about 19.5 kilograms)

8:10
a Jdg 6:5; 7:12;
Isa 9:4

8:11
b Nu 32:42
c Nu 32:35

8:15
d ver 6

8:16
e ver 7

8:17
f ver 9

8:18
g Jos 19:22;
Jdg 4:6

8:21
h ver 26;
Ps 83:11

8:23
i Ex 16:8;
1Sa 8:7;
10:19;
12:12

8:24
j Ge 25:13

8:27
k Jdg 17:5;
18:14

8:27
a Dt 7:16;
Ps 106:39

8:28
b Jdg 5:31

8:29
c Jdg 7:1

8:30
d Jdg 9:2,5,
18,24

8:31
e Jdg 9:1

8:32
f Ge 25:8

8:33
g Jdg 2:11,13,19
h Jdg 9:4
i Jdg 9:27,46

8:34
j Jdg 3:7; Dt 4:9;
Ps 78:11,42

8:35
k Jdg 9:16

9:1
l Jdg 8:31

9:2
m Ge 29:14;
Jdg 8:30

9:4
n Jdg 8:33
o Jdg 11:3;
2Ch 13:7

9:5
p ver 2; Jdg 8:30
q 2Ki 11:2

9:7
r Dt 11:29;
27:12; Jn 4:20

themselves by worshiping it there, and it became a snare[a] to Gideon and his family.

28 Thus Midian was subdued before the Israelites and did not raise its head again. During Gideon's lifetime, the land enjoyed peace[b] forty years.

29 Jerub-Baal[c] son of Joash went back home to live. 30 He had seventy sons[d] of his own, for he had many wives. 31 His concubine, who lived in Shechem, also bore him a son, whom he named Abimelech.[e] 32 Gideon son of Joash died at a good old age[f] and was buried in the tomb of his father Joash in Ophrah of the Abiezrites.

33 No sooner had Gideon died than the Israelites again prostituted themselves to the Baals.[g] They set up Baal-Berith[h] as their god[i] and 34 did not remember[j] the LORD their God, who had rescued them from the hands of all their enemies on every side. 35 They also failed to show kindness to the family of Jerub-Baal (that is, Gideon) for all the good things he had done for them.[k]

Chapter 9 Theme

9 Abimelech[l] son of Jerub-Baal went to his mother's brothers in Shechem and said to them and to all his mother's clan, 2 "Ask all the citizens of Shechem, 'Which is better for you: to have all seventy of Jerub-Baal's sons rule over you, or just one man?' Remember, I am your flesh and blood.[m]"

3 When the brothers repeated all this to the citizens of Shechem, they were inclined to follow Abimelech, for they said, "He is our brother." 4 They gave him seventy shekels[a] of silver from the temple of Baal-Berith,[n] and Abimelech used it to hire reckless adventurers,[o] who became his followers. 5 He went to his father's home in Ophrah and on one stone murdered his seventy brothers,[p] the sons of Jerub-Baal. But Jotham, the youngest son of Jerub-Baal, escaped by hiding.[q] 6 Then all the citizens of Shechem and Beth Millo gathered beside the great tree at the pillar in Shechem to crown Abimelech king.

7 When Jotham was told about this, he climbed up on the top of Mount Gerizim[r] and shouted to them, "Listen to me, citizens of Shechem, so that God may listen to you. 8 One day the trees went out to anoint a king for themselves. They said to the olive tree, 'Be our king.'

9 "But the olive tree answered, 'Should I give up my oil, by which both gods and men are honored, to hold sway over the trees?'

10 "Next, the trees said to the fig tree, 'Come and be our king.'

11 "But the fig tree replied, 'Should I give up my fruit, so good and sweet, to hold sway over the trees?'

12 "Then the trees said to the vine, 'Come and be our king.'

a4 That is, about 1 3/4 pounds (about 0.8 kilogram)

¹³"But the vine answered, 'Should I give up my wine,ᵃ which cheers both gods and men, to hold sway over the trees?'

¹⁴"Finally all the trees said to the thornbush, 'Come and be our king.'

¹⁵"The thornbush said to the trees, 'If you really want to anoint me king over you, come and take refuge in my shade;ᵇ but if not, then let fire come outᶜ of the thornbush and consume the cedars of Lebanon!'ᵈ

¹⁶"Now if you have acted honorably and in good faith when you made Abimelech king, and if you have been fair to Jerub-Baal and his family, and if you have treated him as he deserves— ¹⁷and to think that my father fought for you, risked his life to rescue you from the hand of Midian ¹⁸(but today you have revolted against my father's family, murdered his seventy sonsᵉ on a single stone, and made Abimelech, the son of his slave girl, king over the citizens of Shechem because he is your brother)— ¹⁹if then you have acted honorably and in good faith toward Jerub-Baal and his family today, may Abimelech be your joy, and may you be his, too! ²⁰But if you have not, let fire come outᶠ from Abimelech and consume you, citizens of Shechem and Beth Millo, and let fire come out from you, citizens of Shechem and Beth Millo, and consume Abimelech!"

²¹Then Jotham fled, escaping to Beer, and he lived there because he was afraid of his brother Abimelech.

²²After Abimelech had governed Israel three years, ²³God sent an evil spiritᵍ between Abimelech and the citizens of Shechem, who acted treacherously against Abimelech. ²⁴God did this in order that the crime against Jerub-Baal's seventy sons, the sheddingʰ of their blood, might be avengedⁱ on their brother Abimelech and on the citizens of Shechem, who had helped himʲ murder his brothers. ²⁵In opposition to him these citizens of Shechem set men on the hilltops to ambush and rob everyone who passed by, and this was reported to Abimelech.

²⁶Now Gaal son of Ebed moved with his brothers into Shechem, and its citizens put their confidence in him. ²⁷After they had gone out into the fields and gathered the grapes and troddenᵏ them, they held a festival in the temple of their god.ˡ While they were eating and drinking, they cursed Abimelech. ²⁸Then Gaal son of Ebed said, "Whoᵐ is Abimelech, and who is Shechem, that we should be subject to him? Isn't he Jerub-Baal's son, and isn't Zebul his deputy? Serve the men of Hamor,ⁿ Shechem's father! Why should we serve Abimelech? ²⁹If only this people were under my command!ᵒ Then I would get rid of him. I would say to Abimelech, 'Call out your whole army!'"ᵃ

ᵃ29 Septuagint; Hebrew *him." Then he said to Abimelech, "Call out your whole army!"*

9:13
ᵃ Ecc 2:3

9:15
ᵇ Isa 30:2
ᶜ ver 20
ᵈ Isa 2:13

9:18
ᵉ ver 5-6;
Jdg 8:30

9:20
ᶠ ver 15

9:23
ᵍ 1Sa 16:14,23;
18:10;
1Ki 22:22;
Isa 19:14; 33:1

9:24
ʰ Nu 35:33;
1Ki 2:32
ⁱ ver 56-57
ʲ Dt 27:25

9:27
ᵏ Am 9:13
ˡ Jdg 8:33

9:28
ᵐ 1Sa 25:10;
1Ki 12:16
ⁿ Ge 34:2,6

9:29
ᵒ 2Sa 15:4

9:32
a Jos 8:2

9:33
b 1Sa 10:7

9:35
c Ps 32:7;
Jer 49:10

9:38
d ver 28-29

9:43
e Jdg 7:16

9:45
f ver 20;
2Ki 3:25
g Dt 29:23

9:46
h Jdg 8:33

9:48
i Ps 68:14

³⁰When Zebul the governor of the city heard what Gaal son of Ebed said, he was very angry. ³¹Under cover he sent messengers to Abimelech, saying, "Gaal son of Ebed and his brothers have come to Shechem and are stirring up the city against you. ³²Now then, during the night you and your men should come and lie in wait*a* in the fields. ³³In the morning at sunrise, advance against the city. When Gaal and his men come out against you, do whatever your hand finds to do.*b*"

³⁴So Abimelech and all his troops set out by night and took up concealed positions near Shechem in four companies. ³⁵Now Gaal son of Ebed had gone out and was standing at the entrance to the city gate just as Abimelech and his soldiers came out from their hiding place.*c*

³⁶When Gaal saw them, he said to Zebul, "Look, people are coming down from the tops of the mountains!"

Zebul replied, "You mistake the shadows of the mountains for men."

³⁷But Gaal spoke up again: "Look, people are coming down from the center of the land, and a company is coming from the direction of the soothsayers' tree."

³⁸Then Zebul said to him, "Where is your big talk now, you who said, 'Who is Abimelech that we should be subject to him?' Aren't these the men you ridiculed?*d* Go out and fight them!"

³⁹So Gaal led out*a* the citizens of Shechem and fought Abimelech. ⁴⁰Abimelech chased him, and many fell wounded in the flight—all the way to the entrance to the gate. ⁴¹Abimelech stayed in Arumah, and Zebul drove Gaal and his brothers out of Shechem.

⁴²The next day the people of Shechem went out to the fields, and this was reported to Abimelech. ⁴³So he took his men, divided them into three companies*e* and set an ambush in the fields. When he saw the people coming out of the city, he rose to attack them. ⁴⁴Abimelech and the companies with him rushed forward to a position at the entrance to the city gate. Then two companies rushed upon those in the fields and struck them down. ⁴⁵All that day Abimelech pressed his attack against the city until he had captured it and killed its people. Then he destroyed the city*f* and scattered salt*g* over it.

⁴⁶On hearing this, the citizens in the tower of Shechem went into the stronghold of the temple*h* of El-Berith. ⁴⁷When Abimelech heard that they had assembled there, ⁴⁸he and all his men went up Mount Zalmon.*i* He took an ax and cut off some branches, which he lifted to his shoulders. He ordered the men with him, "Quick! Do what you have seen me do!" ⁴⁹So all the men cut branches and followed Abimelech. They piled them against the stronghold

a 39 Or *Gaal went out in the sight of*

and set it on fire over the people inside. So all the people in the tower of Shechem, about a thousand men and women, also died.

⁵⁰Next Abimelech went to Thebez^a and besieged it and captured it. ⁵¹Inside the city, however, was a strong tower, to which all the men and women—all the people of the city—fled. They locked themselves in and climbed up on the tower roof. ⁵²Abimelech went to the tower and stormed it. But as he approached the entrance to the tower to set it on fire, ⁵³a woman dropped an upper millstone on his head and cracked his skull.^b

⁵⁴Hurriedly he called to his armor-bearer, "Draw your sword and kill me,^c so that they can't say, 'A woman killed him.'" So his servant ran him through, and he died. ⁵⁵When the Israelites saw that Abimelech was dead, they went home.

⁵⁶Thus God repaid the wickedness that Abimelech had done to his father by murdering his seventy brothers. ⁵⁷God also made the men of Shechem pay for all their wickedness.^d The curse of Jotham son of Jerub-Baal came on them.

Chapter 10 Theme

10 After the time of Abimelech a man of Issachar,^e Tola son of Puah,^f the son of Dodo, rose to save^g Israel. He lived in Shamir, in the hill country of Ephraim. ²He led^a Israel twenty-three years; then he died, and was buried in Shamir.

³He was followed by Jair of Gilead, who led Israel twenty-two years. ⁴He had thirty sons, who rode thirty donkeys. They controlled thirty towns in Gilead, which to this day are called Havvoth Jair.^{bh} ⁵When Jair died, he was buried in Kamon.

⁶Again the Israelites did evil in the eyes of the LORD.ⁱ They served the Baals and the Ashtoreths,^j and the gods of Aram, the gods of Sidon, the gods of Moab, the gods of the Ammonites and the gods of the Philistines.^k And because the Israelites forsook the LORD^l and no longer served him, ⁷he became angry^m with them. He sold themⁿ into the hands of the Philistines and the Ammonites, ⁸who that year shattered and crushed them. For eighteen years they oppressed all the Israelites on the east side of the Jordan in Gilead, the land of the Amorites. ⁹The Ammonites also crossed the Jordan to fight against Judah, Benjamin and the house of Ephraim; and Israel was in great distress. ¹⁰Then the Israelites cried out to the LORD, "We have sinned against you, forsaking our God and serving the Baals."^o

¹¹The LORD replied, "When the Egyptians,^p the Amorites, the Ammonites,^q the Philistines,^r ¹²the Sidonians, the Amalekites and the Maonites^c oppressed you^s and you cried to me for help, did I

---

a2 Traditionally *judged*; also in verse 3   b4 Or *called the settlements of Jair*
c12 Hebrew; some Septuagint manuscripts *Midianites*

**Cross references (margin):**

9:50 a 2Sa 11:21

9:53 b 2Sa 11:21

9:54 c 1Sa 31:4; 2Sa 1:9

9:57 d ver 20

10:1 e Ge 30:18 f Ge 46:13 g Jdg 2:16; 6:14

10:4 h Nu 32:41

10:6 i Jdg 2:11 j Jdg 2:13 k Jdg 2:12 l Dt 32:15

10:7 m Dt 31:17 n Dt 32:30; Jdg 2:14; 1Sa 12:9

10:10 o 1Sa 12:10

10:11 p Ex 14:30 q Nu 21:21; Jdg 3:13 r Jdg 3:31

10:12 s Ps 106:42

10:14
a Dt 32:37

10:15
b 1Sa 3:18;
2Sa 15:26

10:16
c Jos 24:23;
Jer 18:8
d Isa 63:9
e Dt 32:36;
Ps 106:44-45

10:17
f Ge 31:49;
Jdg 11:29

10:18
g Jdg 11:8,9

11:1
h Heb 11:32
i Jdg 6:12

11:3
j 2Sa 10:6,8
k Jdg 9:4

11:4
l Jdg 10:9

11:7
m Ge 26:27

11:8
n Jdg 10:18

11:10
o Ge 31:50;
Jer 42:5

11:11
p Jos 11:3;
Jdg 10:17; 20:1;
1Sa 10:17

not save you from their hands? ¹³But you have forsaken me and served other gods, so I will no longer save you. ¹⁴Go and cry out to the gods you have chosen. Let them save you when you are in trouble!ᵃ"

¹⁵But the Israelites said to the LORD, "We have sinned. Do with us whatever you think best,ᵇ but please rescue us now." ¹⁶Then they got rid of the foreign gods among them and served the LORD.ᶜ And he could bear Israel's miseryᵈ no longer.ᵉ

¹⁷When the Ammonites were called to arms and camped in Gilead, the Israelites assembled and camped at Mizpah.ᶠ ¹⁸The leaders of the people of Gilead said to each other, "Whoever will launch the attack against the Ammonites will be the headᵍ of all those living in Gilead."

Chapter 11 Theme _____

11 Jephthahʰ the Gileadite was a mighty warrior.ⁱ His father was Gilead; his mother was a prostitute. ²Gilead's wife also bore him sons, and when they were grown up, they drove Jephthah away. "You are not going to get any inheritance in our family," they said, "because you are the son of another woman." ³So Jephthah fled from his brothers and settled in the land of Tob,ʲ where a group of adventurersᵏ gathered around him and followed him.

⁴Some time later, when the Ammonitesˡ made war on Israel, ⁵the elders of Gilead went to get Jephthah from the land of Tob. ⁶"Come," they said, "be our commander, so we can fight the Ammonites."

⁷Jephthah said to them, "Didn't you hate me and drive me from my father's house?ᵐ Why do you come to me now, when you're in trouble?"

⁸The elders of Gilead said to him, "Nevertheless, we are turning to you now; come with us to fight the Ammonites, and you will be our headⁿ over all who live in Gilead."

⁹Jephthah answered, "Suppose you take me back to fight the Ammonites and the LORD gives them to me—will I really be your head?"

¹⁰The elders of Gilead replied, "The LORD is our witness;ᵒ we will certainly do as you say." ¹¹So Jephthah went with the elders of Gilead, and the people made him head and commander over them. And he repeated all his words before the LORD in Mizpah.ᵖ

¹²Then Jephthah sent messengers to the Ammonite king with the question: "What do you have against us that you have attacked our country?"

¹³The king of the Ammonites answered Jephthah's messengers, "When Israel came up out of Egypt, they took away my land from

the Arnon to the Jabbok,*a* all the way to the Jordan. Now give it back peaceably."

¹⁴Jephthah sent back messengers to the Ammonite king, ¹⁵saying:

"This is what Jephthah says: Israel did not take the land of Moab*b* or the land of the Ammonites.*c* ¹⁶But when they came up out of Egypt, Israel went through the desert to the Red Sea*a d* and on to Kadesh.*e* ¹⁷Then Israel sent messengers*f* to the king of Edom, saying, 'Give us permission to go through your country,'*g* but the king of Edom would not listen. They sent also to the king of Moab, and he refused.*h* So Israel stayed at Kadesh.

¹⁸"Next they traveled through the desert, skirted the lands of Edom*i* and Moab, passed along the eastern side*j* of the country of Moab, and camped on the other side of the Arnon.*k* They did not enter the territory of Moab, for the Arnon was its border.

¹⁹"Then Israel sent messengers to Sihon king of the Amorites, who ruled in Heshbon, and said to him, 'Let us pass through your country to our own place.'*l* ²⁰Sihon, however, did not trust Israel*b* to pass through his territory. He mustered all his men and encamped at Jahaz and fought with Israel.*m*

²¹"Then the LORD, the God of Israel, gave Sihon and all his men into Israel's hands, and they defeated them. Israel took over all the land of the Amorites who lived in that country, ²²capturing all of it from the Arnon to the Jabbok and from the desert to the Jordan.*n*

²³"Now since the LORD, the God of Israel, has driven the Amorites out before his people Israel, what right have you to take it over? ²⁴Will you not take what your god Chemosh*o* gives you? Likewise, whatever the LORD our God has given us, we will possess. ²⁵Are you better than Balak son of Zippor,*p* king of Moab? Did he ever quarrel with Israel or fight with them?*q* ²⁶For three hundred years Israel occupied*r* Heshbon, Aroer, the surrounding settlements and all the towns along the Arnon. Why didn't you retake them during that time? ²⁷I have not wronged you, but you are doing me wrong by waging war against me. Let the LORD, the Judge,*c s* decide*t* the dispute this day between the Israelites and the Ammonites."

²⁸The king of Ammon, however, paid no attention to the message Jephthah sent him.

---

a 16 Hebrew *Yam Suph;* that is, Sea of Reeds   *b 20* Or *however, would not make an agreement for Israel*   *c 27* Or *Ruler*

11:13
a Ge 32:22;
Nu 21:24

11:15
b Dt 2:9
c Dt 2:19

11:16
d Nu 14:25;
Dt 1:40
e Nu 20:1

11:17
f Nu 20:14
g Nu 20:18,21
h Jos 24:9

11:18
i Nu 21:4
j Dt 2:8
k Nu 21:13

11:19
l Nu 21:21-22;
Dt 2:26-27

11:20
m Nu 21:23;
Dt 2:32

11:22
n Dt 2:36

11:24
o Nu 21:29;
Jos 3:10;
1Ki 11:7

11:25
p Nu 22:2
q Jos 24:9

11:26
r Nu 21:25

11:27
s Ge 18:25
t Ge 16:5; 31:53;
1Sa 24:12,15

11:29
a Nu 11:25;
Jdg 3:10; 6:34;
14:6,19; 15:14;
1Sa 11:6; 16:13;
Isa 11:2

²⁹Then the Spirit*a* of the LORD came upon Jephthah. He crossed Gilead and Manasseh, passed through Mizpah of Gilead, and from there he advanced against the Ammonites. ³⁰And Jephthah made a vow*b* to the LORD: "If you give the Ammonites into my hands, ³¹whatever comes out of the door of my house to meet me when I return in triumph from the Ammonites will be the LORD's, and I will sacrifice it as a burnt offering."

11:30
b Ge 28:20

³²Then Jephthah went over to fight the Ammonites, and the LORD gave them into his hands. ³³He devastated twenty towns from Aroer to the vicinity of Minnith,*c* as far as Abel Keramim. Thus Israel subdued Ammon.

11:33
c Eze 27:17

³⁴When Jephthah returned to his home in Mizpah, who should come out to meet him but his daughter, dancing to the sound of tambourines!*d* She was an only child. Except for her he had neither son nor daughter. ³⁵When he saw her, he tore his clothes and cried, "Oh! My daughter! You have made me miserable and wretched, because I have made a vow to the LORD that I cannot break.*e*"

11:34
d Ex 15:20;
Jer 31:4

³⁶"My father," she replied, "you have given your word to the LORD. Do to me just as you promised,*f* now that the LORD has avenged you of your enemies,*g* the Ammonites. ³⁷But grant me this one request," she said. "Give me two months to roam the hills and weep with my friends, because I will never marry."

³⁸"You may go," he said. And he let her go for two months. She and the girls went into the hills and wept because she would never marry. ³⁹After the two months, she returned to her father and he did to her as he had vowed. And she was a virgin.

11:35
e Nu 30:2;
Ecc 5:2,4,5

From this comes the Israelite custom ⁴⁰that each year the young women of Israel go out for four days to commemorate the daughter of Jephthah the Gileadite.

Chapter 12 Theme

11:36
f Lk 1:38
g 2Sa 18:19

12 The men of Ephraim called out their forces, crossed over to Zaphon and said to Jephthah, "Why did you go to fight the Ammonites without calling us to go with you?*h* We're going to burn down your house over your head."

²Jephthah answered, "I and my people were engaged in a great struggle with the Ammonites, and although I called, you didn't save me out of their hands. ³When I saw that you wouldn't help, I took my life in my hands*i* and crossed over to fight the Ammonites, and the LORD gave me the victory over them. Now why have you come up today to fight me?"

12:1
h Jdg 8:1

⁴Jephthah then called together the men of Gilead and fought against Ephraim. The Gileadites struck them down because the Ephraimites had said, "You Gileadites are renegades from Ephraim

12:3
i 1Sa 19:5; 28:21;
Job 13:14

and Manasseh." [5]The Gileadites captured the fords of the Jordan[a] leading to Ephraim, and whenever a survivor of Ephraim said, "Let me cross over," the men of Gilead asked him, "Are you an Ephraimite?" If he replied, "No," [6]they said, "All right, say 'Shibboleth.'" If he said, "Sibboleth," because he could not pronounce the word correctly, they seized him and killed him at the fords of the Jordan. Forty-two thousand Ephraimites were killed at that time.

[7]Jephthah led[a] Israel six years. Then Jephthah the Gileadite died, and was buried in a town in Gilead.

[8]After him, Ibzan of Bethlehem led Israel. [9]He had thirty sons and thirty daughters. He gave his daughters away in marriage to those outside his clan, and for his sons he brought in thirty young women as wives from outside his clan. Ibzan led Israel seven years. [10]Then Ibzan died, and was buried in Bethlehem.

[11]After him, Elon the Zebulunite led Israel ten years. [12]Then Elon died, and was buried in Aijalon in the land of Zebulun.

[13]After him, Abdon son of Hillel, from Pirathon, led Israel. [14]He had forty sons and thirty grandsons,[b] who rode on seventy donkeys.[c] He led Israel eight years. [15]Then Abdon son of Hillel died, and was buried at Pirathon in Ephraim, in the hill country of the Amalekites.[d]

Chapter 13 Theme

13 Again the Israelites did evil in the eyes of the Lord, so the Lord delivered them into the hands of the Philistines[e] for forty years.

[2]A certain man of Zorah,[f] named Manoah, from the clan of the Danites, had a wife who was sterile and remained childless. [3]The angel of the Lord[g] appeared to her[h] and said, "You are sterile and childless, but you are going to conceive and have a son.[i] [4]Now see to it that you drink no wine or other fermented drink and that you do not eat anything unclean,[j] [5]because you will conceive and give birth to a son. No razor[k] may be used on his head, because the boy is to be a Nazirite,[l] set apart to God from birth, and he will begin[m] the deliverance of Israel from the hands of the Philistines."

[6]Then the woman went to her husband and told him, "A man of God[n] came to me. He looked like an angel of God,[o] very awesome. I didn't ask him where he came from, and he didn't tell me his name. [7]But he said to me, 'You will conceive and give birth to a son. Now then, drink no wine or other fermented drink and do not eat anything unclean, because the boy will be a Nazirite of God from birth until the day of his death.'"

a 7 Traditionally *judged*; also in verses 8-14

Cross references

12:5
a Jos 22:11;
Jdg 3:28

12:14
b Jdg 10:4
c Jdg 5:10

12:15
d Jdg 5:14

13:1
e Jdg 2:11;
1Sa 12:9

13:2
f Jos 15:33;
19:41

13:3
g ver 6,8;
Jdg 6:12
h ver 10
i Lk 1:13

13:4
j ver 14;
Nu 6:2-4;
Lk 1:15

13:5
k Nu 6:5;
1Sa 1:11
l Nu 6:2,13
m 1Sa 7:13

13:6
n ver 8;
1Sa 2:27; 9:6
o ver 17-18;
Mt 28:3

13:14
a Nu 6:4
b ver 4

13:15
c ver 3;
Jdg 6:19

13:16
d Jdg 6:20

13:17
e Ge 32:29

13:18
f Isa 9:6

13:19
g Jdg 6:20

13:20
h Lev 9:24
i 1Ch 21:16;
Eze 1:28;
Mt 17:6

13:21
j ver 16;
Jdg 6:22

13:22
k Dt 5:26
l Ge 32:30;
Jdg 6:22

13:23
m Ps 25:14

13:24
n Heb 11:32
o 1Sa 3:19
p Lk 1:80

13:25
q Jdg 3:10
r Jdg 18:12

⁸Then Manoah prayed to the LORD: "O Lord, I beg you, let the man of God you sent to us come again to teach us how to bring up the boy who is to be born."

⁹God heard Manoah, and the angel of God came again to the woman while she was out in the field; but her husband Manoah was not with her. ¹⁰The woman hurried to tell her husband, "He's here! The man who appeared to me the other day!"

¹¹Manoah got up and followed his wife. When he came to the man, he said, "Are you the one who talked to my wife?"

"I am," he said.

¹²So Manoah asked him, "When your words are fulfilled, what is to be the rule for the boy's life and work?"

¹³The angel of the LORD answered, "Your wife must do all that I have told her. ¹⁴She must not eat anything that comes from the grapevine, nor drink any wine or other fermented drink*a* nor eat anything unclean.*b* She must do everything I have commanded her."

¹⁵Manoah said to the angel of the LORD, "We would like you to stay until we prepare a young goat*c* for you."

¹⁶The angel of the LORD replied, "Even though you detain me, I will not eat any of your food. But if you prepare a burnt offering,*d* offer it to the LORD." (Manoah did not realize that it was the angel of the LORD.)

¹⁷Then Manoah inquired of the angel of the LORD, "What is your name,*e* so that we may honor you when your word comes true?"

¹⁸He replied, "Why do you ask my name?*f* It is beyond understanding.ª" ¹⁹Then Manoah took a young goat, together with the grain offering, and sacrificed it on a rock*g* to the LORD. And the LORD did an amazing thing while Manoah and his wife watched: ²⁰As the flame*h* blazed up from the altar toward heaven, the angel of the LORD ascended in the flame. Seeing this, Manoah and his wife fell with their faces to the ground.*i* ²¹When the angel of the LORD did not show himself again to Manoah and his wife, Manoah realized*j* that it was the angel of the LORD.

²²"We are doomed*k* to die!" he said to his wife. "We have seen*l* God!"

²³But his wife answered, "If the LORD had meant to kill us, he would not have accepted a burnt offering and grain offering from our hands, nor shown us all these things or now told us this."*m*

²⁴The woman gave birth to a boy and named him Samson.*n* He grew*o* and the LORD blessed him,*p* ²⁵and the Spirit of the LORD began to stir*q* him while he was in Mahaneh Dan,*r* between Zorah and Eshtaol.

ª 18 Or *is wonderful*

417

Chapter 14 Theme

14 Samson went down to Timnah[a] and saw there a young Philistine woman. [2]When he returned, he said to his father and mother, "I have seen a Philistine woman in Timnah; now get her for me as my wife."[b]

[3]His father and mother replied, "Isn't there an acceptable woman among your relatives or among all our people?[c] Must you go to the uncircumcised[d] Philistines to get a wife?[e]"

But Samson said to his father, "Get her for me. She's the right one for me." [4](His parents did not know that this was from the LORD, who was seeking an occasion to confront the Philistines;[f] for at that time they were ruling over Israel.)[g] [5]Samson went down to Timnah together with his father and mother. As they approached the vineyards of Timnah, suddenly a young lion came roaring toward him. [6]The Spirit of the LORD came upon him in power[h] so that he tore the lion apart with his bare hands as he might have torn a young goat. But he told neither his father nor his mother what he had done. [7]Then he went down and talked with the woman, and he liked her.

[8]Some time later, when he went back to marry her, he turned aside to look at the lion's carcass. In it was a swarm of bees and some honey, [9]which he scooped out with his hands and ate as he went along. When he rejoined his parents, he gave them some, and they too ate it. But he did not tell them that he had taken the honey from the lion's carcass.

[10]Now his father went down to see the woman. And Samson made a feast there, as was customary for bridegrooms. [11]When he appeared, he was given thirty companions.

[12]"Let me tell you a riddle,[i]" Samson said to them. "If you can give me the answer within the seven days of the feast,[j] I will give you thirty linen garments and thirty sets of clothes.[k] [13]If you can't tell me the answer, you must give me thirty linen garments and thirty sets of clothes."

"Tell us your riddle," they said. "Let's hear it."
[14]He replied,

> "Out of the eater, something to eat;
>   out of the strong, something sweet."

For three days they could not give the answer.

[15]On the fourth[a] day, they said to Samson's wife, "Coax[l] your husband into explaining the riddle for us, or we will burn you and your father's household to death.[m] Did you invite us here to rob us?"

---

a 15 Some Septuagint manuscripts and Syriac; Hebrew *seventh*

14:1
a Ge 38:12

14:2
b Ge 21:21; 34:4

14:3
c Ge 24:4
d Dt 7:3
e Ex 34:16

14:4
f Jos 11:20
g Jdg 13:1

14:6
h Jdg 3:10; 13:25

14:12
i 1Ki 10:1; Eze 17:2
j Ge 29:27
k Ge 45:22; 2Ki 5:5

14:15
l Jdg 16:5; Ecc 7:26
m Jdg 15:6

14:16
a Jdg 16:15

¹⁶Then Samson's wife threw herself on him, sobbing, "You hate me! You don't really love me.^a You've given my people a riddle, but you haven't told me the answer."

"I haven't even explained it to my father or mother," he replied, "so why should I explain it to you?" ¹⁷She cried the whole seven days^b of the feast. So on the seventh day he finally told her, because she continued to press him. She in turn explained the riddle to her people.

14:17
b Est 1:5

¹⁸Before sunset on the seventh day the men of the town said to him,

> "What is sweeter than honey?
> What is stronger than a lion?"^c

Samson said to them,

14:18
c ver 14

> "If you had not plowed with my heifer,
> you would not have solved my riddle."

¹⁹Then the Spirit of the LORD came upon him in power.^d He went down to Ashkelon, struck down thirty of their men, stripped them of their belongings and gave their clothes to those who had explained the riddle. Burning with anger,^e he went up to his father's house. ²⁰And Samson's wife was given to the friend^f who had attended him at his wedding.

14:19
d Nu 11:25;
Jdg 3:10;
6:34; 11:29;
13:25; 15:14;
1Sa 11:6;
16:13;
1Ki 18:46;
2Ch 24:20;
Isa 11:2
e 1Sa 11:6

Chapter 15 Theme _____

15 Later on, at the time of wheat harvest, Samson took a young goat^g and went to visit his wife. He said, "I'm going to my wife's room." But her father would not let him go in.

14:20
f Jdg 15:2,6;
Jn 3:29

²"I was so sure you thoroughly hated her," he said, "that I gave her to your friend.^h Isn't her younger sister more attractive? Take her instead."

³Samson said to them, "This time I have a right to get even with the Philistines; I will really harm them." ⁴So he went out and caught three hundred foxes and tied them tail to tail in pairs. He then fastened a torch to every pair of tails, ⁵lit the torches and let the foxes loose in the standing grain of the Philistines. He burned up the shocks and standing grain, together with the vineyards and olive groves.

15:1
g Ge 38:17

⁶When the Philistines asked, "Who did this?" they were told, "Samson, the Timnite's son-in-law, because his wife was given to his friend."

15:2
h Jdg 14:20

So the Philistines went up and burned her and her father to death.ⁱ ⁷Samson said to them, "Since you've acted like this, I won't stop until I get my revenge on you." ⁸He attacked them viciously and slaughtered many of them. Then he went down and stayed in a cave in the rock of Etam.

15:6
i Jdg 14:15

⁹The Philistines went up and camped in Judah, spreading out near Lehi.ᵃ ¹⁰The men of Judah asked, "Why have you come to fight us?"

"We have come to take Samson prisoner," they answered, "to do to him as he did to us."

¹¹Then three thousand men from Judah went down to the cave in the rock of Etam and said to Samson, "Don't you realize that the Philistines are rulers over us?ᵇ What have you done to us?"

He answered, "I merely did to them what they did to me."

¹²They said to him, "We've come to tie you up and hand you over to the Philistines."

Samson said, "Swear to me that you won't kill me yourselves."

¹³"Agreed," they answered. "We will only tie you up and hand you over to them. We will not kill you." So they bound him with two new ropes and led him up from the rock. ¹⁴As he approached Lehi, the Philistines came toward him shouting. The Spirit of the LORD came upon him in power.ᶜ The ropes on his arms became like charred flax, and the bindings dropped from his hands. ¹⁵Finding a fresh jawbone of a donkey, he grabbed it and struck down a thousand men.ᵈ

¹⁶Then Samson said,

> "With a donkey's jawbone
> I have made donkeys of them.ᵃ
> With a donkey's jawbone
> I have killed a thousand men."

¹⁷When he finished speaking, he threw away the jawbone; and the place was called Ramath Lehi.ᵇ

¹⁸Because he was very thirsty, he cried out to the LORD,ᵉ "You have given your servant this great victory. Must I now die of thirst and fall into the hands of the uncircumcised?" ¹⁹Then God opened up the hollow place in Lehi, and water came out of it. When Samson drank, his strength returned and he revived.ᶠ So the spring was called En Hakkore,ᶜ and it is still there in Lehi.

²⁰Samson ledᵈ Israel for twenty yearsᵍ in the days of the Philistines.

Chapter 16 Theme

16 One day Samson went to Gaza, where he saw a prostitute. He went in to spend the night with her. ²The people of Gaza were told, "Samson is here!" So they surrounded the place and lay in wait for him all night at the city gate.ʰ They made no move during the night, saying, "At dawn we'll kill him."

ᵃ 16 Or *made a heap or two*; the Hebrew for *donkey* sounds like the Hebrew for *heap.*
ᵇ 17 *Ramath Lehi* means *jawbone hill.* ᶜ 19 *En Hakkore* means *caller's spring.*
ᵈ 20 Traditionally *judged*

15:9
ᵃ ver 14,17,19

15:11
ᵇ Jdg 13:1; 14:4;
Ps 106:40-42

15:14
ᶜ Jdg 3:10;
14:19;
1Sa 11:6

15:15
ᵈ Lev 26:8;
Jos 23:10;
Jdg 3:31

15:18
ᵉ Jdg 16:28

15:19
ᶠ Ge 45:27;
Isa 40:29

15:20
ᵍ Jdg 13:1;
16:31;
Heb 11:32

16:2
ʰ 1Sa 23:26;
Ps 118:10-12;
Ac 9:24

16:3
a Jos 10:36

³But Samson lay there only until the middle of the night. Then he got up and took hold of the doors of the city gate, together with the two posts, and tore them loose, bar and all. He lifted them to his shoulders and carried them to the top of the hill that faces Hebron.ᵃ

16:4
b Ge 24:67

⁴Some time later, he fell in loveᵇ with a woman in the Valley of Sorek whose name was Delilah. ⁵The rulers of the Philistinesᶜ went to her and said, "See if you can lureᵈ him into showing you the secret of his great strength and how we can overpower him so we may tie him up and subdue him. Each one of us will give you eleven hundred shekelsᵃ of silver."ᵉ

16:5
c Jos 13:3
d Ex 10:7;
Jdg 14:15
e ver 18

⁶So Delilah said to Samson, "Tell me the secret of your great strength and how you can be tied up and subdued."

⁷Samson answered her, "If anyone ties me with seven fresh thongsᵇ that have not been dried, I'll become as weak as any other man."

⁸Then the rulers of the Philistines brought her seven fresh thongs that had not been dried, and she tied him with them. ⁹With men hidden in the room,ᶠ she called to him, "Samson, the Philistines are upon you!" But he snapped the thongs as easily as a piece of string snaps when it comes close to a flame. So the secret of his strength was not discovered.

16:9
f ver 12

¹⁰Then Delilah said to Samson, "You have made a fool of me;ᵍ you lied to me. Come now, tell me how you can be tied."

¹¹He said, "If anyone ties me securely with new ropesʰ that have never been used, I'll become as weak as any other man."

16:10
g ver 13

¹²So Delilah took new ropes and tied him with them. Then, with men hidden in the room, she called to him, "Samson, the Philistines are upon you!" But he snapped the ropes off his arms as if they were threads.

¹³Delilah then said to Samson, "Until now, you have been making a fool of me and lying to me. Tell me how you can be tied."

16:11
h Jdg 15:13

He replied, "If you weave the seven braids of my head into the fabric ⌊on the loom⌋ and tighten it with the pin, I'll become as weak as any other man." So while he was sleeping, Delilah took the seven braids of his head, wove them into the fabric ¹⁴andᶜ tightened it with the pin.

16:14
i ver 9,20

Again she called to him, "Samson, the Philistines are upon you!"ⁱ He awoke from his sleep and pulled up the pin and the loom, with the fabric.

¹⁵Then she said to him, "How can you say, 'I love you,'ʲ when you won't confide in me? This is the third timeᵏ you have made a fool of me and haven't told me the secret of your great strength.ˡ"

16:15
j Jdg 14:16
k Nu 24:10
l ver 5

a 5 That is, about 28 pounds (about 13 kilograms)   b 7 Or *bowstrings*; also in verses 8 and 9   c 13,14 Some Septuagint manuscripts; Hebrew "⌊*I can*⌋ *if you weave the seven braids of my head into the fabric* ⌊*on the loom*⌋." ¹⁴*So she*

¹⁶With such nagging she prodded him day after day until he was tired to death.

¹⁷So he told her everything.^a "No razor has ever been used on my head," he said, "because I have been a Nazirite^b set apart to God since birth. If my head were shaved, my strength would leave me, and I would become as weak as any other man."

¹⁸When Delilah saw that he had told her everything, she sent word to the rulers of the Philistines,^c "Come back once more; he has told me everything." So the rulers of the Philistines returned with the silver in their hands. ¹⁹Having put him to sleep on her lap, she called a man to shave off the seven braids of his hair, and so began to subdue him.^a And his strength left him.^d

²⁰Then she called, "Samson, the Philistines are upon you!"

He awoke from his sleep and thought, "I'll go out as before and shake myself free." But he did not know that the LORD had left him.^e

²¹Then the Philistines^f seized him, gouged out his eyes^g and took him down to Gaza. Binding him with bronze shackles, they set him to grinding^h in the prison. ²²But the hair on his head began to grow again after it had been shaved.

²³Now the rulers of the Philistines assembled to offer a great sacrifice to Dagonⁱ their god and to celebrate, saying, "Our god has delivered Samson, our enemy, into our hands."

²⁴When the people saw him, they praised their god,^j saying,

"Our god has delivered our enemy
    into our hands,^k
the one who laid waste our land
    and multiplied our slain."

²⁵While they were in high spirits,^l they shouted, "Bring out Samson to entertain us." So they called Samson out of the prison, and he performed for them.

When they stood him among the pillars, ²⁶Samson said to the servant who held his hand, "Put me where I can feel the pillars that support the temple, so that I may lean against them." ²⁷Now the temple was crowded with men and women; all the rulers of the Philistines were there, and on the roof^m were about three thousand men and women watching Samson perform. ²⁸Then Samson prayed to the LORD,ⁿ "O Sovereign LORD, remember me. O God, please strengthen me just once more, and let me with one blow get revenge^o on the Philistines for my two eyes." ²⁹Then Samson reached toward the two central pillars on which the temple stood. Bracing himself against them, his right hand on the one and his left hand on the other, ³⁰Samson said, "Let me die with the Philistines!" Then he pushed with all his might, and down came

---

^a 19 Hebrew; some Septuagint manuscripts *and he began to weaken*

16:17
^a Mic 7:5
^b Nu 6:2,5;
Jdg 13:5

16:18
^c Jos 13:3;
1Sa 5:8

16:19
^d Pr 7:26-27

16:20
^e Nu 14:42;
Jos 7:12;
1Sa 16:14;
18:12; 28:15

16:21
^f Jer 47:1
^g Nu 16:14
^h Job 31:10;
Isa 47:2

16:23
ⁱ 1Sa 5:2;
1Ch 10:10

16:24
^j Da 5:4
^k 1Sa 31:9;
1Ch 10:9

16:25
^l Jdg 9:27;
Ru 3:7;
Est 1:10

16:27
^m Dt 22:8;
Jos 2:8

16:28
ⁿ Jdg 15:18
^o Jer 15:15

16:31
a Jdg 13:2
b Ru 1:1;
1Sa 4:18
c Jdg 15:20

the temple on the rulers and all the people in it. Thus he killed many more when he died than while he lived.

³¹Then his brothers and his father's whole family went down to get him. They brought him back and buried him between Zorah and Eshtaol in the tomb of Manoah*a* his father. He had led*ab* Israel twenty years.*c*

17:1
d Jdg 18:2,13

Chapter 17 Theme

17:2
e Ru 2:20;
1Sa 15:13;
2Sa 2:5

17 Now a man named Micah*d* from the hill country of Ephraim ²said to his mother, "The eleven hundred shekels*b* of silver that were taken from you and about which I heard you utter a curse—I have that silver with me; I took it."

Then his mother said, "The LORD bless you,*e* my son!"

17:3
f Ex 20:4,23;
34:17; Lev 19:4

³When he returned the eleven hundred shekels of silver to his mother, she said, "I solemnly consecrate my silver to the LORD for my son to make a carved image and a cast idol.*f* I will give it back to you."

17:4
g Ex 32:4;
Isa 17:8

⁴So he returned the silver to his mother, and she took two hundred shekels*c* of silver and gave them to a silversmith, who made them into the image and the idol.*g* And they were put in Micah's house.

17:5
h Isa 44:13;
Eze 8:10
i Jdg 8:27
j Ge 31:19;
Jdg 18:14
k Nu 16:10
l Ex 29:9;
Jdg 18:24

⁵Now this man Micah had a shrine,*h* and he made an ephod*i* and some idols*j* and installed*k* one of his sons as his priest.*l* ⁶In those days Israel had no king;*m* everyone did as he saw fit.*n*

⁷A young Levite from Bethlehem in Judah,*o* who had been living within the clan of Judah, ⁸left that town in search of some other place to stay. On his way*d* he came to Micah's house in the hill country of Ephraim.

17:6
m Jdg 18:1; 19:1;
21:25
n Dt 12:8

⁹Micah asked him, "Where are you from?"

"I'm a Levite from Bethlehem in Judah," he said, "and I'm looking for a place to stay."

17:7
o Jdg 19:1;
Ru 1:1-2;
Mic 5:2; Mt 2:1

¹⁰Then Micah said to him, "Live with me and be my father and priest,*p* and I'll give you ten shekels*e* of silver a year, your clothes and your food." ¹¹So the Levite agreed to live with him, and the young man was to him like one of his sons. ¹²Then Micah installed*q* the Levite, and the young man became his priest and lived in his house. ¹³And Micah said, "Now I know that the LORD will be good to me, since this Levite has become my priest."

17:10
p Jdg 18:19

Chapter 18 Theme

17:12
q Nu 16:10

18 In those days Israel had no king.*r* And in those days the tribe of the Danites was seeking a place of their own where they might settle, because they had not

18:1
r Jdg 17:6; 19:1

a 31 Traditionally *judged*   *b 2* That is, about 28 pounds (about 13 kilograms)   *c 4* That is, about 5 pounds (about 2.3 kilograms)   *d 8* Or *To carry on his profession*   *e 10* That is, about 4 ounces (about 110 grams) yet come into an inheritance among the tribes of Israel.ᵃ ²So the Danitesᵇ sent five warriors from Zorah and Eshtaol to spy out the land and explore it. These men represented all their clans. They told them, "Go, explore the land."ᶜ

The men entered the hill country of Ephraim and came to the house of Micah,ᵈ where they spent the night. ³When they were near Micah's house, they recognized the voice of the young Levite; so they turned in there and asked him, "Who brought you here? What are you doing in this place? Why are you here?"

⁴He told them what Micah had done for him, and said, "He has hired me and I am his priest.ᵉ"

⁵Then they said to him, "Please inquire of Godᶠ to learn whether our journey will be successful."

⁶The priest answered them, "Go in peace.ᵍ Your journey has the LORD's approval."

⁷So the five men left and came to Laish,ʰ where they saw that the people were living in safety, like the Sidonians, unsuspecting and secure. And since their land lacked nothing, they were prosperous.ᵃ Also, they lived a long way from the Sidoniansⁱ and had no relationship with anyone else.ᵇ

⁸When they returned to Zorah and Eshtaol, their brothers asked them, "How did you find things?"

⁹They answered, "Come on, let's attack them! We have seen that the land is very good. Aren't you going to do something? Don't hesitate to go there and take it over.ʲ ¹⁰When you get there, you will find an unsuspecting people and a spacious land that God has put into your hands, a land that lacks nothingᵏ whatever.ˡ"

¹¹Then six hundred menᵐ from the clan of the Danites,ⁿ armed for battle, set out from Zorah and Eshtaol. ¹²On their way they set up camp near Kiriath Jearim in Judah. This is why the place west of Kiriath Jearim is called Mahaneh Danᶜᵒ to this day. ¹³From there they went on to the hill country of Ephraim and came to Micah's house.

¹⁴Then the five men who had spied out the land of Laish said to their brothers, "Do you know that one of these houses has an ephod, other household gods, a carved image and a cast idol?ᵖ Now you know what to do." ¹⁵So they turned in there and went to the house of the young Levite at Micah's place and greeted him. ¹⁶The six hundred Danites,�q armed for battle, stood at the entrance to the gate. ¹⁷The five men who had spied out the land went inside and took the carved image, the ephod, the other household godsʳ and the cast idol while the priest and the six hundred armed men stood at the entrance to the gate.

ᵃ7 The meaning of the Hebrew for this clause is uncertain.   ᵇ7 Hebrew; some Septuagint manuscripts *with the Arameans*   ᶜ12 *Mahaneh Dan* means *Dan's camp.*

**Cross references (margin):**

18:1 ᵃ Jos 19:47

18:2 ᵇ Jdg 13:25; ᶜ Jos 2:1; ᵈ Jdg 17:1

18:4 ᵉ Jdg 17:12

18:5 ᶠ 1Ki 22:5

18:6 ᵍ 1Ki 22:6

18:7 ʰ Jos 19:47; ⁱ ver 28

18:9 ʲ Nu 13:30; 1Ki 22:3

18:10 ᵏ ver 7,27; Dt 8:9; ˡ 1Ch 4:40

18:11 ᵐ ver 16,17; ⁿ Jdg 13:2

18:12 ᵒ Jdg 13:25

18:14 ᵖ Ge 31:19; Jdg 17:5

18:16 �q ver 11

18:17 ʳ Ge 31:19; Mic 5:13

18:18
a Isa 46:2;
Jer 43:11;
Hos 10:5

¹⁸When these men went into Micah's house and took*ᵃ* the carved image, the ephod, the other household gods and the cast idol, the priest said to them, "What are you doing?"

18:19
b Job 21:5;
29:9; 40:4;
Mic 7:16
c Jdg 17:10

¹⁹They answered him, "Be quiet!*ᵇ* Don't say a word. Come with us, and be our father and priest.*ᶜ* Isn't it better that you serve a tribe and clan in Israel as priest rather than just one man's household?" ²⁰Then the priest was glad. He took the ephod, the other household gods and the carved image and went along with the people. ²¹Putting their little children, their livestock and their possessions in front of them, they turned away and left.

²²When they had gone some distance from Micah's house, the men who lived near Micah were called together and overtook the Danites. ²³As they shouted after them, the Danites turned and said to Micah, "What's the matter with you that you called out your men to fight?"

18:26
d Ps 18:17;
35:10

²⁴He replied, "You took the gods I made, and my priest, and went away. What else do I have? How can you ask, 'What's the matter with you?'"

18:27
e ver 7,10
f Ge 49:17;
Jos 19:47

²⁵The Danites answered, "Don't argue with us, or some hot-tempered men will attack you, and you and your family will lose your lives." ²⁶So the Danites went their way, and Micah, seeing that they were too strong for him,*ᵈ* turned around and went back home.

²⁷Then they took what Micah had made, and his priest, and went on to Laish, against a peaceful and unsuspecting people.*ᵉ* They attacked them with the sword and burned down their city.*ᶠ* ²⁸There was no one to rescue them because they lived a long way from Sidon*ᵍ* and had no relationship with anyone else. The city was in a valley near Beth Rehob.*ʰ*

18:28
g ver 7
h Nu 13:21;
2Sa 10:6

The Danites rebuilt the city and settled there. ²⁹They named it Dan*ⁱ* after their forefather Dan, who was born to Israel—though the city used to be called Laish.*ʲ* ³⁰There the Danites set up for themselves the idols, and Jonathan son of Gershom,*ᵏ* the son of Moses,*ᵃ* and his sons were priests for the tribe of Dan until the time of the captivity of the land. ³¹They continued to use the idols Micah had made, all the time the house of God*ˡ* was in Shiloh.*ᵐ*

18:29
i Ge 14:14
j Jos 19:47;
1Ki 15:20

18:30
k Ex 2:22;
Jdg 17:3,5

Chapter 19 Theme

19 In those days Israel had no king. Now a Levite who lived in a remote area in the hill country of Ephraim*ⁿ* took a concubine from Bethlehem in Judah.*ᵒ* ²But she was unfaithful to him. She left him and went back to her father's house in Bethlehem, Judah. After she had been there

18:31
l Jdg 19:18
m Jos 18:1;
Jer 7:14

19:1
n Jdg 18:1
o Ru 1:1

a 30 An ancient Hebrew scribal tradition, some Septuagint manuscripts and Vulgate; Masoretic Text *Manasseh* four months, ³her husband went to her to persuade her to return. He had with him his servant and two donkeys. She took him into her father's house, and when her father saw him, he gladly welcomed him. ⁴His father-in-law, the girl's father, prevailed upon him to stay; so he remained with him three days, eating and drinking,ᵃ and sleeping there.

⁵On the fourth day they got up early and he prepared to leave, but the girl's father said to his son-in-law, "Refresh yourselfᵇ with something to eat; then you can go." ⁶So the two of them sat down to eat and drink together. Afterward the girl's father said, "Please stay tonight and enjoy yourself.ᶜ" ⁷And when the man got up to go, his father-in-law persuaded him, so he stayed there that night. ⁸On the morning of the fifth day, when he rose to go, the girl's father said, "Refresh yourself. Wait till afternoon!" So the two of them ate together.

⁹Then when the man, with his concubine and his servant, got up to leave, his father-in-law, the girl's father, said, "Now look, it's almost evening. Spend the night here; the day is nearly over. Stay and enjoy yourself. Early tomorrow morning you can get up and be on your way home." ¹⁰But, unwilling to stay another night, the man left and went toward Jebusᵈ (that is, Jerusalem), with his two saddled donkeys and his concubine.

¹¹When they were near Jebus and the day was almost gone, the servant said to his master, "Come, let's stop at this city of the Jebusitesᵉ and spend the night."

¹²His master replied, "No. We won't go into an alien city, whose people are not Israelites. We will go on to Gibeah." ¹³He added, "Come, let's try to reach Gibeah or Ramahᶠ and spend the night in one of those places." ¹⁴So they went on, and the sun set as they neared Gibeah in Benjamin.ᵍ ¹⁵There they stopped to spend the night. They went and sat in the city square,ʰ but no one took them into his home for the night.

¹⁶That eveningⁱ an old man from the hill country of Ephraim,ʲ who was living in Gibeah (the men of the place were Benjamites), came in from his work in the fields. ¹⁷When he looked and saw the traveler in the city square, the old man asked, "Where are you going? Where did you come from?"ᵏ

¹⁸He answered, "We are on our way from Bethlehem in Judah to a remote area in the hill country of Ephraim where I live. I have been to Bethlehem in Judah and now I am going to the house of the LORD.ˡ No one has taken me into his house. ¹⁹We have both straw and fodderᵐ for our donkeys and bread and wineⁿ for ourselves your servants—me, your maidservant, and the young man with us. We don't need anything."

²⁰"You are welcome at my house," the old man said. "Let me supply whatever you need. Only don't spend the night in the

Cross-references:
19:4 ᵃEx 32:6
19:5 ᵇver 8; Ge 18:5
19:6 ᶜver 9,22; Jdg 16:25
19:10 ᵈGe 10:16; Jos 15:8; 1Ch 11:4-5
19:11 ᵉJos 3:10
19:13 ᶠJos 18:25
19:14 ᵍ1Sa 10:26; Isa 10:29
19:15 ʰGe 19:2
19:16 ⁱPs 104:23; ʲver 1
19:17 ᵏGe 29:4
19:18 ˡJdg 18:31
19:19 ᵐGe 24:25; ⁿGe 14:18

19:21
a Ge 24:32-33;
Lk 7:44

19:22
b Jdg 16:25
c Dt 13:13
d Ge 19:4-5;
Jdg 20:5;
Ro 1:26-27

19:23
e Ge 19:6
f Ge 34:7;
Lev 19:29;
Dt 22:21;
Jdg 20:6;
2Sa 13:12;
Ro 1:27

19:24
g Ge 19:8;
Dt 21:14

19:25
h 1Sa 31:4

19:29
i Ge 22:6
j Jdg 20:6;
1Sa 11:7

19:30
k Hos 9:9
l Jdg 20:7;
Pr 13:10

20:1
m Jdg 21:5
n 1Sa 3:20;
2Sa 3:10;
1Ki 4:25
o 1Sa 11:7
p 1Sa 7:5

20:2
q Jdg 8:10

20:4
r Jos 15:57
s Jdg 19:15

20:5
t Jdg 19:22
u Jdg 19:25-26

20:6
v Jdg 19:29
w Jos 7:15;
Jdg 19:23

20:7
x Jdg 19:30

square." ²¹So he took him into his house and fed his donkeys. After they had washed their feet, they had something to eat and drink.*a*

²²While they were enjoying themselves,*b* some of the wicked men*c* of the city surrounded the house. Pounding on the door, they shouted to the old man who owned the house, "Bring out the man who came to your house so we can have sex with him.*d*"

²³The owner of the house went outside*e* and said to them, "No, my friends, don't be so vile. Since this man is my guest, don't do this disgraceful thing.*f* ²⁴Look, here is my virgin daughter,*g* and his concubine. I will bring them out to you now, and you can use them and do to them whatever you wish. But to this man, don't do such a disgraceful thing."

²⁵But the men would not listen to him. So the man took his concubine and sent her outside to them, and they raped her and abused her*h* throughout the night, and at dawn they let her go. ²⁶At daybreak the woman went back to the house where her master was staying, fell down at the door and lay there until daylight.

²⁷When her master got up in the morning and opened the door of the house and stepped out to continue on his way, there lay his concubine, fallen in the doorway of the house, with her hands on the threshold. ²⁸He said to her, "Get up; let's go." But there was no answer. Then the man put her on his donkey and set out for home.

²⁹When he reached home, he took a knife*i* and cut up his concubine, limb by limb, into twelve parts and sent them into all the areas of Israel.*j* ³⁰Everyone who saw it said, "Such a thing has never been seen or done, not since the day the Israelites came up out of Egypt.*k* Think about it! Consider it! Tell us what to do!'"

Chapter 20 Theme

20 Then all the Israelites*m* from Dan to Beersheba*n* and from the land of Gilead came out as one man*o* and assembled*p* before the LORD in Mizpah. ²The leaders of all the people of the tribes of Israel took their places in the assembly of the people of God, four hundred thousand soldiers*q* armed with swords. ³(The Benjamites heard that the Israelites had gone up to Mizpah.) Then the Israelites said, "Tell us how this awful thing happened."

⁴So the Levite, the husband of the murdered woman, said, "I and my concubine came to Gibeah*r* in Benjamin to spend the night.*s* ⁵During the night the men of Gibeah came after me and surrounded the house, intending to kill me.*t* They raped my concubine, and she died.*u* ⁶I took my concubine, cut her into pieces and sent one piece to each region of Israel's inheritance,*v* because they committed this lewd and disgraceful act*w* in Israel. ⁷Now, all you Israelites, speak up and give your verdict.*x*"

⁸All the people rose as one man, saying, "None of us will go home. No, not one of us will return to his house. ⁹But now this is what we'll do to Gibeah: We'll go up against it as the lot directs.ᵃ ¹⁰We'll take ten men out of every hundred from all the tribes of Israel, and a hundred from a thousand, and a thousand from ten thousand, to get provisions for the army. Then, when the army arrives at Gibeahᵃ in Benjamin, it can give them what they deserve for all this vileness done in Israel." ¹¹So all the men of Israel got together and united as one manᵇ against the city.

¹²The tribes of Israel sent men throughout the tribe of Benjamin, saying, "What about this awful crime that was committed among you? ¹³Now surrender those wicked menᶜ of Gibeah so that we may put them to death and purge the evil from Israel.ᵈ"

But the Benjamites would not listen to their fellow Israelites. ¹⁴From their towns they came together at Gibeah to fight against the Israelites. ¹⁵At once the Benjamites mobilized twenty-six thousand swordsmen from their towns, in addition to seven hundred chosen men from those living in Gibeah. ¹⁶Among all these soldiers there were seven hundred chosen men who were left-handed,ᵉ each of whom could sling a stone at a hair and not miss.

¹⁷Israel, apart from Benjamin, mustered four hundred thousand swordsmen, all of them fighting men.

¹⁸The Israelites went up to Bethelᵇ and inquired of God.ᶠ They said, "Who of us shall go first to fightᵍ against the Benjamites?"

The LORD replied, "Judah shall go first."

¹⁹The next morning the Israelites got up and pitched camp near Gibeah. ²⁰The men of Israel went out to fight the Benjamites and took up battle positions against them at Gibeah. ²¹The Benjamites came out of Gibeah and cut down twenty-two thousand Israelitesʰ on the battlefield that day. ²²But the men of Israel encouraged one another and again took up their positions where they had stationed themselves the first day. ²³The Israelites went up and wept before the LORD until evening,ⁱ and they inquired of the LORD. They said, "Shall we go up again to battleʲ against the Benjamites, our brothers?"

The LORD answered, "Go up against them."

²⁴Then the Israelites drew near to Benjamin the second day. ²⁵This time, when the Benjamites came out from Gibeah to oppose them, they cut down another eighteen thousand Israelites,ᵏ all of them armed with swords.

²⁶Then the Israelites, all the people, went up to Bethel, and there they sat weeping before the LORD.ˡ They fasted that day until evening and presented burnt offerings and fellowship offeringsᶜ

ᵃ 10 One Hebrew manuscript; most Hebrew manuscripts *Geba*, a variant of *Gibeah*   ᵇ 18 Or *to the house of God*; also in verse 26   ᶜ 26 Traditionally *peace offerings*

20:9
ᵃLev 16:8

20:11
ᵇver 1

20:13
ᶜDt 13:13;
Jdg 19:22
ᵈDt 17:12

20:16
ᵉJdg 3:15;
1Ch 12:2

20:18
ᶠver 26-27;
Nu 27:21
ᵍver 23,28

20:21
ʰver 25

20:23
ⁱJos 7:6
ʲver 18

20:25
ᵏver 21

20:26
ˡver 23

20:26
a Jdg 21:4

20:27
b Jos 18:1

20:28
c Jos 24:33
d Dt 18:5
e Jdg 7:9

20:29
f Jos 8:2,4

20:31
g Jos 8:16

20:32
h ver 39

20:33
i Jos 8:19

20:34
j Jos 8:14
k Isa 47:11

20:35
l 1Sa 9:21

20:36
m Jos 8:15

20:37
n Jos 8:19

20:38
o Jos 8:20

20:39
p ver 32

20:40
q Jos 8:20

to the LORD.*a* [27]And the Israelites inquired of the LORD. (In those days the ark of the covenant of God*b* was there, [28]with Phinehas son of Eleazar,*c* the son of Aaron, ministering before it.)*d* They asked, "Shall we go up again to battle with Benjamin our brother, or not?"

The LORD responded, "Go, for tomorrow I will give them into your hands.*e*"

[29]Then Israel set an ambush*f* around Gibeah. [30]They went up against the Benjamites on the third day and took up positions against Gibeah as they had done before. [31]The Benjamites came out to meet them and were drawn away*g* from the city. They began to inflict casualties on the Israelites as before, so that about thirty men fell in the open field and on the roads—the one leading to Bethel and the other to Gibeah.

[32]While the Benjamites were saying, "We are defeating them as before,"*h* the Israelites were saying, "Let's retreat and draw them away from the city to the roads."

[33]All the men of Israel moved from their places and took up positions at Baal Tamar, and the Israelite ambush charged out of its place*i* on the west*a* of Gibeah.*b* [34]Then ten thousand of Israel's finest men made a frontal attack on Gibeah. The fighting was so heavy that the Benjamites did not realize*j* how near disaster was.*k* [35]The LORD defeated Benjamin*l* before Israel, and on that day the Israelites struck down 25,100 Benjamites, all armed with swords. [36]Then the Benjamites saw that they were beaten.

Now the men of Israel had given way*m* before Benjamin, because they relied on the ambush they had set near Gibeah. [37]The men who had been in ambush made a sudden dash into Gibeah, spread out and put the whole city to the sword.*n* [38]The men of Israel had arranged with the ambush that they should send up a great cloud of smoke*o* from the city, [39]and then the men of Israel would turn in the battle.

The Benjamites had begun to inflict casualties on the men of Israel (about thirty), and they said, "We are defeating them as in the first battle."*p* [40]But when the column of smoke began to rise from the city, the Benjamites turned and saw the smoke of the whole city going up into the sky.*q* [41]Then the men of Israel turned on them, and the men of Benjamin were terrified, because they realized that disaster had come upon them. [42]So they fled before the Israelites in the direction of the desert, but they could not escape the battle. And the men of Israel who came out of the towns cut them down there. [43]They surrounded the Benjamites, chased them and easily*c* overran them in the vicinity of Gibeah

a 33 Some Septuagint manuscripts and Vulgate; the meaning of the Hebrew for this word is uncertain.   *b* 33 Hebrew *Geba*, a variant of *Gibeah*   *c* 43 The meaning of the Hebrew for this word is uncertain.

on the east. ⁴⁴Eighteen thousand Benjamites fell, all of them valiant fighters.ᵃ ⁴⁵As they turned and fled toward the desert to the rock of Rimmon,ᵇ the Israelites cut down five thousand men along the roads. They kept pressing after the Benjamites as far as Gidom and struck down two thousand more.

⁴⁶On that day twenty-five thousand Benjamite swordsmen fell, all of them valiant fighters. ⁴⁷But six hundred men turned and fled into the desert to the rock of Rimmon, where they stayed four months. ⁴⁸The men of Israel went back to Benjamin and put all the towns to the sword, including the animals and everything else they found. All the towns they came across they set on fire.ᶜ

Chapter 21 Theme

21 The men of Israel had taken an oathᵈ at Mizpah:ᵉ "Not one of us will giveᶠ his daughter in marriage to a Benjamite." ²The people went to Bethel,ᵃ where they sat before God until evening, raising their voices and weeping bitterly. ³"O LORD, the God of Israel," they cried, "why has this happened to Israel? Why should one tribe be missing from Israel today?"

⁴Early the next day the people built an altar and presented burnt offerings and fellowship offerings.ᵇᵍ

⁵Then the Israelites asked, "Who from all the tribes of Israelʰ has failed to assemble before the LORD?" For they had taken a solemn oath that anyone who failed to assemble before the LORD at Mizpah should certainly be put to death.

⁶Now the Israelites grieved for their brothers, the Benjamites. "Today one tribe is cut off from Israel," they said. ⁷"How can we provide wives for those who are left, since we have taken an oathⁱ by the LORD not to give them any of our daughters in marriage?" ⁸Then they asked, "Which one of the tribes of Israel failed to assemble before the LORD at Mizpah?" They discovered that no one from Jabesh Gileadʲ had come to the camp for the assembly. ⁹For when they counted the people, they found that none of the people of Jabesh Gilead were there.

¹⁰So the assembly sent twelve thousand fighting men with instructions to go to Jabesh Gilead and put to the sword those living there, including the women and children. ¹¹"This is what you are to do," they said. "Kill every male and every woman who is not a virgin.ᵏ" ¹²They found among the people living in Jabesh Gilead four hundred young women who had never slept with a man, and they took them to the camp at Shilohˡ in Canaan.

¹³Then the whole assembly sent an offer of peaceᵐ to the Benjamites at the rock of Rimmon.ⁿ ¹⁴So the Benjamites returned at

20:44
ᵃPs 76:5

20:45
ᵇJos 15:32;
Jdg 21:13

20:48
ᶜJdg 21:23

21:1
ᵈJos 9:18
ᵉJdg 20:1
ᶠver 7,18

21:4
ᵍJdg 20:26;
2Sa 24:25

21:5
ʰJdg 5:23; 20:1

21:7
ⁱver 1

21:8
ʲ1Sa 11:1; 31:11

21:11
ᵏNu 31:17-18

21:12
ˡJos 18:1

21:13
ᵐDt 20:10
ⁿJdg 20:47

ᵃ2 Or *to the house of God*   ᵇ4 Traditionally *peace offerings*

JUDGE	CHAPTER/ VERSE	YEARS JUDGED	MAJOR FACTS/ACCOMPLISHMENTS	LESSONS FOR MY LIFE

THE JUDGES OF ISRAEL

that time and were given the women of Jabesh Gilead who had been spared. But there were not enough for all of them.

21:15
a ver 6

15The people grieved for Benjamin,*a* because the LORD had made a gap in the tribes of Israel. 16And the elders of the assembly said, "With the women of Benjamin destroyed, how shall we provide wives for the men who are left? 17The Benjamite survivors must have heirs," they said, "so that a tribe of Israel will not be wiped out. 18We can't give them our daughters as wives, since we Israelites have taken this oath: 'Cursed be anyone who gives*b* a wife to a Benjamite.' 19But look, there is the annual festival of the LORD in Shiloh,*c* to the north of Bethel, and east of the road that goes from Bethel to Shechem, and to the south of Lebonah."

21:18
b ver 1

21:19
c Jos 18:1;
Jdg 18:31;
1Sa 1:3

20So they instructed the Benjamites, saying, "Go and hide in the vineyards 21and watch. When the girls of Shiloh come out to join in the dancing,*d* then rush from the vineyards and each of you seize a wife from the girls of Shiloh and go to the land of Benjamin. 22When their fathers or brothers complain to us, we will say to them, 'Do us a kindness by helping them, because we did not get wives for them during the war, and you are innocent, since you did not give*e* your daughters to them.'"

21:21
d Ex 15:20;
Jdg 11:34

21:22
e ver 1,18

23So that is what the Benjamites did. While the girls were dancing, each man caught one and carried her off to be his wife. Then they returned to their inheritance and rebuilt the towns and settled in them.*f*

21:23
f Jdg 20:48

24At that time the Israelites left that place and went home to their tribes and clans, each to his own inheritance.

25In those days Israel had no king; everyone did as he saw fit.*g*

21:25
g Dt 12:8;
Jdg 17:6;
18:1; 19:1

Theme of Judges:

Author:

Date:

Purpose:

Key Words:

Israelites did
evil (Israelites
once again did
evil)

sold (served,
serving, were
subject)

Israelites cried
out (they cried
out, Israelites
cried, they cried
to the Lord)

he raised up for
them a deliverer,
he gave them a
deliverer
(the Lord raised
up a judge)

judge(s)

Segment Divisions	Chapter Themes
	1
	2
	3
	4
	5
	6
	7
	8
	9
	10
	11
	12
	13
	14
	15
	16
	17
	18
	19
	20
	21

RUTH

*T*he book of Ruth is set chronologically in the midst of the dark years of the judges. It offers encouragement and hope to those who decide to follow God. This story of love and dedication revolves around three people who determine in their hearts to walk in integrity, clinging to their God and his precepts—three people who know who their king is and who do what is right in his eyes.

∾ THINGS TO DO

1. As you read Ruth one chapter at a time:

    a. First read each chapter simply to catch the flavor of the lives of these people.

    b. Then read each chapter again, observing the events of that chapter. Examine what you read in light of the five W's and an H, asking questions such as: Who are these people? What can I learn about them? What is happening to them? When is it happening, and where? Why do they do what they do? How will they accomplish their tasks? What will be the end result? Record pertinent insights in the margin.

    c. Watch for and mark the key repeated words listed on the RUTH AT A GLANCE chart on page 441. After you finish marking key words in a chapter, observe what you learn about each. If there is something significant you want to remember, write it in the margin.

2. Determine the theme of each chapter and record it on RUTH AT A GLANCE and on the line next to the chapter number in the text.

3. When you finish reading Ruth and marking every reference to *redeem (redemption), kinsman-redeemer, kinsman,* and *close relative (near of kin, relative):*

    a. List everything you learn about the process of redeeming a close relative. Pay attention to the process in chapter 4.

    b. Look up the laws regarding redemption in Leviticus 25:23-28 and Deuteronomy 25:5-10. You may want to record these cross-references in the margin next to your insights on redemption.

4. Complete RUTH AT A GLANCE.

∾ THINGS TO THINK ABOUT

1. What have you learned about loyalty from the story of Ruth? What does it mean to be loyal to God, to his people, to his precepts, and to trust God to do what he says he will do?

2. As you think of Boaz redeeming Ruth, remember that you have a kinsman-redeemer, the Lord Jesus Christ. Think of how the Lord has acted on your behalf as your kinsman-redeemer by becoming a man so he could break death's hold by paying for your sin (Hebrews 2:14, 15). Remember that you were not redeemed from your empty way of life with silver or gold, but with the precious blood of the Lamb of God, a Lamb without spot or blemish (1 Peter 1:18, 19).

3. The final verses of Ruth show us that Ruth was included in the genealogy of David and therefore in the human lineage of our Lord Jesus Christ. Not only did a sovereign God include the harlot, Rahab, in the genealogy of his Son, but he also chose a Gentile, Ruth. Both of these women chose to believe God when those around them didn't! Consider how their example might apply to your life.

4. In the book of Judges Israel forsook the true God and turned to idols, while in Ruth the opposite is seen. One Gentile woman turns from idols to serve the only true God. In which category do you find yourself?

1:1
a Jdg 2:16-18
b Ge 12:10;
Ps 105:16
c Jdg 3:30

1:2
d Ge 35:19

1:4
e Mt 1:5

1:6
f Ex 4:31;
Jer 29:10;
Zep 2:7
g Ps 132:15;
Mt 6:11

1:8
h Ru 2:20;
2Ti 1:16
i ver 5

1:9
j Ru 3:1

1:11
k Ge 38:11;
Dt 25:5

1:13
l Jdg 2:15;
Job 4:5; 19:21;
Ps 32:4

1:14
m Ru 2:11
n Pr 17:17; 18:24

1:15
o Jos 24:14;
Jdg 11:24

Chapter 1 Theme

1 In the days when the judges ruled,ᵃ ᵃ there was a famine in the land,ᵇ and a man from Bethlehem in Judah, together with his wife and two sons, went to live for a while in the country of Moab.ᶜ ²The man's name was Elimelech, his wife's name Naomi, and the names of his two sons were Mahlon and Kilion. They were Ephrathites from Bethlehem,ᵈ Judah. And they went to Moab and lived there.

³Now Elimelech, Naomi's husband, died, and she was left with her two sons. ⁴They married Moabite women, one named Orpah and the other Ruth.ᵉ After they had lived there about ten years, ⁵both Mahlon and Kilion also died, and Naomi was left without her two sons and her husband.

⁶When she heard in Moab that the LORD had come to the aid of his peopleᶠ by providing foodᵍ for them, Naomi and her daughters-in-law prepared to return home from there. ⁷With her two daughters-in-law she left the place where she had been living and set out on the road that would take them back to the land of Judah.

⁸Then Naomi said to her two daughters-in-law, "Go back, each of you, to your mother's home. May the LORD show kindnessʰ to you, as you have shown to your deadⁱ and to me. ⁹May the LORD grant that each of you will find restʲ in the home of another husband."

Then she kissed them and they wept aloud ¹⁰and said to her, "We will go back with you to your people."

¹¹But Naomi said, "Return home, my daughters. Why would you come with me? Am I going to have any more sons, who could become your husbands?ᵏ ¹²Return home, my daughters; I am too old to have another husband. Even if I thought there was still hope for me—even if I had a husband tonight and then gave birth to sons— ¹³would you wait until they grew up? Would you remain unmarried for them? No, my daughters. It is more bitter for me than for you, because the LORD's hand has gone out against me!ˡ"

¹⁴At this they wept again. Then Orpah kissed her mother-in-lawᵐ good-by, but Ruth clung to her.ⁿ

¹⁵"Look," said Naomi, "your sister-in-law is going back to her people and her gods.ᵒ Go back with her."

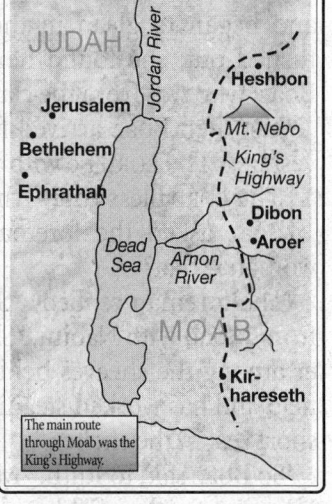

Ruth's Journey from Moab to Bethlehem

The main route through Moab was the King's Highway.

¹⁶But Ruth replied, "Don't urge me to leave you*a* or to turn back from you. Where you go I will go, and where you stay I will stay. Your people will be my people and your God my God.*b* ¹⁷Where you die I will die, and there I will be buried. May the LORD deal with me, be it ever so severely,*c* if anything but death separates you and me." ¹⁸When Naomi realized that Ruth was determined to go with her, she stopped urging her.*d*

¹⁹So the two women went on until they came to Bethlehem. When they arrived in Bethlehem, the whole town was stirred*e* because of them, and the women exclaimed, "Can this be Naomi?"

²⁰"Don't call me Naomi,*a*" she told them. "Call me Mara,*b* because the Almighty*c f* has made my life very bitter.*g* ²¹I went away full, but the LORD has brought me back empty.*h* Why call me Naomi? The LORD has afflicted*d* me; the Almighty has brought misfortune upon me."

²²So Naomi returned from Moab accompanied by Ruth the Moabitess, her daughter-in-law, arriving in Bethlehem as the barley harvest*i* was beginning.*j*

Chapter 2 Theme

2 Now Naomi had a relative*k* on her husband's side, from the clan of Elimelech,*l* a man of standing, whose name was Boaz.*m* ²And Ruth the Moabitess said to Naomi, "Let me go to the fields and pick up the leftover grain*n* behind anyone in whose eyes I find favor."

Naomi said to her, "Go ahead, my daughter." ³So she went out and began to glean in the fields behind the harvesters. As it turned out, she found herself working in a field belonging to Boaz, who was from the clan of Elimelech.

⁴Just then Boaz arrived from Bethlehem and greeted the harvesters, "The LORD be with you!*o*"

"The LORD bless you!*p*" they called back.

⁵Boaz asked the foreman of his harvesters, "Whose young woman is that?"

⁶The foreman replied, "She is the Moabitess*q* who came back from Moab with Naomi. ⁷She said, 'Please let me glean and gather among the sheaves behind the harvesters.' She went into the field and has worked steadily from morning till now, except for a short rest in the shelter."

⁸So Boaz said to Ruth, "My daughter, listen to me. Don't go and glean in another field and don't go away from here. Stay here with my servant girls. ⁹Watch the field where the men are harvesting, and follow along after the girls. I have told the men not

---

a*20 Naomi* means *pleasant*; also in verse 21.   b*20 Mara* means *bitter*.   c*20* Hebrew *Shaddai*; also in verse 21   d*21* Or *has testified against*

Cross references

1:16
a 2Ki 2:2
b Ru 2:11,12

1:17
c 1Sa 3:17; 25:22; 2Sa 19:13; 2Ki 6:31

1:18
d Ac 21:14

1:19
e Mt 21:10

1:20
f Ex 6:3
g ver 13; Job 6:4

1:21
h Job 1:21

1:22
i Ex 9:31; Ru 2:23
j 2Sa 21:9

2:1
k Ru 3:2,12
l Ru 1:2
m Ru 4:21

2:2
n ver 7; Lev 19:9; 23:22; Dt 24:19

2:4
o Jdg 6:12; Lk 1:28; 2Th 3:16
p Ps 129:7-8

2:6
q Ru 1:22

2:10
a 1Sa 25:23
b Ps 41:1
c Dt 15:3

to touch you. And whenever you are thirsty, go and get a drink from the water jars the men have filled."

¹⁰At this, she bowed down with her face to the ground.ᵃ She exclaimed, "Why have I found such favor in your eyes that you notice meᵇ—a foreigner?ᶜ"

¹¹Boaz replied, "I've been told all about what you have done for your mother-in-lawᵈ since the death of your husband—how you left your father and mother and your homeland and came to live with a people you did not know before.ᵉ ¹²May the LORD repay you for what you have done. May you be richly rewarded by the LORD,ᶠ the God of Israel, under whose wingsᵍ you have come to take refuge.ʰ"

2:11
d Ru 1:14
e Ru 1:16-17

¹³"May I continue to find favor in your eyes, my lord," she said. "You have given me comfort and have spoken kindly to your servant—though I do not have the standing of one of your servant girls."

2:12
f 1Sa 24:19
g Ps 17:8; 36:7;
57:1; 61:4;
63:7; 91:4
h Ru 1:16

¹⁴At mealtime Boaz said to her, "Come over here. Have some bread and dip it in the wine vinegar."

When she sat down with the harvesters, he offered her some roasted grain. She ate all she wanted and had some left over.ⁱ ¹⁵As she got up to glean, Boaz gave orders to his men, "Even if she gathers among the sheaves, don't embarrass her. ¹⁶Rather, pull out some stalks for her from the bundles and leave them for her to pick up, and don't rebuke her."

2:14
i ver 18

¹⁷So Ruth gleaned in the field until evening. Then she threshed the barley she had gathered, and it amounted to about an ephah.ᵃ ¹⁸She carried it back to town, and her mother-in-law saw how much she had gathered. Ruth also brought out and gave her what she had left overʲ after she had eaten enough.

2:18
j ver 14

¹⁹Her mother-in-law asked her, "Where did you glean today? Where did you work? Blessed be the man who took notice of you!ᵏ"

Then Ruth told her mother-in-law about the one at whose place she had been working. "The name of the man I worked with today is Boaz," she said.

2:19
k ver 10; Ps 41:1

²⁰"The LORD bless him!" Naomi said to her daughter-in-law. "He has not stopped showing his kindnessˡ to the living and the dead." She added, "That man is our close relative; he is one of our kinsman-redeemers.ᵐ"

²¹Then Ruth the Moabitess said, "He even said to me, 'Stay with my workers until they finish harvesting all my grain.'"

²²Naomi said to Ruth her daughter-in-law, "It will be good for you, my daughter, to go with his girls, because in someone else's field you might be harmed."

2:20
l Ru 3:10;
2Sa 2:5;
Pr 17:17
m Ru 3:9,12;
4:1,14

a 17 That is, probably about 3/5 bushel (about 22 liters)

²³So Ruth stayed close to the servant girls of Boaz to glean until the barley and wheat harvests^a were finished. And she lived with her mother-in-law.

Chapter 3 Theme

3 One day Naomi her mother-in-law said to her, "My daughter, should I not try to find a home^{ab} for you, where you will be well provided for? ²Is not Boaz, with whose servant girls you have been, a kinsman^c of ours? Tonight he will be winnowing barley on the threshing floor. ³Wash and perfume yourself,^d and put on your best clothes. Then go down to the threshing floor, but don't let him know you are there until he has finished eating and drinking. ⁴When he lies down, note the place where he is lying. Then go and uncover his feet and lie down. He will tell you what to do."

⁵"I will do whatever you say,"^e Ruth answered. ⁶So she went down to the threshing floor and did everything her mother-in-law told her to do.

⁷When Boaz had finished eating and drinking and was in good spirits,^f he went over to lie down at the far end of the grain pile. Ruth approached quietly, uncovered his feet and lay down. ⁸In the middle of the night something startled the man, and he turned and discovered a woman lying at his feet.

⁹"Who are you?" he asked.

"I am your servant Ruth," she said. "Spread the corner of your garment^g over me, since you are a kinsman-redeemer.^h"

¹⁰"The LORD bless you, my daughter," he replied. "This kindness is greater than that which you showed earlier: You have not run after the younger men, whether rich or poor. ¹¹And now, my daughter, don't be afraid. I will do for you all you ask. All my fellow townsmen know that you are a woman of noble character.ⁱ ¹²Although it is true that I am near of kin, there is a kinsman-redeemer^j nearer than^k I. ¹³Stay here for the night, and in the morning if he wants to redeem,^l good; let him redeem. But if he is not willing, as surely as the LORD lives^m I will do it. Lie here until morning."

¹⁴So she lay at his feet until morning, but got up before anyone could be recognized; and he said, "Don't let it be known that a woman came to the threshing floor."ⁿ

3:13
lDt 25:5;
Ru 4:5;
Mt 22:24
mJdg 8:19;
Jer 4:2

¹⁵He also said, "Bring me the shawl you are wearing and hold it out." When she did so, he poured into it six measures of barley and put it on her. Then he^b went back to town.

¹⁶When Ruth came to her mother-in-law, Naomi asked, "How did it go, my daughter?"

a 1 Hebrew *find rest* (see Ruth 1:9) b 15 Most Hebrew manuscripts; many Hebrew manuscripts, Vulgate and Syriac *she*

Then she told her everything Boaz had done for her ¹⁷and added, "He gave me these six measures of barley, saying, 'Don't go back to your mother-in-law empty-handed.'"

¹⁸Then Naomi said, "Wait, my daughter, until you find out what happens. For the man will not rest until the matter is settled today."*a*

Chapter 4 Theme

4 Meanwhile Boaz went up to the town gate and sat there. When the kinsman-redeemer he had mentioned*b* came along, Boaz said, "Come over here, my friend, and sit down." So he went over and sat down.

²Boaz took ten of the elders*c* of the town and said, "Sit here," and they did so. ³Then he said to the kinsman-redeemer, "Naomi, who has come back from Moab, is selling the piece of land that belonged to our brother Elimelech. ⁴I thought I should bring the matter to your attention and suggest that you buy it in the presence of these seated here and in the presence of the elders of my people. If you will redeem it, do so. But if you*a* will not, tell me, so I will know. For no one has the right to do it except you,*d* and I am next in line."

"I will redeem it," he said.

⁵Then Boaz said, "On the day you buy the land from Naomi and from Ruth the Moabitess, you acquire*b* the dead man's widow, in order to maintain the name of the dead with his property."*e*

⁶At this, the kinsman-redeemer said, "Then I cannot redeem*f* it because I might endanger my own estate. You redeem it yourself. I cannot do it."

⁷(Now in earlier times in Israel, for the redemption and transfer of property to become final, one party took off his sandal and gave it to the other. This was the method of legalizing transactions in Israel.)*g*

⁸So the kinsman-redeemer said to Boaz, "Buy it yourself." And he removed his sandal.

⁹Then Boaz announced to the elders and all the people, "Today you are witnesses that I have bought from Naomi all the property of Elimelech, Kilion and Mahlon. ¹⁰I have also acquired Ruth the Moabitess, Mahlon's widow, as my wife, in order to maintain the name of the dead with his property, so that his name will not disappear from among his family or from the town records.*h* Today you are witnesses!"

¹¹Then the elders and all those at the gate said, "We are witnesses.*i* May the LORD make the woman who is coming into your

**Cross references (left margin):**

3:18
a Ps 37:3-5

4:1
b Ru 3:12

4:2
c 1Ki 21:8;
Pr 31:23

4:4
d Lev 25:25;
Jer 32:7-8

4:5
e Ge 38:8;
Dt 25:5-6;
Ru 3:13;
Mt 22:24

4:6
f Lev 25:25;
Ru 3:13

4:7
g Dt 25:7-9

4:10
h Dt 25:6

4:11
i Dt 25:9

INSIGHT

The Genealogy of Boaz

Abram + Sarai
(Abraham + Sarah)
↓
Isaac + Rebekah
↓
Jacob + Leah
↓
Judah + Tamar
↓
Perez
↓
Hezron
↓
Ram
↓
Admin
(included in some manuscripts)
↓
Amminadab
↓
Nahshon
↓
Salmon + *Rahab*
(the harlot)
↓
Boaz + *Ruth*
(the Gentile)
↓
Obed
↓
Jesse
↓
David
from whom came "Mary, of whom was born Jesus"

See **The Genealogy of Jesus the Christ** on page 1665.

---

a 4 Many Hebrew manuscripts, Septuagint, Vulgate and Syriac; most Hebrew manuscripts *he*   *b* 5 Hebrew; Vulgate and Syriac *Naomi, you acquire Ruth the Moabitess,* home like Rachel and Leah,[a] who together built up the house of Israel. May you have standing in Ephrathah[b] and be famous in Bethlehem. [12]Through the offspring the LORD gives you by this young woman, may your family be like that of Perez,[c] whom Tamar bore to Judah."

[13]So Boaz took Ruth and she became his wife. Then he went to her, and the LORD enabled her to conceive,[d] and she gave birth to a son. [14]The women[e] said to Naomi: "Praise be to the LORD, who this day has not left you without a kinsman-redeemer. May he become famous throughout Israel! [15]He will renew your life and sustain you in your old age. For your daughter-in-law, who loves you and who is better to you than seven sons,[f] has given him birth."

[16]Then Naomi took the child, laid him in her lap and cared for him. [17]The women living there said, "Naomi has a son." And they named him Obed. He was the father of Jesse,[g] the father of David.

[18]This, then, is the family line of Perez[h]:

Perez was the father of Hezron,
[19]Hezron the father of Ram,
Ram the father of Amminadab,[i]
[20]Amminadab the father of Nahshon,
Nahshon the father of Salmon,[a]
[21]Salmon the father of Boaz,[j]
Boaz the father of Obed,
[22]Obed the father of Jesse,
and Jesse the father of David.

a 20 A few Hebrew manuscripts, some Septuagint manuscripts and Vulgate (see also verse 21 and Septuagint of 1 Chron. 2:11); most Hebrew manuscripts *Salma*

4:11
a Ps 127:3; 128:3
b Ge 35:16

4:12
c ver 18;
Ge 38:29

4:13
d Ge 29:31; 33:5;
Ru 3:11

4:14
e Lk 1:58

4:15
f Ru 1:16-17;
2:11-12;
1Sa 1:8

4:17
g ver 22;
1Sa 16:1,18;
1Ch 2:12,13

4:18
h Mt 1:3-6

4:19
i Ex 6:23

4:21
j Ru 2:1

Theme of Ruth:

Author:

Date:

Purpose:

Key Words:

redeem
(redemption)

close relative
(near of kin,
kinsman,
kinsman-
redeemer,
relative)

Naomi

Ruth

Boaz

Segment Divisions	Chapter Themes
1	
2	
3	
4	

1 SAMUEL

*T*he days of the judges were dark until God raised up Samuel as a prophet, priest, and judge. Samuel would do what was right in God's eyes. But the people weren't satisfied. They cried, "Now appoint a king to lead us, such as all the other nations have!" With that plea they rejected the Lord as their King. What would it be like to live under a monarchy rather than a theocracy? The children of Israel were soon to find out as the times of the kings began. The kingdom, at first united, was divided because of the disobedience of the kings.

The books of 1 and 2 Samuel, 1 and 2 Kings, and 1 and 2 Chronicles record the days of the kings of Israel. Children of God who have been made "to be a kingdom and priests" and who "will reign on the earth" (Revelation 1:6; 5:10) can learn many valuable lessons from these books. The lessons begin in 1 Samuel as God rejects Saul and chooses as king a man after his own heart. And what will such a man be like? Will he live a perfect life? Is this what will make him a man after God's own heart, or are there other reasons?

❧ THINGS TO DO

General Instructions

As you study this book never forget that these are actual people, frail but not without access to God, nor to his precepts and statutes of life. Observe the text prayerfully and carefully, and as you study, note in the margin God's lessons for life. You might want to give these the heading "LFL" (Lessons for Life) and color them in a distinctive way so you can recognize them immediately.

Chapters 1-7: Samuel, the Last Judge

1. As you observe these first seven chapters, mark the following words in a distinctive way and then note in the margin what you learn from observing each word in its context:

    a. *Ark* (of the Lord, of God, of the Lord's covenant), *ephod, judge* (judged, led, was leader, judging), *king, Ichabod,* and *Ebenezer.* The last three words are used only one time in these chapters but are significant. *Ephod* is used only twice in this segment but will have greater significance in the last segment of 1 Samuel. List these key words on an index card you can use as a bookmark for this segment.

    b. Mark selected geographical references on the map on page 497. This will help you gain perspective of events and familiarity with biblical locations.

2. Since 1 Samuel is a historical account, note the focus of each chapter. Who and/or what event does the chapter center on?

    a. In the margin list your insights about the main characters in each chapter. You might note who they are. For example, Elkanah's two wives:

      1) Hannah (childless)
      2) Peninnah (had sons/daughters)

    b. Especially observe the lives of Hannah, Samuel, and Eli, and list what you learn.

    c. In the margin list any progression of events which occurs. For example, in chapter 1 Hannah:

      1) Weeps because barren
      2) Asks for son/makes vow to God
      3) Is confronted by Eli
      4) Conceives
      5) Keeps vow to God

    d. Note in the margin your insights about God and his ways. For instance, in chapter 1 God closes the womb and opens the womb.

3. Record the theme of each chapter on the 1 SAMUEL AT A GLANCE chart on page 496 and in the text next to the chapter number.

Chapters 8-15: From Samuel to Saul, from Judge to King

1. As you observe this segment of 1 Samuel:

    a. Mark the following key words: *judge (judges)*, *king* (don't include foreign kings), *sin (sins, sinned)*, *evil*, *Spirit of God (of the Lord)*, *ark of God*, and *ephod*. Put them on an index card to use as a bookmark.

    b. In the margin list what you learn about Samuel, Saul, King Agag, and the Amalekites.

    c. Note all you learn about God and his ways.

    d. Mark any reference to time (when Saul begins his reign, etc.). Mark these with a symbol.

    e. There are no references to the ark in 1 Samuel after this segment. Review what you learned about the ark in this book and note in the margin where it is last mentioned and its location. (Read "The Ark of the Covenant" on page 2203.)

2. Carefully observe all you learn from marking the word *king*. Watch for the following and record your insights in the margin:

    a. Why the people wanted a king, how they perceived the kingship, and what kind of king they wanted.

    b. How God responded to the people's request, what God desired in a kingship, and how the success or failure of a king was determined.

3. Examine each chapter as you did in the previous segment, watching for and recording the main event of each chapter and any pertinent subpoints. Don't forget to record the chapter theme on 1 SAMUEL AT A GLANCE and in the text.

Chapters 16-31: The Preparation of Another King

1. In this segment:

    a. Make a new bookmark and mark the following key words: *kings (king's)* (not foreign kings), *evil (harm, wrongdoing, mean, disaster, doing wrong, no fault, wrong)*, *evil spirit*, *sin (sinned, wronged)*, *judge*, *covenant*, *inquire (inquired, inquiring, find out)*, and *ephod*. Don't forget to record what you are learning from marking *king* and *ephod*.

    b. Mark all references to time and to geographical locations as before.

2. Observe and record in the margin of each chapter what you learn about Samuel, Saul, and David. Give special attention to all that happens to David and how he responds to God and to man. Watch for and note in the margin the "LFL" (Lessons for Life).

3. In the margin write "Covenant" and list what you have observed from the text. Ask the five W's and an H: Who makes the covenant? How is it made? What is done? What is promised? What are the conditions? When is it made? Where is it made? Why? Remember that you are in covenant with God if you are a child of God (Matthew 26:26-29); watch for any principles which might apply to you. (See the "Insight" on covenant at Genesis 15:10.)

4. As you read each chapter watch for insights about God, note the events of each chapter and the subpoints of the chapter, and record the chapter themes.

5. Complete 1 SAMUEL AT A GLANCE. Watch for any additional segment divisions in 1 Samuel. Look at the chapter themes and see if there is any other way 1 Samuel might be segmented: Can any chapters be grouped in respect to David's relationship to Saul, to Jonathan, to the Philistines, or to others? Or is there any geographical segmentation, such as where Samuel, Saul, and David spend their time?

6. Note the theme of 1 Samuel on 1 SAMUEL AT A GLANCE.

∾ THINGS TO THINK ABOUT

1. What lessons did you learn from Eli's dealings with his sons? Do you see your accountability before God to discipline your children?

2. What do you learn from Samuel, Saul, and David's lives regarding seeking God, listening to him, and obeying him? Are there consequences when you don't?

3. Did you notice how much time has elapsed since David was anointed to be king? Still, as 1 Samuel comes to a close, David is not king over Israel. Think about all that transpired since Samuel anointed David. What can you learn from this about God's promises, his purpose, and his timing? Are you waiting patiently on God for the fulfillment of his promise to you?

4. Review the "Lessons for Life" you observed and the insights you recorded about God in the margins of 1 Samuel. Make these a matter of prayer.

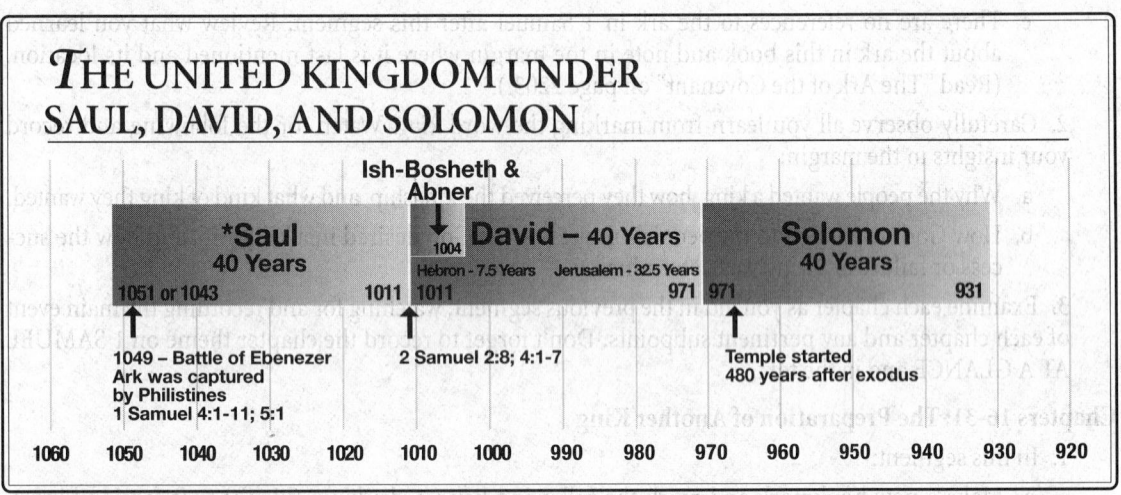

THE UNITED KINGDOM UNDER SAUL, DAVID, AND SOLOMON

First Samuel 13:1 says that Saul was king for thirty-two years.
Acts 13:21 says that Saul was king for forty years.
In Hebrew, numbers from 1-19 are singular and numbers 20 and above are plural.
In this case, the number is plural, so we know it is 20+ years.

In Hebrew, the numbers are missing in 1 Samuel 13:1. Any number given is supplied or guessed.
The first word of 1 Samuel 13:2 is a connector word. It can be used in ten different ways. "And" would be a good translation.
In any case, that connector word tells us Saul was in his thirty-second year when what follows happened.

Chapter 1 Theme

1 There was a certain man from Ramathaim, a Zuphite[a] from the hill country[a] of Ephraim, whose name was Elkanah[b] son of Jeroham, the son of Elihu, the son of Tohu, the son of Zuph, an Ephraimite. ²He had two wives;[c] one was called Hannah and the other Peninnah. Peninnah had children, but Hannah had none. ³Year after year[d] this man went up from his town to worship[e] and sacrifice to the LORD Almighty at Shiloh,[f] where Hophni and Phinehas, the two sons of Eli, were priests of the LORD. ⁴Whenever the day came for Elkanah to sacrifice,[g] he would give portions of the meat to his wife Peninnah and to all her sons and daughters. ⁵But to Hannah he gave a double portion because he loved her,

1:1
a Jos 17:17-18
b 1Ch 6:27,34

1:2
c Dt 21:15-17;
Lk 2:36

1:3
d ver 21;
Ex 23:14; 34:23;
Lk 2:41
e Dt 12:5-7
f Jos 18:1

1:4
g Dt 12:17-18

a 1 Or from Ramathaim Zuphim

1:5
a Ge 16:1; 30:2

1:6
b Job 24:21

1:8
c Ru 4:15

1:9
d 1Sa 3:3

1:10
e Job 7:11

1:11
f Ge 8:1;
28:20; 29:32
g Nu 6:1-21;
Jdg 13:5

1:15
h Ps 42:4; 62:8;
La 2:19

1:17
i Jdg 18:6;
1Sa 25:35;
2Ki 5:19;
Mk 5:34
j Ps 20:3-5

1:18
k Ru 2:13
l Ecc 9:7;
Ro 15:13

1:19
m Ge 4:1;
30:22

1:20
n Ge 41:51-52;
Ex 2:10,22;
Mt 1:21

1:21
o ver 3
p Dt 12:11

1:22
q ver 11,28;
Lk 2:22

1:23
r ver 17;
Nu 30:7

and the LORD had closed her womb.*a* **6**And because the LORD had closed her womb, her rival kept provoking her in order to irritate her.*b* **7**This went on year after year. Whenever Hannah went up to the house of the LORD, her rival provoked her till she wept and would not eat. **8**Elkanah her husband would say to her, "Hannah, why are you weeping? Why don't you eat? Why are you down-hearted? Don't I mean more to you than ten sons?*c*"

9Once when they had finished eating and drinking in Shiloh, Hannah stood up. Now Eli the priest was sitting on a chair by the doorpost of the LORD's temple.*ad* **10**In bitterness of soul*e* Hannah wept much and prayed to the LORD. **11**And she made a vow, saying, "O LORD Almighty, if you will only look upon your servant's misery and remember*f* me, and not forget your servant but give her a son, then I will give him to the LORD for all the days of his life, and no razor*g* will ever be used on his head."

12As she kept on praying to the LORD, Eli observed her mouth. **13**Hannah was praying in her heart, and her lips were moving but her voice was not heard. Eli thought she was drunk **14**and said to her, "How long will you keep on getting drunk? Get rid of your wine."

15"Not so, my lord," Hannah replied, "I am a woman who is deeply troubled. I have not been drinking wine or beer; I was pouring*h* out my soul to the LORD. **16**Do not take your servant for a wicked woman; I have been praying here out of my great anguish and grief."

17Eli answered, "Go in peace,*i* and may the God of Israel grant you what you have asked of him.*j*"

18She said, "May your servant find favor in your eyes.*k*" Then she went her way and ate something, and her face was no longer downcast.*l*

19Early the next morning they arose and worshiped before the LORD and then went back to their home at Ramah. Elkanah lay with Hannah his wife, and the LORD remembered*m* her. **20**So in the course of time Hannah conceived and gave birth to a son. She named*n* him Samuel,*b* saying, "Because I asked the LORD for him."

21When the man Elkanah went up with all his family to offer the annual*o* sacrifice to the LORD and to fulfill his vow,*p* **22**Hannah did not go. She said to her husband, "After the boy is weaned, I will take him and present*q* him before the LORD, and he will live there always."

23"Do what seems best to you," Elkanah her husband told her. "Stay here until you have weaned him; only may the LORD make good*r* his*c* word." So the woman stayed at home and nursed her son until she had weaned him.

INSIGHT

A *Nazirite* (which means "consecration, devotion, and separation") was someone who was bound by a vow of consecration to God's service for either a specific period of time or for life. A Nazirite's devotion to God was evidenced outwardly by not cutting the hair, abstaining from wine and alcoholic drinks, and avoiding contact with the dead. Violation of these brought defilement and need of purification.

a 9 That is, tabernacle   *b* 20 *Samuel* sounds like the Hebrew for *heard of God.*   *c* 23 Masoretic Text; Dead Sea Scrolls, Septuagint and Syriac *your*

445

²⁴After he was weaned, she took the boy with her, young as he was, along with a three-year-old bull,^{aa} an ephah^b of flour and a skin of wine, and brought him to the house of the LORD at Shiloh. ²⁵When they had slaughtered the bull, they brought the boy to Eli, ²⁶and she said to him, "As surely as you live, my lord, I am the woman who stood here beside you praying to the LORD. ²⁷I prayed^b for this child, and the LORD has granted me what I asked of him. ²⁸So now I give him to the LORD. For his whole life^c he will be given over to the LORD." And he worshiped the LORD there.

Chapter 2 Theme

2 Then Hannah prayed and said:^d

"My heart rejoices^e in the LORD;
   in the LORD my horn^{cf} is lifted high.
My mouth boasts over my enemies,
   for I delight in your deliverance.

²"There is no one holy^{dg} like the LORD;
   there is no one besides you;
   there is no Rock^h like our God.

³"Do not keep talking so proudly
   or let your mouth speak such arrogance,ⁱ
for the LORD is a God who knows,
   and by him deeds^j are weighed.^k

⁴"The bows of the warriors are broken,^l
   but those who stumbled are armed with strength.
⁵Those who were full hire themselves out for food,
   but those who were hungry hunger no more.
She who was barren^m has borne seven children,
   but she who has had many sons pines away.

⁶"The LORD brings death and makes alive;ⁿ
   he brings down to the grave^e and raises up.^o
⁷The LORD sends poverty and wealth;^p
   he humbles and he exalts.^q
⁸He raises^r the poor from the dust
   and lifts the needy from the ash heap;
he seats them with princes
   and has them inherit a throne of honor.^s

"For the foundations^t of the earth are the LORD's;
   upon them he has set the world.

^a24 Dead Sea Scrolls, Septuagint and Syriac; Masoretic Text *with three bulls*   ^b24 That is, probably about 3/5 bushel (about 22 liters)   ^c1 *Horn* here symbolizes strength; also in verse 10.   ^d2 Or *no Holy One*   ^e6 Hebrew *Sheol*

1:24
^aNu 15:8-10;
Dt 12:5; Jos 18:1

1:27
^bver 11-13;
Ps 66:19-20

1:28
^cver 11,22;
Ge 24:26,52

2:1
^dLk 1:46-55
^ePs 9:14; 13:5
^fPs 89:17,24;
92:10; Isa 12:2-3

2:2
^gEx 15:11;
Lev 19:2
^hDt 32:30-31;
2Sa 22:2,32

2:3
ⁱPr 8:13
^j1Sa 16:7;
1Ki 8:39
^kPr 16:2;
24:11-12

2:4
^lPs 37:15

2:5
^mPs 113:9;
Jer 15:9

2:6
ⁿDt 32:39
^oIsa 26:19

2:7
^pDt 8:18
^qJob 5:11;
Ps 75:7

2:8
^rPs 113:7-8
^sJob 36:7
^tJob 38:4

2:9
a Ps 91:12
b Mt 8:12
c Ps 33:16-17

2:10
d Ps 2:9
e Ps 18:13
f Ps 96:13
g Ps 21:1
h Ps 89:24

2:11
i ver 18;
1Sa 3:1

2:12
j Jer 2:8; 9:6

2:13
k Lev 7:29-34

2:17
l Mal 2:7-9

2:18
m ver 11;
1Sa 3:1
n ver 28

2:19
o 1Sa 1:3

2:20
p 1Sa 1:11,
27-28; Lk 2:34

2:21
q Ge 21:1
r ver 26;
Jdg 13:24;
1Sa 3:19;
Lk 2:40

2:22
s Ex 38:8

2:25
t Nu 15:30;
Jos 11:20
u Dt 1:17;
1Sa 3:14;
Heb 10:26

⁹"He will guard the feet*a* of his saints,
but the wicked will be silenced in darkness.*b*

"It is not by strength*c* that one prevails;
10 those who oppose the LORD will be shattered.*d*
He will thunder*e* against them from heaven;
the LORD will judge*f* the ends of the earth.

"He will give strength*g* to his king
and exalt the horn*h* of his anointed."

¹¹Then Elkanah went home to Ramah, but the boy ministered*i* before the LORD under Eli the priest.

¹²Eli's sons were wicked men; they had no regard*j* for the LORD. ¹³Now it was the practice of the priests with the people that whenever anyone offered a sacrifice and while the meat*k* was being boiled, the servant of the priest would come with a three-pronged fork in his hand. ¹⁴He would plunge it into the pan or kettle or caldron or pot, and the priest would take for himself whatever the fork brought up. This is how they treated all the Israelites who came to Shiloh. ¹⁵But even before the fat was burned, the servant of the priest would come and say to the man who was sacrificing, "Give the priest some meat to roast; he won't accept boiled meat from you, but only raw."

¹⁶If the man said to him, "Let the fat be burned up first, and then take whatever you want," the servant would then answer, "No, hand it over now; if you don't, I'll take it by force."

¹⁷This sin of the young men was very great in the LORD's sight, for they*a* were treating the LORD's offering with contempt.*l*

¹⁸But Samuel was ministering*m* before the LORD—a boy wearing a linen ephod.*n* ¹⁹Each year his mother made him a little robe and took it to him when she went up with her husband to offer the annual*o* sacrifice. ²⁰Eli would bless Elkanah and his wife, saying, "May the LORD give you children by this woman to take the place of the one she prayed*p* for and gave to the LORD." Then they would go home. ²¹And the LORD was gracious to Hannah;*q* she conceived and gave birth to three sons and two daughters. Meanwhile, the boy Samuel grew*r* up in the presence of the LORD.

²²Now Eli, who was very old, heard about everything his sons were doing to all Israel and how they slept with the women*s* who served at the entrance to the Tent of Meeting. ²³So he said to them, "Why do you do such things? I hear from all the people about these wicked deeds of yours. ²⁴No, my sons; it is not a good report that I hear spreading among the LORD's people. ²⁵If a man sins against another man, God*b* may mediate for him; but if a man sins against the LORD, who will*t* intercede*u* for him?" His sons, however,

INSIGHT

The ***ephod*** was used to seek guidance from God. Described in Exodus 28, it was a linen garment worn by the priest and also by David when he was king (2 Samuel 6:14). The ephod was fastened on each shoulder by onyx clasps which had the names of six tribes engraved on one clasp and six tribes engraved on the other. The ***breastpiece***, which was fastened to the ephod, had a linen pouch which held the ***Urim*** and ***Thummim***, which may have been used as sacred lots to reveal God's will (1 Samuel 28:6).

a 17 Or *men*   *b* 25 Or *the judges*

did not listen to their father's rebuke, for it was the LORD's will to put them to death.

²⁶And the boy Samuel continued to grow[a] in stature and in favor with the LORD and with men.

²⁷Now a man of God[b] came to Eli and said to him, "This is what the LORD says: 'Did I not clearly reveal myself to your father's house when they were in Egypt under Pharaoh? ²⁸I chose[c] your father out of all the tribes of Israel to be my priest, to go up to my altar, to burn incense, and to wear an ephod[d] in my presence. I also gave your father's house all the offerings made with fire by the Israelites. ²⁹Why do you[a] scorn my sacrifice and offering[e] that I prescribed for my dwelling?[f] Why do you honor your sons more than me by fattening yourselves on the choice parts of every offering made by my people Israel?'

³⁰"Therefore the LORD, the God of Israel, declares: 'I promised that your house and your father's house would minister before me forever.[g]' But now the LORD declares: 'Far be it from me! Those who honor me I will honor,[h] but those who despise[i] me will be disdained. ³¹The time is coming when I will cut short your strength and the strength of your father's house, so that there will not be an old man in your family line[j] ³²and you will see distress in my dwelling. Although good will be done to Israel, in your family line there will never be an old man.[k] ³³Every one of you that I do not cut off from my altar will be spared only to blind your eyes with tears and to grieve your heart, and all your descendants will die in the prime of life.

³⁴"'And what happens to your two sons, Hophni and Phinehas, will be a sign to you—they will both die[l] on the same day.[m] ³⁵I will raise up for myself a faithful priest,[n] who will do according to what is in my heart and mind. I will firmly establish his house, and he will minister before my anointed[o] one always. ³⁶Then everyone left in your family line will come and bow down before him for a piece of silver and a crust of bread and plead, "Appoint me to some priestly office so I can have food to eat.[p] "'"

Chapter 3 Theme

3 The boy Samuel ministered[q] before the LORD under Eli. In those days the word of the LORD was rare;[r] there were not many visions.[s]

²One night Eli, whose eyes[t] were becoming so weak that he could barely see, was lying down in his usual place. ³The lamp[u] of God had not yet gone out, and Samuel was lying down in the temple[b] of the LORD, where the ark of God was. ⁴Then the LORD called Samuel.

Samuel answered, "Here I am.[v]" ⁵And he ran to Eli and said, "Here I am; you called me."

a 29 The Hebrew is plural.   b 3 That is, tabernacle

2:26
[a] ver 21;
Lk 2:52

2:27
[b] Ex 4:14-16;
1Ki 13:1

2:28
[c] Ex 28:1
[d] Lev 8:7-8

2:29
[e] ver 12-17
[f] Dt 12:5;
Mt 10:37

2:30
[g] Ex 29:9
[h] Ps 50:23;
91:15
[i] Mal 2:9

2:31
[j] 1Sa 4:11-18;
22:16-20

2:32
[k] 1Ki 2:26-27;
Zec 8:4

2:34
[l] 1Sa 4:11
[m] 1Ki 13:3

2:35
[n] 1Sa 12:3;
1Ki 2:35
[o] 1Sa 16:13;
2Sa 7:11,27;
1Ki 11:38

2:36
[p] 1Ki 2:27

3:1
[q] 1Sa 2:11
[r] Ps 74:9
[s] Am 8:11

3:2
[t] 1Sa 4:15

3:3
[u] Lev 24:1-4

3:4
[v] Isa 6:8

3:7
a Ac 19:12

3:11
b 2Ki 21:12;
Jer 19:3

3:12
c 1Sa 2:27-36

3:13
d 1Sa 2:12,17,
22,29-31

3:14
e Lev 15:30-31;
1Sa 2:25;
Isa 22:14

3:17
f Ru 1:17;
2Sa 3:35

3:18
g Job 2:10;
Isa 39:8

3:19
h Ge 21:22; 39:2
i 1Sa 2:21
j 1Sa 9:6

3:20
k Jdg 20:1

3:21
l ver 10

4:1
m 1Sa 7:12
n Jos 12:18;
1Sa 29:1

But Eli said, "I did not call; go back and lie down." So he went and lay down.

⁶Again the LORD called, "Samuel!" And Samuel got up and went to Eli and said, "Here I am; you called me."

"My son," Eli said, "I did not call; go back and lie down."

⁷Now Samuel did not yet know the LORD: The word of the LORD had not yet been revealed*a* to him.

⁸The LORD called Samuel a third time, and Samuel got up and went to Eli and said, "Here I am; you called me."

Then Eli realized that the LORD was calling the boy. ⁹So Eli told Samuel, "Go and lie down, and if he calls you, say, 'Speak, LORD, for your servant is listening.'" So Samuel went and lay down in his place.

¹⁰The LORD came and stood there, calling as at the other times, "Samuel! Samuel!"

Then Samuel said, "Speak, for your servant is listening."

¹¹And the LORD said to Samuel: "See, I am about to do something in Israel that will make the ears of everyone who hears of it tingle.*b* ¹²At that time I will carry out against Eli everything*c* I spoke against his family—from beginning to end. ¹³For I told him that I would judge his family forever because of the sin he knew about; his sons made themselves contemptible,*a* and he failed to restrain*d* them. ¹⁴Therefore, I swore to the house of Eli, 'The guilt of Eli's house will never be atoned*e* for by sacrifice or offering.'"

¹⁵Samuel lay down until morning and then opened the doors of the house of the LORD. He was afraid to tell Eli the vision, ¹⁶but Eli called him and said, "Samuel, my son."

Samuel answered, "Here I am."

¹⁷"What was it he said to you?" Eli asked. "Do not hide it from me. May God deal with you, be it ever so severely,*f* if you hide from me anything he told you." ¹⁸So Samuel told him everything, hiding nothing from him. Then Eli said, "He is the LORD; let him do what is good in his eyes."*g*

¹⁹The LORD was with*h* Samuel as he grew*i* up, and he let none*j* of his words fall to the ground. ²⁰And all Israel from Dan to Beersheba*k* recognized that Samuel was attested as a prophet of the LORD. ²¹The LORD continued to appear at Shiloh, and there he revealed*l* himself to Samuel through his word.

Chapter 4 Theme

4 And Samuel's word came to all Israel.

Now the Israelites went out to fight against the Philistines. The Israelites camped at Ebenezer,*m* and the Philistines at Aphek.*n* ²The Philistines deployed their forces to meet Israel, and as the

a 13 Masoretic Text; an ancient Hebrew scribal tradition and Septuagint *sons blasphemed God* battle spread, Israel was defeated by the Philistines, who killed about four thousand of them on the battlefield. ³When the soldiers returned to camp, the elders of Israel asked, "Why*a* did the LORD bring defeat upon us today before the Philistines? Let us bring the ark*b* of the LORD's covenant from Shiloh, so that it*a* may go with us and save us from the hand of our enemies."

⁴So the people sent men to Shiloh, and they brought back the ark of the covenant of the LORD Almighty, who is enthroned between the cherubim.*c* And Eli's two sons, Hophni and Phinehas, were there with the ark of the covenant of God.

⁵When the ark of the LORD's covenant came into the camp, all Israel raised such a great shout*d* that the ground shook. ⁶Hearing the uproar, the Philistines asked, "What's all this shouting in the Hebrew camp?"

When they learned that the ark of the LORD had come into the camp, ⁷the Philistines were afraid.*e* "A god has come into the camp," they said. "We're in trouble! Nothing like this has happened before. ⁸Woe to us! Who will deliver us from the hand of these mighty gods? They are the gods who struck the Egyptians with all kinds of plagues in the desert. ⁹Be strong, Philistines! Be men, or you will be subject to the Hebrews, as they*f* have been to you. Be men, and fight!"

¹⁰So the Philistines fought, and the Israelites were defeated*g* and every man fled to his tent. The slaughter was very great; Israel lost thirty thousand foot soldiers. ¹¹The ark of God was captured, and Eli's two sons, Hophni and Phinehas, died.*h*

¹²That same day a Benjamite ran from the battle line and went to Shiloh, his clothes torn and dust*i* on his head. ¹³When he arrived, there was Eli*j* sitting on his chair by the side of the road, watching, because his heart feared for the ark of God. When the man entered the town and told what had happened, the whole town sent up a cry.

¹⁴Eli heard the outcry and asked, "What is the meaning of this uproar?"

The man hurried over to Eli, ¹⁵who was ninety-eight years old and whose eyes*k* were set so that he could not see. ¹⁶He told Eli, "I have just come from the battle line; I fled from it this very day."

Eli asked, "What happened, my son?"

¹⁷The man who brought the news replied, "Israel fled before the Philistines, and the army has suffered heavy losses. Also your two sons, Hophni and Phinehas, are dead, and the ark of God has been captured."

¹⁸When he mentioned the ark of God, Eli fell backward off his chair by the side of the gate. His neck was broken and he died, for he was an old man and heavy. He had led*b l* Israel forty years.

a 3 Or he   b 18 Traditionally judged

4:3
a Jos 7:7;
b Nu 10:35;
Jos 6:7

4:4
c Ex 25:22;
2Sa 6:2

4:5
d Jos 6:5,10

4:7
e Ex 15:14

4:9
f Jdg 13:1;
1Co 16:13

4:10
g ver 2;
Dt 28:25;
2Sa 18:17;
2Ki 14:12

4:11
h 1Sa 2:34;
Ps 78:61,64

4:12
i Jos 7:6;
2Sa 1:2;
15:32;
Ne 9:1;
Job 2:12

4:13
j ver 18;
1Sa 1:9

4:15
k 1Sa 3:2

4:18
l ver 13

Dagon, the chief deity of the Philistines, dates back to Mesopotamia and the third millennium B.C. According to ancient literature Dagon was the father of Baal. (See Judges 16:23; 1 Chronicles 10:10.)

¹⁹His daughter-in-law, the wife of Phinehas, was pregnant and near the time of delivery. When she heard the news that the ark of God had been captured and that her father-in-law and her husband were dead, she went into labor and gave birth, but was overcome by her labor pains. ²⁰As she was dying, the women attending her said, "Don't despair; you have given birth to a son." But she did not respond or pay any attention.

²¹She named the boy Ichabod,ᵃᵃ saying, "The gl8oryᵇ has departed from Israel"—because of the capture of the ark of God and the deaths of her father-in-law and her husband. ²²She said, "The glory has departed from Israel, for the ark of God has been captured."

Chapter 5 Theme

5 After the Philistines had captured the ark of God, they took it from Ebenezerᶜ to Ashdod.ᵈ ²Then they carried the ark into Dagon's temple and set it beside Dagon.ᵉ ³When the people of Ashdod rose early the next day, there was Dagon, fallenᶠ on his face on the ground before the ark of the LORD! They took Dagon and put him back in his place. ⁴But the following morning when they rose, there was Dagon, fallen on his face on the ground before the ark of the LORD! His head and hands had been brokenᵍ off and were lying on the threshold; only his body remained. ⁵That is why to this day neither the priests of Dagon nor any others who enter Dagon's temple at Ashdod step on the threshold.ʰ

⁶The LORD's handⁱ was heavy upon the people of Ashdod and its vicinity; he brought devastationʲ upon them and afflicted them with tumors.ᵇᵏ ⁷When the men of Ashdod saw what was happening, they said, "The ark of the god of Israel must not stay here with us, because his hand is heavy upon us and upon Dagon our god." ⁸So they called together all the rulers of the Philistines and asked them, "What shall we do with the ark of the god of Israel?"

Mediterranean (Great) Sea

The Ark is captured

The Ark was brought into the temple of Dagon

The Ark was kept at Kiriath Jearim until the time of David

Shechem · Aphek · Ebenezer · Shiloh · Bethel · Mizpah · Gilgal · Kiriath Jearim · Jerusalem · Ekron · Ashdod · Gath · Beth Shemesh · Ashkelon · Gaza · Jordan River · Dead Sea

The Wanderings of the Ark
(see page 2703)

ᵃ21 Ichabod means no glory. *ᵇ6 Hebrew; Septuagint and Vulgate tumors. And rats appeared in their land, and death and destruction were throughout the city*

Side references

4:21 ᵃGe 35:18 ᵇPs 26:8; Jer 2:11

5:1 ᶜ1Sa 4:1; 7:12 ᵈJos 13:3

5:2 ᵉJdg 16:23

5:3 ᶠIsa 19:1; 46:7

5:4 ᵍEze 6:6; Mic 1:7

5:5 ʰZep 1:9

5:6 ⁱver 7; Ex 9:3; Ps 32:4; Ac 13:11 ʲver 11; Ps 78:66 ᵏDt 28:27; 1Sa 6:5

451

They answered, "Have the ark of the god of Israel moved to Gath.ᵃ" So they moved the ark of the God of Israel.

⁹But after they had moved it, the LORD's hand was against that city, throwing it into a great panic.ᵇ He afflicted the people of the city, both young and old, with an outbreak of tumors.ᵃ ¹⁰So they sent the ark of God to Ekron.

As the ark of God was entering Ekron, the people of Ekron cried out, "They have brought the ark of the god of Israel around to us to kill us and our people." ¹¹So they called together all the rulersᶜ of the Philistines and said, "Send the ark of the god of Israel away; let it go back to its own place, or itᵇ will kill us and our people." For death had filled the city with panic; God's hand was very heavy upon it. ¹²Those who did not die were afflicted with tumors, and the outcry of the city went up to heaven.

Chapter 6 Theme _____

6 When the ark of the LORD had been in Philistine territory seven months, ²the Philistines called for the priests and the divinersᵈ and said, "What shall we do with the ark of the LORD? Tell us how we should send it back to its place."

³They answered, "If you return the ark of the god of Israel, do not send it away empty,ᵉ but by all means send a guilt offeringᶠ to him. Then you will be healed, and you will know why his handᵍ has not been lifted from you."

⁴The Philistines asked, "What guilt offering should we send to him?"

They replied, "Five gold tumors and five gold rats, according to the numberʰ of the Philistine rulers, because the same plague has struck both you and your rulers. ⁵Make models of the tumorsⁱ and of the rats that are destroying the country, and pay honorʲ to Israel's god. Perhaps he will lift his hand from you and your gods and your land. ⁶Why do you hardenᵏ your hearts as the Egyptians and Pharaoh did? When heᶜ treated them harshly, did theyˡ not send the Israelites out so they could go on their way?

⁷"Now then, get a new cartᵐ ready, with two cows that have calved and have never been yoked.ⁿ Hitch the cows to the cart, but take their calves away and pen them up. ⁸Take the ark of the LORD and put it on the cart, and in a chest beside it put the gold objects you are sending back to him as a guilt offering. Send it on its way, ⁹but keep watching it. If it goes up to its own territory, toward Beth Shemesh,ᵒ then the LORD has brought this great disaster on us. But if it does not, then we will know that it was not his hand that struck us and that it happened to us by chance."

ᵃ9 Or *with tumors in the groin* (see Septuagint)   ᵇ11 Or *he*   ᶜ6 That is, God

5:8
ᵃver 11

5:9
ᵇver 6,11;
Dt 2:15;
1Sa 7:13;
Ps 78:66

5:11
ᶜver 6,8-9

6:2
ᵈGe 41:8;
Ex 7:11;
Isa 2:6

6:3
ᵉEx 23:15;
Dt 16:16
ᶠLev 5:15
ᵍver 9

6:4
ʰver 17-18;
Jos 13:3;
Jdg 3:3

6:5
ⁱ1Sa 5:6-11
ʲJos 7:19;
Isa 42:12;
Jn 9:24;
Rev 14:7

6:6
ᵏEx 7:13;
8:15; 9:34;
14:17
ˡEx 12:31,33

6:7
ᵐ2Sa 6:3
ⁿNu 19:2

6:9
ᵒver 3;
Jos 15:10;
21:16

6:14
a 2Sa 24:22;
1Ki 19:21

6:15
b Jos 3:3

6:17
c ver 4

6:19
d 2Sa 6:7
e Ex 19:21;
Nu 4:5,15,20

6:20
f 2Sa 6:9;
Mal 3:2;
Rev 6:17
g Lev 11:45

6:21
h Jos 9:17;
15:9,60;
1Ch 13:5-6

7:1
i 2Sa 6:3

¹⁰So they did this. They took two such cows and hitched them to the cart and penned up their calves. ¹¹They placed the ark of the Lord on the cart and along with it the chest containing the gold rats and the models of the tumors. ¹²Then the cows went straight up toward Beth Shemesh, keeping on the road and lowing all the way; they did not turn to the right or to the left. The rulers of the Philistines followed them as far as the border of Beth Shemesh.

¹³Now the people of Beth Shemesh were harvesting their wheat in the valley, and when they looked up and saw the ark, they rejoiced at the sight. ¹⁴The cart came to the field of Joshua of Beth Shemesh, and there it stopped beside a large rock. The people chopped up the wood of the cart and sacrificed the cows as a burnt offering*ᵃ* to the Lord. ¹⁵The Levites*ᵇ* took down the ark of the Lord, together with the chest containing the gold objects, and placed them on the large rock. On that day the people of Beth Shemesh offered burnt offerings and made sacrifices to the Lord. ¹⁶The five rulers of the Philistines saw all this and then returned that same day to Ekron.

¹⁷These are the gold tumors the Philistines sent as a guilt offering to the Lord—one each*ᶜ* for Ashdod, Gaza, Ashkelon, Gath and Ekron. ¹⁸And the number of the gold rats was according to the number of Philistine towns belonging to the five rulers—the fortified towns with their country villages. The large rock, on which*ᵃ* they set the ark of the Lord, is a witness to this day in the field of Joshua of Beth Shemesh.

¹⁹But God struck down*ᵈ* some of the men of Beth Shemesh, putting seventy*ᵇ* of them to death because they had looked*ᵉ* into the ark of the Lord. The people mourned because of the heavy blow the Lord had dealt them, ²⁰and the men of Beth Shemesh asked, "Who can stand*ᶠ* in the presence of the Lord, this holy*ᵍ* God? To whom will the ark go up from here?"

²¹Then they sent messengers to the people of Kiriath Jearim,*ʰ* saying, "The Philistines have returned the ark of the Lord. Come down and take it up to your place."

Chapter 7 Theme

7 So the men of Kiriath Jearim came and took up the ark of the Lord. They took it to Abinadab's*ⁱ* house on the hill and consecrated Eleazar his son to guard the ark of the Lord.

²It was a long time, twenty years in all, that the ark remained at Kiriath Jearim, and all the people of Israel mourned and sought after the Lord. ³And Samuel said to the whole house of Israel, "If

a 18 A few Hebrew manuscripts (see also Septuagint); most Hebrew manuscripts *villages as far as Greater Abel, where*   b 19 A few Hebrew manuscripts; most Hebrew manuscripts and Septuagint *50,070* you are returning[a] to the LORD with all your hearts, then rid[b] yourselves of the foreign gods and the Ashtoreths[c] and commit[d] yourselves to the LORD and serve him only,[e] and he will deliver you out of the hand of the Philistines." [4]So the Israelites put away their Baals and Ashtoreths, and served the LORD only.

[5]Then Samuel said, "Assemble all Israel at Mizpah[f] and I will intercede with the LORD for you." [6]When they had assembled at Mizpah, they drew water and poured[g] it out before the LORD. On that day they fasted and there they confessed, "We have sinned against the LORD." And Samuel was leader[a][h] of Israel at Mizpah.

[7]When the Philistines heard that Israel had assembled at Mizpah, the rulers of the Philistines came up to attack them. And when the Israelites heard of it, they were afraid[i] because of the Philistines. [8]They said to Samuel, "Do not stop crying[j] out to the LORD our God for us, that he may rescue us from the hand of the Philistines." [9]Then Samuel[k] took a suckling lamb and offered it up as a whole burnt offering to the LORD. He cried out to the LORD on Israel's behalf, and the LORD answered him.[l]

[10]While Samuel was sacrificing the burnt offering, the Philistines drew near to engage Israel in battle. But that day the LORD thundered[m] with loud thunder against the Philistines and threw them into such a panic[n] that they were routed before the Israelites. [11]The men of Israel rushed out of Mizpah and pursued the Philistines, slaughtering them along the way to a point below Beth Car.

[12]Then Samuel took a stone[o] and set it up between Mizpah and Shen. He named it Ebenezer,[b] saying, "Thus far has the LORD helped us." [13]So the Philistines were subdued[p] and did not invade Israelite territory again.

Throughout Samuel's lifetime, the hand of the LORD was against the Philistines. [14]The towns from Ekron to Gath that the Philistines had captured from Israel were restored to her, and Israel delivered the neighboring territory from the power of the Philistines. And there was peace between Israel and the Amorites.

[15]Samuel[q] continued as judge over Israel all the days of his life. [16]From year to year he went on a circuit from Bethel to Gilgal to Mizpah, judging Israel in all those places. [17]But he always went back to Ramah,[r] where his home was, and there he also judged Israel. And he built an altar[s] there to the LORD.

Chapter 8 Theme

8 When Samuel grew old, he appointed[t] his sons as judges for Israel. [2]The name of his firstborn was Joel and the name of his second was Abijah,[u] and they served at Beersheba.[u] [3]But his

---

a6 Traditionally *judge*   b12 *Ebenezer* means *stone of help.*

### Cross references (margin)

7:3
[a]Dt 30:10;
Isa 55:7;
Hos 6:1
[b]Ge 35:2;
Jos 24:14
[c]Jdg 2:12-13;
1Sa 31:10
[d]Joel 2:12
[e]Dt 6:13;
Mt 4:10;
Lk 4:8

7:5
[f]Jdg 20:1

7:6
[g]Ps 62:8;
La 2:19
[h]Jdg 10:10;
Ne 9:1;
Ps 106:6

7:7
[i]1Sa 17:11

7:8
[j]1Sa 12:19,23;
Isa 37:4;
Jer 15:1

7:9
[k]Ps 99:6
[l]Jer 15:1

7:10
[m]1Sa 2:10;
2Sa 22:14-15
[n]Jos 10:10

7:12
[o]Ge 35:14;
Jos 4:9

7:13
[p]Jdg 13:1,5;
1Sa 13:5

7:15
[q]ver 6;
1Sa 12:11

7:17
[r]1Sa 1:19; 8:4
[s]Jdg 21:4

8:1
[t]Dt 16:18-19

8:2
[u]Ge 22:19;
1Ki 19:3;
Am 5:4-5

8:3
a Ex 23:8;
Dt 16:19;
Ps 15:5

8:4
b 1Sa 7:17

8:5
c Dt 17:14-20

8:6
d 1Sa 15:11

8:7
e Ex 16:8;
1Sa 10:19

8:9
f ver 11-18;
1Sa 10:25

8:11
g 1Sa 10:25;
14:52
h Dt 17:16;
2Sa 15:1

8:12
i 1Sa 22:7

8:14
j Eze 46:18
k 1Ki 21:7,15

8:18
l Pr 1:28;
Isa 1:15;
Mic 3:4

8:19
m Isa 66:4;
Jer 44:16

8:20
n ver 5

8:21
o Jdg 11:11

8:22
p ver 7

9:1
q 1Sa 14:51;
1Ch 8:33; 9:39

sons did not walk in his ways. They turned aside after dishonest gain and accepted bribes*a* and perverted justice.

4So all the elders of Israel gathered together and came to Samuel at Ramah.*b* 5They said to him, "You are old, and your sons do not walk in your ways; now appoint a king*c* to lead*a* us, such as all the other nations have."

6But when they said, "Give us a king to lead us," this displeased*d* Samuel; so he prayed to the LORD. 7And the LORD told him: "Listen to all that the people are saying to you; it is not you they have rejected, but they have rejected me as their king.*e* 8As they have done from the day I brought them up out of Egypt until this day, forsaking me and serving other gods, so they are doing to you. 9Now listen to them; but warn them solemnly and let them know*f* what the king who will reign over them will do."

10Samuel told all the words of the LORD to the people who were asking him for a king. 11He said, "This is what the king who will reign over you will do: He will take*g* your sons and make them serve with his chariots and horses, and they will run in front of his chariots.*h* 12Some he will assign to be commanders*i* of thousands and commanders of fifties, and others to plow his ground and reap his harvest, and still others to make weapons of war and equipment for his chariots. 13He will take your daughters to be perfumers and cooks and bakers. 14He will take the best of your*j* fields and vineyards*k* and olive groves and give them to his attendants. 15He will take a tenth of your grain and of your vintage and give it to his officials and attendants. 16Your menservants and maidservants and the best of your cattle*b* and donkeys he will take for his own use. 17He will take a tenth of your flocks, and you yourselves will become his slaves. 18When that day comes, you will cry out for relief from the king you have chosen, and the LORD will not answer*l* you in that day."

19But the people refused*m* to listen to Samuel. "No!" they said. "We want a king over us. 20Then we will be like all the other nations,*n* with a king to lead us and to go out before us and fight our battles."

21When Samuel heard all that the people said, he repeated*o* it before the LORD. 22The LORD answered, "Listen*p* to them and give them a king."

Then Samuel said to the men of Israel, "Everyone go back to his town."

Chapter 9 Theme

9 There was a Benjamite, a man of standing, whose name was Kish*q* son of Abiel, the son of Zeror, the son of Becorath, the son of Aphiah of Benjamin. 2He had a son named Saul, an impressive

a 5 Traditionally *judge*; also in verses 6 and 20   *b* 16 Septuagint; Hebrew *young men* young man without equal[a] among the Israelites—a head taller[b] than any of the others.

[3]Now the donkeys belonging to Saul's father Kish were lost, and Kish said to his son Saul, "Take one of the servants with you and go and look for the donkeys." [4]So he passed through the hill[c] country of Ephraim and through the area around Shalisha,[d] but they did not find them. They went on into the district of Shaalim, but the donkeys were not there. Then he passed through the territory of Benjamin, but they did not find them.

[5]When they reached the district of Zuph,[e] Saul said to the servant who was with him, "Come, let's go back, or my father will stop thinking about the donkeys and start worrying[f] about us."

[6]But the servant replied, "Look, in this town there is a man of God;[g] he is highly respected, and everything[h] he says comes true. Let's go there now. Perhaps he will tell us what way to take."

[7]Saul said to his servant, "If we go, what can we give the man? The food in our sacks is gone. We have no gift[i] to take to the man of God. What do we have?"

[8]The servant answered him again. "Look," he said, "I have a quarter of a shekel[a] of silver. I will give it to the man of God so that he will tell us what way to take." [9](Formerly in Israel, if a man went to inquire of God, he would say, "Come, let us go to the seer," because the prophet of today used to be called a seer.)[j]

[10]"Good," Saul said to his servant. "Come, let's go." So they set out for the town where the man of God was.

[11]As they were going up the hill to the town, they met some girls coming out to draw[k] water, and they asked them, "Is the seer here?"

[12]"He is," they answered. "He's ahead of you. Hurry now; he has just come to our town today, for the people have a sacrifice[l] at the high place.[m] [13]As soon as you enter the town, you will find him before he goes up to the high place to eat. The people will not begin eating until he comes, because he must bless the sacrifice; afterward, those who are invited will eat. Go up now; you should find him about this time."

[14]They went up to the town, and as they were entering it, there was Samuel, coming toward them on his way up to the high place.

[15]Now the day before Saul came, the LORD had revealed this to Samuel: [16]"About this time tomorrow I will send you a man from the land of Benjamin. Anoint[n] him leader over my people Israel; he will deliver[o] my people from the hand of the Philistines. I have looked upon my people, for their cry has reached me."

[17]When Samuel caught sight of Saul, the LORD said to him, "This[p] is the man I spoke to you about; he will govern my people."

---

a 8 That is, about 1/10 ounce (about 3 grams)

9:2
a 1Sa 10:24
b 1Sa 10:23

9:4
c Jos 24:33
d 2Ki 4:42

9:5
e 1Sa 1:1
f 1Sa 10:2

9:6
g Dt 33:1;
1Ki 13:1
h 1Sa 3:19

9:7
i 1Ki 14:3;
2Ki 5:5,15; 8:8

9:9
j 2Sa 24:11;
2Ki 17:13;
1Ch 9:22;
26:28; 29:29;
Isa 30:10;
Am 7:12

9:11
k Ge 24:11,13

9:12
l Nu 28:11-15;
1Sa 7:17
m Ge 31:54;
1Sa 10:5;
1Ki 3:2

9:16
n 1Sa 10:1
o Ex 3:7-9

9:17
p 1Sa 16:12

¹⁸Saul approached Samuel in the gateway and asked, "Would you please tell me where the seer's house is?"

¹⁹"I am the seer," Samuel replied. "Go up ahead of me to the high place, for today you are to eat with me, and in the morning I will let you go and will tell you all that is in your heart. ²⁰As for the donkeys*a* you lost three days ago, do not worry about them; they have been found. And to whom is all the desire*b* of Israel turned, if not to you and all your father's family?"

²¹Saul answered, "But am I not a Benjamite, from the smallest tribe*c* of Israel, and is not my clan the least of all the clans of the tribe of Benjamin?*d* Why do you say such a thing to me?"

²²Then Samuel brought Saul and his servant into the hall and seated them at the head of those who were invited—about thirty in number. ²³Samuel said to the cook, "Bring the piece of meat I gave you, the one I told you to lay aside."

²⁴So the cook took up the leg*e* with what was on it and set it in front of Saul. Samuel said, "Here is what has been kept for you. Eat, because it was set aside for you for this occasion, from the time I said, 'I have invited guests.'" And Saul dined with Samuel that day.

²⁵After they came down from the high place to the town, Samuel talked with Saul on the roof*f* of his house. ²⁶They rose about daybreak and Samuel called to Saul on the roof, "Get ready, and I will send you on your way." When Saul got ready, he and Samuel went outside together. ²⁷As they were going down to the edge of the town, Samuel said to Saul, "Tell the servant to go on ahead of us"—and the servant did so—"but you stay here awhile, so that I may give you a message from God."

Chapter 10 Theme

10:1
g 1Sa 16:13;
2Ki 9:1,3,6
h Ps 2:12
i Dt 32:9;
Ps 78:62,71

10 Then Samuel took a flask*g* of oil and poured it on Saul's head and kissed him, saying, "Has not the LORD anointed*h* you leader over his inheritance?*a* *i* ²When you leave me today, you will meet two men near Rachel's tomb,*j* at Zelzah on the border of Benjamin. They will say to you, 'The donkeys*k* you set out to look for have been found. And now your father has stopped thinking about them and is worried*l* about you. He is asking, "What shall I do about my son?"'

³"Then you will go on from there until you reach the great tree of Tabor. Three men going up to God at Bethel*m* will meet you there. One will be carrying three young goats, another three loaves of bread, and another a skin of wine. ⁴They will greet you and offer you two loaves of bread, which you will accept from them.

a 1 Hebrew; Septuagint and Vulgate *over his people Israel? You will reign over the LORD's people and save them from the power of their enemies round about. And this will be a sign to you that the LORD has anointed you leader over his inheritance:*

⁵"After that you will go to Gibeah of God, where there is a Philistine outpost.ᵃ As you approach the town, you will meet a procession of prophets coming down from the high placeᵇ with lyres, tambourines, flutes and harpsᶜ being played before them, and they will be prophesying.ᵈ ⁶The Spiritᵉ of the LORD will come upon you in power, and you will prophesy with them; and you will be changed into a different person. ⁷Once these signs are fulfilled, do whateverᶠ your hand finds to do, for God is withᵍ you.

⁸"Go down ahead of me to Gilgal.ʰ I will surely come down to you to sacrifice burnt offerings and fellowship offerings,ᵃ but you must wait seven days until I come to you and tell you what you are to do."

⁹As Saul turned to leave Samuel, God changedⁱ Saul's heart, and all these signs were fulfilled that day. ¹⁰When they arrived at Gibeah, a procession of prophets met him; the Spirit of God came upon him in power, and he joined in their prophesying.ʲ ¹¹When all those who had formerly known him saw him prophesying with the prophets, they asked each other, "What is thisᵏ that has happened to the son of Kish? Is Saul also among the prophets?"ˡ

¹²A man who lived there answered, "And who is their father?" So it became a saying: "Is Saul also among the prophets?" ¹³After Saul stopped prophesying, he went to the high place.

¹⁴Now Saul's uncleᵐ asked him and his servant, "Where have you been?"

"Looking for the donkeys," he said. "But when we saw they were not to be found, we went to Samuel."

¹⁵Saul's uncle said, "Tell me what Samuel said to you."

¹⁶Saul replied, "He assured us that the donkeysⁿ had been found." But he did not tell his uncle what Samuel had said about the kingship.

¹⁷Samuel summoned the people of Israel to the LORD at Mizpahᵒ ¹⁸and said to them, "This is what the LORD, the God of Israel, says: 'I brought Israel up out of Egypt, and I delivered you from the power of Egypt and all the kingdoms that oppressedᵖ you.' ¹⁹But you have now rejected your God, who saves you out of all your calamities and distresses. And you have said, 'No, set a king�q over us.' So now presentʳ yourselves before the LORD by your tribes and clans."

²⁰When Samuel brought all the tribes of Israel near, the tribe of Benjamin was chosen. ²¹Then he brought forward the tribe of Benjamin, clan by clan, and Matri's clan was chosen. Finally Saul son of Kish was chosen. But when they looked for him, he was not to be found. ²²So they inquiredˢ further of the LORD, "Has the man come here yet?"

10:5
ᵃ 1Sa 13:3
ᵇ 1Sa 9:12
ᶜ 2Ki 3:15
ᵈ 1Sa 19:20;
1Co 14:1

10:6
ᵉ ver 10;
Nu 11:25;
1Sa 19:23-24

10:7
ᶠ Ecc 9:10
ᵍ Jos 1:5;
Jdg 6:12;
Heb 13:5

10:8
ʰ 1Sa 11:14-15

10:9
ⁱ ver 6

10:10
ʲ ver 5-6;
1Sa 19:20

10:11
ᵏ Mt 13:54;
Jn 7:15
ˡ 1Sa 19:24

10:14
ᵐ 1Sa 14:50

10:16
ⁿ 1Sa 9:20

10:17
ᵒ Jdg 20:1;
1Sa 7:5

10:18
ᵖ Jdg 6:8-9

10:19
q 1Sa 8:5-7;
12:12
ʳ Jos 7:14;
24:1

10:22
ˢ 1Sa 23:2,4,
9-11

10:23
a 1Sa 9:2

And the LORD said, "Yes, he has hidden himself among the baggage."

²³They ran and brought him out, and as he stood among the people he was a head taller*a* than any of the others. ²⁴Samuel said to all the people, "Do you see the man the LORD has chosen?*b* There is no one like him among all the people."

10:24
b Dt 17:15;
2Sa 21:6
c 1Ki 1:25,34,39

Then the people shouted, "Long live*c* the king!"

²⁵Samuel explained to the people the regulations*d* of the kingship. He wrote them down on a scroll and deposited it before the LORD. Then Samuel dismissed the people, each to his own home.

10:25
d Dt 17:14-20;
1Sa 8:11-18

²⁶Saul also went to his home in Gibeah,*e* accompanied by valiant men whose hearts God had touched. ²⁷But some troublemakers*f* said, "How can this fellow save us?" They despised him and brought him no gifts.*g* But Saul kept silent.

10:26
e 1Sa 11:4

Chapter 11 Theme

10:27
f Dt 13:13
g 1Ki 10:25;
2Ch 17:5

11 Nahash*h* the Ammonite went up and besieged Jabesh Gilead.*i* And all the men of Jabesh said to him, "Make a treaty*j* with us, and we will be subject to you."

²But Nahash the Ammonite replied, "I will make a treaty with you only on the condition that I gouge*k* out the right eye of every one of you and so bring disgrace*l* on all Israel."

11:1
h 1Sa 12:12
i Jdg 21:8
j 1Ki 20:34;
Eze 17:13

³The elders of Jabesh said to him, "Give us seven days so we can send messengers throughout Israel; if no one comes to rescue us, we will surrender to you."

11:2
k Nu 16:14
l 1Sa 17:26

⁴When the messengers came to Gibeah*m* of Saul and reported these terms to the people, they all wept*n* aloud. ⁵Just then Saul was returning from the fields, behind his oxen, and he asked, "What is wrong with the people? Why are they weeping?" Then they repeated to him what the men of Jabesh had said.

11:4
m 1Sa 10:5,26;
15:34
n Jdg 2:4;
1Sa 30:4

Saul's Ascent to Kingship

Saul musters Israelites

Nahash, king of Ammon, besieges Saul

Jabesh Gilead

Bezek

Mahanaim

Saul smites Ammonites

Tirzah

GILEAD

Shechem

Jabbok River

Adam

Ramath Mizpah

Jogbehah

AMMON

Mizpah   Bethel

Gilgal

Gibeon   Gibeah

Rabbah

Beth Shemesh

Jerusalem   Bethlehem

Jordan River

Saul made king

Dead Sea

Israelites
Ammonites

11:6
o Jdg 3:10;
6:34; 13:25;
14:6;
1Sa 10:10;
16:13

⁶When Saul heard their words, the Spirit*o* of God came upon him in power, and he burned with anger. ⁷He took a pair of oxen, cut them into pieces, and sent the pieces by messengers throughout Israel,*p* proclaiming, "This is what will be done to the oxen of anyone*q* who does not follow Saul and Samuel." Then the terror

11:7
p Jdg 19:29
q Jdg 21:5

of the LORD fell on the people, and they turned out as one man. [8]When Saul mustered[a] them at Bezek,[b] the men of Israel numbered three hundred thousand and the men of Judah thirty thousand.

[9]They told the messengers who had come, "Say to the men of Jabesh Gilead, 'By the time the sun is hot tomorrow, you will be delivered.'" When the messengers went and reported this to the men of Jabesh, they were elated. [10]They said to the Ammonites, "Tomorrow we will surrender[c] to you, and you can do to us whatever seems good to you."

[11]The next day Saul separated his men into three divisions;[d] during the last watch of the night they broke into the camp of the Ammonites and slaughtered them until the heat of the day. Those who survived were scattered, so that no two of them were left together.

[12]The people then said to Samuel, "Who[e] was it that asked, 'Shall Saul reign over us?' Bring these men to us and we will put them to death."

[13]But Saul said, "No one shall be put to death today,[f] for this day the LORD has rescued[g] Israel."

[14]Then Samuel said to the people, "Come, let us go to Gilgal[h] and there reaffirm the kingship.[i]" [15]So all the people went to Gilgal[j] and confirmed Saul as king in the presence of the LORD. There they sacrificed fellowship offerings[a] before the LORD, and Saul and all the Israelites held a great celebration.

Chapter 12 Theme

12 Samuel said to all Israel, "I have listened[k] to everything you said to me and have set a king[l] over you. [2]Now you have a king as your leader.[m] As for me, I am old and gray, and my sons are here with you. I have been your leader from my youth until this day. [3]Here I stand. Testify against me in the presence of the LORD and his anointed.[n] Whose ox have I taken? Whose donkey[o] have I taken? Whom have I cheated? Whom have I oppressed? From whose hand have I accepted a bribe[p] to make me shut my eyes? If I have done[q] any of these, I will make it right."

[4]"You have not cheated or oppressed us," they replied. "You have not taken anything from anyone's hand."

[5]Samuel said to them, "The LORD is witness against you, and also his anointed is witness this day, that you have not found anything[r] in my hand.[s]"

"He is witness," they said.

[6]Then Samuel said to the people, "It is the LORD who appointed Moses and Aaron and brought[t] your forefathers up out of Egypt.

a 15 Traditionally *peace offerings*

11:8
a Jdg 20:2
b Jdg 1:4

11:10
c ver 3

11:11
d Jdg 7:16

11:12
e 1Sa 10:27;
Lk 19:27

11:13
f 2Sa 19:22
g Ex 14:13;
1Sa 19:5

11:14
h 1Sa 10:8
i 1Sa 10:25

11:15
j 1Sa 10:8,17

12:1
k 1Sa 8:7
l 1Sa 10:24;
11:15

12:2
m 1Sa 8:5

12:3
n 1Sa 10:1; 24:6;
2Sa 1:14
o Nu 16:15
p Dt 16:19
q Ac 20:33

12:5
r Ac 23:9; 24:20
s Ex 22:4

12:6
t Ex 6:26;
Mic 6:4

12:7
a Isa 1:18;
Mic 6:1-5

12:8
b Ex 2:23
c Ex 3:10; 4:16

12:9
d Jdg 3:7
e Jdg 4:2
f Jdg 10:7; 13:1
g Jdg 3:12

12:10
h Jdg 10:10,15
i Jdg 2:13

12:11
j Jdg 6:14,32
k Jdg 4:6
l Jdg 11:1

12:12
m 1Sa 11:1
n 1Sa 8:5
o Jdg 8:23;
1Sa 8:6,19

12:13
p 1Sa 8:5;
Hos 13:11
q 1Sa 10:24

12:14
r Jos 24:14

12:15
s ver 9;
Jos 24:20;
Isa 1:20

12:16
t Ex 14:13

12:17
u 1Sa 7:9-10
v Jas 5:18
w Pr 26:1
x 1Sa 8:6-7

12:18
y Ex 14:31

12:19
z ver 23;
Ex 9:28;
Jas 5:18;
1Jn 5:16

12:21
a Isa 41:24,29;
Jer 16:19;
Hab 2:18
b Dt 11:16

12:22
c Ps 106:8
d Jos 7:9
e 1Ki 6:13
f Dt 7:7;
1Pe 2:9

⁷Now then, stand here, because I am going to confront*ᵃ* you with evidence before the LORD as to all the righteous acts performed by the LORD for you and your fathers.

⁸"After Jacob entered Egypt, they cried*ᵇ* to the LORD for help, and the LORD sent*ᶜ* Moses and Aaron, who brought your forefathers out of Egypt and settled them in this place.

⁹"But they forgot*ᵈ* the LORD their God; so he sold them into the hand of Sisera,*ᵉ* the commander of the army of Hazor, and into the hands of the Philistines*ᶠ* and the king of Moab,*ᵍ* who fought against them. ¹⁰They cried out to the LORD and said, 'We have sinned; we have forsaken*ʰ* the LORD and served the Baals and the Ashtoreths.*ⁱ* But now deliver us from the hands of our enemies, and we will serve you.' ¹¹Then the LORD sent Jerub-Baal,*ᵃʲ* Barak,*ᵇᵏ* Jephthah*ˡ* and Samuel,*ᶜ* and he delivered you from the hands of your enemies on every side, so that you lived securely.

¹²"But when you saw that Nahash*ᵐ* king*ⁿ* of the Ammonites was moving against you, you said to me, 'No, we want a king to rule*ᵒ* over us'—even though the LORD your God was your king. ¹³Now here is the king*ᵖ* you have chosen, the one you asked*�q* for; see, the LORD has set a king over you. ¹⁴If you fear*ʳ* the LORD and serve and obey him and do not rebel against his commands, and if both you and the king who reigns over you follow the LORD your God—good! ¹⁵But if you do not obey the LORD, and if you rebel against*ˢ* his commands, his hand will be against you, as it was against your fathers.

¹⁶"Now then, stand still and see*ᵗ* this great thing the LORD is about to do before your eyes! ¹⁷Is it not wheat harvest*ᵘ* now? I will call*ᵛ* upon the LORD to send thunder and rain.*ʷ* And you will realize what an evil*ˣ* thing you did in the eyes of the LORD when you asked for a king."

¹⁸Then Samuel called upon the LORD, and that same day the LORD sent thunder and rain. So all the people stood in awe*ʸ* of the LORD and of Samuel.

¹⁹The people all said to Samuel, "Pray*ᶻ* to the LORD your God for your servants so that we will not die, for we have added to all our other sins the evil of asking for a king."

²⁰"Do not be afraid," Samuel replied. "You have done all this evil; yet do not turn away from the LORD, but serve the LORD with all your heart. ²¹Do not turn away after useless*ᵃ* idols.*ᵇ* They can do you no good, nor can they rescue you, because they are useless. ²²For the sake*ᶜ* of his great name*ᵈ* the LORD will not reject*ᵉ* his people, because the LORD was pleased to make*ᶠ* you his own. ²³As for me, far be it from me that I should sin against the LORD by failing

a 11 Also called *Gideon*   *b 11* Some Septuagint manuscripts and Syriac; Hebrew *Bedan*
c 11 Hebrew; some Septuagint manuscripts and Syriac *Samson*

to pray[a] for you. And I will teach[b] you the way that is good and right. [24]But be sure to fear[c] the LORD and serve him faithfully with all your heart; consider[d] what great[e] things he has done for you. [25]Yet if you persist[f] in doing evil, both you and your king will be swept[g] away."

Chapter 13 Theme

13 Saul was ⌊thirty⌋[a] years old when he became king, and he reigned over Israel ⌊forty-⌋[b] two years.

[2]Saul[c] chose three thousand men from Israel; two thousand were with him at Micmash and in the hill country of Bethel, and a thousand were with Jonathan at Gibeah[h] in Benjamin. The rest of the men he sent back to their homes.

[3]Jonathan attacked the Philistine outpost[i] at Geba, and the Philistines heard about it. Then Saul had the trumpet blown throughout the land and said, "Let the Hebrews hear!" [4]So all Israel heard the news: "Saul has attacked the Philistine outpost, and now Israel has become a stench[j] to the Philistines." And the people were summoned to join Saul at Gilgal.

[5]The Philistines assembled to fight Israel, with three thousand[d] chariots, six thousand charioteers, and soldiers as numerous as the sand[k] on the seashore. They went up and camped at Micmash, east of Beth Aven. [6]When the men of Israel saw that their situation was critical and that their army was hard pressed, they hid in caves and thickets, among the rocks, and in pits and cisterns.[l] [7]Some Hebrews even crossed the Jordan to the land of Gad[m] and Gilead.

### Sidebar (left margin)

The Philistines' Attack on the Israelites

(See master map on page 497)

Philistine force to Micmash

Ophrah

SHUAL

Bethel

Rimmon

HILL COUNTRY

Way to Ophrah

Philistines split into troops

Mizpah

Micmash

Way of the Border

Way to Beth Horon

Ramah

Geba

Wadi Suweinit

Jonathan kills Philistine governor

Gibeon

Beeroth

Israelite force from Gilgal

Gibeah of Benjamin

— Israelites
■ Philistines

### Cross-references (right margin)

12:23
[a] Ro 1:9-10; Col 1:9; 2Ti 1:3
[b] 1Ki 8:36; Ps 34:11; Pr 4:11

12:24
[c] Ecc 12:13
[d] Isa 5:12
[e] Dt 10:21

12:25
[f] 1Sa 31:1-5
[g] Jos 24:20

13:2
[h] 1Sa 10:26

13:3
[i] 1Sa 10:5

13:4
[j] Ge 34:30

13:5
[k] Jos 11:4

13:6
[l] Jdg 6:2

13:7
[m] Nu 32:33

Footnotes

[a]1 A few late manuscripts of the Septuagint; Hebrew does not have *thirty*.   [b]1 See the round number in Acts 13:21; Hebrew does not have *forty-*.   [c]1,2 Or *and when he had reigned over Israel two years,* [2]*he*   [d]5 Some Septuagint manuscripts and Syriac; Hebrew *thirty thousand*

13:8
a 1Sa 10:8

13:9
b 2Sa 24:25;
1Ki 3:4

13:10
c 1Sa 15:13

13:11
d ver 2,5,16, 23

13:12
e Jer 26:19

13:13
f 2Ch 16:9
g 1Sa 15:23,24

13:14
h 1Sa 15:28
i Ac 7:46; 13:22
j 2Sa 6:21

13:15
k 1Sa 14:2

13:17
l 1Sa 14:15
m Jos 18:23

13:18
n Jos 18:13-14
o Ne 11:34

13:19
p 2Ki 24:14;
Jer 24:1

13:22
q 1Ch 9:39
r Jdg 5:8

13:23
s 1Sa 14:4

Saul remained at Gilgal, and all the troops with him were quaking with fear. ⁸He waited seven*ᵃ* days, the time set by Samuel; but Samuel did not come to Gilgal, and Saul's men began to scatter. ⁹So he said, "Bring me the burnt offering and the fellowship offerings.ᵃ" And Saul offered*ᵇ* up the burnt offering. ¹⁰Just as he finished making the offering, Samuel*ᶜ* arrived, and Saul went out to greet him.

¹¹"What have you done?" asked Samuel.

Saul replied, "When I saw that the men were scattering, and that you did not come at the set time, and that the Philistines were assembling at Micmash,*ᵈ* ¹²I thought, 'Now the Philistines will come down against me at Gilgal, and I have not sought the LORD's favor.*ᵉ*' So I felt compelled to offer the burnt offering."

¹³"You acted foolishly,*ᶠ*" Samuel said. "You have not kept*ᵍ* the command the LORD your God gave you; if you had, he would have established your kingdom over Israel for all time. ¹⁴But now your kingdom*ʰ* will not endure; the LORD has sought out a man after his own heart*ⁱ* and appointed*ʲ* him leader of his people, because you have not kept the LORD's command."

¹⁵Then Samuel left Gilgal*ᵇ* and went up to Gibeah*ᵏ* in Benjamin, and Saul counted the men who were with him. They numbered about six hundred.

¹⁶Saul and his son Jonathan and the men with them were staying in Gibeah*ᶜ* in Benjamin, while the Philistines camped at Micmash. ¹⁷Raiding*ˡ* parties went out from the Philistine camp in three detachments. One turned toward Ophrah*ᵐ* in the vicinity of Shual, ¹⁸another toward Beth Horon,*ⁿ* and the third toward the borderland overlooking the Valley of Zeboim*ᵒ* facing the desert.

¹⁹Not a blacksmith*ᵖ* could be found in the whole land of Israel, because the Philistines had said, "Otherwise the Hebrews will make swords or spears!" ²⁰So all Israel went down to the Philistines to have their plowshares, mattocks, axes and sickles*ᵈ* sharpened. ²¹The price was two thirds of a shekel*ᵉ* for sharpening plowshares and mattocks, and a third of a shekel*ᶠ* for sharpening forks and axes and for repointing goads.

²²So on the day of the battle not a soldier with Saul and Jonathan*�q* had a sword or spear*ʳ* in his hand; only Saul and his son Jonathan had them.

²³Now a detachment of Philistines had gone out to the pass*ˢ* at Micmash.

a 9 Traditionally *peace offerings*   *b 15* Hebrew; Septuagint *Gilgal and went his way; the rest of the people went after Saul to meet the army, and they went out of Gilgal*   *c 16* Two Hebrew manuscripts *Geba*, a variant of *Gibeah*   *d 20* Septuagint; Hebrew *plowshares*   *e 21* Hebrew *pim*; that is, about 1/4 ounce (about 8 grams)   *f 21* That is, about 1/8 ounce (about 4 grams)

Chapter 14 Theme _____

14 One day Jonathan son of Saul said to the young man bearing his armor, "Come, let's go over to the Philistine outpost on the other side." But he did not tell his father.

Philistines flee to Aijalon

To Gilgal, Jericho

Beth Aven

Micmash

Way of the Border

Philistine camp

Bozez / Seneh (Wadi Suweinit)

Israelite camp

Jonathan surprises Philistine guard

Geba

Gibeah (of Benjamin?)

Gibeah of Saul (?)

Israelites
Philistines

The Battle at Micmash

²Saul was staying on the outskirts of Gibeah[a] under a pomegranate tree in Migron.[b] With him were about six hundred men, ³among whom was Ahijah, who was wearing an ephod. He was a son of Ichabod's[c] brother Ahitub[d] son of Phinehas, the son of Eli,[e] the LORD's priest in Shiloh. No one was aware that Jonathan had left.

⁴On each side of the pass[f] that Jonathan intended to cross to reach the Philistine outpost was a cliff; one was called Bozez, and the other Seneh. ⁵One cliff stood to the north toward Micmash, the other to the south toward Geba.

⁶Jonathan said to his young armor-bearer, "Come, let's go over to the outpost of those uncircumcised[g] fellows. Perhaps the LORD will act in our behalf. Nothing[h] can hinder the LORD from saving, whether by many[i] or by few.[j]"

⁷"Do all that you have in mind," his armor-bearer said. "Go ahead; I am with you heart and soul."

⁸Jonathan said, "Come, then; we will cross over toward the men and let them see us. ⁹If they say to us, 'Wait there until we come to you,' we will stay where we are and not go up to them. ¹⁰But if they say, 'Come up to us,' we will climb up, because that will be our sign[k] that the LORD has given them into our hands."

¹¹So both of them showed themselves to the Philistine outpost. "Look!" said the Philistines. "The Hebrews are crawling out of the holes they were hiding[l] in." ¹²The men of the outpost shouted to Jonathan and his armor-bearer, "Come up to us and we'll teach you a lesson.[m]"

So Jonathan said to his armor-bearer, "Climb up after me; the LORD has given them into the hand[n] of Israel."

¹³Jonathan climbed up, using his hands and feet, with his armor-bearer right behind him. The Philistines fell before Jonathan, and his armor-bearer followed and killed behind him. ¹⁴In that first

14:2
a 1Sa 13:15
b Isa 10:28

14:3
c 1Sa 4:21
d 1Sa 22:11,20
e 1Sa 2:28

14:4
f 1Sa 13:23

14:6
g 1Sa 17:26,36; Jer 9:26
h Heb 11:34
i Jdg 7:4
j 1Sa 17:46-47

14:10
k Ge 24:14; Jdg 6:36-37

14:11
l 1Sa 13:6

14:12
m 1Sa 17:43-44
n 2Sa 5:24

attack Jonathan and his armor-bearer killed some twenty men in an area of about half an acre.ᵃ

14:15
ᵃGe 35:5;
2Ki 7:5-7
ᵇ1Sa 13:17

¹⁵Then panicᵃ struck the whole army—those in the camp and field, and those in the outposts and raidingᵇ parties—and the ground shook. It was a panic sent by God.ᵇ

14:16
ᶜ2Sa 18:24

¹⁶Saul's lookoutsᶜ at Gibeah in Benjamin saw the army melting away in all directions. ¹⁷Then Saul said to the men who were with him, "Muster the forces and see who has left us." When they did, it was Jonathan and his armor-bearer who were not there.

14:18
ᵈ1Sa 30:7

¹⁸Saul said to Ahijah, "Bringᵈ the ark of God." (At that time it was with the Israelites.)ᶜ ¹⁹While Saul was talking to the priest, the tumult in the Philistine camp increased more and more. So Saul said to the priest,ᵉ "Withdraw your hand."

14:19
ᵉNu 27:21

²⁰Then Saul and all his men assembled and went to the battle. They found the Philistines in total confusion, strikingᶠ each other with their swords. ²¹Those Hebrews who had previously been with the Philistines and had gone up with them to their camp wentᵍ over to the Israelites who were with Saul and Jonathan. ²²When all the Israelites who had hiddenʰ in the hill country of Ephraim heard that the Philistines were on the run, they joined the battle in hot pursuit. ²³So the LORD rescuedⁱ Israel that day, and the battle moved on beyond Beth Aven.ʲ

14:20
ᶠJdg 7:22;
2Ch 20:23

14:21
ᵍ1Sa 29:4

²⁴Now the men of Israel were in distress that day, because Saul had bound the people under an oath,ᵏ saying, "Cursed be any man who eats food before evening comes, before I have avenged myself on my enemies!" So none of the troops tasted food.

14:22
ʰ1Sa 13:6

²⁵The entire armyᵈ entered the woods, and there was honey on the ground. ²⁶When they went into the woods, they saw the honey oozing out, yet no one put his hand to his mouth, because they feared the oath. ²⁷But Jonathan had not heard that his father had bound the people with the oath, so he reached out the end of the staff that was in his hand and dipped it into the honeycomb.ˡ He raised his hand to his mouth, and his eyes brightened.ᵉ ²⁸Then one of the soldiers told him, "Your father bound the army under a strict oath, saying, 'Cursed be any man who eats food today!' That is why the men are faint."

14:23
ⁱEx 14:30;
Ps 44:6-7
ʲ1Sa 13:5

14:24
ᵏJos 6:26

²⁹Jonathan said, "My father has made troubleᵐ for the country. See how my eyes brightenedᶠ when I tasted a little of this honey. ³⁰How much better it would have been if the men had eaten today some of the plunder they took from their enemies. Would not the slaughter of the Philistines have been even greater?"

14:27
ˡver 43;
1Sa 30:12

ᵃ14 Hebrew half a yoke; a "yoke" was the land plowed by a yoke of oxen in one day.   ᵇ15 Or a terrible panic   ᶜ18 Hebrew; Septuagint "Bring the ephod." (At that time he wore the ephod before the Israelites.)   ᵈ25 Or Now all the people of the land   ᵉ27 Or his strength was renewed   ᶠ29 Or my strength was renewed

14:29
ᵐJos 7:25;
1Ki 18:18

³¹That day, after the Israelites had struck down the Philistines from Micmash to Aijalon,ᵃ they were exhausted. ³²They pounced on the plunderᵇ and, taking sheep, cattle and calves, they butchered them on the ground and ate them, together with the blood.ᶜ ³³Then someone said to Saul, "Look, the men are sinning against the LORD by eating meat that has blood in it."

"You have broken faith," he said. "Roll a large stone over here at once." ³⁴Then he said, "Go out among the men and tell them, 'Each of you bring me your cattle and sheep, and slaughter them here and eat them. Do not sin against the LORD by eating meat with blood still in it.'"

So everyone brought his ox that night and slaughtered it there. ³⁵Then Saul built an altarᵈ to the LORD; it was the first time he had done this.

³⁶Saul said, "Let us go down after the Philistines by night and plunder them till dawn, and let us not leave one of them alive."

"Do whatever seems best to you," they replied.

But the priest said, "Let us inquire of God here."

³⁷So Saul asked God, "Shall I go down after the Philistines? Will you give them into Israel's hand?" But God did not answerᵉ him that day.

³⁸Saul therefore said, "Come here, all you who are leaders of the army, and let us find out what sin has been committedᶠ today. ³⁹As surely as the LORD who rescues Israel lives,ᵍ even if it lies with my son Jonathan, he must die." But not one of the men said a word.

⁴⁰Saul then said to all the Israelites, "You stand over there; I and Jonathan my son will stand over here."

"Do what seems best to you," the men replied.

⁴¹Then Saul prayed to the LORD, the God of Israel, "Giveʰ me the rightⁱ answer."ᵃ And Jonathan and Saul were taken by lot, and the men were cleared. ⁴²Saul said, "Cast the lot between me and Jonathan my son." And Jonathan was taken.

⁴³Then Saul said to Jonathan, "Tell me what you have done."ʲ

So Jonathan told him, "I merely tasted a little honeyᵏ with the end of my staff. And now must I die?"

⁴⁴Saul said, "May God deal with me, be it ever so severely,ˡ if you do not die, Jonathan.ᵐ"

⁴⁵But the men said to Saul, "Should Jonathan die—he who has brought about this great deliverance in Israel? Never! As surely as the LORD lives, not a hairⁿ of his head will fall to the ground, for he did this today with God's help." So the men rescuedᵒ Jonathan, and he was not put to death.

---

a 41 Hebrew; Septuagint *"Why have you not answered your servant today? If the fault is in me or my son Jonathan, respond with Urim, but if the men of Israel are at fault, respond with Thummim."*

14:31 ᵃ Jos 10:12

14:32 ᵇ 1Sa 15:19; ᶜ Ge 9:4; Lev 3:17; 7:26; 17:10-14; 19:26; Dt 12:16, 23-24

14:35 ᵈ 1Sa 7:17

14:37 ᵉ 1Sa 10:22; 28:6,15

14:38 ᶠ Jos 7:11; 1Sa 10:19

14:39 ᵍ 2Sa 12:5

14:41 ʰ Ac 1:24; ⁱ Pr 16:33

14:43 ʲ Jos 7:19; ᵏ ver 27

14:44 ˡ Ru 1:17; ᵐ ver 39

14:45 ⁿ 1Ki 1:52; Lk 21:18; Ac 27:34; ᵒ 2Sa 14:11

14:47
a 1Sa 11:1-13
b ver 52;
2Sa 10:6

14:48
c 1Sa 15:2,7

14:49
d 1Sa 31:2;
1Ch 8:33
e 1Sa 18:17-20

14:51
f 1Sa 9:1

14:52
g 1Sa 8:11

15:1
h 1Sa 9:16

15:2
i Ex 17:8-14;
Nu 24:20;
Dt 25:17-19

15:3
j Nu 24:20;
Dt 20:16-18;
Jos 6:17;
1Sa 22:19

15:6
k Ex 18:10,19;
Nu 10:29-32;
24:22;
Jdg 1:16; 4:1

⁴⁶Then Saul stopped pursuing the Philistines, and they withdrew to their own land.

⁴⁷After Saul had assumed rule over Israel, he fought against their enemies on every side: Moab, the Ammonites,ᵃ Edom, the kingsᵃ of Zobah,ᵇ and the Philistines. Wherever he turned, he inflicted punishment on them.ᵇ ⁴⁸He fought valiantly and defeated the Amalekites,ᶜ delivering Israel from the hands of those who had plundered them.

⁴⁹Saul's sons were Jonathan, Ishvi and Malki-Shua.ᵈ The name of his older daughter was Merab, and that of the younger was Michal.ᵉ ⁵⁰His wife's name was Ahinoam daughter of Ahimaaz. The name of the commander of Saul's army was Abner son of Ner, and Ner was Saul's uncle. ⁵¹Saul's father Kishᶠ and Abner's father Ner were sons of Abiel.

⁵²All the days of Saul there was bitter war with the Philistines, and whenever Saul saw a mighty or brave man, he tookᵍ him into his service.

Chapter 15 Theme

15 Samuel said to Saul, "I am the one the LORD sent to anointʰ you king over his people Israel; so listen now to the message from the LORD. ²This is what the LORD Almighty says: 'I will punish the Amalekitesⁱ for what they did to Israel when they waylaid them as they came up from Egypt. ³Now go, attack the Amalekites and totallyʲ destroyᶜ everything that belongs to them. Do not spare them; put to death men and women, children and infants, cattle and sheep, camels and donkeys.'"

⁴So Saul summoned the men and mustered them at Telaim—two hundred thousand foot soldiers and ten thousand men from Judah. ⁵Saul went to the city of Amalek and set an ambush in the ravine. ⁶Then he said to the Kenites,ᵏ "Go away, leave the Amalekites so that I do not destroy you along with them; for you showed

a 47 Masoretic Text; Dead Sea Scrolls and Septuagint *king*   b 47 Hebrew; Septuagint *he was victorious*   c 3 The Hebrew term refers to the irrevocable giving over of things or persons to the LORD, often by totally destroying them; also in verses 8, 9, 15, 18, 20 and 21.

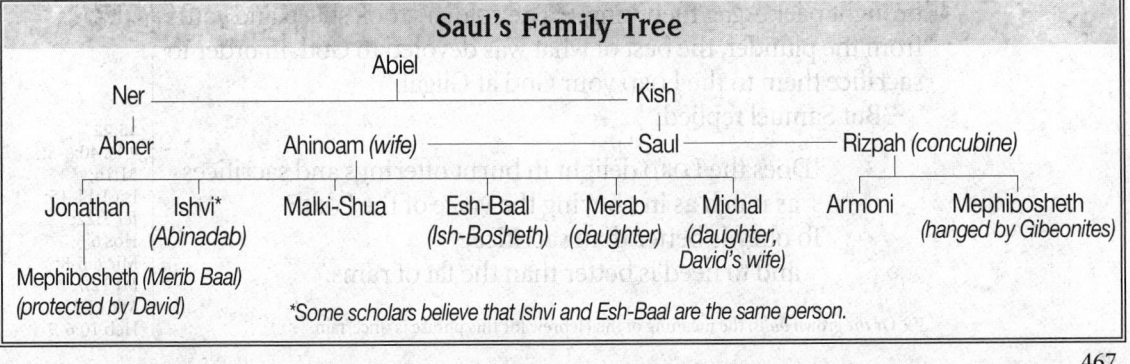

Saul's Family Tree

Some scholars believe that Ishvi and Esh-Baal are the same person.

kindness to all the Israelites when they came up out of Egypt." So the Kenites moved away from the Amalekites.

[7] Then Saul attacked the Amalekites[a] all the way from Havilah to Shur,[b] to the east of Egypt. [8] He took Agag king of the Amalekites alive,[c] and all his people he totally destroyed with the sword. [9] But Saul and the army spared[d] Agag and the best of the sheep and cattle, the fat calves[a] and lambs—everything that was good. These they were unwilling to destroy completely, but everything that was despised and weak they totally destroyed.

[10] Then the word of the LORD came to Samuel: [11] "I am grieved[e] that I have made Saul king, because he has turned[f] away from me and has not carried out my instructions."[g] Samuel was troubled,[h] and he cried out to the LORD all that night.

[12] Early in the morning Samuel got up and went to meet Saul, but he was told, "Saul has gone to Carmel.[i] There he has set up a monument in his own honor and has turned and gone on down to Gilgal."

[13] When Samuel reached him, Saul said, "The LORD bless you! I have carried out the LORD's instructions."

[14] But Samuel said, "What then is this bleating of sheep in my ears? What is this lowing of cattle that I hear?"

[15] Saul answered, "The soldiers brought them from the Amalekites; they spared the best of the sheep and cattle to sacrifice to the LORD your God, but we totally destroyed the rest."

[16] "Stop!" Samuel said to Saul. "Let me tell you what the LORD said to me last night."

"Tell me," Saul replied.

[17] Samuel said, "Although you were once small[j] in your own eyes, did you not become the head of the tribes of Israel? The LORD anointed you king over Israel. [18] And he sent you on a mission, saying, 'Go and completely destroy those wicked people, the Amalekites; make war on them until you have wiped them out.' [19] Why did you not obey the LORD? Why did you pounce on the plunder[k] and do evil in the eyes of the LORD?"

[20] "But I did obey[l] the LORD," Saul said. "I went on the mission the LORD assigned me. I completely destroyed the Amalekites and brought back Agag their king. [21] The soldiers took sheep and cattle from the plunder, the best of what was devoted to God, in order to sacrifice them to the LORD your God at Gilgal."

[22] But Samuel replied:

"Does the LORD delight in burnt offerings and sacrifices
    as much as in obeying the voice of the LORD?
To obey is better than sacrifice,[m]
    and to heed is better than the fat of rams.

[a] 9 Or *the grown bulls;* the meaning of the Hebrew for this phrase is uncertain.

15:7 [a]1Sa 14:48; [b]Ge 16:7; 25:17-18; Ex 15:22
15:8 [c]1Sa 30:1
15:9 [d]ver 3,15
15:11 [e]Ge 6:6; 2Sa 24:16; [f]Jos 22:16; [g]1Sa 13:13; 1Ki 9:6-7; [h]ver 35
15:12 [i]Jos 15:55
15:17 [j]1Sa 9:21
15:19 [k]1Sa 14:32
15:20 [l]ver 13
15:22 [m]Ps 40:6-8; 51:16; Isa 1:11-15; Jer 7:22; Hos 6:6; Mic 6:6-8; Mt 12:7; Mk 12:33; Heb 10:6-9

15:23
a Dt 18:10
b 1Sa 13:13

15:24
c 2Sa 12:13
d Pr 29:25;
Isa 51:12-13

15:25
e Ex 10:17

15:26
f 1Sa 13:14

15:27
g 1Ki 11:11,31

15:28
h 1Sa 28:17;
1Ki 11:31

15:29
i 1Ch 29:11;
Tit 1:2
j Nu 23:19;
Eze 24:14

15:30
k Isa 29:13;
Jn 5:44; 12:43

15:33
l Ge 9:6;
Jdg 1:7

15:34
m 1Sa 7:17
n 1Sa 11:4

15:35
o 1Sa 19:24
p 1Sa 16:1

16:1
q 1Sa 15:35
r 1Sa 15:23
s 2Ki 9:1
t Ru 4:17;
1Sa 9:16
u Ps 78:70;
Ac 13:22

16:3
v Ex 4:15
w Dt 17:15;
1Sa 9:16

²³For rebellion is like the sin of divination,ᵃ
and arrogance like the evil of idolatry.
Because you have rejectedᵇ the word of the LORD,
he has rejected you as king."

²⁴Then Saul said to Samuel, "I have sinned.ᶜ I violated the LORD's command and your instructions. I was afraidᵈ of the people and so I gave in to them. ²⁵Now I beg you, forgiveᵉ my sin and come back with me, so that I may worship the LORD."

²⁶But Samuel said to him, "I will not go back with you. You have rejectedᶠ the word of the LORD, and the LORD has rejected you as king over Israel!"

²⁷As Samuel turned to leave, Saul caught hold of the hem of his robe, and it tore.ᵍ ²⁸Samuel said to him, "The LORD has tornʰ the kingdom of Israel from you today and has given it to one of your neighbors—to one better than you. ²⁹He who is the Glory of Israel does not lieⁱ or changeʲ his mind; for he is not a man, that he should change his mind."

³⁰Saul replied, "I have sinned. But please honorᵏ me before the elders of my people and before Israel; come back with me, so that I may worship the LORD your God." ³¹So Samuel went back with Saul, and Saul worshiped the LORD.

³²Then Samuel said, "Bring me Agag king of the Amalekites."

Agag came to him confidently,ᵃ thinking, "Surely the bitterness of death is past."

³³But Samuel said,

"As your sword has made women childless,
so will your mother be childless among women."ˡ

And Samuel put Agag to death before the LORD at Gilgal.

³⁴Then Samuel left for Ramah,ᵐ but Saul went up to his home in Gibeahⁿ of Saul. ³⁵Until the day Samuelᵒ died, he did not go to see Saul again, though Samuel mournedᵖ for him. And the LORD was grieved that he had made Saul king over Israel.

Chapter 16 Theme

16 The LORD said to Samuel, "How long will you mourn�ۊ for Saul, since I have rejectedʳ him as king over Israel? Fill your horn with oilˢ and be on your way; I am sending you to Jesseᵗ of Bethlehem. I have chosenᵘ one of his sons to be king."

²But Samuel said, "How can I go? Saul will hear about it and kill me."

The LORD said, "Take a heifer with you and say, 'I have come to sacrifice to the LORD.' ³Invite Jesse to the sacrifice, and I will showᵛ you what to do. You are to anointʷ for me the one I indicate."

a 32 Or *him trembling, yet*

⁴Samuel did what the LORD said. When he arrived at Bethlehem,ᵃ the elders of the town trembled when they met him. They asked, "Do you come in peace?ᵇ"

⁵Samuel replied, "Yes, in peace; I have come to sacrifice to the LORD. Consecrateᶜ yourselves and come to the sacrifice with me." Then he consecrated Jesse and his sons and invited them to the sacrifice.

⁶When they arrived, Samuel saw Eliabᵈ and thought, "Surely the LORD's anointed stands here before the LORD."

⁷But the LORD said to Samuel, "Do not consider his appearance or his height, for I have rejected him. The LORD does not look at the things man looks at. Man looks at the outward appearance,ᵉ but the LORD looks at the heart."ᶠ

⁸Then Jesse called Abinadabᵍ and had him pass in front of Samuel. But Samuel said, "The LORD has not chosen this one either." ⁹Jesse then had Shammah pass by, but Samuel said, "Nor has the LORD chosen this one." ¹⁰Jesse had seven of his sons pass before Samuel, but Samuel said to him, "The LORD has not chosen these." ¹¹So he asked Jesse, "Are these allʰ the sons you have?"

"There is still the youngest," Jesse answered, "but he is tending the sheep."

Samuel said, "Send for him; we will not sit downᵃ until he arrives."

¹²So heⁱ sent and had him brought in. He was ruddy, with a fine appearance and handsomeʲ features.

Then the LORD said, "Rise and anoint him; he is the one."

¹³So Samuel took the horn of oil and anointed him in the presence of his brothers, and from that day on the Spirit of the LORDᵏ came upon David in power.ˡ Samuel then went to Ramah.

¹⁴Now the Spirit of the LORD had departedᵐ from Saul, and an evilᵇ spiritⁿ from the LORD tormented him.

¹⁵Saul's attendants said to him, "See, an evil spirit from God is tormenting you. ¹⁶Let our lord command his servants here to search for someone who can play the harp.ᵒ He will play when the evil spirit from God comes upon you, and you will feel better."

¹⁷So Saul said to his attendants, "Find someone who plays well and bring him to me."

¹⁸One of the servants answered, "I have seen a son of Jesse of Bethlehem who knows how to play the harp. He is a brave man and a warrior. He speaks well and is a fine-looking man. And the LORD is withᵖ him."

¹⁹Then Saul sent messengers to Jesse and said, "Send me your son David, who is with the sheep." ²⁰So Jesse took a donkey loaded

---

16:4
ᵃGe 48:7;
Lk 2:4
ᵇ1Ki 2:13;
2Ki 9:17

16:5
ᶜEx 19:10,22

16:6
ᵈ1Sa 17:13

16:7
ᵉPs 147:10
ᶠ1Ki 8:39;
1Ch 28:9;
Isa 55:8

16:8
ᵍ1Sa 17:13

16:11
ʰ1Sa 17:12

16:12
ⁱ1Sa 9:17
ʲGe 39:6;
1Sa 17:42

16:13
ᵏNu 27:18;
Jdg 11:29
ˡ1Sa 10:1,6,
9-10; 11:6

16:14
ᵐJdg 16:20
ⁿJdg 9:23;
1Sa 18:10

16:16
ᵒver 23;
1Sa 18:10;
19:9;
2Ki 3:15

16:18
ᵖ1Sa 3:19;
17:32-37

16:20
a 1Sa 10:27;
Pr 18:16

16:21
b Ge 41:46;
Pr 22:29

16:23
c ver 14-16

17:1
d 1Sa 13:5
e Jos 15:35;
2Ch 28:18

17:2
f 1Sa 21:9

17:4
g Jos 11:21-22;
2Sa 21:19

17:6
h ver 45

17:7
i 2Sa 21:19
j ver 41

17:8
k 1Sa 8:17

17:10
l ver 26,45;
2Sa 21:21

17:12
m Ru 4:17;
1Ch 2:13-15
n Ge 35:19
o 1Sa 16:11

17:13
p 1Sa 16:6
q 1Sa 16:9

17:15
r 1Sa 16:19

with bread,*a* a skin of wine and a young goat and sent them with his son David to Saul.

²¹David came to Saul and entered his service.*b* Saul liked him very much, and David became one of his armor-bearers. ²²Then Saul sent word to Jesse, saying, "Allow David to remain in my service, for I am pleased with him."

²³Whenever the spirit from God came upon Saul, David would take his harp and play. Then relief would come to Saul; he would feel better, and the evil spirit*c* would leave him.

Chapter 17 Theme

17 Now the Philistines gathered their forces for war and assembled*d* at Socoh in Judah. They pitched camp at Ephes Dammim, between Socoh*e* and Azekah. ²Saul and the Israelites assembled and camped in the Valley of Elah*f* and drew up their battle line to meet the Philistines. ³The Philistines occupied one hill and the Israelites another, with the valley between them.

⁴A champion named Goliath,*g* who was from Gath, came out of the Philistine camp. He was over nine feet*a* tall. ⁵He had a bronze helmet on his head and wore a coat of scale armor of bronze weighing five thousand shekels*b*; ⁶on his legs he wore bronze greaves, and a bronze javelin*h* was slung on his back. ⁷His spear shaft was like a weaver's rod,*i* and its iron point weighed six hundred shekels.*c* His shield bearer*j* went ahead of him.

⁸Goliath stood and shouted to the ranks of Israel, "Why do you come out and line up for battle? Am I not a Philistine, and are you not the servants of Saul? Choose*k* a man and have him come down to me. ⁹If he is able to fight and kill me, we will become your subjects; but if I overcome him and kill him, you will become our subjects and serve us." ¹⁰Then the Philistine said, "This day I defy*l* the ranks of Israel! Give me a man and let us fight each other." ¹¹On hearing the Philistine's words, Saul and all the Israelites were dismayed and terrified.

¹²Now David was the son of an Ephrathite named Jesse,*m* who was from Bethlehem*n* in Judah. Jesse had eight*o* sons, and in Saul's time he was old and well advanced in years. ¹³Jesse's three oldest sons had followed Saul to the war: The firstborn was Eliab;*p* the second, Abinadab; and the third, Shammah.*q* ¹⁴David was the youngest. The three oldest followed Saul, ¹⁵but David went back and forth from Saul to tend his father's sheep*r* at Bethlehem.

¹⁶For forty days the Philistine came forward every morning and evening and took his stand.

a 4 Hebrew *was six cubits and a span* (about 3 meters)   *b* 5 That is, about 125 pounds (about 57 kilograms)   *c* 7 That is, about 15 pounds (about 7 kilograms)

¹⁷Now Jesse said to his son David, "Take this ephah^a of roasted grain^a and these ten loaves of bread for your brothers and hurry to their camp. ¹⁸Take along these ten cheeses to the commander of their unit.^b See how your brothers^b are and bring back some assurance^c from them. ¹⁹They are with Saul and all the men of Israel in the Valley of Elah, fighting against the Philistines."

²⁰Early in the morning David left the flock with a shepherd, loaded up and set out, as Jesse had directed. He reached the camp as the army was going out to its battle positions, shouting the war cry. ²¹Israel and the Philistines were drawing up their lines facing each other. ²²David left his things with the keeper of supplies, ran to the battle lines and greeted his brothers. ²³As he was talking with them, Goliath, the Philistine champion from Gath, stepped out from his lines and shouted his usual^c defiance, and David heard it. ²⁴When the Israelites saw the man, they all ran from him in great fear.

²⁵Now the Israelites had been saying, "Do you see how this man keeps coming out? He comes out to defy Israel. The king will give great wealth to the man who kills him. He will also give him his daughter^d in marriage and will exempt his father's family from taxes in Israel."

²⁶David asked the men standing near him, "What will be done for the man who kills this Philistine and removes this disgrace^e from Israel? Who is this uncircumcised^f Philistine that he should defy^g the armies of the living^h God?"

²⁷They repeated to him what they had been saying and told him, "This is what will be done for the man who kills him."

²⁸When Eliab, David's oldest brother, heard him speaking with the men, he burned with angerⁱ at him and asked, "Why have you come down here? And with whom did you leave those few sheep in the desert? I know how conceited you are and how wicked your heart is; you came down only to watch the battle."

²⁹"Now what have I done?" said David. "Can't I even speak?" ³⁰He then turned away to someone else and brought up the same matter, and the men answered him as before. ³¹What David said was overheard and reported to Saul, and Saul sent for him.

³²David said to Saul, "Let no one lose heart^j on account of this Philistine; your servant will go and fight him."

³³Saul replied,^k "You are not able to go out against this Philistine and fight him; you are only a boy, and he has been a fighting man from his youth."

³⁴But David said to Saul, "Your servant has been keeping his father's sheep. When a lion^l or a bear came and carried off a sheep

---

17:17
^a1Sa 25:18

17:18
^bGe 37:14

17:23
^cver 8-10

17:25
^dJos 15:16;
1Sa 18:17

17:26
^e1Sa 11:2
^f1Sa 14:6
^gver 10
^hDt 5:26

17:28
ⁱGe 37:4,8,11;
Pr 18:19;
Mt 10:36

17:32
^jDt 20:3;
1Sa 16:18

17:33
^kNu 13:31

17:34
^lJer 49:19;
Am 3:12

---

^a17 That is, probably about 3/5 bushel (about 22 liters)　^b18 Hebrew *thousand*　^c18 Or *some token*; or *some pledge of spoils*

17:37
a 2Co 1:10
b 2Ti 4:17
c 1Sa 20:13;
1Ch 22:11,16

from the flock, ³⁵I went after it, struck it and rescued the sheep from its mouth. When it turned on me, I seized it by its hair, struck it and killed it. ³⁶Your servant has killed both the lion and the bear; this uncircumcised Philistine will be like one of them, because he has defied the armies of the living God. ³⁷The Lord who delivered[a] me from the paw of the lion[b] and the paw of the bear will deliver me from the hand of this Philistine."

Saul said to David, "Go, and the Lord be with[c] you."

17:42
d 1Sa 16:12
e Ps 123:3-4;
Pr 16:18

³⁸Then Saul dressed David in his own tunic. He put a coat of armor on him and a bronze helmet on his head. ³⁹David fastened on his sword over the tunic and tried walking around, because he was not used to them.

17:43
f 1Sa 24:14;
2Sa 3:8; 9:8;
2Ki 8:13

"I cannot go in these," he said to Saul, "because I am not used to them." So he took them off. ⁴⁰Then he took his staff in his hand, chose five smooth stones from the stream, put them in the pouch of his shepherd's bag and, with his sling in his hand, approached the Philistine.

17:44
g 1Ki 20:10-11

⁴¹Meanwhile, the Philistine, with his shield bearer in front of him, kept coming closer to David. ⁴²He looked David over and saw that he was only a boy, ruddy and handsome,[d] and he despised[e] him. ⁴³He said to David, "Am I a dog,[f] that you come at me with sticks?" And the Philistine cursed David by his gods. ⁴⁴"Come here," he said, "and I'll give your flesh to the birds of the air and the beasts of the field![g]"

17:45
h 2Sa 22:33,35;
2Ch 32:8;
Ps 124:8;
Heb 11:32-34
i ver 10

⁴⁵David said to the Philistine, "You come against me with sword and spear and javelin, but I come against you in the name[h] of the Lord Almighty, the God of the armies of Israel, whom you have defied.[i] ⁴⁶This day the Lord will hand you over to me, and I'll strike you down and cut off your head. Today I will give the carcasses[j] of the Philistine army to the birds of the air and the beasts of the earth, and the whole world[k] will know that there is a God in Israel.[l] ⁴⁷All those gathered here will know that it is not by sword[m] or spear that the Lord saves;[n] for the battle[o] is the Lord's, and he will give all of you into our hands."

17:46
j Dt 28:26
k Jos 4:24;
1Ki 8:43;
Isa 52:10
l 1Ki 18:36;
2Ki 19:19;
Isa 37:20

17:47
m Hos 1:7;
Zec 4:6
n 1Sa 14:6;
2Ch 14:11
o 2Ch 20:15;
Ps 44:6-7

⁴⁸As the Philistine moved closer to attack him, David ran quickly toward the battle line to meet him. ⁴⁹Reaching into his bag and taking out a stone, he slung it and struck the Philistine on the forehead. The stone sank into his forehead, and he fell facedown on the ground.

17:50
p 2Sa 23:21

⁵⁰So David triumphed over the Philistine with a sling[p] and a stone; without a sword in his hand he struck down the Philistine and killed him.

17:51
q Heb 11:34
r 1Sa 21:9

⁵¹David ran and stood over him. He took hold of the Philistine's sword and drew it from the scabbard. After he killed him, he cut[q] off his head with the sword.[r]

When the Philistines saw that their hero was dead, they turned and ran. ⁵²Then the men of Israel and Judah surged forward with a shout and pursued the Philistines to the entrance of Gathᵃ and to the gates of Ekron.ᵃ Their dead were strewn along the Shaaraimᵇ road to Gath and Ekron. ⁵³When the Israelites returned from chasing the Philistines, they plundered their camp. ⁵⁴David took the Philistine's head and brought it to Jerusalem, and he put the Philistine's weapons in his own tent.

⁵⁵As Saul watched Davidᶜ going out to meet the Philistine, he said to Abner, commander of the army, "Abner, whose son is that young man?"

Abner replied, "As surely as you live, O king, I don't know."

⁵⁶The king said, "Find out whose son this young man is."

⁵⁷As soon as David returned from killing the Philistine, Abner took him and brought him before Saul, with David still holding the Philistine's head.

⁵⁸"Whose son are you, young man?" Saul asked him.

David said, "I am the son of your servant Jesseᵈ of Bethlehem."

Chapter 18 Theme

18 After David had finished talking with Saul, Jonathan became one in spirit with David, and he lovedᵉ him as himself.ᶠ ²From that day Saul kept David with him and did not let him return to his father's house. ³And Jonathan made a covenantᵍ with David because he loved him as himself. ⁴Jonathan took off the robeʰ he was wearing and gave it to David, along with his tunic, and even his sword, his bow and his belt.

⁵Whatever Saul sent him to do, David did it so successfullyᵇ that Saul gave him a high rank in the army. This pleased all the people, and Saul's officers as well.

⁶When the men were returning home after David had killed the Philistine, the women came out from all the towns of Israel to meet King Saul with singing and dancing,ⁱ with joyful songs and with tambourinesʲ and lutes. ⁷As they danced, they sang:ᵏ

"Saul has slain his thousands,
and David his tensˡ of thousands."

⁸Saul was very angry; this refrain galled him. "They have credited David with tens of thousands," he thought, "but me with only thousands. What more can he get but the kingdom?ᵐ" ⁹And from that time on Saul kept a jealous eye on David.

¹⁰The next day an evilᶜ spiritⁿ from God came forcefully upon Saul. He was prophesying in his house, while David was playing

Cross references

17:52
ᵃ Jos 15:11
ᵇ Jos 15:36

17:55
ᶜ 1Sa 16:21

17:58
ᵈ ver 12

18:1
ᵉ 2Sa 1:26
ᶠ Ge 44:30

18:3
ᵍ 1Sa 20:8,16, 17,42

18:4
ʰ Ge 41:42

18:6
ⁱ Ex 15:20
ʲ Jdg 11:34; Ps 68:25

18:7
ᵏ Ex 15:21
ˡ 1Sa 21:11; 29:5

18:8
ᵐ 1Sa 15:8

18:10
ⁿ 1Sa 16:14

ᵃ 52 Some Septuagint manuscripts; Hebrew *a valley*   ᵇ 5 Or *wisely*   ᶜ 10 Or *injurious*

18:10
a 1Sa 19:7

18:11
b 1Sa 20:7,33
c 1Sa 19:10

18:12
d ver 15,29
e 1Sa 16:13
f 1Sa 28:15

18:13
g ver 16;
Nu 27:17
h 2Sa 5:2

18:14
i Ge 39:3
j Ge 39:2,23;
Jos 6:27;
1Sa 16:18

18:16
k ver 5

18:17
l 1Sa 17:25
m Nu 21:14;
1Sa 25:28
n ver 25

18:18
o 1Sa 9:21;
2Sa 7:18
p ver 23

18:19
q 2Sa 21:8
r Jdg 7:22

18:20
s ver 28

18:21
t ver 17,26

18:25
u Ge 34:12;
Ex 22:17;
1Sa 14:24
v ver 17

18:27
w ver 13;
2Sa 3:14

the harp, as he usually*a* did. Saul had a spear in his hand ¹¹and he hurled it, saying to himself,*b* "I'll pin David to the wall." But David eluded*c* him twice.

¹²Saul was afraid*d* of David, because the LORD*e* was with*f* David but had left Saul. ¹³So he sent David away from him and gave him command over a thousand men, and David led*g* the troops in their campaigns.*h* ¹⁴In everything he did he had great success,*a i* because the LORD was with*j* him. ¹⁵When Saul saw how successful*b* he was, he was afraid of him. ¹⁶But all Israel and Judah loved David, because he led them in their campaigns.*k*

¹⁷Saul said to David, "Here is my older daughter*l* Merab. I will give her to you in marriage; only serve me bravely and fight the battles*m* of the LORD." For Saul said to himself,*n* "I will not raise a hand against him. Let the Philistines do that!"

¹⁸But David said to Saul, "Who am I,*o* and what is my family or my father's clan in Israel, that I should become the king's son-in-law?*p*" ¹⁹So*c* when the time came for Merab,*q* Saul's daughter, to be given to David, she was given in marriage to Adriel of Meholah.*r*

²⁰Now Saul's daughter Michal*s* was in love with David, and when they told Saul about it, he was pleased. ²¹"I will give her to him," he thought, "so that she may be a snare*t* to him and so that the hand of the Philistines may be against him." So Saul said to David, "Now you have a second opportunity to become my son-in-law."

²²Then Saul ordered his attendants: "Speak to David privately and say, 'Look, the king is pleased with you, and his attendants all like you; now become his son-in-law.'"

²³They repeated these words to David. But David said, "Do you think it is a small matter to become the king's son-in-law? I'm only a poor man and little known."

²⁴When Saul's servants told him what David had said, ²⁵Saul replied, "Say to David, 'The king wants no other price*u* for the bride than a hundred Philistine foreskins, to take revenge on his enemies.'" Saul's plan*v* was to have David fall by the hands of the Philistines.

²⁶When the attendants told David these things, he was pleased to become the king's son-in-law. So before the allotted time elapsed, ²⁷David and his men went out and killed two hundred Philistines. He brought their foreskins and presented the full number to the king so that he might become the king's son-in-law. Then Saul gave him his daughter Michal*w* in marriage.

²⁸When Saul realized that the LORD was with David and that his daughter Michal loved David, ²⁹Saul became still more afraid of him, and he remained his enemy the rest of his days.

a 14 Or *he was very wise*   *b* 15 Or *wise*   *c* 19 Or *However,*

[30]The Philistine commanders continued to go out to battle, and as often as they did, David met with more success[aa] than the rest of Saul's officers, and his name became well known.

Chapter 19 Theme _____

19 Saul told his son Jonathan[b] and all the attendants to kill[c] David. But Jonathan was very fond of David [2]and warned him, "My father Saul is looking for a chance to kill you. Be on your guard tomorrow morning; go into hiding and stay there. [3]I will go out and stand with my father in the field where you are. I'll speak[d] to him about you and will tell you what I find out."

[4]Jonathan spoke[e] well of David to Saul his father and said to him, "Let not the king do wrong[f] to his servant David; he has not wronged you, and what he has done has benefited you greatly. [5]He took his life in his hands when he killed the Philistine. The LORD won a great victory[g] for all Israel, and you saw it and were glad. Why then would you do wrong to an innocent[h] man like David by killing him for no reason?"

[6]Saul listened to Jonathan and took this oath: "As surely as the LORD lives, David will not be put to death."

[7]So Jonathan called David and told him the whole conversation. He brought him to Saul, and David was with Saul as before.[i]

[8]Once more war broke out, and David went out and fought the Philistines. He struck them with such force that they fled before him.

[9]But an evil[b] spirit[j] from the LORD came upon Saul as he was sitting in his house with his spear in his hand. While David was playing the harp, [10]Saul tried to pin him to the wall with his spear, but David eluded[k] him as Saul drove the spear into the wall. That night David made good his escape.

[11]Saul sent men to David's house to watch[l] it and to kill him in the morning. But Michal, David's wife, warned him, "If you don't run for your life tonight, tomorrow you'll be killed." [12]So Michal let David down through a window,[m] and he fled and escaped. [13]Then Michal took an idol[c] and laid it on the bed, covering it with a garment and putting some goats' hair at the head.

[14]When Saul sent the men to capture David, Michal said,[n] "He is ill."

[15]Then Saul sent the men back to see David and told them, "Bring him up to me in his bed so that I may kill him." [16]But when the men entered, there was the idol in the bed, and at the head was some goats' hair.

[17]Saul said to Michal, "Why did you deceive me like this and send my enemy away so that he escaped?"

---

a 30 Or *David acted more wisely*   b 9 Or *injurious*   c 13 Hebrew *teraphim*; also in verse 16

18:30
a ver 5; 2Sa 11:1

19:1
b 1Sa 18:1
c 1Sa 18:9

19:3
d 1Sa 20:12

19:4
e 1Sa 20:32;
Pr 31:8,9;
Jer 18:20
f Ge 42:22;
Pr 17:13

19:5
g 1Sa 11:13;
17:49-50;
1Ch 11:14
h Dt 19:10-13;
1Sa 20:32;
Mt 27:4

19:7
i 1Sa 16:21;
18:2,13

19:9
j 1Sa 16:14;
18:10-11

19:10
k 1Sa 18:11

19:11
l Ps 59 Title

19:12
m Jos 2:15;
Ac 9:25

19:14
n Jos 2:4

Michal told him, "He said to me, 'Let me get away. Why should I kill you?'"

19:18
a 1Sa 7:17

¹⁸When David had fled and made his escape, he went to Samuel at Ramah*a* and told him all that Saul had done to him. Then he and Samuel went to Naioth and stayed there. ¹⁹Word came to Saul: "David is in Naioth at Ramah"; ²⁰so he sent men to capture him. But when they saw a group of prophets*b* prophesying, with Samuel standing there as their leader, the Spirit of God came upon*c* Saul's men and they also prophesied.*d* ²¹Saul was told about it, and he sent more men, and they prophesied too. Saul sent men a third time, and they also prophesied. ²²Finally, he himself left for Ramah and went to the great cistern at Secu. And he asked, "Where are Samuel and David?"

19:20
b ver 11,14;
Jn 7:32,45
c Nu 11:25
d 1Sa 10:5;
Joel 2:28

"Over in Naioth at Ramah," they said.

19:23
e 1Sa 10:13

²³So Saul went to Naioth at Ramah. But the Spirit of God came even upon him, and he walked along prophesying*e* until he came to Naioth. ²⁴He stripped*f* off his robes and also prophesied in Samuel's presence. He lay that way all that day and night. This is why people say, "Is Saul also among the prophets?"*g*

19:24
f 2Sa 6:20;
Isa 20:2; Mic 1:8
g 1Sa 10:11

Chapter 20 Theme _____

20:1
h 1Sa 24:9

20 Then David fled from Naioth at Ramah and went to Jonathan and asked, "What have I done? What is my crime? How have I wronged*h* your father, that he is trying to take my life?"

²"Never!" Jonathan replied. "You are not going to die! Look, my father doesn't do anything, great or small, without confiding in me. Why would he hide this from me? It's not so!"

20:3
i Dt 6:13

³But David took an oath*i* and said, "Your father knows very well that I have found favor in your eyes, and he has said to himself, 'Jonathan must not know this or he will be grieved.' Yet as surely as the LORD lives and as you live, there is only a step between me and death."

20:5
j Nu 10:10;
28:11
k 1Sa 19:2

⁴Jonathan said to David, "Whatever you want me to do, I'll do for you."

⁵So David said, "Look, tomorrow is the New Moon festival,*j* and I am supposed to dine with the king; but let me go and hide*k* in the field until the evening of the day after tomorrow. ⁶If your father misses me at all, tell him, 'David earnestly asked my permission to hurry to Bethlehem,*l* his hometown, because an annual*m* sacrifice is being made there for his whole clan.' ⁷If he says, 'Very well,' then your servant is safe. But if he loses his temper,*n* you can be sure that he is determined to harm me. ⁸As for you, show kindness to your servant, for you have brought him into a covenant*o* with you before the LORD. If I am guilty, then kill*p* me yourself! Why hand me over to your father?"

20:6
l 1Sa 17:58
m Dt 12:5

20:7
n 1Sa 25:17

20:8
o 1Sa 18:3; 23:18
p 2Sa 14:32

⁹"Never!" Jonathan said. "If I had the least inkling that my father was determined to harm you, wouldn't I tell you?"

¹⁰David asked, "Who will tell me if your father answers you harshly?"

¹¹"Come," Jonathan said, "let's go out into the field." So they went there together.

¹²Then Jonathan said to David: "By the LORD, the God of Israel, I will surely sound out my father by this time the day after tomorrow! If he is favorably disposed toward you, will I not send you word and let you know? ¹³But if my father is inclined to harm you, may the LORD deal with me, be it ever so severely,ᵃ if I do not let you know and send you away safely. May the LORD be withᵇ you as he has been with my father. ¹⁴But show me unfailing kindness like that of the LORD as long as I live, so that I may not be killed, ¹⁵and do not ever cut off your kindness from my familyᶜ—not even when the LORD has cut off every one of David's enemies from the face of the earth."

¹⁶So Jonathan made a covenantᵈ with the house of David, saying, "May the LORD call David's enemies to account." ¹⁷And Jonathan had David reaffirm his oathᵉ out of love for him, because he loved him as he loved himself.

¹⁸Then Jonathan said to David: "Tomorrow is the New Moon festival. You will be missed, because your seat will be empty.ᶠ ¹⁹The day after tomorrow, toward evening, go to the place where you hidᵍ when this trouble began, and wait by the stone Ezel. ²⁰I will shoot three arrows to the side of it, as though I were shooting at a target. ²¹Then I will send a boy and say, 'Go, find the arrows.' If I say to him, 'Look, the arrows are on this side of you; bring them here,' then come, because, as surely as the LORD lives, you are safe; there is no danger. ²²But if I say to the boy, 'Look, the arrows are beyondʰ you,' then you must go, because the LORD has sent you away. ²³And about the matter you and I discussed—remember, the LORD is witnessⁱ between you and me forever."

²⁴So David hid in the field, and when the New Moon festival came, the king sat down to eat. ²⁵He sat in his customary place by the wall, opposite Jonathan,ᵃ and Abner sat next to Saul, but David's place was empty.ʲ ²⁶Saul said nothing that day, for he thought, "Something must have happened to David to make him ceremonially unclean—surely he is unclean.ᵏ" ²⁷But the next day, the second day of the month, David's place was empty again. Then Saul said to his son Jonathan, "Why hasn't the son of Jesse come to the meal, either yesterday or today?"

²⁸Jonathan answered, "David earnestly asked me for permissionˡ to go to Bethlehem. ²⁹He said, 'Let me go, because our family is

---

ᵃ 25 Septuagint; Hebrew wall. Jonathan arose

20:13
ᵃ Ru 1:17; 1Sa 3:17
ᵇ Jos 1:5; 1Sa 17:37; 18:12; 1Ch 22:11,16

20:15
ᶜ 2Sa 9:7

20:16
ᵈ 1Sa 25:22

20:17
ᵉ 1Sa 18:3

20:18
ᶠ ver 5,25

20:19
ᵍ 1Sa 19:2

20:22
ʰ ver 37

20:23
ⁱ ver 14-15; Ge 31:50

20:25
ʲ ver 18

20:26
ᵏ Lev 7:20-21; 15:5; 1Sa 16:5

20:28
ˡ ver 6

20:32
a 1Sa 19:4;
Mt 27:23
b Ge 31:36;
Lk 23:22

observing a sacrifice in the town and my brother has ordered me to be there. If I have found favor in your eyes, let me get away to see my brothers.' That is why he has not come to the king's table."

³⁰Saul's anger flared up at Jonathan and he said to him, "You son of a perverse and rebellious woman! Don't I know that you have sided with the son of Jesse to your own shame and to the shame of the mother who bore you? ³¹As long as the son of Jesse lives on this earth, neither you nor your kingdom will be established. Now send and bring him to me, for he must die!"

³²"Why*a* should he be put to death? What*b* has he done?" Jonathan asked his father. ³³But Saul hurled his spear at him to kill him. Then Jonathan knew that his father intended*c* to kill David.

20:33
c ver 7;
1Sa 18:11,17

³⁴Jonathan got up from the table in fierce anger; on that second day of the month he did not eat, because he was grieved at his father's shameful treatment of David.

³⁵In the morning Jonathan went out to the field for his meeting with David. He had a small boy with him, ³⁶and he said to the boy, "Run and find the arrows I shoot." As the boy ran, he shot an arrow beyond him. ³⁷When the boy came to the place where Jonathan's arrow had fallen, Jonathan called out after him, "Isn't the arrow beyond*d* you?" ³⁸Then he shouted, "Hurry! Go quickly! Don't stop!" The boy picked up the arrow and returned to his master. ³⁹(The boy knew nothing of all this; only Jonathan and David knew.) ⁴⁰Then Jonathan gave his weapons to the boy and said, "Go, carry them back to town."

20:37
d ver 22

⁴¹After the boy had gone, David got up from the south side ⌊of the stone⌋ and bowed down before Jonathan three times, with his face to the ground. Then they kissed each other and wept together— but David wept the most.

⁴²Jonathan said to David, "Go in peace,*e* for we have sworn friendship*f* with each other in the name of the LORD, saying, 'The LORD is witness between you and me, and between your descendants and my descendants forever.'" Then David left, and Jonathan went back to the town.

20:42
e ver 22;
1Sa 1:17
f 2Sa 1:26;
Pr 18:24

Chapter 21 Theme _____

21 David went to Nob,*g* to Ahimelech the priest. Ahimelech trembled*h* when he met him, and asked, "Why are you alone? Why is no one with you?"

²David answered Ahimelech the priest, "The king charged me with a certain matter and said to me, 'No one is to know anything about your mission and your instructions.' As for my men, I have told them to meet me at a certain place. ³Now then, what do you have on hand? Give me five loaves of bread, or whatever you can find."

21:1
g 1Sa 14:3;
22:9,19;
Ne 11:32;
Isa 10:32
h 1Sa 16:4

[4]But the priest answered David, "I don't have any ordinary bread[a] on hand; however, there is some consecrated[b] bread here—provided the men have kept[c] themselves from women."

[5]David replied, "Indeed women have been kept from us, as usual whenever[a] I set out. The men's things[b] are holy[d] even on missions that are not holy. How much more so today!" [6]So the priest gave him the consecrated bread,[e] since there was no bread there except the bread of the Presence that had been removed from before the LORD and replaced by hot bread on the day it was taken away.

[7]Now one of Saul's servants was there that day, detained before the LORD; he was Doeg[f] the Edomite,[g] Saul's head shepherd.

[8]David asked Ahimelech, "Don't you have a spear or a sword here? I haven't brought my sword or any other weapon, because the king's business was urgent."

[9]The priest replied, "The sword[h] of Goliath the Philistine, whom you killed in the Valley of Elah,[i] is here; it is wrapped in a cloth behind the ephod. If you want it, take it; there is no sword here but that one."

David said, "There is none like it; give it to me."

[10]That day David fled from Saul and went[j] to Achish king of Gath. [11]But the servants of Achish said to him, "Isn't this David, the king of the land? Isn't he the one they sing about in their dances:

"'Saul has slain his thousands,
and David his tens of thousands'?"[k]

[12]David took these words to heart and was very much afraid of Achish king of Gath. [13]So he pretended to be insane[l] in their presence; and while he was in their hands he acted like a madman, making marks on the doors of the gate and letting saliva run down his beard.

[14]Achish said to his servants, "Look at the man! He is insane! Why bring him to me? [15]Am I so short of madmen that you have to bring this fellow here to carry on like this in front of me? Must this man come into my house?"

Chapter 22 Theme _____

22 David left Gath and escaped to the cave[m] of Adullam. When his brothers and his father's household heard about it, they went down to him there. [2]All those who were in distress or in debt or discontented gathered[n] around him, and he became their leader. About four hundred men were with him.

[3]From there David went to Mizpah in Moab and said to the king of Moab, "Would you let my father and mother come and stay with

---

[a]5 Or *from us in the past few days since* [b]5 Or *bodies*

21:4
[a]Lev 24:8-9
[b]Ex 25:30;
Mt 12:4
[c]Ex 19:15

21:5
[d]1Th 4:4

21:6
[e]Lev 24:8-9;
Mt 12:3-4;
Mk 2:25-28;
Lk 6:1-5

21:7
[f]1Sa 22:9,22
[g]1Sa 14:47;
Ps 52 Title

21:9
[h]1Sa 17:51
[i]1Sa 17:2

21:10
[j]1Sa 27:2

21:11
[k]1Sa 18:7; 29:5;
Ps 56 Title

21:13
[l]Ps 34 Title

22:1
[m]2Sa 23:13;
Ps 57 Title;
142 Title

22:2
[n]1Sa 23:13;
25:13;
2Sa 15:20

22:5
a 2Sa 24:11;
1Ch 21:9; 29:29;
2Ch 29:25

you until I learn what God will do for me?" ⁴So he left them with the king of Moab, and they stayed with him as long as David was in the stronghold.

⁵But the prophet Gad*a* said to David, "Do not stay in the stronghold. Go into the land of Judah." So David left and went to the forest of Hereth.

22:6
b Jdg 4:5
c Ge 21:33

⁶Now Saul heard that David and his men had been discovered. And Saul, spear in hand, was seated*b* under the tamarisk*c* tree on the hill at Gibeah, with all his officials standing around him. ⁷Saul said to them, "Listen, men of Benjamin! Will the son of Jesse give all of you fields and vineyards? Will he make all of you commanders*d* of thousands and commanders of hundreds? ⁸Is that why you have all conspired against me? No one tells me when my son

22:7
d 1Sa 8:14

makes a covenant*e* with the son of Jesse. None of you is concerned*f* about me or tells me that my son has incited my servant to lie in wait for me, as he does today."

22:8
e 1Sa 18:3;
20:16
f 1Sa 23:21

⁹But Doeg*g* the Edomite, who was standing with Saul's officials, said, "I saw the son of Jesse come to Ahimelech son of Ahitub at Nob.*h* ¹⁰Ahimelech inquired*i* of the LORD for him; he also gave him provisions*j* and the sword of Goliath the Philistine."

22:9
g 1Sa 21:7;
Ps 52 Title
h 1Sa 21:1

22:10
i Nu 27:21;
1Sa 10:22
j 1Sa 21:6

¹¹Then the king sent for the priest Ahimelech son of Ahitub and his father's whole family, who were the priests at Nob, and they all came to the king. ¹²Saul said, "Listen now, son of Ahitub."

"Yes, my lord," he answered.

22:13
k ver 8

¹³Saul said to him, "Why have you conspired*k* against me, you and the son of Jesse, giving him bread and a sword and inquiring of God for him, so that he has rebelled against me and lies in wait for me, as he does today?"

¹⁴Ahimelech answered the king, "Who*l* of all your servants is as loyal as David, the king's son-in-law, captain of your bodyguard and highly respected in your household? ¹⁵Was that day the first time I inquired of God for him? Of course not! Let not the king accuse your servant or any of his father's family, for your servant knows nothing at all about this whole affair."

22:14
l 1Sa 19:4

INSIGHT

A *stronghold* was a fortified or secure location.

David's Journeys: 1 Samuel 21–22 *(Numbers on the following maps indicate the progression of David's journey.)*

¹⁶But the king said, "You will surely die, Ahimelech, you and your father's whole family."

¹⁷Then the king ordered the guards at his side: "Turn and kill the priests of the LORD, because they too have sided with David. They knew he was fleeing, yet they did not tell me."

But the king's officials were not willing[a] to raise a hand to strike the priests of the LORD.

¹⁸The king then ordered Doeg, "You turn and strike down the priests." So Doeg the Edomite turned and struck them down. That day he killed eighty-five men who wore the linen ephod.[b] ¹⁹He also put to the sword[c] Nob, the town of the priests, with its men and women, its children and infants, and its cattle, donkeys and sheep.

²⁰But Abiathar,[d] a son of Ahimelech son of Ahitub, escaped and fled to join David.[e] ²¹He told David that Saul had killed the priests of the LORD. ²²Then David said to Abiathar: "That day, when Doeg[f] the Edomite was there, I knew he would be sure to tell Saul. I am responsible for the death of your father's whole family. ²³Stay with me; don't be afraid; the man who is seeking your life[g] is seeking mine also. You will be safe with me."

Chapter 23 Theme

23 When David was told, "Look, the Philistines are fighting against Keilah[h] and are looting the threshing floors," ²he inquired[i] of the LORD, saying, "Shall I go and attack these Philistines?"

The LORD answered him, "Go, attack the Philistines and save Keilah."

³But David's men said to him, "Here in Judah we are afraid. How much more, then, if we go to Keilah against the Philistine forces!"

⁴Once again David inquired of the LORD, and the LORD answered him, "Go down to Keilah, for I am going to give the Philistines into your hand.[j]" ⁵So David and his men went to Keilah, fought the Philistines and carried off their livestock. He inflicted heavy losses on the Philistines and saved the people of Keilah. ⁶(Now Abiathar[k] son of Ahimelech had brought the ephod down with him when he fled to David at Keilah.)

⁷Saul was told that David had gone to Keilah, and he said, "God has handed him over to me, for David has imprisoned himself by entering a town with gates and bars." ⁸And Saul called up all his forces for battle, to go down to Keilah to besiege David and his men.

⁹When David learned that Saul was plotting against him, he said to Abiathar[l] the priest, "Bring the ephod." ¹⁰David said, "O LORD,

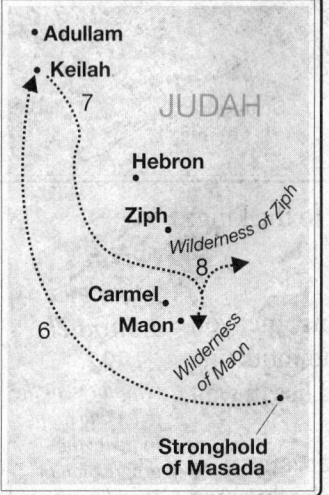

David's Journeys: 1 Samuel 23

- Adullam
- Keilah
- 7
- JUDAH
- Hebron
- Ziph
- Wilderness of Ziph
- 8
- Carmel
- Maon
- Wilderness of Maon
- 6
- Stronghold of Masada

22:17
a Ex 1:17

22:18
b 1Sa 2:18,31

22:19
c 1Sa 15:3

22:20
d 1Sa 23:6,9; 30:7; 1Ki 2:22, 26,27
e 1Sa 2:32

22:22
f 1Sa 21:7

22:23
g 1Ki 2:26

23:1
h Jos 15:44

23:2
i ver 4,12; 1Sa 30:8; 2Sa 5:19,23

23:4
j Jos 8:7; Jdg 7:7

23:6
k 1Sa 22:20

23:9
l ver 6; 1Sa 22:20; 30:7

23:12
a ver 20

23:13
b 1Sa 22:2; 25:13

23:14
c Jos 15:24,55
d Ps 54:3-4
e Ps 32:7

23:16
f 1Sa 30:6

23:17
g 1Sa 20:31;
24:20

23:18
h 1Sa 18:3;
20:16,42;
2Sa 9:1; 21:7

23:19
i 1Sa 26:1
j Ps 54 Title
k 1Sa 26:3

23:20
l ver 12

23:21
m 1Sa 22:8

23:24
n Jos 15:55;
1Sa 25:2

23:26
o Ps 17:9

God of Israel, your servant has heard definitely that Saul plans to come to Keilah and destroy the town on account of me. ¹¹Will the citizens of Keilah surrender me to him? Will Saul come down, as your servant has heard? O Lord, God of Israel, tell your servant."

And the Lord said, "He will."

¹²Again David asked, "Will the citizens of Keilah surrender*a* me and my men to Saul?"

And the Lord said, "They will."

¹³So David and his men,*b* about six hundred in number, left Keilah and kept moving from place to place. When Saul was told that David had escaped from Keilah, he did not go there.

¹⁴David stayed in the desert strongholds and in the hills of the Desert of Ziph.*c* Day after day Saul searched*d* for him, but God did not*e* give David into his hands.

¹⁵While David was at Horesh in the Desert of Ziph, he learned that Saul had come out to take his life. ¹⁶And Saul's son Jonathan went to David at Horesh and helped him find strength*f* in God. ¹⁷"Don't be afraid," he said. "My father Saul will not lay a hand on you. You will be king*g* over Israel, and I will be second to you. Even my father Saul knows this." ¹⁸The two of them made a covenant*h* before the Lord. Then Jonathan went home, but David remained at Horesh.

¹⁹The Ziphites*i* went up to Saul at Gibeah and said, "Is not David hiding among us*j* in the strongholds at Horesh, on the hill of Hakilah,*k* south of Jeshimon? ²⁰Now, O king, come down whenever it pleases you to do so, and we will be responsible for handing*l* him over to the king."

²¹Saul replied, "The Lord bless you for your concern*m* for me. ²²Go and make further preparation. Find out where David usually goes and who has seen him there. They tell me he is very crafty. ²³Find out about all the hiding places he uses and come back to me with definite information.*a* Then I will go with you; if he is in the area, I will track him down among all the clans of Judah."

²⁴So they set out and went to Ziph ahead of Saul. Now David and his men were in the Desert of Maon,*n* in the Arabah south of Jeshimon. ²⁵Saul and his men began the search, and when David was told about it, he went down to the rock and stayed in the Desert of Maon. When Saul heard this, he went into the Desert of Maon in pursuit of David.

²⁶Saul*o* was going along one side of the mountain, and David and his men were on the other side, hurrying to get away from Saul. As Saul and his forces were closing in on David and his men to capture them, ²⁷a messenger came to Saul, saying, "Come quickly! The Philistines are raiding the land." ²⁸Then Saul broke off his pursuit

a 23 Or *me at Nacon*

of David and went to meet the Philistines. That is why they call this place Sela Hammahlekoth.*a* *29*And David went up from there and lived in the strongholds of En Gedi.*a*

Chapter 24 Theme _____

24 After Saul returned from pursuing the Philistines, he was told, "David is in the Desert of En Gedi.*b*" *2*So Saul took three thousand chosen men from all Israel and set out to look*c* for David and his men near the Crags of the Wild Goats.

*3*He came to the sheep pens along the way; a cave*d* was there, and Saul went in to relieve*e* himself. David and his men were far back in the cave. *4*The men said, "This is the day the LORD spoke*f* of when he said*b* to you, 'I will give your enemy into your hands for you to deal with as you wish.' "*g* Then David crept up unnoticed and cut off a corner of Saul's robe.

*5*Afterward, David was conscience-stricken*h* for having cut off a corner of his robe. *6*He said to his men, "The LORD forbid that I should do such a thing to my master, the LORD's anointed,*i* or lift my hand against him; for he is the anointed of the LORD." *7*With these words David rebuked his men and did not allow them to attack Saul. And Saul left the cave and went his way.

*8*Then David went out of the cave and called out to Saul, "My lord the king!" When Saul looked behind him, David bowed down and prostrated himself with his face to the ground.*j* *9*He said to Saul, "Why do you listen when men say, 'David is bent on harming you'? *10*This day you have seen with your own eyes how the LORD delivered you into my hands in the cave. Some urged me to kill you, but I spared you; I said, 'I will not lift my hand against my master, because he is the LORD's anointed.' *11*See, my father, look at this piece of your robe in my hand! I cut off the corner of your robe but did not kill you. Now understand and recognize that I am not guilty*k* of wrongdoing or rebellion. I have not wronged you, but you are hunting*l* me down to take my life. *12*May the LORD judge*m* between you and me. And may the LORD avenge*n* the wrongs you have done to me, but my hand will not touch you. *13*As the old saying goes, 'From evildoers come evil deeds,*o*' so my hand will not touch you.

14"Against whom has the king of Israel come out? Whom are you pursuing? A dead dog?*p* A flea?*q* *15*May the LORD be our judge*r* and decide between us. May he consider my cause and uphold*s* it; may he vindicate*t* me by delivering*u* me from your hand."

a 28 Sela Hammahlekoth means *rock of parting.*   *b 4* Or *"Today the LORD is saying*

David's Journeys: 1 Samuel 24

23:29
a 2Ch 20:2

24:1
b 1Sa 23:28-29

24:2
c 1Sa 26:2

24:3
d Ps 57 Title; 142 Title
e Jdg 3:24

24:4
f 1Sa 25:28-30
g 1Sa 23:17; 26:8

24:5
h 2Sa 24:10

24:6
i 1Sa 26:11

24:8
j 1Sa 25:23-24

24:11
k Ps 7:3
l 1Sa 23:14,23; 1Sa 26:20

24:12
m Ge 16:5; 31:53; Job 5:8
n Jdg 11:27; 1Sa 26:10

24:13
o Mt 7:20

24:14
p 1Sa 17:43; 2Sa 9:8
q 1Sa 26:20

24:15
r ver 12
s Ps 35:1,23; Mic 7:9
t Ps 43:1
u Ps 119:134,154

24:16
a 1Sa 26:17

24:17
b Ge 38:26;
1Sa 26:21
c Mt 5:44

24:18
d 1Sa 26:23

24:20
e 1Sa 23:17
f 1Sa 13:14

24:21
g Ge 21:23;
2Sa 21:1-9
h 1Sa 20:14-15

24:22
i 1Sa 23:29

25:1
j 1Sa 28:3
k Nu 20:29;
Dt 34:8
l Ge 21:21;
2Ch 33:20

25:2
m Jos 15:55;
1Sa 23:24

25:3
n Pr 31:10
o Jos 15:13

25:6
p Ps 122:7;
Lk 10:5
q 1Ch 12:18

25:7
r ver 15

25:8
s Ne 8:10

25:10
t Jdg 9:28

25:11
u Jdg 8:6

[16]When David finished saying this, Saul asked, "Is that your voice,*a* David my son?" And he wept aloud. [17]"You are more righteous than I,"*b* he said. "You have treated me well,*c* but I have treated you badly. [18]You have just now told me of the good you did to me; the LORD delivered*d* me into your hands, but you did not kill me. [19]When a man finds his enemy, does he let him get away unharmed? May the LORD reward you well for the way you treated me today. [20]I know that you will surely be king*e* and that the kingdom*f* of Israel will be established in your hands. [21]Now swear*g* to me by the LORD that you will not cut off my descendants or wipe out my name from my father's family.*h*"

[22]So David gave his oath to Saul. Then Saul returned home, but David and his men went up to the stronghold.*i*

Chapter 25 Theme

25 Now Samuel died,*j* and all Israel assembled and mourned*k* for him; and they buried him at his home in Ramah.*l* Then David moved down into the Desert of Maon.*a*

[2]A certain man in Maon,*m* who had property there at Carmel, was very wealthy. He had a thousand goats and three thousand sheep, which he was shearing in Carmel. [3]His name was Nabal and his wife's name was Abigail.*n* She was an intelligent and beautiful woman, but her husband, a Calebite,*o* was surly and mean in his dealings.

[4]While David was in the desert, he heard that Nabal was shearing sheep. [5]So he sent ten young men and said to them, "Go up to Nabal at Carmel and greet him in my name. [6]Say to him: 'Long life to you! Good health*p* to you and your household! And good health to all that is yours!*q*

[7]" 'Now I hear that it is sheep-shearing time. When your shepherds were with us, we did not mistreat*r* them, and the whole time they were at Carmel nothing of theirs was missing. [8]Ask your own servants and they will tell you. Therefore be favorable toward my young men, since we come at a festive time. Please give your servants and your son David whatever*s* you can find for them.' "

[9]When David's men arrived, they gave Nabal this message in David's name. Then they waited.

[10]Nabal answered David's servants, "Who*t* is this David? Who is this son of Jesse? Many servants are breaking away from their masters these days. [11]Why should I take my bread*u* and water, and

David's Journeys: 1 Samuel 25–27:2

a 1 Some Septuagint manuscripts; Hebrew *Paran*

the meat I have slaughtered for my shearers, and give it to men coming from who knows where?"

¹²David's men turned around and went back. When they arrived, they reported every word. ¹³David said to his men, "Put on your swords!" So they put on their swords, and David put on his. About four hundred men went*ᵃ* up with David, while two hundred stayed with the supplies.*ᵇ*

¹⁴One of the servants told Nabal's wife Abigail: "David sent messengers from the desert to give our master his greetings,*ᶜ* but he hurled insults at them. ¹⁵Yet these men were very good to us. They did not mistreat*ᵈ* us, and the whole time we were out in the fields near them nothing was missing.*ᵉ* ¹⁶Night and day they were a wall*ᶠ* around us all the time we were herding our sheep near them. ¹⁷Now think it over and see what you can do, because disaster is hanging over our master and his whole household. He is such a wicked*ᵍ* man that no one can talk to him."

¹⁸Abigail lost no time. She took two hundred loaves of bread, two skins of wine, five dressed sheep, five seahs*ᵃ* of roasted grain, a hundred cakes of raisins*ʰ* and two hundred cakes of pressed figs, and loaded them on donkeys.*ⁱ* ¹⁹Then she told her servants, "Go on ahead;*ʲ* I'll follow you." But she did not tell her husband Nabal.

²⁰As she came riding her donkey into a mountain ravine, there were David and his men descending toward her, and she met them. ²¹David had just said, "It's been useless—all my watching over this fellow's property in the desert so that nothing of his was missing. He has paid*ᵏ* me back evil for good. ²²May God deal with David,*ᵇ* be it ever so severely,*ˡ* if by morning I leave alive one male*ᵐ* of all who belong to him!"

²³When Abigail saw David, she quickly got off her donkey and bowed down before David with her face to the ground.*ⁿ* ²⁴She fell at his feet and said: "My lord, let the blame be on me alone. Please let your servant speak to you; hear what your servant has to say. ²⁵May my lord pay no attention to that wicked man Nabal. He is just like his name—his name is Fool,*ᵒ* and folly goes with him. But as for me, your servant, I did not see the men my master sent.

²⁶"Now since the LORD has kept you, my master, from bloodshed*ᵖ* and from avenging*�q* yourself with your own hands, as surely as the LORD lives and as you live, may your enemies and all who intend to harm my master be like Nabal.*ʳ* ²⁷And let this gift,*ˢ* which your servant has brought to my master, be given to the men who follow you. ²⁸Please forgive*ᵗ* your servant's offense, for the LORD will certainly make a lasting*ᵘ* dynasty for my master, because he fights the LORD's battles.*ᵛ* Let no wrongdoing*ʷ* be found in you as long as you live. ²⁹Even though someone is pursuing you to take

---

a 18 That is, probably about a bushel (about 37 liters)   *b 22* Some Septuagint manuscripts; Hebrew *with David's enemies*

25:13
a 1Sa 23:13
b 1Sa 30:24

25:14
c 1Sa 13:10

25:15
d ver 7
e ver 21

25:16
f Ex 14:22;
Job 1:10

25:17
g 1Sa 20:7

25:18
h 1Ch 12:40
i 2Sa 16:1

25:19
j Ge 32:20

25:21
k Ps 109:5

25:22
l 1Sa 3:17; 20:13
m 1Ki 14:10;
21:21; 2Ki 9:8

25:23
n 1Sa 20:41

25:25
o Pr 14:16

25:26
p ver 33
q Heb 10:30
r 2Sa 18:32

25:27
s Ge 33:11;
1Sa 30:26

25:28
t ver 24
u 2Sa 7:11,26
v 1Sa 18:17
w 1Sa 24:11

25:29
a Jer 10:18

25:30
b 1Sa 13:14

25:31
c Ge 40:14

25:32
d Ge 24:27;
Ex 18:10;
Lk 1:68

25:33
e ver 26

25:35
f Ge 19:21;
1Sa 20:42;
2Ki 5:19

25:36
g 2Sa 13:23
h Pr 20:1;
Isa 5:11,22;
Hos 4:11
i ver 19

25:38
j 1Sa 26:10;
2Sa 6:7

25:42
k Ge 24:61-67

25:43
l Jos 15:56
m 1Sa 27:3; 30:5

25:44
n 2Sa 3:15
o Isa 10:30

26:1
p 1Sa 23:19
q Ps 54 Title

26:2
r 1Sa 13:2; 24:2

your life, the life of my master will be bound securely in the bundle of the living by the LORD your God. But the lives of your enemies he will hurl*a* away as from the pocket of a sling. ³⁰When the LORD has done for my master every good thing he promised concerning him and has appointed him leader*b* over Israel, ³¹my master will not have on his conscience the staggering burden of needless bloodshed or of having avenged himself. And when the LORD has brought my master success, remember*c* your servant."

³²David said to Abigail, "Praise*d* be to the LORD, the God of Israel, who has sent you today to meet me. ³³May you be blessed for your good judgment and for keeping me from bloodshed*e* this day and from avenging myself with my own hands. ³⁴Otherwise, as surely as the LORD, the God of Israel, lives, who has kept me from harming you, if you had not come quickly to meet me, not one male belonging to Nabal would have been left alive by daybreak."

³⁵Then David accepted from her hand what she had brought him and said, "Go home in peace. I have heard your words and granted*f* your request."

³⁶When Abigail went to Nabal, he was in the house holding a banquet like that of a king. He was in high*g* spirits and very drunk.*h* So she told*i* him nothing until daybreak. ³⁷Then in the morning, when Nabal was sober, his wife told him all these things, and his heart failed him and he became like a stone. ³⁸About ten days later, the LORD struck*j* Nabal and he died.

³⁹When David heard that Nabal was dead, he said, "Praise be to the LORD, who has upheld my cause against Nabal for treating me with contempt. He has kept his servant from doing wrong and has brought Nabal's wrongdoing down on his own head."

Then David sent word to Abigail, asking her to become his wife. ⁴⁰His servants went to Carmel and said to Abigail, "David has sent us to you to take you to become his wife."

⁴¹She bowed down with her face to the ground and said, "Here is your maidservant, ready to serve you and wash the feet of my master's servants." ⁴²Abigail*k* quickly got on a donkey and, attended by her five maids, went with David's messengers and became his wife. ⁴³David had also married Ahinoam*l* of Jezreel, and they both were his wives.*m* ⁴⁴But Saul had given his daughter Michal, David's wife, to Paltiel*a**n* son of Laish, who was from Gallim.*o*

Chapter 26 Theme

26 The Ziphites*p* went to Saul at Gibeah and said, "Is not David hiding*q* on the hill of Hakilah, which faces Jeshimon?" ²So Saul went down to the Desert of Ziph, with his three thousand chosen men of Israel, to search*r* there for David. ³Saul made

a 44 Hebrew *Palti,* a variant of *Paltiel*

his camp beside the road on the hill of Hakilah facing Jeshimon, but David stayed in the desert. When he saw that Saul had followed him there, ⁴he sent out scouts and learned that Saul had definitely arrived.ᵃ

⁵Then David set out and went to the place where Saul had camped. He saw where Saul and Abnerᵃ son of Ner, the commander of the army, had lain down. Saul was lying inside the camp, with the army encamped around him.

⁶David then asked Ahimelech the Hittite and Abishai son of Zeruiah,ᵇ Joab's brother, "Who will go down into the camp with me to Saul?"

"I'll go with you," said Abishai.

⁷So David and Abishai went to the army by night, and there was Saul, lying asleep inside the camp with his spear stuck in the ground near his head. Abner and the soldiers were lying around him.

⁸Abishai said to David, "Today God has delivered your enemy into your hands. Now let me pin him to the ground with one thrust of my spear; I won't strike him twice."

⁹But David said to Abishai, "Don't destroy him! Who can lay a hand on the LORD's anointedᶜ and be guiltless?ᵈ ¹⁰As surely as the LORD lives," he said, "the LORD himself will strikeᵉ him; either his timeᶠ will come and he will die,ᵍ or he will go into battle and perish. ¹¹But the LORD forbid that I should lay a hand on the LORD's anointed. Now get the spear and water jug that are near his head, and let's go."

¹²So David took the spear and water jug near Saul's head, and they left. No one saw or knew about it, nor did anyone wake up. They were all sleeping, because the LORD had put them into a deep sleep.ʰ

¹³Then David crossed over to the other side and stood on top of the hill some distance away; there was a wide space between them. ¹⁴He called out to the army and to Abner son of Ner, "Aren't you going to answer me, Abner?"

Abner replied, "Who are you who calls to the king?"

¹⁵David said, "You're a man, aren't you? And who is like you in Israel? Why didn't you guard your lord the king? Someone came to destroy your lord the king. ¹⁶What you have done is not good. As surely as the LORD lives, you and your men deserve to die, because you did not guard your master, the LORD's anointed. Look around you. Where are the king's spear and water jug that were near his head?"

¹⁷Saul recognized David's voice and said, "Is that your voice,ⁱ David my son?"

David replied, "Yes it is, my lord the king." ¹⁸And he added, "Why is my lord pursuing his servant? What have I done, and what

26:5
ᵃ1Sa 14:50;
17:55

26:6
ᵇJdg 7:10-11;
1Ch 2:16

26:9
ᶜ2Sa 1:14
ᵈ1Sa 24:5

26:10
ᵉ1Sa 25:38;
Ro 12:19
ᶠGe 47:29;
Dt 31:14;
Ps 37:13
ᵍ1Sa 31:6;
2Sa 1:1

26:12
ʰGe 2:21; 15:12

26:17
ⁱ1Sa 24:16

26:18
a 1Sa 24:9,11-14

26:19
b 2Sa 16:11
c 2Sa 14:16

26:20
d 1Sa 24:14

26:21
e Ex 9:27;
1Sa 15:24
f 1Sa 24:17

26:23
g Ps 62:12
h Ps 7:8;
18:20,24

26:24
i Ps 54:7

27:2
j 1Sa 25:13
k 1Sa 21:10
l 1Ki 2:39

27:3
m 1Sa 25:43;
30:3

27:6
n Jos 15:31; 19:5;
Ne 11:28

27:7
o 1Sa 29:3

27:8
p Jos 13:2,13
q Ex 17:8;
1Sa 15:7-8
r Ex 15:22

wrong[a] am I guilty of? [19]Now let my lord the king listen to his servant's words. If the LORD has incited you against me, then may he accept an offering.[b] If, however, men have done it, may they be cursed before the LORD! They have now driven me from my share in the LORD's inheritance[c] and have said, 'Go, serve other gods.' [20]Now do not let my blood fall to the ground far from the presence of the LORD. The king of Israel has come out to look for a flea[d]—as one hunts a partridge in the mountains."

[21]Then Saul said, "I have sinned.[e] Come back, David my son. Because you considered my life precious[f] today, I will not try to harm you again. Surely I have acted like a fool and have erred greatly."

[22]"Here is the king's spear," David answered. "Let one of your young men come over and get it. [23]The LORD rewards[g] every man for his righteousness[h] and faithfulness. The LORD delivered you into my hands today, but I would not lay a hand on the LORD's anointed. [24]As surely as I valued your life today, so may the LORD value my life and deliver[i] me from all trouble."

[25]Then Saul said to David, "May you be blessed, my son David; you will do great things and surely triumph."

So David went on his way, and Saul returned home.

Chapter 27 Theme

27 But David thought to himself, "One of these days I will be destroyed by the hand of Saul. The best thing I can do is to escape to the land of the Philistines. Then Saul will give up searching for me anywhere in Israel, and I will slip out of his hand."

[2]So David and the six hundred men[j] with him left and went[k] over to Achish[l] son of Maoch king of Gath. [3]David and his men settled in Gath with Achish. Each man had his family with him, and David had his two wives:[m] Ahinoam of Jezreel and Abigail of Carmel, the widow of Nabal. [4]When Saul was told that David had fled to Gath, he no longer searched for him.

[5]Then David said to Achish, "If I have found favor in your eyes, let a place be assigned to me in one of the country towns, that I may live there. Why should your servant live in the royal city with you?"

[6]So on that day Achish gave him Ziklag,[n] and it has belonged to the kings of Judah ever since. [7]David lived[o] in Philistine territory a year and four months.

[8]Now David and his men went up and raided the Geshurites,[p] the Girzites and the Amalekites.[q] (From ancient times these peoples had lived in the land extending to Shur[r] and Egypt.) [9]Whenever David attacked an area, he did not leave a man or

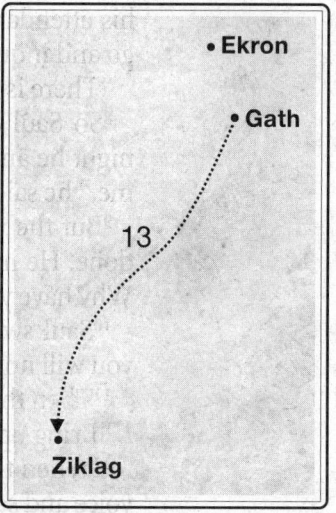

David's Journeys: 1 Samuel 27

woman alive,[a] but took sheep and cattle, donkeys and camels, and clothes. Then he returned to Achish. [10]When Achish asked, "Where did you go raiding today?" David would say, "Against the Negev of Judah" or "Against the Negev of Jerahmeel[b]" or "Against the Negev of the Kenites.[c]" [11]He did not leave a man or woman alive to be brought to Gath, for he thought, "They might inform on us and say, 'This is what David did.'" And such was his practice as long as he lived in Philistine territory. [12]Achish trusted David and said to himself, "He has become so odious to his people, the Israelites, that he will be my servant forever."

Chapter 28 Theme

28

In those days the Philistines gathered[d] their forces to fight against Israel. Achish said to David, "You must understand that you and your men will accompany me in the army."

[2]David said, "Then you will see for yourself what your servant can do."

Achish replied, "Very well, I will make you my bodyguard for life."

[3]Now Samuel was dead,[e] and all Israel had mourned for him and buried him in his own town of Ramah.[f] Saul had expelled the mediums and spiritists[g] from the land.

[4]The Philistines assembled and came and set up camp at Shunem,[h] while Saul gathered all the Israelites and set up camp at Gilboa.[i] [5]When Saul saw the Philistine army, he was afraid; terror filled his heart. [6]He inquired[j] of the LORD, but the LORD did not answer him by dreams[k] or Urim[l] or prophets. [7]Saul then said to his attendants, "Find me a woman who is a medium,[m] so I may go and inquire of her."

"There is one in Endor,[n]" they said.

[8]So Saul disguised[o] himself, putting on other clothes, and at night he and two men went to the woman. "Consult[p] a spirit for me," he said, "and bring up for me the one I name."

[9]But the woman said to him, "Surely you know what Saul has done. He has cut off[q] the mediums and spiritists from the land. Why have you set a trap for my life to bring about my death?"

[10]Saul swore to her by the LORD, "As surely as the LORD lives, you will not be punished for this."

[11]Then the woman asked, "Whom shall I bring up for you?"

"Bring up Samuel," he said.

[12]When the woman saw Samuel, she cried out at the top of her voice and said to Saul, "Why have you deceived me? You are Saul!"

[13]The king said to her, "Don't be afraid. What do you see?"

The woman said, "I see a spirit[a] coming up out of the ground."

a 13 Or see spirits; or see gods

27:9 [a] 1Sa 15:3

27:10 [b] 1Sa 30:29; 1Ch 2:9,25 [c] Jdg 1:16

28:1 [d] 1Sa 29:1

28:3 [e] 1Sa 25:1 [f] 1Sa 7:17 [g] Ex 22:18; Lev 19:31; 20:27; Dt 18:10-11; 1Sa 15:23

28:4 [h] Jos 19:18; 2Ki 4:8 [i] 1Sa 31:1,3

28:6 [j] 1Sa 14:37; 1Ch 10:13-14; Pr 1:28 [k] Nu 12:6 [l] Ex 28:30; Nu 27:21

28:7 [m] Ac 16:16 [n] Jos 17:11

28:8 [o] 2Ch 18:29; 35:22 [p] Dt 18:10-11; 1Ch 10:13; Isa 8:19

28:9 [q] ver 3

28:14
a 1Sa 15:27;
24:8

28:15
b ver 6;
1Sa 18:12

28:17
c 1Sa 15:28

28:18
d 1Sa 15:20
e 1Ki 20:42

28:19
f 1Sa 31:2

28:21
g Jdg 12:3;
1Sa 19:5;
Job 13:14

28:23
h 2Ki 5:13

29:1
i 1Sa 28:1
j Jos 12:18;
1Sa 4:1
k 2Ki 9:30

29:2
l 1Sa 28:2

29:3
m 1Sa 27:7;
Da 6:5

29:4
n 1Ch 12:19

¹⁴"What does he look like?" he asked.

"An old man wearing a robe*a* is coming up," she said.

Then Saul knew it was Samuel, and he bowed down and prostrated himself with his face to the ground.

¹⁵Samuel said to Saul, "Why have you disturbed me by bringing me up?"

"I am in great distress," Saul said. "The Philistines are fighting against me, and God has turned*b* away from me. He no longer answers me, either by prophets or by dreams. So I have called on you to tell me what to do."

¹⁶Samuel said, "Why do you consult me, now that the LORD has turned away from you and become your enemy? ¹⁷The LORD has done what he predicted through me. The LORD has torn*c* the kingdom out of your hands and given it to one of your neighbors—to David. ¹⁸Because you did not obey*d* the LORD or carry out his fierce wrath*e* against the Amalekites, the LORD has done this to you today. ¹⁹The LORD will hand over both Israel and you to the Philistines, and tomorrow you and your sons*f* will be with me. The LORD will also hand over the army of Israel to the Philistines."

²⁰Immediately Saul fell full length on the ground, filled with fear because of Samuel's words. His strength was gone, for he had eaten nothing all that day and night.

²¹When the woman came to Saul and saw that he was greatly shaken, she said, "Look, your maidservant has obeyed you. I took my life*g* in my hands and did what you told me to do. ²²Now please listen to your servant and let me give you some food so you may eat and have the strength to go on your way."

²³He refused*h* and said, "I will not eat."

But his men joined the woman in urging him, and he listened to them. He got up from the ground and sat on the couch.

²⁴The woman had a fattened calf at the house, which she butchered at once. She took some flour, kneaded it and baked bread without yeast. ²⁵Then she set it before Saul and his men, and they ate. That same night they got up and left.

Chapter 29 Theme _____

29 The Philistines gathered*i* all their forces at Aphek,*j* and Israel camped by the spring in Jezreel.*k* ²As the Philistine rulers marched with their units of hundreds and thousands, David and his men were marching at the rear*l* with Achish. ³The commanders of the Philistines asked, "What about these Hebrews?"

Achish replied, "Is this not David, who was an officer of Saul king of Israel? He has already been with me for over a year,*m* and from the day he left Saul until now, I have found no fault in him."

⁴But the Philistine commanders were angry with him and said, "Send*n* the man back, that he may return to the place you assigned

him. He must not go with us into battle, or he will turn[a] against us during the fighting. How better could he regain his master's favor than by taking the heads of our own men? [5]Isn't this the David they sang about in their dances:

> "'Saul has slain his thousands,
> and David his tens of thousands'?"[b]

[6]So Achish called David and said to him, "As surely as the LORD lives, you have been reliable, and I would be pleased to have you serve with me in the army. From the day[c] you came to me until now, I have found no fault in you, but the rulers[d] don't approve of you. [7]Turn back and go in peace; do nothing to displease the Philistine rulers."

[8]"But what have I done?" asked David. "What have you found against your servant from the day I came to you until now? Why can't I go and fight against the enemies of my lord the king?"

[9]Achish answered, "I know that you have been as pleasing in my eyes as an angel[e] of God; nevertheless, the Philistine commanders[f] have said, 'He must not go up with us into battle.' [10]Now get up early, along with your master's servants who have come with you, and leave[g] in the morning as soon as it is light."

[11]So David and his men got up early in the morning to go back to the land of the Philistines, and the Philistines went up to Jezreel.

Chapter 30 Theme

30 David and his men reached Ziklag[h] on the third day. Now the Amalekites[i] had raided the Negev and Ziklag. They had attacked Ziklag and burned it, [2]and had taken captive the women and all who were in it, both young and old. They killed none of them, but carried them off as they went on their way.

[3]When David and his men came to Ziklag, they found it destroyed by fire and their wives and sons and daughters taken captive. [4]So David and his men wept aloud until they had no strength left to weep. [5]David's two wives[j] had been captured— Ahinoam of Jezreel and Abigail, the widow of Nabal of Carmel. [6]David was greatly distressed because the men were talking of stoning[k] him; each one was bitter in spirit because of his sons and daughters. But David found strength[l] in the LORD his God.

[7]Then David said to Abiathar[m] the priest, the son of Ahimelech, "Bring me the ephod.[n]" Abiathar brought it to him, [8]and David inquired[o] of the LORD, "Shall I pursue this raiding party? Will I overtake them?"

"Pursue them," he answered. "You will certainly overtake them and succeed[p] in the rescue."

INSIGHT

The *ephod* was used to seek guidance from God. Described in Exodus 28, it was a linen garment worn by the priest and also by David when he was king (2 Samuel 6:14). The ephod was fastened on each shoulder by onyx clasps which had the names of six tribes engraved on one clasp and six tribes engraved on the other. The *breastpiece*, which was fastened to the ephod, had a linen pouch which held the *Urim* and *Thummim*, which may have been used as sacred lots to reveal God's will (1 Samuel 28:6).

Cross references

29:4
[a] 1Sa 14:21

29:5
[b] 1Sa 18:7; 21:11

29:6
[c] 1Sa 27:8-12
[d] ver 3

29:9
[e] 2Sa 14:17,20; 19:27
[f] ver 4

29:10
[g] 1Ch 12:19

30:1
[h] 1Sa 29:4,11
[i] 1Sa 15:7; 27:8

30:5
[j] 1Sa 25:43; 2Sa 2:2

30:6
[k] Ex 17:4; Jn 8:59
[l] Ps 27:14; 56:3-4,11; Ro 4:20

30:7
[m] 1Sa 22:20
[n] 1Sa 23:9

30:8
[o] 1Sa 23:2
[p] ver 18

30:9
a 1Sa 27:2

30:10
b ver 9,21

30:12
c Jdg 15:19

30:14
d 2Sa 8:18;
1Ki 1:38,44;
Eze 25:16;
Zep 2:5
e ver 16;
Jos 14:13; 15:13
f ver 1

30:16
g Lk 12:19
h ver 14

30:17
i 1Sa 11:11
j 1Sa 15:3

30:18
k Ge 14:16

30:21
l ver 10

⁹David and the six hundred menᵃ with him came to the Besor Ravine, where some stayed behind, ¹⁰for two hundred men were too exhaustedᵇ to cross the ravine. But David and four hundred men continued the pursuit.

¹¹They found an Egyptian in a field and brought him to David. They gave him water to drink and food to eat— ¹²part of a cake of pressed figs and two cakes of raisins. He ate and was revived,ᶜ for he had not eaten any food or drunk any water for three days and three nights.

¹³David asked him, "To whom do you belong, and where do you come from?"

He said, "I am an Egyptian, the slave of an Amalekite. My master abandoned me when I became ill three days ago. ¹⁴We raided the Negev of the Kerethitesᵈ and the territory belonging to Judah and the Negev of Caleb.ᵉ And we burnedᶠ Ziklag."

¹⁵David asked him, "Can you lead me down to this raiding party?"

He answered, "Swear to me before God that you will not kill me or hand me over to my master, and I will take you down to them."

¹⁶He led David down, and there they were, scattered over the countryside, eating, drinking and revelingᵍ because of the great amount of plunderʰ they had taken from the land of the Philistines and from Judah. ¹⁷David foughtⁱ them from dusk until the evening of the next day, and none of them got away, except four hundred young men who rode off on camels and fled.ʲ ¹⁸David recoveredᵏ everything the Amalekites had taken, including his two wives. ¹⁹Nothing was missing: young or old, boy or girl, plunder or anything else they had taken. David brought everything back. ²⁰He took all the flocks and herds, and his men drove them ahead of the other livestock, saying, "This is David's plunder."

²¹Then David came to the two hundred men who had been too exhaustedˡ to follow him and who were left behind at the Besor Ravine. They came out to meet David and the people with him. As David and his men approached, he greeted them. ²²But all the evil men and troublemakers among David's followers said, "Because they did not go out with us, we will not share with them the plunder

Ziklag and the Plunder

we recovered. However, each man may take his wife and children and go."

[23]David replied, "No, my brothers, you must not do that with what the LORD has given us. He has protected us and handed over to us the forces that came against us. [24]Who will listen to what you say? The share of the man who stayed with the supplies is to be the same as that of him who went down to the battle. All will share alike.[a]" [25]David made this a statute and ordinance for Israel from that day to this.

[26]When David arrived in Ziklag, he sent some of the plunder to the elders of Judah, who were his friends, saying, "Here is a present for you from the plunder of the LORD's enemies."

[27]He sent it to those who were in Bethel,[b] Ramoth[c] Negev and Jattir;[d] [28]to those in Aroer,[e] Siphmoth, Eshtemoa[f] [29]and Racal; to those in the towns of the Jerahmeelites[g] and the Kenites;[h] [30]to those in Hormah,[i] Bor Ashan,[j] Athach [31]and Hebron;[k] and to those in all the other places where David and his men had roamed.

Chapter 31 Theme _____

31 Now the Philistines fought against Israel; the Israelites fled before them, and many fell slain on Mount Gilboa.[l] [2]The Philistines pressed hard after Saul and his sons, and they killed his sons Jonathan, Abinadab and Malki-Shua. [3]The fighting grew fierce around Saul, and when the archers overtook him, they wounded[m] him critically.

[4]Saul said to his armor-bearer, "Draw your sword and run me through,[n] or these uncircumcised[o] fellows will come and run me through and abuse me."

But his armor-bearer was terrified and would not do it; so Saul took his own sword and fell on it. [5]When the armor-bearer saw that Saul was dead, he too fell on his sword and died with him. [6]So Saul and his three sons and his armor-bearer and all his men died together that same day.

[7]When the Israelites along the valley and those across the Jordan saw that the Israelite army had fled and that Saul and his sons had died, they abandoned their towns and fled. And the Philistines came and occupied them.

[8]The next day, when the Philistines came to strip the dead, they found Saul and his three sons fallen on Mount Gilboa. [9]They cut off his head and stripped off his armor, and they sent messengers throughout the land of the Philistines to proclaim the news[p] in the temple of their idols and among their people.[q] [10]They put his armor in the temple of the Ashtoreths[r] and fastened his body to the wall of Beth Shan.[s]

Mediterranean (Great) Sea
Mt. Tabor
Endor
Hill of Moreh
Philistine camp
Shunem
Jezreel
Israelite camp
Mt. Gilboa
Death of Saul and his sons
Beth Shan
Socoh
Shechem
Joppa
Aphek
To Ziklag
Gibeah of Saul
Jebus

The Death of Saul and His Sons

30:24
[a]Nu 31:27;
Jos 22:8

30:27
[b]Jos 7:2
[c]Jos 19:8
[d]Jos 15:48

30:28
[e]Jos 13:16
[f]Jos 15:50

30:29
[g]1Sa 27:10
[h]Jdg 1:16;
1Sa 15:6

30:30
[i]Nu 14:45;
Jdg 1:17
[j]Jos 15:42

30:31
[k]Jos 14:13;
2Sa 2:1,4

31:1
[l]1Sa 28:4;
1Ch 10:1-12

31:3
[m]2Sa 1:6

31:4
[n]Jdg 9:54;
2Sa 1:6,10
[o]1Sa 14:6

31:9
[p]2Sa 1:20
[q]Jdg 16:24

31:10
[r]Jdg 2:12-13;
1Sa 7:3
[s]Jos 17:11;
2Sa 21:12

31:11
a 1Sa 11:1

31:12
b 2Sa 2:4-7;
2Ch 16:14;
Am 6:10

[11]When the people of Jabesh Gilead*a* heard of what the Philistines had done to Saul, [12]all their valiant men journeyed through the night to Beth Shan. They took down the bodies of Saul and his sons from the wall of Beth Shan and went to Jabesh, where they burned*b* them. [13]Then they took their bones*c* and buried them under a tamarisk*d* tree at Jabesh, and they fasted*e* seven days.*f*

31:13 *c* 2Sa 21:12-14 *d* 1Sa 22:6 *e* 2Sa 1:12 *f* Ge 50:10

Theme of 1 Samuel:

SEGMENT DIVISIONS

		MAIN DIVISIONS	CHAPTER THEMES
		SAMUEL, THE LAST JUDGE	1	
			2	
			3	
			4	
			5	
			6	
			7	
		FROM SAMUEL TO SAUL / FROM JUDGES TO KINGS	8	
			9	
			10	
			11	
			12	
			13	
			14	
			15	
		THE PREPARATION OF ANOTHER KING	16	
			17	
			18	
			19	
			20	
			21	
			22	
			23	
			24	
			25	
			26	
			27	
			28	
			29	
			30	
			31	

Author:

Date:

Purpose:

Key Words:

This is a full-page map illustration.

Shen–uncertain location where Samuel raised a monument
Beth Car–unidentified place west of Mizpah below which
the stone named *Ebenezer* was raised

Israel in the Days of Samuel, Saul, and David

Mediterranean (Great) Sea

Sidon

Damascus

Tyre

Abel
Dan
Maachah

PHOENICIA

Valley of Mizpah

Sea of Galilee

GESHUR

Hammath

Helam
Tob
Rogelim

Kishon River

ASSHUR

Rehob

Lo Debar

Mt. Gilboa

Jordan River

Jabesh Gilead

Mahanaim
Jabbok River

AMMON

Jazer
Rabbah

GILEAD

Ramah (possibly Ramathaim)

Shiloh

Aphek

Baal Hazor

CANAAN

EPHRAIM

Gittaim

Bethel
Micmash

Kiriath Jearim

Naioth
Beeroth

Geba
Gibeah

Zobah

Nob
Jerusalem

Gilgal

Beth Shemesh

Gibeon
Bethlehem

En Rogel

Baal Perazim

Shaaraim
Ekron

Valley of Elah

Valley of Rephaim

Ashdod

Giloh
Gath

Azekah
Socoh

Tekoa
Keilah

Ashkelon

Adullam

Dead Sea

Gaza

Hebron
Ziph

En Gedi
Forest of Hereth

Ziklag

Forest of Horesh

Jezreel
Maon

MOAB

Beersheba

Wilderness of Maon

JUDAH

Aroer

PHILISTIA

*Wilderness of Shur
(between Egypt and Israel)*

ARABAH

Zered Brook

EDOM

Indicates Saul's wars

497

2 SAMUEL

*T*he LORD is compassionate and gracious, slow to anger, abounding in love. He will not always accuse, nor will he harbor his anger forever. . . . As far as the east is from the west, so far has he removed our transgressions from us. As a father has compassion on his children, so the LORD has compassion on those who fear him; for he knows how we are formed, he remembers that we are dust" (Psalm 103:8, 9, 12-14).

These are the words of David. Were they written before or after he became king? Before or after he sinned with Bathsheba? We don't know, but we do know David understood their meaning. This you will see as you study 2 Samuel.

∾ THINGS TO DO

General Instructions

1. You should study 1 Samuel before you study 2 Samuel. In the Hebrew Scriptures they were written as one book and were not divided until later. Second Samuel records David's life from the time of Saul's death until the account of David's later years and death (which are recorded in 1 Kings). First Chronicles 10 through 29 covers the same period in David's life. As you observe this book keep in mind what you have learned in 1 Samuel.

2. As you study 2 Samuel you need to remember that you are studying a biographical account of a man whose frame is dust, but a man whom God would later say was a man after his own heart. Therefore as you study chapter by chapter:

   a. Observe each chapter in the light of the five W's and an H. Ask questions such as: Who are the main characters in this chapter? What is taking place? Where is this happening? When is it occurring? Why did it happen? Why this response? What are the consequences? How was it handled? How did David (or whoever) respond? Record your insights in the margin.

   b. Mark all references to time with a symbol so these references can be easily recognized. Also mark selected geographical references on the map on page 497.

   c. In chapter 22 and throughout the psalms David wrote about the character of God. Watch for the references to God and note in the margin what you learn about his character and his ways, even as David did.

   d. Watch and see what lessons you can learn for your life. Record these in the margin as you did in 1 Samuel under the heading "LFL" (Lessons for Life).

3. When you finish each chapter record the theme or main event of the chapter on 2 SAMUEL AT A GLANCE on page 545 and on the line next to the chapter number.

Chapters 1-10: David Becomes King of Judah and Then Israel

1. As you read each chapter, in addition to following the general instructions, mark the following key words: *king, (rule), reigned, inquired, ephod, ark, covenant (agreement, compact), before the Lord,* and *evil (wrong)*. Write these key words on an index card you can use as a bookmark. As you mark these words observe what you learn and in the margin record any pertinent insights.

2. When you study chapter 7 give special attention to the Lord's promises to David. Record these in the margin. Then observe what David does and how he responds to the Lord.

3. In 1 Samuel you marked every reference to *covenant*. In 1 Samuel 20 Jonathan and David make a covenant between their "houses" (families). When you study chapters 4 and 9 of 2 Samuel keep

in mind the covenant David and Jonathan made in regard to their houses and notice how David fulfills this covenant. Also when you study Mephibosheth, remember 2 Samuel 5:6-8.

Chapters 11, 12: David's Sins

1. Mark the following key words: *find out (pleaded with)*, *ark*, and *evil (displeased, calamity, sinned, sin)*. Make a new bookmark for this segment.

2. Carefully watch the progression of events in these two chapters. Note in the margin the progression of sin and the things which could have served as admonitions against sin had David heeded them. Also list the consequences of David's sin and how the consequences parallel his sin.

3. Remember to follow the "General Instructions." Don't forget the "Lessons for Life" (LFL).

4. Study Psalm 51. Note when the psalm was written.

Chapters 13-24: Consequences of David's Sins

1. Mark the following key words: *inquires*, *ark*, *covenant (sworn)*, *before the Lord*, *evil (come to ruin, harm, calamities, blame, guilt, guilty, sin, sinned)*, and *Spirit*. Make a new bookmark for this segment.

2. Follow the "General Instructions." Pay attention to who's who in these chapters—there are many key characters. Record their names in the margin along with a brief description of who they are. Observe the consequences of their actions.

3. Note who David's children are and how he deals with them. Watch Absalom carefully and keep a running record in the margin of what you learn about him. Record your "LFL" in the margin.

4. As you study these final chapters give special attention to David's relationship to the Lord and to what David has to say about God even after God told him he would chasten him. Spend time meditating on chapter 22 and 23:1-7. When you come to *covenant (sworn)*, review what you learned in chapter 7 and add any new insights.

5. Then complete 2 SAMUEL AT A GLANCE.

✎ THINGS TO THINK ABOUT

1. What have you learned about sin and its consequences? Did you think that if God forgave you, you would never reap sin's harvest? What do you think now?

2. In light of all you have learned, why do you think God referred to David as a man after his own heart (1 Samuel 13:14; Acts 13:22)? Give this some serious thought. Then think about what such a statement about David, made after his death, would mean to you. If you wanted to be a man, a woman, a teen, a child after God's own heart, what do you think it would require on your part?

3. Review the "Lessons for Life" you marked in the margin. What did you see that you can make a matter of prayer? Did you learn anything about inquiring or sitting before the Lord? Did you learn anything from marking "before the Lord"?

1:1
*a*1Sa 31:6
*b*1Sa 30:17

1 Chapter 1 Theme _____

After the death*a* of Saul, David returned from defeating*b* the Amalekites and stayed in Ziklag two days. [2] On the third day a man*c* arrived from Saul's camp, with his clothes torn and with dust on his head.*d* When he came to David, he fell to the ground to pay him honor.

[3] "Where have you come from?" David asked him.

He answered, "I have escaped from the Israelite camp."

1:2
*c*2Sa 4:10
*d*1Sa 4:12

[4] "What happened?" David asked. "Tell me."

He said, "The men fled from the battle. Many of them fell and died. And Saul and his son Jonathan are dead."

⁵Then David said to the young man who brought him the report, "How do you know that Saul and his son Jonathan are dead?"

⁶"I happened to be on Mount Gilboa,ᵃ" the young man said, "and there was Saul, leaning on his spear, with the chariots and riders almost upon him. ⁷When he turned around and saw me, he called out to me, and I said, 'What can I do?'

⁸"He asked me, 'Who are you?'

"'An Amalekite,ᵇ' I answered.

⁹"Then he said to me, 'Stand over me and kill me! I am in the throes of death, but I'm still alive.'

¹⁰"So I stood over him and killed him, because I knew that after he had fallen he could not survive. And I took the crownᶜ that was on his head and the band on his arm and have brought them here to my lord."

¹¹Then David and all the men with him took hold of their clothes and toreᵈ them. ¹²They mourned and wept and fasted till evening for Saul and his son Jonathan, and for the army of the LORD and the house of Israel, because they had fallen by the sword.

¹³David said to the young man who brought him the report, "Where are you from?"

"I am the son of an alien, an Amalekite,ᵉ" he answered.

¹⁴David asked him, "Why were you not afraid to lift your hand to destroy the LORD's anointed?ᶠ"

¹⁵Then David called one of his men and said, "Go, strike him down!"ᵍ So he struck him down, and he died.ʰ ¹⁶For David had said to him, "Your blood be on your own head.ⁱ Your own mouth testified against you when you said, 'I killed the LORD's anointed.'"

¹⁷David took up this lamentʲ concerning Saul and his son Jonathan, ¹⁸and ordered that the men of Judah be taught this lament of the bow (it is written in the Book of Jashar):ᵏ

¹⁹"Your glory, O Israel, lies slain on your heights.
    How the mighty have fallen!ˡ

²⁰"Tell it not in Gath,ᵐ
    proclaim it not in the streets of Ashkelon,
  lest the daughters of the Philistinesⁿ be glad,
    lest the daughters of the uncircumcised rejoice.ᵒ

²¹"O mountains of Gilboa,ᵖ
    may you have neither dew nor rain,
    nor fields that yield offeringsᑫ ⌊of grain⌋.
  For there the shield of the mighty was defiled,
    the shield of Saul—no longer rubbed with oil.ʳ

INSIGHT

The *Book of Jashar* was a collection of poetical writings of important events in Israel's history which was gathered in the time of David or Solomon. It is often compared to "The Book of the Wars of the Lord." Bible authors are believed to have quoted occasionally from this book.

1:6
ᵃ1Sa 28:4;
31:2-4

1:8
ᵇ1Sa 15:2;
30:13,17

1:10
ᶜJdg 9:54;
2Ki 11:12

1:11
ᵈGe 37:29;
2Sa 3:31; 13:31

1:13
ᵉver 8

1:14
ᶠ1Sa 24:6; 26:9

1:15
ᵍ2Sa 4:12
ʰ2Sa 4:10

1:16
ⁱLev 20:9;
2Sa 3:28-29;
1Ki 2:32;
Mt 27:24-25;
Ac 18:6

1:17
ʲ2Ch 35:25

1:18
ᵏJos 10:13;
1Sa 31:3

1:19
ˡver 27

1:20
ᵐMic 1:10
ⁿ1Sa 31:8
ᵒEx 15:20;
1Sa 18:6

1:21
ᵖver 6;
1Sa 31:1
ᑫEze 31:15
ʳIsa 21:5

1:22
a Isa 34:3,7
b Dt 32:42;
1Sa 18:4

²²From the blood^a of the slain,
>   from the flesh of the mighty,
> the bow^b of Jonathan did not turn back,
>   the sword of Saul did not return unsatisfied.

1:23
c Dt 28:49;
Jer 4:13
d Jdg 14:18

²³"Saul and Jonathan—
>   in life they were loved and gracious,
>   and in death they were not parted.
> They were swifter than eagles,^c
>   they were stronger than lions.^d

1:26
e 1Sa 20:42
f 1Sa 18:1

²⁴"O daughters of Israel,
>   weep for Saul,
> who clothed you in scarlet and finery,
>   who adorned your garments with ornaments of gold.

1:27
g ver 19,25;
1Sa 2:4

²⁵"How the mighty have fallen in battle!
>   Jonathan lies slain on your heights.
> ²⁶I grieve for you, Jonathan my brother;^e
>   you were very dear to me.
> Your love for me was wonderful,^f
>   more wonderful than that of women.

²⁷"How the mighty have fallen!
>   The weapons of war have perished!"^g

Chapter 2 Theme

2:1
h 1Sa 23:2,11-12
i Ge 13:18;
1Sa 30:31

2 In the course of time, David inquired^h of the LORD. "Shall I go up to one of the towns of Judah?" he asked.

The LORD said, "Go up."

2:3
l 1Sa 27:2; 30:9

David asked, "Where shall I go?"

"To Hebron,"ⁱ the LORD answered.

2:2
j 1Sa 25:43; 30:5
k 1Sa 25:42

²So David went up there with his two wives,^j Ahinoam of Jezreel and Abigail,^k the widow of Nabal of Carmel. ³David also took the men who were with him,^l each with his family, and they settled in Hebron and its towns. ⁴Then the men of Judah came to Hebron^m and there they anointedⁿ David king over the house of Judah.

2:4
m 1Sa 30:31
n 1Sa 2:35;
2Sa 5:3-5
o 1Sa 31:11-13

When David was told that it was the men of Jabesh Gilead^o who had buried Saul, ⁵he sent messengers to the men of Jabesh Gilead to say to them, "The LORD bless^p you for showing this kindness to Saul your master by burying him. ⁶May the LORD now show you kindness and faithfulness,^q and I too will show you the same favor because you have done this. ⁷Now then, be strong and brave, for Saul your master is dead, and the house of Judah has anointed me king over them."

2:5
p 1Sa 23:21

2:6
q Ex 34:6;
1Ti 1:16

⁸Meanwhile, Abner^r son of Ner, the commander of Saul's army, had taken Ish-Bosheth son of Saul and brought him over to

2:8
r 1Sa 14:50

Mahanaim.*a* *9*He made him king over Gilead,*b* Ashuri*a c* and Jezreel, and also over Ephraim, Benjamin and all Israel.*d*

*10*Ish-Bosheth son of Saul was forty years old when he became king over Israel, and he reigned two years. The house of Judah, however, followed David. *11*The length of time David was king in Hebron over the house of Judah was seven years and six months.*e*

*12*Abner son of Ner, together with the men of Ish-Bosheth son of Saul, left Mahanaim and went to Gibeon.*f* *13*Joab*g* son of Zeruiah and David's men went out and met them at the pool of Gibeon. One group sat down on one side of the pool and one group on the other side.

*14*Then Abner said to Joab, "Let's have some of the young men get up and fight hand to hand in front of us."

"All right, let them do it," Joab said.

*15*So they stood up and were counted off—twelve men for Benjamin and Ish-Bosheth son of Saul, and twelve for David. *16*Then each man grabbed his opponent by the head and thrust his dagger into his opponent's side, and they fell down together. So that place in Gibeon was called Helkath Hazzurim.*b*

*17*The battle that day was very fierce, and Abner and the men of Israel were defeated*h* by David's men.

*18*The three sons of Zeruiah*i* were there: Joab,*j* Abishai*k* and Asahel.*l* Now Asahel was as fleet-footed as a wild gazelle.*m* *19*He chased Abner, turning neither to the right nor to the left as he pursued him. *20*Abner looked behind him and asked, "Is that you, Asahel?"

"It is," he answered.

*21*Then Abner said to him, "Turn aside to the right or to the left; take on one of the young men and strip him of his weapons." But Asahel would not stop chasing him.

*22*Again Abner warned Asahel, "Stop chasing me! Why should I strike you down? How could I look your brother Joab in the face?"*n*

*23*But Asahel refused to give up the pursuit; so Abner thrust the butt of his spear into Asahel's stomach,*o* and the spear came out through his back. He fell there and died on the spot. And every man stopped when he came to the place where Asahel had fallen and died.*p*

*24*But Joab and Abishai pursued Abner, and as the sun was setting, they came to the hill of Ammah, near Giah on the way to the wasteland of Gibeon. *25*Then the men of Benjamin rallied behind Abner. They formed themselves into a group and took their stand on top of a hill.

*26*Abner called out to Joab, "Must the sword devour*q* forever? Don't you realize that this will end in bitterness? How long before you order your men to stop pursuing their brothers?"

---

a*9* Or *Asher*   b*16* *Helkath Hazzurim* means *field of daggers* or *field of hostilities.*

2:8
*a*Ge 32:2

2:9
*b*Nu 32:26
*c*Jdg 1:32
*d*1Ch 12:29

2:11
*e*2Sa 5:5

2:12
*f*Jos 18:25

2:13
*g*2Sa 8:16;
1Ch 2:16; 11:6

2:17
*h*2Sa 3:1

2:18
*i*2Sa 3:39
*j*2Sa 3:30
*k*1Sa 26:6
*l*1Ch 2:16
*m*1Ch 12:8

2:22
*n*2Sa 3:27

2:23
*o*2Sa 3:27; 4:6
*p*2Sa 20:12

2:26
*q*Dt 32:42;
Jer 46:10,14

2:28
a 2Sa 18:16
b Jdg 3:27

²⁷Joab answered, "As surely as God lives, if you had not spoken, the men would have continued the pursuit of their brothers until morning.^a"

2:29
c ver 8

²⁸So Joab^a blew the trumpet,^b and all the men came to a halt; they no longer pursued Israel, nor did they fight anymore.

²⁹All that night Abner and his men marched through the Arabah. They crossed the Jordan, continued through the whole Bithron^b and came to Mahanaim.^c

2:32
d Ge 49:29

³⁰Then Joab returned from pursuing Abner and assembled all his men. Besides Asahel, nineteen of David's men were found missing. ³¹But David's men had killed three hundred and sixty Benjamites who were with Abner. ³²They took Asahel and buried him in his father's tomb^d at Bethlehem. Then Joab and his men marched all night and arrived at Hebron by daybreak.

3:1
e 1Ki 14:30
f 2Sa 5:10
g 2Sa 2:17

Chapter 3 Theme

3 The war between the house of Saul and the house of David lasted a long time.^e David grew stronger and stronger,^f while the house of Saul grew weaker and weaker.^g

3:2
h 1Sa 25:43;
1Ch 3:1-3

²Sons were born to David in Hebron:

His firstborn was Amnon the son of Ahinoam^h of Jezreel;

³his second, Kileab the son of Abigailⁱ the widow of Nabal of Carmel;

3:3
i 1Sa 25:42
j 2Sa 13:1,28
k 1Sa 27:8;
2Sa 13:37;
14:32; 15:8

the third, Absalom^j the son of Maacah daughter of Talmai king of Geshur;^k

⁴the fourth, Adonijah^l the son of Haggith;

the fifth, Shephatiah the son of Abital;

⁵and the sixth, Ithream the son of David's wife Eglah.

These were born to David in Hebron.

3:4
l 1Ki 1:5,11

⁶During the war between the house of Saul and the house of David, Abner had been strengthening his own position in the house of Saul. ⁷Now Saul had had a concubine^m named Rizpahⁿ daughter of Aiah. And Ish-Bosheth said to Abner, "Why did you sleep with my father's concubine?"

3:7
m 2Sa 16:21-22
n 2Sa 21:8-11

⁸Abner was very angry because of what Ish-Bosheth said and he answered, "Am I a dog's head^o—on Judah's side? This very day I am loyal to the house of your father Saul and to his family and friends. I haven't handed you over to David. Yet now you accuse me of an offense involving this woman! ⁹May God deal with Abner, be it ever so severely, if I do not do for David what the LORD promised^p him on oath ¹⁰and transfer the kingdom from the house of Saul and establish David's throne over Israel

3:8
o 1Sa 24:14;
2Sa 9:8; 16:9

3:9
p 1Sa 15:28;
1Ki 19:2

^a 27 Or *spoken this morning, the men would not have taken up the pursuit of their brothers;* or *spoken, the men would have given up the pursuit of their brothers by morning* ^b 29 Or *morning;* or *ravine;* the meaning of the Hebrew for this word is uncertain.

and Judah from Dan to Beersheba."[a] [11]Ish-Bosheth did not dare to say another word to Abner, because he was afraid of him.

[12]Then Abner sent messengers on his behalf to say to David, "Whose land is it? Make an agreement with me, and I will help you bring all Israel over to you."

[13]"Good," said David. "I will make an agreement with you. But I demand one thing of you: Do not come into my presence unless you bring Michal daughter of Saul when you come to see me."[b] [14]Then David sent messengers to Ish-Bosheth son of Saul, demanding, "Give me my wife Michal,[c] whom I betrothed to myself for the price of a hundred Philistine foreskins."

[15]So Ish-Bosheth gave orders and had her taken away from her husband[d] Paltiel[e] son of Laish. [16]Her husband, however, went with her, weeping behind her all the way to Bahurim.[f] Then Abner said to him, "Go back home!" So he went back.

[17]Abner conferred with the elders[g] of Israel and said, "For some time you have wanted to make David your king. [18]Now do it! For the LORD promised David, 'By my servant David I will rescue my people Israel from the hand of the Philistines[h] and from the hand of all their enemies.[i]'"

[19]Abner also spoke to the Benjamites in person. Then he went to Hebron to tell David everything that Israel and the whole house of Benjamin[j] wanted to do. [20]When Abner, who had twenty men with him, came to David at Hebron, David prepared a feast for him and his men. [21]Then Abner said to David, "Let me go at once and assemble all Israel for my lord the king, so that they may make a compact[k] with you, and that you may rule over all that your heart desires."[l] So David sent Abner away, and he went in peace.

[22]Just then David's men and Joab returned from a raid and brought with them a great deal of plunder. But Abner was no longer with David in Hebron, because David had sent him away, and he had gone in peace. [23]When Joab and all the soldiers with him arrived, he was told that Abner son of Ner had come to the king and that the king had sent him away and that he had gone in peace.

[24]So Joab went to the king and said, "What have you done? Look, Abner came to you. Why did you let him go? Now he is gone! [25]You know Abner son of Ner; he came to deceive you and observe your movements and find out everything you are doing."

[26]Joab then left David and sent messengers after Abner, and they brought him back from the well of Sirah. But David did not know it. [27]Now when Abner[m] returned to Hebron, Joab took him aside into the gateway, as though to speak with him privately. And there, to avenge the blood of his brother Asahel, Joab stabbed him in the stomach, and he died.[n]

3:10 [a]Jdg 20:1; 1Sa 3:20

3:13 [b]Ge 43:5; 1Sa 18:20

3:14 [c]1Sa 18:27

3:15 [d]Dt 24:1-4 [e]1Sa 25:44

3:16 [f]2Sa 16:5; 19:16

3:17 [g]Jdg 11:11

3:18 [h]1Sa 9:16 [i]1Sa 15:28; 2Sa 8:6

3:19 [j]1Sa 10:20-21; 1Ch 12:2,16,29

3:21 [k]ver 10,12 [l]1Ki 11:37

3:27 [m]2Sa 2:8 [n]2Sa 2:22; 20:9-10; 1Ki 2:5

3:28
a ver 37;
Dt 21:9

3:29
b Lev 20:9
c 1Ki 2:31-33
d Lev 15:2

3:31
e 2Sa 1:2,11;
Ps 30:11;
Isa 20:2
f Ge 37:34

3:32
g Nu 14:1;
Pr 24:17

3:33
h 2Sa 1:17

3:35
i Ru 1:17;
1Sa 3:17
j 1Sa 31:13;
2Sa 1:12;
12:17;
Jer 16:7

3:37
k ver 28

3:38
l 2Sa 1:19

3:39
m 2Sa 2:18
n 2Sa 19:5-7
o 1Ki 2:5-6,
33-34;
Ps 41:10;
101:8

4:1
p 2Sa 3:27;
Ezr 4:4

4:2
q Jos 9:17; 18:25

4:3
r Ne 11:33

4:4
s 1Sa 18:1
t 1Sa 31:1-4

²⁸Later, when David heard about this, he said, "I and my kingdom are forever innocent*a* before the LORD concerning the blood of Abner son of Ner. ²⁹May his blood*b* fall upon the head of Joab and upon all his father's house!*c* May Joab's house never be without someone who has a running sore*d* or leprosy*a* or who leans on a crutch or who falls by the sword or who lacks food."

³⁰(Joab and his brother Abishai murdered Abner because he had killed their brother Asahel in the battle at Gibeon.)

³¹Then David said to Joab and all the people with him, "Tear your clothes and put on sackcloth*e* and walk in mourning*f* in front of Abner." King David himself walked behind the bier. ³²They buried Abner in Hebron, and the king wept*g* aloud at Abner's tomb. All the people wept also.

³³The king sang this lament*h* for Abner:

> "Should Abner have died as the lawless die?
> ³⁴   Your hands were not bound,
>   your feet were not fettered.
>   You fell as one falls before wicked men."

And all the people wept over him again.

³⁵Then they all came and urged David to eat something while it was still day; but David took an oath, saying, "May God deal with me, be it ever so severely,*i* if I taste bread*j* or anything else before the sun sets!"

³⁶All the people took note and were pleased; indeed, everything the king did pleased them. ³⁷So on that day all the people and all Israel knew that the king had no part*k* in the murder of Abner son of Ner.

³⁸Then the king said to his men, "Do you not realize that a prince and a great man has fallen*l* in Israel this day? ³⁹And today, though I am the anointed king, I am weak, and these sons of Zeruiah*m* are too strong for me.*n* May the LORD repay*o* the evildoer according to his evil deeds!"

Chapter 4 Theme _____

4 When Ish-Bosheth son of Saul heard that Abner*p* had died in Hebron, he lost courage, and all Israel became alarmed. ²Now Saul's son had two men who were leaders of raiding bands. One was named Baanah and the other Recab; they were sons of Rimmon the Beerothite from the tribe of Benjamin—Beeroth*q* is considered part of Benjamin, ³because the people of Beeroth fled to Gittaim*r* and have lived there as aliens to this day.

⁴(Jonathan*s* son of Saul had a son who was lame in both feet. He was five years old when the news*t* about Saul and Jonathan

a 29 The Hebrew word was used for various diseases affecting the skin—not necessarily leprosy.

came from Jezreel. His nurse picked him up and fled, but as she hurried to leave, he fell and became crippled.[a] His name was Mephibosheth.)[b]

[5]Now Recab and Baanah, the sons of Rimmon the Beerothite, set out for the house of Ish-Bosheth,[c] and they arrived there in the heat of the day while he was taking his noonday rest. [6]They went into the inner part of the house as if to get some wheat, and they stabbed[d] him in the stomach. Then Recab and his brother Baanah slipped away.

[7]They had gone into the house while he was lying on the bed in his bedroom. After they stabbed and killed him, they cut off his head. Taking it with them, they traveled all night by way of the Arabah. [8]They brought the head of Ish-Bosheth to David at Hebron and said to the king, "Here is the head of Ish-Bosheth son of Saul,[e] your enemy, who tried to take your life. This day the LORD has avenged my lord the king against Saul and his offspring."

[9]David answered Recab and his brother Baanah, the sons of Rimmon the Beerothite, "As surely as the LORD lives, who has delivered[f] me out of all trouble, [10]when a man told me, 'Saul is dead,' and thought he was bringing good news, I seized him and put him to death in Ziklag.[g] That was the reward I gave him for his news! [11]How much more—when wicked men have killed an innocent man in his own house and on his own bed—should I not now demand his blood[h] from your hand and rid the earth of you!"

[12]So David gave an order to his men, and they killed them.[i] They cut off their hands and feet and hung the bodies by the pool in Hebron. But they took the head of Ish-Bosheth and buried it in Abner's tomb at Hebron.

Chapter 5 Theme

5 All the tribes of Israel[j] came to David at Hebron and said, "We are your own flesh and blood.[k] [2]In the past, while Saul was king over us, you were the one who led Israel on their military campaigns.[l] And the LORD said to you, 'You will shepherd[m] my people Israel, and you will become their ruler.[n]'"

[3]When all the elders of Israel had come to King David at Hebron, the king made a compact[o] with them at Hebron before the LORD, and they anointed[p] David king over Israel.

[4]David was thirty years old[q] when he became king, and he reigned[r] forty[s] years. [5]In Hebron he reigned over Judah seven years and six months,[t] and in Jerusalem he reigned over all Israel and Judah thirty-three years.

[6]The king and his men marched to Jerusalem[u] to attack the Jebusites,[v] who lived there. The Jebusites said to David, "You will not get in here; even the blind and the lame can ward you off."

4:4
[a] Lev 21:18
[b] 2Sa 9:3,6;
1Ch 8:34; 9:40

4:5
[c] 2Sa 2:8

4:6
[d] 2Sa 2:23

4:8
[e] 1Sa 24:4; 25:29

4:9
[f] Ge 48:16;
1Ki 1:29

4:10
[g] 2Sa 1:2-16

4:11
[h] Ge 9:5;
Ps 9:12

4:12
[i] 2Sa 1:15

5:1
[j] 2Sa 19:43
[k] 1Ch 11:1

5:2
[l] 1Sa 18:5,13,16
[m] 1Sa 16:1;
2Sa 7:7
[n] 1Sa 25:30

5:3
[o] 2Sa 3:21
[p] 2Sa 2:4

5:4
[q] Lk 3:23
[r] 1Ki 2:11;
1Ch 3:4
[s] 1Ch 26:31;
29:27

5:5
[t] 2Sa 2:11;
1Ch 3:4

5:6
[u] Jdg 1:8
[v] Jos 15:8

5:7
a 2Sa 6:12,16;
1Ki 2:10

5:9
b ver 7;
1Ki 9:15,24

5:10
c 2Sa 3:1

5:11
d 1Ki 5:1,18;
1Ch 14:1

5:13
e Dt 17:17;
1Ch 3:9

5:14
f 1Ch 3:5

5:17
g 2Sa 23:14;
1Ch 11:16

5:18
h Jos 15:8; 17:15;
18:16

5:19
i 1Sa 23:2;
2Sa 2:1

5:20
j Isa 28:21

5:21
k Dt 7:5;
1Ch 14:12;
Isa 46:2

5:24
l 2Ki 7:6
m Jdg 4:14

5:25
n Isa 28:21
o 1Ch 14:16

They thought, "David cannot get in here." [7]Nevertheless, David captured the fortress of Zion, the City of David.*a*

[8]On that day, David said, "Anyone who conquers the Jebusites will have to use the water shaft*a* to reach those 'lame and blind' who are David's enemies.*b*" That is why they say, "The 'blind and lame' will not enter the palace."

[9]David then took up residence in the fortress and called it the City of David. He built up the area around it, from the supporting terraces*cb* inward. [10]And he became more and more powerful,*c* because the Lord God Almighty was with him.

[11]Now Hiram*d* king of Tyre sent messengers to David, along with cedar logs and carpenters and stonemasons, and they built a palace for David. [12]And David knew that the Lord had established him as king over Israel and had exalted his kingdom for the sake of his people Israel.

[13]After he left Hebron, David took more concubines and wives*e* in Jerusalem, and more sons and daughters were born to him. [14]These are the names of the children born to him there:*f* Shammua, Shobab, Nathan, Solomon, [15]Ibhar, Elishua, Nepheg, Japhia, [16]Elishama, Eliada and Eliphelet.

[17]When the Philistines heard that David had been anointed king over Israel, they went up in full force to search for him, but David heard about it and went down to the stronghold.*g* [18]Now the Philistines had come and spread out in the Valley of Rephaim;*h* [19]so David inquired*i* of the Lord, "Shall I go and attack the Philistines? Will you hand them over to me?"

The Lord answered him, "Go, for I will surely hand the Philistines over to you."

[20]So David went to Baal Perazim, and there he defeated them. He said, "As waters break out, the Lord has broken out against my enemies before me." So that place was called Baal Perazim.*dj* [21]The Philistines abandoned their idols there, and David and his men carried them off.*k*

[22]Once more the Philistines came up and spread out in the Valley of Rephaim; [23]so David inquired of the Lord, and he answered, "Do not go straight up, but circle around behind them and attack them in front of the balsam trees. [24]As soon as you hear the sound*l* of marching in the tops of the balsam trees, move quickly, because that will mean the Lord has gone out in front*m* of you to strike the Philistine army." [25]So David did as the Lord commanded him, and he struck down the Philistines all the way from Gibeon*en* to Gezer.*o*

a 8 Or *use scaling hooks*   *b* 8 Or *are hated by David*   *c* 9 Or *the Millo*   *d* 20 *Baal Perazim* means *the lord who breaks out.*   *e* 25 Septuagint (see also 1 Chron. 14:16); Hebrew *Geba*

Chapter 6 Theme _____

6 David again brought together out of Israel chosen men, thirty thousand in all. [2]He and all his men set out from Baalah[a] of Judah[a] to bring up from there the ark[b] of God, which is called by the Name,[bc] the name of the LORD Almighty, who is enthroned[d] between the cherubim[e] that are on the ark. [3]They set the ark of God on a new cart[f] and brought it from the house of Abinadab, which was on the hill. Uzzah and Ahio, sons of Abinadab, were guiding the new cart [4]with the ark of God on it,[c] and Ahio was walking in front of it. [5]David and the whole house of Israel were celebrating with all their might before the LORD, with songs[d] and with harps, lyres, tambourines, sistrums and cymbals.[g]

[6]When they came to the threshing floor of Nacon, Uzzah reached out and took hold of[h] the ark of God, because the oxen stumbled. [7]The LORD's anger burned against Uzzah because of his irreverent act;[i] therefore God struck him down[j] and he died there beside the ark of God.

[8]Then David was angry because the LORD's wrath[k] had broken out against Uzzah, and to this day that place is called Perez Uzzah.[el]

[9]David was afraid of the LORD that day and said, "How[m] can the ark of the LORD ever come to me?" [10]He was not willing to take the ark of the LORD to be with him in the City of David. Instead, he took it aside to the house of Obed-Edom[n] the Gittite. [11]The ark of the LORD remained in the house of Obed-Edom the Gittite for three months, and the LORD blessed him and his entire household.[o]

[12]Now King David[p] was told, "The LORD has blessed the household of Obed-Edom and everything he has, because of the ark of God." So David went down and brought up the ark of God from the house of Obed-Edom to the City of David with rejoicing. [13]When those who were carrying the ark of the LORD had taken six steps, he sacrificed[q] a bull and a fattened calf. [14]David, wearing a linen ephod,[r] danced[s] before the LORD with all his might, [15]while he and the entire house of Israel brought up the ark of the LORD with shouts and the sound of trumpets.[t]

[16]As the ark of the LORD was entering the City of David,[u] Michal daughter of Saul watched from a window. And when she saw King David leaping and dancing before the LORD, she despised him in her heart.

[17]They brought the ark of the LORD and set it in its place inside the tent that David had pitched for it,[v] and David sacrificed burnt

a2 That is, Kiriath Jearim; Hebrew Baale Judah, a variant of Baalah of Judah   b2 Hebrew; Septuagint and Vulgate do not have the Name.   c3,4 Dead Sea Scrolls and some Septuagint manuscripts; Masoretic Text cart 4and they brought it with the ark of God from the house of Abinadab, which was on the hill   d5 See Dead Sea Scrolls, Septuagint and 1 Chronicles 13:8; Masoretic Text celebrating before the LORD with all kinds of instruments made of pine.   e8 Perez Uzzah means outbreak against Uzzah.

6:2
a Jos 15:9
b 1Sa 4:4; 7:1
c Lev 24:16;
Isa 63:14
d Ps 99:1
e Ex 25:22;
1Ch 13:5-6

6:3
f Nu 7:4-9;
1Sa 6:7

6:5
g 1Sa 18:6-7;
Ezr 3:10;
Ps 150:5

6:6
h Nu 4:15,
19-20;
1Ch 13:9

6:7
i 1Ch 15:13-15
j Ex 19:22;
1Sa 6:19

6:8
k Ps 7:11
l Ge 38:29

6:9
m Ps 119:120

6:10
n 1Ch 13:13;
26:4-5

6:11
o Ge 30:27; 39:5

6:12
p 1Ki 8:1;
1Ch 15:25

6:13
q 1Ki 8:5,62

6:14
r Ex 19:6;
1Sa 2:18
s Ex 15:20

6:15
t Ps 47:5; 98:6

6:16
u 2Sa 5:7

6:17
v 1Ch 15:1;
2Ch 1:4

6:17
aLev 1:1-17;
1Ki 8:62-64

6:18
b1Ki 8:22

6:19
cHos 3:1
dNe 8:10

6:20
ever 14,16

6:21
f1Sa 13:14;
15:28

7:1
g1Ch 17:1

7:2
h2Sa 5:11
iEx 26:1;
Ac 7:45-46

7:5
j1Ki 8:19;
1Ch 22:8
k1Ki 5:3-5

7:6
lEx 40:18,34
m1Ki 8:16

7:7
nDt 23:14
o2Sa 5:2
pLev 26:11-12

7:8
q1Sa 16:11
r2Sa 6:21
sPs 78:70-72;
2Co 6:18*

7:9
t2Sa 5:10
uPs 18:37-42

7:10
vEx 15:17;
Isa 5:1-7

offerings^a and fellowship offerings^a before the LORD. ¹⁸After he had finished sacrificing^b the burnt offerings and fellowship offerings, he blessed the people in the name of the LORD Almighty. ¹⁹Then he gave a loaf of bread, a cake of dates and a cake of raisins^c to each person in the whole crowd of Israelites, both men and women.^d And all the people went to their homes.

²⁰When David returned home to bless his household, Michal daughter of Saul came out to meet him and said, "How the king of Israel has distinguished himself today, disrobing^e in the sight of the slave girls of his servants as any vulgar fellow would!"

²¹David said to Michal, "It was before the LORD, who chose me rather than your father or anyone from his house when he appointed^f me ruler over the LORD's people Israel—I will celebrate before the LORD. ²²I will become even more undignified than this, and I will be humiliated in my own eyes. But by these slave girls you spoke of, I will be held in honor."

²³And Michal daughter of Saul had no children to the day of her death.

Chapter 7 Theme

7 After the king was settled in his palace^g and the LORD had given him rest from all his enemies around him, ²he said to Nathan the prophet, "Here I am, living in a palace^h of cedar, while the ark of God remains in a tent."ⁱ

³Nathan replied to the king, "Whatever you have in mind, go ahead and do it, for the LORD is with you."

⁴That night the word of the LORD came to Nathan, saying:

⁵"Go and tell my servant David, 'This is what the LORD says: Are you^j the one to build me a house to dwell in?^k ⁶I have not dwelt in a house from the day I brought the Israelites up out of Egypt to this day. I have been moving from place to place with a tent^l as my dwelling.^m ⁷Wherever I have moved with all the Israelites,ⁿ did I ever say to any of their rulers whom I commanded to shepherd^o my people Israel, "Why have you not built me a house of cedar?^p"'

⁸"Now then, tell my servant David, 'This is what the LORD Almighty says: I took you from the pasture and from following the flock^q to be ruler^r over my people Israel.^s ⁹I have been with you wherever you have gone,^t and I have cut off all your enemies from before you.^u Now I will make your name great, like the names of the greatest men of the earth. ¹⁰And I will provide a place for my people Israel and will plant^v them so that they can have a home of their own and no longer be disturbed.

a 17 Traditionally *peace offerings*; also in verse 18

Wicked[a] people will not oppress them anymore,[b] as they did at the beginning [11]and have done ever since the time I appointed leaders[a][c] over my people Israel. I will also give you rest from all your enemies.[d]

"'The LORD declares to you that the LORD himself will establish[e] a house[f] for you: [12]When your days are over and you rest[g] with your fathers, I will raise up your offspring to succeed you, who will come from your own body,[h] and I will establish his kingdom. [13]He is the one who will build a house for my Name,[i] and I will establish the throne of his kingdom forever.[j] [14]I will be his father, and he will be my son.[k] When he does wrong, I will punish him with the rod[l] of men, with floggings inflicted by men. [15]But my love will never be taken away from him, as I took it away from Saul,[m] whom I removed from before you. [16]Your house and your kingdom will endure forever before me[b]; your throne[n] will be established forever.[o]'"

[17]Nathan reported to David all the words of this entire revelation.

[18]Then King David went in and sat before the LORD, and he said:

"Who am I,[p] O Sovereign LORD, and what is my family, that you have brought me this far? [19]And as if this were not enough in your sight, O Sovereign LORD, you have also spoken about the future of the house of your servant. Is this your usual way of dealing with man,[q] O Sovereign LORD?

[20]"What more can David say to you? For you know[r] your servant,[s] O Sovereign LORD. [21]For the sake of your word and according to your will, you have done this great thing and made it known to your servant.

[22]"How great[t] you are,[u] O Sovereign LORD! There is no one like you, and there is no God[v] but you, as we have heard with our own ears.[w] [23]And who is like your people Israel[x]—the one nation on earth that God went out to redeem as a people for himself, and to make a name for himself, and to perform great and awesome wonders[y] by driving out nations and their gods from before your people, whom you redeemed[z] from Egypt?[c] [24]You have established your people Israel as your very own[a] forever, and you, O LORD, have become their God.[b]

[25]"And now, LORD God, keep forever the promise you have made concerning your servant and his house. Do as you promised, [26]so that your name will be great forever. Then men will say, 'The LORD Almighty is God over Israel!' And the house of your servant David will be established before you.

a 11 Traditionally *judges*   b 16 Some Hebrew manuscripts and Septuagint; most Hebrew manuscripts *you*   c 23 See Septuagint and 1 Chron. 17:21; Hebrew *wonders for your land and before your people, whom you redeemed from Egypt, from the nations and their gods.*

7:10
a Ps 89:22-23
b Isa 60:18

7:11
c Jdg 2:16;
1Sa 12:9-11
d ver 1
e 1Sa 25:28
f ver 27

7:12
g 1Ki 2:1
h Ps 132:11-12

7:13
i 1Ki 5:5;
8:19,29
j Isa 9:7

7:14
k Ps 89:26;
Heb 1:5*
l Ps 89:30-33

7:15
m 1Sa 15:23,28

7:16
n Ps 89:36-37
o ver 13

7:18
p Ex 3:11;
1Sa 18:18

7:19
q Isa 55:8-9

7:20
r Jn 21:17
s 1Sa 16:7

7:22
t Ps 48:1;
86:10;
Jer 10:6
u Dt 3:24
v Ex 15:11
w Ex 10:2;
Ps 44:1

7:23
x Dt 4:32-38
y Dt 10:21
z Dt 9:26;
15:15

7:24
a Dt 26:18
b Ex 6:6-7;
Ps 48:14

²⁷"O LORD Almighty, God of Israel, you have revealed this to your servant, saying, 'I will build a house for you.' So your servant has found courage to offer you this prayer. ²⁸O Sovereign LORD, you are God! Your words are trustworthy,^a and you have promised these good things to your servant. ²⁹Now be pleased to bless the house of your servant, that it may continue forever in your sight; for you, O Sovereign LORD, have spoken, and with your blessing^b the house of your servant will be blessed forever."

Chapter 8 Theme

8 In the course of time, David defeated the Philistines and subdued them, and he took Metheg Ammah from the control of the Philistines.

²David also defeated the Moabites.^c He made them lie down on the ground and measured them off with a length of cord. Every two lengths of them were put to death, and the third length was allowed to live. So the Moabites became subject to David and brought tribute.

³Moreover, David fought Hadadezer^d son of Rehob, king of Zobah,^e when he went to restore his control along the Euphrates River. ⁴David captured a thousand of his chariots, seven thousand charioteers^a and twenty thousand foot soldiers. He hamstrung^f all but a hundred of the chariot horses.

⁵When the Arameans of Damascus^g came to help Hadadezer king of Zobah, David struck down twenty-two thousand of them. ⁶He put garrisons in the Aramean kingdom of Damascus, and the Arameans became subject to him and brought tribute. The LORD gave David victory wherever he went.^h

⁷David took the gold shieldsⁱ that belonged to the officers of Hadadezer and brought them to Jerusalem. ⁸From Tebah^b and Berothai,^j towns that belonged to Hadadezer, King David took a great quantity of bronze.

⁹When Tou^c king of Hamath^k heard that David had defeated the entire army of Hadadezer, ¹⁰he sent his son Joram^d to King David to greet him and congratulate him on his victory in battle over Hadadezer, who had been at war with Tou. Joram brought with him articles of silver and gold and bronze.

¹¹King David dedicated^l these articles to the LORD, as he had done with the silver and gold from all the nations he had subdued: ¹²Edom^e and Moab,^m the Ammonitesⁿ and the Philistines,^o

---

7:28
a Ex 34:6; Jn 17:17

7:29
b Nu 6:23-27

8:2
c Ge 19:37; Nu 24:17

8:3
d 2Sa 10:16,19
e 1Sa 14:47

8:4
f Jos 11:9

8:5
g 1Ki 11:24

8:6
h ver 14; 2Sa 3:18; 7:9

8:7
i 1Ki 10:16

8:8
j Eze 47:16

8:9
k 1Ki 8:65; 2Ch 8:4

8:11
l 1Ki 7:51; 1Ch 26:26

8:12
m ver 2
n 2Sa 10:14
o 2Sa 5:25

---

^a4 Septuagint (see also Dead Sea Scrolls and 1 Chron. 18:4); Masoretic Text *captured seventeen hundred of his charioteers*   ^b8 See some Septuagint manuscripts (see also 1 Chron. 18:8); Hebrew *Betah.*   ^c9 Hebrew *Toi,* a variant of *Tou*; also in verse 10   ^d10 A variant of *Hadoram*   ^e12 Some Hebrew manuscripts, Septuagint and Syriac (see also 1 Chron. 18:11); most Hebrew manuscripts *Aram*

and Amalek.*a* He also dedicated the plunder taken from Hadadezer son of Rehob, king of Zobah.

¹³And David became famous*b* after he returned from striking down eighteen thousand Edomites*a* in the Valley of Salt.*c*

¹⁴He put garrisons throughout Edom, and all the Edomites*d* became subject to David.*e* The LORD gave David victory wherever he went.*f*

¹⁵David reigned over all Israel, doing what was just and right for all his people. ¹⁶Joab*g* son of Zeruiah was over the army; Jehoshaphat*h* son of Ahilud was recorder; ¹⁷Zadok*i* son of Ahitub and Ahimelech son of Abiathar were priests; Seraiah was secretary;*j* ¹⁸Benaiah*k* son of Jehoiada was over the Kerethites*l* and Pelethites; and David's sons were royal advisers.*b*

Chapter 9 Theme _____

9 David asked, "Is there anyone still left of the house of Saul to whom I can show kindness for Jonathan's sake?"*m*

²Now there was a servant of Saul's household named Ziba.*n* They called him to appear before David, and the king said to him, "Are you Ziba?"

"Your servant," he replied.

³The king asked, "Is there no one still left of the house of Saul to whom I can show God's kindness?"

Ziba answered the king, "There is still a son of Jonathan;*o* he is crippled*p* in both feet."

a 13 A few Hebrew manuscripts, Septuagint and Syriac (see also 1 Chron. 18:12); most Hebrew manuscripts *Aram* (that is, Arameans)   *b 18* Or *were priests*

8:12
a 1Sa 27:8

8:13
b 2Sa 7:9
c 2Ki 14:7;
1Ch 18:12

8:14
d Nu 24:17-18
e Ge 27:29,37-40
f ver 6

8:16
g 2Sa 19:13;
1Ch 11:6
h 2Sa 20:24;
1Ki 4:3

8:17
i 2Sa 15:24,29;
1Ch 16:39; 24:3
j 1Ki 4:3;
2Ki 12:10

8:18
k 2Sa 20:23;
1Ki 1:8,38;
1Ch 18:17
l 1Sa 30:14

9:1
m 1Sa 20:14-17, 42

9:2
n 2Sa 16:1-4;
19:17,26,29

9:3
o 1Sa 20:14
p 2Sa 4:4

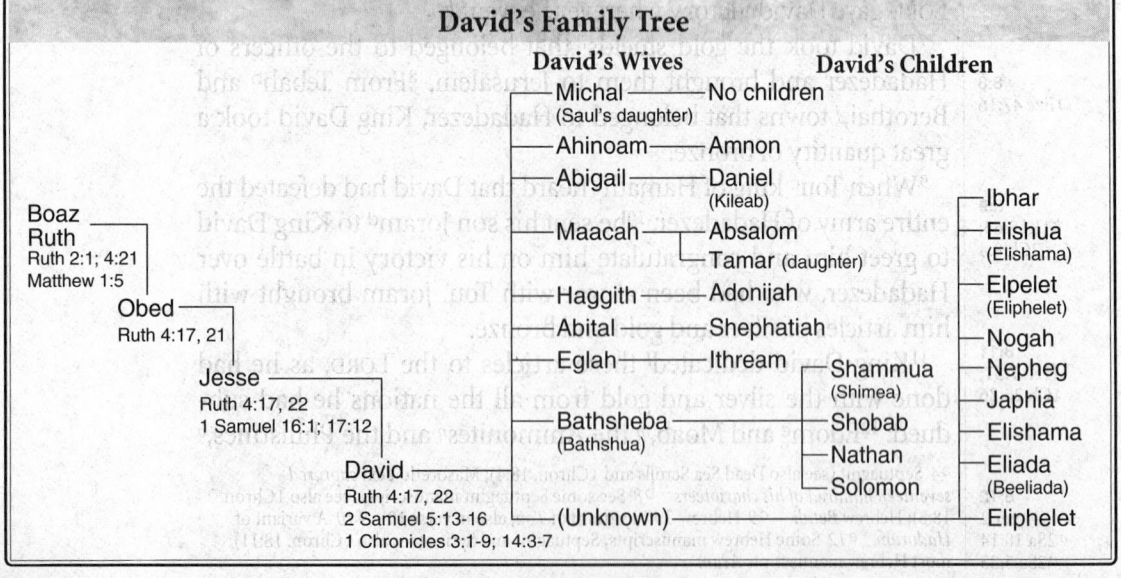

David's Family Tree

David's Wives

- Michal (Saul's daughter) — No children
- Ahinoam — Amnon
- Abigail — Daniel (Kileab)
- Maacah — Absalom / Tamar (daughter)
- Haggith — Adonijah
- Abital — Shephatiah
- Eglah — Ithream
- Bathsheba (Bathshua) — Shammua (Shimea) / Shobab / Nathan / Solomon
- (Unknown)

David's Children

- Ibhar
- Elishua (Elishama)
- Elpelet (Eliphelet)
- Nogah
- Nepheg
- Japhia
- Elishama
- Eliada (Beeliada)
- Eliphelet

Boaz
Ruth
Ruth 2:1; 4:21
Matthew 1:5

Obed
Ruth 4:17, 21

Jesse
Ruth 4:17, 22
1 Samuel 16:1; 17:12

David
Ruth 4:17, 22
2 Samuel 5:13-16
1 Chronicles 3:1-9; 14:3-7

9:4
a 2Sa 17:27-29

9:6
b 2Sa 16:4;
19:24-30

9:7
c ver 1,3;
2Sa 12:8; 19:28;
1Ki 2:7;
2Ki 25:29

9:8
d 2Sa 16:9

9:10
e ver 7,11,13;
2Sa 19:28

9:11
f Job 36:7;
Ps 113:8

9:12
g 1Ch 8:34

10:2
h 1Sa 11:1

10:4
i Lev 19:27;
Isa 15:2;
Jer 48:37
j Isa 20:4

⁴"Where is he?" the king asked.

Ziba answered, "He is at the house of Makir*ᵃ* son of Ammiel in Lo Debar."

⁵So King David had him brought from Lo Debar, from the house of Makir son of Ammiel.

⁶When Mephibosheth son of Jonathan, the son of Saul, came to David, he bowed down to pay him honor.*ᵇ*

David said, "Mephibosheth!"

"Your servant," he replied.

⁷"Don't be afraid," David said to him, "for I will surely show you kindness for the sake of your father Jonathan. I will restore to you all the land that belonged to your grandfather Saul, and you will always eat at my table.*ᶜ*"

⁸Mephibosheth bowed down and said, "What is your servant, that you should notice a dead dog*ᵈ* like me?"

⁹Then the king summoned Ziba, Saul's servant, and said to him, "I have given your master's grandson everything that belonged to Saul and his family. ¹⁰You and your sons and your servants are to farm the land for him and bring in the crops, so that your master's grandson*ᵉ* may be provided for. And Mephibosheth, grandson of your master, will always eat at my table." (Now Ziba had fifteen sons and twenty servants.)

¹¹Then Ziba said to the king, "Your servant will do whatever my lord the king commands his servant to do." So Mephibosheth ate at David's*ᵃ* table like one of the king's sons.*ᶠ*

¹²Mephibosheth had a young son named Mica, and all the members of Ziba's household were servants of Mephibosheth.*ᵍ* ¹³And Mephibosheth lived in Jerusalem, because he always ate at the king's table, and he was crippled in both feet.

Chapter 10 Theme _____

10 In the course of time, the king of the Ammonites died, and his son Hanun succeeded him as king. ²David thought, "I will show kindness to Hanun son of Nahash,*ʰ* just as his father showed kindness to me." So David sent a delegation to express his sympathy to Hanun concerning his father.

When David's men came to the land of the Ammonites, ³the Ammonite nobles said to Hanun their lord, "Do you think David is honoring your father by sending men to you to express sympathy? Hasn't David sent them to you to explore the city and spy it out and overthrow it?" ⁴So Hanun seized David's men, shaved off half of each man's beard,*ⁱ* cut off their garments in the middle at the buttocks,*ʲ* and sent them away.

a 11 Septuagint; Hebrew *my*

10:6
a Ge 34:30
b 2Sa 8:5
c Jdg 18:28
d Dt 3:14

[5]When David was told about this, he sent messengers to meet the men, for they were greatly humiliated. The king said, "Stay at Jericho till your beards have grown, and then come back."

[6]When the Ammonites realized that they had become a stench[a] in David's nostrils, they hired twenty thousand Aramean[b] foot soldiers from Beth Rehob[c] and Zobah, as well as the king of Maacah[d] with a thousand men, and also twelve thousand men from Tob.

[7]On hearing this, David sent Joab out with the entire army of fighting men. [8]The Ammonites came out and drew up in battle formation at the entrance to their city gate, while the Arameans of Zobah and Rehob and the men of Tob and Maacah were by themselves in the open country.

[9]Joab saw that there were battle lines in front of him and behind him; so he selected some of the best troops in Israel and deployed them against the Arameans. [10]He put the rest of the men under the command of Abishai his brother and deployed them against the Ammonites. [11]Joab said, "If the Arameans are too strong for me, then you are to come to my rescue; but if the Ammonites are too strong for you, then I will come to rescue you. [12]Be strong[e] and let us fight bravely for our people and the cities of our God. The LORD will do what is good in his sight."[f]

10:12
e Dt 31:6;
1Co 16:13;
Eph 6:10
f Jdg 10:15;
1Sa 3:18;
Ne 4:14

[13]Then Joab and the troops with him advanced to fight the Arameans, and they fled before him. [14]When the Ammonites saw that the Arameans were fleeing, they fled before Abishai and went inside the city. So Joab returned from fighting the Ammonites and came to Jerusalem.

[15]After the Arameans saw that they had been routed by Israel, they regrouped. [16]Hadadezer had Arameans brought from beyond the River[a]; they went to Helam, with Shobach the commander of Hadadezer's army leading them.

[17]When David was told of this, he gathered all Israel, crossed the Jordan and went to Helam. The Arameans formed their battle lines to meet David and fought against him. [18]But they fled before Israel, and David killed seven hundred of their charioteers and forty thousand of their foot soldiers.[b] He also struck down Shobach the commander of their army, and he died there. [19]When all the kings who were vassals of Hadadezer saw that they had been defeated by Israel, they made peace with the Israelites and became subject[g] to them.

10:19
g 2Sa 8:6
h 1Ki 11:25;
2Ki 5:1

So the Arameans[h] were afraid to help the Ammonites anymore.

Chapter 11 Theme

11 In the spring,[i] at the time when kings go off to war, David sent Joab[j] out with the king's men and the whole Israelite

---

a 16 That is, the Euphrates   b 18 Some Septuagint manuscripts (see also 1 Chron. 19:18); Hebrew *horsemen*

11:1
i 1Ki 20:22,26
j 2Sa 2:18

11:1
a 1Ch 20:1
b 2Sa 12:26-28

11:2
c Dt 22:8;
Jos 2:8
d Mt 5:28

11:3
e 1Ch 3:5
f 2Sa 23:34
g 2Sa 23:39

11:4
h Lev 20:10;
Ps 51 Title;
Jas 1:14-15
i Dt 22:22
j Lev 15:25-30;
18:19

11:6
k 1Ch 11:41

11:8
l Ge 18:4; 43:24;
Lk 7:44

11:11
m 2Sa 7:2

11:14
n 1Ki 21:8

11:15
o 2Sa 12:9
p 2Sa 12:12

11:21
q Jdg 8:31
r Jdg 9:50-54

army.a They destroyed the Ammonites and besieged Rabbah.b But David remained in Jerusalem.

2One evening David got up from his bed and walked around on the roofc of the palace. From the roof he sawd a woman bathing. The woman was very beautiful, 3and David sent someone to find out about her. The man said, "Isn't this Bathsheba,e the daughter of Eliamf and the wife of Uriahg the Hittite?" 4Then David sent messengers to get her.h She came to him, and he slepti with her. (She had purified herself from her uncleanness.)j Thena she went back home. 5The woman conceived and sent word to David, saying, "I am pregnant."

6So David sent this word to Joab: "Send me Uriahk the Hittite." And Joab sent him to David. 7When Uriah came to him, David asked him how Joab was, how the soldiers were and how the war was going. 8Then David said to Uriah, "Go down to your house and wash your feet."l So Uriah left the palace, and a gift from the king was sent after him. 9But Uriah slept at the entrance to the palace with all his master's servants and did not go down to his house.

10When David was told, "Uriah did not go home," he asked him, "Haven't you just come from a distance? Why didn't you go home?" 11Uriah said to David, "The arkm and Israel and Judah are staying in tents, and my master Joab and my lord's men are camped in the open fields. How could I go to my house to eat and drink and lie with my wife? As surely as you live, I will not do such a thing!"

12Then David said to him, "Stay here one more day, and tomorrow I will send you back." So Uriah remained in Jerusalem that day and the next. 13At David's invitation, he ate and drank with him, and David made him drunk. But in the evening Uriah went out to sleep on his mat among his master's servants; he did not go home.

14In the morning David wrote a lettern to Joab and sent it with Uriah. 15In it he wrote, "Put Uriah in the front line where the fighting is fiercest. Then withdraw from him so he will be struck downo and die.p"

16So while Joab had the city under siege, he put Uriah at a place where he knew the strongest defenders were. 17When the men of the city came out and fought against Joab, some of the men in David's army fell; moreover, Uriah the Hittite died.

18Joab sent David a full account of the battle. 19He instructed the messenger: "When you have finished giving the king this account of the battle, 20the king's anger may flare up, and he may ask you, 'Why did you get so close to the city to fight? Didn't you know they would shoot arrows from the wall? 21Who killed Abimelechq son of Jerub-Beshethb? Didn't a woman throw an upper millstone on him from the wall,r so that he died in Thebez? Why

a 4 Or with her. When she purified herself from her uncleanness,   b 21 Also known as Jerub-Baal (that is, Gideon) did you get so close to the wall?' If he asks you this, then say to him, 'Also, your servant Uriah the Hittite is dead.'"

[22] The messenger set out, and when he arrived he told David everything Joab had sent him to say. [23] The messenger said to David, "The men overpowered us and came out against us in the open, but we drove them back to the entrance to the city gate. [24] Then the archers shot arrows at your servants from the wall, and some of the king's men died. Moreover, your servant Uriah the Hittite is dead."

[25] David told the messenger, "Say this to Joab: 'Don't let this upset you; the sword devours one as well as another. Press the attack against the city and destroy it.' Say this to encourage Joab."

[26] When Uriah's wife heard that her husband was dead, she mourned for him. [27] After the time of mourning was over, David had her brought to his house, and she became his wife and bore him a son. But the thing David had done displeased[a] the LORD.

Chapter 12 Theme _____

12 The LORD sent Nathan[b] to David.[c] When he came to him,[d] he said, "There were two men in a certain town, one rich and the other poor. [2] The rich man had a very large number of sheep and cattle, [3] but the poor man had nothing except one little ewe lamb he had bought. He raised it, and it grew up with him and his children. It shared his food, drank from his cup and even slept in his arms. It was like a daughter to him.

[4] "Now a traveler came to the rich man, but the rich man refrained from taking one of his own sheep or cattle to prepare a meal for the traveler who had come to him. Instead, he took the ewe lamb that belonged to the poor man and prepared it for the one who had come to him."

[5] David[e] burned with anger against the man and said to Nathan, "As surely as the LORD lives, the man who did this deserves to die! [6] He must pay for that lamb four times over,[f] because he did such a thing and had no pity."

[7] Then Nathan said to David, "You are the man! This is what the LORD, the God of Israel, says: 'I anointed[g] you[h] king over Israel, and I delivered you from the hand of Saul. [8] I gave your master's house to you,[i] and your master's wives into your arms. I gave you the house of Israel and Judah. And if all this had been too little, I would have given you even more. [9] Why did you despise[j] the word of the LORD by doing what is evil in his eyes? You struck down[k] Uriah the Hittite with the sword and took his wife to be your own. You killed him with the sword of the Ammonites. [10] Now, therefore, the sword[l] will never depart from your house, because you despised me and took the wife of Uriah the Hittite to be your own.'

11:27
a 2Sa 12:9;
Ps 51:4-5

12:1
b 2Sa 7:2;
1Ki 20:35-41
c Ps 51 Title
d 2Sa 14:4

12:5
e 1Ki 20:40

12:6
f Ex 22:1;
Lk 19:8

12:7
g 1Sa 16:13
h 1Ki 20:42

12:8
i 2Sa 9:7

12:9
j Nu 15:31;
1Sa 15:19
k 2Sa 11:15

12:10
l 2Sa 13:28;
18:14-15;
1Ki 2:25

12:11
a Dt 28:30;
2Sa 16:21-22

12:12
b 2Sa 11:4-15
c 2Sa 16:22

12:13
d Ge 13:13;
Nu 22:34;
1Sa 15:24;
2Sa 24:10
e Ps 32:1-5;
51:1,9; 103:12;
Zec 3:4,9
f Pr 28:13;
Mic 7:18-19
g Lev 20:10;
24:17

12:14
h Isa 52:5;
Ro 2:24

12:15
i 1Sa 25:38

12:16
j 2Sa 13:31;
Ps 5:7

12:17
k 2Sa 3:35

12:20
l Mt 6:17
m Job 1:20

12:21
n Jdg 20:26

12:22
o Jnh 3:9
p Isa 38:1-5

12:23
q Ge 37:35
r 1Sa 31:13;
2Sa 13:39;
Job 7:10; 10:21

12:24
s 1Ki 1:11
t 1Ki 1:10;
1Ch 22:9; 28:5;
Mt 1:6

12:25
u Ne 13:26

12:26
v Dt 3:11;
1Ch 20:1-3

¹¹"This is what the LORD says: 'Out of your own household I am going to bring calamity upon you.*a* Before your very eyes I will take your wives and give them to one who is close to you, and he will lie with your wives in broad daylight. ¹²You did it in secret,*b* but I will do this thing in broad daylight*c* before all Israel.'"

¹³Then David said to Nathan, "I have sinned*d* against the LORD."

Nathan replied, "The LORD has taken away*e* your sin.*f* You are not going to die.*g* ¹⁴But because by doing this you have made the enemies of the LORD show utter contempt,*ah* the son born to you will die."

¹⁵After Nathan had gone home, the LORD struck*i* the child that Uriah's wife had borne to David, and he became ill. ¹⁶David pleaded with God for the child. He fasted and went into his house and spent the nights lying*j* on the ground. ¹⁷The elders of his household stood beside him to get him up from the ground, but he refused, and he would not eat any food with them.*k*

¹⁸On the seventh day the child died. David's servants were afraid to tell him that the child was dead, for they thought, "While the child was still living, we spoke to David but he would not listen to us. How can we tell him the child is dead? He may do something desperate."

¹⁹David noticed that his servants were whispering among themselves and he realized the child was dead. "Is the child dead?" he asked.

"Yes," they replied, "he is dead."

²⁰Then David got up from the ground. After he had washed,*l* put on lotions and changed his clothes,*m* he went into the house of the LORD and worshiped. Then he went to his own house, and at his request they served him food, and he ate.

²¹His servants asked him, "Why are you acting this way? While the child was alive, you fasted and wept,*n* but now that the child is dead, you get up and eat!"

²²He answered, "While the child was still alive, I fasted and wept. I thought, 'Who knows?*o* The LORD may be gracious to me and let the child live.'*p* ²³But now that he is dead, why should I fast? Can I bring him back again? I will go to him,*q* but he will not return to me."*r*

²⁴Then David comforted his wife Bathsheba,*s* and he went to her and lay with her. She gave birth to a son, and they named him Solomon.*t* The LORD loved him; ²⁵and because the LORD loved him, he sent word through Nathan the prophet to name him Jedidiah.*bu*

²⁶Meanwhile Joab fought against Rabbah*v* of the Ammonites and captured the royal citadel. ²⁷Joab then sent messengers to

a 14 Masoretic Text; an ancient Hebrew scribal tradition *this you have shown utter contempt for the LORD*   *b* 25 *Jedidiah* means *loved by the LORD*.

David, saying, "I have fought against Rabbah and taken its water supply. ²⁸Now muster the rest of the troops and besiege the city and capture it. Otherwise I will take the city, and it will be named after me."

²⁹So David mustered the entire army and went to Rabbah, and attacked and captured it. ³⁰He took the crown^a from the head of their king^a—its weight was a talent^b of gold, and it was set with precious stones—and it was placed on David's head. He took a great quantity of plunder from the city ³¹and brought out the people who were there, consigning them to labor with saws and with iron picks and axes, and he made them work at brickmaking.^c He did this to all the Ammonite^b towns. Then David and his entire army returned to Jerusalem.

Chapter 13 Theme _____

13 In the course of time, Amnon^c son of David fell in love with Tamar,^d the beautiful sister of Absalom^e son of David. ²Amnon became frustrated to the point of illness on account of his sister Tamar, for she was a virgin, and it seemed impossible for him to do anything to her.

³Now Amnon had a friend named Jonadab son of Shimeah,^f David's brother. Jonadab was a very shrewd man. ⁴He asked Amnon, "Why do you, the king's son, look so haggard morning after morning? Won't you tell me?"

Amnon said to him, "I'm in love with Tamar, my brother Absalom's sister."

⁵"Go to bed and pretend to be ill," Jonadab said. "When your father comes to see you, say to him, 'I would like my sister Tamar to come and give me something to eat. Let her prepare the food in my sight so I may watch her and then eat it from her hand.'"

⁶So Amnon lay down and pretended to be ill. When the king came to see him, Amnon said to him, "I would like my sister Tamar to come and make some special bread in my sight, so I may eat from her hand."

⁷David sent word to Tamar at the palace: "Go to the house of your brother Amnon and prepare some food for him." ⁸So Tamar went to the house of her brother Amnon, who was lying down. She took some dough, kneaded it, made the bread in his sight and baked it. ⁹Then she took the pan and served him the bread, but he refused to eat.

"Send everyone out of here,"^g Amnon said. So everyone left him. ¹⁰Then Amnon said to Tamar, "Bring the food here into my bedroom so I may eat from your hand." And Tamar took the

---

12:30
^a 1Ch 20:2;
Est 8:15;
Ps 21:3; 132:18

12:31
^b 1Sa 14:47

13:1
^c 2Sa 3:2
^d 2Sa 14:27;
1Ch 3:9
^e 2Sa 3:3

13:3
^f 1Sa 16:9

13:9
^g Ge 45:1

---

^a *30* Or *of Milcom* (that is, Molech)   ^b *30* That is, about 75 pounds (about 34 kilograms)
^c *31* The meaning of the Hebrew for this clause is uncertain.

13:11
a Ge 39:12
b Ge 38:16

bread she had prepared and brought it to her brother Amnon in his bedroom. ¹¹But when she took it to him to eat, he grabbed*ᵃ* her and said, "Come to bed with me, my sister."*ᵇ*

13:12
c Lev 20:17;
Jdg 20:6
d Ge 34:7;
Jdg 19:23

¹²"Don't, my brother!" she said to him. "Don't force me. Such a thing should not be done in Israel!*ᶜ* Don't do this wicked thing.*ᵈ* ¹³What about me?*ᵉ* Where could I get rid of my disgrace? And what about you? You would be like one of the wicked fools in Israel. Please speak to the king; he will not keep me from being married to you." ¹⁴But he refused to listen to her, and since he was stronger than she, he raped her.*ᶠ*

13:13
e Ge 20:12;
Lev 18:9;
Dt 22:21,23-24

¹⁵Then Amnon hated her with intense hatred. In fact, he hated her more than he had loved her. Amnon said to her, "Get up and get out!"

¹⁶"No!" she said to him. "Sending me away would be a greater wrong than what you have already done to me."

But he refused to listen to her. ¹⁷He called his personal servant and said, "Get this woman out of here and bolt the door after her." ¹⁸So his servant put her out and bolted the door after her. She was wearing a richly ornamented*ᵃ* robe,*ᵍ* for this was the kind of garment the virgin daughters of the king wore. ¹⁹Tamar put ashes*ʰ* on her head and tore the ornamented*ᵇ* robe she was wearing. She put her hand on her head and went away, weeping aloud as she went.

13:14
f Ge 34:2;
Dt 22:25;
Eze 22:11

13:18
g Ge 37:23;
Jdg 5:30

²⁰Her brother Absalom said to her, "Has that Amnon, your brother, been with you? Be quiet now, my sister; he is your brother. Don't take this thing to heart." And Tamar lived in her brother Absalom's house, a desolate woman.

13:19
h Jos 7:6;
1Sa 4:12;
2Sa 1:2;
Est 4:1;
Da 9:3

²¹When King David heard all this, he was furious.*ⁱ* ²²Absalom never said a word to Amnon, either good or bad;*ʲ* he hated*ᵏ* Amnon because he had disgraced his sister Tamar.

²³Two years later, when Absalom's sheepshearers*ˡ* were at Baal Hazor near the border of Ephraim, he invited all the king's sons to come there. ²⁴Absalom went to the king and said, "Your servant has had shearers come. Will the king and his officials please join me?"

13:21
i Ge 34:7

²⁵"No, my son," the king replied. "All of us should not go; we would only be a burden to you." Although Absalom urged him, he still refused to go, but gave him his blessing.

²⁶Then Absalom said, "If not, please let my brother Amnon come with us."

The king asked him, "Why should he go with you?" ²⁷But Absalom urged him, so he sent with him Amnon and the rest of the king's sons.

13:22
j Ge 31:24
k Lev 19:17-18;
1Jn 2:9-11

13:23
l 1Sa 25:7

a 18 The meaning of the Hebrew for this phrase is uncertain.   *b 19* The meaning of the Hebrew for this word is uncertain.

²⁸Absalom[a] ordered his men, "Listen! When Amnon is in high[b] spirits from drinking wine and I say to you, 'Strike Amnon down,' then kill him. Don't be afraid. Have not I given you this order? Be strong and brave.[c]" ²⁹So Absalom's men did to Amnon what Absalom had ordered. Then all the king's sons got up, mounted their mules and fled.

³⁰While they were on their way, the report came to David: "Absalom has struck down all the king's sons; not one of them is left." ³¹The king stood up, tore[d] his clothes and lay down on the ground; and all his servants stood by with their clothes torn.

³²But Jonadab son of Shimeah, David's brother, said, "My lord should not think that they killed all the princes; only Amnon is dead. This has been Absalom's expressed intention ever since the day Amnon raped his sister Tamar. ³³My lord the king should not be concerned about the report that all the king's sons are dead. Only Amnon is dead."

³⁴Meanwhile, Absalom had fled.

Now the man standing watch looked up and saw many people on the road west of him, coming down the side of the hill. The watchman went and told the king, "I see men in the direction of Horonaim, on the side of the hill."[a]

³⁵Jonadab said to the king, "See, the king's sons are here; it has happened just as your servant said."

³⁶As he finished speaking, the king's sons came in, wailing loudly. The king, too, and all his servants wept very bitterly.

³⁷Absalom fled and went to Talmai[e] son of Ammihud, the king of Geshur. But King David mourned for his son every day.

³⁸After Absalom fled and went to Geshur, he stayed there three years. ³⁹And the spirit of the king[b] longed to go to Absalom,[f] for he was consoled[g] concerning Amnon's death.

Chapter 14 Theme _____

14 Joab[h] son of Zeruiah knew that the king's heart longed for Absalom. ²So Joab sent someone to Tekoa[i] and had a wise woman[j] brought from there. He said to her, "Pretend you are in mourning. Dress in mourning clothes, and don't use any cosmetic lotions.[k] Act like a woman who has spent many days grieving for the dead. ³Then go to the king and speak these words to him." And Joab[l] put the words in her mouth.

⁴When the woman from Tekoa went[c] to the king, she fell with her face to the ground to pay him honor, and she said, "Help me, O king!"

---

a 34 Septuagint; Hebrew does not have this sentence.   b 39 Dead Sea Scrolls and some Septuagint manuscripts; Masoretic Text *But ⌐the spirit of⌐ David the king*   c 4 Many Hebrew manuscripts, Septuagint, Vulgate and Syriac; most Hebrew manuscripts *spoke*

13:28
a 2Sa 3:3;
b Jdg 19:6,9,22;
Ru 3:7;
1Sa 25:36
c 2Sa 12:10

13:31
d Nu 14:6;
2Sa 1:11; 12:16

13:37
e ver 34;
2Sa 3:3;
14:23,32

13:39
f 2Sa 14:13
g 2Sa 12:19-23

14:1
h 2Sa 2:18

14:2
i 2Ch 11:6;
Ne 3:5;
Jer 6:1;
Am 1:1
j 2Sa 20:16
k Ru 3:3;
2Sa 12:20;
Isa 1:6

14:3
l ver 19

14:7
a Nu 35:19
b Mt 21:38
c Dt 19:10-13

14:8
d 1Sa 25:35

14:9
e 1Sa 25:24
f Mt 27:25
g 1Sa 25:28;
1Ki 2:33

14:11
h Nu 35:12,21
i Mt 10:30
j 1Sa 14:45

14:13
k 2Sa 12:7;
1Ki 20:40
l 2Sa 13:38-39

14:14
m Job 14:11;
Ps 58:7;
Isa 19:5
n Job 10:8;
17:13; 30:23;
Ps 22:15;
Heb 9:27
o Nu 35:15,
25-28; Job 34:15

14:16
p Ex 34:9;
1Sa 26:19

14:17
q ver 20;
1Sa 29:9;
2Sa 19:27
r 1Ki 3:9;
Da 2:21

14:19
s ver 3

⁵The king asked her, "What is troubling you?"

She said, "I am indeed a widow; my husband is dead. ⁶I your servant had two sons. They got into a fight with each other in the field, and no one was there to separate them. One struck the other and killed him. ⁷Now the whole clan has risen up against your servant; they say, 'Hand over the one who struck his brother down, so that we may put him to death^a for the life of his brother whom he killed; then we will get rid of the heir^b as well.' They would put out the only burning coal I have left,^c leaving my husband neither name nor descendant on the face of the earth."

⁸The king said to the woman, "Go home,^d and I will issue an order in your behalf."

⁹But the woman from Tekoa said to him, "My lord the king, let the blame^e rest on me and on my father's family,^f and let the king and his throne be without guilt.^g"

¹⁰The king replied, "If anyone says anything to you, bring him to me, and he will not bother you again."

¹¹She said, "Then let the king invoke the LORD his God to prevent the avenger^h of blood from adding to the destruction, so that my son will not be destroyed."

"As surely as the LORD lives," he said, "not one hair^i of your son's head will fall to the ground.^j"

¹²Then the woman said, "Let your servant speak a word to my lord the king."

"Speak," he replied.

¹³The woman said, "Why then have you devised a thing like this against the people of God? When the king says this, does he not convict himself,^k for the king has not brought back his banished son?^l ¹⁴Like water^m spilled on the ground, which cannot be recovered, so we must die.^n But God does not take away life; instead, he devises ways so that a banished person^o may not remain estranged from him.

¹⁵"And now I have come to say this to my lord the king because the people have made me afraid. Your servant thought, 'I will speak to the king; perhaps he will do what his servant asks. ¹⁶Perhaps the king will agree to deliver his servant from the hand of the man who is trying to cut off both me and my son from the inheritance^p God gave us.'

¹⁷"And now your servant says, 'May the word of my lord the king bring me rest, for my lord the king is like an angel^q of God in discerning^r good and evil. May the LORD your God be with you.'"

¹⁸Then the king said to the woman, "Do not keep from me the answer to what I am going to ask you."

"Let my lord the king speak," the woman said.

¹⁹The king asked, "Isn't the hand of Joab^s with you in all this?"

The woman answered, "As surely as you live, my lord the king, no one can turn to the right or to the left from anything my lord the king says. Yes, it was your servant Joab who instructed me to do this and who put all these words into the mouth of your servant. ²⁰Your servant Joab did this to change the present situation. My lord has wisdom*ᵃ* like that of an angel of God—he knows everything that happens in the land.*ᵇ*"

²¹The king said to Joab, "Very well, I will do it. Go, bring back the young man Absalom."

²²Joab fell with his face to the ground to pay him honor, and he blessed the king.*ᶜ* Joab said, "Today your servant knows that he has found favor in your eyes, my lord the king, because the king has granted his servant's request."

²³Then Joab went to Geshur and brought Absalom back to Jerusalem. ²⁴But the king said, "He must go to his own house; he must not see my face." So Absalom went to his own house and did not see the face of the king.

²⁵In all Israel there was not a man so highly praised for his handsome appearance as Absalom. From the top of his head to the sole of his foot there was no blemish in him. ²⁶Whenever he cut the hair of his head*ᵈ*—he used to cut his hair from time to time when it became too heavy for him—he would weigh it, and its weight was two hundred shekels*ᵃ* by the royal standard.

²⁷Three sons*ᵉ* and a daughter were born to Absalom. The daughter's name was Tamar,*ᶠ* and she became a beautiful woman.

²⁸Absalom lived two years in Jerusalem without seeing the king's face. ²⁹Then Absalom sent for Joab in order to send him to the king, but Joab refused to come to him. So he sent a second time, but he refused to come. ³⁰Then he said to his servants, "Look, Joab's field is next to mine, and he has barley*ᵍ* there. Go and set it on fire." So Absalom's servants set the field on fire.

³¹Then Joab did go to Absalom's house and he said to him, "Why have your servants set my field on fire?*ʰ*"

³²Absalom said to Joab, "Look, I sent word to you and said, 'Come here so I can send you to the king to ask, "Why have I come from Geshur?*ⁱ* It would be better for me if I were still there!"' Now then, I want to see the king's face, and if I am guilty of anything, let him put me to death."*ʲ*

³³So Joab went to the king and told him this. Then the king summoned Absalom, and he came in and bowed down with his face to the ground before the king. And the king kissed*ᵏ* Absalom.

Chapter 15 Theme

15 In the course of time,*ˡ* Absalom provided himself with a chariot*ᵐ* and horses and with fifty men to run ahead of

---

ᵃ 26 That is, about 5 pounds (about 2.3 kilograms)

14:20
ᵃ 1Ki 3:12,28;
Isa 28:6
ᵇ ver 17;
2Sa 18:13;
19:27

14:22
ᶜ Ge 47:7

14:26
ᵈ 2Sa 18:9;
Eze 44:20

14:27
ᵉ 2Sa 18:18
ᶠ 2Sa 13:1

14:30
ᵍ Ex 9:31

14:31
ʰ Jdg 15:5

14:32
ⁱ 2Sa 3:3
ʲ 1Sa 20:8

14:33
ᵏ Ge 33:4;
Lk 15:20

15:1
ˡ 2Sa 12:11
ᵐ 1Sa 8:11;
1Ki 1:5

15:2
a Ge 23:10;
2 Sa 19:8

15:3
b Pr 12:2

15:4
c Jdg 9:29

15:6
d Ro 16:18

15:8
e 2 Sa 3:3;
13:37-38
f Ge 28:20

15:10
g 1 Ki 1:34,39;
2 Ki 9:13

15:12
h ver 31,34;
2 Sa 16:15,23;
1 Ch 27:33
i Job 19:14;
Ps 41:9; 55:13;
Jer 9:4
j Jos 15:51
k Ps 3:1

15:14
l 2 Sa 12:11;
1 Ki 2:26;
Ps 132:1;
Ps 3 Title
m 2 Sa 19:9

15:16
n 2 Sa 16:21-22;
20:3

15:18
o 1 Sa 30:14;
2 Sa 8:18;
20:7,23;
1 Ki 1:38,44;
1 Ch 18:17

him. ²He would get up early and stand by the side of the road leading to the city gate.*a* Whenever anyone came with a complaint to be placed before the king for a decision, Absalom would call out to him, "What town are you from?" He would answer, "Your servant is from one of the tribes of Israel." ³Then Absalom would say to him, "Look, your claims are valid and proper, but there is no representative of the king to hear you."*b* ⁴And Absalom would add, "If only I were appointed judge in the land!*c* Then everyone who has a complaint or case could come to me and I would see that he gets justice."

⁵Also, whenever anyone approached him to bow down before him, Absalom would reach out his hand, take hold of him and kiss him. ⁶Absalom behaved in this way toward all the Israelites who came to the king asking for justice, and so he stole the hearts*d* of the men of Israel.

⁷At the end of four*a* years, Absalom said to the king, "Let me go to Hebron and fulfill a vow I made to the LORD. ⁸While your servant was living at Geshur*e* in Aram, I made this vow:*f* 'If the LORD takes me back to Jerusalem, I will worship the LORD in Hebron.*b*'"

⁹The king said to him, "Go in peace." So he went to Hebron.

¹⁰Then Absalom sent secret messengers throughout the tribes of Israel to say, "As soon as you hear the sound of the trumpets,*g* then say, 'Absalom is king in Hebron.'" ¹¹Two hundred men from Jerusalem had accompanied Absalom. They had been invited as guests and went quite innocently, knowing nothing about the matter. ¹²While Absalom was offering sacrifices, he also sent for Ahithophel*h* the Gilonite, David's counselor,*i* to come from Giloh,*j* his hometown. And so the conspiracy gained strength, and Absalom's following kept on increasing.*k*

¹³A messenger came and told David, "The hearts of the men of Israel are with Absalom."

¹⁴Then David said to all his officials who were with him in Jerusalem, "Come! We must flee,*l* or none of us will escape from Absalom.*m* We must leave immediately, or he will move quickly to overtake us and bring ruin upon us and put the city to the sword."

¹⁵The king's officials answered him, "Your servants are ready to do whatever our lord the king chooses."

¹⁶The king set out, with his entire household following him; but he left ten concubines*n* to take care of the palace. ¹⁷So the king set out, with all the people following him, and they halted at a place some distance away. ¹⁸All his men marched past him, along with all the Kerethites*o* and Pelethites; and all the six hundred Gittites who had accompanied him from Gath marched before the king.

a 7 Some Septuagint manuscripts, Syriac and Josephus; Hebrew *forty*   *b* 8 Some Septuagint manuscripts; Hebrew does not have *in Hebron.*

¹⁹The king said to Ittai*a* the Gittite, "Why should you come along with us? Go back and stay with King Absalom. You are a foreigner,*b* an exile from your homeland. ²⁰You came only yesterday. And today shall I make you wander*c* about with us, when I do not know where I am going? Go back, and take your countrymen. May kindness and faithfulness*d* be with you."

²¹But Ittai replied to the king, "As surely as the LORD lives, and as my lord the king lives, wherever my lord the king may be, whether it means life or death, there will your servant be."*e*

²²David said to Ittai, "Go ahead, march on." So Ittai the Gittite marched on with all his men and the families that were with him.

²³The whole countryside wept aloud as all the people passed by. The king also crossed the Kidron Valley,*f* and all the people moved on toward the desert.

²⁴Zadok*g* was there, too, and all the Levites who were with him were carrying the ark*h* of the covenant of God. They set down the ark of God, and Abiathar*i* offered sacrifices*a* until all the people had finished leaving the city.

²⁵Then the king said to Zadok, "Take the ark of God back into the city. If I find favor in the LORD's eyes, he will bring me back and let me see it and his dwelling place*j* again. ²⁶But if he says, 'I am not pleased with you,' then I am ready; let him do to me whatever seems good to him.*k*"

²⁷The king also said to Zadok the priest, "Aren't you a seer?*l* Go back to the city in peace, with your son Ahimaaz and Jonathan*m* son of Abiathar. You and Abiathar take your two sons with you. ²⁸I will wait at the fords*n* in the desert until word comes from you to inform me." ²⁹So Zadok and Abiathar took the ark of God back to Jerusalem and stayed there.

³⁰But David continued up the Mount of Olives, weeping*o* as he went; his head*p* was covered and he was barefoot. All the people with him covered their heads too and were weeping as they went up. ³¹Now David had been told, "Ahithophel*q* is among the conspirators with Absalom." So David prayed, "O LORD, turn Ahithophel's counsel into foolishness."

³²When David arrived at the summit, where people used to worship God, Hushai the Arkite*r* was there to meet him, his robe torn and dust*s* on his head. ³³David said to him, "If you go with me, you will be a burden*t* to me. ³⁴But if you return to the city and say to Absalom, 'I will be your servant, O king; I was your father's servant in the past, but now I will be your servant,'*u* then you can help me by frustrating Ahithophel's advice. ³⁵Won't the priests Zadok and Abiathar be there with you? Tell them anything you hear in the king's palace.*v* ³⁶Their two sons, Ahimaaz

---

a24 Or *Abiathar went up*

15:19
a 2Sa 18:2
b Ge 31:15

15:20
c 1Sa 23:13
d 2Sa 2:6

15:21
e Ru 1:16-17;
Pr 17:17

15:23
f 2Ch 29:16

15:24
g 2Sa 8:17
h Nu 4:15
i 1Sa 22:20

15:25
j Ex 15:13;
Ps 43:3;
Jer 25:30

15:26
k 1Sa 3:18;
2Sa 22:20;
1Ki 10:9

15:27
l 1Sa 9:9
m 2Sa 17:17

15:28
n 2Sa 17:16

15:30
o 2Sa 19:4;
Ps 126:6
p Est 6:12;
Isa 20:2-4

15:31
q ver 12;
2Sa 16:23;
17:14,23

15:32
r Jos 16:2
s 2Sa 1:2

15:33
t 2Sa 19:35

15:34
u 2Sa 16:19

15:35
v 2Sa 17:15-16

15:36
a ver 27;
2Sa 17:17

son of Zadok and Jonathan*a* son of Abiathar, are there with them. Send them to me with anything you hear.”

37 So David's friend Hushai*b* arrived at Jerusalem as Absalom*c* was entering the city.

Chapter 16 Theme _____

15:37
b 2Sa 16:16-17;
1Ch 27:33
c 2Sa 16:15

16 When David had gone a short distance beyond the summit, there was Ziba,*d* the steward of Mephibosheth, waiting to meet him. He had a string of donkeys saddled and loaded with two hundred loaves of bread, a hundred cakes of raisins, a hundred cakes of figs and a skin of wine.*e*

16:1
d 2Sa 9:1-13
e 1Sa 25:18

2 The king asked Ziba, “Why have you brought these?”

Ziba answered, “The donkeys are for the king's household to ride on, the bread and fruit are for the men to eat, and the wine is to refresh*f* those who become exhausted in the desert.”

16:2
f 2Sa 17:27-29

3 The king then asked, “Where is your master's grandson?”*g*

Ziba said to him, “He is staying in Jerusalem, because he thinks, ‘Today the house of Israel will give me back my grandfather's kingdom.’”

16:3
g 2Sa 9:9-10;
19:26-27

4 Then the king said to Ziba, “All that belonged to Mephibosheth is now yours.”

“I humbly bow,” Ziba said. “May I find favor in your eyes, my lord the king.”

16:5
h 2Sa 3:16
i 2Sa 19:16-23;
1Ki 2:8-9, 36,44
j Ex 22:28

5 As King David approached Bahurim,*h* a man from the same clan as Saul's family came out from there. His name was Shimei*i* son of Gera, and he cursed*j* as he came out. 6 He pelted David and all the king's officials with stones, though all the troops and the special guard were on David's right and left. 7 As he cursed, Shimei said, “Get out, get out, you man of blood, you scoundrel! 8 The LORD has repaid you for all the blood you shed in the household of Saul, in whose place you have reigned.*k* The LORD has handed the kingdom over to your son Absalom. You have come to ruin because you are a man of blood!”

16:8
k 2Sa 21:9

9 Then Abishai*l* son of Zeruiah said to the king, “Why should this dead dog curse my lord the king? Let me go over and cut off his head.”*m*

16:9
l 2Sa 9:8
m Ex 22:28;
Lk 9:54

10 But the king said, “What do you and I have in common, you sons of Zeruiah?*n* If he is cursing because the LORD said to him, ‘Curse David,’ who can ask, ‘Why do you do this?’”*o*

16:10
n 2Sa 19:22
o Ro 9:20

11 David then said to Abishai and all his officials, “My son,*p* who is of my own flesh, is trying to take my life. How much more, then, this Benjamite! Leave him alone; let him curse, for the LORD has told him to.*q* 12 It may be that the LORD will see my distress*r* and repay me with good*s* for the cursing I am receiving today.*t*”

16:11
p 2Sa 12:11
q Ge 45:5

13 So David and his men continued along the road while Shimei was going along the hillside opposite him, cursing as he went and

16:12
r Ps 4:1; 25:18
s Dt 23:5;
Ro 8:28
t Ps 109:28

throwing stones at him and showering him with dirt. ¹⁴The king and all the people with him arrived at their destination exhausted.ᵃ And there he refreshed himself.

¹⁵Meanwhile, Absalomᵇ and all the men of Israel came to Jerusalem, and Ahithophelᶜ was with him. ¹⁶Then Hushaiᵈ the Arkite, David's friend, went to Absalom and said to him, "Long live the king! Long live the king!"

¹⁷Absalom asked Hushai, "Is this the love you show your friend? Why didn't you go with your friend?"ᵉ

¹⁸Hushai said to Absalom, "No, the one chosen by the LORD, by these people, and by all the men of Israel—his I will be, and I will remain with him. ¹⁹Furthermore, whom should I serve? Should I not serve the son? Just as I served your father, so I will serve you."ᶠ

²⁰Absalom said to Ahithophel, "Give us your advice. What should we do?"

²¹Ahithophel answered, "Lie with your father's concubines whom he left to take care of the palace. Then all Israel will hear that you have made yourself a stench in your father's nostrils, and the hands of everyone with you will be strengthened." ²²So they pitched a tent for Absalom on the roof, and he lay with his father's concubines in the sight of all Israel.ᵍ

²³Now in those days the adviceʰ Ahithophel gave was like that of one who inquires of God. That was how both Davidⁱ and Absalom regarded all of Ahithophel's advice.

Chapter 17 Theme _____

17 Ahithophel said to Absalom, "I wouldᵃ choose twelve thousand men and set out tonight in pursuit of David. ²I wouldᵇ attack him while he is weary and weak.ʲ I wouldᵇ strike him with terror, and then all the people with him will flee. I wouldᵇ strike down only the kingᵏ ³and bring all the people back to you. The death of the man you seek will mean the return of all; all the people will be unharmed." ⁴This plan seemed good to Absalom and to all the elders of Israel.

⁵But Absalom said, "Summon also Hushaiˡ the Arkite, so we can hear what he has to say." ⁶When Hushai came to him, Absalom said, "Ahithophel has given this advice. Should we do what he says? If not, give us your opinion."

⁷Hushai replied to Absalom, "The advice Ahithophel has given is not good this time. ⁸You know your father and his men; they are fighters, and as fierce as a wild bear robbed of her cubs.ᵐ Besides, your father is an experienced fighter;ⁿ he will not spend the night with the troops. ⁹Even now, he is hidden in a cave or

---

16:14
ᵃ2Sa 17:2

16:15
ᵇ2Sa 15:37
ᶜ2Sa 15:12

16:16
ᵈ2Sa 15:37

16:17
ᵉ2Sa 19:25

16:19
ᶠ2Sa 15:34

16:22
ᵍ2Sa 12:11-12;
15:16

16:23
ʰ2Sa 17:14,23
ⁱ2Sa 15:12

17:2
ʲ2Sa 16:14
ᵏ1Ki 22:31;
Zec 13:7

17:5
ˡ2Sa 15:32

17:8
ᵐHos 13:8
ⁿ1Sa 16:18

ᵃ1 Or *Let me*   ᵇ2 Or *will*

17:9
a Jer 41:9

17:10
b 1Ch 12:8
c Jos 2:9,11;
Eze 21:15
d 2Sa 23:8;
1Ch 11:11

17:11
e Jdg 20:1
f Ge 12:2; 22:17;
Jos 11:4

17:13
g Mic 1:6

17:14
h 2Sa 16:23
i 2Sa 15:12
j 2Sa 15:34;
Ne 4:15
k Ps 9:16
l 2Ch 10:8

17:16
m 2Sa 15:28
n 2Sa 15:35

17:17
o 2Sa 15:27,36
p Jos 15:7; 18:16

17:18
q 2Sa 3:16; 16:5

17:19
r Jos 2:6

17:20
s Ex 1:19;
Jos 2:3-5;
1Sa 19:12-17

17:23
t 2Sa 15:12;
16:23

some other place.*a* If he should attack your troops first,*a* whoever hears about it will say, 'There has been a slaughter among the troops who follow Absalom.' ¹⁰Then even the bravest soldier, whose heart is like the heart of a lion,*b* will melt*c* with fear, for all Israel knows that your father is a fighter and that those with him are brave.*d*

¹¹"So I advise you: Let all Israel, from Dan to Beersheba*e*—as numerous as the sand*f* on the seashore—be gathered to you, with you yourself leading them into battle. ¹²Then we will attack him wherever he may be found, and we will fall on him as dew settles on the ground. Neither he nor any of his men will be left alive. ¹³If he withdraws into a city, then all Israel will bring ropes to that city, and we will drag it down to the valley*g* until not even a piece of it can be found."

¹⁴Absalom and all the men of Israel said, "The advice*h* of Hushai the Arkite is better than that of Ahithophel."*i* For the LORD had determined to frustrate*j* the good advice of Ahithophel in order to bring disaster*k* on Absalom.*l*

¹⁵Hushai told Zadok and Abiathar, the priests, "Ahithophel has advised Absalom and the elders of Israel to do such and such, but I have advised them to do so and so. ¹⁶Now send a message immediately and tell David, 'Do not spend the night at the fords in the desert;*m* cross over without fail, or the king and all the people with him will be swallowed up.'*n*"

¹⁷Jonathan*o* and Ahimaaz were staying at En Rogel.*p* A servant girl was to go and inform them, and they were to go and tell King David, for they could not risk being seen entering the city. ¹⁸But a young man saw them and told Absalom. So the two of them left quickly and went to the house of a man in Bahurim.*q* He had a well in his courtyard, and they climbed down into it. ¹⁹His wife took a covering and spread it out over the opening of the well and scattered grain over it. No one knew anything about it.*r*

²⁰When Absalom's men came to the woman*s* at the house, they asked, "Where are Ahimaaz and Jonathan?"

The woman answered them, "They crossed over the brook."*b* The men searched but found no one, so they returned to Jerusalem.

²¹After the men had gone, the two climbed out of the well and went to inform King David. They said to him, "Set out and cross the river at once; Ahithophel has advised such and such against you." ²²So David and all the people with him set out and crossed the Jordan. By daybreak, no one was left who had not crossed the Jordan.

²³When Ahithophel saw that his advice*t* had not been followed, he saddled his donkey and set out for his house in his hometown.

---

a 9 Or *When some of the men fall at the first attack*   *b 20* Or "*They passed by the sheep pen toward the water.*"

He put his house in order[a] and then hanged himself. So he died and was buried in his father's tomb.

[24]David went to Mahanaim,[b] and Absalom crossed the Jordan with all the men of Israel. [25]Absalom had appointed Amasa[c] over the army in place of Joab. Amasa was the son of a man named Jether,[a][d] an Israelite[b] who had married Abigail,[c] the daughter of Nahash and sister of Zeruiah the mother of Joab. [26]The Israelites and Absalom camped in the land of Gilead.

[27]When David came to Mahanaim, Shobi son of Nahash[e] from Rabbah[f] of the Ammonites, and Makir[g] son of Ammiel from Lo Debar, and Barzillai[h] the Gileadite[i] from Rogelim [28]brought bedding and bowls and articles of pottery. They also brought wheat and barley, flour and roasted grain, beans and lentils,[d] [29]honey and curds, sheep, and cheese from cows' milk for David and his people to eat.[j] For they said, "The people have become hungry and tired and thirsty in the desert.[k]"

Chapter 18 Theme _____

18 David mustered the men who were with him and appointed over them commanders of thousands and commanders of hundreds. [2]David sent the troops out[l]—a third under the command of Joab, a third under Joab's brother Abishai[m] son of Zeruiah, and a third under Ittai[n] the Gittite. The king told the troops, "I myself will surely march out with you."

[3]But the men said, "You must not go out; if we are forced to flee, they won't care about us. Even if half of us die, they won't care; but you are worth ten[o] thousand of us.[e] It would be better now for you to give us support from the city."[p]

[4]The king answered, "I will do whatever seems best to you."

So the king stood beside the gate while all the men marched out in units of hundreds and of thousands. [5]The king commanded Joab, Abishai and Ittai, "Be gentle with the young man Absalom for my sake." And all the troops heard the king giving orders concerning Absalom to each of the commanders.

[6]The army marched into the field to fight Israel, and the battle took place in the forest[q] of Ephraim. [7]There the army of Israel was defeated by David's men, and the casualties that day were great—twenty thousand men. [8]The battle spread out over the whole countryside, and the forest claimed more lives that day than the sword.

---

[a]25 Hebrew *Ithra*, a variant of *Jether*   [b]25 Hebrew and some Septuagint manuscripts; other Septuagint manuscripts (see also 1Chron. 2:17) *Ishmaelite* or *Jezreelite*   [c]25 Hebrew *Abigal*, a variant of *Abigail*   [d]28 Most Septuagint manuscripts and Syriac; Hebrew *lentils, and roasted grain*   [e]3 Two Hebrew manuscripts, some Septuagint manuscripts and Vulgate; most Hebrew manuscripts *care; for now there are ten thousand like us*

17:23
[a]2Ki 20:1;
Mt 27:5

17:24
[b]Ge 32:2;
2Sa 2:8

17:25
[c]2Sa 19:13;
20:4,9-12;
1Ki 2:5,32;
1Ch 12:18
[d]1Ch 2:13-17

17:27
[e]1Sa 11:1
[f]Dt 3:11;
2Sa 10:1-2;
12:26,29
[g]2Sa 9:4
[h]2Sa 19:31-39;
1Ki 2:7
[i]2Sa 19:31;
Ezr 2:61

17:29
[j]1Ch 12:40
[k]2Sa 16:2;
Ro 12:13

18:2
[l]Jdg 7:16;
1Sa 11:11
[m]1Sa 26:6
[n]2Sa 15:19

18:3
[o]1Sa 18:7
[p]2Sa 21:17

18:6
[q]Jos 17:18

18:9
a 2Sa 14:26

⁹Now Absalom happened to meet David's men. He was riding his mule, and as the mule went under the thick branches of a large oak, Absalom's head*ᵃ* got caught in the tree. He was left hanging in midair, while the mule he was riding kept on going.

¹⁰When one of the men saw this, he told Joab, "I just saw Absalom hanging in an oak tree."

18:11
b 2Sa 3:39
c 1Sa 18:4

¹¹Joab said to the man who had told him this, "What! You saw him? Why didn't you strike*ᵇ* him to the ground right there? Then I would have had to give you ten shekels*ᵃ* of silver and a warrior's belt.*ᶜ*"

18:13
d 2Sa 14:19-20

¹²But the man replied, "Even if a thousand shekels*ᵇ* were weighed out into my hands, I would not lift my hand against the king's son. In our hearing the king commanded you and Abishai and Ittai, 'Protect the young man Absalom for my sake.*ᶜ*' ¹³And if I had put my life in jeopardy*ᵈ*—and nothing is hidden from the king*ᵈ*—you would have kept your distance from me."

18:14
e 2Sa 2:18;
14:30

¹⁴Joab*ᵉ* said, "I'm not going to wait like this for you." So he took three javelins in his hand and plunged them into Absalom's heart while Absalom was still alive in the oak tree. ¹⁵And ten of Joab's armor-bearers surrounded Absalom, struck him and killed him.*ᶠ*

18:15
f 2Sa 12:10

¹⁶Then Joab*ᵍ* sounded the trumpet, and the troops stopped pursuing Israel, for Joab halted them. ¹⁷They took Absalom, threw him into a big pit in the forest and piled up*ʰ* a large heap of rocks*ⁱ* over him. Meanwhile, all the Israelites fled to their homes.

18:16
g 2Sa 2:28;
20:22

¹⁸During his lifetime Absalom had taken a pillar and erected it in the King's Valley*ʲ* as a monument*ᵏ* to himself, for he thought, "I have no son*ˡ* to carry on the memory of my name." He named the pillar after himself, and it is called Absalom's Monument to this day.

18:17
h Jos 7:26
i Jos 8:29

¹⁹Now Ahimaaz*ᵐ* son of Zadok said, "Let me run and take the news to the king that the LORD has delivered him from the hand of his enemies.*ⁿ*"

²⁰"You are not the one to take the news today," Joab told him. "You may take the news another time, but you must not do so today, because the king's son is dead."

18:18
j Ge 14:17
k Ge 50:5;
Nu 32:42;
1Sa 15:12
l 2Sa 14:27

²¹Then Joab said to a Cushite, "Go, tell the king what you have seen." The Cushite bowed down before Joab and ran off.

²²Ahimaaz son of Zadok again said to Joab, "Come what may, please let me run behind the Cushite."

But Joab replied, "My son, why do you want to go? You don't have any news that will bring you a reward."

²³He said, "Come what may, I want to run."

18:19
m 2Sa 15:36
n ver 31;
Jdg 11:36

ᵃ 11 That is, about 4 ounces (about 115 grams) ᵇ 12 That is, about 25 pounds (about 11 kilograms) ᶜ 12 A few Hebrew manuscripts, Septuagint, Vulgate and Syriac; most Hebrew manuscripts may be translated *Absalom, whoever you may be.* ᵈ 13 Or *Otherwise, if I had acted treacherously toward him*

So Joab said, "Run!" Then Ahimaaz ran by way of the plain[a] and outran the Cushite.

²⁴While David was sitting between the inner and outer gates, the watchman[a] went up to the roof of the gateway by the wall. As he looked out, he saw a man running alone. ²⁵The watchman called out to the king and reported it.

The king said, "If he is alone, he must have good news." And the man came closer and closer.

²⁶Then the watchman saw another man running, and he called down to the gatekeeper, "Look, another man running alone!"

The king said, "He must be bringing good news,[b] too."

²⁷The watchman said, "It seems to me that the first one runs like[c] Ahimaaz son of Zadok."

"He's a good man," the king said. "He comes with good news."

²⁸Then Ahimaaz called out to the king, "All is well!" He bowed down before the king with his face to the ground and said, "Praise be to the LORD your God! He has delivered up the men who lifted their hands against my lord the king."

²⁹The king asked, "Is the young man Absalom safe?"

Ahimaaz answered, "I saw great confusion just as Joab was about to send the king's servant and me, your servant, but I don't know what it was."

³⁰The king said, "Stand aside and wait here." So he stepped aside and stood there.

³¹Then the Cushite arrived and said, "My lord the king, hear the good news! The LORD has delivered you today from all who rose up against you."

³²The king asked the Cushite, "Is the young man Absalom safe?"

The Cushite replied, "May the enemies of my lord the king and all who rise up to harm you be like that young man."[d]

³³The king was shaken. He went up to the room over the gateway and wept. As he went, he said: "O my son Absalom! My son, my son Absalom! If only I had died[e] instead of you—O Absalom, my son, my son!"[f]

Chapter 19 Theme _____

19 Joab was told, "The king is weeping and mourning for Absalom." ²And for the whole army the victory that day was turned into mourning, because on that day the troops heard it said, "The king is grieving for his son." ³The men stole into the city that day as men steal in who are ashamed when they flee from battle. ⁴The king covered his face and cried aloud, "O my son Absalom! O Absalom, my son, my son!"

a 23 That is, the plain of the Jordan

18:24
a 1Sa 14:16;
2Sa 19:8;
2Ki 9:17;
Jer 51:12

18:26
b 1Ki 1:42;
Isa 52:7; 61:1

18:27
c 2Ki 9:20

18:32
d Jdg 5:31;
1Sa 25:26

18:33
e Ex 32:32;
f Ge 43:14;
2Sa 19:4;
Ro 9:3

19:7
a Pr 14:28

19:8
b 2Sa 15:2

19:9
c 2Sa 8:1-14
d 2Sa 15:14

19:11
e 2Sa 15:24

19:13
f 2Sa 17:25
g Ge 29:14
h Ru 1:17;
1Ki 19:2; 8:16
i 2Sa 2:13

19:15
j Jos 5:9;
1Sa 11:15

19:16
k 2Sa 16:5-13;
1Ki 2:8

19:17
l 2Sa 9:2;
16:1-2
m Ge 43:16

19:19
n 1Sa 22:15;
2Sa 16:6-8

⁵Then Joab went into the house to the king and said, "Today you have humiliated all your men, who have just saved your life and the lives of your sons and daughters and the lives of your wives and concubines. ⁶You love those who hate you and hate those who love you. You have made it clear today that the commanders and their men mean nothing to you. I see that you would be pleased if Absalom were alive today and all of us were dead. ⁷Now go out and encourage your men. I swear by the LORD that if you don't go out, not a man will be left with you by nightfall. This will be worse for you than all the calamities that have come upon you from your youth till now."ᵃ

⁸So the king got up and took his seat in the gateway. When the men were told, "The king is sitting in the gateway,ᵇ" they all came before him.

Meanwhile, the Israelites had fled to their homes. ⁹Throughout the tribes of Israel, the people were all arguing with each other, saying, "The king delivered us from the hand of our enemies; he is the one who rescued us from the hand of the Philistines.ᶜ But now he has fled the country because of Absalom;ᵈ ¹⁰and Absalom, whom we anointed to rule over us, has died in battle. So why do you say nothing about bringing the king back?"

¹¹King David sent this message to Zadokᵉ and Abiathar, the priests: "Ask the elders of Judah, 'Why should you be the last to bring the king back to his palace, since what is being said throughout Israel has reached the king at his quarters? ¹²You are my brothers, my own flesh and blood. So why should you be the last to bring back the king?' ¹³And say to Amasa,ᶠ 'Are you not my own flesh and blood?ᵍ May God deal with me, be it ever so severely,ʰ if from now on you are not the commander of my army in place of Joab.ⁱ'"

¹⁴He won over the hearts of all the men of Judah as though they were one man. They sent word to the king, "Return, you and all your men." ¹⁵Then the king returned and went as far as the Jordan.

Now the men of Judah had come to Gilgalʲ to go out and meet the king and bring him across the Jordan. ¹⁶Shimeiᵏ son of Gera, the Benjamite from Bahurim, hurried down with the men of Judah to meet King David. ¹⁷With him were a thousand Benjamites, along with Ziba,ˡ the steward of Saul's household,ᵐ and his fifteen sons and twenty servants. They rushed to the Jordan, where the king was. ¹⁸They crossed at the ford to take the king's household over and to do whatever he wished.

When Shimei son of Gera crossed the Jordan, he fell prostrate before the king ¹⁹and said to him, "May my lord not hold me guilty. Do not remember how your servant did wrong on the day my lord the king left Jerusalem.ⁿ May the king put it out of his

531

mind. ²⁰For I your servant know that I have sinned, but today I have come here as the first of the whole house of Joseph to come down and meet my lord the king."

²¹Then Abishai*ᵃ* son of Zeruiah said, "Shouldn't Shimei be put to death for this? He cursedᵇ the LORD's anointed."*ᶜ*

²²David replied, "What do you and I have in common, you sons of Zeruiah?ᵈ This day you have become my adversaries! Should anyone be put to death in Israel today?ᵉ Do I not know that today I am king over Israel?" ²³So the king said to Shimei, "You shall not die." And the king promised him on oath.ᶠ

²⁴Mephibosheth,ᵍ Saul's grandson, also went down to meet the king. He had not taken care of his feet or trimmed his mustache or washed his clothes from the day the king left until the day he returned safely. ²⁵When he came from Jerusalem to meet the king, the king asked him, "Why didn't you go with me,ʰ Mephibosheth?"

²⁶He said, "My lord the king, since I your servant am lame,ⁱ I said, 'I will have my donkey saddled and will ride on it, so I can go with the king.' But Zibaʲ my servant betrayed me. ²⁷And he has slandered your servant to my lord the king. My lord the king is like an angelᵏ of God; so do whatever pleases you. ²⁸All my grandfather's descendants deserved nothing but deathˡ from my lord the king, but you gave your servant a place among those who eat at your table.ᵐ So what right do I have to make any more appeals to the king?"

²⁹The king said to him, "Why say more? I order you and Ziba to divide the fields."

³⁰Mephibosheth said to the king, "Let him take everything, now that my lord the king has arrived home safely."

³¹Barzillaiⁿ the Gileadite also came down from Rogelim to cross the Jordan with the king and to send him on his way from there. ³²Now Barzillai was a very old man, eighty years of age. He had provided for the king during his stay in Mahanaim, for he was a very wealthyᵒ man. ³³The king said to Barzillai, "Cross over with me and stay with me in Jerusalem, and I will provide for you."

³⁴But Barzillai answered the king, "How many more years will I live, that I should go up to Jerusalem with the king? ³⁵I am now eightyᵖ years old. Can I tell the difference between what is good and what is not? Can your servant taste what he eats and drinks? Can I still hear the voices of men and women singers?�q Why should your servant be an addedʳ burden to my lord the king? ³⁶Your servant will cross over the Jordan with the king for a short distance, but why should the king reward me in this way? ³⁷Let your servant return, that I may die in my own town near the tomb of my fatherˢ and mother. But here is your servant Kimham.ᵗ Let him cross over with my lord the king. Do for him whatever pleases you."

19:21
a 1Sa 26:6
b Ex 22:28
c 1Sa 12:3; 26:9; 2Sa 16:7-8

19:22
d 2Sa 2:18; 16:10
e 1Sa 11:13

19:23
f 1Ki 2:8,42

19:24
g 2Sa 4:4; 9:6-10

19:25
h 2Sa 16:17

19:26
i Lev 21:18
j 2Sa 9:2

19:27
k 1Sa 29:9; 2Sa 14:17,20

19:28
l 2Sa 16:8; 21:6-9
m 2Sa 9:7,13

19:31
n 2Sa 17:27-29, 27; 1Ki 2:7

19:32
o 1Sa 25:2; 2Sa 17:27

19:35
p Ps 90:10
q 2Ch 35:25; Ezr 2:65; Ecc 2:8; 12:1; Isa 5:11-12
r 2Sa 15:33

19:37
s Ge 49:29; 1Ki 2:7
t ver 40; Jer 41:17

38The king said, "Kimham shall cross over with me, and I will do for him whatever pleases you. And anything you desire from me I will do for you."

39So all the people crossed the Jordan, and then the king crossed over. The king kissed Barzillai and gave him his blessing,*a* and Barzillai returned to his home.

40When the king crossed over to Gilgal, Kimham crossed with him. All the troops of Judah and half the troops of Israel had taken the king over.

41Soon all the men of Israel were coming to the king and saying to him, "Why did our brothers, the men of Judah, steal the king away and bring him and his household across the Jordan, together with all his men?"*b*

42All the men of Judah answered the men of Israel, "We did this because the king is closely related to us. Why are you angry about it? Have we eaten any of the king's provisions? Have we taken anything for ourselves?"

43Then the men of Israel*c* answered the men of Judah, "We have ten shares in the king; and besides, we have a greater claim on David than you have. So why do you treat us with contempt? Were we not the first to speak of bringing back our king?"

But the men of Judah responded even more harshly than the men of Israel.

20:1
d Ge 31:14
e Ge 29:14;
1Ki 12:16
f 1Sa 22:7-8;
2Ch 10:16

Chapter 20 Theme _____

20 Now a troublemaker named Sheba son of Bicri, a Benjamite, happened to be there. He sounded the trumpet and shouted,

> "We have no share*d* in David,*e*
> no part in Jesse's son!*f*
> Every man to his tent, O Israel!"

2So all the men of Israel deserted David to follow Sheba son of Bicri. But the men of Judah stayed by their king all the way from the Jordan to Jerusalem.

3When David returned to his palace in Jerusalem, he took the ten concubines*g* he had left to take care of the palace and put them in a house under guard. He provided for them, but did not lie with them. They were kept in confinement till the day of their death, living as widows.

4Then the king said to Amasa,*h* "Summon the men of Judah to come to me within three days, and be here yourself." **5**But when Amasa went to summon Judah, he took longer than the time the king had set for him.

6David said to Abishai,*i* "Now Sheba son of Bicri will do us more harm than Absalom did. Take your master's men and pursue him, or he will find fortified cities and escape from us." ⁷So Joab's men and the Kerethites*ᵃ* and Pelethites and all the mighty warriors went out under the command of Abishai. They marched out from Jerusalem to pursue Sheba son of Bicri.

⁸While they were at the great rock in Gibeon,*ᵇ* Amasa came to meet them. Joab*ᶜ* was wearing his military tunic, and strapped over it at his waist was a belt with a dagger in its sheath. As he stepped forward, it dropped out of its sheath.

⁹Joab said to Amasa, "How are you, my brother?" Then Joab took Amasa by the beard with his right hand to kiss him. ¹⁰Amasa was not on his guard against the dagger*ᵈ* in Joab's*ᵉ* hand, and Joab plunged it into his belly, and his intestines spilled out on the ground. Without being stabbed again, Amasa died. Then Joab and his brother Abishai pursued Sheba son of Bicri.

¹¹One of Joab's men stood beside Amasa and said, "Whoever favors Joab, and whoever is for David, let him follow Joab!" ¹²Amasa lay wallowing in his blood in the middle of the road, and the man saw that all the troops came to a halt*ᶠ* there. When he realized that everyone who came up to Amasa stopped, he dragged him from the road into a field and threw a garment over him. ¹³After Amasa had been removed from the road, all the men went on with Joab to pursue Sheba son of Bicri.

¹⁴Sheba passed through all the tribes of Israel to Abel Beth Maacah*ᵃ* and through the entire region of the Berites,*ᵍ* who gathered together and followed him. ¹⁵All the troops with Joab came and besieged Sheba in Abel Beth Maacah.*ʰ* They built a siege ramp*ⁱ* up to the city, and it stood against the outer fortifications. While they were battering the wall to bring it down, ¹⁶a wise woman*ʲ* called from the city, "Listen! Listen! Tell Joab to come here so I can speak to him." ¹⁷He went toward her, and she asked, "Are you Joab?"

"I am," he answered.

She said, "Listen to what your servant has to say."

"I'm listening," he said.

¹⁸She continued, "Long ago they used to say, 'Get your answer at Abel,' and that settled it. ¹⁹We are the peaceful*ᵏ* and faithful in Israel. You are trying to destroy a city that is a mother in Israel. Why do you want to swallow up the LORD's inheritance?"*ˡ*

²⁰"Far be it from me!" Joab replied, "Far be it from me to swallow up or destroy! ²¹That is not the case. A man named Sheba son of Bicri, from the hill country of Ephraim, has lifted up his hand against the king, against David. Hand over this one man, and I'll withdraw from the city."

ᵃ 14 Or *Abel, even Beth Maacah;* also in verse 15

20:7
a 1Sa 30:14;
2Sa 8:18;
15:18;
1Ki 1:38

20:8
b Jos 9:3
c 2Sa 2:18

20:10
d Jdg 3:21;
2Sa 2:23; 3:27
e 1Ki 2:5

20:12
f 2Sa 2:23

20:14
g Nu 21:16

20:15
h 1Ki 15:20;
2Ki 15:29
i 2Ki 19:32;
Isa 37:33;
Jer 6:6; 32:24

20:16
j 2Sa 14:2

20:19
k Dt 2:26
l 1Sa 26:19;
2Sa 21:3

Ref	
20:21	a 2Sa 4:8
20:22	b Ecc 9:13
20:23	c 2Sa 2:28; 8:16-18; 24:2
20:24	d 1Ki 4:6; 5:14; 12:18; 2Ch 10:18 e 2Sa 8:16; 1Ki 4:3
20:25	f 1Sa 2:35; 2Sa 8:17
21:1	g Ge 12:10; Dt 32:24 h Ex 32:11
21:2	i Jos 9:15
21:3	j 1Sa 26:19; 2Sa 20:19
21:4	k Nu 35:33-34
21:6	l Nu 25:4 m 1Sa 10:24
21:7	n 2Sa 4:4 o 1Sa 18:3; 20:8,15; 2Sa 9:7
21:8	p 2Sa 3:7 q 1Sa 18:19

The woman said to Joab, "His head[a] will be thrown to you from the wall."

[22]Then the woman went to all the people with her wise advice,[b] and they cut off the head of Sheba son of Bicri and threw it to Joab. So he sounded the trumpet, and his men dispersed from the city, each returning to his home. And Joab went back to the king in Jerusalem.

[23]Joab[c] was over Israel's entire army; Benaiah son of Jehoiada was over the Kerethites and Pelethites; [24]Adoniram[a][d] was in charge of forced labor; Jehoshaphat[e] son of Ahilud was recorder; [25]Sheva was secretary; Zadok[f] and Abiathar were priests; [26]and Ira the Jairite was David's priest.

Chapter 21 Theme

21 During the reign of David, there was a famine[g] for three successive years; so David sought[h] the face of the LORD. The LORD said, "It is on account of Saul and his blood-stained house; it is because he put the Gibeonites to death."

[2]The king summoned the Gibeonites[i] and spoke to them. (Now the Gibeonites were not a part of Israel but were survivors of the Amorites; the Israelites had sworn to ⌊spare⌋ them, but Saul in his zeal for Israel and Judah had tried to annihilate them.) [3]David asked the Gibeonites, "What shall I do for you? How shall I make amends so that you will bless the LORD's inheritance?"[j]

[4]The Gibeonites answered him, "We have no right to demand silver or gold from Saul or his family, nor do we have the right to put anyone in Israel to death."[k]

"What do you want me to do for you?" David asked.

[5]They answered the king, "As for the man who destroyed us and plotted against us so that we have been decimated and have no place anywhere in Israel, [6]let seven of his male descendants be given to us to be killed and exposed[l] before the LORD at Gibeah of Saul—the LORD's chosen[m] one."

So the king said, "I will give them to you."

[7]The king spared Mephibosheth[n] son of Jonathan, the son of Saul, because of the oath[o] before the LORD between David and Jonathan son of Saul. [8]But the king took Armoni and Mephibosheth, the two sons of Aiah's daughter Rizpah,[p] whom she had borne to Saul, together with the five sons of Saul's daughter Merab,[b] whom she had borne to Adriel son of Barzillai the Meholathite.[q] [9]He handed them over to the Gibeonites, who killed and

a 24 Some Septuagint manuscripts (see also 1Kings 4:6 and 5:14); Hebrew *Adoram*   b 8 Two Hebrew manuscripts, some Septuagint manuscripts and Syriac (see also 1Samuel 18:19); most Hebrew and Septuagint manuscripts *Michal* exposed them on a hill before the LORD. All seven of them fell together; they were put to death[a] during the first days of the harvest, just as the barley harvest was beginning.[b]

[10]Rizpah daughter of Aiah took sackcloth and spread it out for herself on a rock. From the beginning of the harvest till the rain poured down from the heavens on the bodies, she did not let the birds of the air touch them by day or the wild animals by night.[c] [11]When David was told what Aiah's daughter Rizpah, Saul's concubine, had done, [12]he went and took the bones of Saul[d] and his son Jonathan from the citizens of Jabesh Gilead. (They had taken them secretly from the public square at Beth Shan,[e] where the Philistines had hung[f] them after they struck Saul down on Gilboa.) [13]David brought the bones of Saul and his son Jonathan from there, and the bones of those who had been killed and exposed were gathered up.

[14]They buried the bones of Saul and his son Jonathan in the tomb of Saul's father Kish, at Zela[g] in Benjamin, and did everything the king commanded. After that,[h] God answered prayer[i] in behalf of the land.

[15]Once again there was a battle between the Philistines[j] and Israel. David went down with his men to fight against the Philistines, and he became exhausted. [16]And Ishbi-Benob, one of the descendants of Rapha, whose bronze spearhead weighed three hundred shekels[a] and who was armed with a new ⌊sword⌋, said he would kill David. [17]But Abishai[k] son of Zeruiah came to David's rescue; he struck the Philistine down and killed him. Then David's men swore to him, saying, "Never again will you go out with us to battle, so that the lamp[l] of Israel will not be extinguished.[m]"

[18]In the course of time, there was another battle with the Philistines, at Gob. At that time Sibbecai[n] the Hushathite killed Saph, one of the descendants of Rapha.

[19]In another battle with the Philistines at Gob, Elhanan son of Jaare-Oregim[b] the Bethlehemite killed Goliath[c] the Gittite, who had a spear with a shaft like a weaver's rod.[o]

[20]In still another battle, which took place at Gath, there was a huge man with six fingers on each hand and six toes on each foot—twenty-four in all. He also was descended from Rapha. [21]When he taunted Israel, Jonathan son of Shimeah,[p] David's brother, killed him.

[22]These four were descendants of Rapha in Gath, and they fell at the hands of David and his men.

---

a 16 That is, about 7 1/2 pounds (about 3.5 kilograms) b 19 Or son of Jair the weaver
c 19 Hebrew and Septuagint; 1 Chron. 20:5 son of Jair killed Lahmi the brother of Goliath

21:9
a 2Sa 16:8
b Ru 1:22

21:10
c ver 8;
Dt 21:23;
1Sa 17:44

21:12
d 1Sa 31:11-13
e Jos 17:11
f 1Sa 31:10

21:14
g Jos 18:28
h Jos 7:26
i 2Sa 24:25

21:15
j 2Sa 5:25

21:17
k 2Sa 20:6
l 1Ki 11:36
m 2Sa 18:3

21:18
n 1Ch 11:29;
20:4; 27:11

21:19
o 1Sa 17:7

21:21
p 1Sa 16:9

22:1
a Ex 15:1;
Jdg 5:1;
Ps 18:2-50

22:2
b Dt 32:4;
Ps 71:3
c Ps 31:3;
91:2
d Ps 144:2

22:3
e Dt 32:37;
Jer 16:19
f Ge 15:1
g Lk 1:69
h Ps 9:9

22:4
i Ps 48:1; 96:4

22:5
j Ps 69:14-15;
93:4;
Jnh 2:3

22:6
k Ps 116:3

22:7
l Ps 120:1
m Ps 34:6,15;
116:4

22:8
n Jdg 5:4;
Ps 97:4
o Ps 77:18
p Job 26:11

22:9
q Ps 97:3;
Heb 12:29

22:10
r 1Ki 8:12;
Na 1:3

22:11
s Ps 104:3

22:13
t ver 9

22:14
u 1Sa 2:10

22:15
v Dt 32:23

22:16
w Na 1:4

Chapter 22 Theme

22 David sang*a* to the LORD the words of this song when the LORD delivered him from the hand of all his enemies and from the hand of Saul. ²He said:

"The LORD is my rock,*b* my fortress*c* and my deliverer;*d*
3   my God is my rock, in whom I take refuge,*e*
   my shield*f* and the horn*a g* of my salvation.
He is my stronghold,*h* my refuge and my savior—
   from violent men you save me.
⁴I call to the LORD, who is worthy*i* of praise,
   and I am saved from my enemies.

⁵"The waves*j* of death swirled about me;
   the torrents of destruction overwhelmed me.
⁶The cords of the grave*b k* coiled around me;
   the snares of death confronted me.
⁷In my distress*l* I called*m* to the LORD;
   I called out to my God.
From his temple he heard my voice;
   my cry came to his ears.

⁸"The earth*n* trembled and quaked,*o*
   the foundations*p* of the heavens*c* shook;
   they trembled because he was angry.
⁹Smoke rose from his nostrils;
   consuming fire*q* came from his mouth,
   burning coals blazed out of it.
¹⁰He parted the heavens and came down;
   dark clouds*r* were under his feet.
¹¹He mounted the cherubim and flew;
   he soared*d* on the wings of the wind.*s*
¹²He made darkness his canopy around him—
   the dark*e* rain clouds of the sky.
¹³Out of the brightness of his presence
   bolts of lightning*t* blazed forth.
¹⁴The LORD thundered*u* from heaven;
   the voice of the Most High resounded.
¹⁵He shot arrows*v* and scattered ⌊the enemies⌋,
   bolts of lightning and routed them.
¹⁶The valleys of the sea were exposed
   and the foundations of the earth laid bare
at the rebuke*w* of the LORD,
   at the blast of breath from his nostrils.

a3 *Horn* here symbolizes strength.   *b6* Hebrew *Sheol*   *c8* Hebrew; Vulgate and Syriac (see also Psalm 18:7) *mountains*   *d11* Many Hebrew manuscripts (see also Psalm 18:10); most Hebrew manuscripts *appeared*   *e12* Septuagint and Vulgate (see also Psalm 18:11); Hebrew *massed*

¹⁷"He reached down from on high[a] and took hold of me;
    he drew[b] me out of deep waters.
¹⁸He rescued me from my powerful enemy,
    from my foes, who were too strong for me.
¹⁹They confronted me in the day of my disaster,
    but the LORD was my support.[c]
²⁰He brought me out into a spacious[d] place;
    he rescued[e] me because he delighted[f] in me.[g]

²¹"The LORD has dealt with me according to my
    righteousness;[h]
    according to the cleanness of my hands[i] he has
    rewarded me.
²²For I have kept[j] the ways of the LORD;
    I have not done evil by turning from my God.
²³All his laws are before me;[k]
    I have not turned[l] away from his decrees.
²⁴I have been blameless[m] before him
    and have kept myself from sin.
²⁵The LORD has rewarded me according to my
    righteousness,[n]
    according to my cleanness[a] in his sight.

²⁶"To the faithful you show yourself faithful,
    to the blameless you show yourself blameless,
²⁷to the pure[o] you show yourself pure,
    but to the crooked you show yourself shrewd.[p]
²⁸You save the humble,[q]
    but your eyes are on the haughty to bring
    them low.[r]
²⁹You are my lamp,[s] O LORD;
    the LORD turns my darkness into light.
³⁰With your help I can advance against a troop[b];
    with my God I can scale a wall.

³¹"As for God, his way is perfect;[t]
    the word of the LORD is flawless.[u]
He is a shield
    for all who take refuge in him.
³²For who is God besides the LORD?
    And who is the Rock[v] except our God?
³³It is God who arms me with strength[c]
    and makes my way perfect.

---

a 25 Hebrew; Septuagint and Vulgate (see also Psalm 18:24) to the cleanness of my hands
b 30 Or can run through a barricade   c 33 Dead Sea Scrolls, some Septuagint manuscripts, Vulgate and Syriac (see also Psalm 18:32); Masoretic Text who is my strong refuge

22:17
a Ps 144:7
b Ex 2:10

22:19
c Ps 23:4

22:20
d Ps 31:8
e Ps 118:5
f Ps 22:8
g 2Sa 15:26

22:21
h 1Sa 26:23
i Ps 24:4

22:22
j Ge 18:19;
Ps 128:1;
Pr 8:32

22:23
k Dt 6:4-9;
Ps 119:30-32
l Ps 119:102

22:24
m Ge 6:9;
Eph 1:4

22:25
n ver 21

22:27
o Mt 5:8
p Lev 26:23-24

22:28
q Ex 3:8;
Ps 72:12-13
r Isa 2:12,17;
5:15

22:29
s Ps 27:1

22:31
t Dt 32:4;
Mt 5:48
u Ps 12:6;
119:140;
Pr 30:5-6

22:32
v 1Sa 2:2

22:34
a Hab 3:19
b Dt 32:13

22:35
c Ps 144:1

22:36
d Eph 6:16

22:37
e Pr 4:11

22:39
f Mal 4:3

22:40
g Ps 44:5

22:41
h Ex 23:27

22:42
i Isa 1:15
j Ps 50:22

22:43
k Mic 7:10
l Isa 10:6;
Mic 7:10

22:44
m 2Sa 3:1
n Dt 28:13
o 2Sa 8:1-14;
Isa 55:3-5

22:45
p Ps 66:3; 81:15

22:46
q Mic 7:17

22:47
r Ps 89:26

22:48
s Ps 94:1; 144:2;
1Sa 25:39

22:49
t Ps 140:1,4

22:50
u Ro 15:9*

22:51
v Ps 144:9-10
w Ps 89:20
x 2Sa 7:13
y Ps 89:24,29

34He makes my feet like the feet of a deer;*a*
　　he enables me to stand on the heights.*b*
35He trains my hands*c* for battle;
　　my arms can bend a bow of bronze.
36You give me your shield*d* of victory;
　　you stoop down to make me great.
37You broaden the path*e* beneath me,
　　so that my ankles do not turn.

38"I pursued my enemies and crushed them;
　　I did not turn back till they were destroyed.
39I crushed*f* them completely, and they could not rise;
　　they fell beneath my feet.
40You armed me with strength for battle;
　　you made my adversaries bow at my feet.*g*
41You made my enemies turn their backs*h* in flight,
　　and I destroyed my foes.
42They cried for help,*i* but there was no one to save them—*j*
　　to the LORD, but he did not answer.
43I beat them as fine as the dust of the earth;
　　I pounded and trampled*k* them like mud*l* in the streets.

44"You have delivered*m* me from the attacks of my people;
　　you have preserved*n* me as the head of nations.
　People*o* I did not know are subject to me,
45　and foreigners come cringing*p* to me;
　　as soon as they hear me, they obey me.
46They all lose heart;
　　they come trembling*a q* from their strongholds.

47"The LORD lives! Praise be to my Rock!
　　Exalted be God, the Rock, my Savior!*r*
48He is the God who avenges me,*s*
　　who puts the nations under me,
49　who sets me free from my enemies.*t*
　You exalted me above my foes;
　　from violent men you rescued me.
50Therefore I will praise you, O LORD, among the nations;
　　I will sing praises to your name.*u*
51He gives his king great victories;*v*
　　he shows unfailing kindness to his anointed,*w*
　　to David*x* and his descendants forever."*y*

a 46 Some Septuagint manuscripts and Vulgate (see also Psalm 18:45); Masoretic Text *they arm themselves.*

539

Chapter 23 Theme

23

These are the last words of David:

"The oracle of David son of Jesse,
 the oracle of the man exalted[a] by the Most High,
the man anointed[b] by the God of Jacob,
 Israel's singer of songs[a]:

[2]"The Spirit[c] of the LORD spoke through me;
 his word was on my tongue.
[3]The God of Israel spoke,
 the Rock[d] of Israel said to me:
'When one rules over men in righteousness,[e]
 when he rules in the fear of God,[f]
[4]he is like the light of morning at sunrise[g]
 on a cloudless morning,
like the brightness after rain
 that brings the grass from the earth.'

[5]"Is not my house right with God?
 Has he not made with me an everlasting covenant,[h]
 arranged and secured in every part?
Will he not bring to fruition my salvation
 and grant me my every desire?
[6]But evil men are all to be cast aside like thorns,[i]
 which are not gathered with the hand.
[7]Whoever touches thorns
 uses a tool of iron or the shaft of a spear;
 they are burned up where they lie."

[8]These are the names of David's mighty men:

Josheb-Basshebeth,[b] a Tahkemonite,[c] was chief of the Three; he raised his spear against eight hundred men, whom he killed[d] in one encounter.

[9]Next to him was Eleazar son of Dodai[j] the Ahohite.[k] As one of the three mighty men, he was with David when they taunted the Philistines gathered ⌊at Pas Dammim⌋[e] for battle. Then the men of Israel retreated, [10]but he stood his ground and struck down the Philistines till his hand grew tired and froze to the sword. The LORD brought about a great victory that day. The troops returned to Eleazar, but only to strip the dead.

[11]Next to him was Shammah son of Agee the Hararite. When the Philistines banded together at a place where there was a field

Cross References

23:1
[a] 2Sa 7:8-9; Ps 78:70-71; 89:27
[b] 1Sa 16:12-13; Ps 89:20

23:2
[c] Mt 22:43; 2Pe 1:21

23:3
[d] Dt 32:4; 2Sa 22:2,32
[e] Ps 72:3
[f] 2Ch 19:7,9; Isa 11:1-5

23:4
[g] Jdg 5:31; Ps 89:36

23:5
[h] Ps 89:29; Isa 55:3

23:6
[i] Mt 13:40-41

23:9
[j] 1Ch 27:4
[k] 1Ch 8:4

---

a 1 Or *Israel's beloved singer* b 8 Hebrew; some Septuagint manuscripts suggest *Ish-Bosheth,* that is, *Esh-Baal* (see also 1 Chron. 11:11 *Jashobeam*). c 8 Probably a variant of *Hacmonite* (see 1 Chron. 11:11) d 8 Some Septuagint manuscripts (see also 1 Chron. 11:11); Hebrew and other Septuagint manuscripts *Three; it was Adino the Eznite who killed eight hundred men*
e 9 See 1 Chron. 11:13; Hebrew *gathered there.*

23:13
a 1Sa 22:1
b 2Sa 5:18

23:14
c 1Sa 22:4-5
d Ru 1:19

23:16
e Ge 35:14

23:17
f Lev 17:10-12

23:18
g 2Sa 10:10,14;
1Ch 11:20

23:20
h 2Sa 8:18; 20:23
i Jos 15:21

23:24
j 2Sa 2:18

23:25
k Jdg 7:1;
1Ch 11:27

23:26
l 1Ch 27:10

23:27
m Jos 21:18

23:28
n 1Ch 27:13
o 2Ki 25:23;
Ne 7:26

full of lentils, Israel's troops fled from them. ¹²But Shammah took his stand in the middle of the field. He defended it and struck the Philistines down, and the LORD brought about a great victory.

¹³During harvest time, three of the thirty chief men came down to David at the cave of Adullam,ᵃ while a band of Philistines was encamped in the Valley of Rephaim.ᵇ ¹⁴At that time David was in the stronghold,ᶜ and the Philistine garrison was at Bethlehem.ᵈ ¹⁵David longed for water and said, "Oh, that someone would get me a drink of water from the well near the gate of Bethlehem!" ¹⁶So the three mighty men broke through the Philistine lines, drew water from the well near the gate of Bethlehem and carried it back to David. But he refused to drink it; instead, he pouredᵉ it out before the LORD. ¹⁷"Far be it from me, O LORD, to do this!" he said. "Is it not the bloodᶠ of men who went at the risk of their lives?" And David would not drink it.

Such were the exploits of the three mighty men.

¹⁸Abishaiᵍ the brother of Joab son of Zeruiah was chief of the Three.ᵃ He raised his spear against three hundred men, whom he killed, and so he became as famous as the Three. ¹⁹Was he not held in greater honor than the Three? He became their commander, even though he was not included among them.

²⁰Benaiahʰ son of Jehoiada was a valiant fighter from Kabzeel,ⁱ who performed great exploits. He struck down two of Moab's best men. He also went down into a pit on a snowy day and killed a lion. ²¹And he struck down a huge Egyptian. Although the Egyptian had a spear in his hand, Benaiah went against him with a club. He snatched the spear from the Egyptian's hand and killed him with his own spear. ²²Such were the exploits of Benaiah son of Jehoiada; he too was as famous as the three mighty men. ²³He was held in greater honor than any of the Thirty, but he was not included among the Three. And David put him in charge of his bodyguard.

²⁴Among the Thirty were:

Asahelʲ the brother of Joab,
Elhanan son of Dodo from Bethlehem,
²⁵Shammah the Harodite,ᵏ
Elika the Harodite,
²⁶Helezˡ the Paltite,
Ira son of Ikkesh from Tekoa,
²⁷Abiezer from Anathoth,ᵐ
Mebunnaiᵇ the Hushathite,
²⁸Zalmon the Ahohite,
Maharaiⁿ the Netophathite,ᵒ

ᵃ18 Most Hebrew manuscripts (see also 1 Chron. 11:20); two Hebrew manuscripts and Syriac *Thirty*   ᵇ27 Hebrew; some Septuagint manuscripts (see also 1 Chron. 11:29) *Sibbecai*

²⁹Heled[a] son of Baanah the Netophathite,
Ithai son of Ribai from Gibeah[a] in Benjamin,
³⁰Benaiah the Pirathonite,[b]
Hiddai[b] from the ravines of Gaash,[c]
³¹Abi-Albon the Arbathite,
Azmaveth the Barhumite,[d]
³²Eliahba the Shaalbonite,
the sons of Jashen,
Jonathan ³³son of[c] Shammah the Hararite,
Ahiam son of Sharar[d] the Hararite,
³⁴Eliphelet son of Ahasbai the Maacathite,
Eliam[e] son of Ahithophel[f] the Gilonite,
³⁵Hezro the Carmelite,[g]
Paarai the Arbite,
³⁶Igal son of Nathan from Zobah,[h]
the son of Hagri,[e]
³⁷Zelek the Ammonite,
Naharai the Beerothite, the armor-bearer of Joab son of Zeruiah,
³⁸Ira the Ithrite,[i]
Gareb the Ithrite
³⁹and Uriah[j] the Hittite.
There were thirty-seven in all.

Chapter 24 Theme

24 Again[k] the anger of the LORD burned against Israel, and he incited David against them, saying, "Go and take a census of[l] Israel and Judah."

²So the king said to Joab[m] and the army commanders[f] with him, "Go throughout the tribes of Israel from Dan to Beersheba[n] and enroll the fighting men, so that I may know how many there are."

³But Joab replied to the king, "May the LORD your God multiply the troops a hundred times over,[o] and may the eyes of my lord the king see it. But why does my lord the king want to do such a thing?"

⁴The king's word, however, overruled Joab and the army commanders; so they left the presence of the king to enroll the fighting men of Israel.

⁵After crossing the Jordan, they camped near Aroer,[p] south of the town in the gorge, and then went through Gad and on to Jazer.[q] ⁶They went to Gilead and the region of Tahtim Hodshi, and

---

a 29 Some Hebrew manuscripts and Vulgate (see also 1 Chron. 11:30); most Hebrew manuscripts *Heleb*   b 30 Hebrew; some Septuagint manuscripts (see also 1 Chron. 11:32) *Hurai*   c 33 Some Septuagint manuscripts (see also 1 Chron. 11:34); Hebrew does not have *son of*.   d 33 Hebrew; some Septuagint manuscripts (see also 1 Chron. 11:35) *Sacar*   e 36 Some Septuagint manuscripts (see also 1 Chron. 11:38); Hebrew *Haggadi*   f 2 Septuagint (see also verse 4 and 1 Chron. 21:2); Hebrew *Joab the army commander*

23:29
a Jos 15:57

23:30
b Jdg 12:13
c Jos 24:30

23:31
d 2Sa 3:16

23:34
e 2Sa 11:3
f 2Sa 15:12

23:35
g Jos 12:22

23:36
h 1Sa 14:47

23:38
i 2Sa 20:26;
1Ch 2:53

23:39
j 2Sa 11:3

24:1
k Jos 9:15
l 1Ch 27:23

24:2
m 2Sa 20:23
n Jdg 20:1;
2Sa 3:10

24:3
o Dt 1:11

24:5
p Dt 2:36;
Jos 13:9
q Nu 21:32

24:6
a Ge 10:19;
Jos 19:28;
Jdg 1:31

24:7
b Jos 19:29
c Ge 21:22-33
d Dt 1:7;
Jos 11:3

24:9
e Nu 1:44-46;
1Ch 21:5

24:10
f 1Sa 24:5
g 2Sa 12:13
h Nu 12:11;
1Sa 13:13

24:11
i 1Sa 22:5
j 1Sa 9:9;
1Ch 29:29

24:13
k Dt 28:38-42,
48; Eze 14:21
l Lev 26:25

24:14
m Ne 9:28;
Ps 51:1;
103:8,13; 130:4

24:15
n 1Ch 27:24

24:16
o Ge 6:6;
1Sa 15:11
p Ex 12:23;
Ac 12:23

24:17
q Ps 74:1
r Jnh 1:12

24:21
s Nu 16:44-50

on to Dan Jaan and around toward Sidon.ᵃ ⁷Then they went toward the fortress of Tyreᵇ and all the towns of the Hivites and Canaanites. Finally, they went on to Beershebaᶜ in the Negevᵈ of Judah.

⁸After they had gone through the entire land, they came back to Jerusalem at the end of nine months and twenty days.

⁹Joab reported the number of the fighting men to the king: In Israel there were eight hundred thousand able-bodied men who could handle a sword, and in Judah five hundred thousand.ᵉ

¹⁰David was conscience-strickenᶠ after he had counted the fighting men, and he said to the Lord, "I have sinnedᵍ greatly in what I have done. Now, O Lord, I beg you, take away the guilt of your servant. I have done a very foolish thing.ʰ"

¹¹Before David got up the next morning, the word of the Lord had come to Gadⁱ the prophet, David's seer:ʲ ¹²"Go and tell David, 'This is what the Lord says: I am giving you three options. Choose one of them for me to carry out against you.'"

¹³So Gad went to David and said to him, "Shall there come upon you threeᵃ years of famineᵏ in your land? Or three months of fleeing from your enemies while they pursue you? Or three days of plagueˡ in your land? Now then, think it over and decide how I should answer the one who sent me."

¹⁴David said to Gad, "I am in deep distress. Let us fall into the hands of the Lord, for his mercyᵐ is great; but do not let me fall into the hands of men."

¹⁵So the Lord sent a plague on Israel from that morning until the end of the time designated, and seventy thousand of the people from Dan to Beersheba died.ⁿ ¹⁶When the angel stretched out his hand to destroy Jerusalem, the Lord was grievedᵒ because of the calamity and said to the angel who was afflicting the people, "Enough! Withdraw your hand." The angel of the Lordᵖ was then at the threshing floor of Araunah the Jebusite.

¹⁷When David saw the angel who was striking down the people, he said to the Lord, "I am the one who has sinned and done wrong. These are but sheep.�q What have they done? Let your hand fall upon me and my family."ʳ

¹⁸On that day Gad went to David and said to him, "Go up and build an altar to the Lord on the threshing floor of Araunah the Jebusite." ¹⁹So David went up, as the Lord had commanded through Gad. ²⁰When Araunah looked and saw the king and his men coming toward him, he went out and bowed down before the king with his face to the ground.

²¹Araunah said, "Why has my lord the king come to his servant?"

"To buy your threshing floor," David answered, "so I can build an altar to the Lord, that the plague on the people may be stopped."ˢ

a 13 Septuagint (see also 1 Chron. 21:12); Hebrew *seven*

²²Araunah said to David, "Let my lord the king take whatever pleases him and offer it up. Here are oxen*ᵃ* for the burnt offering, and here are threshing sledges and ox yokes for the wood. ²³O king, Araunah gives*ᵇ* all this to the king." Araunah also said to him, "May the LORD your God accept you."

²⁴But the king replied to Araunah, "No, I insist on paying you for it. I will not sacrifice to the LORD my God burnt offerings that cost me nothing."*ᶜ*

So David bought the threshing floor and the oxen and paid fifty shekels*ᵃ* of silver for them. ²⁵David built an altar*ᵈ* to the LORD there and sacrificed burnt offerings and fellowship offerings.*ᵇ* Then the LORD answered prayer*ᵉ* in behalf of the land, and the plague on Israel was stopped.

a 24 That is, about 1 1/4 pounds (about 0.6 kilogram)   *b 25* Traditionally *peace offerings*

24:22
a 1Sa 6:14;
1Ki 19:21

24:23
b Eze 20:40-41

24:24
c Mal 1:13-14

24:25
d 1Sa 7:17
e 2Sa 21:14

Theme of 2 Samuel:

SEGMENT DIVISIONS

Author:			CHAPTER THEMES
			1
Date:			2
			3
Purpose:			4
			5
Key Words:			6
			7
			8
			9
			10
			11
			12
			13
			14
			15
			16
			17
			18
			19
			20
			21
			22
			23
			24

1 KINGS

*D*avid—the warrior, the great king, the man loved but chastened by God—was getting old. At the end of his life many people were vying for his throne. First Kings, which records the final events of David's life, begins a new era for Israel, one that begins with untold glory and ends with apostasy.

The account of the kings who followed David is full of wonderful but sobering lessons. It is the history of Israel and their God, who made them a people of his own possession.

We don't know who wrote 1 Kings. We only know that this is God's Word preserved "to teach us, so that through endurance and the encouragement of the Scriptures we might have hope" (Romans 15:4).

∾ THINGS TO DO

General Information

Chapter 12 of 1 Kings records a dramatic, pivotal point in the history of Israel. Therefore as we study 1 Kings, we will divide it into two segments with two sets of instructions.

Chapters 1-11

Read through this first segment of 1 Kings one chapter at a time.

1. Remember, you are studying the lives of real people. Observe the opportunities God gives them, his instructions to them, and how they respond. Watch when they succeed and when they fail; note why—and learn! Ask God to speak to your heart. In the margin of each chapter, if applicable, make a list of these two things: "Lessons for Life" (LFL) and "Insights about God" (△).

2. Mark in a distinctive way the following words and phrases: *word (promise, command)*, or any reference to the *word of the Lord*, *heart (wholeheartedly, hearts, mind, thought)*, *pray (prays, praying, cry, cried, called, declared, shouted)*, *covenant (treaty)*, *wisdom (wise)*, *command (give orders, told, word, commands)*, *promise (word, promises, promised)*, *high places*, *house* (when it refers to God's house, their place of worship), and *sin (commit, wrong, sinned, committed)*. The first occurrence of the word *sin* is in chapter 8.

    a. List the key words on an index card and use it as a bookmark while you study this segment of 1 Kings.

    b. When you read "*and the Lord said,*" "*the Lord said,*" or "*the Lord asked,*" highlight or underline what the Lord said. Then underline anything you want to remember.

3. The main characters of these first chapters are David and Solomon. List in the margins what you learn about them.

    a. When you come to Solomon's reign, read Deuteronomy 7:2-6 and 17:14-20 to understand Solomon's actions as he took over the kingdom. Remember that sin was to be judged and murderers were to be put to death; otherwise the land would be polluted.

    b. Second Chronicles 1 through 9 is an excellent cross-reference on 1 Kings 1 through 11.

4. Mark every reference to time.

5. After you finish reading a chapter, record the theme or subject of that chapter next to the chapter number in the text and on the appropriate place on 1 KINGS AT A GLANCE on page 598.

6. When you finish chapter 11 see if any of the first eleven chapters can be grouped under a common theme or as part of an event: e.g. the building of the temple. These are called segment divisions and can be recorded in the designated place on 1 KINGS AT A GLANCE.

Chapters 12-22

1. As you read chapter 12 study the chart ISRAEL'S DIVISION AND CAPTIVITY on page 575. Note the division of the kingdom which occurred in 931 B.C. Write this date at the beginning of chapter 12. From this point on whenever "Israel" is used you will need to distinguish whether it is a reference to the ten tribes of the northern kingdom (which it will usually be) or to the nation of Israel as a whole.

2. Add *according to, like, as, in accordance with,* and *keeping with* to your key word list. When you come to these phrases, note what was "according to," "in accordance with," or "in keeping with" what. You will gain some important insights. Mark your key words in this section.

3. Watch for insights the Lord gives you about himself, his ways, and about life in general through the example of the kings and God's people. Record these in the margin under "Insights about God" or "Lessons for Life" just as you did in the first segment of 1 Kings.

4. When you read of a king or another key figure consult THE HISTORICAL CHART OF THE KINGS AND PROPHETS OF ISRAEL AND JUDAH, which is located on pages 651 through 653 between 2 Kings and 1 Chronicles.

5. Each time you finish reading about a king, record your insights on the chart THE KINGS OF ISRAEL AND JUDAH on pages 654 and 655 between 2 Kings and 1 Chronicles. Also fill in the information on Solomon.

   a. Make sure you note on the chart whether each king ruled over the northern (Israel) or southern (Judah) kingdom.

   b. Mark every reference to time. You might find it helpful to record in the margin the dates the king reigned. These are on the chart THE KINGS OF ISRAEL AND JUDAH.

6. In chapter 17, when you come to Elijah, in the margin compile a list of everything you learn about this prophet. Also compare 17:1 with Deuteronomy 28:1, 2, 12, 15, 23, 24 and James 5:17, 18. What could be the scriptural basis for Elijah's prayer and word to Ahab? Think about it.

7. Record the chapter themes and any segment divisions you see on 1 KINGS AT A GLANCE. Also fill in any other pertinent information. Choose a theme for 1 Kings which best describes what happens during this period in Israel's history.

8. Second Kings is a continuation of 1 Kings. You will want to study it next.

∾ THINGS TO THINK ABOUT

1. Have you seen God's graciousness and slowness to anger? God doesn't retaliate, but rather brings us to repentance and obedience. What does this provoke in your heart? And how should you live if he is in control of your life?

2. Have you seen how a person can start well in his walk with the Lord and then turn away? What do you think causes this? What can you do to prevent this in your own life? Go back and review what you have listed in the margin regarding the kings and their relationship with the Lord. What lessons have you learned that you can apply to your life?

3. Did you notice the sovereignty of God—how he turns hearts, directs spirits, raises up and puts down kings and others in order to accomplish his purpose and will? Are you living in the light of this truth about God?

4. Have you been thinking that you had to be absolutely perfect before God could use you? Did you see how Elijah was a man "of like passions" just like you and yet God used him? What have you learned in 1 Kings? When David's life was over, didn't God call David a man after his own heart? Frailties and all, David was a man of God because he believed and obeyed God.

David's Family Tree Related to 1 Kings	
David	According to 2 Samuel 5:13-16; 1 Chronicles 3:1-9; 14:3-7, there were fourteen other sons: **Shephatiah, Ithream, Eliphelet, Shammua, Shobab, Nathan, Ibhar, Elishama, Eliphelet, Nogah, Nepheg, Japhia, Eliada, Elishua.**

Amnon —— Daniel —— Absalom —— Adonijah —— Solomon
(killed by Absalom)   (Kileab)   (killed by Joab)   (deposed by Solomon
   (died in youth)   and killed by Benaiah,
                                          son of Jehoiada, by
                                          order of Solomon)

Chapter 1 Theme

1 When King David was old and well advanced in years, he could not keep warm even when they put covers over him. ²So his servants said to him, "Let us look for a young virgin to attend the king and take care of him. She can lie beside him so that our lord the king may keep warm."

³Then they searched throughout Israel for a beautiful girl and found Abishag, a Shunammite,ᵃ and brought her to the king. ⁴The girl was very beautiful; she took care of the king and waited on him, but the king had no intimate relations with her.

⁵Now Adonijah,ᵇ whose mother was Haggith, put himself forward and said, "I will be king." So he got chariotsᶜ and horsesᵃ ready, with fifty men to run ahead of him. ⁶(His father had never interferedᵈ with him by asking, "Why do you behave as you do?" He was also very handsome and was born next after Absalom.)

⁷Adonijah conferred with Joabᵉ son of Zeruiah and with Abiatharᶠ the priest, and they gave him their support. ⁸But Zadokᵍ the priest, Benaiahʰ son of Jehoiada, Nathanⁱ the prophet, Shimeiʲ and Reiᵇ and David's special guardᵏ did not join Adonijah.

⁹Adonijah then sacrificed sheep, cattle and fattened calves at the Stone of Zoheleth near En Rogel.ˡ He invited all his brothers, the king's sons, and all the men of Judah who were royal officials, ¹⁰but he did not invite Nathan the prophet or Benaiah or the special guard or his brother Solomon.ᵐ

¹¹Then Nathan asked Bathsheba,ⁿ Solomon's mother, "Have you not heard that Adonijah,ᵒ the son of Haggith, has become king without our lord David's knowing it? ¹²Now then, let me adviseᵖ you how you can save your own life and the life of your son Solomon. ¹³Go in to King David and say to him, 'My lord the king, did you not swearᑫ to me your servant: "Surely Solomon your son shall be king after me, and he will sit on my throne"? Why then has Adonijah become king?' ¹⁴While you are still there talking to the king, I will come in and confirm what you have said."

1:3 ᵃJos 19:18

1:5 ᵇ2Sa 3:4; ᶜ2Sa 15:1

1:6 ᵈ2Sa 3:3-4

1:7 ᵉ1Ki 2:22,28; 1Ch 11:6; ᶠ1Sa 22:20; 2Sa 20:25

1:8 ᵍ2Sa 20:25; ʰ2Sa 8:18; ⁱ2Sa 12:1; ʲ1Ki 4:18; ᵏ2Sa 23:8

1:9 ˡ2Sa 17:17

1:10 ᵐ2Sa 12:24

1:11 ⁿ2Sa 12:24; ᵒ2Sa 3:4

1:12 ᵖPr 15:22

1:13 ᑫver 30; 1Ch 22:9-13

ᵃ5 Or *charioteers*   ᵇ8 Or *and his friends*

1:15
a ver 1

¹⁵So Bathsheba went to see the aged king in his room, where Abishag*ᵃ* the Shunammite was attending him. ¹⁶Bathsheba bowed low and knelt before the king.

"What is it you want?" the king asked.

1:17
b ver 13,30

¹⁷She said to him, "My lord, you yourself swore*ᵇ* to me your servant by the LORD your God: 'Solomon your son shall be king after me, and he will sit on my throne.' ¹⁸But now Adonijah has become king, and you, my lord the king, do not know about it. ¹⁹He has sacrificed*ᶜ* great numbers of cattle, fattened calves, and sheep, and has invited all the king's sons, Abiathar the priest and Joab the commander of the army, but he has not invited Solomon your servant. ²⁰My lord the king, the eyes of all Israel are on you, to learn from you who will sit on the throne of my lord the king after him. ²¹Otherwise, as soon as my lord the king is laid to rest*ᵈ* with his fathers, I and my son Solomon will be treated as criminals."

1:19
c ver 9

1:21
d Dt 31:16;
1Ki 2:10

²²While she was still speaking with the king, Nathan the prophet arrived. ²³And they told the king, "Nathan the prophet is here." So he went before the king and bowed with his face to the ground.

²⁴Nathan said, "Have you, my lord the king, declared that Adonijah shall be king after you, and that he will sit on your throne? ²⁵Today he has gone down and sacrificed great numbers of cattle, fattened calves, and sheep. He has invited all the king's sons, the commanders of the army and Abiathar the priest. Right now they are eating and drinking with him and saying, 'Long live King Adonijah!' ²⁶But me your servant, and Zadok the priest, and Benaiah son of Jehoiada, and your servant Solomon he did not invite.*ᵉ* ²⁷Is this something my lord the king has done without letting his servants know who should sit on the throne of my lord the king after him?"

1:26
e ver 8,10

1:29
f 2Sa 4:9

²⁸Then King David said, "Call in Bathsheba." So she came into the king's presence and stood before him.

²⁹The king then took an oath: "As surely as the LORD lives, who has delivered me out of every trouble,*ᶠ* ³⁰I will surely carry out today what I swore*ᵍ* to you by the LORD, the God of Israel: Solomon your son shall be king after me, and he will sit on my throne in my place."

1:30
g ver 13,17

³¹Then Bathsheba bowed low with her face to the ground and, kneeling before the king, said, "May my lord King David live forever!"

³²King David said, "Call in Zadok the priest, Nathan the prophet and Benaiah son of Jehoiada." When they came before the king, ³³he said to them: "Take your lord's servants with you and set Solomon my son on my own mule*ʰ* and take him down to Gihon.*ⁱ* ³⁴There have Zadok the priest and Nathan the prophet anoint*ʲ* him king over Israel. Blow the trumpet*ᵏ* and shout, 'Long live King

1:33
h 2Sa 20:6-7
i 2Ch 32:30;
33:14

1:34
j 1Sa 10:1;
16:3,12;
1Ki 19:16;
2Ki 9:3,13
k ver 25;
2Sa 5:3; 15:10

Solomon!' ³⁵Then you are to go up with him, and he is to come and sit on my throne and reign in my place. I have appointed him ruler over Israel and Judah."

³⁶Benaiah son of Jehoiada answered the king, "Amen! May the LORD, the God of my lord the king, so declare it. ³⁷As the LORD was with^a my lord the king, so may he be with^a Solomon to make his throne even greater^b than the throne of my lord King David!"

³⁸So Zadok^c the priest, Nathan the prophet, Benaiah son of Jehoiada, the Kerethites^d and the Pelethites went down and put Solomon on King David's mule and escorted him to Gihon.^e ³⁹Zadok the priest took the horn of oil^f from the sacred tent and anointed Solomon. Then they sounded the trumpet and all the people shouted,^g "Long live King Solomon!" ⁴⁰And all the people went up after him, playing flutes and rejoicing greatly, so that the ground shook with the sound.

⁴¹Adonijah and all the guests who were with him heard it as they were finishing their feast. On hearing the sound of the trumpet, Joab asked, "What's the meaning of all the noise in the city?"

⁴²Even as he was speaking, Jonathan^h son of Abiathar the priest arrived. Adonijah said, "Come in. A worthy man like you must be bringing good news."ⁱ

⁴³"Not at all!" Jonathan answered. "Our lord King David has made Solomon king. ⁴⁴The king has sent with him Zadok the priest, Nathan the prophet, Benaiah son of Jehoiada, the Kerethites and the Pelethites, and they have put him on the king's mule, ⁴⁵and Zadok the priest and Nathan the prophet have anointed him king at Gihon. From there they have gone up cheering, and the city resounds^j with it. That's the noise you hear. ⁴⁶Moreover, Solomon has taken his seat on the royal throne. ⁴⁷Also, the royal officials have come to congratulate our lord King David, saying, 'May your God make Solomon's name more famous than yours and his throne greater^k than yours!' And the king bowed in worship on his bed ⁴⁸and said, 'Praise be to the LORD, the God of Israel, who has allowed my eyes to see a successor^l on my throne today.'"

⁴⁹At this, all Adonijah's guests rose in alarm and dispersed. ⁵⁰But Adonijah, in fear of Solomon, went and took hold of the horns^m of the altar. ⁵¹Then Solomon was told, "Adonijah is afraid of King Solomon and is clinging to the horns of the altar. He says, 'Let King Solomon swear to me today that he will not put his servant to death with the sword.'"

⁵²Solomon replied, "If he shows himself to be a worthy man, not a hairⁿ of his head will fall to the ground; but if evil is found in him, he will die." ⁵³Then King Solomon sent men, and they brought him down from the altar. And Adonijah came and bowed down to King Solomon, and Solomon said, "Go to your home."

1:37 *a* Jos 1:5,17; 1Sa 20:13 *b* ver 47
1:38 *c* ver 8 *d* 2Sa 8:18 *e* ver 33
1:39 *f* Ex 30:23-32; Ps 89:20 *g* ver 34; 1Sa 10:24
1:42 *h* 2Sa 15:27,36 *i* 2Sa 18:26
1:45 *j* ver 40
1:47 *k* ver 37; Ge 47:31
1:48 *l* 2Sa 7:12; 1Ki 3:6
1:50 *m* 1Ki 2:28
1:52 *n* 1Sa 14:45; 2Sa 14:11

Chapter 2 Theme

2 When the time drew near for David to die,[a] he gave a charge to Solomon his son.

[2] "I am about to go the way of all the earth,"[b] he said. "So be strong,[c] show yourself a man, [3] and observe[d] what the LORD your God requires: Walk in his ways, and keep his decrees and commands, his laws and requirements, as written in the Law of Moses, so that you may prosper[e] in all you do and wherever you go, [4] and that the LORD may keep his promise[f] to me: 'If your descendants watch how they live, and if they walk faithfully[g] before me with all their heart and soul, you will never fail to have a man on the throne of Israel.'

[5] "Now you yourself know what Joab[h] son of Zeruiah did to me—what he did to the two commanders of Israel's armies, Abner[i] son of Ner and Amasa[j] son of Jether. He killed them, shedding their blood in peacetime as if in battle, and with that blood stained the belt around his waist and the sandals on his feet. [6] Deal with him according to your wisdom,[k] but do not let his gray head go down to the grave[a] in peace.

[7] "But show kindness to the sons of Barzillai[l] of Gilead and let them be among those who eat at your table.[m] They stood by me when I fled from your brother Absalom.

[8] "And remember, you have with you Shimei[n] son of Gera, the Benjamite from Bahurim, who called down bitter curses on me the day I went to Mahanaim. When he came down to meet me at the Jordan, I swore[o] to him by the LORD: 'I will not put you to death by the sword.' [9] But now, do not consider him innocent. You are a man of wisdom;[p] you will know what to do to him. Bring his gray head down to the grave in blood."

[10] Then David rested with his fathers and was buried[q] in the City of David.[r] [11] He had reigned[s] forty years over Israel—seven years in Hebron and thirty-three in Jerusalem. [12] So Solomon sat on the throne[t] of his father David, and his rule was firmly established.[u]

[13] Now Adonijah, the son of Haggith, went to Bathsheba, Solomon's mother. Bathsheba asked him, "Do you come peacefully?"[v]

He answered, "Yes, peacefully." [14] Then he added, "I have something to say to you."

"You may say it," she replied.

[15] "As you know," he said, "the kingdom was mine. All Israel looked to me as their king. But things changed, and the kingdom has gone to my brother; for it has come to him from the LORD. [16] Now I have one request to make of you. Do not refuse me."

"You may make it," she said.

a6 Hebrew *Sheol*; also in verse 9

Cross-references:
2:1 a Ge 47:29; Dt 31:14
2:2 b Jos 23:14; c Dt 31:7,23; Jos 1:6
2:3 d Dt 17:14-20; Jos 1:7; e 1Ch 22:13
2:4 f 2Sa 7:13,25; 1Ki 8:25; g 2Ki 20:3; Ps 132:12
2:5 h 2Sa 2:18; 18:5,12,14; i 2Sa 3:27; j 2Sa 20:10
2:6 k ver 9
2:7 l 2Sa 17:27; 19:31-39; m 2Sa 9:7
2:8 n 2Sa 16:5-13; o 2Sa 19:18-23
2:9 p ver 6
2:10 q Ac 2:29; 13:36; r 2Sa 5:7
2:11 s 2Sa 5:4,5
2:12 t 1Ch 29:23; u 2Ch 1:1
2:13 v 1Sa 16:4

¹⁷So he continued, "Please ask King Solomon—he will not refuse you—to give me Abishag^a the Shunammite as my wife."

¹⁸"Very well," Bathsheba replied, "I will speak to the king for you."

¹⁹When Bathsheba went to King Solomon to speak to him for Adonijah, the king stood up to meet her, bowed down to her and sat down on his throne. He had a throne brought for the king's mother,^b and she sat down at his right hand.^c

²⁰"I have one small request to make of you," she said. "Do not refuse me."

The king replied, "Make it, my mother; I will not refuse you."

²¹So she said, "Let Abishag^d the Shunammite be given in marriage to your brother Adonijah."

²²King Solomon answered his mother, "Why do you request Abishag^e the Shunammite for Adonijah? You might as well request the kingdom for him—after all, he is my older brother^f—yes, for him and for Abiathar the priest and Joab son of Zeruiah!"

²³Then King Solomon swore by the LORD: "May God deal with me, be it ever so severely,^g if Adonijah does not pay with his life for this request! ²⁴And now, as surely as the LORD lives—he who has established me securely on the throne of my father David and has founded a dynasty for me as he promised^h—Adonijah shall be put to death today!" ²⁵So King Solomon gave orders to Benaiahⁱ son of Jehoiada, and he struck down Adonijah and he died.

²⁶To Abiathar^j the priest the king said, "Go back to your fields in Anathoth.^k You deserve to die, but I will not put you to death now, because you carried the ark^l of the Sovereign LORD before my father David and shared all my father's hardships."^m ²⁷So Solomon removed Abiathar from the priesthood of the LORD, fulfillingⁿ the word the LORD had spoken at Shiloh about the house of Eli.

²⁸When the news reached Joab, who had conspired with Adonijah though not with Absalom, he fled to the tent of the LORD and took hold of the horns^o of the altar. ²⁹King Solomon was told that Joab had fled to the tent of the LORD and was beside the altar. Then Solomon ordered Benaiah^p son of Jehoiada, "Go, strike him down!"

³⁰So Benaiah entered the tent of the LORD and said to Joab, "The king says, 'Come out!^q'"

But he answered, "No, I will die here."

Benaiah reported to the king, "This is how Joab answered me."

³¹Then the king commanded Benaiah, "Do as he says. Strike him down and bury him, and so clear me and my father's house of the guilt of the innocent blood^r that Joab shed. ³²The LORD will repay^s him for the blood he shed,^t because without the knowledge of my father David he attacked two men and killed them

2:17
a 1Ki 1:3

2:19
b 1Ki 15:13
c Ps 45:9

2:21
d 1Ki 1:3

2:22
e 2Sa 12:8;
1Ki 1:3
f 1Ch 3:2

2:23
g Ru 1:17

2:24
h 2Sa 7:11;
1Ch 22:10

2:25
i 2Sa 8:18

2:26
j 1Sa 22:20
k Jos 21:18
l 2Sa 15:24
m 1Sa 23:6

2:27
n 1Sa 2:27-36

2:28
o 1Ki 1:7,50

2:29
p ver 25

2:30
q Ex 21:14

2:31
r Nu 35:33;
Dt 19:13; 21:8-9

2:32
s Jdg 9:57;
Ps 7:16
t Jdg 9:24

2:32
a 2Sa 3:27; 20:10
b 2Ch 21:13

2:35
c 1Ki 4:4
d ver 27;
1Ch 29:22

2:36
e ver 8; 2Sa 16:5

2:37
f 2Sa 15:23
g Lev 20:9;
Jos 2:19;
2Sa 1:16

2:39
h 1Sa 27:2

2:44
i 1Sa 25:39;
2Sa 16:5-13;
Eze 17:19

2:45
j 2Sa 7:13;
Pr 25:5

2:46
k ver 12; 2Ch 1:1

3:1
l 1Ki 7:8
m 1Ki 9:24
n 2Sa 5:7
o 1Ki 7:1;
9:15,19

3:2
p Lev 17:3-5;
Dt 12:2,4-5;
1Ki 22:43

with the sword. Both of them—Abner son of Ner, commander of Israel's army, and Amasa*a* son of Jether, commander of Judah's army—were better*b* men and more upright than he. ³³May the guilt of their blood rest on the head of Joab and his descendants forever. But on David and his descendants, his house and his throne, may there be the LORD's peace forever."

³⁴So Benaiah son of Jehoiada went up and struck down Joab and killed him, and he was buried on his own land*a* in the desert. ³⁵The king put Benaiah*c* son of Jehoiada over the army in Joab's position and replaced Abiathar with Zadok*d* the priest.

³⁶Then the king sent for Shimei*e* and said to him, "Build yourself a house in Jerusalem and live there, but do not go anywhere else. ³⁷The day you leave and cross the Kidron Valley,*f* you can be sure you will die; your blood will be on your own head."*g*

³⁸Shimei answered the king, "What you say is good. Your servant will do as my lord the king has said." And Shimei stayed in Jerusalem for a long time.

³⁹But three years later, two of Shimei's slaves ran off to Achish*h* son of Maacah, king of Gath, and Shimei was told, "Your slaves are in Gath." ⁴⁰At this, he saddled his donkey and went to Achish at Gath in search of his slaves. So Shimei went away and brought the slaves back from Gath.

⁴¹When Solomon was told that Shimei had gone from Jerusalem to Gath and had returned, ⁴²the king summoned Shimei and said to him, "Did I not make you swear by the LORD and warn you, 'On the day you leave to go anywhere else, you can be sure you will die'? At that time you said to me, 'What you say is good. I will obey.' ⁴³Why then did you not keep your oath to the LORD and obey the command I gave you?"

⁴⁴The king also said to Shimei, "You know in your heart all the wrong*i* you did to my father David. Now the LORD will repay you for your wrongdoing. ⁴⁵But King Solomon will be blessed, and David's throne will remain secure*j* before the LORD forever."

⁴⁶Then the king gave the order to Benaiah son of Jehoiada, and he went out and struck Shimei down and killed him.

The kingdom was now firmly established*k* in Solomon's hands.

Chapter 3 Theme

3 Solomon made an alliance with Pharaoh king of Egypt and married*l* his daughter.*m* He brought her to the City of David*n* until he finished building his palace*o* and the temple of the LORD, and the wall around Jerusalem. ²The people, however, were still sacrificing at the high places,*p* because a temple had not yet been built

a 34 Or *buried in his tomb*

for the Name of the LORD. ³Solomon showed his love[a] for the LORD by walking according to the statutes[b] of his father David, except that he offered sacrifices and burned incense on the high places.

⁴The king went to Gibeon[c] to offer sacrifices, for that was the most important high place, and Solomon offered a thousand burnt offerings on that altar. ⁵At Gibeon the LORD appeared[d] to Solomon during the night in a dream,[e] and God said, "Ask for whatever you want me to give you."

⁶Solomon answered, "You have shown great kindness to your servant, my father David, because he was faithful[f] to you and righteous and upright in heart. You have continued this great kindness to him and have given him a son[g] to sit on his throne this very day.

⁷"Now, O LORD my God, you have made your servant king in place of my father David. But I am only a little child[h] and do not know how to carry out my duties. ⁸Your servant is here among the people you have chosen,[i] a great people, too numerous to count or number.[j] ⁹So give your servant a discerning[k] heart to govern your people and to distinguish[l] between right and wrong. For who is able[m] to govern this great people of yours?"

¹⁰The Lord was pleased that Solomon had asked for this. ¹¹So God said to him, "Since you have asked[n] for this and not for long life or wealth for yourself, nor have asked for the death of your enemies but for discernment in administering justice, ¹²I will do what you have asked.[o] I will give you a wise[p] and discerning heart, so that there will never have been anyone like you, nor will there ever be. ¹³Moreover, I will give you what you have not[q] asked for—both riches and honor[r]—so that in your lifetime you will have no equal[s] among kings. ¹⁴And if you walk[t] in my ways and obey my statutes and commands as David your father did, I will give you a long life."[u] ¹⁵Then Solomon awoke[v]—and he realized it had been a dream.

He returned to Jerusalem, stood before the ark of the Lord's covenant and sacrificed burnt offerings[w] and fellowship offerings.[a][x] Then he gave a feast[y] for all his court.

¹⁶Now two prostitutes came to the king and stood before him. ¹⁷One of them said, "My lord, this woman and I live in the same house. I had a baby while she was there with me. ¹⁸The third day after my child was born, this woman also had a baby. We were alone; there was no one in the house but the two of us.

¹⁹"During the night this woman's son died because she lay on him. ²⁰So she got up in the middle of the night and took my son from my side while I your servant was asleep. She put him by her breast and put her dead son by my breast. ²¹The next morning, I

3:3
[a] Dt 6:5;
Ps 31:23;
1Co 8:3
[b] 1Ki 2:3; 9:4;
11:4,6,38

3:4
[c] 1Ch 16:39

3:5
[d] 1Ki 9:2
[e] Nu 12:6;
Mt 1:20

3:6
[f] 1Ki 2:4; 9:4
[g] 1Ki 1:48

3:7
[h] Nu 27:17;
1Ch 29:1

3:8
[i] Dt 7:6
[j] Ge 15:5

3:9
[k] 2Sa 14:17;
Jas 1:5
[l] Pr 2:3-9;
Heb 5:14
[m] Ps 72:1-2

3:11
[n] Jas 4:3

3:12
[o] 1Jn 5:14-15
[p] 1Ki 4:29,30,
31; 5:12; 10:23;
Ecc 1:16

3:13
[q] Mt 6:33;
Eph 3:20
[r] 1Ki 4:21-24;
Pr 3:1-2,16
[s] 1Ki 10:23

3:14
[t] ver 6;
Pr 3:1-2,16
[u] Ps 61:6; 91:16

3:15
[v] Ge 41:7
[w] 1Ki 8:65
[x] Mk 6:21
[y] Est 1:3,9;
Da 5:1

---

a 15 Traditionally *peace offerings*

3:26
a Ge 43:30;
Isa 49:15;
Jer 31:20;
Hos 11:8

got up to nurse my son—and he was dead! But when I looked at him closely in the morning light, I saw that it wasn't the son I had borne."

²²The other woman said, "No! The living one is my son; the dead one is yours."

But the first one insisted, "No! The dead one is yours; the living one is mine." And so they argued before the king.

²³The king said, "This one says, 'My son is alive and your son is dead,' while that one says, 'No! Your son is dead and mine is alive.'"

3:28
b ver 9,11-12;
Col 2:3

²⁴Then the king said, "Bring me a sword." So they brought a sword for the king. ²⁵He then gave an order: "Cut the living child in two and give half to one and half to the other."

²⁶The woman whose son was alive was filled with compassion*a* for her son and said to the king, "Please, my lord, give her the living baby! Don't kill him!"

4:2
c 1Ch 6:10

But the other said, "Neither I nor you shall have him. Cut him in two!"

²⁷Then the king gave his ruling: "Give the living baby to the first woman. Do not kill him; she is his mother."

²⁸When all Israel heard the verdict the king had given, they held the king in awe, because they saw that he had wisdom*b* from God to administer justice.

4:3
d 2Sa 8:16

Chapter 4 Theme _____

4 So King Solomon ruled over all Israel. ²And these were his chief officials:

Azariah*c* son of Zadok—the priest;

³Elihoreph and Ahijah, sons of Shisha—secretaries;

Jehoshaphat*d* son of Ahilud—recorder;

4:4
e 1Ki 2:35
f 1Ki 2:27

⁴Benaiah*e* son of Jehoiada—commander in chief;

Zadok*f* and Abiathar—priests;

⁵Azariah son of Nathan—in charge of the district officers;

Zabud son of Nathan—a priest and personal adviser to the king;

⁶Ahishar—in charge of the palace;

Adoniram son of Abda—in charge of forced labor.

4:8
g Jos 24:33

⁷Solomon also had twelve district governors over all Israel, who supplied provisions for the king and the royal household. Each one had to provide supplies for one month in the year. ⁸These are their names:

Ben-Hur—in the hill country*g* of Ephraim;

4:9
h Jdg 1:35
i Jos 21:16

⁹Ben-Deker—in Makaz, Shaalbim,*h* Beth Shemesh*i* and Elon Bethhanan;

¹⁰Ben-Hesed—in Arubboth (Socoh[a] and all the land of He-pher[b] were his);

¹¹Ben-Abinadab—in Naphoth Dor[ac] (he was married to Ta-phath daughter of Solomon);

¹²Baana son of Ahilud—in Taanach and Megiddo, and in all of Beth Shan[d] next to Zarethan[e] below Jezreel, from Beth Shan to Abel Meholah[f] across to Jokmeam;[g]

¹³Ben-Geber—in Ramoth Gilead (the settlements of Jair[h] son of Manasseh in Gilead were his, as well as the district of Argob in Bashan and its sixty large walled cities[i] with bronze gate bars);

¹⁴Ahinadab son of Iddo—in Mahanaim;[j]

¹⁵Ahimaaz[k]—in Naphtali (he had married Basemath daughter of Solomon);

¹⁶Baana son of Hushai[l]—in Asher and in Aloth;

¹⁷Jehoshaphat son of Pa-ruah—in Issachar;

¹⁸Shimei[m] son of Ela—in Benjamin;

¹⁹Geber son of Uri—in Gilead (the country of Sihon king of the Am-orites and the country of Og[n] king of Ba-shan). He was the only governor over the district.

²⁰The people of Judah and Israel were as numerous as the sand[o] on the seashore; they ate, they drank and they were happy. ²¹And Solomon ruled[p] over all the kingdoms from the River[bq] to the land of the Philistines, as far as the border of Egypt.[r] These coun-tries brought tribute[s] and were Solomon's subjects all his life.

²²Solomon's daily provi-sions were thirty cors[c] of fine flour and sixty cors[d] of meal,

Solomon's Kingdom

a 11 Or in the heights of Dor   b 21 That is, the Euphrates; also in verse 24   c 22 That is, probably about 185 bushels (about 6.6 kiloliters)   d 22 That is, probably about 375 bushels (about 13.2 kiloliters)

4:10
a Jos 15:35
b Jos 12:17

4:11
c Jos 11:2

4:12
d Jos 17:11; Jdg 5:19
e Jos 3:16
f 1Ki 19:16
g 1Ch 6:68

4:13
h Nu 32:41
i Dt 3:4

4:14
j Jos 13:26

4:15
k 2Sa 15:27

4:16
l 2Sa 15:32

4:18
m 1Ki 1:8

4:19
n Dt 3:8-10

4:20
o Ge 22:17; 32:12; 1Ki 3:8

4:21
p 2Ch 9:26; Ps 72:11
q Jos 1:4; Ps 72:8
r Ge 15:18
s Ps 68:29

4:24
a Ps 72:11
b 1Ch 22:9

4:25
c Jdg 20:1
d Jer 23:6
e Mic 4:4;
Zec 3:10

4:26
f 1Ki 10:26;
2Ch 1:14

4:27
g ver 7

4:29
h 1Ki 3:12

4:30
i Ge 25:6
j Ac 7:22

4:31
k 1Ki 3:12;
1Ch 2:6; 6:33;
15:19;
Ps 89 Title

4:32
l Pr 1:1;
Ecc 12:9
m SS 1:1

4:34
n 1Ki 10:1;
2Ch 9:23

5:1
o ver 10,18;
2Sa 5:11;
1Ch 14:1

5:3
p 1Ch 22:8; 28:3

5:4
q 1Ki 4:24;
1Ch 22:9

5:5
r 1Ch 17:12
s 2Sa 7:13;
1Ch 22:10

²³ten head of stall-fed cattle, twenty of pasture-fed cattle and a hundred sheep and goats, as well as deer, gazelles, roebucks and choice fowl. ²⁴For he ruled over all the kingdoms west of the River, from Tiphsah[a] to Gaza, and had peace[b] on all sides. ²⁵During Solomon's lifetime Judah and Israel, from Dan to Beersheba,[c] lived in safety,[d] each man under his own vine and fig tree.[e]

²⁶Solomon had four[a] thousand stalls for chariot horses,[f] and twelve thousand horses.[b]

²⁷The district officers,[g] each in his month, supplied provisions for King Solomon and all who came to the king's table. They saw to it that nothing was lacking. ²⁸They also brought to the proper place their quotas of barley and straw for the chariot horses and the other horses.

²⁹God gave Solomon wisdom[h] and very great insight, and a breadth of understanding as measureless as the sand on the seashore. ³⁰Solomon's wisdom was greater than the wisdom of all the men of the East,[i] and greater than all the wisdom of Egypt.[j] ³¹He was wiser[k] than any other man, including Ethan the Ezrahite—wiser than Heman, Calcol and Darda, the sons of Mahol. And his fame spread to all the surrounding nations. ³²He spoke three thousand proverbs[l] and his songs[m] numbered a thousand and five. ³³He described plant life, from the cedar of Lebanon to the hyssop that grows out of walls. He also taught about animals and birds, reptiles and fish. ³⁴Men of all nations came to listen to Solomon's wisdom, sent by all the kings[n] of the world, who had heard of his wisdom.

Chapter 5 Theme _____

5 When Hiram[o] king of Tyre heard that Solomon had been anointed king to succeed his father David, he sent his envoys to Solomon, because he had always been on friendly terms with David. ²Solomon sent back this message to Hiram:

³"You know that because of the wars[p] waged against my father David from all sides, he could not build a temple for the Name of the LORD his God until the LORD put his enemies under his feet. ⁴But now the LORD my God has given me rest[q] on every side, and there is no adversary or disaster. ⁵I intend, therefore, to build a temple[r] for the Name of the LORD my God, as the LORD told my father David, when he said, 'Your son whom I will put on the throne in your place will build the temple for my Name.'[s]

⁶"So give orders that cedars of Lebanon be cut for me. My men will work with yours, and I will pay you for your men

a 26 Some Septuagint manuscripts (see also 2 Chron. 9:25); Hebrew *forty*   b 26 Or *charioteers* whatever wages you set. You know that we have no one so skilled in felling timber as the Sidonians."

[7]When Hiram heard Solomon's message, he was greatly pleased and said, "Praise be to the LORD today, for he has given David a wise son to rule over this great nation."

[8]So Hiram sent word to Solomon:

"I have received the message you sent me and will do all you want in providing the cedar and pine logs. [9]My men will haul them down from Lebanon to the sea[a], and I will float them in rafts by sea to the place you specify. There I will separate them and you can take them away. And you are to grant my wish by providing food[b] for my royal household."

[10]In this way Hiram kept Solomon supplied with all the cedar and pine logs he wanted, [11]and Solomon gave Hiram twenty thousand cors[a] of wheat as food for his household, in addition to twenty thousand baths[b,c] of pressed olive oil. Solomon continued to do this for Hiram year after year. [12]The LORD gave Solomon wisdom,[c] just as he had promised him. There were peaceful relations between Hiram and Solomon, and the two of them made a treaty.[d]

[13]King Solomon conscripted laborers[e] from all Israel—thirty thousand men. [14]He sent them off to Lebanon in shifts of ten thousand a month, so that they spent one month in Lebanon and two months at home. Adoniram[f] was in charge of the forced labor. [15]Solomon had seventy thousand carriers and eighty thousand stonecutters in the hills, [16]as well as thirty-three hundred[d] foremen[g] who supervised the project and directed the workmen. [17]At the king's command they removed from the quarry[h] large blocks of quality stone[i] to provide a foundation of dressed stone for the temple. [18]The craftsmen of Solomon and Hiram and the men of Gebal[e,j] cut and prepared the timber and stone for the building of the temple.

Chapter 6 Theme

6 In the four hundred and eightieth[f] year after the Israelites had come out of Egypt, in the fourth year of Solomon's reign over Israel, in the month of Ziv, the second month, he began to build the temple of the LORD.[k]

[2]The temple[l] that King Solomon built for the LORD was sixty cubits long, twenty wide and thirty high.[g] [3]The portico at the front of the main hall of the temple extended the width of the temple,

Cross references

5:9
[a]Ezr 3:7
[b]Eze 27:17;
Ac 12:20

5:12
[c]1Ki 3:12
[d]Am 1:9

5:13
[e]1Ki 9:15

5:14
[f]1Ki 4:6;
2Ch 10:18

5:16
[g]1Ki 9:23

5:17
[h]1Ki 6:7
[i]1Ch 22:2

5:18
[j]Jos 13:5

6:1
[k]Ac 7:47

6:2
[l]Eze 41:1

---

[a]11 That is, probably about 125,000 bushels (about 4,400 kiloliters)   [b]11 Septuagint (see also 2 Chron. 2:10); Hebrew *twenty cors*   [c]11 That is, about 115,000 gallons (about 440 kiloliters)   [d]16 Hebrew; some Septuagint manuscripts (see also 2 Chron. 2:2, 18) *thirty-six hundred*   [e]18 That is, Byblos   [f]1 Hebrew; Septuagint *four hundred and fortieth*   [g]2 That is, about 90 feet (about 27 meters) long and 30 feet (about 9 meters) wide and 45 feet (about 13.5 meters) high

The Jewish Calendar

Babylonian names (B) for the months are still used today for the Jewish calendar. Canaanite names (C) were used prior to the Babylonian captivity in 586 B.C. Four are mentioned in the Old Testament. **Adar-Sheni** is an intercalary month used every two to three years or seven times in 19 years.

1st month	2nd month	3rd month	4th month
Nisan (B) Abib (C) March-April	Iyyar (B) Ziv (C) April-May	Sivan (B) May-June	Tammuz (B) June-July
7th month	*8th month*	*9th month*	*10th month*
5th month	**6th month**	**7th month**	**8th month**
Ab (B) July-August	Elul (B) August-September	Tishri (B) Ethanim (C) September-October	Marcheshvan (B) Bul (C) October-November
11th month	*12th month*	*1st month*	*2nd month*
9th month	**10th month**	**11th month**	**12th month**
Chislev (B) November-December	Tebeth (B) December-January	Shebat (B) January-February	Adar (B) February-March
3rd month	*4th month*	*5th month*	*6th month*

Sacred calendar appears in black • Civil calendar appears in gray

6:4
a Eze 40:16; 41:16

that is twenty cubits,[a] and projected ten cubits[b] from the front of the temple. [4]He made narrow clerestory windows[a] in the temple. [5]Against the walls of the main hall and inner sanctuary he built a structure around the building, in which there were side rooms.[b]

6:5
b ver 16,19-21; Eze 41:5-6

[6]The lowest floor was five cubits[c] wide, the middle floor six cubits[d] and the third floor seven.[e] He made offset ledges around the outside of the temple so that nothing would be inserted into the temple walls.

6:7
c Ex 20:25
d Dt 27:5

[7]In building the temple, only blocks dressed[c] at the quarry were used, and no hammer, chisel or any other iron tool[d] was heard at the temple site while it was being built.

6:9
e ver 14,38

[8]The entrance to the lowest[f] floor was on the south side of the temple; a stairway led up to the middle level and from there to the third. [9]So he built the temple and completed it, roofing it with beams and cedar[e] planks. [10]And he built the side rooms all along the temple. The height of each was five cubits, and they were attached to the temple by beams of cedar.

6:12
f 2Sa 7:12-16; 1Ki 2:4; 9:5

[11]The word of the LORD came to Solomon: [12]"As for this temple you are building, if you follow my decrees, carry out my regulations and keep all my commands and obey them, I will fulfill through you the promise[f] I gave to David your father. [13]And I will live among the Israelites and will not abandon[g] my people Israel."

6:13
g Ex 25:8; Lev 26:11; Dt 31:6; Heb 13:5

[14]So Solomon built the temple and completed[h] it. [15]He lined its interior walls with cedar boards, paneling them from the floor of the temple to the ceiling,[i] and covered the floor of the temple

6:14
h ver 9,38

6:15
i 1Ki 7:7

---

a3 That is, about 30 feet (about 9 meters)   b3 That is, about 15 feet (about 4.5 meters)   c6 That is, about 7 1/2 feet (about 2.3 meters); also in verses 10 and 24   d6 That is, about 9 feet (about 2.7 meters)   e6 That is, about 10 1/2 feet (about 3.1 meters)   f8 Septuagint; Hebrew *middle*

Solomon's Temple

Altar of Incense
(Gold or Golden Altar)

Ark of the Covenant *(or Testimony)*

Bronze Basin on Bulls

Bronze Altar

Lampstand

Table

Bronze Stands with Bronze Basins

Temple Furnishings

Table for Consecrated Bread

Altar of Incense *(Gold or Golden Altar)*

Bronze Basin on Bulls

Ark of the Covenant *(or Testimony)*

with planks of pine. ¹⁶He partitioned off twenty cubits*ª* at the rear of the temple with cedar boards from floor to ceiling to form within the temple an inner sanctuary, the Most Holy Place.*ª* ¹⁷The main hall in front of this room was forty cubits,*ᵇ* long. ¹⁸The inside of the temple was cedar,*ᵇ* carved with gourds and open flowers. Everything was cedar; no stone was to be seen.

¹⁹He prepared the inner sanctuary*ᶜ* within the temple to set the ark of the covenant*ᵈ* of the LORD there. ²⁰The inner sanctuary*ᵉ* was twenty cubits long, twenty wide and twenty high.*ᶜ* He overlaid

ª 16 That is, about 30 feet (about 9 meters)   *ᵇ 17* That is, about 60 feet (about 18 meters)
ᶜ 20 That is, about 30 feet (about 9 meters) long, wide and high

6:16
ª Ex 26:33;
Lev 16:2;
1Ki 8:6

6:18
ᵇ 1Ki 7:24;
Ps 74:6

6:19
ᶜ 1Ki 8:6
ᵈ 1Sa 3:3

6:20
ᵉ Eze 41:3-4

6:23
a Ex 37:1-9

the inside with pure gold, and he also overlaid the altar of cedar. ²¹Solomon covered the inside of the temple with pure gold, and he extended gold chains across the front of the inner sanctuary, which was overlaid with gold. ²²So he overlaid the whole interior with gold. He also overlaid with gold the altar that belonged to the inner sanctuary.

6:27
b Ex 25:20; 37:9;
1Ki 8:7; 2Ch 5:8

*Close-up of
Most Holy
Place*

²³In the inner sanctuary he made a pair of cherubim*ᵃ* of olive wood, each ten cubitsᵃ high. ²⁴One wing of the first cherub was five cubits long, and the other wing five cubits—ten cubits from wing tip to wing tip. ²⁵The second cherub also measured ten cubits, for the two cherubim were identical in size and shape. ²⁶The height of each cherub was ten cubits. ²⁷He placed the cherubim*ᵇ* inside the innermost room of the temple, with their wings spread out. The wing of one cherub touched one wall, while the wing of the other touched the other wall, and their wings touched each other in the middle of the room. ²⁸He overlaid the cherubim with gold.

6:29
c ver 32,35

²⁹On the walls all around the temple, in both the inner and outer rooms, he carved cherubim,*ᶜ* palm trees and open flowers. ³⁰He also covered the floors of both the inner and outer rooms of the temple with gold.

6:36
d 1Ki 7:12;
Ezr 6:4

³¹For the entrance of the inner sanctuary he made doors of olive wood with five-sided jambs. ³²And on the two olive wood doors he carved cherubim, palm trees and open flowers, and overlaid the cherubim and palm trees with beaten gold. ³³In the same way he made four-sided jambs of olive wood for the entrance to the main hall. ³⁴He also made two pine doors, each having two leaves that turned in sockets. ³⁵He carved cherubim, palm trees and open flowers on them and overlaid them with gold hammered evenly over the carvings.

6:38
e Heb 8:5

³⁶And he built the inner courtyard of three courses*ᵈ* of dressed stone and one course of trimmed cedar beams.

³⁷The foundation of the temple of the Lᴏʀᴅ was laid in the fourth year, in the month of Ziv. ³⁸In the eleventh year in the month of Bul, the eighth month, the temple was finished in all its details according to its specifications.*ᵉ* He had spent seven years building it.

Chapter 7 Theme _____

7:1
f 1Ki 9:10;
2Ch 8:1

7 It took Solomon thirteen years, however, to complete the construction of his palace.*ᶠ* ²He built the Palace*ᵍ* of the Forest of Lebanon*ʰ* a hundred cubits long, fifty wide and thirty high,ᵇ with four rows of cedar columns supporting trimmed

7:2
g 2Sa 7:2
h 1Ki 10:17;
2Ch 9:16

ᵃ 23 That is, about 15 feet (about 4.5 meters)   ᵇ 2 That is, about 150 feet (about 46 meters) long, 75 feet (about 23 meters) wide and 45 feet (about 13.5 meters) high

7:7
a Ps 122:5;
Pr 20:8
b 1Ki 6:15

cedar beams. ³It was roofed with cedar above the beams that rested on the columns—forty-five beams, fifteen to a row. ⁴Its windows were placed high in sets of three, facing each other. ⁵All the doorways had rectangular frames; they were in the front part in sets of three, facing each other.ᵃ

⁶He made a colonnade fifty cubits long and thirty wide.ᵇ In front of it was a portico, and in front of that were pillars and an overhanging roof.

⁷He built the throne hall, the Hall of Justice, where he was to judge,ᵃ and he covered it with cedar from floor to ceiling.ᶜᵇ ⁸And the palace in which he was to live, set farther back, was similar in design. Solomon also made a palace like this hall for Pharaoh's daughter, whom he had married.ᶜ

7:8
c 1Ki 3:1;
2Ch 8:11

⁹All these structures, from the outside to the great courtyard and from foundation to eaves, were made of blocks of high-grade stone cut to size and trimmed with a saw on their inner and outer faces. ¹⁰The foundations were laid with large stones of good quality, some measuring ten cubitsᵈ and some eight.ᵉ ¹¹Above were high-grade stones, cut to size, and cedar beams. ¹²The great courtyard was surrounded by a wall of three coursesᵈ of dressed stone and one course of trimmed cedar beams, as was the inner courtyard of the temple of the LORD with its portico.

7:12
d 1Ki 6:36

¹³King Solomon sent to Tyre and brought Huram,ᶠᵉ ¹⁴whose mother was a widow from the tribe of Naphtali and whose father was a man of Tyre and a craftsman in bronze. Huram was highly skilledᶠ and experienced in all kinds of bronze work. He came to King Solomon and did allᵍ the work assigned to him.

7:13
e 2Ch 2:13

¹⁵He cast two bronze pillars,ʰ each eighteen cubits high and twelve cubits around,ᵍ by line. ¹⁶He also made two capitalsⁱ of cast bronze to set on the tops of the pillars; each capital was five cubitsʰ high. ¹⁷A network of interwoven chains festooned the capitals on top of the pillars, seven for each capital. ¹⁸He made pomegranates in two rowsⁱ encircling each network to decorate the capitals on top of the pillars.ʲ He did the same for each capital. ¹⁹The capitals on top of the pillars in the portico were in the shape of lilies, four cubitsᵏ high. ²⁰On the capitals of both pillars, above the bowl-shaped part next to the network, were the two hundred pomegranatesʲ in rows all around. ²¹He erected the pillars at the portico of the temple. The pillar to the south he named Jakinˡ and

7:14
f Ex 31:2-5;
35:31; 36:1;
2Ch 2:14
g 2Ch 4:11,16

7:15
h 2Ki 25:17;
2Ch 3:15; 4:12;
52:17,21

7:16
i 2Ki 25:17

ᵃ5 The meaning of the Hebrew for this verse is uncertain.   ᵇ6 That is, about 75 feet (about 23 meters) long and 45 feet (about 13.5 meters) wide   ᶜ7 Vulgate and Syriac; Hebrew *floor*
ᵈ10 That is, about 15 feet (about 4.5 meters)   ᵉ10 That is, about 12 feet (about 3.6 meters)
ᶠ13 Hebrew *Hiram*, a variant of *Huram*; also in verses 40 and 45   ᵍ15 That is, about 27 feet (about 8.1 meters) high and 18 feet (about 5.4 meters) around   ʰ16 That is, about 7 1/2 feet (about 2.3 meters); also in verse 23   ⁱ18 Two Hebrew manuscripts and Septuagint; most Hebrew manuscripts *made the pillars, and there were two rows*   ʲ18 Many Hebrew manuscripts and Syriac; most Hebrew manuscripts *pomegranates*   ᵏ19 That is, about 6 feet (about 1.8 meters); also in verse 38   ˡ21 *Jakin* probably means *he establishes*.

7:20
j 2Ch 3:16; 4:13;
Jer 52:23

7:21
a 1Ki 6:3;
2Ch 3:17

the one to the north Boaz.ªª ²²The capitals on top were in the shape of lilies. And so the work on the pillars was completed.

²³He made the Sea*b* of cast metal, circular in shape, measuring ten cubits*b* from rim to rim and five cubits high. It took a line of thirty cubits*c* to measure around it. ²⁴Below the rim, gourds encircled it—ten to a cubit. The gourds were cast in two rows in one piece with the Sea.

7:23
b 2Ki 25:13;
1Ch 18:8;
Jer 52:17

²⁵The Sea stood on twelve bulls,*c* three facing north, three facing west, three facing south and three facing east. The Sea rested on top of them, and their hindquarters were toward the center. ²⁶It was a handbreadth*d* in thickness, and its rim was like the rim of a cup, like a lily blossom. It held two thousand baths.*e*

Bronze Basin on Bulls

²⁷He also made ten movable stands*d* of bronze; each was four cubits long, four wide and three high.*f* ²⁸This is how the stands were made: They had side panels attached to uprights. ²⁹On the panels between the uprights were lions, bulls and cherubim—and on the uprights as well. Above and below the lions and bulls were wreaths of hammered work. ³⁰Each stand*e* had four bronze wheels with bronze axles, and each had a basin resting on four supports, cast with wreaths on each side. ³¹On the inside of the stand there was an opening that had a circular frame one cubit*g* deep. This opening was round, and with its basework it measured a cubit and a half.*h* Around its opening there was engraving. The panels of the stands were square, not round. ³²The four wheels were under the panels, and the axles of the wheels were attached to the stand. The diameter of each wheel was a cubit and a half. ³³The wheels were made like chariot wheels; the axles, rims, spokes and hubs were all of cast metal.

7:25
c 2Ch 4:4-5;
Jer 52:20

7:27
d ver 38;
2Ch 4:14

³⁴Each stand had four handles, one on each corner, projecting from the stand. ³⁵At the top of the stand there was a circular band half a cubit*i* deep. The supports and panels were attached to the top of the stand. ³⁶He engraved cherubim, lions and palm trees on the surfaces of the supports and on the panels, in every available space, with wreaths all around. ³⁷This is the way he made the ten stands. They were all cast in the same molds and were identical in size and shape.

7:30
e 2Ki 16:17

³⁸He then made ten bronze basins,*f* each holding forty baths*j* and measuring four cubits across, one basin to go on each of the ten stands. ³⁹He placed five of the stands on the south side of the temple and five on the north. He placed the Sea on the south side,

7:38
f Ex 30:18;
2Ch 4:6

---

a 21 Boaz probably means *in him is strength.*   *b 23* That is, about 15 feet (about 4.5 meters)   *c 23* That is, about 45 feet (about 13.5 meters)   *d 26* That is, about 3 inches (about 8 centimeters)   *e 26* That is, probably about 11,500 gallons (about 44 kiloliters); the Septuagint does not have this sentence.   *f 27* That is, about 6 feet (about 1.8 meters) long and wide and about 4 1/2 feet (about 1.3 meters) high   *g 31* That is, about 1 1/2 feet (about 0.5 meter)   *h 31* That is, about 2 1/4 feet (about 0.7 meter); also in verse 32   *i 35* That is, about 3/4 foot (about 0.2 meter)   *j 38* That is, about 230 gallons (about 880 liters)

Bronze Stand with Bronze Basin

at the southeast corner of the temple. ⁴⁰He also made the basins and shovels and sprinkling bowls.

So Huram finished all the work he had undertaken for King Solomon in the temple of the LORD:

⁴¹the two pillars;

the two bowl-shaped capitals on top of the pillars;

the two sets of network decorating the two bowl-shaped capitals on top of the pillars;

⁴²the four hundred pomegranates for the two sets of network (two rows of pomegranates for each network, decorating the bowl-shaped capitals*ᵃ* on top of the pillars);

⁴³the ten stands with their ten basins;

⁴⁴the Sea and the twelve bulls under it;

⁴⁵the pots, shovels and sprinkling bowls.*ᵇ*

All these objects that Huram made for King Solomon for the temple of the LORD were of burnished bronze. ⁴⁶The king had them cast in clay molds in the plain*ᶜ* of the Jordan between Succoth*ᵈ* and Zarethan.*ᵉ* ⁴⁷Solomon left all these things unweighed,*ᶠ* because there were so many; the weight of the bronze was not determined.

⁴⁸Solomon also made all the furnishings that were in the LORD's temple:

the golden altar;

the golden table*ᵍ* on which was the bread of the Presence;*ʰ*

⁴⁹the lampstands*ⁱ* of pure gold (five on the right and five on the left, in front of the inner sanctuary);

the gold floral work and lamps and tongs;

⁵⁰the pure gold basins, wick trimmers, sprinkling bowls, dishes and censers;*ʲ*

and the gold sockets for the doors of the innermost room, the Most Holy Place, and also for the doors of the main hall of the temple.

⁵¹When all the work King Solomon had done for the temple of the LORD was finished, he brought in the things his father David had dedicated*ᵏ*—the silver and gold and the furnishings—and he placed them in the treasuries of the LORD's temple.

Lampstand

Chapter 8 Theme

8 Then King Solomon summoned into his presence at Jerusalem the elders of Israel, all the heads of the tribes and the chiefs*ˡ* of the Israelite families, to bring up the ark*ᵐ* of the LORD's covenant from Zion, the City of David.*ⁿ* ²All the men of Israel came together to King Solomon at the time of the festival*ᵒ* in the month of Ethanim, the seventh month.*ᵖ*

7:42
ᵃ ver 20

7:45
ᵇ Ex 27:3

7:46
ᶜ 2Ch 4:17
ᵈ Ge 33:17;
Jos 13:27
ᵉ Jos 3:16

7:47
ᶠ 1Ch 22:3

7:48
ᵍ Ex 37:10
ʰ Ex 25:30

7:49
ⁱ Ex 25:31-38

7:50
ʲ 2Ki 25:13

7:51
ᵏ 2Sa 8:11

8:1
ˡ Nu 7:2
ᵐ 2Sa 6:17
ⁿ 2Sa 5:7

8:2
ᵒ 2Ch 7:8
ᵖ Lev 23:34

8:3
a Nu 7:9; Jos 3:3

8:4
b 1Ki 3:4;
2Ch 1:3

8:5
c 2Sa 6:13

8:6
d 2Sa 6:17
e 1Ki 6:19,27

8:8
f Ex 25:13-15

8:9
g Ex 24:7-8;
25:21; 40:20;
Dt 10:2-5;
Heb 9:4

8:10
h Ex 40:34-35;
2Ch 7:1-2

8:12
i Ps 18:11; 97:2

8:13
j Ex 15:17;
2Sa 7:13;
Ps 132:13

8:14
k 2Sa 6:18

8:15
l 2Sa 7:12-13;
1Ch 29:10,20;
Ne 9:5; Lk 1:68

8:16
m Dt 12:5
n 1Sa 16:1
o 2Sa 7:4-6,8

8:17
p 2Sa 7:2;
1Ch 17:1

8:19
q 2Sa 7:5
r 2Sa 7:13;
1Ki 5:3,5

8:20
s 1Ch 28:6

³When all the elders of Israel had arrived, the priests*a* took up the ark, ⁴and they brought up the ark of the LORD and the Tent of Meeting*b* and all the sacred furnishings in it. The priests and Levites carried them up, ⁵and King Solomon and the entire assembly of Israel that had gathered about him were before the ark, sacrificing*c* so many sheep and cattle that they could not be recorded or counted.

⁶The priests then brought the ark of the LORD's covenant*d* to its place in the inner sanctuary of the temple, the Most Holy Place, and put it beneath the wings of the cherubim.*e* ⁷The cherubim spread their wings over the place of the ark and overshadowed the ark and its carrying poles. ⁸These poles were so long that their ends could be seen from the Holy Place in front of the inner sanctuary, but not from outside the Holy Place; and they are still there today.*f* ⁹There was nothing in the ark except the two stone tablets*g* that Moses had placed in it at Horeb, where the LORD made a covenant with the Israelites after they came out of Egypt.

¹⁰When the priests withdrew from the Holy Place, the cloud*h* filled the temple of the LORD. ¹¹And the priests could not perform their service because of the cloud, for the glory of the LORD filled his temple.

¹²Then Solomon said, "The LORD has said that he would dwell in a dark cloud;*i* ¹³I have indeed built a magnificent temple for you, a place for you to dwell*j* forever."

¹⁴While the whole assembly of Israel was standing there, the king turned around and blessed*k* them. ¹⁵Then he said:

"Praise be to the LORD,*l* the God of Israel, who with his own hand has fulfilled what he promised with his own mouth to my father David. For he said, ¹⁶'Since the day I brought my people Israel out of Egypt, I have not chosen a city in any tribe of Israel to have a temple built for my Name*m* to be there, but I have chosen*n* David*o* to rule my people Israel.'

¹⁷"My father David had it in his heart to build a temple*p* for the Name of the LORD, the God of Israel. ¹⁸But the LORD said to my father David, 'Because it was in your heart to build a temple for my Name, you did well to have this in your heart. ¹⁹Nevertheless, you*q* are not the one to build the temple, but your son, who is your own flesh and blood—he is the one who will build the temple for my Name.'*r*

²⁰"The LORD has kept the promise he made: I have succeeded David my father and now I sit on the throne of Israel, just as the LORD promised, and I have built*s* the temple for the Name of the LORD, the God of Israel. ²¹I have provided a place there for the ark, in which is the covenant of the LORD that he made with our fathers when he brought them out of Egypt."

INSIGHT

See the illustration of Solomon's Temple on page IISB-36.

²²Then Solomon stood before the altar of the LORD in front of the whole assembly of Israel, spread out his hands[a] toward heaven ²³and said:

"O LORD, God of Israel, there is no God like[b] you in heaven above or on earth below—you who keep your covenant of love[c] with your servants who continue wholeheartedly in your way. ²⁴You have kept your promise to your servant David my father; with your mouth you have promised and with your hand you have fulfilled it—as it is today.

²⁵"Now LORD, God of Israel, keep for your servant David my father the promises[d] you made to him when you said, 'You shall never fail to have a man to sit before me on the throne of Israel, if only your sons are careful in all they do to walk before me as you have done.' ²⁶And now, O God of Israel, let your word that you promised[e] your servant David my father come true.

²⁷"But will God really dwell[f] on earth? The heavens, even the highest heaven, cannot contain[g] you. How much less this temple I have built! ²⁸Yet give attention to your servant's prayer and his plea for mercy, O LORD my God. Hear the cry and the prayer that your servant is praying in your presence this day. ²⁹May your eyes be open[h] toward[i] this temple night and day, this place of which you said, 'My Name[j] shall be there,' so that you will hear the prayer your servant prays toward this place. ³⁰Hear the supplication of your servant and of your people Israel when they pray toward this place. Hear from heaven, your dwelling place, and when you hear, forgive.[k]

³¹"When a man wrongs his neighbor and is required to take an oath and he comes and swears the oath[l] before your altar in this temple, ³²then hear from heaven and act. Judge between your servants, condemning the guilty and bringing down on his own head what he has done. Declare the innocent not guilty, and so establish his innocence.[m]

³³"When your people Israel have been defeated[n] by an enemy because they have sinned[o] against you, and when they turn back to you and confess your name, praying and making supplication to you in this temple, ³⁴then hear from heaven and forgive the sin of your people Israel and bring them back to the land you gave to their fathers.

³⁵"When the heavens are shut up and there is no rain[p] because your people have sinned against you, and when they pray toward this place and confess your name and turn from their sin because you have afflicted them, ³⁶then hear from heaven and forgive the sin of your servants, your people Israel.

8:22
a Ex 9:29;
Ezr 9:5

8:23
b 1Sa 2:2;
2Sa 7:22
c Dt 7:9,12;
Ne 1:5; 9:32;
Da 9:4

8:25
d 1Ki 2:4

8:26
e 2Sa 7:25

8:27
f Ac 7:48
g 2Ch 2:6;
Ps 139:7-16;
Isa 66:1;
Jer 23:24

8:29
h 2Ch 7:15;
Ne 1:6
i Da 6:10
j Dt 12:11

8:30
k Ps 85:2

8:31
l Ex 22:11

8:32
m Dt 25:1

8:33
n Lev 26:17;
Dt 28:25
o Lev 26:39

8:35
p Lev 26:19;
Dt 28:24

8:36
a 1Sa 12:23;
Ps 25:4; 94:12
b Ps 5:8; 27:11;
Jer 6:16

8:37
c Lev 26:26
d Dt 28:22

8:39
e 1Sa 16:7;
1Ch 28:9;
Ps 11:4;
Jer 17:10;
Jn 2:24;
Ac 1:24

8:40
f Ps 130:4

8:42
g Dt 3:24

8:43
h 1Sa 17:46;
2Ki 19:19
i Ps 102:15

8:46
j Pr 20:9;
Ecc 7:20;
Ro 3:9;
1Jn 1:8-10
k Lev 26:33-39;
Dt 28:64

8:47
l Lev 26:40;
Ne 1:6
m Ps 106:6;
Da 9:5

8:48
n Dt 4:29;
Jer 29:12-14
o Da 6:10
p Jnh 2:4

8:50
q 2Ch 30:9;
Ps 106:46

8:51
r Dt 4:20; 9:29;
Ne 1:10
s Jer 11:4

Teach[a] them the right way[b] to live, and send rain on the land you gave your people for an inheritance.

[37]"When famine[c] or plague comes to the land, or blight[d] or mildew, locusts or grasshoppers, or when an enemy besieges them in any of their cities, whatever disaster or disease may come, [38]and when a prayer or plea is made by any of your people Israel—each one aware of the afflictions of his own heart, and spreading out his hands toward this temple— [39]then hear from heaven, your dwelling place. Forgive and act; deal with each man according to all he does, since you know[e] his heart (for you alone know the hearts of all men), [40]so that they will fear[f] you all the time they live in the land you gave our fathers.

[41]"As for the foreigner who does not belong to your people Israel but has come from a distant land because of your name— [42]for men will hear of your great name and your mighty hand[g] and your outstretched arm—when he comes and prays toward this temple, [43]then hear from heaven, your dwelling place, and do whatever the foreigner asks of you, so that all the peoples of the earth may know[h] your name and fear[i] you, as do your own people Israel, and may know that this house I have built bears your Name.

[44]"When your people go to war against their enemies, wherever you send them, and when they pray to the LORD toward the city you have chosen and the temple I have built for your Name, [45]then hear from heaven their prayer and their plea, and uphold their cause.

[46]"When they sin against you—for there is no one who does not sin[j]—and you become angry with them and give them over to the enemy, who takes them captive[k] to his own land, far away or near; [47]and if they have a change of heart in the land where they are held captive, and repent and plead[l] with you in the land of their conquerors and say, 'We have sinned, we have done wrong, we have acted wickedly';[m] [48]and if they turn back to you with all their heart[n] and soul in the land of their enemies who took them captive, and pray[o] to you toward the land you gave their fathers, toward the city you have chosen and the temple[p] I have built for your Name; [49]then from heaven, your dwelling place, hear their prayer and their plea, and uphold their cause. [50]And forgive your people, who have sinned against you; forgive all the offenses they have committed against you, and cause their conquerors to show them mercy;[q] [51]for they are your people and your inheritance,[r] whom you brought out of Egypt, out of that iron-smelting furnace.[s]

[52]"May your eyes be open to your servant's plea and to the plea of your people Israel, and may you listen to them whenever

they cry out to you. ⁵³For you singled them out from all the nations of the world to be your own inheritance,^a just as you declared through your servant Moses when you, O Sovereign LORD, brought our fathers out of Egypt."

⁵⁴When Solomon had finished all these prayers and supplications to the LORD, he rose from before the altar of the LORD, where he had been kneeling with his hands spread out toward heaven. ⁵⁵He stood and blessed^b the whole assembly of Israel in a loud voice, saying:

⁵⁶"Praise be to the LORD, who has given rest^c to his people Israel just as he promised. Not one word has failed of all the good promises^d he gave through his servant Moses. ⁵⁷May the LORD our God be with us as he was with our fathers; may he never leave us nor forsake^e us. ⁵⁸May he turn our hearts^f to him, to walk in all his ways and to keep the commands, decrees and regulations he gave our fathers. ⁵⁹And may these words of mine, which I have prayed before the LORD, be near to the LORD our God day and night, that he may uphold the cause of his servant and the cause of his people Israel according to each day's need, ⁶⁰so that all the peoples^g of the earth may know that the LORD is God and that there is no other.^h ⁶¹But your hearts must be fully committedⁱ to the LORD our God, to live by his decrees and obey his commands, as at this time."

⁶²Then the king and all Israel with him offered sacrifices before the LORD. ⁶³Solomon offered a sacrifice of fellowship offerings^a to the LORD: twenty-two thousand cattle and a hundred and twenty thousand sheep and goats. So the king and all the Israelites dedicated the temple of the LORD.

⁶⁴On that same day the king consecrated the middle part of the courtyard in front of the temple of the LORD, and there he offered burnt offerings, grain offerings and the fat of the fellowship offerings, because the bronze altar^j before the LORD was too small to hold the burnt offerings, the grain offerings and the fat of the fellowship offerings.

⁶⁵So Solomon observed the festival^k at that time, and all Israel with him—a vast assembly, people from Lebo^b Hamath^l to the Wadi of Egypt.^m They celebrated it before the LORD our God for seven days and seven days more, fourteen days in all. ⁶⁶On the following day he sent the people away. They blessed the king and then went home, joyful and glad in heart for all the good things the LORD had done for his servant David and his people Israel.

^a63 Traditionally *peace offerings*; also in verse 64   ^b65 Or *from the entrance to*

8:53
^aEx 19:5;
Dt 9:26-29

8:55
^bver 14;
2Sa 6:18

8:56
^cDt 12:10
^dJos 21:45;
23:15

8:57
^eDt 31:6;
Jos 1:5;
Heb 13:5

8:58
^fPs 119:36

8:60
^gJos 4:24;
1Sa 17:46
^hDt 4:35;
1Ki 18:39;
Jer 10:10-12

8:61
ⁱ1Ki 11:4;
15:3,14;
2Ki 20:3

8:64
^j2Ch 4:1

8:65
^kver 2;
Lev 23:34
^lNu 34:8;
Jos 13:5;
Jdg 3:3;
2Ki 14:25
^mGe 15:18

Chapter 9 Theme

9 When Solomon had finished*a* building the temple of the LORD
and the royal palace, and had achieved all he had desired to
do, **2**the LORD appeared*b* to him a second time, as he had appeared
to him at Gibeon. **3**The LORD said to him:

"I have heard*c* the prayer and plea you have made before
me; I have consecrated this temple, which you have built, by
putting my Name there forever. My eyes*d* and my heart will
always be there.

4"As for you, if you walk before me in integrity of heart*e* and
uprightness, as David*f* your father did, and do all I command
and observe my decrees and laws, **5**I will establish*g* your royal
throne over Israel forever, as I promised David your father
when I said, 'You shall never fail*h* to have a man on the throne
of Israel.'

6"But if you*a* or your sons turn away*i* from me and do not
observe the commands and decrees I have given you*a* and go
off to serve other gods and worship them, **7**then I will cut off
Israel from the land*j* I have given them and will reject this temple I have consecrated for my Name.*k* Israel will then become
a byword*l* and an object of ridicule*m* among all peoples. **8**And
though this temple is now imposing, all who pass by will be
appalled and will scoff and say, 'Why has the LORD done such
a thing to this land and to this temple?'*n* **9**People will answer,
'Because they have forsaken the LORD their God, who brought
their fathers out of Egypt, and have embraced other gods,
worshiping and serving them—that is why the LORD brought
all this disaster on them.'"

9:7
*j*2Ki 17:23;
25:21
*k*Jer 7:14
*l*Ps 44:14
*m*Dt 28:37

10At the end of twenty years, during which Solomon built these
two buildings—the temple of the LORD and the royal palace—
11King Solomon gave twenty towns in Galilee to Hiram king of
Tyre, because Hiram had supplied him with all the cedar and pine
and gold*o* he wanted. **12**But when Hiram went from Tyre to see
the towns that Solomon had given him, he was not pleased with
them. **13**"What kind of towns are these you have given me, my
brother?" he asked. And he called them the Land of Cabul,*bp* a
name they have to this day. **14**Now Hiram had sent to the king 120
talents*c* of gold.

15Here is the account of the forced labor King Solomon conscripted*q* to build the LORD's temple, his own palace, the supporting terraces,*dr* the wall of Jerusalem, and Hazor,*s* Megiddo and

9:15
*q*Jos 16:10;
1Ki 5:13
*r*ver 24;
2Sa 5:9
*s*Jos 19:36

*a*6 The Hebrew is plural.   *b*13 *Cabul* sounds like the Hebrew for *good-for-nothing.*
*c*14 That is, about 4 1/2 tons (about 4 metric tons)   *d*15 Or *the Millo*; also in verse 24

Gezer.*a* ¹⁶(Pharaoh king of Egypt had attacked and captured Gezer. He had set it on fire. He killed its Canaanite inhabitants and then gave it as a wedding gift to his daughter, Solomon's wife. ¹⁷And Solomon rebuilt Gezer.) He built up Lower Beth Horon,*b* ¹⁸Baalath,*c* and Tadmor*a* in the desert, within his land, ¹⁹as well as all his store cities*d* and the towns for his chariots*e* and for his horses*b*—whatever he desired to build in Jerusalem, in Lebanon and throughout all the territory he ruled.

²⁰All the people left from the Amorites, Hittites, Perizzites, Hivites and Jebusites (these peoples were not Israelites), ²¹that is, their descendants*f* remaining in the land, whom the Israelites could not exterminate*cg*—these Solomon conscripted for his slave labor force,*h* as it is to this day. ²²But Solomon did not make slaves*i* of any of the Israelites; they were his fighting men, his government officials, his officers, his captains, and the commanders of his chariots and charioteers. ²³They were also the chief officials*j* in charge of Solomon's projects—550 officials supervising the men who did the work.

²⁴After Pharaoh's daughter*k* had come up from the City of David to the palace Solomon had built for her, he constructed the supporting terraces.*l*

²⁵Three*m* times a year Solomon sacrificed burnt offerings and fellowship offerings*d* on the altar he had built for the LORD, burning incense before the LORD along with them, and so fulfilled the temple obligations.

²⁶King Solomon also built ships*n* at Ezion Geber,*o* which is near Elath in Edom, on the shore of the Red Sea.*e* ²⁷And Hiram sent his men—sailors*p* who knew the sea—to serve in the fleet with Solomon's men. ²⁸They sailed to Ophir*q* and brought back 420 talents*f* of gold, which they delivered to King Solomon.

Chapter 10 Theme

10 When the queen of Sheba*r* heard about the fame of Solomon and his relation to the name of the LORD, she came to test him with hard questions.*s* ²Arriving at Jerusalem with a very great caravan—with camels carrying spices, large quantities of gold, and precious stones—she came to Solomon and talked with him about all that she had on her mind. ³Solomon answered all her questions; nothing was too hard for the king to explain to her. ⁴When the queen of Sheba saw all the wisdom of Solomon and the palace he had built, ⁵the food on his table,*t* the seating of his

---

a 18 The Hebrew may also be read *Tamar*.   b 19 Or *charioteers*   c 21 The Hebrew term refers to the irrevocable giving over of things or persons to the LORD, often by totally destroying them.   d 25 Traditionally *peace offerings*   e 26 Hebrew *Yam Suph*; that is, Sea of Reeds   f 28 That is, about 16 tons (about 14.5 metric tons)

**Cross references (margin):**

9:15 *a* Jos 17:11

9:17 *b* Jos 16:3; 2Ch 8:5

9:18 *c* Jos 19:44

9:19 *d* ver 1 *e* 1Ki 4:26

9:21 *f* Ge 9:25-26 *g* Jos 15:63; 17:12; Jdg 1:21,27,29 *h* Ezr 2:55,58

9:22 *i* Lev 25:39

9:23 *j* 1Ki 5:16

9:24 *k* 1Ki 3:1; 7:8 *l* 2Sa 5:9; 1Ki 11:27; 2Ch 32:5

9:25 *m* Ex 23:14; 2Ch 8:12-13,16

9:26 *n* 1Ki 22:48 *o* Nu 33:35; Dt 2:8

9:27 *p* 1Ki 10:11; Eze 27:8

9:28 *q* 1Ch 29:4

10:1 *r* Ge 10:7,28; Mt 12:42; Lk 11:31 *s* Jdg 14:12

10:5 *t* 1Ch 26:16

10:7
a 1Ch 29:25

officials, the attending servants in their robes, his cupbearers, and the burnt offerings he made at[a] the temple of the LORD, she was overwhelmed.

⁶She said to the king, "The report I heard in my own country about your achievements and your wisdom is true. ⁷But I did not believe these things until I came and saw with my own eyes. Indeed, not even half was told me; in wisdom and wealth[a] you have far exceeded the report I heard. ⁸How happy your men must be! How happy your officials, who continually stand before you and hear[b] your wisdom! ⁹Praise[c] be to the LORD your God, who has delighted in you and placed you on the throne of Israel. Because of the LORD's eternal love for Israel, he has made you king, to maintain justice[d] and righteousness."

10:8
b Pr 8:34

10:9
c 1Ki 5:7
d 2Sa 8:15;
Ps 33:5; 72:2

¹⁰And she gave the king 120 talents[b] of gold,[e] large quantities of spices, and precious stones. Never again were so many spices brought in as those the queen of Sheba gave to King Solomon.

¹¹(Hiram's ships brought gold from Ophir;[f] and from there they brought great cargoes of almugwood[c] and precious stones. ¹²The king used the almugwood to make supports for the temple of the LORD and for the royal palace, and to make harps and lyres for the musicians. So much almugwood has never been imported or seen since that day.)

10:10
e ver 2

¹³King Solomon gave the queen of Sheba all she desired and asked for, besides what he had given her out of his royal bounty. Then she left and returned with her retinue to her own country.

¹⁴The weight of the gold[g] that Solomon received yearly was 666 talents,[d] ¹⁵not including the revenues from merchants and traders and from all the Arabian kings and the governors of the land.

10:11
f Ge 10:29;
1Ki 9:27-28

¹⁶King Solomon made two hundred large shields[h] of hammered gold; six hundred bekas[e] of gold went into each shield. ¹⁷He also made three hundred small shields of hammered gold, with three minas[f] of gold in each shield. The king put them in the Palace of the Forest of Lebanon.[i]

10:14
g 1Ki 9:28

¹⁸Then the king made a great throne inlaid with ivory and overlaid with fine gold. ¹⁹The throne had six steps, and its back had a rounded top. On both sides of the seat were armrests, with a lion standing beside each of them. ²⁰Twelve lions stood on the six steps, one at either end of each step. Nothing like it had ever been made for any other kingdom. ²¹All King Solomon's goblets were gold, and all the household articles in the Palace of the Forest of Lebanon were pure gold. Nothing was made of silver, because silver was considered of little value in Solomon's days. ²²The king

10:16
h 1Ki 14:26-28

10:17
i 1Ki 7:2

a 5 Or the ascent by which he went up to   b 10 That is, about 4 1/2 tons (about 4 metric tons)
c 11 Probably a variant of algumwood; also in verse 12   d 14 That is, about 25 tons (about 23 metric tons)   e 16 That is, about 7 1/2 pounds (about 3.5 kilograms)   f 17 That is, about 3 3/4 pounds (about 1.7 kilograms)

had a fleet of trading ships[aa] at sea along with the ships of Hiram. Once every three years it returned, carrying gold, silver and ivory, and apes and baboons.

²³King Solomon was greater in riches[b] and wisdom[c] than all the other kings of the earth. ²⁴The whole world sought audience with Solomon to hear the wisdom[d] God had put in his heart. ²⁵Year after year, everyone who came brought a gift—articles of silver and gold, robes, weapons and spices, and horses and mules.

²⁶Solomon accumulated chariots and horses;[e] he had fourteen hundred chariots and twelve thousand horses,[b] which he kept in the chariot cities and also with him in Jerusalem. ²⁷The king made silver as common[f] in Jerusalem as stones, and cedar as plentiful as sycamore-fig trees in the foothills. ²⁸Solomon's horses were imported from Egypt[c] and from Kue[d]—the royal merchants purchased them from Kue. ²⁹They imported a chariot from Egypt for six hundred shekels[e] of silver, and a horse for a hundred and fifty.[f] They also exported them to all the kings of the Hittites[g] and of the Arameans.

Chapter 11 Theme

11 King Solomon, however, loved many foreign women[h] besides Pharaoh's daughter—Moabites, Ammonites, Edomites, Sidonians and Hittites. ²They were from nations about which the LORD had told the Israelites, "You must not intermarry[i] with them, because they will surely turn your hearts after their gods." Nevertheless, Solomon held fast to them in love. ³He had seven hundred wives of royal birth and three hundred concubines, and his wives led him astray. ⁴As Solomon grew old, his wives turned his heart after other gods, and his heart was not fully devoted[j] to the LORD his God, as the heart of David his father had been. ⁵He followed Ashtoreth[k] the goddess of the Sidonians, and Molech[gl] the detestable god of the Ammonites. ⁶So Solomon did evil in the eyes of the LORD; he did not follow the LORD completely, as David his father had done.

⁷On a hill east[m] of Jerusalem, Solomon built a high place for Chemosh[n] the detestable god of Moab, and for Molech[o] the detestable god of the Ammonites. ⁸He did the same for all his foreign wives, who burned incense and offered sacrifices to their gods.

⁹The LORD became angry with Solomon because his heart had turned away from the LORD, the God of Israel, who had appeared[p] to him twice. ¹⁰Although he had forbidden Solomon to follow other

---

10:22
a 1Ki 9:26

10:23
b 1Ki 3:13
c 1Ki 4:30

10:24
d 1Ki 3:9,12,28

10:26
e Dt 17:16;
1Ki 4:26; 9:19;
2Ch 1:14; 9:25

10:27
f Dt 17:17

10:29
g 2Ki 7:6-7

11:1
h Dt 17:17;
Ne 13:26

11:2
i Ex 34:16;
Dt 7:3-4

11:4
j 1Ki 8:61; 9:4

11:5
k ver 33;
Jdg 2:13;
2Ki 23:13
l ver 7

11:7
m 2Ki 23:13
n Nu 21:29;
Jdg 11:24
o Lev 20:2-5;
Ac 7:43

11:9
p ver 2-3;
1Ki 3:5; 9:2

---

a 22 Hebrew *of ships of Tarshish*   b 26 Or *charioteers*   c 28 Or possibly *Muzur*, a region in Cilicia; also in verse 29   d 28 Probably *Cilicia*   e 29 That is, about 15 pounds (about 7 kilograms)   f 29 That is, about 3 3/4 pounds (about 1.7 kilograms)   g 5 Hebrew *Milcom*; also in verse 33

11:10
a 1Ki 9:6
b 1Ki 6:12

11:11
c ver 31;
1Ki 12:15-16;
2Ki 17:21

11:13
d 1Ki 12:20
e 2Sa 7:15
f Dt 12:11

11:15
g Dt 20:13;
2Sa 8:14;
1Ch 18:12

11:18
h Nu 10:12

11:23
i ver 14
j 2Sa 8:3

11:24
k 2Sa 8:5;
10:8,18

11:25
l 2Sa 10:19

11:26
m 2Sa 20:21;
1Ki 12:2;
2Ch 13:6

gods,*a* Solomon did not keep the LORD's command.*b* ¹¹So the LORD said to Solomon, "Since this is your attitude and you have not kept my covenant and my decrees, which I commanded you, I will most certainly tear*c* the kingdom away from you and give it to one of your subordinates. ¹²Nevertheless, for the sake of David your father, I will not do it during your lifetime. I will tear it out of the hand of your son. ¹³Yet I will not tear the whole kingdom from him, but will give him one tribe*d* for the sake*e* of David my servant and for the sake of Jerusalem, which I have chosen."*f*

¹⁴Then the LORD raised up against Solomon an adversary, Hadad the Edomite, from the royal line of Edom. ¹⁵Earlier when David was fighting with Edom, Joab the commander of the army, who had gone up to bury the dead, had struck down all the men in Edom.*g* ¹⁶Joab and all the Israelites stayed there for six months, until they had destroyed all the men in Edom. ¹⁷But Hadad, still only a boy, fled to Egypt with some Edomite officials who had served his father. ¹⁸They set out from Midian and went to Paran.*h* Then taking men from Paran with them, they went to Egypt, to Pharaoh king of Egypt, who gave Hadad a house and land and provided him with food.

¹⁹Pharaoh was so pleased with Hadad that he gave him a sister of his own wife, Queen Tahpenes, in marriage. ²⁰The sister of Tahpenes bore him a son named Genubath, whom Tahpenes brought up in the royal palace. There Genubath lived with Pharaoh's own children.

²¹While he was in Egypt, Hadad heard that David rested with his fathers and that Joab the commander of the army was also dead. Then Hadad said to Pharaoh, "Let me go, that I may return to my own country."

²²"What have you lacked here that you want to go back to your own country?" Pharaoh asked.

"Nothing," Hadad replied, "but do let me go!"

²³And God raised up against Solomon another adversary,*i* Rezon son of Eliada, who had fled from his master, Hadadezer*j* king of Zobah. ²⁴He gathered men around him and became the leader of a band of rebels when David destroyed the forces*a* ⌊of Zobah⌋; the rebels went to Damascus,*k* where they settled and took control. ²⁵Rezon was Israel's adversary as long as Solomon lived, adding to the trouble caused by Hadad. So Rezon ruled in Aram*l* and was hostile toward Israel.

²⁶Also, Jeroboam son of Nebat rebelled*m* against the king. He was one of Solomon's officials, an Ephraimite from Zeredah, and his mother was a widow named Zeruah.

INSIGHT

Religious Influences of Solomon's Wives

1. The Gods of Egypt (see page 104).
2. Ashtoreth—*Sidonian* (Canaanite) goddess of fertility, love, and war. Later she became the spouse of Baal (2 Kings 23:13).
3. Chemosh—*god of Moab*—meaning "to subdue." Solomon erected a sanctuary for Chemosh on a mountain east of Jerusalem (2 Kings 23:13; Jeremiah 48:7, 13, 46).
4. Molech— (also known as *Milcom*)—*Ammonite* god whose name means "king." At the request of his pagan wives, Solomon built sanctuaries to Molech (Milcom) on the Mount of Olives. Human sacrifices, usually children, were made to Molech. This practice was condemned by God (Leviticus 18:21; 20:3-5; 2 Kings 23:10; Jeremiah 32:35). Compare with 2 Kings 17:31 and Jeremiah 7:31; 19:5.

For more information, look up these names in a Bible dictionary.

a 24 Hebrew *destroyed them*

²⁷Here is the account of how he rebelled against the king: Solomon had built the supporting terraces[a][a] and had filled in the gap in the wall of the city of David his father. ²⁸Now Jeroboam was a man of standing,[b] and when Solomon saw how well[c] the young man did his work, he put him in charge of the whole labor force of the house of Joseph.

²⁹About that time Jeroboam was going out of Jerusalem, and Ahijah[d] the prophet of Shiloh met him on the way, wearing a new cloak. The two of them were alone out in the country, ³⁰and Ahijah took hold of the new cloak he was wearing and tore[e] it into twelve pieces. ³¹Then he said to Jeroboam, "Take ten pieces for yourself, for this is what the LORD, the God of Israel, says: 'See, I am going to tear[f] the kingdom out of Solomon's hand and give you ten tribes. ³²But for the sake of my servant David and the city of Jerusalem, which I have chosen out of all the tribes of Israel, he will have one tribe. ³³I will do this because they have[b] forsaken me and worshiped[g] Ashtoreth the goddess of the Sidonians, Chemosh the god of the Moabites, and Molech the god of the Ammonites, and have not walked in my ways, nor done what is right in my eyes, nor kept my statutes[h] and laws as David, Solomon's father, did.

³⁴"'But I will not take the whole kingdom out of Solomon's hand; I have made him ruler all the days of his life for the sake of David my servant, whom I chose and who observed my commands and statutes. ³⁵I will take the kingdom from his son's hands and give you ten tribes. ³⁶I will give one tribe[i] to his son so that David my servant may always have a lamp[j] before me in Jerusalem, the city where I chose to put my Name. ³⁷However, as for you, I will take you, and you will rule over all that your heart desires;[k] you will be king over Israel. ³⁸If you do whatever I command you and walk in my ways and do what is right in my eyes by keeping my statutes[l] and commands, as David my servant did, I will be with you. I will build you a dynasty[m] as enduring as the one I built for David and will give Israel to you. ³⁹I will humble David's descendants because of this, but not forever.'"

⁴⁰Solomon tried to kill Jeroboam, but Jeroboam fled to Egypt, to Shishak[n] the king, and stayed there until Solomon's death.

⁴¹As for the other events of Solomon's reign—all he did and the wisdom he displayed—are they not written in the book of the annals of Solomon? ⁴²Solomon reigned in Jerusalem over all Israel forty years. ⁴³Then he rested with his fathers and was buried in the city of David his father. And Rehoboam[o] his son succeeded him as king.

---

a27 Or *the Millo*   b33 Hebrew; Septuagint, Vulgate and Syriac *because he has*

11:27
a 1Ki 9:24

11:28
b Ru 2:1
c Pr 22:29

11:29
d 1Ki 12:15;
14:2; 2Ch 9:29

11:30
e 1Sa 15:27

11:31
f ver 11

11:33
g ver 5-7
h 1Ki 3:3

11:36
i ver 13;
1Ki 12:17
j 1Ki 15:4;
2Ki 8:19

11:37
k 2Sa 3:21

11:38
l Dt 17:19
m Jos 1:5;
2Sa 7:11,27

11:40
n 2Ch 12:2

11:43
o 1Ki 14:21;
Mt 1:7

Israel's Division and Captivity

Northern Kingdom of Israel
Ten tribes
Capital: Samaria

Kings: Jeroboam, followed by eighteen bad kings

◄········ 209 years ········►

722 B.C.
Taken captive by Assyria when Hoshea was king of Israel

1043 B.C.

Saul, David, Solomon
United Kingdom, 112 YEARS

931 B.C. **Kingdom Divided**

605 B.C.

538 B.C.
Decree of Cyrus

70-year
Captivity

Zerubbabel, Ezra, Nehemiah

536 B.C.
Started rebuilding the Temple

536 B.C.

when Jehoiakim was king of Judah

when Jehoiachin was king of Judah

when Zedekiah was king of Judah

Southern Kingdom of Judah
Two tribes (Benjamin and Judah)
Capital: Jerusalem

Kings: Rehoboam, followed by eleven bad and eight good kings

Judah taken captive by Babylon 586 B.C.

Daniel and friends

Ezekiel and ten thousand

Jerusalem destroyed

◄··········· 345 years ···············►

605 B.C.

597 B.C.

586 B.C.

Three sieges of Jerusalem by Babylonians

12:2
a 1Ki 11:40

Chapter 12 Theme

12 Rehoboam went to Shechem, for all the Israelites had gone there to make him king. ²When Jeroboam son of Nebat heard this (he was still in Egypt, where he had fled*a* from King Solomon), he returned from*a* Egypt. ³So they sent for Jeroboam, and he and the whole assembly of Israel went to Rehoboam and said to him: ⁴"Your father put a heavy yoke*b* on us, but now lighten the harsh labor and the heavy yoke he put on us, and we will serve you."

12:4
b 1Sa 8:11-18;
1Ki 4:20-28

⁵Rehoboam answered, "Go away for three days and then come back to me." So the people went away.

⁶Then King Rehoboam consulted the elders*c* who had served his father Solomon during his lifetime. "How would you advise me to answer these people?" he asked.

12:6
c 1Ki 4:2

⁷They replied, "If today you will be a servant to these people and serve them and give them a favorable answer,*d* they will always be your servants."

⁸But Rehoboam rejected the advice the elders gave him and consulted the young men who had grown up with him and were serving him. ⁹He asked them, "What is your advice? How should we answer these people who say to me, 'Lighten the yoke your father put on us'?"

¹⁰The young men who had grown up with him replied, "Tell these people who have said to you, 'Your father put a heavy yoke

12:7
d Pr 15:1   a 2 Or he remained in

on us, but make our yoke lighter'—tell them, 'My little finger is thicker than my father's waist. ¹¹My father laid on you a heavy yoke; I will make it even heavier. My father scourged you with whips; I will scourge you with scorpions.'"

¹²Three days later Jeroboam and all the people returned to Rehoboam, as the king had said, "Come back to me in three days." ¹³The king answered the people harshly. Rejecting the advice given him by the elders, ¹⁴he followed the advice of the young men and said, "My father made your yoke heavy; I will make it even heavier. My father scourged*ᵃ* you with whips; I will scourge you with scorpions." ¹⁵So the king did not listen to the people, for this turn of events was from the LORD,*ᵇ* to fulfill the word the LORD had spoken to Jeroboam son of Nebat through Ahijah*ᶜ* the Shilonite.

¹⁶When all Israel saw that the king refused to listen to them, they answered the king:

> "What share do we have in David,
>   what part in Jesse's son?
> To your tents, O Israel!*ᵈ*
>   Look after your own house, O David!"

So the Israelites went home. ¹⁷But as for the Israelites who were living in the towns of Judah,*ᵉ* Rehoboam still ruled over them.

¹⁸King Rehoboam sent out Adoniram,*ᵃᶠ* who was in charge of forced labor, but all Israel stoned him to death. King Rehoboam, however, managed to get into his chariot and escape to Jerusalem. ¹⁹So Israel has been in rebellion against the house of David*ᵍ* to this day.

²⁰When all the Israelites heard that Jeroboam had returned, they sent and called him to the assembly and made him king over all Israel. Only the tribe of Judah remained loyal to the house of David.*ʰ*

²¹When Rehoboam arrived in Jerusalem, he mustered the whole house of Judah and the tribe of Benjamin—a hundred and eighty thousand fighting men—to make war*ⁱ* against the house of Israel and to regain the kingdom for Rehoboam son of Solomon.

²²But this word of God came to Shemaiah*ʲ* the man of God: ²³"Say to Rehoboam son of Solomon king of Judah, to the whole house of Judah and Benjamin, and to the rest of the people, ²⁴'This is what the LORD says: Do not go up to fight against your brothers, the Israelites. Go home, every one of you, for this is my doing.'" So they obeyed the word of the LORD and went home again, as the LORD had ordered.

ᵃ18 Some Septuagint manuscripts and Syriac (see also 1 Kings 4:6 and 5:14); Hebrew *Adoram*

12:14
ᵃEx 1:14; 5:5-9, 16-18

12:15
ᵇver 24;
Dt 2:30;
Jdg 14:4;
2Ch 22:7; 25:20
ᶜ1Ki 11:29

12:16
ᵈ2Sa 20:1

12:17
ᵉ1Ki 11:13,36

12:18
ᶠ2Sa 20:24;
1Ki 4:6; 5:14

12:19
ᵍ2Ki 17:21

12:20
ʰ1Ki 11:13,32

12:21
ⁱ2Ch 11:1

12:22
ʲ2Ch 12:5-7

12:25
a Jdg 9:45
b Jdg 8:8,17

12:27
c Dt 12:5-6

12:28
d Ex 32:4;
2Ki 10:29;
17:16
e Ex 32:8

12:29
f Ge 28:19
g Jdg 18:27-31

12:30
h 1Ki 13:34;
2Ki 17:21

12:31
i 1Ki 13:32
j Nu 3:10;
1Ki 13:33;
2Ki 17:32;
2Ch 11:14-15;
13:9

12:32
k Lev 23:33-34;
Nu 29:12

12:33
l Nu 15:39;
1Ki 13:1;
Am 7:13

13:1
m 2Ki 23:17
n 1Ki 12:32-33

13:2
o 2Ki 23:15-16,
20

13:3
p Jdg 6:17;
Isa 7:14;
Jn 2:11;
1Co 1:22

²⁵Then Jeroboam fortified Shechem^a in the hill country of Ephraim and lived there. From there he went out and built up Peniel.^{ab}

²⁶Jeroboam thought to himself, "The kingdom will now likely revert to the house of David. ²⁷If these people go up to offer sacrifices at the temple of the LORD in Jerusalem,^c they will again give their allegiance to their lord, Rehoboam king of Judah. They will kill me and return to King Rehoboam."

²⁸After seeking advice, the king made two golden calves.^d He said to the people, "It is too much for you to go up to Jerusalem. Here are your gods, O Israel, who brought you up out of Egypt."^e ²⁹One he set up in Bethel,^f and the other in Dan.^g ³⁰And this thing became a sin;^h the people went even as far as Dan to worship the one there.

³¹Jeroboam built shrinesⁱ on high places and appointed priests^j from all sorts of people, even though they were not Levites. ³²He instituted a festival on the fifteenth day of the eighth^k month, like the festival held in Judah, and offered sacrifices on the altar. This he did in Bethel, sacrificing to the calves he had made. And at Bethel he also installed priests at the high places he had made. ³³On the fifteenth day of the eighth month, a month of his own choosing, he offered sacrifices on the altar he had built at Bethel.^l So he instituted the festival for the Israelites and went up to the altar to make offerings.

Chapter 13 Theme _____

13 By the word of the LORD a man of God^m came from Judah to Bethel,ⁿ as Jeroboam was standing by the altar to make an offering. ²He cried out against the altar by the word of the LORD: "O altar, altar! This is what the LORD says: 'A son named Josiah^o will be born to the house of David. On you he will sacrifice the priests of the high places who now make offerings here, and human bones will be burned on you.'" ³That same day the man of God gave a sign:^p "This is the sign the LORD has declared: The altar will be split apart and the ashes on it will be poured out."

⁴When King Jeroboam heard what the man of God cried out against the altar at Bethel, he stretched out his hand from the altar and said, "Seize him!" But the hand he stretched out toward the man shriveled up, so that he could not pull it back. ⁵Also, the altar was split apart and its ashes poured out according to the sign given by the man of God by the word of the LORD.

The Divided Kingdom 931–586 B.C.

a 25 Hebrew *Penuel*, a variant of *Peniel*

⁶Then the king said to the man of God, "Intercede*ᵃ* with the LORD your God and pray for me that my hand may be restored." So the man of God interceded with the LORD, and the king's hand was restored and became as it was before.

⁷The king said to the man of God, "Come home with me and have something to eat, and I will give you a gift."*ᵇ*

⁸But the man of God answered the king, "Even if you were to give me half your possessions,*ᶜ* I would not go with you, nor would I eat bread*ᵈ* or drink water here. ⁹For I was commanded by the word of the LORD: 'You must not eat bread or drink water or return by the way you came.'" ¹⁰So he took another road and did not return by the way he had come to Bethel.

¹¹Now there was a certain old prophet living in Bethel, whose sons came and told him all that the man of God had done there that day. They also told their father what he had said to the king. ¹²Their father asked them, "Which way did he go?" And his sons showed him which road the man of God from Judah had taken. ¹³So he said to his sons, "Saddle the donkey for me." And when they had saddled the donkey for him, he mounted it ¹⁴and rode after the man of God. He found him sitting under an oak tree and asked, "Are you the man of God who came from Judah?"

"I am," he replied.

¹⁵So the prophet said to him, "Come home with me and eat."

¹⁶The man of God said, "I cannot turn back and go with you, nor can I eat bread*ᵉ* or drink water with you in this place. ¹⁷I have been told by the word of the LORD: 'You must not eat bread or drink water there or return by the way you came.'"

¹⁸The old prophet answered, "I too am a prophet, as you are. And an angel said to me by the word of the LORD: 'Bring him back with you to your house so that he may eat bread and drink water.'" (But he was lying*ᶠ* to him.) ¹⁹So the man of God returned with him and ate and drank in his house.

²⁰While they were sitting at the table, the word of the LORD came to the old prophet who had brought him back. ²¹He cried out to the man of God who had come from Judah, "This is what the LORD says: 'You have defied*ᵍ* the word of the LORD and have not kept the command the LORD your God gave you. ²²You came back and ate bread and drank water in the place where he told you not to eat or drink. Therefore your body will not be buried in the tomb of your fathers.'"

²³When the man of God had finished eating and drinking, the prophet who had brought him back saddled his donkey for him. ²⁴As he went on his way, a lion*ʰ* met him on the road and killed him, and his body was thrown down on the road, with both the donkey and the lion standing beside it. ²⁵Some people who passed

13:6
ᵃ Ex 8:8; 9:28; 10:17; Lk 6:27-28; Ac 8:24; Jas 5:16

13:7
ᵇ 1Sa 9:7; 2Ki 5:15

13:8
ᶜ Nu 22:18; 24:13
ᵈ ver 16

13:16
ᵉ ver 8

13:18
ᶠ Dt 13:3

13:21
ᵍ ver 26

13:24
ʰ 1Ki 20:36

13:30
a Jer 22:18

13:31
b 2Ki 23:18

13:32
c ver 2;
Lev 26:30
d 1Ki 16:24,28
e 2Ki 23:16

13:33
f 1Ki 12:31;
2Ch 11:15; 13:9

13:34
g 1Ki 12:30
h 1Ki 14:10

14:2
i 1Sa 28:8;
2Sa 14:2;
1Ki 11:29

14:3
j 1Sa 9:7

14:7
k 2Sa 12:7-8;
1Ki 16:2

14:8
l 1Ki 11:31,
33,38

by saw the body thrown down there, with the lion standing beside the body, and they went and reported it in the city where the old prophet lived.

²⁶When the prophet who had brought him back from his journey heard of it, he said, "It is the man of God who defied the word of the LORD. The LORD has given him over to the lion, which has mauled him and killed him, as the word of the LORD had warned him."

²⁷The prophet said to his sons, "Saddle the donkey for me," and they did so. ²⁸Then he went out and found the body thrown down on the road, with the donkey and the lion standing beside it. The lion had neither eaten the body nor mauled the donkey. ²⁹So the prophet picked up the body of the man of God, laid it on the donkey, and brought it back to his own city to mourn for him and bury him. ³⁰Then he laid the body in his own tomb, and they mourned over him and said, "Oh, my brother!"*a*

³¹After burying him, he said to his sons, "When I die, bury me in the grave where the man of God is buried; lay my bones*b* beside his bones. ³²For the message he declared by the word of the LORD against the altar in Bethel and against all the shrines on the high places*c* in the towns of Samaria*d* will certainly come true."*e*

³³Even after this, Jeroboam did not change his evil ways, but once more appointed priests for the high places from all sorts*f* of people. Anyone who wanted to become a priest he consecrated for the high places. ³⁴This was the sin*g* of the house of Jeroboam that led to its downfall and to its destruction*h* from the face of the earth.

Chapter 14 Theme

14 At that time Abijah son of Jeroboam became ill, ²and Jeroboam said to his wife, "Go, disguise yourself, so you won't be recognized as the wife of Jeroboam. Then go to Shiloh. Ahijah*i* the prophet is there—the one who told me I would be king over this people. ³Take ten loaves of bread*j* with you, some cakes and a jar of honey, and go to him. He will tell you what will happen to the boy." ⁴So Jeroboam's wife did what he said and went to Ahijah's house in Shiloh.

Now Ahijah could not see; his sight was gone because of his age. ⁵But the LORD had told Ahijah, "Jeroboam's wife is coming to ask you about her son, for he is ill, and you are to give her such and such an answer. When she arrives, she will pretend to be someone else."

⁶So when Ahijah heard the sound of her footsteps at the door, he said, "Come in, wife of Jeroboam. Why this pretense? I have been sent to you with bad news. ⁷Go, tell Jeroboam that this is what the LORD, the God of Israel, says: 'I raised you up from among the people and made you a leader*k* over my people Israel. ⁸I tore*l* the kingdom away from the house of David and gave it to you, but

you have not been like my servant David, who kept my commands and followed me with all his heart, doing only what was right[a] in my eyes. [9]You have done more evil than all who lived before you. You have made for yourself other gods, idols[b] made of metal; you have provoked me to anger and thrust me behind your back.[c]

[10]"'Because of this, I am going to bring disaster on the house of Jeroboam. I will cut off from Jeroboam every last male in Israel— slave or free.[d] I will burn up the house of Jeroboam as one burns dung, until it is all gone.[e] [11]Dogs[f] will eat those belonging to Jeroboam who die in the city, and the birds of the air will feed on those who die in the country. The LORD has spoken!'

[12]"As for you, go back home. When you set foot in your city, the boy will die. [13]All Israel will mourn for him and bury him. He is the only one belonging to Jeroboam who will be buried, because he is the only one in the house of Jeroboam in whom the LORD, the God of Israel, has found anything good.[g]

[14]"The LORD will raise up for himself a king over Israel who will cut off the family of Jeroboam. This is the day! What? Yes, even now.[a] [15]And the LORD will strike Israel, so that it will be like a reed swaying in the water. He will uproot[h] Israel from this good land that he gave to their forefathers and scatter them beyond the River,[b] because they provoked[i] the LORD to anger by making Asherah[j] poles.[c] [16]And he will give Israel up because of the sins[k] Jeroboam has committed and has caused Israel to commit."

[17]Then Jeroboam's wife got up and left and went to Tirzah.[l] As soon as she stepped over the threshold of the house, the boy died. [18]They buried him, and all Israel mourned for him, as the LORD had said through his servant the prophet Ahijah.

[19]The other events of Jeroboam's reign, his wars and how he ruled, are written in the book of the annals of the kings of Israel. [20]He reigned for twenty-two years and then rested with his fathers. And Nadab his son succeeded him as king.

[21]Rehoboam son of Solomon was king in Judah. He was forty-one years old when he became king, and he reigned seventeen years in Jerusalem, the city the LORD had chosen out of all the tribes of Israel in which to put his Name. His mother's name was Naamah; she was an Ammonite.[m]

[22]Judah[n] did evil in the eyes of the LORD. By the sins they committed they stirred up his jealous anger[o] more than their fathers had done. [23]They also set up for themselves high places, sacred stones[p] and Asherah poles on every high hill and under every spreading tree.[q] [24]There were even male shrine prostitutes[r] in the land; the people engaged in all the detestable practices of the nations the LORD had driven out before the Israelites.

---

a 14 The meaning of the Hebrew for this sentence is uncertain.   b 15 That is, the Euphrates
c 15 That is, symbols of the goddess Asherah; here and elsewhere in 1 Kings

---

14:8
a 1Ki 15:5

14:9
b Ex 34:17;
1Ki 12:28;
2Ch 11:15
c Ne 9:26;
Ps 50:17;
Eze 23:35

14:10
d Dt 32:36;
1Ki 21:21;
2Ki 9:8-9; 14:26
e 1Ki 15:29

14:11
f 1Ki 16:4; 21:24

14:13
g 2Ch 12:12;
19:3

14:15
h Dt 29:28;
2Ki 15:29; 17:6;
Ps 52:5
i Jos 23:15-16
j Ex 34:13;
Dt 12:3

14:16
k 1Ki 12:30;
13:34; 15:30,34;
16:2

14:17
l ver 12;
1Ki 15:33;
16:6-9

14:21
m ver 31;
1Ki 11:1;
2Ch 12:13

14:22
n 2Ch 12:1
o Dt 32:21;
Ps 78:58;
1Co 10:22

14:23
p Dt 16:22;
2Ki 17:9-10;
Eze 16:24-25
q Dt 12:2;
Isa 57:5

14:24
r Dt 23:17;
1Ki 15:12;
2Ki 23:7

14:25
a 1Ki 11:40;
2Ch 12:2

²⁵In the fifth year of King Rehoboam, Shishak king of Egypt attacked[a] Jerusalem. ²⁶He carried off the treasures of the temple[b] of the LORD and the treasures of the royal palace. He took everything, including all the gold shields[c] Solomon had made. ²⁷So King Rehoboam made bronze shields to replace them and assigned these to the commanders of the guard on duty at the entrance to the royal palace. ²⁸Whenever the king went to the LORD's temple, the guards bore the shields, and afterward they returned them to the guardroom.

14:26
b 1Ki 15:15,18
c 1Ki 10:17

14:30
d 1Ki 12:21; 15:6

²⁹As for the other events of Rehoboam's reign, and all he did, are they not written in the book of the annals of the kings of Judah? ³⁰There was continual warfare[d] between Rehoboam and Jeroboam. ³¹And Rehoboam rested with his fathers and was buried with them in the City of David. His mother's name was Naamah; she was an Ammonite.[e] And Abijah[a] his son succeeded him as king.

14:31
e ver 21;
2Ch 12:16

Chapter 15 Theme

15 In the eighteenth year of the reign of Jeroboam son of Nebat, Abijah[b] became king of Judah, ²and he reigned in Jerusalem three years. His mother's name was Maacah[f] daughter of Abishalom.[c]

15:2
f 2Ch 11:20; 13:2

³He committed all the sins his father had done before him; his heart was not fully devoted[g] to the LORD his God, as the heart of David his forefather had been. ⁴Nevertheless, for David's sake the LORD his God gave him a lamp[h] in Jerusalem by raising up a son to succeed him and by making Jerusalem strong. ⁵For David had done what was right in the eyes of the LORD and had not failed to keep[i] any of the LORD's commands all the days of his life—except in the case of Uriah[j] the Hittite.

15:3
g 1Ki 11:4;
Ps 119:80

15:4
h 2Sa 21:17;
1Ki 11:36;
2Ch 21:7

⁶There was war[k] between Rehoboam[d] and Jeroboam throughout ₍Abijah's₎ lifetime. ⁷As for the other events of Abijah's reign, and all he did, are they not written in the book of the annals of the kings of Judah? There was war between Abijah and Jeroboam. ⁸And Abijah rested with his fathers and was buried in the City of David. And Asa his son succeeded him as king.

15:5
i 1Ki 9:4; 14:8
j 2Sa 11:2-27;
12:9

⁹In the twentieth year of Jeroboam king of Israel, Asa became king of Judah, ¹⁰and he reigned in Jerusalem forty-one years. His grandmother's name was Maacah[l] daughter of Abishalom.

15:6
k 1Ki 14:30

¹¹Asa did what was right in the eyes of the LORD, as his father David had done. ¹²He expelled the male shrine prostitutes[m] from the land and got rid of all the idols his fathers had made. ¹³He even

15:10
l ver 2

15:12
m 1Ki 14:24;
22:46

---

a 31 Some Hebrew manuscripts and Septuagint (see also 2 Chron. 12:16); most Hebrew manuscripts *Abijam* b 1 Some Hebrew manuscripts and Septuagint (see also 2 Chron. 12:16); most Hebrew manuscripts *Abijam*; also in verses 7 and 8 c 2 A variant of *Absalom*; also in verse 10 d 6 Most Hebrew manuscripts; some Hebrew manuscripts and Syriac *Abijam* (that is, Abijah) deposed his grandmother Maacah from her position as queen mother, because she had made a repulsive Asherah pole. Asa cut the pole down[a] and burned it in the Kidron Valley. [14]Although he did not remove the high places, Asa's heart was fully committed[b] to the LORD all his life. [15]He brought into the temple of the LORD the silver and gold and the articles that he and his father had dedicated.[c]

[16]There was war[d] between Asa and Baasha king of Israel throughout their reigns. [17]Baasha king of Israel went up against Judah and fortified Ramah[e] to prevent anyone from leaving or entering the territory of Asa king of Judah.

[18]Asa then took all the silver and gold that was left in the treasuries of the LORD's temple[f] and of his own palace. He entrusted it to his officials and sent[g] them to Ben-Hadad[h] son of Tabrimmon, the son of Hezion, the king of Aram, who was ruling in Damascus. [19]"Let there be a treaty between me and you," he said, "as there was between my father and your father. See, I am sending you a gift of silver and gold. Now break your treaty with Baasha king of Israel so he will withdraw from me."

[20]Ben-Hadad agreed with King Asa and sent the commanders of his forces against the towns of Israel. He conquered[i] Ijon, Dan, Abel Beth Maacah and all Kinnereth in addition to Naphtali. [21]When Baasha heard this, he stopped building Ramah and withdrew to Tirzah. [22]Then King Asa issued an order to all Judah—no one was exempt—and they carried away from Ramah the stones and timber Baasha had been using there. With them King Asa built up Geba[j] in Benjamin, and also Mizpah.

[23]As for all the other events of Asa's reign, all his achievements, all he did and the cities he built, are they not written in the book of the annals of the kings of Judah? In his old age, however, his feet became diseased. [24]Then Asa rested with his fathers and was buried with them in the city of his father David. And Jehoshaphat[k] his son succeeded him as king.

[25]Nadab son of Jeroboam became king of Israel in the second year of Asa king of Judah, and he reigned over Israel two years. [26]He did evil in the eyes of the LORD, walking in the ways of his father[l] and in his sin, which he had caused Israel to commit.

[27]Baasha son of Ahijah of the house of Issachar plotted against him, and he struck him down[m] at Gibbethon,[n] a Philistine town, while Nadab and all Israel were besieging it. [28]Baasha killed Nadab in the third year of Asa king of Judah and succeeded him as king.

[29]As soon as he began to reign, he killed Jeroboam's whole family.[o] He did not leave Jeroboam anyone that breathed, but destroyed them all, according to the word of the LORD given through his servant Ahijah the Shilonite— [30]because of the sins[p] Jeroboam had committed and had caused Israel to commit, and because he provoked the LORD, the God of Israel, to anger.

15:13 [a]Ex 32:20

15:14 [b]ver 3; 1Ki 8:61; 22:43

15:15 [c]1Ki 7:51

15:16 [d]ver 32

15:17 [e]Jos 18:25; 1Ki 12:27

15:18 [f]ver 15; 1Ki 14:26 [g]2Ki 12:18 [h]1Ki 11:23-24

15:20 [i]Jdg 18:29; 2Sa 20:14; 2Ki 15:29

15:22 [j]Jos 18:24; 21:17

15:24 [k]Mt 1:8

15:26 [l]1Ki 12:30; 14:16

15:27 [m]1Ki 14:14 [n]Jos 19:44; 21:23

15:29 [o]1Ki 14:10,14

15:30 [p]1Ki 14:9,16

15:32
a ver 16

15:34
b ver 26;
1Ki 12:28-29;
13:33; 14:16

16:1
c ver 7;
2Ch 19:2; 20:34
d 2Ch 16:7

16:2
e 1Sa 2:8
f 1Ki 14:7-9
g 1Ki 15:34

16:3
h ver 11;
1Ki 14:10;
15:29; 21:22

16:4
i 1Ki 14:11

16:5
j 1Ki 14:19;
15:31

16:6
k 1Ki 14:17;
15:33

16:7
l 1Ki 15:27,29
m ver 1

16:9
n 2Ki 9:30-33
o 1Ki 18:3

16:11
p ver 3

16:13
q Dt 32:21;
1Sa 12:21;
Isa 41:29

³¹As for the other events of Nadab's reign, and all he did, are they not written in the book of the annals of the kings of Israel? ³²There was war*a* between Asa and Baasha king of Israel throughout their reigns.

³³In the third year of Asa king of Judah, Baasha son of Ahijah became king of all Israel in Tirzah, and he reigned twenty-four years. ³⁴He did evil*b* in the eyes of the LORD, walking in the ways of Jeroboam and in his sin, which he had caused Israel to commit.

Chapter 16 Theme _____

16 Then the word of the LORD came to Jehu*c* son of Hanani*d* against Baasha: ²"I lifted you up from the dust*e* and made you leader*f* of my people Israel, but you walked in the ways of Jeroboam and caused*g* my people Israel to sin and to provoke me to anger by their sins. ³So I am about to consume Baasha and his house,*h* and I will make your house like that of Jeroboam son of Nebat. ⁴Dogs*i* will eat those belonging to Baasha who die in the city, and the birds of the air will feed on those who die in the country."

⁵As for the other events of Baasha's reign, what he did and his achievements, are they not written in the book of the annals*j* of the kings of Israel? ⁶Baasha rested with his fathers and was buried in Tirzah.*k* And Elah his son succeeded him as king.

⁷Moreover, the word of the LORD came*l* through the prophet Jehu*m* son of Hanani to Baasha and his house, because of all the evil he had done in the eyes of the LORD, provoking him to anger by the things he did, and becoming like the house of Jeroboam—and also because he destroyed it.

⁸In the twenty-sixth year of Asa king of Judah, Elah son of Baasha became king of Israel, and he reigned in Tirzah two years.

⁹Zimri, one of his officials, who had command of half his chariots, plotted against him. Elah was in Tirzah at the time, getting drunk*n* in the home of Arza, the man in charge*o* of the palace at Tirzah. ¹⁰Zimri came in, struck him down and killed him in the twenty-seventh year of Asa king of Judah. Then he succeeded him as king.

¹¹As soon as he began to reign and was seated on the throne, he killed off Baasha's whole family.*p* He did not spare a single male, whether relative or friend. ¹²So Zimri destroyed the whole family of Baasha, in accordance with the word of the LORD spoken against Baasha through the prophet Jehu— ¹³because of all the sins Baasha and his son Elah had committed and had caused Israel to commit, so that they provoked the LORD, the God of Israel, to anger by their worthless idols.*q*

¹⁴As for the other events of Elah's reign, and all he did, are they not written in the book of the annals of the kings of Israel?

¹⁵In the twenty-seventh year of Asa king of Judah, Zimri reigned in Tirzah seven days. The army was encamped near Gibbethon,ᵃ a Philistine town. ¹⁶When the Israelites in the camp heard that Zimri had plotted against the king and murdered him, they proclaimed Omri, the commander of the army, king over Israel that very day there in the camp. ¹⁷Then Omri and all the Israelites with him withdrew from Gibbethon and laid siege to Tirzah. ¹⁸When Zimri saw that the city was taken, he went into the citadel of the royal palace and set the palace on fire around him. So he died, ¹⁹because of the sins he had committed, doing evil in the eyes of the LORD and walking in the ways of Jeroboam and in the sin he had committed and had caused Israel to commit.

²⁰As for the other events of Zimri's reign, and the rebellion he carried out, are they not written in the book of the annals of the kings of Israel?

²¹Then the people of Israel were split into two factions; half supported Tibni son of Ginath for king, and the other half supported Omri. ²²But Omri's followers proved stronger than those of Tibni son of Ginath. So Tibni died and Omri became king.

²³In the thirty-first year of Asa king of Judah, Omri became king of Israel, and he reigned twelve years, six of them in Tirzah.ᵇ ²⁴He bought the hill of Samaria from Shemer for two talentsᵃ of silver and built a city on the hill, calling it Samaria,ᶜ after Shemer, the name of the former owner of the hill.

²⁵But Omri did evilᵈ in the eyes of the LORD and sinned more than all those before him. ²⁶He walked in all the ways of Jeroboam son of Nebat and in his sin, which he had causedᵉ Israel to commit, so that they provoked the LORD, the God of Israel, to anger by their worthless idols.ᶠ

²⁷As for the other events of Omri's reign, what he did and the things he achieved, are they not written in the book of the annals of the kings of Israel? ²⁸Omri rested with his fathers and was buried in Samaria. And Ahab his son succeeded him as king.

²⁹In the thirty-eighth year of Asa king of Judah, Ahab son of Omri became king of Israel, and he reigned in Samaria over Israel twenty-two years. ³⁰Ahab son of Omri did moreᵍ evil in the eyes of the LORD than any of those before him. ³¹He not only considered it trivial to commit the sins of Jeroboam son of Nebat, but he also marriedʰ Jezebel daughterⁱ of Ethbaal king of the Sidonians, and began to serve Baalʲ and worship him. ³²He set up an altar for Baal in the templeᵏ of Baal that he built in Samaria. ³³Ahab also made an Asherah poleˡ and did moreᵐ to provoke the LORD, the God of Israel, to anger than did all the kings of Israel before him.

ᵃ24 That is, about 150 pounds (about 70 kilograms)

16:15
ᵃJos 19:44;
1Ki 15:27

16:23
ᵇ1Ki 15:21

16:24
ᶜ1Ki 13:32;
Jn 4:4

16:25
ᵈDt 4:25;
Mic 6:16

16:26
ᵉver 19
ᶠDt 32:21

16:30
ᵍver 25;
1Ki 14:9

16:31
ʰDt 7:3;
1Ki 11:2
ⁱJdg 18:7;
2Ki 9:34
ʲ2Ki 10:18;
17:16

16:32
ᵏ2Ki 10:21,27;
11:18

16:33
ˡ2Ki 13:6
ᵐver 29,30;
1Ki 14:9; 21:25

³⁴In Ahab's time, Hiel of Bethel rebuilt Jericho. He laid its foundations at the cost of his firstborn son Abiram, and he set up its gates at the cost of his youngest son Segub, in accordance with the word of the LORD spoken by Joshua son of Nun.*a*

Chapter 17 Theme _____

17:1
b Mal 4:5;
Jas 5:17
c Jdg 12:4
d Dt 10:8;
1Ki 18:1;
2Ki 3:14;
Lk 4:25

17 Now Elijah*b* the Tishbite, from Tishbe*a* in Gilead,*c* said to Ahab, "As the LORD, the God of Israel, lives, whom I serve, there will be neither dew nor rain*d* in the next few years except at my word."

²Then the word of the LORD came to Elijah: ³"Leave here, turn eastward and hide in the Kerith Ravine, east of the Jordan. ⁴You will drink from the brook, and I have ordered the ravens*e* to feed you there."

⁵So he did what the LORD had told him. He went to the Kerith Ravine, east of the Jordan, and stayed there. ⁶The ravens brought him bread and meat in the morning*f* and bread and meat in the evening, and he drank from the brook.

⁷Some time later the brook dried up because there had been no rain in the land. ⁸Then the word of the LORD came to him: ⁹"Go at once to Zarephath*g* of Sidon and stay there. I have commanded a widow*h* in that place to supply you with food." ¹⁰So he went to Zarephath. When he came to the town gate, a widow was there gathering sticks. He called to her and asked, "Would you bring me a little water in a jar so I may have a drink?"*i* ¹¹As she was going to get it, he called, "And bring me, please, a piece of bread."

¹²"As surely as the LORD your God lives," she replied, "I don't have any bread—only a handful of flour in a jar and a little oil*j* in a jug. I am gathering a few sticks to take home and make a meal for myself and my son, that we may eat it—and die."

¹³Elijah said to her, "Don't be afraid. Go home and do as you have said. But first make a small cake of bread for me from what you have and bring it to me, and then make something for yourself and your son. ¹⁴For this is what the LORD, the God of Israel, says: 'The jar of flour will not be used up and the jug of oil will not run dry until the day the LORD gives rain on the land.'"

¹⁵She went away and did as Elijah had told her. So there was food every day for Elijah and for the woman and her family. ¹⁶For the jar of flour was not used up and the jug of oil did not run dry, in keeping with the word of the LORD spoken by Elijah.

¹⁷Some time later the son of the woman who owned the house became ill. He grew worse and worse, and finally stopped breathing. ¹⁸She said to Elijah, "What do you have against me, man of God? Did you come to remind me of my sin*k* and kill my son?"

a *1* Or *Tishbite, of the settlers*

¹⁹"Give me your son," Elijah replied. He took him from her arms, carried him to the upper room where he was staying, and laid him on his bed. ²⁰Then he cried out to the LORD, "O LORD my God, have you brought tragedy also upon this widow I am staying with, by causing her son to die?" ²¹Then he stretched*ᵃ* himself out on the boy three times and cried to the LORD, "O LORD my God, let this boy's life return to him!"

²²The LORD heard Elijah's cry, and the boy's life returned to him, and he lived. ²³Elijah picked up the child and carried him down from the room into the house. He gave him to his mother and said, "Look, your son is alive!"

²⁴Then the woman said to Elijah, "Now I know*ᵇ* that you are a man of God and that the word of the LORD from your mouth is the truth."*ᶜ*

Chapter 18 Theme

18 After a long time, in the third*ᵈ* year, the word of the LORD came to Elijah: "Go and present yourself to Ahab, and I will send rain*ᵉ* on the land." ²So Elijah went to present himself to Ahab.

Now the famine was severe in Samaria, ³and Ahab had summoned Obadiah, who was in charge*ᶠ* of his palace. (Obadiah was a devout believer*ᵍ* in the LORD. ⁴While Jezebel*ʰ* was killing off the LORD's prophets, Obadiah had taken a hundred prophets and hidden*ⁱ* them in two caves, fifty in each, and had supplied them with food and water.) ⁵Ahab had said to Obadiah, "Go through the land to all the springs and valleys. Maybe we can find some grass to keep the horses and mules alive so we will not have to kill any of our animals." ⁶So they divided the land they were to cover, Ahab going in one direction and Obadiah in another.

⁷As Obadiah was walking along, Elijah met him. Obadiah recognized*ʲ* him, bowed down to the ground, and said, "Is it really you, my lord Elijah?"

⁸"Yes," he replied. "Go tell your master, 'Elijah is here.'"

⁹"What have I done wrong," asked Obadiah, "that you are handing your servant over to Ahab to be put to death? ¹⁰As surely as the LORD your God lives, there is not a nation or kingdom where my master has not sent someone to look*ᵏ* for you. And whenever a nation or kingdom claimed you were not there, he made them swear they could not find you. ¹¹But now you tell me to go to my master and say, 'Elijah is here.' ¹²I don't know where the Spirit*ˡ* of the LORD may carry you when I leave you. If I go and tell Ahab and he doesn't find you, he will kill me. Yet I your servant have worshiped the LORD since my youth. ¹³Haven't you heard, my lord, what I did while Jezebel was killing the prophets of the LORD? I hid a hundred of the LORD's prophets in two caves, fifty in each,

17:21
*ᵃ*2Ki 4:34;
Ac 20:10

17:24
*ᵇ*Jn 3:2; 16:30
*ᶜ*Ps 119:43;
Jn 17:17

18:1
*ᵈ*1Ki 17:1;
Lk 4:25; Jas 5:17
*ᵉ*Dt 28:12

18:3
*ᶠ*1Ki 16:9
*ᵍ*Ne 7:2

18:4
*ʰ*2Ki 9:7
*ⁱ*ver 13; Isa 16:3

18:7
*ʲ*2Ki 1:8

18:10
*ᵏ*1Ki 17:3

18:12
*ˡ*2Ki 2:16;
Eze 3:14;
Ac 8:39

18:15
a 1Ki 17:1

and supplied them with food and water. ¹⁴And now you tell me to go to my master and say, 'Elijah is here.' He will kill me!"

¹⁵Elijah said, "As the LORD Almighty lives, whom I serve, I will surely present*a* myself to Ahab today."

18:17
b Jos 7:25;
1Ki 21:20;
Ac 16:20

¹⁶So Obadiah went to meet Ahab and told him, and Ahab went to meet Elijah. ¹⁷When he saw Elijah, he said to him, "Is that you, you troubler*b* of Israel?"

¹⁸"I have not made trouble for Israel," Elijah replied. "But you*c*

18:18
c 1Ki 16:31,33;
21:25
d 2Ch 15:2

and your father's family have. You have abandoned*d* the LORD's commands and have followed the Baals. ¹⁹Now summon the people from all over Israel to meet me on Mount Carmel.*e* And bring the four hundred and fifty prophets of Baal and the four hundred prophets of Asherah, who eat at Jezebel's table."

18:19
e Jos 19:26

²⁰So Ahab sent word throughout all Israel and assembled the prophets on Mount Carmel. ²¹Elijah went before the people and said, "How long will you waver*f* between two opinions? If the LORD is God, follow him; but if Baal is God, follow him."

18:21
f Jos 24:15;
2Ki 17:41;
Mt 6:24

But the people said nothing.

²²Then Elijah said to them, "I am the only one of the LORD's prophets left,*g* but Baal has four hundred and fifty prophets.*h*

18:22
g 1Ki 19:10
h ver 19

²³Get two bulls for us. Let them choose one for themselves, and let them cut it into pieces and put it on the wood but not set fire to it. I will prepare the other bull and put it on the wood but not set fire to it. ²⁴Then you call on the name of your god, and I will call on the name of the LORD. The god who answers by fire*i*—he is God."

18:24
i ver 38;
1Ch 21:26

Then all the people said, "What you say is good."

²⁵Elijah said to the prophets of Baal, "Choose one of the bulls and prepare it first, since there are so many of you. Call on the name of your god, but do not light the fire." ²⁶So they took the bull given them and prepared it.

18:26
j Ps 115:4-5;
Jer 10:5;
1Co 8:4; 12:2

Then they called on the name of Baal from morning till noon. "O Baal, answer us!" they shouted. But there was no response;*j* no one answered. And they danced around the altar they had made.

²⁷At noon Elijah began to taunt them. "Shout louder!" he said. "Surely he is a god! Perhaps he is deep in thought, or busy, or traveling. Maybe he is sleeping and must be awakened."*k* ²⁸So they shouted louder and slashed*l* themselves with swords and spears, as was their custom, until their blood flowed. ²⁹Midday passed, and they continued their frantic prophesying until the time for the evening sacrifice.*m* But there was no response, no one answered, no one paid attention.*n*

18:27
k Hab 2:19

18:28
l Lev 19:28;
Dt 14:1

18:29
m Ex 29:41
n ver 26

³⁰Then Elijah said to all the people, "Come here to me." They came to him, and he repaired the altar*o* of the LORD, which was in ruins. ³¹Elijah took twelve stones, one for each of the tribes descended from Jacob, to whom the word of the LORD had come,

18:30
o 1Ki 19:10

saying, "Your name shall be Israel."ᵃ ³²With the stones he built an altar in the nameᵇ of the LORD, and he dug a trench around it large enough to hold two seahsᵃ of seed. ³³He arrangedᶜ the wood, cut the bull into pieces and laid it on the wood. Then he said to them, "Fill four large jars with water and pour it on the offering and on the wood."

³⁴"Do it again," he said, and they did it again.

"Do it a third time," he ordered, and they did it the third time. ³⁵The water ran down around the altar and even filled the trench.

³⁶At the time of sacrifice, the prophet Elijah stepped forward and prayed: "O LORD, God of Abraham,ᵈ Isaac and Israel, let it be knownᵉ today that you are God in Israel and that I am your servant and have done all these things at your command.ᶠ ³⁷Answer me, O LORD, answer me, so these people will know that you, O LORD, are God, and that you are turning their hearts back again."

³⁸Then the fireᵍ of the LORD fell and burned up the sacrifice, the wood, the stones and the soil, and also licked up the water in the trench.

³⁹When all the people saw this, they fell prostrate and cried, "The LORD—he is God! The LORD—he is God!"ʰ

⁴⁰Then Elijah commanded them, "Seize the prophets of Baal. Don't let anyone get away!" They seized them, and Elijah had them brought down to the Kishon Valleyⁱ and slaughteredʲ there.

⁴¹And Elijah said to Ahab, "Go, eat and drink, for there is the sound of a heavy rain." ⁴²So Ahab went off to eat and drink, but Elijah climbed to the top of Carmel, bent down to the ground and put his face between his knees.ᵏ

⁴³"Go and look toward the sea," he told his servant. And he went up and looked.

"There is nothing there," he said.

Seven times Elijah said, "Go back."

⁴⁴The seventh time the servant reported, "A cloudˡ as small as a man's hand is rising from the sea."

So Elijah said, "Go and tell Ahab, 'Hitch up your chariot and go down before the rain stops you.'"

⁴⁵Meanwhile, the sky grew black with clouds, the wind rose, a heavy rain came on and Ahab rode off to Jezreel. ⁴⁶The powerᵐ of the LORD came upon Elijah and, tucking his cloak into his belt,ⁿ he ran ahead of Ahab all the way to Jezreel.

Chapter 19 Theme

19 Now Ahab told Jezebel everything Elijah had done and how he had killedᵒ all the prophets with the sword. ²So Jezebel sent a messenger to Elijah to say, "May the gods deal with

ᵃ 32 That is, probably about 13 quarts (about 15 liters)

18:31 ᵃGe 32:28; 35:10; 2Ki 17:34
18:32 ᵇCol 3:17
18:33 ᶜGe 22:9; Lev 1:6-8
18:36 ᵈEx 3:6; Mt 22:32; ᵉ1Ki 8:43; 2Ki 19:19; ᶠNu 16:28
18:38 ᵍLev 9:24; Jdg 6:21; 1Ch 21:26; 2Ch 7:1; Job 1:16
18:39 ʰver 24
18:40 ⁱJdg 4:7; ʲDt 13:5; 18:20; 2Ki 10:24-25
18:42 ᵏver 19-20; Jas 5:18
18:44 ˡLk 12:54
18:46 ᵐ2Ki 3:15; ⁿ2Ki 4:29; 9:1
19:1 ᵒ1Ki 18:40

19:2
a 1Ki 20:10;
2Ki 6:31;
Ru 1:17

19:3
b Ge 31:21

19:4
c Nu 11:15;
Jer 20:18;
Jnh 4:8

19:5
d Ge 28:11

19:8
e Ex 24:18;
34:28;
Dt 9:9-11,18;
Mt 4:2
f Ex 3:1

19:9
g Ex 33:22

19:10
h Nu 25:13
i 1Ki 18:4,22;
Ro 11:3*

19:11
j Ex 24:12
k Eze 1:4; 37:7

me, be it ever so severely,a if by this time tomorrow I do not make your life like that of one of them.”

³Elijah was afraida and ranb for his life. When he came to Beersheba in Judah, he left his servant there, ⁴while he himself went a day's journey into the desert. He came to a broom tree, sat down under it and prayed that he might die. “I have had enough, LORD,” he said. “Take my life;c I am no better than my ancestors.” ⁵Then he lay down under the tree and fell asleep.d

All at once an angel touched him and said, “Get up and eat.” ⁶He looked around, and there by his head was a cake of bread baked over hot coals, and a jar of water. He ate and drank and then lay down again.

⁷The angel of the LORD came back a second time and touched him and said, “Get up and eat, for the journey is too much for you.” ⁸So he got up and ate and drank. Strengthened by that food, he traveled fortye days and forty nights until he reached Horeb,f the mountain of God. ⁹There he went into a caveg and spent the night.

And the word of the LORD came to him: “What are you doing here, Elijah?”

¹⁰He replied, “I have been very zealoush for the LORD God Almighty. The Israelites have rejected your covenant, broken down your altars, and put your prophets to death with the sword. I am the only one left,i and now they are trying to kill me too.”

¹¹The LORD said, “Go out and stand on the mountainj in the presence of the LORD, for the LORD is about to pass by.”

Then a great and powerful windk tore the mountains apart and shattered the rocks before the LORD, but the LORD was not in the wind. After the wind there was an earthquake, but the LORD was

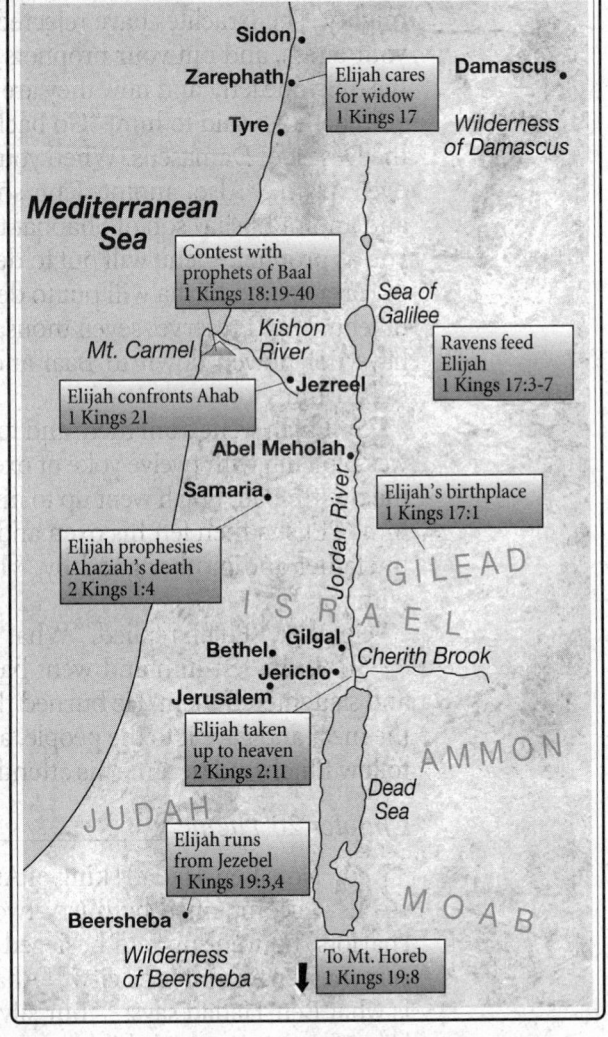

Mediterranean Sea

Sidon
Zarephath
Tyre

Elijah cares for widow
1 Kings 17

Damascus

Wilderness of Damascus

Contest with prophets of Baal
1 Kings 18:19-40

Sea of Galilee

Mt. Carmel
Kishon River
Jezreel

Ravens feed Elijah
1 Kings 17:3-7

Elijah confronts Ahab
1 Kings 21

Abel Meholah

Samaria

Elijah's birthplace
1 Kings 17:1

Jordan River

GILEAD

Elijah prophesies Ahaziah's death
2 Kings 1:4

ISRAEL

Bethel
Gilgal
Jericho
Jerusalem

Cherith Brook

Elijah taken up to heaven
2 Kings 2:11

AMMON

JUDAH

Dead Sea

Elijah runs from Jezebel
1 Kings 19:3,4

Beersheba

Wilderness of Beersheba

To Mt. Horeb
1 Kings 19:8

MOAB

Elijah's Ministry

a 3 Or *Elijah saw*

589

not in the earthquake. ¹²After the earthquake came a fire, but the LORD was not in the fire. And after the fire came a gentle whisper.ᵃ ¹³When Elijah heard it, he pulled his cloak over his faceᵇ and went out and stood at the mouth of the cave.

Then a voice said to him, "What are you doing here, Elijah?"

¹⁴He replied, "I have been very zealous for the LORD God Almighty. The Israelites have rejected your covenant, broken down your altars, and put your prophets to death with the sword. I am the only one left,ᶜ and now they are trying to kill me too."

¹⁵The LORD said to him, "Go back the way you came, and go to the Desert of Damascus. When you get there, anoint Hazaelᵈ king over Aram. ¹⁶Also, anointᵉ Jehu son of Nimshi king over Israel, and anoint Elishaᶠ son of Shaphat from Abel Meholah to succeed you as prophet. ¹⁷Jehu will put to death any who escape the sword of Hazael,ᵍ and Elisha will put to death any who escape the sword of Jehu. ¹⁸Yet I reserveʰ seven thousand in Israel—all whose knees have not bowed down to Baal and all whose mouths have not kissedⁱ him."

¹⁹So Elijah went from there and found Elisha son of Shaphat. He was plowing with twelve yoke of oxen, and he himself was driving the twelfth pair. Elijah went up to him and threw his cloakʲ around him. ²⁰Elisha then left his oxen and ran after Elijah. "Let me kiss my father and mother good-by,"ᵏ he said, "and then I will come with you."

"Go back," Elijah replied. "What have I done to you?"

²¹So Elisha left him and went back. He took his yoke of oxenˡ and slaughtered them. He burned the plowing equipment to cook the meat and gave it to the people, and they ate. Then he set out to follow Elijah and became his attendant.ᵐ

Chapter 20 Theme

20 Now Ben-Hadadⁿ king of Aram mustered his entire army. Accompanied by thirty-two kings with their horses and chariots, he went up and besieged Samaria and attacked it. ²He sent messengers into the city to Ahab king of Israel, saying, "This is what Ben-Hadad says: ³'Your silver and gold are mine, and the best of your wives and children are mine.'"

⁴The king of Israel answered, "Just as you say, my lord the king. I and all I have are yours."

⁵The messengers came again and said, "This is what Ben-Hadad says: 'I sent to demand your silver and gold, your wives and your children. ⁶But about this time tomorrow I am going to send my officials to search your palace and the houses of your officials. They will seize everything you value and carry it away.'"

⁷The king of Israel summoned all the elders of the land and said to them, "See how this man is looking for trouble!ᵒ When he

19:12 ᵃJob 4:16; Zec 4:6

19:13 ᵇver 9; Ex 3:6

19:14 ᶜver 10

19:15 ᵈ2Ki 8:7-15

19:16 ᵉ2Ki 9:1-3,6 ᶠver 21; 2Ki 2:9,15

19:17 ᵍ2Ki 8:12,29; 9:14; 13:3,7,22

19:18 ʰRo 11:4* ⁱHos 13:2

19:19 ʲ2Ki 2:8,14

19:20 ᵏMt 8:21-22; Lk 9:61

19:21 ˡ2Sa 24:22 ᵐver 16

20:1 ⁿ1Ki 15:18; 22:31; 2Ki 6:24

20:7 ᵒ2Ki 5:7

20:10
a 2Sa 22:43;
1Ki 19:2

sent for my wives and my children, my silver and my gold, I did not refuse him.'"

⁸The elders and the people all answered, "Don't listen to him or agree to his demands."

⁹So he replied to Ben-Hadad's messengers, "Tell my lord the king, 'Your servant will do all you demanded the first time, but this demand I cannot meet.'" They left and took the answer back to Ben-Hadad.

20:11
b Pr 27:1;
Jer 9:23

¹⁰Then Ben-Hadad sent another message to Ahab: "May the gods deal with me, be it ever so severely, if enough dustᵃ remains in Samaria to give each of my men a handful."

¹¹The king of Israel answered, "Tell him: 'One who puts on his armor should not boastᵇ like one who takes it off.'"

20:12
c ver 16;
1Ki 16:9

¹²Ben-Hadad heard this message while he and the kings were drinkingᶜ in their tents,ᵃ and he ordered his men: "Prepare to attack." So they prepared to attack the city.

¹³Meanwhile a prophet came to Ahab king of Israel and announced, "This is what the LORD says: 'Do you see this vast army? I will give it into your hand today, and then you will knowᵈ that I am the LORD.'"

¹⁴"But who will do this?" asked Ahab.

The prophet replied, "This is what the LORD says: 'The young officers of the provincial commanders will do it.'"

20:13
d ver 28;
Ex 6:7

"And who will startᵉ the battle?" he asked.

The prophet answered, "You will."

¹⁵So Ahab summoned the young officers of the provincial commanders, 232 men. Then he assembled the rest of the Israelites, 7,000 in all. ¹⁶They set out at noon while Ben-Hadad and the 32 kings allied with him were in their tents getting drunk.ᶠ ¹⁷The young officers of the provincial commanders went out first.

20:14
e Jdg 1:1

Now Ben-Hadad had dispatched scouts, who reported, "Men are advancing from Samaria."

¹⁸He said, "If they have come out for peace, take them alive; if they have come out for war, take them alive."

¹⁹The young officers of the provincial commanders marched out of the city with the army behind them ²⁰and each one struck down his opponent. At that, the Arameans fled, with the Israelites in pursuit. But Ben-Hadad king of Aram escaped on horseback with some of his horsemen. ²¹The king of Israel advanced and overpowered the horses and chariots and inflicted heavy losses on the Arameans.

20:16
f ver 12;
1Ki 16:9

²²Afterward, the prophetᵍ came to the king of Israel and said, "Strengthen your position and see what must be done, because next springʰ the king of Aram will attack you again."

20:22
g ver 13
h ver 26;
2Sa 11:1

a 12 Or in Succoth; also in verse 16

²³Meanwhile, the officials of the king of Aram advised him, "Their gods are gods*ᵃ* of the hills. That is why they were too strong for us. But if we fight them on the plains, surely we will be stronger than they. ²⁴Do this: Remove all the kings from their commands and replace them with other officers. ²⁵You must also raise an army like the one you lost—horse for horse and chariot for chariot—so we can fight Israel on the plains. Then surely we will be stronger than they." He agreed with them and acted accordingly.

²⁶The next spring*ᵇ* Ben-Hadad mustered the Arameans and went up to Aphek*ᶜ* to fight against Israel. ²⁷When the Israelites were also mustered and given provisions, they marched out to meet them. The Israelites camped opposite them like two small flocks of goats, while the Arameans covered the countryside.*ᵈ*

²⁸The man of God came up and told the king of Israel, "This is what the LORD says: 'Because the Arameans think the LORD is a god of the hills and not a god*ᵉ* of the valleys, I will deliver this vast army into your hands, and you will know*ᶠ* that I am the LORD.'"

²⁹For seven days they camped opposite each other, and on the seventh day the battle was joined. The Israelites inflicted a hundred thousand casualties on the Aramean foot soldiers in one day. ³⁰The rest of them escaped to the city of Aphek,*ᵍ* where the wall collapsed on twenty-seven thousand of them. And Ben-Hadad fled to the city and hid*ʰ* in an inner room.

³¹His officials said to him, "Look, we have heard that the kings of the house of Israel are merciful. Let us go to the king of Israel with sackcloth*ⁱ* around our waists and ropes around our heads. Perhaps he will spare your life."

³²Wearing sackcloth around their waists and ropes around their heads, they went to the king of Israel and said, "Your servant Ben-Hadad says: 'Please let me live.'"

The king answered, "Is he still alive? He is my brother."

³³The men took this as a good sign and were quick to pick up his word. "Yes, your brother Ben-Hadad!" they said.

"Go and get him," the king said. When Ben-Hadad came out, Ahab had him come up into his chariot.

³⁴"I will return the cities*ʲ* my father took from your father," Ben-Hadad offered. "You may set up your own market areas in Damascus,*ᵏ* as my father did in Samaria."

⌞Ahab said,⌟ "On the basis of a treaty*ˡ* I will set you free." So he made a treaty with him, and let him go.

³⁵By the word of the LORD one of the sons of the prophets said to his companion, "Strike me with your weapon," but the man refused.*ᵐ*

³⁶So the prophet said, "Because you have not obeyed the LORD, as soon as you leave me a lion*ⁿ* will kill you." And after the man went away, a lion found him and killed him.

20:23 ᵃ1Ki 14:23; Ro 1:21-23

20:26 ᵇver 22 ᶜ2Ki 13:17

20:27 ᵈJdg 6:6; 1Sa 13:6

20:28 ᵉver 23 ᶠver 13

20:30 ᵍver 26 ʰ1Ki 22:25; 2Ch 18:24

20:31 ⁱGe 37:34

20:34 ʲ1Ki 15:20 ᵏJer 49:23-27 ˡEx 23:32

20:35 ᵐ1Ki 13:21; 2Ki 2:3-7

20:36 ⁿ1Ki 13:24

20:39
a 2Ki 10:24

20:42
b Jer 48:10
c ver 39;
Jos 2:14;
1Ki 22:31-37

20:43
d 1Ki 21:4

21:1
e 2Ki 9:21
f 1Ki 18:45-46

21:3
g Lev 25:23;
Nu 36:7;
Eze 46:18

21:4
h 1Ki 20:43

21:7
i 1Sa 8:14

21:8
j Ge 38:18;
Est 3:12; 8:8,10

21:10
k Ac 6:11

³⁷The prophet found another man and said, "Strike me, please." So the man struck him and wounded him. ³⁸Then the prophet went and stood by the road waiting for the king. He disguised himself with his headband down over his eyes. ³⁹As the king passed by, the prophet called out to him, "Your servant went into the thick of the battle, and someone came to me with a captive and said, 'Guard this man. If he is missing, it will be your life for his life,ᵃ or you must pay a talentᵃ of silver.' ⁴⁰While your servant was busy here and there, the man disappeared."

"That is your sentence," the king of Israel said. "You have pronounced it yourself."

⁴¹Then the prophet quickly removed the headband from his eyes, and the king of Israel recognized him as one of the prophets. ⁴²He said to the king, "This is what the Lord says: 'You have set free a man I had determined should die.ᵇᵇ Therefore it is your life for his life,ᶜ your people for his people.'" ⁴³Sullen and angry,ᵈ the king of Israel went to his palace in Samaria.

Chapter 21 Theme

21 Some time later there was an incident involving a vineyard belonging to Nabothᵉ the Jezreelite. The vineyard was in Jezreel,ᶠ close to the palace of Ahab king of Samaria. ²Ahab said to Naboth, "Let me have your vineyard to use for a vegetable garden, since it is close to my palace. In exchange I will give you a better vineyard or, if you prefer, I will pay you whatever it is worth."

³But Naboth replied, "The Lord forbid that I should give you the inheritanceᵍ of my fathers."

⁴So Ahab went home, sullen and angryʰ because Naboth the Jezreelite had said, "I will not give you the inheritance of my fathers." He lay on his bed sulking and refused to eat.

⁵His wife Jezebel came in and asked him, "Why are you so sullen? Why won't you eat?"

⁶He answered her, "Because I said to Naboth the Jezreelite, 'Sell me your vineyard; or if you prefer, I will give you another vineyard in its place.' But he said, 'I will not give you my vineyard.'"

⁷Jezebel his wife said, "Is this how you act as king over Israel? Get up and eat! Cheer up. I'll get you the vineyardⁱ of Naboth the Jezreelite."

⁸So she wrote letters in Ahab's name, placed his sealʲ on them, and sent them to the elders and nobles who lived in Naboth's city with him. ⁹In those letters she wrote:

"Proclaim a day of fasting and seat Naboth in a prominent place among the people. ¹⁰But seat two scoundrelsᵏ opposite

---

a 39 That is, about 75 pounds (about 34 kilograms)   b 42 The Hebrew term refers to the irrevocable giving over of things or persons to the Lord, often by totally destroying them.

him and have them testify that he has cursed[a] both God and the king. Then take him out and stone him to death."

¹¹So the elders and nobles who lived in Naboth's city did as Jezebel directed in the letters she had written to them. ¹²They proclaimed a fast[b] and seated Naboth in a prominent place among the people. ¹³Then two scoundrels came and sat opposite him and brought charges against Naboth before the people, saying, "Naboth has cursed both God and the king." So they took him outside the city and stoned him to death.[c] ¹⁴Then they sent word to Jezebel: "Naboth has been stoned and is dead."

¹⁵As soon as Jezebel heard that Naboth had been stoned to death, she said to Ahab, "Get up and take possession of the vineyard[d] of Naboth the Jezreelite that he refused to sell you. He is no longer alive, but dead." ¹⁶When Ahab heard that Naboth was dead, he got up and went down to take possession of Naboth's vineyard.

¹⁷Then the word of the LORD came to Elijah the Tishbite: ¹⁸"Go down to meet Ahab king of Israel, who rules in Samaria. He is now in Naboth's vineyard, where he has gone to take possession of it. ¹⁹Say to him, 'This is what the LORD says: Have you not murdered a man and seized his property?' Then say to him, 'This is what the LORD says: In the place where dogs licked up Naboth's blood,[e] dogs[f] will lick up your blood—yes, yours!'"

²⁰Ahab said to Elijah, "So you have found me, my enemy!"[g]

"I have found you," he answered, "because you have sold[h] yourself to do evil in the eyes of the LORD. ²¹'I am going to bring disaster on you. I will consume your descendants and cut off from Ahab every last male[i] in Israel—slave or free. ²²I will make your house[j] like that of Jeroboam son of Nebat and that of Baasha son of Ahijah, because you have provoked me to anger and have caused Israel to sin.'[k]

²³"And also concerning Jezebel the LORD says: 'Dogs[l] will devour Jezebel by the wall of[a] Jezreel.'

²⁴"Dogs[m] will eat those belonging to Ahab who die in the city, and the birds of the air will feed on those who die in the country."

²⁵(There was never[n] a man like Ahab, who sold himself to do evil in the eyes of the LORD, urged on by Jezebel his wife. ²⁶He behaved in the vilest manner by going after idols, like the Amorites[o] the LORD drove out before Israel.)

²⁷When Ahab heard these words, he tore his clothes, put on sackcloth[p] and fasted. He lay in sackcloth and went around meekly.

²⁸Then the word of the LORD came to Elijah the Tishbite: ²⁹"Have you noticed how Ahab has humbled himself before me? Because

---

a 23 Most Hebrew manuscripts; a few Hebrew manuscripts, Vulgate and Syriac (see also 2 Kings 9:26) *the plot of ground at*

21:10
a Ex 22:28;
Lev 24:15-16

21:12
b Isa 58:4

21:13
c 2Ki 9:26

21:15
d 1Sa 8:14

21:19
e 2Ki 9:26;
Ps 9:12;
Isa 14:20
f 1Ki 22:38

21:20
g 1Ki 18:17
h ver 25;
2Ki 17:17;
Ro 7:14

21:21
i 1Ki 14:10;
2Ki 9:8

21:22
j 1Ki 15:29; 16:3
k 1Ki 12:30

21:23
l 2Ki 9:10,
34-36

21:24
m 1Ki 14:11;
16:4

21:25
n ver 20;
1Ki 16:33

21:26
o Ge 15:16;
Lev 18:25-30;
2Ki 21:11

21:27
p Ge 37:34;
2Sa 3:31;
2Ki 6:30

21:29
a 2Ki 9:26

he has humbled himself, I will not bring this disaster in his day, but I will bring it on his house in the days of his son."*a*

Chapter 22 Theme _____

22:3
b Dt 4:43;
Jos 21:38

22 For three years there was no war between Aram and Israel. ²But in the third year Jehoshaphat king of Judah went down to see the king of Israel. ³The king of Israel had said to his officials, "Don't you know that Ramoth Gilead*b* belongs to us and yet we are doing nothing to retake it from the king of Aram?"

22:4
c 2Ki 3:7

⁴So he asked Jehoshaphat, "Will you go with me to fight*c* against Ramoth Gilead?"

Jehoshaphat replied to the king of Israel, "I am as you are, my people as your people, my horses as your horses." ⁵But Jehoshaphat also said to the king of Israel, "First seek the counsel*d* of the LORD."

22:5
d Ex 33:7;
2Ki 3:11

⁶So the king of Israel brought together the prophets—about four hundred men—and asked them, "Shall I go to war against Ramoth Gilead, or shall I refrain?"

"Go,"*e* they answered, "for the Lord will give it into the king's hand."

22:6
e 1Ki 18:19

⁷But Jehoshaphat asked, "Is there not a prophet*f* of the LORD here whom we can inquire of?"

⁸The king of Israel answered Jehoshaphat, "There is still one man through whom we can inquire of the LORD, but I hate*g* him because he never prophesies anything good*h* about me, but always bad. He is Micaiah son of Imlah."

22:7
f 2Ki 3:11

"The king should not say that," Jehoshaphat replied.

⁹So the king of Israel called one of his officials and said, "Bring Micaiah son of Imlah at once."

22:8
g Am 5:10
h Isa 5:20

¹⁰Dressed in their royal robes, the king of Israel and Jehoshaphat king of Judah were sitting on their thrones at the threshing floor*i* by the entrance of the gate of Samaria, with all the prophets prophesying before them. ¹¹Now Zedekiah son of Kenaanah had made iron horns*j* and he declared, "This is what the LORD says: 'With these you will gore the Arameans until they are destroyed.'"

22:10
i ver 6

¹²All the other prophets were prophesying the same thing. "Attack Ramoth Gilead and be victorious," they said, "for the LORD will give it into the king's hand."

¹³The messenger who had gone to summon Micaiah said to him, "Look, as one man the other prophets are predicting success for the king. Let your word agree with theirs, and speak favorably."

22:11
j Dt 33:17;
Zec 1:18-21

¹⁴But Micaiah said, "As surely as the LORD lives, I can tell him only what the LORD tells me."*k*

¹⁵When he arrived, the king asked him, "Micaiah, shall we go to war against Ramoth Gilead, or shall I refrain?"

22:14
k Nu 22:18;
24:13;
1Ki 18:10,15

"Attack and be victorious," he answered, "for the LORD will give it into the king's hand."

¹⁶The king said to him, "How many times must I make you swear to tell me nothing but the truth in the name of the Lord?"

¹⁷Then Micaiah answered, "I saw all Israel scattered on the hills like sheep without a shepherd,^a and the Lord said, 'These people have no master. Let each one go home in peace.'"

¹⁸The king of Israel said to Jehoshaphat, "Didn't I tell you that he never prophesies anything good about me, but only bad?"

¹⁹Micaiah continued, "Therefore hear the word of the Lord: I saw the Lord sitting on his throne^b with all the host^c of heaven standing around him on his right and on his left. ²⁰And the Lord said, 'Who will entice Ahab into attacking Ramoth Gilead and going to his death there?'

"One suggested this, and another that. ²¹Finally, a spirit came forward, stood before the Lord and said, 'I will entice him.'

²²"'By what means?' the Lord asked.

"'I will go out and be a lying^d spirit in the mouths of all his prophets,' he said.

"'You will succeed in enticing him,' said the Lord. 'Go and do it.'

²³"So now the Lord has put a lying spirit in the mouths of all these prophets^e of yours. The Lord has decreed disaster for you."

²⁴Then Zedekiah^f son of Kenaanah went up and slapped^g Micaiah in the face. "Which way did the spirit from^a the Lord go when he went from me to speak to you?" he asked.

²⁵Micaiah replied, "You will find out on the day you go to hide^h in an inner room."

²⁶The king of Israel then ordered, "Take Micaiah and send him back to Amon the ruler of the city and to Joash the king's son ²⁷and say, 'This is what the king says: Put this fellow in prisonⁱ and give him nothing but bread and water until I return safely.'"

²⁸Micaiah declared, "If you ever return safely, the Lord has not spoken^j through me." Then he added, "Mark my words, all you people!"

²⁹So the king of Israel and Jehoshaphat king of Judah went up to Ramoth Gilead. ³⁰The king of Israel said to Jehoshaphat, "I will enter the battle in disguise,^k but you wear your royal robes." So the king of Israel disguised himself and went into battle.

³¹Now the king of Aram had ordered his thirty-two chariot commanders, "Do not fight with anyone, small or great, except the king^l of Israel." ³²When the chariot commanders saw Jehoshaphat, they thought, "Surely this is the king of Israel." So they turned to attack him, but when Jehoshaphat cried out, ³³the chariot commanders saw that he was not the king of Israel and stopped pursuing him.

³⁴But someone drew his bow^m at random and hit the king of Israel between the sections of his armor. The king told his chariot driver,

^a 24 Or *Spirit of*

22:17
^a ver 34-36;
Nu 27:17;
Mt 9:36

22:19
^b Isa 6:1;
Eze 1:26;
Da 7:9
^c Job 1:6; 2:1;
Ps 103:20-21;
Mt 18:10;
Heb 1:7,14

22:22
^d Jdg 9:23;
1Sa 16:14;
18:10; 19:9;
Eze 14:9;
2Th 2:11

22:23
^e Eze 14:9

22:24
^f ver 11
^g Ac 23:2

22:25
^h 1Ki 20:30

22:27
ⁱ 2Ch 16:10

22:28
^j Dt 18:22

22:30
^k 2Ch 35:32

22:31
^l 2Sa 17:2

22:34
^m 2Ch 35:23

22:36
a 2Ki 14:12

"Wheel around and get me out of the fighting. I've been wounded." [35]All day long the battle raged, and the king was propped up in his chariot facing the Arameans. The blood from his wound ran onto the floor of the chariot, and that evening he died. [36]As the sun was setting, a cry spread through the army: "Every man to his town; everyone to his land!"[a]

22:38
b 1Ki 21:19

[37]So the king died and was brought to Samaria, and they buried him there. [38]They washed the chariot at a pool in Samaria (where the prostitutes bathed),[a] and the dogs[b] licked up his blood, as the word of the LORD had declared.

22:39
c 2Ch 9:17;
Am 3:15

[39]As for the other events of Ahab's reign, including all he did, the palace he built and inlaid with ivory,[c] and the cities he fortified, are they not written in the book of the annals of the kings of Israel? [40]Ahab rested with his fathers. And Ahaziah his son succeeded him as king.

22:43
d 2Ch 17:3
e 1Ki 3:2;
15:14;
2Ki 12:3

[41]Jehoshaphat son of Asa became king of Judah in the fourth year of Ahab king of Israel. [42]Jehoshaphat was thirty-five years old when he became king, and he reigned in Jerusalem twenty-five years. His mother's name was Azubah daughter of Shilhi. [43]In everything he walked in the ways of his father Asa[d] and did not stray from them; he did what was right in the eyes of the LORD. The high places,[e] however, were not removed, and the people continued to offer sacrifices and burn incense there. [44]Jehoshaphat was also at

22:46
f Dt 23:17;
1Ki 14:24;
15:12

peace with the king of Israel.

[45]As for the other events of Jehoshaphat's reign, the things he achieved and his military exploits, are they not written in the book of the annals of the kings of Judah? [46]He rid the land of the rest of the male shrine prostitutes[f] who remained there even after the reign of his father Asa. [47]There was then no king[g] in Edom; a

22:47
g 2Sa 8:14;
2Ki 3:9; 8:20

deputy ruled.

[48]Now Jehoshaphat built a fleet of trading ships[b][h] to go to Ophir for gold, but they never set sail—they were wrecked at Ezion Geber. [49]At that time Ahaziah son of Ahab said to Jehoshaphat,

22:48
h 1Ki 9:26; 10:22

"Let my men sail with your men," but Jehoshaphat refused.

[50]Then Jehoshaphat rested with his fathers and was buried with them in the city of David his father. And Jehoram his son succeeded him.

[51]Ahaziah son of Ahab became king of Israel in Samaria in the

22:52
i 1Ki 15:26;
21:25

seventeenth year of Jehoshaphat king of Judah, and he reigned over Israel two years. [52]He did evil[i] in the eyes of the LORD, because he walked in the ways of his father and mother and in the ways of Jeroboam son of Nebat, who caused Israel to sin. [53]He served and worshiped Baal[j] and provoked the LORD, the God of Israel, to

22:53
j Jdg 2:11
k 1Ki 16:30-32

anger, just as his father[k] had done.

a 38 Or *Samaria and cleaned the weapons*   b 48 Hebrew *of ships of Tarshish*

1 KINGS AT A GLANCE

Theme of 1 Kings:

SEGMENT DIVISIONS

		CHAPTER THEMES
		1
		2
		3
		4
		5
		6
		7
		8
		9
		10
		11
		12
		13
		14
		15
		16
		17
		18
		19
		20
		21
		22

Author:

Date:

Purpose:

Key Words:

2 KINGS

"Where now is the LORD, the God of Elijah?"

As you study 2 Kings, the continuation of 1 Kings, you will see God at work setting up and removing kings and kingdoms. You will be introduced to his spokesmen, the prophets, who spoke his Word until Israel and then Judah were led into captivity.

∾ THINGS TO DO

1. As you read through 2 Kings one chapter at a time:

   a. Mark the following key repeated words: *according to the word of the Lord (as the Lord had said, in accordance with the word of the Lord), heart (spirit, in accord, mind, wholehearted), sin (sins, which he caused Israel to commit), high places (high place, shrine),* and *covenant.* Always watch for and mark words which are distinctive to a particular chapter such as *practices* in chapter 17. Write these key words on an index card you can use as a bookmark while studying 2 Kings.

   b. Look for what you learn about God: his requirements, his ways, his judgments, and his character. Record your insights in the margin of the text. Be sure to note "Lessons for Life" (LFL).

   c. Watch for any reforms instituted by a king. In the margin note these reforms and the results. As you finish reading about the reign of a king, record what you learn on the chart THE KINGS OF ISRAEL AND JUDAH on pages 654 and 655.

   d. Record the theme or main event of each chapter on 2 KINGS AT A GLANCE on page 650 and in the text next to the chapter number.

2. Second Kings has some key or pivotal events:

   a. In 1:1 through 8:15 the prophetic ministries of Elijah and then Elisha are prominent. List in the margin the miracles accomplished through these men. Several miraculous things occur after 8:15; watch for them.

   b. Second Kings gives the account of the Assyrian invasion and subsequent captivity of the northern kingdom of Israel. Give special attention to the details of this invasion and why it came about. Note these in the margin of the text under the heading "The Assyrian Captivity."

   c. After the Assyrian captivity all that is left is the southern kingdom of Judah. Watch how Judah conducts herself after seeing God's judgment on the northern kingdom. All this came to pass just as God's prophets said it would.

   d. Watch for the account of the Babylonian captivity of the southern kingdom of Judah and the ensuing events. Record this in the margin as you did the Assyrian captivity.

3. There are two charts which identify the major characters and events of 2 Kings.

   a. The first chart, ISRAEL'S DIVISION AND CAPTIVITY, on page 649, gives a broad overview of the division of the kingdom through the three sieges of Jerusalem by the Babylonians.

   b. The second is a three-part chart: THE HISTORICAL CHART OF THE KINGS AND PROPHETS OF ISRAEL AND JUDAH, on pages 651 through 653. This chart shows the relationship of the kings and prophets to one another and to other foreign kings and their kingdoms. You might color these charts so that the kings of the northern and southern kingdoms and the prophets can be readily distinguished from one another.

   c. When you read of key figures or events in 2 Kings consult these charts.

4. Complete the chart 2 KINGS AT A GLANCE. Considering the key events or personages featured in 2 Kings, see which chapters of 2 Kings can be grouped together under a common theme or topic. Record the theme of each segment under "Segment Divisions." Also, you might want to note on the chart the chapters which tell when the Assyrian and Babylonian invasions occur. Remember to record the theme of 2 Kings.

∾ THINGS TO THINK ABOUT

1. As you consider the lives of Elijah and Elisha, what do you learn about faith and trusting God?

2. As you think about the captivity of Israel and Judah, and the reasons for their captivity, what do you learn about the necessity of living a righteous life? What practical applications can you make to your own life? Remember, walking your own way may be pleasurable for awhile, but a just God must hold you accountable.

3. As you studied 1 and 2 Kings you saw that what God says will happen eventually comes to pass. Since his Word stands and none can alter it, can you see how critical it is that you believe God and hold to his Word no matter what others say or do?

∾∾∾∾∾

Chapter 1 Theme _____

1 After Ahab's death, Moab*a* rebelled against Israel. ²Now Ahaziah had fallen through the lattice of his upper room in Samaria and injured himself. So he sent messengers,*b* saying to them, "Go and consult Baal-Zebub,*c* the god of Ekron,*d* to see if I will recover*e* from this injury."

³But the angel*f* of the LORD said to Elijah*g* the Tishbite, "Go up and meet the messengers of the king of Samaria and ask them, 'Is it because there is no God in Israel*h* that you are going off to consult Baal-Zebub, the god of Ekron?' ⁴Therefore this is what the LORD says: 'You will not leave*i* the bed you are lying on. You will certainly die!'" So Elijah went.

⁵When the messengers returned to the king, he asked them, "Why have you come back?"

⁶"A man came to meet us," they replied. "And he said to us, 'Go back to the king who sent you and tell him, "This is what the LORD says: Is it because there is no God in Israel that you are sending men to consult Baal-Zebub, the god of Ekron? Therefore you will not leave the bed you are lying on. You will certainly die!"'"

⁷The king asked them, "What kind of man was it who came to meet you and told you this?"

⁸They replied, "He was a man with a garment of hair*j* and with a leather belt around his waist."

The king said, "That was Elijah the Tishbite."

⁹Then he sent*k* to Elijah a captain*l* with his company of fifty men. The captain went up to Elijah, who was sitting on the top of a hill, and said to him, "Man of God, the king says, 'Come down!'"

1:1
*a*Ge 19:37;
2Sa 8:2; 2Ki 3:5

1:2
*b*ver 16
*c*Mk 3:22
*d*1Sa 6:2;
Isa 2:6; 14:29;
Mt 10:25
*e*Jdg 18:5;
2Ki 8:7-10

1:3
*f*ver 15; Ge 16:7
*g*1Ki 17:1
*h*1Sa 28:8

1:4
*i*ver 6,16;
Ps 41:8

1:8
*j*1Ki 18:7;
Zec 13:4;
Mt 3:4; Mk 1:6

1:9
*k*2Ki 6:14
*l*Ex 18:25;
Isa 3:3

1:10
a 1Ki 18:38;
Lk 9:54;
Rev 11:5; 13:13

[10]Elijah answered the captain, "If I am a man of God, may fire come down from heaven and consume you and your fifty men!" Then fire*a* fell from heaven and consumed the captain and his men.

[11]At this the king sent to Elijah another captain with his fifty men. The captain said to him, "Man of God, this is what the king says, 'Come down at once!'"

1:13
b 1Sa 26:21;
Ps 72:14

[12]"If I am a man of God," Elijah replied, "may fire come down from heaven and consume you and your fifty men!" Then the fire of God fell from heaven and consumed him and his fifty men.

1:15
c ver 3
d Isa 51:12; 57:11;
Jer 1:17;
Eze 2:6

[13]So the king sent a third captain with his fifty men. This third captain went up and fell on his knees before Elijah. "Man of God," he begged, "please have respect for my life*b* and the lives of these fifty men, your servants! [14]See, fire has fallen from heaven and consumed the first two captains and all their men. But now have respect for my life!"

1:16
e ver 2
f ver 4

[15]The angel*c* of the LORD said to Elijah, "Go down with him; do not be afraid*d* of him." So Elijah got up and went down with him to the king.

1:17
g 2Ki 8:15;
Jer 20:6; 28:17
h 2Ki 3:1; 8:16

[16]He told the king, "This is what the LORD says: Is it because there is no God in Israel for you to consult that you have sent messengers*e* to consult Baal-Zebub, the god of Ekron? Because you have done this, you will never leave*f* the bed you are lying on. You will certainly die!" [17]So he died,*g* according to the word of the LORD that Elijah had spoken.

Because Ahaziah had no son, Joram*ah* succeeded him as king in the second year of Jehoram son of Jehoshaphat king of Judah. [18]As for all the other events of Ahaziah's reign, and what he did, are they not written in the book of the annals of the kings of Israel?

Chapter 2 Theme _____

2:1
i Ge 5:24;
Heb 11:5
j ver 11;
1Ki 19:11;
Isa 5:28; 66:15;
Jer 4:13;
Na 1:3
k 1Ki 19:16,21
l Dt 11:30;
2Ki 4:38

2 When the LORD was about to take*i* Elijah up to heaven in a whirlwind,*j* Elijah and Elisha*k* were on their way from Gilgal.*l* [2]Elijah said to Elisha, "Stay here;*m* the LORD has sent me to Bethel."

But Elisha said, "As surely as the LORD lives and as you live, I will not leave you."*n* So they went down to Bethel.

2:2
m ver 6
n Ru 1:16;
1Sa 1:26;
2Ki 4:30

[3]The company*o* of the prophets at Bethel came out to Elisha and asked, "Do you know that the LORD is going to take your master from you today?"

"Yes, I know," Elisha replied, "but do not speak of it."

2:3
o 1Sa 10:5;
2Ki 4:1,38

[4]Then Elijah said to him, "Stay here, Elisha; the LORD has sent me to Jericho.*p*"

And he replied, "As surely as the LORD lives and as you live, I will not leave you." So they went to Jericho.

2:4
p Jos 3:16; 6:26

a 17 Hebrew *Jehoram,* a variant of *Joram*

[5]The company[a] of the prophets at Jericho went up to Elisha and asked him, "Do you know that the LORD is going to take your master from you today?"

"Yes, I know," he replied, "but do not speak of it."

[6]Then Elijah said to him, "Stay here;[b] the LORD has sent me to the Jordan."[c]

And he replied, "As surely as the LORD lives and as you live, I will not leave you."[d] So the two of them walked on.

[7]Fifty men of the company of the prophets went and stood at a distance, facing the place where Elijah and Elisha had stopped at the Jordan. [8]Elijah took his cloak,[e] rolled it up and struck[f] the water with it. The water divided[g] to the right and to the left, and the two of them crossed over on dry[h] ground.

Elisha's Ministry

[9]When they had crossed, Elijah said to Elisha, "Tell me, what can I do for you before I am taken from you?"

"Let me inherit a double[i] portion of your spirit,"[j] Elisha replied.

[10]"You have asked a difficult thing," Elijah said, "yet if you see me when I am taken from you, it will be yours—otherwise not."

[11]As they were walking along and talking together, suddenly a chariot of fire[k] and horses of fire appeared and separated the two of them, and Elijah went up to heaven[l] in a whirlwind.[m] [12]Elisha saw this and cried out, "My father! My father! The chariots[n] and horsemen of Israel!" And Elisha saw him no more. Then he took hold of his own clothes and tore[o] them apart.

[13]He picked up the cloak that had fallen from Elijah and went back and stood on the bank of the Jordan. [14]Then he took the cloak[p] that had fallen from him and struck[q] the water with it. "Where now is the LORD,

Map of Elisha's Ministry:
- Damascus — Elisha prophesies doom on Ben-Hadad (2 Kings 8:7-15)
- Tyre
- Mediterranean Sea
- Elisha brings to life son of woman from Shunem (2 Kings 4:8-37)
- Elisha sends the young man to anoint Jehu (2 Kings 9)
- Sea of Galilee
- Mt. Carmel
- Shunem
- Abel Meholah
- Ramoth Gilead
- Elisha guides Aramean forces from Dothan to Samaria (2 Kings 6:13ff)
- Dothan
- Elisha's native town (1 Kings 19:16)
- ISRAEL
- Jordan River
- Elisha prophesies lifting of siege (2 Kings 6:20-7:20)
- Samaria
- Naaman healed of leprosy (2 Kings 5)
- Elisha removes death from the pot (2 Kings 4:38-41)
- Gilgal
- Bethel
- Jericho
- Elisha becomes Elijah's successor, cleanses waters of Jericho, recovers axe head (2 Kings 2, 6)
- Go up, you baldhead! (2 Kings 2:23)
- Jerusalem
- JUDAH
- AMMON
- Dead Sea
- PHILISTIA
- Arad
- Beersheba
- Kir Moab
- MOAB
- Elisha prophesies flood (2 Kings 3:13-20)
- Way of Edom
- EDOM

Margin cross-references:
2:5 [a]ver 3
2:6 [b]ver 2 [c]Jos 3:15 [d]Ru 1:16
2:8 [e]1Ki 19:19 [f]ver 14 [g]Ex 14:21 [h]Ex 14:22,29
2:9 [i]Dt 21:17 [j]Nu 11:17
2:11 [k]2Ki 6:17; Ps 68:17; 104:3,4; Isa 66:15; Hab 3:8; Zec 6:1 [l]Ge 5:24 [m]ver 1
2:12 [n]2Ki 6:17; 13:14 [o]Ge 37:29
2:14 [p]1Ki 19:19 [q]ver 8

2:15
a ver 7;
1Sa 10:5
b Nu 11:17

the God of Elijah?" he asked. When he struck the water, it divided to the right and to the left, and he crossed over.

15The company*a* of the prophets from Jericho, who were watching, said, "The spirit*b* of Elijah is resting on Elisha." And they went to meet him and bowed to the ground before him. 16"Look," they said, "we your servants have fifty able men. Let them go and look for your master. Perhaps the Spirit*c* of the LORD has picked him up*d* and set him down on some mountain or in some valley."

"No," Elisha replied, "do not send them."

2:16
c 1Ki 18:12
d Ac 8:39

17But they persisted until he was too ashamed*e* to refuse. So he said, "Send them." And they sent fifty men, who searched for three days but did not find him. 18When they returned to Elisha, who was staying in Jericho, he said to them, "Didn't I tell you not to go?"

19The men of the city said to Elisha, "Look, our lord, this town is well situated, as you can see, but the water is bad and the land is unproductive."

2:17
e 2Ki 8:11

20"Bring me a new bowl," he said, "and put salt in it." So they brought it to him.

21Then he went out to the spring and threw*f* the salt into it, saying, "This is what the LORD says: 'I have healed this water. Never again will it cause death or make the land unproductive.'" 22And the water has remained wholesome*g* to this day, according to the word Elisha had spoken.

2:21
f Ex 15:25;
2Ki 4:41; 6:6

2:22
g Ex 15:25

23From there Elisha went up to Bethel. As he was walking along the road, some youths came out of the town and jeered*h* at him. "Go on up, you baldhead!" they said. "Go on up, you baldhead!" 24He turned

2:23
h Ex 22:28;
2Ch 36:16;
Job 19:18;
Ps 31:18

The Cities and Geography of 2 Kings

Mediterranean Sea
To Arpad
Hamath
ARAM
Damascus
LEBANON
Ijon
Abel Beth Maacah
BASHAN
Kedesh
Hazor
Sea of Galilee
Mt. Carmel
Shunem
GILEAD
Megiddo
Jezreel
Dothan
Ramoth Gilead
Samaria
Jordan River
Aphek
Bethel
Jericho
Ekron
Jerusalem
AMMON
Gath
Libnah
Lachish
Dead Sea
Beersheba
MOAB
To Egypt
EDOM

around, looked at them and called down a curse[a] on them in the name[b] of the LORD. Then two bears came out of the woods and mauled forty-two of the youths. [25]And he went on to Mount Carmel[c] and from there returned to Samaria.

Chapter 3 Theme

3 Joram[a][d] son of Ahab became king of Israel in Samaria in the eighteenth year of Jehoshaphat king of Judah, and he reigned twelve years. [2]He did evil[e] in the eyes of the LORD, but not as his father[f] and mother had done. He got rid of the sacred stone[g] of Baal that his father had made. [3]Nevertheless he clung to the sins[h] of Jeroboam son of Nebat, which he had caused Israel to commit; he did not turn away from them.

[4]Now Mesha king of Moab[i] raised sheep, and he had to supply the king of Israel with a hundred thousand lambs[j] and with the wool of a hundred thousand rams. [5]But after Ahab died, the king of Moab rebelled[k] against the king of Israel. [6]So at that time King Joram set out from Samaria and mobilized all Israel. [7]He also sent this message to Jehoshaphat king of Judah: "The king of Moab has rebelled against me. Will you go with me to fight[l] against Moab?"

"I will go with you," he replied. "I am as you are, my people as your people, my horses as your horses."

[8]"By what route shall we attack?" he asked.

"Through the Desert of Edom," he answered.

[9]So the king of Israel set out with the king of Judah and the king of Edom.[m] After a roundabout march of seven days, the army had no more water for themselves or for the animals with them.

[10]"What!" exclaimed the king of Israel. "Has the LORD called us three kings together only to hand us over to Moab?"

[11]But Jehoshaphat asked, "Is there no prophet of the LORD here, that we may inquire[n] of the LORD through him?"

An officer of the king of Israel answered, "Elisha[o] son of Shaphat is here. He used to pour water on the hands of Elijah.[b][p]"

[12]Jehoshaphat said, "The word[q] of the LORD is with him." So the king of Israel and Jehoshaphat and the king of Edom went down to him.

[13]Elisha said to the king of Israel, "What do we have to do with each other? Go to the prophets of your father and the prophets of your mother."

"No," the king of Israel answered, "because it was the LORD who called us three kings together to hand us over to Moab."

---

a 1 Hebrew *Jehoram*, a variant of *Joram*; also in verse 6   b 11 That is, he was Elijah's personal servant.

## Cross references (margin)

2:24
[a]Ge 4:11;
Ne 13:25-27
[b]Dt 18:19

2:25
[c]1Ki 18:20;
2Ki 4:25

3:1
[d]2Ki 1:17

3:2
[e]1Ki 15:26
[f]1Ki 16:30-32
[g]Ex 23:24;
2Ki 10:18,
26-28

3:3
[h]1Ki 12:28-32;
14:9,16

3:4
[i]Ge 19:37;
2Ki 1:1
[j]Ezr 7:17;
Isa 16:1

3:5
[k]2Ki 1:1

3:7
[l]1Ki 22:4

3:9
[m]1Ki 22:47

3:11
[n]Ge 25:22;
1Ki 22:7
[o]Ge 20:7
[p]1Ki 19:16

3:12
[q]Nu 11:17

3:15
a 1Sa 16:23
b Jer 15:17;
Eze 1:3

3:17
c Ps 107:35;
Isa 32:2; 35:6;
41:18

3:18
d Ge 18:14;
2Ki 20:10;
Isa 49:6;
Jer 32:17,27;
Mk 10:27

3:20
e Ex 29:39-40
f Ex 17:6

3:25
g ver 19;
Isa 15:1; 16:7;
Jer 48:31,36

3:27
h Dt 12:31;
2Ki 16:3; 21:6;
2Ch 28:3;
Ps 106:38;
Jer 19:4-5;
Am 2:1;
Mic 6:7

4:1
i 1Sa 10:5;
2Ki 2:3
j Ex 22:26;
Lev 25:39-43;
Ne 5:3-5;
Job 22:6; 24:9

¹⁴Elisha said, "As surely as the LORD Almighty lives, whom I serve, if I did not have respect for the presence of Jehoshaphat king of Judah, I would not look at you or even notice you. ¹⁵But now bring me a harpist."*a*

While the harpist was playing, the hand*b* of the LORD came upon Elisha ¹⁶and he said, "This is what the LORD says: Make this valley full of ditches. ¹⁷For this is what the LORD says: You will see neither wind nor rain, yet this valley will be filled with water,*c* and you, your cattle and your other animals will drink. ¹⁸This is an easy*d* thing in the eyes of the LORD; he will also hand Moab over to you. ¹⁹You will overthrow every fortified city and every major town. You will cut down every good tree, stop up all the springs, and ruin every good field with stones."

²⁰The next morning, about the time*e* for offering the sacrifice, there it was—water flowing from the direction of Edom! And the land was filled with water.*f*

²¹Now all the Moabites had heard that the kings had come to fight against them; so every man, young and old, who could bear arms was called up and stationed on the border. ²²When they got up early in the morning, the sun was shining on the water. To the Moabites across the way, the water looked red—like blood. ²³"That's blood!" they said. "Those kings must have fought and slaughtered each other. Now to the plunder, Moab!"

²⁴But when the Moabites came to the camp of Israel, the Israelites rose up and fought them until they fled. And the Israelites invaded the land and slaughtered the Moabites. ²⁵They destroyed the towns, and each man threw a stone on every good field until it was covered. They stopped up all the springs and cut down every good tree. Only Kir Hareseth*g* was left with its stones in place, but men armed with slings surrounded it and attacked it as well.

²⁶When the king of Moab saw that the battle had gone against him, he took with him seven hundred swordsmen to break through to the king of Edom, but they failed. ²⁷Then he took his firstborn*h* son, who was to succeed him as king, and offered him as a sacrifice on the city wall. The fury against Israel was great; they withdrew and returned to their own land.

Chapter 4 Theme _____

4 The wife of a man from the company*i* of the prophets cried out to Elisha, "Your servant my husband is dead, and you know that he revered the LORD. But now his creditor*j* is coming to take my two boys as his slaves."

²Elisha replied to her, "How can I help you? Tell me, what do you have in your house?"

"Your servant has nothing there at all," she said, "except a little oil."[a]

[3] Elisha said, "Go around and ask all your neighbors for empty jars. Don't ask for just a few. [4] Then go inside and shut the door behind you and your sons. Pour oil into all the jars, and as each is filled, put it to one side."

[5] She left him and afterward shut the door behind her and her sons. They brought the jars to her and she kept pouring. [6] When all the jars were full, she said to her son, "Bring me another one."

But he replied, "There is not a jar left." Then the oil stopped flowing.

[7] She went and told the man of God,[b] and he said, "Go, sell the oil and pay your debts. You and your sons can live on what is left."

[8] One day Elisha went to Shunem.[c] And a well-to-do woman was there, who urged him to stay for a meal. So whenever he came by, he stopped there to eat. [9] She said to her husband, "I know that this man who often comes our way is a holy man of God. [10] Let's make a small room on the roof and put in it a bed and a table, a chair and a lamp for him. Then he can stay[d] there whenever he comes to us."

[11] One day when Elisha came, he went up to his room and lay down there. [12] He said to his servant Gehazi, "Call the Shunammite."[e] So he called her, and she stood before him. [13] Elisha said to him, "Tell her, 'You have gone to all this trouble for us. Now what can be done for you? Can we speak on your behalf to the king or the commander of the army?'"

She replied, "I have a home among my own people."

[14] "What can be done for her?" Elisha asked.

Gehazi said, "Well, she has no son and her husband is old."

[15] Then Elisha said, "Call her." So he called her, and she stood in the doorway. [16] "About this time[f] next year," Elisha said, "you will hold a son in your arms."

"No, my lord," she objected. "Don't mislead your servant, O man of God!"

[17] But the woman became pregnant, and the next year about that same time she gave birth to a son, just as Elisha had told her.

[18] The child grew, and one day he went out to his father, who was with the reapers.[g] [19] "My head! My head!" he said to his father.

His father told a servant, "Carry him to his mother." [20] After the servant had lifted him up and carried him to his mother, the boy sat on her lap until noon, and then he died. [21] She went up and laid him on the bed[h] of the man of God, then shut the door and went out.

[22] She called her husband and said, "Please send me one of the servants and a donkey so I can go to the man of God quickly and return."

4:2
[a] 1Ki 17:12

4:7
[b] 1Ki 12:22

4:8
[c] Jos 19:18

4:10
[d] Mt 10:41;
Ro 12:13

4:12
[e] 2Ki 8:1

4:16
[f] Ge 18:10

4:18
[g] Ru 2:3

4:21
[h] ver 32

4:23
a Nu 10:10;
1Ch 23:31;
Ps 81:3

²³"Why go to him today?" he asked. "It's not the New Moon*a* or the Sabbath."

"It's all right," she said.

²⁴She saddled the donkey and said to her servant, "Lead on; don't slow down for me unless I tell you." ²⁵So she set out and came to the man of God at Mount Carmel.*b*

4:25
b 1Ki 18:20;
2Ki 2:25

When he saw her in the distance, the man of God said to his servant Gehazi, "Look! There's the Shunammite! ²⁶Run to meet her and ask her, 'Are you all right? Is your husband all right? Is your child all right?'"

"Everything is all right," she said.

4:27
c 1Sa 1:15

²⁷When she reached the man of God at the mountain, she took hold of his feet. Gehazi came over to push her away, but the man of God said, "Leave her alone! She is in bitter distress,*c* but the LORD has hidden it from me and has not told me why."

²⁸"Did I ask you for a son, my lord?" she said. "Didn't I tell you, 'Don't raise my hopes'?"

4:29
d 1Ki 18:46;
2Ki 2:8,
14; 9:1
e Ex 4:2;
7:19; 14:16

²⁹Elisha said to Gehazi, "Tuck your cloak into your belt,*d* take my staff*e* in your hand and run. If you meet anyone, do not greet him, and if anyone greets you, do not answer. Lay my staff on the boy's face."

4:32
f ver 21

³⁰But the child's mother said, "As surely as the LORD lives and as you live, I will not leave you." So he got up and followed her.

³¹Gehazi went on ahead and laid the staff on the boy's face, but there was no sound or response. So Gehazi went back to meet Elisha and told him, "The boy has not awakened."

4:33
g 1Ki 17:20;
Mt 6:6

³²When Elisha reached the house, there was the boy lying dead on his couch.*f* ³³He went in, shut the door on the two of them and prayed*g* to the LORD. ³⁴Then he got on the bed and lay upon the boy, mouth to mouth, eyes to eyes, hands to hands. As he stretched*h* himself out upon him, the boy's body grew warm.

4:34
h 1Ki 17:21;
Ac 20:10

³⁵Elisha turned away and walked back and forth in the room and then got on the bed and stretched out upon him once more. The boy sneezed seven times*i* and opened his eyes.*j*

4:35
i Jos 6:15
j 2Ki 8:5

³⁶Elisha summoned Gehazi and said, "Call the Shunammite." And he did. When she came, he said, "Take your son."*k* ³⁷She came in, fell at his feet and bowed to the ground. Then she took her son and went out.

4:36
k Heb 11:35

³⁸Elisha returned to Gilgal*l* and there was a famine*m* in that region. While the company of the prophets was meeting with him, he said to his servant, "Put on the large pot and cook some stew for these men."

4:38
l 2Ki 2:1
m Lev 26:26;
2Ki 8:1

³⁹One of them went out into the fields to gather herbs and found a wild vine. He gathered some of its gourds and filled the fold of his cloak. When he returned, he cut them up into the pot of

INSIGHT

The land of **Baal Shalishah**, meaning "the third," was evidently the tribal territory of Ephraim (1 Samuel 9:4). Modern-day Kefr Thilth may be on the site of the ancient city. However, the exact location of Baal Shalishah has recently been questioned.

stew, though no one knew what they were. ⁴⁰The stew was poured out for the men, but as they began to eat it, they cried out, "O man of God, there is death in the pot!" And they could not eat it.

⁴¹Elisha said, "Get some flour." He put it into the pot and said, "Serve it to the people to eat." And there was nothing harmful in the pot.^a

⁴²A man came from Baal Shalishah,^b bringing the man of God twenty loaves^c of barley bread^d baked from the first ripe grain, along with some heads of new grain. "Give it to the people to eat," Elisha said.

⁴³"How can I set this before a hundred men?" his servant asked.

But Elisha answered, "Give it to the people to eat.^e For this is what the LORD says: 'They will eat and have some left over.^f'" ⁴⁴Then he set it before them, and they ate and had some left over, according to the word of the LORD.

Chapter 5 Theme

⁵ Now Naaman was commander of the army of the king of Aram.^g He was a great man in the sight of his master and highly regarded, because through him the LORD had given victory to Aram. He was a valiant soldier, but he had leprosy.^a ^h

²Now bandsⁱ from Aram had gone out and had taken captive a young girl from Israel, and she served Naaman's wife. ³She said to her mistress, "If only my master would see the prophet^j who is in Samaria! He would cure him of his leprosy."

⁴Naaman went to his master and told him what the girl from Israel had said. ⁵"By all means, go," the king of Aram replied. "I will send a letter to the king of Israel." So Naaman left, taking with him ten talents^b of silver, six thousand shekels^c of gold and ten sets of clothing.^k ⁶The letter that he took to the king of Israel read: "With this letter I am sending my servant Naaman to you so that you may cure him of his leprosy."

⁷As soon as the king of Israel read the letter,^l he tore his robes and said, "Am I God?^m Can I kill and bring back to life?ⁿ Why does this fellow send someone to me to be cured of his leprosy? See how he is trying to pick a quarrel^o with me!"

⁸When Elisha the man of God heard that the king of Israel had torn his robes, he sent him this message: "Why have you torn your robes? Have the man come to me and he will know that there is a prophet^p in Israel." ⁹So Naaman went with his horses and chariots and stopped at the door of Elisha's house. ¹⁰Elisha sent a

### Cross references (margin)

4:41
^aEx 15:25;
2Ki 2:21

4:42
^b1Sa 9:4;
^cMt 14:17;
15:36
^d1Sa 9:7

4:43
^eLk 9:13;
^fMt 14:20;
Jn 6:12

5:1
^gGe 10:22;
2Sa 10:19
^hEx 4:6;
Nu 12:10;
Lk 4:27

5:2
ⁱ2Ki 6:23; 13:20;
24:2

5:3
^jGe 20:7

5:5
^kver 22;
Ge 24:53;
Jdg 14:12;
1Sa 9:7

5:7
^l2Ki 19:14
^mGe 30:2
ⁿDt 32:39;
1Sa 2:6
^o1Ki 20:7

5:8
^p1Ki 22:7

---

^a 1 The Hebrew word was used for various diseases affecting the skin—not necessarily leprosy; also in verses 3, 6, 7, 11 and 27.   ^b 5 That is, about 750 pounds (about 340 kilograms)   ^c 5 That is, about 150 pounds (about 70 kilograms)

5:10
a Jn 9:7
b Ge 33:3;
Lev 14:7

5:11
c Ex 7:19

5:12
d Isa 8:6
e Pr 14:17,29;
19:11; 29:11

5:13
f 2Ki 6:21; 13:14

5:14
g Ge 33:3;
Lev 14:7;
Jos 6:15
h Ex 4:7
i Job 33:25;
Lk 4:27

5:15
j Jos 2:11
k Jos 4:24;
1Sa 17:46;
Da 2:47
l 1Sa 9:7; 25:27

5:16
m ver 20,26;
Ge 14:23;
Da 5:17

5:17
n Ex 20:24

5:18
o 2Ki 7:2

5:19
p 1Sa 1:17;
Ac 15:33

5:20
q Ex 20:7

5:22
r ver 5;
Ge 45:22

messenger to say to him, "Go, wash*a* yourself seven times*b* in the Jordan, and your flesh will be restored and you will be cleansed."

¹¹But Naaman went away angry and said, "I thought that he would surely come out to me and stand and call on the name of the LORD his God, wave his hand*c* over the spot and cure me of my leprosy. ¹²Are not Abana and Pharpar, the rivers of Damascus, better than any of the waters*d* of Israel? Couldn't I wash in them and be cleansed?" So he turned and went off in a rage.*e*

¹³Naaman's servants went to him and said, "My father,*f* if the prophet had told you to do some great thing, would you not have done it? How much more, then, when he tells you, 'Wash and be cleansed'!" ¹⁴So he went down and dipped himself in the Jordan seven times,*g* as the man of God had told him, and his flesh was restored*h* and became clean like that of a young boy.*i*

¹⁵Then Naaman and all his attendants went back to the man of God.*j* He stood before him and said, "Now I know*k* that there is no God in all the world except in Israel. Please accept now a gift*l* from your servant."

¹⁶The prophet answered, "As surely as the LORD lives, whom I serve, I will not accept a thing." And even though Naaman urged him, he refused.*m*

¹⁷"If you will not," said Naaman, "please let me, your servant, be given as much earth*n* as a pair of mules can carry, for your servant will never again make burnt offerings and sacrifices to any other god but the LORD. ¹⁸But may the LORD forgive your servant for this one thing: When my master enters the temple of Rimmon to bow down and he is leaning*o* on my arm and I bow there also— when I bow down in the temple of Rimmon, may the LORD forgive your servant for this."

¹⁹"Go in peace,"*p* Elisha said.

After Naaman had traveled some distance, ²⁰Gehazi, the servant of Elisha the man of God, said to himself, "My master was too easy on Naaman, this Aramean, by not accepting from him what he brought. As surely as the LORD*q* lives, I will run after him and get something from him."

²¹So Gehazi hurried after Naaman. When Naaman saw him running toward him, he got down from the chariot to meet him. "Is everything all right?" he asked.

²²"Everything is all right," Gehazi answered. "My master sent me to say, 'Two young men from the company of the prophets have just come to me from the hill country of Ephraim. Please give them a talent*a* of silver and two sets of clothing.'"*r*

²³"By all means, take two talents," said Naaman. He urged Gehazi to accept them, and then tied up the two talents of silver in

---

INSIGHT

The **Arameans**, the descendants of Noah through Shem, lived in a confederation of towns and settlements in what is now Syria. Some settled as far as Babylon. Jacob's grandfather, Abraham, was Aramean (Deuteronomy 26:5).

---

a 22 That is, about 75 pounds (about 34 kilograms)

two bags, with two sets of clothing. He gave them to two of his servants, and they carried them ahead of Gehazi. [24]When Gehazi came to the hill, he took the things from the servants and put them away in the house. He sent the men away and they left. [25]Then he went in and stood before his master Elisha.

"Where have you been, Gehazi?" Elisha asked.

"Your servant didn't go anywhere," Gehazi answered.

[26]But Elisha said to him, "Was not my spirit with you when the man got down from his chariot to meet you? Is this the time[a] to take money, or to accept clothes, olive groves, vineyards, flocks, herds, or menservants and maidservants?[b] [27]Naaman's leprosy[c] will cling to you and to your descendants forever." Then Gehazi[d] went from Elisha's presence and he was leprous, as white as snow.[e]

Chapter 6 Theme _____

6 The company[f] of the prophets said to Elisha, "Look, the place where we meet with you is too small for us. [2]Let us go to the Jordan, where each of us can get a pole; and let us build a place there for us to live."

And he said, "Go."

[3]Then one of them said, "Won't you please come with your servants?"

"I will," Elisha replied. [4]And he went with them.

They went to the Jordan and began to cut down trees. [5]As one of them was cutting down a tree, the iron axhead fell into the water. "Oh, my lord," he cried out, "it was borrowed!"

[6]The man of God asked, "Where did it fall?" When he showed him the place, Elisha cut a stick and threw[g] it there, and made the iron float. [7]"Lift it out," he said. Then the man reached out his hand and took it.

[8]Now the king of Aram was at war with Israel. After conferring with his officers, he said, "I will set up my camp in such and such a place."

[9]The man of God sent word to the king[h] of Israel: "Beware of passing that place, because the Arameans are going down there." [10]So the king of Israel checked on the place indicated by the man of God. Time and again Elisha warned[i] the king, so that he was on his guard in such places.

[11]This enraged the king of Aram. He summoned his officers and demanded of them, "Will you not tell me which of us is on the side of the king of Israel?"

[12]"None of us, my lord the king,[j]" said one of his officers, "but Elisha, the prophet who is in Israel, tells the king of Israel the very words you speak in your bedroom."

5:26
[a] ver 16
[b] Jer 45:5

5:27
[c] Nu 12:10; 2Ki 15:5
[d] Col 3:5
[e] Ex 4:6

6:1
[f] 1Sa 10:5; 2Ki 4:38

6:6
[g] Ex 15:25; 2Ki 2:21

6:9
[h] ver 12

6:10
[i] Jer 11:18

6:12
[j] ver 9

6:13
a Ge 37:17

6:14
b 2Ki 1:9

6:16
c Ge 15:1
d 2Ch 32:7;
Ps 55:18;
Ro 8:31;
1Jn 4:4

6:17
e 2Ki 2:11,12;
Ps 68:17;
Zec 6:1-7

6:18
f Ge 19:11;
Ac 13:11

6:21
g 2Ki 5:13

6:22
h Dt 20:11;
2Ch 28:8-15;
Ro 12:20

6:23
i 2Ki 5:2

6:24
j 1Ki 15:18; 20:1;
2Ki 8:7
k Dt 28:52

6:25
l Lev 26:26;
Ru 1:1
m Isa 36:12

¹³"Go, find out where he is," the king ordered, "so I can send men and capture him." The report came back: "He is in Dothan."*a* ¹⁴Then he sent*b* horses and chariots and a strong force there. They went by night and surrounded the city.

¹⁵When the servant of the man of God got up and went out early the next morning, an army with horses and chariots had surrounded the city. "Oh, my lord, what shall we do?" the servant asked.

¹⁶"Don't be afraid,"*c* the prophet answered. "Those who are with us are more*d* than those who are with them."

¹⁷And Elisha prayed, "O LORD, open his eyes so he may see." Then the LORD opened the servant's eyes, and he looked and saw the hills full of horses and chariots*e* of fire all around Elisha.

¹⁸As the enemy came down toward him, Elisha prayed to the LORD, "Strike these people with blindness."*f* So he struck them with blindness, as Elisha had asked.

¹⁹Elisha told them, "This is not the road and this is not the city. Follow me, and I will lead you to the man you are looking for." And he led them to Samaria.

²⁰After they entered the city, Elisha said, "LORD, open the eyes of these men so they can see." Then the LORD opened their eyes and they looked, and there they were, inside Samaria.

²¹When the king of Israel saw them, he asked Elisha, "Shall I kill them, my father?*g* Shall I kill them?"

²²"Do not kill them," he answered. "Would you kill men you have captured*h* with your own sword or bow? Set food and water before them so that they may eat and drink and then go back to their master." ²³So he prepared a great feast for them, and after they had finished eating and drinking, he sent them away, and they returned to their master. So the bands*i* from Aram stopped raiding Israel's territory.

²⁴Some time later, Ben-Hadad*j* king of Aram mobilized his entire army and marched up and laid siege*k* to Samaria. ²⁵There was a great famine*l* in the city; the siege lasted so long that a donkey's head sold for eighty shekels*a* of silver, and a quarter of a cab*b* of seed pods*c* *m* for five shekels.*d*

²⁶As the king of Israel was passing by on the wall, a woman cried to him, "Help me, my lord the king!"

²⁷The king replied, "If the LORD does not help you, where can I get help for you? From the threshing floor? From the winepress?" ²⁸Then he asked her, "What's the matter?"

She answered, "This woman said to me, 'Give up your son so we may eat him today, and tomorrow we'll eat my son.' ²⁹So we

---

a 25 That is, about 2 pounds (about 1 kilogram)   *b* 25 That is, probably about 1/2 pint (about 0.3 liter)   *c* 25 Or *of dove's dung*   *d* 25 That is, about 2 ounces (about 55 grams) cooked my son and ate[a] him. The next day I said to her, 'Give up your son so we may eat him,' but she had hidden him."

30When the king heard the woman's words, he tore[b] his robes. As he went along the wall, the people looked, and there, underneath, he had sackcloth[c] on his body. 31He said, "May God deal with me, be it ever so severely, if the head of Elisha son of Shaphat remains on his shoulders today!"

32Now Elisha was sitting in his house, and the elders[d] were sitting with him. The king sent a messenger ahead, but before he arrived, Elisha said to the elders, "Don't you see how this murderer[e] is sending someone to cut off my head?[f] Look, when the messenger comes, shut the door and hold it shut against him. Is not the sound of his master's footsteps behind him?"

33While he was still talking to them, the messenger came down to him. And ⌊the king⌋ said, "This disaster is from the LORD. Why should I wait[g] for the LORD any longer?"

Chapter 7 Theme

7 Elisha said, "Hear the word of the LORD. This is what the LORD says: About this time tomorrow, a seah[a] of flour will sell for a shekel[b] and two seahs[c] of barley for a shekel[h] at the gate of Samaria."

2The officer on whose arm the king was leaning[i] said to the man of God, "Look, even if the LORD should open the floodgates[j] of the heavens, could this happen?"

"You will see it with your own eyes," answered Elisha, "but you will not eat[k] any of it!"

3Now there were four men with leprosy[d][l] at the entrance of the city gate. They said to each other, "Why stay here until we die? 4If we say, 'We'll go into the city'—the famine is there, and we will die. And if we stay here, we will die. So let's go over to the camp of the Arameans and surrender. If they spare us, we live; if they kill us, then we die."

5At dusk they got up and went to the camp of the Arameans. When they reached the edge of the camp, not a man was there, 6for the Lord had caused the Arameans to hear the sound[m] of chariots and horses and a great army, so that they said to one another, "Look, the king of Israel has hired[n] the Hittite[o] and Egyptian kings to attack us!" 7So they got up and fled[p] in the dusk and abandoned their tents and their horses and donkeys. They left the camp as it was and ran for their lives.

a1 That is, probably about 7 quarts (about 7.3 liters); also in verses 16 and 18   b1 That is, about 2/5 ounce (about 11 grams); also in verses 16 and 18   c1 That is, probably about 13 quarts (about 15 liters); also in verses 16 and 18   d3 The Hebrew word is used for various diseases affecting the skin—not necessarily leprosy; also in verse 8.

6:29 [a]Lev 26:29; Dt 28:53-55

6:30 [b]2Ki 18:37; Isa 22:15; [c]Ge 37:34; 1Ki 21:27

6:32 [d]Eze 8:1; 14:1; 20:1; [e]1Ki 18:4; [f]ver 31

6:33 [g]Lev 24:11; Job 2:9; 14:14; Isa 40:31

7:1 [h]ver 16

7:2 [i]2Ki 5:18; [j]ver 19; Ge 7:11; Ps 78:23; Mal 3:10; [k]ver 17

7:3 [l]Lev 13:45-46; Nu 5:1-4

7:6 [m]Ex 14:24; 2Sa 5:24; Eze 1:24; [n]2Sa 10:6; Jer 46:21; [o]Nu 13:29

7:7 [p]Jdg 7:21; Ps 48:4-6; Pr 28:1; Isa 30:17

7:8
a Isa 33:23; 35:6

⁸The men who had leprosy*a* reached the edge of the camp and entered one of the tents. They ate and drank, and carried away silver, gold and clothes, and went off and hid them. They returned and entered another tent and took some things from it and hid them also.

⁹Then they said to each other, "We're not doing right. This is a day of good news and we are keeping it to ourselves. If we wait until daylight, punishment will overtake us. Let's go at once and report this to the royal palace."

7:12
b Jos 8:4;
2Ki 6:25-29

¹⁰So they went and called out to the city gatekeepers and told them, "We went into the Aramean camp and not a man was there—not a sound of anyone—only tethered horses and donkeys, and the tents left just as they were." ¹¹The gatekeepers shouted the news, and it was reported within the palace.

¹²The king got up in the night and said to his officers, "I will tell you what the Arameans have done to us. They know we are starving; so they have left the camp to hide*b* in the countryside, thinking, 'They will surely come out, and then we will take them alive and get into the city.'"

7:16
c Isa 33:4,23
d ver 1

¹³One of his officers answered, "Have some men take five of the horses that are left in the city. Their plight will be like that of all the Israelites left here—yes, they will only be like all these Israelites who are doomed. So let us send them to find out what happened."

¹⁴So they selected two chariots with their horses, and the king sent them after the Aramean army. He commanded the drivers, "Go and find out what has happened." ¹⁵They followed them as far as the Jordan, and they found the whole road strewn with the clothing and equipment the Arameans had thrown away in their headlong flight. So the messengers returned and reported to the king. ¹⁶Then the people went out and plundered*c* the camp of the Arameans. So a seah of flour sold for a shekel, and two seahs of barley sold for a shekel,*d* as the LORD had said.

7:17
e ver 2;
2Ki 6:32

¹⁷Now the king had put the officer on whose arm he leaned in charge of the gate, and the people trampled him in the gateway, and he died,*e* just as the man of God had foretold when the king came down to his house. ¹⁸It happened as the man of God had said to the king: "About this time tomorrow, a seah of flour will sell for a shekel and two seahs of barley for a shekel at the gate of Samaria."

¹⁹The officer had said to the man of God, "Look, even if the LORD should open the floodgates*f* of the heavens, could this happen?" The man of God had replied, "You will see it with your own eyes, but you will not eat any of it!" ²⁰And that is exactly what happened to him, for the people trampled him in the gateway, and he died.

7:19
f ver 2

Chapter 8 Theme

8 Now Elisha had said to the woman[a] whose son he had restored to life, "Go away with your family and stay for a while wherever you can, because the LORD has decreed a famine[b] in the land that will last seven years."[c] [2]The woman proceeded to do as the man of God said. She and her family went away and stayed in the land of the Philistines seven years.

[3]At the end of the seven years she came back from the land of the Philistines and went to the king to beg for her house and land. [4]The king was talking to Gehazi, the servant of the man of God, and had said, "Tell me about all the great things Elisha has done." [5]Just as Gehazi was telling the king how Elisha had restored[d] the dead to life, the woman whose son Elisha had brought back to life came to beg the king for her house and land.

Gehazi said, "This is the woman, my lord the king, and this is her son whom Elisha restored to life." [6]The king asked the woman about it, and she told him.

Then he assigned an official to her case and said to him, "Give back everything that belonged to her, including all the income from her land from the day she left the country until now."

[7]Elisha went to Damascus,[e] and Ben-Hadad[f] king of Aram was ill. When the king was told, "The man of God has come all the way up here," [8]he said to Hazael,[g] "Take a gift[h] with you and go to meet the man of God. Consult[i] the LORD through him; ask him, 'Will I recover from this illness?'"

[9]Hazael went to meet Elisha, taking with him as a gift forty camel-loads of all the finest wares of Damascus. He went in and stood before him, and said, "Your son Ben-Hadad king of Aram has sent me to ask, 'Will I recover from this illness?'"

[10]Elisha answered, "Go and say to him, 'You will certainly recover';[j] but[a] the LORD has revealed to me that he will in fact die." [11]He stared at him with a fixed gaze until Hazael felt ashamed.[k] Then the man of God began to weep.[l]

[12]"Why is my lord weeping?" asked Hazael.

"Because I know the harm[m] you will do to the Israelites," he answered. "You will set fire to their fortified places, kill their young men with the sword, dash[n] their little children[o] to the ground, and rip open[p] their pregnant women."

[13]Hazael said, "How could your servant, a mere dog,[q] accomplish such a feat?"

"The LORD has shown me that you will become king[r] of Aram," answered Elisha.

[14]Then Hazael left Elisha and returned to his master. When Ben-Hadad asked, "What did Elisha say to you?" Hazael replied,

---

a 10 The Hebrew may also be read *Go and say, 'You will certainly not recover,' for.*

8:1
[a] 2Ki 4:8-37
[b] Lev 26:26;
Dt 28:22;
Ru 1:1
[c] Ge 12:10;
Ps 105:16;
Hag 1:11

8:5
[d] 2Ki 4:35

8:7
[e] 2Sa 8:5;
1Ki 11:24
[f] 2Ki 6:24

8:8
[g] 1Ki 19:15
[h] Ge 32:20;
1Sa 9:7;
2Ki 1:2
[i] Jdg 18:5

8:10
[j] Isa 38:1

8:11
[k] Jdg 3:25
[l] Lk 19:41

8:12
[m] 1Ki 19:17;
2Ki 10:32;
12:17; 13:3,7
[n] Ps 137:9;
Isa 13:16;
Hos 13:16;
Na 3:10;
Lk 19:44
[o] Ge 34:29
[p] 2Ki 15:16;
Am 1:13

8:13
[q] 1Sa 17:43;
2Sa 3:8
[r] 1Ki 19:15

8:15
a 2Ki 1:17

8:16
b 2Ki 1:17; 3:1
c 2Ch 21:1-4

8:18
d ver 26;
2Ki 11:1

8:19
e Ge 6:13
f 2Sa 21:17; 7:13;
1Ki 11:36;
Rev 21:23

8:20
g 1Ki 22:47

8:22
h Ge 27:40
i Nu 33:20;
Jos 21:13;
2Ki 19:8

8:25
j 2Ki 9:29

8:26
k ver 18
l 1Ki 16:23

8:27
m 1Ki 16:30
n 1Ki 15:26

8:28
o Dt 4:43;
Ki 22:3,29

8:29
p 2Ki 9:15
q 1Ki 19:15,17

9:1
r 1Sa 10:5
s 2Ki 4:29
t 1Sa 10:1
u 2Ki 8:28

"He told me that you would certainly recover." ¹⁵But the next day he took a thick cloth, soaked it in water and spread it over the king's face, so that he died.*a* Then Hazael succeeded him as king.

¹⁶In the fifth year of Joram*b* son of Ahab king of Israel, when Jehoshaphat was king of Judah, Jehoram*c* son of Jehoshaphat began his reign as king of Judah. ¹⁷He was thirty-two years old when he became king, and he reigned in Jerusalem eight years. ¹⁸He walked in the ways of the kings of Israel, as the house of Ahab had done, for he married a daughter*d* of Ahab. He did evil in the eyes of the LORD. ¹⁹Nevertheless, for the sake of his servant David, the LORD was not willing to destroy*e* Judah. He had promised to maintain a lamp*f* for David and his descendants forever.

²⁰In the time of Jehoram, Edom rebelled against Judah and set up its own king.*g* ²¹So Jehoram*a* went to Zair with all his chariots. The Edomites surrounded him and his chariot commanders, but he rose up and broke through by night; his army, however, fled back home. ²²To this day Edom has been in rebellion*h* against Judah. Libnah*i* revolted at the same time.

²³As for the other events of Jehoram's reign, and all he did, are they not written in the book of the annals of the kings of Judah? ²⁴Jehoram rested with his fathers and was buried with them in the City of David. And Ahaziah his son succeeded him as king.

²⁵In the twelfth*j* year of Joram son of Ahab king of Israel, Ahaziah son of Jehoram king of Judah began to reign. ²⁶Ahaziah was twenty-two years old when he became king, and he reigned in Jerusalem one year. His mother's name was Athaliah,*k* a granddaughter of Omri*l* king of Israel. ²⁷He walked in the ways of the house of Ahab*m* and did evil*n* in the eyes of the LORD, as the house of Ahab had done, for he was related by marriage to Ahab's family.

²⁸Ahaziah went with Joram son of Ahab to war against Hazael king of Aram at Ramoth Gilead.*o* The Arameans wounded Joram; ²⁹so King Joram returned to Jezreel*p* to recover from the wounds the Arameans had inflicted on him at Ramoth*b* in his battle with Hazael*q* king of Aram.

Then Ahaziah son of Jehoram king of Judah went down to Jezreel to see Joram son of Ahab, because he had been wounded.

Chapter 9 Theme

9 The prophet Elisha summoned a man from the company*r* of the prophets and said to him, "Tuck your cloak into your belt,*s* take this flask of oil*t* with you and go to Ramoth Gilead.*u* ²When you get there, look for Jehu son of Jehoshaphat, the son of Nimshi. Go to him, get him away from his companions and take

a 21 Hebrew *Joram,* a variant of *Jehoram;* also in verses 23 and 24   *b* 29 Hebrew *Ramah,* a variant of *Ramoth*

INSIGHT

Zair's exact location is in question. The name means "small." Some believe it was south of the Dead (Salt) Sea near Edom, while others equate it with Zoar (Genesis 13:10) or Zior (Joshua 15:54).

him into an inner room. ³Then take the flask and pour the oil^a on his head and declare, 'This is what the LORD says: I anoint you king over Israel.' Then open the door and run; don't delay!"

⁴So the young man, the prophet, went to Ramoth Gilead. ⁵When he arrived, he found the army officers sitting together. "I have a message for you, commander," he said.

"For which of us?" asked Jehu.

"For you, commander," he replied.

⁶Jehu got up and went into the house. Then the prophet poured the oil^b on Jehu's head and declared, "This is what the LORD, the God of Israel, says: 'I anoint you king over the LORD's people Israel. ⁷You are to destroy the house of Ahab your master, and I will avenge^c the blood of my servants^d the prophets and the blood of all the LORD's servants shed by Jezebel.^e ⁸The whole house^f of Ahab will perish. I will cut off from Ahab every last male^g in Israel—slave or free. ⁹I will make the house of Ahab like the house of Jeroboam^h son of Nebat and like the house of Baashaⁱ son of Ahijah. ¹⁰As for Jezebel, dogs^j will devour her on the plot of ground at Jezreel, and no one will bury her.'" Then he opened the door and ran.

¹¹When Jehu went out to his fellow officers, one of them asked him, "Is everything all right? Why did this madman^k come to you?"

"You know the man and the sort of things he says," Jehu replied.

¹²"That's not true!" they said. "Tell us."

Jehu said, "Here is what he told me: 'This is what the LORD says: I anoint you king over Israel.'"

¹³They hurried and took their cloaks and spread^l them under him on the bare steps. Then they blew the trumpet^m and shouted, "Jehu is king!"

¹⁴So Jehu son of Jehoshaphat, the son of Nimshi, conspired against Joram. (Now Joram and all Israel had been defending Ramoth Gileadⁿ against Hazael king of Aram, ¹⁵but King Joram^a had returned to Jezreel to recover^o from the wounds the Arameans had inflicted on him in the battle with Hazael king of Aram.) Jehu said, "If this is the way you feel, don't let anyone slip out of the city to go and tell the news in Jezreel." ¹⁶Then he got into his chariot and rode to Jezreel, because Joram was resting there and Ahaziah^p king of Judah had gone down to see him.

¹⁷When the lookout^q standing on the tower in Jezreel saw Jehu's troops approaching, he called out, "I see some troops coming."

"Get a horseman," Joram ordered. "Send him to meet them and ask, 'Do you come in peace?^r'"

---

^a 15 Hebrew *Jehoram*, a variant of *Joram*; also in verses 17 and 21-24

9:3
^a 1Ki 19:16

9:6
^b 1Ki 19:16;
2Ch 22:7

9:7
^c Ge 4:24;
Rev 6:10
^d Dt 32:43
^e 1Ki 18:4;
21:15

9:8
^f 2Ki 10:17
^g Dt 32:36;
1Sa 25:22;
1Ki 21:21;
2Ki 14:26

9:9
^h 1Ki 14:10;
15:29; 16:3,11
ⁱ 1Ki 16:3

9:10
^j ver 35-36;
1Ki 21:23

9:11
^k Jer 29:26;
Jn 10:20;
Ac 26:24

9:13
^l Mt 21:8;
Lk 19:36
^m 2Sa 15:10;
1Ki 1:34,39

9:14
ⁿ Dt 4:43;
2Ki 8:28

9:15
^o 2Ki 8:29

9:16
^p 2Ch 22:7

9:17
^q Isa 21:6
^r 1Sa 16:4

9:20
a 2Sa 18:27

¹⁸The horseman rode off to meet Jehu and said, "This is what the king says: 'Do you come in peace?'"

"What do you have to do with peace?" Jehu replied. "Fall in behind me."

The lookout reported, "The messenger has reached them, but he isn't coming back."

9:21
b ver 26;
1Ki 21:1-7,
15-19

¹⁹So the king sent out a second horseman. When he came to them he said, "This is what the king says: 'Do you come in peace?'"

Jehu replied, "What do you have to do with peace? Fall in behind me."

9:22
c 1Ki 16:30-33;
18:19;
2Ch 21:13;
Rev 2:20

²⁰The lookout reported, "He has reached them, but he isn't coming back either. The driving is like^a that of Jehu son of Nimshi—he drives like a madman."

9:23
d 2Ki 11:14

²¹"Hitch up my chariot," Joram ordered. And when it was hitched up, Joram king of Israel and Ahaziah king of Judah rode out, each in his own chariot, to meet Jehu. They met him at the plot of ground that had belonged to Naboth^b the Jezreelite. ²²When Joram saw Jehu he asked, "Have you come in peace, Jehu?"

9:24
e 1Ki 22:34

"How can there be peace," Jehu replied, "as long as all the idolatry and witchcraft of your mother Jezebel^c abound?"

9:25
f 1Ki 21:19-22,
24-29

²³Joram turned about and fled, calling out to Ahaziah, "Treachery,^{d} Ahaziah!"

²⁴Then Jehu drew his bow^e and shot Joram between the shoulders. The arrow pierced his heart and he slumped down in his chariot. ²⁵Jehu said to Bidkar, his chariot officer, "Pick him up and throw him on the field that belonged to Naboth the Jezreelite. Remember how you and I were riding together in chariots behind Ahab his father when the LORD made this prophecy^f about him:

9:26
g 1Ki 21:19
h 1Ki 21:29

²⁶'Yesterday I saw the blood of Naboth^g and the blood of his sons, declares the LORD, and I will surely make you pay for it on this plot of ground, declares the LORD.'^{a} Now then, pick him up and throw him on that plot, in accordance with the word of the LORD."^{h}

9:27
i Jdg 1:27
j 2Ki 23:29

²⁷When Ahaziah king of Judah saw what had happened, he fled up the road to Beth Haggan.^{b} Jehu chased him, shouting, "Kill him too!" They wounded him in his chariot on the way up to Gur near Ibleam,^{i} but he escaped to Megiddo^j and died there. ²⁸His servants took him by chariot^k to Jerusalem and buried him with his fathers in his tomb in the City of David. ²⁹(In the eleventh^l year of Joram son of Ahab, Ahaziah had become king of Judah.)

9:28
k 2Ki 14:20;
23:30

9:29
l 2Ki 8:25

9:30
m Jer 4:30;
Eze 23:40

³⁰Then Jehu went to Jezreel. When Jezebel heard about it, she painted^m her eyes, arranged her hair and looked out of a window. ³¹As Jehu entered the gate, she asked, "Have you come in peace, Zimri,^{n} you murderer of your master?"^{c}

9:31
n 1Ki 16:9-10

a 26 See 1Kings 21:19.   b 27 Or *fled by way of the garden house*   c 31 Or *"Did Zimri have peace, who murdered his master?"*

³²He looked up at the window and called out, "Who is on my side? Who?" Two or three eunuchs looked down at him. ³³"Throw her down!" Jehu said. So they threw her down, and some of her blood spattered the wall and the horses as they trampled her underfoot.ᵃ

³⁴Jehu went in and ate and drank. "Take care of that cursed woman," he said, "and bury her, for she was a king's daughter."ᵇ ³⁵But when they went out to bury her, they found nothing except her skull, her feet and her hands. ³⁶They went back and told Jehu, who said, "This is the word of the Lᴏʀᴅ that he spoke through his servant Elijah the Tishbite: On the plot of ground at Jezreel dogsᶜ will devour Jezebel's flesh.ᵃᵈ ³⁷Jezebel's body will be like refuseᵉ on the ground in the plot at Jezreel, so that no one will be able to say, 'This is Jezebel.'"

Chapter 10 Theme _____

10 Now there were in Samariaᶠ seventy sonsᵍ of the house of Ahab. So Jehu wrote letters and sent them to Samaria: to the officials of Jezreel,ᵇʰ to the elders and to the guardiansⁱ of Ahab's children. He said, ²"As soon as this letter reaches you, since your master's sons are with you and you have chariots and horses, a fortified city and weapons, ³choose the best and most worthy of your master's sons and set him on his father's throne. Then fight for your master's house."

⁴But they were terrified and said, "If two kings could not resist him, how can we?"

⁵So the palace administrator, the city governor, the elders and the guardians sent this message to Jehu: "We are your servantsʲ and we will do anything you say. We will not appoint anyone as king; you do whatever you think best."

⁶Then Jehu wrote them a second letter, saying, "If you are on my side and will obey me, take the heads of your master's sons and come to me in Jezreel by this time tomorrow."

Now the royal princes, seventy of them, were with the leading men of the city, who were rearing them. ⁷When the letter arrived, these men took the princes and slaughtered all seventyᵏ of them. They put their headsˡ in baskets and sent them to Jehu in Jezreel. ⁸When the messenger arrived, he told Jehu, "They have brought the heads of the princes."

Then Jehu ordered, "Put them in two piles at the entrance of the city gate until morning."

⁹The next morning Jehu went out. He stood before all the people and said, "You are innocent. It was I who conspired against my

9:33
ᵃPs 7:5

9:34
ᵇ1Ki 16:31; 21:25

9:36
ᶜPs 68:23; Jer 15:3
ᵈ1Ki 21:23

9:37
ᵉPs 83:10; Isa 5:25; Jer 8:2; 9:22; 16:4; 25:33; Zep 1:17

10:1
ᶠ1Ki 13:32
ᵍJdg 8:30
ʰ1Ki 21:1
ⁱver 5

10:5
ʲJos 9:8; 1Ki 20:4,32

10:7
ᵏ1Ki 21:21
ˡ2Sa 4:8

10:10
a 2Ki 9:7-10
b 1Ki 21:29

10:11
c Hos 1:4
d ver 14;
Job 18:19

10:13
e 2Ki 8:24,29;
2Ch 22:8
f 1Ki 2:19

10:15
g Jer 35:6,
14-19
h 1Ch 2:55;
Jer 35:2
i Ezr 10:19;
Eze 17:18

10:16
j Nu 25:13;
1Ki 19:10

10:17
k 2Ki 9:8

10:18
l Jdg 2:11;
1Ki 16:31-32

10:19
m 1Ki 18:19;
22:6

10:20
n Ex 32:5;
Joel 1:14

10:24
o 1Ki 20:39

master and killed him, but who killed all these? ¹⁰Know then, that not a word the LORD has spoken against the house of Ahab will fail. The LORD has done what he promised*a* through his servant Elijah."*b* ¹¹So Jehu*c* killed everyone in Jezreel who remained of the house of Ahab, as well as all his chief men, his close friends and his priests, leaving him no survivor.*d*

¹²Jehu then set out and went toward Samaria. At Beth Eked of the Shepherds, ¹³he met some relatives of Ahaziah king of Judah and asked, "Who are you?"

They said, "We are relatives of Ahaziah,*e* and we have come down to greet the families of the king and of the queen mother.*f*"

¹⁴"Take them alive!" he ordered. So they took them alive and slaughtered them by the well of Beth Eked—forty-two men. He left no survivor.

¹⁵After he left there, he came upon Jehonadab*g* son of Recab,*h* who was on his way to meet him. Jehu greeted him and said, "Are you in accord with me, as I am with you?"

"I am," Jehonadab answered.

"If so," said Jehu, "give me your hand."*i* So he did, and Jehu helped him up into the chariot. ¹⁶Jehu said, "Come with me and see my zeal*j* for the LORD." Then he had him ride along in his chariot.

¹⁷When Jehu came to Samaria, he killed all who were left there of Ahab's family;*k* he destroyed them, according to the word of the LORD spoken to Elijah.

¹⁸Then Jehu brought all the people together and said to them, "Ahab served*l* Baal a little; Jehu will serve him much. ¹⁹Now summon*m* all the prophets of Baal, all his ministers and all his priests. See that no one is missing, because I am going to hold a great sacrifice for Baal. Anyone who fails to come will no longer live." But Jehu was acting deceptively in order to destroy the ministers of Baal.

²⁰Jehu said, "Call an assembly*n* in honor of Baal." So they proclaimed it. ²¹Then he sent word throughout Israel, and all the ministers of Baal came; not one stayed away. They crowded into the temple of Baal until it was full from one end to the other. ²²And Jehu said to the keeper of the wardrobe, "Bring robes for all the ministers of Baal." So he brought out robes for them.

²³Then Jehu and Jehonadab son of Recab went into the temple of Baal. Jehu said to the ministers of Baal, "Look around and see that no servants of the LORD are here with you—only ministers of Baal." ²⁴So they went in to make sacrifices and burnt offerings. Now Jehu had posted eighty men outside with this warning: "If one of you lets any of the men I am placing in your hands escape, it will be your life for his life."*o*

²⁵As soon as Jehu had finished making the burnt offering, he ordered the guards and officers: "Go in and kill*ᵃ* them; let no one escape."*ᵇ* So they cut them down with the sword. The guards and officers threw the bodies out and then entered the inner shrine of the temple of Baal. ²⁶They brought the sacred stone*ᶜ* out of the temple of Baal and burned it. ²⁷They demolished the sacred stone of Baal and tore down the temple*ᵈ* of Baal, and people have used it for a latrine to this day.

²⁸So Jehu*ᵉ* destroyed Baal worship in Israel. ²⁹However, he did not turn away from the sins*ᶠ* of Jeroboam son of Nebat, which he had caused Israel to commit—the worship of the golden calves*ᵍ* at Bethel*ʰ* and Dan.

³⁰The LORD said to Jehu, "Because you have done well in accomplishing what is right in my eyes and have done to the house of Ahab all I had in mind to do, your descendants will sit on the throne of Israel to the fourth generation."*ⁱ* ³¹Yet Jehu was not careful*ʲ* to keep the law of the LORD, the God of Israel, with all his heart. He did not turn away from the sins*ᵏ* of Jeroboam, which he had caused Israel to commit.

³²In those days the LORD began to reduce*ˡ* the size of Israel. Hazael*ᵐ* overpowered the Israelites throughout their territory ³³east of the Jordan in all the land of Gilead (the region of Gad, Reuben and Manasseh), from Aroer*ⁿ* by the Arnon Gorge through Gilead to Bashan.

³⁴As for the other events of Jehu's reign, all he did, and all his achievements, are they not written in the book of the annals*ᵒ* of the kings of Israel?

³⁵Jehu rested with his fathers and was buried in Samaria. And Jehoahaz his son succeeded him as king. ³⁶The time that Jehu reigned over Israel in Samaria was twenty-eight years.

Chapter 11 Theme _____

11 When Athaliah*ᵖ* the mother of Ahaziah saw that her son was dead, she proceeded to destroy the whole royal family. ²But Jehosheba, the daughter of King Jehoram*ᵃ* and sister of Ahaziah, took Joash*�q* son of Ahaziah and stole him away from among the royal princes, who were about to be murdered. She put him and his nurse in a bedroom to hide him from Athaliah; so he was not killed.*ʳ* ³He remained hidden with his nurse at the temple of the LORD for six years while Athaliah ruled the land.

⁴In the seventh year Jehoiada sent for the commanders of units of a hundred, the Carites*ˢ* and the guards and had them brought to him at the temple of the LORD. He made a covenant with them

a2 Hebrew Joram, a variant of Jehoram

10:25
*ᵃ*Ex 22:20;
2Ki 11:18
*ᵇ*1Ki 18:40

10:26
*ᶜ*1Ki 14:23

10:27
*ᵈ*1Ki 16:32

10:28
*ᵉ*1Ki 19:17

10:29
*ᶠ*1Ki 12:30
*ᵍ*1Ki 12:28-29
*ʰ*1Ki 12:32

10:30
*ⁱ*ver 35;
2Ki 15:12

10:31
*ʲ*Pr 4:23
*ᵏ*1Ki 12:30

10:32
*ˡ*2Ki 13:25
*ᵐ*1Ki 19:17;
2Ki 8:12

10:33
*ⁿ*Nu 32:34;
Dt 2:36;
Jdg 11:26;
Isa 17:2

10:34
*ᵒ*1Ki 15:31

11:1
*ᵖ*2Ki 8:18

11:2
*�q*ver 21;
2Ki 12:1
*ʳ*Jdg 9:5

11:4
*ˢ*ver 19

11:5
a 1Ch 9:25
b 1Ki 14:27

11:10
c 2Sa 8:7;
1Ch 18:7

11:12
d Ex 25:16;
2Ki 23:3;
e 1Sa 9:16;
1Ki 1:39
f Ps 47:1; 98:8;
Isa 55:12
g 1Sa 10:24

11:14
h 1Ki 7:15;
2Ki 23:3;
2Ch 34:31
i 1Ki 1:39
j Ge 37:29
k 2Ki 9:23

11:15
l 1Ki 2:30

11:16
m Ne 3:28;
Jer 31:40
n Ge 4:14

11:17
o Ex 24:8;
2Sa 5:3;
2Ch 15:12; 23:3;
29:10; 34:31;
Ezr 10:3
p 2Ki 23:3;
Jer 34:8

11:18
q 1Ki 16:32
r Dt 12:3
s 1Ki 18:40;
2Ki 10:25; 23:20

and put them under oath at the temple of the LORD. Then he showed them the king's son. ⁵He commanded them, saying, "This is what you are to do: You who are in the three companies that are going on duty on the Sabbath*ᵃ*—a third of you guarding the royal palace,*ᵇ* ⁶a third at the Sur Gate, and a third at the gate behind the guard, who take turns guarding the temple— ⁷and you who are in the other two companies that normally go off Sabbath duty are all to guard the temple for the king. ⁸Station yourselves around the king, each man with his weapon in his hand. Anyone who approaches your ranks*ᵃ* must be put to death. Stay close to the king wherever he goes."

⁹The commanders of units of a hundred did just as Jehoiada the priest ordered. Each one took his men—those who were going on duty on the Sabbath and those who were going off duty—and came to Jehoiada the priest. ¹⁰Then he gave the commanders the spears and shields*ᶜ* that had belonged to King David and that were in the temple of the LORD. ¹¹The guards, each with his weapon in his hand, stationed themselves around the king— near the altar and the temple, from the south side to the north side of the temple.

¹²Jehoiada brought out the king's son and put the crown on him; he presented him with a copy of the covenant*ᵈ* and proclaimed him king. They anointed*ᵉ* him, and the people clapped their hands*ᶠ* and shouted, "Long live the king!"*ᵍ*

¹³When Athaliah heard the noise made by the guards and the people, she went to the people at the temple of the LORD. ¹⁴She looked and there was the king, standing by the pillar,*ʰ* as the custom was. The officers and the trumpeters were beside the king, and all the people of the land were rejoicing and blowing trumpets.*ⁱ* Then Athaliah tore*ʲ* her robes and called out, "Treason! Treason!"*ᵏ*

¹⁵Jehoiada the priest ordered the commanders of units of a hundred, who were in charge of the troops: "Bring her out between the ranks*ᵇ* and put to the sword anyone who follows her." For the priest had said, "She must not be put to death in the temple*ˡ* of the LORD." ¹⁶So they seized her as she reached the place where the horses enter*ᵐ* the palace grounds, and there she was put to death.*ⁿ*

¹⁷Jehoiada then made a covenant*ᵒ* between the LORD and the king and people that they would be the LORD's people. He also made a covenant between the king and the people.*ᵖ* ¹⁸All the people of the land went to the temple*�q* of Baal and tore it down. They smashed*ʳ* the altars and idols to pieces and killed Mattan the priest*ˢ* of Baal in front of the altars.

a 8 Or approaches the precincts   *b 15 Or out from the precincts*

Then Jehoiada the priest posted guards at the temple of the LORD. ¹⁹He took with him the commanders of hundreds, the Carites,ᵃ the guards and all the people of the land, and together they brought the king down from the temple of the LORD and went into the palace, entering by way of the gate of the guards. The king then took his place on the royal throne, ²⁰and all the people of the land rejoiced.ᵇ And the city was quiet, because Athaliah had been slain with the sword at the palace.

²¹Joashᵃ was seven years old when he began to reign.

Chapter 12 Theme _____

12 In the seventh year of Jehu, Joashᵇᶜ became king, and he reigned in Jerusalem forty years. His mother's name was Zibiah; she was from Beersheba. ²Joash did what was right in the eyes of the LORD all the years Jehoiada the priest instructed him. ³The high places,ᵈ however, were not removed; the people continued to offer sacrifices and burn incense there.

⁴Joash said to the priests, "Collectᵉ all the money that is brought as sacred offeringsᶠ to the temple of the LORD—the money collected in the census,ᵍ the money received from personal vows and the money brought voluntarilyʰ to the temple. ⁵Let every priest receive the money from one of the treasurers, and let it be used to repair whatever damage is found in the temple."

⁶But by the twenty-third year of King Joash the priests still had not repaired the temple. ⁷Therefore King Joash summoned Jehoiada the priest and the other priests and asked them, "Why aren't you repairing the damage done to the temple? Take no more money from your treasurers, but hand it over for repairing the temple." ⁸The priests agreed that they would not collect any more money from the people and that they would not repair the temple themselves.

⁹Jehoiada the priest took a chest and bored a hole in its lid. He placed it beside the altar, on the right side as one enters the temple of the LORD. The priests who guarded the entranceⁱ put into the chest all the moneyʲ that was brought to the temple of the LORD. ¹⁰Whenever they saw that there was a large amount of money in the chest, the royal secretaryᵏ and the high priest came, counted the money that had been brought into the temple of the LORD and put it into bags. ¹¹When the amount had been determined, they gave the money to the men appointed to supervise the work on the temple. With it they paid those who worked on the temple of the LORD—the carpenters and builders, ¹²the masons and stonecutters.ˡ They purchased timber and dressed

---

a 21 Hebrew *Jehoash,* a variant of *Joash*   b 1 Hebrew *Jehoash,* a variant of *Joash*; also in verses 2, 4, 6, 7 and 18

11:19
ᵃ ver 4

11:20
ᵇ Pr 11:10; 28:12; 29:2

12:1
ᶜ 2Ki 11:2

12:3
ᵈ 1Ki 3:3; 2Ki 14:4; 15:35; 18:4

12:4
ᵉ 2Ki 22:4
ᶠ Ex 35:5
ᵍ Ex 30:12
ʰ Ex 35:29; 1Ch 29:3-9

12:9
ⁱ Jer 35:4
ʲ 2Ch 24:8; Mk 12:41; Lk 21:1

12:10
ᵏ 2Sa 8:17

12:12
ˡ 2Ki 22:5-6

12:13
a 1Ki 7:48-51;
2Ch 24:14

stone for the repair of the temple of the LORD, and met all the other expenses of restoring the temple.

¹³The money brought into the temple was not spent for making silver basins, wick trimmers, sprinkling bowls, trumpets or any other articles of gold*a* or silver for the temple of the LORD; ¹⁴it was paid to the workmen, who used it to repair the temple. ¹⁵They did not require an accounting from those to whom they gave the money to pay the workers, because they acted with complete honesty.*b* ¹⁶The money from the guilt offerings*c* and sin offerings*d* was not brought into the temple of the LORD; it belonged*e* to the priests.

12:15
b 2Ki 22:7;
1Co 4:2

12:16
c Lev 5:14-19;
Nu 18:9
d Lev 4:1-35
e Lev 7:7

¹⁷About this time Hazael*f* king of Aram went up and attacked Gath and captured it. Then he turned to attack Jerusalem. ¹⁸But Joash king of Judah took all the sacred objects dedicated by his fathers—Jehoshaphat, Jehoram and Ahaziah, the kings of Judah— and the gifts he himself had dedicated and all the gold found in the treasuries of the temple of the LORD and of the royal palace, and he sent*g* them to Hazael king of Aram, who then withdrew*h* from Jerusalem.

12:17
f 2Ki 8:12

12:18
g 1Ki 15:18;
2Ch 21:16-17
h 1Ki 15:21

¹⁹As for the other events of the reign of Joash, and all he did, are they not written in the book of the annals of the kings of Judah? ²⁰His officials*i* conspired against him and assassinated*j* him at Beth Millo,*k* on the road down to Silla. ²¹The officials who murdered him were Jozabad son of Shimeath and Jehozabad son of Shomer. He died and was buried with his fathers in the City of David. And Amaziah his son succeeded him as king.

12:20
i 2Ki 14:5
j 2Ch 24:25
k Jdg 9:6

INSIGHT

Silla's exact location is indefinite, but is believed to be near Jerusalem.

13:2
l 1Ki 12:26-33

Chapter 13 Theme

13 In the twenty-third year of Joash son of Ahaziah king of Judah, Jehoahaz son of Jehu became king of Israel in Samaria, and he reigned seventeen years. ²He did evil*l* in the eyes of the LORD by following the sins of Jeroboam son of Nebat, which he had caused Israel to commit, and he did not turn away from them. ³So the LORD's anger*m* burned against Israel, and for a long time he kept them under the power*n* of Hazael king of Aram and Ben-Hadad*o* his son.

13:3
m Dt 31:17;
Jdg 2:14
n 1Ki 8:12;
12:17; 19:17
o ver 24

⁴Then Jehoahaz sought*p* the LORD's favor, and the LORD listened to him, for he saw*q* how severely the king of Aram was oppressing*r* Israel. ⁵The LORD provided a deliverer*s* for Israel, and they escaped from the power of Aram. So the Israelites lived in their own homes as they had before. ⁶But they did not turn away from the sins*t* of the house of Jeroboam, which he had caused Israel to commit; they continued in them. Also, the Asherah pole*au* remained standing in Samaria.

13:4
p Dt 4:29;
Ps 78:34
q Ex 3:7;
Dt 26:7
r 2Ki 14:26

13:5
s ver 25;
2Ki 14:25,27

13:6
t 1Ki 12:30
u 1Ki 16:33

a 6 That is, a symbol of the goddess Asherah; here and elsewhere in 2 Kings

⁷Nothing had been left[a] of the army of Jehoahaz except fifty horsemen, ten chariots and ten thousand foot soldiers, for the king of Aram had destroyed the rest and made them like the dust[b] at threshing time.

⁸As for the other events of the reign of Jehoahaz, all he did and his achievements, are they not written in the book of the annals of the kings of Israel? ⁹Jehoahaz rested with his fathers and was buried in Samaria. And Jehoash[a] his son succeeded him as king.

¹⁰In the thirty-seventh year of Joash king of Judah, Jehoash son of Jehoahaz became king of Israel in Samaria, and he reigned sixteen years. ¹¹He did evil in the eyes of the LORD and did not turn away from any of the sins of Jeroboam son of Nebat, which he had caused Israel to commit; he continued in them.

¹²As for the other events of the reign of Jehoash, all he did and his achievements, including his war against Amaziah[c] king of Judah, are they not written in the book of the annals[d] of the kings of Israel? ¹³Jehoash[e] rested with his fathers, and Jeroboam[e] succeeded him on the throne. Jehoash was buried in Samaria with the kings of Israel.

¹⁴Now Elisha was suffering from the illness from which he died. Jehoash king of Israel went down to see him and wept over him. "My father! My father!" he cried. "The chariots[f] and horsemen of Israel!"

¹⁵Elisha said, "Get a bow and some arrows,"[g] and he did so. ¹⁶"Take the bow in your hands," he said to the king of Israel. When he had taken it, Elisha put his hands on the king's hands.

¹⁷"Open the east window," he said, and he opened it. "Shoot!"[h] Elisha said, and he shot. "The LORD's arrow of victory, the arrow of victory over Aram!" Elisha declared. "You will completely destroy the Arameans at Aphek."[i]

¹⁸Then he said, "Take the arrows," and the king took them. Elisha told him, "Strike the ground." He struck it three times and stopped. ¹⁹The man of God was angry with him and said, "You should have struck the ground five or six times; then you would have defeated Aram and completely destroyed it. But now you will defeat it only three times."[j]

²⁰Elisha died and was buried.

Now Moabite raiders[k] used to enter the country every spring. ²¹Once while some Israelites were burying a man, suddenly they saw a band of raiders; so they threw the man's body into Elisha's tomb. When the body touched Elisha's bones, the man came to life[l] and stood up on his feet.

²²Hazael king of Aram oppressed[m] Israel throughout the reign of Jehoahaz. ²³But the LORD was gracious to them and had

a 9 Hebrew *Joash*, a variant of *Jehoash*; also in verses 12-14 and 25

13:7
a 2Ki 10:32-33
b 2Sa 22:43

13:12
c 2Ki 14:15
d 1Ki 15:31

13:13
e 2Ki 14:23;
Hos 1:1

13:14
f 2Ki 2:12

13:15
g 1Sa 20:20

13:17
h Jos 8:18
i 1Ki 20:26

13:19
j ver 25

13:20
k 2Ki 3:7;
24:2

13:21
l Mt 27:52

13:22
m 1Ki 19:17;
2Ki 8:12

13:23
a Ge 13:16-17;
Ex 2:24
b Dt 29:20
c Ex 33:15;
2Ki 14:27;
17:18; 24:3,20

compassion and showed concern for them because of his covenant*a* with Abraham, Isaac and Jacob. To this day he has been unwilling to destroy*b* them or banish them from his presence.*c*

²⁴Hazael king of Aram died, and Ben-Hadad*d* his son succeeded him as king. ²⁵Then Jehoash son of Jehoahaz recaptured from Ben-Hadad son of Hazael the towns he had taken in battle from his father Jehoahaz. Three times*e* Jehoash defeated him, and so he recovered*f* the Israelite towns.

13:24
d ver 3

Chapter 14 Theme

13:25
e ver 18,19
f 2Ki 10:32

14 In the second year of Jehoash*a* son of Jehoahaz king of Israel, Amaziah son of Joash king of Judah began to reign. ²He was twenty-five years old when he became king, and he reigned in Jerusalem twenty-nine years. His mother's name was Jehoaddin; she was from Jerusalem. ³He did what was right in the eyes of the LORD, but not as his father David had done. In everything he followed the example of his father Joash. ⁴The high places,*g* however, were not removed; the people continued to offer sacrifices and burn incense there.

14:4
g 2Ki 12:3;
16:4

⁵After the kingdom was firmly in his grasp, he executed*h* the officials*i* who had murdered his father the king. ⁶Yet he did not put the sons of the assassins to death, in accordance with what is written in the Book of the Law*j* of Moses where the LORD commanded: "Fathers shall not be put to death for their children, nor children put to death for their fathers; each is to die for his own sins."b*k*

14:5
h 2Ki 21:24
i 2Ki 12:20

14:6
j Dt 28:61
k Nu 26:11;
Job 21:20;
Jer 31:30;
44:3;
Eze 18:4,20

⁷He was the one who defeated ten thousand Edomites in the Valley of Salt*l* and captured Sela*m* in battle, calling it Joktheel, the name it has to this day.

⁸Then Amaziah sent messengers to Jehoash son of Jehoahaz, the son of Jehu, king of Israel, with the challenge: "Come, meet me face to face."

14:7
l 2Sa 8:13;
2Ch 25:11
m Jdg 1:36

⁹But Jehoash king of Israel replied to Amaziah king of Judah: "A thistle*n* in Lebanon sent a message to a cedar in Lebanon, 'Give your daughter to my son in marriage.' Then a wild beast in Lebanon came along and trampled the thistle underfoot. ¹⁰You have indeed defeated Edom and now you are arrogant.*o* Glory in your victory, but stay at home! Why ask for trouble and cause your own downfall and that of Judah also?"

14:9
n Jdg 9:8-15

14:10
o Dt 8:14;
2Ch 26:16;
32:25

¹¹Amaziah, however, would not listen, so Jehoash king of Israel attacked. He and Amaziah king of Judah faced each other at Beth Shemesh*p* in Judah.

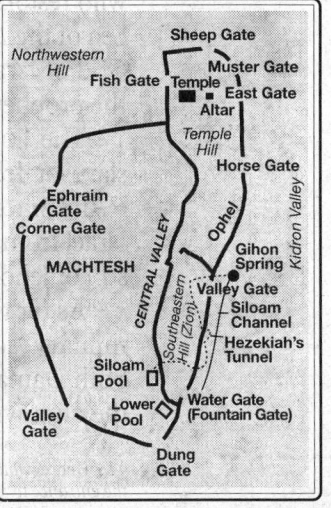

Jerusalem of the Old Testament

14:11
p Jos 15:10

a*1* Hebrew *Joash,* a variant of *Jehoash*; also in verses 13, 23 and 27
b*6* Deut. 24:16

¹²Judah was routed by Israel, and every man fled to his home.ᵃ ¹³Jehoash king of Israel captured Amaziah king of Judah, the son of Joash, the son of Ahaziah, at Beth Shemesh. Then Jehoash went to Jerusalem and broke down the wallᵇ of Jerusalem from the Ephraim Gateᶜ to the Corner Gateᵈ—a section about six hundred feet long.ᵃ ¹⁴He took all the gold and silver and all the articles found in the temple of the LORD and in the treasuries of the royal palace. He also took hostages and returned to Samaria.

¹⁵As for the other events of the reign of Jehoash, what he did and his achievements, including his warᵉ against Amaziah king of Judah, are they not written in the book of the annals of the kings of Israel? ¹⁶Jehoash rested with his fathers and was buried in Samaria with the kings of Israel. And Jeroboam his son succeeded him as king.

¹⁷Amaziah son of Joash king of Judah lived for fifteen years after the death of Jehoash son of Jehoahaz king of Israel. ¹⁸As for the other events of Amaziah's reign, are they not written in the book of the annals of the kings of Judah?

¹⁹They conspiredᶠ against him in Jerusalem, and he fled to Lachish,ᵍ but they sent men after him to Lachish and killed him there. ²⁰He was brought back by horseʰ and was buried in Jerusalem with his fathers, in the City of David.

²¹Then all the people of Judah took Azariah,ᵇⁱ who was sixteen years old, and made him king in place of his father Amaziah. ²²He was the one who rebuilt Elathʲ and restored it to Judah after Amaziah rested with his fathers.

²³In the fifteenth year of Amaziah son of Joash king of Judah, Jeroboamᵏ son of Jehoash king of Israel became king in Samaria, and he reigned forty-one years. ²⁴He did evil in the eyes of the LORD and did not turn away from any of the sins of Jeroboam son of Nebat, which he had caused Israel to commit.ˡ ²⁵He was the one who restored the boundaries of Israel from Leboᶜ Hamathᵐ to the Sea of the Arabah,ᵈⁿ in accordance with the word of the LORD, the God of Israel, spoken through his servant Jonahᵒ son of Amittai, the prophet from Gath Hepher.

²⁶The LORD had seen how bitterly everyone in Israel, whether slave or free,ᵖ was suffering;ᵠ there was no one to help them.ʳ ²⁷And since the LORD had not said he would blot outˢ the name of Israel from under heaven, he savedᵗ them by the hand of Jeroboam son of Jehoash.

²⁸As for the other events of Jeroboam's reign, all he did, and his military achievements, including how he recovered for Israel both Damascusᵘ and Hamath,ᵛ which had belonged to Yaudi,ᵉ are they not written in the book of the annalsʷ of the kings of Israel?

ᵃ13 Hebrew *four hundred cubits* (about 180 meters)   ᵇ21 Also called *Uzziah*   ᶜ25 Or *from the entrance to*   ᵈ25 That is, the Dead Sea   ᵉ28 Or *Judah*

14:12
ᵃ2Sa 18:17

14:13
ᵇ1Ki 3:1;
2Ch 33:14;
36:19;
Jer 39:2
ᶜNe 8:16; 12:39
ᵈ2Ch 25:23;
Jer 31:38;
Zec 14:10

14:15
ᵉ2Ki 13:12

14:19
ᶠ2Ki 12:20
ᵍJos 10:3;
2Ki 18:14,17

14:20
ʰ2Ki 9:28

14:21
ⁱ2Ki 15:1;
2Ch 26:23

14:22
ʲ1Ki 9:26;
2Ki 16:6

14:23
ᵏ2Ki 13:13

14:24
ˡ1Ki 15:30

14:25
ᵐNu 13:21;
1Ki 8:65
ⁿDt 3:17
ᵒJnh 1:1;
Mt 12:39

14:26
ᵖDt 32:36
ᵠ2Ki 13:4
ʳPs 18:41;
22:11; 72:12;
107:12;
Isa 63:5;
La 1:7

14:27
ˢ2Ki 13:23
ᵗJdg 6:14

14:28
ᵘ2Sa 8:5;
1Ki 11:24
ᵛ2Ch 8:3
ʷ1Ki 15:31

15:1
a ver 32;
2Ki 14:21

[29]Jeroboam rested with his fathers, the kings of Israel. And Zechariah his son succeeded him as king.

Chapter 15 Theme

15 In the twenty-seventh year of Jeroboam king of Israel, Azariah[a] son of Amaziah king of Judah began to reign. [2]He was sixteen years old when he became king, and he reigned in Jerusalem fifty-two years. His mother's name was Jecoliah; she was from Jerusalem. [3]He did what was right in the eyes of the LORD, just as his father Amaziah had done. [4]The high places, however, were not removed; the people continued to offer sacrifices and burn incense there.

15:5
b Ge 12:17
c Lev 13:46
d 2Ch 27:1
e Ge 41:40

[5]The LORD afflicted[b] the king with leprosy[a] until the day he died, and he lived in a separate house.[bc] Jotham[d] the king's son had charge of the palace[e] and governed the people of the land.

[6]As for the other events of Azariah's reign, and all he did, are they not written in the book of the annals of the kings of Judah? [7]Azariah rested[f] with his fathers and was buried near them in the City of David. And Jotham[g] his son succeeded him as king.

15:7
f Isa 6:1;
14:28
g ver 5

[8]In the thirty-eighth year of Azariah king of Judah, Zechariah son of Jeroboam became king of Israel in Samaria, and he reigned six months. [9]He did evil[h] in the eyes of the LORD, as his fathers had done. He did not turn away from the sins of Jeroboam son of Nebat, which he had caused Israel to commit.

15:9
h 1Ki 15:26

[a]5 The Hebrew word was used for various diseases affecting the skin—not necessarily leprosy.
[b]5 Or *in a house where he was relieved of responsibility*

Some of the Pagan Gods Worshiped by the Israelites

The god:	Ruled over / description:	Reference:
Adrammelech	War, love	2 Kings 17:31
Anammelech	Demanded child sacrifice	2 Kings 17:31
Asherah	Wife of Baal	2 Kings 13:6
Ashima	God of Hittites	2 Kings 17:30
Ashtoreth (Astarte, Ishtar)	Sex, fertility, queen of heaven	2 Kings 23:13
Baal	Rain, wind, clouds, fertility of land	2 Kings 3:2
Baal-Zebub	God of Ekron	2 Kings 1:2
Chemosh	Provider of land	2 Kings 23:13
Molech (Milcom)	National god of Moabites, worship involved human sacrifice	2 Kings 23:10
Nebo	Wisdom, literature, arts	1 Chronicles 5:8
Nergal	Underworld, death	2 Kings 17:30
Nibhaz	Worshiped by the Avvites (*a people transplanted to Samaria from Assyria*)	2 Kings 17:31
Nisroch	God worshiped in Nineveh	2 Kings 19:37
Rimmon	Thunder, lightning, rain	2 Kings 5:18
Succoth Benoth	Mistress of Marduk, goddess of war	2 Kings 17:30
Tartak	Fertility (worshiped by Avvites)	2 Kings 17:31

[10]Shallum son of Jabesh conspired against Zechariah. He attacked him in front of the people,[a] assassinated[a] him and succeeded him as king. [11]The other events of Zechariah's reign are written in the book of the annals[b] of the kings of Israel. [12]So the word of the LORD spoken to Jehu was fulfilled:[c] "Your descendants will sit on the throne of Israel to the fourth generation."[b]

[13]Shallum son of Jabesh became king in the thirty-ninth year of Uzziah king of Judah, and he reigned in Samaria[d] one month. [14]Then Menahem son of Gadi went from Tirzah[e] up to Samaria. He attacked Shallum son of Jabesh in Samaria, assassinated[f] him and succeeded him as king.

[15]The other events of Shallum's reign, and the conspiracy he led, are written in the book of the annals[g] of the kings of Israel.

[16]At that time Menahem, starting out from Tirzah, attacked Tiphsah[h] and everyone in the city and its vicinity, because they refused to open[i] their gates. He sacked Tiphsah and ripped open all the pregnant women.

[17]In the thirty-ninth year of Azariah king of Judah, Menahem son of Gadi became king of Israel, and he reigned in Samaria ten years. [18]He did evil in the eyes of the LORD. During his entire reign he did not turn away from the sins of Jeroboam son of Nebat, which he had caused Israel to commit.

[19]Then Pul[c][j] king of Assyria invaded the land, and Menahem gave him a thousand talents[d] of silver to gain his support and strengthen his own hold on the kingdom. [20]Menahem exacted this money from Israel. Every wealthy man had to contribute fifty shekels[e] of silver to be given to the king of Assyria. So the king of Assyria withdrew[k] and stayed in the land no longer.

[21]As for the other events of Menahem's reign, and all he did, are they not written in the book of the annals of the kings of Israel? [22]Menahem rested with his fathers. And Pekahiah his son succeeded him as king.

[23]In the fiftieth year of Azariah king of Judah, Pekahiah son of Menahem became king of Israel in Samaria, and he reigned two years. [24]Pekahiah did evil in the eyes of the LORD. He did not turn away from the sins of Jeroboam son of Nebat, which he had caused Israel to commit. [25]One of his chief officers, Pekah[l] son of Remaliah, conspired against him. Taking fifty men of Gilead with him, he assassinated[m] Pekahiah, along with Argob and Arieh, in the citadel of the royal palace at Samaria. So Pekah killed Pekahiah and succeeded him as king.

[26]The other events of Pekahiah's reign, and all he did, are written in the book of the annals of the kings of Israel.

15:10
[a] 2Ki 12:20

15:11
[b] 1Ki 15:31

15:12
[c] 2Ki 10:30

15:13
[d] ver 1,8

15:14
[e] 1Ki 14:17
[f] 2Ki 12:20

15:15
[g] 1Ki 15:31

15:16
[h] 1Ki 4:24
[i] 2Ki 8:12;
Hos 13:16

15:19
[j] 1Ch 5:6,26

15:20
[k] 2Ki 12:18

15:25
[l] 2Ch 28:6;
Isa 7:1
[m] 2Ki 12:20

a 10 Hebrew; some Septuagint manuscripts in Ibleam   b 12 2 Kings 10:30   c 19 Also called Tiglath-Pileser   d 19 That is, about 37 tons (about 34 metric tons)   e 20 That is, about 1 1/4 pounds (about 0.6 kilogram)

15:27
[a] 2Ch 28:6;
Isa 7:1
[b] Isa 7:4

15:29
[c] 2Ki 16:7; 17:6;
1Ch 5:26;
2Ch 28:20;
Jer 50:17
[d] 1Ki 15:20
[e] 2Ki 16:9;
17:24;
2Ch 16:4;
Isa 9:1
[f] 2Ki 24:14-16;
1Ch 5:22;
Isa 14:6,17;
36:17; 45:13

15:30
[g] 2Ki 17:1
[h] 2Ki 12:20

15:32
[i] 1Ch 5:17

15:34
[j] ver 3;
1Ki 14:8;
2Ch 26:4-5

15:35
[k] 2Ki 12:3
[l] 2Ch 23:20

15:37
[m] 2Ki 16:5;
Isa 7:1

16:1
[n] Isa 1:1; 14:28

16:2
[o] 1Ki 14:8

16:3
[p] Lev 18:21;
2Ki 21:6
[q] Lev 18:3;
Dt 9:4; 12:31

16:4
[r] Dt 12:2;
Eze 6:13

16:5
[s] 2Ki 15:37;
Isa 7:1,4

16:6
[t] Isa 9:12
[u] 2Ki 14:22;
2Ch 26:2

²⁷In the fifty-second year of Azariah king of Judah, Pekah[a] son of Remaliah[b] became king of Israel in Samaria, and he reigned twenty years. ²⁸He did evil in the eyes of the LORD. He did not turn away from the sins of Jeroboam son of Nebat, which he had caused Israel to commit.

²⁹In the time of Pekah king of Israel, Tiglath-Pileser[c] king of Assyria came and took Ijon,[d] Abel Beth Maacah, Janoah, Kedesh and Hazor. He took Gilead and Galilee, including all the land of Naphtali,[e] and deported[f] the people to Assyria. ³⁰Then Hoshea[g] son of Elah conspired against Pekah son of Remaliah. He attacked and assassinated[h] him, and then succeeded him as king in the twentieth year of Jotham son of Uzziah.

³¹As for the other events of Pekah's reign, and all he did, are they not written in the book of the annals of the kings of Israel?

³²In the second year of Pekah son of Remaliah king of Israel, Jotham[i] son of Uzziah king of Judah began to reign. ³³He was twenty-five years old when he became king, and he reigned in Jerusalem sixteen years. His mother's name was Jerusha daughter of Zadok. ³⁴He did what was right[j] in the eyes of the LORD, just as his father Uzziah had done. ³⁵The high places,[k] however, were not removed; the people continued to offer sacrifices and burn incense there. Jotham rebuilt the Upper Gate[l] of the temple of the LORD.

³⁶As for the other events of Jotham's reign, and what he did, are they not written in the book of the annals of the kings of Judah? ³⁷(In those days the LORD began to send Rezin[m] king of Aram and Pekah son of Remaliah against Judah.) ³⁸Jotham rested with his fathers and was buried with them in the City of David, the city of his father. And Ahaz his son succeeded him as king.

Chapter 16 Theme

16 In the seventeenth year of Pekah son of Remaliah, Ahaz[n] son of Jotham king of Judah began to reign. ²Ahaz was twenty years old when he became king, and he reigned in Jerusalem sixteen years. Unlike David his father, he did not do what was right[o] in the eyes of the LORD his God. ³He walked in the ways of the kings of Israel and even sacrificed his son[p] in[a] the fire, following the detestable[q] ways of the nations the LORD had driven out before the Israelites. ⁴He offered sacrifices and burned incense at the high places, on the hilltops and under every spreading tree.[r]

⁵Then Rezin[s] king of Aram and Pekah son of Remaliah king of Israel marched up to fight against Jerusalem and besieged Ahaz, but they could not overpower him. ⁶At that time, Rezin[t] king of Aram recovered Elath[u] for Aram by driving out the men of Judah. Edomites then moved into Elath and have lived there to this day.

[a] 3 Or *even made his son pass through*

[7]Ahaz sent messengers to say to Tiglath-Pileser[a] king of Assyria, "I am your servant and vassal. Come up and save[b] me out of the hand of the king of Aram and of the king of Israel, who are attacking me." [8]And Ahaz took the silver and gold found in the temple of the LORD and in the treasuries of the royal palace and sent it as a gift[c] to the king of Assyria. [9]The king of Assyria complied by attacking Damascus[d] and capturing it. He deported its inhabitants to Kir[e] and put Rezin to death.

[10]Then King Ahaz went to Damascus to meet Tiglath-Pileser king of Assyria. He saw an altar in Damascus and sent to Uriah[f] the priest a sketch of the altar, with detailed plans for its construction. [11]So Uriah the priest built an altar in accordance with all the plans that King Ahaz had sent from Damascus and finished it before King Ahaz returned. [12]When the king came back from Damascus and saw the altar, he approached it and presented offerings[a][g] on it. [13]He offered up his burnt offering[h] and grain offering, poured out his drink offering, and sprinkled the blood of his fellowship offerings[b][i] on the altar. [14]The bronze altar[j] that stood before the LORD he brought from the front of the temple—from between the new altar and the temple of the LORD—and put it on the north side of the new altar.

The Assyrian Captivity of Israel

a 12 Or *and went up* b 13 Traditionally *peace offerings*

16:7
[a] 2Ki 15:29
[b] Isa 2:6;
Jer 2:18;
Eze 16:28;
Hos 10:6

16:8
[c] 2Ki 12:18

16:9
[d] 2Ki 15:29
[e] Isa 22:6;
Am 1:5; 9:7

16:10
[f] Isa 8:2

16:12
[g] 2Ch 26:16

16:13
[h] Lev 6:8-13
[i] Lev 7:11-21

16:14
[j] 2Ch 4:1

KEY:
→ Israelite exiles to Assyria
---► Assyrian importees to Samaria

16:15
a Ex 29:38-41
b 1Sa 9:9

16:17
c 1Ki 7:27

16:18
d Eze 16:28

17:1
e 2Ki 15:30

17:3
f 2Ki 18:9-12;
Hos 10:14

17:5
g Hos 13:16

17:6
h Hos 13:16
i Dt 28:36,64;
2Ki 18:10-11
j 1Ch 5:26

17:7
k Jos 23:16;
Jdg 6:10
l Ex 14:15-31

17:8
m Lev 18:3;
Dt 18:9;
2Ki 16:3

17:9
n 2Ki 18:8

¹⁵King Ahaz then gave these orders to Uriah the priest: "On the large new altar, offer the morning^a burnt offering and the evening grain offering, the king's burnt offering and his grain offering, and the burnt offering of all the people of the land, and their grain offering and their drink offering. Sprinkle on the altar all the blood of the burnt offerings and sacrifices. But I will use the bronze altar for seeking guidance."^b ¹⁶And Uriah the priest did just as King Ahaz had ordered.

¹⁷King Ahaz took away the side panels and removed the basins from the movable stands. He removed the Sea from the bronze bulls that supported it and set it on a stone base.^c ¹⁸He took away the Sabbath canopy^a that had been built at the temple and removed the royal entryway outside the temple of the LORD, in deference to the king of Assyria.^d

¹⁹As for the other events of the reign of Ahaz, and what he did, are they not written in the book of the annals of the kings of Judah? ²⁰Ahaz rested with his fathers and was buried with them in the City of David. And Hezekiah his son succeeded him as king.

Chapter 17 Theme

17 In the twelfth year of Ahaz king of Judah, Hoshea^e son of Elah became king of Israel in Samaria, and he reigned nine years. ²He did evil in the eyes of the LORD, but not like the kings of Israel who preceded him.

³Shalmaneser^f king of Assyria came up to attack Hoshea, who had been Shalmaneser's vassal and had paid him tribute. ⁴But the king of Assyria discovered that Hoshea was a traitor, for he had sent envoys to So^b king of Egypt, and he no longer paid tribute to the king of Assyria, as he had done year by year. Therefore Shalmaneser seized him and put him in prison. ⁵The king of Assyria invaded the entire land, marched against Samaria and laid siege^g to it for three years. ⁶In the ninth year of Hoshea, the king of Assyria captured Samaria^h and deported^i the Israelites to Assyria. He settled them in Halah, in Gozan^j on the Habor River and in the towns of the Medes.

⁷All this took place because the Israelites had sinned^k against the LORD their God, who had brought them up out of Egypt^l from under the power of Pharaoh king of Egypt. They worshiped other gods ⁸and followed the practices of the nations^m the LORD had driven out before them, as well as the practices that the kings of Israel had introduced. ⁹The Israelites secretly did things against the LORD their God that were not right. From watchtower to fortified city^n they built themselves high places in all their towns.

a 18 Or *the dais of his throne* (see Septuagint)   b 4 Or *to Sais, to the*; *So* is possibly an abbreviation for *Osorkon.*

¹⁰They set up sacred stones and Asherah poles^a on every high hill and under every spreading tree.^b ¹¹At every high place they burned incense, as the nations whom the LORD had driven out before them had done. They did wicked things that provoked the LORD to anger. ¹²They worshiped idols,^c though the LORD had said, "You shall not do this."^a ¹³The LORD warned Israel and Judah through all his prophets and seers:^d "Turn from your evil ways.^e Observe my commands and decrees, in accordance with the entire Law that I commanded your fathers to obey and that I delivered to you through my servants the prophets."

¹⁴But they would not listen and were as stiff-necked^f as their fathers, who did not trust in the LORD their God. ¹⁵They rejected his decrees and the covenant^g he had made with their fathers and the warnings he had given them. They followed worthless idols^h and themselves became worthless. They imitated the nationsⁱ around them although the LORD had ordered them, "Do not do as they do," and they did the things the LORD had forbidden them to do.

¹⁶They forsook all the commands of the LORD their God and made for themselves two idols cast in the shape of calves,^j and an Asherah^k pole. They bowed down to all the starry hosts,^l and they worshiped Baal.^m ¹⁷They sacrificedⁿ their sons and daughters in^b the fire. They practiced divination and sorcery^o and sold^p themselves to do evil in the eyes of the LORD, provoking him to anger.

¹⁸So the LORD was very angry with Israel and removed them from his presence. Only the tribe of Judah was left, ¹⁹and even Judah did not keep the commands of the LORD their God. They followed the practices Israel had introduced.^q ²⁰Therefore the LORD rejected all the people of Israel; he afflicted them and gave them into the hands of plunderers,^r until he thrust them from his presence.

²¹When he tore^s Israel away from the house of David, they made Jeroboam son of Nebat their king.^t Jeroboam enticed Israel away from following the LORD and caused them to commit a great sin. ²²The Israelites persisted in all the sins of Jeroboam and did not turn away from them ²³until the LORD removed them from his presence, as he had warned through all his servants the prophets. So the people of Israel were taken from their homeland into exile in Assyria, and they are still there.

²⁴The king of Assyria^u brought people from Babylon, Cuthah, Avva, Hamath and Sepharvaim^v and settled them in the towns of Samaria to replace the Israelites. They took over Samaria and lived in its towns. ²⁵When they first lived there, they did not worship the LORD; so he sent lions^w among them and they killed some of

INSIGHT

Cuthah (or Cuth), located in Mesopotamia about eighteen miles northeast of Babylon, was the center of worship for Nergal, the god of death or the underworld. The Assyrians took the people of Cuthah captive and exiled them to Israel (2 Kings 17:24). There they made an idol to Nergal (2 Kings 17:30), and became yet another influence upon the people's tendency to worship other gods alongside Yahweh of Israel.

17:10
^aEx 34:13;
Mic 5:14
^b1Ki 14:23

17:12
^cEx 20:4

17:13
^d1Sa 9:9
^eJer 18:11;
25:5; 35:15

17:14
^fEx 32:9;
Dt 31:27;
Ac 7:51

17:15
^gDt 29:25
^hDt 32:21;
Ro 1:21-23
ⁱDt 12:30-31

17:16
^j1Ki 12:28
^k1Ki 14:15,23
^l2Ki 21:3
^m1Ki 16:31

17:17
ⁿDt 18:10-12;
2Ki 16:3
^oLev 19:26
^p1Ki 21:20

17:19
^q1Ki 14:22-23;
2Ki 16:3

17:20
^r2Ki 15:29

17:21
^s1Ki 11:11
^t1Ki 12:20

17:24
^uEzr 4:2,10
^v2Ki 18:34

17:25
^wGe 37:20

^a 12 Exodus 20:4, 5   ^b 17 Or They made their sons and daughters pass through

the people. ²⁶It was reported to the king of Assyria: "The people you deported and resettled in the towns of Samaria do not know what the god of that country requires. He has sent lions among them, which are killing them off, because the people do not know what he requires."

²⁷Then the king of Assyria gave this order: "Have one of the priests you took captive from Samaria go back to live there and teach the people what the god of the land requires." ²⁸So one of the priests who had been exiled from Samaria came to live in Bethel and taught them how to worship the LORD.

²⁹Nevertheless, each national group made its own gods in the several towns^a where they settled, and set them up in the shrines^b the people of Samaria had made at the high places.^c ³⁰The men from Babylon made Succoth Benoth, the men from Cuthah made Nergal, and the men from Hamath made Ashima; ³¹the Avvites made Nibhaz and Tartak, and the Sepharvites burned their children in the fire as sacrifices to Adrammelech^d and Anammelech, the gods of Sepharvaim.^e ³²They worshiped the LORD, but they also appointed all sorts^f of their own people to officiate for them as priests in the shrines at the high places. ³³They worshiped the LORD, but they also served their own gods in accordance with the customs of the nations from which they had been brought.

³⁴To this day they persist in their former practices. They neither worship the LORD nor adhere to the decrees and ordinances, the laws and commands that the LORD gave the descendants of Jacob, whom he named Israel.^g ³⁵When the LORD made a covenant with the Israelites, he commanded them: "Do not worship^h any other gods or bow down to them, serve them or sacrifice to them. ³⁶But the LORD, who brought you up out of Egypt with mighty power and outstretched arm,ⁱ is the one you must worship. To him you shall bow down and to him offer sacrifices. ³⁷You must always be careful^j to keep the decrees and ordinances, the laws and commands he wrote for you. Do not worship other gods. ³⁸Do not forget^k the covenant I have made with you, and do not worship other gods. ³⁹Rather, worship the LORD your God; it is he who will deliver you from the hand of all your enemies."

⁴⁰They would not listen, however, but persisted in their former practices. ⁴¹Even while these people were worshiping the LORD,^l they were serving their idols. To this day their children and grandchildren continue to do as their fathers did.

Chapter 18 Theme

18 In the third year of Hoshea son of Elah king of Israel, Hezekiah^m son of Ahaz king of Judah began to reign. ²He was twenty-five years old when he became king, and he reigned in Jerusalem twenty-nine years.*a* His mother's name was Abijah*a* daughter of Zechariah. ³He did what was right in the eyes of the LORD, just as his father David*b* had done. ⁴He removed*c* the high places, smashed the sacred stones*d* and cut down the Asherah poles. He broke into pieces the bronze snake*e* Moses had made, for up to that time the Israelites had been burning incense to it. (It was called*b* Nehushtan.*c*)

⁵Hezekiah trusted*f* in the LORD, the God of Israel. There was no one like him among all the kings of Judah, either before him or after him. ⁶He held fast*g* to the LORD and did not cease to follow him; he kept the commands the LORD had given Moses. ⁷And the LORD was with him; he was successful*h* in whatever he undertook. He rebelled*i* against the king of Assyria and did not serve him. ⁸From watchtower to fortified city,*j* he defeated the Philistines, as far as Gaza and its territory.

⁹In King Hezekiah's fourth year,*k* which was the seventh year of Hoshea son of Elah king of Israel, Shalmaneser king of Assyria marched against Samaria and laid siege to it. ¹⁰At the end of three years the Assyrians took it. So Samaria was captured in Hezekiah's sixth year, which was the ninth year of Hoshea king of Israel. ¹¹The king*l* of Assyria deported Israel to Assyria and settled them in Halah, in Gozan on the Habor River and in towns of the Medes. ¹²This happened because they had not obeyed the LORD their God, but had violated his covenant*m*—all that Moses the servant of the LORD commanded.*n* They neither listened to the commands*o* nor carried them out.

¹³In the fourteenth year of King Hezekiah's reign, Sennacherib king of Assyria attacked all the fortified cities of Judah*p* and captured them. ¹⁴So Hezekiah king of Judah sent this message to the king of Assyria at Lachish: "I have done wrong.*q* Withdraw from me, and I will pay whatever you demand of me." The king of Assyria exacted from Hezekiah king of Judah three hundred talents*d* of silver and thirty talents*e* of gold. ¹⁵So Hezekiah gave*r* him all the silver that was found in the temple of the LORD and in the treasuries of the royal palace.

¹⁶At this time Hezekiah king of Judah stripped off the gold with which he had covered the doors and doorposts of the temple of the LORD, and gave it to the king of Assyria.

¹⁷The king of Assyria sent his supreme commander,*s* his chief officer and his field commander with a large army, from Lachish to King Hezekiah at Jerusalem. They came up to Jerusalem and stopped at the aqueduct of the Upper Pool,*t* on the road to the

---

18:2
a Isa 38:5

18:3
b Isa 38:5

18:4
c 2Ch 31:1
d Ex 23:24
e Nu 21:9

18:5
f 2Ki 19:10;
23:25

18:6
g Dt 10:20;
Jos 23:8

18:7
h Ge 39:3;
1Sa 18:14
i 2Ki 16:7

18:8
j 2Ki 17:9;
Isa 14:29

18:9
k Isa 1:1

18:11
l Isa 37:12

18:12
m 2Ki 17:15
n Da 9:6,10
o 1Ki 9:6

18:13
p 2Ch 32:1;
Isa 1:7;
Mic 1:9

18:14
q Isa 24:5

18:15
r 1Ki 15:18;
2Ki 16:8

18:17
s Isa 20:1
t 2Ki 20:20;
2Ch 32:4,30;
Isa 7:3

---

a 2 Hebrew *Abi*, a variant of *Abijah*   *b 4* Or *He called it*   *c 4 Nehushtan* sounds like the Hebrew for *bronze* and *snake* and *unclean thing*.   *d 14* That is, about 11 tons (about 10 metric tons)   *e 14* That is, about 1 ton (about 1 metric ton)

Washerman's Field. ¹⁸They called for the king; and Eliakim^a son of Hilkiah the palace administrator, Shebna^b the secretary, and Joah son of Asaph the recorder went out to them.

¹⁹The field commander said to them, "Tell Hezekiah:

"'This is what the great king, the king of Assyria, says: On what are you basing this confidence of yours? ²⁰You say you have strategy and military strength—but you speak only empty words. On whom are you depending, that you rebel against me? ²¹Look now, you are depending on Egypt,^c that splintered reed of a staff,^d which pierces a man's hand and wounds him if he leans on it! Such is Pharaoh king of Egypt to all who depend on him. ²²And if you say to me, "We are depending on the LORD our God"—isn't he the one whose high places and altars Hezekiah removed, saying to Judah and Jerusalem, "You must worship before this altar in Jerusalem"?

²³"'Come now, make a bargain with my master, the king of Assyria: I will give you two thousand horses—if you can put riders on them! ²⁴How can you repulse one officer^e of the least of my master's officials, even though you are depending on Egypt for chariots and horsemen^a? ²⁵Furthermore, have I come to attack and destroy this place without word from the LORD?^f The LORD himself told me to march against this country and destroy it.'"

²⁶Then Eliakim son of Hilkiah, and Shebna and Joah said to the field commander, "Please speak to your servants in Aramaic,^g since we understand it. Don't speak to us in Hebrew in the hearing of the people on the wall."

²⁷But the commander replied, "Was it only to your master and you that my master sent me to say these things, and not to the men sitting on the wall—who, like you, will have to eat their own filth and drink their own urine?"

²⁸Then the commander stood and called out in Hebrew: "Hear the word of the great king, the king of Assyria! ²⁹This is what the king says: Do not let Hezekiah deceive^h you. He cannot deliver you from my hand. ³⁰Do not let Hezekiah persuade you to trust in the LORD when he says, 'The LORD will surely deliver us; this city will not be given into the hand of the king of Assyria.'

³¹"Do not listen to Hezekiah. This is what the king of Assyria says: Make peace with me and come out to me. Then every one of you will eat from his own vine and fig treeⁱ and drink water from his own cistern,^j ³²until I come and take you to a land like your own, a land of grain and new wine, a land of bread and vineyards, a land of olive trees and honey. Choose life^k and not death!

18:18
^a 2Ki 19:2;
Isa 22:20
^b Isa 22:15

18:21
^c Isa 20:5;
Eze 29:6
^d Isa 30:5,7

18:24
^e Isa 10:8

18:25
^f 2Ki 19:6,22

18:26
^g Ezr 4:7

18:29
^h 2Ki 19:10

18:31
ⁱ Nu 13:23;
1Ki 4:25
^j Jer 14:3;
La 4:4

18:32
^k Dt 8:7-9; 30:19

a 24 Or *charioteers*

"Do not listen to Hezekiah, for he is misleading you when he says, 'The LORD will deliver us.' ³³Has the god*a* of any nation ever delivered his land from the hand of the king of Assyria? ³⁴Where are the gods of Hamath*b* and Arpad?*c* Where are the gods of Sepharvaim, Hena and Ivvah? Have they rescued Samaria from my hand? ³⁵Who of all the gods of these countries has been able to save his land from me? How then can the LORD deliver Jerusalem from my hand?"*d*

³⁶But the people remained silent and said nothing in reply, because the king had commanded, "Do not answer him."

³⁷Then Eliakim son of Hilkiah the palace administrator, Shebna the secretary and Joah son of Asaph the recorder went to Hezekiah, with their clothes torn,*e* and told him what the field commander had said.

Chapter 19 Theme

19 When King Hezekiah heard this, he tore*f* his clothes and put on sackcloth and went into the temple of the LORD. ²He sent Eliakim the palace administrator, Shebna the secretary and the leading priests, all wearing sackcloth, to the prophet Isaiah*g* son of Amoz. ³They told him, "This is what Hezekiah says: This day is a day of distress and rebuke and disgrace, as when children come to the point of birth and there is no strength to deliver them. ⁴It may be that the LORD your God will hear all the words of the field commander, whom his master, the king of Assyria, has sent to ridicule*h* the living God, and that he will rebuke*i* him for the words the LORD your God has heard. Therefore pray for the remnant that still survives."

⁵When King Hezekiah's officials came to Isaiah, ⁶Isaiah said to them, "Tell your master, 'This is what the LORD says: Do not be afraid of what you have heard—those words with which the underlings of the king of Assyria have blasphemed*j* me. ⁷Listen! I am going to put such a spirit in him that when he hears a certain report, he will return to his own country, and there I will have him cut down with the sword.*k*'"

⁸When the field commander heard that the king of Assyria had left Lachish,*l* he withdrew and found the king fighting against Libnah.

⁹Now Sennacherib received a report that Tirhakah, the Cushite*a* king ⌊of Egypt⌋, was marching out to fight against him. So he again sent messengers to Hezekiah with this word: ¹⁰"Say to Hezekiah king of Judah: Do not let the god you depend*m* on deceive*n* you when he says, 'Jerusalem will not be handed over to

---

INSIGHT

Ivvah (also spelled Ava or Avva) refers to the people the Assyrians conquered and took to Israel to replace the people taken into exile (2 Kings 17:24). Since the gods of the Ivvahian people did not come to their rescue against the Assyrians, they were used by Sennacherib as an example to call Jerusalem to surrender in 701 B.C. (2 Kings 18:34). Ivvah is believed to have been in Syria. Sennacherib used the same ploy against the city of Hena, which could possibly have been Ana or Anat on the Euphrates River.

18:33 *a* 2Ki 19:12; Isa 10:10-11

18:34 *b* 2Ki 17:24; 19:13 *c* Isa 10:9

18:35 *d* Ps 2:1-2

18:37 *e* 2Ki 6:30

19:1 *f* Ge 37:34; 1Ki 21:27; 2Ch 32:20-22

19:2 *g* Isa 1:1

19:4 *h* 2Ki 18:35 *i* 2Sa 16:12

19:6 *j* 2Ki 18:25

19:7 *k* ver 37

19:8 *l* 2Ki 18:14

19:10 *m* 2Ki 18:5 *n* 2Ki 18:29

---

a 9 That is, from the upper Nile region

"With the soles of my feet
I have dried up all the streams of Egypt."

25"'Have you not heard?[a]
Long ago I ordained it.
In days of old I planned[b] it;
now I have brought it to pass,
that you have turned fortified cities
into piles of stone.[c]
26Their people, drained of power,
are dismayed[d] and put to shame.
They are like plants in the field,
like tender green shoots,[e]
like grass sprouting on the roof,
scorched[f] before it grows up.

27"'But I know[g] where you stay
and when you come and go
and how you rage against me.
28Because you rage against me
and your insolence has reached my ears,
I will put my hook[h] in your nose
and my bit[i] in your mouth,
and I will make you return[j]
by the way you came.'

29"This will be the sign[k] for you, O Hezekiah:

"This year you will eat what grows by itself,[l]
and the second year what springs from that.
But in the third year sow and reap,
plant vineyards[m] and eat their fruit.
30Once more a remnant of the house of Judah
will take root[n] below and bear fruit above.
31For out of Jerusalem will come a remnant,
and out of Mount Zion a band of survivors.

The zeal[o] of the LORD Almighty will accomplish this.

32"Therefore this is what the LORD says concerning the king of Assyria:

"He will not enter this city
or shoot an arrow here.
He will not come before it with shield
or build a siege ramp against it.
33By the way that he came he will return;[p]
he will not enter this city,

declares the LORD.

19:25
[a] Isa 40:21,28
[b] Isa 10:5; 45:7
[c] Mic 1:6

19:26
[d] Ps 6:10
[e] Isa 4:2
[f] Ps 129:6

19:27
[g] Ps 139:1-4

19:28
[h] Eze 19:9, 29:4
[i] Isa 30:28
[j] ver 33

19:29
[k] 2Ki 20:8-9;
Lk 2:12
[l] Lev 25:5
[m] Ps 107:37

19:30
[n] 2Ch 32:22-23

19:31
[o] Isa 9:7

19:33
[p] ver 28

the king of Assyria.' ¹¹Surely you have heard what the kings of Assyria have done to all the countries, destroying them completely. And will you be delivered? ¹²Did the gods of the nations that were destroyed by my forefathers deliver[a] them: the gods of Gozan,[b] Haran,[c] Rezeph and the people of Eden who were in Tel Assar? ¹³Where is the king of Hamath, the king of Arpad, the king of the city of Sepharvaim, or of Hena or Ivvah?"[d]

¹⁴Hezekiah received the letter from the messengers and read it. Then he went up to the temple of the Lord and spread it out before the Lord. ¹⁵And Hezekiah prayed to the Lord: "O Lord, God of Israel, enthroned between the cherubim,[e] you alone are God over all the kingdoms of the earth. You have made heaven and earth. ¹⁶Give ear,[f] O Lord, and hear;[g] open your eyes,[h] O Lord, and see; listen to the words Sennacherib has sent to insult the living God.

¹⁷"It is true, O Lord, that the Assyrian kings have laid waste these nations and their lands. ¹⁸They have thrown their gods into the fire and destroyed them, for they were not gods[i] but only wood and stone, fashioned by men's hands.[j] ¹⁹Now, O Lord our God, deliver us from his hand, so that all kingdoms[k] on earth may know[l] that you alone, O Lord, are God."

²⁰Then Isaiah son of Amoz sent a message to Hezekiah: "This is what the Lord, the God of Israel, says: I have heard[m] your prayer concerning Sennacherib king of Assyria. ²¹This is the word that the Lord has spoken against him:

"'The Virgin Daughter[n] of Zion
  despises you and mocks[o] you.
The Daughter of Jerusalem
  tosses her head[p] as you flee.
²²Who is it you have insulted and blasphemed?
  Against whom have you raised your voice
and lifted your eyes in pride?
  Against the Holy One[q] of Israel!
²³By your messengers
  you have heaped insults on the Lord.
And you have said,[r]
  "With my many chariots[s]
I have ascended the heights of the mountains,
  the utmost heights of Lebanon.
I have cut down its tallest cedars,
  the choicest of its pines.
I have reached its remotest parts,
  the finest of its forests.
²⁴I have dug wells in foreign lands
  and drunk the water there.

19:12 [a]2Ki 18:33; [b]2Ki 17:6; [c]Ge 11:31
19:13 [d]2Ki 18:34
19:15 [e]Ex 25:22
19:16 [f]Ps 31:2; [g]1Ki 8:29; [h]ver 4; 2Ch 6:40
19:18 [i]Isa 44:9-11; Jer 10:3-10; [j]Ps 115:4; Ac 17:29
19:19 [k]1Ki 8:43; [l]Ps 83:18
19:20 [m]2Ki 20:5
19:21 [n]Jer 14:17; La 2:13; [o]Ps 22:7-8; [p]Job 16:4; Ps 109:25
19:22 [q]Ps 71:22; Isa 5:24
19:23 [r]Isa 10:18; [s]Ps 20:7

19:34
a 2Ki 20:6
b 1Ki 11:12-13

³⁴I will defend*a* this city and save it,
    for my sake and for the sake of David*b* my servant.' "

³⁵That night the angel of the LORD*c* went out and put to death a hundred and eighty-five thousand men in the Assyrian camp. When the people got up the next morning—there were all the dead bodies!*d* ³⁶So Sennacherib king of Assyria broke camp and withdrew. He returned to Nineveh*e* and stayed there.

19:35
c Ex 12:23
d Job 24:24

³⁷One day, while he was worshiping in the temple of his god Nisroch, his sons Adrammelech and Sharezer cut him down with the sword,*f* and they escaped to the land of Ararat.*g* And Esarhaddon*h* his son succeeded him as king.

19:36
e Ge 10:11;
Jnh 1:2

Chapter 20 Theme _____

19:37
f ver 7
g Ge 8:4
h Ezr 4:2

20 In those days Hezekiah became ill and was at the point of death. The prophet Isaiah son of Amoz went to him and said, "This is what the LORD says: Put your house in order, because you are going to die; you will not recover."

²Hezekiah turned his face to the wall and prayed to the LORD, ³"Remember,*i* O LORD, how I have walked before you faithfully*j* and with wholehearted devotion and have done what is good in your eyes." And Hezekiah wept bitterly.

20:3
i Ne 13:22
j 2Ki 18:3-6

⁴Before Isaiah had left the middle court, the word of the LORD came to him: ⁵"Go back and tell Hezekiah, the leader of my people, 'This is what the LORD, the God of your father David, says: I have heard*k* your prayer and seen your tears;*l* I will heal you. On the third day from now you will go up to the temple of the LORD. ⁶I will add fifteen years to your life. And I will deliver you and this city from the hand of the king of Assyria. I will defend*m* this city for my sake and for the sake of my servant David.' "

20:5
k 1Sa 9:16;
1Ki 9:3;
2Ki 19:20
l Ps 39:12; 56:8

⁷Then Isaiah said, "Prepare a poultice of figs." They did so and applied it to the boil,*n* and he recovered.

20:6
m 2Ki 19:34

⁸Hezekiah had asked Isaiah, "What will be the sign that the LORD will heal me and that I will go up to the temple of the LORD on the third day from now?"

⁹Isaiah answered, "This is the LORD's sign*o* to you that the LORD will do what he has promised: Shall the shadow go forward ten steps, or shall it go back ten steps?"

20:7
n Isa 38:21

¹⁰"It is a simple matter for the shadow to go forward ten steps," said Hezekiah. "Rather, have it go back ten steps."

¹¹Then the prophet Isaiah called upon the LORD, and the LORD made the shadow go back*p* the ten steps it had gone down on the stairway of Ahaz.

20:9
o Dt 13:2;
Jer 44:29

¹²At that time Merodach-Baladan son of Baladan king of Babylon sent Hezekiah letters and a gift, because he had heard of Hezekiah's illness. ¹³Hezekiah received the messengers and

20:11
p Jos 10:13

showed them all that was in his storehouses—the silver, the gold, the spices and the fine oil—his armory and everything found among his treasures. There was nothing in his palace or in all his kingdom that Hezekiah did not show them.

¹⁴Then Isaiah the prophet went to King Hezekiah and asked, "What did those men say, and where did they come from?"

"From a distant land," Hezekiah replied. "They came from Babylon."

¹⁵The prophet asked, "What did they see in your palace?"

"They saw everything in my palace," Hezekiah said. "There is nothing among my treasures that I did not show them."

¹⁶Then Isaiah said to Hezekiah, "Hear the word of the LORD: ¹⁷The time will surely come when everything in your palace, and all that your fathers have stored up until this day, will be carried off to Babylon.ᵃ Nothing will be left, says the LORD. ¹⁸And some of your descendants,ᵇ your own flesh and blood, that will be born to you, will be taken away, and they will become eunuchs in the palace of the king of Babylon."

¹⁹"The word of the LORD you have spoken is good," Hezekiah replied. For he thought, "Will there not be peace and security in my lifetime?"

²⁰As for the other events of Hezekiah's reign, all his achievements and how he made the poolᶜ and the tunnel by which he brought water into the city, are they not written in the book of the annals of the kings of Judah? ²¹Hezekiah rested with his fathers. And Manasseh his son succeeded him as king.

Chapter 21 Theme _____

21 Manasseh was twelve years old when he became king, and he reigned in Jerusalem fifty-five years. His mother's name was Hephzibah.ᵈ ²He did evilᵉ in the eyes of the LORD, following the detestable practicesᶠ of the nations the LORD had driven out before the Israelites. ³He rebuilt the high placesᵍ his father Hezekiah had destroyed; he also erected altars to Baalʰ and made an Asherah pole, as Ahab king of Israel had done. He bowed down to all the starry hostsⁱ and worshiped them. ⁴He built altarsʲ in the temple of the LORD, of which the LORD had said, "In Jerusalem I will put my Name."ᵏ ⁵In both courtsˡ of the temple of the LORD, he built altars to all the starry hosts. ⁶He sacrificed his own sonᵐ inᵃ the fire, practiced sorcery and divination, and consulted mediums and spiritists.ⁿ He did much evil in the eyes of the LORD, provoking him to anger.

ᵃ6 Or *He made his own son pass through*

20:17
ᵃ2Ki 24:13; 25:13; 2Ch 36:10; Jer 27:22; 52:17-23

20:18
ᵇ2Ki 24:15; 2Ch 33:11; Da 1:3

20:20
ᶜNe 3:16

21:1
ᵈIsa 62:4

21:2
ᵉJer 15:4
ᶠ2Ki 16:3

21:3
ᵍ2Ki 18:4
ʰJdg 6:28; 1Ki 16:32
ⁱDt 17:3; 2Ki 17:16

21:4
ʲJer 32:34
ᵏ2Sa 7:13; 1Ki 8:29

21:5
ˡ1Ki 7:12; 2Ki 23:12

21:6
ᵐLev 18:21; Dt 18:10; 2Ki 16:3; 17:17
ⁿLev 19:31

21:7
a Dt 16:21;
2Ki 23:4
b 2Sa 7:13;
1Ki 8:29; 9:3;
2Ki 23:27;
Jer 32:34

21:8
c 2Sa 7:10
d 2Ki 18:12

21:9
e Pr 29:12
f Dt 9:4

21:11
g 2Ki 24:3-4
h Ge 15:16;
1Ki 21:26

21:12
i 2Ki 23:26; 24:3;
Jer 15:4
j 1Sa 3:11;
Jer 19:3

21:13
k Isa 34:11;
La 2:8;
Am 7:7-9
l 2Ki 23:27

21:14
m Ps 78:58-60
n 2Ki 19:4;
Mic 2:12

21:15
o Ex 32:22
p Jer 25:7

21:16
q 2Ki 24:4

21:18
r ver 26

21:20
s ver 2-6

21:22
t 1Ki 11:33

21:23
u 2Ki 12:20;
2Ch 33:24-25

21:24
v 2Ki 14:5

[7]He took the carved Asherah pole[a] he had made and put it in the temple, of which the LORD had said to David and to his son Solomon, "In this temple and in Jerusalem, which I have chosen out of all the tribes of Israel, I will put my Name[b] forever. [8]I will not again[c] make the feet of the Israelites wander from the land I gave their forefathers, if only they will be careful to do everything I commanded them and will keep the whole Law that my servant Moses[d] gave them." [9]But the people did not listen. Manasseh led them astray, so that they did more evil[e] than the nations[f] the LORD had destroyed before the Israelites.

[10]The LORD said through his servants the prophets: [11]"Manasseh king of Judah has committed these detestable sins. He has done more evil[g] than the Amorites[h] who preceded him and has led Judah into sin with his idols. [12]Therefore this is what the LORD, the God of Israel, says: I am going to bring such disaster[i] on Jerusalem and Judah that the ears of everyone who hears of it will tingle.[j] [13]I will stretch out over Jerusalem the measuring line used against Samaria and the plumb line[k] used against the house of Ahab. I will wipe[l] out Jerusalem as one wipes a dish, wiping it and turning it upside down. [14]I will forsake[m] the remnant[n] of my inheritance and hand them over to their enemies. They will be looted and plundered by all their foes, [15]because they have done evil[o] in my eyes and have provoked[p] me to anger from the day their forefathers came out of Egypt until this day."

[16]Moreover, Manasseh also shed so much innocent blood[q] that he filled Jerusalem from end to end—besides the sin that he had caused Judah to commit, so that they did evil in the eyes of the LORD.

[17]As for the other events of Manasseh's reign, and all he did, including the sin he committed, are they not written in the book of the annals of the kings of Judah? [18]Manasseh rested with his fathers and was buried in his palace garden,[r] the garden of Uzza. And Amon his son succeeded him as king.

[19]Amon was twenty-two years old when he became king, and he reigned in Jerusalem two years. His mother's name was Meshullemeth daughter of Haruz; she was from Jotbah. [20]He did evil[s] in the eyes of the LORD, as his father Manasseh had done. [21]He walked in all the ways of his father; he worshiped the idols his father had worshiped, and bowed down to them. [22]He forsook the LORD, the God of his fathers, and did not walk[t] in the way of the LORD.

[23]Amon's officials conspired against him and assassinated[u] the king in his palace. [24]Then the people of the land killed[v] all who had plotted against King Amon, and they made Josiah his son king in his place.

²⁵As for the other events of Amon's reign, and what he did, are they not written in the book of the annals of the kings of Judah? ²⁶He was buried in his grave in the garden*ᵃ* of Uzza. And Josiah his son succeeded him as king.

Chapter 22 Theme _____

22 Josiah was eight years old when he became king, and he reigned in Jerusalem thirty-one years. His mother's name was Jedidah daughter of Adaiah; she was from Bozkath.*ᵇ* ²He did what was right*ᶜ* in the eyes of the LORD and walked in all the ways of his father David, not turning aside to the right*ᵈ* or to the left.

³In the eighteenth year of his reign, King Josiah sent the secretary, Shaphan*ᵉ* son of Azaliah, the son of Meshullam, to the temple of the LORD. He said: ⁴"Go up to Hilkiah the high priest and have him get ready the money that has been brought into the temple of the LORD, which the doorkeepers have collected*ᶠ* from the people. ⁵Have them entrust it to the men appointed to supervise the work on the temple. And have these men pay the workers who repair*ᵍ* the temple of the LORD— ⁶the carpenters, the builders and the masons. Also have them purchase timber and dressed stone to repair the temple.*ʰ* ⁷But they need not account for the money entrusted to them, because they are acting faithfully."*ⁱ*

⁸Hilkiah the high priest said to Shaphan the secretary, "I have found the Book of the Law*ʲ* in the temple of the LORD." He gave it to Shaphan, who read it. ⁹Then Shaphan the secretary went to the king and reported to him: "Your officials have paid out the money that was in the temple of the LORD and have entrusted it to the workers and supervisors at the temple." ¹⁰Then Shaphan the secretary informed the king, "Hilkiah the priest has given me a book." And Shaphan read from it in the presence of the king.*ᵏ*

¹¹When the king heard the words of the Book of the Law, he tore his robes. ¹²He gave these orders to Hilkiah the priest, Ahikam*ˡ* son of Shaphan, Acbor son of Micaiah, Shaphan the secretary and Asaiah the king's attendant: ¹³"Go and inquire of the LORD for me and for the people and for all Judah about what is written in this book that has been found. Great is the LORD's anger*ᵐ* that burns against us because our fathers have not obeyed the words of this book; they have not acted in accordance with all that is written there concerning us."

¹⁴Hilkiah the priest, Ahikam, Acbor, Shaphan and Asaiah went to speak to the prophetess Huldah, who was the wife of Shallum son of Tikvah, the son of Harhas, keeper of the wardrobe. She lived in Jerusalem, in the Second District.

¹⁵She said to them, "This is what the LORD, the God of Israel, says: Tell the man who sent you to me, ¹⁶'This is what the LORD

21:26 *ᵃ*ver 18

22:1 *ᵇ*Jos 15:39

22:2 *ᶜ*Dt 17:19 *ᵈ*Dt 5:32

22:3 *ᵉ*2Ch 34:20; Jer 39:14

22:4 *ᶠ*2Ki 12:4-5

22:5 *ᵍ*2Ki 12:5, 11-14

22:6 *ʰ*2Ki 12:11-12

22:7 *ⁱ*2Ki 12:15

22:8 *ʲ*Dt 31:24

22:10 *ᵏ*Jer 36:21

22:12 *ˡ*2Ki 25:22; Jer 26:24

22:13 *ᵐ*Dt 29:24-28; 31:17

22:16
a Dt 31:29;
Jos 23:15
b Dt 29:27;
Da 9:11

22:17
c Dt 29:25-27

22:18
d 2Ch 34:26;
Jer 21:2

22:19
e Ex 10:3;
1Ki 21:29;
Ps 51:17;
Isa 57:15;
Mic 6:8
f Jer 26:6
g Lev 26:31

22:20
h Isa 57:1

23:2
i Dt 31:11;
2Ki 22:8

23:3
j 2Ki 11:14,17
k Dt 13:4

23:4
l 2Ki 25:18
m 2Ki 21:7

23:5
n 2Ki 21:3;
Jer 8:2

23:6
o Jer 26:23

23:7
p 1Ki 14:24;
15:12;
Eze 16:16

says: I am going to bring disaster*a* on this place and its people, according to everything written in the book*b* the king of Judah has read. ¹⁷Because they have forsaken*c* me and burned incense to other gods and provoked me to anger by all the idols their hands have made,ᵃ my anger will burn against this place and will not be quenched.' ¹⁸Tell the king of Judah, who sent you to inquire*d* of the LORD, 'This is what the LORD, the God of Israel, says concerning the words you heard: ¹⁹Because your heart was responsive and you humbled*e* yourself before the LORD when you heard what I have spoken against this place and its people, that they would become accursed*f* and laid waste,*g* and because you tore your robes and wept in my presence, I have heard you, declares the LORD. ²⁰Therefore I will gather you to your fathers, and you will be buried in peace.*h* Your eyes will not see all the disaster I am going to bring on this place.' "

So they took her answer back to the king.

Chapter 23 Theme _____

23 Then the king called together all the elders of Judah and Jerusalem. ²He went up to the temple of the LORD with the men of Judah, the people of Jerusalem, the priests and the prophets—all the people from the least to the greatest. He read*i* in their hearing all the words of the Book of the Covenant, which had been found in the temple of the LORD. ³The king stood by the pillar and renewed the covenant*j* in the presence of the LORD—to follow*k* the LORD and keep his commands, regulations and decrees with all his heart and all his soul, thus confirming the words of the covenant written in this book. Then all the people pledged themselves to the covenant.

⁴The king ordered Hilkiah the high priest, the priests next in rank and the doorkeepers*l* to remove*m* from the temple of the LORD all the articles made for Baal and Asherah and all the starry hosts. He burned them outside Jerusalem in the fields of the Kidron Valley and took the ashes to Bethel. ⁵He did away with the pagan priests appointed by the kings of Judah to burn incense on the high places of the towns of Judah and on those around Jerusalem—those who burned incense to Baal, to the sun and moon, to the constellations and to all the starry hosts.*n* ⁶He took the Asherah pole from the temple of the LORD to the Kidron Valley outside Jerusalem and burned it there. He ground it to powder and scattered the dust over the graves of the common people.*o* ⁷He also tore down the quarters of the male shrine prostitutes,*p* which were in the temple of the LORD and where women did weaving for Asherah.

a 17 Or *by everything they have done*

643

8Josiah brought all the priests from the towns of Judah and desecrated the high places, from Geba[a] to Beersheba, where the priests had burned incense. He broke down the shrines[a] at the gates—at the entrance to the Gate of Joshua, the city governor, which is on the left of the city gate. 9Although the priests of the high places did not serve[b] at the altar of the LORD in Jerusalem, they ate unleavened bread with their fellow priests.

10He desecrated Topheth,[c] which was in the Valley of Ben Hinnom,[d] so no one could use it to sacrifice his son[e] or daughter in[b] the fire to Molech. 11He removed from the entrance to the temple of the LORD the horses that the kings of Judah had dedicated to the sun. They were in the court near the room of an official named Nathan-Melech. Josiah then burned the chariots dedicated to the sun.[f]

12He pulled down the altars the kings of Judah had erected on the roof[g] near the upper room of Ahaz, and the altars Manasseh had built in the two courts[h] of the temple of the LORD. He removed them from there, smashed them to pieces and threw the rubble into the Kidron Valley. 13The king also desecrated the high places that were east of Jerusalem on the south of the Hill of Corruption—the ones Solomon[i] king of Israel had built for Ashtoreth the vile goddess of the Sidonians, for Chemosh the vile god of Moab, and for Molech[c] the detestable god of the people of Ammon. 14Josiah smashed[j] the sacred stones and cut down the Asherah poles and covered the sites with human bones.

15Even the altar[k] at Bethel, the high place made by Jeroboam[l] son of Nebat, who had caused Israel to sin—even that altar and high place he demolished. He burned the high place and ground it to powder, and burned the Asherah pole also. 16Then Josiah[m] looked around, and when he saw the tombs that were there on the hillside, he had the bones removed from them and burned on the altar to defile it, in accordance with the word of the LORD proclaimed by the man of God who foretold these things.

17The king asked, "What is that tombstone I see?"

The men of the city said, "It marks the tomb of the man of God who came from Judah and pronounced against the altar of Bethel the very things you have done to it."

18"Leave it alone," he said. "Don't let anyone disturb his bones[n]." So they spared his bones and those of the prophet who had come from Samaria.

19Just as he had done at Bethel, Josiah removed and defiled all the shrines at the high places that the kings of Israel had built in the towns of Samaria that had provoked the LORD to anger. 20Josiah slaughtered[o] all the priests of those high places on the altars and burned human bones[p] on them. Then he went back to Jerusalem.

---

a8 Or high places   b10 Or to make his son or daughter pass through   c13 Hebrew Milcom

23:8
[a]1Ki 15:22

23:9
[b]Eze 44:10-14

23:10
[c]Isa 30:33;
Jer 7:31,32;
19:6
[d]Jos 15:8
[e]Lev 18:21;
Dt 18:10

23:11
[f]Dt 4:19

23:12
[g]Jer 19:13;
Zep 1:5
[h]2Ki 21:5

23:13
[i]1Ki 11:7

23:14
[j]Ex 23:24;
Dt 7:5,25

23:15
[k]1Ki 13:1-3
[l]1Ki 12:33

23:16
[m]1Ki 13:2

23:18
[n]1Ki 13:31

23:20
[o]Ex 22:20;
2Ki 10:25; 11:18
[p]1Ki 13:2

23:21
a Ex 12:11;
Nu 9:2;
Dt 16:1-8

²¹The king gave this order to all the people: "Celebrate the Passover^a to the LORD your God, as it is written in this Book of the Covenant." ²²Not since the days of the judges who led Israel, nor throughout the days of the kings of Israel and the kings of Judah, had any such Passover been observed. ²³But in the eighteenth year of King Josiah, this Passover was celebrated to the LORD in Jerusalem.

23:24
b Lev 19:31;
Dt 18:11;
2Ki 21:6
c Ge 31:19

²⁴Furthermore, Josiah got rid of the mediums and spiritists,^b the household gods,^c the idols and all the other detestable things seen in Judah and Jerusalem. This he did to fulfill the requirements of the law written in the book that Hilkiah the priest had discovered in the temple of the LORD. ²⁵Neither before nor after Josiah was there a king like him who turned^d to the LORD as he did—with all his heart and with all his soul and with all his strength, in accordance with all the Law of Moses.

23:25
d 2Ki 18:5

23:26
e 2Ki 21:12;
Jer 15:4

²⁶Nevertheless, the LORD did not turn away from the heat of his fierce anger, which burned against Judah because of all that Manasseh^e had done to provoke him to anger. ²⁷So the LORD said, "I will remove^f Judah also from my presence^g as I removed Israel, and I will reject Jerusalem, the city I chose, and this temple, about which I said, 'There shall my Name be.'^a"

23:27
f 2Ki 21:13
g 2Ki 18:11

²⁸As for the other events of Josiah's reign, and all he did, are they not written in the book of the annals of the kings of Judah?

23:29
h Jer 46:2
i Zec 12:11

²⁹While Josiah was king, Pharaoh Neco^h king of Egypt went up to the Euphrates River to help the king of Assyria. King Josiah marched out to meet him in battle, but Neco faced him and killed him at Megiddo.ⁱ ³⁰Josiah's servants brought his body in a chariot^j from Megiddo to Jerusalem and buried him in his own tomb. And the people of the land took Jehoahaz son of Josiah and anointed him and made him king in place of his father.

23:30
j 2Ki 9:28

³¹Jehoahaz^k was twenty-three years old when he became king, and he reigned in Jerusalem three months. His mother's name was Hamutal^l daughter of Jeremiah; she was from Libnah. ³²He did evil in the eyes of the LORD, just as his fathers had done. ³³Pharaoh Neco put him in chains at Riblah^m in the land of Hamath^{bn} so that he might not reign in Jerusalem, and he imposed on Judah a levy of a hundred talents^c of silver and a talent^d of gold. ³⁴Pharaoh Neco made Eliakim^o son of Josiah king in place of his father Josiah and changed Eliakim's name to Jehoiakim. But he took Jehoahaz and carried him off to Egypt, and there he died.^p ³⁵Jehoiakim paid Pharaoh Neco the silver and gold he demanded. In order to do so, he taxed the land and

23:31
k 1Ch 3:15;
Jer 22:11
l 2Ki 24:18

23:33
m 2Ki 25:6
n 1Ki 8:65

23:34
o 1Ch 3:15;
2Ch 36:5-8
p Jer 22:12;
Eze 19:3-4

^a27 1 Kings 8:29   ^b33 Hebrew; Septuagint (see also 2 Chron. 36:3) *Neco at Riblah in Hamath removed him*   ^c33 That is, about 3 3/4 tons (about 3.4 metric tons)   ^d33 That is, about 75 pounds (about 34 kilograms)

exacted the silver and gold from the people of the land according to their assessments.[a]

[36] Jehoiakim[b] was twenty-five years old when he became king, and he reigned in Jerusalem eleven years. His mother's name was Zebidah daughter of Pedaiah; she was from Rumah. [37] And he did evil in the eyes of the LORD, just as his fathers had done.

Chapter 24 Theme _____

24 During Jehoiakim's reign, Nebuchadnezzar[c] king of Babylon invaded the land, and Jehoiakim became his vassal for three years. But then he changed his mind and rebelled against Nebuchadnezzar. [2] The LORD sent Babylonian,[a] Aramean,[d] Moabite and Ammonite raiders against him. He sent them to destroy[e] Judah, in accordance with the word of the LORD proclaimed by his servants the prophets. [3] Surely these things happened to Judah according to the LORD's command,[f] in order to remove them from his presence because of the sins of Manasseh[g] and all he had done, [4] including the shedding of innocent blood.[h] For he had filled Jerusalem with innocent blood, and the LORD was not willing to forgive.

[5] As for the other events of Jehoiakim's reign, and all he did, are they not written in the book of the annals of the kings of Judah? [6] Jehoiakim rested[i] with his fathers. And Jehoiachin his son succeeded him as king.

[7] The king of Egypt[j] did not march out from his own country again, because the king of Babylon[k] had taken all his territory, from the Wadi of Egypt to the Euphrates River.

[8] Jehoiachin[l] was eighteen years old when he became king, and he reigned in Jerusalem three months. His mother's name was Nehushta daughter of Elnathan; she was from Jerusalem. [9] He did evil in the eyes of the LORD, just as his father had done.

[10] At that time the officers of Nebuchadnezzar[m] king of Babylon advanced on Jerusalem and laid siege to it, [11] and Nebuchadnezzar himself came up to the city while his officers were besieging it. [12] Jehoiachin king of Judah, his mother, his attendants, his nobles and his officials all surrendered[n] to him.

In the eighth year of the reign of the king of Babylon, he took Jehoiachin prisoner. [13] As the LORD had declared,[o] Nebuchadnezzar removed all the treasures[p] from the temple of the LORD and from the royal palace, and took away all the gold articles[q] that Solomon[r] king of Israel had made for the temple of the LORD. [14] He carried into exile[s] all Jerusalem: all the officers and fighting men, and all the craftsmen and artisans—a total of ten thousand. Only the poorest[t] people of the land were left.

a 2 Or Chaldean

Marginal references

23:35
[a] ver 33

23:36
[b] Jer 26:1

24:1
[c] Jer 25:1,9;
Da 1:1

24:2
[d] Jer 35:11
[e] Jer 25:9

24:3
[f] 2Ki 18:25
[g] 2Ki 21:12;
23:26

24:4
[h] 2Ki 21:16

24:6
[i] Jer 22:19

24:7
[j] Ge 15:18
[k] Jer 37:5-7; 46:2

24:8
[l] 1Ch 3:16

24:10
[m] Da 1:1

24:12
[n] 2Ki 25:27;
Jer 22:24-30;
24:1; 25:1; 29:2;
52:28

24:13
[o] 2Ki 20:17
[p] 2Ki 25:15;
Isa 39:6
[q] 2Ki 25:14;
Jer 20:5
[r] 1Ki 7:51

24:14
[s] Jer 24:1; 52:28
[t] 2Ki 25:12;
Jer 40:7; 52:16

24:15
a Jer 22:24-28
b Est 2:6;
Eze 17:12-14

24:16
c Jer 52:28

24:17
d 1Ch 3:15;
2Ch 36:11;
Jer 37:1

24:18
e Jer 52:1
f 2Ki 23:31

24:20
g Dt 4:26;
29:27

25:1
h Jer 34:1-7
i Eze 24:2

25:3
j Jer 14:18;
La 4:9

25:4
k Eze 33:21
l Jer 4:17

25:5
m Eze 12:14

25:6
n Jer 34:21-22
o 2Ki 23:33

25:7
p Jer 21:7; 32:4-5;
Eze 12:11

¹⁵Nebuchadnezzar took Jehoiachin captive to Babylon. He also took from Jerusalem to Babylon the king's mother,*a* his wives, his officials and the leading men*b* of the land. ¹⁶The king of Babylon also deported to Babylon the entire force of seven thousand fighting men, strong and fit for war, and a thousand craftsmen and artisans.*c*

¹⁷He made Mattaniah, Jehoiachin's uncle, king in his place and changed his name to Zedekiah.*d*

¹⁸Zedekiah*e* was twenty-one years old when he became king, and he reigned in Jerusalem eleven years. His mother's name was Hamutal*f* daughter of Jeremiah; she was from Libnah. ¹⁹He did evil in the eyes of the LORD, just as Jehoiakim had done. ²⁰It was because of the LORD's anger that all this happened to Jerusalem and Judah, and in the end he thrust*g* them from his presence.

Now Zedekiah rebelled against the king of Babylon.

Exiles of Judah to Babylon

Chapter 25 Theme

25 So in the ninth year of Zedekiah's reign, on the tenth day of the tenth month, Nebuchadnezzar*h* king of Babylon marched against Jerusalem with his whole army. He encamped outside the city and built siege works*i* all around it. ²The city was kept under siege until the eleventh year of King Zedekiah. ³By the ninth day of the ⌊fourth⌋*a* month the famine*j* in the city had become so severe that there was no food for the people to eat. ⁴Then the city wall was broken through,*k* and the whole army fled at night through the gate between the two walls near the king's garden, though the Babylonians*b* were surrounding*l* the city. They fled toward the Arabah,*c* ⁵but the Babylonian*d* army pursued the king and overtook him in the plains of Jericho. All his soldiers were separated from him and scattered,*m* ⁶and he was captured.*n* He was taken to the king of Babylon at Riblah,*o* where sentence was pronounced on him. ⁷They killed the sons of Zedekiah before his eyes. Then they put out his eyes, bound him with bronze shackles and took him to Babylon.*p*

⁸On the seventh day of the fifth month, in the nineteenth year of Nebuchadnezzar king of Babylon, Nebuzaradan commander

a 3 See Jer. 52:6.   *b* 4 Or *Chaldeans*; also in verses 13, 25 and 26   *c* 4 Or *the Jordan Valley*
d 5 Or *Chaldean*; also in verses 10 and 24

of the imperial guard, an official of the king of Babylon, came to Jerusalem. [9]He set fire[a] to the temple of the LORD, the royal palace and all the houses of Jerusalem. Every important building he burned down.[b] [10]The whole Babylonian army, under the commander of the imperial guard, broke down the walls[c] around Jerusalem. [11]Nebuzaradan the commander of the guard carried into exile[d] the people who remained in the city, along with the rest of the populace and those who had gone over to the king of Babylon.[e] [12]But the commander left behind some of the poorest people[f] of the land to work the vineyards and fields.

[13]The Babylonians broke up the bronze pillars, the movable stands and the bronze Sea that were at the temple of the LORD and they carried the bronze to Babylon. [14]They also took away the pots, shovels, wick trimmers, dishes and all the bronze articles[g] used in the temple service. [15]The commander of the imperial guard took away the censers and sprinkling bowls—all that were made of pure gold or silver.

[16]The bronze from the two pillars, the Sea and the movable stands, which Solomon had made for the temple of the LORD, was more than could be weighed. [17]Each pillar[h] was twenty-seven feet[a] high. The bronze capital on top of one pillar was four and a half feet[b] high and was decorated with a network and pomegranates of bronze all around. The other pillar, with its network, was similar.

[18]The commander of the guard took as prisoners Seraiah[i] the chief priest, Zephaniah[j] the priest next in rank and the three doorkeepers. [19]Of those still in the city, he took the officer in charge of the fighting men and five royal advisers. He also took the secretary who was chief officer in charge of conscripting the people of the land and sixty of his men who were found in the city. [20]Nebuzaradan the commander took them all and brought them to the king of Babylon at Riblah. [21]There at Riblah, in the land of Hamath, the king had them executed.

So Judah went into captivity, away from her land.[k]

[22]Nebuchadnezzar king of Babylon appointed Gedaliah[l] son of Ahikam, the son of Shaphan, to be over the people he had left behind in Judah. [23]When all the army officers and their men heard that the king of Babylon had appointed Gedaliah as governor, they came to Gedaliah at Mizpah—Ishmael son of Nethaniah, Johanan son of Kareah, Seraiah son of Tanhumeth the Netophathite, Jaazaniah the son of the Maacathite, and their men. [24]Gedaliah took an oath to reassure them and their men. "Do not be afraid of the Babylonian officials," he said. "Settle down in the land and serve the king of Babylon, and it will go well with you."

a 17 Hebrew *eighteen cubits* (about 8.1 meters) b 17 Hebrew *three cubits* (about 1.3 meters)

25:9
[a] Isa 60:7
[b] Ps 74:3-8;
Jer 2:15;
Am 2:5;
Mic 3:12

25:10
[c] Ne 1:3

25:11
[d] 2Ki 24:14
[e] 2Ki 24:1

25:12
[f] 2Ki 24:14

25:14
[g] Ex 27:3;
1Ki 7:47-50

25:17
[h] 1Ki 7:15-22

25:18
[i] 1Ch 6:14;
Ezr 7:1;
Ne 11:11
[j] Jer 21:1;
29:25

25:21
[k] Ge 12:7;
Dt 28:64;
Jos 23:13;
2Ki 23:27

25:22
[l] Jer 39:14;
40:5,7

25:26
a Isa 30:2;
Jer 43:7

25:27
b 2Ki 24:12;
Jer 52:31-34

25:28
c Ezr 5:5;
Ne 2:1;
Da 2:48

25:29
d 2Sa 9:7

25:30
e Est 2:9;
Jer 28:4

²⁵In the seventh month, however, Ishmael son of Nethaniah, the son of Elishama, who was of royal blood, came with ten men and assassinated Gedaliah and also the men of Judah and the Babylonians who were with him at Mizpah. ²⁶At this, all the people from the least to the greatest, together with the army officers, fled to Egypt*a* for fear of the Babylonians.

²⁷In the thirty-seventh year of the exile of Jehoiachin king of Judah, in the year Evil-Merodach*a* became king of Babylon, he released Jehoiachin*b* from prison on the twenty-seventh day of the twelfth month. ²⁸He spoke kindly to him and gave him a seat of honor*c* higher than those of the other kings who were with him in Babylon. ²⁹So Jehoiachin put aside his prison clothes and for the rest of his life ate regularly at the king's table.*d* ³⁰Day by day the king gave Jehoiachin a regular allowance as long as he lived.*e*

a 27 Also called *Amel-Marduk*

Israel's Division and Captivity

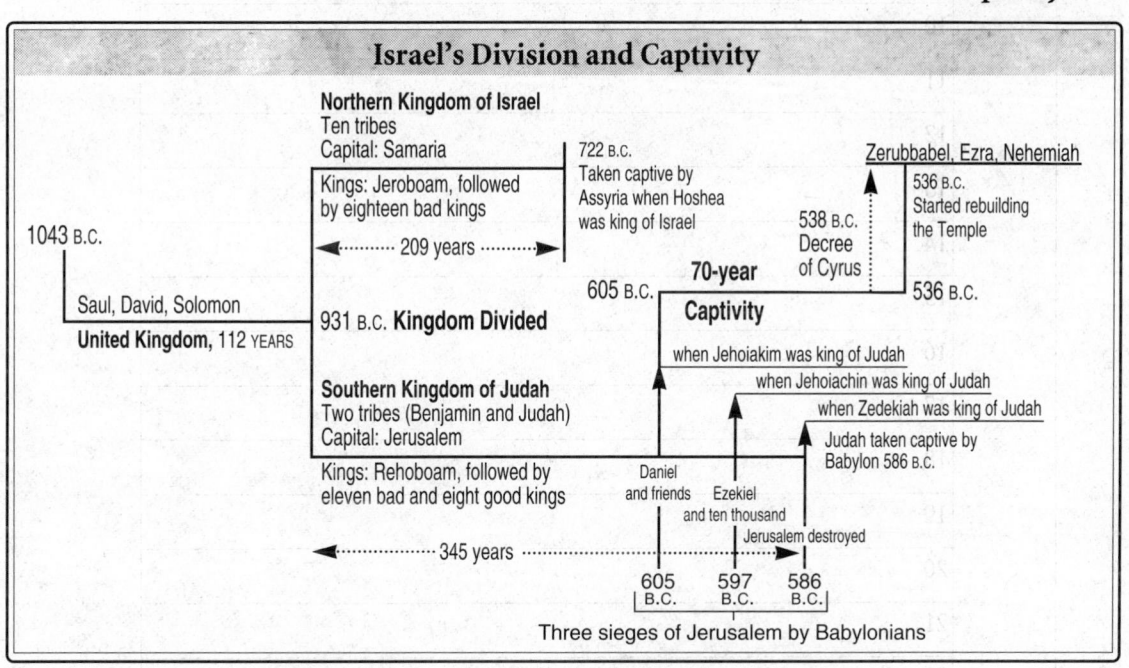

Israel's Division and Captivity

1043 B.C.

Saul, David, Solomon
United Kingdom, 112 YEARS

Northern Kingdom of Israel
Ten tribes
Capital: Samaria

Kings: Jeroboam, followed
by eighteen bad kings

◄·········· 209 years ··········►

722 B.C.
Taken captive by
Assyria when Hoshea
was king of Israel

931 B.C. **Kingdom Divided**

Southern Kingdom of Judah
Two tribes (Benjamin and Judah)
Capital: Jerusalem

Kings: Rehoboam, followed by
eleven bad and eight good kings

605 B.C.

70-year
Captivity

when Jehoiakim was king of Judah
when Jehoiachin was king of Judah
when Zedekiah was king of Judah
Judah taken captive by
Babylon 586 B.C.

538 B.C.
Decree
of Cyrus

Zerubbabel, Ezra, Nehemiah
536 B.C.
Started rebuilding
the Temple

536 B.C.

◄················ 345 years ················►

Daniel
and friends

Ezekiel
and ten thousand

Jerusalem destroyed

605
B.C.

597
B.C.

586
B.C.

Three sieges of Jerusalem by Babylonians

Theme of 2 Kings:

SEGMENT DIVISIONS

		CHAPTER THEMES
		1
		2
		3
		4
		5
		6
		7
		8
		9
		10
		11
		12
		13
		14
		15
		16
		17
		18
		19
		20
		21
		22
		23
		24
		25

Author:

Date:

Purpose:

Key Words:

THE HISTORICAL CHART OF THE KINGS AND PROPHETS OF ISRAEL AND JUDAH

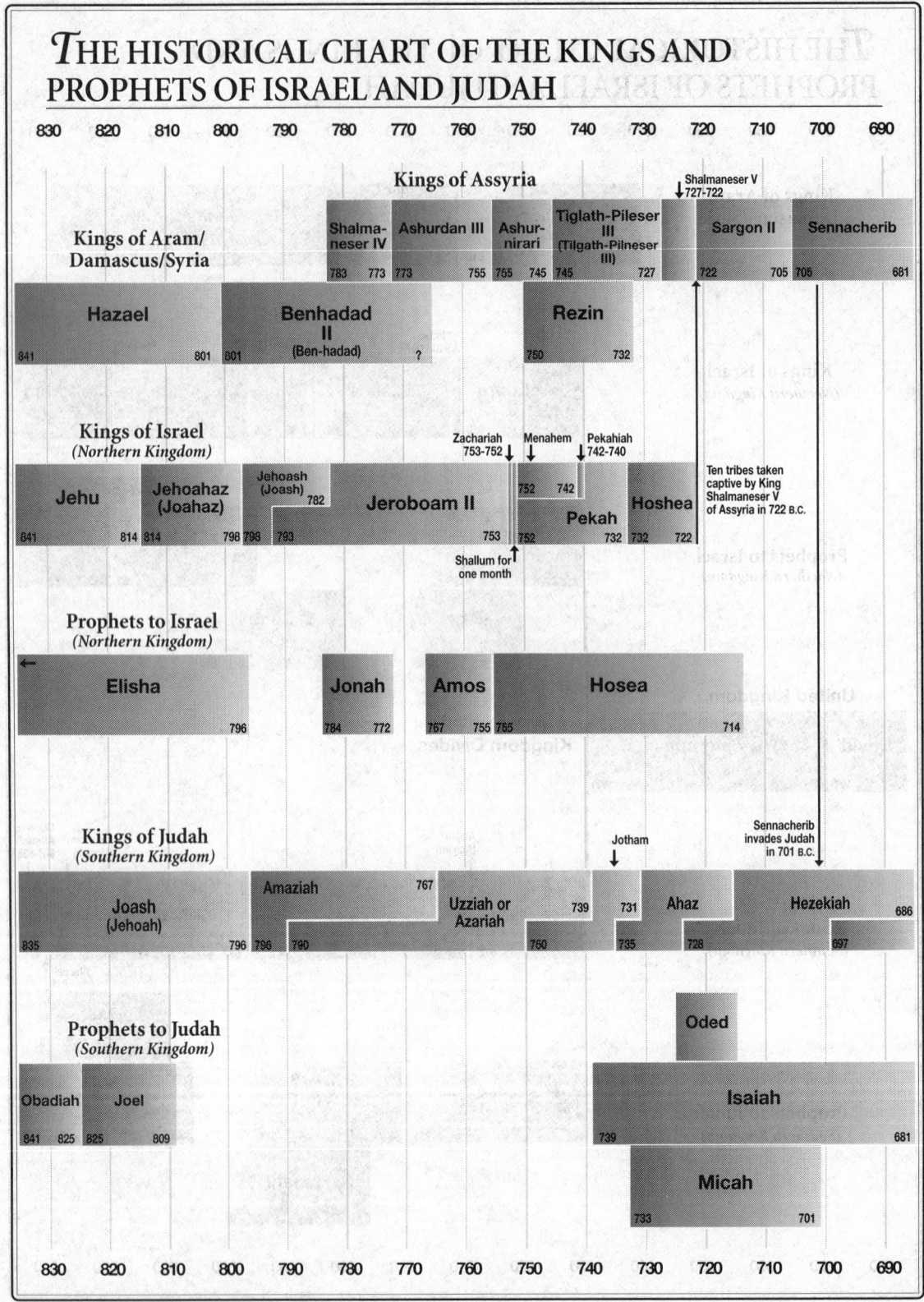

THE HISTORICAL CHART OF THE KINGS AND PROPHETS OF ISRAEL AND JUDAH

| 830 | 820 | 810 | 800 | 790 | 780 | 770 | 760 | 750 | 740 | 730 | 720 | 710 | 700 | 690 |

Kings of Assyria

Shalmaneser V 727-722

| Shalma-neser IV | Ashurdan III | Ashur-nirari | Tiglath-Pileser III (Tilgath-Pilneser III) | | Sargon II | Sennacherib |
| 783 | 773 | 773 | 755 | 755 | 745 | 745 | 727 | 722 | 705 | 705 | 681 |

Kings of Aram/ Damascus/Syria

| Hazael | | Benhadad II (Ben-hadad) | | Rezin |
| 841 | 801 | 801 | ? | 750 | 732 |

Kings of Israel (Northern Kingdom)

Zachariah 753-752

Menahem

Pekahiah 742-740

| Jehu | Jehoahaz (Joahaz) | Jehoash (Joash) | Jeroboam II | | | Pekah | Hoshea |
| 841 | 814 | 814 | 798 | 798 | 793 | 782 | 753 | 752 | 742 | 752 | 732 | 732 | 722 |

Shallum for one month

Ten tribes taken captive by King Shalmaneser V of Assyria in 722 B.C.

Prophets to Israel (Northern Kingdom)

← | Elisha | | Jonah | | Amos | | Hosea |
| 796 | 784 | 772 | 757 | 755 | 765 | 714 |

Kings of Judah (Southern Kingdom)

Jotham

Sennacherib invades Judah in 701 B.C.

| Joash (Jehoah) | | Amaziah | 767 | Uzziah or Azariah | 739 | 731 | Ahaz | | Hezekiah | 686 |
| 835 | 796 | 796 | 790 | | 760 | | 735 | 728 | 697 |

Prophets to Judah (Southern Kingdom)

Oded

| Obadiah | Joel | | Isaiah | |
| 841 | 825 | 825 | 809 | 739 | 681 |

| Micah |
| 733 | 701 |

| 830 | 820 | 810 | 800 | 790 | 780 | 770 | 760 | 750 | 740 | 730 | 720 | 710 | 700 | 690 |

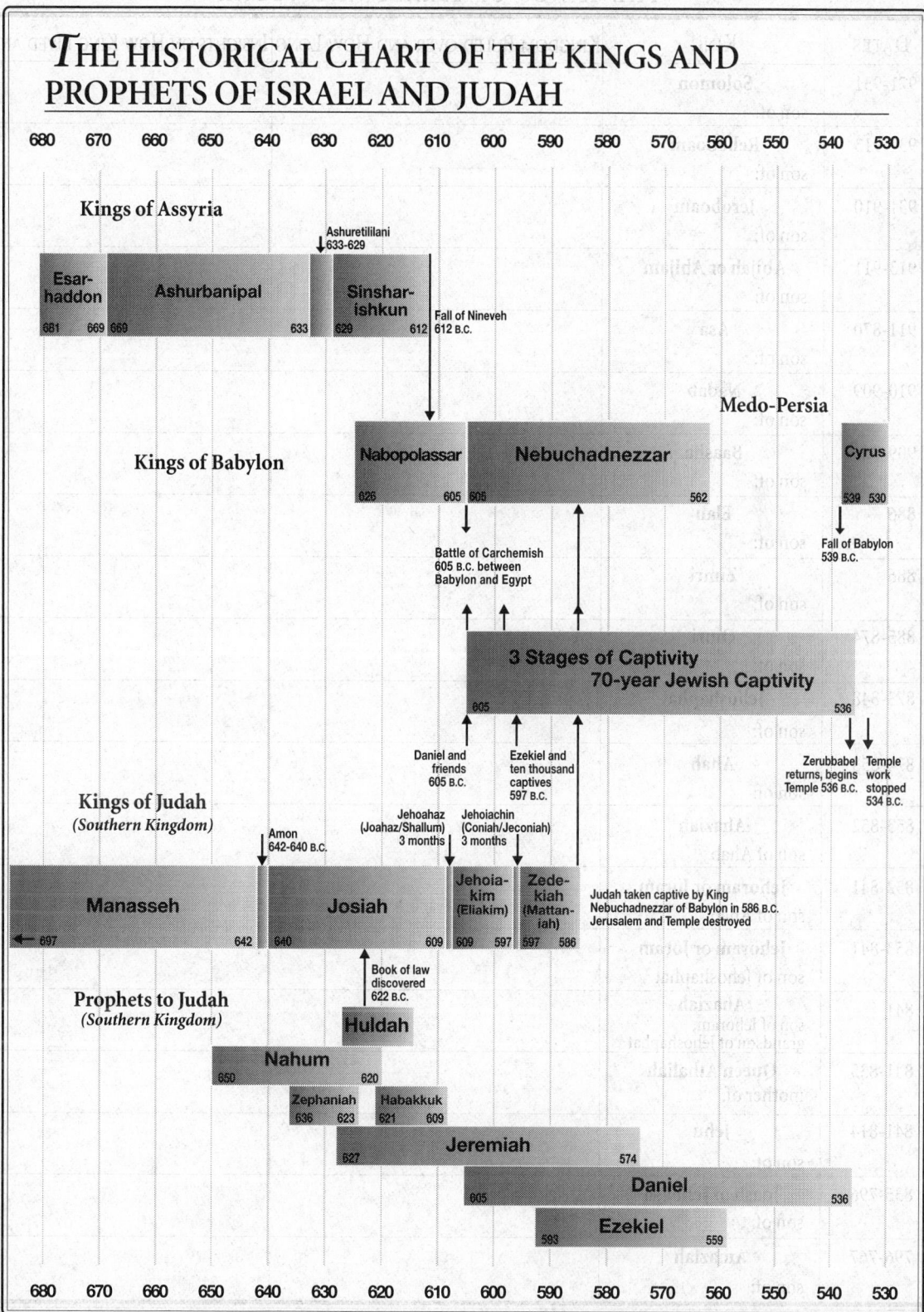

THE HISTORICAL CHART OF THE KINGS AND PROPHETS OF ISRAEL AND JUDAH

680 670 660 650 640 630 620 610 600 590 580 570 560 550 540 530

Kings of Assyria

Ashuretililani
↓ 633-629

| Esar-haddon | Ashurbanipal | Sinshar-ishkun |
681 669 | 669   633 | 629 612 |

Fall of Nineveh
612 B.C.

Medo-Persia

Kings of Babylon

| Nabopolassar | Nebuchadnezzar | Cyrus |
626   605 | 605   562 | 539 530 |

Battle of Carchemish
605 B.C. between
Babylon and Egypt

Fall of Babylon
539 B.C.

3 Stages of Captivity
70-year Jewish Captivity
605   536

Daniel and
friends
605 B.C.

Ezekiel and
ten thousand
captives
597 B.C.

Zerubbabel
returns, begins
Temple 536 B.C.

Temple
work
stopped
534 B.C.

Jehoahaz
(Joahaz/Shallum)
3 months

Jehoiachin
(Coniah/Jeconiah)
3 months

Kings of Judah
(Southern Kingdom)

Amon
642-640 B.C.

| Manasseh | Josiah | Jehoia-kim (Eliakim) | Zede-kiah (Mattan-iah) |
← 697   642 | 640   609 | 609 597 | 597 586 |

Judah taken captive by King
Nebuchadnezzar of Babylon in 586 B.C.
Jerusalem and Temple destroyed

Book of law
discovered
622 B.C.

Prophets to Judah
(Southern Kingdom)

Huldah

Nahum
650   620

Zephaniah
636 623

Habakkuk
621 609

Jeremiah
627   574

Daniel
605   536

Ezekiel
593   559

680 670 660 650 640 630 620 610 600 590 580 570 560 550 540 530

DATES	KING	KINGDOM RULED OVER AND HOW LONG	INSIGHTS ON HOW KING LIVED AND DIED
971-931	**Solomon** son of:		
931-913	**Rehoboam** son of:		
931-910	**Jeroboam** son of:		
913-911	**Abijah** or **Abijam** son of:		
911-870	**Asa** son of:		
910-909	**Nadab** son of:		
909-886	**Baasha** son of:		
886	**Elah** son of:		
886	**Zimri** son of:		
885-874	**Omri** son of:		
873-848	**Jehoshaphat** son of:		
874-853	**Ahab** son of:		
853-852	**Ahaziah** son of Ahab		
852-841	**Jehoram** or **Joram** son of Ahab		
853-841	**Jehoram** or **Joram** son of Jehoshaphat		
841	**Ahaziah** son of Jehoram, grandson of Jehoshaphat		
841-835	**Queen Athaliah** mother of:		
841-814	**Jehu** son of:		
835-796	**Joash** or **Jehoash** son of:		
796-767	**Amaziah** son of:		

If a king ruled for any portion of a year, customarily that year was included as part of his reign.
An overlap in reigns indicates a co-regency, such as a son ruling alongside his father.

THE KINGS OF ISRAEL AND JUDAH

DATES	KING	KINGDOM RULED OVER AND HOW LONG	INSIGHTS ON HOW KING LIVED AND DIED
814-798	**Jehoahaz** or **Joahaz** son of:		
798-782	**Jehoash** or **Joash** son of:		
790-739	**Azariah** or **Uzziah** son of:		
793-753	**Jeroboam II** son of:		
753-752	**Zechariah** son of:		
752	**Shallum** son of:		
752-742	**Menahem** son of:		
742-740	**Pekahiah** son of:		
752-732	**Pekah** son of:		
750-731	**Jotham** son of:		
735-715	**Ahaz** son of:		
732-722	**Hoshea** son of:		
728-686	**Hezekiah** son of:		
697-642	**Manasseh** son of:		
642-640	**Amon** son of:		
640-609	**Josiah** son of:		
609	**Jehoahaz** or **Joahaz** **or Shallum** son of:		
609-597	**Jehoiakim** or **Eliakim** son of:		
597	**Jehoiachin** or **Coniah** or **Jeconiah** son of:		
597-586	**Zedekiah** or **Mattaniah** son of:		

If a king ruled for any portion of a year, customarily that year was included as part of his reign.
An overlap in reigns indicates a co-regency, such as a son ruling alongside his father.

1 CHRONICLES

*J*udah had watched Assyria capture Israel in 722 B.C. In 586 B.C., when the Babylonians besieged Jerusalem for the third and final time, Judah lost her temple, the city of David, and the reign of the sons of David came to a halt. All seemed lost. Judah was held captive for 70 years. Then a Persian king, Cyrus, sent out a decree telling the exiles they could return and rebuild Jerusalem and their temple.

But if they did, could they be assured that the God of Abraham, Isaac, and Jacob would be with them? Had he abandoned his people and his promise to Abraham because of their sin? Would the northern and southern kingdoms ever be united again? Would God still send Messiah? Would David have a descendant who would sit on the throne of David forever?

And the temple? Between the time of Solomon and the Babylonian captivity, king after king had neglected it or desecrated it with idols. If they were to restore it, would it do any good?

And what of the prophets? What was God's Word, the prophets' message, regarding Israel, Judah, and their future? Would the Word of God change? Would the messages of the prophets be valid after Israel and Judah had so grievously sinned?

Having returned from captivity, God's people had to be reminded of "the events or annals of the days, the years," and so Chronicles was written. We don't know for certain who wrote it; perhaps it was Ezra. However, we do know that it was part of God's plan, for God included it in the canon of Scripture.

∾ THINGS TO DO

General Instructions

1. If possible, study 1 and 2 Samuel and then 1 and 2 Kings before you study 1 and 2 Chronicles. Chronicles is to these other historical books what John is to the synoptic Gospels (Matthew, Mark, and Luke). Both John and Chronicles are supplemental and yet bring unique insight and understanding. Study the HISTORICAL PARALLEL OF SAMUEL, KINGS, AND CHRONICLES on page 659.

2. First and 2 Chronicles have time gaps in them. Keep this in mind as you study. When you wonder about the timing of something, look at the HISTORICAL PARALLEL again.

3. As you read 1 Chronicles watch for references to time, to any mention of dates or periods of time as well as who is reigning at the time. Mark these with an appropriate symbol.

4. When you finish observing each chapter, record its theme on 1 CHRONICLES AT A GLANCE on page 715 and on the line next to the chapter number in the text.

Chapters 1-9: The Genealogies of the Nation of Israel

1. This section may seem boring because it is primarily genealogies with a few historical sidelights. However, remember that this information has a purpose, and that is why God included it in his Word. Some genealogies, such as 4:1-23, are not included anywhere else.

   a. Don't skip this section; you will gain valuable insights which will help you in the study of the rest of the book.

   b. To discover the scope of the genealogies, read verses 1:1 and 9:1, 2. Then write in the margin of 1:1 when the genealogies begin and end according to the historical events they represent. Keeping in mind what was said in the introduction to 1 Chronicles, notice in 9:2 the words "the first to resettle on their own property in their own towns."

2. In this segment the key words to mark or underline are the names of people who play vital roles in Israel's history.

a. Mark the following key words in a distinctive way: *Adam, Noah,* and Noah's three sons: *Shem, Ham,* and *Japheth.* Then mark the phrases *the sons of Japheth, the sons of Ham,* and *the sons of Shem.*

b. Mark *the sons of Abraham: Isaac and Ishmael,* and *Abraham was the father of Isaac,* and *the sons of Isaac: Esau and Israel* (remember that Israel was called Jacob until God changed his name to Israel).

c. In chapter 2 mark *these were the sons of Israel.* Then count the sons. How many were there? They became the heads of the tribes of Israel. Record their names on an index card and look for any place where they are repeated in this segment. Use this card as a bookmark.

   1) Read Genesis 49:1-28 where Jacob (Israel) gives a prophetic blessing to each of these men.

   2) Look at the "Insight" on page 662 which shows the birth order and mother of each of Israel's sons.

d. In 2:3-15 mark *the sons of Judah (the people of Judah),* and then look for *David.* In the margin list David's genealogy from Judah through David's immediate father, Jesse. Remember that the author of Chronicles gives the genealogy of Judah before the other sons of Israel. Why? What would be important to the exiles who now repossessed their cities? Wouldn't it be God's promises to David? Keep this in mind as you study the second-to-the-last segment of 1 Chronicles.

e. In 3:1 mark the names of the sons of David, then list their names in the margin.

f. First Chronicles 3:10-16 gives the line of kings which come from David through Solomon.

   1) List these names in the margin.

   2) Then turn to the "Insight" next to Jeremiah 1:2-9 and look at this partial list of kings and note their alternate names. Write these names next to the names you listed in the margin of 1 Chronicles 3:10-16.

g. First Chronicles 3:17-24 lists the genealogy through Jeconiah (Jehoiachin). He was the king who reigned three months and ten days before he was taken into exile in Babylon, put in prison, and then released. See 2 Kings 24:8-16 and 2 Chronicles 36:9, 10.

3. When you read chapters 4 through 9 watch for any mention of the twelve sons of Israel and their genealogy. As you do:

a. Notice that not all twelve are mentioned in chapters 4 through 9.

b. Joseph's sons Manasseh and Ephraim are mentioned in Scripture as part of the twelve tribes of Israel. The reason for this is given in 1 Chronicles 5:1, 2. Take special note of this.

   1) Write "Joseph's son" next to any mention of Manasseh and/or Ephraim.

   2) Manasseh is named twice. The tribe split when Canaan was divided. Half the tribe of Manasseh took land east of the Jordan and the other half went west of the Jordan; thus the reference to the "half-tribe of Manasseh."

4. Read the section on the sons of Levi carefully and either underline what they were to do or note it in the margin. Also observe and note what Aaron and his sons were to do. This will help when you come to the final chapters of 1 Chronicles.

5. Don't forget to record the chapter themes in the text and on 1 CHRONICLES AT A GLANCE.

Chapters 10-19: God Turns the Kingdom to David

1. As you read this segment see how it fits with 1 and 2 Samuel. To do this consult the chart THE HISTORICAL PARALLEL OF SAMUEL, KINGS, AND CHRONICLES on page 659.

a. Read 1 Chronicles 10, mark any reference to *kingdom,* and list the events of that chapter.

b. Also note where it says whose son David was. Keep in mind what you just studied in the first segment.

1 CHRONICLES

    c. Note in the margin why Saul died, who died with him, and what happened to Saul's body.

2. Read this segment chapter by chapter and do the following:

    a. Mark the following key words: *City of David, ark,* and *covenant (compact).* Observe what you learn from these words and record your insights in the margin.

    b. Ask the five W's and an H as you read each chapter. Who are the key characters? What happens? When? (Draw a symbol next to any mention of time.) Where do events occur? Why do they occur? How do things happen? Record your insights in the margin.

    c. Don't forget to record chapter themes on 1 CHRONICLES AT A GLANCE and in the text next to the chapter number.

3. Watch for any prophecies (promises), speeches, songs, or psalms of praise. Who gives them? Why? What is said in each? Record your insights in the margin. Also ask: How can I apply these truths in my life?

Chapters 20-29: David Builds an Altar and Prepares for God's House

1. Note where this portion of 1 Chronicles comes in respect to 2 Samuel.

    a. When you read chapter 20, compare the wording of verse 1 with 2 Samuel 11:1. Then as you look at the content of 2 Samuel 11, 12, note what the author of Chronicles leaves out.

    b. Now compare 1 Chronicles 21 with 2 Samuel 24. Why was this event included in 1 Chronicles when David's other sin was omitted? See the "Insight" on page 700 next to 1 Chronicles 22. Remember, the temple is very important to the returning exiles.

2. As you read each chapter, mark the following key words and note in the margin what you learn from each: *house (temple, family, palatial structure, sanctuary), ark, heart (hearts, wholehearted, wholeheartedly), Levi (Levite, Levites),* and *Aaron.*

    a. The word *house* has been used numerous times in 1 Chronicles; however, with one or two exceptions "house" referred to someone's family, such as the house of David. In this segment it is used primarily for the house of the Lord. As you mark it note what you learn. Keep in mind that this is the book for the exiles who had returned to rebuild the temple and thus the emphasis is on the house of God and its importance. When difficulties arose this historical account would affirm God's enduring purpose and promises.

    b. As you mark the references to the Levites and to Aaron and his sons, observe carefully the types of duties they were to perform and which Levite family was to perform each type of duty. Also go back and review what you marked in the first segment regarding Levi, Aaron, and Aaron's other sons.

3. Read each chapter as you did in the last segment, asking the five W's and an H. Note in the margin what you observe. Also as you did in the last segment, watch for any speeches, prophecies, etc., and note the same things you looked for previously.

4. Complete 1 CHRONICLES AT A GLANCE. There are two lines for any additional segment divisions you might see and want to mark.

❧ THINGS TO THINK ABOUT

1. Second Timothy 2:13 says, "If we are faithless, he will remain faithful, for he cannot disown himself." What have you seen of the faithfulness of God in the book of 1 Chronicles? What assurance does this give you for your life?

2. You marked the word *heart* in this last segment. Go back over these references in chapter 29 and review what you observed about the heart. Also review what you observed as David blessed the Lord.

Think about your own heart. What is your heart like in respect to the Lord? How can you turn what David did into a prayer to the Lord?

3. As you think about all you learned about the priests and their duties and you think of yourself and other Christians as a kingdom of priests unto God (Revelation 1 and 5), do you see any application you can make to your responsibilities as a priest unto God?

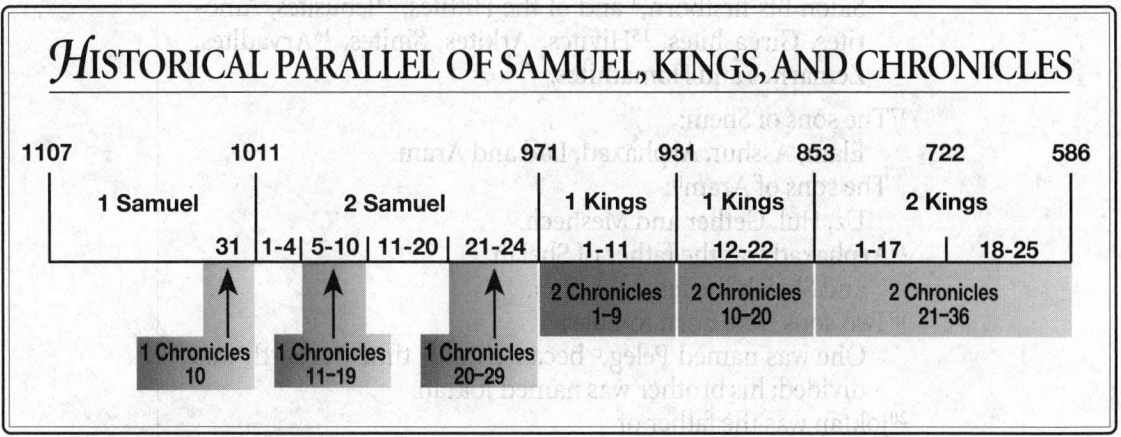

ℋISTORICAL PARALLEL OF SAMUEL, KINGS, AND CHRONICLES

1107	1011	971	931	853	722	586

1 Samuel	2 Samuel	1 Kings	1 Kings	2 Kings
31	1-4 | 5-10 | 11-20 | 21-24	1-11	12-22	1-17 | 18-25

| 1 Chronicles 10 | 1 Chronicles 11-19 | 1 Chronicles 20-29 | 2 Chronicles 1-9 | 2 Chronicles 10-20 | 2 Chronicles 21-36 |

~~~~~~

Chapter 1 Theme

1:1
a Ge 5:1-32;
Lk 3:36-38

1 Adam,*a* Seth, Enosh, ²Kenan,*b* Mahalalel,*c* Jared,*d* ³Enoch,*e* Methuselah, *f* Lamech,*g* Noah.*h*

⁴The sons of Noah:*ai*
  Shem, Ham and Japheth.*j*

1:2
b Ge 5:9
c Ge 5:12
d Ge 5:15

⁵The sons*b* of Japheth:
  Gomer, Magog, Madai, Javan, Tubal, Meshech and Tiras.
⁶The sons of Gomer:
  Ashkenaz, Riphath*c* and Togarmah.
⁷The sons of Javan:
  Elishah, Tarshish, the Kittim and the Rodanim.

⁸The sons of Ham:
  Cush, Mizraim,*d* Put and Canaan.

1:3
e Ge 5:18;
Jude 14
f Ge 5:21
g Ge 5:25
h Ge 5:29

⁹The sons of Cush:
  Seba, Havilah, Sabta, Raamah and Sabteca.
  The sons of Raamah:
  Sheba and Dedan.
¹⁰Cush was the father*e* of
  Nimrod, who grew to be a mighty warrior on earth.

---

*a*4 Septuagint; Hebrew does not have *The sons of Noah:*   *b*5 *Sons* may mean *descendants* or *successors* or *nations*; also in verses 6-10, 17 and 20.   *c*6 Many Hebrew manuscripts and Vulgate (see also Septuagint and Gen. 10:3); most Hebrew manuscripts *Diphath*   *d*8 That is, Egypt; also in verse 11   *e*10 *Father* may mean *ancestor* or *predecessor* or *founder*; also in verses 11, 13, 18 and 20.

1:4
i Ge 6:10; 10:1
j Ge 5:32

¹¹Mizraim was the father of
the Ludites, Anamites, Lehabites, Naphtuhites, ¹²Pathrusites, Casluhites (from whom the Philistines came) and Caphtorites.
¹³Canaan was the father of
Sidon his firstborn,^a and of the Hittites, ¹⁴Jebusites, Amorites, Girgashites, ¹⁵Hivites, Arkites, Sinites, ¹⁶Arvadites, Zemarites and Hamathites.

¹⁷The sons of Shem:
Elam, Asshur, Arphaxad, Lud and Aram.
The sons of Aram^b:
Uz, Hul, Gether and Meshech.
¹⁸Arphaxad was the father of Shelah,
and Shelah the father of Eber.
¹⁹Two sons were born to Eber:
One was named Peleg,^c because in his time the earth was divided; his brother was named Joktan.
²⁰Joktan was the father of
Almodad, Sheleph, Hazarmaveth, Jerah, ²¹Hadoram, Uzal, Diklah, ²²Obal,^d Abimael, Sheba, ²³Ophir, Havilah and Jobab. All these were sons of Joktan.

²⁴Shem,^a Arphaxad,^e Shelah,
²⁵Eber, Peleg, Reu,
²⁶Serug, Nahor, Terah
²⁷and Abram (that is, Abraham).

²⁸The sons of Abraham:
Isaac and Ishmael.
²⁹These were their descendants:
Nebaioth the firstborn of Ishmael, Kedar, Adbeel, Mibsam, ³⁰Mishma, Dumah, Massa, Hadad, Tema, ³¹Jetur, Naphish and Kedemah. These were the sons of Ishmael.

³²The sons born to Keturah, Abraham's concubine:^b
Zimran, Jokshan, Medan, Midian, Ishbak and Shuah.
The sons of Jokshan:
Sheba and Dedan.^c
³³The sons of Midian:
Ephah, Epher, Hanoch, Abida and Eldaah.
All these were descendants of Keturah.

³⁴Abraham^d was the father of Isaac.^e
The sons of Isaac:
Esau and Israel.^f

1:24 ^aGe 10:21-25; Lk 3:34-36

1:32 ^bGe 22:24 ^cGe 10:7

1:34 ^dLk 3:34 ^eGe 21:2-3; Mt 1:2; Ac 7:8 ^fGe 17:5; 25:25-26

a 13 Or of the Sidonians, the foremost   b 17 One Hebrew manuscript and some Septuagint manuscripts (see also Gen. 10:23); most Hebrew manuscripts do not have this line.   c 19 Peleg means division.   d 22 Some Hebrew manuscripts and Syriac (see also Gen. 10:28); most Hebrew manuscripts Ebal   e 24 Hebrew; some Septuagint manuscripts Arphaxad, Cainan (see also note at Gen. 11:10)

1:35
a Ge 36:19
b Ge 36:4

35The sons of Esau:*a*

Eliphaz, Reuel,*b* Jeush, Jalam and Korah.

36The sons of Eliphaz:

Teman, Omar, Zepho,*a* Gatam and Kenaz;

by Timna: Amalek.*bc*

37The sons of Reuel:*d*

Nahath, Zerah, Shammah and Mizzah.

38The sons of Seir:

Lotan, Shobal, Zibeon, Anah, Dishon, Ezer and Dishan.

39The sons of Lotan:

Hori and Homam. Timna was Lotan's sister.

1:36
c Ex 17:14

40The sons of Shobal:

Alvan,*c* Manahath, Ebal, Shepho and Onam.

The sons of Zibeon:

Aiah and Anah.*e*

41The son of Anah:

Dishon.

The sons of Dishon:

Hemdan,*d* Eshban, Ithran and Keran.

42The sons of Ezer:

Bilhan, Zaavan and Akan.*e*

The sons of Dishan*f*:

Uz and Aran.

1:37
d Ge 36:17

43These were the kings who reigned in Edom before any Israelite king reigned*g*:

Bela son of Beor, whose city was named Dinhabah.

44When Bela died, Jobab son of Zerah from Bozrah succeeded him as king.

45When Jobab died, Husham from the land of the Temanites*f* succeeded him as king.

46When Husham died, Hadad son of Bedad, who defeated Midian in the country of Moab, succeeded him as king. His city was named Avith.

1:40
e Ge 36:2

47When Hadad died, Samlah from Masrekah succeeded him as king.

48When Samlah died, Shaul from Rehoboth on the river*h* succeeded him as king.

49When Shaul died, Baal-Hanan son of Acbor succeeded him as king.

---

a 36 Many Hebrew manuscripts, some Septuagint manuscripts and Syriac (see also Gen. 36:11); most Hebrew manuscripts *Zephi*   *b 36* Some Septuagint manuscripts (see also Gen. 36:12); Hebrew *Gatam, Kenaz, Timna and Amalek*   *c 40* Many Hebrew manuscripts and some Septuagint manuscripts (see also Gen. 36:23); most Hebrew manuscripts *Alian*   *d 41* Many Hebrew manuscripts and some Septuagint manuscripts (see also Gen. 36:26); most Hebrew manuscripts *Hamran*   *e 42* Many Hebrew and Septuagint manuscripts (see also Gen. 36:27); most Hebrew manuscripts *Zaavan, Jaakan*   *f 42* Hebrew *Dishon*, a variant of *Dishan*   *g 43* Or *before an Israelite king reigned over them*   *h 48* Possibly the Euphrates

1:45
f Ge 36:11

50When Baal-Hanan died, Hadad succeeded him as king. His city was named Pau,[a] and his wife's name was Mehetabel daughter of Matred, the daughter of Me-Zahab. 51Hadad also died.

The chiefs of Edom were:

Timna, Alvah, Jetheth, 52Oholibamah, Elah, Pinon, 53Kenaz, Teman, Mibzar, 54Magdiel and Iram. These were the chiefs of Edom.

INSIGHT

The Birth Order of Jacob's (Israel's) Sons

Mother	Son
Leah	Reuben (born 1921 B.C.)
	Simeon
	Levi
	Judah
Bilhah (Rachel's maid-servant)	Dan
	Naphtali
Zilpah (Leah's maid-servant)	Gad
	Asher
Leah	Issachar
	Zebulun
Rachel	Joseph (born 1914 B.C.)
	Benjamin

Chapter 2 Theme

2 These were the sons of Israel:
Reuben, Simeon, Levi, Judah, Issachar, Zebulun, 2Dan, Joseph, Benjamin, Naphtali, Gad and Asher.

3The sons of Judah:[a]
Er, Onan and Shelah.[b] These three were born to him by a Canaanite woman, the daughter of Shua.[c] Er, Judah's first-born, was wicked in the LORD's sight; so the LORD put him to death.[d] 4Tamar,[e] Judah's daughter-in-law,[f] bore him Perez[g] and Zerah. Judah had five sons in all.

5The sons of Perez:[h]
Hezron[i] and Hamul.

6The sons of Zerah:
Zimri, Ethan, Heman, Calcol and Darda[b]—five in all.

7The son of Carmi:
Achar,[c][j] who brought trouble on Israel by violating the ban on taking devoted things.[d][k]

8The son of Ethan:
Azariah.

9The sons born to Hezron[l] were:
Jerahmeel, Ram and Caleb.[e]

10Ram[m] was the father of
Amminadab,[n] and Amminadab the father of Nahshon,[o] the leader of the people of Judah. 11Nahshon was the father of Salmon,[f] Salmon the father of Boaz, 12Boaz[p] the father of Obed and Obed the father of Jesse.[q]

13Jesse[r] was the father of
Eliab[s] his firstborn; the second son was Abinadab, the third Shimea, 14the fourth Nethanel, the fifth Raddai, 15the sixth Ozem and the seventh David. 16Their sisters were Zeruiah[t]

a50 Many Hebrew manuscripts, some Septuagint manuscripts, Vulgate and Syriac (see also Gen. 36:39); most Hebrew manuscripts *Pai* b6 Many Hebrew manuscripts, some Septuagint manuscripts and Syriac (see also 1 Kings 4:31); most Hebrew manuscripts *Dara* c7 *Achar* means *trouble*; *Achar* is called *Achan* in Joshua. d7 The Hebrew term refers to the irrevocable giving over of things or persons to the LORD, often by totally destroying them. e9 Hebrew *Kelubai*, a variant of *Caleb* f11 Septuagint (see also Ruth 4:21); Hebrew *Salma*

Cross-references:
2:3 aGe 29:35; 38:2-10 bGe 38:5 cGe 38:2 dNu 26:19
2:4 eGe 38:11-30 fGe 11:31 gGe 38:29
2:5 hGe 46:12 iNu 26:21
2:7 jJos 7:1 kJos 6:18
2:9 lNu 26:21
2:10 mLk 3:32-33 nEx 6:23 oNu 1:7
2:12 pRu 2:1 qRu 4:17
2:13 rRu 4:17 s1Sa 16:6
2:16 t1Sa 26:6

2:16
a 2Sa 2:18
b 2Sa 2:13
and Abigail. Zeruiah's*a* three sons were Abishai, Joab*b* and Asahel. **17**Abigail was the mother of Amasa,*c* whose father was Jether the Ishmaelite.

18Caleb son of Hezron had children by his wife Azubah (and by Jerioth). These were her sons: Jesher, Shobab and Ardon. **19**When Azubah died, Caleb*d* married Ephrath, who bore him Hur. **20**Hur was the father of Uri, and Uri the father of Bezalel.*e*

2:17
c 2Sa 17:25

21Later, Hezron lay with the daughter of Makir the father of Gilead*f* (he had married her when he was sixty years old), and she bore him Segub. **22**Segub was the father of Jair, who controlled twenty-three towns in Gilead. **23**(But Geshur and Aram captured Havvoth Jair,*ag* as well as Kenath*h* with its surrounding settlements—sixty towns.) All these were descendants of Makir the father of Gilead.

2:19
d ver 42,50

24After Hezron died in Caleb Ephrathah, Abijah the wife of Hezron bore him Ashhur*i* the father*b* of Tekoa.

25The sons of Jerahmeel the firstborn of Hezron:
Ram his firstborn, Bunah, Oren, Ozem and*c* Ahijah. **26**Jerahmeel had another wife, whose name was Atarah; she was the mother of Onam.

2:20
e Ex 31:2

27The sons of Ram the firstborn of Jerahmeel:
Maaz, Jamin and Eker.
28The sons of Onam:
Shammai and Jada.
The sons of Shammai:
Nadab and Abishur.

2:21
f Nu 27:1

29Abishur's wife was named Abihail, who bore him Ahban and Molid.
30The sons of Nadab:
Seled and Appaim. Seled died without children.
31The son of Appaim:
Ishi, who was the father of Sheshan.
Sheshan was the father of Ahlai.

2:23
g Nu 32:41;
Dt 3:14;
Jos 13:30
h Nu 32:42

32The sons of Jada, Shammai's brother:
Jether and Jonathan. Jether died without children.
33The sons of Jonathan:
Peleth and Zaza.
These were the descendants of Jerahmeel.
34Sheshan had no sons—only daughters.
He had an Egyptian servant named Jarha. **35**Sheshan gave

2:24
i 1Ch 4:5
a 23 Or *captured the settlements of Jair* *b* 24 *Father* may mean *civic leader* or *military leader*; also in verses 42, 45, 49-52 and possibly elsewhere. *c* 25 Or *Oren and Ozem, by*

his daughter in marriage to his servant Jarha, and she bore him Attai.

³⁶Attai was the father of Nathan,
Nathan the father of Zabad,ᵃ

³⁷Zabad the father of Ephlal,
Ephlal the father of Obed,

³⁸Obed the father of Jehu,
Jehu the father of Azariah,

³⁹Azariah the father of Helez,
Helez the father of Eleasah,

⁴⁰Eleasah the father of Sismai,
Sismai the father of Shallum,

⁴¹Shallum the father of Jekamiah,
and Jekamiah the father of Elishama.

⁴²The sons of Calebᵇ the brother of Jerahmeel:
Mesha his firstborn, who was the father of Ziph, and his son Mareshah,ᵃ who was the father of Hebron.

⁴³The sons of Hebron:
Korah, Tappuah, Rekem and Shema. ⁴⁴Shema was the father of Raham, and Raham the father of Jorkeam. Rekem was the father of Shammai. ⁴⁵The son of Shammai was Maonᶜ, and Maon was the father of Beth Zur.ᵈ

⁴⁶Caleb's concubine Ephah was the mother of Haran, Moza and Gazez. Haran was the father of Gazez.

⁴⁷The sons of Jahdai:
Regem, Jotham, Geshan, Pelet, Ephah and Shaaph.

⁴⁸Caleb's concubine Maacah was the mother of Sheber and Tirhanah. ⁴⁹She also gave birth to Shaaph the father of Madmannahᵉ and to Sheva the father of Macbenah and Gibea. Caleb's daughter was Acsah.ᶠ ⁵⁰These were the descendants of Caleb.

The sons of Hurᵍ the firstborn of Ephrathah:
Shobal the father of Kiriath Jearim,ʰ ⁵¹Salma the father of Bethlehem, and Hareph the father of Beth Gader.

⁵²The descendants of Shobal the father of Kiriath Jearim were:
Haroeh, half the Manahathites, ⁵³and the clans of Kiriath Jearim: the Ithrites,ⁱ Puthites, Shumathites and Mishraites. From these descended the Zorathites and Eshtaolites.

⁵⁴The descendants of Salma:
Bethlehem, the Netophathites,ʲ Atroth Beth Joab, half the Manahathites, the Zorites, ⁵⁵and the clans of scribesᵇ who lived at Jabez: the Tirathites, Shimeathites and Sucathites.

ᵃ42 The meaning of the Hebrew for this phrase is uncertain.   ᵇ55 Or *of the Sopherites*

2:36 ᵃ1Ch 11:41

2:42 ᵇver 19

2:45 ᶜJos 15:55
ᵈJos 15:58

2:49 ᵉJos 15:31
ᶠJos 15:16

2:50 ᵍ1Ch 4:4
ʰver 19

2:53 ⁱ2Sa 23:38

2:54 ʲEzr 2:22;
Ne 7:26; 12:28

2:55
a Ge 15:19;
Jdg 1:16;
Jdg 4:11
b Jos 19:35
c Ki 10:15, 23;
Jer 35:2-19

3:1
d 1Ch 14:3; 28:5
e Jos 15:56
f 1Sa 25:42

3:2
g 1Ki 2:22

3:4
h 2Sa 5:4;
1Ch 29:27
i 2Sa 2:11; 5:5

3:5
j 2Sa 11:3; 12:24

3:9
k 2Sa 13:1
l 1Ch 14:4

3:10
m 1Ki 11:43;
14:21-31;
2Ch 12:16
n 2Ch 17:1–21:3

3:11
o 2Ki 8:16-24;
2Ch 21:1
p 2Ch 22:1-10
q 2Ki 11:1–
12:21

3:12
r 2Ki 14:1-22;
2Ch 25:1-28
s Isa 1:1;
Hos 1:1;
Mic 1:1

3:13
t 2Ki 16:1-20;
2Ch 28:1;
Isa 7:1
u 2Ki 18:1–20:21;
2Ch 29:1;
Jer 26:19
v 2Ch 33:1

3:14
w 2Ki 21:19-26;
2Ch 33:21;
Zep 1:1
x 2Ch 34:1;
Jer 1:2; 3:6; 25:3

3:15
y 2Ki 23:34
z Jer 37:1
a 2Ki 23:31

These are the Kenites[a] who came from Hammath,[b] the father of the house of Recab.[ac]

Chapter 3 Theme

3 These were the sons of David[d] born to him in Hebron:
The firstborn was Amnon the son of Ahinoam of Jezreel;[e]
the second, Daniel the son of Abigail [f] of Carmel;
[2] the third, Absalom the son of Maacah daughter of Talmai king of Geshur;
the fourth, Adonijah[g] the son of Haggith;
[3] the fifth, Shephatiah the son of Abital;
and the sixth, Ithream, by his wife Eglah.
[4] These six were born to David in Hebron,[h] where he reigned seven years and six months.[i]

David reigned in Jerusalem thirty-three years, [5] and these were the children born to him there:
Shammua,[b] Shobab, Nathan and Solomon. These four were by Bathsheba[cj] daughter of Ammiel. [6] There were also Ibhar, Elishua,[d] Eliphelet, [7] Nogah, Nepheg, Japhia, [8] Elishama, Eliada and Eliphelet—nine in all. [9] All these were the sons of David, besides his sons by his concubines. And Tamar[k] was their sister.[l]

[10] Solomon's son was Rehoboam,[m]
Abijah his son,
Asa his son,
Jehoshaphat[n] his son,
[11] Jehoram[eo] his son,
Ahaziah[p] his son,
Joash[q] his son,
[12] Amaziah[r] his son,
Azariah his son,
Jotham[s] his son,
[13] Ahaz[t] his son,
Hezekiah[u] his son,
Manasseh[v] his son,
[14] Amon[w] his son,
Josiah[x] his son.
[15] The sons of Josiah:
Johanan the firstborn,
Jehoiakim[y] the second son,
Zedekiah[z] the third,
Shallum[a] the fourth.

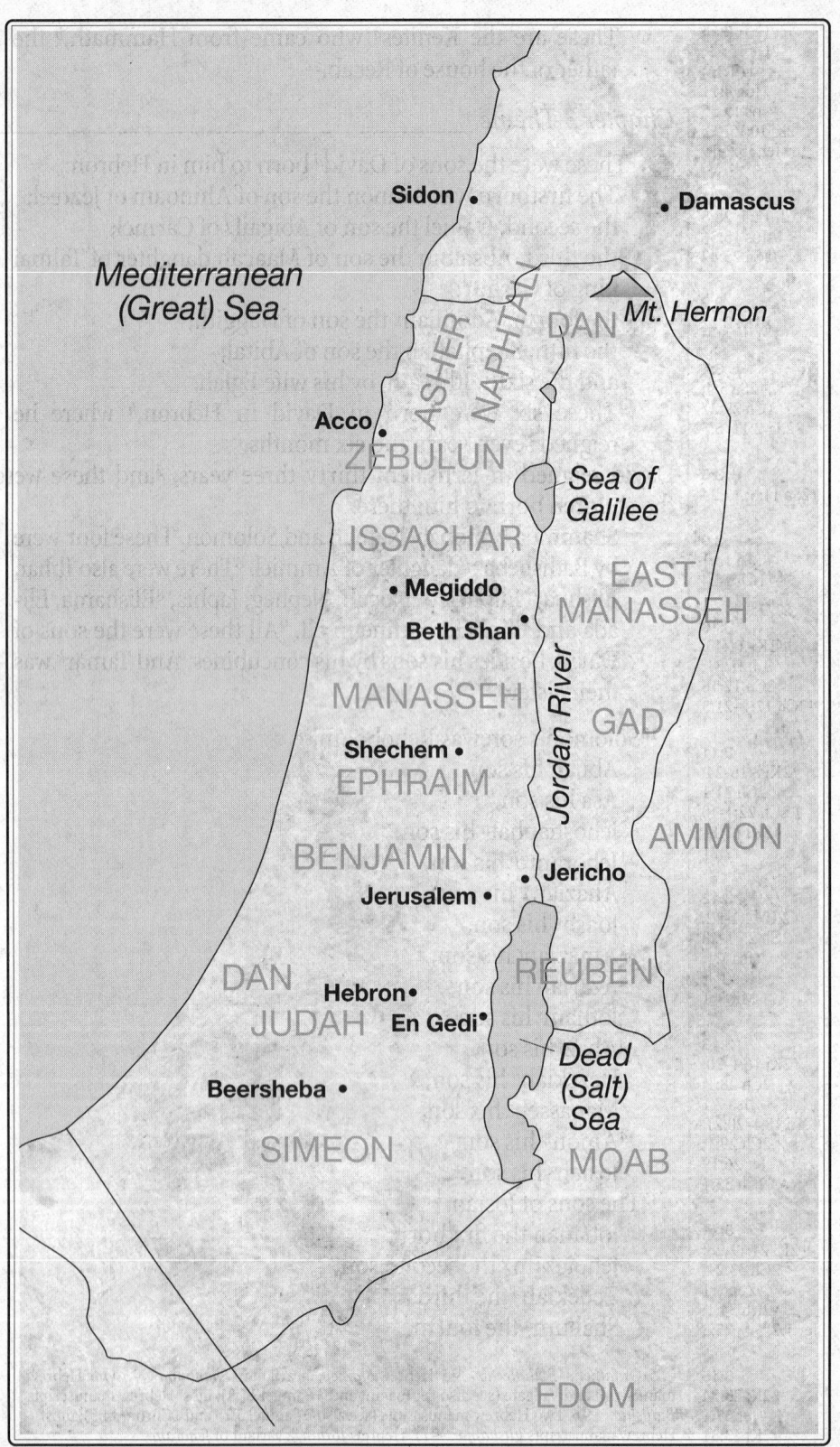

The Land
Allotted to the
Twelve Tribes

Sidon

Damascus

Mediterranean
(Great) Sea

ASHER

NAPHTALI

DAN

Mt. Hermon

Acco

ZEBULUN

Sea of
Galilee

ISSACHAR

EAST
MANASSEH

Megiddo

Beth Shan

Jordan River

MANASSEH

GAD

Shechem

EPHRAIM

AMMON

BENJAMIN

Jericho

Jerusalem

REUBEN

DAN

Hebron

JUDAH

En Gedi

Dead
(Salt)
Sea

Beersheba

SIMEON

MOAB

EDOM

3:16
a 2Ki 24:6,8;
Mt 1:11
b 2Ki 24:18

¹⁶The successors of Jehoiakim:
> Jehoiachin^a ^a his son,
> and Zedekiah.^b

¹⁷The descendants of Jehoiachin the captive:
> Shealtiel^c his son, ¹⁸Malkiram, Pedaiah, Shenazzar,^d Jeka-
> miah, Hoshama and Nedabiah.^e

3:17
c Ezr 3:2

¹⁹The sons of Pedaiah:
> Zerubbabel^f and Shimei.

> The sons of Zerubbabel:
> Meshullam and Hananiah.
> Shelomith was their sister.

3:18
d Ezr 1:8; 5:14
e Jer 22:30

²⁰There were also five others:
> Hashubah, Ohel, Berekiah, Hasadiah and Jushab-Hesed.

²¹The descendants of Hananiah:
> Pelatiah and Jeshaiah, and the sons of Rephaiah, of Arnan,
> of Obadiah and of Shecaniah.

²²The descendants of Shecaniah:
> Shemaiah and his sons:
> Hattush,^g Igal, Bariah, Neariah and Shaphat—six in all.

3:19
f Ezr 2:2;
3:2; 5:2;
Ne 7:7; 12:1;
Hag 1:1; 2:2;
Zec 4:6

²³The sons of Neariah:
> Elioenai, Hizkiah and Azrikam—three in all.

²⁴The sons of Elioenai:
> Hodaviah, Eliashib, Pelaiah, Akkub, Johanan, Delaiah and
> Anani—seven in all.

Chapter 4 Theme

3:22
g Ezr 8:2-3

4 The descendants of Judah:^h
> Perez, Hezron,ⁱ Carmi, Hur and Shobal.

²Reaiah son of Shobal was the father of Jahath, and Jahath the father of Ahumai and Lahad. These were the clans of the Zorathites.

³These were the sons^b of Etam:
> Jezreel, Ishma and Idbash. Their sister was named Hazze-lelponi. ⁴Penuel was the father of Gedor, and Ezer the father of Hushah.

> These were the descendants of Hur,^j the firstborn of Ephra-thah and father^c of Bethlehem.^k

4:1
h Ge 29:35;
46:12;
1Ch 2:3
i Nu 26:21

⁵Ashhur^l the father of Tekoa had two wives, Helah and Naarah.

⁶Naarah bore him Ahuzzam, Hepher, Temeni and Haa-hashtari. These were the descendants of Naarah.

⁷The sons of Helah:
> Zereth, Zohar, Ethnan, ⁸and Koz, who was the father of

4:4
j 1Ch 2:50
k Ru 1:19

4:5
l 1Ch 2:24

a 16 Hebrew *Jeconiah,* a variant of *Jehoiachin;* also in verse 17   b 3 Some Septuagint manuscripts (see also Vulgate); Hebrew *father*   c 4 *Father* may mean *civic leader* or *military leader;* also in verses 12, 14, 17, 18 and possibly elsewhere.

Anub and Hazzobebah and of the clans of Aharhel son of Harum.

⁹Jabez was more honorable than his brothers. His mother had named him Jabez,ᵃ saying, "I gave birth to him in pain." ¹⁰Jabez cried out to the God of Israel, "Oh, that you would bless me and enlarge my territory! Let your hand be with me, and keep me from harm so that I will be free from pain." And God granted his request.

¹¹Kelub, Shuhah's brother, was the father of Mehir, who was the father of Eshton. ¹²Eshton was the father of Beth Rapha, Paseah and Tehinnah the father of Ir Nahash.ᵇ These were the men of Recah.

¹³The sons of Kenaz:
Othnielᵃ and Seraiah.
The sons of Othniel:
Hathath and Meonothai.ᶜ ¹⁴Meonothai was the father of Ophrah.
Seraiah was the father of Joab,
the father of Ge Harashim.ᵈ It was called this because its people were craftsmen.
¹⁵The sons of Caleb son of Jephunneh:
Iru, Elah and Naam.
The son of Elah:
Kenaz.
¹⁶The sons of Jehallelel:
Ziph, Ziphah, Tiria and Asarel.
¹⁷The sons of Ezrah:
Jether, Mered, Epher and Jalon. One of Mered's wives gave birth to Miriam,ᵇ Shammai and Ishbah the father of Eshtemoa. ¹⁸(His Judean wife gave birth to Jered the father of Gedor, Heber the father of Soco, and Jekuthiel the father of Zanoah.ᶜ) These were the children of Pharaoh's daughter Bithiah, whom Mered had married.
¹⁹The sons of Hodiah's wife, the sister of Naham:
the father of Keilahᵈ the Garmite, and Eshtemoa the Maacathite.ᵉ
²⁰The sons of Shimon:
Amnon, Rinnah, Ben-Hanan and Tilon.
The descendants of Ishi:
Zoheth and Ben-Zoheth.

ᵃ9 *Jabez* sounds like the Hebrew for *pain.* ᵇ12 Or *of the city of Nahash* ᶜ13 Some Septuagint manuscripts and Vulgate; Hebrew does not have *and Meonothai.* ᵈ14 *Ge Harashim* means *valley of craftsmen.*

4:13
ᵃJos 15:17

4:17
ᵇEx 15:20

4:18
ᶜJos 15:34

4:19
ᵈJos 15:44
ᵉDt 3:14

4:21
aGe 38:5

4:24
bGe 29:33
cNu 26:12

4:28
dGe 21:14
eJos 15:26

4:29
fJos 15:29

4:30
gNu 14:45

4:31
hJos 15:36

4:32
iNu 34:11
jJos 15:42

4:39
kJos 15:58

4:40
lJdg 18:7-10

4:41
m2Ch 20:1; 26:7

4:42
nGe 14:6

4:43
o1Sa 15:8;
30:17;
2Sa 8:12;
Est 3:1; 9:16

²¹The sons of Shelah*a* son of Judah:

Er the father of Lecah, Laadah the father of Mareshah and the clans of the linen workers at Beth Ashbea, ²²Jokim, the men of Cozeba, and Joash and Saraph, who ruled in Moab and Jashubi Lehem. (These records are from ancient times.) ²³They were the potters who lived at Netaim and Gederah; they stayed there and worked for the king.

²⁴The descendants of Simeon:*b*

Nemuel, Jamin, Jarib,*c* Zerah and Shaul;

²⁵Shallum was Shaul's son, Mibsam his son and Mishma his son.

²⁶The descendants of Mishma:

Hammuel his son, Zaccur his son and Shimei his son.

²⁷Shimei had sixteen sons and six daughters, but his brothers did not have many children; so their entire clan did not become as numerous as the people of Judah. ²⁸They lived in Beersheba,*d* Moladah,*e* Hazar Shual, ²⁹Bilhah, Ezem,*f* Tolad, ³⁰Bethuel, Hormah,*g* Ziklag, ³¹Beth Marcaboth, Hazar Susim, Beth Biri and Shaaraim.*h* These were their towns until the reign of David. ³²Their surrounding villages were Etam, Ain,*i* Rimmon, Token and Ashan*j*—five towns— ³³and all the villages around these towns as far as Baalath.*a* These were their settlements. And they kept a genealogical record.

³⁴Meshobab, Jamlech, Joshah son of Amaziah, ³⁵Joel, Jehu son of Joshibiah, the son of Seraiah, the son of Asiel, ³⁶also Elioenai, Jaakobah, Jeshohaiah, Asaiah, Adiel, Jesimiel, Benaiah, ³⁷and Ziza son of Shiphi, the son of Allon, the son of Jedaiah, the son of Shimri, the son of Shemaiah.

³⁸The men listed above by name were leaders of their clans. Their families increased greatly, ³⁹and they went to the outskirts of Gedor*k* to the east of the valley in search of pasture for their flocks. ⁴⁰They found rich, good pasture, and the land was spacious, peaceful and quiet.*l* Some Hamites had lived there formerly.

⁴¹The men whose names were listed came in the days of Hezekiah king of Judah. They attacked the Hamites in their dwellings and also the Meunites*m* who were there and completely destroyed*b* them, as is evident to this day. Then they settled in their place, because there was pasture for their flocks. ⁴²And five hundred of these Simeonites, led by Pelatiah, Neariah, Rephaiah and Uzziel, the sons of Ishi, invaded the hill country of Seir.*n* ⁴³They killed the remaining Amalekites*o* who had escaped, and they have lived there to this day.

---

a 33 Some Septuagint manuscripts (see also Joshua 19:8); Hebrew *Baal*   *b 41* The Hebrew term refers to the irrevocable giving over of things or persons to the LORD, often by totally destroying them.

Chapter 5 Theme _____

5 The sons of Reuben[a] the firstborn of Israel (he was the first-born, but when he defiled his father's marriage bed,[b] his rights as firstborn were given to the sons of Joseph[c] son of Israel;[d] so he could not be listed in the genealogical record in accordance with his birthright,[e] ²and though Judah[f] was the strongest of his brothers and a ruler[g] came from him, the rights of the firstborn[h] belonged to Joseph)— ³the sons of Reuben[i] the firstborn of Israel:

Hanoch, Pallu,[j] Hezron and Carmi.

⁴The descendants of Joel:

Shemaiah his son, Gog his son,
Shimei his son, ⁵Micah his son,
Reaiah his son, Baal his son,

⁶and Beerah his son, whom Tiglath-Pileser[a][k] king of Assyria took into exile. Beerah was a leader of the Reubenites.

⁷Their relatives by clans,[l] listed according to their genealogical records:

Jeiel the chief, Zechariah, ⁸and Bela son of Azaz, the son of Shema, the son of Joel. They settled in the area from Aroer[m] to Nebo and Baal Meon.[n] ⁹To the east they occupied the land up to the edge of the desert that extends to the Euphrates River, because their livestock had increased in Gilead.[o]

¹⁰During Saul's reign they waged war against the Hagrites[p], who were defeated at their hands; they occupied the dwellings of the Hagrites throughout the entire region east of Gilead.

¹¹The Gadites[q] lived next to them in Bashan, as far as Salecah:[r]

¹²Joel was the chief, Shapham the second, then Janai and Shaphat, in Bashan.

¹³Their relatives, by families, were:

Michael, Meshullam, Sheba, Jorai, Jacan, Zia and Eber— seven in all.

¹⁴These were the sons of Abihail son of Huri, the son of Jaroah, the son of Gilead, the son of Michael, the son of Jeshishai, the son of Jahdo, the son of Buz.

¹⁵Ahi son of Abdiel, the son of Guni, was head of their family.

¹⁶The Gadites lived in Gilead, in Bashan and its outlying villages, and on all the pasturelands of Sharon as far as they extended.

¹⁷All these were entered in the genealogical records during the reigns of Jotham[s] king of Judah and Jeroboam[t] king of Israel.

¹⁸The Reubenites, the Gadites and the half-tribe of Manasseh had 44,760 men ready for military service[u]—able-bodied men

---

5:1
a Ge 29:32
b Ge 35:22; 49:4
c Ge 48:16,22; 49:26
d Ge 48:5
e 1Ch 26:10

5:2
f Ge 49:10,12
g 1Sa 9:16; 12:12; 2Sa 6:21; 1Ch 11:2; 2Ch 7:18; Ps 60:7; Mic 5:2; Mt 2:6
h Ge 25:31

5:3
i Ge 29:32; 46:9; Ex 6:14; Nu 26:5-11
j Nu 26:5

5:6
k ver 26; 2Ki 15:19; 16:10; 2Ch 28:20

5:7
l ver 17

5:8
m Nu 32:34
n Jos 13:17

5:9
o Nu 32:26; Jos 22:9

5:10
p ver 18-21

5:11
q Jos 13:24-28
r Dt 3:10; Jos 13:11

5:17
s 2Ki 15:32
t 2Ki 14:16,28

5:18
u Nu 1:3

---

a 6 Hebrew *Tilgath-Pilneser*, a variant of *Tiglath-Pileser*; also in verse 26

5:19
a ver 10;
Ge 25:15;
1Ch 1:31

5:20
b Ps 37:40
c 1Ki 8:44;
2Ch 13:14;
14:11;
Ps 20:7-9;
22:5
d Ps 26:1;
Da 6:23

5:22
e 2Ch 32:8
f 2Ki 15:29; 17:6

5:23
g Dt 3:8,9;
SS 4:8

5:25
h Dt 32:15-18;
2Ki 17:7;
1Ch 9:1;
2Ch 26:16
i Ex 34:15

5:26
j 2Ki 15:19
k 2Ki 15:29
l 2Ki 17:6; 18:11

6:1
m Ge 46:11;
Ex 6:16;
Nu 26:57;
1Ch 23:6

6:3
n Lev 10:1

6:8
o 2Sa 8:17;
15:27; Ezr 7:2

who could handle shield and sword, who could use a bow, and who were trained for battle. ¹⁹They waged war against the Hagrites, Jetur,*a* Naphish and Nodab. ²⁰They were helped*b* in fighting them, and God handed the Hagrites and all their allies over to them, because they cried*c* out to him during the battle. He answered their prayers, because they trusted*d* in him. ²¹They seized the livestock of the Hagrites—fifty thousand camels, two hundred fifty thousand sheep and two thousand donkeys. They also took one hundred thousand people captive, ²²and many others fell slain, because the battle*e* was God's. And they occupied the land until the exile.*f*

²³The people of the half-tribe of Manasseh were numerous; they settled in the land from Bashan to Baal Hermon, that is, to Senir (Mount Hermon).*g*

²⁴These were the heads of their families: Epher, Ishi, Eliel, Azriel, Jeremiah, Hodaviah and Jahdiel. They were brave warriors, famous men, and heads of their families. ²⁵But they were unfaithful*h* to the God of their fathers and prostituted*i* themselves to the gods of the peoples of the land, whom God had destroyed before them. ²⁶So the God of Israel stirred up the spirit of Pul*j* king of Assyria (that is, Tiglath-Pileser*k* king of Assyria), who took the Reubenites, the Gadites and the half-tribe of Manasseh into exile. He took them to Halah,*l* Habor, Hara and the river of Gozan, where they are to this day.

Chapter 6 Theme _____

6 The sons of Levi:*m*
　　Gershon, Kohath and Merari.
²The sons of Kohath:
　　Amram, Izhar, Hebron and Uzziel.
³The children of Amram:
　　Aaron, Moses and Miriam.
　The sons of Aaron:
　　Nadab, Abihu,*n* Eleazar and Ithamar.
⁴Eleazar was the father of Phinehas,
　　Phinehas the father of Abishua,
⁵Abishua the father of Bukki,
　　Bukki the father of Uzzi,
⁶Uzzi the father of Zerahiah,
　　Zerahiah the father of Meraioth,
⁷Meraioth the father of Amariah,
　　Amariah the father of Ahitub,
⁸Ahitub the father of Zadok,*o*
　　Zadok the father of Ahimaaz,
⁹Ahimaaz the father of Azariah,
　　Azariah the father of Johanan,

¹⁰Johanan the father of Azariah^a (it was he who served as priest in the temple Solomon built in Jerusalem),

¹¹Azariah the father of Amariah,
Amariah the father of Ahitub,

¹²Ahitub the father of Zadok,
Zadok the father of Shallum,

¹³Shallum the father of Hilkiah,^b
Hilkiah the father of Azariah,

¹⁴Azariah the father of Seraiah,^c
and Seraiah the father of Jehozadak.

¹⁵Jehozadak^d was deported when the Lord sent Judah and Jerusalem into exile by the hand of Nebuchadnezzar.

¹⁶The sons of Levi:^e
Gershon,^a Kohath and Merari.^f

¹⁷These are the names of the sons of Gershon:
Libni and Shimei.

¹⁸The sons of Kohath:
Amram, Izhar, Hebron and Uzziel.

¹⁹The sons of Merari:^g
Mahli and Mushi.

These are the clans of the Levites listed according to their fathers:

²⁰Of Gershon:
Libni his son, Jehath his son,
Zimmah his son, ²¹Joah his son,
Iddo his son, Zerah his son
and Jeatherai his son.

²²The descendants of Kohath:
Amminadab his son, Korah^h his son,
Assir his son, ²³Elkanah his son,
Ebiasaph his son, Assir his son,

²⁴Tahath his son, Urielⁱ his son,
Uzziah his son and Shaul his son.

²⁵The descendants of Elkanah:
Amasai, Ahimoth,

²⁶Elkanah his son,^b Zophai his son,
Nahath his son, ²⁷Eliab his son,
Jeroham his son, Elkanah^j his son
and Samuel^k his son.^c

²⁸The sons of Samuel:
Joel^{dl} the firstborn
and Abijah the second son.

6:10 ^a1Ki 4:2; 6:1; 2Ch 3:1; 26:17-18

6:13 ^b2Ki 22:1-20; 2Ch 34:9; 35:8

6:14 ^c2Ki 25:18; Ezr 2:2; Ne 11:11

6:15 ^d2Ki 25:18; Ne 12:1; Hag 1:1,14; 2:2,4; Zec 6:11

6:16 ^eGe 29:34; Ex 6:16; Nu 3:17-20 ^fNu 26:57

6:19 ^gGe 46:11; 1Ch 23:21; 24:26

6:22 ^hEx 6:24

6:24 ⁱ1Ch 15:5

6:27 ^j1Sa 1:1 ^k1Sa 1:20

6:28 ^lver 33; 1Sa 8:2

---

^a16 Hebrew *Gershom*, a variant of *Gershon*; also in verses 17, 20, 43, 62 and 71   ^b26 Some Hebrew manuscripts, Septuagint and Syriac; most Hebrew manuscripts *Ahimoth* ²⁶*and Elkanah. The sons of Elkanah:*   ^c27 Some Septuagint manuscripts (see also 1 Samuel 1:19,20 and 1 Chron. 6:33,34); Hebrew does not have *and Samuel his son.*   ^d28 Some Septuagint manuscripts and Syriac (see also 1 Samuel 8:2 and 1 Chron. 6:33); Hebrew does not have *Joel.*

6:31
a 1Ch 25:1;
2Ch 29:25-26;
Ne 12:45
b 1Ch 9:33;
15:19;
Ezr 3:10;
Ps 68:25

²⁹The descendants of Merari:
> Mahli, Libni his son,
> Shimei his son, Uzzah his son,
> ³⁰Shimea his son, Haggiah his son
> and Asaiah his son.

³¹These are the men^a David put in charge of the music^b in the house of the LORD after the ark came to rest there. ³²They ministered with music before the tabernacle, the Tent of Meeting, until Solomon built the temple of the LORD in Jerusalem. They performed their duties according to the regulations laid down for them.

³³Here are the men who served, together with their sons:
> From the Kohathites:
> Heman,^c the musician,
> the son of Joel,^d the son of Samuel,
> ³⁴the son of Elkanah,^e the son of Jeroham,
> the son of Eliel, the son of Toah,
> ³⁵the son of Zuph, the son of Elkanah,
> the son of Mahath, the son of Amasai,
> ³⁶the son of Elkanah, the son of Joel,
> the son of Azariah, the son of Zephaniah,
> ³⁷the son of Tahath, the son of Assir,
> the son of Ebiasaph, the son of Korah,^f
> ³⁸the son of Izhar,^g the son of Kohath,
> the son of Levi, the son of Israel;
> ³⁹and Heman's associate Asaph,^h who served at his right hand:
> Asaph son of Berekiah, the son of Shimea,ⁱ
> ⁴⁰the son of Michael, the son of Baaseiah,^a
> the son of Malkijah, ⁴¹the son of Ethni,
> the son of Zerah, the son of Adaiah,
> ⁴²the son of Ethan, the son of Zimmah,
> the son of Shimei, ⁴³the son of Jahath,
> the son of Gershon, the son of Levi;
> ⁴⁴and from their associates, the Merarites, at his left hand:
> Ethan son of Kishi, the son of Abdi,
> the son of Malluch, ⁴⁵the son of Hashabiah,
> the son of Amaziah, the son of Hilkiah,
> ⁴⁶the son of Amzi, the son of Bani,
> the son of Shemer, ⁴⁷the son of Mahli,
> the son of Mushi, the son of Merari,
> the son of Levi.

⁴⁸Their fellow Levites^j were assigned to all the other duties of the tabernacle, the house of God. ⁴⁹But Aaron and his descendants

6:33
c 1Ki 4:31;
1Ch 15:17;
25:1
d ver 28

6:34
e 1Sa 1:1

6:37
f Ex 6:24

6:38
g Ex 6:21

6:39
h 1Ch 25:1,9;
2Ch 29:13;
Ne 11:17
i 1Ch 15:17

6:48
j 1Ch 23:32

^a40 Most Hebrew manuscripts; some Hebrew manuscripts, one Septuagint manuscript and Syriac *Maaseiah*

were the ones who presented offerings on the altar[a] of burnt offering and on the altar of incense[b] in connection with all that was done in the Most Holy Place, making atonement for Israel, in accordance with all that Moses the servant of God had commanded.

⁵⁰These were the descendants of Aaron:

Eleazar his son, Phinehas his son,
Abishua his son, ⁵¹Bukki his son,
Uzzi his son, Zerahiah his son,
⁵²Meraioth his son, Amariah his son,
Ahitub his son, ⁵³Zadok[c] his son
and Ahimaaz his son.

⁵⁴These were the locations of their settlements[d] allotted as their territory (they were assigned to the descendants of Aaron who were from the Kohathite clan, because the first lot was for them):

⁵⁵They were given Hebron in Judah with its surrounding pasturelands. ⁵⁶But the fields and villages around the city were given to Caleb son of Jephunneh.[e]

⁵⁷So the descendants of Aaron were given Hebron (a city of refuge), and Libnah,[a][f] Jattir,[g] Eshtemoa, ⁵⁸Hilen, Debir,[h] ⁵⁹Ashan,[i] Juttah[b] and Beth Shemesh, together with their pasturelands. ⁶⁰And from the tribe of Benjamin they were given Gibeon,[c] Geba, Alemeth and Anathoth,[j] together with their pasturelands.

These towns, which were distributed among the Kohathite clans, were thirteen in all.

⁶¹The rest of Kohath's descendants were allotted ten towns from the clans of half the tribe of Manasseh.

⁶²The descendants of Gershon, clan by clan, were allotted thirteen towns from the tribes of Issachar, Asher and Naphtali, and from the part of the tribe of Manasseh that is in Bashan.

⁶³The descendants of Merari, clan by clan, were allotted twelve towns from the tribes of Reuben, Gad and Zebulun.

⁶⁴So the Israelites gave the Levites these towns[k] and their pasturelands. ⁶⁵From the tribes of Judah, Simeon and Benjamin they allotted the previously named towns.

⁶⁶Some of the Kohathite clans were given as their territory towns from the tribe of Ephraim.

⁶⁷In the hill country of Ephraim they were given Shechem (a city of refuge), and Gezer,[d][l] ⁶⁸Jokmeam,[m] Beth Horon,[n] ⁶⁹Aijalon[o] and Gath Rimmon,[p] together with their pasturelands.

6:49
[a] Ex 27:1-8
[b] Ex 30:1-7,10; 2Ch 26:18

6:53
[c] 2Sa 8:17

6:54
[d] Nu 31:10

6:56
[e] Jos 14:13; 15:13

6:57
[f] Nu 33:20
[g] Jos 15:48

6:58
[h] Jos 10:3

6:59
[i] Jos 15:42

6:60
[j] Jer 1:1

6:64
[k] Nu 35:1-8; Jos 21:3, 41-42

6:67
[l] Jos 10:33

6:68
[m] 1Ki 4:12
[n] Jos 10:10

6:69
[o] Jos 10:12
[p] Jos 19:45

---

[a] 57 See Joshua 21:13; Hebrew *given the cities of refuge: Hebron, Libnah*.   [b] 59 Syriac (see also Septuagint and Joshua 21:16); Hebrew does not have *Juttah*.   [c] 60 See Joshua 21:17; Hebrew does not have *Gibeon*.   [d] 67 See Joshua 21:21; Hebrew *given the cities of refuge: Shechem, Gezer*.

6:71
a 1Ch 23:7
b Jos 20:8

[70]And from half the tribe of Manasseh the Israelites gave Aner and Bileam, together with their pasturelands, to the rest of the Kohathite clans.

[71]The Gershonites*a* received the following:
From the clan of the half-tribe of Manasseh
they received Golan in Bashan*b* and also Ashtaroth, together with their pasturelands;

6:72
c Jos 19:12

[72]from the tribe of Issachar
they received Kedesh, Daberath,*c* [73]Ramoth and Anem, together with their pasturelands;

6:74
d Jos 19:28

[74]from the tribe of Asher
they received Mashal, Abdon,*d* [75]Hukok*e* and Rehob,*f* together with their pasturelands;

6:75
e Jos 19:34
f Nu 13:21

[76]and from the tribe of Naphtali
they received Kedesh in Galilee, Hammon*g* and Kiriatha-im,*h* together with their pasturelands.

[77]The Merarites (the rest of the Levites) received the following:
From the tribe of Zebulun
they received Jokneam, Kartah,*a* Rimmono and Tabor, together with their pasturelands;

6:76
g Jos 19:28
h Nu 32:37

[78]from the tribe of Reuben across the Jordan east of Jericho
they received Bezer*i* in the desert, Jahzah, [79]Kedemoth*j* and Mephaath, together with their pasturelands;

6:78
i Jos 20:8

[80]and from the tribe of Gad
they received Ramoth in Gilead,*k* Mahanaim,*l* [81]Heshbon and Jazer,*m* together with their pasturelands.*n*

6:79
j Dt 2:26

Chapter 7 Theme _____

7

The sons of Issachar:*o*
Tola, Puah,*p* Jashub and Shimron—four in all.
[2]The sons of Tola:

6:80
k Jos 20:8
l Ge 32:2

Uzzi, Rephaiah, Jeriel, Jahmai, Ibsam and Samuel—heads of their families. During the reign of David, the descendants of Tola listed as fighting men in their genealogy numbered 22,600.
[3]The son of Uzzi:
Izrahiah.

6:81
m Nu 21:32
n 2Ch 11:14

The sons of Izrahiah:
Michael, Obadiah, Joel and Isshiah. All five of them were chiefs. [4]According to their family genealogy, they had 36,000 men ready for battle, for they had many wives and children.

7:1
o Ge 30:18;
Nu 26:23
p Ge 46:13

a 77 See Septuagint and Joshua 21:34; Hebrew does not have *Jokneam, Kartah.*

⁵The relatives who were fighting men belonging to all the clans of Issachar, as listed in their genealogy, were 87,000 in all.

⁶Three sons of Benjamin:ᵃ
Bela, Beker and Jediael.

⁷The sons of Bela:
Ezbon, Uzzi, Uzziel, Jerimoth and Iri, heads of families—five in all. Their genealogical record listed 22,034 fighting men.

⁸The sons of Beker:
Zemirah, Joash, Eliezer, Elioenai, Omri, Jeremoth, Abijah, Anathoth and Alemeth. All these were the sons of Beker. ⁹Their genealogical record listed the heads of families and 20,200 fighting men.

¹⁰The son of Jediael:
Bilhan.

The sons of Bilhan:
Jeush, Benjamin, Ehud, Kenaanah, Zethan, Tarshish and Ahishahar. ¹¹All these sons of Jediael were heads of families. There were 17,200 fighting men ready to go out to war.

¹²The Shuppites and Huppites were the descendants of Ir, and the Hushites the descendants of Aher.

¹³The sons of Naphtali:ᵇ
Jahziel, Guni, Jezer and Shillemᵃ—the descendants of Bilhah.

¹⁴The descendants of Manasseh:ᶜ
Asriel was his descendant through his Aramean concubine. She gave birth to Makir the father of Gilead.ᵈ ¹⁵Makir took a wife from among the Huppites and Shuppites. His sister's name was Maacah.

Another descendant was named Zelophehad,ᵉ who had only daughters.

¹⁶Makir's wife Maacah gave birth to a son and named him Peresh. His brother was named Sheresh, and his sons were Ulam and Rakem.

¹⁷The son of Ulam:
Bedan.

These were the sons of Giladᶠ son of Makir, the son of Manasseh. ¹⁸His sister Hammoleketh gave birth to Ishhod, Abiezerᵍ and Mahlah.

¹⁹The sons of Shemida were:
Ahian, Shechem, Likhi and Aniam.

²⁰The descendants of Ephraim:ʰ
Shuthelah, Bered his son,
Tahath his son, Eleadah his son,

7:6
ᵃGe 46:21;
Nu 26:38;
1Ch 8:1-40

7:13
ᵇGe 30:8; 46:24

7:14
ᶜGe 41:51;
Jos 17:1;
1Ch 5:23
ᵈNu 26:30

7:15
ᵉNu 26:33;
36:1-12

7:17
ᶠNu 26:30;
1Sa 12:11

7:18
ᵍJos 17:2

7:20
ʰGe 41:52;
Nu 1:33; 26:35

ᵃ13 Some Hebrew and Septuagint manuscripts (see also Gen. 46:24 and Num. 26:49); most Hebrew manuscripts *Shallum*

7:24
a Jos 10:10;
16:3,5

Tahath his son, ²¹Zabad his son
and Shuthelah his son.

Ezer and Elead were killed by the native-born men of Gath, when they went down to seize their livestock. ²²Their father Ephraim mourned for them many days, and his relatives came to comfort him. ²³Then he lay with his wife again, and she became pregnant and gave birth to a son. He named him Beriah,ᵃ because there had been misfortune in his family. ²⁴His daughter was Sheerah, who built Lower and Upper Beth Horonᵃ as well as Uzzen Sheerah.

²⁵Rephah was his son, Resheph his son,ᵇ
Telah his son, Tahan his son,
²⁶Ladan his son, Ammihud his son,
Elishama his son, ²⁷Nun his son
and Joshua his son.

7:28
b Jos 10:33; 16:7

²⁸Their lands and settlements included Bethel and its surrounding villages, Naaran to the east, Gezerᵇ and its villages to the west, and Shechem and its villages all the way to Ayyah and its villages. ²⁹Along the borders of Manasseh were Beth Shan,ᶜ Taanach, Megiddo and Dor,ᵈ together with their villages. The descendants of Joseph son of Israel lived in these towns.

³⁰The sons of Asher:ᵉ
Imnah, Ishvah, Ishvi and Beriah. Their sister was Serah.
³¹The sons of Beriah:
Heber and Malkiel, who was the father of Birzaith.
³²Heber was the father of Japhlet, Shomer and Hotham and of their sister Shua.
³³The sons of Japhlet:
Pasach, Bimhal and Ashvath.
These were Japhlet's sons.

7:29
c Jos 17:11
d Jos 11:2

³⁴The sons of Shomer:
Ahi, Rohgah,ᶜ Hubbah and Aram.
³⁵The sons of his brother Helem:
Zophah, Imna, Shelesh and Amal.
³⁶The sons of Zophah:
Suah, Harnepher, Shual, Beri, Imrah, ³⁷Bezer, Hod, Shamma, Shilshah, Ithranᵈ and Beera.
³⁸The sons of Jether:
Jephunneh, Pispah and Ara.
³⁹The sons of Ulla:
Arah, Hanniel and Rizia.

⁴⁰All these were descendants of Asher—heads of families, choice men, brave warriors and outstanding leaders. The number of men ready for battle, as listed in their genealogy, was 26,000.

7:30
e Ge 46:17;
Nu 1:40; 26:44

ᵃ 23 *Beriah* sounds like the Hebrew for *misfortune.*   ᵇ 25 Some Septuagint manuscripts; Hebrew does not have *his son.*   ᶜ 34 Or *of his brother Shomer: Rohgah*   ᵈ 37 Possibly a variant of *Jether*

Chapter 8 Theme _____

8 Benjamin[a] was the father of Bela his firstborn,
  Ashbel the second son, Aharah the third,
  ²Nohah the fourth and Rapha the fifth.

³The sons of Bela were:

  Addar,[b] Gera, Abihud,[a] ⁴Abishua, Naaman, Ahoah,[c] ⁵Gera, Shephuphan and Huram.

⁶These were the descendants of Ehud,[d] who were heads of families of those living in Geba and were deported to Manahath:

  ⁷Naaman, Ahijah, and Gera, who deported them and who was the father of Uzza and Ahihud.

⁸Sons were born to Shaharaim in Moab after he had divorced his wives Hushim and Baara. ⁹By his wife Hodesh he had Jobab, Zibia, Mesha, Malcam, ¹⁰Jeuz, Sakia and Mirmah. These were his sons, heads of families. ¹¹By Hushim he had Abitub and Elpaal.

¹²The sons of Elpaal:

  Eber, Misham, Shemed (who built Ono[e] and Lod with its surrounding villages), ¹³and Beriah and Shema, who were heads of families of those living in Aijalon[f] and who drove out the inhabitants of Gath.[g]

¹⁴Ahio, Shashak, Jeremoth, ¹⁵Zebadiah, Arad, Eder, ¹⁶Michael, Ishpah and Joha were the sons of Beriah.

¹⁷Zebadiah, Meshullam, Hizki, Heber, ¹⁸Ishmerai, Izliah and Jobab were the sons of Elpaal.

¹⁹Jakim, Zicri, Zabdi, ²⁰Elienai, Zillethai, Eliel, ²¹Adaiah, Beraiah and Shimrath were the sons of Shimei.

²²Ishpan, Eber, Eliel, ²³Abdon, Zicri, Hanan, ²⁴Hananiah, Elam, Anthothijah, ²⁵Iphdeiah and Penuel were the sons of Shashak.

²⁶Shamsherai, Shehariah, Athaliah, ²⁷Jaareshiah, Elijah and Zicri were the sons of Jeroham.

²⁸All these were heads of families, chiefs as listed in their genealogy, and they lived in Jerusalem.

²⁹Jeiel[b] the father[c] of Gibeon lived in Gibeon.[h]

  His wife's name was Maacah, ³⁰and his firstborn son was Abdon, followed by Zur, Kish, Baal, Ner,[d] Nadab, ³¹Gedor, Ahio, Zeker ³²and Mikloth, who was the father of Shimeah. They too lived near their relatives in Jerusalem.

---

[a] 3 Or *Gera the father of Ehud*   [b] 29 Some Septuagint manuscripts (see also 1 Chron. 9:35); Hebrew does not have *Jeiel*.   [c] 29 *Father* may mean *civic leader* or *military leader*.   [d] 30 Some Septuagint manuscripts (see also 1 Chron. 9:36); Hebrew does not have *Ner*.

8:1
[a] Ge 46:21;
1Ch 7:6

8:3
[b] Ge 46:21

8:4
[c] 2Sa 23:9

8:6
[d] Jdg 3:12-30;
1Ch 2:52

8:12
[e] Ezr 2:33;
Ne 6:2; 7:37;
11:35

8:13
[f] Jos 10:12
[g] Jos 11:22

8:29
[h] Jos 9:3

8:33
a 1Sa 28:19
b 1Sa 9:1
c 1Sa 14:49
d 2Sa 2:8

³³Ner*a* was the father of Kish,*b* Kish the father of Saul*c*, and Saul the father of Jonathan, Malki-Shua, Abinadab and Esh-Baal.*a d*

³⁴The son of Jonathan:*e*

Merib-Baal,*b f* who was the father of Micah.

³⁵The sons of Micah:

Pithon, Melech, Tarea and Ahaz.

³⁶Ahaz was the father of Jehoaddah, Jehoaddah was the father of Alemeth, Azmaveth and Zimri, and Zimri was the father of Moza. ³⁷Moza was the father of Binea; Raphah was his son, Eleasah his son and Azel his son.

8:34
e 2Sa 9:12
f 2Sa 4:4

³⁸Azel had six sons, and these were their names:

Azrikam, Bokeru, Ishmael, Sheariah, Obadiah and Hanan. All these were the sons of Azel.

³⁹The sons of his brother Eshek:

Ulam his firstborn, Jeush the second son and Eliphelet the third. ⁴⁰The sons of Ulam were brave warriors who could handle the bow. They had many sons and grandsons— 150 in all.

8:40
g Nu 26:38

All these were the descendants of Benjamin.*g*

Chapter 9 Theme

9 All Israel was listed in the genealogies recorded in the book of the kings of Israel.

The people of Judah were taken captive to Babylon because of their unfaithfulness.*h* ²Now the first to resettle on their own property in their own towns*i* were some Israelites, priests, Levites and temple servants.*j*

9:1
h 1Ch 5:25

³Those from Judah, from Benjamin, and from Ephraim and Manasseh who lived in Jerusalem were:

⁴Uthai son of Ammihud, the son of Omri, the son of Imri, the son of Bani, a descendant of Perez son of Judah.*k*

⁵Of the Shilonites:

Asaiah the firstborn and his sons.

9:2
i Jos 9:27;
Ezr 2:70
j Ezr 2:43,58;
8:20;
Ne 7:60

⁶Of the Zerahites:

Jeuel.

The people from Judah numbered 690.

⁷Of the Benjamites:

Sallu son of Meshullam, the son of Hodaviah, the son of Hassenuah;

⁸Ibneiah son of Jeroham; Elah son of Uzzi, the son of Micri; and Meshullam son of Shephatiah, the son of Reuel, the son of Ibnijah.

9:4
k Ge 38:29;
46:12

a 33 Also known as *Ish-Bosheth*   *b 34* Also known as *Mephibosheth*

⁹The people from Benjamin, as listed in their genealogy, numbered 956. All these men were heads of their families. ¹⁰Of the priests:

Jedaiah; Jehoiarib; Jakin;

¹¹Azariah son of Hilkiah, the son of Meshullam, the son of Zadok, the son of Meraioth, the son of Ahitub, the official in charge of the house of God;

¹²Adaiah son of Jeroham, the son of Pashhur,ᵃ the son of Malkijah; and Maasai son of Adiel, the son of Jahzerah, the son of Meshullam, the son of Meshillemith, the son of Immer.

¹³The priests, who were heads of families, numbered 1,760. They were able men, responsible for ministering in the house of God.

¹⁴Of the Levites:

Shemaiah son of Hasshub, the son of Azrikam, the son of Hashabiah, a Merarite; ¹⁵Bakbakkar, Heresh, Galal and Mattaniahᵇ son of Mica, the son of Zicri, the son of Asaph; ¹⁶Obadiah son of Shemaiah, the son of Galal, the son of Jeduthun; and Berekiah son of Asa, the son of Elkanah, who lived in the villages of the Netophathites.ᶜ

¹⁷The gatekeepers:ᵈ

Shallum, Akkub, Talmon, Ahiman and their brothers, Shallum their chief ¹⁸being stationed at the King's Gateᵉ on the east, up to the present time. These were the gatekeepers belonging to the camp of the Levites. ¹⁹Shallumᶠ son of Kore, the son of Ebiasaph, the son of Korah, and his fellow gatekeepers from his family (the Korahites) were responsible for guarding the thresholds of the Tentᵃ just as their fathers had been responsible for guarding the entrance to the dwelling of the LORD. ²⁰In earlier times Phinehasᵍ son of Eleazar was in charge of the gatekeepers, and the LORD was with him. ²¹Zechariahʰ son of Meshelemiah was the gatekeeper at the entrance to the Tent of Meeting.

²²Altogether, those chosen to be gatekeepersⁱ at the thresholds numbered 212. They were registered by genealogy in their villages. The gatekeepers had been assigned to their positions of trust by David and Samuel the seer.ʲ ²³They and their descendants were in charge of guarding the gates of the house of the LORD—the house called the Tent. ²⁴The gatekeepers were on the four sides: east, west, north and south. ²⁵Their brothers in their villages had to come from time to time and share their duties for seven-dayᵏ periods. ²⁶But the four principal gatekeepers, who were Levites, were entrusted with the responsibility for the rooms and treasuriesˡ

a 19 That is, the temple; also in verses 21 and 23

9:12
ᵃ Ezr 2:38; 10:22; Ne 10:3; Jer 21:1; 38:1

9:15
ᵇ 2Ch 20:14; Ne 11:22

9:16
ᶜ Ne 12:28

9:17
ᵈ ver 22; 1Ch 26:1; 2Ch 8:14; 31:14; Ezr 2:42; Ne 7:45

9:18
ᵉ 1Ch 26:14; Eze 43:1; 46:1

9:19
ᶠ Jer 35:4

9:20
ᵍ Nu 25:7-13

9:21
ʰ 1Ch 26:2,14

9:22
ⁱ ver 17; 1Ch 26:1-2; 2Ch 31:15,18
ʲ 1Sa 9:9

9:25
ᵏ 2Ki 11:5; 2Ch 23:8

9:26
ˡ 1Ch 26:22

9:27
a Nu 3:38;
1Ch 23:30-32
b Isa 22:22

in the house of God. [27]They would spend the night stationed around the house of God,[a] because they had to guard it; and they had charge of the key[b] for opening it each morning.

[28]Some of them were in charge of the articles used in the temple service; they counted them when they were brought in and when they were taken out. [29]Others were assigned to take care of the furnishings and all the other articles of the sanctuary,[c] as well as the flour and wine, and the oil, incense and spices. [30]But some[d] of the priests took care of mixing the spices. [31]A Levite named Mattithiah, the firstborn son of Shallum the Korahite, was entrusted with the responsibility for baking the offering bread. [32]Some of their Kohathite brothers were in charge of preparing for every Sabbath the bread set out on the table.[e]

9:29
c Nu 3:28;
1Ch 23:29

9:30
d Ex 30:23-25

[33]Those who were musicians,[f] heads of Levite families, stayed in the rooms of the temple and were exempt from other duties because they were responsible for the work day and night.[g]

[34]All these were heads of Levite families, chiefs as listed in their genealogy, and they lived in Jerusalem.

9:32
e Lev 24:5-8;
1Ch 23:29;
2Ch 13:11

[35]Jeiel[h] the father[a] of Gibeon lived in Gibeon.

His wife's name was Maacah, [36]and his firstborn son was Abdon, followed by Zur, Kish, Baal, Ner, Nadab, [37]Gedor, Ahio, Zechariah and Mikloth. [38]Mikloth was the father of Shimeam. They too lived near their relatives in Jerusalem.

[39]Ner[i] was the father of Kish,[j] Kish the father of Saul, and Saul the father of Jonathan,[k] Malki-Shua, Abinadab and Esh-Baal.[b][l]

9:33
f 1Ch 6:31;
25:1-31
g Ps 134:1

[40]The son of Jonathan:

Merib-Baal,[c][m] who was the father of Micah.

[41]The sons of Micah:

Pithon, Melech, Tahrea and Ahaz.[d]

9:35
h 1Ch 8:29

[42]Ahaz was the father of Jadah, Jadah[e] was the father of Alemeth, Azmaveth and Zimri, and Zimri was the father of Moza. [43]Moza was the father of Binea; Rephaiah was his son, Eleasah his son and Azel his son.

[44]Azel had six sons, and these were their names:

Azrikam, Bokeru, Ishmael, Sheariah, Obadiah and Hanan. These were the sons of Azel.

9:39
i 1Ch 8:33
j 1Sa 9:1
k 1Sa 13:22
l 2Sa 2:8

Chapter 10 Theme

10 Now the Philistines fought against Israel; the Israelites fled before them, and many fell slain on Mount Gilboa. [2]The Philistines pressed hard after Saul and his sons, and they killed

---

a 35 *Father* may mean *civic leader* or *military leader.* b 39 Also known as *Ish-Bosheth*
c 40 Also known as *Mephibosheth* d 41 Vulgate and Syriac (see also Septuagint and 1 Chron. 8:35); Hebrew does not have *and Ahaz.* e 42 Some Hebrew manuscripts and Septuagint (see also 1 Chron. 8:36); most Hebrew manuscripts *Jarah, Jarah*

9:40
m 2Sa 4:4

his sons Jonathan, Abinadab and Malki-Shua. ³The fighting grew fierce around Saul, and when the archers overtook him, they wounded him.

⁴Saul said to his armor-bearer, "Draw your sword and run me through, or these uncircumcised fellows will come and abuse me."

But his armor-bearer was terrified and would not do it; so Saul took his own sword and fell on it. ⁵When the armor-bearer saw that Saul was dead, he too fell on his sword and died. ⁶So Saul and his three sons died, and all his house died together.

⁷When all the Israelites in the valley saw that the army had fled and that Saul and his sons had died, they abandoned their towns and fled. And the Philistines came and occupied them.

⁸The next day, when the Philistines came to strip the dead, they found Saul and his sons fallen on Mount Gilboa. ⁹They stripped him and took his head and his armor, and sent messengers throughout the land of the Philistines to proclaim the news among their idols and their people. ¹⁰They put his armor in the temple of their gods and hung up his head in the temple of Dagon.ᵃ

¹¹When all the inhabitants of Jabesh Gileadᵇ heard of everything the Philistines had done to Saul, ¹²all their valiant men went and took the bodies of Saul and his sons and brought them to Jabesh. Then they buried their bones under the great tree in Jabesh, and they fasted seven days.

¹³Saul diedᶜ because he was unfaithfulᵈ to the Lord; he did not keepᵉ the word of the Lord and even consulted a mediumᶠ for guidance, ¹⁴and did not inquire of the Lord. So the Lord put him to death and turnedᵍ the kingdomʰ over to David son of Jesse.

Chapter 11 Theme

11 All Israelⁱ came together to David at Hebronʲ and said, "We are your own flesh and blood. ²In the past, even while Saul was king, you were the one who led Israel on their military campaigns.ᵏ And the Lord your God said to you, 'You will shepherdˡ my people Israel, and you will become their ruler.ᵐ' "

³When all the elders of Israel had come to King David at Hebron, he made a compact with them at Hebron before the Lord, and they anointedⁿ David king over Israel, as the Lord had promised through Samuel.

⁴David and all the Israelites marched to Jerusalem (that is, Jebus). The Jebusitesᵒ who lived there ⁵said to David, "You will not get in here." Nevertheless, David captured the fortress of Zion, the City of David.

⁶David had said, "Whoever leads the attack on the Jebusites will become commander-in-chief." Joabᵖ son of Zeruiah went up first, and so he received the command.

10:10
ᵃJdg 16:23

10:11
ᵇJdg 21:8

10:13
ᶜ2Sa 1:1
ᵈ1Sa 15:23;
1Ch 5:25
ᵉ1Sa 13:13
ᶠLev 19:31;
20:6;
Dt 18:9-14;
1Sa 28:7

10:14
ᵍ1Ch 12:23
ʰ1Sa 13:14;
15:28

11:1
ⁱ1Ch 9:1
ʲGe 13:18;
23:19

11:2
ᵏ1Sa 18:5,16
ˡPs 78:71;
Mt 2:6
ᵐ1Ch 5:2

11:3
ⁿ1Sa 16:1-13

11:4
ᵒGe 10:16;
15:18-21;
Jos 3:10; 15:8;
Jdg 1:21; 19:10

11:6
ᵖ2Sa 2:13; 8:16

11:8
a 2Sa 5:9;
2Ch 32:5

11:9
b 2Sa 3:1;
Est 9:4

11:10
c ver 1
d ver 3;
1Ch 12:23

11:11
e 2Sa 17:10

11:14
f Ex 14:30;
1Sa 11:13

11:15
g 1Ch 14:9;
Isa 17:5

11:16
h 2Sa 5:17

11:18
i Dt 12:16

11:20
j 1Sa 26:6

11:22
k Jos 15:21
l 1Sa 17:36

11:23
m 1Sa 17:7

[7]David then took up residence in the fortress, and so it was called the City of David. [8]He built up the city around it, from the supporting terraces[a][a] to the surrounding wall, while Joab restored the rest of the city. [9]And David became more and more powerful,[b] because the LORD Almighty was with him.

[10]These were the chiefs of David's mighty men—they, together with all Israel,[c] gave his kingship strong support to extend it over the whole land, as the LORD had promised[d]— [11]this is the list of David's mighty men:[e]

Jashobeam,[b] a Hacmonite, was chief of the officers[c]; he raised his spear against three hundred men, whom he killed in one encounter.

[12]Next to him was Eleazar son of Dodai the Ahohite, one of the three mighty men. [13]He was with David at Pas Dammim when the Philistines gathered there for battle. At a place where there was a field full of barley, the troops fled from the Philistines. [14]But they took their stand in the middle of the field. They defended it and struck the Philistines down, and the LORD brought about a great victory.[f]

[15]Three of the thirty chiefs came down to David to the rock at the cave of Adullam, while a band of Philistines was encamped in the Valley[g] of Rephaim. [16]At that time David was in the stronghold,[h] and the Philistine garrison was at Bethlehem. [17]David longed for water and said, "Oh, that someone would get me a drink of water from the well near the gate of Bethlehem!" [18]So the Three broke through the Philistine lines, drew water from the well near the gate of Bethlehem and carried it back to David. But he refused to drink it; instead, he poured[i] it out before the LORD. [19]"God forbid that I should do this!" he said. "Should I drink the blood of these men who went at the risk of their lives?" Because they risked their lives to bring it back, David would not drink it.

Such were the exploits of the three mighty men.

[20]Abishai[j] the brother of Joab was chief of the Three. He raised his spear against three hundred men, whom he killed, and so he became as famous as the Three. [21]He was doubly honored above the Three and became their commander, even though he was not included among them.

[22]Benaiah son of Jehoiada was a valiant fighter from Kabzeel,[k] who performed great exploits. He struck down two of Moab's best men. He also went down into a pit on a snowy day and killed a lion.[l] [23]And he struck down an Egyptian who was seven and a half feet[d] tall. Although the Egyptian had a spear like a weaver's rod[m] in his hand, Benaiah went against him with a club. He snatched the spear from the Egyptian's hand and killed him with his own

a 8 Or *the Millo*   *b* 11 Possibly a variant of *Jashob-Baal*   *c* 11 Or *Thirty*; some Septuagint manuscripts *Three* (see also 2 Samuel 23:8)   *d* 23 Hebrew *five cubits* (about 2.3 meters) spear. ²⁴Such were the exploits of Benaiah son of Jehoiada; he too was as famous as the three mighty men. ²⁵He was held in greater honor than any of the Thirty, but he was not included among the Three. And David put him in charge of his bodyguard.

²⁶The mighty men were:

Asahel[a] the brother of Joab,

Elhanan son of Dodo from Bethlehem,

²⁷Shammoth[b] the Harorite,

Helez the Pelonite,

²⁸Ira son of Ikkesh from Tekoa,

Abiezer[c] from Anathoth,

²⁹Sibbecai[d] the Hushathite,

Ilai the Ahohite,

³⁰Maharai the Netophathite,

Heled son of Baanah the Netophathite,

³¹Ithai son of Ribai from Gibeah in Benjamin,

Benaiah[e] the Pirathonite,[f]

³²Hurai from the ravines of Gaash,

Abiel the Arbathite,

³³Azmaveth the Baharumite,

Eliahba the Shaalbonite,

³⁴the sons of Hashem the Gizonite,

Jonathan son of Shagee the Hararite,

³⁵Ahiam son of Sacar the Hararite,

Eliphal son of Ur,

³⁶Hepher the Mekerathite,

Ahijah the Pelonite,

³⁷Hezro the Carmelite,

Naarai son of Ezbai,

³⁸Joel the brother of Nathan,

Mibhar son of Hagri,

³⁹Zelek the Ammonite,

Naharai the Berothite, the armor-bearer of Joab son of Zeruiah,

⁴⁰Ira the Ithrite,

Gareb the Ithrite,

⁴¹Uriah[g] the Hittite,

Zabad[h] son of Ahlai,

⁴²Adina son of Shiza the Reubenite, who was chief of the Reubenites, and the thirty with him,

⁴³Hanan son of Maacah,

Joshaphat the Mithnite,

⁴⁴Uzzia the Ashterathite,[i]

Shama and Jeiel the sons of Hotham the Aroerite,

11:26
[a] 2Sa 2:18

11:27
[b] 1Ch 27:8

11:28
[c] 1Ch 27:12

11:29
[d] 2Sa 21:18

11:31
[e] 1Ch 27:14
[f] Jdg 12:13

11:41
[g] 2Sa 11:6
[h] 1Ch 2:36

11:44
[i] Dt 1:4

12:1
a Jos 15:31;
1Sa 27:2-6

12:2
b Jdg 3:15; 20:16
c 2Sa 3:19

12:4
d Jos 15:36

12:7
e Jos 15:58

12:8
f Ge 30:11
g 2Sa 17:10
h 2Sa 2:18

12:14
i Lev 26:8
j Dt 32:30

12:15
k Jos 3:15

12:16
l 2Sa 3:19

⁴⁵Jediael son of Shimri,
   his brother Joha the Tizite,
⁴⁶Eliel the Mahavite,
   Jeribai and Joshaviah the sons of Elnaam,
   Ithmah the Moabite,
⁴⁷Eliel, Obed and Jaasiel the Mezobaite.

Chapter 12 Theme _____

12 These were the men who came to David at Ziklag,ᵃ while he was banished from the presence of Saul son of Kish (they were among the warriors who helped him in battle; ²they were armed with bows and were able to shoot arrows or to sling stones right-handed or left-handed;ᵇ they were kinsmen of Saulᶜ from the tribe of Benjamin):

³Ahiezer their chief and Joash the sons of Shemaah the Gibeathite; Jeziel and Pelet the sons of Azmaveth; Beracah, Jehu the Anathothite, ⁴and Ishmaiah the Gibeonite, a mighty man among the Thirty, who was a leader of the Thirty; Jeremiah, Jahaziel, Johanan, Jozabad the Gederathite,ᵈ ⁵Eluzai, Jerimoth, Bealiah, Shemariah and Shephatiah the Haruphite; ⁶Elkanah, Isshiah, Azarel, Joezer and Jashobeam the Korahites; ⁷and Joelah and Zebadiah the sons of Jeroham from Gedor.ᵉ

⁸Some Gaditesᶠ defected to David at his stronghold in the desert. They were brave warriors, ready for battle and able to handle the shield and spear. Their faces were the faces of lions,ᵍ and they were as swift as gazellesʰ in the mountains.

⁹Ezer was the chief,
   Obadiah the second in command, Eliab the third,
¹⁰Mishmannah the fourth, Jeremiah the fifth,
¹¹Attai the sixth, Eliel the seventh,
¹²Johanan the eighth, Elzabad the ninth,
¹³Jeremiah the tenth and Macbannai the eleventh.

¹⁴These Gadites were army commanders; the least was a match for a hundred,ⁱ and the greatest for a thousand.ʲ ¹⁵It was they who crossed the Jordan in the first month when it was overflowing all its banks,ᵏ and they put to flight everyone living in the valleys, to the east and to the west.

¹⁶Other Benjamitesˡ and some men from Judah also came to David in his stronghold. ¹⁷David went out to meet them and said to them, "If you have come to me in peace, to help me, I am ready to have you unite with me. But if you have come to betray me to my enemies when my hands are free from violence, may the God of our fathers see it and judge you."

¹⁸Then the Spirit^a came upon Amasai,^b chief of the Thirty, and he said:

> "We are yours, O David!
>   We are with you, O son of Jesse!
> Success,^c success to you,
>   and success to those who help you,
>   for your God will help you."

So David received them and made them leaders of his raiding bands.

¹⁹Some of the men of Manasseh defected to David when he went with the Philistines to fight against Saul. (He and his men did not help the Philistines because, after consultation, their rulers sent him away. They said, "It will cost us our heads if he deserts to his master Saul.")^d ²⁰When David went to Ziklag,^e these were the men of Manasseh who defected to him: Adnah, Jozabad, Jediael, Michael, Jozabad, Elihu and Zillethai, leaders of units of a thousand in Manasseh. ²¹They helped David against raiding bands, for all of them were brave warriors, and they were commanders in his army. ²²Day after day men came to help David, until he had a great army, like the army of God.^a

²³These are the numbers of the men armed for battle who came to David at Hebron^f to turn^g Saul's kingdom over to him, as the LORD had said:^h

²⁴men of Judah, carrying shield and spear—6,800 armed for battle;

²⁵men of Simeon, warriors ready for battle—7,100;

²⁶men of Levi—4,600, ²⁷including Jehoiada, leader of the family of Aaron, with 3,700 men, ²⁸and Zadok,ⁱ a brave young warrior, with 22 officers from his family;

²⁹men of Benjamin,^j Saul's kinsmen—3,000, most^k of whom had remained loyal to Saul's house until then;

³⁰men of Ephraim, brave warriors, famous in their own clans—20,800;

³¹men of half the tribe of Manasseh, designated by name to come and make David king—18,000;

³²men of Issachar, who understood the times and knew what Israel should do^l—200 chiefs, with all their relatives under their command;

³³men of Zebulun, experienced soldiers prepared for battle with every type of weapon, to help David with undivided loyalty—50,000;

³⁴men of Naphtali—1,000 officers, together with 37,000 men carrying shields and spears;

³⁵men of Dan, ready for battle—28,600;

a 22 Or *a great and mighty army*

12:18
a Jdg 3:10; 6:34;
1Ch 28:12;
2Ch 15:1; 20:14;
24:20
b 2Sa 17:25
c 1Sa 25:5-6

12:19
d 1Sa 29:2-11

12:20
e 1Sa 27:6

12:23
f 2Sa 2:3-4
g 1Ch 10:14
h 1Sa 16:1;
1Ch 11:10

12:28
i 2Sa 8:17;
1Ch 6:8; 15:11;
16:39; 27:17

12:29
j 2Sa 3:19
k 2Sa 2:8-9

12:32
l Est 1:13

12:38
a 2Sa 5:1-3;
1Ch 9:1

12:39
b 2Sa 3:20;
Isa 25:6-8

12:40
c 2Sa 16:1;
17:29
d 1Sa 25:18
e 1Ch 29:22

13:3
f 1Sa 7:1-2
g 2Ch 1:5

13:5
h 1Ch 11:1; 15:3
i Jos 13:3
j Nu 13:21
k 1Sa 6:21; 7:2

13:6
l Jos 15:9;
2Sa 6:2
m Ex 25:22;
2Ki 19:15

13:7
n Nu 4:15;
1Sa 7:1

³⁶men of Asher, experienced soldiers prepared for battle—40,000;

³⁷and from east of the Jordan, men of Reuben, Gad and the half-tribe of Manasseh, armed with every type of weapon—120,000.

³⁸All these were fighting men who volunteered to serve in the ranks. They came to Hebron fully determined to make David king over all Israel.ᵃ All the rest of the Israelites were also of one mind to make David king. ³⁹The men spent three days there with David, eating and drinking,ᵇ for their families had supplied provisions for them. ⁴⁰Also, their neighbors from as far away as Issachar, Zebulun and Naphtali came bringing food on donkeys, camels, mules and oxen. There were plentiful suppliesᶜ of flour, fig cakes, raisinᵈ cakes, wine, oil, cattle and sheep, for there was joyᵉ in Israel.

Chapter 13 Theme

13 David conferred with each of his officers, the commanders of thousands and commanders of hundreds. ²He then said to the whole assembly of Israel, "If it seems good to you and if it is the will of the LORD our God, let us send word far and wide to the rest of our brothers throughout the territories of Israel, and also to the priests and Levites who are with them in their towns and pasturelands, to come and join us. ³Let us bring the ark of our God back to us,ᶠ for we did not inquireᵍ ofᵃ itᵇ during the reign of Saul." ⁴The whole assembly agreed to do this, because it seemed right to all the people.

⁵So David assembled all the Israelites,ʰ from the Shihor Riverⁱ in Egypt to Leboᶜ Hamath,ʲ to bring the ark of God from Kiriath Jearim.ᵏ ⁶David and all the Israelites with him went to Baalahˡ of Judah (Kiriath Jearim) to bring up from there the ark of God the LORD, who is enthroned between the cherubimᵐ—the ark that is called by the Name.

⁷They moved the ark of God from Abinadab'sⁿ house on a new cart, with Uzzah and Ahio guiding it. ⁸David and all the Israelites

The Wanderings of the Ark
(see page 2203)

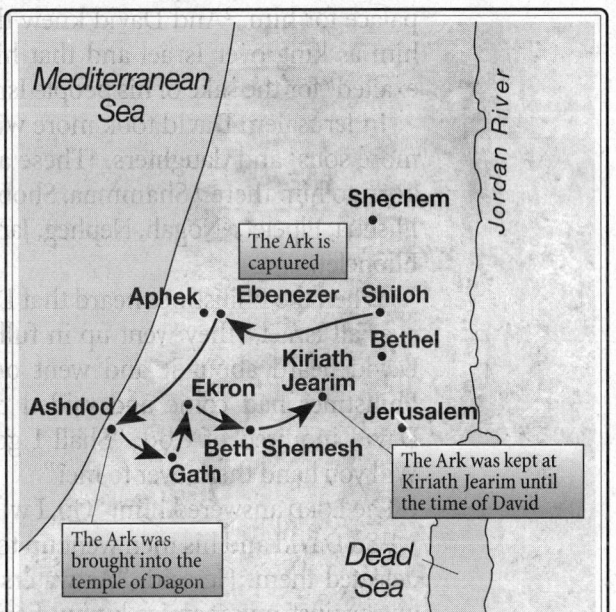

Mediterranean Sea

Jordan River

Shechem

The Ark is captured

Aphek   Ebenezer   Shiloh

Bethel

Kiriath Jearim

Ekron   Jerusalem

Ashdod

Beth Shemesh

Gath

The Ark was kept at Kiriath Jearim until the time of David

The Ark was brought into the temple of Dagon

Dead Sea

a 3 Or *we neglected*   b 3 Or *him*   c 5 Or *to the entrance to*

687

were celebrating with all their might before God, with songs and with harps, lyres, tambourines, cymbals and trumpets.[a]

⁹When they came to the threshing floor of Kidon, Uzzah reached out his hand to steady the ark, because the oxen stumbled. ¹⁰The LORD's anger[b] burned against Uzzah, and he struck him down[c] because he had put his hand on the ark. So he died there before God.

¹¹Then David was angry because the LORD's wrath had broken out against Uzzah, and to this day that place is called Perez Uzzah.[ad]

¹²David was afraid of God that day and asked, "How can I ever bring the ark of God to me?" ¹³He did not take the ark to be with him in the City of David. Instead, he took it aside to the house of Obed-Edom[e] the Gittite. ¹⁴The ark of God remained with the family of Obed-Edom in his house for three months, and the LORD blessed his household[f] and everything he had.

Chapter 14 Theme

14 Now Hiram king of Tyre sent messengers to David, along with cedar logs,[g] stonemasons and carpenters to build a palace for him. ²And David knew that the LORD had established him as king over Israel and that his kingdom had been highly exalted[h] for the sake of his people Israel.

³In Jerusalem David took more wives and became the father of more sons[i] and daughters. ⁴These are the names of the children born to him there:[j] Shammua, Shobab, Nathan, Solomon, ⁵Ibhar, Elishua, Elpelet, ⁶Nogah, Nepheg, Japhia, ⁷Elishama, Beeliada[b] and Eliphelet.

⁸When the Philistines heard that David had been anointed king over all Israel,[k] they went up in full force to search for him, but David heard about it and went out to meet them. ⁹Now the Philistines had come and raided the Valley[l] of Rephaim; ¹⁰so David inquired of God: "Shall I go and attack the Philistines? Will you hand them over to me?"

The LORD answered him, "Go, I will hand them over to you."

¹¹So David and his men went up to Baal Perazim,[m] and there he defeated them. He said, "As waters break out, God has broken out against my enemies by my hand." So that place was called Baal Perazim.[c] ¹²The Philistines had abandoned their gods there, and David gave orders to burn[n] them in the fire.[o]

¹³Once more the Philistines raided the valley;[p] ¹⁴so David inquired of God again, and God answered him, "Do not go straight up, but circle around them and attack them in front of the balsam trees. ¹⁵As soon as you hear the sound of marching in the tops of

---

a11 *Perez Uzzah* means *outbreak against Uzzah.*   b7 A variant of *Eliada*   c11 *Baal Perazim* means *the lord who breaks out.*

13:8
a 2Sa 6:5;
1Ch 15:16,
19,24;
2Ch 5:12;
Ps 92:3

13:10
b 1Ch 15:13,15
c Lev 10:2

13:11
d 1Ch 15:13;
Ps 7:11

13:13
e 1Ch 15:18,
24; 16:38;
26:4-5,15

13:14
f 2Sa 6:11;
1Ch 26:4-5

14:1
g 2Ch 2:3;
Ezr 3:7

14:2
h Nu 24:7;
Dt 26:19

14:3
i 1Ch 3:1

14:4
j 1Ch 3:9

14:8
k 1Ch 11:1

14:9
l ver 13;
Jos 15:8;
1Ch 11:15

14:11
m Isa 28:21

14:12
n Ex 32:20
o Jos 7:15

14:13
p ver 9

the balsam trees, move out to battle, because that will mean God has gone out in front of you to strike the Philistine army." [16]So David did as God commanded him, and they struck down the Philistine army, all the way from Gibeon*[a]* to Gezer.*[b]*

[17]So David's fame*[c]* spread throughout every land, and the LORD made all the nations fear*[d]* him.

Chapter 15 Theme

15 After David had constructed buildings for himself in the City of David, he prepared*[e]* a place for the ark of God and pitched*[f]* a tent for it. [2]Then David said, "No one but the Levites*[g]* may carry*[h]* the ark of God, because the LORD chose them to carry the ark of the LORD and to minister*[i]* before him forever."

[3]David assembled all Israel*[j]* in Jerusalem to bring up the ark of the LORD to the place he had prepared for it. [4]He called together the descendants of Aaron and the Levites:

[5]From the descendants of Kohath,
 Uriel the leader and 120 relatives;
[6]from the descendants of Merari,
 Asaiah the leader and 220 relatives;
[7]from the descendants of Gershon,*[a]*
 Joel the leader and 130 relatives;
[8]from the descendants of Elizaphan,*[k]*
 Shemaiah the leader and 200 relatives;
[9]from the descendants of Hebron,*[l]*
 Eliel the leader and 80 relatives;
[10]from the descendants of Uzziel,
 Amminadab the leader and 112 relatives.

[11]Then David summoned Zadok*[m]* and Abiathar*[n]* the priests, and Uriel, Asaiah, Joel, Shemaiah, Eliel and Amminadab the Levites. [12]He said to them, "You are the heads of the Levitical families; you and your fellow Levites are to consecrate*[o]* yourselves and bring up the ark of the LORD, the God of Israel, to the place I have prepared for it. [13]It was because you, the Levites,*[p]* did not bring it up the first time that the LORD our God broke out in anger against us.*[q]* We did not inquire of him about how to do it in the prescribed way." [14]So the priests and Levites consecrated themselves in order to bring up the ark of the LORD, the God of Israel. [15]And the Levites carried the ark of God with the poles on their shoulders, as Moses had commanded*[r]* in accordance with the word of the LORD.

[16]David told the leaders of the Levites to appoint their brothers as singers*[s]* to sing joyful songs, accompanied by musical instruments: lyres, harps and cymbals.*[t]*

---

a 7 Hebrew *Gershom,* a variant of *Gershon*

Cross references

14:16
a Jos 9:3
b Jos 10:33

14:17
c Jos 6:27;
2Ch 26:8
d Ex 15:14-16;
Dt 2:25

15:1
e Ps 132:1-18
f 1Ch 16:1; 17:1

15:2
g Nu 4:15;
Dt 10:8; 2Ch 5:5
h Dt 31:9
i 1Ch 23:13

15:3
j 1Ki 8:1;
1Ch 13:5

15:8
k Ex 6:22

15:9
l Ex 6:18

15:11
m 1Ch 12:28
n 1Sa 22:20

15:12
o Ex 19:14-15;
Lev 11:44;
2Ch 35:6

15:13
p 1Ki 8:4
q 2Sa 6:3;
1Ch 13:7-10

15:15
r Ex 25:14;
Nu 4:5,15

15:16
s Ps 68:25
t 1Ch 13:8; 25:1;
Ne 12:27,36

¹⁷So the Levites appointed Heman*ᵃ* son of Joel; from his brothers, Asaph*ᵇ* son of Berekiah; and from their brothers the Merarites,*ᶜ* Ethan son of Kushaiah; ¹⁸and with them their brothers next in rank: Zechariah,*ᵃ* Jaaziel, Shemiramoth, Jehiel, Unni, Eliab, Benaiah, Maaseiah, Mattithiah, Eliphelehu, Mikneiah, Obed-Edom*ᵈ* and Jeiel,*ᵇ* the gatekeepers.

¹⁹The musicians Heman,*ᵉ* Asaph and Ethan were to sound the bronze cymbals; ²⁰Zechariah, Aziel, Shemiramoth, Jehiel, Unni, Eliab, Maaseiah and Benaiah were to play the lyres according to *alamoth*,*ᶜ* ²¹and Mattithiah, Eliphelehu, Mikneiah, Obed-Edom, Jeiel and Azaziah were to play the harps, directing according to *sheminith*.*ᶜ* ²²Kenaniah the head Levite was in charge of the singing; that was his responsibility because he was skillful at it.

²³Berekiah and Elkanah were to be doorkeepers for the ark. ²⁴Shebaniah, Joshaphat, Nethanel, Amasai, Zechariah, Benaiah and Eliezer the priests were to blow trumpets*ᶠ* before the ark of God. Obed-Edom and Jehiah were also to be doorkeepers for the ark.

²⁵So David and the elders of Israel and the commanders of units of a thousand went to bring up the ark*ᵍ* of the covenant of the LORD from the house of Obed-Edom, with rejoicing. ²⁶Because God had helped the Levites who were carrying the ark of the covenant of the LORD, seven bulls and seven rams*ʰ* were sacrificed. ²⁷Now David was clothed in a robe of fine linen, as were all the Levites who were carrying the ark, and as were the singers, and Kenaniah, who was in charge of the singing of the choirs. David also wore a linen ephod. ²⁸So all Israel brought up the ark of the covenant of the LORD with shouts, with the sounding of rams' horns*ⁱ* and trumpets, and of cymbals, and the playing of lyres and harps.

²⁹As the ark of the covenant of the LORD was entering the City of David, Michal daughter of Saul watched from a window. And when she saw King David dancing and celebrating, she despised him in her heart.

Robe of the Ephod

Chapter 16 Theme

16 They brought the ark of God and set it inside the tent that David had pitched*ʲ* for it, and they presented burnt offerings and fellowship offerings*ᵈ* before God. ²After David had finished sacrificing the burnt offerings and fellowship offerings, he blessed*ᵏ* the people in the name of the LORD. ³Then he gave a loaf of bread, a cake of dates and a cake of raisins to each Israelite man and woman.

⁴He appointed some of the Levites to minister*ˡ* before the ark of the LORD, to make petition, to give thanks, and to praise the LORD, the God of Israel: ⁵Asaph was the chief, Zechariah second, then

---

a 18 Three Hebrew manuscripts and most Septuagint manuscripts (see also verse 20 and 1 Chron. 16:5); most Hebrew manuscripts *Zechariah son and* or *Zechariah, Ben and*
b 18 Hebrew; Septuagint (see also verse 21) *Jeiel and Azaziah*   *c 20,21* Probably a musical term
d 1 Traditionally *peace offerings*; also in verse 2

15:17
a 1Ch 6:33
b 1Ch 6:39
c 1Ch 6:44

15:18
d 1Ch 26:4-5

15:19
e 1Ch 25:6

15:24
f ver 28; 1Ch 16:6; 2Ch 7:6

15:25
g 1Ch 13:13; 2Ch 1:4

15:26
h Nu 23:1-4,29

15:28
i 1Ch 13:8

16:1
j 1Ch 15:1

16:2
k Ex 39:43

16:4
l 1Ch 15:2

16:7
a 2Sa 23:1

Jeiel, Shemiramoth, Jehiel, Mattithiah, Eliab, Benaiah, Obed-Edom and Jeiel. They were to play the lyres and harps, Asaph was to sound the cymbals, ⁶and Benaiah and Jahaziel the priests were to blow the trumpets regularly before the ark of the covenant of God.

⁷That day David first committed to Asaph and his associates this psalm[a] of thanks to the LORD:

16:8
b ver 34;
Ps 136:1
c 2Ki 19:19

16:9
d Ex 15:1

⁸Give thanks[b] to the LORD, call on his name;
  make known among the nations[c] what he has done.
⁹Sing to him, sing praise[d] to him;
  tell of all his wonderful acts.
¹⁰Glory in his holy name;
  let the hearts of those who seek the LORD rejoice.

16:11
e 1Ch 28:9;
2Ch 7:14;
Ps 24:6;
119:2,58

¹¹Look to the LORD and his strength;
  seek[e] his face always.
¹²Remember[f] the wonders he has done,
  his miracles,[g] and the judgments he pronounced,
¹³O descendants of Israel his servant,
  O sons of Jacob, his chosen ones.

16:12
f Ps 77:11
g Ps 78:43

16:14
h Isa 26:9

¹⁴He is the LORD our God;
  his judgments[h] are in all the earth.
¹⁵He remembers[a] his covenant forever,
  the word he commanded, for a thousand generations,

16:16
i Ge 12:7; 15:18;
17:2; 22:16-18;
26:3; 28:13;
35:11

¹⁶the covenant[i] he made with Abraham,
  the oath he swore to Isaac.
¹⁷He confirmed it to Jacob[j] as a decree,
  to Israel as an everlasting covenant:

16:17
j Ge 35:9-12

¹⁸"To you I will give the land of Canaan[k]
  as the portion you will inherit."

16:18
k Ge 13:14-17

¹⁹When they were but few in number,[l]
  few indeed, and strangers in it,
²⁰they[b] wandered from nation to nation,
  from one kingdom to another.
²¹He allowed no man to oppress them;
  for their sake he rebuked kings:[m]

16:19
l Ge 34:30;
Dt 7:7

²²"Do not touch my anointed ones;
  do my prophets[n] no harm."

16:21
m Ge 12:17;
20:3;
Ex 7:15-18

²³Sing to the LORD, all the earth;
  proclaim his salvation day after day.
²⁴Declare his glory among the nations,

16:22
n Ge 20:7

a 15 Some Septuagint manuscripts (see also Psalm 105:8); Hebrew *Remember* b 18-20 One Hebrew manuscript, Septuagint and Vulgate (see also Psalm 105:12); most Hebrew manuscripts *inherit, / ¹⁹though you are but few in number, / few indeed, and strangers in it." / ²⁰They* his marvelous deeds among all peoples.

25For great is the LORD and most worthy of praise;a
he is to be fearedb above all gods.c
26For all the gods of the nations are idols,
but the LORD made the heavens.d
27Splendor and majesty are before him;
strength and joy in his dwelling place.
28Ascribe to the LORD, O families of nations,
ascribe to the LORD glory and strength,e
29 ascribe to the LORD the glory due his name.
Bring an offering and come before him;
worship the LORD in the splendor of hisa holiness.f
30Trembleg before him, all the earth!
The world is firmly established; it cannot be moved.
31Let the heavens rejoice, let the earth be glad;h
let them say among the nations, "The LORD reigns!i"
32Let the sea resound, and all that is in it;j
let the fields be jubilant, and everything in them!
33Then the treesk of the forest will sing,
they will sing for joy before the LORD,
for he comes to judgel the earth.

34Give thanksm to the LORD, for he is good;n
his love endures forever.o
35Cry out, "Save us, O God our Savior;p
gather us and deliver us from the nations,
that we may give thanks to your holy name,
that we may glory in your praise."
36Praise be to the LORD, the God of Israel,q
from everlasting to everlasting.

Then all the people said "Amen" and "Praise the LORD."

37David left Asaph and his associates before the ark of the covenant of the LORD to minister there regularly, according to each day's requirements.r 38He also left Obed-Edoms and his sixty-eight associates to minister with them. Obed-Edom son of Jeduthun, and also Hosah,t were gatekeepers.

39David left Zadoku the priest and his fellow priests before the tabernacle of the LORD at the high place in Gibeonv 40to present burnt offerings to the LORD on the altar of burnt offering regularly, morning and evening, in accordance with everything written in the Laww of the LORD, which he had given Israel. 41With them were Hemanx and Jeduthun and the rest of those chosen and designated by name to give thanks to the LORD, "for his love endures forever." 42Heman and Jeduthun were responsible for the sounding of the

a 29 Or LORD with the splendor of

16:25
aPs 48:1
bPs 76:7; 89:7
cDt 32:39

16:26
dLev 19:4;
Ps 102:25

16:28
ePs 29:1-2

16:29
fPs 29:1-2

16:30
gPs 114:7

16:31
hIsa 44:23;
49:13
iPs 93:1

16:32
jPs 98:7

16:33
kIsa 55:12
lPs 96:10;
98:9

16:34
mver 8
nNa 1:7
o2Ch 5:13; 7:3;
Ezr 3:11;
Ps 136:1-26;
Jer 33:11

16:35
pMic 7:7

16:36
qDt 27:15;
1Ki 8:15;
Ps 72:18-19

16:37
r2Ch 8:14

16:38
s1Ch 13:13
t1Ch 26:10

16:39
u2Sa 8:17;
1Ch 15:11
v1Ki 3:4;
2Ch 1:3

16:40
wEx 29:38;
Nu 28:1-8

16:41
x1Ch 6:33;
25:1-6;
2Ch 5:13

16:42
a 2Ch 7:6

trumpets and cymbals and for the playing of the other instruments for sacred song.^a The sons of Jeduthun were stationed at the gate.

⁴³Then all the people left, each for his own home, and David returned home to bless his family.

Chapter 17 Theme _____

17:1
b 1Ch 15:1

17 After David was settled in his palace, he said to Nathan the prophet, "Here I am, living in a palace of cedar, while the ark of the covenant of the Lord is under a tent.^b"

17:2
c 2Ch 6:7

²Nathan replied to David, "Whatever you have in mind,^c do it, for God is with you."

³That night the word of God came to Nathan, saying:

⁴"Go and tell my servant David, 'This is what the Lord says: You^d are not the one to build me a house to dwell in. ⁵I have not

17:4
d 1Ch 28:3

dwelt in a house from the day I brought Israel up out of Egypt to this day. I have moved from one tent site to another, from one dwelling place to another. ⁶Wherever I have moved with all the Israelites, did I ever say to any of their leaders^a whom I commanded to shepherd my people, "Why have you not built me a house of cedar?"'

17:7
e 2Sa 6:21

⁷"Now then, tell my servant David, 'This is what the Lord Almighty says: I took you from the pasture and from following the flock, to be ruler^e over my people Israel. ⁸I have been with you wherever you have gone, and I have cut off all your enemies from before you. Now I will make your name like the names of the greatest men of the earth. ⁹And I will provide a place for my people Israel and will plant them so that they can have a home of their own and no longer be disturbed. Wicked people will not oppress them anymore, as they did at the begin-

17:10
f Jdg 2:16

ning ¹⁰and have done ever since the time I appointed leaders^f over my people Israel. I will also subdue all your enemies.

17:12
g 1Ki 5:5
h 2Ch 7:18

"'I declare to you that the Lord will build a house for you: ¹¹When your days are over and you go to be with your fathers, I will raise up your offspring to succeed you, one of your own sons, and I will establish his kingdom. ¹²He is the one who will build^g a house for me, and I will establish his throne forever.^h

17:13
i 2Co 6:18
j Lk 1:32;
Heb 1:5*

¹³I will be his father,ⁱ and he will be my son.^j I will never take my love away from him, as I took it away from your predecessor. ¹⁴I will set him over my house and my kingdom forever; his throne^k will be established forever.^l'"

¹⁵Nathan reported to David all the words of this entire revelation. ¹⁶Then King David went in and sat before the Lord, and he said:

17:14
k 1Ki 2:12;
1Ch 28:5
l Ps 132:11;
Jer 33:17

a 6 Traditionally *judges*; also in verse 10

"Who am I, O Lord God, and what is my family, that you have brought me this far? [17]And as if this were not enough in your sight, O God, you have spoken about the future of the house of your servant. You have looked on me as though I were the most exalted of men, O Lord God.

[18]"What more can David say to you for honoring your servant? For you know your servant, [19]O Lord. For the sake[a] of your servant and according to your will, you have done this great thing and made known all these great promises.[b]

[20]"There is no one like you, O Lord, and there is no God but you,[c] as we have heard with our own ears. [21]And who is like your people Israel—the one nation on earth whose God went out to redeem[d] a people for himself, and to make a name for yourself, and to perform great and awesome wonders by driving out nations from before your people, whom you redeemed from Egypt? [22]You made your people Israel your very own forever,[e] and you, O Lord, have become their God.

[23]"And now, Lord, let the promise[f] you have made concerning your servant and his house be established forever. Do as you promised, [24]so that it will be established and that your name will be great forever. Then men will say, 'The Lord Almighty, the God over Israel, is Israel's God!' And the house of your servant David will be established before you.

[25]"You, my God, have revealed to your servant that you will build a house for him. So your servant has found courage to pray to you. [26]O Lord, you are God! You have promised these good things to your servant. [27]Now you have been pleased to bless the house of your servant, that it may continue forever in your sight;[g] for you, O Lord, have blessed it, and it will be blessed forever."

Chapter 18 Theme _____

18 In the course of time, David defeated the Philistines and subdued them, and he took Gath and its surrounding villages from the control of the Philistines.

[2]David also defeated the Moabites,[h] and they became subject to him and brought tribute.

[3]Moreover, David fought Hadadezer king of Zobah,[i] as far as Hamath, when he went to establish his control along the Euphrates River.[j] [4]David captured a thousand of his chariots, seven thousand charioteers and twenty thousand foot soldiers. He hamstrung[k] all but a hundred of the chariot horses.

[5]When the Arameans of Damascus[l] came to help Hadadezer king of Zobah, David struck down twenty-two thousand of them. [6]He put garrisons in the Aramean kingdom of Damascus, and

17:19
a 2Sa 7:16-17;
2Ki 20:6;
Isa 9:7;
37:35; 55:3
b 2Sa 7:25

17:20
c Ex 8:10;
9:14; 15:11;
Isa 44:6; 46:9

17:21
d Ex 6:6

17:22
e Ex 19:5-6

17:23
f 1Ki 8:25

17:27
g Ps 16:11; 21:6

18:2
h Nu 21:29

18:3
i 1Ch 19:6
j Ge 2:14

18:4
k Ge 49:6

18:5
l 2Ki 16:9;
1Ch 19:6

the Arameans became subject to him and brought tribute. The LORD gave David victory everywhere he went.

[7]David took the gold shields carried by the officers of Hadadezer and brought them to Jerusalem. [8]From Tebah[a] and Cun, towns that belonged to Hadadezer, David took a great quantity of bronze, which Solomon used to make the bronze Sea,[a] the pillars and various bronze articles.

[9]When Tou king of Hamath heard that David had defeated the entire army of Hadadezer king of Zobah, [10]he sent his son Hadoram to King David to greet him and congratulate him on his victory in battle over Hadadezer, who had been at war with Tou. Hadoram brought all kinds of articles of gold and silver and bronze.

[11]King David dedicated these articles to the LORD, as he had done with the silver and gold he had taken from all these nations: Edom[b] and Moab, the Ammonites and the Philistines, and Amalek.[c]

[12]Abishai son of Zeruiah struck down eighteen thousand Edomites[d] in the Valley of Salt. [13]He put garrisons in Edom, and all the Edomites became subject to David. The LORD gave David victory everywhere he went.

[14]David reigned[e] over all Israel,[f] doing what was just and right for all his people.

[15]Joab[g] son of Zeruiah was over the army; Jehoshaphat son of Ahilud was recorder; [16]Zadok[h] son of Ahitub and Ahimelech[b][i] son of Abiathar were priests; Shavsha was secretary; [17]Benaiah son of Jehoiada was over the Kerethites and Pelethites;[j] and David's sons were chief officials at the king's side.

The Borders of David's Empire

**Side notes:**

18:8
a 1Ki 7:23;
2Ch 4:12,
15-16

18:11
b Nu 24:18
c Nu 24:20

18:12
d 1Ki 11:15

18:14
e 1Ch 29:26
f 1Ch 11:1

18:15
g 2Sa 5:6-8;
1Ch 11:6

18:16
h 2Sa 8:17;
1Ch 6:8
i 1Ch 24:6

18:17
j 1Sa 30:14;
2Sa 8:18;
15:18

a 8 Hebrew *Tibhath*, a variant of *Tebah* b 16 Some Hebrew manuscripts, Vulgate and Syriac (see also 2 Samuel 8:17); most Hebrew manuscripts *Abimelech*

695

Chapter 19 Theme _____

19 In the course of time, Nahash king of the Ammonites*a* died, and his son succeeded him as king. ²David thought, "I will show kindness to Hanun son of Nahash, because his father showed kindness to me." So David sent a delegation to express his sympathy to Hanun concerning his father.

When David's men came to Hanun in the land of the Ammonites to express sympathy to him, ³the Ammonite nobles said to Hanun, "Do you think David is honoring your father by sending men to you to express sympathy? Haven't his men come to you to explore and spy out*b* the country and overthrow it?" ⁴So Hanun seized David's men, shaved them, cut off their garments in the middle at the buttocks, and sent them away.

⁵When someone came and told David about the men, he sent messengers to meet them, for they were greatly humiliated. The king said, "Stay at Jericho till your beards have grown, and then come back."

⁶When the Ammonites realized that they had become a stench*c* in David's nostrils, Hanun and the Ammonites sent a thousand talents*a* of silver to hire chariots and charioteers from Aram Naharaim,*b* Aram Maacah and Zobah.*d* ⁷They hired thirty-two thousand chariots and charioteers, as well as the king of Maacah with his troops, who came and camped near Medeba,*e* while the Ammonites were mustered from their towns and moved out for battle.

⁸On hearing this, David sent Joab out with the entire army of fighting men. ⁹The Ammonites came out and drew up in battle formation at the entrance to their city, while the kings who had come were by themselves in the open country.

¹⁰Joab saw that there were battle lines in front of him and behind him; so he selected some of the best troops in Israel and deployed them against the Arameans. ¹¹He put the rest of the men under the command of Abishai*f* his brother, and they were deployed against the Ammonites. ¹²Joab said, "If the Arameans are too strong for me, then you are to rescue me; but if the Ammonites are too strong for you, then I will rescue you. ¹³Be strong and let us fight bravely for our people and the cities of our God. The LORD will do what is good in his sight."

¹⁴Then Joab and the troops with him advanced to fight the Arameans, and they fled before him. ¹⁵When the Ammonites saw that the Arameans were fleeing, they too fled before his brother Abishai and went inside the city. So Joab went back to Jerusalem.

¹⁶After the Arameans saw that they had been routed by Israel, they sent messengers and had Arameans brought from beyond the

19:1
a Ge 19:38;
Jdg 10:17–
11:33;
2Ch 20:1-2;
Zep 2:8-11

19:3
b Nu 21:32

19:6
c Ge 34:30
d 1Ch 18:3,5,9

19:7
e Nu 21:30;
Jos 13:9,16

19:11
f 1Sa 26:6

a 6 That is, about 37 tons (about 34 metric tons)   *b* 6 That is, Northwest Mesopotamia

River,ᵃ with Shophach the commander of Hadadezer's army leading them.

¹⁷When David was told of this, he gathered all Israelᵃ and crossed the Jordan; he advanced against them and formed his battle lines opposite them. David formed his lines to meet the Arameans in battle, and they fought against him. ¹⁸But they fled before Israel, and David killed seven thousand of their charioteers and forty thousand of their foot soldiers. He also killed Shophach the commander of their army.

¹⁹When the vassals of Hadadezer saw that they had been defeated by Israel, they made peace with David and became subject to him.

So the Arameans were not willing to help the Ammonites anymore.

Chapter 20 Theme _____

20 In the spring, at the time when kings go off to war, Joab led out the armed forces. He laid waste the land of the Ammonites and went to Rabbahᵇ and besieged it, but David remained in Jerusalem. Joab attacked Rabbah and left it in ruins.ᶜ ²David took the crown from the head of their kingᵇ—its weight was found to be a talentᶜ of gold, and it was set with precious stones—and it was placed on David's head. He took a great quantity of plunder from the city ³and brought out the people who were there, consigning them to labor with saws and with iron picks and axes.ᵈ David did this to all the Ammonite towns. Then David and his entire army returned to Jerusalem.

⁴In the course of time, war broke out with the Philistines, at Gezer.ᵉ At that time Sibbecai the Hushathite killed Sippai, one of the descendants of the Rephaites,ᶠ and the Philistines were subjugated.

⁵In another battle with the Philistines, Elhanan son of Jair killed Lahmi the brother of Goliath the Gittite, who had a spear with a shaft like a weaver's rod.ᵍ

⁶In still another battle, which took place at Gath, there was a huge man with six fingers on each hand and six toes on each foot—twenty-four in all. He also was descended from Rapha. ⁷When he taunted Israel, Jonathan son of Shimea, David's brother, killed him.

⁸These were descendants of Rapha in Gath, and they fell at the hands of David and his men.

Chapter 21 Theme _____

21 Satanʰ rose up against Israel and incited David to take a censusⁱ of Israel. ²So David said to Joab and the commanders of the troops, "Go and countʲ the Israelites from Beersheba to

ᵃ*16* That is, the Euphrates   ᵇ*2* Or *of Milcom,* that is, Molech   ᶜ*2* That is, about 75 pounds (about 34 kilograms)

Dan. Then report back to me so that I may know how many there are."

³But Joab replied, "May the LORD multiply his troops a hundred times over.ᵃ My lord the king, are they not all my lord's subjects? Why does my lord want to do this? Why should he bring guilt on Israel?"

⁴The king's word, however, overruled Joab; so Joab left and went throughout Israel and then came back to Jerusalem. ⁵Joab reported the number of the fighting men to David: In all Israelᵇ there were one million one hundred thousand men who could handle a sword, including four hundred and seventy thousand in Judah.

⁶But Joab did not include Levi and Benjamin in the numbering, because the king's command was repulsive to him. ⁷This command was also evil in the sight of God; so he punished Israel.

⁸Then David said to God, "I have sinned greatly by doing this. Now, I beg you, take away the guilt of your servant. I have done a very foolish thing."

⁹The LORD said to Gad,ᶜ David's seer,ᵈ ¹⁰"Go and tell David, 'This is what the LORD says: I am giving you three options. Choose one of them for me to carry out against you.'"

¹¹So Gad went to David and said to him, "This is what the LORD says: 'Take your choice: ¹²three years of famine,ᵉ three months of being swept awayᵃ before your enemies, with their swords overtaking you, or three days of the swordᶠ of the LORDᵍ—days of plague in the land, with the angel of the LORD ravaging every part of Israel.' Now then, decide how I should answer the one who sent me."

¹³David said to Gad, "I am in deep distress. Let me fall into the hands of the LORD, for his mercyʰ is very great; but do not let me fall into the hands of men."

¹⁴So the LORD sent a plague on Israel, and seventy thousand men of Israel fell dead.ⁱ ¹⁵And God sent an angelʲ to destroy Jerusalem.ᵏ But as the angel was doing so, the LORD saw it and was grievedˡ because of the calamity and said to the angel who was destroyingᵐ the people, "Enough! Withdraw your hand." The angel of the LORD was then standing at the threshing floor of Araunahᵇ the Jebusite.

¹⁶David looked up and saw the angel of the LORD standing between heaven and earth, with a drawn sword in his hand extended over Jerusalem. Then David and the elders, clothed in sackcloth, fell facedown.ⁿ

¹⁷David said to God, "Was it not I who ordered the fighting men to be counted? I am the one who has sinned and done wrong. These are but sheep.ᵒ What have they done? O LORD my God, let

ᵃ12 Hebrew; Septuagint and Vulgate (see also 2 Samuel 24:13) of fleeing   ᵇ15 Hebrew Ornan, a variant of Araunah; also in verses 18-28

Cross references: 21:3 ᵃDt 1:11; 21:5 ᵇ1Ch 9:1; 21:9 ᶜ1Sa 22:5 ᵈ1Sa 9:9; 21:12 ᵉDt 32:24 ᶠEze 30:25 ᵍGe 19:13; 21:13 ʰPs 6:4; 86:15; 130:4,7; 21:14 ⁱ1Ch 27:24; 21:15 ʲGe 32:1 ᵏPs 125:2 ˡGe 6:6; Ex 32:14 ᵐGe 19:13; 21:16 ⁿNu 14:5; Jos 7:6; 21:17 ᵒ2Sa 7:8; Ps 74:1

21:17
a Jnh 1:12

your hand fall upon me and my family,*a* but do not let this plague remain on your people."

¹⁸Then the angel of the LORD ordered Gad to tell David to go up and build an altar to the LORD on the threshing floor*b* of Araunah the Jebusite. ¹⁹So David went up in obedience to the word that Gad had spoken in the name of the LORD.

21:18
b 2Ch 3:1

²⁰While Araunah was threshing wheat,*c* he turned and saw the angel; his four sons who were with him hid themselves. ²¹Then David approached, and when Araunah looked and saw him, he left the threshing floor and bowed down before David with his face to the ground.

21:20
c Jdg 6:11

²²David said to him, "Let me have the site of your threshing floor so I can build an altar to the LORD, that the plague on the people may be stopped. Sell it to me at the full price."

INSIGHT

See 2 Chronicles 3:1 for what happened at this threshing floor.

²³Araunah said to David, "Take it! Let my lord the king do whatever pleases him. Look, I will give the oxen for the burnt offerings, the threshing sledges for the wood, and the wheat for the grain offering. I will give all this."

21:26
d Lev 9:24;
Jdg 6:21

²⁴But King David replied to Araunah, "No, I insist on paying the full price. I will not take for the LORD what is yours, or sacrifice a burnt offering that costs me nothing."

²⁵So David paid Araunah six hundred shekels^a of gold for the site. ²⁶David built an altar to the LORD there and sacrificed burnt offerings and fellowship offerings.^b He called on the LORD, and the LORD answered him with fire^d from heaven on the altar of burnt offering.

21:29
e 1Ki 3:4;
1Ch 16:39

²⁷Then the LORD spoke to the angel, and he put his sword back into its sheath. ²⁸At that time, when David saw that the LORD had answered him on the threshing floor of Araunah the Jebusite, he offered sacrifices there. ²⁹The tabernacle of the LORD, which Moses had made in the desert, and the altar of burnt offering were at that time on the high place at Gibeon.^e ³⁰But David could not go before it to inquire of God, because he was afraid of the sword of the angel of the LORD.

22:1
f Ge 28:17;
1Ch 21:18-29;
2Ch 3:1

Chapter 22 Theme

<big>**22**</big> Then David said, "The house of the LORD God*f* is to be here, and also the altar of burnt offering for Israel."

22:2
g 1Ki 9:21;
Isa 56:6
h 1Ki 5:17-18

²So David gave orders to assemble the aliens*g* living in Israel, and from among them he appointed stonecutters*h* to prepare dressed stone for building the house of God. ³He provided a large amount of iron to make nails for the doors of the gateways and for the fittings, and more bronze than could be weighed.ⁱ ⁴He also provided

22:3
i ver 14;
1Ki 7:47;
1Ch 29:2-5

^a25 That is, about 15 pounds (about 7 kilograms)   ^b26 Traditionally *peace offerings*

INSIGHT

There were basically three historical temples: *Solomon's* (pre-exilic), *Zerubbabel's*, called the second temple (post-exilic), and *Herod's* (New Testament). Since Herod's Temple was an expansion/rebuilding of the second temple, it is often referred to as the second temple rather than "the third." All were located on a hill north of David's capital city, which he took from the Jebusites (2 Samuel 5:6, 7). David acquired the temple hill to build an altar and offer sacrifices (2 Samuel 24:18-25). Second Chronicles identifies this hill with Mount Moriah, where Abraham was willing to offer Isaac (2 Chronicles 3:1; Genesis 22:1-14).

more cedar logs^a than could be counted, for the Sidonians and Tyrians had brought large numbers of them to David.

⁵David said, "My son Solomon is young^b and inexperienced, and the house to be built for the LORD should be of great magnificence and fame and splendor in the sight of all the nations. Therefore I will make preparations for it." So David made extensive preparations before his death.

⁶Then he called for his son Solomon and charged him to build^c a house for the LORD, the God of Israel. ⁷David said to Solomon: "My son, I had it in my heart^d to build^e a house for the Name^f of the LORD my God. ⁸But this word of the LORD came to me: 'You have shed much blood and have fought many wars.^g You are not to build a house for my Name,^h because you have shed much blood on the earth in my sight. ⁹But you will have a son who will be a man of peaceⁱ and rest, and I will give him rest from all his enemies on every side. His name will be Solomon,^{a j} and I will grant Israel peace and quiet^k during his reign. ¹⁰He is the one who will build a house for my Name.^l He will be my son,^m and I will be his father. And I will establish the throne of his kingdom over Israel forever.'ⁿ

¹¹"Now, my son, the LORD be with^o you, and may you have success and build the house of the LORD your God, as he said you would. ¹²May the LORD give you discretion and understanding^p when he puts you in command over Israel, so that you may keep the law of the LORD your God. ¹³Then you will have success if you are careful to observe the decrees and laws^q that the LORD gave Moses for Israel. Be strong and courageous.^r Do not be afraid or discouraged.

¹⁴"I have taken great pains to provide for the temple of the LORD a hundred thousand talents^b of gold, a million talents^c of silver, quantities of bronze and iron too great to be weighed, and wood and stone. And you may add to them.^s ¹⁵You have many workmen: stonecutters, masons and carpenters, as well as men skilled in every kind of work ¹⁶in gold and silver, bronze and iron—craftsmen^t beyond number. Now begin the work, and the LORD be with you."

¹⁷Then David ordered^u all the leaders of Israel to help his son Solomon. ¹⁸He said to them, "Is not the LORD your God with you? And has he not granted you rest^v on every side?^w For he has handed the inhabitants of the land over to me, and the land is subject to the LORD and to his people. ¹⁹Now devote your heart and soul to seeking the LORD your God.^x Begin to build the sanctuary of the LORD God, so that you may bring the ark of the covenant of the

---

22:4
^a1Ki 5:6

22:5
^b1Ki 3:7;
1Ch 29:1

22:6
^cAc 7:47

22:7
^d1Ch 17:2
^e2Sa 7:2;
1Ki 8:17
^fDt 12:5,11

22:8
^g1Ki 5:3
^h1Ch 28:3

22:9
ⁱ1Ki 5:4
^j2Sa 12:24
^k1Ki 4:20

22:10
^l1Ch 17:12
^m2Sa 7:13
ⁿ2Sa 7:14;
2Ch 6:15

22:11
^over 16

22:12
^p1Ki 3:9-12;
2Ch 1:10

22:13
^q1Ch 28:7
^rDt 31:6;
Jos 1:6-9;
1Ch 28:20

22:14
^sver 3;
1Ch 29:2-5,19

22:16
^tver 11;
2Ch 2:7

22:17
^u1Ch 28:1-6

22:18
^vver 9;
1Ch 23:25
^w2Sa 7:1

22:19
^xver 7;
1Ki 8:6;
1Ch 28:9;
2Ch 5:7; 7:14

---

^a9 *Solomon* sounds like and may be derived from the Hebrew for *peace.*   ^b14 That is, about 3,750 tons (about 3,450 metric tons)   ^c14 That is, about 37,500 tons (about 34,500 metric tons)

LORD and the sacred articles belonging to God into the temple that will be built for the Name of the LORD."

Chapter 23 Theme

23 When David was old and full of years, he made his son Solomon[a] king over Israel.[b]

[2] He also gathered together all the leaders of Israel, as well as the priests and Levites. [3] The Levites thirty years old or more[c] were counted, and the total number of men was thirty-eight thousand.[d] [4] David said, "Of these, twenty-four thousand are to supervise[e] the work of the temple of the LORD and six thousand are to be officials and judges.[f] [5] Four thousand are to be gatekeepers and four thousand are to praise the LORD with the musical instruments[g] I have provided for that purpose."[h]

[6] David divided[i] the Levites into groups corresponding to the sons of Levi: Gershon, Kohath and Merari.

[7] Belonging to the Gershonites:
Ladan and Shimei.

[8] The sons of Ladan:
Jehiel the first, Zetham and Joel—three in all.

[9] The sons of Shimei:
Shelomoth, Haziel and Haran—three in all.
These were the heads of the families of Ladan.

[10] And the sons of Shimei:
Jahath, Ziza,[a] Jeush and Beriah.
These were the sons of Shimei—four in all.

[11] Jahath was the first and Ziza the second, but Jeush and Beriah did not have many sons; so they were counted as one family with one assignment.

[12] The sons of Kohath:[j]
Amram, Izhar, Hebron and Uzziel—four in all.

[13] The sons of Amram:[k]
Aaron and Moses.

Aaron was set apart,[l] he and his descendants forever, to consecrate the most holy things, to offer sacrifices before the LORD, to minister before him and to pronounce blessings[m] in his name forever. [14] The sons of Moses the man[n] of God were counted as part of the tribe of Levi.

[15] The sons of Moses:
Gershom and Eliezer.[o]

[16] The descendants of Gershom:[p]
Shubael was the first.

Cross references
23:1
a 1Ki 1:33-39; 1Ch 28:5
b 1Ki 1:30; 1Ch 29:28

23:3
c ver 24; Nu 8:24
d Nu 4:3-49

23:4
e Ezr 3:8
f 1Ch 26:29; 2Ch 19:8

23:5
g 1Ch 15:16
h Ne 12:45

23:6
i 2Ch 8:14; 29:25

23:12
j Ex 6:18

23:13
k Ex 6:20; 28:1
l Ex 30:7-10; Dt 21:5
m Nu 6:23

23:14
n Dt 33:1

23:15
o Ex 18:4

23:16
p 1Ch 26:24-28

a 10 One Hebrew manuscript, Septuagint and Vulgate (see also verse 11); most Hebrew manuscripts *Zina*

¹⁷The descendants of Eliezer:

Rehabiah was the first.

Eliezer had no other sons, but the sons of Rehabiah were very numerous.

¹⁸The sons of Izhar:

Shelomith was the first.

¹⁹The sons of Hebron:[a]

Jeriah the first, Amariah the second, Jahaziel the third and Jekameam the fourth.

²⁰The sons of Uzziel:

Micah the first and Isshiah the second.

²¹The sons of Merari:[b]

Mahli and Mushi.

The sons of Mahli:

Eleazar and Kish.

²²Eleazar died without having sons: he had only daughters. Their cousins, the sons of Kish, married them.

²³The sons of Mushi:

Mahli, Eder and Jerimoth—three in all.

²⁴These were the descendants of Levi by their families—the heads of families as they were registered under their names and counted individually, that is, the workers twenty years old or more[c] who served in the temple of the LORD. ²⁵For David had said, "Since the LORD, the God of Israel, has granted rest[d] to his people and has come to dwell in Jerusalem forever, ²⁶the Levites no longer need to carry the tabernacle or any of the articles used in its service."[e] ²⁷According to the last instructions of David, the Levites were counted from those twenty years old or more.

²⁸The duty of the Levites was to help Aaron's descendants in the service of the temple of the LORD: to be in charge of the courtyards, the side rooms, the purification[f] of all sacred things and the performance of other duties at the house of God. ²⁹They were in charge of the bread set out on the table,[g] the flour for the grain offerings,[h] the unleavened wafers, the baking and the mixing, and all measurements of quantity and size.[i] ³⁰They were also to stand every morning to thank and praise the LORD. They were to do the same in the evening[j] ³¹and whenever burnt offerings were presented to the LORD on Sabbaths and at New Moon[k] festivals and at appointed feasts.[l] They were to serve before the LORD regularly in the proper number and in the way prescribed for them.

³²And so the Levites[m] carried out their responsibilities for the Tent of Meeting,[n] for the Holy Place and, under their brothers the descendants of Aaron, for the service of the temple of the LORD.[o]

23:19
[a] 1Ch 24:23

23:21
[b] 1Ch 24:26

23:24
[c] Nu 4:3; 10:17,21

23:25
[d] 1Ch 22:9

23:26
[e] Nu 4:5,15; 7:9; Dt 10:8

23:28
[f] 2Ch 29:15; Ne 13:9; Mal 3:3

23:29
[g] Ex 25:30
[h] Lev 2:4-7; 6:20-23
[i] Lev 19:35-36; 1Ch 9:29,32

23:30
[j] 1Ch 9:33; Ps 134:1

23:31
[k] 2Ki 4:23
[l] Lev 23:4; Nu 28:9–29:39; Isa 1:13-14; Col 2:16

23:32
[m] Nu 1:53; 1Ch 6:48
[n] Nu 3:6-8,38
[o] 2Ch 23:18; 31:2; Eze 44:14

24:1
*a*1Ch 23:6;
28:13;
2Ch 5:11;
8:14; 23:8;
31:2; 35:4,5;
Ezr 6:18
*b*Nu 3:2-4
*c*Ex 6:23

24:2
*d*Lev 10:1-2;
Nu 3:4

24:3
*e*2Sa 8:17

24:5
*f*ver 31;
1Ch 25:8

24:6
*g*1Ch 18:16

24:7
*h*Ezr 2:36;
Ne 12:6

24:8
*i*Ezr 2:39;
Ne 10:5

24:10
*j*Ne 12:4,17;
Lk 1:5

24:14
*k*Jer 20:1

24:15
*l*Ne 10:20

Chapter 24 Theme

24 These were the divisions*a* of the sons of Aaron:*b* The sons of Aaron were Nadab, Abihu, Eleazar and Ithamar.*c* ²But Nadab and Abihu died before their father did,*d* and they had no sons; so Eleazar and Ithamar served as the priests. ³With the help of Zadok*e* a descendant of Eleazar and Ahimelech a descendant of Ithamar, David separated them into divisions for their appointed order of ministering. ⁴A larger number of leaders were found among Eleazar's descendants than among Ithamar's, and they were divided accordingly: sixteen heads of families from Eleazar's descendants and eight heads of families from Ithamar's descendants. ⁵They divided them impartially by drawing lots,*f* for there were officials of the sanctuary and officials of God among the descendants of both Eleazar and Ithamar.

⁶The scribe Shemaiah son of Nethanel, a Levite, recorded their names in the presence of the king and of the officials: Zadok the priest, Ahimelech*g* son of Abiathar and the heads of families of the priests and of the Levites—one family being taken from Eleazar and then one from Ithamar.

⁷The first lot fell to Jehoiarib,
  the second to Jedaiah,*h*
⁸the third to Harim,*i*
  the fourth to Seorim,
⁹the fifth to Malkijah,
  the sixth to Mijamin,
¹⁰the seventh to Hakkoz,
  the eighth to Abijah,*j*
¹¹the ninth to Jeshua,
  the tenth to Shecaniah,
¹²the eleventh to Eliashib,
  the twelfth to Jakim,
¹³the thirteenth to Huppah,
  the fourteenth to Jeshebeab,
¹⁴the fifteenth to Bilgah,
  the sixteenth to Immer,*k*
¹⁵the seventeenth to Hezir,*l*
  the eighteenth to Happizzez,
¹⁶the nineteenth to Pethahiah,
  the twentieth to Jehezkel,
¹⁷the twenty-first to Jakin,
  the twenty-second to Gamul,
¹⁸the twenty-third to Delaiah
  and the twenty-fourth to Maaziah.

¹⁹This was their appointed order of ministering when they entered the temple of the LORD, according to the regulations prescribed for them by their forefather Aaron, as the LORD, the God of Israel, had commanded him.

²⁰As for the rest of the descendants of Levi:*ᵃ*

from the sons of Amram: Shubael;

from the sons of Shubael: Jehdeiah.

²¹As for Rehabiah,*ᵇ* from his sons:

Isshiah was the first.

²²From the Izharites: Shelomoth;

from the sons of Shelomoth: Jahath.

²³The sons of Hebron:*ᶜ* Jeriah the first,ᵃ Amariah the second,

Jahaziel the third and Jekameam the fourth.

²⁴The son of Uzziel: Micah;

from the sons of Micah: Shamir.

²⁵The brother of Micah: Isshiah;

from the sons of Isshiah: Zechariah.

²⁶The sons of Merari:*ᵈ* Mahli and Mushi.

The son of Jaaziah: Beno.

²⁷The sons of Merari:

from Jaaziah: Beno, Shoham, Zaccur and Ibri.

²⁸From Mahli: Eleazar, who had no sons.

²⁹From Kish: the son of Kish:

Jerahmeel.

³⁰And the sons of Mushi: Mahli, Eder and Jerimoth.

These were the Levites, according to their families. ³¹They also cast lots,*ᵉ* just as their brothers the descendants of Aaron did, in the presence of King David and of Zadok, Ahimelech, and the heads of families of the priests and of the Levites. The families of the oldest brother were treated the same as those of the youngest.

Chapter 25 Theme

25 David, together with the commanders of the army, set apart some of the sons of Asaph,*ᶠ* Heman*ᵍ* and Jeduthun*ʰ* for the ministry of prophesying,*ⁱ* accompanied by harps, lyres and cymbals.*ʲ* Here is the list of the men*ᵏ* who performed this service:*ˡ*

²From the sons of Asaph:

Zaccur, Joseph, Nethaniah and Asarelah. The sons of Asaph were under the supervision of Asaph, who prophesied under the king's supervision.

³As for Jeduthun, from his sons:*ᵐ*

Gedaliah, Zeri, Jeshaiah, Shimei,ᵇHashabiah and Mattithiah,

ᵃ*23* Two Hebrew manuscripts and some Septuagint manuscripts (see also 1 Chron. 23:19); most Hebrew manuscripts *The sons of Jeriah:*   ᵇ*3* One Hebrew manuscript and some Septuagint manuscripts (see also verse 17); most Hebrew manuscripts do not have *Shimei.*

24:20
*ᵃ*1Ch 23:6

24:21
*ᵇ*1Ch 23:17

24:23
*ᶜ*1Ch 23:19

24:26
*ᵈ*1Ch 6:19;
23:21

24:31
*ᵉ*ver 5

25:1
*ᶠ*1Ch 6:39
*ᵍ*1Ch 6:33
*ʰ*1Ch 16:41,42;
Ne 11:17
*ⁱ*1Sa 10:5;
2Ki 3:15
*ʲ*1Ch 15:16
*ᵏ*1Ch 6:31
*ˡ*2Ch 5:12; 8:14;
34:12; 35:15;
Ezr 3:10

25:3
*ᵐ*1Ch 16:41-42

25:3
a Ge 4:21;
Ps 33:2

six in all, under the supervision of their father Jeduthun, who prophesied, using the harp[a] in thanking and praising the LORD. [4]As for Heman, from his sons:

Bukkiah, Mattaniah, Uzziel, Shubael and Jerimoth; Hananiah, Hanani, Eliathah, Giddalti and Romamti-Ezer; Joshbekashah, Mallothi, Hothir and Mahazioth. [5]All these were sons of Heman the king's seer. They were given him through the promises of God to exalt him.[a] God gave Heman fourteen sons and three daughters.

[6]All these men were under the supervision of their fathers[b] for the music of the temple of the LORD, with cymbals, lyres and harps, for the ministry at the house of God. Asaph, Jeduthun and Heman[c] were under the supervision of the king.[d] [7]Along with their relatives—all of them trained and skilled in music for the LORD—they numbered 288. [8]Young and old alike, teacher as well as student, cast lots[e] for their duties.

25:6
b 1Ch 15:16
c 1Ch 15:19
d 2Ch 23:18;
29:25

[9]The first lot, which was for Asaph,[f] fell to Joseph,
  his sons and relatives,[b]   12[c]
  the second to Gedaliah,
  he and his relatives and sons,   12
[10]the third to Zaccur,
  his sons and relatives,   12
[11]the fourth to Izri,[d]
  his sons and relatives,   12
[12]the fifth to Nethaniah,
  his sons and relatives,   12
[13]the sixth to Bukkiah,
  his sons and relatives,   12
[14]the seventh to Jesarelah,[e]
  his sons and relatives,   12

25:8
e 1Ch 26:13

[15]the eighth to Jeshaiah,
  his sons and relatives,   12
[16]the ninth to Mattaniah,
  his sons and relatives,   12
[17]the tenth to Shimei,
  his sons and relatives,   12
[18]the eleventh to Azarel,[f]
  his sons and relatives,   12
[19]the twelfth to Hashabiah,
  his sons and relatives,   12
[20]the thirteenth to Shubael,
  his sons and relatives,   12

25:9
f 1Ch 6:39

a 5 Hebrew *exalt the horn*   b 9 See Septuagint; Hebrew does not have *his sons and relatives.*   c 9 See the total in verse 7; Hebrew does not have *twelve.*   d 11 A variant of *Zeri*   e 14 A variant of *Asarelah*   f 18 A variant of *Uzziel*

²¹the fourteenth to Mattithiah,
his sons and relatives,   12
²²the fifteenth to Jerimoth,
his sons and relatives,   12
²³the sixteenth to Hananiah,
his sons and relatives,   12
²⁴the seventeenth to Joshbekashah,
his sons and relatives,   12
²⁵the eighteenth to Hanani,
his sons and relatives,   12
²⁶the nineteenth to Mallothi,
his sons and relatives,   12
²⁷the twentieth to Eliathah,
his sons and relatives,   12
²⁸the twenty-first to Hothir,
his sons and relatives,   12
²⁹the twenty-second to Giddalti,
his sons and relatives,   12
³⁰the twenty-third to Mahazioth,
his sons and relatives,   12
³¹the twenty-fourth to Romamti-Ezer,
his sons and relatives,   12ᵃ

Chapter 26 Theme _____

26

The divisions of the gatekeepers:ᵇ

From the Korahites: Meshelemiah son of Kore, one of the sons of Asaph.

²Meshelemiah had sons:
Zechariahᶜ the firstborn,
Jediael the second,
Zebadiah the third,
Jathniel the fourth,
³Elam the fifth,
Jehohanan the sixth
and Eliehoenai the seventh.
⁴Obed-Edom also had sons:
Shemaiah the firstborn,
Jehozabad the second,
Joah the third,
Sacar the fourth,
Nethanel the fifth,
⁵Ammiel the sixth,
Issachar the seventh
and Peullethai the eighth.
(For God had blessed Obed-Edom.ᵈ)

25:31
ᵃ1Ch 9:33

26:1
ᵇ1Ch 9:17

26:2
ᶜ1Ch 9:21

26:5
ᵈ2Sa 6:10;
1Ch 13:13;
16:38

26:10
a Dt 21:16;
1Ch 5:1

26:12
b 1Ch 9:22

26:13
c 1Ch 24:5,31;
25:8

26:14
d 1Ch 9:18
e 1Ch 9:21

26:15
f 1Ch 13:13;
2Ch 25:24

26:19
g 2Ch 35:15;
Ne 7:1;
Eze 44:11

26:20
h 2Ch 24:5
i 1Ch 28:12

26:21
j 1Ch 23:7; 29:8

26:22
k 1Ch 9:26

26:23
l Nu 3:27

26:24
m 1Ch 23:16

26:25
n 1Ch 23:18

⁶His son Shemaiah also had sons, who were leaders in their father's family because they were very capable men. ⁷The sons of Shemaiah: Othni, Rephael, Obed and Elzabad; his relatives Elihu and Semakiah were also able men. ⁸All these were descendants of Obed-Edom; they and their sons and their relatives were capable men with the strength to do the work—descendants of Obed-Edom, 62 in all.

⁹Meshelemiah had sons and relatives, who were able men— 18 in all.

¹⁰Hosah the Merarite had sons: Shimri the first (although he was not the firstborn, his father had appointed him the first),ᵃ ¹¹Hilkiah the second, Tabaliah the third and Zechariah the fourth. The sons and relatives of Hosah were 13 in all.

¹²These divisions of the gatekeepers, through their chief men, had duties for ministeringᵇ in the temple of the LORD, just as their relatives had. ¹³Lotsᶜ were cast for each gate, according to their families, young and old alike.

¹⁴The lot for the East Gateᵈ fell to Shelemiah.ᵃ Then lots were cast for his son Zechariah,ᵉ a wise counselor, and the lot for the North Gate fell to him. ¹⁵The lot for the South Gate fell to Obed-Edom,ᶠ and the lot for the storehouse fell to his sons. ¹⁶The lots for the West Gate and the Shalleketh Gate on the upper road fell to Shuppim and Hosah.

Guard was alongside of guard: ¹⁷There were six Levites a day on the east, four a day on the north, four a day on the south and two at a time at the storehouse. ¹⁸As for the court to the west, there were four at the road and two at the court itself.

¹⁹These were the divisions of the gatekeepers who were descendants of Korah and Merari.ᵍ

²⁰Their fellow Levitesʰ wereᵇ in charge of the treasuries of the house of God and the treasuries for the dedicated things.ⁱ

²¹The descendants of Ladan, who were Gershonites through Ladan and who were heads of families belonging to Ladan the Gershonite,ʲ were Jehieli, ²²the sons of Jehieli, Zetham and his brother Joel. They were in charge of the treasuriesᵏ of the temple of the LORD.

²³From the Amramites, the Izharites, the Hebronites and the Uzzielites:ˡ

²⁴Shubael,ᵐ a descendant of Gershom son of Moses, was the officer in charge of the treasuries. ²⁵His relatives through Eliezer: Rehabiah his son, Jeshaiah his son, Joram his son, Zicri his son and Shelomithⁿ his son. ²⁶Shelomith and his

a 14 A variant of *Meshelemiah*   b 20 Septuagint; Hebrew *As for the Levites, Ahijah was* relatives were in charge of all the treasuries for the things dedicated[a] by King David, by the heads of families who were the commanders of thousands and commanders of hundreds, and by the other army commanders. 27Some of the plunder taken in battle they dedicated for the repair of the temple of the LORD. 28And everything dedicated by Samuel the seer[b] and by Saul son of Kish, Abner son of Ner and Joab son of Zeruiah, and all the other dedicated things were in the care of Shelomith and his relatives.

29From the Izharites: Kenaniah and his sons were assigned duties away from the temple, as officials and judges[c] over Israel.

30From the Hebronites: Hashabiah[d] and his relatives—seventeen hundred able men—were responsible in Israel west of the Jordan for all the work of the LORD and for the king's service. 31As for the Hebronites,[e] Jeriah was their chief according to the genealogical records of their families. In the fortieth[f] year of David's reign a search was made in the records, and capable men among the Hebronites were found at Jazer in Gilead. 32Jeriah had twenty-seven hundred relatives, who were able men and heads of families, and King David put them in charge of the Reubenites, the Gadites and the half-tribe of Manasseh for every matter pertaining to God and for the affairs of the king.

Chapter 27 Theme

27 This is the list of the Israelites—heads of families, commanders of thousands and commanders of hundreds, and their officers, who served the king in all that concerned the army divisions that were on duty month by month throughout the year. Each division consisted of 24,000 men.

2In charge of the first division, for the first month, was Jashobeam[g] son of Zabdiel. There were 24,000 men in his division. 3He was a descendant of Perez and chief of all the army officers for the first month.

4In charge of the division for the second month was Dodai[h] the Ahohite; Mikloth was the leader of his division. There were 24,000 men in his division.

5The third army commander, for the third month, was Benaiah[i] son of Jehoiada the priest. He was chief and there were 24,000 men in his division. 6This was the Benaiah who was a mighty man among the Thirty and was over the Thirty. His son Ammizabad was in charge of his division.

26:26
[a] 2Sa 8:11

26:28
[b] 1Sa 9:9

26:29
[c] Dt 17:8-13;
1Ch 23:4;
Ne 11:16

26:30
[d] 1Ch 27:17

26:31
[e] 1Ch 23:19
[f] 2Sa 5:4

27:2
[g] 2Sa 23:8;
1Ch 11:11

27:4
[h] 2Sa 23:9

27:5
[i] 2Sa 23:20

27:7
a 2Sa 2:18;
1Ch 11:26

27:8
b 1Ch 11:27

27:9
c 2Sa 23:26;
1Ch 11:28

27:10
d 2Sa 23:26;
1Ch 11:27

27:11
e 2Sa 21:18

27:12
f 2Sa 23:27;
1Ch 11:28

27:13
g 2Sa 23:28;
1Ch 11:30

27:14
h 1Ch 11:31

27:15
i 2Sa 23:29
j Jos 15:17

27:17
k 1Ch 26:30
l 2Sa 8:17;
1Ch 12:28

27:23
m 1Ch 21:2-5
n Ge 15:5

27:24
o 2Sa 24:15;
1Ch 21:7

⁷The fourth, for the fourth month, was Asahel*ᵃ* the brother of Joab; his son Zebadiah was his successor. There were 24,000 men in his division.

⁸The fifth, for the fifth month, was the commander Shamhuth*ᵇ* the Izrahite. There were 24,000 men in his division.

⁹The sixth, for the sixth month, was Ira*ᶜ* the son of Ikkesh the Tekoite. There were 24,000 men in his division.

¹⁰The seventh, for the seventh month, was Helez*ᵈ* the Pelonite, an Ephraimite. There were 24,000 men in his division.

¹¹The eighth, for the eighth month, was Sibbecai*ᵉ* the Hushathite, a Zerahite. There were 24,000 men in his division.

¹²The ninth, for the ninth month, was Abiezer*ᶠ* the Anathothite, a Benjamite. There were 24,000 men in his division.

¹³The tenth, for the tenth month, was Maharai*ᵍ* the Netophathite, a Zerahite. There were 24,000 men in his division.

¹⁴The eleventh, for the eleventh month, was Benaiah*ʰ* the Pirathonite, an Ephraimite. There were 24,000 men in his division.

¹⁵The twelfth, for the twelfth month, was Heldai*ⁱ* the Netophathite, from the family of Othniel.*ʲ* There were 24,000 men in his division.

¹⁶The officers over the tribes of Israel:

over the Reubenites: Eliezer son of Zicri;
over the Simeonites: Shephatiah son of Maacah;
¹⁷over Levi: Hashabiah*ᵏ* son of Kemuel;
over Aaron: Zadok;*ˡ*
¹⁸over Judah: Elihu, a brother of David;
over Issachar: Omri son of Michael;
¹⁹over Zebulun: Ishmaiah son of Obadiah;
over Naphtali: Jerimoth son of Azriel;
²⁰over the Ephraimites: Hoshea son of Azaziah;
over half the tribe of Manasseh: Joel son of Pedaiah;
²¹over the half-tribe of Manasseh in Gilead: Iddo son of Zechariah;
over Benjamin: Jaasiel son of Abner;
²²over Dan: Azarel son of Jeroham.

These were the officers over the tribes of Israel.

²³David did not take the number of the men twenty years old or less,*ᵐ* because the LORD had promised to make Israel as numerous as the stars*ⁿ* in the sky. ²⁴Joab son of Zeruiah began to count the men but did not finish. Wrath came on Israel on account of this numbering,*ᵒ* and the number was not entered in the book*ᵃ* of the annals of King David.

a 24 Septuagint; Hebrew number

²⁵Azmaveth son of Adiel was in charge of the royal storehouses.

Jonathan son of Uzziah was in charge of the storehouses in the outlying districts, in the towns, the villages and the watchtowers.

²⁶Ezri son of Kelub was in charge of the field workers who farmed the land.

²⁷Shimei the Ramathite was in charge of the vineyards.

Zabdi the Shiphmite was in charge of the produce of the vineyards for the wine vats.

²⁸Baal-Hanan the Gederite was in charge of the olive and sycamore-fig^a trees in the western foothills.

Joash was in charge of the supplies of olive oil.

²⁹Shitrai the Sharonite was in charge of the herds grazing in Sharon.

Shaphat son of Adlai was in charge of the herds in the valleys.

³⁰Obil the Ishmaelite was in charge of the camels.

Jehdeiah the Meronothite was in charge of the donkeys.

³¹Jaziz the Hagrite^b was in charge of the flocks.

All these were the officials in charge of King David's property.

³²Jonathan, David's uncle, was a counselor, a man of insight and a scribe. Jehiel son of Hacmoni took care of the king's sons.

³³Ahithophel^c was the king's counselor.

Hushai^d the Arkite was the king's friend. ³⁴Ahithophel was succeeded by Jehoiada son of Benaiah and by Abiathar.^{e}

Joab^f was the commander of the royal army.

Chapter 28 Theme

28 David summoned all the officials^g of Israel to assemble at Jerusalem: the officers over the tribes, the commanders of the divisions in the service of the king, the commanders of thousands and commanders of hundreds, and the officials in charge of all the property and livestock belonging to the king and his sons, together with the palace officials, the mighty men and all the brave warriors.

²King David rose to his feet and said: "Listen to me, my brothers and my people. I had it in my heart^h to build a house as a place of rest for the ark of the covenant of the LORD, for the footstool^i of our God, and I made plans to build it. ³But God said to me,^{j} 'You are not to build a house for my Name,^{k} because you are a warrior and have shed blood.'^{l}

⁴"Yet the LORD, the God of Israel, chose me^m from my whole family^n to be king over Israel forever. He chose Judah^o as leader, and from the house of Judah he chose my family, and from my father's sons he was pleased to make me king over all Israel. ⁵Of all my sons—and the LORD has given me many^p—he has chosen

27:28 ^{a}1Ki 10:27; 2Ch 1:15
27:31 ^{b}1Ch 5:10
27:33 ^{c}2Sa 15:12; ^{d}2Sa 15:37
27:34 ^{e}1Ki 1:7; ^{f}1Ch 11:6
28:1 ^{g}1Ch 11:10; 27:1-31
28:2 ^{h}1Ch 17:2; ^{i}Ps 99:5; 132:7
28:3 ^{j}2Sa 7:5; ^{k}1Ch 22:8; ^{l}1Ki 5:3; 1Ch 17:4
28:4 ^{m}1Ch 17:23,27; 2Ch 6:6; ^{n}1Sa 16:1-13; ^{o}Ge 49:10; 1Ch 5:2
28:5 ^{p}1Ch 3:1

28:5
*a*1Ch 22:9; 23:1

28:6
*b*2Sa 7:13;
1Ch 22:9-10

28:7
*c*1Ch 22:13

28:8
*d*Dt 6:1
*e*Dt 4:1

28:9
*f*1Ch 29:19
*g*1Sa 16:7;
Ps 7:9
*h*Ps 40:16;
Jer 29:13
*i*Jos 24:20;
2Ch 15:2
*j*Ps 44:23

28:11
*k*Ex 25:9

28:12
*l*1Ch 12:18
*m*1Ch 26:20

28:13
*n*1Ch 24:1

28:15
*o*Ex 25:31

28:16
*p*Ex 25:23

28:17
*q*Ex 27:3

28:18
*r*Ex 30:1-10
*s*Ex 25:18-22
*t*Ex 25:20

28:19
*u*1Ki 6:38
*v*Ex 25:9

28:20
*w*Dt 31:6;
1Ch 22:13;
2Ch 19:11;
Hag 2:4

my son Solomon*a* to sit on the throne of the kingdom of the LORD over Israel. **6**He said to me: 'Solomon your son is the one who will build my house and my courts, for I have chosen him to be my son,*b* and I will be his father. **7**I will establish his kingdom forever if he is unswerving in carrying out my commands and laws,*c* as is being done at this time.'

8"So now I charge you in the sight of all Israel and of the assembly of the LORD, and in the hearing of our God: Be careful to follow all the commands*d* of the LORD your God, that you may possess this good land and pass it on as an inheritance to your descendants forever.*e*

9"And you, my son Solomon, acknowledge the God of your father, and serve him with wholehearted devotion*f* and with a willing mind, for the LORD searches every heart*g* and understands every motive behind the thoughts. If you seek him,*h* he will be found by you; but if you forsake*i* him, he will reject*j* you forever. **10**Consider now, for the LORD has chosen you to build a temple as a sanctuary. Be strong and do the work."

11Then David gave his son Solomon the plans*k* for the portico of the temple, its buildings, its storerooms, its upper parts, its inner rooms and the place of atonement. **12**He gave him the plans of all that the Spirit*l* had put in his mind for the courts of the temple of the LORD and all the surrounding rooms, for the treasuries of the temple of God and for the treasuries for the dedicated things.*m* **13**He gave him instructions for the divisions*n* of the priests and Levites, and for all the work of serving in the temple of the LORD, as well as for all the articles to be used in its service. **14**He designated the weight of gold for all the gold articles to be used in various kinds of service, and the weight of silver for all the silver articles to be used in various kinds of service: **15**the weight of gold for the gold lampstands*o* and their lamps, with the weight for each lampstand and its lamps; and the weight of silver for each silver lampstand and its lamps, according to the use of each lampstand; **16**the weight of gold for each table*p* for consecrated bread; the weight of silver for the silver tables; **17**the weight of pure gold for the forks, sprinkling bowls*q* and pitchers; the weight of gold for each gold dish; the weight of silver for each silver dish; **18**and the weight of the refined gold for the altar of incense.*r* He also gave him the plan for the chariot,*s* that is, the cherubim of gold that spread their wings and shelter*t* the ark of the covenant of the LORD.

19"All this," David said, "I have in writing from the hand of the LORD upon me, and he gave me understanding in all the details*u* of the plan.*v* "

20David also said to Solomon his son, "Be strong and courageous,*w* and do the work. Do not be afraid or discouraged, for the

LORD God, my God, is with you. He will not fail you or forsake[a] you until all the work for the service of the temple of the LORD is finished.[b] [21]The divisions of the priests and Levites are ready for all the work on the temple of God, and every willing man skilled[c] in any craft will help you in all the work. The officials and all the people will obey your every command."

Chapter 29 Theme

29 Then King David said to the whole assembly: "My son Solomon, the one whom God has chosen, is young and inexperienced.[d] The task is great, because this palatial structure is not for man but for the LORD God. [2]With all my resources I have provided for the temple of my God—gold[e] for the gold work, silver for the silver, bronze for the bronze, iron for the iron and wood for the wood, as well as onyx for the settings, turquoise,[a][f] stones of various colors, and all kinds of fine stone and marble—all of these in large quantities.[g] [3]Besides, in my devotion to the temple of my God I now give my personal treasures of gold and silver for the temple of my God, over and above everything I have provided[h] for this holy temple: [4]three thousand talents[b] of gold (gold of Ophir)[i] and seven thousand talents[c] of refined silver,[j] for the overlaying of the walls of the buildings, [5]for the gold work and the silver work, and for all the work to be done by the craftsmen. Now, who is willing to consecrate himself today to the LORD?"

[6]Then the leaders of families, the officers of the tribes of Israel, the commanders of thousands and commanders of hundreds, and the officials[k] in charge of the king's work gave willingly.[l] [7]They[m] gave toward the work on the temple of God five thousand talents[d] and ten thousand darics[e] of gold, ten thousand talents[f] of silver, eighteen thousand talents[g] of bronze and a hundred thousand talents[h] of iron. [8]Any who had precious stones[n] gave them to the treasury of the temple of the LORD in the custody of Jehiel the Gershonite.[o] [9]The people rejoiced at the willing response of their leaders, for they had given freely and wholeheartedly[p] to the LORD. David the king also rejoiced greatly.

[10]David praised the LORD in the presence of the whole assembly, saying,

"Praise be to you, O LORD,
    God of our father Israel,
    from everlasting to everlasting.

---

a2 The meaning of the Hebrew for this word is uncertain.   b4 That is, about 110 tons (about 100 metric tons)   c4 That is, about 260 tons (about 240 metric tons)   d7 That is, about 190 tons (about 170 metric tons)   e7 That is, about 185 pounds (about 84 kilograms)   f7 That is, about 375 tons (about 345 metric tons)   g7 That is, about 675 tons (about 610 metric tons)   h7 That is, about 3,750 tons (about 3,450 metric tons)

28:20
a Dt 4:31;
Jos 24:20
b 1Ki 6:14;
2Ch 7:11

28:21
c Ex 35:25—36:5

29:1
d 1Ki 3:7;
1Ch 22:5;
2Ch 13:7

29:2
e ver 7,14,16;
Ezr 1:4; 6:5;
Hag 2:8
f Isa 54:11
g 1Ch 22:2-5

29:3
h 2Ch 24:10;
31:3; 35:8

29:4
i Ge 10:29
j 1Ch 22:14

29:6
k 1Ch 27:1; 28:1
l ver 9;
Ex 25:1-8;
35:20-29; 36:2;
2Ch 24:10;
Ezr 7:15

29:7
m Ex 25:2;
Ne 7:70-71

29:8
n Ex 35:27
o 1Ch 26:21

29:9
p 1Ki 8:61;
2Co 9:7

29:11
a Ps 24:8; 59:17;
62:11
b Ps 89:11
c Rev 5:12-13

29:12
d 2Ch 1:12
e 2Ch 20:6;
Ro 11:36

29:15
f Ps 39:12;
Heb 11:13
g Job 14:2

29:17
h Ps 139:23;
Pr 15:11; 17:3;
Jer 11:20; 17:10
i 1Ch 28:9;
Ps 15:1-5

29:19
j 1Ch 28:9
k Ps 72:1
l 1Ch 22:14

29:21
m 1Ki 8:62

29:22
n 1Ch 23:1
o 1Ki 1:33-39

29:23
p 1Ki 2:12

29:25
q 2Ch 1:1,12
r 1Ki 3:13;
Ecc 2:9

[11]"Yours, O LORD, is the greatness and the power[a]
and the glory and the majesty and the splendor,
for everything in heaven and earth is yours.[b]
Yours, O LORD, is the kingdom;
you are exalted as head over all.[c]
[12]Wealth and honor[d] come from you;
you are the ruler[e] of all things.
In your hands are strength and power
to exalt and give strength to all.
[13]Now, our God, we give you thanks,
and praise your glorious name.

[14]"But who am I, and who are my people, that we should be able to give as generously as this? Everything comes from you, and we have given you only what comes from your hand. [15]We are aliens and strangers[f] in your sight, as were all our forefathers. Our days on earth are like a shadow,[g] without hope. [16]O LORD our God, as for all this abundance that we have provided for building you a temple for your Holy Name, it comes from your hand, and all of it belongs to you. [17]I know, my God, that you test the heart[h] and are pleased with integrity. All these things have I given willingly and with honest intent. And now I have seen with joy how willingly your people who are here have given to you.[i] [18]O LORD, God of our fathers Abraham, Isaac and Israel, keep this desire in the hearts of your people forever, and keep their hearts loyal to you. [19]And give my son Solomon the wholehearted devotion[j] to keep your commands, requirements and decrees[k] and to do everything to build the palatial structure for which I have provided."[l]

[20]Then David said to the whole assembly, "Praise the LORD your God." So they all praised the LORD, the God of their fathers; they bowed low and fell prostrate before the LORD and the king.

[21]The next day they made sacrifices to the LORD and presented burnt offerings to him:[m] a thousand bulls, a thousand rams and a thousand male lambs, together with their drink offerings, and other sacrifices in abundance for all Israel. [22]They ate and drank with great joy[n] in the presence of the LORD that day.

Then they acknowledged Solomon son of David as king a second time, anointing him before the LORD to be ruler and Zadok[o] to be priest. [23]So Solomon sat on the throne[p] of the LORD as king in place of his father David. He prospered and all Israel obeyed him. [24]All the officers and mighty men, as well as all of King David's sons, pledged their submission to King Solomon.

[25]The LORD highly exalted Solomon in the sight of all Israel and bestowed on him royal splendor[q] such as no king over Israel ever had before.[r]

²⁶David son of Jesse was king*a* over all Israel. ²⁷He ruled over Israel forty years—seven in Hebron and thirty-three in Jerusalem.*b* ²⁸He died*c* at a good old age, having enjoyed long life, wealth and honor. His son Solomon succeeded him as king.*d*

²⁹As for the events of King David's reign, from beginning to end, they are written in the records of Samuel the seer,*e* the records of Nathan*f* the prophet and the records of Gad*g* the seer, ³⁰together with the details of his reign and power, and the circumstances that surrounded him and Israel and the kingdoms of all the other lands.

29:26
a 1Ch 18:14

29:27
b 2Sa 5:4-5;
1Ki 2:11;
1Ch 3:4

29:28
c Ge 15:15;
Ac 13:36
d 1Ch 23:1

29:29
e 1Sa 9:9
f 2Sa 7:2
g 1Sa 22:5

Theme of 1 Chronicles:

	SEGMENT DIVISIONS	MAIN DIVISIONS		CHAPTER THEMES
Author:				
		THE GENEALOGIES OF ISRAEL	1	
Date:			2	
			3	
			4	
Purpose:			5	
			6	
			7	
Key Words:			8	
			9	
		GOD TURNS KINGDOM TO DAVID	10	
			11	
			12	
			13	
			14	
			15	
			16	
			17	
			18	
			19	
		DAVID BUILDS ALTAR, PREPARES FOR GOD'S TEMPLE	20	
			21	
			22	
			23	
			24	
			25	
			26	
			27	
			28	
			29	

2 CHRONICLES

King David wanted to build a house for the Lord, but instead the Lord promised David he would establish David's house forever and that David's son would build God's house. At this point in the record of David's life the writers of the Septuagint divided Chronicles. Second Chronicles tells of the house of David and of the house that David's son built for the Lord.

∾ THINGS TO DO

If you haven't already done so, study 1 Chronicles (at the very least read the introduction to 1 Chronicles) before you begin your study of 2 Chronicles.

Second Chronicles is filled with truths and lessons for life which, if heeded, will help you in your pursuit of holiness. Second Chronicles focuses on the reigns of the kings of Judah and their relationship to God and his house from the time of Solomon until the Babylonian exile. Read all the instructions before you begin.

1. Examine every chapter in the light of the five W's and an H. Record your insights in the margin.

   a. Look for three *who's:* the king, the prophet, and the Lord. Of the three, the Lord and the king are most prominent. Ask: Who are the associates of the king? Who influences, opposes, or assists him?

   b. Look for *what* each king does, *what* God does in respect to that king, and *what* role the prophet plays, if any. In 2 Chronicles the "house" of God takes center stage; therefore, in each reign observe what the king's relationship is to the Lord and to his house.

   c. Also keep track of *when* events occur. Don't forget to note references to time with a symbol.

   d. Because this is a historical book, also watch *where* things occur.

   e. Observing *why* events occur will bring insight into the character and sovereignty of God in the affairs of men and nations. Keep asking why. If the king does evil, ask why.

   f. Ask *how*. How did the king seek the Lord? How did the king do evil? How did God respond?

2. Record your insights on the kings mentioned in 2 Chronicles. Transfer these insights to the chart THE KINGS OF ISRAEL AND JUDAH located on pages 654 and 655 between 2 Kings and 1 Chronicles.

3. On an index card make a list of the key repeated words printed on the 2 CHRONICLES AT A GLANCE chart on page 771. Use this list as a bookmark while you study 2 Chronicles.

   a. In the margin record all you learn from marking each of these key words. Note that after chapter 8, *ark,* one of the key words, is used once more in chapter 35.

   b. You will also observe key words and phrases which will play a major role in only one or two chapters. Don't miss these. They will come to the surface as you prayerfully read and meditate on a chapter.

4. As you study each chapter take notes in the margin of all you learn about God. You will gain rich and perhaps surprising insights. Also mark and record any lessons for life ("LFL").

5. Remember that 1 and 2 Chronicles were written as one book. Second Chronicles is a continuation of 1 Chronicles. Chronicles has a number of speeches, prophecies, and prayers, some of which are not mentioned in Samuel or Kings. Watch for these and pay attention to what is said, by whom, and why. Highlight or note your insights in the margin.

6. When you finish reading each chapter, record its theme on 2 CHRONICLES AT A GLANCE and on the line next to the chapter number. Also watch for the major historical events which occur in 2 Chronicles. Highlight these on the chart.

7. Complete 2 CHRONICLES AT A GLANCE. As you review the chapter themes you have recorded, see how this book could be segmented and record this under "Segment Divisions." Also, record the book's theme.

∾ THINGS TO THINK ABOUT

1. Many lessons about prayer and seeking God can be learned from this book. Review what you have seen from marking the key words. Think about what you learned regarding sin, prayer, confession, and repentance in 2 Chronicles 6.

2. Second Chronicles is filled with illustrations of how people dealt with difficulties and testings. How did you relate to these people? What did you learn from their lives—men such as Asa, Jehoshaphat, Hezekiah, Uzziah? As you studied them, did God prick your heart? With what warnings or cautions?

3. What did you learn about the heart from this book? Do you serve the Lord wholeheartedly or half-heartedly? What did you learn about crying to the Lord? What happened to those who cried out to him? Did they always deserve to be heard?

4. What did you learn about the sovereignty of God? How active or involved is God in the affairs of men? What were the different ways God afflicted those who disobeyed? Do you have a healthy fear of God?

∾∾∾∾∾

Chapter 1 Theme _____

1 Solomon son of David established[a] himself firmly over his kingdom, for the LORD his God was with[b] him and made him exceedingly great.[c]

[1:1]
a 1Ki 2:12,26; 2Ch 12:1
b Ge 21:22; 39:2; Nu 14:43
c 1Ch 29:25

²Then Solomon spoke to all Israel[d]—to the commanders of thousands and commanders of hundreds, to the judges and to all the leaders in Israel, the heads of families— ³and Solomon and the whole assembly went to the high place at Gibeon, for God's Tent of Meeting[e] was there, which Moses[f] the LORD's servant had made in the desert. ⁴Now David had brought up the ark[g] of God from Kiriath Jearim to the place he had prepared for it, because he had pitched a tent[h] for it in Jerusalem. ⁵But the bronze altar[i] that Bezalel[j] son of Uri, the son of Hur, had made was in Gibeon in front of the tabernacle of the LORD; so Solomon and the assembly inquired[k] of him there. ⁶Solomon went up to the bronze altar before the LORD in the Tent of Meeting and offered a thousand burnt offerings on it.

[1:2]
d 1Ch 9:1; 28:1

[1:3]
e Ex 36:8
f Ex 40:18

[1:4]
g 2Sa 6:2; 1Ch 15:25
h 2Sa 6:17; 1Ch 15:1

[1:5]
i Ex 38:2
j Ex 31:2
k 1Ch 13:3

⁷That night God appeared[l] to Solomon and said to him, "Ask for whatever you want me to give you."

[1:7]
l 2Ch 7:12

⁸Solomon answered God, "You have shown great kindness to David my father and have made me[m] king in his place. ⁹Now, LORD God, let your promise[n] to my father David be confirmed, for you have made me king over a people who are as numerous as the dust

[1:8]
m 1Ch 23:1; 28:5

[1:9]
n 2Sa 7:25; 1Ki 8:25

I N S I G H T

Read **The Ark of the Covenant** on page 2203.

∾∾∾

of the earth.*a* [10]Give me wisdom and knowledge, that I may lead*b* this people, for who is able to govern this great people of yours?"

[11]God said to Solomon, "Since this is your heart's desire and you have not asked for wealth,*c* riches or honor, nor for the death of your enemies, and since you have not asked for a long life but for wisdom and knowledge to govern my people over whom I have made you king, [12]therefore wisdom and knowledge will be given you. And I will also give you wealth, riches and honor,*d* such as no king who was before you ever had and none after you will have.*e*"

[13]Then Solomon went to Jerusalem from the high place at Gibeon, from before the Tent of Meeting. And he reigned over Israel.

[14]Solomon accumulated chariots*f* and horses; he had fourteen hundred chariots and twelve thousand horses,*a* which he kept in the chariot cities and also with him in Jerusalem. [15]The king made silver and gold*g* as common in Jerusalem as stones, and cedar as plentiful as sycamore-fig trees in the foothills. [16]Solomon's horses were imported from Egypt*b* and from Kue*c*—the royal merchants purchased them from Kue. [17]They imported a chariot*h* from Egypt for six hundred shekels*d* of silver, and a horse for a hundred and fifty.*e* They also exported them to all the kings of the Hittites and of the Arameans.

Chapter 2 Theme

2 Solomon gave orders to build a temple*i* for the Name of the LORD and a royal palace for himself.*j* [2]He conscripted seventy thousand men as carriers and eighty thousand as stonecutters in the hills and thirty-six hundred as foremen over them.*k*

[3]Solomon sent this message to Hiram*fl* king of Tyre:

"Send me cedar logs*m* as you did for my father David when you sent him cedar to build a palace to live in. [4]Now I am about to build a temple*n* for the Name of the LORD my God and to dedicate it to him for burning fragrant incense*o* before him, for setting out the consecrated bread*p* regularly, and for making burnt offerings*q* every morning and evening and on Sabbaths*r* and New Moons and at the appointed feasts of the LORD our God. This is a lasting ordinance for Israel.

[5]"The temple I am going to build will be great,*s* because our God is greater than all other gods.*t* [6]But who is able to build a temple for him, since the heavens, even the highest heavens, cannot contain him?*u* Who then am I*v* to build a temple for him, except as a place to burn sacrifices before him?

---

a 14 Or *charioteers*   *b 16* Or possibly *Muzur*, a region in Cilicia; also in verse 17
c 16 Probably Cilicia   *d 17* That is, about 15 pounds (about 7 kilograms)   *e 17* That is, about
3 3/4 pounds (about 1.7 kilograms)   *f 3* Hebrew *Huram*, a variant of *Hiram*; also in
verses 11 and 12

1:9
a Ge 12:2

1:10
b Nu 27:17;
2Sa 5:2;
Pr 8:15-16

1:11
c Dt 17:17

1:12
d 1Ch 29:12
e 1Ch 29:25;
2Ch 9:22;
Ne 13:26

1:14
f 1Sa 8:11;
1Ki 4:26; 9:19

1:15
g 1Ki 9:28;
Isa 60:5

1:17
h SS 1:9

2:1
i Dt 12:5
j Ecc 2:4

2:2
k ver 18;
2Ch 10:4

2:3
l 2Sa 5:11
m 1Ch 14:1

2:4
n ver 1; Dt 12:5
o Ex 30:7
p Ex 25:30
q Ex 29:42;
2Ch 13:11
r Nu 28:9-10

2:5
s 1Ch 22:5;
Ps 135:5
t 1Ch 16:25

2:6
u 1Ki 8:27;
2Ch 6:18;
Jer 23:24
v Ex 3:11

2:7
a ver 13-14;
Ex 35:31;
1Ch 22:16

2:10
b Ezr 3:7

2:11
c 1Ki 10:9;
2Ch 9:8

2:12
d Ne 9:6; Ps 8:3;
33:6; 102:25

2:13
e 1Ki 7:13

2:14
f Ex 31:6
g Ex 35:31
h Ex 35:35

2:15
i ver 10; Ezr 3:7

2:16
j Jos 19:46;
Jnh 1:3

2:17
k 1Ch 22:2
l 2Sa 24:2

2:18
m ver 2;
1Ch 22:2;
2Ch 8:8

7"Send me, therefore, a man skilled to work in gold and silver, bronze and iron, and in purple, crimson and blue yarn, and experienced in the art of engraving, to work in Judah and Jerusalem with my skilled craftsmen,*a* whom my father David provided.

8"Send me also cedar, pine and algum*a* logs from Lebanon, for I know that your men are skilled in cutting timber there. My men will work with yours 9to provide me with plenty of lumber, because the temple I build must be large and magnificent. 10I will give your servants, the woodsmen who cut the timber, twenty thousand cors*b* of ground wheat, twenty thousand cors of barley, twenty thousand baths*c* of wine and twenty thousand baths of olive oil.*b*"

11Hiram king of Tyre replied by letter to Solomon:

"Because the LORD loves*c* his people, he has made you their king."

12And Hiram added:

"Praise be to the LORD, the God of Israel, who made heaven and earth!*d* He has given King David a wise son, endowed with intelligence and discernment, who will build a temple for the LORD and a palace for himself.

13"I am sending you Huram-Abi,*e* a man of great skill, 14whose mother was from Dan*f* and whose father was from Tyre. He is trained*g* to work in gold and silver, bronze and iron, stone and wood, and with purple and blue*h* and crimson yarn and fine linen. He is experienced in all kinds of engraving and can execute any design given to him. He will work with your craftsmen and with those of my lord, David your father.

15"Now let my lord send his servants the wheat and barley and the olive oil*i* and wine he promised, 16and we will cut all the logs from Lebanon that you need and will float them in rafts by sea down to Joppa.*j* You can then take them up to Jerusalem."

17Solomon took a census of all the aliens*k* who were in Israel, after the census*l* his father David had taken; and they were found to be 153,600. 18He assigned*m* 70,000 of them to be carriers and 80,000 to be stonecutters in the hills, with 3,600 foremen over them to keep the people working.

Cedar from Lebanon

a 8 Probably a variant of *almug*; possibly juniper   *b* 10 That is, probably about 125,000 bushels (about 4,400 kiloliters)   *c* 10 That is, probably about 115,000 gallons (about 440 kiloliters)

Chapter 3 Theme _____

3 Then Solomon began to build[a] the temple of the LORD[b] in Jerusalem on Mount Moriah, where the LORD had appeared to his father David. It was on the threshing floor of Araunah[ac] the Jebusite, the place provided by David. [2]He began building on the second day of the second month in the fourth year of his reign.[d]

[3]The foundation Solomon laid for building the temple of God was sixty cubits long and twenty cubits wide[be] (using the cubit of the old standard). [4]The portico at the front of the temple was twenty cubits[c] long across the width of the building and twenty cubits[d] high.

He overlaid the inside with pure gold. [5]He paneled the main hall with pine and covered it with fine gold and decorated it with palm tree[f] and chain designs. [6]He adorned the temple with precious stones. And the gold he used was gold of Parvaim. [7]He overlaid the ceiling beams, doorframes, walls and doors of the temple with gold, and he carved cherubim[g] on the walls.

[8]He built the Most Holy Place,[h] its length corresponding to the width of the temple—twenty cubits long and twenty cubits wide. He overlaid the inside with six hundred talents[e] of fine gold. [9]The gold nails[i] weighed fifty shekels.[f] He also overlaid the upper parts with gold.

[10]In the Most Holy Place he made a pair[j] of sculptured cherubim and overlaid them with gold. [11]The total wingspan of the cherubim was twenty cubits. One wing of the first cherub was five cubits[g] long and touched the temple wall, while its other wing, also five cubits long, touched the wing of the other cherub. [12]Similarly one wing of the second cherub was five cubits long and touched the other temple wall, and its other wing, also five cubits long, touched the wing of the first cherub. [13]The wings of these cherubim[k] extended twenty cubits. They stood on their feet, facing the main hall.[h]

[14]He made the curtain[l] of blue, purple and crimson yarn and fine linen, with cherubim[m] worked into it.

[15]In the front of the temple he made two pillars,[n] which ⌊together⌋ were thirty-five cubits[i] long, each with a capital[o] on top measuring five cubits. [16]He made interwoven chains[jp] and put them on top of the pillars. He also made a hundred pomegranates[q] and attached them to the chains. [17]He erected the pillars in the front of

Close-up of Most Holy Place

---

a1 Hebrew *Ornan,* a variant of *Araunah*   b3 That is, about 90 feet (about 27 meters) long and 30 feet (about 9 meters) wide   c4 That is, about 30 feet (about 9 meters); also in verses 8, 11 and 13   d4 Some Septuagint and Syriac manuscripts; Hebrew *and a hundred and twenty*   e8 That is, about 23 tons (about 21 metric tons)   f9 That is, about 1 1/4 pounds (about 0.6 kilogram)   g11 That is, about 7 1/2 feet (about 2.3 meters); also in verse 15   h13 Or *facing inward*   i15 That is, about 52 feet (about 16 meters)   j16 Or possibly *made chains in the inner sanctuary;* the meaning of the Hebrew for this phrase is uncertain.

3:1
a Ac 7:47
b Ge 28:17
c 2Sa 24:18;
1Ch 21:18

3:2
d Ezr 5:11

3:3
e Eze 41:2

3:5
f Eze 40:16

3:7
g Ge 3:24;
1Ki 6:29-35;
Eze 41:18

3:8
h Ex 26:33

3:9
i Ex 26:32

3:10
j Ex 25:18

3:13
k Ex 25:18

3:14
l Ex 26:31,33;
Heb 9:3
m Ge 3:24

3:15
n 1Ki 7:15;
Rev 3:12
o 1Ki 7:22

3:16
p 1Ki 7:17
q 1Ki 7:20

the temple, one to the south and one to the north. The one to the south he named Jakin[a] and the one to the north Boaz.[b]

Chapter 4 Theme

4 He made a bronze altar[a] twenty cubits long, twenty cubits wide and ten cubits high.[c] ²He made the Sea[b] of cast metal, circular in shape, measuring ten cubits from rim to rim and five cubits[d] high. It took a line of thirty cubits[e] to measure around it. ³Below the rim, figures of bulls encircled it—ten to a cubit.[f] The bulls were cast in two rows in one piece with the Sea.

Bronze Altar

⁴The Sea stood on twelve bulls, three facing north, three facing west, three facing south and three facing east.[c] The Sea rested on top of them, and their hindquarters were toward the center. ⁵It was a handbreadth[g] in thickness, and its rim was like the rim of a cup, like a lily blossom. It held three thousand baths.[h]

⁶He then made ten basins[d] for washing and placed five on the south side and five on the north. In them the things to be used for the burnt offerings[e] were rinsed, but the Sea was to be used by the priests for washing.

Bronze Basin on Bulls

⁷He made ten gold lampstands[f] according to the specifications[g] for them and placed them in the temple, five on the south side and five on the north.

⁸He made ten tables[h] and placed them in the temple, five on the south side and five on the north. He also made a hundred gold sprinkling bowls.[i]

⁹He made the courtyard[j] of the priests, and the large court and the doors for the court, and overlaid the doors with bronze. ¹⁰He placed the Sea on the south side, at the southeast corner.

¹¹He also made the pots and shovels and sprinkling bowls.

So Huram finished[k] the work he had undertaken for King Solomon in the temple of God:

Bronze Stand with Bronze Basin

¹²the two pillars;

the two bowl-shaped capitals on top of the pillars;

the two sets of network decorating the two bowl-shaped capitals on top of the pillars;

¹³the four hundred pomegranates for the two sets of network (two rows of pomegranates for each network, decorating the bowl-shaped capitals on top of the pillars);

¹⁴the stands[l] with their basins;

¹⁵the Sea and the twelve bulls under it;

¹⁶the pots, shovels, meat forks and all related articles.

Table

4:1 *a* Ex 20:24; 27:1-2; 40:6; 1Ki 8:64; 2Ki 16:14

4:2 *b* Rev 4:6; 15:2

4:4 *c* Nu 2:3-25; Eze 48:30-34; Rev 21:13

4:6 *d* Ex 30:18; *e* Ne 13:5,9; Eze 40:38

4:7 *f* Ex 25:31; *g* Ex 25:40

4:8 *h* Ex 25:23; *i* Nu 4:14

4:9 *j* 1Ki 6:36; 2Ki 21:5; 2Ch 33:5

4:11 *k* 1Ki 7:14

4:14 *l* 1Ki 7:27-30

Footnotes

a 17 Jakin probably means *he establishes.*   *b 17* Boaz probably means *in him is strength.*   *c 1* That is, about 30 feet (about 9 meters) long and wide, and about 15 feet (about 4.5 meters) high   *d 2* That is, about 7 1/2 feet (about 2.3 meters)   *e 2* That is, about 45 feet (about 13.5 meters)   *f 3* That is, about 1 1/2 feet (about 0.5 meter)   *g 5* That is, about 3 inches (about 8 centimeters)   *h 5* That is, about 17,500 gallons (about 66 kiloliters)

All the objects that Huram-Abi*a* made for King Solomon for the temple of the LORD were of polished bronze. [17]The king had them cast in clay molds in the plain of the Jordan between Succoth*b* and Zarethan.*a* [18]All these things that Solomon made amounted to so much that the weight of the bronze*c* was not determined.

[19]Solomon also made all the furnishings that were in God's temple:

the golden altar;
the tables*d* on which was the bread of the Presence;
[20]the lampstands*e* of pure gold with their lamps, to burn in front of the inner sanctuary as prescribed;
[21]the gold floral work and lamps and tongs (they were solid gold);
[22]the pure gold wick trimmers, sprinkling bowls, dishes*f* and censers;*g* and the gold doors of the temple: the inner doors to the Most Holy Place and the doors of the main hall.

Lampstand

Chapter 5 Theme

5 When all the work Solomon had done for the temple of the LORD was finished,*h* he brought in the things his father David had dedicated*i*—the silver and gold and all the furnishings—and he placed them in the treasuries of God's temple.

[2]Then Solomon summoned to Jerusalem the elders of Israel, all the heads of the tribes and the chiefs of the Israelite families, to bring up the ark*j* of the LORD's covenant from Zion, the City of David. [3]And all the men of Israel*k* came together to the king at the time of the festival in the seventh month.

[4]When all the elders of Israel had arrived, the Levites took up the ark, [5]and they brought up the ark and the Tent of Meeting and all the sacred furnishings in it. The priests, who were Levites,*l* carried them up; [6]and King Solomon and the entire assembly of Israel that had gathered about him were before the ark, sacrificing so many sheep and cattle that they could not be recorded or counted.

[7]The priests then brought the ark*m* of the LORD's covenant to its place in the inner sanctuary of the temple, the Most Holy Place, and put it beneath the wings of the cherubim. [8]The cherubim*n* spread their wings over the place of the ark and covered the ark and its carrying poles. [9]These poles were so long that their ends, extending from the ark, could be seen from in front of the inner sanctuary, but not from outside the Holy Place; and they are still there today. [10]There was nothing in the ark except*o* the two tablets*p* that Moses had placed in it at Horeb, where the LORD made a covenant with the Israelites after they came out of Egypt.

Ark
of the Covenant
(or Testimony)

a 17 Hebrew *Zeredatha*, a variant of *Zarethan*

4:16
a 1Ki 7:13

4:17
b Ge 33:17

4:18
c 1Ki 7:23

4:19
d Ex 25:23,30

4:20
e Ex 25:31

4:22
f Nu 7:14
g Lev 10:1

5:1
h 1Ki 6:14
i 2Sa 8:11

5:2
j Nu 3:31;
2Sa 6:12;
1Ch 15:25

5:3
k 1Ch 9:1;
2Ch 7:8-10

5:5
l Nu 3:31;
1Ch 15:2

5:7
m Rev 11:19

5:8
n Ge 3:24

5:10
o Heb 9:4
p Ex 16:34;
Dt 10:2

¹¹The priests then withdrew from the Holy Place. All the priests who were there had consecrated themselves, regardless of their divisions.*a* ¹²All the Levites who were musicians*b*—Asaph, Heman, Jeduthun and their sons and relatives—stood on the east side of the altar, dressed in fine linen and playing cymbals, harps and lyres. They were accompanied by 120 priests sounding trumpets.*c* ¹³The trumpeters and singers joined in unison, as with one voice, to give praise and thanks to the LORD. Accompanied by trumpets, cymbals and other instruments, they raised their voices in praise to the LORD and sang:

5:12
b 1Ki 10:12;
1Ch 25:1;
Ps 68:25
c 1Ch 13:8;
15:24

> "He is good;
>   his love endures forever."*d*

Then the temple of the LORD was filled with a cloud, ¹⁴and the priests could not perform*e* their service because of the cloud,*f* for the glory*g* of the LORD filled the temple of God.

5:13
d 1Ch 16:34, 41;
2Ch 7:3; 20:21;
Ezr 3:11;
Ps 100:5;
136:1;
Jer 33:11

Chapter 6 Theme

6 Then Solomon said, "The LORD has said that he would dwell in a dark cloud;*h* ²I have built a magnificent temple for you, a place for you to dwell forever.'"

³While the whole assembly of Israel was standing there, the king turned around and blessed them. ⁴Then he said:

5:14
e Ex 40:35;
Rev 15:8
f Ex 19:16
g Ex 29:43;
2Ch 7:2

"Praise be to the LORD, the God of Israel, who with his hands has fulfilled what he promised with his mouth to my father David. For he said, ⁵'Since the day I brought my people out of Egypt, I have not chosen a city in any tribe of Israel to have a temple built for my Name to be there, nor have I chosen anyone to be the leader over my people Israel. ⁶But now I have chosen Jerusalem*j* for my Name*k* to be there, and I have chosen David*l* to rule my people Israel.'

⁷"My father David had it in his heart*m* to build a temple for the Name of the LORD, the God of Israel. ⁸But the LORD said to my father David, 'Because it was in your heart to build a temple for my Name, you did well to have this in your heart. ⁹Nevertheless, you are not the one to build the temple, but your son, who is your own flesh and blood—he is the one who will build the temple for my Name.'

6:6
j Dt 12:5;
Isa 14:1
k Ex 20:24;
2Ch 12:13
l 1Ch 28:4

¹⁰"The LORD has kept the promise he made. I have succeeded David my father and now I sit on the throne of Israel, just as the LORD promised, and I have built the temple for the Name of the LORD, the God of Israel. ¹¹There I have placed the ark, in which is the covenant*n* of the LORD that he made with the people of Israel."

INSIGHT

See the illustration of Solomon's Temple on page IISB-36.

¹²Then Solomon stood before the altar of the LORD in front of the whole assembly of Israel and spread out his hands. ¹³Now he had made a bronze platform,ᵃ five cubitsᵃ long, five cubits wide and three cubitsᵇ high, and had placed it in the center of the outer court. He stood on the platform and then knelt downᵇ before the whole assembly of Israel and spread out his hands toward heaven. ¹⁴He said:

"O LORD, God of Israel, there is no God like youᶜ in heaven or on earth—you who keep your covenant of loveᵈ with your servants who continue wholeheartedly in your way. ¹⁵You have kept your promise to your servant David my father; with your mouth you have promisedᵉ and with your hand you have fulfilled it—as it is today.

¹⁶"Now LORD, God of Israel, keep for your servant David my father the promises you made to him when you said, 'You shall never failᶠ to have a man to sit before me on the throne of Israel, if only your sons are careful in all they do to walk before me according to my law,ᵍ as you have done.' ¹⁷And now, O LORD, God of Israel, let your word that you promised your servant David come true.

¹⁸"But will God really dwellʰ on earth with men? The heavens,ⁱ even the highest heavens, cannot contain you. How much less this temple I have built! ¹⁹Yet give attention to your servant's prayer and his plea for mercy, O LORD my God. Hear the cry and the prayer that your servant is praying in your presence. ²⁰May your eyesʲ be open toward this temple day and night, this place of which you said you would put your Nameᵏ there. May you hearˡ the prayer your servant prays toward this place. ²¹Hear the supplications of your servant and of your people Israel when they pray toward this place. Hear from heaven, your dwelling place; and when you hear, forgive.ᵐ

²²"When a man wrongs his neighbor and is required to take an oathⁿ and he comes and swears the oath before your altar in this temple, ²³then hear from heaven and act. Judge between your servants, repayingᵒ the guilty by bringing down on his own head what he has done. Declare the innocent not guilty and so establish his innocence.

²⁴"When your people Israel have been defeatedᵖ by an enemy because they have sinned against you and when they turn back and confess your name, praying and making supplication before you in this temple, ²⁵then hear from heaven and forgive the sin of your people Israel and bring them back to the land you gave to them and their fathers.

6:13
ᵃNe 8:4
ᵇPs 95:6

6:14
ᶜEx 8:10; 15:11
ᵈDt 7:9

6:15
ᵉ1Ch 22:10

6:16
ᶠ2Sa 7:13,15;
1Ki 2:4;
2Ch 7:18; 23:3
ᵍPs 132:12

6:18
ʰRev 21:3
ⁱ2Ch 2:6;
Ps 11:4;
Isa 40:22; 66:1;
Ac 7:49

6:20
ʲEx 3:16;
Ps 34:15
ᵏDt 12:11
ˡ2Ch 7:14;
30:20

6:21
ᵐPs 51:1;
Isa 33:24; 40:2;
43:25; 44:22;
55:7; Mic 7:18

6:22
ⁿEx 22:11

6:23
ᵒIsa 3:11; 65:6;
Mt 16:27

6:24
ᵖLev 26:17

ᵃ 13 That is, about 7 1/2 feet (about 2.3 meters)   ᵇ 13 That is, about 4 1/2 feet (about 1.3 meters)

6:26
a Lev 26:19;
Dt 11:17; 28:24;
2Sa 1:21;
1Ki 17:1

6:27
b ver 30,39;
2Ch 7:14

6:28
c 2Ch 20:9

6:30
d ver 27
e 1Sa 16:7;
1Ch 28:9;
Ps 7:9; 44:21;
Pr 16:2; 17:3

6:31
f Ps 103:11, 13;
Pr 8:13

6:32
g 2Ch 9:6;
Jn 12:20;
Ac 8:27
h Ex 3:19,20

6:33
i 2Ch 7:14

6:34
j Dt 28:7
k 1Ch 5:20

6:36
l Job 15:14;
Ps 143:2;
Ecc 7:20;
Jer 17:9;
Jas 3:1;
1Jn 1:8-10
m Lev 26:44

6:37
n 2Ch 7:14;
33:12,19,23;
Jer 29:13

26"When the heavens are shut up and there is no rain[a] because your people have sinned against you, and when they pray toward this place and confess your name and turn from their sin because you have afflicted them, 27then hear from heaven and forgive[b] the sin of your servants, your people Israel. Teach them the right way to live, and send rain on the land you gave your people for an inheritance.

28"When famine[c] or plague comes to the land, or blight or mildew, locusts or grasshoppers, or when enemies besiege them in any of their cities, whatever disaster or disease may come, 29and when a prayer or plea is made by any of your people Israel—each one aware of his afflictions and pains, and spreading out his hands toward this temple— 30then hear from heaven, your dwelling place. Forgive,[d] and deal with each man according to all he does, since you know his heart (for you alone know the hearts of men),[e] 31so that they will fear you[f] and walk in your ways all the time they live in the land you gave our fathers.

32"As for the foreigner who does not belong to your people Israel but has come[g] from a distant land because of your great name and your mighty hand[h] and your outstretched arm— when he comes and prays toward this temple, 33then hear from heaven, your dwelling place, and do whatever the foreigner[i] asks of you, so that all the peoples of the earth may know your name and fear you, as do your own people Israel, and may know that this house I have built bears your Name.

34"When your people go to war against their enemies,[j] wherever you send them, and when they pray[k] to you toward this city you have chosen and the temple I have built for your Name, 35then hear from heaven their prayer and their plea, and uphold their cause.

36"When they sin against you—for there is no one who does not sin[l]—and you become angry with them and give them over to the enemy, who takes them captive[m] to a land far away or near; 37and if they have a change of heart[n] in the land where they are held captive, and repent and plead with you in the land of their captivity and say, 'We have sinned, we have done wrong and acted wickedly'; 38and if they turn back to you with all their heart and soul in the land of their captivity where they were taken, and pray toward the land you gave their fathers, toward the city you have chosen and toward the temple I have built for your Name; 39then from heaven, your dwelling place, hear their prayer and their pleas, and uphold their cause. And forgive your people, who have sinned against you.

⁴⁰"Now, my God, may your eyes be open and your ears atten-
tiveᵃ to the prayers offered in this place.

⁴¹"Now arise,ᵇ O Lord God, and come to your resting place,ᶜ
you and the ark of your might.
May your priests,ᵈ O Lord God, be clothed with salvation,
may your saints rejoice in your goodness.ᵉ
⁴²O Lord God, do not reject your anointed one.
Remember the great loveᶠ promised to
David your servant."

Chapter 7 Theme

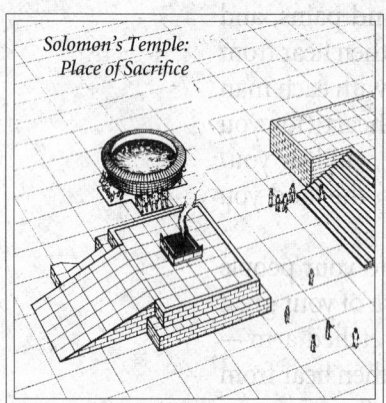

Solomon's Temple:
Place of Sacrifice

7 When Solomon finished praying, fireᵍ came
down from heaven and consumed the burnt
offering and the sacrifices, and the glory of the
Lord filledʰ the temple.ⁱ ²The priests could not
enterʲ the temple of the Lord because the gloryᵏ
of the Lord filled it. ³When all the Israelites saw
the fire coming down and the glory of the Lord
above the temple, they knelt on the pavement
with their faces to the ground, and they worshiped and gave thanks to the Lord, saying,

"He is good;
his love endures forever."ˡ

⁴Then the king and all the people offered sacrifices before the
Lord. ⁵And King Solomon offered a sacrifice of twenty-two thousand head of cattle and a hundred and twenty thousand sheep
and goats. So the king and all the people dedicated the temple of
God. ⁶The priests took their positions, as did the Levitesᵐ with
the Lord's musical instruments,ⁿ which King David had made
for praising the Lord and which were used when he gave thanks,
saying, "His love endures forever." Opposite the Levites, the
priests blew their trumpets, and all the Israelites were standing.

⁷Solomon consecrated the middle part of the courtyard in front
of the temple of the Lord, and there he offered burnt offerings
and the fat of the fellowship offerings,ᵃ because the bronze altar
he had made could not hold the burnt offerings, the grain offerings and the fat portions.

⁸So Solomon observed the festivalᵒ at that time for seven days,
and all Israel with him—a vast assembly, people from Leboᵇ
Hamath to the Wadi of Egypt.ᵖ ⁹On the eighth day they held an
assembly, for they had celebrated the dedication of the altar for
seven days and the festivalᵠ for seven days more. ¹⁰On the twenty-
third day of the seventh month he sent the people to their homes,

ᵃ7 Traditionally *peace offerings*   ᵇ8 Or *from the entrance to*

6:40
ᵃ2Ch 7:15;
Ne 1:6,11;
Ps 17:1,6

6:41
ᵇIsa 33:10
ᶜ1Ch 28:2
ᵈPs 132:16
ᵉPs 116:12

6:42
ᶠPs 89:24,28;
Isa 55:3

7:1
ᵍLev 9:24;
1Ki 18:38
ʰEx 16:10
ⁱPs 26:8

7:2
ʲ1Ki 8:11
ᵏEx 29:43;
40:35; 2Ch 5:14

7:3
ˡ1Ch 16:34;
2Ch 5:13; 20:21

7:6
ᵐ1Ch 15:16
ⁿ2Ch 5:12

7:8
ᵒ2Ch 30:26
ᵖGe 15:18

7:9
ᵠLev 23:36

7:12
a Dt 12:5

7:13
b 2Ch 6:26-28;
Am 4:7

7:14
c Lev 26:41;
2Ch 6:37;
Jas 4:10
d 1Ch 16:11
e Isa 55:7;
Zec 1:4
f 2Ch 6:27
g 2Ch 30:20;
Isa 30:26; 57:18

7:15
h 2Ch 6:40

7:16
i ver 12; 2Ch 6:6

7:17
j 1Ki 9:4

7:18
k 2Ch 6:16
l 2Sa 7:13;
2Ch 13:5

7:19
m Dt 28:15
n Lev 26:14,33

7:20
o Dt 29:28
p 1Ki 14:15
q Dt 28:37

7:21
r Dt 29:24

8:5
s 1Ch 7:24;
2Ch 14:7

joyful and glad in heart for the good things the Lord had done for David and Solomon and for his people Israel.

[11]When Solomon had finished the temple of the Lord and the royal palace, and had succeeded in carrying out all he had in mind to do in the temple of the Lord and in his own palace, [12]the Lord appeared to him at night and said:

"I have heard your prayer and have chosen this place for myself[a] as a temple for sacrifices.

[13]"When I shut up the heavens so that there is no rain,[b] or command locusts to devour the land or send a plague among my people, [14]if my people, who are called by my name, will humble[c] themselves and pray and seek my face[d] and turn[e] from their wicked ways, then will I hear from heaven and will forgive[f] their sin and will heal[g] their land. [15]Now my eyes will be open and my ears attentive to the prayers offered in this place.[h] [16]I have chosen[i] and consecrated this temple so that my Name may be there forever. My eyes and my heart will always be there.

[17]"As for you, if you walk before me[j] as David your father did, and do all I command, and observe my decrees and laws, [18]I will establish your royal throne, as I covenanted with David your father when I said, 'You shall never fail to have a man[k] to rule over Israel.'[l]

[19]"But if you[a] turn away[m] and forsake[n] the decrees and commands I have given you[a] and go off to serve other gods and worship them, [20]then I will uproot[o] Israel from my land,[p] which I have given them, and will reject this temple I have consecrated for my Name. I will make it a byword and an object of ridicule[q] among all peoples. [21]And though this temple is now so imposing, all who pass by will be appalled and say,[r] 'Why has the Lord done such a thing to this land and to this temple?' [22]People will answer, 'Because they have forsaken the Lord, the God of their fathers, who brought them out of Egypt, and have embraced other gods, worshiping and serving them—that is why he brought all this disaster on them.'"

Chapter 8 Theme

8 At the end of twenty years, during which Solomon built the temple of the Lord and his own palace, [2]Solomon rebuilt the villages that Hiram[b] had given him, and settled Israelites in them. [3]Solomon then went to Hamath Zobah and captured it. [4]He also built up Tadmor in the desert and all the store cities he had built in Hamath. [5]He rebuilt Upper Beth Horon[s] and Lower Beth Horon

a 19 The Hebrew is plural.   b 2 Hebrew *Huram*, a variant of *Hiram*; also in verse 18 as fortified cities, with walls and with gates and bars, [6]as well as Baalath and all his store cities, and all the cities for his chariots and for his horses[a]—whatever he desired to build in Jerusalem, in Lebanon and throughout all the territory he ruled.

[7]All the people left from the Hittites, Amorites, Perizzites, Hivites and Jebusites[a] (these peoples were not Israelites), [8]that is, their descendants remaining in the land, whom the Israelites had not destroyed—these Solomon conscripted[b] for his slave labor force, as it is to this day. [9]But Solomon did not make slaves of the Israelites for his work; they were his fighting men, commanders of his captains, and commanders of his chariots and charioteers. [10]They were also King Solomon's chief officials—two hundred and fifty officials supervising the men.

[11]Solomon brought Pharaoh's daughter[c] up from the City of David to the palace he had built for her, for he said, "My wife must not live in the palace of David king of Israel, because the places the ark of the LORD has entered are holy."

[12]On the altar[d] of the LORD that he had built in front of the portico, Solomon sacrificed burnt offerings to the LORD, [13]according to the daily requirement[e] for offerings commanded by Moses for Sabbaths,[f] New Moons and the three[g] annual feasts—the Feast of Unleavened Bread, the Feast of Weeks[h] and the Feast of Tabernacles. [14]In keeping with the ordinance of his father David, he appointed the divisions[i] of the priests for their duties, and the Levites[j] to lead the praise and to assist the priests according to each day's requirement. He also appointed the gatekeepers[k] by divisions for the various gates, because this was what David the man of God[l] had ordered.[m] [15]They did not deviate from the king's commands to the priests or to the Levites in any matter, including that of the treasuries.

[16]All Solomon's work was carried out, from the day the foundation of the temple of the LORD was laid until its completion. So the temple of the LORD was finished.

[17]Then Solomon went to Ezion Geber and Elath on the coast of Edom. [18]And Hiram sent him ships commanded by his own officers, men who knew the sea. These, with Solomon's men, sailed to Ophir and brought back four hundred and fifty talents[b] of gold,[n] which they delivered to King Solomon.

Chapter 9 Theme _____

9 When the queen of Sheba[o] heard of Solomon's fame, she came to Jerusalem to test him with hard questions. Arriving with a very great caravan—with camels carrying spices, large quantities of gold, and precious stones—she came to Solomon and talked with him about all she had on her mind. [2]Solomon answered all

---

a6 Or *charioteers*   b18 That is, about 17 tons (about 16 metric tons)

8:7
[a]Ge 10:16

8:8
[b]1Ki 4:6; 9:21

8:11
[c]1Ki 3:1; 7:8

8:12
[d]1Ki 8:64;
2Ch 4:1; 15:8

8:13
[e]Ex 29:38;
Nu 28:3
[f]Nu 28:9
[g]Ex 23:14;
Dt 16:16
[h]Ex 23:16

8:14
[i]1Ch 24:1
[j]1Ch 25:1
[k]1Ch 9:17; 26:1
[l]Ne 12:24,36
[m]1Ch 23:6;
Ne 12:45

8:18
[n]2Ch 9:9

9:1
[o]Ge 10:7;
Eze 23:42;
Mt 12:42;
Lk 11:31

9:3
a 1Ki 5:12

9:6
b 2Ch 6:32

9:8
c 1Ki 2:12;
1Ch 17:14;
28:5; 29:23;
2Ch 13:8
d 2Ch 2:11

9:9
e 2Ch 8:18

9:10
f 2Ch 8:18

9:14
g 2Ch 17:11;
Isa 21:13;
Jer 25:24;
Eze 27:21; 30:5

9:16
h 2Ch 12:9
i 1Ki 7:2

9:17
j 1Ki 22:39

her questions; nothing was too hard for him to explain to her. ³When the queen of Sheba saw the wisdom of Solomon,ᵃ as well as the palace he had built, ⁴the food on his table, the seating of his officials, the attending servants in their robes, the cupbearers in their robes and the burnt offerings he made atᵃ the temple of the LORD, she was overwhelmed.

⁵She said to the king, "The report I heard in my own country about your achievements and your wisdom is true. ⁶But I did not believe what they said until I cameᵇ and saw with my own eyes. Indeed, not even half the greatness of your wisdom was told me; you have far exceeded the report I heard. ⁷How happy your men must be! How happy your officials, who continually stand before you and hear your wisdom! ⁸Praise be to the LORD your God, who has delighted in you and placed you on his throneᶜ as king to rule for the LORD your God. Because of the love of your God for Israel and his desire to uphold them forever, he has made you kingᵈ over them, to maintain justice and righteousness."

⁹Then she gave the king 120 talentsᵇ of gold,ᵉ large quantities of spices, and precious stones. There had never been such spices as those the queen of Sheba gave to King Solomon.

¹⁰(The men of Hiram and the men of Solomon brought gold from Ophir;ᶠ they also brought algumwoodᶜ and precious stones. ¹¹The king used the algumwood to make steps for the temple of the LORD and for the royal palace, and to make harps and lyres for the musicians. Nothing like them had ever been seen in Judah.)

¹²King Solomon gave the queen of Sheba all she desired and asked for; he gave her more than she had brought to him. Then she left and returned with her retinue to her own country.

¹³The weight of the gold that Solomon received yearly was 666 talents,ᵈ ¹⁴not including the revenues brought in by merchants and traders. Also all the kings of Arabiaᵍ and the governors of the land brought gold and silver to Solomon.

¹⁵King Solomon made two hundred large shields of hammered gold; six hundred bekasᵉ of hammered gold went into each shield. ¹⁶He also made three hundred small shieldsʰ of hammered gold, with three hundred bekasᶠ of gold in each shield. The king put them in the Palace of the Forest of Lebanon.ⁱ

¹⁷Then the king made a great throne inlaid with ivoryʲ and overlaid with pure gold. ¹⁸The throne had six steps, and a footstool of gold was attached to it. On both sides of the seat were armrests, with a lion standing beside each of them. ¹⁹Twelve lions stood on the six steps, one at either end of each step. Nothing like it had ever

---

ᵃ 4 Or *the ascent by which he went up to*   ᵇ 9 That is, about 4 1/2 tons (about 4 metric tons)
ᶜ 10 Probably a variant of *almugwood*   ᵈ 13 That is, about 25 tons (about 23 metric tons)
ᵉ 15 That is, about 7 1/2 pounds (about 3.5 kilograms)   ᶠ 16 That is, about 3 3/4 pounds (about 1.7 kilograms)

been made for any other kingdom. ²⁰All King Solomon's goblets were gold, and all the household articles in the Palace of the Forest of Lebanon were pure gold. Nothing was made of silver, because silver was considered of little value in Solomon's day. ²¹The king had a fleet of trading ships[a] manned by Hiram's[b] men. Once every three years it returned, carrying gold, silver and ivory, and apes and baboons.

²²King Solomon was greater in riches and wisdom than all the other kings of the earth.[a] ²³All the kings[b] of the earth sought audience with Solomon to hear the wisdom God had put in his heart. ²⁴Year after year, everyone who came brought a gift[c]—articles of silver and gold, and robes, weapons and spices, and horses and mules.

²⁵Solomon had four thousand stalls for horses and chariots,[d] and twelve thousand horses,[c] which he kept in the chariot cities and also with him in Jerusalem. ²⁶He ruled[e] over all the kings from the River[df] to the land of the Philistines, as far as the border of Egypt.[g] ²⁷The king made silver as common in Jerusalem as stones, and cedar as plentiful as sycamore-fig trees in the foothills. ²⁸Solomon's horses were imported from Egypt[e] and from all other countries.

²⁹As for the other events of Solomon's reign, from beginning to end, are they not written in the records of Nathan[h] the prophet, in the prophecy of Ahijah[i] the Shilonite and in the visions of Iddo the seer concerning Jeroboam[j] son of Nebat? ³⁰Solomon reigned in Jerusalem over all Israel forty years. ³¹Then he rested with his fathers and was buried in the city of David[k] his father. And Rehoboam his son succeeded him as king.

Chapter 10 Theme _____

10

Rehoboam went to Shechem, for all the Israelites had gone there to make him king. ²When Jeroboam[l] son of Nebat heard this (he was in Egypt, where he had fled[m] from King Solomon), he returned from Egypt. ³So they sent for Jeroboam, and he and all Israel[n] went to Rehoboam and said to him: ⁴"Your father put a heavy yoke on us,[o] but now lighten the harsh labor and the heavy yoke he put on us, and we will serve you."

⁵Rehoboam answered, "Come back to me in three days." So the people went away.

⁶Then King Rehoboam consulted the elders[p] who had served his father Solomon during his lifetime. "How would you advise me to answer these people?" he asked.

⁷They replied, "If you will be kind to these people and please them and give them a favorable answer,[q] they will always be your servants."

---

a 21 Hebrew *of ships that could go to Tarshish*   b 21 Hebrew *Huram*, a variant of *Hiram*
c 25 Or *charioteers*   d 26 That is, the Euphrates   e 28 Or possibly *Muzur*, a region in Cilicia

---

9:22
a 1Ki 3:13;
2Ch 1:12

9:23
b 1Ki 4:34

9:24
c 2Ch 32:23;
Ps 45:12; 68:29;
72:10; Isa 18:7

9:25
d 1Sa 8:11;
1Ki 4:26

9:26
e 1Ki 4:21
f Ps 72:8-9
g Ge 15:18-21

9:29
h 2Sa 7:2;
1Ch 29:29
i 1Ki 11:29
j 2Ch 10:2

9:31
k 1Ki 2:10

10:2
l 2Ch 9:29
m 1Ki 11:40

10:3
n 1Ch 9:1

10:4
o 2Ch 2:2

10:6
p Job 8:8-9;
12:12; 15:10;
32:7

10:7
q Pr 15:1

10:8
a 2Sa 17:14
b Pr 13:20

[8]But Rehoboam rejected[a] the advice the elders[b] gave him and consulted the young men who had grown up with him and were serving him. [9]He asked them, "What is your advice? How should we answer these people who say to me, 'Lighten the yoke your father put on us'?"

[10]The young men who had grown up with him replied, "Tell the people who have said to you, 'Your father put a heavy yoke on us, but make our yoke lighter'—tell them, 'My little finger is thicker than my father's waist. [11]My father laid on you a heavy yoke; I will make it even heavier. My father scourged you with whips; I will scourge you with scorpions.'"

10:15
c 2Ch 11:4;
25:16-20
d 1Ki 11:29

[12]Three days later Jeroboam and all the people returned to Rehoboam, as the king had said, "Come back to me in three days." [13]The king answered them harshly. Rejecting the advice of the elders, [14]he followed the advice of the young men and said, "My father made your yoke heavy; I will make it even heavier. My father scourged you with whips; I will scourge you with scorpions." [15]So the king did not listen to the people, for this turn of events was from God,[c] to fulfill the word the LORD had spoken to Jeroboam son of Nebat through Ahijah the Shilonite.[d]

10:16
e 1Ch 9:1
f ver 19; 2Sa 20:1

[16]When all Israel[e] saw that the king refused to listen to them, they answered the king:

> "What share do we have in David,[f]
>   what part in Jesse's son?
> To your tents, O Israel!
> Look after your own house, O David!"

10:18
g 1Ki 5:14

So all the Israelites went home. [17]But as for the Israelites who were living in the towns of Judah, Rehoboam still ruled over them.

[18]King Rehoboam sent out Adoniram,[a][g] who was in charge of forced labor, but the Israelites stoned him to death. King Rehoboam, however, managed to get into his chariot and escape to Jerusalem. [19]So Israel has been in rebellion against the house of David to this day.

Chapter 11 Theme _____

11:1
h 1Ki 12:21

11 When Rehoboam arrived in Jerusalem,[h] he mustered the house of Judah and Benjamin—a hundred and eighty thousand fighting men—to make war against Israel and to regain the kingdom for Rehoboam.

[2]But this word of the LORD came to Shemaiah[i] the man of God: [3]"Say to Rehoboam son of Solomon king of Judah and to all the Israelites in Judah and Benjamin, [4]'This is what the LORD says:

11:2
i 2Ch 12:5-7, 15

a 18 Hebrew *Hadoram*, a variant of *Adoniram*

Do not go up to fight against your brothers.[a] Go home, every one of you, for this is my doing.'" So they obeyed the words of the LORD and turned back from marching against Jeroboam.

The Divided Kingdom 931–586 B.C.

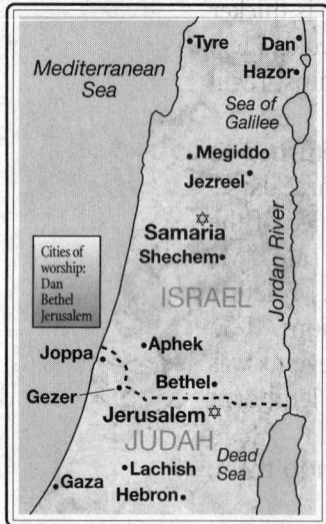

Cities of worship: Dan Bethel Jerusalem

[5] Rehoboam lived in Jerusalem and built up towns for defense in Judah: [6] Bethlehem, Etam, Tekoa, [7] Beth Zur, Soco, Adullam, [8] Gath, Mareshah, Ziph, [9] Adoraim, Lachish, Azekah, [10] Zorah, Aijalon and Hebron. These were fortified cities in Judah and Benjamin. [11] He strengthened their defenses and put commanders in them, with supplies of food, olive oil and wine. [12] He put shields and spears in all the cities, and made them very strong. So Judah and Benjamin were his.

[13] The priests and Levites from all their districts throughout Israel sided with him. [14] The Levites[b] even abandoned their pasturelands and property,[c] and came to Judah and Jerusalem because Jeroboam and his sons had rejected them as priests of the LORD. [15] And he appointed[d] his own priests[e] for the high places and for the goat[f] and calf[g] idols he had made. [16] Those from every tribe of Israel[h] who set their hearts on seeking the LORD, the God of Israel, followed the Levites to Jerusalem to offer sacrifices to the LORD, the God of their fathers. [17] They strengthened[i] the kingdom of Judah and supported Rehoboam son of Solomon three years, walking in the ways of David and Solomon during this time.

[18] Rehoboam married Mahalath, who was the daughter of David's son Jerimoth and of Abihail, the daughter of Jesse's son Eliab. [19] She bore him sons: Jeush, Shemariah and Zaham. [20] Then he married Maacah[j] daughter of Absalom, who bore him Abijah,[k] Attai, Ziza and Shelomith. [21] Rehoboam loved Maacah daughter of Absalom more than any of his other wives and concubines. In all, he had eighteen wives[l] and sixty concubines, twenty-eight sons and sixty daughters.

[22] Rehoboam appointed Abijah[m] son of Maacah to be the chief prince among his brothers, in order to make him king. [23] He acted wisely, dispersing some of his sons throughout the districts of Judah and Benjamin, and to all the fortified cities. He gave them abundant provisions and took many wives for them.

Chapter 12 Theme _____

12 After Rehoboam's position as king was established[n] and he had become strong,[o] he and all Israel[a] with him abandoned the law of the LORD. [2] Because they had been unfaithful[p] to the LORD, Shishak[q] king of Egypt attacked Jerusalem in the fifth

---

11:4
[a] 2Ch 28:8-11

11:14
[b] Nu 35:2-5
[c] 2Ch 13:9

11:15
[d] 1Ki 13:33
[e] 1Ki 12:31
[f] Lev 17:7
[g] 1Ki 12:28; 2Ch 13:8

11:16
[h] 2Ch 15:9

11:17
[i] 2Ch 12:1

11:20
[j] 1Ki 15:2
[k] 2Ch 13:2

11:21
[l] Dt 17:17

11:22
[m] Dt 21:15-17

12:1
[n] ver 13
[o] 2Ch 11:17

12:2
[p] 1Ki 14:22-24
[q] 1Ki 11:40

---

[a] 1 That is, Judah, as frequently in 2 Chronicles

12:3
a 2Ch 16:8;
Na 3:9

12:4
b 2Ch 11:10

12:5
c 2Ch 11:2
d Dt 28:15;
2Ch 15:2

12:6
e Ex 9:27;
Da 9:14

12:7
f 1Ki 21:29;
Ps 78:38

12:8
g Dt 28:48

12:9
h 2Ch 9:16

12:12
i 1Ki 14:13;
2Ch 19:3

12:13
j Dt 12:5;
2Ch 6:6

12:15
k 2Ch 9:29; 11:2

12:16
l 2Ch 11:20

year of King Rehoboam. ³With twelve hundred chariots and sixty thousand horsemen and the innumerable troops of Libyans, Sukkites and Cushites*ᵃ* that came with him from Egypt, ⁴he captured the fortified cities*ᵇ* of Judah and came as far as Jerusalem.

⁵Then the prophet Shemaiah*ᶜ* came to Rehoboam and to the leaders of Judah who had assembled in Jerusalem for fear of Shishak, and he said to them, "This is what the LORD says, 'You have abandoned me; therefore, I now abandon*ᵈ* you to Shishak.'"

⁶The leaders of Israel and the king humbled themselves and said, "The LORD is just."*ᵉ*

⁷When the LORD saw that they humbled themselves, this word of the LORD came to Shemaiah: "Since they have humbled themselves, I will not destroy them but will soon give them deliverance.*ᶠ* My wrath will not be poured out on Jerusalem through Shishak. ⁸They will, however, become subject*ᵍ* to him, so that they may learn the difference between serving me and serving the kings of other lands."

⁹When Shishak king of Egypt attacked Jerusalem, he carried off the treasures of the temple of the LORD and the treasures of the royal palace. He took everything, including the gold shields*ʰ* Solomon had made. ¹⁰So King Rehoboam made bronze shields to replace them and assigned these to the commanders of the guard on duty at the entrance to the royal palace. ¹¹Whenever the king went to the LORD's temple, the guards went with him, bearing the shields, and afterward they returned them to the guardroom.

¹²Because Rehoboam humbled himself, the LORD's anger turned from him, and he was not totally destroyed. Indeed, there was some good*ⁱ* in Judah.

¹³King Rehoboam established himself firmly in Jerusalem and continued as king. He was forty-one years old when he became king, and he reigned seventeen years in Jerusalem, the city the LORD had chosen out of all the tribes of Israel in which to put his Name.*ʲ* His mother's name was Naamah; she was an Ammonite. ¹⁴He did evil because he had not set his heart on seeking the LORD.

¹⁵As for the events of Rehoboam's reign, from beginning to end, are they not written in the records of Shemaiah*ᵏ* the prophet and of Iddo the seer that deal with genealogies? There was continual warfare between Rehoboam and Jeroboam. ¹⁶Rehoboam rested with his fathers and was buried in the City of David. And Abijah*ˡ* his son succeeded him as king.

Chapter 13 Theme

13 In the eighteenth year of the reign of Jeroboam, Abijah became king of Judah, ²and he reigned in Jerusalem three

a 3 That is, people from the upper Nile region

years. His mother's name was Maacah,[a] a daughter[b] of Uriel of Gibeah.

There was war between Abijah[a] and Jeroboam.[b] ³Abijah went into battle with a force of four hundred thousand able fighting men, and Jeroboam drew up a battle line against him with eight hundred thousand able troops.

⁴Abijah stood on Mount Zemaraim,[c] in the hill country of Ephraim, and said, "Jeroboam and all Israel,[d] listen to me! ⁵Don't you know that the LORD, the God of Israel, has given the kingship of Israel to David and his descendants forever[e] by a covenant of salt?[f] ⁶Yet Jeroboam son of Nebat, an official of Solomon son of David, rebelled[g] against his master. ⁷Some worthless scoundrels[h] gathered around him and opposed Rehoboam son of Solomon when he was young and indecisive and not strong enough to resist them.

⁸"And now you plan to resist the kingdom of the LORD, which is in the hands of David's descendants. You are indeed a vast army and have with you the golden calves[i] that Jeroboam made to be your gods. ⁹But didn't you drive out the priests of the LORD,[j] the sons of Aaron, and the Levites, and make priests of your own as the peoples of other lands do? Whoever comes to consecrate himself with a young bull[k] and seven rams may become a priest of what are not gods.[l]

¹⁰"As for us, the LORD is our God, and we have not forsaken him. The priests who serve the LORD are sons of Aaron, and the Levites assist them. ¹¹Every morning and evening[m] they present burnt offerings and fragrant incense to the LORD. They set out the bread on the ceremonially clean table[n] and light the lamps on the gold lampstand every evening. We are observing the requirements of the LORD our God. But you have forsaken him. ¹²God is with us; he is our leader. His priests with their trumpets will sound the battle cry against you.[o] Men of Israel, do not fight against the LORD,[p] the God of your fathers, for you will not succeed."

¹³Now Jeroboam had sent troops around to the rear, so that while he was in front of Judah the ambush[q] was behind them. ¹⁴Judah turned and saw that they were being attacked at both front and rear. Then they cried out[r] to the LORD. The priests blew their trumpets ¹⁵and the men of Judah raised the battle cry. At the sound of their battle cry, God routed Jeroboam and all Israel[s] before Abijah and Judah. ¹⁶The Israelites fled before Judah, and God delivered[t] them into their hands. ¹⁷Abijah and his men inflicted heavy losses on them, so that there were five hundred thousand casualties among Israel's able men. ¹⁸The men of Israel were subdued on that occasion, and the men of Judah were victorious because they relied[u] on the LORD, the God of their fathers.

ᵃ2 Most Septuagint manuscripts and Syriac (see also 2 Chron. 11:20 and 1 Kings 15:2); Hebrew *Micaiah* ᵇ2 Or *granddaughter*

13:2
ᵃ2Ch 11:20
ᵇ1Ki 15:6

13:4
ᶜJos 18:22
ᵈ1Ch 11:1

13:5
ᵉ2Sa 7:13
ᶠLev 2:13
Nu 18:19

13:6
ᵍ1Ki 11:26

13:7
ʰJdg 9:4

13:8
ⁱ1Ki 12:28
2Ch 11:15

13:9
ʲ2Ch 11:14-15
ᵏEx 29:35-36
ˡJer 2:11

13:11
ᵐEx 29:39
2Ch 2:4
ⁿ2Lev 24:5-9

13:12
ᵒNu 10:8-9
ᵖAc 5:39

13:13
�q Jos 8:9

13:14
ʳ2Ch 14:11

13:15
ˢ2Ch 14:12

13:16
ᵗ2Ch 16:8

13:18
ᵘ1Ch 5:20;
2Ch 14:11;
Ps 22:5

¹⁹Abijah pursued Jeroboam and took from him the towns of Bethel, Jeshanah and Ephron, with their surrounding villages. ²⁰Jeroboam did not regain power during the time of Abijah. And the LORD struck him down and he died.

²¹But Abijah grew in strength. He married fourteen wives and had twenty-two sons and sixteen daughters.

²²The other events of Abijah's reign, what he did and what he said, are written in the annotations of the prophet Iddo.

Chapter 14 Theme

14 And Abijah rested with his fathers and was buried in the City of David. Asa his son succeeded him as king, and in his days the country was at peace for ten years.

²Asa did what was good and right in the eyes of the LORD his God. ³He removed the foreign altars and the high places, smashed the sacred stones and cut down the Asherah poles.ᵃᵃ ⁴He commanded Judah to seek the LORD, the God of their fathers, and to obey his laws and commands. ⁵He removed the high places and incense altarsᵇ in every town in Judah, and the kingdom was at peace under him. ⁶He built up the fortified cities of Judah, since the land was at peace. No one was at war with him during those years, for the LORD gave him rest.ᶜ

⁷"Let us build up these towns," he said to Judah, "and put walls around them, with towers, gates and bars. The land is still ours, because we have sought the LORD our God; we sought him and he has given us rest on every side." So they built and prospered.

⁸Asa had an army of three hundred thousand men from Judah, equipped with large shields and with spears, and two hundred and eighty thousand from Benjamin, armed with small shields and with bows. All these were brave fighting men.

⁹Zerah the Cushiteᵈ marched out against them with a vast armyᵇ and three hundred chariots, and came as far as Mareshah.ᵉ ¹⁰Asa went out to meet him, and they took up battle positions in the Valley of Zephathah near Mareshah.

¹¹Then Asa calledᶠ to the LORD his God and said, "LORD, there is no one like you to help the powerless against the mighty. Help us, O LORD our God, for we relyᵍ on you, and in your nameʰ we have come against this vast army. O LORD, you are our God; do not let man prevailⁱ against you."

¹²The LORD struck downʲ the Cushites before Asa and Judah. The Cushites fled, ¹³and Asa and his army pursued them as far as Gerar.ᵏ Such a great number of Cushites fell that they could not

14:3 ᵃEx 34:13; Dt 7:5; 1Ki 15:12-14

14:5 ᵇ2Ch 34:4,7

14:6 ᶜ1Ch 22:9; 2Ch 15:15

14:9 ᵈ2Ch 12:3; 16:8 ᵉ2Ch 11:8

14:11 ᶠ2Ch 13:14 ᵍ2Ch 13:18 ʰ1Sa 17:45 ⁱ1Sa 14:6; Ps 9:19

14:12 ʲ2Ch 13:15

14:13 ᵏGe 10:19

ᵃ3 That is, symbols of the goddess Asherah; here and elsewhere in 2 Chronicles   ᵇ9 Hebrew *with an army of a thousand thousands* or *with an army of thousands upon thousands* recover; they were crushed before the LORD and his forces. The men of Judah carried off a large amount of plunder. ¹⁴They destroyed all the villages around Gerar, for the terror[a] of the LORD had fallen upon them. They plundered all these villages, since there was much booty there. ¹⁵They also attacked the camps of the herdsmen and carried off droves of sheep and goats and camels. Then they returned to Jerusalem.

Chapter 15 Theme

15 The Spirit of God came upon[b] Azariah son of Oded. ²He went out to meet Asa and said to him, "Listen to me, Asa and all Judah and Benjamin. The LORD is with you[c] when you are with him.[d] If you seek[e] him, he will be found by you, but if you forsake him, he will forsake you.[f] ³For a long time Israel was without the true God, without a priest to teach[g] and without the law.[h] ⁴But in their distress they turned to the LORD, the God of Israel, and sought him,[i] and he was found by them. ⁵In those days it was not safe to travel about,[j] for all the inhabitants of the lands were in great turmoil. ⁶One nation was being crushed by another and one city by another,[k] because God was troubling them with every kind of distress. ⁷But as for you, be strong[l] and do not give up, for your work will be rewarded."[m]

⁸When Asa heard these words and the prophecy of Azariah son of[a] Oded the prophet, he took courage. He removed the detestable idols from the whole land of Judah and Benjamin and from the towns he had captured[n] in the hills of Ephraim. He repaired the altar[o] of the LORD that was in front of the portico of the LORD's temple.

⁹Then he assembled all Judah and Benjamin and the people from Ephraim, Manasseh and Simeon who had settled among them, for large numbers[p] had come over to him from Israel when they saw that the LORD his God was with him.

¹⁰They assembled at Jerusalem in the third month of the fifteenth year of Asa's reign. ¹¹At that time they sacrificed to the LORD seven hundred head of cattle and seven thousand sheep and goats from the plunder[q] they had brought back. ¹²They entered into a covenant[r] to seek the LORD,[s] the God of their fathers, with all their heart and soul. ¹³All who would not seek the LORD, the God of Israel, were to be put to death,[t] whether small or great, man or woman. ¹⁴They took an oath to the LORD with loud acclamation, with shouting and with trumpets and horns. ¹⁵All Judah rejoiced about the oath because they had sworn it wholeheartedly. They sought God[u] eagerly, and he was found by them. So the LORD gave them rest[v] on every side.

a8 Vulgate and Syriac (see also Septuagint and verse 1); Hebrew does not have *Azariah son of*.

14:14
a Ge 35:5;
2Ch 17:10

15:1
b Nu 11:25,26;
24:2;
2Ch 20:14;
24:20

15:2
c ver 4,15;
2Ch 20:17
d Jas 4:8
e Jer 29:13
f 1Ch 28:9;
2Ch 24:20

15:3
g Lev 10:11
h 2Ch 17:9;
La 2:9

15:4
i Dt 4:29

15:5
j Jdg 5:6

15:6
k Mt 24:7

15:7
l Jos 1:7,9
m Ps 58:11

15:8
n 2Ch 13:19
o 2Ch 8:12

15:9
p 2Ch 11:16-17

15:11
q 2Ch 14:13

15:12
r 2Ki 11:17;
2Ch 23:16;
34:31
s 1Ch 16:11

15:13
t Ex 22:20;
Dt 13:9-16

15:15
u Dt 4:29
v 1Ch 22:9;
2Ch 14:7

15:16
a Ex 34:13;
2Ch 14:2-5

[16] King Asa also deposed his grandmother Maacah from her position as queen mother, because she had made a repulsive Asherah pole.*a* Asa cut the pole down, broke it up and burned it in the Kidron Valley. [17] Although he did not remove the high places from Israel, Asa's heart was fully committed ⌊to the LORD⌋ all his life. [18] He brought into the temple of God the silver and gold and the articles that he and his father had dedicated.

[19] There was no more war until the thirty-fifth year of Asa's reign.

Chapter 16 Theme _____

16:1
b Jer 41:9

16 In the thirty-sixth year of Asa's reign Baasha*b* king of Israel went up against Judah and fortified Ramah to prevent anyone from leaving or entering the territory of Asa king of Judah.

[2] Asa then took the silver and gold out of the treasuries of the LORD's temple and of his own palace and sent it to Ben-Hadad king of Aram, who was ruling in Damascus. [3] "Let there be a treaty*c* between me and you," he said, "as there was between my father and your father. See, I am sending you silver and gold. Now break your treaty with Baasha king of Israel so he will withdraw from me."

16:3
c 2Ch 20:35

[4] Ben-Hadad agreed with King Asa and sent the commanders of his forces against the towns of Israel. They conquered Ijon, Dan, Abel Maim*a* and all the store cities of Naphtali. [5] When Baasha heard this, he stopped building Ramah and abandoned his work. [6] Then King Asa brought all the men of Judah, and they carried away from Ramah the stones and timber Baasha had been using. With them he built up Geba and Mizpah.

16:7
d 1Ki 16:1

[7] At that time Hanani*d* the seer came to Asa king of Judah and said to him: "Because you relied on the king of Aram and not on the LORD your God, the army of the king of Aram has escaped from your hand. [8] Were not the Cushites*be* and Libyans a mighty army with great numbers of chariots and horsemen*c*? Yet when you relied on the LORD, he delivered*f* them into your hand. [9] For the eyes*g* of the LORD range throughout the earth to strengthen those whose hearts are fully committed to him. You have done a foolish*h* thing, and from now on you will be at war."

16:8
e 2Ch 12:3; 14:9
f 2Ch 13:16

[10] Asa was angry with the seer because of this; he was so enraged that he put him in prison. At the same time Asa brutally oppressed some of the people.

[11] The events of Asa's reign, from beginning to end, are written in the book of the kings of Judah and Israel. [12] In the thirty-ninth year of his reign Asa was afflicted with a disease in his feet. Though his disease was severe, even in his illness he did not seek help from the

16:9
g Pr 15:3;
Jer 16:17;
Zec 4:10
h 1Sa 13:13

a 4 Also known as *Abel Beth Maacah*   b 8 That is, people from the upper Nile region
c 8 Or *charioteers*

LORD,[a] but only from the physicians. [13]Then in the forty-first year of his reign Asa died and rested with his fathers. [14]They buried him in the tomb that he had cut out for himself in the City of David. They laid him on a bier covered with spices and various blended perfumes,[b] and they made a huge fire[c] in his honor.

Chapter 17 Theme

17 Jehoshaphat his son succeeded him as king and strengthened himself against Israel. [2]He stationed troops in all the fortified cities of Judah and put garrisons in Judah and in the towns of Ephraim that his father Asa had captured.[d]

[3]The LORD was with Jehoshaphat because in his early years he walked in the ways his father David[e] had followed. He did not consult the Baals [4]but sought[f] the God of his father and followed his commands rather than the practices of Israel. [5]The LORD established the kingdom under his control; and all Judah brought gifts[g] to Jehoshaphat, so that he had great wealth and honor.[h] [6]His heart was devoted[i] to the ways of the LORD; furthermore, he removed the high places[j] and the Asherah poles[k] from Judah.[l]

[7]In the third year of his reign he sent his officials Ben-Hail, Obadiah, Zechariah, Nethanel and Micaiah to teach[m] in the towns of Judah. [8]With them were certain Levites[n]—Shemaiah, Nethaniah, Zebadiah, Asahel, Shemiramoth, Jehonathan, Adonijah, Tobijah and Tob-Adonijah—and the priests Elishama and Jehoram. [9]They taught throughout Judah, taking with them the Book of the Law[o] of the LORD; they went around to all the towns of Judah and taught the people.

[10]The fear[p] of the LORD fell on all the kingdoms of the lands surrounding Judah, so that they did not make war with Jehoshaphat. [11]Some Philistines brought Jehoshaphat gifts and silver as tribute, and the Arabs[q] brought him flocks:[r] seven thousand seven hundred rams and seven thousand seven hundred goats.

[12]Jehoshaphat became more and more powerful; he built forts and store cities in Judah [13]and had large supplies in the towns of Judah. He also kept experienced fighting men in Jerusalem. [14]Their enrollment[s] by families was as follows:

From Judah, commanders of units of 1,000:
Adnah the commander, with 300,000 fighting men;
[15]next, Jehohanan the commander, with 280,000;
[16]next, Amasiah son of Zicri, who volunteered[t] himself for the service of the LORD, with 200,000.
[17]From Benjamin:[u]
Eliada, a valiant soldier, with 200,000 men armed with bows and shields;
[18]next, Jehozabad, with 180,000 men armed for battle.

16:12 a Jer 17:5-6
16:14 b Ge 50:2; Jn 19:39-40 c 2Ch 21:19; Jer 34:5
17:2 d 2Ch 15:8
17:3 e 1Ki 22:43
17:4 f 1Ki 12:28; 2Ch 22:9
17:5 g 1Sa 10:27 h 2Ch 18:1
17:6 i 1Ki 8:61; 2Ch 15:17 j 1Ki 15:14; 2Ch 19:3; 20:33 k Ex 34:13 l 2Ch 21:12
17:7 m Lev 10:11; Dt 6:4-9; 2Ch 15:3; 35:3
17:8 n 2Ch 19:8; Ne 8:7-8
17:9 o Dt 6:4-9; 28:61
17:10 p Ge 35:5; Dt 2:25; 2Ch 14:14
17:11 q 2Ch 9:14; 26:8 r 2Ch 21:16
17:14 s 2Sa 24:2
17:16 t Jdg 5:9; 1Ch 29:9
17:17 u Nu 1:36

17:19
a 2Ch 11:10
b 2Ch 25:5

[19]These were the men who served the king, besides those he stationed in the fortified cities*a* throughout Judah.*b*

Chapter 18 Theme

18 Now Jehoshaphat had great wealth and honor,*c* and he allied*d* himself with Ahab*e* by marriage. [2]Some years later he went down to visit Ahab in Samaria. Ahab slaughtered many sheep and cattle for him and the people with him and urged him to attack Ramoth Gilead. [3]Ahab king of Israel asked Jehoshaphat king of Judah, "Will you go with me against Ramoth Gilead?"

Jehoshaphat replied, "I am as you are, and my people as your people; we will join you in the war." [4]But Jehoshaphat also said to the king of Israel, "First seek the counsel of the LORD."

18:1
c 2Ch 17:5
d 2Ch 19:1-3;
22:3
e 2Ch 21:6

[5]So the king of Israel brought together the prophets—four hundred men—and asked them, "Shall we go to war against Ramoth Gilead, or shall I refrain?"

"Go," they answered, "for God will give it into the king's hand."

[6]But Jehoshaphat asked, "Is there not a prophet of the LORD here whom we can inquire of?"

[7]The king of Israel answered Jehoshaphat, "There is still one man through whom we can inquire of the LORD, but I hate him because he never prophesies anything good about me, but always bad. He is Micaiah son of Imlah."

"The king should not say that," Jehoshaphat replied.

[8]So the king of Israel called one of his officials and said, "Bring Micaiah son of Imlah at once."

[9]Dressed in their royal robes, the king of Israel and Jehoshaphat king of Judah were sitting on their thrones at the threshing floor by the entrance to the gate of Samaria, with all the prophets prophesying before them. [10]Now Zedekiah son of Kenaanah had made iron horns, and he declared, "This is what the LORD says: 'With these you will gore the Arameans until they are destroyed.'"

18:11
f 2Ch 22:5

[11]All the other prophets were prophesying the same thing. "Attack Ramoth Gilead*f* and be victorious," they said, "for the LORD will give it into the king's hand."

[12]The messenger who had gone to summon Micaiah said to him, "Look, as one man the other prophets are predicting success for the king. Let your word agree with theirs, and speak favorably."

[13]But Micaiah said, "As surely as the LORD lives, I can tell him only what my God says."*g*

[14]When he arrived, the king asked him, "Micaiah, shall we go to war against Ramoth Gilead, or shall I refrain?"

"Attack and be victorious," he answered, "for they will be given into your hand."

18:13
g Nu 22:18,
20,35

[15]The king said to him, "How many times must I make you swear to tell me nothing but the truth in the name of the LORD?"

¹⁶Then Micaiah answered, "I saw all Israel*a* scattered on the hills like sheep without a shepherd,*b* and the LORD said, 'These people have no master. Let each one go home in peace.'"

¹⁷The king of Israel said to Jehoshaphat, "Didn't I tell you that he never prophesies anything good about me, but only bad?"

¹⁸Micaiah continued, "Therefore hear the word of the LORD: I saw the LORD sitting on his throne*c* with all the host of heaven standing on his right and on his left. ¹⁹And the LORD said, 'Who will entice Ahab king of Israel into attacking Ramoth Gilead and going to his death there?'

"One suggested this, and another that. ²⁰Finally, a spirit came forward, stood before the LORD and said, 'I will entice him.'

"'By what means?' the LORD asked.

²¹"'I will go and be a lying spirit*d* in the mouths of all his prophets,' he said.

"'You will succeed in enticing him,' said the LORD. 'Go and do it.'

²²"So now the LORD has put a lying spirit in the mouths of these prophets of yours.*e* The LORD has decreed disaster for you."

²³Then Zedekiah son of Kenaanah went up and slapped*f* Micaiah in the face. "Which way did the spirit from*a* the LORD go when he went from me to speak to you?" he asked.

²⁴Micaiah replied, "You will find out on the day you go to hide in an inner room."

²⁵The king of Israel then ordered, "Take Micaiah and send him back to Amon the ruler of the city and to Joash the king's son, ²⁶and say, 'This is what the king says: Put this fellow in prison*g* and give him nothing but bread and water until I return safely.'"

²⁷Micaiah declared, "If you ever return safely, the LORD has not spoken through me." Then he added, "Mark my words, all you people!"

²⁸So the king of Israel and Jehoshaphat king of Judah went up to Ramoth Gilead. ²⁹The king of Israel said to Jehoshaphat, "I will enter the battle in disguise, but you wear your royal robes." So the king of Israel disguised*h* himself and went into battle.

³⁰Now the king of Aram had ordered his chariot commanders, "Do not fight with anyone, small or great, except the king of Israel." ³¹When the chariot commanders saw Jehoshaphat, they thought, "This is the king of Israel." So they turned to attack him, but Jehoshaphat cried out,*i* and the LORD helped him. God drew them away from him, ³²for when the chariot commanders saw that he was not the king of Israel, they stopped pursuing him.

³³But someone drew his bow at random and hit the king of Israel between the sections of his armor. The king told the chariot driver, "Wheel around and get me out of the fighting. I've been

a 23 Or Spirit of

18:16
a 1Ch 9:1
b Nu 27:17;
Eze 34:5-8

18:18
c Da 7:9

18:21
d 1Ch 21:1;
Job 1:6;
Zec 3:1;
Jn 8:44

18:22
e Job 12:16;
Isa 19:14;
Eze 14:9

18:23
f Jer 20:2;
Mk 14:65;
Ac 23:2

18:26
g 2Ch 16:10;
Heb 11:36

18:29
h 1Sa 28:8

18:31
i 2Ch 13:14

18:34
a 2Ch 22:5

19:2
b 1Ki 16:1
c 2Ch 16:2-9
d Ps 139:21-22
e 2Ch 24:18;
32:25; Ps 7:11

19:3
f 1Ki 14:13;
2Ch 12:12
g 2Ch 17:6
h 2Ch 18:1;
20:35; 25:7;
Ezr 7:10

19:5
i Ge 47:6;
Ex 18:26

19:6
j Lev 19:15
k Dt 1:17;
16:18-20;
17:8-13

19:7
l Ge 18:25;
Dt 32:4
m Dt 10:17;
Job 34:19;
Ro 2:11;
Col 3:25

19:8
n 2Ch 17:8-9

19:10
o Dt 17:8-13

19:11
p 1Ch 28:20

20:1
q 1Ch 4:41

wounded." ³⁴All day long the battle raged, and the king of Israel propped himself up in his chariot facing the Arameans until evening. Then at sunset he died.ᵃ

Chapter 19 Theme _____

19 When Jehoshaphat king of Judah returned safely to his palace in Jerusalem, ²Jehuᵇ the seer, the son of Hanani, went out to meet him and said to the king, "Should you help the wickedᶜ and loveᵃ those who hate the Lord?ᵈ Because of this, the wrathᵉ of the Lord is upon you. ³There is, however, some goodᶠ in you, for you have rid the land of the Asherah polesᵍ and have set your heart on seeking God.ʰ"

⁴Jehoshaphat lived in Jerusalem, and he went out again among the people from Beersheba to the hill country of Ephraim and turned them back to the Lord, the God of their fathers. ⁵He appointed judgesⁱ in the land, in each of the fortified cities of Judah. ⁶He told them, "Consider carefully what you do,ʲ because you are not judging for manᵏ but for the Lord, who is with you whenever you give a verdict. ⁷Now let the fear of the Lord be upon you. Judge carefully, for with the Lord our God there is no injusticeˡ or partialityᵐ or bribery."

⁸In Jerusalem also, Jehoshaphat appointed some of the Levites, priests and heads of Israelite families to administerⁿ the law of the Lord and to settle disputes. And they lived in Jerusalem. ⁹He gave them these orders: "You must serve faithfully and wholeheartedly in the fear of the Lord. ¹⁰In every case that comes before you from your fellow countrymen who live in the cities—whether bloodshed or other concerns of the law, commands, decrees or ordinances—you are to warn them not to sin against the Lord;ᵒ otherwise his wrath will come on you and your brothers. Do this, and you will not sin.

¹¹"Amariah the chief priest will be over you in any matter concerning the Lord, and Zebadiah son of Ishmael, the leader of the tribe of Judah, will be over you in any matter concerning the king, and the Levites will serve as officials before you. Act with courage,ᵖ and may the Lord be with those who do well."

Chapter 20 Theme _____

20 After this, the Moabites and Ammonites with some of the Meunitesᵇ �q came to make war on Jehoshaphat. ²Some men came and told Jehoshaphat, "A vast army is coming against you from Edom,ᶜ from the other side of the Sea.ᵈ It is

a 2 Or *and make alliances with*   b 1 Some Septuagint manuscripts; Hebrew *Ammonites*
c 2 One Hebrew manuscript; most Hebrew manuscripts, Septuagint and Vulgate *Aram*
d 2 That is, the Dead Sea

already in Hazazon Tamar[a]" (that is, En Gedi). [3]Alarmed, Jehoshaphat resolved to inquire of the LORD, and he proclaimed a fast[b] for all Judah. [4]The people of Judah came together to seek help from the LORD; indeed, they came from every town in Judah to seek him.

[5]Then Jehoshaphat stood up in the assembly of Judah and Jerusalem at the temple of the LORD in the front of the new courtyard [6]and said:

"O LORD, God of our fathers,[c] are you not the God who is in heaven?[d] You rule over all the kingdoms[e] of the nations. Power and might are in your hand, and no one can withstand you. [7]O our God, did you not drive out the inhabitants of this land before your people Israel and give it forever to the descendants of Abraham your friend?[f] [8]They have lived in it and have built in it a sanctuary[g] for your Name, saying, [9]'If calamity comes upon us, whether the sword of judgment, or plague or famine,[h] we will stand in your presence before this temple that bears your Name and will cry out to you in our distress, and you will hear us and save us.'

[10]"But now here are men from Ammon, Moab and Mount Seir, whose territory you would not allow Israel to invade when they came from Egypt;[i] so they turned away from them and did not destroy them. [11]See how they are repaying us by coming to drive us out of the possession[j] you gave us as an inheritance. [12]O our God, will you not judge them?[k] For we have no power to face this vast army that is attacking us. We do not know what to do, but our eyes are upon you.[l]"

[13]All the men of Judah, with their wives and children and little ones, stood there before the LORD.

[14]Then the Spirit[m] of the LORD came upon Jahaziel son of Zechariah, the son of Benaiah, the son of Jeiel, the son of Mattaniah, a Levite and descendant of Asaph, as he stood in the assembly.

[15]He said: "Listen, King Jehoshaphat and all who live in Judah and Jerusalem! This is what the LORD says to you: 'Do not be afraid or discouraged[n] because of this vast army. For the battle[o] is not yours, but God's. [16]Tomorrow march down against them. They will be climbing up by the Pass of Ziz, and you will find them at the end of the gorge in the Desert of Jeruel. [17]You will not have to fight this battle. Take up your positions; stand firm and see[p] the deliverance the LORD will give you, O Judah and Jerusalem. Do not be afraid; do not be discouraged. Go out to face them tomorrow, and the LORD will be with you.'"

[18]Jehoshaphat bowed[q] with his face to the ground, and all the people of Judah and Jerusalem fell down in worship before the LORD. [19]Then some Levites from the Kohathites and Korahites

20:2
[a] Ge 14:7

20:3
[b] 1Sa 7:6;
2Ch 19:3;
Ezr 8:21;
Jer 36:9;
Jnh 3:5,7

20:6
[c] Mt 6:9
[d] Dt 4:39
[e] 1Ch 29:11-12

20:7
[f] Isa 41:8;
Jas 2:23

20:8
[g] 2Ch 6:20

20:9
[h] 2Ch 6:28

20:10
[i] Nu 20:14-21;
Dt 2:4-6,9,
18-19

20:11
[j] Ps 83:1-12

20:12
[k] Jdg 11:27
[l] Ps 25:15;
121:1-2

20:14
[m] 2Ch 15:1

20:15
[n] 2Ch 32:7
[o] Ex 14:13-14;
1Sa 17:47

20:17
[p] Ex 14:13;
2Ch 15:2

20:18
[q] Ex 4:31

20:20
a Isa 7:9
b Ge 39:3;
Pr 16:3

stood up and praised the LORD, the God of Israel, with very loud voice.

²⁰Early in the morning they left for the Desert of Tekoa. As they set out, Jehoshaphat stood and said, "Listen to me, Judah and people of Jerusalem! Have faith*ᵃ* in the LORD your God and you will be upheld; have faith in his prophets and you will be successful.*ᵇ*" ²¹After consulting the people, Jehoshaphat appointed men to sing to the LORD and to praise him for the splendor of his*ᵃ* holiness*ᶜ* as they went out at the head of the army, saying:

20:21
c 1Ch 16:29;
Ps 29:2
d 2Ch 5:13;
Ps 136:1

> "Give thanks to the LORD,
>   for his love endures forever."*ᵈ*

²²As they began to sing and praise, the LORD set ambushes*ᵉ* against the men of Ammon and Moab and Mount Seir who were invading Judah, and they were defeated. ²³The men of Ammon*ᶠ* and Moab rose up against the men from Mount Seir*ᵍ* to destroy and annihilate them. After they finished slaughtering the men from Seir, they helped to destroy one another.*ʰ*

20:22
e Jdg 7:22;
2Ch 13:13

20:23
f Ge 19:38
g 2Ch 21:8
h Jdg 7:22;
1Sa 14:20;
Eze 38:21

²⁴When the men of Judah came to the place that overlooks the desert and looked toward the vast army, they saw only dead bodies lying on the ground; no one had escaped. ²⁵So Jehoshaphat and his men went to carry off their plunder, and they found among them a great amount of equipment and clothing*ᵇ* and also articles of value—more than they could take away. There was so much plunder that it took three days to collect it. ²⁶On the fourth day they assembled in the Valley of Beracah, where they praised the LORD. This is why it is called the Valley of Beracah*ᶜ* to this day.

²⁷Then, led by Jehoshaphat, all the men of Judah and Jerusalem returned joyfully to Jerusalem, for the LORD had given them cause to rejoice over their enemies. ²⁸They entered Jerusalem and went to the temple of the LORD with harps and lutes and trumpets.

20:29
i Ge 35:5;
Dt 2:25;
2Ch 14:14; 17:10
j Ex 14:14

²⁹The fear*ⁱ* of God came upon all the kingdoms of the countries when they heard how the LORD had fought*ʲ* against the enemies of Israel. ³⁰And the kingdom of Jehoshaphat was at peace, for his God had given him rest*ᵏ* on every side.

20:30
k 1Ch 22:9;
2Ch 14:6-7;
15:15

³¹So Jehoshaphat reigned over Judah. He was thirty-five years old when he became king of Judah, and he reigned in Jerusalem twenty-five years. His mother's name was Azubah daughter of Shilhi. ³²He walked in the ways of his father Asa and did not stray from them; he did what was right in the eyes of the LORD. ³³The high places,*ˡ* however, were not removed, and the people still had not set their hearts on the God of their fathers.

20:33
l 2Ch 17:6;
19:3

a 21 Or *him with the splendor of*   *b 25* Some Hebrew manuscripts and Vulgate; most Hebrew manuscripts *corpses*   *c 26* *Beracah* means *praise.*

³⁴The other events of Jehoshaphat's reign, from beginning to end, are written in the annals of Jehuᵃ son of Hanani, which are recorded in the book of the kings of Israel.

³⁵Later, Jehoshaphat king of Judah made an allianceᵇ with Ahaziah king of Israel, who was guilty of wickedness.ᶜ ³⁶He agreed with him to construct a fleet of trading ships.ᵃ After these were built at Ezion Geber, ³⁷Eliezer son of Dodavahu of Mareshah prophesied against Jehoshaphat, saying, "Because you have made an alliance with Ahaziah, the LORD will destroy what you have made." The shipsᵈ were wrecked and were not able to set sail to trade.ᵇ

Chapter 21 Theme

21 Then Jehoshaphat rested with his fathers and was buried with them in the City of David. And Jehoramᵉ his son succeeded him as king. ²Jehoram's brothers, the sons of Jehoshaphat, were Azariah, Jehiel, Zechariah, Azariahu, Michael and Shephatiah. All these were sons of Jehoshaphat king of Israel.ᶜ ³Their father had given them many giftsᶠ of silver and gold and articles of value, as well as fortified citiesᵍ in Judah, but he had given the kingdom to Jehoram because he was his firstborn son.

⁴When Jehoram establishedʰ himself firmly over his father's kingdom, he put all his brothersⁱ to the sword along with some of the princes of Israel. ⁵Jehoram was thirty-two years old when he became king, and he reigned in Jerusalem eight years. ⁶He walked in the ways of the kings of Israel,ʲ as the house of Ahab had done, for he married a daughter of Ahab.ᵏ He did evil in the eyes of the LORD. ⁷Nevertheless, because of the covenant the LORD had made with David,ˡ the LORD was not willing to destroy the house of David.ᵐ He had promised to maintain a lampⁿ for him and his descendants forever.

⁸In the time of Jehoram, Edomᵒ rebelled against Judah and set up its own king. ⁹So Jehoram went there with his officers and all his chariots. The Edomites surrounded him and his chariot commanders, but he rose up and broke through by night. ¹⁰To this day Edom has been in rebellion against Judah.

Libnahᵖ revolted at the same time, because Jehoram had forsaken the LORD, the God of his fathers. ¹¹He had also built high places on the hills of Judah and had caused the people of Jerusalem to prostitute themselves and had led Judah astray.

¹²Jehoram received a letter from Elijahᑫ the prophet, which said:

"This is what the LORD, the God of your fatherʳ David, says: 'You have not walked in the ways of your father Jehoshaphat or

20:34	ᵃ 1Ki 16:1
20:35	ᵇ 2Ch 16:3 ᶜ 2Ch 19:1-3
20:37	ᵈ 1Ki 9:26; 2Ch 9:21
21:1	ᵉ 1Ch 3:11
21:3	ᶠ 2Ch 11:23 ᵍ 2Ch 11:10
21:4	ʰ 1Ki 2:12 ⁱ Jdg 9:5
21:6	ʲ 1Ki 12:28-30 ᵏ 2Ch 18:1; 22:3
21:7	ˡ 2Sa 7:13 ᵐ 2Sa 7:15; 2Ch 23:3 ⁿ 2Sa 21:17; 1Ki 11:36
21:8	ᵒ 2Ch 20:22-23
21:10	ᵖ Nu 33:20
21:12	ᑫ 2Ki 1:16-17 ʳ 2Ch 17:3-6

ᵃ 36 Hebrew *of ships that could go to Tarshish*   ᵇ 37 Hebrew *sail for Tarshish*   ᶜ 2 That is, Judah, as frequently in 2 Chronicles

21:12
a 2Ch 14:2

21:13
b ver 6,11;
1Ki 16:29-33
c ver 4;
1Ki 2:32

21:15
d ver 18-19;
Nu 12:10

21:16
e 2Ch 17:10-11;
22:1; 26:7

21:17
f 2Ki 12:18;
2Ch 22:1;
25:23;
Joel 3:5

21:19
g 2Ch 16:14

21:20
h 2Ch 24:25;
28:27; 33:20;
Jer 22:18,28

22:1
i 2Ch 33:25; 36:1
j 2Ch 23:20-21;
26:1
k 2Ch 21:16-17

22:3
l 2Ch 18:1
m 2Ch 21:6

22:5
n 2Ch 18:11,34

22:6
o 1Ki 19:15;
2Ki 8:13-15;
9:15

of Asa*a* king of Judah. ¹³But you have walked in the ways of the kings of Israel, and you have led Judah and the people of Jerusalem to prostitute themselves, just as the house of Ahab did.*b* You have also murdered your own brothers, members of your father's house, men who were better*c* than you. ¹⁴So now the LORD is about to strike your people, your sons, your wives and everything that is yours, with a heavy blow. ¹⁵You yourself will be very ill with a lingering disease*d* of the bowels, until the disease causes your bowels to come out.'"

¹⁶The LORD aroused against Jehoram the hostility of the Philistines and of the Arabs*e* who lived near the Cushites. ¹⁷They attacked Judah, invaded it and carried off all the goods found in the king's palace, together with his sons and wives. Not a son was left to him except Ahaziah,*a* the youngest.*f*

¹⁸After all this, the LORD afflicted Jehoram with an incurable disease of the bowels. ¹⁹In the course of time, at the end of the second year, his bowels came out because of the disease, and he died in great pain. His people made no fire in his honor,*g* as they had for his fathers.

²⁰Jehoram was thirty-two years old when he became king, and he reigned in Jerusalem eight years. He passed away, to no one's regret, and was buried*h* in the City of David, but not in the tombs of the kings.

Chapter 22 Theme

22 The people*i* of Jerusalem*j* made Ahaziah, Jehoram's youngest son, king in his place, since the raiders,*k* who came with the Arabs into the camp, had killed all the older sons. So Ahaziah son of Jehoram king of Judah began to reign.

²Ahaziah was twenty-two*b* years old when he became king, and he reigned in Jerusalem one year. His mother's name was Athaliah, a granddaughter of Omri.

³He too walked*l* in the ways of the house of Ahab,*m* for his mother encouraged him in doing wrong. ⁴He did evil in the eyes of the LORD, as the house of Ahab had done, for after his father's death they became his advisers, to his undoing. ⁵He also followed their counsel when he went with Joram*c* son of Ahab king of Israel to war against Hazael king of Aram at Ramoth Gilead.*n* The Arameans wounded Joram; ⁶so he returned to Jezreel to recover from the wounds they had inflicted on him at Ramoth*d* in his battle with Hazael*o* king of Aram.

a 17 Hebrew *Jehoahaz*, a variant of *Ahaziah*   b 2 Some Septuagint manuscripts and Syriac (see also 2 Kings 8:26); Hebrew *forty-two*   c 5 Hebrew *Jehoram*, a variant of *Joram*; also in verses 6 and 7   d 6 Hebrew *Ramah*, a variant of *Ramoth*

Then Ahaziah[a] son of Jehoram king of Judah went down to Jezreel to see Joram son of Ahab because he had been wounded.

[7]Through Ahaziah's[a] visit to Joram, God brought about Ahaziah's downfall. When Ahaziah arrived, he went out with Joram to meet Jehu son of Nimshi, whom the LORD had anointed to destroy the house of Ahab. [8]While Jehu was executing judgment on the house of Ahab,[b] he found the princes of Judah and the sons of Ahaziah's relatives, who had been attending Ahaziah, and he killed them. [9]He then went in search of Ahaziah, and his men captured him while he was hiding[c] in Samaria. He was brought to Jehu and put to death. They buried him, for they said, "He was a son of Jehoshaphat, who sought[d] the LORD with all his heart." So there was no one in the house of Ahaziah powerful enough to retain the kingdom.

[10]When Athaliah the mother of Ahaziah saw that her son was dead, she proceeded to destroy the whole royal family of the house of Judah. [11]But Jehosheba,[b] the daughter of King Jehoram, took Joash son of Ahaziah and stole him away from among the royal princes who were about to be murdered and put him and his nurse in a bedroom. Because Jehosheba,[b] the daughter of King Jehoram and wife of the priest Jehoiada, was Ahaziah's sister, she hid the child from Athaliah so she could not kill him. [12]He remained hidden with them at the temple of God for six years while Athaliah ruled the land.

Chapter 23 Theme _____

23 In the seventh year Jehoiada showed his strength. He made a covenant with the commanders of units of a hundred: Azariah son of Jeroham, Ishmael son of Jehohanan, Azariah son of Obed, Maaseiah son of Adaiah, and Elishaphat son of Zicri. [2]They went throughout Judah and gathered the Levites[e] and the heads of Israelite families from all the towns. When they came to Jerusalem, [3]the whole assembly made a covenant[f] with the king at the temple of God.

Jehoiada said to them, "The king's son shall reign, as the LORD promised concerning the descendants of David.[g] [4]Now this is what you are to do: A third of you priests and Levites who are going on duty on the Sabbath are to keep watch at the doors, [5]a third of you at the royal palace and a third at the Foundation Gate, and all the other men are to be in the courtyards of the temple of the LORD. [6]No one is to enter the temple of the LORD except the priests and Levites on duty; they may enter because they are consecrated, but all the other men are to guard[h] what the LORD has assigned to

---

22:7
[a] 2Ki 9:16;
2Ch 10:15

22:8
[b] 2Ki 10:13

22:9
[c] Jdg 9:5
[d] 2Ch 17:4

23:2
[e] Nu 35:2-5

23:3
[f] 2Ki 11:17
[g] 2Sa 7:12;
1Ki 2:4;
2Ch 6:16;
7:18; 21:7

23:6
[h] 1Ch 23:28-29;
Zec 3:7

---

[a]6 Some Hebrew manuscripts, Septuagint, Vulgate and Syriac (see also 2 Kings 8:29); most Hebrew manuscripts *Azariah* [b]11 Hebrew *Jehoshabeath*, a variant of *Jehosheba*

23:8
a 2Ki 11:9
b 1Ch 24:1

them.*a* ⁷The Levites are to station themselves around the king, each man with his weapons in his hand. Anyone who enters the temple must be put to death. Stay close to the king wherever he goes."

⁸The Levites and all the men of Judah did just as Jehoiada the priest ordered.*a* Each one took his men—those who were going on duty on the Sabbath and those who were going off duty—for Jehoiada the priest had not released any of the divisions.*b* ⁹Then he gave the commanders of units of a hundred the spears and the large and small shields that had belonged to King David and that were in the temple of God. ¹⁰He stationed all the men, each with his weapon in his hand, around the king—near the altar and the temple, from the south side to the north side of the temple.

23:11
c Ex 25:16;
Dt 17:18;
1Sa 10:24

¹¹Jehoiada and his sons brought out the king's son and put the crown on him; they presented him with a copy*c* of the covenant and proclaimed him king. They anointed him and shouted, "Long live the king!"

¹²When Athaliah heard the noise of the people running and cheering the king, she went to them at the temple of the Lord.

23:13
d 1Ki 1:41
e 1Ki 7:15

¹³She looked, and there was the king,*d* standing by his pillar*e* at the entrance. The officers and the trumpeters were beside the king, and all the people of the land were rejoicing and blowing trumpets, and singers with musical instruments were leading the praises. Then Athaliah tore her robes and shouted, "Treason! Treason!"

23:15
f Ne 3:28;
Jer 31:40

¹⁴Jehoiada the priest sent out the commanders of units of a hundred, who were in charge of the troops, and said to them: "Bring her out between the ranks*b* and put to the sword anyone who follows her." For the priest had said, "Do not put her to death at the temple of the Lord." ¹⁵So they seized her as she reached the entrance of the Horse Gate*f* on the palace grounds, and there they put her to death.

23:16
g 2Ch 29:10;
34:31; Ne 9:38

¹⁶Jehoiada then made a covenant*g* that he and the people and the king*c* would be the Lord's people. ¹⁷All the people went to the temple of Baal and tore it down. They smashed the altars and idols and killed*h* Mattan the priest of Baal in front of the altars.

23:17
h Dt 13:6-9

¹⁸Then Jehoiada placed the oversight of the temple of the Lord in the hands of the priests, who were Levites,*i* to whom David had made assignments in the temple,*j* to present the burnt offerings of the Lord as written in the Law of Moses, with rejoicing and singing, as David had ordered. ¹⁹He also stationed doorkeepers*k* at the gates of the Lord's temple so that no one who was in any way unclean might enter.

23:18
i 1Ch 23:28-32;
2Ch 5:5
j 1Ch 23:6; 25:6

²⁰He took with him the commanders of hundreds, the nobles, the rulers of the people and all the people of the land and brought

23:19
k 1Ch 9:22

a 6 Or *to observe the Lord's command* ⌊*not to enter*⌋   *b* 14 Or *out from the precincts*   *c* 16 Or *covenant between* ⌊*the Lord*⌋ *and the people and the king that they* (see 2 Kings 11:17) the king down from the temple of the LORD. They went into the palace through the Upper Gate[a] and seated the king on the royal throne, 21and all the people of the land rejoiced. And the city was quiet, because Athaliah had been slain with the sword.[b]

Chapter 24 Theme

24 Joash was seven years old when he became king, and he reigned in Jerusalem forty years. His mother's name was Zibiah; she was from Beersheba. 2Joash did what was right in the eyes of the LORD[c] all the years of Jehoiada the priest. 3Jehoiada chose two wives for him, and he had sons and daughters.

4Some time later Joash decided to restore the temple of the LORD. 5He called together the priests and Levites and said to them, "Go to the towns of Judah and collect the money[d] due annually from all Israel,[e] to repair the temple of your God. Do it now." But the Levites[f] did not act at once.

6Therefore the king summoned Jehoiada the chief priest and said to him, "Why haven't you required the Levites to bring in from Judah and Jerusalem the tax imposed by Moses the servant of the LORD and by the assembly of Israel for the Tent of the Testimony?"[g]

7Now the sons of that wicked woman Athaliah had broken into the temple of God and had used even its sacred objects for the Baals.

8At the king's command, a chest was made and placed outside, at the gate of the temple of the LORD. 9A proclamation was then issued in Judah and Jerusalem that they should bring to the LORD the tax that Moses the servant of God had required of Israel in the desert. 10All the officials and all the people brought their contributions gladly,[h] dropping them into the chest until it was full. 11Whenever the chest was brought in by the Levites to the king's officials and they saw that there was a large amount of money, the royal secretary and the officer of the chief priest would come and empty the chest and carry it back to its place. They did this regularly and collected a great amount of money. 12The king and Jehoiada gave it to the men who carried out the work required for the temple of the LORD. They hired[i] masons and carpenters to restore the LORD's temple, and also workers in iron and bronze to repair the temple.

13The men in charge of the work were diligent, and the repairs progressed under them. They rebuilt the temple of God according to its original design and reinforced it. 14When they had finished, they brought the rest of the money to the king and Jehoiada, and with it were made articles for the LORD's temple: articles for the service and for the burnt offerings, and also dishes and other objects of gold and silver. As long as Jehoiada lived, burnt offerings were presented continually in the temple of the LORD.

23:20
[a] 2Ki 15:35

23:21
[b] 2Ch 22:1

24:2
[c] 2Ch 25:2; 26:5

24:5
[d] Ex 30:16;
Ne 10:32-33;
Mt 17:24
[e] 1Ch 11:1
[f] 1Ch 26:20

24:6
[g] Ex 30:12-16;
Nu 1:50

24:10
[h] Ex 25:2;
1Ch 29:3,6,9

24:12
[i] 2Ch 34:11

24:18
a ver 4;
Jos 24:20;
2Ch 7:19
b Ex 34:13;
1Ki 14:23;
2Ch 33:3;
Jer 17:2
c Jos 22:20;
2Ch 19:2

24:19
d Nu 11:29;
Jer 7:25;
Zec 1:4

24:20
e Jdg 3:10;
1Ch 12:18;
2Ch 20:14
f Mt 23:35;
Lk 11:51
g Nu 14:41
h Dt 31:17;
2Ch 15:2

24:21
i Jos 7:25;
Ac 7:58-59
j Ne 9:26;
Jer 26:21
k Jer 20:2;
Mt 23:35

24:22
l Ge 9:5

24:23
m 2Ki 12:17-18

24:24
n 2Ch 14:9; 16:8;
20:2,12
o Lev 26:23-25;
Dt 28:25

24:25
p 2Ch 21:20

24:26
q 2Ki 12:21
r Ru 1:4

25:2
s ver 14;
1Ki 8:61;
2Ch 24:2

¹⁵Now Jehoiada was old and full of years, and he died at the age of a hundred and thirty. ¹⁶He was buried with the kings in the City of David, because of the good he had done in Israel for God and his temple.

¹⁷After the death of Jehoiada, the officials of Judah came and paid homage to the king, and he listened to them. ¹⁸They abandoned*a* the temple of the LORD, the God of their fathers, and worshiped Asherah poles and idols.*b* Because of their guilt, God's anger *c* came upon Judah and Jerusalem. ¹⁹Although the LORD sent prophets to the people to bring them back to him, and though they testified against them, they would not listen.*d*

²⁰Then the Spirit*e* of God came upon Zechariah*f* son of Jehoiada the priest. He stood before the people and said, "This is what God says: 'Why do you disobey the LORD's commands? You will not prosper.*g* Because you have forsaken the LORD, he has forsaken*h* you.'"

²¹But they plotted against him, and by order of the king they stoned*i* him to death*j* in the courtyard of the LORD's temple.*k* ²²King Joash did not remember the kindness Zechariah's father Jehoiada had shown him but killed his son, who said as he lay dying, "May the LORD see this and call you to account."*l*

²³At the turn of the year,*a* the army of Aram marched against Joash; it invaded Judah and Jerusalem and killed all the leaders of the people.*m* They sent all the plunder to their king in Damascus. ²⁴Although the Aramean army had come with only a few men,*n* the LORD delivered into their hands a much larger army.*o* Because Judah had forsaken the LORD, the God of their fathers, judgment was executed on Joash. ²⁵When the Arameans withdrew, they left Joash severely wounded. His officials conspired against him for murdering the son of Jehoiada the priest, and they killed him in his bed. So he died and was buried*p* in the City of David, but not in the tombs of the kings.

²⁶Those who conspired against him were Zabad,*b* son of Shimeath an Ammonite woman, and Jehozabad, son of Shimrith*c q* a Moabite woman.*r* ²⁷The account of his sons, the many prophecies about him, and the record of the restoration of the temple of God are written in the annotations on the book of the kings. And Amaziah his son succeeded him as king.

Chapter 25 Theme

25 Amaziah was twenty-five years old when he became king, and he reigned in Jerusalem twenty-nine years. His mother's name was Jehoaddin*d*; she was from Jerusalem. ²He did what was right in the eyes of the LORD, but not wholeheartedly.*s* ³After the

---

a 23 Probably in the spring   *b 26* A variant of *Jozabad*   *c 26* A variant of *Shomer*
d 1 Hebrew *Jehoaddan*, a variant of *Jehoaddin*

kingdom was firmly in his control, he executed the officials who had murdered his father the king. ⁴Yet he did not put their sons to death, but acted in accordance with what is written in the Law, in the Book of Moses,ᵃ where the LORD commanded: "Fathers shall not be put to death for their children, nor children put to death for their fathers; each is to die for his own sins."ᵃᵇ

⁵Amaziah called the people of Judah together and assigned them according to their families to commanders of thousands and commanders of hundreds for all Judah and Benjamin. He then musteredᶜ those twenty years oldᵈ or more and found that there were three hundred thousand men ready for military service,ᵉ able to handle the spear and shield. ⁶He also hired a hundred thousand fighting men from Israel for a hundred talentsᵇ of silver.

⁷But a man of God came to him and said, "O king, these troops from Israelᶠ must not march with you, for the LORD is not with Israel—not with any of the people of Ephraim. ⁸Even if you go and fight courageously in battle, God will overthrow you before the enemy, for God has the power to help or to overthrow."ᵍ

⁹Amaziah asked the man of God, "But what about the hundred talents I paid for these Israelite troops?"

The man of God replied, "The LORD can give you much more than that."ʰ

¹⁰So Amaziah dismissed the troops who had come to him from Ephraim and sent them home. They were furious with Judah and left for home in a great rage.ⁱ

¹¹Amaziah then marshaled his strength and led his army to the Valley of Salt, where he killed ten thousand men of Seir. ¹²The army of Judah also captured ten thousand men alive, took them to the top of a cliff and threw them down so that all were dashed to pieces.ʲ

¹³Meanwhile the troops that Amaziah had sent back and had not allowed to take part in the war raided Judean towns from Samaria to Beth Horon. They killed three thousand people and carried off great quantities of plunder.

¹⁴When Amaziah returned from slaughtering the Edomites, he brought back the gods of the people of Seir. He set them up as his own gods,ᵏ bowed down to them and burned sacrifices to them. ¹⁵The anger of the LORD burned against Amaziah, and he sent a prophet to him, who said, "Why do you consult this people's gods, which could not saveˡ their own people from your hand?"

¹⁶While he was still speaking, the king said to him, "Have we appointed you an adviser to the king? Stop! Why be struck down?"

So the prophet stopped but said, "I know that God has determined to destroy you, because you have done this and have not listened to my counsel."

ᵃ4 Deut. 24:16   ᵇ6 That is, about 3 3/4 tons (about 3.4 metric tons); also in verse 9

25:4 ᵃDt 28:61; ᵇNu 26:11; Dt 24:16
25:5 ᶜ2Sa 24:2; ᵈEx 30:14; ᵉNu 1:3; 1Ch 21:1; 2Ch 17:14-19
25:7 ᶠ2Ch 16:2-9; 19:1-3
25:8 ᵍ2Ch 14:11; 20:6
25:9 ʰDt 8:18; Pr 10:22
25:10 ⁱver 13
25:12 ʲPs 141:6; Ob 3
25:14 ᵏEx 20:3; 2Ch 28:23; Isa 44:15
25:15 ˡPs 96:5; Isa 36:20

25:18
a Jdg 9:8-15

¹⁷After Amaziah king of Judah consulted his advisers, he sent this challenge to Jehoash^a son of Jehoahaz, the son of Jehu, king of Israel: "Come, meet me face to face."

¹⁸But Jehoash king of Israel replied to Amaziah king of Judah: "A thistle^a in Lebanon sent a message to a cedar in Lebanon, 'Give your daughter to my son in marriage.' Then a wild beast in Lebanon came along and trampled the thistle underfoot. ¹⁹You say to yourself that you have defeated Edom, and now you are arrogant and proud. But stay at home! Why ask for trouble and cause your own downfall and that of Judah also?"

25:20
b 1Ki 12:15;
2Ch 10:15; 22:7

²⁰Amaziah, however, would not listen, for God so worked that he might hand them over to ⌊Jehoash⌋, because they sought the gods of Edom.^b ²¹So Jehoash king of Israel attacked. He and Amaziah king of Judah faced each other at Beth Shemesh in Judah. ²²Judah was routed by Israel, and every man fled to his home. ²³Jehoash king of Israel captured Amaziah king of Judah, the son of Joash, the son of Ahaziah,^b at Beth Shemesh. Then Jehoash brought him to Jerusalem and broke down the wall of Jerusalem from the Ephraim Gate^c to the Corner Gate^d—a section about six hundred feet^c long. ²⁴He took all the gold and silver and all the articles found in the temple of God that had been in the care of Obed-Edom,^e together with the palace treasures and the hostages, and returned to Samaria.

25:23
c 2Ki 14:13;
Ne 8:16; 12:39
d 2Ch 26:9;
Jer 31:38

²⁵Amaziah son of Joash king of Judah lived for fifteen years after the death of Jehoash son of Jehoahaz king of Israel. ²⁶As for the other events of Amaziah's reign, from beginning to end, are they not written in the book of the kings of Judah and Israel? ²⁷From the time that Amaziah turned away from following the LORD, they conspired against him in Jerusalem and he fled to Lachish,^f but they sent men after him to Lachish and killed him there. ²⁸He was brought back by horse and was buried with his fathers in the City of Judah.

25:24
e 1Ch 26:15

Chapter 26 Theme _____

25:27
f Jos 10:3

26 Then all the people of Judah^g took Uzziah,^d who was sixteen years old, and made him king in place of his father Amaziah. ²He was the one who rebuilt Elath and restored it to Judah after Amaziah rested with his fathers.

³Uzziah was sixteen years old when he became king, and he reigned in Jerusalem fifty-two years. His mother's name was Jecoliah; she was from Jerusalem. ⁴He did what was right in the eyes of the LORD, just as his father Amaziah had done. ⁵He sought God

26:1
g 2Ch 22:1

^a *17* Hebrew *Joash,* a variant of *Jehoash;* also in verses 18, 21, 23 and 25   ^b *23* Hebrew *Jehoahaz,* a variant of *Ahaziah*   ^c *23* Hebrew *four hundred cubits* (about 180 meters)   ^d *1* Also called *Azariah*

during the days of Zechariah, who instructed him in the fear[a] of God.[a] As long as he sought the LORD, God gave him success.[b]

[6]He went to war against the Philistines[c] and broke down the walls of Gath, Jabneh and Ashdod.[d] He then rebuilt towns near Ashdod and elsewhere among the Philistines. [7]God helped him against the Philistines and against the Arabs[e] who lived in Gur Baal and against the Meunites.[f] [8]The Ammonites[g] brought tribute to Uzziah, and his fame spread as far as the border of Egypt, because he had become very powerful.

[9]Uzziah built towers in Jerusalem at the Corner Gate,[h] at the Valley Gate[i] and at the angle of the wall, and he fortified them. [10]He also built towers in the desert and dug many cisterns, because he had much livestock in the foothills and in the plain. He had people working his fields and vineyards in the hills and in the fertile lands, for he loved the soil.

[11]Uzziah had a well-trained army, ready to go out by divisions according to their numbers as mustered by Jeiel the secretary and Maaseiah the officer under the direction of Hananiah, one of the royal officials. [12]The total number of family leaders over the fighting men was 2,600. [13]Under their command was an army of 307,500 men trained for war, a powerful force to support the king against his enemies. [14]Uzziah provided shields, spears, helmets, coats of armor, bows and slingstones for the entire army.[j] [15]In Jerusalem he made machines designed by skillful men for use on the towers and on the corner defenses to shoot arrows and hurl large stones. His fame spread far and wide, for he was greatly helped until he became powerful.

[16]But after Uzziah became powerful, his pride[k] led to his downfall.[l] He was unfaithful[m] to the LORD his God, and entered the temple of the LORD to burn incense[n] on the altar of incense. [17]Azariah[o] the priest with eighty other courageous priests of the LORD followed him in. [18]They confronted him and said, "It is not right for you, Uzziah, to burn incense to the LORD. That is for the priests,[p] the descendants[q] of Aaron,[r] who have been consecrated to burn incense.[s] Leave the sanctuary, for you have been unfaithful; and you will not be honored by the LORD God."

[19]Uzziah, who had a censer in his hand ready to burn incense, became angry. While he was raging at the priests in their presence before the incense altar in the LORD's temple, leprosy[b][t] broke out on his forehead. [20]When Azariah the chief priest and all the other priests looked at him, they saw that he had leprosy on his forehead, so they hurried him out. Indeed, he himself was eager to leave, because the LORD had afflicted him.

[a]5 Many Hebrew manuscripts, Septuagint and Syriac; other Hebrew manuscripts *vision*
[b]19 The Hebrew word was used for various diseases affecting the skin—not necessarily leprosy; also in verses 20, 21 and 23.

26:5 [a]2Ch15:2; 24:2; Da 1:17 [b]2Ch 27:6
26:6 [c]Isa 2:6; 11:14; 14:29; Jer 25:20 [d]Am 1:8; 3:9
26:7 [e]2Ch 21:16 [f]2Ch 20:1
26:8 [g]Ge 19:38; 2Ch 17:11
26:9 [h]2Ki 14:13; 2Ch 25:23 [i]Ne 2:13; 3:13
26:14 [j]Jer 46:4
26:16 [k]2Ki 14:10 [l]Dt 32:15; 2Ch 25:19 [m]1Ch 5:25 [n]2Ki 16:12
26:17 [o]1Ki 4:2; 1Ch 6:10
26:18 [p]Nu 16:39 [q]Nu 18:1-7 [r]Ex 30:7 [s]1Ch 6:49
26:19 [t]Nu 12:10; 2Ki 5:25-27

26:21
a Ex 4:6;
Lev 13:46; 14:8;
Nu 5:2; 19:12

²¹King Uzziah had leprosy until the day he died. He lived in a separate house*ᵃᵃ*—leprous, and excluded from the temple of the LORD. Jotham his son had charge of the palace and governed the people of the land.

26:22
b 2Ki 15:1;
Isa 1:1; 6:1

²²The other events of Uzziah's reign, from beginning to end, are recorded by the prophet Isaiah*ᵇ* son of Amoz. ²³Uzziah*ᶜ* rested with his fathers and was buried near them in a field for burial that belonged to the kings, for people said, "He had leprosy." And Jotham his son succeeded him as king.*ᵈ*

Chapter 27 Theme _____

26:23
c Isa 1:1; 6:1
d 2Ki 14:21;
15:7; Am 1:1

27 Jotham*ᵉ* was twenty-five years old when he became king, and he reigned in Jerusalem sixteen years. His mother's name was Jerusha daughter of Zadok. ²He did what was right in the eyes of the LORD, just as his father Uzziah had done, but unlike him he did not enter the temple of the LORD. The people, however, continued their corrupt practices. ³Jotham rebuilt the Upper Gate of the temple of the LORD and did extensive work on the wall at the hill of Ophel.*ᶠ* ⁴He built towns in the Judean hills and forts and towers in the wooded areas.

27:1
e 2Ki 15:5,32;
1Ch 3:12

⁵Jotham made war on the king of the Ammonites*ᵍ* and conquered them. That year the Ammonites paid him a hundred talents*ᵇ* of silver, ten thousand cors*ᶜ* of wheat and ten thousand cors of barley. The Ammonites brought him the same amount also in the second and third years.

27:3
f 2Ch 33:14;
Ne 3:26

⁶Jotham grew powerful*ʰ* because he walked steadfastly before the LORD his God.

27:5
g Ge 19:38

⁷The other events in Jotham's reign, including all his wars and the other things he did, are written in the book of the kings of Israel and Judah. ⁸He was twenty-five years old when he became king, and he reigned in Jerusalem sixteen years. ⁹Jotham rested with his fathers and was buried in the City of David. And Ahaz his son succeeded him as king.

27:6
h 2Ch 26:5

Chapter 28 Theme _____

28:1
i 1Ch 3:13;
Isa 1:1

28 Ahaz*ⁱ* was twenty years old when he became king, and he reigned in Jerusalem sixteen years. Unlike David his father, he did not do what was right in the eyes of the LORD. ²He walked in the ways of the kings of Israel and also made cast idols*ʲ* for worshiping the Baals. ³He burned sacrifices in the Valley of Ben Hinnom*ᵏ* and sacrificed his sons*ˡ* in the fire, following the detestable*ᵐ* ways of the nations the LORD had driven out before the Israelites. ⁴He offered sacrifices and burned incense at the high places, on the hilltops and under every spreading tree.

28:2
j Ex 34:17;
2Ch 22:3

28:3
k Jos 15:8;
2Ki 23:10
l Lev 18:21;
2Ki 3:27;
2Ch 33:6;
Eze 20:26
m Dt 18:9;
2Ch 33:2

a 21 Or *in a house where he was relieved of responsibilities*   *b 5* That is, about 3 3/4 tons (about 3.4 metric tons)   *c 5* That is, probably about 62,000 bushels (about 2,200 kiloliters)

⁵Therefore the LORD his God handed him over to the king of Aram.ᵃ The Arameans defeated him and took many of his people as prisoners and brought them to Damascus.

He was also given into the hands of the king of Israel, who inflicted heavy casualties on him. ⁶In one day Pekahᵇ son of Remaliah killed a hundred and twenty thousand soldiers in Judahᶜ—because Judah had forsaken the LORD, the God of their fathers. ⁷Zicri, an Ephraimite warrior, killed Maaseiah the king's son, Azrikam the officer in charge of the palace, and Elkanah, second to the king. ⁸The Israelites took captive from their kinsmenᵈ two hundred thousand wives, sons and daughters. They also took a great deal of plunder, which they carried back to Samaria.ᵉ

⁹But a prophet of the LORD named Oded was there, and he went out to meet the army when it returned to Samaria. He said to them, "Because the LORD, the God of your fathers, was angryᶠ with Judah, he gave them into your hand. But you have slaughtered them in a rage that reaches to heaven.ᵍ ¹⁰And now you intend to make the men and women of Judah and Jerusalem your slaves.ʰ But aren't you also guilty of sins against the LORD your God? ¹¹Now listen to me! Send back your fellow countrymen you have taken as prisoners, for the LORD's fierce anger rests on you.ⁱ"

¹²Then some of the leaders in Ephraim—Azariah son of Jehohanan, Berekiah son of Meshillemoth, Jehizkiah son of Shallum, and Amasa son of Hadlai—confronted those who were arriving from the war. ¹³"You must not bring those prisoners here," they said, "or we will be guilty before the LORD. Do you intend to add to our sin and guilt? For our guilt is already great, and his fierce anger rests on Israel."

¹⁴So the soldiers gave up the prisoners and plunder in the presence of the officials and all the assembly. ¹⁵The men designated by name took the prisoners, and from the plunder they clothed all who were naked. They provided them with clothes and sandals, food and drink,ʲ and healing balm. All those who were weak they put on donkeys. So they took them back to their fellow countrymen at Jericho, the City of Palms,ᵏ and returned to Samaria.

¹⁶At that time King Ahaz sent to the kingᵃ of Assyriaˡ for help. ¹⁷The Edomitesᵐ had again come and attacked Judah and carried away prisoners,ⁿ ¹⁸while the Philistinesᵒ had raided towns in the foothills and in the Negev of Judah. They captured and occupied Beth Shemesh, Aijalonᵖ and Gederoth, as well as Soco, Timnah and Gimzo, with their surrounding villages. ¹⁹The LORD had humbled Judah because of Ahaz king of Israel,ᵇ for he had promoted wickedness in Judah and had been most unfaithful�q to the LORD.

ᵃ16 One Hebrew manuscript, Septuagint and Vulgate (see also 2 Kings 16:7); most Hebrew manuscripts *kings*   ᵇ19 That is, Judah, as frequently in 2 Chronicles

28:5
ᵃ Isa 7:1

28:6
ᵇ 2Ki 15:25,27
ᶜ ver 8;
Isa 9:21;
11:13

28:8
ᵈ Dt 28:25-41;
2Ch 11:4
ᵉ 2Ch 29:9

28:9
ᶠ 2Ch 25:15;
Isa 10:6; 47:6;
Zec 1:15
ᵍ Ezr 9:6;
Rev 18:5

28:10
ʰ Lev 25:39-46

28:11
ⁱ 2Ch 11:4;
Jas 2:13

28:15
ʲ 2Ki 6:22;
Pr 25:21-22
ᵏ Dt 34:3;
Jdg 1:16

28:16
ˡ 2Ki 16:7

28:17
ᵐ Ps 137:7;
Isa 34:5
ⁿ 2Ch 29:9

28:18
ᵒ Eze 16:27,57
ᵖ Jos 10:12

28:19
q 2Ch 21:2

28:20
a 2Ki 15:29;
1Ch 5:6
b 2Ki 16:7

28:22
c Jer 5:3

28:23
d 2Ch 25:14
e Jer 44:17-18

28:24
f 2Ki 16:18
g 2Ch 29:7
h 2Ch 30:14

28:27
i Isa 14:28-32
j 2Ch 21:20;
24:25

29:1
k 1Ch 3:13

29:2
l 2Ch 28:1;
34:2

29:3
m 2Ch 28:24

29:5
n 2Ch 35:6

29:6
o Ps 106:6-47;
Jer 2:27
p 1Ch 5:25;
Eze 8:16

29:8
q Dt 28:25;
2Ch 24:18
r Jer 18:16;
19:8; 25:9,18

29:9
s 2Ch 28:5-8, 17

29:10
t 2Ch 15:12;
23:16

²⁰Tiglath-Pileser*a a* king of Assyria came to him, but he gave him trouble instead of help.*b* ²¹Ahaz took some of the things from the temple of the LORD and from the royal palace and from the princes and presented them to the king of Assyria, but that did not help him.

²²In his time of trouble King Ahaz became even more unfaithful*c* to the LORD. ²³He offered sacrifices to the gods*d* of Damascus, who had defeated him; for he thought, "Since the gods of the kings of Aram have helped them, I will sacrifice to them so they will help me."*e* But they were his downfall and the downfall of all Israel.

²⁴Ahaz gathered together the furnishings from the temple of God*f* and took them away.*b* He shut the doors*g* of the LORD's temple and set up altars*h* at every street corner in Jerusalem. ²⁵In every town in Judah he built high places to burn sacrifices to other gods and provoked the LORD, the God of his fathers, to anger.

²⁶The other events of his reign and all his ways, from beginning to end, are written in the book of the kings of Judah and Israel. ²⁷Ahaz rested*i* with his fathers and was buried*j* in the city of Jerusalem, but he was not placed in the tombs of the kings of Israel. And Hezekiah his son succeeded him as king.

Chapter 29 Theme

29 Hezekiah*k* was twenty-five years old when he became king, and he reigned in Jerusalem twenty-nine years. His mother's name was Abijah daughter of Zechariah. ²He did what was right in the eyes of the LORD, just as his father David*l* had done.

³In the first month of the first year of his reign, he opened the doors of the temple of the LORD and repaired*m* them. ⁴He brought in the priests and the Levites, assembled them in the square on the east side ⁵and said: "Listen to me, Levites! Consecrate*n* yourselves now and consecrate the temple of the LORD, the God of your fathers. Remove all defilement from the sanctuary. ⁶Our fathers*o* were unfaithful;*p* they did evil in the eyes of the LORD our God and forsook him. They turned their faces away from the LORD's dwelling place and turned their backs on him. ⁷They also shut the doors of the portico and put out the lamps. They did not burn incense or present any burnt offerings at the sanctuary to the God of Israel. ⁸Therefore, the anger of the LORD has fallen on Judah and Jerusalem; he has made them an object of dread and horror*q* and scorn,*r* as you can see with your own eyes. ⁹This is why our fathers have fallen by the sword and why our sons and daughters and our wives are in captivity.*s* ¹⁰Now I intend to make a covenant*t* with the LORD, the God of Israel, so that his fierce anger will turn away from

a 20 Hebrew *Tilgath-Pilneser,* a variant of *Tiglath-Pileser*   *b 24* Or *and cut them up* us. ¹¹My sons, do not be negligent now, for the LORD has chosen you to stand before him and serve him,ᵃ to ministerᵇ before him and to burn incense."

¹²Then these Levitesᶜ set to work:

from the Kohathites,
Mahath son of Amasai and Joel son of Azariah;
from the Merarites,
Kish son of Abdi and Azariah son of Jehallelel;
from the Gershonites,
Joah son of Zimmah and Edenᵈ son of Joah;
¹³from the descendants of Elizaphan,
Shimri and Jeiel;
from the descendants of Asaph,ᵉ
Zechariah and Mattaniah;
¹⁴from the descendants of Heman,
Jehiel and Shimei;
from the descendants of Jeduthun,
Shemaiah and Uzziel.

¹⁵When they had assembled their brothers and consecrated themselves, they went in to purifyᶠ the temple of the LORD, as the king had ordered, following the word of the LORD. ¹⁶The priests went into the sanctuary of the LORD to purify it. They brought out to the courtyard of the LORD's temple everything unclean that they found in the temple of the LORD. The Levites took it and carried it out to the Kidron Valley.ᵍ ¹⁷They began the consecration on the first day of the first month, and by the eighth day of the month they reached the portico of the LORD. For eight more days they consecrated the temple of the LORD itself, finishing on the sixteenth day of the first month.

¹⁸Then they went in to King Hezekiah and reported: "We have purified the entire temple of the LORD, the altar of burnt offering with all its utensils, and the table for setting out the consecrated bread, with all its articles. ¹⁹We have prepared and consecrated all the articlesʰ that King Ahaz removed in his unfaithfulness while he was king. They are now in front of the LORD's altar."

²⁰Early the next morning King Hezekiah gathered the city officials together and went up to the temple of the LORD. ²¹They brought seven bulls, seven rams, seven male lambs and seven male goats as a sin offeringⁱ for the kingdom, for the sanctuary and for Judah. The king commanded the priests, the descendants of Aaron, to offer these on the altar of the LORD. ²²So they slaughtered the bulls, and the priests took the blood and sprinkled it on the altar; next they slaughtered the rams and sprinkled their blood on the altar; then they slaughtered the lambs and sprinkled their bloodʲ on the altar. ²³The goats for the sin offering were brought before

29:11
ᵃNu 3:6; 8:6,14
ᵇ1Ch 15:2

29:12
ᶜNu 3:17-20
ᵈ2Ch 31:15

29:13
ᵉ1Ch 6:39

29:15
ᶠver 5;
1Ch 23:28;
2Ch 30:12

29:16
ᵍ2Sa 15:23

29:19
ʰ2Ch 28:24

29:21
ⁱLev 4:13-14

29:22
ʲLev 4:18

the king and the assembly, and they laid their hands*a* on them. ²⁴The priests then slaughtered the goats and presented their blood on the altar for a sin offering to atone*b* for all Israel, because the king had ordered the burnt offering and the sin offering for all Israel.

²⁵He stationed the Levites in the temple of the LORD with cymbals, harps and lyres in the way prescribed by David*c* and Gad*d* the king's seer and Nathan the prophet; this was commanded by the LORD through his prophets. ²⁶So the Levites stood ready with David's instruments,*e* and the priests with their trumpets.*f*

²⁷Hezekiah gave the order to sacrifice the burnt offering on the altar. As the offering began, singing to the LORD began also, accompanied by trumpets and the instruments*g* of David king of Israel. ²⁸The whole assembly bowed in worship, while the singers sang and the trumpeters played. All this continued until the sacrifice of the burnt offering was completed.

²⁹When the offerings were finished, the king and everyone present with him knelt down and worshiped.*h* ³⁰King Hezekiah and his officials ordered the Levites to praise the LORD with the words of David and of Asaph the seer. So they sang praises with gladness and bowed their heads and worshiped.

³¹Then Hezekiah said, "You have now dedicated yourselves to the LORD. Come and bring sacrifices*i* and thank offerings to the temple of the LORD." So the assembly brought sacrifices and thank offerings, and all whose hearts were willing*j* brought burnt offerings.

³²The number of burnt offerings the assembly brought was seventy bulls, a hundred rams and two hundred male lambs—all of them for burnt offerings to the LORD. ³³The animals consecrated as sacrifices amounted to six hundred bulls and three thousand sheep and goats. ³⁴The priests, however, were too few to skin all the burnt offerings;*k* so their kinsmen the Levites helped them until the task was finished and until other priests had been consecrated,*l* for the Levites had been more conscientious in consecrating themselves than the priests had been. ³⁵There were burnt offerings in abundance, together with the fat*m* of the fellowship offerings*a n* and the drink offerings*o* that accompanied the burnt offerings.

So the service of the temple of the LORD was reestablished. ³⁶Hezekiah and all the people rejoiced at what God had brought about for his people, because it was done so quickly.

Chapter 30 Theme

30 Hezekiah sent word to all Israel and Judah and also wrote letters to Ephraim and Manasseh,*p* inviting them to come to the temple of the LORD in Jerusalem and celebrate the Passover*q*

29:23
a Lev 4:15

29:24
b Ex 29:36;
Lev 4:26

29:25
c 1Ch 25:6;
2Ch 8:14
d 1Sa 22:5;
2Sa 24:11

29:26
e 1Ch 15:16
f 1Ch 15:24;
23:5; 2Ch 5:12

29:27
g 2Ch 23:18

29:29
h 2Ch 20:18

29:31
i Heb 13:15-16
j Ex 25:2; 35:22

29:34
k 2Ch 35:11
l 2Ch 30:3,15

29:35
m Ex 29:13;
Lev 3:16
n Lev 7:11-21
o Nu 15:5-10

30:1
p Ge 41:52
q Ex 12:11;
Nu 28:16

---

a 35 Traditionally *peace offerings*

to the LORD, the God of Israel. ²The king and his officials and the whole assembly in Jerusalem decided to celebrate[a] the Passover in the second month. ³They had not been able to celebrate it at the regular time because not enough priests had consecrated[b] themselves and the people had not assembled in Jerusalem. ⁴The plan seemed right both to the king and to the whole assembly. ⁵They decided to send a proclamation throughout Israel, from Beersheba to Dan,[c] calling the people to come to Jerusalem and celebrate the Passover to the LORD, the God of Israel. It had not been celebrated in large numbers according to what was written.

⁶At the king's command, couriers went throughout Israel and Judah with letters from the king and from his officials, which read:

"People of Israel, return to the LORD, the God of Abraham, Isaac and Israel, that he may return to you who are left, who have escaped from the hand of the kings of Assyria. ⁷Do not be like your fathers[d] and brothers, who were unfaithful to the LORD, the God of their fathers, so that he made them an object of horror,[e] as you see. ⁸Do not be stiff-necked,[f] as your fathers were; submit to the LORD. Come to the sanctuary, which he has consecrated forever. Serve the LORD your God, so that his fierce anger[g] will turn away from you. ⁹If you return[h] to the LORD, then your brothers and your children will be shown compassion[i] by their captors and will come back to this land, for the LORD your God is gracious and compassionate.[j] He will not turn his face from you if you return to him."

¹⁰The couriers went from town to town in Ephraim and Manasseh, as far as Zebulun, but the people scorned and ridiculed[k] them. ¹¹Nevertheless, some men of Asher, Manasseh and Zebulun humbled themselves and went to Jerusalem.[l] ¹²Also in Judah the hand of God was on the people to give them unity[m] of mind to carry out what the king and his officials had ordered, following the word of the LORD.

¹³A very large crowd of people assembled in Jerusalem to celebrate the Feast of Unleavened Bread[n] in the second month. ¹⁴They removed the altars[o] in Jerusalem and cleared away the incense altars and threw them into the Kidron Valley.[p]

¹⁵They slaughtered the Passover lamb on the fourteenth day of the second month. The priests and the Levites were ashamed and consecrated[q] themselves and brought burnt offerings to the temple of the LORD. ¹⁶Then they took up their regular positions[r] as prescribed in the Law of Moses the man of God. The priests sprinkled the blood handed to them by the Levites. ¹⁷Since many in the crowd had not consecrated themselves, the Levites had to kill[s] the Passover lambs for all those who were not ceremonially clean and

---

30:2
[a] Nu 9:10

30:3
[b] 2Ch 29:34

30:5
[c] Jdg 20:1

30:7
[d] Ps 78:8,57; 106:6; Eze 20:18
[e] 2Ch 29:8

30:8
[f] Ex 32:9
[g] Nu 25:4; 2Ch 29:10

30:9
[h] Dt 30:2-5; Isa 1:16; 55:7
[i] 1Ki 8:50; Ps 106:46
[j] Ex 34:6-7; Dt 4:31; Mic 7:18

30:10
[k] 2Ch 36:16

30:11
[l] ver 25

30:12
[m] Jer 32:39; Eze 11:19; Php 2:13

30:13
[n] Nu 28:16

30:14
[o] 2Ch 28:24
[p] 2Sa 15:23

30:15
[q] 2Ch 29:34

30:16
[r] 2Ch 35:10

30:17
[s] 2Ch 29:34

30:18
a Ex 12:43-49;
Nu 9:6-10

30:20
b 2Ch 6:20
c 2Ch 7:14;
Mal 4:2
d Jas 5:16

30:21
e Ex 12:15,17;
13:6

30:23
f 1Ki 8:65;
2Ch 7:9

30:24
g 1Ki 8:5;
2Ch 29:34; 35:7;
Ezr 6:17; 8:35

30:25
h ver 11

30:26
i 2Ch 7:8

30:27
j Ex 39:43;
Nu 6:23;
Dt 26:15;
2Ch 23:18;
Ps 68:5

31:1
k 2Ki 18:4;
2Ch 32:12;
Isa 36:7

31:2
l 2Ch 29:9
m 1Ch 24:1
n 1Ch 15:2
o Ps 7:17; 9:2;
47:6; 71:22
p 1Ch 23:28-32

31:3
q 1Ch 29:3;
2Ch 35:7;
Eze 45:17

could not consecrate ⌊their lambs⌋ to the LORD. ¹⁸Although most of the many people who came from Ephraim, Manasseh, Issachar and Zebulun had not purified themselves,*a* yet they ate the Passover, contrary to what was written. But Hezekiah prayed for them, saying, "May the LORD, who is good, pardon everyone ¹⁹who sets his heart on seeking God—the LORD, the God of his fathers—even if he is not clean according to the rules of the sanctuary." ²⁰And the LORD heard*b* Hezekiah and healed*c* the people.*d*

²¹The Israelites who were present in Jerusalem celebrated the Feast of Unleavened Bread*e* for seven days with great rejoicing, while the Levites and priests sang to the LORD every day, accompanied by the LORD's instruments of praise.*a*

²²Hezekiah spoke encouragingly to all the Levites, who showed good understanding of the service of the LORD. For the seven days they ate their assigned portion and offered fellowship offerings*b* and praised the LORD, the God of their fathers.

²³The whole assembly then agreed to celebrate*f* the festival seven more days; so for another seven days they celebrated joyfully. ²⁴Hezekiah king of Judah provided*g* a thousand bulls and seven thousand sheep and goats for the assembly, and the officials provided them with a thousand bulls and ten thousand sheep and goats. A great number of priests consecrated themselves. ²⁵The entire assembly of Judah rejoiced, along with the priests and Levites and all who had assembled from Israel*h*, including the aliens who had come from Israel and those who lived in Judah. ²⁶There was great joy in Jerusalem, for since the days of Solomon*i* son of David king of Israel there had been nothing like this in Jerusalem. ²⁷The priests and the Levites stood to bless*j* the people, and God heard them, for their prayer reached heaven, his holy dwelling place.

Chapter 31 Theme _____

31
When all this had ended, the Israelites who were there went out to the towns of Judah, smashed the sacred stones and cut down*k* the Asherah poles. They destroyed the high places and the altars throughout Judah and Benjamin and in Ephraim and Manasseh. After they had destroyed all of them, the Israelites returned to their own towns and to their own property.

²Hezekiah*l* assigned the priests and Levites to divisions*m*—each of them according to their duties as priests or Levites—to offer burnt offerings and fellowship offerings,*b* to minister,*n* to give thanks and to sing praises*o* at the gates of the LORD's dwelling.*p* ³The king contributed*q* from his own possessions for the morning

a 21 Or *priests praised the LORD every day with resounding instruments belonging to the LORD*
b 22, 2 Traditionally *peace offerings*

and evening burnt offerings and for the burnt offerings on the Sabbaths, New Moons and appointed feasts as written in the Law of the LORD.*a* *4*He ordered the people living in Jerusalem to give the portion*b* due the priests and Levites so they could devote themselves to the Law of the LORD. *5*As soon as the order went out, the Israelites generously gave the firstfruits*c* of their grain, new wine,*d* oil and honey and all that the fields produced. They brought a great amount, a tithe of everything. *6*The men of Israel and Judah who lived in the towns of Judah also brought a tithe*e* of their herds and flocks and a tithe of the holy things dedicated to the LORD their God, and they piled them in heaps.*f* *7*They began doing this in the third month and finished in the seventh month.*g* *8*When Hezekiah and his officials came and saw the heaps, they praised the LORD and blessed*h* his people Israel.

*9*Hezekiah asked the priests and Levites about the heaps; *10*and Azariah the chief priest, from the family of Zadok,*i* answered, "Since the people began to bring their contributions to the temple of the LORD, we have had enough to eat and plenty to spare, because the LORD has blessed his people, and this great amount is left over."*j*

*11*Hezekiah gave orders to prepare storerooms in the temple of the LORD, and this was done. *12*Then they faithfully brought in the contributions, tithes and dedicated gifts. Conaniah,*k* a Levite, was in charge of these things, and his brother Shimei was next in rank. *13*Jehiel, Azaziah, Nahath, Asahel, Jerimoth, Jozabad,*l* Eliel, Ismakiah, Mahath and Benaiah were supervisors under Conaniah and Shimei his brother, by appointment of King Hezekiah and Azariah the official in charge of the temple of God.

*14*Kore son of Imnah the Levite, keeper of the East Gate, was in charge of the freewill offerings given to God, distributing the contributions made to the LORD and also the consecrated gifts. *15*Eden,*m* Miniamin, Jeshua, Shemaiah, Amariah and Shecaniah assisted him faithfully in the towns*n* of the priests, distributing to their fellow priests according to their divisions, old and young alike.

*16*In addition, they distributed to the males three years old or more whose names were in the genealogical records*o*—all who would enter the temple of the LORD to perform the daily duties of their various tasks, according to their responsibilities and their divisions. *17*And they distributed to the priests enrolled by their families in the genealogical records and likewise to the Levites twenty years old or more, according to their responsibilities and their divisions. *18*They included all the little ones, the wives, and the sons and daughters of the whole community listed in these genealogical records. For they were faithful in consecrating themselves.

31:3
*a*Nu 28:1–29:40

31:4
*b*Nu 18:8;
Dt 18:8;
Ne 13:10;
Mal 2:7

31:5
*c*Nu 18:12,24;
Ne 13:12;
Eze 44:30
*d*Dt 12:17

31:6
*e*Lev 27:30;
Ne 13:10-12
*f*Dt 14:28;
Ru 3:7

31:7
*g*Ex 23:16

31:8
*h*Ps 144:13-15

31:10
*i*2Sa 8:17
*j*Ex 36:5;
Eze 44:30;
Mal 3:10-12

31:12
*k*2Ch 35:9

31:13
*l*2Ch 35:9

31:15
*m*2Ch 29:12
*n*Jos 21:9-19

31:16
*o*1Ch 23:3;
Ezr 3:4

31:19
a ver 12-15;
Lev 25:34;
Nu 35:2-5

31:20
b 2Ki 20:3; 22:2

31:21
c Dt 29:9

32:1
d 2Ki 18:13-19;
Isa 36:1;
37:9,17,37

32:2
e Isa 22:7;
Jer 1:15

32:4
f 2Ki 18:17;
20:20;
Isa 22:9,11;
Na 3:14

32:5
g 2Ch 25:23;
Isa 22:10
h 1Ki 9:24;
1Ch 11:8
i Isa 22:8

32:7
j Dt 31:6;
1Ch 22:13
k 2Ch 20:15
l Nu 14:9;
2Ki 6:16

32:8
m Job 40:9;
Isa 52:10;
Jer 17:5; 32:21
n Dt 3:22;
1Sa 17:45;
2Ch 13:12
o 1Ch 5:22;
2Ch 20:17;
Ps 20:7;
Isa 28:6

32:9
p Jos 10:3,31

32:10
q Eze 29:16

32:11
r Isa 37:10

¹⁹As for the priests, the descendants of Aaron, who lived on the farm lands around their towns or in any other towns,ᵃ men were designated by name to distribute portions to every male among them and to all who were recorded in the genealogies of the Levites.

²⁰This is what Hezekiah did throughout Judah, doing what was good and right and faithfulᵇ before the LORD his God. ²¹In everything that he undertook in the service of God's temple and in obedience to the law and the commands, he sought his God and worked wholeheartedly. And so he prospered.ᶜ

Chapter 32 Theme

32 After all that Hezekiah had so faithfully done, Sennacheribᵈ king of Assyria came and invaded Judah. He laid siege to the fortified cities, thinking to conquer them for himself. ²When Hezekiah saw that Sennacherib had come and that he intended to make war on Jerusalem,ᵉ ³he consulted with his officials and military staff about blocking off the water from the springs outside the city, and they helped him. ⁴A large force of men assembled, and they blocked all the springsᶠ and the stream that flowed through the land. "Why should the kingsᵃ of Assyria come and find plenty of water?" they said. ⁵Then he worked hard repairing all the broken sections of the wallᵍ and building towers on it. He built another wall outside that one and reinforced the supporting terracesᵇʰ of the City of David. He also made large numbers of weaponsⁱ and shields.

⁶He appointed military officers over the people and assembled them before him in the square at the city gate and encouraged them with these words: ⁷"Be strong and courageous.ʲ Do not be afraid or discouragedᵏ because of the king of Assyria and the vast army with him, for there is a greater power with us than with him.ˡ ⁸With him is only the arm of flesh,ᵐ but with usⁿ is the LORD our God to help us and to fight our battles."ᵒ And the people gained confidence from what Hezekiah the king of Judah said.

⁹Later, when Sennacherib king of Assyria and all his forces were laying siege to Lachish,ᵖ he sent his officers to Jerusalem with this message for Hezekiah king of Judah and for all the people of Judah who were there:

¹⁰"This is what Sennacherib king of Assyria says: On what are you basing your confidence,�q that you remain in Jerusalem under siege? ¹¹When Hezekiah says, 'The LORD our God will save us from the hand of the king of Assyria,' he is misleadingʳ you, to let you die of hunger and thirst. ¹²Did not Hezekiah

ᵃ4 Hebrew; Septuagint and Syriac *king*   ᵇ5 Or *the Millo*

himself remove this god's high places and altars, saying to Judah and Jerusalem, 'You must worship before one altar*a* and burn sacrifices on it'?

¹³"Do you not know what I and my fathers have done to all the peoples of the other lands? Were the gods of those nations ever able to deliver their land from my hand?*b* ¹⁴Who of all the gods of these nations that my fathers destroyed has been able to save his people from me? How then can your god deliver you from my hand? ¹⁵Now do not let Hezekiah deceive*c* you and mislead you like this. Do not believe him, for no god of any nation or kingdom has been able to deliver*d* his people from my hand or the hand of my fathers.*e* How much less will your god deliver you from my hand!"

¹⁶Sennacherib's officers spoke further against the LORD God and against his servant Hezekiah. ¹⁷The king also wrote letters*f* insulting*g* the LORD, the God of Israel, and saying this against him: "Just as the gods*h* of the peoples of the other lands did not rescue their people from my hand, so the god of Hezekiah will not rescue his people from my hand." ¹⁸Then they called out in Hebrew to the people of Jerusalem who were on the wall, to terrify them and make them afraid in order to capture the city. ¹⁹They spoke about the God of Jerusalem as they did about the gods of the other peoples of the world—the work of men's hands.*i*

²⁰King Hezekiah and the prophet Isaiah son of Amoz cried out in prayer to heaven about this. ²¹And the LORD sent an angel,*j* who annihilated all the fighting men and the leaders and officers in the camp of the Assyrian king. So he withdrew to his own land in disgrace. And when he went into the temple of his god, some of his sons cut him down with the sword.*k*

²²So the LORD saved Hezekiah and the people of Jerusalem from the hand of Sennacherib king of Assyria and from the hand of all others. He took care of them*a* on every side. ²³Many brought offerings to Jerusalem for the LORD and valuable gifts*l* for Hezekiah king of Judah. From then on he was highly regarded by all the nations.

²⁴In those days Hezekiah became ill and was at the point of death. He prayed to the LORD, who answered him and gave him a miraculous sign. ²⁵But Hezekiah's heart was proud*m* and he did not respond to the kindness shown him; therefore the LORD's wrath*n* was on him and on Judah and Jerusalem. ²⁶Then Hezekiah repented*o* of the pride of his heart, as did the people of Jerusalem; therefore the LORD's wrath did not come upon them during the days of Hezekiah.*p*

a 22 Hebrew; Septuagint and Vulgate *He gave them rest*

32:12
a 2Ch 31:1

32:13
b ver 15

32:15
c Isa 37:10
d Da 3:15
e Ex 5:2

32:17
f Isa 37:14
g Ps 74:22;
Isa 37:4,17
h 2Ki 19:12

32:19
i 2Ki 19:18;
Ps 115:4,4-8;
Isa 2:8; 17:8

32:21
j Ge 19:13
k 2Ki 19:7

32:23
l 2Ch 9:24; 17:5;
Isa 45:14;
Zec 14:16-17

32:25
m 2Ki 14:10;
2Ch 26:16
n 2Ch 19:2;
24:18

32:26
o Jer 26:18-19
p 2Ch 34:27,28;
Isa 39:8

¹⁸Then Shaphan the secretary informed the king, "Hilkiah the priest has given me a book." And Shaphan read from it in the presence of the king.

¹⁹When the king heard the words of the Law,[a] he tore[b] his robes. ²⁰He gave these orders to Hilkiah, Ahikam son of Shaphan[c], Abdon son of Micah,[a] Shaphan the secretary and Asaiah the king's attendant: ²¹"Go and inquire of the LORD for me and for the remnant in Israel and Judah about what is written in this book that has been found. Great is the LORD's anger that is poured out[d] on us because our fathers have not kept the word of the LORD; they have not acted in accordance with all that is written in this book."

²²Hilkiah and those the king had sent with him[b] went to speak to the prophetess[e] Huldah, who was the wife of Shallum son of Tokhath,[c] the son of Hasrah,[d] keeper of the wardrobe. She lived in Jerusalem, in the Second District.

²³She said to them, "This is what the LORD, the God of Israel, says: Tell the man who sent you to me, ²⁴'This is what the LORD says: I am going to bring disaster[f] on this place and its people[g]— all the curses[h] written in the book that has been read in the presence of the king of Judah. ²⁵Because they have forsaken me[i] and burned incense to other gods and provoked me to anger by all that their hands have made,[e] my anger will be poured out on this place and will not be quenched.' ²⁶Tell the king of Judah, who sent you to inquire of the LORD, 'This is what the LORD, the God of Israel, says concerning the words you heard: ²⁷Because your heart was responsive[j] and you humbled[k] yourself before God when you heard what he spoke against this place and its people, and because you humbled yourself before me and tore your robes and wept in my presence, I have heard you, declares the LORD. ²⁸Now I will gather you to your fathers,[l] and you will be buried in peace. Your eyes will not see all the disaster I am going to bring on this place and on those who live here.'"[m]

So they took her answer back to the king.

²⁹Then the king called together all the elders of Judah and Jerusalem. ³⁰He went up to the temple of the LORD[n] with the men of Judah, the people of Jerusalem, the priests and the Levites—all the people from the least to the greatest. He read in their hearing all the words of the Book of the Covenant, which had been found in the temple of the LORD. ³¹The king stood by his pillar[o] and renewed the covenant[p] in the presence of the LORD—to follow[q] the LORD and keep his commands, regulations and decrees with all his heart and all his soul, and to obey the words of the covenant written in this book.

---

a 20 Also called *Acbor son of Micaiah*   b 22 One Hebrew manuscript, Vulgate and Syriac; most Hebrew manuscripts do not have *had sent with him*.   c 22 Also called *Tikvah*   d 22 Also called *Harhas*   e 25 Or *by everything they have done*

34:19
a Dt 28:3-68
b Jos 7:6;
Isa 36:22;
37:1

34:20
c 2Ki 22:3

34:21
d 2Ch 29:8;
La 2:4; 4:11;
Eze 36:18

34:22
e Ex 15:20;
Ne 6:14

34:24
f Pr 16:4;
Isa 3:9;
Jer 40:2;
42:10;
44:2,11
g 2Ch 36:14-20
h Dt 28:15-68

34:25
i 2Ch 33:3-6;
Jer 22:9

34:27
j 2Ch 12:7; 32:26
k Ex 10:3;
2Ch 6:37

34:28
l 2Ch 35:20-25
m 2Ch 32:26

34:30
n 2Ki 23:2;
Ne 8:1-3

34:31
o 1Ki 7:15;
2Ki 11:14
p 2Ki 11:17;
2Ch 23:16;
29:10
q Dt 13:4

34:2
a 2Ch 29:2

34:3
b 1Ki 13:2;
1Ch 16:11;
2Ch 15:2;
33:17,22

34:4
c Ex 34:13
d Ex 32:20;
Lev 26:30;
2Ki 23:11;
Mic 1:5

34:5
e 1Ki 13:2

34:7
f Ex 32:20;
2Ch 31:1

34:9
g 1Ch 6:13;
2Ch 35:8

34:11
h 2Ch 24:12
i 2Ch 33:4-7

34:12
j 2Ki 12:15
k 1Ch 25:1

34:13
l 1Ch 23:4

34:15
m 2Ki 22:8;
Ezr 7:6;
Ne 8:1

right in the eyes of the LORD and walked in the ways of his father David,*a* not turning aside to the right or to the left.

³In the eighth year of his reign, while he was still young, he began to seek the God*b* of his father David. In his twelfth year he began to purge Judah and Jerusalem of high places, Asherah poles, carved idols and cast images. ⁴Under his direction the altars of the Baals were torn down; he cut to pieces the incense altars that were above them, and smashed the Asherah poles,*c* the idols and the images. These he broke to pieces and scattered over the graves of those who had sacrificed to them.*d* ⁵He burned*e* the bones of the priests on their altars, and so he purged Judah and Jerusalem. ⁶In the towns of Manasseh, Ephraim and Simeon, as far as Naphtali, and in the ruins around them, ⁷he tore down the altars and the Asherah poles and crushed the idols to powder*f* and cut to pieces all the incense altars throughout Israel. Then he went back to Jerusalem.

⁸In the eighteenth year of Josiah's reign, to purify the land and the temple, he sent Shaphan son of Azaliah and Maaseiah the ruler of the city, with Joah son of Joahaz, the recorder, to repair the temple of the LORD his God.

⁹They went to Hilkiah*g* the high priest and gave him the money that had been brought into the temple of God, which the Levites who were the doorkeepers had collected from the people of Manasseh, Ephraim and the entire remnant of Israel and from all the people of Judah and Benjamin and the inhabitants of Jerusalem. ¹⁰Then they entrusted it to the men appointed to supervise the work on the LORD's temple. These men paid the workers who repaired and restored the temple. ¹¹They also gave money*h* to the carpenters and builders to purchase dressed stone, and timber for joists and beams for the buildings that the kings of Judah had allowed to fall into ruin.*i*

¹²The men did the work faithfully.*j* Over them to direct them were Jahath and Obadiah, Levites descended from Merari, and Zechariah and Meshullam, descended from Kohath. The Levites—all who were skilled in playing musical instruments—*k* ¹³had charge of the laborers*l* and supervised all the workers from job to job. Some of the Levites were secretaries, scribes and doorkeepers.

¹⁴While they were bringing out the money that had been taken into the temple of the LORD, Hilkiah the priest found the Book of the Law of the LORD that had been given through Moses. ¹⁵Hilkiah said to Shaphan the secretary, "I have found the Book of the Law*m* in the temple of the LORD." He gave it to Shaphan.

¹⁶Then Shaphan took the book to the king and reported to him: "Your officials are doing everything that has been committed to them. ¹⁷They have paid out the money that was in the temple of the LORD and have entrusted it to the supervisors and workers."

¹⁰The LORD spoke to Manasseh and his people, but they paid no attention. ¹¹So the LORD brought against them the army commanders of the king of Assyria, who took Manasseh prisoner,ᵃ put a hook in his nose, bound him with bronze shacklesᵇ and took him to Babylon. ¹²In his distress he sought the favor of the LORD his God and humbledᶜ himself greatly before the God of his fathers. ¹³And when he prayed to him, the LORD was moved by his entreaty and listened to his plea; so he brought him back to Jerusalem and to his kingdom. Then Manasseh knew that the LORD is God.

¹⁴Afterward he rebuilt the outer wall of the City of David, west of the Gihonᵈ spring in the valley, as far as the entrance of the Fish Gateᵉ and encircling the hill of Ophel;ᶠ he also made it much higher. He stationed military commanders in all the fortified cities in Judah.

¹⁵He got rid of the foreign gods and removedᵍ the image from the temple of the LORD, as well as all the altars he had built on the temple hill and in Jerusalem; and he threw them out of the city. ¹⁶Then he restored the altar of the LORD and sacrificed fellowship offeringsᵃ and thank offeringsʰ on it, and told Judah to serve the LORD, the God of Israel. ¹⁷The people, however, continued to sacrifice at the high places, but only to the LORD their God.

¹⁸The other events of Manasseh's reign, including his prayer to his God and the words the seers spoke to him in the name of the LORD, the God of Israel, are written in the annals of the kings of Israel.ᵇ ¹⁹His prayer and how God was moved by his entreaty, as well as all his sins and unfaithfulness, and the sites where he built high places and set up Asherah poles and idols before he humbledⁱ himself—all are written in the records of the seers.ᶜʲ ²⁰Manasseh rested with his fathers and was buriedᵏ in his palace. And Amon his son succeeded him as king.

²¹Amonˡ was twenty-two years old when he became king, and he reigned in Jerusalem two years. ²²He did evil in the eyes of the LORD, as his father Manasseh had done. Amon worshiped and offered sacrifices to all the idols Manasseh had made. ²³But unlike his father Manasseh, he did not humbleᵐ himself before the LORD; Amon increased his guilt.

²⁴Amon's officials conspired against him and assassinated him in his palace. ²⁵Then the peopleⁿ of the land killed all who had plotted against King Amon, and they made Josiah his son king in his place.

Chapter 34 Theme

34 Josiahᵒ was eight years old when he became king,ᵖ and he reigned in Jerusalem thirty-one years. ²He did what was

---

### Cross references (margin)

33:11
ᵃ Dt 28:36
ᵇ Ps 149:8

33:12
ᶜ 2Ch 6:37;
32:26;
1Pe 5:6

33:14
ᵈ 1Ki 1:33
ᵉ Ne 3:3;
12:39;
Zep 1:10
ᶠ 2Ch 27:3;
Ne 3:26

33:15
ᵍ ver 3-7;
2Ki 23:12

33:16
ʰ Lev 7:11-18

33:19
ⁱ 2Ch 6:37
ʲ 2Ki 21:17

33:20
ᵏ 2Ki 21:18;
2Ch 21:20

33:21
ˡ 1Ch 3:14

33:23
ᵐ ver 12;
Ex 10:3;
2Ch 7:14;
Ps 18:27;
147:6;
Pr 3:34

33:25
ⁿ 2Ch 22:1

34:1
ᵒ 1Ch 3:14
ᵖ Zep 1:1

ᵃ16 Traditionally *peace offerings*   ᵇ18 That is, Judah, as frequently in 2 Chronicles   ᶜ19 One Hebrew manuscript and Septuagint; most Hebrew manuscripts *of Hozai*

32:27
a 1Ch 29:12

32:29
b 1Ch 29:12

32:30
c 2Ki 18:17
d 1Ki 1:33

32:31
e Isa 39:1
f ver 24; Isa 38:7
g Ge 22:1;
Dt 8:16

33:1
h 1Ch 3:13

33:2
i Jer 15:4
j Dt 18:9;
2Ch 28:3

33:3
k Dt 16:21-22
l Dt 17:3;
2Ch 31:1

33:4
m 2Ch 7:16

33:5
n 2Ch 4:9

33:6
o Lev 18:21;
Dt 18:10;
2Ch 28:3
p Lev 19:31
q 1Sa 28:13

33:7
r 2Ch 7:16

33:8
s 2Sa 7:10

33:9
t Jer 15:4

²⁷Hezekiah had very great riches and honor,*a* and he made treasuries for his silver and gold and for his precious stones, spices, shields and all kinds of valuables. ²⁸He also made buildings to store the harvest of grain, new wine and oil; and he made stalls for various kinds of cattle, and pens for the flocks. ²⁹He built villages and acquired great numbers of flocks and herds, for God had given him very great riches.*b*

³⁰It was Hezekiah who blocked*c* the upper outlet of the Gihon*d* spring and channeled the water down to the west side of the City of David. He succeeded in everything he undertook. ³¹But when envoys were sent by the rulers of Babylon*e* to ask him about the miraculous sign*f* that had occurred in the land, God left him to test*g* him and to know everything that was in his heart.

³²The other events of Hezekiah's reign and his acts of devotion are written in the vision of the prophet Isaiah son of Amoz in the book of the kings of Judah and Israel. ³³Hezekiah rested with his fathers and was buried on the hill where the tombs of David's descendants are. All Judah and the people of Jerusalem honored him when he died. And Manasseh his son succeeded him as king.

Chapter 33 Theme _____

33 Manasseh*h* was twelve years old when he became king, and he reigned in Jerusalem fifty-five years. ²He did evil in the eyes of the Lord,*i* following the detestable*j* practices of the nations the Lord had driven out before the Israelites. ³He rebuilt the high places his father Hezekiah had demolished; he also erected altars to the Baals and made Asherah poles.*k* He bowed down*l* to all the starry hosts and worshiped them. ⁴He built altars in the temple of the Lord, of which the Lord had said, "My Name*m* will remain in Jerusalem forever." ⁵In both courts of the temple of the Lord,*n* he built altars to all the starry hosts. ⁶He sacrificed his sons*o* in*a* the fire in the Valley of Ben Hinnom, practiced sorcery, divination and witchcraft, and consulted mediums*p* and spiritists.*q* He did much evil in the eyes of the Lord, provoking him to anger.

⁷He took the carved image he had made and put it in God's temple,*r* of which God had said to David and to his son Solomon, "In this temple and in Jerusalem, which I have chosen out of all the tribes of Israel, I will put my Name forever. ⁸I will not again make the feet of the Israelites leave the land*s* I assigned to your forefathers, if only they will be careful to do everything I commanded them concerning all the laws, decrees and ordinances given through Moses." ⁹But Manasseh led Judah and the people of Jerusalem astray, so that they did more evil than the nations the Lord had destroyed before the Israelites.*t*

a 6 Or *He made his sons pass through*

34:33
a ver 3-7;
Dt 18:9

35:1
b Ex 12:1-30;
Nu 9:3; 28:16

35:3
c Dt 33:10;
1Ch 23:26;
2Ch 5:7; 17:7

35:4
d ver 10;
1Ch 9:10-13;
24:1;
2Ch 8:14;
Ezr 6:18

35:6
e Lev 11:44;
2Ch 29:5,15

35:7
f 2Ch 30:24
g 2Ch 31:3

35:8
h 1Ch 29:3;
2Ch 29:31-36
i 1Ch 6:13

35:9
j 2Ch 31:12
k 2Ch 31:13

35:10
l ver 4;
Ezr 6:18
m 2Ch 30:16

35:11
n 2Ch 29:22,34;
30:17

35:13
o Ex 12:2-11;
Lev 6:25;
1Sa 2:13-15

³²Then he had everyone in Jerusalem and Benjamin pledge themselves to it; the people of Jerusalem did this in accordance with the covenant of God, the God of their fathers.

³³Josiah removed all the detestable*a* idols from all the territory belonging to the Israelites, and he had all who were present in Israel serve the LORD their God. As long as he lived, they did not fail to follow the LORD, the God of their fathers.

Chapter 35 Theme

35 Josiah celebrated the Passover*b* to the LORD in Jerusalem, and the Passover lamb was slaughtered on the fourteenth day of the first month. ²He appointed the priests to their duties and encouraged them in the service of the LORD's temple. ³He said to the Levites, who instructed*c* all Israel and who had been consecrated to the LORD: "Put the sacred ark in the temple that Solomon son of David king of Israel built. It is not to be carried about on your shoulders. Now serve the LORD your God and his people Israel. ⁴Prepare yourselves by families in your divisions,*d* according to the directions written by David king of Israel and by his son Solomon.

⁵"Stand in the holy place with a group of Levites for each subdivision of the families of your fellow countrymen, the lay people. ⁶Slaughter the Passover lambs, consecrate yourselves*e* and prepare ⌊the lambs⌋ for your fellow countrymen, doing what the LORD commanded through Moses."

⁷Josiah provided for all the lay people who were there a total of thirty thousand sheep and goats for the Passover offerings,*f* and also three thousand cattle—all from the king's own possessions.*g*

⁸His officials also contributed*h* voluntarily to the people and the priests and Levites. Hilkiah,*i* Zechariah and Jehiel, the administrators of God's temple, gave the priests twenty-six hundred Passover offerings and three hundred cattle. ⁹Also Conaniah*j* along with Shemaiah and Nethanel, his brothers, and Hashabiah, Jeiel and Jozabad,*k* the leaders of the Levites, provided five thousand Passover offerings and five hundred head of cattle for the Levites.

¹⁰The service was arranged and the priests stood in their places with the Levites in their divisions*l* as the king had ordered.*m* ¹¹The Passover lambs were slaughtered,*n* and the priests sprinkled the blood handed to them, while the Levites skinned the animals. ¹²They set aside the burnt offerings to give them to the subdivisions of the families of the people to offer to the LORD, as is written in the Book of Moses. They did the same with the cattle. ¹³They roasted the Passover animals over the fire as prescribed,*o* and boiled the holy offerings in pots, caldrons and pans and served them quickly to all the people. ¹⁴After this, they made preparations for themselves

and for the priests, because the priests, the descendants of Aaron, were sacrificing the burnt offerings and the fat portions[a] until nightfall. So the Levites made preparations for themselves and for the Aaronic priests.

[15] The musicians,[b] the descendants of Asaph, were in the places prescribed by David, Asaph, Heman and Jeduthun the king's seer. The gatekeepers at each gate did not need to leave their posts, because their fellow Levites made the preparations for them.

[16] So at that time the entire service of the LORD was carried out for the celebration of the Passover and the offering of burnt offerings on the altar of the LORD, as King Josiah had ordered. [17] The Israelites who were present celebrated the Passover at that time and observed the Feast of Unleavened Bread for seven days. [18] The Passover had not been observed like this in Israel since the days of the prophet Samuel; and none of the kings of Israel had ever celebrated such a Passover as did Josiah, with the priests, the Levites and all Judah and Israel who were there with the people of Jerusalem. [19] This Passover was celebrated in the eighteenth year of Josiah's reign.

[20] After all this, when Josiah had set the temple in order, Neco king of Egypt went up to fight at Carchemish[c] on the Euphrates,[d] and Josiah marched out to meet him in battle. [21] But Neco sent messengers to him, saying, "What quarrel is there between you and me, O king of Judah? It is not you I am attacking at this time, but the house with which I am at war. God has told[e] me to hurry; so stop opposing God, who is with me, or he will destroy you."

[22] Josiah, however, would not turn away from him, but disguised[f] himself to engage him in battle. He would not listen to what Neco had said at God's command but went to fight him on the plain of Megiddo.

[23] Archers[g] shot King Josiah, and he told his officers, "Take me away; I am badly wounded." [24] So they took him out of his chariot, put him in the other chariot he had and brought him to Jerusalem, where he died. He was buried in the tombs of his fathers, and all Judah and Jerusalem mourned for him.

[25] Jeremiah composed laments for Josiah, and to this day all the men and women singers commemorate Josiah in the laments.[h] These became a tradition in Israel and are written in the Laments.

[26] The other events of Josiah's reign and his acts of devotion, according to what is written in the Law of the LORD— [27] all the events, from beginning to end, are written in the book of the kings of Israel and Judah.

Chapter 36 Theme

36 And the people of the land took Jehoahaz son of Josiah and made him king in Jerusalem in place of his father.

35:14
[a] Ex 29:13

35:15
[b] 1Ch 25:1;
26:12-19;
2Ch 29:30;
Ne 12:46;
Ps 68:25

35:20
[c] Isa 10:9;
Jer 46:2
[d] Ge 2:14

35:21
[e] 1Ki 13:18;
2Ki 18:25

35:22
[f] Jdg 5:19;
1Sa 28:8;
2Ch 18:29

35:23
[g] 1Ki 22:34

35:25
[h] Jer 22:10,
15-16

36:4
a Jer 22:10-12

36:5
b Jer 22:18;
26:1; 35:1

36:6
c Jer 25:9; 27:6;
Eze 29:18
d 2Ch 33:11;
Eze 19:9;
Da 1:1

36:7
e 2Ki 24:13;
Ezr 1:7;
Da 1:2

36:9
f Jer 22:24-28;
52:31

36:10
g ver 18;
2Ki 20:17;
Ezr 1:7;
Jer 22:25;
24:1; 29:1;
37:1;
Eze 17:12

36:11
h 2Ki 24:17;
Jer 27:1; 28:1

36:12
i Jer 37:1-39:18
j Dt 8:3;
2Ch 7:14;
2Ch 33:23;
Jer 21:3-7

36:13
k Eze 17:13
l 2Ki 17:14;
2Ch 30:8

36:14
m 1Ch 5:25

36:15
n Isa 5:4;
44:26;
Jer 7:25;
Hag 1:13;
Zec 1:4;
Mal 2:7; 3:1
o Jer 7:13,25;
25:3-4;
35:14,15;
44:4-6

36:16
p 2Ki 2:23;
Pr 1:25;
Jer 5:13
q Ezr 5:12;
Pr 1:30-31
r 2Ch 30:10;
Pr 29:1;
Zec 1:2

²Jehoahaz[a] was twenty-three years old when he became king, and he reigned in Jerusalem three months. ³The king of Egypt dethroned him in Jerusalem and imposed on Judah a levy of a hundred talents[b] of silver and a talent[c] of gold. ⁴The king of Egypt made Eliakim, a brother of Jehoahaz, king over Judah and Jerusalem and changed Eliakim's name to Jehoiakim. But Neco[a] took Eliakim's brother Jehoahaz and carried him off to Egypt.

⁵Jehoiakim[b] was twenty-five years old when he became king, and he reigned in Jerusalem eleven years. He did evil in the eyes of the LORD his God. ⁶Nebuchadnezzar[c] king of Babylon attacked him and bound him with bronze shackles to take him to Babylon.[d] ⁷Nebuchadnezzar also took to Babylon articles from the temple of the LORD and put them in his temple[d] there.[e]

⁸The other events of Jehoiakim's reign, the detestable things he did and all that was found against him, are written in the book of the kings of Israel and Judah. And Jehoiachin his son succeeded him as king.

⁹Jehoiachin[f] was eighteen[e] years old when he became king, and he reigned in Jerusalem three months and ten days. He did evil in the eyes of the LORD. ¹⁰In the spring, King Nebuchadnezzar sent for him and brought him to Babylon,[g] together with articles of value from the temple of the LORD, and he made Jehoiachin's uncle,[f] Zedekiah, king over Judah and Jerusalem.

¹¹Zedekiah[h] was twenty-one years old when he became king, and he reigned in Jerusalem eleven years. ¹²He did evil in the eyes of the LORD[i] his God and did not humble[j] himself before Jeremiah the prophet, who spoke the word of the LORD. ¹³He also rebelled against King Nebuchadnezzar, who had made him take an oath[k] in God's name. He became stiff-necked[l] and hardened his heart and would not turn to the LORD, the God of Israel. ¹⁴Furthermore, all the leaders of the priests and the people became more and more unfaithful,[m] following all the detestable practices of the nations and defiling the temple of the LORD, which he had consecrated in Jerusalem.

¹⁵The LORD, the God of their fathers, sent word to them through his messengers[n] again and again,[o] because he had pity on his people and on his dwelling place. ¹⁶But they mocked God's messengers, despised his words and scoffed[p] at his prophets until the wrath[q] of the LORD was aroused against his people and there was no remedy.[r] ¹⁷He brought up against them the king of the Babylonians,[g] who killed their young men with the sword in the sanctuary, and spared

---

a 2 Hebrew *Joahaz*, a variant of *Jehoahaz*; also in verse 4   b 3 That is, about 3 3/4 tons (about 3.4 metric tons)   c 3 That is, about 75 pounds (about 34 kilograms)   d 7 Or *palace*   e 9 One Hebrew manuscript, some Septuagint manuscripts and Syriac (see also 2 Kings 24:8); most Hebrew manuscripts *eight*   f 10 Hebrew *brother*, that is, relative (see 2 Kings 24:17)   g 17 Or *Chaldeans* neither young man[a] nor young woman, old man or aged. God handed all of them over to Nebuchadnezzar.[b] [18]He carried to Babylon all the articles[c] from the temple of God, both large and small, and the treasures of the LORD's temple and the treasures of the king and his officials. [19]They set fire[d] to God's temple[e] and broke down the wall[f] of Jerusalem; they burned all the palaces and destroyed[g] everything of value there.[h]

[20]He carried into exile[i] to Babylon the remnant, who escaped from the sword, and they became servants[j] to him and his sons until the kingdom of Persia came to power. [21]The land enjoyed its sabbath rests;[k] all the time of its desolation it rested,[l] until the seventy years[m] were completed in fulfillment of the word of the LORD spoken by Jeremiah.

[22]In the first year of Cyrus[n] king of Persia, in order to fulfill the word of the LORD spoken by Jeremiah, the LORD moved the heart of Cyrus king of Persia to make a proclamation throughout his realm and to put it in writing:

[23]"This is what Cyrus king of Persia says:

"'The LORD, the God of heaven, has given me all the kingdoms of the earth and he has appointed[o] me to build a temple for him at Jerusalem in Judah. Anyone of his people among you—may the LORD his God be with him, and let him go up.'"

36:22 [n] Isa 44:28; 45:1,13; Jer 25:12; 29:10; Da 1:21; 6:28; 10:1   36:23 [o] Jdg 4:10

36:17
[a] Jer 6:11
[b] Ezr 5:12; Jer 32:28

36:18
[c] ver 7,10

36:19
[d] Jer 11:16; 17:27; 21:10,14; 22:7; 32:29; 39:8; La 4:11; Eze 20:47; Am 2:5; Zec 11:1;
[e] 1Ki 9:8-9
[f] 2Ki 14:13
[g] La 2:6
[h] Ps 79:1-3

36:20
[i] Lev 26:44; 2Ki 24:14; Ezr 2:1; Ne 7:6
[j] Jer 27:7

36:21
[k] Lev 25:4; 26:34
[l] 1Ch 22:9
[m] Jer 1:1; 25:11; 27:22; 29:10; 40:1; Da 9:2; Zec 1:12; 7:5

Theme of 2 Chronicles:

			SEGMENT DIVISIONS	CHAPTER THEMES

Author:

Date:

Purpose:

Key Words:

  temple

  palace

  ark

  covenant

  cry (cried)

  seek, seeking,
  consult, inquire
  of, sought
  (inquired of,
  took, in search
  of)

  heart

  pray
  (prayer[s],
  prayed, prays)

  prophet(s)

Segment Divisions			Chapter
			1
			2
			3
			4
			5
			6
			7
			8
			9
			10
			11
			12
			13
			14
			15
			16
			17
			18
			19
			20
			21
			22
			23
			24
			25
			26
			27
			28
			29
			30
			31
			32
			33
			34
			35
			36

EZRA

*E*very seventh year the land was to lie fallow. This was God's ordinance to his people, part of his law by which they were to govern their lives.

However, for 490 years God's people had not paid attention to this statute, nor to others. The land had missed 70 Sabbaths. As prophesied by Jeremiah, God would exact 70 years for the land. Then the Spirit of God would move on behalf of his people. He would stir up the spirit of Cyrus, king of Persia, so that Cyrus would send out a written decree proclaiming, "The LORD, the God of heaven, has given me all the kingdoms of the earth and he has appointed me to build a temple for him at Jerusalem in Judah. Anyone of his people among you—may the LORD his God be with him, and let him go up" (2 Chronicles 36:23).

And so a remnant returned from the land of exile to the land promised to Abraham, Isaac, and Jacob as an everlasting possession. Ezra tells us what happened.

∾ THINGS TO DO

To better understand Ezra, look at Isaiah's prophecy in 44:28–45:7. This was written about 175 years before Cyrus was born.

Ezra falls into two main segments: chapters 1 through 6 and chapters 7 through 10. There is a lapse of approximately 58 to 60 years between these two segments.

Chapters 1-6

1. Read this segment chapter by chapter and do the following:

   a. In a distinctive way mark in the text the key words listed on the EZRA AT A GLANCE chart on page 791.

   b. Pay attention to any references to time. Mark these in a way that will enable you to spot them immediately. You may want to put a symbol in the margin next to the references to time.

   c. When you come to a reference of a particular king, consult the historical chart THE TIMES OF EZRA, NEHEMIAH, AND ESTHER, on page 774. This will help you appreciate the historical setting of the book of Ezra and see the relationship of Ezra to Esther and Nehemiah, who were contemporaries of Ezra.

   d. If specific people play a significant role, record their names in the margin and briefly describe what they did.

2. There are seven official documents or letters in the book of Ezra, all of which (except the first) were written in Aramaic, the international language of the times. The first document, written by Cyrus, the Persian king, is in Hebrew. These documents or letters are found in Ezra 1:2-4; 4:11-16; 4:17-22; 5:7-17; 6:2-5; and 6:6-12. The last one is in the second segment of the book, 7:12-26.

As you come to each document or letter in the text, underline who presented it. Then in the margin list the major points of the document or letter. This information will help you keep track of the opposition the Jews faced and how God moved on their behalf.

3. After you finish reading each chapter, identify the main subject, theme, or event and record it on the line next to the chapter number and on EZRA AT A GLANCE.

4. The book of Ezra records when the temple construction began and when it was completed. Write this information in the margin in bold print so you can easily find it.

5. For a better understanding of the Jewish feasts, consult the chart THE FEASTS OF ISRAEL on pages 210 and 211.

Chapters 7-10

1. This is the first time Ezra's name appears in this book. Note how he is described. Observe this man and the lessons you can learn from his life. List your insights in the margin under LFL, "Lessons for Life."

2. Don't forget to mark the key words listed on EZRA AT A GLANCE. Also, note your insights on the last official document in 7:12-26.

3. Watch for and mark references to time and to kings. Note these as you did before.

4. Record the theme of each chapter as you did in the first segment of Ezra.

5. How does the second segment of Ezra, chapters 7 through 10, differ from the first?

   a. Record the theme or subject of the first six chapters on EZRA AT A GLANCE under "Segment Divisions." Do the same for the last segment, chapters 7 through 10.

   b. On the second line for segment divisions write in the name(s) of the central character(s) of each segment.

   c. Consult the historical chart THE TIMES OF EZRA, NEHEMIAH, AND ESTHER on page 774 and then record on the chart the number of years covered in each segment.

6. What is the theme or teaching of Ezra? Record this and any other requested information in the appropriate place on EZRA AT A GLANCE.

∾ THINGS TO THINK ABOUT

1. How did the people in Ezra's time deal with their sin? What showed you whether their sorrow led to repentance or simply regret? How do you deal with sin in your own life? How is it dealt with within your church congregation?

2. What did you learn about prayer and fasting? Are either of these integral parts of your walk with the Lord? Why?

3. As you review what you have learned in Ezra, what have you learned about your God, his promises, and his ways? What difference can this knowledge make in your life?

∾∾∾∾∾∾

Chapter 1 Theme _____

1:1
a Jer 25:11-12; 29:10-14
b 2Ch 36:22,23

1 In the first year of Cyrus king of Persia, in order to fulfill the word of the LORD spoken by Jeremiah,a the LORD moved the heartb of Cyrus king of Persia to make a proclamation throughout his realm and to put it in writing:

1:2
c Isa 44:28; 45:13
d Ezr 5:13

2"This is what Cyrus king of Persia says:

" 'The LORD, the God of heaven, has given me all the kingdoms of the earth and he has appointedc me to buildd a temple for him at Jerusalem in Judah. 3Anyone of his people among you—may his God be with him, and let him go up to Jerusalem in Judah and build the temple of the LORD, the God of Israel, the God who is in Jerusalem. 4And the people of any

1:4
e Isa 10:20-22

place where survivorse may now be living are to provide him

THE TIMES OF EZRA, NEHEMIAH, AND ESTHER

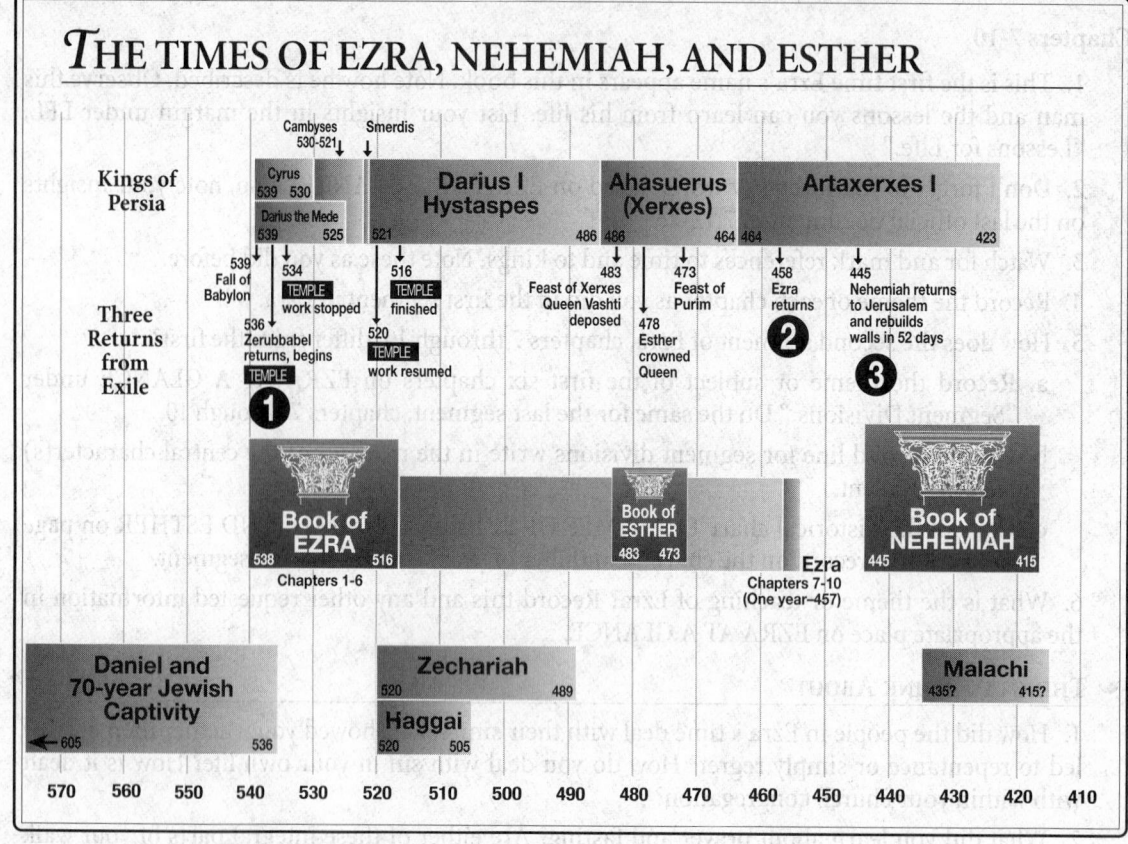

Kings of Persia			
Cyrus 539 530 / Darius the Mede 539 525	Cambyses 530-521 / Smerdis	Darius I Hystaspes 521 486	Ahasuerus (Xerxes) 486 464	Artaxerxes I 464 423

Three Returns from Exile

- 539 Fall of Babylon
- 536 Zerubbabel returns, begins TEMPLE **1**
- 534 TEMPLE work stopped
- 520 TEMPLE work resumed
- 516 TEMPLE finished
- 483 Feast of Xerxes Queen Vashti deposed
- 478 Esther crowned Queen
- 473 Feast of Purim
- 458 Ezra returns **2**
- 445 Nehemiah returns to Jerusalem and rebuilds walls in 52 days **3**

Book of EZRA 538 516
Chapters 1-6

Book of ESTHER 483 473

Book of NEHEMIAH 445 415

Ezra Chapters 7-10 (One year–457)

Daniel and 70-year Jewish Captivity ←605 536

Zechariah 520 489

Haggai 520 505

Malachi 435? 415?

570 560 550 540 530 520 510 500 490 480 470 460 450 440 430 420 410

---

with silver and gold, with goods and livestock, and with free-will offerings[a] for the temple of God in Jerusalem.'"[b]

[5]Then the family heads of Judah and Benjamin,[c] and the priests and Levites—everyone whose heart God had moved[d]—prepared to go up and build the house[e] of the LORD in Jerusalem. [6]All their neighbors assisted them with articles of silver and gold, with goods and livestock, and with valuable gifts, in addition to all the freewill offerings. [7]Moreover, King Cyrus brought out the articles belonging to the temple of the LORD, which Nebuchadnezzar had carried away from Jerusalem and had placed in the temple of his god.[a][f] [8]Cyrus king of Persia had them brought by Mithredath the treasurer, who counted them out to Sheshbazzar[g] the prince of Judah.

[9]This was the inventory:

gold dishes	30
silver dishes	1,000
silver pans[b]	29

[a]7 Or *gods*   [b]9 The meaning of the Hebrew for this word is uncertain.

1:4 [a]Nu 15:3; Ps 50:14; 54:6; 116:17 [b]Ezr 4:3; 5:13; 6:3,14

1:5 [c]Ezr 4:1; Ne 11:4 [d]ver 1; Ex 35:20-22; 2Ch 36:22; Hag 1:14; Php 2:13 [e]Ps 127:1

1:7 [f]2Ki 24:13; 2Ch 36:7,10; Ezr 5:14; 6:5

1:8 [g]Ezr 5:14

2:1
*a*2Ch 36:20;
Ne 7:6
*b*2Ki 24:16;
25:12
*c*Ne 7:73

¹⁰gold bowls   30

matching silver bowls   410

other articles   1,000

¹¹In all, there were 5,400 articles of gold and of silver. Sheshbazzar brought all these along when the exiles came up from Babylon to Jerusalem.

Chapter 2 Theme

2 Now these are the people of the province who came up from the captivity of the exiles,*a* whom Nebuchadnezzar king of Babylon*b* had taken captive to Babylon (they returned to Jerusalem and Judah, each to his own town,*c* ²in company with Zerubbabel,*d* Jeshua,*e* Nehemiah, Seraiah,*f* Reelaiah, Mordecai, Bilshan, Mispar, Bigvai, Rehum and Baanah):

2:2
*d*1Ch 3:19
*e*Ezr 3:2
*f*Ne 10:2

The list of the men of the people of Israel:

³the descendants of Parosh*g*	2,172
⁴of Shephatiah	372
⁵of Arah	775
⁶of Pahath-Moab (through the line of Jeshua and Joab)	2,812
⁷of Elam	1,254
⁸of Zattu	945
⁹of Zaccai	760
¹⁰of Bani	642
¹¹of Bebai	623
¹²of Azgad	1,222
¹³of Adonikam*h*	666
¹⁴of Bigvai	2,056
¹⁵of Adin	454
¹⁶of Ater (through Hezekiah)	98
¹⁷of Bezai	323
¹⁸of Jorah	112
¹⁹of Hashum	223
²⁰of Gibbar	95
²¹the men of Bethlehem*i*	123
²²of Netophah	56
²³of Anathoth	128
²⁴of Azmaveth	42
²⁵of Kiriath Jearim,*a* Kephirah and Beeroth	743
²⁶of Ramah*j* and Geba	621
²⁷of Micmash	122

2:3
*g*Ezr 8:3

2:13
*h*Ezr 8:13

2:21
*i*Mic 5:2

2:26
*j*Jos 18:25

*a*25 See Septuagint (see also Neh. 7:29); Hebrew *Kiriath Arim.*

²⁸of Bethel and Ai*a*	223
²⁹of Nebo	52
³⁰of Magbish	156
³¹of the other Elam	1,254
³²of Harim	320
³³of Lod, Hadid and Ono	725
³⁴of Jericho*b*	345
³⁵of Senaah	3,630

³⁶The priests:

the descendants of Jedaiah*c* (through the family of Jeshua)	973
³⁷of Immer*d*	1,052
³⁸of Pashhur*e*	1,247
³⁹of Harim*f*	1,017

⁴⁰The Levites:*g*

the descendants of Jeshua*h* and Kadmiel (through the line of Hodaviah)	74

⁴¹The singers:*i*

the descendants of Asaph	128

⁴²The gatekeepers*j* of the temple:

the descendants of Shallum, Ater, Talmon, Akkub, Hatita and Shobai	139

⁴³The temple servants:*k*

the descendants of
Ziha, Hasupha, Tabbaoth,
⁴⁴Keros, Siaha, Padon,
⁴⁵Lebanah, Hagabah, Akkub,
⁴⁶Hagab, Shalmai, Hanan,
⁴⁷Giddel, Gahar, Reaiah,
⁴⁸Rezin, Nekoda, Gazzam,
⁴⁹Uzza, Paseah, Besai,
⁵⁰Asnah, Meunim, Nephussim,
⁵¹Bakbuk, Hakupha, Harhur,
⁵²Bazluth, Mehida, Harsha,
⁵³Barkos, Sisera, Temah,
⁵⁴Neziah and Hatipha

⁵⁵The descendants of the servants of Solomon:

the descendants of
Sotai, Hassophereth, Peruda,

2:28
a Ge 12:8

2:34
b 1Ki 16:34; 2Ch 28:15

2:36
c 1Ch 24:7

2:37
d 1Ch 24:14

2:38
e 1Ch 9:12

2:39
f 1Ch 24:8

2:40
g Ge 29:34; Nu 3:9; Dt 18:6-7; 1Ch 16:4; Ezr 7:7; 8:15; Ne 12:24
h Ezr 3:9

2:41
i 1Ch 15:16

2:42
j 1Sa 3:15; 1Ch 9:17

2:43
k 1Ch 9:2; Ne 11:21

2:58
a 1Ki 9:21;
1Ch 9:2

2:59
b Nu 1:18

2:61
c 2Sa 17:27

2:62
d Nu 3:10;
16:39-40

2:63
e Lev 2:3,10
f Ex 28:30;
Nu 27:21

2:65
g 2Sa 19:35

2:66
h Isa 66:20

2:68
i Ex 25:2

2:70
j ver 1;
1Ch 9:2;
Ne 11:3-4

3:1
k Ne 7:73; 8:1
l Lev 23:24

3:2
m Ezr 2:2;
Ne 12:1,8;
Hag 2:2
n Hag 1:1;
Zec 6:11
o 1Ch 3:17

⁵⁶Jaala, Darkon, Giddel,
⁵⁷Shephatiah, Hattil,
Pokereth-Hazzebaim and Ami

⁵⁸The temple servants*a* and the descendants
of the servants of Solomon   392

⁵⁹The following came up from the towns of Tel Melah, Tel Harsha, Kerub, Addon and Immer, but they could not show that their families were descended*b* from Israel:

⁶⁰The descendants of
Delaiah, Tobiah and Nekoda   652

⁶¹And from among the priests:

The descendants of
Hobaiah, Hakkoz and Barzillai (a man who had
married a daughter of Barzillai the Gileadite*c* and was
called by that name).

⁶²These searched for their family records, but they could not find them and so were excluded from the priesthood*d* as unclean. ⁶³The governor ordered them not to eat any of the most sacred food*e* until there was a priest ministering with the Urim and Thummim.*f*

⁶⁴The whole company numbered 42,360, ⁶⁵besides their 7,337 menservants and maidservants; and they also had 200 men and women singers.*g* ⁶⁶They had 736 horses,*h* 245 mules, ⁶⁷435 camels and 6,720 donkeys.

⁶⁸When they arrived at the house of the LORD in Jerusalem, some of the heads of the families*i* gave freewill offerings toward the rebuilding of the house of God on its site. ⁶⁹According to their ability they gave to the treasury for this work 61,000 drachmas*a* of gold, 5,000 minas*b* of silver and 100 priestly garments.

⁷⁰The priests, the Levites, the singers, the gatekeepers and the temple servants settled in their own towns, along with some of the other people, and the rest of the Israelites settled in their towns.*j*

Chapter 3 Theme

3 When the seventh month came and the Israelites had settled in their towns,*k* the people assembled*l* as one man in Jerusalem. ²Then Jeshua*m* son of Jozadak*n* and his fellow priests and Zerubbabel son of Shealtiel*o* and his associates began to build the altar of the God of Israel to sacrifice burnt offerings on it, in accordance

a 69 That is, about 1,100 pounds (about 500 kilograms)   b 69 That is, about 3 tons (about 2.9 metric tons) with what is written in the Law of Moses*a* the man of God. ³Despite their fear*b* of the peoples around them, they built the altar on its foundation and sacrificed burnt offerings on it to the LORD, both the morning and evening sacrifices.*c* ⁴Then in accordance with what is written, they celebrated the Feast of Tabernacles*d* with the required number of burnt offerings prescribed for each day. ⁵After that, they presented the regular burnt offerings, the New Moon*e* sacrifices and the sacrifices for all the appointed sacred feasts of the LORD,*f* as well as those brought as freewill offerings to the LORD. ⁶On the first day of the seventh month they began to offer burnt offerings to the LORD, though the foundation of the LORD's temple had not yet been laid.

⁷Then they gave money to the masons and carpenters, and gave food and drink and oil to the people of Sidon and Tyre, so that they would bring cedar logs*g* by sea from Lebanon*h* to Joppa, as authorized by Cyrus*i* king of Persia.

⁸In the second month of the second year after their arrival at the house of God in Jerusalem, Zerubbabel*j* son of Shealtiel, Jeshua son of Jozadak and the rest of their brothers (the priests and the Levites and all who had returned from the captivity to Jerusalem) began the work, appointing Levites twenty*k* years of age and older to supervise the building of the house of the LORD. ⁹Jeshua*l* and his sons and brothers and Kadmiel and his sons (descendants of Hodaviah*a*) and the sons of Henadad and their sons and brothers—all Levites—joined together in supervising those working on the house of God.

¹⁰When the builders laid*m* the foundation of the temple of the LORD, the priests in their vestments and with trumpets,*n* and the Levites (the sons of Asaph) with cymbals, took their places to praise*o* the LORD, as prescribed by David*p* king of Israel.*q* ¹¹With praise and thanksgiving they sang to the LORD:

> "He is good;
> his love to Israel endures forever."*r*

And all the people gave a great shout*s* of praise to the LORD, because the foundation of the house of the LORD was laid. ¹²But many of the older priests and Levites and family heads, who had seen the former temple,*t* wept aloud when they saw the foundation of this temple being laid, while many others shouted for joy. ¹³No one could distinguish the sound of the shouts of joy*u* from the sound of weeping, because the people made so much noise. And the sound was heard far away.

a9 Hebrew *Yehudah*, probably a variant of *Hodaviah*

3:2
a Ex 20:24;
Dt 12:5-6

3:3
b Ezr 4:4;
Da 9:25
c Ex 29:39;
Nu 28:1-8

3:4
d Ex 23:16;
Nu 29:12-38;
Ne 8:14-18;
Zec 14:16-19

3:5
e Nu 28:3,11,14;
Col 2:16
f Lev 23:1-44;
Nu 29:39

3:7
g 1Ch 14:1
h Isa 35:2
i Ezr 1:2-4; 6:3

3:8
j Zec 4:9
k 1Ch 23:24

3:9
l Ezr 2:40

3:10
m Ezr 5:16
n Nu 10:2;
1Ch 16:6
o 1Ch 25:1
p 1Ch 6:31
q Zec 6:12

3:11
r 1Ch 16:34,41;
2Ch 7:3;
Ps 107:1;
118:1
s Ne 12:24

3:12
t Hag 2:3,9

3:13
u Job 8:21;
Ps 27:6; Isa 16:9

4:2
a 2Ki 17:24;
19:37
b 2Ki 17:41

4:3
c Ezr 1:1-4;
Ne 2:20

4:4
d Ezr 3:3

4:6
e Est 1:1;
Da 9:1
f Est 3:13; 9:5

4:7
g Ezr 7:1;
Ne 2:1
h 2Ki 18:26;
Isa 36:11;
Da 2:4

4:9
i Ezr 5:6;
6:6,13

4:10
j ver 17;
Ne 4:2

4:12
k Ezr 5:3,9

4:13
l Ezr 7:24;
Ne 5:4

Chapter 4 Theme

4 When the enemies of Judah and Benjamin heard that the exiles were building a temple for the LORD, the God of Israel, ²they came to Zerubbabel and to the heads of the families and said, "Let us help you build because, like you, we seek your God and have been sacrificing to him since the time of Esarhaddon*a* king of Assyria, who brought us here."*b*

³But Zerubbabel, Jeshua and the rest of the heads of the families of Israel answered, "You have no part with us in building a temple to our God. We alone will build it for the LORD, the God of Israel, as King Cyrus, the king of Persia, commanded us."*c*

⁴Then the peoples around them set out to discourage the people of Judah and make them afraid to go on building.*a d* ⁵They hired counselors to work against them and frustrate their plans during the entire reign of Cyrus king of Persia and down to the reign of Darius king of Persia.

⁶At the beginning of the reign of Xerxes,*b e* they lodged an accusation against the people of Judah and Jerusalem.*f*

⁷And in the days of Artaxerxes*g* king of Persia, Bishlam, Mithredath, Tabeel and the rest of his associates wrote a letter to Artaxerxes. The letter was written in Aramaic script and in the Aramaic*h* language.*c,d*

⁸Rehum the commanding officer and Shimshai the secretary wrote a letter against Jerusalem to Artaxerxes the king as follows:

⁹Rehum the commanding officer and Shimshai the secretary, together with the rest of their associates *i* —the judges and officials over the men from Tripolis, Persia,*e* Erech and Babylon, the Elamites of Susa, ¹⁰and the other people whom the great and honorable Ashurbanipal*f* deported and settled in the city of Samaria and elsewhere in Trans-Euphrates.*j*

¹¹(This is a copy of the letter they sent him.)

To King Artaxerxes,

From your servants, the men of Trans-Euphrates:

¹²The king should know that the Jews who came up to us from you have gone to Jerusalem and are rebuilding that rebellious and wicked city. They are restoring the walls and repairing the foundations.*k*

¹³Furthermore, the king should know that if this city is built and its walls are restored, no more taxes, tribute or duty*l* will

a4 Or *and troubled them as they built*   *b6* Hebrew *Ahasuerus,* a variant of Xerxes' Persian name   *c7* Or *written in Aramaic and translated*   *d7* The text of Ezra 4:8—6:18 is in Aramaic.   *e9* Or *officials, magistrates and governors over the men from*   *f10* Aramaic *Osnappar,* a variant of *Ashurbanipal* be paid, and the royal revenues will suffer. [14]Now since we are under obligation to the palace and it is not proper for us to see the king dishonored, we are sending this message to inform the king, [15]so that a search may be made in the archives[a] of your predecessors. In these records you will find that this city is a rebellious city, troublesome to kings and provinces, a place of rebellion from ancient times. That is why this city was destroyed.[b] [16]We inform the king that if this city is built and its walls are restored, you will be left with nothing in Trans-Euphrates.

[17]The king sent this reply:

To Rehum the commanding officer, Shimshai the secretary and the rest of their associates living in Samaria and elsewhere in Trans-Euphrates:[c]

Greetings.

[18]The letter you sent us has been read and translated in my presence. [19]I issued an order and a search was made, and it was found that this city has a long history of revolt[d] against kings and has been a place of rebellion and sedition. [20]Jerusalem has had powerful kings ruling over the whole of Trans-Euphrates,[e] and taxes, tribute and duty were paid to them. [21]Now issue an order to these men to stop work, so that this city will not be rebuilt until I so order. [22]Be careful not to neglect this matter. Why let this threat grow, to the detriment of the royal interests?[f]

[23]As soon as the copy of the letter of King Artaxerxes was read to Rehum and Shimshai the secretary and their associates,[g] they went immediately to the Jews in Jerusalem and compelled them by force to stop.

[24]Thus the work on the house of God in Jerusalem came to a standstill until the second year of the reign of Darius[h] king of Persia.

Chapter 5 Theme _____

5 Now Haggai[i] the prophet and Zechariah[j] the prophet, a descendant of Iddo, prophesied[k] to the Jews in Judah and Jerusalem in the name of the God of Israel, who was over them. [2]Then Zerubbabel[l] son of Shealtiel and Jeshua[m] son of Jozadak set to work[n] to rebuild the house of God in Jerusalem. And the prophets of God were with them, helping them.

[3]At that time Tattenai,[o] governor of Trans-Euphrates, and Shethar-Bozenai[p] and their associates went to them and asked, "Who authorized you to rebuild this temple and restore this

---

4:15
[a]Ezr 5:17; 6:1
[b]Est 3:8

4:17
[c]ver 10

4:19
[d]2Ki 18:7

4:20
[e]Ge 15:18-21;
Ex 23:31;
Jos 1:4;
1Ki 4:21;
1Ch 18:3;
Ps 72:8-11

4:22
[f]Da 6:2

4:23
[g]ver 9

4:24
[h]Ne 2:1-8;
Da 9:25;
Hag 1:1,15;
Zec 1:1

5:1
[i]Ezr 6:14;
Hag 1:1,3,12;
2:1,10,20
[j]Zec 1:1; 7:1
[k]Hag 1:14–2:9;
Zec 4:9-10; 8:9

5:2
[l]1Ch 3:19;
Hag 1:14; 2:21;
Zec 4:6-10
[m]Ezr 2:2; 3:2
[n]ver 8;
Hag 2:2-5

5:3
[o]Ezr 6:6
[p]Ezr 6:6

5:3
aver 9;
Ezr 1:3;
4:12

structure?"a 4They also asked, "What are the names of the men constructing this building?"a 5But the eye of their Godb was watching over the elders of the Jews, and they were not stopped until a report could go to Darius and his written reply be received.

6This is a copy of the letter that Tattenai, governor of Trans-Euphrates, and Shethar-Bozenai and their associates, the officials of Trans-Euphrates, sent to King Darius. 7The report they sent him read as follows:

5:5
b2Ki 25:28;
Ezr 7:6,9,28;
8:18,22,31;
Ne 2:8,18;
Ps 33:18;
Isa 66:14

To King Darius:

Cordial greetings.

8The king should know that we went to the district of Judah, to the temple of the great God. The people are building it with large stones and placing the timbers in the walls. The workc is being carried on with diligence and is making rapid progress under their direction.

5:8
cver 2

9We questioned the elders and asked them, "Who authorized you to rebuild this temple and restore this structure?"d 10We also asked them their names, so that we could write down the names of their leaders for your information.

5:9
dEzr 4:12

11This is the answer they gave us:

"We are the servants of the God of heaven and earth, and we are rebuilding the templee that was built many years ago, one that a great king of Israel built and finished. 12But because our fathers angeredf the God of heaven, he handed them over to Nebuchadnezzar the Chaldean, king of Babylon, who destroyed this temple and deported the people to Babylon.g

5:11
e1Ki 6:1;
2Ch 3:1-2

5:12
f2Ch 36:16
gDt 21:10;
28:36; 2Ki 24:1;
25:8,9,11;
Jer 1:3

13"However, in the first year of Cyrus king of Babylon, King Cyrus issued a decreeh to rebuild this house of God. 14He even removed from the templeb of Babylon the gold and silver articles of the house of God, which Nebuchadnezzar had taken from the temple in Jerusalem and brought to the templeb in Babylon.i

5:13
hEzr 1:1

"Then King Cyrus gave them to a man named Sheshbazzar,j whom he had appointed governor, 15and he told him, 'Take these articles and go and deposit them in the temple in Jerusalem. And rebuild the house of God on its site.' 16So this Sheshbazzar came and laid the foundations of the house of Godk in Jerusalem. From that day to the present it has been under construction but is not yet finished."

5:14
iEzr 1:7; 6:5;
Da 5:2
j1Ch 3:18

5:16
kEzr 3:10; 6:15

17Now if it pleases the king, let a search be made in the royal archivesl of Babylon to see if King Cyrus did in fact issue a

5:17
lEzr 4:15; 6:1,2

a4 See Septuagint; Aramaic 4We told them the names of the men constructing this building. b14 Or palace

781

decree to rebuild this house of God in Jerusalem. Then let the king send us his decision in this matter.

Chapter 6 Theme _____

6 King Darius then issued an order, and they searched in the archives*ᵃ* stored in the treasury at Babylon. ²A scroll was found in the citadel of Ecbatana in the province of Media, and this was written on it:

Memorandum:

³In the first year of King Cyrus, the king issued a decree concerning the temple of God in Jerusalem:

Let the temple be rebuilt as a place to present sacrifices, and let its foundations be laid.*ᵇ* It is to be ninety feet*ᵃ* high and ninety feet wide, ⁴with three courses*ᶜ* of large stones and one of timbers. The costs are to be paid by the royal treasury.*ᵈ* ⁵Also, the gold*ᵉ* and silver articles of the house of God, which Nebuchadnezzar took from the temple in Jerusalem and brought to Babylon, are to be returned to their places in the temple in Jerusalem; they are to be deposited in the house of God.*ᶠ*

⁶Now then, Tattenai,*ᵍ* governor of Trans-Euphrates, and Shethar-Bozenai*ʰ* and you, their fellow officials of that province, stay away from there. ⁷Do not interfere with the work on this temple of God. Let the governor of the Jews and the Jewish elders rebuild this house of God on its site.

⁸Moreover, I hereby decree what you are to do for these elders of the Jews in the construction of this house of God:

The expenses of these men are to be fully paid out of the royal treasury,*ⁱ* from the revenues*ʲ* of Trans-Euphrates, so that the work will not stop. ⁹Whatever is needed—young bulls, rams, male lambs for burnt offerings*ᵏ* to the God of heaven, and wheat, salt, wine and oil, as requested by the priests in Jerusalem—must be given them daily without fail, ¹⁰so that they may offer sacrifices pleasing to the God of heaven and pray for the well-being of the king and his sons.*ˡ*

¹¹Furthermore, I decree that if anyone changes this edict, a beam is to be pulled from his house and he is to be lifted up and impaled*ᵐ* on it. And for this crime his house is to be made a pile of rubble.*ⁿ* ¹²May God, who has caused his Name to dwell there,*ᵒ* overthrow any king or people who lifts a hand to change this decree or to destroy this temple in Jerusalem.

I Darius*ᵖ* have decreed it. Let it be carried out with diligence.

ᵃ3 Aramaic *sixty cubits* (about 27 meters)

6:1
ᵃ Ezr 4:15; 5:17

6:3
ᵇ Ezr 3:10; Hag 2:3

6:4
ᶜ 1Ki 6:36
ᵈ ver 8; Ezr 7:20

6:5
ᵉ 1Ch 29:2
ᶠ Ezr 1:7; 5:14

6:6
ᵍ Ezr 5:3
ʰ Ezr 5:3

6:8
ⁱ ver 4
ʲ 1Sa 9:20

6:9
ᵏ Lev 1:3,10

6:10
ˡ Ezr 7:23; 1Ti 2:1-2

6:11
ᵐ Dt 21:22-23; Est 2:23; 5:14; 9:14
ⁿ Ezr 7:26; Da 2:5; 3:29

6:12
ᵒ Ex 20:24; Dt 12:5; 1Ki 9:3; 2Ch 6:2
ᵖ ver 14

6:13
a Ezr 4:9

6:14
b Ezr 5:1
c Ezr 1:1-4
d ver 12
e Ezr 7:1;
Ne 2:1

6:15
f Zec 1:1; 4:9

6:16
g 1Ki 8:63;
2Ch 7:5

6:17
h 2Sa 6:13;
2Ch 29:21;
30:24;
Ezr 8:35

6:18
i 1Ch 23:6;
2Ch 35:4;
Lk 1:5
j 1Ch 24:1
k Nu 3:6-9;
8:9-11;
18:1-32

6:19
l Ex 12:11;
Nu 28:16

6:20
m 2Ch 30:15,
17; 35:11

6:21
n Ezr 9:1;
Ne 9:2
o Dt 18:9;
Ezr 9:11;
Eze 36:25
p 1Ch 22:19;
Ps 14:2

6:22
q Ex 12:17
r Ezr 1:1

7:1
s Ezr 4:7; 6:14;
Ne 2:1
t 2Ki 22:4

7:2
u 1Ki 1:8;
1Ch 6:8
v Ne 11:11

7:6
w Ne 12:36
x Ezr 5:5;
Isa 41:20

7:7
y Ezr 8:1

¹³Then, because of the decree King Darius had sent, Tattenai, governor of Trans-Euphrates, and Shethar-Bozenai and their associates*a* carried it out with diligence. ¹⁴So the elders of the Jews continued to build and prosper under the preaching*b* of Haggai the prophet and Zechariah, a descendant of Iddo. They finished building the temple according to the command of the God of Israel and the decrees of Cyrus,*c* Darius*d* and Artaxerxes,*e* kings of Persia. ¹⁵The temple was completed on the third day of the month Adar, in the sixth year of the reign of King Darius.*f*

¹⁶Then the people of Israel—the priests, the Levites and the rest of the exiles—celebrated the dedication*g* of the house of God with joy. ¹⁷For the dedication of this house of God they offered*h* a hundred bulls, two hundred rams, four hundred male lambs and, as a sin offering for all Israel, twelve male goats, one for each of the tribes of Israel. ¹⁸And they installed the priests in their divisions*i* and the Levites in their groups*j* for the service of God at Jerusalem, according to what is written in the Book of Moses.*k*

¹⁹On the fourteenth day of the first month, the exiles celebrated the Passover.*l* ²⁰The priests and Levites had purified themselves and were all ceremonially clean. The Levites slaughtered*m* the Passover lamb for all the exiles, for their brothers the priests and for themselves. ²¹So the Israelites who had returned from the exile ate it, together with all who had separated themselves*n* from the unclean practices*o* of their Gentile neighbors in order to seek the LORD,*p* the God of Israel. ²²For seven days they celebrated with joy the Feast of Unleavened Bread,*q* because the LORD had filled them with joy by changing the attitude*r* of the king of Assyria, so that he assisted them in the work on the house of God, the God of Israel.

Chapter 7 Theme

7 After these things, during the reign of Artaxerxes*s* king of Persia, Ezra son of Seraiah, the son of Azariah, the son of Hilkiah,*t* ²the son of Shallum, the son of Zadok,*u* the son of Ahitub,*v* ³the son of Amariah, the son of Azariah, the son of Meraioth, ⁴the son of Zerahiah, the son of Uzzi, the son of Bukki, ⁵the son of Abishua, the son of Phinehas, the son of Eleazar, the son of Aaron the chief priest— ⁶this Ezra*w* came up from Babylon. He was a teacher well versed in the Law of Moses, which the LORD, the God of Israel, had given. The king had granted him everything he asked, for the hand of the LORD his God was on him.*x* ⁷Some of the Israelites, including priests, Levites, singers, gatekeepers and temple servants, also came up to Jerusalem in the seventh year of King Artaxerxes.*y*

⁸Ezra arrived in Jerusalem in the fifth month of the seventh year of the king. ⁹He had begun his journey from Babylon on the

first day of the first month, and he arrived in Jerusalem on the first day of the fifth month, for the gracious hand of his God was on him.[a] ¹⁰For Ezra had devoted himself to the study and observance of the Law of the LORD, and to teaching[b] its decrees and laws in Israel.

¹¹This is a copy of the letter King Artaxerxes had given to Ezra the priest and teacher, a man learned in matters concerning the commands and decrees of the LORD for Israel:

¹²ᵃArtaxerxes, king of kings,[c]

To Ezra the priest, a teacher of the Law of the God of heaven:

Greetings.

¹³Now I decree that any of the Israelites in my kingdom, including priests and Levites, who wish to go to Jerusalem with you, may go. ¹⁴You are sent by the king and his seven advisers[d] to inquire about Judah and Jerusalem with regard to the Law of your God, which is in your hand. ¹⁵Moreover, you are to take with you the silver and gold that the king and his advisers have freely given[e] to the God of Israel, whose dwelling[f] is in Jerusalem, ¹⁶together with all the silver and gold[g] you may obtain from the province of Babylon, as well as the freewill offerings of the people and priests for the temple of their God in Jerusalem.[h] ¹⁷With this money be sure to buy bulls, rams and male lambs,[i] together with their grain offerings and drink offerings,[j] and sacrifice[k] them on the altar of the temple of your God in Jerusalem.

¹⁸You and your brother Jews may then do whatever seems best with the rest of the silver and gold, in accordance with the will of your God. ¹⁹Deliver[l] to the God of Jerusalem all the articles entrusted to you for worship in the temple of your God. ²⁰And anything else needed for the temple of your God that you may have occasion to supply, you may provide from the royal treasury.[m]

²¹Now I, King Artaxerxes, order all the treasurers of Trans-Euphrates to provide with diligence whatever Ezra the priest, a teacher of the Law of the God of heaven, may ask of you— ²²up to a hundred talents[b] of silver, a hundred cors[c] of wheat, a hundred baths[d] of wine, a hundred baths[d] of olive oil, and salt without limit. ²³Whatever the God of heaven has prescribed, let it be done with diligence for the temple of the God of heaven. Why should there be wrath against the realm of the king

---

7:9
ᵃ ver 6

7:10
ᵇ ver 25;
Dt 33:10;
Ne 8:1-8

7:12
ᶜ Eze 26:7;
Da 2:37

7:14
ᵈ Est 1:14

7:15
ᵉ 1Ch 29:6
ᶠ 1Ch 29:6,9;
2Ch 6:2

7:16
ᵍ Ezr 8:25
ʰ Zec 6:10

7:17
ⁱ 2Ki 3:4
ʲ Nu 15:5-12
ᵏ Dt 12:5-11

7:19
ˡ Ezr 5:14;
Jer 27:22

7:20
ᵐ Ezr 6:4

ᵃ 12 The text of Ezra 7:12-26 is in Aramaic.   ᵇ 22 That is, about 3 3/4 tons (about 3.4 metric tons)   ᶜ 22 That is, probably about 600 bushels (about 22 kiloliters)   ᵈ 22 That is, probably about 600 gallons (about 2.2 kiloliters)

7:23
a Ezr 6:10

7:24
b Ezr 4:13
c Ezr 8:36

7:25
d Ex 18:21,26;
Dt 16:18
e ver 10;
Lev 10:11

7:26
f Ezr 6:11

7:27
g Ezr 1:1; 6:22
h 1Ch 29:12

7:28
i 2Ki 25:28
j Ezr 5:5; 9:9

8:1
k Ezr 7:7

8:3
l 1Ch 3:22
m Ezr 2:3

8:4
n Ezr 2:6

8:6
o Ezr 2:15;
Ne 7:20; 10:16

and of his sons?[a] [24]You are also to know that you have no authority to impose taxes, tribute or duty[b] on any of the priests, Levites, singers, gatekeepers, temple servants or other workers at this house of God.[c]

[25]And you, Ezra, in accordance with the wisdom of your God, which you possess, appoint[d] magistrates and judges to administer justice to all the people of Trans-Euphrates—all who know the laws of your God. And you are to teach[e] any who do not know them. [26]Whoever does not obey the law of your God and the law of the king must surely be punished by death, banishment, confiscation of property, or imprisonment.[f]

[27]Praise be to the LORD, the God of our fathers, who has put it into the king's heart[g] to bring honor[h] to the house of the LORD in Jerusalem in this way [28]and who has extended his good favor[i] to me before the king and his advisers and all the king's powerful officials. Because the hand of the LORD my God was on me,[j] I took courage and gathered leading men from Israel to go up with me.

Chapter 8 Theme

8 These are the family heads and those registered with them who came up with me from Babylon during the reign of King Artaxerxes:[k]

[2]of the descendants of Phinehas, Gershom;
of the descendants of Ithamar, Daniel;
of the descendants of David, Hattush [3]of the descendants of Shecaniah;[l]

of the descendants of Parosh,[m] Zechariah, and with him were registered 150 men;
[4]of the descendants of Pahath-Moab,[n] Eliehoenai son of Zerahiah, and with him 200 men;
[5]of the descendants of Zattu,[a] Shecaniah son of Jahaziel, and with him 300 men;
[6]of the descendants of Adin,[o] Ebed son of Jonathan, and with him 50 men;
[7]of the descendants of Elam, Jeshaiah son of Athaliah, and with him 70 men;
[8]of the descendants of Shephatiah, Zebadiah son of Michael, and with him 80 men;
[9]of the descendants of Joab, Obadiah son of Jehiel, and with him 218 men;
[10]of the descendants of Bani,[b] Shelomith son of Josiphiah, and with him 160 men;

a 5 Some Septuagint manuscripts (also 1 Esdras 8:32); Hebrew does not have Zattu. b 10 Some Septuagint manuscripts (also 1 Esdras 8:36); Hebrew does not have Bani.

¹¹of the descendants of Bebai, Zechariah son of Bebai, and with him 28 men;

¹²of the descendants of Azgad, Johanan son of Hakkatan, and with him 110 men;

¹³of the descendants of Adonikam,^a the last ones, whose names were Eliphelet, Jeuel and Shemaiah, and with them 60 men;

¹⁴of the descendants of Bigvai, Uthai and Zaccur, and with them 70 men.

¹⁵I assembled them at the canal that flows toward Ahava,^b and we camped there three days. When I checked among the people and the priests, I found no Levites^c there. ¹⁶So I summoned Eliezer, Ariel, Shemaiah, Elnathan, Jarib, Elnathan, Nathan, Zechariah and Meshullam, who were leaders, and Joiarib and Elnathan, who were men of learning, ¹⁷and I sent them to Iddo, the leader in Casiphia. I told them what to say to Iddo and his kinsmen, the temple servants^d in Casiphia, so that they might bring attendants to us for the house of our God. ¹⁸Because the gracious hand of our God was on us,^e they brought us Sherebiah, a capable man, from the descendants of Mahli son of Levi, the son of Israel, and Sherebiah's sons and brothers, 18 men; ¹⁹and Hashabiah, together with Jeshaiah from the descendants of Merari, and his brothers and nephews, 20 men. ²⁰They also brought 220 of the temple servants^f—a body that David and the officials had established to assist the Levites. All were registered by name.

²¹There, by the Ahava Canal,^g I proclaimed a fast, so that we might humble ourselves before our God and ask him for a safe journey^h for us and our children, with all our possessions. ²²I was ashamed to ask the king for soldiersⁱ and horsemen to protect us from enemies on the road, because we had told the king, "The gracious hand of our God is on everyone^j who looks to him, but his great anger is against all who forsake him.^k" ²³So we fasted^l and petitioned our God about this, and he answered our prayer.

²⁴Then I set apart twelve of the leading priests, together with Sherebiah,^m Hashabiah and ten of their brothers, ²⁵and I weighed outⁿ to them the offering of silver and gold and the articles that the king, his advisers, his officials and all Israel present there had donated for the house of our God. ²⁶I weighed out to them 650 talents^a of silver, silver articles weighing 100 talents,^b 100 talents^b of gold, ²⁷20 bowls of gold valued at 1,000 darics,^c and two fine articles of polished bronze, as precious as gold.

²⁸I said to them, "You as well as these articles are consecrated to the LORD.^o The silver and gold are a freewill offering to the LORD,

---

^a26 That is, about 25 tons (about 22 metric tons)   ^b26 That is, about 3 3/4 tons (about 3.4 metric tons)   ^c27 That is, about 19 pounds (about 8.5 kilograms)

8:13
^aEzr 2:13

8:15
^bver 21,31
^cEzr 2:40; 7:7

8:17
^dEzr 2:43

8:18
^eEzr 5:5

8:20
^f1Ch 9:2;
Ezr 2:43

8:21
^gver 15;
2Ch 20:3
^hPs 5:8; 107:7

8:22
ⁱNe 2:9;
Ezr 7:6,9,28
^jEzr 5:5
^kDt 31:17;
2Ch 15:2

8:23
^l2Ch 20:3;
33:13

8:24
^mver 18

8:25
ⁿver 33;
Ezr 7:15,16

8:28
^oLev 21:6;
22:2-3

8:31
a ver 15

8:32
b Ge 40:13;
Ne 2:11

8:33
c Ne 3:4,21
d Ne 3:24

8:35
e 2Ch 29:21;
Ezr 6:17

8:36
f Ezr 7:21-24
g Est 9:3

9:1
h Ezr 6:21;
Ne 9:2
i Ge 19:38
j Ex 13:5

9:2
k Ex 34:16
l Ex 22:31
m Ezr 10:2

9:4
n Ezr 10:3

9:5
o Ex 29:41

the God of your fathers. ²⁹Guard them carefully until you weigh them out in the chambers of the house of the Lord in Jerusalem before the leading priests and the Levites and the family heads of Israel." ³⁰Then the priests and Levites received the silver and gold and sacred articles that had been weighed out to be taken to the house of our God in Jerusalem.

³¹On the twelfth day of the first month we set out from the Ahava Canal*a* to go to Jerusalem. The hand of our God was on us, and he protected us from enemies and bandits along the way. ³²So we arrived in Jerusalem, where we rested three days.*b*

³³On the fourth day, in the house of our God, we weighed out the silver and gold and the sacred articles into the hands of Meremoth*c* son of Uriah, the priest. Eleazar son of Phinehas was with him, and so were the Levites Jozabad son of Jeshua and Noadiah son of Binnui.*d* ³⁴Everything was accounted for by number and weight, and the entire weight was recorded at that time.

³⁵Then the exiles who had returned from captivity sacrificed burnt offerings to the God of Israel: twelve bulls for all Israel, ninety-six rams, seventy-seven male lambs and, as a sin offering, twelve male goats.*e* All this was a burnt offering to the Lord. ³⁶They also delivered the king's orders*f* to the royal satraps and to the governors of Trans-Euphrates, who then gave assistance to the people and to the house of God.*g*

Chapter 9 Theme

9 After these things had been done, the leaders came to me and said, "The people of Israel, including the priests and the Levites, have not kept themselves separate*h* from the neighboring peoples with their detestable practices, like those of the Canaanites, Hittites, Perizzites, Jebusites, Ammonites,*i* Moabites, Egyptians and Amorites.*j* ²They have taken some of their daughters*k* as wives for themselves and their sons, and have mingled the holy race*l* with the peoples around them. And the leaders and officials have led the way in this unfaithfulness."*m*

³When I heard this, I tore my tunic and cloak, pulled hair from my head and beard and sat down appalled. ⁴Then everyone who trembled*n* at the words of the God of Israel gathered around me because of this unfaithfulness of the exiles. And I sat there appalled until the evening sacrifice.

⁵Then, at the evening sacrifice,*o* I rose from my self-abasement, with my tunic and cloak torn, and fell on my knees with my hands spread out to the Lord my God ⁶and prayed:

"O my God, I am too ashamed and disgraced to lift up my face to you, my God, because our sins are higher than our heads and our guilt has reached to the heavens.[a] [7]From the days of our forefathers[b] until now, our guilt has been great. Because of our sins, we and our kings and our priests have been subjected to the sword[c] and captivity,[d] to pillage and humiliation[e] at the hand of foreign kings, as it is today.

[8]"But now, for a brief moment, the LORD our God has been gracious[f] in leaving us a remnant[g] and giving us a firm place[h] in his sanctuary, and so our God gives light to our eyes[i] and a little relief in our bondage. [9]Though we are slaves,[j] our God has not deserted us in our bondage. He has shown us kindness[k] in the sight of the kings of Persia: He has granted us new life to rebuild the house of our God and repair its ruins,[l] and he has given us a wall of protection in Judah and Jerusalem.

[10]"But now, O our God, what can we say after this? For we have disregarded the commands[m] [11]you gave through your servants the prophets when you said: 'The land you are entering to possess is a land polluted[n] by the corruption of its peoples. By their detestable practices[o] they have filled it with their impurity from one end to the other. [12]Therefore, do not give your daughters in marriage to their sons or take their daughters for your sons. Do not seek a treaty of friendship with them[p] at any time, that you may be strong and eat the good things of the land and leave it to your children as an everlasting inheritance.'

[13]"What has happened to us is a result of our evil deeds and our great guilt, and yet, our God, you have punished us less than our sins have deserved[q] and have given us a remnant like this. [14]Shall we again break your commands and intermarry[r] with the peoples who commit such detestable practices? Would you not be angry enough with us to destroy us,[s] leaving us no remnant[t] or survivor? [15]O LORD, God of Israel, you are righteous![u] We are left this day as a remnant. Here we are before you in our guilt, though because of it not one of us can stand[v] in your presence.[w]"

Chapter 10 Theme

10 While Ezra was praying and confessing,[x] weeping and throwing himself down before the house of God, a large crowd of Israelites—men, women and children—gathered around him. They too wept bitterly. [2]Then Shecaniah son of Jehiel, one of the descendants of Elam, said to Ezra, "We have been unfaithful[y] to our God by marrying foreign women from the peoples around us. But in spite of this, there is still hope for Israel.[z] [3]Now let us make a covenant[a] before our God to send away[b] all these women and their children, in accordance with the counsel of my lord and of those who fear the commands of our God. Let it be done

9:6
[a] 2Ch 28:9;
Job 42:6;
Ps 38:4;
Rev 18:5

9:7
[b] 2Ch 29:6
[c] Eze 21:1-32
[d] Dt 28:64
[e] Dt 28:37

9:8
[f] Ps 25:16;
Isa 33:2
[g] Ge 45:7
[h] Ecc 12:11;
Isa 22:23
[i] Ps 13:3

9:9
[j] Ex 1:14;
Ne 9:36
[k] Ezr 7:28
[l] Ps 69:35;
Isa 43:1;
Jer 32:44

9:10
[m] Dt 11:8;
Isa 1:19-20

9:11
[n] Lev 18:25-28
[o] Dt 9:4

9:12
[p] Ex 34:15;
Dt 7:3; 23:6

9:13
[q] Job 11:6;
Ps 103:10

9:14
[r] Ne 13:27
[s] Dt 9:8
[t] Dt 9:14

9:15
[u] Ge 18:25;
Ps 51:4;
Jer 12:1;
Da 9:7
[v] Ne 9:33;
Ps 130:3;
Mal 3:2
[w] 1Ki 8:47

10:1
[x] 2Ch 20:9;
Da 9:20

10:2
[y] Ezr 9:2;
Ne 13:27
[z] Dt 30:8-10

10:3
[a] 2Ch 34:31
[b] Ex 34:16;
Dt 7:2-3;
Ezr 9:4

10:5
a Ne 5:12; 13:25

10:6
b Ex 34:28;
Dt 9:18

10:9
c Ezr 1:5

10:11
d ver 3;
Dt 24:1;
Ne 9:2;
Mal 2:10-16

10:12
e Jos 6:5

10:14
f Dt 16:18
g Nu 25:4;
2Ch 29:10;
30:8

10:15
h Ne 11:16

10:18
i Jdg 3:6
j Ezr 2:2

according to the Law. [4]Rise up; this matter is in your hands. We will support you, so take courage and do it."

[5]So Ezra rose up and put the leading priests and Levites and all Israel under oath*a* to do what had been suggested. And they took the oath. [6]Then Ezra withdrew from before the house of God and went to the room of Jehohanan son of Eliashib. While he was there, he ate no food and drank no water,*b* because he continued to mourn over the unfaithfulness of the exiles.

[7]A proclamation was then issued throughout Judah and Jerusalem for all the exiles to assemble in Jerusalem. [8]Anyone who failed to appear within three days would forfeit all his property, in accordance with the decision of the officials and elders, and would himself be expelled from the assembly of the exiles.

[9]Within the three days, all the men of Judah and Benjamin*c* had gathered in Jerusalem. And on the twentieth day of the ninth month, all the people were sitting in the square before the house of God, greatly distressed by the occasion and because of the rain. [10]Then Ezra the priest stood up and said to them, "You have been unfaithful; you have married foreign women, adding to Israel's guilt. [11]Now make confession to the LORD, the God of your fathers, and do his will. Separate yourselves from the peoples around you and from your foreign wives."*d*

[12]The whole assembly responded with a loud voice:*e* "You are right! We must do as you say. [13]But there are many people here and it is the rainy season; so we cannot stand outside. Besides, this matter cannot be taken care of in a day or two, because we have sinned greatly in this thing. [14]Let our officials act for the whole assembly. Then let everyone in our towns who has married a foreign woman come at a set time, along with the elders and judges*f* of each town, until the fierce anger*g* of our God in this matter is turned away from us." [15]Only Jonathan son of Asahel and Jahzeiah son of Tikvah, supported by Meshullam and Shabbethai*h* the Levite, opposed this.

[16]So the exiles did as was proposed. Ezra the priest selected men who were family heads, one from each family division, and all of them designated by name. On the first day of the tenth month they sat down to investigate the cases, [17]and by the first day of the first month they finished dealing with all the men who had married foreign women.

[18]Among the descendants of the priests, the following had married foreign women:*i*

From the descendants of Jeshua*j* son of Jozadak, and his brothers: Maaseiah, Eliezer, Jarib and Gedaliah. [19](They all gave their hands*a* in pledge to put away their wives, and for their guilt they each presented a ram from the flock as a guilt offering.)*b*

²⁰From the descendants of Immer:*c*

Hanani and Zebadiah.

²¹From the descendants of Harim:*d*

Maaseiah, Elijah, Shemaiah, Jehiel and Uzziah.

²²From the descendants of Pashhur:*e*

Elioenai, Maaseiah, Ishmael, Nethanel, Jozabad and Elasah.

²³Among the Levites:*f*

Jozabad, Shimei, Kelaiah (that is, Kelita), Pethahiah, Judah and Eliezer.

²⁴From the singers:

Eliashib.*g*

From the gatekeepers:

Shallum, Telem and Uri.

²⁵And among the other Israelites:

From the descendants of Parosh:*h*

Ramiah, Izziah, Malkijah, Mijamin, Eleazar, Malkijah and Benaiah.

²⁶From the descendants of Elam:*i*

Mattaniah, Zechariah, Jehiel, Abdi, Jeremoth and Elijah.

²⁷From the descendants of Zattu:

Elioenai, Eliashib, Mattaniah, Jeremoth, Zabad and Aziza.

²⁸From the descendants of Bebai:

Jehohanan, Hananiah, Zabbai and Athlai.

²⁹From the descendants of Bani:

Meshullam, Malluch, Adaiah, Jashub, Sheal and Jeremoth.

³⁰From the descendants of Pahath-Moab:

Adna, Kelal, Benaiah, Maaseiah, Mattaniah, Bezalel, Binnui and Manasseh.

³¹From the descendants of Harim:

Eliezer, Ishijah, Malkijah, Shemaiah, Shimeon, ³²Benjamin, Malluch and Shemariah.

³³From the descendants of Hashum:

Mattenai, Mattattah, Zabad, Eliphelet, Jeremai, Manasseh and Shimei.

³⁴From the descendants of Bani:

Maadai, Amram, Uel, ³⁵Benaiah, Bedeiah, Keluhi, ³⁶Vaniah, Meremoth, Eliashib, ³⁷Mattaniah, Mattenai and Jaasu.

³⁸From the descendants of Binnui:*a*

Shimei, ³⁹Shelemiah, Nathan, Adaiah, ⁴⁰Macnadebai, Shashai,

a 37,38 See Septuagint (also 1 Esdras 9:34); Hebrew Jaasu ³⁸and Bani and Binnui,

---

10:19
a 2Ki 10:15
b Lev 5:15; 6:6

10:20
c 1Ch 24:14

10:21
d 1Ch 24:8

10:22
e 1Ch 9:12

10:23
f Ne 8:7; 9:4

10:24
g Ne 3:1; 12:10; 13:7,28

10:25
h Ezr 2:3

10:26
i ver 2

NEHEMIAH

Since the third millennium B.C. the cities of the Middle East were surrounded by walls of stones while guarded gates acted as sentinels opening to or shutting out all who wanted to enter. From the tops of these walls, watchmen could survey the landscape for great distances, seeing everyone who approached the city either as visitors or invaders.

The city fathers would gather at the city gates to carry out their business transactions and pass their judgments on civic affairs. The condition of the walls of the city was a matter of either pride or reproach.

Jerusalem's walls had been destroyed during the Babylonian invasion. The walls and its many gates stood in ruins, a rebuke to the newly returned exiles and a cause of mourning to Nehemiah, although he was over 600 miles away serving as cupbearer to Artaxerxes. Nehemiah had not forgotten his beloved city or people.

While Ezra gives the account of the rebuilding of the temple under Zerubbabel, Nehemiah (Ezra's contemporary) gives the account of the rebuilding of Jerusalem's walls. His account begins in 445 B.C. in Susa, the Persian capital.

∾ THINGS TO DO

1. Nehemiah is a continuation of Ezra. As a matter of fact, Ezra and Nehemiah were treated as one book in the earliest Hebrew manuscripts. Therefore to put this book into context, study the historical chart THE TIMES OF EZRA, NEHEMIAH, AND ESTHER on page 793.

2. As you read Nehemiah chapter by chapter:

   a. Look for the theme of each chapter. Record this next to the chapter number on the NEHE-MIAH AT A GLANCE chart on page 818 and record it in the text next to the chapter number.

   b. Read each chapter again. This time make a list of the points you want to remember about the main topic or event within each chapter.

   1) For example, in chapter 1 the theme is Nehemiah's concern for Jerusalem. In the margin opposite the first three verses you could write "Remnant's Distress." Then underneath it write "walls broken down, gates burned."

   2) Then next to verses 4 through 11 you could write "Nehemiah's Prayer" and list the main parts or points of his prayer; for example, a) weeps, mourns, fasts, b) reminds God of who he is and his covenant, and c) confesses his and Israel's sins.

   3) As you summarize each chapter, list what you learn about God.

   c. While there are many key repeated words you could mark—such as *wall, gate, rebuilding, repairs,* etc.—you may want to observe them without marking them because of the nature of Nehemiah's writing. Some key words are used so many times within specific chapters that you may become overwhelmed by all the markings.

   1) However, you will find it beneficial to mark every occurrence of *remember* and *remember me* and then in the margin note what or who is to be remembered and why.

   2) Also mark *commands (ordinances, gave, over, regulations, law, laws)* and note in the margin what you learn from marking these words.

Sharai, [41]Azarel, Shelemiah, Shemariah, [42]Shallum, Amariah and Joseph.

[43]From the descendants of Nebo:

Jeiel, Mattithiah, Zabad, Zebina, Jaddai, Joel and Benaiah.

[44]All these had married foreign women, and some of them had children by these wives.[a]

[a]44 Or *and they sent them away with their children*

EZRA AT A GLANCE

Theme of Ezra:

	SEGMENT DIVISIONS		
Author:	YEARS COVERED	CENTRAL CHARACTERS	CHAPTER THEMES
Date:			1
			2
Purpose:			3
			4
Key Words:			
house, temple (or any reference to God's house)			5
			6
decree (decrees, order, authorized, letter)			7
			8
the law, the Law (of Moses, of the Lord, of your God)			9
commands			10

   d. Note any references to time by drawing a symbol next to the verse.

   e. As you read through Nehemiah, note in the margin when the wall is started, when it is completed, and when it is dedicated.

3. There are valuable lessons to be learned from observing how Nehemiah handled situations. As you see how Nehemiah related to God in each situation, how he dealt with the people (including those who opposed him), and the example he set, you will see principles you can apply to your life. As you study, record your insights on the chart LESSONS FROM THE LIFE OF NEHEMIAH on page 819.

4. When you finish recording the theme of every chapter on NEHEMIAH AT A GLANCE, look for the main division of the book, where one emphasis ends and another begins. On the line under the chapter themes, record this division and the theme or subject of the two segments of the book. Also fill in the rest of the chart and record the theme of Nehemiah.

❧ THINGS TO THINK ABOUT

1. Read Nehemiah chapter 9 again and think about the character of God and how he dealt with Israel. What can you learn about God and also about Israel's behavior that you can apply to your own life?

2. Have you thought about what could happen if the congregation of a church gathered together and publicly confessed their sins and then the sins of their nation?

3. What have you learned from Nehemiah's life? How are you going to apply it to your life in a practical way?

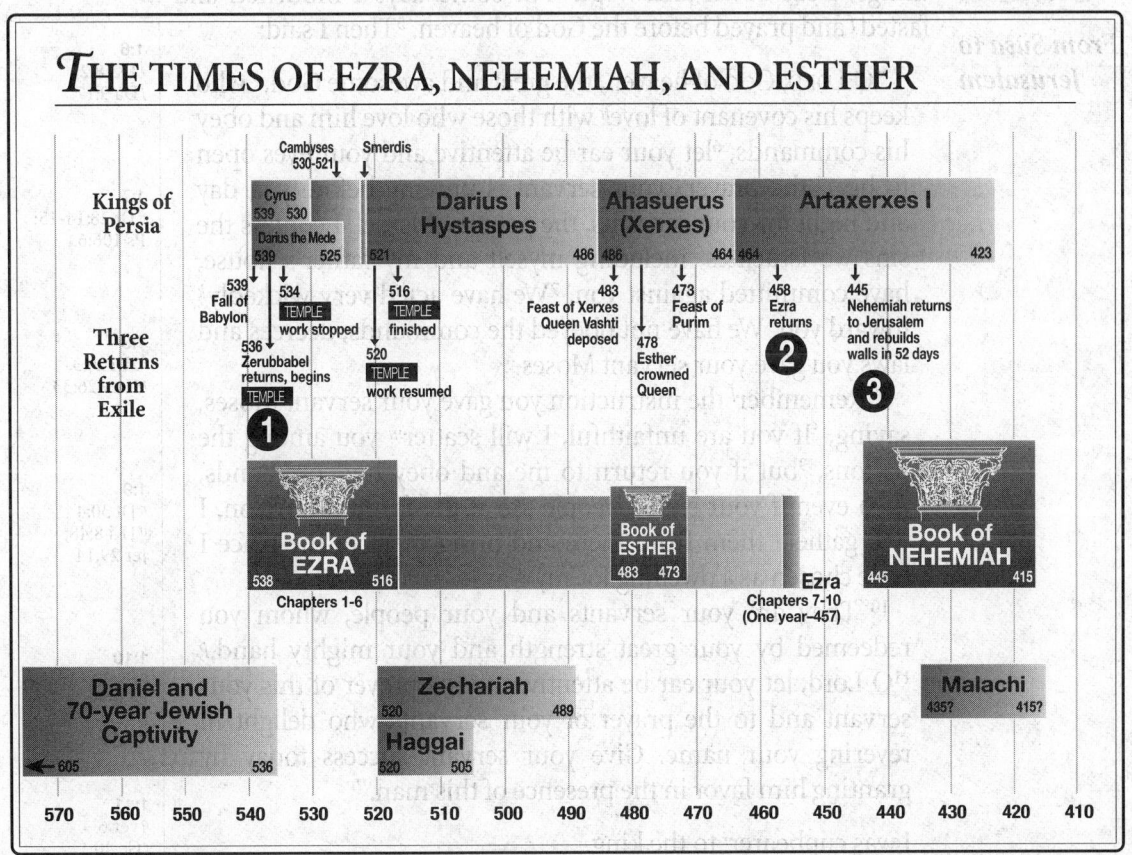

THE TIMES OF EZRA, NEHEMIAH, AND ESTHER

Chapter 1 Theme _____

1 The words of Nehemiah son of Hacaliah:[a]

In the month of Kislev[a] in the twentieth year, while I was in the citadel of Susa, [2]Hanani,[b] one of my brothers, came from Judah with some other men, and I questioned them about the Jewish remnant[c] that survived the exile, and also about Jerusalem.

[3]They said to me, "Those who survived the exile and are back in the province are in great trouble and disgrace. The wall of Jerusalem is broken down, and its gates have been burned with fire.[d]"

[4]When I heard these things, I sat down and wept.[e] For some days I mourned and fasted[f] and prayed before the God of heaven. [5]Then I said:

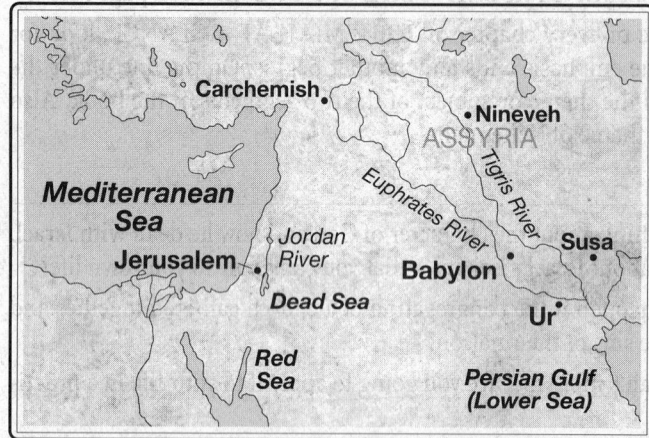

From Susa to Jerusalem

"O LORD, God of heaven, the great and awesome God,[g] who keeps his covenant of love[h] with those who love him and obey his commands, [6]let your ear be attentive and your eyes open to hear[i] the prayer[j] your servant is praying before you day and night for your servants, the people of Israel. I confess the sins we Israelites, including myself and my father's house, have committed against you. [7]We have acted very wickedly[k] toward you. We have not obeyed the commands, decrees and laws you gave your servant Moses.

[8]"Remember[l] the instruction you gave your servant Moses, saying, 'If you are unfaithful, I will scatter[m] you among the nations, [9]but if you return to me and obey my commands, then even if your exiled people are at the farthest horizon, I will gather[n] them from there and bring them to the place I have chosen as a dwelling for my Name.'[o]

[10]"They are your servants and your people, whom you redeemed by your great strength and your mighty hand.[p] [11]O Lord, let your ear be attentive[q] to the prayer of this your servant and to the prayer of your servants who delight in revering your name. Give your servant success today by granting him favor in the presence of this man."

I was cupbearer[r] to the king.

1:1 [a]Ne 10:1; Zec 7:1

1:2 [b]Ne 7:2; [c]Jer 52:28

1:3 [d]2Ki 25:10; Ne 2:3,13,17

1:4 [e]Ps 137:1; [f]Ezr 9:4

1:5 [g]Dt 7:21; Ne 4:14; [h]Ex 20:6; Da 9:4

1:6 [i]1Ki 8:29; [j]Da 9:17

1:7 [k]Dt 28:14-15; Ps 106:6

1:8 [l]2Ki 20:3; [m]Lev 26:33

1:9 [n]Dt 30:4; [o]1Ki 8:48; Jer 29:14

1:10 [p]Ex 32:11; Dt 9:29

1:11 [q]ver 6; [r]Ge 40:1

2:1
a Ezr 7:1

Chapter 2 Theme

2 In the month of Nisan in the twentieth year of King Artaxerxes,*a* when wine was brought for him, I took the wine and gave it to the king. I had not been sad in his presence before; ²so the king asked me, "Why does your face look so sad when you are not ill? This can be nothing but sadness of heart."

I was very much afraid, ³but I said to the king, "May the king live forever!*b* Why should my face not look sad when the city*c* where my fathers are buried lies in ruins, and its gates have been destroyed by fire?*d*"

⁴The king said to me, "What is it you want?"

Then I prayed to the God of heaven, ⁵and I answered the king, "If it pleases the king and if your servant has found favor in his sight, let him send me to the city in Judah where my fathers are buried so that I can rebuild it."

⁶Then the king*e*, with the queen sitting beside him, asked me, "How long will your journey take, and when will you get back?" It pleased the king to send me; so I set a time.

⁷I also said to him, "If it pleases the king, may I have letters to the governors of Trans-Euphrates,*f* so that they will provide me safe-conduct until I arrive in Judah? ⁸And may I have a letter to Asaph, keeper of the king's forest, so he will give me timber to make beams for the gates of the citadel*g* by the temple and for the city wall and for the residence I will occupy?" And because the gracious hand of my God was upon me,*h* the king granted my requests. ⁹So I went to the governors of Trans-Euphrates and gave them the king's letters. The king had also sent army officers and cavalry*i* with me.

¹⁰When Sanballat*j* the Horonite and Tobiah*k* the Ammonite official heard about this, they were very much disturbed that someone had come to promote the welfare of the Israelites.*l*

¹¹I went to Jerusalem, and after staying there three days*m* ¹²I set out during the night with a few men. I had not told anyone what my God had put in my heart to do for Jerusalem. There were no mounts with me except the one I was riding on.

¹³By night I went out through the Valley Gate*n* toward the Jackal*a* Well and the Dung Gate,*o* examining the walls*p* of Jerusalem, which had been broken down, and its gates, which had been destroyed by fire. ¹⁴Then I moved on toward the Fountain Gate*q* and the King's Pool,*r* but there was not enough room for my mount to get through; ¹⁵so I went up the valley by night, examining the wall. Finally, I turned back and reentered through the Valley Gate. ¹⁶The officials did not know where I had gone or what I

2:3
b 1Ki 1:31;
Da 2:4; 5:10;
6:6,21
c Ps 137:6
d Ne 1:3

2:6
e Ne 5:14; 13:6

2:7
f Ezr 8:36

2:8
g Ne 7:2
h ver 18;
Ezr 5:5; 7:6

2:9
i Ezr 8:22

2:10
j ver 19; Ne 4:1,7
k Ne 4:3; 13:4-7
l Est 10:3

2:11
m Ge 40:13

2:13
n 2Ch 26:9
o Ne 3:13
p Ne 1:3

2:14
q Ne 3:15
r 2Ki 18:17

a 13 Or *Serpent* or *Fig*

was doing, because as yet I had said nothing to the Jews or the priests or nobles or officials or any others who would be doing the work.

[17] Then I said to them, "You see the trouble we are in: Jerusalem lies in ruins, and its gates have been burned with fire.[a] Come, let us rebuild the wall[b] of Jerusalem, and we will no longer be in disgrace.[c]" [18] I also told them about the gracious hand of my God upon me[d] and what the king had said to me.

They replied, "Let us start rebuilding." So they began this good work.

[19] But when Sanballat the Horonite, Tobiah the Ammonite official and Geshem[e] the Arab heard about it, they mocked and ridiculed us.[f] "What is this you are doing?" they asked. "Are you rebelling against the king?"

[20] I answered them by saying, "The God of heaven will give us success. We his servants will start rebuilding, but as for you, you have no share[g] in Jerusalem or any claim or historic right to it."

Chapter 3 Theme

3 Eliashib[h] the high priest and his fellow priests went to work and rebuilt[i] the Sheep Gate.[j] They dedicated it and set its doors in place, building as far as the Tower of the Hundred, which they dedicated, and as far as the Tower of Hananel.[k] [2] The men of Jericho[l] built the adjoining section, and Zaccur son of Imri built next to them.

The Gates in Nehemiah's Time

[3] The Fish Gate[m] was rebuilt by the sons of Hassenaah. They laid its beams and put its doors and bolts and bars in place. [4] Meremoth son of Uriah, the son of Hakkoz, repaired the next section. Next to him Meshullam son of Berekiah, the son of Meshezabel, made repairs, and next to him Zadok son of Baana also made repairs. [5] The next section was repaired by the men of Tekoa,[n] but their nobles would not put their shoulders to the work under their supervisors.[a]

[6] The Jeshanah[b] Gate[o] was repaired by Joiada son of Paseah and Meshullam son of Besodeiah. They laid its beams and put its doors and bolts and bars in place. [7] Next to them, repairs were made by men from Gibeon[p] and Mizpah—Melatiah of Gibeon and Jadon of Meronoth—places under the authority of the governor of Trans-Euphrates. [8] Uzziel son of Harhaiah, one of the goldsmiths, repaired the next section; and Hananiah, one of the perfume-makers, made repairs next to that. They restored[c]

2:17
[a] Ne 1:3
[b] Ps 102:16;
Isa 30:13; 58:12
[c] Eze 5:14

2:18
[d] 2Sa 2:7

2:19
[e] Ne 6:1,2,6
[f] Ps 44:13-16

2:20
[g] Ezr 4:3

3:1
[h] Ezr 10:24
[i] Isa 58:12
[j] ver 32;
Ne 12:39
[k] Ne 12:39;
Jer 31:38;
Zec 14:10

3:2
[l] Ne 7:36

3:3
[m] 2Ch 33:14;
Ne 12:39

3:5
[n] 2Sa 14:2

3:6
[o] Ne 12:39

3:7
[p] Jos 9:3; Ne 2:7

---

[a] 5 Or *their Lord* or *the governor*   [b] 6 Or *Old*   [c] 8 Or *They left out part of*

a Ne 12:38

b Ne 12:38

c 2Ch 26:9
d Jos 15:34
e Ne 2:13

f Jer 6:1

g Isa 8:6; Jn 9:7

h Jos 15:58
i Ac 2:29

j Jos 15:44

k Ezr 8:33

l Ezr 8:33

Jerusalem as far as the Broad Wall.*a* ⁹Rephaiah son of Hur, ruler of a half-district of Jerusalem, repaired the next section. ¹⁰Adjoining this, Jedaiah son of Harumaph made repairs opposite his house, and Hattush son of Hashabneiah made repairs next to him. ¹¹Malkijah son of Harim and Hasshub son of Pahath-Moab repaired another section and the Tower of the Ovens.*b* ¹²Shallum son of Hallohesh, ruler of a half-district of Jerusalem, repaired the next section with the help of his daughters.

¹³The Valley Gate*c* was repaired by Hanun and the residents of Zanoah.*d* They rebuilt it and put its doors and bolts and bars in place. They also repaired five hundred yards*a* of the wall as far as the Dung Gate.*e*

¹⁴The Dung Gate was repaired by Malkijah son of Recab, ruler of the district of Beth Hakkerem.*f* He rebuilt it and put its doors and bolts and bars in place.

¹⁵The Fountain Gate was repaired by Shallun son of Col-Hozeh, ruler of the district of Mizpah. He rebuilt it, roofing it over and putting its doors and bolts and bars in place. He also repaired the wall of the Pool of Siloam,*b g* by the King's Garden, as far as the steps going down from the City of David. ¹⁶Beyond him, Nehemiah son of Azbuk, ruler of a half-district of Beth Zur,*h* made repairs up to a point opposite the tombs*c i* of David, as far as the artificial pool and the House of the Heroes.

¹⁷Next to him, the repairs were made by the Levites under Rehum son of Bani. Beside him, Hashabiah, ruler of half the district of Keilah,*j* carried out repairs for his district. ¹⁸Next to him, the repairs were made by their countrymen under Binnui*d* son of Henadad, ruler of the other half-district of Keilah. ¹⁹Next to him, Ezer son of Jeshua, ruler of Mizpah, repaired another section, from a point facing the ascent to the armory as far as the angle. ²⁰Next to him, Baruch son of Zabbai zealously repaired another section, from the angle to the entrance of the house of Eliashib the high priest. ²¹Next to him, Meremoth*k* son of Uriah, the son of Hakkoz, repaired another section, from the entrance of Eliashib's house to the end of it.

²²The repairs next to him were made by the priests from the surrounding region. ²³Beyond them, Benjamin and Hasshub made repairs in front of their house; and next to them, Azariah son of Maaseiah, the son of Ananiah, made repairs beside his house. ²⁴Next to him, Binnui*l* son of Henadad repaired another

a 13 Hebrew *a thousand cubits* (about 450 meters)   b 15 Hebrew *Shelah*, a variant of *Shiloah*, that is, Siloam   c 16 Hebrew; Septuagint, some Vulgate manuscripts and Syriac *tomb*   d 18 Two Hebrew manuscripts and Syriac (see also Septuagint and verse 24); most Hebrew manuscripts *Bavvai*

797

section, from Azariah's house to the angle and the corner, [25]and Palal son of Uzai worked opposite the angle and the tower projecting from the upper palace near the court of the guard.[a] Next to him, Pedaiah son of Parosh[b] [26]and the temple servants[c] living on the hill of Ophel[d] made repairs up to a point opposite the Water Gate[e] toward the east and the projecting tower. [27]Next to them, the men of Tekoa[f] repaired another section, from the great projecting tower[g] to the wall of Ophel.

[28]Above the Horse Gate,[h] the priests made repairs, each in front of his own house. [29]Next to them, Zadok son of Immer made repairs opposite his house. Next to him, Shemaiah son of Shecaniah, the guard at the East Gate, made repairs. [30]Next to him, Hananiah son of Shelemiah, and Hanun, the sixth son of Zalaph, repaired another section. Next to them, Meshullam son of Berekiah made repairs opposite his living quarters. [31]Next to him, Malkijah, one of the goldsmiths, made repairs as far as the house of the temple servants and the merchants, opposite the Inspection Gate, and as far as the room above the corner; [32]and between the room above the corner and the Sheep Gate[i] the goldsmiths and merchants made repairs.

Chapter 4 Theme

4 When Sanballat[j] heard that we were rebuilding the wall, he became angry and was greatly incensed. He ridiculed the Jews, [2]and in the presence of his associates[k] and the army of Samaria, he said, "What are those feeble Jews doing? Will they restore their wall? Will they offer sacrifices? Will they finish in a day? Can they bring the stones back to life from those heaps of rubble[l]—burned as they are?"

[3]Tobiah[m] the Ammonite, who was at his side, said, "What they are building—if even a fox climbed up on it, he would break down their wall of stones!"[n]

[4]Hear us, O our God, for we are despised.[o] Turn their insults back on their own heads. Give them over as plunder in a land of captivity. [5]Do not cover up their guilt[p] or blot out their sins from your sight,[q] for they have thrown insults in the face of[a] the builders.

[6]So we rebuilt the wall till all of it reached half its height, for the people worked with all their heart.

[7]But when Sanballat, Tobiah,[r] the Arabs, the Ammonites and the men of Ashdod heard that the repairs to Jerusalem's walls had gone ahead and that the gaps were being closed, they were very angry. [8]They all plotted together[s] to come and fight against

a5 Or *have provoked you to anger before*

3:25
[a] Jer 32:2; 37:21; 39:14
[b] Ezr 2:3

3:26
[c] Ne 7:46; 11:21
[d] 2Ch 33:14
[e] Ne 8:1,3,16; 12:37

3:27
[f] ver 5
[g] Ps 48:12

3:28
[h] 2Ki 11:16; 2Ch 23:15; Jer 31:40

3:32
[i] ver 1; Jn 5:2

4:1
[j] Ne 2:10

4:2
[k] Ezr 4:9-10
[l] Ps 79:1; Jer 26:18

4:3
[m] Ne 2:10
[n] Job 13:12; 15:3

4:4
[o] Ps 44:13; 79:12; 123:3-4; Jer 33:24

4:5
[p] Isa 2:9; La 1:22
[q] 2Ki 14:27; Ps 51:1; 69:27-28; 109:14; Jer 18:23

4:7
[r] Ne 2:10

4:8
[s] Ps 2:2; 83:1-18

4:10
a 1Ch 23:4

Jerusalem and stir up trouble against it. ⁹But we prayed to our God and posted a guard day and night to meet this threat.

¹⁰Meanwhile, the people in Judah said, "The strength of the laborers*ᵃ* is giving out, and there is so much rubble that we cannot rebuild the wall."

¹¹Also our enemies said, "Before they know it or see us, we will be right there among them and will kill them and put an end to the work."

4:14
b Ge 28:15;
Nu 14:9; Dt 1:29
c Ne 1:8
d Ne 1:5
e 2Sa 10:12

¹²Then the Jews who lived near them came and told us ten times over, "Wherever you turn, they will attack us."

¹³Therefore I stationed some of the people behind the lowest points of the wall at the exposed places, posting them by families, with their swords, spears and bows. ¹⁴After I looked things over, I stood up and said to the nobles, the officials and the rest of the people, "Don't be afraid*ᵇ* of them. Remember*ᶜ* the Lord, who is great and awesome,*ᵈ* and fight*ᵉ* for your brothers, your sons and your daughters, your wives and your homes."

4:15
f 2Sa 17:14;
Job 5:12

¹⁵When our enemies heard that we were aware of their plot and that God had frustrated it,*ᶠ* we all returned to the wall, each to his own work.

¹⁶From that day on, half of my men did the work, while the other half were equipped with spears, shields, bows and armor. The officers posted themselves behind all the people of Judah ¹⁷who were building the wall. Those who carried materials did their work with one hand and held a weapon*ᵍ* in the other, ¹⁸and each of the builders wore his sword at his side as he worked. But the man who sounded the trumpet*ʰ* stayed with me.

4:17
g Ps 149:6

¹⁹Then I said to the nobles, the officials and the rest of the people, "The work is extensive and spread out, and we are widely separated from each other along the wall. ²⁰Wherever you hear the sound of the trumpet,*ⁱ* join us there. Our God will fight*ʲ* for us!"

²¹So we continued the work with half the men holding spears, from the first light of dawn till the stars came out. ²²At that time I also said to the people, "Have every man and his helper stay inside Jerusalem at night, so they can serve us as guards by night and workmen by day." ²³Neither I nor my brothers nor my men nor the guards with me took off our clothes; each had his weapon, even when he went for water.ᵃ

4:18
h Nu 10:2

Chapter 5 Theme

5 Now the men and their wives raised a great outcry against their Jewish brothers. ²Some were saying, "We and our sons and daughters are numerous; in order for us to eat and stay alive, we must get grain."

4:20
i Eze 33:3
j Ex 14:14;
Dt 1:30; 20:4;
Jos 10:14

a 23 The meaning of the Hebrew for this clause is uncertain.

³Others were saying, "We are mortgaging our fields,ᵃ our vineyards and our homes to get grain during the famine."ᵇ

⁴Still others were saying, "We have had to borrow money to pay the king's taxᶜ on our fields and vineyards. ⁵Although we are of the same flesh and bloodᵈ as our countrymen and though our sons are as good as theirs, yet we have to subject our sons and daughters to slavery.ᵉ Some of our daughters have already been enslaved, but we are powerless, because our fields and our vineyards belong to others."ᶠ

⁶When I heard their outcry and these charges, I was very angry. ⁷I pondered them in my mind and then accused the nobles and officials. I told them, "You are exacting usuryᵍ from your own countrymen!" So I called together a large meeting to deal with them ⁸and said: "As far as possible,we have boughtʰ back our Jewish brothers who were sold to the Gentiles. Now you are selling your brothers, only for them to be sold back to us!" They kept quiet, because they could find nothing to say.ⁱ

⁹So I continued, "What you are doing is not right. Shouldn't you walk in the fear of our God to avoid the reproachʲ of our Gentile enemies? ¹⁰I and my brothers and my men are also lending the people money and grain. But let the exacting of usury stop!ᵏ ¹¹Give back to them immediately their fields, vineyards, olive groves and houses, and also the usuryˡ you are charging them—the hundredth part of the money, grain, new wine and oil."

¹²"We will give it back," they said. "And we will not demand anything more from them. We will do as you say."

Then I summoned the priests and made the nobles and officials take an oathᵐ to do what they had promised. ¹³I also shookⁿ out the folds of my robe and said, "In this way may God shake out of his house and possessions every man who does not keep this promise. So may such a man be shaken out and emptied!"

At this the whole assembly said, "Amen,"ᵒ and praised the LORD. And the people did as they had promised.

¹⁴Moreover, from the twentieth year of King Artaxerxes,ᵖ when I was appointed to be their governor�q in the land of Judah, until his thirty-second year—twelve years—neither I nor my brothers ate the food allotted to the governor. ¹⁵But the earlier governors—those preceding me—placed a heavy burden on the people and took forty shekelsᵃ of silver from them in addition to food and wine. Their assistants also lorded it over the people. But out of reverence for Godʳ I did not act like that. ¹⁶Instead,ˢ I devoted myself to the work on this wall. All my men were assembled there for the work; weᵇ did not acquire any land.

ᵃ15 That is, about 1 pound (about 0.5 kilogram)   ᵇ16 Most Hebrew manuscripts; some Hebrew manuscripts, Septuagint, Vulgate and Syriac I

5:3
ᵃPs 109:11
ᵇGe 47:23

5:4
ᶜEzr 4:13

5:5
ᵈGe 29:14
ᵉLev 25:39-43, 47; 2Ki 4:1; Isa 50:1
ᶠDt 15:7-11; 2Ki 4:1

5:7
ᵍEx 22:25-27; Lev 25:35-37; Dt 23:19-20; 24:10-13

5:8
ʰLev 25:47
ⁱJer 34:8

5:9
ʲIsa 52:5

5:10
ᵏEx 22:25

5:11
ˡIsa 58:6

5:12
ᵐEzr 10:5

5:13
ⁿMt 10:14; Ac 18:6
ᵒDt 27:15-26

5:14
ᵖNe 2:6; 13:6
qGe 42:6; Ezr 6:7; Jer 40:7; Hag 1:1

5:15
ʳGe 20:11

5:16
ˢ2Th 3:7-10

5:18
a 1Ki 4:23

¹⁷Furthermore, a hundred and fifty Jews and officials ate at my table, as well as those who came to us from the surrounding nations. ¹⁸Each day one ox, six choice sheep and some poultry*ᵃ* were prepared for me, and every ten days an abundant supply of wine of all kinds. In spite of all this, I never demanded the food allotted to the governor, because the demands were heavy on these people.

5:19
b Ge 8:1;
2Ki 20:3;
Ne 1:8;
13:14,22,31

¹⁹Remember*ᵇ* me with favor, O my God, for all I have done for these people.

Chapter 6 Theme _____

6:1
c Ne 2:10
d Ne 2:19

6 When word came to Sanballat, Tobiah,*ᶜ* Geshem*ᵈ* the Arab and the rest of our enemies that I had rebuilt the wall and not a gap was left in it—though up to that time I had not set the doors in the gates— ²Sanballat and Geshem sent me this message: "Come, let us meet together in one of the villages*ᵃ* on the plain of Ono.*ᵉ*"

But they were scheming to harm me; ³so I sent messengers to them with this reply: "I am carrying on a great project and cannot go down. Why should the work stop while I leave it and go down to you?" ⁴Four times they sent me the same message, and each time I gave them the same answer.

6:2
e 1Ch 8:12

⁵Then, the fifth time, Sanballat*ᶠ* sent his aide to me with the same message, and in his hand was an unsealed letter ⁶in which was written:

"It is reported among the nations—and Geshem*ᵇ ᵍ* says it is true—that you and the Jews are plotting to revolt, and therefore you are building the wall. Moreover, according to these reports you are about to become their king ⁷and have even appointed prophets to make this proclamation about you in Jerusalem: 'There is a king in Judah!' Now this report will get back to the king; so come, let us confer together."

6:5
f Ne 2:10

⁸I sent him this reply: "Nothing like what you are saying is happening; you are just making it up out of your head."

⁹They were all trying to frighten us, thinking, "Their hands will get too weak for the work, and it will not be completed."

⌊But I prayed,⌋ "Now strengthen my hands."

6:6
g Ne 2:19

¹⁰One day I went to the house of Shemaiah son of Delaiah, the son of Mehetabel, who was shut in at his home. He said, "Let us meet in the house of God, inside the temple*ʰ*, and let us close the temple doors, because men are coming to kill you—by night they are coming to kill you."

6:10
h Nu 18:7

a 2 Or *in Kephirim*   *b* 6 Hebrew *Gashmu*, a variant of *Geshem*

¹¹But I said, "Should a man like me run away? Or should one like me go into the temple to save his life? I will not go!" ¹²I realized that God had not sent him, but that he had prophesied against me[a] because Tobiah and Sanballat[b] had hired him. ¹³He had been hired to intimidate me so that I would commit a sin by doing this, and then they would give me a bad name to discredit me.[c]

¹⁴Remember[d] Tobiah and Sanballat,[e] O my God, because of what they have done; remember also the prophetess[f] Noadiah and the rest of the prophets[g] who have been trying to intimidate me.

¹⁵So the wall was completed on the twenty-fifth of Elul, in fifty-two days. ¹⁶When all our enemies heard about this, all the surrounding nations were afraid and lost their self-confidence, because they realized that this work had been done with the help of our God.

¹⁷Also, in those days the nobles of Judah were sending many letters to Tobiah, and replies from Tobiah kept coming to them. ¹⁸For many in Judah were under oath to him, since he was son-in-law to Shecaniah son of Arah, and his son Jehohanan had married the daughter of Meshullam son of Berekiah. ¹⁹Moreover, they kept reporting to me his good deeds and then telling him what I said. And Tobiah sent letters to intimidate me.

Chapter 7 Theme

7 After the wall had been rebuilt and I had set the doors in place, the gatekeepers[h] and the singers[i] and the Levites[j] were appointed. ²I put in charge of Jerusalem my brother Hanani,[k] along with[a] Hananiah[l] the commander of the citadel,[m] because he was a man of integrity and feared[n] God more than most men do. ³I said to them, "The gates of Jerusalem are not to be opened until the sun is hot. While the gatekeepers are still on duty, have them shut the doors and bar them. Also appoint residents of Jerusalem as guards, some at their posts and some near their own houses."

⁴Now the city was large and spacious, but there were few people in it,[o] and the houses had not yet been rebuilt. ⁵So my God put it into my heart to assemble the nobles, the officials and the common people for registration by families. I found the genealogical record of those who had been the first to return. This is what I found written there:

⁶These are the people of the province who came up from the captivity of the exiles[p] whom Nebuchadnezzar king of

a2 Or *Hanani, that is,*

6:12
a Eze 13:22-23
b Ne 2:10

6:13
c Jer 20:10

6:14
d Ne 1:8
e Ne 2:10
f Ex 15:20;
Eze 13:17-23;
Ac 21:9;
Rev 2:20
g Ne 13:29;
Jer 23:9-40;
Zec 13:2-3

7:1
h 1Ch 9:27;
26:12-19;
Ne 6:1,15
i Ps 68:25
j Ne 8:9

7:2
k Ne 1:2
l Ne 10:23
m Ne 2:8
n 1Ki 18:3

7:4
o Ne 11:1

7:6
p 2Ch 36:20;
Ezr 2:1-70;
Ne 1:2

Babylon had taken captive (they returned to Jerusalem and Judah, each to his own town, [7]in company with Zerubbabel,[a] Jeshua, Nehemiah, Azariah, Raamiah, Nahamani, Mordecai, Bilshan, Mispereth, Bigvai, Nehum and Baanah):

The list of the men of Israel:

[8]the descendants of Parosh	2,172
[9]of Shephatiah	372
[10]of Arah	652
[11]of Pahath-Moab (through the line of Jeshua and Joab)	2,818
[12]of Elam	1,254
[13]of Zattu	845
[14]of Zaccai	760
[15]of Binnui	648
[16]of Bebai	628
[17]of Azgad	2,322
[18]of Adonikam	667
[19]of Bigvai	2,067
[20]of Adin[b]	655
[21]of Ater (through Hezekiah)	98
[22]of Hashum	328
[23]of Bezai	324
[24]of Hariph	112
[25]of Gibeon	95
[26]the men of Bethlehem and Netophah[c]	188
[27]of Anathoth[d]	128
[28]of Beth Azmaveth	42
[29]of Kiriath Jearim, Kephirah[e] and Beeroth[f]	743
[30]of Ramah and Geba	621
[31]of Micmash	122
[32]of Bethel and Ai[g]	123
[33]of the other Nebo	52
[34]of the other Elam	1,254
[35]of Harim	320
[36]of Jericho[h]	345
[37]of Lod, Hadid and Ono[i]	721
[38]of Senaah	3,930

[39]The priests:

the descendants of Jedaiah (through the family of Jeshua)	973
[40]of Immer	1,052
[41]of Pashhur	1,247
[42]of Harim	1,017

7:7 [a] 1Ch 3:19; Ezr 2:2

7:20 [b] Ezr 8:6

7:26 [c] 2Sa 23:28; 1Ch 2:54

7:27 [d] Jos 21:18

7:29 [e] Jos 18:26 [f] Jos 18:25

7:32 [g] Ge 12:8

7:36 [h] Ne 3:2

7:37 [i] 1Ch 8:12

⁴³The Levites:

the descendants of Jeshua
(through Kadmiel through the line of Hodaviah)   74

⁴⁴The singers:*ᵃ*

the descendants of Asaph   148

⁴⁵The gatekeepers:*ᵇ*

the descendants of
Shallum, Ater, Talmon, Akkub, Hatita and Shobai   138

⁴⁶The temple servants:*ᶜ*

the descendants of
Ziha, Hasupha, Tabbaoth,
⁴⁷Keros, Sia, Padon,
⁴⁸Lebana, Hagaba, Shalmai,
⁴⁹Hanan, Giddel, Gahar,
⁵⁰Reaiah, Rezin, Nekoda,
⁵¹Gazzam, Uzza, Paseah,
⁵²Besai, Meunim, Nephussim,
⁵³Bakbuk, Hakupha, Harhur,
⁵⁴Bazluth, Mehida, Harsha,
⁵⁵Barkos, Sisera, Temah,
⁵⁶Neziah and Hatipha

⁵⁷The descendants of the servants of Solomon:

the descendants of
Sotai, Sophereth, Perida,
⁵⁸Jaala, Darkon, Giddel,
⁵⁹Shephatiah, Hattil,
Pokereth-Hazzebaim and Amon

⁶⁰The temple servants and the descendants of the servants of
Solomon*ᵈ*   392

⁶¹The following came up from the towns of Tel Melah, Tel Harsha, Kerub, Addon and Immer, but they could not show that their families were descended from Israel:

⁶²the descendants of
Delaiah, Tobiah and Nekoda   642

⁶³And from among the priests:

the descendants of
Hobaiah, Hakkoz and Barzillai (a man who had married a daughter of Barzillai the Gileadite and was called by that name).

7:44
ᵃ Ne 11:23

7:45
ᵇ 1Ch 9:17

7:46
ᶜ Ne 3:26

7:60
ᵈ 1Ch 9:2

7:65
a Ex 28:30;
Ne 8:9

7:71
b 1Ch 29:7

7:72
c Ex 25:2

7:73
d Ne 1:10;
Ps 34:22;
103:21; 113:1;
135:1
e Ezr 3:1;
Ne 11:1
f Ezr 3:1

8:1
g Ne 3:26
h Dt 28:61;
2Ch 34:15;
Ezr 7:6

8:2
i Lev 23:23-25;
Nu 29:1-6
j Dt 31:11

8:3
k Ne 3:26

8:4
l 2Ch 6:13

8:5
m Jdg 3:20

⁶⁴These searched for their family records, but they could not find them and so were excluded from the priesthood as unclean. ⁶⁵The governor, therefore, ordered them not to eat any of the most sacred food until there should be a priest ministering with the Urim and Thummim.*a*

⁶⁶The whole company numbered 42,360, ⁶⁷besides their 7,337 menservants and maidservants; and they also had 245 men and women singers. ⁶⁸There were 736 horses, 245 mules,*a* ⁶⁹435 camels and 6,720 donkeys.

⁷⁰Some of the heads of the families contributed to the work. The governor gave to the treasury 1,000 drachmas*b* of gold, 50 bowls and 530 garments for priests. ⁷¹Some of the heads of the families*b* gave to the treasury for the work 20,000 drachmas*c* of gold and 2,200 minas*d* of silver. ⁷²The total given by the rest of the people was 20,000 drachmas of gold, 2,000 minas*e* of silver and 67 garments for priests.*c*

⁷³The priests, the Levites, the gatekeepers, the singers and the temple servants,*d* along with certain of the people and the rest of the Israelites, settled in their own towns.*e*

Chapter 8 Theme

8 When the seventh month came and the Israelites had settled in their towns,*f* ¹all the people assembled as one man in the square before the Water Gate.*g* They told Ezra the scribe to bring out the Book of the Law of Moses,*h* which the LORD had commanded for Israel.

²So on the first day of the seventh month*i* Ezra the priest brought the Law*j* before the assembly, which was made up of men and women and all who were able to understand. ³He read it aloud from daybreak till noon as he faced the square before the Water Gate*k* in the presence of the men, women and others who could understand. And all the people listened attentively to the Book of the Law.

⁴Ezra the scribe stood on a high wooden platform*l* built for the occasion. Beside him on his right stood Mattithiah, Shema, Anaiah, Uriah, Hilkiah and Maaseiah; and on his left were Pedaiah, Mishael, Malkijah, Hashum, Hashbaddanah, Zechariah and Meshullam.

⁵Ezra opened the book. All the people could see him because he was standing*m* above them; and as he opened it, the people all

a 68 Some Hebrew manuscripts (see also Ezra 2:66); most Hebrew manuscripts do not have this verse.   *b* 70 That is, about 19 pounds (about 8.5 kilograms)   *c* 71 That is, about 375 pounds (about 170 kilograms); also in verse 72   *d* 71 That is, about 1 1/3 tons (about 1.2 metric tons)   *e* 72 That is, about 1 1/4 tons (about 1.1 metric tons) stood up. [6]Ezra praised the LORD, the great God; and all the people lifted their hands[a] and responded, "Amen! Amen!" Then they bowed down and worshiped the LORD with their faces to the ground.

[7]The Levites[b]—Jeshua, Bani, Sherebiah, Jamin, Akkub, Shabbethai, Hodiah, Maaseiah, Kelita, Azariah, Jozabad, Hanan and Pelaiah—instructed[c] the people in the Law while the people were standing there. [8]They read from the Book of the Law of God, making it clear[a] and giving the meaning so that the people could understand what was being read.

[9]Then Nehemiah the governor, Ezra the priest and scribe, and the Levites[d] who were instructing the people said to them all, "This day is sacred to the LORD your God. Do not mourn or weep."[e] For all the people had been weeping as they listened to the words of the Law.

[10]Nehemiah said, "Go and enjoy choice food and sweet drinks, and send some to those who have nothing[f] prepared. This day is sacred to our Lord. Do not grieve, for the joy[g] of the LORD is your strength."

[11]The Levites calmed all the people, saying, "Be still, for this is a sacred day. Do not grieve."

[12]Then all the people went away to eat and drink, to send portions of food and to celebrate with great joy,[h] because they now understood the words that had been made known to them.

[13]On the second day of the month, the heads of all the families, along with the priests and the Levites, gathered around Ezra the scribe to give attention to the words of the Law. [14]They found written in the Law, which the LORD had commanded through Moses, that the Israelites were to live in booths during the feast of the seventh month [15]and that they should proclaim this word and spread it throughout their towns and in Jerusalem: "Go out into the hill country and bring back branches from olive and wild olive trees, and from myrtles, palms and shade trees, to make booths"—as it is written.[b]

[16]So the people went out and brought back branches and built themselves booths on their own roofs, in their courtyards, in the courts of the house of God and in the square by the Water Gate and the one by the Gate of Ephraim.[i] [17]The whole company that had returned from exile built booths and lived in them. From the days of Joshua son of Nun until that day, the Israelites had not celebrated[j] it like this. And their joy was very great.

[18]Day after day, from the first day to the last, Ezra read[k] from the Book of the Law of God. They celebrated the feast for seven

8:6
[a]Ex 4:31;
Ezr 9:5; 1Ti 2:8

8:7
[b]Ezr 10:23
[c]Lev 10:11;
2Ch 17:7

8:9
[d]Ne 7:1,65,70
[e]Dt 12:7,12;
16:14-15

8:10
[f]1Sa 25:8;
Lk 14:12-14
[g]Lev 23:40;
Dt 12:18;
16:11,14-15

8:12
[h]Est 9:22

8:16
[i]2Ki 14:13;
Ne 12:39

8:17
[j]2Ch 7:8; 8:13;
30:21

8:18
[k]Dt 31:11

a 8 Or God, translating it   b 15 See Lev. 23:37-40.

8:18
a Lev 23:36,40;
Nu 29:35

9:1
b Jos 7:6;
1Sa 4:12

9:2
c Ne 13:3,30
d Ezr 10:11;
Ps 106:6

9:4
e Ezr 10:23

9:5
f Ps 78:4

9:6
g Dt 6:4
h 2Ki 19:15
i Ge 1:1;
Isa 37:16
j Ps 95:5
k Dt 10:14

9:7
l Ge 11:31
m Ge 17:5

9:8
n Ge 15:18-21
o Jos 21:45
p Ge 15:6;
Ezr 9:15

9:9
q Ex 3:7
r Ex 14:10-30

9:10
s Ex 10:1
t Jer 32:20;
Da 9:15

9:11
u Ex 14:21;
Ps 78:13
v Ex 15:4-5,10;
Heb 11:29

9:12
w Ex 15:13
x Ex 13:21

9:13
y Ex 19:11
z Ex 19:19
a Ps 119:137
b Ex 20:1

days, and on the eighth day, in accordance with the regulation,[a] there was an assembly.

Chapter 9 Theme

9 On the twenty-fourth day of the same month, the Israelites gathered together, fasting and wearing sackcloth and having dust on their heads.[b] 2Those of Israelite descent had separated themselves from all foreigners.[c] They stood in their places and confessed their sins and the wickedness of their fathers.[d] 3They stood where they were and read from the Book of the Law of the LORD their God for a quarter of the day, and spent another quarter in confession and in worshiping the LORD their God. 4Standing on the stairs were the Levites[e]—Jeshua, Bani, Kadmiel, Shebaniah, Bunni, Sherebiah, Bani and Kenani—who called with loud voices to the LORD their God. 5And the Levites—Jeshua, Kadmiel, Bani, Hashabneiah, Sherebiah, Hodiah, Shebaniah and Pethahiah—said: "Stand up and praise the LORD your God,[f] who is from everlasting to everlasting.[a]"

"Blessed be your glorious name, and may it be exalted above all blessing and praise. 6You alone are the LORD.[g] You made the heavens,[h] even the highest heavens, and all their starry host, the earth[i] and all that is on it, the seas[j] and all that is in them.[k] You give life to everything, and the multitudes of heaven worship you.

7"You are the LORD God, who chose Abram and brought him out of Ur of the Chaldeans[l] and named him Abraham.[m] 8You found his heart faithful to you, and you made a covenant with him to give to his descendants the land of the Canaanites, Hittites, Amorites, Perizzites, Jebusites and Girgashites.[n] You have kept your promise[o] because you are righteous.[p]

9"You saw the suffering of our forefathers in Egypt;[q] you heard their cry at the Red Sea.[b][r] 10You sent miraculous signs[s] and wonders against Pharaoh, against all his officials and all the people of his land, for you knew how arrogantly the Egyptians treated them. You made a name[t] for yourself, which remains to this day. 11You divided the sea before them,[u] so that they passed through it on dry ground, but you hurled their pursuers into the depths, like a stone into mighty waters.[v] 12By day you led[w] them with a pillar of cloud,[x] and by night with a pillar of fire to give them light on the way they were to take.

13"You came down on Mount Sinai;[y] you spoke[z] to them from heaven. You gave them regulations and laws that are just[a] and right, and decrees and commands that are good.[b]

a5 Or *God for ever and ever*   b9 Hebrew *Yam Suph*; that is, Sea of Reeds

¹⁴You made known to them your holy Sabbath*ᵃ* and gave them commands, decrees and laws through your servant Moses. ¹⁵In their hunger you gave them bread from heaven*ᵇ* and in their thirst you brought them water from the rock;*ᶜ* you told them to go in and take possession of the land you had sworn with uplifted hand to give them.*ᵈ*

¹⁶"But they, our forefathers, became arrogant and stiff-necked, and did not obey your commands.*ᵉ* ¹⁷They refused to listen and failed to remember*ᶠ* the miracles you performed among them. They became stiff-necked and in their rebellion appointed a leader in order to return to their slavery.*ᵍ* But you are a forgiving God, gracious and compassionate, slow to anger*ʰ* and abounding in love.*ⁱ* Therefore you did not desert them,*ʲ* ¹⁸even when they cast for themselves an image of a calf*ᵏ* and said, 'This is your god, who brought you up out of Egypt,' or when they committed awful blasphemies.

¹⁹"Because of your great compassion you did not abandon them in the desert. By day the pillar of cloud did not cease to guide them on their path, nor the pillar of fire by night to shine on the way they were to take. ²⁰You gave your good Spirit*ˡ* to instruct them. You did not withhold your manna*ᵐ* from their mouths, and you gave them water*ⁿ* for their thirst. ²¹For forty years you sustained them in the desert; they lacked nothing,*ᵒ* their clothes did not wear out nor did their feet become swollen.*ᵖ*

²²"You gave them kingdoms and nations, allotting to them even the remotest frontiers. They took over the country of Sihon*ᵃ* *�q* king of Heshbon and the country of Og king of Bashan.*ʳ* ²³You made their sons as numerous as the stars in the sky, and you brought them into the land that you told their fathers to enter and possess. ²⁴Their sons went in and took possession of the land.*ˢ* You subdued before them the Canaanites, who lived in the land; you handed the Canaanites over to them, along with their kings and the peoples of the land, to deal with them as they pleased. ²⁵They captured fortified cities and fertile land; they took possession of houses filled with all kinds of good things, wells already dug, vineyards, olive groves and fruit trees in abundance. They ate to the full and were well-nourished;*ᵗ* they reveled in your great goodness.*ᵘ*

²⁶"But they were disobedient and rebelled against you; they put your law behind their backs.*ᵛ* They killed your prophets,*ʷ* who had admonished them in order to turn them back to you; they committed awful blasphemies.*ˣ* ²⁷So you handed them over to their enemies,*ʸ* who oppressed them. But when they

a 22 One Hebrew manuscript and Septuagint; most Hebrew manuscripts *Sihon, that is, the country of the*

9:14
ᵃ Ge 2:3;
Ex 20:8-11

9:15
ᵇ Ex 16:4;
Jn 6:31
ᶜ Ex 17:6;
Nu 20:7-13
ᵈ Dt 1:8,21

9:16
ᵉ Dt 1:26-33;
31:29

9:17
ᶠ Ps 78:42
ᵍ Nu 14:1-4
ʰ Ex 34:6
ⁱ Nu 14:17-19
ʲ Ps 78:11

9:18
ᵏ Ex 32:4

9:20
ˡ Nu 11:17;
Isa 63:11,14
ᵐ Ex 16:15
ⁿ Ex 17:6

9:21
ᵒ Dt 2:7
ᵖ Dt 8:4

9:22
q Nu 21:21
ʳ Nu 21:33

9:24
ˢ Jos 11:23

9:25
ᵗ Dt 6:10-12
ᵘ Nu 13:27;
Dt 32:12-15

9:26
ᵛ 1Ki 14:9
ʷ Mt 21:35-36
ˣ Jdg 2:12-13

9:27
ʸ Jdg 2:14

9:27
a Ps 106:45

9:28
b Ps 106:43

9:29
c Ps 5:5; Isa 2:11;
Jer 43:2
d Dt 30:16
e Zec 7:11-12

9:30
f 2Ki 17:13-18;
2Ch 36:16

9:31
g Isa 48:9;
Jer 4:27

9:32
h Ps 24:8
i Dt 7:9

9:33
j Ge 18:25
k Jer 44:3;
Da 9:7-8,14

9:34
l 2Ki 23:11
m Jer 44:17

9:35
n Isa 63:7
o Dt 28:45-48

9:36
p Dt 28:48;
Ezr 9:9

9:37
q Dt 28:33;
La 5:5

9:38
r 2Ch 23:16
s Isa 44:5

were oppressed they cried out to you. From heaven you heard them, and in your great compassion*a* you gave them deliverers, who rescued them from the hand of their enemies.

²⁸"But as soon as they were at rest, they again did what was evil in your sight. Then you abandoned them to the hand of their enemies so that they ruled over them. And when they cried out to you again, you heard from heaven, and in your compassion you delivered them*b* time after time.

²⁹"You warned them to return to your law, but they became arrogant*c* and disobeyed your commands. They sinned against your ordinances, by which a man will live if he obeys them.*d* Stubbornly they turned their backs on you, became stiff-necked and refused to listen.*e* ³⁰For many years you were patient with them. By your Spirit you admonished them through your prophets.*f* Yet they paid no attention, so you handed them over to the neighboring peoples. ³¹But in your great mercy you did not put an end*g* to them or abandon them, for you are a gracious and merciful God.

³²"Now therefore, O our God, the great, mighty*h* and awesome God, who keeps his covenant of love,*i* do not let all this hardship seem trifling in your eyes—the hardship that has come upon us, upon our kings and leaders, upon our priests and prophets, upon our fathers and all your people, from the days of the kings of Assyria until today. ³³In all that has happened to us, you have been just;*j* you have acted faithfully, while we did wrong.*k* ³⁴Our kings,*l* our leaders, our priests and our fathers*m* did not follow your law; they did not pay attention to your commands or the warnings you gave them. ³⁵Even while they were in their kingdom, enjoying your great goodness*n* to them in the spacious and fertile land you gave them, they did not serve you*o* or turn from their evil ways.

³⁶"But see, we are slaves*p* today, slaves in the land you gave our forefathers so they could eat its fruit and the other good things it produces. ³⁷Because of our sins, its abundant harvest goes to the kings you have placed over us. They rule over our bodies and our cattle as they please. We are in great distress.*q*

³⁸"In view of all this, we are making a binding agreement,*r* putting it in writing,*s* and our leaders, our Levites and our priests are affixing their seals to it."

Chapter 10 Theme _____

10 Those who sealed it were:

Nehemiah the governor, the son of Hacaliah.

Zedekiah, [2]Seraiah,[a] Azariah, Jeremiah, [3]Pashhur,[b] Amariah, Malkijah, [4]Hattush, Shebaniah, Malluch, [5]Harim,[c] Meremoth, Obadiah, [6]Daniel, Ginnethon, Baruch, [7]Meshullam, Abijah, Mijamin, [8]Maaziah, Bilgai and Shemaiah.

These were the priests.

[9]The Levites:[d]

Jeshua son of Azaniah, Binnui of the sons of Henadad, Kadmiel, [10]and their associates: Shebaniah, Hodiah, Kelita, Pelaiah, Hanan, [11]Mica, Rehob, Hashabiah, [12]Zaccur, Sherebiah, Shebaniah, [13]Hodiah, Bani and Beninu.

[14]The leaders of the people:

Parosh, Pahath-Moab, Elam, Zattu, Bani, [15]Bunni, Azgad, Bebai, [16]Adonijah, Bigvai, Adin,[e] [17]Ater, Hezekiah, Azzur, [18]Hodiah, Hashum, Bezai, [19]Hariph, Anathoth, Nebai, [20]Magpiash, Meshullam, Hezir,[f] [21]Meshezabel, Zadok, Jaddua, [22]Pelatiah, Hanan, Anaiah, [23]Hoshea, Hananiah,[g] Hasshub, [24]Hallohesh, Pilha, Shobek, [25]Rehum, Hashabnah, Maaseiah, [26]Ahiah, Hanan, Anan, [27]Malluch, Harim and Baanah.

[28]"The rest of the people—priests, Levites, gatekeepers, singers, temple servants[h] and all who separated themselves from the neighboring peoples[i] for the sake of the Law of God, together with their wives and all their sons and daughters who are able to understand— [29]all these now join their brothers the nobles, and bind themselves with a curse and an oath[j] to follow the Law of God given through Moses the servant of God and to obey carefully all the commands, regulations and decrees of the LORD our Lord.

[30]"We promise not to give our daughters in marriage to the peoples around us or take their daughters for our sons.[k]

10:2
[a] Ezr 2:2

10:3
[b] 1Ch 9:12

10:5
[c] 1Ch 24:8

10:9
[d] Ne 12:1

10:16
[e] Ezr 8:6

10:20
[f] 1Ch 24:15

10:23
[g] Ne 7:2

10:28
[h] Ps 135:1
[i] 2Ch 6:26;
Ne 9:2

10:29
[j] Nu 5:21;
Ps 119:106

10:30
[k] Ex 34:16;
Dt 7:3; Ne 13:23

10:31
a Ne 13:16,18;
Jer 17:27;
Eze 23:38;
Am 8:5
b Ex 23:11;
Lev 25:1-7
c Dt 15:1

31"When the neighboring peoples bring merchandise or grain to sell on the Sabbath,a we will not buy from them on the Sabbath or on any holy day. Every seventh year we will forgo working the landb and will cancel all debts.c

32"We assume the responsibility for carrying out the commands to give a third of a shekela each year for the service of the house of our God: 33for the bread set out on the table;d for the regular grain offerings and burnt offerings; for the offerings on the Sabbaths, New Moone festivals and appointed feasts; for the holy offerings; for sin offerings to make atonement for Israel; and for all the duties of the house of our God.f

10:33
d Lev 24:6
e Nu 10:10;
Ps 81:3; Isa 1:14
f 2Ch 24:5

34"We—the priests, the Levites and the people—have cast lotsg to determine when each of our families is to bring to the house of our God at set times each year a contribution of woodh to burn on the altar of the LORD our God, as it is written in the Law.

10:34
g Lev 16:8
h Ne 13:31

35"We also assume responsibility for bringing to the house of the LORD each year the firstfruitsi of our crops and of every fruit tree.j

10:35
i Ex 22:29;
23:19; Nu 18:12
j Dt 26:1-11

36"As it is also written in the Law, we will bring the firstbornk of our sons and of our cattle, of our herds and of our flocks to the house of our God, to the priests ministering there.l

10:36
k Ex 13:2;
Nu 18:14-16
l Ne 13:31

37"Moreover, we will bring to the storerooms of the house of our God, to the priests, the first of our ground meal, of our ⌊grain⌋ offerings, of the fruit of all our trees and of our new wine and oil.m And we will bring a tithen of our crops to the Levites,o for it is the Levites who collect the tithes in all the towns where we work.p 38A priest descended from Aaron is to accompany the Levites when they receive the tithes, and the Levites are to bring a tenth of the tithesq up to the house of our God, to the storerooms of the treasury. 39The people of Israel, including the Levites, are to bring their contributions of grain, new wine and oil to the storerooms where the articles for the sanctuary are kept and where the ministering priests, the gatekeepers and the singers stay.

10:37
m Lev 23:17;
Nu 18:12
n Lev 27:30;
Nu 18:21
o Dt 14:22-29
p Eze 44:30

10:38
q Nu 18:26

"We will not neglect the house of our God."r

10:39
r Dt 12:6;
Ne 13:11,12

Chapter 11 Theme

11 Now the leaders of the people settled in Jerusalem, and the rest of the people cast lots to bring one out of every ten to live in Jerusalem,s the holy city,t while the remaining nine were to stay in their own towns.u 2The people commended all the men who volunteered to live in Jerusalem.

11:1
s Ne 7:4
t ver 18;
Isa 48:2; 52:1;
64:10;
Zec 14:20-21
u Ne 7:73

a 32 That is, about 1/8 ounce (about 4 grams)

³These are the provincial leaders who settled in Jerusalem (now some Israelites, priests, Levites, temple servants and descendants of Solomon's servants lived in the towns of Judah, each on his own property in the various towns,^a ⁴while other people from both Judah and Benjamin^b lived in Jerusalem):^c

From the descendants of Judah:

Athaiah son of Uzziah, the son of Zechariah, the son of Amariah, the son of Shephatiah, the son of Mahalalel, a descendant of Perez; ⁵and Maaseiah son of Baruch, the son of Col-Hozeh, the son of Hazaiah, the son of Adaiah, the son of Joiarib, the son of Zechariah, a descendant of Shelah. ⁶The descendants of Perez who lived in Jerusalem totaled 468 able men.

⁷From the descendants of Benjamin:

Sallu son of Meshullam, the son of Joed, the son of Pedaiah, the son of Kolaiah, the son of Maaseiah, the son of Ithiel, the son of Jeshaiah, ⁸and his followers, Gabbai and Sallai—928 men. ⁹Joel son of Zicri was their chief officer, and Judah son of Hassenuah was over the Second District of the city.

¹⁰From the priests:

Jedaiah; the son of Joiarib; Jakin; ¹¹Seraiah^d son of Hilkiah, the son of Meshullam, the son of Zadok, the son of Meraioth, the son of Ahitub,^e supervisor in the house of God, ¹²and their associates, who carried on work for the temple—822 men; Adaiah son of Jeroham, the son of Pelaliah, the son of Amzi, the son of Zechariah, the son of Pashhur, the son of Malkijah, ¹³and his associates, who were heads of families—242 men; Amashsai son of Azarel, the son of Ahzai, the son of Meshillemoth, the son of Immer, ¹⁴and his^a associates, who were able men—128. Their chief officer was Zabdiel son of Haggedolim.

¹⁵From the Levites:

Shemaiah son of Hasshub, the son of Azrikam, the son of Hashabiah, the son of Bunni; ¹⁶Shabbethai^f and Jozabad,^g two of the heads of the Levites, who had charge of the outside work of the house of God; ¹⁷Mattaniah^h son of Mica, the son of Zabdi, the son of Asaph,ⁱ the director who led in thanksgiving and prayer; Bakbukiah, second among his associates; and Abda son of Shammua, the son of Galal, the son of Jeduthun.^j ¹⁸The Levites in the holy city^k totaled 284.

^a14 Most Septuagint manuscripts; Hebrew *their*

11:3
^a1Ch 9:2-3; Ezr 2:1

11:4
^bEzr 1:5
^cEzr 2:70

11:11
^d2Ki 25:18; Ezr 2:2
^eEzr 7:2

11:16
^fEzr 10:15
^gEzr 8:33

11:17
^h1Ch 9:15; Ne 12:8
ⁱ2Ch 5:12
^j1Ch 25:1

11:18
^kRev 21:2

¹⁹The gatekeepers:

Akkub, Talmon and their associates, who kept watch at the gates—172 men.

²⁰The rest of the Israelites, with the priests and Levites, were in all the towns of Judah, each on his ancestral property.

²¹The temple servants^a lived on the hill of Ophel, and Ziha and Gishpa were in charge of them.

²²The chief officer of the Levites in Jerusalem was Uzzi son of Bani, the son of Hashabiah, the son of Mattaniah,^b the son of Mica. Uzzi was one of Asaph's descendants, who were the singers responsible for the service of the house of God. ²³The singers^c were under the king's orders, which regulated their daily activity.

²⁴Pethahiah son of Meshezabel, one of the descendants of Zerah^d son of Judah, was the king's agent in all affairs relating to the people.

²⁵As for the villages with their fields, some of the people of Judah lived in Kiriath Arba^e and its surrounding settlements, in Dibon^f and its settlements, in Jekabzeel and its villages, ²⁶in Jeshua, in Moladah, in Beth Pelet,^g ²⁷in Hazar Shual, in Beersheba^h and its settlements, ²⁸in Ziklag,ⁱ in Meconah and its settlements, ²⁹in En Rimmon, in Zorah,^j in Jarmuth,^k ³⁰Zanoah, Adullam^l and their villages, in Lachish^m and its fields, and in Azekahⁿ and its settlements. So they were living all the way from Beersheba^o to the Valley of Hinnom.

³¹The descendants of the Benjamites from Geba^p lived in Micmash,^q Aija, Bethel and its settlements, ³²in Anathoth,^r Nob^s and Ananiah, ³³in Hazor,^t Ramah and Gittaim,^u ³⁴in Hadid, Zeboim^v and Neballat, ³⁵in Lod and Ono,^w and in the Valley of the Craftsmen.

³⁶Some of the divisions of the Levites of Judah settled in Benjamin.

Chapter 12 Theme

12 These were the priests^x and Levites who returned with Zerubbabel^y son of Shealtiel and with Jeshua:^z

Seraiah,^a Jeremiah, Ezra,
²Amariah, Malluch, Hattush,
³Shecaniah, Rehum, Meremoth,
⁴Iddo,^b Ginnethon,^a Abijah,^c
⁵Mijamin,^b Moadiah, Bilgah,
⁶Shemaiah, Joiarib, Jedaiah,^d
⁷Sallu, Amok, Hilkiah and Jedaiah.

These were the leaders of the priests and their associates in the days of Jeshua.

**Cross references (left margin):**

11:21 *a*Ezr 2:43; Ne 3:26

11:22 *b*1Ch 9:15

11:23 *c*Ne 7:44

11:24 *d*Ge 38:30

11:25 *e*Ge 35:27; Jos 14:15 *f*Nu 21:30

11:26 *g*Jos 15:27

11:27 *h*Ge 21:14

11:28 *i*1Sa 27:6

11:29 *j*Jos 15:33 *k*Jos 10:3

11:30 *l*Jos 15:35 *m*Jos 10:3 *n*Jos 10:10 *o*Jos 15:28

11:31 *p*Jos 21:17; Isa 10:29 *q*1Sa 13:2

11:32 *r*Jos 21:18; Isa 10:30 *s*1Sa 21:1

11:33 *t*Jos 11:1 *u*2Sa 4:3

11:34 *v*1Sa 13:18

11:35 *w*1Ch 8:12

12:1 *x*Ne 10:1-8 *y*1Ch 3:19 *z*Ezr 2:2 *a*Ezr 2:2

12:4 *b*Zec 1:1 *c*Lk 1:5

12:6 *d*1Ch 24:7

---

^a4 Many Hebrew manuscripts and Vulgate (see also Neh. 12:16); most Hebrew manuscripts *Ginnethoi* ^b5 A variant of *Miniamin*

⁸The Levites were Jeshua, Binnui, Kadmiel, Sherebiah, Judah, and also Mattaniah,ᵃ who, together with his associates, was in charge of the songs of thanksgiving. ⁹Bakbukiah and Unni, their associates, stood opposite them in the services.

¹⁰Jeshua was the father of Joiakim, Joiakim the father of Eliashib,ᵇ Eliashib the father of Joiada, ¹¹Joiada the father of Jonathan, and Jonathan the father of Jaddua.

¹²In the days of Joiakim, these were the heads of the priestly families:

of Seraiah's family, Meraiah;

of Jeremiah's, Hananiah;

¹³of Ezra's, Meshullam;

of Amariah's, Jehohanan;

¹⁴of Malluch's, Jonathan;

of Shecaniah's,ᵃ Joseph;

¹⁵of Harim's, Adna;

of Meremoth's,ᵇ Helkai;

¹⁶of Iddo's,ᶜ Zechariah;

of Ginnethon's, Meshullam;

¹⁷of Abijah's, Zicri;

of Miniamin's and of Moadiah's, Piltai;

¹⁸of Bilgah's, Shammua;

of Shemaiah's, Jehonathan;

¹⁹of Joiarib's, Mattenai;

of Jedaiah's, Uzzi;

²⁰of Sallu's, Kallai;

of Amok's, Eber;

²¹of Hilkiah's, Hashabiah;

of Jedaiah's, Nethanel.

²²The family heads of the Levites in the days of Eliashib, Joiada, Johanan and Jaddua, as well as those of the priests, were recorded in the reign of Darius the Persian. ²³The family heads among the descendants of Levi up to the time of Johanan son of Eliashib were recorded in the book of the annals. ²⁴And the leaders of the Levitesᵈ were Hashabiah, Sherebiah, Jeshua son of Kadmiel, and their associates, who stood opposite them to give praise and thanksgiving, one section responding to the other, as prescribed by David the man of God.

²⁵Mattaniah, Bakbukiah, Obadiah, Meshullam, Talmon and Akkub were gatekeepers who guarded the storerooms at the gates. ²⁶They served in the days of Joiakim son of Jeshua, the son of Jozadak, and in the days of Nehemiah the governor and of Ezra the priest and scribe.

ᵃ14 Very many Hebrew manuscripts, some Septuagint manuscripts and Syriac (see also Neh. 12:3); most Hebrew manuscripts *Shebaniah's*   ᵇ15 Some Septuagint manuscripts (see also Neh. 12:3); Hebrew *Meraioth's*

ᵃ 12:8
Ne 11:17

ᵇ 12:10
Ezr 10:24

ᶜ 12:16
ver 4

ᵈ 12:24
Ezr 2:40

12:27
a Dt 20:5
b 2Sa 6:5
c 1Ch 15:16,28;
25:6; Ps 92:3

12:28
d 1Ch 2:54; 9:16

12:30
e Ex 19:10;
Job 1:5

12:31
f Ne 2:13

12:34
g Ezr 1:5

12:35
h Ezr 3:10

12:36
i 1Ch 15:16
j 2Ch 8:14
k Ezr 7:6

12:37
l Ne 2:14; 3:15
m Ne 3:26

12:38
n Ne 3:11
o Ne 3:8

12:39
p 2Ki 14:13;
Ne 8:16
q Ne 3:6
r 2Ch 33:14;
Ne 3:3
s Ne 3:1
t Ne 3:1
u Ne 3:1

12:44
v Ne 13:4,13
w Lev 27:30
x Dt 18:8

²⁷At the dedication*a* of the wall of Jerusalem, the Levites were sought out from where they lived and were brought to Jerusalem to celebrate joyfully the dedication with songs of thanksgiving and with the music of cymbals,*b* harps and lyres.*c* ²⁸The singers also were brought together from the region around Jerusalem—from the villages of the Netophathites,*d* ²⁹from Beth Gilgal, and from the area of Geba and Azmaveth, for the singers had built villages for themselves around Jerusalem. ³⁰When the priests and Levites had purified themselves ceremonially, they purified the people,*e* the gates and the wall.

³¹I had the leaders of Judah go up on top*a* of the wall. I also assigned two large choirs to give thanks. One was to proceed on top*b* of the wall to the right, toward the Dung Gate.*f* ³²Hoshaiah and half the leaders of Judah followed them, ³³along with Azariah, Ezra, Meshullam, ³⁴Judah, Benjamin,*g* Shemaiah, Jeremiah, ³⁵as well as some priests with trumpets,*h* and also Zechariah son of Jonathan, the son of Shemaiah, the son of Mattaniah, the son of Micaiah, the son of Zaccur, the son of Asaph, ³⁶and his associates—Shemaiah, Azarel, Milalai, Gilalai, Maai, Nethanel, Judah and Hanani—with musical instruments*i* ⌞prescribed by⌟ David the man of God.*j* Ezra*k* the scribe led the procession. ³⁷At the Fountain Gate*l* they continued directly up the steps of the City of David on the ascent to the wall and passed above the house of David to the Water Gate*m* on the east.

³⁸The second choir proceeded in the opposite direction. I followed them on top*c* of the wall, together with half the people— past the Tower of the Ovens*n* to the Broad Wall,*o* ³⁹over the Gate of Ephraim,*p* the Jeshanah*d* Gate,*q* the Fish Gate,*r* the Tower of Hananel*s* and the Tower of the Hundred,*t* as far as the Sheep Gate.*u* At the Gate of the Guard they stopped.

⁴⁰The two choirs that gave thanks then took their places in the house of God; so did I, together with half the officials, ⁴¹as well as the priests—Eliakim, Maaseiah, Miniamin, Micaiah, Elioenai, Zechariah and Hananiah with their trumpets— ⁴²and also Maaseiah, Shemaiah, Eleazar, Uzzi, Jehohanan, Malkijah, Elam and Ezer. The choirs sang under the direction of Jezrahiah. ⁴³And on that day they offered great sacrifices, rejoicing because God had given them great joy. The women and children also rejoiced. The sound of rejoicing in Jerusalem could be heard far away.

⁴⁴At that time men were appointed to be in charge of the storerooms*v* for the contributions, firstfruits and tithes.*w* From the fields around the towns they were to bring into the storerooms the portions required by the Law for the priests and the Levites, for Judah was pleased with the ministering priests and Levites.*x*

a 31 Or *go alongside*   *b* 31 Or *proceed alongside*   *c* 38 Or *them alongside*   *d* 39 Or *Old*

⁴⁵They performed the service of their God and the service of purification, as did also the singers and gatekeepers, according to the commands of David[a] and his son Solomon.[b] ⁴⁶For long ago, in the days of David and Asaph,[c] there had been directors for the singers and for the songs of praise[d] and thanksgiving to God. ⁴⁷So in the days of Zerubbabel and of Nehemiah, all Israel contributed the daily portions for the singers and gatekeepers. They also set aside the portion for the other Levites, and the Levites set aside the portion for the descendants of Aaron.[e]

Chapter 13 Theme _____

13 On that day the Book of Moses was read aloud in the hearing of the people and there it was found written that no Ammonite or Moabite should ever be admitted into the assembly of God,[f] ²because they had not met the Israelites with food and water but had hired Balaam[g] to call a curse down on them.[h] (Our God, however, turned the curse into a blessing.)[i] ³When the people heard this law, they excluded from Israel all who were of foreign descent.[j]

⁴Before this, Eliashib the priest had been put in charge of the storerooms[k] of the house of our God. He was closely associated with Tobiah,[l] ⁵and he had provided him with a large room formerly used to store the grain offerings and incense and temple articles, and also the tithes[m] of grain, new wine and oil prescribed for the Levites, singers and gatekeepers, as well as the contributions for the priests.

⁶But while all this was going on, I was not in Jerusalem, for in the thirty-second year of Artaxerxes[n] king of Babylon I had returned to the king. Some time later I asked his permission ⁷and came back to Jerusalem. Here I learned about the evil thing Eliashib[o] had done in providing Tobiah a room in the courts of the house of God. ⁸I was greatly displeased and threw all Tobiah's household goods out of the room.[p] ⁹I gave orders to purify the rooms,[q] and then I put back into them the equipment of the house of God, with the grain offerings and the incense.

¹⁰I also learned that the portions assigned to the Levites had not been given to them,[r] and that all the Levites and singers responsible for the service had gone back to their own fields. ¹¹So I rebuked the officials and asked them, "Why is the house of God neglected?"[s] Then I called them together and stationed them at their posts.

¹²All Judah brought the tithes[t] of grain, new wine and oil into the storerooms.[u] ¹³I put Shelemiah the priest, Zadok the scribe, and a Levite named Pedaiah in charge of the storerooms and made Hanan son of Zaccur, the son of Mattaniah, their assistant, because these men were considered trustworthy. They were made responsible for distributing the supplies to their brothers.[v]

12:45
a 1Ch 25:1;
2Ch 8:14
b 1Ch 6:31; 23:5

12:46
c 2Ch 35:15
d 2Ch 29:27;
Ps 137:4

12:47
e Nu 18:21;
Dt 18:8

13:1
f ver 23; Dt 23:3

13:2
g Nu 22:3-11
h Nu 23:7;
Dt 23:3
i Nu 23:11;
Dt 23:4-5

13:3
j ver 23; Ne 9:2

13:4
k Ne 12:44
l Ne 2:10

13:5
m Lev 27:30;
Nu 18:21

13:6
n Ne 2:6; 5:14

13:7
o Ezr 10:24

13:8
p Mt 21:12-13;
Jn 2:13-16

13:9
q 1Ch 23:28;
2Ch 29:5

13:10
r Dt 12:19

13:11
s Ne 10:37-39;
Hag 1:1-9

13:12
t 2Ch 31:6
u 1Ki 7:51;
Ne 10:37-39;
Mal 3:10

13:13
v Ne 12:44;
Ac 6:1-5

13:14
a Ge 8:1

[14]Remember[a] me for this, O my God, and do not blot out what I have so faithfully done for the house of my God and its services.

13:15
b Ex 20:8-11;
34:21;
Dt 5:12-15;
Ne 10:31

[15]In those days I saw men in Judah treading winepresses on the Sabbath and bringing in grain and loading it on donkeys, together with wine, grapes, figs and all other kinds of loads. And they were bringing all this into Jerusalem on the Sabbath.[b] Therefore I warned them against selling food on that day. [16]Men from Tyre who lived in Jerusalem were bringing in fish and all kinds of merchandise and selling them in Jerusalem on the Sabbath[c] to the people of Judah. [17]I rebuked the nobles of Judah and said to them, "What is this wicked thing you are doing—desecrating the Sabbath day? [18]Didn't your forefathers do the same things, so that our God brought all this calamity upon us and upon this city? Now you are stirring up more wrath against Israel by desecrating the Sabbath."[d]

13:16
c Ne 10:31

13:18
d Ne 10:31;
Jer 17:21-23

[19]When evening shadows fell on the gates of Jerusalem before the Sabbath,[e] I ordered the doors to be shut and not opened until the Sabbath was over. I stationed some of my own men at the gates so that no load could be brought in on the Sabbath day. [20]Once or twice the merchants and sellers of all kinds of goods spent the night outside Jerusalem. [21]But I warned them and said, "Why do you spend the night by the wall? If you do this again, I will lay hands on you." From that time on they no longer came on the Sabbath. [22]Then I commanded the Levites to purify themselves and go and guard the gates in order to keep the Sabbath day holy.

13:19
e Lev 23:32

13:22
f Ge 8:1;
Ne 12:30

Remember[f] me for this also, O my God, and show mercy to me according to your great love.

13:23
g Ezr 9:1-2;
Mal 2:11
h ver 1; Ne 10:30

[23]Moreover, in those days I saw men of Judah who had married[g] women from Ashdod, Ammon and Moab.[h] [24]Half of their children spoke the language of Ashdod or the language of one of the other peoples, and did not know how to speak the language of Judah. [25]I rebuked them and called curses down on them. I beat some of the men and pulled out their hair. I made them take an oath[i] in God's name and said: "You are not to give your daughters in marriage to their sons, nor are you to take their daughters in marriage for your sons or for yourselves. [26]Was it not because of marriages like these that Solomon king of Israel sinned? Among the many nations there was no king like him.[j] He was loved by his God,[k] and God made him king over all Israel, but even he was led into sin by foreign women.[l] [27]Must we hear now that you too are doing all this terrible wickedness and are being unfaithful to our God by marrying[m] foreign women?"

13:25
i Ezr 10:5

13:26
j 1Ki 3:13;
2Ch 1:12
k 2Sa 12:25
l 1Ki 11:3

13:27
m Ezr 9:14; 10:2

²⁸One of the sons of Joiada son of Eliashib*a* the high priest was son-in-law to Sanballat*b* the Horonite. And I drove him away from me.

²⁹Remember*c* them, O my God, because they defiled the priestly office and the covenant of the priesthood and of the Levites.

³⁰So I purified the priests and the Levites of everything foreign,*d* and assigned them duties, each to his own task. ³¹I also made provision for contributions of wood*e* at designated times, and for the firstfruits.

Remember*f* me with favor, O my God.

13:28
a Ezr 10:24
b Ne 2:10

13:29
c Ne 6:14

13:30
d Ne 10:30

13:31
e Ne 10:34
f ver 14,22;
Ge 8:1

NEHEMIAH AT A GLANCE

Theme of Nehemiah:

SEGMENT DIVISIONS

			CHAPTER THEMES	
		1		Author:
		2		Date:
		3		
		4		Purpose:
		5		
		6		Key Words:
		7		
		8		
		9		
		10		
		11		
		12		
		13		

LESSONS FROM THE LIFE OF NEHEMIAH

THE SITUATION	HOW NEHEMIAH RELATED TO GOD	HOW NEHEMIAH RELATED TO PEOPLE	NEHEMIAH'S EXAMPLE

ESTHER

*T*hroughout time people have attempted to destroy the nation of Israel, the "apple of his eye." Why? Because from the Jews came the covenants, the promises, the law, and the Messiah—salvation for the world. The people of God are the enemy of Satan, the prince of this world.

While a remnant from Judah returned to the land promised to Abraham, Isaac, and Jacob, other Jews remained in the cities of their captivity. Some were welcomed as valuable members of their communities, but others were despised and hated. Some were even targeted for extermination.

Esther tells the story. The book of Esther records a ten-year span during the 58- to 60-year interlude in the book of Ezra. Esther tells us of the inauguration of a feast which has endured over 2000 years because of one woman who, for the sake of her people, was willing to say, "If I perish, I perish."

❧ THINGS TO DO

Esther is a story of intrigue—a divinely inspired one. It reveals the sovereignty of God, although God is never mentioned in this book. As you read:

1. Consult the historical chart THE TIMES OF EZRA, NEHEMIAH, AND ESTHER on page 821 in order to see the setting of Esther.

2. Observe the main events which occur in each chapter. Examine each chapter under the scrutiny of the five W's and an H: Who? What? When? Where? Why? and How? Ask: Who was involved? What happened? When did it occur? Where did it take place and why? How did it come about? etc.

   a. List in the margin the major points you want to remember about each event under the heading you give that event. For example, Esther 1:3, 4 could be titled "King Ahasuerus' Banquet." Then under the heading you could list these major points: 1) attended by his princes, attendants, etc., 2) given to display riches, 3) lasted 180 days.

   b. While the main event of each chapter will not always be a banquet, banquets play an important role in Esther. So mark in a distinctive way each use of the words *banquet, dinner, feast,* or *feasting.* Ask the five W's and an H about each banquet and list your insights in the margin.

   c. Make sure you underline or mark in a distinctive way the main characters in each chapter.

3. Mark every reference to time with a symbol so it can be seen immediately. This will help you see the timing of the events. Also consult the calendar on page 822 so you can keep track of the references to the various months.

4. Mark every occurrence of the words *Jew* or *Jews* (with their pronouns and synonyms, such as *her people, her kindred, people, nationality, my family, her family background*). *Jews* was a term used to describe the people who came from Judah.

5. Carefully observe the timing of events, such as when the king can't sleep and needs something to read. Remember the truth in Daniel 4:34, 35.

6. When you finish studying each chapter, record the theme of that chapter in the appropriate place on the ESTHER AT A GLANCE chart on page 834. Also record this in the text next to the chapter number.

7. In a chapter margin, list all you learn about Esther and then list all you learn about Mordecai.

8. When you finish reading Esther, complete ESTHER AT A GLANCE. See if any of the chapters can be grouped according to events. If so, record these segment divisions on the AT A GLANCE chart.

❧ THINGS TO THINK ABOUT

1. What can you learn from the lives of each of the main characters of this historical event? Review what you have listed about Esther and Mordecai. Have you ever realized that you too have come to the

kingdom for such a time as this? What are the good works that God would have you do? Read John 15:16 and Ephesians 2:8-10.

2. Have you thought about why Mordecai was unwilling to bow before Haman? Have you "bowed" to someone or something and in so doing compromised your calling and position as a child of God? Read Galatians 1:10.

3. Esther and Mordecai relied heavily on fasting and prayer to turn the tide of events. What about you?

THE TIMES OF EZRA, NEHEMIAH, AND ESTHER

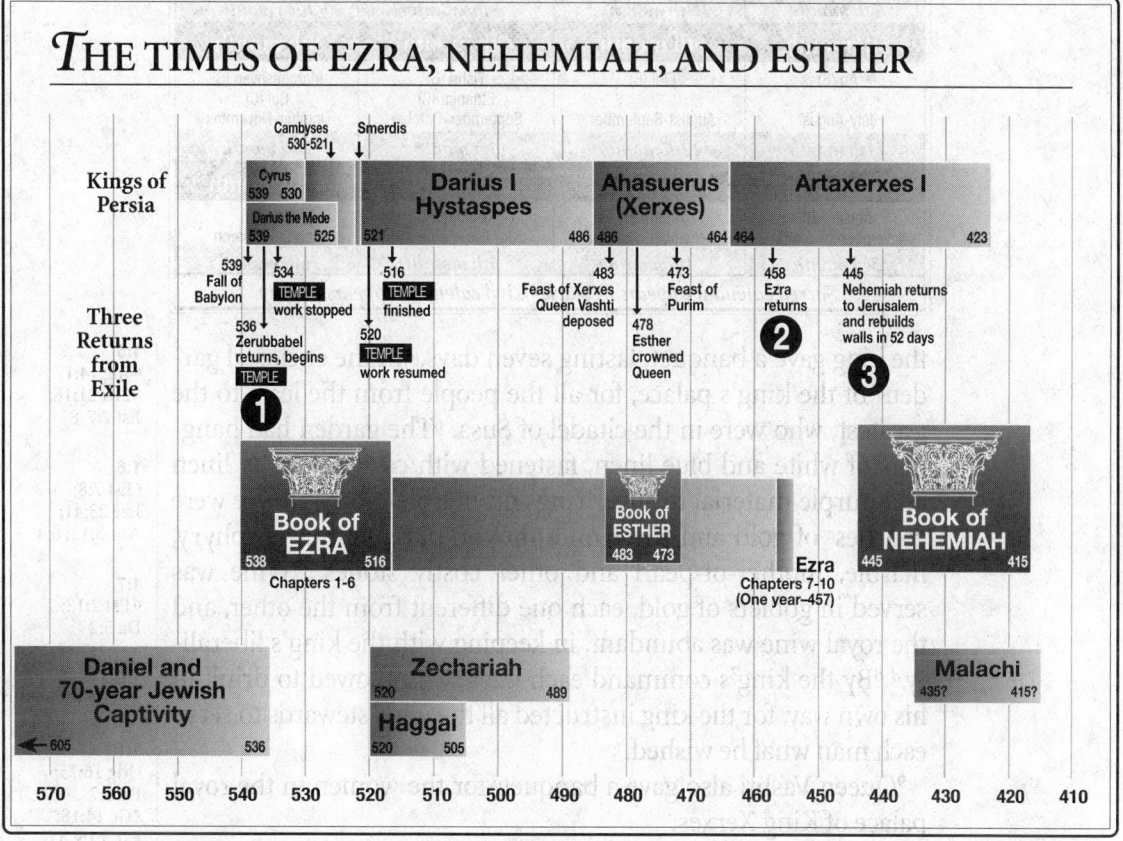

Chapter 1 Theme

1:1
a Ezr 4:6;
Da 9:1
b Est 9:30;
Da 3:2; 6:1
c Est 8:9

1 This is what happened during the time of Xerxes,ᵃᵃ the Xerxes who ruled over 127 provincesᵇ stretching from India to Cushᵇ:ᶜ ²At that time King Xerxes reigned from his royal throne in the citadel of Susa,ᵈ ³and in the third year of his reign he gave a banquetᵉ for all his nobles and officials. The military leaders of Persia and Media, the princes, and the nobles of the provinces were present.

1:2
d Ezr 4:9;
Ne 1:1;
Est 2:8

⁴For a full 180 days he displayed the vast wealth of his kingdom and the splendor and glory of his majesty. ⁵When these days were over,

1:3
e 1Ki 3:15;
Est 2:18

a 1 Hebrew *Ahasuerus*, a variant of Xerxes' Persian name; here and throughout Esther
b 1 That is, the upper Nile region

The Jewish Calendar

Babylonian names (B) for the months are still used today for the Jewish calendar. Canaanite names (C) were used prior to the Babylonian captivity in 586 B.C. Four are mentioned in the Old Testament. **Adar-Sheni** is an intercalary month used every two to three years or seven times in 19 years.

1st month	2nd month	3rd month	4th month
Nisan (B) Abib (C) March-April	Iyyar (B) Ziv (C) April-May	Sivan (B) May-June	Tammuz (B) June-July
7th month	*8th month*	*9th month*	*10th month*
5th month	**6th month**	**7th month**	**8th month**
Ab (B) July-August	Elul (B) August-September	Tishri (B) Ethanim (C) September-October	Marcheshvan (B) Bul (C) October-November
11th month	*12th month*	*1st month*	*2nd month*
9th month	**10th month**	**11th month**	**12th month**
Chislev (B) November-December	Tebeth (B) December-January	Shebat (B) January-February	Adar (B) February-March
3rd month	*4th month*	*5th month*	*6th month*

Sacred calendar appears in black • Civil calendar appears in gray

the king gave a banquet, lasting seven days,[a] in the enclosed garden[b] of the king's palace, for all the people from the least to the greatest, who were in the citadel of Susa. [6]The garden had hangings of white and blue linen, fastened with cords of white linen and purple material to silver rings on marble pillars. There were couches[c] of gold and silver on a mosaic pavement of porphyry, marble, mother-of-pearl and other costly stones. [7]Wine was served in goblets of gold, each one different from the other, and the royal wine was abundant, in keeping with the king's liberality.[d] [8]By the king's command each guest was allowed to drink in his own way, for the king instructed all the wine stewards to serve each man what he wished.

[9]Queen Vashti also gave a banquet[e] for the women in the royal palace of King Xerxes.

[10]On the seventh day, when King Xerxes was in high spirits[f] from wine,[g] he commanded the seven eunuchs who served him— Mehuman, Biztha, Harbona,[h] Bigtha, Abagtha, Zethar and Carcas— [11]to bring[i] before him Queen Vashti, wearing her royal crown, in order to display her beauty[j] to the people and nobles, for she was lovely to look at. [12]But when the attendants delivered the king's command, Queen Vashti refused to come. Then the king became furious and burned with anger.[k]

[13]Since it was customary for the king to consult experts in matters of law and justice, he spoke with the wise men who understood the times[l] [14]and were closest to the king—Carshena, Shethar, Admatha, Tarshish, Meres, Marsena and Memucan, the seven nobles[m] of Persia and Media who had special access to the king and were highest in the kingdom.

1:5
a Jdg 14:17
b 2Ki 21:18;
Est 7:7-8

1:6
c Est 7:8;
Eze 23:41;
Am 3:12; 6:4

1:7
d Est 2:18;
Da 5:2

1:9
e 1Ki 3:15

1:10
f Jdg 16:25;
Ru 3:7
g Ge 14:18;
Est 3:15; 5:6;
7:2; Pr 31:4-7;
Da 5:1-4
h Est 7:9

1:11
i SS 2:4
j Ps 45:11;
Eze 16:14

1:12
k Ge 39:19;
Est 2:21; 7:7;
Pr 19:12

1:13
l 1Ch 12:32;
Jer 10:7; Da 2:12

1:14
m 2Ki 25:19;
Ezr 7:14

1:18
a Pr 19:13; 27:15

¹⁵"According to law, what must be done to Queen Vashti?" he asked. "She has not obeyed the command of King Xerxes that the eunuchs have taken to her."

¹⁶Then Memucan replied in the presence of the king and the nobles, "Queen Vashti has done wrong, not only against the king but also against all the nobles and the peoples of all the provinces of King Xerxes. ¹⁷For the queen's conduct will become known to all the women, and so they will despise their husbands and say, 'King Xerxes commanded Queen Vashti to be brought before him, but she would not come.' ¹⁸This very day the Persian and Median women of the nobility who have heard about the queen's conduct will respond to all the king's nobles in the same way. There will be no end of disrespect and discord.*a*

1:19
b Ecc 8:4
c Est 8:8;
Da 6:8,12

¹⁹"Therefore, if it pleases the king,*b* let him issue a royal decree and let it be written in the laws of Persia and Media, which cannot be repealed,*c* that Vashti is never again to enter the presence of King Xerxes. Also let the king give her royal position to someone else who is better than she. ²⁰Then when the king's edict is proclaimed throughout all his vast realm, all the women will respect their husbands, from the least to the greatest."

1:22
d Ne 13:24;
Est 8:9;
Eph 5:22-24;
1Ti 2:12

²¹The king and his nobles were pleased with this advice, so the king did as Memucan proposed. ²²He sent dispatches to all parts of the kingdom, to each province in its own script and to each people in its own language,*d* proclaiming in each people's tongue that every man should be ruler over his own household.

Chapter 2 Theme

2:1
e Est 1:19-20;
7:10

2 Later when the anger of King Xerxes had subsided,*e* he remembered Vashti and what she had done and what he had decreed about her. ²Then the king's personal attendants proposed, "Let a search be made for beautiful young virgins for the king. ³Let the king appoint commissioners in every province of his realm to bring all these beautiful girls into the harem at the citadel of Susa. Let them be placed under the care of Hegai, the king's eunuch, who is in charge of the women; and let beauty treatments be given to them. ⁴Then let the girl who pleases the king be queen instead of Vashti." This advice appealed to the king, and he followed it.

2:5
f 1Sa 9:1; Est 3:2

⁵Now there was in the citadel of Susa a Jew of the tribe of Benjamin, named Mordecai son of Jair, the son of Shimei, the son of Kish,*f* ⁶who had been carried into exile from Jerusalem by Nebuchadnezzar king of Babylon, among those taken captive with Jehoiachin*a**g* king of Judah.*h* ⁷Mordecai had a cousin named

2:6
g 2Ki 24:6,15;
2Ch 36:10,20
h Da 1:1-5; 5:13

a 6 Hebrew *Jeconiah,* a variant of *Jehoiachin*

Hadassah, whom he had brought up because she had neither father nor mother. This girl, who was also known as Esther,[a] was lovely[b] in form and features, and Mordecai had taken her as his own daughter when her father and mother died.

[8]When the king's order and edict had been proclaimed, many girls were brought to the citadel of Susa[c] and put under the care of Hegai. Esther also was taken to the king's palace and entrusted to Hegai, who had charge of the harem. [9]The girl pleased him and won his favor.[d] Immediately he provided her with her beauty treatments and special food.[e] He assigned to her seven maids selected from the king's palace and moved her and her maids into the best place in the harem.

[10]Esther had not revealed her nationality and family background, because Mordecai had forbidden her to do so.[f] [11]Every day he walked back and forth near the courtyard of the harem to find out how Esther was and what was happening to her.

[12]Before a girl's turn came to go in to King Xerxes, she had to complete twelve months of beauty treatments prescribed for the women, six months with oil of myrrh and six with perfumes[g] and cosmetics. [13]And this is how she would go to the king: Anything she wanted was given her to take with her from the harem to the king's palace. [14]In the evening she would go there and in the morning return to another part of the harem to the care of Shaashgaz, the king's eunuch who was in charge of the concubines.[h] She would not return to the king unless he was pleased with her and summoned her by name.[i]

[15]When the turn came for Esther (the girl Mordecai had adopted, the daughter of his uncle Abihail[j]) to go to the king,[k] she asked for nothing other than what Hegai, the king's eunuch who was in charge of the harem, suggested. And Esther won the favor[l] of everyone who saw her. [16]She was taken to King Xerxes in the royal residence in the tenth month, the month of Tebeth, in the seventh year of his reign.

[17]Now the king was attracted to Esther more than to any of the other women, and she won his favor and approval more than any of the other virgins. So he set a royal crown on her head and made her queen[m] instead of Vashti. [18]And the king gave a great banquet,[n] Esther's banquet, for all his nobles and officials.[o] He proclaimed a holiday throughout the provinces and distributed gifts with royal liberality.[p]

[19]When the virgins were assembled a second time, Mordecai was sitting at the king's gate.[q] [20]But Esther had kept secret her family background and nationality just as Mordecai had told her to do, for she continued to follow Mordecai's instructions as she had done when he was bringing her up.[r]

2:7
[a]Ge 41:45
[b]Ge 39:6

2:8
[c]ver 3,15;
Ne 1:1; Est 1:2;
Da 8:2

2:9
[d]Ge 39:21
[e]ver 3,12;
Ge 37:3;
1Sa 9:22-24;
2Ki 25:30;
Eze 16:9-13;
Da 1:5

2:10
[f]ver 20

2:12
[g]Pr 27:9; SS 1:3;
Isa 3:24

2:14
[h]1Ki 11:3;
SS 6:8; Da 5:2
[i]Est 4:11

2:15
[j]Est 9:29
[k]Ps 45:14
[l]Ge 18:3; 30:27;
Est 5:8

2:17
[m]Est 1:11;
Eze 16:9-13

2:18
[n]1Ki 3:15;
Est 1:3
[o]Ge 40:20
[p]Est 1:7

2:19
[q]ver 21;
Est 3:2; 4:2; 5:13

2:20
[r]ver 10

2:21
a Ge 40:2;
Est 6:2
b Est 1:12; 3:5;
5:9; 7:7

2:23
c Ge 40:19;
Ps 7:14-16;
Pr 26:27
d Est 6:1; 10:2

3:1
e ver 10;
Ex 17:8-16;
Nu 24:7;
Dt 25:17-19;
1Sa 14:48;
Est 5:11

3:3
f Est 5:9; Da 3:12

3:4
g Ge 39:10

3:5
h Est 2:21; 5:9

3:6
i Pr 16:25
j Ps 74:8; 83:4
k Est 9:24

3:7
l Est 9:24,26
m Lev 16:8;
1Sa 10:21
n ver 13;
Ezr 6:15;
Est 9:19

3:8
o Ac 16:20-21
p Jer 29:7;
Da 6:13
q Ezr 4:15

3:9
r Est 7:4

3:10
s Ge 41:42;
Est 7:6; 8:2

²¹During the time Mordecai was sitting at the king's gate, Bigthana*a* and Teresh, two of the king's officers*a* who guarded the doorway, became angry*b* and conspired to assassinate King Xerxes. ²²But Mordecai found out about the plot and told Queen Esther, who in turn reported it to the king, giving credit to Mordecai. ²³And when the report was investigated and found to be true, the two officials were hanged*c* on a gallows.*b* All this was recorded in the book of the annals*d* in the presence of the king.

Chapter 3 Theme _____

3 After these events, King Xerxes honored Haman son of Hammedatha, the Agagite,*e* elevating him and giving him a seat of honor higher than that of all the other nobles. ²All the royal officials at the king's gate knelt down and paid honor to Haman, for the king had commanded this concerning him. But Mordecai would not kneel down or pay him honor.

³Then the royal officials at the king's gate asked Mordecai, "Why do you disobey the king's command?"*f* ⁴Day after day they spoke to him but he refused to comply.*g* Therefore they told Haman about it to see whether Mordecai's behavior would be tolerated, for he had told them he was a Jew.

⁵When Haman saw that Mordecai would not kneel down or pay him honor, he was enraged.*h* ⁶Yet having learned who Mordecai's people were, he scorned the idea of killing only Mordecai. Instead Haman looked for a way*i* to destroy*j* all Mordecai's people, the Jews,*k* throughout the whole kingdom of Xerxes.

⁷In the twelfth year of King Xerxes, in the first month, the month of Nisan, they cast the *pur*ˡ (that is, the lot*m*) in the presence of Haman to select a day and month. And the lot fell on*c* the twelfth month, the month of Adar.*n*

⁸Then Haman said to King Xerxes, "There is a certain people dispersed and scattered among the peoples in all the provinces of your kingdom whose customs*o* are different from those of all other people and who do not obey*p* the king's laws; it is not in the king's best interest to tolerate them.*q* ⁹If it pleases the king, let a decree be issued to destroy them, and I will put ten thousand talents*d* of silver into the royal treasury for the men who carry out this business."*r*

¹⁰So the king took his signet ring*s* from his finger and gave it to Haman son of Hammedatha, the Agagite, the enemy of the Jews. ¹¹"Keep the money," the king said to Haman, "and do with the people as you please."

INSIGHT

Agagite, possibly a synonym for Amalekite, is a reference to a descendant of Agag. Agag was king of the Amalekites, a tribal people whom the Lord ordered King Saul to destroy completely. However, Saul spared King Agag. Haman, the arch villain in Esther, was an Agagite.

a 21 Hebrew *Bigthan*, a variant of *Bigthana*   *b 23* Or *were hung* (or *impaled*) *on poles*; similarly elsewhere in Esther   *c 7* Septuagint; Hebrew does not have *And the lot fell on.*   *d 9* That is, about 375 tons (about 345 metric tons)

825

¹²Then on the thirteenth day of the first month the royal secretaries were summoned. They wrote out in the script of each province and in the language[a] of each people all Haman's orders to the king's satraps, the governors of the various provinces and the nobles of the various peoples. These were written in the name of King Xerxes himself and sealed[b] with his own ring. ¹³Dispatches were sent by couriers to all the king's provinces with the order to destroy, kill and annihilate all the Jews[c]—young and old, women and little children—on a single day, the thirteenth day of the twelfth month, the month of Adar,[d] and to plunder[e] their goods. ¹⁴A copy of the text of the edict was to be issued as law in every province and made known to the people of every nationality so they would be ready for that day.[f]

¹⁵Spurred on by the king's command, the couriers went out, and the edict was issued in the citadel of Susa.[g] The king and Haman sat down to drink,[h] but the city of Susa was bewildered.[i]

Chapter 4 Theme _____

4 When Mordecai learned of all that had been done, he tore his clothes,[j] put on sackcloth and ashes,[k] and went out into the city, wailing[l] loudly and bitterly. ²But he went only as far as the king's gate,[m] because no one clothed in sackcloth was allowed to enter it. ³In every province to which the edict and order of the king came, there was great mourning among the Jews, with fasting, weeping and wailing. Many lay in sackcloth and ashes.

⁴When Esther's maids and eunuchs came and told her about Mordecai, she was in great distress. She sent clothes for him to put on instead of his sackcloth, but he would not accept them. ⁵Then Esther summoned Hathach, one of the king's eunuchs assigned to attend her, and ordered him to find out what was troubling Mordecai and why.

⁶So Hathach went out to Mordecai in the open square of the city in front of the king's gate. ⁷Mordecai told him everything that had happened to him, including the exact amount of money Haman had promised to pay into the royal treasury for the destruction of the Jews.[n] ⁸He also gave him a copy of the text of the edict for their annihilation, which had been published in Susa, to show to Esther and explain it to her, and he told him to urge her to go into the king's presence to beg for mercy and plead with him for her people.

⁹Hathach went back and reported to Esther what Mordecai had said. ¹⁰Then she instructed him to say to Mordecai, ¹¹"All the king's officials and the people of the royal provinces know that for any man or woman who approaches the king in the inner court without being summoned[o] the king has but one law:[p] that

3:12
[a] Ne 13:24
[b] Ge 38:18;
1Ki 21:8;
Est 8:8-10

3:13
[c] 1Sa 15:3;
Ezr 4:6;
Est 8:10-14
[d] ver 7
[e] Est 8:11; 9:10

3:14
[f] Est 8:8; 9:1

3:15
[g] Est 8:14
[h] Est 1:10
[i] Est 8:15

4:1
[j] Nu 14:6
[k] 2Sa 13:19;
Eze 27:30-31;
Jnh 3:5-6
[l] Ex 11:6;
Ps 30:11

4:2
[m] Est 2:19

4:7
[n] Est 3:9; 7:4

4:11
[o] Est 2:14
[p] Da 2:9

4:11
a Est 5:1,2; 8:4

4:14
b Ecc 3:7;
Isa 62:1;
Am 5:13
c Est 9:16,22
d Ge 45:7;
Dt 28:29
e Ge 50:20

4:16
f 2Ch 20:3;
Est 9:31
g Ge 43:14

5:1
h Est 4:16;
Eze 16:13
i Est 6:4; Pr 21:1

5:2
j Est 4:11; 8:4;
Pr 21:1

5:3
k Est 7:2;
Da 5:16;
Mk 6:23

5:6
l Est 1:10
m Mk 6:23
n Est 7:2; 9:12

5:8
o Est 2:15;
7:3; 8:5
p 1Ki 3:15;
Est 6:14

5:9
q Est 2:21;
Pr 14:17
r Est 3:3,5

he be put to death. The only exception to this is for the king to extend the gold scepter[a] to him and spare his life. But thirty days have passed since I was called to go to the king."

[12]When Esther's words were reported to Mordecai, [13]he sent back this answer: "Do not think that because you are in the king's house you alone of all the Jews will escape. [14]For if you remain silent[b] at this time, relief[c] and deliverance[d] for the Jews will arise from another place, but you and your father's family will perish. And who knows but that you have come to royal position for such a time as this?"[e]

[15]Then Esther sent this reply to Mordecai: [16]"Go, gather together all the Jews who are in Susa, and fast[f] for me. Do not eat or drink for three days, night or day. I and my maids will fast as you do. When this is done, I will go to the king, even though it is against the law. And if I perish, I perish."[g]

[17]So Mordecai went away and carried out all of Esther's instructions.

Chapter 5 Theme

5 On the third day Esther put on her royal robes[h] and stood in the inner court of the palace, in front of the king's[i] hall. The king was sitting on his royal throne in the hall, facing the entrance. [2]When he saw Queen Esther standing in the court, he was pleased with her and held out to her the gold scepter that was in his hand. So Esther approached and touched the tip of the scepter.[j]

[3]Then the king asked, "What is it, Queen Esther? What is your request? Even up to half the kingdom,[k] it will be given you."

[4]"If it pleases the king," replied Esther, "let the king, together with Haman, come today to a banquet I have prepared for him."

[5]"Bring Haman at once," the king said, "so that we may do what Esther asks."

So the king and Haman went to the banquet Esther had prepared. [6]As they were drinking wine,[l] the king again asked Esther, "Now what is your petition? It will be given you. And what is your request? Even up to half the kingdom,[m] it will be granted."[n]

[7]Esther replied, "My petition and my request is this: [8]If the king regards me with favor[o] and if it pleases the king to grant my petition and fulfill my request, let the king and Haman come tomorrow to the banquet[p] I will prepare for them. Then I will answer the king's question."

[9]Haman went out that day happy and in high spirits. But when he saw Mordecai at the king's gate and observed that he neither rose nor showed fear in his presence, he was filled with rage[q] against Mordecai.[r] [10]Nevertheless, Haman restrained himself and went home.

Calling together his friends and Zeresh,[a] his wife, [11]Haman boasted[b] to them about his vast wealth, his many sons,[c] and all the ways the king had honored him and how he had elevated him above the other nobles and officials. [12]"And that's not all," Haman added. "I'm the only person[d] Queen Esther invited to accompany the king to the banquet she gave. And she has invited me along with the king tomorrow. [13]But all this gives me no satisfaction as long as I see that Jew Mordecai sitting at the king's gate.[e]"

[14]His wife Zeresh and all his friends said to him, "Have a gallows built, seventy-five feet[a] high,[f] and ask the king in the morning to have Mordecai hanged[g] on it. Then go with the king to the dinner and be happy." This suggestion delighted Haman, and he had the gallows built.

Chapter 6 Theme

6 That night the king could not sleep;[h] so he ordered the book of the chronicles,[i] the record of his reign, to be brought in and read to him. [2]It was found recorded there that Mordecai had exposed Bigthana and Teresh, two of the king's officers who guarded the doorway, who had conspired to assassinate King Xerxes.

[3]"What honor and recognition has Mordecai received for this?" the king asked.

"Nothing has been done for him,"[j] his attendants answered.

[4]The king said, "Who is in the court?" Now Haman had just entered the outer court of the palace to speak to the king about hanging Mordecai on the gallows he had erected for him.

[5]His attendants answered, "Haman is standing in the court."

"Bring him in," the king ordered.

[6]When Haman entered, the king asked him, "What should be done for the man the king delights to honor?"

Now Haman thought to himself, "Who is there that the king would rather honor than me?" [7]So he answered the king, "For the man the king delights to honor, [8]have them bring a royal robe[k] the king has worn and a horse[l] the king has ridden, one with a royal crest placed on its head. [9]Then let the robe and horse be entrusted to one of the king's most noble princes. Let them robe the man the king delights to honor, and lead him on the horse through the city streets, proclaiming before him, 'This is what is done for the man the king delights to honor!'[m]"

[10]"Go at once," the king commanded Haman. "Get the robe and the horse and do just as you have suggested for Mordecai the Jew, who sits at the king's gate. Do not neglect anything you have recommended."

a 14 Hebrew *fifty cubits* (about 23 meters)

5:10
[a] Est 6:13

5:11
[b] Pr 13:16
[c] Est 9:7-10,13

5:12
[d] Job 22:29;
Pr 16:18; 29:23

5:13
[e] Est 2:19

5:14
[f] Est 7:9
[g] Ezr 6:11;
Est 6:4

6:1
[h] Da 2:1; 6:18
[i] Est 2:23; 10:2

6:3
[j] Ecc 9:13-16

6:8
[k] Ge 41:42;
Isa 52:1
[l] 1Ki 1:33

6:9
[m] Ge 41:43

6:11
a Ge 41:42

6:12
b 2Sa 15:30;
Jer 14:3,4;
Mic 3:7

6:13
c Est 5:10
d Ps 57:6;
Pr 26:27; 28:18

6:14
e 1Ki 3:15;
Est 5:8

7:1
f Ge 40:20-22;
Mt 22:1-14

7:2
g Est 1:10
h Est 5:3
i Est 9:12

7:3
j Est 2:15

7:4
k Est 3:9

7:7
l Ge 34:7;
Est 1:12;
Pr 19:12; 20:1-2
m 2Ki 21:18
n Est 6:13

7:8
o Est 1:6
p Ge 39:14
q Ge 34:7
r Est 6:12

7:9
s Est 1:10
t Est 5:14

¹¹So Haman got*a* the robe and the horse. He robed Mordecai, and led him on horseback through the city streets, proclaiming before him, "This is what is done for the man the king delights to honor!"

¹²Afterward Mordecai returned to the king's gate. But Haman rushed home, with his head covered*b* in grief, ¹³and told Zeresh*c* his wife and all his friends everything that had happened to him.

His advisers and his wife Zeresh said to him, "Since Mordecai, before whom your downfall*d* has started, is of Jewish origin, you cannot stand against him—you will surely come to ruin!" ¹⁴While they were still talking with him, the king's eunuchs arrived and hurried Haman away to the banquet*e* Esther had prepared.

Chapter 7 Theme

7 So the king and Haman went to dine*f* with Queen Esther, ²and as they were drinking wine*g* on that second day, the king again asked, "Queen Esther, what is your petition? It will be given you. What is your request? Even up to half the kingdom,*h* it will be granted.*i*"

³Then Queen Esther answered, "If I have found favor*j* with you, O king, and if it pleases your majesty, grant me my life—this is my petition. And spare my people—this is my request. ⁴For I and my people have been sold for destruction and slaughter and annihilation.*k* If we had merely been sold as male and female slaves, I would have kept quiet, because no such distress would justify disturbing the king.*a*"

⁵King Xerxes asked Queen Esther, "Who is he? Where is the man who has dared to do such a thing?"

⁶Esther said, "The adversary and enemy is this vile Haman."

Then Haman was terrified before the king and queen. ⁷The king got up in a rage,*l* left his wine and went out into the palace garden.*m* But Haman, realizing that the king had already decided his fate,*n* stayed behind to beg Queen Esther for his life.

⁸Just as the king returned from the palace garden to the banquet hall, Haman was falling on the couch*o* where Esther was reclining.*p*

The king exclaimed, "Will he even molest the queen while she is with me in the house?"*q*

As soon as the word left the king's mouth, they covered Haman's face.*r* ⁹Then Harbona,*s* one of the eunuchs attending the king, said, "A gallows seventy-five feet*b* high*t* stands by Haman's house. He had it made for Mordecai, who spoke up to help the king."

a 4 Or *quiet, but the compensation our adversary offers cannot be compared with the loss the king would suffer*   *b* 9 Hebrew *fifty cubits* (about 23 meters)

The king said, "Hang him on it!"[a] [10]So they hanged Haman[b] on the gallows[c] he had prepared for Mordecai.[d] Then the king's fury subsided.[e]

Chapter 8 Theme

8 That same day King Xerxes gave Queen Esther the estate of Haman,[f] the enemy of the Jews. And Mordecai came into the presence of the king, for Esther had told how he was related to her. [2]The king took off his signet ring,[g] which he had reclaimed from Haman, and presented it to Mordecai. And Esther appointed him over Haman's estate.[h]

[3]Esther again pleaded with the king, falling at his feet and weeping. She begged him to put an end to the evil plan of Haman the Agagite, which he had devised against the Jews. [4]Then the king extended the gold scepter[i] to Esther and she arose and stood before him.

[5]"If it pleases the king," she said, "and if he regards me with favor and thinks it the right thing to do, and if he is pleased with me, let an order be written overruling the dispatches that Haman son of Hammedatha, the Agagite, devised and wrote to destroy the Jews in all the king's provinces. [6]For how can I bear to see disaster fall on my people? How can I bear to see the destruction of my family?"[j]

[7]King Xerxes replied to Queen Esther and to Mordecai the Jew, "Because Haman attacked the Jews, I have given his estate to Esther, and they have hanged him on the gallows. [8]Now write another decree[k] in the king's name in behalf of the Jews as seems best to you, and seal it with the king's signet ring[l]—for no document written in the king's name and sealed with his ring can be revoked."[m]

[9]At once the royal secretaries were summoned—on the twenty-third day of the third month, the month of Sivan. They wrote out all Mordecai's orders to the Jews, and to the satraps, governors and nobles of the 127 provinces stretching from India to Cush.[a][n] These orders were written in the script of each province and the language of each people and also to the Jews in their own script and language.[o] [10]Mordecai wrote in the name of King Xerxes, sealed the dispatches with the king's signet ring, and sent them by mounted couriers, who rode fast horses especially bred for the king.

[11]The king's edict granted the Jews in every city the right to assemble and protect themselves; to destroy, kill and annihilate any armed force of any nationality or province that might attack them and their women and children; and to plunder[p] the property

---

[a]9 That is, the upper Nile region

Cross references

7:9
[a] Ps 7:14-16; 9:16; Pr 11:5-6; 26:27; Mt 7:2

7:10
[b] Pr 10:28
[c] Est 9:25
[d] Da 6:24
[e] Est 2:1

8:1
[f] Est 2:7; 7:6; Pr 22:22-23

8:2
[g] Ge 41:42; Est 3:10
[h] Pr 13:22; Da 2:48

8:4
[i] Est 4:11; 5:2

8:6
[j] Est 7:4; 9:1

8:8
[k] Est 3:12-14
[l] Ge 41:42
[m] Est 1:19; Da 6:15

8:9
[n] Est 1:1
[o] Est 1:22

8:11
[p] Est 9:10, 15,16

8:12
a Est 3:13; 9:1

8:13
b Est 3:14

8:15
c Est 9:4
d Ge 41:42
e Est 3:15

8:16
f Ps 97:10-12
g Ps 112:4

8:17
h Est 9:19,27;
Ps 35:27;
Pr 11:10
i Ex 15:14,16;
Dt 11:25
j Est 9:3

9:1
k Est 8:12
l Jer 29:4-7
m Est 3:12-14;
Pr 22:22-23

9:2
n ver 15-18
o Est 8:11,17;
Ps 71:13,24

9:3
p Ezr 8:36

9:4
q Ex 11:3
r 2Sa 3:1;
1Ch 11:9

9:5
s Ezr 4:6

9:10
t Est 5:11
u Ge 14:23;
1Sa 14:32;
Est 3:13; 8:11

9:12
v Est 5:6; 7:2

of their enemies. [12]The day appointed for the Jews to do this in all the provinces of King Xerxes was the thirteenth day of the twelfth month, the month of Adar.a [13]A copy of the text of the edict was to be issued as law in every province and made known to the people of every nationality so that the Jews would be ready on that dayb to avenge themselves on their enemies.

[14]The couriers, riding the royal horses, raced out, spurred on by the king's command. And the edict was also issued in the citadel of Susa.

[15]Mordecaic left the king's presence wearing royal garments of blue and white, a large crown of gold and a purple robe of fine linen.d And the city of Susa held a joyous celebration.e [16]For the Jews it was a time of happiness and joy,f gladness and honor.g [17]In every province and in every city, wherever the edict of the king went, there was joyh and gladness among the Jews, with feasting and celebrating. And many people of other nationalities became Jews because feari of the Jews had seized them.j

Chapter 9 Theme

9 On the thirteenth day of the twelfth month, the month of Adar,k the edict commanded by the king was to be carried out. On this day the enemies of the Jews had hoped to overpower them, but now the tables were turned and the Jews got the upper handl over those who hated them.m [2]The Jews assembled in their citiesn in all the provinces of King Xerxes to attack those seeking their destruction. No one could stand against them,o because the people of all the other nationalities were afraid of them. [3]And all the nobles of the provinces, the satraps, the governors and the king's administrators helped the Jews,p because fear of Mordecai had seized them. [4]Mordecai was prominentq in the palace; his reputation spread throughout the provinces, and he became more and more powerful.r

[5]The Jews struck down all their enemies with the sword, killing and destroying them,s and they did what they pleased to those who hated them. [6]In the citadel of Susa, the Jews killed and destroyed five hundred men. [7]They also killed Parshandatha, Dalphon, Aspatha, [8]Poratha, Adalia, Aridatha, [9]Parmashta, Arisai, Aridai and Vaizatha, [10]the ten sonst of Haman son of Hammedatha, the enemy of the Jews. But they did not lay their hands on the plunder.u

[11]The number of those slain in the citadel of Susa was reported to the king that same day. [12]The king said to Queen Esther, "The Jews have killed and destroyed five hundred men and the ten sons of Haman in the citadel of Susa. What have they done in the rest of the king's provinces? Now what is your petition? It will be given you. What is your request? It will also be granted."v

¹³"If it pleases the king," Esther answered, "give the Jews in Susa permission to carry out this day's edict tomorrow also, and let Haman's ten sons^a be hanged^b on gallows."

¹⁴So the king commanded that this be done. An edict was issued in Susa, and they hanged^c the ten sons of Haman. ¹⁵The Jews in Susa came together on the fourteenth day of the month of Adar, and they put to death in Susa three hundred men, but they did not lay their hands on the plunder.^d

¹⁶Meanwhile, the remainder of the Jews who were in the king's provinces also assembled to protect themselves and get relief^e from their enemies.^f They killed seventy-five thousand of them^g but did not lay their hands on the plunder. ¹⁷This happened on the thirteenth day of the month of Adar, and on the fourteenth they rested and made it a day of feasting^h and joy.

¹⁸The Jews in Susa, however, had assembled on the thirteenth and fourteenth, and then on the fifteenth they rested and made it a day of feasting and joy.

¹⁹That is why rural Jews—those living in villages—observe the fourteenth of the month of Adarⁱ as a day of joy and feasting, a day for giving presents to each other.^j

²⁰Mordecai recorded these events, and he sent letters to all the Jews throughout the provinces of King Xerxes, near and far, ²¹to have them celebrate annually the fourteenth and fifteenth days of the month of Adar ²²as the time when the Jews got relief^k from their enemies, and as the month when their sorrow was turned into joy and their mourning into a day of celebration.^l He wrote them to observe the days as days of feasting and joy and giving presents of food^m to one another and gifts to the poor.

²³So the Jews agreed to continue the celebration they had begun, doing what Mordecai had written to them. ²⁴For Haman son of Hammedatha, the Agagite,ⁿ the enemy of all the Jews, had plotted against the Jews to destroy them and had cast the *pur*^o (that is, the lot^p) for their ruin and destruction. ²⁵But when the plot came to the king's attention,^a he issued written orders that the evil scheme Haman had devised against the Jews should come back onto his own head,^q and that he and his sons should be hanged^r on the gallows.^s ²⁶(Therefore these days were called Purim, from the word *pur.*^t) Because of everything written in this letter and because of what they had seen and what had happened to them, ²⁷the Jews took it upon themselves to establish the custom that they and their descendants and all who join them should without fail observe these two days every year, in the way prescribed and at the time appointed. ²⁸These days should be

---

^a 25 Or *when Esther came before the king*

9:13
^a Est 5:11
^b Dt 21:22-23

9:14
^c Ezr 6:11

9:15
^d Ge 14:23;
Est 8:11

9:16
^e Est 4:14
^f Dt 25:19
^g 1Ch 4:43

9:17
^h 1Ki 3:15

9:19
ⁱ Est 3:7
^j ver 22;
Dt 16:11,14;
Ne 8:10,12;
Est 2:9;
Rev 11:10

9:22
^k Est 4:14
^l Ne 8:12;
Ps 30:11-12
^m 2Ki 25:30

9:24
ⁿ Ex 17:8-16
^o Est 3:7
^p Lev 16:8

9:25
^q Ps 7:16
^r Dt 21:22-23
^s Est 7:10

9:26
^t ver 20; Est 3:7

remembered and observed in every generation by every family, and in every province and in every city. And these days of Purim should never cease to be celebrated by the Jews, nor should the memory of them die out among their descendants.

²⁹So Queen Esther, daughter of Abihail,^a along with Mordecai the Jew, wrote with full authority to confirm this second letter concerning Purim. ³⁰And Mordecai sent letters to all the Jews in the 127 provinces^b of the kingdom of Xerxes—words of goodwill and assurance— ³¹to establish these days of Purim at their designated times, as Mordecai the Jew and Queen Esther had decreed for them, and as they had established for themselves and their descendants in regard to their times of fasting^c and lamentation.^d ³²Esther's decree confirmed these regulations about Purim, and it was written down in the records.

Chapter 10 Theme

10 King Xerxes imposed tribute throughout the empire, to its distant shores.^e ²And all his acts of power and might, together with a full account of the greatness of Mordecai^f to which the king had raised him,^g are they not written in the book of the annals^h of the kings of Media and Persia? ³Mordecai the Jew was secondⁱ in rank^j to King Xerxes,^k preeminent among the Jews, and held in high esteem by his many fellow Jews, because he worked for the good of his people and spoke up for the welfare of all the Jews.^l

9:29
a Est 2:15

9:30
b Est 1:1

9:31
c Est 4:16
d Est 4:1-3

10:1
e Ps 72:10; 97:1;
Isa 24:15

10:2
f Est 8:15; 9:4
g Ge 41:44
h Est 2:23

10:3
i Da 5:7
j Ge 41:43
k Ge 41:40
l Ne 2:10;
Jer 29:4-7;
Da 6:3

Theme of Esther:

SEGMENT DIVISIONS

		CHAPTER THEMES
		1
		2
		3
		4
		5
		6
		7
		8
		9
		10

Author:

Date:

Purpose:

Key Words:

JOB

*J*ob is a book born out of pain. Job's pain was so crushing he wanted to die; he wished he had never been born. His pain was compounded because his friends wrestled with the reason for his suffering. Job's affliction brought God's character and ways into question. Yet ultimately it brought deeper intimacy with God.

Job, the first and probably oldest of the poetical books of the Bible, is for those who need answers from God, for those who want to say with Job, "Then I would still have this consolation—my joy in unrelenting pain—that I had not denied the words of the Holy One" (6:10).

ᴥ THINGS TO DO

1. Chapters 1 and 2 provide the setting of Job's pain. Read through these two chapters. Mark every reference to Satan and to God. Then on the OBSERVATIONS CHART on page 893:

   a. List what you learn about Satan—his person and his relationship to God and to Job.

   b. List what you learn about God.

   c. List what you learn about Job: what God says about him; what Satan says; how he responds to God, to his pain, and to the counsel of his wife.

2. In order to understand Job and the ensuing discourses of his friends, read Job 1:8 and 2:3, 11-13 again and then Job 42:7-9. Stop and do this before you proceed any further. Pay attention to what God says about Job and to what God says about what Job's three friends said.

3. In chapter 3 Job pours out his anguish, and then in chapters 4 through 42:6 there is a series of discourses given either by Job, his friends, or God himself. Read through this section chapter by chapter and do the following:

   a. At the top of every chapter, on the line next to the chapter number, note who is speaking and to whom. Then record this under chapter themes on the JOB AT A GLANCE chart on page 894.

   b. Job 42:7 says that Job's friends did not speak what was right concerning God. Therefore if one of these three men speaks, in the margin note how his reasoning is wrong in respect to God and to Job's suffering. Watch carefully to see where or how (if it tells) Job's friend came up with his conclusion. Then watch how Job answers each of his friends. Record pertinent notes in the margin.

4. As you read Job 4 through 42 observe what the text says about:

   a. Man and God

   b. What God expects from man and what he does not expect

   c. Nature

   d. Sin and righteousness

   e. Physical life and death

   f. How to deal with those in pain

Record your insights on the OBSERVATIONS CHART on page 893 as you read each chapter.

5. Mark key words or phrases which play a significant role in a particular chapter or which recur throughout the book (for instance, the words *wisdom, victory,* and *insight*). Note in the margin the insights you glean from marking *wisdom* and other key words. Also highlight or underline verses which speak to your heart.

6. Don't fail to compare Job's end with his beginning and to notice what came from Satan's challenge.

7. When you finish reading Job and you have filled in JOB AT A GLANCE, note how the book divides itself into a pattern of discourses. Record this under "Segment Divisions."

1. Think about Job's end compared to his beginning and then ask yourself if Job's suffering was worth it. What about your suffering? What can it produce if you will respond in the proper way? What is the proper way? What did you learn from Job?

2. What have you learned about Satan and Satan's relationship to God from this book? How can those insights comfort you?

3. Read Job 31 again, and if you did not mark it the first time, mark in a distinctive way every *if* and every *if I have*. Think about how Job appealed to his own integrity in various matters of life. Examine those areas carefully. How does your own integrity measure up in those areas? What do you need to remember, do, hold onto, let go of, begin, or stop?

∽∽∽∽∽

Chapter 1 Theme

1 In the land of Uz[a] there lived a man whose name was Job.[b] This man was blameless[c] and upright; he feared God[d] and shunned evil. [2]He had seven sons and three daughters,[e] [3]and he owned seven thousand sheep, three thousand camels, five hundred yoke of oxen and five hundred donkeys, and had a large number of servants. He was the greatest man[f] among all the people of the East.

[4]His sons used to take turns holding feasts in their homes, and they would invite their three sisters to eat and drink with them. [5]When a period of feasting had run its course, Job would send and have them purified. Early in the morning he would sacrifice a burnt offering[g] for each of them, thinking, "Perhaps my children have sinned[h] and cursed God[i] in their hearts." This was Job's regular custom.

[6]One day the angels[a][j] came to present themselves before the LORD, and Satan[b] also came with them.[k] [7]The LORD said to Satan, "Where have you come from?"

Satan answered the LORD, "From roaming through the earth and going back and forth in it."[l]

[8]Then the LORD said to Satan, "Have you considered my servant Job?[m] There is no one on earth like him; he is blameless and upright, a man who fears God and shuns evil."[n]

[9]"Does Job fear God for nothing?"[o] Satan replied. [10]"Have you not put a hedge around him and his household and everything he has?[p] You have blessed the work of his hands, so that his flocks and herds are spread throughout the land.[q] [11]But stretch out your hand and strike everything he has,[r] and he will surely curse you to your face."[s]

[12]The LORD said to Satan, "Very well, then, everything he has is in your hands, but on the man himself do not lay a finger."

Then Satan went out from the presence of the LORD.

---

a6 Hebrew *the sons of God* b6 *Satan* means *accuser*.

1:1
a Jer 25:20
b Eze 14:14, 20; Jas 5:11
c Ge 6:9; 17:1
d Ge 22:12; Ex 18:21

1:2
e Job 42:13

1:3
f Job 29:25

1:5
g Ge 8:20; Job 42:8
h Job 8:4
i 1Ki 21:10,13

1:6
j Job 38:7
k Job 2:1

1:7
l 1Pe 5:8

1:8
m Jos 1:7; Job 42:7-8
n ver 1

1:9
o 1Ti 6:5

1:10
p Ps 34:7
q ver 3; Job 29:6; 31:25; Ps 128:1-2

1:11
r Job 19:21
s Job 2:5

1:15
aGe 10:7;
Job 6:19

1:16
bGe 19:24
cLev 10:2;
Nu 11:1-3

1:17
dGe 11:28,31

1:19
eJer 4:11; 13:24

1:20
fGe 37:29
g1Pe 5:6

1:21
hEcc 5:15;
1Ti 6:7
i1Sa 2:7
jJob 2:10;
Eph 5:20;
1Th 5:18

1:22
kJob 2:10

2:1
lJob 1:6

2:3
mJob 1:1,8
nJob 27:6
oJob 9:17

2:5
pJob 19:20
qJob 1:11

¹³One day when Job's sons and daughters were feasting and drinking wine at the oldest brother's house, ¹⁴a messenger came to Job and said, "The oxen were plowing and the donkeys were grazing nearby, ¹⁵and the Sabeans*a* attacked and carried them off. They put the servants to the sword, and I am the only one who has escaped to tell you!"

¹⁶While he was still speaking, another messenger came and said, "The fire of God fell from the sky*b* and burned up the sheep and the servants,*c* and I am the only one who has escaped to tell you!"

¹⁷While he was still speaking, another messenger came and said, "The Chaldeans*d* formed three raiding parties and swept down on your camels and carried them off. They put the servants to the sword, and I am the only one who has escaped to tell you!"

¹⁸While he was still speaking, yet another messenger came and said, "Your sons and daughters were feasting and drinking wine at the oldest brother's house, ¹⁹when suddenly a mighty wind*e* swept in from the desert and struck the four corners of the house. It collapsed on them and they are dead, and I am the only one who has escaped to tell you!"

²⁰At this, Job got up and tore his robe*f* and shaved his head. Then he fell to the ground in worship*g* ²¹and said:

"Naked I came from my mother's womb,
    and naked I will depart.*ah*
The LORD gave and the LORD has taken away;*i*
    may the name of the LORD be praised."*j*

²²In all this, Job did not sin by charging God with wrongdoing.*k*

Chapter 2 Theme

2 On another day the angels*b* came to present themselves before the LORD, and Satan also came with them*l* to present himself before him. ²And the LORD said to Satan, "Where have you come from?"

Satan answered the LORD, "From roaming through the earth and going back and forth in it."

³Then the LORD said to Satan, "Have you considered my servant Job? There is no one on earth like him; he is blameless and upright, a man who fears God and shuns evil.*m* And he still maintains his integrity,*n* though you incited me against him to ruin him without any reason."*o*

⁴"Skin for skin!" Satan replied. "A man will give all he has for his own life. ⁵But stretch out your hand and strike his flesh and bones,*p* and he will surely curse you to your face."*q*

a21 Or *will return there*   b1 Hebrew *the sons of God*

⁶The LORD said to Satan, "Very well, then, he is in your hands; but you must spare his life."ᵃ

⁷So Satan went out from the presence of the LORD and afflicted Job with painful sores from the soles of his feet to the top of his head.ᵇ ⁸Then Job took a piece of broken pottery and scraped himself with it as he sat among the ashes.ᶜ

⁹His wife said to him, "Are you still holding on to your integrity? Curse God and die!"

¹⁰He replied, "You are talking like a foolishᵃ woman. Shall we accept good from God, and not trouble?"ᵈ

In all this, Job did not sin in what he said.ᵉ

¹¹When Job's three friends, Eliphaz the Temanite,ᶠ Bildad the Shuhiteᵍ and Zophar the Naamathite, heard about all the troubles that had come upon him, they set out from their homes and met together by agreement to go and sympathize with him and comfort him.ʰ ¹²When they saw him from a distance, they could hardly recognize him; they began to weep aloud, and they tore their robes and sprinkled dust on their heads.ⁱ ¹³Then they sat on the ground with him for seven days and seven nights.ʲ No one said a word to him, because they saw how great his suffering was.

Chapter 3 Theme

3 After this, Job opened his mouth and cursed the day of his birth. ²He said:

³"May the day of my birth perish,
    and the night it was said, 'A boy is born!'ᵏ
⁴That day—may it turn to darkness;
    may God above not care about it;
    may no light shine upon it.
⁵May darkness and deep shadowᵇˡ claim it once more;
    may a cloud settle over it;
    may blackness overwhelm its light.
⁶That night—may thick darknessᵐ seize it;
    may it not be included among the days of the year
    nor be entered in any of the months.
⁷May that night be barren;
    may no shout of joy be heard in it.
⁸May those who curse daysᶜ curse that day,
    those who are ready to rouse Leviathan.ⁿ
⁹May its morning stars become dark;
    may it wait for daylight in vain
    and not see the first rays of dawn,ᵒ

ᵃ10 The Hebrew word rendered *foolish* denotes moral deficiency.   ᵇ5 Or *and the shadow of death*   ᶜ8 Or *the sea*

**Cross references (margin):**

2:6
ᵃJob 1:12

2:7
ᵇDt 28:35;
Job 7:5

2:8
ᶜJob 42:6;
Jer 6:26;
Eze 27:30;
Mt 11:21

2:10
ᵈJob 1:21
ᵉJob 1:22;
Ps 39:1;
Jas 1:12; 5:11

2:11
ᶠGe 36:11;
Jer 49:7
ᵍGe 25:2
ʰJob 42:11;
Ro 12:15

2:12
ⁱJos 7:6;
Ne 9:1;
La 2:10;
Eze 27:30

2:13
ʲGe 50:10;
Eze 3:15

3:3
ᵏJob 10:18-19;
Jer 20:14-18

3:5
ˡJob 10:21,22;
Ps 23:4; Jer 2:6;
13:16

3:6
ᵐJob 23:17

3:8
ⁿJob 41:1,8,
10,25

3:9
ᵒJob 41:18

3:11
a Job 10:18

3:12
b Ge 30:3;
Isa 66:12

3:13
c Job 17:13
d Job 7:8-10,21;
10:22; 14:10-12;
19:27; 21:13,23

3:14
e Job 12:17
f Job 15:28

3:15
g Job 12:21
h Job 27:17

3:16
i Ps 58:8;
Ecc 6:3

3:17
j Job 17:16

3:18
k Job 39:7

3:20
l 1Sa 1:10;
Jer 20:18;
Eze 27:30-31

3:21
m Rev 9:6
n Pr 2:4

3:23
o Job 19:6,8,
12; Ps 88:8;
La 3:7

3:24
p Job 6:7; 33:20
q Ps 42:3,4

3:25
r Job 30:15

3:26
s Job 7:4,14

4:2
t Job 32:20

¹⁰for it did not shut the doors of the womb on me
   to hide trouble from my eyes.

¹¹"Why did I not perish at birth,
   and die as I came from the womb?ᵃ
¹²Why were there knees to receive meᵇ
   and breasts that I might be nursed?
¹³For now I would be lying downᶜ in peace;
   I would be asleep and at rest ᵈ
¹⁴with kings and counselors of the earth,ᵉ
   who built for themselves places now lying in ruins,ᶠ
¹⁵with rulersᵍ who had gold,
   who filled their houses with silver.ʰ
¹⁶Or why was I not hidden in the ground like a
      stillborn child,ⁱ
   like an infant who never saw the light of day?
¹⁷There the wicked cease from turmoil,
   and there the weary are at rest.ʲ
¹⁸Captives also enjoy their ease;
   they no longer hear the slave driver's shout.ᵏ
¹⁹The small and the great are there,
   and the slave is freed from his master.

²⁰"Why is light given to those in misery,
   and life to the bitter of soul,ˡ
²¹to those who long for death that does not come,ᵐ
   who search for it more than for hidden treasure,ⁿ
²²who are filled with gladness
   and rejoice when they reach the grave?
²³Why is life given to a man
   whose way is hidden,
   whom God has hedged in?ᵒ
²⁴For sighing comes to me instead of food;ᵖ
   my groans pour out like water.�q
²⁵What I feared has come upon me;
   what I dreadedʳ has happened to me.
²⁶I have no peace, no quietness;
   I have no rest,ˢ but only turmoil."

Chapter 4 Theme _____

4 Then Eliphaz the Temanite replied:

²"If someone ventures a word with you, will you
      be impatient?
   But who can keep from speaking?ᵗ

³Think how you have instructed many,
  how you have strengthened feeble hands.*a*

⁴Your words have supported those who stumbled;
  you have strengthened faltering knees.*b*

⁵But now trouble comes to you, and you are discouraged;
  it strikes*c* you, and you are dismayed.*d*

⁶Should not your piety be your confidence*e*
  and your blameless*f* ways your hope?

⁷"Consider now: Who, being innocent, has
      ever perished?*g*
  Where were the upright ever destroyed?*h*

⁸As I have observed, those who plow evil*i*
  and those who sow trouble reap it.*j*

⁹At the breath of God*k* they are destroyed;
  at the blast of his anger they perish.*l*

¹⁰The lions may roar and growl,
  yet the teeth of the great lions are broken.*m*

¹¹The lion perishes for lack of prey,*n*
  and the cubs of the lioness are scattered.

¹²"A word was secretly brought to me,
  my ears caught a whisper*o* of it.*p*

¹³Amid disquieting dreams in the night,
  when deep sleep falls on men,*q*

¹⁴fear and trembling seized me
  and made all my bones shake.*r*

¹⁵A spirit glided past my face,
  and the hair on my body stood on end.

¹⁶It stopped,
  but I could not tell what it was.
  A form stood before my eyes,
  and I heard a hushed voice:

¹⁷'Can a mortal be more righteous than God?*s*
  Can a man be more pure than his Maker?*t*

¹⁸If God places no trust in his servants,
  if he charges his angels with error,*u*

¹⁹how much more those who live in houses of clay,*v*
  whose foundations*w* are in the dust,*x*
  who are crushed more readily than a moth!

²⁰Between dawn and dusk they are broken to pieces;
  unnoticed, they perish forever.*y*

²¹Are not the cords of their tent pulled up,*z*
  so that they die without wisdom?'*a a*

---

a 21 Some interpreters end the quotation after verse 17.

4:3
a Isa 35:3;
Heb 12:12

4:4
b Isa 35:3;
Heb 12:12

4:5
c Job 19:21
d Job 6:14

4:6
e Pr 3:26
f Job 1:1

4:7
g Job 36:7
h Job 8:20;
Ps 37:25

4:8
i Job 15:35
j Pr 22:8;
Hos 10:13;
Gal 6:7-8

4:9
k Job 15:30;
Isa 30:33;
2Th 2:8
l Job 40:13

4:10
m Job 5:15;
Ps 58:6

4:11
n Job 27:14;
Ps 34:10

4:12
o Job 26:14
p Job 33:14

4:13
q Job 33:15

4:14
r Jer 23:9;
Hab 3:16

4:17
s Job 9:2
t Job 35:10

4:18
u Job 15:15

4:19
v Job 10:9
w Job 22:16
x Ge 2:7

4:20
y Job 14:2,20;
20:7;
Ps 90:5-6

4:21
z Job 8:22
a Job 18:21;
36:12

5:1
a Job 15:15

5:2
b Pr 12:16

5:3
c Ps 37:35;
Jer 12:2
d Job 24:18

5:4
e Job 4:11
f Am 5:12

5:5
g Job 18:8 -10

5:7
h Job 14:1

5:8
i Ps 35:23; 50:15

5:9
j Job 42:3;
Ps 40:5

5:10
k Job 36:28

5:11
l Ps 113:7-8

5:12
m Ne 4:15;
Ps 33:10

5:13
n 1Co 3:19*

5:14
o Job 12:25
p Dt 28:29

5:15
q Ps 35:10
r Job 4:10

5:16
s Ps 107:42

5:17
t Jas 1:12
u Ps 94:12;
Pr 3:11
v Heb 12:5-11

5:18
w Isa 30:26
x 1Sa 2:6

5:19
y Ps 34:19; 91:10

5:20
z Ps 33:19
a Ps 144:10

Chapter 5 Theme

5 "Call if you will, but who will answer you?
To which of the holy ones[a] will you turn?
²Resentment kills a fool,
and envy slays the simple.[b]
³I myself have seen a fool taking root,[c]
but suddenly his house was cursed.[d]
⁴His children are far from safety,[e]
crushed in court[f] without a defender.
⁵The hungry consume his harvest,[g]
taking it even from among thorns,
and the thirsty pant after his wealth.
⁶For hardship does not spring from the soil,
nor does trouble sprout from the ground.
⁷Yet man is born to trouble[h]
as surely as sparks fly upward.

⁸"But if it were I, I would appeal to God;
I would lay my cause before him.[i]
⁹He performs wonders that cannot be fathomed,[j]
miracles that cannot be counted.
¹⁰He bestows rain on the earth;
he sends water upon the countryside.[k]
¹¹The lowly he sets on high,[l]
and those who mourn are lifted to safety.
¹²He thwarts the plans[m] of the crafty,
so that their hands achieve no success.
¹³He catches the wise in their craftiness,[n]
and the schemes of the wily are swept away.
¹⁴Darkness[o] comes upon them in the daytime;
at noon they grope as in the night.[p]
¹⁵He saves the needy[q] from the sword in their mouth;
he saves them from the clutches of the powerful.[r]
¹⁶So the poor have hope,
and injustice shuts its mouth.[s]

¹⁷"Blessed is the man whom God corrects;[t]
so do not despise the discipline[u] of the Almighty.[a][v]
¹⁸For he wounds, but he also binds up;[w]
he injures, but his hands also heal.[x]
¹⁹From six calamities he will rescue you;
in seven no harm will befall you.[y]
²⁰In famine[z] he will ransom you from death,
and in battle from the stroke of the sword.[a]

a 17 Hebrew *Shaddai*; here and throughout Job

²¹You will be protected from the lash of the tongue,ᵃ
  and need not fearᵇ when destruction comes.
²²You will laugh at destruction and famine,
  and need not fear the beasts of the earth.ᶜ
²³For you will have a covenant with the stonesᵈ of the field,
  and the wild animals will be at peace with you.ᵉ
²⁴You will know that your tent is secure;
  you will take stock of your property and find
    nothing missing.ᶠ
²⁵You will know that your children will be many,ᵍ
  and your descendants like the grass of the earth.ʰ
²⁶You will come to the grave in full vigor,ⁱ
  like sheaves gathered in season.

²⁷"We have examined this, and it is true.
  So hear it and apply it to yourself."

Chapter 6 Theme

6 Then Job replied:
²"If only my anguish could be weighed
  and all my misery be placed on the scales!ʲ
³It would surely outweigh the sandᵏ of the seas—
  no wonder my words have been impetuous.ˡ
⁴The arrowsᵐ of the Almighty are in me,ⁿ
  my spirit drinksᵒ in their poison;
  God's terrorsᵖ are marshaled against me.�q
⁵Does a wild donkey bray when it has grass,
  or an ox bellow when it has fodder?
⁶Is tasteless food eaten without salt,
  or is there flavor in the white of an eggᵃ?
⁷I refuse to touch it;
  such food makes me ill.ʳ

⁸"Oh, that I might have my request,
  that God would grant what I hope for,ˢ
⁹that God would be willing to crush me,
  to let loose his hand and cut me off!ᵗ
¹⁰Then I would still have this consolation—
  my joy in unrelenting pain—
  that I had not denied the wordsᵘ of the Holy One.ᵛ

¹¹"What strength do I have, that I should still hope?
  What prospects, that I should be patient?ʷ

ᵃ6 The meaning of the Hebrew for this phrase is uncertain.

5:21
ᵃ Ps 31:20
ᵇ Ps 91:5

5:22
ᶜ Ps 91:13;
Eze 34:25

5:23
ᵈ Ps 91:12
ᵉ Isa 11:6-9

5:24
ᶠ Job 8:6

5:25
ᵍ Ps 112:2
ʰ Ps 72:16;
Isa 44:3-4

5:26
ⁱ Ge 15:15

6:2
ʲ Job 31:6

6:3
ᵏ Pr 27:3
ˡ Job 23:2

6:4
ᵐ Ps 38:2
ⁿ Job 16:12,13
ᵒ Job 21:20
ᵖ Job 30:15
q Ps 88:15-18

6:7
ʳ Job 3:24

6:8
ˢ Job 14:13

6:9
ᵗ Nu 11:15;
1Ki 19:4

6:10
ᵘ Job 22:22;
23:12
ᵛ Lev 19:2;
Isa 57:15

6:11
ʷ Job 21:4

6:13
a Job 26:2

6:14
b Job 4:5;
c Job 15:4

6:15
d Ps 38:11;
Jer 15:18

6:17
e Job 24:19

6:19
f Ge 25:15;
Isa 21:14

6:20
g Jer 14:3

6:21
h Ps 38:11

6:24
i Ps 39:1

6:25
j Ecc 12:11

6:26
k Job 8:2; 15:3

6:27
l Joel 3:3;
Na 3:10;
2Pe 2:3

6:28
m Job 27:4;
33:1,3; 36:3,4

6:29
n Job 23:7,10;
34:5,36; 42:6

6:30
o Job 27:4
p Job 12:11

¹²Do I have the strength of stone?
Is my flesh bronze?
¹³Do I have any power to help myself,ᵃ
now that success has been driven from me?

¹⁴"A despairing manᵇ should have the devotionᶜ of
his friends,
even though he forsakes the fear of the Almighty.
¹⁵But my brothers are as undependable as
intermittent streams,ᵈ
as the streams that overflow
¹⁶when darkened by thawing ice
and swollen with melting snow,
¹⁷but that cease to flow in the dry season,
and in the heatᵉ vanish from their channels.
¹⁸Caravans turn aside from their routes;
they go up into the wasteland and perish.
¹⁹The caravans of Temaᶠ look for water,
the traveling merchants of Sheba look in hope.
²⁰They are distressed, because they had been confident;
they arrive there, only to be disappointed.ᵍ
²¹Now you too have proved to be of no help;
you see something dreadful and are afraid.ʰ
²²Have I ever said, 'Give something on my behalf,
pay a ransom for me from your wealth,
²³deliver me from the hand of the enemy,
ransom me from the clutches of the ruthless'?

²⁴"Teach me, and I will be quiet;ⁱ
show me where I have been wrong.
²⁵How painful are honest words!ʲ
But what do your arguments prove?
²⁶Do you mean to correct what I say,
and treat the words of a despairing man as wind?ᵏ
²⁷You would even cast lotsˡ for the fatherless
and barter away your friend.

²⁸"But now be so kind as to look at me.
Would I lie to your face?ᵐ
²⁹Relent, do not be unjust;
reconsider, for my integrity is at stake.ᵃⁿ
³⁰Is there any wickedness on my lips?ᵒ
Can my mouth not discernᵖ malice?

a 29 Or *my righteousness still stands*

Chapter 7 Theme _____

7 "Does not man have hard service*a* on earth?*b*
　　Are not his days like those of a hired man?*c*

²Like a slave longing for the evening shadows,
　　or a hired man waiting eagerly for his wages,*d*

³so I have been allotted months of futility,
　　and nights of misery have been assigned to me.*e*

⁴When I lie down I think, 'How long before I get up?'*f*
　　The night drags on, and I toss till dawn.

⁵My body is clothed with worms*g* and scabs,
　　my skin is broken and festering.

⁶"My days are swifter than a weaver's shuttle,*h*
　　and they come to an end without hope.*i*

⁷Remember, O God, that my life is but a breath;*j*
　　my eyes will never see happiness again.*k*

⁸The eye that now sees me will see me no longer;
　　you will look for me, but I will be no more.*l*

⁹As a cloud vanishes and is gone,
　　so he who goes down to the grave*a m* does not return.*n*

¹⁰He will never come to his house again;
　　his place*o* will know him no more.*p*

¹¹"Therefore I will not keep silent;*q*
　　I will speak out in the anguish of my spirit,
　　I will complain in the bitterness of my soul.*r*

¹²Am I the sea, or the monster of the deep,*s*
　　that you put me under guard?

¹³When I think my bed will comfort me
　　and my couch will ease my complaint,*t*

¹⁴even then you frighten me with dreams
　　and terrify*u* me with visions,

¹⁵so that I prefer strangling and death,*v*
　　rather than this body of mine.

¹⁶I despise my life;*w* I would not live forever.
　　Let me alone; my days have no meaning.

¹⁷"What is man that you make so much of him,
　　that you give him so much attention,*x*

¹⁸that you examine him every morning
　　and test him every moment?*y*

¹⁹Will you never look away from me,
　　or let me alone even for an instant?*z*

²⁰If I have sinned, what have I done to you,*a*
　　O watcher of men?

a 9 Hebrew Sheol

Cross references

7:1
a Job 14:14;
Isa 40:2
b Job 5:7
c Job 14:6

7:2
d Lev 19:13

7:3
e Job 16:7; Ps 6:6

7:4
f Dt 28:67

7:5
g Job 17:14;
Isa 14:11

7:6
h Job 9:25
i Job 13:15;
17:11,15

7:7
j Ps 78:39;
Jas 4:14
k Job 9:25

7:8
l Job 20:7,9,21

7:9
m Job 11:8
n 2Sa 12:23;
Job 30:15

7:10
o Job 27:21,23
p Job 8:18

7:11
q Ps 40:9
r 1Sa 1:10

7:12
s Eze 32:2-3

7:13
t Job 9:27

7:14
u Job 9:34

7:15
v 1Ki 19:4

7:16
w Job 9:21; 10:1

7:17
x Ps 8:4; 144:3;
Heb 2:6

7:18
y Job 14:3

7:19
z Job 9:18

7:20
a Job 35:6

7:20
a Job 16:12

7:21
b Job 10:14
c Job 10:9;
Ps 104:29

8:2
d Job 6:26

8:3
e Dt 32:4;
2Ch 19:7;
Ro 3:5
f Ge 18:25

8:4
g Job 1:19

8:5
h Job 11:13

8:6
i Ps 7:6
j Job 5:24

8:7
k Job 42:12

8:8
l Dt 4:32; 32:7;
Job 15:18

8:9
m Ge 47:9
n 1Ch 29:15;
Job 7:6

8:12
o Ps 129:6;
Jer 17:6

8:13
p Ps 9:17
q Job 11:20;
13:16; 15:34;
Pr 10:28

8:14
r Isa 59:5

8:15
s Job 27:18
t Ps 49:11

8:16
u Ps 80:11
v Ps 37:35;
Jer 11:16

Why have you made me your target?[a]
Have I become a burden to you?[a]
²¹Why do you not pardon my offenses
and forgive my sins?[b]
For I will soon lie down in the dust;[c]
you will search for me, but I will be no more."

Chapter 8 Theme

8 Then Bildad the Shuhite replied:

²"How long will you say such things?
Your words are a blustering wind.[d]
³Does God pervert justice?[e]
Does the Almighty pervert what is right?[f]
⁴When your children sinned against him,
he gave them over to the penalty of their sin.[g]
⁵But if you will look to God
and plead[h] with the Almighty,
⁶if you are pure and upright,
even now he will rouse himself on your behalf[i]
and restore you to your rightful place.[j]
⁷Your beginnings will seem humble,
so prosperous[k] will your future be.

⁸"Ask the former generations[l]
and find out what their fathers learned,
⁹for we were born only yesterday and know nothing,[m]
and our days on earth are but a shadow.[n]
¹⁰Will they not instruct you and tell you?
Will they not bring forth words from
their understanding?
¹¹Can papyrus grow tall where there is no marsh?
Can reeds thrive without water?
¹²While still growing and uncut,
they wither more quickly than grass.[o]
¹³Such is the destiny of all who forget God;[p]
so perishes the hope of the godless.[q]
¹⁴What he trusts in is fragile[b];
what he relies on is a spider's web.[r]
¹⁵He leans on his web,[s] but it gives way;
he clings to it, but it does not hold.[t]
¹⁶He is like a well-watered plant in the sunshine,
spreading its shoots[u] over the garden;[v]

a 20 A few manuscripts of the Masoretic Text, an ancient Hebrew scribal tradition and Septuagint; most manuscripts of the Masoretic Text *I have become a burden to myself.*
b 14 The meaning of the Hebrew for this word is uncertain.

¹⁷it entwines its roots around a pile of rocks
   and looks for a place among the stones.
¹⁸But when it is torn from its spot,
   that place disowns it and says, 'I never saw you.'ᵃ
¹⁹Surely its life withersᵇ away,
   andᵃ from the soil other plants grow.ᶜ

²⁰"Surely God does not reject a blamelessᵈ man
   or strengthen the hands of evildoers.ᵉ
²¹He will yet fill your mouth with laughterᶠ
   and your lips with shouts of joy.ᵍ
²²Your enemies will be clothed in shame,ʰ
   and the tents of the wicked will be no more."ⁱ

Chapter 9 Theme _____

9 Then Job replied:

²"Indeed, I know that this is true.
   But how can a mortal be righteous before God?ʲ
³Though one wished to dispute with him,
   he could not answer him one time out of a thousand.ᵏ
⁴His wisdomˡ is profound, his power is vast.ᵐ
   Who has resisted him and come out unscathed?ⁿ
⁵He moves mountains without their knowing it
   and overturns them in his anger.ᵒ
⁶He shakes the earthᵖ from its place
   and makes its pillars tremble.�q
⁷He speaks to the sun and it does not shine;
   he seals off the light of the stars.ʳ
⁸He alone stretches out the heavensˢ
   and treads on the waves of the sea.ᵗ
⁹He is the Maker of the Bear and Orion,
   the Pleiades and the constellations of the south.ᵘ
¹⁰He performs wondersᵛ that cannot be fathomed,
   miracles that cannot be counted.ʷ
¹¹When he passes me, I cannot see him;
   when he goes by, I cannot perceive him.ˣ
¹²If he snatches away, who can stop him?ʸ
   Who can say to him, 'What are you doing?'ᶻ
¹³God does not restrain his anger;
   even the cohorts of Rahabᵃ cowered at his feet.

¹⁴"How then can I dispute with him?
   How can I find words to argue with him?

ᵃ19 Or Surely all the joy it has / is that

8:18
ᵃJob 7:8;
Ps 37:36

8:19
ᵇJob 20:5;
ᶜEcc 1:4

8:20
ᵈJob 1:1;
ᵉJob 21:30

8:21
ᶠJob 5:22
ᵍPs 126:2;
132:16

8:22
ʰPs 35:26;
109:29; 132:18
ⁱJob 18:6,
14,21

9:2
ʲJob 4:17;
Ps 143:2;
Ro 3:20

9:3
ᵏJob 10:2; 40:2

9:4
ˡJob 11:6
ᵐJob 36:5
ⁿ2Ch 13:12

9:5
ᵒMic 1:4

9:6
ᵖIsa 2:21;
Hag 2:6;
Heb 12:26
qJob 26:11

9:7
ʳIsa 13:10;
Eze 32:8

9:8
ˢGe 1:6;
Ps 104:2-3
ᵗJob 38:16;
Ps 77:19

9:9
ᵘGe 1:16;
Job 38:31;
Am 5:8

9:10
ᵛPs 71:15
ʷJob 5:9

9:11
ˣJob 23:8-9;
35:14

9:12
ʸJob 11:10
ᶻIsa 45:9;
Ro 9:20

9:13
ᵃJob 26:12;
Ps 89:10;
Isa 30:7; 51:9

9:15
a Job 10:15
b Job 8:5

9:17
c Job 16:12
d Job 30:22
e Job 16:14
f Job 2:3

9:18
g Job 7:19; 27:2

9:21
h Job 1:1
i Job 7:16

9:22
j Job 10:8;
Ecc 9:2,3;
Eze 21:3

9:23
k Heb 11:36
l Job 24:1,12

9:24
m Job 10:3;
16:11
n Job 12:6

9:25
o Job 7:6

9:26
p Isa 18:2
q Hab 1:8

9:27
r Job 7:11

9:28
s Job 3:25;
Ps 119:120
t Job 7:21

9:29
u Ps 37:33

9:30
v Job 31:7
w Jer 2:22

9:32
x Ro 9:20
y Ps 143:2;
Ecc 6:10

9:33
z 1Sa 2:25

9:34
a Job 13:21;
Ps 39:10

¹⁵Though I were innocent, I could not answer him;^a
    I could only plead^b with my Judge for mercy.
¹⁶Even if I summoned him and he responded,
    I do not believe he would give me a hearing.
¹⁷He would crush me^c with a storm^d
    and multiply^e my wounds for no reason.^f
¹⁸He would not let me regain my breath
    but would overwhelm me with misery.^g
¹⁹If it is a matter of strength, he is mighty!
    And if it is a matter of justice, who will summon him^a?
²⁰Even if I were innocent, my mouth would condemn me;
    if I were blameless, it would pronounce me guilty.

²¹"Although I am blameless,^h
    I have no concern for myself;
    I despise my own life.ⁱ
²²It is all the same; that is why I say,
    'He destroys both the blameless and the wicked.'^j
²³When a scourge^k brings sudden death,
    he mocks the despair of the innocent.^l
²⁴When a land falls into the hands of the wicked,^m
    he blindfolds its judges.ⁿ
    If it is not he, then who is it?

²⁵"My days are swifter than a runner;^o
    they fly away without a glimpse of joy.
²⁶They skim past like boats of papyrus,^p
    like eagles swooping down on their prey.^q
²⁷If I say, 'I will forget my complaint,^r
    I will change my expression, and smile,'
²⁸I still dread^s all my sufferings,
    for I know you will not hold me innocent.^t
²⁹Since I am already found guilty,
    why should I struggle in vain?^u
³⁰Even if I washed myself with soap^b
    and my hands^v with washing soda,^w
³¹you would plunge me into a slime pit
    so that even my clothes would detest me.

³²"He is not a man like me that I might answer him,^x
    that we might confront each other in court.^y
³³If only there were someone to arbitrate between us,^z
    to lay his hand upon us both,
³⁴someone to remove God's rod from me,^a
    so that his terror would frighten me no more.

a 19 See Septuagint; Hebrew *me*.   b 30 Or *snow*

³⁵Then I would speak up without fear of him,
    but as it now stands with me, I cannot.ᵃ

Chapter 10 Theme

10 "I loathe my very life;ᵇ
    therefore I will give free rein to my complaint
    and speak out in the bitterness of my soul.ᶜ
²I will say to God: Do not condemn me,
    but tell me what chargesᵈ you have against me.
³Does it please you to oppress me,ᵉ
    to spurn the work of your hands,ᶠ
    while you smile on the schemes of the wicked?ᵍ
⁴Do you have eyes of flesh?
    Do you see as a mortal sees?ʰ
⁵Are your days like those of a mortal
    or your years like those of a man,ⁱ
⁶that you must search out my faults
    and probe after my sinʲ—
⁷though you know that I am not guilty
    and that no one can rescue me from your hand?

⁸"Your hands shapedᵏ me and made me.
    Will you now turn and destroy me?
⁹Remember that you molded me like clay.ˡ
    Will you now turn me to dust again?ᵐ
¹⁰Did you not pour me out like milk
    and curdle me like cheese,
¹¹clothe me with skin and flesh
    and knit me togetherⁿ with bones and sinews?
¹²You gave me lifeᵒ and showed me kindness,
    and in your providence watched over my spirit.

¹³"But this is what you concealed in your heart,
    and I know that this was in your mind:ᵖ
¹⁴If I sinned, you would be watching me
    and would not let my offense go unpunished.�q
¹⁵If I am guilty—woe to me!ʳ
    Even if I am innocent, I cannot lift my head,ˢ
  for I am full of shame
    and drowned inᵃ my affliction.
¹⁶If I hold my head high, you stalk me like a lionᵗ
    and again display your awesome power against me.ᵘ
¹⁷You bring new witnesses against meᵛ
    and increase your anger toward me;ʷ
    your forces come against me wave upon wave.

ᵃ15 Or *and aware of*

9:35
ᵃJob 13:21

10:1
ᵇ1Ki 19:4
ᶜJob 7:11

10:2
ᵈJob 9:29

10:3
ᵉJob 9:22
ᶠJob 14:15;
Ps 138:8;
Isa 64:8
ᵍJob 21:16;
22:18

10:4
ʰ1Sa 16:7

10:5
ⁱPs 90:2,4;
2Pe 3:8

10:6
ʲJob 14:16

10:8
ᵏPs 119:73

10:9
ˡIsa 64:8
ᵐGe 2:7

10:11
ⁿPs 139:13,15

10:12
ᵒJob 33:4

10:13
ᵖJob 23:13

10:14
qJob 7:21

10:15
ʳJob 9:13;
Isa 3:11
ˢJob 9:15

10:16
ᵗIsa 38:13;
La 3:10
ᵘJob 5:9

10:17
ᵛJob 16:8
ʷRu 1:21

10:18
a Job 3:11

10:20
b Job 14:1
c Job 7:19
d Job 7:16

10:21
e 2Sa 12:23;
Job 3:13; 16:22
f Ps 23:4; 88:12

11:2
g Job 8:2

11:3
h Job 17:2; 21:3

11:4
i Job 6:10
j Job 10:7

11:6
k Job 9:4
l Ezr 9:13;
Job 15:5

11:7
m Ecc 3:11;
Ro 11:33

11:8
n Job 22:12

11:10
o Job 9:12;
Rev 3:7

11:11
p Job 34:21-25;
Ps 10:14

11:13
q 1Sa 7:3;
Ps 78:8
r Ps 88:9

¹⁸"Why then did you bring me out of the womb?ᵃ
I wish I had died before any eye saw me.
¹⁹If only I had never come into being,
or had been carried straight from the womb to
the grave!
²⁰Are not my few daysᵇ almost over?ᶜ
Turn away from meᵈ so I can have a moment's joy
²¹before I go to the place of no return,ᵉ
to the land of gloom and deep shadow,ᵃᶠ
²²to the land of deepest night,
of deep shadow and disorder,
where even the light is like darkness."

Chapter 11 Theme _____

11 Then Zophar the Naamathite replied:

²"Are all these words to go unanswered?ᵍ
Is this talker to be vindicated?
³Will your idle talk reduce men to silence?
Will no one rebuke you when you mock?ʰ
⁴You say to God, 'My beliefs are flawlessⁱ
and I am pureʲ in your sight.'
⁵Oh, how I wish that God would speak,
that he would open his lips against you
⁶and disclose to you the secrets of wisdom,ᵏ
for true wisdom has two sides.
Know this: God has even forgotten some of your sin.ˡ

⁷"Can you fathomᵐ the mysteries of God?
Can you probe the limits of the Almighty?
⁸They are higher than the heavensⁿ—what can you do?
They are deeper than the depths of the graveᵇ—what
can you know?
⁹Their measure is longer than the earth
and wider than the sea.

¹⁰"If he comes along and confines you in prison
and convenes a court, who can oppose him?ᵒ
¹¹Surely he recognizes deceitful men;
and when he sees evil, does he not take note?ᵖ
¹²But a witless man can no more become wise
than a wild donkey's colt can be born a man.ᶜ

¹³"Yet if you devote your heartᵍ to him
and stretch out your hands to him,ʳ

ᵃ21 Or *and the shadow of death; also in verse 22*   ᵇ8 Hebrew *than Sheol*   ᶜ12 Or *wild donkey can be born tame*

¹⁴if you put away the sin that is in your hand
  and allow no evil^a to dwell in your tent,^b
¹⁵then you will lift up your face^c without shame;
  you will stand firm and without fear.
¹⁶You will surely forget your trouble,^d
  recalling it only as waters gone by.^e
¹⁷Life will be brighter than noonday,^f
  and darkness will become like morning.
¹⁸You will be secure, because there is hope;
  you will look about you and take your rest^g in safety.^h
¹⁹You will lie down, with no one to make you afraid,ⁱ
  and many will court your favor.^j
²⁰But the eyes of the wicked will fail,^k
  and escape will elude them;^l
  their hope will become a dying gasp."^m

Chapter 12 Theme

12 Then Job replied:

²"Doubtless you are the people,
  and wisdom will die with you!ⁿ
³But I have a mind as well as you;
  I am not inferior to you.
  Who does not know all these things?^o

⁴"I have become a laughingstock^p to my friends,
  though I called upon God and he answered^q—
  a mere laughingstock, though righteous
    and blameless!^r
⁵Men at ease have contempt for misfortune
  as the fate of those whose feet are slipping.
⁶The tents of marauders are undisturbed,^s
  and those who provoke God are secure^t—
  those who carry their god in their hands.^a

⁷"But ask the animals, and they will teach you,
  or the birds of the air, and they will tell you;
⁸or speak to the earth, and it will teach you,
  or let the fish of the sea inform you.
⁹Which of all these does not know
  that the hand of the Lord has done this?^u
¹⁰In his hand is the life of every creature
  and the breath of all mankind.^v
¹¹Does not the ear test words
  as the tongue tastes food?^w

^a6 Or *secure / in what God's hand brings them*

11:14
^aPs 101:4
^bJob 22:23

11:15
^cJob 22:26;
1Jn 3:21

11:16
^dIsa 65:16
^eJob 22:11

11:17
^fJob 22:28;
Ps 37:6;
Isa 58:8,10

11:18
^gPs 3:5
^hLev 26:6;
Pr 3:24

11:19
ⁱLev 26:6
^jIsa 45:14

11:20
^kDt 28:65;
Job 17:5
^lJob 27:22;
34:22
^mJob 8:13

12:2
ⁿJob 17:10

12:3
^oJob 13:2

12:4
^pJob 21:3
^qPs 91:15
^rJob 6:29

12:6
^sJob 22:18
^tJob 9:24; 21:9

12:9
^uIsa 41:20

12:10
^vJob 27:3; 33:4;
Ac 17:28

12:11
^wJob 34:3

12:12
a Job 15:10
b Job 32:7,9

12:13
c Job 11:6
d Job 9:4
e Job 32:8; 38:36

12:14
f Job 19:10
g Job 37:7; Isa 25:2

12:15
h 1Ki 8:35
i 1Ki 17:1
j Ge 7:11

12:16
k Job 13:7,9

12:17
l Job 19:9
m Job 3:14

12:18
n Ps 116:16

12:19
o Job 24:12,22; 34:20,28; 35:9

12:20
p Job 32:9

12:22
q 1Co 4:5
r Job 3:5
s Da 2:22

12:23
t Jer 25:9
u Ps 107:38; Isa 9:3; 26:15

12:24
v Ps 107:40

12:25
w Job 5:14
x Ps 107:27; Isa 24:20

13:2
y Job 12:3

13:3
z Job 23:3-4

13:4
a Ps 119:69; Jer 23:32

13:5
b Pr 17:28

¹²Is not wisdom found among the aged?ᵃ
  Does not long life bring understanding?ᵇ

¹³"To God belong wisdomᶜ and power;ᵈ
  counsel and understanding are his.ᵉ
¹⁴What he tears down f cannot be rebuilt;ᵍ
  the man he imprisons cannot be released.
¹⁵If he holds back the waters,ʰ there is drought;ⁱ
  if he lets them loose, they devastate the land.ʲ
¹⁶To him belong strength and victory;
  both deceived and deceiver are his.ᵏ
¹⁷He leads counselors away strippedˡ
  and makes fools of judges.ᵐ
¹⁸He takes off the shacklesⁿ put on by kings
  and ties a loinclothᵃ around their waist.
¹⁹He leads priests away stripped
  and overthrows men long established.ᵒ
²⁰He silences the lips of trusted advisers
  and takes away the discernment of elders.ᵖ
²¹He pours contempt on nobles
  and disarms the mighty.
²²He reveals the deep things of darkness�q
  and brings deep shadowsʳ into the light.ˢ
²³He makes nations great, and destroys them;ᵗ
  he enlarges nations,ᵘ and disperses them.
²⁴He deprives the leaders of the earth of their reason;
  he sends them wandering through a trackless waste.ᵛ
²⁵They grope in darkness with no light;ʷ
  he makes them stagger like drunkards.ˣ

Chapter 13 Theme

13 "My eyes have seen all this,
  my ears have heard and understood it.
²What you know, I also know;
  I am not inferior to you.ʸ
³But I desire to speak to the Almighty
  and to argue my case with God.ᶻ
⁴You, however, smear me with lies;ᵃ
  you are worthless physicians, all of you!
⁵If only you would be altogether silent!
  For you, that would be wisdom.ᵇ
⁶Hear now my argument;
  listen to the plea of my lips.

a 18 Or *shackles of kings / and ties a belt*

⁷Will you speak wickedly on God's behalf?
  Will you speak deceitfully for him?^a
⁸Will you show him partiality?^b
  Will you argue the case for God?
⁹Would it turn out well if he examined you?
  Could you deceive him as you might deceive men?^c
¹⁰He would surely rebuke you
  if you secretly showed partiality.
¹¹Would not his splendor^d terrify you?
  Would not the dread of him fall on you?
¹²Your maxims are proverbs of ashes;
  your defenses are defenses of clay.

¹³"Keep silent and let me speak;
  then let come to me what may.
¹⁴Why do I put myself in jeopardy
  and take my life in my hands?
¹⁵Though he slay me, yet will I hope^e in him;^f
  I will surely^a defend my ways to his face.^g
¹⁶Indeed, this will turn out for my deliverance,^h
  for no godless man would dare come before him!
¹⁷Listen carefully to my words;ⁱ
  let your ears take in what I say.
¹⁸Now that I have prepared my case,^j
  I know I will be vindicated.
¹⁹Can anyone bring charges against me?^k
  If so, I will be silent and die.^l

²⁰"Only grant me these two things, O God,
  and then I will not hide from you:
²¹Withdraw your hand^m far from me,
  and stop frightening me with your terrors.
²²Then summon me and I will answer,ⁿ
  or let me speak, and you reply.^o
²³How many wrongs and sins have I committed?^p
  Show me my offense and my sin.
²⁴Why do you hide your face^q
  and consider me your enemy?^r
²⁵Will you torment a windblown leaf?^s
  Will you chase after dry chaff?^t
²⁶For you write down bitter things against me
  and make me inherit the sins of my youth.^u
²⁷You fasten my feet in shackles;^v
  you keep close watch on all my paths
  by putting marks on the soles of my feet.

13:7
^a Job 36:4

13:8
^b Lev 19:15

13:9
^c Job 12:16;
Gal 6:7

13:11
^d Job 31:23

13:15
^e Job 7:6
^f Ps 23:4;
Pr 14:32
^g Job 27:5

13:16
^h Isa 12:1

13:17
ⁱ Job 21:2

13:18
^j Job 23:4

13:19
^k Job 40:4;
Isa 50:8
^l Job 10:8

13:21
^m Ps 39:10

13:22
ⁿ Job 14:15
^o Job 9:16

13:23
^p 1Sa 26:18

13:24
^q Dt 32:20;
Ps 13:1;
Isa 8:17
^r Job 19:11;
La 2:5

13:25
^s Lev 26:36
^t Job 21:18;
Isa 42:3

13:26
^u Ps 25:7

13:27
^v Job 33:11

^a 15 Or *He will surely slay me; I have no hope—* / *yet I will*

28"So man wastes away like something rotten,
like a garment eaten by moths.*a*

Chapter 14 Theme

14:1
b Job 5:7;
Ecc 2:23

14 "Man born of woman
is of few days and full of trouble.*b*

14:2
c Jas 1:10
d Ps 90:5-6
e Job 8:9

2He springs up like a flower*c* and withers away;*d*
like a fleeting shadow,*e* he does not endure.
3Do you fix your eye on such a one?*f*
Will you bring him*a* before you for judgment?*g*
4Who can bring what is pure*h* from the impure?*i*
No one!*j*

14:3
f Ps 8:4; 144:3
g Ps 143:2

5Man's days are determined;
you have decreed the number of his months*k*
and have set limits he cannot exceed.

14:4
h Ps 51:10
i Eph 2:1-3
j Jn 3:6;
Ro 5:12

6So look away from him and let him alone,*l*
till he has put in his time like a hired man.*m*

7"At least there is hope for a tree:
If it is cut down, it will sprout again,
and its new shoots will not fail.

14:5
k Job 21:21

8Its roots may grow old in the ground
and its stump die in the soil,
9yet at the scent of water it will bud
and put forth shoots like a plant.

14:6
l Job 7:19
m Job 7:1,2;
Ps 39:13

10But man dies and is laid low;
he breathes his last and is no more.*n*
11As water disappears from the sea
or a riverbed becomes parched and dry,*o*
12so man lies down and does not rise;
till the heavens are no more,*p* men will not awake
or be roused from their sleep.*q*

14:10
n Job 13:19

14:11
o Isa 19:5

13"If only you would hide me in the grave*b*
and conceal me till your anger has passed!*r*
If only you would set me a time
and then remember me!
14If a man dies, will he live again?
All the days of my hard service
I will wait for my renewal*c* to come.
15You will call and I will answer you;*s*
you will long for the creature your hands have made.
16Surely then you will count my steps*t*
but not keep track of my sin.*u*

14:12
p Rev 20:11;
21:1
q Ac 3:21

14:13
r Isa 26:20

14:15
s Job 13:22

14:16
t Ps 139:1-3;
Pr 5:21;
Jer 32:19
u Job 10:6

a 3 Septuagint, Vulgate and Syriac; Hebrew *me*   *b* 13 Hebrew *Sheol*   *c* 14 Or *release*

¹⁷My offenses will be sealed up in a bag;ᵃ
    you will cover over my sin.ᵇ

¹⁸"But as a mountain erodes and crumbles
    and as a rock is moved from its place,
¹⁹as water wears away stones
    and torrents wash away the soil,
    so you destroy man's hope.ᶜ
²⁰You overpower him once for all, and he is gone;
    you change his countenance and send him away.
²¹If his sons are honored, he does not know it;
    if they are brought low, he does not see it.ᵈ
²²He feels but the pain of his own body
    and mourns only for himself."

Chapter 15 Theme _____

15 Then Eliphaz the Temanite replied:

²"Would a wise man answer with empty notions
    or fill his belly with the hot east wind?ᵉ
³Would he argue with useless words,
    with speeches that have no value?
⁴But you even undermine piety
    and hinder devotion to God.
⁵Your sin prompts your mouth;
    you adopt the tongue of the crafty.ᶠ
⁶Your own mouth condemns you, not mine;
    your own lips testify against you.ᵍ

⁷"Are you the first man ever born?ʰ
    Were you brought forth before the hills?ⁱ
⁸Do you listen in on God's council?ʲ
    Do you limit wisdom to yourself?
⁹What do you know that we do not know?
    What insights do you have that we do not have?ᵏ
¹⁰The gray-haired and the agedˡ are on our side,
    men even older than your father.
¹¹Are God's consolationsᵐ not enough for you,
    wordsⁿ spoken gently to you?ᵒ
¹²Why has your heartᵖ carried you away,
    and why do your eyes flash,
¹³so that you vent your rage against God
    and pour out such words from your mouth?

¹⁴"What is man, that he could be pure,
    or one born of woman,ᑫ that he could be righteous?ʳ

14:17
ᵃ Dt 32:34
ᵇ Hos 13:12

14:19
ᶜ Job 7:6

14:21
ᵈ Ecc 9:5;
Isa 63:16

15:2
ᵉ Job 6:26

15:5
ᶠ Job 5:13

15:6
ᵍ Lk 19:22

15:7
ʰ Job 38:21
ⁱ Ps 90:2; Pr 8:25

15:8
ʲ Ro 11:34;
1Co 2:11

15:9
ᵏ Job 13:2

15:10
ˡ Job 32:6-7

15:11
ᵐ 2Co 1:3-4
ⁿ Zec 1:13
ᵒ Job 36:16

15:12
ᵖ Job 11:13

15:14
ᑫ Job 14:4; 25:4
ʳ Pr 20:9;
Ecc 7:20

15:15
a Job 4:18; 25:5

15:16
b Ps 14:1
c Job 34:7;
Pr 19:28

15:18
d Job 8:8

15:20
e Job 24:1;
27:13-23

15:21
f Job 18:11;
20:25
g Job 27:20;
1 Th 5:3

15:22
h Job 19:29;
27:14

15:23
i Ps 59:15;
109:10
j Job 18:12

15:25
k Job 36:9

15:27
l Ps 17:10

15:28
m Isa 5:9
n Job 3:14

15:29
o Job 27:16-17

15:30
p Job 5:14
q Job 22:20
r Job 4:9

15:31
s Isa 59:4

15:32
t Ecc 7:17
u Job 22:16;
Ps 55:23
v Job 18:16

15:33
w Hab 3:17

¹⁵If God places no trust in his holy ones,
  if even the heavens are not pure in his eyes,^a
¹⁶how much less man, who is vile and corrupt,^b
  who drinks up evil like water!^c

¹⁷"Listen to me and I will explain to you;
  let me tell you what I have seen,
¹⁸what wise men have declared,
  hiding nothing received from their fathers^d
¹⁹(to whom alone the land was given
  when no alien passed among them):
²⁰All his days the wicked man suffers torment,
  the ruthless through all the years stored up for him.^e
²¹Terrifying sounds fill his ears;^f
  when all seems well, marauders attack him.^g
²²He despairs of escaping the darkness;
  he is marked for the sword.^h
²³He wanders aboutⁱ—food for vultures^a;
  he knows the day of darkness is at hand.^j
²⁴Distress and anguish fill him with terror;
  they overwhelm him, like a king poised to attack,
²⁵because he shakes his fist at God
  and vaunts himself against the Almighty,^k
²⁶defiantly charging against him
  with a thick, strong shield.

²⁷"Though his face is covered with fat
  and his waist bulges with flesh,^l
²⁸he will inhabit ruined towns
  and houses where no one lives,^m
  houses crumbling to rubble.ⁿ
²⁹He will no longer be rich and his wealth will
    not endure,^o
  nor will his possessions spread over the land.
³⁰He will not escape the darkness;^p
  a flame^q will wither his shoots,
  and the breath of God's mouth^r will carry him away.
³¹Let him not deceive himself by trusting what
    is worthless,^s
  for he will get nothing in return.
³²Before his time^t he will be paid in full,^u
  and his branches will not flourish.^v
³³He will be like a vine stripped of its unripe grapes,^w
  like an olive tree shedding its blossoms.

a 23 Or *about, looking for food*

³⁴For the company of the godless will be barren,
   and fire will consume the tents of those who
        love bribes.ᵃ
³⁵They conceive trouble and give birth to evil;ᵇ
   their womb fashions deceit."

Chapter 16 Theme _____

16 Then Job replied:

²"I have heard many things like these;
   miserable comforters are you all!ᶜ
³Will your long-winded speeches never end?
   What ails you that you keep on arguing?ᵈ
⁴I also could speak like you,
   if you were in my place;
 I could make fine speeches against you
   and shake my headᵉ at you.
⁵But my mouth would encourage you;
   comfort from my lips would bring you relief.

⁶"Yet if I speak, my pain is not relieved;
   and if I refrain, it does not go away.
⁷Surely, O God, you have worn me out;ᶠ
   you have devastated my entire household.
⁸You have bound me—and it has become a witness;
   my gauntnessᵍ rises up and testifies against me.ʰ
⁹God assails me and tearsⁱ me in his anger
   and gnashes his teeth at me;ʲ
   my opponent fastens on me his piercing eyes.ᵏ
¹⁰Men open their mouthsˡ to jeer at me;
   they strike my cheekᵐ in scorn
   and unite together against me.ⁿ
¹¹God has turned me over to evil men
   and thrown me into the clutches of the wicked.ᵒ
¹²All was well with me, but he shattered me;
   he seized me by the neck and crushed me.ᵖ
 He has made me his target;�q
¹³ his archers surround me.
 Without pity, he piercesʳ my kidneys
   and spills my gall on the ground.
¹⁴Again and againˢ he bursts upon me;
   he rushes at me like a warrior.ᵗ

¹⁵"I have sewed sackclothᵘ over my skin
   and buried my brow in the dust.
¹⁶My face is red with weeping,
   deep shadows ring my eyes;

15:34
ᵃJob 8:22

15:35
ᵇPs 7:14;
Isa 59:4;
Hos 10:13

16:2
ᶜJob 13:4

16:3
ᵈJob 6:26

16:4
ᵉPs 22:7;
109:25;
La 2:15;
Zep 2:15;
Mt 27:39

16:7
ᶠJob 7:3

16:8
ᵍJob 19:20
ʰJob 10:17

16:9
ⁱHos 6:1
ʲPs 35:16;
La 2:16;
Ac 7:54
ᵏJob 13:24

16:10
ˡPs 22:13
ᵐIsa 50:6;
La 3:30;
Mic 5:1;
Ac 23:2
ⁿPs 35:15

16:11
ᵒJob 1:15,17

16:12
ᵖJob 9:17
qLa 3:12

16:13
ʳJob 20:24

16:14
ˢJob 9:17
ᵗJoel 2:7

16:15
ᵘGe 37:34

16:17
a Isa 59:6;
Jnh 3:8

16:18
b Isa 26:21
c Ps 66:18-19

16:19
d Ge 31:50;
Ro 1:9;
1Th 2:5

16:20
e La 2:19

16:21
f Ps 9:4

16:22
g Ecc 12:5

17:1
h Ps 88:3-4

17:2
i 1Sa 1:6-7

17:3
j Ps 119:122
k Pr 6:1
l Isa 38:14

17:5
m Job 11:20

17:6
n Job 30:9

17:7
o Job 16:8

17:8
p Job 22:19

17:9
q Pr 4:18
r Job 22:30

17:10
s Job 12:2

17:11
t Job 7:6

17:13
u Job 3:13

¹⁷yet my hands have been free of violence*a*
  and my prayer is pure.

¹⁸"O earth, do not cover my blood;*b*
  may my cry never be laid to rest!*c*
¹⁹Even now my witness*d* is in heaven;
  my advocate is on high.
²⁰My intercessor is my friend*a*
  as my eyes pour out*e* tears to God;
²¹on behalf of a man he pleads*f* with God
  as a man pleads for his friend.

²²"Only a few years will pass
  before I go on the journey of no return.*g*

Chapter 17 Theme _____

17 My spirit is broken,
    my days are cut short,
    the grave awaits me.*h*
²Surely mockers*i* surround me;
    my eyes must dwell on their hostility.

³"Give me, O God, the pledge you demand.*j*
    Who else will put up security*k* for me?*l*
⁴You have closed their minds to understanding;
    therefore you will not let them triumph.
⁵If a man denounces his friends for reward,
    the eyes of his children will fail.*m*

⁶"God has made me a byword*n* to everyone,
    a man in whose face people spit.
⁷My eyes have grown dim with grief;*o*
    my whole frame is but a shadow.
⁸Upright men are appalled at this;
    the innocent are aroused*p* against the ungodly.
⁹Nevertheless, the righteous*q* will hold to their ways,
    and those with clean hands*r* will grow stronger.

¹⁰"But come on, all of you, try again!
    I will not find a wise man among you.*s*
¹¹My days have passed, my plans are shattered,
    and so are the desires of my heart.*t*
¹²These men turn night into day;
    in the face of darkness they say, 'Light is near.'
¹³If the only home I hope for is the grave,*bu*
    if I spread out my bed in darkness,

a 20 Or *My friends treat me with scorn*   *b 13* Hebrew *Sheol*

¹⁴if I say to corruption,^a 'You are my father,'
    and to the worm,^b 'My mother' or 'My sister,'
¹⁵where then is my hope?^c
    Who can see any hope for me?
¹⁶Will it go down to the gates of death^a?^d
    Will we descend together into the dust?"

Chapter 18 Theme

18 Then Bildad the Shuhite replied:

²"When will you end these speeches?
    Be sensible, and then we can talk.
³Why are we regarded as cattle
    and considered stupid in your sight?^e
⁴You who tear yourself^f to pieces in your anger,
    is the earth to be abandoned for your sake?
    Or must the rocks be moved from their place?

⁵"The lamp of the wicked is snuffed out;^g
    the flame of his fire stops burning.
⁶The light in his tent becomes dark;
    the lamp beside him goes out.
⁷The vigor of his step is weakened;^h
    his own schemesⁱ throw him down.^j
⁸His feet thrust him into a net^k
    and he wanders into its mesh.
⁹A trap seizes him by the heel;
    a snare holds him fast.
¹⁰A noose is hidden for him on the ground;
    a trap lies in his path.
¹¹Terrors startle him on every side^l
    and dog^m his every step.
¹²Calamity is hungryⁿ for him;
    disaster is ready for him when he falls.
¹³It eats away parts of his skin;
    death's firstborn devours his limbs.^o
¹⁴He is torn from the security of his tent^p
    and marched off to the king of terrors.
¹⁵Fire resides^b in his tent;
    burning sulfur^q is scattered over his dwelling.
¹⁶His roots dry up below^r
    and his branches wither above.^s
¹⁷The memory of him perishes from the earth;
    he has no name in the land.^t

a 16 Hebrew *Sheol*   b 15 Or *Nothing he had remains*

17:14
^a Job 13:28;
30:28,30;
Ps 16:10
^b Job 21:26

17:15
^c Job 7:6

17:16
^d Job 3:17-19;
Jnh 2:6

18:3
^e Ps 73:22

18:4
^f Job 13:14

18:5
^g Job 21:17;
Pr 13:9; 20:20;
24:20

18:7
^h Pr 4:12
ⁱ Job 5:13
^j Job 15:6

18:8
^k Job 22:10;
Ps 9:15; 35:7

18:11
^l Job 15:21;
Jer 6:25; 20:3
^m Job 20:8

18:12
ⁿ Isa 8:21

18:13
^o Zec 14:12

18:14
^p Job 8:22

18:15
^q Ps 11:6

18:16
^r Isa 5:24;
Hos 9:1-16;
Am 2:9
^s Job 15:30;
Mal 4:1

18:17
^t Ps 34:16;
Pr 2:22; 10:7

18:18
a Job 5:14

18:19
b Jer 22:30
c Isa 14:22
d Job 27:14-15

18:20
e Ps 37:13;
Jer 50:27,31

18:21
f Job 21:28
g Jer 9:3;
1Th 4:5

19:4
h Job 6:24

19:5
i Ps 35:26; 38:16;
55:12

19:6
j Job 27:2
k Job 18:8

19:7
l Job 30:20
m Job 9:24;
Hab 1:2-4

19:8
n Job 3:23;
La 3:7
o Job 30:26

19:9
p Job 12:17
q Ps 89:39,44;
La 5:16

19:10
r Job 12:14
s Job 7:6
t Job 24:20

19:11
u Job 16:9
v Job 13:24

19:12
w Job 16:13
x Job 30:12

19:13
y Ps 69:8
z Job 16:7;
Ps 88:8

¹⁸He is driven from light into darkness*a*
and is banished from the world.
¹⁹He has no offspring*b* or descendants*c* among his people,
no survivor where once he lived.*d*
²⁰Men of the west are appalled at his fate;*e*
men of the east are seized with horror.
²¹Surely such is the dwelling*f* of an evil man;
such is the place of one who knows not God."*g*

Chapter 19 Theme

19 Then Job replied:

²"How long will you torment me
and crush me with words?
³Ten times now you have reproached me;
shamelessly you attack me.
⁴If it is true that I have gone astray,
my error*h* remains my concern alone.
⁵If indeed you would exalt yourselves above me*i*
and use my humiliation against me,
⁶then know that God has wronged me*j*
and drawn his net*k* around me.

⁷"Though I cry, 'I've been wronged!' I get no response;*l*
though I call for help, there is no justice.*m*
⁸He has blocked my way so I cannot pass;*n*
he has shrouded my paths in darkness.*o*
⁹He has stripped*p* me of my honor
and removed the crown from my head.*q*
¹⁰He tears me down*r* on every side till I am gone;
he uproots my hope*s* like a tree.*t*
¹¹His anger*u* burns against me;
he counts me among his enemies.*v*
¹²His troops advance in force;*w*
they build a siege ramp*x* against me
and encamp around my tent.

¹³"He has alienated my brothers*y* from me;
my acquaintances are completely estranged from me.*z*
¹⁴My kinsmen have gone away;
my friends have forgotten me.
¹⁵My guests and my maidservants count me a stranger;
they look upon me as an alien.
¹⁶I summon my servant, but he does not answer,
though I beg him with my own mouth.
¹⁷My breath is offensive to my wife;
I am loathsome to my own brothers.

¹⁸Even the little boys^a scorn me;
  when I appear, they ridicule me.
¹⁹All my intimate friends^b detest me;^c
  those I love have turned against me.
²⁰I am nothing but skin and bones;^d
  I have escaped with only the skin of my teeth.^a

²¹"Have pity on me, my friends, have pity,
  for the hand of God has struck me.
²²Why do you pursue^e me as God does?
  Will you never get enough of my flesh?^f

²³"Oh, that my words were recorded,
  that they were written on a scroll,^g
²⁴that they were inscribed with an iron tool on^b lead,
  or engraved in rock forever!
²⁵I know that my Redeemer^{ch} lives,ⁱ
  and that in the end he will stand upon the earth.^d
²⁶And after my skin has been destroyed,
  yet^e in^f my flesh I will see God;^j
²⁷I myself will see him
  with my own eyes—I, and not another.
  How my heart yearns^k within me!

²⁸"If you say, 'How we will hound him,
  since the root of the trouble lies in him,^g'
²⁹you should fear the sword yourselves;
  for wrath will bring punishment by the sword,^l
  and then you will know that there is judgment.^h"^m

Chapter 20 Theme

20 Then Zophar the Naamathite replied:

²"My troubled thoughts prompt me to answer
  because I am greatly disturbed.
³I hear a rebukeⁿ that dishonors me,
  and my understanding inspires me to reply.

⁴"Surely you know how it has been from of old,
  ever since manⁱ was placed on the earth,
⁵that the mirth of the wicked is brief,
  the joy of the godless lasts but a moment.^o
⁶Though his pride reaches to the heavens
  and his head touches the clouds,^p

---

^a20 Or only my gums ^b24 Or and ^c25 Or defender ^d25 Or upon my grave ^e26 Or And
after I awake, / though this [body] has been destroyed, / then ^f26 Or / apart from ^g28 Many
Hebrew manuscripts, Septuagint and Vulgate; most Hebrew manuscripts me ^h29 Or / that
you may come to know the Almighty ⁱ4 Or Adam

19:18
^a2Ki 2:23

19:19
^bPs 55:12-13
^cPs 38:11

19:20
^dJob 33:21;
Ps 102:5

19:22
^eJob 13:25;
16:11
^fPs 69:26

19:23
^gIsa 30:8

19:25
^hPs 78:35;
Pr 23:11;
Isa 43:14;
Jer 50:34
ⁱJob 16:19

19:26
^jPs 17:15;
Mt 5:8;
1Co 13:12;
1Jn 3:2

19:27
^kPs 73:26

19:29
^lJob 15:22
^mJob 22:4;
Ps 1:5; 9:7

20:3
ⁿJob 19:3

20:5
^oJob 8:12;
Ps 37:35-36;
73:19

20:6
^pIsa 14:13-14;
Ob 3-4

20:7
a Job 4:20
b Job 7:10; 8:18

20:8
c Ps 73:20
d Job 27:21-23
e Job 18:18
f Ps 90:5

20:9
g Job 7:8

20:10
h Job 5:4
i Job 27:16-17

20:11
j Job 13:26
k Job 21:26

20:13
l Nu 11:18-20

20:16
m Dt 32:32
n Dt 32:24

20:17
o Dt 32:13
p Job 29:6

20:19
q Job 24:4,14; 35:9

20:20
r Ecc 5:12-14

20:21
s Job 15:29

20:23
t Ps 78:30-31

20:24
u Isa 24:18; Am 5:19

20:25
v Job 18:11
w Job 16:13

20:26
x Job 18:18
y Ps 21:9

⁷he will perish forever,ᵃ like his own dung;
  those who have seen him will say, 'Where is he?'ᵇ
⁸Like a dreamᶜ he flies away,ᵈ no more to be found,
  banishedᵉ like a vision of the night.ᶠ
⁹The eye that saw him will not see him again;
  his place will look on him no more.ᵍ
¹⁰His childrenʰ must make amends to the poor;
  his own hands must give back his wealth.ⁱ
¹¹The youthful vigorʲ that fills his bones
  will lie with him in the dust.ᵏ

¹²"Though evil is sweet in his mouth
  and he hides it under his tongue,
¹³though he cannot bear to let it go
  and keeps it in his mouth,ˡ
¹⁴yet his food will turn sour in his stomach;
  it will become the venom of serpents within him.
¹⁵He will spit out the riches he swallowed;
  God will make his stomach vomit them up.
¹⁶He will suck the poisonᵐ of serpents;
  the fangs of an adder will kill him.ⁿ
¹⁷He will not enjoy the streams,
  the rivers flowing with honeyᵒ and cream.ᵖ
¹⁸What he toiled for he must give back uneaten;
  he will not enjoy the profit from his trading.
¹⁹For he has oppressed the poor and left them destitute;�q
  he has seized houses he did not build.

²⁰"Surely he will have no respite from his craving;ʳ
  he cannot save himself by his treasure.
²¹Nothing is left for him to devour;
  his prosperity will not endure.ˢ
²²In the midst of his plenty, distress will overtake him;
  the full force of misery will come upon him.
²³When he has filled his belly,
  God will vent his burning anger against him
  and rain down his blows upon him.ᵗ
²⁴Though he fleesᵘ from an iron weapon,
  a bronze-tipped arrow pierces him.
²⁵He pulls it out of his back,
  the gleaming point out of his liver.
  Terrorsᵛ will come over him;ʷ
²⁶ total darknessˣ lies in wait for his treasures.
  A fire unfanned will consume himʸ
  and devour what is left in his tent.

²⁷The heavens will expose his guilt;
    the earth will rise up against him.ᵃ
²⁸A flood will carry off his house,ᵇ
    rushing watersᵃ on the day of God's wrath.ᶜ
²⁹Such is the fate God allots the wicked,
    the heritage appointed for them by God."ᵈ

Chapter 21 Theme

21 Then Job replied:

²"Listen carefully to my words;
    let this be the consolation you give me.
³Bear with me while I speak,
    and after I have spoken, mock on.ᵉ

⁴"Is my complaint directed to man?
    Why should I not be impatient?ᶠ
⁵Look at me and be astonished;
    clap your hand over your mouth.ᵍ
⁶When I think about this, I am terrified;
    trembling seizes my body.
⁷Why do the wicked live on,
    growing old and increasing in power?ʰ
⁸They see their children established around them,
    their offspring before their eyes.ⁱ
⁹Their homes are safe and free from fear;ʲ
    the rod of God is not upon them.
¹⁰Their bulls never fail to breed;
    their cows calve and do not miscarry.ᵏ
¹¹They send forth their children as a flock;
    their little ones dance about.
¹²They sing to the music of tambourine and harp;
    they make merry to the sound of the flute.ˡ
¹³They spend their years in prosperityᵐ
    and go down to the graveᵇ in peace.ᶜ
¹⁴Yet they say to God, 'Leave us alone!ⁿ
    We have no desire to know your ways.ᵒ
¹⁵Who is the Almighty, that we should serve him?
    What would we gain by praying to him?'ᵖ
¹⁶But their prosperity is not in their own hands,
    so I stand aloof from the counsel of the wicked.

¹⁷"Yet how often is the lamp of the wicked snuffed out?�q
    How often does calamity come upon them,
    the fate God allots in his anger?

ᵃ28 Or *The possessions in his house will be carried off, / washed away*   ᵇ13 Hebrew *Sheol*
ᶜ13 Or *in an instant*

20:27
ᵃDt 31:28

20:28
ᵇDt 28:31
ᶜJob 21:17,
20,30

20:29
ᵈJob 27:13

21:3
ᵉJob 16:10

21:4
ᶠJob 6:11

21:5
ᵍJdg 18:19;
Job 29:9; 40:4

21:7
ʰJob 12:6;
Ps 73:3;
Jer 12:1;
Hab 1:13

21:8
ⁱPs 17:14

21:9
ʲPs 73:5

21:10
ᵏEx 23:26

21:12
ˡPs 81:2

21:13
ᵐJob 36:11

21:14
ⁿJob 22:17
ᵒPr 1:29

21:15
ᵖEx 5:2;
Job 34:9;
Mal 3:14

21:17
qJob 18:5

21:18
a Job 13:25;
Ps 1:4

21:19
b Ex 20:5;
Jer 31:29;
Eze 18:2

21:20
c Ps 75:8;
Isa 51:17
d Jer 25:15;
Rev 14:10

21:21
e Job 14:5

21:22
f Job 35:11;
36:22;
Isa 40:13-14;
Ro 11:34
g Ps 82:1

21:24
h Pr 3:8

21:26
i Job 24:20;
Ecc 9:2-3;
Isa 14:11

21:28
j Job 1:3; 12:21;
31:37
k Job 8:22

21:30
l Pr 16:4
m Job 20:22,28;
2Pe 2:9

21:33
n Job 3:22;
17:16; 24:24
o Job 3:19

21:34
p Job 16:2

22:2
q Lk 17:10

¹⁸How often are they like straw before the wind,
  like chaff*a* swept away by a gale?
¹⁹⌊It is said,⌋ 'God stores up a man's punishment for his sons.'*b*
  Let him repay the man himself, so that he will know it!
²⁰Let his own eyes see his destruction;
  let him drink*c* of the wrath of the Almighty.*a* *d*
²¹For what does he care about the family he leaves behind
  when his allotted months*e* come to an end?

²²"Can anyone teach knowledge to God,*f*
  since he judges even the highest?*g*
²³One man dies in full vigor,
  completely secure and at ease,
²⁴his body*b* well nourished,
  his bones rich with marrow.*h*
²⁵Another man dies in bitterness of soul,
  never having enjoyed anything good.
²⁶Side by side they lie in the dust,
  and worms cover them both.*i*

²⁷"I know full well what you are thinking,
  the schemes by which you would wrong me.
²⁸You say, 'Where now is the great man's*j* house,
  the tents where wicked men lived?'*k*
²⁹Have you never questioned those who travel?
  Have you paid no regard to their accounts—
³⁰that the evil man is spared from the day of calamity,*l*
  that he is delivered from*c* the day of wrath?*m*
³¹Who denounces his conduct to his face?
  Who repays him for what he has done?
³²He is carried to the grave,
  and watch is kept over his tomb.
³³The soil in the valley is sweet to him;*n*
  all men follow after him,
  and a countless throng goes*d* before him.*o*

³⁴"So how can you console me*p* with your nonsense?
  Nothing is left of your answers but falsehood!"

Chapter 22 Theme

22
Then Eliphaz the Temanite replied:

²"Can a man be of benefit to God?*q*
  Can even a wise man benefit him?

a 17-20 Verses 17 and 18 may be taken as exclamations and 19 and 20 as declarations.
b 24 The meaning of the Hebrew for this word is uncertain.   *c* 30 Or *man is reserved for the day of calamity, / that he is brought forth to*   *d* 33 Or / *as a countless throng went*

³What pleasure would it give the Almighty if you
    were righteous?
  What would he gain if your ways were blameless?

⁴"Is it for your piety that he rebukes you
    and brings charges against you?ᵃ
⁵Is not your wickedness great?
    Are not your sinsᵇ endless?
⁶You demanded securityᶜ from your brothers for
    no reason;
    you stripped men of their clothing, leaving
    them naked.
⁷You gave no water to the weary
    and you withheld food from the hungry,ᵈ
⁸though you were a powerful man, owning land—
    an honored man,ᵉ living on it.
⁹And you sent widows away empty-handed ᶠ
    and broke the strength of the fatherless.
¹⁰That is why snares are all around you,
    why sudden peril terrifies you,
¹¹why it is so darkᵍ you cannot see,
    and why a flood of water covers you.ʰ

¹²"Is not God in the heights of heaven?ⁱ
    And see how lofty are the highest stars!
¹³Yet you say, 'What does God know?ʲ
    Does he judge through such darkness?ᵏ
¹⁴Thick cloudsˡ veil him, so he does not see us
    as he goes about in the vaulted heavens.'
¹⁵Will you keep to the old path
    that evil men have trod?
¹⁶They were carried off before their time,ᵐ
    their foundations washed away by a flood.ⁿ
¹⁷They said to God, 'Leave us alone!
    What can the Almighty do to us?'ᵒ
¹⁸Yet it was he who filled their houses with good things,ᵖ
    so I stand aloof from the counsel of the wicked.�q

¹⁹"The righteous see their ruin and rejoice;ʳ
    the innocent mockˢ them, saying,
²⁰'Surely our foes are destroyed,
    and fireᵗ devours their wealth.'

²¹"Submit to God and be at peace with him;
    in this way prosperity will come to you.ᵘ
²²Accept instruction from his mouth
    and lay up his words in your heart.

22:4 ᵃJob 14:3; 19:29; Ps 143:2

22:5 ᵇJob 11:6; 15:5

22:6 ᶜEx 22:26; Dt 24:6,17; Eze 18:12,16

22:7 ᵈJob 31:17, 21,31

22:8 ᵉIsa 3:3; 9:15

22:9 ᶠJob 24:3,21

22:11 ᵍJob 5:14 ʰPs 69:1-2; 124:4-5; La 3:54

22:12 ⁱJob 11:8

22:13 ʲPs 10:11; Isa 29:15 ᵏEze 8:12

22:14 ˡJob 26:9

22:16 ᵐJob 15:32 ⁿJob 14:19; Mt 7:26-27

22:17 ᵒJob 21:15

22:18 ᵖJob 12:6 qJob 21:16

22:19 ʳPs 58:10; 107:42 ˢPs 52:6

22:20 ᵗJob 15:30

22:21 ᵘPs 34:8-10

22:23
a Job 8:5;
Isa 31:6;
Zec 1:3
b Isa 19:22;
Ac 20:32
c Job 11:14

22:24
d Job 31:25

22:25
e Isa 33:6

22:26
f Job 27:10;
Isa 58:14

22:27
g Job 33:26;
34:28;
Isa 58:9

22:29
h Mt 23:12;
1Pe 5:5

22:30
i Job 42:7-8

23:2
j Job 7:11
k Job 6:3

23:4
l Job 13:18

23:6
m Job 9:4

23:7
n Job 13:3

23:9
o Job 9:11

23:10
p Ps 66:10;
139:1-3
q 1Pe 1:7

23:11
r Ps 17:5
s Ps 44:18

23:12
t Job 6:10
u Jn 4:32,34

²³If you return *a* to the Almighty, you will be restored: *b*
   If you remove wickedness far from your tent *c*
²⁴and assign your nuggets to the dust,
   your gold of Ophir to the rocks in the ravines, *d*
²⁵then the Almighty will be your gold,
   the choicest silver for you. *e*
²⁶Surely then you will find delight in the Almighty *f*
   and will lift up your face to God.
²⁷You will pray to him, *g* and he will hear you,
   and you will fulfill your vows.
²⁸What you decide on will be done,
   and light will shine on your ways.
²⁹When men are brought low and you say, 'Lift them up!'
   then he will save the downcast. *h*
³⁰He will deliver even one who is not innocent,
   who will be delivered through the cleanness of
      your hands." *i*

Chapter 23 Theme

23 Then Job replied:

²"Even today my complaint *j* is bitter; *k*
   his hand *a* is heavy in spite of *b* my groaning.
³If only I knew where to find him;
   if only I could go to his dwelling!
⁴I would state my case *l* before him
   and fill my mouth with arguments.
⁵I would find out what he would answer me,
   and consider what he would say.
⁶Would he oppose me with great power? *m*
   No, he would not press charges against me.
⁷There an upright man could present his case before him, *n*
   and I would be delivered forever from my judge.

⁸"But if I go to the east, he is not there;
   if I go to the west, I do not find him.
⁹When he is at work in the north, I do not see him;
   when he turns to the south, I catch no glimpse of him. *o*
¹⁰But he knows the way that I take;
   when he has tested me, *p* I will come forth as gold. *q*
¹¹My feet have closely followed his steps; *r*
   I have kept to his way without turning aside. *s*
¹²I have not departed from the commands of his lips; *t*
   I have treasured the words of his mouth more than my
      daily bread. *u*

a 2 Septuagint and Syriac; Hebrew *I the hand on me*   *b* 2 Or *heavy on me in*

¹³"But he stands alone, and who can oppose him?
He does whatever he pleases.ᵃ
¹⁴He carries out his decree against me,
and many such plans he still has in store.ᵇ
¹⁵That is why I am terrified before him;
when I think of all this, I fear him.
¹⁶God has made my heart faint;ᶜ
the Almightyᵈ has terrified me.
¹⁷Yet I am not silenced by the darkness,ᵉ
by the thick darkness that covers my face.

Chapter 24 Theme

24 "Why does the Almighty not set times for judgment?ᶠ
Why must those who know him look in vain for
such days?ᵍ
²Men move boundary stones;ʰ
they pasture flocks they have stolen.
³They drive away the orphan's donkey
and take the widow's ox in pledge.ⁱ
⁴They thrust the needy from the path
and force all the poorʲ of the land into hiding.ᵏ
⁵Like wild donkeys in the desert,
the poor go about their laborˡ of foraging food;
the wasteland provides food for their children.
⁶They gather fodder in the fields
and glean in the vineyards of the wicked.
⁷Lacking clothes, they spend the night naked;
they have nothing to cover themselves in the cold.ᵐ
⁸They are drenched by mountain rains
and hugⁿ the rocks for lack of shelter.
⁹The fatherlessᵒ child is snatched from the breast;
the infant of the poor is seized for a debt.
¹⁰Lacking clothes, they go about naked;
they carry the sheaves, but still go hungry.
¹¹They crush olives among the terracesᵃ;
they tread the winepresses, yet suffer thirst.
¹²The groans of the dying rise from the city,
and the souls of the wounded cry out for help.ᵖ
But God charges no one with wrongdoing.�q

¹³"There are those who rebel against the light,ʳ
who do not know its ways
or stay in its paths.ˢ
¹⁴When daylight is gone, the murderer rises up

ᵃ 11 Or *olives between the millstones*; the meaning of the Hebrew for this word is uncertain.

23:13
ᵃPs 115:3

23:14
ᵇ1Th 3:3

23:16
ᶜDt 20:3;
Ps 22:14;
Jer 51:46
ᵈJob 27:2

23:17
ᵉJob 19:8

24:1
ᶠJer 46:10
ᵍAc 1:7

24:2
ʰDt 19:14;
27:17;
Pr 23:10

24:3
ⁱDt 24:6,10,
12,17;
Job 22:6

24:4
ʲJob 29:12;
30:25;
Ps 41:1
ᵏPr 28:28

24:5
ˡPs 104:23

24:7
ᵐEx 22:27;
Job 22:6

24:8
ⁿLa 4:5

24:9
ᵒDt 24:17

24:12
ᵖEze 26:15
qJob 9:23

24:13
ʳJn 3:19-20
ˢIsa 5:20

24:14
a Ps 10:9

and kills the poor and needy;
in the night he steals forth like a thief.ᵃ

24:15
b Pr 7:8-9
c Ps 10:11

¹⁵The eye of the adulterer watches for dusk;ᵇ
he thinks, 'No eye will see me,'ᶜ
and he keeps his face concealed.

24:16
d Ex 22:2;
Mt 6:19
e Jn 3:20

¹⁶In the dark, men break into houses,ᵈ
but by day they shut themselves in;
they want nothing to do with the light.ᵉ
¹⁷For all of them, deep darkness is their morningᵃ;
they make friends with the terrors of darkness.ᵇ

24:18
f Job 9:26
g Job 22:16

¹⁸"Yet they are foamᶠ on the surface of the water;ᵍ
their portion of the land is cursed,
so that no one goes to the vineyards.

24:19
h Job 6:17
i Job 21:13

¹⁹As heat and drought snatch away the melted snow,ʰ
so the graveᶜ ⁱ snatches away those who have sinned.
²⁰The womb forgets them,
the worm feasts on them;
evil men are no longer remembered ʲ
but are broken like a tree.ᵏ

24:20
j Job 18:17;
Pr 10:7
k Ps 31:12;
Da 4:14

²¹They prey on the barren and childless woman,
and to the widow show no kindness.ˡ

24:21
l Job 22:9

²²But God drags away the mighty by his power;
though they become established, they have no
assurance of life.ᵐ

24:22
m Dt 28:66

²³He may let them rest in a feeling of security,ⁿ
but his eyes are on their ways.ᵒ
²⁴For a little while they are exalted, and then they
are gone;ᵖ
they are brought low and gathered up like all others;
they are cut off like heads of grain.�vq

24:23
n Job 12:6
o Job 11:11

²⁵"If this is not so, who can prove me false
and reduce my words to nothing?"ʳ

24:24
p Job 14:21;
Ps 37:10
q Isa 17:5

Chapter 25 Theme

25 Then Bildad the Shuhite replied:

²"Dominion and awe belong to God;ˢ
he establishes order in the heights of heaven.
³Can his forces be numbered?
Upon whom does his light not rise?ᵗ
⁴How then can a man be righteous before God?
How can one born of woman be pure?ᵘ

24:25
r Job 6:28; 27:4

25:2
s Job 9:4;
Rev 1:6

25:3
t Jas 1:17

25:4
u Job 4:17; 14:4

a 17 Or them, their morning is like the shadow of death   b 17 Or of the shadow of death
c 19 Hebrew Sheol

867

⁵"If even the moon^a is not bright
　　and the stars are not pure in his eyes,^b
⁶how much less man, who is but a maggot—
　　a son of man,^c who is only a worm!"^d

Chapter 26 Theme _____

26

Then Job replied:

²"How you have helped the powerless!^e
　　How you have saved the arm that is feeble!^f
³What advice you have offered to one without wisdom!
　　And what great insight you have displayed!
⁴Who has helped you utter these words?
　　And whose spirit spoke from your mouth?

⁵"The dead are in deep anguish,^g
　　those beneath the waters and all that live in them.
⁶Death^{a h} is naked before God;
　　Destruction^b lies uncovered.ⁱ
⁷He spreads out the northern ₍skies₎^j over empty space;
　　he suspends the earth over nothing.
⁸He wraps up the waters^k in his clouds,^l
　　yet the clouds do not burst under their weight.
⁹He covers the face of the full moon,
　　spreading his clouds^m over it.
¹⁰He marks out the horizon on the face of the watersⁿ
　　for a boundary between light and darkness.^o
¹¹The pillars of the heavens quake,
　　aghast at his rebuke.
¹²By his power he churned up the sea;^p
　　by his wisdom^q he cut Rahab to pieces.
¹³By his breath the skies became fair;
　　his hand pierced the gliding serpent.^r
¹⁴And these are but the outer fringe of his works;
　　how faint the whisper we hear of him!
　　Who then can understand the thunder of his power?"^s

Chapter 27 Theme _____

27

And Job continued his discourse:^t

²"As surely as God lives, who has denied me justice,^u
　　the Almighty, who has made me taste bitterness
　　　　of soul,^v

---

^a6 Hebrew *Sheol*　^b6 Hebrew *Abaddon*

25:5
^aJob 31:26
^bJob 15:15

25:6
^cJob 7:17
^dPs 22:6

26:2
^eJob 6:12
^fPs 71:9

26:5
^gPs 88:10

26:6
^hPs 139:8
ⁱJob 41:11;
Pr 15:11;
Heb 4:13

26:7
^jJob 9:8

26:8
^kPr 30:4
^lJob 37:11

26:9
^mJob 22:14;
Ps 97:2

26:10
ⁿPr 8:27,29
^oJob 38:8-11

26:12
^pEx 14:21;
Isa 51:15;
Jer 31:35
^qJob 12:13

26:13
^rIsa 27:1

26:14
^sJob 36:29

27:1
^tJob 29:1

27:2
^uJob 34:5
^vJob 9:18

27:3
a Job 32:8; 33:4

27:4
b Job 6:28

27:5
c Job 2:9; 13:15

27:6
d Job 2:3

27:8
e Job 8:13
f Job 11:20;
Lk 12:20

27:9
g Job 35:12;
Pr 1:28;
Isa 1:15;
Jer 14:12;
Mic 3:4

27:10
h Job 22:26

27:13
i Job 15:20;
20:29

27:14
j Dt 28:41;
Job 15:22;
Hos 9:13
k Job 20:10

27:15
l Ps 78:64

27:16
m Zec 9:3

27:17
n Pr 28:8;
Ecc 2:26

27:18
o Job 8:14
p Isa 1:8

27:19
q Job 7:8

27:20
r Job 15:21
s Job 20:8

27:21
t Job 7:10; 21:18

27:22
u Jer 13:14;
Eze 5:11; 24:14
v Job 11:20

27:23
w Job 18:18

³as long as I have life within me,
  the breath of God *a* in my nostrils,
⁴my lips will not speak wickedness,
  and my tongue will utter no deceit. *b*
⁵I will never admit you are in the right;
  till I die, I will not deny my integrity. *c*
⁶I will maintain my righteousness and never let go of it;
  my conscience will not reproach me as long as I live. *d*

⁷"May my enemies be like the wicked,
  my adversaries like the unjust!
⁸For what hope has the godless *e* when he is cut off,
  when God takes away his life? *f*
⁹Does God listen to his cry
  when distress comes upon him? *g*
¹⁰Will he find delight in the Almighty? *h*
  Will he call upon God at all times?

¹¹"I will teach you about the power of God;
  the ways of the Almighty I will not conceal.
¹²You have all seen this yourselves.
  Why then this meaningless talk?

¹³"Here is the fate God allots to the wicked,
  the heritage a ruthless man receives from
    the Almighty: *i*
¹⁴However many his children, their fate is the sword; *j*
  his offspring will never have enough to eat. *k*
¹⁵The plague will bury those who survive him,
  and their widows will not weep for them. *l*
¹⁶Though he heaps up silver like dust
  and clothes like piles of clay, *m*
¹⁷what he lays up the righteous will wear, *n*
  and the innocent will divide his silver.
¹⁸The house he builds is like a moth's cocoon, *o*
  like a hut *p* made by a watchman.
¹⁹He lies down wealthy, but will do so no more; *q*
  when he opens his eyes, all is gone.
²⁰Terrors overtake him like a flood; *r*
  a tempest snatches him away in the night. *s*
²¹The east wind carries him off, and he is gone;
  it sweeps him out of his place. *t*
²²It hurls itself against him without mercy *u*
  as he flees headlong from its power. *v*
²³It claps its hands in derision
  and hisses him out of his place. *w*

Chapter 28 Theme _____

28 "There is a mine for silver
　　and a place where gold is refined.
²Iron is taken from the earth,
　　and copper is smelted from ore.ᵃ
³Man puts an end to the darkness;ᵇ
　　he searches the farthest recesses
　　for ore in the blackest darkness.
⁴Far from where people dwell he cuts a shaft,
　　in places forgotten by the foot of man;
　　far from men he dangles and sways.
⁵The earth, from which food comes,ᶜ
　　is transformed below as by fire;
⁶sapphiresᵃ come from its rocks,
　　and its dust contains nuggets of gold.
⁷No bird of prey knows that hidden path,
　　no falcon's eye has seen it.
⁸Proud beasts do not set foot on it,
　　and no lion prowls there.
⁹Man's hand assaults the flinty rock
　　and lays bare the roots of the mountains.
¹⁰He tunnels through the rock;
　　his eyes see all its treasures.
¹¹He searchesᵇ the sources of the rivers
　　and brings hidden things to light.

¹²"But where can wisdom be found?ᵈ
　　Where does understanding dwell?
¹³Man does not comprehend its worth;ᵉ
　　it cannot be found in the land of the living.
¹⁴The deep says, 'It is not in me';
　　the sea says, 'It is not with me.'
¹⁵It cannot be bought with the finest gold,
　　nor can its price be weighed in silver.ᶠ
¹⁶It cannot be bought with the gold of Ophir,
　　with precious onyx or sapphires.
¹⁷Neither gold nor crystal can compare with it,
　　nor can it be had for jewels of gold.ᵍ
¹⁸Coral and jasper are not worthy of mention;
　　the price of wisdom is beyond rubies.ʰ
¹⁹The topaz of Cush cannot compare with it;
　　it cannot be bought with pure gold.ⁱ

²⁰"Where then does wisdom come from?
　　Where does understanding dwell?ʲ

ᵃ6 Or *lapis lazuli*; also in verse 16 　ᵇ11 Septuagint, Aquila and Vulgate; Hebrew *He dams up*

28:2
ᵃDt 8:9

28:3
ᵇEcc 1:13

28:5
ᶜPs 104:14

28:12
ᵈEcc 7:24

28:13
ᵉPr 3:15;
Mt 13:44-46

28:15
ᶠPr 3:13-14;
8:10-11; 16:16

28:17
ᵍPr 16:16

28:18
ʰPr 3:15

28:19
ⁱPr 8:19

28:20
ʲver 23,28

²¹It is hidden from the eyes of every living thing,
    concealed even from the birds of the air.
²²Destruction^{a a} and Death say,
    'Only a rumor of it has reached our ears.'
²³God understands the way to it
    and he alone knows where it dwells,^b
²⁴for he views the ends of the earth^c
    and sees everything under the heavens.^d
²⁵When he established the force of the wind
    and measured out the waters,^e
²⁶when he made a decree for the rain
    and a path for the thunderstorm,^f
²⁷then he looked at wisdom and appraised it;
    he confirmed it and tested it.
²⁸And he said to man,
    'The fear of the Lord—that is wisdom,
    and to shun evil is understanding.^g'"

Chapter 29 Theme

29 Job continued his discourse:^h

²"How I long for the months gone by,
    for the days when God watched over me,ⁱ
³when his lamp shone upon my head
    and by his light I walked through darkness!^j
⁴Oh, for the days when I was in my prime,
    when God's intimate friendship blessed my house,^k
⁵when the Almighty was still with me
    and my children were around me,
⁶when my path was drenched with cream^l
    and the rock^m poured out for me streams of olive oil.ⁿ

⁷"When I went to the gate^o of the city
    and took my seat in the public square,
⁸the young men saw me and stepped aside
    and the old men rose to their feet;
⁹the chief men refrained from speaking
    and covered their mouths with their hands;^p
¹⁰the voices of the nobles were hushed,
    and their tongues stuck to the roof of their mouths.^q
¹¹Whoever heard me spoke well of me,
    and those who saw me commended me,
¹²because I rescued the poor^r who cried for help,
    and the fatherless^s who had none to assist him.^t

Cross references:
28:22 a Job 26:6
28:23 b Pr 8:22-31
28:24 c Ps 33:13-14; d Pr 15:3
28:25 e Job 12:15; Ps 135:7
28:26 f Job 37:3,8,11; 38:25,27
28:28 g Dt 4:6; Ps 111:10; Pr 1:7; 9:10
29:1 h Job 13:12; 27:1
29:2 i Jer 31:28
29:3 j Job 11:17
29:4 k Ps 25:14; Pr 3:32
29:6 l Job 20:17; m Ps 81:16; n Dt 32:13
29:7 o Job 31:21
29:9 p Job 21:5
29:10 q Ps 137:6
29:12 r Job 24:4; s Job 31:17,21; t Ps 72:12; Pr 21:13

^a 22 Hebrew *Abaddon*

¹³The man who was dying blessed me;*a*
    I made the widow's*b* heart sing.
¹⁴I put on righteousness*c* as my clothing;
    justice was my robe and my turban.
¹⁵I was eyes*d* to the blind
    and feet to the lame.
¹⁶I was a father to the needy;*e*
    I took up the case of the stranger.
¹⁷I broke the fangs of the wicked
    and snatched the victims from their teeth.*f*

¹⁸"I thought, 'I will die in my own house,
    my days as numerous as the grains of sand.*g*
¹⁹My roots will reach to the water,*h*
    and the dew will lie all night on my branches.
²⁰My glory will remain fresh in me,
    the bow*i* ever new in my hand.'*j*

²¹"Men listened to me expectantly,
    waiting in silence for my counsel.
²²After I had spoken, they spoke no more;
    my words fell gently on their ears.*k*
²³They waited for me as for showers
    and drank in my words as the spring rain.
²⁴When I smiled at them, they scarcely believed it;
    the light of my face was precious to them.*a*
²⁵I chose the way for them and sat as their chief;
    I dwelt as a king*l* among his troops;
    I was like one who comforts mourners.*m*

Chapter 30 Theme _____

30 "But now they mock me,*n*
    men younger than I,
whose fathers I would have disdained
    to put with my sheep dogs.
²Of what use was the strength of their hands to me,
    since their vigor had gone from them?
³Haggard from want and hunger,
    they roamed*b* the parched land
    in desolate wastelands at night.
⁴In the brush they gathered salt herbs,
    and their food*c* was the root of the broom tree.
⁵They were banished from their fellow men,
    shouted at as if they were thieves.

a 24 The meaning of the Hebrew for this clause is uncertain.   *b 3* Or *gnawed*   *c 4* Or *fuel*

29:13
a Job 31:20
b Job 22:9

29:14
c Job 27:6;
Ps 132:9;
Isa 59:17; 61:10;
Eph 6:14

29:15
d Nu 10:31

29:16
e Job 24:4;
Pr 29:7

29:17
f Ps 3:7

29:18
g Ps 30:6

29:19
h Job 18:16;
Jer 17:8

29:20
i Ps 18:34
j Ge 49:24

29:22
k Dt 32:2

29:25
l Job 1:3; 31:37
m Job 4:4

30:1
n Job 12:4

30:9
a Ps 69:11
b Job 12:4;
La 3:14,63
c Job 17:6

30:10
d Nu 12:14;
Dt 25:9;
Isa 50:6;
Mt 26:67

30:11
e Ru 1:21
f Ps 32:9

30:12
g Ps 140:4-5
h Job 19:12

30:13
i Isa 3:12

30:15
j Job 31:23;
Ps 55:4-5
k Job 3:25;
Hos 13:3

30:16
l Job 3:24;
Ps 22:14; 42:4

30:19
m Ps 69:2,14

30:20
n Job 19:7

30:21
o Job 19:6,22
p Job 16:9,14
q Job 10:3

30:22
r Job 27:21
s Job 9:17

30:23
t Job 9:22; 10:8
u Job 3:19

30:24
v Job 19:7

⁶They were forced to live in the dry stream beds,
  among the rocks and in holes in the ground.
⁷They brayed among the bushes
  and huddled in the undergrowth.
⁸A base and nameless brood,
  they were driven out of the land.

⁹"And now their sons mock me*a* in song;*b*
  I have become a byword*c* among them.
¹⁰They detest me and keep their distance;
  they do not hesitate to spit in my face.*d*
¹¹Now that God has unstrung my bow and afflicted me,*e*
  they throw off restraint*f* in my presence.
¹²On my right the tribe*a* attacks;
  they lay snares for my feet,*g*
  they build their siege ramps against me.*h*
¹³They break up my road;*i*
  they succeed in destroying me—
  without anyone's helping them.*b*
¹⁴They advance as through a gaping breach;
  amid the ruins they come rolling in.
¹⁵Terrors overwhelm me;*j*
  my dignity is driven away as by the wind,
  my safety vanishes like a cloud.*k*

¹⁶"And now my life ebbs away;*l*
  days of suffering grip me.
¹⁷Night pierces my bones;
  my gnawing pains never rest.
¹⁸In his great power ˻God˼ becomes like clothing to me*c*;
  he binds me like the neck of my garment.
¹⁹He throws me into the mud,*m*
  and I am reduced to dust and ashes.

²⁰"I cry out to you, O God, but you do not answer;*n*
  I stand up, but you merely look at me.
²¹You turn on me ruthlessly;*o*
  with the might of your hand*p* you attack me.*q*
²²You snatch me up and drive me before the wind;*r*
  you toss me about in the storm.*s*
²³I know you will bring me down to death,*t*
  to the place appointed for all the living.*u*

²⁴"Surely no one lays a hand on a broken man
  when he cries for help in his distress.*v*

a 12 The meaning of the Hebrew for this word is uncertain.   *b* 13 Or *me. / 'No one can help him,' ˻they say˼.*   *c* 18 Hebrew; Septuagint *˻God˼ grasps my clothing*

²⁵Have I not wept for those in trouble?
  Has not my soul grieved for the poor?^a
²⁶Yet when I hoped for good, evil came;
  when I looked for light, then came darkness.^b
²⁷The churning inside me never stops;^c
  days of suffering confront me.
²⁸I go about blackened,^d but not by the sun;
  I stand up in the assembly and cry for help.^e
²⁹I have become a brother of jackals,^f
  a companion of owls.^g
³⁰My skin grows black and peels;^h
  my body burns with fever.ⁱ
³¹My harp is tuned to mourning,^j
  and my flute to the sound of wailing.

Chapter 31 Theme

31 "I made a covenant with my eyes
  not to look lustfully at a girl.^k
²For what is man's lot from God above,
  his heritage from the Almighty on high?^l
³Is it not ruin^m for the wicked,
  disaster for those who do wrong?ⁿ
⁴Does he not see my ways^o
  and count my every step?^p

⁵"If I have walked in falsehood
  or my foot has hurried after deceit^q—
⁶let God weigh me in honest scales^r
  and he will know that I am blameless—
⁷if my steps have turned from the path,^s
  if my heart has been led by my eyes,
  or if my hands^t have been defiled,
⁸then may others eat what I have sown,^u
  and may my crops be uprooted.^v

⁹"If my heart has been enticed^w by a woman,
  or if I have lurked at my neighbor's door,
¹⁰then may my wife grind another man's grain,
  and may other men sleep with her.^x
¹¹For that would have been shameful,
  a sin to be judged.^y
¹²It is a fire^z that burns to Destruction^a;^a
  it would have uprooted my harvest.^b

^a12 Hebrew *Abaddon*

Cross references

30:25
^aJob 24:4;
Ps 35:13-14;
Ro 12:15

30:26
^bJob 3:25-26;
19:8; Jer 8:15

30:27
^cLa 2:11

30:28
^dPs 38:6; 42:9;
43:2
^eJob 19:7

30:29
^fPs 44:19
^gPs 102:6;
Mic 1:8

30:30
^hLa 4:8
ⁱPs 102:3

30:31
^jIsa 24:8

31:1
^kMt 5:28

31:2
^lJob 20:29

31:3
^mJob 21:30
ⁿJob 34:22

31:4
^o2Ch 16:9
^pPr 5:21

31:5
^qMic 2:11

31:6
^rJob 6:2; 27:5-6

31:7
^sJob 23:11
^tJob 9:30

31:8
^uLev 26:16;
Job 20:18
^vMic 6:15

31:9
^wJob 24:15

31:10
^xDt 28:30;
Jer 8:10

31:11
^yGe 38:24;
Lev 20:10;
Dt 22:22-24

31:12
^zJob 15:30
^aJob 26:6
^bJob 20:28

13"If I have denied justice to my menservants
        and maidservants
    when they had a grievance against me,a

31:15
b Job 10:3

14what will I do when God confronts me?
    What will I answer when called to account?
15Did not he who made me in the womb make them?
    Did not the same one form us both within
        our mothers?b

31:16
c Job 5:16; 20:19
d Job 22:9

16"If I have denied the desires of the poorc
    or let the eyes of the widowd grow weary,

31:17
e Job 22:7; 29:12

17if I have kept my bread to myself,
    not sharing it with the fatherlesse—

31:19
f Job 22:6
g Job 24:4

18but from my youth I reared him as would a father,
    and from my birth I guided the widow—
19if I have seen anyone perishing for lack of clothing, f
    or a needyg man without a garment,

31:21
h Job 22:9

20and his heart did not bless me
    for warming him with the fleece from my sheep,
21if I have raised my hand against the fatherless,h
    knowing that I had influence in court,

31:22
i Job 38:15

22then let my arm fall from the shoulder,
    let it be broken off at the joint.i

31:23
j Job 13:11

23For I dreaded destruction from God,
    and for fear of his splendorj I could not do
        such things.

31:24
k Job 22:25
l Mt 6:24;
Mk 10:24

24"If I have put my trust in goldk
    or said to pure gold, 'You are my security,'l

31:25
m Ps 62:10

25if I have rejoiced over my great wealth,m
    the fortune my hands had gained,

31:26
n Eze 8:16

26if I have regarded the sunn in its radiance
    or the moon moving in splendor,
27so that my heart was secretly enticed
    and my hand offered them a kiss of homage,

31:28
o Dt 17:2-7

28then these also would be sins to be judged,o
    for I would have been unfaithful to God on high.

31:29
p Ob 12
q Pr 17:5;
24:17-18

29"If I have rejoiced at my enemy's misfortunep
    or gloated over the trouble that came to himq—
30I have not allowed my mouth to sin
    by invoking a curse against his life—

31:31
r Job 22:7

31if the men of my household have never said,
    'Who has not had his fill of Job's meat?'r—

31:32
s Ge 19:2-3;
Ro 12:13

32but no stranger had to spend the night in the street,
    for my door was always open to the travelers—

³³if I have concealed*a* my sin as men do,^a
    by hiding*b* my guilt in my heart
³⁴because I so feared the crowd*c*
    and so dreaded the contempt of the clans
    that I kept silent and would not go outside

³⁵("Oh, that I had someone to hear me!*d*
    I sign now my defense—let the Almighty answer me;
    let my accuser*e* put his indictment in writing.
³⁶Surely I would wear it on my shoulder,
    I would put it on like a crown.
³⁷I would give him an account of my every step;
    like a prince*f* I would approach him.)—

³⁸"if my land cries out against me*g*
    and all its furrows are wet with tears,
³⁹if I have devoured its yield without payment*h*
    or broken the spirit of its tenants,*i*
⁴⁰then let briers*j* come up instead of wheat
    and weeds instead of barley."

The words of Job are ended.

Chapter 32 Theme

32 So these three men stopped answering Job, because he was righteous in his own eyes.*k* ²But Elihu son of Barakel the Buzite,*l* of the family of Ram, became very angry with Job for justifying himself rather than God.*m* ³He was also angry with the three friends, because they had found no way to refute Job, and yet had condemned him.*b* ⁴Now Elihu had waited before speaking to Job because they were older than he. ⁵But when he saw that the three men had nothing more to say, his anger was aroused.

⁶So Elihu son of Barakel the Buzite said:

"I am young in years,
    and you are old;*n*
that is why I was fearful,
    not daring to tell you what I know.
⁷I thought, 'Age should speak;
    advanced years should teach wisdom.'
⁸But it is the spirit*c* in a man,
    the breath of the Almighty,*o* that gives him
      understanding.*p*
⁹It is not only the old*d* who are wise,*q*
    not only the aged who understand what is right.

31:33
a Pr 28:13
b Ge 3:8

31:34
c Ex 23:2

31:35
d Job 19:7; 30:28
e Job 27:7; 35:14

31:37
f Job 1:3; 29:25

31:38
g Ge 4:10

31:39
h 1Ki 21:19
i Lev 19:13;
Jas 5:4

31:40
j Ge 3:18

32:1
k Job 10:7; 33:9

32:2
l Ge 22:21
m Job 27:5;
30:21

32:6
n Job 15:10

32:8
o Job 27:3; 33:4
p Pr 2:6

32:9
q 1Co 1:26

a 33 Or *as Adam did* *b 3* Masoretic Text; an ancient Hebrew scribal tradition *Job, and so had condemned God* *c 8* Or *Spirit*; also in verse 18 *d 9* Or *many*; or *great*

32:13
a Jer 9:23

¹⁰"Therefore I say: Listen to me;
   I too will tell you what I know.
¹¹I waited while you spoke,
   I listened to your reasoning;
 while you were searching for words,

32:21
b Lev 19:15;
Job 13:10
c Mt 22:16

¹²   I gave you my full attention.
  But not one of you has proved Job wrong;
   none of you has answered his arguments.
¹³Do not say, 'We have found wisdom;*a*
   let God refute him, not man.'
¹⁴But Job has not marshaled his words against me,
   and I will not answer him with your arguments.

33:1
d Job 13:6

¹⁵"They are dismayed and have no more to say;
   words have failed them.
¹⁶Must I wait, now that they are silent,
   now that they stand there with no reply?
¹⁷I too will have my say;
   I too will tell what I know.

33:3
e Job 6:28; 27:4;
36:4

¹⁸For I am full of words,
   and the spirit within me compels me;
¹⁹inside I am like bottled-up wine,
   like new wineskins ready to burst.
²⁰I must speak and find relief;
   I must open my lips and reply.

33:4
f Ge 2:7;
Job 10:3
g Job 27:3

²¹I will show partiality*b* to no one,*c*
   nor will I flatter any man;
²²for if I were skilled in flattery,
   my Maker would soon take me away.

Chapter 33 Theme

33:5
h ver 32
i Job 13:18

33 "But now, Job, listen to my words;
   pay attention to everything I say.*d*
²I am about to open my mouth;
   my words are on the tip of my tongue.
³My words come from an upright heart;
   my lips sincerely speak what I know.*e*

33:6
j Job 4:19

⁴The Spirit of God has made me;*f*
   the breath of the Almighty*g* gives me life.
⁵Answer me*h* then, if you can;
   prepare*i* yourself and confront me.
⁶I am just like you before God;
   I too have been taken from clay.*j*

33:7
k Job 9:34;
13:21; 2Co 2:4

⁷No fear of me should alarm you,
   nor should my hand be heavy upon you.*k*

8"But you have said in my hearing—
    I heard the very words—
9'I am pure^a and without sin;^b
    I am clean and free from guilt.
10Yet God has found fault with me;
    he considers me his enemy.^c
11He fastens my feet in shackles;^d
    he keeps close watch on all my paths.'^e

12"But I tell you, in this you are not right,
    for God is greater than man.^f
13Why do you complain to him^g
    that he answers none of man's words^a?
14For God does speak^h—now one way, now another—
    though man may not perceive it.
15In a dream,ⁱ in a vision of the night,
    when deep sleep falls on men
    as they slumber in their beds,
16he may speak^j in their ears
    and terrify them with warnings,
17to turn man from wrongdoing
    and keep him from pride,
18to preserve his soul from the pit,^{bk}
    his life from perishing by the sword.^{cl}
19Or a man may be chastened on a bed of pain
    with constant distress in his bones,^m
20so that his very being finds foodⁿ repulsive
    and his soul loathes the choicest meal.^o
21His flesh wastes away to nothing,
    and his bones, once hidden, now stick out.^p
22His soul draws near to the pit,^d
    and his life to the messengers of death.^{eq}

23"Yet if there is an angel on his side
    as a mediator, one out of a thousand,
    to tell a man what is right for him,^r
24to be gracious to him and say,
    'Spare him from going down to the pit^f;^s
    I have found a ransom for him'—
25then his flesh is renewed like a child's;
    it is restored as in the days of his youth.^t
26He prays to God and finds favor with him,^u
    he sees God's face and shouts for joy;^v
    he is restored by God to his righteous state.^w

---

^a13 Or that he does not answer for any of his actions   ^b18 Or preserve him from the grave
^c18 Or from crossing the River   ^d22 Or He draws near to the grave   ^e22 Or to the dead
^f24 Or grave

33:9
^aJob 10:7
^bJob 13:23;
16:17

33:10
^cJob 13:24

33:11
^dJob 13:27
^eJob 14:16

33:12
^fEcc 7:20

33:13
^gJob 40:2;
Isa 45:9

33:14
^hPs 62:11

33:15
ⁱJob 4:13

33:16
^jJob 36:10,15

33:18
^kver 22,24,
28,30
^lJob 15:22

33:19
^mJob 30:17

33:20
ⁿPs 107:18
^oJob 3:24; 6:6

33:21
^pJob 16:8; 19:20

33:22
^qPs 88:3

33:23
^rMic 6:8

33:24
^sIsa 38:17

33:25
^t2Ki 5:14

33:26
^uJob 34:28
^vJob 22:26
^wPs 50:15;
51:12

<table>
<tr><td>

33:27
a 2Sa 12:13
b Lk 15:21
c Ro 6:21

33:28
d Job 22:28

33:29
e 1Co 12:6;
Eph 1:11;
Php 2:13

33:30
f Ps 56:13

33:33
g Ps 34:11

34:3
h Job 12:11

34:4
i 1Th 5:21

34:5
j Job 33:9
k Job 27:2

34:6
l Job 6:4

34:7
m Job 15:16

34:8
n Job 22:15;
Ps 50:18

34:9
o Job 21:15; 35:3

34:10
p Ge 18:25
q Dt 32:4;
Job 8:3;
Ro 9:14

34:11
r Ps 62:12;
Mt 16:27;
Ro 2:6;
2 Co 5:10
s Jer 32:19;
Eze 33:20

</td><td>

²⁷Then he comes to men and says,
  'I sinned,*a* and perverted what was right,*b*
  but I did not get what I deserved.*c*
²⁸He redeemed my soul from going down to the pit,*a*
  and I will live to enjoy the light.'*d*

²⁹"God does all these things to a man*e*—
  twice, even three times—
³⁰to turn back his soul from the pit,*b*
  that the light of life *f* may shine on him.

³¹"Pay attention, Job, and listen to me;
  be silent, and I will speak.
³²If you have anything to say, answer me;
  speak up, for I want you to be cleared.
³³But if not, then listen to me;
  be silent, and I will teach you wisdom.*g*"

Chapter 34 Theme

34 Then Elihu said:
²"Hear my words, you wise men;
  listen to me, you men of learning.
³For the ear tests words
  as the tongue tastes food.*h*
⁴Let us discern for ourselves what is right;
  let us learn together what is good.*i*

⁵"Job says, 'I am innocent,*j*
  but God denies me justice.*k*
⁶Although I am right,
  I am considered a liar;
 although I am guiltless,
  his arrow inflicts an incurable wound.'*l*
⁷What man is like Job,
  who drinks scorn like water?*m*
⁸He keeps company with evildoers;
  he associates with wicked men.*n*
⁹For he says, 'It profits a man nothing
  when he tries to please God.'*o*

¹⁰"So listen to me, you men of understanding.
  Far be it from God to do evil,*p*
  from the Almighty to do wrong.*q*
¹¹He repays a man for what he has done;*r*
  he brings upon him what his conduct deserves.*s*

</td></tr>
</table>

a 28 Or *redeemed me from going down to the grave*   *b* 30 Or *turn him back from the grave*

¹²It is unthinkable that God would do wrong,
    that the Almighty would pervert justice.*ᵃ*
¹³Who appointed him over the earth?
    Who put him in charge of the whole world?*ᵇ*
¹⁴If it were his intention
    and he withdrew his spiritᵃ and breath,*ᶜ*
¹⁵all mankind would perish together
    and man would return to the dust.*ᵈ*

¹⁶"If you have understanding, hear this;
    listen to what I say.
¹⁷Can he who hates justice govern?*ᵉ*
    Will you condemn the just and mighty One?*ᶠ*
¹⁸Is he not the One who says to kings, 'You are worthless,'
    and to nobles, 'You are wicked,'*ᵍ*
¹⁹who shows no partiality*ʰ* to princes
    and does not favor the rich over the poor,*ⁱ*
    for they are all the work of his hands?*ʲ*
²⁰They die in an instant, in the middle of the night;*ᵏ*
    the people are shaken and they pass away;
    the mighty are removed without human hand.*ˡ*

²¹"His eyes are on the ways of men;
    he sees their every step.*ᵐ*
²²There is no dark place,*ⁿ* no deep shadow,*ᵒ*
    where evildoers can hide.
²³God has no need to examine men further,
    that they should come before him for judgment.*ᵖ*
²⁴Without inquiry he shatters the mighty*�q*
    and sets up others in their place.*ʳ*
²⁵Because he takes note of their deeds,
    he overthrows them in the night and they are crushed.
²⁶He punishes them for their wickedness
    where everyone can see them,
²⁷because they turned from following him*ˢ*
    and had no regard for any of his ways.*ᵗ*
²⁸They caused the cry of the poor to come before him,
    so that he heard the cry of the needy.*ᵘ*
²⁹But if he remains silent, who can condemn him?
    If he hides his face, who can see him?
  Yet he is over man and nation alike,
³⁰ to keep a godless man from ruling,
    from laying snares for the people.*ᵛ*

³¹"Suppose a man says to God,
    'I am guilty but will offend no more.

ᵃ 14 Or *Spirit*

34:12
ᵃ Job 8:3

34:13
ᵇ Job 38:4,6

34:14
ᶜ Ps 104:29

34:15
ᵈ Ge 3:19;
Job 9:22

34:17
ᵉ 2Sa 23:3-4
ᶠ Job 40:8

34:18
ᵍ Ex 22:28

34:19
ʰ Dt 10:17;
Ac 10:34
ⁱ Lev 19:15
ʲ Job 10:3

34:20
ᵏ Ex 12:29
ˡ Job 12:19

34:21
ᵐ Job 31:4;
Pr 15:3

34:22
ⁿ Ps 139:12
ᵒ Am 9:2-3

34:23
ᵖ Job 11:11

34:24
q Job 12:19
ʳ Da 2:21

34:27
ˢ Ps 28:5;
Isa 5:12
ᵗ 1Sa 15:11

34:28
ᵘ Ex 22:23;
Job 35:9;
Jas 5:4

34:30
ᵛ Pr 29:2-12

34:32
a Job 35:11;
Ps 25:4
b Job 33:27

34:33
c Job 41:11

34:35
d Job 35:16; 38:2

34:36
e Job 22:15

34:37
f Job 27:23
g Job 23:2

35:3
h Job 9:29-31;
34:9

35:5
i Ge 15:5
j Job 22:12

35:6
k Pr 8:36

35:7
l Ro 11:35
m Pr 9:12
n Job 22:2-3;
Lk 17:10

35:9
o Ex 2:23
p Job 12:19

35:10
q Job 27:10;
Isa 51:13
r Ps 42:8; 149:5;
Ac 16:25

35:11
s Ps 94:12

35:12
t Pr 1:28

35:13
u Job 27:9;
Pr 15:29;
Isa 1:15;
Jer 11:11

³²Teach me what I cannot see;^a
 if I have done wrong, I will not do so again.'^b
³³Should God then reward you on your terms,
 when you refuse to repent?^c
 You must decide, not I;
 so tell me what you know.

³⁴"Men of understanding declare,
 wise men who hear me say to me,
³⁵'Job speaks without knowledge;^d
 his words lack insight.'
³⁶Oh, that Job might be tested to the utmost
 for answering like a wicked man!^e
³⁷To his sin he adds rebellion;
 scornfully he claps his hands^f among us
 and multiplies his words against God."^g

Chapter 35 Theme _____

35 Then Elihu said:

²"Do you think this is just?
 You say, 'I will be cleared by God.^a'
³Yet you ask him, 'What profit is it to me,^b
 and what do I gain by not sinning?'^h

⁴"I would like to reply to you
 and to your friends with you.
⁵Look up at the heavensⁱ and see;
 gaze at the clouds so high above you.^j
⁶If you sin, how does that affect him?
 If your sins are many, what does that do to him?^k
⁷If you are righteous, what do you give to him,^l
 or what does he receive^m from your hand?ⁿ
⁸Your wickedness affects only a man like yourself,
 and your righteousness only the sons of men.

⁹"Men cry out^o under a load of oppression;
 they plead for relief from the arm of the powerful.^p
¹⁰But no one says, 'Where is God my Maker,^q
 who gives songs in the night,^r
¹¹who teaches^s more to us than to^c the beasts of the earth
 and makes us wiser than^d the birds of the air?'
¹²He does not answer^t when men cry out
 because of the arrogance of the wicked.
¹³Indeed, God does not listen to their empty plea;
 the Almighty pays no attention to it.^u

a 2 Or *My righteousness is more than God's*   b 3 Or *you*   c 11 Or *teaches us by*   d 11 Or *us wise by*

¹⁴How much less, then, will he listen
  when you say that you do not see him,^a
that your case^b is before him
  and you must wait for him,
¹⁵and further, that his anger never punishes
  and he does not take the least notice of wickedness.^a
¹⁶So Job opens his mouth with empty talk;
  without knowledge he multiplies words."^c

Chapter 36 Theme

36 Elihu continued:
²"Bear with me a little longer and I will show you
  that there is more to be said in God's behalf.
³I get my knowledge from afar;
  I will ascribe justice to my Maker.^d
⁴Be assured that my words are not false;^e
  one perfect in knowledge^f is with you.

⁵"God is mighty, but does not despise men;^g
  he is mighty, and firm in his purpose.^h
⁶He does not keep the wicked aliveⁱ
  but gives the afflicted their rights.^j
⁷He does not take his eyes off the righteous;^k
  he enthrones them with kings^l
  and exalts them forever.
⁸But if men are bound in chains,^m
  held fast by cords of affliction,
⁹he tells them what they have done—
  that they have sinned arrogantly.ⁿ
¹⁰He makes them listen^o to correction
  and commands them to repent of their evil.^p
¹¹If they obey and serve him,^q
  they will spend the rest of their days in prosperity
  and their years in contentment.
¹²But if they do not listen,
  they will perish by the sword^{b r}
  and die without knowledge.^s

¹³"The godless in heart^t harbor resentment;
  even when he fetters them, they do not cry for help.
¹⁴They die in their youth,
  among male prostitutes of the shrines.^u

---

^a15 Symmachus, Theodotion and Vulgate; the meaning of the Hebrew for this word is uncertain. ^b12 Or *will cross the River*

Cross references
35:14 ^aJob 9:11 ^bPs 37:6
35:16 ^cJob 34:35,37
36:3 ^dJob 8:3; 37:23
36:4 ^eJob 33:3 ^fJob 37:5, 16,23
36:5 ^gPs 22:24 ^hJob 12:13
36:6 ⁱJob 8:22 ^jJob 5:15
36:7 ^kPs 33:18 ^lPs 113:8
36:8 ^mPs 107:10,14
36:9 ⁿJob 15:25
36:10 ^oJob 33:16 ^p2Ki 17:13
36:11 ^qIsa 1:19
36:12 ^rJob 15:22 ^sJob 4:21
36:13 ^tRo 2:5
36:14 ^uDt 23:17

36:16
a Hos 2:14
b Ps 23:5

36:17
c Job 22:11

36:18
d Job 34:33

36:20
e Job 34:20,25

36:21
f Ps 66:18
g Heb 11:25

36:22
h Isa 40:13;
1Co 2:16

36:23
i Job 34:13
j Job 8:3

36:24
k Ps 92:5; 138:5
l Ps 59:16;
Rev 15:3

36:26
m 1Co 13:12
n Job 10:5;
Ps 90:2; 102:24;
Heb 1:12

36:27
o Job 38:28;
Ps 147:8

36:28
p Job 5:10

36:29
q Job 26:14;
37:16

36:31
r Job 37:13
s Ps 136:25;
Ac 14:17

36:32
t Job 37:12,15

¹⁵But those who suffer he delivers in their suffering;
he speaks to them in their affliction.

¹⁶"He is wooing^a you from the jaws of distress
to a spacious place free from restriction,
to the comfort of your table^b laden with choice food.
¹⁷But now you are laden with the judgment due
the wicked;
judgment and justice have taken hold of you.^c
¹⁸Be careful that no one entices you by riches;
do not let a large bribe turn you aside.^d
¹⁹Would your wealth
or even all your mighty efforts
sustain you so you would not be in distress?
²⁰Do not long for the night,^e
to drag people away from their homes.^a
²¹Beware of turning to evil,^f
which you seem to prefer to affliction.^g

²²"God is exalted in his power.
Who is a teacher like him?^h
²³Who has prescribed his ways for him,ⁱ
or said to him, 'You have done wrong'?^j
²⁴Remember to extol his work,^k
which men have praised in song.^l
²⁵All mankind has seen it;
men gaze on it from afar.
²⁶How great is God—beyond our understanding!^m
The number of his years is past finding out.ⁿ

²⁷"He draws up the drops of water,
which distill as rain to the streams^{b;o}
²⁸the clouds pour down their moisture
and abundant showers fall on mankind.^p
²⁹Who can understand how he spreads out the clouds,
how he thunders from his pavilion?^q
³⁰See how he scatters his lightning about him,
bathing the depths of the sea.
³¹This is the way he governs^c the nations^r
and provides food in abundance.^s
³²He fills his hands with lightning
and commands it to strike its mark.^t
³³His thunder announces the coming storm;
even the cattle make known its approach.^d

a 20 The meaning of the Hebrew for verses 18-20 is uncertain.   b 27 Or distill from the mist as rain   c 31 Or nourishes   d 33 Or announces his coming— / the One zealous against evil

Chapter 37 Theme

37 ¹"At this my heart pounds
   and leaps from its place.
²Listen! Listen to the roar of his voice,
   to the rumbling that comes from his mouth.ᵃ
³He unleashes his lightning beneath the whole heaven
   and sends it to the ends of the earth.
⁴After that comes the sound of his roar;
   he thunders with his majestic voice.
  When his voice resounds,
   he holds nothing back.
⁵God's voice thunders in marvelous ways;
   he does great things beyond our understanding.ᵇ
⁶He says to the snow,ᶜ 'Fall on the earth,'
   and to the rain shower, 'Be a mighty downpour.'ᵈ
⁷So that all men he has made may know his work,
   he stops every man from his labor.ᵃ ᵉ
⁸The animals take cover;
   they remain in their dens.ᶠ
⁹The tempest comes out from its chamber,
   the cold from the driving winds.
¹⁰The breath of God produces ice,
   and the broad waters become frozen.ᵍ
¹¹He loads the clouds with moisture;
   he scatters his lightning through them.ʰ
¹²At his direction they swirl around
   over the face of the whole earth
   to do whatever he commands them.ⁱ
¹³He brings the clouds to punish men,ʲ
   or to water his earthᵇ and show his love.ᵏ

¹⁴"Listen to this, Job;
   stop and consider God's wonders.
¹⁵Do you know how God controls the clouds
   and makes his lightning flash?
¹⁶Do you know how the clouds hang poised,
   those wonders of him who is perfect in knowledge?ˡ
¹⁷You who swelter in your clothes
   when the land lies hushed under the south wind,
¹⁸can you join him in spreading out the skies,ᵐ
   hard as a mirror of cast bronze?

¹⁹"Tell us what we should say to him;
   we cannot draw up our case because of our darkness.

a7 Or / he fills all men with fear by his power   b13 Or to favor them

Side references:
37:2 ᵃPs 29:3-9
37:5 ᵇJob 5:9
37:6 ᶜJob 38:22; ᵈJob 36:27
37:7 ᵉJob 12:14
37:8 ᶠJob 38:40; Ps 104:22
37:10 ᵍJob 38:29-30; Ps 147:17
37:11 ʰJob 36:27,29
37:12 ⁱPs 148:8
37:13 ʲ1Sa 12:17; ᵏEx 9:18; 1Ki 18:45; Job 38:27
37:16 ˡJob 36:4
37:18 ᵐJob 9:8; Ps 104:2; Isa 44:24

²⁰Should he be told that I want to speak?
Would any man ask to be swallowed up?
²¹Now no one can look at the sun,
bright as it is in the skies
after the wind has swept them clean.
²²Out of the north he comes in golden splendor;
God comes in awesome majesty.
²³The Almighty is beyond our reach and exalted
in power;^a
in his justice^b and great righteousness, he does
not oppress.^c
²⁴Therefore, men revere him,^d
for does he not have regard for all the wise^e in heart?^a"

Chapter 38 Theme

38 Then the LORD answered Job out of the storm.^f He said:

²"Who is this that darkens my counsel
with words without knowledge?^g
³Brace yourself like a man;
I will question you,
and you shall answer me.^h

⁴"Where were you when I laid the earth's foundation?ⁱ
Tell me, if you understand.
⁵Who marked off its dimensions?^j Surely you know!
Who stretched a measuring line across it?
⁶On what were its footings set,
or who laid its cornerstone^k—
⁷while the morning stars sang together
and all the angels^b shouted for joy?

⁸"Who shut up the sea behind doors^l
when it burst forth from the womb,^m
⁹when I made the clouds its garment
and wrapped it in thick darkness,
¹⁰when I fixed limits for itⁿ
and set its doors and bars in place,^o
¹¹when I said, 'This far you may come and no farther;
here is where your proud waves halt'?^p

¹²"Have you ever given orders to the morning,
or shown the dawn its place,
¹³that it might take the earth by the edges
and shake the wicked^q out of it?

37:23 ^aJob 9:4; 36:4; 1Ti 6:16 ^bJob 8:3 ^cIsa 63:9; Eze 18:23,32

37:24 ^dMt 10:28 ^eMt 11:25

38:1 ^fJob 40:6

38:2 ^gJob 35:16; 42:3; 1Ti 1:7

38:3 ^hJob 40:7

38:4 ⁱPs 104:5; Pr 8:29

38:5 ^jPr 8:29; Isa 40:12

38:6 ^kJob 26:7

38:8 ^lJer 5:22 ^mGe 1:9-10

38:10 ⁿPs 33:7; 104:9 ^oJob 26:10

38:11 ^pPs 89:9

38:13 ^qPs 104:35

a 24 Or for he does not have regard for any who think they are wise. b 7 Hebrew the sons of God

¹⁴The earth takes shape like clay under a seal;
  its features stand out like those of a garment.
¹⁵The wicked are denied their light,^a
  and their upraised arm is broken.^b

¹⁶"Have you journeyed to the springs of the sea
  or walked in the recesses of the deep?^c
¹⁷Have the gates of death^d been shown to you?
  Have you seen the gates of the shadow of death^a?
¹⁸Have you comprehended the vast expanses of the earth?^e
  Tell me, if you know all this.

¹⁹"What is the way to the abode of light?
  And where does darkness reside?
²⁰Can you take them to their places?
  Do you know the paths^f to their dwellings?
²¹Surely you know, for you were already born!^g
  You have lived so many years!

²²"Have you entered the storehouses of the snow^h
  or seen the storehouses of the hail,
²³which I reserve for times of trouble,ⁱ
  for days of war and battle?^j
²⁴What is the way to the place where the lightning
    is dispersed,
  or the place where the east winds are scattered over
    the earth?
²⁵Who cuts a channel for the torrents of rain,
  and a path for the thunderstorm,^k
²⁶to water^l a land where no man lives,
  a desert with no one in it,
²⁷to satisfy a desolate wasteland
  and make it sprout with grass?^m
²⁸Does the rain have a father?ⁿ
  Who fathers the drops of dew?
²⁹From whose womb comes the ice?
  Who gives birth to the frost from the heavens^o
³⁰when the waters become hard as stone,
  when the surface of the deep is frozen?^p

³¹"Can you bind the beautiful^b Pleiades?
  Can you loose the cords of Orion?^q
³²Can you bring forth the constellations in their seasons^c
  or lead out the Bear^d with its cubs?

---

^a17 Or *gates of deep shadows*   ^b31 Or *the twinkling;* or *the chains of the*   ^c32 Or *the morning star in its season*   ^d32 Or *out Leo*

Cross references:
38:15 ^aJob 18:5; ^bPs 10:15
38:16 ^cPs 77:19
38:17 ^dPs 9:13
38:18 ^eJob 28:24
38:20 ^fJob 26:10
38:21 ^gJob 15:7
38:22 ^hJob 37:6
38:23 ⁱIsa 30:30; Eze 13:11; ^jEx 9:18; Jos 10:11; Rev 16:21
38:25 ^kJob 28:26
38:26 ^lJob 36:27
38:27 ^mPs 104:14; 107:35
38:28 ⁿPs 147:8; Jer 14:22
38:29 ^oPs 147:16-17
38:30 ^pJob 37:10
38:31 ^qJob 9:9; Am 5:8

38:33
*a*Ps 148:6;
Jer 31:36

³³Do you know the laws^{*a*} of the heavens?
　　Can you set up ⌊God's^{*a*}⌋ dominion over the earth?

³⁴"Can you raise your voice to the clouds
　　and cover yourself with a flood of water?^{*b*}

38:34
*b*Job 22:11;
36:27-28

³⁵Do you send the lightning bolts on their way?^{*c*}
　　Do they report to you, 'Here we are'?
³⁶Who endowed the heart^{*b*} with wisdom^{*d*}
　　or gave understanding^{*e*} to the mind^{*b*}?

38:35
*c*Job 36:32; 37:3

³⁷Who has the wisdom to count the clouds?
　　Who can tip over the water jars of the heavens
³⁸when the dust becomes hard
　　and the clods of earth stick together?

38:36
*d*Job 9:4
*e*Job 32:8;
Ps 51:6;
Ecc 2:26

³⁹"Do you hunt the prey for the lioness
　　and satisfy the hunger of the lions^{*f*}
⁴⁰when they crouch in their dens^{*g*}
　　or lie in wait in a thicket?

38:39
*f*Ps 104:21

⁴¹Who provides food for the raven^{*h*}
　　when its young cry out to God
　　and wander about for lack of food?^{*i*}

38:40
*g*Job 37:8

Chapter 39 Theme _____

39
"Do you know when the mountain goats^{*j*}
　　　　give birth?
　　Do you watch when the doe bears her fawn?
²Do you count the months till they bear?
　　Do you know the time they give birth?
³They crouch down and bring forth their young;
　　their labor pains are ended.
⁴Their young thrive and grow strong in the wilds;
　　they leave and do not return.

38:41
*h*Lk 12:24
*i*Ps 147:9;
Mt 6:26

39:1
*j*Dt 14:5

⁵"Who let the wild donkey^{*k*} go free?
　　Who untied his ropes?
⁶I gave him the wasteland^{*l*} as his home,
　　the salt flats as his habitat.^{*m*}
⁷He laughs at the commotion in the town;
　　he does not hear a driver's shout.^{*n*}
⁸He ranges the hills for his pasture
　　and searches for any green thing.

39:5
*k*Job 6:5; 11:12;
24:5

39:6
*l*Job 24:5;
Ps 107:34;
Jer 2:24
*m*Hos 8:9

⁹"Will the wild ox^{*o*} consent to serve you?
　　Will he stay by your manger at night?
¹⁰Can you hold him to the furrow with a harness?
　　Will he till the valleys behind you?

39:7
*n*Job 3:18

39:9
*o*Nu 23:22;
Dt 33:17

a 33 Or *his*; or *their*　　*b* 36 The meaning of the Hebrew for this word is uncertain.

¹¹Will you rely on him for his great strength?
　　Will you leave your heavy work to him?
¹²Can you trust him to bring in your grain
　　and gather it to your threshing floor?

¹³"The wings of the ostrich flap joyfully,
　　but they cannot compare with the pinions and
　　　　feathers of the stork.
¹⁴She lays her eggs on the ground
　　and lets them warm in the sand,
¹⁵unmindful that a foot may crush them,
　　that some wild animal may trample them.
¹⁶She treats her young harshly,^a as if they were not hers;
　　she cares not that her labor was in vain,
¹⁷for God did not endow her with wisdom
　　or give her a share of good sense.^b
¹⁸Yet when she spreads her feathers to run,
　　she laughs at horse and rider.

¹⁹"Do you give the horse his strength
　　or clothe his neck with a flowing mane?
²⁰Do you make him leap like a locust,^c
　　striking terror with his proud snorting?^d
²¹He paws fiercely, rejoicing in his strength,
　　and charges into the fray.^e
²²He laughs at fear, afraid of nothing;
　　he does not shy away from the sword.
²³The quiver rattles against his side,
　　along with the flashing spear and lance.
²⁴In frenzied excitement he eats up the ground;
　　he cannot stand still when the trumpet sounds.^f
²⁵At the blast of the trumpet^g he snorts, 'Aha!'
　　He catches the scent of battle from afar,
　　the shout of commanders and the battle cry.^h

²⁶"Does the hawk take flight by your wisdom
　　and spread his wings toward the south?
²⁷Does the eagle soar at your command
　　and build his nest on high?ⁱ
²⁸He dwells on a cliff and stays there at night;
　　a rocky crag is his stronghold.
²⁹From there he seeks out his food;^j
　　his eyes detect it from afar.
³⁰His young ones feast on blood,
　　and where the slain are, there is he."^k

39:16
^aLa 4:3

39:17
^bJob 35:11

39:20
^cJoel 2:4-5
^dJer 8:16

39:21
^eJer 8:6

39:24
^fJer 4:5,19;
Eze 7:14;
Am 3:6

39:25
^gJos 6:5
^hAm 1:14; 2:2

39:27
ⁱJer 49:16; Ob 4

39:29
^jJob 9:26

39:30
^kMt 24:28;
Lk 17:37

Chapter 40 Theme

40 The LORD said to Job:[a]

²"Will the one who contends with the Almighty
    correct him?
    Let him who accuses God answer him!"

³Then Job answered the LORD:

⁴"I am unworthy[b]—how can I reply to you?
    I put my hand over my mouth.[c]

⁵I spoke once, but I have no answer[d]—
    twice, but I will say no more."[e]

⁶Then the LORD spoke to Job out of the storm:[f]

⁷"Brace yourself like a man;
    I will question you,
    and you shall answer me.[g]

⁸"Would you discredit my justice?[h]
    Would you condemn me to justify yourself?

⁹Do you have an arm like God's,[i]
    and can your voice thunder like his?[j]

¹⁰Then adorn yourself with glory and splendor,
    and clothe yourself in honor and majesty.[k]

¹¹Unleash the fury of your wrath,[l]
    look at every proud man and bring him low,[m]

¹²look at every proud man and humble him,[n]
    crush[o] the wicked where they stand.

¹³Bury them all in the dust together;
    shroud their faces in the grave.

¹⁴Then I myself will admit to you
    that your own right hand can save you.[p]

¹⁵"Look at the behemoth,[a]
    which I made along with you
    and which feeds on grass like an ox.

¹⁶What strength he has in his loins,
    what power in the muscles of his belly!

¹⁷His tail[b] sways like a cedar;
    the sinews of his thighs are close-knit.

¹⁸His bones are tubes of bronze,
    his limbs like rods of iron.

¹⁹He ranks first among the works of God,[q]
    yet his Maker can approach him with his sword.

a 15 Possibly the hippopotamus or the elephant   b 17 Possibly trunk

²⁰The hills bring him their produce,^a
>   and all the wild animals play^b nearby.
²¹Under the lotus plants he lies,
>   hidden among the reeds in the marsh.
²²The lotuses conceal him in their shadow;
>   the poplars by the stream^c surround him.
²³When the river rages, he is not alarmed;
>   he is secure, though the Jordan should surge against
>   his mouth.
²⁴Can anyone capture him by the eyes,^a
>   or trap him and pierce his nose?^d

Chapter 41 Theme

41 "Can you pull in the leviathan^{b e} with a fishhook
>   or tie down his tongue with a rope?
²Can you put a cord through his nose
>   or pierce his jaw with a hook?^f
³Will he keep begging you for mercy?
>   Will he speak to you with gentle words?
⁴Will he make an agreement with you
>   for you to take him as your slave for life?^g
⁵Can you make a pet of him like a bird
>   or put him on a leash for your girls?
⁶Will traders barter for him?
>   Will they divide him up among the merchants?
⁷Can you fill his hide with harpoons
>   or his head with fishing spears?
⁸If you lay a hand on him,
>   you will remember the struggle and never do it again!
⁹Any hope of subduing him is false;
>   the mere sight of him is overpowering.
¹⁰No one is fierce enough to rouse him.^h
>   Who then is able to stand against me?ⁱ
¹¹Who has a claim against me that I must pay?^j
>   Everything under heaven belongs to me.^k

¹²"I will not fail to speak of his limbs,
>   his strength and his graceful form.
¹³Who can strip off his outer coat?
>   Who would approach him with a bridle?
¹⁴Who dares open the doors of his mouth,
>   ringed about with his fearsome teeth?
¹⁵His back has^c rows of shields
>   tightly sealed together;

a 24 Or *by a water hole* b 1 Possibly the crocodile c 15 Or *His pride is his*

40:20
a Ps 104:14
b Ps 104:26

40:22
c Isa 44:4

40:24
d Job 41:2,7,26

41:1
e Job 3:8;
Ps 104:26;
Isa 27:1

41:2
f Isa 37:29

41:4
g Ex 21:6

41:10
h Job 3:8
i Jer 50:44

41:11
j Ro 11:35
k Ex 19:5;
Dt 10:14;
Ps 24:1; 50:12;
1Co 10:26

41:18
a Job 3:9

¹⁶each is so close to the next
    that no air can pass between.
¹⁷They are joined fast to one another;
    they cling together and cannot be parted.
¹⁸His snorting throws out flashes of light;
    his eyes are like the rays of dawn.^a
¹⁹Firebrands stream from his mouth;
    sparks of fire shoot out.

41:21
b Isa 40:7
c Ps 18:8

²⁰Smoke pours from his nostrils
    as from a boiling pot over a fire of reeds.
²¹His breath^b sets coals ablaze,
    and flames dart from his mouth.^c
²²Strength resides in his neck;
    dismay goes before him.

41:30
d Isa 41:15

²³The folds of his flesh are tightly joined;
    they are firm and immovable.
²⁴His chest is hard as rock,
    hard as a lower millstone.
²⁵When he rises up, the mighty are terrified;
    they retreat before his thrashing.
²⁶The sword that reaches him has no effect,
    nor does the spear or the dart or the javelin.

41:33
e Job 40:19

²⁷Iron he treats like straw
    and bronze like rotten wood.
²⁸Arrows do not make him flee;
    slingstones are like chaff to him.
²⁹A club seems to him but a piece of straw;
    he laughs at the rattling of the lance.

41:34
f Job 28:8

³⁰His undersides are jagged potsherds,
    leaving a trail in the mud like a threshing sledge.^d
³¹He makes the depths churn like a boiling caldron
    and stirs up the sea like a pot of ointment.
³²Behind him he leaves a glistening wake;
    one would think the deep had white hair.
³³Nothing on earth is his equal^e—
    a creature without fear.

42:2
g Ge 18:14;
Mt 19:26
h 2Ch 20:6

³⁴He looks down on all that are haughty;
    he is king over all that are proud.^f"

Chapter 42 Theme

42 Then Job replied to the LORD:

²"I know that you can do all things;^g
    no plan of yours can be thwarted.^h
³⌊You asked,⌋ 'Who is this that obscures my counsel
    without knowledge?'ⁱ

42:3
i Job 38:2

Surely I spoke of things I did not understand,
things too wonderful for me to know.*a*

4 ⌊"You said,⌋ 'Listen now, and I will speak;
I will question you,
and you shall answer me.'*b*
5 My ears had heard of you*c*
but now my eyes have seen you.*d*
6 Therefore I despise myself*e*
and repent in dust and ashes."*f*

7 After the LORD had said these things to Job, he said to Eliphaz the Temanite, "I am angry with you and your two friends,*g* because you have not spoken of me what is right, as my servant Job has. 8 So now take seven bulls and seven rams*h* and go to my servant Job and sacrifice a burnt offering*i* for yourselves. My servant Job will pray for you, and I will accept his prayer*j* and not deal with you according to your folly.*k* You have not spoken of me what is right, as my servant Job has." 9 So Eliphaz the Temanite, Bildad the Shuhite and Zophar the Naamathite did what the LORD told them; and the LORD accepted Job's prayer.

10 After Job had prayed for his friends, the LORD made him prosperous again*l* and gave him twice as much as he had before.*m* 11 All his brothers and sisters and everyone who had known him before*n* came and ate with him in his house. They comforted and consoled him over all the trouble the LORD had brought upon him, and each one gave him a piece of silver*a* and a gold ring.

12 The LORD blessed the latter part of Job's life more than the first. He had fourteen thousand sheep, six thousand camels, a thousand yoke of oxen and a thousand donkeys. 13 And he also had seven sons and three daughters. 14 The first daughter he named Jemimah, the second Keziah and the third Keren-Happuch. 15 Nowhere in all the land were there found women as beautiful as Job's daughters, and their father granted them an inheritance along with their brothers.

16 After this, Job lived a hundred and forty years; he saw his children and their children to the fourth generation. 17 And so he died, old and full of years.*o*

a 11 Hebrew ; a kesitah was a unit of money of unknown weight and value.

42:3
a Ps 40:5; 131:1;
139:6

42:4
b Job 38:3;
40:7

42:5
c Job 26:14;
Ro 10:17
d Jdg 13:22;
Isa 6:5;
Eph 1:17-18

42:6
e Job 40:4
f Ezr 9:6

42:7
g Job 32:3

42:8
h Nu 23:1,29
i Job 1:5
j Ge 20:17;
Jas 5:15-16;
1Jn 5:16
k Job 22:30

42:10
l Dt 30:3;
Ps 14:7
m Job 1:3;
Ps 85:1-3;
126:5-6

42:11
n Job 19:13

42:17
o Ge 15:15; 25:8

JOB OBSERVATIONS CHART

INSIGHTS REGARDING SATAN	INSIGHTS REGARDING JOB
Character	Character
Tactics	Relationship to God
Power	Relationship to His Friends

INSIGHTS REGARDING GOD	WHAT GOD SAYS REGARDING
His Character	Job
	Job's Friends
	INSIGHTS REGARDING GOD'S EXPECTATIONS OF MAN
His Ways	
His Power	
Over Satan	
	INSIGHTS INTO LIFE AND DEATH
Over Nature	
Over Man	

Lessons I Learned about Dealing with Those in Pain

Theme of Job:

SEGMENT DIVISIONS

			CHAPTER THEMES
		1	
		2	
		3	
		4	
		5	
		6	
		7	
		8	
		9	
		10	
		11	
		12	
		13	
		14	
		15	
		16	
		17	
		18	
		19	
		20	
		21	
		22	
		23	
		24	
		25	
		26	
		27	
		28	
		29	
		30	
		31	
		32	
		33	
		34	
		35	
		36	
		37	
		38	
		39	
		40	
		41	
		42	

Author:

Date:

Purpose:

Key Words:

PSALMS

$\mathcal{M}$an needs to communicate with God in prayer and in song. He needs to come before him and honestly present that which is on his heart—whether it be distress or joy, confusion or confidence.

Man needs to lift up his voice in worship, to speak to God and to others in psalms and hymns and spiritual songs, singing and making melody with his heart to the Lord (see Ephesians 5:19).

Thus the psalms—praises, prayers, and songs—are to be accompanied on stringed instruments. So David, writer of many psalms, appointed Levites over the service of song in the house of the Lord. They ministered with song before the tabernacle of the tent of meeting until Solomon built the house of the Lord in Jerusalem (see 1 Chronicles 6:31, 32).

Receiving worship is befitting to God alone. Psalms is a book of prayer and praise, written by men but inspired by God. "For from him and through him and to him are all things. To him be the glory forever! Amen" (Romans 11:36).

∾ THINGS TO DO

1. As you study Psalms, remember that the psalms are poetry whether they are prayers or songs. Hebrew poetry does not contain rhyme and meter. Rather, its distinctive feature is parallelism of some form, where one line relates to another in various ways. Usually the poetic lines are composed of two (or sometimes three) balanced segments in which the second is shorter than the first and repeats, contrasts, or completes the first segment.

The psalms vary in design. Nine are alphabetical, with each stanza beginning with the next letter from the Hebrew alphabet. The alphabetical psalms are 9, 10, 25, 34, 37, 111, 112, 119, and 145.

2. The majority of the psalms have a superscription at the beginning, which designates one or several things: the composer, the occasion of the psalm, who it is for, how it is to be accompanied, and what kind of psalm it is. If a psalm has a superscription, read it and consult the cross-references (if it is referenced). This will help put the psalm into context.

3. Watch for the theme of the psalm and how it is developed. Sometimes the theme will be stated at the very beginning of the psalm, while at other times the key thematic scheme will be found in the center of the psalm. Each will have a theme and will be developed in accordance with the author's design for the psalm.

   a. Some of the psalms give insights into the history of Israel, such as Psalm 78. Study these carefully. Note the events, God's intervention, and God's watchful care.

   b. If a psalm makes reference to a person or circumstance which is discussed in one of the historical books of the Bible, you might go back to that book and record the psalm that applies to that person or circumstance. For instance, in the margin of 2 Samuel 12, note "Psalm 51" as a cross-reference.

4. Key words bring out the theme of the psalm's song or prayer. Sometimes a key phrase will open and close the psalm. Watch for and mark these phrases. Also watch for the following key words and mark them in a distinctive way: *righteous (right, righteousness), wicked (evil, vile, evildoers), sin (sins, condemns him, malice, iniquity, wrong, iniquities, affliction, sinful, crime), prayer (prayers, pray, plea), praise (praises, glorify, commend, extol), sing (shout, make music, cry out, jubilant song with music), fear (dread, afraid, be afraid), refuge (stronghold, shelter, hide), hope (hopes, wait for, trust in), save (saves, victory, deliver, saved, salvation, deliverance, Savior, deliverer, victories),* and *cry (call, called, cried).* Write these key words on an index card and use it as a bookmark when you study and meditate on the psalms.

5. Don't miss the central focus of these psalms—God. There is so much to be learned about him, and

then he is to be worshiped and adored. Observe his names, his titles, his attributes, and how man is to respond to him.

    a. Don't forget to look for Jesus, who is God, one with the Father, for he said, "Everything must be fulfilled that is written about me in the Law of Moses, the Prophets and the Psalms" (Luke 24:44).

    b. The psalms are for the heart and soul, but they also address the mind. In the margin record your insights about God (use a △ as a heading). As you do this, meditate on what you learn. Spend time in praise and prayer. Let the book of Psalms help you love the Lord your God with all your heart, mind, body, soul, and strength.

6. When you finish each psalm, record the theme of that psalm on the line in the text next to the number of the psalm and on the PSALMS AT A GLANCE chart on pages 1061 through 1066.

7. Psalms has five segments, which are marked on PSALMS AT A GLANCE.

    a. Give each segment a title or record its theme.

    b. Read Psalms 41:13; 72:18, 19; 89:52; 106:48; and 150:6. Notice what is said and how each segment concludes.

    c. Complete PSALMS AT A GLANCE.

∾ THINGS TO THINK ABOUT
───

1. When you are distressed, confused, afraid, or hurt, or when you need to talk with someone who will understand, turn to Psalms. With the psalmist, be still (cease striving) and know that he is God.

2. Think about the practical value of Psalms and let it serve as your primary counselor when you need wisdom and understanding. Remember, blessed is the man who does not walk in the counsel of the wicked, but whose delight is in the law of the Lord, and who meditates in that law day and night (see Psalm 1).

3. Have you thought about ending each day as the book of Psalms ends—with a psalm of praise? "Let the saints rejoice in this honor and sing for joy on their beds. May the praise of God be in their mouths. . . . Let everything that has breath praise the LORD. Praise the LORD" (Psalm 149:5, 6; Psalm 150:6). Try it and see what God does.

BOOK I

Psalms 1–41

Psalm 1

*Psalm 1 Theme*_____

¹Blessed is the man
    who does not walk*ᵃ* in the counsel of the wicked
    or stand in the way of sinners
    or sit*ᵇ* in the seat of mockers.
²But his delight*ᶜ* is in the law of the LORD,*ᵈ*
    and on his law he meditates*ᵉ* day and night.
³He is like a tree*ᶠ* planted by streams of water,*ᵍ*
    which yields its fruit*ʰ* in season

1:1
a Pr 4:14
b Ps 26:4;
Jer 15:17

1:2
c Ps 119:16,35
d Ps 119:1
e Jos 1:8

1:3
f Ps 128:3
g Jer 17:8
h Eze 47:12

^{12}Kiss the Son,^{a} lest he be angry
and you be destroyed in your way,
for his wrath^b can flare up in a moment.
Blessed are all who take refuge^c in him.

Psalm 3

A psalm of David. When he fled from his son Absalom.^{d}

Psalm 3 Theme _____

^{1}O Lord, how many are my foes!
How many rise up against me!
^{2}Many are saying of me,
"God will not deliver him.^{e}"

Selah^a

^{3}But you are a shield^f around me, O Lord;
you bestow glory on me and lift^b up my head.^{g}
^{4}To the Lord I cry aloud,
and he answers me from his holy hill.^{h}

Selah

^{5}I lie down and sleep;^{i}
I wake again, because the Lord sustains me.
^{6}I will not fear^j the tens of thousands
drawn up against me on every side.

^{7}Arise,^{k} O Lord!
Deliver me,^{l} O my God!
Strike^m all my enemies on the jaw;
break the teeth^n of the wicked.

^{8}From the Lord comes deliverance.^{o}
May your blessing be on your people.

Selah

Psalm 4

For the director of music. With stringed instruments. A psalm of David.

Psalm 4 Theme _____

^{1}Answer me when I call to you,
O my righteous God.
Give me relief from my distress;
be merciful ^{p} to me and hear my prayer.^{q}

2:12
^{a}Jn 5:23
^{b}Rev 6:16
^{c}Ps 34:8;
Ro 9:33

3:Title
^{d}2Sa 15:14

3:2
^{e}Ps 71:11

3:3
^{f}Ge 15:1;
Ps 28:7
^{g}Ps 27:6

3:4
^{h}Ps 2:6

3:5
^{i}Lev 26:6;
Pr 3:24

3:6
^{j}Ps 27:3

3:7
^{k}Ps 7:6
^{l}Ps 6:4
^{m}Job 16:10
^{n}Ps 58:6

3:8
^{o}Isa 43:3,11

4:1
^{p}Ps 25:16
^{q}Ps 17:6

---

^{a}2 A word of uncertain meaning, occurring frequently in the Psalms; possibly a musical term
^{b}3 Or Lord, / my Glorious One, who lifts

1:3
a Ge 39:3

1:4
b Job 21:18;
Isa 17:13

1:5
c Ps 5:5
d Ps 9:7-8,16

1:6
e Ps 37:18;
2Ti 2:19
f Ps 9:6

and whose leaf does not wither.
>Whatever he does prospers.*a*

[4] Not so the wicked!
>They are like chaff*b*
>that the wind blows away.
[5] Therefore the wicked will not stand*c* in the judgment,*d*
>nor sinners in the assembly of the righteous.

[6] For the LORD watches over*e* the way of the righteous,
>but the way of the wicked will perish.*f*

Psalm 2

*Psalm 2 Theme*_____

2:1
g Ps 21:11

[1] Why do the nations conspire*a*
>and the peoples plot*g* in vain?
[2] The kings*h* of the earth take their stand
>and the rulers gather together
> against the LORD
>and against his Anointed*i* One.*bj*
[3] "Let us break their chains," they say,
>"and throw off their fetters."*k*

2:2
h Ps 48:4
i Jn 1:41
j Ps 74:18,23;
Ac 4:25-26*

2:3
k Jer 5:5

[4] The One enthroned in heaven laughs;*l*
>the Lord scoffs at them.
[5] Then he rebukes them in his anger
>and terrifies them in his wrath,*m* saying,
[6] "I have installed my King*c*
>on Zion, my holy hill."

2:4
l Ps 37:13; 59:8;
Pr 1:26

2:5
m Ps 21:9;
78:49-50

[7] I will proclaim the decree of the LORD:

>He said to me, "You are my Son*d*;
>today I have become your Father.*en*
[8] Ask of me,
>and I will make the nations your inheritance,
>the ends of the earth*o* your possession.
[9] You will rule them with an iron scepter*f*;*p*
>you will dash them to pieces*q* like pottery.*r*"

2:7
n Ac 13:33*;
Heb 1:5*

2:8
o Ps 22:27

[10] Therefore, you kings, be wise;
>be warned, you rulers of the earth.
[11] Serve the LORD with fear
>and rejoice*s* with trembling.*t*

2:9
p Rev 12:5
q Ps 89:23
r Rev 2:27*

2:11
s Heb 12:28
t Ps 119:119-120

a 1 Hebrew; Septuagint *rage*   *b 2* Or *anointed one*   *c 6* Or *king*   *d 7* Or *son;* also in verse 12   *e 7* Or *have begotten you*   *f 9* Or *will break them with a rod of iron*

4:2
a Ps 31:6

²How long, O men, will you turn my glory into shame*a*?
How long will you love delusions and seek
false gods*b*?*a*   *Selah*

4:3
b Ps 31:23
c Ps 6:8

³Know that the LORD has set apart the godly*b* for himself;
the LORD will hear*c* when I call to him.

4:4
d Eph 4:26*
e Ps 77:6

⁴In your anger do not sin;*d*
when you are on your beds,*e*
search your hearts and be silent.   *Selah*
⁵Offer right sacrifices
and trust in the LORD.*f*

4:5
f Dt 33:19;
Ps 37:3

⁶Many are asking, "Who can show us any good?"
Let the light of your face shine upon us,*g* O LORD.
⁷You have filled my heart*h* with greater joy*i*
than when their grain and new wine abound.

4:6
g Nu 6:25

⁸I will lie down and sleep*j* in peace,
for you alone, O LORD,
make me dwell in safety.*k*

4:7
h Ac 14:17
i Isa 9:3

Psalm 5

For the director of music. For flutes. A psalm of David.

4:8
j Ps 3:5
k Lev 25:18

Psalm 5 Theme_____

¹Give ear to my words, O LORD,
consider my sighing.

5:2
l Ps 3:4
m Ps 84:3

²Listen to my cry for help,*l*
my King and my God,*m*
for to you I pray.

5:3
n Ps 88:13

³In the morning,*n* O LORD, you hear my voice;
in the morning I lay my requests before you
and wait in expectation.

5:4
o Ps 11:5; 92:15

⁴You are not a God who takes pleasure in evil;
with you the wicked*o* cannot dwell.
⁵The arrogant*p* cannot stand*q* in your presence;
you hate*r* all who do wrong.

5:5
p Ps 73:3
q Ps 1:5
r Ps 11:5

⁶You destroy those who tell lies;*s*
bloodthirsty and deceitful men
the LORD abhors.

⁷But I, by your great mercy,
will come into your house;

5:6
s Ps 55:23;
Rev 21:8

a 2 Or you dishonor my Glorious One   *b 2 Or seek lies*

in reverence will I bow down*a*
   toward your holy temple.
8Lead me, O Lord, in your righteousness*b*
   because of my enemies—
   make straight your way*c* before me.

9Not a word from their mouth can be trusted;
   their heart is filled with destruction.
Their throat is an open grave;*d*
   with their tongue they speak deceit.*e*
10Declare them guilty, O God!
   Let their intrigues be their downfall.
Banish them for their many sins,*f*
   for they have rebelled*g* against you.

11But let all who take refuge in you be glad;
   let them ever sing for joy.*h*
Spread your protection over them,
   that those who love your name*i* may rejoice in you.*j*
12For surely, O Lord, you bless the righteous;
   you surround them*k* with your favor as with a shield.

Psalm 6

For the director of music. With stringed instruments. According to *sheminith*.ᵃ
A psalm of David.

Psalm 6 Theme_____

1O Lord, do not rebuke me in your anger*l*
   or discipline me in your wrath.
2Be merciful to me, Lord, for I am faint;
   O Lord, heal me,*m* for my bones are in agony.*n*
3My soul is in anguish.*o*
   How long,*p* O Lord, how long?

4Turn, O Lord, and deliver me;
   save me because of your unfailing love.*q*
5No one remembers you when he is dead.
   Who praises you from the grave*b*?*r*

6I am worn out*s* from groaning;
   all night long I flood my bed with weeping
   and drench my couch with tears.*t*
7My eyes grow weak*u* with sorrow;
   they fail because of all my foes.

aTitle: Probably a musical term   b5 Hebrew *Sheol*

Side references:

5:7 *a*Ps 138:2

5:8 *b*Ps 31:1 *c*Ps 27:11

5:9 *d*Lk 11:44 *e*Ro 3:13*

5:10 *f*Ps 9:16 *g*Ps 107:11

5:11 *h*Ps 2:12 *i*Ps 69:36 *j*Isa 65:13

5:12 *k*Ps 32:7

6:1 *l*Ps 38:1

6:2 *m*Hos 6:1 *n*Ps 22:14; 31:10

6:3 *o*Jn 12:27 *p*Ps 90:13

6:4 *q*Ps 17:13

6:5 *r*Ps 30:9; 88:10-12; Ecc 9:10; Isa 38:18

6:6 *s*Ps 69:3 *t*Ps 42:3

6:7 *u*Ps 31:9

6:8
a Ps 119:115
b Mt 7:23;
Lk 13:27

⁸Away from me,^a all you who do evil,^b
  for the LORD has heard my weeping.
⁹The LORD has heard my cry for mercy;^c
  the LORD accepts my prayer.
¹⁰All my enemies will be ashamed and dismayed;
  they will turn back in sudden disgrace.^d

6:9
c Ps 116:1

Psalm 7

6:10
d Ps 71:24; 73:19

A *shiggaion*^a of David, which he sang to the LORD concerning Cush, a Benjamite.

Psalm 7 Theme

7:1
e Ps 31:15

¹O LORD my God, I take refuge in you;
  save and deliver me from all who pursue me,^e
²or they will tear me like a lion^f
  and rip me to pieces with no one to rescue^g me.

7:2
f Isa 38:13
g Ps 50:22

³O LORD my God, if I have done this
  and there is guilt on my hands^h—
⁴if I have done evil to him who is at peace with me
  or without cause have robbed my foe—
⁵then let my enemy pursue and overtake me;
  let him trample my life to the ground
  and make me sleep in the dust.

7:3
h 1Sa 24:11;
Isa 59:3

     Selah

⁶Arise,ⁱ O LORD, in your anger;
  rise up against the rage of my enemies.^j
  Awake,^k my God; decree justice.
⁷Let the assembled peoples gather around you.
  Rule over them from on high;
⁸ let the LORD judge the peoples.
 Judge me, O LORD, according to my righteousness,^l
  according to my integrity, O Most High.
⁹O righteous God,^m
  who searches minds and hearts,ⁿ
 bring to an end the violence of the wicked
  and make the righteous secure.^o

7:6
i Ps 94:2
j Ps 138:7
k Ps 44:23

7:8
l Ps 18:20; 96:13

7:9
m Jer 11:20
n 1Ch 28:9;
Ps 26:2;
Rev 2:23
o Ps 37:23

¹⁰My shield^b is God Most High,
  who saves the upright in heart.^p
¹¹God is a righteous judge,^q
  a God who expresses his wrath every day.
¹²If he does not relent,
  he^c will sharpen his sword;^r

7:10
p Ps 125:4

7:11
q Ps 50:6

7:12
r Dt 32:41

^aTitle: Probably a literary or musical term   ^b*10* Or *sovereign*   ^c*12* Or *If a man does not repent, / God*

he will bend and string his bow.
13He has prepared his deadly weapons;
 he makes ready his flaming arrows.

14He who is pregnant with evil
 and conceives trouble gives birth*a* to disillusionment.
15He who digs a hole and scoops it out
 falls into the pit he has made.*b*
16The trouble he causes recoils on himself;
 his violence comes down on his own head.

17I will give thanks to the LORD because of his
 righteousness*c*
and will sing praise*d* to the name of the LORD
 Most High.

Psalm 8

For the director of music. According to *gittith*.*ᵃ* A psalm of David.

Psalm 8 Theme

1O LORD, our Lord,
 how majestic is your name in all the earth!

You have set your glory
 above the heavens.*e*
2From the lips of children and infants
 you have ordained praise*bf*
because of your enemies,
 to silence the foe*g* and the avenger.

3When I consider your heavens,*h*
 the work of your fingers,
the moon and the stars,*i*
 which you have set in place,
4what is man that you are mindful of him,
 the son of man that you care for him?*j*
5You made him a little lower than the heavenly beings*c*
 and crowned him with glory and honor.*k*

6You made him ruler*l* over the works of your hands;
 you put everything under his feet:*mn*
7all flocks and herds,
 and the beasts of the field,

a Title: Probably a musical term *b*2 Or *strength* *c*5 Or *than God*

7:14
a Job 15:35;
Isa 59:4;
Jas 1:15

7:15
b Job 4:8

7:17
c Ps 71:15-16
d Ps 9:2

8:1
e Ps 57:5; 113:4;
148:13

8:2
f Mt 21:16*
g Ps 44:16;
1Co 1:27

8:3
h Ps 89:11
i Ps 136:9

8:4
j Job 7:17;
Ps 144:3;
Heb 2:6

8:5
k Ps 21:5; 103:4

8:6
l Ge 1:28
m Heb 2:6-8*
n 1Co 15:25,27*;
Eph 1:22

8the birds of the air,
  and the fish of the sea,
  all that swim the paths of the seas.

9O Lord, our Lord,
  how majestic is your name in all the earth!*a*

Psalm 9*a*

For the director of music. To ⌊the tune of⌋ "The Death of the Son." A psalm of David.

*Psalm 9 Theme*_____

1I will praise you, O Lord, with all my heart;*b*
  I will tell of all your wonders.*c*
2I will be glad and rejoice*d* in you;
  I will sing praise to your name,*e* O Most High.

3My enemies turn back;
  they stumble and perish before you.
4For you have upheld my right and my cause;*f*
  you have sat on your throne, judging righteously.*g*
5You have rebuked the nations and destroyed the wicked;
  you have blotted out their name*h* for ever and ever.
6Endless ruin has overtaken the enemy,
  you have uprooted their cities;
  even the memory of them*i* has perished.

7The Lord reigns forever;
  he has established his throne*j* for judgment.
8He will judge the world in righteousness;*k*
  he will govern the peoples with justice.
9The Lord is a refuge for the oppressed,
  a stronghold in times of trouble.*l*
10Those who know your name*m* will trust in you,
  for you, Lord, have never forsaken*n* those who
    seek you.

11Sing praises to the Lord, enthroned in Zion;*o*
  proclaim among the nations*p* what he has done.*q*
12For he who avenges blood*r* remembers;
  he does not ignore the cry of the afflicted.

13O Lord, see how my enemies*s* persecute me!
  Have mercy and lift me up from the gates of death,
14that I may declare your praises*t*

a Psalms 9 and 10 may have been originally a single acrostic poem, the stanzas of which begin
with the successive letters of the Hebrew alphabet. In the Septuagint they constitute one psalm.

8:9
a ver 1

9:1
b Ps 86:12
c Ps 26:7

9:2
d Ps 5:11
e Ps 92:1; 83:18

9:4
f Ps 140:12
g 1Pe 2:23

9:5
h Pr 10:7

9:6
i Ps 34:16

9:7
j Ps 89:14

9:8
k Ps 96:13

9:9
l Ps 32:7

9:10
m Ps 91:14
n Ps 37:28

9:11
o Ps 76:2
p Ps 107:22
q Ps 105:1

9:12
r Ge 9:5

9:13
s Ps 38:19

9:14
t Ps 106:2

in the gates of the Daughter of Zion
  and there rejoice in your salvation.*a*

¹⁵The nations have fallen into the pit they have dug;*b*
  their feet are caught in the net they have hidden.*c*
¹⁶The LORD is known by his justice;
  the wicked are ensnared by the work of their hands.
                    *Higgaion.*ᵃ *Selah*

¹⁷The wicked return to the grave,*bd*
  all the nations that forget God.*e*
¹⁸But the needy will not always be forgotten,
  nor the hope*f* of the afflicted*g* ever perish.

¹⁹Arise, O LORD, let not man triumph;
  let the nations be judged in your presence.
²⁰Strike them with terror, O LORD;
  let the nations know they are but men.*h*   *Selah*

Psalm 10*c*

Psalm 10 Theme

¹Why, O LORD, do you stand far off?*i*
  Why do you hide yourself*j* in times of trouble?

²In his arrogance the wicked man hunts down the weak,
  who are caught in the schemes he devises.
³He boasts*k* of the cravings of his heart;
  he blesses the greedy and reviles the LORD.
⁴In his pride the wicked does not seek him;
  in all his thoughts there is no room for God.*l*
⁵His ways are always prosperous;
  he is haughty and your laws are far from him;
  he sneers at all his enemies.
⁶He says to himself, "Nothing will shake me;
  I'll always be happy*m* and never have trouble."
⁷His mouth is full of curses*n* and lies and threats;*o*
  trouble and evil are under his tongue.*p*
⁸He lies in wait near the villages;
  from ambush he murders the innocent,*q*
  watching in secret for his victims.
⁹He lies in wait like a lion in cover;
  he lies in wait to catch the helpless;*r*
  he catches the helpless and drags them off in his net.
¹⁰His victims are crushed, they collapse;
  they fall under his strength.

a 16 Or *Meditation*; possibly a musical notation   *b 17* Hebrew *Sheol*   *c* Psalms 9 and 10 may have been originally a single acrostic poem, the stanzas of which begin with the successive letters of the Hebrew alphabet. In the Septuagint they constitute one psalm.

9:14
a Ps 13:5; 51:12

9:15
b Ps 7:15-16
c Ps 35:8; 57:6

9:17
d Ps 49:14
e Job 8:13;
Ps 50:22

9:18
f Ps 71:5;
Pr 23:18
g Ps 12:5

9:20
h Ps 62:9;
Isa 31:3

10:1
i Ps 22:1,11
j Ps 13:1

10:3
k Ps 94:4

10:4
l Ps 14:1; 36:1

10:6
m Rev 18:7

10:7
n Ro 3:14*
o Ps 73:8
p Ps 140:3

10:8
q Ps 94:6

10:9
r Ps 17:12; 59:3;
140:5

¹¹He says to himself, "God has forgotten;^a
    he covers his face and never sees."

10:11
a Job 22:13

¹²Arise, LORD! Lift up your hand,^b O God.
    Do not forget the helpless.^c
¹³Why does the wicked man revile God?
    Why does he say to himself,
    "He won't call me to account"?

10:12
b Ps 17:7;
Mic 5:9
c Ps 9:12

¹⁴But you, O God, do see trouble^d and grief;
    you consider it to take it in hand.
  The victim commits himself to you;^e
    you are the helper^f of the fatherless.

10:14
d Ps 22:11
e Ps 37:5
f Ps 68:5

¹⁵Break the arm of the wicked and evil man;^g
    call him to account for his wickedness
    that would not be found out.

10:15
g Ps 37:17

¹⁶The LORD is King for ever and ever;^h
    the nationsⁱ will perish from his land.
¹⁷You hear, O LORD, the desire of the afflicted;^j
    you encourage them, and you listen to their cry,
¹⁸defending the fatherless^k and the oppressed,^l
    in order that man, who is of the earth, may terrify
      no more.

10:16
h Ps 29:10
i Dt 8:20

10:17
j 1Ch 29:18;
Ps 34:15

10:18
k Ps 82:3
l Ps 9:9

Psalm 11

For the director of music. Of David.

*Psalm 11 Theme*_____

11:1
m Ps 56:11

¹In the LORD I take refuge.^m
  How then can you say to me:
    "Flee like a bird to your mountain.
²For look, the wicked bend their bows;
    they set their arrowsⁿ against the strings
  to shoot from the shadows
    at the upright in heart.^o
³When the foundations^p are being destroyed,
    what can the righteous do^a?"

11:2
n Ps 7:13
o Ps 64:3-4

11:3
p Ps 82:5

⁴The LORD is in his holy temple;^q
    the LORD is on his heavenly throne.^r
  He observes the sons of men;^s
    his eyes examine^t them.
⁵The LORD examines the righteous,^u

11:4
q Ps 18:6
r Ps 103:19
s Ps 33:13
t Ps 34:15-16

11:5
u Ge 22:1;
Jas 1:12

a 3 Or *what is the Righteous One doing*

but the wicked[a] and those who love violence
his soul hates.[a]
⁶On the wicked he will rain
fiery coals and burning sulfur;[b]
a scorching wind[c] will be their lot.

⁷For the LORD is righteous,[d]
he loves justice;[e]
upright men will see his face.[f]

Psalm 12

For the director of music. According to *sheminith*.[b] A psalm of David.

Psalm 12 Theme _____

¹Help, LORD, for the godly are no more;[g]
the faithful have vanished from among men.
²Everyone lies to his neighbor;
their flattering lips speak with deception.[h]

³May the LORD cut off all flattering lips
and every boastful tongue[i]
⁴that says, "We will triumph with our tongues;
we own our lips[c]—who is our master?"

⁵"Because of the oppression of the weak
and the groaning of the needy,
I will now arise," says the LORD.
"I will protect them[j] from those who malign them."
⁶And the words of the LORD are flawless,[k]
like silver refined in a furnace of clay,
purified seven times.

⁷O LORD, you will keep us safe
and protect us from such people forever.[l]
⁸The wicked freely strut[m] about
when what is vile is honored among men.

Psalm 13

For the director of music. A psalm of David.

Psalm 13 Theme _____

¹How long, O LORD? Will you forget me forever?
How long will you hide your face[n] from me?

11:5 [a]Ps 5:5
11:6 [b]Eze 38:22 [c]Jer 4:11-12
11:7 [d]Ps 7:9,11; 45:7 [e]Ps 33:5 [f]Ps 17:15
12:1 [g]Isa 57:1
12:2 [h]Ps 10:7; 41:6; 55:21; Ro 16:18
12:3 [i]Da 7:8; Rev 13:5
12:5 [j]Ps 10:18; 34:6
12:6 [k]2Sa 22:31; Ps 18:30; Pr 30:5
12:7 [l]Ps 37:28
12:8 [m]Ps 55:10-11
13:1 [n]Job 13:24; Ps 44:24

a5 Or *The LORD, the Righteous One, examines the wicked,* / b Title: Probably a musical term
c4 Or / *our lips are our plowshares*

²How long must I wrestle with my thoughts*a*
    and every day have sorrow in my heart?
    How long will my enemy triumph over me?*b*

³Look on me and answer,*c* O Lᴏʀᴅ my God.
    Give light to my eyes,*d* or I will sleep in death;*e*
⁴my enemy will say, "I have overcome him,*f*"
    and my foes will rejoice when I fall.

⁵But I trust in your unfailing love;*g*
    my heart rejoices in your salvation.*h*
⁶I will sing*i* to the Lᴏʀᴅ,
    for he has been good to me.

Psalm 14

For the director of music. Of David.

Psalm 14 Theme

¹The fool*a* says in his heart,
    "There is no God."*j*
They are corrupt, their deeds are vile;
    there is no one who does good.

²The Lᴏʀᴅ looks down from heaven*k*
    on the sons of men
to see if there are any who understand,*l*
    any who seek God.
³All have turned aside,
    they have together become corrupt;*m*
there is no one who does good,*n*
    not even one.*o*

⁴Will evildoers never learn—*p*
    those who devour my people*q* as men eat bread
    and who do not call on the Lᴏʀᴅ?*r*
⁵There they are, overwhelmed with dread,
    for God is present in the company of the righteous.
⁶You evildoers frustrate the plans of the poor,
    but the Lᴏʀᴅ is their refuge.*s*

⁷Oh, that salvation for Israel would come out of Zion!
    When the Lᴏʀᴅ restores the fortunes*t* of his people,
    let Jacob rejoice and Israel be glad!

a 1 The Hebrew words rendered *fool* in Psalms denote one who is morally deficient.

Psalm 15

A psalm of David.

Psalm 15 Theme _____

15:1
a Ps 27:5-6
b Ps 24:3-5

¹LORD, who may dwell in your sanctuary?*a*
  Who may live on your holy hill?*b*

²He whose walk is blameless
  and who does what is righteous,
who speaks the truth*c* from his heart

15:2
c Ps 24:4;
Zec 8:3,16;
Eph 4:25

3 and has no slander*d* on his tongue,
who does his neighbor no wrong
  and casts no slur on his fellowman,

15:3
d Ex 23:1

⁴who despises a vile man
  but honors*e* those who fear the LORD,
who keeps his oath*f*
  even when it hurts,

15:4
e Ac 28:10
f Jdg 11:35

⁵who lends his money without usury*g*
  and does not accept a bribe*h* against the innocent.

He who does these things
  will never be shaken.*i*

15:5
g Ex 22:25
h Ex 23:8;
Dt 16:19
i 2Pe 1:10

Psalm 16

*A miktam*ᵃ *of David.*

16:1
j Ps 17:8
k Ps 7:1

Psalm 16 Theme _____

¹Keep me safe,*j* O God,
  for in you I take refuge.*k*

²I said to the LORD, "You are my Lord;
  apart from you I have no good thing."*l*

16:2
l Ps 73:25

³As for the saints who are in the land,*m*
  they are the glorious ones in whom is all my delight.*b*

16:3
m Ps 101:6

⁴The sorrows*n* of those will increase
  who run after other gods.*o*
I will not pour out their libations of blood
  or take up their names*p* on my lips.

16:4
n Ps 32:10
o Ps 106:37-38
p Ex 23:13

⁵LORD, you have assigned me my portion*q* and my cup;*r*
  you have made my lot secure.

16:5
q Ps 73:26
r Ps 23:5

ᵃ Title: Probably a literary or musical term   *b* 3 Or *As for the pagan priests who are in the land /
and the nobles in whom all delight, I said:*

16:6
a Ps 78:55;
Jer 3:19

[6]The boundary lines have fallen for me in pleasant places;
　　surely I have a delightful inheritance.*a*

[7]I will praise the LORD, who counsels me;*b*
　　even at night*c* my heart instructs me.
[8]I have set the LORD always before me.
　　Because he is at my right hand,*d*
　　I will not be shaken.

16:7
b Ps 73:24
c Ps 77:6

16:8
d Ps 73:23

[9]Therefore my heart is glad*e* and my tongue rejoices;
　　my body also will rest secure,*f*
[10]because you will not abandon me to the grave,*a*
　　nor will you let your Holy One*b* see decay.*g*
[11]You have made*c* known to me the path of life;*h*
　　you will fill me with joy in your presence,*i*
　　with eternal pleasures*j* at your right hand.

16:9
e Ps 4:7; 30:11
f Ps 4:8

16:10
g Ac 13:35*

Psalm 17

A prayer of David.

16:11
h Mt 7:14
i Ac 2:25-28*
j Ps 36:7-8

Psalm 17 Theme

[1]Hear, O LORD, my righteous plea;
　　listen to my cry.*k*
　Give ear to my prayer—
　　it does not rise from deceitful lips.*l*
[2]May my vindication come from you;
　　may your eyes see what is right.

17:1
k Ps 61:1
l Isa 29:13

[3]Though you probe my heart and examine me at night,
　　though you test me,*m* you will find nothing;*n*
　I have resolved that my mouth will not sin.*o*
[4]As for the deeds of men—
　　by the word of your lips
　I have kept myself
　　from the ways of the violent.
[5]My steps have held to your paths;*p*
　　my feet have not slipped.*q*

17:3
m Ps 26:2; 66:10
n Job 23:10;
Jer 50:20
o Ps 39:1

17:5
p Ps 44:18;
119:133
q Ps 18:36

[6]I call on you, O God, for you will answer me;*r*
　　give ear to me*s* and hear my prayer.*t*
[7]Show the wonder of your great love,*u*
　　you who save by your right hand*v*
　　those who take refuge in you from their foes.

17:6
r Ps 86:7
s Ps 116:2
t Ps 88:2

17:7
u Ps 31:21
v Ps 20:6

a 10 Hebrew *Sheol*　　*b 10* Or *your faithful one*　　*c 11* Or *You will make*

909

⁸Keep me as the apple of your eye;^a
  hide me in the shadow of your wings
⁹from the wicked who assail me,
  from my mortal enemies who surround me.^b

¹⁰They close up their callous hearts,^c
  and their mouths speak with arrogance.^d
¹¹They have tracked me down, they now surround me,^e
  with eyes alert, to throw me to the ground.
¹²They are like a lion^f hungry for prey,
  like a great lion crouching in cover.

¹³Rise up, O LORD, confront them, bring them down;^g
  rescue me from the wicked by your sword.
¹⁴O LORD, by your hand save me from such men,
  from men of this world^h whose reward is in this life.

You still the hunger of those you cherish;
  their sons have plenty,
  and they store up wealthⁱ for their children.
¹⁵And I—in righteousness I will see your face;
  when I awake, I will be satisfied with seeing your
    likeness.^j

Psalm 18

For the director of music. Of David the servant of the LORD. He sang to the LORD the words of this song when the LORD delivered him from the hand of all his enemies and from the hand of Saul. He said:

*Psalm 18 Theme*_____

¹I love you, O LORD, my strength.

²The LORD is my rock,^k my fortress and my deliverer;
  my God is my rock, in whom I take refuge.
  He is my shield^l and the horn^a of my salvation,^m
    my stronghold.
³I call to the LORD, who is worthy of praise,ⁿ
  and I am saved from my enemies.

⁴The cords of death^o entangled me;
  the torrents^p of destruction overwhelmed me.
⁵The cords of the grave^b coiled around me;
  the snares of death^q confronted me.
⁶In my distress I called to the LORD;
  I cried to my God for help.

17:8
^aDt 32:10

17:9
^bPs 31:20; 109:3

17:10
^cPs 73:7
^d1Sa 2:3

17:11
^ePs 37:14; 88:17

17:12
^fPs 7:2; 10:9

17:13
^gPs 7:12; 22:20; 73:18

17:14
^hLk 16:8
ⁱPs 73:3-7

17:15
^jNu 12:8;
Ps 4:6-7; 16:11;
1Jn 3:2

18:2
^kPs 19:14
^lPs 59:11
^mPs 75:10

18:3
ⁿPs 48:1

18:4
^oPs 116:3
^pPs 124:4

18:5
^qPs 116:3

---

a2 *Horn* here symbolizes strength.   b5 Hebrew *Sheol*

18:6
a Ps 34:15

From his temple he heard my voice;[a]
  my cry came before him, into his ears.

18:7
b Jdg 5:4
c Ps 68:7-8

[7]The earth trembled and quaked,[b]
  and the foundations of the mountains shook;
  they trembled because he was angry.[c]

18:8
d Ps 50:3

[8]Smoke rose from his nostrils;
  consuming fire[d] came from his mouth,
  burning coals blazed out of it.

18:9
e Ps 144:5

[9]He parted the heavens and came down;[e]
  dark clouds were under his feet.

18:10
f Ps 80:1
g Ps 104:3

[10]He mounted the cherubim[f] and flew;
  he soared on the wings of the wind.[g]

18:11
h Dt 4:11;
Ps 97:2

[11]He made darkness his covering,[h] his canopy
      around him—
  the dark rain clouds of the sky.

18:12
i Ps 104:2
j Ps 97:3

[12]Out of the brightness of his presence[i] clouds advanced,
  with hailstones and bolts of lightning.[j]

[13]The LORD thundered[k] from heaven;
  the voice of the Most High resounded.[a]

18:13
k Ps 29:3; 104:7

[14]He shot his arrows and scattered ⌊the enemies⌋,
  great bolts of lightning and routed them.[l]

18:14
l Ps 144:6

[15]The valleys of the sea were exposed
  and the foundations of the earth laid bare
at your rebuke,[m] O LORD,
  at the blast of breath from your nostrils.

18:15
m Ps 76:6; 106:9

[16]He reached down from on high and took hold of me;
  he drew me out of deep waters.[n]

18:16
n Ps 144:7

[17]He rescued me from my powerful enemy,
  from my foes, who were too strong for me.[o]

18:17
o Ps 35:10

[18]They confronted me in the day of my disaster,
  but the LORD was my support.[p]

18:18
p Ps 59:16

[19]He brought me out into a spacious place;[q]
  he rescued me because he delighted in me.[r]

18:19
q Ps 31:8
r Ps 118:5

[20]The LORD has dealt with me according to
      my righteousness;
  according to the cleanness of my hands[s] he has
      rewarded me.

18:20
s Ps 24:4

[21]For I have kept the ways of the LORD;[t]
  I have not done evil by turning[u] from my God.
[22]All his laws are before me;[v]
  I have not turned away from his decrees.

18:21
t 2Ch 34:33
u Ps 119:102

18:22
v Ps 119:30

a 13 Some Hebrew manuscripts and Septuagint (see also 2 Samuel 22:14); most Hebrew manuscripts *resounded, / amid hailstones and bolts of lightning*

²³I have been blameless before him
    and have kept myself from sin.
²⁴The LORD has rewarded me according to my
      righteousness,^a
    according to the cleanness of my hands in his sight.

²⁵To the faithful^b you show yourself faithful,
    to the blameless you show yourself blameless,
²⁶to the pure you show yourself pure,
    but to the crooked you show yourself shrewd.^c
²⁷You save the humble
    but bring low those whose eyes are haughty.^d
²⁸You, O LORD, keep my lamp burning;
    my God turns my darkness into light.^e
²⁹With your help^f I can advance against a troop^a;
    with my God I can scale a wall.

³⁰As for God, his way is perfect;^g
    the word of the LORD is flawless.^h
  He is a shield
    for all who take refugeⁱ in him.
³¹For who is God besides the LORD?^j
    And who is the Rock^k except our God?
³²It is God who arms me with strength^l
    and makes my way perfect.
³³He makes my feet like the feet of a deer;^m
    he enables me to stand on the heights.ⁿ
³⁴He trains my hands for battle;^o
    my arms can bend a bow of bronze.
³⁵You give me your shield of victory,
    and your right hand sustains^p me;
    you stoop down to make me great.
³⁶You broaden the path beneath me,
    so that my ankles do not turn.

³⁷I pursued my enemies^q and overtook them;
    I did not turn back till they were destroyed.
³⁸I crushed them so that they could not rise;^r
    they fell beneath my feet.^s
³⁹You armed me with strength for battle;
    you made my adversaries bow at my feet.
⁴⁰You made my enemies turn their backs^t in flight,
    and I destroyed^u my foes.
⁴¹They cried for help, but there was no one to
      save them^v—
    to the LORD, but he did not answer.^w

^a 29 Or *can run through a barricade*

18:24
^a 1Sa 26:23

18:25
^b 1Ki 8:32;
Ps 62:12; Mt 5:7

18:26
^c Pr 3:34

18:27
^d Pr 6:17

18:28
^e Job 18:6; 29:3

18:29
^f Heb 11:34

18:30
^g Dt 32:4;
Rev 15:3
^h Ps 12:6
ⁱ Ps 17:7

18:31
^j Dt 32:39; 86:8;
Isa 45:5,6,14,
18,21
^k Dt 32:31;
1Sa 2:2

18:32
^l Isa 45:5

18:33
^m Hab 3:19
ⁿ Dt 32:13

18:34
^o Ps 144:1

18:35
^p Ps 119:116

18:37
^q Ps 37:20; 44:5

18:38
^r Ps 36:12
^s Ps 47:3

18:40
^t Ps 21:12
^u Ps 94:23

18:41
^v Ps 50:22
^w Job 27:9;
Pr 1:28

18:43
a 2Sa 8:1-14
b Isa 52:15; 55:5

⁴²I beat them as fine as dust borne on the wind;
  I poured them out like mud in the streets.

⁴³You have delivered me from the attacks of the people;
  you have made me the head of nations;[a]
  people I did not know[b] are subject to me.

18:44
c Ps 66:3

⁴⁴As soon as they hear me, they obey me;
  foreigners[c] cringe before me.

⁴⁵They all lose heart;
  they come trembling from their strongholds.[d]

18:45
d Mic 7:17

⁴⁶The LORD lives! Praise be to my Rock!
  Exalted be God my Savior![e]

18:46
e Ps 51:14

⁴⁷He is the God who avenges me,
  who subdues nations[f] under me,
⁴⁸ who saves[g] me from my enemies.
You exalted me above my foes;
  from violent men you rescued me.

18:47
f Ps 47:3

⁴⁹Therefore I will praise you among the nations, O LORD;
  I will sing[h] praises to your name.[i]
⁵⁰He gives his king great victories;
  he shows unfailing kindness to his anointed,
  to David[j] and his descendants forever.[k]

18:48
g Ps 59:1

Psalm 19

18:49
h Ps 108:1
i Ro 15:9*

For the director of music. A psalm of David.

Psalm 19 Theme

18:50
j Ps 144:10
k Ps 89:4

¹The heavens[l] declare[m] the glory of God;
  the skies proclaim the work of his hands.
²Day after day they pour forth speech;
  night after night they display knowledge.[n]
³There is no speech or language
  where their voice is not heard.[a]
⁴Their voice[b] goes out into all the earth,
  their words to the ends of the world.[o]

19:1
l Isa 40:22
m Ps 50:6;
Ro 1:19

In the heavens he has pitched a tent[p] for the sun,
⁵ which is like a bridegroom coming forth from
    his pavilion,
  like a champion rejoicing to run his course.
⁶It rises at one end of the heavens

19:2
n Ps 74:16

19:4
o Ro 10:18*
p Ps 104:2

a 3 Or *They have no speech, there are no words; / no sound is heard from them*   b 4 Septuagint, Jerome and Syriac; Hebrew *line*

and makes its circuit to the other;[a]
nothing is hidden from its heat.

[7]The law of the LORD is perfect,
    reviving the soul.[b]
The statutes of the LORD are trustworthy,[c]
    making wise the simple.[d]
[8]The precepts of the LORD are right,[e]
    giving joy to the heart.
The commands of the LORD are radiant,
    giving light to the eyes.
[9]The fear of the LORD is pure,
    enduring forever.
The ordinances of the LORD are sure
    and altogether righteous.[f]
[10]They are more precious than gold,[g]
    than much pure gold;
they are sweeter than honey,
    than honey from the comb.
[11]By them is your servant warned;
    in keeping them there is great reward.

[12]Who can discern his errors?
    Forgive my hidden faults.[h]
[13]Keep your servant also from willful sins;
    may they not rule over me.
Then will I be blameless,
    innocent of great transgression.

[14]May the words of my mouth and the meditation of my
        heart
    be pleasing[i] in your sight,
    O LORD, my Rock[j] and my Redeemer.[k]

Psalm 20

For the director of music. A psalm of David.

Psalm 20 Theme _____

[1]May the LORD answer you when you are in distress;
    may the name of the God of Jacob[l] protect you.[m]
[2]May he send you help from the sanctuary[n]
    and grant you support from Zion.
[3]May he remember[o] all your sacrifices
    and accept your burnt offerings.[p]   *Selah*

19:6
[a] Ps 113:3;
Ecc 1:5

19:7
[b] Ps 23:3
[c] Ps 93:5; 111:7
[d] Ps 119:98-100

19:8
[e] Ps 12:6;
119:128

19:9
[f] Ps 119:138,142

19:10
[g] Pr 8:10

19:12
[h] Ps 51:2; 90:8;
139:6

19:14
[i] Ps 104:34
[j] Ps 18:2
[k] Isa 47:4

20:1
[l] Ps 46:7,11
[m] Ps 91:14

20:2
[n] Ps 3:4

20:3
[o] Ac 10:4
[p] Ps 51:19

20:4
a Ps 21:2;
145:16,19

⁴May he give you the desire of your heart*a*
  and make all your plans succeed.
⁵We will shout for joy when you are victorious
  and will lift up our banners*b* in the name of our God.
  May the LORD grant all your requests.*c*

20:5
b Ps 9:14; 60:4
c 1Sa 1:17

⁶Now I know that the LORD saves his anointed;*d*
  he answers him from his holy heaven
  with the saving power of his right hand.
⁷Some trust in chariots and some in horses,*e*
  but we trust in the name of the LORD our God.*f*
⁸They are brought to their knees and fall,
  but we rise up*g* and stand firm.*h*

20:6
d Ps 28:8; 41:11;
Isa 58:9

20:7
e Ps 33:17;
Isa 31:1
f 2Ch 32:8

⁹O LORD, save the king!
  Answer*a* us*i* when we call!

20:8
g Mic 7:8
h Ps 37:23

Psalm 21

For the director of music. A psalm of David.

20:9
i Ps 3:7; 17:6

Psalm 21 Theme

21:1
j Ps 59:16-17

¹O LORD, the king rejoices in your strength.
  How great is his joy in the victories you give!*j*
²You have granted him the desire of his heart*k*
  and have not withheld the request of his lips.   *Selah*

21:2
k Ps 37:4

³You welcomed him with rich blessings
  and placed a crown of pure gold*l* on his head.
⁴He asked you for life, and you gave it to him—
  length of days, for ever and ever.*m*
⁵Through the victories*n* you gave, his glory is great;
  you have bestowed on him splendor and majesty.
⁶Surely you have granted him eternal blessings
  and made him glad with the joy*o* of your presence.*p*
⁷For the king trusts in the LORD;
  through the unfailing love of the Most High
  he will not be shaken.

21:3
l 2Sa 12:30

21:4
m Ps 61:5-6;
91:16; 133:3

21:5
n Ps 18:50

21:6
o Ps 43:4
p 1Ch 17:27

⁸Your hand will lay hold*q* on all your enemies;
  your right hand will seize your foes.
⁹At the time of your appearing
  you will make them like a fiery furnace.
  In his wrath the LORD will swallow them up,
  and his fire will consume them.*r*

21:8
q Isa 10:10

21:9
r Ps 50:3;
La 2:2;
Mal 4:1

a 9 Or *save! / O King, answer*

¹⁰You will destroy their descendants from the earth,
  their posterity from mankind.^a
¹¹Though they plot evil^b against you
  and devise wicked schemes,^c they cannot succeed;
¹²for you will make them turn their backs^d
  when you aim at them with drawn bow.

¹³Be exalted, O Lord, in your strength;
  we will sing and praise your might.

Psalm 22

For the director of music. To ₗthe tune ofₗ "The Doe of the Morning."
A psalm of David.

Psalm 22 Theme

¹My God, my God, why have you forsaken me?^e
  Why are you so far^f from saving me,
  so far from the words of my groaning?
²O my God, I cry out by day, but you do not answer,
  by night,^g and am not silent.

³Yet you are enthroned as the Holy One;^h
  you are the praiseⁱ of Israel.^a
⁴In you our fathers put their trust;
  they trusted and you delivered them.
⁵They cried to you and were saved;
  in you they trusted and were not disappointed.^j

⁶But I am a worm^k and not a man,
  scorned by men^l and despised^m by the people.
⁷All who see me mock me;
  they hurl insults,ⁿ shaking their heads:^o
⁸"He trusts in the Lord;
  let the Lord rescue him.^p
Let him deliver him,
  since he delights^q in him."

⁹Yet you brought me out of the womb;^r
  you made me trust in you
  even at my mother's breast.
¹⁰From birth^s I was cast upon you;
  from my mother's womb you have been my God.
¹¹Do not be far from me,
  for trouble is near
  and there is no one to help.^t

a 3 Or *Yet you are holy, / enthroned on the praises of Israel*

21:10
^a Dt 28:18;
Ps 37:28

21:11
^b Ps 2:1
^c Ps 10:2

21:12
^d Ps 7:12-13;
18:40

22:1
^e Mt 27:46*;
Mk 15:34*
^f Ps 10:1

22:2
^g Ps 42:3

22:3
^h Ps 99:9
ⁱ Dt 10:21

22:5
^j Isa 49:23

22:6
^k Job 25:6;
Isa 41:14
^l Ps 31:11
^m Isa 49:7; 53:3

22:7
ⁿ Mt 27:39,44
^o Mk 15:29

22:8
^p Ps 91:14
^q Mt 27:43

22:9
^r Ps 71:6

22:10
^s Isa 46:3

22:11
^t Ps 72:12

22:12
a Ps 68:30
b Dt 32:14

22:13
c Ps 17:12
d Ps 35:21

22:14
e Ps 31:10
f Job 30:16;
Da 5:6

22:15
g Ps 38:10;
Jn 19:28
h Ps 104:29

22:16
i Ps 59:6
j Isa 53:5;
Zec 12:10;
Jn 19:34

22:17
k Lk 23:35
l Lk 23:27

22:18
m Mt 27:35*;
Lk 23:34;
Jn 19:24*

22:19
n Ps 70:5

22:20
o Ps 35:17

22:22
p Heb 2:12*

22:23
q Ps 86:12;
135:19
r Ps 33:8

22:24
s Ps 69:17
t Heb 5:7

22:25
u Ps 35:18
v Ecc 5:4

22:26
w Ps 107:9
x Ps 40:16

22:27
y Ps 2:8
z Ps 86:9

¹²Many bulls*a* surround me;
　　strong bulls of Bashan*b* encircle me.
¹³Roaring lions*c* tearing their prey
　　open their mouths wide*d* against me.
¹⁴I am poured out like water,
　　and all my bones are out of joint.*e*
　My heart has turned to wax;
　　it has melted away*f* within me.
¹⁵My strength is dried up like a potsherd,
　　and my tongue sticks to the roof of my mouth;*g*
　　you lay me*a* in the dust*h* of death.
¹⁶Dogs*i* have surrounded me;
　　a band of evil men has encircled me,
　　they have pierced*b j* my hands and my feet.
¹⁷I can count all my bones;
　　people stare*k* and gloat over me.*l*
¹⁸They divide my garments among them
　　and cast lots*m* for my clothing.

¹⁹But you, O Lᴏʀᴅ, be not far off;
　　O my Strength, come quickly*n* to help me.
²⁰Deliver my life from the sword,
　　my precious life*o* from the power of the dogs.
²¹Rescue me from the mouth of the lions;
　　save*c* me from the horns of the wild oxen.

²²I will declare your name to my brothers;
　　in the congregation I will praise you.*p*
²³You who fear the Lᴏʀᴅ, praise him!*q*
　　All you descendants of Jacob, honor him!
　　Revere him,*r* all you descendants of Israel!
²⁴For he has not despised or disdained
　　the suffering of the afflicted one;
　he has not hidden his face*s* from him
　　but has listened to his cry for help.*t*

²⁵From you comes the theme of my praise in the great
　　　　assembly;*u*
　　before those who fear you*d* will I fulfill my vows.*v*
²⁶The poor will eat*w* and be satisfied;
　　they who seek the Lᴏʀᴅ will praise him—*x*
　　may your hearts live forever!
²⁷All the ends of the earth*y*
　　will remember and turn to the Lᴏʀᴅ,
　and all the families of the nations
　　will bow down before him,*z*

a 15 Or / I am laid *b 16 Some Hebrew manuscripts, Septuagint and Syriac; most Hebrew manuscripts / like the lion,* *c 21 Or / you have heard* *d 25 Hebrew him*

²⁸for dominion belongs to the LORD*a*
  and he rules over the nations.

²⁹All the rich*b* of the earth will feast and worship;
  all who go down to the dust*c* will kneel before him—
  those who cannot keep themselves alive.
³⁰Posterity*d* will serve him;
  future generations will be told about the Lord.
³¹They will proclaim his righteousness
  to a people yet unborn*e*—
  for he has done it.

Psalm 23

A psalm of David.

Psalm 23 Theme _____

¹The LORD is my shepherd,*f* I shall not be in want.*g*
² He makes me lie down in green pastures,
  he leads me beside quiet waters,*h*
³ he restores my soul.*i*
  He guides me in paths of righteousness*j*
  for his name's sake.
⁴Even though I walk
  through the valley of the shadow of death,*a k*
  I will fear no evil,*l*
  for you are with me;*m*
  your rod and your staff,
  they comfort me.

⁵You prepare a table before me
  in the presence of my enemies.
  You anoint my head with oil;*n*
  my cup*o* overflows.
⁶Surely goodness and love will follow me
  all the days of my life,
  and I will dwell in the house of the LORD forever.

Psalm 24

Of David. A psalm.

Psalm 24 Theme _____

¹The earth is the LORD's,*p* and everything in it,
  the world, and all who live in it;*q*

a 4 Or *through the darkest valley*

22:28
a Ps 47:7-8

22:29
b Ps 45:12
c Isa 26:19

22:30
d Ps 102:28

22:31
e Ps 78:6

23:1
f Isa 40:11;
Jn 10:11;
1Pe 2:25
g Php 4:19

23:2
h Eze 34:14;
Rev 7:17

23:3
i Ps 19:7
j Ps 5:8; 85:13

23:4
k Job 10:21-22
l Ps 3:6; 27:1
m Isa 43:2

23:5
n Ps 92:10
o Ps 16:5

24:1
p Ex 9:29;
Job 41:11;
Ps 89:11
q 1Co 10:26*

24:3
a Ps 2:6
b Ps 15:1; 65:4

²for he founded it upon the seas
  and established it upon the waters.

³Who may ascend the hill*a* of the LORD?
  Who may stand in his holy place?*b*
⁴He who has clean hands*c* and a pure heart,*d*
  who does not lift up his soul to an idol
  or swear by what is false.*a*

24:4
c Job 17:9
d Mt 5:8

⁵He will receive blessing from the LORD
  and vindication from God his Savior.
⁶Such is the generation of those who seek him,
  who seek your face,*e* O God of Jacob.*b*   *Selah*

24:6
e Ps 27:8

⁷Lift up your heads, O you gates;*f*
  be lifted up, you ancient doors,
  that the King of glory*g* may come in.
⁸Who is this King of glory?
  The LORD strong and mighty,
  the LORD mighty in battle.*h*
⁹Lift up your heads, O you gates;
  lift them up, you ancient doors,
  that the King of glory may come in.
¹⁰Who is he, this King of glory?
  The LORD Almighty—
  he is the King of glory.   *Selah*

24:7
f Isa 26:2
g Ps 97:6;
1Co 2:8

24:8
h Ps 76:3-6

Psalm 25*c*

Of David.

Psalm 25 Theme

25:1
i Ps 86:4

¹To you, O LORD, I lift up my soul;*i*
² in you I trust,*j* O my God.
  Do not let me be put to shame,
  nor let my enemies triumph over me.
³No one whose hope is in you
  will ever be put to shame,*k*
  but they will be put to shame
  who are treacherous without excuse.

25:2
j Ps 41:11

25:3
k Isa 49:23

⁴Show me your ways, O LORD,
  teach me your paths;*l*
⁵guide me in your truth and teach me,
  for you are God my Savior,
  and my hope is in you all day long.

25:4
l Ex 33:13

a 4 Or *swear falsely*   b 6 Two Hebrew manuscripts and Syriac (see also Septuagint); most Hebrew manuscripts *face, Jacob*   c This psalm is an acrostic poem, the verses of which begin with the successive letters of the Hebrew alphabet.

⁶Remember, O Lᴏʀᴅ, your great mercy and love,ᵃ
  for they are from of old.
⁷Remember not the sins of my youthᵇ
  and my rebellious ways;
according to your loveᶜ remember me,
  for you are good, O Lᴏʀᴅ.

⁸Good and uprightᵈ is the Lᴏʀᴅ;
  therefore he instructsᵉ sinners in his ways.
⁹He guidesᶠ the humble in what is right
  and teaches themᵍ his way.
¹⁰All the ways of the Lᴏʀᴅ are loving and faithfulʰ
  for those who keep the demands of his covenant.ⁱ
¹¹For the sake of your name,ʲ O Lᴏʀᴅ,
  forgive my iniquity, though it is great.
¹²Who, then, is the man that fears the Lᴏʀᴅ?
  He will instruct him in the wayᵏ chosen for him.
¹³He will spend his days in prosperity,ˡ
  and his descendants will inherit the land.ᵐ
¹⁴The Lᴏʀᴅ confidesⁿ in those who fear him;
  he makes his covenant knownᵒ to them.
¹⁵My eyes are ever on the Lᴏʀᴅ,ᵖ
  for only he will release my feet from the snare.

¹⁶Turn to me�q and be gracious to me,
  for I am lonely and afflicted.
¹⁷The troubles of my heart have multiplied;
  free me from my anguish.ʳ
¹⁸Look upon my affliction and my distressˢ
  and take away all my sins.
¹⁹See how my enemiesᵗ have increased
  and how fiercely they hate me!
²⁰Guard my life ᵘ and rescue me;
  let me not be put to shame,
  for I take refuge in you.
²¹May integrity ᵛ and uprightness protect me,
  because my hope is in you.

²²Redeem Israel,ʷ O God,
  from all their troubles!

Psalm 26

Of David.

*Psalm 26 Theme*_____

¹Vindicate me, O Lᴏʀᴅ,
  for I have led a blameless life;ˣ

25:6
ᵃPs 103:17;
Isa 63:7,15

25:7
ᵇJob 13:26;
Jer 3:25
ᶜPs 51:1

25:8
ᵈPs 92:15
ᵉPs 32:8

25:9
ᶠPs 23:3
ᵍPs 27:11

25:10
ʰPs 40:11
ⁱPs 103:18

25:11
ʲPs 31:3; 79:9

25:12
ᵏPs 37:23

25:13
ˡPr 19:23
ᵐPs 37:11

25:14
ⁿPr 3:32
ᵒJn 7:17

25:15
ᵖPs 141:8

25:16
qPs 69:16

25:17
ʳPs 107:6

25:18
ˢ2Sa 16:12

25:19
ᵗPs 3:1

25:20
ᵘPs 86:2

25:21
ᵛPs 41:12

25:22
ʷPs 130:8

26:1
ˣPs 7:8;
Pr 20:7

I have trusted[a] in the LORD
    without wavering.[b]
[2]Test me,[c] O LORD, and try me,
    examine my heart and my mind;[d]
[3]for your love is ever before me,
    and I walk continually[e] in your truth.
[4]I do not sit[f] with deceitful men,
    nor do I consort with hypocrites;
[5]I abhor[g] the assembly of evildoers
    and refuse to sit with the wicked.
[6]I wash my hands in innocence,[h]
    and go about your altar, O LORD,
[7]proclaiming aloud your praise
    and telling of all your wonderful deeds.[i]
[8]I love[j] the house where you live, O LORD,
    the place where your glory dwells.

[9]Do not take away my soul along with sinners,
    my life with bloodthirsty men,[k]
[10]in whose hands are wicked schemes,
    whose right hands are full of bribes.[l]
[11]But I lead a blameless life;
    redeem me[m] and be merciful to me.

[12]My feet stand on level ground;[n]
    in the great assembly[o] I will praise the LORD.

Psalm 27

Of David.

Psalm 27 Theme

[1]The LORD is my light[p] and my salvation[q]—
    whom shall I fear?
The LORD is the stronghold of my life—
    of whom shall I be afraid?[r]
[2]When evil men advance against me
    to devour my flesh,[a]
when my enemies and my foes attack me,
    they will stumble and fall.[s]
[3]Though an army besiege me,
    my heart will not fear;[t]
though war break out against me,
    even then will I be confident.[u]

26:1
a Ps 28:7
b 2Ki 20:3;
Heb 10:23

26:2
c Ps 17:3
d Ps 7:9

26:3
e 2Ki 20:3

26:4
f Ps 1:1

26:5
g Ps 31:6; 139:21

26:6
h Ps 73:13

26:7
i Ps 9:1

26:8
j Ps 27:4

26:9
k Ps 28:3

26:10
l 1Sa 8:3

26:11
m Ps 69:18

26:12
n Ps 27:11; 40:2
o Ps 22:22

27:1
p Isa 60:19
q Ex 15:2
r Ps 118:6

27:2
s Ps 9:3; 14:4

27:3
t Ps 3:6
u Job 4:6

a 2 Or to slander me

⁴One thing^a I ask of the Lord,
 this is what I seek:
that I may dwell in the house of the Lord
 all the days of my life,^b
to gaze upon the beauty of the Lord
 and to seek him in his temple.
⁵For in the day of trouble
 he will keep me safe in his dwelling;
he will hide me^c in the shelter of his tabernacle
 and set me high upon a rock.^d
⁶Then my head will be exalted^e
 above the enemies who surround me;
at his tabernacle will I sacrifice^f with shouts of joy;
 I will sing and make music to the Lord.

⁷Hear my voice when I call, O Lord;
 be merciful to me and answer me.^g
⁸My heart says of you, "Seek his^a face!"
 Your face, Lord, I will seek.
⁹Do not hide your face^h from me,
 do not turn your servant away in anger;
 you have been my helper.
Do not reject me or forsake me,
 O God my Savior.
¹⁰Though my father and mother forsake me,
 the Lord will receive me.
¹¹Teach me your way, O Lord;
 lead me in a straight pathⁱ
 because of my oppressors.
¹²Do not turn me over to the desire of my foes,
 for false witnesses^j rise up against me,
 breathing out violence.

¹³I am still confident of this:
 I will see the goodness of the Lord^k
 in the land of the living.^l
¹⁴Wait^m for the Lord;
 be strong and take heart
 and wait for the Lord.

Psalm 28

Of David.

Psalm 28 Theme _____

¹To you I call, O Lord my Rock;
 do not turn a deaf ear to me.

^a8 Or *To you, O my heart, he has said, "Seek my*

27:4
^aPs 90:17
^bPs 23:6; 26:8

27:5
^cPs 17:8; 31:20
^dPs 40:2

27:6
^ePs 3:3
^fPs 107:22

27:7
^gPs 13:3

27:9
^hPs 69:17

27:11
ⁱPs 5:8; 25:4; 86:11

27:12
^jMt 26:60; Ac 9:1

27:13
^kPs 31:19
^lJer 11:19; Eze 26:20

27:14
^mPs 40:1

28:1
a Ps 83:1
b Ps 88:4

For if you remain silent,*a*
　　I will be like those who have gone down to the pit.*b*
2Hear my cry for mercy*c*
　　as I call to you for help,
　　as I lift up my hands
　　toward your Most Holy Place.*d*

28:2
c Ps 138:2; 140:6
d Ps 5:7

3Do not drag me away with the wicked,
　　with those who do evil,
　　who speak cordially with their neighbors
　　but harbor malice in their hearts.*e*

28:3
e Ps 12:2;
Ps 26:9; Jer 9:8

4Repay them for their deeds
　　and for their evil work;
　　repay them for what their hands have done*f*
　　and bring back upon them what they deserve.*g*
5Since they show no regard for the works of the Lord
　　and what his hands have done,*h*
　　he will tear them down
　　and never build them up again.

28:4
f 2Ti 4:14;
Rev 22:12
g Rev 18:6

28:5
h Isa 5:12

6Praise be to the Lord,
　　for he has heard my cry for mercy.
7The Lord is my strength*i* and my shield;
　　my heart trusts*j* in him, and I am helped.
　　My heart leaps for joy
　　and I will give thanks to him in song.*k*

28:7
i Ps 18:1
j Ps 13:5
k Ps 40:3; 69:30

8The Lord is the strength of his people,
　　a fortress of salvation for his anointed one.*l*
9Save your people and bless your inheritance;*m*
　　be their shepherd*n* and carry them*o* forever.

28:8
l Ps 20:6

28:9
m Dt 9:29;
Ezr 1:4
n Isa 40:11
o Dt 1:31; 32:11

Psalm 29

A psalm of David.

Psalm 29 Theme _____

29:1
p 1Ch 16:28
q Ps 96:7-9

1Ascribe to the Lord,*p* O mighty ones,
　　ascribe to the Lord glory*q* and strength.
2Ascribe to the Lord the glory due his name;
　　worship the Lord in the splendor of his*a* holiness.*r*

29:2
r 2Ch 20:21

3The voice*s* of the Lord is over the waters;
　　the God of glory thunders,*t*
　　the Lord thunders over the mighty waters.

29:3
s Job 37:5
t Ps 18:13

a 2 Or Lord *with the splendor of*

⁴The voice of the L<small>ORD</small> is powerful;^a
    the voice of the L<small>ORD</small> is majestic.
⁵The voice of the L<small>ORD</small> breaks the cedars;
    the L<small>ORD</small> breaks in pieces the cedars of Lebanon.^b
⁶He makes Lebanon skip^c like a calf,
    Sirion^{a d} like a young wild ox.
⁷The voice of the L<small>ORD</small> strikes
    with flashes of lightning.
⁸The voice of the L<small>ORD</small> shakes the desert;
    the L<small>ORD</small> shakes the Desert of Kadesh.^e
⁹The voice of the L<small>ORD</small> twists the oaks^b
    and strips the forests bare.
  And in his temple all cry, "Glory!"^f

¹⁰The L<small>ORD</small> sits^c enthroned over the flood;^g
    the L<small>ORD</small> is enthroned as King forever.^h
¹¹The L<small>ORD</small> gives strength to his people;ⁱ
    the L<small>ORD</small> blesses his people with peace.^j

Psalm 30

A psalm. A song. For the dedication of the temple.^d Of David.

Psalm 30 Theme _____

¹I will exalt you, O Lord,
    for you lifted me out of the depths
    and did not let my enemies gloat over me.^k
²O L<small>ORD</small> my God, I called to you for help^l
    and you healed me.^m
³O L<small>ORD</small>, you brought me up from the grave^e;
    you spared me from going down into the pit.ⁿ

⁴Sing to the L<small>ORD</small>, you saints^o of his;
    praise his holy name.^p
⁵For his anger^q lasts only a moment,
    but his favor lasts a lifetime;
  weeping may remain for a night,
    but rejoicing comes in the morning.^r

⁶When I felt secure, I said,
    "I will never be shaken."
⁷O L<small>ORD</small>, when you favored me,
    you made my mountain^f stand firm;
  but when you hid your face,^s
    I was dismayed.

^a 6 That is, Mount Hermon ^b 9 Or L<small>ORD</small> *makes the deer give birth* ^c 10 Or *sat* ^d Title: Or *palace* ^e 3 Hebrew *Sheol* ^f 7 Or *hill country*

29:4
^a Ps 68:33

29:5
^b Jdg 9:15

29:6
^c Ps 114:4
^d Dt 3:9

29:8
^e Nu 13:26

29:9
^f Ps 26:8

29:10
^g Ge 6:17
^h Ps 10:16

29:11
ⁱ Ps 28:8
^j Ps 37:11

30:1
^k Ps 25:2; 28:9

30:2
^l Ps 88:13
^m Ps 6:2

30:3
ⁿ Ps 28:1; 86:13

30:4
^o Ps 149:1
^p Ps 97:12

30:5
^q Ps 103:9
^r 2Co 4:17

30:7
^s Dt 31:17;
Ps 104:29

30:9
a Ps 6:5

30:11
b Ps 4:7;
Jer 31:4,13

30:12
c Ps 16:9
d Ps 44:8

31:2
e Ps 18:2

31:3
f Ps 18:2
g Ps 23:3

31:4
h Ps 25:15

31:5
i Lk 23:46;
Ac 7:59

31:6
j Jnh 2:8

31:7
k Ps 90:14
l Ps 10:14;
Jn 10:27

31:8
m Dt 32:30

31:9
n Ps 6:7

⁸To you, O Lord, I called;
   to the Lord I cried for mercy:
⁹"What gain is there in my destruction,ᵃ
   in my going down into the pit?
Will the dust praise you?
   Will it proclaim your faithfulness?ᵃ
¹⁰Hear, O Lord, and be merciful to me;
   O Lord, be my help."

¹¹You turned my wailing into dancing;
   you removed my sackcloth and clothed me with joy,ᵇ
¹²that my heart may sing to you and not be silent.
   O Lord my God, I will give you thanksᶜ forever.ᵈ

Psalm 31

For the director of music. A psalm of David.

Psalm 31 Theme _____

¹In you, O Lord, I have taken refuge;
   let me never be put to shame;
   deliver me in your righteousness.
²Turn your ear to me,
   come quickly to my rescue;
 be my rock of refuge,ᵉ
   a strong fortress to save me.
³Since you are my rock and my fortress,ᶠ
   for the sake of your nameᵍ lead and guide me.
⁴Free me from the trap that is set for me,
   for you are my refuge.ʰ
⁵Into your hands I commit my spirit;ⁱ
   redeem me, O Lord, the God of truth.

⁶I hate those who cling to worthless idols;
   I trust in the Lord.ʲ
⁷I will be glad and rejoice in your love,
   for you saw my afflictionᵏ
   and knew the anguishˡ of my soul.
⁸You have not handed me overᵐ to the enemy
   but have set my feet in a spacious place.

⁹Be merciful to me, O Lord, for I am in distress;
   my eyes grow weak with sorrow,ⁿ
   my soul and my body with grief.

ᵃ 9 Or *there if I am silenced*

925

¹⁰My life is consumed by anguish
    and my years by groaning;^a
my strength fails because of my affliction,^a
    and my bones grow weak.^b
¹¹Because of all my enemies,
    I am the utter contempt of my neighbors;^c
I am a dread to my friends—
    those who see me on the street flee from me.
¹²I am forgotten by them as though I were dead;^d
    I have become like broken pottery.
¹³For I hear the slander of many;
    there is terror on every side;^e
they conspire against me
    and plot to take my life.^f

¹⁴But I trust^g in you, O Lord;
    I say, "You are my God."
¹⁵My times^h are in your hands;
    deliver me from my enemies
    and from those who pursue me.
¹⁶Let your face shineⁱ on your servant;
    save me in your unfailing love.
¹⁷Let me not be put to shame,^j O Lord,
    for I have cried out to you;
but let the wicked be put to shame
    and lie silent^k in the grave.^b
¹⁸Let their lying lips^l be silenced,
    for with pride and contempt
    they speak arrogantly^m against the righteous.

¹⁹How great is your goodness,ⁿ
    which you have stored up for those who fear you,
which you bestow in the sight of men^o
    on those who take refuge in you.
²⁰In the shelter of your presence you hide^p them
    from the intrigues of men;^q
in your dwelling you keep them safe
    from accusing tongues.

²¹Praise be to the Lord,
    for he showed his wonderful love^r to me
    when I was in a besieged city.^s
²²In my alarm^t I said,
    "I am cut off from your sight!"
Yet you heard my cry^u for mercy
    when I called to you for help.

^a*10* Or *guilt*   ^b*17* Hebrew *Sheol*

31:10
^aPs 13:2
^bPs 38:3; 39:11

31:11
^cJob 19:13;
Ps 38:11; 64:8;
Isa 53:4

31:12
^dPs 88:4

31:13
^eJer 20:3,10;
La 2:22
^fMt 27:1

31:14
^gPs 140:6

31:15
^hJob 24:1;
Ps 143:9

31:16
ⁱNu 6:25; Ps 4:6

31:17
^jPs 25:2-3
^kPs 115:17

31:18
^lPs 120:2
^mPs 94:4

31:19
ⁿRo 11:22
^oIsa 64:4

31:20
^pPs 27:5
^qJob 5:21

31:21
^rPs 17:7
^s1Sa 23:7

31:22
^tPs 116:11
^uLa 3:54

31:23
a Ps 34:9
b Ps 145:20
c Ps 94:2

²³Love the LORD, all his saints!*ᵃ*
  The LORD preserves the faithful,*ᵇ*
  but the proud he pays back*ᶜ* in full.
²⁴Be strong and take heart,*ᵈ*
  all you who hope in the LORD.

31:24
d Ps 27:14

Psalm 32

Of David. A *maskil.*ᵃ

32:1
e Ps 85:2

Psalm 32 Theme

¹Blessed is he
  whose transgressions are forgiven,
  whose sins are covered. *ᵉ*
²Blessed is the man
  whose sin the LORD does not count against him*ᶠ*
  and in whose spirit is no deceit.*ᵍ*

32:2
f Ro 4:7-8*;
2Co 5:19
g Jn 1:47

³When I kept silent,
  my bones wasted away*ʰ*
  through my groaning all day long.
⁴For day and night
  your hand was heavy*ⁱ* upon me;
my strength was sapped
  as in the heat of summer.   *Selah*

32:3
h Ps 31:10

32:4
i Job 33:7

⁵Then I acknowledged my sin to you
  and did not cover up my iniquity.
I said, "I will confess*ʲ*
  my transgressions*ᵏ* to the LORD"—
and you forgave
  the guilt of my sin.*ˡ*   *Selah*

32:5
j Pr 28:13
k Ps 103:12
l Lev 26:40

⁶Therefore let everyone who is godly pray to you
  while you may be found;*ᵐ*
surely when the mighty waters rise,
  they will not reach him.*ⁿ*
⁷You are my hiding place;
  you will protect me from trouble*ᵒ*
  and surround me with songs of deliverance.*ᵖ* *Selah*

32:6
m Ps 69:13;
Isa 55:6
n Isa 43:2

32:7
o Ps 9:9
p Ex 15:1

⁸I will instruct*q* you and teach you in the way
    you should go;
  I will counsel you and watch over*ʳ* you.

32:8
q Ps 25:8
r Ps 33:18

ᵃ Title: Probably a literary or musical term

⁹Do not be like the horse or the mule,
  which have no understanding
but must be controlled by bit and bridle[a]
  or they will not come to you.
¹⁰Many are the woes of the wicked,[b]
  but the LORD's unfailing love
  surrounds the man who trusts[c] in him.

¹¹Rejoice in the LORD[d] and be glad, you righteous;
  sing, all you who are upright in heart!

Psalm 33

Psalm 33 Theme _____

¹Sing joyfully to the LORD, you righteous;
  it is fitting[e] for the upright[f] to praise him.
²Praise the LORD with the harp;
  make music to him on the ten-stringed lyre.[g]
³Sing to him a new song;[h]
  play skillfully, and shout for joy.

⁴For the word of the LORD is right[i] and true;
  he is faithful in all he does.
⁵The LORD loves righteousness and justice;[j]
  the earth is full of his unfailing love.[k]

⁶By the word[l] of the LORD were the heavens made,
  their starry host by the breath of his mouth.
⁷He gathers the waters of the sea into jars[a];
  he puts the deep into storehouses.
⁸Let all the earth fear the LORD;
  let all the people of the world revere him.[m]
⁹For he spoke, and it came to be;
  he commanded,[n] and it stood firm.
¹⁰The LORD foils the plans of the nations;[o]
  he thwarts the purposes of the peoples.
¹¹But the plans of the LORD stand firm forever,
  the purposes[p] of his heart through all generations.

¹²Blessed is the nation whose God is the LORD,[q]
  the people he chose[r] for his inheritance.
¹³From heaven the LORD looks down
  and sees all mankind;[s]
¹⁴from his dwelling place[t] he watches
  all who live on earth—

a 7 Or *sea as into a heap*

32:9
a Pr 26:3

32:10
b Ro 2:9
c Pr 16:20

32:11
d Ps 64:10

33:1
e Ps 147:1
f Ps 32:11

33:2
g Ps 92:3

33:3
h Ps 96:1

33:4
i Ps 19:8

33:5
j Ps 11:7
k Ps 119:64

33:6
l Heb 11:3

33:8
m Ps 67:7; 96:9

33:9
n Ge 1:3;
Ps 148:5

33:10
o Isa 8:10

33:11
p Job 23:13

33:12
q Ps 144:15
r Ex 19:5; Dt 7:6

33:13
s Job 28:24;
Ps 11:4

33:14
t 1Ki 8:39

33:15
a Job 10:8
b Jer 32:19

33:16
c Ps 44:6

33:17
d Ps 20:7;
Pr 21:31

33:18
e Job 36:7;
Ps 34:15
f Ps 147:11

33:19
g Job 5:20

33:20
h Ps 130:6

33:21
i Zec 10:7;
Jn 16:22

34:1
j Ps 71:6;
Eph 5:20

34:2
k Jer 9:24;
1Co 1:31
l Ps 119:74

34:3
m Lk 1:46

34:4
n Mt 7:7

34:5
o Ps 36:9
p Ps 25:3

34:7
q 2Ki 6:17;
Da 6:22

34:8
r 1Pe 2:3
s Ps 2:12

[15]he who forms[a] the hearts of all,
who considers everything they do.[b]
[16]No king is saved by the size of his army;[c]
no warrior escapes by his great strength.
[17]A horse[d] is a vain hope for deliverance;
despite all its great strength it cannot save.
[18]But the eyes[e] of the LORD are on those who fear him,
on those whose hope is in his unfailing love,[f]
[19]to deliver them from death
and keep them alive in famine.[g]

[20]We wait[h] in hope for the LORD;
he is our help and our shield.
[21]In him our hearts rejoice,[i]
for we trust in his holy name.
[22]May your unfailing love rest upon us, O LORD,
even as we put our hope in you.

Psalm 34[a]

Of David. When he pretended to be insane before Abimelech,
who drove him away, and he left.

*Psalm 34 Theme*_____

[1]I will extol the LORD at all times;[j]
his praise will always be on my lips.
[2]My soul will boast[k] in the LORD;
let the afflicted hear and rejoice.[l]
[3]Glorify the LORD with me;
let us exalt[m] his name together.

[4]I sought the LORD,[n] and he answered me;
he delivered me from all my fears.
[5]Those who look to him are radiant;[o]
their faces are never covered with shame.[p]
[6]This poor man called, and the LORD heard him;
he saved him out of all his troubles.
[7]The angel of the LORD[q] encamps around those
who fear him,
and he delivers them.

[8]Taste and see that the LORD is good;[r]
blessed is the man who takes refuge[s] in him.

a This psalm is an acrostic poem, the verses of which begin with the successive letters of the Hebrew alphabet.

⁹Fear the LORD, you his saints,
　for those who fear him lack nothing.ᵃ
¹⁰The lions may grow weak and hungry,
　but those who seek the LORD lack no good thing.ᵇ

¹¹Come, my children, listen to me;
　I will teach youᶜ the fear of the LORD.
¹²Whoever of you loves lifeᵈ
　and desires to see many good days,
¹³keep your tongue from evil
　and your lips from speaking lies.ᵉ
¹⁴Turn from evil and do good;ᶠ
　seek peaceᵍ and pursue it.

¹⁵The eyes of the LORDʰ are on the righteousⁱ
　and his ears are attentive to their cry;
¹⁶the face of the LORD is againstʲ those who do evil,ᵏ
　to cut off the memoryˡ of them from the earth.

¹⁷The righteous cry out, and the LORD hearsᵐ them;
　he delivers them from all their troubles.
¹⁸The LORD is closeⁿ to the brokenheartedᵒ
　and saves those who are crushed in spirit.

¹⁹A righteous man may have many troubles,ᵖ
　but the LORD delivers him from them all;�q
²⁰he protects all his bones,
　not one of them will be broken.ʳ

²¹Evil will slay the wicked;ˢ
　the foes of the righteous will be condemned.
²²The LORD redeemsᵗ his servants;
　no one will be condemned who takes refuge in him.

Psalm 35

Of David.

Psalm 35 Theme

¹Contend, O LORD, with those who contend with me;
　fightᵘ against those who fight against me.
²Take up shield and buckler;
　ariseᵛ and come to my aid.
³Brandish spear and javelinᵃ
　against those who pursue me.
　Say to my soul,
　　"I am your salvation."

ᵃ3 Or *and block the way*

34:9
ᵃPs 23:1

34:10
ᵇPs 84:11

34:11
ᶜPs 32:8

34:12
ᵈ1Pe 3:10

34:13
ᵉ1Pe 2:22

34:14
ᶠPs 37:27
ᵍHeb 12:14

34:15
ʰPs 33:18
ⁱJob 36:7

34:16
ʲLev 17:10;
Jer 44:11
ᵏ1Pe 3:10-12*
ˡPr 10:7

34:17
ᵐPs 145:19

34:18
ⁿPs 145:18
ᵒIsa 57:15

34:19
ᵖver 17
qver 4,6;
Pr 24:16

34:20
ʳJn 19:36*

34:21
ˢPs 94:23

34:22
ᵗ1Ki 1:29;
Ps 71:23

35:1
ᵘPs 43:1

35:2
ᵛPs 62:2

⁴May those who seek my life
    be disgraced^a and put to shame;
may those who plot my ruin
    be turned back in dismay.
⁵May they be like chaff^b before the wind,
    with the angel of the LORD driving them away;
⁶may their path be dark and slippery,
    with the angel of the LORD pursuing them.
⁷Since they hid their net for me without cause
    and without cause dug a pit for me,
⁸may ruin overtake them by surprise—^c
    may the net they hid entangle them,
    may they fall into the pit,^d to their ruin.
⁹Then my soul will rejoice^e in the LORD
    and delight in his salvation.^f
¹⁰My whole being will exclaim,
    "Who is like you,^g O LORD?
You rescue the poor from those too strong^h for them,
    the poor and needyⁱ from those who rob them."

¹¹Ruthless witnesses^j come forward;
    they question me on things I know nothing about.
¹²They repay me evil for good^k
    and leave my soul forlorn.
¹³Yet when they were ill, I put on sackcloth
    and humbled myself with fasting.^l
When my prayers returned to me unanswered,
¹⁴ I went about mourning
    as though for my friend or brother.
I bowed my head in grief
    as though weeping for my mother.
¹⁵But when I stumbled, they gathered in glee;
    attackers gathered against me when I was unaware.
    They slandered^m me without ceasing.
¹⁶Like the ungodly they maliciously mocked^a;
    they gnashed their teethⁿ at me.
¹⁷O Lord, how long^o will you look on?
    Rescue my life from their ravages,
    my precious life^p from these lions.
¹⁸I will give you thanks in the great assembly;^q
    among throngs of people I will praise you.^r

¹⁹Let not those gloat over me
    who are my enemies without cause;

35:4
^a Ps 70:2

35:5
^b Job 21:18;
Ps 1:4; Isa 29:5

35:8
^c 1Th 5:3
^d Ps 9:15

35:9
^e Lk 1:47
^f Isa 61:10

35:10
^g Ex 15:11
^h Ps 18:17
ⁱ Ps 37:14

35:11
^j Ps 27:12

35:12
^k Jn 10:32

35:13
^l Job 30:25;
Ps 69:10

35:15
^m Job 30:1,8

35:16
ⁿ Job 16:9;
La 2:16

35:17
^o Hab 1:13
^p Ps 22:20

35:18
^q Ps 22:25
^r Ps 22:22

---

^a 16 Septuagint; Hebrew may mean *ungodly circle of mockers.*

　　let not those who hate me without reason[a]
　　　maliciously wink the eye.[b]
20They do not speak peaceably,
　　but devise false accusations
　　against those who live quietly in the land.
21They gape[c] at me and say, "Aha! Aha![d]
　　With our own eyes we have seen it."

22O LORD, you have seen[e] this; be not silent.
　　Do not be far[f] from me, O Lord.
23Awake,[g] and rise to my defense!
　　Contend for me, my God and Lord.
24Vindicate me in your righteousness, O LORD my God;
　　do not let them gloat over me.
25Do not let them think, "Aha, just what we wanted!"
　　or say, "We have swallowed him up."[h]

26May all who gloat over my distress
　　be put to shame[i] and confusion;
　　may all who exalt themselves over me[j]
　　be clothed with shame and disgrace.
27May those who delight in my vindication[k]
　　shout for joy[l] and gladness;
　　may they always say, "The LORD be exalted,
　　who delights[m] in the well-being of his servant."
28My tongue will speak of your righteousness[n]
　　and of your praises all day long.

Psalm 36

For the director of music. Of David the servant of the LORD.

*Psalm 36 Theme*_____

1An oracle is within my heart
　　concerning the sinfulness of the wicked:[a]
　　There is no fear of God
　　　before his eyes.[o]
2For in his own eyes he flatters himself
　　too much to detect or hate his sin.
3The words of his mouth[p] are wicked and deceitful;
　　he has ceased to be wise[q] and to do good.[r]
4Even on his bed he plots evil;[s]
　　he commits himself to a sinful course[t]
　　and does not reject what is wrong.[u]

a 1 Or *heart: / Sin proceeds from the wicked.*

35:19
a Ps 38:19; 69:4;
Jn 15:25*
b Ps 13:4;
Pr 6:13

35:21
c Ps 22:13
d Ps 40:15

35:22
e Ex 3:7
f Ps 10:1; 28:1

35:23
g Ps 44:23

35:25
h La 2:16

35:26
i Ps 40:14;
109:29
j Ps 38:16

35:27
k Ps 9:4
l Ps 32:11
m Ps 40:16;
147:11

35:28
n Ps 51:14

36:1
o Ro 3:18*

36:3
p Ps 10:7
q Ps 94:8
r Jer 4:22

36:4
s Pr 4:16;
Mic 2:1
t Isa 65:2
u Ps 52:3;
Ro 12:9

36:6
a Job 11:8;
Ps 77:19;
Ro 11:33

36:7
b Ru 2:12;
Ps 17:8

36:8
c Ps 65:4
d Job 20:17;
Rev 22:1

36:9
e Jer 2:13
f 1Pe 2:9

36:12
g Ps 140:10

37:1
h Pr 23:17-18
i Ps 73:3

37:2
j Ps 90:6

37:3
k Dt 30:20
l Isa 40:11;
Jn 10:9

37:4
m Isa 58:14

37:5
n Ps 4:5;
Ps 55:22;
Pr 16:3; 1Pe 5:7

37:6
o Mic 7:9
p Job 11:17

37:7
q Ps 62:5;
La 3:26
r Ps 40:1

⁵Your love, O LORD, reaches to the heavens,
your faithfulness to the skies.
⁶Your righteousness is like the mighty mountains,
your justice like the great deep.ᵃ
O LORD, you preserve both man and beast.
⁷ How priceless is your unfailing love!
Both high and low among men
findᵃ refuge in the shadow of your wings.ᵇ
⁸They feast on the abundance of your house;ᶜ
you give them drink from your riverᵈ of delights.
⁹For with you is the fountain of life;ᵉ
in your lightᶠ we see light.

¹⁰Continue your love to those who know you,
your righteousness to the upright in heart.
¹¹May the foot of the proud not come against me,
nor the hand of the wicked drive me away.
¹²See how the evildoers lie fallen—
thrown down, not able to rise!ᵍ

Psalm 37ᵇ

Of David.

Psalm 37 Theme

¹Do not fret because of evil men
or be enviousʰ of those who do wrong;ⁱ
²for like the grass they will soon wither,
like green plants they will soon die away.ʲ

³Trust in the LORD and do good;
dwell in the landᵏ and enjoy safe pasture.ˡ
⁴Delightᵐ yourself in the LORD
and he will give you the desires of your heart.

⁵Commit your way to the LORD;
trust in himⁿ and he will do this:
⁶He will make your righteousnessᵒ shine like the dawn,ᵖ
the justice of your cause like the noonday sun.

⁷Be stillᵍ before the LORD and wait patientlyʳ for him;
do not fret when men succeed in their ways,
when they carry out their wicked schemes.

ᵃ 7 Or love, O God! / Men find; or love! / Both heavenly beings and men / find   ᵇ This psalm is an acrostic poem, the stanzas of which begin with the successive letters of the Hebrew alphabet.

⁸Refrain from anger^a and turn from wrath;
 do not fret—it leads only to evil.
⁹For evil men will be cut off,
 but those who hope in the LORD will inherit the land.^b

¹⁰A little while, and the wicked will be no more;^c
 though you look for them, they will not be found.
¹¹But the meek will inherit the land^d
 and enjoy great peace.

¹²The wicked plot against the righteous
 and gnash their teeth^e at them;
¹³but the Lord laughs at the wicked,
 for he knows their day is coming.^f

¹⁴The wicked draw the sword
 and bend the bow^g
to bring down the poor and needy,^h
 to slay those whose ways are upright.
¹⁵But their swords will pierce their own hearts,ⁱ
 and their bows will be broken.

¹⁶Better the little that the righteous have
 than the wealth^j of many wicked;
¹⁷for the power of the wicked will be broken,^k
 but the LORD upholds the righteous.

¹⁸The days of the blameless are known to the LORD,^l
 and their inheritance will endure forever.
¹⁹In times of disaster they will not wither;
 in days of famine they will enjoy plenty.

²⁰But the wicked will perish:
 The LORD's enemies will be like the beauty
  of the fields,
 they will vanish—vanish like smoke.^m

²¹The wicked borrow and do not repay,
 but the righteous give generously;ⁿ
²²those the LORD blesses will inherit the land,
 but those he curses^o will be cut off.

²³If the LORD delights^p in a man's way,
 he makes his steps firm;^q
²⁴though he stumble, he will not fall,^r
 for the LORD upholds^s him with his hand.

²⁵I was young and now I am old,
 yet I have never seen the righteous forsaken^t
 or their children begging bread.
²⁶They are always generous and lend freely;
 their children will be blessed.^u

**Cross references (margin):**

37:8 [a] Eph 4:31; Col 3:8
37:9 [b] Isa 57:13; 60:21
37:10 [c] Job 7:10; 24:24
37:11 [d] Mt 5:5
37:12 [e] Ps 35:16
37:13 [f] 1Sa 26:10; Ps 2:4
37:14 [g] Ps 11:2 [h] Ps 35:10
37:15 [i] Ps 9:16
37:16 [j] Pr 15:16
37:17 [k] Job 38:15; Ps 10:15
37:18 [l] Ps 1:6
37:20 [m] Ps 102:3
37:21 [n] Ps 112:5
37:22 [o] Job 5:3; Pr 3:33
37:23 [p] Ps 147:11 [q] 1Sa 2:9
37:24 [r] Pr 24:16 [s] Ps 145:14; 147:6
37:25 [t] Heb 13:5
37:26 [u] Ps 147:13

²For your arrows[a] have pierced me,
   and your hand has come down upon me.
³Because of your wrath there is no health in my body;
   my bones[b] have no soundness because of my sin.
⁴My guilt has overwhelmed me
   like a burden too heavy to bear.[c]

⁵My wounds fester and are loathsome
   because of my sinful folly.[d]
⁶I am bowed down and brought very low;
   all day long I go about mourning.[e]
⁷My back is filled with searing pain;[f]
   there is no health in my body.
⁸I am feeble and utterly crushed;
   I groan[g] in anguish of heart.

⁹All my longings lie open before you, O Lord;
   my sighing[h] is not hidden from you.
¹⁰My heart pounds, my strength fails[i] me;
   even the light has gone from my eyes.[j]
¹¹My friends and companions avoid me because
      of my wounds;[k]
   my neighbors stay far away.
¹²Those who seek my life set their traps,[l]
   those who would harm me talk of my ruin;[m]
   all day long they plot deception.[n]

¹³I am like a deaf man, who cannot hear,
   like a mute, who cannot open his mouth;
¹⁴I have become like a man who does not hear,
   whose mouth can offer no reply.
¹⁵I wait[o] for you, O LORD;
   you will answer,[p] O Lord my God.
¹⁶For I said, "Do not let them gloat[q]
   or exalt themselves over me when my foot slips."[r]

¹⁷For I am about to fall,
   and my pain is ever with me.
¹⁸I confess my iniquity;[s]
   I am troubled by my sin.
¹⁹Many are those who are my vigorous enemies;[t]
   those who hate me without reason[u] are numerous.
²⁰Those who repay my good with evil[v]
   slander me when I pursue what is good.

²¹O LORD, do not forsake me;
   be not far[w] from me, O my God.
²²Come quickly to help me,[x]
   O Lord my Savior.[y]

38:2 a Job 6:4; Ps 32:4

38:3 b Ps 6:2; Isa 1:6

38:4 c Ezr 9:6

38:5 d Ps 69:5

38:6 e Job 30:28; Ps 35:14; 42:9

38:7 f Ps 102:3

38:8 g Ps 22:1

38:9 h Job 3:24; Ps 6:6; 10:17

38:10 i Ps 31:10
j Ps 6:7

38:11 k Ps 31:11

38:12 l Ps 140:5
m Ps 35:4; 54:3
n Ps 35:20

38:15 o Ps 39:7
p Ps 17:6

38:16 q Ps 35:26
r Ps 13:4

38:18 s Ps 32:5

38:19 t Ps 18:17
u Ps 35:19

38:20 v Ps 35:12; 1Jn 3:12

38:21 w Ps 35:22

38:22 x Ps 40:13
y Ps 27:1

37:27
a Ps 34:14

37:28
b Ps 21:10;
Isa 14:20

37:29
c ver 9; Pr 2:21

37:31
d Dt 6:6; Ps 40:8;
Isa 51:7
e ver 23

37:32
f Ps 10:8

37:33
g Ps 109:31;
2Pe 2:9

37:34
h Ps 27:14
i Ps 52:6

37:35
j Job 5:3

37:36
k Job 20:5

37:37
l Isa 57:1-2

37:38
m Ps 1:4

37:39
n Ps 3:8
o Ps 9:9

37:40
p 1Ch 5:20
q Isa 31:5

38:1
r Ps 6:1

[27]Turn from evil and do good;[a]
   then you will dwell in the land forever.
[28]For the LORD loves the just
   and will not forsake his faithful ones.

They will be protected forever,
   but the offspring of the wicked will be cut off;[b]
[29]the righteous will inherit the land[c]
   and dwell in it forever.

[30]The mouth of the righteous man utters wisdom,
   and his tongue speaks what is just.
[31]The law of his God is in his heart;[d]
   his feet do not slip.[e]

[32]The wicked lie in wait[f] for the righteous,
   seeking their very lives;
[33]but the LORD will not leave them in their power
   or let them be condemned when brought to trial.[g]

[34]Wait for the LORD[h]
   and keep his way.
He will exalt you to inherit the land;
   when the wicked are cut off, you will see[i] it.

[35]I have seen a wicked and ruthless man
   flourishing[j] like a green tree in its native soil,
[36]but he soon passed away and was no more;
   though I looked for him, he could not be found.[k]

[37]Consider the blameless, observe the upright;
   there is a future[a] for the man of peace.[l]
[38]But all sinners will be destroyed;
   the future[b] of the wicked will be cut off.[m]

[39]The salvation[n] of the righteous comes from the LORD;
   he is their stronghold in time of trouble.[o]
[40]The LORD helps[p] them and delivers[q] them;
   he delivers them from the wicked and saves them,
   because they take refuge in him.

Psalm 38

A psalm of David. A petition.

Psalm 38 Theme _____

[1]O LORD, do not rebuke me in your anger
   or discipline me in your wrath.[r]

a 37 Or *there will be posterity*   b 38 Or *posterity*

Psalm 39

For the director of music. For Jeduthun. A psalm of David.

Psalm 39 Theme

39:1
a 1Ki 2:4
b Job 2:10;
Jas 3:2

[1] I said, "I will watch my ways[a]
and keep my tongue from sin;[b]
I will put a muzzle on my mouth
as long as the wicked are in my presence."

39:2
c Ps 38:13

[2] But when I was silent[c] and still,
not even saying anything good,
my anguish increased.

39:4
d Ps 90:12
e Ps 103:14

[3] My heart grew hot within me,
and as I meditated, the fire burned;
then I spoke with my tongue:

39:5
f Ps 89:45
g Ps 62:9

[4] "Show me, O LORD, my life's end
and the number of my days;[d]
let me know how fleeting is my life.[e]
[5] You have made my days[f] a mere handbreadth;
the span of my years is as nothing before you.
Each man's life is but a breath.[g]   *Selah*

39:6
h 1Pe 1:24
i Ps 127:2
j Lk 12:20

[6] Man is a mere phantom[h] as he goes to and fro:
He bustles about, but only in vain;[i]
he heaps up wealth, not knowing who will get it.[j]

39:7
k Ps 38:15

[7] "But now, Lord, what do I look for?
My hope is in you.[k]

39:8
l Ps 51:9
m Ps 44:13

[8] Save me[l] from all my transgressions;[m]
do not make me the scorn of fools.

39:9
n Job 2:10

[9] I was silent; I would not open my mouth,[n]
for you are the one who has done this.

39:10
o Job 9:34;
Ps 32:4

[10] Remove your scourge from me;
I am overcome by the blow of your hand.[o]

39:11
p 2Pe 2:16
q Job 13:28

[11] You rebuke[p] and discipline men for their sin;
you consume their wealth like a moth[q]—
each man is but a breath.   *Selah*

39:12
r 1Pe 2:11
s Heb 11:13

[12] "Hear my prayer, O LORD,
listen to my cry for help;
be not deaf to my weeping.
For I dwell with you as an alien,[r]
a stranger,[s] as all my fathers were.

39:13
t Job 10:21;
14:10

[13] Look away from me, that I may rejoice again
before I depart and am no more."[t]

Psalm 40

For the director of music. Of David. A psalm.

Psalm 40 Theme

¹I waited patiently[a] for the LORD;
  he turned to me and heard my cry.[b]
²He lifted me out of the slimy pit,
  out of the mud and mire;[c]
he set my feet on a rock[d]
  and gave me a firm place to stand.
³He put a new song[e] in my mouth,
  a hymn of praise to our God.
Many will see and fear
  and put their trust in the LORD.

⁴Blessed is the man[f]
  who makes the LORD his trust,[g]
who does not look to the proud,
  to those who turn aside to false gods.[a]
⁵Many, O LORD my God,
  are the wonders[h] you have done.
The things you planned for us
  no one can recount[i] to you;
were I to speak and tell of them,
  they would be too many to declare.

⁶Sacrifice and offering you did not desire,[j]
  but my ears you have pierced[b,c];
burnt offerings[k] and sin offerings
  you did not require.
⁷Then I said, "Here I am, I have come—
  it is written about me in the scroll.[d]
⁸I desire to do your will,[l] O my God;
  your law is within my heart."[m]

⁹I proclaim righteousness in the great assembly;[n]
  I do not seal my lips,
  as you know,[o] O LORD.
¹⁰I do not hide your righteousness in my heart;
  I speak of your faithfulness[p] and salvation.
I do not conceal your love and your truth
  from the great assembly.[q]

¹¹Do not withhold your mercy from me, O LORD;
  may your love[r] and your truth[s] always protect me.

---

a4 Or *to falsehood*   b6 Hebrew; Septuagint *but a body you have prepared for me* (see also Symmachus and Theodotion)   c6 Or *opened*   d7 Or *come / with the scroll written for me*

40:1
a Ps 27:14
b Ps 34:15

40:2
c Ps 69:14
d Ps 27:5

40:3
e Ps 33:3

40:4
f Ps 34:8
g Ps 84:12

40:5
h Ps 136:4
i Ps 139:18;
Isa 55:8

40:6
j 1Sa 15:22;
Am 5:22
k Isa 1:11

40:8
l Jn 4:34
m Ps 37:31

40:9
n Ps 22:25
o Jos 22:22;
Ps 119:13

40:10
p Ps 89:1
q Ac 20:20

40:11
r Pr 20:28
s Ps 43:3

40:12
a Ps 116:3
b Ps 38:4
c Ps 69:4
d Ps 73:26

¹²For troubles*a* without number surround me;
my sins have overtaken me, and I cannot see.*b*
They are more than the hairs of my head,*c*
and my heart fails*d* within me.

40:13
e Ps 70:1

¹³Be pleased, O Lord, to save me;
O Lord, come quickly to help me.*e*
¹⁴May all who seek to take my life
be put to shame and confusion;
may all who desire my ruin*f*
be turned back in disgrace.

40:14
f Ps 35:4

¹⁵May those who say to me, "Aha! Aha!"
be appalled at their own shame.
¹⁶But may all who seek you
rejoice and be glad in you;
may those who love your salvation always say,
"The Lord be exalted!"*g*

40:16
g Ps 35:27

40:17
h Ps 70:5

¹⁷Yet I am poor and needy;
may the Lord think of me.
You are my help and my deliverer;
O my God, do not delay.*h*

Psalm 41

For the director of music. A psalm of David.

41:1
i Ps 82:3-4;
Pr 14:21

Psalm 41 Theme

41:2
j Ps 37:22
k Ps 27:12

¹Blessed is he who has regard for the weak;*i*
the Lord delivers him in times of trouble.
²The Lord will protect him and preserve his life;
he will bless him in the land*j*
and not surrender him to the desire of his foes.*k*
³The Lord will sustain him on his sickbed
and restore him from his bed of illness.

41:4
l Ps 6:2
m Ps 51:4

⁴I said, "O Lord, have mercy*l* on me;
heal me, for I have sinned*m* against you."
⁵My enemies say of me in malice,
"When will he die and his name perish?*n*"

41:5
n Ps 38:12

41:6
o Ps 12:2
p Pr 26:24

⁶Whenever one comes to see me,
he speaks falsely,*o* while his heart gathers slander;*p*
then he goes out and spreads it abroad.

41:7
q Ps 56:5;
71:10-11

⁷All my enemies whisper together*q* against me;
they imagine the worst for me, saying,

⁸"A vile disease has beset him;
  he will never get up from the place where he lies."
⁹Even my close friend,^a whom I trusted,
  he who shared my bread,
  has lifted up his heel against me.^b

¹⁰But you, O LORD, have mercy on me;
  raise me up,^c that I may repay them.
¹¹I know that you are pleased with me,^d
  for my enemy does not triumph over me.^e
¹²In my integrity you uphold me^f
  and set me in your presence forever.^g

¹³Praise be to the LORD, the God of Israel,^h
  from everlasting to everlasting.
      Amen and Amen.ⁱ

BOOK II

Psalms 42-72

Psalm 42^a

For the director of music. A *maskil* ^b of the Sons of Korah.

Psalm 42 Theme _____

¹As the deer pants for streams of water,
  so my soul pants^j for you, O God.
²My soul thirsts^k for God, for the living God.^l
  When can I go^m and meet with God?
³My tearsⁿ have been my food
  day and night,
while men say to me all day long,
  "Where is your God?"^o
⁴These things I remember
  as I pour out my soul:
how I used to go with the multitude,
  leading the procession to the house of God,^p
with shouts of joy and thanksgiving^q
  among the festive throng.

⁵Why are you downcast,^r O my soul?
  Why so disturbed within me?
Put your hope in God,^s
  for I will yet praise him,
  my Savior^t and ⁶my God.

---

^aIn many Hebrew manuscripts Psalms 42 and 43 constitute one psalm.   ^bTitle: Probably a literary or musical term

41:9
^a2Sa 15:12;
Ps 55:12
^bJob 19:19;
Ps 55:20;
Mt 26:23;
Jn 13:18*

41:10
^cPs 3:3

41:11
^dPs 147:11
^ePs 25:2

41:12
^fPs 37:17
^gJob 36:7

41:13
^hPs 72:18
ⁱPs 89:52;
106:48

42:1
^jPs 119:131

42:2
^kPs 63:1
^lJer 10:10
^mPs 43:4

42:3
ⁿPs 80:5
^oPs 79:10

42:4
^pIsa 30:29
^qPs 100:4

42:5
^rPs 38:6; 77:3
^sLa 3:24
^tPs 44:3

My[a] soul is downcast within me;
    therefore I will remember you
from the land of the Jordan,
    the heights of Hermon—from Mount Mizar.
[7]Deep calls to deep
    in the roar of your waterfalls;
all your waves and breakers
    have swept over me.[a]

[8]By day the LORD directs his love,[b]
    at night[c] his song[d] is with me—
    a prayer to the God of my life.

[9]I say to God my Rock,
    "Why have you forgotten me?
Why must I go about mourning,[e]
    oppressed by the enemy?"
[10]My bones suffer mortal agony
    as my foes taunt me,
saying to me all day long,
    "Where is your God?"

[11]Why are you downcast, O my soul?
    Why so disturbed within me?
Put your hope in God,
    for I will yet praise him,
    my Savior and my God.[f]

Psalm 43[b]

Psalm 43 Theme

[1]Vindicate me, O God,
    and plead my cause[g] against an ungodly nation;
    rescue me from deceitful and wicked men.[h]
[2]You are God my stronghold.
    Why have you rejected[i] me?
Why must I go about mourning,
    oppressed by the enemy?[j]
[3]Send forth your light[k] and your truth,
    let them guide me;
let them bring me to your holy mountain,[l]
    to the place where you dwell.[m]
[4]Then will I go to the altar[n] of God,
    to God, my joy and my delight.

**Cross references (left margin):**

42:7
[a] Ps 88:7; Jnh 2:3

42:8
[b] Ps 57:3
[c] Job 35:10
[d] Ps 63:6; 149:5

42:9
[e] Ps 38:6

42:11
[f] Ps 43:5

43:1
[g] 1Sa 24:15; Ps 26:1; 35:1
[h] Ps 5:6

43:2
[i] Ps 44:9
[j] Ps 42:9

43:3
[k] Ps 36:9
[l] Ps 42:4
[m] Ps 84:1

43:4
[n] Ps 26:6

[a] 5,6 A few Hebrew manuscripts, Septuagint and Syriac; most Hebrew manuscripts *praise him for his saving help.* / [6] *O my God, my*   [b] In many Hebrew manuscripts Psalms 42 and 43 constitute one psalm.

I will praise you with the harp,[a]
O God, my God.

[5]Why are you downcast, O my soul?
Why so disturbed within me?
Put your hope in God,
for I will yet praise him,
my Savior and my God.[b]

Psalm 44

For the director of music. Of the Sons of Korah. A *maskil*.[a]

Psalm 44 Theme _____

[1]We have heard with our ears, O God;
our fathers have told us[c]
what you did in their days,
in days long ago.
[2]With your hand you drove out[d] the nations
and planted[e] our fathers;
you crushed the peoples
and made our fathers flourish.[f]
[3]It was not by their sword[g] that they won the land,
nor did their arm bring them victory;
it was your right hand, your arm,[h]
and the light of your face, for you loved[i] them.

[4]You are my King[j] and my God,
who decrees[b] victories for Jacob.
[5]Through you we push back our enemies;
through your name we trample[k] our foes.
[6]I do not trust in my bow,[l]
my sword does not bring me victory;
[7]but you give us victory[m] over our enemies,
you put our adversaries to shame.[n]
[8]In God we make our boast[o] all day long,
and we will praise your name forever.[p]   *Selah*

[9]But now you have rejected[q] and humbled us;
you no longer go out with our armies.[r]
[10]You made us retreat[s] before the enemy,
and our adversaries have plundered us.
[11]You gave us up to be devoured like sheep[t]
and have scattered us among the nations.[u]

[a] Title: Probably a literary or musical term   [b] 4 Septuagint, Aquila and Syriac; Hebrew *King, O God; / command*

Cross-references:
43:4 [a] Ps 33:2
43:5 [b] Ps 42:6
44:1 [c] Ex 12:26; Ps 78:3
44:2 [d] Ps 78:55 [e] Ex 15:17 [f] Ps 80:9
44:3 [g] Dt 8:17; Jos 24:12 [h] Ps 77:15 [i] Dt 4:37; 7:7-8
44:4 [j] Ps 74:12
44:5 [k] Ps 108:13
44:6 [l] Ps 33:16
44:7 [m] Ps 136:24 [n] Ps 53:5
44:8 [o] Ps 34:2 [p] Ps 30:12
44:9 [q] Ps 74:1 [r] Ps 60:1,10
44:10 [s] Lev 26:17; Jos 7:8; Ps 89:41
44:11 [t] Ro 8:36 [u] Dt 4:27; 28:64; Ps 106:27

¹²You sold your people for a pittance,^a
    gaining nothing from their sale.

¹³You have made us a reproach to our neighbors,^b
    the scorn^c and derision of those around us.
¹⁴You have made us a byword among the nations;
    the peoples shake their heads^d at us.
¹⁵My disgrace is before me all day long,
    and my face is covered with shame
¹⁶at the taunts of those who reproach and revile^e me,
    because of the enemy, who is bent on revenge.

¹⁷All this happened to us,
    though we had not forgotten^f you
    or been false to your covenant.
¹⁸Our hearts had not turned^g back;
    our feet had not strayed from your path.
¹⁹But you crushed^h us and made us a haunt for jackals
    and covered us over with deep darkness.ⁱ

²⁰If we had forgotten^j the name of our God
    or spread out our hands to a foreign god,^k
²¹would not God have discovered it,
    since he knows the secrets of the heart?^l
²²Yet for your sake we face death all day long;
    we are considered as sheep to be slaughtered.^m

²³Awake,ⁿ O Lord! Why do you sleep?^o
    Rouse yourself! Do not reject us forever.^p
²⁴Why do you hide your face^q
    and forget our misery and oppression?^r

²⁵We are brought down to the dust;^s
    our bodies cling to the ground.
²⁶Rise up^t and help us;
    redeem^u us because of your unfailing love.

Psalm 45

For the director of music. To ⌊the tune of⌋ "Lilies." Of the Sons of Korah. A *maskil*.^a
A wedding song.

Psalm 45 Theme

¹My heart is stirred by a noble theme
    as I recite my verses for the king;
    my tongue is the pen of a skillful writer.

^aTitle: Probably a literary or musical term

44:12 ^aIsa 52:3; Jer 15:13
44:13 ^bPs 79:4; 80:6 ^cDt 28:37
44:14 ^dPs 109:25; Jer 24:9
44:16 ^ePs 74:10
44:17 ^fPs 78:7,57; Da 9:13
44:18 ^gJob 23:11
44:19 ^hPs 51:8 ⁱJob 3:5
44:20 ^jPs 78:11 ^kDt 6:14; Ps 81:9
44:21 ^lPs 139:1-2; Jer 17:10
44:22 ^mIsa 53:7; Ro 8:36*
44:23 ⁿPs 7:6 ^oPs 78:65 ^pPs 77:7
44:24 ^qJob 13:24 ^rPs 42:9
44:25 ^sPs 119:25
44:26 ^tPs 35:2 ^uPs 25:22

²You are the most excellent of men
and your lips have been anointed with grace,^a
since God has blessed you forever.
³Gird your sword^b upon your side, O mighty one;^c
clothe yourself with splendor and majesty.
⁴In your majesty ride forth victoriously^d
in behalf of truth, humility and righteousness;
let your right hand display awesome deeds.
⁵Let your sharp arrows pierce the hearts of the
king's enemies;
let the nations fall beneath your feet.
⁶Your throne, O God, will last for ever and ever;^e
a scepter of justice will be the scepter of
your kingdom.
⁷You love righteousness^f and hate wickedness;
therefore God, your God, has set you above
your companions
by anointing^g you with the oil of joy.^h
⁸All your robes are fragrantⁱ with myrrh and aloes
and cassia;
from palaces adorned with ivory
the music of the strings makes you glad.
⁹Daughters of kings^j are among your honored women;
at your right hand^k is the royal bride in gold of Ophir.

¹⁰Listen, O daughter, consider and give ear:
Forget your people^l and your father's house.
¹¹The king is enthralled by your beauty;
honor^m him, for he is your lord.ⁿ
¹²The Daughter of Tyre will come with a gift,^{a o}
men of wealth will seek your favor.

¹³All glorious^p is the princess within ⌊her chamber⌋;
her gown is interwoven with gold.
¹⁴In embroidered garments she is led to the king;^q
her virgin companions follow her
and are brought to you.
¹⁵They are led in with joy and gladness;
they enter the palace of the king.

¹⁶Your sons will take the place of your fathers;
you will make them princes throughout the land.
¹⁷I will perpetuate your memory through all generations;^r
therefore the nations will praise you^s for ever and ever.

a 12 Or *A Tyrian robe is among the gifts*

45:2
^aLk 4:22

45:3
^bHeb 4:12;
Rev 1:16
^cIsa 9:6

45:4
^dRev 6:2

45:6
^ePs 93:2; 98:9

45:7
^fPs 33:5
^gIsa 61:1
^hPs 21:6;
Heb 1:8-9*

45:8
ⁱSS 1:3

45:9
^jSS 6:8
^k1Ki 2:19

45:10
^lDt 21:13

45:11
^mPs 95:6
ⁿIsa 54:5

45:12
^oPs 22:29;
Isa 49:23

45:13
^pIsa 61:10

45:14
^qSS 1:4

45:17
^rMal 1:11
^sPs 138:4

Psalm 46

For the director of music. Of the Sons of Korah. According to *alamoth*.^a A song.

Psalm 46 Theme _____

¹God is our refuge^a and strength,
an ever-present^b help in trouble.
²Therefore we will not fear,^c though the earth give way^d
and the mountains fall^e into the heart of the sea,
³though its waters roar^f and foam
and the mountains quake with their surging.   *Selah*

⁴There is a river whose streams make glad the
city of God,^g
the holy place where the Most High dwells.
⁵God is within her,^h she will not fall;
God will helpⁱ her at break of day.
⁶Nations^j are in uproar, kingdoms^k fall;
he lifts his voice, the earth melts.^l

⁷The LORD Almighty is with us;^m
the God of Jacob is our fortress.ⁿ   *Selah*

⁸Come and see the works of the LORD,^o
the desolations^p he has brought on the earth.
⁹He makes wars^q cease to the ends of the earth;
he breaks the bow^r and shatters the spear,
he burns the shields^b with fire.^s
¹⁰"Be still, and know that I am God;^t
I will be exalted^u among the nations,
I will be exalted in the earth."

¹¹The LORD Almighty is with us;
the God of Jacob is our fortress.   *Selah*

Psalm 47

For the director of music. Of the Sons of Korah. A psalm.

Psalm 47 Theme _____

¹Clap your hands,^v all you nations;
shout to God with cries of joy.^w
²How awesome^x is the LORD Most High,
the great King^y over all the earth!

^a Title: Probably a musical term   ^b 9 Or *chariots*

46:1
a Ps 9:9; 14:6
b Dt 4:7

46:2
c Ps 23:4
d Ps 82:5
e Ps 18:7

46:3
f Ps 93:3

46:4
g Ps 48:1,8;
Isa 60:14

46:5
h Isa 12:6;
Eze 43:7
i Ps 37:40

46:6
j Ps 2:1
k Ps 68:32
l Mic 1:4

46:7
m 2Ch 13:12
n Ps 9:9

46:8
o Ps 66:5
p Isa 61:4

46:9
q Isa 2:4
r Ps 76:3
s Eze 39:9

46:10
t Ps 100:3
u Isa 2:11

47:1
v Ps 98:8;
Isa 55:12
w Ps 106:47

47:2
x Dt 7:21
y Mal 1:14

³He subdued*ᵃ* nations under us,
 peoples under our feet.
⁴He chose our inheritance*ᵇ* for us,
 the pride of Jacob, whom he loved.   *Selah*

⁵God has ascended amid shouts of joy,
 the LORD amid the sounding of trumpets.*ᶜ*
⁶Sing praises*ᵈ* to God, sing praises;
 sing praises to our King, sing praises.

⁷For God is the King of all the earth;*ᵉ*
 sing to him a psalm*ᵃᶠ* of praise.
⁸God reigns*ᵍ* over the nations;
 God is seated on his holy throne.
⁹The nobles of the nations assemble
 as the people of the God of Abraham,
for the kings*ᵇ* of the earth belong to God;*ʰ*
 he is greatly exalted.*ⁱ*

Psalm 48

A song. A psalm of the Sons of Korah.

Psalm 48 Theme

¹Great is the LORD,*ʲ* and most worthy of praise,
 in the city of our God,*ᵏ* his holy mountain.*ˡ*
²It is beautiful*ᵐ* in its loftiness,
 the joy of the whole earth.
 Like the utmost heights of Zaphon*ᶜ* is Mount Zion,
 the*ᵈ* city of the Great King.*ⁿ*
³God is in her citadels;
 he has shown himself to be her fortress.*ᵒ*

⁴When the kings joined forces,
 when they advanced together,*ᵖ*
⁵they saw ⌊her⌋ and were astounded;
 they fled in terror.*�q*
⁶Trembling seized them there,
 pain like that of a woman in labor.
⁷You destroyed them like ships of Tarshish
 shattered by an east wind.*ʳ*

⁸As we have heard,
 so have we seen

---

a7 Or *a maskil* (probably a literary or musical term)   b9 Or *shields*   c2 *Zaphon* can refer to a
sacred mountain or the direction north.   d2 Or *earth, / Mount Zion, on the northern side / of the*

47:3
*ᵃ*Ps 18:39,47

47:4
*ᵇ*1Pe 1:4

47:5
*ᶜ*Ps 68:33; 98:6

47:6
*ᵈ*Ps 68:4; 89:18

47:7
*ᵉ*Zec 14:9
*ᶠ*Col 3:16

47:8
*ᵍ*1Ch 16:31

47:9
*ʰ*Ps 72:11; 89:18
*ⁱ*Ps 97:9

48:1
*ʲ*Ps 96:4
*ᵏ*Ps 46:4
*ˡ*Isa 2:2-3;
Mic 4:1; Zec 8:3

48:2
*ᵐ*Ps 50:2;
La 2:15
*ⁿ*Mt 5:35

48:3
*ᵒ*Ps 46:7

48:4
*ᵖ*2Sa 10:1-19

48:5
*q*Ex 15:16

48:7
*ʳ*Jer 18:17;
Eze 27:26

in the city of the LORD Almighty,
in the city of our God:
God makes her secure forever.*a* Selah

⁹Within your temple, O God,
we meditate on your unfailing love.*b*
¹⁰Like your name,*c* O God,
your praise reaches to the ends of the earth;*d*
your right hand is filled with righteousness.
¹¹Mount Zion rejoices,
the villages of Judah are glad
because of your judgments.*e*

¹²Walk about Zion, go around her,
count her towers,
¹³consider well her ramparts,
view her citadels,*f*
that you may tell of them to the next generation.*g*
¹⁴For this God is our God for ever and ever;
he will be our guide*h* even to the end.

Psalm 49

For the director of music. Of the Sons of Korah. A psalm.

Psalm 49 Theme

¹Hear this, all you peoples;*i*
listen, all who live in this world,*j*
²both low and high,
rich and poor alike:
³My mouth will speak words of wisdom;*k*
the utterance from my heart will give understanding.*l*
⁴I will turn my ear to a proverb;*m*
with the harp I will expound my riddle:*n*

⁵Why should I fear*o* when evil days come,
when wicked deceivers surround me—
⁶those who trust in their wealth*p*
and boast of their great riches?
⁷No man can redeem the life of another
or give to God a ransom for him—
⁸the ransom for a life is costly,
no payment is ever enough—*q*
⁹that he should live on*r* forever
and not see decay.

Side notes:
48:8 *a* Ps 87:5
48:9 *b* Ps 26:3
48:10 *c* Dt 28:58; Jos 7:9 *d* Isa 41:10
48:11 *e* Ps 97:8
48:13 *f* ver 3; Ps 122:7 *g* Ps 78:6
48:14 *h* Ps 23:4
49:1 *i* Ps 78:1 *j* Ps 33:8
49:3 *k* Ps 37:30 *l* Ps 119:130
49:4 *m* Ps 78:2 *n* Nu 12:8
49:5 *o* Ps 23:4
49:6 *p* Job 31:24
49:8 *q* Mt 16:26
49:9 *r* Ps 22:29; 89:48

947

¹⁰For all can see that wise men die;^a
    the foolish and the senseless alike perish
    and leave their wealth to others.^b
¹¹Their tombs will remain their houses^a forever,
    their dwellings for endless generations,
    though they had^b named^c lands after themselves.

¹²But man, despite his riches, does not endure;
    he is^c like the beasts that perish.

¹³This is the fate of those who trust in themselves,^d
    and of their followers, who approve their sayings.
                    Selah

¹⁴Like sheep they are destined for the grave,^{d e}
    and death will feed on them.
 The upright will rule^f over them in the morning;
    their forms will decay in the grave,^d
    far from their princely mansions.
¹⁵But God will redeem my life^e from the grave;^g
    he will surely take me to himself.^h
                    Selah

¹⁶Do not be overawed when a man grows rich,
    when the splendor of his house increases;
¹⁷for he will take nothing with him when he dies,
    his splendor will not descend with him.ⁱ
¹⁸Though while he lived he counted himself blessed—^j
    and men praise you when you prosper—
¹⁹he will join the generation of his fathers,^k
    who will never see the light^l ⌊of life⌋.

²⁰A man who has riches without understanding
    is like the beasts that perish.^m

Psalm 50

A psalm of Asaph.

*Psalm 50 Theme*_____

¹The Mighty One, God, the LORD,ⁿ
    speaks and summons the earth
    from the rising of the sun to the place where it sets.^o
²From Zion, perfect in beauty,^p
    God shines forth.^q

---

^a *11* Septuagint and Syriac; Hebrew *In their thoughts their houses will remain*   ^b *11* Or / *for they have*   ^c *12* Hebrew; Septuagint and Syriac read verse 12 the same as verse 20.   ^d *14* Hebrew *Sheol*; also in verse 15   ^e *15* Or *soul*

49:10
^a Ecc 2:16
^b Ecc 2:18,21

49:11
^c Ge 4:17;
Dt 3:14

49:13
^d Lk 12:20

49:14
^e Job 24:19;
Ps 9:17
^f Da 7:18;
Mal 4:3;
1Co 6:2;
Rev 2:26

49:15
^g Ps 56:13;
Hos 13:14
^h Ps 73:24

49:17
ⁱ Ps 17:14;
1Ti 6:7

49:18
^j Dt 29:19;
Lk 12:19

49:19
^k Ge 15:15
^l Job 33:30

49:20
^m Ecc 3:19

50:1
ⁿ Jos 22:22
^o Ps 113:3

50:2
^p Ps 48:2
^q Dt 33:2;
Ps 80:1

50:3
a Ps 96:13
b Ps 97:3;
Da 7:10

50:4
c Dt 4:26;
Isa 1:2

50:5
d Ps 30:4
e Ex 24:7

50:6
f Ps 89:5
g Ps 75:7

50:7
h Ps 81:8
i Ex 20:2

50:8
j Ps 40:6;
Hos 6:6

50:9
k Ps 69:31

50:10
l Ps 104:24

50:12
m Ex 19:5

50:14
n Heb 13:15
o Dt 23:21

50:15
p Ps 81:7
q Ps 22:23

50:16
r Isa 29:13

50:17
s Ne 9:26;
Ro 2:21-22

50:18
t Ro 1:32;
1 Ti 5:22

50:19
u Ps 10:7; 52:2

50:20
v Mt 10:21

50:21
w Ecc 8:11;
Isa 42:14
x Ps 90:8

³Our God comes[a] and will not be silent;
　a fire devours before him,[b]
　and around him a tempest rages.
⁴He summons the heavens above,
　and the earth,[c] that he may judge his people:
⁵"Gather to me my consecrated ones,[d]
　who made a covenant[e] with me by sacrifice."
⁶And the heavens proclaim[f] his righteousness,
　for God himself is judge.[g]　　　　　　　　　*Selah*

⁷"Hear, O my people, and I will speak,
　O Israel, and I will testify[h] against you:
　I am God, your God.[i]
⁸I do not rebuke you for your sacrifices
　or your burnt offerings,[j] which are ever before me.
⁹I have no need of a bull[k] from your stall
　or of goats from your pens,
¹⁰for every animal of the forest is mine,
　and the cattle on a thousand hills.[l]
¹¹I know every bird in the mountains,
　and the creatures of the field are mine.
¹²If I were hungry I would not tell you,
　for the world[m] is mine, and all that is in it.
¹³Do I eat the flesh of bulls
　or drink the blood of goats?
¹⁴Sacrifice thank offerings[n] to God,
　fulfill your vows[o] to the Most High,
¹⁵and call[p] upon me in the day of trouble;
　I will deliver you, and you will honor[q] me."

¹⁶But to the wicked, God says:

　"What right have you to recite my laws
　　or take my covenant on your lips?[r]
¹⁷You hate my instruction
　and cast my words behind[s] you.
¹⁸When you see a thief, you join[t] with him;
　you throw in your lot with adulterers.
¹⁹You use your mouth for evil
　and harness your tongue to deceit.[u]
²⁰You speak continually against your brother[v]
　and slander your own mother's son.
²¹These things you have done and I kept silent;[w]
　you thought I was altogether[a] like you.
　But I will rebuke you
　and accuse[x] you to your face.

a 21 Or *thought the 'I AM' was*

949

22"Consider this, you who forget God,[a]
　or I will tear you to pieces, with none to rescue:[b]
23He who sacrifices thank offerings honors me,
　and he prepares the way[c]
　so that I may show him[a] the salvation of God.[d]"

Psalm 51

For the director of music. A psalm of David. When the prophet Nathan came to him after David had committed adultery with Bathsheba.

Psalm 51 Theme _____

1Have mercy on me, O God,
　according to your unfailing love;
　according to your great compassion
　blot out[e] my transgressions.[f]
2Wash away[g] all my iniquity
　and cleanse[h] me from my sin.

3For I know my transgressions,
　and my sin is always before me.[i]
4Against you, you only, have I sinned
　and done what is evil in your sight,[j]
　so that you are proved right when you speak
　and justified when you judge.[k]
5Surely I was sinful[l] at birth,
　sinful from the time my mother conceived me.
6Surely you desire truth in the inner parts[b];
　you teach[c] me wisdom[m] in the inmost place.[n]

7Cleanse me with hyssop,[o] and I will be clean;
　wash me, and I will be whiter than snow.[p]
8Let me hear joy and gladness;[q]
　let the bones you have crushed rejoice.
9Hide your face from my sins[r]
　and blot out all my iniquity.

10Create in me a pure heart,[s] O God,
　and renew a steadfast spirit within me.[t]
11Do not cast me from your presence
　or take your Holy Spirit[u] from me.
12Restore to me the joy of your salvation[v]
　and grant me a willing spirit, to sustain me.

13Then I will teach transgressors your ways,[w]
　and sinners will turn back to you.[x]

---

a 23 Or *and to him who considers his way / I will show*　b 6 The meaning of the Hebrew for this phrase is uncertain.　c 6 Or *you desired . . . ; / you taught*

50:22
a Job 8:13;
Ps 9:17
b Ps 7:2

50:23
c Ps 85:13
d Ps 91:16

51:1
e Ac 3:19
f Isa 43:25;
Col 2:14

51:2
g 1Jn 1:9
h Heb 9:14

51:3
i Isa 59:12

51:4
j Ge 20:6;
Lk 15:21
k Ro 3:4*

51:5
l Job 14:4

51:6
m Pr 2:6
n Ps 15:2

51:7
o Lev 14:4;
Heb 9:19
p Isa 1:18

51:8
q Isa 35:10

51:9
r Jer 16:17

51:10
s Ps 78:37;
Ac 15:9
t Eze 18:31

51:11
u Eph 4:30

51:12
v Ps 13:5

51:13
w Ac 9:21-22
x Ps 22:27

¹⁴Save me from bloodguilt,^a O God,
  the God who saves me,^b
  and my tongue will sing of your righteousness.^c
¹⁵O Lord, open my lips,^d
  and my mouth will declare your praise.
¹⁶You do not delight in sacrifice,^e or I would bring it;
  you do not take pleasure in burnt offerings.
¹⁷The sacrifices of God are^a a broken spirit;
  a broken and contrite heart,^f
  O God, you will not despise.

¹⁸In your good pleasure make Zion^g prosper;
  build up the walls of Jerusalem.
¹⁹Then there will be righteous sacrifices,^h
  whole burnt offeringsⁱ to delight you;
  then bulls^j will be offered on your altar.

Psalm 52

For the director of music. A *maskil* ^b of David. When Doeg the Edomite^k had gone to Saul and told him: "David has gone to the house of Ahimelech."

Psalm 52 Theme

¹Why do you boast of evil, you mighty man?
  Why do you boast^l all day long,
  you who are a disgrace in the eyes of God?
²Your tongue plots destruction;
  it is like a sharpened razor,^m
  you who practice deceit.ⁿ
³You love evil rather than good,
  falsehood^o rather than speaking the truth.   *Selah*
⁴You love every harmful word,
  O you deceitful tongue!^p

⁵Surely God will bring you down to everlasting ruin:
  He will snatch you up and tear^q you from your tent;
  he will uproot^r you from the land of the living.^s   *Selah*
⁶The righteous will see and fear;
  they will laugh^t at him, saying,
⁷"Here now is the man
  who did not make God his stronghold
 but trusted in his great wealth ^u
  and grew strong by destroying others!"

⁸But I am like an olive tree^v
  flourishing in the house of God;

51:14
a 2Sa 12:9
b Ps 25:5
c Ps 35:28

51:15
d Ps 9:14

51:16
e 1Sa 15:22;
Ps 40:6

51:17
f Ps 34:18

51:18
g Ps 102:16;
Isa 51:3

51:19
h Ps 4:5
i Ps 66:13
j Ps 66:15

52: Title
k 1Sa 22:9

52:1
l Ps 94:4

52:2
m Ps 57:4
n Ps 50:19

52:3
o Jer 9:5

52:4
p Ps 120:2,3

52:5
q Isa 22:19
r Pr 2:22
s Ps 27:13

52:6
t Job 22:19;
Ps 37:34; 40:3

52:7
u Ps 49:6

52:8
v Jer 11:16

---

a 17 Or *My sacrifice, O God, is*   *b* Title: Probably a literary or musical term

I trust[a] in God's unfailing love
    for ever and ever.
[9]I will praise you forever[b] for what you have done;
    in your name I will hope, for your name is good.[c]
I will praise you in the presence of your saints.

Psalm 53

For the director of music. According to *mahalath*.[a] A *maskil*[b] of David.

Psalm 53 Theme _____

[1]The fool[d] says in his heart,
    "There is no God."[e]
They are corrupt, and their ways are vile;
    there is no one who does good.

[2]God looks down from heaven[f]
    on the sons of men
to see if there are any who understand,
    any who seek God.[g]
[3]Everyone has turned away,
    they have together become corrupt;
there is no one who does good,
    not even one.[h]

[4]Will the evildoers never learn—
    those who devour my people as men eat bread
    and who do not call on God?
[5]There they were, overwhelmed with dread,
    where there was nothing to dread.[i]
God scattered the bones[j] of those who attacked you;
    you put them to shame, for God despised them.

[6]Oh, that salvation for Israel would come out of Zion!
    When God restores the fortunes of his people,
    let Jacob rejoice and Israel be glad!

Psalm 54

For the director of music. With stringed instruments. A *maskil*[b] of David. When the Ziphites had gone to Saul and said, "Is not David hiding among us?"

Psalm 54 Theme _____

[1]Save me, O God, by your name;[k]
    vindicate me by your might.[l]

a Title: Probably a musical term   b Title: Probably a literary or musical term

52:8
a Ps 13:5

52:9
b Ps 30:12
c Ps 54:6

53:1
d Ps 14:1-7;
Ro 3:10
e Ps 10:4

53:2
f Ps 33:13
g 2Ch 15:2

53:3
h Ro 3:10-12*

53:5
i Lev 26:17
j Eze 6:5

54:1
k Ps 20:1
l 2Ch 20:6

54:2
a Ps 5:1; 55:1

54:3
b Ps 86:14
c Ps 40:14
d Ps 36:1

54:4
e Ps 118:7
f Ps 41:12

54:5
g Ps 94:23
h Ps 89:49;
143:12

54:6
i Ps 50:14
j Ps 52:9

54:7
k Ps 34:6
l Ps 59:10

55:1
m Ps 27:9; 61:1

55:2
n Ps 66:19
o Ps 77:3;
Isa 38:14

55:3
p 2Sa 16:6-8;
Ps 17:9
q Ps 71:11

55:4
r Ps 116:3

55:5
s Job 21:6;
Ps 119:120

55:8
t Isa 4:6

55:9
u Jer 6:7

²Hear my prayer, O God;a
listen to the words of my mouth.

³Strangers are attacking me;b
ruthless men seek my lifec—
men without regard for God.d   Selah

⁴Surely God is my help;e
the Lord is the one who sustains me.f

⁵Let evil recoilg on those who slander me;
in your faithfulnessh destroy them.

⁶I will sacrifice a freewill offeringi to you;
I will praise your name, O LORD,
for it is good.j
⁷For he has delivered mek from all my troubles,
and my eyes have looked in triumph on my foes.l

Psalm 55

For the director of music. With stringed instruments. A *maskil* a of David.

Psalm 55 Theme

¹Listen to my prayer, O God,
do not ignore my plea;m
² hear me and answer me.n
My thoughts trouble me and I am distraughto
³ at the voice of the enemy,
at the stares of the wicked;
for they bring down suffering upon mep
and revile me in their anger.q

⁴My heart is in anguish within me;
the terrorsr of death assail me.
⁵Fear and tremblings have beset me;
horror has overwhelmed me.
⁶I said, "Oh, that I had the wings of a dove!
I would fly away and be at rest—
⁷I would flee far away
and stay in the desert;   Selah
⁸I would hurry to my place of shelter,
far from the tempest and storm."

⁹Confuse the wicked, O Lord, confound their speech,
for I see violence and strife u in the city.

a Title: Probably a literary or musical term

953

¹⁰Day and night they prowl about on its walls;
    malice and abuse are within it.
¹¹Destructive forces[a] are at work in the city;
    threats and lies[b] never leave its streets.

¹²If an enemy were insulting me,
    I could endure it;
if a foe were raising himself against me,
    I could hide from him.
¹³But it is you, a man like myself,
    my companion, my close friend,[c]
¹⁴with whom I once enjoyed sweet fellowship
    as we walked with the throng at the house of God.[d]

¹⁵Let death take my enemies by surprise;[e]
    let them go down alive to the grave,[a][f]
    for evil finds lodging among them.

¹⁶But I call to God,
    and the LORD saves me.
¹⁷Evening,[g] morning[h] and noon
    I cry out in distress,
    and he hears my voice.
¹⁸He ransoms me unharmed
    from the battle waged against me,
    even though many oppose me.
¹⁹God, who is enthroned forever,[i]
    will hear[j] them and afflict them—   *Selah*
men who never change their ways
    and have no fear of God.

²⁰My companion attacks his friends;[k]
    he violates his covenant.[l]
²¹His speech is smooth as butter,
    yet war is in his heart;
his words are more soothing than oil,[m]
    yet they are drawn swords.[n]

²²Cast your cares on the LORD
    and he will sustain you;[o]
    he will never let the righteous fall.[p]
²³But you, O God, will bring down the wicked
    into the pit[q] of corruption;
bloodthirsty and deceitful men[r]
    will not live out half their days.[s]

But as for me, I trust in you.[t]

a 15 Hebrew *Sheol*

55:11
a Ps 5:9
b Ps 10:7

55:13
c 2Sa 15:12;
Ps 41:9

55:14
d Ps 42:4

55:15
e Ps 64:7
f Nu 16:30,33

55:17
g Ps 141:2;
Ac 3:1
h Ps 5:3

55:19
i Dt 33:27
j Ps 78:59

55:20
k Ps 7:4
l Ps 89:34

55:21
m Pr 5:3
n Ps 28:3;
Ps 57:4; 59:7

55:22
o Ps 37:5;
Mt 6:25-34;
1Pe 5:7
p Ps 37:24

55:23
q Ps 73:18
r Ps 5:6
s Job 15:32;
Pr 10:27
t Ps 25:2

Psalm 56

For the director of music. To ⌊the tune of⌋ "A Dove on Distant Oaks." Of David.
A *miktam.*[a] When the Philistines had seized him in Gath.

Psalm 56 Theme

¹Be merciful to me, O God, for men hotly pursue me;[a]
  all day long they press their attack.
²My slanderers pursue me all day long;[b]
  many are attacking me in their pride.[c]

³When I am afraid,[d]
  I will trust in you.
⁴In God, whose word I praise,
  in God I trust; I will not be afraid.
  What can mortal man do to me?[e]

⁵All day long they twist my words;[f]
  they are always plotting to harm me.
⁶They conspire,[g] they lurk,
  they watch my steps,
  eager to take my life.[h]

⁷On no account let them escape;
  in your anger, O God, bring down the nations.[i]
⁸Record my lament;
  list my tears on your scroll[b]—
  are they not in your record?[j]

⁹Then my enemies will turn back[k]
  when I call for help.[l]
  By this I will know that God is for me.[m]
¹⁰In God, whose word I praise,
  in the LORD, whose word I praise—
¹¹in God I trust; I will not be afraid.
  What can man do to me?

¹²I am under vows[n] to you, O God;
  I will present my thank offerings to you.
¹³For you have delivered me[c] from death[o]
  and my feet from stumbling,
  that I may walk before God
  in the light of life.[d][p]

Cross references

56:1 a Ps 57:1-3
56:2 b Ps 57:3; c Ps 35:1
56:3 d Ps 55:4-5
56:4 e Ps 118:6; Heb 13:6
56:5 f Ps 41:7
56:6 g Ps 59:3; h Ps 71:10
56:7 i Ps 36:12; 55:23
56:8 j Mal 3:16
56:9 k Ps 9:3; l Ps 102:2; m Ro 8:31
56:12 n Ps 50:14
56:13 o Ps 116:8; p Job 33:30

Footnotes

a Title: Probably a literary or musical term   b 8 Or / put my tears in your wineskin   c 13 Or my soul   d 13 Or the land of the living

Psalm 57

For the director of music. ⌊To the tune of⌋ "Do Not Destroy." Of David. A *miktam*.ᵃ
When he had fled from Saul into the cave.

Psalm 57 Theme _____

¹Have mercy on me, O God, have mercy on me,
    for in you my soul takes refuge.ᵃ
I will take refuge in the shadow of your wingsᵇ
    until the disaster has passed.ᶜ

²I cry out to God Most High,
    to God, who fulfills ⌊his purpose⌋ for me.ᵈ
³He sends from heaven and saves me,ᵉ
    rebuking those who hotly pursue me;ᶠ   *Selah*
God sends his love and his faithfulness.ᵍ

⁴I am in the midst of lions;ʰ
    I lie among ravenous beasts—
men whose teeth are spears and arrows,
    whose tongues are sharp swords.ⁱ

⁵Be exalted, O God, above the heavens;
    let your glory be over all the earth. ʲ

⁶They spread a net for my feet—
    I was bowed downᵏ in distress.
They dug a pitˡ in my path—
    but they have fallen into it themselves.ᵐ   *Selah*

⁷My heart is steadfast, O God,
    my heart is steadfast;ⁿ
I will sing and make music.
⁸Awake, my soul!
    Awake, harp and lyre!ᵒ
    I will awaken the dawn.

⁹I will praise you, O Lord, among the nations;
    I will sing of you among the peoples.
¹⁰For great is your love, reaching to the heavens;
    your faithfulness reaches to the skies.ᵖ

¹¹Be exalted, O God, above the heavens;
    let your glory be over all the earth.�q

ᵃ Title: Probably a literary or musical term

57:1
a Ps 2:12
b Ps 17:8
c Isa 26:20

57:2
d Ps 138:8

57:3
e Ps 18:9,16
f Ps 56:1
g Ps 40:11

57:4
h Ps 35:17
i Ps 55:21;
Pr 30:14

57:5
j Ps 108:5

57:6
k Ps 145:14
l Ps 35:7
m Ps 7:15;
Pr 28:10

57:7
n Ps 108:1

57:8
o Ps 16:9; 30:12;
150:3

57:10
p Ps 36:5; 103:11

57:11
q ver 5

Psalm 58

58:1
a Ps 82:2

For the director of music. ⌊To the tune of⌋ "Do Not Destroy." Of David. A *miktam*.ᵃ

Psalm 58 Theme

58:2
b Ps 94:20;
Mal 3:15

¹Do you rulers indeed speak justly?ᵃ
    Do you judge uprightly among men?
²No, in your heart you devise injustice,
    and your hands mete out violence on the earth.ᵇ

58:4
c Ps 140:3;
Ecc 10:11

³Even from birth the wicked go astray;
    from the womb they are wayward and speak lies.
⁴Their venom is like the venom of a snake,ᶜ
    like that of a cobra that has stopped its ears,

58:6
d Ps 3:7
e Job 4:10

⁵that will not heed the tune of the charmer,
    however skillful the enchanter may be.

⁶Break the teeth in their mouths, O God;ᵈ
    tear out, O Lᴏʀᴅ, the fangs of the lions!ᵉ

58:7
f Jos 7:5;
Ps 112:10
g Ps 64:3

⁷Let them vanish like water that flows away;ᶠ
    when they draw the bow, let their arrows be blunted.ᵍ
⁸Like a slug melting away as it moves along,
    like a stillborn child,ʰ may they not see the sun.

58:8
h Job 3:16

⁹Before your pots can feel ⌊the heat of⌋ the thornsⁱ—
    whether they be green or dry—the wicked will be
        swept away.ᵇʲ

58:9
i Ps 118:12
j Pr 10:25

¹⁰The righteous will be glad when they are avenged,ᵏ
    when they bathe their feet in the blood of the wicked.ˡ
¹¹Then men will say,
    "Surely the righteous still are rewarded;
    surely there is a God who judges the earth."ᵐ

58:10
k Ps 64:10; 91:8
l Ps 68:23

Psalm 59

58:11
m Ps 9:8; 18:20

For the director of music. ⌊To the tune of⌋ "Do Not Destroy." Of David. A *miktam*.ᵃ
When Saul had sent men to watch David's house in order to kill him.

Psalm 59 Theme

59:1
n Ps 143:9

¹Deliver me from my enemies, O God;ⁿ
    protect me from those who rise up against me.
²Deliver me from evildoers
    and save me from bloodthirsty men.ᵒ

59:2
o Ps 139:19

ᵃ Title: Probably a literary or musical term   ᵇ 9 The meaning of the Hebrew for this verse is uncertain.

³See how they lie in wait for me!
    Fierce men conspire^a against me
    for no offense or sin of mine, O LORD.
⁴I have done no wrong, yet they are ready to attack me.^b
    Arise to help me; look on my plight!
⁵O LORD God Almighty, the God of Israel,
    rouse yourself to punish all the nations;
    show no mercy to wicked traitors.^c   *Selah*

⁶They return at evening,
    snarling like dogs,^d
    and prowl about the city.
⁷See what they spew from their mouths—
    they spew out swords^e from their lips,
    and they say, "Who can hear us?"^f
⁸But you, O LORD, laugh at them;^g
    you scoff at all those nations.^h

⁹O my Strength, I watch for you;
    you, O God, are my fortress,ⁱ ¹⁰my loving God.

God will go before me
    and will let me gloat over those who slander me.
¹¹But do not kill them, O Lord our shield,^{aj}
    or my people will forget.^k
In your might make them wander about,
    and bring them down.^l
¹²For the sins of their mouths,^m
    for the words of their lips,ⁿ
    let them be caught in their pride.^o
For the curses and lies they utter,
¹³   consume them in wrath,
    consume them till they are no more.^p
Then it will be known to the ends of the earth
    that God rules over Jacob.^q   *Selah*

¹⁴They return at evening,
    snarling like dogs,
    and prowl about the city.
¹⁵They wander about for food^r
    and howl if not satisfied.
¹⁶But I will sing of your strength,^s
    in the morning^t I will sing of your love;^u
    for you are my fortress,
    my refuge in times of trouble.^v

¹⁷O my Strength, I sing praise to you;
    you, O God, are my fortress, my loving God.

a 11 Or *sovereign*

59:3
a Ps 56:6

59:4
b Ps 35:19,23

59:5
c Jer 18:23

59:6
d ver 14

59:7
e Ps 57:4
f Ps 10:11

59:8
g Ps 37:13;
Pr 1:26
h Ps 2:4

59:9
i Ps 9:9; 62:2

59:11
j Ps 84:9
k Dt 4:9
l Ps 106:27

59:12
m Ps 10:7
n Pr 12:13
o Zep 3:11

59:13
p Ps 104:35
q Ps 83:18

59:15
r Job 15:23

59:16
s Ps 21:13
t Ps 88:13
u Ps 101:1
v Ps 46:1

Psalm 60

For the director of music. To [the tune of] "The Lily of the Covenant." A *miktam*[a] of David. For teaching. When he fought Aram Naharaim[b] and Aram Zobah,[c] and when Joab returned and struck down twelve thousand Edomites in the Valley of Salt.

*Psalm 60 Theme*_____

[1]You have rejected us,[a] O God, and burst forth upon us;
 you have been angry[b]—now restore us![c]
[2]You have shaken the land[d] and torn it open;
 mend its fractures,[e] for it is quaking.
[3]You have shown your people desperate times;[f]
 you have given us wine that makes us stagger.[g]

[4]But for those who fear you, you have raised a banner
 to be unfurled against the bow.   *Selah*

[5]Save us and help us with your right hand,[h]
 that those you love[i] may be delivered.
[6]God has spoken from his sanctuary:
 "In triumph I will parcel out Shechem[j]
 and measure off the Valley of Succoth.
[7]Gilead[k] is mine, and Manasseh is mine;
 Ephraim is my helmet,
 Judah[l] my scepter.[m]
[8]Moab is my washbasin,
 upon Edom I toss my sandal;
 over Philistia I shout in triumph.[n]"

[9]Who will bring me to the fortified city?
 Who will lead me to Edom?
[10]Is it not you, O God, you who have rejected us
 and no longer go out with our armies?[o]
[11]Give us aid against the enemy,
 for the help of man is worthless.[p]
[12]With God we will gain the victory,
 and he will trample down our enemies.[q]

Psalm 61

For the director of music. With stringed instruments. Of David.

*Psalm 61 Theme*_____

[1]Hear my cry, O God;[r]
 listen to my prayer.[s]

Side notes:

60:1 a 2Sa 5:20; Ps 44:9; b Ps 79:5; c Ps 80:3
60:2 d Ps 18:7; e 2Ch 7:14
60:3 f Ps 71:20; g Isa 51:17; Jer 25:16
60:5 h Ps 17:7; 108:6; i Ps 127:2
60:6 j Ge 12:6
60:7 k Jos 13:31; l Dt 33:17; m Ge 49:10
60:8 n 2Sa 8:1
60:10 o Jos 7:12; Ps 44:9; 108:11
60:11 p Ps 146:3
60:12 q Nu 24:18; Ps 44:5
61:1 r Ps 64:1; s Ps 86:6

a Title: Probably a literary or musical term   b Title: That is, Arameans of Northwest Mesopotamia   c Title: That is, Arameans of central Syria

²From the ends of the earth I call to you,
    I call as my heart grows faint;ᵃ
    lead me to the rockᵇ that is higher than I.
³For you have been my refuge,ᶜ
    a strong tower against the foe.ᵈ

⁴I long to dwellᵉ in your tent forever
    and take refuge in the shelter of your wings. ᶠ   *Selah*
⁵For you have heard my vows,ᵍ O God;
    you have given me the heritage of those who fear
        your name.ʰ

⁶Increase the days of the king's life,
    his years for many generations.ⁱ
⁷May he be enthroned in God's presence forever;ʲ
    appoint your love and faithfulness to protect him.ᵏ

⁸Then will I ever sing praise to your nameˡ
    and fulfill my vows day after day.

Psalm 62

For the director of music. For Jeduthun. A psalm of David.

Psalm 62 Theme _____

¹My soul finds restᵐ in God alone;
    my salvation comes from him.
²He alone is my rockⁿ and my salvation;
    he is my fortress, I will never be shaken.

³How long will you assault a man?
    Would all of you throw him down—
    this leaning wall,ᵒ this tottering fence?
⁴They fully intend to topple him
    from his lofty place;
    they take delight in lies.
    With their mouths they bless,
    but in their hearts they curse.ᵖ   *Selah*

⁵Find rest, O my soul, in God alone;
    my hope comes from him.
⁶He alone is my rock and my salvation;
    he is my fortress, I will not be shaken.
⁷My salvation and my honor depend on Godᵃ;
    he is my mighty rock, my refuge.�q

ᵃ 7 Or / *God Most High is my salvation and my honor*

61:2
ᵃ Ps 77:3
ᵇ Ps 18:2

61:3
ᶜ Ps 62:7
ᵈ Pr 18:10

61:4
ᵉ Ps 23:6
ᶠ Ps 91:4

61:5
ᵍ Ps 56:12
ʰ Ps 86:11

61:6
ⁱ Ps 21:4

61:7
ʲ Ps 41:12
ᵏ Ps 40:11

61:8
ˡ Ps 65:1; 71:22

62:1
ᵐ Ps 33:20

62:2
ⁿ Ps 89:26

62:3
ᵒ Isa 30:13

62:4
ᵖ Ps 28:3

62:7
q Ps 46:1; 85:9;
Jer 3:23

62:8
a 1Sa 1:15;
Ps 42:4; La 2:19

⁸Trust in him at all times, O people;
　　pour out your hearts to him,ᵃ
　　for God is our refuge.　　　　　　　　*Selah*

62:9
b Ps 39:5,11
c Isa 40:15

⁹Lowborn men are but a breath,ᵇ
　　the highborn are but a lie;
　if weighed on a balance,ᶜ they are nothing;
　　together they are only a breath.

62:10
d Isa 61:8
e Job 31:25;
1Ti 6:6-10

¹⁰Do not trust in extortion
　　or take pride in stolen goods;ᵈ
　though your riches increase,
　　do not set your heart on them.ᵉ

62:12
f Job 34:11;
Mt 16:27

¹¹One thing God has spoken,
　　two things have I heard:
　that you, O God, are strong,
¹²　　and that you, O Lord, are loving.
　Surely you will reward each person
　　according to what he has done.ᶠ

63:1
g Ps 42:2; 84:2

Psalm 63

A psalm of David. When he was in the Desert of Judah.

63:2
h Ps 27:4

Psalm 63 Theme

63:3
i Ps 69:16

¹O God, you are my God,
　　earnestly I seek you;
　my soul thirsts for you,ᵍ
　　my body longs for you,
　in a dry and weary land
　　where there is no water.

63:4
j Ps 104:33
k Ps 28:2

²I have seen you in the sanctuaryʰ
　　and beheld your power and your glory.
³Because your love is better than life,ⁱ
　　my lips will glorify you.
⁴I will praise you as long as I live,ʲ
　　and in your name I will lift up my hands.ᵏ

63:5
l Ps 36:8

⁵My soul will be satisfied as with the richest of foods;ˡ
　　with singing lips my mouth will praise you.

63:6
m Ps 42:8

⁶On my bed I remember you;
　　I think of you through the watches of the night.ᵐ

63:7
n Ps 27:9

⁷Because you are my help,ⁿ
　　I sing in the shadow of your wings.
⁸My soul clings to you;

63:8
o Ps 18:35

　　your right hand upholds me.ᵒ

⁹They who seek my life will be destroyed;ᵃ
  they will go down to the depths of the earth.ᵇ
¹⁰They will be given over to the sword
  and become food for jackals.

¹¹But the king will rejoice in God;
  all who swear by God's name will praise him,ᶜ
  while the mouths of liars will be silenced.

Psalm 64

For the director of music. A psalm of David.

*Psalm 64 Theme*_____

¹Hear me, O God, as I voice my complaint;ᵈ
  protect my life from the threat of the enemy.ᵉ
²Hide me from the conspiracy of the wicked,ᶠ
  from that noisy crowd of evildoers.

³They sharpen their tongues like swords
  and aim their words like deadly arrows.ᵍ
⁴They shoot from ambush at the innocent man;ʰ
  they shoot at him suddenly, without fear.ⁱ

⁵They encourage each other in evil plans,
  they talk about hiding their snares;
  they say, "Who will see themᵃ?"ʲ
⁶They plot injustice and say,
  "We have devised a perfect plan!"
  Surely the mind and heart of man are cunning.

⁷But God will shoot them with arrows;
  suddenly they will be struck down.
⁸He will turn their own tongues against themᵏ
  and bring them to ruin;
  all who see them will shake their headsˡ in scorn.

⁹All mankind will fear;
  they will proclaim the works of God
  and ponder what he has done.ᵐ
¹⁰Let the righteous rejoice in the Lord
  and take refuge in him;ⁿ
  let all the upright in heart praise him!ᵒ

a5 Or us

63:9 a Ps 40:14; b Ps 55:15
63:11 c Dt 6:13; Ps 21:1; Isa 45:23
64:1 d Ps 55:2; e Ps 140:1
64:2 f Ps 56:6; 59:2
64:3 g Ps 58:7
64:4 h Ps 11:2; i Ps 55:19
64:5 j Ps 10:11
64:8 k Ps 9:3; Pr 18:7; l Ps 22:7
64:9 m Jer 51:10
64:10 n Ps 25:20; o Ps 32:11

Psalm 65

For the director of music. A psalm of David. A song.

Psalm 65 Theme

65:1
a Ps 116:18

¹Praise awaits*a* you, O God, in Zion;
  to you our vows will be fulfilled.*a*

65:2
b Isa 66:23

²O you who hear prayer,
  to you all men will come.*b*

65:3
c Ps 38:4
d Heb 9:14

³When we were overwhelmed by sins,*c*
  you forgave*b* our transgressions.*d*

⁴Blessed are those you choose*e*
  and bring near to live in your courts!
We are filled with the good things of your house,*f*
  of your holy temple.

65:4
e Ps 4:3; 33:12
f Ps 36:8

⁵You answer us with awesome deeds of righteousness,
  O God our Savior,*g*
the hope of all the ends of the earth
  and of the farthest seas,*h*

65:5
g Ps 85:4
h Ps 107:23

⁶who formed the mountains by your power,
  having armed yourself with strength,*i*
⁷who stilled the roaring of the seas,*j*
  the roaring of their waves,
  and the turmoil of the nations.*k*

65:6
i Ps 93:1

⁸Those living far away fear your wonders;
  where morning dawns and evening fades
  you call forth songs of joy.

65:7
j Mt 8:26
k Isa 17:12-13

⁹You care for the land and water it;*l*
  you enrich it abundantly.
The streams of God are filled with water
  to provide the people with grain,*m*
  for so you have ordained it.*c*

¹⁰You drench its furrows
  and level its ridges;
you soften it with showers
  and bless its crops.

65:9
l Ps 68:9-10
m Ps 46:4;
104:14

¹¹You crown the year with your bounty,
  and your carts overflow with abundance.
¹²The grasslands of the desert overflow;*n*
  the hills are clothed with gladness.

65:12
n Job 28:26

a 1 Or *befits*; the meaning of the Hebrew for this word is uncertain.   *b* 3 Or *made atonement for*
c 9 Or *for that is how you prepare the land*

¹³The meadows are covered with flocks^a
and the valleys are mantled with grain;^b
they shout for joy and sing.^c

Psalm 66

For the director of music. A song. A psalm.

Psalm 66 Theme _____

¹Shout with joy to God, all the earth!^d
² Sing the glory of his name;^e
make his praise glorious!
³Say to God, "How awesome are your deeds!^f
So great is your power
that your enemies cringe^g before you.
⁴All the earth bows down^h to you;
they sing praiseⁱ to you,
they sing praise to your name."   *Selah*

⁵Come and see what God has done,
how awesome his works^j in man's behalf!
⁶He turned the sea into dry land,^k
they passed through the waters on foot—
come, let us rejoice in him.
⁷He rules forever^l by his power,
his eyes watch^m the nations—
let not the rebelliousⁿ rise up against him.   *Selah*

⁸Praise^o our God, O peoples,
let the sound of his praise be heard;
⁹he has preserved our lives
and kept our feet from slipping.^p
¹⁰For you, O God, tested us;
you refined us like silver.^q
¹¹You brought us into prison
and laid burdens^r on our backs.
¹²You let men ride over our heads;^s
we went through fire and water,
but you brought us to a place of abundance.^t

¹³I will come to your temple with burnt offerings
and fulfill my vows^u to you—
¹⁴vows my lips promised and my mouth spoke
when I was in trouble.
¹⁵I will sacrifice fat animals to you
and an offering of rams;
I will offer bulls and goats.^v   *Selah*

65:13
^aPs 144:13
^bPs 72:16
^cPs 98:8;
Isa 55:12

66:1
^dPs 100:1

66:2
^ePs 79:9

66:3
^fPs 65:5
^gPs 18:44

66:4
^hPs 22:27
ⁱPs 67:3

66:5
^jPs 106:22

66:6
^kEx 14:22

66:7
^lPs 145:13
^mPs 11:4
ⁿPs 140:8

66:8
^oPs 98:4

66:9
^pPs 121:3

66:10
^qPs 17:3;
Isa 48:10;
Zec 13:9;
1Pe 1:6-7

66:11
^rLa 1:13

66:12
^sIsa 51:23
^tIsa 43:2

66:13
^uEcc 5:4

66:15
^vNu 6:14;
Ps 51:19

66:16
a Ps 34:11
b Ps 71:15,24

¹⁶Come and listen,*a* all you who fear God;
　let me tell*b* you what he has done for me.
¹⁷I cried out to him with my mouth;
　his praise was on my tongue.

66:18
c Job 36:21;
Isa 1:15; Jas 4:3

¹⁸If I had cherished sin in my heart,
　the Lord would not have listened;*c*
¹⁹but God has surely listened
　and heard my voice*d* in prayer.

66:19
d Ps 116:1-2

²⁰Praise be to God,
　who has not rejected*e* my prayer
　or withheld his love from me!

Psalm 67

66:20
e Ps 22:24; 68:35

For the director of music. With stringed instruments. A psalm. A song.

Psalm 67 Theme _____

67:1
f Nu 6:24-26;
Ps 4:6

¹May God be gracious to us and bless us
　and make his face shine upon us,*f*　　　　*Selah*
²that your ways may be known on earth,
　your salvation*g* among all nations.*h*

67:2
g Isa 52:10
h Tit 2:11

³May the peoples praise you, O God;
　may all the peoples praise you.
⁴May the nations be glad and sing for joy,
　for you rule the peoples justly*i*

67:4
i Ps 96:10-13

　and guide the nations of the earth.　　　　*Selah*
⁵May the peoples praise you, O God;
　may all the peoples praise you.

67:6
j Lev 26:4;
Ps 85:12;
Eze 34:27

⁶Then the land will yield its harvest,*j*
　and God, our God, will bless us.
⁷God will bless us,
　and all the ends of the earth will fear him.*k*

Psalm 68

67:7
k Ps 33:8

For the director of music. Of David. A psalm. A song.

68:1
l Nu 10:35;
Isa 33:3

Psalm 68 Theme _____

¹May God arise, may his enemies be scattered;
　may his foes flee*l* before him.
²As smoke*m* is blown away by the wind,
　may you blow them away;

68:2
m Hos 13:3

as wax melts[a] before the fire,
may the wicked perish before God.
[3]But may the righteous be glad
and rejoice[b] before God;
may they be happy and joyful.

[4]Sing to God, sing praise to his name,[c]
extol him who rides on the clouds[a][d]—
his name is the LORD[e]—
and rejoice before him.
[5]A father to the fatherless,[f] a defender of widows,[g]
is God in his holy dwelling.[h]
[6]God sets the lonely in families,[b][i]
he leads forth the prisoners[j] with singing;
but the rebellious live in a sun-scorched land.[k]

[7]When you went out[l] before your people, O God,
when you marched through the wasteland,   *Selah*
[8]the earth shook,
the heavens poured down rain,[m]
before God, the One of Sinai,[n]
before God, the God of Israel.
[9]You gave abundant showers,[o] O God;
you refreshed your weary inheritance.
[10]Your people settled in it,
and from your bounty, O God, you provided[p]
for the poor.

[11]The Lord announced the word,
and great was the company of those who
proclaimed it:
[12]"Kings and armies flee[q] in haste;
in the camps men divide the plunder.
[13]Even while you sleep among the campfires,[c][r]
the wings of ⌊my⌋ dove are sheathed with silver,
its feathers with shining gold."
[14]When the Almighty[d] scattered[s] the kings in the land,
it was like snow fallen on Zalmon.

[15]The mountains of Bashan are majestic mountains;
rugged are the mountains of Bashan.
[16]Why gaze in envy, O rugged mountains,
at the mountain where God chooses[t] to reign,
where the LORD himself will dwell forever?

---

[a]4 Or *I prepare the way for him who rides through the deserts*   [b]6 Or *the desolate in a homeland*   [c]13 Or *saddlebags*   [d]14 Hebrew *Shaddai*

68:2
[a]Isa 9:18;
Mic 1:4

68:3
[b]Ps 32:11

68:4
[c]Ps 66:2
[d]Dt 33:26
[e]Ex 6:3;
Ps 83:18

68:5
[f]Ps 10:14
[g]Dt 10:18
[h]Dt 26:15

68:6
[i]Ps 113:9
[j]Ac 12:6
[k]Ps 107:34

68:7
[l]Ex 13:21;
Jdg 4:14

68:8
[m]Jdg 5:4
[n]Ex 19:16,18

68:9
[o]Dt 11:11

68:10
[p]Ps 74:19

68:12
[q]Jos 10:16

68:13
[r]Ge 49:14

68:14
[s]Jos 10:10

68:16
[t]Dt 12:5

68:17
a Dt 33:2;
Da 7:10

68:18
b Jdg 5:12
c Eph 4:8*

68:19
d Ps 65:5
e Ps 55:22

68:20
f Ps 56:13

68:21
g Ps 110:5;
Hab 3:13

68:22
h Nu 21:33

68:23
i Ps 58:10
j 1Ki 21:19

68:24
k Ps 63:2

68:25
l Jdg 11:34;
1Ch 13:8

68:26
m Ps 26:12;
Isa 48:1

68:27
n 1Sa 9:21

68:29
o Ps 72:10

68:30
p Ps 22:12
q Ps 89:10

68:31
r Isa 19:19;
45:14

¹⁷The chariots of God are tens of thousands
and thousands of thousands;*a*
the Lord ⌊has come⌋ from Sinai into his sanctuary.
¹⁸When you ascended on high,
you led captives*b* in your train;
you received gifts from men,*c*
even from*a* the rebellious—
that you,*b* O LORD God, might dwell there.

¹⁹Praise be to the Lord, to God our Savior,*d*
who daily bears our burdens.*e*   Selah
²⁰Our God is a God who saves;
from the Sovereign LORD comes escape from death.*f*

²¹Surely God will crush the heads*g* of his enemies,
the hairy crowns of those who go on in their sins.
²²The Lord says, "I will bring them from Bashan;
I will bring them from the depths of the sea,*h*
²³that you may plunge your feet in the blood of your foes,*i*
while the tongues of your dogs*j* have their share."

²⁴Your procession has come into view, O God,
the procession of my God and King into
the sanctuary.*k*
²⁵In front are the singers, after them the musicians;
with them are the maidens playing tambourines.*l*
²⁶Praise God in the great congregation;
praise the LORD in the assembly of Israel.*m*
²⁷There is the little tribe*n* of Benjamin, leading them,
there the great throng of Judah's princes,
and there the princes of Zebulun and of Naphtali.

²⁸Summon your power, O God*c*;
show us your strength, O God, as you have
done before.
²⁹Because of your temple at Jerusalem
kings will bring you gifts.*o*
³⁰Rebuke the beast among the reeds,
the herd of bulls*p* among the calves of the nations.
Humbled, may it bring bars of silver.
Scatter the nations*q* who delight in war.
³¹Envoys will come from Egypt;*r*
Cush*d* will submit herself to God.

a 18 Or *gifts for men, / even*   *b 18* Or *they*   *c 28* Many Hebrew manuscripts, Septuagint and Syriac; most Hebrew manuscripts *Your God has summoned power for you*   *d 31* That is, the upper Nile region

³²Sing to God, O kingdoms of the earth,
  sing praise to the Lord,   *Selah*
³³to him who rides^a the ancient skies above,
  who thunders with mighty voice.^b
³⁴Proclaim the power^c of God,
  whose majesty is over Israel,
  whose power is in the skies.
³⁵You are awesome, O God, in your sanctuary;
  the God of Israel gives power and strength to
    his people.^d

Praise be to God!^e

Psalm 69

For the director of music. To ₁the tune of₁ "Lilies." Of David.

Psalm 69 Theme _____

¹Save me, O God,
  for the waters have come up to my neck.^f
²I sink in the miry depths,^g
  where there is no foothold.
I have come into the deep waters;
  the floods engulf me.
³I am worn out calling for help;^h
  my throat is parched.
My eyes fail,ⁱ
  looking for my God.
⁴Those who hate me without reason^j
  outnumber the hairs of my head;
many are my enemies without cause,^k
  those who seek to destroy me.
I am forced to restore
  what I did not steal.

⁵You know my folly,^l O God;
  my guilt is not hidden from you.^m

⁶May those who hope in you
  not be disgraced because of me,
  O Lord, the LORD Almighty;
may those who seek you
  not be put to shame because of me,
  O God of Israel.
⁷For I endure scorn for your sake,ⁿ
  and shame covers my face.^o

68:33
^aPs 18:10
^bPs 29:4

68:34
^cPs 29:1

68:35
^dPs 29:11
^ePs 66:20

69:1
^fJnh 2:5

69:2
^gPs 40:2

69:3
^hPs 6:6
ⁱPs 119:82;
Isa 38:14

69:4
^jJn 15:25*
^kPs 35:19; 38:19

69:5
^lPs 38:5
^mPs 44:21

69:7
ⁿJer 15:15
^oPs 44:15

69:8
a Ps 31:11;
Isa 53:3

69:9
b Jn 2:17*
c Ps 89:50-51;
Ro 15:3*

69:10
d Ps 35:13

69:11
e Ps 35:13

69:12
f Job 30:9

69:13
g Isa 49:8;
2Co 6:2
h Ps 51:1

69:14
i ver 2; Ps 144:7

69:15
j Ps 124:4-5
k Nu 16:33

69:16
l Ps 63:3

69:17
m Ps 27:9
n Ps 66:14

69:18
o Ps 49:15

69:19
p Ps 22:6

69:20
q Job 16:2
r Isa 63:5

69:21
s Mt 27:34;
Mk 15:23;
Jn 19:28-30

69:23
t Isa 6:9-10;
Ro 11:9-10*

69:24
u Ps 79:6

69:25
v Mt 23:38
w Ac 1:20*

⁸I am a stranger to my brothers,
an alien to my own mother's sons;ᵃ
⁹for zeal for your house consumes me,ᵇ
and the insults of those who insult you fall on me.ᶜ
¹⁰When I weep and fast,ᵈ
I must endure scorn;
¹¹when I put on sackcloth,ᵉ
people make sport of me.
¹²Those who sit at the gate mock me,
and I am the song of the drunkards.ᶠ

¹³But I pray to you, O Lord,
in the time of your favor;ᵍ
in your great love,ʰ O God,
answer me with your sure salvation.
¹⁴Rescue me from the mire,
do not let me sink;
deliver me from those who hate me,
from the deep waters.ⁱ
¹⁵Do not let the floodwatersʲ engulf me
or the depths swallow me upᵏ
or the pit close its mouth over me.
¹⁶Answer me, O Lord, out of the goodness of your love;ˡ
in your great mercy turn to me.
¹⁷Do not hide your faceᵐ from your servant;
answer me quickly, for I am in trouble.ⁿ
¹⁸Come near and rescue me;
redeemᵒ me because of my foes.

¹⁹You know how I am scorned,ᵖ disgraced and shamed;
all my enemies are before you.
²⁰Scorn has broken my heart
and has left me helpless;
I looked for sympathy, but there was none,
for comforters,�q but I found none.ʳ
²¹They put gall in my food
and gave me vinegar for my thirst.ˢ

²²May the table set before them become a snare;
may it become retribution andᵃ a trap.
²³May their eyes be darkened so they cannot see,
and their backs be bent forever.ᵗ
²⁴Pour out your wrathᵘ on them;
let your fierce anger overtake them.
²⁵May their place be deserted;ᵛ
let there be no one to dwell in their tents.ʷ

ᵃ22 Or snare / and their fellowship become

²⁶For they persecute those you wound
    and talk about the pain of those you hurt.*ᵃ*
²⁷Charge them with crime upon crime;*ᵇ*
    do not let them share in your salvation.*ᶜ*
²⁸May they be blotted out of the book of life*ᵈ*
    and not be listed with the righteous.*ᵉ*

²⁹I am in pain and distress;
    may your salvation, O God, protect me.*ᶠ*

³⁰I will praise God's name in song*ᵍ*
    and glorify him*ʰ* with thanksgiving.
³¹This will please the Lord more than an ox,
    more than a bull with its horns and hoofs.*ⁱ*
³²The poor will see and be glad*ʲ*—
    you who seek God, may your hearts live!*ᵏ*
³³The Lord hears the needy*ˡ*
    and does not despise his captive people.

³⁴Let heaven and earth praise him,
    the seas and all that move in them,*ᵐ*
³⁵for God will save Zion*ⁿ*
    and rebuild the cities of Judah.*ᵒ*
Then people will settle there and possess it;
³⁶   the children of his servants will inherit it,
    and those who love his name will dwell there.*ᵖ*

Psalm 70

For the director of music. Of David. A petition.

Psalm 70 Theme _____

¹Hasten, O God, to save me;
    O Lord, come quickly to help me.*�q*
²May those who seek my life*ʳ*
    be put to shame and confusion;
  may all who desire my ruin
    be turned back in disgrace.*ˢ*
³May those who say to me, "Aha! Aha!"
    turn back because of their shame.
⁴But may all who seek you
    rejoice and be glad in you;
  may those who love your salvation always say,
    "Let God be exalted!"

69:26
ᵃ Isa 53:4;
Zec 1:15

69:27
ᵇ Ne 4:5
ᶜ Ps 109:14;
Isa 26:10

69:28
ᵈ Ex 32:32-33;
Lk 10:20;
Php 4:3
ᵉ Eze 13:9

69:29
ᶠ Ps 59:1; 70:5

69:30
ᵍ Ps 28:7
ʰ Ps 34:3

69:31
ⁱ Ps 50:9-13

69:32
ʲ Ps 34:2
ᵏ Ps 22:26

69:33
ˡ Ps 12:5; 68:6

69:34
ᵐ Ps 96:11;
148:1; Isa 44:23;
49:13; 55:12

69:35
ⁿ Ob 17
ᵒ Ps 51:18;
Isa 44:26

69:36
ᵖ Ps 37:29;
102:28

70:1
q Ps 40:13

70:2
ʳ Ps 35:4
ˢ Ps 35:26

70:5
a Ps 40:17
b Ps 141:1

71:1
c Ps 25:2-3; 31:1

71:2
d Ps 17:6

71:3
e Ps 18:2; 31:2-3;
44:4

71:4
f Ps 140:4

71:5
g Job 4:6;
Jer 17:7

71:6
h Ps 22:10
i Ps 22:9;
Isa 46:3
j Ps 9:1; 34:1;
52:9; 119:164;
145:2

71:7
k Isa 8:18;
1Co 4:9
l 2Sa 22:3;
Ps 61:3

71:8
m Ps 51:15; 63:5
n Ps 35:28; 96:6;
104:1

71:9
o Ps 51:11
p ver 18;
Ps 92:14;
Isa 46:4

71:10
q Ps 10:8; 59:3;
Pr 1:18
r Ps 31:13; 56:6;
Mt 12:14

71:11
s Ps 7:2

71:12
t Ps 35:22; 38:21
u Ps 38:22; 70:1

71:13
v ver 24

71:14
w Ps 130:7

71:15
x Ps 35:28; 40:5

5 Yet I am poor and needy;[a]
    come quickly to me,[b] O God.
You are my help and my deliverer;
    O LORD, do not delay.

Psalm 71

Psalm 71 Theme _____

1 In you, O LORD, I have taken refuge;
    let me never be put to shame.[c]
2 Rescue me and deliver me in your righteousness;
    turn your ear[d] to me and save me.
3 Be my rock of refuge,
    to which I can always go;
  give the command to save me,
    for you are my rock and my fortress.[e]
4 Deliver me, O my God, from the hand of the wicked,[f]
    from the grasp of evil and cruel men.

5 For you have been my hope, O Sovereign LORD,
    my confidence[g] since my youth.
6 From birth[h] I have relied on you;
    you brought me forth from my mother's womb.[i]
    I will ever praise[j] you.
7 I have become like a portent[k] to many,
    but you are my strong refuge.[l]
8 My mouth[m] is filled with your praise,
    declaring your splendor[n] all day long.

9 Do not cast[o] me away when I am old;[p]
    do not forsake me when my strength is gone.
10 For my enemies speak against me;
    those who wait to kill[q] me conspire[r] together.
11 They say, "God has forsaken him;
    pursue him and seize him,
    for no one will rescue[s] him."
12 Be not far[t] from me, O God;
    come quickly, O my God, to help[u] me.
13 May my accusers perish in shame;
    may those who want to harm me
    be covered with scorn and disgrace.[v]

14 But as for me, I will always have hope;[w]
    I will praise you more and more.
15 My mouth will tell[x] of your righteousness,
    of your salvation all day long,
    though I know not its measure.

¹⁶I will come and proclaim your mighty acts,*a*
    O Sovereign LORD;
  I will proclaim your righteousness, yours alone.
¹⁷Since my youth, O God, you have taught*b* me,
  and to this day I declare your marvelous deeds.*c*
¹⁸Even when I am old and gray,*d*
    do not forsake me, O God,
  till I declare your power to the next generation,
    your might to all who are to come.*e*

¹⁹Your righteousness reaches to the skies,*f* O God,
    you who have done great things.*g*
    Who, O God, is like you?*h*
²⁰Though you have made me see troubles,*i* many
      and bitter,
    you will restore*j* my life again;
  from the depths of the earth
    you will again bring me up.
²¹You will increase my honor*k*
  and comfort*l* me once again.

²²I will praise you with the harp*m*
    for your faithfulness, O my God;
  I will sing praise to you with the lyre,*n*
    O Holy One of Israel.*o*
²³My lips will shout for joy
    when I sing praise to you—
  I, whom you have redeemed.*p*
²⁴My tongue will tell of your righteous acts
    all day long,*q*
  for those who wanted to harm me*r*
    have been put to shame and confusion.

Psalm 72

Of Solomon.

Psalm 72 Theme

¹Endow the king with your justice, O God,
  the royal son with your righteousness.
²He will*a* judge your people in righteousness,*s*
  your afflicted ones with justice.
³The mountains will bring prosperity to the people,
  the hills the fruit of righteousness.

---

a 2 Or May he; similarly in verses 3-11 and 17

71:16
a Ps 106:2

71:17
b Dt 4:5
c Ps 26:7

71:18
d ver 9
e Ps 22:30,31;
78:4

71:19
f Ps 36:5; 57:10
g Ps 126:2;
Lk 1:49
h Ps 35:10

71:20
i Ps 60:3
j Hos 6:2

71:21
k Ps 18:35
l Ps 23:4; 86:17;
Isa 12:1; 49:13

71:22
m Ps 33:2
n Ps 92:3; 144:9
o 2Ki 19:22

71:23
p Ps 103:4

71:24
q Ps 35:28
r ver 13

72:2
s Isa 9:7; 11:4-5;
32:1

72:4
a Isa 11:4

⁴He will defend the afflicted among the people
    and save the children of the needy;ᵃ
    he will crush the oppressor.

72:6
b Dt 32:2;
Hos 6:3

⁵He will endureᵃ as long as the sun,
    as long as the moon, through all generations.
⁶He will be like rainᵇ falling on a mown field,
    like showers watering the earth.
⁷In his days the righteous will flourish;ᶜ
    prosperity will abound till the moon is no more.

72:7
c Ps 92:12;
Isa 2:4

⁸He will rule from sea to sea
    and from the River ᵈᵇ to the ends of the earth.ᶜ ᵉ
⁹The desert tribes will bow before him
    and his enemies will lick the dust.

72:8
d Ex 23:31
e Zec 9:10

¹⁰The kings of Tarshish and of distant shores
    will bring tribute to him;
    the kings of Shebaᶠ and Seba
    will present him gifts.ᵍ
¹¹All kings will bow down to him
    and all nations will serve him.

72:10
f Ge 10:7
g 2Ch 9:24

¹²For he will deliver the needy who cry out,
    the afflicted who have no one to help.
¹³He will take pity on the weak and the needy
    and save the needy from death.
¹⁴He will rescueʰ them from oppression and violence,
    for preciousⁱ is their blood in his sight.

72:14
h Ps 69:18
i 1Sa 26:21;
Ps 116:15

¹⁵Long may he live!
    May gold from Sheba ʲ be given him.
    May people ever pray for him
    and bless him all day long.
¹⁶Let grain abound throughout the land;
    on the tops of the hills may it sway.
    Let its fruit flourish like Lebanon;ᵏ
    let it thrive like the grass of the field.
¹⁷May his name endure forever;ˡ
    may it continue as long as the sun.ᵐ

72:15
j Isa 60:6

72:16
k Ps 104:16

All nations will be blessed through him,
    and they will call him blessed.ⁿ

72:17
l Ex 3:15
m Ps 89:36
n Ge 12:3;
Lk 1:48

¹⁸Praise be to the LORD God, the God of Israel,ᵒ
    who alone does marvelous deeds.ᵖ
¹⁹Praise be to his glorious name forever;

72:18
o 1Ch 29:10;
Ps 41:13; 106:48
p Job 5:9

ᵃ5 Septuagint; Hebrew *You will be feared* ᵇ8 That is, the Euphrates ᶜ8 Or *the end of the land*

may the whole earth be filled with his glory.*a*
Amen and Amen.*b*

20This concludes the prayers of David son of Jesse.

BOOK III

Psalms 73–89

Psalm 73

A psalm of Asaph.

Psalm 73 Theme _____

1Surely God is good to Israel,
 to those who are pure in heart.*c*

2But as for me, my feet had almost slipped;
 I had nearly lost my foothold.
3For I envied*d* the arrogant
 when I saw the prosperity of the wicked.*e*

4They have no struggles;
 their bodies are healthy and strong.*a*
5They are free*f* from the burdens common to man;
 they are not plagued by human ills.
6Therefore pride is their necklace;*g*
 they clothe themselves with violence.*h*
7From their callous hearts*i* comes iniquity*b*;
 the evil conceits of their minds know no limits.
8They scoff, and speak with malice;
 in their arrogance*j* they threaten oppression.
9Their mouths lay claim to heaven,
 and their tongues take possession of the earth.
10Therefore their people turn to them
 and drink up waters in abundance.*c*
11They say, "How can God know?
 Does the Most High have knowledge?"

12This is what the wicked are like—
 always carefree, they increase in wealth.*k*

13Surely in vain*l* have I kept my heart pure;
 in vain have I washed my hands in innocence.*m*
14All day long I have been plagued;
 I have been punished every morning.

---

a4 With a different word division of the Hebrew; Masoretic Text *struggles at their death; / their bodies are healthy*   b7 Syriac (see also Septuagint); Hebrew *Their eyes bulge with fat*   c10 The meaning of the Hebrew for this verse is uncertain.

72:19
a Nu 14:21;
Ne 9:5
b Ps 41:13

73:1
c Mt 5:8

73:3
d Ps 37:1;
Pr 23:17
e Job 21:7;
Jer 12:1

73:5
f Job 21:9

73:6
g Ge 41:42
h Ps 109:18

73:7
i Ps 17:10

73:8
j Ps 17:10;
Jude 16

73:12
k Ps 49:6

73:13
l Job 21:15; 34:9
m Ps 26:6

73:16
a Ecc 8:17

73:17
b Ps 77:13
c Ps 37:38

73:18
d Ps 35:6

73:19
e Isa 47:11

73:20
f Job 20:8
g Ps 78:65

73:22
h Ps 49:10; 92:6
i Ecc 3:18

73:24
j Ps 48:14
k Ps 32:8

73:25
l Php 3:8

73:26
m Ps 84:2
n Ps 40:12

73:27
o Ps 119:155

73:28
p Heb 10:22;
Jas 4:8
q Ps 40:5

74:1
r Dt 29:20;
Ps 44:23
s Ps 79:13; 95:7;
100:3

¹⁵If I had said, "I will speak thus,"
  I would have betrayed your children.
¹⁶When I tried to understand*ᵃ* all this,
  it was oppressive to me
¹⁷till I entered the sanctuary*ᵇ* of God;
  then I understood their final destiny.*ᶜ*

¹⁸Surely you place them on slippery ground;*ᵈ*
  you cast them down to ruin.
¹⁹How suddenly*ᵉ* are they destroyed,
  completely swept away by terrors!
²⁰As a dream *ᶠ* when one awakes,*ᵍ*
  so when you arise, O Lord,
  you will despise them as fantasies.

²¹When my heart was grieved
  and my spirit embittered,
²²I was senseless*ʰ* and ignorant;
  I was a brute beast*ⁱ* before you.

²³Yet I am always with you;
  you hold me by my right hand.
²⁴You guide*ʲ* me with your counsel,*ᵏ*
  and afterward you will take me into glory.
²⁵Whom have I in heaven but you?
  And earth has nothing I desire besides you.*ˡ*
²⁶My flesh and my heart*ᵐ* may fail,*ⁿ*
  but God is the strength of my heart
  and my portion forever.

²⁷Those who are far from you will perish;*ᵒ*
  you destroy all who are unfaithful to you.
²⁸But as for me, it is good to be near God.*ᵖ*
  I have made the Sovereign LORD my refuge;
  I will tell of all your deeds.*�q*

Psalm 74

A *maskil*ᵃ of Asaph.

Psalm 74 Theme _____

¹Why have you rejected us forever,*ʳ* O God?
  Why does your anger smolder against the sheep
  of your pasture?*ˢ*

ᵃ Title: Probably a literary or musical term

²Remember the people you purchased[a] of old,[b]
  the tribe of your inheritance, whom you redeemed[c]—
  Mount Zion, where you dwelt.[d]
³Turn your steps toward these everlasting ruins,
  all this destruction the enemy has brought on
    the sanctuary.

⁴Your foes roared[e] in the place where you met with us;
  they set up their standards[f] as signs.
⁵They behaved like men wielding axes
  to cut through a thicket of trees.[g]
⁶They smashed all the carved[h] paneling
  with their axes and hatchets.
⁷They burned your sanctuary to the ground;
  they defiled the dwelling place of your Name.
⁸They said in their hearts, "We will crush[i] them
    completely!"
  They burned every place where God was
    worshiped in the land.
⁹We are given no miraculous signs;
  no prophets[j] are left,
  and none of us knows how long this will be.

¹⁰How long will the enemy mock you, O God?
  Will the foe revile[k] your name forever?
¹¹Why do you hold back your hand, your right hand?[l]
  Take it from the folds of your garment and
    destroy them!

¹²But you, O God, are my king[m] from of old;
  you bring salvation upon the earth.
¹³It was you who split open the sea[n] by your power;
  you broke the heads of the monster[o] in the waters.
¹⁴It was you who crushed the heads of Leviathan
  and gave him as food to the creatures of the desert.
¹⁵It was you who opened up springs[p] and streams;
  you dried up[q] the ever flowing rivers.
¹⁶The day is yours, and yours also the night;
  you established the sun and moon.[r]
¹⁷It was you who set all the boundaries[s] of the earth;
  you made both summer and winter.[t]

¹⁸Remember how the enemy has mocked you, O LORD,
  how foolish people[u] have reviled your name.
¹⁹Do not hand over the life of your dove to wild beasts;
  do not forget the lives of your afflicted[v]
    people forever.

74:2
[a] Ex 15:16
[b] Dt 32:7
[c] Ex 15:13
[d] Ps 68:16

74:4
[e] La 2:7
[f] Nu 2:2

74:5
[g] Jer 46:22

74:6
[h] 1Ki 6:18

74:8
[i] Ps 83:4

74:9
[j] 1Sa 3:1

74:10
[k] Ps 44:16

74:11
[l] La 2:3

74:12
[m] Ps 44:4

74:13
[n] Ex 14:21
[o] Isa 51:9;
Eze 29:3

74:15
[p] Ex 17:6;
Nu 20:11
[q] Jos 2:10; 3:13

74:16
[r] Ge 1:16;
Ps 136:7-9

74:17
[s] Dt 32:8;
Ac 17:26
[t] Ge 8:22

74:18
[u] Dt 32:6;
Ps 39:8

74:19
[v] Ps 9:18

74:20
a Ge 17:7;
Ps 106:45

²⁰Have regard for your covenant,*a*

because haunts of violence fill the dark places of
the land.

²¹Do not let the oppressed*b* retreat in disgrace;

may the poor and needy*c* praise your name.

74:21
b Ps 103:6
c Ps 35:10

²²Rise up, O God, and defend your cause;

remember how fools*d* mock you all day long.

²³Do not ignore the clamor of your adversaries,*e*

the uproar of your enemies, which rises continually.

74:22
d Ps 53:1

74:23
e Ps 65:7

Psalm 75

For the director of music. ₍To the tune of₎ "Do Not Destroy." A psalm of Asaph.
A song.

75:1
f Ps 145:18
g Ps 44:1; 71:16

Psalm 75 Theme

¹We give thanks to you, O God,

we give thanks, for your Name is near;*f*

men tell of your wonderful deeds.*g*

75:3
h Isa 24:19
i 1Sa 2:8

²You say, "I choose the appointed time;

it is I who judge uprightly.

³When the earth and all its people quake,*h*

it is I who hold its pillars*i* firm.   *Selah*

75:4
j Zec 1:21

⁴To the arrogant I say, 'Boast no more,'

and to the wicked, 'Do not lift up your horns.*j*

⁵Do not lift your horns against heaven;

do not speak with outstretched neck.' "

75:7
k Ps 50:6
l 1Sa 2:7;
Ps 147:6;
Da 2:21

⁶No one from the east or the west

or from the desert can exalt a man.

⁷But it is God who judges:*k*

He brings one down, he exalts another.*l*

75:8
m Pr 23:30
n Job 21:20;
Jer 25:15

⁸In the hand of the LORD is a cup

full of foaming wine mixed*m* with spices;

he pours it out, and all the wicked of the earth

drink it down to its very dregs.*n*

75:9
o Ps 40:10

⁹As for me, I will declare*o* this forever;

I will sing praise to the God of Jacob.

75:10
p Ps 89:17;
92:10; 148:14

¹⁰I will cut off the horns of all the wicked,

but the horns of the righteous will be lifted up. *p*

Psalm 76

For the director of music. With stringed instruments. A psalm of Asaph. A song.

Psalm 76 Theme _____

[1] In Judah God is known;
    his name is great in Israel.
[2] His tent is in Salem,[a]
    his dwelling place in Zion.
[3] There he broke the flashing arrows,
    the shields and the swords, the weapons of war.[b]   _Selah_

[4] You are resplendent with light,
    more majestic than mountains rich with game.
[5] Valiant men lie plundered,
    they sleep their last sleep;[c]
not one of the warriors
    can lift his hands.
[6] At your rebuke, O God of Jacob,
    both horse and chariot[d] lie still.
[7] You alone are to be feared.[e]
    Who can stand[f] before you when you are angry?[g]
[8] From heaven you pronounced judgment,
    and the land feared[h] and was quiet—
[9] when you, O God, rose up to judge,[i]
    to save all the afflicted of the land.   _Selah_
[10] Surely your wrath against men brings you praise,[j]
    and the survivors of your wrath are restrained.[a]

[11] Make vows to the LORD your God and fulfill them;[k]
    let all the neighboring lands
    bring gifts[l] to the One to be feared.
[12] He breaks the spirit of rulers;
    he is feared by the kings of the earth.

Psalm 77

For the director of music. For Jeduthun. Of Asaph. A psalm.

Psalm 77 Theme _____

[1] I cried out to God[m] for help;
    I cried out to God to hear me.

---

[a] 10 Or _Surely the wrath of men brings you praise,/ and with the remainder of wrath you arm yourself_

76:2
[a] Ge 14:18

76:3
[b] Ps 46:9

76:5
[c] Ps 13:3

76:6
[d] Ex 15:1

76:7
[e] 1Ch 16:25
[f] Ezr 9:15;
Rev 6:17
[g] Ps 2:5; Na 1:6

76:8
[h] 1Ch 16:30;
2Ch 20:29-30

76:9
[i] Ps 9:8

76:10
[j] Ex 9:16;
Ro 9:17

76:11
[k] Ps 50:14;
Ecc 5:4-5
[l] 2Ch 32:23;
Ps 68:29

77:1
[m] Ps 3:4

77:2
a Ps 50:15;
Isa 26:9,16
b Job 11:13
c Ge 37:35

²When I was in distress,*a* I sought the Lord;
  at night I stretched out untiring hands*b*
  and my soul refused to be comforted.*c*

77:3
d Ps 143:4

³I remembered you, O God, and I groaned;
  I mused, and my spirit grew faint.*d*   *Selah*

⁴You kept my eyes from closing;
  I was too troubled to speak.

77:5
e Dt 32:7;
Ps 44:1; 143:5;
Isa 51:9

⁵I thought about the former days,*e*
  the years of long ago;
⁶I remembered my songs in the night.
  My heart mused and my spirit inquired:

77:7
f Ps 85:1

⁷"Will the Lord reject forever?
  Will he never show his favor*f* again?

77:8
g 2Pe 3:9

⁸Has his unfailing love vanished forever?
  Has his promise*g* failed for all time?

77:9
h Ps 25:6; 40:11;
51:1
i Isa 49:15

⁹Has God forgotten to be merciful?*h*
  Has he in anger withheld his compassion?*i*"   *Selah*

77:10
j Ps 31:22

¹⁰Then I thought, "To this I will appeal:
  the years of the right hand*j* of the Most High."
¹¹I will remember the deeds of the LORD;
  yes, I will remember your miracles*k* of long ago.

77:11
k Ps 143:5

¹²I will meditate on all your works
  and consider all your mighty deeds.

77:13
l Ex 15:11;
Ps 71:19; 86:8

¹³Your ways, O God, are holy.
  What god is so great as our God?*l*
¹⁴You are the God who performs miracles;
  you display your power among the peoples.

77:15
m Ex 6:6;
Dt 9:29

¹⁵With your mighty arm you redeemed your people,*m*
  the descendants of Jacob and Joseph.   *Selah*

77:16
n Ex 14:21,28;
Hab 3:8
o Ps 114:4;
Hab 3:10

¹⁶The waters*n* saw you, O God,
  the waters saw you and writhed;*o*
  the very depths were convulsed.

77:17
p Jdg 5:4

¹⁷The clouds poured down water,*p*
  the skies resounded with thunder;
  your arrows flashed back and forth.

77:18
q Jdg 5:4

¹⁸Your thunder was heard in the whirlwind,
  your lightning lit up the world;
  the earth trembled and quaked.*q*

77:19
r Hab 3:15

¹⁹Your path led through the sea,*r*
  your way through the mighty waters,
  though your footprints were not seen.

77:20
s Ex 13:21
t Ps 78:52;
Isa 63:11

²⁰You led your people*s* like a flock*t*
  by the hand of Moses and Aaron.

Psalm 78

A maskil [a] *of Asaph.*

*Psalm 78 Theme*_____

¹O my people, hear my teaching;[a]
  listen to the words of my mouth.
²I will open my mouth in parables,[b]
  I will utter hidden things, things from of old—
³what we have heard and known,
  what our fathers have told us.[c]
⁴We will not hide them from their children;[d]
  we will tell the next generation
the praiseworthy deeds[e] of the LORD,
  his power, and the wonders he has done.
⁵He decreed statutes[f] for Jacob[g]
  and established the law in Israel,
which he commanded our forefathers
  to teach their children,
⁶so the next generation would know them,
  even the children yet to be born,[h]
  and they in turn would tell their children.
⁷Then they would put their trust in God
  and would not forget[i] his deeds
  but would keep his commands.[j]
⁸They would not be like their forefathers[k]—
  a stubborn[l] and rebellious[m] generation,
whose hearts were not loyal to God,
  whose spirits were not faithful to him.

⁹The men of Ephraim, though armed with bows,[n]
  turned back on the day of battle;[o]
¹⁰they did not keep God's covenant[p]
  and refused to live by his law.
¹¹They forgot what he had done,[q]
  the wonders he had shown them.
¹²He did miracles[r] in the sight of their fathers
  in the land of Egypt,[s] in the region of Zoan.[t]
¹³He divided the sea[u] and led them through;
  he made the water stand firm like a wall.[v]
¹⁴He guided them with the cloud by day
  and with light from the fire all night.[w]
¹⁵He split the rocks[x] in the desert
  and gave them water as abundant as the seas;

a Title: Probably a literary or musical term

78:1
a Isa 51:4; 55:3

78:2
b Ps 49:4;
Mt 13:35*

78:3
c Ps 44:1

78:4
d Dt 11:19
e Ps 26:7; 71:17

78:5
f Ps 19:7; 81:5
g Ps 147:19

78:6
h Ps 22:31;
102:18

78:7
i Dt 6:12
j Dt 5:29

78:8
k 2Ch 30:7
l Ex 32:9
m ver 37;
Isa 30:9

78:9
n ver 57;
1Ch 12:2
o Jdg 20:39

78:10
p 2Ki 17:15

78:11
q Ps 106:13

78:12
r Ps 106:22
s Ex 7-12
t Nu 13:22

78:13
u Ex 14:21;
Ps 136:13
v Ex 15:8

78:14
w Ex 13:21;
Ps 105:39

78:15
x Nu 20:11;
1Co 10:4

78:17
a Dt 9:22;
Isa 63:10;
Heb 3:16

78:18
b 1Co 10:9
c Ex 16:2;
Nu 11:4

78:19
d Nu 21:5

78:20
e Nu 20:11
f Nu 11:18

78:21
g Nu 11:1

78:22
h Dt 1:32;
Heb 3:19

78:23
i Ge 7:11;
Mal 3:10

78:24
j Ex 16:4;
Jn 6:31*

78:26
k Nu 11:31

78:29
l Nu 11:20

78:30
m Nu 11:33

78:31
n Isa 10:16

78:32
o ver 11
p ver 22

78:33
q Nu 14:29,35

78:34
r Hos 5:15

78:35
s Dt 32:4
t Dt 9:26

¹⁶he brought streams out of a rocky crag
    and made water flow down like rivers.

¹⁷But they continued to sin*a* against him,
    rebelling in the desert against the Most High.
¹⁸They willfully put God to the test*b*
    by demanding the food they craved.*c*
¹⁹They spoke against God,*d* saying,
    "Can God spread a table in the desert?
²⁰When he struck the rock, water gushed out,*e*
    and streams flowed abundantly.
  But can he also give us food?
    Can he supply meat*f* for his people?"
²¹When the LORD heard them, he was very angry;
    his fire broke out*g* against Jacob,
    and his wrath rose against Israel,
²²for they did not believe in God
    or trust*h* in his deliverance.
²³Yet he gave a command to the skies above
    and opened the doors of the heavens;*i*
²⁴he rained down manna*j* for the people to eat,
    he gave them the grain of heaven.
²⁵Men ate the bread of angels;
    he sent them all the food they could eat.
²⁶He let loose the east wind*k* from the heavens
    and led forth the south wind by his power.
²⁷He rained meat down on them like dust,
    flying birds like sand on the seashore.
²⁸He made them come down inside their camp,
    all around their tents.
²⁹They ate till they had more than enough,*l*
    for he had given them what they craved.
³⁰But before they turned from the food they craved,
    even while it was still in their mouths,*m*
³¹God's anger rose against them;
    he put to death the sturdiest*n* among them,
    cutting down the young men of Israel.

³²In spite of all this, they kept on sinning;
    in spite of his wonders,*o* they did not believe.*p*
³³So he ended their days in futility*q*
    and their years in terror.
³⁴Whenever God slew them, they would seek*r* him;
    they eagerly turned to him again.
³⁵They remembered that God was their Rock,*s*
    that God Most High was their Redeemer.*t*

³⁶But then they would flatter him with their mouths,ᵃ
    lying to him with their tongues;
³⁷their hearts were not loyalᵇ to him,
    they were not faithful to his covenant.
³⁸Yet he was merciful;ᶜ
    he forgaveᵈ their iniquitiesᵉ
    and did not destroy them.
  Time after time he restrained his anger
    and did not stir up his full wrath.
³⁹He remembered that they were but flesh,ᶠ
    a passing breezeᵍ that does not return.

⁴⁰How often they rebelledʰ against him in the desertⁱ
    and grieved himʲ in the wasteland!
⁴¹Again and again they put God to the test;ᵏ
    they vexed the Holy One of Israel.ˡ
⁴²They did not remember his power—
    the day he redeemed them from the oppressor,
⁴³the day he displayed his miraculous signs in Egypt,
    his wonders in the region of Zoan.
⁴⁴He turned their rivers to blood;ᵐ
    they could not drink from their streams.
⁴⁵He sent swarms of flies ⁿ that devoured them,
    and frogsᵒ that devastated them.
⁴⁶He gave their crops to the grasshopper,
    their produce to the locust.ᵖ
⁴⁷He destroyed their vines with hailۥᵠ
    and their sycamore-figs with sleet.
⁴⁸He gave over their cattle to the hail,
    their livestockʳ to bolts of lightning.
⁴⁹He unleashed against them his hot anger,ˢ
    his wrath, indignation and hostility—
    a band of destroying angels.
⁵⁰He prepared a path for his anger;
    he did not spare them from death
    but gave them over to the plague.
⁵¹He struck down all the firstborn of Egypt,ᵗ
    the firstfruits of manhood in the tents of Ham.ᵘ
⁵²But he brought his people out like a flock;ᵛ
    he led them like sheep through the desert.
⁵³He guided them safely, so they were unafraid;
    but the sea engulfedʷ their enemies.ˣ
⁵⁴Thus he brought them to the border of his holy land,
    to the hill country his right handʸ had taken.
⁵⁵He drove out nationsᶻ before them
    and allotted their lands to them as an inheritance;ᵃ
    he settled the tribes of Israel in their homes.

78:36 ᵃEze 33:31

78:37 ᵇver 8; Ac 8:21

78:38 ᶜEx 34:6 ᵈIsa 48:10 ᵉNu 14:18,20

78:39 ᶠGe 6:3; Ps 103:14 ᵍJob 7:7; Jas 4:14

78:40 ʰHeb 3:16 ⁱPs 95:8; 106:14 ʲEph 4:30

78:41 ᵏNu 14:22 ˡ2Ki 19:22; Ps 89:18

78:44 ᵐEx 7:20-21; Ps 105:29

78:45 ⁿEx 8:24; Ps 105:31 ᵒEx 8:2,6

78:46 ᵖEx 10:13

78:47 ᵠEx 9:23; Ps 105:32

78:48 ʳEx 9:25

78:49 ˢEx 15:7

78:51 ᵗEx 12:29; Ps 135:8 ᵘPs 105:23; 106:22

78:52 ᵛPs 77:20

78:53 ʷEx 14:28 ˣPs 106:10

78:54 ʸEx 15:17; Ps 44:3

78:55 ᶻPs 44:2 ᵃJos 13:7

78:57
a Eze 20:27
b Hos 7:16

78:58
c Jdg 2:12
d Lev 26:30
e Ex 20:4;
Dt 32:21

78:59
f Dt 32:19

78:60
g Jos 18:1

78:61
h Ps 132:8
i 1Sa 4:17

78:63
j Nu 11:1
k Jer 7:34; 16:9

78:64
l 1Sa 4:17; 22:18

78:65
m Ps 44:23

78:66
n 1Sa 5:6

78:68
o Ps 87:2

78:70
p 1Sa 16:1

78:71
q 2Sa 5:2;
Ps 28:9

78:72
r 1Ki 9:4

79:1
s Ps 74:2
t 2Ki 25:9

56But they put God to the test
and rebelled against the Most High;
they did not keep his statutes.
57Like their fathers a they were disloyal and faithless,
as unreliable as a faulty bow. b
58They angered him c with their high places; d
they aroused his jealousy with their idols. e
59When God heard them, he was very angry;
he rejected Israel f completely.
60He abandoned the tabernacle of Shiloh, g
the tent he had set up among men.
61He sent ₍the ark of₎ his might h into captivity, i
his splendor into the hands of the enemy.
62He gave his people over to the sword;
he was very angry with his inheritance.
63Fire consumed j their young men,
and their maidens had no wedding songs; k
64their priests were put to the sword, l
and their widows could not weep.

65Then the Lord awoke as from sleep, m
as a man wakes from the stupor of wine.
66He beat back his enemies;
he put them to everlasting shame. n
67Then he rejected the tents of Joseph,
he did not choose the tribe of Ephraim;
68but he chose the tribe of Judah,
Mount Zion, o which he loved.
69He built his sanctuary like the heights,
like the earth that he established forever.
70He chose David p his servant
and took him from the sheep pens;
71from tending the sheep he brought him
to be the shepherd q of his people Jacob,
of Israel his inheritance.
72And David shepherded them with integrity of heart; r
with skillful hands he led them.

Psalm 79

A psalm of Asaph.

*Psalm 79 Theme*_____

1O God, the nations have invaded your inheritance; s
they have defiled your holy temple,
they have reduced Jerusalem to rubble. t

²They have given the dead bodies of
  your servants
    as food to the birds of the air,
    the flesh of your saints to the beasts of
      the earth.ᵃ
³They have poured out blood like water
    all around Jerusalem,
    and there is no one to bury the dead.ᵇ
⁴We are objects of reproach to our neighbors,
    of scorn and derision to those around us.ᶜ

⁵How long,ᵈ O Lord? Will you be angryᵉ forever?
    How long will your jealousy burn like fire?ᶠ
⁶Pour out your wrathᵍ on the nations
    that do not acknowledgeʰ you,
  on the kingdoms
    that do not call on your name;ⁱ
⁷for they have devoured Jacob
    and destroyed his homeland.
⁸Do not hold against us the sins of the fathers;ʲ
    may your mercy come quickly to meet us,
    for we are in desperate need.ᵏ

⁹Help us,ˡ O God our Savior,
    for the glory of your name;
  deliver us and forgive our sins
    for your name's sake.ᵐ
¹⁰Why should the nations say,
    "Where is their God?"ⁿ
  Before our eyes, make known among
      the nations
    that you avengeᵒ the outpoured blood of
      your servants.
¹¹May the groans of the prisoners come before you;
    by the strength of your arm
    preserve those condemned to die.

¹²Pay back into the lapsᵖ of our neighbors seven timesᵠ
    the reproach they have hurled at you, O Lord.
¹³Then we your people, the sheep of your pasture,ʳ
    will praise you forever;ˢ
  from generation to generation
    we will recount your praise.

79:2
ᵃDt 28:26;
Jer 7:33

79:3
ᵇJer 16:4

79:4
ᶜPs 44:13; 80:6

79:5
ᵈPs 74:10
ᵉPs 74:1; 85:5
ᶠDt 29:20;
Ps 89:46;
Zep 3:8

79:6
ᵍPs 69:24;
Rev 16:1
ʰJer 10:25;
2Th 1:8
ⁱPs 14:4

79:8
ʲIsa 64:9
ᵏPs 116:6; 142:6

79:9
ˡ2Ch 14:11
ᵐPs 25:11; 31:3;
Jer 14:7

79:10
ⁿPs 42:10
ᵒPs 94:1

79:12
ᵖIsa 65:6;
Jer 32:18
ᵠGe 4:15

79:13
ʳPs 74:1; 95:7
ˢPs 44:8

Psalm 80

For the director of music. To ⌊the tune of⌋ "The Lilies of the Covenant."
Of Asaph. A psalm.

*Psalm 80 Theme*_____

¹Hear us, O Shepherd of Israel,
  you who lead Joseph like a flock;[a]
you who sit enthroned between the cherubim,[b]
    shine forth
² before Ephraim, Benjamin and Manasseh.[c]
Awaken[d] your might;
  come and save us.

³Restore[e] us,[f] O God;
  make your face shine upon us,
  that we may be saved.

⁴O LORD God Almighty,
  how long will your anger smolder
  against the prayers of your people?
⁵You have fed them with the bread of tears;
  you have made them drink tears by the bowlful.[g]
⁶You have made us a source of contention to
      our neighbors,
  and our enemies mock us.[h]

⁷Restore us, O God Almighty;
  make your face shine upon us,
  that we may be saved.

⁸You brought a vine[i] out of Egypt;
  you drove out[j] the nations and planted it.
⁹You cleared the ground for it,
  and it took root and filled the land.
¹⁰The mountains were covered with its shade,
  the mighty cedars with its branches.
¹¹It sent out its boughs to the Sea,[a]
  its shoots as far as the River.[b][k]

¹²Why have you broken down its walls[l]
  so that all who pass by pick its grapes?
¹³Boars from the forest ravage[m] it
  and the creatures of the field feed on it.

**Cross references (left margin):**

80:1
a Ps 77:20
b Ex 25:22

80:2
c Nu 2:18-24
d Ps 35:23

80:3
e Ps 85:4;
La 5:21
f Nu 6:25

80:5
g Ps 42:3;
Isa 30:20

80:6
h Ps 79:4

80:8
i Isa 5:1-2;
Jer 2:21
j Jos 13:6;
Ac 7:45

80:11
k Ps 72:8

80:12
l Ps 89:40;
Isa 5:5

80:13
m Jer 5:6

a 11 Probably the Mediterranean   b 11 That is, the Euphrates

¹⁴Return to us, O God Almighty!
    Look down from heaven and see!^a
    Watch over this vine,
¹⁵   the root your right hand has planted,
    the son^a you have raised up for yourself.

¹⁶Your vine is cut down, it is burned with fire;
    at your rebuke^b your people perish.
¹⁷Let your hand rest on the man at your right hand,
    the son of man you have raised up for yourself.
¹⁸Then we will not turn away from you;
    revive us, and we will call on your name.

¹⁹Restore us, O Lᴏʀᴅ God Almighty;
    make your face shine upon us,
    that we may be saved.

Psalm 81

For the director of music. According to *gittith*.^b Of Asaph.

Psalm 81 Theme

¹Sing for joy to God our strength;
    shout aloud to the God of Jacob!^c
²Begin the music, strike the tambourine,^d
    play the melodious harp^e and lyre.

³Sound the ram's horn at the New Moon,
    and when the moon is full, on the day of our Feast;
⁴this is a decree for Israel,
    an ordinance of the God of Jacob.
⁵He established it as a statute for Joseph
    when he went out against Egypt,^f
    where we heard a language we did not understand.^{c g}

⁶He says, "I removed the burden from their shoulders;^h
    their hands were set free from the basket.
⁷In your distress you calledⁱ and I rescued you,
    I answered^j you out of a thundercloud;
    I tested you at the waters of Meribah.^k   *Selah*

⁸"Hear, O my people,^l and I will warn you—
    if you would but listen to me, O Israel!
⁹You shall have no foreign god^m among you;
    you shall not bow down to an alien god.

---

^a15 Or *branch* ^bTitle: Probably a musical term ^c5 Or *l and we heard a voice we had not known*

Cross references

80:14
^aIsa 63:15

80:16
^bPs 39:11; 76:6

81:1
^cPs 66:1

81:2
^dEx 15:20
^ePs 92:3

81:5
^fEx 11:4
^gPs 114:1

81:6
^hIsa 9:4

81:7
ⁱEx 2:23;
Ps 50:15
^jEx 19:19
^kEx 17:7

81:8
^lPs 50:7

81:9
^mEx 20:3;
Dt 32:12;
Isa 43:12

¹⁰I am the LORD your God,
  who brought you up out of Egypt.*a*
  Open wide your mouth and I will fill*b* it.

¹¹"But my people would not listen to me;
  Israel would not submit to me.*c*
¹²So I gave them over*d* to their stubborn hearts
  to follow their own devices.

¹³"If my people would but listen to me,*e*
  if Israel would follow my ways,
¹⁴how quickly would I subdue*f* their enemies
  and turn my hand against*g* their foes!
¹⁵Those who hate the LORD would cringe before him,
  and their punishment would last forever.
¹⁶But you would be fed with the finest of wheat;*h*
  with honey from the rock I would satisfy you."

Psalm 82

A psalm of Asaph.

Psalm 82 Theme _____

¹God presides in the great assembly;
  he gives judgment*i* among the "gods":

²"How long will you*a* defend the unjust
  and show partiality*j* to the wicked?*k*   *Selah*
³Defend the cause of the weak and fatherless;*l*
  maintain the rights of the poor*m* and oppressed.
⁴Rescue the weak and needy;
  deliver them from the hand of the wicked.

⁵"They know nothing, they understand nothing.*n*
  They walk about in darkness;*o*
  all the foundations*p* of the earth are shaken.

⁶"I said, 'You are "gods";*q*
  you are all sons of the Most High.'
⁷But you will die*r* like mere men;
  you will fall like every other ruler."

⁸Rise up,*s* O God, judge the earth,
  for all the nations are your inheritance.*t*

*Cross references (left margin):*

81:10
a Ex 20:2
b Ps 107:9

81:11
c Ex 32:1-6

81:12
d Ac 7:42;
Ro 1:24

81:13
e Dt 5:29;
Isa 48:18

81:14
f Ps 47:3
g Am 1:8

81:16
h Dt 32:14

82:1
i Ps 58:11;
Isa 3:13

82:2
j Dt 1:17
k Ps 58:1-2;
Pr 18:5

82:3
l Dt 24:17
m Jer 22:16

82:5
n Ps 14:4;
Mic 3:1
o Isa 59:9
p Ps 11:3

82:6
q Jn 10:34*

82:7
r Ps 49:12;
Eze 31:14

82:8
s Ps 12:5
t Ps 2:8;
Rev 11:15

a 2 The Hebrew is plural.

Psalm 83

A song. A psalm of Asaph.

Psalm 83 Theme

¹O God, do not keep silent;ᵃ
  be not quiet, O God, be not still.
²See how your enemies are astir,ᵇ
  how your foes rear their heads.ᶜ
³With cunning they conspireᵈ against your people;
  they plot against those you cherish.
⁴"Come," they say, "let us destroyᵉ them as a nation,
  that the name of Israel be rememberedᶠ no more."

⁵With one mind they plot together;ᵍ
  they form an alliance against you—
⁶the tents of Edomʰ and the Ishmaelites,
  of Moabⁱ and the Hagrites,ʲ
⁷Gebal,ᵃ ᵏ Ammon and Amalek,
  Philistia, with the people of Tyre.ˡ
⁸Even Assyria has joined them
  to lend strength to the descendants of Lot.ᵐ   *Selah*

⁹Do to them as you did to Midian,ⁿ
  as you did to Sisera and Jabin at the river Kishon,ᵒ
¹⁰who perished at Endor
  and became like refuseᵖ on the ground.
¹¹Make their nobles like Oreb and Zeeb,�q
  all their princes like Zebah and Zalmunna,ʳ
¹²who said, "Let us take possessionˢ
  of the pasturelands of God."

¹³Make them like tumbleweed, O my God,
  like chaffᵗ before the wind.
¹⁴As fire consumes the forest
  or a flame sets the mountains ablaze,ᵘ
¹⁵so pursue them with your tempest
  and terrify them with your storm.ᵛ
¹⁶Cover their faces with shameʷ
  so that men will seek your name, O LORD.

¹⁷May they ever be ashamed and dismayed;
  may they perish in disgrace.ˣ
¹⁸Let them know that you, whose name is the LORD—
  that you alone are the Most High over all the earth.ʸ

ᵃ 7 That is, Byblos

83:1
ᵃ Ps 28:1; 35:22

83:2
ᵇ Ps 2:1;
Isa 17:12
ᶜ Jdg 8:28;
Ps 81:15

83:3
ᵈ Ps 31:13

83:4
ᵉ Est 3:6
ᶠ Jer 11:19

83:5
ᵍ Ps 2:2

83:6
ʰ Ps 137:7
ⁱ 2Ch 20:1
ʲ Ge 25:16

83:7
ᵏ Jos 13:5
ˡ Eze 27:3

83:8
ᵐ Dt 2:9

83:9
ⁿ Jdg 7:1-23
ᵒ Jdg 4:23-24

83:10
ᵖ Zep 1:17

83:11
q Jdg 7:25
ʳ Jdg 8:12,21

83:12
ˢ 2Ch 20:11

83:13
ᵗ Ps 35:5;
Isa 17:13

83:14
ᵘ Dt 32:22;
Isa 9:18

83:15
ᵛ Job 9:17

83:16
ʷ Ps 109:29;
132:18

83:17
ˣ Ps 35:4

83:18
ʸ Ps 59:13

Psalm 84

84:1
a Ps 27:4; 43:3;
132:5

For the director of music. According to *gittith*.[a] Of the Sons of Korah. A psalm.

Psalm 84 Theme

84:2
b Ps 42:1-2

[1] How lovely is your dwelling place,[a]
    O LORD Almighty!
[2] My soul yearns,[b] even faints,
    for the courts of the LORD;
my heart and my flesh cry out
    for the living God.

84:3
c Ps 43:4
d Ps 5:2

[3] Even the sparrow has found a home,
    and the swallow a nest for herself,
    where she may have her young—
a place near your altar,[c]
    O LORD Almighty, my King and my God.[d]
[4] Blessed are those who dwell in your house;
    they are ever praising you.   *Selah*

84:5
e Ps 81:1
f Jer 31:6

[5] Blessed are those whose strength[e] is in you,
    who have set their hearts on pilgrimage.[f]

84:6
g Joel 2:23

[6] As they pass through the Valley of Baca,
    they make it a place of springs;
    the autumn[g] rains also cover it with pools.[b]

84:7
h Pr 4:18
i Dt 16:16

[7] They go from strength to strength,[h]
    till each appears[i] before God in Zion.

84:9
j Ps 59:11
k 1Sa 16:6;
Ps 2:2; 132:17

[8] Hear my prayer, O LORD God Almighty;
    listen to me, O God of Jacob.   *Selah*
[9] Look upon our shield,[c][j] O God;
    look with favor on your anointed one.[k]

84:10
l 1Ch 23:5

[10] Better is one day in your courts
    than a thousand elsewhere;
I would rather be a doorkeeper[l] in the house of my God
    than dwell in the tents of the wicked.
[11] For the LORD God is a sun[m] and shield;[n]
    the LORD bestows favor and honor;
no good thing does he withhold[o]
    from those whose walk is blameless.

84:11
m Isa 60:19;
Rev 21:23
n Ge 15:1
o Ps 34:10

[12] O LORD Almighty,
    blessed[p] is the man who trusts in you.

84:12
p Ps 2:12

a Title: Probably a musical term   b 6 Or *blessings*   c 9 Or *sovereign*

Psalm 85

For the director of music. Of the Sons of Korah. A psalm.

Psalm 85 Theme _____

¹You showed favor to your land, O LORD;
    you restored the fortunes*a* of Jacob.
²You forgave*b* the iniquity*c* of your people
    and covered all their sins.   *Selah*
³You set aside all your wrath*d*
    and turned from your fierce anger.*e*

⁴Restore*f* us again, O God our Savior,
    and put away your displeasure toward us.
⁵Will you be angry with us forever?*g*
    Will you prolong your anger through all generations?
⁶Will you not revive*h* us again,
    that your people may rejoice in you?
⁷Show us your unfailing love, O LORD,
    and grant us your salvation.

⁸I will listen to what God the LORD will say;
    he promises peace*i* to his people, his saints—
    but let them not return to folly.
⁹Surely his salvation*j* is near those who fear him,
    that his glory*k* may dwell in our land.

¹⁰Love and faithfulness*l* meet together;
    righteousness*m* and peace kiss each other.
¹¹Faithfulness springs forth from the earth,
    and righteousness*n* looks down from heaven.
¹²The LORD will indeed give what is good,*o*
    and our land will yield*p* its harvest.
¹³Righteousness goes before him
    and prepares the way for his steps.

Psalm 86

A prayer of David.

Psalm 86 Theme _____

¹Hear, O LORD, and answer*q* me,
    for I am poor and needy.
²Guard my life, for I am devoted to you.
    You are my God; save your servant
    who trusts in you.*r*

85:1
a Ps 14:7;
Jer 30:18;
Eze 39:25

85:2
b Nu 14:19
c Ps 78:38

85:3
d Ps 106:23
e Ex 32:12;
Dt 13:17;
Ps 78:38;
Jnh 3:9

85:4
f Ps 80:3,7

85:5
g Ps 79:5

85:6
h Ps 80:18;
Hab 3:2

85:8
i Zec 9:10

85:9
j Isa 46:13
k Zec 2:5

85:10
l Ps 89:14; Pr 3:3
m Ps 72:2-3;
Isa 32:17

85:11
n Isa 45:8

85:12
o Ps 84:11;
Jas 1:17
p Lev 26:4;
Ps 67:6;
Zec 8:12

86:1
q Ps 17:6

86:2
r Ps 25:2; 31:14

86:3
a Ps 4:1; 57:1
b Ps 88:9

³Have mercy^a on me, O Lord,
for I call^b to you all day long.
⁴Bring joy to your servant,
for to you, O Lord,
I lift^c up my soul.

86:4
c Ps 25:1; 143:8

⁵You are forgiving and good, O Lord,
abounding in love^d to all who call to you.
⁶Hear my prayer, O LORD;
listen to my cry for mercy.
⁷In the day of my trouble^e I will call to you,
for you will answer me.

86:5
d Ex 34:6;
Ne 9:17;
Ps 103:8; 145:8;
Joel 2:13;
Jnh 4:2

86:7
e Ps 50:15

⁸Among the gods there is none like you,^f O Lord;
no deeds can compare with yours.
⁹All the nations you have made
will come and worship^g before you, O Lord;
they will bring glory^h to your name.
¹⁰For you are great and do marvelous deeds;ⁱ
you alone^j are God.

86:8
f Ex 15:11;
Dt 3:24; Ps 89:6

86:9
g Ps 66:4;
Rev 15:4
h Isa 43:7

¹¹Teach me your way,^k O LORD,
and I will walk in your truth;
give me an undivided^l heart,
that I may fear your name.
¹²I will praise you, O Lord my God, with all
my heart;
I will glorify your name forever.
¹³For great is your love toward me;
you have delivered me from the depths of
the grave.^a

86:10
i Ps 72:18
j Dt 6:4;
Mk 12:29;
1Co 8:4

¹⁴The arrogant are attacking me, O God;
a band of ruthless men seeks my life—
men without regard for you.^m
¹⁵But you, O Lord, are a compassionate and
graciousⁿ God,
slow to anger, abounding in love and faithfulness.^o
¹⁶Turn to me and have mercy on me;
grant your strength to your servant
and save the son of your maidservant.^{b p}
¹⁷Give me a sign of your goodness,
that my enemies may see it and be put to shame,
for you, O LORD, have helped me and
comforted me.

86:11
k Ps 25:5
l Jer 32:39

86:14
m Ps 54:3

86:15
n Ps 103:8
o Ex 34:6;
Ne 9:17;
Joel 2:13

86:16
p Ps 116:16

a 13 Hebrew *Sheol*   *b 16* Or *save your faithful son*

Psalm 87

Of the Sons of Korah. A psalm. A song.

Psalm 87 Theme_____

¹He has set his foundation on the holy mountain;
² the LORD loves the gates of Zion *a*
more than all the dwellings of Jacob.
³Glorious things are said of you,
O city of God:*b*　　　　　　　　　　*Selah*
⁴"I will record Rahab*ac* and Babylon
among those who acknowledge me—
Philistia too, and Tyre*d*, along with Cush*b*—
and will say, 'This*c* one was born in Zion.*e*'"

⁵Indeed, of Zion it will be said,
"This one and that one were born in her,
and the Most High himself will establish her."
⁶The LORD will write in the register*f* of the peoples:
"This one was born in Zion."　　　　*Selah*
⁷As they make music*g* they will sing,
"All my fountains*h* are in you."

Psalm 88

A song. A psalm of the Sons of Korah. For the director of music. According to
*mahalath leannoth.*d A *maskil*e of Heman the Ezrahite.

Psalm 88 Theme_____

¹O LORD, the God who saves me,*i*
day and night I cry out*j* before you.
²May my prayer come before you;
turn your ear to my cry.

³For my soul is full of trouble
and my life draws near the grave.*fk*
⁴I am counted among those who go down to the pit;*l*
I am like a man without strength.
⁵I am set apart with the dead,
like the slain who lie in the grave,
whom you remember no more,
who are cut off*m* from your care.

a4 A poetic name for Egypt　b4 That is, the upper Nile region　c4 Or "O Rahab and
Babylon, / Philistia, Tyre and Cush, / I will record concerning those who acknowledge me: / 'This
d Title: Possibly a tune, "The Suffering of Affliction"　e Title: Probably a literary or musical
term　f3 Hebrew *Sheol*

Cross references: 87:2 *a*Ps 78:68; 87:3 *b*Ps 46:4; Isa 60:1; 87:4 *c*Job 9:13 *d*Ps 45:12 *e*Isa 19:25; 87:6 *f*Ps 69:28; Isa 4:3; Eze 13:9; 87:7 *g*Ps 149:3 *h*Ps 36:9; 88:1 *i*Ps 51:14 *j*Ps 22:2; 27:9; Lk 18:7; 88:3 *k*Ps 107:18,26; 88:4 *l*Ps 28:1; 88:5 *m*Ps 31:22; Isa 53:8

88:6
a Ps 69:15;
La 3:55

⁶You have put me in the lowest pit,
  in the darkest depths.^a
⁷Your wrath lies heavily upon me;
  you have overwhelmed me with all your waves.^b

Selah

88:7
b Ps 42:7

⁸You have taken from me my closest friends^c
  and have made me repulsive to them.
I am confined^d and cannot escape;
⁹ my eyes^e are dim with grief.

88:8
c Job 19:13;
Ps 31:11
d Jer 32:2

I call^f to you, O LORD, every day;
  I spread out my hands^g to you.
¹⁰Do you show your wonders to the dead?
  Do those who are dead rise up and praise you?^h

Selah

88:9
e Ps 38:10
f Ps 86:3
g Job 11:13;
Ps 143:6

¹¹Is your love declared in the grave,
  your faithfulnessⁱ in Destruction^a?
¹²Are your wonders known in the place of darkness,
  or your righteous deeds in the land of oblivion?

88:10
h Ps 6:5

¹³But I cry to you for help, ^j O LORD;
  in the morning^k my prayer comes before you.^l
¹⁴Why, O LORD, do you reject^m me
  and hide your faceⁿ from me?

88:11
i Ps 30:9

¹⁵From my youth I have been afflicted and close to death;
  I have suffered your terrors^o and am in despair.
¹⁶Your wrath has swept over me;
  your terrors have destroyed me.
¹⁷All day long they surround me like a flood;^p
  they have completely engulfed me.
¹⁸You have taken my companions^q and loved ones from me;
  the darkness is my closest friend.

88:13
j Ps 30:2
k Ps 5:3
l Ps 119:147

88:14
m Ps 43:2
n Job 13:24;
Ps 13:1

88:15
o Job 6:4

Psalm 89

A *maskil* ^b of Ethan the Ezrahite.

88:17
p Ps 22:16; 124:4

88:18
q ver 8;
Job 19:13;
Ps 38:11

Psalm 89 Theme _____

¹I will sing^r of the LORD's great love forever;
  with my mouth I will make your faithfulness known^s
    through all generations.
²I will declare that your love stands firm forever,
  that you established your faithfulness in heaven itself.^t

89:1
r Ps 59:16;
Ps 101:1
s Ps 36:5; 40:10

89:2
t Ps 36:5

a 11 Hebrew *Abaddon*   b Title: Probably a literary or musical term

³You said, "I have made a covenant with my chosen one,
  I have sworn to David my servant,
⁴'I will establish your line forever
  and make your throne firm through all generations.'"ᵃ
                                                    Selah

⁵The heavensᵇ praise your wonders, O LORD,
  your faithfulness too, in the assembly of the holy ones.
⁶For who in the skies above can compare with the LORD?
  Who is like the LORD among the heavenly beings?ᶜ
⁷In the council of the holy ones God is greatly feared;
  he is more awesome than all who surround him.ᵈ
⁸O LORD God Almighty, who is like you?ᵉ
  You are mighty, O LORD, and your faithfulness
    surrounds you.

⁹You rule over the surging sea;
  when its waves mount up, you still them.ᶠ
¹⁰You crushed Rahabᵍ like one of the slain;
  with your strong arm you scatteredʰ your enemies.
¹¹The heavens are yours, and yours also the earth;ⁱ
  you founded the world and all that is in it.ʲ
¹²You created the north and the south;
  Taborᵏ and Hermonˡ sing for joyᵐ at your name.
¹³Your arm is endued with power;
  your hand is strong, your right hand exalted.

¹⁴Righteousness and justice are the foundation of
    your throne;ⁿ
  love and faithfulness go before you.
¹⁵Blessed are those who have learned to acclaim you,
  who walk in the lightᵒ of your presence, O LORD.
¹⁶They rejoice in your nameᵖ all day long;
  they exult in your righteousness.
¹⁷For you are their glory and strength,
  and by your favor you exalt our horn.ᵃ �q
¹⁸Indeed, our shieldᵇ belongs to the LORD,
  our kingʳ to the Holy One of Israel.

¹⁹Once you spoke in a vision,
  to your faithful people you said:
"I have bestowed strength on a warrior;
  I have exalted a young man from among the people.
²⁰I have found Davidˢ my servant;ᵗ
  with my sacred oil I have anointedᵘ him.

ᵃ*17* *Horn* here symbolizes strong one.   ᵇ*18* Or *sovereign*

Reference	
89:4	*a* 2Sa 7:12-16; 1Ki 8:16; Ps 132:11-12; Isa 9:7; Lk 1:33
89:5	*b* Ps 19:1
89:6	*c* Ps 113:5
89:7	*d* Ps 47:2
89:8	*e* Ps 71:19
89:9	*f* Ps 65:7
89:10	*g* Ps 87:4; *h* Ps 68:1
89:11	*i* 1Ch 29:11; Ps 24:1; *j* Ge 1:1
89:12	*k* Jos 19:22; *l* Dt 3:8; Jos 12:1; *m* Ps 98:8
89:14	*n* Ps 97:2
89:15	*o* Ps 44:3
89:16	*p* Ps 105:3
89:17	*q* Ps 75:10; 92:10; 148:14
89:18	*r* Ps 47:9
89:20	*s* Ac 13:22; *t* Ps 78:70; *u* 1Sa 16:1,12

89:21
a Ps 18:35

89:22
b 2Sa 7:10

89:23
c Ps 18:40
d 2Sa 7:9

89:24
e 2Sa 7:15

89:25
f Ps 72:8

89:26
g 2Sa 7:14
h 2Sa 22:47

89:27
i Col 1:18
j Nu 24:7
k Rev 1:5; 19:16

89:28
l ver 33-34;
Isa 55:3

89:29
m ver 4,36;
Dt 11:21;
Jer 33:17

89:32
n 2Sa 7:14

89:33
o 2Sa 7:15

89:34
p Nu 23:19

89:38
q Dt 32:19;
1Ch 28:9;
Ps 44:9

89:39
r La 5:16

89:40
s Ps 80:12
t La 2:2

89:41
u Ps 44:13

²¹My hand will sustain him;
    surely my arm will strengthen him.*ᵃ*
²²No enemy will subject him to tribute;
    no wicked man will oppress*ᵇ* him.
²³I will crush his foes before him*ᶜ*
    and strike down his adversaries.*ᵈ*
²⁴My faithful love will be with him,*ᵉ*
    and through my name his horn*ᵃ* will be exalted.
²⁵I will set his hand over the sea,
    his right hand over the rivers.*ᶠ*
²⁶He will call out to me, 'You are my Father,*ᵍ*
    my God, the Rock my Savior.'*ʰ*
²⁷I will also appoint him my firstborn,*ⁱ*
    the most exalted *ʲ* of the kings*ᵏ* of the earth.
²⁸I will maintain my love to him forever,
    and my covenant with him will never fail.*ˡ*
²⁹I will establish his line forever,
    his throne as long as the heavens endure.*ᵐ*

³⁰"If his sons forsake my law
    and do not follow my statutes,
³¹if they violate my decrees
    and fail to keep my commands,
³²I will punish their sin with the rod,
    their iniquity with flogging;*ⁿ*
³³but I will not take my love from him,*ᵒ*
    nor will I ever betray my faithfulness.
³⁴I will not violate my covenant
    or alter what my lips have uttered.*ᵖ*
³⁵Once for all, I have sworn by my holiness—
    and I will not lie to David—
³⁶that his line will continue forever
    and his throne endure before me like the sun;
³⁷it will be established forever like the moon,
    the faithful witness in the sky."   *Selah*

³⁸But you have rejected,*�q* you have spurned,
    you have been very angry with your anointed one.
³⁹You have renounced the covenant with your servant
    and have defiled his crown in the dust.*ʳ*
⁴⁰You have broken through all his walls*ˢ*
    and reduced his strongholds*ᵗ* to ruins.
⁴¹All who pass by have plundered him;
    he has become the scorn of his neighbors.*ᵘ*

a 24 Horn here symbolizes strength.

⁴²You have exalted the right hand of his foes;
  you have made all his enemies rejoice.^a
⁴³You have turned back the edge of his sword
  and have not supported him in battle.^b
⁴⁴You have put an end to his splendor
  and cast his throne to the ground.
⁴⁵You have cut short the days of his youth;
  you have covered him with a mantle of shame.^c

                                                    Selah

⁴⁶How long, O LORD? Will you hide yourself forever?
  How long will your wrath burn like fire?^d
⁴⁷Remember how fleeting is my life.^e
  For what futility you have created all men!
⁴⁸What man can live and not see death,
  or save himself from the power of the grave^a?^f

                                                    Selah

⁴⁹O Lord, where is your former great love,
  which in your faithfulness you swore to David?
⁵⁰Remember, Lord, how your servant has^b been mocked,^g
  how I bear in my heart the taunts of all the nations,
⁵¹the taunts with which your enemies have mocked,
    O LORD,
  with which they have mocked every step of your
    anointed one.^h

⁵²Praise be to the LORD forever!
    Amen and Amen.ⁱ

BOOK IV

Psalms 90–106

Psalm 90

A prayer of Moses the man of God.

Psalm 90 Theme _____

¹Lord, you have been our dwelling place^j
  throughout all generations.
²Before the mountains were born^k
  or you brought forth the earth and the world,
  from everlasting to everlasting you are God.^l

³You turn men back to dust,
  saying, "Return to dust, O sons of men."^m

---

^a48 Hebrew *Sheol*   ^b50 Or *your servants have*

Cross references

89:42 ^aPs 13:2; 80:6

89:43 ^bPs 44:10

89:45 ^cPs 44:15; 109:29

89:46 ^dPs 79:5

89:47 ^eJob 7:7; Ps 39:5

89:48 ^fPs 22:29; 49:9

89:50 ^gPs 69:19

89:51 ^hPs 74:10

89:52 ⁱPs 41:13; 72:19

90:1 ^jDt 33:27; Eze 11:16

90:2 ^kJob 15:7; Pr 8:25 ^lPs 102:24-27

90:3 ^mGe 3:19; Job 34:15

90:4
a 2Pe 3:8

90:5
b Ps 73:20;
Isa 40:6

90:6
c Mt 6:30;
Jas 1:10

90:8
d Ps 19:12

90:9
e Ps 78:33

90:10
f Job 20:8

90:11
g Ps 76:7

90:12
h Ps 39:4
i Dt 32:29

90:13
j Ps 6:3
k Dt 32:36;
Ps 135:14

90:14
l Ps 103:5
m Ps 85:6
n Ps 31:7

90:16
o Ps 44:1;
Hab 3:2

90:17
p Isa 26:12

91:1
q Ps 31:20
r Ps 17:8

91:2
s Ps 142:5

[4]For a thousand years in your sight
    are like a day that has just gone by,
    or like a watch in the night.[a]
[5]You sweep men away[b] in the sleep of death;
    they are like the new grass of the morning—
[6]though in the morning it springs up new,
    by evening it is dry and withered.[c]

[7]We are consumed by your anger
    and terrified by your indignation.
[8]You have set our iniquities before you,
    our secret sins[d] in the light of your presence.
[9]All our days pass away under your wrath;
    we finish our years with a moan.[e]
[10]The length of our days is seventy years—
    or eighty, if we have the strength;
    yet their span[a] is but trouble and sorrow,
    for they quickly pass, and we fly away.[f]

[11]Who knows the power of your anger?
    For your wrath is as great as the fear that is due you.[g]
[12]Teach us to number our days[h] aright,
    that we may gain a heart of wisdom.[i]

[13]Relent, O LORD! How long[j] will it be?
    Have compassion on your servants.[k]
[14]Satisfy[l] us in the morning with your unfailing love,
    that we may sing for joy[m] and be glad all our days.[n]
[15]Make us glad for as many days as you have afflicted us,
    for as many years as we have seen trouble.
[16]May your deeds be shown to your servants,
    your splendor to their children.[o]

[17]May the favor[b] of the Lord our God rest upon us;
    establish the work of our hands for us—
    yes, establish the work of our hands.[p]

Psalm 91

*Psalm 91 Theme*_____

[1]He who dwells in the shelter[q] of the Most High
    will rest in the shadow[r] of the Almighty.[c]
[2]I will say[d] of the LORD, "He is my refuge[s] and
        my fortress,
    my God, in whom I trust."

a 10 Or yet the best of them   *b 17 Or beauty*   *c 1 Hebrew Shaddai*   *d 2 Or He says*

³Surely he will save you from the fowler's snare^a
and from the deadly pestilence.^b
⁴He will cover you with his feathers,
and under his wings you will find refuge;^c
his faithfulness will be your shield^d and rampart.
⁵You will not fear^e the terror of night,
nor the arrow that flies by day,
⁶nor the pestilence that stalks in the darkness,
nor the plague that destroys at midday.
⁷A thousand may fall at your side,
ten thousand at your right hand,
but it will not come near you.
⁸You will only observe with your eyes
and see the punishment of the wicked.^f

⁹If you make the Most High your dwelling—
even the LORD, who is my refuge—
¹⁰then no harm^g will befall you,
no disaster will come near your tent.
¹¹For he will command his angels^h concerning you
to guard you in all your ways;ⁱ
¹²they will lift you up in their hands,
so that you will not strike your foot against a stone.^j
¹³You will tread upon the lion and the cobra;
you will trample the great lion and the serpent.^k

¹⁴"Because he loves me," says the LORD, "I will rescue him;
I will protect him, for he acknowledges my name.
¹⁵He will call upon me, and I will answer him;
I will be with him in trouble,
I will deliver him and honor him.^l
¹⁶With long life^m will I satisfy him
and show him my salvation.ⁿ"

Psalm 92

A psalm. A song. For the Sabbath day.

Psalm 92 Theme

¹It is good to praise the LORD
and make music to your name,^o O Most High,^p
²to proclaim your love in the morning^q
and your faithfulness at night,
³to the music of the ten-stringed lyre
and the melody of the harp.^r

91:3
^aPs 124:7;
Pr 6:5
^b1Ki 8:37

91:4
^cPs 17:8
^dPs 35:2

91:5
^eJob 5:21

91:8
^fPs 37:34; 58:10;
Mal 1:5

91:10
^gPr 12:21

91:11
^hHeb 1:14
ⁱPs 34:7

91:12
^jMt 4:6*;
Lk 4:10-11*

91:13
^kDa 6:22;
Lk 10:19

91:15
^l1Sa 2:30;
Ps 50:15;
Jn 12:26

91:16
^mDt 6:2; Ps 21:4
ⁿPs 50:23

92:1
^oPs 147:1
^pPs 135:3

92:2
^qPs 89:1

92:3
^r1Sa 10:5;
Ne 12:27;
Ps 33:2

92:4
a Ps 8:6; 143:5

92:5
b Rev 15:3
c Ps 40:5;
139:17;
Isa 28:29;
Ro 11:33

92:6
d Ps 73:22

92:9
e Ps 68:1; 89:10

92:10
f Ps 89:17
g Ps 23:5

92:11
h Ps 54:7; 91:8

92:12
i Ps 1:3; 52:8;
Jer 17:8;
Hos 14:6

92:13
j Ps 100:4

92:14
k Jn 15:2

92:15
l Job 34:10

93:1
m Ps 97:1
n Ps 104:1
o Ps 65:6
p Ps 96:10

93:2
q Ps 45:6

93:3
r Ps 96:11

93:4
s Ps 65:7

⁴For you make me glad by your deeds, O Lord;
  I sing for joy at the works of your hands.ᵃ
⁵How great are your works,ᵇ O Lord,
  how profound your thoughts!ᶜ
⁶The senseless manᵈ does not know,
  fools do not understand,
⁷that though the wicked spring up like grass
  and all evildoers flourish,
 they will be forever destroyed.

⁸But you, O Lord, are exalted forever.

⁹For surely your enemies, O Lord,
  surely your enemies will perish;
  all evildoers will be scattered.ᵉ
¹⁰You have exalted my hornᵃ ᶠ like that of a wild ox;
  fine oilsᵍ have been poured upon me.
¹¹My eyes have seen the defeat of my adversaries;
  my ears have heard the rout of my wicked foes.ʰ

¹²The righteous will flourish like a palm tree,
  they will grow like a cedar of Lebanon;ⁱ
¹³planted in the house of the Lord,
  they will flourish in the courts of our God.ʲ
¹⁴They will still bear fruitᵏ in old age,
  they will stay fresh and green,
¹⁵proclaiming, "The Lord is upright;
  he is my Rock, and there is no wickedness in him.ˡ"

Psalm 93

Psalm 93 Theme

¹The Lord reigns,ᵐ he is robed in majesty;ⁿ
  the Lord is robed in majesty
  and is armed with strength.ᵒ
 The world is firmly established;
  it cannot be moved.ᵖ
²Your throne was established long ago;
  you are from all eternity.�q

³The seasʳ have lifted up, O Lord,
  the seas have lifted up their voice;
  the seas have lifted up their pounding waves.
⁴Mightier than the thunderˢ of the great waters,
  mightier than the breakers of the sea—
  the Lord on high is mighty.

a 10 *Horn* here symbolizes strength.

⁵Your statutes stand firm;
　holiness[a] adorns your house
　for endless days, O LORD.

Psalm 94

Psalm 94 Theme _____

¹O LORD, the God who avenges,[b]
　O God who avenges, shine forth.[c]
²Rise up, O Judge[d] of the earth;
　pay back[e] to the proud what they deserve.
³How long will the wicked, O LORD,
　how long will the wicked be jubilant?

⁴They pour out arrogant[f] words;
　all the evildoers are full of boasting.[g]
⁵They crush your people,[h] O LORD;
　they oppress your inheritance.
⁶They slay the widow and the alien;
　they murder the fatherless.
⁷They say, "The LORD does not see;[i]
　the God of Jacob pays no heed."

⁸Take heed, you senseless ones[j] among the people;
　you fools, when will you become wise?
⁹Does he who implanted the ear not hear?
　Does he who formed the eye not see?[k]
¹⁰Does he who disciplines nations not punish?
　Does he who teaches[l] man lack knowledge?
¹¹The LORD knows the thoughts of man;
　he knows that they are futile.[m]

¹²Blessed is the man you discipline,[n] O LORD,
　the man you teach[o] from your law;
¹³you grant him relief from days of trouble,
　till a pit[p] is dug for the wicked.
¹⁴For the LORD will not reject his people;[q]
　he will never forsake his inheritance.
¹⁵Judgment will again be founded on righteousness,[r]
　and all the upright in heart will follow it.

¹⁶Who will rise up[s] for me against the wicked?
　Who will take a stand for me against evildoers?[t]
¹⁷Unless the LORD had given me help,[u]
　I would soon have dwelt in the silence of death.
¹⁸When I said, "My foot is slipping,[v]"
　your love, O LORD, supported me.

93:5
[a] Ps 29:2

94:1
[b] Na 1:2;
Ro 12:19
[c] Ps 80:1

94:2
[d] Ge 18:25
[e] Ps 31:23

94:4
[f] Ps 31:18
[g] Ps 52:1

94:5
[h] Isa 3:15

94:7
[i] Job 22:14;
Ps 10:11

94:8
[j] Ps 92:6

94:9
[k] Ex 4:11;
Pr 20:12

94:10
[l] Job 35:11;
Isa 28:26

94:11
[m] 1Co 3:20*

94:12
[n] Job 5:17;
Heb 12:5
[o] Dt 8:3

94:13
[p] Ps 55:23

94:14
[q] 1Sa 12:22;
Ps 37:28;
Ro 11:2

94:15
[r] Ps 97:2

94:16
[s] Nu 10:35;
Ps 17:13
[t] Ps 59:2

94:17
[u] Ps 124:2

94:18
[v] Ps 38:16

94:20
a Ps 58:2

¹⁹When anxiety was great within me,
  your consolation brought joy to my soul.

94:21
b Ps 56:6
c Ps 106:38;
Pr 17:15,26

²⁰Can a corrupt throne be allied with you—
  one that brings on misery by its decrees?*a*
²¹They band together*b* against the righteous
  and condemn the innocent*c* to death.

94:22
d Ps 18:2; 59:9

²²But the LORD has become my fortress,
  and my God the rock in whom I take refuge.*d*

94:23
e Ps 7:16

²³He will repay*e* them for their sins
  and destroy them for their wickedness;
  the LORD our God will destroy them.

95:1
f Ps 81:1
g 2Sa 22:47

Psalm 95

95:2
h Mic 6:6
i Ps 81:2;
Eph 5:19

Psalm 95 Theme _____

¹Come, let us sing for joy to the LORD;
  let us shout aloud*f* to the Rock*g* of our salvation.
²Let us come before him*h* with thanksgiving
  and extol him with music*i* and song.

95:3
j Ps 48:1; 145:3
k Ps 96:4; 97:9

³For the LORD is the great God,*j*
  the great King above all gods.*k*

95:5
l Ge 1:9;
Ps 146:6

⁴In his hand are the depths of the earth,
  and the mountain peaks belong to him.
⁵The sea is his, for he made it,
  and his hands formed the dry land.*l*

95:6
m Php 2:10
n 2Ch 6:13
o Ps 100:3;
149:2; Isa 17:7;
Da 6:10-11;
Hos 8:14

⁶Come, let us bow down*m* in worship,
  let us kneel*n* before the LORD our Maker;*o*

95:7
p Ps 74:1; 79:13

⁷for he is our God
  and we are the people of his pasture,*p*
  the flock under his care.

95:8
q Ex 17:7

  Today, if you hear his voice,
⁸ do not harden your hearts as you did at Meribah,*a**q*
  as you did that day at Massah*b* in the desert,

95:9
r Nu 14:22;
Ps 78:18;
1Co 10:9

⁹where your fathers tested*r* and tried me,
  though they had seen what I did.

95:10
s Ac 7:36;
Heb 3:17

¹⁰For forty years*s* I was angry with that generation;
  I said, "They are a people whose hearts go astray,
  and they have not known my ways."

95:11
t Nu 14:23
u Dt 1:35;
Heb 4:3*

¹¹So I declared on oath*t* in my anger,
  "They shall never enter my rest."*u*

a 8 *Meribah* means *quarreling.*   *b* 8 *Massah* means *testing.*

Psalm 96

Psalm 96 Theme_____

¹Sing to the LORD[a] a new song;
    sing to the LORD, all the earth.
²Sing to the LORD, praise his name;
    proclaim his salvation[b] day after day.
³Declare his glory among the nations,
    his marvelous deeds among all peoples.

⁴For great is the LORD and most worthy of praise;[c]
    he is to be feared[d] above all gods.[e]
⁵For all the gods of the nations are idols,
    but the LORD made the heavens.[f]
⁶Splendor and majesty are before him;
    strength and glory[g] are in his sanctuary.

⁷Ascribe to the LORD,[h] O families of nations,[i]
    ascribe to the LORD glory and strength.
⁸Ascribe to the LORD the glory due his name;
    bring an offering[j] and come into his courts.
⁹Worship the LORD in the splendor of his[a] holiness;[k]
    tremble[l] before him, all the earth.[m]

¹⁰Say among the nations, "The LORD reigns.[n]"
    The world is firmly established, it cannot be moved;[o]
    he will judge the peoples with equity.[p]
¹¹Let the heavens rejoice, let the earth be glad;[q]
    let the sea resound, and all that is in it;
¹²   let the fields be jubilant, and everything in them.
    Then all the trees of the forest[r] will sing for joy;[s]
¹³   they will sing before the LORD, for he comes,
    he comes to judge[t] the earth.
    He will judge the world in righteousness
    and the peoples in his truth.

Psalm 97

Psalm 97 Theme_____

¹The LORD reigns,[u] let the earth be glad;[v]
    let the distant shores rejoice.

²Clouds and thick darkness[w] surround him;
    righteousness and justice are the foundation of
        his throne.[x]

a 9 Or LORD with the splendor of

96:1
a 1Ch 16:23

96:2
b Ps 71:15

96:4
c Ps 18:3; 145:3
d Ps 89:7
e Ps 95:3

96:5
f Ps 115:15

96:6
g Ps 29:1

96:7
h Ps 29:1
i Ps 22:27

96:8
j Ps 45:12; 72:10

96:9
k Ps 29:2
l Ps 114:7
m Ps 33:8

96:10
n Ps 97:1
o Ps 93:1
p Ps 67:4

96:11
q Ps 97:1; 98:7;
Isa 49:13

96:12
r Isa 44:23
s Ps 65:13

96:13
t Rev 19:11

97:1
u Ps 96:10
v Ps 96:11

97:2
w Ex 19:9;
Ps 18:11
x Ps 89:14

97:3
a Da 7:10
b Hab 3:5
c Ps 18:8

³Fire[a] goes before[b] him
  and consumes[c] his foes on every side.
⁴His lightning lights up the world;
  the earth sees and trembles.[d]

97:4
d Ps 104:32

⁵The mountains melt[e] like wax before the LORD,
  before the Lord of all the earth.[f]
⁶The heavens proclaim his righteousness,[g]
  and all the peoples see his glory.[h]

97:5
e Ps 46:2,6;
Mic 1:4
f Jos 3:11

⁷All who worship images[i] are put to shame,[j]
  those who boast in idols—
  worship him,[k] all you gods!

97:6
g Ps 50:6
h Ps 19:1

⁸Zion hears and rejoices
  and the villages of Judah are glad
  because of your judgments,[l] O LORD.
⁹For you, O LORD, are the Most High over all the earth;[m]
  you are exalted[n] far above all gods.

97:7
i Lev 26:1
j Jer 10:14
k Heb 1:6

97:8
l Ps 48:11

¹⁰Let those who love the LORD hate evil,[o]
  for he guards the lives of his faithful ones[p]
  and delivers[q] them from the hand of the wicked.[r]
¹¹Light is shed[s] upon the righteous
  and joy on the upright in heart.
¹²Rejoice in the LORD, you who are righteous,
  and praise his holy name.[t]

97:9
m Ps 83:18; 95:3
n Ex 18:11

97:10
o Ps 34:14;
Am 5:15;
Ro 12:9
p Pr 2:8
q Da 3:28
r Ps 37:40;
Jer 15:21

Psalm 98

A psalm.

97:11
s Job 22:28

Psalm 98 Theme _____

97:12
t Ps 30:4

¹Sing to the LORD a new song,[u]
  for he has done marvelous things;[v]
his right hand[w] and his holy arm[x]
  have worked salvation for him.
²The LORD has made his salvation known[y]
  and revealed his righteousness to the nations.
³He has remembered[z] his love
  and his faithfulness to the house of Israel;
all the ends of the earth have seen
  the salvation of our God.

98:1
u Ps 96:1
v Ps 96:3
w Ex 15:6
x Isa 52:10

98:2
y Isa 52:10

98:3
z Lk 1:54

⁴Shout for joy[a] to the LORD, all the earth,
  burst into jubilant song with music;

98:4
a Isa 44:23

⁵make music to the L<small>ORD</small> with the harp,^a
  with the harp and the sound of singing,^b
⁶with trumpets^c and the blast of the ram's horn—
  shout for joy before the L<small>ORD</small>, the King.^d

⁷Let the sea resound, and everything in it,
  the world, and all who live in it.^e
⁸Let the rivers clap their hands,
  let the mountains^f sing together for joy;
⁹let them sing before the L<small>ORD</small>,
  for he comes to judge the earth.
He will judge the world in righteousness
  and the peoples with equity.^g

Psalm 99

Psalm 99 Theme _____

¹The L<small>ORD</small> reigns,^h
  let the nations tremble;
he sits enthroned between the cherubim,ⁱ
  let the earth shake.
²Great is the L<small>ORD</small>^j in Zion;
  he is exalted^k over all the nations.
³Let them praise your great and awesome name^l—
  he is holy.

⁴The King is mighty, he loves justice^m—
  you have established equity;ⁿ
 in Jacob you have done
  what is just and right.
⁵Exalt^o the L<small>ORD</small> our God
  and worship at his footstool;
  he is holy.

⁶Moses^p and Aaron were among his priests,
  Samuel^q was among those who called on his name;
 they called on the L<small>ORD</small>
  and he answered^r them.
⁷He spoke to them from the pillar of cloud;^s
  they kept his statutes and the decrees he gave them.

⁸O L<small>ORD</small> our God,
  you answered them;
 you were to Israel^a a forgiving God,^t
  though you punished their misdeeds.^b

^a8 Hebrew *them*   ^b8 Or / *an avenger of the wrongs done to them*

98:5
a Ps 92:3
b Isa 51:3

98:6
c Nu 10:10
d Ps 47:7

98:7
e Ps 24:1

98:8
f Isa 55:12

98:9
g Ps 96:10

99:1
h Ps 97:1
i Ex 25:22

99:2
j Ps 48:1
k Ps 97:9; 113:4

99:3
l Ps 76:1

99:4
m Ps 11:7
n Ps 98:9

99:5
o Ps 132:7

99:6
p Ex 24:6
q Jer 15:1
r 1Sa 7:9

99:7
s Ex 33:9

99:8
t Nu 14:20

100:1
a Ps 98:4

⁹Exalt the LORD our God
    and worship at his holy mountain,
    for the LORD our God is holy.

Psalm 100

100:2
b Ps 95:2

A psalm. For giving thanks.

Psalm 100 Theme _____

100:3
c Ps 46:10
d Job 10:3
e Ps 74:1;
Eze 34:31

¹Shout for joy^a to the LORD, all the earth.
² Worship the LORD with gladness;
    come before him^b with joyful songs.
³Know that the LORD is God.^c
    It is he who made us,^d and we are his^a;
    we are his people, the sheep of his pasture.^e

100:4
f Ps 116:17

⁴Enter his gates with thanksgiving
    and his courts with praise;
    give thanks to him and praise his name.^f
⁵For the LORD is good^g and his love endures forever;^h
    his faithfulnessⁱ continues through all generations.

100:5
g 1Ch 16:34;
Ps 25:8
h Ezr 3:11;
Ps 106:1
i Ps 119:90

Psalm 101

Of David. A psalm.

Psalm 101 Theme _____

101:1
j Ps 51:14; 89:1;
145:7

¹I will sing of your love^j and justice;
    to you, O LORD, I will sing praise.
²I will be careful to lead a blameless life—
    when will you come to me?

I will walk in my house
    with blameless heart.

101:3
k Dt 15:9
l Ps 40:4

³I will set before my eyes
    no vile thing.^k

The deeds of faithless men I hate;^l
    they will not cling to me.

101:4
m Pr 11:20

⁴Men of perverse heart^m shall be far from me;
    I will have nothing to do with evil.

⁵Whoever slanders his neighborⁿ in secret,
    him will I put to silence;

101:5
n Ps 50:20

a 3 Or *and not we ourselves*

whoever has haughty eyes[a] and a proud heart,
    him will I not endure.

[6]My eyes will be on the faithful in the land,
    that they may dwell with me;
he whose walk is blameless[b]
    will minister to me.

[7]No one who practices deceit
    will dwell in my house;
no one who speaks falsely
    will stand in my presence.

[8]Every morning[c] I will put to silence
    all the wicked[d] in the land;
I will cut off every evildoer[e]
    from the city of the LORD.[f]

Psalm 102

A prayer of an afflicted man. When he is faint and pours out
his lament before the LORD.

Psalm 102 Theme

[1]Hear my prayer, O LORD;
    let my cry for help[g] come to you.
[2]Do not hide your face[h] from me
    when I am in distress.
Turn your ear to me;
    when I call, answer me quickly.

[3]For my days vanish like smoke;[i]
    my bones burn like glowing embers.
[4]My heart is blighted and withered like grass;[j]
    I forget to eat my food.
[5]Because of my loud groaning
    I am reduced to skin and bones.
[6]I am like a desert owl,[k]
    like an owl among the ruins.
[7]I lie awake;[l] I have become
    like a bird alone[m] on a roof.
[8]All day long my enemies taunt me;
    those who rail against me use my name as a curse.
[9]For I eat ashes as my food
    and mingle my drink with tears[n]

101:5
[a] Ps 10:5;
Pr 6:17

101:6
[b] Ps 119:1

101:8
[c] Jer 21:12
[d] Ps 75:10
[e] Ps 118:10-12
[f] Ps 46:4

102:1
[g] Ex 2:23

102:2
[h] Ps 69:17

102:3
[i] Jas 4:14

102:4
[j] Ps 37:2

102:6
[k] Job 30:29;
Isa 34:11

102:7
[l] Ps 77:4
[m] Ps 38:11

102:9
[n] Ps 42:3

102:10
a Ps 38:3

[10]because of your great wrath,[a]
  for you have taken me up and thrown me aside.

102:11
b Job 14:2

[11]My days are like the evening shadow;[b]
  I wither away like grass.

102:12
c Ps 9:7
d Ps 135:13

[12]But you, O Lord, sit enthroned forever;[c]
  your renown endures[d] through all generations.

102:13
e Isa 60:10

[13]You will arise and have compassion[e] on Zion,
  for it is time to show favor to her;
  the appointed time has come.
[14]For her stones are dear to your servants;
  her very dust moves them to pity.

102:15
f 1Ki 8:43
g Ps 138:4

[15]The nations will fear[f] the name of the Lord,
  all the kings[g] of the earth will revere your glory.

102:16
h Isa 60:1-2

[16]For the Lord will rebuild Zion
  and appear in his glory.[h]

102:17
i Ne 1:6

[17]He will respond to the prayer[i] of the destitute;
  he will not despise their plea.

102:18
j Ro 15:4
k Ps 22:31

[18]Let this be written[j] for a future generation,
  that a people not yet created[k] may praise the Lord:

102:19
l Dt 26:15

[19]"The Lord looked down[l] from his sanctuary on high,
  from heaven he viewed the earth,

102:20
m Ps 79:11

[20]to hear the groans of the prisoners[m]
  and release those condemned to death."

102:21
n Ps 22:22

[21]So the name of the Lord will be declared[n] in Zion
  and his praise in Jerusalem
[22]when the peoples and the kingdoms
  assemble to worship the Lord.

102:24
o Ps 90:2;
Isa 38:10

[23]In the course of my life[a] he broke my strength;
  he cut short my days.
[24]So I said:

"Do not take me away, O my God, in the midst of
  my days;

102:25
p Ge 1:1;
Heb 1:10-12*

  your years go on[o] through all generations.
[25]In the beginning[p] you laid the foundations of the earth,
  and the heavens are the work of your hands.

102:26
q Isa 34:4;
Mt 24:35;
2Pe 3:7-10;
Rev 20:11

[26]They will perish,[q] but you remain;
  they will all wear out like a garment.
  Like clothing you will change them
  and they will be discarded.

102:27
r Mal 3:6;
Heb 13:8;
Jas 1:17

[27]But you remain the same,[r]
  and your years will never end.
[28]The children of your servants[s] will live in your presence;
  their descendants[t] will be established before you."

102:28
s Ps 69:36
t Ps 89:4

a 23 Or *By his power*

Psalm 103

Of David.

Psalm 103 Theme _____

¹Praise the LORD, O my soul;[a]
  all my inmost being, praise his holy name.
²Praise the LORD, O my soul,
  and forget not all his benefits—
³who forgives all your sins[b]
  and heals[c] all your diseases,
⁴who redeems your life from the pit
  and crowns you with love and compassion,
⁵who satisfies your desires with good things
  so that your youth is renewed like the eagle's.[d]

⁶The LORD works righteousness
  and justice for all the oppressed.

⁷He made known[e] his ways[f] to Moses,
  his deeds[g] to the people of Israel:
⁸The LORD is compassionate and gracious,[h]
  slow to anger, abounding in love.
⁹He will not always accuse,
  nor will he harbor his anger forever;[i]
¹⁰he does not treat us as our sins deserve[j]
  or repay us according to our iniquities.
¹¹For as high as the heavens are above the earth,
  so great is his love[k] for those who fear him;
¹²as far as the east is from the west,
  so far has he removed our transgressions[l] from us.
¹³As a father has compassion[m] on his children,
  so the LORD has compassion on those who fear him;
¹⁴for he knows how we are formed,[n]
  he remembers that we are dust.
¹⁵As for man, his days are like grass,[o]
  he flourishes like a flower[p] of the field;
¹⁶the wind blows[q] over it and it is gone,
  and its place[r] remembers it no more.
¹⁷But from everlasting to everlasting
  the LORD's love is with those who fear him,
  and his righteousness with their children's children—
¹⁸with those who keep his covenant
  and remember to obey his precepts.[s]

¹⁹The LORD has established his throne in heaven,
  and his kingdom rules[t] over all.

103:1
[a] Ps 104:1

103:3
[b] Ps 130:8
[c] Ex 15:26

103:5
[d] Isa 40:31

103:7
[e] Ps 99:7; 147:19
[f] Ex 33:13
[g] Ps 106:22

103:8
[h] Ex 34:6;
Ps 86:15;
Jas 5:11

103:9
[i] Ps 30:5;
Isa 57:16;
Jer 3:5,12;
Mic 7:18

103:10
[j] Ezr 9:13

103:11
[k] Ps 57:10

103:12
[l] 2Sa 12:13

103:13
[m] Mal 3:17

103:14
[n] Isa 29:16

103:15
[o] Ps 90:5
[p] Job 14:2;
Jas 1:10;
1Pe 1:24

103:16
[q] Isa 40:7
[r] Job 7:10

103:18
[s] Dt 7:9

103:19
[t] Ps 47:2

103:20
a Ps 148:2;
Heb 1:14
b Ps 29:1

²⁰Praise the L<small>ORD</small>, you his angels,*a*
  you mighty ones*b* who do his bidding,
  who obey his word.

²¹Praise the L<small>ORD</small>, all his heavenly hosts,*c*
  you his servants who do his will.

103:21
c 1Ki 22:19

²²Praise the L<small>ORD</small>, all his works*d*
  everywhere in his dominion.

Praise the L<small>ORD</small>, O my soul.

103:22
d Ps 145:10

Psalm 104

104:1
e Ps 103:22

Psalm 104 Theme

¹Praise the L<small>ORD</small>, O my soul.*e*

O L<small>ORD</small> my God, you are very great;
  you are clothed with splendor and majesty.

104:2
f Da 7:9
g Isa 40:22

²He wraps*f* himself in light as with a garment;
  he stretches out the heavens*g* like a tent

³ and lays the beams*h* of his upper chambers on
      their waters.

He makes the clouds*i* his chariot
  and rides on the wings of the wind.*j*

104:3
h Am 9:6
i Isa 19:1
j Ps 18:10

⁴He makes winds his messengers,*a**k*
  flames of fire*l* his servants.

104:4
k Ps 148:8;
Heb 1:7*
l 2Ki 2:11

⁵He set the earth*m* on its foundations;
  it can never be moved.

104:5
m Job 26:7;
Ps 24:1-2

⁶You covered it*n* with the deep*o* as with a garment;
  the waters stood above the mountains.

⁷But at your rebuke*p* the waters fled,
  at the sound of your thunder they took to flight;

104:6
n Ge 7:19
o Ge 1:2

⁸they flowed over the mountains,
  they went down into the valleys,
  to the place you assigned*q* for them.

⁹You set a boundary they cannot cross;
  never again will they cover the earth.

104:7
p Ps 18:15

104:8
q Ps 33:7

¹⁰He makes springs*r* pour water into the ravines;
  it flows between the mountains.

¹¹They give water to all the beasts of the field;
  the wild donkeys quench their thirst.

104:10
r Ps 107:33;
Isa 41:18

¹²The birds of the air*s* nest by the waters;
  they sing among the branches.

104:12
s Mt 8:20

¹³He waters the mountains*t* from his upper chambers;
  the earth is satisfied by the fruit of his work.

104:13
t Ps 147:8;
Jer 10:13

a 4 Or *angels*

¹⁴He makes grass grow^a for the cattle,
    and plants for man to cultivate—
    bringing forth food^b from the earth:
¹⁵wine^c that gladdens the heart of man,
    oil^d to make his face shine,
    and bread that sustains his heart.
¹⁶The trees of the Lord are well watered,
    the cedars of Lebanon that he planted.
¹⁷There the birds^e make their nests;
    the stork has its home in the pine trees.
¹⁸The high mountains belong to the wild goats;
    the crags are a refuge for the coneys.^{af}

¹⁹The moon marks off the seasons,^g
    and the sun^h knows when to go down.
²⁰You bring darkness,ⁱ it becomes night,^j
    and all the beasts of the forest^k prowl.
²¹The lions roar for their prey
    and seek their food from God.^l
²²The sun rises, and they steal away;
    they return and lie down in their dens.^m
²³Then man goes out to his work,ⁿ
    to his labor until evening.

²⁴How many are your works,^o O Lord!
    In wisdom you made^p them all;
    the earth is full of your creatures.
²⁵There is the sea,^q vast and spacious,
    teeming with creatures beyond number—
    living things both large and small.
²⁶There the ships^r go to and fro,
    and the leviathan,^s which you formed to frolic there.

²⁷These all look to you
    to give them their food^t at the proper time.
²⁸When you give it to them,
    they gather it up;
when you open your hand,
    they are satisfied^u with good things.
²⁹When you hide your face,^v
    they are terrified;
when you take away their breath,
    they die and return to the dust.^w
³⁰When you send your Spirit,
    they are created,
    and you renew the face of the earth.

a18 That is, the hyrax or rock badger

104:14
^aJob 38:27;
Ps 147:8
^bGe 1:30;
Job 28:5

104:15
^cJdg 9:13
^dPs 23:5; 92:10;
Lk 7:46

104:17
^ever 12

104:18
^fPr 30:26

104:19
^gGe 1:14
^hPs 19:6

104:20
ⁱIsa 45:7
^jPs 74:16
^kPs 50:10

104:21
^lJob 38:39;
Ps 145:15;
Joel 1:20

104:22
^mJob 37:8

104:23
ⁿGe 3:19

104:24
^oPs 40:5
^pPr 3:19

104:25
^qPs 69:34

104:26
^rPs 107:23;
Eze 27:9
^sJob 41:1

104:27
^tJob 36:31;
Ps 136:25;
145:15; 147:9

104:28
^uPs 145:16

104:29
^vDt 31:17
^wJob 34:14;
Ecc 12:7

PSALM 105

104:31
a Ge 1:31

104:32
b Ps 97:4
c Ex 19:18
d Ps 144:5

104:33
e Ps 63:4

104:34
f Ps 9:2

104:35
g Ps 37:38
h Ps 105:45;
106:48

105:1
i 1Ch 16:34
j Ps 99:6

105:2
k Ps 96:1

105:4
l Ps 27:8

105:5
m Ps 40:5
n Ps 77:11

105:6
o ver 42
p Ps 106:5

105:8
q Ps 106:45;
Lk 1:72

105:9
r Ge 12:7; 17:2;
22:16-18;
Gal 3:15-18

105:10
s Ge 28:13-15

105:11
t Ge 13:15;
15:18

105:12
u Ge 34:30;
Dt 7:7
v Ge 23:4;
Heb 11:9

³¹May the glory of the LORD endure forever;
　　may the LORD rejoice in his works*a*—
³²he who looks at the earth, and it trembles,*b*
　　who touches the mountains,*c* and they smoke.*d*

³³I will sing*e* to the LORD all my life;
　　I will sing praise to my God as long as I live.
³⁴May my meditation be pleasing to him,
　　as I rejoice*f* in the LORD.
³⁵But may sinners vanish*g* from the earth
　　and the wicked be no more.

Praise the LORD, O my soul.

Praise the LORD.*a**h*

Psalm 105

*Psalm 105 Theme*_____

¹Give thanks to the LORD,*i* call on his name;*j*
　　make known among the nations what he has done.
²Sing to him,*k* sing praise to him;
　　tell of all his wonderful acts.
³Glory in his holy name;
　　let the hearts of those who seek the LORD rejoice.
⁴Look to the LORD and his strength;
　　seek his face*l* always.

⁵Remember the wonders*m* he has done,
　　his miracles, and the judgments he pronounced,*n*
⁶O descendants of Abraham his servant,*o*
　　O sons of Jacob, his chosen*p* ones.
⁷He is the LORD our God;
　　his judgments are in all the earth.

⁸He remembers his covenant*q* forever,
　　the word he commanded, for a thousand generations,
⁹the covenant he made with Abraham,*r*
　　the oath he swore to Isaac.
¹⁰He confirmed it*s* to Jacob as a decree,
　　to Israel as an everlasting covenant:
¹¹"To you I will give the land of Canaan*t*
　　as the portion you will inherit."

¹²When they were but few in number,*u*
　　few indeed, and strangers in it,*v*

a 35 Hebrew *Hallelu Yah*; in the Septuagint this line stands at the beginning of Psalm 105.

1011

¹³they wandered from nation to nation,
  from one kingdom to another.
¹⁴He allowed no one to oppress[a] them;
  for their sake he rebuked kings:[b]
¹⁵"Do not touch[c] my anointed ones;
  do my prophets no harm."

¹⁶He called down famine[d] on the land
  and destroyed all their supplies of food;
¹⁷and he sent a man before them—
  Joseph, sold as a slave.[e]
¹⁸They bruised his feet with shackles,[f]
  his neck was put in irons,
¹⁹till what he foretold[g] came to pass,
  till the word of the LORD proved him true.
²⁰The king sent and released him,
  the ruler of peoples set him free.[h]
²¹He made him master of his household,
  ruler over all he possessed,
²²to instruct his princes[i] as he pleased
  and teach his elders wisdom.

²³Then Israel entered Egypt;[j]
  Jacob lived as an alien in the land of Ham.
²⁴The LORD made his people very fruitful;
  he made them too numerous[k] for their foes,
²⁵whose hearts he turned[l] to hate his people,
  to conspire[m] against his servants.
²⁶He sent Moses[n] his servant,
  and Aaron, whom he had chosen.[o]
²⁷They performed[p] his miraculous signs among them,
  his wonders in the land of Ham.
²⁸He sent darkness[q] and made the land dark—
  for had they not rebelled against his words?
²⁹He turned their waters into blood,[r]
  causing their fish to die.[s]
³⁰Their land teemed with frogs,[t]
  which went up into the bedrooms of their rulers.
³¹He spoke, and there came swarms of flies,[u]
  and gnats[v] throughout their country.
³²He turned their rain into hail,[w]
  with lightning throughout their land;
³³he struck down their vines[x] and fig trees
  and shattered the trees of their country.
³⁴He spoke, and the locusts came,[y]
  grasshoppers without number;

105:14
a Ge 35:5
b Ge 12:17-20

105:15
c Ge 26:11

105:16
d Ge 41:54;
Lev 26:26;
Isa 3:1; Eze 4:16

105:17
e Ge 37:28; 45:5;
Ac 7:9

105:18
f Ge 40:15

105:19
g Ge 40:20-22

105:20
h Ge 41:14

105:22
i Ge 41:43-44

105:23
j Ge 46:6;
Ac 13:17

105:24
k Ex 1:7,9

105:25
l Ex 4:21
m Ex 1:6-10;
Ac 7:19

105:26
n Ex 3:10
o Nu 16:5;
17:5-8

105:27
p Ex 7:8–12:51

105:28
q Ex 10:22

105:29
r Ps 78:44
s Ex 7:21

105:30
t Ex 8:2,6

105:31
u Ex 8:21-24
v Ex 8:16-18

105:32
w Ex 9:22-25

105:33
x Ps 78:47

105:34
y Ex 10:4,12-15

105:36
a Ex 12:29

105:37
b Ex 12:35

105:38
c Ex 12:33; 15:16

105:39
d Ex 13:21
e Ne 9:12;
Ps 78:14

105:40
f Ps 78:18,24
g Ex 16:13
h Jn 6:31

105:41
i Ex 17:6;
Nu 20:11;
Ps 78:15-16;
1Co 10:4

105:42
j Ge 15:13-16

105:43
k Ex 15:1-18;
Ps 106:12

105:44
l Jos 13:6-7

105:45
m Dt 4:40;
6:21-24

106:1
n Ps 100:5; 105:1

106:2
o Ps 145:4,12

106:3
p Ps 15:2

106:4
q Ps 119:132

106:5
r Ps 1:3
s Ps 118:15

35they ate up every green thing in their land,
ate up the produce of their soil.
36Then he struck down all the firstborn*a* in their land,
the firstfruits of all their manhood.

37He brought out Israel, laden with silver and gold,*b*
and from among their tribes no one faltered.
38Egypt was glad when they left,
because dread of Israel*c* had fallen on them.
39He spread out a cloud*d* as a covering,
and a fire to give light at night.*e*
40They asked,*f* and he brought them quail*g*
and satisfied them with the bread of heaven.*h*
41He opened the rock,*i* and water gushed out;
like a river it flowed in the desert.

42For he remembered his holy promise*j*
given to his servant Abraham.
43He brought out his people with rejoicing,*k*
his chosen ones with shouts of joy;
44he gave them the lands of the nations,*l*
and they fell heir to what others had toiled for—
45that they might keep his precepts
and observe his laws.*m*

Praise the LORD.*a*

Psalm 106

Psalm 106 Theme

1Praise the LORD.*b*

Give thanks to the LORD, for he is good;*n*
his love endures forever.
2Who can proclaim the mighty acts*o* of the LORD
or fully declare his praise?
3Blessed are they who maintain justice,
who constantly do what is right.*p*
4Remember me,*q* O LORD, when you show favor to
your people,
come to my aid when you save them,
5that I may enjoy the prosperity*r* of your chosen ones,
that I may share in the joy*s* of your nation
and join your inheritance in giving praise.

a 45 Hebrew *Hallelu Yah*   b 1 Hebrew *Hallelu Yah*; also in verse 48

⁶We have sinned,ᵃ even as our fathers did;
　we have done wrong and acted wickedly.
⁷When our fathers were in Egypt,
　they gave no thought to your miracles;
they did not rememberᵇ your many kindnesses,
　and they rebelled by the sea,ᶜ the Red Sea.ᵃ
⁸Yet he saved them for his name's sake,ᵈ
　to make his mighty power known.
⁹He rebukedᵉ the Red Sea, and it dried up;ᶠ
　he led them throughᵍ the depths as through a desert.
¹⁰He saved themʰ from the hand of the foe;
　from the hand of the enemy he redeemed them.ⁱ
¹¹The waters coveredʲ their adversaries;
　not one of them survived.
¹²Then they believed his promises
　and sang his praise.ᵏ

¹³But they soon forgotˡ what he had done
　and did not wait for his counsel.
¹⁴In the desert they gave in to their craving;
　in the wasteland they put God to the test.ᵐ
¹⁵So he gave themⁿ what they asked for,
　but sent a wasting diseaseᵒ upon them.

¹⁶In the camp they grew enviousᵖ of Moses
　and of Aaron, who was consecrated to the LORD.
¹⁷The earth openedᵠ up and swallowed Dathan;
　it buried the company of Abiram.
¹⁸Fire blazedʳ among their followers;
　a flame consumed the wicked.

¹⁹At Horeb they made a calfˢ
　and worshiped an idol cast from metal.
²⁰They exchanged their Gloryᵗ
　for an image of a bull, which eats grass.
²¹They forgot the Godᵘ who saved them,
　who had done great thingsᵛ in Egypt,
²²miraclesᵂ in the land of Hamᵂ
　and awesome deeds by the Red Sea.
²³So he said he would destroyˣ them—
　had not Moses, his chosen one,
stood in the breachʸ before him
　to keep his wrath from destroying them.

²⁴Then they despised the pleasant land;ᶻ
　they did not believeᵃ his promise.

a7 Hebrew *Yam Suph*; that is, Sea of Reeds; also in verses 9 and 22

106:6
ᵃDa 9:5

106:7
ᵇPs 78:11,42
ᶜEx 14:11-12

106:8
ᵈEx 9:16

106:9
ᵉPs 18:15
ᶠEx 14:21;
Na 1:4
ᵍIsa 63:11-14

106:10
ʰEx 14:30
ⁱPs 107:2

106:11
ʲEx 14:28; 15:5

106:12
ᵏEx 15:1-21

106:13
ˡEx 15:24

106:14
ᵐ1Co 10:9

106:15
ⁿNu 11:31
ᵒIsa 10:16

106:16
ᵖNu 16:1-3

106:17
ᵠDt 11:6

106:18
ʳNu 16:35

106:19
ˢEx 32:4

106:20
ᵗJer 2:11;
Ro 1:23

106:21
ᵘPs 78:11
ᵛDt 10:21

106:22
ᵂPs 105:27

106:23
ˣEx 32:10
ʸEx 32:11-14

106:24
ᶻDt 8:7;
Eze 20:6
ᵃHeb 3:18-19

106:25
a Nu 14:2

106:26
b Eze 20:15;
Heb 3:11
c Nu 14:28-35

106:27
d Lev 26:33;
Ps 44:11

106:28
e Nu 25:2-3;
Hos 9:10

106:30
f Nu 25:8

106:31
g Nu 25:11-13

106:32
h Nu 20:2-13;
Ps 81:7

106:33
i Nu 20:8-12

106:34
j Jdg 1:21
k Dt 7:16

106:35
l Jdg 3:5-6

106:36
m Jdg 2:12

106:37
n 2Ki 16:3; 17:17

106:38
o Nu 35:33

106:39
p Eze 20:18
q Lev 17:7;
Nu 15:39

106:40
r Jdg 2:14;
Ps 78:59
s Dt 9:29

106:41
t Jdg 2:14;
Ne 9:27

106:43
u Jdg 2:16-19

²⁵They grumbled^a in their tents
   and did not obey the LORD.
²⁶So he swore^b to them with uplifted hand
   that he would make them fall in the desert,^c
²⁷make their descendants fall among the nations
   and scatter^d them throughout the lands.

²⁸They yoked themselves to the Baal of Peor^e
   and ate sacrifices offered to lifeless gods;
²⁹they provoked the LORD to anger by their wicked deeds,
   and a plague broke out among them.
³⁰But Phinehas stood up and intervened,
   and the plague was checked.^f
³¹This was credited to him^g as righteousness
   for endless generations to come.

³²By the waters of Meribah^h they angered the LORD,
   and trouble came to Moses because of them;
³³for they rebelled against the Spirit of God,
   and rash words came from Moses' lips.^{a i}

³⁴They did not destroy^j the peoples
   as the LORD had commanded^k them,
³⁵but they mingled^l with the nations
   and adopted their customs.
³⁶They worshiped their idols,^m
   which became a snare to them.
³⁷They sacrificed their sonsⁿ
   and their daughters to demons.
³⁸They shed innocent blood,
   the blood of their sons^o and daughters,
   whom they sacrificed to the idols of Canaan,
   and the land was desecrated by their blood.
³⁹They defiled themselves^p by what they did;
   by their deeds they prostituted^q themselves.

⁴⁰Therefore the LORD was angry^r with his people
   and abhorred his inheritance.^s
⁴¹He handed them over^t to the nations,
   and their foes ruled over them.
⁴²Their enemies oppressed them
   and subjected them to their power.
⁴³Many times he delivered them,
   but they were bent on rebellion^u
   and they wasted away in their sin.

⁴⁴But he took note of their distress
  when he heard their cry;ᵃ
⁴⁵for their sake he remembered his covenantᵇ
  and out of his great loveᶜ he relented.
⁴⁶He caused them to be pitiedᵈ
  by all who held them captive.

⁴⁷Save us, O LORD our God,
  and gather usᵉ from the nations,
that we may give thanks to your holy name
  and glory in your praise.

⁴⁸Praise be to the LORD, the God of Israel,
  from everlasting to everlasting.
Let all the people say, "Amen!"ᶠ

Praise the LORD.

BOOK V

Psalms 107–150

Psalm 107

*Psalm 107 Theme*_____

¹Give thanks to the LORD,ᵍ for he is good;
  his love endures forever.
²Let the redeemedʰ of the LORD say this—
  those he redeemed from the hand of the foe,
³those he gatheredⁱ from the lands,
  from east and west, from north and south.ᵃ

⁴Some wandered in desertʲ wastelands,
  finding no way to a city where they could settle.
⁵They were hungry and thirsty,
  and their lives ebbed away.
⁶Then they cried outᵏ to the LORD in their trouble,
  and he delivered them from their distress.
⁷He led them by a straight wayˡ
  to a city where they could settle.
⁸Let them give thanks to the LORD for his unfailing love
  and his wonderful deeds for men,
⁹for he satisfiesᵐ the thirsty
  and fills the hungry with good things.ⁿ

¹⁰Some sat in darknessᵒ and the deepest gloom,
  prisoners suffering in iron chains,ᵖ
¹¹for they had rebelled�q against the words of God
  and despised the counselʳ of the Most High.

ᵃ3 Hebrew *north and the sea*

106:44
ᵃJdg 3:9; 10:10

106:45
ᵇLev 26:42;
Ps 105:8
ᶜJdg 2:18

106:46
ᵈEzr 9:9;
Jer 42:12

106:47
ᵉPs 147:2

106:48
ᶠPs 41:13

107:1
ᵍPs 106:1

107:2
ʰPs 106:10

107:3
ⁱPs 106:47;
Isa 43:5-6

107:4
ʲNu 14:33;
32:13

107:6
ᵏPs 50:15

107:7
ˡEzr 8:21

107:9
ᵐPs 22:26;
Lk 1:53
ⁿPs 34:10

107:10
ᵒLk 1:79
ᵖJob 36:8

107:11
qPs 106:7;
La 3:42
ʳ2Ch 36:16

107:12
a Ps 22:11

107:14
b Ps 116:16;
Lk 13:16;
Ac 12:7

107:17
c Isa 65:6-7;
La 3:39

107:18
d Job 33:20
e Job 33:22;
Ps 9:13; 88:3

107:20
f Mt 8:8
g Ps 103:3
h Job 33:28
i Ps 30:3; 49:15

107:22
j Lev 7:12;
Ps 50:14; 116:17
k Ps 9:11; 73:28;
118:17

107:25
l Ps 105:31
m Jnh 1:4
n Ps 93:3

107:26
o Ps 22:14

107:29
p Mt 8:26
q Ps 89:9

107:32
r Ps 22:22,25;
35:18

¹²So he subjected them to bitter labor;
    they stumbled, and there was no one to help.ᵃ
¹³Then they cried to the LORD in their trouble,
    and he saved them from their distress.
¹⁴He brought them out of darkness and the deepest gloom
    and broke away their chains.ᵇ
¹⁵Let them give thanks to the LORD for his unfailing love
    and his wonderful deeds for men,
¹⁶for he breaks down gates of bronze
    and cuts through bars of iron.

¹⁷Some became fools through their rebellious ways
    and suffered afflictionᶜ because of their iniquities.
¹⁸They loathed all foodᵈ
    and drew near the gates of death.ᵉ
¹⁹Then they cried to the LORD in their trouble,
    and he saved them from their distress.
²⁰He sent forth his wordᶠ and healed them;ᵍ
    he rescuedʰ them from the grave.ⁱ
²¹Let them give thanks to the LORD for his unfailing love
    and his wonderful deeds for men.
²²Let them sacrifice thank offeringsʲ
    and tell of his worksᵏ with songs of joy.

²³Others went out on the sea in ships;
    they were merchants on the mighty waters.
²⁴They saw the works of the LORD,
    his wonderful deeds in the deep.
²⁵For he spokeˡ and stirred up a tempestᵐ
    that lifted high the waves.ⁿ
²⁶They mounted up to the heavens and went down to
        the depths;
    in their peril their courage meltedᵒ away.
²⁷They reeled and staggered like drunken men;
    they were at their wits' end.
²⁸Then they cried out to the LORD in their trouble,
    and he brought them out of their distress.
²⁹He stilled the stormᵖ to a whisper;
    the waves�vᵍ of the sea were hushed.
³⁰They were glad when it grew calm,
    and he guided them to their desired haven.
³¹Let them give thanks to the LORD for his unfailing love
    and his wonderful deeds for men.
³²Let them exalt him in the assemblyʳ of the people
    and praise him in the council of the elders.

³³He turned rivers into a desert,ᵃ
　　flowing springs into thirsty ground,
³⁴and fruitful land into a salt waste,ᵇ
　　because of the wickedness of those who lived there.
³⁵He turned the desert into pools of waterᶜ
　　and the parched ground into flowing springs;
³⁶there he brought the hungry to live,
　　and they founded a city where they could settle.
³⁷They sowed fields and planted vineyardsᵈ
　　that yielded a fruitful harvest;
³⁸he blessed them, and their numbers greatly increased,ᵉ
　　and he did not let their herds diminish.

³⁹Then their numbers decreased,ᶠ and they were humbled
　　by oppression, calamity and sorrow;
⁴⁰he who pours contempt on noblesᵍ
　　made them wander in a trackless waste.ʰ
⁴¹But he lifted the needyⁱ out of their affliction
　　and increased their families like flocks.
⁴²The upright see and rejoice,ʲ
　　but all the wicked shut their mouths.ᵏ

⁴³Whoever is wise,ˡ let him heed these things
　　and consider the great loveᵐ of the LORD.

Psalm 108

A song. A psalm of David.

Psalm 108 Theme _____

¹My heart is steadfast, O God;
　　I will sing and make music with all my soul.
²Awake, harp and lyre!
　　I will awaken the dawn.
³I will praise you, O LORD, among the nations;
　　I will sing of you among the peoples.
⁴For great is your love, higher than the heavens;
　　your faithfulness reaches to the skies.
⁵Be exalted, O God, above the heavens,
　　and let your glory be over all the earth.ⁿ

⁶Save us and help us with your right hand,
　　that those you love may be delivered.
⁷God has spoken from his sanctuary:
　　"In triumph I will parcel out Shechem
　　and measure off the Valley of Succoth.

107:33
ᵃ 1Ki 17:1;
Ps 74:15

107:34
ᵇ Ge 13:10; 14:3;
19:25

107:35
ᶜ Ps 114:8;
Isa 41:18

107:37
ᵈ Isa 65:21

107:38
ᵉ Ge 12:2;
17:16,20; Ex 1:7

107:39
ᶠ 2Ki 10:32;
Eze 5:12

107:40
ᵍ Job 12:21
ʰ Job 12:24

107:41
ⁱ 1Sa 2:8;
Ps 113:7-9

107:42
ʲ Job 22:19
ᵏ Job 5:16;
Ps 63:11;
Ro 3:19

107:43
ˡ Jer 9:12;
Hos 14:9
ᵐ Ps 64:9

108:5
ⁿ Ps 57:5

108:8
a Ge 49:10

108:11
b Ps 44:9

109:1
c Ps 83:1

109:2
d Ps 52:4; 120:2

109:3
e Ps 69:4
f Ps 35:7;
Jn 15:25

109:4
g Ps 69:13

109:5
h Ps 35:12; 38:20

109:6
i Zec 3:1

109:7
j Pr 28:9

109:8
k Ac 1:20*

109:9
l Ex 22:24

⁸Gilead is mine, Manasseh is mine;
  Ephraim is my helmet,
  Judah*a* my scepter.
⁹Moab is my washbasin,
  upon Edom I toss my sandal;
  over Philistia I shout in triumph."

¹⁰Who will bring me to the fortified city?
  Who will lead me to Edom?
¹¹Is it not you, O God, you who have rejected us
  and no longer go out with our armies?*b*
¹²Give us aid against the enemy,
  for the help of man is worthless.
¹³With God we will gain the victory,
  and he will trample down our enemies.

Psalm 109

For the director of music. Of David. A psalm.

Psalm 109 Theme _____

¹O God, whom I praise,
  do not remain silent,*c*
²for wicked and deceitful men
  have opened their mouths against me;
  they have spoken against me with lying tongues.*d*
³With words of hatred*e* they surround me;
  they attack me without cause.*f*
⁴In return for my friendship they accuse me,
  but I am a man of prayer.*g*
⁵They repay me evil for good,*h*
  and hatred for my friendship.

⁶Appoint*a* an evil man*b* to oppose him;
  let an accuser*c*i stand at his right hand.
⁷When he is tried, let him be found guilty,
  and may his prayers condemn*j* him.
⁸May his days be few;
  may another take his place*k* of leadership.
⁹May his children be fatherless
  and his wife a widow.*l*
¹⁰May his children be wandering beggars;
  may they be driven*d* from their ruined homes.

a6 Or ₗThey say:ⱼ "Appoint (with quotation marks at the end of verse 19)   b6 Or the Evil One
c6 Or let Satan   d10 Septuagint; Hebrew sought

¹¹May a creditor seize all he has;
  may strangers plunder the fruits of his labor.^a
¹²May no one extend kindness to him
  or take pity^b on his fatherless children.
¹³May his descendants be cut off,^c
  their names blotted out^d from the next generation.
¹⁴May the iniquity of his fathers^e be remembered before
    the LORD;
  may the sin of his mother never be blotted out.
¹⁵May their sins always remain before the LORD,
  that he may cut off the memory^f of them from
    the earth.

¹⁶For he never thought of doing a kindness,
  but hounded to death the poor
  and the needy^g and the brokenhearted.^h
¹⁷He loved to pronounce a curse—
  may it^a come on him;ⁱ
he found no pleasure in blessing—
  may it be^b far from him.
¹⁸He wore cursing^j as his garment;
  it entered into his body like water,^k
  into his bones like oil.
¹⁹May it be like a cloak wrapped about him,
  like a belt tied forever around him.
²⁰May this be the LORD's payment^l to my accusers,
  to those who speak evil^m of me.

²¹But you, O Sovereign LORD,
  deal well with me for your name's sake;ⁿ
  out of the goodness of your love,^o deliver me.
²²For I am poor and needy,
  and my heart is wounded within me.
²³I fade away like an evening shadow;^p
  I am shaken off like a locust.
²⁴My knees give^q way from fasting;
  my body is thin and gaunt.
²⁵I am an object of scorn^r to my accusers;
  when they see me, they shake their heads.^s

²⁶Help me,^t O LORD my God;
  save me in accordance with your love.
²⁷Let them know^u that it is your hand,
  that you, O LORD, have done it.
²⁸They may curse,^v but you will bless;

109:11
a Job 5:5

109:12
b Isa 9:17

109:13
c Job 18:19;
Ps 37:28
d Pr 10:7

109:14
e Ex 20:5;
Ne 4:5; Jer 18:23

109:15
f Job 18:17;
Ps 34:16

109:16
g Ps 37:14,32
h Ps 34:18

109:17
i Pr 14:14;
Eze 35:6

109:18
j Ps 73:6
k Nu 5:22

109:20
l Ps 94:23;
2Ti 4:14
m Ps 71:10

109:21
n Ps 79:9
o Ps 69:16

109:23
p Ps 102:11

109:24
q Heb 12:12

109:25
r Ps 22:6
s Mt 27:39;
Mk 15:29

109:26
t Ps 119:86

109:27
u Job 37:7

109:28
v 2Sa 16:12

---

a 17 Or curse, / and it has   b 17 Or blessing, / and it is

when they attack they will be put to shame,
but your servant will rejoice.[a]

²⁹My accusers will be clothed with disgrace
and wrapped in shame[b] as in a cloak.

³⁰With my mouth I will greatly extol the LORD;
in the great throng[c] I will praise him.

³¹For he stands at the right hand[d] of the needy one,
to save his life from those who condemn him.

Psalm 110

Of David. A psalm.

Psalm 110 Theme _____

¹The LORD says[e] to my Lord:
"Sit at my right hand
until I make your enemies
a footstool for your feet."[f]

²The LORD will extend your mighty scepter[g] from Zion;
you will rule in the midst of your enemies.

³Your troops will be willing
on your day of battle.
Arrayed in holy majesty,[h]
from the womb of the dawn
you will receive the dew of your youth.[a]

⁴The LORD has sworn
and will not change his mind:[i]
"You are a priest forever,[j]
in the order of Melchizedek.[k]"

⁵The Lord is at your right hand;[l]
he will crush kings[m] on the day of his wrath.[n]
⁶He will judge the nations,[o] heaping up the dead[p]
and crushing the rulers[q] of the whole earth.
⁷He will drink from a brook beside the way[b];
therefore he will lift up his head.[r]

Psalm 111[c]

Psalm 111 Theme _____

¹Praise the LORD.[d]

I will extol the LORD with all my heart
in the council of the upright and in the assembly.

---

a3 Or *I your young men will come to you like the dew*   b7 Or *I The One who grants succession will set him in authority*   cThis psalm is an acrostic poem, the lines of which begin with the successive letters of the Hebrew alphabet.   d1 Hebrew *Hallelu Yah*

**Cross-references (left margin):**

109:28
a Isa 65:14

109:29
b Ps 35:26; 132:18

109:30
c Ps 35:18; 111:1

109:31
d Ps 16:8; 73:23; 121:5

110:1
e Mt 22:44*; Mk 12:36*; Lk 20:42*; Ac 2:34*
f 1Co 15:25

110:2
g Ps 45:6

110:3
h Jdg 5:2; Ps 96:9

110:4
i Nu 23:19
j Heb 5:6*; 7:21*
k Heb 7:15-17*

110:5
l Ps 16:8
m Ps 2:12
n Ps 2:5; Ro 2:5

110:6
o Isa 2:4
p Isa 66:24
q Ps 68:21

110:7
r Ps 27:6

²Great are the works^a of the LORD;
    they are pondered by all who delight in them.
³Glorious and majestic are his deeds,
    and his righteousness endures forever.
⁴He has caused his wonders to be remembered;
    the LORD is gracious and compassionate.^b
⁵He provides food^c for those who fear him;
    he remembers his covenant forever.
⁶He has shown his people the power of his works,
    giving them the lands of other nations.
⁷The works of his hands are faithful and just;
    all his precepts are trustworthy.^d
⁸They are steadfast for ever^e and ever,
    done in faithfulness and uprightness.
⁹He provided redemption^f for his people;
    he ordained his covenant forever—
    holy and awesome^g is his name.

¹⁰The fear of the LORD is the beginning of wisdom;^h
    all who follow his precepts have good understanding.^i
    To him belongs eternal praise.^j

Psalm 112^a

Psalm 112 Theme _____

¹Praise the LORD.^b

Blessed is the man who fears the LORD,^k
    who finds great delight^l in his commands.

²His children will be mighty in the land;
    the generation of the upright will be blessed.
³Wealth and riches are in his house,
    and his righteousness endures forever.
⁴Even in darkness light dawns^m for the upright,
    for the gracious and compassionate and
    righteous^n man.^c
⁵Good will come to him who is generous and
    lends freely,^o
    who conducts his affairs with justice.
⁶Surely he will never be shaken;
    a righteous man will be remembered^p forever.
⁷He will have no fear of bad news;
    his heart is steadfast,^q trusting in the LORD.

^a This psalm is an acrostic poem, the lines of which begin with the successive letters of the Hebrew alphabet.   ^b 1 Hebrew *Hallelu Yah*   ^c 4 Or / *for ⌊the LORD⌋ is gracious and compassionate and righteous*

111:2 ^a Ps 92:5; 143:5
111:4 ^b Ps 103:8
111:5 ^c Mt 6:26,31-33
111:7 ^d Ps 19:7; Rev 15:3
111:8 ^e Isa 40:8; Mt 5:18
111:9 ^f Lk 1:68; ^g Ps 99:3; Lk 1:49
111:10 ^h Pr 9:10; ^i Ecc 12:13; ^j Ps 145:2
112:1 ^k Ps 128:1; ^l Ps 119:14,16,47,92
112:4 ^m Job 11:17; ^n Ps 97:11
112:5 ^o Ps 37:21,26
112:6 ^p Pr 10:7
112:7 ^q Ps 57:7; Pr 1:33

112:8
aPs 59:10

⁸His heart is secure, he will have no fear;
   in the end he will look in triumph on his foes.ᵃ

⁹He has scattered abroad his gifts to the poor,ᵇ

112:9
b2Co 9:9*
cPs 75:10

   his righteousness endures forever;
   his hornᵃ will be liftedᶜ high in honor.

¹⁰The wicked man will seeᵈ and be vexed,

112:10
dPs 86:17
ePs 37:12
fPs 58:7-8
gPr 11:7

   he will gnash his teethᵉ and waste away;ᶠ
   the longings of the wicked will come to nothing.ᵍ

Psalm 113

113:1
hPs 135:1

Psalm 113 Theme _____

¹Praise the LORD.ᵇ

113:2
iDa 2:20

Praise, O servants of the LORD,ʰ
   praise the name of the LORD.
²Let the name of the LORD be praised,
   both now and forevermore.ⁱ

113:3
jIsa 59:19;
Mal 1:11

³From the rising of the sunʲ to the place where it sets,
   the name of the LORD is to be praised.

113:4
kPs 99:2
lPs 8:1; 97:9

⁴The LORD is exaltedᵏ over all the nations,
   his glory above the heavens.ˡ
⁵Who is like the LORD our God,ᵐ
   the One who sits enthronedⁿ on high,
⁶who stoops down to lookᵒ
   on the heavens and the earth?

113:5
mPs 89:6
nPs 103:19

113:6
oPs 11:4; 138:6;
Isa 57:15

⁷He raises the poorᵖ from the dust
   and lifts the needy�q from the ash heap;
⁸he seats themʳ with princes,
   with the princes of their people.
⁹He settles the barrenˢ woman in her home
   as a happy mother of children.

113:7
p1Sa 2:8
qPs 107:41

Praise the LORD.

Psalm 114

113:8
rJob 36:7

Psalm 114 Theme _____

¹When Israel came out of Egypt,ᵗ
   the house of Jacob from a people of foreign tongue,
²Judah became God's sanctuary,
   Israel his dominion.

114:1
tEx 13:3

a9 *Horn* here symbolizes dignity.   b1 Hebrew *Hallelu Yah*; also in verse 9

³The sea looked and fled,*ᵃ*
  the Jordan turned back;*ᵇ*
⁴the mountains skipped like rams,
  the hills like lambs.

⁵Why was it, O sea, that you fled,
  O Jordan, that you turned back,
⁶you mountains, that you skipped like rams,
  you hills, like lambs?

⁷Tremble, O earth,*ᶜ* at the presence of the Lord,
  at the presence of the God of Jacob,
⁸who turned the rock into a pool,
  the hard rock into springs of water.*ᵈ*

Psalm 115

Psalm 115 Theme _____

¹Not to us, O Lᴏʀᴅ, not to us
  but to your name be the glory,*ᵉ*
  because of your love and faithfulness.

²Why do the nations say,
  "Where is their God?"*ᶠ*
³Our God is in heaven;*ᵍ*
  he does whatever pleases him.*ʰ*
⁴But their idols are silver and gold,
  made by the hands of men.*ⁱ*
⁵They have mouths, but cannot speak,*ʲ*
  eyes, but they cannot see;
⁶they have ears, but cannot hear,
  noses, but they cannot smell;
⁷they have hands, but cannot feel,
  feet, but they cannot walk;
  nor can they utter a sound with their throats.
⁸Those who make them will be like them,
  and so will all who trust in them.

⁹O house of Israel, trust in the Lᴏʀᴅ—
  he is their help and shield.
¹⁰O house of Aaron,*ᵏ* trust in the Lᴏʀᴅ—
  he is their help and shield.
¹¹You who fear him, trust in the Lᴏʀᴅ—
  he is their help and shield.

¹²The Lᴏʀᴅ remembers us and will bless us:
  He will bless the house of Israel,
  he will bless the house of Aaron,

114:3
*ᵃ*Ex 14:21;
Ps 77:16
*ᵇ*Jos 3:16

114:7
*ᶜ*Ps 96:9

114:8
*ᵈ*Ex 17:6;
Nu 20:11;
Ps 107:35

115:1
*ᵉ*Ps 96:8;
Isa 48:11;
Eze 36:32

115:2
*ᶠ*Ps 42:3; 79:10

115:3
*ᵍ*Ps 103:19
*ʰ*Ps 135:6;
Da 4:35

115:4
*ⁱ*Dt 4:28;
Jer 10:3-5

115:5
*ʲ*Jer 10:5

115:10
*ᵏ*Ps 118:3

¹³he will bless those who fear^a the LORD—
　　small and great alike.

¹⁴May the LORD make you increase,^b
　　both you and your children.
¹⁵May you be blessed by the LORD,
　　the Maker of heaven^c and earth.

¹⁶The highest heavens belong to the LORD,^d
　　but the earth he has given^e to man.
¹⁷It is not the dead^f who praise the LORD,
　　those who go down to silence;
¹⁸it is we who extol the LORD,
　　both now and forevermore.^g

Praise the LORD.^a

Psalm 116

Psalm 116 Theme _____

¹I love the LORD,^h for he heard my voice;
　　he heard my cryⁱ for mercy.
²Because he turned his ear^j to me,
　　I will call on him as long as I live.

³The cords of death^k entangled me,
　　the anguish of the grave^b came upon me;
　　I was overcome by trouble and sorrow.
⁴Then I called on the name^l of the LORD:
　　"O LORD, save me!^m"

⁵The LORD is gracious and righteous;ⁿ
　　our God is full of compassion.
⁶The LORD protects the simplehearted;
　　when I was in great need,^o he saved me.

⁷Be at rest^p once more, O my soul,
　　for the LORD has been good^q to you.

⁸For you, O LORD, have delivered my soul^r from death,
　　my eyes from tears,
　　my feet from stumbling,
⁹that I may walk before the LORD
　　in the land of the living.^s
¹⁰I believed;^t therefore^c I said,
　　"I am greatly afflicted."

115:13 *a* Ps 128:1,4

115:14 *b* Dt 1:11

115:15 *c* Ge 1:1; 14:19; Ps 96:5

115:16 *d* Ps 89:11 *e* Ps 8:6-8

115:17 *f* Ps 6:5; 88:10-12; Isa 38:18

115:18 *g* Ps 113:2; Da 2:20

116:1 *h* Ps 18:1 *i* Ps 66:19

116:2 *j* Ps 40:1

116:3 *k* Ps 18:4-5

116:4 *l* Ps 118:5 *m* Ps 22:20

116:5 *n* Ezr 9:15; Ne 9:8; Ps 103:8; 145:17

116:6 *o* Ps 19:7; 79:8

116:7 *p* Jer 6:16; Mt 11:29 *q* Ps 13:6

116:8 *r* Ps 56:13

116:9 *s* Ps 27:13

116:10 *t* 2Co 4:13*

---

a 18 Hebrew *Hallelu Yah*　*b 3* Hebrew *Sheol*　*c 10* Or *believed even when*

¹¹And in my dismay I said,
"All men are liars."ᵃ

¹²How can I repay the LORD
for all his goodness to me?
¹³I will lift up the cup of salvation
and call on the nameᵇ of the LORD.
¹⁴I will fulfill my vowsᶜ to the LORD
in the presence of all his people.

¹⁵Precious in the sightᵈ of the LORD
is the death of his saints.
¹⁶O LORD, truly I am your servant;ᵉ
I am your servant, the son of your maidservantᵃ;ᶠ
you have freed me from my chains.

¹⁷I will sacrifice a thank offeringᵍ to you
and call on the name of the LORD.
¹⁸I will fulfill my vows to the LORD
in the presence of all his people,
¹⁹in the courtsʰ of the house of the LORD—
in your midst, O Jerusalem.

Praise the LORD.ᵇ

Psalm 117

Psalm 117 Theme _____

¹Praise the LORD, all you nations;ⁱ
extol him, all you peoples.
²For great is his love toward us,
and the faithfulness of the LORDʲ endures forever.

Praise the LORD.ᵇ

Psalm 118

Psalm 118 Theme _____

¹Give thanks to the LORD,ᵏ for he is good;
his love endures forever.ˡ

²Let Israel say:ᵐ
"His love endures forever."
³Let the house of Aaron say:
"His love endures forever."
⁴Let those who fear the LORD say:
"His love endures forever."

ᵃ16 Or *servant, your faithful son*   ᵇ19,2 Hebrew *Hallelu Yah*

116:11
ᵃ Ro 3:4

116:13
ᵇ Ps 16:5; 80:18

116:14
ᶜ Ps 22:25;
Jnh 2:9

116:15
ᵈ Ps 72:14

116:16
ᵉ Ps 119:125;
143:12
ᶠ Ps 86:16

116:17
ᵍ Lev 7:12;
Ps 50:14

116:19
ʰ Ps 96:8; 135:2

117:1
ⁱ Ro 15:11*

117:2
ʲ Ps 100:5

118:1
ᵏ 1Ch 16:8
ˡ Ps 106:1; 136:1

118:2
ᵐ Ps 115:9

118:5
a Ps 120:1
b Ps 18:19

118:6
c Heb 13:6*
d Ps 27:1; 56:4

118:7
e Ps 54:4
f Ps 59:10

118:8
g Ps 40:4
h Jer 17:5

118:9
i Ps 146:3

118:10
j Ps 18:40

118:11
k Ps 88:17
l Ps 3:6

118:12
m Dt 1:44
n Ps 58:9

118:13
o Ps 86:17; 140:4

118:14
p Ex 15:2
q Isa 12:2

118:15
r Ps 68:3
s Ps 89:13

118:17
t Ps 6:5;
Hab 1:12
u Ex 15:6;
Ps 73:28

118:18
v 2Co 6:9

118:19
w Isa 26:2

118:20
x Ps 24:7;
Isa 35:8;
Rev 22:14

118:21
y Ps 116:1

118:22
z Mt 21:42;
Mk 12:10;
Lk 20:17*;
Ac 4:11*;
1Pe 2:7*

5 In my anguish[a] I cried to the LORD,
     and he answered[b] by setting me free.
6 The LORD is with me;[c] I will not be afraid.
     What can man do to me?[d]
7 The LORD is with me; he is my helper.[e]
     I will look in triumph on my enemies.[f]

8 It is better to take refuge in the LORD[g]
     than to trust in man.[h]
9 It is better to take refuge in the LORD
     than to trust in princes.[i]

10 All the nations surrounded me,
     but in the name of the LORD I cut them off.[j]
11 They surrounded me[k] on every side,[l]
     but in the name of the LORD I cut them off.
12 They swarmed around me like bees,[m]
     but they died out as quickly as burning thorns;[n]
     in the name of the LORD I cut them off.

13 I was pushed back and about to fall,
     but the LORD helped me.[o]
14 The LORD is my strength[p] and my song;
     he has become my salvation.[q]

15 Shouts of joy[r] and victory
     resound in the tents of the righteous:
     "The LORD's right hand[s] has done mighty things!
16   The LORD's right hand is lifted high;
     the LORD's right hand has done mighty things!"

17 I will not die[t] but live,
     and will proclaim[u] what the LORD has done.
18 The LORD has chastened me severely,
     but he has not given me over to death.[v]

19 Open for me the gates[w] of righteousness;
     I will enter and give thanks to the LORD.
20 This is the gate of the LORD
     through which the righteous may enter.[x]
21 I will give you thanks, for you answered me;[y]
     you have become my salvation.

22 The stone the builders rejected
     has become the capstone;[z]
23 the LORD has done this,
     and it is marvelous in our eyes.
24 This is the day the LORD has made;
     let us rejoice and be glad in it.

²⁵O LORD, save us;
    O LORD, grant us success.
²⁶Blessed is he who comes^a in the name of the LORD.
    From the house of the LORD we bless you.^a
²⁷The LORD is God,
    and he has made his light shine^b upon us.
    With boughs in hand, join in the festal procession
    up^b to the horns of the altar.

²⁸You are my God, and I will give you thanks;
    you are my God,^c and I will exalt^d you.

²⁹Give thanks to the LORD, for he is good;
    his love endures forever.

Psalm 119^c

Psalm 119 Theme _____

א Aleph

¹Blessed are they whose ways are blameless,
    who walk^e according to the law of the LORD.
²Blessed are they who keep his statutes
    and seek him with all their heart.^f
³They do nothing wrong;^g
    they walk in his ways.
⁴You have laid down precepts
    that are to be fully obeyed.
⁵Oh, that my ways were steadfast
    in obeying your decrees!
⁶Then I would not be put to shame
    when I consider all your commands.
⁷I will praise you with an upright heart
    as I learn your righteous laws.
⁸I will obey your decrees;
    do not utterly forsake me.

ב Beth

⁹How can a young man keep his way pure?
    By living according to your word.^h
¹⁰I seek you with all my heart;ⁱ
    do not let me stray from your commands.^j

---

a 26 The Hebrew is plural.   b 27 Or *Bind the festal sacrifice with ropes / and take it*
c This psalm is an acrostic poem; the verses of each stanza begin with the same letter of the
Hebrew alphabet.

118:26
a Mt 21:9*;
Mk 11:9*;
Lk 13:35*;
19:38*;
Jn 12:13*

118:27
b 1Pe 2:9

118:28
c Isa 25:1
d Ex 15:2

119:1
e Ps 128:1

119:2
f Dt 6:5

119:3
g 1Jn 3:9; 5:18

119:9
h 2Ch 6:16

119:10
i 2Ch 15:15
j ver 21,118

11 I have hidden your word in my heart^a
    that I might not sin against you.
12 Praise be to you, O LORD;
    teach me your decrees.^b
13 With my lips I recount
    all the laws that come from your mouth.^c
14 I rejoice in following your statutes
    as one rejoices in great riches.
15 I meditate on your precepts^d
    and consider your ways.
16 I delight^e in your decrees;
    I will not neglect your word.

ℷ Gimel

17 Do good to your servant,^f and I will live;
    I will obey your word.
18 Open my eyes that I may see
    wonderful things in your law.
19 I am a stranger on earth;^g
    do not hide your commands from me.
20 My soul is consumed^h with longing
    for your lawsⁱ at all times.
21 You rebuke the arrogant, who are cursed
    and who stray^j from your commands.
22 Remove from me scorn^k and contempt,
    for I keep your statutes.
23 Though rulers sit together and slander me,
    your servant will meditate on your decrees.
24 Your statutes are my delight;
    they are my counselors.

ד Daleth

25 I am laid low in the dust;^l
    preserve my life^m according to your word.
26 I recounted my ways and you answered me;
    teach me your decrees.ⁿ
27 Let me understand the teaching of your precepts;
    then I will meditate on your wonders.^o
28 My soul is weary with sorrow;^p
    strengthen me^q according to your word.
29 Keep me from deceitful ways;
    be gracious to me through your law.
30 I have chosen the way of truth;
    I have set my heart on your laws.

**Cross references (left margin):**

119:11   a Ps 37:31; Lk 2:19,51

119:12   b ver 26

119:13   c Ps 40:9

119:15   d Ps 1:2

119:16   e Ps 1:2

119:17   f Ps 13:6; 116:7

119:19   g 1Ch 29:15; Ps 39:12; 2Co 5:6; Heb 11:13

119:20   h Ps 42:2; 84:2   i Ps 63:1

119:21   j ver 10

119:22   k Ps 39:8

119:25   l Ps 44:25   m Ps 143:11

119:26   n Ps 25:4; 27:11; 86:11

119:27   o Ps 145:5

119:28   p Ps 107:26   q Ps 20:2; 1Pe 5:10

³¹I hold fast *a* to your statutes, O LORD;
 do not let me be put to shame.
³²I run in the path of your commands,
 for you have set my heart free.

ה He

³³Teach me,*b* O LORD, to follow your decrees;
 then I will keep them to the end.
³⁴Give me understanding, and I will keep your law
 and obey it with all my heart.
³⁵Direct me in the path of your commands,
 for there I find delight.

119:36
c 1Ki 8:58
d Eze 33:31;
Mk 7:21-22;
Lk 12:15;
Heb 13:5

³⁶Turn my heart*c* toward your statutes
 and not toward selfish gain.*d*
³⁷Turn my eyes away from worthless things;
 preserve my life*e* according to your word.*a*
³⁸Fulfill your promise*f* to your servant,
 so that you may be feared.
³⁹Take away the disgrace I dread,
 for your laws are good.

⁴⁰How I long*g* for your precepts!
 Preserve my life in your righteousness.

ו Waw

⁴¹May your unfailing love come to me, O LORD,
 your salvation according to your promise;
⁴²then I will answer*h* the one who taunts me,
 for I trust in your word.

⁴³Do not snatch the word of truth from my mouth,
 for I have put my hope in your laws.
⁴⁴I will always obey your law,
 for ever and ever.
⁴⁵I will walk about in freedom,
 for I have sought out your precepts.

⁴⁶I will speak of your statutes before kings*i*
 and will not be put to shame,
⁴⁷for I delight in your commands
 because I love them.
⁴⁸I lift up my hands to*b* your commands, which I love,
 and I meditate on your decrees.

ז Zayin

⁴⁹Remember your word to your servant,
 for you have given me hope.

a 37 Two manuscripts of the Masoretic Text and Dead Sea Scrolls; most manuscripts of the Masoretic Text *life in your way*   *b 48* Or *for*

119:50
a Ro 15:4

119:51
b Jer 20:7
c ver 157;
Job 23:11;
Ps 44:18

119:52
d Ps 103:18

119:53
e Ezr 9:3
f Ps 89:30

119:55
g Ps 63:6

119:57
h Ps 16:5;
La 3:24

119:58
i 1Ki 13:6
j ver 41

119:59
k Lk 15:17-18

119:61
l Ps 140:5

119:62
m Ac 16:25

119:63
n Ps 101:6-7

119:64
o Ps 33:5

119:67
p Jer 31:18-19;
Heb 12:11

119:68
q Ps 106:1;
107:1; Mt 19:17
r ver 12

119:69
s Job 13:4;
Ps 109:2

⁵⁰My comfort in my suffering is this:
    Your promise preserves my life.*a*
⁵¹The arrogant mock me*b* without restraint,
    but I do not turn*c* from your law.
⁵²I remember*d* your ancient laws, O LORD,
    and I find comfort in them.
⁵³Indignation grips me*e* because of the wicked,
    who have forsaken your law.*f*
⁵⁴Your decrees are the theme of my song
    wherever I lodge.
⁵⁵In the night I remember*g* your name, O LORD,
    and I will keep your law.
⁵⁶This has been my practice:
    I obey your precepts.

ח Heth

⁵⁷You are my portion,*h* O LORD;
    I have promised to obey your words.
⁵⁸I have sought your face with all my heart;
    be gracious to me*i* according to your promise.*j*
⁵⁹I have considered my ways*k*
    and have turned my steps to your statutes.
⁶⁰I will hasten and not delay
    to obey your commands.
⁶¹Though the wicked bind me with ropes,
    I will not forget*l* your law.
⁶²At midnight*m* I rise to give you thanks
    for your righteous laws.
⁶³I am a friend to all who fear you,*n*
    to all who follow your precepts.
⁶⁴The earth is filled with your love,*o* O LORD;
    teach me your decrees.

ט Teth

⁶⁵Do good to your servant
    according to your word, O LORD.
⁶⁶Teach me knowledge and good judgment,
    for I believe in your commands.
⁶⁷Before I was afflicted I went astray,*p*
    but now I obey your word.
⁶⁸You are good,*q* and what you do is good;
    teach me your decrees.*r*
⁶⁹Though the arrogant have smeared me with lies,*s*
    I keep your precepts with all my heart.

⁷⁰Their hearts are callous^a and unfeeling,
  but I delight in your law.
⁷¹It was good for me to be afflicted
  so that I might learn your decrees.
⁷²The law from your mouth is more precious to me
  than thousands of pieces of silver and gold.^b

ן Yodh

⁷³Your hands made me^c and formed me;
  give me understanding to learn your commands.
⁷⁴May those who fear you rejoice^d when they see me,
  for I have put my hope in your word.
⁷⁵I know, O LORD, that your laws are righteous,
  and in faithfulness^e you have afflicted me.
⁷⁶May your unfailing love be my comfort,
  according to your promise to your servant.
⁷⁷Let your compassion^f come to me that I may live,
  for your law is my delight.
⁷⁸May the arrogant^g be put to shame for wronging me
    without cause;^h
  but I will meditate on your precepts.
⁷⁹May those who fear you turn to me,
  those who understand your statutes.
⁸⁰May my heart be blameless toward your decrees,
  that I may not be put to shame.

כ Kaph

⁸¹My soul faintsⁱ with longing for your salvation,
  but I have put my hope in your word.
⁸²My eyes fail,^j looking for your promise;
  I say, "When will you comfort me?"
⁸³Though I am like a wineskin in the smoke,
  I do not forget your decrees.
⁸⁴How long^k must your servant wait?
  When will you punish my persecutors?
⁸⁵The arrogant dig pitfalls^l for me,
  contrary to your law.
⁸⁶All your commands are trustworthy;^m
  help me,ⁿ for men persecute me without cause.^o
⁸⁷They almost wiped me from the earth,
  but I have not forsaken^p your precepts.
⁸⁸Preserve my life according to your love,
  and I will obey the statutes of your mouth.

119:70
^aPs 17:10;
Isa 6:10;
Ac 28:27

119:72
^bPs 19:10;
Pr 8:10-11,19

119:73
^cJob 10:8;
Ps 100:3; 138:8;
139:13-16

119:74
^dPs 34:2

119:75
^eHeb 12:5-11

119:77
^fver 41

119:78
^gJer 50:32
^hver 86,161

119:81
ⁱPs 84:2

119:82
^jPs 69:3; La 2:11

119:84
^kPs 39:4;
Rev 6:10

119:85
^lPs 35:7;
Jer 18:20,22

119:86
^mPs 35:19
ⁿPs 109:26
^over 78

119:87
^pIsa 58:2

119:89
a Mt 24:34-35;
1 Pe 1:25

119:90
b Ps 36:5
c Ps 148:6;
Ecc 1:4

119:91
d Jer 33:25

119:97
e Ps 1:2

119:98
f Dt 4:6

119:100
g Job 32:7-9

119:101
h Pr 1:15

119:103
i Ps 19:10;
Pr 8:11
j Pr 24:13-14

119:104
k ver 128

119:105
l Pr 6:23

119:106
m Ne 10:29

ל Lamedh

89Your word, O LORD, is eternal;*a*
  it stands firm in the heavens.
90Your faithfulness*b* continues through all generations;
  you established the earth, and it endures.*c*
91Your laws endure*d* to this day,
  for all things serve you.
92If your law had not been my delight,
  I would have perished in my affliction.
93I will never forget your precepts,
  for by them you have preserved my life.
94Save me, for I am yours;
  I have sought out your precepts.
95The wicked are waiting to destroy me,
  but I will ponder your statutes.
96To all perfection I see a limit;
  but your commands are boundless.

מ Mem

97Oh, how I love your law!
  I meditate*e* on it all day long.
98Your commands make me wiser*f* than my enemies,
  for they are ever with me.
99I have more insight than all my teachers,
  for I meditate on your statutes.
100I have more understanding than the elders,
  for I obey your precepts.*g*
101I have kept my feet*h* from every evil path
  so that I might obey your word.
102I have not departed from your laws,
  for you yourself have taught me.
103How sweet are your words to my taste,
  sweeter than honey*i* to my mouth!*j*
104I gain understanding from your precepts;
  therefore I hate every wrong path.*k*

נ Nun

105Your word is a lamp to my feet
  and a light*l* for my path.
106I have taken an oath*m* and confirmed it,
  that I will follow your righteous laws.
107I have suffered much;
  preserve my life, O LORD, according to your word.

^{108}Accept, O Lord, the willing praise of my mouth,^{a}
    and teach me your laws.
^{109}Though I constantly take my life in my hands,^{b}
    I will not forget your law.
^{110}The wicked have set a snare^c for me,
    but I have not strayed^d from your precepts.
^{111}Your statutes are my heritage forever;
    they are the joy of my heart.
^{112}My heart is set on keeping your decrees
    to the very end.^{e}

ס Samekh

^{113}I hate double-minded men,^{f}
    but I love your law.
^{114}You are my refuge and my shield;^{g}
    I have put my hope^h in your word.
^{115}Away from me,^{i} you evildoers,
    that I may keep the commands of my God!
^{116}Sustain me^j according to your promise, and I will live;
    do not let my hopes be dashed.^{k}
^{117}Uphold me, and I will be delivered;
    I will always have regard for your decrees.
^{118}You reject all who stray from your decrees,
    for their deceitfulness is in vain.
^{119}All the wicked of the earth you discard like dross;^{l}
    therefore I love your statutes.
^{120}My flesh trembles^m in fear of you;
    I stand in awe of your laws.

ע Ayin

^{121}I have done what is righteous and just;
    do not leave me to my oppressors.
^{122}Ensure your servant's well-being;^{n}
    let not the arrogant oppress me.
^{123}My eyes fail, looking for your salvation,
    looking for your righteous promise.^{o}
^{124}Deal with your servant according to your love
    and teach me your decrees.^{p}
^{125}I am your servant;^{q} give me discernment
    that I may understand your statutes.
^{126}It is time for you to act, O Lord;
    your law is being broken.
^{127}Because I love your commands
    more than gold,^{r} more than pure gold,

119:108
^{a}Hos 14:2;
Heb 13:15

119:109
^{b}Jdg 12:3;
Job 13:14

119:110
^{c}Ps 140:5; 141:9
^{d}ver 10

119:112
^{e}ver 33

119:113
^{f}Jas 1:8

119:114
^{g}Ps 32:7; 91:1
^{h}ver 74

119:115
^{i}Ps 6:8; 139:19;
Mt 7:23

119:116
^{j}Ps 54:4
^{k}Ps 25:2;
Ro 5:5; 9:33

119:119
^{l}Eze 22:18,19

119:120
^{m}Hab 3:16

119:122
^{n}Job 17:3

119:123
^{o}ver 82

119:124
^{p}ver 12

119:125
^{q}Ps 116:16

119:127
^{r}Ps 19:10

119:128
a ver 104,163

[128]and because I consider all your precepts right,
   I hate every wrong path.[a]

ב Pe

119:130
b Pr 6:23
c Ps 19:7

[129]Your statutes are wonderful;
   therefore I obey them.
[130]The unfolding of your words gives light;[b]
   it gives understanding to the simple.[c]

119:131
d Ps 42:1
e ver 20

[131]I open my mouth and pant,[d]
   longing for your commands.[e]

119:132
f Ps 25:16; 106:4

[132]Turn to me and have mercy[f] on me,
   as you always do to those who love your name.

119:133
g Ps 17:5
h Ps 19:13;
Ro 6:12

[133]Direct my footsteps according to your word;[g]
   let no sin rule[h] over me.
[134]Redeem me from the oppression of men,[i]
   that I may obey your precepts.

119:134
i Ps 142:6;
Lk 1:74

[135]Make your face shine[j] upon your servant
   and teach me your decrees.
[136]Streams of tears[k] flow from my eyes,
   for your law is not obeyed.[l]

119:135
j Nu 6:25; Ps 4:6

צ Tsadhe

119:136
k Jer 9:1,18
l Eze 9:4

[137]Righteous are you,[m] O LORD,
   and your laws are right.[n]
[138]The statutes you have laid down are righteous;[o]
   they are fully trustworthy.

119:137
m Ezr 9:15;
Jer 12:1
n Ne 9:13

[139]My zeal wears me out,[p]
   for my enemies ignore your words.
[140]Your promises have been thoroughly tested,[q]
   and your servant loves them.

119:138
o Ps 19:7

[141]Though I am lowly and despised,[r]
   I do not forget your precepts.
[142]Your righteousness is everlasting
   and your law is true.[s]

119:139
p Ps 69:9;
Jn 2:17

[143]Trouble and distress have come upon me,
   but your commands are my delight.

119:140
q Ps 12:6

[144]Your statutes are forever right;
   give me understanding[t] that I may live.

119:141
r Ps 22:6

ק Qoph

119:142
s Ps 19:7

[145]I call with all my heart; answer me, O LORD,
   and I will obey your decrees.
[146]I call out to you; save me
   and I will keep your statutes.

119:144
t Ps 19:9

147I rise before dawn*a* and cry for help;
    I have put my hope in your word.
148My eyes stay open through the watches of the night,*b*
    that I may meditate on your promises.
149Hear my voice in accordance with your love;
    preserve my life, O LORD, according to your laws.
150Those who devise wicked schemes are near,
    but they are far from your law.
151Yet you are near,*c* O LORD,
    and all your commands are true.*d*
152Long ago I learned from your statutes
    that you established them to last forever.*e*

ר Resh

153Look upon my suffering*f* and deliver me,
    for I have not forgotten*g* your law.
154Defend my cause*h* and redeem me;*i*
    preserve my life according to your promise.
155Salvation is far from the wicked,
    for they do not seek out*j* your decrees.
156Your compassion is great, O LORD;
    preserve my life*k* according to your laws.
157Many are the foes who persecute me,*l*
    but I have not turned from your statutes.
158I look on the faithless with loathing,*m*
    for they do not obey your word.
159See how I love your precepts;
    preserve my life, O LORD, according to your love.
160All your words are true;
    all your righteous laws are eternal.

שׂ Sin and Shin

161Rulers persecute me*n* without cause,
    but my heart trembles at your word.
162I rejoice in your promise
    like one who finds great spoil.*o*
163I hate and abhor falsehood
    but I love your law.
164Seven times a day I praise you
    for your righteous laws.
165Great peace*p* have they who love your law,
    and nothing can make them stumble.
166I wait for your salvation,*q* O LORD,
    and I follow your commands.

119:147 *a* Ps 5:3; 57:8; 108:2
119:148 *b* Ps 63:6
119:151 *c* Ps 34:18; 145:18 *d* ver 142
119:152 *e* Lk 21:33
119:153 *f* La 5:1 *g* Pr 3:1
119:154 *h* Mic 7:9 *i* 1Sa 24:15
119:155 *j* Job 5:4
119:156 *k* 2Sa 24:14
119:157 *l* Ps 7:1
119:158 *m* Ps 139:21
119:161 *n* 1Sa 24:11
119:162 *o* 1Sa 30:16
119:165 *p* Pr 3:2; Isa 26:3,12; 32:17
119:166 *q* Ge 49:18

167I obey your statutes,
for I love them greatly.
168I obey your precepts and your statutes,
for all my ways are known[a] to you.

ת Taw

169May my cry come[b] before you, O Lord;
give me understanding according to your word.
170May my supplication come[c] before you;
deliver me[d] according to your promise.
171May my lips overflow with praise,[e]
for you teach me[f] your decrees.
172May my tongue sing of your word,
for all your commands are righteous.
173May your hand be ready to help[g] me,
for I have chosen[h] your precepts.
174I long for your salvation,[i] O Lord,
and your law is my delight.
175Let me live[j] that I may praise you,
and may your laws sustain me.
176I have strayed like a lost sheep.[k]
Seek your servant,
for I have not forgotten your commands.

Psalm 120

A song of ascents.

Psalm 120 Theme _____

1I call on the Lord in my distress,[l]
and he answers me.
2Save me, O Lord, from lying lips[m]
and from deceitful tongues.[n]

3What will he do to you,
and what more besides, O deceitful tongue?
4He will punish you with a warrior's sharp arrows,[o]
with burning coals of the broom tree.

5Woe to me that I dwell in Meshech,
that I live among the tents of Kedar![p]
6Too long have I lived
among those who hate peace.
7I am a man of peace;
but when I speak, they are for war.

Margin references:
119:168 a Pr 5:21
119:169 b Ps 18:6
119:170 c Ps 28:2 d Ps 31:2
119:171 e Ps 51:15 f Ps 94:12
119:173 g Ps 37:24 h Jos 24:22
119:174 i ver 166
119:175 j Isa 55:3
119:176 k Isa 53:6
120:1 l Ps 102:2; Jnh 2:2
120:2 m Pr 12:22 n Ps 52:4
120:4 o Ps 45:5
120:5 p Ge 25:13; Jer 49:28

Psalm 121

A song of ascents.

<u>Psalm 121 Theme</u>_____

¹I lift up my eyes to the hills—
  where does my help come from?
²My help comes from the LORD,
  the Maker of heaven and earth.*a*

³He will not let your foot slip—
  he who watches over you will not slumber;
⁴indeed, he who watches over Israel
  will neither slumber nor sleep.

⁵The LORD watches over*b* you—
  the LORD is your shade at your right hand;
⁶the sun*c* will not harm you by day,
  nor the moon by night.

⁷The LORD will keep you from all harm*d*—
  he will watch over your life;
⁸the LORD will watch over your coming and going
  both now and forevermore.*e*

Psalm 122

A song of ascents. Of David.

<u>Psalm 122 Theme</u>_____

¹I rejoiced with those who said to me,
  "Let us go to the house of the LORD."
²Our feet are standing
  in your gates, O Jerusalem.

³Jerusalem is built like a city
  that is closely compacted together.
⁴That is where the tribes go up,
  the tribes of the LORD,
to praise the name of the LORD
  according to the statute given to Israel.
⁵There the thrones for judgment stand,
  the thrones of the house of David.

⁶Pray for the peace of Jerusalem:
  "May those who love*f* you be secure.

121:2
a Ps 115:15;
124:8

121:5
b Isa 25:4

121:6
c Ps 91:5;
Isa 49:10;
Rev 7:16

121:7
d Ps 41:2;
91:10-12

121:8
e Dt 28:6

122:6
f Ps 51:18

122:9
a Ne 2:10

⁷May there be peace within your walls
  and security within your citadels."
⁸For the sake of my brothers and friends,
  I will say, "Peace be within you."
⁹For the sake of the house of the LORD our God,
  I will seek your prosperity.*ᵃ*

Psalm 123

A song of ascents.

123:1
b Ps 11:4; 121:1;
141:8

Psalm 123 Theme _____

¹I lift up my eyes to you,
  to you whose throne*ᵇ* is in heaven.
²As the eyes of slaves look to the hand of their master,
  as the eyes of a maid look to the hand of her mistress,
so our eyes look to the LORD*ᶜ* our God,
  till he shows us his mercy.

³Have mercy on us, O LORD, have mercy on us,
  for we have endured much contempt.
⁴We have endured much ridicule from the proud,
  much contempt from the arrogant.

123:2
c Ps 25:15

Psalm 124

A song of ascents. Of David.

Psalm 124 Theme _____

¹If the LORD had not been on our side—
  let Israel say*ᵈ*—
²if the LORD had not been on our side
  when men attacked us,
³when their anger flared against us,
  they would have swallowed us alive;
⁴the flood would have engulfed us,
  the torrent would have swept over us,
⁵the raging waters
  would have swept us away.

124:1
d Ps 129:1

⁶Praise be to the LORD,
  who has not let us be torn by their teeth.
⁷We have escaped like a bird
  out of the fowler's snare;*ᵉ*

124:7
e Ps 91:3; Pr 6:5

the snare has been broken,
and we have escaped.
[8]Our help is in the name of the LORD,
the Maker of heaven[a] and earth.

Psalm 125

A song of ascents.

Psalm 125 Theme _____

[1]Those who trust in the LORD are like Mount Zion,
which cannot be shaken[b] but endures forever.
[2]As the mountains surround Jerusalem,
so the LORD surrounds[c] his people
both now and forevermore.

[3]The scepter of the wicked will not remain[d]
over the land allotted to the righteous,
for then the righteous might use
their hands to do evil.[e]

[4]Do good, O LORD,[f] to those who are good,
to those who are upright in heart.[g]
[5]But those who turn[h] to crooked ways[i]
the LORD will banish with the evildoers.

Peace be upon Israel.[j]

Psalm 126

A song of ascents.

Psalm 126 Theme _____

[1]When the LORD brought back[k] the captives to[a] Zion,
we were like men who dreamed.[b]
[2]Our mouths were filled with laughter,
our tongues with songs of joy.[l]
Then it was said among the nations,
"The LORD has done great things[m] for them."
[3]The LORD has done great things for us,
and we are filled with joy.[n]

[4]Restore our fortunes,[c] O LORD,
like streams in the Negev.[o]

a1 Or LORD *restored the fortunes of*   b1 Or *men restored to health*   c4 Or *Bring back our captives*

124:8
[a]Ge 1:1;
Ps 121:2; 134:3

125:1
[b]Ps 46:5

125:2
[c]Ps 121:8;
Zec 2:4-5

125:3
[d]Ps 89:22;
Pr 22:8;
Isa 14:5
[e]1Sa 24:10;
Ps 55:20

125:4
[f]Ps 119:68
[g]Ps 7:10; 36:10;
94:15

125:5
[h]Job 23:11
[i]Pr 2:15;
Isa 59:8
[j]Ps 128:6

126:1
[k]Ps 85:1;
Hos 6:11

126:2
[l]Job 8:21;
Ps 51:14
[m]Ps 71:19

126:3
[n]Isa 25:9

126:4
[o]Isa 35:6; 43:19

126:5
a Isa 35:10

⁵Those who sow in tears
 will reap with songs of joy.*a*
⁶He who goes out weeping,
 carrying seed to sow,
will return with songs of joy,
 carrying sheaves with him.

Psalm 127

A song of ascents. Of Solomon.

127:1
b Ps 78:69
c Ps 121:4

Psalm 127 Theme _____

127:2
d Ge 3:17
e Job 11:18

¹Unless the Lord builds*b* the house,
 its builders labor in vain.
 Unless the Lord watches*c* over the city,
 the watchmen stand guard in vain.
²In vain you rise early
 and stay up late,
 toiling for food*d* to eat—
 for he grants sleep*e* to*a* those he loves.

127:3
f Ge 33:5

³Sons are a heritage from the Lord,
 children a reward*f* from him.
⁴Like arrows in the hands of a warrior
 are sons born in one's youth.

127:5
g Pr 27:11

⁵Blessed is the man
 whose quiver is full of them.
 They will not be put to shame
 when they contend with their enemies*g* in the gate.

Psalm 128

A song of ascents.

128:1
h Ps 112:1
i Ps 119:1-3

Psalm 128 Theme _____

128:2
j Isa 3:10
k Ecc 8:12

¹Blessed are all who fear the Lord,*h*
 who walk in his ways.*i*
²You will eat the fruit of your labor;*j*
 blessings and prosperity*k* will be yours.
³Your wife will be like a fruitful vine*l*
 within your house;
 your sons will be like olive shoots*m*
 around your table.

128:3
l Eze 19:10
m Ps 52:8;
144:12

a 2 Or *eat— / for while they sleep he provides for*

⁴Thus is the man blessed
    who fears the LORD.

⁵May the LORD bless you from Zion*a*
    all the days of your life;
may you see the prosperity of Jerusalem,
⁶   and may you live to see your children's children.*b*

Peace be upon Israel.*c*

Psalm 129

A song of ascents.

Psalm 129 Theme _____

¹They have greatly oppressed me from my youth*d*—
    let Israel say*e*—
²they have greatly oppressed me from my youth,
    but they have not gained the victory*f* over me.
³Plowmen have plowed my back
    and made their furrows long.
⁴But the LORD is righteous;*g*
    he has cut me free from the cords of the wicked.

⁵May all who hate Zion*h*
    be turned back in shame.*i*
⁶May they be like grass on the roof,
    which withers*j* before it can grow;
⁷with it the reaper cannot fill his hands,
    nor the one who gathers fill his arms.
⁸May those who pass by not say,
    "The blessing of the LORD be upon you;
we bless you*k* in the name of the LORD."

Psalm 130

A song of ascents.

Psalm 130 Theme _____

¹Out of the depths*l* I cry to you, O LORD;
²   O Lord, hear my voice.*m*
Let your ears be attentive*n*
    to my cry for mercy.

³If you, O LORD, kept a record of sins,
    O Lord, who could stand?*o*

128:5
a Ps 20:2; 134:3

128:6
b Ge 50:23;
Job 42:16
c Ps 125:5

129:1
d Ps 88:15;
Hos 2:15
e Ps 124:1

129:2
f Mt 16:18

129:4
g Ps 119:137

129:5
h Mic 4:11
i Ps 71:13

129:6
j Ps 37:2

129:8
k Ru 2:4;
Ps 118:26

130:1
l Ps 42:7; 69:2;
La 3:55

130:2
m Ps 28:2
n 2Ch 6:40;
Ps 64:1

130:3
o Ps 76:7; 143:2

130:4
a Ex 34:7;
Isa 55:7;
Jer 33:8
b 1Ki 8:40

⁴But with you there is forgiveness;*a*
   therefore you are feared.*b*

⁵I wait for the Lord,*c* my soul waits,
   and in his word*d* I put my hope.
⁶My soul waits for the Lord
   more than watchmen*e* wait for the morning,
   more than watchmen wait for the morning.*f*

130:5
c Ps 27:14;
33:20; Isa 8:17
d Ps 119:81

⁷O Israel, put your hope*g* in the Lord,
   for with the Lord is unfailing love
   and with him is full redemption.
⁸He himself will redeem*h* Israel
   from all their sins.

Psalm 131

130:6
e Ps 63:6
f Ps 119:147

A song of ascents. Of David.

130:7
g Ps 131:3

Psalm 131 Theme _____

¹My heart is not proud,*i* O Lord,
   my eyes are not haughty;
 I do not concern myself with great matters
   or things too wonderful for me.
²But I have stilled and quieted my soul;
   like a weaned child with its mother,
   like a weaned child is my soul*j* within me.

130:8
h Lk 1:68

³O Israel, put your hope*k* in the Lord
   both now and forevermore.

Psalm 132

131:1
i Ps 101:5;
Ro 12:16

A song of ascents.

Psalm 132 Theme _____

131:2
j Mt 18:3;
1Co 14:20

¹O Lord, remember David
   and all the hardships he endured.

²He swore an oath to the Lord
   and made a vow to the Mighty One of Jacob:*l*
³"I will not enter my house
   or go to my bed—
⁴I will allow no sleep to my eyes,
   no slumber to my eyelids,

131:3
k Ps 130:7

132:2
l Ge 49:24

⁵till I find a place[a] for the LORD,
    a dwelling for the Mighty One of Jacob."

⁶We heard it in Ephrathah,[b]
    we came upon it in the fields of Jaar[a;b]c

⁷"Let us go to his dwelling place;[d]
    let us worship at his footstool[e]—

⁸arise, O LORD,[f] and come to your resting place,
    you and the ark of your might.

⁹May your priests be clothed with righteousness;[g]
    may your saints sing for joy."

¹⁰For the sake of David your servant,
    do not reject your anointed one.

¹¹The LORD swore an oath to David,[h]
    a sure oath that he will not revoke:
"One of your own descendants[i]
    I will place on your throne—
¹²if your sons keep my covenant
    and the statutes I teach them,
then their sons will sit
    on your throne[j] for ever and ever."

¹³For the LORD has chosen Zion,[k]
    he has desired it for his dwelling:
¹⁴"This is my resting place for ever and ever;[l]
    here I will sit enthroned, for I have desired it—
¹⁵I will bless her with abundant provisions;
    her poor will I satisfy with food.[m]
¹⁶I will clothe her priests[n] with salvation,
    and her saints will ever sing for joy.

¹⁷"Here I will make a horn[c] grow[o] for David
    and set up a lamp[p] for my anointed one.
¹⁸I will clothe his enemies with shame,[q]
    but the crown on his head will be resplendent."

Psalm 133

A song of ascents. Of David.

Psalm 133 Theme _____

¹How good and pleasant it is
    when brothers live together[r] in unity!

a6 That is, Kiriath Jearim   b6 Or *heard of it in Ephrathah, / we found it in the fields of Jaar.*
(And no quotes around verses 7-9)   c17 *Horn* here symbolizes strong one, that is, king.

**Cross-references (right margin):**

132:5
a Ac 7:46

132:6
b 1Sa 17:12
c 1Sa 7:2

132:7
d Ps 5:7
e Ps 99:5

132:8
f Nu 10:35;
Ps 78:61

132:9
g Job 29:14;
Isa 61:3,10

132:11
h Ps 89:3-4,35
i 2Sa 7:12

132:12
j Lk 1:32;
Ac 2:30

132:13
k Ps 48:1-2

132:14
l Ps 68:16

132:15
m Ps 107:9;
147:14

132:16
n 2Ch 6:41

132:17
o Eze 29:21;
Lk 1:69
p 1Ki 11:36;
2Ch 21:7

132:18
q Ps 35:26;
109:29

133:1
r Ge 13:8;
Heb 13:1

133:2
a Ex 30:25

133:3
b Dt 4:48
c Lev 25:21;
Dt 28:8
d Ps 42:8

134:1
e Ps 135:1-2
f 1Ch 9:33

134:2
g Ps 28:2; 1Ti 2:8

134:3
h Ps 124:8
i Ps 128:5

135:1
j Ps 113:1; 134:1

135:2
k Lk 2:37
l Ps 116:19

135:3
m Ps 119:68
n Ps 147:1

135:4
o Dt 10:15;
1Pe 2:9
p Ex 19:5; Dt 7:6

135:5
q Ps 48:1
r Ps 97:9

135:6
s Ps 115:3

135:7
t Jer 10:13;
Zec 10:1
u Job 28:25
v Job 38:22

[2] It is like precious oil poured on the head,[a]
    running down on the beard,
    running down on Aaron's beard,
    down upon the collar of his robes.
[3] It is as if the dew of Hermon[b]
    were falling on Mount Zion.
For there the LORD bestows his blessing,[c]
    even life forevermore.[d]

Psalm 134

A song of ascents.

Psalm 134 Theme _____

[1] Praise the LORD, all you servants[e] of the LORD
    who minister by night[f] in the house of the LORD.
[2] Lift up your hands[g] in the sanctuary
    and praise the LORD.

[3] May the LORD, the Maker of heaven[h] and earth,
    bless you from Zion.[i]

Psalm 135

Psalm 135 Theme _____

[1] Praise the LORD.[a]

Praise the name of the LORD;
    praise him, you servants[j] of the LORD,
[2] you who minister in the house[k] of the LORD,
    in the courts[l] of the house of our God.

[3] Praise the LORD, for the LORD is good;[m]
    sing praise to his name, for that is pleasant.[n]
[4] For the LORD has chosen Jacob[o] to be his own,
    Israel to be his treasured possession.[p]

[5] I know that the LORD is great,[q]
    that our Lord is greater than all gods.[r]
[6] The LORD does whatever pleases him,[s]
    in the heavens and on the earth,
    in the seas and all their depths.
[7] He makes clouds rise from the ends of the earth;
    he sends lightning with the rain[t]
    and brings out the wind[u] from his storehouses.[v]

a 1 Hebrew *Hallelu Yah*; also in verses 3 and 21

⁸He struck down the firstborn*a* of Egypt,
  the firstborn of men and animals.
⁹He sent his signs*b* and wonders into your midst, O Egypt,
  against Pharaoh and all his servants.*c*
¹⁰He struck down many*d* nations
  and killed mighty kings—
¹¹Sihon*e* king of the Amorites,
  Og king of Bashan
  and all the kings of Canaan*f*—
¹²and he gave their land as an inheritance,*g*
  an inheritance to his people Israel.

¹³Your name, O LORD, endures forever,*h*
  your renown,*i* O LORD, through all generations.
¹⁴For the LORD will vindicate his people
  and have compassion on his servants.*j*

¹⁵The idols of the nations are silver and gold,
  made by the hands of men.
¹⁶They have mouths, but cannot speak,
  eyes, but they cannot see;
¹⁷they have ears, but cannot hear,
  nor is there breath in their mouths.
¹⁸Those who make them will be like them,
  and so will all who trust in them.

¹⁹O house of Israel, praise the LORD;
  O house of Aaron, praise the LORD;
²⁰O house of Levi, praise the LORD;
  you who fear him, praise the LORD.
²¹Praise be to the LORD from Zion,*k*
  to him who dwells in Jerusalem.

  Praise the LORD.

Psalm 136

Psalm 136 Theme _____

¹Give thanks to the LORD, for he is good.*l*
            *His love endures forever.*m*
²Give thanks to the God of gods.*n*
            His love endures forever.
³Give thanks to the Lord of lords:
            His love endures forever.
⁴to him who alone does great wonders,*o*
            His love endures forever.

Cross-references:
135:8 *a*Ex 12:12; Ps 78:51
135:9 *b*Dt 6:22 *c*Ps 136:10-15
135:10 *d*Nu 21:21-25; Ps 136:17-21
135:11 *e*Nu 21:21 *f*Jos 12:7-24
135:12 *g*Ps 78:55
135:13 *h*Ex 3:15 *i*Ps 102:12
135:14 *j*Dt 32:36
135:21 *k*Ps 134:3
136:1 *l*Ps 106:1 *m*1Ch 16:34; 2Ch 20:21
136:2 *n*Dt 10:17
136:4 *o*Ps 72:18

136:5
a Pr 3:19;
Jer 51:15
b Ge 1:1

136:6
c Ge 1:9;
Jer 10:12
d Ps 24:2

136:7
e Ge 1:14,16

136:8
f Ge 1:16

136:10
g Ex 12:29;
Ps 135:8

136:11
h Ex 6:6; 12:51

136:12
i Dt 4:34; Ps 44:3

136:13
j Ex 14:21;
Ps 78:13

136:14
k Ex 14:22

136:15
l Ex 14:27;
Ps 135:9

136:16
m Ex 13:18

136:17
n Ps 135:9-12

136:18
o Dt 29:7

136:19
p Nu 21:21-25

136:21
q Jos 12:1

136:23
r Ps 113:7

136:24
s Ps 107:2

[5]who by his understanding[a] made the heavens,[b]
His love endures forever.

[6]who spread out the earth[c] upon the waters,[d]
His love endures forever.

[7]who made the great lights[e]—
His love endures forever.

[8]the sun to govern[f] the day,
His love endures forever.

[9]the moon and stars to govern the night;
His love endures forever.

[10]to him who struck down the firstborn[g] of Egypt
His love endures forever.

[11]and brought Israel out[h] from among them
His love endures forever.

[12]with a mighty hand and outstretched arm;[i]
His love endures forever.

[13]to him who divided the Red Sea[a][j] asunder
His love endures forever.

[14]and brought Israel through[k] the midst of it,
His love endures forever.

[15]but swept Pharaoh and his army into the Red Sea;[l]
His love endures forever.

[16]to him who led his people through the desert,[m]
His love endures forever.

[17]who struck down great kings,[n]
His love endures forever.

[18]and killed mighty kings[o]—
His love endures forever.

[19]Sihon king of the Amorites[p]
His love endures forever.

[20]and Og king of Bashan—
His love endures forever.

[21]and gave their land[q] as an inheritance,
His love endures forever.

[22]an inheritance to his servant Israel;
His love endures forever.

[23]to the One who remembered us[r] in our low estate
His love endures forever.

[24]and freed us from our enemies,[s]
His love endures forever.

a 13 Hebrew *Yam Suph*; that is, Sea of Reeds; also in verse 15

²⁵and who gives food*a* to every creature.

His love endures forever.

²⁶Give thanks to the God of heaven.

His love endures forever.

Psalm 137

Psalm 137 Theme _____

¹By the rivers of Babylon*b* we sat and wept*c*
  when we remembered Zion.
²There on the poplars
  we hung our harps,
³for there our captors asked us for songs,
  our tormentors demanded*d* songs of joy;
  they said, "Sing us one of the songs of Zion!"

⁴How can we sing the songs of the LORD
  while in a foreign land?
⁵If I forget you, O Jerusalem,
  may my right hand forget ⌊its skill⌋.
⁶May my tongue cling to the roof*e* of my mouth
  if I do not remember you,
  if I do not consider Jerusalem
  my highest joy.

⁷Remember, O LORD, what the Edomites*f* did
  on the day Jerusalem fell.*g*
"Tear it down," they cried,
  "tear it down to its foundations!"

⁸O Daughter of Babylon, doomed to destruction,*h*
  happy is he who repays you
  for what you have done to us—
⁹he who seizes your infants
  and dashes them*i* against the rocks.

Psalm 138

Of David.

Psalm 138 Theme _____

¹I will praise you, O LORD, with all my heart;
  before the "gods"*j* I will sing your praise.
²I will bow down toward your holy temple*k*
  and will praise your name

136:25
*a*Ps 104:27;
145:15

137:1
*b*Eze 1:1,3
*c*Ne 1:4

137:3
*d*Ps 80:6

137:6
*e*Eze 3:26

137:7
*f*Jer 49:7;
La 4:21-22;
Eze 25:12
*g*Ob 11

137:8
*h*Isa 13:1,19;
Jer 25:12,26;
Jer 50:15;
Rev 18:6

137:9
*i*2Ki 8:12;
Isa 13:16

138:1
*j*Ps 95:3; 96:4

138:2
*k*1Ki 8:29;
Ps 5:7; 28:2

138:2
a Isa 42:21

138:3
b Ps 28:7

138:4
c Ps 102:15

138:6
d Ps 113:6;
Isa 57:15
e Pr 3:34; Jas 4:6

138:7
f Ps 23:4
g Jer 51:25
h Ps 20:6
i Ps 71:20

138:8
j Ps 57:2;
Php 1:6
k Job 10:3,8;
14:15

139:1
l Ps 17:3
m Jer 12:3

139:2
n 2Ki 19:27
o Mt 9:4; Jn 2:24

139:3
p Job 31:4

139:4
q Heb 4:13

139:5
r Ps 34:7

139:6
s Job 42:3;
Ro 11:33

139:7
t Jer 23:24;
Jnh 1:3

139:8
u Am 9:2-3
v Pr 15:11

for your love and your faithfulness,
for you have exalted above all things
   your name and your word.*a*
³When I called, you answered me;
   you made me bold and stouthearted.*b*

⁴May all the kings of the earth*c* praise you, O LORD,
   when they hear the words of your mouth.
⁵May they sing of the ways of the LORD,
   for the glory of the LORD is great.

⁶Though the LORD is on high, he looks upon the lowly,*d*
   but the proud*e* he knows from afar.
⁷Though I walk*f* in the midst of trouble,
   you preserve my life;
you stretch out your hand against the anger of my foes,*g*
   with your right hand*h* you save me.*i*
⁸The LORD will fulfill ⌊his purpose⌋*j* for me;
   your love, O LORD, endures forever—
   do not abandon the works of your hands.*k*

Psalm 139

For the director of music. Of David. A psalm.

Psalm 139 Theme _____

¹O LORD, you have searched me*l*
   and you know*m* me.
²You know when I sit and when I rise;*n*
   you perceive my thoughts*o* from afar.
³You discern my going out and my lying down;
   you are familiar with all my ways.*p*
⁴Before a word is on my tongue
   you know it completely,*q* O LORD.

⁵You hem me in*r*—behind and before;
   you have laid your hand upon me.
⁶Such knowledge is too wonderful for me,
   too lofty*s* for me to attain.

⁷Where can I go from your Spirit?
   Where can I flee*t* from your presence?
⁸If I go up to the heavens,*u* you are there;
   if I make my bed*v* in the depths,*a* you are there.

a 8 Hebrew *Sheol*

⁹If I rise on the wings of the dawn,
   if I settle on the far side of the sea,
¹⁰even there your hand will guide me,ᵃ
   your right hand will hold me fast.

¹¹If I say, "Surely the darkness will hide me
   and the light become night around me,"
¹²even the darkness will not be darkᵇ to you;
   the night will shine like the day,
   for darkness is as light to you.

¹³For you created my inmost being;ᶜ
   you knit me togetherᵈ in my mother's womb.
¹⁴I praise you because I am fearfully and wonderfully
      made;
   your works are wonderful,ᵉ
   I know that full well.
¹⁵My frame was not hidden from you
   when I was made in the secret place.
   When I was woven togetherᶠ in the depths of the earth,ᵍ
¹⁶   your eyes saw my unformed body.
   All the days ordained for me
      were written in your book
      before one of them came to be.

¹⁷How precious toᵃ me are your thoughts, O God!ʰ
   How vast is the sum of them!
¹⁸Were I to count them,
   they would outnumber the grains of sand.
   When I awake,
   I am still with you.

¹⁹If only you would slay the wicked,ⁱ O God!
   Away from me,ʲ you bloodthirsty men!
²⁰They speak of you with evil intent;
   your adversaries misuse your name.ᵏ
²¹Do I not hate thoseˡ who hate you, O LORD,
   and abhor those who rise up against you?
²²I have nothing but hatred for them;
   I count them my enemies.

²³Search me,ᵐ O God, and know my heart;ⁿ
   test me and know my anxious thoughts.
²⁴See if there is any offensive way in me,
   and lead meᵒ in the way everlasting.

ᵃ 17 Or concerning

| 139:10 |
| ᵃ Ps 23:3 |

| 139:12 |
| ᵇ Job 34:22; Da 2:22 |

| 139:13 |
| ᶜ Ps 119:73 |
| ᵈ Job 10:11 |

| 139:14 |
| ᵉ Ps 40:5 |

| 139:15 |
| ᶠ Job 10:11 |
| ᵍ Ps 63:9 |

| 139:17 |
| ʰ Ps 40:5 |

| 139:19 |
| ⁱ Isa 11:4 |
| ʲ Ps 119:115 |

| 139:20 |
| ᵏ Jude 15 |

| 139:21 |
| ˡ 2Ch 19:2; Ps 31:6; 119:113; Ps 119:158 |

| 139:23 |
| ᵐ Job 31:6; Ps 26:2 |
| ⁿ Jer 11:20 |

| 139:24 |
| ᵒ Ps 5:8; 143:10; Pr 15:9 |

Psalm 140

For the director of music. A psalm of David.

Psalm 140 Theme _____

[1] Rescue me,[a] O L<small>ORD</small>, from evil men;
   protect me from men of violence,[b]

[2] who devise evil plans[c] in their hearts
   and stir up war every day.

[3] They make their tongues as sharp as[d] a serpent's;
   the poison of vipers[e] is on their lips.   *Selah*

[4] Keep me,[f] O L<small>ORD</small>, from the hands of the wicked;[g]
   protect me from men of violence
   who plan to trip my feet.

[5] Proud men have hidden a snare for me;
   they have spread out the cords of their net
   and have set traps[h] for me along my path.   *Selah*

[6] O L<small>ORD</small>, I say to you, "You are my God."[i]
   Hear, O L<small>ORD</small>, my cry for mercy.[j]

[7] O Sovereign L<small>ORD</small>,[k] my strong deliverer,
   who shields my head in the day of battle—

[8] do not grant the wicked[l] their desires, O L<small>ORD</small>;
   do not let their plans succeed,
   or they will become proud.   *Selah*

[9] Let the heads of those who surround me
   be covered with the trouble their lips have caused.[m]

[10] Let burning coals fall upon them;
   may they be thrown into the fire,[n]
   into miry pits, never to rise.

[11] Let slanderers not be established in the land;
   may disaster hunt down men of violence.[o]

[12] I know that the L<small>ORD</small> secures justice for the poor
   and upholds the cause[p] of the needy.[q]

[13] Surely the righteous will praise your name[r]
   and the upright will live[s] before you.

Psalm 141

A psalm of David.

Psalm 141 Theme _____

[1] O L<small>ORD</small>, I call to you; come quickly[t] to me.
   Hear my voice[u] when I call to you.

²May my prayer be set before you like incense;^a
    may the lifting up of my hands^b be like the evening
        sacrifice.^c

³Set a guard over my mouth, O Lord;
    keep watch over the door of my lips.
⁴Let not my heart be drawn to what is evil,
    to take part in wicked deeds
with men who are evildoers;
    let me not eat of their delicacies.^d

⁵Let a righteous man^a strike me—it is a kindness;
    let him rebuke me^e—it is oil on my head.^f
    My head will not refuse it.

Yet my prayer is ever against the deeds of evildoers;
⁶ their rulers will be thrown down from the cliffs,
    and the wicked will learn that my words were
        well spoken.
⁷⌊They will say,⌋ "As one plows and breaks up the earth,
    so our bones have been scattered at the mouth^g of
        the grave.^b"

⁸But my eyes are fixed^h on you, O Sovereign Lord;
    in you I take refugeⁱ—do not give me over to death.
⁹Keep me^j from the snares they have laid for me,
    from the traps set^k by evildoers.
¹⁰Let the wicked fall^l into their own nets,
    while I pass by in safety.

Psalm 142

A *maskil*^c of David. When he was in the cave. A prayer.

Psalm 142 Theme

¹I cry aloud to the Lord;
    I lift up my voice to the Lord for mercy.^m
²I pour out my complaintⁿ before him;
    before him I tell my trouble.

³When my spirit grows faint^o within me,
    it is you who know my way.
In the path where I walk
    men have hidden a snare for me.

^a5 Or *Let the Righteous One*   ^b7 Hebrew *Sheol*   ^cTitle: Probably a literary or musical term

---

141:2
^aRev 5:8; 8:3
^b1Ti 2:8
^cEx 29:39,41

141:4
^dPr 23:6

141:5
^ePr 9:8
^fPs 23:5

141:7
^gPs 53:5

141:8
^hPs 25:15
ⁱPs 2:12

141:9
^jPs 140:4
^kPs 38:12

141:10
^lPs 35:8

142:1
^mPs 30:8

142:2
ⁿIsa 26:16

142:3
^oPs 140:5;
143:4,7

142:4
a Ps 31:11;
Jer 30:17

⁴Look to my right and see;
    no one is concerned for me.
I have no refuge;
    no one cares*a* for my life.

142:5
b Ps 46:1
c Ps 16:5
d Ps 27:13

⁵I cry to you, O LORD;
    I say, "You are my refuge,*b*
    my portion*c* in the land of the living."*d*
⁶Listen to my cry,*e*
    for I am in desperate need;*f*
rescue me from those who pursue me,
    for they are too strong for me.

142:6
e Ps 17:1
f Ps 79:8; 116:6

⁷Set me free from my prison,*g*
    that I may praise your name.

Then the righteous will gather about me
    because of your goodness to me.*h*

142:7
g Ps 146:7
h Ps 13:6

Psalm 143

A psalm of David.

143:1
i Ps 140:6
j Ps 89:1-2
k Ps 71:2

Psalm 143 Theme _____

¹O LORD, hear my prayer,
    listen to my cry for mercy;*i*
in your faithfulness*j* and righteousness*k*
    come to my relief.

143:2
l Ps 14:3;
Ecc 7:20;
Ro 3:20

²Do not bring your servant into judgment,
    for no one living is righteous*l* before you.

³The enemy pursues me,
    he crushes me to the ground;
he makes me dwell in darkness
    like those long dead.

143:4
m Ps 142:3

⁴So my spirit grows faint within me;
    my heart within me is dismayed.*m*

143:5
n Ps 77:6

⁵I remember*n* the days of long ago;
    I meditate on all your works
    and consider what your hands have done.

143:6
o Ps 63:1; 88:9

⁶I spread out my hands*o* to you;
    my soul thirsts for you like a parched land.   *Selah*

⁷Answer me quickly,*p* O LORD;
    my spirit fails.
Do not hide your face*q* from me
    or I will be like those who go down to the pit.

143:7
p Ps 69:17
q Ps 27:9; 28:1

⁸Let the morning bring me word of your unfailing love,ᵃ
    for I have put my trust in you.
Show me the wayᵇ I should go,
    for to you I lift up my soul.ᶜ
⁹Rescue me from my enemies,ᵈ O LORD,
    for I hide myself in you.
¹⁰Teach me to do your will,
    for you are my God;
may your good Spirit
    leadᵉ me on level ground.

¹¹For your name's sake, O LORD, preserve my life;ᶠ
    in your righteousness,ᵍ bring me out of trouble.
¹²In your unfailing love, silence my enemies;
    destroy all my foes,ʰ
    for I am your servant.ⁱ

Psalm 144

Of David.

Psalm 144 Theme

¹Praise be to the LORD my Rock,ʲ
    who trains my hands for war,
    my fingers for battle.
²He is my loving God and my fortress,ᵏ
    my stronghold and my deliverer,
my shield,ˡ in whom I take refuge,
    who subdues peoplesᵃ under me.

³O LORD, what is manᵐ that you care for him,
    the son of man that you think of him?
⁴Man is like a breath;
    his days are like a fleeting shadow.ⁿ

⁵Part your heavens,ᵒ O LORD, and come down;
    touch the mountains, so that they smoke.ᵖ
⁶Send forth lightning and scatter ⌊the enemies⌋;
    shoot your arrows�q and rout them.
⁷Reach down your hand from on high;
    deliver me and rescue me
from the mighty waters,ʳ
    from the hands of foreignersˢ

ᵃ2 Many manuscripts of the Masoretic Text, Dead Sea Scrolls, Aquila, Jerome and Syriac; most manuscripts of the Masoretic Text *subdues my people*

143:8
ᵃPs 46:5; 90:14
ᵇPs 27:11
ᶜPs 25:1-2

143:9
ᵈPs 31:15

143:10
ᵉNe 9:20;
Ps 23:3; 25:4-5

143:11
ᶠPs 119:25
ᵍPs 31:1

143:12
ʰPs 52:5; 54:5
ⁱPs 116:16

144:1
ʲPs 18:2,34

144:2
ᵏPs 59:9; 91:2
ˡPs 84:9

144:3
ᵐPs 8:4;
Heb 2:6

144:4
ⁿPs 39:11;
102:11

144:5
ᵒPs 18:9;
Isa 64:1
ᵖPs 104:32

144:6
qPs 7:12-13;
18:14

144:7
ʳPs 69:2
ˢPs 18:44

144:8
a Ps 12:2

⁸whose mouths are full of lies,^a
    whose right hands are deceitful.

⁹I will sing a new song to you, O God;
    on the ten-stringed lyre^b I will make music to you,
¹⁰to the One who gives victory to kings,
    who delivers his servant David^c from the
        deadly sword.

144:9
b Ps 33:2-3

144:10
c Ps 18:50

¹¹Deliver me and rescue me
    from the hands of foreigners
  whose mouths are full of lies,
    whose right hands are deceitful.^d

144:11
d Ps 12:2;
Isa 44:20

¹²Then our sons in their youth
    will be like well-nurtured plants,^e
  and our daughters will be like pillars
    carved to adorn a palace.
¹³Our barns will be filled
    with every kind of provision.
  Our sheep will increase by thousands,
    by tens of thousands in our fields;
¹⁴ our oxen will draw heavy loads.^a
  There will be no breaching of walls,
    no going into captivity,
    no cry of distress in our streets.

144:12
e Ps 128:3

144:15
f Ps 33:12

¹⁵Blessed are the people^f of whom this is true;
    blessed are the people whose God is the Lord.

Psalm 145^b

A psalm of praise. Of David.

145:1
g Ps 30:1; 34:1
h Ps 5:2

Psalm 145 Theme _____

145:2
i Ps 71:6

¹I will exalt you,^g my God the King;^h
  I will praise your name for ever and ever.
²Every day I will praiseⁱ you
    and extol your name for ever and ever.

145:3
j Job 5:9;
Ps 147:5;
Ro 11:33

³Great is the Lord and most worthy of praise;
    his greatness no one can fathom.^j
⁴One generation^k will commend your works to another;
    they will tell of your mighty acts.

145:4
k Isa 38:19

a 14 Or *our chieftains will be firmly established*   *b* This psalm is an acrostic poem, the verses of
which (including verse 13b) begin with the successive letters of the Hebrew alphabet.

⁵They will speak of the glorious splendor of your majesty,
    and I will meditate on your wonderful works.ᵃ ᵃ
⁶They will tell of the power of your awesome works,ᵇ
    and I will proclaimᶜ your great deeds.
⁷They will celebrate your abundant goodnessᵈ
    and joyfully sing of your righteousness.ᵉ

⁸The LORD is gracious and compassionate,ᶠ
    slow to anger and rich in love.ᵍ
⁹The LORD is goodʰ to all;
    he has compassion on all he has made.
¹⁰All you have made will praise you,ⁱ O LORD;
    your saints will extol you.ʲ
¹¹They will tell of the glory of your kingdom
    and speak of your might,
¹²so that all men may know of your mighty actsᵏ
    and the glorious splendor of your kingdom.
¹³Your kingdom is an everlasting kingdom,ˡ
    and your dominion endures through all generations.

The LORD is faithful to all his promises
    and loving toward all he has made.ᵇ
¹⁴The LORD upholdsᵐ all those who fall
    and lifts up allⁿ who are bowed down.
¹⁵The eyes of all look to you,
    and you give them their foodᵒ at the proper time.
¹⁶You open your hand
    and satisfy the desiresᵖ of every living thing.

¹⁷The LORD is righteous in all his ways
    and loving toward all he has made.
¹⁸The LORD is nearᑫ to all who call on him,ʳ
    to all who call on him in truth.
¹⁹He fulfills the desiresˢ of those who fear him;
    he hears their cryᵗ and saves them.
²⁰The LORD watches over all who love him,ᵘ
    but all the wicked he will destroy.ᵛ

²¹My mouth will speakʷ in praise of the LORD.
    Let every creatureˣ praise his holy name
    for ever and ever.

ᵃ5 Dead Sea Scrolls and Syriac (see also Septuagint); Masoretic Text *On the glorious splendor of your majesty / and on your wonderful works I will meditate*   ᵇ13 One manuscript of the Masoretic Text, Dead Sea Scrolls and Syriac (see also Septuagint); most manuscripts of the Masoretic Text do not have the last two lines of verse 13.

145:5
ᵃPs 119:27

145:6
ᵇPs 66:3
ᶜDt 32:3

145:7
ᵈIsa 63:7
ᵉPs 51:14

145:8
ᶠPs 86:15
ᵍEx 34:6;
Nu 14:18

145:9
ʰPs 100:5

145:10
ⁱPs 19:1
ʲPs 68:26

145:12
ᵏPs 105:1

145:13
ˡ1Ti 1:17;
2Pe 1:11

145:14
ᵐPs 37:24
ⁿPs 146:8

145:15
ᵒPs 104:27;
136:25

145:16
ᵖPs 104:28

145:18
ᑫDt 4:7
ʳJn 4:24

145:19
ˢPs 37:4
ᵗPr 15:29

145:20
ᵘPs 31:23; 97:10
ᵛPs 9:5

145:21
ʷPs 71:8
ˣPs 65:2

Psalm 146

146:1
a Ps 103:1

Psalm 146 Theme _____

146:2
b Ps 104:33

¹Praise the Lord.ᵃ

Praise the Lord,ᵃ O my soul.
2   I will praise the Lord all my life;ᵇ
    I will sing praise to my God as long as I live.

146:3
c Ps 118:9
d Isa 2:22

³Do not put your trust in princes,ᶜ
    in mortal men,ᵈ who cannot save.
⁴When their spirit departs, they return to the ground;ᵉ
    on that very day their plans come to nothing.ᶠ

146:4
e Ps 104:29;
Ecc 12:7
f Ps 33:10;
1Co 2:6

⁵Blessed is heᵍ whose helpʰ is the God of Jacob,
    whose hope is in the Lord his God,

146:5
g Ps 144:15;
Jer 17:7
h Ps 71:5

⁶the Maker of heavenⁱ and earth,
    the sea, and everything in them—
    the Lord, who remains faithfulʲ forever.
⁷He upholds the cause of the oppressedᵏ
    and gives food to the hungry.ˡ

146:6
i Ps 115:15;
Ac 14:15;
Rev 14:7
j Ps 117:2

The Lord sets prisoners free,ᵐ
8   the Lord gives sight to the blind,ⁿ
the Lord lifts up those who are bowed down,
    the Lord loves the righteous.
⁹The Lord watches over the alien

146:7
k Ps 103:6
l Ps 107:9
m Ps 68:6

    and sustains the fatherless and the widow,ᵒ
    but he frustrates the ways of the wicked.

¹⁰The Lord reignsᵖ forever,
    your God, O Zion, for all generations.

146:8
n Mt 9:30

Praise the Lord.

Psalm 147

146:9
o Ex 22:22;
Dt 10:18;
Ps 68:5

Psalm 147 Theme _____

146:10
p Ex 15:18;
Ps 10:16

¹Praise the Lord.ᵇ

How good it is to sing praises to our God,
    how pleasant�q and fitting to praise him!ʳ

147:1
q Ps 135:3
r Ps 33:1

²The Lord builds up Jerusalem;ˢ
    he gathers the exilesᵗ of Israel.
³He heals the brokenhearted
    and binds up their wounds.

147:2
s Ps 102:16
t Dt 30:3

a 1 Hebrew *Hallelu Yah*; also in verse 10   b 1 Hebrew *Hallelu Yah*; also in verse 20

[4]He determines the number of the stars[a]
and calls them each by name.
[5]Great is our Lord[b] and mighty in power;
his understanding has no limit.[c]
[6]The LORD sustains the humble[d]
but casts the wicked to the ground.

[7]Sing to the LORD[e] with thanksgiving;
make music to our God on the harp.
[8]He covers the sky with clouds;
he supplies the earth with rain[f]
and makes grass grow[g] on the hills.
[9]He provides food[h] for the cattle
and for the young ravens[i] when they call.

[10]His pleasure is not in the strength[j] of the horse,[k]
nor his delight in the legs of a man;
[11]the LORD delights in those who fear him,
who put their hope in his unfailing love.

[12]Extol the LORD, O Jerusalem;
praise your God, O Zion,
[13]for he strengthens the bars of your gates
and blesses your people within you.
[14]He grants peace[l] to your borders
and satisfies you[m] with the finest of wheat.

[15]He sends his command[n] to the earth;
his word runs swiftly.
[16]He spreads the snow[o] like wool
and scatters the frost[p] like ashes.
[17]He hurls down his hail like pebbles.
Who can withstand his icy blast?
[18]He sends his word[q] and melts them;
he stirs up his breezes, and the waters flow.

[19]He has revealed his word to Jacob,
his laws and decrees[r] to Israel.
[20]He has done this for no other nation;[s]
they do not know his laws.

Praise the LORD.

Psalm 148

Psalm 148 Theme _____

[1]Praise the LORD.[a]

Praise the LORD from the heavens,

a1 Hebrew *Hallelu Yah*; also in verse 14

147:4
[a] Isa 40:26

147:5
[b] Ps 48:1
[c] Isa 40:28

147:6
[d] Ps 146:8-9

147:7
[e] Ps 33:3

147:8
[f] Job 38:26
[g] Ps 104:14

147:9
[h] Ps 104:27-28;
Mt 6:26
[i] Job 38:41

147:10
[j] 1Sa 16:7
[k] Ps 33:16-17

147:14
[l] Isa 60:17-18
[m] Ps 132:15

147:15
[n] Job 37:12

147:16
[o] Job 37:6
[p] Job 38:29

147:18
[q] Ps 33:9

147:19
[r] Dt 33:4;
Mal 4:4

147:20
[s] Dt 4:7-8,32-34

praise him in the heights above.
²Praise him, all his angels,[a]
praise him, all his heavenly hosts.
³Praise him, sun and moon,
praise him, all you shining stars.
⁴Praise him, you highest heavens
and you waters above the skies.[b]
⁵Let them praise the name of the LORD,
for he commanded[c] and they were created.
⁶He set them in place for ever and ever;
he gave a decree[d] that will never pass away.

⁷Praise the LORD from the earth,
you great sea creatures[e] and all ocean depths,
⁸lightning and hail, snow and clouds,
stormy winds that do his bidding,[f]
⁹you mountains and all hills,[g]
fruit trees and all cedars,
¹⁰wild animals and all cattle,
small creatures and flying birds,
¹¹kings of the earth and all nations,
you princes and all rulers on earth,
¹²young men and maidens,
old men and children.

¹³Let them praise the name of the LORD,[h]
for his name alone is exalted;
his splendor is above the earth and the heavens.[i]
¹⁴He has raised up for his people a horn,[a][j]
the praise of all his saints,
of Israel, the people close to his heart.

Praise the LORD.

Psalm 149

Psalm 149 Theme _____

¹Praise the LORD.[b][k]

Sing to the LORD a new song,
his praise in the assembly[l] of the saints.

²Let Israel rejoice in their Maker;[m]
let the people of Zion be glad in their King.[n]
³Let them praise his name with dancing
and make music to him with tambourine and harp.[o]

**Cross references (left margin):**

148:2 a Ps 103:20

148:4 b Ge 1:7; 1Ki 8:27

148:5 c Ge 1:1,6; Ps 33:6,9

148:6 d Job 38:33; Ps 89:37; Jer 33:25

148:7 e Ps 74:13-14

148:8 f Ps 147:15-18

148:9 g Isa 44:23; 49:13; 55:12

148:13 h Isa 12:4 i Ps 8:1; 113:4

148:14 j Ps 75:10

149:1 k Ps 33:2 l Ps 35:18

149:2 m Ps 95:6 n Ps 47:6; Zec 9:9

149:3 o Ps 81:2; 150:4

a 14 *Horn* here symbolizes strong one, that is, king.   b 1 Hebrew *Hallelu Yah*; also in verse 9

⁴For the LORD takes delight[a] in his people;
  he crowns the humble with salvation.[b]
⁵Let the saints rejoice[c] in this honor
  and sing for joy on their beds.[d]

⁶May the praise of God be in their mouths[e]
  and a double-edged[f] sword in their hands,
⁷to inflict vengeance on the nations
  and punishment on the peoples,
⁸to bind their kings with fetters,
  their nobles with shackles of iron,
⁹to carry out the sentence written against them.[g]
  This is the glory of all his saints.[h]

Praise the LORD.

Psalm 150

Psalm 150 Theme _____

¹Praise the LORD.[a]

Praise God in his sanctuary;[i]
  praise him in his mighty heavens.[j]
²Praise him for his acts of power;[k]
  praise him for his surpassing greatness.[l]
³Praise him with the sounding of the trumpet,
  praise him with the harp and lyre,[m]
⁴praise him with tambourine and dancing,[n]
  praise him with the strings[o] and flute,
⁵praise him with the clash of cymbals,[p]
  praise him with resounding cymbals.

⁶Let everything[q] that has breath praise the LORD.

Praise the LORD.

a 1 Hebrew *Hallelu Yah*; also in verse 6

149:4
a Ps 35:27
b Ps 132:16

149:5
c Ps 132:16
d Job 35:10

149:6
e Ps 66:17
f Heb 4:12;
Rev 1:16

149:9
g Dt 7:1;
Eze 28:26
h Ps 148:14

150:1
i Ps 102:19
j Ps 19:1

150:2
k Dt 3:24
l Ps 145:5-6

150:3
m Ps 149:3

150:4
n Ex 15:20
o Isa 38:20

150:5
p 1Ch 13:8;
15:16

150:6
q Ps 145:21

Theme of Psalms:

SEGMENT DIVISIONS

		CHAPTER THEMES
		1
		2
		3
		4
		5
		6
		7
		8
		9
		10
		11
		12
		13
		14
		15
		16
		17
		18
		19
		20
		21
		22
		23
		24
		25

Author:

Date:

Purpose:

Key Words:

		CHAPTER THEMES
		26
		27
		28
		29
		30
		31
		32
		33
		34
		35
		36
		37
		38
		39
		40
		41
		42
		43
		44
		45
		46
		47
		48
		49
		50

		CHAPTER THEMES
		51
		52
		53
		54
		55
		56
		57
		58
		59
		60
		61
		62
		63
		64
		65
		66
		67
		68
		69
		70
		71
		72
		73
		74
		75

		CHAPTER THEMES
		76
		77
		78
		79
		80
		81
		82
		83
		84
		85
		86
		87
		88
		89
		90
		91
		92
		93
		94
		95
		96
		97
		98
		99
		100

SEGMENT DIVISIONS

			CHAPTER THEMES
		101	
		102	
		103	
		104	
		105	
		106	
		107	
		108	
		109	
		110	
		111	
		112	
		113	
		114	
		115	
		116	
		117	
		118	
		119	
		120	
		121	
		122	
		123	
		124	
		125	

			Chapter Themes
		126	
		127	
		128	
		129	
		130	
		131	
		132	
		133	
		134	
		135	
		136	
		137	
		138	
		139	
		140	
		141	
		142	
		143	
		144	
		145	
		146	
		147	
		148	
		149	
		150	

PROVERBS

When God appeared to King Solomon in a dream, he said, "Ask for whatever you want me to give you." Solomon asked for an understanding heart so that he could lead the nation of Israel (see 1 Kings 3). In response to that prayer "God gave Solomon wisdom and very great insight, and a breadth of understanding as measureless as the sand on the seashore. Solomon's wisdom was greater than the wisdom of all the men of the East, and greater than all the wisdom of Egypt. He was wiser than any other man. . . . He spoke three thousand proverbs" (1 Kings 4:29-32).

A portion of those proverbs has been preserved for us in the book of Proverbs. A proverb is usually a short saying or maxim which gives insight on life and human behavior.

The book of Proverbs, which is wisdom literature, is a compilation of true sayings which give wisdom and instruction. However, these maxims cannot be interpreted as prophecies, nor can they be held as absolute doctrines. For example, Proverbs says a man's enemies will be at peace with him when his ways please the Lord. We can accept this as a valid proverb which generally proves to be true, though not always. Our Lord's enemies were not at peace with him even though he did only those things which pleased the Father.

The Proverbs are inspired by God. Don't rush through them. Give yourself time for meditation and application. Although Proverbs was written between 971 and 686 B.C., the sayings are timeless. They can equip you for life in the home and the marketplace.

∾ THINGS TO DO

1. Proverbs uses figurative language—similes and metaphors. Read the section called "Figures of Speech" on page 2207 before you study Proverbs.

2. Read Proverbs 1:1-7 and note the author, purpose, and theme of the book in the margin of chapter 1. As you look for the purpose, watch the repeated use of *for*. The theme is also repeated in 9:10. Record these insights on the PROVERBS AT A GLANCE chart on page 1120.

3. A wise person appreciates the wisdom of others. Look at PROVERBS AT A GLANCE and note the major segment divisions of this book. You will see that Solomon respected the wisdom of others. Look up the following verses and note whose words or proverbs follow: Proverbs 10:1; 22:17; 25:1; 30:1; 31:1.

4. Mark the key words listed on PROVERBS AT A GLANCE. Keep a list of what you learn about wisdom, especially in the first nine chapters. Note how wisdom is personified. (An abstraction, such as wisdom, is personified when it takes on the characteristics of a person. Proverbs 1:20 is an example.)

5. Watch for and mark the phrase *my son (O son)*. Then listen as if it is God the Father speaking to you, his own dear child whom he wants to show the path of life.

6. Develop a code for marking the subjects covered throughout Proverbs: sexual morality, finances, discipline, the heart, the tongue, the company we keep, etc. As you read through Proverbs repeatedly you will learn more and more about mankind and will find yourself much wiser when it comes to living in the "fear of the Lord." You will have a collection of insights on the critical issues of life.

7. Record the theme or themes of each chapter on PROVERBS AT A GLANCE and in the text next to the chapter number. You may find this difficult between chapters 10 and 29 because the proverbs are short and varied. However, simply listing the major topics of each chapter will help you find the major topics at a glance. Color coding or marking each topic throughout the book will help you easily spot what Proverbs teaches about a particular subject. This will be a great help as you share these truths with others or need wisdom on a specific topic.

1. Are you walking in the fear of the Lord? To fear God is to have an awesome respect of who he is and a reverential trust in his Word and his character, and to live accordingly.

2. Do you rely on your own understanding or do you seek God's wisdom in the matters of every-day life?

3. What do you need to do or change in light of the insight and wisdom you have learned from these proverbs?

4. Since there are 31 chapters in Proverbs, some people read a chapter a day, month after month. This is good as long as you do not neglect other portions of the Word and as long as you give yourself adequate time to meditate on these proverbs.

   a. After chapter 9 many proverbs are only two to four lines long. You may want to choose one or two proverbs a day, evaluating your life and relationships in the light of them.

   b. Or you may want to select a theme you marked throughout Proverbs, list what you learned from the book as a whole, and then meditate on that theme. For example, you might meditate on what you learned about diligence versus laziness, or about the tongue.

∾∾∾∾∾

Chapter 1 Theme

1:1
a 1Ki 4:29-34
b Pr 10:1; 25:1;
Ecc 1:1

1 The proverbs of Solomon[a] son of David, king of Israel:[b]

²for attaining wisdom and discipline;
  for understanding words of insight;

1:4
c Pr 8:5
d Pr 2:10-11;
8:12

³for acquiring a disciplined and prudent life,
  doing what is right and just and fair;

⁴for giving prudence to the simple,[c]
  knowledge and discretion[d] to the young—

1:5
e Pr 9:9

⁵let the wise listen and add to their learning,[e]
  and let the discerning get guidance—

1:6
f Ps 49:4; 78:2
g Nu 12:8

⁶for understanding proverbs and parables,[f]
  the sayings and riddles[g] of the wise.

1:7
h Job 28:28;
Ps 111:10;
Pr 9:10; 15:33;
Ecc 12:13

⁷The fear of the LORD[h] is the beginning of knowledge,
  but fools[a] despise wisdom and discipline.

INSIGHT

To have **knowledge** is to have under-standing or infor-mation about some-thing. To have **wisdom** is to have the ability to apply knowledge to daily life.

⁸Listen, my son,[i] to your father's instruction
  and do not forsake your mother's teaching.[j]

1:8
i Pr 4:1
j Pr 6:20

⁹They will be a garland to grace your head
  and a chain to adorn your neck.[k]

1:9
k Pr 4:1-9

¹⁰My son, if sinners entice[l] you,
  do not give in[m] to them.[n]

1:10
l Ge 39:7
m Dt 13:8
n Pr 16:29;
Eph 5:11

¹¹If they say, "Come along with us;
  let's lie in wait[o] for someone's blood,
  let's waylay some harmless soul;

1:11
o Ps 10:8

a 7 The Hebrew words rendered *fool* in Proverbs, and often elsewhere in the Old Testament, denote one who is morally deficient.

1:12
a Ps 28:1

1:15
b Ps 119:101
c Ps 1:1;
Pr 4:14

1:16
d Pr 6:18;
Isa 59:7

1:19
e Pr 15:27

1:20
f Pr 8:1;
9:1-3,13-15

1:22
g Pr 8:5;
9:4,16

1:24
h Isa 65:12; 66:4;
Jer 7:13;
Zec 7:11

1:26
i Ps 2:4
j Pr 6:15;
10:24

1:28
k 1Sa 8:18;
Isa 1:15;
Jer 11:11;
Mic 3:4
l Job 27:9;
Pr 8:17;
Eze 8:18;
Zec 7:13

1:29
m Job 21:14

1:30
n ver 25;
Ps 81:11

1:31
o Job 4:8;
Pr 14:14;
Isa 3:11;
Jer 6:19

¹²let's swallow them alive, like the grave,^a
   and whole, like those who go down to the pit;^a
¹³we will get all sorts of valuable things
   and fill our houses with plunder;
¹⁴throw in your lot with us,
   and we will share a common purse"—
¹⁵my son, do not go along with them,
   do not set foot^b on their paths;^c
¹⁶for their feet rush into sin,
   they are swift to shed blood.^d
¹⁷How useless to spread a net
   in full view of all the birds!
¹⁸These men lie in wait for their own blood;
   they waylay only themselves!
¹⁹Such is the end of all who go after ill-gotten gain;
   it takes away the lives of those who get it.^e

²⁰Wisdom calls aloud^f in the street,
   she raises her voice in the public squares;
²¹at the head of the noisy streets^b she cries out,
   in the gateways of the city she makes her speech:

²²"How long will you simple ones^{c g} love your simple ways?
   How long will mockers delight in mockery
   and fools hate knowledge?
²³If you had responded to my rebuke,
   I would have poured out my heart to you
   and made my thoughts known to you.
²⁴But since you rejected me when I called^h
   and no one gave heed when I stretched out my hand,
²⁵since you ignored all my advice
   and would not accept my rebuke,
²⁶I in turn will laughⁱ at your disaster;
   I will mock when calamity overtakes you^j—
²⁷when calamity overtakes you like a storm,
   when disaster sweeps over you like a whirlwind,
   when distress and trouble overwhelm you.

²⁸"Then they will call to me but I will not answer;^k
   they will look for me but will not find me.^l
²⁹Since they hated knowledge
   and did not choose to fear the Lord,^m
³⁰since they would not accept my advice
   and spurned my rebuke,ⁿ
³¹they will eat the fruit of their ways
   and be filled with the fruit of their schemes.^o

^a12 Hebrew *Sheol*   ^b21 Hebrew; Septuagint / *on the tops of the walls*   ^c22 The Hebrew word rendered *simple* in Proverbs generally denotes one without moral direction and inclined to evil.

³²For the waywardness of the simple will kill them,
  and the complacency of fools will destroy them;ᵃ
³³but whoever listens to me will live in safetyᵇ
  and be at ease, without fear of harm."ᶜ

Chapter 2 Theme

2 My son, if you accept my words
  and store up my commands within you,
²turning your ear to wisdom
  and applying your heart to understanding,ᵈ
³and if you call out for insight
  and cry aloud for understanding,
⁴and if you look for it as for silver
  and search for it as for hidden treasure,ᵉ
⁵then you will understand the fear of the Lord
  and find the knowledge of God.ᶠ
⁶For the Lord gives wisdom,ᵍ
  and from his mouth come knowledge and
    understanding.
⁷He holds victory in store for the upright,
  he is a shieldʰ to those whose walk is blameless,ⁱ
⁸for he guards the course of the just
  and protects the way of his faithful ones.ʲ

⁹Then you will understand what is right and just
  and fair—every good path.
¹⁰For wisdom will enter your heart,ᵏ
  and knowledge will be pleasant to your soul.
¹¹Discretion will protect you,
  and understanding will guard you.ˡ

¹²Wisdom will save you from the ways of wicked men,
  from men whose words are perverse,
¹³who leave the straight paths
  to walk in dark ways,ᵐ
¹⁴who delight in doing wrong
  and rejoice in the perverseness of evil,ⁿ
¹⁵whose paths are crookedᵒ
  and who are devious in their ways.ᵖ

¹⁶It will save you also from the adulteress,�q
  from the wayward wife with her seductive words,
¹⁷who has left the partner of her youth
  and ignored the covenant she made before God.ᵃʳ
¹⁸For her house leads down to death
  and her paths to the spirits of the dead.ˢ

ᵃ17 Or covenant of her God

1:32
ᵃ Jer 2:19

1:33
ᵇ Ps 25:12;
Pr 3:23
ᶜ Ps 112:8

2:2
ᵈ Pr 22:17

2:4
ᵉ Job 3:21;
Pr 3:14;
Mt 13:44

2:5
ᶠ Pr 1:7

2:6
ᵍ 1Ki 3:9,12;
Jas 1:5

2:7
ʰ Pr 30:5-6
ⁱ Ps 84:11

2:8
ʲ 1Sa 2:9;
Ps 66:9

2:10
ᵏ Pr 14:33

2:11
ˡ Pr 4:6; 6:22

2:13
ᵐ Pr 4:19;
Jn 3:19

2:14
ⁿ Pr 10:23;
Jer 11:15

2:15
ᵒ Ps 125:5
ᵖ Pr 21:8

2:16
q Pr 5:1-6;
6:20-29;
7:5-27

2:17
ʳ Mal 2:14

2:18
ˢ Pr 7:27

2:19
a Ecc 7:26

2:21
b Ps 37:29

2:22
c Job 18:17;
Ps 37:38
d Dt 28:63;
Pr 10:30

3:1
e Pr 4:5

3:2
f Pr 4:10

3:3
g Ex 13:9;
Pr 6:21; 7:3;
2Co 3:3

3:4
h 1Sa 2:26;
Lk 2:52

3:5
i Ps 37:3,5

3:6
j 1Ch 28:9
k Pr 16:3;
Isa 45:13

3:7
l Ro 12:16
m Job 1:1;
Pr 16:6

3:8
n Pr 4:22
o Job 21:24

3:9
p Ex 22:29;
23:19;
Dt 26:1-15

3:10
q Dt 28:8
r Joel 2:24

3:11
s Job 5:17

3:12
t Pr 13:24;
Rev 3:19
u Dt 8:5;
Heb 12:5-6*

3:14
v Job 28:15;
Pr 8:19; 16:16

3:15
w Job 28:18
x Pr 8:11

¹⁹None who go to her return
   or attain the paths of life.*a*

²⁰Thus you will walk in the ways of good men
   and keep to the paths of the righteous.
²¹For the upright will live in the land,*b*
   and the blameless will remain in it;
²²but the wicked will be cut off from the land,*c*
   and the unfaithful will be torn from it.*d*

Chapter 3 Theme

3 My son, do not forget my teaching,*e*
   but keep my commands in your heart,
²for they will prolong your life many years*f*
   and bring you prosperity.

³Let love and faithfulness never leave you;
   bind them around your neck,
   write them on the tablet of your heart.*g*
⁴Then you will win favor and a good name
   in the sight of God and man.*h*

⁵Trust in the Lord*i* with all your heart
   and lean not on your own understanding;
⁶in all your ways acknowledge him,
   and he will make your paths*j* straight.*a k*

⁷Do not be wise in your own eyes;*l*
   fear the Lord and shun evil.*m*
⁸This will bring health to your body*n*
   and nourishment to your bones.*o*

⁹Honor the Lord with your wealth,
   with the firstfruits*p* of all your crops;
¹⁰then your barns will be filled*q* to overflowing,
   and your vats will brim over with new wine.*r*

¹¹My son, do not despise the Lord's discipline*s*
   and do not resent his rebuke,
¹²because the Lord disciplines those he loves,*t*
   as a father*b* the son he delights in.*u*

¹³Blessed is the man who finds wisdom,
   the man who gains understanding,
¹⁴for she is more profitable than silver
   and yields better returns than gold.*v*
¹⁵She is more precious than rubies;*w*
   nothing you desire can compare with her.*x*

a 6 Or *will direct your paths*   *b* 12 Hebrew; Septuagint / *and he punishes*

¹⁶Long life is in her right hand;
　　in her left hand are riches and honor.^a
¹⁷Her ways are pleasant ways,
　　and all her paths are peace.^b
¹⁸She is a tree of life^c to those who embrace her;
　　those who lay hold of her will be blessed.

¹⁹By wisdom the LORD laid the earth's foundations,^d
　　by understanding he set the heavens^e in place;
²⁰by his knowledge the deeps were divided,
　　and the clouds let drop the dew.

²¹My son, preserve sound judgment and discernment,
　　do not let them out of your sight;^f
²²they will be life for you,
　　an ornament to grace your neck.^g
²³Then you will go on your way in safety,
　　and your foot will not stumble;^h
²⁴when you lie down,ⁱ you will not be afraid;
　　when you lie down, your sleep^j will be sweet.
²⁵Have no fear of sudden disaster
　　or of the ruin that overtakes the wicked,
²⁶for the LORD will be your confidence
　　and will keep your foot^k from being snared.

²⁷Do not withhold good from those who deserve it,
　　when it is in your power to act.
²⁸Do not say to your neighbor,
　　"Come back later; I'll give it tomorrow"—
　　when you now have it with you.^l

²⁹Do not plot harm against your neighbor,
　　who lives trustfully near you.
³⁰Do not accuse a man for no reason—
　　when he has done you no harm.

³¹Do not envy^m a violent man
　　or choose any of his ways,
³²for the LORD detests a perverse manⁿ
　　but takes the upright into his confidence.^o

³³The LORD's curse^p is on the house of the wicked,^q
　　but he blesses the home of the righteous.^r
³⁴He mocks proud mockers
　　but gives grace to the humble.^s
³⁵The wise inherit honor,
　　but fools he holds up to shame.

3:16
a Pr 8:18

3:17
b Pr 16:7;
Mt 11:28-30

3:18
c Ge 2:9;
Pr 11:30;
Rev 2:7

3:19
d Ps 104:24
e Pr 8:27-29

3:21
f Pr 4:20-22

3:22
g Pr 1:8-9

3:23
h Ps 37:24;
Pr 4:12

3:24
i Lev 26:6;
Ps 3:5
j Job 11:18

3:26
k 1Sa 2:9

3:28
l Lev 19:13;
Dt 24:15

3:31
m Ps 37:1;
Pr 24:1-2

3:32
n Pr 11:20
o Job 29:4;
Ps 25:14

3:33
p Dt 11:28;
Mal 2:2
q Zec 5:4
r Ps 1:3

3:34
s Jas 4:6*;
1Pe 5:5*

Chapter 4 Theme _____

4 Listen, my sons,*ᵃ* to a father's instruction;
pay attention and gain understanding.
²I give you sound learning,
so do not forsake my teaching.
³When I was a boy in my father's house,
still tender, and an only child of my mother,
⁴he taught me and said,
"Lay hold of my words with all your heart;
keep my commands and you will live.*ᵇ*
⁵Get wisdom,*ᶜ* get understanding;
do not forget my words or swerve from them.
⁶Do not forsake wisdom, and she will protect you;*ᵈ*
love her, and she will watch over you.
⁷Wisdom is supreme; therefore get wisdom.
Though it cost all*ᵉ* you have,*ᵃ* get understanding.*ᶠ*
⁸Esteem her, and she will exalt you;
embrace her, and she will honor you.*ᵍ*
⁹She will set a garland of grace on your head
and present you with a crown of splendor.*ʰ*"

¹⁰Listen, my son, accept what I say,
and the years of your life will be many.*ⁱ*
¹¹I guide*ʲ* you in the way of wisdom
and lead you along straight paths.
¹²When you walk, your steps will not be hampered;
when you run, you will not stumble.*ᵏ*
¹³Hold on to instruction, do not let it go;
guard it well, for it is your life.*ˡ*
¹⁴Do not set foot on the path of the wicked
or walk in the way of evil men.*ᵐ*
¹⁵Avoid it, do not travel on it;
turn from it and go on your way.
¹⁶For they cannot sleep till they do evil;*ⁿ*
they are robbed of slumber till they make someone fall.
¹⁷They eat the bread of wickedness
and drink the wine of violence.

¹⁸The path of the righteous*ᵒ* is like the first gleam of dawn,
shining ever brighter till the full light of day.*ᵖ*
¹⁹But the way of the wicked is like deep darkness;*�q*
they do not know what makes them stumble.

²⁰My son, pay attention to what I say;
listen closely to my words.*ʳ*

4:4
b Pr 7:2

4:5
c Pr 16:16

4:6
d 2Th 2:10

4:7
e Mt 13:44-46
f Pr 23:23

4:8
g 1Sa 2:30;
Pr 3:18

4:9
h Pr 1:8-9

4:10
i Pr 3:2

4:11
j 1Sa 12:23

4:12
k Job 18:7;
Pr 3:23

4:13
l Pr 3:22

4:14
m Ps 1:1;
Pr 1:15

4:16
n Ps 36:4;
Mic 2:1

4:18
o Isa 26:7
p 2Sa 23:4;
Da 12:3;
Mt 5:14;
Php 2:15

4:19
q Job 18:5;
Pr 2:13;
Isa 59:9-10;
Jn 12:35

4:20
r Pr 5:1

*ᵃ*7 Or *Whatever else you get*

²¹Do not let them out of your sight,^a
    keep them within your heart;
²²for they are life to those who find them
    and health to a man's whole body.^b
²³Above all else, guard your heart,
    for it is the wellspring of life.^c
²⁴Put away perversity from your mouth;
    keep corrupt talk far from your lips.
²⁵Let your eyes look straight ahead,
    fix your gaze directly before you.
²⁶Make level^a paths for your feet^d
    and take only ways that are firm.
²⁷Do not swerve to the right or the left;^e
    keep your foot from evil.

Chapter 5 Theme

5 My son, pay attention to my wisdom,
    listen well to my words^f of insight,
²that you may maintain discretion
    and your lips may preserve knowledge.
³For the lips of an adulteress drip honey,
    and her speech is smoother than oil;^g
⁴but in the end she is bitter as gall,^h
    sharp as a double-edged sword.
⁵Her feet go down to death;
    her steps lead straight to the grave.^{bi}
⁶She gives no thought to the way of life;
    her paths are crooked, but she knows it not.^j

⁷Now then, my sons, listen^k to me;
    do not turn aside from what I say.
⁸Keep to a path far from her,^l
    do not go near the door of her house,
⁹lest you give your best strength to others
    and your years to one who is cruel,
¹⁰lest strangers feast on your wealth
    and your toil enrich another man's house.
¹¹At the end of your life you will groan,
    when your flesh and body are spent.
¹²You will say, "How I hated discipline!
    How my heart spurned correction!^m
¹³I would not obey my teachers
    or listen to my instructors.
¹⁴I have come to the brink of utter ruin
    in the midst of the whole assembly."

---

a 26 Or Consider the   *b 5 Hebrew Sheol*

4:21
a Pr 3:21;
7:1-2

4:22
b Pr 3:8;
12:18

4:23
c Mt 12:34;
Lk 6:45

4:26
d Heb 12:13*

4:27
e Dt 5:32; 28:14

5:1
f Pr 4:20; 22:17

5:3
g Ps 55:21;
Pr 2:16; 7:5

5:4
h Ecc 7:26

5:5
i Pr 7:26-27

5:6
j Pr 30:20

5:7
k Pr 7:24

5:8
l Pr 7:1-27

5:12
m Pr 1:29; 12:1

¹⁵Drink water from your own cistern,
running water from your own well.
¹⁶Should your springs overflow in the streets,
your streams of water in the public squares?

¹⁷Let them be yours alone,
never to be shared with strangers.
¹⁸May your fountain*a* be blessed,
and may you rejoice in the wife of your youth.*b*

5:21
d Ps 119:168;
Hos 7:2
e Job 14:16;
Job 31:4; 34:21;
Pr 15:3;
Jer 16:17; 32:19;
Heb 4:13

¹⁹A loving doe, a graceful deer*c*—
may her breasts satisfy you always,
may you ever be captivated by her love.
²⁰Why be captivated, my son, by an adulteress?
Why embrace the bosom of another man's wife?

²¹For a man's ways are in full view*d* of the LORD,
and he examines all his paths.*e*
²²The evil deeds of a wicked man ensnare him;*f*
the cords of his sin hold him fast.*g*
²³He will die for lack of discipline,*h*
led astray by his own great folly.

Chapter 6 Theme _____

6 My son, if you have put up security for your neighbor,*i*
if you have struck hands in pledge*j* for another,

²if you have been trapped by what you said,
ensnared by the words of your mouth,
³then do this, my son, to free yourself,
since you have fallen into your neighbor's hands:
Go and humble yourself;
press your plea with your neighbor!

⁴Allow no sleep to your eyes,
no slumber to your eyelids.*k*

⁵Free yourself, like a gazelle from the hand of the hunter,
like a bird from the snare of the fowler.*l*

⁶Go to the ant, you sluggard;*m*
consider its ways and be wise!
⁷It has no commander,
no overseer or ruler,

⁸yet it stores its provisions in summer
and gathers its food at harvest.*n*

⁹How long will you lie there, you sluggard?*o*
When will you get up from your sleep?
¹⁰A little sleep, a little slumber,
a little folding of the hands to rest*p*—

^{11}and poverty^a will come on you like a bandit
  and scarcity like an armed man.^{a}

^{12}A scoundrel and villain,
  who goes about with a corrupt mouth,
^{13} who winks with his eye,^{b}
  signals with his feet
  and motions with his fingers,
^{14} who plots evil^c with deceit in his heart—
  he always stirs up dissension.^{d}
^{15}Therefore disaster will overtake him in an instant;
  he will suddenly be destroyed—without remedy.^{e}

^{16}There are six things the LORD hates,
  seven that are detestable to him:
^{17} haughty eyes,
  a lying tongue,^{f}
  hands that shed innocent blood,^{g}
^{18} a heart that devises wicked schemes,
  feet that are quick to rush into evil,^{h}
^{19} a false witness^i who pours out lies
  and a man who stirs up dissension among
    brothers.^{j}

^{20}My son, keep your father's commands
  and do not forsake your mother's teaching.^{k}
^{21}Bind them upon your heart forever;
  fasten them around your neck.^{l}
^{22}When you walk, they will guide you;
  when you sleep, they will watch over you;
  when you awake, they will speak to you.
^{23}For these commands are a lamp,
  this teaching is a light,^{m}
and the corrections of discipline
  are the way to life,
^{24}keeping you from the immoral woman,
  from the smooth tongue of the wayward wife.^{n}
^{25}Do not lust in your heart after her beauty
  or let her captivate you with her eyes,
^{26}for the prostitute reduces you to a loaf of bread,
  and the adulteress preys upon your very life.^{o}
^{27}Can a man scoop fire into his lap
  without his clothes being burned?
^{28}Can a man walk on hot coals
  without his feet being scorched?

6:11
^{a}Pr 24:30-34

6:13
^{b}Ps 35:19

6:14
^{c}Mic 2:1
^{d}ver 16-19

6:15
^{e}2Ch 36:16

6:17
^{f}Ps 120:2;
Pr 12:22
^{g}Dt 19:10;
Isa 1:15; 59:7

6:18
^{h}Ge 6:5

6:19
^{i}Ps 27:12
^{j}ver 12-15

6:20
^{k}Pr 1:8

6:21
^{l}Pr 3:3; 7:1-3

6:23
^{m}Ps 19:8;
119:105

6:24
^{n}Pr 2:16; 7:5

6:26
^{o}Pr 7:22-23;
29:3

^{a} 11 Or *like a vagrant / and scarcity like a beggar*

6:29
a Ex 20:14
b Pr 2:16-19; 5:8

6:31
c Ex 22:1-14

6:32
d Ex 20:14
e Pr 7:7; 9:4,16

6:33
f Pr 5:9-14

6:34
g Nu 5:14
h Ge 34:7

6:35
i Job 31:9-11;
SS 8:7

7:1
j Pr 1:8; 2:1

7:2
k Pr 4:4

7:3
l Dt 6:8;
Pr 3:3

7:5
m ver 21;
Job 31:9;
Pr 2:16; 6:24

7:7
n Pr 1:22; 6:32

7:9
o Job 24:15

7:11
p Pr 9:13;
1Ti 5:13

7:12
q Pr 8:1-36;
23:26-28

7:13
r Ge 39:12
s Pr 1:20

²⁹So is he who sleeps*a* with another man's wife;*b*
no one who touches her will go unpunished.

³⁰Men do not despise a thief if he steals
to satisfy his hunger when he is starving.
³¹Yet if he is caught, he must pay sevenfold,*c*
though it costs him all the wealth of his house.
³²But a man who commits adultery*d* lacks judgment;*e*
whoever does so destroys himself.
³³Blows and disgrace are his lot,
and his shame will never*f* be wiped away;
³⁴for jealousy*g* arouses a husband's fury,*h*
and he will show no mercy when he takes revenge.
³⁵He will not accept any compensation;
he will refuse the bribe, however great it is.*i*

Chapter 7 Theme _____

7 My son,*j* keep my words
and store up my commands within you.
²Keep my commands and you will live;*k*
guard my teachings as the apple of your eye.
³Bind them on your fingers;
write them on the tablet of your heart.*l*
⁴Say to wisdom, "You are my sister,"
and call understanding your kinsman;
⁵they will keep you from the adulteress,
from the wayward wife with her seductive words.*m*

⁶At the window of my house
I looked out through the lattice.
⁷I saw among the simple,
I noticed among the young men,
a youth who lacked judgment.*n*
⁸He was going down the street near her corner,
walking along in the direction of her house
⁹at twilight,*o* as the day was fading,
as the dark of night set in.

¹⁰Then out came a woman to meet him,
dressed like a prostitute and with crafty intent.
¹¹(She is loud*p* and defiant,
her feet never stay at home;
¹²now in the street, now in the squares,
at every corner she lurks.)*q*
¹³She took hold of him*r* and kissed him
and with a brazen face she said:*s*

14"I have fellowship offerings^{aa} at home;
today I fulfilled my vows.
15So I came out to meet you;
I looked for you and have found you!
16I have covered my bed
with colored linens from Egypt.
17I have perfumed my bed^b
with myrrh,^c aloes and cinnamon.
18Come, let's drink deep of love till morning;
let's enjoy ourselves with love!^d
19My husband is not at home;
he has gone on a long journey.
20He took his purse filled with money
and will not be home till full moon."

21With persuasive words she led him astray;
she seduced him with her smooth talk.^e
22All at once he followed her
like an ox going to the slaughter,
like a deer^b stepping into a noose^{cf}
23   till an arrow pierces^g his liver,
like a bird darting into a snare,
little knowing it will cost him his life.^h

24Now then, my sons, listenⁱ to me;
pay attention to what I say.
25Do not let your heart turn to her ways
or stray into her paths.^j
26Many are the victims she has brought down;
her slain are a mighty throng.
27Her house is a highway to the grave,^d
leading down to the chambers of death.^k

Chapter 8 Theme

8 Does not wisdom call out?^l
Does not understanding raise her voice?
2On the heights along the way,
where the paths meet, she takes her stand;
3beside the gates leading into the city,
at the entrances, she cries aloud:^m
4"To you, O men, I call out;
I raise my voice to all mankind.
5You who are simple,ⁿ gain prudence;^o
you who are foolish, gain understanding.

---

^a14 Traditionally *peace offerings*   ^b22 Syriac (see also Septuagint); Hebrew *fool*   ^c22 The meaning of the Hebrew for this line is uncertain.   ^d27 Hebrew *Sheol*

Cross references:
7:14 ^aLev 7:11-18
7:17 ^bEst 1:6; Isa 57:7; Eze 23:41; Am 6:4 ^cGe 37:25
7:18 ^dGe 39:7
7:21 ^ePr 5:3
7:22 ^fJob 18:10
7:23 ^gJob 15:22; 16:13 ^hPr 6:26; Ecc 7:26; 9:12
7:24 ⁱPr 1:8-9; 5:7; 8:32
7:25 ^jPr 5:7-8
7:27 ^kPr 2:18; 5:5; 9:18; Rev 22:15
8:1 ^lPr 1:20; 9:3
8:3 ^mJob 29:7
8:5 ⁿPr 1:22 ^oPr 1:4

8:7
a Ps 37:30;
Jn 8:14

8:10
b Pr 3:14-15

8:11
c Job 28:17-19
d Pr 3:13-15

8:12
e Pr 1:4

8:13
f Pr 16:6
g Jer 44:4

8:14
h Pr 21:22;
Ecc 7:19

8:15
i Da 2:21;
Ro 13:1

8:17
j 1Sa 2:30;
Ps 91:14;
Jn 14:21-24
k Pr 1:28; Jas 1:5

8:18
l Pr 3:16
m Dt 8:18;
Mt 6:33

8:19
n Pr 3:13-14;
10:20

8:21
o Pr 24:4

8:24
p Ge 7:11

8:25
q Job 15:7

8:26
r Ps 90:2

⁶Listen, for I have worthy things to say;
  I open my lips to speak what is right.
⁷My mouth speaks what is true,ᵃ
  for my lips detest wickedness.
⁸All the words of my mouth are just;
  none of them is crooked or perverse.
⁹To the discerning all of them are right;
  they are faultless to those who have knowledge.
¹⁰Choose my instruction instead of silver,
  knowledge rather than choice gold,ᵇ
¹¹for wisdom is more preciousᶜ than rubies,
  and nothing you desire can compare with her.ᵈ

¹²"I, wisdom, dwell together with prudence;
  I possess knowledge and discretion.ᵉ
¹³To fear the LORD is to hate evil;ᶠ
  I hateᵍ pride and arrogance,
  evil behavior and perverse speech.
¹⁴Counsel and sound judgment are mine;
  I have understanding and power.ʰ
¹⁵By me kings reign
  and rulersⁱ make laws that are just;
¹⁶by me princes govern,
  and all nobles who rule on earth.ᵃ
¹⁷I love those who love me,ʲ
  and those who seek me find me.ᵏ
¹⁸With me are riches and honor,ˡ
  enduring wealth and prosperity.ᵐ
¹⁹My fruit is better than fine gold;
  what I yield surpasses choice silver.ⁿ
²⁰I walk in the way of righteousness,
  along the paths of justice,
²¹bestowing wealth on those who love me
  and making their treasuries full.ᵒ

²²"The LORD brought me forth as the first of his works,ᵇ,ᶜ
  before his deeds of old;
²³I was appointedᵈ from eternity,
  from the beginning, before the world began.
²⁴When there were no oceans, I was given birth,
  when there were no springs abounding with water;ᵖ
²⁵before the mountains were settled in place,
  before the hills, I was given birth,�q
²⁶before he made the earth or its fields
  or any of the dust of the world.ʳ

a 16 Many Hebrew manuscripts and Septuagint; most Hebrew manuscripts and nobles—all righteous rulers   b 22 Or way; or dominion   c 22 Or The LORD possessed me at the beginning of his work; or The LORD brought me forth at the beginning of his work   d 23 Or fashioned

^{27}I was there when he set the heavens in place,^{a}
  when he marked out the horizon on the face of the deep,
^{28}when he established the clouds above
  and fixed securely the fountains of the deep,
^{29}when he gave the sea its boundary^b
  so the waters would not overstep his command,^{c}
and when he marked out the foundations of the earth.^{d}
^{30} Then I was the craftsman at his side.^{e}
  I was filled with delight day after day,
    rejoicing always in his presence,
^{31}rejoicing in his whole world
  and delighting in mankind.^{f}

^{32}"Now then, my sons, listen to me;
  blessed are^g those who keep my ways.^{h}
^{33}Listen to my instruction and be wise;
  do not ignore it.
^{34}Blessed is the man who listens^i to me,
  watching daily at my doors,
    waiting at my doorway.
^{35}For whoever finds me^j finds life
  and receives favor from the LORD.^{k}
^{36}But whoever fails to find me harms himself;^{l}
  all who hate me love death."

Chapter 9 Theme _____

9 Wisdom has built^m her house;
  she has hewn out its seven pillars.
^{2}She has prepared her meat and mixed her wine;
  she has also set her table.^{n}
^{3}She has sent out her maids, and she calls^o
  from the highest point of the city.^{p}
^{4}"Let all who are simple come in here!"
  she says to those who lack judgment.^{q}
^{5}"Come, eat my food
  and drink the wine I have mixed.^{r}
^{6}Leave your simple ways and you will live;^{s}
  walk in the way of understanding.

^{7}"Whoever corrects a mocker invites insult;
  whoever rebukes a wicked man incurs abuse.^{t}
^{8}Do not rebuke a mocker^u or he will hate you;
  rebuke a wise man and he will love you.^{v}
^{9}Instruct a wise man and he will be wiser still;
  teach a righteous man and he will add to his learning.^{w}

8:27	^{a} Pr 3:19
8:29	^{b} Ge 1:9; Job 38:10; Ps 16:6 ^{c} Ps 104:9 ^{d} Job 38:5
8:30	^{e} Jn 1:1-3
8:31	^{f} Ps 16:3; 104:1-30
8:32	^{g} Lk 11:28 ^{h} Ps 119:1-2
8:34	^{i} Pr 3:13,18
8:35	^{j} Pr 3:13-18 ^{k} Pr 12:2
8:36	^{l} Pr 15:32
9:1	^{m} Eph 2:20-22; 1Pe 2:5
9:2	^{n} Lk 14:16-23
9:3	^{o} Pr 8:1-3 ^{p} ver 14
9:4	^{q} Pr 6:32
9:5	^{r} Isa 55:1
9:6	^{s} Pr 8:35
9:7	^{t} Pr 23:9
9:8	^{u} Pr 15:12 ^{v} Ps 141:5
9:9	^{w} Pr 1:5,7

9:10
a Job 28:28;
Pr 1:7

9:11
b Pr 3:16;
10:27

9:13
c Pr 7:11
d Pr 5:6

9:14
e ver 3

9:17
f Pr 20:17

9:18
g Pr 2:18;
7:26-27

10:1
h Pr 1:1
i Pr 15:20; 29:3

10:2
j Pr 21:6
k Pr 11:4,19

10:3
l Mt 6:25-34

10:4
m Pr 19:15
n Pr 12:24;
13:4; 21:5

10:6
o ver 8,11,14

10:7
p Ps 112:6
q Ps 109:13
r Ps 9:6

10:8
s Mt 7:24-27

10:9
t Isa 33:15
u Ps 23:4
v Pr 28:18

¹⁰"The fear of the LORD*a* is the beginning of wisdom,
and knowledge of the Holy One is understanding.
¹¹For through me your days will be many,
and years will be added to your life.*b*
¹²If you are wise, your wisdom will reward you;
if you are a mocker, you alone will suffer."

¹³The woman Folly is loud;*c*
she is undisciplined and without knowledge.*d*
¹⁴She sits at the door of her house,
on a seat at the highest point of the city,*e*
¹⁵calling out to those who pass by,
who go straight on their way.
¹⁶"Let all who are simple come in here!"
she says to those who lack judgment.
¹⁷"Stolen water is sweet;
food eaten in secret is delicious!*f*"
¹⁸But little do they know that the dead are there,
that her guests are in the depths of the grave.*ag*

Chapter 10 Theme

10 The proverbs of Solomon:*h*

A wise son brings joy to his father,*i*
but a foolish son grief to his mother.

²Ill-gotten treasures are of no value,*j*
but righteousness delivers from death.*k*

³The LORD does not let the righteous go hungry*l*
but he thwarts the craving of the wicked.

⁴Lazy hands make a man poor,*m*
but diligent hands bring wealth.*n*

⁵He who gathers crops in summer is a wise son,
but he who sleeps during harvest is a disgraceful son.

⁶Blessings crown the head of the righteous,
but violence overwhelms the mouth of the wicked.*bo*

⁷The memory of the righteous*p* will be a blessing,
but the name of the wicked*q* will rot.*r*

⁸The wise in heart accept commands,
but a chattering fool comes to ruin.*s*

⁹The man of integrity*t* walks securely,*u*
but he who takes crooked paths will be found out.*v*

a 18 Hebrew *Sheol*   *b 6* Or *but the mouth of the wicked conceals violence*; also in verse 11

¹⁰He who winks maliciously*ᵃ* causes grief,
  and a chattering fool comes to ruin.

¹¹The mouth of the righteous is a fountain of life,*ᵇ*
  but violence overwhelms the mouth of the wicked.*ᶜ*

¹²Hatred stirs up dissension,
  but love covers over all wrongs.*ᵈ*

¹³Wisdom is found on the lips of the discerning,*ᵉ*
  but a rod is for the back of him who lacks judgment.*ᶠ*

¹⁴Wise men store up knowledge,
  but the mouth of a fool invites ruin.*ᵍ*

¹⁵The wealth of the rich is their fortified city,*ʰ*
  but poverty is the ruin of the poor.*ⁱ*

¹⁶The wages of the righteous bring them life,
  but the income of the wicked brings them punishment.*ʲ*

¹⁷He who heeds discipline shows the way to life,*ᵏ*
  but whoever ignores correction leads others astray.

¹⁸He who conceals his hatred has lying lips,
  and whoever spreads slander is a fool.

¹⁹When words are many, sin is not absent,
  but he who holds his tongue is wise.*ˡ*

²⁰The tongue of the righteous is choice silver,
  but the heart of the wicked is of little value.

²¹The lips of the righteous nourish many,
  but fools die for lack of judgment.*ᵐ*

²²The blessing of the LORD brings wealth,*ⁿ*
  and he adds no trouble to it.

²³A fool finds pleasure in evil conduct,*ᵒ*
  but a man of understanding delights in wisdom.

²⁴What the wicked dreads*ᵖ* will overtake him;
  what the righteous desire will be granted.*�q*

²⁵When the storm has swept by, the wicked are gone,
  but the righteous stand firm*ʳ* forever.*ˢ*

²⁶As vinegar to the teeth and smoke to the eyes,
  so is a sluggard to those who send him.*ᵗ*

²⁷The fear of the LORD adds length to life,*ᵘ*
  but the years of the wicked are cut short.*ᵛ*

10:10
*ᵃ*Ps 35:19

10:11
*ᵇ*Ps 37:30;
Pr 13:12,14,19
*ᶜ*ver 6

10:12
*ᵈ*Pr 17:9;
1Co 13:4-7;
1Pe 4:8

10:13
*ᵉ*ver 31
*ᶠ*Pr 26:3

10:14
*ᵍ*Pr 18:6,7

10:15
*ʰ*Pr 18:11
*ⁱ*Pr 19:7

10:16
*ʲ*Pr 11:18-19

10:17
*ᵏ*Pr 6:23

10:19
*ˡ*Pr 17:28;
Ecc 5:3;
Jas 1:19; 3:2-12

10:21
*ᵐ*Pr 5:22-23;
Hos 4:1,6,14

10:22
*ⁿ*Ge 24:35;
Ps 37:22

10:23
*ᵒ*Pr 2:14; 15:21

10:24
*ᵖ*Isa 66:4
*q*Ps 145:17-19;
Mt 5:6;
1Jn 5:14-15

10:25
*ʳ*Ps 15:5
*ˢ*Pr 12:3,7;
Mt 7:24-27

10:26
*ᵗ*Pr 26:6

10:27
*ᵘ*Pr 9:10-11
*ᵛ*Job 15:32

10:28
a Job 8:13;
Pr 11:7

10:29
b Pr 21:15

10:30
c Ps 37:9,28-29;
Pr 2:20-22

10:31
d Ps 37:30

10:32
e Ecc 10:12

11:1
f Lev 19:36;
Dt 25:13-16;
Pr 20:10,23
g Pr 16:11

11:2
h Pr 16:18
i Pr 18:12;
29:23

11:3
j Pr 13:6

11:4
k Eze 7:19;
Zep 1:18
l Ge 7:1;
Pr 10:2

11:5
m Pr 5:21-23

11:7
n Pr 10:28

11:8
o Pr 21:18

11:10
p Pr 28:12

11:11
q Pr 29:8

11:12
r Pr 14:21

²⁸The prospect of the righteous is joy,
but the hopes of the wicked come to nothing.*a*

²⁹The way of the Lord is a refuge for the righteous,
but it is the ruin of those who do evil.*b*

³⁰The righteous will never be uprooted,
but the wicked will not remain in the land.*c*

³¹The mouth of the righteous brings forth wisdom,*d*
but a perverse tongue will be cut out.

³²The lips of the righteous know what is fitting,*e*
but the mouth of the wicked only what is perverse.

Chapter 11 Theme

11 The Lord abhors dishonest scales,*f*
but accurate weights are his delight.*g*

²When pride comes, then comes disgrace,*h*
but with humility comes wisdom.*i*

³The integrity of the upright guides them,
but the unfaithful are destroyed by their duplicity.*j*

⁴Wealth is worthless in the day of wrath,*k*
but righteousness delivers from death.*l*

⁵The righteousness of the blameless makes a straight way
for them,
but the wicked are brought down by their own
wickedness.*m*

⁶The righteousness of the upright delivers them,
but the unfaithful are trapped by evil desires.

⁷When a wicked man dies, his hope perishes;
all he expected from his power comes to nothing.*n*

⁸The righteous man is rescued from trouble,
and it comes on the wicked instead.*o*

⁹With his mouth the godless destroys his neighbor,
but through knowledge the righteous escape.

¹⁰When the righteous prosper, the city rejoices;*p*
when the wicked perish, there are shouts of joy.

¹¹Through the blessing of the upright a city is exalted,
but by the mouth of the wicked it is destroyed.*q*

¹²A man who lacks judgment derides his neighbor,*r*
but a man of understanding holds his tongue.

¹³A gossip betrays a confidence,ᵃ
but a trustworthy man keeps a secret.

¹⁴For lack of guidance a nation falls,ᵇ
but many advisers make victory sure.ᶜ

¹⁵He who puts up securityᵈ for another will surely suffer,
but whoever refuses to strike hands in pledge is safe.

¹⁶A kindhearted woman gains respect,ᵉ
but ruthless men gain only wealth.

¹⁷A kind man benefits himself,
but a cruel man brings trouble on himself.

¹⁸The wicked man earns deceptive wages,
but he who sows righteousness reaps a sure reward.ᶠ

¹⁹The truly righteous man attains life,
but he who pursues evil goes to his death.

²⁰The LORD detests men of perverse heart
but he delights in those whose ways are blameless.ᵍ

²¹Be sure of this: The wicked will not go unpunished,
but those who are righteous will go free.ʰ

²²Like a gold ring in a pig's snout
is a beautiful woman who shows no discretion.

²³The desire of the righteous ends only in good,
but the hope of the wicked only in wrath.

²⁴One man gives freely, yet gains even more;
another withholds unduly, but comes to poverty.

²⁵A generous man will prosper;
he who refreshes others will himself be refreshed.ⁱ

²⁶People curse the man who hoards grain,
but blessing crowns him who is willing to sell.

²⁷He who seeks good finds goodwill,
but evil comes to him who searches for it.ʲ

²⁸Whoever trusts in his riches will fall,ᵏ
but the righteous will thrive like a green leaf.ˡ

²⁹He who brings trouble on his family will inherit
only wind,
and the fool will be servant to the wise.ᵐ

³⁰The fruit of the righteous is a tree of life,ⁿ
and he who wins souls is wise.

11:13 ᵃLev 19:16; Pr 20:19; 1Ti 5:13
11:14 ᵇPr 20:18 ᶜPr 15:22; 24:6
11:15 ᵈPr 6:1
11:16 ᵉPr 31:31
11:18 ᶠHos 10:12-13
11:20 ᵍ1Ch 29:17; Ps 119:1; Pr 12:2,22
11:21 ʰPr 16:5
11:25 ⁱMt 5:7; 2Co 9:6-9
11:27 ʲEst 7:10; Ps 7:15-16
11:28 ᵏJob 31:24-28; Ps 49:6; 52:7; Mk 10:25; 1Ti 6:17 ˡPs 1:3; 92:12-14; Jer 17:8
11:29 ᵐPr 14:19
11:30 ⁿJas 5:20

³¹If the righteous receive their due^a on earth,
how much more the ungodly and the sinner!

Chapter 12 Theme _____

12 Whoever loves discipline loves knowledge,
but he who hates correction is stupid.^b

²A good man obtains favor from the LORD,
but the LORD condemns a crafty man.

³A man cannot be established through wickedness,
but the righteous cannot be uprooted.^c

⁴A wife of noble character is her husband's crown,
but a disgraceful wife is like decay in his bones.^d

⁵The plans of the righteous are just,
but the advice of the wicked is deceitful.

⁶The words of the wicked lie in wait for blood,
but the speech of the upright rescues them.^e

⁷Wicked men are overthrown and are no more,^f
but the house of the righteous stands firm.^g

⁸A man is praised according to his wisdom,
but men with warped minds are despised.

⁹Better to be a nobody and yet have a servant
than pretend to be somebody and have no food.

¹⁰A righteous man cares for the needs of his animal,
but the kindest acts of the wicked are cruel.

¹¹He who works his land will have abundant food,
but he who chases fantasies lacks judgment.^h

¹²The wicked desire the plunder of evil men,
but the root of the righteous flourishes.

¹³An evil man is trapped by his sinful talk,ⁱ
but a righteous man escapes trouble.^j

¹⁴From the fruit of his lips a man is filled with good things^k
as surely as the work of his hands rewards him.^l

¹⁵The way of a fool seems right to him,^m
but a wise man listens to advice.

¹⁶A fool shows his annoyance at once,
but a prudent man overlooks an insult.ⁿ

¹⁷A truthful witness gives honest testimony,
but a false witness tells lies.^o

11:31
a Pr 13:21;
Jer 25:29;
1Pe 4:18

12:1
b Pr 9:7-9;
15:5,10,12,32

12:3
c Pr 10:25

12:4
d Pr 14:30

12:6
e Pr 14:3

12:7
f Ps 37:36
g Pr 10:25

12:11
h Pr 28:19

12:13
i Pr 18:7
j Pr 21:23;
2Pe 2:9

12:14
k Pr 13:2; 15:23;
18:20
l Isa 3:10-11

12:15
m Pr 14:12;
16:2,25;
Lk 18:11

12:16
n Pr 29:11

12:17
o Pr 14:5,25

¹⁸Reckless words pierce like a sword,ᵃ
  but the tongue of the wise brings healing.ᵇ

¹⁹Truthful lips endure forever,
  but a lying tongue lasts only a moment.

²⁰There is deceit in the hearts of those who plot evil,
  but joy for those who promote peace.

²¹No harm befalls the righteous,ᶜ
  but the wicked have their fill of trouble.

²²The LORD detests lying lips,ᵈ
  but he delights in men who are truthful.ᵉ

²³A prudent man keeps his knowledge to himself,ᶠ
  but the heart of fools blurts out folly.

²⁴Diligent hands will rule,
  but laziness ends in slave labor.ᵍ

²⁵An anxious heart weighs a man down,ʰ
  but a kind word cheers him up.

²⁶A righteous man is cautious in friendship,ᵃ
  but the way of the wicked leads them astray.

²⁷The lazy man does not roastᵇ his game,
  but the diligent man prizes his possessions.

²⁸In the way of righteousness there is life;ⁱ
  along that path is immortality.

Chapter 13 Theme

13 A wise son heeds his father's instruction,
  but a mocker does not listen to rebuke.ʲ

²From the fruit of his lips a man enjoys good things,ᵏ
  but the unfaithful have a craving for violence.

³He who guards his lipsˡ guards his life,ᵐ
  but he who speaks rashly will come to ruin.ⁿ

⁴The sluggard craves and gets nothing,
  but the desires of the diligent are fully satisfied.

⁵The righteous hate what is false,
  but the wicked bring shame and disgrace.

⁶Righteousness guards the man of integrity,
  but wickedness overthrows the sinner.ᵒ

---

a 26 Or *man is a guide to his neighbor*   b 27 The meaning of the Hebrew for this word is uncertain.

12:18
a Ps 57:4
b Pr 15:4

12:21
c Ps 91:10

12:22
d Pr 6:17;
Rev 22:15
e Pr 11:20

12:23
f Pr 10:14; 13:16

12:24
g Pr 10:4

12:25
h Pr 15:13;
Isa 50:4

12:28
i Dt 30:15

13:1
j Pr 10:1

13:2
k Pr 12:14

13:3
l Jas 3:2
m Pr 21:23
n Pr 18:7, 20-21

13:6
o Pr 11:3,5

13:7
a 2Co 6:10

13:9
b Job 18:5;
Pr 4:18-19;
24:20

13:11
c Pr 10:2

13:13
d Nu 15:31;
2Ch 36:16

13:14
e Pr 10:11
f Pr 14:27

13:16
g Pr 12:23

13:17
h Pr 25:13

13:18
i Pr 15:5,31-32

13:20
j Pr 15:31

13:21
k Ps 32:10

13:22
l Job 27:17;
Ecc 2:26

7One man pretends to be rich, yet has nothing;
    another pretends to be poor, yet has great wealth.a

8A man's riches may ransom his life,
    but a poor man hears no threat.

9The light of the righteous shines brightly,
    but the lamp of the wicked is snuffed out.b

10Pride only breeds quarrels,
    but wisdom is found in those who take advice.

11Dishonest money dwindles away,c
    but he who gathers money little by little makes it grow.

12Hope deferred makes the heart sick,
    but a longing fulfilled is a tree of life.

13He who scorns instruction will pay for it,d
    but he who respects a command is rewarded.

14The teaching of the wise is a fountain of life,e
    turning a man from the snares of death.f

15Good understanding wins favor,
    but the way of the unfaithful is hard.a

16Every prudent man acts out of knowledge,
    but a fool exposes his folly.g

17A wicked messenger falls into trouble,
    but a trustworthy envoy brings healing.h

18He who ignores discipline comes to poverty and shame,
    but whoever heeds correction is honored.i

19A longing fulfilled is sweet to the soul,
    but fools detest turning from evil.

20He who walks with the wise grows wise,
    but a companion of fools suffers harm.j

21Misfortune pursues the sinner,
    but prosperity is the reward of the righteous.k

22A good man leaves an inheritance for his children's
    children,
    but a sinner's wealth is stored up for the righteous.l

23A poor man's field may produce abundant food,
    but injustice sweeps it away.

a 15 Or unfaithful does not endure

²⁴He who spares the rod hates his son,
    but he who loves him is careful to discipline him.^a

²⁵The righteous eat to their hearts' content,
    but the stomach of the wicked goes hungry.^b

Chapter 14 Theme

14 The wise woman builds her house,^c
    but with her own hands the foolish one tears hers
        down.

²He whose walk is upright fears the LORD,
    but he whose ways are devious despises him.

³A fool's talk brings a rod to his back,
    but the lips of the wise protect them.^d

⁴Where there are no oxen, the manger is empty,
    but from the strength of an ox comes an
        abundant harvest.

⁵A truthful witness does not deceive,
    but a false witness pours out lies.^e

⁶The mocker seeks wisdom and finds none,
    but knowledge comes easily to the discerning.

⁷Stay away from a foolish man,
    for you will not find knowledge on his lips.

⁸The wisdom of the prudent is to give thought to their ways,
    but the folly of fools is deception.^f

⁹Fools mock at making amends for sin,
    but goodwill is found among the upright.

¹⁰Each heart knows its own bitterness,
    and no one else can share its joy.

¹¹The house of the wicked will be destroyed,
    but the tent of the upright will flourish.^g

¹²There is a way that seems right to a man,^h
    but in the end it leads to death.ⁱ

¹³Even in laughter^j the heart may ache,
    and joy may end in grief.

¹⁴The faithless will be fully repaid for their ways,^k
    and the good man rewarded for his.^l

¹⁵A simple man believes anything,
    but a prudent man gives thought to his steps.

13:24
^aPr 19:18;
22:15;
23:13-14;
29:15,17;
Heb 12:7

13:25
^bPs 34:10;
Pr 10:3

14:1
^cPr 24:3

14:3
^dPr 12:6

14:5
^ePr 6:19; 12:17

14:8
^fver 24

14:11
^gPr 3:33; 12:7

14:12
^hPr 12:15
ⁱPr 16:25

14:13
^jEcc 2:2

14:14
^kPr 1:31
^lPr 12:14

¹⁶A wise man fears the LORD and shuns evil,*a*
but a fool is hotheaded and reckless.

¹⁷A quick-tempered man does foolish things,*b*
and a crafty man is hated.

¹⁸The simple inherit folly,
but the prudent are crowned with knowledge.

¹⁹Evil men will bow down in the presence of the good,
and the wicked at the gates of the righteous.*c*

²⁰The poor are shunned even by their neighbors,
but the rich have many friends.*d*

²¹He who despises his neighbor sins,*e*
but blessed is he who is kind to the needy.*f*

²²Do not those who plot evil go astray?
But those who plan what is good find*a* love
and faithfulness.

²³All hard work brings a profit,
but mere talk leads only to poverty.

²⁴The wealth of the wise is their crown,
but the folly of fools yields folly.

²⁵A truthful witness saves lives,
but a false witness is deceitful.*g*

²⁶He who fears the LORD has a secure fortress,*h*
and for his children it will be a refuge.

²⁷The fear of the LORD is a fountain of life,
turning a man from the snares of death.*i*

²⁸A large population is a king's glory,
but without subjects a prince is ruined.

²⁹A patient man has great understanding,
but a quick-tempered man displays folly.*j*

³⁰A heart at peace gives life to the body,
but envy rots the bones.*k*

³¹He who oppresses the poor shows contempt for
their Maker,*l*
but whoever is kind to the needy honors God.

³²When calamity comes, the wicked are brought down,*m*
but even in death the righteous have a refuge.*n*

a 22 Or *show*

³³Wisdom reposes in the heart of the discerning*a*
and even among fools she lets herself be known.*a*

³⁴Righteousness exalts a nation,*b*
but sin is a disgrace to any people.

³⁵A king delights in a wise servant,
but a shameful servant incurs his wrath.*c*

Chapter 15 Theme

15 A gentle answer turns away wrath,*d*
but a harsh word stirs up anger.

²The tongue of the wise commends knowledge,
but the mouth of the fool gushes folly.*e*

³The eyes*f* of the LORD are everywhere,*g*
keeping watch on the wicked and the good.*h*

⁴The tongue that brings healing is a tree of life,
but a deceitful tongue crushes the spirit.

⁵A fool spurns his father's discipline,
but whoever heeds correction shows prudence.*i*

⁶The house of the righteous contains great treasure,*j*
but the income of the wicked brings them trouble.

⁷The lips of the wise spread knowledge;
not so the hearts of fools.

⁸The LORD detests the sacrifice of the wicked,*k*
but the prayer of the upright pleases him.*l*

⁹The LORD detests the way of the wicked
but he loves those who pursue righteousness.*m*

¹⁰Stern discipline awaits him who leaves the path;
he who hates correction will die.*n*

¹¹Death and Destruction*b* lie open before the LORD*o*—
how much more the hearts of men!*p*

¹²A mocker resents correction;*q*
he will not consult the wise.

¹³A happy heart makes the face cheerful,
but heartache crushes the spirit.*r*

¹⁴The discerning heart seeks knowledge,*s*
but the mouth of a fool feeds on folly.

a 33 Hebrew; Septuagint and Syriac / *but in the heart of fools she is not known*   *b 11* Hebrew
Sheol and Abaddon

14:33 *a* Pr 2:6-10	
14:34 *b* Pr 11:11	
14:35 *c* Mt 24:45-51; 25:14-30	
15:1 *d* Pr 25:15	
15:2 *e* Pr 12:23	
15:3 *f* 2Ch 16:9 *g* Job 31:4; Heb 4:13 *h* Job 34:21; Jer 16:17	
15:5 *i* Pr 13:1	
15:6 *j* Pr 8:21	
15:8 *k* Pr 21:27; Isa 1:11; Jer 6:20 *l* ver 29	
15:9 *m* Pr 21:21; 1Ti 6:11	
15:10 *n* Pr 1:31-32; 5:12	
15:11 *o* Job 26:6; Ps 139:8 *p* 2Ch 6:30; Ps 44:21	
15:12 *q* Am 5:10	
15:13 *r* Pr 12:25; 17:22; 18:14	
15:14 *s* Pr 18:15	

³³The fear of the LORD*ª* teaches a man wisdom,ª
and humility comes before honor.*ᵇ*

Chapter 16 Theme

16 To man belong the plans of the heart,
but from the LORD comes the reply of the tongue.*ᶜ*

²All a man's ways seem innocent to him,
but motives are weighed by the LORD.*ᵈ*

³Commit to the LORD whatever you do,
and your plans will succeed.*ᵉ*

⁴The LORD works out everything for his own ends*ᶠ*—
even the wicked for a day of disaster.*ᵍ*

⁵The LORD detests all the proud of heart.*ʰ*
Be sure of this: They will not go unpunished.*ⁱ*

⁶Through love and faithfulness sin is atoned for;
through the fear of the LORD a man avoids evil.*ʲ*

⁷When a man's ways are pleasing to the LORD,
he makes even his enemies live at peace with him.

⁸Better a little with righteousness
than much gain*ᵏ* with injustice.

⁹In his heart a man plans his course,
but the LORD determines his steps.*ˡ*

¹⁰The lips of a king speak as an oracle,
and his mouth should not betray justice.

¹¹Honest scales and balances are from the LORD;
all the weights in the bag are of his making.*ᵐ*

¹²Kings detest wrongdoing,
for a throne is established through righteousness.*ⁿ*

¹³Kings take pleasure in honest lips;
they value a man who speaks the truth.*ᵒ*

¹⁴A king's wrath is a messenger of death,*ᵖ*
but a wise man will appease it.

¹⁵When a king's face brightens, it means life;*�q*
his favor is like a rain cloud in spring.

¹⁶How much better to get wisdom than gold,
to choose understanding rather than silver!*ʳ*

a 33 Or *Wisdom teaches the fear of the LORD*

15:33
ª Pr 1:7
ᵇ Pr 18:12

16:1
ᶜ Pr 19:21

16:2
ᵈ Pr 21:2

16:3
ᵉ Ps 37:5-6;
Pr 3:5-6

16:4
ᶠ Isa 43:7
ᵍ Ro 9:22

16:5
ʰ Pr 6:16
ⁱ Pr 11:20-21

16:6
ʲ Pr 14:16

16:8
ᵏ Ps 37:16

16:9
ˡ Jer 10:23

16:11
ᵐ Pr 11:1

16:12
ⁿ Pr 25:5

16:13
ᵒ Pr 14:35

16:14
ᵖ Pr 19:12

16:15
q Job 29:24

16:16
ʳ Pr 8:10,19

15:15
a ver 13

15:16
b Ps 37:16-17;
Pr 16:8;
1Ti 6:6

15:17
c Pr 17:1

15:18
d Pr 26:21
e Ge 13:8

15:19
f Pr 22:5

15:20
g Pr 10:1

15:21
h Pr 10:23

15:22
i Pr 11:14

15:23
j Pr 12:14
k Pr 25:11

15:25
l Pr 12:7
m Dt 19:14;
Ps 68:5-6;
Pr 23:10-11

15:26
n Pr 6:16

15:27
o Ex 23:8;
Isa 33:15

15:28
p 1Pe 3:15

15:29
q Ps 145:18-19

15:31
r ver 5

15:32
s Pr 1:7

¹⁵All the days of the oppressed are wretched,
  but the cheerful heart has a continual feast.*a*

¹⁶Better a little with the fear of the LORD
  than great wealth with turmoil.*b*

¹⁷Better a meal of vegetables where there is love
  than a fattened calf with hatred.*c*

¹⁸A hot-tempered man stirs up dissension,*d*
  but a patient man calms a quarrel.*e*

¹⁹The way of the sluggard is blocked with thorns,*f*
  but the path of the upright is a highway.

²⁰A wise son brings joy to his father,*g*
  but a foolish man despises his mother.

²¹Folly delights a man who lacks judgment,*h*
  but a man of understanding keeps a straight course.

²²Plans fail for lack of counsel,
  but with many advisers they succeed.*i*

²³A man finds joy in giving an apt reply*j*—
  and how good is a timely word!*k*

²⁴The path of life leads upward for the wise
  to keep him from going down to the grave.*a*

²⁵The LORD tears down the proud man's house*l*
  but he keeps the widow's boundaries intact.*m*

²⁶The LORD detests the thoughts of the wicked,*n*
  but those of the pure are pleasing to him.

²⁷A greedy man brings trouble to his family,
  but he who hates bribes will live.*o*

²⁸The heart of the righteous weighs its answers,*p*
  but the mouth of the wicked gushes evil.

²⁹The LORD is far from the wicked
  but he hears the prayer of the righteous.*q*

³⁰A cheerful look brings joy to the heart,
  and good news gives health to the bones.

³¹He who listens to a life-giving rebuke
  will be at home among the wise.*r*

³²He who ignores discipline despises himself,*s*
  but whoever heeds correction gains understanding.

a 24 Hebrew *Sheol*

17

Chapter 17 Theme

Better a dry crust with peace and quiet
than a house full of feasting,*a* with strife.*a*

[2] A wise servant will rule over a disgraceful son,
and will share the inheritance as one of the brothers.

[3] The crucible for silver and the furnace for gold,*b*
but the LORD tests the heart.*c*

[4] A wicked man listens to evil lips;
a liar pays attention to a malicious tongue.

[5] He who mocks the poor shows contempt for their Maker;*d*
whoever gloats over disaster*e* will not go unpunished.*f*

[6] Children's children*g* are a crown to the aged,
and parents are the pride of their children.

[7] Arrogant*b* lips are unsuited to a fool—
how much worse lying lips to a ruler!

[8] A bribe is a charm to the one who gives it;
wherever he turns, he succeeds.

[9] He who covers over an offense promotes love,*h*
but whoever repeats the matter separates close friends.*i*

[10] A rebuke impresses a man of discernment
more than a hundred lashes a fool.

[11] An evil man is bent only on rebellion;
a merciless official will be sent against him.

[12] Better to meet a bear robbed of her cubs
than a fool in his folly.

[13] If a man pays back evil*j* for good,
evil will never leave his house.

[14] Starting a quarrel is like breaching a dam;
so drop the matter before a dispute breaks out.*k*

[15] Acquitting the guilty and condemning the innocent*l*—
the LORD detests them both.*m*

[16] Of what use is money in the hand of a fool,
since he has no desire to get wisdom?*n*

[17] A friend loves at all times,
and a brother is born for adversity.

---

a 1 Hebrew *sacrifices*   *b 7* Or *Eloquent*

17:1
a Pr 15:16,17

17:3
b Pr 27:21
c 1Ch 29:17;
Ps 26:2;
Jer 17:10

17:5
d Pr 14:31
e Job 31:29
f Ob 1:12

17:6
g Pr 13:22

17:9
h Pr 10:12
i Pr 16:28

17:13
j Ps 109:4-5;
Jer 18:20

17:14
k Pr 20:3

17:15
l Pr 18:5
m Ex 23:6-7;
Isa 5:23

17:16
n Pr 23:23

17The highway of the upright avoids evil;
  he who guards his way guards his life.

18Pride goes before destruction,
  a haughty spirit before a fall.*a*

19Better to be lowly in spirit and among the oppressed
  than to share plunder with the proud.

20Whoever gives heed to instruction prospers,
  and blessed is he who trusts in the LORD.*b*

21The wise in heart are called discerning,
  and pleasant words promote instruction.*ac*

22Understanding is a fountain of life to those who have it,*d*
  but folly brings punishment to fools.

23A wise man's heart guides his mouth,
  and his lips promote instruction.*b*

24Pleasant words are a honeycomb,
  sweet to the soul and healing to the bones.*e*

25There is a way that seems right to a man,*f*
  but in the end it leads to death.*g*

26The laborer's appetite works for him;
  his hunger drives him on.

27A scoundrel plots evil,
  and his speech is like a scorching fire.*h*

28A perverse man stirs up dissension,*i*
  and a gossip separates close friends.*j*

29A violent man entices his neighbor
  and leads him down a path that is not good.*k*

30He who winks with his eye is plotting perversity;
  he who purses his lips is bent on evil.

31Gray hair is a crown of splendor;*l*
  it is attained by a righteous life.

32Better a patient man than a warrior,
  a man who controls his temper than one who
  takes a city.

33The lot is cast into the lap,
  but its every decision is from the LORD.*m*

16:18 *a*Pr 11:2; 18:12
16:20 *b*Ps 2:12; 34:8; Pr 19:8; Jer 17:7
16:21 *c*ver 23
16:22 *d*Pr 13:14
16:24 *e*Pr 24:13-14
16:25 *f*Pr 12:15 *g*Pr 14:12
16:27 *h*Jas 3:6
16:28 *i*Pr 15:18 *j*Pr 17:9
16:29 *k*Pr 1:10; 12:26
16:31 *l*Pr 20:29
16:33 *m*Pr 18:18; 29:26

a 21 Or words make a man persuasive   *b 23 Or mouth / and makes his lips persuasive*

19:1
a Pr 28:6

19:2
b Pr 29:20

19:4
c Pr 14:20

19:5
d Ex 23:1;
e Dt 19:19;
Pr 21:28

19:6
f Pr 29:26
g Pr 17:8; 18:16

19:7
h ver 4; Ps 38:11

19:8
i Pr 16:20

19:9
j ver 5

19:10
k Pr 26:1
l Pr 30:21-23;
Ecc 10:5-7

19:11
m Pr 16:32

19:12
n Ps 133:3
o Pr 16:14-15

19:13
p Pr 10:1
q Pr 21:9

19:14
r 2Co 12:14
s Pr 18:22

19:15
t Pr 6:9; 10:4

19:16
u Pr 16:17;
Lk 10:28

Chapter 19 Theme _____

19

Better a poor man whose walk is blameless
 than a fool whose lips are perverse.[a]

²It is not good to have zeal without knowledge,
 nor to be hasty and miss the way.[b]

³A man's own folly ruins his life,
 yet his heart rages against the LORD.

⁴Wealth brings many friends,
 but a poor man's friend deserts him.[c]

⁵A false witness[d] will not go unpunished,
 and he who pours out lies will not go free.[e]

⁶Many curry favor with a ruler,[f]
 and everyone is the friend of a man who gives gifts.[g]

⁷A poor man is shunned by all his relatives—
 how much more do his friends avoid him!
Though he pursues them with pleading,
 they are nowhere to be found.[a][h]

⁸He who gets wisdom loves his own soul;
 he who cherishes understanding prospers.[i]

⁹A false witness will not go unpunished,
 and he who pours out lies will perish.[j]

¹⁰It is not fitting for a fool[k] to live in luxury—
 how much worse for a slave to rule over princes![l]

¹¹A man's wisdom gives him patience;[m]
 it is to his glory to overlook an offense.

¹²A king's rage is like the roar of a lion,
 but his favor is like dew[n] on the grass.[o]

¹³A foolish son is his father's ruin,[p]
 and a quarrelsome wife is like a constant dripping.[q]

¹⁴Houses and wealth are inherited from parents,[r]
 but a prudent wife is from the LORD.[s]

¹⁵Laziness brings on deep sleep,
 and the shiftless man goes hungry.[t]

¹⁶He who obeys instructions guards his life,
 but he who is contemptuous of his ways will die.[u]

a 7 The meaning of the Hebrew for this sentence is uncertain.

¹⁷He who is kind to the poor lends to the LORD,
  and he will reward him for what he has done.*a*

¹⁸Discipline your son, for in that there is hope;
  do not be a willing party to his death.*b*

¹⁹A hot-tempered man must pay the penalty;
  if you rescue him, you will have to do it again.

²⁰Listen to advice and accept instruction,*c*
  and in the end you will be wise.*d*

²¹Many are the plans in a man's heart,
  but it is the LORD's purpose that prevails.*e*

²²What a man desires is unfailing love*a*;
  better to be poor than a liar.

²³The fear of the LORD leads to life:
  Then one rests content, untouched by trouble.*f*

²⁴The sluggard buries his hand in the dish;
  he will not even bring it back to his mouth!*g*

²⁵Flog a mocker, and the simple will learn prudence;
  rebuke a discerning man, and he will gain knowledge.*h*

²⁶He who robs his father and drives out his mother*i*
  is a son who brings shame and disgrace.

²⁷Stop listening to instruction, my son,
  and you will stray from the words of knowledge.

²⁸A corrupt witness mocks at justice,
  and the mouth of the wicked gulps down evil.*j*

²⁹Penalties are prepared for mockers,
  and beatings for the backs of fools.*k*

Chapter 20 Theme _____

20 Wine is a mocker and beer a brawler;
  whoever is led astray by them is not wise.*l*

²A king's wrath is like the roar of a lion;*m*
  he who angers him forfeits his life.*n*

³It is to a man's honor to avoid strife,
  but every fool is quick to quarrel.*o*

⁴A sluggard does not plow in season;
  so at harvest time he looks but finds nothing.

a 22 Or A man's greed is his shame

19:17
a Mt 10:42;
2Co 9:6-8

19:18
b Pr 13:24;
23:13-14

19:20
c Pr 4:1
d Pr 12:15

19:21
e Ps 33:11;
Pr 16:9;
Isa 14:24,27

19:23
f Ps 25:13;
Pr 12:21;
1Ti 4:8

19:24
g Pr 26:15

19:25
h Pr 9:9; 21:11

19:26
i Pr 28:24

19:28
j Job 15:16

19:29
k Pr 26:3

20:1
l Pr 31:4

20:2
m Pr 19:12
n Pr 8:36

20:3
o Pr 17:14

20:6
a Ps 12:1

⁵The purposes of a man's heart are deep waters,
but a man of understanding draws them out.

20:7
b Ps 37:25-26;
112:2

⁶Many a man claims to have unfailing love,
but a faithful man who can find?ᵃ

⁷The righteous man leads a blameless life;
blessed are his children after him.ᵇ

20:8
c ver 26;
Pr 25:4-5

⁸When a king sits on his throne to judge,
he winnows out all evil with his eyes.ᶜ

20:9
d 1Ki 8:46;
Ecc 7:20;
1Jn 1:8

⁹Who can say, "I have kept my heart pure;
I am clean and without sin"?ᵈ

¹⁰Differing weights and differing measures—
the Lᴏʀᴅ detests them both.ᵉ

20:10
e ver 23;
Pr 11:1

¹¹Even a child is known by his actions,
by whether his conduct is pureᶠ and right.

20:11
f Mt 7:16

¹²Ears that hear and eyes that see—
the Lᴏʀᴅ has made them both.ᵍ

20:12
g Ps 94:9

¹³Do not love sleep or you will grow poor;ʰ
stay awake and you will have food to spare.

20:13
h Pr 6:11;
19:15

¹⁴"It's no good, it's no good!" says the buyer;
then off he goes and boasts about his purchase.

¹⁵Gold there is, and rubies in abundance,
but lips that speak knowledge are a rare jewel.

20:16
i Ex 22:26
j Pr 27:13

¹⁶Take the garment of one who puts up security for
a stranger;
hold it in pledgeⁱ if he does it for a wayward woman.ʲ

20:17
k Pr 9:17

¹⁷Food gained by fraud tastes sweet to a man,ᵏ
but he ends up with a mouth full of gravel.

20:18
l Pr 11:14;
24:6

¹⁸Make plans by seeking advice;
if you wage war, obtain guidance.ˡ

20:19
m Pr 11:13

¹⁹A gossip betrays a confidence;ᵐ
so avoid a man who talks too much.

²⁰If a man curses his father or mother,ⁿ
his lamp will be snuffed out in pitch darkness.ᵒ

20:20
n Pr 30:11
o Ex 21:17;
Job 18:5

²¹An inheritance quickly gained at the beginning
will not be blessed at the end.

20:22
p Pr 24:29
q Ro 12:19

²²Do not say, "I'll pay you back for this wrong!"ᵖ
Wait for the Lᴏʀᴅ, and he will deliver you.�q

²³The LORD detests differing weights,
and dishonest scales do not please him.ᵃ

²⁴A man's steps are directed by the LORD.
How then can anyone understand his own way?ᵇ

²⁵It is a trap for a man to dedicate something rashly
and only later to consider his vows.ᶜ

²⁶A wise king winnows out the wicked;
he drives the threshing wheel over them.ᵈ

²⁷The lamp of the LORD searches the spirit of a manᵃ;
it searches out his inmost being.

²⁸Love and faithfulness keep a king safe;
through love his throne is made secure.ᵉ

²⁹The glory of young men is their strength,
gray hair the splendor of the old.ᶠ

³⁰Blows and wounds cleanseᵍ away evil,
and beatings purge the inmost being.

Chapter 21 Theme _____

21 The king's heart is in the hand of the LORD;
he directs it like a watercourse wherever he pleases.

²All a man's ways seem right to him,
but the LORD weighs the heart.ʰ

³To do what is right and just
is more acceptable to the LORD than sacrifice.ⁱ

⁴Haughty eyesʲ and a proud heart,
the lamp of the wicked, are sin!

⁵The plans of the diligent lead to profitᵏ
as surely as haste leads to poverty.

⁶A fortune made by a lying tongue
is a fleeting vapor and a deadly snare.ᵇ ˡ

⁷The violence of the wicked will drag them away,
for they refuse to do what is right.

⁸The way of the guilty is devious,ᵐ
but the conduct of the innocent is upright.

⁹Better to live on a corner of the roof
than share a house with a quarrelsome wife.ⁿ

ᵃ27 Or *The spirit of man is the LORD's lamp*   ᵇ6 Some Hebrew manuscripts, Septuagint and
Vulgate; most Hebrew manuscripts *vapor for those who seek death*

20:23
ᵃver 10

20:24
ᵇJer 10:23

20:25
ᶜEcc 5:2,4-5

20:26
ᵈver 8

20:28
ᵉPr 29:14

20:29
ᶠPr 16:31

20:30
ᵍPr 22:15

21:2
ʰPr 16:2;
24:12;
Lk 16:15

21:3
ⁱ1Sa 15:22;
Pr 15:8;
Isa 1:11;
Hos 6:6;
Mic 6:6-8

21:4
ʲPr 6:17

21:5
ᵏPr 10:4;
28:22

21:6
ˡ2Pe 2:3

21:8
ᵐPr 2:15

21:9
ⁿPr 25:24

21:11
a Pr 19:25

21:12
b Pr 14:11

21:13
c Mt 18:30-34;
Jas 2:13

21:14
d Pr 18:16;
19:6

21:15
e Pr 10:29

21:16
f Ps 49:14

21:17
g Pr 23:20-21,
29-35

21:18
h Pr 11:8;
Isa 43:3

21:19
i ver 9

21:21
j Mt 5:6

21:22
k Ecc 9:15-16

21:23
l Jas 3:2
m Pr 12:13;
13:3

21:24
n Ps 1:1;
Pr 1:22;
Isa 16:6;
Jer 48:29

21:25
o Pr 13:4

21:26
p Ps 37:26;
Mt 5:42;
Eph 4:28

21:27
q Isa 66:3;
Jer 6:20;
Am 5:22
r Pr 15:8

[10]The wicked man craves evil;
 his neighbor gets no mercy from him.

[11]When a mocker is punished, the simple gain wisdom;
 when a wise man is instructed, he gets knowledge.[a]

[12]The Righteous One[a] takes note of the house of the wicked
 and brings the wicked to ruin.[b]

[13]If a man shuts his ears to the cry of the poor,
 he too will cry out and not be answered.[c]

[14]A gift given in secret soothes anger,
 and a bribe concealed in the cloak pacifies great wrath.[d]

[15]When justice is done, it brings joy to the righteous
 but terror to evildoers.[e]

[16]A man who strays from the path of understanding
 comes to rest in the company of the dead.[f]

[17]He who loves pleasure will become poor;
 whoever loves wine and oil will never be rich.[g]

[18]The wicked become a ransom[h] for the righteous,
 and the unfaithful for the upright.

[19]Better to live in a desert
 than with a quarrelsome and ill-tempered wife.[i]

[20]In the house of the wise are stores of choice food and oil,
 but a foolish man devours all he has.

[21]He who pursues righteousness and love
 finds life, prosperity[b] and honor.[j]

[22]A wise man attacks the city of the mighty[k]
 and pulls down the stronghold in which they trust.

[23]He who guards his mouth[l] and his tongue
 keeps himself from calamity.[m]

[24]The proud and arrogant[n] man—"Mocker" is his name;
 he behaves with overweening pride.

[25]The sluggard's craving will be the death of him,[o]
 because his hands refuse to work.
[26]All day long he craves for more,
 but the righteous give without sparing.[p]

[27]The sacrifice of the wicked is detestable[q]—
 how much more so when brought with evil intent![r]

a 12 Or The righteous man   *b 21 Or righteousness*

²⁸A false witness will perish,^a
  and whoever listens to him will be destroyed forever.^a

²⁹A wicked man puts up a bold front,
  but an upright man gives thought to his ways.

³⁰There is no wisdom,^b no insight, no plan
  that can succeed against the LORD.^c

³¹The horse is made ready for the day of battle,
  but victory rests with the LORD.^d

Chapter 22 Theme

22 A good name is more desirable than great riches;
  to be esteemed is better than silver or gold.^e

²Rich and poor have this in common:
  The LORD is the Maker of them all.^f

³A prudent man sees danger and takes refuge,^g
  but the simple keep going and suffer for it.^h

⁴Humility and the fear of the LORD
  bring wealth and honor and life.

⁵In the paths of the wicked lie thorns and snares,ⁱ
  but he who guards his soul stays far from them.

⁶Train^b a child in the way he should go,^j
  and when he is old he will not turn from it.

⁷The rich rule over the poor,
  and the borrower is servant to the lender.

⁸He who sows wickedness reaps trouble,^k
  and the rod of his fury will be destroyed.^l

⁹A generous man will himself be blessed,^m
  for he shares his food with the poor.ⁿ

¹⁰Drive out the mocker, and out goes strife;
  quarrels and insults are ended.^o

¹¹He who loves a pure heart and whose speech is gracious
  will have the king for his friend.^p

¹²The eyes of the LORD keep watch over knowledge,
  but he frustrates the words of the unfaithful.

¹³The sluggard says, "There is a lion outside!"^q
  or, "I will be murdered in the streets!"

---

^a28 Or / but the words of an obedient man will live on   ^b6 Or Start

Cross references: 21:28 ^aPr 19:5; 21:30 ^bJer 9:23 ^cIsa 8:10; Ac 5:39; 21:31 ^dPs 3:8; 33:12-19; Isa 31:1; 22:1 ^eEcc 7:1; 22:2 ^fJob 31:15; 22:3 ^gPr 14:16 ^hPr 27:12; 22:5 ⁱPr 15:19; 22:6 ^jEph 6:4; 22:8 ^kJob 4:8 ^lPs 125:3; 22:9 ^m2Co 9:6 ⁿPr 19:17; 22:10 ^oPr 18:6; 26:20; 22:11 ^pPr 16:13; Mt 5:8; 22:13 ^qPr 26:13

22:14
a Pr 2:16;
5:3-5; 7:5;
23:27
b Ecc 7:26

¹⁴The mouth of an adulteress is a deep pit;^a
he who is under the LORD's wrath will fall into it.^b

¹⁵Folly is bound up in the heart of a child,
but the rod of discipline will drive it far from him.^c

22:15
c Pr 13:24;
23:14

¹⁶He who oppresses the poor to increase his wealth
and he who gives gifts to the rich—both come
to poverty.

¹⁷Pay attention and listen to the sayings of the wise;^d
apply your heart to what I teach,

22:17
d Pr 5:1

¹⁸for it is pleasing when you keep them in your heart
and have all of them ready on your lips.
¹⁹So that your trust may be in the LORD,
I teach you today, even you.

22:21
e Lk 1:3-4;
1Pe 3:15

²⁰Have I not written thirty^a sayings for you,
sayings of counsel and knowledge,
²¹teaching you true and reliable words,^e
so that you can give sound answers
to him who sent you?

22:22
f Zec 7:10
g Ex 23:6;
Mal 3:5

²²Do not exploit the poor^f because they are poor
and do not crush the needy in court,^g
²³for the LORD will take up their case^h
and will plunder those who plunder them.ⁱ

22:23
h Ps 12:5
i 1Sa 25:39;
Pr 23:10-11

²⁴Do not make friends with a hot-tempered man,
do not associate with one easily angered,
²⁵or you may learn his ways
and get yourself ensnared.^j

22:25
j 1Co 15:33

²⁶Do not be a man who strikes hands in pledge^k
or puts up security for debts;
²⁷if you lack the means to pay,
your very bed will be snatched from under you.^l

22:26
k Pr 11:15

²⁸Do not move an ancient boundary stone^m
set up by your forefathers.

²⁹Do you see a man skilled in his work?
He will serveⁿ before kings;
he will not serve before obscure men.

22:27
l Pr 17:18

Chapter 23 Theme

22:28
m Dt 19:14;
Pr 23:10

23 When you sit to dine with a ruler,
note well what^b is before you,
²and put a knife to your throat
if you are given to gluttony.

22:29
n Ge 41:46

a 20 Or *not formerly written*; or *not written excellent*   b 1 Or *who*

³Do not crave his delicacies,ᵃ
  for that food is deceptive.

⁴Do not wear yourself out to get rich;
  have the wisdom to show restraint.
⁵Cast but a glance at riches, and they are gone,
  for they will surely sprout wings
  and fly off to the sky like an eagle.ᵇ

⁶Do not eat the food of a stingy man,
  do not crave his delicacies;ᶜ
⁷for he is the kind of man
  who is always thinking about the cost.ᵃ
  "Eat and drink," he says to you,
  but his heart is not with you.
⁸You will vomit up the little you have eaten
  and will have wasted your compliments.

⁹Do not speak to a fool,
  for he will scorn the wisdom of your words.ᵈ

¹⁰Do not move an ancient boundary stoneᵉ
  or encroach on the fields of the fatherless,
¹¹for their Defenderᶠ is strong;
  he will take up their case against you.ᵍ

¹²Apply your heart to instruction
  and your ears to words of knowledge.

¹³Do not withhold discipline from a child;
  if you punish him with the rod, he will not die.
¹⁴Punish him with the rod
  and save his soul from death.ᵇ

¹⁵My son, if your heart is wise,
  then my heart will be glad;
¹⁶my inmost being will rejoice
  when your lips speak what is right.ʰ

¹⁷Do not let your heart envyⁱ sinners,
  but always be zealous for the fear of the LORD.
¹⁸There is surely a future hope for you,
  and your hope will not be cut off.ʲ

¹⁹Listen, my son, and be wise,
  and keep your heart on the right path.
²⁰Do not join those who drink too much wineᵏ
  or gorge themselves on meat,

23:3
ᵃ ver 6-8

23:5
ᵇ Pr 27:24

23:6
ᶜ Ps 141:4

23:9
ᵈ Pr 1:7; 9:7;
Mt 7:6

23:10
ᵉ Dt 19:14;
Pr 22:28

23:11
ᶠ Job 19:25
ᵍ Pr 22:22-23

23:16
ʰ ver 24;
Pr 27:11

23:17
ⁱ Ps 37:1;
Pr 28:14

23:18
ʲ Ps 9:18;
Pr 24:14,19-20

23:20
ᵏ Isa 5:11,22;
Ro 13:13;
Eph 5:18

ᵃ 7 Or *for as he thinks within himself, /so he is*; or *for as he puts on a feast, / so he is*   ᵇ 14 Hebrew *Sheol*

23:21
a Pr 21:17

23:22
b Lev 19:32;
Pr 1:8; 30:17;
Eph 6:1-2

23:23
c Pr 4:7

23:24
d ver 15-16;
Pr 10:1; 15:20

23:26
e Pr 3:1; 5:1-6
f Ps 18:21;
Pr 4:4

23:27
g Pr 22:14

23:28
h Pr 7:11-12;
Ecc 7:26

23:30
i Ps 75:8;
Isa 5:11;
Eph 5:18

24:1
j Ps 37:1; 73:3;
Pr 3:31-32;
23:17-18

24:2
k Ps 10:7

24:3
l Pr 14:1

24:4
m Pr 8:21

²¹for drunkards and gluttons become poor,ᵃ
and drowsiness clothes them in rags.

²²Listen to your father, who gave you life,
and do not despise your mother when she is old.ᵇ
²³Buy the truth and do not sell it;
get wisdom, discipline and understanding.ᶜ
²⁴The father of a righteous man has great joy;
he who has a wise son delights in him.ᵈ
²⁵May your father and mother be glad;
may she who gave you birth rejoice!

²⁶My son,ᵉ give me your heart
and let your eyes keep to my ways,ᶠ
²⁷for a prostitute is a deep pitᵍ
and a wayward wife is a narrow well.
²⁸Like a bandit she lies in wait,ʰ
and multiplies the unfaithful among men.

²⁹Who has woe? Who has sorrow?
Who has strife? Who has complaints?
Who has needless bruises? Who has bloodshot eyes?
³⁰Those who linger over wine,ⁱ
who go to sample bowls of mixed wine.
³¹Do not gaze at wine when it is red,
when it sparkles in the cup,
when it goes down smoothly!
³²In the end it bites like a snake
and poisons like a viper.
³³Your eyes will see strange sights
and your mind imagine confusing things.
³⁴You will be like one sleeping on the high seas,
lying on top of the rigging.
³⁵"They hit me," you will say, "but I'm not hurt!
They beat me, but I don't feel it!
When will I wake up
so I can find another drink?"

Chapter 24 Theme _____

24 Do not envyʲ wicked men,
do not desire their company;
²for their hearts plot violence,
and their lips talk about making trouble.ᵏ

³By wisdom a house is built,ˡ
and through understanding it is established;
⁴through knowledge its rooms are filled
with rare and beautiful treasures.ᵐ

⁵A wise man has great power,
　and a man of knowledge increases strength;
⁶for waging war you need guidance,
　and for victory many advisers.ᵃ

⁷Wisdom is too high for a fool;
　in the assembly at the gate he has nothing to say.

⁸He who plots evil
　will be known as a schemer.
⁹The schemes of folly are sin,
　and men detest a mocker.

¹⁰If you falter in times of trouble,
　how small is your strength!ᵇ

¹¹Rescue those being led away to death;
　hold back those staggering toward slaughter.ᶜ
¹²If you say, "But we knew nothing about this,"
　does not he who weighsᵈ the heart perceive it?
　Does not he who guards your life know it?
　　Will he not repay each person according to what
　　　he has done?ᵉ

¹³Eat honey, my son, for it is good;
　honey from the comb is sweet to your taste.
¹⁴Know also that wisdom is sweet to your soul;
　if you find it, there is a future hope for you,
　and your hope will not be cut off.ᶠ ᵍ

¹⁵Do not lie in wait like an outlaw against a righteous
　　man's house,
　do not raid his dwelling place;
¹⁶for though a righteous man falls seven times, he
　　rises again,
　but the wicked are brought down by calamity.ʰ

¹⁷Do not gloatⁱ when your enemy falls;
　when he stumbles, do not let your heart rejoice,ʲ
¹⁸or the Lᴏʀᴅ will see and disapprove
　and turn his wrath away from him.

¹⁹Do not fretᵏ because of evil men
　or be envious of the wicked,
²⁰for the evil man has no future hope,
　and the lamp of the wicked will be snuffed out.ˡ

²¹Fear the Lᴏʀᴅ and the king,ᵐ my son,
　and do not join with the rebellious,

24:6
ᵃ Pr 11:14;
20:18;
Lk 14:31

24:10
ᵇ Job 4:5;
Jer 51:46;
Heb 12:3

24:11
ᶜ Ps 82:4;
Isa 58:6-7

24:12
ᵈ Pr 21:2
ᵉ Job 34:11;
Ps 62:12;
Ro 2:6*

24:14
ᶠ Ps 119:103;
Pr 16:24
ᵍ Pr 23:18

24:16
ʰ Job 5:19;
Ps 34:19;
Mic 7:8

24:17
ⁱ Ob 1:12
ʲ Job 31:29

24:19
ᵏ Ps 37:1

24:20
ˡ Job 18:5;
Pr 13:9;
23:17-18

24:21
ᵐ Ro 13:1-5;
1Pe 2:17

24:23
a Pr 1:6
b Lev 19:15
c Pr 28:21

²²for those two will send sudden destruction upon them,
and who knows what calamities they can bring?

²³These also are sayings of the wise:ᵃ

To show partialityᵇ in judging is not good:ᶜ

24:24
d Pr 17:15

²⁴Whoever says to the guilty, "You are innocent"ᵈ—
peoples will curse him and nations denounce him.
²⁵But it will go well with those who convict the guilty,
and rich blessing will come upon them.

24:28
e Ps 7:4;
Pr 25:18;
Eph 4:25

²⁶An honest answer
is like a kiss on the lips.

²⁷Finish your outdoor work
and get your fields ready;
after that, build your house.

24:29
f Pr 20:22;
Mt 5:38-41;
Ro 12:17

²⁸Do not testify against your neighbor without cause,ᵉ
or use your lips to deceive.
²⁹Do not say, "I'll do to him as he has done to me;
I'll pay that man back for what he did."ᶠ

24:30
g Pr 6:6-11;
26:13-16

³⁰I went past the field of the sluggard,ᵍ
past the vineyard of the man who lacks judgment;
³¹thorns had come up everywhere,
the ground was covered with weeds,
and the stone wall was in ruins.

24:33
h Pr 6:10

³²I applied my heart to what I observed
and learned a lesson from what I saw:
³³A little sleep, a little slumber,
a little folding of the hands to restʰ—

24:34
i Pr 10:4;
Ecc 10:18

³⁴and poverty will come on you like a bandit
and scarcity like an armed man.ᵃⁱ

Chapter 25 Theme _____

25:1
j 1Ki 4:32
k Pr 1:1

25 These are more proverbsʲ of Solomon, copied by the men of Hezekiah king of Judah:ᵏ

²It is the glory of God to conceal a matter;
to search out a matter is the glory of kings.ˡ

³As the heavens are high and the earth is deep,
so the hearts of kings are unsearchable.

25:2
l Pr 16:10-15

⁴Remove the dross from the silver,
and out comes material forᵇ the silversmith;
⁵remove the wicked from the king's presence,ᵐ
and his throne will be establishedⁿ through
righteousness.ᵒ

25:5
m Pr 20:8
n 2Sa 7:13
o Pr 16:12;
29:14

ᵃ 34 Or like a vagrant / and scarcity like a beggar   ᵇ 4 Or comes a vessel from

⁶Do not exalt yourself in the king's presence,
    and do not claim a place among great men;
⁷it is better for him to say to you, "Come up here,"^a
    than for him to humiliate you before a nobleman.

What you have seen with your eyes
⁸ do not bring^a hastily to court,
for what will you do in the end
    if your neighbor puts you to shame?^b

⁹If you argue your case with a neighbor,
    do not betray another man's confidence,
¹⁰or he who hears it may shame you
    and you will never lose your bad reputation.

¹¹A word aptly spoken
    is like apples of gold in settings of silver.^c

¹²Like an earring of gold or an ornament of fine gold
    is a wise man's rebuke to a listening ear.^d

¹³Like the coolness of snow at harvest time
    is a trustworthy messenger to those who send him;
    he refreshes the spirit of his masters.^e

¹⁴Like clouds and wind without rain
    is a man who boasts of gifts he does not give.

¹⁵Through patience a ruler can be persuaded,^f
    and a gentle tongue can break a bone.^g

¹⁶If you find honey, eat just enough—
    too much of it, and you will vomit.^h
¹⁷Seldom set foot in your neighbor's house—
    too much of you, and he will hate you.

¹⁸Like a club or a sword or a sharp arrow
    is the man who gives false testimony against
      his neighbor.ⁱ

¹⁹Like a bad tooth or a lame foot
    is reliance on the unfaithful in times of trouble.

²⁰Like one who takes away a garment on a cold day,
    or like vinegar poured on soda,
    is one who sings songs to a heavy heart.

²¹If your enemy is hungry, give him food to eat;
    if he is thirsty, give him water to drink.
²²In doing this, you will heap burning coals^j on his head,
    and the LORD will reward you.^k

^a 7,8 Or *nobleman / on whom you had set your eyes. / *⁸Do not go*

25:7
^aLk 14:7-10

25:8
^bMt 5:25-26

25:11
^cver 12;
Pr 15:23

25:12
^dver 11;
Ps 141:5;
Pr 13:18; 15:31

25:13
^ePr 10:26; 13:17

25:15
^fEcc 10:4
^gPr 15:1

25:16
^hver 27

25:18
ⁱPs 57:4;
Pr 12:18

25:22
^jPs 18:8
^k2Sa 16:12;
2Ch 28:15;
Mt 5:44;
Ro 12:20*

25:24
a Pr 21:9

25:25
b Pr 15:30

25:27
c ver 16
d Pr 27:2;
Mt 23:12

26:1
e 1Sa 12:17
f ver 8;
Pr 19:10

26:2
g Nu 23:8;
Dt 23:5

26:3
h Ps 32:9
i Pr 10:13

26:4
j ver 5;
Isa 36:21

26:5
k ver 4;
Pr 3:7

26:6
l Pr 10:26

26:7
m ver 9

26:8
n ver 1

26:9
o ver 7

26:11
p 2Pe 2:22*
q Ex 8:15;
Ps 85:8

26:12
r Pr 3:7
s Pr 29:20

²³As a north wind brings rain,
so a sly tongue brings angry looks.

²⁴Better to live on a corner of the roof
than share a house with a quarrelsome wife.^a

²⁵Like cold water to a weary soul
is good news from a distant land.^b

²⁶Like a muddied spring or a polluted well
is a righteous man who gives way to the wicked.

²⁷It is not good to eat too much honey,^c
nor is it honorable to seek one's own honor.^d

²⁸Like a city whose walls are broken down
is a man who lacks self-control.

Chapter 26 Theme _____

26 Like snow in summer or rain[e] in harvest,
honor is not fitting for a fool.[f]

²Like a fluttering sparrow or a darting swallow,
an undeserved curse does not come to rest.[g]

³A whip for the horse, a halter for the donkey,[h]
and a rod for the backs of fools![i]

⁴Do not answer a fool according to his folly,
or you will be like him yourself.[j]

⁵Answer a fool according to his folly,
or he will be wise in his own eyes.[k]

⁶Like cutting off one's feet or drinking violence
is the sending of a message by the hand of a fool.[l]

⁷Like a lame man's legs that hang limp
is a proverb in the mouth of a fool.[m]

⁸Like tying a stone in a sling
is the giving of honor to a fool.[n]

⁹Like a thornbush in a drunkard's hand
is a proverb in the mouth of a fool.[o]

¹⁰Like an archer who wounds at random
is he who hires a fool or any passer-by.

¹¹As a dog returns to its vomit,[p]
so a fool repeats his folly.[q]

¹²Do you see a man wise in his own eyes?[r]
There is more hope for a fool than for him.[s]

¹³The sluggard says,ᵃ "There is a lion in the road,
  a fierce lion roaming the streets!"ᵇ

¹⁴As a door turns on its hinges,
  so a sluggard turns on his bed.ᶜ

¹⁵The sluggard buries his hand in the dish;
  he is too lazy to bring it back to his mouth.ᵈ

¹⁶The sluggard is wiser in his own eyes
  than seven men who answer discreetly.

¹⁷Like one who seizes a dog by the ears
  is a passer-by who meddles in a quarrel not his own.

¹⁸Like a madman shooting
  firebrands or deadly arrows
¹⁹is a man who deceives his neighbor
  and says, "I was only joking!"

²⁰Without wood a fire goes out;
  without gossip a quarrel dies down.ᵉ

²¹As charcoal to embers and as wood to fire,
  so is a quarrelsome man for kindling strife.ᶠ

²²The words of a gossip are like choice morsels;
  they go down to a man's inmost parts.ᵍ

²³Like a coating of glazeᵃ over earthenware
  are fervent lips with an evil heart.

²⁴A malicious man disguises himself with his lips,ʰ
  but in his heart he harbors deceit.ⁱ

²⁵Though his speech is charming,ʲ do not believe him,
  for seven abominations fill his heart.ᵏ

²⁶His malice may be concealed by deception,
  but his wickedness will be exposed in the assembly.

²⁷If a man digs a pit,ˡ he will fall into it;ᵐ
  if a man rolls a stone, it will roll back on him.ⁿ

²⁸A lying tongue hates those it hurts,
  and a flattering mouthᵒ works ruin.

Chapter 27 Theme

27 Do not boastᵖ about tomorrow,
  for you do not know what a day may bring forth.�q

²Let another praise you, and not your own mouth;
  someone else, and not your own lips.ʳ

---

a 23 With a different word division of the Hebrew; Masoretic Text *of silver dross*

26:13
ᵃ Pr 6:6-11;
24:30-34
ᵇ Pr 22:13

26:14
ᶜ Pr 6:9

26:15
ᵈ Pr 19:24

26:20
ᵉ Pr 22:10

26:21
ᶠ Pr 14:17;
15:18

26:22
ᵍ Pr 18:8

26:24
ʰ Ps 31:18
ⁱ Ps 41:6;
Pr 10:18; 12:20

26:25
ʲ Ps 28:3
ᵏ Jer 9:4-8

26:27
ˡ Ps 7:15
ᵐ Est 6:13
ⁿ Est 2:23; 7:9;
Ps 35:8;
141:10;
Pr 28:10; 29:6;
Isa 50:11

26:28
ᵒ Ps 12:3;
Pr 29:5

27:1
ᵖ 1Ki 20:11
q Mt 6:34;
Lk 12:19-20;
Jas 4:13-16

27:2
ʳ Pr 25:27

27:3
a Job 6:3

27:4
b Nu 5:14

27:6
c Ps 141:5;
Pr 28:23

27:8
d Isa 16:2

27:9
e Est 2:12;
Ps 45:8

27:10
f Pr 17:17;
18:24

27:11
g Pr 10:1;
23:15-16
h Ge 24:60

27:12
i Pr 22:3

27:13
j Pr 20:16

27:15
k Est 1:18;
Pr 19:13

27:18
l 1Co 9:7
m Lk 19:12-27

³Stone is heavy and sand*a* a burden,
  but provocation by a fool is heavier than both.

⁴Anger is cruel and fury overwhelming,
  but who can stand before jealousy?*b*

⁵Better is open rebuke
  than hidden love.

⁶Wounds from a friend can be trusted,
  but an enemy multiplies kisses.*c*

⁷He who is full loathes honey,
  but to the hungry even what is bitter tastes sweet.

⁸Like a bird that strays from its nest*d*
  is a man who strays from his home.

⁹Perfume*e* and incense bring joy to the heart,
  and the pleasantness of one's friend springs from his
    earnest counsel.

¹⁰Do not forsake your friend and the friend of your father,
  and do not go to your brother's house when disaster*f*
    strikes you—
  better a neighbor nearby than a brother far away.

¹¹Be wise, my son, and bring joy to my heart;*g*
  then I can answer anyone who treats me with contempt.*h*

¹²The prudent see danger and take refuge,
  but the simple keep going and suffer for it.*i*

¹³Take the garment of one who puts up security for a
    stranger;
  hold it in pledge if he does it for a wayward woman.*j*

¹⁴If a man loudly blesses his neighbor early in the morning,
  it will be taken as a curse.

¹⁵A quarrelsome wife is like
  a constant dripping*k* on a rainy day;
¹⁶restraining her is like restraining the wind
  or grasping oil with the hand.

¹⁷As iron sharpens iron,
  so one man sharpens another.

¹⁸He who tends a fig tree will eat its fruit,*l*
  and he who looks after his master will be honored.*m*

¹⁹As water reflects a face,
  so a man's heart reflects the man.

²⁰Death and Destruction^a are never satisfied,^a
and neither are the eyes of man.^b

²¹The crucible for silver and the furnace for gold,^c
but man is tested by the praise he receives.

²²Though you grind a fool in a mortar,
grinding him like grain with a pestle,
you will not remove his folly from him.

²³Be sure you know the condition of your flocks,^d
give careful attention to your herds;
²⁴for riches do not endure forever,^e
and a crown is not secure for all generations.
²⁵When the hay is removed and new growth appears
and the grass from the hills is gathered in,
²⁶the lambs will provide you with clothing,
and the goats with the price of a field.
²⁷You will have plenty of goats' milk
to feed you and your family
and to nourish your servant girls.

Chapter 28 Theme _____

28

The wicked man flees^f though no one pursues,^g
but the righteous are as bold as a lion.^h

²When a country is rebellious, it has many rulers,
but a man of understanding and knowledge
maintains order.

³A ruler^b who oppresses the poor
is like a driving rain that leaves no crops.

⁴Those who forsake the law praise the wicked,
but those who keep the law resist them.

⁵Evil men do not understand justice,
but those who seek the LORD understand it fully.

⁶Better a poor man whose walk is blameless
than a rich man whose ways are perverse.ⁱ

⁷He who keeps the law is a discerning son,
but a companion of gluttons disgraces his father.^j

⁸He who increases his wealth by exorbitant interest^k
amasses it for another,^l who will be kind to the poor.^m

⁹If anyone turns a deaf ear to the law,
even his prayers are detestable.ⁿ

a 20 Hebrew *Sheol and Abaddon*   b 3 Or *A poor man*

1112

### Cross-references (margin)

27:20
a Pr 30:15-16;
Hab 2:5
b Ecc 1:8; 6:7

27:21
c Pr 17:3

27:23
d Pr 12:10

27:24
e Pr 23:5

28:1
f 2Ki 7:7
g Lev 26:17;
Ps 53:5
h Ps 138:3

28:6
i Pr 19:1

28:7
j Pr 23:19-21

28:8
k Ex 18:21
l Job 27:17;
Pr 13:22
m Ps 112:9;
Pr 14:31;
Lk 14:12-14

28:9
n Ps 66:18;
109:7;
Pr 15:8;
Isa 1:13

28:10
a Pr 26:27

28:12
b 2Ki 11:20
c Pr 11:10;
29:2

28:13
d Job 31:33
e Ps 32:1-5;
1Jn 1:9

28:17
f Ge 9:6

28:18
g Pr 10:9

28:19
h Pr 12:11

28:20
i ver 22;
Pr 10:6;
1Ti 6:9

28:21
j Pr 18:5
k Eze 13:19

28:22
l ver 20;
Pr 23:6

28:23
m Pr 27:5-6

28:24
n Pr 19:26
o Pr 18:9

28:25
p Pr 29:25

¹⁰He who leads the upright along an evil path
    will fall into his own trap,*a*
    but the blameless will receive a good inheritance.

¹¹A rich man may be wise in his own eyes,
    but a poor man who has discernment sees through him.

¹²When the righteous triumph, there is great elation;*b*
    but when the wicked rise to power, men go into hiding.*c*

¹³He who conceals his sins*d* does not prosper,
    but whoever confesses and renounces them
        finds mercy.*e*

¹⁴Blessed is the man who always fears the LORD,
    but he who hardens his heart falls into trouble.

¹⁵Like a roaring lion or a charging bear
    is a wicked man ruling over a helpless people.

¹⁶A tyrannical ruler lacks judgment,
    but he who hates ill-gotten gain will enjoy a long life.

¹⁷A man tormented by the guilt of murder
    will be a fugitive*f* till death;
    let no one support him.

¹⁸He whose walk is blameless is kept safe,
    but he whose ways are perverse will suddenly fall.*g*

¹⁹He who works his land will have abundant food,
    but the one who chases fantasies will have his fill
        of poverty.*h*

²⁰A faithful man will be richly blessed,
    but one eager to get rich will not go unpunished.*i*

²¹To show partiality is not good*j*—
    yet a man will do wrong for a piece of bread.*k*

²²A stingy man is eager to get rich
    and is unaware that poverty awaits him.*l*

²³He who rebukes a man will in the end gain more favor
    than he who has a flattering tongue.*m*

²⁴He who robs his father or mother*n*
    and says, "It's not wrong"—
    he is partner to him who destroys.*o*

²⁵A greedy man stirs up dissension,
    but he who trusts in the LORD*p* will prosper.

²⁶He who trusts in himself is a fool,^a
  but he who walks in wisdom is kept safe.

²⁷He who gives to the poor will lack nothing,^b
  but he who closes his eyes to them receives
    many curses.

²⁸When the wicked rise to power, people go into hiding;^c
  but when the wicked perish, the righteous thrive.

Chapter 29 Theme _____

29 A man who remains stiff-necked after many rebukes
  will suddenly be destroyed—without remedy.^d

²When the righteous thrive, the people rejoice;^e
  when the wicked rule, the people groan.^f

³A man who loves wisdom brings joy to his father,^g
  but a companion of prostitutes squanders his wealth.^h

⁴By justice a king gives a country stability,ⁱ
  but one who is greedy for bribes tears it down.

⁵Whoever flatters his neighbor
  is spreading a net for his feet.

⁶An evil man is snared by his own sin,^j
  but a righteous one can sing and be glad.

⁷The righteous care about justice for the poor,^k
  but the wicked have no such concern.

⁸Mockers stir up a city,
  but wise men turn away anger.^l

⁹If a wise man goes to court with a fool,
  the fool rages and scoffs, and there is no peace.

¹⁰Bloodthirsty men hate a man of integrity
  and seek to kill the upright.^m

¹¹A fool gives full vent to his anger,
  but a wise man keeps himself under control.ⁿ

¹²If a ruler listens to lies,
  all his officials become wicked.

¹³The poor man and the oppressor have this in common:
  The LORD gives sight to the eyes of both.^o

¹⁴If a king judges the poor with fairness,
  his throne will always be secure.^p

28:26
^aPs 4:5; Pr 3:5

28:27
^bDt 15:7; 24:19;
Pr 19:17; 22:9

28:28
^cver 12

29:1
^d2Ch 36:16;
Pr 6:15

29:2
^eEst 8:15
^fPr 28:12

29:3
^gPr 10:1
^hPr 5:8-10;
Lk 15:11-32

29:4
ⁱPr 8:15-16

29:6
^jEcc 9:12

29:7
^kJob 29:16;
Ps 41:1;
Pr 31:8-9

29:8
^lPr 11:11;
16:14

29:10
^m1Jn 3:12

29:11
ⁿPr 12:16;
19:11

29:13
^oPr 22:2;
Mt 5:45

29:14
^pPs 72:1-5;
Pr 16:12

29:15
*a*Pr 10:1; 13:24;
17:21,25

¹⁵The rod of correction imparts wisdom,
   but a child left to himself disgraces his mother.*a*

¹⁶When the wicked thrive, so does sin,
   but the righteous will see their downfall.*b*

29:16
*b*Ps 37:35-36;
58:10; 91:8;
92:11

¹⁷Discipline your son, and he will give you peace;
   he will bring delight to your soul.*c*

¹⁸Where there is no revelation, the people cast off restraint;
   but blessed is he who keeps the law.*d*

29:17
*c*ver 15;
Pr 10:1

¹⁹A servant cannot be corrected by mere words;
   though he understands, he will not respond.

²⁰Do you see a man who speaks in haste?
   There is more hope for a fool than for him.*e*

29:18
*d*Ps 1:1-2;
119:1-2;
Jn 13:17

²¹If a man pampers his servant from youth,
   he will bring grief*a* in the end.

²²An angry man stirs up dissension,
   and a hot-tempered one commits many sins.*f*

29:20
*e*Pr 26:12;
Jas 1:19

²³A man's pride brings him low,
   but a man of lowly spirit gains honor.*g*

²⁴The accomplice of a thief is his own enemy;
   he is put under oath and dare not testify.*h*

29:22
*f*Pr 14:17; 15:18;
26:21

²⁵Fear of man will prove to be a snare,
   but whoever trusts in the LORD*i* is kept safe.

²⁶Many seek an audience with a ruler,*j*
   but it is from the LORD that man gets justice.

29:23
*g*Pr 11:2; 15:33;
16:18; Isa 66:2;
Mt 23:12

²⁷The righteous detest the dishonest;
   the wicked detest the upright.*k*

29:24
*h*Lev 5:1

Chapter 30 Theme _____

30
The sayings of Agur son of Jakeh—an oracle*b*:

This man declared to Ithiel,
   to Ithiel and to Ucal:*c*

29:25
*i*Pr 28:25

²"I am the most ignorant of men;
   I do not have a man's understanding.

29:26
*j*Pr 19:6

³I have not learned wisdom,
   nor have I knowledge of the Holy One.*l*

29:27
*k*ver 10

---

a21 The meaning of the Hebrew for this word is uncertain.   *b1* Or *Jakeh of Massa*
c1 Masoretic Text; with a different word division of the Hebrew *declared,* "I am weary, O God; /
I am weary, O God, and faint."

30:3
*l*Pr 9:10

4Who has gone up^a to heaven and come down?
Who has gathered up the wind in the hollow^b of
his hands?
Who has wrapped up the waters^c in his cloak?^d
Who has established all the ends of the earth?
What is his name,^e and the name of his son?
Tell me if you know!

5"Every word of God is flawless;^f
he is a shield^g to those who take refuge in him.
6Do not add^h to his words,
or he will rebuke you and prove you a liar.

7"Two things I ask of you, O Lord;
do not refuse me before I die:
8Keep falsehood and lies far from me;
give me neither poverty nor riches,
but give me only my daily bread.ⁱ
9Otherwise, I may have too much and disown^j you
and say, 'Who is the Lord?'^k
Or I may become poor and steal,
and so dishonor the name of my God.^l

10"Do not slander a servant to his master,
or he will curse you, and you will pay for it.

11"There are those who curse their fathers
and do not bless their mothers;^m
12those who are pure in their own eyesⁿ
and yet are not cleansed of their filth;^o
13those whose eyes are ever so haughty,^p
whose glances are so disdainful;
14those whose teeth^q are swords
and whose jaws are set with knives^r
to devour^s the poor^t from the earth,
the needy from among mankind.^u

15"The leech has two daughters.
'Give! Give!' they cry.

"There are three things that are never satisfied,^v
four that never say, 'Enough!':
16the grave,^a ^w the barren womb,
land, which is never satisfied with water,
and fire, which never says, 'Enough!'

17"The eye that mocks^x a father,
that scorns obedience to a mother,

^a 16 Hebrew Sheol

1116

30:4
^aPs 24:1-2;
Jn 3:13;
Eph 4:7-10
^bPs 104:3;
Isa 40:12
^cJob 26:8;
38:8-9
^dGe 1:2
^eRev 19:12

30:5
^fPs 12:6;
18:30
^gGe 15:1;
Ps 84:11

30:6
^hDt 4:2; 12:32;
Rev 22:18

30:8
ⁱMt 6:11

30:9
^jJos 24:27;
Isa 1:4; 59:13
^kDt 6:12;
8:10-14;
Hos 13:6
^lDt 8:12

30:11
^mPr 20:20

30:12
ⁿPr 16:2;
Lk 18:11
^oJer 2:23,35

30:13
^p2Sa 22:28;
Job 41:34;
Ps 131:1;
Pr 6:17

30:14
^qJob 4:11;
29:17;
Ps 3:7
^rPs 57:4
^sJob 24:9;
Ps 14:4
^tAm 8:4;
Mic 2:2
^uJob 19:22

30:15
^vPr 27:20

30:16
^wPr 27:20;
Isa 5:14; 14:9,11;
Hab 2:5

30:17
^xDt 21:18-21;
Pr 23:22

30:17
a Job 15:23

will be pecked out by the ravens of the valley,
 will be eaten by the vultures.*a*

18"There are three things that are too amazing for me,
 four that I do not understand:
19the way of an eagle in the sky,
 the way of a snake on a rock,
the way of a ship on the high seas,
 and the way of a man with a maiden.

30:20
b Pr 5:6

20"This is the way of an adulteress:
 She eats and wipes her mouth
 and says, 'I've done nothing wrong.'*b*

21"Under three things the earth trembles,
 under four it cannot bear up:

30:22
c Pr 19:10;
29:2

22a servant who becomes king,*c*
 a fool who is full of food,
23an unloved woman who is married,
 and a maidservant who displaces her mistress.

24"Four things on earth are small,
 yet they are extremely wise:
25Ants are creatures of little strength,
 yet they store up their food in the summer;*d*

30:25
d Pr 6:6-8

26coneys*a e* are creatures of little power,
 yet they make their home in the crags;
27locusts*f* have no king,
 yet they advance together in ranks;
28a lizard can be caught with the hand,
 yet it is found in kings' palaces.

30:26
e Ps 104:18

29"There are three things that are stately in
 their stride,
 four that move with stately bearing:
30a lion, mighty among beasts,
 who retreats before nothing;
31a strutting rooster, a he-goat,
 and a king with his army around him.*b*

30:27
f Ex 10:4

32"If you have played the fool and exalted yourself,
 or if you have planned evil,
 clap your hand over your mouth!*g*
33For as churning the milk produces butter,
 and as twisting the nose produces blood,
 so stirring up anger produces strife."

30:32
g Job 21:5;
29:9

a 26 That is, the hyrax or rock badger   *b 31* Or *king secure against revolt*

Chapter 31 Theme

31 The sayings[a] of King Lemuel—an oracle[a] his mother taught him:

2 "O my son, O son of my womb,
   O son of my vows,[b][b]
3 do not spend your strength on women,
   your vigor on those who ruin kings.[c]

4 "It is not for kings, O Lemuel—
   not for kings to drink wine,[d]
   not for rulers to crave beer,
5 lest they drink[e] and forget what the law decrees,[f]
   and deprive all the oppressed of their rights.
6 Give beer to those who are perishing,
   wine[g] to those who are in anguish;
7 let them drink[h] and forget their poverty
   and remember their misery no more.

8 "Speak[i] up for those who cannot speak for themselves,
   for the rights of all who are destitute.
9 Speak up and judge fairly;
   defend the rights of the poor and needy."[j]

10 [c]A wife of noble character[k] who can find?[l]
   She is worth far more than rubies.
11 Her husband[m] has full confidence in her
   and lacks nothing of value.[n]
12 She brings him good, not harm,
   all the days of her life.
13 She selects wool and flax
   and works with eager hands.[o]
14 She is like the merchant ships,
   bringing her food from afar.
15 She gets up while it is still dark;
   she provides food for her family
   and portions for her servant girls.
16 She considers a field and buys it;
   out of her earnings she plants a vineyard.
17 She sets about her work vigorously;
   her arms are strong for her tasks.
18 She sees that her trading is profitable,
   and her lamp does not go out at night.
19 In her hand she holds the distaff
   and grasps the spindle with her fingers.

a 1 Or *of Lemuel king of Massa, which*   b 2 Or / *the answer to my prayers*   c 10 Verses 10-31 are an acrostic, each verse beginning with a successive letter of the Hebrew alphabet.

31:1 a Pr 22:17

31:2 b Jdg 11:30; Isa 49:15

31:3 c Dt 17:17; 1Ki 11:3; Ne 13:26; Pr 5:1-14

31:4 d Pr 20:1; Ecc 10:16-17; Isa 5:22

31:5 e 1Ki 16:9 f Pr 16:12; Hos 4:11

31:6 g Ge 14:18

31:7 h Est 1:10

31:8 i 1Sa 19:4; Job 29:12-17

31:9 j Lev 19:15; Dt 1:16; Pr 24:23; 29:7; Isa 1:17; Jer 22:16

31:10 k Ru 3:11; Pr 12:4; 18:22 l Pr 8:35; 19:14

31:11 m Ge 2:18 n Pr 12:4

31:13 o 1Ti 2:9-10

31:20
a Dt 15:11;
Eph 4:28;
Heb 13:16

²⁰She opens her arms to the poor
    and extends her hands to the needy.^a
²¹When it snows, she has no fear for her household;
    for all of them are clothed in scarlet.
²²She makes coverings for her bed;
    she is clothed in fine linen and purple.
²³Her husband is respected at the city gate,
    where he takes his seat among the elders^b of the land.

31:23
b Ex 3:16;
Ru 4:1,11;
Pr 12:4

²⁴She makes linen garments and sells them,
    and supplies the merchants with sashes.
²⁵She is clothed with strength and dignity;
    she can laugh at the days to come.
²⁶She speaks with wisdom,
    and faithful instruction is on her tongue.^c
²⁷She watches over the affairs of her household
    and does not eat the bread of idleness.

31:26
c Pr 10:31

²⁸Her children arise and call her blessed;
    her husband also, and he praises her:
²⁹"Many women do noble things,
    but you surpass them all."
³⁰Charm is deceptive, and beauty is fleeting;
    but a woman who fears the LORD is to be praised.
³¹Give her the reward she has earned,
    and let her works bring her praise^d at the city gate.

31:31
d Pr 11:16

Theme of Proverbs:

SEGMENT DIVISIONS

MAIN DIVISIONS		CHAPTER THEMES	
THE CRY OF WISDOM, KNOWLEDGE, AND UNDERSTANDING		1	
		2	
		3	
		4	
		5	
		6	
		7	
		8	
		9	
THE PROVERBS OF SOLOMON AND WISDOM OF WISE MEN		10	
		11	
		12	
		13	
		14	
		15	
		16	
		17	
		18	
		19	
		20	
		21	
		22	
		23	
		24	
SOLOMON'S PROVERBS TRANSCRIBED		25	
		26	
		27	
		28	
		29	
WORDS & COUNSEL OF OTHERS		30	
		31	

Author:

Date:

Purpose:

Key Words:

wisdom, guidance (wise)

judgment, victory

knowledge

understanding (discerning, insight, discernment)

fear(s)

my son (O son)

command(s)

instruction (discipline, teach, teaching, lesson)

tongue

fool, fool's, foolish (folly, simple way)

ECCLESIASTES

*L*ife seems inconsistent, unpredictable, and unfair at times. No matter the generation, no matter the time in history, the righteous and the wicked have the same experiences, face the same trials, grapple with the same problems. And all end up in the grave!

As people grow older they look back and see what a breath, what a vapor, life is. It passes so quickly. What was its purpose? Was what we strove to attain worth it? Did we live as we should have?

"What does man gain from all his labor at which he toils under the sun?" (Ecclesiastes 1:3). And what is the conclusion of it all? (See Ecclesiastes 12:13.)

∾ THINGS TO DO

General Instructions

1. A careful observation of Ecclesiastes gives insight into why this book is included in the Bible. So as you begin your study of this book, do the following:

   a. Remember that all you read must be considered in the context of the whole counsel of God.

   b. Read 1:1-3 and 12:13, 14 to see how Ecclesiastes begins and ends. Keep these verses in mind as you study.

2. In the margin of chapter 1, list what you learn about the author:

   a. Who and/or what he is; how he describes himself; what he pursued, had, or experienced, and what gain it was to him. This is important. You may want to list your insights on a piece of paper first as you go through Ecclesiastes. Then when you have completed your study, summarize and record them in the margin of chapter 1.

   b. As you read the book, observe what the author has seen, come to know, commends, and concludes. Mark or note these insights in a special way, since these usually include important key repeated phrases.

   c. After chapter 4, watch for and list in the margin the author's commands and warnings. For example, in 5:1 he tells us to guard our steps when we go into the house of God.

3. As you read each chapter mark in a distinctive way the key words listed on the ECCLESIASTES AT A GLANCE chart on page 1138. List these key words on an index card that you can use as a bookmark while observing this book.

4. When you finish observing each chapter:

   a. Look at every reference to God. On a piece of paper list all you learn about him, what he does, and what we are to do in respect to him.

   b. Also mark the contrasting groups of people: the righteous and the wicked, the wise and the foolish. On a separate piece of paper list what you learn about these persons from each chapter.

   c. Also make a list of what you learn about *wealth* and *labor (work, toil, effort)*.

   d. When you have completed your study of the book, summarize in one of the margins what you learned from compiling the above lists.

5. Record the theme of each chapter on ECCLESIASTES AT A GLANCE and on the line next to the chapter number in the text.

Chapters 1-8: Exploring Life's Inconsistencies

1. As you read, mark the key words listed on ECCLESIASTES AT A GLANCE. Also watch for and mark these words: *explore, discover (comprehend), discovered (find),* and *turned.*

2. Mark the word *meaningless*. The word *meaningless* is from the word *hebel*.

    a. *Hebel* appears more in Ecclesiastes than in any other book of the Bible; half of all its occurrences are in Ecclesiastes.

    b. Except for 11:8 and 12:8, all the occurrences of *meaningless* appear in this first section of Ecclesiastes. Therefore after you finish marking each occurrence of these words, list in one of the chapter margins everything you learn from the text about *meaningless*.

Chapters 9-12: Explaining Life's Inconsistencies

1. Read 9:1 and mark the word *concluded*. Do you see how this verse might be used as a pivotal point in the book? If so, watch for any explanations the author might give to life's inconsistencies.

2. When you finish observing chapter 10, review each reference to wisdom that you have marked and in the margin list everything you learned about wisdom from Ecclesiastes.

3. As you read 12:1-7, think of the human body and the effects of age on its members. See if you find any "pictorial descriptions" of the body and what happens as you get old (e.g., "when the grinders cease because they are few" might be a picture of losing some teeth).

4. Complete ECCLESIASTES AT A GLANCE.

∾ THINGS TO THINK ABOUT

1. Where have you been searching for the meaning of life? What have you been pursuing in order to find fulfillment or happiness?

2. Where can the meaning of life be found? Where can't it be found?

3. The author of Ecclesiastes is Solomon, David's son, who was the richest and wisest of men. What do you learn from his experience that can help you?

4. Review all you have learned about God from this book. Since God is going to bring every act to judgment, even those of Christians (2 Corinthians 5:10; Romans 14:10), what are you doing that you should continue to do and what do you need to stop doing? Will you?

∾∾∾∾∾

Chapter 1 Theme _____

1 The words of the Teacher,[a][a] son of David, king in Jerusalem:[b]

2"Meaningless! Meaningless!"
    says the Teacher.
"Utterly meaningless!
    Everything is meaningless."[c]

3What does man gain from all his labor
    at which he toils under the sun?[d]
4Generations come and generations go,
    but the earth remains forever.[e]
5The sun rises and the sun sets,
    and hurries back to where it rises.[f]
6The wind blows to the south
    and turns to the north;

1:1
[a]ver 12;
Ecc 7:27; 12:10
[b]Pr 1:1

1:2
[c]Ps 39:5-6; 62:9;
144:4; Ecc 12:8;
Ro 8:20-21

1:3
[d]Ecc 2:11,22;
3:9; 5:15-16

1:4
[e]Ps 104:5;
119:90

1:5
[f]Ps 19:5-6

---

a 1 Or *leader of the assembly*; also in verses 2 and 12

round and round it goes,
    ever returning on its course.
⁷All streams flow into the sea,
    yet the sea is never full.
To the place the streams come from,
    there they return again.^a
⁸All things are wearisome,
    more than one can say.
The eye never has enough of seeing,^b
    nor the ear its fill of hearing.
⁹What has been will be again,
    what has been done will be done again;^c
    there is nothing new under the sun.
¹⁰Is there anything of which one can say,
    "Look! This is something new"?
It was here already, long ago;
    it was here before our time.
¹¹There is no remembrance of men of old,
    and even those who are yet to come
will not be remembered
    by those who follow.^d

¹²I, the Teacher,^e was king over Israel in Jerusalem. ¹³I devoted myself to study and to explore by wisdom all that is done under heaven. What a heavy burden God has laid on men!^f ¹⁴I have seen all the things that are done under the sun; all of them are meaningless, a chasing after the wind.^g

¹⁵What is twisted cannot be straightened;^h
    what is lacking cannot be counted.

¹⁶I thought to myself, "Look, I have grown and increased in wisdom more than anyone who has ruled over Jerusalem before me;ⁱ I have experienced much of wisdom and knowledge." ¹⁷Then I applied myself to the understanding of wisdom,^j and also of madness and folly,^k but I learned that this, too, is a chasing after the wind.

¹⁸For with much wisdom comes much sorrow;
    the more knowledge, the more grief.^l

Chapter 2 Theme

2 I thought in my heart, "Come now, I will test you with pleasure^m to find out what is good." But that also proved to be meaningless. ²"Laughter,"ⁿ I said, "is foolish. And what does pleasure accomplish?" ³I tried cheering myself with wine,^o and embracing folly^p—my mind still guiding me with wisdom. I

**Cross references (margin):**

1:7 ^aJob 36:28

1:8 ^bPr 27:20

1:9 ^cEcc 2:12; 3:15

1:11 ^dEcc 2:16

1:12 ^ever 1

1:13 ^fGe 3:17; Ecc 3:10

1:14 ^gEcc 2:11,17

1:15 ^hEcc 7:13

1:16 ⁱ1Ki 3:12; 4:30; Ecc 2:9

1:17 ^jEcc 7:23 ^kEcc 2:3,12; 7:25

1:18 ^lEcc 2:23; 12:12

2:1 ^mEcc 7:4; 8:15; Lk 12:19

2:2 ⁿPr 14:13; Ecc 7:6

2:3 ^over 24-25; Ecc 3:12-13 ^pEcc 1:17

wanted to see what was worthwhile for men to do under heaven during the few days of their lives.

[4]I undertook great projects: I built houses for myself[a] and planted vineyards.[b] [5]I made gardens and parks and planted all kinds of fruit trees in them. [6]I made reservoirs to water groves of flourishing trees. [7]I bought male and female slaves and had other slaves who were born in my house. I also owned more herds and flocks than anyone in Jerusalem before me. [8]I amassed silver and gold[c] for myself, and the treasure of kings and provinces. I acquired men and women singers,[d] and a harem[a] as well—the delights of the heart of man. [9]I became greater by far than anyone in Jerusalem before me.[e] In all this my wisdom stayed with me.

[10]I denied myself nothing my eyes desired;
   I refused my heart no pleasure.
My heart took delight in all my work,
   and this was the reward for all my labor.
[11]Yet when I surveyed all that my hands had done
   and what I had toiled to achieve,
everything was meaningless, a chasing after the wind;[f]
   nothing was gained under the sun.[g]

[12]Then I turned my thoughts to consider wisdom,
   and also madness and folly.[h]
What more can the king's successor do
   than what has already been done?[i]
[13]I saw that wisdom[j] is better than folly,[k]
   just as light is better than darkness.
[14]The wise man has eyes in his head,
   while the fool walks in the darkness;
but I came to realize
   that the same fate overtakes them both.[l]

[15]Then I thought in my heart,

"The fate of the fool will overtake me also.
   What then do I gain by being wise?"[m]
I said in my heart,
   "This too is meaningless."
[16]For the wise man, like the fool, will not be long
      remembered;
   in days to come both will be forgotten.[n]
Like the fool, the wise man too must die!

[17]So I hated life, because the work that is done under the sun was grievous to me. All of it is meaningless, a chasing after the wind.[o] [18]I hated all the things I had toiled for under the sun, because I must leave them to the one who comes after me.[p]

---

[a]8 The meaning of the Hebrew for this phrase is uncertain.

2:4
[a]1Ki 7:1-12
[b]SS 8:11

2:8
[c]1Ki 9:28;
10:10,14,21
[d]2Sa 19:35

2:9
[e]1Ch 29:25;
Ecc 1:16

2:11
[f]Ecc 1:14
[g]Ecc 1:3

2:12
[h]Ecc 1:17
[i]Ecc 1:9; 7:25

2:13
[j]Ecc 7:19; 9:18
[k]Ecc 7:11-12

2:14
[l]Ps 49:10;
Pr 17:24;
Ecc 3:19; 6:6;
7:2; 9:3,11-12

2:15
[m]Ecc 6:8

2:16
[n]Ecc 1:11; 9:5

2:17
[o]Ecc 4:2

2:18
[p]Ps 39:6; 49:10

2:22
a Ecc 1:3; 3:9

2:23
b Job 5:7; 14:1;
Ecc 1:18

2:24
c Ecc 8:15;
1Co 15:32
d Ecc 3:22
e Ecc 3:12-13;
5:17-19;
9:7-10

2:26
f Job 27:17
g Pr 13:22

3:1
h ver 11,17;
Ecc 8:6

3:7
i Am 5:13

3:9
j Ecc 1:3

3:10
k Ecc 1:13

3:11
l ver 1
m Job 11:7;
Ecc 8:17
n Job 28:23;
Ro 11:33

3:13
o Ecc 2:3
p Ps 34:12
q Dt 12:7,18;
Ecc 2:24; 5:19

[19] And who knows whether he will be a wise man or a fool? Yet he will have control over all the work into which I have poured my effort and skill under the sun. This too is meaningless. [20] So my heart began to despair over all my toilsome labor under the sun. [21] For a man may do his work with wisdom, knowledge and skill, and then he must leave all he owns to someone who has not worked for it. This too is meaningless and a great misfortune. [22] What does a man get for all the toil and anxious striving with which he labors under the sun?[a] [23] All his days his work is pain and grief;[b] even at night his mind does not rest. This too is meaningless.

[24] A man can do nothing better than to eat and drink[c] and find satisfaction in his work.[d] This too, I see, is from the hand of God,[e] [25] for without him, who can eat or find enjoyment? [26] To the man who pleases him, God gives wisdom, knowledge and happiness, but to the sinner he gives the task of gathering and storing up wealth[f] to hand it over to the one who pleases God.[g] This too is meaningless, a chasing after the wind.

Chapter 3 Theme

3 There is a time[h] for everything,
   and a season for every activity under heaven:

2   a time to be born and a time to die,
     a time to plant and a time to uproot,
3   a time to kill and a time to heal,
     a time to tear down and a time to build,
4   a time to weep and a time to laugh,
     a time to mourn and a time to dance,
5   a time to scatter stones and a time to gather them,
     a time to embrace and a time to refrain,
6   a time to search and a time to give up,
     a time to keep and a time to throw away,
7   a time to tear and a time to mend,
     a time to be silent[i] and a time to speak,
8   a time to love and a time to hate,
     a time for war and a time for peace.

[9] What does the worker gain from his toil?[j] [10] I have seen the burden God has laid on men.[k] [11] He has made everything beautiful in its time.[l] He has also set eternity in the hearts of men; yet they cannot fathom[m] what God has done from beginning to end.[n] [12] I know that there is nothing better for men than to be happy and do good while they live. [13] That everyone may eat and drink,[o] and find satisfaction[p] in all his toil—this is the gift of God.[q] [14] I know that everything God does will endure forever;

1125

nothing can be added to it and nothing taken from it. God does it so that men will revere him.[a]

> [15]Whatever is has already been,[b]
> and what will be has been before;[c]
> and God will call the past to account.[a]

[16]And I saw something else under the sun:

> In the place of judgment—wickedness was there,
> in the place of justice—wickedness was there.

[17]I thought in my heart,

> "God will bring to judgment[d]
> both the righteous and the wicked,
> for there will be a time for every activity,
> a time for every deed."[e]

[18]I also thought, "As for men, God tests them so that they may see that they are like the animals.[f] [19]Man's fate[g] is like that of the animals; the same fate awaits them both: As one dies, so dies the other. All have the same breath[b]; man has no advantage over the animal. Everything is meaningless. [20]All go to the same place; all come from dust, and to dust all return.[h] [21]Who knows if the spirit of man rises upward[i] and if the spirit of the animal[c] goes down into the earth?"

[22]So I saw that there is nothing better for a man than to enjoy his work,[j] because that is his lot.[k] For who can bring him to see what will happen after him?

Chapter 4 Theme

4 Again I looked and saw all the oppression[l] that was taking place under the sun:

> I saw the tears of the oppressed—
> and they have no comforter;
> power was on the side of their oppressors—
> and they have no comforter.[m]
> [2]And I declared that the dead,[n]
> who had already died,
> are happier than the living,
> who are still alive.[o]
> [3]But better than both
> is he who has not yet been,[p]
> who has not seen the evil
> that is done under the sun.[q]

---

[a]15 Or *God calls back the past*   [b]19 Or *spirit*   [c]21 Or *Who knows the spirit of man, which rises upward, or the spirit of the animal, which*

3:14
[a]Job 23:15;
Ecc 5:7; 7:18;
8:12-13; Jas 1:17

3:15
[b]Ecc 6:10
[c]Ecc 1:9

3:17
[d]Job 19:29;
Ecc 11:9;
Mt 16:27;
Ro 2:6-8;
2Th 1:6-7
[e]ver 1

3:18
[f]Ps 73:22

3:19
[g]Ecc 2:14

3:20
[h]Ge 2:7; 3:19;
Job 34:15

3:21
[i]Ecc 12:7

3:22
[j]Ecc 2:24; 5:18
[k]Job 31:2

4:1
[l]Ps 12:5;
Ecc 3:16
[m]La 1:16

4:2
[n]Jer 20:17-18;
22:10
[o]Job 3:17; 10:18

4:3
[p]Job 3:16;
Ecc 6:3
[q]Job 3:22

4:4
a Ecc 1:14

⁴And I saw that all labor and all achievement spring from man's envy of his neighbor. This too is meaningless, a chasing after the wind.ᵃ

⁵The fool folds his handsᵇ
    and ruins himself.
⁶Better one handful with tranquillity
    than two handfuls with toilᶜ
    and chasing after the wind.

⁷Again I saw something meaningless under the sun:

⁸There was a man all alone;
    he had neither son nor brother.
There was no end to his toil,
    yet his eyes were not contentᵈ with his wealth.
"For whom am I toiling," he asked,
    "and why am I depriving myself of enjoyment?"
This too is meaningless—
    a miserable business!

4:5
b Pr 6:10

⁹Two are better than one,
    because they have a good return for their work:
¹⁰If one falls down,
    his friend can help him up.
But pity the man who falls
    and has no one to help him up!
¹¹Also, if two lie down together, they will keep warm.
    But how can one keep warm alone?
¹²Though one may be overpowered,
    two can defend themselves.
A cord of three strands is not quickly broken.

4:6
c Pr 15:16-17;
16:8

¹³Better a poor but wise youth than an old but foolish king who no longer knows how to take warning. ¹⁴The youth may have come from prison to the kingship, or he may have been born in poverty within his kingdom. ¹⁵I saw that all who lived and walked under the sun followed the youth, the king's successor. ¹⁶There was no end to all the people who were before them. But those who came later were not pleased with the successor. This too is meaningless, a chasing after the wind.

4:8
d Pr 27:20

Chapter 5 Theme

5 Guard your steps when you go to the house of God. Go near to listen rather than to offer the sacrifice of fools, who do not know that they do wrong.

²Do not be quick with your mouth,
    do not be hasty in your heart
    to utter anything before God.ᵉ

5:2
e Jdg 11:35

God is in heaven
and you are on earth,
so let your words be few.[a]
[3] As a dream[b] comes when there are many cares,
so the speech of a fool when there are many words.[c]

[4] When you make a vow to God, do not delay in fulfilling it.[d] He has no pleasure in fools; fulfill your vow.[e] [5] It is better not to vow than to make a vow and not fulfill it.[f] [6] Do not let your mouth lead you into sin. And do not protest to the ⌊temple⌋ messenger, "My vow was a mistake." Why should God be angry at what you say and destroy the work of your hands? [7] Much dreaming and many words are meaningless. Therefore stand in awe of God.[g]

[8] If you see the poor oppressed[h] in a district, and justice and rights denied, do not be surprised at such things; for one official is eyed by a higher one, and over them both are others higher still. [9] The increase from the land is taken by all; the king himself profits from the fields.

[10] Whoever loves money never has money enough;
whoever loves wealth is never satisfied with his income.
This too is meaningless.

[11] As goods increase,
so do those who consume them.
And what benefit are they to the owner
except to feast his eyes on them?

[12] The sleep of a laborer is sweet,
whether he eats little or much,
but the abundance of a rich man
permits him no sleep.[i]

[13] I have seen a grievous evil under the sun:[j]

wealth hoarded to the harm of its owner,
[14]   or wealth lost through some misfortune,
so that when he has a son
there is nothing left for him.
[15] Naked a man comes from his mother's womb,
and as he comes, so he departs.[k]
He takes nothing from his labor[l]
that he can carry in his hand.[m]

[16] This too is a grievous evil:

As a man comes, so he departs,
and what does he gain,
since he toils for the wind?[n]

5:2
[a] Job 6:24;
Pr 10:19; 20:25

5:3
[b] Job 20:8
[c] Ecc 10:14

5:4
[d] Dt 23:21;
Jdg 11:35;
Ps 119:60
[e] Nu 30:2;
Ps 66:13-14;
76:11

5:5
[f] Nu 30:2-4;
Pr 20:25;
Jnh 2:9; Ac 5:4

5:7
[g] Ecc 3:14; 12:13

5:8
[h] Ps 12:5;
Ecc 4:1

5:12
[i] Job 20:20

5:13
[j] Ecc 6:1-2

5:15
[k] Job 1:21
[l] Ps 49:17;
1Ti 6:7
[m] Ecc 1:3

5:16
[n] Pr 11:29;
Ecc 1:3

5:18
a Ecc 2:3
b Ecc 2:10,24

5:19
c 1Ch 29:12;
2Ch 1:12
d Ecc 6:2
e Job 31:2
f Ecc 2:24; 3:13

5:20
g Dt 12:7,18

6:2
h Ps 17:14;
Ecc 5:19
i Ecc 5:13

6:3
j Job 3:16;
Ecc 4:3
k Job 3:3

6:7
l Pr 16:26; 27:20

6:8
m Ecc 2:15

6:9
n Ecc 1:14

6:12
o Job 10:20
p Job 14:2;
Ps 39:6; Jas 4:14

17All his days he eats in darkness,
with great frustration, affliction and anger.

18Then I realized that it is good and proper for a man to eat and drink,a and to find satisfaction in his toilsome laborb under the sun during the few days of life God has given him—for this is his lot. 19Moreover, when God gives any man wealth and possessions,c and enables him to enjoy them,d to accept his lote and be happy in his work—this is a gift of God.f 20He seldom reflects on the days of his life, because God keeps him occupied with gladness of heart.g

Chapter 6 Theme

6 I have seen another evil under the sun, and it weighs heavily on men: 2God gives a man wealth, possessions and honor, so that he lacks nothing his heart desires, but God does not enable him to enjoy them,h and a stranger enjoys them instead. This is meaningless, a grievous evil.i

3A man may have a hundred children and live many years; yet no matter how long he lives, if he cannot enjoy his prosperity and does not receive proper burial, I say that a stillbornj child is better off than he.k 4It comes without meaning, it departs in darkness, and in darkness its name is shrouded. 5Though it never saw the sun or knew anything, it has more rest than does that man— 6even if he lives a thousand years twice over but fails to enjoy his prosperity. Do not all go to the same place?

7All man's efforts are for his mouth,
yet his appetite is never satisfied.l
8What advantage has a wise man
over a fool?m
What does a poor man gain
by knowing how to conduct himself before others?
9Better what the eye sees
than the roving of the appetite.
This too is meaningless,
a chasing after the wind.n

10Whatever exists has already been named,
and what man is has been known;
no man can contend
with one who is stronger than he.
11The more the words,
the less the meaning,
and how does that profit anyone?

12For who knows what is good for a man in life, during the few and meaningless dayso he passes through like a shadow?p Who can tell him what will happen under the sun after he is gone?

Chapter 7 Theme _____

7 A good name is better than fine perfume,[a]
and the day of death better than the day of birth.

[2]It is better to go to a house of mourning
than to go to a house of feasting,
for death[b] is the destiny[c] of every man;
the living should take this to heart.

[3]Sorrow is better than laughter,[d]
because a sad face is good for the heart.

[4]The heart of the wise is in the house of mourning,
but the heart of fools is in the house of pleasure.[e]

[5]It is better to heed a wise man's rebuke[f]
than to listen to the song of fools.

[6]Like the crackling of thorns[g] under the pot,
so is the laughter[h] of fools.
This too is meaningless.

[7]Extortion turns a wise man into a fool,
and a bribe[i] corrupts the heart.

[8]The end of a matter is better than its beginning,
and patience[j] is better than pride.

[9]Do not be quickly provoked[k] in your spirit,
for anger resides in the lap of fools.

[10]Do not say, "Why were the old days better than these?"
For it is not wise to ask such questions.

[11]Wisdom, like an inheritance, is a good thing[l]
and benefits those who see the sun.[m]

[12]Wisdom is a shelter
as money is a shelter,
but the advantage of knowledge is this:
that wisdom preserves the life of its possessor.

[13]Consider what God has done:[n]

Who can straighten
what he has made crooked?[o]

[14]When times are good, be happy;
but when times are bad, consider:
God has made the one
as well as the other.
Therefore, a man cannot discover
anything about his future.

[15]In this meaningless life[p] of mine I have seen both of these:

a righteous man perishing in his righteousness,
and a wicked man living long in his wickedness.[q]

7:1
a Pr 22:1; SS 1:3

7:2
b Pr 11:19
c Ps 90:12

7:3
d Pr 14:13

7:4
e Ecc 2:1;
Jer 16:8

7:5
f Ps 141:5;
Pr 13:18;
15:31-32

7:6
g Ps 58:9; 118:12
h Ecc 2:2

7:7
i Ex 18:21; 23:8;
Dt 16:19

7:8
j Pr 14:29;
Gal 5:22;
Eph 4:2

7:9
k Mt 5:22;
Pr 14:17;
Jas 1:19

7:11
l Pr 8:10-11;
Ecc 2:13
m Ecc 11:7

7:13
n Ecc 2:24
o Ecc 1:15

7:15
p Job 7:7
q Ecc 8:12-14;
Jer 12:1

7:17
a Job 15:32;
Ps 55:23

¹⁶Do not be overrighteous,
    neither be overwise—
    why destroy yourself?
¹⁷Do not be overwicked,
    and do not be a fool—
    why die before your time?[a]

7:18
b Ecc 3:14

¹⁸It is good to grasp the one
    and not let go of the other.
    The man who fears God[b] will avoid all ⌊extremes⌋.[a]

7:19
c Ecc 2:13
d Ecc 9:13-18

¹⁹Wisdom[c] makes one wise man more powerful[d]
    than ten rulers in a city.

7:20
e Ps 14:3
f 1Ki 8:46;
2Ch 6:36;
Pr 20:9; Ro 3:23

²⁰There is not a righteous man[e] on earth
    who does what is right and never sins.[f]

²¹Do not pay attention to every word people say,
    or you[g] may hear your servant cursing you—
²²for you know in your heart
    that many times you yourself have cursed others.

7:21
g Pr 30:10

²³All this I tested by wisdom and I said,

    "I am determined to be wise"[h]—
    but this was beyond me.

7:23
h Ecc 1:17;
Ro 1:22

²⁴Whatever wisdom may be,
    it is far off and most profound—
    who can discover it?[i]

7:24
i Job 28:12

²⁵So I turned my mind to understand,
    to investigate and to search out wisdom and the
        scheme of things[j]
    and to understand the stupidity of wickedness
    and the madness of folly.[k]

7:25
j Job 28:3
k Ecc 1:17

²⁶I find more bitter than death
    the woman who is a snare,[l]
    whose heart is a trap
    and whose hands are chains.
    The man who pleases God will escape her,
    but the sinner she will ensnare.[m]

7:26
l Ex 10:7;
Jdg 14:15
m Pr 2:16-19;
5:3-5; 7:23;
22:14

²⁷"Look," says the Teacher,[b][n] "this is what I have discovered:

    "Adding one thing to another to discover the scheme
        of things—
²⁸   while I was still searching
    but not finding—
    I found one ⌊upright⌋ man among a thousand,
    but not one ⌊upright⌋ woman[o] among them all.

7:27
n Ecc 1:1

7:28
o 1Ki 11:3

a 18 Or *will follow them both*   b 27 Or *leader of the assembly*

²⁹This only have I found:
> God made mankind upright,
> but men have gone in search of many schemes."

Chapter 8 Theme _____

8 Who is like the wise man?
> Who knows the explanation of things?
> Wisdom brightens a man's face
> and changes its hard appearance.

²Obey the king's command, I say, because you took an oath before God. ³Do not be in a hurry to leave the king's presence.ᵃ Do not stand up for a bad cause, for he will do whatever he pleases. ⁴Since a king's word is supreme, who can say to him, "What are you doing?ᵇ"

> ⁵Whoever obeys his command will come to no harm,
> and the wise heart will know the proper time and
> procedure.
> ⁶For there is a proper time and procedure for every matter,ᶜ
> though a man's misery weighs heavily upon him.

> ⁷Since no man knows the future,
> who can tell him what is to come?
> ⁸No man has power over the wind to contain itᵃ;
> so no one has power over the day of his death.
> As no one is discharged in time of war,
> so wickedness will not release those who practice it.

⁹All this I saw, as I applied my mind to everything done under the sun. There is a time when a man lords it over others to his ownᵇ hurt. ¹⁰Then too, I saw the wicked buriedᵈ—those who used to come and go from the holy place and receive praiseᶜ in the city where they did this. This too is meaningless.

¹¹When the sentence for a crime is not quickly carried out, the hearts of the people are filled with schemes to do wrong. ¹²Although a wicked man commits a hundred crimes and still lives a long time, I know that it will go betterᵉ with God-fearing men,ᶠ who are reverent before God.ᵍ ¹³Yet because the wicked do not fear God,ʰ it will not go well with them, and their daysⁱ will not lengthen like a shadow.

¹⁴There is something else meaningless that occurs on earth: righteous men who get what the wicked deserve, and wicked men who get what the righteous deserve.ʲ This too, I say, is meaningless.ᵏ ¹⁵So I commend the enjoyment of lifeˡ, because nothing is better for a man under the sun than to eat and drinkᵐ and be

---

8:3
ᵃEcc 10:4

8:4
ᵇJob 9:12;
Est 1:19;
Da 4:35

8:6
ᶜEcc 3:1

8:10
ᵈEcc 1:11

8:12
ᵉDt 12:28;
Ps 37:11,18-19;
Pr 1:32-33;
Isa 3:10-11
ᶠEx 1:20
ᵍEcc 3:14

8:13
ʰEcc 3:14;
Isa 3:11
ⁱDt 4:40;
Job 5:26;
Ps 34:12;
Isa 65:20

8:14
ʲJob 21:7;
Ps 73:14;
Mal 3:15
ᵏEcc 7:15

8:15
ˡPs 42:8
ᵐEx 32:6;
Ecc 2:3

ᵃ8 Or *over his spirit to retain it*   ᵇ9 Or *to their*   ᶜ10 Some Hebrew manuscripts and Septuagint (Aquila); most Hebrew manuscripts *and are forgotten* glad.[a] Then joy will accompany him in his work all the days of the life God has given him under the sun.

[16] When I applied my mind to know wisdom[b] and to observe man's labor on earth[c]—his eyes not seeing sleep day or night— [17] then I saw all that God has done.[d] No one can comprehend what goes on under the sun. Despite all his efforts to search it out, man cannot discover its meaning. Even if a wise man claims he knows, he cannot really comprehend it.[e]

Chapter 9 Theme

9 So I reflected on all this and concluded that the righteous and the wise and what they do are in God's hands, but no man knows whether love or hate awaits him.[f] [2] All share a common destiny—the righteous and the wicked, the good and the bad,[a] the clean and the unclean, those who offer sacrifices and those who do not.

> As it is with the good man,
>   so with the sinner;
> as it is with those who take oaths,
>   so with those who are afraid to take them.[g]

[3] This is the evil in everything that happens under the sun: The same destiny overtakes all.[h] The hearts of men, moreover, are full of evil and there is madness in their hearts while they live,[i] and afterward they join the dead.[j] [4] Anyone who is among the living has hope[b]—even a live dog is better off than a dead lion!

> [5] For the living know that they will die,
>   but the dead know nothing;[k]
> they have no further reward,
>   and even the memory of them[l] is forgotten.[m]
> [6] Their love, their hate
>   and their jealousy have long since vanished;
> never again will they have a part
>   in anything that happens under the sun.[n]

[7] Go, eat your food with gladness, and drink your wine[o] with a joyful heart,[p] for it is now that God favors what you do. [8] Always be clothed in white,[q] and always anoint your head with oil. [9] Enjoy life with your wife,[r] whom you love, all the days of this meaningless life that God has given you under the sun—all your meaningless days. For this is your lot[s] in life and in your toilsome labor under the sun. [10] Whatever[t] your hand finds to do, do it with all your might,[u] for in the grave,[c][v] where you are going, there is neither working nor planning nor knowledge nor wisdom.[w]

8:15
a Ecc 2:24;
3:12-13;
5:18; 9:7

8:16
b Ecc 1:17
c Ecc 1:13

8:17
d Job 28:3
e Job 5:9; 28:23;
Ecc 3:11;
Ro 11:33

9:1
f Dt 33:3;
Job 12:10;
Ecc 10:14

9:2
g Job 9:22;
Ecc 2:14;
6:6; 7:2

9:3
h Job 9:22;
Ecc 2:14
i Jer 11:8; 13:10;
16:12; 17:9
j Job 21:26

9:5
k Job 14:21
l Ps 9:6
m Ecc 1:11; 2:16;
Isa 26:14

9:6
n Job 21:21

9:7
o Nu 6:20
p Ecc 2:24; 8:15

9:8
q Ps 23:5;
Rev 3:4

9:9
r Pr 5:18
s Job 31:2

9:10
t 1Sa 10:7
u Ecc 11:6;
Ro 12:11;
Col 3:23
v Nu 16:33
w Ecc 2:24

---

a 2 Septuagint (Aquila), Vulgate and Syriac; Hebrew does not have *and the bad.*   b 4 Or *What then is to be chosen? With all who live, there is hope*   c 10 Hebrew *Sheol*

[11]I have seen something else under the sun:

> The race is not to the swift
>> or the battle to the strong,[a]
> nor does food come to the wise[b]
>> or wealth to the brilliant
>> or favor to the learned;
> but time and chance[c] happen to them all.[d]

[12]Moreover, no man knows when his hour will come:

> As fish are caught in a cruel net,
>> or birds are taken in a snare,
> so men are trapped by evil times[e]
>> that fall unexpectedly upon them.[f]

[13]I also saw under the sun this example of wisdom[g] that greatly impressed me: [14]There was once a small city with only a few people in it. And a powerful king came against it, surrounded it and built huge siegeworks against it. [15]Now there lived in that city a man poor but wise, and he saved the city by his wisdom. But nobody remembered that poor man.[h] [16]So I said, "Wisdom is better than strength." But the poor man's wisdom is despised, and his words are no longer heeded.[i]

> [17]The quiet words of the wise are more to be heeded
>> than the shouts of a ruler of fools.
> [18]Wisdom[j] is better than weapons of war,
>> but one sinner destroys much good.

Chapter 10 Theme

10
> As dead flies give perfume a bad smell,
>> so a little folly[k] outweighs wisdom and honor.
> [2]The heart of the wise inclines to the right,
>> but the heart of the fool to the left.
> [3]Even as he walks along the road,
>> the fool lacks sense
>> and shows everyone[l] how stupid he is.
> [4]If a ruler's anger rises against you,
>> do not leave your post;[m]
>> calmness can lay great errors to rest.[n]

> [5]There is an evil I have seen under the sun,
>> the sort of error that arises from a ruler:
> [6]Fools are put in many high positions,[o]
>> while the rich occupy the low ones.
> [7]I have seen slaves on horseback,
>> while princes go on foot like slaves.[p]

9:11 [a]Am 2:14-15 [b]Job 32:13; Isa 47:10; Jer 9:23 [c]Ecc 2:14 [d]Dt 8:18

9:12 [e]Pr 29:6 [f]Ps 73:22; Ecc 2:14; 8:7

9:13 [g]2Sa 20:22

9:15 [h]Ge 40:14; Ecc 1:11; 2:16; 4:13

9:16 [i]Pr 21:22; Ecc 7:19

9:18 [j]ver 16

10:1 [k]Pr 13:16; 18:2

10:3 [l]Pr 13:16; 18:2

10:4 [m]Ecc 8:3 [n]Pr 16:14; 25:15

10:6 [o]Pr 29:2

10:7 [p]Pr 19:10

10:8
a Ps 7:15; 57:6;
Pr 26:27
b Est 2:23;
Ps 9:16;
Am 5:19

10:9
c Pr 26:27

10:11
d Ps 58:5; Isa 3:3

10:12
e Pr 10:32
f Pr 10:14; 14:3;
15:2; 18:7

10:14
g Pr 15:2;
Ecc 5:3;
6:12; 8:7
h Ecc 9:1

10:16
i Isa 3:4-5,12

10:17
j Dt 14:26;
1Sa 25:36;
Pr 31:4

10:18
k Pr 20:4;
24:30-34

10:19
l Ge 14:18;
Jdg 9:13

10:20
m Ex 22:28

11:1
n ver 6;
Isa 32:20;
Hos 10:12
o Dt 24:19;
Pr 19:17;
Mt 10:42

⁸Whoever digs a pit may fall into it;[a]
  whoever breaks through a wall may be bitten by
    a snake.[b]
⁹Whoever quarries stones may be injured by them;
  whoever splits logs may be endangered by them.[c]

¹⁰If the ax is dull
    and its edge unsharpened,
  more strength is needed
    but skill will bring success.

¹¹If a snake bites before it is charmed,
  there is no profit for the charmer.[d]

¹²Words from a wise man's mouth are gracious,[e]
  but a fool is consumed by his own lips.[f]
¹³At the beginning his words are folly;
  at the end they are wicked madness—
¹⁴ and the fool multiplies words.[g]

No one knows what is coming—
  who can tell him what will happen after him?[h]

¹⁵A fool's work wearies him;
  he does not know the way to town.

¹⁶Woe to you, O land whose king was a servant[a][i]
  and whose princes feast in the morning.
¹⁷Blessed are you, O land whose king is of noble birth
    and whose princes eat at a proper time—
  for strength and not for drunkenness.[j]

¹⁸If a man is lazy, the rafters sag;
  if his hands are idle, the house leaks.[k]

¹⁹A feast is made for laughter,
    and wine[l] makes life merry,
  but money is the answer for everything.

²⁰Do not revile the king[m] even in your thoughts,
    or curse the rich in your bedroom,
  because a bird of the air may carry your words,
    and a bird on the wing may report what you say.

Chapter 11 Theme

11
Cast[n] your bread upon the waters,
  for after many days you will find it again.[o]

a 16 Or *king is a child*

²Give portions to seven, yes to eight,
    for you do not know what disaster may come
      upon the land.

³If clouds are full of water,
    they pour rain upon the earth.
Whether a tree falls to the south or to the north,
    in the place where it falls, there will it lie.
⁴Whoever watches the wind will not plant;
    whoever looks at the clouds will not reap.

⁵As you do not know the path of the wind,*a*
    or how the body is formed*a* in a mother's womb,*b*
so you cannot understand the work of God,
    the Maker of all things.

⁶Sow your seed in the morning,
    and at evening let not your hands be idle,*c*
for you do not know which will succeed,
    whether this or that,
    or whether both will do equally well.

⁷Light is sweet,
    and it pleases the eyes to see the sun.*d*
⁸However many years a man may live,
    let him enjoy them all.
But let him remember*e* the days of darkness,
    for they will be many.
    Everything to come is meaningless.

⁹Be happy, young man, while you are young,
    and let your heart give you joy in the days of your
      youth.
Follow the ways of your heart
    and whatever your eyes see,
but know that for all these things
    God will bring you to judgment.*f*
¹⁰So then, banish anxiety*g* from your heart
    and cast off the troubles of your body,
    for youth and vigor are meaningless.*h*

Chapter 12 Theme

12
Remember*i* your Creator
    in the days of your youth,
before the days of trouble*j* come
    and the years approach when you will say,
    "I find no pleasure in them"—

---

a 5 Or *know how life* (or *the spirit*) / *enters the body being formed*

11:5
a Jn 3:8-10
b Ps 139:14-16

11:6
c Ecc 9:10

11:7
d Ecc 7:11

11:8
e Ecc 12:1

11:9
f Job 19:29;
Ecc 2:24; 3:17;
12:14;
Ro 14:10

11:10
g Ps 94:19
h Ecc 2:24

12:1
i Ecc 11:8
j 2Sa 19:35

12:4
a Jer 25:10

12:5
b Job 17:13;
10:21
c Jer 9:17;
Am 5:16

12:7
d Ge 3:19;
Job 34:15;
Ps 146:4
e Ecc 3:21
f Job 20:8;
Zec 12:1

12:8
g Ecc 1:2

12:9
h 1Ki 4:32

12:10
i Pr 22:20-21

12:11
j Ezr 9:8

12:12
k Ecc 1:18

12:13
l Dt 4:2; 10:12
m Mic 6:8

12:14
n Ecc 3:17
o Mt 10:26;
1Co 4:5

[2]before the sun and the light
and the moon and the stars grow dark,
and the clouds return after the rain;
[3]when the keepers of the house tremble,
and the strong men stoop,
when the grinders cease because they are few,
and those looking through the windows grow dim;
[4]when the doors to the street are closed
and the sound of grinding fades;
when men rise up at the sound of birds,
but all their songs grow faint;[a]
[5]when men are afraid of heights
and of dangers in the streets;
when the almond tree blossoms
and the grasshopper drags himself along
and desire no longer is stirred.
Then man goes to his eternal home[b]
and mourners[c] go about the streets.

[6]Remember him—before the silver cord is severed,
or the golden bowl is broken;
before the pitcher is shattered at the spring,
or the wheel broken at the well,
[7]and the dust returns[d] to the ground it came from,
and the spirit returns to God[e] who gave it.[f]

[8]"Meaningless! Meaningless!" says the Teacher.[a]
"Everything is meaningless![g]"

[9]Not only was the Teacher wise, but also he imparted knowledge to the people. He pondered and searched out and set in order many proverbs.[h] [10]The Teacher searched to find just the right words, and what he wrote was upright and true.[i]

[11]The words of the wise are like goads, their collected sayings like firmly embedded nails[j]—given by one Shepherd. [12]Be warned, my son, of anything in addition to them.

Of making many books there is no end, and much study wearies the body.[k]

[13]Now all has been heard;
here is the conclusion of the matter:
Fear God and keep his commandments,[l]
for this is the whole ⌊duty⌋ of man.[m]
[14]For God will bring every deed into judgment,[n]
including every hidden thing,[o]
whether it is good or evil.

a 8 Or *the leader of the assembly*; also in verses 9 and 10

Theme of Ecclesiastes:

SEGMENT DIVISIONS

		CHAPTER THEMES
		1
		2
		3
		4
		5
		6
		7
		8
		9
		10
		11
		12

Author:

Date:

Purpose:

Key Words:
God

meaningless

under the sun
(under heaven)

wisdom
(wise, skill)

righteous,
overrighteous
(righteousness,
justice, rights)

wicked,
overwicked
(wickedness)

wise (overwise)

fool(s), fool's

evil (misfortune,
wrong, bad,
crime[s],
trouble)

labor (work[ed],
toil[ed],
effort[s],
toilsome, do
his work)

wealthy, much

SONG OF SONGS

Song of Songs is a love story included in the canon of Scripture. On the eighth day of Passover the Jews would sing portions of the Song of Songs, a book they compared to the Most Holy Place in the temple.

Song of Songs is a book never quoted by our Lord, but one from which many Christians sing, "I am my lover's and my lover is mine" and "his banner over me is love."

Many waters cannot quench love;
  rivers cannot wash it away.
If one were to give all the wealth of his house for love,
  it would be utterly scorned (8:7).

∽ THINGS TO DO

1. The Song of Songs is a unified lyrical poem composed of a variety of songs. There is no other book like it in Scripture. Before you begin to analyze its content sit down and read it through slowly without stopping. Remember, the phrases may seem different or unusual because of the culture of the Eastern people.

2. As you read Song of Songs notice who is speaking when. The reference notes of the NIV identify who speaks. If you prefer to identify the speaker yourself, do the following:

    a. Read the book again and mark every time the "woman" speaks and also when the "man" speaks. Watch for pronouns such as *he, him, his,* and *she* and mark them in a distinctive way.

    b. As you read, you will notice there is a third party referred to in the text as the "daughters of Jerusalem" or "daughters of Zion" and in the reference notes in the margin as "Friends." Note when the "daughters of Jerusalem" or "daughters of Zion" (the friends) intervene. When you see any other parties speaking, mark these as well. Note these under "Segment Divisions" on the SONG OF SONGS AT A GLANCE chart on page 1152.

3. Now read through the Song of Songs again. This time do the following:

    a. When you note from the text whose song this is, record it under "Author" on SONG OF SONGS AT A GLANCE.

    b. As you read, mark the key words listed on SONG OF SONGS AT A GLANCE.

    c. Watch for details about the bride and the bridegroom—their position, family, how they met, where they met, etc. A careful reading of the book as a whole can help you piece together these facts. You might want to write your observations on a piece of paper and then transfer them to the margin of the text.

    d. Watch for other segment divisions in the book. For instance, note when the courtship ends, when the wedding takes place, and what occurs in the marriage and why. (Watch for the word *wedding*.) Record these divisions on SONG OF SONGS AT A GLANCE.

    e. Record the theme of each chapter on SONG OF SONGS AT A GLANCE and then on the line next to the chapter number. Complete the chart.

∽ THINGS TO THINK ABOUT

1. There are many different interpretations about the meaning of this book. Does Song of Songs speak only about the emotional and physical relationship of love and marriage? Or does it symbolize something such as Israel's relationship to God, or the church's relationship to Jesus, their heavenly bridegroom, or the individual's devotion to Christ? If it goes beyond the natural to the spiritual, what would you see that you might apply to your relationship with the Lord Jesus Christ?

2. If this book speaks merely of the physical and emotional bonds of marriage, what do you learn from it that you might apply to your relationship with your mate? Think about the way the bride and bridegroom communicated with each other, what they shared, what their physical relationship was like, what caused problems, and how they solved them.

3. What can you learn from Song of Songs that would help you prepare for marriage? For instance, what can you learn from this book about understanding yourself, your future mate, and the importance of intimacy, purity, and physical oneness?

4. What do you think an adulterous relationship would do to the intimacy between the bride and the bridegroom? James 4:4 tells us that when we become friends with the world (the world system) we are committing spiritual adultery. What does this do to our intimacy with God? Read 2 Corinthians 11:2, 3 and think about it.

∿∿∿∿∿

Chapter 1 Theme _____

1

Solomon's Song of Songs.[a]

Beloved[a]

[2]Let him kiss me with the kisses of his mouth—
  for your love[b] is more delightful than wine.
[3]Pleasing is the fragrance of your perfumes;[c]
  your name[d] is like perfume poured out.
  No wonder the maidens[e] love you!
[4]Take me away with you—let us hurry!
  Let the king bring me into his chambers.[f]

Friends

We rejoice and delight in you[b];
  we will praise your love more than wine.

Beloved

How right they are to adore you!

[5]Dark am I, yet lovely,[g]
  O daughters of Jerusalem,[h]
  dark like the tents of Kedar,
  like the tent curtains of Solomon.[c]
[6]Do not stare at me because I am dark,
  because I am darkened by the sun.
My mother's sons were angry with me
  and made me take care of the vineyards;[i]
  my own vineyard I have neglected.

---

[a] Primarily on the basis of the gender of the Hebrew pronouns used, male and female speakers are indicated in the margins by the captions *Lover* and *Beloved* respectively. The words of others are marked *Friends*. In some instances the divisions and their captions are debatable. [b] 4 The Hebrew is masculine singular. [c] 5 Or *Salma*

1:1
[a] 1Ki 4:32

1:2
[b] SS 4:10

1:3
[c] SS 4:10
[d] Ecc 7:1
[e] Ps 45:14

1:4
[f] Ps 45:15

1:5
[g] SS 2:14; 4:3
[h] SS 2:7; 5:8;
5:16

1:6
[i] Ps 69:8;
SS 8:12

1:7
aSS 3:1-4;
Isa 13:20

⁷Tell me, you whom I love, where you graze your flock
  and where you rest your sheep^a at midday.
Why should I be like a veiled woman
  beside the flocks of your friends?

Friends

1:8
bSS 5:9; 6:1

⁸If you do not know, most beautiful of women,ᵇ
  follow the tracks of the sheep
and graze your young goats
  by the tents of the shepherds.

Lover

1:9
c2Ch 1:17

⁹I liken you, my darling, to a mare
  harnessed to one of the chariotsᶜ of Pharaoh.
¹⁰Your cheeksᵈ are beautiful with earrings,
  your neck with strings of jewels.ᵉ
¹¹We will make you earrings of gold,
  studded with silver.

1:10
dSS 5:13
eIsa 61:10

Beloved

¹²While the king was at his table,
  my perfume spread its fragrance.ᶠ
¹³My lover is to me a sachet of myrrh
  resting between my breasts.
¹⁴My lover is to me a cluster of hennaᵍ blossoms
  from the vineyards of En Gedi.ʰ

1:12
fSS 4:11-14

Lover

1:14
gSS 4:13
h1Sa 23:29

¹⁵How beautifulⁱ you are, my darling!
  Oh, how beautiful!
  Your eyes are doves.ʲ

Beloved

1:15
iSS 4:7
jSS 2:14; 4:1;
5:2,12; 6:9

¹⁶How handsome you are, my lover!
  Oh, how charming!
  And our bed is verdant.

Lover

1:17
k1Ki 6:9

¹⁷The beams of our house are cedars;ᵏ
  our rafters are firs.

Chapter 2 Theme _____

Beloved[a]

2 I am a rose[b][a] of Sharon,[b]
a lily[c] of the valleys.

Lover

[2]Like a lily among thorns
is my darling among the maidens.

Beloved

[3]Like an apple tree among the trees of the forest
is my lover[d] among the young men.
I delight[e] to sit in his shade,
and his fruit is sweet to my taste.[f]
[4]He has taken me to the banquet hall,[g]
and his banner[h] over me is love.
[5]Strengthen me with raisins,
refresh me with apples,[i]
for I am faint with love.[j]
[6]His left arm is under my head,
and his right arm embraces me.[k]
[7]Daughters of Jerusalem, I charge you[l]
by the gazelles and by the does of the field:
Do not arouse or awaken love
until it so desires.[m]

[8]Listen! My lover!
Look! Here he comes,
leaping across the mountains,
bounding over the hills.[n]
[9]My lover is like a gazelle[o] or a young stag.[p]
Look! There he stands behind our wall,
gazing through the windows,
peering through the lattice.
[10]My lover spoke and said to me,
"Arise, my darling,
my beautiful one, and come with me.
[11]See! The winter is past;
the rains are over and gone.
[12]Flowers appear on the earth;
the season of singing has come,
the cooing of doves
is heard in our land.

a 1 Or *Lover* b 1 Possibly a member of the crocus family

2:1
a Isa 35:1
b 1Ch 27:29
c SS 5:13;
Hos 14:5

2:3
d SS 1:14
e SS 1:4
f SS 4:16

2:4
g Est 1:11
h Nu 1:52

2:5
i SS 7:8
j SS 5:8

2:6
k SS 8:3

2:7
l SS 5:8
m SS 3:5; 8:4

2:8
n ver 17;
SS 8:14

2:9
o 2Sa 2:18
p ver 17;
SS 8:14

¹³The fig tree forms its early fruit;^a
the blossoming^b vines spread their fragrance.
Arise, come, my darling;
my beautiful one, come with me."

Lover

¹⁴My dove^c in the clefts of the rock,
in the hiding places on the mountainside,
show me your face,
let me hear your voice;
for your voice is sweet,
and your face is lovely.^d
¹⁵Catch for us the foxes,^e
the little foxes
that ruin the vineyards,^f
our vineyards that are in bloom.^g

Beloved

¹⁶My lover is mine and I am his;^h
he browses among the lilies.ⁱ
¹⁷Until the day breaks
and the shadows flee,^j
turn, my lover,^k
and be like a gazelle
or like a young stag^l
on the rugged hills.^a^m

Chapter 3 Theme

3 All night long on my bed
I lookedⁿ for the one my heart loves;
I looked for him but did not find him.
²I will get up now and go about the city,
through its streets and squares;
I will search for the one my heart loves.
So I looked for him but did not find him.
³The watchmen found me
as they made their rounds in the city.^o
"Have you seen the one my heart loves?"
⁴Scarcely had I passed them
when I found the one my heart loves.
I held him and would not let him go
till I had brought him to my mother's house,^p
to the room of the one who conceived me.^q

2:13
a Isa 28:4;
Jer 24:2;
Hos 9:10;
Mic 7:1;
Na 3:12
b SS 7:12

2:14
c Ge 8:8;
SS 1:15
d SS 1:5; 8:13

2:15
e Jdg 15:4
f SS 1:6
g SS 7:12

2:16
h SS 7:10
i SS 4:5; 6:3

2:17
j SS 4:6
k SS 1:14
l ver 9
m ver 8

3:1
n SS 5:6;
Isa 26:9

3:3
o SS 5:7

3:4
p SS 8:2
q SS 6:9

a 17 Or *the hills of Bether*

⁵Daughters of Jerusalem, I charge you*ᵃ*
    by the gazelles and by the does of the field:
Do not arouse or awaken love
    until it so desires.*ᵇ*

⁶Who is this coming up from the desert*ᶜ*
    like a column of smoke,
perfumed with myrrh*ᵈ* and incense
    made from all the spices*ᵉ* of the merchant?
⁷Look! It is Solomon's carriage,
    escorted by sixty warriors,*ᶠ*
    the noblest of Israel,
⁸all of them wearing the sword,
    all experienced in battle,
each with his sword at his side,
    prepared for the terrors of the night.*ᵍ*
⁹King Solomon made for himself the carriage;
    he made it of wood from Lebanon.
¹⁰Its posts he made of silver,
    its base of gold.
Its seat was upholstered with purple,
    its interior lovingly inlaid
by*ᵃ* the daughters of Jerusalem.
¹¹Come out, you daughters of Zion,*ʰ*
    and look at King Solomon wearing the crown,
    the crown with which his mother crowned him
on the day of his wedding,
    the day his heart rejoiced.*ⁱ*

Chapter 4 Theme

Lover

4 How beautiful you are, my darling!
    Oh, how beautiful!
    Your eyes behind your veil are doves.*ʲ*
Your hair is like a flock of goats
    descending from Mount Gilead.*ᵏ*
²Your teeth are like a flock of sheep just shorn,
    coming up from the washing.
Each has its twin;
    not one of them is alone.*ˡ*
³Your lips are like a scarlet ribbon;
    your mouth*ᵐ* is lovely.
Your temples behind your veil
    are like the halves of a pomegranate.*ⁿ*

ᵃ 10 Or its inlaid interior a gift of love / from

Cross references (right margin):

3:5
ᵃ SS 2:7
ᵇ SS 8:4

3:6
ᶜ SS 8:5
ᵈ SS 1:13; 4:6,14
ᵉ Ex 30:34

3:7
ᶠ 1Sa 8:11

3:8
ᵍ Job 15:22; Ps 91:5

3:11
ʰ Isa 4:4
ⁱ Isa 62:5

4:1
ʲ SS 1:15; 5:12
ᵏ SS 6:5; Mic 7:14

4:2
ˡ SS 6:6

4:3
ᵐ SS 5:16
ⁿ SS 6:7

4:4
a SS 7:4
b Eze 27:10

4:5
c SS 7:3
d Pr 5:19
e SS 2:16; 6:2-3

4:6
f SS 2:17
g ver 14

4:7
h SS 1:15

4:8
i SS 5:1
j Dt 3:9
k 1Ch 5:23

4:9
l Ge 41:42

4:10
m SS 7:6
n SS 1:2

4:11
o Ps 19:10;
SS 5:1
p Hos 14:6

4:12
q Pr 5:15-18

4:13
r SS 6:11; 7:12
s SS 1:14

4:14
t Ex 30:23
u SS 3:6
v SS 1:12

⁴Your neck is like the tower *a* of David,
   built with elegance*a*;
  on it hang a thousand shields,*b*
   all of them shields of warriors.
⁵Your two breasts*c* are like two fawns,
   like twin fawns of a gazelle *d*
   that browse among the lilies.*e*
⁶Until the day breaks
   and the shadows flee,*f*
 I will go to the mountain of myrrh*g*
   and to the hill of incense.
⁷All beautiful*h* you are, my darling;
   there is no flaw in you.

⁸Come with me from Lebanon, my bride,*i*
   come with me from Lebanon.
 Descend from the crest of Amana,
   from the top of Senir,*j* the summit of Hermon,*k*
 from the lions' dens
   and the mountain haunts of the leopards.
⁹You have stolen my heart, my sister, my bride;
   you have stolen my heart
 with one glance of your eyes,
   with one jewel of your necklace.*l*
¹⁰How delightful*m* is your love*n*, my sister, my bride!
   How much more pleasing is your love than wine,
   and the fragrance of your perfume than any spice!
¹¹Your lips drop sweetness as the honeycomb, my bride;
   milk and honey are under your tongue.*o*
   The fragrance of your garments is like that of Lebanon.*p*
¹²You are a garden locked up, my sister, my bride;
   you are a spring enclosed, a sealed fountain.*q*
¹³Your plants are an orchard of pomegranates*r*
   with choice fruits,
   with henna*s* and nard,
¹⁴ nard and saffron,
   calamus and cinnamon,*t*
   with every kind of incense tree,
   with myrrh*u* and aloes
   and all the finest spices.*v*
¹⁵You are*b* a garden fountain,
   a well of flowing water
   streaming down from Lebanon.

a 4 The meaning of the Hebrew for this word is uncertain.   *b* 15 Or *I am* (spoken by the *Beloved*)

Beloved

¹⁶Awake, north wind,
　　and come, south wind!
　Blow on my garden,
　　that its fragrance may spread abroad.
　Let my lover come into his garden
　　and taste its choice fruits.*a*

Chapter 5 Theme _____

Lover

5 I have come into my garden, my sister, my bride;*b*
　　I have gathered my myrrh with my spice.
　I have eaten my honeycomb and my honey;
　　I have drunk my wine and my milk. *c*

Friends

Eat, O friends, and drink;
　drink your fill, O lovers.

Beloved

²I slept but my heart was awake.
　Listen! My lover is knocking:
"Open to me, my sister, my darling,
　my dove, my flawless*d* one.*e*
My head is drenched with dew,
　my hair with the dampness of the night."
³I have taken off my robe—
　must I put it on again?
I have washed my feet—
　must I soil them again?
⁴My lover thrust his hand through the latch-opening;
　my heart began to pound for him.
⁵I arose to open for my lover,
　and my hands dripped with myrrh,*f*
my fingers with flowing myrrh,
　on the handles of the lock.
⁶I opened for my lover,*g*
　but my lover had left; he was gone.*h*
My heart sank at his departure.*a*
I looked*i* for him but did not find him.
I called him but he did not answer.

a6 *Or* heart had gone out to him when he spoke

4:16
a SS 2:3; 5:1

5:1
b SS 4:8
c SS 4:11;
Isa 55:1

5:2
d SS 4:7
e SS 6:9

5:5
f ver 13

5:6
g SS 6:1
h SS 6:2
i SS 3:1

5:7
a SS 3:3

7The watchmen found me
    as they made their rounds in the city.a
They beat me, they bruised me;
    they took away my cloak,
those watchmen of the walls!

5:8
b SS 2:7; 3:5
c SS 2:5

8O daughters of Jerusalem, I charge you b —
    if you find my lover,
what will you tell him?
    Tell him I am faint with love.c

Friends

5:9
d SS 1:8; 6:1

9How is your beloved better than others,
    most beautiful of women?d
How is your beloved better than others,
    that you charge us so?

Beloved

5:10
e Ps 45:2

10My lover is radiant and ruddy,
    outstanding among ten thousand.e

5:12
f SS 1:15; 4:1
g Ge 49:12

11His head is purest gold;
    his hair is wavy
    and black as a raven.
12His eyes are like dovesf
    by the water streams,
washed in milk,g
    mounted like jewels.

5:13
h SS 1:10
i SS 6:2
j SS 2:1

13His cheeksh are like beds of spicei
    yielding perfume.
His lips are like liliesj
    dripping with myrrh.

5:14
k Job 28:6

14His arms are rods of gold
    set with chrysolite.
His body is like polished ivory
    decorated with sapphires.a k

5:15
l 1Ki 4:33;
SS 7:4

15His legs are pillars of marble
    set on bases of pure gold.
His appearance is like Lebanon,l
    choice as its cedars.
16His mouthm is sweetness itself;
    he is altogether lovely.
This is my lover,n this my friend,
    O daughters of Jerusalem.o

5:16
m SS 4:3
n SS 7:9
o SS 1:5

a 14 Or lapis lazuli

Chapter 6 Theme _____

Friends

6

Where has your lover*a* gone,
  most beautiful of women?*b*
Which way did your lover turn,
  that we may look for him with you?

Beloved

²My lover has gone*c* down to his garden,*d*
  to the beds of spices,*e*
to browse in the gardens
  and to gather lilies.
³I am my lover's and my lover is mine;*f*
  he browses among the lilies.*g*

Lover

⁴You are beautiful, my darling, as Tirzah,*h*
  lovely as Jerusalem,*i*
  majestic as troops with banners.*j*
⁵Turn your eyes from me;
  they overwhelm me.
Your hair is like a flock of goats
  descending from Gilead.*k*
⁶Your teeth are like a flock of sheep
  coming up from the washing.
Each has its twin,
  not one of them is alone.*l*
⁷Your temples behind your veil*m*
  are like the halves of a pomegranate.*n*
⁸Sixty queens*o* there may be,
  and eighty concubines,*p*
  and virgins beyond number;
⁹but my dove,*q* my perfect one,*r* is unique,
  the only daughter of her mother,
  the favorite of the one who bore her.*s*
The maidens saw her and called her blessed;
  the queens and concubines praised her.

Friends

¹⁰Who is this that appears like the dawn,
  fair as the moon, bright as the sun,
  majestic as the stars in procession?

6:1
a SS 5:6
b SS 1:8

6:2
c SS 5:6
d SS 4:12
e SS 5:13

6:3
f SS 7:10
g SS 2:16

6:4
h Jos 12:24
i Ps 48:2; 50:2
j ver 10

6:5
k SS 4:1

6:6
l SS 4:2

6:7
m Ge 24:65
n SS 4:3

6:8
o Ps 45:9
p Ge 22:24

6:9
q SS 1:15
r SS 5:2
s SS 3:4

6:11
a SS 7:12

Lover

> [11]I went down to the grove of nut trees
> > to look at the new growth in the valley,
> > to see if the vines had budded
> > or the pomegranates were in bloom.*a*

6:13
b Ex 15:20

> [12]Before I realized it,
> > my desire set me among the royal chariots of my people.*a*

Friends

> [13]Come back, come back, O Shulammite;
> > come back, come back, that we may gaze on you!

7:1
c Ps 45:13

Lover

> Why would you gaze on the Shulammite
> > as on the dance*b* of Mahanaim?

Chapter 7 Theme _____

7:3
d SS 4:5

7

> How beautiful your sandaled feet,
> > O prince's*c* daughter!
> Your graceful legs are like jewels,
> > the work of a craftsman's hands.

7:4
e Ps 144:12;
SS 4:4
f Nu 21:26
g SS 5:15

> [2]Your navel is a rounded goblet
> > that never lacks blended wine.
> Your waist is a mound of wheat
> > encircled by lilies.
> [3]Your breasts*d* are like two fawns,
> > twins of a gazelle.
> [4]Your neck is like an ivory tower.*e*
> Your eyes are the pools of Heshbon*f*
> > by the gate of Bath Rabbim.

7:5
h Isa 35:2

> Your nose is like the tower of Lebanon*g*
> > looking toward Damascus.
> [5]Your head crowns you like Mount Carmel.*h*
> > Your hair is like royal tapestry;
> > the king is held captive by its tresses.

7:6
i SS 1:15
j SS 4:10

> [6]How beautiful*i* you are and how pleasing,
> > O love, with your delights!*j*
> [7]Your stature is like that of the palm,
> > and your breasts*k* like clusters of fruit.
> [8]I said, "I will climb the palm tree;
> > I will take hold of its fruit."
> May your breasts be like the clusters of the vine,

7:7
k SS 4:5

a 12 Or *among the chariots of Amminadab; or among the chariots of the people of the prince*

the fragrance of your breath like apples,[a]
9 and your mouth like the best wine.

Beloved

May the wine go straight to my lover,[b]
flowing gently over lips and teeth.[a]
10 I belong to my lover,
and his desire[c] is for me.[d]
11 Come, my lover, let us go to the countryside,
let us spend the night in the villages.[b]
12 Let us go early to the vineyards[e]
to see if the vines have budded,[f]
if their blossoms[g] have opened,
and if the pomegranates[h] are in bloom[i]—
there I will give you my love.
13 The mandrakes[j] send out their fragrance,
and at our door is every delicacy,
both new and old,
that I have stored up for you, my lover.[k]

Chapter 8 Theme

8 If only you were to me like a brother,
who was nursed at my mother's breasts!
Then, if I found you outside,
I would kiss you,
and no one would despise me.
2 I would lead you
and bring you to my mother's house[l]—
she who has taught me.
I would give you spiced wine to drink,
the nectar of my pomegranates.
3 His left arm is under my head
and his right arm embraces me.[m]
4 Daughters of Jerusalem, I charge you:
Do not arouse or awaken love
until it so desires.[n]

Friends

5 Who is this coming up from the desert[o]
leaning on her lover?

7:8
[a] SS 2:5

7:9
[b] SS 5:16

7:10
[c] Ps 45:11
[d] SS 2:16; 6:3

7:12
[e] SS 1:6
[f] SS 2:15
[g] SS 2:13
[h] SS 4:13
[i] SS 6:11

7:13
[j] Ge 30:14
[k] SS 4:16

8:2
[l] SS 3:4

8:3
[m] SS 2:6

8:4
[n] SS 2:7; 3:5

8:5
[o] SS 3:6

---

[a] 9 Septuagint, Aquila, Vulgate and Syriac; Hebrew *lips of sleepers*   [b] 11 Or *henna bushes*

8:5
a SS 3:4

Beloved

Under the apple tree I roused you;
　　there your mother conceived[a] you,
　　there she who was in labor gave you birth.
[6]Place me like a seal over your heart,
　　like a seal on your arm;
for love[b] is as strong as death,
　　its jealousy[a][c] unyielding as the grave.[b]
It burns like blazing fire,
　　like a mighty flame.[c]

8:6
b SS 1:2
c Nu 5:14

[7]Many waters cannot quench love;
　　rivers cannot wash it away.
If one were to give
　　all the wealth of his house for love,
　　it[d] would be utterly scorned.[d]

Friends

[8]We have a young sister,
　　and her breasts are not yet grown.
What shall we do for our sister
　　for the day she is spoken for?
[9]If she is a wall,
　　we will build towers of silver on her.
If she is a door,
　　we will enclose her with panels of cedar.

8:7
d Pr 6:35

Beloved

[10]I am a wall,
　　and my breasts are like towers.
Thus I have become in his eyes
　　like one bringing contentment.
[11]Solomon had a vineyard[e] in Baal Hamon;
　　he let out his vineyard to tenants.
Each was to bring for its fruit
　　a thousand shekels[e][f] of silver.
[12]But my own vineyard[g] is mine to give;
　　the thousand shekels are for you, O Solomon,
　　and two hundred[f] are for those who tend its fruit.

8:11
e Ecc 2:4
f Isa 7:23

a 6 Or *ardor*　b 6 Hebrew *Sheol*　c 6 Or / *like the very flame of the* LORD　d 7 Or *he*
e 11 That is, about 25 pounds (about 11.5 kilograms); also in verse 12　f 12 That is, about 5
pounds (about 2.3 kilograms)

8:12
g SS 1:6

Lover

¹³You who dwell in the gardens
with friends in attendance,
let me hear your voice!

Beloved

¹⁴Come away, my lover,
and be like a gazelle[a]
or like a young stag[b]
on the spice-laden mountains. [c]

8:14
a Pr 5:19
b SS 2:9
c SS 2:8,17

SONG OF SONGS AT A GLANCE

Theme of Song of Songs:

SEGMENT DIVISIONS

			CHAPTER THEMES
		1	
		2	
		3	
		4	
		5	
		6	
		7	
		8	

Author:

Date:

Purpose:

Key Words:

love (adore)

beloved (lover)

come
(coming, comes)

beautiful
(delightful, fair)

ISAIAH

The messages of the Old Testament prophets addressed the people of Israel and Judah who lived between the years of 840 and 420 B.C. Isaiah is the first of the major prophets. Isaiah's name, *Yeshayahu*, means "Jehovah Saves" or "Salvation of Jehovah." No other prophet gives more prophecies regarding the coming Messiah. Isaiah reveals the Messiah (Christ) as the Suffering Servant and the Conquering King. Under divine inspiration Isaiah announces and declares things that are coming and events which will occur in the future so that God's people might know there is no God besides him.

From Isaiah 37:37, 38 we know Isaiah lived at least until 681 B.C., the year Esarhaddon, the son of Sennacherib, became king of Assyria after his father's death. Tradition says Isaiah was sawn in two by Manasseh, the king of Judah who reigned after Hezekiah (2 Kings 21:16). If tradition is correct, Isaiah might be one of the heroes of faith referred to in Hebrews 11:37.

∾ THINGS TO DO

The basic structure of Isaiah is easy to remember if it is compared to the Bible's structure. The Bible is comprised of 66 books, 39 in the Old Testament and 27 in the New Testament. Isaiah, which focuses on the Holy One of Israel, has 66 chapters which fall into two main divisions: Isaiah 1 through 39 reveals God's character and judgment, and Isaiah 40 through 66 shows God's comfort and redemption. Because Isaiah is a long book filled with discourses and songs, it needs to be studied segment by segment so that you don't miss the wonder of its promises and prophecies. Ask God to help you understand the important message of this book.

General Instructions

1. As you read through Isaiah one chapter at a time, observe each chapter in the light of the five W's and an H. Ask general questions such as: Who does this chapter focus on? What happens or what is this about? When is this happening? Where will it happen? Why is this going to happen and how?

2. Isaiah is a set of discourses or songs rather than a historical chronology of events in the life of Israel. Periodically there are historical interludes which are very important. In these interludes God will often tell Isaiah to do something which will act as a sign to the people. For instance, in Isaiah 8:3 Isaiah is to name his son *Maher-Shalal-Hash-Baz,* which means "quick to the plunder, swift to the spoil." His name pointed the people to the Assyrian invasion, which would come before Maher-Shalal-Hash-Baz would learn to say Momma or Daddy. Observe these interludes carefully.

3. Isaiah recorded many prophecies regarding future events, including the captivity, the birth of Messiah, the reign of Messiah, and the last days. Watch for these prophecies and note them in the margin. Also check the reference notes to see where they are fulfilled.

   a. As you read some of these prophecies you will see that the first and second coming of Messiah (Christ) can be prophesied without any indication that there is an interval of time between these comings. For instance, Isaiah 61:1 through 2a covers the first coming of Jesus Christ. As a matter of fact Jesus read this passage in the synagogue in Nazareth and stopped at this point (Luke 4:18, 19). Why? Because the next part of the verse, "And the day of vengeance of our God," skips to the day of the Lord, which encompasses Christ's judgment and his second coming.

   b. You will find it beneficial to read the section entitled "Guidelines for Interpreting Predictive Prophecy" on page 2205.

      c. On page 1158 is a chart called THE PROPHETIC POINTS OF HISTORY. Keeping these prophetic points in mind as you read Isaiah will help you distinguish the time periods to which Isaiah refers. You may want to draw this chart on a card so you can look at it as you study Isaiah.

4. Mark every reference to *the day of the Lord* or *the last days* in a distinctive way, then list your observations in the margin and on the chart THE DAY OF THE LORD that begins on page 2178. It will become a valuable resource on this critical event. Record the book, chapter, and verse from which you took your information. Do this all the way through Isaiah.

5. Babylon plays a significant prophetic role throughout Scripture, even in the day of the Lord. List what you learn about Babylon in the margin of the text. Then record that information on the chart WHAT THE BIBLE TEACHES ABOUT BABYLON beginning on page 2176. When you record your observations on Babylon note the reference (book, chapter, and verse) from which you took your information. You will want this for future reference.

Isaiah 1-39: God's Character and Judgment

Chapters 1-12: Discourses Regarding Judah and Jerusalem

1. Read Isaiah 1 to get the spiritual and moral condition and the historical setting of this book.

      a. Examine Isaiah 1 carefully under the scrutiny of the five W's and an H: Who? What? When? Where? Why? and How? Ask questions such as: Who wrote this? When was it written? Why was it written? To whom was it written? What do you learn about them? What are they to do and why? What will happen? Interrogating the text with such questions will give you great insight into what is being said in this chapter. Record your insights in the margin of chapter 1.

      b. To put the book into its chronological setting, compare Isaiah 1:1 with the historical chart on page 1159. Record your insights under "Author" and "Date" on the ISAIAH AT A GLANCE chart on page 1277.

2. As you read Isaiah 2 through 12 one chapter at a time:

      a. Mark the following key words in a distinctive way: *remnant, Israel, Judah, Samaria, Assyria (Assyrian), woe, Holy One of Israel,* and *the Lord Almighty.* (Although the last two phrases are titles referring to God, it is helpful to see how each is used, so mark them distinctively.)

      b. Also mark every occurrence of *in the last days* and *in that day.* As you mark *in that day* make sure you know what day it is referring to. For instance, in Isaiah 2 *in that day* refers to the last days. Therefore both can be marked in the same way. However, this may not always be the case, so check the context in which "that day" is used.

      c. Write all these key words on an index card that you can use as a bookmark while you study Isaiah. Color code them so you can mark them quickly.

      d. Watch for key repeated words or phrases which are not on the list but are distinctive to certain chapters.

3. As you read each chapter observe the following and record your insights in the margin:

      a. Notice to whom God is speaking and what he says about their behavior.

      b. Observe the consequences of the behavior.

      c. See if there is an exhortation or plea followed by a promise of how God will cleanse them, bless them, or move on their behalf.

4. Isaiah 6 is a strategic chapter. It records Isaiah's call and commission from the Lord.

      a. To get the historical setting of this chapter read 2 Kings 15. Uzziah is called Azariah in 2 Kings 15:1 (see 2 Chronicles 26:1). On the chart on page 1159, you will notice that the reigns of Uzziah and Jotham overlapped. This is because they served as co-regents for a time.

      b. Observe the progression of events in this chapter and note them in the margin.

5. As you study each chapter, don't forget the "General Instructions." These are an important part of the process of carefully observing the text.

6. When you finish observing each chapter record the theme of that chapter on ISAIAH AT A GLANCE and on the line in the text next to the chapter number.

Chapters 13-23: Oracles Against Various Nations

1. As you read this section chapter by chapter:

   a. Watch for and mark in a distinctive way the key repeated phrase, *an oracle concerning* _____. Note who the oracle concerns and locate each of these on the map at the beginning of chapter 13.

   b. Mark the following key words: *the Lord Almighty, Babylon, day of the Lord,* and *remnant (those who remain, survivors)*. Write these on a new index card to use as a bookmark.

2. As you observe each chapter, note the following in the margin or mark it in the text:

   a. Observe if there is any judgment connected with those to whom the oracle is given and why.

   b. Watch where the judgment comes and if there is any effect on Israel.

   c. Watch for *when* something happens. Note this with a time symbol in the margin.

   d. Notice how God's purposes are being worked out in history.

3. Record the theme of each chapter in the same way you did previously. However, remember that this will not always be easy. The chapter divisions in the Bible are not part of the original Scriptures. Therefore, if you have a hard time summarizing the theme of each chapter, don't be discouraged. When it is not easy to settle on a chapter theme, pick a key verse that the truths of the chapter seem to pivot around, or simply choose some words from the first verse and record these on ISAIAH AT A GLANCE.

Chapters 24-27: Discourses Regarding "That Day"

1. As you read this segment, mark the following key words: *earth('s), in that day, salvation,* and *the Lord Almighty*.

2. As you read each chapter observe the following:

   a. What happens to the earth and its inhabitants (humans and animals)

   b. What the Lord of hosts will do and where he will be

   c. What the people's response will be

3. Record the theme of each chapter on ISAIAH AT A GLANCE and in the text.

Chapters 28-33: Six Woes

1. As you read each chapter watch for and mark the following key words: *woe, the Holy One of Israel, the Lord Almighty, remnant, (the* or *my) Spirit, in that day (on that day),* and *salvation*.

2. As you read each of these chapters, note in the margin or mark in the text the following:

   a. To whom the woe is given

   b. What was done to cause the woe

   c. What the Lord will do and what the result will be

3. Record the chapter themes on ISAIAH AT A GLANCE and in the text.

Chapters 34, 35: God's Recompense and Ransom for Zion

1. As you read these two chapters, mark the following key words: *nations* (and any pronouns), *sword, retribution, glory,* and *ransomed*.

2. Look for and list in the margin on whom God's recompense will come, what it will be, and what will follow. Make sure you note what happens to the ransomed and the redeemed. Also note what this will mean to Zion.

3. Record the chapter themes on ISAIAH AT A GLANCE and in the text.

ISAIAH

Chapters 36-39: Historical Account from the Threat of Assyria to the Threat of Babylon

1. Read these chapters and mark the following words: *Assyria (Assyrian), Sennacherib, his field commander (the field commander, the commander)* (also known as Rabshakeh), *Hezekiah('s), Isaiah, Babylon, remnant, the Lord Almighty (O Lord Almighty),* and *prayer (pray, prayed).*

2. Now read the chapters again, observing the words you marked. In the margin note what you learn about each of the characters and what they do, what happens as a result, and how God intervenes. List what you learn about God from these chapters. Don't miss what happens to Assyria and Babylon. This is a pivotal point in respect to these two powers and the nation of Israel.

3. Record the chapter themes on ISAIAH AT A GLANCE and in the text.

Isaiah 40-66: God's Comfort and Redemption

Chapters 40-48: Behold the Lord, Your Redeemer

1. Mark the following references to God in a distinctive way: *the Lord Almighty, the Holy One of Israel, I am the Lord (God), I the Lord, none besides me (no other god, no god),* and *Redeemer.* Then list in the margin all you see about God that you want to remember for future reference. Note God's character, what he does, and to what or whom he is compared.

2. As you do all this don't simply mark these and move on. Meditate on what you see. Think of what these insights can do for your relationship with God. Remember, he is not only Israel's Redeemer but yours also if you have repented and believed in the Lord Jesus Christ.

3. Also mark *servant.* As you read each chapter, check the context (the surrounding verses) in which *servant* is used. This is vital. Note whether *servant* refers to Israel (Jacob) or to the Lord Jesus Christ. Record your insights in the margin. If it seems to be a prophetic reference to Jesus, check a concordance to find the New Testament verses which correspond to the Old Testament passage and see if they show how this prophecy was fulfilled by Jesus. When you make your list in the margin put it under "Israel the Servant" or "Messiah the Servant."

4. Mark every reference to *redeemed* and list in the margin what you learn about the redeemed. Then mark *who remain* (used only one time in this segment), *glory of the Lord, salvation, nation (nations, Gentiles),* and *Babylon.* In the margin record what you learn about each.

5. Put the key words for this segment on an index card to use as a bookmark in studying the remainder of Isaiah. *Remnant (who remain), none besides me (no other god),* and *Babylon* do not appear after this segment.

6. Record your chapter themes as before. Fill in the second line of the segment division for these chapters: Discourses Regarding _____.

Chapters 49-57: Your Redeemer Will Save

1. As you read through this segment, add the following key words to your bookmark: *covenant, Zion,* and *Jerusalem.* Mark *Zion* and *Jerusalem* in the same way. In the margin note what you observe from marking these words. Don't forget to delete from your card key words which no longer appear.

2. Do everything you did under numbers 1 through 5 in the previous segment. Watch carefully all that the Lord can and will do and note it in the margin. Observe the text carefully to see why this segment is titled "Your Redeemer Will Save." Watch for God's instructions and take them to heart.

3. Watch for prophetic verses which come in the midst of what Isaiah is saying. Give special attention to 50:6 and 52:13 through 53:12. After you observe Isaiah 53, read it through on your knees and substitute your name every time you see *we* or *us.*

4. Look for and record the theme of each chapter. If you think it will be helpful, summarize and list in the margin the subpoints covered in the chapter. Fill in the second line of the segment division for these chapters.

Chapters 58-66: Your Redeemer Will Come

1. Once again mark the key words on your bookmark. Delete *the Lord Almighty,* as it is not mentioned in this segment. *Servant* becomes *servants* in this segment; don't miss it.

2. There is much in this segment about the events that surround or accompany the Lord's coming to reign and what will follow, even in regard to the new heaven and new earth. In the margin list what you observe. Also watch for practical lessons and list what you learn in the margin. For instance, in Isaiah 58 you will gain insights on fasting.

3. Once again continue marking everything as you did under 1 through 5 (Isaiah 40-48).

4. Record your chapter themes and then complete ISAIAH AT A GLANCE. Fill in the second line of the segment division for these chapters. Write in any new segment divisions you have seen.

∾ **THINGS TO THINK ABOUT**

1. God's character never changes; therefore what distressed him in the days of Isaiah still distresses him today. And what he had to judge then, he cannot overlook now. Is there anything in your life you must confess and forsake? And what if you are not willing to do so? Will God be able to overlook it? Think about what you learned about God and his ways.

2. God is sovereign. He ruled over the nations in the days of Israel. Does he do the same today? What then can you know? How will your nation fit into all this?

3. Amos says God doesn't do anything without first revealing it to his servants the prophets (Amos 3:7). Therefore from studying Isaiah what do you know with an absolute certainty is going to come to pass? If the prophecies regarding the first coming of Jesus Christ literally came to pass (and they did), won't the prophecies regarding his second coming be literally fulfilled? How then are you going to live?

∾∾∾∾∾

1:1
a Nu 12:6
b Isa 40:9
c Isa 2:1
d 2Ch 26:22
e 2Ki 16:1

Chapter 1 Theme _____

1 The vision*a* concerning Judah and Jerusalem*b* that Isaiah son of Amoz saw*c* during the reigns of Uzziah,*d* Jotham, Ahaz*e* and Hezekiah, kings of Judah.

²Hear, O heavens! Listen, O earth!
For the LORD has spoken:*f*
"I reared children and brought them up,
but they have rebelled*g* against me.

1:2
f Mic 1:2
g Isa 30:1,9; 65:2

³The ox knows his master,
the donkey his owner's manger,
but Israel does not know,*h*
my people do not understand."

1:3
h Jer 8:7; 9:3,6

⁴Ah, sinful nation,
a people loaded with guilt,
a brood of evildoers,*i*
children given to corruption!
They have forsaken the LORD;
they have spurned the Holy One*j* of Israel
and turned their backs on him.

1:4
i Isa 14:20
j Isa 5:19,24

The Prophetic Points of History

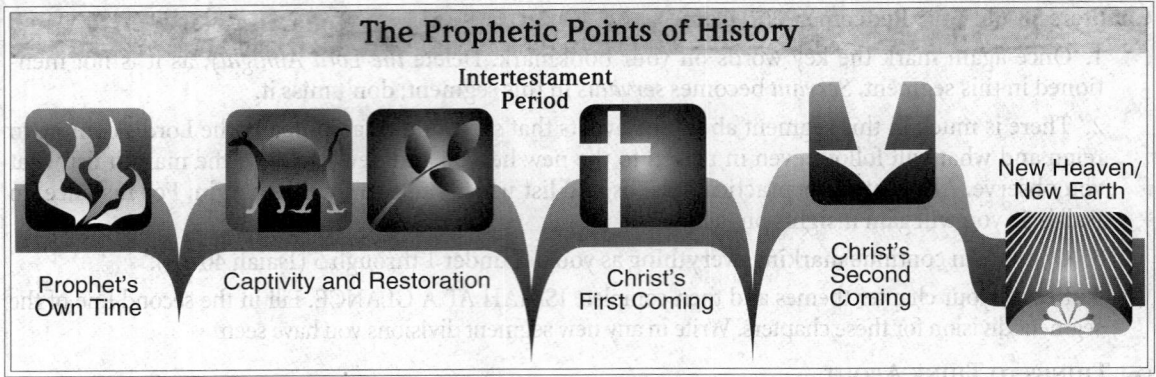

Intertestament Period

New Heaven/ New Earth

Prophet's Own Time

Captivity and Restoration

Christ's First Coming

Christ's Second Coming

⁵Why should you be beaten anymore?
   Why do you persist in rebellion?ᵃ
Your whole head is injured,
   your whole heart afflicted.ᵇ
⁶From the sole of your foot to the top of your head
   there is no soundnessᶜ—
only wounds and welts
   and open sores,
not cleansed or bandagedᵈ
   or soothed with oil.ᵉ

⁷Your country is desolate,ᶠ
   your cities burned with fire;
your fields are being stripped by foreigners
   right before you,
   laid waste as when overthrown by strangers.
⁸The Daughter of Zion is left
   like a shelter in a vineyard,
like a hutᵍ in a field of melons,
   like a city under siege.
⁹Unless the LORD Almighty
   had left us some survivors,ʰ
we would have become like Sodom,
   we would have been like Gomorrah.ⁱ

¹⁰Hear the word of the LORD,ʲ
   you rulers of Sodom;ᵏ
listen to the lawˡ of our God,
   you people of Gomorrah!
¹¹"The multitude of your sacrifices—
   what are they to me?" says the LORD.
"I have more than enough of burnt offerings,
   of rams and the fat of fattened animals;ᵐ
I have no pleasure
   in the blood of bullsⁿ and lambs and goats.ᵒ

1:5
ᵃ Isa 31:6
ᵇ Isa 33:6,24

1:6
ᶜ Ps 38:3
ᵈ Isa 30:26;
Jer 8:22
ᵉ Lk 10:34

1:7
ᶠ Lev 26:34

1:8
ᵍ Job 27:18

1:9
ʰ Isa 10:20-22;
37:4,31-32
ⁱ Ge 19:24;
Ro 9:29*

1:10
ʲ Isa 28:14
ᵏ Isa 3:9;
Eze 16:49;
Ro 9:29;
Rev 11:8
ˡ Isa 8:20

1:11
ᵐ Ps 50:8
ⁿ Jer 6:20
ᵒ 1Sa 15:22;
Mal 1:10

1:12
a Ex 23:17

¹²When you come to appear before me,
who has asked this of you,ᵃ
this trampling of my courts?

1:13
b Isa 66:3
c Jer 7:9
d 1Ch 23:31

¹³Stop bringing meaningless offerings!ᵇ
Your incenseᶜ is detestable to me.
New Moons, Sabbaths and convocationsᵈ—
I cannot bear your evil assemblies.

1:14
e Lev 23:1-44;
Nu 28:11–29:39;
Isa 29:1
f Isa 7:13;
43:22,24

¹⁴Your New Moon festivals and your appointed feastsᵉ
my soul hates.
They have become a burden to me;
I am wearyᶠ of bearing them.

¹⁵When you spread out your hands in prayer,
I will hideᵍ my eyes from you;
even if you offer many prayers,
I will not listen.

1:15
g Isa 8:17; 59:2;
Mic 3:4
h Isa 59:3

Your hands are full of blood;ʰ

¹⁶ wash and make yourselves clean.
Take your evil deeds
out of my sight!ⁱ

1:16
i Isa 52:11
j Isa 55:7;
Jer 25:5

Stop doing wrong,ʲ

¹⁷ learn to do right!
Seek justice,ᵏ
encourage the oppressed.ᵃ

1:17
k Zep 2:3   ᵃ 17 Or / rebuke the oppressor

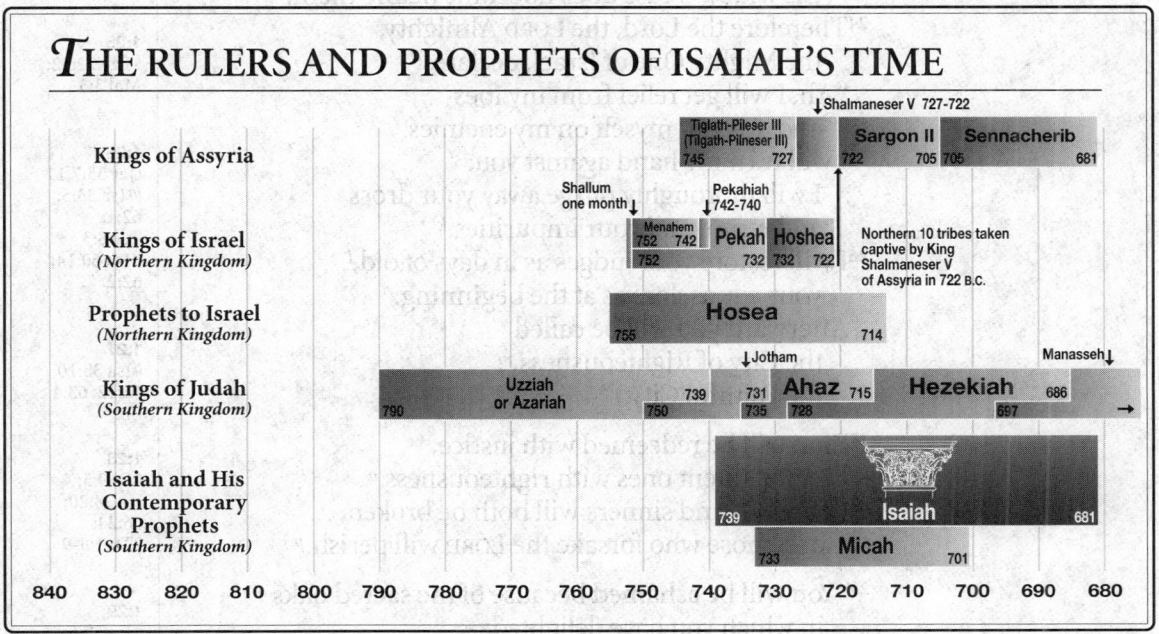

THE RULERS AND PROPHETS OF ISAIAH'S TIME

Kings of Assyria			Tiglath-Pileser III (Tilgath-Pilneser III) 745 727	↓Shalmaneser V 727-722	**Sargon II** 722 705	**Sennacherib** 705 681
Kings of Israel (Northern Kingdom)		Shallum one month ↓ Menahem 752 742 752	**Pekah** 732	Pekahiah ↓742-740 **Hoshea** 732 722	Northern 10 tribes taken captive by King Shalmaneser V of Assyria in 722 B.C.	
Prophets to Israel (Northern Kingdom)		**Hosea** 755		714		
Kings of Judah (Southern Kingdom)	**Uzziah or Azariah** 790	739 750	↓Jotham 731 735 **Ahaz** 728 715	**Hezekiah** 697 686	Manasseh↓ →	
Isaiah and His Contemporary Prophets (Southern Kingdom)			**Isaiah** 739 733 **Micah**	701	681	

| 840 | 830 | 820 | 810 | 800 | 790 | 780 | 770 | 760 | 750 | 740 | 730 | 720 | 710 | 700 | 690 | 680 |

Defend the cause of the fatherless,[a]
    plead the case of the widow.

18"Come now, let us reason together,"[b]
    says the LORD.
"Though your sins are like scarlet,
    they shall be as white as snow;[c]
though they are red as crimson,
    they shall be like wool.
19If you are willing and obedient,
    you will eat the best from the land;[d]
20but if you resist and rebel,
    you will be devoured by the sword."[e]
        For the mouth of the LORD has spoken.[f]

21See how the faithful city
    has become a harlot![g]
She once was full of justice;
    righteousness used to dwell in her—
    but now murderers!
22Your silver has become dross,
    your choice wine is diluted with water.
23Your rulers are rebels,
    companions of thieves;
they all love bribes[h]
    and chase after gifts.
They do not defend the cause of the fatherless;
    the widow's case does not come before them.[i]
24Therefore the Lord, the LORD Almighty,
    the Mighty One of Israel, declares:
"Ah, I will get relief from my foes
    and avenge[j] myself on my enemies.
25I will turn my hand against you;
    I will thoroughly purge away your dross
    and remove all your impurities.[k]
26I will restore your judges as in days of old,[l]
    your counselors as at the beginning.
Afterward you will be called
    the City of Righteousness,[m]
    the Faithful City.[n]"

27Zion will be redeemed with justice,
    her penitent ones with righteousness.[o]
28But rebels and sinners will both be broken,
    and those who forsake the LORD will perish.[p]

29"You will be ashamed because of the sacred oaks[q]
    in which you have delighted;

1:17
[a] Ps 82:3

1:18
[b] Isa 41:1;
43:9,26
[c] Ps 51:7;
Rev 7:14

1:19
[d] Dt 30:15-16;
Isa 55:2

1:20
[e] Isa 3:25;
65:12
[f] Isa 34:16;
40:5; 58:14;
Mic 4:4

1:21
[g] Isa 57:3-9;
Jer 2:20

1:23
[h] Ex 23:8
[i] Isa 10:2;
Jer 5:28;
Eze 22:6-7;
Zec 7:10

1:24
[j] Isa 35:4; 59:17;
61:2; 63:4

1:25
[k] Eze 22:22;
Mal 3:3

1:26
[l] Jer 33:7,11
[m] Isa 33:5;
62:1;
Zec 8:3
[n] Isa 60:14;
62:2

1:27
[o] Isa 35:10;
62:12; 63:4

1:28
[p] Ps 9:5;
Isa 24:20;
66:24;
2Th 1:8-9

1:29
[q] Isa 57:5

1:29
a Isa 65:3; 66:17

you will be disgraced because of the gardens[a]
  that you have chosen.
30 You will be like an oak with fading leaves,
  like a garden without water.
31 The mighty man will become tinder
  and his work a spark;
both will burn together,
  with no one to quench the fire.[b]"

1:31
b Isa 5:24;
9:18-19; 26:11;
33:14;
66:15-16,24

Chapter 2 Theme _____

2:1
c Isa 1:1

2 This is what Isaiah son of Amoz saw concerning Judah and Jerusalem:[c]

2 In the last days

2:2
d Isa 27:13; 56:7;
66:20; Mic 4:7

  the mountain[d] of the LORD's temple will be established
    as chief among the mountains;
  it will be raised above the hills,
    and all nations will stream to it.

3 Many peoples will come and say,

2:3
e Isa 51:4,7
f Lk 24:47

  "Come, let us go up to the mountain of the LORD,
    to the house of the God of Jacob.
  He will teach us his ways,
    so that we may walk in his paths."
  The law[e] will go out from Zion,
    the word of the LORD from Jerusalem.[f]

2:4
g Joel 3:10
h Ps 46:9;
Isa 9:5; 11:6-9;
32:18;
Hos 2:18;
Zec 9:10

4 He will judge between the nations
    and will settle disputes for many peoples.
  They will beat their swords into plowshares
    and their spears into pruning hooks.[g]
  Nation will not take up sword against nation,[h]
    nor will they train for war anymore.

2:5
i Isa 58:1
j Isa 60:1,19-20;
1Jn 1:5,7

5 Come, O house of Jacob,[i]
    let us walk in the light[j] of the LORD.

2:6
k Dt 31:17
l 2Ki 1:2
m Pr 6:1
n 2Ki 16:7

6 You have abandoned[k] your people,
    the house of Jacob.
  They are full of superstitions from the East;
    they practice divination like the Philistines[l]
    and clasp hands[m] with pagans.[n]
7 Their land is full of silver and gold;
    there is no end to their treasures.
  Their land is full of horses;[o]
    there is no end to their chariots.[p]

2:7
o Dt 17:16
p Isa 31:1;
Mic 5:10

⁸Their land is full of idols;ᵃ
    they bow down to the work of their hands,
    to what their fingersᵇ have made.
⁹So man will be brought lowᶜ
    and mankind humbledᵈ—
    do not forgive them.ᵃᵉ

¹⁰Go into the rocks,
    hide in the ground
  from dread of the Lord
    and the splendor of his majesty!ᶠ
¹¹The eyes of the arrogant man will be humbled
    and the prideᵍ of men brought low;
  the Lord alone will be exalted in that day.

¹²The Lord Almighty has a day in store
    for all the proud and lofty,
    for all that is exaltedʰ
    (and they will be humbled),ⁱ
¹³for all the cedars of Lebanon, tall and lofty,
    and all the oaks of Bashan,ʲ
¹⁴for all the towering mountains
    and all the high hills,ᵏ
¹⁵for every lofty tower
    and every fortified wall,ˡ
¹⁶for every trading shipᵇᵐ
    and every stately vessel.
¹⁷The arrogance of man will be brought low
    and the pride of men humbled;
  the Lord alone will be exalted in that day,ⁿ
¹⁸   and the idols will totally disappear.ᵒ

¹⁹Men will flee to caves in the rocks
    and to holes in the ground
  from dread of the Lord
    and the splendor of his majesty,
    when he rises to shake the earth.ᵖ
²⁰In that day men will throw away
    to the rodents and batsᑫ
  their idols of silver and idols of gold,
    which they made to worship.
²¹They will flee to caverns in the rocks
    and to the overhanging crags
  from dread of the Lord
    and the splendor of his majesty,
    when he rises to shake the earth.ʳ

2:8
ᵃ Isa 10:9-11
ᵇ Isa 17:8

2:9
ᶜ Ps 62:9
ᵈ Isa 5:15
ᵉ Ne 4:5

2:10
ᶠ 2Th 1:9;
Rev 6:15-16

2:11
ᵍ Isa 5:15; 37:23

2:12
ʰ Isa 24:4,21;
Mal 4:1
ⁱ Job 40:11

2:13
ʲ Zec 11:2

2:14
ᵏ Isa 30:25; 40:4

2:15
ˡ Isa 25:2,12

2:16
ᵐ 1Ki 10:22

2:17
ⁿ ver 11

2:18
ᵒ Isa 21:9

2:19
ᵖ Heb 12:26

2:20
ᑫ Lev 11:19

2:21
ʳ ver 19

2:22
aPs 146:3;
Jer 17:5
bPs 8:4; 144:3;
Isa 40:15;
Jas 4:14

3:1
cLev 26:26
dIsa 5:13;
Eze 4:16

3:2
eEze 17:13
f2Ki 24:14;
Isa 9:14-15

3:4
gEcc 10:16fn

3:5
hIsa 9:19;
Jer 9:8;
Mic 7:2,6

3:7
iEze 34:4;
Hos 5:13

3:8
jIsa 1:7
kIsa 9:15,17
lPs 73:9,11

3:9
mGe 13:13
nPr 8:36;
Ro 6:23

3:10
oDt 28:1-14
pPs 128:2

3:11
qDt 28:15-68

3:12
rver 4

[22]Stop trusting in man,[a]
who has but a breath in his nostrils.
Of what account is he?[b]

Chapter 3 Theme _____

3

See now, the Lord,
the LORD Almighty,
is about to take from Jerusalem and Judah
both supply and support:
all supplies of food[c] and all supplies of water,[d]
[2] the hero and warrior,[e]
the judge and prophet,
the soothsayer and elder,[f]
[3]the captain of fifty and man of rank,
the counselor, skilled craftsman and clever enchanter.

[4]I will make boys their officials;
mere children will govern them.[g]
[5]People will oppress each other—
man against man, neighbor against neighbor.[h]
The young will rise up against the old,
the base against the honorable.

[6]A man will seize one of his brothers
at his father's home, and say,
"You have a cloak, you be our leader;
take charge of this heap of ruins!"
[7]But in that day he will cry out,
"I have no remedy.[i]
I have no food or clothing in my house;
do not make me the leader of the people."

[8]Jerusalem staggers,
Judah is falling;[j]
their words[k] and deeds are against the LORD,
defying[l] his glorious presence.
[9]The look on their faces testifies against them;
they parade their sin like Sodom;[m]
they do not hide it.
Woe to them!
They have brought disaster[n] upon themselves.

[10]Tell the righteous it will be well[o] with them,
for they will enjoy the fruit of their deeds.[p]
[11]Woe to the wicked! Disaster[q] is upon them!
They will be paid back for what their hands have done.

[12]Youths[r] oppress my people,
women rule over them.

O my people, your guides lead you astray;[a]
    they turn you from the path.

13The Lord takes his place in court;
    he rises to judge[b] the people.
14The Lord enters into judgment[c]
    against the elders and leaders of his people:
"It is you who have ruined my vineyard;
    the plunder[d] from the poor is in your houses.
15What do you mean by crushing my people[e]
    and grinding the faces of the poor?"
        declares the Lord, the Lord Almighty.

16The Lord says,
"The women of Zion[f] are haughty,
walking along with outstretched necks,
    flirting with their eyes,
tripping along with mincing steps,
    with ornaments jingling on their ankles.
17Therefore the Lord will bring sores on the heads of the
    women of Zion;
    the Lord will make their scalps bald."

18In that day the Lord will snatch away their finery: the bangles and headbands and crescent necklaces,[g] 19the earrings and bracelets and veils, 20the headdresses[h] and ankle chains and sashes, the perfume bottles and charms, 21the signet rings and nose rings, 22the fine robes and the capes and cloaks, the purses 23and mirrors, and the linen garments and tiaras and shawls.

24Instead of fragrance[i] there will be a stench;
    instead of a sash,[j] a rope;
instead of well-dressed hair, baldness;[k]
    instead of fine clothing, sackcloth;[l]
    instead of beauty,[m] branding.
25Your men will fall by the sword,[n]
    your warriors in battle.
26The gates of Zion will lament and mourn;[o]
    destitute, she will sit on the ground.[p]

Chapter 4 Theme

4 In that day seven women
    will take hold of one man[q]
and say, "We will eat our own food[r]
    and provide our own clothes;
only let us be called by your name.
    Take away our disgrace!"[s]

3:12 [a] Isa 9:16
3:13 [b] Mic 6:2
3:14 [c] Job 22:4 [d] Job 24:9; Jas 2:6
3:15 [e] Ps 94:5
3:16 [f] SS 3:11
3:18 [g] Jdg 8:21
3:20 [h] Ex 39:28
3:24 [i] Est 2:12 [j] Pr 31:24 [k] Isa 22:12 [l] La 2:10; Eze 27:30-31 [m] 1Pe 3:3
3:25 [n] Isa 1:20
3:26 [o] Jer 14:2 [p] La 2:10
4:1 [q] Isa 13:12 [r] 2Th 3:12 [s] Ge 30:23

4:2
aIsa 11:1-5;
53:2; Jer 23:5-6;
Zec 3:8; 6:12
bPs 72:16

4:3
cRo 11:5
dIsa 52:1; 60:21
eLk 10:20

4:4
fIsa 3:24
gIsa 1:15
hIsa 28:6
iIsa 1:31;
Mt 3:11

4:5
jEx 13:21
kIsa 60:1

4:6
lPs 27:5
mIsa 25:4

5:1
nPs 80:8-9

5:2
oJer 2:21
pMt 21:19;
Mk 11:13;
Lk 13:6

5:3
qMt 21:40

5:4
r2Ch 36:15;
Jer 2:5-7;
Mic 6:3-4;
Mt 23:37

5:5
sPs 80:12
tIsa 28:3,18;
La 1:15;
Lk 21:24

5:6
uIsa 7:23,24;
Heb 6:8

5:7
vPs 80:8

²In that day the Branch of the LORDᵃ will be beautiful and glorious, and the fruitᵇ of the land will be the pride and glory of the survivors in Israel. ³Those who are left in Zion, who remainᶜ in Jerusalem, will be called holy,ᵈ all who are recordedᵉ among the living in Jerusalem. ⁴The Lord will wash away the filthᶠ of the women of Zion; he will cleanse the bloodstainsᵍ from Jerusalem by a spiritᵃ of judgmentʰ and a spiritᵃ of fire.ⁱ ⁵Then the LORD will create over all of Mount Zion and over those who assemble there a cloud of smoke by day and a glow of flaming fire by night;ʲ over all the gloryᵏ will be a canopy. ⁶It will be a shelterˡ and shade from the heat of the day, and a refugeᵐ and hiding place from the storm and rain.

Chapter 5 Theme

5
I will sing for the one I love
  a song about his vineyard:ⁿ
My loved one had a vineyard
  on a fertile hillside.
²He dug it up and cleared it of stones
  and planted it with the choicest vines.ᵒ
He built a watchtower in it
  and cut out a winepress as well.
Then he looked for a crop of good grapes,
  but it yielded only bad fruit.ᵖ

³"Now you dwellers in Jerusalem and men of Judah,
  judge between me and my vineyard. q
⁴What more could have been done for my vineyard
  than I have done for it?ʳ
When I looked for good grapes,
  why did it yield only bad?
⁵Now I will tell you
  what I am going to do to my vineyard:
I will take away its hedge,
  and it will be destroyed;
I will break down its wall,ˢ
  and it will be trampled.ᵗ
⁶I will make it a wasteland,
  neither pruned nor cultivated,
  and briers and thornsᵘ will grow there.
I will command the clouds
  not to rain on it."

⁷The vineyardᵛ of the LORD Almighty
  is the house of Israel,

a 4 Or *the Spirit*

and the men of Judah
are the garden of his delight.
And he looked for justice,[a] but saw bloodshed;
for righteousness, but heard cries of distress.

[8]Woe[b] to you who add house to house
and join field to field[c]
till no space is left
and you live alone in the land.

[9]The LORD Almighty has declared in my hearing:[d]

"Surely the great houses will become desolate,[e]
the fine mansions left without occupants.
[10]A ten-acre[a] vineyard will produce only a bath[b] of wine,
a homer[c] of seed only an ephah[d] of grain."[f]

[11]Woe to those who rise early in the morning
to run after their drinks,
who stay up late at night
till they are inflamed with wine.[g]
[12]They have harps and lyres at their banquets,
tambourines and flutes and wine,
but they have no regard[h] for the deeds of the LORD,
no respect for the work of his hands.[i]
[13]Therefore my people will go into exile[j]
for lack of understanding;[k]
their men of rank will die of hunger
and their masses will be parched with thirst.
[14]Therefore the grave[e][l] enlarges its appetite
and opens its mouth[m] without limit;
into it will descend their nobles and masses
with all their brawlers and revelers.
[15]So man will be brought low[n]
and mankind humbled,[o]
the eyes of the arrogant[p] humbled.
[16]But the LORD Almighty will be exalted by his justice,[q]
and the holy God will show himself holy[r] by his
righteousness.
[17]Then sheep will graze as in their own pasture;[s]
lambs will feed[f] among the ruins of the rich.

[18]Woe to those who draw sin along with cords of deceit,
and wickedness[t] as with cart ropes,

5:7
[a] Isa 59:15

5:8
[b] Jer 22:13
[c] Mic 2:2;
Hab 2:9-12

5:9
[d] Isa 22:14
[e] Isa 6:11-12;
Mt 23:38

5:10
[f] Lev 26:26

5:11
[g] Pr 23:29-30

5:12
[h] Job 34:27
[i] Ps 28:5;
Am 6:5-6

5:13
[j] Hos 4:6
[k] Isa 1:3

5:14
[l] Pr 30:16
[m] Nu 16:30

5:15
[n] Isa 10:33
[o] Isa 2:9
[p] Isa 2:11

5:16
[q] Isa 28:17;
30:18; 33:5; 61:8
[r] Isa 29:23

5:17
[s] Isa 7:25;
Zep 2:6,14

5:18
[t] Isa 59:4-8;
Jer 23:14

---

a 10 Hebrew *ten-yoke,* that is, the land plowed by 10 yoke of oxen in one day   *b 10* That is,
probably about 6 gallons (about 22 liters)   *c 10* That is, probably about 6 bushels (about 220 liters)
d 10 That is, probably about 3/5 bushel (about 22 liters)   *e 14* Hebrew *Sheol*
f 17 Septuagint; Hebrew / *strangers will eat*

5:19
a Jer 17:15;
Eze 12:22;
2Pe 3:4

5:20
b Mt 6:22-23;
Lk 11:34-35
c Am 5:7

5:21
d Pr 3:7;
Ro 12:16;
1Co 3:18-20

5:22
e Pr 23:20

5:23
f Ex 23:8
g Isa 10:2
h Ps 94:21;
Jas 5:6

5:24
i Job 18:16
j Isa 8:6; 30:9,12

5:25
k 2Ki 22:13
l 2Ki 9:37
m Jer 4:8;
Da 9:16
n Isa 9:12,17,
21; 10:4

5:26
o Isa 7:18;
Zec 10:8
p Dt 28:49;
Isa 13:5; 18:3

5:27
q Job 12:18
r Joel 2:7-8

5:28
s Ps 45:5
t Ps 7:12

¹⁹to those who say, "Let God hurry,
    let him hasten his work
      so we may see it.
Let it approach,
    let the plan of the Holy One of Israel come,
      so we may know it."[a]

²⁰Woe to those who call evil good
    and good evil,
who put darkness for light
    and light for darkness,[b]
who put bitter for sweet
    and sweet for bitter.[c]

²¹Woe to those who are wise in their own eyes[d]
    and clever in their own sight.

²²Woe to those who are heroes at drinking wine[e]
    and champions at mixing drinks,
²³who acquit the guilty for a bribe,[f]
    but deny justice[g] to the innocent.[h]
²⁴Therefore, as tongues of fire lick up straw
    and as dry grass sinks down in the flames,
so their roots will decay[i]
    and their flowers blow away like dust;
for they have rejected the law of the LORD Almighty
    and spurned the word[j] of the Holy One of Israel.
²⁵Therefore the LORD's anger[k] burns against his people;
    his hand is raised and he strikes them down.
The mountains shake,
    and the dead bodies are like refuse[l] in the streets.

Yet for all this, his anger is not turned away,[m]
    his hand is still upraised.[n]

²⁶He lifts up a banner for the distant nations,
    he whistles[o] for those at the ends of the earth.[p]
Here they come,
    swiftly and speedily!
²⁷Not one of them grows tired or stumbles,
    not one slumbers or sleeps;
not a belt is loosened at the waist,[q]
    not a sandal thong is broken.[r]
²⁸Their arrows are sharp,[s]
    all their bows[t] are strung;
their horses' hoofs seem like flint,
    their chariot wheels like a whirlwind.

^{29}Their roar is like that of the lion,^{a}
  they roar like young lions;
they growl as they seize^b their prey
  and carry it off with no one to rescue.^{c}
^{30}In that day they will roar over it
  like the roaring of the sea.^{d}
And if one looks at the land,
  he will see darkness and distress;^{e}
  even the light will be darkened^f by the clouds.

Chapter 6 Theme

6 In the year that King Uzziah^g died,^{h} I saw the Lord^i seated on a throne,^{j} high and exalted, and the train of his robe filled the temple. ^{2}Above him were seraphs,^{k} each with six wings: With two wings they covered their faces, with two they covered their feet,^{l} and with two they were flying. ^{3}And they were calling to one another:

  "Holy, holy, holy is the LORD Almighty;
    the whole earth is full of his glory."^{m}

^{4}At the sound of their voices the doorposts and thresholds shook and the temple was filled with smoke.

^{5}"Woe to me!" I cried. "I am ruined! For I am a man of unclean lips, and I live among a people of unclean lips,^{n} and my eyes have seen the King,^{o} the LORD Almighty."

^{6}Then one of the seraphs flew to me with a live coal in his hand, which he had taken with tongs from the altar. ^{7}With it he touched my mouth and said, "See, this has touched your lips;^{p} your guilt is taken away and your sin atoned for.^{q}"

^{8}Then I heard the voice^r of the Lord saying, "Whom shall I send? And who will go for us?"

And I said, "Here am I. Send me!"

^{9}He said, "Go^s and tell this people:

  "'Be ever hearing, but never understanding;
    be ever seeing, but never perceiving.'^{t}
^{10}Make the heart of this people calloused;^{u}
    make their ears dull
    and close their eyes.^{a}
Otherwise they might see with their eyes,
    hear with their ears,^{v}
    understand with their hearts,
  and turn and be healed."^{w}

INSIGHT

For the historical background of King Uzziah (also called Azariah), read 2 Kings 15 and 2 Chronicles 26.

5:29
^{a}Jer 51:38;
Zep 3:3;
Zec 11:3
^{b}Isa 10:6;
49:24-25
^{c}Isa 42:22;
Mic 5:8

5:30
^{d}Lk 21:25
^{e}Isa 8:22;
Jer 4:23-28
^{f}Joel 2:10

6:1
^{g}2Ch 26:22,23
^{h}2Ki 15:7
^{i}Jn 12:41
^{j}Rev 4:2

6:2
^{k}Rev 4:8
^{l}Eze 1:11

6:3
^{m}Ps 72:19;
Rev 4:8

6:5
^{n}Jer 9:3-8
^{o}Jer 51:57

6:7
^{p}Jer 1:9
^{q}1Jn 1:7

6:8
^{r}Ac 9:4

6:9
^{s}Eze 3:11
^{t}Mt 13:15*;
Lk 8:10*

6:10
^{u}Dt 32:15;
Ps 119:70
^{v}Jer 5:21
^{w}Mt 13:13-15;
Mk 4:12*;
Ac 28:26-27*

---

^{a}9,10 Hebrew; Septuagint 'You will be ever hearing, but never understanding; / you will be ever seeing, but never perceiving.' / ^{10}This people's heart has become calloused; / they hardly hear with their ears, / and they have closed their eyes

6:11
a Ps 79:5
b Lev 26:31

[11]Then I said, "For how long, O Lord?"*a*

And he answered:

"Until the cities lie ruined*b*
    and without inhabitant,
until the houses are left deserted
    and the fields ruined and ravaged,

6:12
c Dt 28:64
d Jer 4:29

[12]until the LORD has sent everyone far away*c*
    and the land is utterly forsaken.*d*

6:13
e Isa 1:9
f Job 14:7

[13]And though a tenth remains*e* in the land,
    it will again be laid waste.
But as the terebinth and oak
    leave stumps when they are cut down,
    so the holy seed will be the stump in the land."*f*

Chapter 7 Theme

7:1
g 2Ki 15:37
h 2Ch 28:5
i 2Ki 15:25

7 When Ahaz son of Jotham, the son of Uzziah, was king of Judah, King Rezin*g* of Aram*h* and Pekah*i* son of Remaliah king of Israel marched up to fight against Jerusalem, but they could not overpower it.

7:2
j ver 13;
Isa 22:22
k Isa 9:9

[2]Now the house of David*j* was told, "Aram has allied itself with*a* Ephraim*k*"; so the hearts of Ahaz and his people were shaken, as the trees of the forest are shaken by the wind.

7:3
l 2Ki 18:17;
Isa 36:2

[3]Then the LORD said to Isaiah, "Go out, you and your son Shear-Jashub,*b* to meet Ahaz at the end of the aqueduct of the Upper Pool, on the road to the Washerman's Field.*l* [4]Say to him, 'Be careful, keep calm*m* and don't be afraid.*n* Do not lose heart*o* because of these two smoldering stubs*p* of firewood—because of the fierce anger*q* of Rezin and Aram and of the son of Remaliah. [5]Aram, Ephraim and Remaliah's son have plotted your ruin, saying, [6]"Let us invade Judah; let us tear it apart and divide it among ourselves, and make the son of Tabeel king over it." [7]Yet this is what the Sovereign LORD says:

7:4
m Isa 30:15
n Isa 35:4
o Dt 20:3
p Zec 3:2
q Isa 10:24

7:7
r Isa 8:10;
Ac 4:25

"'It will not take place,
    it will not happen,*r*
[8]for the head of Aram is Damascus,*s*
    and the head of Damascus is only Rezin.
Within sixty-five years
    Ephraim will be too shattered*t* to be a people.

7:8
s Ge 14:15
t Isa 17:1-3

[9]The head of Ephraim is Samaria,
    and the head of Samaria is only Remaliah's son.
If you do not stand firm in your faith,*u*
    you will not stand at all.'"*v*

7:9
u 2Ch 20:20
v Isa 8:6-8;
30:12-14

a 2 Or *has set up camp in*   *b* 3 *Shear-Jashub* means *a remnant will return.*

[10]Again the LORD spoke to Ahaz, [11]"Ask the LORD your God for a sign, whether in the deepest depths or in the highest heights."

[12]But Ahaz said, "I will not ask; I will not put the LORD to the test."

[13]Then Isaiah said, "Hear now, you house of David! Is it not enough to try the patience of men? Will you try the patience of my God[a] also? [14]Therefore the Lord himself will give you[a] a sign: The virgin will be with child and will give birth to a son,[b] and[b] will call him Immanuel.[c c] [15]He will eat curds and honey[d] when he knows enough to reject the wrong and choose the right. [16]But before the boy knows[e] enough to reject the wrong and choose the right, the land of the two kings you dread will be laid waste.[f] [17]The LORD will bring on you and on your people and on the house of your father a time unlike any since Ephraim broke away[g] from Judah—he will bring the king of Assyria.[h]"

[18]In that day the LORD will whistle[i] for flies from the distant streams of Egypt and for bees from the land of Assyria.[j] [19]They will all come and settle in the steep ravines and in the crevices[k] in the rocks, on all the thornbushes and at all the water holes. [20]In that day the Lord will use[l] a razor hired from beyond the River[d]— the king of Assyria[m]—to shave your head and the hair of your legs, and to take off your beards also. [21]In that day, a man will keep alive a young cow and two goats. [22]And because of the abundance of the milk they give, he will have curds to eat. All who remain in the land will eat curds and honey. [23]In that day, in every place where there were a thousand vines worth a thousand silver shekels,[e] there will be only briers and thorns.[n] [24]Men will go there with bow and arrow, for the land will be covered with briers and thorns. [25]As for all the hills once cultivated by the hoe, you will no longer go there for fear of the briers and thorns; they will become places where cattle are turned loose and where sheep run.[o]

Chapter 8 Theme

8 The LORD said to me, "Take a large scroll[p] and write on it with an ordinary pen: Maher-Shalal-Hash-Baz.[f q] [2]And I will call in Uriah[r] the priest and Zechariah son of Jeberekiah as reliable witnesses for me."

[3]Then I went to the prophetess, and she conceived and gave birth to a son. And the LORD said to me, "Name him Maher-Shalal-Hash-Baz. [4]Before the boy knows[s] how to say 'My father' or 'My mother,' the wealth of Damascus and the plunder of Samaria will be carried off by the king of Assyria.[t]"

[5]The LORD spoke to me again:

---

[a]14 The Hebrew is plural.   [b]14 Masoretic Text; Dead Sea Scrolls and he or and they
[c]14 *Immanuel* means *God with us.*   [d]20 That is, the Euphrates   [e]23 That is, about 25 pounds (about 11.5 kilograms)   [f]1 *Maher-Shalal-Hash-Baz* means *quick to the plunder, swift to the spoil*; also in verse 3.

7:13
[a]Isa 25:1

7:14
[b]Lk 1:31
[c]Isa 8:8,10;
Mt 1:23*

7:15
[d]ver 22

7:16
[e]Isa 8:4
[f]Isa 17:3;
Hos 5:9,13;
Am 1:3-5

7:17
[g]1Ki 12:16
[h]2Ch 28:20

7:18
[i]Isa 5:26
[j]Isa 13:5

7:19
[k]Isa 2:19

7:20
[l]Isa 10:15
[m]Isa 8:7; 10:5

7:23
[n]Isa 5:6

7:25
[o]Isa 5:17

8:1
[p]Isa 30:8;
[q]ver 3; Hab 2:2

8:2
[r]2Ki 16:10

8:4
[s]Isa 7:16
[t]Isa 7:8

8:6
a Isa 5:24
b Jn 9:7
c Isa 7:1

8:7
d Isa 17:12-13
e Isa 7:20

8:8
f Isa 7:14

8:9
g Isa 17:12-13
h Joel 3:9

8:10
i Job 5:12
j Isa 7:7
k Isa 7:14;
Ro 8:31

8:11
l Eze 3:14
m Eze 2:8

8:12
n Isa 7:2; 30:1
o 1Pe 3:14*

8:13
p Nu 20:12
q Isa 29:23

8:14
r Isa 4:6;
Eze 11:16
s Lk 2:34;
Ro 9:33*;
1Pe 2:8*
t Isa 24:17-18

8:15
u Isa 28:13;
59:10; Lk 20:18;
Ro 9:32

8:16
v Isa 29:11-12

8:17
w Hab 2:3
x Dt 31:17;
Isa 54:8

⁶"Because this people has rejected[a]
  the gently flowing waters of Shiloah[b]
and rejoices over Rezin
  and the son of Remaliah,[c]
⁷therefore the Lord is about to bring against them
  the mighty floodwaters[d] of the River[a]—
  the king of Assyria[e] with all his pomp.
It will overflow all its channels,
  run over all its banks
⁸and sweep on into Judah, swirling over it,
  passing through it and reaching up to the neck.
Its outspread wings will cover the breadth of your land,
  O Immanuel[b]!"[f]

⁹Raise the war cry,[c][g] you nations, and be shattered!
  Listen, all you distant lands.
Prepare[h] for battle, and be shattered!
  Prepare for battle, and be shattered!
¹⁰Devise your strategy, but it will be thwarted;[i]
  propose your plan, but it will not stand,[j]
  for God is with us.[d][k]

¹¹The Lord spoke to me with his strong hand upon me,[l] warning me not to follow[m] the way of this people. He said:

¹²"Do not call conspiracy[n]
  everything that these people call conspiracy[e];
do not fear what they fear,
  and do not dread it.[o]
¹³The Lord Almighty is the one you are to regard as holy,[p]
  he is the one you are to fear,
  he is the one you are to dread,[q]
¹⁴and he will be a sanctuary;[r]
  but for both houses of Israel he will be
a stone that causes men to stumble
  and a rock that makes them fall.[s]
And for the people of Jerusalem he will be
  a trap and a snare.[t]
¹⁵Many of them will stumble;[u]
  they will fall and be broken,
  they will be snared and captured."

¹⁶Bind up the testimony
  and seal[v] up the law among my disciples.
¹⁷I will wait[w] for the Lord,
  who is hiding[x] his face from the house of Jacob.
  I will put my trust in him.

---

a 7 That is, the Euphrates   b 8 Immanuel means God with us.   c 9 Or Do your worst
d 10 Hebrew Immanuel   e 12 Or Do not call for a treaty / every time these people call for a treaty

[18]Here am I, and the children the LORD has given me.[a] We are signs[b] and symbols in Israel from the LORD Almighty, who dwells on Mount Zion.[c]

[19]When men tell you to consult[d] mediums and spiritists, who whisper and mutter,[e] should not a people inquire of their God? Why consult the dead on behalf of the living? [20]To the law[f] and to the testimony! If they do not speak according to this word, they have no light[g] of dawn. [21]Distressed and hungry, they will roam through the land; when they are famished, they will become enraged and, looking upward, will curse[h] their king and their God. [22]Then they will look toward the earth and see only distress and darkness and fearful gloom, and they will be thrust into utter darkness.[i]

Chapter 9 Theme

9 Nevertheless, there will be no more gloom for those who were in distress. In the past he humbled the land of Zebulun and the land of Naphtali,[j] but in the future he will honor Galilee of the Gentiles, by the way of the sea, along the Jordan—

[2]The people walking in darkness
    have seen a great light;[k]
on those living in the land of the shadow of death[a][l]
    a light has dawned.[m]
[3]You have enlarged the nation
    and increased their joy;
they rejoice before you
    as people rejoice at the harvest,
as men rejoice
    when dividing the plunder.
[4]For as in the day of Midian's defeat,[n]
    you have shattered
the yoke[o] that burdens them,
    the bar across their shoulders,[p]
    the rod of their oppressor.[q]
[5]Every warrior's boot used in battle
    and every garment rolled in blood
will be destined for burning,[r]
    will be fuel for the fire.
[6]For to us a child is born,[s]
    to us a son is given,[t]
and the government[u] will be on his shoulders.
And he will be called
    Wonderful Counselor,[b][v] Mighty God,[w]
    Everlasting Father, Prince of Peace.[x]

a 2 Or land of darkness   b 6 Or Wonderful, Counselor

8:18
[a] Heb 2:13*
[b] Lk 2:34
[c] Ps 9:11

8:19
[d] 1Sa 28:8
[e] Isa 29:4

8:20
[f] Isa 1:10;
Lk 16:29
[g] Mic 3:6

8:21
[h] Rev 16:11

8:22
[i] ver 20; Isa 5:30

9:1
[j] 2Ki 15:29

9:2
[k] Eph 5:8
[l] Lk 1:79
[m] Mt 4:15-16*

9:4
[n] Jdg 7:25
[o] Isa 14:25
[p] Isa 10:27
[q] Isa 14:4; 49:26;
51:13; 54:14

9:5
[r] Isa 2:4

9:6
[s] Isa 53:2;
Lk 2:11
[t] Jn 3:16
[u] Mt 28:18
[v] Isa 28:29
[w] Isa 10:21; 11:2
[x] Isa 26:3,12;
66:12

9:7
a Da 2:44;
Lk 1:33
b Isa 11:4; 16:5;
32:1,16
c Isa 37:32;
59:17

⁷Of the increase of his government and peace
  there will be no end.ᵃ
He will reign on David's throne
  and over his kingdom,
establishing and upholding it
  with justiceᵇ and righteousness
  from that time on and forever.
The zealᶜ of the LORD Almighty
  will accomplish this.

9:9
d Isa 7:9
e Isa 46:12

⁸The Lord has sent a message against Jacob;
  it will fall on Israel.
⁹All the people will know it—
  Ephraim and the inhabitants of Samariaᵈ—
who say with pride
  and arroganceᵉ of heart,

9:11
f Isa 7:8

¹⁰"The bricks have fallen down,
  but we will rebuild with dressed stone;
the fig trees have been felled,
  but we will replace them with cedars."

9:12
g 2Ki 16:6
h 2Ch 28:18
i Ps 79:7
j Isa 5:25

¹¹But the LORD has strengthened Rezin'sᶠ foes against them
  and has spurred their enemies on.
¹²Arameansᵍ from the east and Philistinesʰ from the west
  have devouredⁱ Israel with open mouth.

Yet for all this, his anger is not turned away,
  his hand is still upraised.ʲ

9:13
k Jer 5:3
l Isa 31:1;
Hos 7:7,10

¹³But the people have not returned to him who
      struckᵏ them,
  nor have they soughtˡ the LORD Almighty.

9:14
m Isa 19:15
n Rev 18:8

¹⁴So the LORD will cut off from Israel both head and tail,
  both palm branch and reedᵐ in a single day;ⁿ
¹⁵the eldersᵒ and prominent men are the head,
  the prophets who teach lies are the tail.

9:15
o Isa 3:2-3

¹⁶Those who guideᵖ this people mislead them,
  and those who are guided are led astray.�q
¹⁷Therefore the Lord will take no pleasure in the
      young men,ʳ
  nor will he pityˢ the fatherless and widows,
for everyone is ungodlyᵗ and wicked,ᵘ
  every mouth speaks vileness.ᵛ

9:16
p Mt 15:14;
23:16,24
q Isa 3:12

9:17
r Jer 18:21
s Isa 27:11
t Isa 10:6
u Isa 1:4
v Mt 12:34
w Isa 5:25

Yet for all this, his anger is not turned away,
  his hand is still upraised.ʷ

¹⁸Surely wickedness burns like a fire;ˣ
  it consumes briers and thorns,

9:18
x Mal 4:1

it sets the forest thickets ablaze,[a]
  so that it rolls upward in a column of smoke.
[19]By the wrath[b] of the LORD Almighty
  the land will be scorched
and the people will be fuel for the fire;[c]
  no one will spare his brother.[d]
[20]On the right they will devour,
  but still be hungry;[e]
on the left they will eat,[f]
  but not be satisfied.
Each will feed on the flesh of his own offspring[a]:
[21] Manasseh will feed on Ephraim, and Ephraim on
      Manasseh;
  together they will turn against Judah.[g]

Yet for all this, his anger is not turned away,
  his hand is still upraised.[h]

Chapter 10 Theme

10 Woe to those who make unjust laws,
  to those who issue oppressive decrees,[i]
[2]to deprive[j] the poor of their rights
  and withhold justice from the oppressed of my people,[k]
making widows their prey
  and robbing the fatherless.
[3]What will you do on the day of reckoning,[l]
  when disaster[m] comes from afar?
To whom will you run for help?[n]
  Where will you leave your riches?
[4]Nothing will remain but to cringe among the captives[o]
  or fall among the slain.[p]

Yet for all this, his anger is not turned away,[q]
  his hand is still upraised.

[5]"Woe to the Assyrian,[r] the rod of my anger,
  in whose hand is the club[s] of my wrath![t]
[6]I send him against a godless[u] nation,
  I dispatch him against a people who anger me,[v]
to seize loot and snatch plunder,[w]
  and to trample them down like mud in the streets.
[7]But this is not what he intends,[x]
  this is not what he has in mind;
his purpose is to destroy,
  to put an end to many nations.

a 20 Or *arm*

Cross references (right column):

9:18
a Ps 83:14

9:19
b Isa 13:9,13
c Isa 1:31
d Mic 7:2,6

9:20
e Lev 26:26
f Isa 49:26

9:21
g 2Ch 28:6
h Isa 5:25

10:1
i Ps 58:2

10:2
j Isa 3:14
k Isa 5:23

10:3
l Job 31:14;
  Hos 9:7
m Lk 19:44
n Isa 20:6

10:4
o Isa 24:22
p Isa 22:2; 34:3;
  66:16
q Isa 5:25

10:5
r Isa 14:25;
  Zep 2:13
s Jer 51:20
t Isa 13:3,5,13;
  30:30; 66:14

10:6
u Isa 9:17
v Isa 9:19
w Isa 5:29

10:7
x Ge 50:20;
  Ac 4:23-28

10:8
a 2Ki 18:24

10:9
b Ge 10:10
c 2Ch 35:20
d 2Ki 17:6
e 2Ki 16:9

10:10
f 2Ki 19:18

10:12
g Isa 28:21-22;
65:7
h 2Ki 19:31
i Jer 50:18

10:13
j Isa 37:24;
Da 4:30
k Eze 28:4

10:14
l Jer 49:16; Ob 4
m Job 31:25

10:15
n Isa 45:9;
Ro 9:20-21
o ver 5

10:16
p ver 18; Isa 17:4
q Isa 8:7

10:17
r Isa 31:9
s Isa 37:23
t Nu 11:1-3
u Isa 9:18

10:18
v 2Ki 19:23

10:19
w Isa 21:17

10:20
x Isa 11:10,11

⁸'Are not my commanders*a* all kings?' he says.
⁹   'Has not Calno*b* fared like Carchemish?*c*
Is not Hamath like Arpad,
   and Samaria*d* like Damascus?*e*
¹⁰As my hand seized the kingdoms of the idols,*f*
   kingdoms whose images excelled those of Jerusalem
      and Samaria—
¹¹shall I not deal with Jerusalem and her images
   as I dealt with Samaria and her idols?'"

¹²When the Lord has finished all his work*g* against Mount Zion*h* and Jerusalem, he will say, "I will punish the king of Assyria*i* for the willful pride of his heart and the haughty look in his eyes. ¹³For he says:

"'By the strength of my hand I have done this,*j*
   and by my wisdom, because I have understanding.
I removed the boundaries of nations,
   I plundered their treasures;*k*
   like a mighty one I subdued*a* their kings.
¹⁴As one reaches into a nest,*l*
   so my hand reached for the wealth*m* of the nations;
as men gather abandoned eggs,
   so I gathered all the countries;
not one flapped a wing,
   or opened its mouth to chirp.'"

¹⁵Does the ax raise itself above him who swings it,
   or the saw boast against him who uses it?*n*
As if a rod were to wield him who lifts it up,
   or a club*o* brandish him who is not wood!
¹⁶Therefore, the Lord, the LORD Almighty,
   will send a wasting disease*p* upon his sturdy warriors;
under his pomp*q* a fire will be kindled
   like a blazing flame.
¹⁷The Light of Israel will become a fire,*r*
   their Holy One*s* a flame;
in a single day it will burn and consume
   his thorns*t* and his briers.*u*
¹⁸The splendor of his forests*v* and fertile fields
   it will completely destroy,
   as when a sick man wastes away.
¹⁹And the remaining trees of his forests will be so few*w*
   that a child could write them down.

²⁰In that day*x* the remnant of Israel,
   the survivors of the house of Jacob,

a 13 Or / *I subdued the mighty,*

will no longer rely[a] on him
who struck them down[b]
but will truly rely[c] on the LORD,
the Holy One of Israel.
[21]A remnant[d] will return,[a] a remnant of Jacob
will return to the Mighty God.[e]
[22]Though your people, O Israel, be like the sand by the sea,
only a remnant will return.[f]
Destruction has been decreed,[g]
overwhelming and righteous.
[23]The Lord, the LORD Almighty, will carry out
the destruction decreed upon the whole land.[h]

[24]Therefore, this is what the Lord, the LORD Almighty, says:

"O my people who live in Zion,[i]
do not be afraid of the Assyrians,
who beat[j] you with a rod
and lift up a club against you, as Egypt did.
[25]Very soon[k] my anger against you will end
and my wrath[l] will be directed to their destruction."

[26]The LORD Almighty will lash[m] them with a whip,
as when he struck down Midian[n] at the rock of Oreb;
and he will raise his staff over the waters,[o]
as he did in Egypt.
[27]In that day their burden will be lifted from your shoulders,
their yoke[p] from your neck;[q]
the yoke will be broken
because you have grown so fat.[b]

[28]They enter Aiath;
they pass through Migron;[r]
they store supplies at Micmash.[s]
[29]They go over the pass, and say,
"We will camp overnight at Geba."
Ramah[t] trembles;
Gibeah of Saul flees.
[30]Cry out, O Daughter of Gallim![u]
Listen, O Laishah!
Poor Anathoth![v]
[31]Madmenah is in flight;
the people of Gebim take cover.
[32]This day they will halt at Nob;[w]
they will shake their fist

10:20
a 2Ki 16:7
b 2Ch 28:20
c Isa 17:7

10:21
d Isa 6:13
e Isa 9:6

10:22
f Ro 9:27-28
g Isa 28:22;
Da 9:27

10:23
h Isa 28:22;
Ro 9:27-28*

10:24
i Ps 87:5-6
j Ex 5:14

10:25
k Isa 17:14
l ver 5;
Da 11:36

10:26
m Isa 37:36-38
n Isa 9:4
o Ex 14:16

10:27
p Isa 9:4
q Isa 14:25

10:28
r 1Sa 14:2
s 1Sa 13:2

10:29
t Jos 18:25

10:30
u 1Sa 25:44
v Ne 11:32

10:32
w 1Sa 21:1

a 21 Hebrew shear-jashub; also in verse 22 b 27 Hebrew; Septuagint broken / from your shoulders

10:32
a Jer 6:23

10:33
b Am 2:9

11:1
c ver 10;
Isa 9:7;
Rev 5:5
d Isa 4:2

11:2
e Isa 42:1; 48:16;
61:1;
Mt 3:16;
Jn 1:32-33
f Eph 1:17
g 2Ti 1:7

11:3
h Jn 7:24
i Jn 2:25

11:4
j Ps 72:2
k Isa 9:7
l Isa 3:14
m Mal 4:6
n Job 4:9;
2Th 2:8

11:5
o Isa 25:1
p Eph 6:14

11:6
q Isa 65:25

11:9
r Job 5:23
s Ps 98:2-3;
Isa 52:10
t Isa 45:6,14;
Hab 2:14

11:10
u Jn 12:32
v Isa 49:23;
Lk 2:32
w Ro 15:12*
x Isa 14:3; 28:12;
32:17-18

11:11
y Isa 10:20
z Isa 19:24;
Hos 11:11;
Mic 7:12;
Zec 10:10

at the mount of the Daughter of Zion,[a]
at the hill of Jerusalem.

33See, the Lord, the LORD Almighty,
will lop off the boughs with great power.
The lofty trees will be felled,
the tall[b] ones will be brought low.
34He will cut down the forest thickets with an ax;
Lebanon will fall before the Mighty One.

Chapter 11 Theme

11

A shoot will come up from the stump of Jesse;[c]
from his roots a Branch[d] will bear fruit.
2The Spirit[e] of the LORD will rest on him—
the Spirit of wisdom[f] and of understanding,
the Spirit of counsel and of power,[g]
the Spirit of knowledge and of the fear of the LORD—
3and he will delight in the fear of the LORD.

He will not judge by what he sees with his eyes,[h]
or decide by what he hears with his ears;[i]
4but with righteousness[j] he will judge the needy,
with justice[k] he will give decisions for the poor[l] of
the earth.
He will strike[m] the earth with the rod of his mouth;
with the breath[n] of his lips he will slay the wicked.
5Righteousness will be his belt
and faithfulness[o] the sash around his waist. [p]

6The wolf will live with the lamb,[q]
the leopard will lie down with the goat,
the calf and the lion and the yearling[a] together;
and a little child will lead them.
7The cow will feed with the bear,
their young will lie down together,
and the lion will eat straw like the ox.
8The infant will play near the hole of the cobra,
and the young child put his hand into the viper's nest.
9They will neither harm nor destroy[r]
on all my holy mountain,
for the earth[s] will be full of the knowledge[t] of the LORD
as the waters cover the sea.

10In that day the Root of Jesse will stand as a banner[u] for the peoples; the nations[v] will rally to him,[w] and his place of rest[x] will be glorious. 11In that day[y] the Lord will reach out his hand a second time to reclaim the remnant that is left of his people from Assyria,[z]

a 6 Hebrew; Septuagint *lion will feed*

from Lower Egypt, from Upper Egypt,[a] from Cush,[b] from Elam,[a] from Babylonia,[c] from Hamath and from the islands[b] of the sea.

12He will raise a banner for the nations
    and gather the exiles of Israel;
he will assemble the scattered people[c] of Judah
    from the four quarters of the earth.
13Ephraim's jealousy will vanish,
    and Judah's enemies[d] will be cut off;
Ephraim will not be jealous of Judah,
    nor Judah hostile toward Ephraim.[d]
14They will swoop down on the slopes of Philistia to
        the west;
    together they will plunder the people to the east.
They will lay hands on Edom[e] and Moab,[f]
    and the Ammonites will be subject to them.
15The LORD will dry up
    the gulf of the Egyptian sea;
with a scorching wind he will sweep his hand[g]
    over the Euphrates River.[e][h]
He will break it up into seven streams
    so that men can cross over in sandals.
16There will be a highway[i] for the remnant of his people
        that is left from Assyria,
    as there was for Israel
        when they came up from Egypt.[j]

Chapter 12 Theme _____

12 In that day you will say:

"I will praise[k] you, O LORD.
    Although you were angry with me,
your anger has turned away
    and you have comforted me.
2Surely God is my salvation;
    I will trust[l] and not be afraid.
The LORD, the LORD, is my strength and my song;
    he has become my salvation.[m]"
3With joy you will draw water[n]
    from the wells of salvation.

4In that day you will say:

"Give thanks to the LORD, call on his name;[o]
    make known among the nations what he has done,
    and proclaim that his name is exalted.

11:11
[a]Ge 10:22
[b]Isa 42:4,10,12;
66:19

11:12
[c]Zep 3:10

11:13
[d]Jer 3:18;
Eze 37:16-17,22;
Hos 1:11

11:14
[e]Da 11:41;
Joel 3:19
[f]Isa 16:14; 25:10

11:15
[g]Isa 19:16
[h]Isa 7:20

11:16
[i]Isa 19:23; 62:10
[j]Ex 14:26-31

12:1
[k]Isa 25:1

12:2
[l]Isa 26:3
[m]Ex 15:2;
Ps 118:14

12:3
[n]Jn 4:10,14

12:4
[o]Ps 105:1;
Isa 24:15

---

[a]11 Hebrew *from Pathros*   [b]11 That is, the upper Nile region   [c]11 Hebrew *Shinar*
[d]13 Or *hostility*   [e]15 Hebrew *the River*

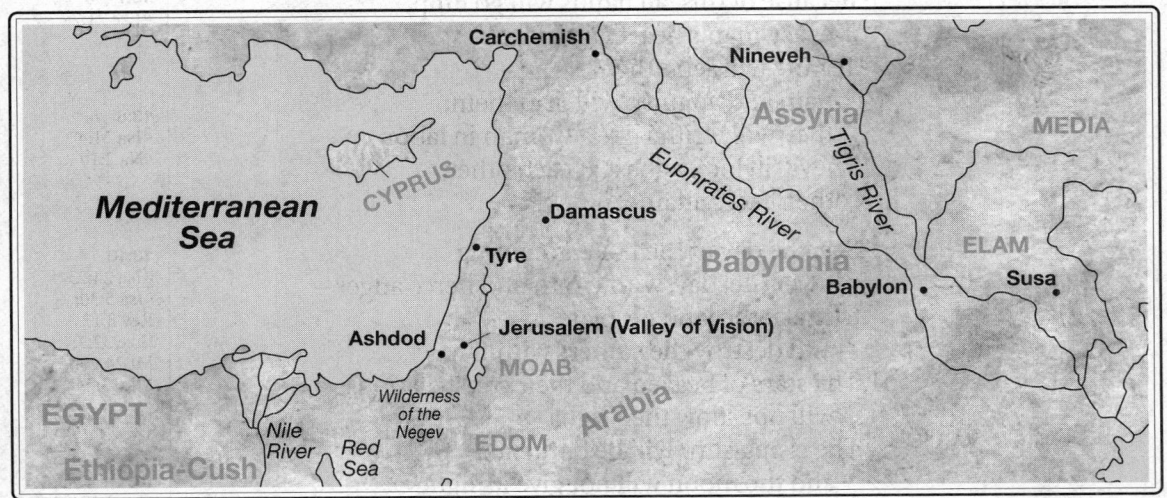

The Nations That Received the Oracles

12:5
a Ex 15:1
b Ps 98:1

⁵Sing*a* to the LORD, for he has done glorious things;*b*
  let this be known to all the world.
⁶Shout aloud and sing for joy, people of Zion,
  for great is the Holy One of Israel*c* among you.*d*"

12:6
c Isa 49:26
d Zep 3:14-17

Chapter 13 Theme

13 An oracle concerning Babylon that Isaiah son of Amoz saw:

²Raise a banner*e* on a bare hilltop,
  shout to them;
 beckon to them
  to enter the gates of the nobles.
³I have commanded my holy ones;
  I have summoned my warriors*f* to carry out my wrath—
  those who rejoice*g* in my triumph.

13:2
e Jer 50:2; 51:27

13:3
f Joel 3:11
g Ps 149:2

⁴Listen, a noise on the mountains,
  like that of a great multitude!*h*
 Listen, an uproar among the kingdoms,
  like nations massing together!
 The LORD Almighty is mustering
  an army for war.
⁵They come from faraway lands,
  from the ends of the heavens*i*—
 the LORD and the weapons of his wrath—
  to destroy*j* the whole country.

13:4
h Joel 3:14

13:5
i Isa 5:26
j Isa 24:1

⁶Wail,*k* for the day*l* of the LORD is near;
  it will come like destruction from the Almighty.*a*

13:6
k Eze 30:2
l Isa 2:12;
Joel 1:15

a 6 Hebrew *Shaddai*

INSIGHT

From 729 B.C. Babylon was part of the Assyrian Empire. The ruler of Assyria assumed the title "King of Babylon." Babylon then became the capital of the Neo-Babylonian Empire which Nebuchadnezzar ruled after the death of his father, Nabopolassar. Nebuchadnezzar first besieged Jerusalem in 605 B.C. In 586 B.C. he destroyed Jerusalem and the temple.

⁷Because of this, all hands will go limp,
  every man's heart will melt.ᵃ
⁸Terrorᵇ will seize them,
  pain and anguish will grip them;
  they will writhe like a woman in labor.
They will look aghast at each other,
  their faces aflame.ᶜ

⁹See, the day of the LORD is coming
  —a cruel day, with wrath and fierce anger—
to make the land desolate
  and destroy the sinners within it.
¹⁰The stars of heaven and their constellations
  will not show their light.
The rising sunᵈ will be darkenedᵉ
  and the moon will not give its light.ᶠ
¹¹I will punishᵍ the world for its evil,
  the wicked for their sins.
I will put an end to the arrogance of the haughty
  and will humble the pride of the ruthless.
¹²I will make manʰ scarcer than pure gold,
  more rare than the gold of Ophir.
¹³Therefore I will make the heavens tremble;ⁱ
  and the earth will shake from its place
at the wrath of the LORD Almighty,
  in the day of his burning anger.

¹⁴Like a hunted gazelle,
  like sheep without a shepherd,ʲ
each will return to his own people,
  each will flee to his native land.ᵏ
¹⁵Whoever is captured will be thrust through;
  all who are caught will fallˡ by the sword.ᵐ
¹⁶Their infantsⁿ will be dashed to pieces before their eyes;
  their houses will be looted and their wives ravished.

¹⁷See, I will stir upᵒ against them the Medes,
  who do not care for silver
  and have no delight in gold.ᵖ
¹⁸Their bows will strike down the young men;
  they will have no mercy on infants
  nor will they look with compassion on children.
¹⁹Babylon, the jewel of kingdoms,
  the glory�q of the Babylonians'ᵃ pride,
will be overthrownʳ by God
  like Sodom and Gomorrah.ˢ

ᵃ19 Or Chaldeans'

Cross references (right column):

13:7
ᵃEze 21:7

13:8
ᵇIsa 21:4
ᶜNa 2:10

13:10
ᵈIsa 24:23
ᵉIsa 5:30;
Rev 8:12
ᶠEze 32:7;
Mt 24:29*;
Mk 13:24*

13:11
ᵍIsa 3:11; 11:4;
26:21

13:12
ʰIsa 4:1

13:13
ⁱIsa 34:4; 51:6;
Hag 2:6

13:14
ʲ1Ki 22:17
ᵏJer 50:16

13:15
ˡJer 51:4
ᵐIsa 14:19;
Jer 50:25

13:16
ⁿPs 137:9

13:17
ᵒJer 51:1
ᵖPr 6:34-35

13:19
qDa 4:30
ʳRev 14:8
ˢGe 19:24

²⁰She will never be inhabited^a
or lived in through all generations;
no Arab^b will pitch his tent there,
no shepherd will rest his flocks there.
²¹But desert creatures^c will lie there,
jackals will fill her houses;
there the owls will dwell,
and there the wild goats will leap about.
²²Hyenas will howl in her strongholds,^d
jackals^e in her luxurious palaces.
Her time is at hand,^f
and her days will not be prolonged.

Chapter 14 Theme

14 The LORD will have compassion^g on Jacob;
once again he will choose^h Israel
and will settle them in their own land.
Aliensⁱ will join them
and unite with the house of Jacob.
²Nations will take them
and bring^j them to their own place.
And the house of Israel will possess the nations^k
as menservants and maidservants in the LORD's land.
They will make captives of their captors
and rule over their oppressors.^l

³On the day the LORD gives you relief^m from suffering and turmoil and cruel bondage, ⁴you will take up this tauntⁿ against the king of Babylon:

How the oppressor^o has come to an end!
How his fury^a has ended!
⁵The LORD has broken the rod of the wicked, ^p
the scepter of the rulers,
⁶which in anger struck down peoples ^q
with unceasing blows,
and in fury subdued nations
with relentless aggression.^r
⁷All the lands are at rest and at peace;
they break into singing.^s
⁸Even the pine trees^t and the cedars of Lebanon
exult over you and say,
"Now that you have been laid low,
no woodsman comes to cut us down."

The cross-reference column:

13:20
a Isa 14:23; 34:10-15
b 2Ch 17:11

13:21
c Rev 18:2

13:22
d Isa 25:2
e Isa 34:13
f Jer 51:33

14:1
g Ps 102:13; Isa 49:10,13; 54:7-8,10
h Isa 41:8; 44:1; 49:7; Zec 1:17; 2:12
i Eph 2:12-19

14:2
j Isa 60:9
k Isa 49:7,23
l Isa 60:14; 61:5

14:3
m Isa 11:10

14:4
n Hab 2:6
o Isa 9:4

14:5
p Ps 125:3

14:6
q Isa 10:14
r Isa 47:6

14:7
s Ps 98:1; 126:1-3

14:8
t Eze 31:16

---

^a 4 Dead Sea Scrolls, Septuagint and Syriac; the meaning of the word in the Masoretic Text is uncertain.

⁹The grave^{a a} below is all astir
    to meet you at your coming;
it rouses the spirits of the departed to greet you—
    all those who were leaders in the world;
it makes them rise from their thrones—
    all those who were kings over the nations.
¹⁰They will all respond,
    they will say to you,
"You also have become weak, as we are;
    you have become like us."^b
¹¹All your pomp has been brought down to the grave,
    along with the noise of your harps;
maggots are spread out beneath you
    and worms^c cover you.

¹²How you have fallen^d from heaven,
    O morning star,^e son of the dawn!
You have been cast down to the earth,
    you who once laid low the nations!
¹³You said in your heart,
    "I will ascend^f to heaven;
I will raise my throne^g
    above the stars of God;
I will sit enthroned on the mount of assembly,
    on the utmost heights of the sacred mountain.^b
¹⁴I will ascend above the tops of the clouds;
    I will make myself like the Most High."^h
¹⁵But you are brought down to the grave,
    to the depthsⁱ of the pit.

¹⁶Those who see you stare at you,
    they ponder your fate:^j
"Is this the man who shook the earth
    and made kingdoms tremble,
¹⁷the man who made the world a desert,^k
    who overthrew its cities
    and would not let his captives go home?"

¹⁸All the kings of the nations lie in state,
    each in his own tomb.
¹⁹But you are cast out^l of your tomb
    like a rejected branch;
you are covered with the slain,
    with those pierced by the sword,
    those who descend to the stones of the pit.^m
Like a corpse trampled underfoot,

14:9
^a Eze 32:21

14:10
^b Eze 32:21

14:11
^c Isa 51:8

14:12
^d Isa 34:4;
Lk 10:18
^e 2Pe 1:19;
Rev 2:28;
8:10; 9:1

14:13
^f Da 5:23; 8:10;
Mt 11:23
^g Eze 28:2;
2Th 2:4

14:14
^h Isa 47:8;
2Th 2:4

14:15
ⁱ Mt 11:23;
Lk 10:15

14:16
^j Jer 50:23

14:17
^k Joel 2:3

14:19
^l Isa 22:16-18
^m Jer 41:7-9

^a 9 Hebrew *Sheol*; also in verses 11 and 15   ^b 13 Or *the north*; Hebrew *Zaphon*

14:20
a Job 18:19
b Isa 1:4
c Ps 21:10

14:21
d Ex 20:5;
Lev 26:39

14:22
e 1Ki 14:10;
Job 18:19

14:23
f Isa 34:11-15;
Zep 2:14

14:24
g Isa 45:23
h Ac 4:28

14:25
i Isa 10:5,12
j Isa 9:4
k Isa 10:27

14:26
l Isa 23:9
m Ex 15:12

14:27
n 2Ch 20:6;
Isa 43:13;
Da 4:35

14:28
o Isa 13:1
p 2Ki 16:20

14:29
q 2Ch 26:6
r Isa 11:8

14:30
s Isa 3:15
t Isa 7:21-22
u Isa 8:21; 9:20;
51:19
v Jer 25:16

14:31
w Isa 3:26
x Jer 1:14

20   you will not join them in burial,
  for you have destroyed your land
    and killed your people.

The offspring[a] of the wicked[b]
  will never be mentioned[c] again.
21Prepare a place to slaughter his sons
  for the sins of their forefathers;[d]
they are not to rise to inherit the land
  and cover the earth with their cities.

22"I will rise up against them,"
  declares the Lord Almighty.
"I will cut off from Babylon her name and survivors,
  her offspring and descendants,[e]"
           declares the Lord.

23"I will turn her into a place for owls[f]
  and into swampland;
I will sweep her with the broom of destruction,"
  declares the Lord Almighty.

24The Lord Almighty has sworn,[g]

  "Surely, as I have planned, so it will be,
    and as I have purposed, so it will stand.[h]
25I will crush the Assyrian[i] in my land;
  on my mountains I will trample him down.
His yoke[j] will be taken from my people,
  and his burden removed from their shoulders.[k]"

26This is the plan[l] determined for the whole world;
  this is the hand[m] stretched out over all nations.
27For the Lord Almighty has purposed, and who can
    thwart him?
  His hand is stretched out, and who can turn it back?[n]

28This oracle[o] came in the year King Ahaz[p] died:

29Do not rejoice, all you Philistines,[q]
  that the rod that struck you is broken;
from the root of that snake will spring up a viper,[r]
  its fruit will be a darting, venomous serpent.
30The poorest of the poor will find pasture,
  and the needy[s] will lie down in safety.[t]
But your root I will destroy by famine;[u]
  it will slay[v] your survivors.

31Wail, O gate![w] Howl, O city!
  Melt away, all you Philistines!
A cloud of smoke comes from the north,[x]
  and there is not a straggler in its ranks.

³²What answer shall be given
    to the envoys^a of that nation?
"The LORD has established Zion,^b
    and in her his afflicted people will find refuge.^c"

Chapter 15 Theme

15 An oracle concerning Moab:^d

Ar in Moab is ruined,^e
    destroyed in a night!
Kir in Moab is ruined,
    destroyed in a night!
²Dibon goes up to its temple,
    to its high places^f to weep;
Moab wails over Nebo and Medeba.
Every head is shaved^g
    and every beard cut off.
³In the streets they wear sackcloth;
    on the roofs and in the public squares^h
they all wail,
    prostrate with weeping.ⁱ
⁴Heshbon and Elealeh^j cry out,
    their voices are heard all the way to Jahaz.
Therefore the armed men of Moab cry out,
    and their hearts are faint.

⁵My heart cries out over Moab;^k
    her fugitives flee as far as Zoar,
    as far as Eglath Shelishiyah.
They go up the way to Luhith,
    weeping as they go;
on the road to Horonaim^l
    they lament their destruction.^m
⁶The waters of Nimrim are dried upⁿ
    and the grass is withered;^o
the vegetation is gone
    and nothing green is left.
⁷So the wealth they have acquired ^p and stored up
    they carry away over the Ravine of the Poplars.
⁸Their outcry echoes along the border of Moab;
    their wailing reaches as far as Eglaim,
    their lamentation as far as Beer Elim.
⁹Dimon's^a waters are full of blood,
    but I will bring still more upon Dimon^a—

INSIGHT

Moab was a narrow strip of land directly east of the Dead (Salt) Sea. Its inhabitants were called Moabites and were neighbors to the Israelites. Moab, the father of the Moabites, was the son of Lot by his firstborn daughter. Ruth, who is in the genealogy of King David, was a Moabitess.

a 9 Masoretic Text; Dead Sea Scrolls, some Septuagint manuscripts and Vulgate *Dibon*

14:32
^a Isa 37:9
^b Ps 87:2,5;
Isa 44:28; 54:11
^c Isa 4:6; Jas 2:5

15:1
^d Isa 11:14
^e Jer 48:24,41

15:2
^f Jer 48:35
^g Lev 21:5

15:3
^h Jer 48:38
ⁱ Isa 22:4

15:4
^j Nu 32:3

15:5
^k Jer 48:31
^l Jer 48:3,34
^m Jer 4:20; 48:5

15:6
ⁿ Isa 19:5-7;
Jer 48:34
^o Joel 1:12

15:7
^p Isa 30:6;
Jer 48:36

15:9
a 2Ki 17:25

> a lion[a] upon the fugitives of Moab
>   and upon those who remain in the land.

Chapter 16 Theme

16:1
b 2Ki 3:4
c 2Ki 14:7
d Isa 10:32

16

> Send lambs[b] as tribute
>   to the ruler of the land,
> from Sela,[c] across the desert,
>   to the mount of the Daughter of Zion.[d]

> [2]Like fluttering birds
>   pushed from the nest,[e]
> so are the women of Moab
>   at the fords of the Arnon.[f]

16:2
e Pr 27:8
f Nu 21:13-14;
Jer 48:20

> [3]"Give us counsel,
>   render a decision.
> Make your shadow like night—
>   at high noon.
> Hide the fugitives,[g]
>   do not betray the refugees.
> [4]Let the Moabite fugitives stay with you;
>   be their shelter from the destroyer."

16:3
g 1Ki 18:4

> The oppressor[h] will come to an end,
>   and destruction will cease;
>   the aggressor will vanish from the land.
> [5]In love a throne[i] will be established;
>   in faithfulness a man will sit on it—
>   one from the house[a] of David[j]—
> one who in judging seeks justice[k]
>   and speeds the cause of righteousness.

16:4
h Isa 9:4

16:5
i Da 7:14;
Mic 4:7
j Lk 1:32
k Isa 9:7

> [6]We have heard of Moab's[l] pride[m]—
>   her overweening pride and conceit,
> her pride and her insolence—
>   but her boasts are empty.
> [7]Therefore the Moabites wail,[n]
>   they wail together for Moab.
> Lament and grieve
>   for the men[b][o] of Kir Hareseth. [p]
> [8]The fields of Heshbon wither,
>   the vines of Sibmah also.
> The rulers of the nations
>   have trampled down the choicest vines,
> which once reached Jazer
>   and spread toward the desert.

16:6
l Am 2:1;
Zep 2:8
m Ob 3;
Zep 2:10

16:7
n Jer 48:20
o 1Ch 16:3
p 2Ki 3:25

a 5 Hebrew *tent*   b 7 Or *"raisin cakes,"* a wordplay

Their shoots spread out
and went as far as the sea.
⁹So I weep,^a as Jazer weeps,
for the vines of Sibmah.
O Heshbon, O Elealeh,
I drench you with tears!
The shouts of joy over your ripened fruit
and over your harvests^b have been stilled.
¹⁰Joy and gladness are taken away from the orchards;^c
no one sings or shouts in the vineyards;
no one treads^d out wine at the presses,^e
for I have put an end to the shouting.
¹¹My heart laments for Moab^f like a harp,
my inmost being^g for Kir Hareseth.
¹²When Moab appears at her high place,
she only wears herself out;
when she goes to her shrine^h to pray,
it is to no avail.ⁱ

¹³This is the word the LORD has already spoken concerning Moab. ¹⁴But now the LORD says: "Within three years, as a servant bound by contract would count them, Moab's splendor and all her many people will be despised,^j and her survivors will be very few and feeble."^k

Chapter 17 Theme

17 An oracle concerning Damascus:^l

"See, Damascus will no longer be a city
but will become a heap of ruins.^m
²The cities of Aroer will be deserted
and left to flocks,ⁿ which will lie down,
with no one to make them afraid.^o
³The fortified city will disappear from Ephraim,
and royal power from Damascus;
the remnant of Aram will be
like the glory^p of the Israelites,"^q
declares the LORD Almighty.

⁴"In that day the glory of Jacob will fade;
the fat of his body will waste^r away.
⁵It will be as when a reaper gathers the standing grain
and harvests^s the grain with his arm—
as when a man gleans heads of grain
in the Valley of Rephaim.
⁶Yet some gleanings will remain,^t
as when an olive tree is beaten,^u

I N S I G H T

Damascus is the capital of Aram (or Syria).

16:9
a Isa 15:3
b Jer 40:12

16:10
c Isa 24:7-8
d Jdg 9:27
e Job 24:11

16:11
f Isa 15:5
g Isa 63:15;
Hos 11:8;
Php 2:1

16:12
h Isa 15:2
i 1Ki 18:29

16:14
j Isa 25:10;
Jer 48:42
k Isa 21:17

17:1
l Ge 14:15;
Jer 49:23; Ac 9:2
m Isa 25:2;
Am 1:3; Zec 9:1

17:2
n Isa 7:21;
Eze 25:5
o Jer 7:33;
Mic 4:4

17:3
p ver 4; Hos 9:11
q Isa 7:8,16; 8:4

17:4
r Isa 10:16

17:5
s ver 11;
Jer 51:33;
Joel 3:13;
Mt 13:30

17:6
t Dt 4:27;
Isa 24:13
u Isa 27:12

leaving two or three olives on the topmost branches,
four or five on the fruitful boughs,"
declares the LORD, the God of Israel.

17:7
a Isa 10:20
b Mic 7:7

7In that day men will look[a] to their Maker
and turn their eyes to the Holy One[b] of Israel.
8They will not look to the altars,
the work of their hands,[c]
and they will have no regard for the Asherah poles[a]
and the incense altars their fingers have made.

17:8
c Isa 2:18,20;
30:22

9In that day their strong cities, which they left because of the Israelites, will be like places abandoned to thickets and undergrowth. And all will be desolation.

17:10
d Isa 51:13
e Ps 68:19;
Isa 12:2

10You have forgotten[d] God your Savior;[e]
you have not remembered the Rock, your fortress.
Therefore, though you set out the finest plants
and plant imported vines,
11though on the day you set them out, you make them grow,
and on the morning[f] when you plant them, you bring
them to bud,
yet the harvest will be as nothing[g]
in the day of disease and incurable pain.[h]

17:11
f Ps 90:6
g Hos 8:7
h Job 4:8

12Oh, the raging of many nations—
they rage like the raging sea![i]
Oh, the uproar of the peoples—
they roar like the roaring of great waters!
13Although the peoples roar like the roar of surging waters,
when he rebukes[j] them they flee[k] far away,
driven before the wind like chaff[l] on the hills,
like tumbleweed before a gale.[m]
14In the evening, sudden terror!
Before the morning, they are gone![n]
This is the portion of those who loot us,
the lot of those who plunder us.

17:12
i Ps 18:4;
Jer 6:23;
Lk 21:25

17:13
j Ps 9:5
k Isa 13:14
l Isa 41:2,
15-16
m Job 21:18

17:14
n 2Ki 19:35

Chapter 18 Theme

18 Woe to the land of whirring wings[b]
along the rivers of Cush,[c][o]
2which sends envoys by sea
in papyrus[p] boats over the water.

18:1
o Isa 20:3-5;
Eze 30:4-5,9;
Zep 2:12; 3:10

Go, swift messengers,
to a people tall and smooth-skinned,

18:2
p Ex 2:3

a 8 That is, symbols of the goddess Asherah   b 1 Or *of locusts*   c 1 That is, the upper Nile region

to a people feared far and wide,
an aggressive[a] nation of strange speech,
whose land is divided by rivers.[b]

[3]All you people of the world,
you who live on the earth,
when a banner[c] is raised on the mountains,
you will see it,
and when a trumpet sounds,
you will hear it.

[4]This is what the LORD says to me:
"I will remain quiet and will look on from my
dwelling place,[d]
like shimmering heat in the sunshine,
like a cloud of dew[e] in the heat of harvest."

[5]For, before the harvest, when the blossom is gone
and the flower becomes a ripening grape,
he will cut off the shoots with pruning knives,
and cut down and take away the spreading
branches.[f]

[6]They will all be left to the mountain birds of prey
and to the wild animals;[g]
the birds will feed on them all summer,
the wild animals all winter.

[7]At that time gifts will be brought to the LORD Almighty

from a people tall and smooth-skinned,
from a people feared far and wide,
an aggressive nation of strange speech,
whose land is divided by rivers—

the gifts will be brought to Mount Zion, the place of the Name of
the LORD Almighty.[h]

Chapter 19 Theme _____

19

An oracle[i] concerning Egypt:[j][k]

See, the LORD rides on a swift cloud[l]
and is coming to Egypt.
The idols of Egypt tremble before him,
and the hearts of the Egyptians melt[m] within them.

[2]"I will stir up Egyptian against Egyptian—
brother will fight against brother,[n]
neighbor against neighbor,
city against city,
kingdom against kingdom.[o]

18:2
[a]Ge 10:8-9;
2Ch 12:3
[b]ver 7

18:3
[c]Isa 5:26

18:4
[d]Isa 26:21;
Hos 5:15
[e]Isa 26:19;
Hos 14:5

18:5
[f]Isa 17:10-11;
Eze 17:6

18:6
[g]Isa 56:9;
Jer 7:33;
Eze 32:4; 39:17

18:7
[h]Ps 68:31

19:1
[i]Isa 13:1;
Jer 43:12
[j]Joel 3:19
[k]Ex 12:12
[l]Ps 18:10; 104:3;
Rev 1:7
[m]Jos 2:11

19:2
[n]Jdg 7:22;
Mt 10:21,36
[o]2Ch 20:23

19:3
a Isa 8:19; 47:13;
Da 2:2,10

³The Egyptians will lose heart,
 and I will bring their plans to nothing;
they will consult the idols and the spirits of the dead,
 the mediums and the spiritists.*a*

19:4
b Isa 20:4;
Jer 46:26;
Eze 29:19

⁴I will hand the Egyptians over
 to the power of a cruel master,
and a fierce king*b* will rule over them,"
 declares the Lord, the LORD Almighty.

19:5
c Jer 51:36

⁵The waters of the river will dry up,*c*
 and the riverbed will be parched and dry.
⁶The canals will stink;*d*
 the streams of Egypt will dwindle and dry up.*e*
The reeds and rushes will wither,*f*

19:6
d Ex 7:18
e Isa 37:25;
Eze 30:12
f Isa 15:6

⁷ also the plants along the Nile,
 at the mouth of the river.
Every sown field*g* along the Nile
 will become parched, will blow away and be no more.
⁸The fishermen*h* will groan and lament,
 all who cast hooks*i* into the Nile;
those who throw nets on the water
 will pine away.

19:7
g Isa 23:3

19:8
h Eze 47:10
i Hab 1:15

⁹Those who work with combed flax will despair,
 the weavers of fine linen*j* will lose hope.
¹⁰The workers in cloth will be dejected,
 and all the wage earners will be sick at heart.

19:9
j Pr 7:16;
Eze 27:7

¹¹The officials of Zoan*k* are nothing but fools;
 the wise counselors of Pharaoh give senseless advice.
How can you say to Pharaoh,
 "I am one of the wise men,*l*
 a disciple of the ancient kings"?

19:11
k Nu 13:22
l 1Ki 4:30;
Ac 7:22

¹²Where are your wise men*m* now?
 Let them show you and make known
what the LORD Almighty
 has planned*n* against Egypt.
¹³The officials of Zoan have become fools,
 the leaders of Memphis*ᵃ ᵒ* are deceived;
the cornerstones of her peoples
 have led Egypt astray.

19:12
m 1Co 1:20
n Isa 14:24;
Ro 9:17

¹⁴The LORD has poured into them
 a spirit of dizziness;*p*
they make Egypt stagger in all that she does,
 as a drunkard staggers around in his vomit.

19:13
o Jer 2:16;
Eze 30:13,16

19:14
p Mt 17:17

a 13 Hebrew *Noph*

1189

¹⁵There is nothing Egypt can do—
head or tail, palm branch or reed.^a

¹⁶In that day the Egyptians will be like women.^b They will shudder with fear^c at the uplifted hand^d that the LORD Almighty raises against them. ¹⁷And the land of Judah will bring terror to the Egyptians; everyone to whom Judah is mentioned will be terrified, because of what the LORD Almighty is planning^e against them.

¹⁸In that day five cities in Egypt will speak the language of Canaan and swear allegiance^f to the LORD Almighty. One of them will be called the City of Destruction.^a

¹⁹In that day there will be an altar^g to the LORD in the heart of Egypt, and a monument^h to the LORD at its border. ²⁰It will be a sign and witness to the LORD Almighty in the land of Egypt. When they cry out to the LORD because of their oppressors, he will send them a savior and defender, and he will rescueⁱ them. ²¹So the LORD will make himself known to the Egyptians, and in that day they will acknowledge^j the LORD. They will worship^k with sacrifices and grain offerings; they will make vows to the LORD and keep them. ²²The LORD will strike^l Egypt with a plague; he will strike them and heal them. They will turn^m to the LORD, and he will respond to their pleas and healⁿ them.

²³In that day there will be a highway^o from Egypt to Assyria. The Assyrians will go to Egypt and the Egyptians to Assyria. The Egyptians and Assyrians will worship^p together. ²⁴In that day Israel will be the third, along with Egypt and Assyria, a blessing on the earth. ²⁵The LORD Almighty will bless them, saying, "Blessed be Egypt my people,^q Assyria my handiwork,^r and Israel my inheritance.^s"

Chapter 20 Theme

20 In the year that the supreme commander,^t sent by Sargon king of Assyria, came to Ashdod and attacked and captured it— ²at that time the LORD spoke through Isaiah son of Amoz.^u He said to him, "Take off the sackcloth^v from your body and the sandals^w from your feet." And he did so, going around stripped^x and barefoot.^y

³Then the LORD said, "Just as my servant Isaiah has gone stripped and barefoot for three years, as a sign^z and portent against Egypt and Cush,^{b a} ⁴so the king^b of Assyria will lead away stripped and barefoot the Egyptian captives and Cushite exiles, young and old, with buttocks bared—to Egypt's shame.^c ⁵Those who trusted in Cush and boasted in Egypt^d will be afraid and put to shame. ⁶In

---

^a*18* Most manuscripts of the Masoretic Text; some manuscripts of the Masoretic Text, Dead Sea Scrolls and Vulgate *City of the Sun* (that is, Heliopolis)   ^b*3* That is, the upper Nile region; also in verse 5

19:15
^aIsa 9:14

19:16
^b51:30; Na 3:13
^cHeb 10:31
^dIsa 11:15

19:17
^eIsa 14:24

19:18
^fZep 3:9

19:19
^gJos 22:10
^hGe 28:18

19:20
ⁱIsa 49:24-26

19:21
^jIsa 11:9
^kIsa 56:7;
Mal 1:11

19:22
^lHeb 12:11
^mIsa 45:14;
Hos 14:1
ⁿDt 32:39

19:23
^oIsa 11:16
^pIsa 27:13

19:25
^qPs 100:3
^rIsa 29:23;
45:11; 60:21;
64:8; Eph 2:10
^sHos 2:23

20:1
^t2Ki 18:17

20:2
^uIsa 13:1
^vZec 13:4;
Mt 3:4
^wEze 24:17,23
^x1Sa 19:24
^yMic 1:8

20:3
^zIsa 8:18
^aIsa 37:9; 43:3

20:4
^bIsa 19:4
^cIsa 47:3;
Jer 13:22,26

20:5
^d2Ki 18:21;
Isa 30:5

20:6
a Isa 10:3
b Jer 30:15-17;
Mt 23:33;
1Th 5:3;
Heb 2:3

that day the people who live on this coast will say, 'See what has happened to those we relied on, those we fled to for help[a] and deliverance from the king of Assyria! How then can we escape?[b]'"

Chapter 21 Theme

21:1
c Isa 13:21;
Jer 51:43
d Zec 9:14

21

An oracle concerning the Desert[c] by the Sea:

Like whirlwinds sweeping through the southland,[d]
    an invader comes from the desert,
    from a land of terror.

21:2
e Ps 60:3
f Isa 33:1
g Isa 22:6;
Jer 49:34

2 A dire[e] vision has been shown to me:
    The traitor betrays,[f] the looter takes loot.
Elam,[g] attack! Media, lay siege!
    I will bring to an end all the groaning she caused.

3 At this my body is racked with pain,
    pangs seize me, like those of a woman in labor;[h]
I am staggered by what I hear,
    I am bewildered by what I see.
4 My heart falters,
    fear makes me tremble;
the twilight I longed for
    has become a horror to me.

21:3
h Ps 48:6;
Isa 26:17

5 They set the tables,
    they spread the rugs,
    they eat, they drink![i]
Get up, you officers,
    oil the shields!

6 This is what the Lord says to me:

"Go, post a lookout
    and have him report what he sees.
7 When he sees chariots[j]
    with teams of horses,
riders on donkeys
    or riders on camels,
let him be alert,
    fully alert."

21:5
i Jer 51:39,57;
Da 5:2

21:7
j ver 9

8 And the lookout[a][k] shouted,

"Day after day, my lord, I stand on the watchtower;
    every night I stay at my post.
9 Look, here comes a man in a chariot
    with a team of horses.

21:8
k Hab 2:1

a 8 Dead Sea Scrolls and Syriac; Masoretic Text A lion

And he gives back the answer:
    'Babylon[a] has fallen,[b] has fallen!
All the images of its gods[c]
    lie shattered on the ground!'"

10O my people, crushed on the threshing floor,[d]
    I tell you what I have heard
from the LORD Almighty,
    from the God of Israel.

11An oracle concerning Dumah[a;e]

Someone calls to me from Seir,[f]
    "Watchman, what is left of the night?
    Watchman, what is left of the night?"
12The watchman replies,
    "Morning is coming, but also the night.
    If you would ask, then ask;
    and come back yet again."

13An oracle[g] concerning Arabia:

You caravans of Dedanites,
    who camp in the thickets of Arabia,
14   bring water for the thirsty;
you who live in Tema,[h]
    bring food for the fugitives.
15They flee[i] from the sword,
    from the drawn sword,
from the bent bow
    and from the heat of battle.

16This is what the Lord says to me: "Within one year, as a servant bound by contract[j] would count it, all the pomp[k] of Kedar[l] will come to an end. 17The survivors of the bowmen, the warriors of Kedar, will be few.[m]" The LORD, the God of Israel, has spoken.

Chapter 22 Theme _____

22 An oracle[n] concerning the Valley[o] of Vision:

What troubles you now,
    that you have all gone up on the roofs,
2O town full of commotion,
    O city of tumult and revelry?[p]
Your slain were not killed by the sword,
    nor did they die in battle.
3All your leaders have fled together;
    they have been captured without using the bow.

a 11 *Dumah* means *silence* or *stillness,* a wordplay on *Edom.*

21:9
a Rev 14:8
b Jer 51:8;
Rev 18:2
c Isa 46:1;
Jer 50:2; 51:44

21:10
d Jer 51:33

21:11
e Ge 25:14
f Ge 32:3

21:13
g Isa 13:1

21:14
h Ge 25:15

21:15
i Isa 13:14

21:16
j Isa 16:14
k Isa 17:3
l Ps 120:5;
Isa 60:7

21:17
m Isa 10:19

22:1
n Isa 13:1
o Ps 125:2;
Jer 21:13;
Joel 3:2,12,14

22:2
p Isa 32:13

22:4
a Isa 15:3;
Lk 19:41
b Jer 9:1

All you who were caught were taken prisoner together,
 having fled while the enemy was still far away.
⁴Therefore I said, "Turn away from me;
 let me weepᵃ bitterly.
Do not try to console me
 over the destruction of my people."ᵇ

22:5
c La 1:5

⁵The Lord, the LORD Almighty, has a day
 of tumult and trampling and terrorᶜ
 in the Valley of Vision,
a day of battering down walls
 and of crying out to the mountains.

22:6
d Isa 21:2
e Jer 49:35
f 2Ki 16:9

⁶Elamᵈ takes up the quiver,ᵉ
 with her charioteers and horses;
 Kirᶠ uncovers the shield.

22:7
g 2Ch 32:1-2

⁷Your choicest valleys are full of chariots,
 and horsemen are posted at the city gates;ᵍ
⁸ the defenses of Judah are stripped away.

22:8
h 2Ch 32:5
i 1Ki 7:2

And you looked in that day
 to the weaponsʰ in the Palace of the Forest;ⁱ
⁹you saw that the City of David
 had many breaches in its defenses;

22:9
j 2Ch 32:4

you stored up water
 in the Lower Pool.ʲ
¹⁰You counted the buildings in Jerusalem
 and tore down houses to strengthen the wall.

22:11
k 2Ki 25:4;
Jer 39:4
l 2Ch 32:4

¹¹You built a reservoir between the two wallsᵏ
 for the water of the Old Pool,ˡ
but you did not look to the One who made it,
 or have regard for the One who planned it long ago.

22:12
m Joel 2:17
n Mic 1:16
o Joel 1:13

¹²The Lord, the LORD Almighty,
 called you on that day
to weepᵐ and to wail,
 to tear out your hairⁿ and put on sackcloth.ᵒ
¹³But see, there is joy and revelry,
 slaughtering of cattle and killing of sheep,
 eating of meat and drinking of wine!ᵖ

22:13
p Isa 5:22;
28:7-8; 56:12;
Lk 17:26-29
q 1Co 15:32*

"Let us eat and drink," you say,
 "for tomorrow we die!"ᵍ

22:14
r Isa 5:9
s Isa 13:11;
26:21;
30:13-14;
Eze 24:13

¹⁴The LORD Almighty has revealed this in my hearing:ʳ "Till your dying day this sin will not be atonedˢ for," says the Lord, the LORD Almighty.

¹⁵This is what the Lord, the LORD Almighty, says:

"Go, say to this steward,
 to Shebna,[a] who is in charge of the palace:
¹⁶What are you doing here and who gave you permission
 to cut out a grave[b] for yourself here,
hewing your grave on the height
 and chiseling your resting place in the rock?

¹⁷"Beware, the LORD is about to take firm hold of you
 and hurl you away, O you mighty man.
¹⁸He will roll you up tightly like a ball
 and throw[c] you into a large country.
There you will die
 and there your splendid chariots will remain—
 you disgrace to your master's house!
¹⁹I will depose you from your office,
 and you will be ousted from your position.

²⁰"In that day I will summon my servant, Eliakim[d] son of Hilki-ah. ²¹I will clothe him with your robe and fasten your sash around him and hand your authority over to him. He will be a father to those who live in Jerusalem and to the house of Judah. ²²I will place on his shoulder the key[e] to the house of David;[f] what he opens no one can shut, and what he shuts no one can open.[g] ²³I will drive him like a peg[h] into a firm place;[i] he will be a seat[a] of honor[j] for the house of his father. ²⁴All the glory of his family will hang on him: its offspring and offshoots—all its lesser vessels, from the bowls to all the jars.

²⁵"In that day," declares the LORD Almighty, "the peg[k] driven into the firm place will give way; it will be sheared off and will fall, and the load hanging on it will be cut down." The LORD has spoken.[l]

Chapter 23 Theme

23 An oracle concerning Tyre:[m]

Wail, O ships[n] of Tarshish![o]
 For Tyre is destroyed
 and left without house or harbor.
From the land of Cyprus[b]
 word has come to them.

²Be silent, you people of the island
 and you merchants of Sidon,
 whom the seafarers have enriched.
³On the great waters
 came the grain of the Shihor;

22:15
a 2Ki 18:18;
Isa 36:3

22:16
b Mt 27:60

22:18
c Isa 17:13

22:20
d 2Ki 18:18;
Isa 36:3

22:22
e Rev 3:7
f Isa 7:2
g Job 12:14

22:23
h Zec 10:4
i Ezr 9:8
j 1Sa 2:7-8;
Job 36:7

22:25
k ver 23
l Isa 46:11;
Mic 4:4

23:1
m Jos 19:29;
1Ki 5:1;
Jer 47:4;
Eze 26,27,28;
Joel 3:4-8;
Am 1:9-10;
Zec 9:2-4
n 1Ki 10:22
o Ge 10:4;
Isa 2:16 fn

a 23 Or *throne* b 1 Hebrew *Kittim*

23:3
a Isa 19:7
b Eze 27:3

the harvest of the Nile*ᵃ ᵃ* was the revenue of Tyre,*ᵇ*
    and she became the marketplace of the nations.

⁴Be ashamed, O Sidon,*ᶜ* and you, O fortress of the sea,
    for the sea has spoken:
"I have neither been in labor nor given birth;
    I have neither reared sons nor brought
        up daughters."

23:4
c Ge 10:15,19

⁵When word comes to Egypt,
    they will be in anguish at the report from Tyre.

⁶Cross over to Tarshish;
    wail, you people of the island.
⁷Is this your city of revelry,*ᵈ*
    the old, old city,
whose feet have taken her
    to settle in far-off lands?

23:7
d Isa 22:2; 32:13

⁸Who planned this against Tyre,
    the bestower of crowns,
whose merchants are princes,
    whose traders are renowned in the earth?
⁹The LORD Almighty planned it,
    to bring low*ᵉ* the pride of all glory
    and to humble*ᶠ* all who are renowned*ᵍ* on the earth.

23:9
e Job 40:11
f Isa 13:11
g Isa 5:13; 9:15

¹⁰Till*ᵇ* your land as along the Nile,
    O Daughter of Tarshish,
    for you no longer have a harbor.
¹¹The LORD has stretched out his hand*ʰ* over the sea
    and made its kingdoms tremble.
He has given an order concerning Phoenicia*ᶜ*
    that her fortresses be destroyed.*ⁱ*
¹²He said, "No more of your reveling,*ʲ*
    O Virgin Daughter*ᵏ* of Sidon, now crushed!

23:11
h Ex 14:21
i Isa 25:2;
Zec 9:3-4

"Up, cross over to Cyprus*ᵈ*;
    even there you will find no rest."
¹³Look at the land of the Babylonians,*ᵉ*
    this people that is now of no account!
The Assyrians*ˡ* have made it
    a place for desert creatures;
they raised up their siege towers,
    they stripped its fortresses bare
    and turned it into a ruin.*ᵐ*

23:12
j Rev 18:22
k Isa 47:1

23:13
l Isa 10:5
m Isa 10:7

a 2,3 Masoretic Text; one Dead Sea Scroll *Sidon, / who cross over the sea; / your envoys* ³*are
on the great waters. / The grain of the Shihor, / the harvest of the Nile,*   *b 10* Dead Sea Scrolls
and some Septuagint manuscripts; Masoretic Text *Go through*   *c 11* Hebrew *Canaan*
d 12 Hebrew *Kittim*   *e 13* Or *Chaldeans*

[14]Wail, you ships of Tarshish;[a]
  your fortress is destroyed!

[15]At that time Tyre[b] will be forgotten for seventy years, the span of a king's life. But at the end of these seventy years, it will happen to Tyre as in the song of the prostitute:

[16]"Take up a harp, walk through the city,
  O prostitute forgotten;
play the harp well, sing many a song,
  so that you will be remembered."

[17]At the end of seventy years, the LORD will deal with Tyre. She will return to her hire as a prostitute[c] and will ply her trade with all the kingdoms on the face of the earth. [18]Yet her profit and her earnings will be set apart for the LORD;[d] they will not be stored up or hoarded. Her profits will go to those who live before the LORD,[e] for abundant food and fine clothes.

Chapter 24 Theme

24 See, the LORD is going to lay waste the earth[f]
  and devastate it;
he will ruin its face
  and scatter its inhabitants—
[2]it will be the same
  for priest as for people,[g]
  for master as for servant,
  for mistress as for maid,
  for seller as for buyer,[h]
  for borrower as for lender,
  for debtor as for creditor.[i]
[3]The earth will be completely laid waste
  and totally plundered.[j]
                  The LORD has spoken this word.

[4]The earth dries up and withers,
  the world languishes and withers,
  the exalted[k] of the earth languish.
[5]The earth is defiled[l] by its people;
  they have disobeyed[m] the laws,
violated the statutes
  and broken the everlasting covenant.
[6]Therefore a curse consumes the earth;
  its people must bear their guilt.
Therefore earth's inhabitants are burned up,[n]
  and very few are left.
[7]The new wine dries up and the vine withers;[o]
  all the merrymakers groan.[p]

Cross references

23:14
[a] Isa 2:16 fn

23:15
[b] Jer 25:22

23:17
[c] Eze 16:26;
Na 3:4; Rev 17:1

23:18
[d] Ex 28:36;
Ps 72:10
[e] Isa 60:5-9;
Mic 4:13

24:1
[f] ver 20;
Isa 2:19-21; 33:9

24:2
[g] Hos 4:9
[h] Eze 7:12
[i] Lev 25:35-37;
Dt 23:19-20

24:3
[j] Isa 6:11-12

24:4
[k] Isa 2:12

24:5
[l] Ge 3:17;
Nu 35:33
[m] Isa 10:6; 59:12

24:6
[n] Isa 1:31

24:7
[o] Joel 1:10-12
[p] Isa 16:8-10

24:8
a Isa 5:12
b Jer 7:34; 16:9;
25:10; Hos 2:11
c Rev 18:22
d Eze 26:13

⁸The gaiety of the tambourines^a is stilled,
   the noise^b of the revelers has stopped,
   the joyful harp^c is silent.^d
⁹No longer do they drink wine^e with a song;
   the beer is bitter^f to its drinkers.
¹⁰The ruined city lies desolate;
   the entrance to every house is barred.

24:9
e Isa 5:11,22
f Isa 5:20

¹¹In the streets they cry out for wine;
   all joy turns to gloom,^g
   all gaiety is banished from the earth.
¹²The city is left in ruins,
   its gate is battered to pieces.

24:11
g Isa 16:10;
32:13; Jer 14:3

¹³So will it be on the earth
   and among the nations,
as when an olive tree is beaten,^h
   or as when gleanings are left after the grape
      harvest.

24:13
h Isa 17:6

¹⁴They raise their voices, they shout for joy;ⁱ
   from the west they acclaim the LORD's majesty.
¹⁵Therefore in the east give glory^j to the LORD;
   exalt^k the name of the LORD, the God of Israel,
   in the islands of the sea.
¹⁶From the ends of the earth we hear singing:
   "Glory^l to the Righteous One."

24:14
i Isa 12:6

But I said, "I waste away, I waste away!
   Woe to me!
The treacherous betray!
   With treachery the treacherous betray!^m"

24:15
j Isa 66:19
k Isa 25:3;
Mal 1:11

¹⁷Terror and pit and snareⁿ await you,
   O people of the earth.
¹⁸Whoever flees at the sound of terror
   will fall into a pit;
whoever climbs out of the pit
   will be caught in a snare.

24:16
l Isa 28:5
m Isa 21:2;
Jer 5:11

The floodgates of the heavens^o are opened,
   the foundations of the earth shake.^p
¹⁹The earth is broken up,
   the earth is split asunder,^q
   the earth is thoroughly shaken.
²⁰The earth reels like a drunkard,^r
   it sways like a hut in the wind;
so heavy upon it is the guilt of its rebellion^s
   that it falls—never to rise again.

24:17
n Jer 48:43

24:18
o Ge 7:11
p Ps 18:7

24:19
q Dt 11:6

24:20
r Isa 19:14
s Isa 1:2,28;
43:27

²¹In that day the LORD will punish^a
the powers in the heavens above
and the kings on the earth below.
²²They will be herded together
like prisoners^b bound in a dungeon;^c
they will be shut up in prison
and be punished^a after many days.^d
²³The moon will be abashed, the sun^e ashamed;
for the LORD Almighty will reign^f
on Mount Zion^g and in Jerusalem,
and before its elders, gloriously.^h

Chapter 25 Theme

25 O LORD, you are my God;
I will exalt you and praise your name,
for in perfect faithfulness
you have done marvelous things,ⁱ
things planned^j long ago.
²You have made the city a heap of rubble,^k
the fortified^l town a ruin,
the foreigners' stronghold^m a city no more;
it will never be rebuilt.
³Therefore strong peoples will honor you;
cities of ruthlessⁿ nations will revere you.
⁴You have been a refuge^o for the poor,
a refuge for the needy in his distress,
a shelter from the storm
and a shade from the heat.
For the breath of the ruthless^p
is like a storm driving against a wall
⁵   and like the heat of the desert.
You silence^q the uproar of foreigners;
as heat is reduced by the shadow of a cloud,
so the song of the ruthless is stilled.

⁶On this mountain^r the LORD Almighty will prepare
a feast^s of rich food for all peoples,
a banquet of aged wine—
the best of meats and the finest of wines.^t
⁷On this mountain he will destroy
the shroud^u that enfolds all peoples,
the sheet that covers all nations;
⁸   he will swallow up death^v forever.
The Sovereign LORD will wipe away the tears^w
from all faces;

a 22 Or *released*

24:21
^aIsa 10:12

24:22
^bIsa 10:4
^cIsa 42:7,22
^dEze 38:8

24:23
^eIsa 13:10
^fRev 22:5
^gHeb 12:22
^hIsa 60:19

25:1
ⁱPs 98:1
^jNu 23:19

25:2
^kIsa 17:1
^lIsa 17:3
^mIsa 13:22

25:3
ⁿIsa 13:11

25:4
^oIsa 4:6; 17:10;
27:5; 33:16
^pIsa 29:5; 49:25

25:5
^qJer 51:55

25:6
^rIsa 2:2
^sIsa 1:19;
Mt 8:11; 22:4
^tPr 9:2

25:7
^u2Co 3:15-16;
Eph 4:18

25:8
^vHos 13:14;
1Co 15:54-55*
^wIsa 30:19;
35:10; 51:11;
65:19; Rev 7:17;
21:4

25:8
a Mt 5:11;
1 Pe 4:14

he will remove the disgrace^a of his people
from all the earth.

The LORD has spoken.

⁹In that day they will say,

25:9
b Isa 40:9
c Ps 20:5;
Isa 33:22; 35:4;
49:25-26; 60:16
d Isa 35:2,10

"Surely this is our God;^b
we trusted in him, and he saved^c us.
This is the LORD, we trusted in him;
let us rejoice^d and be glad in his salvation."

¹⁰The hand of the LORD will rest on this mountain;
but Moab^e will be trampled under him
as straw is trampled down in the manure.

25:10
e Am 2:1-3

¹¹They will spread out their hands in it,
as a swimmer spreads out his hands to swim.
God will bring down^f their pride^g
despite the cleverness^a of their hands.

25:11
f Isa 5:25; 14:26;
16:14
g Job 40:12

¹²He will bring down your high fortified walls
and lay them low;^h
he will bring them down to the ground,
to the very dust.

25:12
h Isa 15:1

Chapter 26 Theme _____

26

In that day this song will be sung in the land of Judah:

We have a strong city;ⁱ
God makes salvation
its walls^j and ramparts.

26:1
i Isa 14:32
j Isa 60:18

²Open the gates
that the righteous^k nation may enter,
the nation that keeps faith.

26:2
k Isa 54:14; 58:8;
62:2

³You will keep in perfect peace
him whose mind is steadfast,
because he trusts in you.

⁴Trust^l in the LORD forever,
for the LORD, the LORD, is the Rock eternal.

26:4
l Isa 12:2; 50:10

⁵He humbles those who dwell on high,
he lays the lofty city low;
he levels it to the ground^m
and casts it down to the dust.

26:5
m Isa 25:12

⁶Feet trample it down—
the feet of the oppressed,
the footsteps of the poor.ⁿ

26:6
n Isa 3:15

a 11 The meaning of the Hebrew for this word is uncertain.

⁷The path of the righteous is level;
    O upright One, you make the way of the
        righteous smooth.^a
⁸Yes, LORD, walking in the way of your laws,^a^b
    we wait for you;
  your name^c and renown
    are the desire of our hearts.
⁹My soul yearns for you in the night;
    in the morning my spirit longs^d for you.
When your judgments come upon the earth,
    the people of the world learn righteousness.^e
¹⁰Though grace is shown to the wicked,
    they do not learn righteousness;
even in a land of uprightness they go on doing evil^f
    and regard^g not the majesty of the LORD.
¹¹O LORD, your hand is lifted high,
    but they do not see^h it.
Let them see your zeal for your people and be put to
        shame;
    let the fireⁱ reserved for your enemies consume them.

¹²LORD, you establish peace for us;
    all that we have accomplished you have done for us.
¹³O LORD, our God, other lords^j besides you have ruled
    over us,
  but your name alone do we honor.^k
¹⁴They are now dead,^l they live no more;
    those departed spirits do not rise.
You punished them and brought them to ruin;^m
    you wiped out all memory of them.
¹⁵You have enlarged the nation, O LORD;
    you have enlarged the nation.
You have gained glory for yourself;
    you have extended all the bordersⁿ of the land.

¹⁶LORD, they came to you in their distress;^o
    when you disciplined them,
    they could barely whisper a prayer.^b
¹⁷As a woman with child and about to give birth ^p
    writhes and cries out in her pain,
    so were we in your presence, O LORD.
¹⁸We were with child, we writhed in pain,
    but we gave birth^q to wind.
We have not brought salvation^r to the earth;
    we have not given birth to people of the world.

26:7
^aIsa 42:16

26:8
^bIsa 56:1
^cIsa 12:4

26:9
^dPs 63:1; 78:34;
Isa 55:6
^eMt 6:33

26:10
^fIsa 32:6
^gIsa 22:12-13;
Hos 11:7;
Jn 5:37-38;
Ro 2:4

26:11
^hIsa 44:9,18
ⁱHeb 10:27

26:13
^jIsa 2:8; 10:5,11
^kIsa 63:7

26:14
^lDt 4:28
^mIsa 10:3

26:15
ⁿIsa 33:17

26:16
^oHos 5:15

26:17
^pJn 16:21

26:18
^qIsa 33:11; 59:4
^rPs 17:14

---

^a8 Or *judgments*   ^b16 The meaning of the Hebrew for this clause is uncertain.

26:19
a Isa 25:8;
Eph 5:14
b Eze 37:1-14;
Da 12:2

[19]But your dead[a] will live;
their bodies will rise.
You who dwell in the dust,
wake up and shout for joy.
Your dew is like the dew of the morning;
the earth will give birth to her dead.[b]

26:20
c Ex 12:23
d Ps 91:1,4
e Ps 30:5;
Isa 54:7-8

[20]Go, my people, enter your rooms
and shut the doors[c] behind you;
hide[d] yourselves for a little while
until his wrath has passed by.[e]

26:21
f Jude 14
g Mic 1:3
h Isa 13:9,11;
30:12-14
i Job 16:18;
Lk 11:50-51

[21]See, the LORD is coming[f] out of his dwelling[g]
to punish[h] the people of the earth for their sins.
The earth will disclose the blood[i] shed upon her;
she will conceal her slain no longer.

Chapter 27 Theme _____

27:1
j Isa 34:6; 66:16
k Job 3:8
l Ps 74:13

27

In that day,

the LORD will punish with his sword,[j]
his fierce, great and powerful sword,
Leviathan[k] the gliding serpent,
Leviathan the coiling serpent;
he will slay the monster[l] of the sea.

27:2
m Jer 2:21

[2]In that day—

"Sing about a fruitful vineyard:[m]

27:3
n Isa 58:11

[3] I, the LORD, watch over it;
I water[n] it continually.
I guard it day and night
so that no one may harm it.

27:4
o Isa 10:17;
Mt 3:12;
Heb 6:8

[4] I am not angry.
If only there were briers and thorns confronting me!
I would march against them in battle;
I would set them all on fire.[o]

27:5
p Isa 25:4
q Job 22:21;
Ro 5:1; 2Co 5:20

[5]Or else let them come to me for refuge;[p]
let them make peace[q] with me,
yes, let them make peace with me."

27:6
r Hos 14:5-6
s Isa 37:31

[6]In days to come Jacob will take root,
Israel will bud and blossom[r]
and fill all the world with fruit.[s]

27:7
t Isa 37:36-38

[7]Has ⌊the LORD⌋ struck her
as he struck[t] down those who struck her?
Has she been killed
as those were killed who killed her?

⁸By warfare[a] and exile[a] you contend with her—
  with his fierce blast he drives her out,
  as on a day the east wind blows.
⁹By this, then, will Jacob's guilt be atoned for,
  and this will be the full fruitage of the removal of
    his sin:[b]
When he makes all the altar stones
  to be like chalk stones crushed to pieces,
  no Asherah poles[bc] or incense altars
  will be left standing.
¹⁰The fortified city stands desolate,[d]
  an abandoned settlement, forsaken like the desert;
there the calves graze,
  there they lie down;[e]
  they strip its branches bare.
¹¹When its twigs are dry, they are broken off
  and women come and make fires with them.
For this is a people without understanding;[f]
  so their Maker has no compassion on them,
  and their Creator[g] shows them no favor.[h]

¹²In that day the LORD will thresh from the flowing Euphrates[c] to the Wadi of Egypt,[i] and you, O Israelites, will be gathered[j] up one by one. ¹³And in that day a great trumpet[k] will sound. Those who were perishing in Assyria and those who were exiled in Egypt[l] will come and worship the LORD on the holy mountain in Jerusalem.

Chapter 28 Theme _____

28 Woe to that wreath, the pride of Ephraim's[m] drunkards,
  to the fading flower, his glorious beauty,
set on the head of a fertile valley[n]—
  to that city, the pride of those laid low by wine![o]
²See, the Lord has one who is powerful[p] and strong.
  Like a hailstorm[q] and a destructive wind,[r]
like a driving rain and a flooding[s] downpour,
  he will throw it forcefully to the ground.
³That wreath, the pride of Ephraim's[t] drunkards,
  will be trampled underfoot.
⁴That fading flower, his glorious beauty,
  set on the head of a fertile valley,[u]
will be like a fig[v] ripe before harvest—
  as soon as someone sees it and takes it in his hand,
  he swallows it.

a 8 See Septuagint; the meaning of the Hebrew for this word is uncertain.   b 9 That is, symbols of the goddess Asherah   c 12 Hebrew *River*

27:8
a Isa 50:1; 54:7

27:9
b Ro 11:27*
c Ex 34:13

27:10
d Isa 32:14;
Jer 26:6
e Isa 17:2

27:11
f Dt 32:28;
Isa 1:3; Jer 8:7
g Dt 32:18;
Isa 43:1,7,15;
44:1-2,21,24
h Isa 9:17

27:12
i Ge 15:18
j Dt 30:4;
Isa 11:12; 17:6

27:13
k Lev 25:9;
Mt 24:31
l Isa 19:21,25

28:1
m ver 3;
Isa 9:9
n ver 4
o Hos 7:5

28:2
p Isa 40:10
q Isa 30:30;
Eze 13:11
r Isa 29:6
s Isa 8:7

28:3
t ver 1

28:4
u ver 1
v Hos 9:10;
Na 3:12

28:5
a Isa 62:3

28:6
b Isa 11:2-4;
32:1,16
c Jn 5:30
d 2Ch 32:8

28:7
e Isa 22:13
f Isa 56:10-12
g Isa 24:2
h Isa 9:15
i Isa 29:11;
Hos 4:11

28:8
j Jer 48:26

28:9
k ver 26;
Isa 30:20; 48:17;
50:4; 54:13
l Ps 131:2
m Heb 5:12-13

28:11
n Isa 33:19
o 1Co 14:21*

28:12
p Isa 11:10;
Mt 11:28-29

28:13
q Mt 21:44
r Isa 8:15

28:14
s Isa 1:10

⁵In that day the Lord Almighty
  will be a glorious crown,ᵃ
a beautiful wreath
  for the remnant of his people.
⁶He will be a spirit of justiceᵇ
  to him who sits in judgment,ᶜ
a source of strength
  to those who turn back the battleᵈ at the gate.

⁷And these also stagger from wineᵉ
  and reelᶠ from beer:
Priests�g and prophetsʰ stagger from beer
  and are befuddled with wine;
they reel from beer,
  they stagger when seeing visions,ⁱ
  they stumble when rendering decisions.
⁸All the tables are covered with vomitʲ
  and there is not a spot without filth.

⁹"Who is it he is trying to teach?ᵏ
  To whom is he explaining his message?
To children weanedˡ from their milk,ᵐ
  to those just taken from the breast?
¹⁰For it is:
  Do and do, do and do,
  rule on rule, rule on ruleᵃ;
  a little here, a little there."

¹¹Very well then, with foreign lips and strange tonguesⁿ
  God will speak to this people,ᵒ
¹²to whom he said,
  "This is the resting place, let the weary rest"; ᵖ
and, "This is the place of repose"—
  but they would not listen.
¹³So then, the word of the Lord to them will become:
  Do and do, do and do,
  rule on rule, rule on rule;
  a little here, a little there—
so that they will go and fall backward,
  be injuredq and snared and captured.ʳ

¹⁴Therefore hear the word of the Lord,ˢ you scoffers
  who rule this people in Jerusalem.
¹⁵You boast, "We have entered into a covenant with death,
  with the graveᵇ we have made an agreement.

ᵃ 10 Hebrew / sav lasav sav lasav / kav lakav kav lakav (possibly meaningless sounds; perhaps a mimicking of the prophet's words); also in verse 13   ᵇ 15 Hebrew Sheol; also in verse 18

1203

When an overwhelming scourge sweeps by,^{a}
    it cannot touch us,
for we have made a lie^b our refuge
    and falsehood^a our hiding place.^{c}"

^{16}So this is what the Sovereign LORD says:

"See, I lay a stone in Zion,
    a tested stone,^{d}
a precious cornerstone for a sure foundation;
    the one who trusts will never be dismayed.^{e}
^{17}I will make justice^f the measuring line
    and righteousness the plumb line;^{g}
hail will sweep away your refuge, the lie,
    and water will overflow your hiding place.
^{18}Your covenant with death will be annulled;
    your agreement with the grave will not stand.^{h}
When the overwhelming scourge sweeps by,^{i}
    you will be beaten down^j by it.
^{19}As often as it comes it will carry you away;^{k}
    morning after morning, by day and by night,
    it will sweep through."

The understanding of this message
    will bring sheer terror.^{l}
^{20}The bed is too short to stretch out on,
    the blanket too narrow to wrap around you.^{m}
^{21}The LORD will rise up as he did at Mount Perazim,^{n}
    he will rouse himself as in the Valley of Gibeon^o—
to do his work,^{p} his strange work,
    and perform his task, his alien task.
^{22}Now stop your mocking,
    or your chains will become heavier;
the Lord, the LORD Almighty, has told me
    of the destruction decreed^q against the whole land.^{r}

^{23}Listen and hear my voice;
    pay attention and hear what I say.
^{24}When a farmer plows for planting, does he plow
        continually?
    Does he keep on breaking up and harrowing the soil?
^{25}When he has leveled the surface,
    does he not sow caraway and scatter cummin?^{s}
Does he not plant wheat in its place,^{b}
    barley in its plot,^{b}
    and spelt^t in its field?

^{a}15 Or *false gods* ^{b}25 The meaning of the Hebrew for this word is uncertain.

28:15
^{a}ver 2,18;
Isa 8:7-8; 30:28;
Da 11:22
^{b}Isa 9:15
^{c}Isa 29:15

28:16
^{d}Ps 118:22;
Isa 8:14-15;
Mt 21:42;
Ac 4:11;
Eph 2:20
^{e}Ro 9:33*;
10:11*; 1Pe 2:6*

28:17
^{f}Isa 5:16
^{g}2Ki 21:13

28:18
^{h}Isa 7:7
^{i}ver 15
^{j}Da 8:13

28:19
^{k}2Ki 24:2
^{l}Job 18:11

28:20
^{m}Isa 59:6

28:21
^{n}1Ch 14:11
^{o}Jos 10:10,12;
1Ch 14:16
^{p}Isa 10:12;
Lk 19:41-44

28:22
^{q}Isa 10:22
^{r}Isa 10:23

28:25
^{s}Mt 23:23
^{t}Ex 9:32

28:29
a Isa 9:6
b Ro 11:33

²⁶His God instructs him
  and teaches him the right way.

²⁷Caraway is not threshed with a sledge,
  nor is a cartwheel rolled over cummin;
caraway is beaten out with a rod,
  and cummin with a stick.

29:1
c Isa 22:12-13
d 2Sa 5:9
e Isa 1:14

²⁸Grain must be ground to make bread;
  so one does not go on threshing it forever.
Though he drives the wheels of his threshing cart over it,
  his horses do not grind it.

²⁹All this also comes from the Lord Almighty,
  wonderful in counsel[a] and magnificent in wisdom.[b]

29:2
f Isa 3:26; La 2:5

Chapter 29 Theme

29
Woe[c] to you, Ariel, Ariel,[d]
  the city where David settled!
Add year to year
  and let your cycle of festivals[e] go on.

29:3
g Lk 19:43-44

²Yet I will besiege Ariel;
  she will mourn and lament,[f]
  she will be to me like an altar hearth.[a]

³I will encamp against you all around;
  I will encircle[g] you with towers
  and set up my siege works against you.

29:4
h Isa 8:19

⁴Brought low, you will speak from the ground;
  your speech will mumble[h] out of the dust.
Your voice will come ghostlike from the earth;
  out of the dust your speech will whisper.

29:5
i Isa 17:13
j Isa 17:14;
1Th 5:3

⁵But your many enemies will become like fine dust,
  the ruthless hordes like blown chaff.[i]
Suddenly,[j] in an instant,
⁶ the Lord Almighty will come
with thunder and earthquake[k] and great noise,
  with windstorm and tempest and flames of a
    devouring fire.

29:6
k Mt 24:7;
Mk 13:8;
Lk 21:11;
Rev 11:19

⁷Then the hordes of all the nations[l] that fight against Ariel,
  that attack her and her fortress and besiege her,
will be as it is with a dream,[m]
  with a vision in the night—

29:7
l Mic 4:11-12;
Zec 12:9
m Job 20:8

⁸as when a hungry man dreams that he is eating,
  but he awakens,[n] and his hunger remains;
as when a thirsty man dreams that he is drinking,
  but he awakens faint, with his thirst unquenched.

29:8
n Ps 73:20

a 2 The Hebrew for *altar hearth* sounds like the Hebrew for *Ariel*.

So will it be with the hordes of all the nations
    that fight against Mount Zion.

9Be stunned and amazed,
    blind yourselves and be sightless;
be drunk,*a* but not from wine,*b*
    stagger, but not from beer.
10The LORD has brought over you a deep sleep:
    He has sealed your eyes*c* (the prophets);*d*
    he has covered your heads (the seers).*e*

11For you this whole vision is nothing but words sealed*f* in a scroll. And if you give the scroll to someone who can read, and say to him, "Read this, please," he will answer, "I can't; it is sealed." 12Or if you give the scroll to someone who cannot read, and say, "Read this, please," he will answer, "I don't know how to read."

13The Lord says:

"These people come near to me with their mouth
    and honor me with their lips,
    but their hearts are far from me.*g*
Their worship of me
    is made up only of rules taught by men.*a h*
14Therefore once more I will astound these people
    with wonder upon wonder;*i*
the wisdom of the wise*j* will perish,
    the intelligence of the intelligent will vanish.*k*"
15Woe to those who go to great depths
    to hide their plans from the LORD,
who do their work in darkness and think,
    "Who sees us?*l* Who will know?"*m*
16You turn things upside down,
    as if the potter were thought to be like the clay!
Shall what is formed say to him who formed it,
    "He did not make me"?
Can the pot say of the potter,*n*
    "He knows nothing"?

17In a very short time, will not Lebanon be turned into a
    fertile field*o*
and the fertile field seem like a forest?*p*
18In that day the deaf*q* will hear the words of the scroll,
    and out of gloom and darkness
    the eyes of the blind will see.*r*
19Once more the humble*s* will rejoice in the LORD;
    the needy*t* will rejoice in the Holy One of Israel.

a 13 Hebrew; Septuagint *They worship me in vain; / their teachings are but rules taught by men*

29:9 *a* Isa 51:17; *b* Isa 51:21-22

29:10 *c* Ps 69:23; Isa 6:9-10; Ro 11:8*; *d* Mic 3:6; *e* 1Sa 9:9

29:11 *f* Isa 8:16; Mt 13:11; Rev 5:1-2

29:13 *g* Eze 33:31; *h* Mt 15:8-9*; Mk 7:6-7*; Col 2:22

29:14 *i* Hab 1:5; *j* Jer 8:9; 49:7; *k* Isa 6:9-10; 1Co 1:19*

29:15 *l* Ps 10:11-13; 94:7; Isa 57:12; *m* Job 22:13

29:16 *n* Isa 45:9; 64:8; Ro 9:20-21*

29:17 *o* Ps 84:6; *p* Isa 32:15

29:18 *q* Mk 7:37; *r* Isa 32:3; 35:5; Mt 11:5

29:19 *s* Isa 61:1; Mt 5:5; 11:29; *t* Isa 14:30; Mt 11:5; Jas 1:9; 2:5

²⁰The ruthless will vanish,
>> the mockers^a will disappear,
>> and all who have an eye for evil^b will be cut down—
²¹those who with a word make a man out to be guilty,
>> who ensnare the defender in court^c
>> and with false testimony deprive the innocent
>>> of justice.^d

²²Therefore this is what the Lord, who redeemed Abraham,^e says to the house of Jacob:

>> "No longer will Jacob be ashamed;^f
>> no longer will their faces grow pale.
²³When they see among them their children,^g
>> the work of my hands,^h
> they will keep my name holy;
>> they will acknowledge the holiness of the Holy One
>>> of Jacob,
>> and will stand in awe of the God of Israel.
²⁴Those who are waywardⁱ in spirit will gain
>>> understanding;^j
>> those who complain will accept instruction."^k

Chapter 30 Theme

30

"Woe^l to the obstinate children,"^m
>> declares the Lord,
> "to those who carry out plans that are not mine,
>> forming an alliance,ⁿ but not by my Spirit,
>> heaping sin upon sin;
²who go down to Egypt^o
>> without consulting^p me;
> who look for help to Pharaoh's protection,^q
>> to Egypt's shade for refuge.
³But Pharaoh's protection will be to your shame,
>> Egypt's shade will bring you disgrace.^r
⁴Though they have officials in Zoan^s
>> and their envoys have arrived in Hanes,
⁵everyone will be put to shame
>> because of a people^t useless to them,
> who bring neither help nor advantage,
>> but only shame and disgrace."

⁶An oracle concerning the animals of the Negev:

>> Through a land of hardship and distress,^u
>> of lions and lionesses,
>> of adders and darting snakes,^v

Cross references (left margin):

- **29:21** c Am 5:10,15 · d Isa 32:7
- **29:22** e Isa 41:8; 63:16 · f Isa 49:23
- **29:23** g Isa 49:20-26 · h Isa 19:25
- **29:24** i Isa 28:7; Heb 5:2 · j Isa 41:20; 60:16 · k Isa 30:21
- **30:1** l Isa 29:15 · m Isa 1:2 · n Isa 8:12
- **30:2** o Isa 31:1 · p Nu 27:21 · q Isa 36:9
- **30:3** r Isa 20:4-5; 36:6
- **30:4** s Isa 19:11
- **30:5** t ver 7
- **30:6** u Ex 5:10,21; Isa 8:22; Jer 11:4 · v Dt 8:15

the envoys carry their riches on donkeys' backs,
　　their treasures[a] on the humps of camels,
to that unprofitable nation,
7　to Egypt, whose help is utterly useless.
Therefore I call her
　　Rahab the Do-Nothing.

8Go now, write it on a tablet for them,
　　inscribe it on a scroll,[b]
that for the days to come
　　it may be an everlasting witness.
9These are rebellious people, deceitful[c] children,
　　children unwilling to listen to the LORD's instruction.[d]
10They say to the seers,
　　"See no more visions[e] !"
and to the prophets,
　　"Give us no more visions of what is right!
Tell us pleasant things,[f]
　　prophesy illusions.[g]
11Leave this way,
　　get off this path,
and stop confronting[h] us
　　with the Holy One of Israel!"

12Therefore, this is what the Holy One of Israel says:

"Because you have rejected this message,[i]
　　relied on oppression[j]
　　and depended on deceit,
13this sin will become for you
　　like a high wall,[k] cracked and bulging,
　　that collapses[l] suddenly,[m] in an instant.
14It will break in pieces like pottery,[n]
　　shattered so mercilessly
that among its pieces not a fragment will be found
　　for taking coals from a hearth
　　or scooping water out of a cistern."

15This is what the Sovereign LORD, the Holy One of Israel, says:

"In repentance and rest is your salvation,
　　in quietness and trust[o] is your strength,
　　but you would have none of it.
16You said, 'No, we will flee on horses.'[p]
　　Therefore you will flee!
You said, 'We will ride off on swift horses.'
　　Therefore your pursuers will be swift!

30:6
[a] Isa 15:7

30:8
[b] Isa 8:1;
Hab 2:2

30:9
[c] Isa 28:15;
59:3-4
[d] Isa 1:10

30:10
[e] Jer 11:21;
Am 7:13
[f] 1Ki 22:8
[g] Eze 13:7;
Ro 16:18

30:11
[h] Job 21:14

30:12
[i] Isa 5:24
[j] Isa 5:7

30:13
[k] Ps 62:3
[l] 1Ki 20:30
[m] Isa 29:5

30:14
[n] Ps 2:9;
Jer 19:10-11

30:15
[o] Isa 32:17

30:16
[p] Isa 31:1,3

30:17
a Lev 26:8;
Jos 23:10
b Lev 26:36;
Dt 28:25

30:18
c Isa 42:14;
2Pe 3:9,15
d Isa 5:16
e Isa 25:9

30:19
f Isa 60:20; 61:3
g Ps 50:15;
Isa 58:9; 65:24;
Mt 7:7-11

30:20
h 1Ki 22:27
i Ps 74:9;
Am 8:11

30:21
j Isa 29:24

30:22
k Ex 32:4

30:23
l Isa 65:21-22
m Ps 65:13

30:24
n Mt 3:12;
Lk 3:17

30:25
o Isa 2:15
p Isa 41:18

30:26
q Isa 24:23;
60:19-20;
Rev 21:23; 22:5
r Dt 32:39;
Isa 1:5

30:27
s Isa 59:19
t Isa 66:14
u Isa 10:5

30:28
v Isa 11:4
w Isa 8:8
x Am 9:9
y 2Ki 19:28;
Isa 37:29

¹⁷A thousand will flee
  at the threat of one;
at the threat of five*a*
  you will all flee*b* away,
till you are left
  like a flagstaff on a mountaintop,
  like a banner on a hill."

¹⁸Yet the LORD longs*c* to be gracious to you;
  he rises to show you compassion.
For the LORD is a God of justice.*d*
  Blessed are all who wait for him!*e*

¹⁹O people of Zion, who live in Jerusalem, you will weep no more.*f* How gracious he will be when you cry for help! As soon as he hears, he will answer*g* you. ²⁰Although the Lord gives you the bread*h* of adversity and the water of affliction, your teachers will be hidden*i* no more; with your own eyes you will see them. ²¹Whether you turn to the right or to the left, your ears will hear a voice*j* behind you, saying, "This is the way; walk in it." ²²Then you will defile your idols*k* overlaid with silver and your images covered with gold; you will throw them away like a menstrual cloth and say to them, "Away with you!"

²³He will also send you rain*l* for the seed you sow in the ground, and the food that comes from the land will be rich and plentiful. In that day your cattle will graze in broad meadows.*m* ²⁴The oxen and donkeys that work the soil will eat fodder and mash, spread out with fork*n* and shovel. ²⁵In the day of great slaughter, when the towers*o* fall, streams of water will flow*p* on every high mountain and every lofty hill. ²⁶The moon will shine like the sun,*q* and the sunlight will be seven times brighter, like the light of seven full days, when the LORD binds up the bruises of his people and heals*r* the wounds he inflicted.

²⁷See, the Name*s* of the LORD comes from afar,
  with burning anger*t* and dense clouds of smoke;
his lips are full of wrath,*u*
  and his tongue is a consuming fire.
²⁸His breath*v* is like a rushing torrent,
  rising up to the neck.*w*
He shakes the nations in the sieve*x* of destruction;
  he places in the jaws of the peoples
  a bit*y* that leads them astray.
²⁹And you will sing
  as on the night you celebrate a holy festival;
your hearts will rejoice
  as when people go up with flutes

to the mountain[a] of the LORD,
    to the Rock of Israel.
[30]The LORD will cause men to hear his majestic voice
    and will make them see his arm coming down
with raging anger and consuming fire,
    with cloudburst, thunderstorm and hail.
[31]The voice of the LORD will shatter Assyria;[b]
    with his scepter he will strike[c] them down.
[32]Every stroke the LORD lays on them
    with his punishing rod
will be to the music of tambourines and harps,
    as he fights them in battle with the blows of his arm.[d]
[33]Topheth[e] has long been prepared;
    it has been made ready for the king.
Its fire pit has been made deep and wide,
    with an abundance of fire and wood;
the breath of the LORD,
    like a stream of burning sulfur,[f]
    sets it ablaze.

Chapter 31 Theme

31 Woe to those who go down to Egypt[g] for help,
    who rely on horses,
who trust in the multitude of their chariots[h]
    and in the great strength of their horsemen,
but do not look to the Holy One of Israel,
    or seek help from the LORD.[i]
[2]Yet he too is wise[j] and can bring disaster;[k]
    he does not take back his words.[l]
He will rise up against the house of the wicked,[m]
    against those who help evildoers.
[3]But the Egyptians[n] are men and not God;[o]
    their horses are flesh and not spirit.
When the LORD stretches out his hand, [p]
    he who helps will stumble,
    he who is helped[q] will fall;
    both will perish together.

[4]This is what the LORD says to me:

"As a lion[r] growls,
    a great lion over his prey—
and though a whole band of shepherds
    is called together against him,
he is not frightened by their shouts
    or disturbed by their clamor—

30:29
[a] Ps 42:4

30:31
[b] Isa 10:5,12
[c] Isa 11:4

30:32
[d] Isa 11:15;
Eze 32:10

30:33
[e] 2Ki 23:10
[f] Ge 19:24

31:1
[g] Dt 17:16;
Isa 30:2,5
[h] Isa 2:7
[i] Ps 20:7;
Da 9:13

31:2
[j] Ro 16:27
[k] Isa 45:7
[l] Nu 23:19
[m] Isa 32:6

31:3
[n] Isa 36:9
[o] Eze 28:9;
2Th 2:4
[p] Isa 9:17,21
[q] Isa 30:5-7

31:4
[r] Nu 24:9;
Hos 11:10;
Am 3:8

31:4
a Isa 42:13

31:5
b Ps 91:4
c Isa 37:35; 38:6

31:7
d Isa 2:20; 30:22

31:8
e Isa 10:12
f Isa 14:25; 37:7
g Ge 49:15

31:9
h Dt 32:31,37
i Isa 10:17

32:1
j Eze 37:24
k Ps 72:1-4;
Isa 9:7

32:2
l Isa 4:6

32:3
m Isa 29:18

32:4
n Isa 29:24

32:5
o 1Sa 25:25

32:6
p Pr 19:3
q Isa 9:17
r Isa 9:16
s Isa 3:15

32:7
t Jer 5:26-28
u Mic 7:3
v Isa 61:1

so the LORD Almighty will come down[a]
> to do battle on Mount Zion and on its heights.
5Like birds hovering overhead,
> the LORD Almighty will shield[b] Jerusalem;
he will shield it and deliver[c] it,
> he will 'pass over' it and will rescue it."

6Return to him you have so greatly revolted against, O Israelites. 7For in that day every one of you will reject the idols of silver and gold[d] your sinful hands have made.

8"Assyria[e] will fall by a sword that is not of man;
> a sword, not of mortals, will devour[f] them.
They will flee before the sword
> and their young men will be put to forced labor.[g]
9Their stronghold[h] will fall because of terror;
> at sight of the battle standard their commanders
> > will panic,"
declares the LORD,
> whose fire[i] is in Zion,
> whose furnace is in Jerusalem.

Chapter 32 Theme _____

32 See, a king[j] will reign in righteousness
> and rulers will rule with justice.[k]
2Each man will be like a shelter[l] from the wind
> and a refuge from the storm,
like streams of water in the desert
> and the shadow of a great rock in a thirsty land.

3Then the eyes of those who see will no longer be closed,[m]
> and the ears of those who hear will listen.
4The mind of the rash will know and understand,[n]
> and the stammering tongue will be fluent and clear.
5No longer will the fool[o] be called noble
> nor the scoundrel be highly respected.
6For the fool speaks folly,[p]
> his mind is busy with evil:
He practices ungodliness[q]
> and spreads error[r] concerning the LORD;
the hungry he leaves empty[s]
> and from the thirsty he withholds water.
7The scoundrel's methods are wicked,[t]
> he makes up evil schemes[u]
to destroy the poor with lies,
> even when the plea of the needy[v] is just.

8But the noble man makes noble plans,
   and by noble deeds[a] he stands.

9You women who are so complacent,
   rise up and listen[b] to me;
you daughters who feel secure,[c]
   hear what I have to say!
10In little more than a year
   you who feel secure will tremble;
the grape harvest will fail,[d]
   and the harvest of fruit will not come.
11Tremble, you complacent women;
   shudder, you daughters who feel secure!
Strip off your clothes,[e]
   put sackcloth around your waists.
12Beat your breasts[f] for the pleasant fields,
   for the fruitful vines
13and for the land of my people,
   a land overgrown with thorns and briers[g]—
yes, mourn for all houses of merriment
   and for this city of revelry.[h]
14The fortress[i] will be abandoned,
   the noisy city deserted;[j]
citadel and watchtower[k] will become a wasteland forever,
   the delight of donkeys,[l] a pasture for flocks,
15till the Spirit[m] is poured upon us from on high,
   and the desert becomes a fertile field,[n]
and the fertile field seems like a forest.[o]
16Justice will dwell in the desert
   and righteousness live in the fertile field.
17The fruit of righteousness will be peace;[p]
   the effect of righteousness will be quietness and
      confidence[q] forever.
18My people will live in peaceful dwelling places,
   in secure homes,
   in undisturbed places of rest.[r]
19Though hail[s] flattens the forest[t]
   and the city is leveled[u] completely,
20how blessed you will be,
   sowing[v] your seed by every stream,
   and letting your cattle and donkeys range free.[w]

Chapter 33 Theme

33 Woe to you, O destroyer,
   you who have not been destroyed!
Woe to you, O traitor,
   you who have not been betrayed!

32:8
[a] Pr 11:25

32:9
[b] Isa 28:23
[c] Isa 47:8;
Am 6:1;
Zep 2:15

32:10
[d] Isa 5:5-6; 24:7

32:11
[e] Isa 47:2

32:12
[f] Na 2:7

32:13
[g] Isa 5:6
[h] Isa 22:2

32:14
[i] Isa 13:22
[j] Isa 6:11; 27:10
[k] Isa 34:13
[l] Ps 104:11

32:15
[m] Isa 11:2;
Joel 2:28
[n] Ps 107:35;
Isa 35:1-2
[o] Isa 29:17

32:17
[p] Ps 119:165;
Ro 14:17;
Jas 3:18
[q] Isa 30:15

32:18
[r] Hos 2:18-23

32:19
[s] Isa 28:17;
30:30
[t] Isa 10:19;
Zec 11:2
[u] Isa 24:10;
27:10

32:20
[v] Ecc 11:1
[w] Isa 30:24

33:1
a Hab 2:8;
Mt 7:2
b Isa 21:2

33:2
c Isa 40:10; 51:9;
59:16
d Isa 25:9

33:3
e Isa 59:16-18

33:5
f Ps 97:9
g Isa 28:6
h Isa 1:26

33:6
i Isa 51:6
j Isa 11:2-3;
Mt 6:33

33:7
k 2Ki 18:37

33:8
l Jdg 5:6;
Isa 35:8

33:9
m Isa 3:26
n Isa 2:13; 35:2
o Isa 24:4

33:10
p Ps 12:5;
Isa 2:21

33:11
q Ps 7:14;
Isa 59:4;
Jas 1:15
r Isa 26:18
s Isa 1:31

33:12
t Isa 10:17

33:13
u Ps 48:10; 49:1
v Isa 49:1

33:14
w Isa 32:11
x Isa 30:30;
Heb 12:29

When you stop destroying,
  you will be destroyed;[a]
when you stop betraying,
  you will be betrayed.[b]

2 O LORD, be gracious to us;
  we long for you.
Be our strength[c] every morning,
  our salvation[d] in time of distress.
3 At the thunder of your voice, the peoples flee;
  when you rise up,[e] the nations scatter.
4 Your plunder, O nations, is harvested as by young locusts;
  like a swarm of locusts men pounce on it.

5 The LORD is exalted,[f] for he dwells on high;
  he will fill Zion with justice[g] and righteousness.[h]
6 He will be the sure foundation for your times,
  a rich store of salvation[i] and wisdom and knowledge;
  the fear[j] of the LORD is the key to this treasure.[a]

7 Look, their brave men cry aloud in the streets;
  the envoys[k] of peace weep bitterly.
8 The highways are deserted,
  no travelers are on the roads.[l]
The treaty is broken,
  its witnesses[b] are despised,
  no one is respected.
9 The land mourns[c][m] and wastes away,
  Lebanon[n] is ashamed and withers;[o]
Sharon is like the Arabah,
  and Bashan and Carmel drop their leaves.

10 "Now will I arise,[p]" says the LORD.
  "Now will I be exalted;
  now will I be lifted up.
11 You conceive[q] chaff,
  you give birth[r] to straw;
  your breath is a fire[s] that consumes you.
12 The peoples will be burned as if to lime;
  like cut thornbushes they will be set ablaze.[t]"

13 You who are far away,[u] hear[v] what I have done;
  you who are near, acknowledge my power!
14 The sinners in Zion are terrified;
  trembling[w] grips the godless:
"Who of us can dwell with the consuming fire?[x]
  Who of us can dwell with everlasting burning?"

a 6 Or *is a treasure from him*   b 8 Dead Sea Scrolls; Masoretic Text / *the cities*   c 9 Or *dries up*

¹⁵He who walks righteously[a]
  and speaks what is right,[b]
who rejects gain from extortion
  and keeps his hand from accepting bribes,
who stops his ears against plots of murder
  and shuts his eyes[c] against contemplating evil—
¹⁶this is the man who will dwell on the heights,
  whose refuge[d] will be the mountain fortress.[e]
His bread will be supplied,
  and water will not fail[f] him.

¹⁷Your eyes will see the king[g] in his beauty
  and view a land that stretches afar.[h]
¹⁸In your thoughts you will ponder the former terror:[i]
  "Where is that chief officer?
  Where is the one who took the revenue?
  Where is the officer in charge of the towers?"
¹⁹You will see those arrogant people no more,
  those people of an obscure speech,
  with their strange, incomprehensible tongue.[j]

²⁰Look upon Zion, the city of our festivals;
  your eyes will see Jerusalem,
  a peaceful abode,[k] a tent that will not be moved;[l]
its stakes will never be pulled up,
  nor any of its ropes broken.
²¹There the LORD will be our Mighty One.
  It will be like a place of broad rivers and streams.[m]
No galley with oars will ride them,
  no mighty ship will sail them.
²²For the LORD is our judge,[n]
  the LORD is our lawgiver,[o]
the LORD is our king;[p]
  it is he who will save[q] us.

²³Your rigging hangs loose:
  The mast is not held secure,
  the sail is not spread.
Then an abundance of spoils will be divided
  and even the lame[r] will carry off plunder.[s]
²⁴No one living in Zion will say, "I am ill";[t]
  and the sins of those who dwell there will be forgiven.[u]

Chapter 34 Theme

34 Come near, you nations, and listen;
  pay attention, you peoples![v]

Cross references (right column):

33:15
[a] Isa 58:8
[b] Ps 15:2; 24:4
[c] Ps 119:37

33:16
[d] Isa 25:4
[e] Isa 26:1
[f] Isa 49:10

33:17
[g] Isa 6:5
[h] Isa 26:15

33:18
[i] Isa 17:14

33:19
[j] Isa 28:11; Jer 5:15

33:20
[k] Isa 32:18
[l] Ps 46:5; 125:1-2

33:21
[m] Isa 41:18; 48:18; 66:12

33:22
[n] Isa 11:4
[o] Isa 2:3; Jas 4:12
[p] Ps 89:18
[q] Isa 25:9

33:23
[r] 2Ki 7:8
[s] 2Ki 7:16

33:24
[t] Isa 30:26
[u] Jer 50:20; 1Jn 1:7-9

34:1
[v] Isa 41:1; 43:9

34:1
a Ps 49:1
b Dt 32:1

34:2
c Isa 13:5
d Isa 30:25

34:3
e Joel 2:20;
Am 4:10
f ver 7;
Eze 14:19; 35:6;
38:22

34:4
g Isa 13:13;
2Pe 3:10
h Eze 32:7-8
i Joel 2:31;
Mt 24:29*;
Rev 6:13

34:5
j Dt 32:41-42;
Jer 46:10;
Eze 21:5
k Am 1:11-12
l Isa 24:6;
Mal 1:4

34:7
m Ps 68:30

34:8
n Isa 63:4

34:10
o Rev 14:10-11;
19:3
p Isa 13:20;
24:1; Eze 29:12;
Mal 1:3

34:11
q Zep 2:14;
Rev 18:2
r 2Ki 21:13;
La 2:8

Let the earth*a* hear, and all that is in it,
the world, and all that comes out of it!*b*
²The LORD is angry with all nations;
his wrath is upon all their armies.
He will totally destroy*a**c* them,
he will give them over to slaughter.*d*
³Their slain will be thrown out,
their dead bodies will send up a stench;*e*
the mountains will be soaked with their blood.*f*
⁴All the stars of the heavens will be dissolved*g*
and the sky rolled up*h* like a scroll;
all the starry host will fall*i*
like withered leaves from the vine,
like shriveled figs from the fig tree.

⁵My sword*j* has drunk its fill in the heavens;
see, it descends in judgment on Edom,*k*
the people I have totally destroyed.*l*
⁶The sword of the LORD is bathed in blood,
it is covered with fat—
the blood of lambs and goats,
fat from the kidneys of rams.
For the LORD has a sacrifice in Bozrah
and a great slaughter in Edom.
⁷And the wild oxen will fall with them,
the bull calves and the great bulls.*m*
Their land will be drenched with blood,
and the dust will be soaked with fat.

⁸For the LORD has a day of vengeance,*n*
a year of retribution, to uphold Zion's cause.
⁹Edom's streams will be turned into pitch,
her dust into burning sulfur;
her land will become blazing pitch!
¹⁰It will not be quenched night and day;
its smoke will rise forever.*o*
From generation to generation it will lie desolate;*p*
no one will ever pass through it again.
¹¹The desert owl*b**q* and screech owl*b* will possess it;
the great owl*b* and the raven will nest there.
God will stretch out over Edom
the measuring line of chaos
and the plumb line*r* of desolation.

a 2 The Hebrew term refers to the irrevocable giving over of things or persons to the LORD, often by totally destroying them; also in verse 5.   *b 11* The precise identification of these birds is uncertain.

¹²Her nobles will have nothing there to be called
    a kingdom,
  all her princes[a] will vanish[b] away.
¹³Thorns will overrun her citadels,
    nettles and brambles her strongholds.[c]
She will become a haunt for jackals,[d]
    a home for owls.
¹⁴Desert creatures will meet with hyenas,[e]
    and wild goats will bleat to each other;
there the night creatures will also repose
    and find for themselves places of rest.
¹⁵The owl will nest there and lay eggs,
    she will hatch them, and care for her young under the
      shadow of her wings;
there also the falcons[f] will gather,
    each with its mate.

¹⁶Look in the scroll[g] of the LORD and read:

None of these will be missing,
    not one will lack her mate.
For it is his mouth[h] that has given the order,
    and his Spirit will gather them together.
¹⁷He allots their portions;[i]
    his hand distributes them by measure.
They will possess it forever
    and dwell there from generation to generation.[j]

Chapter 35 Theme

35 The desert[k] and the parched land will be glad;
    the wilderness will rejoice and blossom.[l]
Like the crocus, ²it will burst into bloom;
    it will rejoice greatly and shout for joy.[m]
The glory of Lebanon[n] will be given to it,
    the splendor of Carmel[o] and Sharon;
they will see the glory of the LORD,
    the splendor of our God.[p]

³Strengthen the feeble hands,
    steady the knees[q] that give way;
⁴say to those with fearful hearts,
    "Be strong, do not fear;
your God will come,
    he will come with vengeance;[r]
with divine retribution
    he will come to save you."

34:12
[a] Jer 27:20; 39:6
[b] Isa 41:11-12

34:13
[c] Isa 13:22; 32:13
[d] Ps 44:19; Jer 9:11; 10:22

34:14
[e] Isa 13:22

34:15
[f] Dt 14:13

34:16
[g] Isa 30:8
[h] Isa 1:20; 58:14

34:17
[i] Isa 17:14; Jer 13:25
[j] ver 10

35:1
[k] Isa 27:10; 41:18-19
[l] Isa 51:3

35:2
[m] Isa 25:9; 55:12
[n] Isa 32:15
[o] SS 7:5
[p] Isa 25:9

35:3
[q] Job 4:4; Heb 12:12

35:4
[r] Isa 1:24; 34:8

35:5
a Mt 11:5;
Jn 9:6-7
b Isa 29:18; 50:4

⁵Then will the eyes of the blind be opened*ᵃ*
  and the ears of the deaf*ᵇ* unstopped.
⁶Then will the lame*ᶜ* leap like a deer,
  and the mute tongue*ᵈ* shout for joy.
Water will gush forth in the wilderness
  and streams*ᵉ* in the desert.

35:6
c Mt 15:30;
Jn 5:8-9; Ac 3:8
d Isa 32:4;
Mt 9:32-33;
12:22; Lk 11:14
e Isa 41:18;
Jn 7:38

⁷The burning sand will become a pool,
  the thirsty ground bubbling springs.*ᶠ*
In the haunts where jackals*ᵍ* once lay,
  grass and reeds and papyrus will grow.

35:7
f Isa 49:10
g Isa 13:22

⁸And a highway*ʰ* will be there;
  it will be called the Way of Holiness.*ⁱ*
The unclean*ʲ* will not journey on it;
  it will be for those who walk in that Way;
  wicked fools will not go about on it.*ᵃ*
⁹No lion*ᵏ* will be there,
  nor will any ferocious beast*ˡ* get up on it;
  they will not be found there.
But only the redeemed*ᵐ* will walk there,
¹⁰ and the ransomed of the LORD will return.
They will enter Zion with singing;
  everlasting joy*ⁿ* will crown their heads.
Gladness and joy will overtake them,
  and sorrow and sighing will flee away.*ᵒ*

35:8
h Isa 11:16; 33:8;
Mt 7:13-14
i Isa 4:3;
1Pe 1:15
j Isa 52:1

35:9
k Isa 30:6
l Isa 34:14
m Isa 51:11;
62:12; 63:4

Chapter 36 Theme

36 In the fourteenth year of King Hezekiah's reign, Sennacherib*ᵖ* king of Assyria attacked all the fortified cities of Judah and captured them. ²Then the king of Assyria sent his field commander with a large army from Lachish to King Hezekiah at Jerusalem. When the commander stopped at the aqueduct of the Upper Pool, on the road to the Washerman's Field,*�q* ³Eliakim*ʳ* son of Hilkiah the palace administrator, Shebna*ˢ* the secretary, and Joah son of Asaph the recorder went out to him.

⁴The field commander said to them, "Tell Hezekiah,

"'This is what the great king, the king of Assyria, says: On what are you basing this confidence of yours? ⁵You say you have strategy and military strength—but you speak only empty words. On whom are you depending, that you rebel*ᵗ* against me? ⁶Look now, you are depending on Egypt,*ᵘ* that splintered reed*ᵛ* of a staff, which pierces a man's hand and wounds him if he leans on it! Such is Pharaoh king of Egypt to all who depend

35:10
n Isa 25:9
o Isa 30:19;
51:11; Rev 7:17;
21:4

36:1
p 2Ch 32:1

36:2
q Isa 7:3

36:3
r Isa 22:20-21
s 2Ki 18:18

36:5
t 2Ki 18:7

36:6
u Isa 30:2,5
v Eze 29:6-7

ᵃ 8 Or / *the simple will not stray from it*

on him. ⁷And if you say to me, "We are depending on the LORD our God"—isn't he the one whose high places and altars Hezekiah removed,ᵃ saying to Judah and Jerusalem, "You must worship before this altar"?ᵇ

⁸"Come now, make a bargain with my master, the king of Assyria: I will give you two thousand horses—if you can put riders on them! ⁹How then can you repulse one officer of the least of my master's officials, even though you are depending on Egyptᶜ for chariots and horsemen?ᵈ ¹⁰Furthermore, have I come to attack and destroy this land without the LORD? The LORD himself toldᵉ me to march against this country and destroy it.'"

¹¹Then Eliakim, Shebna and Joah said to the field commander, "Please speak to your servants in Aramaic,ᶠ since we understand it. Don't speak to us in Hebrew in the hearing of the people on the wall."

¹²But the commander replied, "Was it only to your master and you that my master sent me to say these things, and not to the men sitting on the wall—who, like you, will have to eat their own filth and drink their own urine?"

¹³Then the commander stood and called out in Hebrew,ᵍ "Hear the words of the great king, the king of Assyria! ¹⁴This is what the king says: Do not let Hezekiah deceive you. He cannot deliver you! ¹⁵Do not let Hezekiah persuade you to trust in the LORD when he says, 'The LORD will surely deliver us; this city will not be given into the hand of the king of Assyria.'ʰ

¹⁶"Do not listen to Hezekiah. This is what the king of Assyria says: Make peace with me and come out to me. Then every one of you will eat from his own vine and fig treeⁱ and drink water from his own cistern,ʲ ¹⁷until I come and take you to a land like your own—a land of grain and new wine, a land of bread and vineyards.

¹⁸"Do not let Hezekiah mislead you when he says, 'The LORD will deliver us.' Has the god of any nation ever delivered his land from the hand of the king of Assyria? ¹⁹Where are the gods of Hamath and Arpad? Where are the gods of Sepharvaim? Have they rescued Samaria from my hand? ²⁰Who of all the godsᵏ of these countries has been able to save his land from me? How then can the LORD deliver Jerusalem from my hand?"

²¹But the people remained silent and said nothing in reply, because the king had commanded, "Do not answer him."ˡ

²²Then Eliakim son of Hilkiah the palace administrator, Shebna the secretary, and Joah son of Asaph the recorder went to Hezekiah, with their clothes torn, and told him what the field commander had said.

36:7 ᵃ2Ki 18:4 ᵇDt 12:2-5
36:9 ᶜIsa 31:3 ᵈIsa 30:2-5
36:10 ᵉ1Ki 13:18
36:11 ᶠEzr 4:7
36:13 ᵍ2Ch 32:18
36:15 ʰIsa 37:10
36:16 ⁱ1Ki 4:25; Zec 3:10 ʲPr 5:15
36:20 ᵏ1Ki 20:23
36:21 ˡPr 9:7-8; 26:4

37:2
a Isa 1:1

37:3
b Isa 26:18; 66:9;
Hos 13:13

37:4
c Isa 36:13,
18-20
d Isa 1:9

37:6
e Isa 7:4

37:7
f ver 9

37:8
g Nu 33:20

37:9
h ver 7

37:10
i Isa 36:15

37:11
j Isa 36:18-20

37:12
k 2Ki 18:11
l Ge 11:31;
12:1-4;
Ac 7:2

37:16
m Dt 10:17;
Ps 86:10;
136:2-3

37:17
n 2Ch 6:40
o Da 9:18

Chapter 37 Theme _____

37

When King Hezekiah heard this, he tore his clothes and put on sackcloth and went into the temple of the LORD. ²He sent Eliakim the palace administrator, Shebna the secretary, and the leading priests, all wearing sackcloth, to the prophet Isaiah son of Amoz.*a* ³They told him, "This is what Hezekiah says: This day is a day of distress and rebuke and disgrace, as when children come to the point of birth*b* and there is no strength to deliver them. ⁴It may be that the LORD your God will hear the words of the field commander, whom his master, the king of Assyria, has sent to ridicule the living God, and that he will rebuke him for the words the LORD your God has heard.*c* Therefore pray for the remnant*d* that still survives."

⁵When King Hezekiah's officials came to Isaiah, ⁶Isaiah said to them, "Tell your master, 'This is what the LORD says: Do not be afraid*e* of what you have heard—those words with which the underlings of the king of Assyria have blasphemed me. ⁷Listen! I am going to put a spirit in him so that when he hears a certain report,*f* he will return to his own country, and there I will have him cut down with the sword.'"

⁸When the field commander heard that the king of Assyria had left Lachish, he withdrew and found the king fighting against Libnah.*g*

⁹Now Sennacherib received a report*h* that Tirhakah, the Cushite*a* king ⌊of Egypt⌋, was marching out to fight against him. When he heard it, he sent messengers to Hezekiah with this word: ¹⁰"Say to Hezekiah king of Judah: Do not let the god you depend on deceive you when he says, 'Jerusalem will not be handed over to the king of Assyria.'*i* ¹¹Surely you have heard what the kings of Assyria have done to all the countries, destroying them completely. And will you be delivered?*j* ¹²Did the gods of the nations that were destroyed by my forefathers*k* deliver them—the gods of Gozan, Haran,*l* Rezeph and the people of Eden who were in Tel Assar? ¹³Where is the king of Hamath, the king of Arpad, the king of the city of Sepharvaim, or of Hena or Ivvah?"

¹⁴Hezekiah received the letter from the messengers and read it. Then he went up to the temple of the LORD and spread it out before the LORD. ¹⁵And Hezekiah prayed to the LORD: ¹⁶"O LORD Almighty, God of Israel, enthroned between the cherubim, you alone are God*m* over all the kingdoms of the earth. You have made heaven and earth. ¹⁷Give ear, O LORD, and hear;*n* open your eyes, O LORD, and see;*o* listen to all the words Sennacherib has sent to insult the living God.

a 9 That is, from the upper Nile region

¹⁸"It is true, O Lᴏʀᴅ, that the Assyrian kings have laid waste all these peoples and their lands.ᵃ ¹⁹They have thrown their gods into the fire and destroyed them,ᵇ for they were not godsᶜ but only wood and stone, fashioned by human hands. ²⁰Now, O Lᴏʀᴅ our God, deliver us from his hand, so that all kingdoms on earth may know that you alone, O Lᴏʀᴅ, are God.ᵃᵈ"

²¹Then Isaiah son of Amozᵉ sent a message to Hezekiah: "This is what the Lᴏʀᴅ, the God of Israel, says: Because you have prayed to me concerning Sennacherib king of Assyria, ²²this is the word the Lᴏʀᴅ has spoken against him:

"The Virgin Daughter of Zion
    despises and mocks you.
The Daughter of Jerusalem
    tosses her headᶠ as you flee.
²³Who is it you have insulted and blasphemed?ᵍ
    Against whom have you raised your voice
    and lifted your eyes in pride?ʰ
    Against the Holy One of Israel!
²⁴By your messengers
    you have heaped insults on the Lord.
And you have said,
    'With my many chariots
I have ascended the heights of the mountains,
    the utmost heights of Lebanon.ⁱ
I have cut down its tallest cedars,
    the choicest of its pines.
I have reached its remotest heights,
    the finest of its forests.
²⁵I have dug wells in foreign landsᵇ
    and drunk the water there.
With the soles of my feet
    I have dried up all the streams of Egypt.ʲ'

²⁶"Have you not heard?
    Long ago I ordainedᵏ it.
In days of old I plannedˡ it;
    now I have brought it to pass,
that you have turned fortified cities
    into piles of stone.ᵐ
²⁷Their people, drained of power,
    are dismayed and put to shame.
They are like plants in the field,
    like tender green shoots,

37:18
ᵃ 2Ki 15:29;
Na 2:11-12

37:19
ᵇ Isa 26:14
ᶜ Isa 41:24,29

37:20
ᵈ Ps 46:10

37:21
ᵉ ver 2

37:22
ᶠ Job 16:4

37:23
ᵍ ver 4
ʰ Isa 2:11

37:24
ⁱ Isa 14:8

37:25
ʲ Dt 11:10

37:26
ᵏ Ac 2:23;
4:27-28;
1Pe 2:8
ˡ Isa 10:6; 25:1
ᵐ Isa 25:2

ᵃ 20 Dead Sea Scrolls (see also 2 Kings 19:19); Masoretic Text *alone are the* Lᴏʀᴅ   ᵇ 25 Dead Sea Scrolls (see also 2 Kings 19:24); Masoretic Text does not have *in foreign lands.*

37:27
a Ps 129:6

like grass sprouting on the roof,a
scorcheda before it grows up.

37:28
b Ps 139:1-3
c Ps 2:1

28"But I know where you stay
and when you come and gob
and how you ragec against me.
29Because you rage against me
and because your insolenced has reached my ears,
I will put my hook in your nosee
and my bit in your mouth,
and I will make you return
by the way you came.f

37:29
d Isa 10:12
e Isa 30:28;
Eze 38:4
f ver 34

30"This will be the sign for you, O Hezekiah:

"This year you will eat what grows by itself,
and the second year what springs from that.
But in the third year sow and reap,
plant vineyards and eat their fruit.
31Once more a remnant of the house of Judah
will take root below and bear fruitg above.
32For out of Jerusalem will come a remnant,
and out of Mount Zion a band of survivors.
The zealh of the LORD Almighty
will accomplish this.

37:31
g Isa 27:6

37:32
h Isa 9:7

33"Therefore this is what the LORD says concerning the king of Assyria:

"He will not enter this city
or shoot an arrow here.
He will not come before it with shield
or build a siege ramp against it.
34By the way that he came he will return;i
he will not enter this city,"

declares the LORD.

37:34
i ver 29

35"I will defendj this city and save it,
for my sakek and for the sake of Davidl my servant!"

37:35
j Isa 31:5; 38:6
k Isa 43:25;
48:9,11
l 2Ki 20:6

36Then the angel of the LORD went out and put to death a hundred and eighty-five thousand men in the Assyrianm camp. When the people got up the next morning—there were all the dead bodies! 37So Sennacherib king of Assyria broke camp and withdrew. He returned to Ninevehn and stayed there.

38One day, while he was worshiping in the temple of his god Nisroch, his sons Adrammelech and Sharezer cut him down with

37:36
m Isa 10:12

37:37
n Ge 10:11

a 27 Some manuscripts of the Masoretic Text, Dead Sea Scrolls and some Septuagint manuscripts (see also 2 Kings 19:26); most manuscripts of the Masoretic Text roof / and terraced fields the sword, and they escaped to the land of Ararat.[a] And Esarhaddon his son succeeded him as king.

Chapter 38 Theme _____

38 In those days Hezekiah became ill and was at the point of death. The prophet Isaiah son of Amoz[b] went to him and said, "This is what the LORD says: Put your house in order,[c] because you are going to die; you will not recover."

[2]Hezekiah turned his face to the wall and prayed to the LORD, [3]"Remember, O LORD, how I have walked[d] before you faithfully and with wholehearted devotion[e] and have done what is good in your eyes.[f]" And Hezekiah wept[g] bitterly.

[4]Then the word of the LORD came to Isaiah: [5]"Go and tell Hezekiah, 'This is what the LORD, the God of your father David, says: I have heard your prayer and seen your tears; I will add fifteen years[h] to your life. [6]And I will deliver you and this city from the hand of the king of Assyria. I will defend[i] this city.

[7]"This is the LORD's sign[j] to you that the LORD will do what he has promised: [8]I will make the shadow cast by the sun go back the ten steps it has gone down on the stairway of Ahaz.'" So the sunlight went back the ten steps it had gone down.[k]

[9]A writing of Hezekiah king of Judah after his illness and recovery:

[10]I said, "In the prime of my life[l]
    must I go through the gates of death[a][m]
    and be robbed of the rest of my years?[n]"
[11]I said, "I will not again see the LORD,
    the LORD, in the land of the living;[o]
no longer will I look on mankind,
    or be with those who now dwell in this world.[b]
[12]Like a shepherd's tent[p] my house
    has been pulled down[q] and taken from me.
Like a weaver I have rolled[r] up my life,
    and he has cut me off from the loom;[s]
    day and night[t] you made an end of me.
[13]I waited patiently till dawn,
    but like a lion he broke[u] all my bones;[v]
    day and night you made an end of me.
[14]I cried like a swift or thrush,
    I moaned like a mourning dove.[w]
My eyes grew weak as I looked to the heavens.
    I am troubled; O Lord, come to my aid!"[x]

a 10 Hebrew *Sheol*   b 11 A few Hebrew manuscripts; most Hebrew manuscripts *in the place of cessation*

37:38
[a]Ge 8:4;
Jer 51:27

38:1
[b]Isa 37:2
[c]2Sa 17:23

38:3
[d]Ne 13:14;
Ps 26:3
[e]1Ch 29:19
[f]Dt 6:18
[g]Ps 6:8

38:5
[h]2Ki 18:2

38:6
[i]Isa 31:5; 37:35

38:7
[j]Isa 7:11,14

38:8
[k]Jos 10:13

38:10
[l]Ps 102:24
[m]Ps 107:18;
2Co 1:9
[n]Job 17:11

38:11
[o]Ps 27:13; 116:9

38:12
[p]2Co 5:1,4;
2Pe 1:13-14
[q]Job 4:21
[r]Heb 1:12
[s]Job 7:6
[t]Ps 73:14

38:13
[u]Ps 51:8
[v]Job 10:16;
Da 6:24

38:14
[w]Isa 59:11
[x]Job 17:3

38:15
a Ps 39:9
b 1Ki 21:27
c Job 7:11

¹⁵But what can I say?
>> He has spoken to me, and he himself has done this.^a
> I will walk humbly^b all my years
>> because of this anguish of my soul.^c

38:16
d Ps 119:25

¹⁶Lord, by such things men live;
> and my spirit finds life in them too.
> You restored me to health
>> and let me live.^d

38:17
e Ps 30:3
f Jer 31:34
g Isa 43:25;
Mic 7:19

¹⁷Surely it was for my benefit
>> that I suffered such anguish.
> In your love you kept me
>> from the pit^e of destruction;
> you have put all my sins^f
>> behind your back.^g

38:18
h Ecc 9:10
i Ps 6:5;
88:10-11;
115:17
j Ps 30:9

¹⁸For the grave^{a h} cannot praise you,
>> death cannot sing your praise;ⁱ
> those who go down to the pit^j
>> cannot hope for your faithfulness.
¹⁹The living, the living—they praise^k you,
>> as I am doing today;
> fathers tell their children^l
>> about your faithfulness.

38:19
k Dt 6:7;
Ps 118:17;
119:175
l Dt 11:19

²⁰The Lord will save me,
>> and we will sing^m with stringed instrumentsⁿ
> all the days of our lives^o
>> in the temple^p of the Lord.

38:20
m Ps 68:25
n Ps 33:2
o Ps 116:2
p Ps 116:17-19

²¹Isaiah had said, "Prepare a poultice of figs and apply it to the boil, and he will recover."

²²Hezekiah had asked, "What will be the sign that I will go up to the temple of the Lord?"

Chapter 39 Theme _____

39 At that time Merodach-Baladan son of Baladan king of Babylon^q sent Hezekiah letters and a gift, because he had heard of his illness and recovery. ²Hezekiah received the envoys^r gladly and showed them what was in his storehouses—the silver, the gold,^s the spices, the fine oil, his entire armory and everything found among his treasures. There was nothing in his palace or in all his kingdom that Hezekiah did not show them.

39:1
q 2Ch 32:31

39:2
r 2Ch 32:31
s 2Ki 18:15

³Then Isaiah the prophet went to King Hezekiah and asked, "What did those men say, and where did they come from?"

"From a distant land,^t" Hezekiah replied. "They came to me from Babylon."

39:3
t Dt 28:49

a 18 Hebrew *Sheol*

[4]The prophet asked, "What did they see in your palace?"

"They saw everything in my palace," Hezekiah said. "There is nothing among my treasures that I did not show them."

[5]Then Isaiah said to Hezekiah, "Hear the word of the LORD Almighty: [6]The time will surely come when everything in your palace, and all that your fathers have stored up until this day, will be carried off to Babylon.[a] Nothing will be left, says the LORD. [7]And some of your descendants, your own flesh and blood who will be born to you, will be taken away, and they will become eunuchs in the palace of the king of Babylon.[b]"

[8]"The word of the LORD you have spoken is good," Hezekiah replied. For he thought, "There will be peace and security in my lifetime.[c]"

Chapter 40 Theme

40

Comfort, comfort[d] my people,
    says your God.
[2]Speak tenderly[e] to Jerusalem,
    and proclaim to her
that her hard service has been completed,[f]
    that her sin has been paid for,
that she has received from the LORD's hand
    double[g] for all her sins.

[3]A voice of one calling:
"In the desert prepare
    the way[h] for the LORD[a];
make straight in the wilderness
    a highway for our God.[b][i]
[4]Every valley shall be raised up,
    every mountain and hill made low;
the rough ground shall become level,[j]
    the rugged places a plain.
[5]And the glory of the LORD will be revealed,
    and all mankind together will see it.[k]
        For the mouth of the LORD has spoken."[l]

[6]A voice says, "Cry out."
    And I said, "What shall I cry?"

"All men are like grass,[m]
    and all their glory is like the flowers of the field.
[7]The grass withers and the flowers fall,
    because the breath[n] of the LORD blows on them.
    Surely the people are grass.

---

a 3 Or A voice of one calling in the desert: / "Prepare the way for the LORD   b 3 Hebrew; Septuagint make straight the paths of our God

Side references

39:6
a 2Ki 24:13;
Jer 20:5

39:7
b 2Ki 24:15;
Da 1:1-7

39:8
c 2Ch 32:26

40:1
d Isa 12:1; 49:13;
51:3,12; 52:9;
61:2; 66:13;
Jer 31:13;
Zep 3:14-17;
2Co 1:3

40:2
e Isa 35:4
f Isa 41:11-13;
49:25
g Isa 61:7;
Jer 16:18;
Zec 9:12;
Rev 18:6

40:3
h Mal 3:1
i Mt 3:3*;
Mk 1:3*;
Jn 1:23*

40:4
j Isa 45:2,13

40:5
k Isa 52:10;
Lk 3:4-6*
l Isa 1:20;
58:14

40:6
m Job 14:2

40:7
n Job 41:21

40:8
a Isa 55:11;
59:21
b Mt 5:18;
1Pe 1:24-25*

40:9
c Isa 52:7-10;
61:1; Ro 10:15
d Isa 25:9

40:10
e Rev 22:7
f Isa 59:16
g Isa 9:6-7
h Isa 62:11;
Rev 22:12

40:11
i Eze 34:23;
Mic 5:4;
Jn 10:11

40:12
j Job 38:10
k Pr 30:4
l Heb 1:10-12

40:13
m Ro 11:34*;
1Co 2:16*

40:14
n Job 21:22;
Col 2:3

40:16
o Ps 50:9-11;
Mic 6:7;
Heb 10:5-9

40:17
p Isa 30:28
q Isa 29:7
r Da 4:35

40:18
s Ex 8:10;
1Sa 2:2; Isa 46:5
t Ac 17:29

40:19
u Ps 115:4
v Isa 41:7;
Jer 10:3
w Isa 2:20

⁸The grass withers and the flowers fall,
 but the word*a* of our God stands forever.*b*"

⁹You who bring good tidings*c* to Zion,
 go up on a high mountain.
You who bring good tidings to Jerusalem,*a*
 lift up your voice with a shout,
lift it up, do not be afraid;
 say to the towns of Judah,
 "Here is your God!"*d*

¹⁰See, the Sovereign LORD comes*e* with power,
 and his arm*f* rules*g* for him.
See, his reward*h* is with him,
 and his recompense accompanies him.

¹¹He tends his flock like a shepherd:*i*
 He gathers the lambs in his arms
and carries them close to his heart;
 he gently leads those that have young.

¹²Who has measured the waters*j* in the hollow of his hand,*k*
 or with the breadth of his hand marked off the heavens?*l*
Who has held the dust of the earth in a basket,
 or weighed the mountains on the scales
 and the hills in a balance?
¹³Who has understood the mind*b* of the LORD,
 or instructed him as his counselor?*m*
¹⁴Whom did the LORD consult to enlighten him,
 and who taught him the right way?
Who was it that taught him knowledge*n*
 or showed him the path of understanding?

¹⁵Surely the nations are like a drop in a bucket;
 they are regarded as dust on the scales;
 he weighs the islands as though they were fine dust.
¹⁶Lebanon is not sufficient for altar fires,
 nor its animals*o* enough for burnt offerings.
¹⁷Before him all the nations*p* are as nothing;*q*
 they are regarded by him as worthless
 and less than nothing.*r*

¹⁸To whom, then, will you compare God?*s*
 What image*t* will you compare him to?
¹⁹As for an idol,*u* a craftsman casts it,
 and a goldsmith*v* overlays it with gold*w*
 and fashions silver chains for it.

a 9 Or O Zion, bringer of good tidings, / go up on a high mountain. / O Jerusalem, bringer of good
tidings   b 13 Or Spirit; or spirit

1225

²⁰A man too poor to present such an offering
    selects wood that will not rot.
He looks for a skilled craftsman
    to set up an idol that will not topple.ᵃ

²¹Do you not know?
    Have you not heard?
Has it not been toldᵇ you from the beginning?
    Have you not understoodᶜ since the earth was founded?ᵈ
²²He sits enthroned above the circle of the earth,
    and its people are like grasshoppers.ᵉ
He stretches out the heavens like a canopy,ᶠ
    and spreads them out like a tentᵍ to live in.
²³He brings princesʰ to naught
    and reduces the rulers of this world to nothing.ⁱ
²⁴No sooner are they planted,
    no sooner are they sown,
    no sooner do they take root in the ground,
than he blowsʲ on them and they wither,
    and a whirlwind sweeps them away like chaff.

²⁵"To whom will you compare me?ᵏ
    Or who is my equal?" says the Holy One.
²⁶Lift your eyes and look to the heavens:ˡ
    Who createdᵐ all these?
He who brings out the starry hostⁿ one by one,
    and calls them each by name.
Because of his great power and mighty strength,
    not one of them is missing.ᵒ

²⁷Why do you say, O Jacob,
    and complain, O Israel,
"My way is hidden from the LORD;
    my cause is disregarded by my God"?ᵖ
²⁸Do you not know?
    Have you not heard?ᑫ
The LORD is the everlastingʳ God,
    the Creator of the ends of the earth.
He will not grow tired or weary,
    and his understanding no one can fathom.ˢ
²⁹He gives strength to the wearyᵗ
    and increases the power of the weak.
³⁰Even youths grow tired and weary,
    and young menᵘ stumble and fall;
³¹but those who hopeᵛ in the LORD
    will renew their strength.ʷ

40:20 ᵃ 1Sa 5:3

40:21 ᵇ Ps 19:1; 50:6; Ac 14:17 ᶜ Ro 1:19 ᵈ Isa 48:13; 51:13

40:22 ᵉ Nu 13:33; Ps 104:2; Isa 42:5 ᶠ Job 22:14 ᵍ Job 36:29

40:23 ʰ Isa 34:12 ⁱ Job 12:21; Ps 107:40

40:24 ʲ Isa 41:16

40:25 ᵏ ver 18

40:26 ˡ Isa 51:6 ᵐ Ps 89:11-13; Isa 42:5 ⁿ Ps 147:4 ᵒ Isa 34:16

40:27 ᵖ Job 27:2; Lk 18:7-8

40:28 ᑫ ver 21 ʳ Ps 90:2 ˢ Ps 147:5; Ro 11:33

40:29 ᵗ Isa 50:4; Jer 31:25

40:30 ᵘ Isa 9:17; Jer 6:11; 9:21

40:31 ᵛ Lk 18:1 ʷ 2Co 4:16

They will soar on wings like eagles;[a]
  they will run and not grow weary,
  they will walk and not be faint.[b]

Chapter 41 Theme _____

41 "Be silent[c] before me, you islands![d]
  Let the nations renew their strength!
Let them come forward[e] and speak;
  let us meet together[f] at the place of judgment.

[2]"Who has stirred[g] up one from the east,[h]
  calling him in righteousness to his service[a]
He hands nations over to him
  and subdues kings before him.
He turns them to dust[i] with his sword,
  to windblown chaff[j] with his bow.
[3]He pursues them and moves on unscathed,
  by a path his feet have not traveled before.
[4]Who has done this and carried it through,
  calling forth the generations from the beginning?[k]
I, the LORD—with the first of them
  and with the last[l]—I am he."

[5]The islands[m] have seen it and fear;
  the ends of the earth tremble.
They approach and come forward;
[6] each helps the other
  and says to his brother, "Be strong!"
[7]The craftsman encourages the goldsmith,[n]
  and he who smooths with the hammer
  spurs on him who strikes the anvil.
He says of the welding, "It is good."
  He nails down the idol so it will not topple.

[8]"But you, O Israel, my servant,
  Jacob, whom I have chosen,
  you descendants of Abraham[o] my friend,[p]
[9]I took you from the ends of the earth,[q]
  from its farthest corners I called you.
I said, 'You are my servant';
  I have chosen[r] you and have not rejected you.
[10]So do not fear, for I am with you;[s]
  do not be dismayed, for I am your God.
I will strengthen you and help[t] you;
  I will uphold you with my righteous right hand.

a 2 Or / whom victory meets at every step

Cross references

40:31 a Ex 19:4; Ps 103:5 b 2Co 4:1; Heb 12:1-3
41:1 c Hab 2:20; Zec 2:13 d Isa 11:11 e Isa 48:16 f Isa 1:18; 34:1; 50:8
41:2 g Ezr 1:2 h ver 25; Isa 45:1,13 i 2Sa 22:43 j Isa 40:24
41:4 k ver 26; Isa 46:10 l Isa 44:6; 48:12; Rev 1:8,17; 22:13
41:5 m Eze 26:17-18
41:7 n Isa 40:19
41:8 o Isa 29:22; 51:2; 63:16 p 2Ch 20:7; Jas 2:23
41:9 q Isa 11:12 r Dt 7:6
41:10 s Jos 1:9; Isa 43:2,5; Ro 8:31 t ver 13-14; Isa 44:2; 49:8

11"All who rage*a* against you
  will surely be ashamed and disgraced;*b*
those who oppose*c* you
  will be as nothing and perish.*d*
12Though you search for your enemies,
  you will not find them.*e*
Those who wage war against you
  will be as nothing*f* at all.
13For I am the LORD, your God,
  who takes hold of your right hand*g*
and says to you, Do not fear;
  I will help*h* you.
14Do not be afraid, O worm Jacob,
  O little Israel,
for I myself will help you," declares the LORD,
  your Redeemer, the Holy One of Israel.
15"See, I will make you into a threshing sledge,*i*
  new and sharp, with many teeth.
You will thresh the mountains and crush them,
  and reduce the hills to chaff.
16You will winnow*j* them, the wind will pick them up,
  and a gale will blow them away.
But you will rejoice in the LORD
  and glory*k* in the Holy One of Israel.

17"The poor and needy search for water,*l*
  but there is none;
  their tongues are parched with thirst.
But I the LORD will answer*m* them;
  I, the God of Israel, will not forsake them.
18I will make rivers flow*n* on barren heights,
  and springs within the valleys.
I will turn the desert*o* into pools of water,
  and the parched ground into springs.*p*
19I will put in the desert
  the cedar and the acacia, the myrtle and the olive.
I will set pines in the wasteland,
  the fir and the cypress together,*q*
20so that people may see and know,
  may consider and understand,
that the hand of the LORD has done this,
  that the Holy One of Israel has created*r* it.

21"Present your case," says the LORD.
  "Set forth your arguments," says Jacob's King.*s*
22"Bring in ⌐your idols⌐ to tell us
  what is going to happen.*t*

41:11 *a*Isa 17:12 *b*Isa 45:24 *c*Ex 23:22 *d*Isa 29:8
41:12 *e*Ps 37:35-36 *f*Isa 17:14
41:13 *g*Isa 42:6; 45:1 *h*ver 10
41:15 *i*Mic 4:13
41:16 *j*Jer 51:2 *k*Isa 45:25
41:17 *l*Isa 43:20 *m*Isa 30:19
41:18 *n*Isa 30:25 *o*Isa 43:19 *p*Isa 35:7
41:19 *q*Isa 60:13
41:20 *r*Job 12:9
41:21 *s*Isa 43:15
41:22 *t*Isa 43:9; 45:21

Tell us what the former things were,
  so that we may consider them
  and know their final outcome.
Or declare to us the things to come,[a]
23 tell us what the future holds,
  so we may know[b] that you are gods.
Do something, whether good or bad,[c]
  so that we will be dismayed and filled with fear.
24But you are less than nothing[d]
  and your works are utterly worthless;
  he who chooses you is detestable.[e]

25"I have stirred up one from the north,[f] and he comes—
  one from the rising sun who calls on my name.
He treads[g] on rulers as if they were mortar,
  as if he were a potter treading the clay.
26Who told of this from the beginning, so we could know,
  or beforehand, so we could say, 'He was right'?
No one told of this,
  no one foretold it,
  no one heard any words[h] from you.
27I was the first to tell[i] Zion, 'Look, here they are!'
  I gave to Jerusalem a messenger of good tidings.[j]
28I look but there is no one[k]—
  no one among them to give counsel,[l]
  no one to give answer when I ask them.
29See, they are all false!
  Their deeds amount to nothing;[m]
  their images are but wind[n] and confusion.

Chapter 42 Theme _____

42 "Here is my servant, whom I uphold,
  my chosen one[o] in whom I delight;
I will put my Spirit[p] on him
  and he will bring justice to the nations.
2He will not shout or cry out,
  or raise his voice in the streets.
3A bruised reed he will not break,
  and a smoldering wick he will not snuff out.
In faithfulness he will bring forth justice;[q]
4 he will not falter or be discouraged
  till he establishes justice on earth.
  In his law the islands will put their hope."[r]

5This is what God the LORD says—
  he who created the heavens and stretched them out,
  who spread out the earth and all that comes out of it,[s]

41:22 a Isa 46:10
41:23 b Isa 42:9; 44:7-8; 45:3 c Jer 10:5
41:24 d Isa 37:19; 44:9; 1Co 8:4 e Ps 115:8
41:25 f ver 2 g 2Sa 22:43
41:26 h Hab 2:18-19
41:27 i Isa 48:3,16 j Isa 40:9
41:28 k Isa 50:2; 59:16; 63:5 l Isa 40:13-14
41:29 m ver 24 n Jer 5:13
42:1 o Isa 43:10; Lk 9:35; 1Pe 2:4,6 p Isa 11:2; Mt 3:16-17; Jn 3:34
42:3 q Ps 72:2
42:4 r Ge 49:10; Mt 12:18-21*
42:5 s Ps 24:2

who gives breath[a] to its people,
and life to those who walk on it:
⁶"I, the LORD, have called[b] you in righteousness;[c]
I will take hold of your hand.
I will keep[d] you and will make you
to be a covenant[e] for the people
and a light for the Gentiles,[f]
⁷to open eyes that are blind,[g]
to free[h] captives from prison[i]
and to release from the dungeon those who sit
in darkness.

⁸"I am the LORD; that is my name![j]
I will not give my glory to another[k]
or my praise to idols.
⁹See, the former things have taken place,
and new things I declare;
before they spring into being
I announce them to you."

¹⁰Sing to the LORD a new song,[l]
his praise from the ends of the earth,[m]
you who go down to the sea, and all that is in it,[n]
you islands, and all who live in them.
¹¹Let the desert[o] and its towns raise their voices;
let the settlements where Kedar[p] lives rejoice.
Let the people of Sela sing for joy;
let them shout from the mountaintops.[q]
¹²Let them give glory[r] to the LORD
and proclaim his praise in the islands.
¹³The LORD will march out like a mighty[s] man,
like a warrior he will stir up his zeal;[t]
with a shout[u] he will raise the battle cry
and will triumph over his enemies.[v]

¹⁴"For a long time I have kept silent,
I have been quiet and held myself back.
But now, like a woman in childbirth,
I cry out, I gasp and pant.
¹⁵I will lay waste[w] the mountains and hills
and dry up all their vegetation;
I will turn rivers into islands
and dry up[x] the pools.
¹⁶I will lead[y] the blind[z] by ways they have not known,
along unfamiliar paths I will guide them;
I will turn the darkness into light before them
and make the rough places smooth.[a]

42:5
[a] Ac 17:25

42:6
[b] Isa 43:1
[c] Jer 23:6
[d] Isa 26:3
[e] Isa 49:8
[f] Lk 2:32;
Ac 13:47

42:7
[g] Isa 35:5
[h] Isa 49:9; 61:1
[i] Lk 4:19;
2Ti 2:26;
Heb 2:14-15

42:8
[j] Ex 3:15
[k] Isa 48:11

42:10
[l] Ps 33:3; 40:3;
98:1
[m] Isa 49:6
[n] 1Ch 16:32;
Ps 96:11

42:11
[o] Isa 32:16
[p] Isa 60:7
[q] Isa 52:7;
Na 1:15

42:12
[r] Isa 24:15

42:13
[s] Isa 9:6
[t] Isa 26:11
[u] Hos 11:10
[v] Isa 66:14

42:15
[w] Eze 38:20
[x] Isa 50:2;
Na 1:4-6

42:16
[y] Lk 1:78-79
[z] Isa 32:3
[a] Lk 3:5

42:16
aHeb 13:5

These are the things I will do;
  I will not forsake[a] them.
17But those who trust in idols,
  who say to images, 'You are our gods,'
  will be turned back in utter shame.[b]

42:17
bPs 97:7;
Isa 1:29; 44:11;
45:16

18"Hear, you deaf;[c]
  look, you blind, and see!

42:18
cIsa 35:5

19Who is blind[d] but my servant,[e]
  and deaf like the messenger[f] I send?
Who is blind like the one committed[g] to me,
  blind like the servant of the LORD?
20You have seen many things, but have paid no attention;
  your ears are open, but you hear nothing."[h]

42:19
dIsa 43:8;
Eze 12:2
eIsa 41:8-9
fIsa 44:26
gIsa 26:3

21It pleased the LORD
  for the sake of his righteousness
  to make his law[i] great and glorious.
22But this is a people plundered and looted,
  all of them trapped in pits[j]
  or hidden away in prisons.[k]
They have become plunder,
  with no one to rescue them;
they have been made loot,
  with no one to say, "Send them back."

42:20
hJer 6:10

42:21
iver 4

42:22
jIsa 24:18
kIsa 24:22

23Which of you will listen to this
  or pay close attention[l] in time to come?
24Who handed Jacob over to become loot,
  and Israel to the plunderers?
Was it not the LORD,
  against whom we have sinned?
For they would not follow[m] his ways;
  they did not obey his law.
25So he poured out on them his burning anger,
  the violence of war.
It enveloped them in flames,[n] yet they did not understand;
  it consumed them, but they did not take it to heart.[o]

42:23
lIsa 48:18

42:24
mIsa 30:15

42:25
n2Ki 25:9
oIsa 29:13; 47:7;
57:1,11; Hos 7:9

Chapter 43 Theme _____

43
But now, this is what the LORD says—
  he who created you, O Jacob,
  he who formed[p] you, O Israel:[q]
"Fear not, for I have redeemed[r] you;
  I have summoned you by name;[s] you are mine.
2When you pass through the waters,[t]
  I will be with you;[u]

43:1
pver 7
qGe 32:28;
Isa 44:21
rIsa 44:2,6
sIsa 42:6; 45:3-4

43:2
tIsa 8:7
uDt 31:6,8

and when you pass through the rivers,
   they will not sweep over you.
When you walk through the fire,[a]
   you will not be burned;
   the flames will not set you ablaze.[b]
³For I am the LORD, your God,[c]
   the Holy One of Israel, your Savior;
I give Egypt for your ransom,
   Cush[a][d] and Seba in your stead.[e]
⁴Since you are precious and honored in my sight,
   and because I love[f] you,
I will give men in exchange for you,
   and people in exchange for your life.
⁵Do not be afraid,[g] for I am with you;[h]
   I will bring your children[i] from the east
   and gather you from the west.
⁶I will say to the north, 'Give them up!'
   and to the south,[j] 'Do not hold them back.'
Bring my sons from afar
   and my daughters[k] from the ends of the earth—
⁷everyone who is called by my name,[l]
   whom I created for my glory,
   whom I formed and made.[m]"

⁸Lead out those who have eyes but are blind,[n]
   who have ears but are deaf.[o]
⁹All the nations gather together[p]
   and the peoples assemble.
Which of them foretold[q] this
   and proclaimed to us the former things?
Let them bring in their witnesses to prove they were right,
   so that others may hear and say, "It is true."
¹⁰"You are my witnesses," declares the LORD,
   "and my servant[r] whom I have chosen,
so that you may know and believe me
   and understand that I am he.
Before me no god[s] was formed,
   nor will there be one after me.
¹¹I, even I, am the LORD,
   and apart from me there is no savior.[t]
¹²I have revealed and saved and proclaimed—
   I, and not some foreign god[u] among you.
You are my witnesses,[v]" declares the LORD, "that I am God.

a 3 That is, the upper Nile region

43:2
a Isa 29:6; 30:27
b Ps 66:12;
Da 3:25-27

43:3
c Ex 20:2
d Isa 20:3
e Pr 21:18

43:4
f Isa 63:9

43:5
g Isa 44:2
h Jer 30:10-11
i Isa 41:8

43:6
j Ps 107:3
k 2Co 6:18

43:7
l Isa 56:5; 63:19;
Jas 2:7
m ver 1,21;
Ps 100:3;
Eph 2:10

43:8
n Isa 6:9-10
o Isa 42:20;
Eze 12:2

43:9
p Isa 41:1
q Isa 41:26

43:10
r Isa 41:8-9
s Isa 44:6,8

43:11
t Isa 45:21

43:12
u Dt 32:12;
Ps 81:9
v Isa 44:8

43:13
a Ps 90:2
b Job 9:12;
Isa 14:27

13   Yes, and from ancient days*a* I am he.
No one can deliver out of my hand.
When I act, who can reverse it?"*b*

43:14
c Isa 13:14-15
d Isa 23:13

14This is what the LORD says—
your Redeemer, the Holy One of Israel:
"For your sake I will send to Babylon
and bring down as fugitives*c* all the
Babylonians,*a* *d*
in the ships in which they took pride.
15I am the LORD, your Holy One,
Israel's Creator, your King."

43:16
e Ps 77:19;
Isa 11:15; 51:10

16This is what the LORD says—
he who made a way through the sea,
a path through the mighty waters,*e*

43:17
f Ps 118:12;
Isa 1:31
g Ex 14:9

17who drew out*f* the chariots and horses,
the army and reinforcements together,*g*
and they lay there, never to rise again,
extinguished, snuffed out like a wick:
18"Forget the former things;
do not dwell on the past.

43:19
h 2Co 5:17;
Rev 21:5
i Ex 17:6;
Nu 20:11

19See, I am doing a new thing!*h*
Now it springs up; do you not perceive it?
I am making a way in the desert*i*
and streams in the wasteland.

43:20
j Isa 13:22
k Isa 48:21

20The wild animals honor me,
the jackals*j* and the owls,
because I provide water*k* in the desert
and streams in the wasteland,
to give drink to my people, my chosen,

43:21
l Ps 102:18;
1Pe 2:9

21   the people I formed for myself
that they may proclaim my praise.*l*

43:22
m Isa 30:11

22"Yet you have not called upon me, O Jacob,
you have not wearied yourselves for me, O Israel.*m*

43:23
n Zec 7:5-6;
Mal 1:6-8
o Am 5:25
p Jer 7:22
q Ex 30:35;
Lev 2:1

23You have not brought me sheep for burnt offerings,
nor honored*n* me with your sacrifices.*o*
I have not burdened you with grain offerings
nor wearied you with demands*p* for incense.*q*
24You have not bought any fragrant calamus*r* for me,
or lavished on me the fat of your sacrifices.
But you have burdened me with your sins
and wearied*s* me with your offenses.*t*

43:24
r Ex 30:23
s Isa 1:14; 7:13
t Mal 2:17

a 14 Or *Chaldeans*

²⁵"I, even I, am he who blots out
  your transgressions,ᵃ for my own sake,ᵇ
  and remembers your sins no more.ᶜ
²⁶Review the past for me,
  let us argue the matter together;ᵈ
  state the caseᵉ for your innocence.
²⁷Your first father sinned;
  your spokesmenᶠ rebelled against me.
²⁸So I will disgrace the dignitaries of your temple,
  and I will consign Jacob to destructionᵃ
  and Israel to scorn.ᵍ

Chapter 44 Theme _____

44 "But now listen, O Jacob, my servant,ʰ
  Israel, whom I have chosen.
²This is what the LORD says—
  he who made you, who formed you in the womb,
  and who will helpⁱ you:
Do not be afraid, O Jacob, my servant,
  Jeshurun,ʲ whom I have chosen.
³For I will pour waterᵏ on the thirsty land,
  and streams on the dry ground;
I will pour out my Spiritˡ on your offspring,
  and my blessing on your descendants.ᵐ
⁴They will spring up like grass in a meadow,
  like poplar treesⁿ by flowing streams.ᵒ
⁵One will say, 'I belong to the LORD';
  another will call himself by the name of Jacob;
still another will write on his hand,ᵖ 'The LORD's,'�q
  and will take the name Israel.

⁶"This is what the LORD says—
  Israel's Kingʳ and Redeemer,ˢ the LORD Almighty:
I am the first and I am the last;ᵗ
  apart from me there is no God.
⁷Who then is like me? Let him proclaim it.
  Let him declare and lay out before me
what has happened since I established my ancient people,
  and what is yet to come—
  yes, let him foretellᵘ what will come.
⁸Do not tremble, do not be afraid.
  Did I not proclaim this and foretell it long ago?

ᵃ28 The Hebrew term refers to the irrevocable giving over of things or persons to the LORD, often by totally destroying them.

43:25
ᵃ Ac 3:19
ᵇ Isa 37:35;
Eze 36:22
ᶜ Isa 38:17;
Jer 31:34

43:26
ᵈ Isa 1:18
ᵉ Isa 41:1; 50:8

43:27
ᶠ Isa 9:15; 28:7;
Jer 5:31

43:28
ᵍ Jer 24:9;
Eze 5:15

44:1
ʰ ver 21;
Jer 30:10;
46:27-28

44:2
ⁱ Isa 41:10
ʲ Dt 32:15

44:3
ᵏ Joel 3:18
ˡ Joel 2:28;
Ac 2:17
ᵐ Isa 61:9; 65:23

44:4
ⁿ Lev 23:40
ᵒ Job 40:22

44:5
ᵖ Ex 13:9
q Zec 8:20-22

44:6
ʳ Isa 41:21
ˢ Isa 43:1
ᵗ Isa 41:4;
Rev 1:8,17;
22:13

44:7
ᵘ Isa 41:22,26

You are my witnesses. Is there any God[a] besides me?
No, there is no other Rock;[b] I know not one."

44:8
[a] Isa 43:10
[b] Dt 4:35;
1Sa 2:2

9 All who make idols are nothing,
and the things they treasure are worthless.[c]
Those who would speak up for them are blind;
they are ignorant, to their own shame.

44:9
[c] Isa 41:24

10 Who shapes a god and casts an idol,
which can profit him nothing?[d]

11 He and his kind will be put to shame;[e]
craftsmen are nothing but men.
Let them all come together and take their stand;
they will be brought down to terror and infamy.[f]

44:10
[d] Isa 41:29;
Jer 10:5;
Ac 19:26

12 The blacksmith[g] takes a tool
and works with it in the coals;
he shapes an idol with hammers,
he forges it with the might of his arm.[h]
He gets hungry and loses his strength;
he drinks no water and grows faint.

44:11
[e] Isa 1:29
[f] Isa 42:17

13 The carpenter[i] measures with a line
and makes an outline with a marker;
he roughs it out with chisels
and marks it with compasses.
He shapes it in the form of man,[j]
of man in all his glory,
that it may dwell in a shrine.[k]

44:12
[g] Isa 40:19;
41:6-7
[h] Jer 10:3-5;
Ac 17:29

14 He cut down cedars,
or perhaps took a cypress or oak.
He let it grow among the trees of the forest,
or planted a pine, and the rain made it grow.

15 It is man's fuel[l] for burning;
some of it he takes and warms himself,
he kindles a fire and bakes bread.
But he also fashions a god and worships it;
he makes an idol and bows[m] down to it.

44:13
[i] Isa 41:7
[j] Ps 115:4-7
[k] Jdg 17:4-5

16 Half of the wood he burns in the fire;
over it he prepares his meal,
he roasts his meat and eats his fill.
He also warms himself and says,
"Ah! I am warm; I see the fire."

17 From the rest he makes a god, his idol;
he bows down to it and worships.
He prays[n] to it and says,
"Save[o] me; you are my god."

44:15
[l] ver 19
[m] 2Ch 25:14

18 They know nothing, they understand[p] nothing;
their eyes[q] are plastered over so they cannot see,

44:17
[n] 1Ki 18:26
[o] Isa 45:20

44:18
[p] Isa 1:3
[q] Isa 6:9-10

and their minds closed so they cannot understand.

19No one stops to think,
no one has the knowledge or understanding[a] to say,
"Half of it I used for fuel;
I even baked bread over its coals,
I roasted meat and I ate.
Shall I make a detestable[b] thing from what is left?
Shall I bow down to a block of wood?"

20He feeds on ashes,[c] a deluded[d] heart misleads him;
he cannot save himself, or say,
"Is not this thing in my right hand a lie?[e]"

21"Remember[f] these things, O Jacob,
for you are my servant, O Israel.
I have made you, you are my servant;[g]
O Israel, I will not forget you.[h]

22I have swept away[i] your offenses like a cloud,
your sins like the morning mist.
Return[j] to me,
for I have redeemed[k] you."

23Sing for joy,[l] O heavens, for the LORD has done this;
shout aloud, O earth[m] beneath.
Burst into song, you mountains,[n]
you forests and all your trees,
for the LORD has redeemed Jacob,
he displays his glory[o] in Israel.

24"This is what the LORD says—
your Redeemer,[p] who formed you in the womb:

I am the LORD,
who has made all things,
who alone stretched out the heavens,[q]
who spread out the earth by myself,

25who foils[r] the signs of false prophets
and makes fools of diviners,[s]
who overthrows the learning of the wise[t]
and turns it into nonsense,[u]

26who carries out the words[v] of his servants
and fulfills[w] the predictions of his messengers,

who says of Jerusalem, 'It shall be inhabited,'
of the towns of Judah, 'They shall be built,'
and of their ruins, 'I will restore them,'[x]

27who says to the watery deep, 'Be dry,
and I will dry up your streams,'

44:19
a Isa 5:13; 27:11;
45:20
b Dt 27:15

44:20
c Ps 102:9
d Job 15:31;
Ro 1:21-23,28;
2Th 2:11;
2Ti 3:13
e Isa 59:3,4,13;
Ro 1:25

44:21
f Isa 46:8;
Zec 10:9
g ver 1-2
h Isa 49:15

44:22
i Isa 43:25;
Ac 3:19
j Isa 55:7
k 1Co 6:20

44:23
l Isa 42:10
m Ps 148:7
n Ps 98:8
o Isa 61:3

44:24
p Isa 43:14
q Isa 42:5

44:25
r Ps 33:10
s Isa 47:13
t 1Co 1:27
u 2Sa 15:31;
1Co 1:19-20

44:26
v Zec 1:6
w Isa 55:11;
Mt 5:18
x Isa 49:8-21

44:28
a 2Ch 36:22
b Isa 14:32
c Ezr 1:2-4

²⁸who says of Cyrus,ᵃ 'He is my shepherd
    and will accomplish all that I please;
he will say of Jerusalem,ᵇ "Let it be rebuilt,"
    and of the temple,ᶜ "Let its foundations be laid."'

Chapter 45 Theme

45:1
d Ps 73:23;
Isa 41:13; 42:6
e Jer 50:35

45 "This is what the LORD says to his anointed,
    to Cyrus, whose right hand I take holdᵈ of
to subdue nationsᵉ before him
    and to strip kings of their armor,
to open doors before him
    so that gates will not be shut:

45:2
f Isa 40:4
g Ps 107:16;
Jer 51:30

²I will go before you
    and will levelᶠ the mountainsᵃ;
I will break down gates of bronze
    and cut through bars of iron.ᵍ

45:3
h Jer 50:37
i Jer 41:8
j Isa 41:23
k Ex 33:12;
Isa 43:1

³I will give you the treasuresʰ of darkness,
    riches stored in secret places,ⁱ
so that you may knowʲ that I am the LORD,
    the God of Israel, who summons you by name.ᵏ

45:4
l Isa 41:8-9
m Ac 17:23

⁴For the sake of Jacob my servant,ˡ
    of Israel my chosen,
I summon you by name
    and bestow on you a title of honor,
    though you do not acknowledgeᵐ me.

45:5
n Isa 44:8
o Ps 18:31
p Ps 18:39

⁵I am the LORD, and there is no other;ⁿ
    apart from me there is no God.ᵒ
I will strengthen you,ᵖ
    though you have not acknowledged me,

45:6
q Isa 43:5;
Mal 1:11
r ver 5,18

⁶so that from the rising of the sun
    to the place of its setting�q
men may know there is none besides me.ʳ
    I am the LORD, and there is no other.

45:7
s Isa 31:2;
Am 3:6

⁷I form the light and create darkness,
    I bring prosperity and create disaster;ˢ
    I, the LORD, do all these things.

45:8
t Ps 72:6;
Joel 3:18
u Ps 85:11;
Isa 60:21;
61:10,11;
Hos 10:12
v Isa 12:3

⁸"You heavens above, rainᵗ down righteousness;ᵘ
    let the clouds shower it down.
Let the earth open wide,
    let salvationᵛ spring up,
let righteousness grow with it;
    I, the LORD, have created it.

INSIGHT

This prophecy regarding Cyrus was given 175 years before his birth. In 539 B.C. Babylon was conquered by Cyrus and Darius of the Medo-Persian Empire.

ᵃ 2 Dead Sea Scrolls and Septuagint; the meaning of the word in the Masoretic Text is uncertain.

9"Woe to him who quarrels[a] with his Maker,
    to him who is but a potsherd among the potsherds on
        the ground.
Does the clay say to the potter,[b]
    'What are you making?'
Does your work say,
    'He has no hands'?
10Woe to him who says to his father,
    'What have you begotten?'
or to his mother,
    'What have you brought to birth?'

11"This is what the LORD says—
    the Holy One of Israel, and its Maker:
Concerning things to come,
    do you question me about my children,
    or give me orders about the work of my hands?[c]
12It is I who made the earth
    and created mankind upon it.
My own hands stretched out the heavens;[d]
    I marshaled their starry hosts.[e]
13I will raise up Cyrus[a][f] in my righteousness:
    I will make all his ways straight.
He will rebuild my city
    and set my exiles free,
but not for a price or reward,[g]
    says the LORD Almighty."

14This is what the LORD says:

"The products of Egypt and the merchandise of Cush,[b]
    and those tall Sabeans—
they will come over to you
    and will be yours;
they will trudge behind you,
    coming over to you in chains.[h]
They will bow down before you
    and plead[i] with you, saying,
'Surely God is with you,[j] and there is no other;
    there is no other god.'"

15Truly you are a God who hides[k] himself,
    O God and Savior of Israel.
16All the makers of idols will be put to shame
    and disgraced;[l]
    they will go off into disgrace together.

---

a 13 Hebrew *him*   b 14 That is, the upper Nile region

45:9
a Job 15:25
b Isa 29:16;
Ro 9:20-21*

45:11
c Isa 19:25

45:12
d Ge 2:1;
Isa 42:5
e Ne 9:6

45:13
f 2Ch 36:22;
Isa 41:2
g Isa 52:3

45:14
h Isa 14:1-2
i Jer 16:19;
Zec 8:20-23
j 1Co 14:25

45:15
k Ps 44:24

45:16
l Isa 44:9,11

45:17
a Ro 11:26
b Isa 26:4

[17]But Israel will be saved*a* by the LORD
  with an everlasting salvation;*b*
you will never be put to shame or disgraced,
  to ages everlasting.

45:18
c Ge 1:2
d Ge 1:26;
Isa 42:5
e ver 5

[18]For this is what the LORD says—
he who created the heavens,
  he is God;
he who fashioned and made the earth,
  he founded it;
he did not create it to be empty,*c*
  but formed it to be inhabited*d*—

45:19
f Isa 48:16
g Isa 41:8
h Dt 30:11

he says:
"I am the LORD,
  and there is no other.*e*
[19]I have not spoken in secret,*f*
  from somewhere in a land of darkness;
I have not said to Jacob's descendants,*g*
  'Seek me in vain.'
I, the LORD, speak the truth;
  I declare what is right.*h*

45:20
i Isa 43:9
j Isa 44:19
k Isa 46:1;
Jer 10:5
l Isa 44:17;
46:6-7

[20]"Gather together*i* and come;
  assemble, you fugitives from the nations.
Ignorant*j* are those who carry*k* about idols of wood,
  who pray to gods that cannot save.*l*

45:21
m Isa 41:22
n ver 5

[21]Declare what is to be, present it—
  let them take counsel together.
Who foretold*m* this long ago,
  who declared it from the distant past?
Was it not I, the LORD?
  And there is no God apart from me,*n*
a righteous God and a Savior;
  there is none but me.

45:22
o Zec 12:10
p Nu 21:8-9;
2Ch 20:12
q Isa 49:6,12

[22]"Turn*o* to me and be saved,*p*
  all you ends of the earth;*q*
for I am God, and there is no other.

45:23
r Ge 22:16
s Heb 6:13
t Isa 55:11
u Ps 63:11;
Isa 19:18;
Ro 14:11*;
Php 2:10-11

[23]By myself I have sworn,*r*
  my mouth has uttered in all integrity*s*
  a word that will not be revoked:*t*
Before me every knee will bow;
  by me every tongue will swear.*u*
[24]They will say of me, 'In the LORD alone
  are righteousness*v* and strength.'"
All who have raged against him
  will come to him and be put to shame.*w*

45:24
v Jer 33:16
w Isa 41:11

²⁵But in the LORD all the descendants of Israel
    will be found righteous and will exult.*a*

Chapter 46 Theme _____

46 Bel*b* bows down, Nebo stoops low;
    their idols are borne by beasts of burden.*a*
The images that are carried*c* about are burdensome,
    a burden for the weary.
²They stoop and bow down together;
    unable to rescue the burden,
    they themselves go off into captivity.*d*

³"Listen*e* to me, O house of Jacob,
    all you who remain of the house of Israel,
you whom I have upheld since you were conceived,
    and have carried since your birth.
⁴Even to your old age and gray hairs*f*
    I am he,*g* I am he who will sustain you.
I have made you and I will carry you;
    I will sustain you and I will rescue you.

⁵"To whom will you compare me or count me equal?
    To whom will you liken me that we may be compared?*h*
⁶Some pour out gold from their bags
    and weigh out silver on the scales;
they hire a goldsmith*i* to make it into a god,
    and they bow down and worship it.*j*
⁷They lift it to their shoulders and carry*k* it;
    they set it up in its place, and there it stands.
    From that spot it cannot move.
Though one cries out to it, it does not answer;
    it cannot save*l* him from his troubles.

⁸"Remember*m* this, fix it in mind,
    take it to heart, you rebels.
⁹Remember the former things, those of long ago;*n*
    I am God, and there is no other;
    I am God, and there is none like me.*o*
¹⁰I make known the end from the beginning,
    from ancient times,*p* what is still to come.
I say: My purpose will stand,*q*
    and I will do all that I please.
¹¹From the east I summon a bird of prey;
    from a far-off land, a man to fulfill my purpose.
What I have said, that will I bring about;
    what I have planned, that will I do.

a 1 Or *are but beasts and cattle*

45:25
a Isa 41:16

46:1
b Isa 21:9;
Jer 50:2; 51:44
c Isa 45:20

46:2
d Jdg 18:17-18;
2Sa 5:21

46:3
e ver 12

46:4
f Ps 71:18
g Isa 43:13

46:5
h Isa 40:18,25

46:6
i Isa 40:19
j Isa 44:17

46:7
k ver 1
l Isa 44:17;
Isa 45:20

46:8
m Isa 44:21

46:9
n Dt 32:7
o Isa 45:5,21

46:10
p Isa 45:21
q Pr 19:21;
Ac 5:39

46:12
a ver 3
b Ps 119:150;
Isa 48:1; Jer 2:5

46:13
c Isa 44:23

47:1
d Isa 23:12
e Ps 137:8;
Jer 50:42; 51:33;
Zec 2:7
f Dt 28:56

47:2
g Ex 11:5;
Mt 24:41
h Jdg 16:21
i Ge 24:65
j Isa 32:11

47:3
k Eze 16:37;
Na 3:5
l Isa 20:4
m Isa 34:8

47:4
n Jer 50:34

47:5
o Isa 13:10
p Isa 13:19

47:6
q 2Ch 28:9
r Isa 10:13

47:7
s ver 5; Rev 18:7
t Isa 42:23,25
u Dt 32:29

47:8
v Isa 32:9
w Isa 45:6;
Zep 2:15

[12]Listen[a] to me, you stubborn-hearted,
  you who are far from righteousness.[b]
[13]I am bringing my righteousness near,
  it is not far away;
  and my salvation will not be delayed.
I will grant salvation to Zion,
  my splendor[c] to Israel.

Chapter 47 Theme

47

"Go down, sit in the dust,
  Virgin Daughter[d] of Babylon;
sit on the ground without a throne,
  Daughter of the Babylonians.[a] [e]
No more will you be called
  tender or delicate.[f]
[2]Take millstones[g] and grind[h] flour;
  take off your veil.[i]
Lift up your skirts,[j] bare your legs,
  and wade through the streams.
[3]Your nakedness[k] will be exposed
  and your shame[l] uncovered.
I will take vengeance;[m]
  I will spare no one."

[4]Our Redeemer—the LORD Almighty is his name[n]—
  is the Holy One of Israel.

[5]"Sit in silence, go into darkness,[o]
  Daughter of the Babylonians;
no more will you be called
  queen of kingdoms.[p]
[6]I was angry[q] with my people
  and desecrated my inheritance;
I gave them into your hand,[r]
  and you showed them no mercy.
Even on the aged
  you laid a very heavy yoke.
[7]You said, 'I will continue forever—
  the eternal queen!'[s]
But you did not consider these things
  or reflect[t] on what might happen.[u]

[8]"Now then, listen, you wanton creature,
  lounging in your security[v]
and saying to yourself,
  'I am, and there is none besides me.[w]

I will never be a widow[a]
    or suffer the loss of children.'
[9]Both of these will overtake you
    in a moment,[b] on a single day:
    loss of children[c] and widowhood.
They will come upon you in full measure,
    in spite of your many sorceries[d]
    and all your potent spells.[e]
[10]You have trusted[f] in your wickedness
    and have said, 'No one sees me.'[g]
Your wisdom[h] and knowledge mislead[i] you
    when you say to yourself,
    'I am, and there is none besides me.'
[11]Disaster will come upon you,
    and you will not know how to conjure it away.
A calamity will fall upon you
    that you cannot ward off with a ransom;
a catastrophe you cannot foresee
    will suddenly[j] come upon you.

[12]"Keep on, then, with your magic spells
    and with your many sorceries,[k]
    which you have labored at since childhood.
Perhaps you will succeed,
    perhaps you will cause terror.
[13]All the counsel you have received has only worn you out![l]
    Let your astrologers[m] come forward,
those stargazers who make predictions month by month,
    let them save[n] you from what is coming upon you.
[14]Surely they are like stubble;[o]
    the fire will burn them up.
They cannot even save themselves
    from the power of the flame.[p]
Here are no coals to warm anyone;
    here is no fire to sit by.
[15]That is all they can do for you—
    these you have labored with
    and trafficked[q] with since childhood.
Each of them goes on in his error;
    there is not one that can save you.

Chapter 48 Theme

48 "Listen to this, O house of Jacob,
    you who are called by the name of Israel
    and come from the line of Judah,

Cross references

47:8
[a] Rev 18:7

47:9
[b] Ps 73:19;
1Th 5:3;
Rev 18:8-10
[c] Isa 13:18
[d] Na 3:4
[e] Rev 18:23

47:10
[f] Ps 52:7; 62:10
[g] Isa 29:15
[h] Isa 5:21
[i] Isa 44:20

47:11
[j] 1Th 5:3

47:12
[k] ver 9

47:13
[l] Isa 57:10;
Jer 51:58
[m] Isa 44:25
[n] ver 15

47:14
[o] Isa 5:24;
Na 1:10
[p] Isa 10:17;
Jer 51:30,32,58

47:15
[q] Rev 18:11

48:1
a Isa 58:2
b Jer 4:2

48:2
c Isa 52:1
d Isa 10:20;
Mic 3:11;
Ro 2:17

48:3
e Isa 41:22
f Isa 45:21

48:4
g Dt 31:27
h Ex 32:9;
Ac 7:51
i Eze 3:9

48:5
j Jer 44:15-18

48:8
k Dt 9:7,24;
Ps 58:3

48:9
l Ps 78:38;
Isa 30:18
m Ne 9:31

48:10
n 1Ki 8:51

48:11
o 1Sa 12:22;
Isa 37:35
p Dt 32:27;
Jer 14:7,21;
Eze 20:9,14,
22,44
q Isa 42:8

48:12
r Isa 46:3
s Isa 41:4;
Rev 1:17; 22:13

48:13
t Heb 1:10-12
u Ex 20:11
v Isa 40:26

you who take oaths in the name of the LORD
and invoke[a] the God of Israel—
but not in truth[b] or righteousness—
2 you who call yourselves citizens of the holy city[c]
and rely[d] on the God of Israel—
the LORD Almighty is his name:
3 I foretold the former things[e] long ago,
my mouth announced[f] them and I made them known;
then suddenly I acted, and they came to pass.
4 For I knew how stubborn[g] you were;
the sinews of your neck[h] were iron,
your forehead[i] was bronze.
5 Therefore I told you these things long ago;
before they happened I announced them to you
so that you could not say,
'My idols did them;[j]
my wooden image and metal god ordained them.'
6 You have heard these things; look at them all.
Will you not admit them?

"From now on I will tell you of new things,
of hidden things unknown to you.
7 They are created now, and not long ago;
you have not heard of them before today.
So you cannot say,
'Yes, I knew of them.'
8 You have neither heard nor understood;
from of old your ear has not been open.
Well do I know how treacherous you are;
you were called a rebel[k] from birth.
9 For my own name's sake I delay my wrath;[l]
for the sake of my praise I hold it back from you,
so as not to cut you off.[m]
10 See, I have refined you, though not as silver;
I have tested you in the furnace[n] of affliction.
11 For my own sake,[o] for my own sake, I do this.
How can I let myself be defamed?[p]
I will not yield my glory to another.[q]

12 "Listen[r] to me, O Jacob,
Israel, whom I have called:
I am he;
I am the first and I am the last.[s]
13 My own hand laid the foundations of the earth,[t]
and my right hand spread out the heavens;[u]
when I summon them,
they all stand up together.[v]

¹⁴"Come together,^a all of you, and listen:
  Which of ⌊the idols⌋ has foretold these things?
The LORD's chosen ally
  will carry out his purpose^b against Babylon;
  his arm will be against the Babylonians.^a
¹⁵I, even I, have spoken;
  yes, I have called^c him.
I will bring him,
  and he will succeed in his mission.

¹⁶"Come near^d me and listen to this:

"From the first announcement I have not spoken
    in secret;^e
  at the time it happens, I am there."

And now the Sovereign LORD has sent^f me,
  with his Spirit.

¹⁷This is what the LORD says—
  your Redeemer,^g the Holy One^h of Israel:
"I am the LORD your God,
  who teaches you what is best for you,
  who directsⁱ you in the way^j you should go.
¹⁸If only you had paid attention^k to my commands,
  your peace^l would have been like a river,
  your righteousness^m like the waves of the sea.
¹⁹Your descendants would have been like the sand,
  your children like its numberless grains;ⁿ
their name would never be cut off^o
  nor destroyed from before me."

²⁰Leave Babylon,
  flee^p from the Babylonians!
Announce this with shouts of joy^q
  and proclaim it.
Send it out to the ends of the earth;
  say, "The LORD has redeemed^r his servant Jacob."
²¹They did not thirst^s when he led them through
    the deserts;
  he made water flow^t for them from the rock;
he split the rock
  and water gushed out.^u

²²"There is no peace," says the LORD, "for the wicked."^v

a 14 Or *Chaldeans*; also in verse 20

48:14
a Isa 43:9
b Isa 46:10-11

48:15
c Isa 45:1

48:16
d Isa 41:1
e Isa 45:19
f Zec 2:9,11

48:17
g Isa 49:7
h Isa 43:14
i Isa 49:10
j Ps 32:8

48:18
k Dt 32:29
l Ps 119:165;
Isa 66:12
m Isa 45:8

48:19
n Ge 22:17
o Isa 56:5; 66:22

48:20
p Jer 50:8;
51:6,45;
Zec 2:6-7;
Rev 18:4
q Isa 49:13
r Isa 52:9; 63:9

48:21
s Isa 41:17
t Isa 30:25
u Ex 17:6;
Nu 20:11;
Ps 105:41;
Isa 35:6

48:22
v Isa 57:21

49:1
a Isa 44:24; 46:3;
Mt 1:20
b Isa 7:14; 9:6;
44:2;
Jer 1:5; Gal 1:15

Chapter 49 Theme

49

Listen to me, you islands;
  hear this, you distant nations:
Before I was born[a] the LORD called[b] me;
  from my birth he has made mention of my name.
[2]He made my mouth like a sharpened sword,[c]
  in the shadow of his hand he hid me;
he made me into a polished arrow
  and concealed me in his quiver.
[3]He said to me, "You are my servant,[d]
  Israel, in whom I will display my splendor.[e]"
[4]But I said, "I have labored to no purpose;
  I have spent my strength in vain[f] and for nothing.
Yet what is due me is in the LORD's hand,
  and my reward[g] is with my God."

[5]And now the LORD says—
  he who formed me in the womb to be his servant
to bring Jacob back to him
  and gather Israel[h] to himself,
for I am honored[i] in the eyes of the LORD
  and my God has been my strength—
[6]he says:
"It is too small a thing for you to be my servant
  to restore the tribes of Jacob
  and bring back those of Israel I have kept.
I will also make you a light for the Gentiles,[j]
  that you may bring my salvation to the ends of
    the earth."[k]

[7]This is what the LORD says—
  the Redeemer and Holy One of Israel[l]—
to him who was despised[m] and abhorred by
    the nation,
  to the servant of rulers:
"Kings[n] will see you and rise up,
  princes will see and bow down,
because of the LORD, who is faithful,
  the Holy One of Israel, who has chosen you."

[8]This is what the LORD says:

"In the time of my favor[o] I will answer you,
  and in the day of salvation I will help you;[p]
I will keep[q] you and will make you
  to be a covenant for the people,[r]

49:2
c Isa 11:4;
Rev 1:16

49:3
d Zec 3:8
e Isa 44:23

49:4
f Isa 65:23
g Isa 35:4

49:5
h Isa 11:12
i Isa 43:4

49:6
j Lk 2:32
k Ac 13:47*

49:7
l Isa 48:17
m Ps 22:6; 69:7-9
n Isa 52:15

49:8
o Ps 69:13
p 2Co 6:2*
q Isa 26:3
r Isa 42:6

to restore the land[a]
and to reassign its desolate inheritances,
[9]to say to the captives,[b] 'Come out,'
and to those in darkness, 'Be free!'

"They will feed beside the roads
and find pasture on every barren hill.[c]
[10]They will neither hunger nor thirst,[d]
nor will the desert heat or the sun beat upon them.[e]
He who has compassion[f] on them will guide them
and lead them beside springs[g] of water.
[11]I will turn all my mountains into roads,
and my highways[h] will be raised up.[i]
[12]See, they will come from afar[j]—
some from the north, some from the west,
some from the region of Aswan.[a]"

[13]Shout for joy, O heavens;
rejoice, O earth;
burst into song, O mountains![k]
For the LORD comforts[l] his people
and will have compassion on his afflicted ones.

[14]But Zion said, "The LORD has forsaken me,
the Lord has forgotten me."

[15]"Can a mother forget the baby at her breast
and have no compassion on the child she has borne?
Though she may forget,
I will not forget you![m]
[16]See, I have engraved[n] you on the palms of my hands;
your walls[o] are ever before me.
[17]Your sons hasten back,
and those who laid you waste[p] depart from you.
[18]Lift up your eyes and look around;
all your sons gather[q] and come to you.
As surely as I live,[r]" declares the LORD,
"you will wear[s] them all as ornaments;
you will put them on, like a bride.

[19]"Though you were ruined and made desolate[t]
and your land laid waste,[u]
now you will be too small for your people,[v]
and those who devoured you will be far away.
[20]The children born during your bereavement
will yet say in your hearing,

a 12 Dead Sea Scrolls; Masoretic Text Sinim

49:8
[a] Isa 44:26

49:9
[b] Isa 42:7; 61:1;
Lk 4:19
[c] Isa 41:18

49:10
[d] Isa 33:16
[e] Ps 121:6;
Rev 7:16
[f] Isa 14:1
[g] Isa 35:7

49:11
[h] Isa 11:16
[i] Isa 40:4

49:12
[j] Isa 43:5-6

49:13
[k] Isa 44:23
[l] Isa 40:1

49:15
[m] Isa 44:21

49:16
[n] SS 8:6
[o] Ps 48:12-13;
Isa 62:6

49:17
[p] Isa 10:6

49:18
[q] Isa 43:5; 54:7;
Isa 60:4
[r] Isa 45:23
[s] Isa 52:1

49:19
[t] Isa 54:1,3
[u] Isa 5:6
[v] Zec 10:10

'This place is too small for us;
　　give us more space to live in.'[a]
21Then you will say in your heart,
'Who bore me these?
　　I was bereaved and barren;
　　I was exiled and rejected.[b]
Who brought these up?
　　I was left[c] all alone,
　　but these—where have they come from?'"

22This is what the Sovereign LORD says:

"See, I will beckon to the Gentiles,
　　I will lift up my banner[d] to the peoples;
they will bring your sons in their arms
　　and carry your daughters on their shoulders.[e]
23Kings[f] will be your foster fathers,
　　and their queens your nursing mothers.[g]
They will bow down before you with their faces to the
　　　　ground;
　　they will lick the dust[h] at your feet.
Then you will know that I am the LORD;[i]
　　those who hope in me will not be disappointed."

24Can plunder be taken from warriors,[j]
　　or captives rescued from the fierce[a]?

25But this is what the LORD says:

"Yes, captives[k] will be taken from warriors,[l]
　　and plunder retrieved from the fierce;
I will contend with those who contend with you,
　　and your children I will save.[m]
26I will make your oppressors[n] eat[o] their own flesh;
　　they will be drunk on their own blood,[p] as with wine.
Then all mankind will know[q]
　　that I, the LORD, am your Savior,
　　your Redeemer, the Mighty One of Jacob."

Chapter 50 Theme

50
This is what the LORD says:

"Where is your mother's certificate of divorce[r]
　　with which I sent her away?
Or to which of my creditors
　　did I sell[s] you?

---

a 24 Dead Sea Scrolls, Vulgate and Syriac (see also Septuagint and verse 25); Masoretic Text righteous

### Cross references (margin)

49:20
a Isa 54:1-3

49:21
b Isa 5:13
c Isa 1:8

49:22
d Isa 11:10
e Isa 60:4

49:23
f Isa 60:3,10-11
g Isa 60:16
h Ps 72:9
i Mic 7:17

49:24
j Mt 12:29;
Lk 11:21

49:25
k Isa 14:2
l Jer 50:33-34
m Isa 25:9; 35:4

49:26
n Isa 9:4
o Isa 9:20
p Rev 16:6
q Eze 39:7

50:1
r Dt 24:1;
Jer 3:8; Hos 2:2
s Ne 5:5;
Mt 18:25

Because of your sins you were sold;[a]
   because of your transgressions your mother was
     sent away.
²When I came, why was there no one?
   When I called, why was there no one to answer?[b]
Was my arm too short[c] to ransom you?
   Do I lack the strength[d] to rescue you?
By a mere rebuke I dry up the sea,[e]
   I turn rivers into a desert;
their fish rot for lack of water
   and die of thirst.
³I clothe the sky with darkness
   and make sackcloth[f] its covering."

⁴The Sovereign LORD has given me an instructed tongue,[g]
   to know the word that sustains the weary.[h]
He wakens me morning by morning,[i]
   wakens my ear to listen like one being taught.
⁵The Sovereign LORD has opened my ears,[j]
   and I have not been rebellious;[k]
   I have not drawn back.
⁶I offered my back to those who beat[l] me,
   my cheeks to those who pulled out my beard;
I did not hide my face
   from mocking and spitting.[m]
⁷Because the Sovereign LORD helps[n] me,
   I will not be disgraced.
Therefore have I set my face like flint,[o]
   and I know I will not be put to shame.
⁸He who vindicates me is near.
   Who then will bring charges against me?[p]
   Let us face each other![q]
Who is my accuser?
   Let him confront me!
⁹It is the Sovereign LORD who helps[r] me.
   Who is he that will condemn me?
They will all wear out like a garment;
   the moths[s] will eat them up.

¹⁰Who among you fears the LORD
   and obeys the word of his servant?[t]
Let him who walks in the dark,
   who has no light,
trust[u] in the name of the LORD
   and rely on his God.
¹¹But now, all you who light fires
   and provide yourselves with flaming torches,[v]

50:1
a Dt 32:30;
Isa 52:3

50:2
b Isa 41:28
c Nu 11:23;
Isa 59:1
d Ge 18:14
e Ex 14:22;
Jos 3:16

50:3
f Rev 6:12

50:4
g Ex 4:12
h Mt 11:28
i Ps 5:3; 119:147;
143:8

50:5
j Isa 35:5
k Mt 26:39;
Jn 8:29; 14:31;
15:10; Ac 26:19;
Heb 5:8

50:6
l Isa 53:5;
Mt 27:30;
Mk 14:65;
15:19; Lk 22:63
m La 3:30;
Mt 26:67

50:7
n Isa 42:1
o Eze 3:8-9

50:8
p Isa 43:26;
Ro 8:32-34
q Isa 41:1

50:9
r Isa 41:10
s Job 13:28;
Isa 51:8

50:10
t Isa 49:3
u Isa 26:4

50:11
v Pr 26:18

go, walk in the light of your fires[a]
and of the torches you have set ablaze.
This is what you shall receive from my hand:
You will lie down in torment.[b]

Chapter 51 Theme _____

51 "Listen[c] to me, you who pursue righteousness[d]
and who seek the LORD:
Look to the rock from which you were cut
and to the quarry from which you were hewn;
[2]look to Abraham,[e] your father,
and to Sarah, who gave you birth.
When I called him he was but one,
and I blessed him and made him many.[f]
[3]The LORD will surely comfort[g] Zion
and will look with compassion on all her ruins;[h]
he will make her deserts like Eden,[i]
her wastelands like the garden of the LORD.
Joy and gladness[j] will be found in her,
thanksgiving and the sound of singing.

[4]"Listen to me, my people;[k]
hear me, my nation:
The law will go out from me;
my justice[l] will become a light to the nations.[m]
[5]My righteousness draws near speedily,
my salvation is on the way,[n]
and my arm[o] will bring justice to the nations.
The islands will look to me
and wait in hope for my arm.
[6]Lift up your eyes to the heavens,
look at the earth beneath;
the heavens will vanish like smoke,[p]
the earth will wear out like a garment[q]
and its inhabitants die like flies.
But my salvation will last forever,
my righteousness will never fail.

[7]"Hear me, you who know what is right,[r]
you people who have my law in your hearts:[s]
Do not fear the reproach of men
or be terrified by their insults.[t]
[8]For the moth will eat them up like a garment;[u]
the worm will devour them like wool.
But my righteousness will last forever,[v]
my salvation through all generations."

50:11
[a]Jas 3:6
[b]Isa 65:13-15

51:1
[c]Isa 46:3
[d]ver 7;
Ps 94:15;
Ro 9:30-31

51:2
[e]Isa 29:22;
Ro 4:16;
Heb 11:11
[f]Ge 12:2

51:3
[g]Isa 40:1
[h]Isa 52:9
[i]Ge 2:8
[j]Isa 25:9; 66:10

51:4
[k]Ps 50:7
[l]Isa 2:4
[m]Isa 42:4,6

51:5
[n]Isa 46:13
[o]Isa 40:10;
63:1,5

51:6
[p]Mt 24:35;
2Pe 3:10
[q]Ps 102:25-26

51:7
[r]ver 1
[s]Ps 37:31
[t]Mt 5:11;
Ac 5:41

51:8
[u]Isa 50:9
[v]ver 6

⁹Awake, awake! Clothe yourself with strength,^a
  O arm of the LORD;
awake, as in days gone by,
  as in generations of old.^b
Was it not you who cut Rahab to pieces,
  who pierced that monster^c through?
¹⁰Was it not you who dried up the sea,^d
  the waters of the great deep,
who made a road in the depths of the sea
  so that the redeemed might cross over?
¹¹The ransomed^e of the LORD will return.
  They will enter Zion with singing;
  everlasting joy will crown their heads.
Gladness and joy^f will overtake them,
  and sorrow and sighing will flee away.^g

¹²"I, even I, am he who comforts^h you.
  Who are you that you fear mortal men,ⁱ
  the sons of men, who are but grass,^j
¹³that you forget^k the LORD your Maker,^l
  who stretched out the heavens^m
  and laid the foundations of the earth,
that you live in constant terrorⁿ every day
  because of the wrath of the oppressor,
  who is bent on destruction?
For where is the wrath of the oppressor?
¹⁴ The cowering prisoners will soon be set free;
they will not die in their dungeon,
  nor will they lack bread.^o
¹⁵For I am the LORD your God,
  who churns up the sea^p so that its waves roar—
  the LORD Almighty is his name.
¹⁶I have put my words in your mouth^q
  and covered you with the shadow of my hand^r—
I who set the heavens in place,
  who laid the foundations of the earth,
  and who say to Zion, 'You are my people.' "

¹⁷Awake, awake!^s
  Rise up, O Jerusalem,
you who have drunk from the hand of the LORD
  the cup of his wrath,^t
you who have drained to its dregs
  the goblet that makes men stagger.^u
¹⁸Of all the sons^v she bore
  there was none to guide her;^w
of all the sons she reared
  there was none to take her by the hand.

51:9
^aIsa 52:1
^bDt 4:34
^cPs 74:13

51:10
^dEx 14:22

51:11
^eIsa 35:9
^fJer 33:11
^gRev 7:17

51:12
^h2Co 1:4
ⁱPs 118:6;
Isa 2:22
^jIsa 40:6-7;
1Pe 1:24

51:13
^kIsa 17:10
^lIsa 45:11
^mPs 104:2;
Isa 48:13
ⁿIsa 7:4

51:14
^oIsa 49:10

51:15
^pJer 31:35

51:16
^qDt 18:18;
Isa 59:21
^rEx 33:22

51:17
^sIsa 52:1
^tJob 21:20;
Rev 14:10; 16:19
^uPs 60:3

51:18
^vPs 88:18
^wIsa 49:21

¹⁹These double calamities[a] have come upon you—
who can comfort you?—
ruin and destruction, famine[b] and sword—
who can[a] console you?
²⁰Your sons have fainted;
they lie at the head of every street,[c]
like antelope caught in a net.
They are filled with the wrath of the LORD
and the rebuke of your God.

²¹Therefore hear this, you afflicted one,
made drunk,[d] but not with wine.
²²This is what your Sovereign LORD says,
your God, who defends[e] his people:
"See, I have taken out of your hand
the cup[f] that made you stagger;
from that cup, the goblet of my wrath,
you will never drink again.
²³I will put it into the hands of your tormentors,[g]
who said to you,
'Fall prostrate[h] that we may walk[i] over you.'
And you made your back like the ground,
like a street to be walked over."

Chapter 52 Theme _____

52

Awake, awake,[j] O Zion,
clothe yourself with strength.[k]
Put on your garments of splendor,[l]
O Jerusalem, the holy city.[m]
The uncircumcised and defiled
will not enter you again.[n]
²Shake off your dust;[o]
rise up, sit enthroned, O Jerusalem.
Free yourself from the chains on your neck,
O captive Daughter of Zion.

³For this is what the LORD says:

"You were sold for nothing,[p]
and without money[q] you will be redeemed."

⁴For this is what the Sovereign LORD says:

"At first my people went down to Egypt[r] to live;
lately, Assyria has oppressed them.

⁵"And now what do I have here?" declares the LORD.

51:19
[a] Isa 47:9
[b] Isa 14:30

51:20
[c] Isa 5:25;
Jer 14:16

51:21
[d] ver 17; Isa 29:9

51:22
[e] Isa 49:25
[f] ver 17

51:23
[g] Isa 49:26;
Jer 25:15-17,
26,28; 49:12
[h] Zec 12:2
[i] Jos 10:24

52:1
[j] Isa 51:17
[k] Isa 51:9
[l] Ex 28:2,40;
Ps 110:3;
Zec 3:4
[m] Ne 11:1;
Mt 4:5; Rev 21:2
[n] Na 1:15;
Rev 21:27

52:2
[o] Isa 29:4

52:3
[p] Ps 44:12
[q] Isa 45:13

52:4
[r] Ge 46:6

a 19 Dead Sea Scrolls, Septuagint, Vulgate and Syriac; Masoretic Text / *how can I*

"For my people have been taken away for nothing,
and those who rule them mock,[a]"

declares the LORD.

"And all day long
my name is constantly blasphemed.[a]
⁶Therefore my people will know[b] my name;
therefore in that day they will know
that it is I who foretold it.
Yes, it is I."

⁷How beautiful on the mountains
are the feet of those who bring good news,[c]
who proclaim peace,[d]
who bring good tidings,
who proclaim salvation,
who say to Zion,
"Your God reigns!"[e]
⁸Listen! Your watchmen[f] lift up their voices;
together they shout for joy.
When the LORD returns to Zion,
they will see it with their own eyes.
⁹Burst into songs of joy[g] together,
you ruins[h] of Jerusalem,
for the LORD has comforted his people,
he has redeemed Jerusalem.[i]
¹⁰The LORD will lay bare his holy arm
in the sight of all the nations,[j]
and all the ends of the earth will see
the salvation[k] of our God.

¹¹Depart,[l] depart, go out from there!
Touch no unclean thing![m]
Come out from it and be pure,[n]
you who carry the vessels of the LORD.
¹²But you will not leave in haste[o]
or go in flight;
for the LORD will go before you,[p]
the God of Israel will be your rear guard.[q]

¹³See, my servant[r] will act wisely[b];
he will be raised and lifted up and highly exalted.[s]
¹⁴Just as there were many who were appalled at him[c]—
his appearance was so disfigured beyond that of
any man
and his form marred beyond human likeness—

Cross references

52:5 [a]Eze 36:20; Ro 2:24*

52:6 [b]Isa 49:23

52:7 [c]Isa 40:9; Ro 10:15*
[d]Na 1:15; Eph 6:15
[e]Ps 93:1

52:8 [f]Isa 62:6

52:9 [g]Ps 98:4
[h]Isa 51:3
[i]Isa 48:20

52:10 [j]Isa 66:18
[k]Ps 98:2-3; Lk 3:6

52:11 [l]Isa 48:20
[m]Isa 1:16; 2Co 6:17*
[n]2Ti 2:19

52:12 [o]Ex 12:11
[p]Mic 2:13
[q]Ex 14:19

52:13 [r]Isa 42:1
[s]Isa 57:15; Php 2:9

---

[a]5 Dead Sea Scrolls and Vulgate; Masoretic Text *wail*   [b]13 Or *will prosper*   [c]14 Hebrew *you*

¹⁵so will he sprinkle many nations,^a
 and kings will shut their mouths because of him.
For what they were not told, they will see,
 and what they have not heard, they will understand.^a

Chapter 53 Theme

53 Who has believed our message^b
 and to whom has the arm of the LORD been revealed?^c
²He grew up before him like a tender shoot,
 and like a root out of dry ground.
He had no beauty or majesty to attract us to him,
 nothing in his appearance^d that we should desire him.
³He was despised and rejected by men,
 a man of sorrows, and familiar with suffering.^e
Like one from whom men hide their faces
 he was despised,^f and we esteemed him not.

⁴Surely he took up our infirmities
 and carried our sorrows,^g
yet we considered him stricken by God,^h
 smitten by him, and afflicted.
⁵But he was pierced for our transgressions,ⁱ
 he was crushed for our iniquities;
the punishment that brought us peace was upon him,
 and by his wounds we are healed.^j
⁶We all, like sheep, have gone astray,
 each of us has turned to his own way;
and the LORD has laid on him
 the iniquity of us all.

⁷He was oppressed and afflicted,
 yet he did not open his mouth;^k
he was led like a lamb to the slaughter,
 and as a sheep before her shearers is silent,
 so he did not open his mouth.
⁸By oppression^b and judgment he was taken away.
 And who can speak of his descendants?
For he was cut off from the land of the living;^l
 for the transgression^m of my people he was stricken.^c
⁹He was assigned a grave with the wicked,
 and with the richⁿ in his death,
though he had done no violence,^o
 nor was any deceit in his mouth.^p

52:15
^aRo 15:21*;
Eph 3:4-5

53:1
^bRo 10:16*
^cJn 12:38*

53:2
^dIsa 52:14

53:3
^ever 4,10;
Lk 18:31-33
^fPs 22:6;
Jn 1:10-11

53:4
^gMt 8:17*
^hJn 19:7

53:5
ⁱRo 4:25;
1Co 15:3;
Heb 9:28
^j1Pe 2:24-25

53:7
^kMk 14:61

53:8
^lDa 9:26;
Ac 8:32-33*
^mver 12

53:9
ⁿMt 27:57-60
^oIsa 42:1-3
^p1Pe 2:22*

---

^a15 Hebrew; Septuagint *so will many nations marvel at him*   ^b8 Or *From arrest*   ^c8 Or *away.
/ Yet who of his generation considered / that he was cut off from the land of the living / for the
transgression of my people, / to whom the blow was due?*

¹⁰Yet it was the LORD's will[a] to crush[b] him and cause him
to suffer,[c]
and though the LORD makes[a] his life a guilt offering,
he will see his offspring[d] and prolong his days,
and the will of the LORD will prosper in his hand.
¹¹After the suffering[e] of his soul,
he will see the light ⌊of life⌋[b] and be satisfied[c];
by his knowledge[d] my righteous servant will justify[f] many,
and he will bear their iniquities.
¹²Therefore I will give him a portion among the great,[e][g]
and he will divide the spoils with the strong,[f]
because he poured out his life unto death,[h]
and was numbered with the transgressors.[i]
For he bore the sin of many,
and made intercession for the transgressors.

Chapter 54 Theme

54 "Sing, O barren woman,
you who never bore a child;
burst into song, shout for joy,
you who were never in labor;
because more are the children[j] of the desolate woman
than of her who has a husband,[k]"
says the LORD.

²"Enlarge the place of your tent,[l]
stretch your tent curtains wide,
do not hold back;
lengthen your cords,
strengthen your stakes.[m]
³For you will spread out to the right and to the left;
your descendants will dispossess nations
and settle in their desolate[n] cities.

⁴"Do not be afraid; you will not suffer shame.
Do not fear disgrace; you will not be humiliated.
You will forget the shame of your youth
and remember no more the reproach[o] of your
widowhood.
⁵For your Maker is your husband[p]—
the LORD Almighty is his name—
the Holy One of Israel is your Redeemer;[q]
he is called the God of all the earth.[r]

53:10 [a]Isa 46:10 [b]ver 5 [c]ver 3 [d]Ps 22:30
53:11 [e]Jn 10:14-18 [f]Ro 5:18-19
53:12 [g]Php 2:9 [h]Mt 26:28, 38,39,42 [i]Mk 15:27*; Lk 22:37*; 23:32
54:1 [j]Isa 49:20 [k]1Sa 2:5; Gal 4:27*
54:2 [l]Isa 49:19-20 [m]Ex 35:18; 39:40
54:3 [n]Isa 49:19
54:4 [o]Isa 51:7
54:5 [p]Jer 3:14 [q]Isa 48:17 [r]Isa 6:3

a 10 Hebrew *though you make*   b 11 Dead Sea Scrolls (see also Septuagint); Masoretic Text does not have *the light ⌊of life⌋*.   c 11 Or (with Masoretic Text) ¹¹*He will see the result of the suffering of his soul / and be satisfied*   d 11 Or *by knowledge of him*   e 12 Or *many*   f 12 Or *numerous*

54:6
a Isa 49:14-21
b Isa 50:1-2;
62:4,12

⁶The LORD will call you back*ᵃ*
  as if you were a wife deserted*ᵇ* and distressed in spirit—
a wife who married young,
  only to be rejected," says your God.

54:7
c Isa 26:20
d Isa 49:18

⁷"For a brief moment*ᶜ* I abandoned you,
  but with deep compassion I will bring you back.*ᵈ*
⁸In a surge of anger*ᵉ*
  I hid my face from you for a moment,
but with everlasting kindness*ᶠ*
  I will have compassion on you,"
  says the LORD your Redeemer.

54:8
e Isa 60:10
f ver 10

⁹"To me this is like the days of Noah,
  when I swore that the waters of Noah would never
    again cover the earth.*ᵍ*
So now I have sworn not to be angry*ʰ* with you,
  never to rebuke you again.

54:9
g Ge 8:21
h Isa 12:1

¹⁰Though the mountains be shaken*ⁱ*
  and the hills be removed,
yet my unfailing love for you will not be shaken*ʲ*
  nor my covenant*ᵏ* of peace be removed,"
  says the LORD, who has compassion*ˡ* on you.

54:10
i Ps 46:2
j Isa 51:6
k Ps 89:34
l ver 8

¹¹"O afflicted*ᵐ* city, lashed by storms*ⁿ* and not comforted,*ᵒ*
  I will build you with stones of turquoise,*ᵃ ᵖ*
  your foundations*�q* with sapphires.*ᵇ*
¹²I will make your battlements of rubies,
  your gates of sparkling jewels,
  and all your walls of precious stones.

54:11
m Isa 14:32
n Isa 28:2; 29:6
o Isa 51:19
p 1Ch 29:2;
Rev 21:18
q Isa 28:16;
Rev 21:19-20

¹³All your sons will be taught by the LORD,*ʳ*
  and great will be your children's peace.*ˢ*
¹⁴In righteousness you will be established:
Tyranny*ᵗ* will be far from you;
  you will have nothing to fear.
Terror will be far removed;
  it will not come near you.

54:13
r Jn 6:45*
s Isa 48:18

¹⁵If anyone does attack you, it will not be my doing;
  whoever attacks you will surrender*ᵘ* to you.

54:14
t Isa 9:4

¹⁶"See, it is I who created the blacksmith
  who fans the coals into flame
  and forges a weapon fit for its work.
And it is I who have created the destroyer to work havoc;
¹⁷ no weapon forged against you will prevail,*ᵛ*
  and you will refute*ʷ* every tongue that accuses you.

54:15
u Isa 41:11-16

54:17
v Isa 29:8
w Isa 45:24-25

a 11 The meaning of the Hebrew for this word is uncertain. *b 11* Or *lapis lazuli*

This is the heritage of the servants of the LORD,
　　and this is their vindication from me,"

　　　　　　　　　　　　　　　　　　　declares the LORD.

Chapter 55 Theme

55 "Come, all you who are thirsty,[a]
　　come to the waters;
and you who have no money,
　　come, buy[b] and eat!
Come, buy wine and milk[c]
　　without money and without cost.[d]
[2]Why spend money on what is not bread,
　　and your labor on what does not satisfy?[e]
Listen, listen to me, and eat what is good,[f]
　　and your soul will delight in the richest of fare.
[3]Give ear and come to me;
　　hear me, that your soul may live.[g]
I will make an everlasting covenant[h] with you,
　　my faithful love[i] promised to David.[j]
[4]See, I have made him a witness to the peoples,
　　a leader and commander[k] of the peoples.
[5]Surely you will summon nations[l] you know not,
　　and nations that do not know you will hasten to you,
because of the LORD your God,
　　the Holy One of Israel,
　　for he has endowed you with splendor."[m]

[6]Seek the LORD while he may be found;[n]
　　call[o] on him while he is near.
[7]Let the wicked forsake his way
　　and the evil man his thoughts.[p]
Let him turn[q] to the LORD, and he will have mercy[r] on him,
　　and to our God, for he will freely pardon.[s]

[8]"For my thoughts are not your thoughts,
　　neither are your ways my ways,"[t]

　　　　　　　　　　　　　　　　　　　declares the LORD.

[9]"As the heavens are higher than the earth,[u]
　　so are my ways higher than your ways
　　and my thoughts than your thoughts.
[10]As the rain[v] and the snow
　　come down from heaven,
and do not return to it
　　without watering the earth
and making it bud and flourish,
　　so that it yields seed for the sower and bread for
　　　the eater,[w]

55:1
[a] Jn 4:14; 7:37
[b] La 5:4;
Mt 13:44;
Rev 3:18
[c] SS 5:1
[d] Hos 14:4;
Mt 10:8;
Rev 21:6

55:2
[e] Ps 22:26;
Ecc 6:2;
Hos 8:7
[f] Isa 1:19

55:3
[g] Lev 18:5;
Ro 10:5
[h] Isa 61:8
[i] Isa 54:8
[j] Ac 13:34*

55:4
[k] Jer 30:9;
Eze 34:23-24

55:5
[l] Isa 49:6
[m] Isa 60:9

55:6
[n] Ps 32:6;
Isa 49:8;
2Co 6:1-2
[o] Isa 65:24

55:7
[p] Isa 32:7; 59:7
[q] Isa 44:22
[r] Isa 54:10
[s] Isa 1:18; 40:2

55:8
[t] Isa 53:6

55:9
[u] Ps 103:11

55:10
[v] Isa 30:23
[w] 2Co 9:10

55:11
a Isa 45:23
b Isa 44:26

[11]so is my word that goes out from my mouth:
>> It will not return to me empty,[a]
> but will accomplish what I desire
>> and achieve the purpose[b] for which I sent it.

55:12
c Isa 54:10,13
d 1Ch 16:33
e Ps 98:8

[12]You will go out in joy
>> and be led forth in peace;[c]
> the mountains and hills
>> will burst into song before you,
> and all the trees[d] of the field
>> will clap their hands.[e]

55:13
f Isa 5:6
g Isa 41:19
h Isa 63:12

[13]Instead of the thornbush will grow the pine tree,
>> and instead of briers[f] the myrtle[g] will grow.
> This will be for the LORD's renown,[h]
>> for an everlasting sign,
>> which will not be destroyed."

Chapter 56 Theme

56

This is what the LORD says:

56:1
i Isa 1:17
j Ps 85:9

> "Maintain justice[i]
>> and do what is right,
> for my salvation[j] is close at hand
>> and my righteousness will soon be revealed.
> [2]Blessed[k] is the man who does this,
>> the man who holds it fast,
> who keeps the Sabbath[l] without desecrating it,
>> and keeps his hand from doing any evil."

56:2
k Ps 119:2
l Ex 20:8,10;
Isa 58:13

[3]Let no foreigner who has bound himself to the LORD say,
>> "The LORD will surely exclude me from his people."
> And let not any eunuch[m] complain,
>> "I am only a dry tree."

56:3
m Jer 38:7fn;
Ac 8:27

[4]For this is what the LORD says:

> "To the eunuchs who keep my Sabbaths,
>> who choose what pleases me
>> and hold fast to my covenant—
> [5]to them I will give within my temple and its walls[n]
>> a memorial and a name
>> better than sons and daughters;
> I will give them an everlasting name
>> that will not be cut off.[o]
> [6]And foreigners who bind themselves to the LORD
>> to serve[p] him,
> to love the name of the LORD,
>> and to worship him,

56:5
n Isa 26:1; 60:18
o Isa 48:19;
55:13

56:6
p Isa 60:7,10;
61:5

all who keep the Sabbath[a] without desecrating it
    and who hold fast to my covenant—
[7]these I will bring to my holy mountain[b]
    and give them joy in my house of prayer.
Their burnt offerings and sacrifices[c]
    will be accepted on my altar;
for my house will be called
    a house of prayer for all nations.[d]"[e]
[8]The Sovereign LORD declares—
    he who gathers the exiles of Israel:
"I will gather[f] still others to them
    besides those already gathered."

[9]Come, all you beasts of the field,[g]
    come and devour, all you beasts of the forest!
[10]Israel's watchmen[h] are blind,
    they all lack knowledge;
they are all mute dogs,
    they cannot bark;
they lie around and dream,
    they love to sleep.[i]
[11]They are dogs with mighty appetites;
    they never have enough.
They are shepherds[j] who lack understanding;[k]
    they all turn to their own way,
    each seeks his own gain.[l]
[12]"Come," each one cries, "let me get wine!
    Let us drink our fill of beer!
And tomorrow will be like today,
    or even far better."[m]

Chapter 57 Theme

57

The righteous perish,[n]
    and no one ponders it in his heart;[o]
devout men are taken away,
    and no one understands
that the righteous are taken away
    to be spared from evil.[p]
[2]Those who walk uprightly[q]
    enter into peace;
    they find rest as they lie in death.

[3]"But you—come here, you sons of a sorceress,
    you offspring of adulterers[r] and prostitutes![s]
[4]Whom are you mocking?
    At whom do you sneer
    and stick out your tongue?

56:6
[a] ver 2,4

56:7
[b] Isa 2:2
[c] Ro 12:1;
Heb 13:15
[d] Mt 21:13*;
Lk 19:46*
[e] Mk 11:17*

56:8
[f] Isa 11:12;
60:3-11;
Jn 10:16

56:9
[g] Isa 18:6;
Jer 12:9

56:10
[h] Eze 3:17
[i] Na 3:18

56:11
[j] Eze 34:2
[k] Isa 1:3
[l] Isa 57:17;
Eze 13:19;
Mic 3:11

56:12
[m] Ps 10:6;
Lk 12:18-19

57:1
[n] Ps 12:1
[o] Isa 42:25
[p] 2Ki 22:20

57:2
[q] Isa 26:7

57:3
[r] Mt 16:4
[s] Isa 1:21

Are you not a brood of rebels,
the offspring of liars?
⁵You burn with lust among the oaks
and under every spreading tree;ᵃ
you sacrifice your childrenᵇ in the ravines
and under the overhanging crags.
⁶⌊The idols⌋ᶜ among the smooth stones of the ravines
are your portion;
they, they are your lot.
Yes, to them you have poured out drink offeringsᵈ
and offered grain offerings.
In the light of these things, should I relent?ᵉ
⁷You have made your bed on a high and lofty hill;ᶠ
there you went up to offer your sacrifices.
⁸Behind your doors and your doorposts
you have put your pagan symbols.
Forsaking me, you uncovered your bed,
you climbed into it and opened it wide;
you made a pact with those whose beds you love,ᵍ
and you looked on their nakedness.ʰ
⁹You went to Molechᵃ with olive oil
and increased your perfumes.
You sent your ambassadorsᵇ ⁱ far away;
you descended to the graveᶜ itself!
¹⁰You were wearied by all your ways,
but you would not say, 'It is hopeless.'ʲ
You found renewal of your strength,
and so you did not faint.

¹¹"Whom have you so dreaded and fearedᵏ
that you have been false to me,
and have neither rememberedˡ me
nor pondered this in your hearts?
Is it not because I have long been silentᵐ
that you do not fear me?
¹²I will expose your righteousness and your works,ⁿ
and they will not benefit you.
¹³When you cry outᵒ for help,
let your collection ⌊of idols⌋ save you!
The wind will carry all of them off,
a mere breath will blow them away.
But the man who makes me his refuge
will inherit the land ᵖ
and possess my holy mountain."q

57:5 a 2Ki 16:4 b Lev 18:21; Ps 106:37-38; Eze 16:20
57:6 c Jer 3:9 d Jer 7:18 e Jer 5:9,29; 9:9
57:7 f Jer 3:6; Eze 16:16
57:8 g Eze 16:26; 23:7 h Eze 23:18
57:9 i Eze 23:16,40
57:10 j Jer 2:25; 18:12
57:11 k Pr 29:25 l Jer 2:32; 3:21 m Ps 50:21
57:12 n Isa 29:15; Mic 3:2-4,8
57:13 o Jer 22:20; 30:15 p Ps 37:9 q Isa 65:9-11

a 9 Or to the king   b 9 Or idols   c 9 Hebrew Sheol

1259

¹⁴And it will be said:

> "Build up, build up, prepare the road!
> Remove the obstacles out of the way of my people."^a

¹⁵For this is what the high and lofty^b One says—
> he who lives forever,^c whose name is holy:
> "I live in a high and holy place,
> but also with him who is contrite^d and lowly in spirit,^e
> to revive the spirit of the lowly
> and to revive the heart of the contrite.^f
¹⁶I will not accuse forever,
> nor will I always be angry,^g
> for then the spirit of man would grow faint before me—
> the breath of man that I have created.
¹⁷I was enraged by his sinful greed;^h
> I punished him, and hid my face in anger,
> yet he kept on in his willful ways.ⁱ
¹⁸I have seen his ways, but I will heal^j him;
> I will guide him and restore comfort^k to him,
¹⁹ creating praise on the lips^l of the mourners in Israel.
> Peace, peace,^m to those far and near,"ⁿ
> says the Lord. "And I will heal them."
²⁰But the wicked^o are like the tossing sea,
> which cannot rest,
> whose waves cast up mire and mud.
²¹"There is no peace,"^p says my God, "for the wicked."^q

Chapter 58 Theme

58 "Shout it aloud,^r do not hold back.
> Raise your voice like a trumpet.
> Declare to my people their rebellion^s
> and to the house of Jacob their sins.
²For day after day they seek^t me out;
> they seem eager to know my ways,
> as if they were a nation that does what is right
> and has not forsaken the commands of its God.
> They ask me for just decisions
> and seem eager for God to come near^u them.
³'Why have we fasted,'^v they say,
> 'and you have not seen it?
> Why have we humbled ourselves,
> and you have not noticed?'^w

> "Yet on the day of your fasting, you do as you please^x
> and exploit all your workers.
⁴Your fasting ends in quarreling and strife,^y
> and in striking each other with wicked fists.

57:14
^aIsa 62:10;
Jer 18:15

57:15
^bIsa 52:13
^cDt 33:27
^dPs 147:3
^ePs 34:18;
51:17; Isa 66:2
^fIsa 61:1

57:16
^gPs 85:5; 103:9;
Mic 7:18

57:17
^hIsa 56:11
ⁱIsa 1:4

57:18
^jIsa 30:26
^kIsa 61:1-3

57:19
^lIsa 6:7;
Heb 13:15
^mEph 2:17
ⁿAc 2:39

57:20
^oJob 18:5-21

57:21
^pIsa 59:8
^qIsa 48:22

58:1
^rIsa 40:6
^sIsa 48:8

58:2
^tIsa 48:1;
Tit 1:16; Jas 4:8
^uIsa 29:13

58:3
^vLev 16:29
^wMal 3:14
^xIsa 22:13;
Zec 7:5-6

58:4
^y1Ki 21:9-13;
Isa 59:6

You cannot fast as you do today
   and expect your voice to be heard^a on high.
⁵Is this the kind of fast^b I have chosen,
   only a day for a man to humble^c himself?
Is it only for bowing one's head like a reed
   and for lying on sackcloth and ashes?^d
Is that what you call a fast,
   a day acceptable to the LORD?

⁶"Is not this the kind of fasting I have chosen:
   to loose the chains of injustice^e
   and untie the cords of the yoke,
to set the oppressed^f free
   and break every yoke?
⁷Is it not to share your food with the hungry^g
   and to provide the poor wanderer with shelter^h—
when you see the naked, to clotheⁱ him,
   and not to turn away from your own flesh and blood?^j
⁸Then your light will break forth like the dawn,^k
   and your healing^l will quickly appear;
then your righteousness^a will go before you,
   and the glory of the LORD will be your rear guard.^m
⁹Then you will call,ⁿ and the LORD will answer;
   you will cry for help, and he will say: Here am I.

"If you do away with the yoke of oppression,
   with the pointing finger^o and malicious talk,^p
¹⁰and if you spend yourselves in behalf of the hungry
   and satisfy the needs of the oppressed,^q
then your light^r will rise in the darkness,
   and your night will become like the noonday.^s
¹¹The LORD will guide you always;
   he will satisfy your needs^t in a sun-scorched land
   and will strengthen your frame.
You will be like a well-watered garden,^u
   like a spring^v whose waters never fail.
¹²Your people will rebuild the ancient ruins^w
   and will raise up the age-old foundations;^x
you will be called Repairer of Broken Walls,
   Restorer of Streets with Dwellings.

¹³"If you keep your feet from breaking the Sabbath^y
   and from doing as you please on my holy day,
if you call the Sabbath a delight^z
   and the LORD's holy day honorable,

**Cross references (margin):**

58:4
^aIsa 59:2

58:5
^bZec 7:5
^c1Ki 21:27
^dJob 2:8

58:6
^eNe 5:10-11
^fJer 34:9

58:7
^gEze 18:16;
Lk 3:11
^hIsa 16:4;
Heb 13:2
ⁱJob 31:19-20;
Mt 25:36
^jGe 29:14;
Lk 10:31-32

58:8
^kJob 11:17
^lIsa 30:26
^mEx 14:19

58:9
ⁿPs 50:15
^oPr 6:13
^pPs 12:2;
Isa 59:13

58:10
^qDt 15:7-8
^rIsa 42:16
^sJob 11:17

58:11
^tPs 107:9
^uSS 4:15
^vJn 4:14

58:12
^wIsa 49:8
^xIsa 44:28

58:13
^yIsa 56:2
^zPs 84:2,10

---

^a8 Or *your righteous One*

and if you honor it by not going your own way
and not doing as you please or speaking idle words,
[14]then you will find your joy[a] in the LORD,
and I will cause you to ride on the heights[b] of the land
and to feast on the inheritance of your father Jacob."
The mouth of the LORD has spoken.[c]

Chapter 59 Theme

59 Surely the arm of the LORD is not too short[d] to save,
nor his ear too dull to hear.[e]
[2]But your iniquities have separated
you from your God;
your sins have hidden his face from you,
so that he will not hear.[f]
[3]For your hands are stained with blood,[g]
your fingers with guilt.
Your lips have spoken lies,
and your tongue mutters wicked things.
[4]No one calls for justice;
no one pleads his case with integrity.
They rely on empty arguments and speak lies;
they conceive trouble and give birth to evil.[h]
[5]They hatch the eggs of vipers
and spin a spider's web.[i]
Whoever eats their eggs will die,
and when one is broken, an adder is hatched.
[6]Their cobwebs are useless for clothing;
they cannot cover themselves with what they make.[j]
Their deeds are evil deeds,
and acts of violence[k] are in their hands.
[7]Their feet rush into sin;
they are swift to shed innocent blood.[l]
Their thoughts are evil thoughts;[m]
ruin and destruction mark their ways.[n]
[8]The way of peace they do not know;
there is no justice in their paths.
They have turned them into crooked roads;
no one who walks in them will know peace.[o]

[9]So justice is far from us,
and righteousness does not reach us.
We look for light, but all is darkness;[p]
for brightness, but we walk in deep shadows.
[10]Like the blind[q] we grope along the wall,
feeling our way like men without eyes.
At midday we stumble[r] as if it were twilight;
among the strong, we are like the dead.[s]

58:14
a Job 22:26
b Dt 32:13
c Isa 1:20

59:1
d Nu 11:23;
Isa 50:2
e Isa 58:9; 65:24

59:2
f Isa 1:15; 58:4

59:3
g Isa 1:15

59:4
h Job 15:35;
Ps 7:14

59:5
i Job 8:14

59:6
j Isa 28:20
k Isa 58:4

59:7
l Pr 6:17
m Mk 7:21-22
n Ro 3:15-17*

59:8
o Isa 57:21;
Lk 1:79

59:9
p Isa 5:30; 8:20

59:10
q Dt 28:29
r Isa 8:15
s La 3:6

59:11
a Isa 38:14;
Eze 7:16

¹¹We all growl like bears;
we moan mournfully like doves.ᵃ
We look for justice, but find none;
for deliverance, but it is far away.

59:12
b Ezr 9:6
c Isa 3:9

¹²For our offensesᵇ are many in your sight,
and our sins testifyᶜ against us.
Our offenses are ever with us,
and we acknowledge our iniquities:
¹³rebellion and treachery against the Lᴏʀᴅ,
turning our backsᵈ on our God,
fomenting oppressionᵉ and revolt,
uttering liesᶠ our hearts have conceived.

59:13
d Pr 30:9;
Mt 10:33;
Tit 1:16
e Isa 5:7
f Mk 7:21-22

¹⁴So justice is driven back,
and righteousnessᵍ stands at a distance;
truthʰ has stumbled in the streets,
honesty cannot enter.
¹⁵Truth is nowhere to be found,
and whoever shuns evil becomes a prey.

59:14
g Isa 1:21
h Isa 48:1

The Lᴏʀᴅ looked and was displeased
that there was no justice.
¹⁶He saw that there was no one,ⁱ
he was appalled that there was no one to intervene;
so his own arm worked salvationʲ for him,
and his own righteousness sustained him.

59:16
i Isa 41:28
j Ps 98:1;
Isa 63:5

¹⁷He put on righteousness as his breastplate,ᵏ
and the helmetˡ of salvation on his head;
he put on the garmentsᵐ of vengeance
and wrapped himself in zealⁿ as in a cloak.

59:17
k Eph 6:14
l Eph 6:17;
1Th 5:8
m Isa 63:3
n Isa 9:7

¹⁸According to what they have done,
so will he repay
wrath to his enemies
and retribution to his foes;
he will repay the islands their due.
¹⁹From the west,ᵒ men will fear the name of the Lᴏʀᴅ,
and from the rising of the sun,ᵖ they will revere
his glory.
For he will come like a pent-up flood
that the breath of the Lᴏʀᴅ drives along.ᵃ

59:19
o Isa 49:12
p Ps 113:3

²⁰"The Redeemer will come to Zion,
to those in Jacob who repent of their sins,"�q
declares the Lᴏʀᴅ.

59:20
q Ac 2:38-39;
Ro 11:26-27*

²¹"As for me, this is my covenant with them," says the Lᴏʀᴅ.
"My Spirit,ʳ who is on you, and my words that I have put in your

59:21
r Isa 11:2; 44:3

ᵃ 19 Or *When the enemy comes in like a flood, / the Spirit of the Lᴏʀᴅ will put him to flight* mouth will not depart from your mouth, or from the mouths of your children, or from the mouths of their descendants from this time on and forever," says the LORD.

Chapter 60 Theme _____

60

"Arise,[a] shine, for your light[b] has come,
   and the glory of the LORD rises upon you.
[2]See, darkness covers the earth
   and thick darkness[c] is over the peoples,
but the LORD rises upon you
   and his glory appears over you.
[3]Nations[d] will come to your light,
   and kings[e] to the brightness of your dawn.

[4]"Lift up your eyes and look about you:
   All assemble[f] and come to you;
your sons come from afar,
   and your daughters[g] are carried on the arm.[h]
[5]Then you will look and be radiant,
   your heart will throb and swell with joy;
the wealth on the seas will be brought to you,
   to you the riches of the nations will come.
[6]Herds of camels will cover your land,
   young camels of Midian[i] and Ephah.[j]
And all from Sheba[k] will come,
   bearing gold and incense[l]
   and proclaiming the praise[m] of the LORD.
[7]All Kedar's[n] flocks will be gathered to you,
   the rams of Nebaioth will serve you;
they will be accepted as offerings on my altar,
   and I will adorn my glorious temple.[o]

[8]"Who are these[p] that fly along like clouds,
   like doves to their nests?
[9]Surely the islands[q] look to me;
   in the lead are the ships of Tarshish,[a][r]
bringing[s] your sons from afar,
   with their silver and gold,
to the honor of the LORD your God,
   the Holy One of Israel,
   for he has endowed you with splendor.[t]

[10]"Foreigners[u] will rebuild your walls,
   and their kings[v] will serve you.

a 9 Or *the trading ships*

60:1
a Isa 52:2
b Eph 5:14

60:2
c Jer 13:16;
Col 1:13

60:3
d Isa 45:14;
Rev 21:24
e Isa 49:23

60:4
f Isa 11:12
g Isa 43:6
h Isa 49:20-22

60:6
i Ge 25:2
j Ge 25:4
k Ps 72:10
l Isa 43:23;
Mt 2:11
m Isa 42:10

60:7
n Ge 25:13
o ver 13;
Hag 2:3,7,9

60:8
p Isa 49:21

60:9
q Isa 11:11
r Isa 2:16 fn
s Isa 14:2; 43:6
t Isa 55:5

60:10
u Isa 14:1-2
v Isa 49:23;
Rev 21:24

Though in anger I struck you,
in favor I will show you compassion.[a]
[11] Your gates[b] will always stand open,
they will never be shut, day or night,
so that men may bring you the wealth of the nations[c]—
their kings[d] led in triumphal procession.
[12] For the nation or kingdom that will not serve[e] you
will perish;
it will be utterly ruined.

[13] "The glory of Lebanon[f] will come to you,
the pine, the fir and the cypress together,[g]
to adorn the place of my sanctuary;
and I will glorify the place of my feet.[h]
[14] The sons of your oppressors[i] will come bowing
before you;
all who despise you will bow down[j] at your feet
and will call you the City of the Lord,
Zion[k] of the Holy One of Israel.

[15] "Although you have been forsaken[l] and hated,
with no one traveling[m] through,
I will make you the everlasting pride[n]
and the joy[o] of all generations.
[16] You will drink the milk of nations
and be nursed[p] at royal breasts.
Then you will know that I, the Lord, am your Savior,
your Redeemer,[q] the Mighty One of Jacob.
[17] Instead of bronze I will bring you gold,
and silver in place of iron.
Instead of wood I will bring you bronze,
and iron in place of stones.
I will make peace your governor
and righteousness your ruler.
[18] No longer will violence be heard in your land,
nor ruin or destruction within your borders,
but you will call your walls Salvation[r]
and your gates Praise.
[19] The sun will no more be your light by day,
nor will the brightness of the moon shine on you,
for the Lord will be your everlasting light,[s]
and your God will be your glory.[t]
[20] Your sun[u] will never set again,
and your moon will wane no more;
the Lord will be your everlasting light,
and your days of sorrow[v] will end.

60:10
a Isa 54:8

60:11
b ver 18;
Isa 62:10;
Rev 21:25
c ver 5;
Rev 21:26
d Ps 149:8

60:12
e Isa 14:2

60:13
f Isa 35:2
g Isa 41:19
h 1Ch 28:2;
Ps 132:7

60:14
i Isa 14:2
j Isa 49:23;
Rev 3:9
k Heb 12:22

60:15
l Isa 1:7-9; 6:12
m Isa 33:8
n Isa 4:2
o Isa 65:18

60:16
p Isa 49:23;
66:11,12
q Isa 59:20

60:18
r Isa 26:1

60:19
s Rev 22:5
t Zec 2:5;
Rev 21:23

60:20
u Isa 30:26
v Isa 35:10

²¹Then will all your people be righteous[a]
  and they will possess[b] the land forever.
They are the shoot I have planted,[c]
  the work of my hands,[d]
  for the display of my splendor.[e]
²²The least of you will become a thousand,
  the smallest a mighty nation.
I am the Lord;
  in its time I will do this swiftly."

Chapter 61 Theme

61 The Spirit[f] of the Sovereign Lord is on me,
  because the Lord has anointed[g] me
  to preach good news to the poor.[h]
He has sent me to bind up[i] the brokenhearted,
  to proclaim freedom for the captives[j]
  and release from darkness for the prisoners,[a]
²to proclaim the year of the Lord's favor[k]
  and the day of vengeance[l] of our God,
to comfort[m] all who mourn,
³ and provide for those who grieve in Zion—
to bestow on them a crown of beauty
    instead of ashes,
the oil of gladness
    instead of mourning,
and a garment of praise
    instead of a spirit of despair.
They will be called oaks of righteousness,
  a planting of the Lord
  for the display of his splendor.[n]

⁴They will rebuild the ancient ruins[o]
  and restore the places long devastated;
they will renew the ruined cities
  that have been devastated for generations.
⁵Aliens[p] will shepherd your flocks;
  foreigners will work your fields and vineyards.
⁶And you will be called priests[q] of the Lord,
  you will be named ministers of our God.
You will feed on the wealth[r] of nations,
  and in their riches you will boast.

⁷Instead of their shame
  my people will receive a double[s] portion,

a 1 Hebrew; Septuagint *the blind*

60:21
[a] Rev 21:27
[b] Ps 37:11,22;
Isa 57:13; 61:7
[c] Mt 15:13
[d] Isa 19:25;
29:23;
Eph 2:10
[e] Isa 52:1

61:1
[f] Isa 11:2
[g] Ps 45:7
[h] Mt 11:5;
Lk 7:22
[i] Isa 57:15
[j] Isa 42:7; 49:9

61:2
[k] Isa 49:8;
Lk 4:18-19*
[l] Isa 34:8
[m] Isa 57:18;
Mt 5:4

61:3
[n] Isa 60:20-21

61:4
[o] Isa 49:8;
Eze 36:33;
Am 9:14

61:5
[p] Isa 14:1-2

61:6
[q] Ex 19:6;
1Pe 2:5
[r] Isa 60:11

61:7
[s] Isa 40:2;
Zec 9:12

61:8
a Ps 11:7;
Isa 5:16
b Isa 55:3

and instead of disgrace
    they will rejoice in their inheritance;
and so they will inherit a double portion in their land,
    and everlasting joy will be theirs.

8"For I, the LORD, love justice;*a*
    I hate robbery and iniquity.
In my faithfulness I will reward them
    and make an everlasting covenant*b* with them.
9Their descendants will be known among the nations
    and their offspring among the peoples.
All who see them will acknowledge
    that they are a people the LORD has blessed."

61:10
c Isa 25:9;
Hab 3:18
d Ps 132:9;
Isa 52:1
e Isa 49:18;
Rev 21:2

10I delight greatly in the LORD;
    my soul rejoices*c* in my God.
For he has clothed me with garments of salvation
    and arrayed me in a robe of righteousness,*d*
as a bridegroom adorns his head like a priest,
    and as a bride*e* adorns herself with her jewels.
11For as the soil makes the sprout come up
    and a garden causes seeds to grow,
so the Sovereign LORD will make righteousness*f*
        and praise
    spring up before all nations.

61:11
f Ps 85:11

62:1
g Isa 1:26

Chapter 62 Theme

62 For Zion's sake I will not keep silent,
    for Jerusalem's sake I will not remain quiet,
till her righteousness*g* shines out like the dawn,
    her salvation like a blazing torch.
2The nations*h* will see your righteousness,
    and all kings your glory;
you will be called by a new name*i*
    that the mouth of the LORD will bestow.
3You will be a crown*j* of splendor in the LORD's hand,
    a royal diadem in the hand of your God.
4No longer will they call you Deserted,*k*
    or name your land Desolate.
But you will be called Hephzibah,*a*
    and your land Beulah*b*;
for the LORD will take delight*l* in you,
    and your land will be married.*m*
5As a young man marries a maiden,
    so will your sons*c* marry you;

62:2
h Isa 52:10; 60:3
i ver 4,12

62:3
j Isa 28:5;
Zec 9:16;
1Th 2:19

62:4
k Isa 54:6
l Jer 32:41;
Zep 3:17
m Jer 3:14;
Hos 2:19

a 4 Hephzibah means *my delight is in her.*   *b 4* Beulah means *married.*   *c 5* Or *Builder*

as a bridegroom rejoices over his bride,
    so will your God rejoice[a] over you.

[6]I have posted watchmen[b] on your walls, O Jerusalem;
    they will never be silent day or night.
You who call on the LORD,
    give yourselves no rest,
[7]and give him no rest[c] till he establishes Jerusalem
    and makes her the praise of the earth.

[8]The LORD has sworn by his right hand
    and by his mighty arm:
"Never again will I give your grain[d]
    as food for your enemies,
and never again will foreigners drink the new wine
    for which you have toiled;
[9]but those who harvest it will eat it
    and praise the LORD,
and those who gather the grapes will drink it
    in the courts of my sanctuary."

[10]Pass through, pass through the gates![e]
    Prepare the way for the people.
Build up, build up the highway![f] [g]
    Remove the stones.
Raise a banner[h] for the nations.

[11]The LORD has made proclamation
    to the ends of the earth:
"Say to the Daughter of Zion,[i]
    'See, your Savior comes![j]
See, his reward is with him,
    and his recompense accompanies him.'"[k]
[12]They will be called[l] the Holy People,[m]
    the Redeemed[n] of the LORD;
and you will be called Sought After,
    the City No Longer Deserted.[o]

Chapter 63 Theme

63

Who is this coming from Edom,
    from Bozrah,[p] with his garments stained crimson?
Who is this, robed in splendor,
    striding forward in the greatness of his strength?

"It is I, speaking in righteousness,
    mighty to save."[q]

[2]Why are your garments red,
    like those of one treading the winepress?

62:5
[a]Isa 65:19

62:6
[b]Isa 52:8;
Eze 3:17

62:7
[c]Mt 15:21-28;
Lk 18:1-8

62:8
[d]Dt 28:30-33;
Isa 1:7; Jer 5:17

62:10
[e]Isa 60:11
[f]Isa 57:14
[g]Isa 11:16
[h]Isa 11:10

62:11
[i]Zec 9:9;
Mt 21:5
[j]Rev 22:12
[k]Isa 40:10

62:12
[l]ver 4
[m]1Pe 2:9
[n]Isa 35:9
[o]Isa 42:16

63:1
[p]Am 1:12
[q]Zep 3:17

63:3
a Rev 14:20;
19:15
b Isa 22:5
c Rev 19:13

3"I have trodden the winepress*a* alone;
    from the nations no one was with me.
I trampled them in my anger
    and trod them down in my wrath;*b*
their blood spattered my garments,*c*
    and I stained all my clothing.

63:5
d Isa 41:28
e Ps 44:3; 98:1
f Isa 59:16

4For the day of vengeance was in my heart,
    and the year of my redemption has come.
5I looked, but there was no one*d* to help,
    I was appalled that no one gave support;
so my own arm*e* worked salvation for me,
    and my own wrath sustained me.*f*

63:6
g Isa 29:9
h Isa 34:3

6I trampled the nations in my anger;
    in my wrath I made them drunk*g*
and poured their blood*h* on the ground."

7I will tell of the kindnesses*i* of the LORD,
    the deeds for which he is to be praised,
    according to all the LORD has done for us—

63:7
i Isa 54:8
j Ps 51:1;
Eph 2:4

yes, the many good things he has done
    for the house of Israel,
    according to his compassion*j* and many kindnesses.
8He said, "Surely they are my people,*k*
    sons who will not be false to me";
    and so he became their Savior.

63:8
k Isa 51:4

9In all their distress he too was distressed,
    and the angel of his presence*l* saved them.
In his love and mercy he redeemed*m* them;
    he lifted them up and carried*n* them
    all the days of old.

63:9
l Ex 33:14
m Dt 7:7-8
n Dt 1:31

10Yet they rebelled*o*
    and grieved his Holy Spirit.*p*
So he turned and became their enemy*q*
    and he himself fought against them.

63:10
o Ps 78:40
p Ps 51:11;
Ac 7:51;
Eph 4:30
q Ps 106:40

11Then his people recalled*a* the days of old,
    the days of Moses and his people—
where is he who brought them through the sea,*r*
    with the shepherd of his flock?
Where is he who set
    his Holy Spirit*s* among them,

63:11
r Ex 14:22,30
s Nu 11:17

12who sent his glorious arm of power
    to be at Moses' right hand,
who divided the waters*t* before them,
    to gain for himself everlasting renown,

63:12
t Ex 14:21-22;
Isa 11:15

a 11 Or *But may he recall*

¹³who led^a them through the depths?
>> Like a horse in open country,
>>> they did not stumble;^b
¹⁴like cattle that go down to the plain,
>> they were given rest by the Spirit of the LORD.
> This is how you guided your people
>> to make for yourself a glorious name.

¹⁵Look down from heaven^c and see
>> from your lofty throne,^d holy and glorious.
> Where are your zeal^e and your might?
>> Your tenderness and compassion^f are withheld from us.
¹⁶But you are our Father,
>> though Abraham does not know us
>> or Israel acknowledge^g us;
> you, O LORD, are our Father,
>> our Redeemer^h from of old is your name.
¹⁷Why, O LORD, do you make us wander from your ways
>> and harden our hearts so we do not revereⁱ you?
> Return^j for the sake of your servants,
>> the tribes that are your inheritance.
¹⁸For a little while your people possessed your holy place,
>> but now our enemies have trampled down your
>>> sanctuary.^k
¹⁹We are yours from of old;
>> but you have not ruled over them,
>> they have not been called by your name.^a

Chapter 64 Theme

64 Oh, that you would rend the heavens^l and come down,^m
>> that the mountainsⁿ would tremble before you!
> ²As when fire sets twigs ablaze
>> and causes water to boil,
> come down to make your name known to your enemies
>> and cause the nations to quake^o before you!
> ³For when you did awesome^p things that we
>>> did not expect,
>> you came down, and the mountains trembled
>>> before you.
> ⁴Since ancient times no one has heard,
>> no ear has perceived,
> no eye has seen any God besides you,
>> who acts on behalf of those who wait for him.^q
> ⁵You come to the help of those who gladly do right,^r
>> who remember your ways.

^a 19 Or *We are like those you have never ruled, / like those never called by your name*

63:13
^a Dt 32:12
^b Jer 31:9

63:15
^c Dt 26:15;
Ps 80:14
^d Ps 123:1
^e Isa 9:7; 26:11
^f Jer 31:20;
Hos 11:8

63:16
^g Job 14:21
^h Isa 41:14; 44:6

63:17
ⁱ Isa 29:13
^j Nu 10:36

63:18
^k Ps 74:3-8

64:1
^l Ps 18:9; 144:5
^m Mic 1:3
ⁿ Ex 19:18

64:2
^o Ps 99:1;
Jer 5:22; 33:9

64:3
^p Ps 65:5

64:4
^q Isa 30:18;
1Co 2:9*

64:5
^r Isa 26:8

64:6
a Isa 46:12; 48:1
b Ps 90:5-6

64:7
c Isa 59:4
d Dt 31:18;
Isa 1:15; 54:8
e Isa 9:18

64:8
f Isa 63:16
g Isa 29:16

64:9
h Isa 57:17;
60:10
i Isa 43:25

64:11
j Ps 74:3-7
k La 1:7,10

64:12
l Ps 74:10-11;
Isa 42:14
m Ps 83:1

65:1
n Hos 1:10;
Ro 9:24-26;
10:20*
o Eph 2:12

65:2
p Isa 1:2,23;
Ro 10:21*
q Ps 81:11-12;
Isa 66:18

65:3
r Job 1:11
s Isa 1:29

65:4
t Lev 11:7

65:5
u Mt 9:11;
Lk 7:39;
18:9-12

But when we continued to sin against them,
  you were angry.
  How then can we be saved?
6 All of us have become like one who is unclean,
  and all our righteous[a] acts are like filthy rags;
we all shrivel up like a leaf,[b]
  and like the wind our sins sweep us away.
7 No one[c] calls on your name
  or strives to lay hold of you;
for you have hidden[d] your face from us
  and made us waste away[e] because of our sins.

8 Yet, O LORD, you are our Father.[f]
  We are the clay, you are the potter;[g]
  we are all the work of your hand.
9 Do not be angry[h] beyond measure, O LORD;
  do not remember our sins[i] forever.
Oh, look upon us, we pray,
  for we are all your people.
10 Your sacred cities have become a desert;
  even Zion is a desert, Jerusalem a desolation.
11 Our holy and glorious temple,[j] where our fathers
    praised you,
  has been burned with fire,
  and all that we treasured[k] lies in ruins.
12 After all this, O LORD, will you hold yourself back?[l]
  Will you keep silent[m] and punish us beyond measure?

Chapter 65 Theme

65 "I revealed myself to those who did not ask for me;
  I was found by those who did not seek me.[n]
To a nation[o] that did not call on my name,
  I said, 'Here am I, here am I.'
2 All day long I have held out my hands
  to an obstinate people,[p]
who walk in ways not good,
  pursuing their own imaginations[q]—
3 a people who continually provoke me
  to my very face,[r]
offering sacrifices in gardens[s]
  and burning incense on altars of brick;
4 who sit among the graves
  and spend their nights keeping secret vigil;
who eat the flesh of pigs,[t]
  and whose pots hold broth of unclean meat;
5 who say, 'Keep away; don't come near me,
  for I am too sacred[u] for you!'

Such people are smoke in my nostrils,
 a fire that keeps burning all day.

6"See, it stands written before me:
 I will not keep silent[a] but will pay back[b] in full;
 I will pay it back into their laps[c]—
7both your sins[d] and the sins of your fathers,"[e]
 says the LORD.
"Because they burned sacrifices on the mountains
 and defied me on the hills,[f]
I will measure into their laps
 the full payment for their former deeds."

8This is what the LORD says:

"As when juice is still found in a cluster of grapes
 and men say, 'Don't destroy it,
 there is yet some good in it,'
so will I do in behalf of my servants;
 I will not destroy them all.
9I will bring forth descendants[g] from Jacob,
 and from Judah those who will possess[h] my mountains;
my chosen people will inherit them,
 and there will my servants live.[i]
10Sharon[j] will become a pasture for flocks,
 and the Valley of Achor[k] a resting place for herds,
 for my people who seek[l] me.

11"But as for you who forsake[m] the LORD
 and forget my holy mountain,
who spread a table for Fortune
 and fill bowls of mixed wine for Destiny,
12I will destine you for the sword,[n]
 and you will all bend down for the slaughter;
for I called but you did not answer,[o]
 I spoke but you did not listen.[p]
You did evil in my sight
 and chose what displeases me."

13Therefore this is what the Sovereign LORD says:

"My servants will eat,[q]
 but you will go hungry;
my servants will drink,
 but you will go thirsty;[r]
my servants will rejoice,
 but you will be put to shame.[s]
14My servants will sing
 out of the joy of their hearts,

65:6
a Ps 50:3
b Jer 16:18
c Ps 79:12

65:7
d Isa 22:14
e Ex 20:5
f Isa 57:7

65:9
g Isa 45:19
h Am 9:11-15
i Isa 32:18

65:10
j Isa 35:2
k Jos 7:26
l Isa 51:1

65:11
m Dt 29:24-25;
Isa 1:28

65:12
n Isa 27:1
o Pr 1:24-25;
Isa 41:28;
66:4
p 2Ch 36:15-16;
Jer 7:13

65:13
q Isa 1:19
r Isa 41:17
s Isa 44:9

65:14
a Mt 8:12;
Lk 13:28

but you will cry out[a]
>> from anguish of heart
>> and wail in brokenness of spirit.

[15]You will leave your name
>> to my chosen ones as a curse;[b]
> the Sovereign LORD will put you to death,
>> but to his servants he will give another name.

65:15
b Zec 8:13

[16]Whoever invokes a blessing in the land
>> will do so by the God of truth;[c]
> he who takes an oath in the land
>> will swear[d] by the God of truth.
> For the past troubles will be forgotten
>> and hidden from my eyes.

65:16
c Ps 31:5
d Isa 19:18

[17]"Behold, I will create
>> new heavens and a new earth.[e]
> The former things will not be remembered,[f]
>> nor will they come to mind.

65:17
e Isa 66:22;
2Pe 3:13
f Isa 43:18;
Jer 3:16

[18]But be glad and rejoice[g] forever
>> in what I will create,
> for I will create Jerusalem to be a delight
>> and its people a joy.

65:18
g Ps 98:1-9;
Isa 25:9

[19]I will rejoice[h] over Jerusalem
>> and take delight in my people;
> the sound of weeping and of crying[i]
>> will be heard in it no more.

65:19
h Isa 35:10; 62:5
i Isa 25:8;
Rev 7:17

[20]"Never again will there be in it
>> an infant who lives but a few days,
>> or an old man who does not live out his years;[j]
> he who dies at a hundred
>> will be thought a mere youth;
> he who fails to reach[a] a hundred
>> will be considered accursed.

65:20
j Ecc 8:13

[21]They will build houses[k] and dwell in them;
>> they will plant vineyards and eat their fruit.[l]
[22]No longer will they build houses and others live in them,
>> or plant and others eat.
> For as the days of a tree,[m]
>> so will be the days[n] of my people;
> my chosen ones will long enjoy
>> the works of their hands.

65:21
k Isa 32:18
l Isa 37:30;
Am 9:14

[23]They will not toil in vain
>> or bear children doomed to misfortune;
> for they will be a people blessed[o] by the LORD,
>> they and their descendants[p] with them.

65:22
m Ps 92:12-14
n Ps 21:4; 91:16

65:23
o Dt 28:3-12;
Isa 61:9
p Ac 2:39

a 20 Or *the sinner who reaches*

²⁴Before they call[a] I will answer;
    while they are still speaking[b] I will hear.
²⁵The wolf and the lamb[c] will feed together,
    and the lion will eat straw like the ox,
    but dust will be the serpent's[d] food.
They will neither harm nor destroy
    on all my holy mountain,"

                                            says the LORD.

Chapter 66 Theme _____

66 This is what the LORD says:

"Heaven is my throne,[e]
    and the earth is my footstool.[f]
Where is the house[g] you will build for me?
    Where will my resting place be?
²Has not my hand made all these things,[h]
    and so they came into being?"

                                    declares the LORD.

"This is the one I esteem:
    he who is humble and contrite in spirit,[i]
    and trembles at my word.[j]
³But whoever sacrifices a bull[k]
    is like one who kills a man,
and whoever offers a lamb,
    like one who breaks a dog's neck;
whoever makes a grain offering
    is like one who presents pig's blood,
and whoever burns memorial incense,[l]
    like one who worships an idol.
They have chosen their own ways,[m]
    and their souls delight in their abominations;
⁴so I also will choose harsh treatment for them
    and will bring upon them what they dread.[n]
For when I called, no one answered,[o]
    when I spoke, no one listened.
They did evil[p] in my sight
    and chose what displeases me."[q]

⁵Hear the word of the LORD,
    you who tremble at his word:
"Your brothers who hate[r] you,
    and exclude you because of my name, have said,
'Let the LORD be glorified,
    that we may see your joy!'

65:24
[a] Isa 55:6
[b] Da 9:20-23;
10:12

65:25
[c] Isa 11:6
[d] Ge 3:14;
Mic 7:17

66:1
[e] Mt 23:22
[f] 1Ki 8:27;
Mt 5:34-35
[g] 2Sa 7:7;
Jn 4:20-21;
Ac 7:49*; 17:24

66:2
[h] Isa 40:26;
Ac 7:50*
[i] Isa 57:15;
Mt 5:3-4;
Lk 18:13-14
[j] Ezr 9:4

66:3
[k] Isa 1:11
[l] Lev 2:2
[m] Isa 57:17

66:4
[n] Pr 10:24
[o] Pr 1:24;
Jer 7:13
[p] 2Ki 21:2,4,6
[q] Isa 65:12

66:5
[r] Ps 38:20;
Isa 60:15

66:5
a Lk 13:17

Yet they will be put to shame.[a]

⁶Hear that uproar from the city,
  hear that noise from the temple!
It is the sound of the LORD
  repaying[b] his enemies all they deserve.

66:6
b Isa 65:6;
Joel 3:7

⁷"Before she goes into labor,[c]
  she gives birth;
before the pains come upon her,
  she delivers a son.[d]

66:7
c Isa 54:1
d Rev 12:5

⁸Who has ever heard of such a thing?
  Who has ever seen[e] such things?
Can a country be born in a day
  or a nation be brought forth in a moment?
Yet no sooner is Zion in labor
  than she gives birth to her children.

66:8
e Isa 64:4

⁹Do I bring to the moment of birth[f]
  and not give delivery?" says the LORD.
"Do I close up the womb
  when I bring to delivery?" says your God.

66:9
f Isa 37:3

¹⁰"Rejoice[g] with Jerusalem and be glad for her,
  all you who love[h] her;
rejoice greatly with her,
  all you who mourn over her.

66:10
g Dt 32:43;
Ro 15:10
h Ps 26:8

¹¹For you will nurse[i] and be satisfied
  at her comforting breasts;
you will drink deeply
  and delight in her overflowing abundance."

66:11
i Isa 60:16

¹²For this is what the LORD says:

"I will extend peace to her like a river,[j]
  and the wealth[k] of nations like a flooding stream;
you will nurse and be carried[l] on her arm
  and dandled on her knees.
¹³As a mother comforts her child,
  so will I comfort[m] you;
and you will be comforted over Jerusalem."

66:12
j Isa 48:18
k Ps 72:3;
Isa 60:5; 61:6
l Isa 60:4

66:13
m Isa 40:1;
2Co 1:4

¹⁴When you see this, your heart will rejoice
  and you will flourish like grass;
the hand of the LORD will be made known to his servants,
  but his fury[n] will be shown to his foes.
¹⁵See, the LORD is coming with fire,
  and his chariots[o] are like a whirlwind;
he will bring down his anger with fury,
  and his rebuke[p] with flames of fire.

66:14
n Isa 10:5

66:15
o Ps 68:17
p Ps 9:5

¹⁶For with fire^a and with his sword^b
the LORD will execute judgment upon all men,
and many will be those slain by the LORD.

¹⁷"Those who consecrate and purify themselves to go into the gardens,^c following the one in the midst of^a those who eat the flesh of pigs^d and rats and other abominable things—they will meet their end^e together," declares the LORD.

¹⁸"And I, because of their actions and their imaginations, am about to come^b and gather all nations and tongues, and they will come and see my glory.

¹⁹"I will set a sign^f among them, and I will send some of those who survive to the nations—to Tarshish,^g to the Libyans^c and Lydians^h (famous as archers), to Tubalⁱ and Greece, and to the distant islands^j that have not heard of my fame or seen my glory.^k They will proclaim my glory among the nations. ²⁰And they will bring all your brothers, from all the nations, to my holy mountain in Jerusalem as an offering to the LORD—on horses, in chariots and wagons, and on mules and camels," says the LORD. "They will bring them, as the Israelites bring their grain offerings, to the temple of the LORD in ceremonially clean vessels.^l ²¹And I will select some of them also to be priests^m and Levites," says the LORD.

²²"As the new heavens and the new earthⁿ that I make will endure before me," declares the LORD, "so will your name and descendants endure.^o ²³From one New Moon to another and from one Sabbath^p to another, all mankind will come and bow down^q before me," says the LORD. ²⁴"And they will go out and look upon the dead bodies of those who rebelled against me; their worm^r will not die, nor will their fire be quenched,^s and they will be loathsome to all mankind."

---

a 17 Or *gardens behind one of your temples, and*   b 18 The meaning of the Hebrew for this clause is uncertain.   c 19 Some Septuagint manuscripts *Put* (Libyans); Hebrew *Pul*

66:16
a Isa 30:30
b Isa 27:1

66:17
c Isa 1:29
d Lev 11:7
e Ps 37:20;
Isa 1:28

66:19
f Isa 11:10; 49:22
g Isa 2:16
h Eze 27:10
i Ge 10:2
j Isa 11:11
k 1Ch 16:24;
Isa 24:15

66:20
l Isa 52:11

66:21
m Ex 19:6;
Isa 61:6;
1Pe 2:5,9

66:22
n Isa 65:17;
Heb 12:26-27;
2Pe 3:13;
Rev 21:1
o Jn 10:27-29;
1Pe 1:4-5

66:23
p Eze 46:1-3
q Isa 19:21

66:24
r Isa 14:11
s Isa 1:31;
Mk 9:48*

Theme of Isaiah:

Author:

Date:

Purpose:

Key Words:

SEGMENT DIVISIONS

			CHAPTER THEMES
			1
			2
			3
	Discourses Regarding Jerusalem		4
			5
			6
			7
			8
			9
			10
			11
			12
			13
			14
			15
	Oracles	God's Character and Judgment	16
			17
			18
			19
			20
			21
			22
			23
	Discourses Regarding That Day		24
			25
			26
			27
			28
			29
	Woes		30
			31
			32
			33

SEGMENT DIVISIONS

			CHAPTER THEMES
GOD'S RANSOM	GOD'S CHARACTER AND JUDGMENT	34	
		35	
HISTORICAL INTERLUDE		36	
		37	
		38	
		39	
DISCOURSES REGARDING:	GOD'S COMFORT AND REDEMPTION	40	
		41	
		42	
		43	
		44	
		45	
		46	
		47	
		48	
DISCOURSES REGARDING:		49	
		50	
		51	
		52	
		53	
		54	
		55	
		56	
		57	
DISCOURSES REGARDING:		58	
		59	
		60	
		61	
		62	
		63	
		64	
		65	
		66	

JEREMIAH

*I*saiah lived and prophesied one hundred years before the Babylonian captivity; Jeremiah prophesied just before and during Babylon's three sieges of Judah. Between these two great prophets there was about a 30-year period when God didn't speak. True prophets were silent, but false prophets were very vocal, proclaiming peace rather than judgment—and the people loved it. This occurred during Manasseh's reign, a reign noted for its blasphemy and bloodshed.

Jeremiah was born at this time. However, Jeremiah's ministry as a prophet didn't begin until about 627 B.C., the same time that Nabopolassar began his rule of the Neo-Babylonian Empire. Josiah succeeded Manasseh as ruler over Judah. Revival came when the Word of the Lord was found in the house of God and Josiah called the people to repentance.

Then, in 612 B.C., Nineveh, the capital of Assyria, fell to the Babylonians. In 605 B.C., as Egypt went to engage Babylon in battle at Carchemish, Josiah intercepted Neco, king of Egypt, on the plain of Megiddo. Although Neco had warned Josiah not to try to stop him, Josiah tried anyway, and as a result he was killed in battle (see 2 Chronicles 35:20-27).

The revival came to an end, and like her sister Israel, Judah played the harlot again. Egypt was defeated by Babylon at Carchemish, leaving Babylon the predominant world power, God's rod of judgment for his adulterous wife. And Jeremiah the prophet wept.

∿ THINGS TO DO

Chapter 1: Understanding Jeremiah's Message

To understand Jeremiah's message you must understand Jeremiah's call and commission from the Lord. To do so, become thoroughly familiar with Jeremiah 1 before reading the instructions for Jeremiah 2 through 38.

1. Read the chapter, asking God for insight and understanding. Then read the chapter one more time to become familiar with it as a whole.

2. The first three verses give the historical setting of Jeremiah.

   a. Examine the historical chart at the beginning of Jeremiah on page 1283 in the light of these verses. "When the people of Jerusalem went into exile" (1:3) refers to the final siege and destruction of Jerusalem by Nebuchadnezzar, king of Babylon, in 586 B.C.

   b. Jeremiah contains many references to time, such as in Jeremiah 1:1-3. When you encounter one, consult the chart to see who was reigning at the time and what his relationship was to the other kings. The book of Jeremiah is not strictly chronological, so this will help you keep the timing of events in perspective. Mark every reference to time in a distinctive way.

   c. Fill in "Author" and "Date" on the JEREMIAH AT A GLANCE chart on page 1394.

3. Read Jeremiah 1 again. As you do, ask the five W's and an H. Ask questions such as: Who was Jeremiah? What was Jeremiah called to do or be? To whom was he appointed and by whom? When was he called and why? How did he respond? How will he be able to fulfill his appointment? What was he to say? How would the people respond? What was Jeremiah to do? What if the people didn't respond? What would God do?

   a. On a piece of paper, jot down your answers to these questions and any others you think of while observing the text. Don't read anything into the text, but simply let it speak for itself.

    b. In the margin of Jeremiah 1, list all you learn about Jeremiah, his call, and the specifics of his commission. Record what you observed from examining the chapter in light of the five W's and an H. Be as specific as possible. Read the chapter through several more times.

4. Record the theme of this chapter on JEREMIAH AT A GLANCE and in the text next to the chapter number.

5. The rest of Jeremiah revolves around Jeremiah's call and commission. Everything Jeremiah says and does is rooted in chapter 1. Remember this as you study!

Jeremiah's critical and passionate message consists of discourses and narrative accounts of events in Jeremiah's life and in the history of Israel, Judah, and the nations.

Chapters 2-38: Judah's Sin and God's Warning to Return

Read all the instructions before you begin. Every now and then refresh your memory, since Jeremiah is a long book.

1. Study this segment chapter by chapter doing the following:

    a. When Jeremiah spoke he was to do two things, one negative and one positive, in that order. First, he was to uproot, tear down, destroy, and overthrow. Second, he was to build and plant. As you read, observe how Jeremiah does these two things in regard to Judah.

        1) List their sins, their "wickedness" (1:16), which God has to deal with by uprooting, tearing down, destroying, and overthrowing. Note their sins by writing them in the margin.

        2) Also note any promise of building and planting—restoration. Record in the margin what God will do on their behalf, when he will do it, and why.

    b. Jeremiah had the assurance that God would fulfill his word (1:12). As you read, note in the margin what God says will happen to Judah in the way of judgment.

        1) Watch for how God will bring about this judgment. In several places God has Jeremiah do some symbolic acts in order to get his point across to the people. Watch for these.

        2) Watch for any verse which shows that God fulfilled (accomplished or carried out) what he said he would do. Also note what God has to do because of the covenant (the law) he made with them.

    c. Mark all references to time with a symbol in the margin.

2. Jeremiah was told to speak all God commanded him and that he would be opposed by kings, officials, priests, and people.

    a. Note in the margin any opposition that comes Jeremiah's way. You may want to put it under the heading "Opposition." Observe Jeremiah's struggles and how he handles these. Also note how God rescues Jeremiah as he said he would in 1:8, 18, 19. (The height of Jeremiah's physical suffering is described in chapters 37 through 38.)

    b. Also note what you learn about the leaders, the shepherds (spiritual), and the prophets.

3. In chapter 21 Nebuchadnezzar, king of Babylon, appears on the scene, for "from the north disaster will be poured out on all who live in the land" (1:14). From this point on, Babylon and Nebuchadnezzar are prominent. You might want to summarize your insights about them in the margin under the heading "Babylon."

4. There are many key repeated words. The following list contains suggestions about which words to mark, though you may want to add to or delete from it. Marking key words is helpful as long as you think about how they contribute to the text and what you learn from their occurrence.

    a. Mark every reference to *nation, people,* or *nations*. Observe which nation it is and make a list in the margin of what you learn about it.

b. Watch for any words or synonyms that have to do with uprooting, destroying, building, planting, or restoring. Mark these in a distinctive way or underline them in the text.

c. You also might want to mark the following words and their synonyms in a distinctive way so you can easily recognize their occurrence in the text: *listen (hear, obey, listened, pay any attention), return (repent, come back, go back, send me back, turn, restrain, turns, stop, changed, relent), prostitute (adultery, adulteries), wickedness (disaster, evil, wicked, calamity, worst, guilt, sin, sins, sinning, crimes, wrong), heart (hearts, to themselves, cares, yourself, heart's, minds), forsaken (forsake, deserted, abandoned, rejected, forsook, desert, vanish from), heal (dress the wound, cure, healing, healed, Comforter, incurable),* and *covenant*. Write these on an index card, color code them as you want to mark them in your Bible, and use the card as a bookmark as you study Jeremiah.

5. As you finish observing each chapter, marking its key words, and putting notes in the margin, record the theme of that chapter on JEREMIAH AT A GLANCE. Also record it in the text on the line next to the chapter number.

Chapters 39-45: Jerusalem's Fall and Judah's Uprooting

1. Except for chapter 45, this section is narrative. Therefore as you read each chapter:

a. Note what happens, when it happens (mark references to time), where it happens, and why.

b. Note who is involved. Mark in a distinctive way the main characters in each chapter, and then in the margin list who they are and anything significant you want to remember about them.

c. Mark the key word *listen (obey, hear)* and any other words which are distinctive to each chapter.

2. Record the theme of each chapter as you have done before.

Chapters 46-51: Jeremiah's Prophecy Concerning the Nations

1. As you read, note what the Lord says will happen and why. Also note the end result and if the Lord gives any hope for the future. Watch for and mark time phrases.

2. Mark the key words: *concerning (against), nations (nations'), Medes,* and *north*. Also observe what you learn about Israel from these chapters.

3. These chapters contain critical information about Babylon which will help when you study prophecy and/or the book of Revelation. In the margin list what you learn about Babylon. Also list your insights on the chart WHAT THE BIBLE TEACHES ABOUT BABYLON beginning on page 2176. (Note the book, chapter, and verse from which you gain insights.)

Chapter 52: Judah's Final Days of Exile

1. As you observe this chapter, mark the time phrases and list in the margin what was done to the kings, the city, the temple vessels, and who did it.

2. Record the theme of this chapter on JEREMIAH AT A GLANCE and then complete the chart. Record the segment divisions of Jeremiah.

∽ THINGS TO THINK ABOUT

1. Judah lived like a prostitute. How have you behaved as the bride of Christ? Do you relate to any of Judah's sins? In James 4:4 God calls those who are friends with the world adulteresses. What would he call you?

2. How faithful are you to proclaim God's Word to others? What can you learn from Jeremiah's life in this respect? Do you hesitate to share God's Word with others because of fear or because you think they wouldn't listen? Are you dismayed by their faces? What should you do? Think about all the times you marked *listen (hear, obey, listened)* in Jeremiah. Judah didn't listen to God—only to those prophets who tickled her ears. How carefully do you listen to God's Word?

3. Would God have relented of the calamity he was about to bring on Judah? Why? What do you learn from this?

4. God uses nations as his rod of judgment and yet he holds them accountable for their actions. What does this tell you about God and about your accountability before him?

Chapter 1 Theme _____

1 The words of Jeremiah son of Hilkiah, one of the priests at Anathoth[a] in the territory of Benjamin. [2]The word of the LORD came to him in the thirteenth year of the reign of Josiah son of Amon king of Judah, [3]and through the reign of Jehoiakim[b] son of Josiah king of Judah, down to the fifth month of the eleventh year of Zedekiah[c] son of Josiah king of Judah, when the people of Jerusalem went into exile.[d]

[4]The word of the LORD came to me, saying,

[5]"Before I formed you in the womb I knew[ae] you,
    before you were born[f] I set you apart;
    I appointed you as a prophet to the nations.[g]"

[6]"Ah, Sovereign LORD," I said, "I do not know how to speak;[h] I am only a child."[i]

[7]But the LORD said to me, "Do not say, 'I am only a child.' You must go to everyone I send you to and say whatever I command you. [8]Do not be afraid[j] of them, for I am with you[k] and will rescue you," declares the LORD.

[9]Then the LORD reached out his hand and touched[l] my mouth and said to me, "Now, I have put my words in your mouth.[m] [10]See, today I appoint you over nations and kingdoms to uproot and tear down, to destroy and overthrow, to build and to plant."[n]

[11]The word of the LORD came to me: "What do you see, Jeremiah?"[o]

"I see the branch of an almond tree," I replied.

[12]The LORD said to me, "You have seen correctly, for I am watching[b] to see that my word is fulfilled."

[13]The word of the LORD came to me again: "What do you see?"[p]

"I see a boiling pot, tilting away from the north," I answered.

[14]The LORD said to me, "From the north disaster will be poured out on all who live in the land. [15]I am about to summon all the peoples of the northern kingdoms," declares the LORD.

"Their kings will come and set up their thrones
    in the entrance of the gates of Jerusalem;
they will come against all her surrounding walls
    and against all the towns of Judah.[q]

a 5 Or *chose* b 12 The Hebrew for *watching* sounds like the Hebrew for *almond tree*.

INSIGHT

The Last Kings of Judah

Josiah
640-609 B.C.

Jehoahaz
(also called Joahaz or Shallum)
609 B.C.

Jehoiakim
(also called Eliakim)
609-597 B.C.

Jehoiachin
(also called Coniah or Jeconiah)
597 B.C.

Zedekiah
(also called Mattaniah)
597-586 B.C.

1:1
a Jos 21:18;
1Ch 6:60;
Jer 32:7-9

1:3
b 2Ki 23:34
c 2Ki 24:17;
Jer 39:2
d Jer 52:15

1:5
e Ps 139:16
f Isa 49:1
g ver 10;
Jer 25:15-26

1:6
h Ex 4:10; 6:12
i 1Ki 3:7

1:8
j Eze 2:6
k Jos 1:5;
Jer 15:20

1:9
l Isa 6:7
m Ex 4:12

1:10
n Jer 18:7-10;
24:6; 31:4,28

1:11
o Jer 24:3;
Am 7:8

1:13
p Zec 4:2

1:15
q Jer 4:16; 9:11

THE RULERS AND PROPHETS OF JEREMIAH'S TIME

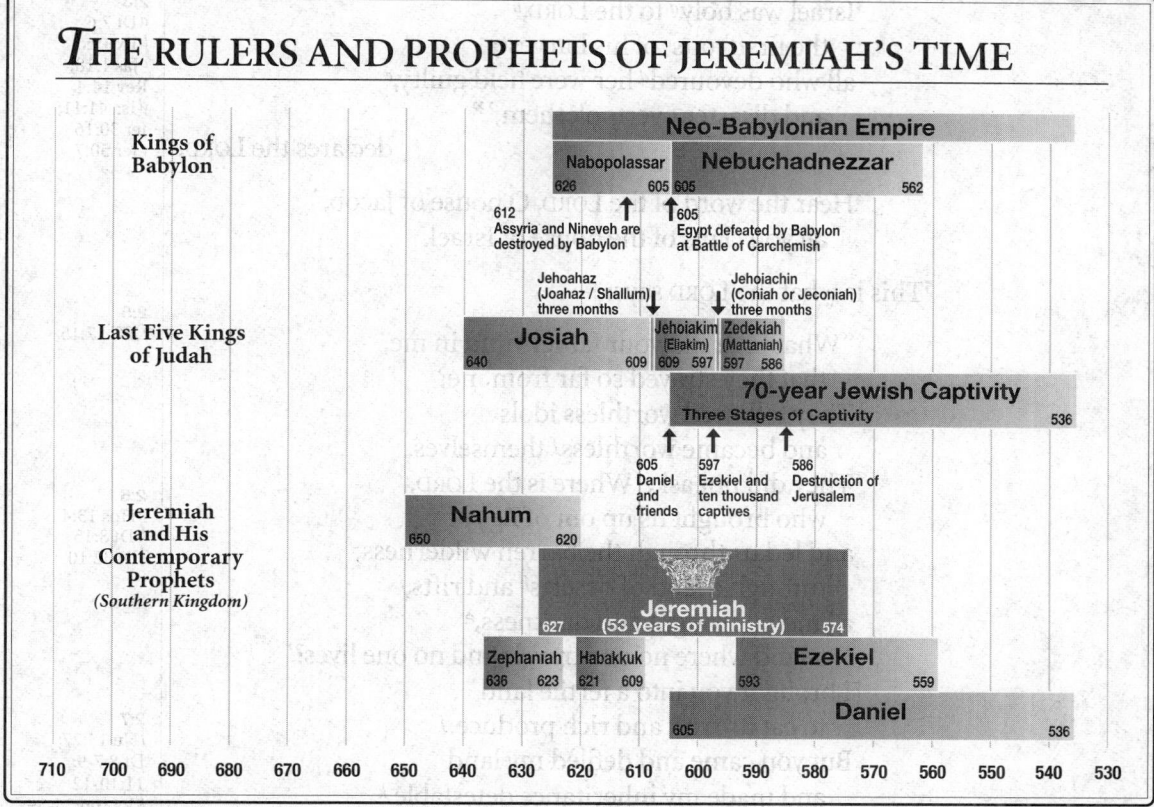

16I will pronounce my judgments on my people
 because of their wickedness*a* in forsaking me,*b*
in burning incense to other gods*c*
 and in worshiping what their hands have made.

17"Get yourself ready! Stand up and say to them whatever I command you. Do not be terrified*d* by them, or I will terrify you before them. **18**Today I have made you*e* a fortified city, an iron pillar and a bronze wall to stand against the whole land—against the kings of Judah, its officials, its priests and the people of the land. **19**They will fight against you but will not overcome you, for I am with you*f* and will rescue*g* you," declares the LORD.

Chapter 2 Theme

2 The word of the LORD came to me: **2**"Go and proclaim in the hearing of Jerusalem:

"'I remember the devotion of your youth,*h*
 how as a bride you loved me
and followed me through the desert,*i*
 through a land not sown.

1:16
a Dt 28:20
b Jer 17:13
c Jer 7:9;
   19:4

1:17
d Eze 2:6

1:18
e Isa 50:7

1:19
f Jer 20:11
g ver 8

2:2
h Eze 16:8-14, 60;
   Hos 2:15
i Dt 2:7

1283

³Israel was holy^a to the LORD,^b
    the firstfruits^c of his harvest;
all who devoured^d her were held guilty,^e
    and disaster overtook them,'"

            declares the LORD.

⁴Hear the word of the LORD, O house of Jacob,
    all you clans of the house of Israel.

⁵This is what the LORD says:

"What fault did your fathers find in me,
    that they strayed so far from me?
They followed worthless idols
    and became worthless^f themselves.
⁶They did not ask, 'Where is the LORD,
    who brought us up out of Egypt^g
and led us through the barren wilderness,
    through a land of deserts^h and rifts,ⁱ
a land of drought and darkness,^a
    a land where no one travels and no one lives?'
⁷I brought you into a fertile land
    to eat its fruit and rich produce.^j
But you came and defiled my land
    and made my inheritance detestable.^k
⁸The priests did not ask,
    'Where is the LORD?'
Those who deal with the law did not know me;^l
    the leaders rebelled against me.
The prophets prophesied by Baal,^m
    following worthless idols.ⁿ

⁹"Therefore I bring charges^o against you again,"

            declares the LORD.

"And I will bring charges against your children's
    children.
¹⁰Cross over to the coasts of Kittim^b and look,
    send to Kedar^c and observe closely;
    see if there has ever been anything like this:
¹¹Has a nation ever changed its gods?
    (Yet they are not gods^p at all.)
But my people have exchanged their^d Glory^q
    for worthless idols.

---

a 6 Or *and the shadow of death*   *b 10* That is, Cyprus and western coastlands   *c 10* The home of Bedouin tribes in the Syro-Arabian desert   *d 11* Masoretic Text; an ancient Hebrew scribal tradition *my*

2:3
a Dt 7:6
b Ex 19:6
c Jas 1:18;
Rev 14:4
d Isa 41:11;
Jer 30:16
e Jer 50:7

2:5
f 2Ki 17:15

2:6
g Hos 13:4
h Dt 8:15
i Dt 32:10

2:7
j Nu 13:27;
Dt 8:7-9;
11:10-12
k Ps 106:34-39;
Jer 16:18

2:8
l Jer 4:22
m Jer 23:13
n Jer 16:19

2:9
o Eze 20:35-36;
Mic 6:2

2:11
p Isa 37:19;
Jer 16:20
q Ps 106:20;
Ro 1:23

¹²Be appalled at this, O heavens,
  and shudder with great horror,"
                                        declares the LORD.

¹³"My people have committed two sins:
  They have forsaken me,
    the spring of living water,^a
  and have dug their own cisterns,
    broken cisterns that cannot hold water.
¹⁴Is Israel a servant, a slave^b by birth?
  Why then has he become plunder?
¹⁵Lions^c have roared;
  they have growled at him.
  They have laid waste^d his land;
    his towns are burned and deserted.
¹⁶Also, the men of Memphis^{ae} and Tahpanhes^f
  have shaved the crown of your head.^b
¹⁷Have you not brought this on yourselves^g
  by forsaking the LORD your God
  when he led you in the way?
¹⁸Now why go to Egypt^h
  to drink water from the Shihor^c?ⁱ
  And why go to Assyria
  to drink water from the River^d?
¹⁹Your wickedness will punish you;
  your backsliding^j will rebuke^k you.
  Consider then and realize
  how evil and bitter^l it is for you
  when you forsake the LORD your God
  and have no awe^m of me,"
                  declares the Lord, the LORD Almighty.

²⁰"Long ago you broke off your yokeⁿ
  and tore off your bonds;
  you said, 'I will not serve you!'
  Indeed, on every high hill^o
  and under every spreading tree^p
  you lay down as a prostitute.
²¹I had planted^q you like a choice vine^r
  of sound and reliable stock.
  How then did you turn against me
  into a corrupt,^s wild vine?
²²Although you wash yourself with soda
  and use an abundance of soap,

*Cross-references (left margin):*

2:13 ^aPs 36:9; Jn 4:14
2:14 ^bEx 4:22
2:15 ^cJer 4:7; 50:17 ^dIsa 1:7
2:16 ^eIsa 19:13 ^fJer 43:7-9
2:17 ^gJer 4:18
2:18 ^hIsa 30:2 ⁱJos 13:3
2:19 ^jJer 3:11,22 ^kIsa 3:9; Hos 5:5 ^lJob 20:14; Am 8:10 ^mPs 36:1
2:20 ⁿLev 26:13 ^oIsa 57:7; Jer 17:2 ^pDt 12:2
2:21 ^qEx 15:17 ^rPs 80:8 ^sIsa 5:4

Footnotes:

^a 16 Hebrew *Noph* ^b 16 Or *have cracked your skull* ^c 18 That is, a branch of the Nile
^d 18 That is, the Euphrates

the stain of your guilt is still before me,"
declares the Sovereign LORD.

²³"How can you say, 'I am not defiled;^a
  I have not run after the Baals'?^b
See how you behaved in the valley;^c
  consider what you have done.
You are a swift she-camel
  running^d here and there,
²⁴a wild donkey^e accustomed to the desert,
  sniffing the wind in her craving—
  in her heat who can restrain her?
Any males that pursue her need not tire themselves;
  at mating time they will find her.
²⁵Do not run until your feet are bare
  and your throat is dry.
But you said, 'It's no use!
  I love foreign gods,^f
  and I must go after them.'

²⁶"As a thief is disgraced^g when he is caught,
  so the house of Israel is disgraced—
they, their kings and their officials,
  their priests and their prophets.
²⁷They say to wood, 'You are my father,'
  and to stone,^h 'You gave me birth.'
They have turned their backs to me
  and not their faces;ⁱ
yet when they are in trouble,^j they say,
  'Come and save us!'
²⁸Where then are the gods^k you made for yourselves?
  Let them come if they can save you
  when you are in trouble!^l
For you have as many gods
  as you have towns,^m O Judah.

²⁹"Why do you bring charges against me?
  You have allⁿ rebelled against me,"
declares the LORD.

³⁰"In vain I punished your people;
  they did not respond to correction.
Your sword has devoured your prophets^o
  like a ravening lion.

³¹"You of this generation, consider the word of the LORD:

"Have I been a desert to Israel
  or a land of great darkness?^p

2:23
^aPr 30:12
^bJer 9:14
^cJer 7:31
^dver 33;
Jer 31:22

2:24
^eJer 14:6

2:25
^fDt 32:16;
Jer 3:13; 14:10

2:26
^gJer 48:27

2:27
^hJer 3:9
ⁱJer 18:17; 32:33
^jJdg 10:10;
Isa 26:16

2:28
^kIsa 45:20
^lDt 32:37
^m2Ki 17:29;
Jer 11:13

2:29
ⁿJer 5:1; 6:13;
Da 9:11

2:30
^oNe 9:26;
Ac 7:52;
1Th 2:15

2:31
^pIsa 45:19

2:34
a 2Ki 21:16
b Ex 22:2

Why do my people say, 'We are free to roam;
    we will come to you no more'?
³²Does a maiden forget her jewelry,
    a bride her wedding ornaments?
Yet my people have forgotten me,
    days without number.

2:35
c Jer 25:31
d 1Jn 1:8,10

³³How skilled you are at pursuing love!
    Even the worst of women can learn from your ways.
³⁴On your clothes men find
    the lifeblood^a of the innocent poor,
    though you did not catch them breaking in.^b
Yet in spite of all this
³⁵ you say, 'I am innocent;
    he is not angry with me.'
But I will pass judgment^c on you
    because you say, 'I have not sinned.'^d

2:36
e Jer 31:22
f Isa 30:2,3,7

³⁶Why do you go about so much,
    changing^e your ways?
You will be disappointed by Egypt^f
    as you were by Assyria.
³⁷You will also leave that place
    with your hands on your head,^g
for the LORD has rejected those you trust;
    you will not be helped^h by them.

2:37
g 2Sa 13:19
h Jer 37:7

Chapter 3 Theme

3 "If a man divorces^i his wife
    and she leaves him and marries another man,
should he return to her again?
    Would not the land be completely defiled?
But you have lived as a prostitute with many lovers^j—
    would you now return to me?"

            declares the LORD.

3:1
i Dt 24:1-4
j Jer 2:20,25;
Eze 16:26,29

²"Look up to the barren heights and see.
    Is there any place where you have not been ravished?
By the roadside^k you sat waiting for lovers,
    sat like a nomad^a in the desert.
You have defiled the land^l
    with your prostitution and wickedness.
³Therefore the showers have been withheld,^m
    and no spring rains^n have fallen.
Yet you have the brazen look of a prostitute;
    you refuse to blush with shame.^o

3:2
k Ge 38:14;
Eze 16:25
l Jer 2:7

3:3
m Lev 26:19
n Jer 14:4
o Jer 6:15; 8:12;
Zep 3:5

a 2 Or an Arab

⁴Have you not just called to me:
'My Father,ᵃ my friend from my youth,ᵇ
⁵will you always be angry?ᶜ
Will your wrath continue forever?'
This is how you talk,
but you do all the evil you can."

⁶During the reign of King Josiah, the LORD said to me, "Have you seen what faithless Israel has done? She has gone up on every high hill and under every spreading treeᵈ and has committed adulteryᵉ there. ⁷I thought that after she had done all this she would return to me but she did not, and her unfaithful sisterᶠ Judah saw it. ⁸I gave faithless Israel her certificate of divorce and sent her away because of all her adulteries. Yet I saw that her unfaithful sister Judah had no fear;ᵍ she also went out and committed adultery. ⁹Because Israel's immorality mattered so little to her, she defiled the landʰ and committed adultery with stoneⁱ and wood.ʲ ¹⁰In spite of all this, her unfaithful sister Judah did not return to me with all her heart, but only in pretense,ᵏ" declares the LORD.

¹¹The LORD said to me, "Faithless Israel is more righteousˡ than unfaithfulᵐ Judah. ¹²Go, proclaim this message toward the north:ⁿ

"'Return,ᵒ faithless Israel,' declares the LORD,
'I will frown on you no longer,
for I am merciful,' declares the LORD,
'I will not be angryᵖ forever.
¹³Only acknowledgeq your guilt—
you have rebelled against the LORD your God,
you have scattered your favors to foreign godsʳ
under every spreading tree,ˢ
and have not obeyedᵗ me,'"

declares the LORD.

¹⁴"Return,ᵘ faithless people," declares the LORD, "for I am your husband. I will choose you—one from a town and two from a clan—and bring you to Zion. ¹⁵Then I will give you shepherdsᵛ after my own heart, who will lead you with knowledge and understanding. ¹⁶In those days, when your numbers have increased greatly in the land," declares the LORD, "men will no longer say, 'The ark of the covenant of the LORD.' It will never enter their minds or be remembered;ʷ it will not be missed, nor will another one be made. ¹⁷At that time they will call Jerusalem The Throneˣ of the LORD, and all nations will gather in Jerusalem to honorʸ the name of the LORD. No longer will they follow the stubbornness of their evil hearts.ᶻ ¹⁸In those days the house of Judah will join the house of Israel,ᵃ and togetherᵇ they will come from a northernᶜ land to the landᵈ I gave your forefathers as an inheritance.

3:4
ᵃver 19
ᵇJer 2:2

3:5
ᶜPs 103:9;
Isa 57:16

3:6
ᵈJer 17:2
ᵉJer 2:20

3:7
ᶠEze 16:46

3:8
ᵍEze 16:47;
23:11

3:9
ʰver 2
ⁱIsa 57:6
ʲJer 2:27

3:10
ᵏJer 12:2

3:11
ˡEze 16:52;
23:11
ᵐver 7

3:12
ⁿ2Ki 17:3-6
ᵒver 14;
Jer 31:21,22;
Eze 33:11
ᵖPs 86:15

3:13
qDt 30:1-3;
Jer 14:20;
1Jn 1:9
ʳJer 2:25
ˢDt 12:2
ᵗver 25

3:14
ᵘHos 2:19

3:15
ᵛAc 20:28

3:16
ʷIsa 65:17

3:17
ˣJer 17:12;
Eze 43:7
ʸIsa 60:9
ᶻJer 11:8

3:18
ᵃHos 1:11
ᵇIsa 11:13;
Jer 50:4
ᶜJer 16:15; 31:8
ᵈAm 9:15

3:19
a ver 4; Isa 63:16

3:21
b ver 2

3:22
c Hos 14:4
d Jer 33:6;
Hos 6:1

3:23
e Ps 3:8;
Jer 17:14

3:24
f Hos 9:10

3:25
g Ezr 9:6
h Jer 22:21

4:1
i Jer 3:1,22;
Joel 2:12
j Jer 35:15

4:2
k Dt 10:20;
Isa 65:16
l Jer 12:16
m Ge 22:18;
Gal 3:8

19"I myself said,

"'How gladly would I treat you like sons
  and give you a desirable land,
  the most beautiful inheritance of any nation.'
I thought you would call me 'Father'*a*
  and not turn away from following me.
20But like a woman unfaithful to her husband,
  so you have been unfaithful to me, O house of Israel,"
                                        declares the Lord.

21A cry is heard on the barren heights,*b*
  the weeping and pleading of the people of Israel,
because they have perverted their ways
  and have forgotten the Lord their God.

22"Return,*c* faithless people;
  I will cure*d* you of backsliding."

"Yes, we will come to you,
  for you are the Lord our God.
23Surely the ⌊idolatrous⌋ commotion on the hills
  and mountains is a deception;
surely in the Lord our God
  is the salvation*e* of Israel.
24From our youth shameful*f* gods have consumed
  the fruits of our fathers' labor—
their flocks and herds,
  their sons and daughters.
25Let us lie down in our shame,*g*
  and let our disgrace cover us.
We have sinned against the Lord our God,
  both we and our fathers;
from our youth*h* till this day
  we have not obeyed the Lord our God."

Chapter 4 Theme

4 "If you will return,*i* O Israel,
    return to me,"
                                        declares the Lord.
  "If you put your detestable idols*j* out of my sight
    and no longer go astray,
  2and if in a truthful, just and righteous way
    you swear,*k* 'As surely as the Lord lives,'*l*
  then the nations will be blessed*m* by him
    and in him they will glory."

INSIGHT

The people set up their idols on hills (see 1 Kings 14:23).

1289

³This is what the LORD says to the men of Judah and to Jerusalem:

"Break up your unplowed ground*a*
and do not sow among thorns.*b*
⁴Circumcise yourselves to the LORD,
circumcise your hearts,*c*
you men of Judah and people of Jerusalem,
or my wrath*d* will break out and burn like fire
because of the evil you have done—
burn with no one to quench*e* it.

⁵"Announce in Judah and proclaim in Jerusalem and say:
'Sound the trumpet throughout the land!'
Cry aloud and say:
'Gather together!
Let us flee to the fortified cities!'*f*
⁶Raise the signal to go to Zion!
Flee for safety without delay!
For I am bringing disaster from the north,*g*
even terrible destruction."

⁷A lion*h* has come out of his lair;
a destroyer of nations has set out.
He has left his place
to lay waste*i* your land.
Your towns will lie in ruins*j*
without inhabitant.
⁸So put on sackcloth,*k*
lament and wail,
for the fierce anger*l* of the LORD
has not turned away from us.

⁹"In that day," declares the LORD,
"the king and the officials will lose heart,
the priests will be horrified,
and the prophets will be appalled."*m*

¹⁰Then I said, "Ah, Sovereign LORD, how completely you have deceived*n* this people and Jerusalem by saying, 'You will have peace,'*o* when the sword is at our throats."

¹¹At that time this people and Jerusalem will be told, "A scorching wind*p* from the barren heights in the desert blows toward my people, but not to winnow or cleanse; ¹²a wind too strong for that comes from me.*a* Now I pronounce my judgments*q* against them."

¹³Look! He advances like the clouds,*r*
his chariots*s* come like a whirlwind,*t*

4:3
a Hos 10:12
b Mk 4:18

4:4
c Dt 10:16;
Jer 9:26;
Ro 2:28-29
d Zep 2:2
e Am 5:6

4:5
f Jos 10:20;
Jer 8:14

4:6
g Jer 1:13-15;
50:3

4:7
h 2Ki 24:1;
Jer 2:15
i Isa 1:7
j Jer 25:9

4:8
k Isa 22:12;
Jer 6:26
l Jer 30:24

4:9
m Isa 29:9

4:10
n 2Th 2:11
o Jer 14:13

4:11
p Eze 17:10;
Hos 13:15

4:12
q Jer 1:16

4:13
r Isa 19:1
s Isa 66:15
t Isa 5:28

---

a 12 Or comes at my command

his horses are swifter than eagles.[a]
    Woe to us! We are ruined!

¹⁴O Jerusalem, wash[b] the evil from your heart and be saved.
    How long will you harbor wicked thoughts?

¹⁵A voice is announcing from Dan,[c]
    proclaiming disaster from the hills of Ephraim.
¹⁶"Tell this to the nations,
    proclaim it to Jerusalem:
'A besieging army is coming from a distant land,
    raising a war cry[d] against the cities of Judah.
¹⁷They surround[e] her like men guarding a field,
    because she has rebelled[f] against me,'"

declares the LORD.

¹⁸"Your own conduct and actions[g]
    have brought this upon you.[h]
This is your punishment.
    How bitter[i] it is!
    How it pierces to the heart!"

¹⁹Oh, my anguish, my anguish![j]
    I writhe in pain.
Oh, the agony of my heart!
    My heart pounds within me,
    I cannot keep silent.[k]
For I have heard the sound of the trumpet;
    I have heard the battle cry.[l]
²⁰Disaster follows disaster;[m]
    the whole land lies in ruins.
In an instant my tents[n] are destroyed,
    my shelter in a moment.
²¹How long must I see the battle standard
    and hear the sound of the trumpet?

²²"My people are fools;[o]
    they do not know me.[p]
They are senseless children;
    they have no understanding.
They are skilled in doing evil;[q]
    they know not how to do good."[r]

²³I looked at the earth,
    and it was formless and empty;[s]
and at the heavens,
    and their light was gone.
²⁴I looked at the mountains,
    and they were quaking;[t]
    all the hills were swaying.

Cross references (margin):

4:13
a Dt 28:49;
Hab 1:8

4:14
b Jas 4:8

4:15
c Jer 8:16

4:16
d Eze 21:22

4:17
e 2Ki 25:1,4
f Jer 5:23

4:18
g Ps 107:17;
Isa 50:1
h Jer 2:17
i Jer 2:19

4:19
j Isa 16:11; 22:4;
Jer 9:10
k Jer 20:9
l Nu 10:9

4:20
m Ps 42:7;
Eze 7:26
n Jer 10:20

4:22
o Jer 10:8
p Jer 2:8
q Jer 13:23;
1Co 14:20
r Ro 16:19

4:23
s Ge 1:2

4:24
t Isa 5:25;
Eze 38:20

²⁵I looked, and there were no people;
　　every bird in the sky had flown away.^a
²⁶I looked, and the fruitful land was a desert;
　　all its towns lay in ruins
　　before the LORD, before his fierce anger.

²⁷This is what the LORD says:

"The whole land will be ruined,
　　though I will not destroy^b it completely.
²⁸Therefore the earth will mourn^c
　　and the heavens above grow dark,^d
because I have spoken and will not relent,^e
　　I have decided and will not turn back.^f"

²⁹At the sound of horsemen and archers^g
　　every town takes to flight.^h
Some go into the thickets;
　　some climb up among the rocks.
All the towns are deserted;ⁱ
　　no one lives in them.

³⁰What are you doing,^j O devastated one?
　　Why dress yourself in scarlet
　　and put on jewels^k of gold?
Why shade your eyes with paint?^l
　　You adorn yourself in vain.
Your lovers^m despise you;
　　they seek your life.

³¹I hear a cry as of a woman in labor,ⁿ
　　a groan as of one bearing her first child—
the cry of the Daughter of Zion gasping for breath,^o
　　stretching out her hands^p and saying,
"Alas! I am fainting;
　　my life is given over to murderers."

Chapter 5 Theme

5 "Go up and down^q the streets of Jerusalem,
　　look around and consider,
　　search through her squares.
If you can find but one person^r
　　who deals honestly and seeks the truth,
　　I will forgive^s this city.
²Although they say, 'As surely as the LORD lives,'^t
　　still they are swearing falsely."

4:25
^aJer 9:10; 12:4;
Zep 1:3

4:27
^bJer 5:10,18;
12:12; 30:11;
46:28

4:28
^cJer 12:4,11;
14:2; Hos 4:3
^dIsa 5:30; 50:3
^eNu 23:19
^fJer 23:20; 30:24

4:29
^gJer 6:23
^h2Ki 25:4
ⁱver 7

4:30
^jIsa 10:3-4
^kEze 23:40
^l2Ki 9:30
^mLa 1:2;
Eze 23:9,22

4:31
ⁿJer 13:21
^oIsa 42:14
^pIsa 1:15;
La 1:17

5:1
^q2Ch 16:9;
Eze 22:30
^rGe 18:32
^sGe 18:24

5:2
^tJer 4:2

5:3
a 2Ch 16:9
b Isa 9:13
c Jer 2:30;
Zep 3:2
d Jer 7:26; 19:15;
Eze 3:8-9

³O LORD, do not your eyes*a* look for truth?
   You struck*b* them, but they felt no pain;
   you crushed them, but they refused correction.*c*
They made their faces harder than stone*d*
   and refused to repent.

⁴I thought, "These are only the poor;
   they are foolish,
for they do not know*e* the way of the LORD,
   the requirements of their God.

5:4
e Jer 8:7

⁵So I will go to the leaders*f*
   and speak to them;
surely they know the way of the LORD,
   the requirements of their God."
But with one accord they too had broken off the yoke
   and torn off the bonds.*g*

5:5
f Mic 3:1,9
g Ps 2:3;
Jer 2:20

⁶Therefore a lion from the forest will attack them,
   a wolf from the desert will ravage them,
a leopard*h* will lie in wait near their towns
   to tear to pieces any who venture out,
for their rebellion is great
   and their backslidings many.*i*

5:6
h Hos 13:7
i Jer 30:14

⁷"Why should I forgive you?
   Your children have forsaken me
   and sworn*j* by gods that are not gods.*k*
I supplied all their needs,
   yet they committed adultery*l*
   and thronged to the houses of prostitutes.

5:7
j Jos 23:7;
Zep 1:5
k Dt 32:21;
Jer 2:11;
Gal 4:8
l Nu 25:1

⁸They are well-fed, lusty stallions,
   each neighing for another man's wife.*m*
⁹Should I not punish them for this?"*n*
   declares the LORD.
"Should I not avenge myself
   on such a nation as this?

5:8
m Jer 29:23;
Eze 22:11

5:9
n ver 29;
Jer 9:9

¹⁰"Go through her vineyards and ravage them,
   but do not destroy them completely.*o*
Strip off her branches,
   for these people do not belong to the LORD.
¹¹The house of Israel and the house of Judah
   have been utterly unfaithful*p* to me,"
                              declares the LORD.

5:10
o Jer 4:27

5:11
p Jer 3:20

¹²They have lied about the LORD;
   they said, "He will do nothing!
No harm will come to us;*q*
   we will never see sword or famine.*r*

5:12
q Jer 23:17
r 2Ch 36:16;
Jer 14:13

¹³The prophets^a are but wind
    and the word is not in them;
    so let what they say be done to them."

¹⁴Therefore this is what the LORD God Almighty says:

"Because the people have spoken these words,
    I will make my words in your mouth^b a fire^c
    and these people the wood it consumes.
¹⁵O house of Israel," declares the LORD,
    "I am bringing a distant nation^d against you—
an ancient and enduring nation,
    a people whose language^e you do not know,
    whose speech you do not understand.
¹⁶Their quivers are like an open grave;
    all of them are mighty warriors.
¹⁷They will devour^{fg} your harvests and food,
    devour^{hi} your sons and daughters;
they will devour^j your flocks and herds,
    devour your vines and fig trees.
With the sword they will destroy
    the fortified cities in which you trust.^k

¹⁸"Yet even in those days," declares the LORD, "I will not destroy^l you completely. ¹⁹And when the people ask,^m 'Why has the LORD our God done all this to us?' you will tell them, 'As you have forsaken me and served foreign godsⁿ in your own land, so now you will serve foreigners^o in a land not your own.'

²⁰"Announce this to the house of Jacob
    and proclaim it in Judah:
²¹Hear this, you foolish and senseless people,
    who have eyes^p but do not see,
    who have ears but do not hear:^q
²²Should you not fear^r me?" declares the LORD.
    "Should you not tremble in my presence?
I made the sand a boundary for the sea,
    an everlasting barrier it cannot cross.
The waves may roll, but they cannot prevail;
    they may roar, but they cannot cross it.
²³But these people have stubborn and rebellious^s hearts;
    they have turned aside and gone away.
²⁴They do not say to themselves,
    'Let us fear the LORD our God,
who gives autumn and spring rains^t in season,
    who assures us of the regular weeks of harvest.'^u
²⁵Your wrongdoings have kept these away;
    your sins have deprived you of good.

5:13 ^aJer 14:15

5:14 ^bJer 1:9;
Hos 6:5
^cJer 23:29

5:15 ^dDt 28:49;
Isa 5:26;
Jer 4:16
^eIsa 28:11

5:17 ^fJer 8:16
^gLev 50:7,16
^hJer 50:7,17
ⁱDt 28:32
^jDt 28:31
^kDt 28:33

5:18 ^lJer 4:27

5:19 ^mDt 29:24-26;
1Ki 9:9
ⁿJer 16:13
^oDt 28:48

5:21 ^pIsa 6:10;
Eze 12:2
^qMt 13:15;
Mk 8:18

5:22 ^rDt 28:58

5:23 ^sDt 21:18

5:24 ^tPs 147:8;
Joel 2:23
^uGe 8:22;
Ac 14:17

5:26
a Ps 10:8;
Pr 1:11

26"Among my people are wicked men
        who lie in wait^a like men who snare birds
        and like those who set traps to catch men.
27Like cages full of birds,
        their houses are full of deceit;^b
    they have become rich^c and powerful

5:27
b Jer 9:6
c Jer 12:1

28   and have grown fat^d and sleek.
    Their evil deeds have no limit;
        they do not plead the case of the fatherless^e to win it,
        they do not defend the rights of the poor.^f

5:28
d Dt 32:15
e Zec 7:10
f Isa 1:23; Jer 7:6

29Should I not punish them for this?"
        declares the LORD.
    "Should I not avenge myself
        on such a nation as this?

30"A horrible^g and shocking thing
        has happened in the land:

5:30
g Jer 23:14;
Hos 6:10

31The prophets prophesy lies,^h
        the priests rule by their own authority,
    and my people love it this way.
        But what will you do in the end?

Chapter 6 Theme _____

5:31
h Eze 13:6;
Mic 2:11

6

    "Flee for safety, people of Benjamin!
        Flee from Jerusalem!
    Sound the trumpet in Tekoa!ⁱ
        Raise the signal over Beth Hakkerem!^j
    For disaster looms out of the north,^k
        even terrible destruction.
2I will destroy the Daughter of Zion,
        so beautiful and delicate.
3Shepherds^l with their flocks will come against her;
        they will pitch their tents around^m her,
        each tending his own portion."

6:1
i 2Ch 11:6
j Ne 3:14
k Jer 4:6

4"Prepare for battle against her!
        Arise, let us attack at noon!ⁿ
    But, alas, the daylight is fading,
        and the shadows of evening grow long.
5So arise, let us attack at night
        and destroy her fortresses!"

6:3
l Jer 12:10
m 2Ki 25:4;
Lk 19:43

6This is what the LORD Almighty says:

    "Cut down the trees^o
        and build siege ramps^p against Jerusalem.
    This city must be punished;
        it is filled with oppression.

6:4
n Jer 15:8

6:6
o Dt 20:19-20
p Jer 32:24

⁷As a well pours out its water,
    so she pours out her wickedness.
Violence^a and destruction^b resound in her;
    her sickness and wounds are ever before me.
⁸Take warning, O Jerusalem,
    or I will turn away^c from you
and make your land desolate
    so no one can live in it."

⁹This is what the LORD Almighty says:

    "Let them glean the remnant of Israel
        as thoroughly as a vine;
    pass your hand over the branches again,
        like one gathering grapes."

¹⁰To whom can I speak and give warning?
    Who will listen to me?
Their ears are closed^{a d}
    so they cannot hear.
The word^e of the LORD is offensive to them;
    they find no pleasure in it.
¹¹But I am full of the wrath^f of the LORD,
    and I cannot hold it in.^g

    "Pour it out on the children in the street
        and on the young men^h gathered together;
    both husband and wife will be caught in it,
        and the old, those weighed down with years.
¹²Their houses will be turned over to others,ⁱ
    together with their fields and their wives,^j
when I stretch out my hand^k
    against those who live in the land,"
                        declares the LORD.
¹³"From the least to the greatest,
    all are greedy for gain;^l
prophets and priests alike,
    all practice deceit.^m
¹⁴They dress the wound of my people
    as though it were not serious.
'Peace, peace,' they say,
    when there is no peace.ⁿ
¹⁵Are they ashamed of their loathsome conduct?
    No, they have no shame at all;
    they do not even know how to blush.^o

a 10 Hebrew *uncircumcised*

6:7
a Ps 55:9;
Eze 7:11,23
b Jer 20:8

6:8
c Eze 23:18;
Hos 9:12

6:10
d Ac 7:51
e Jer 20:8

6:11
f Jer 7:20
g Job 32:20;
Jer 20:9
h Jer 9:21

6:12
i Dt 28:30
j Jer 8:10; 38:22
k Isa 5:25

6:13
l Isa 56:11
m Jer 8:10

6:14
n Jer 4:10; 8:11;
Eze 13:10

6:15
o Jer 3:3; 8:10-12

6:16
a Jer 18:15
b Ps 119:3
c Mt 11:29

6:17
d Eze 3:17
e Jer 11:7-8; 25:4

6:19
f Isa 1:2;
Jer 22:29
g Pr 1:31
h Jer 8:9

6:20
i Ex 30:23
j Am 5:22
k Ps 50:8-10;
Jer 7:21;
Mic 6:7-8
l Isa 1:11

6:21
m Isa 8:14

6:22
n Jer 1:15; 10:22

6:23
o Isa 13:18
p Jer 4:29

6:24
q Jer 4:19
r Jer 4:31;
50:41-43

So they will fall among the fallen;
  they will be brought down when I punish them,"
                                        says the LORD.

¹⁶This is what the LORD says:

"Stand at the crossroads and look;
  ask for the ancient paths,ᵃ
ask where the good wayᵇ is, and walk in it,
  and you will find restᶜ for your souls.
  But you said, 'We will not walk in it.'
¹⁷I appointed watchmenᵈ over you and said,
  'Listen to the sound of the trumpet!'
  But you said, 'We will not listen.'ᵉ
¹⁸Therefore hear, O nations;
  observe, O witnesses,
  what will happen to them.
¹⁹Hear, O earth:ᶠ
  I am bringing disaster on this people,
  the fruit of their schemes,ᵍ
because they have not listened to my words
  and have rejected my law.ʰ
²⁰What do I care about incense from Sheba
  or sweet calamusⁱ from a distant land?
Your burnt offerings are not acceptable;ʲ
  your sacrificesᵏ do not please me."ˡ

²¹Therefore this is what the LORD says:

"I will put obstacles before this people.
  Fathers and sons alike will stumbleᵐ over them;
  neighbors and friends will perish."

²²This is what the LORD says:

"Look, an army is coming
  from the land of the north;ⁿ
a great nation is being stirred up
  from the ends of the earth.
²³They are armed with bow and spear;
  they are cruel and show no mercy.ᵒ
They sound like the roaring sea
  as they ride on their horses;ᵖ
they come like men in battle formation
  to attack you, O Daughter of Zion."

²⁴We have heard reports about them,
  and our hands hang limp.
Anguish�q has gripped us,
  pain like that of a woman in labor.ʳ

²⁵Do not go out to the fields
　　or walk on the roads,
for the enemy has a sword,
　　and there is terror on every side.*ᵃ*

²⁶O my people, put on sackcloth*ᵇ*
　　and roll in ashes;*ᶜ*
mourn with bitter wailing
　　as for an only son,*ᵈ*
for suddenly the destroyer
　　will come upon us.

²⁷"I have made you a tester*ᵉ* of metals
　　and my people the ore,
that you may observe
　　and test their ways.
²⁸They are all hardened rebels,*ᶠ*
　　going about to slander.*ᵍ*
They are bronze and iron;*ʰ*
　　they all act corruptly.
²⁹The bellows blow fiercely
　　to burn away the lead with fire,
but the refining goes on in vain;
　　the wicked are not purged out.
³⁰They are called rejected silver,
　　because the LORD has rejected them."*ⁱ*

Chapter 7 Theme

7 This is the word that came to Jeremiah from the LORD: ²"Stand*ʲ* at the gate of the LORD's house and there proclaim this message:

"'Hear the word of the LORD, all you people of Judah who come through these gates to worship the LORD. ³This is what the LORD Almighty, the God of Israel, says: Reform your ways*ᵏ* and your actions, and I will let you live in this place. ⁴Do not trust in deceptive*ˡ* words and say, "This is the temple of the LORD, the temple of the LORD, the temple of the LORD!" ⁵If you really change your ways and your actions and deal with each other justly,*ᵐ* ⁶if you do not oppress the alien, the fatherless or the widow and do not shed innocent blood*ⁿ* in this place, and if you do not follow other gods*ᵒ* to your own harm, ⁷then I will let you live in this place, in the land*ᵖ* I gave your forefathers for ever and ever. ⁸But look, you are trusting in deceptive words that are worthless.

⁹"'Will you steal and murder, commit adultery and perjury,*ᵃ* burn incense to Baal*�q* and follow other gods*ʳ* you have not known,

ᵃ 9 Or and swear by false gods

6:25	*ᵃ*Jer 49:29
6:26	*ᵇ*Jer 4:8 *ᶜ*Jer 25:34; Mic 1:10 *ᵈ*Zec 12:10
6:27	*ᵉ*Jer 9:7
6:28	*ᶠ*Jer 5:23 *ᵍ*Jer 9:4 *ʰ*Eze 22:18
6:30	*ⁱ*Ps 119:119; Jer 7:29; Hos 9:17
7:2	*ʲ*Jer 17:19
7:3	*ᵏ*Jer 18:11; 26:13
7:4	*ˡ*Mic 3:11
7:5	*ᵐ*Jer 22:3
7:6	*ⁿ*Jer 2:34; 19:4 *ᵒ*Dt 8:19
7:7	*ᵖ*Dt 4:40
7:9	*q*Jer 11:13,17 *ʳ*Ex 20:3

7:10
a Jer 32:34;
Eze 23:38-39

7:11
b Isa 56:7
c Mt 21:13*;
Mk 11:17*;
Lk 19:46*
d Jer 29:23

7:12
e Jos 18:1
f 1Sa 4:10-11,22;
Ps 78:60-64

7:13
g 2Ch 36:15
h Isa 65:12
i Jer 35:17

7:14
j 1Ki 9:7

7:15
k Ps 78:67

7:16
l Ex 32:10;
Dt 9:14;
Jer 15:1

7:18
m Jer 44:17-19
n Jer 19:13
o 1Ki 14:9

7:19
p Jer 9:19

7:20
q Jer 42:18;
La 2:3-5

7:21
r Isa 1:11;
Am 5:21-22
s Hos 8:13

7:22
t 1Sa 15:22;
Ps 51:16;
Hos 6:6

7:23
u Ex 19:5
v Lev 26:12
w Ex 15:26

7:24
x Ps 81:11-12;
Jer 11:8

7:25
y Jer 25:4

7:26
z Jer 16:12

7:27
a Eze 2:7
b Eze 3:7

7:29
c Job 1:20;
Isa 15:2;
Mic 1:16

¹⁰and then come and stand before me in this house,*a* which bears my Name, and say, "We are safe"—safe to do all these detestable things? ¹¹Has this house,*b* which bears my Name, become a den of robbers*c* to you? But I have been watching!*d* declares the LORD.

¹²"'Go now to the place in Shiloh*e* where I first made a dwelling for my Name, and see what I did *f* to it because of the wickedness of my people Israel. ¹³While you were doing all these things, declares the LORD, I spoke to you again and again,*g* but you did not listen;*h* I called you, but you did not answer.*i* ¹⁴Therefore, what I did to Shiloh I will now do to the house that bears my Name,*j* the temple you trust in, the place I gave to you and your fathers. ¹⁵I will thrust you from my presence, just as I did all your brothers, the people of Ephraim.'*k*

¹⁶"So do not pray for this people nor offer any plea*l* or petition for them; do not plead with me, for I will not listen to you. ¹⁷Do you not see what they are doing in the towns of Judah and in the streets of Jerusalem? ¹⁸The children gather wood, the fathers light the fire, and the women knead the dough and make cakes of bread for the Queen of Heaven.*m* They pour out drink offerings*n* to other gods to provoke*o* me to anger. ¹⁹But am I the one they are provoking? declares the LORD. Are they not rather harming themselves, to their own shame?*p*

²⁰"Therefore this is what the Sovereign LORD says: My anger*q* and my wrath will be poured out on this place, on man and beast, on the trees of the field and on the fruit of the ground, and it will burn and not be quenched.

²¹"This is what the LORD Almighty, the God of Israel, says: Go ahead, add your burnt offerings to your other sacrifices*r* and eat*s* the meat yourselves! ²²For when I brought your forefathers out of Egypt and spoke to them, I did not just give them commands about burnt offerings and sacrifices,*t* ²³but I gave them this command: Obey*u* me, and I will be your God and you will be my people.*v* Walk in all the ways I command you, that it may go well*w* with you. ²⁴But they did not listen or pay attention;*x* instead, they followed the stubborn inclinations of their evil hearts. They went backward and not forward. ²⁵From the time your forefathers left Egypt until now, day after day, again and again I sent you my servants the prophets.*y* ²⁶But they did not listen to me or pay attention. They were stiff-necked and did more evil than their forefathers.'*z*

²⁷"When you tell*a* them all this, they will not listen*b* to you; when you call to them, they will not answer. ²⁸Therefore say to them, 'This is the nation that has not obeyed the LORD its God or responded to correction. Truth has perished; it has vanished from their lips. ²⁹Cut off*c* your hair and throw it away; take up a lament

I N S I G H T

Shiloh, the home of the tabernacle, was Israel's religious center for over a century after the conquest of Canaan under Joshua. When they took the ark of the covenant from Shiloh, the Philistines slaughtered 30,000 of Israel's foot soldiers (1 Samuel 4:1-11).

on the barren heights, for the LORD has rejected and abandoned*a* this generation that is under his wrath.

30"'The people of Judah have done evil in my eyes, declares the LORD. They have set up their detestable idols*b* in the house that bears my Name and have defiled*c* it. 31They have built the high places of Topheth*d* in the Valley of Ben Hinnom to burn their sons and daughters*e* in the fire—something I did not command, nor did it enter my mind.*f* 32So beware, the days are coming, declares the LORD, when people will no longer call it Topheth or the Valley of Ben Hinnom, but the Valley of Slaughter,*g* for they will bury*h* the dead in Topheth until there is no more room. 33Then the carcasses of this people will become food*i* for the birds of the air and the beasts of the earth, and there will be no one to frighten them away. 34I will bring an end to the sounds*j* of joy and gladness and to the voices of bride and bridegroom*k* in the towns of Judah and the streets of Jerusalem, for the land will become desolate.*l*

Chapter 8 Theme

8 "'At that time, declares the LORD, the bones of the kings and officials of Judah, the bones of the priests and prophets, and the bones of the people of Jerusalem will be removed from their graves. 2They will be exposed to the sun and the moon and all the stars of the heavens, which they have loved and served*m* and which they have followed and consulted and worshiped. They will not be gathered up or buried, but will be like refuse lying on the ground. 3Wherever I banish them, all the survivors of this evil nation will prefer death to life,*n* declares the LORD Almighty.'

4"Say to them, 'This is what the LORD says:

"'When men fall down, do they not get up?*o*
    When a man turns away, does he not return?
5Why then have these people turned away?
    Why does Jerusalem always turn away?
They cling to deceit;*p*
    they refuse to return.*q*
6I have listened attentively,
    but they do not say what is right.
No one repents*r* of his wickedness,
    saying, "What have I done?"
Each pursues his own course*s*
    like a horse charging into battle.
7Even the stork in the sky
    knows her appointed seasons,
and the dove, the swift and the thrush
    observe the time of their migration.

7:29
a Jer 6:30

7:30
b Eze 7:20-22
c Jer 32:34

7:31
d 2Ki 23:10
e Ps 106:38
f Jer 19:5

7:32
g Jer 19:6
h Jer 19:11

7:33
i Dt 28:26

7:34
j Isa 24:8;
Eze 26:13
k Rev 18:23
l Lev 26:34

8:2
m 2Ki 23:5;
Ac 7:42

8:3
n Job 3:22;
Rev 9:6

8:4
o Pr 24:16

8:5
p Jer 5:27
q Jer 7:24; 9:6

8:6
r Rev 9:20
s Ps 14:1-3

But my people do not know[a]
the requirements of the LORD.

8:7
a Isa 1:3;
Jer 5:4-5

8 "'How can you say, "We are wise,
for we have the law[b] of the LORD,"
when actually the lying pen of the scribes
has handled it falsely?

8:8
b Ro 2:17

9 The wise[c] will be put to shame;
they will be dismayed and trapped.
Since they have rejected the word[d] of the LORD,
what kind of wisdom do they have?

8:9
c Jer 6:15
d Jer 6:19

10 Therefore I will give their wives to other men
and their fields to new owners.[e]
From the least to the greatest,
all are greedy for gain;[f]

8:10
e Jer 6:12
f Isa 56:11

prophets and priests alike,
all practice deceit.
11 They dress the wound of my people
as though it were not serious.
"Peace, peace," they say,
when there is no peace.[g]

8:11
g Jer 6:14

12 Are they ashamed of their loathsome conduct?
No, they have no shame[h] at all;
they do not even know how to blush.
So they will fall among the fallen;
they will be brought down when they are punished,[i]
says the LORD.[j]

8:12
h Jer 3:3
i Ps 52:5-7;
Isa 3:9
j Jer 6:15

13 "'I will take away their harvest,
declares the Lord.
There will be no grapes on the vine.[k]
There will be no figs[l] on the tree,
and their leaves will wither.[m]
What I have given them
will be taken[n] from them.a'"

8:13
k Joel 1:7
l Lk 13:6
m Mt 21:19
n Jer 5:17

14 "Why are we sitting here?
Gather together!
Let us flee to the fortified cities[o]
and perish there!
For the LORD our God has doomed us to perish
and given us poisoned water[p] to drink,
because we have sinned[q] against him.

8:14
o Jer 4:5;
Jer 35:11
p Dt 29:18;
Jer 9:15; 23:15
q Jer 14:7,20

15 We hoped for peace[r]
but no good has come,
for a time of healing
but there was only terror.[s]

8:15
r ver 11
s Jer 14:19

a 13 The meaning of the Hebrew for this sentence is uncertain.

¹⁶The snorting of the enemy's horses
    is heard from Dan;^a
at the neighing of their stallions
    the whole land trembles.
They have come to devour
    the land and everything in it,
    the city and all who live there."

¹⁷"See, I will send venomous snakes^b among you,
    vipers that cannot be charmed,^c
and they will bite you,"
                declares the LORD.

¹⁸O my Comforter^a in sorrow,
    my heart is faint^d within me.
¹⁹Listen to the cry of my people
    from a land far away:^e
"Is the LORD not in Zion?
    Is her King no longer there?"

"Why have they provoked me to anger with their images,
    with their worthless foreign idols?"^f

²⁰"The harvest is past,
    the summer has ended,
    and we are not saved."

²¹Since my people are crushed, I am crushed;
    I mourn,^g and horror grips me.
²²Is there no balm in Gilead?^h
    Is there no physician there?
Why then is there no healingⁱ
    for the wound of my people?

Chapter 9 Theme

9 Oh, that my head were a spring of water
    and my eyes a fountain of tears!
I would weep^j day and night
    for the slain of my people.^k
²Oh, that I had in the desert
    a lodging place for travelers,
so that I might leave my people
    and go away from them;
for they are all adulterers,^l
    a crowd of unfaithful people.

³"They make ready their tongue
    like a bow, to shoot lies;^m

---

^a 18 The meaning of the Hebrew for this word is uncertain.

8:16
^aJer 4:15

8:17
^bNu 21:6;
Dt 32:24
^cPs 58:5

8:18
^dLa 5:17

8:19
^eJer 9:16
^fDt 32:21

8:21
^gJer 14:17

8:22
^hGe 37:25
ⁱJer 30:12

9:1
^jJer 13:17;
La 2:11,18
^kIsa 22:4

9:2
^lJer 5:7-8;
23:10; Hos 4:2

9:3
^mPs 64:3

it is not by truth
that they triumph^a in the land.
They go from one sin to another;
they do not acknowledge me,"

declares the LORD.

^{4}"Beware of your friends;
do not trust your brothers.^{a}
For every brother is a deceiver,^{bb}
and every friend a slanderer.
^{5}Friend deceives friend,
and no one speaks the truth.
They have taught their tongues to lie;
they weary themselves with sinning.
^{6}You^c live in the midst of deception;^{c}
in their deceit they refuse to acknowledge me,"

declares the LORD.

^{7}Therefore this is what the LORD Almighty says:

"See, I will refine^d and test^e them,
for what else can I do
because of the sin of my people?
^{8}Their tongue^f is a deadly arrow;
it speaks with deceit.
With his mouth each speaks cordially to his neighbor,
but in his heart he sets a trap^g for him.
^{9}Should I not punish them for this?"
declares the LORD.
"Should I not avenge^h myself
on such a nation as this?"

^{10}I will weep and wail for the mountains
and take up a lament concerning the desert pastures.
They are desolate and untraveled,
and the lowing of cattle is not heard.
The birds of the air^i have fled
and the animals are gone.

^{11}"I will make Jerusalem a heap of ruins,
a haunt of jackals;^{j}
and I will lay waste the towns of Judah
so no one can live there."^{k}

^{12}What man is wise^l enough to understand this? Who has been instructed by the LORD and can explain it? Why has the land been ruined and laid waste like a desert that no one can cross?

9:4
^{a} Mic 7:5-6
^{b} Ge 27:35

9:6
^{c} Jer 5:27

9:7
^{d} Isa 1:25
^{e} Jer 6:27

9:8
^{f} ver 3
^{g} Jer 5:26

9:9
^{h} Jer 5:9,29

9:10
^{i} Jer 4:25; 12:4; Hos 4:3

9:11
^{j} Isa 34:13
^{k} Isa 25:2; Jer 26:9

9:12
^{l} Ps 107:43; Hos 14:9

---

^{a} 3 Or *lies; / they are not valiant for truth* ^{b} 4 Or *a deceiving Jacob* ^{c} 6 That is, Jeremiah (the Hebrew is singular)

¹³The LORD said, "It is because they have forsaken my law, which I set before them; they have not obeyed me or followed my law.ᵃ ¹⁴Instead, they have followedᵇ the stubbornness of their hearts;ᶜ they have followed the Baals, as their fathers taught them." ¹⁵Therefore, this is what the LORD Almighty, the God of Israel, says: "See, I will make this people eat bitter foodᵈ and drink poisoned water.ᵉ ¹⁶I will scatter them among nationsᶠ that neither they nor their fathers have known,ᵍ and I will pursue them with the swordʰ until I have destroyed them."ⁱ

¹⁷This is what the LORD Almighty says:

"Consider now! Call for the wailing womenʲ to come;
    send for the most skillful of them.
¹⁸Let them come quickly
    and wail over us
till our eyes overflow with tears
    and water streams from our eyelids.ᵏ
¹⁹The sound of wailing is heard from Zion:
    'How ruinedˡ we are!
    How great is our shame!
We must leave our land
    because our houses are in ruins.'"

²⁰Now, O women, hear the word of the LORD;
    open your ears to the words of his mouth.
Teach your daughters how to wail;
    teach one another a lament.ᵐ
²¹Death has climbed in through our windows
    and has entered our fortresses;
it has cut off the children from the streets
    and the young menⁿ from the public squares.

²²Say, "This is what the LORD declares:

"'The dead bodies of men will lie
    like refuseᵒ on the open field,
like cut grain behind the reaper,
    with no one to gather them.'"

²³This is what the LORD says:

"Let not the wise man boast of his wisdomᵖ
    or the strong man boast of his strengthᑫ
    or the rich man boast of his riches,ʳ
²⁴but let him who boasts boastˢ about this:
    that he understands and knows me,

9:13
ᵃ2Ch 7:19;
Ps 89:30-32

9:14
ᵇJer 2:8,23
ᶜJer 7:24

9:15
ᵈLa 3:15
ᵉJer 8:14

9:16
ᶠLev 26:33
ᵍDt 28:64
ʰEze 5:2
ⁱJer 44:27;
Eze 5:12

9:17
ʲ2Ch 35:25;
Ecc 12:5;
Am 5:16

9:18
ᵏJer 14:17

9:19
ˡJer 4:13

9:20
ᵐIsa 32:9-13

9:21
ⁿ2Ch 36:17

9:22
ᵒJer 8:2

9:23
ᵖEcc 9:11
ᑫ1Ki 20:11
ʳEze 28:4-5

9:24
ˢ1Co 1:31*;
Gal 6:14

9:24
a 2Co 10:17*
b Ps 51:1;
Mic 7:18
c Ps 36:6

that I am the LORD,[a] who exercises kindness,[b]
  justice and righteousness[c] on earth,
  for in these I delight,"

declares the LORD.

9:25
d Ro 2:8-9

[25]"The days are coming," declares the LORD, "when I will punish all who are circumcised only in the flesh[d]— [26]Egypt, Judah, Edom, Ammon, Moab and all who live in the desert in distant places.[a][e] For all these nations are really uncircumcised, and even the whole house of Israel is uncircumcised in heart.[f]"

9:26
e Jer 25:23
f Lev 26:41;
Ac 7:51;
Ro 2:28

Chapter 10 Theme _____

10 Hear what the LORD says to you, O house of Israel. [2]This is what the LORD says:

"Do not learn the ways of the nations[g]
  or be terrified by signs in the sky,
  though the nations are terrified by them.

10:2
g Lev 20:23

[3]For the customs of the peoples are worthless;
  they cut a tree out of the forest,
  and a craftsman[h] shapes it with his chisel.

10:3
h Isa 40:19

[4]They adorn it with silver and gold;
  they fasten it with hammer and nails
  so it will not totter.[i]

10:4
i Isa 41:7

[5]Like a scarecrow in a melon patch,
  their idols cannot speak;[j]
they must be carried
  because they cannot walk.[k]
Do not fear them;
  they can do no harm
  nor can they do any good."[l]

10:5
j 1Co 12:2
k Ps 115:5,7
l Isa 41:24;
46:7

[6]No one is like you, O LORD;
  you are great,[m]
  and your name is mighty in power.

10:6
m Ps 48:1

[7]Who should not revere you,
  O King of the nations?[n]
  This is your due.
Among all the wise men of the nations
  and in all their kingdoms,
  there is no one like you.

10:7
n Ps 22:28;
Rev 15:4

[8]They are all senseless and foolish;[o]
  they are taught by worthless wooden idols.
[9]Hammered silver is brought from Tarshish
  and gold from Uphaz.

10:8
o Isa 40:19;
Jer 4:22

a 26 Or *desert and who clip the hair by their foreheads*

What the craftsman and goldsmith have made[a]
  is then dressed in blue and purple—
    all made by skilled workers.
¹⁰But the LORD is the true God;
  he is the living God, the eternal King.
When he is angry, the earth trembles;
  the nations cannot endure his wrath.[b]

¹¹"Tell them this: 'These gods, who did not make the heavens and the earth, will perish[c] from the earth and from under the heavens.'"[a]

¹²But God made the earth by his power;
  he founded the world by his wisdom
    and stretched out the heavens[d] by his understanding.
¹³When he thunders,[e] the waters in the heavens roar;
  he makes clouds rise from the ends of the earth.
He sends lightning with the rain[f]
  and brings out the wind from his storehouses.

¹⁴Everyone is senseless and without knowledge;
  every goldsmith is shamed by his idols.
His images are a fraud;
  they have no breath in them.
¹⁵They are worthless,[g] the objects of mockery;
  when their judgment comes, they will perish.
¹⁶He who is the Portion[h] of Jacob is not like these,
  for he is the Maker of all things,[i]
including Israel, the tribe of his inheritance[j]—
  the LORD Almighty is his name.[k]

¹⁷Gather up your belongings[l] to leave the land,
  you who live under siege.
¹⁸For this is what the LORD says:
  "At this time I will hurl[m] out
    those who live in this land;
I will bring distress on them
  so that they may be captured."

¹⁹Woe to me because of my injury!
  My wound[n] is incurable!
Yet I said to myself,
  "This is my sickness, and I must endure[o] it."
²⁰My tent[p] is destroyed;
  all its ropes are snapped.

a 11 The text of this verse is in Aramaic.

10:9
a Ps 115:4;
Isa 40:19

10:10
b Ps 76:7

10:11
c Ps 96:5;
Isa 2:18

10:12
d Ge 1:1,8;
Job 9:8;
Isa 40:22

10:13
e Job 36:29
f Ps 135:7

10:15
g Isa 41:24;
Jer 14:22

10:16
h Dt 32:9;
Ps 119:57
i ver 12
j Ps 74:2
k Jer 31:35;
32:18

10:17
l Eze 12:3-12

10:18
m 1Sa 25:29

10:19
n Jer 14:17
o Mic 7:9

10:20
p Jer 4:20

10:20
a Jer 31:15;
La 1:5

10:21
b Jer 23:2

10:22
c Jer 9:11

10:23
d Pr 20:24

10:24
e Ps 6:1; 38:1
f Jer 30:11

10:25
g Zep 3:8
h Job 18:21;
Ps 14:4
i Ps 79:7;
Jer 8:16
j Ps 79:6-7

11:3
k Dt 27:26;
Gal 3:10

11:4
l Dt 4:20;
1Ki 8:51
m Ex 24:8
n Jer 7:23; 31:33

11:5
o Ex 13:5;
Dt 7:12;
Ps 105:8-11

11:6
p Dt 15:5;
Ro 2:13;
Jas 1:22

11:7
q 2Ch 36:15

11:8
r Jer 7:26
s Lev 26:14-43

My sons are gone from me and are no more;[a]
>   no one is left now to pitch my tent
>   or to set up my shelter.
[21] The shepherds are senseless
>   and do not inquire of the Lord;
> so they do not prosper
>   and all their flock is scattered.[b]
[22] Listen! The report is coming—
>   a great commotion from the land of the north!
> It will make the towns of Judah desolate,
>   a haunt of jackals.[c]

[23] I know, O Lord, that a man's life is not his own;
>   it is not for man to direct his steps.[d]
[24] Correct me, Lord, but only with justice—
>   not in your anger,[e]
>   lest you reduce me to nothing.[f]
[25] Pour out your wrath on the nations[g]
>   that do not acknowledge you,
>   on the peoples who do not call on your name.[h]
> For they have devoured[i] Jacob;
>   they have devoured him completely
>   and destroyed his homeland.[j]

Chapter 11 Theme

11 This is the word that came to Jeremiah from the Lord: [2]"Listen to the terms of this covenant and tell them to the people of Judah and to those who live in Jerusalem. [3]Tell them that this is what the Lord, the God of Israel, says: 'Cursed[k] is the man who does not obey the terms of this covenant— [4]the terms I commanded your forefathers when I brought them out of Egypt, out of the iron-smelting furnace.[l] I said, 'Obey[m] me and do everything I command you, and you will be my people,[n] and I will be your God. [5]Then I will fulfill the oath I swore[o] to your forefathers, to give them a land flowing with milk and honey'—the land you possess today."

I answered, "Amen, Lord."

[6]The Lord said to me, "Proclaim all these words in the towns of Judah and in the streets of Jerusalem: 'Listen to the terms of this covenant and follow[p] them. [7]From the time I brought your forefathers up from Egypt until today, I warned them again and again,[q] saying, "Obey me." [8]But they did not listen or pay attention;[r] instead, they followed the stubbornness of their evil hearts. So I brought on them all the curses[s] of the covenant I had commanded them to follow but that they did not keep.'"

⁹Then the LORD said to me, "There is a conspiracy[a] among the people of Judah and those who live in Jerusalem. ¹⁰They have returned to the sins of their forefathers,[b] who refused to listen to my words. They have followed other gods[c] to serve them. Both the house of Israel and the house of Judah have broken the covenant I made with their forefathers. ¹¹Therefore this is what the LORD says: 'I will bring on them a disaster[d] they cannot escape. Although they cry[e] out to me, I will not listen[f] to them. ¹²The towns of Judah and the people of Jerusalem will go and cry out to the gods to whom they burn incense,[g] but they will not help them at all when disaster[h] strikes. ¹³You have as many gods as you have towns, O Judah; and the altars you have set up to burn incense[i] to that shameful[j] god Baal are as many as the streets of Jerusalem.'

¹⁴"Do not pray[k] for this people nor offer any plea or petition for them, because I will not listen[l] when they call to me in the time of their distress.

¹⁵"What is my beloved doing in my temple
    as she works out her evil schemes with many?
Can consecrated meat avert ⌊your punishment⌋?
When you engage in your wickedness,
    then you rejoice.[a]"

¹⁶The LORD called you a thriving olive tree
    with fruit beautiful in form.
But with the roar of a mighty storm
    he will set it on fire,[m]
and its branches will be broken.[n]

¹⁷The LORD Almighty, who planted[o] you, has decreed disaster for you, because the house of Israel and the house of Judah have done evil and provoked me to anger by burning incense to Baal.[p]

¹⁸Because the LORD revealed their plot to me, I knew it, for at that time he showed me what they were doing. ¹⁹I had been like a gentle lamb led to the slaughter; I did not realize that they had plotted[q] against me, saying,

"Let us destroy the tree and its fruit;
    let us cut him off from the land of the living,[r]
that his name be remembered[s] no more."

²⁰But, O LORD Almighty, you who judge righteously
    and test the heart and mind,[t]
let me see your vengeance upon them,
    for to you I have committed my cause.

²¹"Therefore this is what the LORD says about the men of Anathoth who are seeking your life[u] and saying, 'Do not prophesy in the

---

11:9
[a] Eze 22:25

11:10
[b] Dt 9:7
[c] Jdg 2:12-13

11:11
[d] 2Ki 22:16
[e] Jer 14:12; Eze 8:18
[f] ver 14; Pr 1:28; Isa 1:15; Zec 7:13

11:12
[g] Jer 44:17
[h] Dt 32:37

11:13
[i] Jer 7:9
[j] Jer 3:24

11:14
[k] Ex 32:10
[l] ver 11

11:16
[m] Jer 21:14
[n] Isa 27:11; Ro 11:17-24

11:17
[o] Isa 5:2; Jer 12:2
[p] Jer 7:9

11:19
[q] Jer 18:18; 20:10
[r] Job 28:13; Isa 53:8
[s] Ps 83:4

11:20
[t] Ps 7:9

11:21
[u] Jer 12:6

---

[a] 15 Or Could consecrated meat avert your punishment? / Then you would rejoice

name of the LORD or you will die[a] by our hands'— ²²therefore this is what the LORD Almighty says: 'I will punish them. Their young men[b] will die by the sword, their sons and daughters by famine. ²³Not even a remnant[c] will be left to them, because I will bring disaster on the men of Anathoth in the year of their punishment.[d]'"

Chapter 12 Theme _____

12 You are always righteous,[e] O LORD,
　　when I bring a case before you.
　Yet I would speak with you about your justice:
　　Why does the way of the wicked prosper?[f]
　　Why do all the faithless live at ease?
　²You have planted[g] them, and they have taken root;
　　they grow and bear fruit.
　You are always on their lips
　　but far from their hearts.[h]
　³Yet you know me, O LORD;
　　you see me and test[i] my thoughts about you.
　Drag them off like sheep to be butchered!
　　Set them apart for the day of slaughter![j]
　⁴How long will the land lie parched[a][k]
　　and the grass in every field be withered?[l]
　Because those who live in it are wicked,
　　the animals and birds have perished.[m]
　Moreover, the people are saying,
　　"He will not see what happens to us."

　⁵"If you have raced with men on foot
　　and they have worn you out,
　　how can you compete with horses?
　If you stumble in safe country,[b]
　　how will you manage in the thickets[n] by[c] the Jordan?
　⁶Your brothers, your own family—
　　even they have betrayed you;
　　they have raised a loud cry against you.[o]
　Do not trust them,
　　though they speak well of you.[p]

　⁷"I will forsake my house,
　　abandon[q] my inheritance;
　I will give the one I love
　　into the hands of her enemies.
　⁸My inheritance has become to me
　　like a lion in the forest.

---

^a4 Or *land mourn*　^b5 Or *If you put your trust in a land of safety*　^c5 Or *the flooding of*

11:21
a Jer 26:8,11;
　38:4

11:22
b Jer 18:21

11:23
c Jer 6:9
d Jer 23:12

12:1
e Ezr 9:15
f Jer 5:27-28

12:2
g Jer 11:17
h Isa 29:13;
　Jer 3:10;
　Mt 15:8;
　Tit 1:16

12:3
i Ps 7:9; 11:5;
　139:1-4;
　Jer 11:20
j Jer 17:18

12:4
k Jer 4:28
l Joel 1:10-12
m Jer 4:25; 9:10

12:5
n Jer 49:19;
　50:44

12:6
o Pr 26:24-25;
　Jer 9:4
p Ps 12:2

12:7
q Jer 7:29

She roars at me;
    therefore I hate her.*a*

⁹Has not my inheritance become to me
    like a speckled bird of prey
    that other birds of prey surround and attack?
Go and gather all the wild beasts;
    bring them to devour.*b*
¹⁰Many shepherds*c* will ruin my vineyard
    and trample down my field;
they will turn my pleasant field
    into a desolate wasteland.*d*
¹¹It will be made a wasteland,
    parched and desolate before me;*e*
the whole land will be laid waste
    because there is no one who cares.
¹²Over all the barren heights in the desert
    destroyers will swarm,
for the sword of the Lord*f* will devour
    from one end of the land to the other;*g*
    no one will be safe.
¹³They will sow wheat but reap thorns;
    they will wear themselves out but gain nothing.*h*
So bear the shame of your harvest
    because of the Lord's fierce anger."*i*

¹⁴This is what the Lord says: "As for all my wicked neighbors who seize the inheritance I gave my people Israel, I will uproot*j* them from their lands and I will uproot the house of Judah from among them. ¹⁵But after I uproot them, I will again have compassion and will bring*k* each of them back to his own inheritance and his own country. ¹⁶And if they learn well the ways of my people and swear by my name, saying, 'As surely as the Lord lives'*l*— even as they once taught my people to swear by Baal*m*—then they will be established among my people.*n* ¹⁷But if any nation does not listen, I will completely uproot and destroy*o* it," declares the Lord.

Chapter 13 Theme

13 This is what the Lord said to me: "Go and buy a linen belt and put it around your waist, but do not let it touch water." ²So I bought a belt, as the Lord directed, and put it around my waist.

³Then the word of the Lord came to me a second time: ⁴"Take the belt you bought and are wearing around your waist, and go now to Perath*a* and hide it there in a crevice in the rocks." ⁵So I went and hid it at Perath, as the Lord told me.*p*

---

*a*4 Or possibly *the Euphrates; also in verses 5-7*

12:8
*a*Hos 9:15;
Am 6:8

12:9
*b*Isa 56:9;
Jer 15:3;
Eze 23:25

12:10
*c*Jer 23:1
*d*Isa 5:1-7

12:11
*e*ver 4;
Isa 42:25;
Jer 23:10

12:12
*f*Jer 47:6
*g*Jer 3:2

12:13
*h*Lev 26:20;
Dt 28:38;
Mic 6:15;
Hag 1:6
*i*Jer 4:26

12:14
*j*Zec 2:7-9

12:15
*k*Am 9:14-15

12:16
*l*Jer 4:2
*m*Jos 23:7
*n*Isa 49:6;
Jer 3:17

12:17
*o*Isa 60:12

13:5
*p*Ex 40:16

13:9
a Lev 26:19

⁶Many days later the LORD said to me, "Go now to Perath and get the belt I told you to hide there." ⁷So I went to Perath and dug up the belt and took it from the place where I had hidden it, but now it was ruined and completely useless.

⁸Then the word of the LORD came to me: ⁹"This is what the LORD says: 'In the same way I will ruin the pride of Judah and the great pride*a* of Jerusalem. ¹⁰These wicked people, who refuse to listen to my words, who follow the stubbornness of their hearts*b* and go after other gods*c* to serve and worship them, will be like this belt—completely useless! ¹¹For as a belt is bound around a man's waist, so I bound the whole house of Israel and the whole house of Judah to me,' declares the LORD, 'to be my people for my renown*d* and praise and honor.*e* But they have not listened.'*f*

13:10
b Jer 11:8; 16:12
c Jer 9:14

13:11
d Jer 32:20; 33:9
e Ex 19:5-6
f Jer 7:26

¹²"Say to them: 'This is what the LORD, the God of Israel, says: Every wineskin should be filled with wine.' And if they say to you, 'Don't we know that every wineskin should be filled with wine?' ¹³then tell them, 'This is what the LORD says: I am going to fill with drunkenness*g* all who live in this land, including the kings who sit on David's throne, the priests, the prophets and all those living in Jerusalem. ¹⁴I will smash them one against the other, fathers and sons alike, declares the LORD. I will allow no pity or mercy or compassion*h* to keep me from destroying*i* them.'"

13:13
g Ps 60:3; 75:8;
Isa 51:17; 63:6;
Jer 51:57

¹⁵Hear and pay attention,
    do not be arrogant,
    for the LORD has spoken.
¹⁶Give glory*j* to the LORD your God
    before he brings the darkness,
  before your feet stumble*k*
    on the darkening hills.
  You hope for light,
    but he will turn it to thick darkness
    and change it to deep gloom.*l*

13:14
h Jer 16:5
i Dt 29:20;
Eze 5:10

¹⁷But if you do not listen,*m*
    I will weep in secret
    because of your pride;
  my eyes will weep bitterly,
    overflowing with tears,*n*
    because the LORD's flock*o* will be taken captive.*p*

13:16
j Jos 7:19
k Jer 23:12
l Isa 59:9

¹⁸Say to the king and to the queen mother,
    "Come down from your thrones,
  for your glorious crowns
    will fall from your heads."
¹⁹The cities in the Negev will be shut up,
    and there will be no one to open them.

13:17
m Mal 2:2
n Jer 9:1
o Ps 80:1;
Jer 23:1
p Jer 14:18

> All Judah[a] will be carried into exile,
>   carried completely away.
>
> ²⁰Lift up your eyes and see
>   those who are coming from the north.[b]
> Where is the flock[c] that was entrusted to you,
>   the sheep of which you boasted?
> ²¹What will you say when ˻the LORD˼ sets over you
>   those you cultivated as your special allies?[d]
> Will not pain grip you
>   like that of a woman in labor?[e]
> ²²And if you ask yourself,
>   "Why has this happened to me?"—
> it is because of your many sins[f]
>   that your skirts have been torn off
>   and your body mistreated.[g]
> ²³Can the Ethiopian[a] change his skin
>   or the leopard its spots?
> Neither can you do good
>   who are accustomed to doing evil.
> ²⁴"I will scatter you like chaff[h]
>   driven by the desert wind.[i]
> ²⁵This is your lot,
>   the portion[j] I have decreed for you,"
>   declares the LORD,
> "because you have forgotten me
>   and trusted in false gods.
> ²⁶I will pull up your skirts over your face
>   that your shame may be seen[k]—
> ²⁷your adulteries and lustful neighings,
>   your shameless prostitution![l]
> I have seen your detestable acts
>   on the hills and in the fields.[m]
> Woe to you, O Jerusalem!
>   How long will you be unclean?"[n]

Chapter 14 Theme

14 This is the word of the LORD to Jeremiah concerning the drought:

> ²"Judah mourns,[o]
>   her cities languish;
> they wail for the land,
>   and a cry goes up from Jerusalem.

a 23 Hebrew *Cushite* (probably a person from the upper Nile region)

13:19 a Jer 20:4; 52:30
13:20 b Jer 6:22; Hab 1:6 c Jer 23:2
13:21 d Jer 38:22 e Jer 4:31
13:22 f Jer 9:2-6; 16:10-12 g Eze 16:37; Na 3:5-6
13:24 h Ps 1:4 i Lev 26:33
13:25 j Job 20:29; Mt 24:51
13:26 k La 1:8; Eze 16:37; Hos 2:10
13:27 l Jer 2:20 m Eze 6:13 n Hos 8:5
14:2 o Isa 3:26; Jer 8:21

14:3
a 2Ki 18:31;
Job 6:19-20
b 2Sa 15:30

³The nobles send their servants for water;
    they go to the cisterns
    but find no water.ᵃ
They return with their jars unfilled;
    dismayed and despairing,
    they cover their heads.ᵇ

14:4
c Jer 3:3

⁴The ground is cracked
    because there is no rain in the land;ᶜ
the farmers are dismayed
    and cover their heads.

14:5
d Isa 15:6

⁵Even the doe in the field
    deserts her newborn fawn
    because there is no grass.ᵈ

14:6
e Job 39:5-6;
Jer 2:24

⁶Wild donkeys stand on the barren heightsᵉ
    and pant like jackals;
their eyesight fails
    for lack of pasture."

14:7
f Hos 5:5
g Jer 5:6
h Jer 8:14

⁷Although our sins testifyᶠ against us,
    O Lᴏʀᴅ, do something for the sake of your name.
For our backslidingᵍ is great;
    we have sinnedʰ against you.

14:8
i Jer 17:13

⁸O Hopeⁱ of Israel,
    its Savior in times of distress,
why are you like a stranger in the land,
    like a traveler who stays only a night?

14:9
j Isa 50:2
k Jer 8:19
l Isa 63:19;
Jer 15:16

⁹Why are you like a man taken by surprise,
    like a warrior powerless to save?ʲ
You are amongᵏ us, O Lᴏʀᴅ,
    and we bear your name;ˡ
    do not forsake us!

14:10
m Ps 119:101;
Jer 2:25
n Jer 6:20;
Am 5:22
o Hos 9:9
p Jer 44:21-23;
Hos 8:13

¹⁰This is what the Lᴏʀᴅ says about this people:

"They greatly love to wander;
    they do not restrain their feet.ᵐ
So the Lᴏʀᴅ does not acceptⁿ them;
    he will now rememberᵒ their wickedness
    and punish them for their sins."ᵖ

14:11
q Ex 32:10

¹¹Then the Lᴏʀᴅ said to me, "Do not pray�q for the well-being of this people. ¹²Although they fast, I will not listen to their cry;ʳ though they offer burnt offeringsˢ and grain offerings, I will not acceptᵗ them. Instead, I will destroy them with the sword, famine and plague."

14:12
r Isa 1:15;
Jer 11:11
s Jer 7:21
t Jer 6:20

¹³But I said, "Ah, Sovereign Lᴏʀᴅ, the prophets keep telling them, 'You will not see the sword or suffer famine.ᵘ Indeed, I will give you lasting peace in this place.'"

14:13
u Jer 5:12

¹⁴Then the LORD said to me, "The prophets are prophesying lies[a] in my name. I have not sent[b] them or appointed them or spoken to them. They are prophesying to you false visions,[c] divinations,[d] idolatries[a] and the delusions of their own minds. ¹⁵Therefore, this is what the LORD says about the prophets who are prophesying in my name: I did not send them, yet they are saying, 'No sword or famine will touch this land.' Those same prophets will perish[e] by sword and famine.[f] ¹⁶And the people they are prophesying to will be thrown out into the streets of Jerusalem because of the famine and sword. There will be no one to bury[g] them or their wives, their sons or their daughters.[h] I will pour out on them the calamity they deserve.[i]

¹⁷"Speak this word to them:

"'Let my eyes overflow with tears[j]
    night and day without ceasing;
for my virgin daughter—my people—
    has suffered a grievous wound,
    a crushing blow.[k]
¹⁸If I go into the country,
    I see those slain by the sword;
if I go into the city,
    I see the ravages of famine.[l]
Both prophet and priest
    have gone to a land they know not.'"

¹⁹Have you rejected Judah completely?[m]
    Do you despise Zion?
Why have you afflicted us
    so that we cannot be healed?[n]
We hoped for peace
    but no good has come,
for a time of healing
    but there is only terror.[o]
²⁰O LORD, we acknowledge our wickedness
    and the guilt of our fathers;
    we have indeed sinned[p] against you.
²¹For the sake of your name[q] do not despise us;
    do not dishonor your glorious throne.[r]
Remember your covenant with us
    and do not break it.
²²Do any of the worthless idols of the nations bring rain?[s]
    Do the skies themselves send down showers?

---

a 14 Or *visions, worthless divinations*

14:14
a Jer 27:14
b Jer 23:21,32
c Jer 23:16
d Eze 12:24

14:15
e Eze 14:9
f Jer 5:12-13

14:16
g Ps 79:3
h Jer 7:33
i Pr 1:31

14:17
j Jer 9:1
k Jer 8:21

14:18
l Eze 7:15

14:19
m Jer 7:29
n Jer 30:12-13
o Jer 8:15

14:20
p Da 9:7-8

14:21
q ver 7
r Jer 3:17

14:22
s Ps 135:7

No, it is you, O LORD our God.
Therefore our hope is in you,
for you are the one who does all this.

Chapter 15 Theme

15 Then the LORD said to me: "Even if Moses[a] and Samuel[b] were to stand before me, my heart would not go out to this people.[c] Send them away from my presence![d] Let them go! [2]And if they ask you, 'Where shall we go?' tell them, 'This is what the LORD says:

"'Those destined for death, to death;
those for the sword, to the sword;[e]
those for starvation, to starvation;[f]
those for captivity, to captivity.'[g]

[3]"I will send four kinds of destroyers[h] against them," declares the LORD, "the sword to kill and the dogs to drag away and the birds[i] of the air and the beasts of the earth to devour and destroy.[j] [4]I will make them abhorrent[k] to all the kingdoms of the earth[l] because of what Manasseh[m] son of Hezekiah king of Judah did in Jerusalem.

[5]"Who will have pity[n] on you, O Jerusalem?
Who will mourn for you?
Who will stop to ask how you are?
[6]You have rejected[o] me," declares the LORD.
"You keep on backsliding.
So I will lay hands[p] on you and destroy you;
I can no longer show compassion.
[7]I will winnow them with a winnowing fork
at the city gates of the land.
I will bring bereavement and destruction on my people,[q]
for they have not changed their ways.
[8]I will make their widows more numerous
than the sand of the sea.
At midday I will bring a destroyer[r]
against the mothers of their young men;
suddenly I will bring down on them
anguish and terror.
[9]The mother of seven will grow faint[s]
and breathe her last.
Her sun will set while it is still day;
she will be disgraced and humiliated.
I will put the survivors to the sword[t]
before their enemies,"
declares the LORD.

INSIGHT

Read 2 Chronicles 33:1-13 to see what Manasseh did.

15:1
[a] Ex 32:11;
Nu 14:13-20
[b] 1Sa 7:9
[c] Jer 7:16;
Eze 14:14,20
[d] 2Ki 17:20

15:2
[e] Jer 43:11
[f] Jer 14:12
[g] Rev 13:10

15:3
[h] Lev 26:16
[i] Dt 28:26
[j] Lev 26:22;
Eze 14:21

15:4
[k] Jer 24:9; 29:18
[l] Dt 28:25
[m] 2Ki 21:2;
23:26-27

15:5
[n] Isa 51:19;
Jer 13:14; 21:7;
Na 3:7

15:6
[o] Jer 6:19; 7:24
[p] Zep 1:4

15:7
[q] Jer 18:21

15:8
[r] Jer 6:4

15:9
[s] 1Sa 2:5
[t] Jer 21:7

¹⁰Alas, my mother, that you gave me birth,^a
    a man with whom the whole land strives and contends!^b
I have neither lent^c nor borrowed,
    yet everyone curses me.

¹¹The LORD said,

    "Surely I will deliver you^d for a good purpose;
        surely I will make your enemies plead^e with you
        in times of disaster and times of distress.

¹²"Can a man break iron—
    iron from the north^f—or bronze?
¹³Your wealth and your treasures
    I will give as plunder, without charge,^g
because of all your sins
    throughout your country.^h
¹⁴I will enslave you to your enemies
    in^a a land you do not know,ⁱ
for my anger will kindle a fire^j
    that will burn against you."

¹⁵You understand, O LORD;
    remember me and care for me.
    Avenge me on my persecutors.^k
You are long-suffering—do not take me away;
    think of how I suffer reproach for your sake.^l
¹⁶When your words came, I ate^m them;
    they were my joy and my heart's delight,ⁿ
for I bear your name,^o
    O LORD God Almighty.
¹⁷I never sat^p in the company of revelers,
    never made merry with them;
I sat alone because your hand was on me
    and you had filled me with indignation.
¹⁸Why is my pain unending
    and my wound grievous and incurable?^q
Will you be to me like a deceptive brook,
    like a spring that fails?^r

¹⁹Therefore this is what the LORD says:

    "If you repent, I will restore you
        that you may serve^s me;
    if you utter worthy, not worthless, words,
        you will be my spokesman.

^a 14 Some Hebrew manuscripts, Septuagint and Syriac (see also Jer. 17:4); most Hebrew manuscripts *I will cause your enemies to bring you / into*

15:10
^aJob 3:1
^bJer 1:19
^cLev 25:36

15:11
^dJer 40:4
^eJer 21:1-2;
37:3; 42:1-3

15:12
^fJer 28:14

15:13
^gPs 44:12
^hJer 17:3

15:14
ⁱDt 28:36;
Jer 16:13
^jDt 32:22;
Ps 21:9

15:15
^kJer 12:3
^lPs 69:7-9

15:16
^mEze 3:3;
Rev 10:10
ⁿPs 119:72,103
^oJer 14:9

15:17
^pPs 1:1; 26:4-5;
Jer 16:8

15:18
^qJer 30:15;
Mic 1:9
^rJob 6:15

15:19
^sZec 3:7

15:20
a Jer 20:11;
Eze 3:8

15:21
b Jer 50:34
c Ge 48:16

16:2
d 1Co 7:26-27

16:3
e Jer 6:21

16:4
f Jer 25:33
g Ps 83:10;
Jer 9:22
h Ps 79:1-3;
Jer 15:3; 34:20

16:6
i Eze 9:5-6
j Lev 19:28
k Jer 41:5; 47:5

16:7
l Eze 24:17;
Hos 9:4

16:8
m Ecc 7:2-4;
Jer 15:17

16:9
n Isa 24:8;
Eze 26:13;
Hos 2:11
o Rev 18:23

16:10
p Dt 29:24;
Jer 5:19

16:11
q Dt 29:25-26;
1Ki 9:9;
Ps 106:35-43;
Jer 22:9

16:12
r Jer 7:26
s Ecc 9:3;
Jer 13:10

16:13
t Dt 28:36;
Jer 5:19
u Dt 4:28
v Jer 15:5

Let this people turn to you,
> but you must not turn to them.
²⁰I will make you a wall to this people,
> a fortified wall of bronze;
they will fight against you
> but will not overcome you,
for I am with you
> to rescue and save you,"*a*

> > declares the LORD.

²¹"I will save you from the hands of the wicked
> and redeem*b* you from the grasp of the cruel."*c*

Chapter 16 Theme

16 Then the word of the LORD came to me: ²"You must not marry*d* and have sons or daughters in this place." ³For this is what the LORD says about the sons and daughters born in this land and about the women who are their mothers and the men who are their fathers:*e* ⁴"They will die of deadly diseases. They will not be mourned or buried*f* but will be like refuse lying on the ground.*g* They will perish by sword and famine, and their dead bodies will become food for the birds of the air and the beasts of the earth."*h*

⁵For this is what the LORD says: "Do not enter a house where there is a funeral meal; do not go to mourn or show sympathy, because I have withdrawn my blessing, my love and my pity from this people," declares the LORD. ⁶"Both high and low will die in this land.*i* They will not be buried or mourned, and no one will cut *j* himself or shave*k* his head for them. ⁷No one will offer food to comfort those who mourn*l* for the dead—not even for a father or a mother—nor will anyone give them a drink to console them.

⁸"And do not enter a house where there is feasting and sit down to eat and drink.*m* ⁹For this is what the LORD Almighty, the God of Israel, says: Before your eyes and in your days I will bring an end to the sounds*n* of joy and gladness and to the voices of bride and bridegroom in this place.*o*

¹⁰"When you tell these people all this and they ask you, 'Why has the LORD decreed such a great disaster against us? What wrong have we done? What sin have we committed against the LORD our God?'*p* ¹¹then say to them, 'It is because your fathers forsook me,' declares the LORD, 'and followed other gods and served and worshiped them. They forsook me and did not keep my law.*q* ¹²But you have behaved more wickedly than your fathers.*r* See how each of you is following the stubbornness of his evil heart*s* instead of obeying me. ¹³So I will throw you out of this land into a land neither you nor your fathers have known,*t* and there you will serve other gods*u* day and night, for I will show you no favor.'*v*

¹⁴"However, the days are coming," declares the LORD, "when men will no longer say, 'As surely as the LORD lives, who brought the Israelites up out of Egypt,'ᵃ ¹⁵but they will say, 'As surely as the LORD lives, who brought the Israelites up out of the land of the north and out of all the countries where he had banished them.'ᵇ For I will restoreᶜ them to the land I gave their forefathers.

¹⁶"But now I will send for many fishermen," declares the LORD, "and they will catch them.ᵈ After that I will send for many hunters, and they will huntᵉ them down on every mountain and hill and from the crevices of the rocks.ᶠ ¹⁷My eyes are on all their ways; they are not hiddenᵍ from me, nor is their sin concealed from my eyes.ʰ ¹⁸I will repay them doubleⁱ for their wickedness and their sin, because they have defiled my landʲ with the lifeless forms of their vile images and have filled my inheritance with their detestable idols."

¹⁹O LORD, my strength and my fortress,
    my refuge in time of distress,
to you the nations will comeᵏ
    from the ends of the earth and say,
"Our fathers possessed nothing but false gods,ˡ
    worthless idols that did them no good.
²⁰Do men make their own gods?
    Yes, but they are not gods!"ᵐ

²¹"Therefore I will teach them—
    this time I will teach them
my power and might.
Then they will know
    that my name is the LORD.

Chapter 17 Theme

17
"Judah's sin is engraved with an iron tool,ⁿ
    inscribed with a flint point,
on the tablets of their heartsᵒ
    and on the horns of their altars.
²Even their children remember
    their altars and Asherah polesᵃ ᵖ
beside the spreading trees
    and on the high hills.�q
³My mountain in the land
    and yourᵇ wealth and all your treasures
I will give away as plunder,ʳ
    together with your high places,ˢ
because of sin throughout your country.ᵗ

ᵃ2 That is, symbols of the goddess Asherah   ᵇ2,3 Or hills / ³and the mountains of the land. / Your

16:14
ᵃDt 15:15;
Jer 23:7-8

16:15
ᵇIsa 11:11;
Jer 23:8
ᶜJer 24:6

16:16
ᵈAm 4:2;
Hab 1:14-15
ᵉAm 9:3;
Mic 7:2
ᶠ1Sa 26:20

16:17
ᵍ1Co 4:5;
Heb 4:13
ʰPr 15:3

16:18
ⁱIsa 40:2;
Rev 18:6
ʲNu 35:34;
Jer 2:7

16:19
ᵏIsa 2:2;
Jer 3:17
ˡPs 4:2

16:20
ᵐPs 115:4-7;
Isa 37:19;
Jer 2:11

17:1
ⁿJob 19:24
ᵒPr 3:3; 2Co 3:3

17:2
ᵖ2Ch 24:18
qJer 2:20

17:3
ʳ2Ki 24:13
ˢJer 26:18;
Mic 3:12
ᵗJer 15:13

17:4
a La 5:2
b Dt 28:48;
Jer 12:7
c Jer 16:13
d Jer 7:20; 15:14

17:5
e Isa 2:22;
30:1-3

17:6
f Dt 29:23;
Job 39:6

17:7
g Ps 34:8; 40:4;
Pr 16:20

17:8
h Jer 14:1-6
i Ps 1:3;
92:12-14

17:9
j Ecc 9:3;
Mt 13:15;
Mk 7:21-22

17:10
k 1Sa 16:7;
Rev 2:23
l Ps 17:3;
139:23;
Jer 11:20;
20:12;
Ro 8:27
m Ps 62:12;
Jer 32:19
n Ro 2:6

17:11
o Lk 12:20

17:12
p Jer 3:17

17:13
q Jer 14:8
r Isa 1:28;
Jer 2:17

17:14
s Ps 109:1

⁴Through your own fault you will lose
the inheritance[a] I gave you.
I will enslave you to your enemies[b]
in a land[c] you do not know,
for you have kindled my anger,
and it will burn[d] forever."

⁵This is what the LORD says:

"Cursed is the one who trusts in man,[e]
who depends on flesh for his strength
and whose heart turns away from the LORD.
⁶He will be like a bush in the wastelands;
he will not see prosperity when it comes.
He will dwell in the parched places of the desert,
in a salt[f] land where no one lives.

⁷"But blessed is the man who trusts[g] in the LORD,
whose confidence is in him.
⁸He will be like a tree planted by the water
that sends out its roots by the stream.
It does not fear when heat comes;
its leaves are always green.
It has no worries in a year of drought[h]
and never fails to bear fruit."[i]

⁹The heart[j] is deceitful above all things
and beyond cure.
Who can understand it?

¹⁰"I the LORD search the heart[k]
and examine the mind,[l]
to reward[m] a man according to his conduct,
according to what his deeds deserve."[n]

¹¹Like a partridge that hatches eggs it did not lay
is the man who gains riches by unjust means.
When his life is half gone, they will desert him,
and in the end he will prove to be a fool.[o]

¹²A glorious throne,[p] exalted from the beginning,
is the place of our sanctuary.
¹³O LORD, the hope[q] of Israel,
all who forsake[r] you will be put to shame.
Those who turn away from you will be written in the dust
because they have forsaken the LORD,
the spring of living water.

¹⁴Heal me, O LORD, and I will be healed;
save me and I will be saved,
for you are the one I praise.[s]

¹⁵They keep saying to me,
"Where is the word of the LORD?
Let it now be fulfilled!"^a
¹⁶I have not run away from being your shepherd;
you know I have not desired the day of despair.
What passes my lips is open before you.
¹⁷Do not be a terror^b to me;
you are my refuge^c in the day of disaster.
¹⁸Let my persecutors be put to shame,
but keep me from shame;
let them be terrified,
but keep me from terror.
Bring on them the day of disaster;
destroy them with double destruction.^d

¹⁹This is what the LORD said to me: "Go and stand at the gate of the people, through which the kings of Judah go in and out; stand also at all the other gates of Jerusalem.^e ²⁰Say to them, 'Hear the word of the LORD, O kings of Judah and all people of Judah and everyone living in Jerusalem^f who come through these gates.^g ²¹This is what the LORD says: Be careful not to carry a load on the Sabbath^h day or bring it through the gates of Jerusalem. ²²Do not bring a load out of your houses or do any work on the Sabbath, but keep the Sabbath day holy, as I commanded your forefathers.ⁱ ²³Yet they did not listen or pay attention;^j they were stiff-necked^k and would not listen or respond to discipline.^l ²⁴But if you are careful to obey me, declares the LORD, and bring no load through the gates of this city on the Sabbath, but keep the Sabbath day holy by not doing any work on it, ²⁵then kings who sit on David's throne^m will come through the gates of this city with their officials. They and their officials will come riding in chariots and on horses, accompanied by the men of Judah and those living in Jerusalem, and this city will be inhabited forever. ²⁶People will come from the towns of Judah and the villages around Jerusalem, from the territory of Benjamin and the western foothills, from the hill country and the Negev,ⁿ bringing burnt offerings and sacrifices, grain offerings, incense and thank offerings to the house of the LORD. ²⁷But if you do not obey^o me to keep the Sabbath day holy by not carrying any load as you come through the gates of Jerusalem on the Sabbath day, then I will kindle an unquenchable fire^p in the gates of Jerusalem that will consume her fortresses.'"^q

Chapter 18 Theme

18 This is the word that came to Jeremiah from the LORD: ²"Go down to the potter's house, and there I will give you my message." ³So I went down to the potter's house, and I saw him

17:15
a Isa 5:19;
2Pe 3:4

17:17
b Ps 88:15-16
c Jer 16:19;
Na 1:7

17:18
d Ps 35:1-8

17:19
e Jer 7:2; 26:2

17:20
f Jer 19:3
g Jer 22:2

17:21
h Nu 15:32-36;
Ne 13:15-21;
Jn 5:10

17:22
i Ex 20:8; 31:13;
Isa 56:2-6;
Eze 20:12

17:23
j Jer 7:26
k Jer 19:15
l Jer 7:28

17:25
m 2Sa 7:13;
Isa 9:7;
Jer 22:2,4;
Lk 1:32

17:26
n Jer 32:44;
33:13; Zec 7:7

17:27
o Jer 22:5
p Jer 7:20
q 2Ki 25:9;
Am 2:5

18:6
a Isa 45:9;
Ro 9:20-21

18:7
b Jer 1:10

18:8
c Jer 26:13;
Jnh 3:8-10
d Eze 18:21;
Hos 11:8-9

18:9
e Jer 1:10; 31:28

18:10
f Eze 33:18
g 1Sa 2:29-30

18:11
h Jer 4:6
i 2Ki 17:13;
Isa 1:16-19
j Jer 7:3

18:12
k Isa 57:10;
Jer 2:25

18:13
l Isa 66:8;
Jer 2:10
m Jer 5:30

18:15
n Jer 10:15
o Jer 6:16
p Isa 57:14;
62:10

18:16
q Jer 25:9
r Jer 19:8
s Ps 22:7

18:17
t Jer 13:24
u Jer 2:27

working at the wheel. [4]But the pot he was shaping from the clay was marred in his hands; so the potter formed it into another pot, shaping it as seemed best to him.

[5]Then the word of the LORD came to me: [6]"O house of Israel, can I not do with you as this potter does?" declares the LORD. "Like clay*a* in the hand of the potter, so are you in my hand, O house of Israel. [7]If at any time I announce that a nation or kingdom is to be uprooted,*b* torn down and destroyed, [8]and if that nation I warned repents of its evil, then I will relent*c* and not inflict on it the disaster*d* I had planned. [9]And if at another time I announce that a nation or kingdom is to be built*e* up and planted, [10]and if it does evil*f* in my sight and does not obey me, then I will reconsider*g* the good I had intended to do for it.

[11]"Now therefore say to the people of Judah and those living in Jerusalem, 'This is what the LORD says: Look! I am preparing a disaster*h* for you and devising a plan against you. So turn*i* from your evil ways,*j* each one of you, and reform your ways and your actions.' [12]But they will reply, 'It's no use.*k* We will continue with our own plans; each of us will follow the stubbornness of his evil heart.'"

[13]Therefore this is what the LORD says:

> "Inquire among the nations:
>   Who has ever heard anything like this?*l*
> A most horrible*m* thing has been done
>   by Virgin Israel.
> [14]Does the snow of Lebanon
>   ever vanish from its rocky slopes?
> Do its cool waters from distant sources
>   ever cease to flow?*a*
> [15]Yet my people have forgotten me;
>   they burn incense to worthless idols,*n*
> which made them stumble in their ways
>   and in the ancient paths.*o*
> They made them walk in bypaths
>   and on roads not built up.*p*
> [16]Their land will be laid waste,*q*
>   an object of lasting scorn;*r*
> all who pass by will be appalled
>   and will shake their heads.*s*
> [17]Like a wind*t* from the east,
>   I will scatter them before their enemies;
> I will show them my back and not my face*u*
>   in the day of their disaster."

---

a 14 The meaning of the Hebrew for this sentence is uncertain.

[18]They said, "Come, let's make plans[a] against Jeremiah; for the teaching of the law by the priest[b] will not be lost, nor will counsel from the wise, nor the word from the prophets.[c] So come, let's attack him with our tongues[d] and pay no attention to anything he says."

[19]Listen to me, O LORD;
   hear what my accusers are saying!
[20]Should good be repaid with evil?
   Yet they have dug a pit[e] for me.
Remember that I stood before you
   and spoke in their behalf[f]
to turn your wrath away from them.
[21]So give their children over to famine;[g]
   hand them over to the power of the sword.
Let their wives be made childless and widows;[h]
   let their men be put to death,
   their young men slain by the sword in battle.
[22]Let a cry[i] be heard from their houses
   when you suddenly bring invaders against them,
for they have dug a pit to capture me
   and have hidden snares[j] for my feet.
[23]But you know, O LORD,
   all their plots to kill[k] me.
Do not forgive[l] their crimes
   or blot out their sins from your sight.
Let them be overthrown before you;
   deal with them in the time of your anger.

Chapter 19 Theme _____

19 This is what the LORD says: "Go and buy a clay jar from a potter.[m] Take along some of the elders[n] of the people and of the priests [2]and go out to the Valley of Ben Hinnom,[o] near the entrance of the Potsherd Gate. There proclaim the words I tell you, [3]and say, 'Hear the word of the LORD, O kings[p] of Judah and people of Jerusalem. This is what the LORD Almighty, the God of Israel, says: Listen! I am going to bring a disaster[q] on this place that will make the ears of everyone who hears of it tingle.[r] [4]For they have forsaken[s] me and made this a place of foreign gods; they have burned sacrifices[t] in it to gods that neither they nor their fathers nor the kings of Judah ever knew, and they have filled this place with the blood of the innocent.[u] [5]They have built the high places of Baal to burn their sons[v] in the fire as offerings to Baal—something I did not command or mention, nor did it enter my mind.[w] [6]So beware, the days are coming, declares the LORD, when people

Cross references

18:18
[a]Jer 11:19
[b]Mal 2:7
[c]Jer 5:13
[d]Ps 52:2

18:20
[e]Ps 35:7; 57:6
[f]Ps 106:23

18:21
[g]Jer 11:22
[h]Ps 109:9

18:22
[i]Jer 6:26
[j]Ps 140:5

18:23
[k]Jer 11:21
[l]Ps 109:14

19:1
[m]Jer 18:2
[n]Nu 11:17

19:2
[o]Jos 15:8

19:3
[p]Jer 17:20
[q]Jer 6:19
[r]1Sa 3:11

19:4
[s]Dt 28:20; Isa 65:11
[t]Lev 18:21
[u]2Ki 21:16; Jer 2:34

19:5
[v]Lev 18:21; Ps 106:37-38
[w]Jer 7:31; 32:35

19:6
a Jos 15:8
b Jer 7:32

19:7
c Lev 26:17;
Dt 28:25
d Jer 16:4; 34:20
e Ps 79:2

19:8
f Jer 18:16

19:9
g Lev 26:29;
Dt 28:49-57;
La 4:10
h Isa 9:20

19:10
i ver 1

19:11
j Ps 2:9;
Isa 30:14
k Jer 7:32

19:13
l Jer 32:29; 52:13
m Dt 4:19;
Ac 7:42
n Jer 7:18;
Eze 20:28

19:14
o 2Ch 20:5;
Jer 26:2

19:15
p Ne 9:16;
Jer 7:26; 17:23

20:1
q 1Ch 24:14
r 2Ki 25:18

20:2
s Jer 1:19
t Job 13:27
u Jer 37:13; 38:7;
Zec 14:10

20:3
v ver 10

20:4
w Jer 29:21
x Jer 21:10
y Jer 52:27

20:5
z Jer 17:3
a 2Ki 20:17

will no longer call this place Topheth or the Valley of Ben Hinnom,ᵃ but the Valley of Slaughter.ᵇ

⁷"'In this place I will ruinᵃ the plans of Judah and Jerusalem. I will make them fall by the sword before their enemies,ᶜ at the hands of those who seek their lives, and I will give their carcassesᵈ as foodᵉ to the birds of the air and the beasts of the earth. ⁸I will devastate this city and make it an object of scorn;ᶠ all who pass by will be appalled and will scoff because of all its wounds. ⁹I will make them eatᵍ the flesh of their sons and daughters, and they will eat one another's flesh during the stress of the siege imposed on them by the enemiesʰ who seek their lives.'

¹⁰"Then break the jarⁱ while those who go with you are watching, ¹¹and say to them, 'This is what the LORD Almighty says: I will smashʲ this nation and this city just as this potter's jar is smashed and cannot be repaired. They will buryᵏ the dead in Topheth until there is no more room. ¹²This is what I will do to this place and to those who live here, declares the LORD. I will make this city like Topheth. ¹³The housesˡ in Jerusalem and those of the kings of Judah will be defiled like this place, Topheth—all the houses where they burned incense on the roofs to all the starry hostsᵐ and poured out drink offeringsⁿ to other gods.'"

¹⁴Jeremiah then returned from Topheth, where the LORD had sent him to prophesy, and stood in the courtᵒ of the LORD's temple and said to all the people, ¹⁵"This is what the LORD Almighty, the God of Israel, says: 'Listen! I am going to bring on this city and the villages around it every disaster I pronounced against them, because they were stiff-neckedᵖ and would not listen to my words.'"

Chapter 20 Theme

20 When the priest Pashhur son of Immer,�q the chief officerʳ in the temple of the LORD, heard Jeremiah prophesying these things, ²he had Jeremiah the prophet beatenˢ and put in the stocksᵗ at the Upper Gate of Benjaminᵘ at the LORD's temple. ³The next day, when Pashhur released him from the stocks, Jeremiah said to him, "The LORD's name for you is not Pashhur, but Magor-Missabib.ᵇᵛ ⁴For this is what the LORD says: 'I will make you a terror to yourself and to all your friends; with your own eyesʷ you will see them fall by the sword of their enemies. I will handˣ all Judah over to the king of Babylon, who will carryʸ them away to Babylon or put them to the sword. ⁵I will hand over to their enemies all the wealthᶻ of this city—all its products, all its valuables and all the treasures of the kings of Judah. They will take it awayᵃ as plunder

a 7 The Hebrew for *ruin* sounds like the Hebrew for *jar* (see verses 1 and 10).
b 3 *Magor-Missabib* means *terror on every side*.

and carry it off to Babylon. ⁶And you, Pashhur, and all who live in your house will go into exile to Babylon. There you will die and be buried, you and all your friends to whom you have prophesied*a* lies.'"

⁷O Lord, you deceived*a* me, and I was deceived*a*;
    you overpowered me and prevailed.
I am ridiculed all day long;
    everyone mocks me.
⁸Whenever I speak, I cry out
    proclaiming violence and destruction.*b*
So the word of the Lord has brought me
    insult and reproach*c* all day long.
⁹But if I say, "I will not mention him
    or speak any more in his name,"
his word is in my heart like a fire,*d*
    a fire shut up in my bones.
I am weary of holding it in;*e*
    indeed, I cannot.
¹⁰I hear many whispering,
    "Terror*f* on every side!
    Report*g* him! Let's report him!"
All my friends*h*
    are waiting for me to slip,*i* saying,
"Perhaps he will be deceived;
    then we will prevail*j* over him
    and take our revenge on him."

¹¹But the Lord*k* is with me like a mighty warrior;
    so my persecutors*l* will stumble and not prevail.*m*
They will fail and be thoroughly disgraced;*n*
    their dishonor will never be forgotten.
¹²O Lord Almighty, you who examine the righteous
    and probe the heart and mind,*o*
let me see your vengeance*p* upon them,
    for to you I have committed*q* my cause.

¹³Sing to the Lord!
    Give praise to the Lord!
He rescues*r* the life of the needy
    from the hands of the wicked.

¹⁴Cursed be the day I was born!*s*
    May the day my mother bore me not be blessed!
¹⁵Cursed be the man who brought my father the news,
    who made him very glad, saying,
    "A child is born to you—a son!"

---

a 7 Or *persuaded*

20:6
a Jer 14:15;
La 2:14

20:8
b Jer 6:7
c 2Ch 36:16;
Jer 6:10

20:9
d Ps 39:3
e Job 32:18-20;
Ac 4:20

20:10
f Ps 31:13;
Jer 6:25
g Isa 29:21
h Ps 41:9
i Lk 11:53-54
j 1Ki 19:2

20:11
k Jer 1:8;
Ro 8:31
l Jer 17:18
m Jer 15:20
n Jer 23:40

20:12
o Jer 17:10
p Ps 54:7;
59:10
q Ps 62:8;
Jer 11:20

20:13
r Ps 35:10

20:14
s Job 3:3;
Jer 15:10

20:16
a Ge 19:25

20:17
b Job 10:18-19

20:18
c Ps 90:9

21:1
d 2Ki 24:18;
Jer 52:1
e Jer 38:1
f 2Ki 25:18;
Jer 29:25; 37:3

21:2
g Jer 37:3,7
h 2Ki 25:1
i Ps 44:1-4;
Jer 32:17

21:4
j Jer 32:5
k Jer 37:8-10

21:5
l Jer 6:12

21:6
m Jer 14:12

21:7
n 2Ki 25:7;
Jer 52:9
o Jer 37:17; 39:5
p 2Ch 36:17;
Eze 7:9; Hab 1:6

21:9
q Jer 14:12
r Jer 38:2,17;
39:18; 45:5

21:10
s Jer 44:11,27;
Am 9:4
t Jer 32:28;
38:2-3
u Jer 52:13

21:11
v Jer 13:18

16May that man be like the towns*a*
  the Lord overthrew without pity.
May he hear wailing in the morning,
  a battle cry at noon.
17For he did not kill me in the womb,*b*
  with my mother as my grave,
  her womb enlarged forever.
18Why did I ever come out of the womb
  to see trouble and sorrow
  and to end my days in shame?*c*

Chapter 21 Theme _____

21 The word came to Jeremiah from the Lord when King Zedekiah*d* sent to him Pashhur*e* son of Malkijah and the priest Zephaniah*f* son of Maaseiah. They said: 2"Inquire*g* now of the Lord for us because Nebuchadnezzar*ah* king of Babylon is attacking us. Perhaps the Lord will perform wonders*i* for us as in times past so that he will withdraw from us."

3But Jeremiah answered them, "Tell Zedekiah, 4'This is what the Lord, the God of Israel, says: I am about to turn*j* against you the weapons of war that are in your hands, which you are using to fight the king of Babylon and the Babylonians*b* who are outside the wall besieging*k* you. And I will gather them inside this city. 5I myself will fight against you with an outstretched hand*l* and a mighty arm in anger and fury and great wrath. 6I will strike down those who live in this city—both men and animals—and they will die of a terrible plague.*m* 7After that, declares the Lord, I will hand over Zedekiah*n* king of Judah, his officials and the people in this city who survive the plague, sword and famine, to Nebuchadnezzar king of Babylon*o* and to their enemies who seek their lives. He will put them to the sword; he will show them no mercy or pity or compassion.'*p*

8"Furthermore, tell the people, 'This is what the Lord says: See, I am setting before you the way of life and the way of death. 9Whoever stays in this city will die by the sword, famine or plague.*q* But whoever goes out and surrenders to the Babylonians who are besieging you will live; he will escape with his life.*r* 10I have determined to do this city harm*s* and not good, declares the Lord. It will be given into the hands*t* of the king of Babylon, and he will destroy it with fire.'*u*

11"Moreover, say to the royal house*v* of Judah, 'Hear the word of the Lord; 12O house of David, this is what the Lord says:

a 2 Hebrew *Nebuchadrezzar,* of which *Nebuchadnezzar* is a variant; here and often in Jeremiah and Ezekiel b 4 Or *Chaldeans*; also in verse 9

"'Administer justice[a] every morning;
　　rescue from the hand of his oppressor
　　the one who has been robbed,
or my wrath will break out and burn like fire
　　because of the evil you have done—
　　burn with no one to quench[b] it.

[13] I am against[c] you, ⌊Jerusalem,⌋
　　you who live above this valley[d]
　　on the rocky plateau,

　　　　　　　　　　　　　declares the LORD—
you who say, "Who can come against us?
　　Who can enter our refuge?"[e]

[14] I will punish you as your deeds[f] deserve,

　　　　　　　　　　　　declares the LORD.
I will kindle a fire[g] in your forests[h]
　　that will consume everything around you.'"

Chapter 22 Theme

22 This is what the LORD says: "Go down to the palace of the king of Judah and proclaim this message there: [2]'Hear the word of the LORD, O king of Judah, you who sit on David's throne[i]—you, your officials and your people who come through these gates.[j] [3]This is what the LORD says: Do what is just[k] and right. Rescue from the hand of his oppressor[l] the one who has been robbed. Do no wrong or violence to the alien, the fatherless or the widow,[m] and do not shed innocent blood in this place. [4]For if you are careful to carry out these commands, then kings[n] who sit on David's throne will come through the gates of this palace, riding in chariots and on horses, accompanied by their officials and their people. [5]But if you do not obey[o] these commands, declares the LORD, I swear[p] by myself that this palace will become a ruin.'"

[6]For this is what the LORD says about the palace of the king of Judah:

"Though you are like Gilead to me,
　　like the summit of Lebanon,
I will surely make you like a desert,[q]
　　like towns not inhabited.

[7] I will send destroyers[r] against you,
　　each man with his weapons,
and they will cut[s] up your fine cedar beams
　　and throw them into the fire.

[8] "People from many nations will pass by this city and will ask one another, 'Why has the LORD done such a thing to this great

Cross references

21:12
[a] Jer 22:3
[b] Isa 1:31

21:13
[c] Eze 13:8
[d] Ps 125:2
[e] Jer 49:4; Ob 3-4

21:14
[f] Isa 3:10-11
[g] 2Ch 36:19; Jer 52:13
[h] Eze 20:47

22:2
[i] Jer 17:25; Lk 1:32
[j] Jer 17:20

22:3
[k] Mic 6:8; Zec 7:9
[l] Ps 72:4; Jer 21:12
[m] Ex 22:22

22:4
[n] Jer 17:25

22:5
[o] Jer 17:27
[p] Heb 6:13

22:6
[q] Mic 3:12

22:7
[r] Jer 4:7
[s] Isa 10:34

22:8
a Dt 29:25-26;
1Ki 9:8-9;
Jer 16:10-11

22:9
b 2Ki 22:17;
2Ch 34:25

22:10
c Ecc 4:2
d ver 18

22:11
e 2Ki 23:31

22:12
f 2Ki 23:34

22:13
g Mic 3:10;
Hab 2:9
h Lev 19:13;
Jas 5:4

22:14
i Isa 5:8-9
j 2Sa 7:2

22:15
k 2Ki 23:25
l Ps 128:2;
Isa 3:10

22:16
m Ps 72:1-4,
12-13

22:17
n 2Ki 24:4

22:19
o Jer 36:30

city?'*a* 9And the answer will be: 'Because they have forsaken the covenant of the LORD their God and have worshiped and served other gods.*b*'"

10Do not weep for the dead*c* ⌊king⌋ or mourn*d* his loss;
    rather, weep bitterly for him who is exiled,
because he will never return
    nor see his native land again.

11For this is what the LORD says about Shallum*ae* son of Josiah, who succeeded his father as king of Judah but has gone from this place: "He will never return. 12He will die*f* in the place where they have led him captive; he will not see this land again."

13"Woe to him who builds*g* his palace by unrighteousness,
    his upper rooms by injustice,
making his countrymen work for nothing,
    not paying*h* them for their labor.
14He says, 'I will build myself a great palace*i*
    with spacious upper rooms.'
So he makes large windows in it,
    panels it with cedar*j*
    and decorates it in red.

15"Does it make you a king
    to have more and more cedar?
Did not your father have food and drink?
    He did what was right and just,*k*
    so all went well*l* with him.
16He defended the cause of the poor and needy,*m*
    and so all went well.
Is that not what it means to know me?"
    declares the LORD.
17"But your eyes and your heart
    are set only on dishonest gain,
on shedding innocent blood*n*
    and on oppression and extortion."

18Therefore this is what the LORD says about Jehoiakim son of Josiah king of Judah:

"They will not mourn for him:
    'Alas, my brother! Alas, my sister!'
They will not mourn for him:
    'Alas, my master! Alas, his splendor!'
19He will have the burial of a donkey—
    dragged away and thrown*o*
    outside the gates of Jerusalem."

a 11 Also called *Jehoahaz*

²⁰"Go up to Lebanon and cry out,
    let your voice be heard in Bashan,
cry out from Abarim,^a
    for all your allies are crushed.
²¹I warned you when you felt secure,
    but you said, 'I will not listen!'
This has been your way from your youth;^b
    you have not obeyed^c me.
²²The wind will drive all your shepherds away,
    and your allies will go into exile.
Then you will be ashamed and disgraced
    because of all your wickedness.
²³You who live in 'Lebanon,^a'
    who are nestled in cedar buildings,
how you will groan when pangs come upon you,
    pain^d like that of a woman in labor!

²⁴"As surely as I live," declares the Lord, "even if you, Jehoiachin^{be} son of Jehoiakim king of Judah, were a signet ring on my right hand, I would still pull you off. ²⁵I will hand you over^f to those who seek your life, those you fear—to Nebuchadnezzar king of Babylon and to the Babylonians.^c ²⁶I will hurl^g you and the mother who gave you birth into another country, where neither of you was born, and there you both will die. ²⁷You will never come back to the land you long to return to."

²⁸Is this man Jehoiachin a despised, broken pot,^h
    an object no one wants?
Why will he and his children be hurledⁱ out,
    cast into a land^j they do not know?
²⁹O land,^k land, land,
    hear the word of the Lord!
³⁰This is what the Lord says:
"Record this man as if childless,^l
    a man who will not prosper^m in his lifetime,
for none of his offspring will prosper,
    none will sit on the throneⁿ of David
    or rule anymore in Judah."

Chapter 23 Theme

23 "Woe to the shepherds^o who are destroying and scattering^p the sheep of my pasture!"^q declares the Lord. ²Therefore this is what the Lord, the God of Israel, says to the shepherds who

^a 23 That is, the palace in Jerusalem (see 1 Kings 7:2)   ^b 24 Hebrew *Coniah*, a variant of *Jehoiachin*; also in verse 28   ^c 25 Or *Chaldeans*

Cross references

22:20
^aNu 27:12

22:21
^bJer 3:25; 32:30
^cJer 7:23-28

22:23
^dJer 4:31

22:24
^e2Ki 24:6,8;
Jer 37:1

22:25
^f2Ki 24:16;
Jer 34:20

22:26
^g2Ki 24:8;
2Ch 36:10

22:28
^hPs 31:12;
Jer 48:38;
Hos 8:8
ⁱJer 15:1
^jJer 17:4

22:29
^kJer 6:19;
Mic 1:2

22:30
^l1Ch 3:18;
Mt 1:12
^mJer 10:21
ⁿPs 94:20

23:1
^oJer 10:21;
Eze 34:1-10;
Zec 11:15-17
^pIsa 56:11
^qEze 34:31

23:2
a Jer 21:12

23:3
b Isa 11:10-12;
Jer 32:37;
Eze 34:11-16

23:4
c Jer 3:15; 31:10;
Eze 34:23
d Jer 30:10;
46:27-28
e Jn 6:39

23:5
f Isa 4:2
g Isa 9:7
h Isa 11:1;
Zec 6:12

23:6
i Jer 33:16;
Mt 1:21-23
j Ro 3:21-22;
1Co 1:30

23:7
k Jer 16:14

23:8
l Isa 43:5-6;
Am 9:14-15

23:9
m Jer 20:8-9

23:10
n Jer 9:2
o Ps 107:34;
Jer 9:10
p Hos 4:2-3

23:11
q Jer 6:13; 8:10;
Zep 3:4
r Jer 7:10

23:12
s Ps 35:6;
Jer 13:16

tend my people: "Because you have scattered my flock and driven them away and have not bestowed care on them, I will bestow punishment on you for the evil[a] you have done," declares the LORD. [3]"I myself will gather the remnant[b] of my flock out of all the countries where I have driven them and will bring them back to their pasture, where they will be fruitful and increase in number. [4]I will place shepherds[c] over them who will tend them, and they will no longer be afraid[d] or terrified, nor will any be missing,[e]" declares the LORD.

[5]"The days are coming," declares the LORD,
  "when I will raise up to David[a] a righteous Branch,[f]
  a King who will reign[g] wisely
    and do what is just and right[h] in the land.
[6]In his days Judah will be saved
    and Israel will live in safety.
  This is the name[i] by which he will be called:
    The LORD Our Righteousness.[j]

[7]"So then, the days are coming," declares the LORD, "when people will no longer say, 'As surely as the LORD lives, who brought the Israelites up out of Egypt,'[k] [8]but they will say, 'As surely as the LORD lives, who brought the descendants of Israel up out of the land of the north and out of all the countries where he had banished them.' Then they will live in their own land."[l]

[9]Concerning the prophets:

  My heart is broken within me;
    all my bones tremble.
  I am like a drunken man,
    like a man overcome by wine,
  because of the LORD
    and his holy words.[m]
[10]The land is full of adulterers;[n]
    because of the curse[b] the land lies parched[c]
    and the pastures[o] in the desert are withered.[p]
  The ⌊prophets⌋ follow an evil course
    and use their power unjustly.

[11]"Both prophet and priest are godless;[q]
    even in my temple[r] I find their wickedness,"
                        declares the LORD.
[12]"Therefore their path will become slippery;[s]
    they will be banished to darkness
    and there they will fall.

a 5 Or up from David's line   b 10 Or because of these things   c 10 Or land mourns

I will bring disaster on them
    in the year they are punished,*a*"

                    declares the LORD.

¹³"Among the prophets of Samaria
    I saw this repulsive thing:
They prophesied by Baal*b*
    and led my people Israel astray.
¹⁴And among the prophets of Jerusalem
    I have seen something horrible:*c*
They commit adultery and live a lie.*d*
They strengthen the hands of evildoers,*e*
    so that no one turns from his wickedness.
They are all like Sodom*f* to me;
    the people of Jerusalem are like Gomorrah."*g*

¹⁵Therefore, this is what the LORD Almighty says concerning the prophets:

"I will make them eat bitter food
    and drink poisoned water,*h*
because from the prophets of Jerusalem
    ungodliness has spread throughout the land."

¹⁶This is what the LORD Almighty says:

"Do not listen*i* to what the prophets are prophesying
    to you;
    they fill you with false hopes.
They speak visions*j* from their own minds,
    not from the mouth*k* of the LORD.
¹⁷They keep saying to those who despise me,
    'The LORD says: You will have peace.'*l*
And to all who follow the stubbornness*m* of their hearts
    they say, 'No harm*n* will come to you.'
¹⁸But which of them has stood in the council of the LORD
    to see or to hear his word?
Who has listened and heard his word?
¹⁹See, the storm*o* of the LORD
    will burst out in wrath,
a whirlwind swirling down
    on the heads of the wicked.
²⁰The anger*p* of the LORD will not turn back*q*
    until he fully accomplishes
    the purposes of his heart.
In days to come
    you will understand it clearly.

23:12
a Jer 11:23

23:13
b Jer 2:8

23:14
c Jer 5:30
d Jer 29:23
e Eze 13:22
f Ge 18:20
g Isa 1:9-10;
Jer 20:16

23:15
h Jer 8:14; 9:15

23:16
i Jer 27:9-10,14;
Mt 7:15
j Jer 14:14
k Jer 9:20

23:17
l Jer 8:11
m Jer 13:10
n Jer 5:12;
Am 9:10;
Mic 3:11

23:19
o Jer 25:32;
30:23

23:20
p 2Ki 23:26
q Jer 30:24

²¹I did not send*ᵃ* these prophets,
yet they have run with their message;
I did not speak to them,
yet they have prophesied.
²²But if they had stood in my council,
they would have proclaimed my words to my people
and would have turned*ᵇ* them from their evil ways
and from their evil deeds.

²³"Am I only a God nearby,*ᶜ*"

declares the LORD,

"and not a God far away?
²⁴Can anyone hide*ᵈ* in secret places
so that I cannot see him?"

declares the LORD.

"Do not I fill heaven and earth?"*ᵉ*

declares the LORD.

²⁵"I have heard what the prophets say who prophesy lies*ᶠ* in my name. They say, 'I had a dream!*ᵍ* I had a dream!' ²⁶How long will this continue in the hearts of these lying prophets, who prophesy the delusions*ʰ* of their own minds? ²⁷They think the dreams they tell one another will make my people forget*ⁱ* my name, just as their fathers forgot*ʲ* my name through Baal worship. ²⁸Let the prophet who has a dream tell his dream, but let the one who has my word speak it faithfully. For what has straw to do with grain?" declares the LORD. ²⁹"Is not my word like fire,"*ᵏ* declares the LORD, "and like a hammer that breaks a rock in pieces?

³⁰"Therefore," declares the LORD, "I am against*ˡ* the prophets*ᵐ* who steal from one another words supposedly from me. ³¹Yes," declares the LORD, "I am against the prophets who wag their own tongues and yet declare, 'The LORD declares.'*ⁿ* ³²Indeed, I am against those who prophesy false dreams,*ᵒ*" declares the LORD. "They tell them and lead my people astray with their reckless lies, yet I did not send or appoint them. They do not benefit*ᵖ* these people in the least," declares the LORD.

³³"When these people, or a prophet or a priest, ask you, 'What is the oracle*ᵃ�q* of the LORD?' say to them, 'What oracle?*ᵇ* I will forsake*ʳ* you, declares the LORD.' ³⁴If a prophet or a priest or anyone else claims, 'This is the oracle*ˢ* of the LORD,' I will punish*ᵗ* that man and his household. ³⁵This is what each of you keeps on saying to his friend or relative: 'What is the LORD's answer?'*ᵘ* or 'What has the LORD spoken?' ³⁶But you must not mention 'the oracle of the LORD' again, because every man's own word becomes his oracle and so

ᵃ 33 Or *burden* (see Septuagint and Vulgate)   *ᵇ* 33 Hebrew; Septuagint and Vulgate '*You are the burden.* (The Hebrew for *oracle* and *burden* is the same.)

you distort[a] the words of the living God, the LORD Almighty, our God. [37]This is what you keep saying to a prophet: 'What is the LORD's answer to you?' or 'What has the LORD spoken?' [38]Although you claim, 'This is the oracle of the LORD,' this is what the LORD says: You used the words, 'This is the oracle of the LORD,' even though I told you that you must not claim, 'This is the oracle of the LORD.' [39]Therefore, I will surely forget you and cast[b] you out of my presence along with the city I gave to you and your fathers. [40]I will bring upon you everlasting disgrace[c]—everlasting shame that will not be forgotten."

Chapter 24 Theme

24 After Jehoiachin[a][d] son of Jehoiakim king of Judah and the officials, the craftsmen and the artisans of Judah were carried into exile from Jerusalem to Babylon by Nebuchadnezzar king of Babylon, the LORD showed me two baskets of figs[e] placed in front of the temple of the LORD. [2]One basket had very good figs, like those that ripen early; the other basket had very poor[f] figs, so bad they could not be eaten.

[3]Then the LORD asked me, "What do you see,[g] Jeremiah?"

"Figs," I answered. "The good ones are very good, but the poor ones are so bad they cannot be eaten."

[4]Then the word of the LORD came to me: [5]"This is what the LORD, the God of Israel, says: 'Like these good figs, I regard as good the exiles from Judah, whom I sent away from this place to the land of the Babylonians.[b] [6]My eyes will watch over them for their good, and I will bring them back[h] to this land. I will build[i] them up and not tear them down; I will plant them and not uproot them. [7]I will give them a heart to know me, that I am the LORD. They will be my people,[j] and I will be their God, for they will return[k] to me with all their heart.[l]

[8]"'But like the poor[m] figs, which are so bad they cannot be eaten,' says the LORD, 'so will I deal with Zedekiah king of Judah, his officials[n] and the survivors[o] from Jerusalem, whether they remain in this land or live in Egypt.[p] [9]I will make them abhorrent[q] and an offense to all the kingdoms of the earth, a reproach and a byword,[r] an object of ridicule and cursing,[s] wherever I banish[t] them. [10]I will send the sword,[u] famine and plague[v] against them until they are destroyed from the land I gave to them and their fathers.'"

Chapter 25 Theme

25 The word came to Jeremiah concerning all the people of Judah in the fourth year of Jehoiakim[w] son of Josiah king

INSIGHT

Read 2 Kings 24:10-17 for the historical account of this time. Jehoiachin is also called Jeconiah.

23:36
[a]Gal 1:7-8;
2Pe 3:16

23:39
[b]Jer 7:15

23:40
[c]Jer 20:11;
Eze 5:14-15

24:1
[d]2Ki 24:16;
2Ch 36:9;
Jer 29:2
[e]Am 8:1-2

24:2
[f]Isa 5:4

24:3
[g]Jer 1:11;
Am 8:2

24:6
[h]Jer 29:10;
Eze 11:17
[i]Jer 33:7; 42:10

24:7
[j]Isa 51:16;
Jer 31:33;
Heb 8:10
[k]Jer 32:40
[l]Eze 11:19

24:8
[m]Jer 29:17
[n]Jer 39:6
[o]Jer 39:9
[p]Jer 44:1,26

24:9
[q]Jer 15:4; 34:17
[r]Dt 28:25;
1Ki 9:7
[s]Jer 29:18
[t]Dt 28:37

24:10
[u]Isa 51:19
[v]Jer 27:8

25:1
[w]2Ki 24:2;
Jer 36:1

[a]1 Hebrew *Jeconiah*, a variant of *Jehoiachin*   [b]5 Or *Chaldeans*

25:1
a 2Ki 24:1

25:2
b Jer 18:11

25:3
c Jer 1:2
d Jer 11:7; 26:5
e Jer 7:26

25:4
f Jer 7:25

25:6
g Dt 8:19

25:7
h Dt 32:21
i 2Ki 21:15

25:9
j Isa 13:3-5
k Jer 1:15
l Jer 27:6
m Jer 18:16

25:10
n Isa 24:8;
Eze 26:13
o Jer 7:34
p Ecc 12:3-4
q Rev 18:22-23

25:11
r Jer 4:26-27;
12:11-12
s 2Ch 36:21

25:12
t Jer 29:10
u Isa 13:19-22;
14:22-23

25:14
v Jer 27:7
w Jer 50:9;
51:27-28
x Jer 51:6

25:15
y Isa 51:17;
Ps 75:8;
Rev 14:10

25:16
z Na 3:11
a Jer 51:7

25:17
b Jer 1:10

25:18
c Jer 24:9
d Jer 44:22

of Judah, which was the first year of Nebuchadnezzar[a] king of Babylon. [2]So Jeremiah the prophet said to all the people of Judah[b] and to all those living in Jerusalem: [3]For twenty-three years—from the thirteenth year of Josiah[c] son of Amon king of Judah until this very day—the word of the LORD has come to me and I have spoken to you again and again,[d] but you have not listened.[e]

[4]And though the LORD has sent all his servants the prophets[f] to you again and again, you have not listened or paid any attention. [5]They said, "Turn now, each of you, from your evil ways and your evil practices, and you can stay in the land the LORD gave to you and your fathers for ever and ever. [6]Do not follow other gods[g] to serve and worship them; do not provoke me to anger with what your hands have made. Then I will not harm you."

[7]"But you did not listen to me," declares the LORD, "and you have provoked me with what your hands have made,[h] and you have brought harm[i] to yourselves."

[8]Therefore the LORD Almighty says this: "Because you have not listened to my words, [9]I will summon[j] all the peoples of the north[k] and my servant[l] Nebuchadnezzar king of Babylon," declares the LORD, "and I will bring them against this land and its inhabitants and against all the surrounding nations. I will completely destroy[a] them and make them an object of horror and scorn,[m] and an everlasting ruin. [10]I will banish from them the sounds[n] of joy and gladness, the voices of bride and bridegroom,[o] the sound of millstones[p] and the light of the lamp.[q] [11]This whole country will become a desolate wasteland,[r] and these nations will serve the king of Babylon seventy years.[s]

[12]"But when the seventy years[t] are fulfilled, I will punish the king of Babylon and his nation, the land of the Babylonians,[b] for their guilt," declares the LORD, "and will make it desolate[u] forever. [13]I will bring upon that land all the things I have spoken against it, all that are written in this book and prophesied by Jeremiah against all the nations. [14]They themselves will be enslaved[v] by many nations[w] and great kings; I will repay[x] them according to their deeds and the work of their hands."

[15]This is what the LORD, the God of Israel, said to me: "Take from my hand this cup[y] filled with the wine of my wrath and make all the nations to whom I send you drink it. [16]When they drink it, they will stagger[z] and go mad[a] because of the sword I will send among them."

[17]So I took the cup from the LORD's hand and made all the nations to whom he sent[b] me drink it: [18]Jerusalem and the towns of Judah, its kings and officials, to make them a ruin and an object of horror and scorn and cursing,[c] as they are today;[d] [19]Pharaoh

a 9 The Hebrew term refers to the irrevocable giving over of things or persons to the LORD, often by totally destroying them.   b 12 Or *Chaldeans* king of Egypt, his attendants, his officials and all his people, ²⁰and all the foreign people there; all the kings of Uz;^a all the kings of the Philistines (those of Ashkelon,^b Gaza, Ekron, and the people left at Ashdod); ²¹Edom, Moab and Ammon;^c ²²all the kings of Tyre and Sidon;^d the kings of the coastlands^e across the sea; ²³Dedan, Tema, Buz and all who are in distant places^a;^f ²⁴all the kings of Arabia^g and all the kings of the foreign people who live in the desert; ²⁵all the kings of Zimri, Elam^h and Media; ²⁶and all the kings of the north,ⁱ near and far, one after the other—all the kingdoms on the face of the earth. And after all of them, the king of Sheshach^b^j will drink it too.

²⁷"Then tell them, 'This is what the LORD Almighty, the God of Israel, says: Drink, get drunk^k and vomit, and fall to rise no more because of the sword^l I will send among you.' ²⁸But if they refuse to take the cup from your hand and drink, tell them, 'This is what the LORD Almighty says: You must drink it! ²⁹See, I am beginning to bring disaster^m on the city that bears my Name,ⁿ and will you indeed go unpunished?^o You will not go unpunished, for I am calling down a sword upon all^p who live on the earth, declares the LORD Almighty.'

³⁰"Now prophesy all these words against them and say to them:

"'The LORD will roar^q from on high;
    he will thunder^r from his holy dwelling
    and roar mightily against his land.
He will shout like those who tread the grapes,
    shout against all who live on the earth.
³¹The tumult will resound to the ends of the earth,
    for the LORD will bring charges^s against the nations;
he will bring judgment on all mankind
    and put the wicked to the sword,'"

declares the LORD.

³²This is what the LORD Almighty says:

"Look! Disaster is spreading
    from nation to nation;^t
a mighty storm^u is rising
    from the ends of the earth."

³³At that time those slain^v by the LORD will be everywhere—from one end of the earth to the other. They will not be mourned or gathered^w up or buried,^x but will be like refuse lying on the ground.

³⁴Weep and wail, you shepherds;
    roll^y in the dust, you leaders of the flock.

---

^a 23 Or *who clip the hair by their foreheads*   ^b 26 *Sheshach* is a cryptogram for Babylon.

25:20
a Job 1:1
b Jer 47:5

25:21
c Jer 49:1

25:22
d Jer 47:4
e Jer 31:10

25:23
f Jer 9:26; 49:32

25:24
g 2Ch 9:14

25:25
h Ge 10:22

25:26
i Jer 50:3,9
j Jer 51:41

25:27
k ver 16,28;
Hab 2:16
l Eze 21:4

25:29
m Jer 13:12-14
n 1Pe 4:17
o Pr 11:31
p ver 30-31

25:30
q Isa 16:10;
42:13
r Joel 3:16;
Am 1:2

25:31
s Hos 4:1;
Joel 3:2;
Mic 6:2

25:32
t Isa 34:2
u Jer 23:19

25:33
v Isa 66:16;
Eze 39:17-20
w Jer 16:4
x Ps 79:3

25:34
y Jer 6:26

25:34
a Isa 34:6;
Jer 50:27

25:35
b Job 11:20

25:38
c Jer 4:7

26:1
d 2Ki 23:36

26:2
e Jer 19:14
f Jer 1:17;
Mt 28:20;
Ac 20:27
g Dt 4:2

26:3
h Jer 36:7
i Jer 18:8

26:4
j Lev 26:14
k 1Ki 9:6

26:5
l Jer 25:4

26:6
m Jos 18:1
n 2Ki 22:19

26:9
o Jer 9:11

26:11
p Dt 18:20;
Jer 18:23; 38:4;
Mt 26:66;
Ac 6:11

For your time to be slaughtered*a* has come;
    you will fall and be shattered like fine pottery.
³⁵The shepherds will have nowhere to flee,
    the leaders of the flock no place to escape.*b*
³⁶Hear the cry of the shepherds,
    the wailing of the leaders of the flock,
    for the LORD is destroying their pasture.
³⁷The peaceful meadows will be laid waste
    because of the fierce anger of the LORD.
³⁸Like a lion*c* he will leave his lair,
    and their land will become desolate
    because of the sword*a* of the oppressor
    and because of the LORD's fierce anger.

Chapter 26 Theme _____

26 Early in the reign of Jehoiakim*d* son of Josiah king of Judah, this word came from the LORD: ²"This is what the LORD says: Stand in the courtyard*e* of the LORD's house and speak to all the people of the towns of Judah who come to worship in the house of the LORD. Tell*f* them everything I command you; do not omit*g* a word. ³Perhaps they will listen and each will turn*h* from his evil way. Then I will relent*i* and not bring on them the disaster I was planning because of the evil they have done. ⁴Say to them, 'This is what the LORD says: If you do not listen*j* to me and follow my law,*k* which I have set before you, ⁵and if you do not listen to the words of my servants the prophets, whom I have sent to you again and again (though you have not listened*l*), ⁶then I will make this house like Shiloh*m* and this city an object of cursing*n* among all the nations of the earth.'"

⁷The priests, the prophets and all the people heard Jeremiah speak these words in the house of the LORD. ⁸But as soon as Jeremiah finished telling all the people everything the LORD had commanded him to say, the priests, the prophets and all the people seized him and said, "You must die! ⁹Why do you prophesy in the LORD's name that this house will be like Shiloh and this city will be desolate and deserted?"*o* And all the people crowded around Jeremiah in the house of the LORD.

¹⁰When the officials of Judah heard about these things, they went up from the royal palace to the house of the LORD and took their places at the entrance of the New Gate of the LORD's house. ¹¹Then the priests and the prophets said to the officials and all the people, "This man should be sentenced to death*p* because he has prophesied against this city. You have heard it with your own ears!"

a 38 Some Hebrew manuscripts and Septuagint (see also Jer. 46:16 and 50:16); most Hebrew manuscripts *anger*

¹²Then Jeremiah said to all the officials^a and all the people: "The LORD sent me to prophesy^b against this house and this city all the things you have heard.^c ¹³Now reform^d your ways and your actions and obey the LORD your God. Then the LORD will relent and not bring the disaster he has pronounced against you. ¹⁴As for me, I am in your hands;^e do with me whatever you think is good and right. ¹⁵Be assured, however, that if you put me to death, you will bring the guilt of innocent blood on yourselves and on this city and on those who live in it, for in truth the LORD has sent me to you to speak all these words in your hearing."

¹⁶Then the officials^f and all the people said to the priests and the prophets, "This man should not be sentenced to death!^g He has spoken to us in the name of the LORD our God."

¹⁷Some of the elders of the land stepped forward and said to the entire assembly of people, ¹⁸"Micah^h of Moresheth prophesied in the days of Hezekiah king of Judah. He told all the people of Judah, 'This is what the LORD Almighty says:

"'Zionⁱ will be plowed like a field,
    Jerusalem will become a heap of rubble,^j
    the temple hill^k a mound overgrown with thickets.'^al

¹⁹"Did Hezekiah king of Judah or anyone else in Judah put him to death? Did not Hezekiah^m fear the LORD and seek his favor? And did not the LORD relent,ⁿ so that he did not bring the disaster^o he pronounced against them? We are about to bring a terrible disaster^p on ourselves!"

²⁰(Now Uriah son of Shemaiah from Kiriath Jearim^q was another man who prophesied in the name of the LORD; he prophesied the same things against this city and this land as Jeremiah did. ²¹When King Jehoiakim^r and all his officers and officials heard his words, the king sought to put him to death. But Uriah heard of it and fled^s in fear to Egypt. ²²King Jehoiakim, however, sent Elnathan^t son of Acbor to Egypt, along with some other men. ²³They brought Uriah out of Egypt and took him to King Jehoiakim, who had him struck down with a sword and his body thrown into the burial place of the common people.)

²⁴Furthermore, Ahikam^u son of Shaphan supported Jeremiah, and so he was not handed over to the people to be put to death.

Chapter 27 Theme _____

27

Early in the reign of Zedekiah^b^v son of Josiah king of Judah, this word came to Jeremiah from the LORD: ²This is what the LORD said to me: "Make a yoke^w out of straps and crossbars

---

a 18 Micah 3:12   b 1 A few Hebrew manuscripts and Syriac (see also Jer. 27:3, 12 and 28:1); most Hebrew manuscripts *Jehoiakim* (Most Septuagint manuscripts do not have this verse.)

**Cross references (margin):**

26:12
a Jer 1:18
b Am 7:15; Ac 4:18-20; 5:29
c ver 2,15

26:13
d Jer 7:5; Joel 2:12-14

26:14
e Jer 38:5

26:16
f Ac 23:9
g Ac 5:34-39; 23:29

26:18
h Mic 1:1
i Isa 2:3
j Ne 4:2; Jer 9:11
k Mic 4:1; Zec 8:3
l Jer 17:3

26:19
m 2Ch 32:24-26; Isa 37:14-20
n Ex 32:14; 2Sa 24:16
o Jer 44:7
p Hab 2:10

26:20
q Jos 9:17

26:21
r 1Ki 19:2
s Mt 10:23

26:22
t Jer 36:12,25

26:24
u 2Ki 22:12

27:1
v 2Ch 36:11

27:2
w Jer 28:10,13

and put it on your neck. ³Then send word to the kings of Edom, Moab, Ammon,ᵃ Tyre and Sidon through the envoys who have come to Jerusalem to Zedekiah king of Judah. ⁴Give them a message for their masters and say, 'This is what the LORD Almighty, the God of Israel, says: "Tell this to your masters: ⁵With my great power and outstretched armᵇ I made the earth and its people and the animals that are on it, and I giveᶜ it to anyone I please. ⁶Now I will hand all your countries over to my servantᵈ Nebuchadnezzarᵉ king of Babylon; I will make even the wild animals subject to him.ᶠ ⁷All nations will serveᵍ him and his son and his grandson until the timeʰ for his land comes; then many nations and great kings will subjugateⁱ him.

⁸"'"If, however, any nation or kingdom will not serve Nebuchadnezzar king of Babylon or bow its neck under his yoke, I will punish that nation with the sword, famine and plague, declares the LORD, until I destroy it by his hand. ⁹So do not listen to your prophets, your diviners, your interpreters of dreams, your mediumsʲ or your sorcerers who tell you, 'You will not serve the king of Babylon.' ¹⁰They prophesy liesᵏ to you that will only serve to remove you far from your lands; I will banish you and you will perish. ¹¹But if any nation will bow its neck under the yokeˡ of the king of Babylon and serve him, I will let that nation remain in its own land to till it and to live there, declares the LORD.""'

¹²I gave the same message to Zedekiah king of Judah. I said, "Bow your neck under the yoke of the king of Babylon; serve him and his people, and you will live. ¹³Why will you and your people dieᵐ by the sword, famine and plague with which the LORD has threatened any nation that will not serve the king of Babylon? ¹⁴Do not listen to the words of the prophets who say to you, 'You will not serve the king of Babylon,' for they are prophesying liesⁿ to you. ¹⁵'I have not sentᵒ them,' declares the LORD. 'They are prophesying lies in my name.ᵖ Therefore, I will banish you and you will perish,�q both you and the prophets who prophesy to you.'"

¹⁶Then I said to the priests and all these people, "This is what the LORD says: Do not listen to the prophets who say, 'Very soon now the articlesʳ from the LORD's house will be brought back from Babylon.' They are prophesying lies to you. ¹⁷Do not listen to them. Serve the king of Babylon, and you will live. Why should this city become a ruin? ¹⁸If they are prophets and have the word of the LORD, let them pleadˢ with the LORD Almighty that the furnishings remaining in the house of the LORD and in the palace of the king of Judah and in Jerusalem not be taken to Babylon. ¹⁹For this is what the LORD Almighty says about the pillars, the Sea,ᵗ the movable stands and the other furnishingsᵘ that are left in this city, ²⁰which Nebuchadnezzar king of Babylon did not take away when

he carried[a] Jehoiachin[ab] son of Jehoiakim king of Judah into exile from Jerusalem to Babylon, along with all the nobles of Judah and Jerusalem— [21]yes, this is what the LORD Almighty, the God of Israel, says about the things that are left in the house of the LORD and in the palace of the king of Judah and in Jerusalem: [22]"They will be taken[c] to Babylon and there they will remain until the day[d] I come for them,' declares the LORD. 'Then I will bring[e] them back and restore them to this place.'"

Chapter 28 Theme

28 In the fifth month of that same year, the fourth year, early in the reign of Zedekiah[f] king of Judah, the prophet Hananiah son of Azzur, who was from Gibeon,[g] said to me in the house of the LORD in the presence of the priests and all the people: [2]"This is what the LORD Almighty, the God of Israel, says: 'I will break the yoke[h] of the king of Babylon. [3]Within two years I will bring back to this place all the articles[i] of the LORD's house that Nebuchadnezzar king of Babylon removed from here and took to Babylon. [4]I will also bring back to this place Jehoiachin[aj] son of Jehoiakim king of Judah and all the other exiles from Judah who went to Babylon,' declares the LORD, 'for I will break the yoke of the king of Babylon.'"

[5]Then the prophet Jeremiah replied to the prophet Hananiah before the priests and all the people who were standing in the house of the LORD. [6]He said, "Amen! May the LORD do so! May the LORD fulfill the words you have prophesied by bringing the articles of the LORD's house and all the exiles back to this place from Babylon. [7]Nevertheless, listen to what I have to say in your hearing and in the hearing of all the people: [8]From early times the prophets who preceded you and me have prophesied war, disaster and plague[k] against many countries and great kingdoms. [9]But the prophet who prophesies peace will be recognized as one truly sent by the LORD only if his prediction comes true.[l]"

[10]Then the prophet Hananiah took the yoke[m] off the neck of the prophet Jeremiah and broke it, [11]and he said[n] before all the people, "This is what the LORD says: 'In the same way will I break the yoke of Nebuchadnezzar king of Babylon off the neck of all the nations within two years.'" At this, the prophet Jeremiah went on his way.

[12]Shortly after the prophet Hananiah had broken the yoke off the neck of the prophet Jeremiah, the word of the LORD came to Jeremiah: [13]"Go and tell Hananiah, 'This is what the LORD says: You have broken a wooden yoke, but in its place you will get a yoke of iron. [14]This is what the LORD Almighty, the God of Israel,

INSIGHT

Read 2 Chronicles 36:11-13 and 2 Kings 24:18–25:7 to see whose prophecy came to pass.

27:20
[a] 2Ch 36:10; Jer 24:1
[b] Jer 22:24

27:22
[c] 2Ki 25:13
[d] 2Ch 36:21
[e] Ezr 1:7; 7:19

28:1
[f] Jer 27:1,3
[g] Jos 9:3

28:2
[h] Jer 27:12

28:3
[i] 2Ki 24:13

28:4
[j] Jer 22:24-27

28:8
[k] Lev 26:14-17; Isa 5:5-7

28:9
[l] Dt 18:22

28:10
[m] Jer 27:2

28:11
[n] Jer 14:14; 27:10

---

[a] 20,4 Hebrew *Jeconiah*, a variant of *Jehoiachin*

28:14
a Dt 28:48
b Jer 25:11
c Jer 27:6

says: I will put an iron yoke*a* on the necks of all these nations to make them serve*b* Nebuchadnezzar king of Babylon, and they will serve him. I will even give him control over the wild animals.*c*'"

28:15
d Jer 29:31
e Jer 20:6;
29:21;
La 2:14;
Eze 13:6

¹⁵Then the prophet Jeremiah said to Hananiah the prophet, "Listen, Hananiah! The LORD has not sent*d* you, yet you have persuaded this nation to trust in lies.*e* ¹⁶Therefore, this is what the LORD says: 'I am about to remove you from the face of the earth.*f* This very year you are going to die, because you have preached rebellion*g* against the LORD.'"

28:16
f Ge 7:4
g Dt 13:5;
Jer 29:32

¹⁷In the seventh month of that same year, Hananiah the prophet died.

Chapter 29 Theme

29:1
h 2Ch 36:10

29 This is the text of the letter that the prophet Jeremiah sent from Jerusalem to the surviving elders among the exiles and to the priests, the prophets and all the other people Nebuchadnezzar had carried into exile from Jerusalem to Babylon.*h* ²(This

29:2
i 2Ki 24:12;
Jer 22:24-28

was after King Jehoiachin*ai* and the queen mother, the court officials and the leaders of Judah and Jerusalem, the craftsmen and the artisans had gone into exile from Jerusalem.) ³He entrusted the letter to Elasah son of Shaphan and to Gemariah son of Hilkiah, whom Zedekiah king of Judah sent to King Nebuchadnezzar in Babylon. It said:

29:4
j Jer 24:5

29:5
k ver 28

⁴This is what the LORD Almighty, the God of Israel, says to all those I carried*j* into exile from Jerusalem to Babylon: ⁵"Build*k* houses and settle down; plant gardens and eat what they produce. ⁶Marry and have sons and daughters; find wives for your sons and give your daughters in marriage, so that they too may have sons and daughters. Increase in number there; do not decrease. ⁷Also, seek the peace and prosperity of the city to which I have carried you into exile. Pray*l* to the LORD for it, because if it prospers, you too will prosper." ⁸Yes, this is what the LORD Almighty, the God of Israel, says: "Do not let the prophets and diviners among you deceive*m* you. Do not listen to the dreams you encourage them to have.*n* ⁹They are prophesying lies*o* to you in my name. I have not sent them," declares the LORD.

29:7
l Ezr 6:10;
1Ti 2:1-2

29:8
m Jer 37:9
n Jer 23:27

29:9
o Jer 14:14;
27:15

29:10
p 2Ch 36:21;
Jer 25:12;
Da 9:2
q Jer 21:22

¹⁰This is what the LORD says: "When seventy years*p* are completed for Babylon, I will come to you and fulfill my gracious promise to bring you back*q* to this place. ¹¹For I know the plans*r* I have for you," declares the LORD, "plans to prosper you and not to harm you, plans to give you hope and a future. ¹²Then you will call upon me and come and pray to me, and I

29:11
r Ps 40:5

a 2 Hebrew *Jeconiah*, a variant of *Jehoiachin*

I N S I G H T

Why 70 years of captivity? Because for 490 years Israel had not given the land its Sabbath rest. See Leviticus 25:1-7; 26:27-35, 40-43; 2 Chronicles 36:20, 21.

will listen[a] to you. [13]You will seek[b] me and find me when you seek me with all your heart.[c] [14]I will be found by you," declares the LORD, "and will bring you back[d] from captivity.[a] I will gather you from all the nations and places where I have banished you," declares the LORD, "and will bring you back to the place from which I carried you into exile."[e]

[15]You may say, "The LORD has raised up prophets for us in Babylon," [16]but this is what the LORD says about the king who sits on David's throne and all the people who remain in this city, your countrymen who did not go with you into exile— [17]yes, this is what the LORD Almighty says: "I will send the sword, famine and plague[f] against them and I will make them like poor figs[g] that are so bad they cannot be eaten. [18]I will pursue them with the sword, famine and plague and will make them abhorrent[h] to all the kingdoms of the earth and an object of cursing and horror,[i] of scorn and reproach, among all the nations where I drive them. [19]For they have not listened to my words,"[j] declares the LORD, "words that I sent to them again and again by my servants the prophets.[k] And you exiles have not listened either," declares the LORD.

[20]Therefore, hear the word of the LORD, all you exiles whom I have sent[l] away from Jerusalem to Babylon. [21]This is what the LORD Almighty, the God of Israel, says about Ahab son of Kolaiah and Zedekiah son of Maaseiah, who are prophesying lies[m] to you in my name: "I will hand them over to Nebuchadnezzar king of Babylon, and he will put them to death before your very eyes. [22]Because of them, all the exiles from Judah who are in Babylon will use this curse: 'The LORD treat you like Zedekiah and Ahab, whom the king of Babylon burned[n] in the fire.' [23]For they have done outrageous things in Israel; they have committed adultery[o] with their neighbors' wives and in my name have spoken lies, which I did not tell them to do. I know[p] it and am a witness to it," declares the LORD.

[24]Tell Shemaiah the Nehelamite, [25]"This is what the LORD Almighty, the God of Israel, says: You sent letters in your own name to all the people in Jerusalem, to Zephaniah[q] son of Maaseiah the priest, and to all the other priests. You said to Zephaniah, [26]'The LORD has appointed you priest in place of Jehoiada to be in charge of the house of the LORD; you should put any madman[r] who acts like a prophet into the stocks[s] and neck-irons. [27]So why have you not reprimanded Jeremiah from Anathoth, who poses as a prophet among you? [28]He has sent this message[t] to us in Babylon: It will be a long time.[u] Therefore build[v] houses and settle down; plant gardens and eat what they produce.'"

a 14 Or *will restore your fortunes*

29:12
a Ps 145:19

29:13
b Mt 7:7
c Dt 4:29;
Jer 24:7

29:14
d Dt 30:3;
Jer 30:3
e Jer 23:3-4

29:17
f Jer 27:8
g Jer 24:8-10

29:18
h Jer 15:4
i Dt 28:25;
Jer 42:18

29:19
j Jer 6:19
k Jer 25:4

29:20
l Jer 24:5

29:21
m ver 9;
Jer 14:14

29:22
n Da 3:6

29:23
o Jer 23:14
p Heb 4:13

29:25
q 2Ki 25:18;
Jer 21:1

29:26
r 2Ki 9:11;
Hos 9:7;
Jn 10:20
s Jer 20:2

29:28
t ver 1
u ver 10
v ver 5

29:31
a ver 24
b Jer 14:14;
28:15

29:32
c 1Sa 2:30-33
d ver 10
e Jer 28:16

30:2
f Isa 30:8

30:3
g Jer 29:14
h Jer 16:15

30:5
i Jer 6:25

30:6
j Jer 4:31

30:7
k Isa 2:12;
Joel 2:11
l Zep 1:15
m ver 10

30:8
n Isa 9:4
o Eze 34:27

30:9
p Isa 55:3-4;
Lk 1:69;
Ac 2:30; 13:23
q Eze 34:23-24;
37:24;
Hos 3:5

30:10
r Isa 43:5;
Jer 46:27-28
s Isa 44:2
t Jer 29:14

[29]Zephaniah the priest, however, read the letter to Jeremiah the prophet. [30]Then the word of the LORD came to Jeremiah: [31]"Send this message to all the exiles: 'This is what the LORD says about Shemaiah[a] the Nehelamite: Because Shemaiah has prophesied to you, even though I did not send[b] him, and has led you to believe a lie, [32]this is what the LORD says: I will surely punish Shemaiah the Nehelamite and his descendants.[c] He will have no one left among this people, nor will he see the good[d] things I will do for my people, declares the LORD, because he has preached rebellion[e] against me.'"

Chapter 30 Theme

30 This is the word that came to Jeremiah from the LORD: [2]"This is what the LORD, the God of Israel, says: 'Write[f] in a book all the words I have spoken to you. [3]The days are coming,' declares the LORD, 'when I will bring[g] my people Israel and Judah back from captivity[a] and restore[h] them to the land I gave their forefathers to possess,' says the LORD."

[4]These are the words the LORD spoke concerning Israel and Judah: [5]"This is what the LORD says:

"'Cries of fear[i] are heard—
    terror, not peace.
[6]Ask and see:
    Can a man bear children?
Then why do I see every strong man
    with his hands on his stomach like a woman in labor,[j]
    every face turned deathly pale?
[7]How awful that day[k] will be!
    None will be like it.
It will be a time of trouble[l] for Jacob,
    but he will be saved[m] out of it.

[8]"'In that day,' declares the LORD Almighty,
    'I will break the yoke[n] off their necks
and will tear off their bonds;
    no longer will foreigners enslave them.[o]
[9]Instead, they will serve the LORD their God
    and David[p] their king,[q]
    whom I will raise up for them.

[10]"'So do not fear,[r] O Jacob my servant;[s]
    do not be dismayed, O Israel,'

                                        declares the LORD.

'I will surely save[t] you out of a distant place,
    your descendants from the land of their exile.

a 3 Or *will restore the fortunes of my people Israel and Judah*

1341

Jacob will again have peace and security,[a]
and no one will make him afraid.
[11]I am with you and will save you,'
declares the LORD.
'Though I completely destroy all the nations
among which I scatter you,
I will not completely destroy[b] you.
I will discipline[c] you but only with justice;
I will not let you go entirely unpunished.'[d]

[12]"This is what the LORD says:

"'Your wound is incurable,
your injury beyond healing.[e]
[13]There is no one to plead your cause,
no remedy for your sore,
no healing[f] for you.
[14]All your allies[g] have forgotten you;
they care nothing for you.
I have struck you as an enemy[h] would
and punished you as would the cruel,[i]
because your guilt is so great
and your sins[j] so many.
[15]Why do you cry out over your wound,
your pain that has no cure?
Because of your great guilt and many sins
I have done these things to you.

[16]"'But all who devour[k] you will be devoured;
all your enemies will go into exile.[l]
Those who plunder[m] you will be plundered;
all who make spoil of you I will despoil.
[17]But I will restore you to health
and heal your wounds,'
declares the LORD,
'because you are called an outcast,[n]
Zion for whom no one cares.'

[18]"This is what the LORD says:

"'I will restore the fortunes[o] of Jacob's tents
and have compassion[p] on his dwellings;
the city will be rebuilt[q] on her ruins,
and the palace will stand in its proper place.
[19]From them will come songs[r] of thanksgiving[s]
and the sound of rejoicing.[t]
I will add to their numbers,[u]
and they will not be decreased;

30:10 [a]Isa 35:9
30:11 [b]Jer 4:27; 46:28 [c]Jer 10:24 [d]Am 9:8
30:12 [e]Jer 15:18
30:13 [f]Jer 8:22; 14:19; 46:11
30:14 [g]Jer 22:20; La 1:2 [h]Job 13:24 [i]Job 30:21 [j]Jer 5:6
30:16 [k]Isa 33:1; Jer 2:3; 10:25 [l]Isa 14:2; Joel 3:4-8 [m]Jer 50:10
30:17 [n]Jer 33:24
30:18 [o]ver 3; Jer 31:23 [p]Ps 102:13 [q]Jer 31:4,24,38
30:19 [r]Isa 35:10; 51:11 [s]Isa 51:3 [t]Ps 126:1-2; Jer 31:4 [u]Jer 33:22

30:19
a Isa 60:9

30:20
b Isa 54:13;
Jer 31:17
c Isa 54:14

30:21
d ver 9
e Nu 16:5

30:23
f Jer 23:19

30:24
g Jer 4:8
h Jer 4:28
i Jer 23:19-20

31:1
j Jer 30:22

31:2
k Nu 14:20
l Ex 33:14

31:3
m Dt 4:37
n Hos 11:4

31:4
o Jer 30:19

31:5
p Jer 50:19
q Isa 65:21;
Am 9:14

I will bring them honor,[a]
and they will not be disdained.
[20]Their children[b] will be as in days of old,
and their community will be established[c] before me;
I will punish all who oppress them.
[21]Their leader[d] will be one of their own;
their ruler will arise from among them.
I will bring him near[e] and he will come close to me,
for who is he who will devote himself
to be close to me?'

declares the LORD.

[22]"So you will be my people,
and I will be your God.'"

[23]See, the storm[f] of the LORD
will burst out in wrath,
a driving wind swirling down
on the heads of the wicked.
[24]The fierce anger[g] of the LORD will not turn back[h]
until he fully accomplishes
the purposes of his heart.
In days to come
you will understand[i] this.

Chapter 31 Theme _____

31 "At that time," declares the LORD, "I will be the God[j] of all the clans of Israel, and they will be my people."
[2]This is what the LORD says:

"The people who survive the sword
will find favor[k] in the desert;
I will come to give rest[l] to Israel."

[3]The LORD appeared to us in the past,[a] saying:

"I have loved[m] you with an everlasting love;
I have drawn[n] you with loving-kindness.
[4]I will build you up again
and you will be rebuilt, O Virgin Israel.
Again you will take up your tambourines
and go out to dance with the joyful.[o]
[5]Again you will plant vineyards
on the hills of Samaria;[p]
the farmers will plant them
and enjoy their fruit.[q]

a 3 Or *Lord has appeared to us from afar*

[6]There will be a day when watchmen cry out
    on the hills of Ephraim,
'Come, let us go up to Zion,
    to the LORD our God.'"[a]

[7]This is what the LORD says:

"Sing with joy for Jacob;
    shout for the foremost[b] of the nations.
Make your praises heard, and say,
    'O LORD, save[c] your people,
    the remnant[d] of Israel.'
[8]See, I will bring them from the land of the north[e]
    and gather[f] them from the ends of the earth.
Among them will be the blind[g] and the lame,[h]
    expectant mothers and women in labor;
    a great throng will return.
[9]They will come with weeping;[i]
    they will pray as I bring them back.
I will lead[j] them beside streams of water
    on a level[k] path where they will not stumble,
because I am Israel's father,[l]
    and Ephraim is my firstborn son.

[10]"Hear the word of the LORD, O nations;
    proclaim it in distant coastlands:[m]
'He who scattered Israel will gather[n] them
    and will watch over his flock like a shepherd.'[o]
[11]For the LORD will ransom Jacob
    and redeem[p] them from the hand of those stronger[q]
    than they.
[12]They will come and shout for joy on the heights[r]
    of Zion;
    they will rejoice in the bounty[s] of the LORD—
the grain, the new wine and the oil,[t]
    the young of the flocks and herds.
They will be like a well-watered garden,[u]
    and they will sorrow[v] no more.
[13]Then maidens will dance and be glad,
    young men and old as well.
I will turn their mourning[w] into gladness;
    I will give them comfort and joy[x] instead
    of sorrow.
[14]I will satisfy[y] the priests with abundance,
    and my people will be filled with my bounty,"
                   declares the LORD.

31:6
[a] Isa 2:3;
Jer 50:4-5;
Mic 4:2

31:7
[b] Dt 28:13;
Isa 61:9
[c] Ps 14:7; 28:9
[d] Isa 37:31

31:8
[e] Jer 3:18; 23:8
[f] Dt 30:4;
Eze 34:12-14
[g] Isa 42:16
[h] Eze 34:16;
Mic 4:6

31:9
[i] Ps 126:5
[j] Isa 63:13
[k] Isa 49:11
[l] Ex 4:22; Jer 3:4

31:10
[m] Isa 66:19;
Jer 25:22
[n] Jer 50:19
[o] Isa 40:11;
Eze 34:12

31:11
[p] Isa 44:23;
48:20
[q] Ps 142:6

31:12
[r] Eze 17:23;
Mic 4:1
[s] Joel 3:18
[t] Hos 2:21-22
[u] Isa 58:11
[v] Isa 65:19;
Jn 16:22;
Rev 7:17

31:13
[w] Isa 61:3
[x] Ps 30:11;
Isa 51:11

31:14
[y] ver 25

31:15
a Jos 18:25
b Ge 37:35
c Jer 10:20;
Mt 2:17-18*

31:16
d Isa 25:8; 30:19
e Ru 2:12
f Jer 30:3;
Eze 11:17

31:18
g Job 5:17
h Hos 4:16
i Ps 80:3

31:19
j Eze 36:31
k Eze 21:12;
Lk 18:13

31:20
l Hos 4:4; 11:8
m Isa 55:7;
63:15; Mic 7:18

31:21
n Jer 50:5
o Isa 52:11
p ver 4

31:22
q Jer 2:23
r Jer 3:6

¹⁵This is what the LORD says:

"A voice is heard in Ramah,ᵃ
  mourning and great weeping,
Rachel weeping for her children
  and refusing to be comforted,ᵇ
because her children are no more."ᶜ

¹⁶This is what the LORD says:

"Restrain your voice from weeping
  and your eyes from tears,ᵈ
for your work will be rewarded,ᵉ"

declares the LORD.
"They will returnᶠ from the land of the enemy.
¹⁷So there is hope for your future,"

declares the LORD.
"Your children will return to their own land.

¹⁸"I have surely heard Ephraim's moaning:
'You disciplinedᵍ me like an unruly calf,ʰ
  and I have been disciplined.
Restoreⁱ me, and I will return,
  because you are the LORD my God.
¹⁹After I strayed,ʲ
  I repented;
after I came to understand,
  I beatᵏ my breast.
I was ashamed and humiliated
  because I bore the disgrace of my youth.'
²⁰Is not Ephraim my dear son,
  the child in whom I delight?
Though I often speak against him,
  I still rememberˡ him.
Therefore my heart yearns for him;
  I have great compassionᵐ for him,"

declares the LORD.

²¹"Set up road signs;
  put up guideposts.
Take note of the highway,ⁿ
  the road that you take.
Return,ᵒ O Virginᵖ Israel,
  return to your towns.
²²How long will you wander,�602
  O unfaithfulʳ daughter?

1345

The LORD will create a new thing on earth—
　　a woman will surround[a] a man."

²³This is what the LORD Almighty, the God of Israel, says: "When I bring them back from captivity,[b][a] the people in the land of Judah and in its towns will once again use these words: 'The LORD bless you, O righteous dwelling,[b] O sacred mountain.'[c] ²⁴People will live[d] together in Judah and all its towns—farmers and those who move about with their flocks. ²⁵I will refresh the weary and satisfy the faint."[e]

²⁶At this I awoke[f] and looked around. My sleep had been pleasant to me.

²⁷"The days are coming," declares the LORD, "when I will plant[g] the house of Israel and the house of Judah with the offspring of men and of animals. ²⁸Just as I watched over them to uproot and tear down, and to overthrow, destroy and bring disaster,[h] so I will watch over them to build and to plant,"[i] declares the LORD. ²⁹"In those days people will no longer say,

'The fathers[j] have eaten sour grapes,
　　and the children's teeth are set on edge.'[k]

³⁰Instead, everyone will die for his own sin;[l] whoever eats sour grapes—his own teeth will be set on edge.

³¹"The time is coming," declares the LORD,
　　"when I will make a new covenant[m]
with the house of Israel
　　and with the house of Judah.
³²It will not be like the covenant[n]
I made with their forefathers[o]
when I took them by the hand
　　to lead them out of Egypt,
because they broke my covenant,
　　though I was a husband to[c] them,[d]"
　　　　　　　　　　　　　　　　　declares the LORD.
³³"This is the covenant I will make with the house of Israel
　　after that time," declares the LORD.
"I will put my law in their minds
　　and write it on their hearts.[p]
I will be their God,
　　and they will be my people.[q]
³⁴No longer will a man teach[r] his neighbor,
　　or a man his brother, saying, 'Know the LORD,'

a22 Or will go about ⌊seeking⌋; or will protect　　b23 Or I restore their fortunes　　c32 Hebrew; Septuagint and Syriac / and I turned away from　　d32 Or was their master

31:23
a Jer 30:18
b Isa 1:26
c Ps 48:1;
Zec 8:3

31:24
d Zec 8:4-8

31:25
e Jn 4:14

31:26
f Zec 4:1

31:27
g Eze 36:9-11;
Hos 2:23

31:28
h Jer 18:8; 44:27
i Jer 1:10

31:29
j La 5:7
k Eze 18:2

31:30
l Isa 3:11;
Gal 6:7

31:31
m Jer 32:40;
Eze 37:26;
Lk 22:20;
Heb 8:8-12*;
10:16-17

31:32
n Ex 24:8
o Dt 5:3

31:33
p 2Co 3:3
q Jer 24:7;
Heb 10:16

31:34
r 1Jn 2:27

31:34
a Jn 6:45
b Isa 54:13;
Jer 33:8; 50:20
c Ro 11:27;
Mic 7:19;
Heb 10:17*

31:35
d Ps 136:7-9
e Ge 1:16
f Jer 10:16

31:36
g Isa 54:9-10;
Jer 33:20-26
h Ps 89:36-37

31:37
i Jer 33:22
j Jer 33:24-26;
Ro 11:1-5

31:38
k Jer 30:18
l Ne 3:1
m 2Ki 14:13;
Zec 14:10

31:40
n Jer 7:31-32
o Jer 8:2
p 2Sa 15:23;
Jn 18:1
q 2Ki 11:16
r Joel 3:17;
Zec 14:21

32:1
s 2Ki 25:1
t Jer 25:1; 39:1

32:2
u Ne 3:25;
Jer 37:21

32:3
v Jer 26:8-9
w ver 28;
Jer 34:2-3

32:4
x Jer 38:18,23;
39:5-7; 52:9

because they will all know*a* me,
from the least of them to the greatest,"
declares the LORD.
"For I will forgive*b* their wickedness
and will remember their sins*c* no more."

35This is what the LORD says,

he who appoints*d* the sun
to shine by day,
who decrees the moon and stars
to shine by night,*e*
who stirs up the sea
so that its waves roar—
the LORD Almighty is his name:*f*
36"Only if these decrees*g* vanish from my sight,"
declares the LORD,
"will the descendants*h* of Israel ever cease
to be a nation before me."

37This is what the LORD says:

"Only if the heavens above can be measured*i*
and the foundations of the earth below be searched out
will I reject*j* all the descendants of Israel
because of all they have done,"
declares the LORD.

38"The days are coming," declares the LORD, "when this city will be rebuilt*k* for me from the Tower of Hananel*l* to the Corner Gate.*m* 39The measuring line will stretch from there straight to the hill of Gareb and then turn to Goah. 40The whole valley*n* where dead bodies*o* and ashes are thrown, and all the terraces out to the Kidron Valley*p* on the east as far as the corner of the Horse Gate,*q* will be holy*r* to the LORD. The city will never again be uprooted or demolished."

Chapter 32 Theme

32 This is the word that came to Jeremiah from the LORD in the tenth*s* year of Zedekiah king of Judah, which was the eighteenth*t* year of Nebuchadnezzar. 2The army of the king of Babylon was then besieging Jerusalem, and Jeremiah the prophet was confined in the courtyard of the guard*u* in the royal palace of Judah.

3Now Zedekiah king of Judah had imprisoned him there, saying, "Why do you prophesy*v* as you do? You say, 'This is what the LORD says: I am about to hand this city over to the king of Babylon, and he will capture*w* it. 4Zedekiah king of Judah will not escape*x* out of

INSIGHT

Read Leviticus 25:23-28 in regard to redeeming the land.

the hands of the Babylonians[a] but will certainly be handed over to the king of Babylon, and will speak with him face to face and see him with his own eyes. [5]He will take[a] Zedekiah to Babylon, where he will remain until I deal with him, declares the LORD. If you fight against the Babylonians, you will not succeed.'"[b]

[6]Jeremiah said, "The word of the LORD came to me: [7]Hanamel son of Shallum your uncle is going to come to you and say, 'Buy my field at Anathoth, because as nearest relative it is your right and duty[c] to buy it.'

[8]"Then, just as the LORD had said, my cousin Hanamel came to me in the courtyard of the guard and said, 'Buy my field at Anathoth in the territory of Benjamin. Since it is your right to redeem it and possess it, buy it for yourself.'

"I knew that this was the word of the LORD; [9]so I bought the field at Anathoth from my cousin Hanamel and weighed out for him seventeen shekels[b] of silver.[d] [10]I signed and sealed the deed, had it witnessed,[e] and weighed out the silver on the scales. [11]I took the deed of purchase—the sealed copy containing the terms and conditions, as well as the unsealed copy— [12]and I gave this deed to Baruch[f] son of Neriah,[g] the son of Mahseiah, in the presence of my cousin Hanamel and of the witnesses who had signed the deed and of all the Jews sitting in the courtyard of the guard.

[13]"In their presence I gave Baruch these instructions: [14]'This is what the LORD Almighty, the God of Israel, says: Take these documents, both the sealed and unsealed copies of the deed of purchase, and put them in a clay jar so they will last a long time. [15]For this is what the LORD Almighty, the God of Israel, says: Houses, fields and vineyards will again be bought in this land.'[h]

[16]"After I had given the deed of purchase to Baruch son of Neriah, I prayed to the LORD:

[17]"Ah, Sovereign LORD,[i] you have made the heavens and the earth by your great power and outstretched arm.[j] Nothing is too hard[k] for you. [18]You show love[l] to thousands but bring the punishment for the fathers' sins into the laps of their children[m] after them. O great and powerful God, whose name is the LORD Almighty,[n] [19]great are your purposes and mighty are your deeds.[o] Your eyes are open to all the ways of men;[p] you reward everyone according to his conduct and as his deeds deserve.[q] [20]You performed miraculous signs and wonders in Egypt[r] and have continued them to this day, both in Israel and among all mankind, and have gained the renown that is still yours. [21]You brought your people Israel out of Egypt with signs and wonders, by a mighty hand[s] and an outstretched arm and with

---

32:5
a Jer 39:7;
Eze 12:13
b Jer 21:4

32:7
c Lev 25:24-25;
Ru 4:3-4;
Mt 27:10*

32:9
d Ge 23:16

32:10
e Ru 4:9

32:12
f ver 16;
Jer 36:4;
43:3,6; 45:1
g Jer 51:59

32:15
h ver 43-44;
Jer 30:18;
Am 9:14-15

32:17
i Jer 1:6
j 2Ki 19:15;
Ps 102:25
k Mt 19:26

32:18
l Dt 5:10
m Ex 20:5
n Jer 10:16

32:19
o Isa 28:29
p Pr 5:21;
Jer 16:17
q Jer 17:10;
Mt 16:27

32:20
r Ex 9:16

32:21
s Ex 6:6;
1Ch 17:21;
Da 9:15

---

a 4 Or *Chaldeans*; also in verses 5, 24, 25, 28, 29 and 43   b 9 That is, about 7 ounces (about 200 grams)

32:21
a Dt 26:8

32:22
b Ex 3:8; Jer 11:5

32:23
c Ps 44:2;
78:54-55
d Ne 9:26;
Jer 11:8
e Da 9:14

32:24
f Jer 14:12
g Dt 4:25-26;
Jos 23:15-16

32:27
h Nu 16:22

32:28
i 2Ch 36:17
j ver 3

32:29
k 2Ch 36:19;
Jer 21:10;
37:8,10; 52:13
l Jer 19:13
m Jer 44:18

32:30
n Jer 22:21
o Jer 8:19
p Jer 25:7

32:31
q 2Ki 23:27; 24:3

32:32
r Isa 1:4-6;
Da 9:8

32:33
s Jer 2:27;
Eze 8:16
t Jer 7:13

32:34
u Jer 7:30

32:35
v Lev 18:21
w Jer 7:31; 19:5

32:36
x ver 24

32:37
y Jer 23:3,6
z Dt 30:3;
Eze 34:28

32:38
a Jer 24:7;
2Co 6:16*

32:39
b Eze 11:19

great terror.a 22You gave them this land you had sworn to give their forefathers, a land flowing with milk and honey.b 23They came in and took possessionc of it, but they did not obey you or follow your law;d they did not do what you commanded them to do. So you brought all this disastere upon them.

24"See how the siege ramps are built up to take the city. Because of the sword, famine and plague,f the city will be handed over to the Babylonians who are attacking it. What you saidg has happened, as you now see. 25And though the city will be handed over to the Babylonians, you, O Sovereign LORD, say to me, 'Buy the field with silver and have the transaction witnessed.'"

26Then the word of the LORD came to Jeremiah: 27"I am the LORD, the God of all mankind.h Is anything too hard for me? 28Therefore, this is what the LORD says: I am about to hand this city over to the Babylonians and to Nebuchadnezzari king of Babylon, who will capture it.j 29The Babylonians who are attacking this city will come in and set it on fire; they will burn it down,k along with the housesl where the people provoked me to anger by burning incense on the roofs to Baal and by pouring out drink offeringsm to other gods.

30"The people of Israel and Judah have done nothing but evil in my sight from their youth;n indeed, the people of Israel have done nothing but provokeo me with what their hands have made,p declares the LORD. 31From the day it was built until now, this city has so aroused my anger and wrath that I must removeq it from my sight. 32The people of Israel and Judah have provoked me by all the evilr they have done—they, their kings and officials, their priests and prophets, the men of Judah and the people of Jerusalem. 33They turned their backss to me and not their faces; though I taughtt them again and again, they would not listen or respond to discipline. 34They set up their abominable idols in the house that bears my Name and defiledu it. 35They built high places for Baal in the Valley of Ben Hinnom to sacrifice their sons and daughtersa to Molech,v though I never commanded, nor did it enter my mind,w that they should do such a detestable thing and so make Judah sin.

36"You are saying about this city, 'By the sword, famine and plaguex it will be handed over to the king of Babylon'; but this is what the LORD, the God of Israel, says: 37I will surely gathery them from all the lands where I banish them in my furious anger and great wrath; I will bring them back to this place and let them live in safety.z 38They will be my people,a and I will be their God. 39I will give them singlenessb of heart and action, so that they will always fear me for their own good and the good of their children after

a 35 Or to make their sons and daughters pass through ⌊the fire⌋

1349

them. ⁴⁰I will make an everlasting covenant*a* with them: I will never stop doing good to them, and I will inspire them to fear me, so that they will never turn away from me.*b* ⁴¹I will rejoice in doing them good*c* and will assuredly plant*d* them in this land with all my heart and soul.

⁴²"This is what the LORD says: As I have brought all this great calamity on this people, so I will give them all the prosperity I have promised*e* them. ⁴³Once more fields will be bought*f* in this land of which you say, 'It is a desolate waste, without men or animals, for it has been handed over to the Babylonians.' ⁴⁴Fields will be bought for silver, and deeds*g* will be signed, sealed and witnessed in the territory of Benjamin, in the villages around Jerusalem, in the towns of Judah and in the towns of the hill country, of the western foothills and of the Negev,*h* because I will restore*i* their fortunes,*a* declares the LORD."

Chapter 33 Theme

33 While Jeremiah was still confined in the courtyard*j* of the guard, the word of the LORD came to him a second time: ²"This is what the LORD says, he who made the earth,*k* the LORD who formed it and established it—the LORD is his name:*l* ³'Call*m* to me and I will answer you and tell you great and unsearchable things you do not know.' ⁴For this is what the LORD, the God of Israel, says about the houses in this city and the royal palaces of Judah that have been torn down to be used against the siege*n* ramps*o* and the sword ⁵in the fight with the Babylonians*b*: 'They will be filled with the dead bodies of the men I will slay in my anger and wrath.*p* I will hide my face*q* from this city because of all its wickedness.

⁶"'Nevertheless, I will bring health and healing to it; I will heal my people and will let them enjoy abundant peace and security. ⁷I will bring Judah*r* and Israel back from captivity*c s* and will rebuild them as they were before.*t* ⁸I will cleanse*u* them from all the sin they have committed against me and will forgive*v* all their sins of rebellion against me. ⁹Then this city will bring me renown, joy, praise*w* and honor*x* before all nations on earth that hear of all the good things I do for it; and they will be in awe and will tremble at the abundant prosperity and peace I provide for it.'

¹⁰"This is what the LORD says: 'You say about this place, "It is a desolate waste, without men or animals."*y* Yet in the towns of Judah and the streets of Jerusalem that are deserted, inhabited by neither men nor animals, there will be heard once more ¹¹the sounds of joy

---

32:40
a Isa 55:3
b Jer 24:7

32:41
c Dt 30:9
d Jer 24:6; 31:28; Am 9:15

32:42
e Jer 31:28

32:43
f ver 15

32:44
g ver 10
h Jer 17:26
i Jer 33:7,11,26

33:1
j Jer 32:2-3; 37:21; 38:28

33:2
k Jer 10:16
l Ex 3:15; 15:3

33:3
m Isa 55:6; Jer 29:12

33:4
n Eze 4:2
o Jer 32:24; Hab 1:10

33:5
p Jer 21:4-7
q Isa 8:17

33:7
r Jer 32:44
s Jer 30:3; Am 9:14
t Isa 1:26

33:8
u Heb 9:13-14
v Jer 31:34; Mic 7:18; Zec 13:1

33:9
w Jer 13:11
x Isa 62:7; Jer 3:17

33:10
y Jer 32:43

---

a 44 Or *will bring them back from captivity*   *b* 5 Or *Chaldeans*   *c* 7 Or *will restore the fortunes of Judah and Israel* and gladness,[a] the voices of bride and bridegroom, and the voices of those who bring thank offerings[b] to the house of the LORD, saying,

> "Give thanks to the LORD Almighty,
>   for the LORD is good;[c]
>   his love endures forever."[d]

For I will restore the fortunes of the land as they were before,' says the LORD.

¹²"This is what the LORD Almighty says: 'In this place, desolate[e] and without men or animals—in all its towns there will again be pastures for shepherds to rest their flocks.[f] ¹³In the towns of the hill country, of the western foothills and of the Negev,[g] in the territory of Benjamin, in the villages around Jerusalem and in the towns of Judah, flocks will again pass under the hand[h] of the one who counts them,' says the LORD.

¹⁴"'The days are coming,' declares the LORD, 'when I will fulfill the gracious promise[i] I made to the house of Israel and to the house of Judah.

> ¹⁵"'In those days and at that time
>   I will make a righteous[j] Branch[k] sprout from
>   David's line;
>   he will do what is just and right in the land.
> ¹⁶In those days Judah will be saved[l]
>   and Jerusalem will live in safety.
> This is the name by which it[a] will be called:
>   The LORD Our Righteousness.'[m]

¹⁷For this is what the LORD says: 'David will never fail[n] to have a man to sit on the throne of the house of Israel, ¹⁸nor will the priests, who are Levites,[o] ever fail to have a man to stand before me continually to offer burnt offerings, to burn grain offerings and to present sacrifices.[p]'"

¹⁹The word of the LORD came to Jeremiah: ²⁰"This is what the LORD says: 'If you can break my covenant with the day[q] and my covenant with the night, so that day and night no longer come at their appointed time, ²¹then my covenant[r] with David my servant—and my covenant with the Levites who are priests ministering before me—can be broken and David will no longer have a descendant to reign on his throne.[s] ²²I will make the descendants of David my servant and the Levites who minister before me as countless[t] as the stars of the sky and as measureless as the sand on the seashore.'"

²³The word of the LORD came to Jeremiah: ²⁴"Have you not noticed that these people are saying, 'The LORD has rejected the two

---

Cross-references (margin):

33:11
a Isa 51:3
b Lev 7:12
c 1Ch 16:8;
    Ps 136:1
d 1Ch 16:34;
    2Ch 5:13;
    Ps 100:4-5

33:12
e Jer 32:43
f Isa 65:10;
    Eze 34:11-15

33:13
g Jer 17:26
h Lev 27:32

33:14
i Jer 29:10

33:15
j Ps 72:2
k Isa 4:2; 11:1;
    Jer 23:5

33:16
l Isa 45:17
m 1Co 1:30

33:17
n 2Sa 7:13;
    1Ki 2:4;
    Ps 89:29-37;
    Lk 1:33

33:18
o Dt 18:1
p Heb 13:15

33:20
q Ps 89:36

33:21
r Ps 89:34
s 2Ch 7:18

33:22
t Ge 15:5

a 16 Or he

kingdoms[a][a] he chose'? So they despise[b] my people and no longer regard them as a nation.[c] [25]This is what the LORD says: 'If I have not established my covenant with day and night[d] and the fixed laws of heaven and earth,[e] [26]then I will reject[f] the descendants of Jacob[g] and David my servant and will not choose one of his sons to rule over the descendants of Abraham, Isaac and Jacob. For I will restore their fortunes[b][h] and have compassion on them.'"

Chapter 34 Theme

34 While Nebuchadnezzar king of Babylon and all his army and all the kingdoms and peoples[i] in the empire he ruled were fighting against Jerusalem[j] and all its surrounding towns, this word came to Jeremiah from the LORD: [2]"This is what the LORD, the God of Israel, says: Go to Zedekiah[k] king of Judah and tell him, 'This is what the LORD says: I am about to hand this city over to the king of Babylon, and he will burn it down.[l] [3]You will not escape from his grasp but will surely be captured and handed over[m] to him. You will see the king of Babylon with your own eyes, and he will speak with you face to face. And you will go to Babylon.

[4]"'Yet hear the promise of the LORD, O Zedekiah king of Judah. This is what the LORD says concerning you: You will not die by the sword; [5]you will die peacefully. As people made a funeral fire[n] in honor of your fathers, the former kings who preceded you, so they will make a fire in your honor and lament, "Alas,[o] O master!" I myself make this promise, declares the LORD.'"

[6]Then Jeremiah the prophet told all this to Zedekiah king of Judah, in Jerusalem, [7]while the army of the king of Babylon was fighting against Jerusalem and the other cities of Judah that were still holding out—Lachish[p] and Azekah.[q] These were the only fortified cities left in Judah.

[8]The word came to Jeremiah from the LORD after King Zedekiah had made a covenant with all the people[r] in Jerusalem to proclaim freedom[s] for the slaves. [9]Everyone was to free his Hebrew slaves, both male and female; no one was to hold a fellow Jew in bondage.[t] [10]So all the officials and people who entered into this covenant agreed that they would free their male and female slaves and no longer hold them in bondage. They agreed, and set them free. [11]But afterward they changed their minds and took back the slaves they had freed and enslaved them again.

[12]Then the word of the LORD came to Jeremiah: [13]"This is what the LORD, the God of Israel, says: I made a covenant with your forefathers[u] when I brought them out of Egypt, out of the land of slavery. I said, [14]'Every seventh year each of you must free any fellow

---

33:24
a Eze 37:22
b Ne 4:4
c Jer 30:17

33:25
d Jer 31:35-36
e Ps 74:16-17

33:26
f Jer 31:37
g Isa 14:1
h ver 7

34:1
i Jer 27:7
j 2Ki 25:1; Jer 39:1

34:2
k 2Ch 36:11
l ver 22; Jer 32:29; 37:8

34:3
m 2Ki 25:7; Jer 21:7; 32:4

34:5
n 2Ch 16:14; 21:19
o Jer 22:18

34:7
p Jos 10:3
q Jos 10:10; 2Ch 11:9

34:8
r 2Ki 11:17
s Ex 21:2; Lev 25:10, 39-41; Ne 5:5-8

34:9
t Lev 25:39-46

34:13
u Ex 24:8

---

a 24 Or *families*   b 26 Or *will bring them back from captivity*

34:14
a Ex 21:2
b Dt 15:12;
2Ki 17:14

34:15
c ver 8
d Jer 7:10-11;
32:34

34:16
e Eze 3:20; 18:24
f Ex 20:7;
Lev 19:12

34:17
g Mt 7:2; Gal 6:7
h Dt 28:25,64;
Jer 29:18

34:18
i Ge 15:10

34:19
j Zep 3:3-4

34:20
k Jer 21:7
l Jer 11:21
m Dt 28:26;
Jer 7:33; 19:7

34:21
n Jer 32:4
o Jer 39:6;
52:24-27
p Jer 37:5

34:22
q Jer 39:1-2
r Jer 39:8

35:1
s 2Ch 36:5

35:2
t 2Ki 10:15;
1Ch 2:55
u 1Ki 6:5

35:4
v Dt 33:1
w 1Ch 9:19
x 2Ki 12:9

35:6
y 2Ki 10:15
z Lev 10:9;
Nu 6:2-4;
Lk 1:15

Hebrew who has sold himself to you. After he has served you six years, you must let him go free.'ᵃ ᵃ Your fathers, however, did not listen to me or pay attentionᵇ to me. ¹⁵Recently you repented and did what is right in my sight: Each of you proclaimed freedom to his countrymen.ᶜ You even made a covenant before me in the house that bears my Name.ᵈ ¹⁶But now you have turned aroundᵉ and profanedᶠ my name; each of you has taken back the male and female slaves you had set free to go where they wished. You have forced them to become your slaves again.

¹⁷"Therefore, this is what the LORD says: You have not obeyed me; you have not proclaimed freedom for your fellow countrymen. So I now proclaim 'freedom' for you,ᵍ declares the LORD— 'freedom' to fall by the sword, plague and famine. I will make you abhorrent to all the kingdoms of the earth.ʰ ¹⁸The men who have violated my covenant and have not fulfilled the terms of the covenant they made before me, I will treat like the calf they cut in two and then walked between its pieces.ⁱ ¹⁹The leaders of Judah and Jerusalem, the court officials,ʲ the priests and all the people of the land who walked between the pieces of the calf, ²⁰I will hand overᵏ to their enemies who seek their lives.ˡ Their dead bodies will become food for the birds of the air and the beasts of the earth.ᵐ

²¹"I will hand Zedekiahⁿ king of Judah and his officialsᵒ over to their enemies who seek their lives, to the army of the king of Babylon, which has withdrawnᵖ from you. ²²I am going to give the order, declares the LORD, and I will bring them back to this city. They will fight against it, takeᑫ it and burnʳ it down. And I will lay waste the towns of Judah so no one can live there."

Chapter 35 Theme

35 This is the word that came to Jeremiah from the LORD during the reign of Jehoiakimˢ son of Josiah king of Judah: ²"Go to the Recabiteᵗ family and invite them to come to one of the side roomsᵘ of the house of the LORD and give them wine to drink."

³So I went to get Jaazaniah son of Jeremiah, the son of Habazziniah, and his brothers and all his sons—the whole family of the Recabites. ⁴I brought them into the house of the LORD, into the room of the sons of Hanan son of Igdaliah the man of God.ᵛ It was next to the room of the officials, which was over that of Maaseiah son of Shallumʷ the doorkeeper.ˣ ⁵Then I set bowls full of wine and some cups before the men of the Recabite family and said to them, "Drink some wine."

⁶But they replied, "We do not drink wine, because our forefather Jonadabʸ son of Recab gave us this command: 'Neither you nor your descendants must ever drink wine.ᶻ ⁷Also you must never

a 14 Deut. 15:12

build houses, sow seed or plant vineyards; you must never have any of these things, but must always live in tents.*a* Then you will live a long time in the land*b* where you are nomads.' **8**We have obeyed everything our forefather*c* Jonadab son of Recab commanded us. Neither we nor our wives nor our sons and daughters have ever drunk wine **9**or built houses to live in or had vineyards, fields or crops.*d* **10**We have lived in tents and have fully obeyed everything our forefather Jonadab commanded us. **11**But when Nebuchadnezzar king of Babylon invaded*e* this land, we said, 'Come, we must go to Jerusalem*f* to escape the Babylonian*a* and Aramean armies.' So we have remained in Jerusalem."

12Then the word of the LORD came to Jeremiah, saying: **13**"This is what the LORD Almighty, the God of Israel, says: Go and tell the men of Judah and the people of Jerusalem, 'Will you not learn a lesson*g* and obey my words?' declares the LORD. **14**'Jonadab son of Recab ordered his sons not to drink wine and this command has been kept. To this day they do not drink wine, because they obey their forefather's command. But I have spoken to you again and again,*h* yet you have not obeyed*i* me. **15**Again and again I sent all my servants the prophets*j* to you. They said, "Each of you must turn*k* from your wicked ways and reform*l* your actions; do not follow other gods to serve them. Then you will live in the land*m* I have given to you and your fathers." But you have not paid attention or listened*n* to me. **16**The descendants of Jonadab son of Recab have carried out the command their forefather*o* gave them, but these people have not obeyed me.'

17"Therefore, this is what the LORD God Almighty, the God of Israel, says: 'Listen! I am going to bring on Judah and on everyone living in Jerusalem every disaster*p* I pronounced against them. I spoke to them, but they did not listen;*q* I called to them, but they did not answer.'"*r*

18Then Jeremiah said to the family of the Recabites, "This is what the LORD Almighty, the God of Israel, says: 'You have obeyed the command of your forefather Jonadab and have followed all his instructions and have done everything he ordered.' **19**Therefore, this is what the LORD Almighty, the God of Israel, says: 'Jonadab son of Recab will never fail*s* to have a man to serve*t* me.'"

Chapter 36 Theme

36 In the fourth year of Jehoiakim*u* son of Josiah king of Judah, this word came to Jeremiah from the LORD: **2**"Take a scroll*v* and write on it all the words I have spoken to you concerning Israel, Judah and all the other nations from the time I began

a 11 Or Chaldean

35:7
a Heb 11:9
b Ex 20:12;
Eph 6:2-3

35:8
c Pr 1:8;
Col 3:20

35:9
d 1Ti 6:6

35:11
e 2Ki 24:1
f Jer 8:14

35:13
g Jer 6:10;
32:33

35:14
h Jer 7:13; 25:3
i Isa 30:9

35:15
j Jer 7:25
k Jer 26:3
l Isa 1:16-17;
Jer 4:1; 18:11;
Eze 18:30
m Jer 25:5
n Jer 7:26

35:16
o Mal 1:6

35:17
p Jos 23:15;
Jer 21:4-7
q Pr 1:24;
Ro 10:21
r Isa 65:12;
66:4;
Jer 7:13

35:19
s Jer 33:17
t Jer 15:19

36:1
u 2Ch 36:5

36:2
v Ex 17:14;
Jer 30:2;
Hab 2:2

36:2
a Jer 1:2; 25:3

speaking to you in the reign of Josiah*a* till now. ³Perhaps*b* when the people of Judah hear*c* about every disaster I plan to inflict on them, each of them will turn*d* from his wicked way; then I will forgive*e* their wickedness and their sin."

36:3
b ver 7; Eze 12:3
c Mk 4:12
d Jer 26:3;
Jnh 3:8; Ac 3:19
e Jer 18:8

⁴So Jeremiah called Baruch*f* son of Neriah, and while Jeremiah dictated*g* all the words the LORD had spoken to him, Baruch wrote them on the scroll.*h* ⁵Then Jeremiah told Baruch, "I am restricted; I cannot go to the LORD's temple. ⁶So you go to the house of the LORD on a day of fasting*i* and read to the people from the scroll the words of the LORD that you wrote as I dictated. Read them to all the people of Judah who come in from their towns. ⁷Perhaps they will bring their petition before the LORD, and each will turn*j* from his wicked ways, for the anger*k* and wrath pronounced against this people by the LORD are great."

36:4
f Jer 32:12
g ver 18
h Eze 2:9

⁸Baruch son of Neriah did everything Jeremiah the prophet told him to do; at the LORD's temple he read the words of the LORD from the scroll. ⁹In the ninth month*l* of the fifth year of Jehoiakim son of Josiah king of Judah, a time of fasting*m* before the LORD was proclaimed for all the people in Jerusalem and those who had come from the towns of Judah. ¹⁰From the room of Gemariah son of Shaphan the secretary,*n* which was in the upper courtyard at the entrance of the New Gate*o* of the temple, Baruch read to all the people at the LORD's temple the words of Jeremiah from the scroll.

36:6
i ver 9

36:7
j Jer 26:3
k Dt 31:17

36:9
l ver 22
m 2Ch 20:3

36:10
n Jer 52:25
o Jer 26:10

¹¹When Micaiah son of Gemariah, the son of Shaphan, heard all the words of the LORD from the scroll, ¹²he went down to the secretary's room in the royal palace, where all the officials were sitting: Elishama the secretary, Delaiah son of Shemaiah, Elnathan*p* son of Acbor, Gemariah son of Shaphan, Zedekiah son of Hananiah, and all the other officials. ¹³After Micaiah told them everything he had heard Baruch read to the people from the scroll, ¹⁴all the officials sent Jehudi*q* son of Nethaniah, the son of Shelemiah, the son of Cushi, to say to Baruch, "Bring the scroll from which you have read to the people and come." So Baruch son of Neriah went to them with the scroll in his hand. ¹⁵They said to him, "Sit down, please, and read it to us."

36:12
p Jer 26:22

36:14
q ver 21

So Baruch read it to them. ¹⁶When they heard all these words, they looked at each other in fear and said to Baruch, "We must report all these words to the king." ¹⁷Then they asked Baruch, "Tell us, how did you come to write all this? Did Jeremiah dictate it?"

36:18
r ver 4

¹⁸"Yes," Baruch replied, "he dictated*r* all these words to me, and I wrote them in ink on the scroll."

36:19
s 1Ki 17:3

¹⁹Then the officials said to Baruch, "You and Jeremiah, go and hide.*s* Don't let anyone know where you are."

²⁰After they put the scroll in the room of Elishama the secretary, they went to the king in the courtyard and reported everything to him. ²¹The king sent Jehudi*t* to get the scroll, and Jehudi brought

36:21
t ver 14

it from the room of Elishama the secretary and read it to the king[a] and all the officials standing beside him. 22It was the ninth month and the king was sitting in the winter apartment,[b] with a fire burning in the firepot in front of him. 23Whenever Jehudi had read three or four columns of the scroll, the king cut them off with a scribe's knife and threw them into the firepot, until the entire scroll was burned in the fire.[c] 24The king and all his attendants who heard all these words showed no fear,[d] nor did they tear their clothes.[e] 25Even though Elnathan, Delaiah and Gemariah urged the king not to burn the scroll, he would not listen to them. 26Instead, the king commanded Jerahmeel, a son of the king, Seraiah son of Azriel and Shelemiah son of Abdeel to arrest[f] Baruch the scribe and Jeremiah the prophet. But the LORD had hidden[g] them.

27After the king burned the scroll containing the words that Baruch had written at Jeremiah's dictation,[h] the word of the LORD came to Jeremiah: 28"Take another scroll and write on it all the words that were on the first scroll, which Jehoiakim king of Judah burned up. 29Also tell Jehoiakim king of Judah, 'This is what the LORD says: You burned that scroll and said, "Why did you write on it that the king of Babylon would certainly come and destroy this land and cut off both men and animals from it?"[i] 30Therefore, this is what the LORD says about Jehoiakim king of Judah: He will have no one to sit on the throne of David; his body will be thrown out[j] and exposed to the heat by day and the frost by night. 31I will punish him and his children and his attendants for their wickedness; I will bring on them and those living in Jerusalem and the people of Judah every disaster[k] I pronounced against them, because they have not listened.'"

32So Jeremiah took another scroll and gave it to the scribe Baruch son of Neriah, and as Jeremiah dictated,[l] Baruch wrote[m] on it all the words of the scroll that Jehoiakim king of Judah had burned[n] in the fire. And many similar words were added to them.

Chapter 37 Theme

37 Zedekiah[o] son of Josiah was made king[p] of Judah by Nebuchadnezzar king of Babylon; he reigned in place of Jehoiachin[a][q] son of Jehoiakim. 2Neither he nor his attendants nor the people of the land paid any attention[r] to the words the LORD had spoken through Jeremiah the prophet.

3King Zedekiah, however, sent Jehucal son of Shelemiah with the priest Zephaniah[s] son of Maaseiah to Jeremiah the prophet with this message: "Please pray[t] to the LORD our God for us."

4Now Jeremiah was free to come and go among the people, for he had not yet been put in prison.[u] 5Pharaoh's army had marched

a 1 Hebrew *Coniah*, a variant of *Jehoiachin*

36:21
a 2Ki 22:10

36:22
b Am 3:15

36:23
c 1Ki 22:8

36:24
d Ps 36:1
e Ge 37:29;
2Ki 22:11;
Isa 37:1

36:26
f Mt 23:34
g Jer 15:21

36:27
h ver 4

36:29
i Isa 30:10

36:30
j Jer 22:19

36:31
k Pr 29:1

36:32
l ver 4
m Ex 34:1
n ver 23

37:1
o 2Ki 24:17
p Eze 17:13
q 2Ki 24:8,12;
2Ch 36:10;
Jer 22:24

37:2
r 2Ki 24:19;
2Ch 36:12,14

37:3
s Jer 29:25; 52:24
t 1Ki 13:6;
Jer 21:1-2; 42:2

37:4
u ver 15; Jer 32:2

37:5
a Eze 17:15
b Jer 34:21
c 2Ki 24:7

out of Egypt,[a] and when the Babylonians[a] who were besieging Jerusalem heard the report about them, they withdrew[b] from Jerusalem.[c]

⁶Then the word of the LORD came to Jeremiah the prophet: ⁷"This is what the LORD, the God of Israel, says: Tell the king of Judah, who sent you to inquire[d] of me, 'Pharaoh's army, which has marched out to support you, will go back to its own land, to Egypt.[e] ⁸Then the Babylonians will return and attack this city; they will capture it and burn[f] it down.'

37:7
d 2Ki 22:18
e Jer 2:36;
La 4:17

⁹"This is what the LORD says: Do not deceive[g] yourselves, thinking, 'The Babylonians will surely leave us.' They will not! ¹⁰Even if you were to defeat the entire Babylonian[b] army that is attacking you and only wounded men were left in their tents, they would come out and burn this city down."

37:8
f Jer 34:22; 39:8

37:9
g Jer 29:8

¹¹After the Babylonian army had withdrawn[h] from Jerusalem because of Pharaoh's army, ¹²Jeremiah started to leave the city to go to the territory of Benjamin to get his share of the property[i] among the people there. ¹³But when he reached the Benjamin Gate, the captain of the guard, whose name was Irijah son of Shelemiah, the son of Hananiah, arrested him and said, "You are deserting to the Babylonians!"

37:11
h ver 5

37:12
i Jer 32:9

¹⁴"That's not true!" Jeremiah said. "I am not deserting to the Babylonians." But Irijah would not listen to him; instead, he arrested[j] Jeremiah and brought him to the officials. ¹⁵They were angry with Jeremiah and had him beaten[k] and imprisoned in the house[l] of Jonathan the secretary, which they had made into a prison.

37:14
j Jer 40:4

¹⁶Jeremiah was put into a vaulted cell in a dungeon, where he remained a long time. ¹⁷Then King Zedekiah sent for him and had him brought to the palace, where he asked[m] him privately,[n] "Is there any word from the LORD?"

37:15
k Jer 20:2
l Jer 38:26

"Yes," Jeremiah replied, "you will be handed over[o] to the king of Babylon."

37:17
m Jer 15:11
n Jer 38:16
o Jer 21:7

¹⁸Then Jeremiah said to King Zedekiah, "What crime[p] have I committed against you or your officials or this people, that you have put me in prison? ¹⁹Where are your prophets who prophesied to you, 'The king of Babylon will not attack you or this land'? ²⁰But now, my lord the king, please listen. Let me bring my petition before you: Do not send me back to the house of Jonathan the secretary, or I will die there."

37:18
p 1Sa 26:18;
Jn 10:32;
Ac 25:8

²¹King Zedekiah then gave orders for Jeremiah to be placed in the courtyard of the guard and given bread from the street of the bakers each day until all the bread[q] in the city was gone.[r] So Jeremiah remained in the courtyard of the guard.[s]

37:21
q Isa 33:16;
Jer 38:9
r 2Ki 25:3;
Jer 52:6
s Jer 32:2;
38:6,13,28

a 5 Or *Chaldeans*; also in verses 8, 9, 13 and 14   b 10 Or *Chaldean*; also in verse 11

Chapter 38 Theme

38 Shephatiah son of Mattan, Gedaliah son of Pashhur, Jehucal son of Shelemiah, and Pashhur son of Malkijah heard what Jeremiah was telling all the people when he said, ²"This is what the LORD says: 'Whoever stays in this city will die by the sword, famine or plague,^b but whoever goes over to the Babylonians^b will live. He will escape with his life; he will live.'^c ³And this is what the LORD says: 'This city will certainly be handed over to the army of the king of Babylon, who will capture it.'"^d

⁴Then the officials^e said to the king, "This man should be put to death.^f He is discouraging the soldiers who are left in this city, as well as all the people, by the things he is saying to them. This man is not seeking the good of these people but their ruin."

⁵"He is in your hands," King Zedekiah answered. "The king can do nothing to oppose you."

⁶So they took Jeremiah and put him into the cistern of Malkijah, the king's son, which was in the courtyard of the guard.^g They lowered Jeremiah by ropes into the cistern; it had no water in it, only mud, and Jeremiah sank down into the mud.

⁷But Ebed-Melech,^h a Cushite,^c an official^{d i} in the royal palace, heard that they had put Jeremiah into the cistern. While the king was sitting in the Benjamin Gate,^j ⁸Ebed-Melech went out of the palace and said to him, ⁹"My lord the king, these men have acted wickedly in all they have done to Jeremiah the prophet. They have thrown him into a cistern, where he will starve to death when there is no longer any bread^k in the city."

¹⁰Then the king commanded Ebed-Melech the Cushite, "Take thirty men from here with you and lift Jeremiah the prophet out of the cistern before he dies."

¹¹So Ebed-Melech took the men with him and went to a room under the treasury in the palace. He took some old rags and worn-out clothes from there and let them down with ropes to Jeremiah in the cistern. ¹²Ebed-Melech the Cushite said to Jeremiah, "Put these old rags and worn-out clothes under your arms to pad the ropes." Jeremiah did so, ¹³and they pulled him up with the ropes and lifted him out of the cistern. And Jeremiah remained in the courtyard of the guard.^l

¹⁴Then King Zedekiah sent for Jeremiah the prophet and had him brought to the third entrance to the temple of the LORD. "I am going to ask you something," the king said to Jeremiah. "Do not hide^m anything from me."

38:1 a Jer 37:3
38:2 b Jer 34:17 c Jer 21:9; 39:18; 45:5
38:3 d Jer 21:4,10; 32:3
38:4 e Jer 36:12 f Jer 26:11
38:6 g Jer 37:21
38:7 h Jer 39:16 i Ac 8:27 j Job 29:7
38:9 k Jer 37:21
38:13 l Jer 37:21
38:14 m 1Sa 3:17

a 1 Hebrew *Jucal*, a variant of *Jehucal*   b 2 Or *Chaldeans*; also in verses 18, 19 and 23   c 7 Probably from the upper Nile region   d 7 Or *a eunuch*

38:16
a Jer 37:17
b Isa 42:5; 57:16
c ver 4

¹⁵Jeremiah said to Zedekiah, "If I give you an answer, will you not kill me? Even if I did give you counsel, you would not listen to me."

¹⁶But King Zedekiah swore this oath secretly*ᵃ* to Jeremiah: "As surely as the LORD lives, who has given us breath,*ᵇ* I will neither kill you nor hand you over to those who are seeking your life."*ᶜ*

38:17
d 2Ki 24:12;
Jer 21:9

¹⁷Then Jeremiah said to Zedekiah, "This is what the LORD God Almighty, the God of Israel, says: 'If you surrender to the officers of the king of Babylon, your life will be spared and this city will not be burned down; you and your family will live.*ᵈ* ¹⁸But if you will not surrender to the officers of the king of Babylon, this city will be handed over*ᵉ* to the Babylonians and they will burn*ᶠ* it down; you yourself will not escape*ᵍ* from their hands.'"

38:18
e ver 3; Jer 34:3
f Jer 37:8
g Jer 24:8; 32:4

¹⁹King Zedekiah said to Jeremiah, "I am afraid*ʰ* of the Jews who have gone over*ⁱ* to the Babylonians, for the Babylonians may hand me over to them and they will mistreat me."

²⁰"They will not hand you over," Jeremiah replied. "Obey*ʲ* the LORD by doing what I tell you. Then it will go well with you, and your life*ᵏ* will be spared. ²¹But if you refuse to surrender, this is what the LORD has revealed to me: ²²All the women*ˡ* left in the palace of the king of Judah will be brought out to the officials of the king of Babylon. Those women will say to you:

38:19
h Isa 51:12;
Jn 12:42
i Jer 39:9

38:20
j Jer 11:4
k Isa 55:3

> "'They misled you and overcame you—
>   those trusted friends of yours.
> Your feet are sunk in the mud;
>   your friends have deserted you.'

²³"All your wives and children*ᵐ* will be brought out to the Babylonians. You yourself will not escape from their hands but will be captured*ⁿ* by the king of Babylon; and this city will*ᵃ* be burned down."

38:22
l Jer 6:12

²⁴Then Zedekiah said to Jeremiah, "Do not let anyone know about this conversation, or you may die. ²⁵If the officials hear that I talked with you, and they come to you and say, 'Tell us what you said to the king and what the king said to you; do not hide it from us or we will kill you,' ²⁶then tell them, 'I was pleading with the king not to send me back to Jonathan's house*ᵒ* to die there.'"

38:23
m 2Ki 25:6
n Jer 41:10

²⁷All the officials did come to Jeremiah and question him, and he told them everything the king had ordered him to say. So they said no more to him, for no one had heard his conversation with the king.

38:26
o Jer 37:15

²⁸And Jeremiah remained in the courtyard of the guard*ᵖ* until the day Jerusalem was captured.

38:28
p Jer 37:21;
39:14

ᵃ 23 Or *and you will cause this city to*

Chapter 39 Theme _____

39 This is how Jerusalem was taken: ¹In the ninth year of Zedekiah king of Judah, in the tenth month, Nebuchadnezzar king of Babylon marched against Jerusalem with his whole army and laid siege[a] to it. ²And on the ninth day of the fourth month of Zedekiah's eleventh year, the city wall was broken through. ³Then all the officials[b] of the king of Babylon came and took seats in the Middle Gate: Nergal-Sharezer of Samgar, Nebo-Sarsekim[a] a chief officer, Nergal-Sharezer a high official and all the other officials of the king of Babylon. ⁴When Zedekiah king of Judah and all the soldiers saw them, they fled; they left the city at night by way of the king's garden, through the gate between the two walls, and headed toward the Arabah.[b]

⁵But the Babylonian[c] army pursued them and overtook Zedekiah[c] in the plains of Jericho. They captured him and took him to Nebuchadnezzar king of Babylon at Riblah[d] in the land of Hamath, where he pronounced sentence on him. ⁶There at Riblah the king of Babylon slaughtered the sons of Zedekiah before his eyes and also killed all the nobles of Judah. ⁷Then he put out Zedekiah's eyes[e] and bound him with bronze shackles to take him to Babylon.[f]

⁸The Babylonians[d] set fire[g] to the royal palace and the houses of the people and broke down the walls[h] of Jerusalem. ⁹Nebuzaradan commander of the imperial guard carried into exile to Babylon the people who remained in the city, along with those who had gone over to him, and the rest of the people.[i] ¹⁰But Nebuzaradan the commander of the guard left behind in the land of Judah some of the poor people, who owned nothing; and at that time he gave them vineyards and fields.

¹¹Now Nebuchadnezzar king of Babylon had given these orders about Jeremiah through Nebuzaradan commander of the imperial guard: ¹²"Take him and look after him; don't harm[j] him but do for him whatever he asks." ¹³So Nebuzaradan the commander of the guard, Nebushazban a chief officer, Nergal-Sharezer a high official and all the other officers of the king of Babylon ¹⁴sent and had Jeremiah taken out of the courtyard of the guard.[k] They turned him over to Gedaliah son of Ahikam,[l] the son of Shaphan, to take him back to his home. So he remained among his own people.[m]

¹⁵While Jeremiah had been confined in the courtyard of the guard, the word of the LORD came to him: ¹⁶"Go and tell Ebed-Melech[n] the Cushite, 'This is what the LORD Almighty, the God of Israel, says: I am about to fulfill my words against this city through disaster,[o] not prosperity. At that time they will be fulfilled before

39:1
a 2Ki 25:1;
Jer 52:4;
Eze 24:2

39:3
b Jer 21:4

39:5
c Jer 32:4
d 2Ki 23:33

39:7
e Eze 12:13
f Jer 32:5

39:8
g Jer 38:18
h Ne 1:3

39:9
i Jer 40:1

39:12
j Pr 16:7;
1Pe 3:13

39:14
k Jer 38:28
l 2Ki 22:12
m Jer 40:5

39:16
n Jer 38:7
o Jer 21:10;
Da 9:12

---

a 3 Or *Nergal-Sharezer, Samgar-Nebo, Sarsekim*   *b 4* Or *the Jordan Valley*   *c 5* Or *Chaldean*
d 8 Or *Chaldeans*

39:17
a Ps 41:1-2

your eyes. ¹⁷But I will rescue[a] you on that day, declares the LORD; you will not be handed over to those you fear. ¹⁸I will save you; you will not fall by the sword[b] but will escape with your life,[c] because you trust[d] in me, declares the LORD.'"

39:18
b Jer 45:5
c Jer 21:9; 38:2
d Jer 17:7

Chapter 40 Theme

40 The word came to Jeremiah from the LORD after Nebuzaradan commander of the imperial guard had released him at Ramah. He had found Jeremiah bound in chains among all the captives from Jerusalem and Judah who were being carried into exile to Babylon. ²When the commander of the guard found Jeremiah, he said to him, "The LORD your God decreed this disaster for this place.[e] ³And now the LORD has brought it about; he has done just as he said he would. All this happened because you people sinned[f] against the LORD and did not obey[g] him. ⁴But today I am freeing you from the chains on your wrists. Come with me to Babylon, if you like, and I will look after you; but if you do not want to, then don't come. Look, the whole country lies before you; go wherever you please."[h] ⁵However, before Jeremiah turned to go,[a] Nebuzaradan added, "Go back to Gedaliah[i] son of Ahikam, the son of Shaphan, whom the king of Babylon has appointed over the towns of Judah, and live with him among the people, or go anywhere else you please."[j]

40:2
e Jer 50:7

40:3
f Da 9:11
g Dt 29:24-28;
Ro 2:5-9

40:4
h Ge 13:9;
Jer 39:11-12

40:5
i 2Ki 25:22
j Jer 39:14

Then the commander gave him provisions and a present and let him go. ⁶So Jeremiah went to Gedaliah son of Ahikam at Mizpah[k] and stayed with him among the people who were left behind in the land.

40:6
k Jdg 20:1;
1Sa 7:5-17

⁷When all the army officers and their men who were still in the open country heard that the king of Babylon had appointed Gedaliah son of Ahikam as governor over the land and had put him in charge of the men, women and children who were the poorest[l] in the land and who had not been carried into exile to Babylon, ⁸they came to Gedaliah at Mizpah[m]—Ishmael[n] son of Nethaniah, Johanan and Jonathan the sons of Kareah, Seraiah son of Tanhumeth, the sons of Ephai the Netophathite,[o] and Jaazaniah[b] the son of the Maacathite,[p] and their men. ⁹Gedaliah son of Ahikam, the son of Shaphan, took an oath to reassure them and their men. "Do not be afraid to serve[q] the Babylonians,[c]" he said. "Settle down in the land and serve the king of Babylon, and it will go well with you.[r] ¹⁰I myself will stay at Mizpah[s] to represent you before the Babylonians who come to us, but you are to harvest the wine, summer fruit and oil, and put them in your storage jars, and live in the towns you have taken over."[t]

40:7
l Jer 39:10

40:8
m ver 13
n ver 14;
Jer 41:1,2
o 2Sa 23:28
p Dt 3:14

40:9
q Jer 27:11
r Jer 38:20

40:10
s ver 6
t Dt 1:39

[a] 5 Or *Jeremiah answered*   [b] 8 Hebrew *Jezaniah,* a variant of *Jaazaniah*   [c] 9 Or *Chaldeans;* also in verse 10

11When all the Jews in Moab,[a] Ammon, Edom and all the other countries heard that the king of Babylon had left a remnant in Judah and had appointed Gedaliah son of Ahikam, the son of Shaphan, as governor over them, 12they all came back to the land of Judah, to Gedaliah at Mizpah, from all the countries where they had been scattered.[b] And they harvested an abundance of wine and summer fruit.

13Johanan son of Kareah and all the army officers still in the open country came to Gedaliah at Mizpah[c] 14and said to him, "Don't you know that Baalis king of the Ammonites[d] has sent Ishmael son of Nethaniah to take your life?" But Gedaliah son of Ahikam did not believe them.

15Then Johanan son of Kareah said privately to Gedaliah in Mizpah, "Let me go and kill Ishmael son of Nethaniah, and no one will know it. Why should he take your life and cause all the Jews who are gathered around you to be scattered and the remnant of Judah to perish?"

16But Gedaliah son of Ahikam said to Johanan son of Kareah, "Don't do such a thing! What you are saying about Ishmael is not true."

Chapter 41 Theme

41 In the seventh month Ishmael[e] son of Nethaniah, the son of Elishama, who was of royal blood and had been one of the king's officers, came with ten men to Gedaliah son of Ahikam at Mizpah. While they were eating together there, 2Ishmael[f] son of Nethaniah and the ten men who were with him got up and struck down Gedaliah son of Ahikam, the son of Shaphan, with the sword, killing the one whom the king of Babylon had appointed[g] as governor over the land.[h] 3Ishmael also killed all the Jews who were with Gedaliah at Mizpah, as well as the Babylonian[a] soldiers who were there.

4The day after Gedaliah's assassination, before anyone knew about it, 5eighty men who had shaved off their beards,[i] torn their clothes and cut themselves came from Shechem,[j] Shiloh[k] and Samaria,[l] bringing grain offerings and incense with them to the house of the Lord.[m] 6Ishmael son of Nethaniah went out from Mizpah to meet them, weeping[n] as he went. When he met them, he said, "Come to Gedaliah son of Ahikam." 7When they went into the city, Ishmael son of Nethaniah and the men who were with him slaughtered them and threw them into a cistern. 8But ten of them said to Ishmael, "Don't kill us! We have wheat and barley, oil and honey, hidden in a field."[o] So he let them alone and

Cross references

40:11 [a] Nu 25:1

40:12 [b] Jer 43:5

40:13 [c] ver 8

40:14 [d] 2Sa 10:1-19; Jer 25:21; 41:10

41:1 [e] Jer 40:8

41:2 [f] Ps 41:9; 109:5 [g] Jer 40:5 [h] 2Sa 3:27; 20:9-10

41:5 [i] Lev 19:27 [j] Ge 33:18; Jdg 9:1-57; 1Ki 12:1 [k] Jos 18:1 [l] 1Ki 16:24 [m] 2Ki 25:9

41:6 [n] 2Sa 3:16

41:8 [o] Isa 45:3

41:9
a 1Ki 15:22;
2Ch 16:6
b Jdg 6:2
c 2Ch 16:1

41:10
d Jer 40:7,12
e Jer 40:14

41:11
f Jer 40:8

41:12
g 2Sa 2:13

41:13
h ver 10

41:15
i Job 21:30;
Pr 28:17

41:16
j Jer 43:4

41:17
k 2Sa 19:37
l Jer 42:14

41:18
m Isa 51:12;
Jer 42:16;
Lk 12:4-5
n Jer 40:5

42:1
o Jer 40:13;
41:11
p Jer 6:13;
44:12

42:2
q Jer 36:7;
Ac 8:24;
Jas 5:16
r Isa 1:9
s Lev 26:22;
La 1:1

42:3
t Ps 86:11; Pr 3:6

42:4
u Ex 8:29;
1Sa 12:23
v 1Ki 22:14;
1Sa 3:17

42:5
w Ge 31:50

did not kill them with the others. ⁹Now the cistern where he threw all the bodies of the men he had killed along with Gedaliah was the one King Asa[a] had made as part of his defense[b] against Baasha[c] king of Israel. Ishmael son of Nethaniah filled it with the dead.

¹⁰Ishmael made captives of all the rest of the people[d] who were in Mizpah—the king's daughters along with all the others who were left there, over whom Nebuzaradan commander of the imperial guard had appointed Gedaliah son of Ahikam. Ishmael son of Nethaniah took them captive and set out to cross over to the Ammonites.[e]

¹¹When Johanan[f] son of Kareah and all the army officers who were with him heard about all the crimes Ishmael son of Nethaniah had committed, ¹²they took all their men and went to fight Ishmael son of Nethaniah. They caught up with him near the great pool[g] in Gibeon. ¹³When all the people[h] Ishmael had with him saw Johanan son of Kareah and the army officers who were with him, they were glad. ¹⁴All the people Ishmael had taken captive at Mizpah turned and went over to Johanan son of Kareah. ¹⁵But Ishmael son of Nethaniah and eight of his men escaped[i] from Johanan and fled to the Ammonites.

¹⁶Then Johanan son of Kareah and all the army officers who were with him led away all the survivors[j] from Mizpah whom he had recovered from Ishmael son of Nethaniah after he had assassinated Gedaliah son of Ahikam: the soldiers, women, children and court officials he had brought from Gibeon. ¹⁷And they went on, stopping at Geruth Kimham[k] near Bethlehem on their way to Egypt[l] ¹⁸to escape the Babylonians.[a] They were afraid[m] of them because Ishmael son of Nethaniah had killed Gedaliah[n] son of Ahikam, whom the king of Babylon had appointed as governor over the land.

Chapter 42 Theme _____

42 Then all the army officers, including Johanan[o] son of Kareah and Jezaniah[b] son of Hoshaiah, and all the people from the least to the greatest[p] approached ²Jeremiah the prophet and said to him, "Please hear our petition and pray[q] to the LORD your God for this entire remnant.[r] For as you now see, though we were once many, now only a few[s] are left. ³Pray that the LORD your God will tell us where we should go and what we should do."[t]

⁴"I have heard you," replied Jeremiah the prophet. "I will certainly pray[u] to the LORD your God as you have requested; I will tell you everything the LORD says and will keep nothing back from you."[v]

⁵Then they said to Jeremiah, "May the LORD be a true and faithful witness[w] against us if we do not act in accordance with everything the LORD your God sends you to tell us. ⁶Whether it is favorable or

unfavorable, we will obey the LORD our God, to whom we are sending you, so that it will go well[a] with us, for we will obey[b] the LORD our God."

[7] Ten days later the word of the LORD came to Jeremiah. [8] So he called together Johanan son of Kareah and all the army officers[c] who were with him and all the people from the least to the greatest. [9] He said to them, "This is what the LORD, the God of Israel, to whom you sent me to present your petition, says:[d] [10] 'If you stay in this land, I will build[e] you up and not tear you down; I will plant[f] you and not uproot you,[g] for I am grieved over the disaster I have inflicted on you.[h] [11] Do not be afraid of the king of Babylon,[i] whom you now fear.[j] Do not be afraid of him, declares the LORD, for I am with you and will save[k] you and deliver you from his hands.[l] [12] I will show you compassion so that he will have compassion on you and restore you to your land.'[m]

[13] "However, if you say, 'We will not stay in this land,' and so disobey[n] the LORD your God, [14] and if you say, 'No, we will go and live in Egypt,[o] where we will not see war or hear the trumpet or be hungry for bread,' [15] then hear the word of the LORD, O remnant of Judah. This is what the LORD Almighty, the God of Israel, says: 'If you are determined to go to Egypt and you do go to settle there, [16] then the sword[p] you fear will overtake you there, and the famine you dread will follow you into Egypt, and there you will die. [17] Indeed, all who are determined to go to Egypt to settle there will die by the sword, famine and plague;[q] not one of them will survive or escape the disaster I will bring on them.' [18] This is what the LORD Almighty, the God of Israel, says: 'As my anger and wrath[r] have been poured out on those who lived in Jerusalem,[s] so will my wrath be poured out on you when you go to Egypt. You will be an object of cursing and horror,[t] of condemnation and reproach; you will never see this place again.'[u]

[19] "O remnant of Judah, the LORD has told you, 'Do not go to Egypt.'[v] Be sure of this: I warn you today [20] that you made a fatal mistake[a] when you sent me to the LORD your God and said, 'Pray to the LORD our God for us; tell us everything he says and we will do it.'[w] [21] I have told you today, but you still have not obeyed the LORD your God in all he sent me to tell you.[x] [22] So now, be sure of this: You will die by the sword, famine and plague[y] in the place where you want to go to settle."[z]

Chapter 43 Theme _____

43 When Jeremiah finished telling the people all the words of the LORD their God—everything the LORD had sent him to tell them[a]— [2] Azariah son of Hoshaiah and Johanan[b] son of

---

a 20 Or you erred in your hearts

42:6
a Dt 5:29; 6:3;
Jer 7:23
b Ex 24:7;
Jos 24:24

42:8
c ver 1

42:9
d 2Ki 22:15

42:10
e Jer 24:6
f Jer 31:28
g Eze 36:36
h Jer 18:8

42:11
i Jer 27:11
j Nu 14:9
k Isa 43:5
l Jer 1:8;
Ro 8:31

42:12
m Ps 106:44-46

42:13
n Jer 44:16

42:14
o Nu 11:4-5

42:16
p Eze 11:8

42:17
q ver 22;
Jer 44:13

42:18
r Dt 29:18-20;
Jer 7:20
s 2Ch 36:19;
Jer 39:1-9
t Jer 29:18
u Jer 22:10

42:19
v Dt 17:16;
Isa 30:7

42:20
w ver 2

42:21
x Eze 2:7;
Zec 7:11-12

42:22
y ver 17;
Eze 6:11
z Hos 9:6

43:1
a Jer 26:8;
42:9-22

43:2
b Jer 42:1

43:3
a Jer 38:4

43:4
b Jer 42:5-6
c Jer 42:10

43:5
d Jer 40:12

43:7
e Jer 2:16; 44:1

43:8
f Jer 2:16

43:10
g Isa 44:28;
Jer 25:9; 27:6

43:11
h Jer 46:13-26;
Eze 29:19-20
i Jer 15:2; 44:13;
Zec 11:9

43:12
j Jer 46:25;
Eze 30:13
k Ps 104:2;
109:18-19

44:1
l Ex 14:2
m Jer 43:7,8
n Isa 19:13
o Isa 11:11;
Jer 46:14

44:2
p Isa 6:11;
Jer 9:11; 34:22

44:3
q ver 8;
Dt 13:6-11;
29:26
r Dt 32:17;
Jer 19:4

44:4
s Jer 7:13
t Jer 7:25; 25:4;
26:5

Kareah and all the arrogant men said to Jeremiah, "You are lying! The LORD our God has not sent you to say, 'You must not go to Egypt to settle there.' ³But Baruch son of Neriah is inciting you against us to hand us over to the Babylonians,ᵃ so they may kill us or carry us into exile to Babylon."ᵃ

⁴So Johanan son of Kareah and all the army officers and all the people disobeyed the LORD's commandᵇ to stay in the land of Judah.ᶜ ⁵Instead, Johanan son of Kareah and all the army officers led away all the remnant of Judah who had come back to live in the land of Judah from all the nations where they had been scattered.ᵈ ⁶They also led away all the men, women and children and the king's daughters whom Nebuzaradan commander of the imperial guard had left with Gedaliah son of Ahikam, the son of Shaphan, and Jeremiah the prophet and Baruch son of Neriah. ⁷So they entered Egypt in disobedience to the LORD and went as far as Tahpanhes.ᵉ

⁸In Tahpanhesᶠ the word of the LORD came to Jeremiah: ⁹"While the Jews are watching, take some large stones with you and bury them in clay in the brick pavement at the entrance to Pharaoh's palace in Tahpanhes. ¹⁰Then say to them, 'This is what the LORD Almighty, the God of Israel, says: I will send for my servantᵍ Nebuchadnezzar king of Babylon, and I will set his throne over these stones I have buried here; he will spread his royal canopy above them. ¹¹He will come and attack Egypt,ʰ bringing death to those destined for death, captivity to those destined for captivity, and the sword to those destined for the sword.ⁱ ¹²Heᵇ will set fire to the temples of the godsʲ of Egypt; he will burn their temples and take their gods captive. As a shepherd wrapsᵏ his garment around him, so will he wrap Egypt around himself and depart from there unscathed. ¹³There in the temple of the sunᶜ in Egypt he will demolish the sacred pillars and will burn down the temples of the gods of Egypt.'"

Chapter 44 Theme

44 This word came to Jeremiah concerning all the Jews living in Lower Egypt—in Migdol,ˡ Tahpanhesᵐ and Memphisᵈ ⁿ—and in Upper Egyptᵉ:ᵒ ²"This is what the LORD Almighty, the God of Israel, says: You saw the great disaster I brought on Jerusalem and on all the towns of Judah. Today they lie deserted and in ruinsᵖ ³because of the evil they have done. They provoked me to anger by burning incense and by worshiping other godsᵠ that neither they nor you nor your fathersʳ ever knew. ⁴Again and againˢ I sent my servants the prophets,ᵗ who said, 'Do not do this

INSIGHT

Jeremiah's ministry ended sometime after 586 B.C., possibly about 574 B.C., when, according to tradition, he was stoned to death in Egypt. Jeremiah 43:6, 7 tells us that Jeremiah's last days were spent in Egypt.

ᵃ3 Or *Chaldeans* ᵇ12 Or *I* ᶜ13 Or *in Heliopolis* ᵈ1 Hebrew *Noph* ᵉ1 Hebrew *in Pathros* detestable thing that I hate!' ⁵But they did not listen or pay attention; they did not turn from their wickedness or stop burning incense to other gods.ᵃ ⁶Therefore, my fierce anger was poured out; it raged against the towns of Judah and the streets of Jerusalem and made them the desolate ruins they are today.

⁷"Now this is what the LORD God Almighty, the God of Israel, says: Why bring such great disasterᵇ on yourselves by cutting off from Judah the men and women,ᶜ the children and infants, and so leave yourselves without a remnant? ⁸Why provoke me to anger with what your hands have made,ᵈ burning incense to other gods in Egypt, where you have come to live?ᵉ You will destroy yourselves and make yourselves an object of cursing and reproachᶠ among all the nations on earth. ⁹Have you forgotten the wickedness committed by your fathers and by the kings and queens of Judah and the wickedness committed by you and your wives in the land of Judah and the streets of Jerusalem?ᵍ ¹⁰To this day they have not humbled themselves or shown reverence, nor have they followed my lawʰ and the decrees I set before you and your fathers.ⁱ

¹¹"Therefore, this is what the LORD Almighty, the God of Israel, says: I am determined to bring disasterʲ on you and to destroy all Judah. ¹²I will take away the remnantᵏ of Judah who were determined to go to Egypt to settle there. They will all perish in Egypt; they will fall by the sword or die from famine. From the least to the greatest, they will die by sword or famine.ˡ They will become an object of cursing and horror, of condemnation and reproach.ᵐ ¹³I will punish those who live in Egypt with the sword, famine and plague,ⁿ as I punished Jerusalem. ¹⁴None of the remnant of Judah who have gone to live in Egypt will escape or survive to return to the land of Judah, to which they long to return and live; none will return except a few fugitives."ᵒ

¹⁵Then all the men who knew that their wives were burning incense to other gods, along with all the women who were present—a large assembly—and all the people living in Lower and Upper Egypt,ᵃ said to Jeremiah, ¹⁶"We will not listenᵖ to the message you have spoken to us in the name of the LORD! ¹⁷We will certainly do everything we said we would: We will burn incense to the Queen of Heavenʳ and will pour out drink offerings to her just as we and our fathers, our kings and our officials did in the towns of Judah and in the streets of Jerusalem. At that time we had plenty of food and were well off and suffered no harm.ˢ ¹⁸But ever since we stopped burning incense to the Queen of Heaven and pouring out drink offerings to her, we have had nothing and have been perishing by sword and famine.ᵗ"

ᵃ 15 Hebrew *in Egypt and Pathros*

44:5
ᵃ Jer 11:8-10

44:7
ᵇ Jer 26:19
ᶜ Jer 51:22

44:8
ᵈ Jer 25:6-7
ᵉ 1Co 10:22
ᶠ Jer 42:18

44:9
ᵍ ver 17,21

44:10
ʰ Jos 1:7
ⁱ 1Ki 9:6-9

44:11
ʲ Jer 21:10; Am 9:4

44:12
ᵏ ver 7
ˡ Isa 1:28
ᵐ Jer 29:18; 42:15-18

44:13
ⁿ Jer 42:17

44:14
ᵒ ver 28; Jer 22:24-27; Ro 9:27

44:16
ᵖ Jer 11:8-10

44:17
ᵠ Dt 23:23
ʳ ver 25; Jer 7:18
ˢ Hos 2:5-13

44:18
ᵗ Mal 3:13-15

44:19
a Jer 7:18

44:21
b Isa 64:9;
Jer 14:10
c Jer 11:13
d ver 9
e Ps 79:8

44:22
f Jer 25:18
g Ge 19:13;
Ps 107:33-34

44:23
h Jer 40:2
i 1Ki 9:9;
Jer 7:13-15;
Da 9:11-12

44:24
j ver 15
k Jer 43:7

44:25
l ver 17
m Eze 20:39

44:26
n Ge 22:16;
Isa 48:1;
Heb 6:13-17
o Dt 32:40;
Ps 50:16

44:27
p Jer 31:28

44:28
q ver 13-14;
Isa 10:19
r ver 17,25-26

44:29
s Pr 19:21

44:30
t Jer 46:26;
Eze 30:21
u 2Ki 25:1-7
v Jer 39:5

45:1
w Jer 32:12;
36:4,18,32
x 2Ch 36:5

¹⁹The women added, "When we burned incense to the Queen of Heaven*a* and poured out drink offerings to her, did not our husbands know that we were making cakes like her image and pouring out drink offerings to her?"

²⁰Then Jeremiah said to all the people, both men and women, who were answering him, ²¹"Did not the LORD remember*b* and think about the incense*c* burned in the towns of Judah and the streets of Jerusalem*d* by you and your fathers,*e* your kings and your officials and the people of the land? ²²When the LORD could no longer endure your wicked actions and the detestable things you did, your land became an object of cursing*f* and a desolate waste without inhabitants, as it is today.*g* ²³Because you have burned incense and have sinned against the LORD and have not obeyed him or followed his law or his decrees or his stipulations, this disaster*h* has come upon you, as you now see."*i*

²⁴Then Jeremiah said to all the people, including the women,*j* "Hear the word of the LORD, all you people of Judah in Egypt.*k* ²⁵This is what the LORD Almighty, the God of Israel, says: You and your wives have shown by your actions what you promised when you said, 'We will certainly carry out the vows we made to burn incense and pour out drink offerings to the Queen of Heaven.'*l*

"Go ahead then, do what you promised! Keep your vows!*m* ²⁶But hear the word of the LORD, all Jews living in Egypt: 'I swear*n* by my great name,' says the LORD, 'that no one from Judah living anywhere in Egypt will ever again invoke my name or swear, "As surely as the Sovereign LORD lives."*o* ²⁷For I am watching over them for harm,*p* not for good; the Jews in Egypt will perish by sword and famine until they are all destroyed. ²⁸Those who escape the sword and return to the land of Judah from Egypt will be very few.*q* Then the whole remnant of Judah who came to live in Egypt will know whose word will stand—mine or theirs.*r*

²⁹"'This will be the sign to you that I will punish you in this place,' declares the LORD, 'so that you will know that my threats of harm against you will surely stand.'*s* ³⁰This is what the LORD says: 'I am going to hand Pharaoh*t* Hophra king of Egypt over to his enemies who seek his life, just as I handed Zedekiah*u* king of Judah over to Nebuchadnezzar king of Babylon, the enemy who was seeking his life.'"*v*

Chapter 45 Theme

45 This is what Jeremiah the prophet told Baruch*w* son of Neriah in the fourth year of Jehoiakim*x* son of Josiah king of Judah, after Baruch had written on a scroll the words Jeremiah was then dictating: ²"This is what the LORD, the God of Israel, says

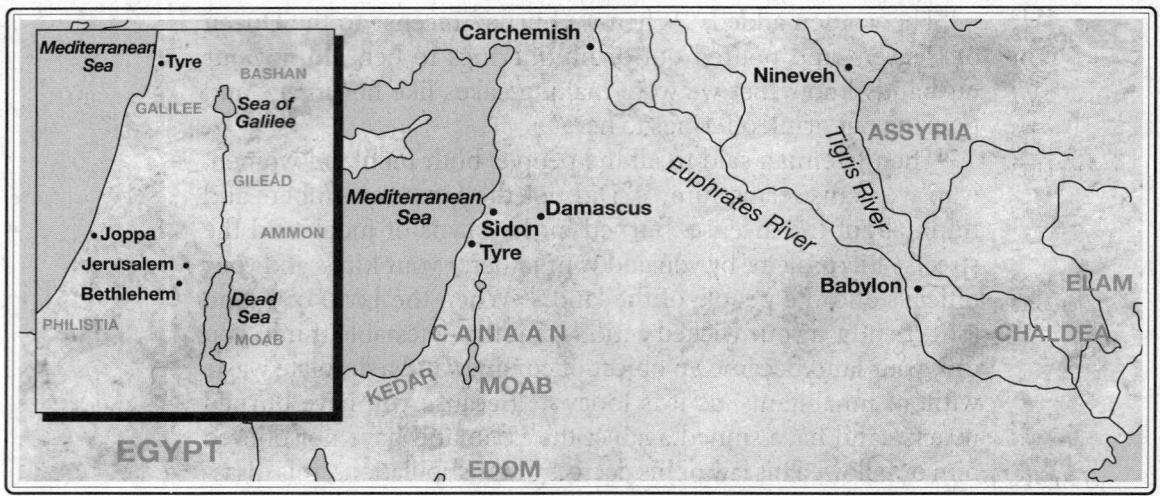

to you, Baruch: [3]You said, 'Woe to me! The LORD has added sorrow to my pain; I am worn out with groaning[a] and find no rest.'"

[4]⌊The LORD said,⌋ "Say this to him: 'This is what the LORD says: I will overthrow what I have built and uproot what I have planted,[b] throughout the land.[c] [5]Should you then seek great things for yourself? Seek them not.[d] For I will bring disaster on all people, declares the LORD, but wherever you go I will let you escape with your life.'"[e]

Chapter 46 Theme

46
This is the word of the LORD that came to Jeremiah the prophet concerning the nations:[f]

[2]Concerning Egypt:

This is the message against the army of Pharaoh Neco[g] king of Egypt, which was defeated at Carchemish[h] on the Euphrates River by Nebuchadnezzar king of Babylon in the fourth year of Jehoiakim[i] son of Josiah king of Judah:

[3]"Prepare your shields,[j] both large and small,
　　and march out for battle!
[4]Harness the horses,
　　mount the steeds!
Take your positions
　　with helmets on!
Polish[k] your spears,
　　put on your armor![l]
[5]What do I see?
　　They are terrified,

45:3
[a] Ps 69:3

45:4
[b] Jer 11:17
[c] Isa 5:5-7;
Jer 18:7-10

45:5
[d] Mt 6:25-27,33
[e] Jer 21:9; 38:2;
39:18

46:1
[f] Jer 1:10;
25:15-38

46:2
[g] 2Ki 23:29
[h] 2Ch 35:20
[i] Jer 45:1

46:3
[j] Isa 21:5;
Jer 51:11-12

46:4
[k] Eze 21:9-11
[l] 1Sa 17:5,38;
2Ch 26:14;
Ne 4:16

46:5
a ver 21
b Jer 49:29

they are retreating,
their warriors are defeated.
They flee*a* in haste
without looking back,
and there is terror*b* on every side,"

declares the LORD.

46:6
c Isa 30:16
d ver 12,16;
Da 11:19

6"The swift cannot flee*c*
nor the strong escape.
In the north by the River Euphrates
they stumble and fall.*d*

46:7
e Jer 47:2

7"Who is this that rises like the Nile,
like rivers of surging waters?*e*
8Egypt rises like the Nile,
like rivers of surging waters.
She says, 'I will rise and cover the earth;
I will destroy cities and their people.'

46:9
f Jer 47:3
g Isa 66:19

9Charge, O horses!
Drive furiously, O charioteers!*f*
March on, O warriors—
men of Cush*a* and Put who carry shields,
men of Lydia*g* who draw the bow.

46:10
h Joel 1:15
i Dt 32:42
j Zep 1:7

10But that day*h* belongs to the Lord, the LORD Almighty—
a day of vengeance, for vengeance on his foes.
The sword will devour*i* till it is satisfied,
till it has quenched its thirst with blood.
For the Lord, the LORD Almighty, will offer sacrifice*j*
in the land of the north by the River Euphrates.

46:11
k Jer 8:22
l Isa 47:1
m Jer 30:13;
Mic 1:9

11"Go up to Gilead and get balm,*k*
O Virgin*l* Daughter of Egypt.
But you multiply remedies in vain;
there is no healing*m* for you.
12The nations will hear of your shame;
your cries will fill the earth.

46:12
n Isa 19:4;
Na 3:8-10

One warrior will stumble over another;
both will fall*n* down together."

13This is the message the LORD spoke to Jeremiah the prophet about the coming of Nebuchadnezzar king of Babylon to attack Egypt:*o*

46:13
o Isa 19:1

14"Announce this in Egypt, and proclaim it in Migdol;
proclaim it also in Memphis*b* and Tahpanhes:*p*
'Take your positions and get ready,
for the sword devours those around you.'

46:14
p Jer 43:8

a 9 That is, the upper Nile region   b 14 Hebrew *Noph*; also in verse 19

¹⁵Why will your warriors be laid low?
　　They cannot stand, for the LORD will push them down.^a
¹⁶They will stumble^b repeatedly;
　　they will fall^c over each other.
　They will say, 'Get up, let us go back
　　to our own people and our native lands,
　　away from the sword of the oppressor.'
¹⁷There they will exclaim,
　　'Pharaoh king of Egypt is only a loud noise;
　he has missed his opportunity.^d'

¹⁸"As surely as I live," declares the King,^e
　　whose name is the LORD Almighty,
　"one will come who is like Tabor^f among the mountains,
　　like Carmel^g by the sea.
¹⁹Pack your belongings for exile,^h
　　you who live in Egypt,
　for Memphis will be laid waste
　　and lie in ruins without inhabitant.

²⁰"Egypt is a beautiful heifer,
　　but a gadfly is coming
　　against her from the north.ⁱ
²¹The mercenaries^j in her ranks
　　are like fattened calves.
　They too will turn and flee^k together,
　　they will not stand their ground,
　for the day^l of disaster is coming upon them,
　　the time for them to be punished.
²²Egypt will hiss like a fleeing serpent
　　as the enemy advances in force;
　they will come against her with axes,
　　like men who cut down trees.
²³They will chop down her forest,"

　　　　　　　　　　declares the LORD,
　"dense though it be.
　They are more numerous than locusts,^m
　　they cannot be counted.
²⁴The Daughter of Egypt will be put to shame,
　　handed over to the people of the north.ⁿ"

²⁵The LORD Almighty, the God of Israel, says: "I am about to bring punishment on Amon god of Thebes,^{a o} on Pharaoh, on Egypt and her gods^p and her kings, and on those who rely^q on Pharaoh. ²⁶I will hand them over^r to those who seek their lives, to Nebuchadnezzar

^a 25 Hebrew *No*

46:15	^a Isa 66:15-16
46:16	^b Lev 26:37 ^c ver 6
46:17	^d Isa 19:11-16
46:18	^e Jer 48:15 ^f Jos 19:22 ^g 1Ki 18:42
46:19	^h Isa 20:4
46:20	ⁱ ver 24; Jer 47:2
46:21	^j 2Ki 7:6 ^k ver 5 ^l Ps 37:13
46:23	^m Jdg 7:12
46:24	ⁿ Jer 1:15
46:25	^o Eze 30:14; Na 3:8 ^p Jer 43:12 ^q Isa 20:6
46:26	^r Jer 44:30

46:26
a Eze 32:11
b Eze 29:11-16

king*a* of Babylon and his officers. Later, however, Egypt will be inhabited*b* as in times past," declares the LORD.

> ²⁷"Do not fear,*c* O Jacob my servant;
>   do not be dismayed, O Israel.
> I will surely save you out of a distant place,
>   your descendants from the land of their exile.*d*

46:27
c Isa 41:13; 43:5
d Isa 11:11;
    Jer 50:19

> Jacob will again have peace and security,
>   and no one will make him afraid.
> ²⁸Do not fear, O Jacob my servant,
>   for I am with you,"*e* declares the LORD.
> "Though I completely destroy*f* all the nations
>   among which I scatter you,
> I will not completely destroy you.

46:28
e Isa 8:9-10
f Jer 4:27

> I will discipline you but only with justice;
>   I will not let you go entirely unpunished."

Chapter 47 Theme

47 This is the word of the LORD that came to Jeremiah the prophet concerning the Philistines before Pharaoh attacked Gaza:*g*

47:1
g Ge 10:19;
    Am 1:6;
    Zec 9:5-7

²This is what the LORD says:

> "See how the waters are rising in the north;*h*
>   they will become an overflowing torrent.
> They will overflow the land and everything in it,
>   the towns and those who live in them.
> The people will cry out;
>   all who dwell in the land will wail
> ³at the sound of the hoofs of galloping steeds,
>   at the noise of enemy chariots
>   and the rumble of their wheels.
> Fathers will not turn to help their children;
>   their hands will hang limp.

47:2
h Isa 8:7; 14:31

> ⁴For the day has come
>   to destroy all the Philistines
> and to cut off all survivors
>   who could help Tyre*i* and Sidon.*j*
> The LORD is about to destroy the Philistines,*k*
>   the remnant from the coasts of Caphtor.*a l*
> ⁵Gaza will shave*m* her head in mourning;
>   Ashkelon*n* will be silenced.
> O remnant on the plain,
>   how long will you cut yourselves?

47:4
i Am 1:9-10;
    Zec 9:2-4
j Jer 25:22
k Ge 10:14;
    Joel 3:4
l Dt 2:23

47:5
m Jer 41:5;
    Mic 1:16
n Jer 25:20

a 4 That is, Crete

6"'Ah, sword[a] of the LORD,' ⌊you cry,⌋
    'how long till you rest?
  Return to your scabbard;
    cease and be still.'
7But how can it rest
    when the LORD has commanded it,
  when he has ordered it
    to attack Ashkelon and the coast?"

Chapter 48 Theme _____

48

Concerning Moab:

This is what the LORD Almighty, the God of Israel, says:

"Woe to Nebo,[b] for it will be ruined.
  Kiriathaim[c] will be disgraced and captured;
    the stronghold[a] will be disgraced and shattered.
2Moab will be praised[d] no more;
  in Heshbon[be] men will plot her downfall:
    'Come, let us put an end to that nation.'
  You too, O Madmen,[c] will be silenced;
    the sword will pursue you.
3Listen to the cries from Horonaim,[f]
  cries of great havoc and destruction.
4Moab will be broken;
  her little ones will cry out.[d]
5They go up the way to Luhith,[g]
  weeping bitterly as they go;
 on the road down to Horonaim
  anguished cries over the destruction are heard.
6Flee! Run for your lives;
  become like a bush[e] in the desert.[h]
7Since you trust in your deeds and riches,
  you too will be taken captive,
 and Chemosh[i] will go into exile,[j]
  together with his priests and officials.
8The destroyer will come against every town,
  and not a town will escape.
 The valley will be ruined
  and the plateau destroyed,
  because the LORD has spoken.
9Put salt on Moab,
  for she will be laid waste[f];

47:6
[a] Jer 12:12

48:1
[b] Nu 32:38
[c] Nu 32:37

48:2
[d] Isa 16:14
[e] Nu 21:25

48:3
[f] Isa 15:5

48:5
[g] Isa 15:5

48:6
[h] Jer 17:6

48:7
[i] Nu 21:29
[j] Isa 46:1-2;
Jer 49:3

---

[a]1 Or / *Misgab*   [b]2 The Hebrew for *Heshbon* sounds like the Hebrew for *plot*.   [c]2 The name of the Moabite town Madmen sounds like the Hebrew for *be silenced*.   [d]4 Hebrew; Septuagint / *proclaim it to Zoar*   [e]6 Or *like Aroer*   [f]9 Or *Give wings to Moab, / for she will fly away*

her towns will become desolate,
with no one to live in them.

¹⁰"A curse on him who is lax in doing the LORD's work!
A curse on him who keeps his sword^a from
bloodshed!^b

¹¹"Moab has been at rest^c from youth,
like wine left on its dregs,^d
not poured from one jar to another—
she has not gone into exile.
So she tastes as she did,
and her aroma is unchanged.
¹²But days are coming,"
declares the LORD,
"when I will send men who pour from jars,
and they will pour her out;
they will empty her jars
and smash her jugs.
¹³Then Moab will be ashamed^e of Chemosh,
as the house of Israel was ashamed
when they trusted in Bethel.

¹⁴"How can you say, 'We are warriors,^f
men valiant in battle'?
¹⁵Moab will be destroyed and her towns invaded;
her finest young men will go down in the slaughter,^g"
declares the King,^h whose name is the LORD Almighty.ⁱ
¹⁶"The fall of Moab is at hand;^j
her calamity will come quickly.
¹⁷Mourn for her, all who live around her,
all who know her fame;
say, 'How broken is the mighty scepter,
how broken the glorious staff!'

¹⁸"Come down from your glory
and sit on the parched ground,^k
O inhabitants of the Daughter of Dibon,^l
for he who destroys Moab
will come up against you
and ruin your fortified cities.^m
¹⁹Stand by the road and watch,
you who live in Aroer.ⁿ
Ask the man fleeing and the woman escaping,
ask them, 'What has happened?'
²⁰Moab is disgraced, for she is shattered.
Wail^o and cry out!

**Cross references (left margin):**

48:10
a Jer 47:6
b 1Ki 20:42;
2Ki 13:15-19

48:11
c Zec 1:15
d Zep 1:12

48:13
e Hos 10:6

48:14
f Ps 33:16

48:15
g Jer 50:27
h Jer 46:18
i Jer 51:57

48:16
j Isa 13:22

48:18
k Isa 47:1
l Nu 21:30;
Jos 13:9
m ver 8

48:19
n Dt 2:36

48:20
o Isa 16:7

INSIGHT

Chemosh was a Moabite god who was believed to provide the people with land. During his reforms King Josiah desecrated a temple built by Solomon for Chemosh (2 Kings 23:13).

Announce by the Arnon[a]
    that Moab is destroyed.
[21]Judgment has come to the plateau—
    to Holon, Jahzah[b] and Mephaath,[c]
[22] to Dibon,[d] Nebo and Beth Diblathaim,
[23] to Kiriathaim, Beth Gamul and Beth Meon,[e]
[24] to Kerioth[f] and Bozrah—
    to all the towns of Moab, far and near.
[25]Moab's horn[a][g] is cut off;
    her arm[h] is broken,"

                      declares the LORD.

[26]"Make her drunk,[i]
    for she has defied the LORD.
Let Moab wallow in her vomit;
    let her be an object of ridicule.
[27]Was not Israel the object of your ridicule?[j]
    Was she caught among thieves,
that you shake your head[k] in scorn[l]
    whenever you speak of her?
[28]Abandon your towns and dwell among the rocks,
    you who live in Moab.
Be like a dove[m] that makes its nest
    at the mouth of a cave.[n]

[29]"We have heard of Moab's pride[o]—
    her overweening pride and conceit,
her pride and arrogance
    and the haughtiness of her heart.
[30]I know her insolence but it is futile,"

                      declares the LORD,

    "and her boasts accomplish nothing.
[31]Therefore I wail[p] over Moab,
    for all Moab I cry out,
    I moan for the men of Kir Hareseth.[q]
[32]I weep for you, as Jazer weeps,
    O vines of Sibmah.[r]
Your branches spread as far as the sea;
    they reached as far as the sea of Jazer.
The destroyer has fallen
    on your ripened fruit and grapes.
[33]Joy and gladness are gone
    from the orchards and fields of Moab.
I have stopped the flow of wine[s] from the presses;
    no one treads them with shouts of joy.[t]

a 25 *Horn* here symbolizes strength.

48:20
a Nu 21:13

48:21
b Nu 21:23;
Isa 15:4
c Jos 13:18

48:22
d Jos 13:9,17

48:23
e Jos 13:17

48:24
f Am 2:2

48:25
g Ps 75:10
h Ps 10:15;
Eze 30:21

48:26
i Jer 25:16,27

48:27
j Jer 2:26
k Job 16:4;
Jer 18:16
l Mic 7:8-10

48:28
m Ps 55:6-7
n Jdg 6:2

48:29
o Job 40:12;
Isa 16:6

48:31
p Isa 15:5-8
q 2Ki 3:25

48:32
r Isa 16:8-9

48:33
s Isa 16:10
t Joel 1:12

Although there are shouts,
  they are not shouts of joy.

34"The sound of their cry rises
  from Heshbon to Elealeh[a] and Jahaz,[b]
from Zoar[c] as far as Horonaim[d] and Eglath Shelishiyah,
  for even the waters of Nimrim are dried up.[e]
35In Moab I will put an end
  to those who make offerings on the high places[f]
  and burn incense[g] to their gods,"
                                                  declares the LORD.

36"So my heart laments[h] for Moab like a flute;
  it laments like a flute for the men of Kir Hareseth.
  The wealth they acquired[i] is gone.
37Every head is shaved[j]
  and every beard cut off;
every hand is slashed
  and every waist is covered with sackcloth.[k]
38On all the roofs in Moab
  and in the public squares
there is nothing but mourning,
  for I have broken Moab
  like a jar[l] that no one wants,"
                                                  declares the LORD.

39"How shattered she is! How they wail!
  How Moab turns her back in shame!
Moab has become an object of ridicule,
  an object of horror to all those around her."

40This is what the LORD says:

"Look! An eagle is swooping[m] down,
  spreading its wings[n] over Moab.
41Kerioth[a] will be captured
  and the strongholds taken.
In that day the hearts of Moab's warriors
  will be like the heart of a woman in labor.[o]
42Moab will be destroyed[p] as a nation[q]
  because she defied[r] the LORD.
43Terror and pit and snare[s] await you,
  O people of Moab,"
                                                  declares the LORD.

44"Whoever flees[t] from the terror
  will fall into a pit,
whoever climbs out of the pit
  will be caught in a snare;

48:34
a Nu 32:3
b Isa 15:4
c Ge 13:10
d Isa 15:5
e Isa 15:6

48:35
f Isa 15:2; 16:12
g Jer 11:13

48:36
h Isa 16:11
i Isa 15:7

48:37
j Isa 15:2;
Jer 41:5
k Ge 37:34

48:38
l Jer 22:28

48:40
m Dt 28:49;
Hab 1:8
n Isa 8:8

48:41
o Isa 21:3

48:42
p Ps 83:4;
Isa 16:14
q ver 2
r ver 26

48:43
s Isa 24:17

48:44
t 1Ki 19:17;
Isa 24:18

a 41 Or The cities

1375

for I will bring upon Moab
the year[a] of her punishment,"

declares the LORD.

[45]"In the shadow of Heshbon
the fugitives stand helpless,
for a fire has gone out from Heshbon,
a blaze from the midst of Sihon;[b]
it burns the foreheads of Moab,
the skulls[c] of the noisy boasters.
[46]Woe to you, O Moab![d]
The people of Chemosh are destroyed;
your sons are taken into exile
and your daughters into captivity.

[47]"Yet I will restore[e] the fortunes of Moab
in days to come,"

declares the LORD.

Here ends the judgment on Moab.

Chapter 49 Theme _____

49
Concerning the Ammonites:[f]

This is what the LORD says:

"Has Israel no sons?
Has she no heirs?
Why then has Molech[a] taken possession of Gad?
Why do his people live in its towns?
[2]But the days are coming,"
declares the LORD,
"when I will sound the battle cry[g]
against Rabbah[h] of the Ammonites;
it will become a mound of ruins,
and its surrounding villages will be set on fire.
Then Israel will drive out
those who drove her out,[i]"

says the LORD.

[3]"Wail, O Heshbon, for Ai[j] is destroyed!
Cry out, O inhabitants of Rabbah!
Put on sackcloth and mourn;
rush here and there inside the walls,
for Molech will go into exile,[k]
together with his priests and officials.
[4]Why do you boast of your valleys,
boast of your valleys so fruitful?

INSIGHT

Molech was the national god of Ammon. When King Solomon was old he worshiped Molech on the high places he built just outside Jerusalem. King Josiah desecrated these high places during his reforms. Molech is also called *Milcom* or *Malcam*. (1 Kings 11:1-8, 33; 2 Kings 23:13).

48:44
[a] Jer 11:23

48:45
[b] Nu 21:21, 26-28
[c] Nu 24:17

48:46
[d] Nu 21:29

48:47
[e] Jer 12:15; 49:6,39

49:1
[f] Am 1:13; Zep 2:8-9

49:2
[g] Jer 4:19
[h] Dt 3:11
[i] Isa 14:2; Eze 21:28-32; 25:2-11

49:3
[j] Jos 8:28
[k] Jer 48:7

[a] 1 Or *their king*; Hebrew *malcam*; also in verse 3

O unfaithful daughter,
    you trust in your riches*a* and say,
    'Who will attack me?'*b*
⁵I will bring terror on you
    from all those around you,"
                    declares the Lord, the LORD Almighty.
"Every one of you will be driven away,
    and no one will gather the fugitives.

⁶"Yet afterward, I will restore*c* the fortunes of
    the Ammonites,"
                    declares the LORD.

⁷Concerning Edom:*d*

This is what the LORD Almighty says:

"Is there no longer wisdom in Teman?*e*
    Has counsel perished from the prudent?
    Has their wisdom decayed?
⁸Turn and flee, hide in deep caves,
    you who live in Dedan,*f*
    for I will bring disaster on Esau
        at the time I punish him.
⁹If grape pickers came to you,
    would they not leave a few grapes?
    If thieves came during the night,
    would they not steal only as much as they wanted?
¹⁰But I will strip Esau bare;
    I will uncover his hiding places,
        so that he cannot conceal himself.
    His children, relatives and neighbors will perish,
        and he will be no more.*g*
¹¹Leave your orphans;*h* I will protect their lives.
    Your widows too can trust in me."

¹²This is what the LORD says: "If those who do not deserve to drink the cup*i* must drink it, why should you go unpunished?*j* You will not go unpunished, but must drink it. ¹³I swear*k* by myself," declares the LORD, "that Bozrah*l* will become a ruin and an object of horror, of reproach and of cursing; and all its towns will be in ruins forever."

¹⁴I have heard a message from the LORD:
    An envoy was sent to the nations to say,
"Assemble yourselves to attack it!
    Rise up for battle!"

Marginal cross-references (left column):

49:4
a Jer 9:23;
1Ti 6:17
b Jer 21:13

49:6
c ver 39;
Jer 48:47

49:7
d Ge 25:30;
Eze 25:12
e Ge 36:11,15,34

49:8
f Jer 25:23

49:10
g Mal 1:2-5

49:11
h Hos 14:3

49:12
i Jer 25:15
j Jer 25:28-29

49:13
k Ge 22:16
l Ge 36:33;
Isa 34:6

¹⁵"Now I will make you small among the nations,
   despised among men.
¹⁶The terror you inspire
   and the pride of your heart have deceived you,
you who live in the clefts of the rocks,
   who occupy the heights of the hill.
Though you build your nest*a* as high as the eagle's,
   from there I will bring you down,"

                                        declares the LORD.

¹⁷"Edom will become an object of horror;*b*
   all who pass by will be appalled and will scoff
   because of all its wounds.*c*
¹⁸As Sodom and Gomorrah*d* were overthrown,
   along with their neighboring towns,"

                                        says the LORD,

   "so no one will live there;
   no man will dwell*e* in it.

¹⁹"Like a lion coming up from Jordan's thickets*f*
   to a rich pastureland,
I will chase Edom from its land in an instant.
   Who is the chosen one I will appoint for this?
Who is like me and who can challenge me?*g*
   And what shepherd can stand against me?"
²⁰Therefore, hear what the LORD has planned against Edom,
   what he has purposed*h* against those who live in Teman:
The young of the flock*i* will be dragged away;
   he will completely destroy*j* their pasture because of them.
²¹At the sound of their fall the earth will tremble;*k*
   their cry*l* will resound to the Red Sea.*a*
²²Look! An eagle will soar and swoop*m* down,
   spreading its wings over Bozrah.
In that day the hearts of Edom's warriors
   will be like the heart of a woman in labor.*n*

²³Concerning Damascus:*o*

"Hamath*p* and Arpad*q* are dismayed,
   for they have heard bad news.
They are disheartened,
   troubled like*b* the restless sea.*r*
²⁴Damascus has become feeble,
   she has turned to flee
   and panic has gripped her;
anguish and pain have seized her,
   pain like that of a woman in labor.

a 21 Hebrew *Yam Suph*; that is, Sea of Reeds   *b 23* Hebrew *on or by*

49:16
a Job 39:27;
Am 9:2

49:17
b ver 13
c Jer 50:13;
Eze 35:7

49:18
d Ge 19:24;
Dt 29:23
e ver 33

49:19
f Jer 12:5
g Jer 50:44

49:20
h Isa 14:27
i Jer 50:45
j Mal 1:3-4

49:21
k Eze 26:15
l Jer 50:46;
Eze 26:18

49:22
m Hos 8:1
n Isa 13:8;
Jer 48:40-41

49:23
o Ge 14:15;
2Ch 16:2;
Ac 9:2
p Isa 10:9;
Am 6:2;
Zec 9:2
q 2Ki 18:34
r Ge 49:4;
Isa 57:20

25Why has the city of renown not been abandoned,
the town in which I delight?
26Surely, her young men will fall in the streets;
all her soldiers will be silenced*a* in that day,"
declares the LORD Almighty.

27"I will set fire*b* to the walls of Damascus;
it will consume the fortresses of Ben-Hadad.*c*"

28Concerning Kedar*d* and the kingdoms of Hazor, which Nebuchadnezzar king of Babylon attacked:

This is what the LORD says:

"Arise, and attack Kedar
and destroy the people of the East.*e*
29Their tents and their flocks will be taken;
their shelters will be carried off
with all their goods and camels.
Men will shout to them,
'Terror*f* on every side!'

30"Flee quickly away!
Stay in deep caves, you who live in Hazor,"
declares the LORD.
"Nebuchadnezzar king of Babylon has plotted against you;
he has devised a plan against you.

31"Arise and attack a nation at ease,
which lives in confidence,"
declares the LORD,
"a nation that has neither gates nor bars;*g*
its people live alone.
32Their camels will become plunder,
and their large herds will be booty.
I will scatter to the winds those who are in distant places*a h*
and will bring disaster on them from every side,"
declares the LORD.

33"Hazor will become a haunt of jackals,
a desolate*i* place forever.
No one will live there;
no man will dwell*j* in it."

34This is the word of the LORD that came to Jeremiah the prophet concerning Elam,*k* early in the reign of Zedekiah*l* king of Judah:

35This is what the LORD Almighty says:

"See, I will break the bow*m* of Elam,
the mainstay of their might.

49:26 *a* Jer 50:30
49:27 *b* Jer 43:12; Am 1:4 *c* 1Ki 15:18
49:28 *d* Ge 25:13 *e* Jdg 6:3
49:29 *f* Jer 6:25; 46:5
49:31 *g* Eze 38:11
49:32 *h* Jer 9:26
49:33 *i* Jer 10:22 *j* ver 18; Jer 51:37
49:34 *k* Ge 10:22 *l* 2Ki 24:18
49:35 *m* Isa 22:6

a 32 Or *who clip the hair by their foreheads*

1379

³⁶I will bring against Elam the four winds*ᵃ*
   from the four quarters of the heavens;
I will scatter them to the four winds,
   and there will not be a nation
   where Elam's exiles do not go.
³⁷I will shatter Elam before their foes,
   before those who seek their lives;
I will bring disaster upon them,
   even my fierce anger,"ᵇ

                  declares the LORD.

"I will pursue them with the swordᶜ
   until I have made an end of them.
³⁸I will set my throne in Elam
   and destroy her king and officials,"

                  declares the LORD.

³⁹"Yet I will restoreᵈ the fortunes of Elam
   in days to come,"

                  declares the LORD.

Chapter 50 Theme

INSIGHT

Marduk and *Bel* were Babylonian deities. Bel was the Babylonian equivalent of Baal, acknowledged as the lord of heaven.

50 This is the word the LORD spoke through Jeremiah the prophet concerning Babylonᵉ and the land of the Babyloniansᵃ:

²"Announce and proclaimᶠ among the nations,
   lift up a banner and proclaim it;
   keep nothing back, but say,
'Babylon will be captured;ᵍ
   Belʰ will be put to shame,
   Mardukⁱ filled with terror.
Her images will be put to shame
   and her idols filled with terror.'
³A nation from the north will attack her
   and lay waste her land.
No one will liveʲ in it;
   both men and animalsᵏ will flee away.

⁴"In those days, at that time,"
   declares the LORD,
"the people of Israel and the people of Judah togetherˡ
   will go in tearsᵐ to seekⁿ the LORD their God.
⁵They will ask the way to Zion
   and turn their faces toward it.

a 1 Or *Chaldeans*; also in verses 8, 25, 35 and 45

49:36
ᵃ ver 32

49:37
ᵇ Jer 30:24
ᶜ Jer 9:16

49:39
ᵈ Jer 48:47

50:1
ᵉ Ge 10:10;
Isa 13:1

50:2
ᶠ Jer 4:16
ᵍ Jer 51:31
ʰ Isa 46:1
ⁱ Jer 51:47

50:3
ʲ ver 13;
Isa 14:22-23
ᵏ Zep 1:3

50:4
ˡ Jer 3:18;
Hos 1:11
ᵐ Ezr 3:12;
Jer 31:9
ⁿ Hos 3:5

50:5
a Jer 33:7
b Isa 55:3;
Jer 32:40;
Heb 8:6-10

They will come[a] and bind themselves to the LORD
    in an everlasting covenant[b]
    that will not be forgotten.

⁶"My people have been lost sheep;[c]
    their shepherds have led them astray
    and caused them to roam on the mountains.
They wandered over mountain and hill[d]
    and forgot their own resting place.[e]

50:6
c Isa 53:6;
Mt 9:36; 10:6
d Jer 3:6;
Eze 34:6
e ver 19

⁷Whoever found them devoured them;
    their enemies said, 'We are not guilty,[f]
for they sinned against the LORD, their true pasture,
    the LORD, the hope[g] of their fathers.'

⁸"Flee[h] out of Babylon;
    leave the land of the Babylonians,
    and be like the goats that lead the flock.

50:7
f Jer 2:3
g Jer 14:8

⁹For I will stir up and bring against Babylon
    an alliance of great nations from the land of the north.
They will take up their positions against her,
    and from the north she will be captured.
Their arrows will be like skilled warriors
    who do not return empty-handed.

50:8
h Isa 48:20;
Jer 51:6;
Rev 18:4

¹⁰So Babylonia[a] will be plundered;
    all who plunder her will have their fill,"
                    declares the LORD.

¹¹"Because you rejoice and are glad,
    you who pillage my inheritance,[i]
because you frolic like a heifer threshing grain
    and neigh like stallions,

50:11
i Isa 47:6

¹²your mother will be greatly ashamed;
    she who gave you birth will be disgraced.
She will be the least of the nations—
    a wilderness, a dry land, a desert.
¹³Because of the LORD's anger she will not be inhabited
    but will be completely desolate.
All who pass Babylon will be horrified and scoff[j]
    because of all her wounds.[k]

50:13
j Jer 18:16
k Jer 49:17

¹⁴"Take up your positions around Babylon,
    all you who draw the bow.[l]
Shoot at her! Spare no arrows,
    for she has sinned against the LORD.

50:14
l ver 29,42

¹⁵Shout[m] against her on every side!
    She surrenders, her towers fall,
    her walls[n] are torn down.

50:15
m Jer 51:14
n Jer 51:44,58

a 10 Or *Chaldea*

Since this is the vengeance[a] of the LORD,
 take vengeance on her;
 do to her[b] as she has done to others.
16Cut off from Babylon the sower,
 and the reaper with his sickle at harvest.
Because of the sword[c] of the oppressor
 let everyone return to his own people,[d]
 let everyone flee to his own land.[e]

17"Israel is a scattered flock
 that lions[f] have chased away.
The first to devour him
 was the king[g] of Assyria;
the last to crush his bones
 was Nebuchadnezzar[h] king[i] of Babylon."

18Therefore this is what the LORD Almighty, the God of Israel, says:

"I will punish the king of Babylon and his land
 as I punished the king[j] of Assyria.[k]
19But I will bring[l] Israel back to his own pasture
 and he will graze on Carmel and Bashan;
his appetite will be satisfied
 on the hills[m] of Ephraim and Gilead.
20In those days, at that time,"
 declares the LORD,
"search will be made for Israel's guilt,
 but there will be none,
and for the sins[n] of Judah,
 but none will be found,
for I will forgive[o] the remnant[p] I spare.

21"Attack the land of Merathaim
 and those who live in Pekod.[q]
Pursue, kill and completely destroy[a] them,"
       declares the LORD.
"Do everything I have commanded you.
22The noise[r] of battle is in the land,
 the noise of great destruction!
23How broken and shattered
 is the hammer of the whole earth!
How desolate[s] is Babylon
 among the nations!
24I set a trap[t] for you, O Babylon,
 and you were caught before you knew it;

---

a 21 The Hebrew term refers to the irrevocable giving over of things or persons to the LORD, often by totally destroying them; also in verse 26.

50:15
a Jer 51:6
b Ps 137:8;
Rev 18:6

50:16
c Jer 25:38
d Isa 13:14
e Jer 51:9

50:17
f Jer 2:15
g 2Ki 17:6
h 2Ki 24:10,14
i 2Ki 25:7

50:18
j Isa 10:12
k Eze 31:3

50:19
l Jer 31:10;
Eze 34:13
m Jer 31:5; 33:12

50:20
n Mic 7:18,19
o Jer 31:34
p Isa 1:9

50:21
q Eze 23:23

50:22
r Jer 4:19-21;
51:54

50:23
s Isa 14:16

50:24
t Da 5:30-31

you were found and captured[a]
    because you opposed[b] the LORD.
[25]The LORD has opened his arsenal
    and brought out the weapons[c] of his wrath,
for the Sovereign LORD Almighty has work to do
    in the land of the Babylonians.[d]
[26]Come against her from afar.
    Break open her granaries;
    pile her up like heaps of grain.
Completely destroy[e] her
    and leave her no remnant.
[27]Kill all her young bulls;
    let them go down to the slaughter!
Woe to them! For their day has come,
    the time for them to be punished.
[28]Listen to the fugitives and refugees from Babylon
        declaring in Zion[f]
how the LORD our God has taken vengeance,[g]
    vengeance for his temple.

[29]"Summon archers against Babylon,
    all those who draw the bow.[h]
Encamp all around her;
    let no one escape.
Repay[i] her for her deeds;[j]
    do to her as she has done.
For she has defied[k] the LORD,
    the Holy One of Israel.
[30]Therefore, her young men[l] will fall in the streets;
    all her soldiers will be silenced in that day,"
                                        declares the LORD.
[31]"See, I am against[m] you, O arrogant one,"
        declares the Lord, the LORD Almighty,
    "for your day has come,
        the time for you to be punished.
[32]The arrogant one will stumble and fall
    and no one will help her up;
I will kindle a fire[n] in her towns
    that will consume all who are around her."

[33]This is what the LORD Almighty says:

"The people of Israel are oppressed,[o]
    and the people of Judah as well.
All their captors hold them fast,
    refusing to let them go.[p]
[34]Yet their Redeemer is strong;
    the LORD Almighty[q] is his name.

50:24
[a] Jer 51:31
[b] Job 9:4

50:25
[c] Isa 13:5
[d] Jer 51:25,55

50:26
[e] Isa 14:22-23

50:28
[f] Isa 48:20; Jer 51:10
[g] ver 15

50:29
[h] ver 14
[i] Rev 18:6
[j] Jer 51:56
[k] Isa 47:10

50:30
[l] Isa 13:18; Jer 49:26

50:31
[m] Jer 21:13

50:32
[n] Jer 21:14; 49:27

50:33
[o] Isa 58:6
[p] Isa 14:17

50:34
[q] Jer 51:19

He will vigorously defend their cause[a]
  so that he may bring rest[b] to their land,
  but unrest to those who live in Babylon.

35"A sword[c] against the Babylonians!"
  declares the LORD—
"against those who live in Babylon
  and against her officials and wise[d] men!
36A sword against her false prophets!
  They will become fools.
A sword against her warriors![e]
  They will be filled with terror.
37A sword against her horses and chariots[f]
  and all the foreigners in her ranks!
  They will become women.[g]
A sword against her treasures!
  They will be plundered.
38A drought on[a] her waters!
  They will dry[h] up.
For it is a land of idols,[i]
  idols that will go mad with terror.

39"So desert creatures and hyenas will live there,
  and there the owl will dwell.
It will never again be inhabited
  or lived in from generation to generation.[j]
40As God overthrew Sodom and Gomorrah[k]
  along with their neighboring towns,"
             declares the LORD,
"so no one will live there;
  no man will dwell in it.

41"Look! An army is coming from the north;[l]
  a great nation and many kings
  are being stirred up from the ends of the earth.[m]
42They are armed with bows[n] and spears;
  they are cruel and without mercy.[o]
They sound like the roaring sea[p]
  as they ride on their horses;
they come like men in battle formation
  to attack you, O Daughter of Babylon.[q]
43The king of Babylon has heard reports about them,
  and his hands hang limp.
Anguish has gripped him,
  pain like that of a woman in labor.

a 38 Or A sword against

50:34
a Jer 15:21;
51:36
b Isa 14:7

50:35
c Jer 47:6
d Da 5:7

50:36
e Jer 49:22

50:37
f Jer 51:21
g Jer 51:30;
Na 3:13

50:38
h Jer 51:36
i ver 2

50:39
j Isa 13:19-22;
34:13-15;
Jer 51:37;
Rev 18:2

50:40
k Ge 19:24

50:41
l Jer 6:22
m Isa 13:4;
Jer 51:22-28

50:42
n ver 14
o Isa 13:18
p Isa 5:30
q Jer 6:23

50:44
a Nu 16:5
b Job 41:10;
Isa 46:9;
Jer 49:19

44Like a lion coming up from Jordan's thickets
　　to a rich pastureland,
I will chase Babylon from its land in an instant.
　　Who is the chosen[a] one I will appoint for this?
Who is like me and who can challenge me?[b]
　　And what shepherd can stand against me?"

50:45
c Ps 33:11;
Isa 14:24;
Jer 51:11

45Therefore, hear what the LORD has planned against
　　Babylon,
　　what he has purposed[c] against the land of the
　　　Babylonians:
The young of the flock will be dragged away;
　　he will completely destroy their pasture because of
　　　them.

50:46
d Rev 18:9-10

46At the sound of Babylon's capture the earth will tremble;
　　its cry[d] will resound among the nations.

Chapter 51 Theme

51:2
e Isa 41:16;
Jer 15:7;
Mt 3:12

51 This is what the LORD says:

"See, I will stir up the spirit of a destroyer
　　against Babylon and the people of Leb Kamai.[a]

51:3
f Jer 50:29
g Jer 46:4

2I will send foreigners to Babylon
　　to winnow[e] her and to devastate her land;
they will oppose her on every side
　　in the day of her disaster.
3Let not the archer string his bow,[f]
　　nor let him put on his armor.[g]
Do not spare her young men;
　　completely destroy[b] her army.

51:4
h Isa 13:15
i Jer 49:26; 50:30

4They will fall[h] down slain in Babylon,[c]
　　fatally wounded in her streets.[i]

51:5
j Isa 54:6-8
k Hos 4:1

5For Israel and Judah have not been forsaken[j]
　　by their God, the LORD Almighty,
though their land[d] is full of guilt[k]
　　before the Holy One of Israel.

51:6
l Jer 50:8
m Nu 16:26;
Rev 18:4
n Jer 50:15
o Jer 25:14

6"Flee[l] from Babylon!
　　Run for your lives!
Do not be destroyed because of her sins.[m]
It is time for the LORD's vengeance;[n]
　　he will pay[o] her what she deserves.
7Babylon was a gold cup[p] in the LORD's hand;
　　she made the whole earth drunk.

51:7
p Jer 25:15-16;
Rev 14:8-10;
17:4

a 1 *Leb Kamai* is a cryptogram for Chaldea, that is, Babylonia.　b 3 The Hebrew term refers to the irrevocable giving over of things or persons to the LORD, often by totally destroying them.　c 4 Or *Chaldea*　d 5 Or *l and the land lof the Babylonians l*

The nations drank her wine;
    therefore they have now gone mad.
[8]Babylon will suddenly fall[a] and be broken.
    Wail over her!
Get balm[b] for her pain;
    perhaps she can be healed.

[9]"'We would have healed Babylon,
    but she cannot be healed;
let us leave[c] her and each go to his own land,
    for her judgment[d] reaches to the skies,
    it rises as high as the clouds.'

[10]"'The LORD has vindicated[e] us;
    come, let us tell in Zion
    what the LORD our God has done.'[f]

[11]"Sharpen the arrows,[g]
    take up the shields![h]
The LORD has stirred up the kings of the Medes,[i]
    because his purpose[j] is to destroy Babylon.
The LORD will take vengeance,
    vengeance for his temple.[k]
[12]Lift up a banner against the walls of Babylon!
    Reinforce the guard,
station the watchmen,
    prepare an ambush!
The LORD will carry out his purpose,
    his decree against the people of Babylon.
[13]You who live by many waters[l]
    and are rich in treasures,[m]
your end has come,
    the time for you to be cut off.
[14]The LORD Almighty has sworn by himself:[n]
    I will surely fill you with men, as with a swarm
      of locusts,[o]
and they will shout[p] in triumph over you.

[15]"He made the earth by his power;
    he founded the world by his wisdom
    and stretched[q] out the heavens by his understanding.
[16]When he thunders,[r] the waters in the heavens roar;
    he makes clouds rise from the ends of the earth.
He sends lightning with the rain
    and brings out the wind from his storehouses.[s]

[17]"Every man is senseless and without knowledge;
    every goldsmith is shamed by his idols.

51:8 [a]Isa 21:9; Rev 14:8 [b]Jer 46:11

51:9 [c]Isa 13:14; Jer 50:16 [d]Rev 18:4-5

51:10 [e]Mic 7:9 [f]Jer 50:28

51:11 [g]Jer 50:9 [h]Jer 46:4 [i]ver 28 [j]Jer 50:45 [k]Jer 50:28

51:13 [l]Rev 17:1,15 [m]Isa 45:3; Hab 2:9

51:14 [n]Am 6:8 [o]ver 27; Na 3:15 [p]Jer 50:15

51:15 [q]Ge 1:1; Job 9:8; Ps 104:2

51:16 [r]Ps 18:11-13 [s]Ps 135:7; Jnh 1:4

His images are a fraud;*a*
they have no breath in them.
[18]They are worthless,*b* the objects of mockery;
when their judgment comes, they will perish.
[19]He who is the Portion of Jacob is not like these,
for he is the Maker of all things,
including the tribe of his inheritance—
the LORD Almighty is his name.

[20]"You are my war club,*c*
my weapon for battle—
with you I shatter*d* nations,
with you I destroy kingdoms,
[21]with you I shatter horse and rider,*e*
with you I shatter chariot and driver,
[22]with you I shatter man and woman,
with you I shatter old man and youth,
with you I shatter young man and maiden,*f*
[23]with you I shatter shepherd and flock,
with you I shatter farmer and oxen,
with you I shatter governors and officials.*g*

[24]"Before your eyes I will repay*h* Babylon and all who live in Babylonia*a* for all the wrong they have done in Zion," declares the LORD.

[25]"I am against you, O destroying mountain,
you who destroy the whole earth,"
declares the LORD.
"I will stretch out my hand against you,
roll you off the cliffs,
and make you a burned-out mountain.*i*
[26]No rock will be taken from you for a cornerstone,
nor any stone for a foundation,
for you will be desolate*j* forever,"
declares the LORD.

[27]"Lift up a banner*k* in the land!
Blow the trumpet among the nations!
Prepare the nations for battle against her;
summon against her these kingdoms:*l*
Ararat,*m* Minni and Ashkenaz.*n*
Appoint a commander against her;
send up horses like a swarm of locusts.
[28]Prepare the nations for battle against her—
the kings of the Medes,*o*
their governors and all their officials,
and all the countries they rule.

51:17
a Isa 44:20;
Hab 2:18-19

51:18
b Jer 18:15

51:20
c Isa 10:5
d Mic 4:13

51:21
e Ex 15:1

51:22
f 2Ch 36:17;
Isa 13:17-18

51:23
g ver 57

51:24
h Jer 50:15

51:25
i Zec 4:7

51:26
j ver 29;
Isa 13:19-22;
Jer 50:12

51:27
k Isa 13:2;
Jer 50:2
l Jer 25:14
m Ge 8:4
n Ge 10:3

51:28
o ver 11

a 24 Or *Chaldea*; also in verse 35

²⁹The land trembles and writhes,
for the LORD's purposes against Babylon stand—
to lay waste the land of Babylon
so that no one will live there.ᵃ

³⁰Babylon's warriorsᵇ have stopped fighting;
they remain in their strongholds.
Their strength is exhausted;
they have become like women.ᶜ
Her dwellings are set on fire;
the barsᵈ of her gates are broken.

³¹One courierᵉ follows another
and messenger follows messenger
to announce to the king of Babylon
that his entire city is captured,

³²the river crossings seized,
the marshes set on fire,
and the soldiers terrified.ᶠ"

³³This is what the LORD Almighty, the God of Israel, says:

"The Daughter of Babylon is like a threshing floorᵍ
at the time it is trampled;
the time to harvestʰ her will soon come."

³⁴"Nebuchadnezzarⁱ king of Babylon has devoured us,
he has thrown us into confusion,
he has made us an empty jar.
Like a serpent he has swallowed us
and filled his stomach with our delicacies,
and then has spewed us out.

³⁵May the violence done to our fleshᵃ be upon Babylon,"
say the inhabitants of Zion.
"May our blood be on those who live in Babylonia,"
says Jerusalem.ʲ

³⁶Therefore, this is what the LORD says:

"See, I will defend your causeᵏ
and avengeˡ you;
I will dry upᵐ her sea
and make her springs dry.

³⁷Babylon will be a heap of ruins,
a hauntⁿ of jackals,
an object of horror and scorn,
a place where no one lives.ᵒ

³⁸Her people all roar like young lions,
they growl like lion cubs.

ᵃ 35 Or *done to us and to our children*

51:29
ᵃ ver 43;
Isa 13:20

51:30
ᵇ Jer 50:36
ᶜ Isa 19:16
ᵈ Isa 45:2;
La 2:9; Na 3:13

51:31
ᵉ 2Sa 18:19-31

51:32
ᶠ Jer 50:36

51:33
ᵍ Isa 21:10
ʰ Isa 17:5;
Hos 6:11

51:34
ⁱ Jer 50:17

51:35
ʲ ver 24; Ps 137:8

51:36
ᵏ Ps 140:12;
Jer 50:34;
La 3:58
ˡ ver 6; Ro 12:19
ᵐ Jer 50:38

51:37
ⁿ Isa 13:22;
Rev 18:2
ᵒ Jer 50:13,39

51:39
a ver 57

³⁹But while they are aroused,
 I will set out a feast for them
 and make them drunk,
so that they shout with laughter—
 then sleep forever and not awake,"
declares the L<small>ORD</small>.^a

51:41
b Jer 25:26
c Isa 13:19

⁴⁰"I will bring them down
 like lambs to the slaughter,
 like rams and goats.

51:42
d Isa 8:7

⁴¹"How Sheshach^{ab} will be captured,^c
 the boast of the whole earth seized!
What a horror Babylon will be
 among the nations!

51:43
e ver 29,62;
Isa 13:20;
Jer 2:6

⁴²The sea will rise over Babylon;
 its roaring waves^d will cover her.
⁴³Her towns will be desolate,
 a dry and desert land,
 a land where no one lives,
 through which no man travels.^e

51:44
f Isa 46:1
g ver 34
h ver 58;
Jer 50:15

⁴⁴I will punish Bel^f in Babylon
 and make him spew out^g what he has swallowed.
The nations will no longer stream to him.
 And the wall^h of Babylon will fall.

51:45
i Rev 18:4
j ver 6; Isa 48:20;
Jer 50:8

⁴⁵"Come outⁱ of her, my people!
 Run^j for your lives!
 Run from the fierce anger of the L<small>ORD</small>.
⁴⁶Do not lose heart or be afraid^k
 when rumors^l are heard in the land;
one rumor comes this year, another the next,
 rumors of violence in the land
 and of ruler against ruler.

51:46
k Jer 46:27
l 2Ki 19:7

⁴⁷For the time will surely come
 when I will punish the idols^m of Babylon;
her whole land will be disgracedⁿ
 and her slain will all lie fallen within her.

51:47
m ver 52;
Isa 46:1-2;
Jer 50:2
n Jer 50:12

⁴⁸Then heaven and earth and all that is in them
 will shout^o for joy over Babylon,
for out of the north^p
 destroyers will attack her,"
declares the L<small>ORD</small>.

51:48
o Isa 44:23;
Rev 18:20
p ver 11

⁴⁹"Babylon must fall because of Israel's slain,
 just as the slain in all the earth
 have fallen because of Babylon.^q

51:49
q Ps 137:8;
Jer 50:29

^a *41* **Sheshach** is a cryptogram for Babylon.

⁵⁰You who have escaped the sword,
    leave^a and do not linger!
Remember^b the LORD in a distant land,
    and think on Jerusalem."

⁵¹"We are disgraced,^c
    for we have been insulted
    and shame covers our faces,
because foreigners have entered
    the holy places of the LORD's house."^d

⁵²"But days are coming," declares the LORD,
    "when I will punish her idols,^e
and throughout her land
    the wounded will groan.
⁵³Even if Babylon reaches the sky^f
    and fortifies her lofty stronghold,
    I will send destroyers^g against her,"

declares the LORD.

⁵⁴"The sound of a cry comes from Babylon,
    the sound of great destruction^h
    from the land of the Babylonians.^a
⁵⁵The LORD will destroy Babylon;
    he will silence her noisy din.
Wavesⁱ ⌊of enemies⌋ will rage like great waters;
    the roar of their voices will resound.
⁵⁶A destroyer^j will come against Babylon;
    her warriors will be captured,
    and their bows will be broken.^k
For the LORD is a God of retribution;
    he will repay^l in full.
⁵⁷I will make her officials and wise men drunk,
    her governors, officers and warriors as well;
they will sleep^m forever and not awake,"
    declares the King,ⁿ whose name is the LORD Almighty.

⁵⁸This is what the LORD Almighty says:

"Babylon's thick wall^o will be leveled
    and her high gates set on fire;
the peoples^p exhaust themselves for nothing,
    the nations' labor is only fuel for the flames."^q

⁵⁹This is the message Jeremiah gave to the staff officer Seraiah son of Neriah,^r the son of Mahseiah, when he went to Babylon with Zedekiah^s king of Judah in the fourth^t year of his reign. ⁶⁰Jeremiah

^a54 Or *Chaldeans*

51:50
^aver 45
^bPs 137:6

51:51
^cPs 44:13-16; 79:4
^dLa 1:10

51:52
^ever 47

51:53
^fGe 11:4; Isa 14:13-14
^gJer 49:16

51:54
^hJer 50:22

51:55
ⁱPs 18:4

51:56
^jver 48
^kPs 46:9
^lver 6; Ps 94:1-2; Hab 2:8

51:57
^mPs 76:5; Jer 25:27
ⁿJer 46:18; 48:15

51:58
^over 44
^pver 64
^qHab 2:13

51:59
^rJer 36:4
^sJer 52:1
^tJer 28:1

51:60
a Jer 30:2; 36:2

51:62
b Isa 13:20;
Jer 50:13,39

51:64
c ver 58
d Job 31:40

52:1
e 2Ki 24:17
f Jos 10:29;
2Ki 8:22

52:2
g Jer 36:30

52:3
h Isa 3:1
i Eze 17:12-16

52:4
j Zec 8:19
k 2Ki 25:1-7;
Jer 39:1
l Eze 24:1-2

52:6
m Isa 3:1

52:9
n Jer 32:4
o Nu 34:11
p Nu 13:21

52:10
q Jer 22:30

52:11
r Eze 12:13

52:12
s Zec 7:5; 8:19
t Jer 39:9

had written on a scroll[a] about all the disasters that would come upon Babylon—all that had been recorded concerning Babylon. [61]He said to Seraiah, "When you get to Babylon, see that you read all these words aloud. [62]Then say, 'O LORD, you have said you will destroy this place, so that neither man nor animal will live in it; it will be desolate[b] forever.' [63]When you finish reading this scroll, tie a stone to it and throw it into the Euphrates. [64]Then say, 'So will Babylon sink to rise no more because of the disaster I will bring upon her. And her people[c] will fall.'"

The words of Jeremiah end[d] here.

Chapter 52 Theme

52 Zedekiah[e] was twenty-one years old when he became king, and he reigned in Jerusalem eleven years. His mother's name was Hamutal daughter of Jeremiah; she was from Libnah.[f] [2]He did evil in the eyes of the LORD, just as Jehoiakim[g] had done. [3]It was because of the LORD's anger that all this happened to Jerusalem and Judah,[h] and in the end he thrust them from his presence.

Now Zedekiah rebelled[i] against the king of Babylon.

[4]So in the ninth year of Zedekiah's reign, on the tenth[j] day of the tenth month, Nebuchadnezzar king of Babylon marched against Jerusalem[k] with his whole army. They camped outside the city and built siege works all around it.[l] [5]The city was kept under siege until the eleventh year of King Zedekiah.

[6]By the ninth day of the fourth month the famine in the city had become so severe that there was no food for the people to eat.[m] [7]Then the city wall was broken through, and the whole army fled. They left the city at night through the gate between the two walls near the king's garden, though the Babylonians[a] were surrounding the city. They fled toward the Arabah,[b] [8]but the Babylonian[c] army pursued King Zedekiah and overtook him in the plains of Jericho. All his soldiers were separated from him and scattered, [9]and he was captured.[n]

He was taken to the king of Babylon at Riblah[o] in the land of Hamath,[p] where he pronounced sentence on him. [10]There at Riblah the king of Babylon slaughtered the sons[q] of Zedekiah before his eyes; he also killed all the officials of Judah. [11]Then he put out Zedekiah's eyes, bound him with bronze shackles and took him to Babylon, where he put him in prison till the day of his death.[r]

[12]On the tenth day of the fifth[s] month, in the nineteenth year of Nebuchadnezzar king of Babylon, Nebuzaradan[t] commander of the imperial guard, who served the king of Babylon, came to

a 7 Or *Chaldeans*; also in verse 17   b 7 Or *the Jordan Valley*   c 8 Or *Chaldean*; also in verse 14

Jerusalem. [13]He set fire[a] to the temple[b] of the Lord, the royal palace and all the houses of Jerusalem. Every important building he burned down. [14]The whole Babylonian army under the commander of the imperial guard broke down all the walls[c] around Jerusalem. [15]Nebuzaradan the commander of the guard carried into exile some of the poorest people and those who remained in the city, along with the rest of the craftsmen[a] and those who had gone over to the king of Babylon. [16]But Nebuzaradan left behind[d] the rest of the poorest people of the land to work the vineyards and fields.

[17]The Babylonians broke up the bronze pillars,[e] the movable stands[f] and the bronze Sea[g] that were at the temple of the Lord and they carried all the bronze to Babylon.[h] [18]They also took away the pots, shovels, wick trimmers, sprinkling bowls, dishes and all the bronze articles used in the temple service.[i] [19]The commander of the imperial guard took away the basins, censers,[j] sprinkling bowls, pots, lampstands, dishes and bowls used for drink offerings—all that were made of pure gold or silver.

[20]The bronze from the two pillars, the Sea and the twelve bronze bulls under it, and the movable stands, which King Solomon had made for the temple of the Lord, was more than could be weighed.[k] [21]Each of the pillars was eighteen cubits high and twelve cubits in circumference[b]; each was four fingers thick, and hollow.[l] [22]The bronze capital[m] on top of the one pillar was five cubits[c] high and was decorated with a network and pomegranates of bronze all around. The other pillar, with its pomegranates, was similar. [23]There were ninety-six pomegranates on the sides; the total number of pomegranates[n] above the surrounding network was a hundred.

[24]The commander of the guard took as prisoners Seraiah[o] the chief priest, Zephaniah[p] the priest next in rank and the three doorkeepers. [25]Of those still in the city, he took the officer in charge of the fighting men, and seven royal advisers. He also took the secretary who was chief officer in charge of conscripting the people of the land and sixty of his men who were found in the city. [26]Nebuzaradan[q] the commander took them all and brought them to the king of Babylon at Riblah. [27]There at Riblah, in the land of Hamath, the king had them executed.

So Judah went into captivity, away[r] from her land. [28]This is the number of the people Nebuchadnezzar carried into exile:[s]

in the seventh year, 3,023 Jews;
[29]in Nebuchadnezzar's eighteenth year,
832 people from Jerusalem;

52:13
[a]2Ch 36:19;
Ps 74:8;
La 2:6
[b]Ps 79:1;
Mic 3:12

52:14
[c]Ne 1:3

52:16
[d]Jer 40:6

52:17
[e]1Ki 7:15
[f]1Ki 7:27-37
[g]1Ki 7:23
[h]Jer 27:19-22

52:18
[i]Ex 27:3;
1Ki 7:45

52:19
[j]1Ki 7:50

52:20
[k]1Ki 7:47

52:21
[l]1Ki 7:15

52:22
[m]1Ki 7:16

52:23
[n]1Ki 7:20

52:24
[o]2Ki 25:18
[p]Jer 21:1; 37:3

52:26
[q]ver 12

52:27
[r]Jer 20:4

52:28
[s]2Ki 24:14-16;
2Ch 36:20

---

[a]15 Or *populace*   [b]21 That is, about 27 feet (about 8.1 meters) high and 18 feet (about 5.4 meters) in circumference   [c]22 That is, about 7 1/2 feet (about 2.3 meters)

52:33
a 2Sa 9:7

³⁰in his twenty-third year,

745 Jews taken into exile by Nebuzaradan the commander of the imperial guard.

There were 4,600 people in all.

³¹In the thirty-seventh year of the exile of Jehoiachin king of Judah, in the year Evil-Merodach*a* became king of Babylon, he released Jehoiachin king of Judah and freed him from prison on the twenty-fifth day of the twelfth month. ³²He spoke kindly to him and gave him a seat of honor higher than those of the other kings who were with him in Babylon. ³³So Jehoiachin put aside his prison clothes and for the rest of his life ate regularly at the king's table.*a* ³⁴Day by day the king of Babylon gave Jehoiachin a regular allowance*b* as long as he lived, till the day of his death.

52:34
b 2Sa 9:10

a 31 Also called *Amel-Marduk*

Theme of Jeremiah:

		Chapter Themes
		1
		2
		3
		4
		5
		6
		7
		8
		9
		10
		11
		12
		13
		14
		15
		16
		17
		18
		19
		20
		21
		22
		23
		24
		25
		26

Author:

Date:

Purpose:

Key Words:

SEGMENT DIVISIONS

		CHAPTER THEMES
		27
		28
		29
		30
		31
		32
		33
		34
		35
		36
		37
		38
		39
		40
		41
		42
		43
		44
		45
		46
		47
		48
		49
		50
		51
		52

LAMENTATIONS

*L*amentations is a book of wailings that were read annually by the Jews as a reminder of the fall of Jerusalem and destruction of the temple. They were a reminder of an avoidable tragedy caused by sin—a reminder of a God who judges but who keeps his covenant forever.

These expressions of grief were written sometime between the destruction of Jerusalem and the return of the remnant after 70 years of captivity. Judah's plight is desperate but not hopeless when the people remember, "Because of the LORD's great love we are not consumed, for his compassions never fail. They are new every morning; great is your faithfulness" (3:22, 23).

∾ THINGS TO DO

1. There are five laments in this book; each begins a new chapter. Lamentations is written as poetry. Each chapter, except chapter 3, is 22 verses long—a verse for every letter of the Hebrew alphabet. As you read chapter by chapter note how each lament begins and who or what the lament centers on.

2. Mark the key words listed on LAMENTATIONS AT A GLANCE on page 1411.

3. Note the personification of Jerusalem and Judah. Jerusalem is personified as a woman. The personification is seen in the first lines of Lamentations: "How deserted lies the city . . . like a widow is she." List what happened to Jerusalem and why; this is key. Note her emotions, the anguish because of her children, the thoughts and memories she has to deal with.

4. Carefully observe and list what you learn about God, his character, his judgments, and why he acts as he does. For example, 1:5 states that God caused Judah grief because of Judah's sin. God brought about Judah's captivity because of Judah's transgressions.

5. Lamentations gives a more definitive understanding of what took place during the Babylonian siege of Jerusalem. In the margin of the text, list what you learn. For example, 1:10 says the nations entered the sanctuary, the house of God where only Jewish priests were to go. Verse 11 reveals there was a famine—people were seeking bread and giving away their treasures in order to get it.

6. Determine the theme of each chapter. Write the theme next to each chapter number and on LAMENTATIONS AT A GLANCE.

7. Complete LAMENTATIONS AT A GLANCE.

∾ THINGS TO THINK ABOUT

1. Have you become more aware of the consequences of sin?

2. God's judgment can take many forms. The sovereign God rules. None can stay his hand or say to him, "What have you done?" for he does according to his will in the army of heaven and among the inhabitants of the earth (Daniel 4:34, 35). Do you think you can sin and go unchastened by God? Judgment must begin at the house of God. Look at 1 Corinthians 11:31, 32.

3. Why do you think God deals with sin as he does? How should you respond? Read chapter 3 on your knees, so your "dancing" need not be turned into "mourning."

THE TIME OF LAMENTATIONS

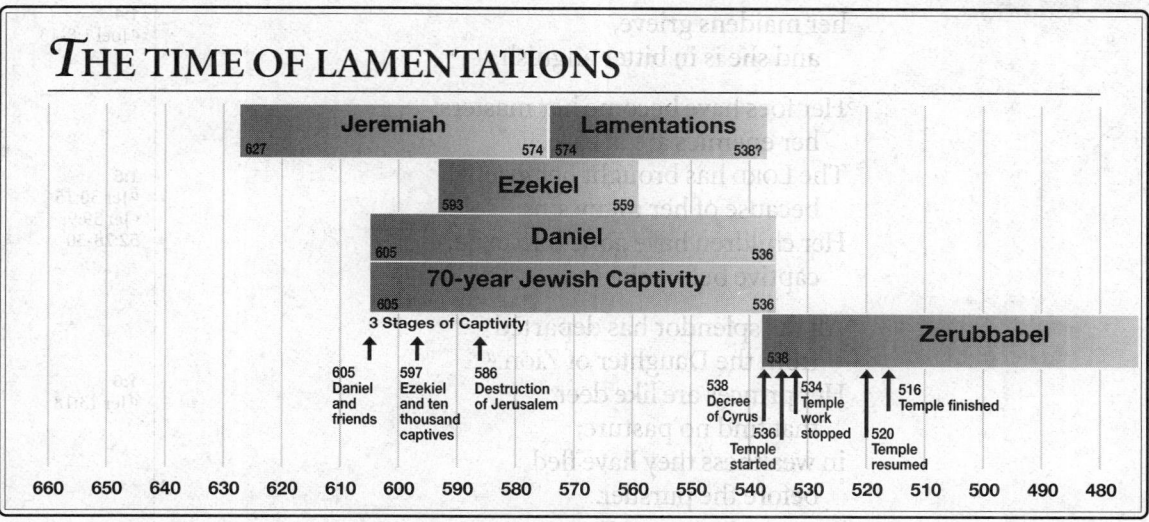

Chapter 1 Theme

1:1
a Isa 47:8
b 1Ki 4:21
c Isa 3:26;
Jer 40:9

1^a How deserted lies the city,
  once so full of people!
How like a widow*a* is she,
  who once was great*b* among the nations!
She who was queen among the provinces
  has now become a slave.*c*

1:2
d Ps 6:6
e Jer 3:1
f Jer 4:30;
Mic 7:5
g ver 16

²Bitterly she weeps*d* at night,
  tears are upon her cheeks.
Among all her lovers*e*
  there is none to comfort her.
All her friends have betrayed*f* her;
  they have become her enemies.*g*

1:3
h Jer 13:19
i Dt 28:65

³After affliction and harsh labor,
  Judah has gone into exile.*h*
She dwells among the nations;
  she finds no resting place.*i*
All who pursue her have overtaken her
  in the midst of her distress.

⁴The roads to Zion mourn,
  for no one comes to her appointed feasts.
All her gateways are desolate,*j*
  her priests groan,

1:4
j Jer 9:11

a This chapter is an acrostic poem, the verses of which begin with the successive letters of the Hebrew alphabet.

1397

her maidens grieve,
and she is in bitter anguish.*a*

5Her foes have become her masters;
her enemies are at ease.
The LORD has brought her grief*b*
because of her many sins.
Her children have gone into exile,*c*
captive before the foe.

6All the splendor has departed
from the Daughter of Zion.*d*
Her princes are like deer
that find no pasture;
in weakness they have fled
before the pursuer.

7In the days of her affliction and wandering
Jerusalem remembers all the treasures
that were hers in days of old.
When her people fell into enemy hands,
there was no one to help her.*e*
Her enemies looked at her
and laughed at her destruction.

8Jerusalem has sinned*f* greatly
and so has become unclean.
All who honored her despise her,
for they have seen her nakedness;*g*
she herself groans*h*
and turns away.

9Her filthiness clung to her skirts;
she did not consider her future.*i*
Her fall*j* was astounding;
there was none to comfort*k* her.
"Look, O LORD, on my affliction,*l*
for the enemy has triumphed."

10The enemy laid hands
on all her treasures;*m*
she saw pagan nations
enter her sanctuary*n*—
those you had forbidden*o*
to enter your assembly.

11All her people groan*p*
as they search for bread;*q*

1:4
a Joel 1:8-13

1:5
b Jer 30:15
c Jer 39:9;
52:28-30

1:6
d Jer 13:18

1:7
e Jer 37:7;
La 4:17

1:8
f ver 20;
Isa 59:2-13
g Jer 13:22,26
h ver 21,22

1:9
i Dt 32:28-29;
Isa 47:7;
Eze 24:13
j Jer 13:18
k Ecc 4:1;
Jer 16:7
l Ps 25:18

1:10
m Isa 64:11
n Ps 74:7-8;
Jer 51:51
o Dt 23:3

1:11
p Ps 38:8
q Jer 52:6

1:12
a Jer 18:16
b ver 18
c Isa 13:13;
Jer 30:24

they barter their treasures for food
to keep themselves alive.
"Look, O LORD, and consider,
for I am despised."

¹²"Is it nothing to you, all you who pass by?*a*
Look around and see.
Is any suffering like my suffering*b*
that was inflicted on me,
that the LORD brought on me
in the day of his fierce anger?*c*

1:13
d Job 30:30
e Jer 44:6
f Hab 3:16

¹³"From on high he sent fire,
sent it down into my bones.*d*
He spread a net for my feet
and turned me back.
He made me desolate,*e*
faint*f* all the day long.

1:14
g Dt 28:48;
Isa 47:6
h Jer 32:5

¹⁴"My sins have been bound into a yoke*a*;*g*
by his hands they were woven together.
They have come upon my neck
and the Lord has sapped my strength.
He has handed me over*h*
to those I cannot withstand.

1:15
i Jer 37:10
j Isa 41:2
k Isa 28:18;
Jer 18:21

¹⁵"The Lord has rejected
all the warriors in my midst;*i*
he has summoned an army*j* against me
to*b* crush my young men.*k*
In his winepress the Lord has trampled
the Virgin Daughter of Judah.

1:16
l La 2:11,18;
3:48-49
m Ps 69:20;
Ecc 4:1
n ver 2;
Jer 13:17; 14:17

¹⁶"This is why I weep
and my eyes overflow with tears.*l*
No one is near to comfort*m* me,
no one to restore my spirit.
My children are destitute
because the enemy has prevailed."*n*

1:17
o Jer 4:31

¹⁷Zion stretches out her hands,*o*
but there is no one to comfort her.
The LORD has decreed for Jacob
that his neighbors become his foes;
Jerusalem has become
an unclean thing among them.

^a 14 Most Hebrew manuscripts; Septuagint *He kept watch over my sins*   ^b 15 Or *has set a time for me / when he will*

18"The LORD is righteous,
    yet I rebelled[a] against his command.
Listen, all you peoples;
    look upon my suffering.[b]
My young men and maidens
    have gone into exile.[c]

19"I called to my allies
    but they betrayed me.
My priests and my elders
    perished[d] in the city
while they searched for food
    to keep themselves alive.

20"See, O LORD, how distressed[e] I am!
    I am in torment[f] within,
and in my heart I am disturbed,
    for I have been most rebellious.
Outside, the sword bereaves;
    inside, there is only death.[g]

21"People have heard my groaning,[h]
    but there is no one to comfort me.[i]
All my enemies have heard of my distress;
    they rejoice[j] at what you have done.
May you bring the day[k] you have announced
    so they may become like me.

22"Let all their wickedness come before you;
    deal with them
as you have dealt with me
    because of all my sins.[l]
My groans are many
    and my heart is faint."

Chapter 2 Theme

2[a] How the Lord has covered the Daughter of Zion
    with the cloud of his anger[b]![m]
He has hurled down the splendor of Israel
    from heaven to earth;
he has not remembered his footstool[n]
    in the day of his anger.

2Without pity[o] the Lord has swallowed[p] up
    all the dwellings of Jacob;

---

a This chapter is an acrostic poem, the verses of which begin with the successive letters of the Hebrew alphabet.   b 1 Or *How the Lord in his anger / has treated the Daughter of Zion with contempt*

1:18
a 1Sa 12:14
b ver 12
c Dt 28:32,41

1:19
d Jer 14:15;
La 2:20

1:20
e Jer 4:19
f La 2:11
g Dt 32:25;
Eze 7:15

1:21
h ver 8
i ver 4
j La 2:15
k Isa 47:11;
Jer 30:16

1:22
l Ne 4:5

2:1
m La 3:44
n Ps 99:5; 132:7

2:2
o La 3:43
p Ps 21:9

in his wrath he has torn down
the strongholds*a* of the Daughter of Judah.
He has brought her kingdom and its princes
down to the ground*b* in dishonor.

³In fierce anger he has cut off
every horn*ac* of Israel.
He has withdrawn his right hand*d*
at the approach of the enemy.
He has burned in Jacob like a flaming fire
that consumes everything around it.*e*

⁴Like an enemy he has strung his bow;*f*
his right hand is ready.
Like a foe he has slain
all who were pleasing to the eye;*g*
he has poured out his wrath like fire*h*
on the tent of the Daughter of Zion.

⁵The Lord is like an enemy;*i*
he has swallowed up Israel.
He has swallowed up all her palaces
and destroyed her strongholds.*j*
He has multiplied mourning and lamentation
for the Daughter of Judah.*k*

⁶He has laid waste his dwelling like a garden;
he has destroyed his place of meeting.*l*
The Lord has made Zion forget
her appointed feasts and her Sabbaths;*m*
in his fierce anger he has spurned
both king and priest.*n*

⁷The Lord has rejected his altar
and abandoned his sanctuary.
He has handed over to the enemy
the walls of her palaces;*o*
they have raised a shout in the house of the Lord
as on the day of an appointed feast.

⁸The Lord determined to tear down
the wall around the Daughter of Zion.
He stretched out a measuring line*p*
and did not withhold his hand from destroying.
He made ramparts and walls lament;
together they wasted away.*q*

2:2
a Ps 89:39-40;
Mic 5:11
b Isa 25:12

2:3
c Ps 75:5,10
d Ps 74:11
e Isa 42:25;
Jer 21:4-5,14

2:4
f Job 16:13;
La 3:12-13
g Eze 24:16,25
h Isa 42:25;
Jer 7:20

2:5
i Jer 30:14
j ver 2
k Jer 9:17-20

2:6
l Jer 52:13
m La 1:4;
Zep 3:18
n La 4:16

2:7
o Ps 74:7-8;
Isa 64:11;
Jer 33:4-5

2:8
p 2Ki 21:13;
Isa 34:11
q Isa 3:26

a 3 Or / all the strength; or every king; horn here symbolizes strength.

⁹Her gates^a have sunk into the ground;
    their bars he has broken and destroyed.
Her king and her princes are exiled^b among the nations,
    the law^c is no more,
and her prophets no longer find
    visions^d from the Lord.

¹⁰The elders of the Daughter of Zion
    sit on the ground in silence;
they have sprinkled dust on their heads^e
    and put on sackcloth.^f
The young women of Jerusalem
    have bowed their heads to the ground.^g

¹¹My eyes fail from weeping,^h
    I am in torment within,ⁱ
my heart is poured out^j on the ground
    because my people are destroyed,
because children and infants faint^k
    in the streets of the city.

¹²They say to their mothers,
    "Where is bread and wine?"
as they faint like wounded men
    in the streets of the city,
as their lives ebb away
    in their mothers' arms.^l

¹³What can I say for you?
    With what can I compare you,
    O Daughter of Jerusalem?
To what can I liken you,
    that I may comfort you,
    O Virgin Daughter of Zion?^m
Your wound is as deep as the sea.ⁿ
    Who can heal you?

¹⁴The visions of your prophets
    were false and worthless;
they did not expose your sin
    to ward off your captivity.^o
The oracles they gave you
    were false and misleading.^p

¹⁵All who pass your way
    clap their hands at you;^q
they scoff^r and shake their heads
    at the Daughter of Jerusalem:

2:9
^aNe 1:3
^bDt 28:36;
2Ki 24:15
^c2Ch 15:3
^dJer 14:14

2:10
^eJob 2:12
^fIsa 15:3
^gJob 2:13;
Isa 3:26

2:11
^hLa 1:16;
3:48-51
ⁱLa 1:20
^jver 19; Ps 22:14
^kLa 4:4

2:12
^lLa 4:4

2:13
^mIsa 37:22
ⁿJer 14:17;
La 1:12

2:14
^oIsa 58:1
^pJer 2:8;
23:25-32,
33-40; 29:9;
Eze 13:3; 22:28

2:15
^qEze 25:6
^rJer 19:8

"Is this the city that was called
    the perfection of beauty,^a
    the joy of the whole earth?"^b

¹⁶All your enemies open their mouths
    wide against you;^c
they scoff and gnash their teeth^d
    and say, "We have swallowed her up.^e
This is the day we have waited for;
    we have lived to see it."

¹⁷The LORD has done what he planned;
    he has fulfilled his word,
    which he decreed long ago.^f
He has overthrown you without pity,^g
    he has let the enemy gloat over you,
    he has exalted the horn^a of your foes.^h

¹⁸The hearts of the people
    cry out to the Lord.ⁱ
O wall of the Daughter of Zion,
    let your tears^j flow like a river
    day and night;^k
give yourself no relief,
    your eyes no rest.^l

¹⁹Arise, cry out in the night,
    as the watches of the night begin;
pour out your heart^m like water
    in the presence of the Lord.ⁿ
Lift up your hands to him
    for the lives of your children,
who faint^o from hunger
    at the head of every street.

²⁰"Look, O LORD, and consider:
    Whom have you ever treated like this?
Should women eat their offspring,^p
    the children they have cared for?^q
Should priest and prophet be killed^r
    in the sanctuary of the Lord?

²¹"Young and old lie together
    in the dust of the streets;
my young men and maidens
    have fallen by the sword.^s

2:15
^a Ps 50:2
^b Ps 48:2

2:16
^c Ps 56:2;
La 3:46
^d Job 16:9
^e Ps 35:25

2:17
^f Dt 28:15-45
^g ver 2; Eze 5:11
^h Ps 89:42

2:18
ⁱ Ps 119:145
^j La 1:16
^k Jer 9:1
^l La 3:49

2:19
^m 1Sa 1:15;
Ps 62:8
ⁿ Isa 26:9
^o Isa 51:20

2:20
^p Dt 28:53;
Jer 19:9
^q La 4:10
^r Ps 78:64;
Jer 14:15

2:21
^s 2Ch 36:17;
Ps 78:62-63;
Jer 6:11

---

^a 17 *Horn* here symbolizes strength.

You have slain them in the day of your anger;
  you have slaughtered them without pity.[a]

²²"As you summon to a feast day,
  so you summoned against me terrors[b] on every side.
In the day of the LORD's anger
    no one escaped or survived;
those I cared for and reared,[c]
  my enemy has destroyed."

Chapter 3 Theme

3[a] I am the man who has seen affliction
    by the rod of his wrath.[d]
²He has driven me away and made me walk
    in darkness[e] rather than light;
³indeed, he has turned his hand against me[f]
    again and again, all day long.

⁴He has made my skin and my flesh grow old
    and has broken my bones.[g]
⁵He has besieged me and surrounded me
    with bitterness[h] and hardship.[i]
⁶He has made me dwell in darkness
    like those long dead.[j]

⁷He has walled me in so I cannot escape;[k]
    he has weighed me down with chains.[l]
⁸Even when I call out or cry for help,
    he shuts out my prayer.[m]
⁹He has barred my way with blocks of stone;
    he has made my paths crooked.[n]

¹⁰Like a bear lying in wait,
    like a lion in hiding,
¹¹he dragged me from the path and mangled[o] me
    and left me without help.
¹²He drew his bow[p]
    and made me the target[q] for his arrows.[r]

¹³He pierced my heart
    with arrows from his quiver.[s]
¹⁴I became the laughingstock[t] of all my people;
    they mock me in song[u] all day long.
¹⁵He has filled me with bitter herbs
    and sated me with gall.[v]

---

[a] This chapter is an acrostic poem; the verses of each stanza begin with the successive letters of the Hebrew alphabet, and the verses within each stanza begin with the same letter.

2:21
[a] Jer 13:14;
La 3:43;
Zec 11:6

2:22
[b] Ps 31:13;
Jer 6:25
[c] Hos 9:13

3:1
[d] Job 19:21;
Ps 88:7

3:2
[e] Jer 4:23

3:3
[f] Isa 5:25

3:4
[g] Ps 51:8;
Isa 38:13;
Jer 50:17

3:5
[h] ver 19
[i] Jer 23:15

3:6
[j] Ps 88:5-6

3:7
[k] Job 3:23
[l] Jer 40:4

3:8
[m] Job 30:20;
Ps 22:2

3:9
[n] Isa 63:17;
Hos 2:6

3:11
[o] Hos 6:1

3:12
[p] La 2:4
[q] Job 7:20
[r] Ps 7:12-13;
38:2

3:13
[s] Job 6:4

3:14
[t] Jer 20:7
[u] Job 30:9

3:15
[v] Jer 9:15

3:16
a Pr 20:17

3:18
b Job 17:15

3:20
c Ps 42:5
d Ps 42:11

3:22
e Ps 78:38;
Mal 3:6

3:23
f Zep 3:5

3:24
g Ps 16:5

3:25
h Isa 25:9; 30:18

3:26
i Ps 37:7; 40:1

3:28
j Jer 15:17

3:29
k Jer 31:17

3:30
l Job 16:10;
Isa 50:6

3:31
m Ps 94:14;
Isa 54:7

3:32
n Ps 78:38;
Hos 11:8

3:33
o Eze 33:11

3:36
p Jer 22:3;
Hab 1:13

¹⁶He has broken my teeth with gravel;*ᵃ*
   he has trampled me in the dust.
¹⁷I have been deprived of peace;
   I have forgotten what prosperity is.
¹⁸So I say, "My splendor is gone
   and all that I had hoped from the LORD."*ᵇ*

¹⁹I remember my affliction and my wandering,
   the bitterness and the gall.
²⁰I well remember them,
   and my soul is downcast*ᶜ* within me.*ᵈ*
²¹Yet this I call to mind
   and therefore I have hope:

²²Because of the LORD's great love we are not consumed,
   for his compassions never fail.*ᵉ*
²³They are new every morning;
   great is your faithfulness.*ᶠ*
²⁴I say to myself, "The LORD is my portion;*ᵍ*
   therefore I will wait for him."

²⁵The LORD is good to those whose hope is in him,
   to the one who seeks him;*ʰ*
²⁶it is good to wait quietly
   for the salvation of the LORD.*ⁱ*
²⁷It is good for a man to bear the yoke
   while he is young.

²⁸Let him sit alone in silence,*ʲ*
   for the LORD has laid it on him.
²⁹Let him bury his face in the dust—
   there may yet be hope.*ᵏ*
³⁰Let him offer his cheek to one who would strike him,*ˡ*
   and let him be filled with disgrace.

³¹For men are not cast off
   by the Lord forever.*ᵐ*
³²Though he brings grief, he will show compassion,
   so great is his unfailing love.*ⁿ*
³³For he does not willingly bring affliction
   or grief to the children of men.*ᵒ*

³⁴To crush underfoot
   all prisoners in the land,
³⁵to deny a man his rights
   before the Most High,
³⁶to deprive a man of justice—
   would not the Lord see such things?*ᵖ*

37Who can speak and have it happen
  if the Lord has not decreed it?*a*

38Is it not from the mouth of the Most High
  that both calamities and good things come?*b*

39Why should any living man complain
  when punished for his sins?*c*

40Let us examine our ways and test them,*d*
  and let us return to the LORD.*e*

41Let us lift up our hearts and our hands
  to God in heaven,*f* and say:

42"We have sinned and rebelled*g*
  and you have not forgiven.*h*

43"You have covered yourself with anger and pursued us;
  you have slain without pity.*i*

44You have covered yourself with a cloud*j*
  so that no prayer*k* can get through.

45You have made us scum*l* and refuse
  among the nations.

46"All our enemies have opened their mouths
  wide against us.*m*

47We have suffered terror and pitfalls,*n*
  ruin and destruction.*o*"

48Streams of tears flow from my eyes*p*
  because my people are destroyed.*q*

49My eyes will flow unceasingly,
  without relief,*r*

50until the LORD looks down
  from heaven and sees.*s*

51What I see brings grief to my soul
  because of all the women of my city.

52Those who were my enemies without cause
  hunted me like a bird.*t*

53They tried to end my life in a pit*u*
  and threw stones at me;

54the waters closed over my head,*v*
  and I thought I was about to be cut off.

55I called on your name, O LORD,
  from the depths of the pit.*w*

56You heard my plea:*x* "Do not close your ears
  to my cry for relief."

57You came near when I called you,
  and you said, "Do not fear."*y*

3:37 *a* Ps 33:9-11

3:38 *b* Job 2:10; Isa 45:7; Jer 32:42

3:39 *c* Jer 30:15; Mic 7:9

3:40 *d* 2Co 13:5 *e* Ps 119:59; 139:23-24

3:41 *f* Ps 25:1; 28:2

3:42 *g* Da 9:5 *h* Jer 5:7-9

3:43 *i* La 2:2,17,21

3:44 *j* Ps 97:2 *k* ver 8

3:45 *l* 1Co 4:13

3:46 *m* La 2:16

3:47 *n* Jer 48:43 *o* Isa 24:17-18; 51:19

3:48 *p* La 1:16, *q* La 2:11

3:49 *r* Jer 14:17

3:50 *s* Isa 63:15

3:52 *t* Ps 35:7

3:53 *u* Jer 37:16

3:54 *v* Ps 69:2; Jnh 2:3-5

3:55 *w* Ps 130:1; Jnh 2:2

3:56 *x* Ps 55:1

3:57 *y* Isa 41:10

⁵⁸O Lord, you took up my case;^a
    you redeemed my life.^b
⁵⁹You have seen, O LORD, the wrong done to me.^c
    Uphold my cause!
⁶⁰You have seen the depth of their vengeance,
    all their plots against me.^d

⁶¹O LORD, you have heard their insults,
    all their plots against me—
⁶²what my enemies whisper and mutter
    against me all day long.^e
⁶³Look at them! Sitting or standing,
    they mock me in their songs.

⁶⁴Pay them back what they deserve, O LORD,
    for what their hands have done.^f
⁶⁵Put a veil over their hearts,^g
    and may your curse be on them!
⁶⁶Pursue them in anger and destroy them
    from under the heavens of the LORD.

Chapter 4 Theme

4^a How the gold has lost its luster,
    the fine gold become dull!
The sacred gems are scattered
    at the head of every street.^h

²How the precious sons of Zion,
    once worth their weight in gold,
are now considered as pots of clay,
    the work of a potter's hands!

³Even jackals offer their breasts
    to nurse their young,
but my people have become heartless
    like ostriches in the desert.ⁱ

⁴Because of thirst the infant's tongue
    sticks to the roof of its mouth;^j
the children beg for bread,
    but no one gives it to them.^k

⁵Those who once ate delicacies
    are destitute in the streets.
Those nurtured in purple^l
    now lie on ash heaps.^m

3:58
a Jer 51:36
b Ps 34:22;
Jer 50:34

3:59
c Jer 18:19-20

3:60
d Jer 11:20;
18:18

3:62
e Eze 36:3

3:64
f Ps 28:4

3:65
g Isa 6:10

4:1
h Eze 7:19

4:3
i Job 39:16

4:4
j Ps 22:15
k La 2:11,12

4:5
l Jer 6:2
m Am 6:3-7

---

^a This chapter is an acrostic poem, the verses of which begin with the successive letters of the Hebrew alphabet.

⁶The punishment of my people
    is greater than that of Sodom,ᵃ
which was overthrown in a moment
    without a hand turned to help her.

⁷Their princes were brighter than snow
    and whiter than milk,
their bodies more ruddy than rubies,
    their appearance like sapphires.ᵃ

⁸But now they are blackerᵇ than soot;
    they are not recognized in the streets.
Their skin has shriveled on their bones;ᶜ
    it has become as dry as a stick.

⁹Those killed by the sword are better off
    than those who die of famine;
racked with hunger, they waste away
    for lack of food from the field.ᵈ

¹⁰With their own hands compassionate women
    have cooked their own children,ᵉ
who became their food
    when my people were destroyed.

¹¹The Lᴏʀᴅ has given full vent to his wrath;
    he has poured out his fierce anger.
He kindled a fireᶠ in Zion
    that consumed her foundations.ᵍ

¹²The kings of the earth did not believe,
    nor did any of the world's people,
that enemies and foes could enter
    the gates of Jerusalem.ʰ

¹³But it happened because of the sins of her prophets
    and the iniquities of her priests,ⁱ
who shed within her
    the blood of the righteous.

¹⁴Now they grope through the streets
    like men who are blind.ʲ
They are so defiled with bloodᵏ
    that no one dares to touch their garments.

¹⁵"Go away! You are unclean!" men cry to them.
    "Away! Away! Don't touch us!"
When they flee and wander about,

---

a 7 Or *lapis lazuli*

4:6
ᵃGe 19:25

4:8
ᵇJob 30:28
ᶜPs 102:3-5

4:9
ᵈJer 15:2; 16:4

4:10
ᵉLev 26:29;
Dt 28:53-57;
Jer 19:9;
La 2:20;
Eze 5:10

4:11
ᶠJer 17:27
ᵍDt 32:22;
Jer 7:20;
Eze 22:31

4:12
ʰ1Ki 9:9;
Jer 21:13

4:13
ⁱJer 5:31; 6:13;
Eze 22:28;
Mic 3:11

4:14
ʲIsa 59:10
ᵏJer 2:34; 19:4

4:15
a Lev 13:46

4:16
b Isa 9:14-16
c La 5:12

4:17
d Isa 20:5;
Eze 29:16
e La 1:7
f Jer 37:7

4:18
g Eze 7:2-12;
Am 8:2

4:19
h Dt 28:49
i Isa 5:26-28

4:20
j 2Sa 19:21
k Jer 39:5;
Eze 12:12-13;
19:4,8

4:21
l Jer 25:15
m Isa 34:6-10;
Am 1:11-12;
Ob 16

4:22
n Isa 40:2;
Jer 33:8
o Ps 137:7;
Mal 1:4

5:1
p Ps 44:13-16;
89:50

5:2
q Ps 79:1
r Zep 1:13

5:3
s Jer 15:8; 18:21

5:4
t Isa 3:1

people among the nations say,
"They can stay here no longer."*a*

¹⁶The LORD himself has scattered them;
he no longer watches over them.*b*
The priests are shown no honor,
the elders*c* no favor.

¹⁷Moreover, our eyes failed,
looking in vain*d* for help;*e*
from our towers we watched
for a nation*f* that could not save us.

¹⁸Men stalked us at every step,
so we could not walk in our streets.
Our end was near, our days were numbered,
for our end had come.*g*

¹⁹Our pursuers were swifter
than eagles*h* in the sky;
they chased us*i* over the mountains
and lay in wait for us in the desert.

²⁰The LORD's anointed,*j* our very life breath,
was caught in their traps.*k*
We thought that under his shadow
we would live among the nations.

²¹Rejoice and be glad, O Daughter of Edom,
you who live in the land of Uz.
But to you also the cup*l* will be passed;
you will be drunk and stripped naked.*m*

²²O Daughter of Zion, your punishment will end;*n*
he will not prolong your exile.
But, O Daughter of Edom, he will punish your sin
and expose your wickedness.*o*

Chapter 5 Theme

5 Remember, O LORD, what has happened to us;
look, and see our disgrace.*p*
²Our inheritance*q* has been turned over to aliens,
our homes*r* to foreigners.
³We have become orphans and fatherless,
our mothers like widows.*s*
⁴We must buy the water we drink;
our wood can be had only at a price.*t*

⁵Those who pursue us are at our heels;
  we are weary*a* and find no rest.
⁶We submitted to Egypt and Assyria*b*
  to get enough bread.
⁷Our fathers sinned and are no more,
  and we bear their punishment.*c*
⁸Slaves*d* rule over us,
  and there is none to free us from their hands.*e*
⁹We get our bread at the risk of our lives
  because of the sword in the desert.
¹⁰Our skin is hot as an oven,
  feverish from hunger.*f*
¹¹Women have been ravished*g* in Zion,
  and virgins in the towns of Judah.
¹²Princes have been hung up by their hands;
  elders are shown no respect.*h*
¹³Young men toil at the millstones;
  boys stagger under loads of wood.
¹⁴The elders are gone from the city gate;
  the young men have stopped their music.*i*
¹⁵Joy is gone from our hearts;
  our dancing has turned to mourning.*j*
¹⁶The crown*k* has fallen from our head.
  Woe to us, for we have sinned!*l*
¹⁷Because of this our hearts*m* are faint,
  because of these things our eyes*n* grow dim
¹⁸for Mount Zion, which lies desolate,*o*
  with jackals prowling over it.

¹⁹You, O LORD, reign forever;
  your throne endures*p* from generation to generation.
²⁰Why do you always forget us?*q*
  Why do you forsake us so long?
²¹Restore*r* us to yourself, O LORD, that we may return;
  renew our days as of old
²²unless you have utterly rejected us
  and are angry with us beyond measure.*s*

5:5
a Ne 9:37

5:6
b Hos 9:3

5:7
c Jer 14:20;
16:12

5:8
d Ne 5:15
e Zec 11:6

5:10
f La 4:8-9

5:11
g Zec 14:2

5:12
h La 4:16

5:14
i Isa 24:8;
Jer 7:34

5:15
j Jer 25:10

5:16
k Ps 89:39
l Isa 3:11

5:17
m Isa 1:5,
n Ps 6:7

5:18
o Mic 3:12

5:19
p Ps 45:6;
102:12,24-27

5:20
q Ps 13:1; 44:24

5:21
r Ps 80:3

5:22
s Isa 64:9

Theme of Lamentations:

SEGMENT DIVISIONS	CHAPTER THEMES
1	
2	
3	
4	
5	

Author:

Date:

Purpose:

Key Words:

  how, what

  Zion (Jerusalem, the city)

  anger (wrath)

  sin, punishment (wickedness)

  destroy, tear down (destroyed, destruction)

  affliction

  desolate (destitute, without help)

EZEKIEL

*I*n 622 B.C. the book of the law was found in the house of the Lord. When it was brought to King Josiah, he wept, for he saw the awfulness of Judah's sin and knew that God's wrath burned against them. Although Josiah was determined that Judah would walk after the Lord and keep his commandments, the prophetess Huldah told him that after his death God would have to bring judgment upon Judah, for they had forsaken God and burned incense to other gods (see 2 Kings 22).

God's judgment on Judah began when King Josiah tried to stop Pharaoh Neco, king of Egypt, on his way to Carchemish on the Euphrates in 609 B.C. (see 2 Chronicles 35:20-27). Neco killed Josiah on the plain of Megiddo. Then four years later, in 605 B.C., Neco was defeated at Carchemish by Nebuchadnezzar, king of Babylon (see Jeremiah 46:2).

Ezekiel was eighteen years old when a handful of the nobles and princes were captured by King Nebuchadnezzar and taken from Judah to Babylon. Among them was a fifteen-year-old boy named Daniel, and his three friends, Hananiah, Mishael, and Azariah. Ezekiel, however, was left behind. At age 30 he would be eligible for the priesthood and would spend his life in service to God in the temple at Jerusalem. Or so it seemed.

For over ten years things were relatively quiet in Judah. The prophets were bringing good news prophesying peace. The people loved it and continued in their sin. Only one lonely voice disturbed their peace—the voice of Jeremiah.

Then Jehoiakim, king of Judah, rebelled against Nebuchadnezzar (2 Kings 23:36–24:4). When Jehoiakim died, Jehoiachin became king, and in 597 B.C. Nebuchadnezzar once again besieged Jerusalem. This time 10,000 people were taken captive into Babylon and Ezekiel, who would soon have been eligible for the priesthood, was among them. Never again would he see Jerusalem or the temple where he was to serve. Both would be destroyed by Nebuchadnezzar in 586 B.C.

But Ezekiel would see another temple and another Jerusalem—one which would be called Jehovah-shammah, the Lord is there! At age 30, Ezekiel had a vision.

⮕ THINGS TO DO

In order to understand the depth and magnitude of the book of Ezekiel, you need to study it again and again. However, if you do the following, you will gain a good understanding of the message of Ezekiel.

General Instructions

1. Ezekiel has many references to time. These are important and need to be marked in a distinctive way with a color and/or symbol. Ezekiel 1:1, 2 establishes the historical setting of Ezekiel's ministry. The other references to time give you the historical timing of his visions and prophecies.

   a. Every time you mark references to time look at the calendar on page 1416 at the beginning of Ezekiel 1 to see what month Ezekiel is referring to. (Follow the sacred calendar highlighted in black.)

   b. Ezekiel 1:2 is a parenthesis and serves as an explanation of the timing of verse 2. Read 2 Kings 24:8 through 25:21 for a good overview of the historical setting. This will help you understand the timing of Ezekiel's prophecies.

      1) As you read, look for Jehoiachin's name, mark it in a distinctive way, and watch when he goes into exile. Also note who is made king when Jehoiachin goes into exile.

      2) In the margins of 2 Kings 24, 25, record the dates of Jerusalem's first, second, and third sieges. (Jehoiachin was taken captive when Nebuchadnezzar besieged Jerusalem the second time.) The first siege is recorded in 2 Kings 24:1-7 and occurred in 605 B.C. The second siege is recorded

EZEKIEL

in 2 Kings 24:10-16 and occurred in 597 B.C. (Ezekiel was taken captive during the second siege.) The third and final siege is recorded in 2 Kings 25:1-21. It began in 588 B.C. and in 586 B.C. the city was captured and destroyed.

3) Read Ezekiel 1:1-3 and record what you learn about Ezekiel under "Author" on the EZEKIEL AT A GLANCE chart on page 1498.

4) Now read Numbers 4:3 and observe at what age a man began his priestly service. Then look at Ezekiel 1 and compare this with the way Ezekiel is described and the year he had his first visions from God. Verse 2 tells you what year it was in relationship to the second siege of Jerusalem, the year when Jehoiachin went into exile.

2. Now that you have the historical setting, as you read the dates of all the other visions or prophecies in Ezekiel, you can know that the dates are calculated from the time of Jehoiachin's and Ezekiel's exile in 597 B.C.

3. Key repeated words and phrases to mark throughout the book are listed on EZEKIEL AT A GLANCE. Write them on an index card, color code each in a distinctive way, and then use the card as a bookmark while you study Ezekiel.

Chapters 1-3: Ezekiel's Call

1. Read chapters 1 through 3 and mark the key repeated words.

2. As you go through these chapters one at a time, interrogate the text with the five W's and an H. Ask questions such as: What does Ezekiel see? How are they described? Where are they? Where is Ezekiel? What is he told to do? Why is he told to do it? When is Ezekiel to speak?

3. In the margin of each chapter record your observations. Note what Ezekiel is called to do and how he is to do it. Also note to whom he is sent and why.

4. In summary form list everything you observe from the text about Ezekiel, the people to whom he was sent, and the glory of the Lord.

5. Record the theme of each chapter on EZEKIEL AT A GLANCE and in the text next to the chapter number.

Chapters 4-24: Prophecies about Judah and Jerusalem

1. Read through this segment one chapter at a time. On the first reading of a chapter, mark every reference to the time of a vision. Also mark the key words that are on your bookmark.

    a. Watch for and mark the phrase know that I am the Lord (know that I the Lord made them). This is a key phrase used throughout the remainder of Ezekiel, so add this to your bookmark. Every time you see this phrase, in the margin note who is going to know and how they will know it.

    b. When you mark Spirit, heart (hearts, courage), and the glory of the God of Israel (the glory of the Lord), list in the margin what you learn about each from that chapter.

    c. Add covenant (treaty) to your list of key words. When they are used in a chapter, list what you learn about them in the margin. Also watch for additional key repeated words.

2. Now read through each chapter again. Watch for every reference to the son of man. In the margin note God's instructions to Ezekiel, the son of man. Note to whom or to what he was to speak and how. Note whether it was by symbolic acts, messages, visions, parables, or signs. Also note why he was to speak in that way and the significance of his action. Also notice when Ezekiel's mouth is shut and then later opened. This is important.

3. Record the theme of each chapter as you have done previously.

EZEKIEL

Chapters 25-32: Prophecies about the Nations

1. Read through this segment one chapter at a time. On the first reading mark the key words. When you mark the phrases *know that I am the Lord* and *know that I am the Sovereign Lord,* note in the margin who is going to know and how they will know it.

2. On the second reading of the chapter, identify and record in the margin the nation to whom the prophecy is given and the ruler—if he is mentioned. Also observe and note what will happen to the nation and why.

3. Make sure you note or mark *when* the word of the Lord came to Ezekiel.

4. Record the theme of each chapter as you have done previously.

Chapters 33-39: Prophecies about Israel's Restoration

1. Read each chapter and once again:

   a. Mark every reference to time. Do not miss when the visions or prophecies were given to Ezekiel.

   b. Mark every key word. In the margin list what you learn from marking *covenant* and then compare it with what you observed about covenant in Ezekiel 16 and 17.

   c. Continue noting the same observations from marking every occurrence of *know that I am the Lord* or *know that I the Lord am the Holy One.* Also list what you learn about the *Spirit, heart (hearts, courage),* and *the glory of the God of Israel (the glory of the Lord).*

2. Read the chapter again. List God's instructions to Ezekiel ("the son of man"). Note to whom or to what he was to speak and what the message was to be. As you look at the prophecy, list what is going to happen, to whom or what it will happen, and when it will happen. Put a symbol next to any indication of timing. Also note any symbolic acts he was to perform and why.

3. List the theme of each chapter as before.

Chapters 40-48: Prophecies about the Temple

1. As you begin observing this final segment, read 40:1-5. In a distinctive way, mark when this final vision is given. Then in the margin list who gives it, how, where, and what Ezekiel is to do.

2. Read each chapter carefully and do the following:

   a. Mark key words as before; however, add to your list *temple (sanctuary, house, wall), holy (sacred), offering (offerings, special gift),* and *gate (gateways, entrance, gateposts).* The phrase "know that I am the Lord" is not used in this final segment.

   b. Watch for and record the reason for the vision of the temple and its measurements. Also note what you learn about *the glory of the Lord* and *the Spirit,* and their relationship to the temple or sanctuary. Compare this with what you saw in Ezekiel 8 through 11.

   c. Warning: This last segment of Ezekiel may seem a little boring after the first 39 chapters. Don't get bogged down in all the temple measurements. Don't miss the last verse of Ezekiel, since it names the city.

   d. In the margin list the main points, instructions, or events of each chapter.

3. Record the theme of these chapters as you have done before. Then complete EZEKIEL AT A GLANCE. Go back to each vision Ezekiel had, note the year when it occurred, and from your calendar on page 1416 record the name of the month and the day. (Follow the sacred calendar highlighted in black.) Then transfer this information to the segment division portion of EZEKIEL AT A GLANCE.

∿ THINGS TO THINK ABOUT

1. As you think about God's call upon Ezekiel's life, what do you see about Ezekiel's responsibility as a watchman that you could apply to your own life? If the people wouldn't listen, was Ezekiel still to

speak (Ezekiel 2, 3, 33)? Remember that the things in the Old Testament were written for our example, encouragement, and endurance (1 Corinthians 10:6, 11 and Romans 15:4).

2. Before Ezekiel ever shared God's message he was told to eat it, to take it to heart, and to listen closely to the Lord (Ezekiel 3). What lessons can you learn from his example? How would what you are doing in this inductive study Bible help you? What do you need to remember as you work your way through the Bible?

3. What have you learned about God and his ways from studying Ezekiel? God took Israel as his wife. Christians are espoused to Jesus Christ, their heavenly Bridegroom (2 Corinthians 11:2, 3). Have you, like Israel, played the prostitute spiritually and grieved God's heart (Ezekiel 6:9; James 4:4)? If so, what do you need to do? If not, what should you do so that you never do?

4. In Ezekiel 20:33 God tells Israel, "As surely as I live, I will rule over you with a mighty hand and an outstretched arm and with outpoured wrath." Think about this verse in the light of the character and position of God and in the light of Philippians 2:5-11. Have you genuinely confessed Jesus Christ as your Lord, your King who has a right to rule over you?

5. Think about what you have observed from marking the word *covenant*. What have you learned about the heart of stone and the Spirit dwelling within (Ezekiel 36)? Read 2 Corinthians 3 and see how this parallels what Ezekiel says. Do you have a heart of stone or a heart of flesh? Where is the Spirit of God in relationship to you? Is he within? Read Ezekiel 36:26, 27.

6. What have you learned about prophecy from Ezekiel that you could use in sharing God's Word with the Jews? What about the prophecies of Ezekiel 36 and 37 and the way they already are being fulfilled? And what do you learn about Israel's future in respect to Ezekiel 38 through 39? This is of great interest to Jews.

7. What have you learned about the holiness of God? What effect will it have on your life?

Chapter 1 Theme

1 In the[a] thirtieth year, in the fourth month on the fifth day, while I was among the exiles[a] by the Kebar River, the heavens were opened[b] and I saw visions[c] of God.

593 B.C.

[2] On the fifth of the month—it was the fifth year of the exile of King Jehoiachin[d]— [3] the word of the LORD came to Ezekiel the priest, the son of Buzi,[b] by the Kebar River in the land of the Babylonians.[c] There the hand of the LORD was upon him.[e]

[4] I looked, and I saw a windstorm coming out of the north[f]—an immense cloud with flashing lightning and surrounded by brilliant light. The center of the fire looked like glowing metal,[g] [5] and in the fire was what looked like four living creatures.[h] In appearance their form was that of a man,[i] [6] but each of them had four faces[j] and four wings. [7] Their legs were straight; their feet were like those of a calf and gleamed like burnished bronze.[k] [8] Under their wings on their four sides they had the hands of a man.[l] All four of them had faces and wings, [9] and their wings touched one another. Each one went straight ahead; they did not turn as they moved.[m]

INSIGHT

According to Numbers 4:3, men entered the priestly service at the age of thirty.

### Cross references (margin)

1:1
a Eze 11:24-25
b Mt 3:16; Ac 7:56
c Ex 24:10

1:2
d 2Ki 24:15

1:3
e 2Ki 3:15; Eze 3:14,22

1:4
f Jer 1:14
g Eze 8:2

1:5
h Rev 4:6
i ver 26

1:6
j Eze 10:14

1:7
k Da 10:6; Rev 1:15

1:8
l Eze 10:8

1:9
m Eze 10:22

a 1 Or ⌊my⌋   b 3 Or *Ezekiel son of Buzi the priest*   c 3 Or *Chaldeans*

The Jewish Calendar

Babylonian names (B) for the months are still used today for the Jewish calendar. Canaanite names (C) were used prior to the Babylonian captivity in 586 B.C. Four are mentioned in the Old Testament. **Adar-Sheni** is an intercalary month used every two to three years or seven times in 19 years.

1st month	2nd month	3rd month	4th month
Nisan (B) Abib (C) March-April	Iyyar (B) Ziv (C) April-May	Sivan (B) May-June	Tammuz (B) June-July
7th month	*8th month*	*9th month*	*10th month*
5th month	**6th month**	**7th month**	**8th month**
Ab (B) July-August	Elul (B) August-September	Tishri (B) Ethanim (C) September-October	Marcheshvan (B) Bul (C) October-November
11th month	*12th month*	*1st month*	*2nd month*
9th month	**10th month**	**11th month**	**12th month**
Chislev (B) November-December	Tebeth (B) December-January	Shebat (B) January-February	Adar (B) February-March
3rd month	*4th month*	*5th month*	*6th month*

Sacred calendar appears in black • Civil calendar appears in gray

¹⁰Their faces looked like this: Each of the four had the face of a man, and on the right side each had the face of a lion, and on the left the face of an ox; each also had the face of an eagle.ᵃ ¹¹Such were their faces. Their wingsᵇ were spread out upward; each had two wings, one touching the wing of another creature on either side, and two wings covering its body. ¹²Each one went straight ahead. Wherever the spirit would go, they would go, without turning as they went. ¹³The appearance of the living creatures was like burning coals of fire or like torches. Fire moved back and forth among the creatures; it was bright, and lightningᶜ flashed out of it. ¹⁴The creatures sped back and forth like flashes of lightning.ᵈ

¹⁵As I looked at the living creatures, I saw a wheel on the ground beside each creature with its four faces. ¹⁶This was the appearance and structure of the wheels: They sparkled like chrysolite,ᵉ and all four looked alike. Each appeared to be made like a wheel intersecting a wheel. ¹⁷As they moved, they would go in any one of the four directions the creatures faced; the wheels did not turnᶠ aboutᵃ as the creatures went. ¹⁸Their rims were high and awesome, and all four rims were full of eyesᵍ all around.

¹⁹When the living creatures moved, the wheels beside them moved; and when the living creatures rose from the ground, the wheels also rose. ²⁰Wherever the spirit would go, they would go,ʰ and the wheels would rise along with them, because the spirit of the living creatures was in the wheels. ²¹When the creatures moved, they also moved; when the creatures stood still, they also stood still; and when the creatures rose from the ground, the wheels rose along with them, because the spirit of the living creatures was in the wheels.ⁱ

ᵃ17 Or *aside*

1:10
ᵃEze 10:14;
Rev 4:7

1:11
ᵇIsa 6:2

1:13
ᶜRev 4:5

1:14
ᵈPs 29:7

1:16
ᵉEze 10:9-11;
Da 10:6

1:17
ᶠver 9

1:18
ᵍEze 10:12;
Rev 4:6

1:20
ʰver 12

1:21
ⁱEze 10:17

THE RULERS AND PROPHETS OF EZEKIEL'S TIME

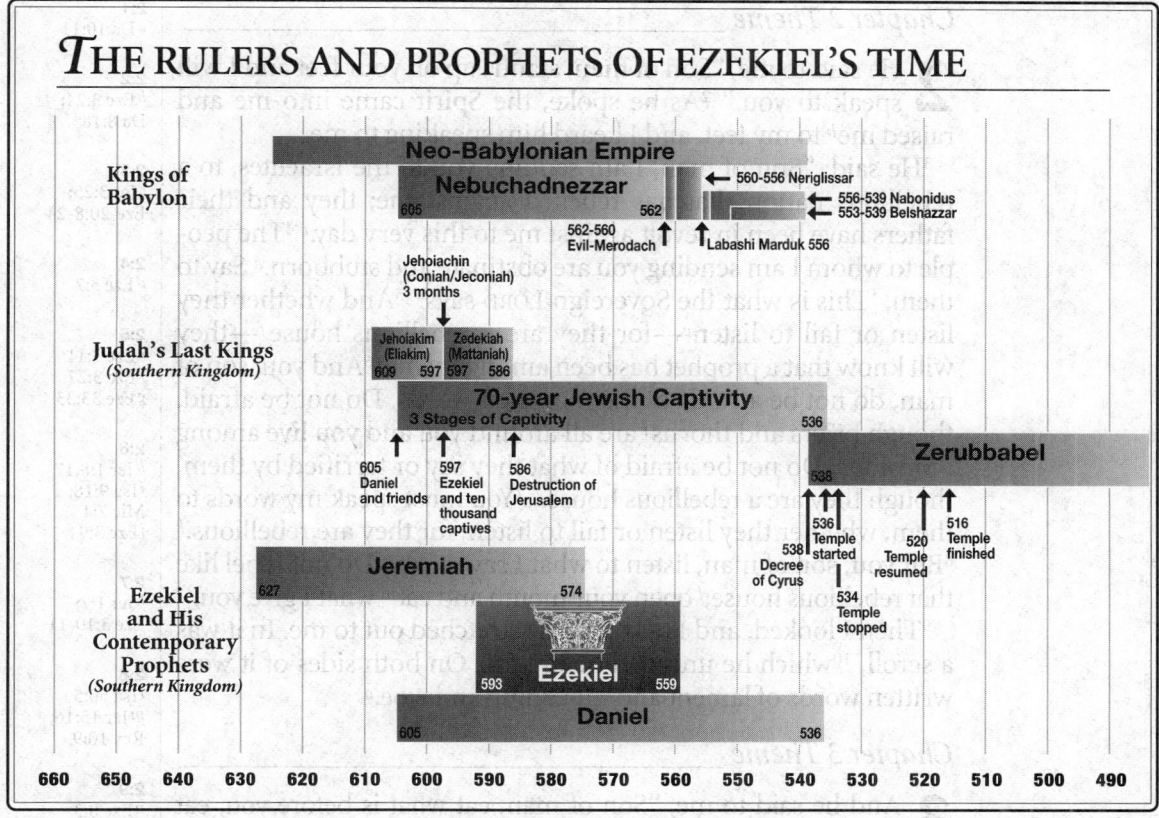

Kings of Babylon

Neo-Babylonian Empire

Nebuchadnezzar — 605 — 562

560-556 Neriglissar
556-539 Nabonidus
553-539 Belshazzar

562-560 Evil-Merodach
Labashi Marduk 556

Judah's Last Kings *(Southern Kingdom)*

Jehoiachin (Coniah/Jeconiah) 3 months

Jehoiakim (Eliakim) 609 — 597
Zedekiah (Mattaniah) 597 — 586

70-year Jewish Captivity
3 Stages of Captivity — 536

605 Daniel and friends
597 Ezekiel and ten thousand captives
586 Destruction of Jerusalem

Zerubbabel — 538

538 Decree of Cyrus
536 Temple started
534 Temple stopped
520 Temple resumed
516 Temple finished

Ezekiel and His Contemporary Prophets *(Southern Kingdom)*

Jeremiah 627 — 574

Ezekiel 593 — 559

Daniel 605 — 536

660 650 640 630 620 610 600 590 580 570 560 550 540 530 520 510 500 490

1:22
aEze 10:1

1:24
bEze 10:5; 43:2; Da 10:6; Rev 1:15; 19:6
c2Ki 7:6

1:26
dEx 24:10; Eze 10:1
eRev 1:13

1:27
fEze 8:2

1:28
gGe 9:13; Rev 10:1
hRev 4:2
iEze 8:4
jEze 3:23; Da 8:17; Rev 1:17

22Spread out above the heads of the living creatures was what looked like an expanse,a sparkling like ice, and awesome. 23Under the expanse their wings were stretched out one toward the other, and each had two wings covering its body. 24When the creatures moved, I heard the sound of their wings, like the roar of rushing waters, like the voiceb of the Almighty,a like the tumult of an army.c When they stood still, they lowered their wings.

25Then there came a voice from above the expanse over their heads as they stood with lowered wings. 26Above the expanse over their heads was what looked like a throne of sapphire,bd and high above on the throne was a figure like that of a man.e 27I saw that from what appeared to be his waist up he looked like glowing metal, as if full of fire, and that from there down he looked like fire; and brilliant light surrounded him.f 28Like the appearance of a rainbowg in the clouds on a rainy day, so was the radiance around him.h

This was the appearance of the likeness of the gloryi of the LORD. When I saw it, I fell facedown,j and I heard the voice of one speaking.

a24 Hebrew *Shaddai*   b26 Or *lapis lazuli*

2:1
a Da 10:11

2:2
b Eze 3:24;
Da 8:18

2:3
c Jer 3:25;
Eze 20:8-24

2:4
d Eze 3:7

2:5
e Eze 3:11
f Eze 3:27
g Eze 33:33

2:6
h Jer 1:8,17
i Isa 9:18;
Mic 7:4
j Eze 3:9

2:7
k Jer 1:7;
Eze 3:10-11

2:8
l Isa 50:5
m Jer 15:16;
Rev 10:9

2:9
n Eze 8:3

2:10
o Rev 8:13

3:3
p Jer 15:16
q Ps 19:10;
Ps 119:103;
Rev 10:9-10

3:5
r Isa 28:11;
Jnh 1:2

3:6
s Mt 11:21-23

3:7
t Eze 2:4;
Jn 15:20-23

3:8
u Jer 1:18

3:9
v Isa 50:7;
Eze 2:6; Mic 3:8

3:11
w Eze 2:4-5,7

Chapter 2 Theme

2 He said to me, "Son of man, stand[a] up on your feet and I will speak to you." [2]As he spoke, the Spirit came into me and raised me[b] to my feet, and I heard him speaking to me.

[3]He said: "Son of man, I am sending you to the Israelites, to a rebellious nation that has rebelled against me; they and their fathers have been in revolt against me to this very day.[c] [4]The people to whom I am sending you are obstinate and stubborn.[d] Say to them, 'This is what the Sovereign LORD says.' [5]And whether they listen or fail to listen[e]—for they are a rebellious house[f]—they will know that a prophet has been among them.[g] [6]And you, son of man, do not be afraid[h] of them or their words. Do not be afraid, though briers and thorns[i] are all around you and you live among scorpions. Do not be afraid of what they say or terrified by them, though they are a rebellious house.[j] [7]You must speak my words to them, whether they listen or fail to listen, for they are rebellious.[k] [8]But you, son of man, listen to what I say to you. Do not rebel like that rebellious house;[l] open your mouth and eat[m] what I give you."

[9]Then I looked, and I saw a hand[n] stretched out to me. In it was a scroll, [10]which he unrolled before me. On both sides of it were written words of lament and mourning and woe.[o]

Chapter 3 Theme

3 And he said to me, "Son of man, eat what is before you, eat this scroll; then go and speak to the house of Israel." [2]So I opened my mouth, and he gave me the scroll to eat.

[3]Then he said to me, "Son of man, eat this scroll I am giving you and fill your stomach with it." So I ate[p] it, and it tasted as sweet as honey[q] in my mouth.

[4]He then said to me: "Son of man, go now to the house of Israel and speak my words to them. [5]You are not being sent to a people of obscure speech and difficult language,[r] but to the house of Israel— [6]not to many peoples of obscure speech and difficult language, whose words you cannot understand. Surely if I had sent you to them, they would have listened to you.[s] [7]But the house of Israel is not willing to listen to you because they are not willing to listen to me, for the whole house of Israel is hardened and obstinate.[t] [8]But I will make you as unyielding and hardened as they are.[u] [9]I will make your forehead like the hardest stone, harder than flint. Do not be afraid of them or terrified by them, though they are a rebellious house.[v]"

[10]And he said to me, "Son of man, listen carefully and take to heart all the words I speak to you. [11]Go now to your countrymen in exile and speak to them. Say to them, 'This is what the Sovereign LORD says,' whether they listen or fail to listen.[w]"

3:12
a Eze 8:3;
Ac 8:39

3:13
b Eze 1:24;
10:5,16-17

3:15
c Ps 137:1
d Job 2:13

3:16
e Jer 42:7

3:17
f Isa 52:8;
Jer 6:17;
Eze 33:7-9

3:18
g ver 20;
Eze 33:6

3:19
h 2Ki 17:13;
Eze 14:14,20;
Ac 18:6; 20:26;
1Ti 4:14-16

3:20
i Ps 125:5;
Eze 18:24;
33:12,18

3:21
j Ac 20:31

3:22
k Eze 1:3
l Ac 9:6
m Eze 8:4

3:23
n Eze 1:1
o Eze 1:28

3:24
p Eze 2:2

3:25
q Eze 4:8

3:26
r Eze 2:5; 24:27;
33:22

3:27
s ver 11
t Eze 12:3;
24:27; 33:22

4:2
u Jer 6:6

¹²Then the Spirit lifted me up,ᵃ and I heard behind me a loud rumbling sound—May the glory of the LORD be praised in his dwelling place!— ¹³the sound of the wings of the living creatures brushing against each other and the sound of the wheels beside them, a loud rumbling sound.ᵇ ¹⁴The Spirit then lifted me up and took me away, and I went in bitterness and in the anger of my spirit, with the strong hand of the LORD upon me. ¹⁵I came to the exiles who lived at Tel Abib near the Kebar River.ᶜ And there, where they were living, I sat among them for seven daysᵈ—overwhelmed.

¹⁶At the end of seven days the word of the LORD came to me:ᵉ ¹⁷"Son of man, I have made you a watchmanᶠ for the house of Israel; so hear the word I speak and give them warning from me. ¹⁸When I say to a wicked man, 'You will surely die,' and you do not warn him or speak out to dissuade him from his evil ways in order to save his life, that wicked man will die forᵃ his sin, and I will hold you accountable for his blood.ᵍ ¹⁹But if you do warn the wicked man and he does not turn from his wickedness or from his evil ways, he will die for his sin; but you will have saved yourself.ʰ

²⁰"Again, when a righteous man turns from his righteousness and does evil, and I put a stumbling block before him, he will die. Since you did not warn him, he will die for his sin. The righteous things he did will not be remembered, and I will hold you accountable for his blood.ⁱ ²¹But if you do warn the righteous man not to sin and he does not sin, he will surely live because he took warning, and you will have saved yourself.ʲ"

²²The hand of the LORDᵏ was upon me there, and he said to me, "Get up and goˡ out to the plain,ᵐ and there I will speak to you." ²³So I got up and went out to the plain. And the glory of the LORD was standing there, like the glory I had seen by the Kebar River,ⁿ and I fell facedown.ᵒ

²⁴Then the Spirit came into me and raised meᵖ to my feet. He spoke to me and said: "Go, shut yourself inside your house. ²⁵And you, son of man, they will tie with ropes; you will be bound so that you cannot go out among the people.q ²⁶I will make your tongue stick to the roof of your mouth so that you will be silent and unable to rebuke them, though they are a rebellious house.r ²⁷But when I speak to you, I will open your mouth and you shall say to them, 'This is what the Sovereign LORD says.'ˢ Whoever will listen let him listen, and whoever will refuse let him refuse; for they are a rebellious house.ᵗ

Chapter 4 Theme

4 "Now, son of man, take a clay tablet, put it in front of you and draw the city of Jerusalem on it. ²Then lay siege to it: Erect siege works against it, build a rampᵘ up to it, set up camps against it and

---

a 18 Or in; also in verses 19 and 20

put battering rams around it.*a* ³Then take an iron pan, place it as an iron wall between you and the city and turn your face toward it. It will be under siege, and you shall besiege it. This will be a sign*b* to the house of Israel.*c*

⁴"Then lie on your left side and put the sin of the house of Israel upon yourself.*a* You are to bear their sin for the number of days you lie on your side. ⁵I have assigned you the same number of days as the years of their sin. So for 390 days you will bear the sin of the house of Israel.

⁶"After you have finished this, lie down again, this time on your right side, and bear the sin of the house of Judah. I have assigned you 40 days, a day for each year.*d* ⁷Turn your face toward the siege of Jerusalem and with bared arm prophesy against her. ⁸I will tie you up with ropes so that you cannot turn from one side to the other until you have finished the days of your siege.*e*

⁹"Take wheat and barley, beans and lentils, millet and spelt;*f* put them in a storage jar and use them to make bread for yourself. You are to eat it during the 390 days you lie on your side. ¹⁰Weigh out twenty shekels*b* of food to eat each day and eat it at set times. ¹¹Also measure out a sixth of a hin*c* of water and drink it at set times. ¹²Eat the food as you would a barley cake; bake it in the sight of the people, using human excrement*g* for fuel." ¹³The LORD said, "In this way the people of Israel will eat defiled food among the nations where I will drive them."*h*

¹⁴Then I said, "Not so, Sovereign LORD!*i* I have never defiled myself. From my youth until now I have never eaten anything found dead *j* or torn by wild animals. No unclean meat has ever entered my mouth.*k*"

¹⁵"Very well," he said, "I will let you bake your bread over cow manure instead of human excrement."

¹⁶He then said to me: "Son of man, I will cut off*l* the supply of food in Jerusalem. The people will eat rationed food in anxiety and drink rationed water in despair,*m* ¹⁷for food and water will be scarce. They will be appalled at the sight of each other and will waste away because of*d* their sin.*n*

Chapter 5 Theme

5 "Now, son of man, take a sharp sword and use it as a barber's razor*o* to shave*p* your head and your beard.*q* Then take a set of scales and divide up the hair. ²When the days of your siege come to an end, burn a third of the hair with fire inside the city. Take a third and strike it with the sword all around the city. And scatter a third to the wind. For I will pursue them with drawn sword.*r* ³But take a few strands of hair and tuck them away in the

a 4 Or *your side*   *b 10* That is, about 8 ounces (about 0.2 kilogram)   *c 11* That is, about 2/3 quart (about 0.6 liter)   *d 17* Or *away in*

4:2
a Eze 21:22

4:3
b Isa 8:18; 20:3; Eze 12:3-6; 24:24,27
c Jer 39:1

4:6
d Nu 14:34; Da 9:24-26; 12:11-12

4:8
e Eze 3:25

4:9
f Isa 28:25

4:12
g Isa 36:12

4:13
h Hos 9:3

4:14
i Jer 1:6; Eze 9:8; 20:49
j Lev 11:39
k Ex 22:31; Dt 14:3; Ac 10:14

4:16
l Ps 105:16; Eze 5:16
m ver 10-11; Lev 26:26; Isa 3:1; Eze 12:19

4:17
n Lev 26:39; Eze 24:23; 33:10

5:1
o Isa 7:20
p Eze 44:20
q Lev 21:5

5:2
r ver 12; Lev 26:33

folds of your garment.[a] [4]Again, take a few of these and throw them into the fire and burn them up. A fire will spread from there to the whole house of Israel.

[5]"This is what the Sovereign LORD says: This is Jerusalem, which I have set in the center of the nations, with countries all around her. [6]Yet in her wickedness she has rebelled against my laws and decrees more than the nations and countries around her. She has rejected my laws and has not followed my decrees.[b]

[7]"Therefore this is what the Sovereign LORD says: You have been more unruly than the nations around you and have not followed my decrees or kept my laws. You have not even[a] conformed to the standards of the nations around you.[c]

[8]"Therefore this is what the Sovereign LORD says: I myself am against you, Jerusalem, and I will inflict punishment on you in the sight of the nations.[d] [9]Because of all your detestable idols, I will do to you what I have never done before and will never do again.[e] [10]Therefore in your midst fathers will eat their children, and children will eat their fathers.[f] I will inflict punishment on you and will scatter all your survivors to the winds.[g] [11]Therefore as surely as I live, declares the Sovereign LORD, because you have defiled my sanctuary with all your vile images[h] and detestable practices,[i] I myself will withdraw my favor; I will not look on you with pity or spare you.[j] [12]A third of your people will die of the plague or perish by famine inside you; a third will fall by the sword outside your walls; and a third I will scatter to the winds and pursue with drawn sword.[k]

[13]"Then my anger will cease and my wrath[l] against them will subside, and I will be avenged.[m] And when I have spent my wrath upon them, they will know that I the LORD have spoken in my zeal.

[14]"I will make you a ruin and a reproach among the nations around you, in the sight of all who pass by.[n] [15]You will be a reproach and a taunt, a warning and an object of horror to the nations around you when I inflict punishment on you in anger and in wrath and with stinging rebuke.[o] I the LORD have spoken.[p] [16]When I shoot at you with my deadly and destructive arrows of famine, I will shoot to destroy you. I will bring more and more famine upon you and cut off your supply of food.[q] [17]I will send famine and wild beasts against you, and they will leave you childless. Plague and bloodshed[r] will sweep through you, and I will bring the sword against you. I the LORD have spoken.[s]"

Chapter 6 Theme

6 The word of the LORD came to me: [2]"Son of man, set your face against the mountains[t] of Israel; prophesy against them [3]and say: 'O mountains of Israel, hear the word of the Sovereign

---

5:3
[a] Jer 39:10

5:6
[b] Jer 11:10; Eze 16:47-51; Zec 7:11

5:7
[c] 2Ch 33:9; Jer 2:10-11; Eze 16:47

5:8
[d] Eze 15:7

5:9
[e] Da 9:12; Mt 24:21

5:10
[f] Lev 26:29; La 2:20
[g] Lev 26:33; Ps 44:11; Eze 12:14; Zec 2:6

5:11
[h] Eze 7:20
[i] 2Ch 36:14; Eze 8:6
[j] Eze 7:4,9

5:12
[k] ver 2,17; Jer 15:2; 21:9; Eze 6:11-12; 12:14

5:13
[l] Eze 21:17; 36:6
[m] Isa 1:24

5:14
[n] Lev 26:32; Ne 2:17; Ps 74:3-10; 79:1-4

5:15
[o] 1Ki 9:7; Jer 22:8-9; 24:9
[p] Eze 25:17

5:16
[q] Dt 32:24

5:17
[r] Eze 38:22
[s] Eze 14:21

6:2
[t] Eze 36:1

---

[a] 7 Most Hebrew manuscripts; some Hebrew manuscripts and Syriac *You have*

LORD. This is what the Sovereign LORD says to the mountains and hills, to the ravines and valleys:*a* I am about to bring a sword against you, and I will destroy your high places.*b* *4*Your altars will be demolished and your incense altars*c* will be smashed; and I will slay your people in front of your idols. *5*I will lay the dead bodies of the Israelites in front of their idols, and I will scatter your bones*d* around your altars. *6*Wherever you live, the towns will be laid waste and the high places demolished, so that your altars will be laid waste and devastated, your idols*e* smashed and ruined, your incense altars*f* broken down, and what you have made wiped out.*g* *7*Your people will fall slain among you, and you will know that I am the LORD.

8"But I will spare some, for some of you will escape*h* the sword when you are scattered among the lands and nations.*i* *9*Then in the nations where they have been carried captive, those who escape will remember me—how I have been grieved *j* by their adulterous hearts, which have turned away from me, and by their eyes, which have lusted after their idols.*k* They will loathe themselves for the evil they have done and for all their detestable practices.*l* *10*And they will know that I am the LORD; I did not threaten in vain to bring this calamity on them.

11"This is what the Sovereign LORD says: Strike your hands together and stamp your feet and cry out "Alas!" because of all the wicked and detestable practices of the house of Israel, for they will fall by the sword, famine and plague.*m* *12*He that is far away will die of the plague, and he that is near will fall by the sword, and he that survives and is spared will die of famine. So will I spend my wrath upon them.*n* *13*And they will know that I am the LORD, when their people lie slain among their idols around their altars, on every high hill and on all the mountaintops, under every spreading tree and every leafy oak*o*—places where they offered fragrant incense to all their idols.*p* *14*And I will stretch out my hand*q* against them and make the land a desolate waste from the desert to Diblah*a*—wherever they live. Then they will know that I am the LORD.*r*'"

Chapter 7 Theme

7 The word of the LORD came to me: *2*"Son of man, this is what the Sovereign LORD says to the land of Israel: The end!*s* The end has come upon the four corners*t* of the land. *3*The end is now upon you and I will unleash my anger against you. I will judge you according to your conduct and repay you for all your detestable practices. *4*I will not look on you with pity*u* or spare you; I will surely repay you for your conduct and the detestable practices

a 14 Most Hebrew manuscripts; a few Hebrew manuscripts *Riblah*

6:3
a Eze 36:4
b Lev 26:30

6:4
c 2Ch 14:5

6:5
d Jer 8:1-2

6:6
e Mic 1:7;
Zec 13:2
f Lev 26:30
g Isa 6:11;
Eze 5:14

6:8
h Jer 44:28
i Isa 6:13;
Jer 44:14;
Eze 12:16; 14:22

6:9
j Ps 78:40;
Isa 7:13
k Eze 20:7,24
l Eze 20:43;
36:31

6:11
m Eze 5:12;
21:14,17; 25:6

6:12
n Eze 5:12

6:13
o Isa 57:5
p 1Ki 14:23;
Jer 2:20;
Eze 20:28;
Hos 4:13

6:14
q Isa 5:25
r Eze 14:13

7:2
s Am 8:2,10
t Rev 7:1; 20:8

7:4
u Eze 5:11

7:5
a 2Ki 21:12

7:7
b Eze 12:23;
Zep 1:14

7:8
c Isa 42:25;
Eze 9:8; 14:19;
Na 1:6
d Eze 20:8,21;
36:19

7:10
e Ps 89:32;
Isa 10:5

7:11
f Jer 16:6;
Zep 1:18

7:12
g ver 7;
Isa 5:13-14;
Eze 30:3

7:13
h Lev 25:24-28

7:15
i Dt 32:25;
Jer 14:18;
La 1:20;
Eze 5:12

7:16
j Isa 59:11
k Ezr 9:15;
Eze 6:8

7:17
l Isa 13:7;
Eze 21:7; 22:14

7:18
m Ps 55:5
n Isa 15:2-3;
Eze 27:31;
Am 8:10

7:19
o Eze 13:5;
Zep 1:7,18
p Eze 14:3
q Pr 11:4

7:20
r Jer 7:30

7:21
s 2Ki 24:13

7:22
t Eze 39:23-24

7:23
u 2Ki 21:16

among you. Then you will know that I am the LORD.

⁵"This is what the Sovereign LORD says: Disaster!ᵃ An unheard-ofᵃ disaster is coming. ⁶The end has come! The end has come! It has roused itself against you. It has come! ⁷Doom has come upon you—you who dwell in the land. The time has come, the day is near;ᵇ there is panic, not joy, upon the mountains. ⁸I am about to pour out my wrathᶜ on you and spend my anger against you; I will judge you according to your conduct and repay you for all your detestable practices.ᵈ ⁹I will not look on you with pity or spare you; I will repay you in accordance with your conduct and the detestable practices among you. Then you will know that it is I the LORD who strikes the blow.

¹⁰"The day is here! It has come! Doom has burst forth, the rodᵉ has budded, arrogance has blossomed! ¹¹Violence has grown intoᵇ a rod to punish wickedness; none of the people will be left, none of that crowd—no wealth, nothing of value.ᶠ ¹²The time has come, the day has arrived. Let not the buyer rejoice nor the seller grieve, for wrath is upon the whole crowd.ᵍ ¹³The seller will not recover the land he has sold as long as both of them live, for the vision concerning the whole crowd will not be reversed. Because of their sins, not one of them will preserve his life.ʰ ¹⁴Though they blow the trumpet and get everything ready, no one will go into battle, for my wrath is upon the whole crowd.

¹⁵"Outside is the sword, inside are plague and famine; those in the country will die by the sword, and those in the city will be devoured by famine and plague.ⁱ ¹⁶All who survive and escape will be in the mountains, moaning like dovesʲ of the valleys, each because of his sins.ᵏ ¹⁷Every hand will go limp,ˡ and every knee will become as weak as water. ¹⁸They will put on sackcloth and be clothed with terror.ᵐ Their faces will be covered with shame and their heads will be shaved.ⁿ ¹⁹They will throw their silver into the streets, and their gold will be an unclean thing. Their silver and gold will not be able to save them in the day of the LORD's wrath.ᵒ They will not satisfy their hunger or fill their stomachs with it, for it has made them stumbleᵖ into sin.ᵠ ²⁰They were proud of their beautiful jewelry and used it to make their detestable idols and vile images.ʳ Therefore I will turn these into an unclean thing for them. ²¹I will hand it all over as plunder to foreigners and as loot to the wicked of the earth, and they will defile it.ˢ ²²I will turn my faceᵗ away from them, and they will desecrate my treasured place; robbers will enter it and desecrate it.

²³"Prepare chains, because the land is full of bloodshedᵘ and the city is full of violence. ²⁴I will bring the most wicked of the nations

---

ᵃ 5 Most Hebrew manuscripts; some Hebrew manuscripts and Syriac *Disaster after*
ᵇ 11 Or *The violent one has become*

to take possession of their houses; I will put an end to the pride of the mighty, and their sanctuaries[a] will be desecrated.[b] 25When terror comes, they will seek peace, but there will be none.[c] 26Calamity upon calamity[d] will come, and rumor upon rumor. They will try to get a vision from the prophet; the teaching of the law by the priest will be lost, as will the counsel of the elders.[e] 27The king will mourn, the prince will be clothed with despair,[f] and the hands of the people of the land will tremble. I will deal with them according to their conduct,[g] and by their own standards I will judge them. Then they will know that I am the LORD.[h]"

Chapter 8 Theme

592 B.C.

8 In the sixth year, in the sixth month on the fifth day, while I was sitting in my house and the elders[i] of Judah were sitting before[j] me, the hand of the Sovereign LORD came upon me there.[k] 2I looked, and I saw a figure like that of a man.[a] From what appeared to be his waist down he was like fire, and from there up his appearance was as bright as glowing metal.[l] 3He stretched out what looked like a hand and took me by the hair of my head. The Spirit lifted me up[m] between earth and heaven and in visions of God he took me to Jerusalem, to the entrance to the north gate of the inner court, where the idol that provokes to jealousy[n] stood. 4And there before me was the glory[o] of the God of Israel, as in the vision I had seen in the plain.[p]

5Then he said to me, "Son of man, look toward the north." So I looked, and in the entrance north of the gate of the altar I saw this idol[q] of jealousy.

6And he said to me, "Son of man, do you see what they are doing—the utterly detestable[r] things the house of Israel is doing here, things that will drive me far from my sanctuary? But you will see things that are even more detestable."

7Then he brought me to the entrance to the court. I looked, and I saw a hole in the wall. 8He said to me, "Son of man, now dig into the wall." So I dug into the wall and saw a doorway there. 9And he said to me, "Go in and see the wicked and detestable things they are doing here." 10So I went in and looked, and I saw portrayed all over the walls all kinds of crawling things and detestable animals and all the idols of the house of Israel.[s] 11In front of them stood seventy elders of the house of Israel, and Jaazaniah son of Shaphan was standing among them. Each had a censer[t] in his hand, and a fragrant cloud of incense[u] was rising.

12He said to me, "Son of man, have you seen what the elders of the house of Israel are doing in the darkness, each at the shrine of his own idol? They say, 'The LORD does not see[v] us; the LORD has

a2 Or *saw a fiery figure*

7:24 a Eze 24:21; b 2Ch 7:20; Eze 28:7

7:25 c Eze 13:10,16

7:26 d Jer 4:20; e Isa 47:11; Eze 20:1-3; Mic 3:6

7:27 f Ps 109:19; Eze 26:16; g Eze 18:20; h ver 4

8:1 i Eze 14:1; j Eze 33:31; k Eze 1:1-3

8:2 l Eze 1:4,26-27

8:3 m Eze 3:12; 11:1; n Ex 20:5; Dt 32:16

8:4 o Eze 1:28; p Eze 3:22

8:5 q Ps 78:58; Jer 32:34

8:6 r Eze 5:11

8:10 s Ex 20:4

8:11 t Nu 16:17; u Nu 16:35

8:12 v Ps 10:11; Isa 29:15; Eze 9:9

8:16
a Joel 2:17
b Dt 4:19; 17:3;
Job 31:28;
Jer 2:27;
Eze 11:1,12

8:17
c Eze 9:9
d Eze 16:26

8:18
e Eze 9:10; 24:14
f Isa 1:15;
Jer 11:11;
Mic 3:4;
Zec 7:13

9:2
g Lev 16:4;
Eze 10:2;
Rev 15:6

9:3
h Eze 10:4
i Eze 11:22

9:4
j Ex 12:7;
2Co 1:22;
Rev 7:3; 9:4
k Ps 119:136;
Jer 13:17;
Eze 21:6
l Ps 119:53

9:5
m Eze 5:11

9:6
n Eze 8:11-13,16
o 2Ch 36:17;
Jer 25:29;
1Pe 4:17

9:8
p Jos 7:6
q Eze 11:13;
Am 7:1-6

9:9
r Eze 22:29

forsaken the land.'" [13]Again, he said, "You will see them doing things that are even more detestable."

[14]Then he brought me to the entrance to the north gate of the house of the LORD, and I saw women sitting there, mourning for Tammuz. [15]He said to me, "Do you see this, son of man? You will see things that are even more detestable than this."

[16]He then brought me into the inner court of the house of the LORD, and there at the entrance to the temple, between the portico and the altar,[a] were about twenty-five men. With their backs toward the temple of the LORD and their faces toward the east, they were bowing down to the sun in the east.[b]

[17]He said to me, "Have you seen this, son of man? Is it a trivial matter for the house of Judah to do the detestable things they are doing here? Must they also fill the land with violence[c] and continually provoke me to anger?[d] Look at them putting the branch to their nose! [18]Therefore I will deal with them in anger; I will not look on them with pity[e] or spare them. Although they shout in my ears, I will not listen[f] to them."

Chapter 9 Theme

9 Then I heard him call out in a loud voice, "Bring the guards of the city here, each with a weapon in his hand." [2]And I saw six men coming from the direction of the upper gate, which faces north, each with a deadly weapon in his hand. With them was a man clothed in linen[g] who had a writing kit at his side. They came in and stood beside the bronze altar.

[3]Now the glory[h] of the God of Israel went up from above the cherubim,[i] where it had been, and moved to the threshold of the temple. Then the LORD called to the man clothed in linen who had the writing kit at his side [4]and said to him, "Go throughout the city of Jerusalem and put a mark[j] on the foreheads of those who grieve and lament[k] over all the detestable things that are done in it.[l]"

[5]As I listened, he said to the others, "Follow him through the city and kill, without showing pity[m] or compassion. [6]Slaughter old men, young men and maidens, women and children, but do not touch anyone who has the mark. Begin at my sanctuary." So they began with the elders[n] who were in front of the temple.[o]

[7]Then he said to them, "Defile the temple and fill the courts with the slain. Go!" So they went out and began killing throughout the city. [8]While they were killing and I was left alone, I fell facedown,[p] crying out, "Ah, Sovereign LORD! Are you going to destroy the entire remnant of Israel in this outpouring of your wrath on Jerusalem?[q]"

[9]He answered me, "The sin of the house of Israel and Judah is exceedingly great; the land is full of bloodshed and the city is full of injustice.[r] They say, 'The LORD has forsaken the land; the LORD

does not see.'*a* **10**So I will not look on them with pity*b* or spare them, but I will bring down on their own heads what they have done.*c*"

11Then the man in linen with the writing kit at his side brought back word, saying, "I have done as you commanded."

Chapter 10 Theme _____

10 I looked, and I saw the likeness of a throne*d* of sapphire*ae* above the expanse*f* that was over the heads of the cherubim. **2**The LORD said to the man clothed in linen,*g* "Go in among the wheels*h* beneath the cherubim. Fill*i* your hands with burning coals from among the cherubim and scatter them over the city." And as I watched, he went in.

3Now the cherubim were standing on the south side of the temple when the man went in, and a cloud filled the inner court. **4**Then the glory of the LORD*j* rose from above the cherubim and moved to the threshold of the temple. The cloud filled the temple, and the court was full of the radiance of the glory of the LORD. **5**The sound of the wings of the cherubim could be heard as far away as the outer court, like the voice*k* of God Almighty*b* when he speaks.

6When the LORD commanded the man in linen, "Take fire from among the wheels, from among the cherubim," the man went in and stood beside a wheel. **7**Then one of the cherubim reached out his hand to the fire that was among them. He took up some of it and put it into the hands of the man in linen, who took it and went out. **8**(Under the wings of the cherubim could be seen what looked like the hands of a man.)*l*

9I looked, and I saw beside the cherubim four wheels, one beside each of the cherubim; the wheels sparkled like chrysolite.*m* **10**As for their appearance, the four of them looked alike; each was like a wheel intersecting a wheel. **11**As they moved, they would go in any one of the four directions the cherubim faced; the wheels did not turn about*c* as the cherubim went. The cherubim went in whatever direction the head faced, without turning as they went. **12**Their entire bodies, including their backs, their hands and their wings, were completely full of eyes,*n* as were their four wheels.*o* **13**I heard the wheels being called "the whirling wheels." **14**Each of the cherubim*p* had four faces:*q* One face was that of a cherub, the second the face of a man, the third the face of a lion, and the fourth the face of an eagle.*r*

15Then the cherubim rose upward. These were the living creatures*s* I had seen by the Kebar River. **16**When the cherubim moved, the wheels beside them moved; and when the cherubim spread their wings to rise from the ground, the wheels did not leave their side. **17**When the cherubim stood still, they also stood still; and

a1 Or *lapis lazuli*　*b5* Hebrew *El-Shaddai*　*c11* Or *aside*

9:9
a Job 22:13;
Eze 8:12

9:10
b Eze 7:4; 8:18
c Isa 65:6;
Eze 11:21

10:1
d Rev 4:2
e Ex 24:10
f Eze 1:22

10:2
g Eze 9:2
h Eze 1:15
i Rev 8:5

10:4
j Eze 1:28; 9:3

10:5
k Job 40:9;
Eze 1:24

10:8
l Eze 1:8

10:9
m Eze 1:15-16;
Rev 21:20

10:12
n Rev 4:6-8
o Eze 1:15-21

10:14
p 1Ki 7:36
q Eze 1:6
r Eze 1:10;
Rev 4:7

10:15
s Eze 1:3,5

10:17
a Eze 1:20-21

10:18
b Ps 18:10

10:19
c Eze 11:1,22

10:20
d Eze 1:1

10:21
e Eze 41:18
f Eze 1:6

11:1
g Eze 8:16;
10:19; 43:4-5

11:3
h Jer 1:13;
Eze 24:3
i ver 7,11

11:4
j Eze 3:4,17

11:5
k Jer 17:10

11:6
l Eze 7:23; 22:6

11:7
m Eze 24:3-13;
Mic 3:2-3

11:8
n Pr 10:24

11:9
o Ps 106:41
p Dt 28:36;
Eze 5:8

11:10
q 2Ki 14:25

11:11
r ver 3

11:12
s Lev 18:4;
Eze 18:9
t Eze 8:10

when the cherubim rose, they rose with them, because the spirit of the living creatures was in them.a

18Then the glory of the LORD departed from over the threshold of the temple and stopped above the cherubim.b 19While I watched, the cherubim spread their wings and rose from the ground, and as they went, the wheels went with them.c They stopped at the entrance to the east gate of the LORD's house, and the glory of the God of Israel was above them.

20These were the living creatures I had seen beneath the God of Israel by the Kebar River,d and I realized that they were cherubim. 21Each had four facese and four wings,f and under their wings was what looked like the hands of a man. 22Their faces had the same appearance as those I had seen by the Kebar River. Each one went straight ahead.

Chapter 11 Theme _____

11 Then the Spirit lifted me up and brought me to the gate of the house of the LORD that faces east. There at the entrance to the gate were twenty-five men, and I saw among them Jaazaniah son of Azzur and Pelatiah son of Benaiah, leaders of the people.g 2The LORD said to me, "Son of man, these are the men who are plotting evil and giving wicked advice in this city. 3They say, 'Will it not soon be time to build houses?a This city is a cooking pot,h and we are the meat.'i 4Therefore prophesyj against them; prophesy, son of man."

5Then the Spirit of the LORD came upon me, and he told me to say: "This is what the LORD says: That is what you are saying, O house of Israel, but I know what is going through your mind.k 6You have killed many people in this city and filled its streets with the dead.l

7"Therefore this is what the Sovereign LORD says: The bodies you have thrown there are the meat and this city is the pot, but I will drive you out of it.m 8You fear the sword, and the sword is what I will bring against you, declares the Sovereign LORD.n 9I will drive you out of the city and hand you overo to foreigners and inflict punishment on you.p 10You will fall by the sword, and I will execute judgment on you at the borders of Israel.q Then you will know that I am the LORD. 11This city will not be a potr for you, nor will you be the meat in it; I will execute judgment on you at the borders of Israel. 12And you will know that I am the LORD, for you have not followed my decreess or kept my laws but have conformed to the standards of the nations around you.t"

a 3 Or *This is not the time to build houses.*

¹³Now as I was prophesying, Pelatiah*a* son of Benaiah died. Then I fell facedown and cried out in a loud voice, "Ah, Sovereign LORD! Will you completely destroy the remnant of Israel?*b*"

¹⁴The word of the LORD came to me: ¹⁵"Son of man, your brothers—your brothers who are your blood relatives*a* and the whole house of Israel—are those of whom the people of Jerusalem have said, 'They are*b* far away from the LORD; this land was given to us as our possession.'*c*

¹⁶"Therefore say: 'This is what the Sovereign LORD says: Although I sent them far away among the nations and scattered them among the countries, yet for a little while I have been a sanctuary*d* for them in the countries where they have gone.'

¹⁷"Therefore say: 'This is what the Sovereign LORD says: I will gather you from the nations and bring you back from the countries where you have been scattered, and I will give you back the land of Israel again.'*e*

¹⁸"They will return to it and remove all its vile images*f* and detestable idols.*g* ¹⁹I will give them an undivided heart*h* and put a new spirit in them; I will remove from them their heart of stone*i* and give them a heart of flesh.*j* ²⁰Then they will follow my decrees and be careful to keep my laws.*k* They will be my people, and I will be their God.*l* ²¹But as for those whose hearts are devoted to their vile images and detestable idols, I will bring down on their own heads what they have done, declares the Sovereign LORD.*m*"

²²Then the cherubim, with the wheels beside them, spread their wings, and the glory of the God of Israel was above them.*n* ²³The glory*o* of the LORD went up from within the city and stopped above the mountain*p* east of it. ²⁴The Spirit*q* lifted me up and brought me to the exiles in Babylonia*c* in the vision*r* given by the Spirit of God.

Then the vision I had seen went up from me, ²⁵and I told the exiles everything the LORD had shown me.*s*

Chapter 12 Theme

12 The word of the LORD came to me: ²"Son of man, you are living among a rebellious people. They have eyes to see but do not see and ears to hear but do not hear, for they are a rebellious people.*t*

³"Therefore, son of man, pack your belongings for exile and in the daytime, as they watch, set out and go from where you are to another place. Perhaps*u* they will understand,*v* though they are a rebellious house.*w* ⁴During the daytime, while they watch, bring out your belongings packed for exile. Then in the evening, while they are watching, go out like those who go into exile.*x* ⁵While

---

11:13
a ver 1
b Eze 9:8

11:15
c Eze 33:24

11:16
d Ps 90:1; 91:9; Isa 8:14

11:17
e Jer 3:18; 24:5-6; Eze 28:25; 34:13

11:18
f Eze 5:11
g Eze 37:23

11:19
h Jer 32:39
i Zec 7:12
j Eze 18:31; 36:26; 2Co 3:3

11:20
k Ps 105:45
l Eze 14:11; 36:26-28

11:21
m Eze 9:10; 16:43

11:22
n Eze 10:19

11:23
o Eze 8:4; 10:4
p Zec 14:4

11:24
q Eze 8:3
r 2Co 12:2-4

11:25
s Eze 3:4,11

12:2
t Isa 6:10; Eze 2:6-8; Mt 13:15

12:3
u Jer 36:3
v Jer 26:3
w 2Ti 2:25-26

12:4
x ver 12; Jer 39:4

---

a 15 Or *are in exile with you* (see Septuagint and Syriac)   *b* 15 Or *those to whom the people of Jerusalem have said, 'Stay*   *c* 24 Or *Chaldea*

12:6
a ver 12;
Isa 8:18; 20:3;
Eze 4:3; 24:24

12:7
b Eze 24:18;
37:10

12:9
c Eze 17:12;
20:49; 24:19

12:11
d 2Ki 25:7;
Jer 15:2;
52:15

12:12
e Jer 39:4
f Jer 52:7

12:13
g Eze 17:20;
19:8;
Hos 7:12
h Isa 24:17-18
i Jer 39:7
j Jer 52:11;
Eze 17:16

12:14
k 2Ki 25:5;
Eze 5:10,12

12:16
l Jer 22:8-9;
Eze 6:8-10;
14:22

12:18
m La 5:9;
Eze 4:16

12:19
n Eze 6:6-14;
Mic 7:13;
Zec 7:14
o Eze 4:16;
23:33

12:20
p Isa 7:23-24;
Jer 4:7

12:22
q Eze 11:3;
Am 6:3;
2Pe 3:4

12:23
r Ps 37:13;
Joel 2:1;
Zep 1:14

12:24
s Jer 14:14;
Eze 13:23;
Zec 13:2-4

they watch, dig through the wall and take your belongings out through it. ⁶Put them on your shoulder as they are watching and carry them out at dusk. Cover your face so that you cannot see the land, for I have made you a sign*a* to the house of Israel."

⁷So I did as I was commanded.*b* During the day I brought out my things packed for exile. Then in the evening I dug through the wall with my hands. I took my belongings out at dusk, carrying them on my shoulders while they watched.

⁸In the morning the word of the LORD came to me: ⁹"Son of man, did not that rebellious house of Israel ask you, 'What are you doing?'*c*

¹⁰"Say to them, 'This is what the Sovereign LORD says: This oracle concerns the prince in Jerusalem and the whole house of Israel who are there.' ¹¹Say to them, 'I am a sign to you.'

"As I have done, so it will be done to them. They will go into exile as captives.*d*

¹²"The prince among them will put his things on his shoulder at dusk*e* and leave, and a hole will be dug in the wall for him to go through. He will cover his face so that he cannot see the land.*f* ¹³I will spread my net*g* for him, and he will be caught in my snare;*h* I will bring him to Babylonia, the land of the Chaldeans, but he will not see*i* it, and there he will die.*j* ¹⁴I will scatter to the winds all those around him—his staff and all his troops—and I will pursue them with drawn sword.*k*

¹⁵"They will know that I am the LORD, when I disperse them among the nations and scatter them through the countries. ¹⁶But I will spare a few of them from the sword, famine and plague, so that in the nations where they go they may acknowledge all their detestable practices. Then they will know that I am the LORD.*l*"

¹⁷The word of the LORD came to me: ¹⁸"Son of man, tremble as you eat your food,*m* and shudder in fear as you drink your water. ¹⁹Say to the people of the land: 'This is what the Sovereign LORD says about those living in Jerusalem and in the land of Israel: They will eat their food in anxiety and drink their water in despair, for their land will be stripped of everything*n* in it because of the violence of all who live there.*o* ²⁰The inhabited towns will be laid waste and the land will be desolate. Then you will know that I am the LORD.*p*'"

²¹The word of the LORD came to me: ²²"Son of man, what is this proverb you have in the land of Israel: 'The days go by and every vision comes to nothing'?*q* ²³Say to them, 'This is what the Sovereign LORD says: I am going to put an end to this proverb, and they will no longer quote it in Israel.' Say to them, 'The days are near when every vision will be fulfilled.*r* ²⁴For there will be no more false visions or flattering divinations*s* among the people of Israel.

²⁵But I the LORD will speak what I will, and it shall be fulfilled without delay. For in your days, you rebellious house, I will fulfill whatever I say, declares the Sovereign LORD.ᵃ'"

²⁶The word of the LORD came to me: ²⁷"Son of man, the house of Israel is saying, 'The vision he sees is for many years from now, and he prophesies about the distant future.'ᵇ

²⁸"Therefore say to them, 'This is what the Sovereign LORD says: None of my words will be delayed any longer; whatever I say will be fulfilled, declares the Sovereign LORD.'"

Chapter 13 Theme

13 The word of the LORD came to me: ²"Son of man, prophesy against the prophets of Israel who are now prophesying. Say to those who prophesy out of their own imagination: 'Hear the word of the LORD!ᶜ ³This is what the Sovereign LORD says: Woe to the foolishᵃ prophetsᵈ who follow their own spirit and have seen nothing!ᵉ ⁴Your prophets, O Israel, are like jackals among ruins. ⁵You have not gone up to the breaks in the wall to repairᶠ it for the house of Israel so that it will stand firm in the battle on the day of the LORD.ᵍ ⁶Their visions are false and their divinations a lie. They say, "The LORD declares," when the LORD has not sent them; yet they expect their words to be fulfilled.ʰ ⁷Have you not seen false visions and uttered lying divinations when you say, "The LORD declares," though I have not spoken?

⁸"'Therefore this is what the Sovereign LORD says: Because of your false words and lying visions, I am against you, declares the Sovereign LORD. ⁹My hand will be against the prophets who see false visions and utter lying divinations. They will not belong to the council of my people or be listed in the recordsⁱ of the house of Israel, nor will they enter the land of Israel. Then you will know that I am the Sovereign LORD.ʲ

¹⁰"'Because they lead my people astray,ᵏ saying, "Peace," when there is no peace, and because, when a flimsy wall is built, they cover it with whitewash,ˡ ¹¹therefore tell those who cover it with whitewash that it is going to fall. Rain will come in torrents, and I will send hailstones hurtling down, and violent winds will burst forth.ᵐ ¹²When the wall collapses, will people not ask you, "Where is the whitewash you covered it with?"

¹³"'Therefore this is what the Sovereign LORD says: In my wrath I will unleash a violent wind, and in my anger hailstonesⁿ and torrents of rain will fall with destructive fury.ᵒ ¹⁴I will tear down the wall you have covered with whitewash and will level it to the ground so that its foundationᵖ will be laid bare. When itᵇ falls,�q you will

ᵃ3 Or *wicked*   ᵇ14 Or *the city*

12:25
ᵃIsa 14:24;
Hab 1:5

12:27
ᵇDa 10:14

13:2
ᶜver 17;
Jer 23:16; 37:19

13:3
ᵈLa 2:14
ᵉJer 23:25-32

13:5
ᶠIsa 58:12;
Eze 22:30
ᵍEze 7:19

13:6
ʰJer 28:15;
Eze 22:28

13:9
ⁱJer 17:13
ʲEze 20:38

13:10
ᵏJer 50:6
ˡEze 7:25; 22:28

13:11
ᵐEze 38:22

13:13
ⁿRev 11:19;
16:21
ᵒEx 9:25;
Isa 30:30

13:14
ᵖMic 1:6
qJer 6:15

13:16
a Isa 57:21;
Jer 6:14

13:17
b Rev 2:20
c ver 2

13:19
d Eze 20:39;
22:26
e Pr 28:21

13:21
f Ps 91:3

13:22
g Jer 23:14;
Eze 33:14-16

13:23
h ver 6;
Eze 12:24
i Mic 3:6

14:1
j Eze 8:1; 20:1

14:3
k ver 7; Eze 7:19
l Isa 1:15;
Eze 20:31

14:5
m Zec 11:8
n Jer 2:11

14:6
o Isa 2:20; 30:22

14:7
p Ex 12:48; 20:10

be destroyed in it; and you will know that I am the LORD. ¹⁵So I will spend my wrath against the wall and against those who covered it with whitewash. I will say to you, "The wall is gone and so are those who whitewashed it, ¹⁶those prophets of Israel who prophesied to Jerusalem and saw visions of peace for her when there was no peace, declares the Sovereign LORD.*a*"'

¹⁷"Now, son of man, set your face against the daughters*b* of your people who prophesy out of their own imagination. Prophesy against them*c* ¹⁸and say, 'This is what the Sovereign LORD says: Woe to the women who sew magic charms on all their wrists and make veils of various lengths for their heads in order to ensnare people. Will you ensnare the lives of my people but preserve your own? ¹⁹You have profaned*d* me among my people for a few handfuls of barley and scraps of bread. By lying to my people, who listen to lies, you have killed those who should not have died and have spared those who should not live.*e*

²⁰"'Therefore this is what the Sovereign LORD says: I am against your magic charms with which you ensnare people like birds and I will tear them from your arms; I will set free the people that you ensnare like birds. ²¹I will tear off your veils and save my people from your hands, and they will no longer fall prey to your power. Then you will know that I am the LORD.*f* ²²Because you disheartened the righteous with your lies, when I had brought them no grief, and because you encouraged the wicked not to turn from their evil ways and so save their lives,*g* ²³therefore you will no longer see false visions or practice divination.*h* I will save my people from your hands. And then you will know that I am the LORD.*i*'"

Chapter 14 Theme

14 Some of the elders of Israel came to me and sat down in front of me.*j* ²Then the word of the LORD came to me: ³"Son of man, these men have set up idols in their hearts and put wicked stumbling blocks*k* before their faces. Should I let them inquire of me at all?*l* ⁴Therefore speak to them and tell them, 'This is what the Sovereign LORD says: When any Israelite sets up idols in his heart and puts a wicked stumbling block before his face and then goes to a prophet, I the LORD will answer him myself in keeping with his great idolatry. ⁵I will do this to recapture the hearts of the people of Israel, who have all deserted*m* me for their idols.'*n*

⁶"Therefore say to the house of Israel, 'This is what the Sovereign LORD says: Repent! Turn from your idols and renounce all your detestable practices!*o*

⁷"'When any Israelite or any alien*p* living in Israel separates himself from me and sets up idols in his heart and puts a wicked stumbling block before his face and then goes to a prophet to

inquire of me, I the LORD will answer him myself. [8]I will set my face against[a] that man and make him an example and a byword.[b] I will cut him off from my people. Then you will know that I am the LORD.

[9]"And if the prophet[c] is enticed[d] to utter a prophecy, I the LORD have enticed that prophet, and I will stretch out my hand against him and destroy him from among my people Israel.[e] [10]They will bear their guilt—the prophet will be as guilty as the one who consults him. [11]Then the people of Israel will no longer stray[f] from me, nor will they defile themselves anymore with all their sins. They will be my people, and I will be their God, declares the Sovereign LORD.[g] '"

[12]The word of the LORD came to me: [13]"Son of man, if a country sins against me by being unfaithful and I stretch out my hand against it to cut off its food supply[h] and send famine upon it and kill its men and their animals,[i] [14]even if these three men—Noah,[j] Daniel[a][k] and Job[l]—were in it, they could save only themselves by their righteousness,[m] declares the Sovereign LORD.

[15]"Or if I send wild beasts[n] through that country and they leave it childless and it becomes desolate so that no one can pass through it because of the beasts,[o] [16]as surely as I live, declares the Sovereign LORD, even if these three men were in it, they could not save their own sons or daughters. They alone would be saved, but the land would be desolate.[p]

[17]"Or if I bring a sword[q] against that country and say, 'Let the sword pass throughout the land,' and I kill its men and their animals,[r] [18]as surely as I live, declares the Sovereign LORD, even if these three men were in it, they could not save their own sons or daughters. They alone would be saved.

[19]"Or if I send a plague into that land and pour out my wrath[s] upon it through bloodshed, killing its men and their animals,[t] [20]as surely as I live, declares the Sovereign LORD, even if Noah, Daniel and Job were in it, they could save neither son nor daughter. They would save only themselves by their righteousness.[u]

[21]"For this is what the Sovereign LORD says: How much worse will it be when I send against Jerusalem my four dreadful judgments—sword and famine and wild beasts and plague—to kill its men and their animals![v] [22]Yet there will be some survivors—sons and daughters who will be brought out of it.[w] They will come to you, and when you see their conduct[x] and their actions, you will be consoled regarding the disaster I have brought upon Jerusalem—every disaster I have brought upon it. [23]You will be consoled when you see their conduct and their actions, for you will know that I have done nothing in it without cause, declares the Sovereign LORD.[y] "

---

a 14 Or Danel; the Hebrew spelling may suggest a person other than the prophet Daniel; also in verse 20.

14:8
[a] Eze 15:7
[b] Eze 5:15

14:9
[c] Jer 14:15
[d] Jer 4:10
[e] 1Ki 22:23

14:11
[f] Eze 48:11
[g] Eze 11:19-20; 37:23

14:13
[h] Lev 26:26
[i] Eze 5:16; 6:14; 15:8

14:14
[j] Ge 6:8
[k] ver 20; Eze 28:3; Da 1:6; 6:13
[l] Job 1:1
[m] Job 42:9; Jer 15:1; Eze 18:20

14:15
[n] Eze 5:17
[o] Lev 26:22

14:16
[p] Eze 18:20

14:17
[q] Lev 26:25; Eze 5:12; 21:3-4
[r] Eze 25:13; Zep 1:3

14:19
[s] Eze 7:8
[t] Eze 38:22

14:20
[u] ver 14

14:21
[v] Jer 15:3; Eze 5:17; 33:27; Am 4:6-10; Rev 6:8

14:22
[w] Eze 12:16
[x] Eze 20:43

14:23
[y] Jer 22:8-9

15:2
aIsa 5:1-7;
Jer 2:21;
Hos 10:1

15:4
bEze 19:14;
Jn 15:6

15:7
cPs 34:16;
Eze 14:8
dIsa 24:18;
Am 9:1-4

15:8
eEze 14:13
fEze 17:20

16:2
gEze 20:4; 22:2

16:3
hEze 21:30
iver 45

16:4
jHos 2:3

16:6
kEx 19:4

16:7
lDt 1:10
mEx 1:7

16:8
nRu 3:9
oJer 2:2;
Hos 2:7,19-20

16:9
pRu 3:3

16:10
qEx 26:36
rEze 27:16
sver 18

16:11
tEze 23:40

Chapter 15 Theme

15 The word of the LORD came to me: ²"Son of man, how is the wood of a vine[a] better than that of a branch on any of the trees in the forest? ³Is wood ever taken from it to make anything useful? Do they make pegs from it to hang things on? ⁴And after it is thrown on the fire as fuel and the fire burns both ends and chars the middle, is it then useful for anything?[b] ⁵If it was not useful for anything when it was whole, how much less can it be made into something useful when the fire has burned it and it is charred?

⁶"Therefore this is what the Sovereign LORD says: As I have given the wood of the vine among the trees of the forest as fuel for the fire, so will I treat the people living in Jerusalem. ⁷I will set my face against[c] them. Although they have come out of the fire, the fire will yet consume them. And when I set my face against them, you will know that I am the LORD.[d] ⁸I will make the land desolate[e] because they have been unfaithful,[f] declares the Sovereign LORD."

Chapter 16 Theme

16 The word of the LORD came to me: ²"Son of man, confront Jerusalem with her detestable practices[g] ³and say, 'This is what the Sovereign LORD says to Jerusalem: Your ancestry[h] and birth were in the land of the Canaanites; your father was an Amorite and your mother a Hittite.[i] ⁴On the day you were born[j] your cord was not cut, nor were you washed with water to make you clean, nor were you rubbed with salt or wrapped in cloths. ⁵No one looked on you with pity or had compassion enough to do any of these things for you. Rather, you were thrown out into the open field, for on the day you were born you were despised.

⁶"Then I passed by and saw you kicking about in your blood, and as you lay there in your blood I said to you, "Live!"[a][k] ⁷I made you grow[l] like a plant of the field. You grew up and developed and became the most beautiful of jewels.[b] Your breasts were formed and your hair grew, you who were naked and bare.[m]

⁸"Later I passed by, and when I looked at you and saw that you were old enough for love, I spread the corner of my garment[n] over you and covered your nakedness. I gave you my solemn oath and entered into a covenant with you, declares the Sovereign LORD, and you became mine.[o]

⁹"I bathed[c] you with water and washed[p] the blood from you and put ointments on you. ¹⁰I clothed you with an embroidered[q] dress and put leather sandals on you. I dressed you in fine linen[r] and covered you with costly garments.[s] ¹¹I adorned you with jewelry:[t]

a6 A few Hebrew manuscripts, Septuagint and Syriac; most Hebrew manuscripts *"Live!" And as you lay there in your blood I said to you, "Live!"* b7 Or *became mature* c9 Or *I had bathed*

I put bracelets*a* on your arms and a necklace*b* around your neck, ¹²and I put a ring on your nose,*c* earrings on your ears and a beautiful crown*d* on your head. ¹³So you were adorned with gold and silver; your clothes were of fine linen and costly fabric and embroidered cloth. Your food was fine flour, honey and olive oil.*e* You became very beautiful and rose to be a queen.*f* ¹⁴And your fame*g* spread among the nations on account of your beauty,*h* because the splendor I had given you made your beauty perfect, declares the Sovereign LORD.

¹⁵"'But you trusted in your beauty and used your fame to become a prostitute. You lavished your favors on anyone who passed by*i* and your beauty became his.*a j* ¹⁶You took some of your garments to make gaudy high places, where you carried on your prostitution.*k* Such things should not happen, nor should they ever occur. ¹⁷You also took the fine jewelry I gave you, the jewelry made of my gold and silver, and you made for yourself male idols and engaged in prostitution with them.*l* ¹⁸And you took your embroidered clothes to put on them, and you offered my oil and incense before them. ¹⁹Also the food I provided for you—the fine flour, olive oil and honey I gave you to eat—you offered as fragrant incense before them. That is what happened, declares the Sovereign LORD.*m*

²⁰"'And you took your sons and daughters*n* whom you bore to me*o* and sacrificed them as food to the idols. Was your prostitution not enough?*p* ²¹You slaughtered my children and sacrificed them*b* to the idols.*q* ²²In all your detestable practices and your prostitution you did not remember the days of your youth,*r* when you were naked and bare, kicking about in your blood.*s*

²³"'Woe! Woe to you, declares the Sovereign LORD. In addition to all your other wickedness, ²⁴you built a mound for yourself and made a lofty shrine*t* in every public square.*u* ²⁵At the head of every street you built your lofty shrines and degraded your beauty, offering your body with increasing promiscuity to anyone who passed by.*v* ²⁶You engaged in prostitution with the Egyptians, your lustful neighbors, and provoked*w* me to anger with your increasing promiscuity.*x* ²⁷So I stretched out my hand*y* against you and reduced your territory; I gave you over to the greed of your enemies, the daughters of the Philistines,*z* who were shocked by your lewd conduct. ²⁸You engaged in prostitution with the Assyrians*a* too, because you were insatiable; and even after that, you still were not satisfied. ²⁹Then you increased your promiscuity to include Babylonia,*c b* a land of merchants, but even with this you were not satisfied.

---

a 15 Most Hebrew manuscripts; one Hebrew manuscript (see some Septuagint manuscripts) *by. Such a thing should not happen* *b 21* Or *and made them pass through* ⌊*the fire*⌋ *c 29* Or *Chaldea*

16:11
a Isa 3:19;
Eze 23:42
b Ge 41:42

16:12
c Isa 3:21
d Isa 28:5;
Jer 13:18

16:13
e 1Sa 10:1
f Dt 32:13-14;
1Ki 4:21

16:14
g 1Ki 10:24
h La 2:15

16:15
i ver 25
j Isa 57:8;
Jer 2:20;
Eze 23:3; 27:3

16:16
k 2Ki 23:7

16:17
l Eze 7:20

16:19
m Hos 2:8

16:20
n Jer 7:31
o Ex 13:2
p Ps 106:37-38;
Isa 57:5;
Eze 23:37

16:21
q 2Ki 17:17;
Jer 19:5

16:22
r Jer 2:2;
Hos 11:1
s ver 6

16:24
t ver 31; Isa 57:7
u Ps 78:58;
Jer 2:20; 3:2;
Eze 20:28

16:25
v ver 15; Pr 9:14

16:26
w Eze 8:17
x Eze 20:8;
23:19-21

16:27
y Eze 20:33
z 2Ch 28:18

16:28
a 2Ki 16:7

16:29
b Eze 23:14-17

16:30
a Jer 3:3

16:31
b ver 24

16:33
c Isa 30:6; 57:9
d Hos 8:9-10

16:36
e Jer 19:5;
Eze 23:10

16:37
f Jer 13:22

16:38
g Eze 23:45
h Lev 20:10;
Eze 23:25

16:39
i Eze 23:26;
Hos 2:3

16:40
j Jn 8:5,7

16:41
k Dt 13:16
l Eze 23:10
m Eze 23:27,48

16:42
n Isa 54:9;
Eze 5:13; 39:29

16:43
o Ps 78:42
p Eze 22:31
q ver 22;
Eze 11:21

16:45
r Eze 23:2

16:46
s Ge 13:10-13;
Eze 23:4

³⁰"'How weak-willed you are, declares the Sovereign LORD, when you do all these things, acting like a brazen prostitute!ᵃ ³¹When you built your mounds at the head of every street and made your lofty shrinesᵇ in every public square, you were unlike a prostitute, because you scorned payment.

³²"'You adulterous wife! You prefer strangers to your own husband! ³³Every prostitute receives a fee, but you give giftsᶜ to all your lovers, bribing them to come to you from everywhere for your illicit favors.ᵈ ³⁴So in your prostitution you are the opposite of others; no one runs after you for your favors. You are the very opposite, for you give payment and none is given to you.

³⁵"'Therefore, you prostitute, hear the word of the LORD! ³⁶This is what the Sovereign LORD says: Because you poured out your wealthᵃ and exposed your nakedness in your promiscuity with your lovers, and because of all your detestable idols, and because you gave them your children's blood,ᵉ ³⁷therefore I am going to gather all your lovers, with whom you found pleasure, those you loved as well as those you hated. I will gather them against you from all around and will strip you in front of them, and they will see all your nakedness.ᶠ ³⁸I will sentence you to the punishment of women who commit adultery and who shed blood;ᵍ I will bring upon you the blood vengeance of my wrath and jealous anger.ʰ ³⁹Then I will hand you over to your lovers, and they will tear down your mounds and destroy your lofty shrines. They will strip you of your clothes and take your fine jewelry and leave you naked and bare.ⁱ ⁴⁰They will bring a mob against you, who will stoneʲ you and hack you to pieces with their swords. ⁴¹They will burn downᵏ your houses and inflict punishment on you in the sight of many women.ˡ I will put a stopᵐ to your prostitution, and you will no longer pay your lovers. ⁴²Then my wrath against you will subside and my jealous anger will turn away from you; I will be calm and no longer angry.ⁿ

⁴³"'Because you did not rememberᵒ the days of your youth but enraged me with all these things, I will surely bring downᵖ on your head what you have done, declares the Sovereign LORD. Did you not add lewdness to all your other detestable practices?�q

⁴⁴"'Everyone who quotes proverbs will quote this proverb about you: "Like mother, like daughter." ⁴⁵You are a true daughter of your mother, who despised her husband and her children; and you are a true sister of your sisters, who despised their husbands and their children. Your mother was a Hittite and your father an Amorite.ʳ ⁴⁶Your older sister was Samaria, who lived to the north of you with her daughters; and your younger sister, who lived to the south of you with her daughters, was Sodom.ˢ ⁴⁷You not only walked in their ways and copied their detestable practices, but in all your

a 36 Or lust

ways you soon became more depraved than they.*a* *48*As surely as I live, declares the Sovereign LORD, your sister Sodom and her daughters never did what you and your daughters have done.*b*

49"'Now this was the sin of your sister Sodom:*c* She and her daughters were arrogant,*d* overfed and unconcerned; they did not help the poor and needy.*e* *50*They were haughty and did detestable things before me. Therefore I did away with them as you have seen.*f* *51*Samaria did not commit half the sins you did. You have done more detestable things than they, and have made your sisters seem righteous by all these things you have done.*g* *52*Bear your disgrace, for you have furnished some justification for your sisters. Because your sins were more vile than theirs, they appear more righteous than you. So then, be ashamed and bear your disgrace, for you have made your sisters appear righteous.

53"'However, I will restore*h* the fortunes of Sodom and her daughters and of Samaria and her daughters, and your fortunes along with them, *54*so that you may bear your disgrace*i* and be ashamed of all you have done in giving them comfort. *55*And your sisters, Sodom with her daughters and Samaria with her daughters, will return to what they were before; and you and your daughters will return to what you were before.*j* *56*You would not even mention your sister Sodom in the day of your pride, *57*before your wickedness was uncovered. Even so, you are now scorned by the daughters of Edom*a k* and all her neighbors and the daughters of the Philistines—all those around you who despise you. *58*You will bear the consequences of your lewdness and your detestable practices, declares the LORD.*l*

59"'This is what the Sovereign LORD says: I will deal with you as you deserve, because you have despised my oath by breaking the covenant.*m* *60*Yet I will remember the covenant I made with you in the days of your youth, and I will establish an everlasting covenant*n* with you. *61*Then you will remember your ways and be ashamed*o* when you receive your sisters, both those who are older than you and those who are younger. I will give them to you as daughters, but not on the basis of my covenant with you. *62*So I will establish my covenant with you, and you will know that I am the LORD.*p* *63*Then, when I make atonement*q* for you for all you have done, you will remember and be ashamed and never again open your mouth*r* because of your humiliation, declares the Sovereign LORD.*s*'"

Chapter 17 Theme

17 The word of the LORD came to me: *2*"Son of man, set forth an allegory and tell the house of Israel a parable.*t* *3*Say to them, 'This is what the Sovereign LORD says: A great eagle*u* with

16:47
a 2Ki 21:9;
Eze 5:7

16:48
b Mt 10:15;
11:23-24

16:49
c Ge 13:13
d Ps 138:6
e Eze 18:7,12,16;
Lk 12:16-20

16:50
f Ge 18:20-21;
19:5

16:51
g Jer 3:8-11

16:53
h Isa 19:24-25

16:54
i Jer 2:26;
Eze 14:22

16:55
j Mal 3:4

16:57
k 2Ki 16:6

16:58
l Eze 23:49

16:59
m Eze 17:19

16:60
n Jer 32:40;
Eze 37:26

16:61
o Eze 20:43

16:62
p Jer 24:7;
Eze 20:37, 43-44;
Hos 2:19-20

16:63
q Ps 65:3; 79:9
r Ro 3:19
s Ps 39:9;
Da 9:7-8

17:2
t Eze 20:49

17:3
u Hos 8:1

a 57 Many Hebrew manuscripts and Syriac; most Hebrew manuscripts, Septuagint and Vulgate *Aram*

17:3
a Jer 22:23

17:5
b Dt 8:7-9;
Isa 44:4

17:7
c Eze 31:4

17:10
d Hos 13:15

17:12
e Eze 12:9
f 2Ki 24:15
g Eze 24:19

17:13
h 2Ch 36:13

17:14
i Eze 29:14

17:15
j Jer 52:3
k Dt 17:16
l Jer 34:3; 38:18

17:16
m Jer 52:11;
Eze 12:13
n 2Ki 24:17

17:17
o Jer 37:7
p Eze 4:2
q Isa 36:6;
Jer 37:5;
Eze 29:6-7

17:18
r 1Ch 29:24

17:19
s Eze 16:59

17:20
t Eze 12:13; 32:3
u Jer 2:35;
Eze 20:36

17:21
v Eze 12:14
w 2Ki 25:11

powerful wings, long feathers and full plumage of varied colors came to Lebanon.*a* Taking hold of the top of a cedar, 4he broke off its topmost shoot and carried it away to a land of merchants, where he planted it in a city of traders.

5"He took some of the seed of your land and put it in fertile soil. He planted it like a willow by abundant water,*b* 6and it sprouted and became a low, spreading vine. Its branches turned toward him, but its roots remained under it. So it became a vine and produced branches and put out leafy boughs.

7"But there was another great eagle with powerful wings and full plumage. The vine now sent out its roots toward him from the plot where it was planted and stretched out its branches to him for water.*c* 8It had been planted in good soil by abundant water so that it would produce branches, bear fruit and become a splendid vine.'

9"Say to them, 'This is what the Sovereign LORD says: Will it thrive? Will it not be uprooted and stripped of its fruit so that it withers? All its new growth will wither. It will not take a strong arm or many people to pull it up by the roots. 10Even if it*d* is transplanted, will it thrive? Will it not wither completely when the east wind strikes it—wither away in the plot where it grew?'"

11Then the word of the LORD came to me: 12"Say to this rebellious house, 'Do you not know what these things mean?*e* ' Say to them: 'The king of Babylon went to Jerusalem and carried off her king and her nobles,*f* bringing them back with him to Babylon.*g* 13Then he took a member of the royal family and made a treaty with him, putting him under oath.*h* He also carried away the leading men of the land, 14so that the kingdom would be brought low,*i* unable to rise again, surviving only by keeping his treaty. 15But the king rebelled*j* against him by sending his envoys to Egypt to get horses and a large army.*k* Will he succeed? Will he who does such things escape? Will he break the treaty and yet escape?*l*

16"'As surely as I live, declares the Sovereign LORD, he shall die*m* in Babylon, in the land of the king who put him on the throne, whose oath he despised and whose treaty he broke.*n* 17Pharaoh*o* with his mighty army and great horde will be of no help to him in war, when ramps*p* are built and siege works erected to destroy many lives.*q* 18He despised the oath by breaking the covenant. Because he had given his hand in pledge*r* and yet did all these things, he shall not escape.

19"'Therefore this is what the Sovereign LORD says: As surely as I live, I will bring down on his head my oath that he despised and my covenant that he broke.*s* 20I will spread my net*t* for him, and he will be caught in my snare. I will bring him to Babylon and execute judgment*u* upon him there because he was unfaithful to me. 21All his fleeing troops will fall by the sword,*v* and the survivors*w* will be scattered to the winds.*a* Then you will know that I the LORD have spoken.

22"'This is what the Sovereign LORD says: I myself will take a shoot from the very top of a cedar and plant it; I will break off a tender sprig from its topmost shoots and plant it on a high and lofty mountain.*b* 23On the mountain heights of Israel I will plant it; it will produce branches and bear fruit and become a splendid cedar. Birds of every kind will nest in it; they will find shelter in the shade of its branches.*c* 24All the trees of the field*d* will know that I the LORD bring down the tall tree and make the low tree grow tall. I dry up the green tree and make the dry tree flourish.

"'I the LORD have spoken, and I will do it.*e*'"

Chapter 18 Theme

18 The word of the LORD came to me: 2"What do you people mean by quoting this proverb about the land of Israel:

"'The fathers eat sour grapes,
    and the children's teeth are set on edge'?*f*

3"As surely as I live, declares the Sovereign LORD, you will no longer quote this proverb in Israel. 4For every living soul belongs to me, the father as well as the son—both alike belong to me. The soul who sins is the one who will die.*g*

5"Suppose there is a righteous man
    who does what is just and right.
6He does not eat at the mountain*h* shrines
    or look to the idols*i* of the house of Israel.
He does not defile his neighbor's wife
    or lie with a woman during her period.
7He does not oppress*j* anyone,
    but returns what he took in pledge*k* for a loan.
He does not commit robbery
    but gives his food to the hungry
    and provides clothing for the naked.*l*
8He does not lend at usury
    or take excessive interest.*a m*
He withholds his hand from doing wrong
    and judges fairly*n* between man and man.
9He follows my decrees
    and faithfully keeps my laws.
That man is righteous;*o*
    he will surely live,*p*
                                    declares the Sovereign LORD.

a 8 Or take interest; similarly in verses 13 and 17

17:21
a 2Ki 25:5

17:22
b Jer 23:5;
Eze 20:40;
36:1,36;
37:22

17:23
c Ps 92:12;
Isa 2:2;
Eze 31:6;
Da 4:12;
Hos 14:5-7;
Mt 13:32

17:24
d Ps 96:12
e Eze 19:12;
21:26; 22:14;
Am 9:11

18:2
f Isa 3:15;
Jer 31:29;
La 5:7

18:4
g ver 20;
Isa 42:5;
Ro 6:23

18:6
h Eze 22:9
i Dt 4:19;
Eze 6:13; 20:24

18:7
j Ex 22:21
k Ex 22:26;
Dt 24:12
l Dt 15:11;
Mt 25:36

18:8
m Ex 22:25;
Lev 25:35-37;
Dt 23:19-20
n Zec 8:16

18:9
o Hab 2:4
p Lev 18:5;
Eze 20:11;
Am 5:4

18:10
a Ex 21:12

¹⁰"Suppose he has a violent son, who sheds blood^a or does any of these other things^a ¹¹(though the father has done none of them):

> "He eats at the mountain shrines.
> He defiles his neighbor's wife.
> ¹²He oppresses the poor^b and needy.
> He commits robbery.
> He does not return what he took in pledge.
> He looks to the idols.
> He does detestable things.^c
> ¹³He lends at usury and takes excessive interest.^d

18:12
b Am 4:1
c 2Ki 21:11;
Isa 59:6-7;
Jer 22:17;
Eze 8:6,17

Will such a man live? He will not! Because he has done all these detestable things, he will surely be put to death and his blood will be on his own head.^e

18:13
d Ex 22:25
e Eze 33:4-5

¹⁴"But suppose this son has a son who sees all the sins his father commits, and though he sees them, he does not do such things:^f

> ¹⁵"He does not eat at the mountain shrines
> or look to the idols of the house of Israel.
> He does not defile his neighbor's wife.
> ¹⁶He does not oppress anyone
> or require a pledge for a loan.
> He does not commit robbery
> but gives his food to the hungry
> and provides clothing for the naked.^g
> ¹⁷He withholds his hand from sin^b
> and takes no usury or excessive interest.
> He keeps my laws and follows my decrees.

18:14
f 2Ch 34:21;
Pr 23:24

18:16
g Ps 41:1;
Isa 58:10

18:19
h Ex 20:5;
Dt 5:9; Jer 15:4;
Zec 1:3-6

He will not die for his father's sin; he will surely live. ¹⁸But his father will die for his own sin, because he practiced extortion, robbed his brother and did what was wrong among his people.

¹⁹"Yet you ask, 'Why does the son not share the guilt of his father?' Since the son has done what is just and right and has been careful to keep all my decrees, he will surely live.^h ²⁰The soul who sins is the one who will die. The son will not share the guilt of the father, nor will the father share the guilt of the son. The righteousness of the righteous man will be credited to him, and the wickedness of the wicked will be charged against him.ⁱ

18:20
i Dt 24:16;
1Ki 8:32;
2Ki 14:6;
Isa 3:11;
Mt 16:27;
Ro 2:9

²¹"But if a wicked man turns away from all the sins he has committed and keeps all my decrees and does what is just and right, he will surely live; he will not die.^j ²²None of the offenses he has committed will be remembered against him. Because of the righteous things he has done, he will live.^k ²³Do I take any pleasure in

18:21
j Eze 33:12,19

18:22
k Ps 18:20-24;
Isa 43:25;
Mic 7:19

a 10 Or *things to a brother*   b 17 Septuagint (see also verse 8); Hebrew *from the poor* the death of the wicked? declares the Sovereign LORD. Rather, am I not pleased[a] when they turn from their ways and live?[b]

24"But if a righteous man turns from his righteousness and commits sin and does the same detestable things the wicked man does, will he live? None of the righteous things he has done will be remembered. Because of the unfaithfulness he is guilty of and because of the sins he has committed, he will die.[c]

25"Yet you say, 'The way of the Lord is not just.' Hear, O house of Israel: Is my way unjust?[d] Is it not your ways that are unjust? 26If a righteous man turns from his righteousness and commits sin, he will die for it; because of the sin he has committed he will die. 27But if a wicked man turns away from the wickedness he has committed and does what is just and right, he will save his life.[e] 28Because he considers all the offenses he has committed and turns away from them, he will surely live; he will not die. 29Yet the house of Israel says, 'The way of the Lord is not just.' Are my ways unjust, O house of Israel? Is it not your ways that are unjust?

30"Therefore, O house of Israel, I will judge you, each one according to his ways, declares the Sovereign LORD. Repent![f] Turn away from all your offenses; then sin will not be your downfall.[g] 31Rid yourselves of all the offenses you have committed, and get a new heart[h] and a new spirit. Why will you die, O house of Israel?[i] 32For I take no pleasure in the death of anyone, declares the Sovereign LORD. Repent and live![j]

Chapter 19 Theme

19 "Take up a lament[k] concerning the princes[l] of Israel 2and say:

"'What a lioness was your mother
among the lions!
She lay down among the young lions
and reared her cubs.
3She brought up one of her cubs,
and he became a strong lion.
He learned to tear the prey
and he devoured men.
4The nations heard about him,
and he was trapped in their pit.
They led him with hooks
to the land of Egypt.[m]

5"'When she saw her hope unfulfilled,
her expectation gone,
she took another of her cubs

18:23
a Ps 147:11
b Eze 33:11;
1Ti 2:4

18:24
c 1Sa 15:11;
2Ch 24:17-20;
Eze 3:20; 20:27;
2Pe 2:20-22

18:25
d Ge 18:25;
Jer 12:1;
Eze 33:17;
Zep 3:5;
Mal 2:17; 3:13-15

18:27
e Isa 1:18

18:30
f Mt 3:2
g Eze 7:3; 33:20;
Hos 12:6

18:31
h Ps 51:10
i Isa 1:16-17;
Eze 11:19; 36:26

18:32
j Eze 33:11

19:1
k Eze 26:17;
27:2,32
l 2Ki 24:6

19:4
m 2Ki 23:33-34;
2Ch 36:4

and made him a strong lion.[a]

6He prowled among the lions,
  for he was now a strong lion.
He learned to tear the prey
  and he devoured men.[b]
7He broke down[a] their strongholds
  and devastated[c] their towns.
The land and all who were in it
  were terrified by his roaring.
8Then the nations[d] came against him,
  those from regions round about.
They spread their net for him,
  and he was trapped in their pit.[e]
9With hooks they pulled him into a cage
  and brought him to the king of Babylon.[f]
They put him in prison,
  so his roar was heard no longer
  on the mountains of Israel.[g]

10"'Your mother was like a vine in your vineyard[b]
  planted by the water;
it was fruitful and full of branches
  because of abundant water.[h]
11Its branches were strong,
  fit for a ruler's scepter.
It towered high
  above the thick foliage,
conspicuous for its height
  and for its many branches.[i]
12But it was uprooted[j] in fury
  and thrown to the ground.
The east wind made it shrivel,
  it was stripped of its fruit;
its strong branches withered
  and fire consumed them.[k]
13Now it is planted in the desert,[l]
  in a dry and thirsty land.[m]
14Fire spread from one of its main[c] branches
  and consumed[n] its fruit.
No strong branch is left on it
  fit for a ruler's scepter.'[o]

This is a lament and is to be used as a lament."

**Cross references (left margin):**

19:5
[a] 2Ki 23:34

19:6
[b] 2Ki 24:9;
2Ch 36:9

19:7
[c] Eze 30:12

19:8
[d] 2Ki 24:2
[e] 2Ki 24:11

19:9
[f] 2Ch 36:6
[g] 2Ki 24:15

19:10
[h] Ps 80:8-11

19:11
[i] Eze 31:3;
Da 4:11

19:12
[j] Eze 17:10
[k] Isa 27:11;
Eze 28:17;
Hos 13:15

19:13
[l] Eze 20:35
[m] Hos 2:3

19:14
[n] Eze 20:47
[o] Eze 15:4

Footnotes:

[a] 7 Targum (see Septuagint); Hebrew *He knew*   [b] 10 Two Hebrew manuscripts; most Hebrew manuscripts *your blood*   [c] 14 Or *from under its*

Chapter 20 Theme

20 In the seventh year, in the fifth month on the tenth day, some of the elders of Israel came to inquire of the LORD, and they sat down in front of me.*a*

²Then the word of the LORD came to me: ³"Son of man, speak to the elders of Israel and say to them, 'This is what the Sovereign LORD says: Have you come to inquire*b* of me? As surely as I live, I will not let you inquire of me, declares the Sovereign LORD.*c*

⁴"Will you judge them? Will you judge them, son of man? Then confront them with the detestable practices of their fathers*d* ⁵and say to them: 'This is what the Sovereign LORD says: On the day I chose*e* Israel, I swore with uplifted hand to the descendants of the house of Jacob and revealed myself to them in Egypt. With uplifted hand I said to them, "I am the LORD your God.*f*" ⁶On that day I swore to them that I would bring them out of Egypt into a land I had searched out for them, a land flowing with milk and honey,*g* the most beautiful of all lands.*h* ⁷And I said to them, "Each of you, get rid of the vile images*i* you have set your eyes on, and do not defile yourselves with the idols of Egypt. I am the LORD your God.*j*"

⁸"But they rebelled against me and would not listen to me; they did not get rid of the vile images they had set their eyes on, nor did they forsake the idols of Egypt.*k* So I said I would pour out my wrath on them and spend my anger against them in Egypt.*l* ⁹But for the sake of my name I did what would keep it from being profaned in the eyes of the nations they lived among and in whose sight I had revealed myself to the Israelites by bringing them out of Egypt.*m* ¹⁰Therefore I led them out of Egypt and brought them into the desert.*n* ¹¹I gave them my decrees and made known to them my laws, for the man who obeys them will live by them.*o* ¹²Also I gave them my Sabbaths as a sign*p* between us, so they would know that I the LORD made them holy.

¹³"Yet the people of Israel rebelled*q* against me in the desert. They did not follow my decrees but rejected my laws—although the man who obeys them will live by them—and they utterly desecrated my Sabbaths. So I said I would pour out my wrath*r* on them and destroy them in the desert.*s* ¹⁴But for the sake of my name I did what would keep it from being profaned in the eyes of the nations in whose sight I had brought them out.*t* ¹⁵Also with uplifted hand I swore to them in the desert that I would not bring them into the land I had given them—a land flowing with milk and honey, most beautiful of all lands*u*— ¹⁶because they rejected my laws and did not follow my decrees and desecrated my Sabbaths. For their hearts*v* were devoted to their idols.*w* ¹⁷Yet I looked on them with pity and did not destroy them or put an end to them in the desert. ¹⁸I said to their children in the desert, "Do

20:1
a Eze 8:1

20:3
b Eze 14:3
c Mic 3:7

20:4
d Eze 16:2; 22:2;
Mt 23:32

20:5
e Dt 7:6
f Ex 6:7

20:6
g Ex 3:8;
Jer 32:22
h Dt 8:7; Ps 48:2;
Da 8:9

20:7
i Ex 20:4
j Ex 20:2;
Lev 18:3;
Dt 29:18

20:8
k Eze 7:8
l Isa 63:10

20:9
m Eze 36:22;
39:7

20:10
n Ex 13:18

20:11
o Lev 18:5;
Dt 4:7-8;
Ro 10:5

20:12
p Ex 31:13

20:13
q Ps 78:40
r Dt 9:8
s Nu 14:29;
Ps 95:8-10;
Isa 56:6

20:14
t Eze 36:23

20:15
u Ps 95:11;
106:26

20:16
v Nu 15:39
w Am 5:26

20:18
a Zec 1:4

20:19
b Ex 20:2
c Dt 5:32-33;
6:1-2; 8:1;
11:1; 12:1

20:20
d Jer 17:22

20:22
e Ps 78:38

20:23
f Lev 26:33;
Dt 28:64

20:24
g ver 13
h Eze 6:9
i ver 16

20:25
j Ps 81:12
k 2Th 2:11

20:26
l 2Ki 17:17

20:27
m Ro 2:24
n Eze 18:24

20:28
o Ps 78:55,58
p Eze 6:13

20:30
q ver 43
r Jer 16:12

20:31
s Eze 16:20
t Ps 106:37-39;
Jer 7:31

20:33
u Jer 21:5

20:34
v 2Co 6:17*

not follow the statutes of your fathers[a] or keep their laws or defile yourselves with their idols. [19]I am the LORD your God;[b] follow my decrees and be careful to keep my laws.[c] [20]Keep my Sabbaths holy, that they may be a sign between us. Then you will know that I am the LORD your God.[d]"

[21]"But the children rebelled against me: They did not follow my decrees, they were not careful to keep my laws—although the man who obeys them will live by them—and they desecrated my Sabbaths. So I said I would pour out my wrath on them and spend my anger against them in the desert. [22]But I withheld[e] my hand, and for the sake of my name I did what would keep it from being profaned in the eyes of the nations in whose sight I had brought them out. [23]Also with uplifted hand I swore to them in the desert that I would disperse them among the nations and scatter[f] them through the countries, [24]because they had not obeyed my laws but had rejected my decrees and desecrated my Sabbaths,[g] and their eyes ⌊lusted⌋ after[h] their fathers' idols.[i] [25]I also gave them over[j] to statutes that were not good and laws they could not live by;[k] [26]I let them become defiled through their gifts—the sacrifice of every firstborn[a]—that I might fill them with horror so they would know that I am the LORD.[l] '

[27]"Therefore, son of man, speak to the people of Israel and say to them, 'This is what the Sovereign LORD says: In this also your fathers blasphemed[m] me by forsaking me:[n] [28]When I brought them into the land[o] I had sworn to give them and they saw any high hill or any leafy tree, there they offered their sacrifices, made offerings that provoked me to anger, presented their fragrant incense and poured out their drink offerings.[p] [29]Then I said to them: What is this high place you go to?'" (It is called Bamah[b] to this day.)

[30]"Therefore say to the house of Israel: 'This is what the Sovereign LORD says: Will you defile yourselves[q] the way your fathers did and lust after their vile images?[r] [31]When you offer your gifts—the sacrifice of your sons[s] in[c] the fire—you continue to defile yourselves with all your idols to this day. Am I to let you inquire of me, O house of Israel? As surely as I live, declares the Sovereign LORD, I will not let you inquire of me.[t]

[32]"You say, "We want to be like the nations, like the peoples of the world, who serve wood and stone." But what you have in mind will never happen. [33]As surely as I live, declares the Sovereign LORD, I will rule over you with a mighty hand and an outstretched arm and with outpoured wrath.[u] [34]I will bring you from the nations[v] and gather you from the countries where you have been scattered—with a mighty hand and an outstretched arm and with

a 26 Or —making every firstborn pass through ⌊the fire⌋   b 29 Bamah means high place.
c 31 Or —making your sons pass through

outpoured wrath.*a* **35**I will bring you into the desert of the nations and there, face to face, I will execute judgment*b* upon you. **36**As I judged your fathers in the desert of the land of Egypt, so I will judge you, declares the Sovereign LORD.*c* **37**I will take note of you as you pass under my rod,*d* and I will bring you into the bond of the covenant.*e* **38**I will purge*f* you of those who revolt and rebel against me. Although I will bring them out of the land where they are living, yet they will not enter the land of Israel. Then you will know that I am the LORD.*g*

39"'As for you, O house of Israel, this is what the Sovereign LORD says: Go and serve your idols,*h* every one of you! But afterward you will surely listen to me and no longer profane my holy name with your gifts and idols.*i* **40**For on my holy mountain, the high mountain of Israel, declares the Sovereign LORD, there in the land the entire house of Israel will serve me, and there I will accept them. There I will require your offerings*j* and your choice gifts,*a* along with all your holy sacrifices.*k* **41**I will accept you as fragrant incense when I bring you out from the nations and gather you from the countries where you have been scattered, and I will show myself holy*l* among you in the sight of the nations.*m* **42**Then you will know that I am the LORD,*n* when I bring you into the land of Israel,*o* the land I had sworn with uplifted hand to give to your fathers. **43**There you will remember your conduct and all the actions by which you have defiled yourselves, and you will loathe yourselves for all the evil you have done.*p* **44**You will know that I am the LORD, when I deal with you for my name's sake*q* and not according to your evil ways and your corrupt practices, O house of Israel, declares the Sovereign LORD.*r*'"

45The word of the LORD came to me: **46**"Son of man, set your face toward the south; preach against the south and prophesy against*s* the forest of the southland.*t* **47**Say to the southern forest: 'Hear the word of the LORD. This is what the Sovereign LORD says: I am about to set fire to you, and it will consume all your trees, both green and dry. The blazing flame will not be quenched, and every face from south to north will be scorched by it.*u* **48**Everyone will see that I the LORD have kindled it; it will not be quenched.*v*'"

49Then I said, "Ah, Sovereign LORD! They are saying of me, 'Isn't he just telling parables?*w*'"

Chapter 21 Theme _____

21 The word of the LORD came to me: **2**"Son of man, set your face against Jerusalem and preach against the sanctuary. Prophesy against*x* the land of Israel **3**and say to her: 'This is what

a 40 Or and the gifts of your firstfruits

20:34
*a*Isa 27:12-13;
Jer 44:6; La 2:4

20:35
*b*Jer 2:35

20:36
*c*Nu 11:1-35;
1Co 10:5-10

20:37
*d*Lev 27:32;
Jer 33:13
*e*Eze 16:62

20:38
*f*Eze 34:17-22;
Am 9:9-10
*g*Ps 95:11;
Jer 44:14;
Eze 13:9;
Mal 3:3;
Heb 4:3

20:39
*h*Jer 44:25
*i*Isa 1:13;
Eze 43:7;
Am 4:4

20:40
*j*Isa 60:7
*k*Isa 56:7;
Mal 3:4

20:41
*l*Eze 28:25;
36:23
*m*Eze 11:17

20:42
*n*Eze 38:23
*o*Eze 34:13;
36:24

20:43
*p*Eze 6:9; 16:61;
Hos 5:15

20:44
*q*Eze 36:22
*r*Eze 24:24

20:46
*s*Eze 21:2;
Am 7:16
*t*Isa 30:6;
Jer 13:19

20:47
*u*Isa 9:18-19;
13:8; Jer 21:14

20:48
*v*Jer 7:20

20:49
*w*Mt 13:13;
Jn 16:25

21:2
*x*Eze 20:46

21:3
a Jer 21:13
b ver 9-11;
Job 9:22

the LORD says: I am against you.*a* I will draw my sword from its scabbard and cut off from you both the righteous and the wicked.*b* ⁴Because I am going to cut off the righteous and the wicked, my sword will be unsheathed against everyone from south to north.*c* ⁵Then all people will know that I the LORD have drawn my sword from its scabbard; it will not return*d* again.'*e*

21:4
c Eze 20:47

⁶"Therefore groan, son of man! Groan before them with broken heart and bitter grief.*f* ⁷And when they ask you, 'Why are you groaning?' you shall say, 'Because of the news that is coming. Every heart will melt and every hand go limp;*g* every spirit will become faint and every knee become as weak as water.' It is coming! It will surely take place, declares the Sovereign LORD."

21:5
d ver 30
e Na 1:9

⁸The word of the LORD came to me: ⁹"Son of man, prophesy and say, 'This is what the Lord says:

21:6
f Isa 22:4

> "'A sword, a sword,
>   sharpened and polished—
> ¹⁰sharpened for the slaughter,*h*
>   polished to flash like lightning!

"'Shall we rejoice in the scepter of my son ⌞Judah⌟? The sword despises every such stick.

21:7
g Eze 22:14; 7:17

> ¹¹"'The sword is appointed to be polished,*i*
>   to be grasped with the hand;
> it is sharpened and polished,
>   made ready for the hand of the slayer.
> ¹²Cry out and wail, son of man,
>   for it is against my people;
>   it is against all the princes of Israel.
> They are thrown to the sword
>   along with my people.
> Therefore beat your breast.*j*

21:10
h Ps 110:5-6;
Isa 34:5-6

21:11
i Jer 46:4

¹³"'Testing will surely come. And what if the scepter ⌞of Judah⌟, which the sword despises, does not continue? declares the Sovereign LORD.'

21:12
j Jer 31:19

> ¹⁴"So then, son of man, prophesy
>   and strike your hands*k* together.
> Let the sword strike twice,
>   even three times.
> It is a sword for slaughter—
>   a sword for great slaughter,
>   closing in on them from every side.*l*
> ¹⁵So that hearts may melt*m*
>   and the fallen be many,

21:14
k Nu 24:10

21:14
l Eze 6:11; 30:24

21:15
m 2Sa 17:10

I have stationed the sword for slaughter[a]
    at all their gates.
Oh! It is made to flash like lightning,
    it is grasped for slaughter.[a]
[16]O sword, slash to the right,
    then to the left,
    wherever your blade is turned.
[17]I too will strike my hands[b] together,
    and my wrath[c] will subside.
I the LORD have spoken."

[18]The word of the LORD came to me: [19]"Son of man, mark out two roads for the sword of the king of Babylon to take, both starting from the same country. Make a signpost where the road branches off to the city. [20]Mark out one road for the sword to come against Rabbah of the Ammonites[d] and another against Judah and fortified Jerusalem. [21]For the king of Babylon will stop at the fork in the road, at the junction of the two roads, to seek an omen: He will cast lots[e] with arrows, he will consult his idols, he will examine the liver.[f] [22]Into his right hand will come the lot for Jerusalem, where he is to set up battering rams, to give the command to slaughter, to sound the battle cry, to set battering rams against the gates, to build a ramp and to erect siege works.[g] [23]It will seem like a false omen to those who have sworn allegiance to him, but he will remind[h] them of their guilt and take them captive.

[24]"Therefore this is what the Sovereign LORD says: 'Because you people have brought to mind your guilt by your open rebellion, revealing your sins in all that you do—because you have done this, you will be taken captive.

[25]"'O profane and wicked prince of Israel, whose day has come, whose time of punishment has reached its climax,[i] [26]this is what the Sovereign LORD says: Take off the turban, remove the crown.[j] It will not be as it was: The lowly will be exalted and the exalted will be brought low.[k] [27]A ruin! A ruin! I will make it a ruin! It will not be restored until he comes to whom it rightfully belongs; to him I will give it.'[l]

[28]"And you, son of man, prophesy and say, 'This is what the Sovereign LORD says about the Ammonites[m] and their insults:

"'A sword,[n] a sword,
    drawn for the slaughter,
polished to consume
    and to flash like lightning!
[29]Despite false visions concerning you
    and lying divinations about you,

21:15
[a] Ps 22:14

21:17
[b] ver 14;
Eze 22:13
[c] Eze 5:13

21:20
[d] Dt 3:11;
Jer 49:2;
Am 1:14

21:21
[e] Pr 16:33
[f] Nu 22:7; 23:23

21:22
[g] Eze 4:2; 26:9

21:23
[h] Nu 5:15

21:25
[i] Eze 35:5

21:26
[j] Jer 13:18
[k] Ps 75:7;
Eze 17:24

21:27
[l] Ps 2:6;
Jer 23:5-6;
Eze 37:24;
Hag 2:21-22

21:28
[m] Zep 2:8
[n] Jer 12:12

a 15 Septuagint; the meaning of the Hebrew for this word is uncertain.

21:29
a ver 25;
Eze 22:28; 35:5

21:30
b Jer 47:6
c Eze 16:3

21:31
d Eze 22:20-21
e Jer 51:20-23

21:32
f Mal 4:1
g Eze 25:10

22:2
h Eze 24:6,9;
Na 3:1
i Eze 16:2

22:3
j ver 6,13,27;
Eze 23:37,45

22:4
k 2Ki 21:16
l Eze 21:25
m Eze 5:14

22:6
n Isa 1:23

22:7
o Dt 5:16; 27:16
p Ex 22:21-22

22:8
q Eze 23:38-39

22:9
r Lev 19:16
s Eze 18:11
t Hos 4:10,14

22:10
u Lev 18:8,19

22:11
v Lev 18:15
w Lev 18:9;
2Sa 13:14

22:12
x Dt 27:25;
Mic 7:3
y Lev 19:13

it will be laid on the necks
  of the wicked who are to be slain,
whose day has come,
  whose time of punishment has reached its climax.[a]
³⁰Return the sword to its scabbard.[b]
  In the place where you were created,
in the land of your ancestry,[c]
  I will judge you.
³¹I will pour out my wrath upon you
  and breathe out my fiery anger[d] against you;
I will hand you over to brutal men,
  men skilled in destruction.[e]
³²You will be fuel for the fire,[f]
  your blood will be shed in your land,
you will be remembered[g] no more;
  for I the LORD have spoken.'"

Chapter 22 Theme

22 The word of the LORD came to me: ²"Son of man, will you judge her? Will you judge this city of bloodshed?[h] Then confront her with all her detestable practices[i] ³and say: 'This is what the Sovereign LORD says: O city that brings on herself doom by shedding blood[j] in her midst and defiles herself by making idols, ⁴you have become guilty because of the blood you have shed[k] and have become defiled by the idols you have made. You have brought your days to a close, and the end of your years has come.[l] Therefore I will make you an object of scorn to the nations and a laughingstock to all the countries.[m] ⁵Those who are near and those who are far away will mock you, O infamous city, full of turmoil.

⁶"'See how each of the princes of Israel who are in you uses his power to shed blood.[n] ⁷In you they have treated father and mother with contempt;[o] in you they have oppressed the alien and mistreated the fatherless and the widow.[p] ⁸You have despised my holy things and desecrated my Sabbaths.[q] ⁹In you are slanderous men[r] bent on shedding blood; in you are those who eat at the mountain shrines[s] and commit lewd acts.[t] ¹⁰In you are those who dishonor their fathers' bed; in you are those who violate women during their period, when they are ceremonially unclean.[u] ¹¹In you one man commits a detestable offense with his neighbor's wife, another shamefully defiles his daughter-in-law,[v] and another violates his sister,[w] his own father's daughter. ¹²In you men accept bribes[x] to shed blood; you take usury and excessive interest[a] and make unjust gain from your neighbors[y] by extortion. And you have forgotten me, declares the Sovereign LORD.

a 12 Or usury and interest

13"'I will surely strike my hands^a together at the unjust gain^b you have made and at the blood^c you have shed in your midst. ¹⁴Will your courage endure or your hands be strong in the day I deal with you? I the LORD have spoken,^d and I will do it.^e ¹⁵I will disperse you among the nations and scatter^f you through the countries; and I will put an end to your uncleanness.^g ¹⁶When you have been defiled^a in the eyes of the nations, you will know that I am the LORD.'"

¹⁷Then the word of the LORD came to me: ¹⁸"Son of man, the house of Israel has become dross^h to me; all of them are the copper, tin, iron and lead left inside a furnace. They are but the dross of silver.ⁱ ¹⁹Therefore this is what the Sovereign LORD says: 'Because you have all become dross, I will gather you into Jerusalem. ²⁰As men gather silver, copper, iron, lead and tin into a furnace to melt it with a fiery blast, so will I gather you in my anger and my wrath and put you inside the city and melt you.^j ²¹I will gather you and I will blow on you with my fiery wrath, and you will be melted inside her. ²²As silver is melted^k in a furnace, so you will be melted inside her, and you will know that I the LORD have poured out my wrath upon you.'"^l

²³Again the word of the LORD came to me: ²⁴"Son of man, say to the land, 'You are a land that has had no rain or showers^b in the day of wrath.'^m ²⁵There is a conspiracyⁿ of her princes^c within her like a roaring lion tearing its prey; they devour people,^o take treasures and precious things and make many widows^p within her. ²⁶Her priests do violence to my law^q and profane my holy things; they do not distinguish between the holy and the common;^r they teach that there is no difference between the unclean and the clean;^s and they shut their eyes to the keeping of my Sabbaths, so that I am profaned among them.^t ²⁷Her officials within her are like wolves tearing their prey; they shed blood and kill people to make unjust gain.^u ²⁸Her prophets whitewash^v these deeds for them by false visions and lying divinations. They say, 'This is what the Sovereign LORD says'—when the LORD has not spoken.^w ²⁹The people of the land practice extortion and commit robbery; they oppress the poor and needy and mistreat the alien,^x denying them justice.^y

³⁰"I looked for a man among them who would build up the wall^z and stand before me in the gap on behalf of the land so I would not have to destroy it, but I found none.^a ³¹So I will pour out my wrath on them and consume them with my fiery anger, bringing down^b on their own heads all they have done, declares the Sovereign LORD."^c

^a16 Or *When I have allotted you your inheritance*   ^b24 Septuagint; Hebrew *has not been cleansed or rained on*   ^c25 Septuagint; Hebrew *prophets*

22:13 ^aEze 21:17 ^bIsa 33:15 ^cver 3
22:14 ^dEze 24:14 ^eEze 17:24; 21:7
22:15 ^fDt 4:27; Zec 7:14 ^gEze 23:27
22:18 ^hPs 119:119; Isa 1:22 ⁱJer 6:28-30
22:20 ^jMal 3:2
22:22 ^kIsa 1:25 ^lEze 20:8,33
22:24 ^mEze 24:13
22:25 ⁿJer 11:9 ^oHos 6:9 ^pJer 15:8
22:26 ^qMal 2:7-8 ^rEze 44:23 ^sLev 10:10 ^t1Sa 2:12-17; Jer 2:8,26; Hag 2:11-14
22:27 ^uIsa 1:23
22:28 ^vEze 13:10 ^wEze 13:2,6-7
22:29 ^xEx 22:21; 23:9 ^yIsa 5:7
22:30 ^zEze 13:5 ^aPs 106:23; Jer 5:1
22:31 ^bEze 16:43 ^cEze 7:8-9; 9:10; Ro 2:8

23:2
a Jer 3:7;
Eze 16:45

23:3
b Jos 24:14
c Lev 17:7

23:5
d 2Ki 16:7;
Hos 5:13
e Hos 8:9

23:7
f Hos 5:3; 6:10

23:8
g Ex 32:4
h Eze 16:15

23:9
i 2Ki 18:11
j Hos 11:5

23:10
k Hos 2:10
l Eze 16:41
m Eze 16:36

23:11
n Jer 3:8-11;
Eze 16:51

23:12
o 2Ki 16:7-15;
2Ch 28:16

23:14
p Eze 8:10
q Jer 22:14

23:18
r Ps 78:59;
106:40; Jer 6:8
s Jer 12:8;
Am 5:21

23:21
t Eze 16:26

Chapter 23 Theme

23 The word of the Lord came to me: ²"Son of man, there were two women, daughters of the same mother.*a* ³They became prostitutes in Egypt,*b* engaging in prostitution*c* from their youth. In that land their breasts were fondled and their virgin bosoms caressed. ⁴The older was named Oholah, and her sister was Oholibah. They were mine and gave birth to sons and daughters. Oholah is Samaria, and Oholibah is Jerusalem.

⁵"Oholah engaged in prostitution while she was still mine; and she lusted after her lovers, the Assyrians*d*—warriors*e* ⁶clothed in blue, governors and commanders, all of them handsome young men, and mounted horsemen. ⁷She gave herself as a prostitute to all the elite of the Assyrians and defiled herself with all the idols of everyone she lusted after.*f* ⁸She did not give up the prostitution she began in Egypt,*g* when during her youth men slept with her, caressed her virgin bosom and poured out their lust upon her.*h*

⁹"Therefore I handed her over*i* to her lovers, the Assyrians, for whom she lusted. *j* ¹⁰They stripped*k* her naked, took away her sons and daughters and killed her with the sword. She became a byword among women,*l* and punishment was inflicted on her.*m*

¹¹"Her sister Oholibah saw this, yet in her lust and prostitution she was more depraved than her sister.*n* ¹²She too lusted after the Assyrians—governors and commanders, warriors in full dress, mounted horsemen, all handsome young men.*o* ¹³I saw that she too defiled herself; both of them went the same way.

¹⁴"But she carried her prostitution still further. She saw men portrayed on a wall,*p* figures of Chaldeansa portrayed in red,*q* ¹⁵with belts around their waists and flowing turbans on their heads; all of them looked like Babylonian chariot officers, natives of Chaldea.b ¹⁶As soon as she saw them, she lusted after them and sent messengers to them in Chaldea. ¹⁷Then the Babylonians came to her, to the bed of love, and in their lust they defiled her. After she had been defiled by them, she turned away from them in disgust. ¹⁸When she carried on her prostitution openly and exposed her nakedness, I turned away*r* from her in disgust, just as I had turned away from her sister.*s* ¹⁹Yet she became more and more promiscuous as she recalled the days of her youth, when she was a prostitute in Egypt. ²⁰There she lusted after her lovers, whose genitals were like those of donkeys and whose emission was like that of horses. ²¹So you longed for the lewdness of your youth, when in Egypt your bosom was caressed and your young breasts fondled.c*t*

a 14 Or *Babylonians*   b 15 Or *Babylonia*; also in verse 16   c 21 Syriac (see also verse 3); Hebrew *caressed because of your young breasts*

²²"Therefore, Oholibah, this is what the Sovereign LORD says: I will stir up your lovers against you, those you turned away from in disgust, and I will bring them against you from every side^a— ²³the Babylonians^b and all the Chaldeans, the men of Pekod^c and Shoa and Koa, and all the Assyrians with them, handsome young men, all of them governors and commanders, chariot officers and men of high rank, all mounted on horses.^d ²⁴They will come against you with weapons,^a chariots and wagons^e and with a throng of people; they will take up positions against you on every side with large and small shields and with helmets. I will turn you over to them for punishment,^f and they will punish you according to their standards. ²⁵I will direct my jealous anger against you, and they will deal with you in fury. They will cut off your noses and your ears, and those of you who are left will fall by the sword. They will take away your sons and daughters,^g and those of you who are left will be consumed by fire.^h ²⁶They will also stripⁱ you of your clothes and take your fine jewelry.^j ²⁷So I will put a stop^k to the lewdness and prostitution you began in Egypt. You will not look on these things with longing or remember Egypt anymore.

²⁸"For this is what the Sovereign LORD says: I am about to hand you over^l to those you hate, to those you turned away from in disgust. ²⁹They will deal with you in hatred and take away everything you have worked for. They will leave you naked and bare, and the shame of your prostitution will be exposed. Your lewdness and promiscuity^m ³⁰have brought this upon you, because you lusted after the nations and defiled yourself with their idols.ⁿ ³¹You have gone the way of your sister; so I will put her cup^o into your hand.^p

³²"This is what the Sovereign LORD says:

> "You will drink your sister's cup,
>   a cup large and deep;
> it will bring scorn and derision,
>   for it holds so much.^q
> ³³You will be filled with drunkenness and sorrow,
>   the cup of ruin and desolation,
>   the cup of your sister Samaria.^r
> ³⁴You will drink it^s and drain it dry;
>   you will dash it to pieces
>   and tear your breasts.

I have spoken, declares the Sovereign LORD.

³⁵"Therefore this is what the Sovereign LORD says: Since you have forgotten^t me and thrust me behind your back,^u you must bear the consequences of your lewdness and prostitution."

---

^a24 The meaning of the Hebrew for this word is uncertain.

23:22
^a Eze 16:37

23:23
^b 2Ki 20:14-18
^c Jer 50:21
^d 2Ki 24:2

23:24
^e Jer 47:3;
Eze 26:7,10;
Na 2:4
^f Jer 39:5-6

23:25
^g ver 47
^h Eze 20:47-48

23:26
ⁱ Jer 13:22
^j Isa 3:18-23;
Eze 16:39

23:27
^k Eze 16:41

23:28
^l Jer 34:20

23:29
^m Dt 28:48

23:30
ⁿ Eze 6:9

23:31
^o Jer 25:15
^p 2Ki 21:13

23:32
^q Ps 60:3;
Isa 51:17;
Jer 25:15

23:33
^r Jer 25:15-16

23:34
^s Ps 75:8;
Isa 51:17

23:35
^t Isa 17:10;
Jer 3:21
^u 1Ki 14:9

23:36
a Eze 16:2
b Isa 58:1;
Eze 22:2;
Mic 3:8

23:37
c Eze 16:36

23:39
d 2Ki 21:4
e Jer 7:10

23:40
f Isa 57:9
g 2Ki 9:30
h Jer 4:30;
Eze 16:13-19

23:41
i Est 1:6; Pr 7:17;
Am 6:4
j Isa 65:11;
Eze 44:16

23:42
k Ge 24:30
l Eze 16:11-12

23:43
m ver 3

23:45
n Lev 20:10;
Eze 16:38;
Hos 6:5

23:46

³⁶The Lord said to me: "Son of man, will you judge Oholah and Oholibah? Then confront[a] them with their detestable practices,[b] ³⁷for they have committed adultery and blood is on their hands. They committed adultery with their idols; they even sacrificed their children, whom they bore to me,[a] as food for them.[c] ³⁸They have also done this to me: At that same time they defiled my sanctuary and desecrated my Sabbaths. ³⁹On the very day they sacrificed their children to their idols, they entered my sanctuary and desecrated[d] it. That is what they did in my house.[e]

⁴⁰"They even sent messengers for men who came from far away,[f] and when they arrived you bathed yourself for them, painted your eyes[g] and put on your jewelry.[h] ⁴¹You sat on an elegant couch,[i] with a table[j] spread before it on which you had placed the incense and oil that belonged to me.

⁴²"The noise of a carefree crowd was around her; Sabeans[b] were brought from the desert along with men from the rabble, and they put bracelets[k] on the arms of the woman and her sister and beautiful crowns on their heads.[l] ⁴³Then I said about the one worn out by adultery, 'Now let them use her as a prostitute,[m] for that is all she is.' ⁴⁴And they slept with her. As men sleep with a prostitute, so they slept with those lewd women, Oholah and Oholibah. ⁴⁵But righteous men will sentence them to the punishment of women who commit adultery and shed blood, because they are adulterous and blood is on their hands.[n]

⁴⁶"This is what the Sovereign Lord

Fill it with the best of these bones;
⁵ take the pick of the flock.^a
Pile wood beneath it for the bones;
bring it to a boil
and cook the bones in it.^b

⁶"'For this is what the Sovereign Lord says:

"'Woe to the city of bloodshed,^c
to the pot now encrusted,
whose deposit will not go away!
Empty it piece by piece
without casting lots^d for them.

⁷"'For the blood she shed is in her midst:
She poured it on the bare rock;
she did not pour it on the ground,
where the dust would cover it.^e
⁸To stir up wrath and take revenge
I put her blood on the bare rock,
so that it would not be covered.

⁹"'Therefore this is what the Sovereign Lord says:

"'Woe to the city of bloodshed!
I, too, will pile the wood high.
¹⁰So heap on the wood

24:5
^a Jer 52:10
^b Jer 52:24-27

24:6
^c Eze 22:2
^d Ob 1:11;
Na 3:10

24:7
^e Lev 17:13

24:16
a Jer 13:17; 16:5;
22:10

24:17
b Jer 16:7

24:19
c Eze 12:9; 37:18

24:21
d Ps 27:4
e Eze 23:25
f Jer 7:14,15;
Eze 23:47

24:22
g Jer 16:7

24:23
h Job 27:15
i Ps 78:64

24:24
j Isa 20:3;
Eze 4:3; 12:11

24:25
k Jer 11:22

do not lament or weep or shed any tears.*a* ¹⁷Groan quietly; do not mourn for the dead. Keep your turban fastened and your sandals on your feet; do not cover the lower part of your face or eat the customary food ⌊of mourners⌋.*b*"

¹⁸So I spoke to the people in the morning, and in the evening my wife died. The next morning I did as I had been commanded.

¹⁹Then the people asked me, "Won't you tell us what these things have to do with us?*c*"

²⁰So I said to them, "The word of the LORD came to me: ²¹Say to the house of Israel, 'This is what the Sovereign LORD says: I am about to desecrate my sanctuary—the stronghold in which you take pride, the delight of your eyes,*d* the object of your affection. The sons and daughters*e* you left behind will fall by the sword.*f* ²²And you will do as I have done. You will not cover the lower part of your face or eat the customary food ⌊of mourners⌋.*g* ²³You will keep your turbans on your heads and your sandals on your feet. You will not mourn*h* or weep but will waste away because of*a* your sins and groan among yourselves.*i* ²⁴Ezekiel will be a sign*j* to you; you will do just as he has done. When this happens, you will know that I am the Sovereign LORD.'

²⁵"And you, son of man, on the day I take away their stronghold, their joy and glory, the delight of their eyes, their heart's desire, and their sons and daughters*k* as well— ²⁶on that day a fugitive

a 23 Or *away in*

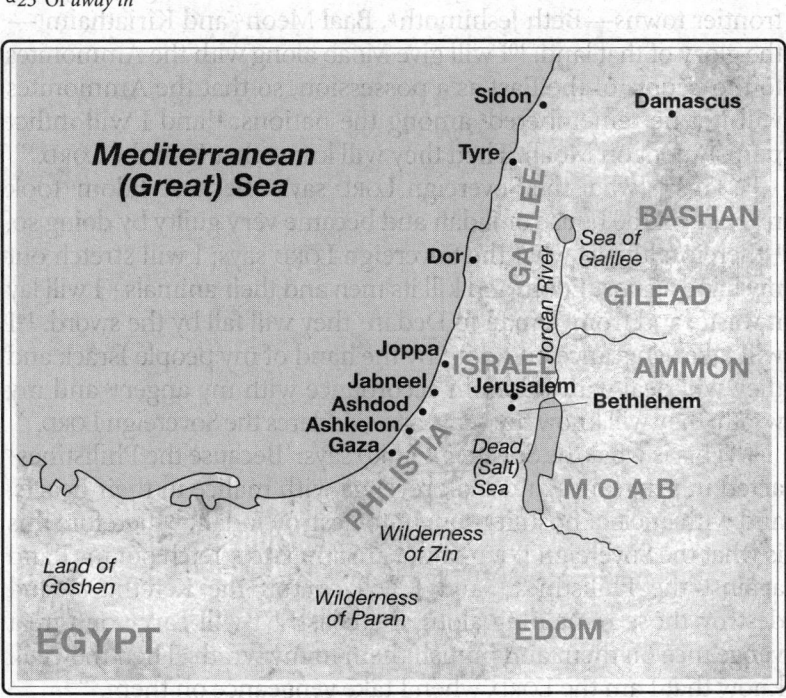

The Nations of Ezekiel's Prophecies

will come to tell you[a] the news. [27]At that time your mouth will be opened; you will speak with him and will no longer be silent. So you will be a sign to them, and they will know that I am the LORD.[b]"

Chapter 25 Theme _____

25 The word of the LORD came to me: [2]"Son of man, set your face against the Ammonites[c] and prophesy against them.[d] [3]Say to them, 'Hear the word of the Sovereign LORD. This is what the Sovereign LORD says: Because you said "Aha![e]" over my sanctuary when it was desecrated and over the land of Israel when it was laid waste and over the people of Judah when they went into exile,[f] [4]therefore I am going to give you to the people of the East[g] as a possession. They will set up their camps and pitch their tents among you; they will eat your fruit and drink your milk.[h] [5]I will turn Rabbah[i] into a pasture for camels and Ammon into a resting place for sheep.[j] Then you will know that I am the LORD. [6]For this is what the Sovereign LORD says: Because you have clapped your hands and stamped your feet, rejoicing with all the malice of your heart against the land of Israel,[k] [7]therefore I will stretch out my hand[l] against you and give you as plunder to the nations. I will cut you off from the nations and exterminate you from the countries. I will destroy[m] you, and you will know that I am the LORD.[n]'"

[8]"This is what the Sovereign LORD says: 'Because Moab[o] and Seir said, "Look, the house of Judah has become like all the other nations," [9]therefore I will expose the flank of Moab, beginning at its frontier towns—Beth Jeshimoth[p], Baal Meon[q] and Kiriathaim[r]—the glory of that land. [10]I will give Moab along with the Ammonites to the people of the East as a possession, so that the Ammonites will not be remembered[s] among the nations; [11]and I will inflict punishment on Moab. Then they will know that I am the LORD.'"

[12]"This is what the Sovereign LORD says: 'Because Edom[t] took revenge on the house of Judah and became very guilty by doing so, [13]therefore this is what the Sovereign LORD says: I will stretch out my hand against Edom and kill its men and their animals.[u] I will lay it waste, and from Teman to Dedan[v] they will fall by the sword. [14]I will take vengeance on Edom by the hand of my people Israel, and they will deal with Edom in accordance with my anger[w] and my wrath; they will know my vengeance, declares the Sovereign LORD.'"

[15]"This is what the Sovereign LORD says: 'Because the Philistines[x] acted in vengeance and took revenge with malice in their hearts, and with ancient hostility sought to destroy Judah, [16]therefore this is what the Sovereign LORD says: I am about to stretch out my hand against the Philistines,[y] and I will cut off the Kerethites[z] and destroy those remaining along the coast. [17]I will carry out great vengeance on them and punish them in my wrath. Then they will know that I am the LORD, when I take vengeance on them.'"

24:26
[a]1Sa 4:12; Job 1:15-19

24:27
[b]Eze 3:26; 33:22

25:2
[c]Eze 21:28; Zep 2:8-9
[d]Jer 49:1-6

25:3
[e]Eze 26:2; 36:2
[f]Pr 17:5

25:4
[g]Jdg 6:3
[h]Dt 28:33,51; Jdg 6:33

25:5
[i]Dt 3:11; Eze 21:20
[j]Isa 17:2

25:6
[k]Ob 1:12; Zep 2:8

25:7
[l]Zep 1:4
[m]Eze 21:31
[n]Am 1:14-15

25:8
[o]Jer 48:1; Am 2:1

25:9
[p]Nu 33:49
[q]Nu 32:3; Jos 13:17
[r]Nu 32:37; Jos 13:19

25:10
[s]Eze 21:32

25:12
[t]2Ch 28:17

25:13
[u]Eze 29:8
[v]Jer 25:23

25:14
[w]Eze 35:11

25:15
[x]2Ch 28:18

25:16
[y]Jer 47:1-7
[z]1Sa 30:14; Zep 2:4-5

587-586 B.C.

Chapter 26 Theme _____

26 In the eleventh year, on the first day of the month, the word of the LORD came to me: [2]"Son of man, because Tyre[a] has said of Jerusalem, 'Aha![b] The gate to the nations is broken, and its doors have swung open to me; now that she lies in ruins I will prosper,' [3]therefore this is what the Sovereign LORD says: I am against you, O Tyre, and I will bring many nations against you, like the sea[c] casting up its waves. [4]They will destroy[d] the walls of Tyre[e] and pull down her towers; I will scrape away her rubble and make her a bare rock. [5]Out in the sea[f] she will become a place to spread fishnets, for I have spoken, declares the Sovereign LORD. She will become plunder[g] for the nations, [6]and her settlements on the mainland will be ravaged by the sword. Then they will know that I am the LORD.

[7]"For this is what the Sovereign LORD says: From the north I am going to bring against Tyre Nebuchadnezzar[a][h] king of Babylon, king of kings,[i] with horses and chariots,[j] with horsemen and a great army. [8]He will ravage your settlements on the mainland with the sword; he will set up siege works[k] against you, build a ramp[l] up to your walls and raise his shields against you. [9]He will direct the blows of his battering rams against your walls and demolish your towers with his weapons. [10]His horses will be so many that they will cover you with dust. Your walls will tremble at the noise of the war horses, wagons and chariots[m] when he enters your gates as men enter a city whose walls have been broken through. [11]The hoofs[n] of his horses will trample all your streets; he will kill your people with the sword, and your strong pillars[o] will fall to the ground.[p] [12]They will plunder your wealth and loot your merchandise; they will break down your walls and demolish your fine houses and throw your stones, timber and rubble into the sea.[q] [13]I will put an end[r] to your noisy songs, and the music of your harps[s] will be heard no more.[t] [14]I will make you a bare rock, and you will become a place to spread fishnets. You will never be rebuilt,[u] for I the LORD have spoken, declares the Sovereign LORD.

[15]"This is what the Sovereign LORD says to Tyre: Will not the coastlands[v] tremble[w] at the sound of your fall, when the wounded groan and the slaughter takes place in you? [16]Then all the princes of the coast will step down from their thrones and lay aside their robes and take off their embroidered garments. Clothed[x] with terror, they will sit on the ground, trembling[y] every moment, appalled[z] at you. [17]Then they will take up a lament[a] concerning you and say to you:

> "'How you are destroyed, O city of renown,
>   peopled by men of the sea!

---

a 7 Hebrew *Nebuchadrezzar*, of which *Nebuchadnezzar* is a variant; here and often in Ezekiel and Jeremiah

---

Cross-references (left margin):

26:2
a 2Sa 5:11;
Isa 23
b Eze 25:3

26:3
c Isa 5:30;
Jer 50:42; 51:42

26:4
d Isa 23:1,11
e Am 1:10

26:5
f Eze 27:32
g Eze 29:19

26:7
h Jer 27:6
i Ezr 7:12;
Da 2:37
j Eze 23:24;
Na 2:3-4

26:8
k Jer 6:6
l Eze 21:22

26:10
m Jer 4:13

26:11
n Isa 5:28
o Jer 43:13
p Isa 26:5

26:12
q Isa 23:8;
Eze 27:3-27;
28:8

26:13
r Jer 7:34
s Isa 14:11
t Jer 25:10;
Rev 18:22

26:14
u Job 12:14;
Mal 1:4

26:15
v Eze 27:35
w Jer 49:21

26:16
x Job 8:22
y Hos 11:10
z Eze 32:10

26:17
a Eze 19:1; 27:32

You were a power on the seas,
  you and your citizens;
you put your terror
  on all who lived there.[a]
[18]Now the coastlands tremble
  on the day of your fall;
the islands in the sea
  are terrified at your collapse.'[b]

[19]"This is what the Sovereign LORD says: When I make you a desolate city, like cities no longer inhabited, and when I bring the ocean depths over you and its vast waters cover you,[c] [20]then I will bring you down with those who go down to the pit,[d] to the people of long ago. I will make you dwell in the earth below, as in ancient ruins, with those who go down to the pit, and you will not return or take your place[a] in the land of the living.[e] [21]I will bring you to a horrible end and you will be no more. You will be sought, but you will never again be found, declares the Sovereign LORD."[f]

Chapter 27 Theme

27 The word of the LORD came to me: [2]"Son of man, take up a lament concerning Tyre. [3]Say to Tyre, situated at the gateway to the sea,[g] merchant of peoples on many coasts, 'This is what the Sovereign LORD says:

"'You say, O Tyre,
  "I am perfect in beauty."[h]'
[4]Your domain was on the high seas;
  your builders brought your beauty to perfection.
[5]They made all your timbers
  of pine trees from Senir[b];[i]
they took a cedar from Lebanon
  to make a mast for you.
[6]Of oaks[j] from Bashan
  they made your oars;
of cypress wood[c] from the coasts of Cyprus[d][k]
  they made your deck, inlaid with ivory.
[7]Fine embroidered linen from Egypt was your sail
  and served as your banner;
your awnings were of blue and purple[l]
  from the coasts of Elishah.
[8]Men of Sidon and Arvad[m] were your oarsmen;
  your skilled men, O Tyre, were aboard as your seamen.[n]
[9]Veteran craftsmen of Gebal[e][o] were on board
  as shipwrights to caulk your seams.

---

[a]20 Septuagint; Hebrew *return, and I will give glory*   [b]5 That is, Hermon   [c]6 Targum; the Masoretic Text has a different division of the consonants.   [d]6 Hebrew *Kittim*   [e]9 That is, Byblos

26:17
[a]Isa 14:12

26:18
[b]Isa 23:5; 41:5;
Eze 27:35

26:19
[c]Isa 8:7-8

26:20
[d]Eze 32:18;
Am 9:2;
Jnh 2:2,6
[e]Eze 32:24,30

26:21
[f]Eze 27:36;
28:19; Rev 18:21

27:3
[g]ver 33
[h]Eze 28:2

27:5
[i]Dt 3:9

27:6
[j]Nu 21:33;
Jer 22:20;
Zec 11:2
[k]Ge 10:4;
Isa 23:12

27:7
[l]Ex 25:4;
Jer 10:9

27:8
[m]Ge 10:18
[n]1Ki 9:27

27:9
[o]Jos 13:5;
1Ki 5:18

27:10
a Eze 38:5
b Eze 30:5

27:12
c Ge 10:4
d ver 18,33

27:13
e Ge 10:2;
Isa 66:19;
Eze 38:2
f Rev 18:13

27:14
g Ge 10:3;
Eze 38:6

27:15
h Ge 10:7
i Jer 25:22
j 1Ki 10:22;
Rev 18:12

27:16
k Jdg 10:6;
Isa 7:1-8
l Eze 28:13

27:17
m Jdg 11:33

27:18
n Ge 14:15;
Eze 47:16-18

27:21
o Ge 25:13;
Isa 60:7

27:22
p Ge 10:7,28;
1Ki 10:1-2;
Isa 60:6
q Ge 43:11

27:23
r 2Ki 19:12
s Isa 37:12

All the ships of the sea and their sailors
came alongside to trade for your wares.

¹⁰ "'Men of Persia,*a* Lydia and Put*b*
served as soldiers in your army.
They hung their shields and helmets on your walls,
bringing you splendor.
¹¹ Men of Arvad and Helech
manned your walls on every side;
men of Gammad
were in your towers.
They hung their shields around your walls;
they brought your beauty to perfection.

¹² "'Tarshish*c* did business with you because of your great wealth of goods;*d* they exchanged silver, iron, tin and lead for your merchandise.

¹³ "'Greece, Tubal and Meshech*e* traded with you; they exchanged slaves*f* and articles of bronze for your wares.

¹⁴ "'Men of Beth Togarmah*g* exchanged work horses, war horses and mules for your merchandise.

¹⁵ "'The men of Rhodes*a* *h* traded with you, and many coastlands*i* were your customers; they paid you with ivory*j* tusks and ebony.

¹⁶ "'Aram*b* *k* did business with you because of your many products; they exchanged turquoise,*l* purple fabric, embroidered work, fine linen, coral and rubies for your merchandise.

¹⁷ "'Judah and Israel traded with you; they exchanged wheat from Minnith*m* and confections,*c* honey, oil and balm for your wares.

¹⁸ "'Damascus,*n* because of your many products and great wealth of goods, did business with you in wine from Helbon and wool from Zahar.

¹⁹ "'Danites and Greeks from Uzal bought your merchandise; they exchanged wrought iron, cassia and calamus for your wares.

²⁰ "'Dedan traded in saddle blankets with you.

²¹ "'Arabia and all the princes of Kedar*o* were your customers; they did business with you in lambs, rams and goats.

²² "'The merchants of Sheba*p* and Raamah traded with you; for your merchandise they exchanged the finest of all kinds of spices*q* and precious stones, and gold.

²³ "'Haran,*r* Canneh and Eden*s* and merchants of Sheba, Asshur and Kilmad traded with you. ²⁴ In your marketplace they traded with you beautiful garments, blue fabric, embroidered work and multicolored rugs with cords twisted and tightly knotted.

a 15 Septuagint; Hebrew *Dedan*   *b* 16 Most Hebrew manuscripts; some Hebrew manuscripts and Syriac *Edom*   *c* 17 The meaning of the Hebrew for this word is uncertain.

25 "'The ships of Tarshish[a] serve
    as carriers for your wares.
You are filled with heavy cargo
    in the heart of the sea.
26 Your oarsmen take you
    out to the high seas.
But the east wind[b] will break you to pieces
    in the heart of the sea.
27 Your wealth,[c] merchandise and wares,
    your mariners, seamen and shipwrights,
your merchants and all your soldiers,
    and everyone else on board
will sink into the heart of the sea
    on the day of your shipwreck.
28 The shorelands will quake[d]
    when your seamen cry out.
29 All who handle the oars
    will abandon their ships;
the mariners and all the seamen
    will stand on the shore.
30 They will raise their voice
    and cry bitterly over you;
they will sprinkle dust[e] on their heads
    and roll[f] in ashes.[g]
31 They will shave their heads because of you
    and will put on sackcloth.
They will weep[h] over you with anguish of soul
    and with bitter mourning.[i]
32 As they wail and mourn over you,
    they will take up a lament[j] concerning you:
"Who was ever silenced like Tyre,
    surrounded by the sea?"
33 When your merchandise went out on the seas,
    you satisfied many nations;
with your great wealth[k] and your wares
    you enriched the kings of the earth.
34 Now you are shattered by the sea
    in the depths of the waters;
your wares and all your company
    have gone down with you.[l]
35 All who live in the coastlands[m]
    are appalled at you;
their kings shudder with horror
    and their faces are distorted with fear.

27:25
[a] Isa 2:16 fn

27:26
[b] Ps 48:7;
Jer 18:17

27:27
[c] Pr 11:4

27:28
[d] Eze 26:15

27:30
[e] 2Sa 1:2
[f] Jer 6:26
[g] Rev 18:18-19

27:31
[h] Isa 16:9
[i] Isa 22:12;
Eze 7:18

27:32
[j] Eze 26:17

27:33
[k] ver 12;
Eze 28:4-5

27:34
[l] Zec 9:4

27:35
[m] Eze 26:15

27:36
a Jer 18:16; 19:8;
49:17; 50:13;
Zep 2:15
b Ps 37:10,36;
Eze 26:21

³⁶The merchants among the nations hiss at you;*a*
    you have come to a horrible end
    and will be no more.*b*' "

Chapter 28 Theme _____

28 The word of the LORD came to me: ²"Son of man, say to the ruler of Tyre, 'This is what the Sovereign LORD says:

28:2
c Isa 14:13
d Ps 9:20; 82:6-7;
Isa 31:3; 2Th 2:4

"'In the pride of your heart
    you say, "I am a god;
I sit on the throne*c* of a god
    in the heart of the seas."
But you are a man and not a god,
    though you think you are as wise as a god.*d*

28:3
e Da 1:20; 5:11-12

³Are you wiser than Daniel*a*?*e*
    Is no secret hidden from you?
⁴By your wisdom and understanding
    you have gained wealth for yourself
and amassed gold and silver
    in your treasuries.*f*

28:4
f Zec 9:3

⁵By your great skill in trading
    you have increased your wealth,
and because of your wealth
    your heart has grown proud.*g*

28:5
g Job 31:25;
Ps 52:7; 62:10;
Hos 12:8; 13:6

⁶"'Therefore this is what the Sovereign LORD says:

"'Because you think you are wise,
    as wise as a god,
⁷I am going to bring foreigners against you,
    the most ruthless of nations;*h*
they will draw their swords against your beauty
        and wisdom
    and pierce your shining splendor.

28:7
h Eze 30:11;
31:12; 32:12;
Hab 1:6

⁸They will bring you down to the pit,*i*
    and you will die a violent death
    in the heart of the seas.*j*
⁹Will you then say, "I am a god,"
    in the presence of those who kill you?
You will be but a man, not a god,
    in the hands of those who slay you.

28:8
i Eze 32:30
j Eze 27:27

¹⁰You will die the death of the uncircumcised*k*
    at the hands of foreigners.

I have spoken, declares the Sovereign LORD.'"

28:10
k Eze 31:18;
32:19,24

a 3 Or *Danel*; the Hebrew spelling may suggest a person other than the prophet Daniel.

[11] The word of the LORD came to me: [12] "Son of man, take up a lament[a] concerning the king of Tyre and say to him: 'This is what the Sovereign LORD says:

"'You were the model of perfection,
    full of wisdom and perfect in beauty.[b]
[13] You were in Eden,[c]
    the garden of God;[d]
every precious stone adorned you:
    ruby, topaz and emerald,
    chrysolite, onyx and jasper,
    sapphire,[a] turquoise[e] and beryl.[b]
Your settings and mountings[c] were made of gold;
    on the day you were created they were prepared.
[14] You were anointed[f] as a guardian cherub,[g]
    for so I ordained you.
You were on the holy mount of God;
    you walked among the fiery stones.
[15] You were blameless in your ways
    from the day you were created
    till wickedness was found in you.
[16] Through your widespread trade
    you were filled with violence,[h]
    and you sinned.
So I drove you in disgrace from the mount of God,
    and I expelled you, O guardian cherub,[i]
    from among the fiery stones.
[17] Your heart became proud[j]
    on account of your beauty,
and you corrupted your wisdom
    because of your splendor.
So I threw you to the earth;
    I made a spectacle of you before kings.
[18] By your many sins and dishonest trade
    you have desecrated your sanctuaries.
So I made a fire come out from you,
    and it consumed you,
and I reduced you to ashes[k] on the ground
    in the sight of all who were watching.
[19] All the nations who knew you
    are appalled at you;
you have come to a horrible end
    and will be no more.[l]'"

---

[a] 13 Or *lapis lazuli*   [b] 13 The precise identification of some of these precious stones is uncertain.   [c] 13 The meaning of the Hebrew for this phrase is uncertain.

28:12
[a] Eze 19:1
[b] Eze 27:2-4

28:13
[c] Ge 2:8
[d] Eze 31:8-9
[e] Eze 27:16

28:14
[f] Ex 30:26; 40:9
[g] Ex 25:17-20

28:16
[h] Hab 2:17
[i] Ge 3:24

28:17
[j] Eze 31:10

28:18
[k] Mal 4:3

28:19
[l] Jer 51:64;
Eze 26:21; 27:36

28:21
a Eze 6:2
b Ge 10:15;
Jer 25:22

²⁰The word of the LORD came to me: ²¹"Son of man, set your face against^{*a*} Sidon;^{*b*} prophesy against her ²²and say: 'This is what the Sovereign LORD says:

28:22
c Eze 39:13
d Eze 30:19

> "'I am against you, O Sidon,
>   and I will gain glory^{*c*} within you.
> They will know that I am the LORD,
>   when I inflict punishment^{*d*} on her
>   and show myself holy within her.

28:23
e Eze 38:22

> ²³I will send a plague upon her
>   and make blood flow in her streets.
> The slain will fall within her,
>   with the sword against her on every side.
> Then they will know that I am the LORD.^{*e*}

28:24
f Nu 33:55;
Jos 23:13;
Eze 2:6

²⁴"'No longer will the people of Israel have malicious neighbors who are painful briers and sharp thorns.^{*f*} Then they will know that I am the Sovereign LORD.

28:25
g Ps 106:47;
Jer 32:37
h Isa 11:12
i Eze 20:41
j Jer 23:8;
Eze 11:17;
34:27; 37:25

²⁵"'This is what the Sovereign LORD says: When I gather^{*g*} the people of Israel from the nations where they have been scattered,^{*h*} I will show myself holy^{*i*} among them in the sight of the nations. Then they will live in their own land, which I gave to my servant Jacob.^{*j*} ²⁶They will live there in safety^{*k*} and will build houses and plant vineyards; they will live in safety when I inflict punishment on all their neighbors who maligned them. Then they will know that I am the LORD their God.'"

28:26
k Jer 23:6
l Isa 65:21;
Jer 32:15;
Eze 38:8;
Am 9:14-15

Chapter 29 Theme

29

In the tenth year, in the tenth month on the twelfth day, the word of the LORD came to me:^{*m*} ²"Son of man, set your face against Pharaoh king of Egypt^{*n*} and prophesy against him and against all Egypt.^{*o*} ³Speak to him and say: 'This is what the Sovereign LORD says:

587 B.C.

29:1
m ver 17;
Eze 26:1

29:2
n Jer 25:19
o Isa 19:1-17;
Jer 46:2;
Eze 30:1-26;
31:1-18; 32:1-32

> "'I am against you, Pharaoh^{*p*} king of Egypt,
>   you great monster^{*q*} lying among your streams.
> You say, "The Nile is mine;
>   I made it for myself."

29:3
p Jer 44:30
q Ps 74:13;
Isa 27:1;
Eze 32:2

> ⁴But I will put hooks^{*r*} in your jaws
>   and make the fish of your streams stick to your scales.
> I will pull you out from among your streams,
>   with all the fish sticking to your scales.^{*s*}
> ⁵I will leave you in the desert,
>   you and all the fish of your streams.
> You will fall on the open field
>   and not be gathered or picked up.

29:4
r 2Ki 19:28
s Eze 38:4

> I will give you as food
> to the beasts of the earth and the birds of the air.[a]

[6]Then all who live in Egypt will know that I am the LORD.

"'You have been a staff of reed[b] for the house of Israel. [7]When they grasped you with their hands, you splintered[c] and you tore open their shoulders; when they leaned on you, you broke and their backs were wrenched.[a][d]

[8]"'Therefore this is what the Sovereign LORD says: I will bring a sword against you and kill your men and their animals.[e] [9]Egypt will become a desolate wasteland. Then they will know that I am the LORD.

"'Because you said, "The Nile is mine; I made it,[f]" [10]therefore I am against you and against your streams, and I will make the land of Egypt a ruin and a desolate waste from Migdol to Aswan,[g] as far as the border of Cush.[b] [11]No foot of man or animal will pass through it; no one will live there for forty years.[h] [12]I will make the land of Egypt desolate among devastated lands, and her cities will lie desolate forty years among ruined cities. And I will disperse the Egyptians among the nations and scatter them through the countries.[i]

[13]"'Yet this is what the Sovereign LORD says: At the end of forty years I will gather the Egyptians from the nations where they were scattered. [14]I will bring them back from captivity and return them to Upper Egypt,[c][j] the land of their ancestry. There they will be a lowly[k] kingdom. [15]It will be the lowliest of kingdoms and will never again exalt itself above the other nations.[l] I will make it so weak that it will never again rule over the nations. [16]Egypt will no longer be a source of confidence[m] for the people of Israel but will be a reminder of their sin in turning to her for help. Then they will know that I am the Sovereign LORD.[n]'"

571 B.C. [17]In the twenty-seventh year, in the first month on the first day, the word of the LORD came to me:[o] [18]"Son of man, Nebuchadnezzar[p] king of Babylon drove his army in a hard campaign against Tyre; every head was rubbed bare[q] and every shoulder made raw. Yet he and his army got no reward from the campaign he led against Tyre. [19]Therefore this is what the Sovereign LORD says: I am going to give Egypt to Nebuchadnezzar king of Babylon, and he will carry off its wealth. He will loot and plunder the land as pay for his army.[r] [20]I have given him Egypt as a reward for his efforts because he and his army did it for me, declares the Sovereign LORD.[s]

[21]"On that day I will make a horn[d][t] grow for the house of Israel, and I will open your mouth[u] among them. Then they will know that I am the LORD.[v]"

a 7 Syriac (see also Septuagint and Vulgate); Hebrew *and you caused their backs to stand*
b 10 That is, the upper Nile region   c 14 Hebrew *to Pathros*   d 21 *Horn* here symbolizes strength.

29:5
a Jer 7:33; 34:20; Eze 32:4-6; 39:4

29:6
b 2Ki 18:21; Isa 36:6

29:7
c Isa 36:6
d Eze 17:15-17

29:8
e Eze 14:17; 32:11-13

29:9
f Eze 30:7-8,13-19

29:10
g Eze 30:6

29:11
h Eze 32:13

29:12
i Jer 46:19; Eze 30:7,23,26

29:14
j Eze 30:14
k Eze 17:14

29:15
l Zec 10:11

29:16
m Isa 36:4,6
n Isa 30:2; Hos 8:13

29:17
o Eze 24:1

29:18
p Jer 27:6; Eze 26:7-8
q Jer 48:37

29:19
r Jer 43:10-13; Eze 30:4,10,24-25

29:20
s Isa 10:6-7; 45:1; Jer 25:9

29:21
t Ps 132:17
u Eze 33:22
v Eze 24:27

30:2
a Isa 13:6

30:3
b Eze 7:7;
Joel 2:1,11;
Ob 1:15
c ver 18;
Eze 7:12,19

30:4
d Eze 29:19

30:5
e Eze 27:10
f Jer 25:20

30:6
g Eze 29:10

30:7
h Eze 29:12

30:9
i Isa 18:1-2
j Isa 23:5
k Eze 32:9-10

30:10
l Eze 29:19

30:11
m Eze 28:7

30:12
n Isa 19:6
o Eze 29:9

Chapter 30 Theme _____

30 The word of the LORD came to me: [2]"Son of man, prophesy and say: 'This is what the Sovereign LORD says:

"'Wail[a] and say,
  "Alas for that day!"
[3]For the day is near,[b]
  the day of the LORD[c] is near—
a day of clouds,
  a time of doom for the nations.
[4]A sword will come against Egypt,
  and anguish will come upon Cush.[a]
When the slain fall in Egypt,
  her wealth will be carried away
  and her foundations torn down.[d]

[5]Cush and Put,[e] Lydia and all Arabia, Libya[b] and the people[f] of the covenant land will fall by the sword along with Egypt.

[6]"'This is what the LORD says:

"'The allies of Egypt will fall
  and her proud strength will fail.
From Migdol to Aswan[g]
  they will fall by the sword within her,
        declares the Sovereign LORD.
[7]"'They will be desolate
  among desolate lands,
and their cities will lie
  among ruined cities.[h]
[8]Then they will know that I am the LORD,
  when I set fire to Egypt
  and all her helpers are crushed.

[9]"'On that day messengers will go out from me in ships to frighten Cush[i] out of her complacency. Anguish[j] will take hold of them on the day of Egypt's doom, for it is sure to come.[k]

[10]"'This is what the Sovereign LORD says:

"'I will put an end to the hordes of Egypt
  by the hand of Nebuchadnezzar king of Babylon.[l]
[11]He and his army—the most ruthless of nations[m]—
  will be brought in to destroy the land.
They will draw their swords against Egypt
  and fill the land with the slain.
[12]I will dry up[n] the streams of the Nile[o]
  and sell the land to evil men;

a4 That is, the upper Nile region; also in verses 5 and 9   b5 Hebrew *Cub*

1463

by the hand of foreigners
I will lay waste the land and everything in it.

I the LORD have spoken.

13"'This is what the Sovereign LORD says:

"'I will destroy the idols[a]
and put an end to the images in Memphis.[a][b]
No longer will there be a prince in Egypt,[c]
and I will spread fear throughout the land.
14I will lay[d] waste Upper Egypt,[b]
set fire to Zoan[e]
and inflict punishment on Thebes.[c][f]
15I will pour out my wrath on Pelusium,[d]
the stronghold of Egypt,
and cut off the hordes of Thebes.
16I will set fire to Egypt;
Pelusium will writhe in agony.
Thebes will be taken by storm;
Memphis will be in constant distress.
17The young men of Heliopolis[e][g] and Bubastis[f]
will fall by the sword,
and the cities themselves will go into captivity.
18Dark will be the day at Tahpanhes
when I break the yoke of Egypt;[h]
there her proud strength will come to an end.
She will be covered with clouds,
and her villages will go into captivity.[i]
19So I will inflict punishment on Egypt,
and they will know that I am the LORD.'"

587 B.C. 20In the eleventh year, in the first month on the seventh day, the word of the LORD came to me:[j] 21"Son of man, I have broken the arm[k] of Pharaoh king of Egypt. It has not been bound up for healing[l] or put in a splint so as to become strong enough to hold a sword. 22Therefore this is what the Sovereign LORD says: I am against Pharaoh king of Egypt.[m] I will break both his arms, the good arm as well as the broken one, and make the sword fall from his hand.[n] 23I will disperse the Egyptians among the nations and scatter them through the countries.[o] 24I will strengthen[p] the arms of the king of Babylon and put my sword[q] in his hand, but I will break the arms of Pharaoh, and he will groan before him like a mortally wounded man. 25I will strengthen the arms of the king of

a 13 Hebrew Noph; also in verse 16   b 14 Hebrew waste Pathros   c 14 Hebrew No; also in verses 15 and 16   d 15 Hebrew Sin; also in verse 16   e 17 Hebrew Awen (or On)   f 17 Hebrew Pi Beseth

30:13
a Jer 43:12
b Isa 19:13
c Zec 10:11

30:14
d Eze 29:14
e Ps 78:12,43
f Jer 46:25

30:17
g Ge 41:45

30:18
h Lev 26:13
i ver 3

30:20
j Eze 26:1; 29:17; 31:1

30:21
k Jer 48:25
l Jer 30:13; 46:11

30:22
m Jer 46:25
n Ps 37:17

30:23
o Eze 29:12

30:24
p Zec 10:6,12
q Eze 21:14; Zep 2:12

30:26
a Eze 29:12

Babylon, but the arms of Pharaoh will fall limp. Then they will know that I am the LORD, when I put my sword into the hand of the king of Babylon and he brandishes it against Egypt. ²⁶I will disperse the Egyptians among the nations and scatter them through the countries. Then they will know that I am the LORD.*a*"

Chapter 31 Theme

31:1
b Jer 52:5
c Eze 30:20

31 In the eleventh year,*b* in the third month on the first day, the word of the LORD came to me:*c* ²"Son of man, say to Pharaoh king of Egypt and to his hordes:

587 B.C.

"'Who can be compared with you in majesty?
³Consider Assyria, once a cedar in Lebanon,
  with beautiful branches overshadowing the forest;
it towered on high,
  its top above the thick foliage.*d*

31:3
d Isa 10:34

⁴The waters nourished it,
  deep springs made it grow tall;
their streams flowed
  all around its base
and sent their channels
  to all the trees of the field.
⁵So it towered higher
  than all the trees of the field;
its boughs increased
  and its branches grew long,
    spreading because of abundant waters.*e*

31:5
e Eze 17:5

⁶All the birds of the air
  nested in its boughs,
all the beasts of the field
  gave birth under its branches;
all the great nations
  lived in its shade.*f*

31:6
f Eze 17:23;
Mt 13:32

⁷It was majestic in beauty,
  with its spreading boughs,
for its roots went down
  to abundant waters.
⁸The cedars*g* in the garden of God
  could not rival it,
nor could the pine trees
  equal its boughs,
nor could the plane trees
  compare with its branches—
no tree in the garden of God
  could match its beauty.*h*

31:8
g Ps 80:10
h Ge 2:8-9

⁹I made it beautiful
  with abundant branches,
  the envy of all the trees of Eden[a]
  in the garden of God.[b]

¹⁰"Therefore this is what the Sovereign LORD says: Because it towered on high, lifting its top above the thick foliage, and because it was proud[c] of its height, ¹¹I handed it over to the ruler of the nations, for him to deal with according to its wickedness. I cast it aside,[d] ¹²and the most ruthless of foreign nations[e] cut it down and left it. Its boughs fell on the mountains and in all the valleys;[f] its branches lay broken in all the ravines of the land. All the nations of the earth came out from under its shade and left it.[g] ¹³All the birds of the air settled on the fallen tree, and all the beasts of the field were among its branches.[h] ¹⁴Therefore no other trees by the waters are ever to tower proudly on high, lifting their tops above the thick foliage. No other trees so well-watered are ever to reach such a height; they are all destined for death,[i] for the earth below, among mortal men, with those who go down to the pit.[j]

¹⁵"This is what the Sovereign LORD says: On the day it was brought down to the grave[a] I covered the deep springs with mourning for it; I held back its streams, and its abundant waters were restrained. Because of it I clothed Lebanon with gloom, and all the trees of the field withered away. ¹⁶I made the nations tremble[k] at the sound of its fall when I brought it down to the grave with those who go down to the pit. Then all the trees[l] of Eden, the choicest and best of Lebanon, all the trees that were well-watered, were consoled[m] in the earth below.[n] ¹⁷Those who lived in its shade, its allies among the nations, had also gone down to the grave with it, joining those killed by the sword.[o]

¹⁸"Which of the trees of Eden can be compared with you in splendor and majesty? Yet you, too, will be brought down with the trees of Eden to the earth below; you will lie among the uncircumcised,[p] with those killed by the sword.

"'This is Pharaoh and all his hordes, declares the Sovereign LORD.'"

Chapter 32 Theme

585 B.C. **32** In the twelfth year, in the twelfth month on the first day, the word of the LORD came to me:[q] ²"Son of man, take up a lament[r] concerning Pharaoh king of Egypt and say to him:

"'You are like a lion[s] among the nations;
  you are like a monster in the seas

[a] 15 Hebrew *Sheol*; also in verses 16 and 17

31:9
[a] Ge 2:8
[b] Ge 13:10;
Eze 28:13

31:10
[c] Isa 14:13-14;
Eze 28:17

31:11
[d] Da 5:20

31:12
[e] Eze 28:7
[f] Eze 32:5; 35:8
[g] Eze 32:11-12;
Da 4:14

31:13
[h] Isa 18:6;
Eze 29:5; 32:4

31:14
[i] Ps 82:7
[j] Ps 63:9;
Eze 26:20; 32:24

31:16
[k] Eze 26:15
[l] Isa 14:8
[m] Eze 14:22;
32:31
[n] Isa 14:15;
Eze 32:18

31:17
[o] Ps 9:17

31:18
[p] Jer 9:26;
Eze 32:19,21

32:1
[q] Eze 31:1; 33:21

32:2
[r] Eze 19:1; 27:2
[s] Eze 19:3,6;
Na 2:11-13

32:2
a Eze 29:3; 34:18

thrashing about in your streams,
churning the water with your feet
and muddying the streams.*a*

³"'This is what the Sovereign LORD says:

32:3
b Eze 12:13

"'With a great throng of people
I will cast my net over you,
and they will haul you up in my net.*b*
⁴I will throw you on the land
and hurl you on the open field.

32:4
c Isa 18:6;
Eze 31:12-13

I will let all the birds of the air settle on you
and all the beasts of the earth gorge themselves on you.*c*
⁵I will spread your flesh on the mountains
and fill the valleys*d* with your remains.
⁶I will drench the land with your flowing blood*e*

32:5
d Eze 31:12

all the way to the mountains,
and the ravines will be filled with your flesh.
⁷When I snuff you out, I will cover the heavens
and darken their stars;

32:6
e Isa 34:3

I will cover the sun with a cloud,
and the moon will not give its light.*f*
⁸All the shining lights in the heavens
I will darken over you;
I will bring darkness over your land,
declares the Sovereign LORD.

32:7
f Isa 13:10; 34:4;
Eze 30:3;
Joel 2:2,31; 3:15;
Mt 24:29;
Rev 8:12

⁹I will trouble the hearts of many peoples
when I bring about your destruction among the
nations,
among*a* lands you have not known.
¹⁰I will cause many peoples to be appalled at you,
and their kings will shudder with horror because of you
when I brandish my sword before them.

32:10
g Jer 46:10
h Eze 26:16;
27:35

On the day*g* of your downfall
each of them will tremble
every moment for his life.*h*

¹¹"'For this is what the Sovereign LORD says:

32:11
i Jer 46:26

"'The sword of the king of Babylon*i*
will come against you.
¹²I will cause your hordes to fall
by the swords of mighty men—
the most ruthless of all nations.*j*
They will shatter the pride of Egypt,
and all her hordes will be overthrown.*k*

32:12
j Eze 28:7
k Eze 31:11-12

a 9 Hebrew; Septuagint *bring you into captivity among the nations, / to*

> [13]I will destroy all her cattle
> from beside abundant waters
> no longer to be stirred by the foot of man
> or muddied by the hoofs of cattle.*a*
>
> [14]Then I will let her waters settle
> and make her streams flow like oil,
> declares the Sovereign LORD.
>
> [15]When I make Egypt desolate
> and strip the land of everything in it,
> when I strike down all who live there,
> then they will know that I am the LORD.*b*

[16]"This is the lament*c* they will chant for her. The daughters of the nations will chant it; for Egypt and all her hordes they will chant it, declares the Sovereign LORD."

586-585 B.C. [17]In the twelfth year, on the fifteenth day of the month, the word of the LORD came to me:*d* [18]"Son of man, wail for the hordes of Egypt and consign*e* to the earth below both her and the daughters of mighty nations, with those who go down to the pit.*f* [19]Say to them, 'Are you more favored than others? Go down and be laid among the uncircumcised.'*g* [20]They will fall among those killed by the sword. The sword is drawn; let her be dragged*h* off with all her hordes. [21]From within the grave*a i* the mighty leaders will say of Egypt and her allies, 'They have come down and they lie with the uncircumcised, with those killed by the sword.'

[22]"Assyria is there with her whole army; she is surrounded by the graves of all her slain, all who have fallen by the sword. [23]Their graves are in the depths of the pit*j* and her army lies around her grave. All who had spread terror in the land of the living are slain, fallen by the sword.

[24]"Elam*k* is there, with all her hordes around her grave. All of them are slain, fallen by the sword.*l* All who had spread terror in the land of the living*m* went down uncircumcised to the earth below. They bear their shame with those who go down to the pit.*n* [25]A bed is made for her among the slain, with all her hordes around her grave. All of them are uncircumcised, killed by the sword. Because their terror had spread in the land of the living, they bear their shame with those who go down to the pit; they are laid among the slain.

[26]"Meshech and Tubal*o* are there, with all their hordes around their graves. All of them are uncircumcised, killed by the sword because they spread their terror in the land of the living. [27]Do they not lie with the other uncircumcised warriors who have fallen, who went down to the grave with their weapons of war, whose

---

32:13
a Eze 29:8,11

32:15
b Ex 7:5;
14:4,18;
Ps 107:33-34;
Eze 6:7

32:16
c 2Sa 1:17;
2Ch 35:25;
Eze 26:17

32:17
d ver 1

32:18
e Jer 1:10
f Eze 31:14,16;
Mic 1:8

32:19
g ver 29-30;
Eze 28:10; 31:18

32:20
h Ps 28:3

32:21
i Isa 14:9

32:23
j Isa 14:15

32:24
k Ge 10:22
l Jer 49:37
m Job 28:13
n Eze 26:20

32:26
o Ge 10:2;
Eze 27:13

---

a 21 Hebrew *Sheol*; also in verse 27

swords were placed under their heads? The punishment for their sins rested on their bones, though the terror of these warriors had stalked through the land of the living. ²⁸"You too, O Pharaoh, will be broken and will lie among the uncircumcised, with those killed by the sword.

²⁹"Edom*a* is there, her kings and all her princes; despite their power, they are laid with those killed by the sword. They lie with the uncircumcised, with those who go down to the pit.*b*

³⁰"All the princes of the north*c* and all the Sidonians*d* are there; they went down with the slain in disgrace despite the terror caused by their power. They lie uncircumcised with those killed by the sword and bear their shame with those who go down to the pit.

³¹"Pharaoh—he and all his army—will see them and he will be consoled*e* for all his hordes that were killed by the sword, declares the Sovereign LORD. ³²Although I had him spread terror in the land of the living, Pharaoh and all his hordes will be laid among the uncircumcised, with those killed by the sword, declares the Sovereign LORD."

Chapter 33 Theme

33 The word of the LORD came to me: ²"Son of man, speak to your countrymen and say to them: 'When I bring the sword*f* against a land, and the people of the land choose one of their men and make him their watchman,*g* ³and he sees the sword coming against the land and blows the trumpet*h* to warn the people, ⁴then if anyone hears the trumpet but does not take warning*i* and the sword comes and takes his life, his blood will be on his own head.*j* ⁵Since he heard the sound of the trumpet but did not take warning, his blood will be on his own head. If he had taken warning, he would have saved himself. ⁶But if the watchman sees the sword coming and does not blow the trumpet to warn the people and the sword comes and takes the life of one of them, that man will be taken away because of his sin, but I will hold the watchman accountable for his blood.'*k*

**Cross References (left margin):**

32:29
a Isa 34:5-15;
Jer 49:7;
Eze 35:15;
Ob 1:1
b Eze 25:12-14

32:30
c Jer 25:26;
Eze 38:6; 39:2
d Jer 25:22;
Eze 28:21

32:31
e Eze 14:22;
31:16

33:2
f Jer 12:12
g Eze 3:11

33:3
h Hos 8:1

33:4
i 2Ch 25:16
j Jer 6:17;
Eze 18:13;
Zec 1:4; Ac 18:6

33:6
k Eze 3:18

The Prophetic Points of History

Prophet's Own Time — Captivity and Restoration — Intertestament Period — Christ's First Coming — Christ's Second Coming — New Heaven/New Earth

7"Son of man, I have made you a watchman for the house of Israel; so hear the word I speak and give them warning from me.[a] 8When I say to the wicked, 'O wicked man, you will surely die,[b]' and you do not speak out to dissuade him from his ways, that wicked man will die for[a] his sin, and I will hold you accountable for his blood.[c] 9But if you do warn the wicked man to turn from his ways and he does not do so, he will die for his sin, but you will have saved yourself.[d]

10"Son of man, say to the house of Israel, 'This is what you are saying: "Our offenses and sins weigh us down, and we are wasting away[e] because of[b] them. How then can we live?[f]"' 11Say to them, 'As surely as I live, declares the Sovereign LORD, I take no pleasure in the death of the wicked, but rather that they turn from their ways and live.[g] Turn! Turn from your evil ways! Why will you die, O house of Israel?'[h]

12"Therefore, son of man, say to your countrymen, 'The righteousness of the righteous man will not save him when he disobeys, and the wickedness of the wicked man will not cause him to fall when he turns from it. The righteous man, if he sins, will not be allowed to live because of his former righteousness.'[i] 13If I tell the righteous man that he will surely live, but then he trusts in his righteousness and does evil, none of the righteous things he has done will be remembered; he will die for the evil he has done.[j] 14And if I say to the wicked man, 'You will surely die,' but he then turns away from his sin and does what is just[k] and right— 15if he gives back what he took in pledge for a loan, returns what he has stolen,[l] follows the decrees that give life, and does no evil, he will surely live; he will not die.[m] 16None of the sins he has committed will be remembered against him. He has done what is just and right; he will surely live.[n]

17"Yet your countrymen say, 'The way of the Lord is not just.' But it is their way that is not just. 18If a righteous man turns from his righteousness and does evil, he will die for it.[o] 19And if a wicked man turns away from his wickedness and does what is just and right, he will live by doing so. 20Yet, O house of Israel, you say, 'The way of the Lord is not just.' But I will judge each of you according to his own ways."

585 B.C. 21In the twelfth year of our exile, in the tenth month on the fifth day, a man who had escaped[p] from Jerusalem came to me and said, "The city has fallen!"[q] 22Now the evening before the man arrived, the hand of the LORD was upon me,[r] and he opened my mouth[s] before the man came to me in the morning. So my mouth was opened and I was no longer silent.[t]

23Then the word of the LORD came to me: 24"Son of man, the people living in those ruins[u] in the land of Israel are saying,

---

a8 Or in; also in verse 9   b10 Or away in

33:7
a Jer 26:2; Eze 3:17

33:8
b ver 14
c Eze 18:4

33:9
d Eze 3:17-19

33:10
e Eze 24:23
f Lev 26:39; Eze 4:17

33:11
g Eze 18:32; 2Pe 3:9
h Eze 18:23

33:12
i 2Ch 7:14; Eze 3:20

33:13
j Eze 18:24; Heb 10:38; 2Pe 2:20-21

33:14
k Eze 18:27

33:15
l Ex 22:1-4; Lev 6:2-5
m Eze 20:11; Lk 19:8

33:16
n Isa 43:25; Eze 18:22

33:18
o Eze 3:20; Eze 18:26

33:21
p Eze 24:26
q 2Ki 25:4,10; Jer 39:1-2; Eze 32:1

33:22
r Eze 1:3
s Lk 1:64
t Eze 3:26-27; 24:27

33:24
u Eze 36:4

'Abraham was only one man, yet he possessed the land. But we are many; surely the land has been given to us as our possession.'[a] [25]Therefore say to them, 'This is what the Sovereign LORD says: Since you eat meat with the blood[b] still in it and look to your idols and shed blood, should you then possess the land?[c] [26]You rely on your sword, you do detestable things, and each of you defiles his neighbor's wife.[d] Should you then possess the land?'

[27]"Say this to them: 'This is what the Sovereign LORD says: As surely as I live, those who are left in the ruins will fall by the sword, those out in the country I will give to the wild animals to be devoured, and those in strongholds and caves will die of a plague.[e] [28]I will make the land a desolate waste, and her proud strength will come to an end, and the mountains of Israel will become desolate so that no one will cross them. [29]Then they will know that I am the LORD, when I have made the land a desolate waste because of all the detestable things they have done.'

[30]"As for you, son of man, your countrymen are talking together about you by the walls and at the doors of the houses, saying to each other, 'Come and hear the message that has come from the LORD.' [31]My people come to you, as they usually do, and sit before[f] you to listen to your words, but they do not put them into practice. With their mouths they express devotion, but their hearts are greedy for unjust gain.[g] [32]Indeed, to them you are nothing more than one who sings love songs with a beautiful voice and plays an instrument well, for they hear your words but do not put them into practice.[h]

[33]"When all this comes true—and it surely will—then they will know that a prophet has been among them.[i]"

Chapter 34 Theme

34 The word of the LORD came to me: [2]"Son of man, prophesy against the shepherds of Israel; prophesy and say to them: 'This is what the Sovereign LORD says: Woe to the shepherds of Israel who only take care of themselves! Should not shepherds take care of the flock?[j] [3]You eat the curds, clothe yourselves with the wool and slaughter the choice animals, but you do not take care of the flock.[k] [4]You have not strengthened the weak or healed the sick or bound up the injured. You have not brought back the strays or searched for the lost. You have ruled them harshly and brutally.[l] [5]So they were scattered because there was no shepherd,[m] and when they were scattered they became food for all the wild animals.[n] [6]My sheep wandered over all the mountains and on every high hill. They were scattered over the whole earth, and no one searched or looked for them.[o]

[7]"Therefore, you shepherds, hear the word of the LORD: [8]As surely as I live, declares the Sovereign LORD, because my flock lacks

33:24 [a]Isa 51:2; Jer 40:7; Eze 11:15; Ac 7:5

33:25 [b]Ge 9:4; Dt 12:16 [c]Jer 7:9-10; Eze 22:6,27

33:26 [d]Eze 22:11

33:27 [e]1Sa 13:6; Isa 2:19; Jer 42:22; Eze 39:4

33:31 [f]Eze 8:1 [g]Ps 78:36-37; Isa 29:13; Eze 22:27; Mt 13:22; 1Jn 3:18

33:32 [h]Mk 6:20

33:33 [i]1Sa 3:20; Jer 28:9; Eze 2:5

34:2 [j]Ps 78:70-72; Isa 40:11; Jer 3:15; 23:1; Mic 3:11; Jn 10:11; 21:15-17

34:3 [k]Isa 56:11; Eze 22:27; Zec 11:16

34:4 [l]Zec 11:15-17

34:5 [m]Nu 27:17 [n]ver 28; Isa 56:9

34:6 [o]Ps 142:4; 1Pe 2:25

a shepherd and so has been plundered and has become food for all the wild animals, and because my shepherds did not search for my flock but cared for themselves rather than for my flock, ⁹therefore, O shepherds, hear the word of the LORD: ¹⁰This is what the Sovereign LORD says: I am against*ᵃ* the shepherds and will hold them accountable for my flock. I will remove them from tending the flock so that the shepherds can no longer feed themselves. I will rescue*ᵇ* my flock from their mouths, and it will no longer be food for them.*ᶜ*

¹¹"'For this is what the Sovereign LORD says: I myself will search for my sheep and look after them. ¹²As a shepherd*ᵈ* looks after his scattered flock when he is with them, so will I look after my sheep. I will rescue them from all the places where they were scattered on a day of clouds and darkness.*ᵉ* ¹³I will bring them out from the nations and gather them from the countries, and I will bring them into their own land. I will pasture them on the mountains of Israel, in the ravines and in all the settlements in the land.*ᶠ* ¹⁴I will tend them in a good pasture, and the mountain heights of Israel*ᵍ* will be their grazing land. There they will lie down in good grazing land, and there they will feed in a rich pasture*ʰ* on the mountains of Israel.*ⁱ* ¹⁵I myself will tend my sheep and have them lie down, declares the Sovereign LORD.*ʲ* ¹⁶I will search for the lost and bring back the strays. I will bind up the injured and strengthen the weak,*ᵏ* but the sleek and the strong I will destroy. I will shepherd the flock with justice.*ˡ*

¹⁷"'As for you, my flock, this is what the Sovereign LORD says: I will judge between one sheep and another, and between rams and goats.*ᵐ* ¹⁸Is it not enough for you to feed on the good pasture? Must you also trample the rest of your pasture with your feet? Is it not enough for you to drink clear water? Must you also muddy the rest with your feet? ¹⁹Must my flock feed on what you have trampled and drink what you have muddied with your feet?

²⁰"'Therefore this is what the Sovereign LORD says to them: See, I myself will judge between the fat sheep and the lean sheep. ²¹Because you shove with flank and shoulder, butting all the weak sheep with your horns*ⁿ* until you have driven them away, ²²I will save my flock, and they will no longer be plundered. I will judge between one sheep and another.*ᵒ* ²³I will place over them one shepherd, my servant David, and he will tend*ᵖ* them; he will tend them and be their shepherd. ²⁴I the LORD will be their God,*ᑫ* and my servant David will be prince among them. I the LORD have spoken.*ʳ*

²⁵"'I will make a covenant of peace with them and rid the land of wild beasts*ˢ* so that they may live in the desert and sleep in the forests in safety.*ᵗ* ²⁶I will bless*ᵘ* them and the places surrounding

---

34:10
ᵃ Jer 21:13
ᵇ Ps 72:14
ᶜ 1Sa 2:29-30;
Zec 10:3

34:12
ᵈ Isa 40:11;
Jer 31:10;
Lk 19:10
ᵉ Eze 30:3

34:13
ᶠ Jer 23:3

34:14
ᵍ Eze 20:40
ʰ Ps 23:2
ⁱ Eze 36:29-30

34:15
ʲ Ps 23:1-2

34:16
ᵏ Mic 4:6
ˡ Isa 10:16;
Lk 5:32

34:17
ᵐ Mt 25:32-33

34:21
ⁿ Dt 33:17

34:22
ᵒ Ps 72:12-14;
Jer 23:2-3

34:23
ᵖ Isa 40:11

34:24
ᑫ Eze 36:28
ʳ Jer 30:9

34:25
ˢ Lev 26:6
ᵗ Isa 11:6-9;
Hos 2:18

34:26
ᵘ Ge 12:2

34:26
a Ps 68:9
b Dt 11:13-15;
Isa 44:3

34:27
c Lev 26:13
d Jer 30:8

34:28
e Jer 30:10;
Eze 39:26

34:29
f Isa 4:2
g Eze 36:29
h Eze 36:6
i Eze 36:15

34:30
j Eze 14:11;
37:27

34:31
k Ps 100:3;
Jer 23:1

35:3
l Jer 6:12
m Eze 25:12-14

35:4
n ver 9

35:5
o Ps 137:7;
Eze 21:29

35:6
p Isa 63:2-6

35:8
q Eze 31:12

35:9
r Jer 49:13

35:10
s Ps 83:12;
Eze 36:2,5

35:11
t Eze 25:14
u Ps 9:16; Mt 7:2

35:12
v Jer 50:7

my hill.*a* I will send down showers in season;*a* there will be showers of blessing.*b* 27 The trees of the field will yield their fruit and the ground will yield its crops; the people will be secure in their land. They will know that I am the LORD, when I break the bars of their yoke*c* and rescue them from the hands of those who enslaved them.*d* 28 They will no longer be plundered by the nations, nor will wild animals devour them. They will live in safety, and no one will make them afraid.*e* 29 I will provide for them a land renowned*f* for its crops, and they will no longer be victims of famine*g* in the land or bear the scorn*h* of the nations.*i* 30 Then they will know that I, the LORD their God, am with them and that they, the house of Israel, are my people, declares the Sovereign LORD.*j* 31 You my sheep, the sheep of my pasture,*k* are people, and I am your God, declares the Sovereign LORD.'"

Chapter 35 Theme _____

35 The word of the LORD came to me: 2 "Son of man, set your face against Mount Seir; prophesy against it 3 and say: 'This is what the Sovereign LORD says: I am against you, Mount Seir, and I will stretch out my hand*l* against you and make you a desolate waste.*m* 4 I will turn your towns into ruins and you will be desolate. Then you will know that I am the LORD.*n*

5 "'Because you harbored an ancient hostility and delivered the Israelites over to the sword at the time of their calamity, the time their punishment reached its climax,*o* 6 therefore as surely as I live, declares the Sovereign LORD, I will give you over to bloodshed and it will pursue you.*p* Since you did not hate bloodshed, bloodshed will pursue you. 7 I will make Mount Seir a desolate waste and cut off from it all who come and go. 8 I will fill your mountains with the slain; those killed by the sword will fall on your hills and in your valleys and in all your ravines.*q* 9 I will make you desolate forever; your towns will not be inhabited. Then you will know that I am the LORD.*r*

10 "'Because you have said, "These two nations and countries will be ours and we will take possession*s* of them," even though I the LORD was there, 11 therefore as surely as I live, declares the Sovereign LORD, I will treat you in accordance with the anger*t* and jealousy you showed in your hatred of them and I will make myself known among them when I judge you.*u* 12 Then you will know that I the LORD have heard all the contemptible things you have said against the mountains of Israel. You said, "They have been laid waste and have been given over to us to devour."*v* 13 You boasted against me and spoke against me without restraint, and I

a 26 Or *I will make them and the places surrounding my hill a blessing* heard it.[a] [14]This is what the Sovereign LORD says: While the whole earth rejoices, I will make you desolate.[b] [15]Because you rejoiced[c] when the inheritance of the house of Israel became desolate, that is how I will treat you. You will be desolate, O Mount Seir,[d] you and all of Edom.[e] Then they will know that I am the LORD.'"

INSIGHT

See **Major Events in Israel's History** on page 2189. Notice the section from 1948 through modern times.

Chapter 36 Theme

36 "Son of man, prophesy to the mountains of Israel and say, 'O mountains of Israel, hear the word of the LORD. [2]This is what the Sovereign LORD says: The enemy said of you, "Aha![f] The ancient heights[g] have become our possession."[h]' [3]Therefore prophesy and say, 'This is what the Sovereign LORD says: Because they ravaged and hounded you from every side so that you became the possession of the rest of the nations and the object of people's malicious talk and slander,[i] [4]therefore, O mountains of Israel, hear the word of the Sovereign LORD: This is what the Sovereign LORD says to the mountains and hills, to the ravines and valleys,[j] to the desolate ruins and the deserted towns that have been plundered and ridiculed by the rest of the nations around you[k]— [5]this is what the Sovereign LORD says: In my burning zeal I have spoken against the rest of the nations, and against all Edom, for with glee and with malice in their hearts they made my land their own possession so that they might plunder its pastureland.'[l] [6]Therefore prophesy concerning the land of Israel and say to the mountains and hills, to the ravines and valleys: 'This is what the Sovereign LORD says: I speak in my jealous wrath because you have suffered the scorn of the nations.[m] [7]Therefore this is what the Sovereign LORD says: I swear with uplifted hand that the nations around you will also suffer scorn.

[8]"But you, O mountains of Israel, will produce branches and fruit[n] for my people Israel, for they will soon come home. [9]I am concerned for you and will look on you with favor; you will be plowed and sown, [10]and I will multiply the number of people upon you, even the whole house of Israel. The towns will be inhabited and the ruins rebuilt.[o] [11]I will increase the number of men and animals upon you, and they will be fruitful and become numerous. I will settle people on you as in the past[p] and will make you prosper more than before.[q] Then you will know that I am the LORD. [12]I will cause people, my people Israel, to walk upon you. They will possess you, and you will be their inheritance;[r] you will never again deprive them of their children.

[13]"This is what the Sovereign LORD says: Because people say to you, "You devour men[s] and deprive your nation of its children," [14]therefore you will no longer devour men or make your nation childless, declares the Sovereign LORD. [15]No longer will I make you

35:13
[a] Da 11:36

35:14
[b] Jer 51:48

35:15
[c] Ob 1:12
[d] ver 3
[e] Isa 34:5-6,11;
Jer 50:11-13;
La 4:21

36:2
[f] Eze 25:3
[g] Dt 32:13
[h] Eze 35:10

36:3
[i] Ps 44:13-14

36:4
[j] Eze 6:3
[k] Dt 11:11;
Ps 79:4;
Eze 34:28

36:5
[l] Jer 50:11;
Eze 25:12-14;
35:10,15

36:6
[m] Ps 123:3-4;
Eze 34:29

36:8
[n] Isa 27:6

36:10
[o] ver 33;
Isa 49:17-23

36:11
[p] Mic 7:14
[q] Jer 31:28;
Eze 16:55

36:12
[r] Eze 47:14,22

36:13
[s] Nu 13:32

36:15
a Ps 89:50-51;
Eze 34:29

36:17
b Jer 2:7

36:18
c 2Ch 34:21

36:19
d Dt 28:64
e Eze 39:24

36:20
f Ro 2:24
g Isa 52:5;
Jer 33:24;
Eze 12:16

36:21
h Ps 74:18;
Isa 48:9

36:22
i Ro 2:24*
j Ps 106:8

36:23
k Eze 20:41
l Ps 126:2;
Isa 5:16

36:24
m Eze 34:13;
37:21

36:25
n Heb 9:13;
10:22
o Ps 51:2,7
p Zec 13:2

36:26
q Jer 24:7
r Ps 51:10;
Eze 11:19

36:27
s Eze 37:14

36:28
t Jer 30:22
u Eze 14:11;
37:14,27

36:29
v Eze 34:29

36:30
w Lev 26:4-5;
Eze 34:27;
Hos 2:21-22

36:31
x Eze 6:9; 20:43

36:32
y Dt 9:5

hear the taunts of the nations, and no longer will you suffer the scorn of the peoples or cause your nation to fall, declares the Sovereign Lord.*a*'"

16Again the word of the Lord came to me: 17"Son of man, when the people of Israel were living in their own land, they defiled it by their conduct and their actions. Their conduct was like a woman's monthly uncleanness in my sight.*b* 18So I poured out*c* my wrath on them because they had shed blood in the land and because they had defiled it with their idols. 19I dispersed them among the nations, and they were scattered*d* through the countries; I judged them according to their conduct and their actions.*e* 20And wherever they went among the nations they profaned*f* my holy name, for it was said of them, 'These are the Lord's people, and yet they had to leave his land.'*g* 21I had concern for my holy name, which the house of Israel profaned among the nations where they had gone.*h*

22"Therefore say to the house of Israel, 'This is what the Sovereign Lord says: It is not for your sake, O house of Israel, that I am going to do these things, but for the sake of my holy name, which you have profaned*i* among the nations where you have gone.*j* 23I will show the holiness of my great name, which has been profaned among the nations, the name you have profaned among them. Then the nations will know that I am the Lord, declares the Sovereign Lord, when I show myself holy*k* through you before their eyes.*l*

24"'For I will take you out of the nations; I will gather you from all the countries and bring you back into your own land.*m* 25I will sprinkle*n* clean water on you, and you will be clean; I will cleanse*o* you from all your impurities and from all your idols.*p* 26I will give you a new heart*q* and put a new spirit in you; I will remove from you your heart of stone and give you a heart of flesh.*r* 27And I will put my Spirit*s* in you and move you to follow my decrees and be careful to keep my laws. 28You will live in the land I gave your forefathers; you will be my people,*t* and I will be your God.*u* 29I will save you from all your uncleanness. I will call for the grain and make it plentiful and will not bring famine*v* upon you. 30I will increase the fruit of the trees and the crops of the field, so that you will no longer suffer disgrace among the nations because of famine.*w* 31Then you will remember your evil ways and wicked deeds, and you will loathe yourselves for your sins and detestable practices.*x* 32I want you to know that I am not doing this for your sake, declares the Sovereign Lord. Be ashamed and disgraced for your conduct, O house of Israel!*y*

33"'This is what the Sovereign Lord says: On the day I cleanse you from all your sins, I will resettle your towns, and the ruins will be rebuilt. 34The desolate land will be cultivated instead of lying desolate in the sight of all who pass through it. 35They will say,

"This land that was laid waste has become like the garden of Eden;[a] the cities that were lying in ruins, desolate and destroyed, are now fortified and inhabited.[b]" [36]Then the nations around you that remain will know that I the LORD have rebuilt what was destroyed and have replanted what was desolate. I the LORD have spoken, and I will do it.'[c]

[37]"This is what the Sovereign LORD says: Once again I will yield to the plea of the house of Israel and do this for them: I will make their people as numerous as sheep, [38]as numerous as the flocks for offerings[d] at Jerusalem during her appointed feasts. So will the ruined cities be filled with flocks of people. Then they will know that I am the LORD."

Chapter 37 Theme

37 The hand of the LORD was upon me,[e] and he brought me out by the Spirit[f] of the LORD and set me in the middle of a valley;[g] it was full of bones.[h] [2]He led me back and forth among them, and I saw a great many bones on the floor of the valley, bones that were very dry. [3]He asked me, "Son of man, can these bones live?"

I said, "O Sovereign LORD, you alone know.[i]"

[4]Then he said to me, "Prophesy to these bones and say to them, 'Dry bones, hear the word of the LORD![j] [5]This is what the Sovereign LORD says to these bones: I will make breath[a] enter you, and you will come to life.[k] [6]I will attach tendons to you and make flesh come upon you and cover you with skin; I will put breath in you, and you will come to life. Then you will know that I am the LORD.[l]'"

[7]So I prophesied as I was commanded. And as I was prophesying, there was a noise, a rattling sound, and the bones came together, bone to bone. [8]I looked, and tendons and flesh appeared on them and skin covered them, but there was no breath in them.

[9]Then he said to me, "Prophesy to the breath;[m] prophesy, son of man, and say to it, 'This is what the Sovereign LORD says: Come from the four winds, O breath, and breathe into these slain, that they may live.'" [10]So I prophesied as he commanded me, and breath entered them; they came to life and stood up on their feet— a vast army.[n]

[11]Then he said to me: "Son of man, these bones are the whole house of Israel. They say, 'Our bones are dried up and our hope is gone; we are cut off.'[o] [12]Therefore prophesy and say to them: 'This is what the Sovereign LORD says: O my people, I am going to open your graves and bring you up from them; I will bring you back to the land of Israel.[p] [13]Then you, my people, will know that I am the

36:35 [a]Joel 2:3; [b]Isa 51:3

36:36 [c]Eze 17:22; 22:14; 37:14; 39:27-28

36:38 [d]1Ki 8:63; 2Ch 35:7-9

37:1 [e]Eze 1:3; 8:3 [f]Eze 11:24; Lk 4:1; Ac 8:39 [g]Jer 7:32 [h]Jer 8:2; Eze 40:1

37:3 [i]Dt 32:39; 1Sa 2:6; Isa 26:19

37:4 [j]Jer 22:29

37:5 [k]Ge 2:7; Ps 104:29-30

37:6 [l]Eze 38:23; Joel 2:27; 3:17

37:9 [m]Ps 104:30

37:10 [n]Rev 11:11

37:11 [o]La 3:54

37:12 [p]Dt 32:39; 1Sa 2:6; Isa 26:19; Hos 13:14; Am 9:14-15

[a]5 The Hebrew for this word can also mean *wind* or *spirit* (see verses 6-14).

37:14
a Joel 2:28-29
b Eze 36:27-28,36

37:16
c 1Ki 12:20;
2Ch 10:17-19
d Nu 17:2-3;
2Ch 15:9

37:17
e ver 24;
Isa 11:13;
Jer 50:4;
Hos 1:11

37:18
f Eze 24:19

37:19
g Zec 10:6

37:21
h Isa 43:5-6;
Eze 36:24; 39:27

37:22
i Isa 11:13;
Jer 3:18;
Hos 1:11

37:23
j Eze 36:25; 43:7
k Eze 11:18;
36:28

37:24
l Hos 3:5
m Isa 40:11;
Eze 34:23
n Ps 78:70-71

37:25
o Eze 28:25
p Am 9:15
q Isa 11:1

37:26
r Isa 55:3
s Jer 30:19
t Eze 16:62

37:27
u Lev 26:11;
Jn 1:14
v 2Co 6:16*

37:28
w Ex 31:13;
Eze 20:12

38:2
x Ge 10:2
y Rev 20:8

LORD, when I open your graves and bring you up from them. ¹⁴I will put my Spirit^a in you and you will live, and I will settle you in your own land. Then you will know that I the LORD have spoken, and I have done it, declares the LORD.^b'"

¹⁵The word of the LORD came to me: ¹⁶"Son of man, take a stick of wood and write on it, 'Belonging to Judah and the Israelites^c associated with him.^d' Then take another stick of wood, and write on it, 'Ephraim's stick, belonging to Joseph and all the house of Israel associated with him.' ¹⁷Join them together into one stick so that they will become one in your hand.^e

¹⁸"When your countrymen ask you, 'Won't you tell us what you mean by this?'^f ¹⁹say to them, 'This is what the Sovereign LORD says: I am going to take the stick of Joseph—which is in Ephraim's hand—and of the Israelite tribes associated with him, and join it to Judah's stick, making them a single stick of wood, and they will become one in my hand.'^g ²⁰Hold before their eyes the sticks you have written on ²¹and say to them, 'This is what the Sovereign LORD says: I will take the Israelites out of the nations where they have gone. I will gather them from all around and bring them back into their own land.^h ²²I will make them one nation in the land, on the mountains of Israel. There will be one king over all of them and they will never again be two nations or be divided into two kingdoms.ⁱ ²³They will no longer defile^j themselves with their idols and vile images or with any of their offenses, for I will save them from all their sinful backsliding,^a and I will cleanse them. They will be my people, and I will be their God.^k

²⁴"'My servant David^l will be king over them, and they will all have one shepherd.^m They will follow my laws and be careful to keep my decrees.ⁿ ²⁵They will live in the land I gave to my servant Jacob, the land where your fathers lived.^o They and their children and their children's children will live there forever,^p and David my servant will be their prince forever.^q ²⁶I will make a covenant of peace^r with them; it will be an everlasting covenant. I will establish them and increase their numbers,^s and I will put my sanctuary among them forever.^t ²⁷My dwelling place^u will be with them; I will be their God, and they will be my people.^v ²⁸Then the nations will know that I the LORD make Israel holy,^w when my sanctuary is among them forever.'"

Chapter 38 Theme

38 The word of the LORD came to me: ²"Son of man, set your face against Gog, of the land of Magog,^x the chief prince of^b Meshech and Tubal;^y prophesy against him ³and say: 'This is what the Sovereign LORD says: I am against you, O Gog, chief prince

^a23 Many Hebrew manuscripts (see also Septuagint); most Hebrew manuscripts *all their dwelling places where they sinned*   ^b2 Or *the prince of Rosh,*

of^a Meshech and Tubal.^a ⁴I will turn you around, put hooks^b in your jaws and bring you out with your whole army—your horses, your horsemen fully armed, and a great horde with large and small shields, all of them brandishing their swords.^c ⁵Persia, Cush^b ^d and Put^e will be with them, all with shields and helmets, ⁶also Gomer^f with all its troops, and Beth Togarmah^g from the far north with all its troops—the many nations with you.

⁷"'Get ready; be prepared,^h you and all the hordes gathered about you, and take command of them. ⁸After many daysⁱ you will be called to arms. In future years you will invade a land that has recovered from war, whose people were gathered from many nations^j to the mountains of Israel, which had long been desolate. They had been brought out from the nations, and now all of them live in safety.^k ⁹You and all your troops and the many nations with you will go up, advancing like a storm;^l you will be like a cloud^m covering the land.

¹⁰"'This is what the Sovereign LORD says: On that day thoughts will come into your mind and you will devise an evil scheme.ⁿ ¹¹You will say, "I will invade a land of unwalled villages; I will attack a peaceful and unsuspecting people—all of them living without walls and without gates and bars.^o ¹²I will plunder and loot and turn my hand against the resettled ruins and the people gathered from the nations, rich in livestock and goods, living at the center of the land." ¹³Sheba^p and Dedan and the merchants of Tarshish and all her villages^c will say to you, "Have you come to plunder? Have you gathered your hordes to loot, to carry off silver and gold, to take away livestock and goods and to seize much plunder?^q"'

¹⁴"Therefore, son of man, prophesy and say to Gog: 'This is what the Sovereign LORD says: In that day, when my people Israel are living in safety,^r will you not take notice of it? ¹⁵You will come from your place in the far north, you and many nations with you, all of them riding on horses, a great horde, a mighty army.^s ¹⁶You will advance against my people Israel like a cloud^t that covers the land. In days to come, O Gog, I will bring you against my land, so that the nations may know me when I show myself holy through you before their eyes.^u

¹⁷"'This is what the Sovereign LORD says: Are you not the one I spoke of in former days by my servants the prophets of Israel? At that time they prophesied for years that I would bring you against them. ¹⁸This is what will happen in that day: When Gog attacks the land of Israel, my hot anger will be aroused, declares the Sovereign LORD. ¹⁹In my zeal and fiery wrath I declare that at that time there shall be a great earthquake in the land of Israel.^v ²⁰The fish of the sea, the birds of the air, the beasts of the field, every creature that

---

a 3 Or *Gog, prince of Rosh,*   b 5 That is, the upper Nile region   c 13 Or *her strong lions*

38:3
^a Eze 39:1

38:4
^b 2Ki 19:28
^c Eze 29:4;
Da 11:40

38:5
^d Ge 10:6
^e Eze 27:10

38:6
^f Ge 10:2
^g Eze 27:14

38:7
^h Isa 8:9

38:8
ⁱ Isa 24:22
^j Isa 11:11
^k Jer 23:6

38:9
^l Isa 28:2
^m Jer 4:13;
Joel 2:2

38:10
ⁿ Ps 36:4;
Mic 2:1

38:11
^o Jer 49:31;
Zec 2:4

38:13
^p Eze 27:22
^q Isa 10:6;
Jer 15:13

38:14
^r ver 8; Zec 2:5

38:15
^s Eze 39:2

38:16
^t ver 9
^u Isa 29:23;
Eze 39:21

38:19
^v Ps 18:7;
Eze 5:13;
Hag 2:6,21

moves along the ground, and all the people on the face of the earth will tremble at my presence. The mountains will be overturned, the cliffs will crumble and every wall will fall to the ground.*a* 21I will summon a sword*b* against Gog on all my mountains, declares the Sovereign LORD. Every man's sword will be against his brother.*c* 22I will execute judgment*d* upon him with plague and bloodshed; I will pour down torrents of rain, hailstones*e* and burning sulfur on him and on his troops and on the many nations with him. 23And so I will show my greatness and my holiness, and I will make myself known in the sight of many nations. Then they will know that I am the LORD.*f*'

Chapter 39 Theme

39 "Son of man, prophesy against Gog and say: 'This is what the Sovereign LORD says: I am against you, O Gog, chief prince of*a* Meshech and Tubal.*g* 2I will turn you around and drag you along. I will bring you from the far north and send you against the mountains of Israel. 3Then I will strike your bow*h* from your left hand and make your arrows*i* drop from your right hand. 4On the mountains of Israel you will fall, you and all your troops and the nations with you. I will give you as food to all kinds of carrion birds and to the wild animals.*j* 5You will fall in the open field, for I have spoken, declares the Sovereign LORD. 6I will send fire*k* on Magog and on those who live in safety in the coastlands,*l* and they will know that I am the LORD.

7"'I will make known my holy name among my people Israel. I will no longer let my holy name be profaned,*m* and the nations will know that I the LORD am the Holy One in Israel.*n* 8It is coming! It will surely take place, declares the Sovereign LORD. This is the day I have spoken of.

9"'Then those who live in the towns of Israel will go out and use the weapons for fuel and burn them up—the small and large shields, the bows and arrows, the war clubs and spears. For seven years they will use them for fuel.*o* 10They will not need to gather wood from the fields or cut it from the forests, because they will use the weapons for fuel. And they will plunder those who plundered them and loot those who looted them, declares the Sovereign LORD.*p*

11"'On that day I will give Gog a burial place in Israel, in the valley of those who travel east toward*b* the Sea.*c* It will block the way of travelers, because Gog and all his hordes will be buried there. So it will be called the Valley of Hamon Gog.*d q*

12"'For seven months the house of Israel will be burying them in order to cleanse the land.*r* 13All the people of the land will bury

---

38:20
a Hos 4:3;
Na 1:5

38:21
b Eze 14:17
c 1Sa 14:20;
2Ch 20:23;
Hag 2:22

38:22
d Isa 66:16;
Jer 25:31
e Ps 18:12;
Rev 16:21

38:23
f Eze 36:23

39:1
g Eze 38:2,3

39:3
h Hos 1:5
i Ps 76:3

39:4
j ver 17-20;
Eze 29:5; 33:27

39:6
k Eze 30:8;
Am 1:4
l Jer 25:22

39:7
m Ex 20:7
n Isa 12:6;
Eze 36:16,23

39:9
o Ps 46:9

39:10
p Isa 14:2; 33:1;
Hab 2:8

39:11
q Eze 38:2

39:12
r Dt 21:23

---

a 1 Or *Gog, prince of Rosh,*   *b 11* Or *of*   *c 11* That is, the Dead Sea   *d 11* *Hamon Gog* means *hordes of Gog.*

them, and the day I am glorified[a] will be a memorable day for them, declares the Sovereign LORD.

¹⁴"'Men will be regularly employed to cleanse the land. Some will go throughout the land and, in addition to them, others will bury those that remain on the ground. At the end of the seven months they will begin their search. ¹⁵As they go through the land and one of them sees a human bone, he will set up a marker beside it until the gravediggers have buried it in the Valley of Hamon Gog. ¹⁶(Also a town called Hamonah[a] will be there.) And so they will cleanse the land.'

¹⁷"Son of man, this is what the Sovereign LORD says: Call out to every kind of bird[b] and all the wild animals: 'Assemble and come together from all around to the sacrifice I am preparing for you, the great sacrifice on the mountains of Israel. There you will eat flesh and drink blood. ¹⁸You will eat the flesh of mighty men and drink the blood of the princes of the earth as if they were rams and lambs, goats and bulls—all of them fattened animals from Bashan.[c] ¹⁹At the sacrifice I am preparing for you, you will eat fat till you are glutted and drink blood till you are drunk. ²⁰At my table you will eat your fill of horses and riders, mighty men and soldiers of every kind,' declares the Sovereign LORD.[d]

²¹"I will display my glory among the nations, and all the nations will see the punishment I inflict and the hand I lay upon them.[e] ²²From that day forward the house of Israel will know that I am the LORD their God. ²³And the nations will know that the people of Israel went into exile for their sin, because they were unfaithful to me. So I hid my face from them and handed them over to their enemies, and they all fell by the sword.[f] ²⁴I dealt with them according to their uncleanness and their offenses, and I hid my face from them.[g]

²⁵"Therefore this is what the Sovereign LORD says: I will now bring Jacob back from captivity[b][h] and will have compassion[i] on all the people of Israel, and I will be zealous for my holy name.[j] ²⁶They will forget their shame and all the unfaithfulness they showed toward me when they lived in safety[k] in their land with no one to make them afraid.[l] ²⁷When I have brought them back from the nations and have gathered them from the countries of their enemies, I will show myself holy through them in the sight of many nations.[m] ²⁸Then they will know that I am the LORD their God, for though I sent them into exile among the nations, I will gather them to their own land, not leaving any behind. ²⁹I will no longer hide my face from them, for I will pour out my Spirit[n] on the house of Israel, declares the Sovereign LORD."

a 16 *Hamonah* means *horde.* b 25 Or *now restore the fortunes of Jacob*

39:13
a Eze 28:22

39:17
b Rev 19:17

39:18
c Ps 22:12;
Jer 51:40

39:20
d Rev 19:17-18

39:21
e Ex 9:16;
Isa 37:20;
Eze 38:16

39:23
f Isa 1:15; 59:2;
Jer 22:8-9; 44:23

39:24
g Jer 2:17,19;
4:18; Eze 36:19

39:25
h Jer 33:7;
Eze 34:13
i Jer 30:18
j Isa 27:12-13

39:26
k 1Ki 4:25
l Isa 17:2;
Eze 34:28;
Mic 4:4

39:27
m Eze 36:23-24;
37:21; 38:16

39:29
n Joel 2:28;
Ac 2:17

Chapter 40 Theme

40:1
a 2Ki 25:7;
Jer 39:1-10;
52:4-11;
Eze 33:21
b Eze 1:3

40 In the twenty-fifth year of our exile, at the beginning of the year, on the tenth of the month, in the fourteenth year after the fall of the city[a]—on that very day the hand of the LORD was upon me[b] and he took me there. [2]In visions[c] of God he took me to the land of Israel and set me on a very high mountain,[d] on whose south side were some buildings that looked like a city. [3]He took me there, and I saw a man whose appearance was like bronze;[e] he was standing in the gateway with a linen cord and a measuring rod[f] in his hand. [4]The man said to me, "Son of man, look with your eyes and hear with your ears and pay attention to everything I am going to show you, for that is why you have been brought here. Tell[g] the house of Israel everything you see.[h]"

40:2
c Da 7:1,7
d Eze 17:22;
Rev 21:10

[5]I saw a wall completely surrounding the temple area. The length of the measuring rod in the man's hand was six long cubits, each of which was a cubit[a] and a handbreadth.[b] He measured[i] the wall; it was one measuring rod thick and one rod high.

40:3
e Eze 1:7;
Da 10:6;
Rev 1:15
f Eze 47:3;
Zec 2:1-2;
Rev 11:1; 21:15

[6]Then he went to the gate facing east.[j] He climbed its steps and measured the threshold of the gate; it was one rod deep.[c] [7]The alcoves[k] for the guards were one rod long and one rod wide, and the projecting walls between the alcoves were five cubits thick. And the threshold of the gate next to the portico facing the temple was one rod deep.

40:4
g Jer 26:2
h Eze 44:5

[8]Then he measured the portico of the gateway; [9]it[d] was eight cubits deep and its jambs were two cubits thick. The portico of the gateway faced the temple.

40:5
i Eze 42:20

[10]Inside the east gate were three alcoves on each side; the three had the same measurements, and the faces of the projecting walls on each side had the same measurements. [11]Then he measured the width of the entrance to the gateway; it was ten cubits and its length was thirteen cubits. [12]In front of each alcove was a wall one cubit high, and the alcoves were six cubits square. [13]Then he measured the gateway from the top of the rear wall of one alcove to the top of the opposite one; the distance was twenty-five cubits from one parapet opening to the opposite one. [14]He measured along the faces of the projecting walls all around the inside of the gateway— sixty cubits. The measurement was up to the portico[e] facing the courtyard.[f l] [15]The distance from the entrance of the gateway to the far end of its portico was fifty cubits. [16]The alcoves and the projecting walls inside the gateway were surmounted by narrow parapet openings all around, as was the portico; the openings all around

40:6
j Eze 8:16

40:7
k ver 36

40:14
l Ex 27:9

a 5 The common cubit was about 1 1/2 feet (about 0.5 meter).   b 5 That is, about 3 inches (about 8 centimeters)   c 6 Septuagint; Hebrew *deep, the first threshold, one rod deep*   d 8,9 Many Hebrew manuscripts, Septuagint, Vulgate and Syriac; most Hebrew manuscripts *gateway facing the temple; it was one rod deep.* 9 *Then he measured the portico of the gateway; it*   e 14 Septuagint; Hebrew *projecting wall*   f 14 The meaning of the Hebrew for this verse is uncertain.

faced inward. The faces of the projecting walls were decorated with palm trees.[a]

[17] Then he brought me into the outer court.[b] There I saw some rooms and a pavement that had been constructed all around the court; there were thirty rooms[c] along the pavement.[d] [18] It abutted the sides of the gateways and was as wide as they were long; this was the lower pavement. [19] Then he measured the distance from the inside of the lower gateway to the outside of the inner court;[e] it was a hundred cubits[f] on the east side as well as on the north.

[20] Then he measured the length and width of the gate facing north, leading into the outer court. [21] Its alcoves[g]—three on each side—its projecting walls and its portico had the same measurements as those of the first gateway. It was fifty cubits long and twenty-five cubits wide. [22] Its openings, its portico[h] and its palm tree decorations had the same measurements as those of the gate facing east. Seven steps led up to it, with its portico opposite them. [23] There was a gate to the inner court facing the north gate, just as there was on the east. He measured from one gate to the opposite one; it was a hundred cubits.[i]

[24] Then he led me to the south side and I saw a gate facing south. He measured its jambs and its portico, and they had the same measurements as the others. [25] The gateway and its portico had narrow openings all around, like the openings of the others. It was fifty cubits long and twenty-five cubits wide.[j] [26] Seven steps led up to it, with its portico opposite them; it had palm tree decorations on the faces of the projecting walls on each side.[k] [27] The inner court[l] also had a gate facing south, and he measured from this gate to the outer gate on the south side; it was a hundred cubits.

[28] Then he brought me into the inner court through the south gate, and he measured the south gate; it had the same measurements[m] as the others. [29] Its alcoves, its projecting walls and its portico had the same measurements as the others. The gateway and its portico had openings all around. It was fifty cubits long and twenty-five cubits wide. [30] (The porticoes[n] of the gateways around the inner court were twenty-five cubits wide and five cubits deep.) [31] Its portico[o] faced the outer court; palm trees decorated its jambs, and eight steps led up to it.

[32] Then he brought me to the inner court on the east side, and he measured the gateway; it had the same measurements as the others. [33] Its alcoves, its projecting walls and its portico had the same measurements as the others. The gateway and its portico had openings all around. It was fifty cubits long and twenty-five cubits wide. [34] Its portico[p] faced the outer court; palm trees decorated the jambs on either side, and eight steps led up to it.

[35] Then he brought me to the north gate[q] and measured it. It had the same measurements as the others, [36] as did its alcoves,[r] its

40:16	[a] ver 21-22; 2Ch 3:5; Eze 41:26
40:17	[b] Rev 11:2 [c] Eze 41:6 [d] Eze 42:1
40:19	[e] Eze 46:1 [f] ver 23,27
40:21	[g] ver 7
40:22	[h] ver 49
40:23	[i] ver 19
40:25	[j] ver 33
40:26	[k] ver 22
40:27	[l] ver 32
40:28	[m] ver 35
40:30	[n] ver 21
40:31	[o] ver 22
40:34	[p] ver 22
40:35	[q] Eze 44:4; 47:2
40:36	[r] ver 7

40:38
a 2Ch 4:6;
Eze 42:13

projecting walls and its portico, and it had openings all around. It was fifty cubits long and twenty-five cubits wide. ³⁷Its portico^a faced the outer court; palm trees decorated the jambs on either side, and eight steps led up to it.

40:39
b Eze 46:2
c Lev 4:3,28
d Lev 7:1

³⁸A room with a doorway was by the portico in each of the inner gateways, where the burnt offerings^a were washed. ³⁹In the portico of the gateway were two tables on each side, on which the burnt offerings,^b sin offerings^c and guilt offerings^d were slaughtered. ⁴⁰By the outside wall of the portico of the gateway, near the steps at the entrance to the north gateway were two tables, and on the other side of the steps were two tables. ⁴¹So there were four tables on one side of the gateway and four on the other—eight tables in all—on which the sacrifices were slaughtered. ⁴²There were also four tables of dressed stone^e for the burnt offerings, each a cubit and a half long, a cubit and a half wide and a cubit high. On them were placed the utensils for slaughtering the burnt offerings and the other sacrifices.^f ⁴³And double-pronged hooks, each a handbreadth long, were attached to the wall all around. The tables were for the flesh of the offerings.

40:42
e Ex 20:25
f ver 39

40:45
g 1Ch 9:23

⁴⁴Outside the inner gate, within the inner court, were two rooms, one^b at the side of the north gate and facing south, and another at the side of the south^c gate and facing north. ⁴⁵He said to me, "The room facing south is for the priests who have charge of the temple,^g ⁴⁶and the room facing north^h is for the priests who have charge of the altar.ⁱ These are the sons of Zadok,^j who are the only Levites who may draw near to the LORD to minister before him.^k"

40:46
h Eze 42:13
i Nu 18:5
j 1Ki 2:35
k Nu 16:5;
Eze 43:19;
44:15; 45:4;
48:11

⁴⁷Then he measured the court: It was square—a hundred cubits long and a hundred cubits wide. And the altar was in front of the temple.

⁴⁸He brought me to the portico of the temple^l and measured the jambs of the portico; they were five cubits wide on either side. The width of the entrance was fourteen cubits and its projecting walls were^d three cubits wide on either side. ⁴⁹The portico^m was twenty cubits wide, and twelve^e cubits from front to back. It was reached by a flight of stairs,^f and there were pillarsⁿ on each side of the jambs.

40:48
l 1Ki 6:2

Chapter 41 Theme _____

40:49
m ver 22; 1Ki 6:3
n 1Ki 7:15

41 Then the man brought me to the outer sanctuary^o and measured the jambs; the width of the jambs was six cubits^g on each side.^h ²The entrance was ten cubits wide, and the projecting walls on each side of it were five cubits wide. He also measured the outer sanctuary; it was forty cubits long and twenty cubits wide.^p

41:1
o ver 23

41:2
p 2Ch 3:3

a 37 Septuagint (see also verses 31 and 34); Hebrew *jambs*   b 44 Septuagint; Hebrew *were rooms for singers, which were*   c 44 Septuagint; Hebrew *east*   d 48 Septuagint; Hebrew *entrance was*   e 49 Septuagint; Hebrew *eleven*   f 49 Hebrew; Septuagint *Ten steps led up to it*   g 1 The common cubit was about 1 1/2 feet (about 0.5 meter).   h 1 One Hebrew manuscript and Septuagint; most Hebrew manuscripts *side, the width of the tent*

³Then he went into the inner sanctuary and measured the jambs of the entrance; each was two cubits wide. The entrance was six cubits wide, and the projecting walls on each side of it were seven cubits wide. ⁴And he measured the length of the inner sanctuary; it was twenty cubits, and its width was twenty cubits across the end of the outer sanctuary.ᵃ He said to me, "This is the Most Holy Place.ᵇ"

⁵Then he measured the wall of the temple; it was six cubits thick, and each side room around the temple was four cubits wide. ⁶The side rooms were on three levels, one above another, thirtyᶜ on each level. There were ledges all around the wall of the temple to serve as supports for the side rooms, so that the supports were not inserted into the wall of the temple.ᵈ ⁷The side rooms all around the temple were wider at each successive level. The structure surrounding the temple was built in ascending stages, so that the rooms widened as one went upward. A stairwayᵉ went up from the lowest floor to the top floor through the middle floor.

⁸I saw that the temple had a raised base all around it, forming the foundation of the side rooms. It was the length of the rod, six long cubits. ⁹The outer wall of the side rooms was five cubits thick. The open area between the side rooms of the temple ¹⁰and the ⌊priests'⌋ rooms was twenty cubits wide all around the temple. ¹¹There were entrances to the side rooms from the open area, one on the north and another on the south; and the base adjoining the open area was five cubits wide all around.

¹²The building facing the temple courtyard on the west side was seventy cubits wide. The wall of the building was five cubits thick all around, and its length was ninety cubits.

¹³Then he measured the temple; it was a hundred cubits long, and the temple courtyard and the building with its walls were also a hundred cubits long. ¹⁴The width of the temple courtyard on the east, including the front of the temple, was a hundred cubits.ᶠ

¹⁵Then he measured the length of the building facing the courtyard at the rear of the temple, including its galleriesᵍ on each side; it was a hundred cubits.

The outer sanctuary, the inner sanctuary and the portico facing the court, ¹⁶as well as the thresholds and the narrow windowsʰ and galleries around the three of them—everything beyond and including the threshold was covered with wood. The floor, the wall up to the windows, and the windows were covered.ⁱ ¹⁷In the space above the outside of the entrance to the inner sanctuary and on the walls at regular intervals all around the inner and outer sanctuary ¹⁸were carvedʲ cherubimᵏ and palm trees.ˡ Palm trees alternated with cherubim. Each cherub had two faces:ᵐ ¹⁹the face of a man toward the palm tree on one side and the face of a lion toward the

41:4 ᵃ1Ki 6:20 ᵇEx 26:33; Heb 9:3-8
41:6 ᶜEze 40:17 ᵈ1Ki 6:5
41:7 ᵉ1Ki 6:8
41:14 ᶠEze 40:47
41:15 ᵍEze 42:3
41:16 ʰ1Ki 6:4 ⁱver 25-26; 1Ki 6:15; Eze 42:3
41:18 ʲ1Ki 6:18 ᵏEx 37:7; 2Ch 3:7 ˡ1Ki 6:29; 7:36 ᵐEze 10:21

41:19
a Eze 10:14

41:21
b ver 1

41:22
c Ex 30:1
d Ex 25:23;
Eze 23:41; 44:16;
Mal 1:7,12

41:23
e ver 1
f 1Ki 6:32

41:24
g 1Ki 6:34

41:26
h ver 15-16;
Eze 40:16

42:1
i ver 13
j Eze 41:12-14
k Eze 40:17

42:3
l Eze 41:15
m Eze 41:16

42:4
n Eze 46:19

42:9
o Eze 44:5; 46:19

42:10
p ver 1

palm tree on the other. They were carved all around the whole temple.*a* ²⁰From the floor to the area above the entrance, cherubim and palm trees were carved on the wall of the outer sanctuary.

²¹The outer sanctuary*b* had a rectangular doorframe, and the one at the front of the Most Holy Place was similar. ²²There was a wooden altar*c* three cubits high and two cubits square*a*; its corners, its base*b* and its sides were of wood. The man said to me, "This is the table*d* that is before the Lord." ²³Both the outer sanctuary*e* and the Most Holy Place had double doors.*f* ²⁴Each door had two leaves—two hinged leaves*g* for each door. ²⁵And on the doors of the outer sanctuary were carved cherubim and palm trees like those carved on the walls, and there was a wooden overhang on the front of the portico. ²⁶On the sidewalls of the portico were narrow windows with palm trees carved on each side. The side rooms of the temple also had overhangs.*h*

Chapter 42 Theme

42 Then the man led me northward into the outer court and brought me to the rooms*i* opposite the temple courtyard*j* and opposite the outer wall on the north side.*k* ²The building whose door faced north was a hundred cubits*c* long and fifty cubits wide. ³Both in the section twenty cubits from the inner court and in the section opposite the pavement of the outer court, gallery*l* faced gallery at the three levels.*m* ⁴In front of the rooms was an inner passageway ten cubits wide and a hundred cubits*d* long. Their doors were on the north.*n* ⁵Now the upper rooms were narrower, for the galleries took more space from them than from the rooms on the lower and middle floors of the building. ⁶The rooms on the third floor had no pillars, as the courts had; so they were smaller in floor space than those on the lower and middle floors. ⁷There was an outer wall parallel to the rooms and the outer court; it extended in front of the rooms for fifty cubits. ⁸While the row of rooms on the side next to the outer court was fifty cubits long, the row on the side nearest the sanctuary was a hundred cubits long. ⁹The lower rooms had an entrance*o* on the east side as one enters them from the outer court.

¹⁰On the south side*e* along the length of the wall of the outer court, adjoining the temple courtyard and opposite the outer wall, were rooms*p* ¹¹with a passageway in front of them. These were like the rooms on the north; they had the same length and width, with similar exits and dimensions. Similar to the doorways on the north ¹²were the doorways of the rooms on the south. There was

---

a 22 Septuagint; Hebrew *long*   *b* 22 Septuagint; Hebrew *length*   *c* 2 The common cubit was about 1 1/2 feet (about 0.5 meter).   *d* 4 Septuagint and Syriac; Hebrew *and one cubit*   *e* 10 Septuagint; Hebrew *Eastward* a doorway at the beginning of the passageway that was parallel to the corresponding wall extending eastward, by which one enters the rooms.

¹³Then he said to me, "The north*ᵃ* and south rooms facing the temple courtyard are the priests' rooms, where the priests who approach the LORD will eat the most holy offerings. There they will put the most holy offerings—the grain offerings, the sin offerings*ᵇ* and the guilt offerings*ᶜ*—for the place is holy.*ᵈ* ¹⁴Once the priests enter the holy precincts, they are not to go into the outer court until they leave behind the garments*ᵉ* in which they minister, for these are holy. They are to put on other clothes before they go near the places that are for the people.*ᶠ*"

¹⁵When he had finished measuring what was inside the temple area, he led me out by the east gate*ᵍ* and measured the area all around: ¹⁶He measured the east side with the measuring rod; it was five hundred cubits.*ᵃ* ¹⁷He measured the north side; it was five hundred cubits*ᵇ* by the measuring rod. ¹⁸He measured the south side; it was five hundred cubits by the measuring rod. ¹⁹Then he turned to the west side and measured; it was five hundred cubits by the measuring rod. ²⁰So he measured*ʰ* the area on all four sides. It had a wall around it,*ⁱ* five hundred cubits long and five hundred cubits wide,*ʲ* to separate the holy from the common.*ᵏ*

Chapter 43 Theme

43 Then the man brought me to the gate facing east,*ˡ* ²and I saw the glory of the God of Israel coming from the east. His voice was like the roar of rushing waters,*ᵐ* and the land was radiant with his glory.*ⁿ* ³The vision I saw was like the vision I had seen when he*ᶜ* came to destroy the city and like the visions I had seen by the Kebar River, and I fell facedown. ⁴The glory*ᵒ* of the LORD entered the temple through the gate facing east.*ᵖ* ⁵Then the Spirit*�q* lifted me up*ʳ* and brought me into the inner court, and the glory of the LORD filled the temple.

⁶While the man was standing beside me, I heard someone speaking to me from inside the temple. ⁷He said: "Son of man, this is the place of my throne and the place for the soles of my feet. This is where I will live among the Israelites forever. The house of Israel will never again defile my holy name—neither they nor their kings—by their prostitution*ᵈ* and the lifeless idols*ᵉ* of their kings at their high places.*ˢ* ⁸When they placed their threshold next to my threshold and their doorposts beside my doorposts, with only a wall between me and them, they defiled my holy name by their

---

42:13
ᵃ Eze 40:46
ᵇ Lev 10:17; 6:25
ᶜ Lev 14:13
ᵈ Ex 29:31; Lev 6:29; 7:6; 10:12-13; Nu 18:9-10

42:14
ᵉ Eze 44:19
ᶠ Ex 29:9; Lev 8:7-9

42:15
ᵍ Eze 43:1

42:20
ʰ Eze 40:5
ⁱ Zec 2:5
ʲ Eze 45:2; Rev 21:16
ᵏ Eze 22:26

43:1
ˡ Eze 10:19; 42:15; 44:1; 46:1

43:2
ᵐ Rev 1:15
ⁿ Isa 6:3; Eze 11:23; Rev 18:1

43:4
ᵒ Eze 1:28
ᵖ Eze 10:19

43:5
q Eze 11:24
ʳ Eze 3:12; 8:3

43:7
ˢ Lev 26:30

ᵃ 16 See Septuagint of verse 17; Hebrew *rods*; also in verses 18 and 19.   *ᵇ* 17 Septuagint; Hebrew *rods*   *ᶜ* 3 Some Hebrew manuscripts and Vulgate; most Hebrew manuscripts *I*   *ᵈ* 7 Or *their spiritual adultery*; also in verse 9   *ᵉ* 7 Or *the corpses*; also in verse 9

43:9
ᵃEze 37:26-28

43:10
ᵇEze 16:61

43:11
ᶜEze 44:5

43:12
ᵈEze 40:2

43:13
ᵉ2Ch 4:1

43:15
ᶠEx 27:2

43:17
ᵍEx 20:26

43:18
ʰEx 40:29
ⁱLev 1:5,11;
Heb 9:21-22

43:19
ʲLev 4:3;
Eze 45:18-19
ᵏEze 44:15
ˡNu 16:40;
Eze 40:46

43:20
ᵐver 17
ⁿLev 16:19

43:21
ᵒEx 29:14;
Heb 13:11

43:23
ᵖEx 29:1

43:24
�q Lev 2:13;
Mk 9:49-50

43:25
ʳLev 8:33

detestable practices. So I destroyed them in my anger. ⁹Now let them put away from me their prostitution and the lifeless idols of their kings, and I will live among them forever.ᵃ

¹⁰"Son of man, describe the temple to the people of Israel, that they may be ashamedᵇ of their sins. Let them consider the plan, ¹¹and if they are ashamed of all they have done, make known to them the design of the temple—its arrangement, its exits and entrances—its whole design and all its regulationsᵃ and laws. Write these down before them so that they may be faithful to its design and follow all its regulations.ᶜ

¹²"This is the law of the temple: All the surrounding areaᵈ on top of the mountain will be most holy. Such is the law of the temple.

¹³"These are the measurements of the altarᵉ in long cubits, that cubit being a cubitᵇ and a handbreadthᶜ: Its gutter is a cubit deep and a cubit wide, with a rim of one spanᵈ around the edge. And this is the height of the altar: ¹⁴From the gutter on the ground up to the lower ledge it is two cubits high and a cubit wide, and from the smaller ledge up to the larger ledge it is four cubits high and a cubit wide. ¹⁵The altar hearth is four cubits high, and four hornsᶠ project upward from the hearth. ¹⁶The altar hearth is square, twelve cubits long and twelve cubits wide. ¹⁷The upper ledge also is square, fourteen cubits long and fourteen cubits wide, with a rim of half a cubit and a gutter of a cubit all around. The stepsᵍ of the altar face east."

¹⁸Then he said to me, "Son of man, this is what the Sovereign Lord says: These will be the regulations for sacrificing burnt offeringsʰ and sprinkling bloodⁱ upon the altar when it is built: ¹⁹You are to give a young bullʲ as a sin offering to the priests, who are Levites, of the family of Zadok,ᵏ who come nearˡ to minister before me, declares the Sovereign Lord. ²⁰You are to take some of its blood and put it on the four horns of the altar and on the four corners of the upper ledgeᵐ and all around the rim, and so purify the altarⁿ and make atonement for it. ²¹You are to take the bull for the sin offering and burn it in the designated part of the temple area outside the sanctuary.ᵒ

²²"On the second day you are to offer a male goat without defect for a sin offering, and the altar is to be purified as it was purified with the bull. ²³When you have finished purifying it, you are to offer a young bull and a ram from the flock, both without defect.ᵖ ²⁴You are to offer them before the Lord, and the priests are to sprinkle salt�q on them and sacrifice them as a burnt offering to the Lord.

²⁵"For seven daysʳ you are to provide a male goat daily for a sin offering; you are also to provide a young bull and a ram from the

ᵃ 11 Some Hebrew manuscripts and Septuagint; most Hebrew manuscripts *regulations and its whole design*   ᵇ 13 The common cubit was about 1 1/2 feet (about 0.5 meter).   ᶜ 13 That is, about 3 inches (about 8 centimeters)   ᵈ 13 That is, about 9 inches (about 22 centimeters) flock, both without defect.ᵃ ²⁶For seven days they are to make atonement for the altar and cleanse it; thus they will dedicate it. ²⁷At the end of these days, from the eighth dayᵇ on, the priests are to present your burnt offerings and fellowship offeringsᵃ ᶜ on the altar. Then I will accept you, declares the Sovereign Lᴏʀᴅ."

Chapter 44 Theme

44 Then the man brought me back to the outer gate of the sanctuary, the one facing east,ᵈ and it was shut. ²The Lᴏʀᴅ said to me, "This gate is to remain shut. It must not be opened; no one may enter through it.ᵉ It is to remain shut because the Lᴏʀᴅ, the God of Israel, has entered through it. ³The prince himself is the only one who may sit inside the gateway to eat in the presenceᶠ of the Lᴏʀᴅ. He is to enter by way of the portico of the gateway and go out the same way.ᵍ"

⁴Then the man brought me by way of the north gate to the front of the temple. I looked and saw the glory of the Lᴏʀᴅ filling the templeʰ of the Lᴏʀᴅ, and I fell facedown.ⁱ

⁵The Lᴏʀᴅ said to me, "Son of man, look carefully, listen closely and give attention to everything I tell you concerning all the regulations regarding the temple of the Lᴏʀᴅ. Give attention to the entrance of the temple and all the exits of the sanctuary.ʲ ⁶Say to the rebellious houseᵏ of Israel, 'This is what the Sovereign Lᴏʀᴅ says: Enough of your detestable practices, O house of Israel! ⁷In addition to all your other detestable practices, you brought foreigners uncircumcised in heartˡ and flesh into my sanctuary, desecrating my temple while you offered me food, fat and blood, and you broke my covenant.ᵐ ⁸Instead of carrying out your duty in regard to my holy things, you put others in charge of my sanctuary.ⁿ ⁹This is what the Sovereign Lᴏʀᴅ says: No foreigner uncircumcised in heart and flesh is to enter my sanctuary, not even the foreigners who live among the Israelites.ᵒ

¹⁰"'The Levites who went far from me when Israel went astrayᵖ and who wandered from me after their idols must bear the consequences of their sin.ᑫ ¹¹They may serve in my sanctuary, having charge of the gates of the temple and serving in it; they may slaughter the burnt offeringsʳ and sacrifices for the people and stand before the people and serve them.ˢ ¹²But because they served them in the presence of their idols and made the house of Israel fall into sin, therefore I have sworn with uplifted handᵗ that they must bear the consequences of their sin, declares the Sovereign Lᴏʀᴅ.ᵘ ¹³They are not to come near to serve me as priests or come near any of my holy things or my most holy offerings; they

ᵃ27 Traditionally *peace offerings*

43:25 ᵃEx 29:37
43:27 ᵇLev 9:1 ᶜLev 17:5
44:1 ᵈEze 43:1
44:2 ᵉEze 43:4-5
44:3 ᶠEx 24:9-11 ᵍEze 46:2,8
44:4 ʰIsa 6:4; Rev 15:8 ⁱEze 1:28; 3:23
44:5 ʲEze 40:4; 43:10-11
44:6 ᵏEze 3:9
44:7 ˡLev 26:41 ᵐGe 17:14; Ex 12:48; Lev 22:25
44:8 ⁿLev 22:2; Nu 18:7
44:9 ᵒJoel 3:17; Zec 14:21
44:10 ᵖ2Ki 23:8 ᑫNu 18:23
44:11 ʳ2Ch 29:34 ˢNu 3:5-37; 16:9; 1Ch 26:12-19
44:12 ᵗPs 106:26 ᵘ2Ki 16:10-16

44:13
a Eze 16:61
b Nu 18:3

44:14
c Nu 18:4;
1Ch 23:28-32

44:15
d Jer 33:18;
Eze 40:46;
Zec 3:7

44:16
e Eze 41:22
f Nu 18:5

44:17
g Ex 39:27-28;
Rev 19:8

44:18
h Ex 28:39;
Isa 3:20
i Ex 28:42
j Lev 16:4

44:19
k Lev 6:27;
Eze 46:20
l Lev 6:10-11;
Eze 42:14

44:20
m Lev 21:5;
Nu 6:5

44:21
n Lev 10:9

44:22
o Lev 21:7

44:23
p Eze 22:26
q Mal 2:7

44:24
r Dt 17:8-9;
1Ch 23:4
s 2Ch 19:8

44:25
t Lev 21:1-4

44:26
u Nu 19:14

44:28
v Nu 18:20;
Dt 10:9; 18:1-2;
Jos 13:33

44:29
w Lev 27:21
x Nu 18:9,14

44:30
y Nu 18:12-13

must bear the shame[a] of their detestable practices.[b] [14]Yet I will put them in charge of the duties of the temple and all the work that is to be done in it.[c]

[15]"'But the priests, who are Levites and descendants of Zadok and who faithfully carried out the duties of my sanctuary when the Israelites went astray from me, are to come near to minister before me; they are to stand before me to offer sacrifices of fat and blood, declares the Sovereign LORD.[d] [16]They alone are to enter my sanctuary; they alone are to come near my table[e] to minister before me and perform my service.[f]

[17]"'When they enter the gates of the inner court, they are to wear linen clothes;[g] they must not wear any woolen garment while ministering at the gates of the inner court or inside the temple. [18]They are to wear linen turbans[h] on their heads and linen undergarments[i] around their waists. They must not wear anything that makes them perspire.[j] [19]When they go out into the outer court where the people are, they are to take off the clothes they have been ministering in and are to leave them in the sacred rooms, and put on other clothes, so that they do not consecrate[k] the people by means of their garments.[l]

[20]"'They must not shave their heads or let their hair grow long, but they are to keep the hair of their heads trimmed.[m] [21]No priest is to drink wine when he enters the inner court.[n] [22]They must not marry widows or divorced women; they may marry only virgins of Israelite descent or widows of priests.[o] [23]They are to teach my people the difference between the holy and the common[p] and show them how to distinguish between the unclean and the clean.[q]

[24]"'In any dispute, the priests are to serve as judges[r] and decide it according to my ordinances. They are to keep my laws and my decrees for all my appointed feasts, and they are to keep my Sabbaths holy.[s]

[25]"'A priest must not defile himself by going near a dead person; however, if the dead person was his father or mother, son or daughter, brother or unmarried sister, then he may defile himself.[t] [26]After he is cleansed, he must wait seven days.[u] [27]On the day he goes into the inner court of the sanctuary to minister in the sanctuary, he is to offer a sin offering for himself, declares the Sovereign LORD.

[28]"'I am to be the only inheritance[v] the priests have. You are to give them no possession in Israel; I will be their possession. [29]They will eat the grain offerings, the sin offerings and the guilt offerings; and everything in Israel devoted[a] to the LORD[w] will belong to them.[x] [30]The best of all the firstfruits[y] and of all your special gifts will belong to the priests. You are to give them the first portion of

---

[a] 29 The Hebrew term refers to the irrevocable giving over of things or persons to the LORD.

your ground meal*a* so that a blessing*b* may rest on your household.*c* [31]The priests must not eat anything, bird or animal, found dead or torn by wild animals.*d*

Chapter 45 Theme _____

45 "'When you allot the land as an inheritance,*e* you are to present to the LORD a portion of the land as a sacred district, 25,000 cubits long and 20,000*a* cubits wide; the entire area will be holy.*f* [2]Of this, a section 500 cubits square*g* is to be for the sanctuary, with 50 cubits around it for open land. [3]In the sacred district, measure off a section 25,000 cubits*b* long and 10,000 cubits*c* wide. In it will be the sanctuary, the Most Holy Place. [4]It will be the sacred portion of the land for the priests,*h* who minister in the sanctuary and who draw near to minister before the LORD. It will be a place for their houses as well as a holy place for the sanctuary.*i* [5]An area 25,000 cubits long and 10,000 cubits wide will belong to the Levites, who serve in the temple, as their possession for towns to live in.*d j*

[6]"'You are to give the city as its property an area 5,000 cubits wide and 25,000 cubits long, adjoining the sacred portion; it will belong to the whole house of Israel.*k*

[7]"'The prince will have the land bordering each side of the area formed by the sacred district and the property of the city. It will extend westward from the west side and eastward from the east side, running lengthwise from the western to the eastern border parallel to one of the tribal portions.*l* [8]This land will be his possession in Israel. And my princes will no longer oppress my people but will allow the house of Israel to possess the land according to their tribes.*m*

[9]"'This is what the Sovereign LORD says: You have gone far enough, O princes of Israel! Give up your violence and oppression and do what is just and right.*n* Stop dispossessing my people, declares the Sovereign LORD. [10]You are to use accurate scales,*o* an accurate ephah*e p* and an accurate bath.*f* [11]The ephah*q* and the bath are to be the same size, the bath containing a tenth of a homer*g* and the ephah a tenth of a homer; the homer is to be the standard measure for both. [12]The shekel*h* is to consist of twenty gerahs.*r* Twenty shekels plus twenty-five shekels plus fifteen shekels equal one mina.*i*

[13]"'This is the special gift you are to offer: a sixth of an ephah from each homer of wheat and a sixth of an ephah from each

---

*a*1 Septuagint (see also verses 3 and 5 and 48:9); Hebrew *10,000*   *b*3 That is, about 7 miles (about 12 kilometers)   *c*3 That is, about 3 miles (about 5 kilometers)   *d*5 Septuagint; Hebrew *temple; they will have as their possession 20 rooms*   *e*10 An ephah was a dry measure.   *f*10 A bath was a liquid measure.   *g*11 A homer was a dry measure.   *h*12 A shekel weighed about 2/5 ounce (about 11.5 grams).   *i*12 That is, 60 shekels; the common mina was 50 shekels.

44:30
a Nu 15:18-21
b Mal 3:10
c Ne 10:35-37

44:31
d Ex 22:31;
Lev 22:8

45:1
e Eze 47:21-22
f Eze 48:8-9,29

45:2
g Eze 42:20

45:4
h Eze 40:46
i Eze 48:10-11

45:5
j Eze 48:13

45:6
k Eze 48:15-18

45:7
l Eze 48:21

45:8
m Nu 26:53;
Eze 46:18

45:9
n Jer 22:3;
Zec 7:9-10; 8:16

45:10
o Dt 25:15;
Pr 11:1;
Am 8:4-6;
Mic 6:10-11
p Lev 19:36

45:11
q Isa 5:10

45:12
r Ex 30:13;
Lev 27:25;
Nu 3:47

45:15
a Lev 1:4
b Lev 6:30

45:17
c Lev 23:38;
Isa 66:23
d 1Ki 8:62;
2Ch 31:3;
Eze 46:4-12

45:18
e Ex 12:2
f Lev 22:20;
Heb 9:14
g Lev 16:16,33

45:19
h Eze 43:17
i Lev 16:18-19;
Eze 43:20

45:20
j Lev 4:27

45:21
k Ex 12:11;
Lev 23:5-6

45:22
l Lev 4:14

45:23
m Job 42:8
n Nu 28:16-25

45:24
o Nu 28:12-13
p Eze 46:5-7

45:25
q Dt 16:13
r Lev 23:34-43;
Nu 29:12-38

46:1
s Eze 40:19
t 1Ch 9:18
u ver 6;
Isa 66:23

46:2
v ver 8

homer of barley. [14]The prescribed portion of oil, measured by the bath, is a tenth of a bath from each cor (which consists of ten baths or one homer, for ten baths are equivalent to a homer). [15]Also one sheep is to be taken from every flock of two hundred from the well-watered pastures of Israel. These will be used for the grain offerings, burnt offerings[a] and fellowship offerings[a] to make atonement[b] for the people, declares the Sovereign LORD. [16]All the people of the land will participate in this special gift for the use of the prince in Israel. [17]It will be the duty of the prince to provide the burnt offerings, grain offerings and drink offerings at the festivals, the New Moons and the Sabbaths[c]—at all the appointed feasts of the house of Israel. He will provide the sin offerings, grain offerings, burnt offerings and fellowship offerings to make atonement for the house of Israel.[d]

[18]"'This is what the Sovereign LORD says: In the first month[e] on the first day you are to take a young bull without defect[f] and purify the sanctuary.[g] [19]The priest is to take some of the blood of the sin offering and put it on the doorposts of the temple, on the four corners of the upper ledge[h] of the altar[i] and on the gateposts of the inner court. [20]You are to do the same on the seventh day of the month for anyone who sins unintentionally[j] or through ignorance; so you are to make atonement for the temple.

[21]"'In the first month on the fourteenth day you are to observe the Passover,[k] a feast lasting seven days, during which you shall eat bread made without yeast. [22]On that day the prince is to provide a bull as a sin offering for himself and for all the people of the land.[l] [23]Every day during the seven days of the Feast he is to provide seven bulls and seven rams[m] without defect as a burnt offering to the LORD, and a male goat for a sin offering.[n] [24]He is to provide as a grain offering[o] an ephah for each bull and an ephah for each ram, along with a hin[b] of oil for each ephah.[p]

[25]"'During the seven days of the Feast,[q] which begins in the seventh month on the fifteenth day, he is to make the same provision for sin offerings, burnt offerings, grain offerings and oil.[r]

Chapter 46 Theme

46 "'This is what the Sovereign LORD says: The gate of the inner court[s] facing east[t] is to be shut on the six working days, but on the Sabbath day and on the day of the New Moon[u] it is to be opened. [2]The prince is to enter from the outside through the portico[v] of the gateway and stand by the gatepost. The priests are to sacrifice his burnt offering and his fellowship offerings.[c] He is to worship at the threshold of the gateway and then go out, but

---

a 15 Traditionally *peace offerings*; also in verse 17   *b 24* That is, probably about 4 quarts (about 4 liters)   *c 2* Traditionally *peace offerings*; also in verse 12 the gate will not be shut until evening.[a] [3]On the Sabbaths and New Moons the people of the land are to worship in the presence of the LORD at the entrance to that gateway.[b] [4]The burnt offering the prince brings to the LORD on the Sabbath day is to be six male lambs and a ram, all without defect. [5]The grain offering given with the ram is to be an ephah,[a] and the grain offering with the lambs is to be as much as he pleases, along with a hin[b] of oil for each ephah.[c] [6]On the day of the New Moon[d] he is to offer a young bull, six lambs and a ram, all without defect. [7]He is to provide as a grain offering one ephah with the bull, one ephah with the ram, and with the lambs as much as he wants to give, along with a hin of oil with each ephah.[e] [8]When the prince enters, he is to go in through the portico[f] of the gateway, and he is to come out the same way.[g]

[9]"'When the people of the land come before the LORD at the appointed feasts,[h] whoever enters by the north gate to worship is to go out the south gate; and whoever enters by the south gate is to go out the north gate. No one is to return through the gate by which he entered, but each is to go out the opposite gate. [10]The prince is to be among them, going in when they go in and going out when they go out.[i]

[11]"'At the festivals and the appointed feasts, the grain offering is to be an ephah with a bull, an ephah with a ram, and with the lambs as much as one pleases, along with a hin of oil for each ephah.[j] [12]When the prince provides[k] a freewill offering[l] to the LORD—whether a burnt offering or fellowship offerings—the gate facing east is to be opened for him. He shall offer his burnt offering or his fellowship offerings as he does on the Sabbath day. Then he shall go out, and after he has gone out, the gate will be shut.[m]

[13]"'Every day you are to provide a year-old lamb without defect for a burnt offering to the LORD; morning by morning you shall provide it.[n] [14]You are also to provide with it morning by morning a grain offering, consisting of a sixth of an ephah with a third of a hin of oil to moisten the flour. The presenting of this grain offering to the LORD is a lasting ordinance.[o] [15]So the lamb and the grain offering and the oil shall be provided morning by morning for a regular[p] burnt offering.[q]

[16]"'This is what the Sovereign LORD says: If the prince makes a gift from his inheritance to one of his sons, it will also belong to his descendants; it is to be their property by inheritance.[r] [17]If, however, he makes a gift from his inheritance to one of his servants, the servant may keep it until the year of freedom;[s] then it will revert to the prince. His inheritance belongs to his sons only; it is theirs. [18]The prince must not take any of the inheritance[t] of the people,

---

a5 That is, probably about 3/5 bushel (about 22 liters)   b5 That is, probably about 4 quarts (about 4 liters)

46:2
[a] ver 12;
Eze 44:3

46:3
[b] Lk 1:10

46:5
[c] ver 11;
Eze 45:24

46:6
[d] ver 1;
Nu 10:10

46:7
[e] Eze 45:24

46:8
[f] ver 2
[g] Eze 44:3

46:9
[h] Ex 23:14;
34:20

46:10
[i] 2Sa 6:14-15;
Ps 42:4

46:11
[j] ver 5

46:12
[k] Eze 45:17
[l] Lev 7:16
[m] ver 2

46:13
[n] Ex 29:38;
Nu 28:3

46:14
[o] Da 8:11

46:15
[p] Ex 29:42
[q] Ex 29:38;
Nu 28:5-6

46:16
[r] 2Ch 21:3

46:17
[s] Lev 25:10

46:18
[t] Lev 25:23;
Eze 45:8;
Mic 2:1-2

46:19
a Eze 42:9

driving them off their property. He is to give his sons their inheritance out of his own property, so that none of my people will be separated from his property.'"

46:20
b Lev 6:27
c Zec 14:20

¹⁹Then the man brought me through the entrance *a* at the side of the gate to the sacred rooms facing north, which belonged to the priests, and showed me a place at the western end. ²⁰He said to me, "This is the place where the priests will cook the guilt offering and the sin offering and bake the grain offering, to avoid bringing them into the outer court and consecrating *b* the people." *c*

²¹He then brought me to the outer court and led me around to its four corners, and I saw in each corner another court. ²²In the four corners of the outer court were enclosed *a* courts, forty cubits long and thirty cubits wide; each of the courts in the four corners was the same size. ²³Around the inside of each of the four courts was a ledge of stone, with places for fire built all around under the ledge. ²⁴He said to me, "These are the kitchens where those who minister at the temple will cook the sacrifices of the people."

47:1
d Isa 55:1
e Ps 46:4;
Joel 3:18;
Rev 22:1

47:3
f Eze 40:3

Chapter 47 Theme

47
The man brought me back to the entrance of the temple, and I saw water *d* coming out from under the threshold of the temple toward the east (for the temple faced east). The water was coming down from under the south side of the temple, south of the altar. *e* ²He then brought me out through the north gate and led me around the outside to the outer gate facing east, and the water was flowing from the south side.

47:5
g Isa 11:9;
Hab 2:14

³As the man went eastward with a measuring line *f* in his hand, he measured off a thousand cubits *b* and then led me through water that was ankle-deep. ⁴He measured off another thousand cubits and led me through water that was knee-deep. He measured off another thousand and led me through water that was up to the waist. ⁵He measured off another thousand, but now it was a river that I could not cross, because the water had risen and was deep enough to swim in—a river that no one could cross. *g* ⁶He asked me, "Son of man, do you see this?"

47:7
h ver 12;
Rev 22:2

Then he led me back to the bank of the river. ⁷When I arrived there, I saw a great number of trees on each side of the river. *h* ⁸He said to me, "This water flows toward the eastern region and goes down into the Arabah, *c i* where it enters the Sea. *d* When it empties into the Sea, *d* the water there becomes fresh. *j* ⁹Swarms of living creatures will live wherever the river flows. There will be large numbers of fish, because this water flows there and makes the salt water fresh; so where the river flows everything will live. *k* ¹⁰Fishermen *l*

47:8
i Dt 3:17;
Jos 3:16
j Isa 41:18

47:9
k Isa 12:3; 55:1;
Jn 4:14; 7:37-38

47:10
l Mt 4:19

a 22 The meaning of the Hebrew for this word is uncertain.   *b* 3 That is, about 1,500 feet (about 450 meters)   *c* 8 Or *the Jordan Valley*   *d* 8 That is, the Dead Sea will stand along the shore; from En Gedi[a] to En Eglaim there will be places for spreading nets.[b] The fish will be of many kinds[c]—like the fish of the Great Sea.[a][d] ¹¹But the swamps and marshes will not become fresh; they will be left for salt.[e] ¹²Fruit trees of all kinds will grow on both banks of the river.[f] Their leaves will not wither, nor will their fruit[g] fail. Every month they will bear, because the water from the sanctuary flows to them. Their fruit will serve for food and their leaves for healing.[h]"

The Tribes, the Prince's Portion, the City, the Sanctuary

Mediterranean (Great) Sea

● Sidon DAN
ASHER
● Tyre NAPHTALI
MANASSEH
EPHRAIM

REUBEN

8.3 mi

Levites' portion

6.6 mi

Priests' portion
(Sanctuary)

City land | City | City land

JUDAH

Prince's portion

BENJAMIN
SIMEON
ISSACHAR
ZEBULUN
GAD

Dead (Salt) Sea

¹³This is what the Sovereign LORD says: "These are the boundaries[i] by which you are to divide the land for an inheritance among the twelve tribes of Israel, with two portions for Joseph.[j] ¹⁴You are to divide it equally among them. Because I swore with uplifted hand to give it to your forefathers, this land will become your inheritance.[k]

¹⁵"This is to be the boundary of the land:

"On the north side it will run from the Great Sea by the Hethlon road[l] past Lebo[b] Hamath to Zedad, ¹⁶Berothah[c][m] and Sibraim (which lies on the border between Damascus and Hamath),[n] as far as Hazer Hatticon, which is on the border of Hauran. ¹⁷The boundary will extend from the sea to Hazar Enan,[d] along the northern border of Damascus, with the border of Hamath to the north. This will be the north boundary.[o]

¹⁸"On the east side the boundary will run between Hauran and Damascus, along the Jordan between Gilead and the land of Israel, to the eastern sea and as far as Tamar.[e] This will be the east boundary.

¹⁹"On the south side it will run from Tamar as far as the waters of Meribah Kadesh,[p] then along the Wadi ⌊of Egypt⌋[q] to the Great Sea.[r] This will be the south boundary.

²⁰"On the west side, the Great Sea will be the boundary to a point opposite Lebo[f] Hamath.[s] This will be the west boundary.[t]

47:10 a Jos 15:62; b Eze 26:5; c Ps 104:25; Mt 13:47; d Nu 34:6

47:11 e Dt 29:23

47:12 f ver 7; Rev 22:2; g Ps 1:3; h Ge 2:9; Jer 17:8

47:13 i Nu 34:2-12; j Ge 48:5

47:14 k Ge 12:7; Dt 1:8; Eze 20:5-6

47:15 l Eze 48:1

47:16 m 2Sa 8:8; n Nu 13:21; Eze 48:1

47:17 o Eze 48:1

47:19 p Dt 32:51; q Isa 27:12; r Eze 48:28

47:20 s Eze 48:1; t Nu 34:6

---

a 10 That is, the Mediterranean; also in verses 15, 19 and 20   b 15 Or *past the entrance to*   c 15,16 *See Septuagint and Ezekiel 48:1; Hebrew road to go into Zedad,* ¹⁶*Hamath, Berothah*   d 17 Hebrew *Enon,* a variant of *Enan*   e 18 Septuagint and Syriac; Hebrew *Israel. You will measure to the eastern sea*   f 20 Or *opposite the entrance to*

47:22
a Isa 14:1
b Nu 26:55-56;
Isa 56:6-7;
Ro 10:12;
Eph 2:12-16;
3:6; Col 3:11

48:1
c Ge 30:6
d Eze 47:15-17
e Eze 47:20

48:2
f Jos 19:24-31

48:3
g Jos 19:32-39

48:4
h Jos 17:1-11

48:5
i Jos 16:5-9
j Jos 17:7-10
k Jos 17:17

48:6
l Jos 13:15-21

48:7
m Jos 15:1-63

48:8
n ver 21

48:9
o Eze 45:1

48:10
p ver 21;
Eze 45:3-4

48:11
q 2Sa 8:17
r Lev 8:35
s Eze 14:11;
44:15

48:13
t Eze 45:5

21"You are to distribute this land among yourselves according to the tribes of Israel. 22You are to allot it as an inheritance for yourselves and for the aliens[a] who have settled among you and who have children. You are to consider them as native-born Israelites; along with you they are to be allotted an inheritance among the tribes of Israel.[b] 23In whatever tribe the alien settles, there you are to give him his inheritance," declares the Sovereign LORD.

Chapter 48 Theme _____

48 "These are the tribes, listed by name: At the northern frontier, Dan[c] will have one portion; it will follow the Hethlon road[d] to Lebo[a] Hamath;[e] Hazar Enan and the northern border of Damascus next to Hamath will be part of its border from the east side to the west side.

2"Asher[f] will have one portion; it will border the territory of Dan from east to west.

3"Naphtali[g] will have one portion; it will border the territory of Asher from east to west.

4"Manasseh[h] will have one portion; it will border the territory of Naphtali from east to west.

5"Ephraim[i] will have one portion; it will border the territory of Manasseh[j] from east to west.[k]

6"Reuben[l] will have one portion; it will border the territory of Ephraim from east to west.

7"Judah[m] will have one portion; it will border the territory of Reuben from east to west.

8"Bordering the territory of Judah from east to west will be the portion you are to present as a special gift. It will be 25,000 cubits[b] wide, and its length from east to west will equal one of the tribal portions; the sanctuary will be in the center of it.[n]

9"The special portion you are to offer to the LORD will be 25,000 cubits long and 10,000 cubits[c] wide.[o] 10This will be the sacred portion for the priests. It will be 25,000 cubits long on the north side, 10,000 cubits wide on the west side, 10,000 cubits wide on the east side and 25,000 cubits long on the south side. In the center of it will be the sanctuary of the LORD.[p] 11This will be for the consecrated priests, the Zadokites,[q] who were faithful in serving me[r] and did not go astray as the Levites did when the Israelites went astray.[s] 12It will be a special gift to them from the sacred portion of the land, a most holy portion, bordering the territory of the Levites.

13"Alongside the territory of the priests, the Levites will have an allotment 25,000 cubits long and 10,000 cubits wide. Its total length will be 25,000 cubits and its width 10,000 cubits.[t] 14They

a 1 Or to the entrance to   b 8 That is, about 7 miles (about 12 kilometers)   c 9 That is, about 3 miles (about 5 kilometers) must not sell or exchange any of it. This is the best of the land and must not pass into other hands, because it is holy to the LORD.[a]

¹⁵"The remaining area, 5,000 cubits wide and 25,000 cubits long, will be for the common use of the city, for houses and for pastureland. The city will be in the center of it ¹⁶and will have these measurements: the north side 4,500 cubits, the south side 4,500 cubits, the east side 4,500 cubits, and the west side 4,500 cubits.[b] ¹⁷The pastureland for the city will be 250 cubits on the north, 250 cubits on the south, 250 cubits on the east, and 250 cubits on the west. ¹⁸What remains of the area, bordering on the sacred portion and running the length of it, will be 10,000 cubits on the east side and 10,000 cubits on the west side. Its produce will supply food for the workers of the city.[c] ¹⁹The workers from the city who farm it will come from all the tribes of Israel. ²⁰The entire portion will be a square, 25,000 cubits on each side. As a special gift you will set aside the sacred portion, along with the property of the city.

²¹"What remains on both sides of the area formed by the sacred portion and the city property will belong to the prince. It will extend eastward from the 25,000 cubits of the sacred portion to the eastern border, and westward from the 25,000 cubits to the western border. Both these areas running the length of the tribal portions will belong to the prince, and the sacred portion with the temple sanctuary will be in the center of them.[d] ²²So the property of the Levites and the property of the city will lie in the center of the area that belongs to the prince. The area belonging to the prince will lie between the border of Judah and the border of Benjamin.

²³"As for the rest of the tribes: Benjamin[e] will have one portion; it will extend from the east side to the west side.

²⁴"Simeon[f] will have one portion; it will border the territory of Benjamin from east to west.

²⁵"Issachar[g] will have one portion; it will border the territory of Simeon from east to west.

²⁶"Zebulun[h] will have one portion; it will border the territory of Issachar from east to west.

²⁷"Gad[i] will have one portion; it will border the territory of Zebulun from east to west.

²⁸"The southern boundary of Gad will run south from Tamar[j] to the waters of Meribah Kadesh, then along the Wadi [of Egypt] to the Great Sea.[a][k]

²⁹"This is the land you are to allot as an inheritance to the tribes of Israel, and these will be their portions," declares the Sovereign LORD.

³⁰"These will be the exits of the city: Beginning on the north side, which is 4,500 cubits long, ³¹the gates of the city will be named after

a 28 That is, the Mediterranean

48:14
[a] Lev 25:34; 27:10,28

48:16
[b] Rev 21:16

48:18
[c] Eze 45:6

48:21
[d] ver 8,10; Eze 45:7

48:23
[e] Jos 18:11-28

48:24
[f] Ge 29:33; Jos 19:1-9

48:25
[g] Jos 19:17-23

48:26
[h] Jos 19:10-16

48:27
[i] Jos 13:24-28

48:28
[j] Ge 14:7
[k] Eze 47:19

48:35
a Isa 12:6; 24:23;
Jer 3:17; 14:9;
Jer 33:16;
Joel 3:21;
Zec 2:10;
Rev 21:3

the tribes of Israel. The three gates on the north side will be the gate of Reuben, the gate of Judah and the gate of Levi.

³²"On the east side, which is 4,500 cubits long, will be three gates: the gate of Joseph, the gate of Benjamin and the gate of Dan.

³³"On the south side, which measures 4,500 cubits, will be three gates: the gate of Simeon, the gate of Issachar and the gate of Zebulun.

³⁴"On the west side, which is 4,500 cubits long, will be three gates: the gate of Gad, the gate of Asher and the gate of Naphtali.

³⁵"The distance all around will be 18,000 cubits.

"And the name of the city from that time on will be:

THE LORD IS THERE.*a*"

Theme of Ezekiel:

SEGMENT DIVISIONS

		CHAPTER THEMES	Author:
		1	
		2	Date:
		3	
		4	
		5	Purpose:
		6	
		7	Key Words:
		8	son of man
		9	covenant
		10	vision(s)
		11	glory (most beautiful, splendor)
		12	Spirit (spirit)
		13	know that I am the Lord (know that I the Lord made them)
		14	sin(s) (guilt[y], doing wrong, evil, wicked)
		15	
		16	rebelled (rebel, rebellious)
		17	wrath (anger, fury)
		18	
		19	heart(s) (courage, think, wise)
		20	prostitute(s), prostitution (promiscuous, promiscuity, illicit favors, favors, adultery, adulterous)
		21	
		22	
		23	
		24	

SEGMENT DIVISIONS

	CHAPTER THEMES
25	
26	
27	
28	
29	
30	
31	
32	
33	
34	
35	
36	
37	
38	
39	
40	
41	
42	
43	
44	
45	
46	
47	
48	

DANIEL

$\mathcal{D}$aniel's prophetic ministry began and ended in Babylon. When Nebuchadnezzar first besieged Jerusalem in 605 B.C., Daniel, who was about fifteen years old, was among the captives taken to Babylon.

As Moses predicted, Israel lost her place of supremacy among the nations because she did not obey God. Instead of being the head, Israel became the tail to be wagged by the Gentiles (Deuteronomy 28). Yet, because the gifts and calling of God are irrevocable, when the fullness of the Gentiles is complete, then all Israel will be saved, for the deliverer will come out of Zion and take away Israel's sin (see Romans 11:25-30). All this becomes evident as the prophecies of Daniel unfold.

∾ THINGS TO DO

What the skeleton is to the body, Daniel is to prophecy. All the other prophecies in the Old and New Testament add flesh to Daniel's bones. If you carefully and thoroughly observe Daniel and discover exactly what the text says, you will find that Daniel's prophecies will become increasingly clear and more exciting with every new observation.

General Instructions

Read through Daniel one chapter at a time. Don't hurry. Simply do the following assignment on each chapter. Record all your notes in the margin of the chapter. As you read, answer the following questions and record the answers in the margin of the text:

1. When do the events of this chapter occur? Mark every reference to time with a symbol or with a distinctive color so you can see it immediately.

2. What king/kingdom is ruling at the time? Record this in the margin along with a notation of the "when" of the chapter. For instance, in the margin of chapter 1 you would put the following:

> Third year of Jehoiakim, king of Judah
> Nebuchadnezzar was king of Babylon

3. Who are the main characters in the chapter?

4. What, in general, is the chapter about?

5. Record the theme or event of the chapter on the DANIEL AT A GLANCE chart on page 1530 and on the line in the text next to the chapter number. Then in the margin list the key points or happenings connected with the main event of the chapter.

6. If a vision or dream is recorded, note in the margin who had the vision or dream and what the vision or dream was about. Also, sketch or draw on another piece of paper so you will better remember and understand the dream or vision.

7. When you finish the above, read "From 931 B.C. Until the Birth of Christ" beginning on page 2191 in the section called "Major Events in Israel's History."

Chapters 1-6

1. Read Daniel 1 through 6 again chapter by chapter. This time do the following:

   a. Mark every reference to God in a distinctive way. Watch for the repeated reference to God as the "Most High" and mark this. Then in the margin list what you learn about God from marking those references to him. Note what he is called or how he is referred to. Then meditate on what you have learned about God and how you can apply these truths to your own life.

b. In the margins list everything you learn about Daniel: his character, his relationship to God and to others, and how he handles and responds to various situations.

c. Mark in a distinctive way the following key repeated words: *kingdom (dominion, reign)*, *rules (ruler, sovereign)*, *dream*, *mystery (mysteries)*, and *Nebuchadnezzar* (including pronouns). Put these on an index card and use it as a bookmark. Also watch for and mark key repeated words which appear in individual chapters. If there is room in the margin, summarize what you learn about Nebuchadnezzar.

2. Study the historical chart on page 1504. In the light of what you have observed in the text and on the chart, see if the first six chapters of Daniel come in chronological order.

Chapters 7-12

1. As you prepare to go through these final chapters of Daniel, review what you have observed in chapters 7 through 12 and what you recorded on DANIEL AT A GLANCE. Do you see any difference between the first six chapters of Daniel and the last six?

a. Are the last six chapters chronological?

b. Who had the dreams/visions in each of these major segments?

c. Record your insights to these two questions on DANIEL AT A GLANCE under "Segment Divisions." Show the chronology or lack of it on one line, and then on the other write the main theme or emphasis of these two major divisions of Daniel.

2. Read Daniel 7 through 12 again chapter by chapter. Do the following:

a. As you read each chapter mark the following key words: *vision, kingdom (sovereign power, king, empire, dominion, authority, power), horn (horns, two-horned), saints, you who are highly esteemed (man highly esteemed), end (fulfilled, appointed time, time of the end), covenant, Michael,* and *Gabriel.* Write these on an index card you can use as a bookmark.

b. Mark every reference to God in a distinctive way. Then make a list in the margin of everything you learn about him.

c. List everything you learn about Daniel from observing the text.

Understanding the Visions and Dreams in Daniel

1. When you come to a vision, observe the details of the vision carefully. See if the text interprets the vision. Read it over and over until you see exactly what the text is saying.

2. After you observe chapter 7, compare it with chapter 2.

a. If you didn't do a sketch of the vision in chapter 2, stop and do it. Then do a sketch of the vision in chapter 7. What parallels do you see? Which chapter gives more details of the events encompassed in the vision? Pay attention to those details when you sketch out the vision.

b. Mark any references to time with a symbol. In Jewish reckoning "time, times and half a time" is the equivalent of 3 1/2 years. Note what precedes a period of time and what brings it to an end.

3. When you observe chapter 8, list in the margin everything you learn about the ram and the goat. In a distinctive way mark every pronoun which refers to "another horn, which started small" of 8:9. Then list everything you observe from the text about this horn. Ask the five W's and an H: Where did it come from? What does it do and where? When does it happen? How long does it last?

4. When you observe Daniel 9:24-27, follow those verses chronologically.

a. Number from 1 to 6 in the text the six things in Daniel 9:24 which will be accomplished, or list them in the margin.

b. Observe who the 70 weeks pertain to. Read the reference note regarding *sevens*. Then on a piece of paper draw a line and put in the sequence of events. For example:

|Seven sevens| (you complete the drawing).
Decree

Note when the prophecy begins (what starts it) and what happens at each interval of time. Note what happens after the seven sevens and 62 sevens and what happens during the last seven (the seventieth seven) mentioned in 9:27.

   c. Observe who destroys the city and the sanctuary, and their relationship to the prince who is to come in 9:27. A historical fact that might help is that Jerusalem was destroyed in A.D. 70 by Titus, a Roman general.

5. Read chapters 10 through 12 as one unit and then concentrate on the message and vision of chapters 11 through 12.

   a. Mark every reference to time, including the word *then*, which shows the sequence of events.

   b. Chapter 11 is not an easy chapter to understand apart from a grasp of history. It was written years before the fact, but many people are not familiar with this period of time. When you read of the kings of the south and the north, keep in mind that they are so named because of their geographical relationship to Israel, the Beautiful Land.

   c. As you read through the chapter, consult the chart HISTORY OF ISRAEL'S RELATIONSHIP TO THE KINGS OF DANIEL 11 on page 1524. In 11:1-35 there are approximately 135 prophetic statements which have all been fulfilled. The accuracy of Daniel's prophecies regarding the Gentile nations and their relationship to Israel has staggered the minds of some theologians. Many even say that because of its historical accuracy, Daniel had to be written sometime after the Maccabean period in the second century B.C. However, the book of Daniel clearly refers to Daniel as the author, and so does our Lord Jesus Christ (see Matthew 24:15).

   d. If you have not done so, make a list in the margin of everything you learned about the contemptible person in Daniel 11:22-35. Then list the similarities between the description of the contemptible person of 11:22-35 and Antiochus IV Epiphanes (see history section on pages 2193, 2194 for information on Antiochus IV Epiphanes). To date, no person in history has yet fulfilled the description given in 11:36-45.

   e. Reading *Josephus, the Essential Writings* (Kregel, 1988) will help you understand the intertestament period, the 400 silent years from Malachi to Matthew. It also gives insight into Rome's role in Israel's history and tells more about the various kings mentioned in Daniel 11:1-35, especially Antiochus IV Epiphanes.

   f. In chapter 12 observe the transition from 11:45 to 12:1 chronologically. Mark all references to time and the events connected with them. Observe this chapter very carefully.

6. When you study the dreams and visions in Daniel, remember that Nebuchadnezzar's dream in chapter 2 gives a broad overview and that every vision which follows begins to fill in the details. Now that you have finished observing Daniel, you might want to study the chart PROPHETIC OVERVIEW OF DANIEL on page 1529 and see how it compares with the text and your understanding of it.

7. Finally, determine how the book of Daniel can be segmented. Note these under "Segment Divisions" on DANIEL AT A GLANCE. Then complete the chart.

∾ THINGS TO THINK ABOUT

1. Keeping in mind the meaning of Daniel's name, "God is my judge," think about how Daniel lived. Review what you observed of his life and character and determine to be a Daniel. You have God's Spirit; you have his grace (John 14:17; 1 Corinthians 15:10).

2. What did Daniel know about God that would help him accept what happened to him? How does this understanding of God help you deal with the situations and circumstances of your life?

3. How does your understanding of future events help you understand and deal with what is happening in history? Have you thought about using Daniel as a tool in sharing the gospel with others? Many times prophecy will open the door when nothing else will.

〜〜〜〜〜〜

Chapter 1 Theme

1 In the third year of the reign of Jehoiakim king of Judah, Nebuchadnezzar[a] king of Babylon came to Jerusalem and besieged it.[b] 2And the Lord delivered Jehoiakim king of Judah into his hand, along with some of the articles from the temple of God. These he carried off to the temple of his god in Babylonia[a] and put in the treasure house of his god.[c]

3Then the king ordered Ashpenaz, chief of his court officials, to bring in some of the Israelites from the royal family and the nobility[d]— 4young men without any physical defect, handsome, showing aptitude for every kind of learning, well informed, quick to understand, and qualified to serve in the king's palace. He was to teach them the language and literature of the Babylonians.[b] 5The king assigned them a daily amount of food and wine[e] from the king's table. They were to be trained for three years, and after that they were to enter the king's service.[f]

6Among these were some from Judah: Daniel,[g] Hananiah, Mishael and Azariah. 7The chief official gave them new names: to Daniel, the name Belteshazzar;[h] to Hananiah, Shadrach; to Mishael, Meshach; and to Azariah, Abednego.[i]

8But Daniel resolved not to defile[j] himself with the royal food and wine, and he asked the chief official for permission not to defile himself this way. 9Now God had caused the official to show favor[k] and sympathy[l] to Daniel, 10but the official told Daniel, "I am afraid of my lord the king, who has assigned your[c] food and drink. Why should he see you looking worse than the other young men your age? The king would then have my head because of you."

11Daniel then said to the guard whom the chief official had appointed over Daniel, Hananiah, Mishael and Azariah, 12"Please test your servants for ten days: Give us nothing but vegetables to eat and water to drink. 13Then compare our appearance with that of the young men who eat the royal food, and treat your servants in accordance with what you see." 14So he agreed to this and tested them for ten days.

15At the end of the ten days they looked healthier and better nourished than any of the young men who ate the royal food.[m] 16So the guard took away their choice food and the wine they were to drink and gave them vegetables instead.[n]

Cross references

1:1
[a] 2Ki 24:1
[b] 2Ch 36:6

1:2
[c] 2Ch 36:7;
Jer 27:19-20;
Zec 5:5-11

1:3
[d] 2Ki 20:18;
24:15;
Isa 39:7

1:5
[e] ver 8,10
[f] ver 19

1:6
[g] Eze 14:14

1:7
[h] Da 4:8; 5:12
[i] Da 2:49; 3:12

1:8
[j] Eze 4:13-14

1:9
[k] Ge 39:21;
Pr 16:7
[l] 1Ki 8:50;
Ps 106:46

1:15
[m] Ex 23:25

1:16
[n] ver 12-13

---

[a]2 Hebrew *Shinar*   [b]4 Or *Chaldeans*   [c]10 The Hebrew for *your* and *you* in this verse is plural.

[17]To these four young men God gave knowledge and understanding[a] of all kinds of literature and learning.[b] And Daniel could understand visions and dreams of all kinds.[c]

[18]At the end of the time[d] set by the king to bring them in, the chief official presented them to Nebuchadnezzar. [19]The king talked with them, and he found none equal to Daniel, Hananiah, Mishael and Azariah; so they entered the king's service.[e] [20]In every matter of wisdom and understanding about which the king questioned them, he found them ten times better than all the magicians and enchanters in his whole kingdom.[f]

[21]And Daniel remained there until the first year of King Cyrus.[g]

Chapter 2 Theme

2 In the second year of his reign, Nebuchadnezzar had dreams;[h] his mind was troubled[i] and he could not sleep.[j] [2]So the king summoned the magicians,[k] enchanters, sorcerers[l] and astrologers[a][m] to tell him what he had dreamed.[n] When they came in and stood before the king, [3]he said to them, "I have had a dream that troubles[o] me and I want to know what it means.[b]"

a 2 Or *Chaldeans*; also in verses 4, 5 and 10   b 3 Or *was*

1:17
a 1Ki 3:12
b Da 2:23; Jas 1:5
c Da 2:19,30; 7:1; 8:1

1:18
d ver 5

1:19
e Ge 41:46

1:20
f 1Ki 4:30; Da 2:13,28

1:21
g Da 6:28; 10:1

2:1
h Job 33:15,18; Da 4:5
i Ge 41:8
j Est 6:1; Da 6:18

2:2
k Ge 41:8
l Ex 7:11
m ver 10; Da 5:7
n Da 4:6

2:3
o Da 4:5

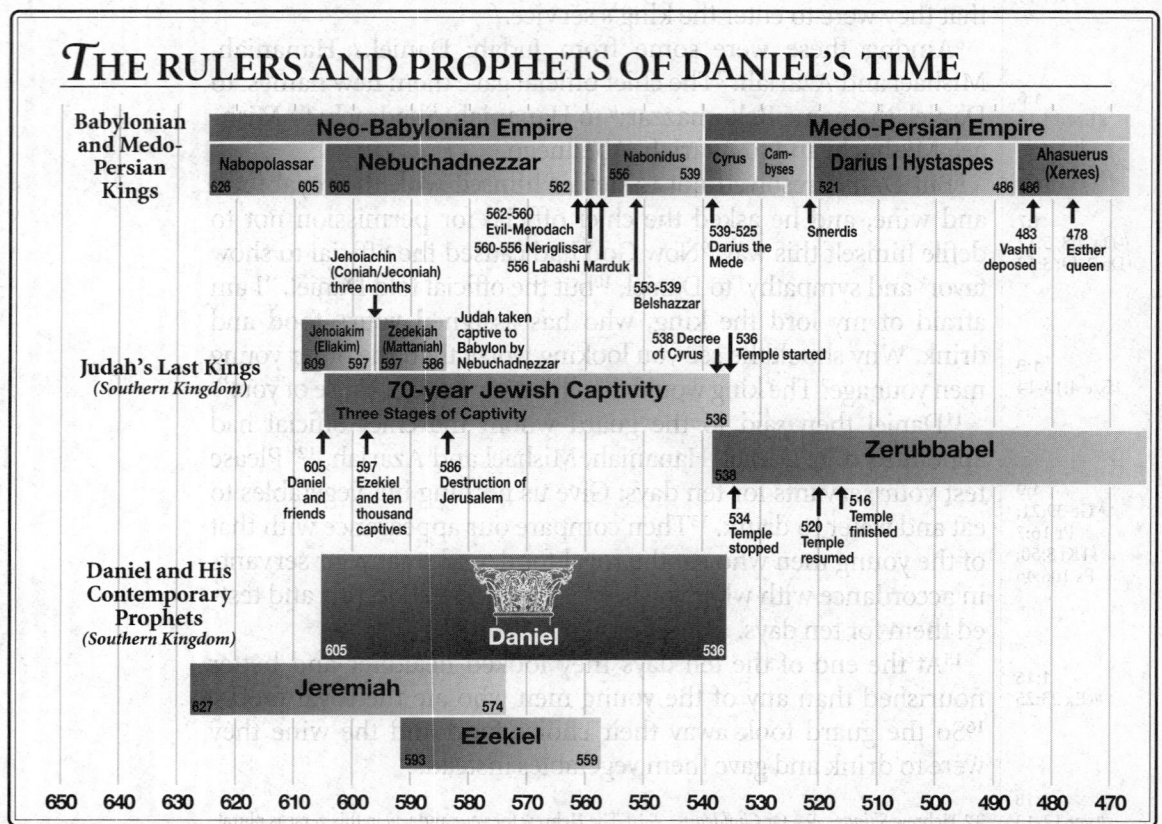

THE RULERS AND PROPHETS OF DANIEL'S TIME

Daniel was written in Aramaic and Hebrew. The Aramaic portion was from 2:4 through 7:28.

2:4
a Ezr 4:7
b Da 3:9; 5:10

2:5
c ver 12
d Ezr 6:11;
  Da 3:29

2:6
e ver 48;
  Da 5:7,16

2:9
f Est 4:11
g Isa 41:22-24

2:10
h ver 27

2:11
i Da 5:11

2:12
j Da 3:13,19
k ver 5

2:13
l Da 1:20

2:17
m Da 1:6

2:18
n Isa 37:4
o Jer 33:3

2:19
p ver 28
q Job 33:15;
  Da 1:17

2:20
r Ps 113:2;
  145:1-2
s Jer 32:19

2:21
t Da 7:25
u Job 12:19;
  Ps 75:6-7

⁴Then the astrologers answered the king in Aramaic,ᵃᵃ "O king, live forever!ᵇ Tell your servants the dream, and we will interpret it."

⁵The king replied to the astrologers, "This is what I have firmly decided: If you do not tell me what my dream was and interpret it, I will have you cut into piecesᶜ and your houses turned into piles of rubble.ᵈ ⁶But if you tell me the dream and explain it, you will receive from me gifts and rewards and great honor.ᵉ So tell me the dream and interpret it for me."

⁷Once more they replied, "Let the king tell his servants the dream, and we will interpret it."

⁸Then the king answered, "I am certain that you are trying to gain time, because you realize that this is what I have firmly decided: ⁹If you do not tell me the dream, there is just one penaltyᶠ for you. You have conspired to tell me misleading and wicked things, hoping the situation will change. So then, tell me the dream, and I will know that you can interpret it for me."ᵍ

¹⁰The astrologers answered the king, "There is not a man on earth who can do what the king asks! No king, however great and mighty, has ever asked such a thing of any magician or enchanter or astrologer.ʰ ¹¹What the king asks is too difficult. No one can reveal it to the king except the gods,ⁱ and they do not live among men."

¹²This made the king so angry and furiousʲ that he ordered the executionᵏ of all the wise men of Babylon. ¹³So the decree was issued to put the wise men to death, and men were sent to look for Daniel and his friends to put them to death.ˡ

¹⁴When Arioch, the commander of the king's guard, had gone out to put to death the wise men of Babylon, Daniel spoke to him with wisdom and tact. ¹⁵He asked the king's officer, "Why did the king issue such a harsh decree?" Arioch then explained the matter to Daniel. ¹⁶At this, Daniel went in to the king and asked for time, so that he might interpret the dream for him.

¹⁷Then Daniel returned to his house and explained the matter to his friends Hananiah, Mishael and Azariah.ᵐ ¹⁸He urged them to plead for mercyⁿ from the God of heaven concerning this mystery,ᵒ so that he and his friends might not be executed with the rest of the wise men of Babylon. ¹⁹During the night the mysteryᵖ was revealed to Daniel in a vision.ᵠ Then Daniel praised the God of heaven ²⁰and said:

> "Praise be to the name of God for ever and ever;ʳ
>   wisdom and powerˢ are his.
> ²¹He changes times and seasons;ᵗ
>   he sets up kings and deposesᵘ them.

ᵃ4 The text from here through chapter 7 is in Aramaic.

He gives wisdom[a] to the wise
and knowledge to the discerning.
[22]He reveals deep and hidden things;[b]
he knows what lies in darkness,[c]
and light[d] dwells with him.
[23]I thank and praise you, O God of my fathers:[e]
You have given me wisdom[f] and power,
you have made known to me what we asked of you,
you have made known to us the dream of the king."

[24]Then Daniel went to Arioch,[g] whom the king had appointed to execute the wise men of Babylon, and said to him, "Do not execute the wise men of Babylon. Take me to the king, and I will interpret his dream for him."

[25]Arioch took Daniel to the king at once and said, "I have found a man among the exiles from Judah[h] who can tell the king what his dream means."

[26]The king asked Daniel (also called Belteshazzar),[i] "Are you able to tell me what I saw in my dream and interpret it?"

[27]Daniel replied, "No wise man, enchanter, magician or diviner can explain to the king the mystery he has asked about,[j] [28]but there is a God in heaven who reveals mysteries.[k] He has shown King Nebuchadnezzar what will happen in days to come.[l] Your dream and the visions that passed through your mind[m] as you lay on your bed are these:

[29]"As you were lying there, O king, your mind turned to things to come, and the revealer of mysteries showed you what is going to happen. [30]As for me, this mystery has been revealed[n] to me, not because I have greater wisdom than other living men, but so that you, O king, may know the interpretation and that you may understand what went through your mind.

[31]"You looked, O king, and there before you stood a large statue—an enormous, dazzling statue,[o] awesome in appearance. [32]The head of the statue was made of pure gold, its chest and arms of silver, its belly and thighs of bronze, [33]its legs of iron, its feet partly of iron and partly of baked clay. [34]While you were watching, a rock was cut out, but not by human hands.[p] It struck the statue on its feet of iron and clay and smashed them.[q] [35]Then the iron, the clay, the bronze, the silver and the gold were broken to pieces at the same time and became like chaff on a threshing floor in the summer. The wind swept them away[r] without leaving a trace. But the rock that struck the statue became a huge mountain[s] and filled the whole earth.

[36]"This was the dream, and now we will interpret it to the king. [37]You, O king, are the king of kings.[t] The God of heaven has given you dominion[u] and power and might and glory; [38]in your hands

Cross references:
2:21 [a] Jas 1:5
2:22 [b] Job 12:22; Ps 25:14; Da 5:11 [c] Ps 139:11-12; Jer 23:24; Heb 4:13 [d] Isa 45:7; Jas 1:17
2:23 [e] Ex 3:15 [f] Da 1:17
2:24 [g] ver 14
2:25 [h] Da 1:6; 5:13; 6:13
2:26 [i] Da 1:7
2:27 [j] ver 10
2:28 [k] Ge 40:8; Am 4:13 [l] Ge 49:1; Da 10:14 [m] Da 4:5
2:30 [n] Isa 45:3; Da 1:17; Am 4:13
2:31 [o] Hab 1:7
2:34 [p] Zec 4:6 [q] ver 44-45; Ps 2:9; Isa 60:12; Da 8:25
2:35 [r] Ps 1:4; 37:10; Isa 17:13 [s] Isa 2:3; Mic 4:1
2:37 [t] Eze 26:7 [u] Jer 27:7

he has placed mankind and the beasts of the field and the birds of the air. Wherever they live, he has made you ruler over them all.[a] You are that head of gold.

39"After you, another kingdom will rise, inferior to yours. Next, a third kingdom, one of bronze, will rule over the whole earth. **40**Finally, there will be a fourth kingdom, strong as iron—for iron breaks and smashes everything—and as iron breaks things to pieces, so it will crush and break all the others.[b] **41**Just as you saw that the feet and toes were partly of baked clay and partly of iron, so this will be a divided kingdom; yet it will have some of the strength of iron in it, even as you saw iron mixed with clay. **42**As the toes were partly iron and partly clay, so this kingdom will be partly strong and partly brittle. **43**And just as you saw the iron mixed with baked clay, so the people will be a mixture and will not remain united, any more than iron mixes with clay.

44"In the time of those kings, the God of heaven will set up a kingdom that will never be destroyed, nor will it be left to another people. It will crush[c] all those kingdoms[d] and bring them to an end, but it will itself endure forever.[e] **45**This is the meaning of the vision of the rock[f] cut out of a mountain, but not by human hands[g]—a rock that broke the iron, the bronze, the clay, the silver and the gold to pieces.

"The great God has shown the king what will take place in the future. The dream is true and the interpretation is trustworthy."

46Then King Nebuchadnezzar fell prostrate[h] before Daniel and paid him honor and ordered that an offering[i] and incense be presented to him. **47**The king said to Daniel, "Surely your God is the God of gods[j] and the Lord of kings[k] and a revealer of mysteries,[l] for you were able to reveal this mystery."

48Then the king placed Daniel in a high position and lavished many gifts on him. He made him ruler over the entire province of Babylon and placed him in charge of all its wise men.[m] **49**Moreover, at Daniel's request the king appointed Shadrach, Meshach and Abednego administrators over the province of Babylon,[n] while Daniel himself remained at the royal court.

Chapter 3 Theme

3 King Nebuchadnezzar made an image[o] of gold, ninety feet high and nine feet[a] wide, and set it up on the plain of Dura in the province of Babylon. **2**He then summoned the satraps, prefects, governors, advisers, treasurers, judges, magistrates and all the other provincial officials[p] to come to the dedication of the image he had set up. **3**So the satraps, prefects, governors, advisers, treasurers, judges, magistrates and all the other provincial officials assembled

INSIGHT

For a clear understanding of the empires represented in the statue, consult the timeline on pages IISB-45 through IISB-48, and the historical account on pages 2191 through 2198.

Cross references

2:38
a Jer 27:6;
Da 4:21-22

2:40
b Da 7:7,23

2:44
c Ps 2:9;
1Co 15:24
d Isa 60:12
e Ps 145:13;
Isa 9:7;
Da 4:34; 6:26;
7:14,27;
Mic 4:7,13;
Lk 1:33

2:45
f Isa 28:16
g Da 8:25

2:46
h Da 8:17;
Ac 10:25
i Ac 14:13

2:47
j Da 11:36
k Da 4:25
l ver 22,28

2:48
m ver 6;
Da 4:9; 5:11

2:49
n Da 1:7

3:1
o Isa 46:6;
Jer 16:20;
Hab 2:19

3:2
p ver 27; Da 6:7

a 1 Aramaic *sixty cubits high and six cubits wide* (about 27 meters high and 2.7 meters wide) for the dedication of the image that King Nebuchadnezzar had set up, and they stood before it.

[4]Then the herald loudly proclaimed, "This is what you are commanded to do, O peoples, nations and men of every language:[a] [5]As soon as you hear the sound of the horn, flute, zither, lyre, harp, pipes and all kinds of music, you must fall down and worship the image of gold that King Nebuchadnezzar has set up.[b] [6]Whoever does not fall down and worship will immediately be thrown into a blazing furnace."[c]

[7]Therefore, as soon as they heard the sound of the horn, flute, zither, lyre, harp and all kinds of music, all the peoples, nations and men of every language fell down and worshiped the image of gold that King Nebuchadnezzar had set up.[d]

[8]At this time some astrologers[ae] came forward and denounced the Jews. [9]They said to King Nebuchadnezzar, "O king, live forever![f] [10]You have issued a decree,[g] O king, that everyone who hears the sound of the horn, flute, zither, lyre, harp, pipes and all kinds of music must fall down and worship the image of gold,[h] [11]and that whoever does not fall down and worship will be thrown into a blazing furnace. [12]But there are some Jews whom you have set over the affairs of the province of Babylon—Shadrach, Meshach and Abednego[i]—who pay no attention[j] to you, O king. They neither serve your gods nor worship the image of gold you have set up."[k]

[13]Furious[l] with rage, Nebuchadnezzar summoned Shadrach, Meshach and Abednego. So these men were brought before the king, [14]and Nebuchadnezzar said to them, "Is it true, Shadrach, Meshach and Abednego, that you do not serve my gods[m] or worship the image[n] of gold I have set up? [15]Now when you hear the

[a]8 Or Chaldeans

3:4 [a]Da 4:1; 6:25
3:5 [b]ver 10,15
3:6 [c]ver 11,15,21; Jer 29:22; Da 6:7; Mt 13:42,50; Rev 13:15
3:7 [d]ver 5
3:8 [e]Da 2:10
3:9 [f]Ne 2:3; Da 5:10; 6:6
3:10 [g]Da 6:12 [h]ver 4-6
3:12 [i]Da 2:49 [j]Da 6:13 [k]Est 3:3
3:13 [l]Da 2:12
3:14 [m]Isa 46:1; Jer 50:2 [n]ver 1

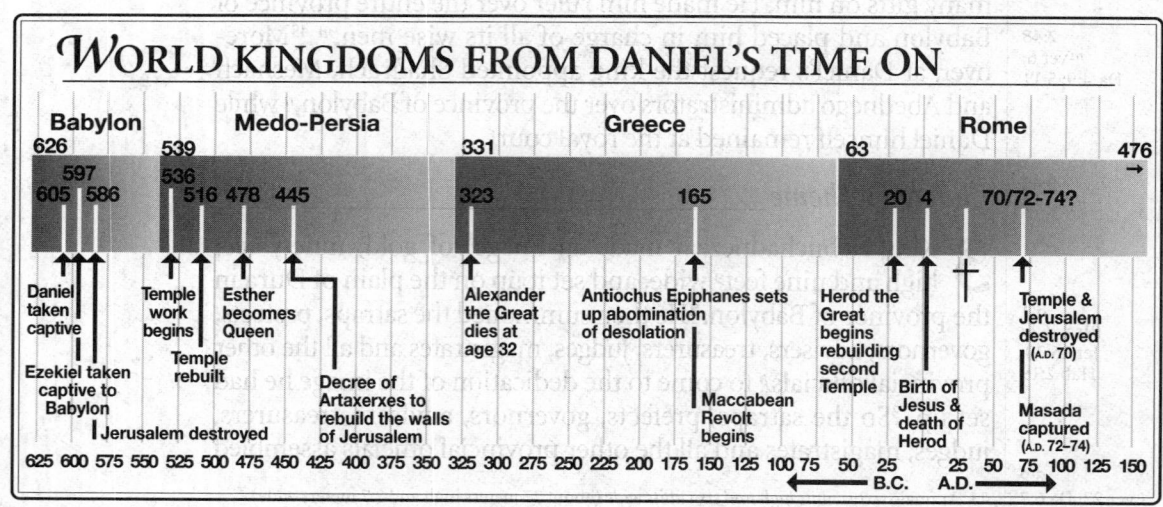

WORLD KINGDOMS FROM DANIEL'S TIME ON

3:15
a Isa 36:18-20
b Ex 5:2;
2Ch 32:15

3:16
c Da 1:7

3:17
d Ps 27:1-2
e Job 5:19;
Jer 1:8

3:18
f ver 28;
Jos 24:15

3:19
g Lev 26:18-28

3:22
h Da 1:7

3:26
i Da 4:2,34

3:27
j ver 2
k Isa 43:2;
Heb 11:32-34
l Da 6:23

3:28
m Ps 34:7;
Da 6:22;
Ac 5:19
n Job 13:15;
Ps 26:1; 84:12;
Jer 17:7
o ver 18

3:29
p Da 6:26

sound of the horn, flute, zither, lyre, harp, pipes and all kinds of music, if you are ready to fall down and worship the image I made, very good. But if you do not worship it, you will be thrown immediately into a blazing furnace. Then what god[a] will be able to rescue[b] you from my hand?"

[16]Shadrach, Meshach and Abednego[c] replied to the king, "O Nebuchadnezzar, we do not need to defend ourselves before you in this matter. [17]If we are thrown into the blazing furnace, the God we serve is able to save[d] us from it, and he will rescue[e] us from your hand, O king. [18]But even if he does not, we want you to know, O king, that we will not serve your gods or worship the image of gold you have set up.[f]"

[19]Then Nebuchadnezzar was furious with Shadrach, Meshach and Abednego, and his attitude toward them changed. He ordered the furnace heated seven[g] times hotter than usual [20]and commanded some of the strongest soldiers in his army to tie up Shadrach, Meshach and Abednego and throw them into the blazing furnace. [21]So these men, wearing their robes, trousers, turbans and other clothes, were bound and thrown into the blazing furnace. [22]The king's command was so urgent and the furnace so hot that the flames of the fire killed the soldiers who took up Shadrach, Meshach and Abednego,[h] [23]and these three men, firmly tied, fell into the blazing furnace.

[24]Then King Nebuchadnezzar leaped to his feet in amazement and asked his advisers, "Weren't there three men that we tied up and threw into the fire?"

They replied, "Certainly, O king."

[25]He said, "Look! I see four men walking around in the fire, unbound and unharmed, and the fourth looks like a son of the gods."

[26]Nebuchadnezzar then approached the opening of the blazing furnace and shouted, "Shadrach, Meshach and Abednego, servants of the Most High God,[i] come out! Come here!"

So Shadrach, Meshach and Abednego came out of the fire, [27]and the satraps, prefects, governors and royal advisers[j] crowded around them.[k] They saw that the fire[l] had not harmed their bodies, nor was a hair of their heads singed; their robes were not scorched, and there was no smell of fire on them.

[28]Then Nebuchadnezzar said, "Praise be to the God of Shadrach, Meshach and Abednego, who has sent his angel[m] and rescued his servants! They trusted[n] in him and defied the king's command and were willing to give up their lives rather than serve or worship any god except their own God.[o] [29]Therefore I decree[p] that the people of any nation or language who say anything against the God of Shadrach, Meshach and Abednego be cut into pieces and

their houses be turned into piles of rubble,[a] for no other god can save[b] in this way."

[30]Then the king promoted Shadrach, Meshach and Abednego in the province of Babylon.[c]

Chapter 4 Theme

4 King Nebuchadnezzar,

To the peoples, nations and men of every language,[d] who live in all the world:

May you prosper greatly![e]

[2]It is my pleasure to tell you about the miraculous signs[f] and wonders that the Most High God[g] has performed for me.

[3]How great are his signs,
   how mighty his wonders![h]
His kingdom is an eternal kingdom;
   his dominion endures[i] from generation
      to generation.

[4]I, Nebuchadnezzar, was at home in my palace, contented[j] and prosperous. [5]I had a dream[k] that made me afraid. As I was lying in my bed, the images and visions that passed through my mind[l] terrified me. [6]So I commanded that all the wise men of Babylon be brought before me to interpret[m] the dream for me. [7]When the magicians,[n] enchanters, astrologers[a] and diviners[o] came, I told them the dream, but they could not interpret it for me.[p] [8]Finally, Daniel came into my presence and I told him the dream. (He is called Belteshazzar,[q] after the name of my god, and the spirit of the holy gods[r] is in him.)

[9]I said, "Belteshazzar, chief[s] of the magicians, I know that the spirit of the holy gods[t] is in you, and no mystery is too difficult for you. Here is my dream; interpret it for me. [10]These are the visions I saw while lying in my bed:[u] I looked, and there before me stood a tree in the middle of the land. Its height was enormous.[v] [11]The tree grew large and strong and its top touched the sky; it was visible to the ends of the earth. [12]Its leaves were beautiful, its fruit abundant, and on it was food for all. Under it the beasts of the field found shelter, and the birds of the air lived in its branches;[w] from it every creature was fed.

[13]"In the visions I saw while lying in my bed,[x] I looked, and there before me was a messenger,[b] a holy one,[y] coming down from heaven. [14]He called in a loud voice: 'Cut down the tree and trim off its branches; strip off its leaves and scatter its

---

3:29
[a] Ezr 6:11
[b] Da 6:27

3:30
[c] Da 2:49

4:1
[d] Da 3:4
[e] Da 6:25

4:2
[f] Ps 74:9
[g] Da 3:26

4:3
[h] Ps 105:27;
Da 6:27
[i] Da 2:44

4:4
[j] Ps 30:6

4:5
[k] Da 2:1
[l] Da 2:28

4:6
[m] Da 2:2

4:7
[n] Ge 41:8
[o] Isa 44:25;
Da 2:2
[p] Da 2:10

4:8
[q] Da 1:7
[r] Da 5:11,14

4:9
[s] Da 2:48
[t] Da 5:11-12

4:10
[u] ver 5
[v] Eze 31:3-4

4:12
[w] Eze 17:23;
Mt 13:32

4:13
[x] Da 7:1
[y] ver 23;
Dt 33:2;
Da 8:13

---

[a] 7 Or *Chaldeans*   [b] 13 Or *watchman*; also in verses 17 and 23

4:14
a Eze 31:12;
Mt 3:10

4:16
b ver 23,32

4:17
c ver 2,25;
Ps 83:18
d Jer 27:5-7;
Da 2:21;
5:18-21
e Da 11:21

4:18
f Ge 41:8;
Da 5:8,15
g Ge 41:15
h ver 7-9

4:19
i Da 7:15,28;
8:27; 10:16-17

4:22
j 2Sa 12:7
k Jer 27:7;
Da 2:37-38;
5:18-19

4:23
l ver 13
m Da 5:21

4:24
n Job 40:12;
Ps 107:40

4:25
o ver 17;
Ps 83:18
p Jer 27:5;
Da 5:21

4:26
q ver 15
r Da 2:37

fruit. Let the animals flee from under it and the birds from its branches.[a] [15]But let the stump and its roots, bound with iron and bronze, remain in the ground, in the grass of the field.

" 'Let him be drenched with the dew of heaven, and let him live with the animals among the plants of the earth. [16]Let his mind be changed from that of a man and let him be given the mind of an animal, till seven times[a] pass by for him.[b]

[17]" 'The decision is announced by messengers, the holy ones declare the verdict, so that the living may know that the Most High[c] is sovereign[d] over the kingdoms of men and gives them to anyone he wishes and sets over them the lowliest[e] of men.'

[18]"This is the dream that I, King Nebuchadnezzar, had. Now, Belteshazzar, tell me what it means, for none of the wise men in my kingdom can interpret it for me.[f] But you can,[g] because the spirit of the holy gods is in you."[h]

[19]Then Daniel (also called Belteshazzar) was greatly perplexed for a time, and his thoughts terrified[i] him. So the king said, "Belteshazzar, do not let the dream or its meaning alarm you."

Belteshazzar answered, "My lord, if only the dream applied to your enemies and its meaning to your adversaries! [20]The tree you saw, which grew large and strong, with its top touching the sky, visible to the whole earth, [21]with beautiful leaves and abundant fruit, providing food for all, giving shelter to the beasts of the field, and having nesting places in its branches for the birds of the air— [22]you, O king, are that tree![j] You have become great and strong; your greatness has grown until it reaches the sky, and your dominion extends to distant parts of the earth.[k]

[23]"You, O king, saw a messenger, a holy one,[l] coming down from heaven and saying, 'Cut down the tree and destroy it, but leave the stump, bound with iron and bronze, in the grass of the field, while its roots remain in the ground. Let him be drenched with the dew of heaven; let him live like the wild animals, until seven times pass by for him.'[m]

[24]"This is the interpretation, O king, and this is the decree[n] the Most High has issued against my lord the king: [25]You will be driven away from people and will live with the wild animals; you will eat grass like cattle and be drenched with the dew of heaven. Seven times will pass by for you until you acknowledge that the Most High[o] is sovereign over the kingdoms of men and gives them to anyone he wishes.[p] [26]The command to leave the stump of the tree with its roots[q] means that your kingdom will be restored to you when you acknowledge that Heaven rules.[r]

a 16 Or years; also in verses 23, 25 and 32

[27]Therefore, O king, be pleased to accept my advice: Renounce your sins by doing what is right, and your wickedness by being kind to the oppressed.[a] It may be that then your prosperity will continue.[b]"

[28]All this happened[c] to King Nebuchadnezzar. [29]Twelve months later, as the king was walking on the roof of the royal palace of Babylon, [30]he said, "Is not this the great Babylon I have built as the royal residence, by my mighty power and for the glory of my majesty?"[d]

[31]The words were still on his lips when a voice came from heaven, "This is what is decreed for you, King Nebuchadnezzar: Your royal authority has been taken from you. [32]You will be driven away from people and will live with the wild animals; you will eat grass like cattle. Seven times will pass by for you until you acknowledge that the Most High is sovereign over the kingdoms of men and gives them to anyone he wishes."

[33]Immediately what had been said about Nebuchadnezzar was fulfilled. He was driven away from people and ate grass like cattle. His body was drenched with the dew of heaven until his hair grew like the feathers of an eagle and his nails like the claws of a bird.[e]

[34]At the end of that time, I, Nebuchadnezzar, raised my eyes toward heaven, and my sanity was restored. Then I praised the Most High; I honored and glorified him who lives forever.[f]

His dominion is an eternal dominion;
    his kingdom endures from generation to generation.[g]
[35]All the peoples of the earth
    are regarded as nothing.[h]
He does as he pleases[i]
    with the powers of heaven
    and the peoples of the earth.
No one can hold back his hand
    or say to him: "What have you done?"[j]

[36]At the same time that my sanity was restored, my honor and splendor were returned to me for the glory of my kingdom.[k] My advisers and nobles sought me out, and I was restored to my throne and became even greater than before. [37]Now I, Nebuchadnezzar, praise and exalt and glorify the King of heaven, because everything he does is right and all his ways are just.[l] And those who walk in pride he is able to humble.[m]

Chapter 5 Theme

5 King Belshazzar gave a great banquet[n] for a thousand of his nobles and drank wine with them. [2]While Belshazzar was

---

4:27
[a] Isa 55:6-7
[b] 1Ki 21:29;
Ps 41:3;
Eze 18:22

4:28
[c] Nu 23:19

4:30
[d] Isa 37:24-25;
Da 5:20;
Hab 2:4

4:33
[e] Da 5:20-21

4:34
[f] Da 12:7;
Rev 4:10
[g] Ps 145:13;
Da 2:44;
5:21; 6:26;
Lk 1:33

4:35
[h] Isa 40:17
[i] Ps 115:3;
135:6
[j] Isa 45:9;
Ro 9:20

4:36
[k] Pr 22:4

4:37
[l] Dt 32:4;
Ps 33:4-5
[m] Ex 18:11;
Job 40:11-12;
Da 5:20,23

5:1
[n] Est 1:3

5:2
a 2Ki 24:13;
Jer 52:19
b Est 1:7;
Da 1:2

5:4
c Ps 135:15-18;
Hab 2:19;
Rev 9:20

5:6
d Da 4:5
e Eze 7:17

5:7
f Isa 44:25
g Da 4:6-7
h Ge 41:42
i Da 2:5-6,48;
6:2-3

5:8
j Da 2:10,27

5:9
k Isa 21:4

5:10
l Da 3:9

5:11
m Da 4:8-9,19
n ver 14;
Da 1:17
o Da 2:47-48

5:12
p Da 1:7
q ver 14-16;
Da 6:3

5:13
r Da 6:13

drinking his wine, he gave orders to bring in the gold and silver goblets[a] that Nebuchadnezzar his father[a] had taken from the temple in Jerusalem, so that the king and his nobles, his wives and his concubines might drink from them.[b] 3So they brought in the gold goblets that had been taken from the temple of God in Jerusalem, and the king and his nobles, his wives and his concubines drank from them. 4As they drank the wine, they praised the gods of gold and silver, of bronze, iron, wood and stone.[c]

5Suddenly the fingers of a human hand appeared and wrote on the plaster of the wall, near the lampstand in the royal palace. The king watched the hand as it wrote. 6His face turned pale and he was so frightened[d] that his knees knocked together and his legs gave way.[e]

7The king called out for the enchanters, astrologers[b] and diviners[f] to be brought and said to these wise[g] men of Babylon, "Whoever reads this writing and tells me what it means will be clothed in purple and have a gold chain placed around his neck,[h] and he will be made the third highest ruler in the kingdom."[i]

8Then all the king's wise men came in, but they could not read the writing or tell the king what it meant.[j] 9So King Belshazzar became even more terrified[k] and his face grew more pale. His nobles were baffled.

10The queen,[c] hearing the voices of the king and his nobles, came into the banquet hall. "O king, live forever!"[l] she said. "Don't be alarmed! Don't look so pale! 11There is a man in your kingdom who has the spirit of the holy gods[m] in him. In the time of your father he was found to have insight and intelligence and wisdom[n] like that of the gods. King Nebuchadnezzar your father—your father the king, I say—appointed him chief of the magicians, enchanters, astrologers and diviners.[o] 12This man Daniel, whom the king called Belteshazzar,[p] was found to have a keen mind and knowledge and understanding, and also the ability to interpret dreams, explain riddles and solve difficult problems.[q] Call for Daniel, and he will tell you what the writing means."

13So Daniel was brought before the king, and the king said to him, "Are you Daniel, one of the exiles my father the king brought from Judah?[r] 14I have heard that the spirit of the gods is in you and that you have insight, intelligence and outstanding wisdom. 15The wise men and enchanters were brought before me to read this writing and tell me what it means, but they could not explain it. 16Now I have heard that you are able to give interpretations and to solve difficult problems. If you can read this writing and tell me what it means, you will be clothed in purple and have a gold chain

a 2 Or *ancestor;* or *predecessor;* also in verses 11, 13 and 18   *b* 7 Or *Chaldeans;* also in verse 11
c 10 Or *queen mother*

placed around your neck, and you will be made the third highest ruler in the kingdom."

¹⁷Then Daniel answered the king, "You may keep your gifts for yourself and give your rewards to someone else.ᵃ Nevertheless, I will read the writing for the king and tell him what it means.

¹⁸"O king, the Most High God gave your father Nebuchadnezzar sovereignty and greatness and glory and splendor.ᵇ ¹⁹Because of the high position he gave him, all the peoples and nations and men of every language dreaded and feared him. Those the king wanted to put to death, he put to death;ᶜ those he wanted to spare, he spared; those he wanted to promote, he promoted; and those he wanted to humble, he humbled. ²⁰But when his heart became arrogant and hardened with pride,ᵈ he was deposed from his royal throne and strippedᵉ of his glory.ᶠ ²¹He was driven away from people and given the mind of an animal; he lived with the wild donkeys and ate grass like cattle; and his body was drenched with the dew of heaven, until he acknowledged that the Most High God is sovereignᵍ over the kingdoms of men and sets over them anyone he wishes.ʰ

²²"But you his son,ᵃ O Belshazzar, have not humbledⁱ yourself, though you knew all this. ²³Instead, you have set yourself up againstʲ the Lord of heaven. You had the goblets from his temple brought to you, and you and your nobles, your wives and your concubines drank wine from them. You praised the gods of silver and gold, of bronze, iron, wood and stone, which cannot see or hear or understand.ᵏ But you did not honor the God who holds in his hand your lifeˡ and all your ways.ᵐ ²⁴Therefore he sent the hand that wrote the inscription.

²⁵"This is the inscription that was written:

MENE, MENE, TEKEL, PARSINᵇ

²⁶"This is what these words mean:

*Mene*ᶜ: God has numbered the daysⁿ of your reign and brought it to an end.ᵒ

²⁷*Tekel*ᵈ: You have been weighed on the scales and found wanting.ᵖ

²⁸*Peres*ᵉ: Your kingdom is divided and given to the Medes�q and Persians."ʳ

²⁹Then at Belshazzar's command, Daniel was clothed in purple, a gold chain was placed around his neck, and he was proclaimed the third highest ruler in the kingdom.

ᵃ22 Or *descendant*; or *successor*   ᵇ25 Aramaic *UPARSIN* (that is, *AND PARSIN*)   ᶜ26 *Mene* can mean *numbered* or *mina* (a unit of money).   ᵈ27 *Tekel* can mean *weighed* or *shekel*.
ᵉ28 *Peres* (the singular of *Parsin*) can mean *divided* or *Persia* or *a half mina* or *a half shekel*.

5:17
ᵃ2Ki 5:16

5:18
ᵇJer 27:7;
Da 2:37-38

5:19
ᶜDa 2:12-13; 3:6

5:20
ᵈDa 4:30
ᵉJer 13:18
ᶠJob 40:12;
Isa 14:13-15

5:21
ᵍEze 17:24
ʰDa 4:16-17,35

5:22
ⁱEx 10:3;
2Ch 33:23

5:23
ʲJer 50:29
ᵏPs 115:4-8;
Hab 2:19
ˡJob 12:10
ᵐJob 31:4;
Jer 10:23

5:26
ⁿJer 27:7
ᵒIsa 13:6

5:27
ᵖPs 62:9

5:28
qIsa 13:17
ʳDa 6:28

5:30
a ver 1
b Isa 21:9;
Jer 51:31

5:31
c Da 6:1; 9:1

6:1
d Da 5:31
e Est 1:1

6:2
f Da 2:48-49
g Ezr 4:22

6:3
h Ge 41:41;
Est 10:3;
Da 5:12-14

6:5
i Ac 24:13-16

6:6
j Ne 2:3;
Da 2:4

6:7
k Da 3:2
l Ps 59:3; 64:2-6;
Da 3:6

6:8
m Est 1:19

6:10
n 1Ki 8:48-49
o Ps 95:6
p Ac 5:29

6:12
q Est 1:19;
Da 3:8-12

6:13
r Da 2:25; 5:13
s Est 3:8;
Da 3:12

6:14
t Mk 6:26

³⁰That very night Belshazzar,ᵃ king of the Babylonians,ᵃ was slain,ᵇ ³¹and Dariusᶜ the Mede took over the kingdom, at the age of sixty-two.

Chapter 6 Theme _____

6 It pleased Dariusᵈ to appoint 120 satrapsᵉ to rule throughout the kingdom, ²with three administrators over them, one of whom was Daniel.ᶠ The satraps were made accountableᵍ to them so that the king might not suffer loss. ³Now Daniel so distinguished himself among the administrators and the satraps by his exceptional qualities that the king planned to set him over the whole kingdom.ʰ ⁴At this, the administrators and the satraps tried to find grounds for charges against Daniel in his conduct of government affairs, but they were unable to do so. They could find no corruption in him, because he was trustworthy and neither corrupt nor negligent. ⁵Finally these men said, "We will never find any basis for charges against this man Daniel unless it has something to do with the law of his God."ⁱ

⁶So the administrators and the satraps went as a group to the king and said: "O King Darius, live forever!ʲ ⁷The royal administrators, prefects, satraps, advisers and governorsᵏ have all agreed that the king should issue an edict and enforce the decree that anyone who prays to any god or man during the next thirty days, except to you, O king, shall be thrown into the lions' den.ˡ ⁸Now, O king, issue the decree and put it in writing so that it cannot be altered—in accordance with the laws of the Medes and Persians, which cannot be repealed."ᵐ ⁹So King Darius put the decree in writing.

¹⁰Now when Daniel learned that the decree had been published, he went home to his upstairs room where the windows opened towardⁿ Jerusalem. Three times a day he got down on his kneesᵒ and prayed, giving thanks to his God, just as he had done before.ᵖ ¹¹Then these men went as a group and found Daniel praying and asking God for help. ¹²So they went to the king and spoke to him about his royal decree: "Did you not publish a decree that during the next thirty days anyone who prays to any god or man except to you, O king, would be thrown into the lions' den?"

The king answered, "The decree stands—in accordance with the laws of the Medes and Persians, which cannot be repealed."ᑫ

¹³Then they said to the king, "Daniel, who is one of the exiles from Judah,ʳ pays no attentionˢ to you, O king, or to the decree you put in writing. He still prays three times a day." ¹⁴When the king heard this, he was greatly distressed;ᵗ he was determined to rescue Daniel and made every effort until sundown to save him.

a 30 Or *Chaldeans*

[15]Then the men went as a group to the king and said to him, "Remember, O king, that according to the law of the Medes and Persians no decree or edict that the king issues can be changed."[a]

[16]So the king gave the order, and they brought Daniel and threw him into the lions' den.[b] The king said to Daniel, "May your God, whom you serve continually, rescue[c] you!"

[17]A stone was brought and placed over the mouth of the den, and the king sealed[d] it with his own signet ring and with the rings of his nobles, so that Daniel's situation might not be changed. [18]Then the king returned to his palace and spent the night without eating[e] and without any entertainment being brought to him. And he could not sleep.[f]

[19]At the first light of dawn, the king got up and hurried to the lions' den. [20]When he came near the den, he called to Daniel in an anguished voice, "Daniel, servant of the living God, has your God, whom you serve continually, been able to rescue you from the lions?"[g]

[21]Daniel answered, "O king, live forever![h] [22]My God sent his angel,[i] and he shut the mouths of the lions.[j] They have not hurt me, because I was found innocent in his sight.[k] Nor have I ever done any wrong before you, O king."

[23]The king was overjoyed and gave orders to lift Daniel out of the den. And when Daniel was lifted from the den, no wound[l] was found on him, because he had trusted[m] in his God.

[24]At the king's command, the men who had falsely accused Daniel were brought in and thrown into the lions' den,[n] along with their wives and children.[o] And before they reached the floor of the den, the lions overpowered them and crushed all their bones.[p]

[25]Then King Darius wrote to all the peoples, nations and men of every language throughout the land:

"May you prosper greatly!"[q]

[26]"I issue a decree that in every part of my kingdom people must fear and reverence the God of Daniel.[r]

"For he is the living God
    and he endures forever;
his kingdom will not be destroyed,
    his dominion will never end.[s]
[27]He rescues and he saves;
    he performs signs and wonders[t]
    in the heavens and on the earth.
He has rescued Daniel
    from the power of the lions."[u]

6:15 [a] Est 8:8

6:16 [b] ver 7; [c] Job 5:19; Ps 37:39-40

6:17 [d] Mt 27:66

6:18 [e] 2Sa 12:17; [f] Est 6:1; Da 2:1

6:20 [g] Da 3:17

6:21 [h] Da 2:4

6:22 [i] Da 3:28; [j] Ps 91:11-13; Heb 11:33; [k] Ac 12:11; 2Ti 4:17

6:23 [l] Da 3:27; [m] 1Ch 5:20

6:24 [n] Dt 19:18-19; Est 7:9-10; Ps 54:5; [o] Dt 24:16; 2Ki 14:6; [p] Isa 38:13

6:25 [q] Da 4:1

6:26 [r] Ps 99:1-3; Da 3:29; [s] Da 2:44; 4:34

6:27 [t] Da 4:3; [u] ver 22

6:28
a 2Ch 36:22;
Da 1:21

[28] So Daniel prospered during the reign of Darius and the reign of Cyrus[aa] the Persian.

Chapter 7 Theme _____

7:1
b Da 5:1
c Da 1:17
d Jer 36:4

7 In the first year of Belshazzar[b] king of Babylon, Daniel had a dream, and visions passed through his mind[c] as he was lying on his bed. He wrote[d] down the substance of his dream.

[2] Daniel said: "In my vision at night I looked, and there before me were the four winds of heaven[e] churning up the great sea. [3] Four great beasts,[f] each different from the others, came up out of the sea.

7:2
e Rev 7:1

[4] "The first was like a lion,[g] and it had the wings of an eagle.[h] I watched until its wings were torn off and it was lifted from the ground so that it stood on two feet like a man, and the heart of a man was given to it.

7:3
f Rev 13:1

[5] "And there before me was a second beast, which looked like a bear. It was raised up on one of its sides, and it had three ribs in its mouth between its teeth. It was told, 'Get up and eat your fill of flesh!'[i]

7:4
g Jer 4:7
h Eze 17:3

[6] "After that, I looked, and there before me was another beast, one that looked like a leopard.[j] And on its back it had four wings like those of a bird. This beast had four heads, and it was given authority to rule.

7:5
i Da 2:39

[7] "After that, in my vision at night I looked, and there before me was a fourth beast—terrifying and frightening and very powerful. It had large iron[k] teeth; it crushed and devoured its victims and trampled underfoot whatever was left. It was different from all the former beasts, and it had ten horns.[l]

7:6
j Rev 13:2

[8] "While I was thinking about the horns, there before me was another horn, a little[m] one, which came up among them; and three of the first horns were uprooted before it. This horn had eyes like the eyes of a man[n] and a mouth that spoke boastfully.[o]

7:7
k Da 2:40
l Rev 12:3

[9] "As I looked,

7:8
m Da 8:9
n Rev 9:7
o Ps 12:3;
Rev 13:5-6

"thrones were set in place,
    and the Ancient of Days took his seat.
His clothing was as white as snow;
    the hair of his head was white like wool.[p]
His throne was flaming with fire,
    and its wheels[q] were all ablaze.
[10] A river of fire[r] was flowing,
    coming out from before him.[s]
Thousands upon thousands attended him;
    ten thousand times ten thousand stood before him.
The court was seated,
    and the books[t] were opened.

7:9
p Rev 1:14
q Eze 1:15;
10:6

7:10
r Ps 50:3; 97:3;
Isa 30:27
s Dt 33:2;
Ps 68:17;
Rev 5:11
t Rev 20:11-15

a 28 Or Darius, that is, the reign of Cyrus

¹¹"Then I continued to watch because of the boastful words the horn was speaking. I kept looking until the beast was slain and its body destroyed and thrown into the blazing fire.ᵃ ¹²(The other beasts had been stripped of their authority, but were allowed to live for a period of time.)

¹³"In my vision at night I looked, and there before me was one like a son of man,ᵇ coming with the clouds of heaven.ᶜ He approached the Ancient of Days and was led into his presence. ¹⁴He was given authority,ᵈ glory and sovereign power; all peoples, nations and men of every language worshiped him.ᵉ His dominion is an everlasting dominion that will not pass away, and his kingdom is one that will never be destroyed.ᶠ

¹⁵"I, Daniel, was troubled in spirit, and the visions that passed through my mind disturbed me.ᵍ ¹⁶I approached one of those standing there and asked him the true meaning of all this.

"So he told me and gave me the interpretationʰ of these things: ¹⁷'The four great beasts are four kingdoms that will rise from the earth. ¹⁸But the saints of the Most High will receive the kingdom and will possess it forever—yes, for ever and ever.'ⁱ

¹⁹"Then I wanted to know the true meaning of the fourth beast, which was different from all the others and most terrifying, with its iron teeth and bronze claws—the beast that crushed and devoured its victims and trampled underfoot whatever was left. ²⁰I also wanted to know about the ten horns on its head and about the other horn that came up, before which three of them fell—the horn that looked more imposing than the others and that had eyes and a mouth that spoke boastfully. ²¹As I watched, this horn was waging war against the saints and defeating them,ʲ ²²until the Ancient of Days came and pronounced judgment in favor of the saints of the Most High, and the time came when they possessed the kingdom.

²³"He gave me this explanation: 'The fourth beast is a fourth kingdom that will appear on earth. It will be different from all the other kingdoms and will devour the whole earth, trampling it down and crushing it.ᵏ ²⁴The ten hornsˡ are ten kings who will come from this kingdom. After them another king will arise, different from the earlier ones; he will subdue three kings. ²⁵He will speak against the Most Highᵐ and oppress his saints and try to change the set timesⁿ and the laws. The saints will be handed over to him for a time, times and half a time.ᵃᵒ

²⁶"'But the court will sit, and his power will be taken away and completely destroyed forever. ²⁷Then the sovereignty, power and greatness of the kingdoms under the whole heaven will be handed over to the saints, the people of the Most High. His kingdom will be an everlastingᵖ kingdom, and all rulers will worshipᵠ and obey him.'

ᵃ25 Or for a year, two years and half a year

7:11 ᵃRev 19:20
7:13 ᵇMt 8:20*; Rev 1:13*; ᶜMt 24:30; Rev 1:7
7:14 ᵈMt 28:18; ᵉPs 72:11; 102:22; 1Co 15:27; Eph 1:22; ᶠDa 2:44; Heb 12:28; Rev 11:15
7:15 ᵍDa 4:19
7:16 ʰDa 8:16; 9:22; Zec 1:9
7:18 ⁱIsa 60:12-14; Rev 2:26; 20:4
7:21 ʲRev 13:7
7:23 ᵏDa 2:40
7:24 ˡRev 17:12
7:25 ᵐIsa 37:23; Da 11:36; ⁿDa 2:21; ᵒDa 8:24; 12:7; Rev 12:14
7:27 ᵖDa 2:44; 4:34; Lk 1:33; Rev 11:15; 22:5; ᵠPs 22:27; 72:11; 86:9

28"This is the end of the matter. I, Daniel, was deeply troubled*a* by my thoughts, and my face turned pale, but I kept the matter to myself."

Chapter 8 Theme

8 In the third year of King Belshazzar's reign, I, Daniel, had a vision, after the one that had already appeared to me. ²In my vision I saw myself in the citadel of Susa*b* in the province of Elam;*c* in the vision I was beside the Ulai Canal. ³I looked up,*d* and there before me was a ram with two horns, standing beside the canal, and the horns were long. One of the horns was longer than the other but grew up later. ⁴I watched the ram as he charged toward the west and the north and the south. No animal could stand against him, and none could rescue from his power. He did as he pleased*e* and became great.

8:3
d Da 10:5

8:4
e Da 11:3,16

8:7
f Da 7:7

⁵As I was thinking about this, suddenly a goat with a prominent horn between his eyes came from the west, crossing the whole earth without touching the ground. ⁶He came toward the two-horned ram I had seen standing beside the canal and charged at him in great rage. ⁷I saw him attack the ram furiously, striking the ram and shattering his two horns. The ram was powerless to stand against him; the goat knocked him to the ground and trampled on him,*f* and none could rescue the ram from his power. ⁸The goat became very great, but at the height of his power his large horn was broken off,*g* and in its place four prominent horns grew up toward the four winds of heaven.*h*

8:8
g 2Ch 26:16-21;
Da 5:20
h Da 7:2;
Rev 7:1

8:9
i Da 11:16

⁹Out of one of them came another horn, which started small but grew in power to the south and to the east and toward the Beautiful Land.*i* ¹⁰It grew until it reached*j* the host of the heavens, and it threw some of the starry host down to the earth*k* and trampled*l* on them. ¹¹It set itself up to be as great as the Prince of the host;*m* it took away the daily sacrifice*n* from him, and the place of his sanctuary was brought low.*o* ¹²Because of rebellion, the host ₍of the saints₎*a* and the daily sacrifice were given over to it. It prospered in everything it did, and truth was thrown to the ground.

8:10
j Isa 14:13
k Rev 12:4
l Da 7:7

8:11
m Da 11:36-37
n Eze 46:13-14
o Da 11:31;
12:11

¹³Then I heard a holy one*p* speaking, and another holy one said to him, "How long will it take for the vision to be fulfilled*q*—the vision concerning the daily sacrifice, the rebellion that causes desolation, and the surrender of the sanctuary and of the host that will be trampled*r* underfoot?"

¹⁴He said to me, "It will take 2,300 evenings and mornings; then the sanctuary will be reconsecrated."*s*

¹⁵While I, Daniel, was watching the vision*t* and trying to understand it, there before me stood one who looked like a man.*u*

a 12 Or rebellion, the armies

INSIGHT

The maps on pages 2310, 2311 show the boundaries of the Babylonian, Persian, Greek, and Roman Empires as they relate to the nations today.

¹⁶And I heard a man's voice from the Ulai calling, "Gabriel,^a tell this man the meaning of the vision."

¹⁷As he came near the place where I was standing, I was terrified and fell prostrate.^b "Son of man," he said to me, "understand that the vision concerns the time of the end."^c

¹⁸While he was speaking to me, I was in a deep sleep, with my face to the ground.^d Then he touched me and raised me to my feet.^e

¹⁹He said: "I am going to tell you what will happen later in the time of wrath, because the vision concerns the appointed time of the end.^{af} ²⁰The two-horned ram that you saw represents the kings of Media and Persia. ²¹The shaggy goat is the king of Greece,^g and the large horn between his eyes is the first king.^h ²²The four horns that replaced the one that was broken off represent four kingdoms that will emerge from his nation but will not have the same power.

²³"In the latter part of their reign, when rebels have become completely wicked, a stern-faced king, a master of intrigue, will arise. ²⁴He will become very strong, but not by his own power. He will cause astounding devastation and will succeed in whatever he does. He will destroy the mighty men and the holy people.ⁱ ²⁵He will cause deceit to prosper, and he will consider himself superior. When they feel secure, he will destroy many and take his stand against the Prince of princes.^j Yet he will be destroyed, but not by human power.^k

²⁶"The vision of the evenings and mornings that has been given you is true,^l but seal^m up the vision, for it concerns the distant future."ⁿ

²⁷I, Daniel, was exhausted and lay ill for several days. Then I got up and went about the king's business.^o I was appalled^p by the vision; it was beyond understanding.

Chapter 9 Theme

9 In the first year of Darius^q son of Xerxes^b (a Mede by descent), who was made ruler over the Babylonian^c kingdom— ²in the first year of his reign, I, Daniel, understood from the Scriptures, according to the word of the LORD given to Jeremiah the prophet, that the desolation of Jerusalem would last seventy^r years. ³So I turned to the Lord God and pleaded with him in prayer and petition, in fasting, and in sackcloth and ashes.^s

⁴I prayed to the LORD my God and confessed:

"O Lord, the great and awesome God,^t who keeps his covenant of love^u with all who love him and obey his commands, ⁵we have sinned and done wrong.^v We have been wicked and have rebelled; we have turned away^w from your

---

8:16
^aDa 9:21;
Lk 1:19

8:17
^bEze 1:28;
Da 2:46;
Rev 1:17
^cHab 2:3

8:18
^dDa 10:9
^eEze 2:2;
Da 10:16-18

8:19
^fHab 2:3

8:21
^gDa 10:20
^hDa 11:3

8:24
ⁱDa 7:25; 11:36

8:25
^jDa 11:36
^kDa 2:34; 11:21

8:26
^lDa 10:1
^mRev 22:10
ⁿDa 10:14

8:27
^oDa 2:48
^pDa 7:28

9:1
^qDa 5:31

9:2
^r2Ch 36:21;
Jer 29:10;
Zec 7:5

9:3
^sNe 1:4;
Jer 29:12

9:4
^tDt 7:21
^uDt 7:9

9:5
^vPs 106:6
^wIsa 53:6

---

^a 19 Or *because the end will be at the appointed time*   ^b 1 Hebrew *Ahasuerus*   ^c 1 Or *Chaldean*

9:5
a ver 11;
La 1:20

9:6
b 2Ch 36:16;
Jer 44:5

9:7
c Ps 44:15
d Dt 4:27;
Am 9:9
e Jer 3:25

9:9
f Ps 130:4
g Ne 9:17;
Jer 14:7

9:10
h 2Ki 17:13-15;
18:12

9:11
i Isa 1:4-6;
Jer 8:5-10

9:12
j Isa 44:26;
Zec 1:6
k Jer 44:2-6;
Eze 5:9

9:13
l Isa 9:13;
Jer 2:30

9:14
m Jer 44:27
n Ne 9:33

9:15
o Jer 32:21
p Ne 9:10

9:16
q Ps 31:1
r Jer 32:32
s Zec 8:3
t Eze 5:14

9:17
u Nu 6:24-26;
Ps 80:19

9:18
v Ps 80:14
w Isa 37:17;
Jer 7:10-12;
25:29

9:19
x Ps 44:23

9:20
y ver 3;
Ps 145:18;
Isa 58:9

9:21
z Da 8:16;
Lk 1:19

commands and laws.*a* [6]We have not listened to your servants the prophets,*b* who spoke in your name to our kings, our princes and our fathers, and to all the people of the land.

[7]"Lord, you are righteous, but this day we are covered with shame*c*—the men of Judah and people of Jerusalem and all Israel, both near and far, in all the countries where you have scattered*d* us because of our unfaithfulness to you.*e* [8]O Lord, we and our kings, our princes and our fathers are covered with shame because we have sinned against you. [9]The Lord our God is merciful and forgiving,*f* even though we have rebelled against him;*g* [10]we have not obeyed the Lord our God or kept the laws he gave us through his servants the prophets.*h* [11]All Israel has transgressed your law and turned away, refusing to obey you.

"Therefore the curses and sworn judgments written in the Law of Moses, the servant of God, have been poured out on us, because we have sinned*i* against you. [12]You have fulfilled*j* the words spoken against us and against our rulers by bringing upon us great disaster. Under the whole heaven nothing has ever been done like what has been done to Jerusalem.*k* [13]Just as it is written in the Law of Moses, all this disaster has come upon us, yet we have not sought the favor of the Lord our God by turning from our sins and giving attention to your truth.*l* [14]The Lord did not hesitate to bring the disaster*m* upon us, for the Lord our God is righteous in everything he does; yet we have not obeyed him.*n*

[15]"Now, O Lord our God, who brought your people out of Egypt with a mighty hand*o* and who made for yourself a name*p* that endures to this day, we have sinned, we have done wrong. [16]O Lord, in keeping with all your righteous acts,*q* turn away your anger and your wrath from Jerusalem,*r* your city, your holy hill.*s* Our sins and the iniquities of our fathers have made Jerusalem and your people an object of scorn*t* to all those around us.

[17]"Now, our God, hear the prayers and petitions of your servant. For your sake, O Lord, look with favor*u* on your desolate sanctuary. [18]Give ear, O God, and hear; open your eyes and see*v* the desolation of the city that bears your Name.*w* We do not make requests of you because we are righteous, but because of your great mercy. [19]O Lord, listen! O Lord, forgive!*x* O Lord, hear and act! For your sake, O my God, do not delay, because your city and your people bear your Name."

[20]While I was speaking and praying, confessing my sin and the sin of my people Israel and making my request to the Lord my God for his holy hill*y*— [21]while I was still in prayer, Gabriel,*z* the

man I had seen in the earlier vision, came to me in swift flight about the time of the evening sacrifice.[a] [22]He instructed me and said to me, "Daniel, I have now come to give you insight and understanding. [23]As soon as you began to pray, an answer was given, which I have come to tell you, for you are highly esteemed.[b] Therefore, consider the message and understand the vision:[c]

[24]"Seventy 'sevens'[a] are decreed for your people and your holy city to finish[b] transgression, to put an end to sin, to atone[d] for wickedness, to bring in everlasting righteousness,[e] to seal up vision and prophecy and to anoint the most holy.[c]

[25]"Know and understand this: From the issuing of the decree[d] to restore and rebuild[f] Jerusalem until the Anointed One,[e][g] the ruler, comes, there will be seven 'sevens,' and sixty-two 'sevens.' It will be rebuilt with streets and a trench, but in times of trouble. [26]After the sixty-two 'sevens,' the Anointed One will be cut off[h] and will have nothing.[f] The people of the ruler who will come will destroy the city and the sanctuary. The end will come like a flood:[i] War will continue until the end, and desolations have been decreed. [27]He will confirm a covenant with many for one 'seven.'[g] In the middle of the 'seven'[g] he will put an end to sacrifice and offering. And on a wing ⌊of the temple⌋ he will set up an abomination that causes desolation, until the end that is decreed[j] is poured out on him.[h]"[i]

Chapter 10 Theme

10 In the third year of Cyrus[k] king of Persia, a revelation was given to Daniel (who was called Belteshazzar).[l] Its message was true[m] and it concerned a great war.[j] The understanding of the message came to him in a vision.

[2]At that time I, Daniel, mourned[n] for three weeks. [3]I ate no choice food; no meat or wine touched my lips; and I used no lotions at all until the three weeks were over.

[4]On the twenty-fourth day of the first month, as I was standing on the bank of the great river, the Tigris,[o] [5]I looked up and there before me was a man dressed in linen,[p] with a belt of the finest gold[q] around his waist. [6]His body was like chrysolite, his face like lightning,[r] his eyes like flaming torches,[s] his arms and legs like the gleam of burnished bronze,[t] and his voice like the sound of a multitude.

[7]I, Daniel, was the only one who saw the vision; the men with me did not see it,[u] but such terror overwhelmed them that they

---

INSIGHT

The word *sevens* in Hebrew is *sāvûōt*. There is no indication whether the "sevens" refer to seven days, weeks, months, or years. Seventy sevens (or weeks) is 490. So, if the six things of Daniel 9:24 were not completed within 490 days, weeks, or months, it would be logical to assume that the *sevens* refers to sevens of years. A decree to rebuild and restore Jerusalem was issued by King Artaxerxes of Medo-Persia in 445 B.C. (see Nehemiah 1:1–2:8). This began the 490 years.

9:21
[a]Ex 29:39

9:23
[b]Da 10:19;
Lk 1:28
[c]Da 10:11-12;
Mt 24:15

9:24
[d]Isa 53:10
[e]Isa 56:1

9:25
[f]Ezr 4:24
[g]Jn 4:25

9:26
[h]Isa 53:8
[i]Na 1:8

9:27
[j]Isa 10:22

10:1
[k]Da 1:21
[l]Da 1:7
[m]Da 8:26

10:2
[n]Ezr 9:4

10:4
[o]Ge 2:14

10:5
[p]Eze 9:2;
Rev 15:6
[q]Jer 10:9

10:6
[r]Mt 17:2
[s]Rev 19:12
[t]Rev 1:15

10:7
[u]2Ki 6:17-20;
Ac 9:7

---

[a]24 Or 'weeks'; also in verses 25 and 26   [b]24 Or restrain   [c]24 Or Most Holy Place; or most holy One   [d]25 Or word   [e]25 Or an anointed one; also in verse 26   [f]26 Or off and will have no one; or off, but not for himself   [g]27 Or 'week'   [h]27 Or it   [i]27 Or And one who causes desolation will come upon the pinnacle of the abominable ⌊temple⌋, until the end that is decreed is poured out on the desolated ⌊city⌋   [j]1 Or true and burdensome

10:8
a Ge 32:24
b Da 8:27
c Hab 3:16

10:9
d Da 8:18

10:10
e Jer 1:9
f Rev 1:17

10:11
g Da 9:23
h Eze 2:1

10:12
i Da 9:3
j Da 9:20

10:13
k ver 21;
Da 12:1;
Jude 9

10:14
l Da 9:22
m Da 2:28; 8:26;
Hab 2:3

10:15
n Eze 24:27;
Lk 1:20

10:16
o Isa 6:7;
Jer 1:9;
Da 8:15-18
p Isa 21:3

10:17
q Da 4:19

10:18
r ver 16

10:19
s Jdg 6:23;
Isa 35:4
t Jos 1:9
u Isa 6:1-8

10:20
v Da 8:21; 11:2

10:21
w Da 11:2
x ver 13;
Jude 9

11:1
y Da 5:31

11:2
z Da 10:21
a Da 10:20

fled and hid themselves. **8**So I was left alone,*a* gazing at this great vision; I had no strength left,*b* my face turned deathly pale and I was helpless.*c* **9**Then I heard him speaking, and as I listened to him, I fell into a deep sleep, my face to the ground.*d*

10A hand touched me*e* and set me trembling on my hands and knees.*f* **11**He said, "Daniel, you who are highly esteemed,*g* consider carefully the words I am about to speak to you, and stand up,*h* for I have now been sent to you." And when he said this to me, I stood up trembling.

12Then he continued, "Do not be afraid, Daniel. Since the first day that you set your mind to gain understanding and to humble*i* yourself before your God, your words were heard, and I have come in response to them.*j* **13**But the prince of the Persian kingdom resisted me twenty-one days. Then Michael,*k* one of the chief princes, came to help me, because I was detained there with the king of Persia. **14**Now I have come to explain*l* to you what will happen to your people in the future, for the vision concerns a time yet to come.*m*"

15While he was saying this to me, I bowed with my face toward the ground and was speechless.*n* **16**Then one who looked like a man*a* touched my lips, and I opened my mouth and began to speak.*o* I said to the one standing before me, "I am overcome with anguish*p* because of the vision, my lord, and I am helpless. **17**How can I, your servant, talk with you, my lord? My strength is gone and I can hardly breathe."*q*

18Again the one who looked like a man touched*r* me and gave me strength. **19**"Do not be afraid, O man highly esteemed," he said. "Peace!*s* Be strong now; be strong."*t*

When he spoke to me, I was strengthened and said, "Speak, my lord, since you have given me strength."*u*

20So he said, "Do you know why I have come to you? Soon I will return to fight against the prince of Persia, and when I go, the prince of Greece*v* will come; **21**but first I will tell you what is written in the Book of Truth.*w* (No one supports me against them except Michael,*x* your prince.

Chapter 11 Theme

11 And in the first year of Darius*y* the Mede, I took my stand to support and protect him.)

2"Now then, I tell you the truth:*z* Three more kings will appear in Persia, and then a fourth, who will be far richer than all the others. When he has gained power by his wealth, he will stir up everyone against the kingdom of Greece.*a* **3**Then a mighty king will appear,

a 16 Most manuscripts of the Masoretic Text; one manuscript of the Masoretic Text, Dead Sea Scrolls and Septuagint *Then something that looked like a man's hand*

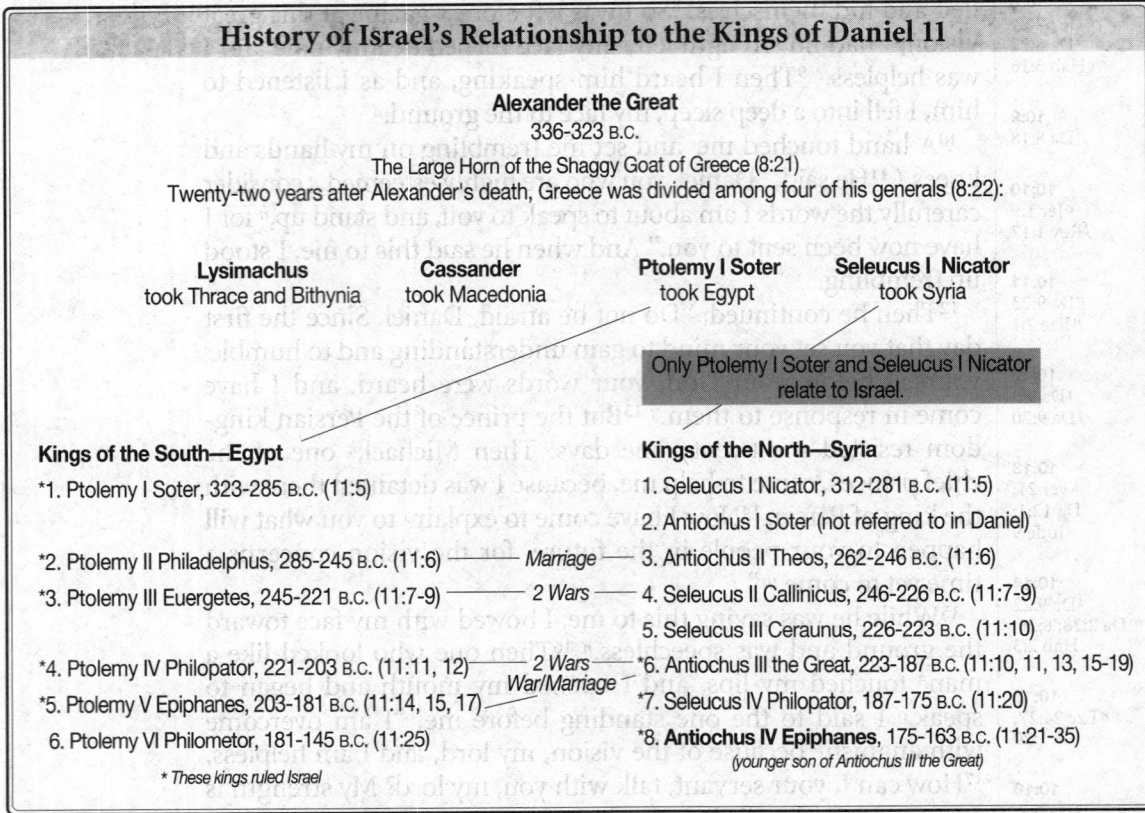

History of Israel's Relationship to the Kings of Daniel 11

Alexander the Great
336-323 B.C.

The Large Horn of the Shaggy Goat of Greece (8:21)
Twenty-two years after Alexander's death, Greece was divided among four of his generals (8:22):

Lysimachus	**Cassander**	**Ptolemy I Soter**	**Seleucus I Nicator**
took Thrace and Bithynia	took Macedonia	took Egypt	took Syria

Only Ptolemy I Soter and Seleucus I Nicator relate to Israel.

Kings of the South—Egypt

*1. Ptolemy I Soter, 323-285 B.C. (11:5)

*2. Ptolemy II Philadelphus, 285-245 B.C. (11:6) — Marriage —

*3. Ptolemy III Euergetes, 245-221 B.C. (11:7-9) — 2 Wars —

*4. Ptolemy IV Philopator, 221-203 B.C. (11:11, 12) — 2 Wars / War/Marriage

*5. Ptolemy V Epiphanes, 203-181 B.C. (11:14, 15, 17)

6. Ptolemy VI Philometor, 181-145 B.C. (11:25)

These kings ruled Israel

Kings of the North—Syria

1. Seleucus I Nicator, 312-281 B.C. (11:5)

2. Antiochus I Soter (not referred to in Daniel)

3. Antiochus II Theos, 262-246 B.C. (11:6)

4. Seleucus II Callinicus, 246-226 B.C. (11:7-9)

5. Seleucus III Ceraunus, 226-223 B.C. (11:10)

*6. Antiochus III the Great, 223-187 B.C. (11:10, 11, 13, 15-19)

*7. Seleucus IV Philopator, 187-175 B.C. (11:20)

*8. **Antiochus IV Epiphanes**, 175-163 B.C. (11:21-35)
(younger son of Antiochus III the Great)

---

who will rule with great power and do as he pleases.[a] ⁴After he has appeared, his empire will be broken up and parceled out toward the four winds of heaven.[b] It will not go to his descendants, nor will it have the power he exercised, because his empire will be uprooted and given to others.

⁵"The king of the South will become strong, but one of his commanders will become even stronger than he and will rule his own kingdom with great power. ⁶After some years, they will become allies. The daughter of the king of the South will go to the king of the North to make an alliance, but she will not retain her power, and he and his power[a] will not last. In those days she will be handed over, together with her royal escort and her father[b] and the one who supported her.

⁷"One from her family line will arise to take her place. He will attack the forces of the king of the North[c] and enter his fortress; he will fight against them and be victorious. ⁸He will also seize their gods,[d] their metal images and their valuable articles of silver and gold and carry them off to Egypt.[e] For some years he will leave the

11:3
[a] Da 8:4,21

11:4
[b] Da 7:2; 8:22

11:7
[c] ver 6

11:8
[d] Isa 37:19; 46:1-2
[e] Jer 43:12

a6 Or *offspring*   b6 Or *child* (see Vulgate and Syriac)

11:10
a Isa 8:8;
Jer 46:8;
Da 9:26

11:11
b Da 8:7-8

11:15
c Eze 4:2

11:16
d Da 8:4
e Jos 1:5;
Da 8:7
f Da 8:9

11:17
g Ps 20:4

11:18
h Isa 66:19;
Jer 25:22
i Hos 12:14

11:19
j Ps 27:2
k Ps 37:36;
Eze 26:21

11:20
l Isa 60:17

11:21
m Da 4:17
n Da 8:25

11:22
o Da 8:10-11

11:23
p Da 8:25

11:24
q Ne 9:25

king of the North alone. ⁹Then the king of the North will invade the realm of the king of the South but will retreat to his own country. ¹⁰His sons will prepare for war and assemble a great army, which will sweep on like an irresistible flood*a* and carry the battle as far as his fortress.

¹¹"Then the king of the South will march out in a rage and fight against the king of the North, who will raise a large army, but it will be defeated.*b* ¹²When the army is carried off, the king of the South will be filled with pride and will slaughter many thousands, yet he will not remain triumphant. ¹³For the king of the North will muster another army, larger than the first; and after several years, he will advance with a huge army fully equipped.

¹⁴"In those times many will rise against the king of the South. The violent men among your own people will rebel in fulfillment of the vision, but without success. ¹⁵Then the king of the North will come and build up siege ramps*c* and will capture a fortified city. The forces of the South will be powerless to resist; even their best troops will not have the strength to stand. ¹⁶The invader will do as he pleases;*d* no one will be able to stand against him.*e* He will establish himself in the Beautiful Land and will have the power to destroy it.*f* ¹⁷He will determine to come with the might of his entire kingdom and will make an alliance with the king of the South. And he will give him a daughter in marriage in order to overthrow the kingdom, but his plans*a* will not succeed*g* or help him. ¹⁸Then he will turn his attention to the coastlands*h* and will take many of them, but a commander will put an end to his insolence and will turn his insolence back upon him.*i* ¹⁹After this, he will turn back toward the fortresses of his own country but will stumble and fall,*j* to be seen no more.*k*

²⁰"His successor will send out a tax collector to maintain the royal splendor.*l* In a few years, however, he will be destroyed, yet not in anger or in battle.

²¹"He will be succeeded by a contemptible*m* person who has not been given the honor of royalty.*n* He will invade the kingdom when its people feel secure, and he will seize it through intrigue. ²²Then an overwhelming army will be swept away before him; both it and a prince of the covenant will be destroyed.*o* ²³After coming to an agreement with him, he will act deceitfully,*p* and with only a few people he will rise to power. ²⁴When the richest provinces feel secure, he will invade them and will achieve what neither his fathers nor his forefathers did. He will distribute plunder, loot and wealth among his followers.*q* He will plot the overthrow of fortresses—but only for a time.

a 17 Or *but she*

25"With a large army he will stir up his strength and courage against the king of the South. The king of the South will wage war with a large and very powerful army, but he will not be able to stand because of the plots devised against him. 26Those who eat from the king's provisions will try to destroy him; his army will be swept away, and many will fall in battle. 27The two kings, with their hearts bent on evil,[a] will sit at the same table and lie[b] to each other, but to no avail, because an end will still come at the appointed time.[c] 28The king of the North will return to his own country with great wealth, but his heart will be set against the holy covenant. He will take action against it and then return to his own country.

29"At the appointed time he will invade the South again, but this time the outcome will be different from what it was before. 30Ships of the western coastlands[a][d] will oppose him, and he will lose heart. Then he will turn back and vent his fury against the holy covenant. He will return and show favor to those who forsake the holy covenant.

31"His armed forces will rise up to desecrate the temple fortress and will abolish the daily sacrifice. Then they will set up the abomination that causes desolation.[e] 32With flattery he will corrupt those who have violated the covenant, but the people who know their God will firmly resist[f] him.

33"Those who are wise will instruct[g] many, though for a time they will fall by the sword or be burned or captured or plundered.[h] 34When they fall, they will receive a little help, and many who are not sincere[i] will join them. 35Some of the wise will stumble, so that they may be refined,[j] purified and made spotless until the time of the end, for it will still come at the appointed time.

36"The king will do as he pleases. He will exalt and magnify himself above every god and will say unheard-of things[k] against the God of gods.[l] He will be successful until the time of wrath[m] is completed, for what has been determined must take place. 37He will show no regard for the gods of his fathers or for the one desired by women, nor will he regard any god, but will exalt himself above them all. 38Instead of them, he will honor a god of fortresses; a god unknown to his fathers he will honor with gold and silver, with precious stones and costly gifts. 39He will attack the mightiest fortresses with the help of a foreign god and will greatly honor those who acknowledge him. He will make them rulers over many people and will distribute the land at a price.[b]

40"At the time of the end the king of the South[n] will engage him in battle, and the king of the North will storm[o] out against him with chariots and cavalry and a great fleet of ships. He will invade many countries and sweep through them like a flood.[p] 41He will

---

a 30 Hebrew of Kittim   b 39 Or land for a reward

11:27
a Ps 64:6
b Ps 12:2;
Jer 9:5
c Hab 2:3

11:30
d Ge 10:4

11:31
e Da 8:11-13;
9:27;
Mt 24:15*;
Mk 13:14*

11:32
f Mic 5:7-9

11:33
g Mal 2:7
h Mt 24:9;
Jn 16:2;
Heb 11:32-38

11:34
i Mt 7:15;
Ro 16:18

11:35
j Ps 78:38;
Da 12:10;
Zec 13:9;
Jn 15:2

11:36
k Rev 13:5-6
l Dt 10:17;
Isa 14:13-14;
Da 7:25;
8:11-12,25;
2Th 2:4
m Isa 10:25;
26:20

11:40
n Isa 21:1
o Isa 5:28
p Eze 38:4

11:41
a Isa 11:14
b Jer 48:47

11:43
c Eze 30:4
d 2Ch 12:3;
Na 3:9

12:1
e Da 10:13
f Da 9:12;
Mt 24:21;
Mk 13:19;
Rev 16:18
g Ex 32:32;
Ps 56:8
h Jer 30:7

12:2
i Isa 26:19;
Mt 25:46;
Jn 5:28-29

12:3
j Da 11:33
k Mt 13:43;
Jn 5:35
l 1Co 15:42

12:4
m Isa 8:16
n ver 9,13;
Rev 22:10

12:5
o Da 10:4

12:6
p Eze 9:2
q Da 8:13

12:7
r Rev 10:5-6
s Da 7:25
t Da 8:24
u Lk 21:24;
Rev 10:7

12:9
v ver 4

12:10
w Da 11:35
x Isa 32:7;
Rev 22:11
y Hos 14:9

12:11
z Da 8:11; 9:27;
Mt 24:15*;
Mk 13:14*

also invade the Beautiful Land. Many countries will fall, but Edom,*a* Moab*b* and the leaders of Ammon will be delivered from his hand. 42He will extend his power over many countries; Egypt will not escape. 43He will gain control of the treasures of gold and silver and all the riches of Egypt,*c* with the Libyans*d* and Nubians in submission. 44But reports from the east and the north will alarm him, and he will set out in a great rage to destroy and annihilate many. 45He will pitch his royal tents between the seas at*a* the beautiful holy mountain. Yet he will come to his end, and no one will help him.

Chapter 12 Theme

12 "At that time Michael,*e* the great prince who protects your people, will arise. There will be a time of distress*f* such as has not happened from the beginning of nations until then. But at that time your people—everyone whose name is found written in the book*g*—will be delivered.*h* 2Multitudes who sleep in the dust of the earth will awake: some to everlasting life, others to shame and everlasting contempt.*i* 3Those who are wise*b**j* will shine*k* like the brightness of the heavens, and those who lead many to righteousness, like the stars for ever and ever.*l* 4But you, Daniel, close up and seal*m* the words of the scroll until the time of the end.*n* Many will go here and there to increase knowledge."

5Then I, Daniel, looked, and there before me stood two others, one on this bank of the river and one on the opposite bank.*o* 6One of them said to the man clothed in linen,*p* who was above the waters of the river, "How long will it be before these astonishing things are fulfilled?"*q*

7The man clothed in linen, who was above the waters of the river, lifted his right hand and his left hand toward heaven, and I heard him swear by him who lives forever,*r* saying, "It will be for a time, times and half a time.*c**s* When the power of the holy people*t* has been finally broken, all these things will be completed.*u*"

8I heard, but I did not understand. So I asked, "My lord, what will the outcome of all this be?"

9He replied, "Go your way, Daniel, because the words are closed up and sealed until the time of the end.*v* 10Many will be purified, made spotless and refined,*w* but the wicked will continue to be wicked.*x* None of the wicked will understand, but those who are wise will understand.*y*

11"From the time that the daily sacrifice is abolished and the abomination that causes desolation*z* is set up, there will be 1,290

*a*45 Or *the sea and*   *b*3 Or *who impart wisdom*   *c*7 Or *a year, two years and half a year* days. ¹²Blessed is the one who waits^a for and reaches the end of the 1,335 days.^b

¹³"As for you, go your way till the end. You will rest,^c and then at the end of the days you will rise to receive your allotted inheritance.^d"

12:12
^a Isa 30:18
^b Da 8:14

12:13
^c Isa 57:2
^d Ps 16:5;
Rev 14:13

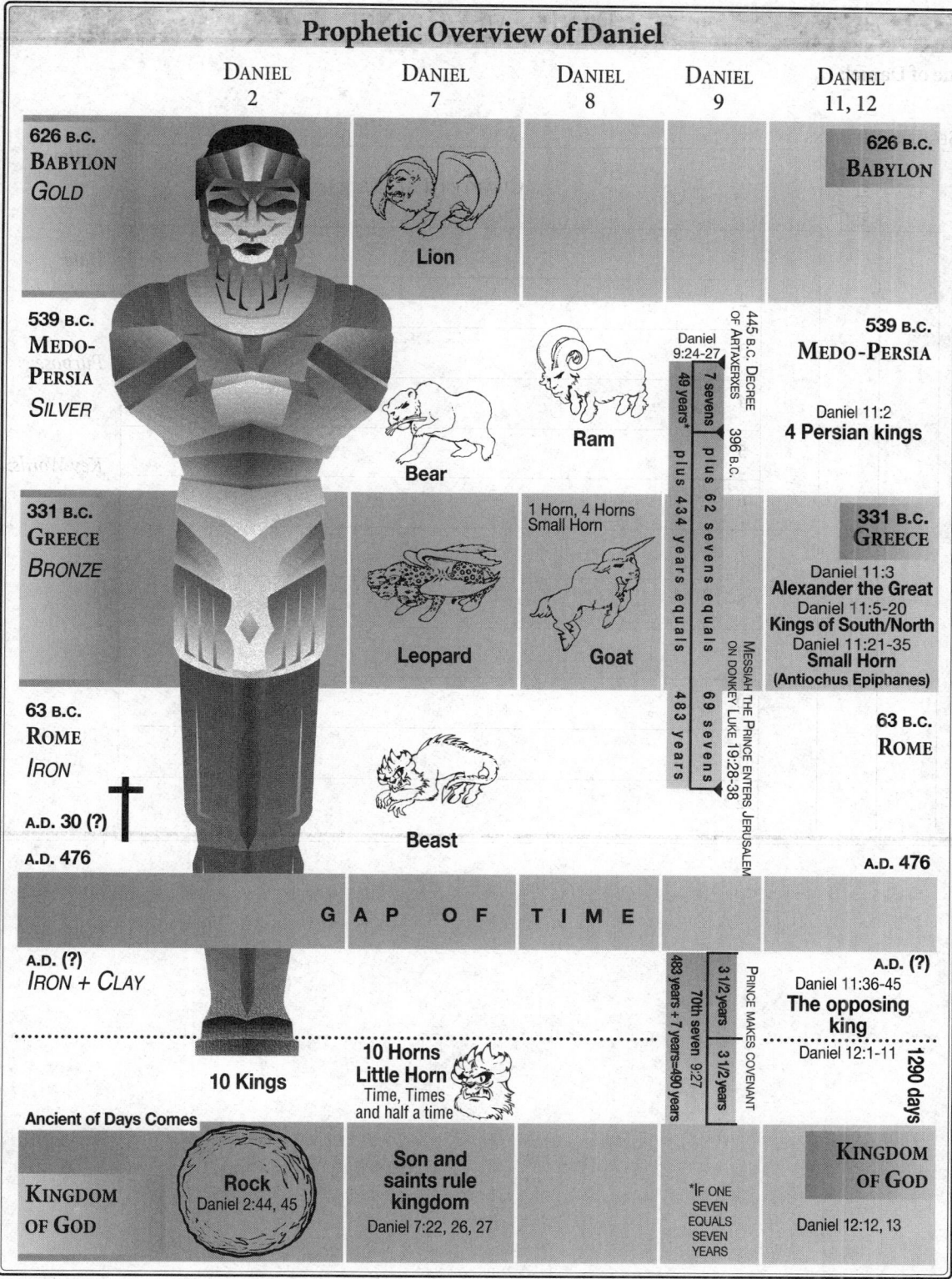

Prophetic Overview of Daniel

DANIEL 2	DANIEL 7	DANIEL 8	DANIEL 9	DANIEL 11, 12

626 B.C. BABYLON *GOLD*

Lion

626 B.C. BABYLON

539 B.C. MEDO-PERSIA *SILVER*

Bear

Ram

Daniel 9:24-27

539 B.C. MEDO-PERSIA

Daniel 11:2
4 Persian kings

331 B.C. GREECE *BRONZE*

Leopard

1 Horn, 4 Horns
Small Horn

Goat

445 B.C. DECREE OF ARTAXERXES

49 years* — 7 sevens — plus 62 sevens equals — plus 434 years equals — 69 sevens — 483 years

396 B.C.

MESSIAH THE PRINCE ENTERS JERUSALEM ON DONKEY LUKE 19:28-38

331 B.C. GREECE
Daniel 11:3
Alexander the Great
Daniel 11:5-20
Kings of South/North
Daniel 11:21-35
Small Horn
(Antiochus Epiphanes)

63 B.C. ROME *IRON*

Beast

63 B.C. ROME

A.D. 30 (?)

A.D. 476

A.D. 476

G A P   O F   T I M E

A.D. (?) *IRON + CLAY*

483 years + 7 years=490 years

70th seven 9:27

3 1/2 years

3 1/2 years

PRINCE MAKES COVENANT

A.D. (?)
Daniel 11:36-45
The opposing king

Daniel 12:1-11

1290 days

10 Kings

**10 Horns
Little Horn**
Time, Times
and half a time

Ancient of Days Comes

KINGDOM OF GOD

Rock
Daniel 2:44, 45

Son and saints rule kingdom
Daniel 7:22, 26, 27

*IF ONE
SEVEN
EQUALS
SEVEN
YEARS

KINGDOM OF GOD

Daniel 12:12, 13

Theme of Daniel:

SEGMENT DIVISIONS

		KINGS/ KINGDOM	CHAPTER THEMES
			1
			2
			3
			4
			5
			6
			7
			8
			9
			10
			11
			12

Author:

Date:

Purpose:

Key Words:

HOSEA

God had entered into a covenant with Israel. Yet from the time of Jeroboam's reign of the northern kingdom through Jeroboam II's reign, Israel continued to play the prostitute. God begged her to return to him, but she would not listen. God's heart hurt. If only Israel could understand, if only she could see what she was doing to the one who had betrothed her to himself. If only she could see what her infidelity was doing to her children! Then the word of the Lord came to Hosea: "Go, take to yourself an adulterous wife and children of unfaithfulness."

∾ THINGS TO DO

Chapters 1-3

1. The first three chapters of Hosea provide the setting for Hosea's prophetic message to the northern kingdom of Israel. Read these three chapters as you would a story, but remember that it is a true story.

2. Read through Hosea 1 again. As you read:

   a. Mark every occurrence of the word *adulterous (adultery, unfaithfulness)*.

   b. In the margin, draw a simple family tree which shows whom Hosea married and the names of their children. Under each family member write a brief description of what the person was like or what his or her name meant. Consult the reference notes in the margin if you have problems discerning the meanings of the children's names.

   c. In the margin, list what this chapter teaches about the sons of Israel and the sons of Judah.

3. Now go back and read the introduction which precedes "Things to Do." Then:

   a. Read 1 Kings 11:26-40, where God tells Jeroboam what he will do after King Solomon's death. Notice why God does what he does.

   b. Read 1 Kings 12, which tells of the fulfillment of God's word to Jeroboam. This chapter describes how the kingdom of Israel was divided into the northern kingdom, consisting of ten tribes, and the southern kingdom, consisting of two tribes. Pay attention to what Jeroboam does, since the northern kingdom no longer has access to Jerusalem and the temple, where they were to worship God.

   c. Read Hosea 1:2 again, and then Hosea 3:1. Watch the word *as* in 3:1.

   d. In the margin of chapter 1 write why Hosea was told by God to marry Gomer. This will help you see why chapters 1 through 3 provide the setting for Hosea's message to the northern kingdom of Israel.

4. Keeping in mind what you have seen thus far, read Hosea 2 and do the following:

   a. Mark every occurrence of the words *adulterous* and *adultery* and the phrase *in that day*.

   b. Carefully observe what the children are to say to their mother and why.

   c. Read chapters 1 and 2 and underline every occurrence of *the Lord said* or *declares the Lord*. Then highlight or mark in a distinctive way every occurrence of *I will*. Then decide who is speaking throughout chapter 2 and who the *her* and *she* refer to.

   d. Finally, read each *I will* in chapter 2. Watch the sequence of events and summarize the type of action taken in these "I wills." Also watch what happens to *her*. Record your insights in the margin of chapter 2.

   e. When you come to 2:23 read the reference notes on this verse and compare this with 1:6, 9; 2:1.

5. In the light of all you have seen in chapters 1 and 2, read chapter 3 and do the following:

    a. In a distinctive way mark the word *love*.

    b. In the margin, summarize what God tells Hosea to do and why.

    c. Read 3:5 and mark the reference to *in the last days,* but before you choose how to mark it, see if you notice any parallel to *in that day* in chapter 2. If you think any of these references pertain to the day of the Lord, record your insights on the chart THE DAY OF THE LORD beginning on page 2178.

6. Write the themes of each of the first three chapters on the HOSEA AT A GLANCE chart on page 1553. Then record the chapter theme next to the chapter number in the text.

Chapters 4-14

1. Keeping in mind the setting of Hosea 1 through 3, read through Hosea chapter by chapter. As you do:

    a. Mark in a distinctive way the following key words (with their synonyms or pronouns): *prostitution (commit adultery, been unfaithful), knowledge (acknowledgment), covenant (treaty), return (go back, repent), iniquity (sin, sins, guilt, wicked, wickedness, evildoers).* Also mark the phrases *I will, from me,* and *against me (unfaithful to me* [the Lord]). Write these words on an index card and use it as a bookmark.

    b. Also mark *Judah (Judah's), Israel (Israel's, Israelites),* and *Ephraim (Ephraim's)* each in its own distinctive way. As you do, remember that Ephraim was one of the ten tribes which comprised the northern kingdom of Israel. After Pekah took the throne in Israel, Tiglath-Pileser, king of Assyria, came against him and took all of the kingdom captive in 733 B.C. except Ephraim and western Manasseh. Ten years later the remainder of the northern kingdom was completely destroyed by the Assyrians in 722 B.C. Thus Ephraim refers to what remained of Israel in those last ten years.

2. After you read a chapter and mark key words and the references to Judah, Israel, and Ephraim, compile your insights on the chart GOD'S RESPONSE TO ISRAEL'S SIN on page 1552.

3. As you read through the remainder of Hosea, remember that this is a passionate discourse because of God's relationship to Israel, the relationship of a husband to his wife (Ezekiel 16; Jeremiah 3:6-8), and of a father to his children (Hosea 11:1-3; Jeremiah 31:20). Remember also that because it is passionate, there is quite a bit of repetition, but not without purpose.

4. As you finish reading each chapter, summarize the theme of each one and record it on HOSEA AT A GLANCE and in the text. Also, when you finish the book, decide on its theme and record it on the chart. Then fill in the remainder of the chart.

ଵ THINGS TO THINK ABOUT

In 2 Corinthians 11:2 Paul wrote, "I am jealous for you with a godly jealousy. I promised you to one husband, to Christ, so that I might present you as a pure virgin to him."

1. Are there any similarities between your relationship to Jesus Christ and Israel's relationship to God? How are you pleasing your heavenly Bridegroom? Are you breaking God's heart in any way?

2. What do you need to do?

3. How do you think God will respond, and why?

ᔦᔦᔦᔦᔦ

Chapter 1 Theme _____

1 The word of the LORD that came to Hosea son of Beeri during the reigns of Uzziah, Jotham, Ahaz and Hezekiah, kings of Judah,[a] and during the reign of Jeroboam[b] son of Jehoash[a] king of Israel:[c]

a 1 Hebrew *Joash,* a variant of *Jehoash*

1:1
a Isa 1:1; Mic 1:1
b 2Ki 13:13
c Am 1:1

THE RULERS AND PROPHETS OF HOSEA'S TIME

Kings of Assyria
- Ashur-nirari (755–745)
- Tiglath-Pileser III (Tilgath-Pilneser III) (745–727)
- Shalmaneser V ↓727–722
- Sargon II (722–705)
- Sennacherib (705–681)

Kings of Israel (Northern Kingdom)
- Jeroboam II (793–753)
- Zechariah
- Shallum one month
- Menahem (752–742)
- Pekahiah 742–740
- Pekah (752–732)
- Hoshea (732–722)
- Northern ten tribes taken captive by King Shalmaneser V of Assyria in 722 B.C.

Hosea and His Contemporary Prophets (Northern Kingdom)
- Jonah (784–772)
- Amos (767–755)
- Hosea (755–714)

Kings of Judah (Southern Kingdom)
- Uzziah or Azariah (790–739)
- Jotham ↓ (750–731 / 735)
- Ahaz (735–728 / 715)
- Hezekiah (715–686)

Prophets to Judah (Southern Kingdom)
- Isaiah (739–681)
- Micah (733–701)

Timeline scale: 840 830 820 810 800 790 780 770 760 750 740 730 720 710 700 690 680

---

²When the LORD began to speak through Hosea, the LORD said to him, "Go, take to yourself an adulterous*ᵃ* wife and children of unfaithfulness, because the land is guilty of the vilest adultery*ᵇ* in departing from the LORD." ³So he married Gomer daughter of Diblaim, and she conceived and bore him a son.

⁴Then the LORD said to Hosea, "Call him Jezreel,*ᶜ* because I will soon punish the house of Jehu for the massacre at Jezreel, and I will put an end to the kingdom of Israel. ⁵In that day I will break Israel's bow in the Valley of Jezreel.*ᵈ*"

⁶Gomer*ᵉ* conceived again and gave birth to a daughter. Then the LORD said to Hosea, "Call her Lo-Ruhamah,*ᵃ* for I will no longer show love to the house of Israel,*ᶠ* that I should at all forgive them. ⁷Yet I will show love to the house of Judah; and I will save them— not by bow,*ᵍ* sword or battle, or by horses and horsemen, but by the LORD their God.*ʰ*"

⁸After she had weaned Lo-Ruhamah, Gomer had another son. ⁹Then the LORD said, "Call him Lo-Ammi,*ᵇ* for you are not my people, and I am not your God.

1:2
a Jer 3:1;
Hos 2:2,5;
3:1
b Dt 31:16;
Jer 3:14;
Eze 23:3-21;
Hos 5:3

1:4
c 2Ki 10:1-14;
Hos 2:22

1:5
d 2Ki 15:29

1:6
e ver 3
f Hos 2:4

1:7
g Ps 44:6
h Zec 4:6

ᵃ6 *Lo-Ruhamah* means *not loved.* ᵇ9 *Lo-Ammi* means *not my people.*

INSIGHT

Only one Israelite king, Jeroboam (often referred to as Jeroboam II), is mentioned in Hosea 1:1. Because Hosea mentions the names of the kings of Judah, we can know the other kings who ruled Israel during Hosea's ministry.

¹⁰"Yet the Israelites will be like the sand on the seashore, which cannot be measured or counted.ᵃ In the place where it was said to them, 'You are not my people,' they will be called 'sons of the living God.'ᵇ ¹¹The people of Judah and the people of Israel will be reunited,ᶜ and they will appoint one leaderᵈ and will come up out of the land,ᵉ for great will be the day of Jezreel.

Chapter 2 Theme _____

2 "Say of your brothers, 'My people,' and of your sisters, 'My loved one.'ᶠ

²"Rebuke your mother,ᵍ rebuke her,
    for she is not my wife,
    and I am not her husband.
Let her remove the adulterousʰ look from her face
    and the unfaithfulness from between her breasts.
³Otherwise I will strip her naked
    and make her as bare as on the day she was born;ⁱ
I will make her like a desert,ʲ
    turn her into a parched land,
    and slay her with thirst.
⁴I will not show my love to her children,ᵏ
    because they are the children of adultery.
⁵Their mother has been unfaithful
    and has conceived them in disgrace.
She said, 'I will go after my lovers,ˡ
    who give me my food and my water,
    my wool and my linen, my oil and my drink.'ᵐ
⁶Therefore I will block her path with thornbushes;
    I will wall her in so that she cannot find her way.ⁿ
⁷She will chase after her lovers but not catch them;
    she will look for them but not find them.ᵒ
Then she will say,
    'I will go back to my husband as at first,ᵖ
    for then I was better offᵠ than now.'
⁸She has not acknowledgedʳ that I was the one
    who gave her the grain, the new wine and oil,
who lavished on her the silver and gold—
    which they used for Baal.ˢ

⁹"Therefore I will take away my grainᵗ when it ripens,
    and my new wineᵘ when it is ready.
I will take back my wool and my linen,
    intended to cover her nakedness.
¹⁰So now I will expose her lewdness
    before the eyes of her lovers;
    no one will take her out of my hands.ᵛ

INSIGHT

Baal, which meant "lord, owner, possessor," or "husband," was the Canaanite god of fertility. **Baal** was part of several compound names for locations where Canaanite deities were worshiped, such as Baal Peor.

1:10
ᵃ Ge 22:17;
Jer 33:22
ᵇ ver 9;
Ro 9:26*

1:11
ᶜ Isa 11:12,13
ᵈ Jer 23:5-8
ᵉ Eze 37:15-28

2:1
ᶠ ver 23

2:2
ᵍ ver 5;
Isa 50:1;
Hos 1:2
ʰ Eze 23:45

2:3
ⁱ Eze 16:4,22
ʲ Isa 32:13-14

2:4
ᵏ Eze 8:18

2:5
ˡ Jer 3:6
ᵐ Jer 44:17-18

2:6
ⁿ Job 3:23; 19:8;
La 3:9

2:7
ᵒ Hos 5:13
ᵖ Jer 2:2; 3:1
ᵠ Eze 16:8

2:8
ʳ Isa 1:3
ˢ Eze 16:15-19;
Hos 8:4

2:9
ᵗ Hos 8:7
ᵘ Hos 9:2

2:10
ᵛ Eze 16:37

2:11
a Jer 7:34
b Isa 1:14;
Jer 16:9;
Hos 3:4;
Am 8:10

¹¹I will stop^a all her celebrations:
   her yearly festivals, her New Moons,
   her Sabbath days—all her appointed feasts.^b
¹²I will ruin her vines^c and her fig trees,
   which she said were her pay from her lovers;
  I will make them a thicket,^d
   and wild animals will devour them.^e

2:12
c Isa 7:23;
Jer 8:13
d Isa 5:6
e Hos 13:8

¹³I will punish her for the days
   she burned incense to the Baals;^f
  she decked herself with rings and jewelry,^g
   and went after her lovers,^h
   but me she forgot,ⁱ"

                 declares the LORD.

2:13
f Hos 11:2
g Eze 16:17
h Hos 4:13
i Hos 4:6;
8:14; 13:6

¹⁴"Therefore I am now going to allure her;
   I will lead her into the desert
   and speak tenderly to her.

¹⁵There I will give her back her vineyards,
   and will make the Valley of Achor^{a j} a door of hope.
  There she will sing^{b k} as in the days of her youth,^l
   as in the day she came up out of Egypt.^m

2:15
j Jos 7:24,26
k Ex 15:1-18
l Jer 2:2
m Hos 12:9

¹⁶"In that day," declares the LORD,
   "you will call me 'my husband';
   you will no longer call me 'my master.^c'
¹⁷I will remove the names of the Baals from her lips;ⁿ
   no longer will their names be invoked.^o

2:17
n Ex 23:13;
Ps 16:4
o Jos 23:7

¹⁸In that day I will make a covenant for them
   with the beasts of the field and the birds of the air
   and the creatures that move along the ground.^p
  Bow and sword and battle
   I will abolish^q from the land,
   so that all may lie down in safety.^r

2:18
p Job 5:22
q Isa 2:4
r Jer 23:6;
Eze 34:25

¹⁹I will betroth^s you to me forever;
   I will betroth you in^d righteousness and justice,^t
   in^e love and compassion.
²⁰I will betroth you in faithfulness,
   and you will acknowledge^u the LORD.

2:19
s Isa 62:4
t Isa 1:27

²¹"In that day I will respond,"
   declares the LORD—
  "I will respond^v to the skies,
   and they will respond to the earth;
²²and the earth will respond to the grain,
   the new wine and oil,^w

2:20
u Jer 31:34;
Hos 6:6; 13:4

2:21
v Isa 55:10;
Zec 8:12

2:22
w Jer 31:12;
Joel 2:19

^a 15 *Achor* means *trouble.*   ^b 15 Or *respond*   ^c 16 Hebrew *baal*   ^d 19 Or *with;* also in verse 20
^e 19 Or *with*

and they will respond to Jezreel.*a*

²³I will plant*a* her for myself in the land;
 I will show my love to the one I called 'Not
 my loved one.*b* *b*'
 I will say to those called 'Not my people,*c*' 'You are
 my people';*c*
 and they will say, 'You are my God.*d*'"

Chapter 3 Theme _____

3 The LORD said to me, "Go, show your love to your wife again,
 though she is loved by another and is an adulteress.*e* Love her
as the LORD loves the Israelites, though they turn to other gods
and love the sacred raisin cakes.*f*"

²So I bought her for fifteen shekels*d* of silver and about a homer
and a letheke*e* of barley. ³Then I told her, "You are to live with*f* me
many days; you must not be a prostitute or be intimate with any
man, and I will live with*f* you."

⁴For the Israelites will live many days without king or prince,*g*
without sacrifice*h* or sacred stones, without ephod or idol.*i* ⁵After-
ward the Israelites will return and seek the LORD their God and
David their king.*j* They will come trembling to the LORD and to
his blessings in the last days.*k*

Chapter 4 Theme _____

4 Hear the word of the LORD, you Israelites,
 because the LORD has a charge to bring
 against you who live in the land:
"There is no faithfulness, no love,
 no acknowledgment*l* of God in the land.
²There is only cursing,*g* lying*m* and murder,*n*
 stealing*o* and adultery;
they break all bounds,
 and bloodshed follows bloodshed.
³Because of this the land mourns,*h* *p*
 and all who live in it waste away;*q*
the beasts of the field and the birds of the air
 and the fish of the sea are dying.*r*

⁴"But let no man bring a charge,
 let no man accuse another,
for your people are like those
 who bring charges against a priest.*s*

---

a*22 Jezreel* means *God plants.*   b*23* Hebrew *Lo-Ruhamah*   c*23* Hebrew *Lo-Ammi*
d*2* That is, about 6 ounces (about 170 grams)   e*2* That is, probably about 10 bushels (about
330 liters)   f*3* Or *wait for*   g*2* That is, to pronounce a curse upon   h*3* Or *dries up*

2:23
a Jer 31:27
b Hos 1:6
c Hos 1:10
d Ro 9:25*;
1Pe 2:10

3:1
e Hos 1:2
f 2Sa 6:19

3:4
g Hos 13:11
h Da 11:31;
Hos 2:11
i Jdg 17:5-6;
Zec 10:2

3:5
j Eze 34:23-24
k Jer 50:4-5

4:1
l Jer 7:28

4:2
m Hos 7:3; 10:4
n Hos 6:9
o Hos 7:1

4:3
p Jer 4:28
q Isa 33:9
r Jer 4:25;
Zep 1:3

4:4
s Dt 17:12;
Eze 3:26

4:5
a Eze 14:7
b Hos 2:2

[5] You stumble[a] day and night,
  and the prophets stumble with you.
So I will destroy your mother[b]—
[6] my people are destroyed from lack of knowledge.[c]

4:6
c Hos 2:13;
Mal 2:7-8
d Hos 8:1,12

"Because you have rejected knowledge,
  I also reject you as my priests;
because you have ignored the law[d] of your God,
  I also will ignore your children.
[7] The more the priests increased,
  the more they sinned against me;

4:7
e Hab 2:16
f Hos 10:1,6;
13:6

  they exchanged[a] their[b] Glory[e] for something
    disgraceful.[f]
[8] They feed on the sins of my people
  and relish their wickedness.[g]
[9] And it will be: Like people, like priests.[h]

4:8
g Isa 56:11;
Mic 3:11

  I will punish both of them for their ways
  and repay them for their deeds.[i]

[10] "They will eat but not have enough;[j]
  they will engage in prostitution but not increase,
because they have deserted[k] the LORD

4:9
h Isa 24:2
i Jer 5:31;
Hos 8:13; 9:9,15

  to give themselves [11]to prostitution,[l]
to old wine and new,
  which take away the understanding[m] [12]of my people.
They consult a wooden idol[n]
  and are answered by a stick of wood.[o]

4:10
j Lev 26:26;
Mic 6:14
k Hos 7:14; 9:17

A spirit of prostitution leads them astray;[p]
  they are unfaithful to their God.
[13] They sacrifice on the mountaintops
  and burn offerings on the hills,
under oak,[q] poplar and terebinth,
  where the shade is pleasant.[r]

4:11
l Hos 5:4
m Pr 20:1

Therefore your daughters turn to prostitution[s]
  and your daughters-in-law to adultery.[t]

[14] "I will not punish your daughters
  when they turn to prostitution,
nor your daughters-in-law
  when they commit adultery,

4:12
n Jer 2:27
o Hab 2:19
p Isa 44:20

because the men themselves consort with harlots[u]
  and sacrifice with shrine prostitutes—
  a people without understanding will come to ruin!

4:13
q Isa 1:29
r Jer 3:6;
Hos 11:2
s Jer 2:20;
Am 7:17
t Hos 2:13

[15] "Though you commit adultery, O Israel,
  let not Judah become guilty.

4:14
u ver 11

a 7 Syriac and an ancient Hebrew scribal tradition; Masoretic Text *I will exchange*
b 7 Masoretic Text; an ancient Hebrew scribal tradition *my*

INSIGHT

After Pekah took the throne in Israel, Tiglath-Pileser, king of Assyria, came against him in 733 B.C. and took captive all of the kingdom except Ephraim and western Manasseh. Ten years later the remainder of the northern kingdom was completely destroyed by the Assyrians in 722 B.C. Thus Ephraim is a reference to what remained of Israel in those last ten years.

"Do not go to Gilgal;[a]
   do not go up to Beth Aven.[a]
   And do not swear, 'As surely as the LORD lives!'
[16]The Israelites are stubborn,
   like a stubborn heifer.
How then can the LORD pasture them
   like lambs[b] in a meadow?
[17]Ephraim is joined to idols;
   leave him alone!
[18]Even when their drinks are gone,
   they continue their prostitution;
   their rulers dearly love shameful ways.
[19]A whirlwind[c] will sweep them away,
   and their sacrifices will bring them shame.[d]

Chapter 5 Theme

5 "Hear this, you priests!
   Pay attention, you Israelites!
Listen, O royal house!
   This judgment is against you:
You have been a snare[e] at Mizpah,
   a net spread out on Tabor.
[2]The rebels are deep in slaughter.[f]
   I will discipline all of them.[g]
[3]I know all about Ephraim;
   Israel is not hidden from me.
Ephraim, you have now turned to prostitution;
   Israel is corrupt.[h]

[4]"Their deeds do not permit them
   to return to their God.
A spirit of prostitution[i] is in their heart;
   they do not acknowledge[j] the LORD.
[5]Israel's arrogance testifies[k] against them;
   the Israelites, even Ephraim, stumble in their sin;
   Judah also stumbles with them.
[6]When they go with their flocks and herds
   to seek the LORD,[l]
they will not find him;
   he has withdrawn[m] himself from them.
[7]They are unfaithful[n] to the LORD;
   they give birth to illegitimate[o] children.
Now their New Moon festivals
   will devour[p] them and their fields.

a 15 *Beth Aven* means *house of wickedness* (a name for Bethel, which means *house of God*).

4:15
a Hos 9:15;
12:11;
Am 4:4

4:16
b Isa 5:17; 7:25

4:19
c Hos 12:1;
13:15
d Isa 1:29

5:1
e Hos 6:9; 9:8

5:2
f Hos 4:2
g Hos 9:15

5:3
h Hos 6:10

5:4
i Hos 4:11
j Hos 4:6

5:5
k Hos 7:10

5:6
l Mic 6:6-7
m Pr 1:28;
Isa 1:15; Eze 8:6

5:7
n Hos 6:7
o Hos 2:4
p Hos 2:11-12

5:8
a Hos 9:9; 10:9
b Isa 10:29
c Hos 4:15

8 "Sound the trumpet in Gibeah,*a*
    the horn in Ramah.*b*
Raise the battle cry in Beth Aven*ᵃ;c*
    lead on, O Benjamin.

5:9
d Isa 37:3;
Hos 9:11-17
e Isa 46:10;
Zec 1:6

9 Ephraim will be laid waste
    on the day of reckoning.*d*
Among the tribes of Israel
    I proclaim what is certain.*e*
10 Judah's leaders are like those
    who move boundary stones.*f*

5:10
f Dt 19:14
g Eze 7:8

I will pour out my wrath*g* on them
    like a flood of water.
11 Ephraim is oppressed,
    trampled in judgment,
    intent on pursuing idols.*ᵇh*

5:11
h Hos 9:16;
Mic 6:16

12 I am like a moth*i* to Ephraim,
    like rot to the people of Judah.

13 "When Ephraim saw his sickness,
    and Judah his sores,

5:12
i Isa 51:8

then Ephraim turned to Assyria,*j*
    and sent to the great king for help.*k*
But he is not able to cure*l* you,
    not able to heal your sores.*m*

5:13
j Hos 7:11; 8:9
k Hos 10:6
l Hos 14:3
m Jer 30:12

14 For I will be like a lion*n* to Ephraim,
    like a great lion to Judah.
I will tear them to pieces and go away;
    I will carry them off, with no one to rescue them.*o*
15 Then I will go back to my place
    until they admit their guilt.

5:14
n Am 3:4
o Mic 5:8

And they will seek my face;*p*
    in their misery*q* they will earnestly seek me.*r*"

Chapter 6 Theme

5:15
p Hos 3:5
q Jer 2:27
r Isa 64:9

6 "Come, let us return to the LORD.
    He has torn us to pieces*s*
        but he will heal us;
    he has injured us
        but he will bind up our wounds.*t*

6:1
s Hos 5:14
t Dt 32:39;
Jer 30:17;
Hos 14:4

2 After two days he will revive us;*u*
    on the third day he will restore us,
    that we may live in his presence.
3 Let us acknowledge the LORD;
    let us press on to acknowledge him.

6:2
u Ps 30:5

ᵃ 8 Beth Aven means *house of wickedness* (a name for Bethel, which means *house of God*). *ᵇ 11* The meaning of the Hebrew for this word is uncertain.

As surely as the sun rises,
 he will appear;
he will come to us like the winter rains,*a*
 like the spring rains that water the earth.*b*"

⁴"What can I do with you, Ephraim?*c*
 What can I do with you, Judah?
Your love is like the morning mist,
 like the early dew that disappears.*d*
⁵Therefore I cut you in pieces with my prophets,
 I killed you with the words of my mouth;*e*
 my judgments flashed like lightning upon you.*f*
⁶For I desire mercy, not sacrifice,*g*
 and acknowledgment*h* of God rather
  than burnt offerings.
⁷Like Adam,*a* they have broken the covenant*i*—
 they were unfaithful*j* to me there.
⁸Gilead is a city of wicked men,
 stained with footprints of blood.
⁹As marauders lie in ambush for a man,
 so do bands of priests;
they murder on the road to Shechem,
 committing shameful crimes.*k*
¹⁰I have seen a horrible*l* thing
 in the house of Israel.
 There Ephraim is given to prostitution
 and Israel is defiled.*m*

¹¹"Also for you, Judah,
 a harvest*n* is appointed.

Chapter 7 Theme

7

"Whenever I would restore the fortunes of my people,
 whenever I would heal Israel,
the sins of Ephraim are exposed
 and the crimes of Samaria revealed.*o*
They practice deceit,*p*
 thieves break into houses,*q*
 bandits rob in the streets;
²but they do not realize
 that I remember*r* all their evil deeds.
Their sins engulf them;*s*
 they are always before me.

---

a 7 Or *As at Adam;* or *Like men*

Cross references (right column):

6:3
a Joel 2:23
b Ps 72:6

6:4
c Hos 11:8
d Hos 7:1; 13:3

6:5
e Jer 1:9-10;
23:29
f Heb 4:12

6:6
g Isa 1:11;
Mt 9:13*; 12:7*
h Hos 2:20

6:7
i Hos 8:1
j Hos 5:7

6:9
k Jer 7:9-10;
Eze 22:9;
Hos 7:1

6:10
l Jer 5:30
m Hos 5:3

6:11
n Jer 51:33;
Joel 3:13

7:1
o Hos 6:4
p ver 13
q Hos 4:2

7:2
r Jer 14:10;
Hos 8:13
s Jer 2:19

7:3
a Hos 4:2;
Mic 7:3

³"They delight the king with their wickedness,
    the princes with their lies.*ᵃ*
⁴They are all adulterers,*ᵇ*
    burning like an oven
  whose fire the baker need not stir
    from the kneading of the dough till it rises.

7:4
b Jer 9:2

⁵On the day of the festival of our king
    the princes become inflamed with wine,*ᶜ*
    and he joins hands with the mockers.
⁶Their hearts are like an oven;*ᵈ*
    they approach him with intrigue.
  Their passion smolders all night;
    in the morning it blazes like a flaming fire.

7:5
c Isa 28:1,7

7:6
d Ps 21:9

⁷All of them are hot as an oven;
    they devour their rulers.
  All their kings fall,
    and none of them calls*ᵉ* on me.

7:7
e ver 16

⁸"Ephraim mixes*ᶠ* with the nations;
    Ephraim is a flat cake not turned over.
⁹Foreigners sap his strength,*ᵍ*
    but he does not realize it.
  His hair is sprinkled with gray,
    but he does not notice.

7:8
f ver 11;
Ps 106:35;
Hos 5:13

¹⁰Israel's arrogance testifies against him,*ʰ*
    but despite all this
  he does not return to the LORD his God
    or search*ⁱ* for him.

7:9
g Isa 1:7;
Hos 8:7

7:10
h Hos 5:5
i Isa 9:13

¹¹"Ephraim is like a dove,*ʲ*
    easily deceived and senseless—
  now calling to Egypt,
    now turning to Assyria.*ᵏ*
¹²When they go, I will throw my net*ˡ*
        over them;
    I will pull them down like birds of the air.
  When I hear them flocking together,
    I will catch them.

7:11
j Hos 11:11
k Hos 5:13; 12:1

7:12
l Eze 12:13

¹³Woe*ᵐ* to them,
    because they have strayed*ⁿ* from me!
  Destruction to them,
    because they have rebelled against me!
  I long to redeem them
    but they speak lies against me.*ᵒ*
¹⁴They do not cry out to me from their hearts*ᵖ*
    but wail upon their beds.

7:13
m Hos 9:12
n Jer 14:10;
Eze 34:4-6;
Hos 9:17
o ver 1;
Mt 23:37

7:14
p Jer 3:10

They gather together[a] for grain and new wine[a]
   but turn away from me.[b]
[15]I trained them and strengthened them,
   but they plot evil[c] against me.
[16]They do not turn to the Most High;
   they are like a faulty bow.[d]
Their leaders will fall by the sword
   because of their insolent words.
For this they will be ridiculed[e]
   in the land of Egypt.[f]

Chapter 8 Theme

8 "Put the trumpet to your lips!
   An eagle[g] is over the house of the LORD
because the people have broken my covenant
   and rebelled against my law.[h]
[2]Israel cries out to me,
   'O our God, we acknowledge you!'
[3]But Israel has rejected what is good;
   an enemy will pursue him.
[4]They set up kings without my consent;
   they choose princes without my approval.[i]
With their silver and gold
   they make idols[j] for themselves
   to their own destruction.
[5]Throw out your calf-idol, O Samaria![k]
   My anger burns against them.
How long will they be incapable of purity?[l]
[6] They are from Israel!
This calf—a craftsman has made it;
   it is not God.
It will be broken in pieces,
   that calf of Samaria.

[7]"They sow the wind
   and reap the whirlwind.[m]
The stalk has no head;
   it will produce no flour.
Were it to yield grain,
   foreigners would swallow it up.[n]
[8]Israel is swallowed up;[o]
   now she is among the nations
   like a worthless[p] thing.

a 14 Most Hebrew manuscripts; some Hebrew manuscripts and Septuagint *They slash themselves*

7:14
[a] Am 2:8
[b] Hos 13:16

7:15
[c] Na 1:9,11

7:16
[d] Ps 78:9,57
[e] Eze 23:32
[f] Hos 9:3

8:1
[g] Dt 28:49;
Jer 4:13
[h] Hos 4:6; 6:7

8:4
[i] Hos 13:10
[j] Hos 2:8

8:5
[k] Hos 10:5
[l] Jer 13:27

8:7
[m] Pr 22:8;
Isa 66:15;
Hos 10:12-13;
Na 1:3
[n] Hos 2:9

8:8
[o] Jer 51:34
[p] Jer 22:28

8:10
a Eze 16:37;
22:20
b Jer 42:2

⁹For they have gone up to Assyria
  like a wild donkey wandering alone.
  Ephraim has sold herself to lovers.
¹⁰Although they have sold themselves among the nations,
  I will now gather them together.ᵃ
They will begin to waste awayᵇ
  under the oppression of the mighty king.

8:11
c Hos 10:1;
12:11

¹¹"Though Ephraim built many altars for sin offerings,
  these have become altars for sinning.ᶜ
¹²I wrote for them the many things of my law,
  but they regarded them as something alien.

8:13
d Jer 7:21
e Hos 7:2
f Hos 4:9
g Hos 9:3,6

¹³They offer sacrifices given to me
  and they eatᵈ the meat,
  but the LORD is not pleased with them.
Now he will rememberᵉ their wickedness
  and punish their sins:ᶠ
  They will return to Egypt.ᵍ

8:14
h Dt 32:18;
Hos 2:13
i Jer 17:27

¹⁴Israel has forgottenʰ his Maker
  and built palaces;
  Judah has fortified many towns.
But I will send fire upon their cities
  that will consume their fortresses."ⁱ

9:1
j Isa 22:12-13
k Hos 10:5

Chapter 9 Theme _____

9

Do not rejoice, O Israel;
  do not be jubilantʲ like the other nations.
For you have been unfaithfulᵏ to your God;
  you love the wages of a prostitute
  at every threshing floor.

9:2
l Hos 2:9

²Threshing floors and winepresses will not feed the people;
  the new wineˡ will fail them.

9:3
m Lev 25:23
n Hos 8:13
o Eze 4:13;
Hos 7:11

³They will not remainᵐ in the LORD's land;
  Ephraim will return to Egyptⁿ
  and eat uncleanᵃ food in Assyria.ᵒ
⁴They will not pour out wine offerings to the LORD,
  nor will their sacrifices pleaseᵖ him.

9:4
p Jer 6:20;
Hos 8:13
q Hag 2:13-14

Such sacrifices will be to them like the bread of mourners;
  all who eat them will be unclean.�q
This food will be for themselves;
  it will not come into the temple of the LORD.

⁵What will you doʳ on the day of your appointed feasts,ˢ
  on the festival days of the LORD?

9:5
r Isa 10:3;
Jer 5:31
s Hos 2:11

a 3 That is, ceremonially unclean

⁶Even if they escape from destruction,
  Egypt will gather them,
  and Memphis^a will bury them.
Their treasures of silver will be taken over by briers,
  and thorns^b will overrun their tents.
⁷The days of punishment^c are coming,
  the days of reckoning are at hand.
  Let Israel know this.
Because your sins^d are so many
  and your hostility so great,
the prophet is considered a fool,^e
  the inspired man a maniac.
⁸The prophet, along with my God,
  is the watchman over Ephraim,^a
yet snares^f await him on all his paths,
  and hostility in the house of his God.
⁹They have sunk deep into corruption,
  as in the days of Gibeah.^g
God will remember^h their wickedness
  and punish them for their sins.

¹⁰"When I found Israel,
  it was like finding grapes in the desert;
when I saw your fathers,
  it was like seeing the early fruit on the fig tree.
But when they came to Baal Peor,ⁱ
  they consecrated themselves to that
    shameful idol^j
  and became as vile as the thing they loved.
¹¹Ephraim's glory will fly away like a bird^k—
  no birth, no pregnancy, no conception.^l
¹²Even if they rear children,
  I will bereave them of every one.
Woe^m to them
  when I turn away from them!ⁿ
¹³I have seen Ephraim, like Tyre,
  planted in a pleasant place.^o
But Ephraim will bring out
  their children to the slayer."

¹⁴Give them, O LORD—
  what will you give them?
Give them wombs that miscarry
  and breasts that are dry.^p

9:6
^aIsa 19:13
^bIsa 5:6;
Hos 10:8

9:7
^cIsa 34:8;
Jer 10:15;
Mic 7:4
^dJer 16:18
^eIsa 44:25;
La 2:14;
Eze 14:9-10

9:8
^fHos 5:1

9:9
^gJdg 19:16-30;
Hos 5:8; 10:9
^hHos 8:13

9:10
ⁱNu 25:1-5;
Ps 106:28-29
^jJer 11:13;
Hos 4:14

9:11
^kHos 4:7; 10:5
^lver 14

9:12
^mHos 7:13
ⁿDt 31:17

9:13
^oEze 27:3

9:14
^pver 11;
Lk 23:29

^a 8 Or *The prophet is the watchman over Ephraim, / the people of my God*

9:15
a Hos 4:15
b Hos 7:2
c Isa 1:23;
Hos 4:9; 5:2

¹⁵"Because of all their wickedness in Gilgal,^a
    I hated them there.
Because of their sinful deeds,^b
    I will drive them out of my house.
I will no longer love them;
    all their leaders are rebellious.^c

9:16
d Hos 5:11
e Hos 8:7
f ver 12

¹⁶Ephraim^d is blighted,
    their root is withered,
    they yield no fruit.^e
Even if they bear children,
    I will slay^f their cherished offspring."

9:17
g Hos 4:10
h Dt 28:65;
Hos 7:13

¹⁷My God will reject them
    because they have not obeyed^g him;
    they will be wanderers among the nations.^h

Chapter 10 Theme _____

10 Israel was a spreading vine;ⁱ
    he brought forth fruit for himself.
As his fruit increased,
    he built more altars;^j
as his land prospered,
    he adorned his sacred stones.^k

10:1
i Eze 15:2
j 1Ki 14:23
k Hos 8:11;
12:11

²Their heart is deceitful,^l
    and now they must bear their guilt.^m
The LORD will demolish their altarsⁿ
    and destroy their sacred stones.^o

10:2
l 1Ki 18:21
m Hos 13:16
n ver 8
o Mic 5:13

³Then they will say, "We have no king
    because we did not revere the LORD.
But even if we had a king,
    what could he do for us?"

⁴They make many promises,
    take false oaths^p
    and make agreements;^q
therefore lawsuits spring up
    like poisonous weeds in a plowed field.

10:4
p Hos 4:2
q Eze 17:19;
Am 5:7

⁵The people who live in Samaria fear
    for the calf-idol of Beth Aven.^a ^r
Its people will mourn over it,
    and so will its idolatrous priests,^s
those who had rejoiced over its splendor,
    because it is taken from them into exile.^t

10:5
r Hos 5:8
s 2Ki 23:5
t Hos 8:5;
9:1,3,11

⁶It will be carried to Assyria^u
    as tribute for the great king.^v

10:6
u Hos 11:5
v Hos 5:13

^a 5 _Beth Aven_ means _house of wickedness_ (a name for Bethel, which means _house of God_).

Ephraim will be disgraced;[a]
 Israel will be ashamed of its wooden idols.[a]

[7] Samaria and its king will float away[b]
 like a twig on the surface of the waters.

[8] The high places of wickedness[b][c] will be destroyed—
 it is the sin of Israel.

Thorns[d] and thistles will grow up
 and cover their altars.[e]

Then they will say to the mountains, "Cover us!"
 and to the hills, "Fall on us!"[f]

[9] "Since the days of Gibeah,[g] you have sinned, O Israel,
 and there you have remained.[c]

Did not war overtake
 the evildoers in Gibeah?

[10] When I please, I will punish[h] them;
 nations will be gathered against them
 to put them in bonds for their double sin.

[11] Ephraim is a trained heifer
 that loves to thresh;

so I will put a yoke
 on her fair neck.

I will drive Ephraim,
 Judah must plow,
 and Jacob must break up the ground.

[12] Sow for yourselves righteousness,[i]
 reap the fruit of unfailing love,
 and break up your unplowed ground;[j]

for it is time to seek[k] the LORD,
 until he comes
 and showers righteousness[l] on you.

[13] But you have planted wickedness,
 you have reaped evil,[m]
 you have eaten the fruit of deception.

Because you have depended on your own strength
 and on your many warriors,[n]

[14] the roar of battle will rise against your people,
 so that all your fortresses will be devastated[o]—

as Shalman devastated Beth Arbel on the day of battle,
 when mothers were dashed to the ground with
 their children. [p]

[15] Thus will it happen to you, O Bethel,
 because your wickedness is great.

---

a6 Or *its counsel*   b8 Hebrew *aven*, a reference to Beth Aven (a derogatory name for Bethel)
c9 Or *there a stand was taken*

10:6
a Isa 30:3;
Hos 4:7

10:7
b Hos 13:11

10:8
c 1Ki 12:28-30;
Hos 4:13
d Hos 9:6
e ver 2;
Isa 32:13
f Lk 23:30*;
Rev 6:16

10:9
g Hos 5:8

10:10
h Eze 5:13;
Hos 4:9

10:12
i Pr 11:18
j Jer 4:3
k Hos 12:6
l Isa 45:8

10:13
m Job 4:8;
Hos 7:3; 11:12;
Gal 6:7-8
n Ps 33:16

10:14
o Isa 17:3
p Hos 13:16

10:15
a ver 7

When that day dawns,
the king of Israel will be completely destroyed.*a*

Chapter 11 Theme _____

11:1
b Ex 4:22;
Hos 12:9,13;
13:4;
Mt 2:15*

11 "When Israel was a child, I loved him,
and out of Egypt I called my son.*b*
²But the more I*a* called Israel,
the further they went from me.*b*
They sacrificed to the Baals*c*
and they burned incense to images.*d*
³It was I who taught Ephraim to walk,
taking them by the arms;*e*
but they did not realize
it was I who healed*f* them.
⁴I led them with cords of human kindness,
with ties of love;*g*
I lifted the yoke*h* from their neck
and bent down to feed*i* them.

11:2
c Hos 2:13
d 2Ki 17:15;
Isa 65:7;
Jer 18:15

11:3
e Dt 1:31;
Hos 7:15
f Jer 30:17

11:4
g Jer 31:2-3
h Lev 26:13
i Ex 16:32;
Ps 78:25

⁵"Will they not return to Egypt*j*
and will not Assyria*k* rule over them
because they refuse to repent?
⁶Swords*l* will flash in their cities,
will destroy the bars of their gates
and put an end to their plans.
⁷My people are determined to turn from me.*m*
Even if they call to the Most High,
he will by no means exalt them.

11:5
j Hos 7:16
k Hos 10:6

11:6
l Hos 13:16

⁸"How can I give you up, Ephraim?*n*
How can I hand you over, Israel?
How can I treat you like Admah?
How can I make you like Zeboiim?*o*
My heart is changed within me;
all my compassion is aroused.
⁹I will not carry out my fierce anger,*p*
nor will I turn and devastate*q* Ephraim.
For I am God, and not man*r*—
the Holy One among you.
I will not come in wrath.*c*
¹⁰They will follow the LORD;
he will roar like a lion.
When he roars,
his children will come trembling from the west.*s*

11:7
m Jer 3:6-7; 8:5

11:8
n Hos 6:4
o Ge 14:8

11:9
p Dt 13:17;
Jer 30:11
q Mal 3:6
r Nu 23:19

11:10
s Hos 6:1-3

a 2 Some Septuagint manuscripts; Hebrew *they*   *b* 2 Septuagint; Hebrew *them*   *c* 9 Or *come against any city*

¹¹They will come trembling
    like birds from Egypt,
    like doves from Assyria.[a]
I will settle them in their homes,"[b]
    declares the LORD.

¹²Ephraim has surrounded me with lies,[c]
    the house of Israel with deceit.
And Judah is unruly against God,
    even against the faithful Holy One.

Chapter 12 Theme _____

12 Ephraim feeds on the wind;[d]
    he pursues the east wind all day
    and multiplies lies and violence.
He makes a treaty with Assyria
    and sends olive oil to Egypt.[e]
²The LORD has a charge[f] to bring against Judah;
    he will punish Jacob[a] according to his ways
    and repay him according to his deeds.[g]
³In the womb he grasped his brother's heel;[h]
    as a man he struggled[i] with God.
⁴He struggled with the angel and overcame him;
    he wept and begged for his favor.
He found him at Bethel[j]
    and talked with him there—
⁵the LORD God Almighty,
    the LORD is his name[k] of renown!
⁶But you must return to your God;
    maintain love and justice,[l]
    and wait for your God always.[m]

⁷The merchant uses dishonest scales;[n]
    he loves to defraud.
⁸Ephraim boasts,
    "I am very rich; I have become wealthy.[o]
With all my wealth they will not find in me
    any iniquity or sin."

⁹"I am the LORD your God,
    ⌊who brought you⌋ out of[b] Egypt;[p]
I will make you live in tents[q] again,
    as in the days of your appointed feasts.
¹⁰I spoke to the prophets,
    gave them many visions
    and told parables[r] through them."[s]

---

^a2 *Jacob* means *he grasps the heel* (figuratively, *he deceives*).   ^b9 Or *God / ever since you were in*

Cross-references

11:11
a Isa 11:11
b Eze 28:26

11:12
c Hos 4:2

12:1
d Eze 17:10
e 2Ki 17:4

12:2
f Mic 6:2
g Hos 4:9

12:3
h Ge 25:26
i Ge 32:24-29

12:4
j Ge 28:12-15;
35:15

12:5
k Ex 3:15

12:6
l Mic 6:8
m Hos 6:1-3;
10:12;
Mic 7:7

12:7
n Am 8:5

12:8
o Ps 62:10;
Rev 3:17

12:9
p Lev 23:43; Hos
11:1
q Ne 8:17

12:10
r Eze 20:49
s 2Ki 17:13;
Jer 7:25

12:11
a Hos 6:8
b Hos 4:15
c Hos 8:11

¹¹Is Gilead wicked?*ᵃ*
  Its people are worthless!
Do they sacrifice bulls in Gilgal?*ᵇ*
  Their altars will be like piles of stones
  on a plowed field.*ᶜ*

12:12
d Ge 28:5
e Ge 29:18

¹²Jacob fled to the country of Aram*ᵃ;ᵈ*
  Israel served to get a wife,
  and to pay for her he tended sheep.*ᵉ*
¹³The Lord used a prophet to bring Israel up from Egypt,
  by a prophet he cared for him.*ᶠ*

12:13
f Ex 13:3;
Isa 63:11-14

¹⁴But Ephraim has bitterly provoked him to anger;
  his Lord will leave upon him the guilt of
      his bloodshed*ᵍ*
  and will repay him for his contempt.*ʰ*

12:14
g Eze 18:13
h Da 11:18

Chapter 13 Theme _____

13
When Ephraim spoke, men trembled;*ⁱ*
  he was exalted *ʲ* in Israel.
  But he became guilty of Baal worship*ᵏ* and died.
²Now they sin more and more;
  they make idols for themselves from their silver,*ˡ*
cleverly fashioned images,
  all of them the work of craftsmen.
It is said of these people,
  "They offer human sacrifice
  and kiss*ᵇ* the calf-idols.*ᵐ*"

13:1
i Jdg 12:1
j Jdg 8:1
k Hos 11:2

³Therefore they will be like the morning mist,
  like the early dew that disappears,*ⁿ*
  like chaff*ᵒ* swirling from a threshing floor,*ᵖ*
  like smoke*�q* escaping through a window.

13:2
l Isa 46:6;
Jer 10:4
m Isa 44:17-20

⁴"But I am the Lord your God,
  ⌊who brought you⌋ out of*ᶜ* Egypt.*ʳ*
You shall acknowledge no God but me,*ˢ*
  no Savior*ᵗ* except me.
⁵I cared for you in the desert,
  in the land of burning heat.
⁶When I fed them, they were satisfied;
  when they were satisfied, they became proud;
  then they forgot me.*ᵘ*

13:3
n Hos 6:4
o Isa 17:13
p Da 2:35
q Ps 68:2

⁷So I will come upon them like a lion,
  like a leopard I will lurk by the path.
⁸Like a bear robbed of her cubs,*ᵛ*
  I will attack them and rip them open.

13:4
r Hos 12:9
s Ex 20:3
t Isa 43:11;
45:21-22

13:6
u Dt 32:12-15;
Hos 2:13

13:8
v 2Sa 17:8

ᵃ 12 That is, Northwest Mesopotamia   *ᵇ 2* Or *"Men who sacrifice / kiss*   *ᶜ 4* Or *God / ever since you were in*

Like a lion I will devour them;
  a wild animal will tear them apart.*a*

⁹"You are destroyed, O Israel,
  because you are against me,*b* against your helper.*c*
¹⁰Where is your king,*d* that he may save you?
  Where are your rulers in all your towns,
of whom you said,
  'Give me a king and princes'?*e*
¹¹So in my anger I gave you a king,
  and in my wrath I took him away.*f*
¹²The guilt of Ephraim is stored up,
  his sins are kept on record.*g*
¹³Pains as of a woman in childbirth*h* come to him,
  but he is a child without wisdom;
when the time arrives,
  he does not come to the opening of the womb.*i*

¹⁴"I will ransom them from the power of the grave*a*;*j*
  I will redeem them from death.
Where, O death, are your plagues?
  Where, O grave,*a* is your destruction?*k*

"I will have no compassion,
¹⁵ even though he thrives*l* among his brothers.
An east wind*m* from the LORD will come,
  blowing in from the desert;
his spring will fail
  and his well dry up.*n*
His storehouse will be plundered*o*
  of all its treasures.
¹⁶The people of Samaria must bear their guilt,*p*
  because they have rebelled*q* against their God.
They will fall by the sword;*r*
  their little ones will be dashed*s* to the ground,
  their pregnant women*t* ripped open."

Chapter 14 Theme

14 Return, O Israel, to the LORD your God.
  Your sins have been your downfall!*u*
²Take words with you
  and return to the LORD.
Say to him:
  "Forgive all our sins
and receive us graciously,*v*
  that we may offer the fruit of our lips.*b*,*w*

a 14 Hebrew *Sheol*   b 2 Or *offer our lips as sacrifices of bulls*

13:8
a Ps 50:22

13:9
b Jer 2:17-19
c Dt 33:29

13:10
d 2Ki 17:4
e 1Sa 8:6;
Hos 8:4

13:11
f 1Ki 14:10;
Hos 10:7

13:12
g Dt 32:34

13:13
h Isa 13:8;
Mic 4:9-10
i Isa 66:9

13:14
j Ps 49:15;
Eze 37:12-13
k 1Co 15:55*

13:15
l Hos 10:1
m Eze 19:12
n Jer 51:36
o Jer 20:5

13:16
p Hos 10:2
q Hos 7:14
r Hos 11:6
s 2Ki 8:12;
Hos 10:14
t 2Ki 15:16;
Isa 13:16

14:1
u Hos 5:5

14:2
v Mic 7:18-19
w Heb 13:15

14:3
a Ps 33:17;
Isa 31:1
b Hos 8:6
c Ps 10:14; 68:5

14:4
d Hos 6:1
e Zep 3:17

14:5
f SS 2:1
g Isa 35:2
h Job 29:19

14:6
i Ps 52:8;
Jer 11:16
j SS 4:11

14:7
k Ps 91:1-4
l Hos 2:22
m Eze 17:23

14:8
n ver 3

14:9
o Ps 107:43
p Pr 10:29;
Isa 1:28
q Ps 111:7-8;
Zep 3:5;
Ac 13:10
r Isa 26:7

³Assyria cannot save us;
  we will not mount war-horses.*a*
We will never again say 'Our gods'*b*
  to what our own hands have made,
  for in you the fatherless*c* find compassion."

⁴"I will heal*d* their waywardness
  and love them freely,*e*
  for my anger has turned away from them.
⁵I will be like the dew to Israel;
  he will blossom like a lily.*f*
Like a cedar of Lebanon*g*
  he will send down his roots;*h*
⁶ his young shoots will grow.
His splendor will be like an olive tree,*i*
  his fragrance like a cedar of Lebanon.*j*
⁷Men will dwell again in his shade.*k*
  He will flourish like the grain.
He will blossom like a vine,
  and his fame will be like the wine*l* from Lebanon.*m*
⁸O Ephraim, what more have I*a* to do with idols?*n*
  I will answer him and care for him.
I am like a green pine tree;
  your fruitfulness comes from me."

⁹Who is wise?*o* He will realize these things.
  Who is discerning? He will understand them.*p*
The ways of the LORD are right;*q*
  the righteous walk*r* in them,
  but the rebellious stumble in them.

a 8 Or *What more has Ephraim*

GOD'S RESPONSE TO ISRAEL'S SIN

THEIR SIN (INIQUITY)	THE IMMEDIATE OR LONG-RANGE CONSEQUENCES

THEIR FUTURE OR HOPE

Theme of Hosea:

Author:

Date:

Purpose:

Key Words:

SEGMENT DIVISIONS	CHAPTER THEMES
	1
	2
	3
	4
	5
	6
	7
	8
	9
	10
	11
	12
	13
	14

JOEL

Although we know nothing about Joel, nor the exact time of his writing other than what we read in this short prophetic book, Joel's message is significant. When Peter preached on Pentecost, he explained Pentecost in the light of a prophecy in Joel (Acts 2:14-21; Joel 2:28-32).

Joel uses a present-day plague to call God's people to repentance. As he does this, Joel, like the other prophets, warns them of the coming day of the Lord—a day that is as sure as the promises of God.

∾ THINGS TO DO

1. Read through Joel and mark the key words listed on the JOEL AT A GLANCE chart on page 1562.

2. To correctly interpret Joel, you must pay attention to the time when certain events occur. Joel switches from the present to the future. To pick this up, watch for and mark the words *then* and *now*. Put a symbol next to any references to time. Also, watch the sequence of events.

3. As you read through Joel, note the following and record what you learn in the appropriate section on the JOEL OBSERVATIONS CHART on page 1563:

   a. What is going to happen to the people, the land, the nations, and the animals and who or what is going to do it.

   b. What the people are to do and why.

   c. How God will respond and the effect it will have on the people.

   d. When applicable, note when any of the above will happen.

4. Record the theme of each chapter on JOEL AT A GLANCE as well as in the text next to the chapter number. Then fill in the rest of the chart. Be sure to record the theme or message of Joel.

5. The day of the Lord is an important day prophetically. Beginning on page 2178 you will find the chart THE DAY OF THE LORD. Record your insights from Joel on the day of the Lord. As you do so, note the reference (book, chapter, and verse) that you took your information from so you can find it later.

∾ THINGS TO THINK ABOUT

1. What do you see happening in the world, in your nation? Could it be the judgment of the Lord? What could you and others learn from Joel's exhortations? What could you do?

2. Have you failed God in any way? According to what you have seen in Joel, is there a chance to return to him? What could you do? How can you apply the message of Joel to your life? What do you think would happen if your church collectively repented and returned to the Lord in this manner? Think about it and ask God what to do.

∾∾∾∾∾∾

Chapter 1 Theme _____

1 The word of the LORD that came[a] to Joel[b] son of Pethuel.

> [2]Hear this,[c] you elders;
>   listen, all who live in the land.[d]
> Has anything like this ever happened in your days
>   or in the days of your forefathers?[e]
> [3]Tell it to your children,[f]
>   and let your children tell it to their children,
>   and their children to the next generation.

1:1
a Jer 1:2
b Ac 2:16

1:2
c Hos 5:1
d Hos 4:1
e Joel 2:2

1:3
f Ex 10:2;
Ps 78:4

⁴What the locust swarm has left
  the great locusts have eaten;
what the great locusts have left
  the young locusts have eaten;
what the young locusts have left
  other locusts*a* have eaten.*a*

⁵Wake up, you drunkards, and weep!
  Wail, all you drinkers of wine;*b*
wail because of the new wine,
  for it has been snatched from your lips.
⁶A nation has invaded my land,
  powerful and without number;*c*
it has the teeth*d* of a lion,
  the fangs of a lioness.
⁷It has laid waste*e* my vines
  and ruined my fig trees.*f*
It has stripped off their bark
  and thrown it away,
  leaving their branches white.

⁸Mourn like a virgin*b* in sackcloth*g*
  grieving for the husband*c* of her youth.
⁹Grain offerings and drink offerings*h*
  are cut off from the house of the LORD.

Cross references

1:4
a Dt 28:39;
Na 3:15

1:5
b Joel 3:3

1:6
c Joel 2:2,11,25
d Rev 9:8

1:7
e Isa 5:6
f Am 4:9

1:8
g ver 13;
Isa 22:12;
Am 8:10

1:9
h Hos 9:4;
Joel 2:14,17

a 4 The precise meaning of the four Hebrew words used here for locusts is uncertain.
b 8 Or *young woman*   *c* 8 Or *betrothed*

THE RULERS AND PROPHETS OF JOEL'S TIME

Kings of Israel *(Northern Kingdom)*
Jehoram (Joram) 852–841 | Jehu 841–814 | Jehoahaz (Joahaz) 814–798

Prophets to Israel *(Northern Kingdom)*
Elisha 852–796

Kings of Judah *(Southern Kingdom)*
Jehoram (Joram) 853–841 | Ahaziah 841 | Queen Athaliah 841–835 | Joash (Jehoash) 835–796

Joel and His Contemporary Prophets *(Southern Kingdom)*
Obadiah 841–825 | Joel 825–809 | Jahaziel 865–835

930 920 910 900 890 880 870 860 850 840 830 820 810 800 790 780 770

The priests are in mourning,
 those who minister before the Lord.
¹⁰The fields are ruined,
 the ground is dried up[a];[a]
the grain is destroyed,
 the new wine[b] is dried up,
 the oil fails.
¹¹Despair, you farmers,[c]
 wail, you vine growers;
grieve for the wheat and the barley,
 because the harvest of the field is destroyed.[d]
¹²The vine is dried up
 and the fig tree is withered;
the pomegranate, the palm and the apple tree—
 all the trees of the field—are dried up.[e]
Surely the joy of mankind
 is withered away.

¹³Put on sackcloth,[f] O priests, and mourn;
 wail, you who minister[g] before the altar.
Come, spend the night in sackcloth,
 you who minister before my God;
for the grain offerings and drink offerings[h]
 are withheld from the house of your God.
¹⁴Declare a holy fast;[i]
 call a sacred assembly.
Summon the elders
 and all who live in the land
to the house of the Lord your God,
 and cry out[j] to the Lord.

¹⁵Alas for that[k] day!
For the day of the Lord[l] is near;
 it will come like destruction from the Almighty.[b]

¹⁶Has not the food been cut off[m]
 before our very eyes—
joy and gladness
 from the house of our God?[n]
¹⁷The seeds are shriveled
 beneath the clods.[c][o]
The storehouses are in ruins,
 the granaries have been broken down,
 for the grain has dried up.

---

a 10 Or *ground mourns* b 15 Hebrew *Shaddai* c 17 The meaning of the Hebrew for this
word is uncertain.

1:10
a Isa 24:4
b Hos 9:2

1:11
c Jer 14:3-4;
Am 5:16
d Isa 17:11

1:12
e Hag 2:19

1:13
f Jer 4:8
g Joel 2:17
h ver 9

1:14
i 2Ch 20:3
j Jnh 3:8

1:15
k Jer 30:7
l Isa 13:6,9;
Joel 2:1,11,31

1:16
m Isa 3:7
n Dt 12:7

1:17
o Isa 17:10-11

1:19
a Ps 50:15
b Am 7:4
c Jer 9:10

1:20
d Ps 104:21
e 1Ki 17:7

2:1
f Jer 4:5
g ver 15
h Joel 1:15;
Zep 1:14-16
i Ob 1:15

2:2
j Am 5:18
k Da 9:12
l Joel 1:6
m Joel 1:2

2:3
n Ge 2:8
o Ps 105:34-35

2:4
p Rev 9:7

2:5
q Rev 9:9
r Isa 5:24;
30:30

2:6
s Isa 13:8
t Na 2:10

2:7
u Isa 5:27

¹⁸How the cattle moan!
> The herds mill about
because they have no pasture;
> even the flocks of sheep are suffering.

¹⁹To you, O Lord, I call,^a
> for fire^b has devoured the open pastures^c
> and flames have burned up all the trees of the field.
²⁰Even the wild animals pant for you;^d
> the streams of water have dried up^e
> and fire has devoured the open pastures.

Chapter 2 Theme

2 Blow the trumpet^f in Zion;^g
> sound the alarm on my holy hill.
Let all who live in the land tremble,
> for the day of the Lord^h is coming.
It is close at handⁱ—
2   a day of darkness^j and gloom,^k
> a day of clouds and blackness.
Like dawn spreading across the mountains
> a large and mighty army^l comes,
such as never was of old^m
> nor ever will be in ages to come.

³Before them fire devours,
> behind them a flame blazes.
Before them the land is like the garden of Eden,ⁿ
> behind them, a desert waste^o—
> nothing escapes them.
⁴They have the appearance of horses;^p
> they gallop along like cavalry.
⁵With a noise like that of chariots^q
> they leap over the mountaintops,
like a crackling fire^r consuming stubble,
> like a mighty army drawn up for battle.

⁶At the sight of them, nations are in anguish;^s
> every face turns pale.^t
⁷They charge like warriors;
> they scale walls like soldiers.
They all march in line,
> not swerving^u from their course.
⁸They do not jostle each other;
> each marches straight ahead.
They plunge through defenses
> without breaking ranks.

⁹They rush upon the city;
　　they run along the wall.
They climb into the houses;
　　like thieves they enter through the windows.ᵃ

¹⁰Before them the earth shakes,ᵇ
　　the sky trembles,
the sun and moon are darkened,ᶜ
　　and the stars no longer shine.ᵈ
¹¹The Lordᵉ thunders
　　at the head of his army;
his forces are beyond number,
　　and mighty are those who obey his command.
The day of the Lord is great;ᶠ
　　it is dreadful.
Who can endure it?ᵍ

¹²"Even now," declares the Lord,
　　"returnʰ to me with all your heart,
　　with fasting and weeping and mourning."

¹³Rend your heartⁱ
　　and not your garments.ʲ
Return to the Lord your God,
　　for he is gracious and compassionate,
slow to anger and abounding in love,ᵏ
　　and he relents from sending calamity.ˡ
¹⁴Who knows? He may turnᵐ and have pity
　　and leave behind a blessingⁿ—
grain offerings and drink offeringsᵒ
　　for the Lord your God.

¹⁵Blow the trumpetᵖ in Zion,
　　declare a holy fast,�q
　　call a sacred assembly.ʳ
¹⁶Gather the people,
　　consecrateˢ the assembly;
bring together the elders,
　　gather the children,
　　those nursing at the breast.
Let the bridegroomᵗ leave his room
　　and the bride her chamber.
¹⁷Let the priests, who minister before the Lord,
　　weep between the temple porch and the altar.ᵘ
Let them say, "Spare your people, O Lord.
　　Do not make your inheritance an object of scorn,ᵛ
　　a byword among the nations.

2:9
ᵃ Jer 9:21

2:10
ᵇ Ps 18:7
ᶜ Mt 24:29
ᵈ Isa 13:10;
Eze 32:8

2:11
ᵉ Joel 1:15
ᶠ Zep 1:14;
Rev 18:8
ᵍ Eze 22:14

2:12
ʰ Jer 4:1;
Hos 12:6

2:13
ⁱ Ps 34:18;
Isa 57:15
ʲ Job 1:20
ᵏ Ex 34:6
ˡ Jer 18:8

2:14
ᵐ Jer 26:3
ⁿ Hag 2:19
ᵒ Joel 1:13

2:15
ᵖ Nu 10:2
q Jer 36:9
ʳ Joel 1:14

2:16
ˢ Ex 19:10,22
ᵗ Ps 19:5

2:17
ᵘ Eze 8:16;
Mt 23:35
ᵛ Dt 9:26-29;
Ps 44:13

2:17
a Ps 42:3

Why should they say among the peoples,
　　'Where is their God?ᵃ'"

2:18
b Zec 1:14

¹⁸Then the Lᴏʀᴅ will be jealousᵇ for his land
　　and take pity on his people.

¹⁹The Lᴏʀᴅ will replyᵃ to them:

2:19
c Jer 31:12
d Eze 34:29

"I am sending you grain, new wine and oil,ᶜ
　　enough to satisfy you fully;
never again will I make you
　　an object of scornᵈ to the nations.

²⁰"I will drive the northern armyᵉ far from you,
　　pushing it into a parched and barren land,
with its front columns going into the eastern ᶠ seaᵇ
　　and those in the rear into the western sea.ᶜ

2:20
e Jer 1:14-15
f Zec 14:8
g Isa 34:3

And its stenchᵍ will go up;
　　its smell will rise."

Surely he has done great things.ᵈ

2:21
h Isa 54:4;
Zep 3:16-17
i Ps 126:3

²¹　Be not afraid,ʰ O land;
　　be glad and rejoice.
Surely the Lᴏʀᴅ has done great things.ⁱ
²²　Be not afraid, O wild animals,
　　for the open pastures are becoming green.ʲ
The trees are bearing their fruit;
　　the fig tree and the vine yield their riches.ᵏ

2:22
j Ps 65:12
k Joel 1:18-20

²³Be glad, O people of Zion,
　　rejoiceˡ in the Lᴏʀᴅ your God,
for he has given you
　　the autumn rains in righteousness.ᵉ

2:23
l Ps 149:2;
Isa 12:6; 41:16;
Hab 3:18;
Zec 10:7
m Lev 26:4

He sends you abundant showers,
　　both autumn and spring rains,ᵐ as before.
²⁴The threshing floors will be filled with grain;
　　the vats will overflowⁿ with new wineᵒ and oil.

²⁵"I will repay you for the years the locusts have eaten—
　　the great locust and the young locust,
　　the other locusts and the locust swarmᶠ—
my great army that I sent among you.

2:24
n Lev 26:10;
Mal 3:10
o Am 9:13

²⁶You will have plenty to eat, until you are full,ᵖ
　　and you will praiseᵠ the name of the Lᴏʀᴅ your God,
　　who has worked wondersʳ for you;
never again will my people be shamed.

2:26
p Lev 26:5
q Isa 62:9
r Ps 126:3;
Isa 25:1

ᵃ 18,19 Or Lᴏʀᴅ was jealous . . . / and took pity . . . / ¹⁹The Lᴏʀᴅ replied　ᵇ 20 That is, the Dead
Sea　ᶜ 20 That is, the Mediterranean　ᵈ 20 Or rise. / Surely it has done great things."
ᵉ 23 Or / the teacher for righteousness:　ᶠ 25 The precise meaning of the four Hebrew words
used here for locusts is uncertain.

²⁷Then you will know that I am in Israel,
   that I am the Lord ᵃ your God,
   and that there is no other;
never again will my people be shamed.

²⁸"And afterward,
   I will pour out my Spirit ᵇ on all people.
Your sons and daughters will prophesy,
   your old men will dream dreams,
   your young men will see visions.
²⁹Even on my servants, ᶜ both men and women,
   I will pour out my Spirit in those days.
³⁰I will show wonders in the heavens ᵈ
   and on the earth, ᵉ
   blood and fire and billows of smoke.
³¹The sun will be turned to darkness ᶠ
   and the moon to blood
   before the coming of the great and dreadful day of
      the Lord. ᵍ
³²And everyone who calls
   on the name of the Lord will be saved; ʰ
for on Mount Zion ⁱ and in Jerusalem
   there will be deliverance, ʲ
   as the Lord has said,
among the survivors ᵏ
   whom the Lord calls.

Chapter 3 Theme

The Valley of Jehoshaphat

3 "In those days and at that time,
   when I restore the fortunes ˡ of Judah and Jerusalem,
   ²I will gather all nations
      and bring them down to the Valley
         of Jehoshaphat. ᵃ
There I will enter into judgment ᵐ against them
   concerning my inheritance, my people Israel,
for they scattered my people among the nations
   and divided up my land.
³They cast lots for my people
   and traded boys for prostitutes;
they sold girls for wine ⁿ
   that they might drink.

⁴"Now what have you against me, O Tyre and Sidon ᵒ
and all you regions of Philistia? Are you repaying me
for something I have done? If you are paying me back,
I will swiftly and speedily return on your own heads

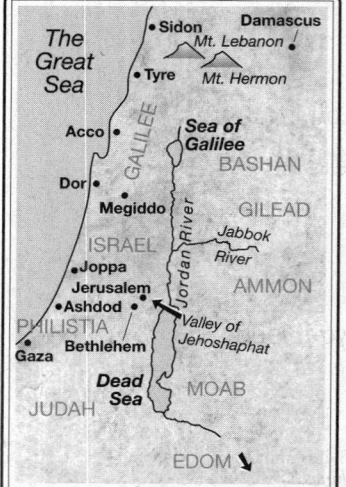

The Valley of Jehoshaphat

The Great Sea — Sidon • Damascus • Mt. Lebanon • Tyre • Mt. Hermon • Acco • GALILEE • Sea of Galilee • BASHAN • Dor • Megiddo • GILEAD • Jabbok River • Jordan River • ISRAEL • Joppa • Jerusalem • Ashdod • AMMON • PHILISTIA • Valley of Jehoshaphat • Bethlehem • Gaza • Dead Sea • MOAB • JUDAH • EDOM

ᵃ2 *Jehoshaphat* means *the Lord judges;* also in verse 12.

Ref	Cross-reference
2:27	ᵃ Joel 3:17
2:28	ᵇ Eze 39:29
2:29	ᶜ 1Co 12:13; Gal 3:28
2:30	ᵈ Lk 21:11; ᵉ Mk 13:24-25
2:31	ᶠ Mt 24:29; ᵍ Isa 13:9-10; Mal 4:1,5
2:32	ʰ Ac 2:17-21*; Ro 10:13*; ⁱ Isa 46:13; ʲ Ob 1:17; ᵏ Isa 11:11; Mic 4:7; Ro 9:27
3:1	ˡ Jer 16:15
3:2	ᵐ Eze 36:5
3:3	ⁿ Am 2:6
3:4	ᵒ Mt 11:21

what you have done.*a* **5**For you took my silver and my gold and carried off my finest treasures to your temples.*b* **6**You sold the people of Judah and Jerusalem to the Greeks, that you might send them far from their homeland.

7"See, I am going to rouse them out of the places to which you sold them,*c* and I will return on your own heads what you have done. **8**I will sell your sons*d* and daughters to the people of Judah,*e* and they will sell them to the Sabeans, a nation far away." The LORD has spoken.

> **9**Proclaim this among the nations:
>   Prepare for war!*f*
> Rouse the warriors!*g*
>   Let all the fighting men draw near and attack.
> **10**Beat your plowshares into swords
>   and your pruning hooks*h* into spears.
> Let the weakling*i* say,
>   "I am strong!"
> **11**Come quickly, all you nations from every side,
>   and assemble*j* there.
>
> Bring down your warriors,*k* O LORD!
>
> **12**"Let the nations be roused;
>   let them advance into the Valley of Jehoshaphat,
> for there I will sit
>   to judge*l* all the nations on every side.
> **13**Swing the sickle,
>   for the harvest*m* is ripe.
> Come, trample the grapes,
>   for the winepress*n* is full
>   and the vats overflow—
> so great is their wickedness!"
>
> **14**Multitudes, multitudes
>   in the valley of decision!
> For the day of the LORD*o* is near
>   in the valley of decision.
> **15**The sun and moon will be darkened,
>   and the stars no longer shine.
> **16**The LORD will roar from Zion
>   and thunder from Jerusalem; *p*
>   the earth and the sky will tremble.*q*
> But the LORD will be a refuge for his people,
>   a stronghold*r* for the people of Israel.
>
> **17**"Then you will know that I, the LORD your God,*s*
>   dwell in Zion,*t* my holy hill.
> Jerusalem will be holy;
>   never again will foreigners invade her.

**Margin references (left column):**

3:4
a Isa 34:8

3:5
b 2Ch 21:16-17

3:7
c Isa 43:5-6;
Jer 23:8

3:8
d Isa 60:14
e Isa 14:2

3:9
f Isa 8:9
g Jer 46:4

3:10
h Isa 2:4;
Mic 4:3
i Zec 12:8

3:11
j Eze 38:15-16;
Zep 3:8
k Isa 13:3

3:12
l Isa 2:4

3:13
m Hos 6:11;
Mt 13:39;
Rev 14:15-19
n Rev 14:20

3:14
o Isa 34:2-8;
Joel 1:15

3:16
p Am 1:2
q Eze 38:19
r Jer 16:19

3:17
s Joel 2:27
t Isa 4:3

INSIGHT box (right column):

INSIGHT

Sabeans are the descendants of Seba, the son of Cush or possibly of Sheba, the son of Raamah (see Genesis 10:7). Sabeans destroyed Job's flocks, herds, and servants. They were known as traveling merchants. The term *Sabeans* could have been adapted to refer to foreign or nomadic merchants.

18"In that day the mountains will drip new wine,
  and the hills will flow with milk;[a]
  all the ravines of Judah will run with water.[b]
A fountain will flow out of the LORD's house[c]
  and will water the valley of acacias.[a][d]
19But Egypt will be desolate,
  Edom a desert waste,
  because of violence[e] done to the people of Judah,
    in whose land they shed innocent blood.
20Judah will be inhabited forever[f]
  and Jerusalem through all generations.
21Their bloodguilt, which I have not pardoned,
  I will pardon.[g]"

The LORD dwells in Zion!

a 18 Or *Valley of Shittim*

3:18
a Ex 3:8
b Isa 30:25; 35:6
c Rev 22:1-2
d Eze 47:1;
  Am 9:13

3:19
e Ob 1:10

3:20
f Am 9:15

3:21
g Eze 36:25

JOEL AT A GLANCE

Theme of Joel:

SEGMENT DIVISIONS

		CHAPTER THEMES
		1
		2
		3

Author:

Date:

Purpose:

Key Words:
  locust(s)
  Zion
  day of the Lord
  (in that day,
  those days)
  return
  I will (will I)
  never again
  then
  now
  nations
  (nation and
  its pronouns)

JOEL OBSERVATIONS CHART

What Happens to the People	What the People Are to Do	What Is the Effect on People

What Happens to the Land Before and During Judgment	What Happens to the Land After Judgment

What Happens to the Animals

What Happens to the Nations and Why

How Will God Respond

AMOS

While the cows of Bashan (the best of breeds raised in Canaan) grazed and were pampered in the northern Transjordan region, the Israelites of the northern kingdom went up to worship at Bethel. There at Bethel the higher echelon would burn incense and present their sacrifices at the altar.

Bethel was the place where Jeroboam I, the first king of Israel (the northern kingdom), had set up the golden calves (see 1 Kings 12-13). He felt he had to. When the twelve tribes divided into two kingdoms, those of the northern kingdom were cut off from Jerusalem. Jerusalem now belonged to the two tribes of the southern kingdom, Judah and Benjamin. If Jeroboam's people went to celebrate the feasts in Jerusalem at the temple as God commanded, they might defect to the southern kingdom.

So Jeroboam commissioned his own priests and instituted his own feast. The people would worship as they pleased, where they pleased. Those who did not go to Bethel could go to Gilgal, another principal place of worship. In Gilgal they could present their thank offerings with leaven, proclaim their freewill offerings, and even worship other gods.

Israel became prosperous and politically secure. Jeroboam died, and later Jeroboam II reigned. It was a golden era. Surely God was pleased with Israel—or that is what they supposed until a shepherd from the small city of Tekoa, just ten miles south of Jerusalem, appeared on the scene.

Then the word of the Lord came.

∾ THINGS TO DO

General Instructions

In order to understand the historical setting of Amos, do the following:

1. Read Amos 1:1 and then record what you learn about Amos on the AMOS AT A GLANCE chart on page 1581 under "Author." Then under "Date" record the information that gives you a clue as to the time of these visions (see Zechariah 14:5). Under "Purpose" fill in Amos's reason for writing (see Amos 1:1).

2. Study the historical chart on page 1566 which shows Amos's relationship to the kings of Israel and Judah. Remember, Amos is a prophet to the northern kingdom.

3. Read 2 Chronicles 26:1-23 and 2 Kings 14:23 through 15:7. When you come across Azariah, remember that this is another name for King Uzziah, who ruled over the southern kingdom.

As you read through Amos, you will find three key phrases which divide the book into three segments. Therefore your instructions will be divided accordingly.

Chapters 1, 2

1. Read Amos 1 and 2 and mark each occurrence of the phrase *This is what the Lord says, for three sins of* _____ *even for four*. Note whose transgressions God is going to deal with in each incident.

2. Read what follows each of the statements you have marked. Look for another key repeated phrase, then mark or color it in a distinctive way.

3. Then observe why God will not revoke their punishment, and what the punishment will be. Note their punishment by marking each occurrence of *I will*.

4. In 2:4, 6 God deals with the southern kingdom, Judah, and with the northern kingdom, Israel. To understand why God speaks to them separately, look at Amos 1:1 and notice to whom Amos was sent as a prophet. (This information is also on the historical chart on page 1566.) It is important to keep this in mind as you study the rest of Amos.

5. Record the theme of the first two chapters on AMOS AT A GLANCE and in the text next to the chapter numbers.

Chapters 3-6

1. The second key repeated phrase is *hear this word*. Read Amos 3 through 6 and distinctively mark each occurrence of this phrase. Also mark every *Israel (Israelites)* (and every reference to Israel throughout Amos). Then list in the margin all you learn from marking *Israel*.

2. Read Amos 3 through 6 a second time, chapter by chapter. As you read these messages from the Lord, ask the five W's and an H. Ask questions such as: Who is speaking? To whom? What is being said? What is going to happen? When will it happen? Where will it take place? Why will it happen? How will it happen? (Remember, you won't always find answers to every question.)

3. Mark in a distinctive way key repeated words or phrases. For instance, marking every *I will* as it refers to God and asking the five W's and an H will help you see what God is going to do. Watch for *yet* in chapter 4 and *seek* in chapter 5. Mark every reference to *the day of the Lord*. Then in the margin list everything you learn about this day.

4. In the margin list important insights about God, Israel, what the people are doing wrong, and what they don't like.

5. When you finish studying a chapter, decide on the theme or topic of that chapter and record it on AMOS AT A GLANCE and in the text next to the chapter number.

Chapters 7-9

1. The key repeated phrase which sets off the last segment of Amos is *This is what the Sovereign Lord showed me*. Read these last three chapters and distinctively mark each occurrence of this phrase.

2. As you read through this final segment of Amos, watch what Amos was shown, and how he responds. Also observe the response to Amos's prophecy and how Amos deals with this.

3. In chapter 8 you see one final *hear this*. Pay careful attention to what God is going to do. Compare 8:8 with 1:1.

4. Although the phrase *This is what the Sovereign Lord showed me* is not used in 9:1, can you see that *I saw the Lord…and he said* could be Amos's fifth vision, which parallels those you marked in chapters 7 and 8? If so, mark it as you did the others.

5. Mark the *I will*'s of God and any other key words or phrases.

6. In the chapter margins record your insights about God and Israel.

7. Record the chapter themes as you did before and complete AMOS AT A GLANCE. Make sure you also record the theme of Amos.

8. Beginning on page 2178 you will find the chart called THE DAY OF THE LORD. Record your insights from Amos on the day of the Lord on this chart. As you do, note the reference (book, chapter, and verse) from which you took your information so you can find it later.

9. Finally, watch the closing words of Amos. What is God's promise? Remember any reference to the land. Has this promise regarding the land of Israel been fulfilled? Think of Israel's history. Read the section called "Major Events in Israel's History" on page 2189. Then answer the question.

❧ THINGS TO THINK ABOUT

1. Has wealth, the ease of life, the possession of things, the pursuit of happiness led to complacency in your worship? Are you worshiping God his way or your way?

2. As you review the list of Israel's sins, are you guilty of any of these? According to what you read in Amos, could Israel or the other nations sin and not reap the consequences? Can you?

3. What is the purpose of God's judgments? When God decides to judge, what can we do? What can we expect?

THE RULERS AND PROPHETS OF AMOS'S TIME

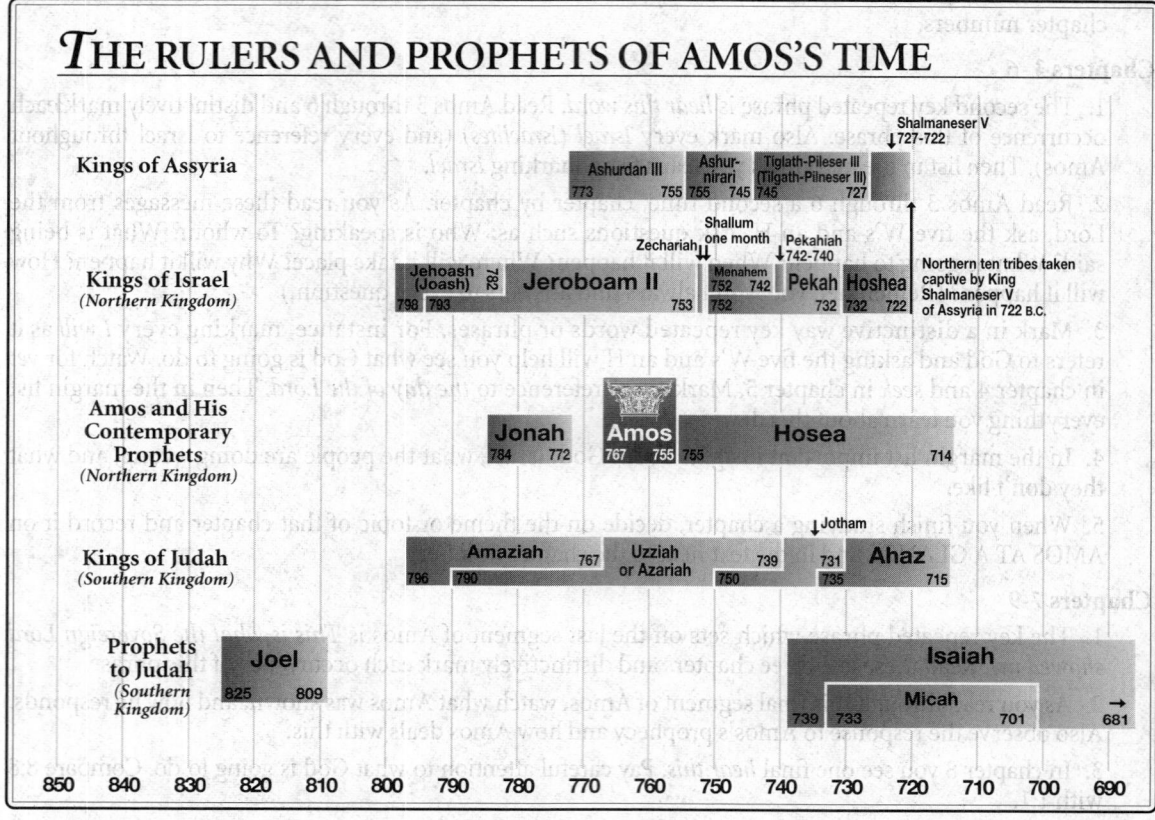

Kings of Assyria	Ashurdan III 773 · 755	Ashur-nirari 755 · 745	Tiglath-Pileser III (Tilgath-Pileser III) 745 · 727		Shalmaneser V ↓ 727-722	

Kings of Israel (Northern Kingdom)
Jehoash (Joash) 798 · 793 | 782 | Jeroboam II 753 | Zechariah | Shallum one month | Menahem 752 · 742 | Pekahiah ↓742-740 | Pekah 752 · 732 | Hoshea 732 · 722

Northern ten tribes taken captive by King Shalmaneser V of Assyria in 722 B.C.

Amos and His Contemporary Prophets (Northern Kingdom)
Jonah 784 · 772 | Amos 767 · 755 · 755 | Hosea 714

Kings of Judah (Southern Kingdom)
Amaziah 796 · 790 | 767 | Uzziah or Azariah 750 · 739 | ↓ Jotham 731 · 735 | Ahaz 715

Prophets to Judah (Southern Kingdom)
Joel 825 · 809 | Isaiah | Micah 739 · 733 · 701 · 681 →

850 840 830 820 810 800 790 780 770 760 750 740 730 720 710 700 690

Chapter 1 Theme

1 The words of Amos, one of the shepherds of Tekoa[a]—what he saw concerning Israel two years before the earthquake,[b] when Uzziah[c] was king of Judah and Jeroboam[d] son of Jehoash[a] was king of Israel.[e]

²He said:

"The LORD roars[f] from Zion
    and thunders from Jerusalem;[g]
the pastures of the shepherds dry up,[h]
    and the top of Carmel[h] withers."[i]

³This is what the LORD says:

"For three sins of Damascus,[j]
    even for four, I will not turn back ⌊my wrath⌋,[k]
Because she threshed Gilead
    with sledges having iron teeth,

INSIGHT

There are two Zions referred to in the Scriptures: the earthly Zion, Jerusalem, and the heavenly Zion, where God's throne is. Zion is also referred to as the city of God.

1:1
a 2Sa 14:2
b Zec 14:5
c 2Ch 26:23
d 2Ki 14:23
e Hos 1:1

1:2
f Isa 42:13
g Joel 3:16
h Am 9:3
i Jer 12:4

1:3
j Isa 8:4; 17:1-3
k Am 2:6

a 1 Hebrew *Joash,* a variant of *Jehoash*   b 2 Or *shepherds mourn*

1:4
a Jer 49:27
b Jer 17:27
c 1Ki 20:1;
2Ki 6:24

⁴I will send fire *a* upon the house of Hazael
    that will consume the fortresses *b* of Ben-Hadad. *c*
⁵I will break down the gate *d* of Damascus;
    I will destroy the king who is in *a* the Valley of Aven *b*
and the one who holds the scepter in Beth Eden.
    The people of Aram will go into exile to Kir, *e*"
                                    says the LORD.

1:5
d Jer 51:30
e 2Ki 16:9

⁶This is what the LORD says:

"For three sins of Gaza, *f*
    even for four, I will not turn back ⌊my wrath⌋.
Because she took captive whole communities
    and sold them to Edom, *g*

1:6
f 1Sa 6:17;
Zep 2:4
g Ob 11

⁷I will send fire upon the walls of Gaza
    that will consume her fortresses.
⁸I will destroy the king *c* of Ashdod *h*
    and the one who holds the scepter in Ashkelon.
I will turn my hand *i* against Ekron,
    till the last of the Philistines *j* is dead,"
                        says the Sovereign LORD. *k*

1:8
h 2Ch 26:6
i Ps 81:14
j Eze 25:16
k Isa 14:28-32;
Zep 2:4-7

⁹This is what the LORD says:

"For three sins of Tyre, *l*
    even for four, I will not turn back
        ⌊my wrath⌋.
Because she sold whole communities of
        captives to Edom,
    disregarding a treaty of brotherhood,
¹⁰I will send fire upon the walls of Tyre
    that will consume her fortresses. *m*"

1:9
l 1Ki 5:1;
9:11-14;
Isa 23:1-18;
Jer 25:22;
Joel 3:4;
Mt 11:21

¹¹This is what the LORD says:

"For three sins of Edom, *n*
    even for four, I will not turn back
        ⌊my wrath⌋.
Because he pursued his brother with a sword, *d*
    stifling all compassion, *d*
because his anger raged continually
    and his fury flamed unchecked, *o*
¹²I will send fire upon Teman *p*
    that will consume the fortresses of Bozrah."

1:10
m Zec 9:1-4

1:11
n Nu 20:14-21;
2Ch 28:17;
Jer 49:7-22
o Eze 25:12-14

¹³This is what the LORD says:

"For three sins of Ammon, *q*
    even for four, I will not turn back ⌊my wrath⌋.

1:12
p Ob 9-10

1:13
q Jer 49:1-6;
Eze 21:28; 25:2-7

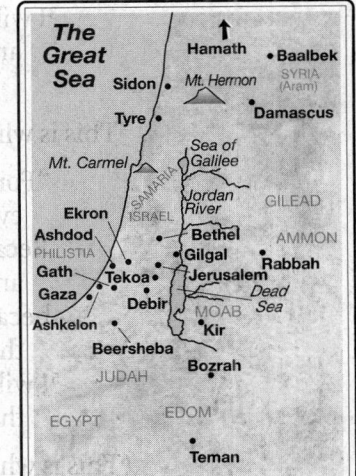

This Is What the Lord Says

The Great Sea — Sidon, Tyre, Mt. Carmel, Ekron, Ashdod, Gath, Gaza, Ashkelon, PHILISTIA, ISRAEL, SAMARIA, Beersheba, JUDAH, EGYPT, Hamath, Baalbek, SYRIA (Aram), Mt. Hermon, Damascus, Sea of Galilee, Jordan River, GILEAD, Bethel, Gilgal, Tekoa, Jerusalem, Debir, Kir, MOAB, Dead Sea, AMMON, Rabbah, Bozrah, EDOM, Teman

a 5 Or *the inhabitants of*   b 5 *Aven* means *wickedness.*   c 8 Or *inhabitants*   d 11 Or *sword /*
and destroyed his allies

Because he ripped open the pregnant women[a] of Gilead
    in order to extend his borders,
¹⁴I will set fire to the walls of Rabbah[b]
    that will consume her fortresses
    amid war cries[c] on the day of battle,
        amid violent winds on a stormy day.
¹⁵Her king[a] will go into exile,
    he and his officials together,"

                says the LORD.

Chapter 2 Theme

2 This is what the LORD says:

"For three sins of Moab,
    even for four, I will not turn back ⌊my wrath⌋.
Because he burned, as if to lime,
    the bones of Edom's king,
²I will send fire upon Moab
    that will consume the fortresses of Kerioth.[b]
Moab will go down in great tumult
    amid war cries and the blast of the trumpet.
³I will destroy her ruler[d]
    and kill all her officials with him,"[e]

                says the LORD.

⁴This is what the LORD says:

"For three sins of Judah,[f]
    even for four, I will not turn back ⌊my wrath⌋.
Because they have rejected the law[g] of the LORD
    and have not kept his decrees,[h]
because they have been led astray[i] by false gods,[c][j]
    the gods[d] their ancestors followed,[k]
⁵I will send fire upon Judah
    that will consume the fortresses of Jerusalem.[l]"

⁶This is what the LORD says:

"For three sins of Israel,
    even for four, I will not turn back ⌊my wrath⌋.
They sell the righteous for silver,
    and the needy for a pair of sandals.[m]
⁷They trample on the heads of the poor
    as upon the dust of the ground
    and deny justice to the oppressed.
Father and son use the same girl
    and so profane my holy name.[n]

### Cross-references (margin)

1:13 [a]Hos 13:16

1:14 [b]Dt 3:11 [c]Am 2:2

2:3 [d]Ps 2:10 [e]Isa 40:23

2:4 [f]2Ki 17:19; Hos 12:2 [g]Jer 6:19 [h]Eze 20:24 [i]Isa 9:16 [j]Isa 28:15 [k]2Ki 22:13; Jer 16:12

2:5 [l]Jer 17:27; Hos 8:14

2:6 [m]Joel 3:3; Am 8:6

2:7 [n]Am 5:11-12; 8:4

---

[a]15 Or / Molech; Hebrew *malcam* [b]2 Or *of her cities* [c]4 Or *by lies* [d]4 Or *lies*

2:8
a Ex 22:26
b Am 4:1; 6:6

8They lie down beside every altar
  on garments taken in pledge.*a*
In the house of their god
  they drink wine*b* taken as fines.

2:9
c Nu 21:23-26;
Jos 10:12
d Eze 17:9;
Mal 4:1

9"I destroyed the Amorite*c* before them,
  though he was tall as the cedars
  and strong as the oaks.
I destroyed his fruit above
  and his roots*d* below.

2:10
e Ex 20:2;
Am 3:1
f Dt 2:7
g Ex 3:8;
Am 9:7

10"I brought you up out of Egypt,*e*
  and I led you forty years in the desert*f*
  to give you the land of the Amorites.*g*
11I also raised up prophets*h* from among your sons
  and Nazirites*i* from among your young men.
Is this not true, people of Israel?"

declares the L ORD.

2:11
h Dt 18:18;
Jer 7:25
i Nu 6:2-3;
Jdg 13:5

12"But you made the Nazirites drink wine
  and commanded the prophets not to prophesy.*j*

2:12
j Isa 30:10;
Jer 11:21;
Am 7:12-13;
Mic 2:6

13"Now then, I will crush you
  as a cart crushes when loaded with grain.
14The swift will not escape,
  the strong*k* will not muster their strength,
  and the warrior will not save his life.*l*

2:14
k Jer 9:23
l Ps 33:16;
Isa 30:16-17

15The archer*m* will not stand his ground,
  the fleet-footed soldier will not get away,
  and the horseman will not save his life.
16Even the bravest warriors*n*
  will flee naked on that day,"

declares the L ORD.

2:15
m Eze 39:3

Chapter 3 Theme

2:16
n Jer 48:41

3 Hear this word the L ORD has spoken against you, O people of
Israel—against the whole family I brought up out of Egypt:*o*

2"You only have I chosen*p*
  of all the families of the earth;
therefore I will punish you
  for all your sins.*q*"

3:1
o Am 2:10

3Do two walk together
  unless they have agreed to do so?
4Does a lion roar in the thicket
  when he has no prey?*r*
Does he growl in his den
  when he has caught nothing?

3:2
p Dt 7:6;
Lk 12:47
q Jer 14:10

3:4
r Ps 104:21;
Hos 5:14

⁵Does a bird fall into a trap on the ground
    where no snare has been set?
Does a trap spring up from the earth
    when there is nothing to catch?
⁶When a trumpet sounds in a city,
    do not the people tremble?
When disaster comes to a city,
    has not the LORD caused it? *a*

⁷Surely the Sovereign LORD does nothing
    without revealing his plan *b*
    to his servants the prophets. *c*

⁸The lion has roared—
    who will not fear?
The Sovereign LORD has spoken—
    who can but prophesy? *d*

⁹Proclaim to the fortresses of Ashdod
    and to the fortresses of Egypt:
"Assemble yourselves on the mountains of Samaria; *e*
    see the great unrest within her
    and the oppression among her people."

¹⁰"They do not know how to do right, *f* " declares the LORD,
    "who hoard plunder*g* and loot in their fortresses." *h*

¹¹Therefore this is what the Sovereign LORD says:

"An enemy will overrun the land;
    he will pull down your strongholds
    and plunder your fortresses. *i* "

¹²This is what the LORD says:

"As a shepherd saves from the lion's *j* mouth
    only two leg bones or a piece of an ear,
so will the Israelites be saved,
those who sit in Samaria
    on the edge of their beds
    and in Damascus on their couches. *a* *k* "

¹³"Hear this and testify*l* against the house of Jacob," declares
the Lord, the LORD God Almighty.

¹⁴"On the day I punish Israel for her sins,
    I will destroy the altars of Bethel; *m*
the horns of the altar will be cut off
    and fall to the ground.

a 12 The meaning of the Hebrew for this line is uncertain.

3:6
a Isa 14:24-27;
45:7

3:7
b Ge 18:17;
Da 9:22;
Jn 15:15;
Rev 10:7
c Jer 23:22

3:8
d Jer 20:9;
Jnh 1:1-3;
3:1-3;
Ac 4:20

3:9
e Am 4:1; 6:1

3:10
f Jer 4:22;
Am 5:7; 6:12
g Hab 2:8
h Zep 1:9

3:11
i Am 2:5; 6:14

3:12
j 1Sa 17:34
k Am 6:4

3:13
l Eze 2:7

3:14
m Am 5:5-6

3:15
a Jer 36:22
b Jdg 3:20
c 1Ki 22:39

¹⁵I will tear down the winter house*a*
   along with the summer house;*b*
the houses adorned with ivory*c* will be destroyed
   and the mansions will be demolished,"
                    declares the LORD.

Chapter 4 Theme _____

4:1
d Ps 22:12;
Eze 39:18
e Am 3:9
f Am 2:8;
5:11; 8:6

4 Hear this word, you cows of Bashan*d* on Mount Samaria,*e*
   you women who oppress the poor and crush the needy
   and say to your husbands, "Bring us some drinks! *f* "
²The Sovereign LORD has sworn by his holiness:
   "The time will surely come
   when you will be taken away*g* with hooks,
      the last of you with fishhooks.

4:2
g Am 6:8

³You will each go straight out
   through breaks in the wall,*h*
   and you will be cast out toward Harmon,*a* "
                    declares the LORD.

4:3
h Eze 12:5

⁴"Go to Bethel and sin;
   go to Gilgal*i* and sin yet more.
Bring your sacrifices every morning,*j*
   your tithes*k* every three years.*b l*

4:4
i Hos 4:15
j Nu 28:3
k Dt 14:28
l Eze 20:39;
Am 5:21-22

⁵Burn leavened bread*m* as a thank offering
   and brag about your freewill offerings*n*—
boast about them, you Israelites,
   for this is what you love to do,"
                    declares the Sovereign LORD.

4:5
m Lev 7:13
n Lev 22:18-21

⁶"I gave you empty stomachs*c* in every city
   and lack of bread in every town,
   yet you have not returned to me,"
                    declares the LORD.*o*

4:6
o Isa 3:1;
Jer 5:3;
Hag 2:17

⁷"I also withheld rain from you
   when the harvest was still three months away.
I sent rain on one town,
   but withheld it from another. *p*
One field had rain;
   another had none and dried up.

4:7
p Ex 9:4,26;
Dt 11:17;
2Ch 7:13

⁸People staggered from town to town for water*q*
   but did not get enough to drink,
   yet you have not returned*r* to me,"
                    declares the LORD.*s*

4:8
q Eze 4:16-17
r Jer 3:7
s Jer 14:4

a 3 Masoretic Text; with a different word division of the Hebrew (see Septuagint) *out,*
O mountain of oppression *b 4* Or *tithes on the third day* *c 6* Hebrew *you cleanness of teeth*

9"Many times I struck your gardens and vineyards,
    I struck them with blight and mildew.ᵃ
Locusts devoured your fig and olive trees,ᵇ
    yet you have not returnedᶜ to me,"
                            declares the LORD.

10"I sent plaguesᵈ among you
    as I did to Egypt.
I killed your young men with the sword,
    along with your captured horses.
I filled your nostrils with the stench of your camps,
    yet you have not returned to me,"
                            declares the LORD.ᵉ

11"I overthrew some of you
    as Iᵃ overthrew Sodom and Gomorrah.ᶠ
You were like a burning stick snatched from the fire,
    yet you have not returned to me,"
                            declares the LORD.

12"Therefore this is what I will do to you, Israel,
    and because I will do this to you,
    prepare to meet your God, O Israel."

13He who forms the mountains,ᵍ
    creates the wind,
    and reveals his thoughtsʰ to man,
he who turns dawn to darkness,
    and treads the high places of the earthⁱ—
    the LORD God Almighty is his name.ʲ

Chapter 5 Theme _____

5 Hear this word, O house of Israel, this lamentᵏ I take up concerning you:

2"Fallen is Virginˡ Israel,
    never to rise again,
deserted in her own land,
    with no one to lift her up.ᵐ"

3This is what the Sovereign LORD says:

"The city that marches out a thousand strong for Israel
    will have only a hundred left;
the town that marches out a hundred strong
    will have only ten left.ⁿ"

4This is what the LORD says to the house of Israel:

ᵃ11 Hebrew God

4:9
ᵃ Dt 28:22
ᵇ Joel 1:7
ᶜ Jer 3:10;
Hag 2:17

4:10
ᵈ Ex 9:3;
Dt 28:27
ᵉ Isa 9:13

4:11
ᶠ Ge 19:24;
Jer 23:14

4:13
ᵍ Ps 65:6
ʰ Da 2:28
ⁱ Mic 1:3
ʲ Isa 47:4;
Am 5:8,27; 9:6

5:1
ᵏ Eze 19:1

5:2
ˡ Jer 14:17
ᵐ Jer 50:32;
Am 8:14

5:3
ⁿ Isa 6:13;
Am 6:9

5:4
a Isa 55:3;
Jer 29:13

"Seek me and live;^a

5 do not seek Bethel,
do not go to Gilgal,^b
do not journey to Beersheba.^c
For Gilgal will surely go into exile,
and Bethel will be reduced to nothing.^{a d}"

5:5
b 1Sa 11:14;
Am 4:4
c Am 8:14
d 1Sa 7:16

⁶Seek^e the LORD and live,^f
or he will sweep through the house of Joseph like a fire;^g
it will devour,
and Bethel^h will have no one to quench it.

5:6
e Isa 55:6
f ver 14
g Dt 4:24
h Am 3:14

⁷You who turn justice into bitternessⁱ
and cast righteousness to the ground
⁸(he who made the Pleiades and Orion,^j
who turns blackness into dawn^k
and darkens day into night,^l
who calls for the waters of the sea
and pours them out over the face of the land—
the LORD is his name^m—

5:7
i Am 6:12

⁹he flashes destruction on the stronghold
and brings the fortified city to ruin),ⁿ
¹⁰you hate the one who reproves in court^o
and despise him who tells the truth.^p

5:8
j Job 9:9
k Isa 42:16
l Ps 104:20;
Am 8:9
m Ps 104:6-9;
Am 4:13

¹¹You trample on the poor^q
and force him to give you grain.
Therefore, though you have built stone mansions,^r
you will not live in them;
though you have planted lush vineyards,
you will not drink their wine.^s

5:9
n Mic 5:11

¹²For I know how many are your offenses
and how great your sins.

You oppress the righteous and take bribes
and you deprive the poor of justice in the courts.^t
¹³Therefore the prudent man keeps quiet in such times,
for the times are evil.

5:10
o Isa 29:21
p 1Ki 22:8

¹⁴Seek good, not evil,
that you may live.
Then the LORD God Almighty will be with you,
just as you say he is.
¹⁵Hate evil,^u love good;
maintain justice in the courts.
Perhaps the LORD God Almighty will have mercy^v
on the remnant^w of Joseph.

5:11
q Am 8:6
r Am 3:15
s Mic 6:15

5:12
t Isa 5:23;
Am 2:6-7

5:15
u Ps 97:10;
Ro 12:9
v Joel 2:14
w Mic 5:7,8

a 5 Or grief; or wickedness; Hebrew aven, a reference to Beth Aven (a derogatory name for Bethel)

¹⁶Therefore this is what the Lord, the L<small>ORD</small> God Almighty, says:

"There will be wailing^a in all the streets
    and cries of anguish in every public square.
The farmers^b will be summoned to weep
    and the mourners to wail.
¹⁷There will be wailing in all the vineyards,
    for I will pass through^c your midst,"

              says the L<small>ORD</small>.^d

¹⁸Woe to you who long
    for the day of the L<small>ORD</small>!^e
Why do you long for the day of the L<small>ORD</small>?
    That day will be darkness,^f not light.^g
¹⁹It will be as though a man fled from a lion
    only to meet a bear,
as though he entered his house
    and rested his hand on the wall
    only to have a snake bite him.^h
²⁰Will not the day of the L<small>ORD</small> be darkness, not light—
    pitch-dark, without a ray of brightness?ⁱ

²¹"I hate, I despise your religious feasts;^j
    I cannot stand your assemblies.^k
²²Even though you bring me burnt offerings and
        grain offerings,
    I will not accept them.
Though you bring choice fellowship offerings,^a
    I will have no regard for them.^{l m}
²³Away with the noise of your songs!
    I will not listen to the music of your harps.ⁿ
²⁴But let justice^o roll on like a river,
    righteousness like a never-failing stream!^p

²⁵"Did you bring me sacrifices^q and offerings
    forty years^r in the desert, O house of Israel?
²⁶You have lifted up the shrine of your king,
    the pedestal of your idols,
    the star of your god^b—
    which you made for yourselves.
²⁷Therefore I will send you into exile beyond Damascus,"
    says the L<small>ORD</small>, whose name is God Almighty.^s

Chapter 6 Theme

6 Woe to you^t who are complacent in Zion,
    and to you who feel secure on Mount Samaria,

---

^a22 Traditionally *peace offerings*   ^b26 Or *lifted up Sakkuth your king / and Kaiwan your idols, / your star-gods*; Septuagint *lifted up the shrine of Molech / and the star of your god Rephan, / their idols*

¹⁶
^aJer 9:17
^bJoel 1:11

5:17
^cEx 12:12
^dIsa 16:10;
Jer 48:33

5:18
^eJoel 1:15
^fJoel 2:2
^gIsa 5:19,30;
Jer 30:7

5:19
^hJob 20:24;
Isa 24:17-18;
Jer 15:2-3; 48:44

5:20
ⁱIsa 13:10;
Zep 1:15

5:21
^jLev 26:31
^kIsa 1:11-16

5:22
^lAm 4:4;
Mic 6:6-7
^mIsa 66:3

5:23
ⁿAm 6:5

5:24
^oJer 22:3
^pMic 6:8

5:25
^qIsa 43:23
^rDt 32:17

5:27
^sAm 4:13;
Ac 7:42-43*

6:1
^tLk 6:24

6:1
a Isa 32:9-11

6:2
b Ge 10:10
c 2Ki 18:34
d 2Ch 26:6
e Na 3:8

6:3
f Isa 56:12;
Am 9:10

6:4
g Eze 34:2-3;
Am 3:12

6:5
h Isa 5:12;
Am 5:23
i 1Ch 15:16

6:6
j Am 2:8
k Eze 9:4

6:8
l Ge 22:16;
Heb 6:13
m Lev 26:30
n Ps 47:4
o Am 4:2
p Dt 32:19

6:9
q Am 5:3

6:10
r 1Sa 31:12
s Am 8:3

6:11
t Am 3:15
u Isa 55:11

6:12
v Hos 10:4
w Am 5:7

6:13
x Job 8:15;
Isa 28:14-15

you notable men of the foremost nation,
to whom the people of Israel come!*a*
²Go to Calneh*b* and look at it;
go from there to great Hamath,*c*
and then go down to Gath*d* in Philistia.
Are they better off than*e* your two kingdoms?
Is their land larger than yours?
³You put off the evil day
and bring near a reign of terror.*f*
⁴You lie on beds inlaid with ivory
and lounge on your couches.
You dine on choice lambs
and fattened calves.*g*
⁵You strum away on your harps*h* like David
and improvise on musical instruments.*i*
⁶You drink wine*j* by the bowlful
and use the finest lotions,
but you do not grieve*k* over the ruin of Joseph.
⁷Therefore you will be among the first to go into exile;
your feasting and lounging will end.

⁸The Sovereign Lord has sworn by himself*l*—the Lord God Almighty declares:

"I abhor*m* the pride of Jacob*n*
and detest his fortresses;
I will deliver up*o* the city
and everything in it.*p*"

⁹If ten*q* men are left in one house, they too will die. ¹⁰And if a relative who is to burn the bodies*r* comes to carry them out of the house and asks anyone still hiding there, "Is anyone with you?" and he says, "No," then he will say, "Hush!*s* We must not mention the name of the Lord."

¹¹For the Lord has given the command,
and he will smash the great house*t* into pieces
and the small house into bits.*u*

¹²Do horses run on the rocky crags?
Does one plow there with oxen?
But you have turned justice into poison*v*
and the fruit of righteousness into bitterness*w*—
¹³you who rejoice in the conquest of Lo Debar*a*
and say, "Did we not take Karnaim*b* by our own strength?*x*"

a 13 *Lo Debar* means *nothing.*   *b* 13 *Karnaim* means *horns; horn* here symbolizes strength.

[14] For the Lord God Almighty declares,
"I will stir up a nation[a] against you, O house of Israel,
that will oppress you all the way
from Lebo[a] Hamath[b] to the valley of the Arabah.[c]"

Chapter 7 Theme _____

7 This is what the Sovereign Lord showed me:[d] He was preparing swarms of locusts[e] after the king's share had been harvested and just as the second crop was coming up. [2] When they had stripped the land clean,[f] I cried out, "Sovereign Lord, forgive! How can Jacob survive?[g] He is so small![h]"

[3] So the Lord relented.[i]

"This will not happen," the Lord said.[j]

[4] This is what the Sovereign Lord showed me: The Sovereign Lord was calling for judgment by fire;[k] it dried up the great deep and devoured[l] the land. [5] Then I cried out, "Sovereign Lord, I beg you, stop! How can Jacob survive? He is so small![m]"

[6] So the Lord relented.[n]

"This will not happen either," the Sovereign Lord said.

[7] This is what he showed me: The Lord was standing by a wall that had been built true to plumb, with a plumb line in his hand. [8] And the Lord asked me, "What do you see,[o] Amos?[p]"

"A plumb line,[q]" I replied.

Then the Lord said, "Look, I am setting a plumb line among my people Israel; I will spare them no longer.[r]

[9] "The high places of Isaac will be destroyed
and the sanctuaries[s] of Israel will be ruined;
with my sword I will rise against the house of
Jeroboam.[t]"

[10] Then Amaziah the priest of Bethel[u] sent a message to Jeroboam[v] king of Israel: "Amos is raising a conspiracy[w] against you in the very heart of Israel. The land cannot bear all his words.[x] [11] For this is what Amos is saying:

"'Jeroboam will die by the sword,
and Israel will surely go into exile,
away from their native land.'"

[12] Then Amaziah said to Amos, "Get out, you seer! Go back to the land of Judah. Earn your bread there and do your prophesying there.[y] [13] Don't prophesy anymore at Bethel, because this is the king's sanctuary and the temple of the kingdom.[z]"

[14] Amos answered Amaziah, "I was neither a prophet[a] nor a

---

a 14 Or *from the entrance to*

6:14
a Jer 5:15
b 1Ki 8:65
c Am 3:11

7:1
d Am 8:1
e Joel 1:4

7:2
f Ex 10:15
g Isa 37:4
h Eze 11:13

7:3
i Dt 32:36;
Jer 26:19;
Jnh 3:10
j Hos 11:8

7:4
k Isa 66:16
l Dt 32:22

7:5
m ver 1-2;
Joel 2:17

7:6
n Jnh 3:10

7:8
o Jer 1:11,13
p Isa 28:17;
La 2:8;
Am 8:2
q 2Ki 21:13
r Jer 15:6;
Eze 7:2-9

7:9
s Lev 26:31
t 2Ki 15:9;
Isa 63:18;
Hos 10:8

7:10
u 1Ki 12:32
v 2Ki 14:23
w Jer 38:4
x Jer 26:8-11

7:12
y Mt 8:34

7:13
z Am 2:12;
Ac 4:18

7:14
a 2Ki 2:5; 4:38

7:15
a 2Sa 7:8
b Jer 7:1-2;
Eze 2:3-4

prophet's son, but I was a shepherd, and I also took care of syc-amore-fig trees. ¹⁵But the LORD took me from tending the flock*a* and said to me, 'Go, prophesy to my people Israel.'*b* ¹⁶Now then, hear the word of the LORD. You say,

7:16
c Eze 20:46;
Mic 2:6

> "'Do not prophesy against*c* Israel,
> and stop preaching against the house of Isaac.'

¹⁷"Therefore this is what the LORD says:

7:17
d Hos 4:13
e 2Ki 17:6;
Eze 4:13;
Hos 9:3

> "'Your wife will become a prostitute*d* in the city,
> and your sons and daughters will fall by the sword.
> Your land will be measured and divided up,
> and you yourself will die in a pagan*a* country.
> And Israel will certainly go into exile,
> away from their native land.*e*'"

Chapter 8 Theme

8:2
f Jer 24:3
g Am 7:8
h Eze 7:2-9

8 This is what the Sovereign LORD showed me: a basket of ripe fruit. ²"What do you see,*f* Amos?*g*" he asked.

"A basket of ripe fruit," I answered.

Then the LORD said to me, "The time is ripe for my people Israel; I will spare them no longer.*h*

8:3
i Am 5:16
j Am 5:23; 6:10

³"In that day," declares the Sovereign LORD, "the songs in the temple will turn to wailing.*bi* Many, many bodies—flung every-where! Silence!*j*"

8:4
k Pr 30:14
l Ps 14:4;
Am 2:7

> ⁴Hear this, you who trample the needy
> and do away with the poor*k* of the land,*l*

⁵saying,

8:5
m 2Ki 4:23;
Ne 13:15-16;
Hos 12:7;
Mic 6:10-11

> "When will the New Moon be over
> that we may sell grain,
> and the Sabbath be ended
> that we may market wheat?"—
> skimping the measure,
> boosting the price
> and cheating with dishonest scales,*m*

8:6
n Am 2:6

> ⁶buying the poor with silver
> and the needy for a pair of sandals,
> selling even the sweepings with the wheat.*n*

8:7
o Am 6:8
p Hos 8:13

⁷The LORD has sworn by the Pride of Jacob:*o* "I will never forget*p* anything they have done.

> ⁸"Will not the land tremble*q* for this,
> and all who live in it mourn?

8:8
q Hos 4:3

a 17 Hebrew *an unclean*   *b 3* Or *"the temple singers will wail*

The whole land will rise like the Nile;
    it will be stirred up and then sink
    like the river of Egypt.*a*

9"In that day," declares the Sovereign LORD,

"I will make the sun go down at noon
    and darken the earth in broad daylight.*b*
10I will turn your religious feasts into mourning
    and all your singing into weeping.
I will make all of you wear sackcloth*c*
    and shave your heads.
I will make that time like mourning for an only son*d*
    and the end of it like a bitter day.*e*

11"The days are coming," declares the Sovereign LORD,
    "when I will send a famine through the land—
not a famine of food or a thirst for water,
    but a famine of hearing the words of the LORD.*f*
12Men will stagger from sea to sea
    and wander from north to east,
searching for the word of the LORD,
    but they will not find it.*g*

13"In that day

"the lovely young women and strong young men
    will faint because of thirst.*h*
14They who swear by the shame*a* of Samaria,
    or say, 'As surely as your god lives, O Dan,'*i*
    or, 'As surely as the god*b* of Beersheba *j* lives'—
they will fall,
    never to rise again.*k*"

Chapter 9 Theme

9 I saw the Lord standing by the altar, and he said:

"Strike the tops of the pillars
    so that the thresholds shake.
Bring them down on the heads*l* of all the people;
    those who are left I will kill with the sword.
Not one will get away,
    none will escape.
2Though they dig down to the depths of the grave,*cm*
    from there my hand will take them.
Though they climb up to the heavens,*n*
    from there I will bring them down.*o*

---

*a*14 Or *by Ashima; or by the idol*   *b*14 Or *power*   *c*2 Hebrew *to Sheol*

8:8
*a*Ps 18:7;
Jer 46:8;
Am 9:5

8:9
*b*Job 5:14;
Isa 59:9-10;
Jer 15:9;
Am 5:8;
Mic 3:6

8:10
*c*Jer 48:37
*d*Jer 6:26;
Zec 12:10
*e*Eze 7:18

8:11
*f*1Sa 3:1;
2Ch 15:3;
Eze 7:26

8:12
*g*Eze 20:3,31

8:13
*h*Isa 41:17;
Hos 2:3

8:14
*i*1Ki 12:29
*j*Am 5:5
*k*Am 5:2

9:1
*l*Ps 68:21

9:2
*m*Ps 139:8
*n*Jer 51:53
*o*Ob 4

³Though they hide themselves on the top of Carmel,*a*
  there I will hunt them down and seize them.*b*
Though they hide from me at the bottom of the sea,
  there I will command the serpent to bite them.*c*
⁴Though they are driven into exile by their enemies,
  there I will command the sword*d* to slay them.
I will fix my eyes upon them
  for evil*e* and not for good.*f*"*g*

9:4
d Lev 26:33;
Eze 5:12
e Jer 21:10
f Jer 39:16
g Jer 44:11

⁵The Lord, the LORD Almighty,
  he who touches the earth and it melts,*h*
  and all who live in it mourn—
the whole land rises like the Nile,
  then sinks like the river of Egypt*i*—

⁶he who builds his lofty palace*a* in the heavens
  and sets its foundation*b* on the earth,
who calls for the waters of the sea
  and pours them out over the face of the land—
  the LORD is his name.*j*

⁷"Are not you Israelites
  the same to me as the Cushites*c*?"*k*
                                    declares the LORD.

"Did I not bring Israel up from Egypt,
  the Philistines from Caphtor*d l*
  and the Arameans from Kir?*m*

9:7
k Isa 20:4; 43:3
l Dt 2:23;
Jer 47:4
m 2Ki 16:9;
Isa 22:6;
Am 1:5; 2:10

⁸"Surely the eyes of the Sovereign LORD
  are on the sinful kingdom.
I will destroy it
  from the face of the earth—
yet I will not totally destroy
  the house of Jacob,"
                                    declares the LORD.*n*

⁹"For I will give the command,
  and I will shake the house of Israel
    among all the nations
as grain*o* is shaken in a sieve,*p*
  and not a pebble will reach the ground.
¹⁰All the sinners among my people
  will die by the sword,
all those who say,
  'Disaster will not overtake or meet us.'*q*

¹¹"In that day I will restore
  David's fallen tent.

a 6 The meaning of the Hebrew for this phrase is uncertain.   *b* 6 The meaning of the Hebrew for this word is uncertain.   *c* 7 That is, people from the upper Nile region   *d* 7 That is, Crete

I will repair its broken places,
　　restore its ruins,
　　and build it as it used to be,^{a}
^{12}so that they may possess the remnant of Edom^b
　　and all the nations that bear my name,^{ac}"
　　　declares the LORD, who will do these things.^{d}

^{13}"The days are coming," declares the LORD,

"when the reaper will be overtaken by the plowman^e
　　and the planter by the one treading grapes.
New wine will drip from the mountains
　　and flow from all the hills.^{f}
^{14}I will bring back my exiled^b people Israel;
　　they will rebuild the ruined cities^g and live in them.
They will plant vineyards and drink their wine;
　　they will make gardens and eat their fruit.^{h}
^{15}I will plant^i Israel in their own land,
　　never again to be uprooted
　　from the land I have given them,"
　　　　　　　　　　　　says the LORD your God.^{j}

^{a} 12 Hebrew; Septuagint *so that the remnant of men / and all the nations that bear my name may seek* ⌊*the Lord*⌋　^{b} 14 Or *will restore the fortunes of my*

9:11
^{a} Ps 80:12

9:12
^{b} Nu 24:18
^{c} Isa 43:7
^{d} Ac 15:16-17*

9:13
^{e} Lev 26:5
^{f} Joel 3:18

9:14
^{g} Isa 61:4
^{h} Jer 30:18;
31:28;
Eze 28:25-26

9:15
^{i} Isa 60:21
^{j} Jer 24:6;
Eze 34:25-28;
37:12,25

Theme of Amos:

SEGMENT DIVISIONS

Author:

Date:

Purpose:

Key Words:

		CHAPTER THEMES
		1
		2
		3
		4
		5
		6
		7
		8
		9

OBADIAH

G od said that whoever touched Israel touched the apple (pupil) of his eye. According to Obadiah 1:10-14, Edom had touched God's eye.

Scholars are divided about whether the incident referred to in these verses occurred during the reign of Jehoram (853-841 B.C.), when the Philistines and the Arabs invaded Jerusalem or during Babylon's sieges of Jerusalem (between 605 and 586 B.C.). However, the exact date is not critical to the message of the book. What we do know is that in both instances Edom did not respond as God wanted, and thus comes this report from the Lord. It came as a word through "the Lord's servant," which is the meaning of Obadiah's name.

∾ THINGS TO DO

1. Read this book once without stopping in order to get an overview of Obadiah's message.

2. Read through Obadiah, and in a distinctive way mark the key words listed on the OBADIAH AT A GLANCE chart on page 1586.

3. Remember that Jacob and Esau were brothers, born to Rebekah and Isaac. If you want to refresh your memory, read Genesis 27:1–28:9 and 32:1–33:20; Romans 9:10-13; and Numbers 20:14-21. Genesis 36 gives the genealogy of Esau and says, "Esau (that is, Edom)." It also names Esau as the father of the Edomites.

Although the people of Edom (descendants of Esau) and Israel (descendants of Jacob) are related (Amos 1:11, 12), biblical history records many conflicts between them. Look at the map on page 1584 and notice the proximity of Edom to Israel. Edom was a constant threat to Israel, repeatedly thwarting the nation and blocking Judean access to the Gulf of Aqaba.

4. Now read through Obadiah again, asking the five W's and an H. Ask questions such as: Who is writing? To whom? Why? What is being written about? What is going to happen? To whom? How? Summarize your observations in the margin of the text.

5. Look at the map and find the Negev and the other places mentioned at the end of Obadiah. These are real lands and real people, and what God says will happen to them *will* happen.

6. Since Obadiah is just one chapter, record the theme (subject) of each paragraph on OBADIAH AT A GLANCE and then fill in the rest of the chart, including the theme of Obadiah.

7. The day of the Lord is an important day prophetically. Beginning on page 2178 you will find a chart titled THE DAY OF THE LORD. Record your insights on the day of the Lord on this chart. As you do so, note the reference (book, chapter, and verse) that you took your information from so you can find it later.

∾ THINGS TO THINK ABOUT

1. Sometimes when tragic and unjust things happen, we wonder where God is. If he is righteous, just, and omnipotent, why doesn't he intervene? What do you learn from Obadiah that helps answer these questions? What do you learn from this for your own life?

2. How should we respond to the tragedies of others, the dark hours of our enemies? What does God think when we use their tragedy to our advantage?

1:15
a Jer 50:29;
Hab 2:8

As you have done, it will be done to you;
  your deeds*a* will return upon your own head.
¹⁶Just as you drank on my holy hill,
  so all the nations will drink*b* continually;
they will drink and drink
  and be as if they had never been.

1:16
b Jer 25:15;
49:12

¹⁷But on Mount Zion will be deliverance;*c*
  it will be holy,*d*
and the house of Jacob
  will possess its inheritance.
¹⁸The house of Jacob will be a fire
  and the house of Joseph a flame;
the house of Esau will be stubble,
  and they will set it on fire and consume*e* it.
There will be no survivors
  from the house of Esau."

1:17
c Am 9:11-15
d Isa 4:3

1:18
e Zec 12:6

                              The Lord has spoken.

¹⁹People from the Negev will occupy
  the mountains of Esau,
and people from the foothills will possess
  the land of the Philistines.*f*
They will occupy the fields of Ephraim and Samaria,*g*
  and Benjamin will possess Gilead.

1:19
f Isa 11:14
g Jer 31:5

²⁰This company of Israelite exiles who are in Canaan
  will possess ˻the land˼ as far as Zarephath;*h*
the exiles from Jerusalem who are in Sepharad
  will possess the towns of the Negev.*i*
²¹Deliverers will go up on*a* Mount Zion
  to govern the mountains of Esau.
  And the kingdom will be the Lord's.*j*

1:20
h 1Ki 17:9-10
i Jer 33:13

1:21
j Ps 22:28;
Zec 14:9,16;
Rev 11:15

a 21 Or *from*

Theme of Obadiah:

SEGMENT DIVISIONS

		PARAGRAPH THEMES
		VERSES 1-9
		VERSES 10-14
		VERSES 15-21

Author:

Date:

Purpose:

Key Words:

  the day

  Esau, Esau's (Edom)

  Jacob (Judah)

  the nations (all nations)

  Mount Zion (my holy hill)

  declares the Lord (or any phrase having to do with the Lord speaking or reporting)

JONAH

*J*ust before God commissioned Amos and then Hosea as prophets to the northern kingdom to warn Israel of the impending invasion by the Assyrians, he appointed the prophet Jonah to go to Nineveh, the capital of Assyria. Fifty years later, in 722 B.C., Assyria would take the northern kingdom into captivity.

God knew what Assyria would do. Why then did he bother to send Jonah to the wicked city of Nineveh? Because of who God is. The focus of Jonah is not a man trapped in the belly of a great fish; the focus is people engraved on the heart of God.

∽ THINGS TO DO

1. Before you read through Jonah, look up 2 Kings 14:23-27, which mentions Jonah and his ministry during the reign of Jeroboam II, king of Israel. At that time Shalmaneser IV was king of Assyria.

2. In the margin of each chapter list everything you learn about God. Note his character and ways as well as his response to a sinful people and a "wrong-way" prophet.

3. In a distinctive way mark the key words listed on the JONAH AT A GLANCE chart on page 1591.

4. Record the theme of each chapter on JONAH AT A GLANCE and in the text next to the chapter number. Then fill in the rest of the chart.

5. Contrast Jonah's heart with God's heart. Record your insights in the margin of chapter 4.

∽ THINGS TO THINK ABOUT

1. What or who evokes compassion in your heart? How does your heart compare with God's? Does it long for the same things? Why?

2. Is there something that you know God wants you to do that you haven't done? What can you learn from Jonah's life?

3. How did Jesus view the story of Jonah? Read Matthew 12:39-41; 16:4. Will you accept as truth what Jesus accepted as fact—or did Jesus compare his resurrection to a mythological tale?

∽∽∽∽∽∽

Chapter 1 Theme _____

1:1
a Mt 12:39-41
b 2Ki 14:25

1 The word of the LORD came to Jonah*a* son of Amittai:*b* 2"Go to the great city of Nineveh*c* and preach against it, because its wickedness has come up before me."

1:2
c Ge 10:11

3But Jonah ran*d* away from the LORD and headed for Tarshish. He went down to Joppa,*e* where he found a ship bound for that port. After paying the fare, he went aboard and sailed for Tarshish to flee from the LORD.

1:3
d Ps 139:7
e Jos 19:46;
Ac 9:36,43

4Then the LORD sent a great wind on the sea, and such a violent storm arose that the ship threatened to break up.*f* 5All the sailors were afraid and each cried out to his own god. And they threw the cargo into the sea to lighten the ship.*g*

1:4
f Ps 107:23-26

But Jonah had gone below deck, where he lay down and fell into a deep sleep. 6The captain went to him and said, "How can you

1:5
g Ac 27:18-19

1587

sleep? Get up and call[a] on your god! Maybe he will take notice of us, and we will not perish."[b]

7Then the sailors said to each other, "Come, let us cast lots to find out who is responsible for this calamity."[c] They cast lots and the lot fell on Jonah.

8So they asked him, "Tell us, who is responsible for making all this trouble for us? What do you do? Where do you come from? What is your country? From what people are you?"

9He answered, "I am a Hebrew and I worship the LORD, the God of heaven,[d] who made the sea and the land.[e]"

10This terrified them and they asked, "What have you done?" (They knew he was running away from the LORD, because he had already told them so.)

Jonah's Journey

11The sea was getting rougher and rougher. So they asked him, "What should we do to you to make the sea calm down for us?"

12"Pick me up and throw me into the sea," he replied, "and it will become calm. I know that it is my fault that this great storm has come upon you."[f]

13Instead, the men did their best to row back to land. But they could not, for the sea grew even wilder than before.[g] 14Then they cried to the LORD, "O LORD, please do not let us die for taking this man's life. Do not hold us accountable for killing an innocent man,[h] for you, O LORD, have done as you pleased."[i] 15Then they took Jonah and threw him overboard, and the raging sea grew calm.[j] 16At this the men greatly feared[k] the LORD, and they offered a sacrifice to the LORD and made vows to him.

17But the LORD provided a great fish to swallow Jonah,[l] and Jonah was inside the fish three days and three nights.

Chapter 2 Theme

2 From inside the fish Jonah prayed to the LORD his God. 2He said:

"In my distress I called to the LORD,[m]
  and he answered me.
From the depths of the grave[a] I called for help,
  and you listened to my cry.

[a]2 Hebrew *Sheol*

1:6
[a]Jnh 3:8
[b]Ps 107:28

1:7
[c]Jos 7:10-18;
1Sa 14:42

1:9
[d]Ac 17:24
[e]Ps 146:6

1:12
[f]2Sa 24:17;
1Ch 21:17

1:13
[g]Pr 21:30

1:14
[h]Dt 21:8
[i]Ps 115:3

1:15
[j]Ps 107:29;
Lk 8:24

1:16
[k]Mk 4:41

1:17
[l]Mt 12:40; 16:4;
Lk 11:30

2:2
[m]Ps 18:6; 120:1

³You hurled me into the deep,*a*
   into the very heart of the seas,
   and the currents swirled about me;
 all your waves and breakers
   swept over me.*b*
⁴I said, 'I have been banished
   from your sight;*c*
 yet I will look again
   toward your holy temple.'
⁵The engulfing waters threatened me,*a*
   the deep surrounded me;
   seaweed was wrapped around my head.*d*
⁶To the roots of the mountains I sank down;
   the earth beneath barred me in forever.
 But you brought my life up from the pit,
   O L*ord* my God.

⁷"When my life was ebbing away,
   I remembered*e* you, L*ord*,

2:4
c Ps 31:22

2:5
d Ps 69:1-2

2:7
e Ps 77:11-12   *a* 5 Or *waters were at my throat*

THE RULERS AND PROPHETS OF JONAH'S TIME

Kings of Assyria	Shalman-eser 783 773 / Ashurdan III 773 755 / Ashur-nirari 755 745 / Tiglath-Pileser III (Tiglath-Pileser III) 745 727	Shalmaneser V ↓727-722		Nineveh fell to Babylon in 612 B.C.
Kings of Israel (Northern Kingdom)	Jehoash (Joash) ↓ 782 / Jeroboam II 798 793 753 / Zechariah ↓↓ Shallum one month ↓↓ Menahem 752 742 / Pekahiah ↓742-740 / Pekah 752 732 / Hoshea 732 722	Northern ten tribes taken captive by King Shalmaneser V of Assyria in 722 B.C.		
Jonah and His Contemporary Prophets (Northern Kingdom)	← Elisha 796 / Jonah 784 772 / Amos 767 755 / Hosea 755 714			
Kings of Judah (Southern Kingdom)	Amaziah 796 790 767 / Uzziah or Azariah 750 739 / ↓Jotham 731 / Ahaz 715			
Prophets to Judah (Southern Kingdom)	Joel 825 809 / Isaiah 739 / Micah 733 701 681			

850	840	830	820	810	800	790	780	770	760	750	740	730	720	710	700	690

1589

and my prayer^a rose to you,
to your holy temple.^b

⁸"Those who cling to worthless idols^c
forfeit the grace that could be theirs.
⁹But I, with a song of thanksgiving,
will sacrifice^d to you.
What I have vowed^e I will make good.
Salvation^f comes from the LORD."

¹⁰And the LORD commanded the fish, and it vomited Jonah onto dry land.

Chapter 3 Theme _____

3 Then the word of the LORD came to Jonah^g a second time: ²"Go to the great city of Nineveh and proclaim to it the message I give you."

³Jonah obeyed the word of the LORD and went to Nineveh. Now Nineveh was a very important city—a visit required three days. ⁴On the first day, Jonah started into the city. He proclaimed: "Forty more days and Nineveh will be overturned." ⁵The Ninevites believed God. They declared a fast, and all of them, from the greatest to the least, put on sackcloth.^h

⁶When the news reached the king of Nineveh, he rose from his throne, took off his royal robes, covered himself with sackcloth and sat down in the dust.ⁱ ⁷Then he issued a proclamation in Nineveh:

"By the decree of the king and his nobles:

Do not let any man or beast, herd or flock, taste anything; do not let them eat or drink.^j ⁸But let man and beast be covered with sackcloth. Let everyone call^k urgently on God. Let them give up their evil ways and their violence. ⁹Who knows?^l God may yet relent and with compassion turn^m from his fierce anger so that we will not perish."

¹⁰When God saw what they did and how they turned from their evil ways, he had compassionⁿ and did not bring upon them the destruction^o he had threatened.^p

Chapter 4 Theme _____

4 But Jonah was greatly displeased and became angry.^q ²He prayed to the LORD, "O LORD, is this not what I said when I was still at home? That is why I was so quick to flee to Tarshish. I knew^r that you are a gracious and compassionate God, slow to anger and abounding in love,^s a God who relents from sending calamity.^t ³Now, O LORD, take away my life,^u for it is better for me to die^v than to live."

2:7
^a 2Ch 30:27
^b Ps 11:4; 18:6

2:8
^c 2Ki 17:15;
Jer 10:8

2:9
^d Ps 50:14,23;
Hos 14:2
^e Ecc 5:4-5
^f Ps 3:8

3:1
^g Jnh 1:1

3:5
^h Da 9:3;
Lk 11:32

3:6
ⁱ Job 2:8,13;
Eze 27:30-31

3:7
^j 2Ch 20:3

3:8
^k Ps 130:1;
Jnh 1:6

3:9
^l 2Sa 12:22
^m Joel 2:14

3:10
ⁿ Am 7:6
^o Jer 18:8
^p Ex 32:14

4:1
^q ver 4;
Lk 15:28

4:2
^r Jer 20:7-8
^s Ex 34:6;
Ps 86:5,15
^t Joel 2:13

4:3
^u 1Ki 19:4
^v Job 7:15

4:4
aMt 20:11-15

⁴But the LORD replied, "Have you any right to be angry?"*a*

⁵Jonah went out and sat down at a place east of the city. There he made himself a shelter, sat in its shade and waited to see what would happen to the city. ⁶Then the LORD God provided a vine and made it grow up over Jonah to give shade for his head to ease his discomfort, and Jonah was very happy about the vine. ⁷But at dawn the next day God provided a worm, which chewed the vine so that it withered.*b* ⁸When the sun rose, God provided a scorching east wind, and the sun blazed on Jonah's head so that he grew faint. He wanted to die, and said, "It would be better for me to die than to live."

4:7
bJoel 1:12

⁹But God said to Jonah, "Do you have a right to be angry about the vine?"

"I do," he said. "I am angry enough to die."

¹⁰But the LORD said, "You have been concerned about this vine, though you did not tend it or make it grow. It sprang up overnight and died overnight. ¹¹But Nineveh*c* has more than a hundred and twenty thousand people who cannot tell their right hand from their left, and many cattle as well. Should I not be concerned*d* about that great city?"

4:11
cJnh 1:2; 3:2
dJnh 3:10

JONAH AT A GLANCE

Theme of Jonah:

	SEGMENT DIVISIONS		
Author:		CHAPTER THEMES	
Date:			
		1	
Purpose:			
Key Words:			
concerned (compassionate)		2	
relent(s)			
turn, give up (turned)			
prayer (prayed)		3	
perish (die)			
Lord			
cried to the Lord (called to the Lord)		4	

MICAH

Micah knew his calling and was ready to fulfill it, for Micah knew his God. What a contrast he is to the prophet Jonah! Micah, whose name means "who is like Jehovah," reminds a rebellious people that "the Lord is coming from his dwelling place."

∾ THINGS TO DO

1. Micah 1:1 gives the historical setting of Micah. Read it carefully and answer as many of the five W's and an H as you can concerning the who, when, where, why, what, and how of this book. Consult the historical chart at the beginning of Micah to see the book in context.

You will note that the reign of the three kings of Judah covers the years 750-686 B.C. Remember that Assyria conquered the northern kingdom in 722 B.C. and Babylon conquered the southern kingdom in 586 B.C.

2. For the historical background of the kings of Judah mentioned in Micah 1:1, read 2 Kings 15:32 through 20:21 and 2 Chronicles 27:1 through 33:20.

3. Read one chapter at a time. As you observe the text of each chapter:

   a. Mark the key words listed on the MICAH AT A GLANCE chart on page 1605. You will find it helpful to record these on an index card that you can use as a bookmark while you study Micah.

   b. Watch for references to time, such as *when, then, in that day, in the last days.* You might want to draw a symbol or note in some other way the references to time.

   c. Since Micah's prophecy concerns Samaria (representing the northern kingdom of Israel) and Jerusalem (representing the southern kingdom of Judah), next to the word *Samaria* in Micah 1:1 put "NK" for northern kingdom. Next to the word *Jerusalem* put "SK" for southern kingdom.

   As you observe the text, watch which kingdom Micah is referring to. Observe what is said regarding their sins, the consequences of their sin, their future, and the remnant. If it will help, list your insights in the margin.

   d. Watch what God is going to do and to whom. Always note to whom Micah is referring.

   e. In the margin list everything you learn about Micah and what he is to do.

   f. Record the theme or subject of each chapter on the line next to the chapter number in the text and on MICAH AT A GLANCE. When you finish the last chapter of Micah, complete the chart.

4. Beginning on page 2178 you will find a chart titled THE DAY OF THE LORD. Record your insights from Micah on the last days if you think these pertain to the day of the Lord. As you do so, note the reference (book, chapter, and verse) from which you took your information so you can find it later.

∾ THINGS TO THINK ABOUT

1. Review what you have learned about God the Father and the Son in this book. Meditate on these truths. Tell God you want to know him more intimately and ask him to open the eyes of your understanding. Ask him to show you how to live in light of who he is.

2. Micah 4:12 says the nations do not know the thoughts of the Lord, nor do they understand his plan. Yet the child of God can know these things through studying his Word. Amos said, "Surely the Sovereign LORD does nothing without revealing his plan to his servants the prophets" (3:7). God's

secret counsel and his plan for the future is in the Word of God. Are you ordering your life in such a way that you take time to study his Word?

3. What have you learned about the unchanging love and compassion of God in pardoning your sins? Are you living accordingly?

4. Although you may not be able to trust in others, can you trust in God? Are you? Can he trust you? In Micah 6:6-8 God tells you how to approach him and what he requires. Will you live accordingly?

Chapter 1 Theme

1 The word of the LORD that came to Micah of Moresheth[a] during the reigns of Jotham,[b] Ahaz[c] and Hezekiah, kings of Judah[d]— the vision[e] he saw concerning Samaria and Jerusalem.

[2]Hear, O peoples, all of you,[f]
　　listen, O earth[g] and all who are in it,
　that the Sovereign LORD may witness[h] against you,
　　the Lord from his holy temple.[i]
[3]Look! The LORD is coming from his dwelling[j] place;
　　he comes down and treads the
　　　　high places of the earth.[k]
[4]The mountains melt[l] beneath him
　　and the valleys split apart,[m]
　like wax before the fire,
　　like water rushing down a slope.
[5]All this is because of Jacob's transgression,
　　because of the sins of the house of Israel.
　What is Jacob's transgression?
　　Is it not Samaria?[n]
　What is Judah's high place?
　　Is it not Jerusalem?

[6]"Therefore I will make Samaria a heap of rubble,
　　a place for planting vineyards.
　I will pour her stones[o] into the valley
　　and lay bare her foundations.[p]
[7]All her idols[q] will be broken to pieces;
　　all her temple gifts will be burned with fire;
　　I will destroy all her images.[r]
　Since she gathered her gifts from the wages of prostitutes,[s]
　　as the wages of prostitutes they will again be used."

[8]Because of this I will weep[t] and wail;
　　I will go about barefoot and naked.
　I will howl like a jackal
　　and moan like an owl.

Cross references

1:1 a Jer 26:18; b 1Ch 3:12; c 1Ch 3:13; d Hos 1:1; e Isa 1:1
1:2 f Ps 50:7; g Jer 6:19; h Ge 31:50; Dt 4:26; Isa 1:2; i Ps 11:4
1:3 j Isa 18:4; k Am 4:13
1:4 l Ps 46:2,6; m Nu 16:31; Na 1:5
1:5 n Am 8:14
1:6 o Am 5:11; p Eze 13:14
1:7 q Eze 6:6; r Dt 9:21; s Dt 23:17-18
1:8 t Isa 15:3

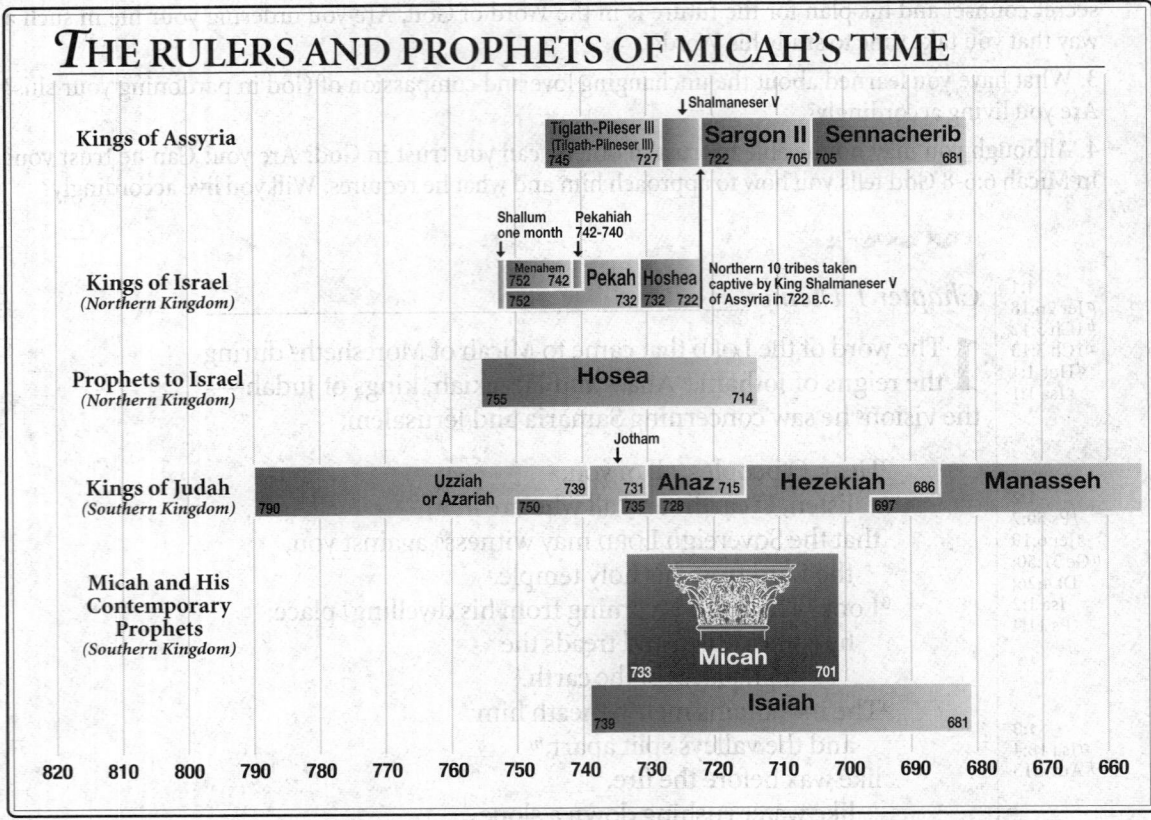

THE RULERS AND PROPHETS OF MICAH'S TIME

Kings of Assyria
Tiglath-Pileser III (Tilgath-Pileser III) 745 — 727 | Shalmaneser V | Sargon II 722 — 705 | Sennacherib 705 — 681

Kings of Israel (Northern Kingdom)
Shallum one month | Pekahiah 742-740 | Menahem 752 — 742 | 752 | Pekah | Hoshea 732 — 722 | 732 | Northern 10 tribes taken captive by King Shalmaneser V of Assyria in 722 B.C.

Prophets to Israel (Northern Kingdom)
Hosea 755 — 714

Kings of Judah (Southern Kingdom)
Jotham | Uzziah or Azariah 790 — 750 | 739 | 731 735 | Ahaz 715 728 | Hezekiah 686 697 | Manasseh

Micah and His Contemporary Prophets (Southern Kingdom)
Micah 733 — 701 | Isaiah 739 — 681

820 810 800 790 780 770 760 750 740 730 720 710 700 690 680 670 660

⁹For her wound*a* is incurable;
  it has come to Judah.*b*
It*a* has reached the very gate*c* of my people,
  even to Jerusalem itself.
¹⁰Tell it not in Gath*b*;
  weep not at all.*c*
In Beth Ophrah*d*
  roll in the dust.
¹¹Pass on in nakedness*d* and shame,
  you who live in Shaphir.*e*
Those who live in Zaanan*f*
  will not come out.
Beth Ezel is in mourning;
  its protection is taken from you.
¹²Those who live in Maroth*g* writhe in pain,
  waiting for relief,*e*

a9 Or *He*   *b10 Gath* sounds like the Hebrew for *tell*.   *c10* Hebrew; Septuagint may suggest *not in Acco*. The Hebrew for *in Acco* sounds like the Hebrew for *weep*.   *d10 Beth Ophrah* means *house of dust*.   *e11 Shaphir* means *pleasant*.   *f11 Zaanan* sounds like the Hebrew for *come out*.   *g12 Maroth* sounds like the Hebrew for *bitter*.

1:9
a Jer 46:11
b 2Ki 18:13
c Isa 3:26

1:11
d Eze 23:29

1:12
e Jer 14:19

1:13
a Jos 10:3

because disaster has come from the LORD,
    even to the gate of Jerusalem.
¹³You who live in Lachish,^a^a
    harness the team to the chariot.
You were the beginning of sin
    to the Daughter of Zion,
for the transgressions of Israel
    were found in you.

1:14
b 2Ki 16:8
c Jos 15:44
d Jer 15:18

¹⁴Therefore you will give parting gifts^b
    to Moresheth Gath.
The town of Aczib^{bc} will prove deceptive^d
    to the kings of Israel.

1:15
e Jos 15:44
f Jos 12:15

¹⁵I will bring a conqueror against you
    who live in Mareshah.^c^e
He who is the glory of Israel
    will come to Adullam.^f

1:16
g Job 1:20

¹⁶Shave^g your heads in mourning
    for the children in whom you delight;
make yourselves as bald as the vulture,
    for they will go from you into exile.

Chapter 2 Theme

2 Woe to those who plan iniquity,
    to those who plot evil on their beds!^h
At morning's light they carry it out
    because it is in their power to do it.

2:1
h Ps 36:4

²They covet fieldsⁱ and seize them,
    and houses, and take them.
They defraud^j a man of his home,
    a fellowman of his inheritance.

2:2
i Isa 5:8
j Jer 22:17

³Therefore, the LORD says:

    "I am planning disaster^k against this people,
        from which you cannot save yourselves.
    You will no longer walk proudly,^l
        for it will be a time of calamity.
⁴In that day men will ridicule you;
    they will taunt you with this mournful song:
'We are utterly ruined;^m
    my people's possession is divided up.
He takes it from me!
    He assigns our fields to traitors.'"

2:3
k Jer 18:11;
Am 3:1-2
l Isa 2:12

2:4
m Jer 4:13

^a 13 *Lachish* sounds like the Hebrew for *team*.   ^b 14 *Aczib* means *deception*.   ^c 15 *Mareshah* sounds like the Hebrew for *conqueror*.

⁵Therefore you will have no one in the assembly of the Lord
    to divide the land[a] by lot.

⁶"Do not prophesy," their prophets say.
    "Do not prophesy about these things;
    disgrace[b] will not overtake us.[c]"
⁷Should it be said, O house of Jacob:
    "Is the Spirit of the Lord angry?
    Does he do such things?"

    "Do not my words do good[d]
    to him whose ways are upright?[e]
⁸Lately my people have risen up
    like an enemy.
You strip off the rich robe
    from those who pass by without a care,
    like men returning from battle.
⁹You drive the women of my people
    from their pleasant homes.[f]
You take away my blessing
    from their children forever.
¹⁰Get up, go away!
    For this is not your resting place,[g]
because it is defiled,[h]
    it is ruined, beyond all remedy.
¹¹If a liar and deceiver[i] comes and says,
    'I will prophesy for you plenty of wine and beer,'
    he would be just the prophet for this people![j]

¹²"I will surely gather all of you, O Jacob;
    I will surely bring together the remnant[k] of Israel.
I will bring them together like sheep in a pen,
    like a flock in its pasture;
    the place will throng with people.
¹³One who breaks open the way will go up before[l] them;
    they will break through the gate and go out.
Their king will pass through before them,
    the Lord at their head."

Chapter 3 Theme

3 Then I said,

    "Listen, you leaders[m] of Jacob,
    you rulers of the house of Israel.
Should you not know justice,
 ² you who hate good and love evil;
who tear the skin from my people
    and the flesh from their bones;[n]

2:5
[a] Jos 18:4

2:6
[b] Mic 6:16
[c] Am 2:12

2:7
[d] Ps 119:65
[e] Ps 15:2; 84:11

2:9
[f] Jer 10:20

2:10
[g] Dt 12:9
[h] Lev 18:25-29;
Ps 106:38-39

2:11
[i] Jer 5:31
[j] Isa 30:10

2:12
[k] Mic 4:7;
5:7; 7:18

2:13
[l] Isa 52:12

3:1
[m] Jer 5:5

3:2
[n] Ps 53:4;
Eze 22:27

³who eat my people's flesh,^a
    strip off their skin
    and break their bones in pieces;^b
who chop them up like meat for the pan,
    like flesh for the pot?^c"

3:3
^aPs 14:4
^bZep 3:3
^cEze 11:7

⁴Then they will cry out to the LORD,
    but he will not answer them.^d
At that time he will hide his face^e from them
    because of the evil they have done.

3:4
^dPs 18:41;
Isa 1:15
^eDt 31:17

⁵This is what the LORD says:

"As for the prophets
    who lead my people astray,^f
if one feeds them,
    they proclaim 'peace';
if he does not,
    they prepare to wage war against him.

3:5
^fIsa 3:12; 9:16

⁶Therefore night will come over you, without visions,
    and darkness, without divination.^g
The sun will set for the prophets,^h
    and the day will go dark for them.

3:6
^gIsa 8:19-22
^hIsa 29:10

⁷The seers will be ashamedⁱ
    and the diviners disgraced.^j
They will all cover their faces
    because there is no answer from God."

3:7
ⁱMic 7:16
^jIsa 44:25

⁸But as for me, I am filled with power,
    with the Spirit of the LORD,
    and with justice and might,
to declare to Jacob his transgression,
    to Israel his sin.^k

3:8
^kIsa 58:1

⁹Hear this, you leaders of the house of Jacob,
    you rulers of the house of Israel,
who despise justice
    and distort all that is right;^l

3:9
^lPs 58:1-2;
Isa 1:23

¹⁰who build^m Zion with bloodshed,ⁿ
    and Jerusalem with wickedness.^o

3:10
^mJer 22:13
ⁿHab 2:12
^oEze 22:27

¹¹Her leaders judge for a bribe,
    her priests teach for a price,
    and her prophets tell fortunes for money.^p
Yet they lean upon the LORD and say,
    "Is not the LORD among us?
    No disaster will come upon us."^q

3:11
^pIsa 1:23;
Jer 6:13;
Hos 4:8,18
^qJer 7:4

¹²Therefore because of you,
    Zion will be plowed like a field,

Jerusalem will become a heap of rubble,[a]
    the temple hill a mound overgrown with thickets.

Chapter 4 Theme

4 In the last days

the mountain[b] of the Lord's temple will be established
    as chief among the mountains;
it will be raised above the hills,[c]
    and peoples will stream to it.[d]

2Many nations will come and say,

"Come, let us go up to the mountain of the LORD,[e]
    to the house of the God of Jacob.[f]
He will teach us his ways,[g]
    so that we may walk in his paths."
The law will go out from Zion,
    the word of the LORD from Jerusalem.
3He will judge between many peoples
    and will settle disputes for strong nations far and wide.[h]
They will beat their swords into plowshares
    and their spears into pruning hooks.[i]
Nation will not take up sword against nation,
    nor will they train for war anymore.[j]
4Every man will sit under his own vine
    and under his own fig tree,[k]
and no one will make them afraid,[l]
    for the LORD Almighty has spoken.[m]
5All the nations may walk
    in the name of their gods;[n]
we will walk in the name of the LORD
    our God for ever and ever.[o]

6"In that day," declares the LORD,

"I will gather the lame;
    I will assemble the exiles[p]
    and those I have brought to grief.[q]
7I will make the lame a remnant,[r]
    those driven away a strong nation.
The LORD will rule over them in Mount Zion
    from that day and forever.[s]
8As for you, O watchtower of the flock,
    O stronghold[a] of the Daughter of Zion,

a8 Or hill

Cross references

3:12
[a] Jer 26:18

4:1
[b] Zec 8:3
[c] Eze 17:22
[d] Ps 22:27;
86:9;
Jer 3:17

4:2
[e] Jer 31:6
[f] Zec 2:11;
14:16
[g] Ps 25:8-9;
Isa 54:13

4:3
[h] Isa 11:4
[i] Joel 3:10
[j] Isa 2:4

4:4
[k] 1Ki 4:25
[l] Lev 26:6
[m] Isa 1:20;
Zec 3:10

4:5
[n] 2Ki 17:29
[o] Jos 24:14-15;
Isa 26:8;
Zec 10:12

4:6
[p] Ps 147:2
[q] Eze 34:13,16;
37:21;
Zep 3:19

4:7
[r] Mic 2:12
[s] Da 7:14;
Lk 1:33;
Rev 11:15

4:8
a Isa 1:26

the former dominion will be restored[a] to you;
kingship will come to the Daughter of Jerusalem."

[9] Why do you now cry aloud—
have you no king?[b]
Has your counselor perished,
that pain seizes you like that of a woman in labor?[c]

4:9
b Jer 8:19
c Jer 30:6

[10] Writhe in agony, O Daughter of Zion,
like a woman in labor,
for now you must leave the city
to camp in the open field.
You will go to Babylon;[d]
there you will be rescued.
There the LORD will redeem[e] you
out of the hand of your enemies.

4:10
d 2Ki 20:18;
Isa 43:14
e Isa 48:20

[11] But now many nations
are gathered against you.
They say, "Let her be defiled,
let our eyes gloat[f] over Zion!"
[12] But they do not know
the thoughts of the LORD;
they do not understand his plan,[g]
he who gathers them like sheaves to the threshing floor.

4:11
f La 2:16;
Ob 1:12

[13] "Rise and thresh, O Daughter of Zion,
for I will give you horns of iron;
I will give you hoofs of bronze
and you will break to pieces many nations."[h]

You will devote their ill-gotten gains to the LORD,
their wealth to the Lord of all the earth.

4:12
g Isa 55:8;
Ro 11:33-34

Chapter 5 Theme _____

4:13
h Da 2:44

5 Marshal your troops, O city of troops,[a]
for a siege is laid against us.
They will strike Israel's ruler
on the cheek[i] with a rod.

5:1
i La 3:30

[2] "But you, Bethlehem[j] Ephrathah,[k]
though you are small among the clans[b] of Judah,
out of you will come for me
one who will be ruler over Israel,
whose origins[c] are from of old,[l]
from ancient times.[d]"[m]

5:2
j Jn 7:42
k Ge 48:7
l Ps 102:25
m Mt 2:6*

a 1 Or *Strengthen your walls, O walled city*   b 2 Or *rulers*   c 2 Hebrew *goings out*
d 2 Or *from days of eternity*

³Therefore Israel will be abandoned
  until the time when she who is in labor gives birth
and the rest of his brothers return
  to join the Israelites.

⁴He will stand and shepherd his flock*a*
  in the strength of the LORD,
  in the majesty of the name of the LORD his God.
And they will live securely, for then his greatness*b*
  will reach to the ends of the earth.
⁵ And he will be their peace.*c*

When the Assyrian invades*d* our land
  and marches through our fortresses,
we will raise against him seven shepherds,
  even eight leaders of men.*e*
⁶They will rule*a* the land of Assyria with the sword,
  the land of Nimrod*f* with drawn sword.*bg*
He will deliver us from the Assyrian
  when he invades our land
  and marches into our borders.*h*

⁷The remnant*i* of Jacob will be
  in the midst of many peoples
like dew from the LORD,
  like showers on the grass,*j*
which do not wait for man
  or linger for mankind.
⁸The remnant of Jacob will be among the nations,
  in the midst of many peoples,
like a lion among the beasts of the forest,*k*
  like a young lion among flocks of sheep,
which mauls and mangles*l* as it goes,
  and no one can rescue.*m*
⁹Your hand will be lifted up*n* in triumph
    over your enemies,
  and all your foes will be destroyed.

¹⁰"In that day," declares the LORD,

"I will destroy your horses from among you
  and demolish your chariots.*o*
¹¹I will destroy the cities*p* of your land
  and tear down all your strongholds.*q*
¹²I will destroy your witchcraft
  and you will no longer cast spells.*r*

a6 Or *crush*   b6 Or *Nimrod in its gates*

5:4
a Isa 40:11; 49:9;
Eze 34:11-15,23;
Mic 7:14
b Isa 52:13;
Lk 1:32

5:5
c Isa 9:6;
Lk 2:14;
Col 1:19-20
d Isa 8:7
e Isa 10:24-27

5:6
f Ge 10:8
g Zep 2:13
h Na 2:11-13

5:7
i Mic 2:12
j Isa 44:4

5:8
k Ge 49:9
l Mic 4:13;
Zec 10:5
m Ps 50:22;
Hos 5:14

5:9
n Ps 10:12

5:10
o Hos 14:3;
Zec 9:10

5:11
p Isa 6:11
q Hos 10:14;
Am 5:9

5:12
r Dt 18:10-12;
Isa 2:6; 8:19

5:13
a Eze 6:9;
Zec 13:2

¹³I will destroy your carved images
    and your sacred stones from among you;
you will no longer bow down
    to the work of your hands.*a*

5:14
b Ex 34:13

¹⁴I will uproot from among you your Asherah poles*ab*
    and demolish your cities.

5:15
c Isa 65:12

¹⁵I will take vengeance*c* in anger and wrath
    upon the nations that have not obeyed me."

Chapter 6 Theme

6:1
d Ps 50:1;
Eze 6:2

6 Listen to what the LORD says:

"Stand up, plead your case before the mountains;*d*
    let the hills hear what you have to say.

6:2
e Dt 32:1
f Hos 12:2
g Ps 50:7

²Hear,*e* O mountains, the LORD's accusation;*f*
    listen, you everlasting foundations of the earth.
For the LORD has a case against his people;
    he is lodging a charge*g* against Israel.

6:3
h Jer 2:5

³"My people, what have I done to you?
    How have I burdened*h* you? Answer me.

6:4
i Dt 7:8
j Ex 4:16
k Ps 77:20
l Ex 15:20

⁴I brought you up out of Egypt
    and redeemed you from the land of slavery.*i*
I sent Moses*j* to lead you,
    also Aaron*k* and Miriam.*l*

⁵My people, remember
    what Balak*m* king of Moab counseled
    and what Balaam son of Beor answered.

6:5
m Nu 22:5-6
n Nu 25:1
o Jos 5:9-10
p Jdg 5:11;
1Sa 12:7

Remember ⌊your journey⌋ from Shittim*n* to Gilgal,*o*
    that you may know the righteous acts*p* of the LORD."

⁶With what shall I come before the LORD
    and bow down before the exalted God?
Shall I come before him with burnt offerings,
    with calves a year old?*q*

6:6
q Ps 40:6-8;
51:16-17

⁷Will the LORD be pleased with thousands of rams,*r*
    with ten thousand rivers of oil?*s*
Shall I offer my firstborn*t* for my transgression,
    the fruit of my body for the sin of my soul?*u*

6:7
r Isa 40:16
s Ps 50:8-10
t Lev 18:21
u 2Ki 16:3

⁸He has showed you, O man, what is good.
    And what does the LORD require of you?
To act justly*v* and to love mercy
    and to walk humbly*w* with your God.*x*

6:8
v Isa 1:17;
Jer 22:3
w Isa 57:15
x Dt 10:12-13;
1Sa 15:22;
Hos 6:6

⁹Listen! The LORD is calling to the city—
    and to fear your name is wisdom—

a 14 That is, symbols of the goddess Asherah

"Heed the rod and the One who appointed it.ᵃ

¹⁰Am I still to forget, O wicked house,
  your ill-gotten treasures
  and the short ephah,ᵇ which is accursed?ᵃ
¹¹Shall I acquit a man with dishonest scales,ᵇ
  with a bag of false weights?
¹²Her rich men are violent;ᶜ
  her people are liarsᵈ
  and their tongues speak deceitfully.ᵉ
¹³Therefore, I have begun to destroyᶠ you,
  to ruin you because of your sins.
¹⁴You will eat but not be satisfied;ᵍ
  your stomach will still be empty.ᶜ
 You will store up but save nothing,ʰ
  because what you save I will give to the sword.
¹⁵You will plant but not harvest;ⁱ
  you will press olives but not use the oil on yourselves,
  you will crush grapes but not drink the wine.ʲ
¹⁶You have observed the statutes of Omriᵏ
  and all the practices of Ahab'sˡ house,
  and you have followed their traditions.ᵐ
 Therefore I will give you over to ruinⁿ
  and your people to derision;
  you will bear the scornᵒ of the nations.ᵈ"

Chapter 7 Theme

7 What misery is mine!
 I am like one who gathers summer fruit
  at the gleaning of the vineyard;
 there is no cluster of grapes to eat,
  none of the early figs that I crave.
²The godly have been swept from the land;ᵖ
  not one upright man remains.
 All men lie in wait to shed blood;�q
  each hunts his brother with a net.ʳ
³Both hands are skilled in doing evil;ˢ
  the ruler demands gifts,
 the judge accepts bribes,
  the powerful dictate what they desire—
  they all conspire together.
⁴The best of them is like a brier,ᵗ
  the most upright worse than a thorn hedge.

ᵃ9 The meaning of the Hebrew for this line is uncertain. ᵇ10 An ephah was a dry measure.
ᶜ14 The meaning of the Hebrew for this word is uncertain. ᵈ16 Septuagint; Hebrew *scorn due
my people*

6:10
ᵃEze 45:9-10;
Am 3:10;
8:4-6

6:11
ᵇLev 19:36;
Hos 12:7

6:12
ᶜIsa 1:23
ᵈIsa 3:8
ᵉJer 9:3

6:13
ᶠIsa 1:7;
6:11

6:14
ᵍIsa 9:20
ʰIsa 30:6

6:15
ⁱDt 28:38;
Jer 12:13
ʲAm 5:11;
Zep 1:13

6:16
ᵏ1Ki 16:25
ˡ1Ki 16:29-33
ᵐJer 7:24
ⁿJer 25:9
ᵒJer 51:51

7:2
ᵖPs 12:1
qMic 3:10
ʳJer 5:26

7:3
ˢPr 4:16

7:4
ᵗEze 2:6

7:4
a Isa 22:5;
Hos 9:7

The day of your watchmen has come,
    the day God visits you.
    Now is the time of their confusion.[a]
5 Do not trust a neighbor;
    put no confidence in a friend.[b]
Even with her who lies in your embrace
    be careful of your words.

7:5
b Jer 9:4

6 For a son dishonors his father,
    a daughter rises up against her mother,[c]
a daughter-in-law against her mother-in-law—
    a man's enemies are the members
        of his own household.[d]

7:6
c Eze 22:7
d Mt 10:35-36*

7 But as for me, I watch in hope[e] for the LORD,
    I wait for God my Savior;
    my God will hear[f] me.

7:7
e Ps 130:5;
Isa 25:9
f Ps 4:3

8 Do not gloat over me,[g] my enemy!
    Though I have fallen, I will rise.[h]
Though I sit in darkness,
    the LORD will be my light.[i]

7:8
g Pr 24:17
h Ps 37:24;
Am 9:11
i Isa 9:2

9 Because I have sinned against him,
    I will bear the LORD's wrath,[j]
until he pleads my case
    and establishes my right.
He will bring me out into the light;
    I will see his righteousness.[k]

7:9
j La 3:39-40
k Isa 46:13

10 Then my enemy will see it
    and will be covered with shame,[l]
she who said to me,
    "Where is the LORD your God?"
My eyes will see her downfall;[m]
    even now she will be trampled[n] underfoot
    like mire in the streets.

7:10
l Ps 35:26
m Isa 51:23
n Zec 10:5

11 The day for building your walls[o] will come,
    the day for extending your boundaries.
12 In that day people will come to you
    from Assyria and the cities of Egypt,
even from Egypt to the Euphrates
    and from sea to sea
    and from mountain to mountain.[p]

7:11
o Isa 54:11

7:12
p Isa 19:23-25

13 The earth will become desolate because
      of its inhabitants,
    as the result of their deeds.[q]

7:13
q Isa 3:10-11

14 Shepherd[r] your people with your staff,[s]
    the flock of your inheritance,

7:14
r Mic 5:4
s Ps 23:4

which lives by itself in a forest,
    in fertile pasturelands.[a]
Let them feed in Bashan and Gilead[a]
    as in days long ago.

15"As in the days when you came out of Egypt,
    I will show them my wonders.[b]"

16Nations will see and be ashamed,[c]
    deprived of all their power.
They will lay their hands on their mouths
    and their ears will become deaf.
17They will lick dust like a snake,
    like creatures that crawl on the ground.
They will come trembling out of their dens;
    they will turn in fear[d] to the LORD our God
    and will be afraid of you.
18Who is a God like you,
    who pardons sin[e] and forgives[f] the transgression
    of the remnant[g] of his inheritance?[h]
You do not stay angry[i] forever
    but delight to show mercy.[j]
19You will again have compassion on us;
    you will tread our sins underfoot
    and hurl all our iniquities[k] into the depths of the sea.[l]
20You will be true to Jacob,
    and show mercy to Abraham,
as you pledged on oath to our fathers[m]
    in days long ago.

a 14 Or *in the middle of Carmel*

7:14
a Jer 50:19

7:15
b Ex 3:20;
Ps 78:12

7:16
c Isa 26:11

7:17
d Isa 25:3;
49:23; 59:19

7:18
e Isa 43:25;
Jer 50:20
f Ps 103:8-13
g Mic 2:12
h Ex 34:9
i Ps 103:9
j Jer 32:41

7:19
k Isa 43:25
l Jer 31:34

7:20
m Dt 7:8;
Lk 1:72

Theme of Micah:

SEGMENT DIVISIONS		CHAPTER THEMES
Author:		1
Date:		
Purpose:		2
Key Words:		
Samaria		
Jerusalem		3
Jacob (Jacob's)		
Israel (Israel's)		
Judah (Judah's)		
Zion		4
Assyrian		
demolish (destroy, ruin, ruined)		
remnant		5
in that day (in the last days)		
my (his, your) people('s) (mark these phrases only when they are referring to God)		6
		7

NAHUM

One hundred years had passed since Jonah went to Nineveh to proclaim its destruction. Now another prophet, Nahum, proclaims his vision from God regarding Nineveh, the capital of Assyria. What a sharp contrast between Nahum's prophetic message and the meaning of his name—comforter!

Assyria sat smugly on her throne. Under Shalmaneser V, Assyria had conquered Israel in 722 B.C. In 701 B.C. under Sennacherib's rule the Assyrians had invaded Judah. Sennacherib's field commander (Rabshakeh) had boasted to Judah that no gods of the nations they had conquered had been able to deliver their people. To Hezekiah, king of Judah, he proclaimed, "Do not let the god you depend on deceive you when he says, 'Jerusalem will not be handed over to the king of Assyria.' Surely you have heard what the kings of Assyria have done to all the countries, destroying them completely. And will you be delivered?" (2 Kings 19:10, 11).

But God did spare Judah. Sennacherib, king of Assyria, returned to Nineveh and died there.

Yet that wasn't the end of the story. God had a message for Nineveh, the capital of Assyria, who at the time of Nahum's prophecy sat at the pinnacle of wealth and power, secure behind her impregnable walls. Or so she thought.

∾ Things to Do

1. If you have time, read Jonah to see what God said to the people of Nineveh 100 years earlier and how they responded.

2. Read Nahum and mark the key words listed on the NAHUM AT A GLANCE chart on page 1612.

3. Study the historical chart on page 1607 to see the context of the book.

4. Now read Nahum chapter by chapter and do the following:

   a. Nahum tells us much about God. Carefully observe the text and then in the margin summarize what you learn about God. For instance, in 1:4 it says that God rules over nature. Write that in your list in the margin under the title "God" (△).

   b. Observe all you can about Nineveh. Watch for the repeated use of *Nineveh* and the pronouns which refer to Nineveh, such as *you* and *your*. Mark any reference to Nineveh that you missed. Then in the margin list what you learn about "Nineveh's Sin."

   c. Make a third list in the margin, "What Will Happen to Nineveh?"

5. Record the theme or subject of each chapter on NAHUM AT A GLANCE and in the text on the line next to the chapter number. Also record the theme of the book and complete any other information requested on the chart.

∾ Things to Think About

1. What do you learn about the justice of God and the certainty of his Word from this book? Is this the kind of God you can trust? Why?

2. Is there anything that can stop God from doing what he says or plans?

3. Can compassionate people deliver this kind of a message? What if you were impressed by God to bring this kind of warning to others? Would you? What would motivate you or hinder you? By the way, remember the meaning of Nahum's name.

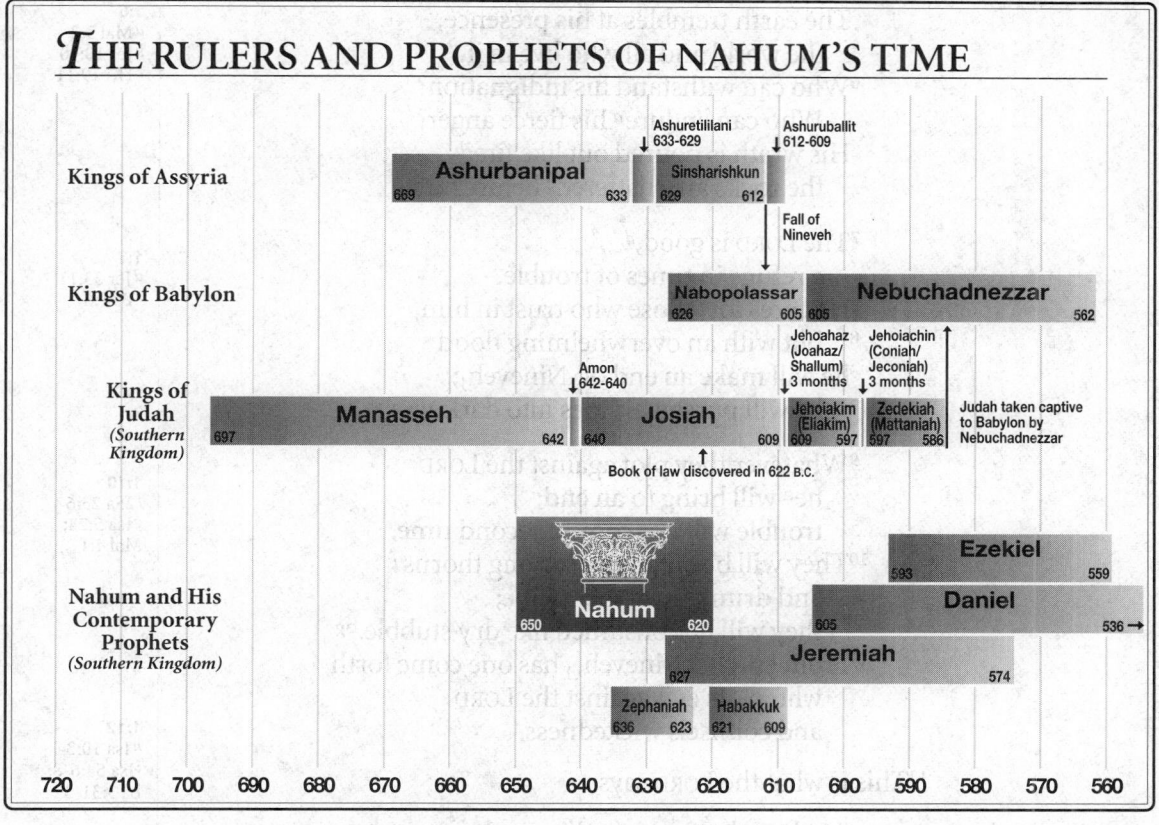

THE RULERS AND PROPHETS OF NAHUM'S TIME

Kings of Assyria

Ashuretililani ↓ 633-629   Ashuruballit ↓ 612-609

| Ashurbanipal | | Sinsharishkun | |
669 · 633 · 629 · 612

Fall of Nineveh

Kings of Babylon

| Nabopolassar | Nebuchadnezzar |
626 · 605 · 605 · 562

Kings of Judah (Southern Kingdom)

Amon ↓ 642-640

Jehoahaz (Joahaz/Shallum) ↓ 3 months   Jehoiachin (Coniah/Jeconiah) ↓ 3 months

| Manasseh | Josiah | Jehoiakim (Eliakim) | Zedekiah (Mattaniah) |
697 · 642 · 640 · 609 · 609 · 597 · 597 · 586

Judah taken captive to Babylon by Nebuchadnezzar

Book of law discovered in 622 B.C.

Nahum and His Contemporary Prophets (Southern Kingdom)

Nahum 650 · 620

Ezekiel 593 · 559

Daniel 605 · 536 →

Jeremiah 627 · 574

Zephaniah 636 · 623   Habakkuk 621 · 609

720 710 700 690 680 670 660 650 640 630 620 610 600 590 580 570 560

1:1
a Isa 13:1; 19:1;
Jer 23:33-34
b Jnh 1:2;
Na 2:8;
Zep 2:13

Chapter 1 Theme _____

1 An oracle[a] concerning Nineveh.[b] The book of the vision of Nahum the Elkoshite.

²The LORD is a jealous[c] and avenging God;
  the LORD takes vengeance[d] and is filled with wrath.
The LORD takes vengeance on his foes
  and maintains his wrath against his enemies.
³The LORD is slow to anger[e] and great in power;
  the LORD will not leave the guilty unpunished.[f]
His way is in the whirlwind and the storm,
  and clouds[g] are the dust of his feet.
⁴He rebukes the sea and dries it up;
  he makes all the rivers run dry.
Bashan and Carmel[h] wither
  and the blossoms of Lebanon fade.
⁵The mountains quake[i] before him
  and the hills melt away.[j]

1:2
c Ex 20:5
d Dt 32:41;
Ps 94:1

1:3
e Ne 9:17
f Ex 34:7
g Ps 104:3

1:4
h Isa 33:9

1:5
i Ex 19:18
j Mic 1:4

The earth trembles at his presence,
the world and all who live in it.
⁶Who can withstand his indignation?
Who can endure*a* his fierce anger?
His wrath is poured out like fire;*b*
the rocks are shattered*c* before him.

⁷The LORD is good,*d*
a refuge in times of trouble.
He cares for*e* those who trust in him,
⁸ but with an overwhelming flood
he will make an end of ⌊Nineveh⌋;
he will pursue his foes into darkness.

⁹Whatever they plot against the LORD
he*a* will bring to an end;
trouble will not come a second time.
¹⁰They will be entangled among thorns*f*
and drunk from their wine;
they will be consumed like dry stubble.*bg*
¹¹From you, ⌊O Nineveh,⌋ has one come forth
who plots evil against the LORD
and counsels wickedness.

¹²This is what the LORD says:

"Although they have allies and are numerous,
they will be cut off*h* and pass away.
Although I have afflicted you, ⌊O Judah,⌋
I will afflict you no more.*i*
¹³Now I will break their yoke*j* from your neck
and tear your shackles away."

¹⁴The LORD has given a command concerning you,
⌊Nineveh⌋:
"You will have no descendants to bear your name.*k*
I will destroy the carved images*l* and cast idols
that are in the temple of your gods.
I will prepare your grave,*m*
for you are vile."

¹⁵Look, there on the mountains,
the feet of one who brings good news,*n*
who proclaims peace!*o*
Celebrate your festivals, *p* O Judah,
and fulfill your vows.

a 9 Or *What do you foes plot against the Lord? / He*   *b 10* The meaning of the Hebrew for this verse is uncertain.

Cross references (right column):

1:6
a Mal 3:2
b Jer 10:10
c 1Ki 19:11

1:7
d Jer 33:11
e Ps 1:6

1:10
f 2Sa 23:6
g Isa 5:24;
Mal 4:1

1:12
h Isa 10:34
i Isa 54:6-8;
La 3:31-32

1:13
j Isa 9:4

1:14
k Isa 14:22
l Mic 5:13
m Eze 32:22-23

1:15
n Isa 40:9;
Ro 10:15
o Isa 52:7
p Lev 23:2-4

> No more will the wicked invade you;[a]
>   they will be completely destroyed.

Chapter 2 Theme _____

2 An attacker[b] advances against you, ⌊Nineveh⌋.
  Guard the fortress,
    watch the road,
    brace yourselves,
    marshal all your strength!

[2]The LORD will restore[c] the splendor[d] of Jacob
    like the splendor of Israel,
  though destroyers have laid them waste
    and have ruined their vines.

[3]The shields of his soldiers are red;
    the warriors are clad in scarlet.[e]
  The metal on the chariots flashes
    on the day they are made ready;
    the spears of pine are brandished.[a]
[4]The chariots[f] storm through the streets,
    rushing back and forth through the squares.
  They look like flaming torches;
    they dart about like lightning.

[5]He summons his picked troops,
    yet they stumble[g] on their way.
  They dash to the city wall;
    the protective shield is put in place.
[6]The river gates[h] are thrown open
    and the palace collapses.
[7]It is decreed[b] that ⌊the city⌋
    be exiled and carried away.
  Its slave girls moan[i] like doves
    and beat upon their breasts.[j]
[8]Nineveh is like a pool,
    and its water is draining away.
  "Stop! Stop!" they cry,
    but no one turns back.
[9]Plunder the silver!
    Plunder the gold!
  The supply is endless,
    the wealth from all its treasures!

Cross references (left margin):
1:15 [a] Isa 52:1
2:1 [b] Jer 51:20
2:2 [c] Eze 37:23 [d] Isa 60:15
2:3 [e] Eze 23:14-15
2:4 [f] Jer 4:13
2:5 [g] Jer 46:12
2:6 [h] Na 3:13
2:7 [i] Isa 59:11 [j] Isa 32:12

[a] 3 Hebrew; Septuagint and Syriac / *the horsemen rush to and fro*   [b] 7 The meaning of the Hebrew for this word is uncertain.

¹⁰She is pillaged, plundered, stripped!
    Hearts melt, knees give way,
      bodies tremble, every face grows pale.ᵃ

¹¹Where now is the lions' den,ᵇ
    the place where they fed their young,
  where the lion and lioness went,
    and the cubs, with nothing to fear?
¹²The lion killedᶜ enough for his cubs
    and strangled the prey for his mate,
  filling his lairs with the kill
    and his dens with the prey.

¹³"I am againstᵈ you,"
    declares the Lᴏʀᴅ Almighty.
"I will burn up your chariots in smoke,ᵉ
    and the sword will devour your young lions.
  I will leave you no prey on the earth.
The voices of your messengers
    will no longer be heard."

Chapter 3 Theme

3   Woe to the city of blood,ᶠ
    full of lies,
full of plunder,
    never without victims!
²The crack of whips,
    the clatter of wheels,
galloping horses
    and jolting chariots!
³Charging cavalry,
    flashing swords
    and glittering spears!
Many casualties,
    piles of dead,
bodies without number,
    people stumbling over the corpsesᵍ—
⁴all because of the wanton lust of a harlot,
    alluring, the mistress of sorceries,ʰ
who enslaved nations by her prostitutionⁱ
    and peoples by her witchcraft.

⁵"I am against ʲ you," declares the Lᴏʀᴅ Almighty.
    "I will lift your skirtsᵏ over your face.
I will show the nations your nakednessˡ
    and the kingdoms your shame.

2:10
ᵃIsa 29:22

2:11
ᵇIsa 5:29

2:12
ᶜJer 51:34

2:13
ᵈJer 21:13;
Na 3:5
ᵉPs 46:9

3:1
ᶠEze 22:2;
Mic 3:10

3:3
ᵍ2Ki 19:35;
Isa 34:3

3:4
ʰIsa 47:9
ⁱIsa 23:17;
Eze 16:25-29

3:5
ʲNa 2:13
ᵏJer 13:22
ˡIsa 47:3

3:6
a Job 9:31
b 1Sa 2:30;
Jer 51:37
c Isa 14:16

3:7
d Na 1:1
e Jer 15:5
f Isa 51:19

3:8
g Am 6:2
h Jer 46:25
i Isa 19:6-9

3:9
j 2Ch 12:3
k Eze 27:10
l Eze 30:5

3:10
m Isa 20:4
n Isa 13:16;
Hos 13:16

3:11
o Isa 49:26
p Isa 2:10

3:12
q Isa 28:4

3:13
r Isa 19:16;
Jer 50:37
s Na 2:6
t Isa 45:2

3:14
u 2Ch 32:4
v Na 2:1

3:15
w Joel 1:4

⁶I will pelt you with filth,ᵃ
   I will treat you with contemptᵇ
   and make you a spectacle.ᶜ
⁷All who see you will flee from you and say,
   'Ninevehᵈ is in ruins—who will mourn for her?'ᵉ
   Where can I find anyone to comfortᶠ you?"

⁸Are you better thanᵍ Thebes,ᵃ ʰ
   situated on the Nile,ⁱ
   with water around her?
The river was her defense,
   the waters her wall.
⁹Cushᵇ ʲ and Egypt were her boundless strength;
   Putᵏ and Libyaˡ were among her allies.
¹⁰Yet she was taken captiveᵐ
   and went into exile.
Her infants were dashedⁿ to pieces
   at the head of every street.
Lots were cast for her nobles,
   and all her great men were put in chains.
¹¹You too will become drunk;ᵒ
   you will go into hiding ᵖ
   and seek refuge from the enemy.

¹²All your fortresses are like fig trees
   with their first ripe fruit;
when they are shaken,
   the figsᑫ fall into the mouth of the eater.
¹³Look at your troops—
   they are all women!ʳ
The gatesˢ of your land
   are wide open to your enemies;
   fire has consumed their bars.ᵗ

¹⁴Draw water for the siege,ᵘ
   strengthen your defenses!ᵛ
Work the clay,
   tread the mortar,
   repair the brickwork!
¹⁵There the fire will devour you;
   the sword will cut you down
   and, like grasshoppers, consume you.
Multiply like grasshoppers,
   multiply like locusts! ʷ
¹⁶You have increased the number of your merchants
   till they are more than the stars of the sky,

INSIGHT

Thebes refers to
No Amon, the
Hebrew name for
No, the capital of
Egypt. Since
Nahum reminds
Nineveh of the fall
of Thebes (No
Amon), his
prophecy had to
come after 661 B.C.
and before Nine-
veh was destroyed
in 612 B.C. by the
Babylonians,
Medes, and
Scythians.

ᵃ8 Hebrew *No Amon* ᵇ9 That is, the upper Nile region

but like locusts they strip the land
and then fly away.
[17]Your guards are like locusts,[a]
your officials like swarms of locusts
that settle in the walls on a cold day—
but when the sun appears they fly away,
and no one knows where.

[18]O king of Assyria, your shepherds[a] slumber;[b]
your nobles lie down to rest.[c]
Your people are scattered[d] on the mountains
with no one to gather them.
[19]Nothing can heal your wound;[e]
your injury is fatal.
Everyone who hears the news about you
claps his hands[f] at your fall,
for who has not felt
your endless cruelty?

[a] 18 Or *rulers*

3:17
[a] Jer 51:27

3:18
[b] Ps 76:5-6
[c] Isa 56:10
[d] 1Ki 22:17

3:19
[e] Jer 30:13;
Mic 1:9
[f] Job 27:23;
La 2:15;
Zep 2:15

NAHUM AT A GLANCE

Theme of Nahum:

SEGMENT
DIVISIONS

		CHAPTER THEMES
1		
2		
3		

Author:

Date:

Purpose:

Key Words:
I am against you

I will

Nineveh (Assyria)

Judah (Jacob, Israel)

HABAKKUK

"T he righteous will live by his faith." This verse, which pierced Martin Luther's heart and as a result brought about a reformation, is from Habakkuk 2:4. Paul echoed it in Romans and Galatians, but its roots are in the Old Testament, where God affirms that salvation has always been by faith and faith alone.

And what is the setting of the verse that unshackled Luther and brought him into a vital relationship with the living God? You will discover this as you study Habakkuk, a book which ends with a crescendo of faith in anticipation of Judah's darkest of hours.

∾ THINGS TO DO

General Instructions

As you read Habakkuk it is critical for you to know whether God is speaking or Habakkuk is speaking. Since the book is only three chapters long, read through Habakkuk and note in the margin when God speaks or when Habakkuk speaks. Try it on your own, then look at the HABAKKUK AT A GLANCE chart on page 1620 for the segment divisions which show who is speaking when.

Chapter 1

1. An "oracle" can be translated "a burden." What is Habakkuk's burden; what is bothering him? Note this in the margin of chapter 1 where it is described.

2. Read through Habakkuk 1 and mark every reference to God (God, the Holy One, Lord, etc.) and every personal pronoun which refers to him. Then in the margin list everything you learn about God as a personality and note what he is going to do.

3. The Chaldeans, another name for the Babylonians, invaded the southern kingdom of Judah three times. In 605 B.C., Daniel and many nobles were taken captive. Then in 597 B.C., Ezekiel was taken captive. The third and final siege occurred in 586 B.C., when Jerusalem and the temple were destroyed. List in the margin everything you learn about the Chaldeans—what they will do and what will happen to them.

4. Study the historical chart on page 1615 and notice the relationship between the time of Habakkuk's writing and the Babylonian invasion.

Chapter 2

1. Mark every word that describes a proud man (e.g., *puffed up, arrogant, greedy,* etc). Also mark the pronouns. Then in the margin list what he is like and with whom he is contrasted.

2. Mark each use of the word *woe* and then observe to whom the woe is going to come, why it will come, and what will happen when it comes. If you want to, summarize this in the margin.

3. List in the margin what you learn about God.

Chapter 3

1. Habakkuk's prayer is written in a poetic form which is intensely emotional. A statement is made and then is followed by a similar statement which heightens the meaning or repeats the truth in another way. Read the prayer again, keeping its form in mind.

2. As you read, ask the five W's and an H: Who is doing what? To whom or what? When will it be done? Why will it be done? What specifically is going to happen? How? In the margin, list everything you learn about God from this chapter.

3. What does this chapter say about Habakkuk and his relationship to God? List it in the margin. Then compare what you write with 2:4. How is Habakkuk going to live? Have his circumstances changed?

4. Fill in the appropriate sections of HABAKKUK AT A GLANCE, recording the theme of each paragraph, each chapter, and the book itself. Fill in any other information asked for on the chart. Also record the theme of each chapter on the line in the text next to the chapter number.

❧ THINGS TO THINK ABOUT

1. What do you learn about God? His ways, his Word, his character? If he is the same yesterday, today, and forever, how would such insight into God influence your relationship to him and to his Word? How would this affect your response to your circumstances?

2. What have you learned about the haughty or proud? God says in James 4 that he opposes the proud. Can you understand why? Can you see any element of pride or haughtiness in your life which you need to deal with?

3. Review what you learned about the woes pronounced by God. Ask God to search your heart. Would these woes be applicable to you because of your lifestyle? Do you need to confess anything to God and receive his forgiveness and cleansing (see 1 John 1:9)?

4. As you look at how Habakkuk begins and ends, think about what produced the difference in Habakkuk and then apply it to your own life. Are you questioning, doubting God and his ways, and is it causing despair? What do you need to do?

〰〰〰〰〰

Chapter 1 Theme _____

1

The oracle *a* that Habakkuk the prophet received.

²How long, O LORD, must I call for help,
   but you do not listen? *b*
Or cry out to you, "Violence!"
   but you do not save? *c*
³Why do you make me look at injustice?
   Why do you tolerate *d* wrong?
Destruction and violence *e* are before me;
   there is strife, *f* and conflict abounds.
⁴Therefore the law *g* is paralyzed,
   and justice never prevails.
The wicked hem in the righteous,
   so that justice is perverted. *h*

⁵"Look at the nations and watch—
   and be utterly amazed. *i*
For I am going to do something in your days
   that you would not believe,
   even if you were told. *j*
⁶I am raising up the Babylonians, *a k*
   that ruthless and impetuous people,

---

a6 Or Chaldeans

1:1
a Na 1:1

1:2
b Ps 13:1-2;
22:1-2
c Jer 14:9

1:3
d ver 13
e Jer 20:8
f Ps 55:9

1:4
g Ps 119:126
h Job 19:7;
Isa 1:23; 5:20;
Eze 9:9

1:5
i Isa 29:9
j Ac 13:41*

1:6
k 2Ki 24:2

who sweep across the whole earth
  to seize dwelling places not their own.*a*
7They are a feared and dreaded people;*b*
  they are a law to themselves
  and promote their own honor.
8Their horses are swifter*c* than leopards,
  fiercer than wolves at dusk.
  Their cavalry gallops headlong;
  their horsemen come from afar.
  They fly like a vulture swooping to devour;
9 they all come bent on violence.
  Their hordes*a* advance like a desert wind
  and gather prisoners*d* like sand.
10They deride kings
  and scoff at rulers.*e*
  They laugh at all fortified cities;
  they build earthen ramps and capture them.
11Then they sweep past like the wind*f* and go on—
  guilty men, whose own strength is their god."*g*

1:6
a Jer 13:20

1:7
b Isa 18:7;
Jer 39:5-9

1:8
c Jer 4:13

1:9
d Hab 2:5

1:10
e 2Ch 36:6

1:11
f Jer 4:11-12
g Da 4:30

a 9 The meaning of the Hebrew for this word is uncertain.

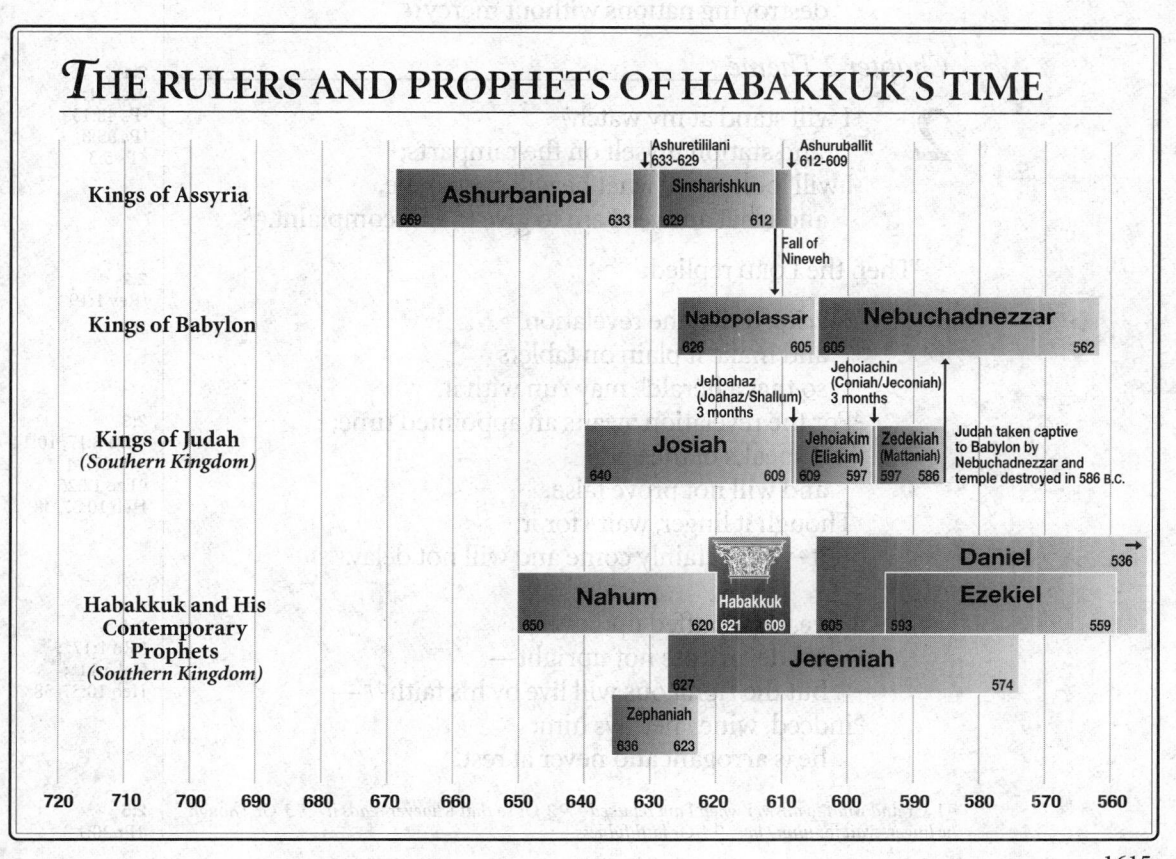

THE RULERS AND PROPHETS OF HABAKKUK'S TIME

1615

¹²O LORD, are you not from everlasting?
  My God, my Holy One,*a* we will not die.
 O LORD, you have appointed*b* them to execute judgment;
  O Rock, you have ordained them to punish.
¹³Your eyes are too pure to look on evil;
  you cannot tolerate wrong.*c*
 Why then do you tolerate the treacherous?
  Why are you silent while the wicked
 swallow up those more righteous than themselves?
¹⁴You have made men like fish in the sea,
  like sea creatures that have no ruler.
¹⁵The wicked foe pulls all of them up with hooks,*d*
  he catches them in his net,*e*
 he gathers them up in his dragnet;
  and so he rejoices and is glad.
¹⁶Therefore he sacrifices to his net
  and burns incense*f* to his dragnet,
 for by his net he lives in luxury
  and enjoys the choicest food.
¹⁷Is he to keep on emptying his net,
  destroying nations without mercy?*g*

Chapter 2 Theme

2 I will stand at my watch*h*
  and station myself on the ramparts;*i*
 I will look to see what he will say*j* to me,
  and what answer I am to give to this complaint.*a k*

²Then the LORD replied:

 "Write*l* down the revelation
  and make it plain on tablets
  so that a herald*b* may run with it.
³For the revelation awaits an appointed time;
  it speaks of the end*m*
  and will not prove false.
 Though it linger, wait*n* for it;
  it*c* will certainly come and will not delay.*o*

⁴"See, he is puffed up;
  his desires are not upright—
  but the righteous will live by his faith*d p*—
⁵indeed, wine*q* betrays him;
  he is arrogant and never at rest.

1:12
a Isa 31:1
b Isa 10:6

1:13
c La 3:34-36

1:15
d Isa 19:8
e Jer 16:16

1:16
f Jer 44:8

1:17
g Isa 14:6; 19:8

2:1
h Isa 21:8
i Ps 48:13
j Ps 85:8
k Ps 5:3

2:2
l Rev 1:19

2:3
m Da 8:17; 10:14
n Ps 27:14
o Eze 12:25;
Heb 10:37-38

2:4
p Ro 1:17*;
Gal 3:11*;
Heb 10:37-38*

2:5
q Pr 20:1

a 1 Or *and what to answer when I am rebuked*   *b* 2 Or *so that whoever reads it*   *c* 3 Or *Though he linger, wait for him; / he*   *d* 4 Or *faithfulness*

Because he is as greedy as the grave^a
and like death is never satisfied,^a
he gathers to himself all the nations
and takes captive all the peoples.
⁶"Will not all of them taunt^b him with ridicule and scorn, saying,

"'Woe to him who piles up stolen goods
and makes himself wealthy by extortion!^c
How long must this go on?'
⁷Will not your debtors^b suddenly arise?
Will they not wake up and make you tremble?
Then you will become their victim.^d
⁸Because you have plundered many nations,
the peoples who are left will plunder you.^e
For you have shed man's blood;^f
you have destroyed lands and cities and
everyone in them.

⁹"Woe to him who builds^g his realm by unjust gain
to set his nest on high,
to escape the clutches of ruin!
¹⁰You have plotted the ruin^h of many peoples,
shamingⁱ your own house and forfeiting your life.
¹¹The stones^j of the wall will cry out,
and the beams of the woodwork will echo it.

¹²"Woe to him who builds a city with bloodshed^k
and establishes a town by crime!
¹³Has not the LORD Almighty determined
that the people's labor is only fuel for the fire,^l
that the nations exhaust themselves for nothing?^m
¹⁴For the earth will be filled with the knowledge of the
gloryⁿ of the LORD,
as the waters cover the sea.^o

¹⁵"Woe to him who gives drink to his neighbors,
pouring it from the wineskin till they are drunk,
so that he can gaze on their naked bodies.
¹⁶You will be filled with shame^p instead of glory.
Now it is your turn! Drink and be exposed^c!^q
The cup^r from the LORD's right hand is coming
around to you,
and disgrace will cover your glory.
¹⁷The violence^s you have done to Lebanon will
overwhelm you,
and your destruction of animals will terrify you.^t

2:5 ^a Pr 27:20; 30:15-16
2:6 ^b Isa 14:4 ^c Am 2:8
2:7 ^d Pr 29:1
2:8 ^e Isa 33:1; Zec 2:8-9 ^f ver 17
2:9 ^g Jer 22:13
2:10 ^h Jer 26:19 ⁱ ver 16
2:11 ^j Jos 24:27; Lk 19:40
2:12 ^k Mic 3:10
2:13 ^l Isa 50:11 ^m Isa 47:13
2:14 ⁿ Nu 14:21 ^o Isa 11:9
2:16 ^p ver 10 ^q La 4:21 ^r Isa 51:22
2:17 ^s Jer 51:35 ^t Jer 50:15

^a 5 Hebrew *Sheol*   ^b 7 Or *creditors*   ^c 16 Masoretic Text; Dead Sea Scrolls, Aquila, Vulgate
and Syriac (see also Septuagint) *and stagger*

For you have shed man's blood;[a]
  you have destroyed lands and cities and
    everyone in them.

[18]"Of what value is an idol,[b] since a man has carved it?
  Or an image that teaches lies?
For he who makes it trusts in his own creation;
  he makes idols that cannot speak.[c]
[19]Woe to him who says to wood, 'Come to life!'
  Or to lifeless stone, 'Wake up!'[d]
Can it give guidance?
  It is covered with gold and silver;[e]
  there is no breath in it.
[20]But the LORD is in his holy temple;[f]
  let all the earth be silent[g] before him."

Chapter 3 Theme

3 A prayer of Habakkuk the prophet. On *shigionoth*.[a]

[2]LORD, I have heard[h] of your fame;
  I stand in awe[i] of your deeds, O LORD.
Renew[j] them in our day,
  in our time make them known;
  in wrath remember mercy.[k]

[3]God came from Teman,
  the Holy One from Mount Paran.   *Selah*[b]
His glory covered the heavens
  and his praise filled the earth.[l]
[4]His splendor was like the sunrise;
  rays flashed from his hand,
  where his power was hidden.
[5]Plague went before him;
  pestilence followed his steps.
[6]He stood, and shook the earth;
  he looked, and made the nations tremble.
The ancient mountains crumbled
  and the age-old hills collapsed.[m]
  His ways are eternal.
[7]I saw the tents of Cushan in distress,
  the dwellings of Midian[n] in anguish.[o]

[8]Were you angry with the rivers,[p] O LORD?
  Was your wrath against the streams?

### Cross references (right margin)

2:17
  [a] ver 8

2:18
  [b] Jer 5:21
  [c] Ps 115:4-5;
  Jer 10:14

2:19
  [d] 1Ki 18:27
  [e] Jer 10:4

2:20
  [f] Ps 11:4
  [g] Isa 41:1

3:2
  [h] Ps 44:1
  [i] Ps 119:120
  [j] Ps 85:6
  [k] Isa 54:8

3:3
  [l] Ps 48:10

3:6
  [m] Ps 114:1-6

3:7
  [n] Jdg 7:24-25
  [o] Ex 15:14

3:8
  [p] Ex 7:20

---

[a] 1 Probably a literary or musical term   [b] 3 A word of uncertain meaning; possibly a musical term; also in verses 9 and 13

3:8
a Ps 68:17

Did you rage against the sea
 when you rode with your horses
 and your victorious chariots?*a*

3:9
b Ps 7:12-13

⁹You uncovered your bow,
 you called for many arrows.*b*   *Selah*
You split the earth with rivers;
¹⁰ the mountains saw you and writhed.

3:10
c Ps 98:7
d Ps 93:3

Torrents of water swept by;
 the deep roared*c*
 and lifted its waves*d* on high.

¹¹Sun and moon stood still*e* in the heavens
 at the glint of your flying arrows,*f*
 at the lightning of your flashing spear.

3:11
e Jos 10:13
f Ps 18:14

¹²In wrath you strode through the earth
 and in anger you threshed*g* the nations.

3:12
g Isa 41:15

¹³You came out to deliver*h* your people,
 to save your anointed one.
You crushed*i* the leader of the land of wickedness,
 you stripped him from head to foot.   *Selah*

3:13
h Ps 20:6; 28:8
i Ps 68:21; 110:6

¹⁴With his own spear you pierced his head
 when his warriors stormed out to scatter us,*j*
gloating as though about to devour
 the wretched*k* who were in hiding.

3:14
j Jdg 7:22
k Ps 64:2-5

¹⁵You trampled the sea with your horses,
 churning the great waters.*l*

¹⁶I heard and my heart pounded,
 my lips quivered at the sound;
decay crept into my bones,
 and my legs trembled.

3:15
l Ex 15:8;
Ps 77:19

Yet I will wait patiently for the day of calamity
 to come on the nation invading us.

¹⁷Though the fig tree does not bud
 and there are no grapes on the vines,
though the olive crop fails
 and the fields produce no food,*m*

3:17
m Joel 1:10-12,18
n Jer 5:17

though there are no sheep in the pen
 and no cattle in the stalls,*n*
¹⁸yet I will rejoice in the Lord,*o*
 I will be joyful in God my Savior.

3:18
o Isa 61:10;
Php 4:4

¹⁹The Sovereign Lord is my strength;*p*
 he makes my feet like the feet of a deer,
 he enables me to go on the heights.*q*

3:19
p Dt 33:29;
Ps 46:1-5
q Dt 32:13;
2Sa 22:34;
Ps 18:33

For the director of music. On my stringed instruments.

Theme of Habakkuk:

SEGMENT DIVISIONS

	Who Is Speaking	Paragraph Themes	Chapter Themes	
				Author:
	Habakkuk Speaks	1:1-4	1	
				Date:
	God Speaks	1:5-11		
	Habakkuk Speaks	1:12-17		Purpose:
		2:1-3	2	
				Key Words:
		2:4, 5		
	God Speaks	2:6-8		
		2:9-11		
		2:12-14		
		2:15-17		
		2:18-20		
		3:1, 2	3	
	Habakkuk Prays	3:3-7		
		3:8-15		
		3:16-19		

ZEPHANIAH

*D*uring the latter years of King Josiah's reign, Israel was a spiritual oasis which was surrounded by apostasy—an abandonment of faith.

We do not know exactly when Zephaniah's prophecy came, although it was during Josiah's reign (640-609 B.C.). However, some argument can be made from the text that Zephaniah prophesied before the reforms Josiah made sometime between 622 and 621 B.C. Whenever it came, it came full gale, a stormy blast calling God's people to humility and righteousness in the face of the day of the Lord's anger.

∾ THINGS TO DO

1. Zephaniah 1:1 gives the genealogy of Zephaniah and also the historical setting of the book. Record your insights about the author on the ZEPHANIAH AT A GLANCE chart on page 1629. If you want a more thorough picture of the historical setting of Zephaniah, read 2 Kings 22:1 through 23:30 and 2 Chronicles 34:1–35:27.

2. Consult the historical chart on page 1622 to see the relationship of his prophecy to the Babylonian captivity and the destruction of Nineveh.

3. Read Zephaniah paragraph by paragraph, watching carefully for the references to the different peoples and places. Mark these references and note what is said about each one.

   a. Be careful to note when there is a change of subject. Watch carefully what happens in 3:1. Although Jerusalem is not mentioned by name at the beginning of chapter 3, the prophecy changes from Nineveh (the Assyrian capital) to Jerusalem.

   b. Decide on the theme or subject covered in each paragraph and record this under "Paragraph Themes" on ZEPHANIAH AT A GLANCE.

4. Now read Zephaniah chapter by chapter and mark the key words listed on ZEPHANIAH AT A GLANCE.

   a. Watch for any other key words as you read chapter by chapter and mark these.

   b. As you mark *the day* or *that day* notice what will happen in that day and how it relates, if at all, to the day of the Lord. (Remember, prophecy can have a near and a distant fulfillment. If you are not familiar with interpreting prophecy, you can read "Guidelines for Interpreting Predictive Prophecy" on page 2205.)

   c. In the margin of each chapter list what you learn from the key words you marked. Note what God will do, to whom, and why. Also note what effect it will have on Israel.

5. Beginning on page 2178 is the chart titled THE DAY OF THE LORD on which you can record what you learn about the day of the Lord. Note the reference (book, chapter, and verse) that you took your information from so you can find it later.

6. Fill in ZEPHANIAH AT A GLANCE. Record the theme of each chapter and of the book in the designated spaces. Then record the chapter theme in the text next to the chapter number.

∾ THINGS TO THINK ABOUT

1. The day of the Lord is also mentioned in the New Testament. One such reference is in 1 Thessalonians 5:1-11. If the day of the Lord is yet future, what should you be doing to prepare for the time of its approaching?

2. What do you learn about the nation of Israel and its future? Are you using these truths in sharing the good news of Jesus Christ with God's people, the Jews?

3. Think about what you have learned about God from Zephaniah and how such knowledge should affect the way you live.

THE RULERS AND PROPHETS OF ZEPHANIAH'S TIME

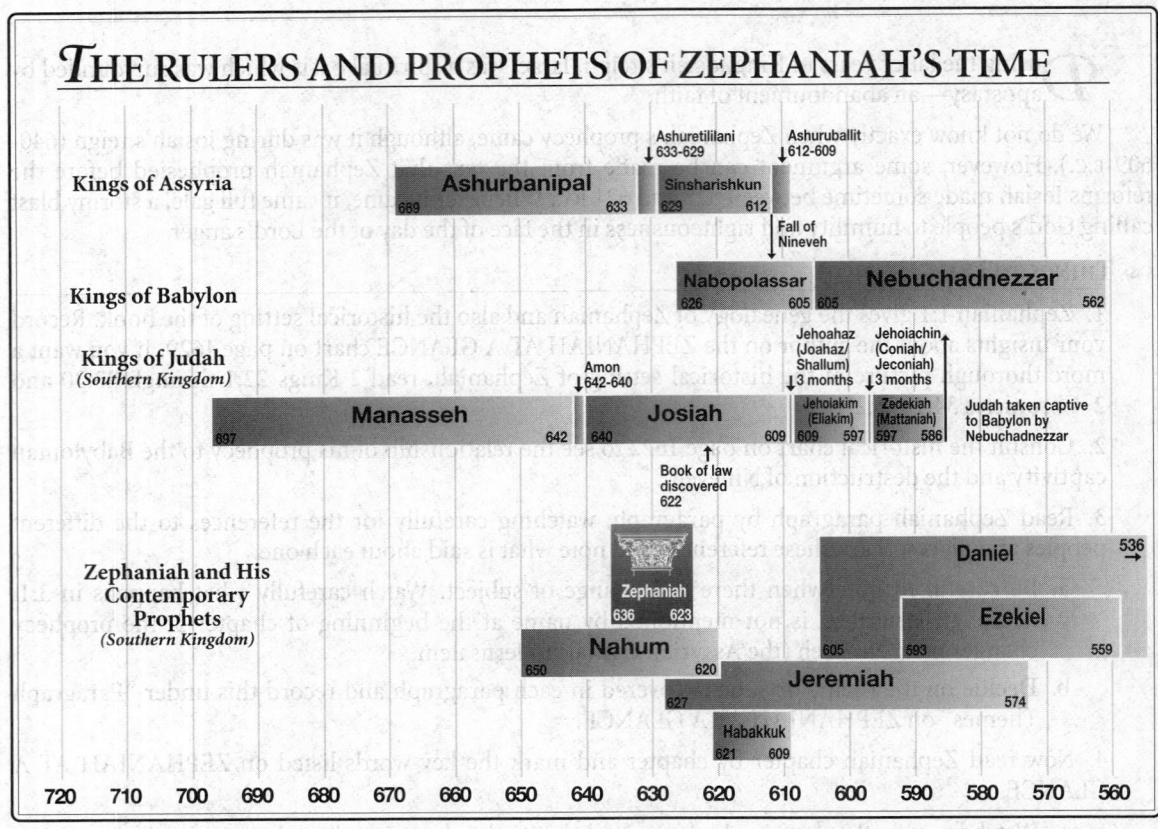

Kings of Assyria	Ashurbanipal (689–633) • Sinsharishkun (629–612) • Ashuretililani ↓633–629 • Ashuruballit ↓612–609 • Fall of Nineveh	
Kings of Babylon	Nabopolassar (626–605) • Nebuchadnezzar (605–562)	
Kings of Judah *(Southern Kingdom)*	Manasseh (697–642) • Amon ↓642–640 • Josiah (640–609) • Jehoahaz (Joahaz/Shallum) ↓3 months • Jehoiakim (Eliakim) 609–597 • Jehoiachin (Coniah/Jeconiah) ↓3 months • Zedekiah (Mattaniah) 597–586 • Book of law discovered 622 • Judah taken captive to Babylon by Nebuchadnezzar	
Zephaniah and His Contemporary Prophets *(Southern Kingdom)*	Zephaniah 636–623 • Nahum 650–620 • Jeremiah 627–574 • Habakkuk 621–609 • Daniel 605–536 • Ezekiel 593–559	

720 710 700 690 680 670 660 650 640 630 620 610 600 590 580 570 560

Chapter 1 Theme

1 The word of the LORD that came to Zephaniah son of Cushi, the son of Gedaliah, the son of Amariah, the son of Hezekiah, during the reign of Josiah[a] son of Amon king of Judah:

²"I will sweep away everything
   from the face of the earth,"[b]

                                        declares the LORD.

³"I will sweep away both men and animals;
   I will sweep away the birds of the air[c]
   and the fish of the sea.
The wicked will have only heaps of rubble[a]
   when I cut off man from the face of the earth,"[d]

                                        declares the LORD.

1:1 [a]2Ki 22:1; 2Ch 34:1–35:25

1:2 [b]Ge 6:7

1:3 [c]Jer 4:25 [d]Hos 4:3

[a]3 The meaning of the Hebrew for this line is uncertain.

1:4
a Jer 6:12
b Mic 5:13
c Hos 10:5

1:5
d Jer 5:7

1:6
e Isa 1:4;
Jer 2:13
f Isa 9:13
g Hos 7:7

1:7
h Hab 2:20;
Zec 2:13
i ver 14;
Isa 13:6
j Isa 34:6;
Jer 46:10

1:8
k Isa 24:21
l Jer 39:6

1:9
m Am 3:10

1:10
n 2Ch 33:14

1:11
o Jas 5:1
p Hos 9:6

1:12
q Am 6:1
r Jer 48:11
s Eze 8:12

1:13
t Jer 15:13
u Dt 28:30,39;
Am 5:11;
Mic 6:15

1:14
v ver 7;
Joel 1:15
w Eze 7:7

⁴"I will stretch out my hand[a] against Judah
 and against all who live in Jerusalem.
I will cut off from this place every remnant of Baal,[b]
 the names of the pagan and the idolatrous priests[c]—
⁵those who bow down on the roofs
 to worship the starry host,
those who bow down and swear by the LORD
 and who also swear by Molech,[a][d]
⁶those who turn back from following[e] the LORD
 and neither seek[f] the LORD nor inquire[g] of him.
⁷Be silent[h] before the Sovereign LORD,
 for the day of the LORD[i] is near.
The LORD has prepared a sacrifice;[j]
 he has consecrated those he has invited.
⁸On the day of the LORD's sacrifice
 I will punish[k] the princes
 and the king's sons[l]
and all those clad
 in foreign clothes.
⁹On that day I will punish
 all who avoid stepping on the threshold,[b]
who fill the temple of their gods
 with violence and deceit.[m]

¹⁰"On that day," declares the LORD,
 "a cry will go up from the Fish Gate,[n]
 wailing from the New Quarter,
 and a loud crash from the hills.
¹¹Wail,[o] you who live in the market district[c];
 all your merchants will be wiped out,
 all who trade with[d] silver will be ruined.[p]
¹²At that time I will search Jerusalem with lamps
 and punish those who are complacent,[q]
 who are like wine left on its dregs,[r]
who think, 'The LORD will do nothing,[s]
 either good or bad.'
¹³Their wealth will be plundered,[t]
 their houses demolished.
They will build houses
 but not live in them;
they will plant vineyards
 but not drink the wine.[u]

¹⁴"The great day of the LORD[v] is near[w]
 near and coming quickly.

---

a 5 Hebrew *Malcam*, that is, Milcom   b 9 See 1 Samuel 5:5.   c 11 Or *the Mortar*   d 11 Or *in*

Listen! The cry on the day of the LORD will be bitter,
the shouting of the warrior there.

¹⁵That day will be a day of wrath,
a day of distress and anguish,
a day of trouble and ruin,
a day of darkness and gloom,
a day of clouds and blackness,[a]

¹⁶a day of trumpet and battle cry[b]
against the fortified cities
and against the corner towers.[c]

¹⁷I will bring distress on the people
and they will walk like blind[d] men,
because they have sinned against the LORD.
Their blood will be poured out[e] like dust
and their entrails like filth.[f]

¹⁸Neither their silver nor their gold
will be able to save them
on the day of the LORD's wrath.[g]
In the fire of his jealousy
the whole world will be consumed,[h]
for he will make a sudden end
of all who live in the earth.[i]"

The Nations of the Lord's Anger

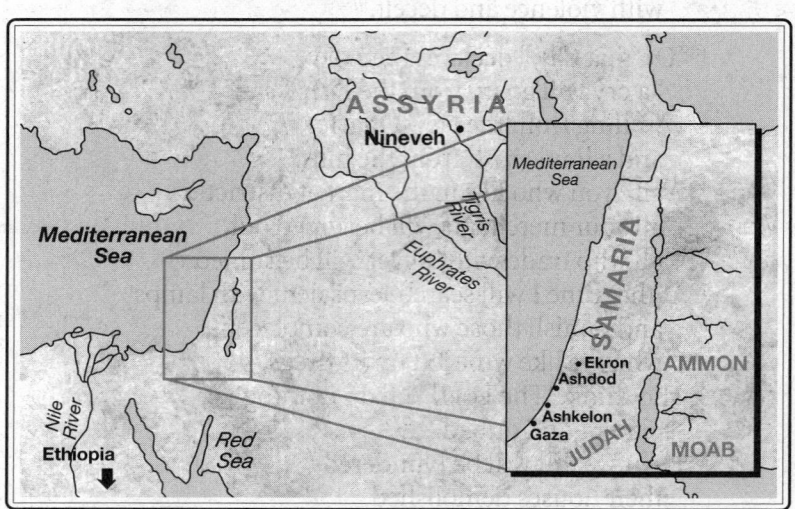

Chapter 2 Theme

2 Gather together,[j] gather together,
O shameful[k] nation,

²before the appointed time arrives
and that day sweeps on like chaff,[l]
before the fierce anger[m] of the LORD comes upon you,
before the day of the LORD's wrath comes upon you.

1:15
[a] Isa 22:5;
Joel 2:2

1:16
[b] Jer 4:19
[c] Isa 2:15

1:17
[d] Isa 59:10
[e] Ps 79:3
[f] Jer 9:22

1:18
[g] Eze 7:19
[h] ver 2-3;
Zep 3:8
[i] Ge 6:7

2:1
[j] 2Ch 20:4;
Joel 1:14
[k] Jer 3:3; 6:15

2:2
[l] Isa 17:13;
Hos 13:3
[m] La 4:11

2:3
a Am 5:6
b Ps 45:4;
Am 5:14-15
c Ps 57:1

2:4
d Am 1:6,7-8;
Zec 9:5-7

2:5
e Eze 25:16
f Am 3:1
g Isa 14:30

2:6
h Isa 5:17

2:7
i Ps 126:4;
Jer 32:44

2:8
j Jer 48:27
k Eze 25:3

2:9
l Isa 15:1-16:14;
Jer 48:1-47
m Dt 29:23
n Jer 49:1-6;
Eze 25:1-7
o Isa 11:14
p Am 2:1-3

2:10
q Isa 16:6
r Jer 48:27

2:11
s Joel 2:11
t Zep 1:4
u Zep 3:9

³Seek^a the LORD, all you humble of the land,
  you who do what he commands.
Seek righteousness, seek humility;^b
  perhaps you will be sheltered^c
  on the day of the LORD's anger.

⁴Gaza^d will be abandoned
  and Ashkelon left in ruins.
At midday Ashdod will be emptied
  and Ekron uprooted.
⁵Woe to you who live by the sea,
  O Kerethite^e people;
the word of the LORD is against you,^f
  O Canaan, land of the Philistines.

"I will destroy you,
  and none will be left."^g

⁶The land by the sea, where the Kerethites^a dwell,
  will be a place for shepherds and sheep pens.^h
⁷It will belong to the remnant of the house of Judah;
  there they will find pasture.
In the evening they will lie down
  in the houses of Ashkelon.
The LORD their God will care for them;
  he will restore their fortunes.^b ⁱ

⁸"I have heard the insults^j of Moab
  and the taunts of the Ammonites,
who insulted^k my people
  and made threats against their land.
⁹Therefore, as surely as I live,"
  declares the LORD Almighty, the God of Israel,
"surely Moab^l will become like Sodom,^m
  the Ammonitesⁿ like Gomorrah—
a place of weeds and salt pits,
  a wasteland forever.
The remnant of my people will plunder^o them;
  the survivors of my nation will inherit their land.^p"

¹⁰This is what they will get in return for their pride,^q
  for insulting^r and mocking the people of the
    LORD Almighty.
¹¹The LORD will be awesome^s to them
  when he destroys all the gods^t of the land.
The nations on every shore will worship him,^u
  every one in its own land.

ZEPHANIAH 2

INSIGHT

The *Kerethites* were probably paid soldiers of the Philistines. David used some of these soldiers as personal bodyguards. Both Ezekiel and Zephaniah pronounced judgment on them.

a 6 The meaning of the Hebrew for this word is uncertain.   b 7 Or *will bring back their captives*

¹²"You too, O Cushites,ᵃ ᵃ
    will be slain by my sword.ᵇ"

¹³He will stretch out his hand against the north
    and destroy Assyria,
leaving Ninevehᶜ utterly desolate
    and dry as the desert.ᵈ
¹⁴Flocks and herds will lie down there,
    creatures of every kind.
The desert owlᵉ and the screech owl
    will roost on her columns.
Their calls will echo through the windows,
    rubble will be in the doorways,
    the beams of cedar will be exposed.
¹⁵This is the carefreeᶠ city
    that lived in safety.ᵍ
She said to herself,
    "I am, and there is none besides me."ʰ
What a ruin she has become,
    a lair for wild beasts!
All who pass by her scoffⁱ
    and shake their fists.

Chapter 3 Theme

3 Woe to the city of oppressors,ʲ
    rebellious and defiled!ᵏ
²She obeysˡ no one,
    she accepts no correction.ᵐ
She does not trust in the Lᴏʀᴅ,
    she does not draw nearⁿ to her God.
³Her officials are roaring lions,
    her rulers are evening wolves,ᵒ
    who leave nothing for the morning.
⁴Her prophets are arrogant;
    they are treacherousᵖ men.
Her priests profane the sanctuary
    and do violence to the law.�q
⁵The Lᴏʀᴅ within her is righteous;
    he does no wrong.ʳ
Morning by morning he dispenses his justice,
    and every new day he does not fail,
    yet the unrighteous know no shame.

⁶"I have cut off nations;
    their strongholds are demolished.
I have left their streets deserted,

Cross references

2:12
ᵃ Isa 18:1; 20:4
ᵇ Jer 46:10

2:13
ᶜ Na 1:1
ᵈ Mic 5:6

2:14
ᵉ Isa 14:23

2:15
ᶠ Isa 32:9
ᵍ Isa 47:8
ʰ Eze 28:2
ⁱ Na 3:19

3:1
ʲ Jer 6:6
ᵏ Eze 23:30

3:2
ˡ Jer 22:21
ᵐ Jer 7:28
ⁿ Ps 73:28;
Jer 5:3

3:3
ᵒ Eze 22:27

3:4
ᵖ Jer 9:4
q Eze 22:26

3:5
ʳ Dt 32:4

ᵃ12 That is, people from the upper Nile region

with no one passing through.
Their cities are destroyed;[a]
    no one will be left—no one at all.

[7] I said to the city,
    'Surely you will fear me
    and accept correction!'
Then her dwelling would not be cut off,
    nor all my punishments come upon her.
But they were still eager
    to act corruptly[b] in all they did.

[8] Therefore wait[c] for me," declares the LORD,
    "for the day I will stand up to testify.[a]
I have decided to assemble the nations,[d]
    to gather the kingdoms
and to pour out my wrath on them—
    all my fierce anger.
The whole world will be consumed[e]
    by the fire of my jealous anger.

[9] "Then will I purify the lips of the peoples,
    that all of them may call[f] on the name of the LORD
    and serve[g] him shoulder to shoulder.
[10] From beyond the rivers of Cush[b][h]
    my worshipers, my scattered people,
    will bring me offerings.[i]
[11] On that day you will not be put to shame[j]
    for all the wrongs you have done to me,
because I will remove from this city
    those who rejoice in their pride.
Never again will you be haughty
    on my holy hill.
[12] But I will leave within you
    the meek[k] and humble,
    who trust[l] in the name of the LORD.
[13] The remnant[m] of Israel will do no wrong;[n]
    they will speak no lies,[o]
    nor will deceit be found in their mouths.
They will eat and lie down[p]
    and no one will make them afraid.[q]"

[14] Sing, O Daughter of Zion;[r]
    shout aloud,[s] O Israel!
Be glad and rejoice with all your heart,
    O Daughter of Jerusalem!
[15] The LORD has taken away your punishment,
    he has turned back your enemy.

3:6
a Lev 26:31

3:7
b Hos 9:9

3:8
c Ps 27:14
d Joel 3:2
e Zep 1:18

3:9
f Zep 2:11
g Isa 19:18

3:10
h Ps 68:31
i Isa 60:7

3:11
j Joel 2:26-27

3:12
k Isa 14:32
l Na 1:7

3:13
m Isa 10:21;
    Mic 4:7
n Ps 119:3
o Rev 14:5
p Eze 34:15;
    Zep 2:7
q Eze 34:25-28

3:14
r Zec 2:10
s Isa 12:6

---

a 8 Septuagint and Syriac; Hebrew *will rise up to plunder*   b 10 That is, the upper Nile region

The LORD, the King of Israel, is with you;*a*

never again will you fear*b* any harm.

¹⁶On that day they will say to Jerusalem,

"Do not fear, O Zion;

do not let your hands hang limp.*c*

¹⁷The LORD your God is with you,

he is mighty to save.*d*

He will take great delight*e* in you,

he will quiet you with his love,

he will rejoice over you with singing."

¹⁸"The sorrows for the appointed feasts

I will remove from you;

they are a burden and a reproach to you.*a*

¹⁹At that time I will deal

with all who oppressed you;

I will rescue the lame

and gather those who have been scattered.*f*

I will give them praise*g* and honor

in every land where they were put to shame.

²⁰At that time I will gather you;

at that time I will bring*h* you home.

I will give you honor*i* and praise

among all the peoples of the earth

when I restore your fortunes*bj*

before your very eyes,"

says the LORD.

---

a 18 Or "*I will gather you who mourn for the appointed feasts;* / *your reproach is a burden to you*
b 20 Or *I bring back your captives*

3:15	*a* Eze 37:26-28
	b Isa 54:14
3:16	*c* Job 4:3; Isa 35:3-4; Heb 12:12
3:17	*d* Isa 63:1
	e Isa 62:4
3:19	*f* Eze 34:16; Mic 4:6
	g Isa 60:18
3:20	*h* Jer 29:14; Eze 37:12
	i Isa 56:5; 66:22
	j Joel 3:1

Theme of Zephaniah:

Author:

Date:

Purpose:

Key Words:

I will (will I)
(the Lord will,
he will, he does)

the day of
the Lord
(the day, in or
on that day)

remnant

SEGMENT DIVISIONS	PARAGRAPH THEMES	CHAPTER THEMES
	1:1-6	1
	1:7-13	
	1:14-18	
	2:1-3	2
	2:4-7	
	2:8-11	
	2:12-15	
	3:1-7	3
	3:8-13	
	3:14-20	

HAGGAI

Discouragement reigned. Only a remnant returned to Jerusalem after the 70 years of exile—a small remnant in comparison to the number of people taken captive. Many Jews were reluctant to leave Babylon to return to Jerusalem. The land of their captors had become home. The Babylonians had allowed them to establish businesses. They had built their houses. Their children, while born in captivity, were secure. Why should they leave?

A small remnant returned to rebuild the temple, soon to become a discouraging task. Their zeal dwindled. What was enthusiastically begun was forgotten before God's house was completed. For about sixteen years the temple stood unfinished and ignored.

Then around 520 B.C. the word of the Lord came to Haggai.

∞ THINGS TO DO

1. Read Haggai in one sitting in order to familiarize yourself with the pattern of the book. Then do the following:

   a. In a distinctive way, mark every reference to time throughout the book so you can spot it immediately. Also mark every use of the phrase *the word of the Lord came through the prophet Haggai*. Each occurrence of this phrase begins a message and will help you see the structure of Haggai.

   b. To get the historical setting of Haggai, read Ezra 4:24–6:22. Then study the two charts at the beginning of Haggai on pages 1631 and 1632. The first gives the historical setting of Haggai. Note who Darius is and also note Darius is mentioned in Haggai. Also note when the temple work started and stopped under Ezra and then when it resumed under Haggai.

   The second chart is a Jewish calendar which will help you discern when Haggai received his message from the Lord. (Follow the sacred calendar.)

2. As you read Haggai a second time, concentrate on one message at a time and do the following:

   a. As you read chapter 1, mark 1:13 the same way you marked the other phrases saying that the word of the Lord came by Haggai the prophet. Scholars debate whether this should be considered a separate message from the first part of the chapter. If so, the book would contain five messages rather than four. See what you think.

   b. As you study each message (which begins with "the word of the LORD came"), watch for and mark in a distinctive way the key repeated words used throughout Haggai. These are listed on the HAGGAI AT A GLANCE chart on page 1634. Mark any other key words you observe.

   c. After you have read each message and marked key words, observe the content of each message by asking the five W's and an H. Ask: What is the specific message and to whom was it given? What has happened? To whom? Why? What is going to happen? What are they to believe or do? Summarize and record what you learn about each message in the section for "Paragraph Themes" on HAGGAI AT A GLANCE.

3. Now go back through Haggai and list the truths you learned about God, the people, and the temple. You may want to record these lists in the margins of Haggai.

4. Complete HAGGAI AT A GLANCE. Record the theme of each chapter in the appropriate places. Then record the chapter theme in the text next to the chapter number. Finally, write out the theme of the book and fill in any other information needed.

∾ THINGS TO THINK ABOUT
_____

1. Have you given too much attention and time to your personal affairs and needs but neglected the things of God that are important for the spreading of the gospel or the furtherance of his work?

2. What might God be trying to say when cataclysmic events take place? Do you take advantage of these things to turn people's attention and thoughts to God?

3. When discouraged in your service to God, do you quit, or do you courageously persevere, determined to be faithful and to leave the outcome to God?

THE RULERS AND PROPHETS OF HAGGAI'S TIME

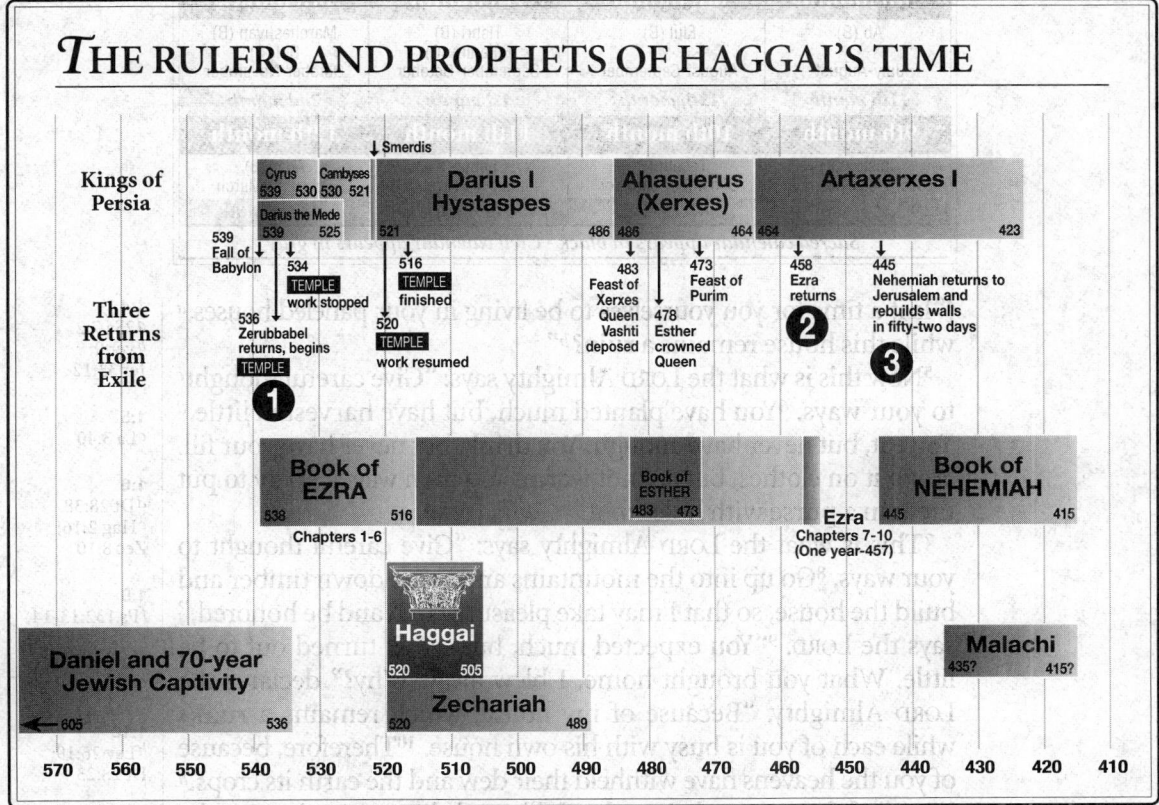

1:1
a Ezr 4:24
b Ezr 5:1
c Mt 1:12-13
d Ezr 5:3
e Ezr 2:2
f 1Ch 6:15;
Ezr 3:2

Chapter 1 Theme
_____

1 In the second year of King Darius,ᵃ on the first day of the sixth month, the word of the LORD came through the prophet Haggaiᵇ to Zerubbabelᶜ son of Shealtiel, governorᵈ of Judah, and to Joshuaᵃ ᵉ son of Jehozadak, ᶠ the high priest:

²This is what the LORD Almighty says: "These people say, 'The time has not yet come for the LORD's house to be built.'"

³Then the word of the LORD came through the prophet Haggai:ᵍ

1:3
g Ezr 5:1

a 1 A variant of Jeshua; here and elsewhere in Haggai

The Jewish Calendar

Babylonian names (B) for the months are still used today for the Jewish calendar. Canaanite names (C) were used prior to the Babylonian captivity in 586 B.C. Four are mentioned in the Old Testament. **Adar-Sheni** is an intercalary month used every two to three years or seven times in 19 years.

1st month	2nd month	3rd month	4th month
Nisan (B) Abib (C) March-April	Iyyar (B) Ziv (C) April-May	Sivan (B) May-June	Tammuz (B) June-July
7th month	*8th month*	*9th month*	*10th month*
5th month	**6th month**	**7th month**	**8th month**
Ab (B) July-August	Elul (B) August-September	Tishri (B) Ethanim (C) September-October	Marcheshvan (B) Bul (C) October-November
11th month	*12th month*	*1st month*	*2nd month*
9th month	**10th month**	**11th month**	**12th month**
Chislev (B) November-December	Tebeth (B) December-January	Shebat (B) January-February	Adar (B) February-March
3rd month	*4th month*	*5th month*	*6th month*

Sacred calendar appears in black • Civil calendar appears in gray

⁴"Is it a time for you yourselves to be living in your paneled houses,ᵃ while this house remains a ruin?ᵇ"

⁵Now this is what the LORD Almighty says: "Give careful thoughtᶜ to your ways. ⁶You have planted much, but have harvested little.ᵈ You eat, but never have enough. You drink, but never have your fill. You put on clothes, but are not warm. You earn wages,ᵉ only to put them in a purse with holes in it."

⁷This is what the LORD Almighty says: "Give careful thought to your ways. ⁸Go up into the mountains and bring down timber and build the house, so that I may take pleasureᶠ in it and be honored," says the LORD. ⁹"You expected much, but see, it turned out to be little. What you brought home, I blew away. Why?" declares the LORD Almighty. "Because of my house, which remains a ruin,ᵍ while each of you is busy with his own house. ¹⁰Therefore, because of you the heavens have withheld their dew and the earth its crops.ʰ ¹¹I called for a droughtⁱ on the fields and the mountains, on the grain, the new wine, the oil and whatever the ground produces, on men and cattle, and on the labor of your hands.ʲ"

¹²Then Zerubbabelᵏ son of Shealtiel, Joshua son of Jehozadak, the high priest, and the whole remnantˡ of the people obeyedᵐ the voice of the LORD their God and the message of the prophet Haggai, because the LORD their God had sent him. And the people fearedⁿ the LORD.

¹³Then Haggai, the LORD's messenger, gave this message of the LORD to the people: "I am withᵒ you," declares the LORD. ¹⁴So the LORD stirred up the spirit of Zerubbabelᵖ son of Shealtiel, governor of Judah, and the spirit of Joshua son of Jehozadak, the high priest, and the spirit of the whole remnant�q of the people. They came and

1:4
ᵃ 2Sa 7:2
ᵇ ver 9;
Jer 33:12

1:5
ᶜ La 3:40

1:6
ᵈ Dt 28:38
ᵉ Hag 2:16;
Zec 8:10

1:8
ᶠ Ps 132:13-14

1:9
ᵍ ver 4

1:10
ʰ Lev 26:19;
Dt 28:23

1:11
ⁱ Dt 28:22;
1Ki 17:1
ʲ Hag 2:17

1:12
ᵏ ver 1
ˡ ver 14;
Isa 1:9;
Hag 2:2
ᵐ Isa 50:10
ⁿ Dt 31:12

1:13
ᵒ Mt 28:20;
Ro 8:31

1:14
ᵖ Ezr 5:2
q ver 12

1:15
a ver 1

2:3
b Ezr 3:12
c Zec 4:10

2:4
d 1Ch 28:20;
Zec 8:9;
Eph 6:10
e 2Sa 5:10;
Ac 7:9

2:5
f Ex 29:46
g Ne 9:20;
Isa 63:11

2:6
h Isa 10:25
i Heb 12:26*

2:7
j Isa 60:7

2:9
k Ps 85:9

2:10
l ver 1

2:11
m Lev 10:10-11;
Dt 17:8-11;
Mal 2:7

2:12
n Lev 6:27;
Mt 23:19

2:13
o Lev 22:4-6

2:14
p Isa 1:13

2:15
q Hag 1:5
r Ezr 3:10
s Ezr 4:24

2:16
t Hag 1:6

2:17
u Hag 1:11
v Dt 28:22;
1Ki 8:37;
Am 4:9

began to work on the house of the Lord Almighty, their God, ¹⁵on the twenty-fourth day of the sixth month*a* in the second year of King Darius.

Chapter 2 Theme

2 On the twenty-first day of the seventh month, the word of the Lord came through the prophet Haggai: ²"Speak to Zerubbabel son of Shealtiel, governor of Judah, to Joshua son of Jehozadak, the high priest, and to the remnant of the people. Ask them, ³'Who of you is left who saw this house*b* in its former glory? How does it look to you now? Does it not seem to you like nothing?*c* ⁴But now be strong, O Zerubbabel,' declares the Lord. 'Be strong,*d* O Joshua son of Jehozadak, the high priest. Be strong, all you people of the land,' declares the Lord, 'and work. For I am with*e* you,' declares the Lord Almighty. ⁵'This is what I covenanted with you when you came out of Egypt.*f* And my Spirit*g* remains among you. Do not fear.'

⁶"This is what the Lord Almighty says: 'In a little while*h* I will once more shake the heavens and the earth,*i* the sea and the dry land. ⁷I will shake all nations, and the desired of all nations will come, and I will fill this house*j* with glory,' says the Lord Almighty. ⁸'The silver is mine and the gold is mine,' declares the Lord Almighty. ⁹'The glory*k* of this present house will be greater than the glory of the former house,' says the Lord Almighty. 'And in this place I will grant peace,' declares the Lord Almighty."

¹⁰On the twenty-fourth day of the ninth month,*l* in the second year of Darius, the word of the Lord came to the prophet Haggai: ¹¹"This is what the Lord Almighty says: 'Ask the priests*m* what the law says: ¹²If a person carries consecrated meat in the fold of his garment, and that fold touches some bread or stew, some wine, oil or other food, does it become consecrated?*n*'"

The priests answered, "No."

¹³Then Haggai said, "If a person defiled by contact with a dead body touches one of these things, does it become defiled?"

"Yes," the priests replied, "it becomes defiled.*o*"

¹⁴Then Haggai said, "'So it is with this people and this nation in my sight,' declares the Lord. 'Whatever they do and whatever they offer*p* there is defiled.

¹⁵"'Now give careful thought*q* to this from this day on*a*—consider how things were before one stone was laid*r* on another in the Lord's temple.*s* ¹⁶When anyone came to a heap of twenty measures, there were only ten. When anyone went to a wine vat to draw fifty measures, there were only twenty.*t* ¹⁷I struck all the work of your hands*u* with blight,*v* mildew and hail, yet you did not turn to me,'

---

a 15 Or to the days past

declares the LORD.[a] [18]'From this day on, from this twenty-fourth day of the ninth month, give careful thought to the day when the foundation[b] of the LORD's temple was laid. Give careful thought: [19]Is there yet any seed left in the barn? Until now, the vine and the fig tree, the pomegranate and the olive tree have not borne fruit.

" 'From this day on I will bless you.' "

[20]The word of the LORD came to Haggai a second time on the twenty-fourth day of the month: [21]"Tell Zerubbabel[c] governor of Judah that I will shake the heavens and the earth. [22]I will overturn royal thrones and shatter the power of the foreign kingdoms.[d] I will overthrow chariots[e] and their drivers; horses and their riders will fall, each by the sword of his brother.[f]

[23]"On that day,' declares the LORD Almighty, 'I will take you, my servant[g] Zerubbabel son of Shealtiel,' declares the LORD, 'and I will make you like my signet ring, for I have chosen you,' declares the LORD Almighty."

	2:17
	[a] Am 4:6
	2:18
	[b] Zec 8:9
	2:21
	[c] Ezr 5:2
	2:22
	[d] Da 2:44
	[e] Mic 5:10
	[f] Jdg 7:22
	2:23
	[g] Isa 43:10

HAGGAI AT A GLANCE

Theme of Haggai:

SEGMENT DIVISIONS

PARAGRAPH THEMES		CHAPTER THEMES
1:1-12		1
1:13-15		
2:1-9		2
2:10-19		
2:20-23		

Author:

Date:

Purpose:

Key Words:

day of the month

the word of the Lord came

house (temple)

people (and pronouns)

give careful thought

shake

ZECHARIAH

*T*he earth was peaceful and quiet. All the nations, except for Israel, were at rest. From Israel's per-spective, it looked as if God had abandoned his people and forgotten his holy city, Jerusalem. Jerusalem's walls were torn down, Solomon's temple had been destroyed, and now a partially rebuilt temple stood on its site. Even if this temple were completed, it would not begin to equal Solomon's.

The majority of God's people had settled in their land of exile and were reluctant to return to Jerusalem. Only a remnant had come back, and they were a discouraged lot who soon abandoned the rebuilding of the house of God until the word of the Lord first came through Haggai and then Zechariah.

Born in Babylon, Zechariah was among the remnant who returned to Jerusalem under the leadership of Zerubbabel and Joshua. Although Zechariah belonged to the priestly line, he, like Haggai his predecessor, was to be God's prophet to the returned and discouraged remnant.

And so, about 520 to 519 B.C., the word of the Lord came to Zechariah—a needed word, an encouraging word.

∾ THINGS TO DO

General Instructions

If you are going to have a good understanding of Zechariah, it will help to put the book into its historical context. Although this will take extra study, it will be worthwhile.

Ezra gives the historical setting of Zechariah; therefore if you have not studied Ezra, read it before you start Zechariah. Ezra, like Zechariah, is a post-exilic book, which simply means it was written after the Jews were sent into exile under the Babylonians (Chaldeans) in 586 B.C. Ezra records the return of a remnant to Jerusalem under the reign and decree of Cyrus, a Persian king who ruled from 539 to 530 B.C. The Babylonians conquered Judah, then the Medes and Persians conquered the Babylonians.

1. As you read Ezra, observe what is said regarding rebuilding the temple, since the temple plays a key role in Ezra and in Zechariah. Also watch for any reference to Zerubbabel and to Jeshua, who is called Joshua in Zechariah. Joshua is also called Jeshua in Nehemiah, another post-exilic book which focuses on rebuilding the walls of Jerusalem.

2. If you have not studied Haggai, study it next, since Haggai and Zechariah are contemporaries.

Chapters 1-8

1. The book of Zechariah divides into two segments: chapters 1 through 8 and chapters 9 through 14. As you read the first segment, mark every occurrence of the phrase *the word of the Lord came.* There will be slight variations to the wording (e.g. *the word of the Lord Almighty came*). However, mark each occurrence the same way. Then in the margin, note the main point of the Lord's message. Also, if the text tells you when the word came, draw a time symbol in the text. Consult the historical chart on page 1637 for the chronological setting of these messages.

2. As you read, also watch for the phrases, *what do you see?, the Lord showed me, I had,* or *I lifted up* or *I looked.* In the margin write "Vision," and then note briefly what the vision was. As you do this, you will see many correlations between the *word of the Lord* and the vision.

3. Watch for and mark in a distinctive way the following key words or phrases, along with their syn-onyms or pronouns: *listen (stopped up their ears), return (turn), again (further, added), temple (house,*

1635

house of the Lord), nations, Judah, Jerusalem, I will live among you (I will be its glory within or reference to the Lord's coming), and *seventy years.*

Record these key words and phrases on an index card and use it as a bookmark as you study Zechariah. You will find it helpful to color or mark these phrases in the same way you mark them in the text.

4. Zechariah contains many prophecies regarding the Messiah's first and final comings, the nation of Israel and Jerusalem, and the future of the nations. Therefore, as you read Zechariah chapter by chapter, watch for these prophecies and note them under the appropriate columns on the chart ZECHARIAH'S PROPHETIC REVELATIONS on page 1653.

5. God's name, Jehovah-sabaoth, Lord of hosts, is used repeatedly. Mark these occurrences. Then as you study Zechariah, on a separate piece of paper keep a list of all you learn about God. When you finish Zechariah, record this list in the margin of Zechariah.

6. After you study each chapter, record its theme (subject) on the ZECHARIAH AT A GLANCE chart on page 1654 under the appropriate chapter number and then in the text next to the chapter number.

Chapters 9-14

1. As you read through this segment, watch for the same key words and/or phrases you marked in chapters 1 through 8, but add to your list *in that day* and any reference to the Lord as *King*.

2. Also mark the phrase *this is the word of the Lord*. The occurrences of this phrase divide these final chapters of Zechariah into segments.

3. After you mark the key words and phrases in this segment, list in the margin or on the chart ZECHARIAH'S PROPHETIC REVELATIONS what you learn about each. If you believe *that day* refers to the day of the Lord, also record your insights on the chart THE DAY OF THE LORD beginning on page 2178.

4. When you read chapter 13, watch what will happen to the two parts and the *third (one-third)*. Watch the pronouns *they* and *them*, and then list in the margin all you learn about the *third (one-third)*—the remnant that survives.

5. In chapter 14 you will see a reference to the Feast of Booths. On pages 210 and 211, you will find a chart called THE FEASTS OF ISRAEL. As you look at the chart, note the significance of the Feast of Booths (or Tabernacles, as it is sometimes referred to).

6. Record the theme of each chapter as you did previously. Then when you finish, write the theme of Zechariah on ZECHARIAH AT A GLANCE. Record the main theme of the two major segment divisions and fill in the other information called for on the chart.

7. Since Haggai and Zechariah were contemporaries, it would be interesting to note how the messages given by the Lord to these two prophets correlate in time. After you have studied both books, look at the "time symbols" in both books and note when the messages came in relationship to each other. List the messages in the order of their occurrence, using the space at the end of Zechariah 14.

❧ THINGS TO THINK ABOUT

1. As you have studied Zechariah, have you been touched by the awesomeness of God's sovereignty? What does it mean to you personally to realize that God reigns supreme over the nations? That he has declared things before they have come to pass, and that as he has purposed, so it shall be? If he can handle nations, can he handle your life?

2. Do you take time to listen—really listen—to what God says in his Word? If you have not listened, God's invitation to return to him is still there in Zechariah for you. Believe him . . . and return.

3. How can you apply the truth of Zechariah 4:6, 7 to your own life? Remember the things that were written in the Old Testament were written for our encouragement and perseverance. They are not simply historical records; they are the bread of life by which we live.

4. God said, "I am coming, and I will live among you." Are you prepared? According to 1 John 3:2, 3 the coming of the Lord is a purifying hope. What do you need to do in order not to be ashamed at his coming?

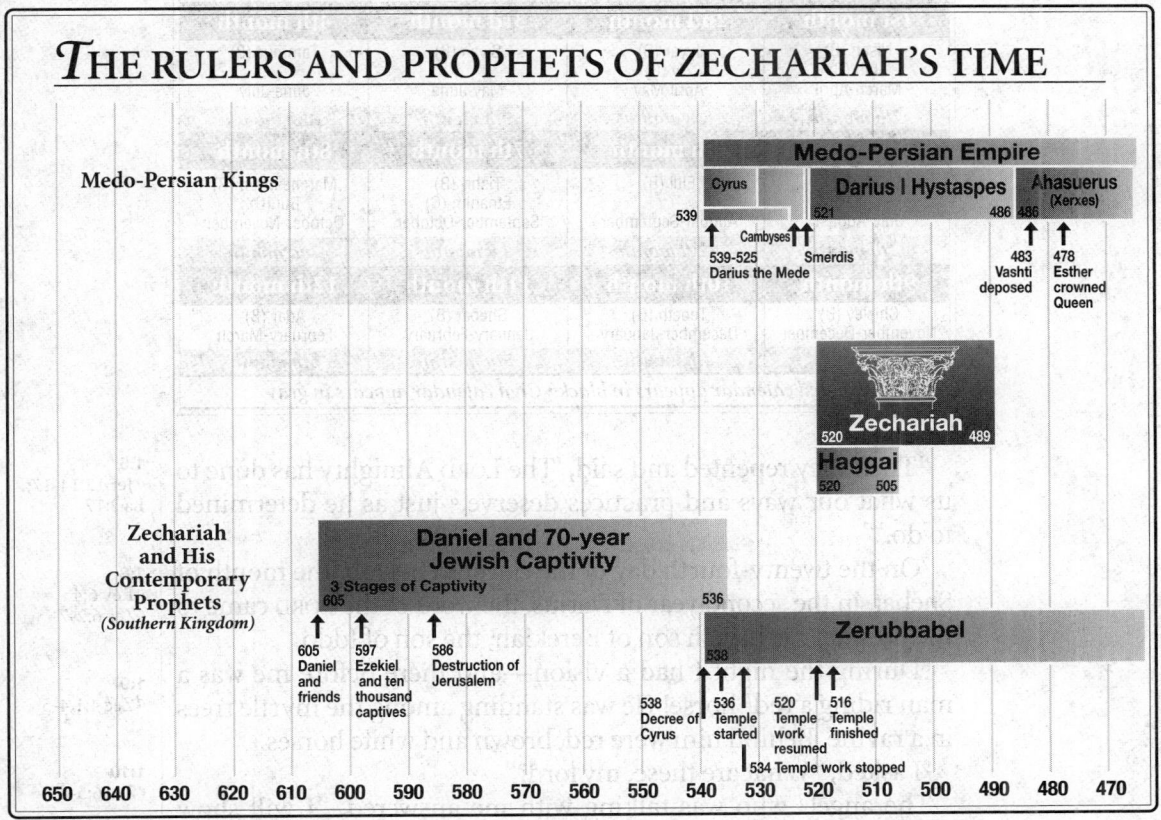

THE RULERS AND PROPHETS OF ZECHARIAH'S TIME

Medo-Persian Kings

Medo-Persian Empire

Cyrus | Darius I Hystaspes | Ahasuerus (Xerxes)

539 | 521 | 486 | 486

Cambyses
539–525 Smerdis
Darius the Mede

483 Vashti deposed
478 Esther crowned Queen

Zechariah
520 — 489

Haggai
520 — 505

Zechariah and His Contemporary Prophets (Southern Kingdom)

Daniel and 70-year Jewish Captivity
3 Stages of Captivity
605 — 536

605 Daniel and friends
597 Ezekiel and ten thousand captives
586 Destruction of Jerusalem

538 Decree of Cyrus

Zerubbabel
538

536 Temple started
520 Temple work resumed
516 Temple finished

534 Temple work stopped

650 640 630 620 610 600 590 580 570 560 550 540 530 520 510 500 490 480 470

1:1
a Ezr 4:24; 6:15
b Ezr 5:1
c Mt 23:35; Lk 11:51
d ver 7; Ne 12:4

1:2
e 2Ch 36:16

1:3
f Mal 3:7; Jas 4:8

1:4
g 2Ch 36:15
h Ps 106:6
i 2Ch 24:19; Ps 78:8; Jer 6:17

Chapter 1 Theme

1 In the eighth month of the second year of Darius,[a] the word of the LORD came to the prophet Zechariah[b] son of Berekiah,[c] the son of Iddo:[d]

[2] "The LORD was very angry[e] with your forefathers. [3]Therefore tell the people: This is what the LORD Almighty says: 'Return to me,' declares the LORD Almighty, 'and I will return to you,'[f] says the LORD Almighty. [4]Do not be like your forefathers,[g] to whom the earlier prophets proclaimed: This is what the LORD Almighty says: 'Turn from your evil ways[h] and your evil practices.' But they would not listen or pay attention to me,[i] declares the LORD. [5]Where are your forefathers now? And the prophets, do they live forever? [6]But did not my words and my decrees, which I commanded my servants the prophets, overtake your forefathers?

The Jewish Calendar

Babylonian names (B) for the months are still used today for the Jewish calendar. Canaanite names (C) were used prior to the Babylonian captivity in 586 B.C. Four are mentioned in the Old Testament. **Adar-Sheni** is an intercalary month used every two to three years or seven times in 19 years.

1st month	2nd month	3rd month	4th month
Nisan (B) Abib (C) March-April	Iyyar (B) Ziv (C) April-May	Sivan (B) May-June	Tammuz (B) June-July
7th month	*8th month*	*9th month*	*10th month*

5th month	6th month	7th month	8th month
Ab (B) July-August	Elul (B) August-September	Tishri (B) Ethanim (C) September-October	Marcheshvan (B) Bul (C) October-November
11th month	*12th month*	*1st month*	*2nd month*

9th month	10th month	11th month	12th month
Chislev (B) November-December	Tebeth (B) December-January	Shebat (B) January-February	Adar (B) February-March
3rd month	*4th month*	*5th month*	*6th month*

Sacred calendar appears in black • Civil calendar appears in gray

"Then they repented and said, 'The LORD Almighty has done to us what our ways and practices deserve,[a] just as he determined to do.'"

[7]On the twenty-fourth day of the eleventh month, the month of Shebat, in the second year of Darius, the word of the LORD came to the prophet Zechariah son of Berekiah, the son of Iddo.

[8]During the night I had a vision—and there before me was a man riding a red[b] horse! He was standing among the myrtle trees in a ravine. Behind him were red, brown and white horses.[c]

[9]I asked, "What are these, my lord?"

The angel[d] who was talking with me answered, "I will show you what they are."

[10]Then the man standing among the myrtle trees explained, "They are the ones the LORD has sent to go throughout the earth."[e]

[11]And they reported to the angel of the LORD, who was standing among the myrtle trees, "We have gone throughout the earth and found the whole world at rest and in peace."[f]

[12]Then the angel of the LORD said, "LORD Almighty, how long will you withhold mercy from Jerusalem and from the towns of Judah, which you have been angry with these seventy[g] years?"

[13]So the LORD spoke kind and comforting words to the angel who talked with me.[h]

[14]Then the angel who was speaking to me said, "Proclaim this word: This is what the LORD Almighty says: 'I am very jealous[i] for Jerusalem and Zion, [15]but I am very angry with the nations that feel secure.[j] I was only a little angry, but they added to the calamity.'[k]

[16]"Therefore, this is what the LORD says: 'I will return[l] to Jerusalem with mercy, and there my house will be rebuilt. And the

1:6
a Jer 12:14-17;
La 2:17

1:8
b Rev 6:4
c Zec 6:2-7

1:9
d Zec 4:1,4-5

1:10
e Zec 6:5-8

1:11
f Isa 14:7

1:12
g Da 9:2

1:13
h Zec 4:1

1:14
i Joel 2:18;
Zec 8:2

1:15
j Jer 48:11
k Ps 123:3-4;
Am 1:11

1:16
l Zec 8:3

1:16
a Zec 2:1-2

1:17
b Isa 51:3
c Isa 14:1
d Zec 2:12

1:19
e Am 6:13

1:21
f Ps 75:4
g Ps 75:10

2:2
h Eze 40:3;
Rev 21:15

2:4
i Eze 38:11
j Isa 49:20;
Jer 30:19; 33:22

2:5
k Isa 26:1
l Rev 21:23

2:6
m Eze 17:21

2:7
n Isa 48:20

2:8
o Dt 32:10

2:9
p Isa 14:2
q Zec 4:9

2:10
r Zep 3:14
s Zec 9:9
t Lev 26:12;
Zec 8:3

2:12
u Dt 32:9;
Ps 33:12;
Jer 10:16
v Zec 1:17

2:13
w Hab 2:20

measuring line*a* will be stretched out over Jerusalem,' declares the LORD Almighty.

¹⁷"Proclaim further: This is what the LORD Almighty says: 'My towns will again overflow with prosperity, and the LORD will again comfort*b* Zion and choose*c* Jerusalem.'"*d*

¹⁸Then I looked up—and there before me were four horns! ¹⁹I asked the angel who was speaking to me, "What are these?"

He answered me, "These are the horns*e* that scattered Judah, Israel and Jerusalem."

²⁰Then the LORD showed me four craftsmen. ²¹I asked, "What are these coming to do?"

He answered, "These are the horns that scattered Judah so that no one could raise his head, but the craftsmen have come to terrify them and throw down these horns of the nations who lifted up their horns*f* against the land of Judah to scatter its people."*g*

Chapter 2 Theme

2 Then I looked up—and there before me was a man with a measuring line in his hand! ²I asked, "Where are you going?"

He answered me, "To measure Jerusalem, to find out how wide and how long it is."*h*

³Then the angel who was speaking to me left, and another angel came to meet him ⁴and said to him: "Run, tell that young man, 'Jerusalem will be a city without walls*i* because of the great number*j* of men and livestock in it. ⁵And I myself will be a wall*k* of fire around it,' declares the LORD, 'and I will be its glory*l* within.'

⁶"Come! Come! Flee from the land of the north," declares the LORD, "for I have scattered you to the four winds of heaven,"*m* declares the LORD.

⁷"Come, O Zion! Escape, you who live in the Daughter of Babylon!"*n* ⁸For this is what the LORD Almighty says: "After he has honored me and has sent me against the nations that have plundered you—for whoever touches you touches the apple of his eye*o*— ⁹I will surely raise my hand against them so that their slaves will plunder them.*a* *p* Then you will know that the LORD Almighty has sent me.*q*

¹⁰"Shout and be glad, O Daughter of Zion.*r* For I am coming,*s* and I will live among you," *t* declares the LORD. ¹¹"Many nations will be joined with the LORD in that day and will become my people. I will live among you and you will know that the LORD Almighty has sent me to you. ¹²The LORD will inherit*u* Judah as his portion in the holy land and will again choose*v* Jerusalem. ¹³Be still*w* before the LORD, all mankind, because he has roused himself from his holy dwelling."

a 8,9 Or *says after . . . eye:* ⁹*"I . . . plunder them."*

Chapter 3 Theme

3 Then he showed me Joshua[a] [a] the high priest standing before the angel of the LORD, and Satan[b] [b] standing at his right side to accuse him. [2]The LORD said to Satan, "The LORD rebuke you,[c] Satan! The LORD, who has chosen[d] Jerusalem, rebuke you! Is not this man a burning stick snatched from the fire?"[e]

[3]Now Joshua was dressed in filthy clothes as he stood before the angel. [4]The angel said to those who were standing before him, "Take off his filthy clothes."

Then he said to Joshua, "See, I have taken away your sin,[f] and I will put rich garments[g] on you."

[5]Then I said, "Put a clean turban[h] on his head." So they put a clean turban on his head and clothed him, while the angel of the LORD stood by.

[6]The angel of the LORD gave this charge to Joshua: [7]"This is what the LORD Almighty says: 'If you will walk in my ways and keep my requirements, then you will govern my house[i] and have charge of my courts, and I will give you a place among these standing here.

[8]"'Listen, O high priest Joshua and your associates seated before you, who are men symbolic[j] of things to come: I am going to bring my servant, the Branch.[k] [9]See, the stone I have set in front of Joshua! There are seven eyes[c] on that one stone,[l] and I will engrave an inscription on it,' says the LORD Almighty, 'and I will remove the sin[m] of this land in a single day.

[10]"'In that day each of you will invite his neighbor to sit under his vine and fig tree,[n] declares the LORD Almighty."

Chapter 4 Theme

4 Then the angel who talked with me returned and wakened[o] me, as a man is wakened from his sleep.[p] [2]He asked me, "What do you see?"[q]

I answered, "I see a solid gold lampstand[r] with a bowl at the top and seven lights[s] on it, with seven channels to the lights. [3]Also there are two olive trees[t] by it, one on the right of the bowl and the other on its left."

[4]I asked the angel who talked with me, "What are these, my lord?"

[5]He answered, "Do you not know what these are?"

"No, my lord," I replied.[u]

[6]So he said to me, "This is the word of the LORD to Zerubbabel:[v] 'Not by might nor by power, but by my Spirit,'[w] says the LORD Almighty.

---

[a]1 A variant of *Jeshua*; here and elsewhere in Zechariah [b]1 *Satan* means *accuser*. [c]9 Or *facets*

3:1
[a] Hag 1:1; Zec 6:11
[b] Ps 109:6

3:2
[c] Jude 9
[d] Isa 14:1
[e] Am 4:11; Jude 23

3:4
[f] Eze 36:25; Mic 7:18
[g] Isa 52:1; Rev 19:8

3:5
[h] Ex 29:6

3:7
[i] Dt 17:8-11; Eze 44:15-16

3:8
[j] Eze 12:11
[k] Isa 4:2

3:9
[l] Isa 28:16
[m] Jer 50:20

3:10
[n] 1Ki 4:25; Mic 4:4

4:1
[o] Da 8:18
[p] Jer 31:26

4:2
[q] Jer 1:13
[r] Ex 25:31; Rev 1:12
[s] Rev 4:5

4:3
[t] ver 11; Rev 11:4

4:5
[u] Zec 1:9

4:6
[v] Ezr 5:2
[w] Isa 11:2-4; Hos 1:7

4:7
a Jer 51:25
b Ps 118:22

4:9
c Ezr 3:11
d Ezr 3:8; 6:15;
Zec 6:12
e Zec 2:9

4:10
f Hag 2:3
g Zec 3:9;
Rev 5:6

4:11
h ver 3; Rev 11:4

4:14
i Ex 29:7; 40:15;
Da 9:24-26;
Zec 3:1-7

5:1
j Eze 2:9; Rev 5:1

5:3
k Isa 24:6; 43:28;
Mal 3:9; 4:6
l Ex 20:15;
Mal 3:8
m Isa 48:1

5:4
n Lev 14:34-45;
Hab 2:9-11;
Mal 3:5

5:8
o Mic 6:11

5:9
p Lev 11:19

[7]"What[a] are you, O mighty mountain? Before Zerubbabel you will become level ground.[a] Then he will bring out the capstone[b] to shouts of 'God bless it! God bless it!'"

[8]Then the word of the LORD came to me: [9]"The hands of Zerubbabel have laid the foundation[c] of this temple; his hands will also complete it.[d] Then you will know that the LORD Almighty has sent me[e] to you.

[10]"Who despises the day of small things?[f] Men will rejoice when they see the plumb line in the hand of Zerubbabel.

"(These seven are the eyes[g] of the LORD, which range throughout the earth.)"

[11]Then I asked the angel, "What are these two olive trees[h] on the right and the left of the lampstand?"

[12]Again I asked him, "What are these two olive branches beside the two gold pipes that pour out golden oil?"

[13]He replied, "Do you not know what these are?"

"No, my lord," I said.

[14]So he said, "These are the two who are anointed[i] to[b] serve the Lord of all the earth."

Chapter 5 Theme

5 I looked again—and there before me was a flying scroll![j] [2]He asked me, "What do you see?"

I answered, "I see a flying scroll, thirty feet long and fifteen feet wide.[c]"

[3]And he said to me, "This is the curse[k] that is going out over the whole land; for according to what it says on one side, every thief[l] will be banished, and according to what it says on the other, everyone who swears falsely[m] will be banished. [4]The LORD Almighty declares, 'I will send it out, and it will enter the house of the thief and the house of him who swears falsely by my name. It will remain in his house and destroy it, both its timbers and its stones.[n]'"

[5]Then the angel who was speaking to me came forward and said to me, "Look up and see what this is that is appearing."

[6]I asked, "What is it?"

He replied, "It is a measuring basket.[d]" And he added, "This is the iniquity[e] of the people throughout the land."

[7]Then the cover of lead was raised, and there in the basket sat a woman! [8]He said, "This is wickedness," and he pushed her back into the basket and pushed the lead cover down over its mouth.[o]

[9]Then I looked up—and there before me were two women, with the wind in their wings! They had wings like those of a stork,[p] and they lifted up the basket between heaven and earth.

a 7 Or *Who* *b* 14 Or *two who bring oil and* *c* 2 Hebrew *twenty cubits long and ten cubits wide* (about 9 meters long and 4.5 meters wide) *d* 6 Hebrew *an ephah*; also in verses 7-11 *e* 6 Or *appearance*

¹⁰"Where are they taking the basket?" I asked the angel who was speaking to me.

¹¹He replied, "To the country of Babylonia^{a a} to build a house^b for it. When it is ready, the basket will be set there in its place."^c

Chapter 6 Theme _____

6 I looked up again—and there before me were four chariots^d coming out from between two mountains—mountains of bronze! ²The first chariot had red horses, the second black,^e ³the third white,^f and the fourth dappled—all of them powerful. ⁴I asked the angel who was speaking to me, "What are these, my lord?"

⁵The angel answered me, "These are the four spirits^{b g} of heaven, going out from standing in the presence of the Lord of the whole world. ⁶The one with the black horses is going toward the north country, the one with the white horses toward the west,^c and the one with the dappled horses toward the south."

⁷When the powerful horses went out, they were straining to go throughout the earth.^h And he said, "Go throughout the earth!" So they went throughout the earth.

⁸Then he called to me, "Look, those going toward the north country have given my Spirit^d restⁱ in the land of the north."

⁹The word of the Lord came to me: ¹⁰"Take ⌊silver and gold⌋ from the exiles Heldai, Tobijah and Jedaiah, who have arrived from Babylon.^j Go the same day to the house of Josiah son of Zephaniah. ¹¹Take the silver and gold and make a crown,^k and set it on the head of the high priest, Joshua^l son of Jehozadak.^m ¹²Tell him this is what the Lord Almighty says: 'Here is the man whose name is the Branch,ⁿ and he will branch out from his place and build the temple of the Lord.^o ¹³It is he who will build the temple of the Lord, and he will be clothed with majesty and will sit and rule on his throne. And he will be a priest^p on his throne. And there will be harmony between the two.' ¹⁴The crown will be given to Heldai,^e Tobijah, Jedaiah and Hen^f son of Zephaniah as a memorial in the temple of the Lord. ¹⁵Those who are far away will come and help to build the temple of the Lord,^q and you will know that the Lord Almighty has sent me to you.^r This will happen if you diligently obey^s the Lord your God."

Chapter 7 Theme _____

7 In the fourth year of King Darius, the word of the Lord came to Zechariah on the fourth day of the ninth month, the month of Kislev.^t ²The people of Bethel had sent Sharezer and

^a11 Hebrew *Shinar*   ^b5 Or *winds*   ^c6 Or *horses after them*   ^d8 Or *spirit*   ^e14 Syriac; Hebrew *Helem*   ^f14 Or *and the gracious one, the*

5:11 ^aGe 10:10 ^bJer 29:5,28 ^cDa 1:2

6:1 ^dver 5

6:2 ^eRev 6:5

6:3 ^fRev 6:2

6:5 ^gEze 37:9; Mt 24:31; Rev 7:1

6:7 ^hZec 1:10

6:8 ⁱEze 5:13; 24:13

6:10 ^jEzr 7:14-16; Jer 28:6

6:11 ^kPs 21:3 ^lZec 3:1 ^mEzr 3:2

6:12 ⁿIsa 4:2; Zec 3:8 ^oEzr 3:8-10; Zec 4:6-9

6:13 ^pPs 110:4

6:15 ^qIsa 60:10 ^rZec 2:9-11 ^sIsa 58:12; Jer 7:23; Zec 3:7

7:1 ^tNe 1:1

Regem-Melech, together with their men, to entreat[a] the LORD ³by asking the priests of the house of the LORD Almighty and the prophets, "Should I mourn[b] and fast in the fifth[c] month, as I have done for so many years?"

⁴Then the word of the LORD Almighty came to me: ⁵"Ask all the people of the land and the priests, 'When you fasted[d] and mourned in the fifth and seventh months for the past seventy years, was it really for me that you fasted? ⁶And when you were eating and drinking, were you not just feasting for yourselves? ⁷Are these not the words the LORD proclaimed through the earlier prophets[e] when Jerusalem and its surrounding towns were at rest[f] and prosperous, and the Negev and the western foothills[g] were settled?'"

⁸And the word of the LORD came again to Zechariah: ⁹"This is what the LORD Almighty says: 'Administer true justice;[h] show mercy and compassion to one another. ¹⁰Do not oppress the widow or the fatherless, the alien[i] or the poor. In your hearts do not think evil of each other.'[j]

¹¹"But they refused to pay attention; stubbornly they turned their backs and stopped up their ears.[k] ¹²They made their hearts as hard as flint[l] and would not listen to the law or to the words that the LORD Almighty had sent by his Spirit through the earlier prophets.[m] So the LORD Almighty was very angry.[n]

¹³"'When I called, they did not listen;[o] so when they called, I would not listen,'[p] says the LORD Almighty.[q] ¹⁴'I scattered[r] them with a whirlwind[s] among all the nations, where they were strangers. The land was left so desolate behind them that no one could come or go. This is how they made the pleasant land desolate.'"[t]

Chapter 8 Theme

8 Again the word of the LORD Almighty came to me. ²This is what the LORD Almighty says: "I am very jealous for Zion; I am burning with jealousy for her."

³This is what the LORD says: "I will return[u] to Zion and dwell in Jerusalem.[v] Then Jerusalem will be called the City of Truth, and the mountain of the LORD Almighty will be called the Holy Mountain."

⁴This is what the LORD Almighty says: "Once again men and women of ripe old age will sit in the streets of Jerusalem,[w] each with cane in hand because of his age. ⁵The city streets will be filled with boys and girls playing there.[x]"

⁶This is what the LORD Almighty says: "It may seem marvelous to the remnant of this people at that time,[y] but will it seem marvelous to me?[z]" declares the LORD Almighty.

⁷This is what the LORD Almighty says: "I will save my people from the countries of the east and the west.[a] ⁸I will bring them back[b] to live in Jerusalem; they will be my people,[c] and I will be faithful and righteous to them as their God."

7:2
a Jer 26:19;
Zec 8:21

7:3
b Zec 12:12-14
c Jer 52:12-14;
Zec 8:19

7:5
d Isa 58:5

7:7
e Zec 1:4
f Jer 22:21
g Jer 17:26

7:9
h Zec 8:16

7:10
i Ex 22:21
j Ex 22:22;
Isa 1:17

7:11
k Jer 8:5;
11:10;
17:23

7:12
l Jer 17:1;
Eze 11:19
m Ne 9:29
n Da 9:12

7:13
o Pr 1:24
p Isa 1:15;
Jer 11:11;
14:12;
Mic 3:4
q Pr 1:28

7:14
r Dt 4:27;
28:64-67
s Jer 23:19
t Jer 44:6

8:3
u Zec 1:16
v Zec 2:10

8:4
w Isa 65:20

8:5
x Jer 30:20;
31:13

8:6
y Ps 118:23;
126:1-3
z Jer 32:17,27

8:7
a Ps 107:3;
Isa 11:11; 43:5

8:8
b Zec 10:10
c Eze 11:19-20;
36:28;
Zec 2:11

[9]This is what the LORD Almighty says: "You who now hear these words spoken by the prophets[a] who were there when the foundation was laid for the house of the LORD Almighty, let your hands be strong[b] so that the temple may be built. [10]Before that time there were no wages[c] for man or beast. No one could go about his business safely because of his enemy, for I had turned every man against his neighbor. [11]But now I will not deal with the remnant of this people as I did in the past,"[d] declares the LORD Almighty.

[12]"The seed will grow well, the vine will yield its fruit,[e] the ground will produce its crops,[f] and the heavens will drop their dew.[g] I will give all these things as an inheritance[h] to the remnant of this people. [13]As you have been an object of cursing[i] among the nations, O Judah and Israel, so will I save you, and you will be a blessing.[j] Do not be afraid, but let your hands be strong."

[14]This is what the LORD Almighty says: "Just as I had determined to bring disaster[k] upon you and showed no pity when your fathers angered me," says the LORD Almighty, [15]"so now I have determined to do good[l] again to Jerusalem and Judah. Do not be afraid. [16]These are the things you are to do: Speak the truth[m] to each other, and render true and sound judgment in your courts;[n] [17]do not plot evil[o] against your neighbor, and do not love to swear falsely.[p] I hate all this," declares the LORD.

[18]Again the word of the LORD Almighty came to me. [19]This is what the LORD Almighty says: "The fasts of the fourth,[q] fifth,[r] seventh[s] and tenth[t] months will become joyful[u] and glad occasions and happy festivals for Judah. Therefore love truth[v] and peace."

[20]This is what the LORD Almighty says: "Many peoples and the inhabitants of many cities will yet come, [21]and the inhabitants of one city will go to another and say, 'Let us go at once to entreat[w] the LORD and seek the LORD Almighty. I myself am going.' [22]And many peoples and powerful nations will come to Jerusalem to seek the LORD Almighty and to entreat him."[x]

[23]This is what the LORD Almighty says: "In those days ten men from all languages and nations will take firm hold of one Jew by the hem of his robe and say, 'Let us go with you, because we have heard that God is with you.'"[y]

Chapter 9 Theme

An Oracle

9 The word of the LORD is against the land of Hadrach
    and will rest upon Damascus[z]—
for the eyes of men and all the tribes of Israel
    are on the LORD—[a]

---

[a] *1 Or Damascus. / For the eye of the LORD is on all mankind, / as well as on the tribes of Israel,*

Cross references

8:9
[a] Ezr 5:1
[b] Hag 2:4

8:10
[c] Hag 1:6

8:11
[d] Isa 12:1

8:12
[e] Joel 2:22
[f] Ps 67:6
[g] Ge 27:28
[h] Ob 1:17

8:13
[i] Jer 42:18
[j] Ge 12:2

8:14
[k] Jer 31:28;
Eze 24:14

8:15
[l] ver 13;
Jer 29:11;
Mic 7:18-20

8:16
[m] Ps 15:2;
Eph 4:25
[n] Zec 7:9

8:17
[o] Pr 3:29
[p] Pr 6:16-19

8:19
[q] Jer 39:2
[r] Jer 52:12
[s] 2Ki 25:25
[t] Jer 52:4
[u] Ps 30:11
[v] ver 16

8:21
[w] Zec 7:2

8:22
[x] Ps 117:1;
Isa 60:3;
Zec 2:11

8:23
[y] Isa 45:14;
1Co 14:25

9:1
[z] Isa 17:1

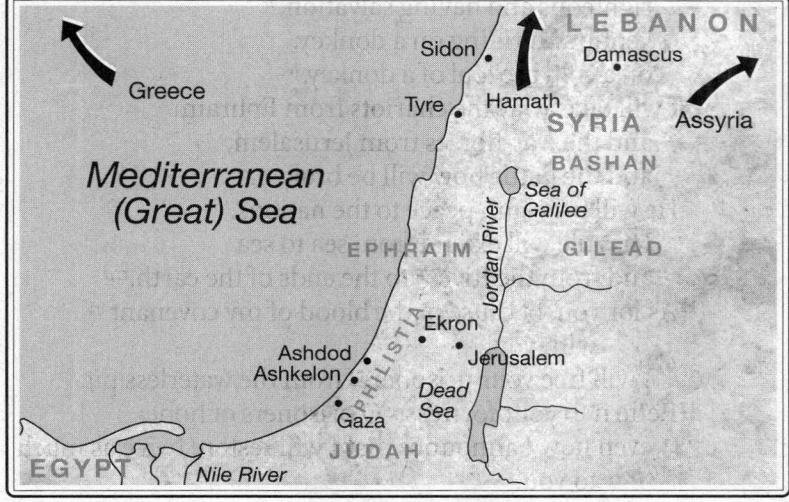

9:2
a Jer 49:23
b Eze 28:1-19

9:3
c Job 27:16;
Eze 28:4

9:4
d Isa 23:1;
Eze 26:3-5;
28:18

²and upon Hamath*ᵃ* too, which borders on it,
  and upon Tyre*ᵇ* and Sidon, though they are
    very skillful.
³Tyre has built herself a stronghold;
  she has heaped up silver like dust,
  and gold like the dirt of the streets.*ᶜ*
⁴But the Lord will take away her possessions
  and destroy her power on the sea,
  and she will be consumed by fire.*ᵈ*
⁵Ashkelon will see it and fear;
  Gaza will writhe in agony,
  and Ekron too, for her hope will wither.
 Gaza will lose her king
  and Ashkelon will be deserted.
⁶Foreigners will occupy Ashdod,
  and I will cut off the pride of the Philistines.
⁷I will take the blood from their mouths,
  the forbidden food from between their teeth.
 Those who are left will belong to our God
  and become leaders in Judah,
  and Ekron will be like the Jebusites.
⁸But I will defend my house
  against marauding forces.
 Never again will an oppressor overrun my people,
  for now I am keeping watch.*ᵉ*

⁹Rejoice greatly, O Daughter of Zion!
  Shout, Daughter of Jerusalem!
 See, your king*ᵃ* comes to you,

9:8
e Isa 52:1; 54:14 | *a* 9 Or *King*

1645

righteous and having salvation, *a*
gentle and riding on a donkey,
on a colt, the foal of a donkey. *b*

¹⁰I will take away the chariots from Ephraim
and the war-horses from Jerusalem,
and the battle bow will be broken.*c*

He will proclaim peace to the nations.
His rule will extend from sea to sea
and from the River*a* to the ends of the earth.*b d*

¹¹As for you, because of the blood of my covenant *e*
with you,
I will free your prisoners *f* from the waterless pit.

¹²Return to your fortress,*g* O prisoners of hope;
even now I announce that I will restore twice as much
to you.

¹³I will bend Judah as I bend my bow
and fill it with Ephraim.*h*

I will rouse your sons, O Zion,
against your sons, O Greece,*i*
and make you like a warrior's sword. *j*

¹⁴Then the LORD will appear over them;*k*
his arrow will flash like lightning.*l*

The Sovereign LORD will sound the trumpet;
he will march in the storms *m* of the south,

¹⁵   and the LORD Almighty will shield*n* them.

They will destroy
and overcome with slingstones.

They will drink and roar as with wine;
they will be full like a bowl
used for sprinkling*c* the corners*o* of the altar.

¹⁶The LORD their God will save them on that day
as the flock of his people.

They will sparkle in his land
like jewels in a crown. *p*

¹⁷How attractive and beautiful they will be!
Grain will make the young men thrive,
and new wine the young women.

Chapter 10 Theme _____

10 Ask the LORD for rain in the springtime;
it is the LORD who makes the storm clouds.

He gives showers of rain to men,
and plants of the field to everyone.

---

a 10 That is, the Euphrates   b 10 Or *the end of the land*   c 15 Or *bowl, / like*

9:9
*a*Isa 9:6-7;
43:3-11;
Jer 23:5-6;
Zep 3:14-15;
Zec 2:10
*b*Mt 21:5*;
Jn 12:15*

9:10
*c*Hos 1:7; 2:18;
Mic 4:3; 5:10;
Zec 10:4
*d*Ps 72:8

9:11
*e*Ex 24:8
*f*Isa 42:7

9:12
*g*Joel 3:16

9:13
*h*Isa 49:2
*i*Joel 3:6
*j*Jer 51:20

9:14
*k*Isa 31:5
*l*Ps 18:14;
Hab 3:11
*m*Isa 21:1; 66:15

9:15
*n*Isa 37:35;
Zec 12:8
*o*Ex 27:2

9:16
*p*Isa 62:3;
Jer 31:11

10:2
a Eze 21:21
b Eze 34:5;
Hos 3:4;
Mt 9:36

²The idols[a] speak deceit,
diviners see visions that lie;
they tell dreams that are false,
they give comfort in vain.
Therefore the people wander like sheep
oppressed for lack of a shepherd.[b]

10:3
c Jer 25:34

³"My anger burns against the shepherds,
and I will punish the leaders;[c]
for the LORD Almighty will care
for his flock, the house of Judah,
and make them like a proud horse in battle.

10:4
d Isa 22:23
e Zec 9:10

⁴From Judah will come the cornerstone,
from him the tent peg,[d]
from him the battle bow,[e]
from him every ruler.
⁵Together they[a] will be like mighty men
trampling the muddy streets in battle.[f]
Because the LORD is with them,
they will fight and overthrow the horsemen.[g]

10:5
f 2Sa 22:43
g Am 2:15;
Hag 2:22

⁶"I will strengthen the house of Judah
and save the house of Joseph.
I will restore them
because I have compassion on them.[h]
They will be as though
I had not rejected them,
for I am the LORD their God
and I will answer[i] them.

10:6
h Zec 8:7-8
i Zec 13:9

⁷The Ephraimites will become like mighty men,
and their hearts will be glad as with wine.[j]
Their children will see it and be joyful;
their hearts will rejoice in the LORD.

10:7
j Zec 9:15

⁸I will signal[k] for them
and gather them in.
Surely I will redeem them;
they will be as numerous[l] as before.
⁹Though I scatter them among the peoples,
yet in distant lands they will remember me.[m]

10:8
k Isa 5:26
l Jer 33:22;
Eze 36:11

They and their children will survive,
and they will return.
¹⁰I will bring them back from Egypt
and gather them from Assyria.[n]
I will bring them to Gilead[o] and Lebanon,
and there will not be room[p] enough for them.

10:9
m Eze 6:9

10:10
n Isa 11:11
o Jer 50:19
p Isa 49:19

a 4,5 Or *ruler, all of them together.* / ⁵*They*

¹¹They will pass through the sea of trouble;
    the surging sea will be subdued
    and all the depths of the Nile will dry up.*^a*
Assyria's pride*^b* will be brought down
    and Egypt's scepter*^c* will pass away.
¹²I will strengthen them in the LORD
    and in his name they will walk,*^d*"

                 declares the LORD.

Chapter 11 Theme _____

11

Open your doors, O Lebanon,*^e*
    so that fire may devour your cedars!
²Wail, O pine tree, for the cedar has fallen;
    the stately trees are ruined!
Wail, oaks of Bashan;
    the dense forest*^f* has been cut down!
³Listen to the wail of the shepherds;
    their rich pastures are destroyed!
Listen to the roar of the lions;
    the lush thicket of the Jordan is ruined!*^g*

⁴This is what the LORD my God says: "Pasture the flock marked for slaughter. ⁵Their buyers slaughter them and go unpunished. Those who sell them say, 'Praise the LORD, I am rich!' Their own shepherds do not spare them.*^h* ⁶For I will no longer have pity on the people of the land," declares the LORD. "I will hand everyone over to his neighbor*ⁱ* and his king. They will oppress the land, and I will not rescue them from their hands."*^j*

⁷So I pastured the flock marked for slaughter, particularly the oppressed of the flock. Then I took two staffs and called one Favor and the other Union, and I pastured the flock. ⁸In one month I got rid of the three shepherds.

The flock detested me, and I grew weary of them ⁹and said, "I will not be your shepherd. Let the dying die, and the perishing perish.*^k* Let those who are left eat one another's flesh."

¹⁰Then I took my staff called Favor*^l* and broke it, revoking*^m* the covenant I had made with all the nations. ¹¹It was revoked on that day, and so the afflicted of the flock who were watching me knew it was the word of the LORD.

¹²I told them, "If you think it best, give me my pay; but if not, keep it." So they paid me thirty pieces of silver.*ⁿ*

¹³And the LORD said to me, "Throw it to the potter"—the handsome price at which they priced me! So I took the thirty pieces of silver and threw them into the house of the LORD to the potter.*^o*

¹⁴Then I broke my second staff called Union, breaking the brotherhood between Judah and Israel.

10:11
a Isa 19:5-7; 51:10
b Zep 2:13
c Eze 30:13

10:12
d Mic 4:5

11:1
e Eze 31:3

11:2
f Isa 32:19

11:3
g Jer 2:15; 50:44

11:5
h Jer 50:7; Eze 34:2-3

11:6
i Zec 14:13
j Isa 9:19-21; Jer 13:14; Mic 5:8; 7:2-6

11:9
k Jer 15:2; 43:11

11:10
l ver 7
m Ps 89:39; Jer 14:21

11:12
n Ex 21:32; Mt 26:15

11:13
o Mt 27:9-10*; Ac 1:18-19

Cross References

11:17
a Jer 23:1
b Eze 30:21-22
c Jer 23:1

12:1
d Isa 42:5;
Jer 51:15
e Ps 102:25;
Heb 1:10
f Isa 57:16

12:2
g Ps 75:8
h Isa 51:23
i Zec 14:14

12:3
j Zec 14:2
k Da 2:34-35
l Mt 21:44

12:4
m Ps 76:6

12:6
n Isa 10:17-18;
Zec 11:1
o Ob 1:18

12:7
p Jer 30:18;
Am 9:11

12:8
q Joel 3:16;
Zec 9:15
r Ps 82:6
s Mic 7:8

12:9
t Zec 14:2-3

12:10
u Isa 44:3;
Eze 39:29;
Joel 2:28-29
v Jn 19:34,37*;
Rev 1:7

[15]Then the LORD said to me, "Take again the equipment of a foolish shepherd. [16]For I am going to raise up a shepherd over the land who will not care for the lost, or seek the young, or heal the injured, or feed the healthy, but will eat the meat of the choice sheep, tearing off their hoofs.

[17]"Woe to the worthless shepherd,a
who deserts the flock!
May the sword strike his armb and his right eye!
May his arm be completely withered,
his right eye totally blinded!"c

Chapter 12 Theme

An Oracle

12 This is the word of the LORD concerning Israel. The LORD, who stretches out the heavens,d who lays the foundation of the earth,e and who forms the spirit of man f within him, declares: [2]"I am going to make Jerusalem a cupg that sends all the surrounding peoples reeling.h Judahi will be besieged as well as Jerusalem. [3]On that day, when all the nationsj of the earth are gathered against her, I will make Jerusalem an immovable rockk for all the nations. All who try to move it will injurel themselves. [4]On that day I will strike every horse with panic and its rider with madness," declares the LORD. "I will keep a watchful eye over the house of Judah, but I will blind all the horses of the nations.m [5]Then the leaders of Judah will say in their hearts, 'The people of Jerusalem are strong, because the LORD Almighty is their God.'

[6]"On that day I will make the leaders of Judah like a firepotn in a woodpile, like a flaming torch among sheaves. They will consumeo right and left all the surrounding peoples, but Jerusalem will remain intact in her place.

[7]"The LORD will save the dwellings of Judah first, so that the honor of the house of David and of Jerusalem's inhabitants may not be greater than that of Judah.p [8]On that day the LORD will shieldq those who live in Jerusalem, so that the feeblest among them will be like David, and the house of David will be like God,r like the Angel of the LORD going befores them. [9]On that day I will set out to destroy all the nations that attack Jerusalem.t

[10]"And I will pour out on the house of David and the inhabitants of Jerusalem a spirita of grace and supplication.u They will look onb me, the one they have pierced,v and they will mourn for him as one mourns for an only child, and grieve bitterly for him as one grieves for a firstborn son. [11]On that day the weeping in Jerusalem

will be great, like the weeping of Hadad Rimmon in the plain of Megiddo.[a] [12]The land will mourn,[b] each clan by itself, with their wives by themselves: the clan of the house of David and their wives, the clan of the house of Nathan and their wives, [13]the clan of the house of Levi and their wives, the clan of Shimei and their wives, [14]and all the rest of the clans and their wives.

Chapter 13 Theme _____

13 "On that day a fountain[c] will be opened to the house of David and the inhabitants of Jerusalem, to cleanse[d] them from sin and impurity.

[2]"On that day, I will banish the names of the idols[e] from the land, and they will be remembered no more," declares the LORD Almighty. "I will remove both the prophets[f] and the spirit of impurity from the land. [3]And if anyone still prophesies, his father and mother, to whom he was born, will say to him, 'You must die, because you have told lies in the LORD's name.' When he prophesies, his own parents will stab him.[g]

[4]"On that day every prophet will be ashamed[h] of his prophetic vision. He will not put on a prophet's garment[i] of hair[j] in order to deceive. [5]He will say, 'I am not a prophet. I am a farmer; the land has been my livelihood since my youth.[a][k] [6]If someone asks him, 'What are these wounds on your body[b]?' he will answer, 'The wounds I was given at the house of my friends.'

[7]"Awake, O sword,[l] against my shepherd,[m]
    against the man who is close to me!"
    declares the LORD Almighty.
  "Strike the shepherd,
    and the sheep will be scattered,[n]
    and I will turn my hand against the little ones.
[8]In the whole land," declares the LORD,
  "two-thirds will be struck down and perish;
    yet one-third will be left in it.[o]
[9]This third I will bring into the fire;[p]
  I will refine them like silver[q]
  and test them like gold.
  They will call[r] on my name
    and I will answer[s] them;
  I will say, 'They are my people,'[t]
    and they will say, 'The LORD is our God.[u]'"

Chapter 14 Theme _____

14 A day of the LORD[v] is coming when your plunder will be divided among you.

[a]5 Or *farmer; a man sold me in my youth*   [b]6 Or *wounds between your hands*

12:11
[a] 2Ki 23:29

12:12
[b] Mt 24:30;
Rev 1:7

13:1
[c] Jer 17:13
[d] Ps 51:2;
Heb 9:14

13:2
[e] Ex 23:13;
Eze 36:25;
Hos 2:17
[f] 1Ki 22:22;
Jer 23:14-15

13:3
[g] Dt 13:6-11;
18:20;
Jer 23:34;
Eze 14:9

13:4
[h] Jer 6:15;
Mic 3:6-7
[i] Mt 3:4
[j] 2Ki 1:8;
Isa 20:2

13:5
[k] Am 7:14

13:7
[l] Jer 47:6
[m] Isa 40:11;
53:4;
Eze 37:24
[n] Mt 26:31*;
Mk 14:27*

13:8
[o] Eze 5:2-4,12

13:9
[p] Mal 3:2
[q] Isa 48:10;
1Pe 1:6-7
[r] Ps 50:15
[s] Zec 10:6
[t] Jer 30:22
[u] Jer 29:12

14:1
[v] Isa 13:9;
Mal 4:1

14:2
a Isa 13:6;
Zec 13:8

14:3
b Zec 9:14-15

14:4
c Eze 11:23

14:5
d Am 1:1
e Isa 29:6;
66:15-16
f Mt 16:27; 25:31

14:6
g Isa 13:10;
Jer 4:23

14:7
h Jer 30:7
i Rev 21:23-25;
22:5
j Isa 30:26

14:8
k Eze 47:1-12;
Jn 7:38;
Rev 22:1-2
l Joel 2:20

14:9
m Dt 6:4;
Isa 45:24;
Rev 11:15
n Eph 4:5-6

14:10
o 1Ki 15:22
p Jer 30:18;
Am 9:11
q Zec 12:6

14:11
r Eze 34:25-28

14:12
s Lev 26:16;
Dt 28:22

14:13
t Zec 11:6

14:14
u Zec 12:2
v Isa 23:18

14:15
w ver 12

14:16
x Isa 60:6-9

14:17
y Jer 14:4;
Am 4:7

[2]I will gather all the nations to Jerusalem to fight against it; the city will be captured, the houses ransacked, and the women raped. Half of the city will go into exile, but the rest of the people will not be taken from the city.[a]

[3]Then the LORD will go out and fight[b] against those nations, as he fights in the day of battle. [4]On that day his feet will stand on the Mount of Olives,[c] east of Jerusalem, and the Mount of Olives will be split in two from east to west, forming a great valley, with half of the mountain moving north and half moving south. [5]You will flee by my mountain valley, for it will extend to Azel. You will flee as you fled from the earthquake[a][d] in the days of Uzziah king of Judah. Then the LORD my God will come,[e] and all the holy ones with him. [f]

[6]On that day there will be no light,[g] no cold or frost. [7]It will be a unique[h] day, without daytime or nighttime[i]—a day known to the LORD. When evening comes, there will be light. [j]

[8]On that day living water[k] will flow out from Jerusalem, half to the eastern[l] sea[b] and half to the western sea,[c] in summer and in winter.

[9]The LORD will be king over the whole earth.[m] On that day there will be one LORD, and his name the only name.[n]

[10]The whole land, from Geba[o] to Rimmon, south of Jerusalem, will become like the Arabah. But Jerusalem will be raised up[p] and remain in its place,[q] from the Benjamin Gate to the site of the First Gate, to the Corner Gate, and from the Tower of Hananel to the royal winepresses. [11]It will be inhabited; never again will it be destroyed. Jerusalem will be secure.[r]

[12]This is the plague with which the LORD will strike all the nations that fought against Jerusalem: Their flesh will rot while they are still standing on their feet, their eyes will rot in their sockets, and their tongues will rot in their mouths.[s] [13]On that day men will be stricken by the LORD with great panic. Each man will seize the hand of another, and they will attack each other.[t] [14]Judah[u] too will fight at Jerusalem. The wealth of all the surrounding nations will be collected[v]—great quantities of gold and silver and clothing. [15]A similar plague[w] will strike the horses and mules, the camels and donkeys, and all the animals in those camps.

[16]Then the survivors from all the nations that have attacked Jerusalem will go up year after year to worship the King, the LORD Almighty, and to celebrate the Feast of Tabernacles.[x] [17]If any of the peoples of the earth do not go up to Jerusalem to worship the King, the LORD Almighty, they will have no rain. [y] [18]If the Egyptian people do not go up and take part, they will have no rain. The LORD[d]

---

[a]5 Or *5My mountain valley will be blocked and will extend to Azel. It will be blocked as it was blocked because of the earthquake*   [b]8 That is, the Dead Sea   [c]8 That is, the Mediterranean   [d]18 Or *part, then the LORD*

will bring on them the plague he inflicts on the nations that do not go up to celebrate the Feast of Tabernacles.[a] [19]This will be the punishment of Egypt and the punishment of all the nations that do not go up to celebrate the Feast of Tabernacles.

[20]On that day HOLY TO THE LORD will be inscribed on the bells of the horses, and the cooking pots[b] in the LORD's house will be like the sacred bowls[c] in front of the altar. [21]Every pot in Jerusalem and Judah will be holy[d] to the LORD Almighty, and all who come to sacrifice will take some of the pots and cook in them. And on that day[e] there will no longer be a Canaanite[a][f] in the house of the LORD Almighty.[g]

a 21 Or merchant

14:18
a ver 12

14:20
b Eze 46:20
c Zec 9:15

14:21
d Ro 14:6-7;
1Co 10:31
e Ne 8:10
f Zec 9:8
g Eze 44:9

Zechariah's Prophetic Revelations

Concerning Messiah, Judah, and Jerusalem	Concerning the Nations	Concerning Messiah, the Savior and King

Theme of Zechariah:

SEGMENT DIVISIONS

		CHAPTER THEMES	Author:
		1	
		2	Date:
		3	Purpose:
		4	
		5	Key Words:
		6	
		7	
		8	
		9	
		10	
		11	
		12	
		13	
		14	

MALACHI

Because they had not obeyed the word of the Lord, in 586 B.C. the children of Israel were taken into captivity. The nation that was once the head became the tail, just as God had spoken through his prophet Moses. And just as God had spoken through Jeremiah the prophet, the children of Israel's captivity lasted for 70 years.

In 538 B.C. Cyrus, king of Persia, issued a decree allowing the children of Israel to return to Jerusalem and rebuild their temple. It was just as God had said when Isaiah gave this prophecy 175 years before Cyrus was born. In 516 B.C. Zerubbabel finished the temple, just as God promised. In 445 B.C. the Persian King Artaxerxes permitted Nehemiah to return to Jerusalem and rebuild its walls, just as Daniel had prophesied.

Over and over the children of Israel saw that God stood by his word. Just as Solomon wrote in Proverbs, the hearts of kings were in God's hands and he could turn them wherever he wanted. Why then did the remnant of Israel think that they could live and worship any way they wanted once they had returned from their 70 years of exile and had settled again in Israel? Had they grown tired of waiting for the fulfillment of the prophecies which promised that the Messiah would reign as King over all the earth? Had God abandoned them as he had Esau's descendants? Did they think he would allow the heathen nations who had come against them to go unpunished? Or were they entertaining thoughts that God really did not love them, that he would not keep his covenant promises?

Whatever it was, once again the remnant became apathetic in their relationship with God. So he spoke one more time through Malachi, whose name means "my messenger." It was sometime around 433 B.C.

∾ THINGS TO DO

1. Since Malachi is a short book, read it without interruption so you can get a perspective of the book before you observe it chapter by chapter. As you read, catch the atmosphere of this book. Remember, this was written to people who had been sent into exile because of disobedience and then had returned to their land just as God had promised.

2. Now read through Malachi one chapter at a time, doing the following:

   a. In a distinctive way or color mark the key words listed on the MALACHI AT A GLANCE chart on page 1661. Write these key words on an index card you can use as a bookmark while you study Malachi.

   b. As you mark every reference to *you say, you ask, saying* or *said,* watch what the priests and/or the people say and how God answers.

   c. Note in the margin with whom God is upset, why he is upset, and what he tells them to do or what he is going to do as a result.

   d. Take note of what will happen to those who fear his name and to those who do not. Record your insights in the margin.

   e. Note God's call to return to him, how they are to return, and what will happen if they do.

3. When you finish each chapter, decide what the main subject or theme of that chapter is and then record it on MALACHI AT A GLANCE and next to the chapter number in the text.

4. As you read the final chapter of Malachi, read Deuteronomy 28-30 which speaks of the blessings or curses upon those who obey or disobey the law given by Moses.

5. God was silent for 400 years after he spoke through his prophet Malachi. His silence was broken when an angel appeared to Zacharias with the news that he and Elizabeth would give birth to a son.

Read Luke 1:5-17 and Matthew 11:2-15 and see how these passages relate to God's final promise in Malachi. Record the essence of that promise in the margin of Malachi 4 and then write next to it the cross-references in Luke and Matthew.

6. Beginning on page 2178 is a chart called THE DAY OF THE LORD. Record on it what you learn from Malachi about that day. Note the reference (book, chapter, and verse) that you took your information from so you can find it later.

❧ THINGS TO THINK ABOUT

1. What do you learn from God's word to the priests that you can apply to your own life? Read through the list you compiled on "the priests" and remember that if you belong to the Lord Jesus Christ you are part of a kingdom of priests unto God. What kind of a priest are you? In principle do you think God expects anything less of you as a Christian? For instance, what do you offer the Lord of your time and talents, your tithe and offering? Do you give others instructions according to the Word of the Lord or according to the current philosophy of the world? What about your covenant relationship with your mate?

2. Are you tired of serving God? Do you fear him? If so, what is God's promise to you?

〰〰〰〰〰

Chapter 1 Theme

1 An oracle:[a] The word[b] of the LORD to Israel through Malachi.[a]

²"I have loved[c] you," says the LORD.

"But you ask, 'How have you loved us?'"

"Was not Esau Jacob's brother?" the LORD says. "Yet I have loved Jacob,[d] ³but Esau I have hated, and I have turned his mountains into a wasteland[e] and left his inheritance to the desert jackals.[f]"

⁴Edom may say, "Though we have been crushed, we will rebuild[g] the ruins."

But this is what the LORD Almighty says: "They may build, but I will demolish. They will be called the Wicked Land, a people always under the wrath of the LORD.[h] ⁵You will see it with your own eyes and say, 'Great[i] is the LORD—even beyond the borders of Israel!'[j]

⁶"A son honors his father, and a servant his master. If I am a father, where is the honor due me? If I am a master, where is the respect[k] due me?" says the LORD Almighty.[l] "It is you, O priests, who show contempt for my name.

"But you ask, 'How have we shown contempt for your name?'"

⁷"You place defiled food[m] on my altar.

"But you ask, 'How have we defiled you?'"

"By saying that the LORD's table is contemptible. ⁸When you bring blind animals for sacrifice, is that not wrong? When you sacrifice crippled or diseased animals,[n] is that not wrong? Try offering them to your governor! Would he be pleased with you? Would he accept you?" says the LORD Almighty.[o]

⁹"Now implore God to be gracious to us. With such offerings[p] from your hands, will he accept you?"—says the LORD Almighty.

a 1 Malachi means my messenger.

1:1
[a] Na 1:1
[b] 1Pe 4:11

1:2
[c] Dt 4:37
[d] Ro 9:13*

1:3
[e] Isa 34:10
[f] Eze 35:3-9

1:4
[g] Isa 9:10
[h] Eze 25:12-14

1:5
[i] Ps 35:27;
Mic 5:4
[j] Am 1:11-12

1:6
[k] Isa 1:2
[l] Job 5:17

1:7
[m] ver 12;
Lev 21:6

1:8
[n] Lev 22:22;
Dt 15:21
[o] Isa 43:23

1:9
[p] Lev 23:33-44

THE RULERS AND PROPHETS OF MALACHI'S TIME

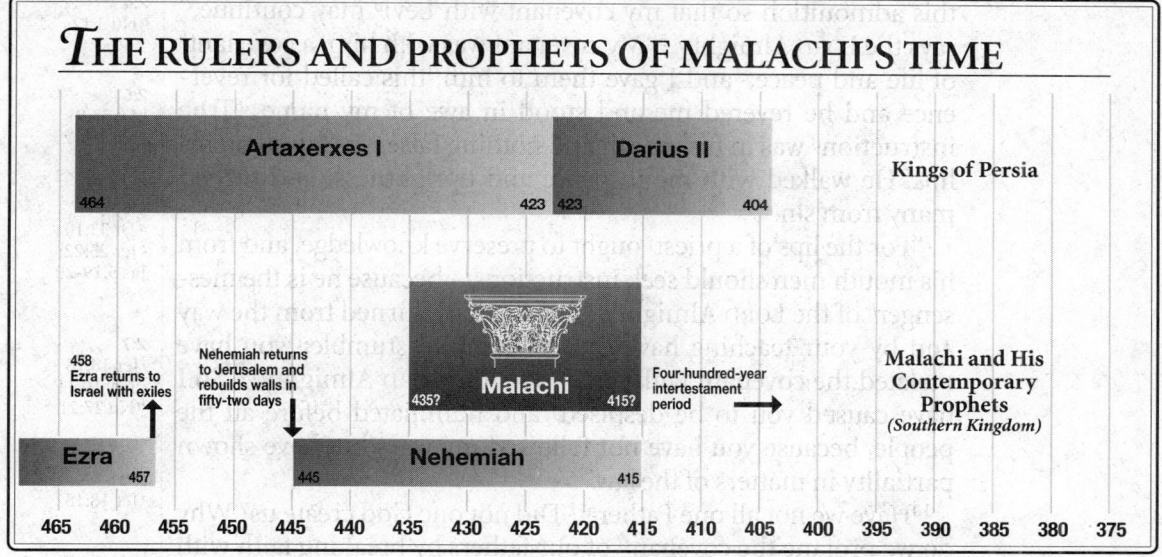

| Artaxerxes I | Darius II | Kings of Persia |

| 464 | 423 | 423 | 404 |

Malachi
435? — 415?

458 Ezra returns to Israel with exiles

Nehemiah returns to Jerusalem and rebuilds walls in fifty-two days

Four-hundred-year intertestament period

Malachi and His Contemporary Prophets
(Southern Kingdom)

Ezra 457

Nehemiah 445 — 415

465 460 455 450 445 440 435 430 425 420 415 410 405 400 395 390 385 380 375

1:10
a Hos 5:6
b Isa 1:11-14;
Jer 14:12

¹⁰"Oh, that one of you would shut the temple doors, so that you would not light useless fires on my altar! I am not pleased*a* with you," says the LORD Almighty, "and I will accept no offering*b* from your hands. ¹¹My name will be great among the nations, from the rising to the setting of the sun. In every place incense*c* and pure offerings will be brought to my name, because my name will be great among the nations," says the LORD Almighty.

1:11
c Isa 60:6-7;
Rev 8:3

¹²"But you profane it by saying of the Lord's table, 'It is defiled,' and of its food,*d* 'It is contemptible.' ¹³And you say, 'What a burden!'*e* and you sniff at it contemptuously," says the LORD Almighty.

1:12
d ver 7

"When you bring injured, crippled or diseased animals and offer them as sacrifices, should I accept them from your hands?" says the LORD. ¹⁴"Cursed is the cheat who has an acceptable male in his flock and vows to give it, but then sacrifices a blemished animal*f* to the Lord. For I am a great king,*g*" says the LORD Almighty, "and my name is to be feared among the nations.

1:13
e Isa 43:22-24

1:14
f Lev 22:18-21
g 1 Ti 6:15

Chapter 2 Theme

2:1
h ver 7

2 "And now this admonition is for you, O priests.*h* ²If you do not listen, and if you do not set your heart to honor my name," says the LORD Almighty, "I will send a curse*i* upon you, and I will curse your blessings. Yes, I have already cursed them, because you have not set your heart to honor me.

2:2
i Dt 28:20

³"Because of you I will rebuke*a* your descendants*b*; I will spread on your faces the offal*j* from your festival sacrifices, and you will be carried off with it.*k* ⁴And you will know that I have sent you

2:3
j Ex 29:14
k 1 Ki 14:10

a 3 Or *cut off* (see Septuagint) *b* 3 Or *will blight your grain* this admonition so that my covenant with Levi[a] may continue," says the LORD Almighty. [5]"My covenant was with him, a covenant[b] of life and peace,[c] and I gave them to him; this called for reverence and he revered me and stood in awe of my name. [6]True instruction[d] was in his mouth and nothing false was found on his lips. He walked with me in peace and uprightness, and turned many from sin.[e]

[7]"For the lips of a priest[f] ought to preserve knowledge, and from his mouth men should seek instruction[g]—because he is the messenger[h] of the LORD Almighty. [8]But you have turned from the way and by your teaching have caused many to stumble;[i] you have violated the covenant with Levi," says the LORD Almighty. [9]"So I have caused you to be despised[j] and humiliated before all the people, because you have not followed my ways but have shown partiality in matters of the law."

[10]Have we not all one Father[a?k] Did not one God create us? Why do we profane the covenant[l] of our fathers by breaking faith with one another?

[11]Judah has broken faith. A detestable thing has been committed in Israel and in Jerusalem: Judah has desecrated the sanctuary the LORD loves, by marrying[m] the daughter of a foreign god.[n] [12]As for the man who does this, whoever he may be, may the LORD cut him off[o] from the tents of Jacob[b]—even though he brings offerings[p] to the LORD Almighty.

[13]Another thing you do: You flood the LORD's altar with tears. You weep and wail because he no longer pays attention[q] to your offerings or accepts them with pleasure from your hands. [14]You ask, "Why?" It is because the LORD is acting as the witness between you and the wife of your youth,[r] because you have broken faith with her, though she is your partner, the wife of your marriage covenant.

[15]Has not ⌊the LORD⌋ made them one?[s] In flesh and spirit they are his. And why one? Because he was seeking godly offspring.[c t] So guard yourself in your spirit, and do not break faith with the wife of your youth.

[16]"I hate divorce,[u]" says the LORD God of Israel, "and I hate a man's covering himself[d] with violence as well as with his garment," says the LORD Almighty.

So guard yourself in your spirit, and do not break faith.

[17]You have wearied[v] the LORD with your words.

"How have we wearied him?" you ask.

By saying, "All who do evil are good in the eyes of the LORD, and he is pleased with them" or "Where is the God of justice?"

---

a 10 Or *father*   b 12 Or *12May the LORD cut off from the tents of Jacob anyone who gives testimony in behalf of the man who does this*   c 15 Or *15But the one ⌊who is our father⌋ did not do this, not as long as life remained in him. And what was he seeking? An offspring from God*   d 16 Or *his wife*

2:4
a Nu 3:12

2:5
b Dt 33:9
c Nu 25:12

2:6
d Dt 33:10
e Jer 23:22;
Jas 5:19-20

2:7
f Jer 18:18
g Lev 10:11
h Nu 27:21

2:8
i Jer 18:15

2:9
j 1Sa 2:30

2:10
k 1Co 8:6
l Ex 19:5

2:11
m Ne 13:23
n Ezr 9:1;
Jer 3:7-9

2:12
o Eze 24:21
p Mal 1:10

2:13
q Jer 14:12

2:14
r Pr 5:18

2:15
s Ge 2:24;
Mt 19:4-6
t 1Co 7:14

2:16
u Dt 24:1;
Mt 5:31-32;
19:4-9

2:17
v Isa 43:24

3:1
a Isa 40:3;
Mt 11:10*;
Mk 1:2*;
Lk 7:27*

3:2
b Eze 22:14;
Rev 6:17
c Zec 13:9;
Mt 3:10-12

3:3
d Da 12:10
e Isa 1:25

3:4
f 2Ch 7:12;
Ps 51:19;
Mal 1:11
g 2Ch 7:3

3:5
h Jer 7:9
i Lev 19:13;
Jas 5:4
j Ex 22:22

3:6
k Nu 23:19;
Jas 1:17

3:7
l Jer 7:26;
Ac 7:51
m Zec 1:3

3:8
n Ne 13:10-12

3:10
o Ne 13:12
p 2Ki 7:2

3:12
q Isa 61:9
r Isa 62:4

3:13
s Mal 2:17

3:14
t Ps 73:13
u Isa 58:3

3:15
v Jer 7:10

3:16
w Ps 34:15
x Ps 56:8

Chapter 3 Theme

3 "See, I will send my messenger, who will prepare the way before me.[a] Then suddenly the Lord you are seeking will come to his temple; the messenger of the covenant, whom you desire, will come," says the LORD Almighty.

²But who can endure[b] the day of his coming? Who can stand when he appears? For he will be like a refiner's fire[c] or a launderer's soap. ³He will sit as a refiner and purifier of silver;[d] he will purify[e] the Levites and refine them like gold and silver. Then the LORD will have men who will bring offerings in righteousness, ⁴and the offerings [f] of Judah and Jerusalem will be acceptable to the LORD, as in days gone by, as in former years.[g]

⁵"So I will come near to you for judgment. I will be quick to testify against sorcerers, adulterers and perjurers,[h] against those who defraud laborers of their wages,[i] who oppress the widows[j] and the fatherless, and deprive aliens of justice, but do not fear me," says the LORD Almighty.

⁶"I the LORD do not change.[k] So you, O descendants of Jacob, are not destroyed. ⁷Ever since the time of your forefathers you have turned away[l] from my decrees and have not kept them. Return to me, and I will return to you,"[m] says the LORD Almighty.

"But you ask, 'How are we to return?'

⁸"Will a man rob God? Yet you rob me.

"But you ask, 'How do we rob you?'

"In tithes[n] and offerings. ⁹You are under a curse—the whole nation of you—because you are robbing me. ¹⁰Bring the whole tithe into the storehouse,[o] that there may be food in my house. Test me in this," says the LORD Almighty, "and see if I will not throw open the floodgates[p] of heaven and pour out so much blessing that you will not have room enough for it. ¹¹I will prevent pests from devouring your crops, and the vines in your fields will not cast their fruit," says the LORD Almighty. ¹²"Then all the nations will call you blessed,[q] for yours will be a delightful land,"[r] says the LORD Almighty.

¹³"You have said harsh things[s] against me," says the LORD.

"Yet you ask, 'What have we said against you?'

¹⁴"You have said, 'It is futile[t] to serve God. What did we gain by carrying out his requirements and going about like mourners[u] before the LORD Almighty? ¹⁵But now we call the arrogant blessed. Certainly the evildoers[v] prosper, and even those who challenge God escape.'"

¹⁶Then those who feared the LORD talked with each other, and the LORD listened and heard.[w] A scroll[x] of remembrance was written in his presence concerning those who feared the LORD and honored his name.

[17]"They will be mine," says the LORD Almighty, "in the day when I make up my treasured possession.[a] [a] I will spare[b] them, just as in compassion a man spares his son who serves him. [18]And you will again see the distinction between the righteous[c] and the wicked, between those who serve God and those who do not.

Chapter 4 Theme

4 "Surely the day is coming;[d] it will burn like a furnace. All the arrogant and every evildoer will be stubble,[e] and that day that is coming will set them on fire," says the LORD Almighty. "Not a root or a branch will be left to them. [2]But for you who revere my name, the sun of righteousness[f] will rise with healing[g] in its wings. And you will go out and leap[h] like calves released from the stall. [3]Then you will trample[i] down the wicked; they will be ashes[j] under the soles of your feet on the day when I do these things," says the LORD Almighty.

[4]"Remember the law[k] of my servant Moses, the decrees and laws I gave him at Horeb for all Israel.

[5]"See, I will send you the prophet Elijah[l] before that great and dreadful day of the LORD comes.[m] [6]He will turn the hearts of the fathers to their children,[n] and the hearts of the children to their fathers; or else I will come and strike[o] the land with a curse."[p]

a 17 Or Almighty, "my treasured possession, in the day when I act

3:17
a Dt 7:6
b Ps 103:13;
Isa 26:20

3:18
c Ge 18:25

4:1
d Joel 2:31
e Isa 5:24; Ob 18

4:2
f Lk 1:78;
Eph 5:14
g Isa 30:26
h Isa 35:6

4:3
i Job 40:12
j Eze 28:18

4:4
k Ps 147:19

4:5
l Mt 11:14;
Lk 1:17
m Joel 2:31

4:6
n Lk 1:17
o Isa 11:4;
Rev 19:15
p Zec 5:3

THE NEW
TESTAMENT

LLSB

THE GENEALOGY OF JESUS THE CHRIST

As proof of his right to the throne of David through Mary

FOR THE GENERATIONS FROM ADAM TO ABRAHAM, SEE LUKE 3:34-38

David

Abraham	Nathan	Solomon
Isaac	Mattatha	Rehoboam
Jacob	Menna	Abijah
Judah	Melea	Asa
Perez	Eliakim	Jehoshaphat
Hezron	Jonam	Joram (Jehoram)
Ram	Joseph	Ahaziah
Admin	Judah	Joash
Amminadab	Simeon	Amaziah
Nahshon	Levi	Uzziah (Azariah)
Salmon—Rahab	Matthat	Jotham
Boaz—Ruth	Jorim	Ahaz
Obed	Eliezer	Hezekiah
Jesse	Joshua	Manasseh
	Er	Amon
	Elmadam	Josiah
	Cosam	Jehoiakim
	Addi	Jeconiah (Jehoiachin)
	Melki	Shealtiel
	Neri	Zerubbabel
	Shealtiel	Abiud
	Zerubbabel	Eliakim
	Rhesa	Azor
	Joanan	Zadok
	Joda	Akim
	Josech	Eliud
	Semein	Eleazar
	Mattathias	Matthan
	Maath	Jacob
	Naggai	Joseph
	Esli	
	Nahum	
	Amos	
	Mattathias	
	Joseph	
	Jannai	
	Melki	
	Levi	
	Matthat	
	Heli	
	Mary	

This information is taken from
1 Chronicles 3
Matthew 1
Luke 3

The Holy Spirit
Luke 1:35

Jesus
("He was the son, so it
was thought, of Joseph"
[Luke 3:23])

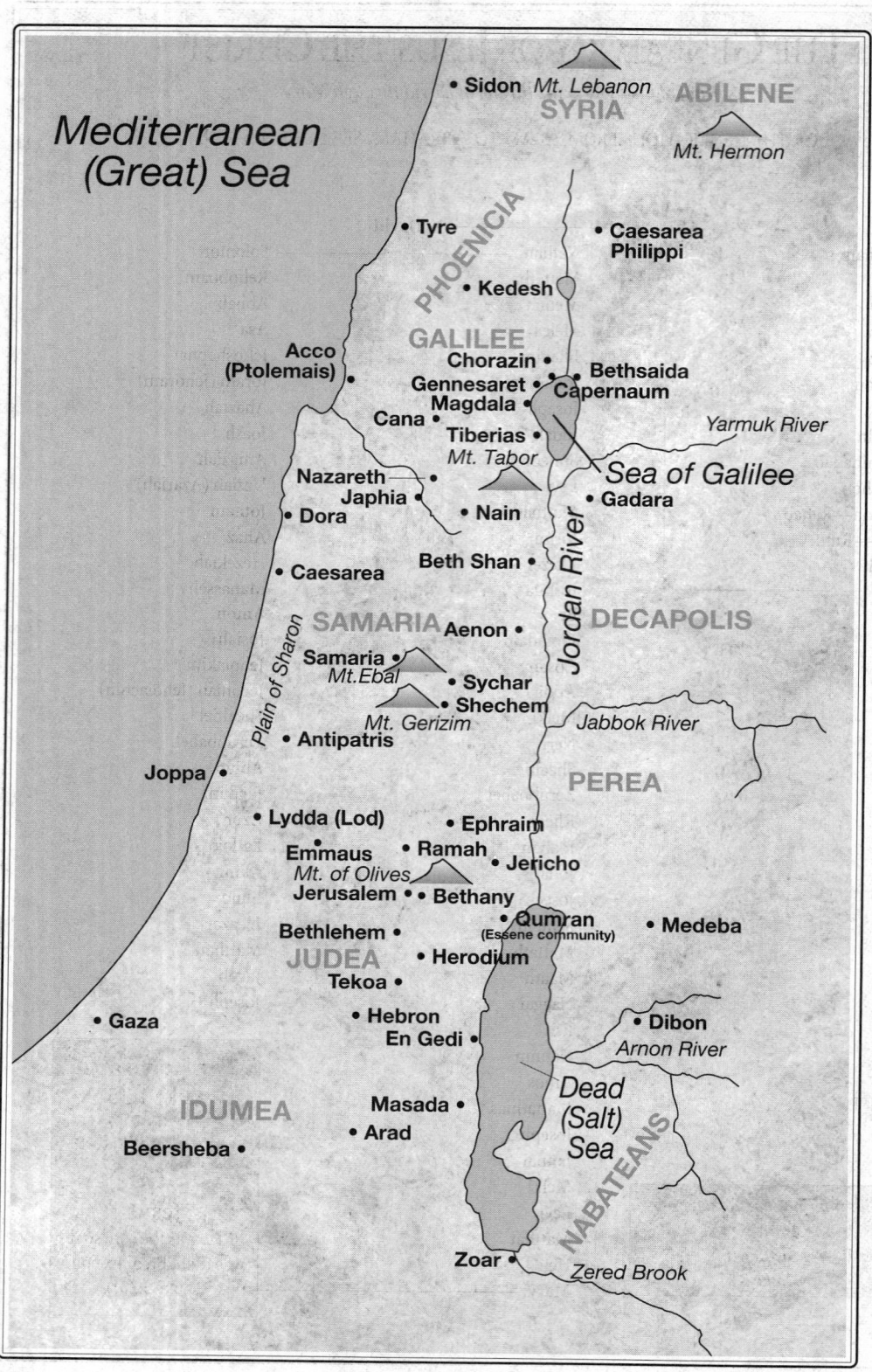

Mediterranean
(Great) Sea

**Bible Cities
in the Time
of Jesus**

• Sidon *Mt. Lebanon* **ABILENE**
SYRIA
Mt. Hermon

• Tyre   • **Caesarea
                            Philippi**

PHOENICIA

• **Kedesh**

GALILEE

Acco
(Ptolemais) •

Chorazin
                    • **Bethsaida**
Gennesaret • **Capernaum**
Magdala
Cana •   *Yarmuk River*
      • **Tiberias**
Mt. Tabor

Nazareth   **Sea of Galilee**
Japhia •   • **Nain**
• **Dora**   • **Gadara**

                    Jordan River

• **Caesarea**

                    DECAPOLIS

SAMARIA **Aenon** •

Plain of Sharon

Samaria • *Mt.Ebal*
                • **Sychar**
                • **Shechem**   *Jabbok River*
Mt. Gerizim

• **Antipatris**

Joppa •   **PEREA**

• **Lydda (Lod)**
                • **Ephraim**
Emmaus   • **Ramah**
Mt. of Olives   • **Jericho**
Jerusalem • • **Bethany**

Bethlehem •   • **Qumran**
                    (Essene community)   • **Medeba**
JUDEA   • **Herodium**
Tekoa •

• **Hebron**   • **Dibon**
En Gedi •   *Arnon River*

• **Gaza**

IDUMEA   **Masada** •   *Dead
                                  (Salt)
Beersheba •   • **Arad**   Sea*

                                  NABATEANS

                Zoar •   *Zered Brook*

MATTHEW

God promised Abraham that through his seed all the nations of the earth would be blessed (Genesis 12:3; 15:1-6). Where was this son of Abraham?

God promised Isaiah that a child would be born, a son would be given, and the government would rest on his shoulders. His name would be Wonderful Counselor, Mighty God, Everlasting Father, Prince of Peace. There would be no end to the increase of his government or of peace. He would occupy the throne of David (Isaiah 9:6, 7). Where was this son of David?

No one knew until a baby's cry went up from Bethlehem Ephrathah. The Magi from the East arrived in Jerusalem saying, "Where is the one who has been born king of the Jews?" The one who was to be ruler in Israel (Micah 5:2), the son of David, the son of Abraham, had been born. Matthew tells us about him, the king of the Jews.

✎ THINGS TO DO

1. From the first verse Matthew's purpose is clear: to show that Jesus was the long-awaited king, the son of David, the Messiah whose coming was prophesied throughout the Old Testament.

There is a pattern to Matthew that repeats itself and divides the Gospel into six segments. Matthew presents certain facts concerning the person and work of Jesus which he then follows with an account of Jesus' teaching. Each teaching account is brought to a conclusion with one of the following phrases: "When Jesus had finished saying these things," "finished instructing," "finished these parables," "when Jesus had finished saying these things," or "when Jesus had finished saying all these things."

Therefore before you read through Matthew chapter by chapter, mark in a distinctive way each occurrence of a dividing phrase in 7:28; 11:1; 13:53; 19:1; and 26:1. Remember, these phrases conclude that particular teaching. Then the cycle begins again.

2. Now read Matthew chapter by chapter, keeping in mind these six segments. As you read:

   a. In a distinctive way mark in the text the key words listed on the MATTHEW AT A GLANCE chart on page 1722.

      1) List in the margin what you learn about the kingdom from the references where you marked the key words *king* and the *kingdom of heaven/God.*

      2) In addition to these key words, watch for other key words or phrases. Reread the observation section in "How to Use The International Inductive Study Bible" on page IISB-15.

   b. Using the same color pen each time, underline each reference to or quotation from an Old Testament prophecy which shows Jesus as the promised king. Then note in the margin how Jesus fulfills that prophecy. (You can recognize Old Testament quotes easily because the NIV text is indented on both sides.)

   c. Watch for the events, works, or facts which demonstrate who Jesus Christ is. You may want to note these in the margin.

   d. When you read Jesus' teaching on a particular subject, in the margin make a list of the main points covered in his teaching. If it is a prophetic teaching, pay attention to time phrases or indicators, including *then, therefore, at that time, when, after, as soon as, while, if, now, as,* and *before.* Watch for the progression of events.

   e. Record the main theme or event of each chapter in the text next to the chapter number and on MATTHEW AT A GLANCE.

3. Chapters 26 through 28 give an account of the final events in the life of Jesus. Record the progression of events on the charts titled THE ARREST, TRIAL, AND CRUCIFIXION OF JESUS CHRIST on

page 1862 and/or THE ACCOUNT OF JESUS' RESURRECTION on page 1863. You may want to first record these insights on notebook paper and then transfer them to the charts. Note the chapter and verse of each insight for future reference.

    a. When you record the circumstances surrounding the resurrection of Jesus Christ, also note any postresurrection appearances which are recorded in Matthew. After you do this for all four Gospels you will have comprehensive notes on all that took place.

    b. As you do this, remember that Luke gives the consecutive order of events, and therefore, Luke becomes a plumb line for the other Gospel records.

4. A chart titled WHAT THE GOSPELS TEACH ABOUT THE KINGDOM OF GOD/THE KINGDOM OF HEAVEN is on pages 1864 and 1865. List and consolidate everything you learn from Matthew about the kingdom on a piece of notebook paper. Then transfer this to the chart. Be sure to note the chapter and verse for future reference.

5. Complete MATTHEW AT A GLANCE. Under "Segment Divisions," record the theme of each segment of Matthew. There is also a blank column for any other segment divisions you might see.

THINGS TO THINK ABOUT

1. Have you bowed your knee to Jesus as king in your life? Read Matthew 7:21-27 and think about the difference between *merely hearing* something and *hearing and living accordingly*. Which best describes you?

2. Can you explain from Scripture to another person why Jesus is the king of the promised kingdom?

3. Do you realize that Jesus' final words to his disciples in Matthew 28:19, 20 are your responsibility also? What are you doing in order to fulfill his Great Commission? As you go, are you making disciples? Are you teaching them to observe all that he has commanded?

Chapter 1 Theme

1 A record of the genealogy of Jesus Christ the son of David,[a] the son of Abraham:[b]

[2] Abraham was the father of Isaac,[c]
Isaac the father of Jacob,[d]
Jacob the father of Judah and his brothers,[e]
[3] Judah the father of Perez and Zerah, whose mother was Tamar,[f]
Perez the father of Hezron,
Hezron the father of Ram,
[4] Ram the father of Amminadab,
Amminadab the father of Nahshon,
Nahshon the father of Salmon,
[5] Salmon the father of Boaz, whose mother was Rahab,
Boaz the father of Obed, whose mother was Ruth,
Obed the father of Jesse,
[6] and Jesse the father of King David.[g]

David was the father of Solomon, whose mother had been Uriah's wife,[h]

INSIGHT

See **The Genealogy of Jesus the Christ** on page 1665.

1:1 a 2Sa 7:12-16; Isa 9:6,7; 11:1; Jer 23:5,6; Mt 9:27; Lk 1:32,69; Ro 1:3; Rev 22:16
b Ge 22:18; Gal 3:16

1:2 c Ge 21:3,12 d Ge 25:26 e Ge 29:35

1:3 f Ge 38:27-30

1:6 g 1Sa 16:1; 17:12 h 2Sa 12:24

1:10
a 2Ki 20:21

⁷Solomon the father of Rehoboam,
  Rehoboam the father of Abijah,
  Abijah the father of Asa,
⁸Asa the father of Jehoshaphat,
  Jehoshaphat the father of Jehoram,
  Jehoram the father of Uzziah,
⁹Uzziah the father of Jotham,
  Jotham the father of Ahaz,
  Ahaz the father of Hezekiah,
¹⁰Hezekiah the father of Manasseh,*a*
  Manasseh the father of Amon,
  Amon the father of Josiah,
¹¹and Josiah the father of Jeconiah*a* and his brothers at the
  time of the exile to Babylon.*b*

1:11
b 2Ki 24:14-16;
Jer 27:20;
Da 1:1,2

1:12
c 1Ch 3:17
d 1Ch 3:19;
Ezr 3:2

¹²After the exile to Babylon:
  Jeconiah was the father of Shealtiel,*c*
  Shealtiel the father of Zerubbabel,*d*
¹³Zerubbabel the father of Abiud,
  Abiud the father of Eliakim,
  Eliakim the father of Azor,
¹⁴Azor the father of Zadok,
  Zadok the father of Akim,
  Akim the father of Eliud,
¹⁵Eliud the father of Eleazar,
  Eleazar the father of Matthan,
  Matthan the father of Jacob,
¹⁶and Jacob the father of Joseph, the husband of Mary,*e* of
  whom was born Jesus, who is called Christ.*f*

1:16
e Lk 1:27
f Mt 27:17

¹⁷Thus there were fourteen generations in all from Abraham to David, fourteen from David to the exile to Babylon, and fourteen from the exile to the Christ.*b*

1:18
g Lk 1:35

¹⁸This is how the birth of Jesus Christ came about: His mother Mary was pledged to be married to Joseph, but before they came together, she was found to be with child through the Holy Spirit.*g* ¹⁹Because Joseph her husband was a righteous man and did not want to expose her to public disgrace, he had in mind to divorce*h* her quietly.

1:19
h Dt 24:1

²⁰But after he had considered this, an angel of the Lord appeared to him in a dream and said, "Joseph son of David, do not be afraid to take Mary home as your wife, because what is conceived in her is from the Holy Spirit. ²¹She will give birth to a son, and you are to give him the name Jesus,*c i* because he will save his people from their sins."*j*

1:21
i Lk 1:31
j Lk 2:11;
Ac 5:31;
13:23,28

a *11* That is, Jehoiachin; also in verse 12   b *17* Or *Messiah*. "The Christ" (Greek) and "the Messiah" (Hebrew) both mean "the Anointed One."   c *21* *Jesus* is the Greek form of *Joshua*, which means *the LORD saves.*

Herod's Family Tree

Herod the Great
(died 4 B.C.)
Mt. 2:1-22; Lk. 1:5

Son of Doris

Antipater
(executed 4 B.C.)

Sons of Mariamne I
(Miriam)

Aristobulus
(executed 7 B.C.)

Alexander
(executed 7 B.C.)

**Sons of Malthace,
a Samaritan**

Herod Antipas
Tetrarch of
Galilee & Perea
(died A.D. 39)
Mt. 14:1-11; Lk. 3:1, 19;
13:31-33; 23:7-12

Archelaus
Governor of Judea,
Samaria, & Idumea
(died A.D. 6)
Mt. 2:22

Son of Cleopatra

Herod Philip II
Tetrarch of Iturea
and Trachonitis
(died A.D. 34)

**Son of Mariamne II
of Simon**

Herod Philip I
(first husband
of Herodias)
(died about A.D. 34)
Lk. 3:19; Mt. 14:3

Herod of Chalcis
(died A.D. 48)

Herodias
(wife of
Herod Antipas)
Mt. 14:3; Lk. 3:19

Herod Agrippa I
King of Judea
(died A.D. 44)
Acts 12:1-24

Salome

Bernice
(consort to
her brother)
Acts 25:13

Herod Agrippa II
Tetrarch of Chalcis,
A.D. 44; King, A.D. 48-100
(died about A.D. 100)
Acts 25:13–26:32

Drusilla
(married Felix,
procurator
of Judea)

22All this took place to fulfill what the Lord had said through the prophet: **23**"The virgin will be with child and will give birth to a son, and they will call him Immanuel"[a][a]—which means, "God with us."

24When Joseph woke up, he did what the angel of the Lord had commanded him and took Mary home as his wife. **25**But he had no union with her until she gave birth to a son. And he gave him the name Jesus.[b]

Chapter 2 Theme

2 After Jesus was born in Bethlehem in Judea,[c] during the time of King Herod,[d] Magi[b] from the east came to Jerusalem **2**and asked, "Where is the one who has been born king of the Jews?[e] We saw his star[f] in the east[c] and have come to worship him."

3When King Herod heard this he was disturbed, and all Jerusalem with him. **4**When he had called together all the people's chief priests and teachers of the law, he asked them where the Christ[d] was to be born. **5**"In Bethlehem[g] in Judea," they replied, "for this is what the prophet has written:

6"'But you, Bethlehem, in the land of Judah,
    are by no means least among the rulers of Judah;
  for out of you will come a ruler
    who will be the shepherd of my people Israel.'[e]"[h]

1:23
[a]Isa 7:14; 8:8,10

1:25
[b]ver 21

2:1
[c]Lk 2:4-7
[d]Lk 1:5

2:2
[e]Jer 23:5;
Mt 27:11;
Mk 15:2;
Jn 1:49; 18:33-37
[f]Nu 24:17

2:5
[g]Jn 7:42

2:6
[h]Mic 5:2;
2Sa 5:2

[a]23 Isaiah 7:14   [b]1 Traditionally *Wise Men*   [c]2 Or *star when it rose*   [d]4 Or *Messiah*
[e]6 Micah 5:2

2:11
a Isa 60:3
b Ps 72:10

7Then Herod called the Magi secretly and found out from them the exact time the star had appeared. 8He sent them to Bethlehem and said, "Go and make a careful search for the child. As soon as you find him, report to me, so that I too may go and worship him."

2:12
c Heb 11:7
d ver 13,19,22;
Mt 27:19

9After they had heard the king, they went on their way, and the star they had seen in the east a went ahead of them until it stopped over the place where the child was. 10When they saw the star, they were overjoyed. 11On coming to the house, they saw the child with his mother Mary, and they bowed down and worshiped him. a Then they opened their treasures and presented him with gifts b of gold and of incense and of myrrh. 12And having been warned c in a dream d not to go back to Herod, they returned to their country by another route.

2:13
e Ac 5:19
f ver 12,19,22

13When they had gone, an angel e of the Lord appeared to Joseph in a dream. f "Get up," he said, "take the child and his mother and escape to Egypt. Stay there until I tell you, for Herod is going to search for the child to kill him."

2:15
g Hos 11:1;
Ex 4:22,23

14So he got up, took the child and his mother during the night and left for Egypt, 15where he stayed until the death of Herod. And so was fulfilled what the Lord had said through the prophet: "Out of Egypt I called my son." b g

16When Herod realized that he had been outwitted by the Magi, he was furious, and he gave orders to kill all the boys in Bethlehem and its vicinity who were two years old and under, in accordance with the time he had learned from the Magi. 17Then what was said through the prophet Jeremiah was fulfilled:

2:18
h Jer 31:15

18"A voice is heard in Ramah,
     weeping and great mourning,
Rachel weeping for her children
     and refusing to be comforted,
because they are no more." c h

2:19
i ver 12,13,22

19After Herod died, an angel of the Lord appeared in a dream i to Joseph in Egypt 20and said, "Get up, take the child and his mother and go to the land of Israel, for those who were trying to take the child's life are dead."

2:22
j ver 12,13,19;
Mt 27:19
k Lk 2:39

21So he got up, took the child and his mother and went to the land of Israel. 22But when he heard that Archelaus was reigning in Judea in place of his father Herod, he was afraid to go there. Having been warned in a dream, j he withdrew to the district of Galilee, k 23and he went and lived in a town called Nazareth. l So was fulfilled m what was said through the prophets: "He will be called a Nazarene." n

2:23
l Lk 1:26;
Jn 1:45,46
m Mt 1:22
n Mk 1:24

a 9 Or seen when it rose   b 15 Hosea 11:1   c 18 Jer. 31:15

Chapter 3 Theme

3 In those days John the Baptist[a] came, preaching in the Desert of Judea ²and saying, "Repent, for the kingdom of heaven[b] is near." ³This is he who was spoken of through the prophet Isaiah:

> "A voice of one calling in the desert,
> 'Prepare the way for the Lord,
>   make straight paths for him.'"[a c]

⁴John's clothes were made of camel's hair, and he had a leather belt around his waist.[d] His food was locusts[e] and wild honey. ⁵People went out to him from Jerusalem and all Judea and the whole region of the Jordan. ⁶Confessing their sins, they were baptized by him in the Jordan River.

⁷But when he saw many of the Pharisees and Sadducees coming to where he was baptizing, he said to them: "You brood of vipers![f] Who warned you to flee from the coming wrath?[g] ⁸Produce fruit in keeping with repentance.[h] ⁹And do not think you can say to yourselves, 'We have Abraham as our father.' I tell you that out of these stones God can raise up children for Abraham. ¹⁰The ax is already at the root of the trees, and every tree that does not produce good fruit will be cut down and thrown into the fire.[i]

¹¹"I baptize you with[b] water for repentance. But after me will come one who is more powerful than I, whose sandals I am not fit to carry. He will baptize you with the Holy Spirit[j] and with fire.[k] ¹²His winnowing fork is in his hand, and he will clear his threshing floor, gathering his wheat into the barn and burning up the chaff with unquenchable fire."[l]

¹³Then Jesus came from Galilee to the Jordan to be baptized by John.[m] ¹⁴But John tried to deter him, saying, "I need to be baptized by you, and do you come to me?"

¹⁵Jesus replied, "Let it be so now; it is proper for us to do this to fulfill all righteousness." Then John consented.

¹⁶As soon as Jesus was baptized, he went up out of the water. At that moment heaven was opened, and he saw the Spirit of God[n] descending like a dove and lighting on him. ¹⁷And a voice from heaven[o] said, "This is my Son,[p] whom I love; with him I am well pleased."[q]

Chapter 4 Theme

4 Then Jesus was led by the Spirit into the desert to be tempted by the devil. ²After fasting forty days and forty nights,[r] he was hungry. ³The tempter[s] came to him and said, "If you are the Son of God,[t] tell these stones to become bread."

a3 Isaiah 40:3   b11 Or *in*

3:1
[a] Lk 1:13,57-66;
3:2-19

3:2
[b] Da 2:44;
Mt 4:17; 6:10;
Lk 11:20; 21:31;
Jn 3:3,5;
Ac 1:3,6

3:3
[c] Isa 40:3;
Mal 3:1;
Lk 1:76;
Jn 1:23

3:4
[d] 2Ki 1:8
[e] Lev 11:22

3:7
[f] Mt 12:34;
23:33
[g] Ro 1:18;
1Th 1:10

3:8
[h] Ac 26:20

3:10
[i] Mt 7:19;
Lk 13:6-9;
Jn 15:2,6

3:11
[j] Mk 1:8
[k] Isa 4:4;
Ac 2:3,4

3:12
[l] Mt 13:30

3:13
[m] Mk 1:4

3:16
[n] Isa 11:2; 42:1

3:17
[o] Mt 17:5;
Jn 12:28
[p] Ps 2:7;
2Pe 1:17,18
[q] Isa 42:1;
Mt 12:18; 17:5;
Mk 1:11; 9:7;
Lk 9:35

4:2
[r] Ex 34:28;
1Ki 19:8

4:3
[s] 1Th 3:5
[t] Mt 3:17;
Jn 5:25;
Ac 9:20

4:4
aDt 8:3

4:5
bNe 11:1;
Da 9:24;
Mt 27:53

4:6
cPs 91:11,12

4:7
dDt 6:16

4:10
eICh 21:1
fDt 6:13

4:11
gMt 26:53;
Lk 22:43;
Heb 1:14

4:12
hMt 14:3
iMk 1:14

4:13
jMk 1:21;
Lk 4:23,31;
Jn 2:12; 4:46,47

4:16
kIsa 9:1,2;
Lk 2:32

4:17
lMt 3:2

4:18
mMt 15:29;
Mk 7:31;
Jn 6:1
nMt 16:17,18

4:19
oMk 10:21,
28,52

4:21
pMt 20:20

[4]Jesus answered, "It is written: 'Man does not live on bread alone, but on every word that comes from the mouth of God.'a"a

[5]Then the devil took him to the holy cityb and had him stand on the highest point of the temple. [6]"If you are the Son of God," he said, "throw yourself down. For it is written:

> "'He will command his angels concerning you,
>   and they will lift you up in their hands,
> so that you will not strike your foot against a stone.'b"c

[7]Jesus answered him, "It is also written: 'Do not put the Lord your God to the test.'c"d

[8]Again, the devil took him to a very high mountain and showed him all the kingdoms of the world and their splendor. [9]"All this I will give you," he said, "if you will bow down and worship me."

[10]Jesus said to him, "Away from me, Satan!e For it is written: 'Worship the Lord your God, and serve him only.'d"f

[11]Then the devil left him, and angels came and attended him.g

[12]When Jesus heard that John had been put in prison,h he returned to Galilee.i [13]Leaving Nazareth, he went and lived in Capernaum,j which was by the lake in the area of Zebulun and Naphtali— [14]to fulfill what was said through the prophet Isaiah:

> [15]"Land of Zebulun and land of Naphtali,
>   the way to the sea, along the Jordan,
>   Galilee of the Gentiles—
> [16]the people living in darkness
>   have seen a great light;
> on those living in the land of the shadow of death
>   a light has dawned."e k

[17]From that time on Jesus began to preach, "Repent, for the kingdom of heavenl is near."

[18]As Jesus was walking beside the Sea of Galilee,m he saw two brothers, Simon called Petern and his brother Andrew. They were casting a net into the lake, for they were fishermen. [19]"Come, follow me,"o Jesus said, "and I will make you fishers of men." [20]At once they left their nets and followed him.

[21]Going on from there, he saw two other brothers, James son of Zebedee and his brother John.p They were in

Israel in the Time of Christ

a4 Deut. 8:3   b6 Psalm 91:11,12   c7 Deut. 6:16   d10 Deut. 6:13   e16 Isaiah 9:1,2 a boat with their father Zebedee, preparing their nets. Jesus called them, ²²and immediately they left the boat and their father and followed him.

²³Jesus went throughout Galilee,*a* teaching in their synagogues,*b* preaching the good news*c* of the kingdom,*d* and healing every disease and sickness among the people.*e* ²⁴News about him spread all over Syria,*f* and people brought to him all who were ill with various diseases, those suffering severe pain, the demon-possessed,*g* those having seizures,*h* and the paralyzed,*i* and he healed them. ²⁵Large crowds from Galilee, the Decapolis,*a* Jerusalem, Judea and the region across the Jordan followed him.*j*

Chapter 5 Theme

5 Now when he saw the crowds, he went up on a mountainside and sat down. His disciples came to him, ²and he began to teach them, saying:

³"Blessed are the poor in spirit,
　　for theirs is the kingdom of heaven.*k*
⁴Blessed are those who mourn,
　　for they will be comforted.*l*
⁵Blessed are the meek,
　　for they will inherit the earth.*m*
⁶Blessed are those who hunger and thirst
　　　for righteousness,
　　for they will be filled.*n*
⁷Blessed are the merciful,
　　for they will be shown mercy.
⁸Blessed are the pure in heart,*o*
　　for they will see God.*p*
⁹Blessed are the peacemakers,
　　for they will be called sons of God.*q*
¹⁰Blessed are those who are persecuted because
　　　of righteousness,*r*
　　for theirs is the kingdom of heaven.

¹¹"Blessed are you when people insult you,*s* persecute you and falsely say all kinds of evil against you because of me. ¹²Rejoice and be glad,*t* because great is your reward in heaven, for in the same way they persecuted the prophets who were before you.*u*

¹³"You are the salt of the earth. But if the salt loses its saltiness, how can it be made salty again? It is no longer good for anything, except to be thrown out and trampled by men.*v*

¹⁴"You are the light of the world.*w* A city on a hill cannot be hidden. ¹⁵Neither do people light a lamp and put it under a bowl.

a 25 That is, the Ten Cities

4:23
a Mk 1:39;
Lk 4:15,44
b Mt 9:35; 13:54;
Mk 1:21;
Lk 4:15;
Jn 6:59
c Mk 1:14
d Mt 3:2;
Ac 20:25
e Mt 8:16; 15:30;
Ac 10:38

4:24
f Lk 2:2
g Mt 8:16,28;
9:32; 15:22;
Mk 1:32;
5:15,16,18
h Mt 17:15
i Mt 8:6; 9:2;
Mk 2:3

4:25
j Mk 3:7,8;
Lk 6:17

5:3
k ver 10,19;
Mt 25:34

5:4
l Isa 61:2,3;
Rev 7:17

5:5
m Ps 37:11;
Ro 4:13

5:6
n Isa 55:1,2

5:8
o Ps 24:3,4
p Heb 12:14;
Rev 22:4

5:9
q ver 44,45;
Ro 8:14

5:10
r 1Pe 3:14

5:11
s 1Pe 4:14

5:12
t Ac 5:41;
1Pe 4:13,16
u Mt 23:31,37;
Ac 7:52;
1Th 2:15

5:13
v Mk 9:50;
Lk 14:34,35

5:14
w Jn 8:12

5:15
a Mk 4:21;
Lk 8:16

5:16
b Mt 9:8

5:17
c Ro 3:31

5:18
d Lk 16:17

5:19
e Jas 2:10

5:21
f Ex 20:13;
Dt 5:17

5:22
g 1Jn 3:15
h Mt 26:59
i Jas 3:6

5:27
j Ex 20:14;
Dt 5:18

5:28
k Pr 6:25

5:29
l Mt 18:6,8,9;
Mk 9:42-47

5:31
m Dt 24:1-4

5:32
n Lk 16:18

5:33
o Lev 19:12

Instead they put it on its stand, and it gives light to everyone in the house.[a] [16]In the same way, let your light shine before men, that they may see your good deeds and praise[b] your Father in heaven.

[17]"Do not think that I have come to abolish the Law or the Prophets; I have not come to abolish them but to fulfill them.[c] [18]I tell you the truth, until heaven and earth disappear, not the smallest letter, not the least stroke of a pen, will by any means disappear from the Law until everything is accomplished.[d] [19]Anyone who breaks one of the least of these commandments[e] and teaches others to do the same will be called least in the kingdom of heaven, but whoever practices and teaches these commands will be called great in the kingdom of heaven. [20]For I tell you that unless your righteousness surpasses that of the Pharisees and the teachers of the law, you will certainly not enter the kingdom of heaven.

[21]"You have heard that it was said to the people long ago, 'Do not murder,[a][f] and anyone who murders will be subject to judgment.' [22]But I tell you that anyone who is angry with his brother[b] will be subject to judgment.[g] Again, anyone who says to his brother, 'Raca,[c]' is answerable to the Sanhedrin.[h] But anyone who says, 'You fool!' will be in danger of the fire of hell.[i]

[23]"Therefore, if you are offering your gift at the altar and there remember that your brother has something against you, [24]leave your gift there in front of the altar. First go and be reconciled to your brother; then come and offer your gift.

[25]"Settle matters quickly with your adversary who is taking you to court. Do it while you are still with him on the way, or he may hand you over to the judge, and the judge may hand you over to the officer, and you may be thrown into prison. [26]I tell you the truth, you will not get out until you have paid the last penny.[d]

[27]"You have heard that it was said, 'Do not commit adultery.'[e][j] [28]But I tell you that anyone who looks at a woman lustfully has already committed adultery with her in his heart.[k] [29]If your right eye causes you to sin,[l] gouge it out and throw it away. It is better for you to lose one part of your body than for your whole body to be thrown into hell. [30]And if your right hand causes you to sin, cut it off and throw it away. It is better for you to lose one part of your body than for your whole body to go into hell.

[31]"It has been said, 'Anyone who divorces his wife must give her a certificate of divorce.'[f][m] [32]But I tell you that anyone who divorces his wife, except for marital unfaithfulness, causes her to become an adulteress, and anyone who marries the divorced woman commits adultery.[n]

[33]"Again, you have heard that it was said to the people long ago, 'Do not break your oath,[o] but keep the oaths you have made to

the Lord.'[a] [34]But I tell you, Do not swear at all:[b] either by heaven, for it is God's throne;[c] [35]or by the earth, for it is his footstool; or by Jerusalem, for it is the city of the Great King.[d] [36]And do not swear by your head, for you cannot make even one hair white or black. [37]Simply let your 'Yes' be 'Yes,' and your 'No,' 'No';[e] anything beyond this comes from the evil one.[f]

[38]"You have heard that it was said, 'Eye for eye, and tooth for tooth.'[a][g] [39]But I tell you, Do not resist an evil person. If someone strikes you on the right cheek, turn to him the other also.[h] [40]And if someone wants to sue you and take your tunic, let him have your cloak as well. [41]If someone forces you to go one mile, go with him two miles. [42]Give to the one who asks you, and do not turn away from the one who wants to borrow from you.[i]

[43]"You have heard that it was said, 'Love your neighbor[b][j] and hate your enemy.'[k] [44]But I tell you: Love your enemies[c] and pray for those who persecute you,[l] [45]that you may be sons[m] of your Father in heaven. He causes his sun to rise on the evil and the good, and sends rain on the righteous and the unrighteous.[n] [46]If you love those who love you, what reward will you get?[o] Are not even the tax collectors doing that? [47]And if you greet only your brothers, what are you doing more than others? Do not even pagans do that? [48]Be perfect, therefore, as your heavenly Father is perfect.[p]

Chapter 6 Theme _____

6 "Be careful not to do your 'acts of righteousness' before men, to be seen by them.[q] If you do, you will have no reward from your Father in heaven.

[2]"So when you give to the needy, do not announce it with trumpets, as the hypocrites do in the synagogues and on the streets, to be honored by men. I tell you the truth, they have received their reward in full. [3]But when you give to the needy, do not let your left hand know what your right hand is doing, [4]so that your giving may be in secret. Then your Father, who sees what is done in secret, will reward you.[r]

[5]"And when you pray, do not be like the hypocrites, for they love to pray standing[s] in the synagogues and on the street corners to be seen by men. I tell you the truth, they have received their reward in full. [6]But when you pray, go into your room, close the door and pray to your Father,[t] who is unseen. Then your Father, who sees what is done in secret, will reward you. [7]And when you pray, do not keep on babbling[u] like pagans, for they think they

---

[a]38 Exodus 21:24; Lev. 24:20; Deut. 19:21 [b]43 Lev. 19:18 [c]44 Some late manuscripts
enemies, bless those who curse you, do good to those who hate you

---

5:33
[a]Nu 30:2;
Dt 23:21;
Mt 23:16-22

5:34
[b]Jas 5:12
[c]Isa 66:1;
Mt 23:22

5:35
[d]Ps 48:2

5:37
[e]Jas 5:12
[f]Mt 6:13;
13:19,38;
Jn 17:15;
2Th 3:3;
1Jn 2:13,14;
3:12; 5:18,19

5:38
[g]Ex 21:24;
Lev 24:20;
Dt 19:21

5:39
[h]Lk 6:29;
Ro 12:17,19;
1Co 6:7;
1Pe 3:9

5:42
[i]Dt 15:8;
Lk 6:30

5:43
[j]Lev 19:18
[k]Dt 23:6

5:44
[l]Lk 6:27,28;
23:34;
Ac 7:60;
Ro 12:14;
1Co 4:12;
1Pe 2:23

5:45
[m]ver 9
[n]Job 25:3

5:46
[o]Lk 6:32

5:48
[p]Lev 19:2;
1Pe 1:16

6:1
[q]Mt 23:5

6:4
[r]ver 6,18;
Col 3:23,24

6:5
[s]Mk 11:25;
Lk 18:10-14

6:6
[t]2Ki 4:33

6:7
[u]Ecc 5:2

6:7
a 1Ki 18:26-29

6:8
b ver 32

6:10
c Mt 3:2
d Mt 26:39

6:11
e Pr 30:8

6:12
f Mt 18:21-35

6:13
g Jas 1:13
h Mt 5:37

6:14
i Mt 18:21-35;
Mk 11:25,26;
Eph 4:32;
Col 3:13

6:15
j Mt 18:35

6:16
k Isa 58:5

6:18
l ver 4,6

6:19
m Pr 23:4;
Heb 13:5
n Jas 5:2,3

6:20
o Mt 19:21;
Lk 12:33; 18:22;
1Ti 6:19
p Lk 12:33

6:21
q Lk 12:34

6:24
r Lk 16:13

6:25
s ver 27,28,31,34;
Lk 10:41;
12:11,22;
Php 4:6;
1Pe 5:7

6:26
t Job 38:41;
Ps 147:9
u Mt 10:29-31

6:27
v Ps 39:5

will be heard because of their many words.*a* ⁸Do not be like them, for your Father knows what you need*b* before you ask him.

⁹"This, then, is how you should pray:

"'Our Father in heaven,
    hallowed be your name,
¹⁰your kingdom*c* come,
    your will be done*d*
    on earth as it is in heaven.
¹¹Give us today our daily bread.*e*
¹²Forgive us our debts,
    as we also have forgiven our debtors.*f*
¹³And lead us not into temptation,*g*
    but deliver us from the evil one.ᵃ'*h*

¹⁴For if you forgive men when they sin against you, your heavenly Father will also forgive you.*i* ¹⁵But if you do not forgive men their sins, your Father will not forgive your sins.*j*

¹⁶"When you fast, do not look somber*k* as the hypocrites do, for they disfigure their faces to show men they are fasting. I tell you the truth, they have received their reward in full. ¹⁷But when you fast, put oil on your head and wash your face, ¹⁸so that it will not be obvious to men that you are fasting, but only to your Father, who is unseen; and your Father, who sees what is done in secret, will reward you.*l*

¹⁹"Do not store up for yourselves treasures on earth,*m* where moth and rust destroy,*n* and where thieves break in and steal. ²⁰But store up for yourselves treasures in heaven,*o* where moth and rust do not destroy, and where thieves do not break in and steal.*p* ²¹For where your treasure is, there your heart will be also.*q*

²²"The eye is the lamp of the body. If your eyes are good, your whole body will be full of light. ²³But if your eyes are bad, your whole body will be full of darkness. If then the light within you is darkness, how great is that darkness!

²⁴"No one can serve two masters. Either he will hate the one and love the other, or he will be devoted to the one and despise the other. You cannot serve both God and Money.*r*

²⁵"Therefore I tell you, do not worry*s* about your life, what you will eat or drink; or about your body, what you will wear. Is not life more important than food, and the body more important than clothes? ²⁶Look at the birds of the air; they do not sow or reap or store away in barns, and yet your heavenly Father feeds them.*t* Are you not much more valuable than they?*u* ²⁷Who of you by worrying can add a single hour to his life*b*?*v*

ᵃ 13 Or *from evil; some late manuscripts* one, / *for yours is the kingdom and the power and the glory forever. Amen.*   ᵇ 27 Or *single cubit to his height*

²⁸"And why do you worry about clothes? See how the lilies of the field grow. They do not labor or spin. ²⁹Yet I tell you that not even Solomon in all his splendor*ᵃ* was dressed like one of these. ³⁰If that is how God clothes the grass of the field, which is here today and tomorrow is thrown into the fire, will he not much more clothe you, O you of little faith?*ᵇ* ³¹So do not worry, saying, 'What shall we eat?' or 'What shall we drink?' or 'What shall we wear?' ³²For the pagans run after all these things, and your heavenly Father knows that you need them.*ᶜ* ³³But seek first his kingdom and his righteousness, and all these things will be given to you as well.*ᵈ* ³⁴Therefore do not worry about tomorrow, for tomorrow will worry about itself. Each day has enough trouble of its own.

Chapter 7 Theme _____

7 "Do not judge, or you too will be judged.*ᵉ* ²For in the same way you judge others, you will be judged, and with the measure you use, it will be measured to you.*ᶠ*

³"Why do you look at the speck of sawdust in your brother's eye and pay no attention to the plank in your own eye? ⁴How can you say to your brother, 'Let me take the speck out of your eye,' when all the time there is a plank in your own eye? ⁵You hypocrite, first take the plank out of your own eye, and then you will see clearly to remove the speck from your brother's eye.

⁶"Do not give dogs what is sacred; do not throw your pearls to pigs. If you do, they may trample them under their feet, and then turn and tear you to pieces.

⁷"Ask and it will be given to you;*ᵍ* seek and you will find; knock and the door will be opened to you. ⁸For everyone who asks receives; he who seeks finds;*ʰ* and to him who knocks, the door will be opened.

⁹"Which of you, if his son asks for bread, will give him a stone? ¹⁰Or if he asks for a fish, will give him a snake? ¹¹If you, then, though you are evil, know how to give good gifts to your children, how much more will your Father in heaven give good gifts to those who ask him! ¹²So in everything, do to others what you would have them do to you,*ⁱ* for this sums up the Law and the Prophets.*ʲ*

¹³"Enter through the narrow gate.*ᵏ* For wide is the gate and broad is the road that leads to destruction, and many enter through it. ¹⁴But small is the gate and narrow the road that leads to life, and only a few find it.

¹⁵"Watch out for false prophets.*ˡ* They come to you in sheep's clothing, but inwardly they are ferocious wolves.*ᵐ* ¹⁶By their fruit you will recognize them.*ⁿ* Do people pick grapes from thornbushes, or figs from thistles?*ᵒ* ¹⁷Likewise every good tree bears good fruit, but a bad tree bears bad fruit. ¹⁸A good tree cannot

6:29
*ᵃ*1Ki 10:4-7

6:30
*ᵇ*Mt 8:26; 14:31;
16:8

6:32
*ᶜ*ver 8

6:33
*ᵈ*Mt 19:29;
Mk 10:29-30

7:1
*ᵉ*Lk 6:37;
Ro 14:4,10,13;
1Co 4:5;
Jas 4:11,12

7:2
*ᶠ*Mk 4:24;
Lk 6:38

7:7
*ᵍ*Mt 21:22;
Mk 11:24;
Jn 14:13,14;
15:7,16;
16:23,24;
Jas 1:5-8; 4:2,3;
1Jn 3:22;
5:14,15

7:8
*ʰ*Pr 8:17;
Jer 29:12,13

7:12
*ⁱ*Lk 6:31
*ʲ*Ro 13:8-10;
Gal 5:14

7:13
*ᵏ*Lk 13:24

7:15
*ˡ*Jer 23:16;
Mt 24:24;
Mk 13:22;
Lk 6:26;
2Pe 2:1;
1Jn 4:1;
Rev 16:13
*ᵐ*Ac 20:29

7:16
*ⁿ*Mt 12:33;
Lk 6:44
*ᵒ*Jas 3:12

7:19
a Mt 3:10

7:21
b Hos 8:2;
Mt 25:11
c Ro 2:13;
Jas 1:22

7:22
d Mt 10:15
e 1Co 13:1-3

7:23
f Ps 6:8;
Mt 25:12,41;
Lk 13:25-27

7:24
g Jas 1:22-25

7:28
h Mt 11:1;
13:53; 19:1; 26:1
i Mt 13:54;
Mk 1:22; 6:2;
Lk 4:32;
Jn 7:46

8:2
j Lk 5:12
k Mt 9:18; 15:25;
18:26; 20:20

8:4
l Mt 9:30;
Mk 5:43; 7:36;
8:30
m Lev 14:2-32

8:8
n Ps 107:20

8:10
o Mt 15:28

bear bad fruit, and a bad tree cannot bear good fruit. ¹⁹Every tree that does not bear good fruit is cut down and thrown into the fire.*a* ²⁰Thus, by their fruit you will recognize them.

²¹"Not everyone who says to me, 'Lord, Lord,'*b* will enter the kingdom of heaven, but only he who does the will of my Father who is in heaven.*c* ²²Many will say to me on that day,*d* 'Lord, Lord, did we not prophesy in your name, and in your name drive out demons and perform many miracles?'*e* ²³Then I will tell them plainly, 'I never knew you. Away from me, you evildoers!'*f*

²⁴"Therefore everyone who hears these words of mine and puts them into practice*g* is like a wise man who built his house on the rock. ²⁵The rain came down, the streams rose, and the winds blew and beat against that house; yet it did not fall, because it had its foundation on the rock. ²⁶But everyone who hears these words of mine and does not put them into practice is like a foolish man who built his house on sand. ²⁷The rain came down, the streams rose, and the winds blew and beat against that house, and it fell with a great crash."

²⁸When Jesus had finished saying these things,*h* the crowds were amazed at his teaching,*i* ²⁹because he taught as one who had authority, and not as their teachers of the law.

Chapter 8 Theme

8 When he came down from the mountainside, large crowds followed him. ²A man with leprosy*a* *j* came and knelt before him*k* and said, "Lord, if you are willing, you can make me clean."

³Jesus reached out his hand and touched the man. "I am willing," he said. "Be clean!" Immediately he was cured*b* of his leprosy. ⁴Then Jesus said to him, "See that you don't tell anyone.*l* But go, show yourself to the priest and offer the gift Moses commanded,*m* as a testimony to them."

⁵When Jesus had entered Capernaum, a centurion came to him, asking for help. ⁶"Lord," he said, "my servant lies at home paralyzed and in terrible suffering."

⁷Jesus said to him, "I will go and heal him."

⁸The centurion replied, "Lord, I do not deserve to have you come under my roof. But just say the word, and my servant will be healed.*n* ⁹For I myself am a man under authority, with soldiers under me. I tell this one, 'Go,' and he goes; and that one, 'Come,' and he comes. I say to my servant, 'Do this,' and he does it."

¹⁰When Jesus heard this, he was astonished and said to those following him, "I tell you the truth, I have not found anyone in Israel with such great faith.*o* ¹¹I say to you that many will come

a 2 The Greek word was used for various diseases affecting the skin—not necessarily leprosy.
b 3 Greek *made clean*

from the east and the west,[a] and will take their places at the feast with Abraham, Isaac and Jacob in the kingdom of heaven.[b] 12But the subjects of the kingdom[c] will be thrown outside, into the darkness, where there will be weeping and gnashing of teeth."[d]

13Then Jesus said to the centurion, "Go! It will be done just as you believed it would."[e] And his servant was healed at that very hour.

14When Jesus came into Peter's house, he saw Peter's mother-in-law lying in bed with a fever. 15He touched her hand and the fever left her, and she got up and began to wait on him.

16When evening came, many who were demon-possessed were brought to him, and he drove out the spirits with a word and healed all the sick.[f] 17This was to fulfill[g] what was spoken through the prophet Isaiah:

"He took up our infirmities
    and carried our diseases."[a][h]

18When Jesus saw the crowd around him, he gave orders to cross to the other side of the lake.[i] 19Then a teacher of the law came to him and said, "Teacher, I will follow you wherever you go."

20Jesus replied, "Foxes have holes and birds of the air have nests, but the Son of Man[j] has no place to lay his head."

21Another disciple said to him, "Lord, first let me go and bury my father."

22But Jesus told him, "Follow me,[k] and let the dead bury their own dead."

23Then he got into the boat and his disciples followed him. 24Without warning, a furious storm came up on the lake, so that the waves swept over the boat. But Jesus was sleeping. 25The disciples went and woke him, saying, "Lord, save us! We're going to drown!"

26He replied, "You of little faith,[l] why are you so afraid?" Then he got up and rebuked the winds and the waves, and it was completely calm.[m]

27The men were amazed and asked, "What kind of man is this? Even the winds and the waves obey him!"

28When he arrived at the other side in the region of the Gadarenes,[b] two demon-possessed[n] men coming from the tombs met him. They were so violent that no one could pass that way. 29"What do you want

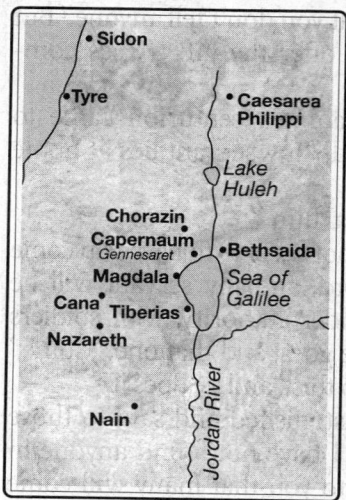

Galilee

- Sidon
- Tyre
- Caesarea Philippi
- Lake Huleh
- Chorazin
- Capernaum
- Gennesaret
- Bethsaida
- Magdala
- Sea of Galilee
- Cana
- Tiberias
- Nazareth
- Jordan River
- Nain

8:11
a Ps 107:3;
Isa 49:12; 59:19;
Mal 1:11
b Lk 13:29

8:12
c Mt 13:38
d Mt 13:42,50;
22:13; 24:51;
25:30;
Lk 13:28

8:13
e Mt 9:22

8:16
f Mt 4:23,24

8:17
g Mt 1:22
h Isa 53:4

8:18
i Mk 4:35

8:20
j Da 7:13;
Mt 12:8,32,40;
16:13,27,28;
17:9; 19:28;
Mk 2:10; 8:31

8:22
k Mt 4:19

8:26
l Mt 6:30
m Ps 65:7; 89:9;
107:29

8:28
n Mt 4:24

a 17 Isaiah 53:4   b 28 Some manuscripts *Gergesenes*; others *Gerasenes*

8:29
a Jdg 11:12;
2Sa 16:10;
1Ki 17:18;
Mk 1:24;
Lk 4:34;
Jn 2:4
b 2Pe 2:4

8:34
c Lk 5:8;
Ac 16:39

9:1
d Mt 4:13

9:2
e Mt 4:24
f ver 22
g Jn 16:33
h Lk 7:48

9:3
i Mt 26:65;
Jn 10:33

9:4
j Ps 94:11;
Mt 12:25;
Lk 6:8; 9:47;
11:17

9:6
k Mt 8:20

9:8
l Mt 5:16; 15:31;
Lk 7:16; 13:13;
17:15; 23:47;
Jn 15:8;
Ac 4:21; 11:18;
21:20

9:11
m Mt 11:19;
Lk 5:30; 15:2;
Gal 2:15

9:13
n Hos 6:6;
Mic 6:6-8;
Mt 12:7
o 1Ti 1:15

9:14
p Lk 18:12

9:15
q Jn 3:29
r Ac 13:2,3;
14:23

with us,[a] Son of God?" they shouted. "Have you come here to torture us before the appointed time?"[b]

³⁰Some distance from them a large herd of pigs was feeding. ³¹The demons begged Jesus, "If you drive us out, send us into the herd of pigs."

³²He said to them, "Go!" So they came out and went into the pigs, and the whole herd rushed down the steep bank into the lake and died in the water. ³³Those tending the pigs ran off, went into the town and reported all this, including what had happened to the demon-possessed men. ³⁴Then the whole town went out to meet Jesus. And when they saw him, they pleaded with him to leave their region.[c]

Chapter 9 Theme _____

9 Jesus stepped into a boat, crossed over and came to his own town.[d] ²Some men brought to him a paralytic,[e] lying on a mat. When Jesus saw their faith,[f] he said to the paralytic, "Take heart,[g] son; your sins are forgiven."[h]

³At this, some of the teachers of the law said to themselves, "This fellow is blaspheming!"[i]

⁴Knowing their thoughts,[j] Jesus said, "Why do you entertain evil thoughts in your hearts? ⁵Which is easier: to say, 'Your sins are forgiven,' or to say, 'Get up and walk'? ⁶But so that you may know that the Son of Man[k] has authority on earth to forgive sins. . . ." Then he said to the paralytic, "Get up, take your mat and go home." ⁷And the man got up and went home. ⁸When the crowd saw this, they were filled with awe; and they praised God,[l] who had given such authority to men.

⁹As Jesus went on from there, he saw a man named Matthew sitting at the tax collector's booth. "Follow me," he told him, and Matthew got up and followed him.

¹⁰While Jesus was having dinner at Matthew's house, many tax collectors and "sinners" came and ate with him and his disciples. ¹¹When the Pharisees saw this, they asked his disciples, "Why does your teacher eat with tax collectors and 'sinners'?"[m]

¹²On hearing this, Jesus said, "It is not the healthy who need a doctor, but the sick. ¹³But go and learn what this means: 'I desire mercy, not sacrifice.'[a][n] For I have not come to call the righteous, but sinners."[o]

¹⁴Then John's disciples came and asked him, "How is it that we and the Pharisees fast,[p] but your disciples do not fast?"

¹⁵Jesus answered, "How can the guests of the bridegroom mourn while he is with them?[q] The time will come when the bridegroom will be taken from them; then they will fast.[r]

a 13 Hosea 6:6

16"No one sews a patch of unshrunk cloth on an old garment, for the patch will pull away from the garment, making the tear worse. 17Neither do men pour new wine into old wineskins. If they do, the skins will burst, the wine will run out and the wineskins will be ruined. No, they pour new wine into new wineskins, and both are preserved."

18While he was saying this, a ruler came and knelt before him*a* and said, "My daughter has just died. But come and put your hand on her,*b* and she will live." 19Jesus got up and went with him, and so did his disciples.

20Just then a woman who had been subject to bleeding for twelve years came up behind him and touched the edge of his cloak.*c* 21She said to herself, "If I only touch his cloak, I will be healed."

22Jesus turned and saw her. "Take heart, daughter," he said, "your faith has healed you."*d* And the woman was healed from that moment.*e*

23When Jesus entered the ruler's house and saw the flute players and the noisy crowd,*f* 24he said, "Go away. The girl is not dead*g* but asleep."*h* But they laughed at him. 25After the crowd had been put outside, he went in and took the girl by the hand, and she got up. 26News of this spread through all that region.*i*

27As Jesus went on from there, two blind men followed him, calling out, "Have mercy on us, Son of David!"*j*

28When he had gone indoors, the blind men came to him, and he asked them, "Do you believe that I am able to do this?"

"Yes, Lord," they replied.

29Then he touched their eyes and said, "According to your faith will it be done to you";*k* 30and their sight was restored. Jesus warned them sternly, "See that no one knows about this."*l* 31But they went out and spread the news about him all over that region.*m*

32While they were going out, a man who was demon-possessed*n* and could not talk*o* was brought to Jesus. 33And when the demon was driven out, the man who had been mute spoke. The crowd was amazed and said, "Nothing like this has ever been seen in Israel."*p*

34But the Pharisees said, "It is by the prince of demons that he drives out demons."*q*

35Jesus went through all the towns and villages, teaching in their synagogues, preaching the good news of the kingdom and healing every disease and sickness.*r* 36When he saw the crowds, he had compassion on them,*s* because they were harassed and helpless, like sheep without a shepherd.*t* 37Then he said to his disciples, "The harvest*u* is plentiful but the workers are few.*v* 38Ask the Lord of the harvest, therefore, to send out workers into his harvest field."

9:18
a Mt 8:2
b Mk 5:23

9:20
c Mt 14:36;
Mk 3:10

9:22
d Mk 10:52;
Lk 7:50;
17:19; 18:42
e Mt 15:28

9:23
f 2Ch 35:25;
Jer 9:17,18

9:24
g Ac 20:10
h Jn 11:11-14

9:26
i Mt 4:24

9:27
j Mt 15:22;
Mk 10:47;
Lk 18:38-39

9:29
k ver 22

9:30
l Mt 8:4

9:31
m ver 26;
Mk 7:36

9:32
n Mt 4:24
o Mt 12:22-24

9:33
p Mk 2:12

9:34
q Mt 12:24;
Lk 11:15

9:35
r Mt 4:23

9:36
s Mt 14:14
t Nu 27:17;
Eze 34:5,6;
Zec 10:2;
Mk 6:34

9:37
u Jn 4:35
v Lk 10:2

10:1
a Mk 3:13-15;
Lk 9:1

10:4
b Mt 26:14-16,
25,47;
Jn 13:2,26,27

10:5
c 2Ki 17:24;
Lk 9:52;
Jn 4:4-26,39,40;
Ac 8:5,25

10:6
d Jer 50:6;
Mt 15:24

10:7
e Mt 3:2

10:9
f Lk 22:35

10:10
g 1Ti 5:18

10:12
h 1Sa 25:6

10:14
i Ne 5:13;
Lk 10:11;
Ac 13:51

10:15
j 2Pe 2:6
k Mt 12:36;
2Pe 2:9;
1Jn 4:17
l Mt 11:22,24

10:16
m Lk 10:3
n Ro 16:19

10:17
o Mt 5:22
p Mt 23:34;
Mk 13:9;
Ac 5:40; 26:11

10:18
q Ac 25:24-26

10:19
r Ex 4:12

10:20
s Ac 4:8

10:21
t ver 35,36;
Mic 7:6

10:22
u Mt 24:13;
Mk 13:13

10:24
v Lk 6:40;
Jn 13:16; 15:20

Chapter 10 Theme

10 He called his twelve disciples to him and gave them authority to drive out evil*a* spirits*a* and to heal every disease and sickness.

²These are the names of the twelve apostles: first, Simon (who is called Peter) and his brother Andrew; James son of Zebedee, and his brother John; ³Philip and Bartholomew; Thomas and Matthew the tax collector; James son of Alphaeus, and Thaddaeus; ⁴Simon the Zealot and Judas Iscariot, who betrayed him.*b*

⁵These twelve Jesus sent out with the following instructions: "Do not go among the Gentiles or enter any town of the Samaritans.*c* ⁶Go rather to the lost sheep of Israel.*d* ⁷As you go, preach this message: 'The kingdom of heaven*e* is near.' ⁸Heal the sick, raise the dead, cleanse those who have leprosy,*b* drive out demons. Freely you have received, freely give. ⁹Do not take along any gold or silver or copper in your belts;*f* ¹⁰take no bag for the journey, or extra tunic, or sandals or a staff; for the worker is worth his keep.*g*

¹¹"Whatever town or village you enter, search for some worthy person there and stay at his house until you leave. ¹²As you enter the home, give it your greeting.*h* ¹³If the home is deserving, let your peace rest on it; if it is not, let your peace return to you. ¹⁴If anyone will not welcome you or listen to your words, shake the dust off your feet*i* when you leave that home or town. ¹⁵I tell you the truth, it will be more bearable for Sodom and Gomorrah*j* on the day of judgment*k* than for that town.*l* ¹⁶I am sending you out like sheep among wolves.*m* Therefore be as shrewd as snakes and as innocent as doves.*n*

¹⁷"Be on your guard against men; they will hand you over to the local councils*o* and flog you in their synagogues.*p* ¹⁸On my account you will be brought before governors and kings*q* as witnesses to them and to the Gentiles. ¹⁹But when they arrest you, do not worry about what to say or how to say it.*r* At that time you will be given what to say, ²⁰for it will not be you speaking, but the Spirit of your Father*s* speaking through you.

²¹"Brother will betray brother to death, and a father his child; children will rebel against their parents*t* and have them put to death. ²²All men will hate you because of me, but he who stands firm to the end will be saved.*u* ²³When you are persecuted in one place, flee to another. I tell you the truth, you will not finish going through the cities of Israel before the Son of Man comes.

²⁴"A student is not above his teacher, nor a servant above his master.*v* ²⁵It is enough for the student to be like his teacher, and

a 1 Greek *unclean*   *b 8* The Greek word was used for various diseases affecting the skin—not necessarily leprosy.

the servant like his master. If the head of the house has been called Beelzebub,[a][a] how much more the members of his household!

26"So do not be afraid of them. There is nothing concealed that will not be disclosed, or hidden that will not be made known.[b] 27What I tell you in the dark, speak in the daylight; what is whispered in your ear, proclaim from the roofs. 28Do not be afraid of those who kill the body but cannot kill the soul. Rather, be afraid of the One[c] who can destroy both soul and body in hell. 29Are not two sparrows sold for a penny[b]? Yet not one of them will fall to the ground apart from the will of your Father. 30And even the very hairs of your head are all numbered.[d] 31So don't be afraid; you are worth more than many sparrows.[e]

32"Whoever acknowledges me before men,[f] I will also acknowledge him before my Father in heaven. 33But whoever disowns me before men, I will disown him before my Father in heaven.[g]

34"Do not suppose that I have come to bring peace to the earth. I did not come to bring peace, but a sword. 35For I have come to turn

> "'a man against his father,
>   a daughter against her mother,
>   a daughter-in-law against her mother-in-law[h]—
> 36   a man's enemies will be the members of
>   his own household.'[c][i]

37"Anyone who loves his father or mother more than me is not worthy of me; anyone who loves his son or daughter more than me is not worthy of me;[j] 38and anyone who does not take his cross and follow me is not worthy of me.[k] 39Whoever finds his life will lose it, and whoever loses his life for my sake will find it.[l]

40"He who receives you receives me,[m] and he who receives me receives the one who sent me.[n] 41Anyone who receives a prophet because he is a prophet will receive a prophet's reward, and anyone who receives a righteous man because he is a righteous man will receive a righteous man's reward. 42And if anyone gives even a cup of cold water to one of these little ones because he is my disciple, I tell you the truth, he will certainly not lose his reward."[o]

Chapter 11 Theme

11 After Jesus had finished instructing his twelve disciples,[p] he went on from there to teach and preach in the towns of Galilee.[d]

2When John heard in prison[q] what Christ was doing, he sent his disciples 3to ask him, "Are you the one who was to come,[r] or should we expect someone else?"

a25 Greek *Beezeboul* or *Beelzeboul*   b29 Greek *an assarion*   c36 Micah 7:6   d1 Greek *in their towns*

10:25
[a]Mk 3:22

10:26
[b]Mk 4:22;
Lk 8:17

10:28
[c]Isa 8:12,13;
Heb 10:31

10:30
[d]1Sa 14:45;
2Sa 14:11;
Lk 21:18;
Ac 27:34

10:31
[e]Mt 12:12

10:32
[f]Ro 10:9

10:33
[g]Mk 8:38;
2Ti 2:12

10:35
[h]ver 21

10:36
[i]Mic 7:6

10:37
[j]Lk 14:26

10:38
[k]Mt 16:24;
Lk 14:27

10:39
[l]Lk 17:33;
Jn 12:25

10:40
[m]Mt 18:5;
Gal 4:14
[n]Lk 9:48;
Jn 12:44; 13:20

10:42
[o]Mt 25:40;
Mk 9:41;
Heb 6:10

11:1
[p]Mt 7:28

11:2
[q]Mt 14:3

11:3
[r]Ps 118:26;
Jn 11:27;
Heb 10:37

11:5
aIsa 35:4-6;
61:1;
Lk 4:18,19

11:6
bMt 13:21

11:7
cMt 3:1

11:9
dMt 21:26;
Lk 1:76

11:10
eMal 3:1;
Mk 1:2

11:14
fMal 4:5;
Mt 17:10-13;
Mk 9:11-13;
Lk 1:17;
Jn 1:21

11:15
gMt 13:9,43;
Mk 4:23;
Lk 14:35;
Rev 2:7

11:18
hMt 3:4
iLk 1:15

11:19
jMt 9:11

11:21
kMk 6:45;
Lk 9:10;
Jn 12:21
lMt 15:21;
Lk 6:17;
Ac 12:20
mJnh 3:5-9

11:22
nver 24;
Mt 10:15

11:23
oMt 4:13
pIsa 14:13-15

⁴Jesus replied, "Go back and report to John what you hear and see: ⁵The blind receive sight, the lame walk, those who have leprosyᵃ are cured, the deaf hear, the dead are raised, and the good news is preached to the poor.ᵃ ⁶Blessed is the man who does not fall away on account of me."ᵇ

⁷As John'sᶜ disciples were leaving, Jesus began to speak to the crowd about John: "What did you go out into the desert to see? A reed swayed by the wind? ⁸If not, what did you go out to see? A man dressed in fine clothes? No, those who wear fine clothes are in kings' palaces. ⁹Then what did you go out to see? A prophet?ᵈ Yes, I tell you, and more than a prophet. ¹⁰This is the one about whom it is written:

> "'I will send my messenger ahead of you,
> who will prepare your way before you.'ᵇᵉ

¹¹I tell you the truth: Among those born of women there has not risen anyone greater than John the Baptist; yet he who is least in the kingdom of heaven is greater than he. ¹²From the days of John the Baptist until now, the kingdom of heaven has been forcefully advancing, and forceful men lay hold of it. ¹³For all the Prophets and the Law prophesied until John. ¹⁴And if you are willing to accept it, he is the Elijah who was to come.ᶠ ¹⁵He who has ears, let him hear.ᵍ

¹⁶"To what can I compare this generation? They are like children sitting in the marketplaces and calling out to others:

> ¹⁷"'We played the flute for you,
> and you did not dance;
> we sang a dirge,
> and you did not mourn.'

¹⁸For John came neither eatingʰ nor drinking,ⁱ and they say, 'He has a demon.' ¹⁹The Son of Man came eating and drinking, and they say, 'Here is a glutton and a drunkard, a friend of tax collectors and "sinners."'ʲ But wisdom is proved right by her actions."

²⁰Then Jesus began to denounce the cities in which most of his miracles had been performed, because they did not repent. ²¹"Woe to you, Korazin! Woe to you, Bethsaida!ᵏ If the miracles that were performed in you had been performed in Tyre and Sidon,ˡ they would have repented long ago in sackcloth and ashes.ᵐ ²²But I tell you, it will be more bearable for Tyre and Sidon on the day of judgment than for you.ⁿ ²³And you, Capernaum,ᵒ will you be lifted up to the skies? No, you will go down to the depths.ᶜᵖ If the miracles that were performed in you had been

---

a5 The Greek word was used for various diseases affecting the skin—not necessarily leprosy.
b10 Mal. 3:1   c23 Greek Hades

performed in Sodom, it would have remained to this day. [24]But I tell you that it will be more bearable for Sodom on the day of judgment than for you."[a]

[25]At that time Jesus said, "I praise you, Father,[b] Lord of heaven and earth, because you have hidden these things from the wise and learned, and revealed them to little children.[c] [26]Yes, Father, for this was your good pleasure.

[27]"All things have been committed to me[d] by my Father.[e] No one knows the Son except the Father, and no one knows the Father except the Son and those to whom the Son chooses to reveal him.[f]

[28]"Come to me,[g] all you who are weary and burdened, and I will give you rest. [29]Take my yoke upon you and learn from me,[h] for I am gentle and humble in heart, and you will find rest for your souls.[i] [30]For my yoke is easy and my burden is light."[j]

Chapter 12 Theme

12 At that time Jesus went through the grainfields on the Sabbath. His disciples were hungry and began to pick some heads of grain[k] and eat them. [2]When the Pharisees saw this, they said to him, "Look! Your disciples are doing what is unlawful on the Sabbath."[l]

[3]He answered, "Haven't you read what David did when he and his companions were hungry?[m] [4]He entered the house of God, and he and his companions ate the consecrated bread—which was not lawful for them to do, but only for the priests.[n] [5]Or haven't you read in the Law that on the Sabbath the priests in the temple desecrate the day[o] and yet are innocent? [6]I tell you that one[a] greater than the temple is here.[p] [7]If you had known what these words mean, 'I desire mercy, not sacrifice,'[b][q] you would not have condemned the innocent. [8]For the Son of Man[r] is Lord of the Sabbath."

[9]Going on from that place, he went into their synagogue, [10]and a man with a shriveled hand was there. Looking for a reason to accuse Jesus, they asked him, "Is it lawful to heal on the Sabbath?"[s]

[11]He said to them, "If any of you has a sheep and it falls into a pit on the Sabbath, will you not take hold of it and lift it out?[t] [12]How much more valuable is a man than a sheep![u] Therefore it is lawful to do good on the Sabbath."

[13]Then he said to the man, "Stretch out your hand." So he stretched it out and it was completely restored, just as sound as the other. [14]But the Pharisees went out and plotted how they might kill Jesus.[v]

a 6 Or *something*; also in verses 41 and 42   b 7 Hosea 6:6

11:24
a Mt 10:15

11:25
b Lk 22:42;
Jn 11:41
c 1Co 1:26-29

11:27
d Mt 28:18
e Jn 3:35; 13:3;
17:2
f Jn 10:15

11:28
g Jn 7:37

11:29
h Jn 13:15;
Php 2:5;
1Pe 2:21;
1Jn 2:6
i Jer 6:16

11:30
j 1Jn 5:3

12:1
k Dt 23:25

12:2
l ver 10;
Lk 13:14; 14:3;
Jn 5:10; 7:23;
9:16

12:3
m 1Sa 21:6

12:4
n Lev 24:5,9

12:5
o Nu 28:9,10;
Jn 7:22,23

12:6
p ver 41,42

12:7
q Hos 6:6;
Mic 6:6-8;
Mt 9:13

12:8
r Mt 8:20

12:10
s ver 2; Lk 13:14;
14:3; Jn 9:16

12:11
t Lk 14:5

12:12
u Mt 10:31

12:14
v Mt 26:4; 27:1;
Mk 3:6;
Lk 6:11;
Jn 5:18; 11:53

12:15
a Mt 4:23

12:16
b Mt 8:4

12:18
c Mt 3:17

12:21
d Isa 42:1-4

12:22
e Mt 4:24;
9:32-33

12:23
f Mt 9:27

12:24
g Mk 3:22
h Mt 9:34

12:25
i Mt 9:4

12:26
j Mt 4:10

12:27
k Ac 19:13

12:30
l Mk 9:40;
Lk 11:23

12:31
m Mk 3:28,29;
Lk 12:10

12:32
n Tit 2:12
o Mk 10:30;
Lk 20:34,35;
Eph 1:21;
Heb 6:5

12:33
p Mt 7:16,17;
Lk 6:43,44

12:34
q Mt 3:7; 23:33
r Mt 15:18;
Lk 6:45

¹⁵Aware of this, Jesus withdrew from that place. Many followed him, and he healed all their sick,^a ¹⁶warning them not to tell who he was.^b ¹⁷This was to fulfill what was spoken through the prophet Isaiah:

> ¹⁸"Here is my servant whom I have chosen,
>   the one I love, in whom I delight;^c
> I will put my Spirit on him,
>   and he will proclaim justice to the nations.
> ¹⁹He will not quarrel or cry out;
>   no one will hear his voice in the streets.
> ²⁰A bruised reed he will not break,
>   and a smoldering wick he will not snuff out,
> till he leads justice to victory.
> ²¹   In his name the nations will put their hope."^{a d}

²²Then they brought him a demon-possessed man who was blind and mute, and Jesus healed him, so that he could both talk and see.^e ²³All the people were astonished and said, "Could this be the Son of David?"^f

²⁴But when the Pharisees heard this, they said, "It is only by Beelzebub,^{b g} the prince of demons, that this fellow drives out demons."^h

²⁵Jesus knew their thoughtsⁱ and said to them, "Every kingdom divided against itself will be ruined, and every city or household divided against itself will not stand. ²⁶If Satan^j drives out Satan, he is divided against himself. How then can his kingdom stand? ²⁷And if I drive out demons by Beelzebub, by whom do your people^k drive them out? So then, they will be your judges. ²⁸But if I drive out demons by the Spirit of God, then the kingdom of God has come upon you.

²⁹"Or again, how can anyone enter a strong man's house and carry off his possessions unless he first ties up the strong man? Then he can rob his house.

³⁰"He who is not with me is against me, and he who does not gather with me scatters.^l ³¹And so I tell you, every sin and blasphemy will be forgiven men, but the blasphemy against the Spirit will not be forgiven.^m ³²Anyone who speaks a word against the Son of Man will be forgiven, but anyone who speaks against the Holy Spirit will not be forgiven, either in this ageⁿ or in the age to come.^o

³³"Make a tree good and its fruit will be good, or make a tree bad and its fruit will be bad, for a tree is recognized by its fruit.^p ³⁴You brood of vipers,^q how can you who are evil say anything good? For out of the overflow of the heart the mouth speaks.^r ³⁵The good man brings good things out of the good stored up in

a 21 Isaiah 42:1-4   b 24 Greek *Beezeboul* or *Beelzeboul*; also in verse 27 him, and the evil man brings evil things out of the evil stored up in him. ³⁶But I tell you that men will have to give account on the day of judgment for every careless word they have spoken. ³⁷For by your words you will be acquitted, and by your words you will be condemned."

³⁸Then some of the Pharisees and teachers of the law said to him, "Teacher, we want to see a miraculous sign from you."ᵃ

³⁹He answered, "A wicked and adulterous generation asks for a miraculous sign! But none will be given it except the sign of the prophet Jonah.ᵇ ⁴⁰For as Jonah was three days and three nights in the belly of a huge fish,ᶜ so the Son of Manᵈ will be three days and three nights in the heart of the earth.ᵉ ⁴¹The men of Ninevehᶠ will stand up at the judgment with this generation and condemn it; for they repented at the preaching of Jonah,ᵍ and now oneᵃ greater than Jonah is here. ⁴²The Queen of the South will rise at the judgment with this generation and condemn it; for she cameʰ from the ends of the earth to listen to Solomon's wisdom, and now one greater than Solomon is here.

⁴³"When an evilᵇ spirit comes out of a man, it goes through arid places seeking rest and does not find it. ⁴⁴Then it says, 'I will return to the house I left.' When it arrives, it finds the house unoccupied, swept clean and put in order. ⁴⁵Then it goes and takes with it seven other spirits more wicked than itself, and they go in and live there. And the final condition of that man is worse than the first.ⁱ That is how it will be with this wicked generation."

⁴⁶While Jesus was still talking to the crowd, his motherʲ and brothersᵏ stood outside, wanting to speak to him. ⁴⁷Someone told him, "Your mother and brothers are standing outside, wanting to speak to you."ᶜ

⁴⁸He replied to him, "Who is my mother, and who are my brothers?" ⁴⁹Pointing to his disciples, he said, "Here are my mother and my brothers. ⁵⁰For whoever does the will of my Father in heavenˡ is my brother and sister and mother."

INSIGHT

See the section on *Parables*, under **Figures of Speech**, on page 2209.

Chapter 13 Theme

13 That same day Jesus went out of the houseᵐ and sat by the lake. ²Such large crowds gathered around him that he got into a boatⁿ and sat in it, while all the people stood on the shore. ³Then he told them many things in parables, saying: "A farmer went out to sow his seed. ⁴As he was scattering the seed, some fell along the path, and the birds came and ate it up. ⁵Some fell on rocky places, where it did not have much soil. It sprang up quickly, because the soil was shallow. ⁶But when the sun came up, the

---

ᵃ41 Or *something*; also in verse 42   ᵇ43 Greek *unclean*   ᶜ47 Some manuscripts do not have verse 47.

12:38
ᵃMt 16:1;
Mk 8:11,12;
Lk 11:16;
Jn 2:18; 6:30;
1Co 1:22

12:39
ᵇMt 16:4;
Lk 11:29

12:40
ᶜJnh 1:17
ᵈMt 8:20
ᵉMt 16:21

12:41
ᶠJnh 1:2
ᵍJnh 3:5

12:42
ʰ1Ki 10:1;
2Ch 9:1

12:45
ⁱ2Pe 2:20

12:46
ʲMt 1:18;
2:11,13,14,20;
Lk 1:43;
2:33,34,48,51;
Jn 2:1,5;
19:25,26
ᵏMt 13:55;
Jn 2:12; 7:3,5;
Ac 1:14;
1Co 9:5;
Gal 1:19

12:50
ˡJn 15:14

13:1
ᵐver 36;
Mt 9:28

13:2
ⁿLk 5:3

²⁴Jesus told them another parable: "The kingdom of heaven is like*ᵃ* a man who sowed good seed in his field. ²⁵But while everyone was sleeping, his enemy came and sowed weeds among the wheat, and went away. ²⁶When the wheat sprouted and formed heads, then the weeds also appeared.

²⁷"The owner's servants came to him and said, 'Sir, didn't you sow good seed in your field? Where then did the weeds come from?'

²⁸"'An enemy did this,' he replied.

"The servants asked him, 'Do you want us to go and pull them up?'

²⁹"'No,' he answered, 'because while you are pulling the weeds, you may root up the wheat with them. ³⁰Let both grow together until the harvest. At that time I will tell the harvesters: First collect the weeds and tie them in bundles to be burned; then gather the wheat and bring it into my barn.'"*ᵇ*

³¹He told them another parable: "The kingdom of heaven is like*ᶜ* a mustard seed,*ᵈ* which a man took and planted in his field. ³²Though it is the smallest of all your seeds, yet when it grows, it is the largest of garden plants and becomes a tree, so that the birds of the air come and perch in its branches."*ᵉ*

³³He told them still another parable: "The kingdom of heaven is like*ᶠ* yeast that a woman took and mixed into a large amount*ᵃ* of flour*ᵍ* until it worked all through the dough."*ʰ*

³⁴Jesus spoke all these things to the crowd in parables; he did not say anything to them without using a parable.*ⁱ* ³⁵So was fulfilled what was spoken through the prophet:

> "I will open my mouth in parables,
> I will utter things hidden since the creation
> of the world."*ᵇ ʲ*

³⁶Then he left the crowd and went into the house. His disciples came to him and said, "Explain to us the parable*ᵏ* of the weeds in the field."

³⁷He answered, "The one who sowed the good seed is the Son of Man.*ˡ* ³⁸The field is the world, and the good seed stands for the sons of the kingdom. The weeds are the sons of the evil one,*ᵐ* ³⁹and the enemy who sows them is the devil. The harvest*ⁿ* is the end of the age,*ᵒ* and the harvesters are angels.*ᵖ*

⁴⁰"As the weeds are pulled up and burned in the fire, so it will be at the end of the age. ⁴¹The Son of Man*ᵠ* will send out his angels,*ʳ* and they will weed out of his kingdom everything that causes sin and all who do evil. ⁴²They will throw them into the fiery furnace, where there will be weeping and gnashing of teeth.*ˢ*

13:24
*ᵃ*ver 31,33,45,47;
Mt 18:23; 20:1;
22:2; 25:1;
Mk 4:26,30

13:30
*ᵇ*Mt 3:12

13:31
*ᶜ*ver 24
*ᵈ*Mt 17:20;
Lk 17:6

13:32
*ᵉ*Ps 104:12;
Eze 17:23; 31:6;
Da 4:12

13:33
*ᶠ*ver 24
*ᵍ*Ge 18:6
*ʰ*Gal 5:9

13:34
*ⁱ*Mk 4:33;
Jn 16:25

13:35
*ʲ*Ps 78:2;
Ro 16:25,26;
1Co 2:7;
Eph 3:9;
Col 1:26

13:36
*ᵏ*Mt 15:15

13:37
*ˡ*Mt 8:20

13:38
*ᵐ*Jn 8:44,45;
1Jn 3:10

13:39
*ⁿ*Joel 3:13
*ᵒ*Mt 24:3; 28:20
*ᵖ*Rev 14:15

13:41
*ᵠ*Mt 8:20
*ʳ*Mt 24:31

13:42
*ˢ*ver 50;
Mt 8:12

ᵃ 33 Greek *three satas* (probably about 1/2 bushel or 22 liters)   *ᵇ 35* Psalm 78:2

plants were scorched, and they withered because they had no root. ⁷Other seed fell among thorns, which grew up and choked the plants. ⁸Still other seed fell on good soil, where it produced a crop—a hundred,^a sixty or thirty times what was sown. ⁹He who has ears, let him hear."^b

¹⁰The disciples came to him and asked, "Why do you speak to the people in parables?"

¹¹He replied, "The knowledge of the secrets of the kingdom of heaven has been given to you,^c but not to them. ¹²Whoever has will be given more, and he will have an abundance. Whoever does not have, even what he has will be taken from him.^d ¹³This is why I speak to them in parables:

> "Though seeing, they do not see;
> though hearing, they do not hear or understand.^e

¹⁴In them is fulfilled the prophecy of Isaiah:

> " 'You will be ever hearing but never understanding;
> you will be ever seeing but never perceiving.
> ¹⁵For this people's heart has become calloused;
> they hardly hear with their ears,
> and they have closed their eyes.
> Otherwise they might see with their eyes,
> hear with their ears,
> understand with their hearts
> and turn, and I would heal them.'^a^f

¹⁶But blessed are your eyes because they see, and your ears because they hear.^g ¹⁷For I tell you the truth, many prophets and righteous men longed to see what you see^h but did not see it, and to hear what you hear but did not hear it.

¹⁸"Listen then to what the parable of the sower means: ¹⁹When anyone hears the message about the kingdomⁱ and does not understand it, the evil one^j comes and snatches away what was sown in his heart. This is the seed sown along the path. ²⁰The one who received the seed that fell on rocky places is the man who hears the word and at once receives it with joy. ²¹But since he has no root, he lasts only a short time. When trouble or persecution comes because of the word, he quickly falls away.^k ²²The one who received the seed that fell among the thorns is the man who hears the word, but the worries of this life and the deceitfulness of wealth^l choke it, making it unfruitful. ²³But the one who received the seed that fell on good soil is the man who hears the word and understands it. He produces a crop, yielding a hundred, sixty or thirty times what was sown."^m

---

13:8 ^a Ge 26:12

13:9 ^b Mt 11:15

13:11 ^c Mt 11:25; 16:17; 19:11; Jn 6:65; 1Co 2:10,14; Col 1:27; 1Jn 2:20,27

13:12 ^d Mt 25:29; Lk 19:26

13:13 ^e Dt 29:4; Jer 5:21; Eze 12:2

13:15 ^f Isa 6:9,10; Jn 12:40; Ac 28:26,27; Ro 11:8

13:16 ^g Mt 16:17

13:17 ^h Jn 8:56; Heb 11:13; 1Pe 1:10-12

13:19 ⁱ Mt 4:23 ^j Mt 5:37

13:21 ^k Mt 11:6

13:22 ^l Mt 19:23; 1Ti 6:9,10,17

13:23 ^m ver 8

^a 15 Isaiah 6:9,10

13:43
aDa 12:3
bMt 11:15

13:44
cver 24
dIsa 55:1;
Php 3:7,8

13:45
ever 24

13:47
fver 24
gMt 22:10

13:49
hMt 25:32

13:50
iMt 8:12

13:53
jMt 7:28

13:54
kMt 4:23
lMt 7:28

13:55
mLk 3:23;
Jn 6:42
nMt 12:46

13:57
oJn 6:61
pLk 4:24;
Jn 4:44

14:1
qMk 8:15;
Lk 3:1,19; 13:31;
23:7,8;
Ac 4:27; 12:1
rLk 9:7-9

14:2
sMt 3:1

14:3
tMt 4:12; 11:2
uLk 3:19,20

14:4
vLev 18:16;
20:21

14:5
wMt 11:9

43Then the righteous will shine like the sun[a] in the kingdom of their Father. He who has ears, let him hear.[b]

44"The kingdom of heaven is like[c] treasure hidden in a field. When a man found it, he hid it again, and then in his joy went and sold all he had and bought that field.[d]

45"Again, the kingdom of heaven is like[e] a merchant looking for fine pearls. 46When he found one of great value, he went away and sold everything he had and bought it.

47"Once again, the kingdom of heaven is like[f] a net that was let down into the lake and caught all kinds[g] of fish. 48When it was full, the fishermen pulled it up on the shore. Then they sat down and collected the good fish in baskets, but threw the bad away. 49This is how it will be at the end of the age. The angels will come and separate the wicked from the righteous[h] 50and throw them into the fiery furnace, where there will be weeping and gnashing of teeth.[i]

51"Have you understood all these things?" Jesus asked.

"Yes," they replied.

52He said to them, "Therefore every teacher of the law who has been instructed about the kingdom of heaven is like the owner of a house who brings out of his storeroom new treasures as well as old."

53When Jesus had finished these parables,[j] he moved on from there. 54Coming to his hometown, he began teaching the people in their synagogue,[k] and they were amazed.[l] "Where did this man get this wisdom and these miraculous powers?" they asked. 55"Isn't this the carpenter's son?[m] Isn't his mother's[n] name Mary, and aren't his brothers James, Joseph, Simon and Judas? 56Aren't all his sisters with us? Where then did this man get all these things?" 57And they took offense[o] at him.

But Jesus said to them, "Only in his hometown and in his own house is a prophet without honor."[p]

58And he did not do many miracles there because of their lack of faith.

Chapter 14 Theme

14 At that time Herod[q] the tetrarch heard the reports about Jesus,[r] 2and he said to his attendants, "This is John the Baptist;[s] he has risen from the dead! That is why miraculous powers are at work in him."

3Now Herod had arrested John and bound him and put him in prison[t] because of Herodias, his brother Philip's wife,[u] 4for John had been saying to him: "It is not lawful for you to have her."[v] 5Herod wanted to kill John, but he was afraid of the people, because they considered him a prophet.[w]

[6]On Herod's birthday the daughter of Herodias danced for them and pleased Herod so much [7]that he promised with an oath to give her whatever she asked. [8]Prompted by her mother, she said, "Give me here on a platter the head of John the Baptist." [9]The king was distressed, but because of his oaths and his dinner guests, he ordered that her request be granted [10]and had John beheaded[a] in the prison. [11]His head was brought in on a platter and given to the girl, who carried it to her mother. [12]John's disciples came and took his body and buried it.[b] Then they went and told Jesus.

[13]When Jesus heard what had happened, he withdrew by boat privately to a solitary place. Hearing of this, the crowds followed him on foot from the towns. [14]When Jesus landed and saw a large crowd, he had compassion on them[c] and healed their sick.[d]

[15]As evening approached, the disciples came to him and said, "This is a remote place, and it's already getting late. Send the crowds away, so they can go to the villages and buy themselves some food."

[16]Jesus replied, "They do not need to go away. You give them something to eat."

[17]"We have here only five loaves[e] of bread and two fish," they answered.

[18]"Bring them here to me," he said. [19]And he directed the people to sit down on the grass. Taking the five loaves and the two fish and looking up to heaven, he gave thanks and broke the loaves.[f] Then he gave them to the disciples, and the disciples gave them to the people. [20]They all ate and were satisfied, and the disciples picked up twelve basketfuls of broken pieces that were left over. [21]The number of those who ate was about five thousand men, besides women and children.

[22]Immediately Jesus made the disciples get into the boat and go on ahead of him to the other side, while he dismissed the crowd. [23]After he had dismissed them, he went up on a mountainside by himself to pray.[g] When evening came, he was there alone, [24]but the boat was already a considerable distance[a] from land, buffeted by the waves because the wind was against it.

[25]During the fourth watch of the night Jesus went out to them, walking on the lake. [26]When the disciples saw him walking on the lake, they were terrified. "It's a ghost,"[h] they said, and cried out in fear.

[27]But Jesus immediately said to them: "Take courage![i] It is I. Don't be afraid."[j]

[28]"Lord, if it's you," Peter replied, "tell me to come to you on the water."

[29]"Come," he said.

14:10 [a]Mt 17:12

14:12 [b]Ac 8:2

14:14 [c]Mt 9:36 [d]Mt 4:23

14:17 [e]Mt 16:9

14:19 [f]1Sa 9:13; Mt 26:26; Mk 8:6; Lk 24:30; Ac 2:42; 27:35; 1Ti 4:4

14:23 [g]Lk 3:21

14:26 [h]Lk 24:37

14:27 [i]Mt 9:2; Ac 23:11; [j]Da 10:12; Mt 17:7; 28:10; Lk 1:13,30; 2:10; Ac 18:9; 23:11; Rev 1:17

---

a 24 Greek *many stadia*

14:31
a Mt 6:30

Then Peter got down out of the boat, walked on the water and came toward Jesus. [30]But when he saw the wind, he was afraid and, beginning to sink, cried out, "Lord, save me!"

[31]Immediately Jesus reached out his hand and caught him. "You of little faith,"*a* he said, "why did you doubt?"

14:33
b Ps 2:7;
Mt 4:3

[32]And when they climbed into the boat, the wind died down. [33]Then those who were in the boat worshiped him, saying, "Truly you are the Son of God."*b*

14:36
c Mt 9:20

[34]When they had crossed over, they landed at Gennesaret. [35]And when the men of that place recognized Jesus, they sent word to all the surrounding country. People brought all their sick to him [36]and begged him to let the sick just touch the edge of his cloak,*c* and all who touched him were healed.

15:2
d Lk 11:38

Chapter 15 Theme

15 Then some Pharisees and teachers of the law came to Jesus from Jerusalem and asked, [2]"Why do your disciples break the tradition of the elders? They don't wash their hands before they eat!"*d*

15:4
e Ex 20:12;
Dt 5:16;
Eph 6:2
f Ex 21:17;
Lev 20:9

[3]Jesus replied, "And why do you break the command of God for the sake of your tradition? [4]For God said, 'Honor your father and mother'*a e* and 'Anyone who curses his father or mother must be put to death.'*b f* [5]But you say that if a man says to his father or mother, 'Whatever help you might otherwise have received from me is a gift devoted to God,' [6]he is not to 'honor his father'*c* with it. Thus you nullify the word of God for the sake of your tradition. [7]You hypocrites! Isaiah was right when he prophesied about you:

15:9
g Col 2:20-22
h Isa 29:13;
Mal 2:2

[8]"'These people honor me with their lips,
      but their hearts are far from me.
[9]They worship me in vain;
      their teachings are but rules taught by men.'*g d h*"

15:11
i Ac 10:14,15
j ver 18

[10]Jesus called the crowd to him and said, "Listen and understand. [11]What goes into a man's mouth does not make him 'unclean,'*i* but what comes out of his mouth, that is what makes him 'unclean.'"*j*

15:13
k Isa 60:21; 61:3;
Jn 15:2

[12]Then the disciples came to him and asked, "Do you know that the Pharisees were offended when they heard this?"

[13]He replied, "Every plant that my heavenly Father has not planted*k* will be pulled up by the roots. [14]Leave them; they are blind guides.*e l* If a blind man leads a blind man, both will fall into a pit."*m*

15:14
l Mt 23:16,24;
Ro 2:19
m Lk 6:39

[15]Peter said, "Explain the parable to us."*n*

15:15
n Mt 13:36

a 4 Exodus 20:12; Deut. 5:16   *b* 4 Exodus 21:17; Lev. 20:9   *c* 6 Some manuscripts *father or his mother*   *d* 9 Isaiah 29:13   *e* 14 Some manuscripts *guides of the blind*

¹⁶"Are you still so dull?"ᵃ Jesus asked them. ¹⁷"Don't you see that whatever enters the mouth goes into the stomach and then out of the body? ¹⁸But the things that come out of the mouth come from the heart,ᵇ and these make a man 'unclean.' ¹⁹For out of the heart come evil thoughts, murder, adultery, sexual immorality, theft, false testimony, slander.ᶜ ²⁰These are what make a man 'unclean';ᵈ but eating with unwashed hands does not make him 'unclean.'"

²¹Leaving that place, Jesus withdrew to the region of Tyre and Sidon.ᵉ ²²A Canaanite woman from that vicinity came to him, crying out, "Lord, Son of David,ᶠ have mercy on me! My daughter is suffering terribly from demon-possession."ᵍ

²³Jesus did not answer a word. So his disciples came to him and urged him, "Send her away, for she keeps crying out after us."

²⁴He answered, "I was sent only to the lost sheep of Israel."ʰ

²⁵The woman came and knelt before him.ⁱ "Lord, help me!" she said.

²⁶He replied, "It is not right to take the children's bread and toss it to their dogs."

²⁷"Yes, Lord," she said, "but even the dogs eat the crumbs that fall from their masters' table."

²⁸Then Jesus answered, "Woman, you have great faith!ʲ Your request is granted." And her daughter was healed from that very hour.

²⁹Jesus left there and went along the Sea of Galilee. Then he went up on a mountainside and sat down. ³⁰Great crowds came to him, bringing the lame, the blind, the crippled, the mute and many others, and laid them at his feet; and he healed them.ᵏ ³¹The people were amazed when they saw the mute speaking, the crippled made well, the lame walking and the blind seeing. And they praised the God of Israel.ˡ

³²Jesus called his disciples to him and said, "I have compassion for these people;ᵐ they have already been with me three days and have nothing to eat. I do not want to send them away hungry, or they may collapse on the way."

³³His disciples answered, "Where could we get enough bread in this remote place to feed such a crowd?"

³⁴"How many loaves do you have?" Jesus asked.

"Seven," they replied, "and a few small fish."

³⁵He told the crowd to sit down on the ground. ³⁶Then he took the seven loaves and the fish, and when he had given thanks, he broke themⁿ and gave them to the disciples, and they in turn to the people. ³⁷They all ate and were satisfied. Afterward the disciples picked up seven basketfuls of broken pieces that were left over.ᵒ ³⁸The number of those who ate was four thousand, besides women and children. ³⁹After Jesus had sent the crowd away, he got into the boat and went to the vicinity of Magadan.

15:16
ᵃ Mt 16:9

15:18
ᵇ Mt 12:34;
Lk 6:45;
Jas 3:6

15:19
ᶜ Gal 5:19-21

15:20
ᵈ Ro 14:14

15:21
ᵉ Mt 11:21

15:22
ᶠ Mt 9:27
ᵍ Mt 4:24

15:24
ʰ Mt 10:6,23;
Ro 15:8

15:25
ⁱ Mt 8:2

15:28
ʲ Mt 9:22

15:30
ᵏ Mt 4:23

15:31
ˡ Mt 9:8

15:32
ᵐ Mt 9:36

15:36
ⁿ Mt 14:19

15:37
ᵒ Mt 16:10

16:1
a Ac 4:1
b Mt 12:38

16:3
c Lk 12:54-56

16:4
d Mt 12:39

16:6
e Lk 12:1

16:8
f Mt 6:30

16:9
g Mt 14:17-21

16:10
h Mt 15:34-38

16:12
i Ac 4:1

16:14
j Mt 3:1; 14:2
k Mk 6:15;
Jn 1:21

16:16
l Mt 4:3;
Ps 42:2;
Jn 11:27;
Ac 14:15;
2Co 6:16;
1Th 1:9;
1Ti 3:15;
Heb 10:31;
12:22

16:17
m 1Co 15:50;
Gal 1:16;
Eph 6:12;
Heb 2:14

16:18
n Jn 1:42
o Eph 2:20

16:19
p Isa 22:22;
Rev 3:7
q Mt 18:18;
Jn 20:23

16:20
r Mk 8:30

16:21
s Mk 10:34;
Lk 17:25

Chapter 16 Theme _____

16

The Pharisees and Sadducees*a* came to Jesus and tested him by asking him to show them a sign from heaven.*b*

²He replied,*a* "When evening comes, you say, 'It will be fair weather, for the sky is red,' ³and in the morning, 'Today it will be stormy, for the sky is red and overcast.' You know how to interpret the appearance of the sky, but you cannot interpret the signs of the times.*c* ⁴A wicked and adulterous generation looks for a miraculous sign, but none will be given it except the sign of Jonah."*d* Jesus then left them and went away.

⁵When they went across the lake, the disciples forgot to take bread. ⁶"Be careful," Jesus said to them. "Be on your guard against the yeast of the Pharisees and Sadducees."*e*

⁷They discussed this among themselves and said, "It is because we didn't bring any bread."

⁸Aware of their discussion, Jesus asked, "You of little faith,*f* why are you talking among yourselves about having no bread? ⁹Do you still not understand? Don't you remember the five loaves for the five thousand, and how many basketfuls you gathered?*g* ¹⁰Or the seven loaves for the four thousand, and how many basketfuls you gathered?*h* ¹¹How is it you don't understand that I was not talking to you about bread? But be on your guard against the yeast of the Pharisees and Sadducees." ¹²Then they understood that he was not telling them to guard against the yeast used in bread, but against the teaching of the Pharisees and Sadducees.*i*

¹³When Jesus came to the region of Caesarea Philippi, he asked his disciples, "Who do people say the Son of Man is?"

¹⁴They replied, "Some say John the Baptist;*j* others say Elijah; and still others, Jeremiah or one of the prophets."*k*

¹⁵"But what about you?" he asked. "Who do you say I am?"

¹⁶Simon Peter answered, "You are the Christ,*b* the Son of the living God."*l*

¹⁷Jesus replied, "Blessed are you, Simon son of Jonah, for this was not revealed to you by man,*m* but by my Father in heaven. ¹⁸And I tell you that you are Peter,*c n* and on this rock I will build my church,*o* and the gates of Hades*d* will not overcome it.*e* ¹⁹I will give you the keys*p* of the kingdom of heaven; whatever you bind on earth will be*f* bound in heaven, and whatever you loose on earth will be*f* loosed in heaven."*q* ²⁰Then he warned his disciples not to tell anyone*r* that he was the Christ.

²¹From that time on Jesus began to explain to his disciples that he must go to Jerusalem and suffer many things*s* at the hands of

---

a 2 Some early manuscripts do not have the rest of verse 2 and all of verse 3.   *b* 16 Or *Messiah*; also in verse 20   *c* 18 *Peter* means *rock*.   *d* 18 Or *hell*   *e* 18 Or *not prove stronger than it*
f 19 Or *have been*

the elders, chief priests and teachers of the law, and that he must be killed and on the third day[a] be raised to life.[b]

[22]Peter took him aside and began to rebuke him. "Never, Lord!" he said. "This shall never happen to you!"

[23]Jesus turned and said to Peter, "Get behind me, Satan![c] You are a stumbling block to me; you do not have in mind the things of God, but the things of men."

[24]Then Jesus said to his disciples, "If anyone would come after me, he must deny himself and take up his cross and follow me.[d] [25]For whoever wants to save his life[a] will lose it, but whoever loses his life for me will find it.[e] [26]What good will it be for a man if he gains the whole world, yet forfeits his soul? Or what can a man give in exchange for his soul? [27]For the Son of Man[f] is going to come[g] in his Father's glory with his angels, and then he will reward each person according to what he has done.[h] [28]I tell you the truth, some who are standing here will not taste death before they see the Son of Man coming in his kingdom."

Chapter 17 Theme

17 After six days Jesus took with him Peter, James and John the brother of James, and led them up a high mountain by themselves. [2]There he was transfigured before them. His face shone like the sun, and his clothes became as white as the light. [3]Just then there appeared before them Moses and Elijah, talking with Jesus.

[4]Peter said to Jesus, "Lord, it is good for us to be here. If you wish, I will put up three shelters—one for you, one for Moses and one for Elijah."

[5]While he was still speaking, a bright cloud enveloped them, and a voice from the cloud said, "This is my Son, whom I love; with him I am well pleased.[i] Listen to him!"[j]

[6]When the disciples heard this, they fell facedown to the ground, terrified. [7]But Jesus came and touched them. "Get up," he said. "Don't be afraid."[k] [8]When they looked up, they saw no one except Jesus.

[9]As they were coming down the mountain, Jesus instructed them, "Don't tell anyone[l] what you have seen, until the Son of Man[m] has been raised from the dead."[n]

[10]The disciples asked him, "Why then do the teachers of the law say that Elijah must come first?"

[11]Jesus replied, "To be sure, Elijah comes and will restore all things.[o] [12]But I tell you, Elijah has already come,[p] and they did not recognize him, but have done to him everything they wished.[q] In the same way the Son of Man is going to suffer[r] at their hands."

16:21
[a]Jn 2:19
[b]Mt 17:22,23;
Mk 9:31;
Lk 9:22;
18:31-33; 24:6,7

16:23
[c]Mt 4:10

16:24
[d]Mt 10:38;
Lk 14:27

16:25
[e]Jn 12:25

16:27
[f]Mt 8:20
[g]Ac 1:11
[h]Job 34:11;
Ps 62:12;
Jer 17:10;
Ro 2:6;
2Co 5:10;
Rev 22:12

17:5
[i]Mt 3:17;
2Pe 1:17
[j]Ac 3:22,23

17:7
[k]Mt 14:27

17:9
[l]Mk 8:30
[m]Mt 8:20
[n]Mt 16:21

17:11
[o]Mal 4:6;
Lk 1:16,17

17:12
[p]Mt 11:14
[q]Mt 14:3,10
[r]Mt 16:21

---

a 25 The Greek word means either *life* or *soul*; also in verse 26.

17:15
a Mt 4:24

17:20
b Mt 21:21
c Mt 13:31;
Mk 11:23;
Lk 17:6
d 1Co 13:2

17:22
e Mt 8:20

17:23
f Ac 2:23; 3:13
g Mt 16:21
h Mt 16:21

17:24
i Ex 30:13

17:25
j Mt 22:17-21;
Ro 13:7

17:27
k Jn 6:61

18:3
l Mt 19:14;
1Pe 2:2
m Mt 3:2

18:4
n Mk 9:35

13Then the disciples understood that he was talking to them about John the Baptist.

14When they came to the crowd, a man approached Jesus and knelt before him. 15"Lord, have mercy on my son," he said. "He has seizures[a] and is suffering greatly. He often falls into the fire or into the water. 16I brought him to your disciples, but they could not heal him."

17"O unbelieving and perverse generation," Jesus replied, "how long shall I stay with you? How long shall I put up with you? Bring the boy here to me." 18Jesus rebuked the demon, and it came out of the boy, and he was healed from that moment.

19Then the disciples came to Jesus in private and asked, "Why couldn't we drive it out?"

20He replied, "Because you have so little faith. I tell you the truth, if you have faith[b] as small as a mustard seed,[c] you can say to this mountain, 'Move from here to there' and it will move.[d] Nothing will be impossible for you.[a]"

22When they came together in Galilee, he said to them, "The Son of Man[e] is going to be betrayed into the hands of men. 23They will kill him,[f] and on the third day[g] he will be raised to life."[h] And the disciples were filled with grief.

24After Jesus and his disciples arrived in Capernaum, the collectors of the two-drachma tax[i] came to Peter and asked, "Doesn't your teacher pay the temple tax[b]?"

25"Yes, he does," he replied.

When Peter came into the house, Jesus was the first to speak. "What do you think, Simon?" he asked. "From whom do the kings of the earth collect duty and taxes[j]—from their own sons or from others?"

26"From others," Peter answered.

"Then the sons are exempt," Jesus said to him. 27"But so that we may not offend[k] them, go to the lake and throw out your line. Take the first fish you catch; open its mouth and you will find a four-drachma coin. Take it and give it to them for my tax and yours."

Chapter 18 Theme _____

18 At that time the disciples came to Jesus and asked, "Who is the greatest in the kingdom of heaven?"

2He called a little child and had him stand among them. 3And he said: "I tell you the truth, unless you change and become like little children,[l] you will never enter the kingdom of heaven.[m] 4Therefore, whoever humbles himself like this child is the greatest in the kingdom of heaven.[n]

a 20 Some manuscripts *you.* 21*But this kind does not go out except by prayer and fasting.*
b 24 Greek *the two drachmas*

⁵"And whoever welcomes a little child like this in my name welcomes me.ᵃ ⁶But if anyone causes one of these little ones who believe in me to sin,ᵇ it would be better for him to have a large millstone hung around his neck and to be drowned in the depths of the sea.ᶜ

⁷"Woe to the world because of the things that cause people to sin! Such things must come, but woe to the man through whom they come!ᵈ ⁸If your hand or your foot causes you to sin,ᵉ cut it off and throw it away. It is better for you to enter life maimed or crippled than to have two hands or two feet and be thrown into eternal fire. ⁹And if your eye causes you to sin,ᶠ gouge it out and throw it away. It is better for you to enter life with one eye than to have two eyes and be thrown into the fire of hell.ᵍ

¹⁰"See that you do not look down on one of these little ones. For I tell you that their angelsʰ in heaven always see the face of my Father in heaven.ᵃ

¹²"What do you think? If a man owns a hundred sheep, and one of them wanders away, will he not leave the ninety-nine on the hills and go to look for the one that wandered off? ¹³And if he finds it, I tell you the truth, he is happier about that one sheep than about the ninety-nine that did not wander off. ¹⁴In the same way your Father in heaven is not willing that any of these little ones should be lost.

¹⁵"If your brother sins against you,ᵇ go and show him his fault,ⁱ just between the two of you. If he listens to you, you have won your brother over. ¹⁶But if he will not listen, take one or two others along, so that 'every matter may be established by the testimony of two or three witnesses.'ᶜʲ ¹⁷If he refuses to listen to them, tell it to the church;ᵏ and if he refuses to listen even to the church, treat him as you would a pagan or a tax collector.ˡ

¹⁸"I tell you the truth, whatever you bind on earth will beᵈ bound in heaven, and whatever you loose on earth will beᵈ loosed in heaven.ᵐ

¹⁹"Again, I tell you that if two of you on earth agree about anything you ask for, it will be done for youⁿ by my Father in heaven. ²⁰For where two or three come together in my name, there am I with them."

²¹Then Peter came to Jesus and asked, "Lord, how many times shall I forgive my brother when he sins against me?ᵒ Up to seven times?"ᵖ

²²Jesus answered, "I tell you, not seven times, but seventy-seven times.ᵉ�q

---

18:5
ᵃMt 10:40

18:6
ᵇMt 5:29
ᶜMk 9:42;
Lk 17:2

18:7
ᵈLk 17:1

18:8
ᵉMt 5:29;
Mk 9:43,45

18:9
ᶠMt 5:29
ᵍMt 5:22

18:10
ʰGe 48:16;
Ps 34:7;
Ac 12:11,15;
Heb 1:14

18:15
ⁱLev 19:17;
Lk 17:3;
Gal 6:1;
Jas 5:19,20

18:16
ʲNu 35:30;
Dt 17:6; 19:15;
Jn 8:17;
2Co 13:1;
1Ti 5:19;
Heb 10:28

18:17
ᵏ1Co 6:1-6
ˡRo 16:17;
2Th 3:6,14

18:18
ᵐMt 16:19;
Jn 20:23

18:19
ⁿMt 7:7

18:21
ᵒMt 6:14
ᵖLk 17:4

18:22
qGe 4:24

18:23
a Mt 13:24
b Mt 25:19

²³"Therefore, the kingdom of heaven is like*ᵃ* a king who wanted to settle accounts*ᵇ* with his servants. ²⁴As he began the settlement, a man who owed him ten thousand talents*ᵃ* was brought to him. ²⁵Since he was not able to pay,*ᶜ* the master ordered that he and his wife and his children and all that he had be sold*ᵈ* to repay the debt.

18:25
c Lk 7:42
d Lev 25:39;
2Ki 4:1;
Ne 5:5,8

²⁶"The servant fell on his knees before him.*ᵉ* 'Be patient with me,' he begged, 'and I will pay back everything.' ²⁷The servant's master took pity on him, canceled the debt and let him go.

²⁸"But when that servant went out, he found one of his fellow servants who owed him a hundred denarii.*ᵇ* He grabbed him and began to choke him. 'Pay back what you owe me!' he demanded.

18:26
e Mt 8:2

²⁹"His fellow servant fell to his knees and begged him, 'Be patient with me, and I will pay you back.'

³⁰"But he refused. Instead, he went off and had the man thrown into prison until he could pay the debt. ³¹When the other servants saw what had happened, they were greatly distressed and went and told their master everything that had happened.

³²"Then the master called the servant in. 'You wicked servant,' he said, 'I canceled all that debt of yours because you begged me to. ³³Shouldn't you have had mercy on your fellow servant just as I had on you?' ³⁴In anger his master turned him over to the jailers to be tortured, until he should pay back all he owed.

18:35
f Mt 6:14;
Jas 2:13

³⁵"This is how my heavenly Father will treat each of you unless you forgive your brother from your heart."*ᶠ*

Chapter 19 Theme

19:1
g Mt 7:28

19 When Jesus had finished saying these things,*ᵍ* he left Galilee and went into the region of Judea to the other side of the Jordan. ²Large crowds followed him, and he healed them*ʰ* there.

19:2
h Mt 4:23

³Some Pharisees came to him to test him. They asked, "Is it lawful for a man to divorce his wife*ⁱ* for any and every reason?"

19:3
i Mt 5:31

⁴"Haven't you read," he replied, "that at the beginning the Creator 'made them male and female,'*ᶜ ʲ* ⁵and said, 'For this reason a man will leave his father and mother and be united to his wife, and the two will become one flesh'*ᵈ*?*ᵏ* ⁶So they are no longer two, but one. Therefore what God has joined together, let man not separate."

19:4
j Ge 1:27; 5:2

Judea

19:5
k Ge 2:24;
1Co 6:16;
Eph 5:31

a 24 That is, millions of dollars   b 28 That is, a few dollars   c 4 Gen. 1:27   f 5 Gen. 2:24

⁷"Why then," they asked, "did Moses command that a man give his wife a certificate of divorce and send her away?"ᵃ

⁸Jesus replied, "Moses permitted you to divorce your wives because your hearts were hard. But it was not this way from the beginning. ⁹I tell you that anyone who divorces his wife, except for marital unfaithfulness, and marries another woman commits adultery."ᵇ

¹⁰The disciples said to him, "If this is the situation between a husband and wife, it is better not to marry."

¹¹Jesus replied, "Not everyone can accept this word, but only those to whom it has been given.ᶜ ¹²For some are eunuchs because they were born that way; others were made that way by men; and others have renounced marriageᵃ because of the kingdom of heaven. The one who can accept this should accept it."

¹³Then little children were brought to Jesus for him to place his hands on themᵈ and pray for them. But the disciples rebuked those who brought them.

¹⁴Jesus said, "Let the little children come to me, and do not hinder them, for the kingdom of heaven belongsᵉ to such as these."ᶠ ¹⁵When he had placed his hands on them, he went on from there.

¹⁶Now a man came up to Jesus and asked, "Teacher, what good thing must I do to get eternal lifeᵍ?"ʰ

¹⁷"Why do you ask me about what is good?" Jesus replied. "There is only One who is good. If you want to enter life, obey the commandments."ⁱ

¹⁸"Which ones?" the man inquired.

Jesus replied, "'Do not murder, do not commit adultery,ʲ do not steal, do not give false testimony, ¹⁹honor your father and mother,'ᵇᵏ and 'love your neighbor as yourself.'ᶜ"ˡ

²⁰"All these I have kept," the young man said. "What do I still lack?"

²¹Jesus answered, "If you want to be perfect,ᵐ go, sell your possessions and give to the poor,ⁿ and you will have treasure in heaven.ᵒ Then come, follow me."

²²When the young man heard this, he went away sad, because he had great wealth.

²³Then Jesus said to his disciples, "I tell you the truth, it is hard for a rich manᵖ to enter the kingdom of heaven. ²⁴Again I tell you, it is easier for a camel to go through the eye of a needle than for a rich man to enter the kingdom of God."

²⁵When the disciples heard this, they were greatly astonished and asked, "Who then can be saved?"

²⁶Jesus looked at them and said, "With man this is impossible, but with God all things are possible."q

---

19:7 aDt 24:1-4; Mt 5:31

19:9 bMt 5:32; Lk 16:18

19:11 cMt 13:11; 1Co 7:7-9,17

19:13 dMk 5:23

19:14 eMt 25:34; fMt 18:3; 1Pe 2:2

19:16 gMt 25:46; hLk 10:25

19:17 iLev 18:5

19:18 jJas 2:11

19:19 kEx 20:12-16; Dt 5:16-20; lLev 19:18; Mt 5:43

19:21 mMt 5:48; nLk 12:33; Ac 2:45; 4:34-35; oMt 6:20

19:23 pMt 13:22; 1Ti 6:9,10

19:26 qGe 18:14; Job 42:2; Jer 32:17; Zec 8:6; Lk 1:37; 18:27; Ro 4:21

ª 12 Or *have made themselves eunuchs*   ᵇ 19 Exodus 20:12-16; Deut. 5:16-20   ᶜ 19 Lev. 19:18

19:27
a Mt 4:19

²⁷Peter answered him, "We have left everything to follow you!ᵃ What then will there be for us?"

19:28
b Mt 20:21;
25:31
c Lk 22:28-30;
Rev 3:21; 4:4;
20:4

²⁸Jesus said to them, "I tell you the truth, at the renewal of all things, when the Son of Man sits on his glorious throne,ᵇ you who have followed me will also sit on twelve thrones, judging the twelve tribes of Israel.ᶜ ²⁹And everyone who has left houses or brothers or sisters or father or motherᵃ or children or fields for my sake will receive a hundred times as much and will inherit eternal life.ᵈ ³⁰But many who are first will be last, and many who are last will be first.ᵉ

19:29
d Mt 6:33; 25:46

Chapter 20 Theme

19:30
e Mt 20:16;
Mk 10:31;
Lk 13:30

20 "For the kingdom of heaven is likeᶠ a landowner who went out early in the morning to hire men to work in his vineyard.ᵍ ²He agreed to pay them a denarius for the day and sent them into his vineyard.

20:1
f Mt 13:24
g Mt 21:28,33

³"About the third hour he went out and saw others standing in the marketplace doing nothing. ⁴He told them, 'You also go and work in my vineyard, and I will pay you whatever is right.' ⁵So they went.

"He went out again about the sixth hour and the ninth hour and did the same thing. ⁶About the eleventh hour he went out and found still others standing around. He asked them, 'Why have you been standing here all day long doing nothing?'

20:8
h Lev 19:13;
Dt 24:15

⁷"'Because no one has hired us,' they answered.

"He said to them, 'You also go and work in my vineyard.'

⁸"When evening came,ʰ the owner of the vineyard said to his foreman, 'Call the workers and pay them their wages, beginning with the last ones hired and going on to the first.'

20:11
i Jnh 4:1

⁹"The workers who were hired about the eleventh hour came and each received a denarius. ¹⁰So when those came who were hired first, they expected to receive more. But each one of them also received a denarius. ¹¹When they received it, they began to grumbleⁱ against the landowner. ¹²'These men who were hired last worked only one hour,' they said, 'and you have made them equal to us who have borne the burden of the work and the heatʲ of the day.'

20:12
j Jnh 4:8;
Lk 12:55;
Jas 1:11

¹³"But he answered one of them, 'Friend,ᵏ I am not being unfair to you. Didn't you agree to work for a denarius? ¹⁴Take your pay and go. I want to give the man who was hired last the same as I gave you. ¹⁵Don't I have the right to do what I want with my own money? Or are you envious because I am generous?'ˡ

20:13
k Mt 22:12;
26:50

20:15
l Dt 15:9;
Mk 7:22

¹⁶"So the last will be first, and the first will be last."ᵐ

20:16
m Mt 19:30

a 29 Some manuscripts *mother or wife*

[17]Now as Jesus was going up to Jerusalem, he took the twelve disciples aside and said to them, [18]"We are going up to Jerusalem,[a] and the Son of Man[b] will be betrayed to the chief priests and the teachers of the law.[c] They will condemn him to death [19]and will turn him over to the Gentiles to be mocked and flogged[d] and crucified.[e] On the third day[f] he will be raised to life!"[g]

[20]Then the mother of Zebedee's sons[h] came to Jesus with her sons and, kneeling down,[i] asked a favor of him.

[21]"What is it you want?" he asked.

She said, "Grant that one of these two sons of mine may sit at your right and the other at your left in your kingdom."[j]

[22]"You don't know what you are asking," Jesus said to them. "Can you drink the cup[k] I am going to drink?"

"We can," they answered.

[23]Jesus said to them, "You will indeed drink from my cup,[l] but to sit at my right or left is not for me to grant. These places belong to those for whom they have been prepared by my Father."

[24]When the ten heard about this, they were indignant[m] with the two brothers. [25]Jesus called them together and said, "You know that the rulers of the Gentiles lord it over them, and their high officials exercise authority over them. [26]Not so with you. Instead, whoever wants to become great among you must be your servant,[n] [27]and whoever wants to be first must be your slave— [28]just as the Son of Man[o] did not come to be served, but to serve,[p] and to give his life as a ransom[q] for many."

[29]As Jesus and his disciples were leaving Jericho, a large crowd followed him. [30]Two blind men were sitting by the roadside, and when they heard that Jesus was going by, they shouted, "Lord, Son of David,[r] have mercy on us!"

[31]The crowd rebuked them and told them to be quiet, but they shouted all the louder, "Lord, Son of David, have mercy on us!"

[32]Jesus stopped and called them. "What do you want me to do for you?" he asked.

[33]"Lord," they answered, "we want our sight."

[34]Jesus had compassion on them and touched their eyes. Immediately they received their sight and followed him.

Chapter 21 Theme

21 As they approached Jerusalem and came to Bethphage on the Mount of Olives,[s] Jesus sent two disciples, [2]saying to them, "Go to the village ahead of you, and at once you will find a donkey tied there, with her colt by her. Untie them and bring them to me. [3]If anyone says anything to you, tell him that the Lord needs them, and he will send them right away."

[4]This took place to fulfill what was spoken through the prophet:

20:18
[a] Lk 9:51
[b] Mt 8:20
[c] Mt 16:21; 27:1,2

20:19
[d] Mt 16:21
[e] Ac 2:23
[f] Mt 16:21
[g] Mt 16:21

20:20
[h] Mt 4:21
[i] Mt 8:2

20:21
[j] Mt 19:28

20:22
[k] Isa 51:17,22; Jer 49:12; Mt 26:39,42; Mk 14:36; Lk 22:42; Jn 18:11

20:23
[l] Ac 12:2; Rev 1:9

20:24
[m] Lk 22:24,25

20:26
[n] Mt 23:11; Mk 9:35

20:28
[o] Mt 8:20
[p] Lk 22:27; Jn 13:13-16; 2Co 8:9; Php 2:7
[q] Isa 53:10; Mt 26:28; 1Ti 2:6; Tit 2:14; Heb 9:28; 1Pe 1:18,19

20:30
[r] Mt 9:27

21:1
[s] Mt 24:3; 26:30; Mk 14:26; Lk 19:37; 21:37; 22:39; Jn 8:1; Ac 1:12

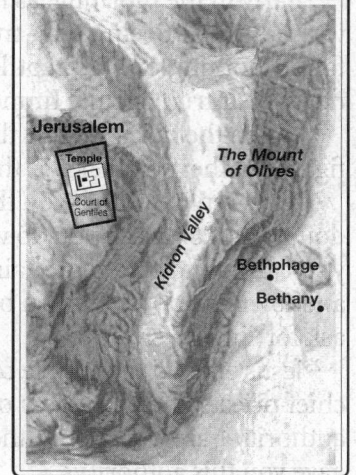
From Bethany, Bethphage across the Mount of Olives into Jerusalem

21:5
a Zec 9:9;
Isa 62:11

5 "Say to the Daughter
    of Zion,
    'See, your king comes
        to you,
    gentle and riding on
        a donkey,
    on a colt, the foal of
        a donkey.'"*a*

21:8
b 2Ki 9:13

6 The disciples went and did as Jesus had instructed them. 7 They brought the donkey and the colt, placed their cloaks on them, and Jesus sat on them. 8 A very large crowd spread their cloaks*b* on the road, while others cut branches

21:9
c ver 15;
Mt 9:27
d Ps 118:26;
Mt 23:39
e Lk 2:14

from the trees and spread them on the road. 9 The crowds that went ahead of him and those that followed shouted,

"Hosanna*b* to the Son of David!"*c*

"Blessed is he who comes in the name of the Lord!"*c* *d*

21:11
f Lk 7:16,39;
24:19;
Jn 1:21,25;
6:14; 7:40

"Hosanna*b* in the highest!"*e*

21:12
g Dt 14:26
h Ex 30:13
i Lev 1:14

10 When Jesus entered Jerusalem, the whole city was stirred and asked, "Who is this?"

11 The crowds answered, "This is Jesus, the prophet*f* from Nazareth in Galilee."

12 Jesus entered the temple area and drove out all who were buying*g* and selling there. He overturned the tables of the money changers*h* and the benches of those selling doves.*i* 13 "It is written," he said to them, "'My house will be called a house of prayer,'*d* *j* but you are making it a 'den of robbers.'*e*"*k*

21:13
j Isa 56:7
k Jer 7:11

14 The blind and the lame came to him at the temple, and he healed them.*l* 15 But when the chief priests and the teachers of the law saw the wonderful things he did and the children shouting in the temple area, "Hosanna to the Son of David,"*m* they were indignant.*n*

21:14
l Mt 4:23

21:15
m ver 9;
Mt 9:27
n Lk 19:39

16 "Do you hear what these children are saying?" they asked him.

"Yes," replied Jesus, "have you never read,

"'From the lips of children and infants
    you have ordained praise'*f*?"*o*

21:16
o Ps 8:2

17 And he left them and went out of the city to Bethany,*p* where he spent the night.

21:17
p Mt 26:6;
Mk 11:1;
Lk 24:50;
Jn 11:1,18; 12:1

a 5 Zech. 9:9   *b* 9 A Hebrew expression meaning "Save!" which became an exclamation of praise; also in verse 15   *c* 9 Psalm 118:26   *d* 13 Isaiah 56:7   *e* 13 Jer. 7:11   *f* 16 Psalm 8:2

[18]Early in the morning, as he was on his way back to the city, he was hungry. [19]Seeing a fig tree by the road, he went up to it but found nothing on it except leaves. Then he said to it, "May you never bear fruit again!" Immediately the tree withered.*a*

[20]When the disciples saw this, they were amazed. "How did the fig tree wither so quickly?" they asked.

[21]Jesus replied, "I tell you the truth, if you have faith and do not doubt,*b* not only can you do what was done to the fig tree, but also you can say to this mountain, 'Go, throw yourself into the sea,' and it will be done. [22]If you believe, you will receive whatever you ask for*c* in prayer."

[23]Jesus entered the temple courts, and, while he was teaching, the chief priests and the elders of the people came to him. "By what authority*d* are you doing these things?" they asked. "And who gave you this authority?"

[24]Jesus replied, "I will also ask you one question. If you answer me, I will tell you by what authority I am doing these things. [25]John's baptism—where did it come from? Was it from heaven, or from men?"

They discussed it among themselves and said, "If we say, 'From heaven,' he will ask, 'Then why didn't you believe him?' [26]But if we say, 'From men'—we are afraid of the people, for they all hold that John was a prophet."*e*

[27]So they answered Jesus, "We don't know."

Then he said, "Neither will I tell you by what authority I am doing these things.

[28]"What do you think? There was a man who had two sons. He went to the first and said, 'Son, go and work today in the vineyard.'*f*

[29]" 'I will not,' he answered, but later he changed his mind and went.

[30]"Then the father went to the other son and said the same thing. He answered, 'I will, sir,' but he did not go.

[31]"Which of the two did what his father wanted?"

"The first," they answered.

Jesus said to them, "I tell you the truth, the tax collectors*g* and the prostitutes*h* are entering the kingdom of God ahead of you. [32]For John came to you to show you the way of righteousness,*i* and you did not believe him, but the tax collectors*j* and the prostitutes*k* did. And even after you saw this, you did not repent*l* and believe him.

[33]"Listen to another parable: There was a landowner who planted*m* a vineyard. He put a wall around it, dug a winepress in it and built a watchtower.*n* Then he rented the vineyard to some farmers and went away on a journey.*o* [34]When the harvest time approached, he sent his servants*p* to the tenants to collect his fruit.

21:19
a Isa 34:4;
Jer 8:13

21:21
b Mt 17:20;
Lk 17:6;
1Co 13:2;
Jas 1:6

21:22
c Mt 7:7

21:23
d Ac 4:7; 7:27

21:26
e Mt 11:9;
Mk 6:20

21:28
f ver 33;
Mt 20:1

21:31
g Lk 7:29
h Lk 7:50

21:32
i Mt 3:1-12
j Lk 3:12,13;
7:29
k Lk 7:36-50
l Lk 7:30

21:33
m Ps 80:8
n Isa 5:1-7
o Mt 25:14,15

21:34
p Mt 22:3

21:35
a 2Ch 24:21;
Mt 23:34,37;
Heb 11:36,37

21:36
b Mt 22:4

21:38
c Heb 1:2
d Mt 12:14
e Ps 2:8

21:41
f Mt 8:11,12
g Ac 13:46; 18:6;
28:28

21:42
h Ps 118:22,23;
Ac 4:11;
1Pe 2:7

21:43
i Mt 8:12

21:44
j Lk 2:34

21:46
k ver 11,26

22:2
l Mt 13:24

22:3
m Mt 21:34

22:4
n Mt 21:36

22:7
o Lk 19:27

35"The tenants seized his servants; they beat one, killed another, and stoned a third.a 36Then he sent other servantsb to them, more than the first time, and the tenants treated them the same way. 37Last of all, he sent his son to them. 'They will respect my son,' he said.

38"But when the tenants saw the son, they said to each other, 'This is the heir.c Come, let's kill himd and take his inheritance.'e 39So they took him and threw him out of the vineyard and killed him.

40"Therefore, when the owner of the vineyard comes, what will he do to those tenants?"

41"He will bring those wretches to a wretched end,"f they replied, "and he will rent the vineyard to other tenants,g who will give him his share of the crop at harvest time."

42Jesus said to them, "Have you never read in the Scriptures:

" 'The stone the builders rejected
has become the capstonea;
the Lord has done this,
and it is marvelous in our eyes'b?h

43"Therefore I tell you that the kingdom of God will be taken away from youi and given to a people who will produce its fruit. 44He who falls on this stone will be broken to pieces, but he on whom it falls will be crushed."cj

45When the chief priests and the Pharisees heard Jesus' parables, they knew he was talking about them. 46They looked for a way to arrest him, but they were afraid of the crowd because the people held that he was a prophet.k

Chapter 22 Theme _____

22 Jesus spoke to them again in parables, saying: 2"The kingdom of heaven is likel a king who prepared a wedding banquet for his son. 3He sent his servantsm to those who had been invited to the banquet to tell them to come, but they refused to come.

4"Then he sent some more servantsn and said, 'Tell those who have been invited that I have prepared my dinner: My oxen and fattened cattle have been butchered, and everything is ready. Come to the wedding banquet.'

5"But they paid no attention and went off—one to his field, another to his business. 6The rest seized his servants, mistreated them and killed them. 7The king was enraged. He sent his army and destroyed those murdererso and burned their city.

a 42 Or cornerstone   b 42 Psalm 118:22,23   c 44 Some manuscripts do not have verse 44.

⁸"Then he said to his servants, 'The wedding banquet is ready, but those I invited did not deserve to come. ⁹Go to the street corners[a] and invite to the banquet anyone you find.' ¹⁰So the servants went out into the streets and gathered all the people they could find, both good and bad,[b] and the wedding hall was filled with guests.

¹¹"But when the king came in to see the guests, he noticed a man there who was not wearing wedding clothes. ¹²'Friend,'[c] he asked, 'how did you get in here without wedding clothes?' The man was speechless.

¹³"Then the king told the attendants, 'Tie him hand and foot, and throw him outside, into the darkness, where there will be weeping and gnashing of teeth.'[d]

¹⁴"For many are invited, but few are chosen."[e]

¹⁵Then the Pharisees went out and laid plans to trap him in his words. ¹⁶They sent their disciples to him along with the Herodians.[f] "Teacher," they said, "we know you are a man of integrity and that you teach the way of God in accordance with the truth. You aren't swayed by men, because you pay no attention to who they are. ¹⁷Tell us then, what is your opinion? Is it right to pay taxes[g] to Caesar or not?"

¹⁸But Jesus, knowing their evil intent, said, "You hypocrites, why are you trying to trap me? ¹⁹Show me the coin used for paying the tax." They brought him a denarius, ²⁰and he asked them, "Whose portrait is this? And whose inscription?"

²¹"Caesar's," they replied.

Then he said to them, "Give to Caesar what is Caesar's,[h] and to God what is God's."

²²When they heard this, they were amazed. So they left him and went away.[i]

²³That same day the Sadducees,[j] who say there is no resurrection,[k] came to him with a question. ²⁴"Teacher," they said, "Moses told us that if a man dies without having children, his brother must marry the widow and have children for him.[l] ²⁵Now there were seven brothers among us. The first one married and died, and since he had no children, he left his wife to his brother. ²⁶The same thing happened to the second and third brother, right on down to the seventh. ²⁷Finally, the woman died. ²⁸Now then, at the resurrection, whose wife will she be of the seven, since all of them were married to her?"

²⁹Jesus replied, "You are in error because you do not know the Scriptures[m] or the power of God. ³⁰At the resurrection people will neither marry nor be given in marriage;[n] they will be like the angels in heaven. ³¹But about the resurrection of the dead—have you not read what God said to you, ³²'I am the God of Abraham,

22:9
[a] Eze 21:21

22:10
[b] Mt 13:47,48

22:12
[c] Mt 20:13; 26:50

22:13
[d] Mt 8:12

22:14
[e] Rev 17:14

22:16
[f] Mk 3:6

22:17
[g] Mt 17:25

22:21
[h] Ro 13:7

22:22
[i] Mk 12:12

22:23
[j] Ac 4:1
[k] Ac 23:8; 1Co 15:12

22:24
[l] Dt 25:5,6

22:29
[m] Jn 20:9

22:30
[n] Mt 24:38

22:32
aEx 3:6;
Ac 7:32

22:33
bMt 7:28

22:34
cAc 4:1

22:35
dLk 7:30; 10:25;
11:45; 14:3

22:37
eDt 6:5

22:39
fLev 19:18;
Mt 5:43; 19:19;
Gal 5:14

22:40
gMt 7:12

22:42
hMt 9:27

22:44
iPs 110:1;
Ac 2:34,35;
1Co 15:25;
Heb 1:13; 10:13

22:46
jMk 12:34;
Lk 20:40

23:2
kEzr 7:6,25;
Ne 8:4

23:4
lLk 11:46;
Ac 15:10;
Gal 6:13

23:5
mMt 6:1,2,5,16
nEx 13:9;
Dt 6:8
oNu 15:38;
Dt 22:12

23:6
pLk 11:43; 14:7;
20:46

23:7
qver 8;
Mk 9:5; 10:51;
Jn 1:38,49

the God of Isaac, and the God of Jacob'?ᵃ He is not the God of the dead but of the living."

³³When the crowds heard this, they were astonished at his teaching.ᵇ

³⁴Hearing that Jesus had silenced the Sadducees,ᶜ the Pharisees got together. ³⁵One of them, an expert in the law,ᵈ tested him with this question: ³⁶"Teacher, which is the greatest commandment in the Law?"

³⁷Jesus replied: "'Love the Lord your God with all your heart and with all your soul and with all your mind.'ᵇᵉ ³⁸This is the first and greatest commandment. ³⁹And the second is like it: 'Love your neighbor as yourself.'ᶜᶠ ⁴⁰All the Law and the Prophets hang on these two commandments."ᵍ

⁴¹While the Pharisees were gathered together, Jesus asked them, ⁴²"What do you think about the Christᵈ? Whose son is he?"

"The son of David,"ʰ they replied.

⁴³He said to them, "How is it then that David, speaking by the Spirit, calls him 'Lord'? For he says,

⁴⁴"'The Lord said to my Lord:
  "Sit at my right hand
    until I put your enemies
      under your feet."'ᵉⁱ

⁴⁵If then David calls him 'Lord,' how can he be his son?" ⁴⁶No one could say a word in reply, and from that day on no one dared to ask him any more questions.ʲ

Chapter 23 Theme _____

23 Then Jesus said to the crowds and to his disciples: ²"The teachers of the lawᵏ and the Pharisees sit in Moses' seat. ³So you must obey them and do everything they tell you. But do not do what they do, for they do not practice what they preach. ⁴They tie up heavy loads and put them on men's shoulders, but they themselves are not willing to lift a finger to move them.ˡ

⁵"Everything they do is done for men to see:ᵐ They make their phylacteriesᶠⁿ wide and the tassels on their garmentsᵒ long; ⁶they love the place of honor at banquets and the most important seats in the synagogues;ᵖ ⁷they love to be greeted in the marketplaces and to have men call them 'Rabbi.'�q

⁸"But you are not to be called 'Rabbi,' for you have only one Master and you are all brothers. ⁹And do not call anyone on earth

a32 Exodus 3:6 b37 Deut. 6:5 c39 Lev. 19:18 d42 Or Messiah e44 Psalm 110:1
f5 That is, boxes containing Scripture verses, worn on forehead and arm

'father,' for you have one Father,^a and he is in heaven. ¹⁰Nor are you to be called 'teacher,' for you have one Teacher, the Christ.^a ¹¹The greatest among you will be your servant.^b ¹²For whoever exalts himself will be humbled, and whoever humbles himself will be exalted.^c

¹³"Woe to you, teachers of the law and Pharisees, you hypocrites!^d You shut the kingdom of heaven in men's faces. You yourselves do not enter, nor will you let those enter who are trying to.^{b e}

¹⁵"Woe to you, teachers of the law and Pharisees, you hypocrites! You travel over land and sea to win a single convert,^f and when he becomes one, you make him twice as much a son of hell^g as you are.

¹⁶"Woe to you, blind guides!^h You say, 'If anyone swears by the temple, it means nothing; but if anyone swears by the gold of the temple, he is bound by his oath.'ⁱ ¹⁷You blind fools! Which is greater: the gold, or the temple that makes the gold sacred?^j ¹⁸You also say, 'If anyone swears by the altar, it means nothing; but if anyone swears by the gift on it, he is bound by his oath.' ¹⁹You blind men! Which is greater: the gift, or the altar that makes the gift sacred?^k ²⁰Therefore, he who swears by the altar swears by it and by everything on it. ²¹And he who swears by the temple swears by it and by the one who dwells^l in it. ²²And he who swears by heaven swears by God's throne and by the one who sits on it.^m

²³"Woe to you, teachers of the law and Pharisees, you hypocrites! You give a tenthⁿ of your spices—mint, dill and cummin. But you have neglected the more important matters of the law—justice, mercy and faithfulness.^o You should have practiced the latter, without neglecting the former. ²⁴You blind guides!^p You strain out a gnat but swallow a camel.

²⁵"Woe to you, teachers of the law and Pharisees, you hypocrites! You clean the outside of the cup and dish,^q but inside they are full of greed and self-indulgence.^r ²⁶Blind Pharisee! First clean the inside of the cup and dish, and then the outside also will be clean.

²⁷"Woe to you, teachers of the law and Pharisees, you hypocrites! You are like whitewashed tombs,^s which look beautiful on the outside but on the inside are full of dead men's bones and everything unclean. ²⁸In the same way, on the outside you appear to people as righteous but on the inside you are full of hypocrisy and wickedness.

²⁹"Woe to you, teachers of the law and Pharisees, you hypocrites! You build tombs for the prophets^t and decorate the graves of the

23:9 ^aMal 1:6; Mt 7:11
23:11 ^bMt 20:26; Mk 9:35
23:12 ^cLk 14:11
23:13 ^dver 15,23, 25,27,29 ^eLk 11:52
23:15 ^fAc 2:11; 6:5; 13:43 ^gMt 5:22
23:16 ^hver 24; Mt 15:14 ⁱMt 5:33-35
23:17 ^jEx 30:29
23:19 ^kEx 29:37
23:21 ^l1Ki 8:13; Ps 26:8
23:22 ^mPs 11:4; Mt 5:34
23:23 ⁿLev 27:30 ^oMic 6:8; Lk 11:42
23:24 ^pver 16
23:25 ^qMk 7:4 ^rLk 11:39
23:27 ^sLk 11:44; Ac 23:3
23:29 ^tLk 11:47,48

^a10 Or *Messiah* ^b13 Some manuscripts *to.* ¹⁴*Woe to you, teachers of the law and Pharisees, you hypocrites! You devour widows' houses and for a show make lengthy prayers. Therefore you will be punished more severely.*

23:31
a Ac 7:51-52

23:32
b 1Th 2:16

23:33
c Mt 3:7; 12:34
d Mt 5:22

23:34
e 2Ch 36:15,16;
Lk 11:49
f Mt 10:17
g Mt 10:23

23:35
h Ge 4:8;
Heb 11:4
i Zec 1:1
j 2Ch 24:21

23:36
k Mt 10:23;
24:34

23:37
l 2Ch 24:21;
Mt 5:12

23:38
m 1Ki 9:7,8;
Jer 22:5

23:39
n Ps 118:26;
Mt 21:9

24:2
o Lk 19:44

24:3
p Mt 21:1

24:5
q ver 11,23,24;
1Jn 2:18

24:7
r Isa 19:2
s Ac 11:28

24:9
t Mt 10:17
u Jn 16:2

24:11
v Mt 7:15

righteous. [30]And you say, 'If we had lived in the days of our forefathers, we would not have taken part with them in shedding the blood of the prophets.' [31]So you testify against yourselves that you are the descendants of those who murdered the prophets.[a] [32]Fill up, then, the measure[b] of the sin of your forefathers!

[33]"You snakes! You brood of vipers![c] How will you escape being condemned to hell?[d] [34]Therefore I am sending you prophets and wise men and teachers. Some of them you will kill and crucify;[e] others you will flog in your synagogues[f] and pursue from town to town.[g] [35]And so upon you will come all the righteous blood that has been shed on earth, from the blood of righteous Abel[h] to the blood of Zechariah son of Berekiah,[i] whom you murdered between the temple and the altar.[j] [36]I tell you the truth, all this will come upon this generation.[k]

[37]"O Jerusalem, Jerusalem, you who kill the prophets and stone those sent to you,[l] how often I have longed to gather your children together, as a hen gathers her chicks under her wings, but you were not willing. [38]Look, your house is left to you desolate.[m] [39]For I tell you, you will not see me again until you say, 'Blessed is he who comes in the name of the Lord.'[a]"[n]

Chapter 24 Theme

24 Jesus left the temple and was walking away when his disciples came up to him to call his attention to its buildings. [2]"Do you see all these things?" he asked. "I tell you the truth, not one stone here will be left on another;[o] every one will be thrown down."

[3]As Jesus was sitting on the Mount of Olives,[p] the disciples came to him privately. "Tell us," they said, "when will this happen, and what will be the sign of your coming and of the end of the age?"

[4]Jesus answered: "Watch out that no one deceives you. [5]For many will come in my name, claiming, 'I am the Christ,'[b] and will deceive many.[q] [6]You will hear of wars and rumors of wars, but see to it that you are not alarmed. Such things must happen, but the end is still to come. [7]Nation will rise against nation, and kingdom against kingdom.[r] There will be famines[s] and earthquakes in various places. [8]All these are the beginning of birth pains.

[9]"Then you will be handed over to be persecuted[t] and put to death,[u] and you will be hated by all nations because of me. [10]At that time many will turn away from the faith and will betray and hate each other, [11]and many false prophets[v] will appear and deceive many people. [12]Because of the increase of wickedness,

INSIGHT

See the illustration of the temple mount on IISB-40.

a 39 Psalm 118:26   b 5 Or *Messiah*; also in verse 23

the love of most will grow cold, ¹³but he who stands firm to the end will be saved.ᵃ ¹⁴And this gospel of the kingdomᵇ will be preached in the whole worldᶜ as a testimony to all nations, and then the end will come.

¹⁵"So when you see standing in the holy placeᵈ 'the abomination that causes desolation,'ᵃᵉ spoken of through the prophet Daniel—let the reader understand— ¹⁶then let those who are in Judea flee to the mountains. ¹⁷Let no one on the roof of his houseᶠ go down to take anything out of the house. ¹⁸Let no one in the field go back to get his cloak. ¹⁹How dreadful it will be in those days for pregnant women and nursing mothers!ᵍ ²⁰Pray that your flight will not take place in winter or on the Sabbath. ²¹For then there will be great distress, unequaled from the beginning of the world until now—and never to be equaled again.ʰ ²²If those days had not been cut short, no one would survive, but for the sake of the electⁱ those days will be shortened. ²³At that time if anyone says to you, 'Look, here is the Christ!' or, 'There he is!' do not believe it.ʲ ²⁴For false Christs and false prophets will appear and perform great signs and miraclesᵏ to deceive even the elect—if that were possible. ²⁵See, I have told you ahead of time.

²⁶"So if anyone tells you, 'There he is, out in the desert,' do not go out; or, 'Here he is, in the inner rooms,' do not believe it. ²⁷For as lightningˡ that comes from the east is visible even in the west, so will be the coming of the Son of Man.ᵐ ²⁸Wherever there is a carcass, there the vultures will gather.ⁿ

²⁹"Immediately after the distress of those days

"'the sun will be darkened,
  and the moon will not give its light;
the stars will fall from the sky,
  and the heavenly bodies will be shaken.'ᵇᵒ

³⁰"At that time the sign of the Son of Man will appear in the sky, and all the nations of the earth will mourn. They will see the Son of Man coming on the clouds of the sky,ᵖ with power and great glory. ³¹And he will send his angelsᵠ with a loud trumpet call,ʳ and they will gather his elect from the four winds, from one end of the heavens to the other.

³²"Now learn this lesson from the fig tree: As soon as its twigs get tender and its leaves come out, you know that summer is near. ³³Even so, when you see all these things, you know that itᶜ is near, right at the door.ˢ ³⁴I tell you the truth, this generationᵈ will certainly not pass away until all these things have happened.ᵗ ³⁵Heaven and earth will pass away, but my words will never pass away.ᵘ

ᵃ15 Daniel 9:27; 11:31; 12:11 ᵇ29 Isaiah 13:10; 34:4 ᶜ33 Or he ᵈ34 Or race

24:13 ᵃMt 10:22
24:14 ᵇMt 4:23; ᶜRo 10:18; Col 1:6,23; Lk 2:1; 4:5; Ac 11:28; 17:6; Rev 3:10; 16:14
24:15 ᵈAc 6:13; ᵉDa 9:27; 11:31; 12:11
24:17 ᶠ1Sa 9:25; Mt 10:27; Lk 12:3; Ac 10:9
24:19 ᵍLk 23:29
24:21 ʰDa 12:1; Joel 2:2
24:22 ⁱver 24,31
24:23 ʲLk 17:23; 21:8
24:24 ᵏ2Th 2:9-11; Rev 13:13
24:27 ˡLk 17:24; ᵐMt 8:20
24:28 ⁿLk 17:37
24:29 ᵒIsa 13:10; 34:4; Eze 32:7; Joel 2:10,31; Zep 1:15; Rev 6:12,13; 8:12
24:30 ᵖDa 7:13; Rev 1:7
24:31 ᵠMt 13:41; ʳIsa 27:13; Zec 9:14; 1Co 15:52; 1Th 4:16; Rev 8:2; 10:7; 11:15
24:33 ˢJas 5:9
24:34 ᵗMt 16:28; 23:36
24:35 ᵘMt 5:18

24:36
a Ac 1:7

24:37
b Ge 6:5; 7:6-23

24:38
c Mt 22:30

24:40
d Lk 17:34

24:41
e Lk 17:35

24:42
f Mt 25:13;
Lk 12:40

24:43
g Lk 12:39

24:44
h 1Th 5:6

24:45
i Mt 25:21,23

24:46
j Rev 16:15

24:47
k Mt 25:21,23

24:49
l Lk 21:34

24:51
m Mt 8:12

25:1
n Mt 13:24
o Lk 12:35-38;
Ac 20:8;
Rev 4:5
p Rev 19:7;
21:2

25:2
q Mt 24:45

25:5
r 1Th 5:6

25:8
s Lk 12:35

36"No one knows about that day or hour, not even the angels in heaven, nor the Son,*a* but only the Father.*a* **37**As it was in the days of Noah,*b* so it will be at the coming of the Son of Man. **38**For in the days before the flood, people were eating and drinking, marrying and giving in marriage,*c* up to the day Noah entered the ark; **39**and they knew nothing about what would happen until the flood came and took them all away. That is how it will be at the coming of the Son of Man. **40**Two men will be in the field; one will be taken and the other left.*d* **41**Two women will be grinding with a hand mill; one will be taken and the other left.*e*

42"Therefore keep watch, because you do not know on what day your Lord will come.*f* **43**But understand this: If the owner of the house had known at what time of night the thief was coming,*g* he would have kept watch and would not have let his house be broken into. **44**So you also must be ready,*h* because the Son of Man will come at an hour when you do not expect him.

45"Who then is the faithful and wise servant,*i* whom the master has put in charge of the servants in his household to give them their food at the proper time? **46**It will be good for that servant whose master finds him doing so when he returns.*j* **47**I tell you the truth, he will put him in charge of all his possessions.*k* **48**But suppose that servant is wicked and says to himself, 'My master is staying away a long time,' **49**and he then begins to beat his fellow servants and to eat and drink with drunkards.*l* **50**The master of that servant will come on a day when he does not expect him and at an hour he is not aware of. **51**He will cut him to pieces and assign him a place with the hypocrites, where there will be weeping and gnashing of teeth.*m*

Chapter 25 Theme _____

25 "At that time the kingdom of heaven will be like*n* ten virgins who took their lamps*o* and went out to meet the bridegroom.*p* **2**Five of them were foolish and five were wise.*q* **3**The foolish ones took their lamps but did not take any oil with them. **4**The wise, however, took oil in jars along with their lamps. **5**The bridegroom was a long time in coming, and they all became drowsy and fell asleep.*r*

6"At midnight the cry rang out: 'Here's the bridegroom! Come out to meet him!'

7"Then all the virgins woke up and trimmed their lamps. **8**The foolish ones said to the wise, 'Give us some of your oil; our lamps are going out.'*s*

9"'No,' they replied, 'there may not be enough for both us and you. Instead, go to those who sell oil and buy some for yourselves.'

a 36 Some manuscripts do not have *nor the Son*.

¹⁰"But while they were on their way to buy the oil, the bridegroom arrived. The virgins who were ready went in with him to the wedding banquet.ᵃ And the door was shut.

¹¹"Later the others also came. 'Sir! Sir!' they said. 'Open the door for us!'

¹²"But he replied, 'I tell you the truth, I don't know you.'

¹³"Therefore keep watch, because you do not know the day or the hour.ᵇ

¹⁴"Again, it will be like a man going on a journey,ᶜ who called his servants and entrusted his property to them. ¹⁵To one he gave five talentsᵃ of money, to another two talents, and to another one talent, each according to his ability.ᵈ Then he went on his journey. ¹⁶The man who had received the five talents went at once and put his money to work and gained five more. ¹⁷So also, the one with the two talents gained two more. ¹⁸But the man who had received the one talent went off, dug a hole in the ground and hid his master's money.

¹⁹"After a long time the master of those servants returned and settled accounts with them.ᵉ ²⁰The man who had received the five talents brought the other five. 'Master,' he said, 'you entrusted me with five talents. See, I have gained five more.'

²¹"His master replied, 'Well done, good and faithful servant! You have been faithful with a few things; I will put you in charge of many things.ᶠ Come and share your master's happiness!'

²²"The man with the two talents also came. 'Master,' he said, 'you entrusted me with two talents; see, I have gained two more.'

²³"His master replied, 'Well done, good and faithful servant! You have been faithful with a few things; I will put you in charge of many things.ᵍ Come and share your master's happiness!'

²⁴"Then the man who had received the one talent came. 'Master,' he said, 'I knew that you are a hard man, harvesting where you have not sown and gathering where you have not scattered seed. ²⁵So I was afraid and went out and hid your talent in the ground. See, here is what belongs to you.'

²⁶"His master replied, 'You wicked, lazy servant! So you knew that I harvest where I have not sown and gather where I have not scattered seed? ²⁷Well then, you should have put my money on deposit with the bankers, so that when I returned I would have received it back with interest.

²⁸"'Take the talent from him and give it to the one who has the ten talents. ²⁹For everyone who has will be given more, and he will have an abundance. Whoever does not have, even what he has will be taken from him.ʰ ³⁰And throw that worthless servant outside, into the darkness, where there will be weeping and gnashing of teeth.'ⁱ

ᵃ15 A talent was worth more than a thousand dollars.

25:10
ᵃRev 19:9

25:13
ᵇMt 24:42,44;
Mk 13:35;
Lk 12:40

25:14
ᶜMt 21:33;
Lk 19:12

25:15
ᵈMt 18:24,25

25:19
ᵉMt 18:23

25:21
ᶠver 23;
Mt 24:45,47;
Lk 16:10

25:23
ᵍver 21

25:29
ʰMt 13:12;
Mk 4:25;
Lk 8:18; 19:26

25:30
ⁱMt 8:12

[31]"When the Son of Man comes[a] in his glory, and all the angels with him, he will sit on his throne[b] in heavenly glory. [32]All the nations will be gathered before him, and he will separate[c] the people one from another as a shepherd separates the sheep from the goats.[d] [33]He will put the sheep on his right and the goats on his left.

[34]"Then the King will say to those on his right, 'Come, you who are blessed by my Father; take your inheritance, the kingdom[e] prepared for you since the creation of the world.[f] [35]For I was hungry and you gave me something to eat, I was thirsty and you gave me something to drink, I was a stranger and you invited me in,[g] [36]I needed clothes and you clothed me,[h] I was sick and you looked after me,[i] I was in prison and you came to visit me.'[j]

[37]"Then the righteous will answer him, 'Lord, when did we see you hungry and feed you, or thirsty and give you something to drink? [38]When did we see you a stranger and invite you in, or needing clothes and clothe you? [39]When did we see you sick or in prison and go to visit you?'

[40]"The King will reply, 'I tell you the truth, whatever you did for one of the least of these brothers of mine, you did for me.'[k]

[41]"Then he will say to those on his left, 'Depart from me,[l] you who are cursed, into the eternal fire[m] prepared for the devil and his angels.[n] [42]For I was hungry and you gave me nothing to eat, I was thirsty and you gave me nothing to drink, [43]I was a stranger and you did not invite me in, I needed clothes and you did not clothe me, I was sick and in prison and you did not look after me.'

[44]"They also will answer, 'Lord, when did we see you hungry or thirsty or a stranger or needing clothes or sick or in prison, and did not help you?'

[45]"He will reply, 'I tell you the truth, whatever you did not do for one of the least of these, you did not do for me.'[o]

[46]"Then they will go away to eternal punishment, but the righteous to eternal life.[p]"[q]

Chapter 26 Theme

26 When Jesus had finished saying all these things,[r] he said to his disciples, [2]"As you know, the Passover[s] is two days away—and the Son of Man will be handed over to be crucified."

[3]Then the chief priests and the elders of the people assembled[t] in the palace of the high priest, whose name was Caiaphas,[u] [4]and they plotted to arrest Jesus in some sly way and kill him.[v] [5]"But not during the Feast," they said, "or there may be a riot[w] among the people."

[6]While Jesus was in Bethany[x] in the home of a man known as Simon the Leper, [7]a woman came to him with an alabaster jar of

INSIGHT

See the chart **The Feasts of Israel** located on pages 210, 211.

very expensive perfume, which she poured on his head as he was reclining at the table.

⁸When the disciples saw this, they were indignant. "Why this waste?" they asked. ⁹"This perfume could have been sold at a high price and the money given to the poor."

¹⁰Aware of this, Jesus said to them, "Why are you bothering this woman? She has done a beautiful thing to me. ¹¹The poor you will always have with you,ᵃ but you will not always have me. ¹²When she poured this perfume on my body, she did it to prepare me for burial.ᵇ ¹³I tell you the truth, wherever this gospel is preached throughout the world, what she has done will also be told, in memory of her."

¹⁴Then one of the Twelve—the one called Judas Iscariotᶜ—went to the chief priests ¹⁵and asked, "What are you willing to give me if I hand him over to you?" So they counted out for him thirty silver coins.ᵈ ¹⁶From then on Judas watched for an opportunity to hand him over.

¹⁷On the first day of the Feast of Unleavened Bread,ᵉ the disciples came to Jesus and asked, "Where do you want us to make preparations for you to eat the Passover?"

¹⁸He replied, "Go into the city to a certain man and tell him, 'The Teacher says: My appointed timeᶠ is near. I am going to celebrate the Passover with my disciples at your house.'" ¹⁹So the disciples did as Jesus had directed them and prepared the Passover.

²⁰When evening came, Jesus was reclining at the table with the Twelve. ²¹And while they were eating, he said, "I tell you the truth, one of you will betray me."ᵍ

²²They were very sad and began to say to him one after the other, "Surely not I, Lord?"

²³Jesus replied, "The one who has dipped his hand into the bowl with me will betray me.ʰ ²⁴The Son of Man will go just as it is written about him.ⁱ But woe to that man who betrays the Son of Man! It would be better for him if he had not been born."

²⁵Then Judas, the one who would betray him, said, "Surely not I, Rabbi?"ʲ

Jesus answered, "Yes, it is you."ᵃ

²⁶While they were eating, Jesus took bread, gave thanks and broke it,ᵏ and gave it to his disciples, saying, "Take and eat; this is my body."

²⁷Then he took the cup, gave thanks and offered it to them, saying, "Drink from it, all of you. ²⁸This is my blood of theᵇ covenant,ˡ which is poured out for many for the forgiveness of sins.ᵐ ²⁹I tell you, I will not drink of this fruit of the vine from now on until that day when I drink it anew with youⁿ in my Father's kingdom."

ᵃ 25 Or "You yourself have said it"   ᵇ 28 Some manuscripts *the new*

26:11
ᵃDt 15:11

26:12
ᵇJn 19:40

26:14
ᶜver 25,47;
Mt 10:4

26:15
ᵈEx 21:32;
Zec 11:12

26:17
ᵉEx 12:18-20

26:18
ᶠJn 7:6,8,30;
12:23; 13:1; 17:1

26:21
ᵍLk 22:21-23;
Jn 13:21

26:23
ʰPs 41:9;
Jn 13:18

26:24
ⁱIsa 53; Da 9:26;
Mk 9:12;
Lk 24:25-27,46;
Ac 17:2,3;
26:22,23

26:25
ʲMt 23:7

26:26
ᵏMt 14:19;
1Co 10:16

26:28
ˡEx 24:6-8;
Heb 9:20
ᵐMt 20:28;
Mk 1:4

26:29
ⁿAc 10:41

26:30
a Mt 21:1;
Mk 14:26

26:31
b Mt 11:6
c Zec 13:7;
Jn 16:32

26:32
d Mt 28:7,10,16

26:34
e ver 75;
Jn 13:38

26:35
f Jn 13:37

26:37
g Mt 4:21

26:38
h Jn 12:27
i ver 40,41

26:39
j Mt 20:22
k ver 42;
Ps 40:6-8;
Isa 50:5;
Jn 5:30; 6:38

26:40
l ver 38

26:41
m Mt 6:13

26:45
n ver 18

26:49
o ver 25

26:50
p Mt 20:13;
22:12

³⁰When they had sung a hymn, they went out to the Mount of Olives.*a*

³¹Then Jesus told them, "This very night you will all fall away on account of me,*b* for it is written:

"'I will strike the shepherd,
  and the sheep of the flock will be scattered.'*ac*

³²But after I have risen, I will go ahead of you into Galilee."*d*

³³Peter replied, "Even if all fall away on account of you, I never will."

³⁴"I tell you the truth," Jesus answered, "this very night, before the rooster crows, you will disown me three times."*e*

³⁵But Peter declared, "Even if I have to die with you,*f* I will never disown you." And all the other disciples said the same.

³⁶Then Jesus went with his disciples to a place called Gethsemane, and he said to them, "Sit here while I go over there and pray." ³⁷He took Peter and the two sons of Zebedee*g* along with him, and he began to be sorrowful and troubled. ³⁸Then he said to them, "My soul is overwhelmed with sorrow*h* to the point of death. Stay here and keep watch with me."*i*

³⁹Going a little farther, he fell with his face to the ground and prayed, "My Father, if it is possible, may this cup*j* be taken from me. Yet not as I will, but as you will."*k*

⁴⁰Then he returned to his disciples and found them sleeping. "Could you men not keep watch with me*l* for one hour?" he asked Peter. ⁴¹"Watch and pray so that you will not fall into temptation.*m* The spirit is willing, but the body is weak."

⁴²He went away a second time and prayed, "My Father, if it is not possible for this cup to be taken away unless I drink it, may your will be done."

⁴³When he came back, he again found them sleeping, because their eyes were heavy. ⁴⁴So he left them and went away once more and prayed the third time, saying the same thing.

⁴⁵Then he returned to the disciples and said to them, "Are you still sleeping and resting? Look, the hour*n* is near, and the Son of Man is betrayed into the hands of sinners. ⁴⁶Rise, let us go! Here comes my betrayer!"

⁴⁷While he was still speaking, Judas, one of the Twelve, arrived. With him was a large crowd armed with swords and clubs, sent from the chief priests and the elders of the people. ⁴⁸Now the betrayer had arranged a signal with them: "The one I kiss is the man; arrest him." ⁴⁹Going at once to Jesus, Judas said, "Greetings, Rabbi!"*o* and kissed him.

⁵⁰Jesus replied, "Friend,*p* do what you came for."*b*

Then the men stepped forward, seized Jesus and arrested him.

a 31 Zech. 13:7   *b 50* Or *"Friend, why have you come?"*

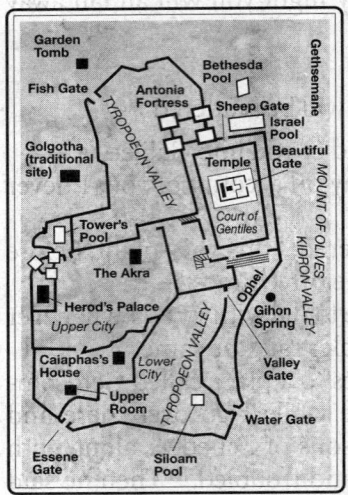

Labels on map: Garden Tomb; Gethsemane; Bethesda Pool; Fish Gate; Antonia Fortress; Sheep Gate; Israel Pool; Beautiful Gate; Golgotha (traditional site); Temple; MOUNT OF OLIVES; TYROPOEON VALLEY; Court of Gentiles; KIDRON VALLEY; Tower's Pool; The Akra; Ophel; Herod's Palace; Gihon Spring; Upper City; Caiaphas's House; Lower City; Valley Gate; Upper Room; Water Gate; Essene Gate; Siloam Pool

51With that, one of Jesus' companions reached for his sword,[a] drew it out and struck the servant of the high priest, cutting off his ear.[b]

52"Put your sword back in its place," Jesus said to him, "for all who draw the sword will die by the sword.[c] 53Do you think I cannot call on my Father, and he will at once put at my disposal more than twelve legions of angels?[d] 54But how then would the Scriptures be fulfilled[e] that say it must happen in this way?"

55At that time Jesus said to the crowd, "Am I leading a rebellion, that you have come out with swords and clubs to capture me? Every day I sat in the temple courts teaching,[f] and you did not arrest me. 56But this has all taken place that the writings of the prophets might be fulfilled."[g] Then all the disciples deserted him and fled.

57Those who had arrested Jesus took him to Caiaphas,[h] the high priest, where the teachers of the law and the elders had assembled. 58But Peter followed him at a distance, right up to the courtyard of the high priest.[i] He entered and sat down with the guards[j] to see the outcome.

59The chief priests and the whole Sanhedrin[k] were looking for false evidence against Jesus so that they could put him to death. 60But they did not find any, though many false witnesses[l] came forward.

Finally two[m] came forward 61and declared, "This fellow said, 'I am able to destroy the temple of God and rebuild it in three days.'"[n]

62Then the high priest stood up and said to Jesus, "Are you not going to answer? What is this testimony that these men are bringing against you?" 63But Jesus remained silent.[o]

The high priest said to him, "I charge you under oath[p] by the living God:[q] Tell us if you are the Christ,[a] the Son of God."

64"Yes, it is as you say," Jesus replied. "But I say to all of you: In the future you will see the Son of Man sitting at the right hand of the Mighty One[r] and coming on the clouds of heaven."[s]

65Then the high priest tore his clothes[t] and said, "He has spoken blasphemy! Why do we need any more witnesses? Look, now you have heard the blasphemy. 66What do you think?"

"He is worthy of death,"[u] they answered.

a 63 Or *Messiah*; also in verse 68

26:51
[a] Lk 22:36,38
[b] Jn 18:10

26:52
[c] Ge 9:6;
Rev 13:10

26:53
[d] 2Ki 6:17;
Da 7:10;
Mt 4:11

26:54
[e] ver 24

26:55
[f] Mk 12:35;
Lk 21:37;
Jn 7:14,28;
18:20

26:56
[g] ver 24

26:57
[h] ver 3

26:58
[i] Jn 18:15
[j] Jn 7:32,45,46

26:59
[k] Mt 5:22

26:60
[l] Ps 27:12; 35:11;
Ac 6:13
[m] Dt 19:15

26:61
[n] Jn 2:19

26:63
[o] Mt 27:12,14
[p] Lev 5:1
[q] Mt 16:16

26:64
[r] Ps 110:1
[s] Da 7:13;
Rev 1:7

26:65
[t] Mk 14:63

26:66
[u] Lev 24:16;
Jn 19:7

26:67
a Mt 16:21;
27:30

26:68
b Lk 22:63-65

26:75
c ver 34;
Jn 13:38

27:1
d Mt 12:14;
Mk 15:1;
Lk 22:66

27:2
e Mt 20:19
f Mk 15:1;
Lk 13:1;
Ac 3:13;
1 Ti 6:13

27:3
g Mt 10:4
h Mt 26:14,15

27:4
i ver 24

27:5
j Lk 1:9,21
k Ac 1:18

27:8
l Ac 1:19

27:9
m Mt 1:22

27:10
n Zec 11:12,13;
Jer 32:6-9

27:11
o Mt 2:2

27:12
p Mt 26:63;
Mk 14:61;
Jn 19:9

[67] Then they spit in his face and struck him with their fists.[a] Others slapped him [68] and said, "Prophesy to us, Christ. Who hit you?"[b]

[69] Now Peter was sitting out in the courtyard, and a servant girl came to him. "You also were with Jesus of Galilee," she said.

[70] But he denied it before them all. "I don't know what you're talking about," he said.

[71] Then he went out to the gateway, where another girl saw him and said to the people there, "This fellow was with Jesus of Nazareth."

[72] He denied it again, with an oath: "I don't know the man!"

[73] After a little while, those standing there went up to Peter and said, "Surely you are one of them, for your accent gives you away."

[74] Then he began to call down curses on himself and he swore to them, "I don't know the man!"

Immediately a rooster crowed. [75] Then Peter remembered the word Jesus had spoken: "Before the rooster crows, you will disown me three times."[c] And he went outside and wept bitterly.

Chapter 27 Theme

27 Early in the morning, all the chief priests and the elders of the people came to the decision to put Jesus to death.[d] [2] They bound him, led him away and handed him over[e] to Pilate, the governor.[f]

[3] When Judas, who had betrayed him,[g] saw that Jesus was condemned, he was seized with remorse and returned the thirty silver coins[h] to the chief priests and the elders. [4] "I have sinned," he said, "for I have betrayed innocent blood."

"What is that to us?" they replied. "That's your responsibility."[i]

[5] So Judas threw the money into the temple[j] and left. Then he went away and hanged himself.[k]

[6] The chief priests picked up the coins and said, "It is against the law to put this into the treasury, since it is blood money." [7] So they decided to use the money to buy the potter's field as a burial place for foreigners. [8] That is why it has been called the Field of Blood[l] to this day. [9] Then what was spoken by Jeremiah the prophet was fulfilled:[m] "They took the thirty silver coins, the price set on him by the people of Israel, [10] and they used them to buy the potter's field, as the Lord commanded me."[a][n]

[11] Meanwhile Jesus stood before the governor, and the governor asked him, "Are you the king of the Jews?"[o]

"Yes, it is as you say," Jesus replied.

[12] When he was accused by the chief priests and the elders, he gave no answer.[p] [13] Then Pilate asked him, "Don't you hear the

a 10 See Zech. 11:12, 13; Jer. 19:1-13; 32:6-9.

testimony they are bringing against you?"*a* *14*But Jesus made no reply,*b* not even to a single charge—to the great amazement of the governor.

*15*Now it was the governor's custom at the Feast to release a prisoner*c* chosen by the crowd. *16*At that time they had a notorious prisoner, called Barabbas. *17*So when the crowd had gathered, Pilate asked them, "Which one do you want me to release to you: Barabbas, or Jesus who is called Christ?"*d* *18*For he knew it was out of envy that they had handed Jesus over to him.

*19*While Pilate was sitting on the judge's seat,*e* his wife sent him this message: "Don't have anything to do with that innocent*f* man, for I have suffered a great deal today in a dream*g* because of him."

*20*But the chief priests and the elders persuaded the crowd to ask for Barabbas and to have Jesus executed.*h*

21"Which of the two do you want me to release to you?" asked the governor.

"Barabbas," they answered.

22"What shall I do, then, with Jesus who is called Christ?"*i* Pilate asked.

They all answered, "Crucify him!"

23"Why? What crime has he committed?" asked Pilate.

But they shouted all the louder, "Crucify him!"

*24*When Pilate saw that he was getting nowhere, but that instead an uproar*j* was starting, he took water and washed his hands*k* in front of the crowd. "I am innocent of this man's blood,"*l* he said. "It is your responsibility!"*m*

*25*All the people answered, "Let his blood be on us and on our children!"*n*

*26*Then he released Barabbas to them. But he had Jesus flogged,*o* and handed him over to be crucified.

*27*Then the governor's soldiers took Jesus into the Praetorium*p* and gathered the whole company of soldiers around him. *28*They stripped him and put a scarlet robe on him,*q* *29*and then twisted together a crown of thorns and set it on his head. They put a staff in his right hand and knelt in front of him and mocked him. "Hail, king of the Jews!" they said.*r* *30*They spit on him, and took the staff and struck him on the head again and again.*s* *31*After they had mocked him, they took off the robe and put his own clothes on him. Then they led him away to crucify him.*t*

*32*As they were going out,*u* they met a man from Cyrene,*v* named Simon, and they forced him to carry the cross.*w* *33*They came to a place called Golgotha (which means The Place of the Skull).*x* *34*There they offered Jesus wine to drink, mixed with gall;*y* but after tasting it, he refused to drink it. *35*When they had crucified

INSIGHT

The palace of the Roman governor (the *Praetorium*) was either a building next to Herod's palace or the Antonia Fortress beside the temple mount complex. See the map on page 1716 and the illustration of the temple mount on page IISB-40.

27:13 *a* Mt 26:62
27:14 *b* Mk 14:61
27:15 *c* Jn 18:39
27:17 *d* ver 22; Mt 1:16
27:19 *e* Jn 19:13 *f* ver 24 *g* Ge 20:6; Nu 12:6; 1Ki 3:5; Job 33:14-16; Mt 1:20; 2:12,13,19,22
27:20 *h* Ac 3:14
27:22 *i* Mt 1:16
27:24 *j* Mt 26:5 *k* Ps 26:6 *l* Dt 21:6-8 *m* ver 4
27:25 *n* Jos 2:19; Ac 5:28
27:26 *o* Isa 53:5; Jn 19:1
27:27 *p* Jn 18:28,33; 19:9
27:28 *q* Jn 19:2
27:29 *r* Isa 53:3; Jn 19:2,3
27:30 *s* Mt 16:21; 26:67
27:31 *t* Isa 53:7
27:32 *u* Heb 13:12 *v* Ac 2:10; 6:9; 11:20; 13:1 *w* Mk 15:21; Lk 23:26
27:33 *x* Jn 19:17
27:34 *y* ver 48; Ps 69:21

27:35
a Ps 22:18

27:36
b ver 54

27:38
c Isa 53:12

27:39
d Ps 22:7; 109:25;
La 2:15

27:40
e Mt 26:61;
Jn 2:19
f ver 42
g Mt 4:3,6

27:42
h Jn 1:49; 12:13
i Jn 3:15

27:43
j Ps 22:8

27:45
k Am 8:9

27:46
l Ps 22:1

27:48
m ver 34;
Ps 69:21

27:50
n Jn 19:30

27:51
o Ex 26:31-33;
Heb 9:3,8
p ver 54

27:53
q Mt 4:5

27:54
r ver 36
s Mt 4:3; 17:5

27:55
t Lk 8:2,3

27:56
u Mk 15:47;
Lk 24:10;
Jn 19:25

him, they divided up his clothes by casting lots.*a* *a* 36And sitting down, they kept watch *b* over him there. 37Above his head they placed the written charge against him: THIS IS JESUS, THE KING OF THE JEWS. 38Two robbers were crucified with him,*c* one on his right and one on his left. 39Those who passed by hurled insults at him, shaking their heads*d* 40and saying, "You who are going to destroy the temple and build it in three days,*e* save yourself!*f* Come down from the cross, if you are the Son of God!"*g*

41In the same way the chief priests, the teachers of the law and the elders mocked him. 42"He saved others," they said, "but he can't save himself! He's the King of Israel!*h* Let him come down now from the cross, and we will believe*i* in him. 43He trusts in God. Let God rescue him*j* now if he wants him, for he said, 'I am the Son of God.'" 44In the same way the robbers who were crucified with him also heaped insults on him.

45From the sixth hour until the ninth hour darkness*k* came over all the land. 46About the ninth hour Jesus cried out in a loud voice, *"Eloi, Eloi,*b* lama sabachthani?"*—which means, "My God, my God, why have you forsaken me?"*c* *l*

47When some of those standing there heard this, they said, "He's calling Elijah."

48Immediately one of them ran and got a sponge. He filled it with wine vinegar,*m* put it on a stick, and offered it to Jesus to drink. 49The rest said, "Now leave him alone. Let's see if Elijah comes to save him."

50And when Jesus had cried out again in a loud voice, he gave up his spirit.*n*

51At that moment the curtain of the temple*o* was torn in two from top to bottom. The earth shook and the rocks split.*p* 52The tombs broke open and the bodies of many holy people who had died were raised to life. 53They came out of the tombs, and after Jesus' resurrection they went into the holy city*q* and appeared to many people.

54When the centurion and those with him who were guarding*r* Jesus saw the earthquake and all that had happened, they were terrified, and exclaimed, "Surely he was the Son*d* of God!"*s*

55Many women were there, watching from a distance. They had followed Jesus from Galilee to care for his needs.*t* 56Among them were Mary Magdalene, Mary the mother of James and Joses, and the mother of Zebedee's sons.*u*

57As evening approached, there came a rich man from Arimathea, named Joseph, who had himself become a disciple of Jesus. 58Going to Pilate, he asked for Jesus' body, and Pilate ordered that

a 35 A few late manuscripts *lots that the word spoken by the prophet might be fulfilled: "They divided my garments among themselves and cast lots for my clothing"* (Psalm 22:18)   *b 46* Some manuscripts *Eli, Eli*   *c 46* Psalm 22:1   *d 54* Or *a son* it be given to him. ⁵⁹Joseph took the body, wrapped it in a clean linen cloth, ⁶⁰and placed it in his own new tomb*ᵃ* that he had cut out of the rock. He rolled a big stone in front of the entrance to the tomb and went away. ⁶¹Mary Magdalene and the other Mary were sitting there opposite the tomb.

⁶²The next day, the one after Preparation Day, the chief priests and the Pharisees went to Pilate. ⁶³"Sir," they said, "we remember that while he was still alive that deceiver said, 'After three days I will rise again.'ᵇ ⁶⁴So give the order for the tomb to be made secure until the third day. Otherwise, his disciples may come and steal the body and tell the people that he has been raised from the dead. This last deception will be worse than the first."

⁶⁵"Take a guard,"ᶜ Pilate answered. "Go, make the tomb as secure as you know how." ⁶⁶So they went and made the tomb secure by putting a sealᵈ on the stoneᵉ and posting the guard.ᶠ

Chapter 28 Theme

28 After the Sabbath, at dawn on the first day of the week, Mary Magdalene and the other Maryᵍ went to look at the tomb.

²There was a violent earthquake,ʰ for an angelⁱ of the Lord came down from heaven and, going to the tomb, rolled back the stone and sat on it. ³His appearance was like lightning, and his clothes were white as snow.ʲ ⁴The guards were so afraid of him that they shook and became like dead men.

⁵The angel said to the women, "Do not be afraid,ᵏ for I know that you are looking for Jesus, who was crucified. ⁶He is not here; he has risen, just as he said.ˡ Come and see the place where he lay. ⁷Then go quickly and tell his disciples: 'He has risen from the dead and is going ahead of you into Galilee.ᵐ There you will see him.' Now I have told you."

⁸So the women hurried away from the tomb, afraid yet filled with joy, and ran to tell his disciples. ⁹Suddenly Jesus met them.ⁿ "Greetings," he said. They came to him, clasped his feet and worshiped him. ¹⁰Then Jesus said to them, "Do not be afraid. Go and tell my brothersᵒ to go to Galilee; there they will see me."

¹¹While the women were on their way, some of the guardsᵖ went into the city and reported to the chief priests everything that had happened. ¹²When the chief priests had met with the elders and devised a plan, they gave the soldiers a large sum of money, ¹³telling them, "You are to say, 'His disciples came during the night and stole him away while we were asleep.' ¹⁴If this report gets to the governor,�q we will satisfy him and keep you out of trouble." ¹⁵So the soldiers took the money and did as they were instructed. And this story has been widely circulated among the Jews to this very day.

27:60
a Mt 27:66;
28:2; Mk 16:4

27:63
b Mt 16:21

27:65
c ver 66;
Mt 28:11

27:66
d Da 6:17
e ver 60;
Mt 28:2
f Mt 28:11

28:1
g Mt 27:56

28:2
h Mt 27:51
i Jn 20:12

28:3
j Da 10:6;
Mk 9:3;
Jn 20:12

28:5
k ver 10;
Mt 14:27

28:6
l Mt 16:21

28:7
m ver 10,16;
Mt 26:32

28:9
n Jn 20:14-18

28:10
o Jn 20:17;
Ro 8:29;
Heb 2:11-13,17

28:11
p Mt 27:65,66

28:14
q Mt 27:2

28:16
a ver 7,10;
Mt 26:32

28:18
b Da 7:13,14;
Lk 10:22;
Jn 3:35; 17:2;
1Co 15:27;
Eph 1:20-22;
Php 2:9,10

28:19
c Mk 16:15,16;
Lk 24:47;
Ac 1:8; 14:21
d Ac 2:38; 8:16;
Ro 6:3,4

¹⁶Then the eleven disciples went to Galilee, to the mountain where Jesus had told them to go.*a* ¹⁷When they saw him, they worshiped him; but some doubted. ¹⁸Then Jesus came to them and said, "All authority in heaven and on earth has been given to me.*b* ¹⁹Therefore go and make disciples of all nations,*c* baptizing them in*a* the name of the Father and of the Son and of the Holy Spirit,*d* ²⁰and teaching*e* them to obey everything I have commanded you. And surely I am with you*f* always, to the very end of the age."*g*

*a*19 Or *into*; see Acts 8:16; 19:5; Romans 6:3; 1Cor. 1:13; 10:2 and Gal. 3:27.

28:20 *e*Ac 2:42 *f*Mt 18:20; Ac 18:10 *g*Mt 13:39

Theme of Matthew:

SEGMENT DIVISIONS

		CHAPTER THEMES
		1
		2
		3
		4
		5
		6
		7
		8
		9
		10
		11
		12
		13
		14
		15
		16
		17
		18
		19
		20
		21
		22
		23
		24
		25
		26
		27
		28

Author:

Date:

Purpose:

Key Words:

king (mark only when referring to Jesus as king) (kingdom, kingdom of heaven, kingdom of God)

fulfill, fulfilled

mark every reference to the devil or demons

covenant

Inside Herod's Temple

SOUTHWESTERN TOWER

NORTHWESTERN TOWER

THE TEMPLE

MOST HOLY PLACE

SANCTUARY

PORTICO

GATE OF KINDLING

CHAMBER OF THE HEARTHSTONE

GATE OF FIRSTLINGS

OFFERING GATE

WATER GATE

PRIESTS' COURT

GATE OF THE FLAME

BASIN

RAMP   ALTAR

SLAUGHTERHOUSE

COURT OF THE ISRAELITES

SOUTHERN WALL

NORTHERN WALL

CHAMBER OF OILS

NICANOR'S GATE

CHAMBER OF LEPERS

GATE

WOMEN'S   COURT

GATE

FOUR LAMPSTANDS FOR THE FEAST OF TABERNACLES

CHAMBER OF NAZIRITES

CHAMBER OF WOOD

THE BEAUTIFUL GATE

SOUTHEASTERN TOWER

NORTHEASTERN TOWER

EASTERN WALL

MARK

*J*esus was clearly born to be king of the Jews, as Matthew points out. However, the gospel was not just for the Jews; it was for the whole world. Before Jesus would reign as King of kings, he would be servant of all by dying for mankind. Mark tells of the works and authority of the one who came not to be served but to serve and to give his life as a ransom for many.

∾ THINGS TO DO

Mark is a fast-paced Gospel which emphasizes the works of Jesus rather than the teachings of Jesus. Although Jesus is referred to as a teacher a number of times, Mark shows Jesus' power and authority through the works he does as he goes about his Father's business.

In reading this Gospel you will notice the repeated use of the words *immediately, at once, without delay, quickly, as soon as, just as,* and *shortly* as Mark takes his reader from one event in the life of Jesus to another. These events and the works of Jesus show the reader Jesus' power and authority as the servant of God and man.

Chapters 1-13

Read through all of the instructions before you begin working on chapters 1-13.

1. Although the emphasis in the Gospel of Mark is on the works of Jesus that show his divine power, Mark opens his Gospel by declaring the deity of Jesus Christ. He also gives an account of the events that took place prior to and in preparation for Jesus' ministry. Read Mark 1:1-13 and list in the margin of the text the following:

    a. The facts that declare the deity of Jesus Christ.

    b. The events that took place in Jesus' life prior to his public ministry.

2. Now read Mark chapter by chapter, and in a distinctive way mark in the text the key words listed on the MARK AT A GLANCE chart on page 1758.

    a. Record these key words on an index card and use it as a bookmark while you study this Gospel.

    b. Also underline in the text each geographical location, whether it is a city, a region, or a place such as the temple or the synagogue. Noting these will help in your overall understanding of these events in Jesus' life.

3. Chapters 1-3 cover events (including healings and miracles) that demonstrate Jesus' authority.

    a. As you look at each event, observe how it demonstrates Jesus' authority, how the people respond, and what Jesus has authority over.

    b. Record your insights in the margin by listing the event, then under that event noting how the people, religious leaders, disciples, and others responded. For example:

Healing on Sabbath

Pharisees counsel to destroy him

    c. After you have recorded these demonstrations and responses, be sure to record the scope of Jesus' authority. For example, next to the illustration above, you might write, "Authority over Sabbath." Watch for Jesus' power over nature, demons, disease, and so on. Ask God to show you how this demonstration of Jesus' power declares his deity. Also, notice how these events portray Jesus as a servant.

d. Throughout these chapters, Jesus faces the accusations and rejection of the Jewish religious leaders of his day. Each time the scribes, Pharisees, or Sadducees accuse Jesus, he reasons with them. Note that conflict in the margin.

4. Also list in the margin the main points of Jesus' teachings, whether the teaching comes as a result of healing, casting out demons, working a miracle, or responding to a question from either the disciples or the multitude. Also note the response of those who hear the teaching.

5. Look at every reference you marked to the kingdom of God and do the following:

   a. Note in the margin when Jesus increases his emphasis on the kingdom of God.

   b. Underline every prediction of Jesus' death and resurrection and note how it coincides with Jesus' emphasis on the kingdom of God.

   c. Observe that in the first part of Mark, Jesus defines the kingdom of God, then at chapter 9 the emphasis shifts to how to enter the kingdom.

   d. Compile the *main* teachings from Mark about the kingdom of God on the chart titled WHAT THE GOSPELS TEACH ABOUT THE KINGDOM OF GOD/THE KINGDOM OF HEAVEN on pages 1864, 1865. It would be good to do this on notebook paper first and then consolidate your insights and transfer them to the chart. Note the chapter and verse beside each insight for future reference.

6. After you finish reading and marking each chapter, record the theme of that chapter on MARK AT A GLANCE. Also record it in the text on the line next to the chapter number.

Chapters 14-16

1. When you read Mark's account of the trial, death, burial, and resurrection of Jesus Christ, record the progression of events on the appropriate charts: THE ARREST, TRIAL, AND CRUCIFIXION OF JESUS CHRIST on page 1862 and THE ACCOUNT OF JESUS' RESURRECTION on page 1863. Once again, do this on notebook paper before transferring the information to the chart and note the chapter and verse beside each insight.

   a. When you record the circumstances surrounding the resurrection of Jesus Christ, also note any postresurrection appearances recorded in Mark. After you do this for all four Gospels you will have comprehensive notes on everything that took place at this time in our Lord's life.

   b. As you do this, remember that because Luke gives the consecutive order of events, it is a plumb line for the other Gospel records.

2. Complete MARK AT A GLANCE. Fill in any segment divisions you have seen from studying the book.

∾ THINGS TO THINK ABOUT

1. People often say that Mark shows the servant aspect of Jesus' ministry. Although the word *servant* is used only seven times, Mark 10:45 says that Jesus "did not come to be served, but to serve, and to give his life as a ransom for many." How like your Lord are you in that respect? Would others regard you as a servant? Or do they see you as having to be "number one"? What is it to be "number one" in God's eyes?

2. Jesus talks about discipleship in this Gospel. According to Jesus, what is required of disciples? Can you consider yourself a true disciple of Jesus Christ? Why? Think about Mark 8:34-36 and 10:28-31.

3. Can you say with Peter, "You are the Christ, the Son of the living God"? And will you listen to Jesus as the Father commands?

Chapter 1 Theme _____

1 The beginning of the gospel about Jesus Christ, the Son of God.ᵃ ᵃ

²It is written in Isaiah the prophet:

"I will send my messenger ahead of you,
    who will prepare your way"ᵇ ᵇ—
³"a voice of one calling in the desert,
'Prepare the way for the Lord,
    make straight paths for him.'"ᶜ ᶜ

⁴And so Johnᵈ came, baptizing in the desert region and preaching a baptism of repentanceᵉ for the forgiveness of sins.ᶠ ⁵The whole Judean countryside and all the people of Jerusalem went out to him. Confessing their sins, they were baptized by him in the Jordan River. ⁶John wore clothing made of camel's hair, with a leather belt around his waist, and he ate locustsᵍ and wild honey. ⁷And this was his message: "After me will come one more powerful than I, the thongs of whose sandals I am not worthy to stoop down and untie.ʰ ⁸I baptize you withᵈ water, but he will baptize you with the Holy Spirit."ⁱ

⁹At that time Jesus came from Nazarethʲ in Galilee and was baptized by John in the Jordan. ¹⁰As Jesus was coming up out of the water, he saw heaven being torn open and the Spirit descending on him like a dove. ᵏ ¹¹And a voice came from heaven: "You are my Son,ˡ whom I love; with you I am well pleased."

¹²At once the Spirit sent him out into the desert, ¹³and he was in the desert forty days, being tempted by Satan.ᵐ He was with the wild animals, and angels attended him.

¹⁴After John was put in prison, Jesus went into Galilee,ⁿ proclaiming the good news of God.ᵒ ¹⁵"The time has come,"ᵖ he said. "The kingdom of God is near. Repent and believe the good news!"�q

¹⁶As Jesus walked beside the Sea of Galilee, he saw Simon and his brother Andrew casting a net into the lake, for they were fishermen. ¹⁷"Come, follow me," Jesus said, "and I will make you fishers of men." ¹⁸At once they left their nets and followed him.

¹⁹When he had gone a little farther, he saw James son of Zebedee and his brother John in a boat, preparing their nets. ²⁰Without delay he called them, and they left their father Zebedee in the boat with the hired men and followed him.

²¹They went to Capernaum, and when the Sabbath came, Jesus went into the synagogue and began to teach.ʳ ²²The people were

1:1
ᵃ Mt 4:3

1:2
ᵇ Mal 3:1;
Mt 11:10;
Lk 7:27

1:3
ᶜ Isa 40:3;
Jn 1:23

1:4
ᵈ Mt 3:1
ᵉ Ac 13:24
ᶠ Lk 1:77

1:6
ᵍ Lev 11:22

1:7
ʰ Ac 13:25

1:8
ⁱ Isa 44:3;
Joel 2:28;
Ac 1:5; 2:4;
11:16; 19:4-6

1:9
ʲ Mt 2:23

1:10
ᵏ Jn 1:32

1:11
ˡ Mt 3:17

1:13
ᵐ Mt 4:10

1:14
ⁿ Mt 4:12
ᵒ Mt 4:23

1:15
ᵖ Gal 4:4;
Eph 1:10
q Ac 20:21

1:21
ʳ Mt 4:23;
Mk 10:1

ᵃ *1* Some manuscripts do not have *the Son of God.*   ᵇ *2* Mal. 3:1   ᶜ *3* Isaiah 40:3   ᵈ *8* Or *in*

1:22
a Mt 7:28,29

1:24
b Mt 8:29
c Mt 2:23;
Lk 24:19;
Ac 24:5
d Lk 1:35;
Jn 6:69;
Ac 3:14

1:25
e ver 34

1:26
f Mk 9:20

1:27
g Mk 10:24,32

1:28
h Mt 9:26

1:29
i ver 21,23

1:31
j Lk 7:14

1:32
k Mt 4:24

1:34
l Mt 4:23
m Mk 3:12;
Ac 16:17,18

1:35
n Lk 3:21

1:38
o Isa 61:1

1:39
p Mt 4:23
q Mt 4:24

1:40
r Mk 10:17

1:44
s Mt 8:4
t Lev 13:49
u Lev 14:1-32

1:45
v Lk 5:15,16
w Mk 2:13;
Lk 5:17;
Jn 6:2

amazed at his teaching, because he taught them as one who had authority, not as the teachers of the law.*a* 23Just then a man in their synagogue who was possessed by an evil*a* spirit cried out, 24"What do you want with us,*b* Jesus of Nazareth?*c* Have you come to destroy us? I know who you are—the Holy One of God!"*d*

25"Be quiet!" said Jesus sternly. "Come out of him!"*e* 26The evil spirit shook the man violently and came out of him with a shriek.*f*

27The people were all so amazed*g* that they asked each other, "What is this? A new teaching—and with authority! He even gives orders to evil spirits and they obey him." 28News about him spread quickly over the whole region*h* of Galilee.

29As soon as they left the synagogue,*i* they went with James and John to the home of Simon and Andrew. 30Simon's mother-in-law was in bed with a fever, and they told Jesus about her. 31So he went to her, took her hand and helped her up.*j* The fever left her and she began to wait on them.

32That evening after sunset the people brought to Jesus all the sick and demon-possessed.*k* 33The whole town gathered at the door, 34and Jesus healed many who had various diseases.*l* He also drove out many demons, but he would not let the demons speak because they knew who he was.*m*

35Very early in the morning, while it was still dark, Jesus got up, left the house and went off to a solitary place, where he prayed.*n* 36Simon and his companions went to look for him, 37and when they found him, they exclaimed: "Everyone is looking for you!"

38Jesus replied, "Let us go somewhere else—to the nearby villages—so I can preach there also. That is why I have come."*o* 39So he traveled throughout Galilee, preaching in their synagogues*p* and driving out demons.*q*

40A man with leprosy*b* came to him and begged him on his knees,*r* "If you are willing, you can make me clean."

41Filled with compassion, Jesus reached out his hand and touched the man. "I am willing," he said. "Be clean!" 42Immediately the leprosy left him and he was cured.

43Jesus sent him away at once with a strong warning: 44"See that you don't tell this to anyone.*s* But go, show yourself to the priest*t* and offer the sacrifices that Moses commanded for your cleansing,*u* as a testimony to them." 45Instead he went out and began to talk freely, spreading the news. As a result, Jesus could no longer enter a town openly but stayed outside in lonely places.*v* Yet the people still came to him from everywhere.*w*

a 23 Greek *unclean*; also in verses 26 and 27   *b 40* The Greek word was used for various diseases affecting the skin—not necessarily leprosy.

Chapter 2 Theme

2 A few days later, when Jesus again entered Capernaum, the people heard that he had come home. [2]So many[a] gathered that there was no room left, not even outside the door, and he preached the word to them. [3]Some men came, bringing to him a paralytic,[b] carried by four of them. [4]Since they could not get him to Jesus because of the crowd, they made an opening in the roof above Jesus and, after digging through it, lowered the mat the paralyzed man was lying on. [5]When Jesus saw their faith, he said to the paralytic, "Son, your sins are forgiven."[c]

[6]Now some teachers of the law were sitting there, thinking to themselves, [7]"Why does this fellow talk like that? He's blaspheming! Who can forgive sins but God alone?"[d]

[8]Immediately Jesus knew in his spirit that this was what they were thinking in their hearts, and he said to them, "Why are you thinking these things? [9]Which is easier: to say to the paralytic, 'Your sins are forgiven,' or to say, 'Get up, take your mat and walk'? [10]But that you may know that the Son of Man[e] has authority on earth to forgive sins. . . ." He said to the paralytic, [11]"I tell you, get up, take your mat and go home." [12]He got up, took his mat and walked out in full view of them all. This amazed everyone and they praised God,[f] saying, "We have never seen anything like this!"[g]

[13]Once again Jesus went out beside the lake. A large crowd came to him,[h] and he began to teach them. [14]As he walked along, he saw Levi son of Alphaeus sitting at the tax collector's booth. "Follow me,"[i] Jesus told him, and Levi got up and followed him.

[15]While Jesus was having dinner at Levi's house, many tax collectors and "sinners" were eating with him and his disciples, for there were many who followed him. [16]When the teachers of the law who were Pharisees[j] saw him eating with the "sinners" and tax collectors, they asked his disciples: "Why does he eat with tax collectors and 'sinners'?"[k]

[17]On hearing this, Jesus said to them, "It is not the healthy who need a doctor, but the sick. I have not come to call the righteous, but sinners."[l]

[18]Now John's disciples and the Pharisees were fasting.[m] Some people came and asked Jesus, "How is it that John's disciples and the disciples of the Pharisees are fasting, but yours are not?"

[19]Jesus answered, "How can the guests of the bridegroom fast while he is with them? They cannot, so long as they have him with them. [20]But the time will come when the bridegroom will be taken from them,[n] and on that day they will fast.

[21]"No one sews a patch of unshrunk cloth on an old garment. If he does, the new piece will pull away from the old, making the

Cross references

2:2
a ver 13;
Mk 1:45

2:3
b Mt 4:24

2:5
c Lk 7:48

2:7
d Isa 43:25

2:10
e Mt 8:20

2:12
f Mt 9:8
g Mt 9:33

2:13
h Mk 1:45;
Lk 5:15;
Jn 6:2

2:14
i Mt 4:19

2:16
j Ac 23:9
k Mt 9:11

2:17
l Lk 19:10;
1Ti 1:15

2:18
m Mt 6:16-18;
Ac 13:2

2:20
n Lk 17:22

2:23
a Dt 23:25

2:24
b Mt 12:2

2:26
c 1Ch 24:6;
2Sa 8:17
d Lev 24:5-9
e 1Sa 21:1-6

2:27
f Ex 23:12;
Dt 5:14
g Col 2:16

2:28
h Mt 8:20

3:1
i Mt 4:23;
Mk 1:21

3:2
j Mt 12:10
k Lk 14:1

3:6
l Mt 22:16;
Mk 12:13
m Mt 12:14

3:7
n Mt 4:25

3:8
o Mt 11:21

3:10
p Mt 4:23
q Mt 9:20

3:11
r Mt 4:3;
Mk 1:23,24

3:12
s Mt 8:4;
Mk 1:24, 25,34;
Ac 16:17,18

3:13
t Mt 5:1

3:14
u Mk 6:30

tear worse. ²²And no one pours new wine into old wineskins. If he does, the wine will burst the skins, and both the wine and the wineskins will be ruined. No, he pours new wine into new wineskins."

²³One Sabbath Jesus was going through the grainfields, and as his disciples walked along, they began to pick some heads of grain.*a* ²⁴The Pharisees said to him, "Look, why are they doing what is unlawful on the Sabbath?"*b*

²⁵He answered, "Have you never read what David did when he and his companions were hungry and in need? ²⁶In the days of Abiathar the high priest,*c* he entered the house of God and ate the consecrated bread, which is lawful only for priests to eat.*d* And he also gave some to his companions."*e*

²⁷Then he said to them, "The Sabbath was made for man,*f* not man for the Sabbath.*g* ²⁸So the Son of Man*h* is Lord even of the Sabbath."

Chapter 3 Theme

3 Another time he went into the synagogue,*i* and a man with a shriveled hand was there. ²Some of them were looking for a reason to accuse Jesus, so they watched him closely*j* to see if he would heal him on the Sabbath.*k* ³Jesus said to the man with the shriveled hand, "Stand up in front of everyone."

⁴Then Jesus asked them, "Which is lawful on the Sabbath: to do good or to do evil, to save life or to kill?" But they remained silent.

⁵He looked around at them in anger and, deeply distressed at their stubborn hearts, said to the man, "Stretch out your hand." He stretched it out, and his hand was completely restored. ⁶Then the Pharisees went out and began to plot with the Herodians*l* how they might kill Jesus.*m*

⁷Jesus withdrew with his disciples to the lake, and a large crowd from Galilee followed.*n* ⁸When they heard all he was doing, many people came to him from Judea, Jerusalem, Idumea, and the regions across the Jordan and around Tyre and Sidon.*o* ⁹Because of the crowd he told his disciples to have a small boat ready for him, to keep the people from crowding him. ¹⁰For he had healed many,*p* so that those with diseases were pushing forward to touch him.*q* ¹¹Whenever the evil*a* spirits saw him, they fell down before him and cried out, "You are the Son of God."*r* ¹²But he gave them strict orders not to tell who he was.*s*

¹³Jesus went up on a mountainside and called to him those he wanted, and they came to him.*t* ¹⁴He appointed twelve—designating them apostles*b* *u*—that they might be with him and that he

---

a 11 Greek *unclean*; also in verse 30   *b* 14 Some manuscripts do not have *designating them apostles*.

might send them out to preach [15]and to have authority to drive out demons.[a] [16]These are the twelve he appointed: Simon (to whom he gave the name Peter);[b] [17]James son of Zebedee and his brother John (to them he gave the name Boanerges, which means Sons of Thunder); [18]Andrew, Philip, Bartholomew, Matthew, Thomas, James son of Alphaeus, Thaddaeus, Simon the Zealot [19]and Judas Iscariot, who betrayed him.

[20]Then Jesus entered a house, and again a crowd gathered,[c] so that he and his disciples were not even able to eat.[d] [21]When his family heard about this, they went to take charge of him, for they said, "He is out of his mind."[e]

[22]And the teachers of the law who came down from Jerusalem[f] said, "He is possessed by Beelzebub[a]![g] By the prince of demons he is driving out demons."[h]

[23]So Jesus called them and spoke to them in parables:[i] "How can Satan[j] drive out Satan? [24]If a kingdom is divided against itself, that kingdom cannot stand. [25]If a house is divided against itself, that house cannot stand. [26]And if Satan opposes himself and is divided, he cannot stand; his end has come. [27]In fact, no one can enter a strong man's house and carry off his possessions unless he first ties up the strong man. Then he can rob his house.[k] [28]I tell you the truth, all the sins and blasphemies of men will be forgiven them. [29]But whoever blasphemes against the Holy Spirit will never be forgiven; he is guilty of an eternal sin."[l]

[30]He said this because they were saying, "He has an evil spirit."

[31]Then Jesus' mother and brothers arrived.[m] Standing outside, they sent someone in to call him. [32]A crowd was sitting around him, and they told him, "Your mother and brothers are outside looking for you."

[33]"Who are my mother and my brothers?" he asked.

[34]Then he looked at those seated in a circle around him and said, "Here are my mother and my brothers! [35]Whoever does God's will is my brother and sister and mother."

The Region of the Tetrarchs

Mediterranean Sea — Sidon, Tyre, ABILENE, ITUREA, TRACHONITIS, GALILEE, Sea of Galilee, SAMARIA, Jordan River, PEREA, JUDEA, IDUMEA, Dead Sea

a 22 Greek *Beezeboul* or *Beelzeboul*

3:15
a Mt 10:1

3:16
b Jn 1:42

3:20
c ver 7
d Mk 6:31

3:21
e Jn 10:20;
Ac 26:24

3:22
f Mt 15:1
g Mt 10:25;
11:18; 12:24;
Jn 7:20;
8:48,52;
10:20
h Mt 9:34

3:23
i Mk 4:2
j Mt 4:10

3:27
k Isa 49:24,25

3:29
l Mt 12:31,32;
Lk 12:10

3:31
m ver 21

Chapter 4 Theme _____

4 Again Jesus began to teach by the lake.[a] The crowd that gathered around him was so large that he got into a boat and sat in it out on the lake, while all the people were along the shore at the water's edge. [2]He taught them many things by parables,[b] and in his teaching said: [3]"Listen! A farmer went out to sow his seed.[c] [4]As he was scattering the seed, some fell along the path, and the birds came and ate it up. [5]Some fell on rocky places, where it did not have much soil. It sprang up quickly, because the soil was shallow. [6]But when the sun came up, the plants were scorched, and they withered because they had no root. [7]Other seed fell among thorns, which grew up and choked the plants, so that they did not bear grain. [8]Still other seed fell on good soil. It came up, grew and produced a crop, multiplying thirty, sixty, or even a hundred times."[d]

[9]Then Jesus said, "He who has ears to hear, let him hear."[e]

[10]When he was alone, the Twelve and the others around him asked him about the parables. [11]He told them, "The secret of the kingdom of God[f] has been given to you. But to those on the outside[g] everything is said in parables [12]so that,

> "'they may be ever seeing but never perceiving,
> and ever hearing but never understanding;
> otherwise they might turn and be forgiven!'[a]"[h]

[13]Then Jesus said to them, "Don't you understand this parable? How then will you understand any parable? [14]The farmer sows the word.[i] [15]Some people are like seed along the path, where the word is sown. As soon as they hear it, Satan[j] comes and takes away the word that was sown in them. [16]Others, like seed sown on rocky places, hear the word and at once receive it with joy. [17]But since they have no root, they last only a short time. When trouble or persecution comes because of the word, they quickly fall away. [18]Still others, like seed sown among thorns, hear the word; [19]but the worries of this life, the deceitfulness of wealth[k] and the desires for other things come in and choke the word, making it unfruitful. [20]Others, like seed sown on good soil, hear the word, accept it, and produce a crop—thirty, sixty or even a hundred times what was sown."

[21]He said to them, "Do you bring in a lamp to put it under a bowl or a bed? Instead, don't you put it on its stand?[l] [22]For whatever is hidden is meant to be disclosed, and whatever is concealed is meant to be brought out into the open.[m] [23]If anyone has ears to hear, let him hear."[n]

4:1
a Mk 2:13; 3:7

4:2
b ver 11;
Mk 3:23

4:3
c ver 26

4:8
d Jn 15:5;
Col 1:6

4:9
e ver 23;
Mt 11:15

4:11
f Mt 3:2
g 1Co 5:12,13;
Col 4:5;
1Th 4:12;
1Ti 3:7

4:12
h Isa 6:9,10;
Mt 13:13-15

4:14
i Mk 16:20;
Lk 1:2;
Ac 4:31; 8:4;
16:6; 17:11;
Php 1:14

4:15
j Mt 4:10

4:19
k Mt 19:23;
1Ti 6:9,10,17;
1Jn 2:15-17

4:21
l Mt 5:15

4:22
m Jer 16:17;
Mt 10:26;
Lk 8:17; 12:2

4:23
n ver 9;
Mt 11:15

INSIGHT

See the section on
Parables, under
**Figures of
Speech**, on page
2209.

a 12 Isaiah 6:9,10

²⁴"Consider carefully what you hear," he continued. "With the measure you use, it will be measured to you—and even more.ᵃ ²⁵Whoever has will be given more; whoever does not have, even what he has will be taken from him."ᵇ

²⁶He also said, "This is what the kingdom of God is like.ᶜ A man scatters seed on the ground. ²⁷Night and day, whether he sleeps or gets up, the seed sprouts and grows, though he does not know how. ²⁸All by itself the soil produces grain—first the stalk, then the head, then the full kernel in the head. ²⁹As soon as the grain is ripe, he puts the sickle to it, because the harvest has come."ᵈ

³⁰Again he said, "What shall we say the kingdom of God is like,ᵉ or what parable shall we use to describe it? ³¹It is like a mustard seed, which is the smallest seed you plant in the ground. ³²Yet when planted, it grows and becomes the largest of all garden plants, with such big branches that the birds of the air can perch in its shade."

³³With many similar parables Jesus spoke the word to them, as much as they could understand.ᶠ ³⁴He did not say anything to them without using a parable.ᵍ But when he was alone with his own disciples, he explained everything.

³⁵That day when evening came, he said to his disciples, "Let us go over to the other side." ³⁶Leaving the crowd behind, they took him along, just as he was, in the boat.ʰ There were also other boats with him. ³⁷A furious squall came up, and the waves broke over the boat, so that it was nearly swamped. ³⁸Jesus was in the stern, sleeping on a cushion. The disciples woke him and said to him, "Teacher, don't you care if we drown?"

³⁹He got up, rebuked the wind and said to the waves, "Quiet! Be still!" Then the wind died down and it was completely calm.

⁴⁰He said to his disciples, "Why are you so afraid? Do you still have no faith?"ⁱ

⁴¹They were terrified and asked each other, "Who is this? Even the wind and the waves obey him!"

Chapter 5 Theme

5 They went across the lake to the region of the Gerasenes.ᵃ ²When Jesus got out of the boat,ʲ a man with an evilᵇ spiritᵏ came from the tombs to meet him. ³This man lived in the tombs, and no one could bind him any more, not even with a chain. ⁴For he had often been chained hand and foot, but he tore the chains apart and broke the irons on his feet. No one was strong enough to subdue him. ⁵Night and day among the tombs and in the hills he would cry out and cut himself with stones.

ᵃ1 Some manuscripts *Gadarenes*; other manuscripts *Gergesenes* ᵇ2 Greek *unclean*; also in verses 8 and 13

4:24
ᵃ Mt 7:2;
Lk 6:38

4:25
ᵇ Mt 13:12;
25:29

4:26
ᶜ Mt 13:24

4:29
ᵈ Rev 14:15

4:30
ᵉ Mt 13:24

4:33
ᶠ Jn 16:12

4:34
ᵍ Jn 16:25

4:36
ʰ ver 1;
Mk 3:9;
5:2,21;
6:32,45

4:40
ⁱ Mt 14:31;
Mk 16:14

5:2
ʲ Mk 4:1
ᵏ Mk 1:23

5:7
aMt 8:29
bMt 4:3;
Lk 1:32; 6:35;
Ac 16:17;
Heb 7:1

5:9
cver 15

5:15
dver 9
ever 16,18;
Mt 4:24

5:19
fMt 8:4

5:20
gMt 4:25;
Mk 7:31

5:21
hMt 9:1 iMk 4:1

5:22
jver 35,36,38;
Lk 13:14;
Ac 13:15;
18:8,17

5:23
kMt 19:13;
Mk 6:5; 7:32;
8:23; 16:18;
Lk 4:40; 13:13;
Ac 6:6

5:25
lLev 15:25-30

5:28
mMt 9:20

5:29
nver 34

5:30
oLk 5:17; 6:19

6When he saw Jesus from a distance, he ran and fell on his knees in front of him. 7He shouted at the top of his voice, "What do you want with me,a Jesus, Son of the Most High God?b Swear to God that you won't torture me!" 8For Jesus had said to him, "Come out of this man, you evil spirit!"

9Then Jesus asked him, "What is your name?"

"My name is Legion,"c he replied, "for we are many." 10And he begged Jesus again and again not to send them out of the area.

11A large herd of pigs was feeding on the nearby hillside. 12The demons begged Jesus, "Send us among the pigs; allow us to go into them." 13He gave them permission, and the evil spirits came out and went into the pigs. The herd, about two thousand in number, rushed down the steep bank into the lake and were drowned.

14Those tending the pigs ran off and reported this in the town and countryside, and the people went out to see what had happened. 15When they came to Jesus, they saw the man who had been possessed by the legiond of demons,e sitting there, dressed and in his right mind; and they were afraid. 16Those who had seen it told the people what had happened to the demon-possessed man—and told about the pigs as well. 17Then the people began to plead with Jesus to leave their region.

18As Jesus was getting into the boat, the man who had been demon-possessed begged to go with him. 19Jesus did not let him, but said, "Go home to your family and tell themf how much the Lord has done for you, and how he has had mercy on you." 20So the man went away and began to tell in the Decapolisa g how much Jesus had done for him. And all the people were amazed.

21When Jesus had again crossed over by boat to the other side of the lake,h a large crowd gathered around him while he was by the lake.i 22Then one of the synagogue rulers,j named Jairus, came there. Seeing Jesus, he fell at his feet 23and pleaded earnestly with him, "My little daughter is dying. Please come and put your hands onk her so that she will be healed and live." 24So Jesus went with him.

A large crowd followed and pressed around him. 25And a woman was there who had been subject to bleedingl for twelve years. 26She had suffered a great deal under the care of many doctors and had spent all she had, yet instead of getting better she grew worse. 27When she heard about Jesus, she came up behind him in the crowd and touched his cloak, 28because she thought, "If I just touch his clothes,m I will be healed." 29Immediately her bleeding stopped and she felt in her body that she was freed from her suffering.n

30At once Jesus realized that powero had gone out from him. He turned around in the crowd and asked, "Who touched my clothes?"

a20 That is, the Ten Cities

³¹"You see the people crowding against you," his disciples answered, "and yet you can ask, 'Who touched me?'"

³²But Jesus kept looking around to see who had done it. ³³Then the woman, knowing what had happened to her, came and fell at his feet and, trembling with fear, told him the whole truth. ³⁴He said to her, "Daughter, your faith has healed you.ᵃ Go in peaceᵇ and be freed from your suffering."

³⁵While Jesus was still speaking, some men came from the house of Jairus, the synagogue ruler.ᶜ "Your daughter is dead," they said. "Why bother the teacher any more?"

³⁶Ignoring what they said, Jesus told the synagogue ruler, "Don't be afraid; just believe."

³⁷He did not let anyone follow him except Peter, James and John the brother of James.ᵈ ³⁸When they came to the home of the synagogue ruler,ᵉ Jesus saw a commotion, with people crying and wailing loudly. ³⁹He went in and said to them, "Why all this commotion and wailing? The child is not dead but asleep."ᶠ ⁴⁰But they laughed at him.

After he put them all out, he took the child's father and mother and the disciples who were with him, and went in where the child was. ⁴¹He took her by the handᵍ and said to her, "Talitha koum!" (which means, "Little girl, I say to you, get up!").ʰ ⁴²Immediately the girl stood up and walked around (she was twelve years old). At this they were completely astonished. ⁴³He gave strict orders not to let anyone know about this,ⁱ and told them to give her something to eat.

Chapter 6 Theme

6 Jesus left there and went to his hometown,ʲ accompanied by his disciples. ²When the Sabbath came,ᵏ he began to teach in the synagogue,ˡ and many who heard him were amazed.ᵐ

"Where did this man get these things?" they asked. "What's this wisdom that has been given him, that he even does miracles! ³Isn't this the carpenter? Isn't this Mary's son and the brother of James, Joseph,ᵃ Judas and Simon?ⁿ Aren't his sisters here with us?" And they took offense at him.ᵒ

⁴Jesus said to them, "Only in his hometown, among his relatives and in his own house is a prophet without honor."ᵖ ⁵He could not do any miracles there, except lay his hands on�q a few sick people and heal them. ⁶And he was amazed at their lack of faith.

Then Jesus went around teaching from village to village.ʳ ⁷Calling the Twelve to him,ˢ he sent them out two by twoᵗ and gave them authority over evilᵇ spirits.ᵘ

ᵃ3 Greek *Joses*, a variant of *Joseph*   ᵇ7 Greek *unclean*

**Cross-references (margin):**

5:34
ᵃ Mt 9:22
ᵇ Ac 15:33

5:35
ᶜ ver 22

5:37
ᵈ Mt 4:21

5:38
ᵉ ver 22

5:39
ᶠ Mt 9:24

5:41
ᵍ Mk 1:31
ʰ Lk 7:14; Ac 9:40

5:43
ⁱ Mt 8:4

6:1
ʲ Mt 2:23

6:2
ᵏ Mk 1:21
ˡ Mt 4:23
ᵐ Mt 7:28

6:3
ⁿ Mt 12:46
ᵒ Mt 11:6; Jn 6:61

6:4
ᵖ Lk 4:24; Jn 4:44

6:5
q Mk 5:23

6:6
ʳ Mt 9:35; Mk 1:39; Lk 13:22

6:7
ˢ Mk 3:13
ᵗ Dt 17:6; Lk 10:1
ᵘ Mt 10:1

6:11
a Mt 10:14

6:12
b Lk 9:6

6:13
c Jas 5:14

6:14
d Mt 3:1

6:15
e Mal 4:5
f Mt 21:11
g Mt 16:14;
Mk 8:28

6:17
h Mt 4:12; 11:2;
Lk 3:19, 20

6:18
i Lev 18:16;
20:21

6:20
j Mt 11:9;
21:26

6:21
k Est 1:3; 2:18
l Lk 3:1

6:23
m Est 5:3,6; 7:2

[8]These were his instructions: "Take nothing for the journey except a staff—no bread, no bag, no money in your belts. [9]Wear sandals but not an extra tunic. [10]Whenever you enter a house, stay there until you leave that town. [11]And if any place will not welcome you or listen to you, shake the dust off your feet[a] when you leave, as a testimony against them."

[12]They went out and preached that people should repent.[b] [13]They drove out many demons and anointed many sick people with oil[c] and healed them.

[14]King Herod heard about this, for Jesus' name had become well known. Some were saying,[a] "John the Baptist[d] has been raised from the dead, and that is why miraculous powers are at work in him."

[15]Others said, "He is Elijah."[e]

And still others claimed, "He is a prophet,[f] like one of the prophets of long ago."[g]

[16]But when Herod heard this, he said, "John, the man I beheaded, has been raised from the dead!"

[17]For Herod himself had given orders to have John arrested, and he had him bound and put in prison.[h] He did this because of Herodias, his brother Philip's wife, whom he had married. [18]For John had been saying to Herod, "It is not lawful for you to have your brother's wife."[i] [19]So Herodias nursed a grudge against John and wanted to kill him. But she was not able to, [20]because Herod feared John and protected him, knowing him to be a righteous and holy man.[j] When Herod heard John, he was greatly puzzled[b]; yet he liked to listen to him.

[21]Finally the opportune time came. On his birthday Herod gave a banquet[k] for his high officials and military commanders and the leading men of Galilee.[l] [22]When the daughter of Herodias came in and danced, she pleased Herod and his dinner guests.

The king said to the girl, "Ask me for anything you want, and I'll give it to you." [23]And he promised her with an oath, "Whatever you ask I will give you, up to half my kingdom."[m]

[24]She went out and said to her mother, "What shall I ask for?"

"The head of John the Baptist," she answered.

[25]At once the girl hurried in to the king with the request: "I want you to give me right now the head of John the Baptist on a platter."

[26]The king was greatly distressed, but because of his oaths and his dinner guests, he did not want to refuse her. [27]So he immediately sent an executioner with orders to bring John's head. The man went, beheaded John in the prison, [28]and brought back his head on a platter. He presented it to the girl, and she gave it to her mother. [29]On hearing of this, John's disciples came and took his body and laid it in a tomb.

a 14 Some early manuscripts *He was saying*   b 20 Some early manuscripts *he did many things*

[30]The apostles[a] gathered around Jesus and reported to him all they had done and taught.[b] [31]Then, because so many people were coming and going that they did not even have a chance to eat,[c] he said to them, "Come with me by yourselves to a quiet place and get some rest."

[32]So they went away by themselves in a boat[d] to a solitary place. [33]But many who saw them leaving recognized them and ran on foot from all the towns and got there ahead of them. [34]When Jesus landed and saw a large crowd, he had compassion on them, because they were like sheep without a shepherd.[e] So he began teaching them many things.

[35]By this time it was late in the day, so his disciples came to him. "This is a remote place," they said, "and it's already very late. [36]Send the people away so they can go to the surrounding countryside and villages and buy themselves something to eat."

[37]But he answered, "You give them something to eat."[f]

They said to him, "That would take eight months of a man's wages[a]! Are we to go and spend that much on bread and give it to them to eat?"

[38]"How many loaves do you have?" he asked. "Go and see."

When they found out, they said, "Five—and two fish."[g]

[39]Then Jesus directed them to have all the people sit down in groups on the green grass. [40]So they sat down in groups of hundreds and fifties. [41]Taking the five loaves and the two fish and looking up to heaven, he gave thanks and broke the loaves.[h] Then he gave them to his disciples to set before the people. He also divided the two fish among them all. [42]They all ate and were satisfied, [43]and the disciples picked up twelve basketfuls of broken pieces of bread and fish. [44]The number of the men who had eaten was five thousand.

[45]Immediately Jesus made his disciples get into the boat[i] and go on ahead of him to Bethsaida,[j] while he dismissed the crowd. [46]After leaving them, he went up on a mountainside to pray.[k]

[47]When evening came, the boat was in the middle of the lake, and he was alone on land. [48]He saw the disciples straining at the oars, because the wind was against them. About the fourth watch of the night he went out to them, walking on the lake. He was about to pass by them, [49]but when they saw him walking on the lake, they thought he was a ghost.[l] They cried out, [50]because they all saw him and were terrified.

Immediately he spoke to them and said, "Take courage! It is I. Don't be afraid."[m] [51]Then he climbed into the boat[n] with them, and the wind died down.[o] They were completely amazed, [52]for they had not understood about the loaves; their hearts were hardened.[p]

a 37 Greek take two hundred denarii

6:30
a Mt 10:2;
Lk 9:10; 17:5;
22:14; 24:10;
Ac 1:2,26
b Lk 9:10

6:31
c Mk 3:20

6:32
d ver 45;
Mk 4:36

6:34
e Mt 9:36

6:37
f 2Ki 4:42-44

6:38
g Mt 15:34;
Mk 8:5

6:41
h Mt 14:19

6:45
i ver 32
j Mt 11:21

6:46
k Lk 3:21

6:49
l Lk 24:37

6:50
m Mt 14:27

6:51
n ver 32
o Mk 4:39

6:52
p Mk 8:17-21

6:53
a Jn 6:24,25

6:56
b Mt 9:20

7:2
c Ac 10:14, 28;
11:8;
Ro 14:14

7:3
d ver 5,8,9,13;
Lk 11:38

7:4
e Mt 23:25;
Lk 11:39

7:5
f ver 3;
Gal 1:14;
Col 2:8

7:7
g Isa 29:13

7:8
h ver 3

7:9
i ver 3

7:10
j Ex 20:12;
Dt 5:16
k Ex 21:17;
Lev 20:9

7:11
l Mt 23:16,18

7:13
m Heb 4:12
n ver 3

⁵³When they had crossed over, they landed at Gennesaret and anchored there.*a* ⁵⁴As soon as they got out of the boat, people recognized Jesus. ⁵⁵They ran throughout that whole region and carried the sick on mats to wherever they heard he was. ⁵⁶And wherever he went—into villages, towns or countryside—they placed the sick in the marketplaces. They begged him to let them touch even the edge of his cloak,*b* and all who touched him were healed.

Chapter 7 Theme _____

7 The Pharisees and some of the teachers of the law who had come from Jerusalem gathered around Jesus and ²saw some of his disciples eating food with hands that were "unclean,"*c* that is, unwashed. ³(The Pharisees and all the Jews do not eat unless they give their hands a ceremonial washing, holding to the tradition of the elders.*d* ⁴When they come from the marketplace they do not eat unless they wash. And they observe many other traditions, such as the washing of cups, pitchers and kettles.*a*)*e*

⁵So the Pharisees and teachers of the law asked Jesus, "Why don't your disciples live according to the tradition of the elders*f* instead of eating their food with 'unclean' hands?"

⁶He replied, "Isaiah was right when he prophesied about you hypocrites; as it is written:

" 'These people honor me with their lips,
    but their hearts are far from me.
⁷They worship me in vain;
    their teachings are but rules taught by men.'*b* *g*

⁸You have let go of the commands of God and are holding on to the traditions of men."*h*

⁹And he said to them: "You have a fine way of setting aside the commands of God in order to observe*c* your own traditions!*i* ¹⁰For Moses said, 'Honor your father and your mother,'*d* *j* and, 'Anyone who curses his father or mother must be put to death.'*e* *k* ¹¹But you say*l* that if a man says to his father or mother: 'Whatever help you might otherwise have received from me is Corban' (that is, a gift devoted to God), ¹²then you no longer let him do anything for his father or mother. ¹³Thus you nullify the word of God*m* by your tradition*n* that you have handed down. And you do many things like that."

¹⁴Again Jesus called the crowd to him and said, "Listen to me, everyone, and understand this. ¹⁵Nothing outside a man can make

a 4 Some early manuscripts *pitchers, kettles and dining couches*   *b 6,7* Isaiah 29:13   *c 9* Some manuscripts *set up*   *d 10* Exodus 20:12; Deut. 5:16   *e 10* Exodus 21:17; Lev. 20:9

him 'unclean' by going into him. Rather, it is what comes out of a man that makes him 'unclean.'ᵃ"

¹⁷After he had left the crowd and entered the house, his disciples asked himᵃ about this parable. ¹⁸"Are you so dull?" he asked. "Don't you see that nothing that enters a man from the outside can make him 'unclean'? ¹⁹For it doesn't go into his heart but into his stomach, and then out of his body." (In saying this, Jesus declared all foodsᵇ "clean.")ᶜ

²⁰He went on: "What comes out of a man is what makes him 'unclean.' ²¹For from within, out of men's hearts, come evil thoughts, sexual immorality, theft, murder, adultery, ²²greed,ᵈ malice, deceit, lewdness, envy, slander, arrogance and folly. ²³All these evils come from inside and make a man 'unclean.'"

²⁴Jesus left that place and went to the vicinity of Tyre.ᵇᵉ He entered a house and did not want anyone to know it; yet he could not keep his presence secret. ²⁵In fact, as soon as she heard about him, a woman whose little daughter was possessed by an evilᶜ spiritᶠ came and fell at his feet. ²⁶The woman was a Greek, born in Syrian Phoenicia. She begged Jesus to drive the demon out of her daughter.

²⁷"First let the children eat all they want," he told her, "for it is not right to take the children's bread and toss it to their dogs."

²⁸"Yes, Lord," she replied, "but even the dogs under the table eat the children's crumbs."

²⁹Then he told her, "For such a reply, you may go; the demon has left your daughter."

³⁰She went home and found her child lying on the bed, and the demon gone.

³¹Then Jesus left the vicinity of Tyreᵍ and went through Sidon, down to the Sea of Galileeʰ and into the region of the Decapolis.ᵈ ⁱ ³²There some people brought to him a man who was deaf and could hardly talk,ʲ and they begged him to place his hand onᵏ the man.

³³After he took him aside, away from the crowd, Jesus put his fingers into the man's ears. Then he spitˡ and touched the man's tongue. ³⁴He looked up to heavenᵐ and with a deep sighⁿ said to him, "Ephphatha!" (which means, "Be opened!"). ³⁵At this, the man's ears were opened, his tongue was loosened and he began to speak plainly.ᵒ

³⁶Jesus commanded them not to tell anyone.ᵖ But the more he did so, the more they kept talking about it. ³⁷People were overwhelmed with amazement. "He has done everything well," they said. "He even makes the deaf hear and the mute speak."

ᵃ15 Some early manuscripts 'unclean.' ¹⁶If anyone has ears to hear, let him hear. ᵇ24 Many early manuscripts Tyre and Sidon ᶜ25 Greek unclean ᵈ31 That is, the Ten Cities

7:17 ᵃMk 9:28

7:19 ᵇRo 14:1-12; Col 2:16; 1Ti 4:3-5 ᶜAc 10:15

7:22 ᵈMt 20:15

7:24 ᵉMt 11:21

7:25 ᶠMt 4:24

7:31 ᵍver 24; Mt 11:21 ʰMt 4:18 ⁱMt 4:25; Mk 5:20

7:32 ʲMt 9:32; Lk 11:14 ᵏMk 5:23

7:33 ˡMk 8:23

7:34 ᵐMk 6:41; Jn 11:41 ⁿMk 8:12

7:35 ᵒIsa 35:5,6

7:36 ᵖMt 8:4

Chapter 8 Theme _____

8:2
a Mt 9:36

8 During those days another large crowd gathered. Since they had nothing to eat, Jesus called his disciples to him and said, [2]"I have compassion for these people;*a* they have already been with me three days and have nothing to eat. [3]If I send them home hungry, they will collapse on the way, because some of them have come a long distance."

[4]His disciples answered, "But where in this remote place can anyone get enough bread to feed them?"

[5]"How many loaves do you have?" Jesus asked.

"Seven," they replied.

[6]He told the crowd to sit down on the ground. When he had taken the seven loaves and given thanks, he broke them and gave them to his disciples to set before the people, and they did so. [7]They had a few small fish as well; he gave thanks for them also and told the disciples to distribute them.*b* [8]The people ate and were satisfied. Afterward the disciples picked up seven basketfuls of broken pieces that were left over.*c* [9]About four thousand men were present. And having sent them away, [10]he got into the boat with his disciples and went to the region of Dalmanutha.

[11]The Pharisees came and began to question Jesus. To test him, they asked him for a sign from heaven.*d* [12]He sighed deeply*e* and said, "Why does this generation ask for a miraculous sign? I tell you the truth, no sign will be given to it." [13]Then he left them, got back into the boat and crossed to the other side.

[14]The disciples had forgotten to bring bread, except for one loaf they had with them in the boat. [15]"Be careful," Jesus warned them. "Watch out for the yeast*f* of the Pharisees*g* and that of Herod."*h*

[16]They discussed this with one another and said, "It is because we have no bread."

[17]Aware of their discussion, Jesus asked them: "Why are you talking about having no bread? Do you still not see or understand? Are your hearts hardened?*i* [18]Do you have eyes but fail to see, and ears but fail to hear? And don't you remember? [19]When I broke the five loaves for the five thousand, how many basketfuls of pieces did you pick up?"

"Twelve,"*j* they replied.

[20]"And when I broke the seven loaves for the four thousand, how many basketfuls of pieces did you pick up?"

They answered, "Seven."*k*

[21]He said to them, "Do you still not understand?"*l*

[22]They came to Bethsaida,*m* and some people brought a blind man*n* and begged Jesus to touch him. [23]He took the blind man by the hand and led him outside the village. When he had spit*o* on

8:7
b Mt 14:19

8:8
c ver 20

8:11
d Mt 12:38

8:12
e Mk 7:34

8:15
f 1Co 5:6-8
g Lk 12:1
h Mt 14:1;
Mk 12:13

8:17
i Isa 6:9,10;
Mk 6:52

8:19
j Mt 14:20;
Mk 6:41-44;
Lk 9:17;
Jn 6:13

8:20
k ver 6-9;
Mt 15:37

8:21
l Mk 6:52

8:22
m Mt 11:21
n Mk 10:46;
Jn 9:1

8:23
o Mk 7:33

INSIGHT

The exact location of *Dalmanutha* is unknown. However, it is believed to be another name for Magdala or the name for a nearby region.

〰〰〰〰

Galilee

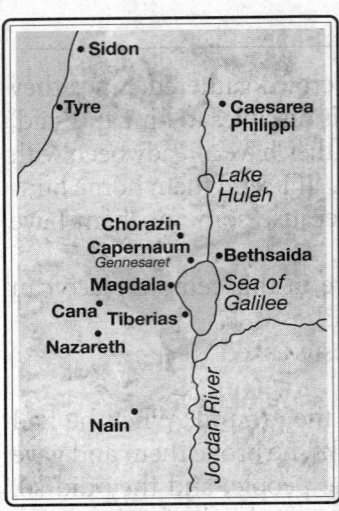

• Sidon
• Tyre
• Caesarea Philippi
Lake Huleh
Chorazin
Capernaum
Gennesaret
• Bethsaida
Magdala•
Sea of Galilee
Cana • Tiberias
Nazareth
Jordan River
• Nain

the man's eyes and put his hands on[a] him, Jesus asked, "Do you see anything?"

[8:23] [a] Mk 5:23

24 He looked up and said, "I see people; they look like trees walking around."

25 Once more Jesus put his hands on the man's eyes. Then his eyes were opened, his sight was restored, and he saw everything clearly. 26 Jesus sent him home, saying, "Don't go into the village.[a]"

[8:28] [b] Mt 3:1 [c] Mal 4:5

27 Jesus and his disciples went on to the villages around Caesarea Philippi. On the way he asked them, "Who do people say I am?"

[8:29] [d] Jn 6:69; 11:27

28 They replied, "Some say John the Baptist;[b] others say Elijah;[c] and still others, one of the prophets."

29 "But what about you?" he asked. "Who do you say I am?" Peter answered, "You are the Christ.[b]"[d]

30 Jesus warned them not to tell anyone about him.[e]

[8:30] [e] Mt 8:4; 16:20; 17:9; Mk 9:9; Lk 9:21

31 He then began to teach them that the Son of Man[f] must suffer many things[g] and be rejected by the elders, chief priests and teachers of the law,[h] and that he must be killed[i] and after three days[j] rise again.[k] 32 He spoke plainly[l] about this, and Peter took him aside and began to rebuke him.

[8:31] [f] Mt 8:20 [g] Mt 16:21 [h] Mt 27:1,2 [i] Ac 2:23; 3:13 [j] Mt 16:21 [k] Mt 16:21

[8:32] [l] Jn 18:20

33 But when Jesus turned and looked at his disciples, he rebuked Peter. "Get behind me, Satan!"[m] he said. "You do not have in mind the things of God, but the things of men."

[8:33] [m] Mt 4:10

34 Then he called the crowd to him along with his disciples and said: "If anyone would come after me, he must deny himself and take up his cross and follow me.[n] 35 For whoever wants to save his life[c] will lose it, but whoever loses his life for me and for the gospel will save it.[o] 36 What good is it for a man to gain the whole world, yet forfeit his soul? 37 Or what can a man give in exchange for his soul? 38 If anyone is ashamed of me and my words in this adulterous and sinful generation, the Son of Man[p] will be ashamed of him[q] when he comes[r] in his Father's glory with the holy angels."

[8:34] [n] Mt 10:38; Lk 14:27

[8:35] [o] Jn 12:25

[8:38] [p] Mt 8:20 [q] Mt 10:33; Lk 12:9 [r] 1Th 2:19

Chapter 9 Theme _____

9 And he said to them, "I tell you the truth, some who are standing here will not taste death before they see the kingdom of God come[s] with power."[t]

[9:1] [s] Mk 13:30; Lk 22:18 [t] Mt 24:30; 25:31

[a] 26 Some manuscripts *Don't go and tell anyone in the village* [b] 29 Or *Messiah*. "The Christ" (Greek) and "the Messiah" (Hebrew) both mean "the Anointed One." [c] 35 The Greek word means either *life* or *soul*; also in verse 36.

²After six days Jesus took Peter, James and John[a] with him and led them up a high mountain, where they were all alone. There he was transfigured before them. ³His clothes became dazzling white,[b] whiter than anyone in the world could bleach them. ⁴And there appeared before them Elijah and Moses, who were talking with Jesus.

⁵Peter said to Jesus, "Rabbi,[c] it is good for us to be here. Let us put up three shelters—one for you, one for Moses and one for Elijah." ⁶(He did not know what to say, they were so frightened.)

⁷Then a cloud appeared and enveloped them, and a voice came from the cloud:[d] "This is my Son, whom I love. Listen to him!"[e]

⁸Suddenly, when they looked around, they no longer saw anyone with them except Jesus.

⁹As they were coming down the mountain, Jesus gave them orders not to tell anyone[f] what they had seen until the Son of Man[g] had risen from the dead. ¹⁰They kept the matter to themselves, discussing what "rising from the dead" meant.

¹¹And they asked him, "Why do the teachers of the law say that Elijah must come first?"

¹²Jesus replied, "To be sure, Elijah does come first, and restores all things. Why then is it written that the Son of Man[h] must suffer much[i] and be rejected?[j] ¹³But I tell you, Elijah has come,[k] and they have done to him everything they wished, just as it is written about him."

¹⁴When they came to the other disciples, they saw a large crowd around them and the teachers of the law arguing with them. ¹⁵As soon as all the people saw Jesus, they were overwhelmed with wonder and ran to greet him.

¹⁶"What are you arguing with them about?" he asked.

¹⁷A man in the crowd answered, "Teacher, I brought you my son, who is possessed by a spirit that has robbed him of speech. ¹⁸Whenever it seizes him, it throws him to the ground. He foams at the mouth, gnashes his teeth and becomes rigid. I asked your disciples to drive out the spirit, but they could not."

¹⁹"O unbelieving generation," Jesus replied, "how long shall I stay with you? How long shall I put up with you? Bring the boy to me."

²⁰So they brought him. When the spirit saw Jesus, it immediately threw the boy into a convulsion. He fell to the ground and rolled around, foaming at the mouth.[l]

²¹Jesus asked the boy's father, "How long has he been like this?"

"From childhood," he answered. ²²"It has often thrown him into fire or water to kill him. But if you can do anything, take pity on us and help us."

²³"'If you can'?" said Jesus. "Everything is possible for him who believes."[m]

²⁴Immediately the boy's father exclaimed, "I do believe; help me overcome my unbelief!"

²⁵When Jesus saw that a crowd was running to the scene,ᵃ he rebuked the evilᵃ spirit. "You deaf and mute spirit," he said, "I command you, come out of him and never enter him again."

²⁶The spirit shrieked, convulsed him violently and came out. The boy looked so much like a corpse that many said, "He's dead." ²⁷But Jesus took him by the hand and lifted him to his feet, and he stood up.

²⁸After Jesus had gone indoors, his disciples asked him privately,ᵇ "Why couldn't we drive it out?"

²⁹He replied, "This kind can come out only by prayer.ᵇ"

³⁰They left that place and passed through Galilee. Jesus did not want anyone to know where they were, ³¹because he was teaching his disciples. He said to them, "The Son of Manᶜ is going to be betrayed into the hands of men. They will kill him,ᵈ and after three daysᵉ he will rise."ᶠ ³²But they did not understand what he meantᵍ and were afraid to ask him about it.

³³They came to Capernaum.ʰ When he was in the house,ⁱ he asked them, "What were you arguing about on the road?" ³⁴But they kept quiet because on the way they had argued about who was the greatest.ʲ

³⁵Sitting down, Jesus called the Twelve and said, "If anyone wants to be first, he must be the very last, and the servant of all."ᵏ

³⁶He took a little child and had him stand among them. Taking him in his arms,ˡ he said to them, ³⁷"Whoever welcomes one of these little children in my name welcomes me; and whoever welcomes me does not welcome me but the one who sent me."ᵐ

³⁸"Teacher," said John, "we saw a man driving out demons in your name and we told him to stop, because he was not one of us."ⁿ

³⁹"Do not stop him," Jesus said. "No one who does a miracle in my name can in the next moment say anything bad about me, ⁴⁰for whoever is not against us is for us.ᵒ ⁴¹I tell you the truth, anyone who gives you a cup of water in my name because you belong to Christ will certainly not lose his reward.ᵖ

⁴²"And if anyone causes one of these little ones who believe in me to sin,�q it would be better for him to be thrown into the sea with a large millstone tied around his neck.ʳ ⁴³If your hand causes you to sin,ˢ cut it off. It is better for you to enter life maimed than with two hands to go into hell,ᵗ where the fire never goes out.ᶜ ᵘ ⁴⁵And if your foot causes you to sin,ᵛ cut it off. It is better for you to enter life crippled than to have two feet and be thrown into hell.ᵈ ʷ

ᵃ 25 Greek *unclean*   ᵇ 29 Some manuscripts *prayer and fasting*   ᶜ 43 Some manuscripts *out,* ⁴⁴*where / "'their worm does not die, / and the fire is not quenched.'*   ᵈ 45 Some manuscripts *hell,* ⁴⁶*where / "'their worm does not die, / and the fire is not quenched.'*

1742

9:25
ᵃ ver 15

9:28
ᵇ Mk 7:17

9:31
ᶜ Mt 8:20
ᵈ ver 12; Ac 2:23; 3:13
ᵉ Mt 16:21
ᶠ Mt 16:21

9:32
ᵍ Lk 2:50; 9:45; 18:34; Jn 12:16

9:33
ʰ Mt 4:13
ⁱ Mk 1:29

9:34
ʲ Lk 22:24

9:35
ᵏ Mt 18:4; 20:26; Mk 10:43; Lk 22:26

9:36
ˡ Mk 10:16

9:37
ᵐ Mt 10:40

9:38
ⁿ Nu 11:27-29

9:40
ᵒ Mt 12:30; Lk 11:23

9:41
ᵖ Mt 10:42

9:42
q Mt 5:29
ʳ Mt 18:6; Lk 17:2

9:43
ˢ Mt 5:29
ᵗ Mt 5:30; 18:8
ᵘ Mt 25:41

9:45
ᵛ Mt 5:29
ʷ Mt 18:8

9:47
a Mt 5:29
b Mt 5:29; 18:9

9:48
c Isa 66:24;
Mt 25:41

9:49
d Lev 2:13

9:50
e Mt 5:13;
Lk 14:34,35
f Col 4:6
g Ro 12:18;
2Co 13:11;
1Th 5:13

10:1
h Mk 1:5;
Jn 10:40; 11:7
i Mt 4:23;
Mk 2:13; 4:2;
6:6,34

10:2
j Mk 2:16

10:4
k Dt 24:1-4;
Mt 5:31

10:5
l Ps 95:8;
Heb 3:15

10:6
m Ge 1:27; 5:2

10:8
n Ge 2:24;
1Co 6:16

10:11
o Mt 5:32;
Lk 16:18

10:12
p Ro 7:3;
1Co 7:10,11

10:14
q Mt 25:34

10:15
r Mt 18:3

10:16
s Mk 9:36

10:17
t Mk 1:40
u Lk 10:25;
Ac 20:32

⁴⁷And if your eye causes you to sin,a pluck it out. It is better for you to enter the kingdom of God with one eye than to have two eyes and be thrown into hell,b ⁴⁸where

> " 'their worm does not die,
>   and the fire is not quenched.'a c

⁴⁹Everyone will be saltedd with fire.

⁵⁰"Salt is good, but if it loses its saltiness, how can you make it salty again?e Have salt in yourselves,f and be at peace with each other."g

Chapter 10 Theme _____

10 Jesus then left that place and went into the region of Judea and across the Jordan.h Again crowds of people came to him, and as was his custom, he taught them.i

²Some Phariseesj came and tested him by asking, "Is it lawful for a man to divorce his wife?"

³"What did Moses command you?" he replied.

⁴They said, "Moses permitted a man to write a certificate of divorce and send her away."k

⁵"It was because your hearts were hardl that Moses wrote you this law," Jesus replied. ⁶"But at the beginning of creation God 'made them male and female.'b m ⁷For this reason a man will leave his father and mother and be united to his wife,c ⁸and the two will become one flesh.'d n So they are no longer two, but one. ⁹Therefore what God has joined together, let man not separate."

¹⁰When they were in the house again, the disciples asked Jesus about this. ¹¹He answered, "Anyone who divorces his wife and marries another woman commits adultery against her.o ¹²And if she divorces her husband and marries another man, she commits adultery."p

¹³People were bringing little children to Jesus to have him touch them, but the disciples rebuked them. ¹⁴When Jesus saw this, he was indignant. He said to them, "Let the little children come to me, and do not hinder them, for the kingdom of God belongs to such as these.q ¹⁵I tell you the truth, anyone who will not receive the kingdom of God like a little child will never enter it."r ¹⁶And he took the children in his arms,s put his hands on them and blessed them.

¹⁷As Jesus started on his way, a man ran up to him and fell on his kneest before him. "Good teacher," he asked, "what must I do to inherit eternal life?"u

a48 Isaiah 66:24   b6 Gen. 1:27   c7 Some early manuscripts do not have *and be united to his wife*.   d8 Gen. 2:24

¹⁸"Why do you call me good?" Jesus answered. "No one is good—except God alone. ¹⁹You know the commandments: 'Do not murder, do not commit adultery, do not steal, do not give false testimony, do not defraud, honor your father and mother.'a"^a

²⁰"Teacher," he declared, "all these I have kept since I was a boy."

²¹Jesus looked at him and loved him. "One thing you lack," he said. "Go, sell everything you have and give to the poor,^b and you will have treasure in heaven.^c Then come, follow me."^d

²²At this the man's face fell. He went away sad, because he had great wealth.

²³Jesus looked around and said to his disciples, "How hard it is for the rich^e to enter the kingdom of God!"

²⁴The disciples were amazed at his words. But Jesus said again, "Children, how hard it is^b to enter the kingdom of God! ^f ²⁵It is easier for a camel to go through the eye of a needle than for a rich man to enter the kingdom of God."^g

²⁶The disciples were even more amazed, and said to each other, "Who then can be saved?"

²⁷Jesus looked at them and said, "With man this is impossible, but not with God; all things are possible with God."^h

²⁸Peter said to him, "We have left everything to follow you!"ⁱ

²⁹"I tell you the truth," Jesus replied, "no one who has left home or brothers or sisters or mother or father or children or fields for me and the gospel ³⁰will fail to receive a hundred times as much^j in this present age (homes, brothers, sisters, mothers, children and fields—and with them, persecutions) and in the age to come,^k eternal life.^l ³¹But many who are first will be last, and the last first."^m

³²They were on their way up to Jerusalem, with Jesus leading the way, and the disciples were astonished, while those who followed were afraid. Again he took the Twelveⁿ aside and told them what was going to happen to him. ³³"We are going up to Jerusalem,"^o he said, "and the Son of Man^p will be betrayed to the chief priests and teachers of the law.^q They will condemn him to death and will hand him over to the Gentiles, ³⁴who will mock him and spit on him, flog him^r and kill him.^s Three days later^t he will rise."^u

³⁵Then James and John, the sons of Zebedee, came to him. "Teacher," they said, "we want you to do for us whatever we ask."

³⁶"What do you want me to do for you?" he asked.

³⁷They replied, "Let one of us sit at your right and the other at your left in your glory."^v

³⁸"You don't know what you are asking,"^w Jesus said. "Can you drink the cup^x I drink or be baptized with the baptism I am baptized with?"^y

---

10:19
a Ex 20:12-16;
Dt 5:16-20

10:21
b Ac 2:45
c Mt 6:20;
Lk 12:33
d Mt 4:19

10:23
e Ps 52:7; 62:10;
1Ti 6:9,10,17

10:24
f Mt 7:13,14

10:25
g Lk 12:16-20

10:27
h Mt 19:26

10:28
i Mt 4:19

10:30
j Mt 6:33
k Mt 12:32
l Mt 25:46

10:31
m Mt 19:30

10:32
n Mk 3:16-19

10:33
o Lk 9:51
p Mt 8:20
q Mt 27:1,2

10:34
r Mt 16:21
s Ac 2:23; 3:13
t Mt 16:21
u Mt 16:21

10:37
v Mt 19:28

10:38
w Job 38:2
x Mt 20:22
y Lk 12:50

---

a 19 Exodus 20:12-16; Deut. 5:16-20   b 24 Some manuscripts *is for those who trust in riches*

10:39
a Ac 12:2;
Rev 1:9

³⁹"We can," they answered.

Jesus said to them, "You will drink the cup I drink and be baptized with the baptism I am baptized with,ᵃ ⁴⁰but to sit at my right or left is not for me to grant. These places belong to those for whom they have been prepared."

10:43
b Mk 9:35

⁴¹When the ten heard about this, they became indignant with James and John. ⁴²Jesus called them together and said, "You know that those who are regarded as rulers of the Gentiles lord it over them, and their high officials exercise authority over them. ⁴³Not so with you. Instead, whoever wants to become great among you must be your servant,ᵇ ⁴⁴and whoever wants to be first must be

10:45
c Mt 20:28
d Mt 20:28

slave of all. ⁴⁵For even the Son of Man did not come to be served, but to serve,ᶜ and to give his life as a ransom for many."ᵈ

⁴⁶Then they came to Jericho. As Jesus and his disciples, together with a large crowd, were leaving the city, a blind man, Bartimaeus (that is, the Son of Timaeus), was sitting by the roadside begging.

10:47
e Mk 1:24
f Mt 9:27

⁴⁷When he heard that it was Jesus of Nazareth,ᵉ he began to shout, "Jesus, Son of David,ᶠ have mercy on me!"

⁴⁸Many rebuked him and told him to be quiet, but he shouted all the more, "Son of David, have mercy on me!"

⁴⁹Jesus stopped and said, "Call him."

So they called to the blind man, "Cheer up! On your feet! He's

10:51
g Mt 23:7

calling you." ⁵⁰Throwing his cloak aside, he jumped to his feet and came to Jesus.

⁵¹"What do you want me to do for you?" Jesus asked him.

The blind man said, "Rabbi,ᵍ I want to see."

10:52
h Mt 9:22
i Mt 4:19

⁵²"Go," said Jesus, "your faith has healed you."ʰ Immediately he received his sight and followedⁱ Jesus along the road.

Chapter 11 Theme

11:1
j Mt 21:17
k Mt 21:1

11 As they approached Jerusalem and came to Bethphage and Bethanyʲ at the Mount of Olives,ᵏ Jesus sent two of his disciples, ²saying to them, "Go to the village ahead of you, and just as you enter it, you will find a colt tied there, which no one has ever ridden.ˡ Untie it and bring it here. ³If anyone asks you, 'Why are you doing this?' tell him, 'The Lord needs it and will send it back here shortly.'"

11:2
l Nu 19:2;
Dt 21:3;
1Sa 6:7

⁴They went and found a colt outside in the street, tied at a doorway.ᵐ As they untied it, ⁵some people standing there asked, "What are you doing, untying that colt?" ⁶They answered as Jesus had told them to, and the people let them go. ⁷When they brought the colt to Jesus and threw their cloaks over it, he sat on it. ⁸Many people spread their cloaks on the road, while others spread branches they had cut in the fields. ⁹Those who went ahead and those who followed shouted,

11:4
m Mk 14:16

"Hosanna!ᵃ"

"Blessed is he who comes in the name of the Lord!"ᵇ ᵃ

¹⁰"Blessed is the coming kingdom of our father David!"

"Hosanna in the highest!"ᵇ

¹¹Jesus entered Jerusalem and went to the temple. He looked around at everything, but since it was already late, he went out to Bethany with the Twelve.ᶜ

From Bethany, Bethphage across the Mount of Olives into Jerusalem

¹²The next day as they were leaving Bethany, Jesus was hungry. ¹³Seeing in the distance a fig tree in leaf, he went to find out if it had any fruit. When he reached it, he found nothing but leaves, because it was not the season for figs.ᵈ ¹⁴Then he said to the tree, "May no one ever eat fruit from you again." And his disciples heard him say it.

¹⁵On reaching Jerusalem, Jesus entered the temple area and began driving out those who were buying and selling there. He overturned the tables of the money changers and the benches of those selling doves, ¹⁶and would not allow anyone to carry merchandise through the temple courts. ¹⁷And as he taught them, he said, "Is it not written:

" 'My house will be called
    a house of prayer for all nations'ᶜ?ᵉ

But you have made it 'a den of robbers.'ᵈ"ᶠ

¹⁸The chief priests and the teachers of the law heard this and began looking for a way to kill him, for they feared him,ᵍ because the whole crowd was amazed at his teaching.ʰ

¹⁹When evening came, theyᵉ went out of the city.ⁱ

²⁰In the morning, as they went along, they saw the fig tree withered from the roots. ²¹Peter remembered and said to Jesus, "Rabbi,ʲ look! The fig tree you cursed has withered!"

²²"Haveᶠ faith in God," Jesus answered. ²³"I tell you the truth, if anyone says to this mountain, 'Go, throw yourself into the sea,' and does not doubt in his heart but believes that what he says will happen, it will be done for him.ᵏ ²⁴Therefore I tell you, whatever you ask for in prayer, believe that you have received it, and it will be yours.ˡ ²⁵And when you stand praying, if you hold anything

11:9
ᵃPs 118:25,26;
Mt 23:39

11:10
ᵇLk 2:14

11:11
ᶜMt 21:12,17

11:13
ᵈLk 13:6-9

11:17
ᵉIsa 56:7
ᶠJer 7:11

11:18
ᵍMt 21:46;
Mk 12:12;
Lk 20:19
ʰMt 7:28

11:19
ⁱLk 21:37

11:21
ʲMt 23:7

11:23
ᵏMt 21:21

11:24
ˡMt 7:7

ᵃ9 A Hebrew expression meaning "Save!" which became an exclamation of praise; also in verse 10   ᵇ9 Psalm 118:25,26   ᶜ17 Isaiah 56:7   ᵈ17 Jer. 7:11   ᵉ19 Some early manuscripts he   ᶠ22 Some early manuscripts If you have against anyone, forgive him, so that your Father in heaven may forgive you your sins.ᵃ"ᵃ

²⁷They arrived again in Jerusalem, and while Jesus was walking in the temple courts, the chief priests, the teachers of the law and the elders came to him. ²⁸"By what authority are you doing these things?" they asked. "And who gave you authority to do this?"

²⁹Jesus replied, "I will ask you one question. Answer me, and I will tell you by what authority I am doing these things. ³⁰John's baptism—was it from heaven, or from men? Tell me!"

³¹They discussed it among themselves and said, "If we say, 'From heaven,' he will ask, 'Then why didn't you believe him?' ³²But if we say, 'From men'. . . ." (They feared the people, for everyone held that John really was a prophet.)ᵇ

³³So they answered Jesus, "We don't know."

Jesus said, "Neither will I tell you by what authority I am doing these things."

Chapter 12 Theme _____

12 He then began to speak to them in parables: "A man planted a vineyard.ᶜ He put a wall around it, dug a pit for the winepress and built a watchtower. Then he rented the vineyard to some farmers and went away on a journey. ²At harvest time he sent a servant to the tenants to collect from them some of the fruit of the vineyard. ³But they seized him, beat him and sent him away empty-handed. ⁴Then he sent another servant to them; they struck this man on the head and treated him shamefully. ⁵He sent still another, and that one they killed. He sent many others; some of them they beat, others they killed.

⁶"He had one left to send, a son, whom he loved. He sent him last of all,ᵈ saying, 'They will respect my son.'

⁷"But the tenants said to one another, 'This is the heir. Come, let's kill him, and the inheritance will be ours.' ⁸So they took him and killed him, and threw him out of the vineyard.

⁹"What then will the owner of the vineyard do? He will come and kill those tenants and give the vineyard to others. ¹⁰Haven't you read this scripture:

" 'The stone the builders rejected
    has become the capstoneᵇ;ᵉ
¹¹the Lord has done this,
    and it is marvelous in our eyes'ᶜ?"ᶠ

¹²Then they looked for a way to arrest him because they knew he had spoken the parable against them. But they were afraid of the crowd;ᵍ so they left him and went away.ʰ

### Cross references (margin)

11:25 ᵃMt 6:14

11:32 ᵇMt 11:9

12:1 ᶜIsa 5:1-7

12:6 ᵈHeb 1:1-3

12:10 ᵉAc 4:11

12:11 ᶠPs 118:22,23

12:12 ᵍMk 11:18
    ʰMt 22:22

ᵃ25 Some manuscripts *sins.* ²⁶*But if you do not forgive, neither will your Father who is in heaven forgive your sins.*   ᵇ10 Or *cornerstone*   ᶜ11 Psalm 118:22,23

¹³Later they sent some of the Pharisees and Herodians*ᵃ* to Jesus to catch him*ᵇ* in his words. ¹⁴They came to him and said, "Teacher, we know you are a man of integrity. You aren't swayed by men, because you pay no attention to who they are; but you teach the way of God in accordance with the truth. Is it right to pay taxes to Caesar or not? ¹⁵Should we pay or shouldn't we?"

But Jesus knew their hypocrisy. "Why are you trying to trap me?" he asked. "Bring me a denarius and let me look at it." ¹⁶They brought the coin, and he asked them, "Whose portrait is this? And whose inscription?"

"Caesar's," they replied.

¹⁷Then Jesus said to them, "Give to Caesar what is Caesar's and to God what is God's."*ᶜ*

And they were amazed at him.

¹⁸Then the Sadducees,*ᵈ* who say there is no resurrection,*ᵉ* came to him with a question. ¹⁹"Teacher," they said, "Moses wrote for us that if a man's brother dies and leaves a wife but no children, the man must marry the widow and have children for his brother.*ᶠ* ²⁰Now there were seven brothers. The first one married and died without leaving any children. ²¹The second one married the widow, but he also died, leaving no child. It was the same with the third. ²²In fact, none of the seven left any children. Last of all, the woman died too. ²³At the resurrection*ᵃ* whose wife will she be, since the seven were married to her?"

²⁴Jesus replied, "Are you not in error because you do not know the Scriptures*ᵍ* or the power of God? ²⁵When the dead rise, they will neither marry nor be given in marriage; they will be like the angels in heaven.*ʰ* ²⁶Now about the dead rising—have you not read in the book of Moses, in the account of the bush, how God said to him, 'I am the God of Abraham, the God of Isaac, and the God of Jacob'*ᵇ*?*ⁱ* ²⁷He is not the God of the dead, but of the living. You are badly mistaken!"

²⁸One of the teachers of the law*ʲ* came and heard them debating. Noticing that Jesus had given them a good answer, he asked him, "Of all the commandments, which is the most important?"

²⁹"The most important one," answered Jesus, "is this: 'Hear, O Israel, the Lord our God, the Lord is one.*ᶜ* ³⁰Love the Lord your God with all your heart and with all your soul and with all your mind and with all your strength.'*ᵈ ᵏ* ³¹The second is this: 'Love your neighbor as yourself.'*ᵉ ˡ* There is no commandment greater than these."

³²"Well said, teacher," the man replied. "You are right in saying that God is one and there is no other but him.*ᵐ* ³³To love him with

---

Cross references:

12:13 *ᵃ*Mt 22:16; Mk 3:6 *ᵇ*Mt 12:10

12:17 *ᶜ*Ro 13:7

12:18 *ᵈ*Ac 4:1 *ᵉ*Ac 23:8; 1Co 15:12

12:19 *ᶠ*Dt 25:5

12:24 *ᵍ*2Ti 3:15-17

12:25 *ʰ*1Co 15:42, 49,52

12:26 *ⁱ*Ex 3:6

12:28 *ʲ*Lk 10:25-28; 20:39

12:30 *ᵏ*Dt 6:4,5

12:31 *ˡ*Lev 19:18; Mt 5:43

12:32 *ᵐ*Dt 4:35,39; Isa 45:6,14; 46:9

ᵃ23 Some manuscripts *resurrection, when men rise from the dead,* *ᵇ26* Exodus 3:6 *ᶜ29* Or *the Lord our God is one Lord* *ᵈ30* Deut. 6:4,5 *ᵉ31* Lev. 19:18

12:33
a 1Sa 15:22;
Hos 6:6;
Mic 6:6-8;
Heb 10:8

all your heart, with all your understanding and with all your strength, and to love your neighbor as yourself is more important than all burnt offerings and sacrifices."*a*

³⁴When Jesus saw that he had answered wisely, he said to him, "You are not far from the kingdom of God."*b* And from then on no one dared ask him any more questions.*c*

12:34
b Mt 3:2
c Mt 22:46;
Lk 20:40

³⁵While Jesus was teaching in the temple courts,*d* he asked, "How is it that the teachers of the law say that the Christ*a* is the son of David?*e* ³⁶David himself, speaking by the Holy Spirit,*f* declared:

12:35
d Mt 26:55
e Mt 9:27

" 'The Lord said to my Lord:
"Sit at my right hand
until I put your enemies
under your feet." '*bg*

³⁷David himself calls him 'Lord.' How then can he be his son?"

The large crowd*h* listened to him with delight.

12:36
f 2Sa 23:2
g Ps 110:1;
Mt 22:44

³⁸As he taught, Jesus said, "Watch out for the teachers of the law. They like to walk around in flowing robes and be greeted in the marketplaces, ³⁹and have the most important seats in the synagogues and the places of honor at banquets.*i* ⁴⁰They devour widows' houses and for a show make lengthy prayers. Such men will be punished most severely."

12:37
h Jn 12:9

⁴¹Jesus sat down opposite the place where the offerings were put*j* and watched the crowd putting their money into the temple treasury. Many rich people threw in large amounts. ⁴²But a poor widow came and put in two very small copper coins,*c* worth only a fraction of a penny.*d*

12:39
i Lk 11:43

⁴³Calling his disciples to him, Jesus said, "I tell you the truth, this poor widow has put more into the treasury than all the others. ⁴⁴They all gave out of their wealth; but she, out of her poverty, put in everything—all she had to live on."*k*

12:41
j 2Ki 12:9;
Jn 8:20

Chapter 13 Theme

12:44
k 2Co 8:12

13 As he was leaving the temple, one of his disciples said to him, "Look, Teacher! What massive stones! What magnificent buildings!"

²"Do you see all these great buildings?" replied Jesus. "Not one stone here will be left on another; every one will be thrown down."*l*

13:2
l Lk 19:44

³As Jesus was sitting on the Mount of Olives*m* opposite the temple, Peter, James, John*n* and Andrew asked him privately, ⁴"Tell us, when will these things happen? And what will be the sign that they are all about to be fulfilled?"

13:3
m Mt 21:1
n Mt 4:21

INSIGHT

The treasury was in the women's court of the temple, where there were thirteen trumpet-shaped offering receptacles. See the illustration of the floor plan of Herod's Temple on page 1723, and see the illustration of Herod's Temple on page IISB-38.

a 35 Or *Messiah*   b 36 Psalm 110:1   c 42 Greek *two lepta*   d 42 Greek *kodrantes*

⁵Jesus said to them: "Watch out that no one deceives you.ᵃ ⁶Many will come in my name, claiming, 'I am he,' and will deceive many. ⁷When you hear of wars and rumors of wars, do not be alarmed. Such things must happen, but the end is still to come. ⁸Nation will rise against nation, and kingdom against kingdom. There will be earthquakes in various places, and famines. These are the beginning of birth pains.

⁹"You must be on your guard. You will be handed over to the local councils and flogged in the synagogues.ᵇ On account of me you will stand before governors and kings as witnesses to them. ¹⁰And the gospel must first be preached to all nations. ¹¹Whenever you are arrested and brought to trial, do not worry beforehand about what to say. Just say whatever is given you at the time, for it is not you speaking, but the Holy Spirit.ᶜ

¹²"Brother will betray brother to death, and a father his child. Children will rebel against their parents and have them put to death.ᵈ ¹³All men will hate you because of me,ᵉ but he who stands firm to the end will be saved.ᶠ

¹⁴"When you see 'the abomination that causes desolation'ᵃᵍ standing where itᵇ does not belong—let the reader understand—then let those who are in Judea flee to the mountains. ¹⁵Let no one on the roof of his house go down or enter the house to take anything out. ¹⁶Let no one in the field go back to get his cloak. ¹⁷How dreadful it will be in those days for pregnant women and nursing mothers!ʰ ¹⁸Pray that this will not take place in winter, ¹⁹because those will be days of distress unequaled from the beginning, when God created the world,ⁱ until now—and never to be equaled again.ʲ ²⁰If the Lord had not cut short those days, no one would survive. But for the sake of the elect, whom he has chosen, he has shortened them. ²¹At that time if anyone says to you, 'Look, here is the Christᶜ!' or, 'Look, there he is!' do not believe it.ᵏ ²²For false Christs and false prophetsˡ will appear and perform signs and miraclesᵐ to deceive the elect—if that were possible. ²³So be on your guard;ⁿ I have told you everything ahead of time.

²⁴"But in those days, following that distress,

" 'the sun will be darkened,
    and the moon will not give its light;
²⁵the stars will fall from the sky,
    and the heavenly bodies will be shaken.'ᵈᵒ

²⁶"At that time men will see the Son of Man coming in cloudsᵖ with great power and glory. ²⁷And he will send his angels and gather his elect from the four winds, from the ends of the earth to the ends of the heavens.�q

---

ᵃ14 Daniel 9:27; 11:31; 12:11 ᵇ14 Or he; also in verse 29 ᶜ21 Or Messiah ᵈ25 Isaiah 13:10; 34:4

13:5
ᵃver 22;
Jer 29:8;
Eph 5:6;
2Th 2:3,10-12;
1Ti 4:1;
2Ti 3:13;
1Jn 4:6

13:9
ᵇMt 10:17

13:11
ᶜMt 10:19,20;
Lk 12:11,12

13:12
ᵈMic 7:6;
Mt 10:21;
Lk 12:51-53

13:13
ᵉJn 15:21
ᶠMt 10:22

13:14
ᵍDa 9:27; 11:31;
12:11

13:17
ʰLk 23:29

13:19
ⁱMk 10:6
ʲDa 9:26; 12:1;
Joel 2:2

13:21
ᵏLk 17:23; 21:8

13:22
ˡMt 7:15
ᵐJn 4:48;
2Th 2:9,10

13:23
ⁿ2Pe 3:17

13:25
ᵒIsa 13:10; 34:4;
Mt 24:29

13:26
ᵖDa 7:13;
Mt 16:27;
Rev 1:7

13:27
qZec 2:6

13:30
a Mk 9:1
b Lk 17:25

28"Now learn this lesson from the fig tree: As soon as its twigs get tender and its leaves come out, you know that summer is near. 29Even so, when you see these things happening, you know that it is near, right at the door. 30I tell you the truth, this generation*a *a* will certainly not pass away until all these things have happened.*b* 31Heaven and earth will pass away, but my words will never pass away.*c*

13:31
c Mt 5:18

32"No one knows about that day or hour, not even the angels in heaven, nor the Son, but only the Father.*d* 33Be on guard! Be alert*b!e* You do not know when that time will come. 34It's like a man going away: He leaves his house and puts his servants*f* in charge, each with his assigned task, and tells the one at the door to keep watch.

13:32
d Ac 1:7;
1Th 5:1,2

35"Therefore keep watch because you do not know when the owner of the house will come back—whether in the evening, or at midnight, or when the rooster crows, or at dawn. 36If he comes suddenly, do not let him find you sleeping. 37What I say to you, I say to everyone: 'Watch!'"*g*

13:33
e 1Th 5:6

13:34
f Mt 25:14

Chapter 14 Theme

13:37
g Lk 12:35-40

14 Now the Passover*h* and the Feast of Unleavened Bread were only two days away, and the chief priests and the teachers of the law were looking for some sly way to arrest Jesus and kill him.*i* 2"But not during the Feast," they said, "or the people may riot."

14:1
h Jn 11:55; 13:1
i Mt 12:14

3While he was in Bethany,*j* reclining at the table in the home of a man known as Simon the Leper, a woman came with an alabaster jar of very expensive perfume, made of pure nard. She broke the jar and poured the perfume on his head.*k*

14:3
j Mt 21:17
k Lk 7:37-39

4Some of those present were saying indignantly to one another, "Why this waste of perfume? 5It could have been sold for more than a year's wages*c* and the money given to the poor." And they rebuked her harshly.

14:7
l Dt 15:11

6"Leave her alone," said Jesus. "Why are you bothering her? She has done a beautiful thing to me. 7The poor you will always have with you, and you can help them any time you want.*l* But you will not always have me. 8She did what she could. She poured perfume on my body beforehand to prepare for my burial.*m* 9I tell you the truth, wherever the gospel is preached throughout the world,*n* what she has done will also be told, in memory of her."

14:8
m Jn 19:40

10Then Judas Iscariot, one of the Twelve,*o* went to the chief priests to betray Jesus to them.*p* 11They were delighted to hear this and promised to give him money. So he watched for an opportunity to hand him over.

14:9
n Mt 24:14;
Mk 16:15

14:10
o Mk 3:16-19
p Mt 10:4

a 30 Or *race*   b 33 Some manuscripts *alert and pray*   c 5 Greek *than three hundred denarii*

¹²On the first day of the Feast of Unleavened Bread, when it was customary to sacrifice the Passover lamb,ᵃ Jesus' disciples asked him, "Where do you want us to go and make preparations for you to eat the Passover?"

¹³So he sent two of his disciples, telling them, "Go into the city, and a man carrying a jar of water will meet you. Follow him. ¹⁴Say to the owner of the house he enters, 'The Teacher asks: Where is my guest room, where I may eat the Passover with my disciples?' ¹⁵He will show you a large upper room,ᵇ furnished and ready. Make preparations for us there."

¹⁶The disciples left, went into the city and found things just as Jesus had told them. So they prepared the Passover.

¹⁷When evening came, Jesus arrived with the Twelve. ¹⁸While they were reclining at the table eating, he said, "I tell you the truth, one of you will betray me—one who is eating with me."

¹⁹They were saddened, and one by one they said to him, "Surely not I?"

²⁰"It is one of the Twelve," he replied, "one who dips bread into the bowl with me.ᶜ ²¹The Son of Manᵈ will go just as it is written about him. But woe to that man who betrays the Son of Man! It would be better for him if he had not been born."

²²While they were eating, Jesus took bread, gave thanks and broke it,ᵉ and gave it to his disciples, saying, "Take it; this is my body."

²³Then he took the cup, gave thanks and offered it to them, and they all drank from it.ᶠ

²⁴"This is my blood of theᵃ covenant,ᵍ which is poured out for many," he said to them. ²⁵"I tell you the truth, I will not drink again of the fruit of the vine until that day when I drink it anew in the kingdom of God."ʰ

²⁶When they had sung a hymn, they went out to the Mount of Olives.ⁱ

²⁷"You will all fall away," Jesus told them, "for it is written:

> " 'I will strike the shepherd,
>   and the sheep will be scattered.'ᵇʲ

²⁸But after I have risen, I will go ahead of you into Galilee."ᵏ

²⁹Peter declared, "Even if all fall away, I will not."

³⁰"I tell you the truth," Jesus answered, "today—yes, tonight—before the rooster crows twiceᶜ you yourself will disown me three times."ˡ

³¹But Peter insisted emphatically, "Even if I have to die with you,ᵐ I will never disown you." And all the others said the same.

ᵃ24 Some manuscripts *the new*   ᵇ27 Zech. 13:7   ᶜ30 Some early manuscripts do not have *twice*.

14:12
ᵃEx 12:1-11;
Dt 16:1-4;
1Co 5:7

14:15
ᵇAc 1:13

14:20
ᶜJn 13:18-27

14:21
ᵈMt 8:20

14:22
ᵉMt 14:19

14:23
ᶠ1Co 10:16

14:24
ᵍMt 26:28

14:25
ʰMt 3:2

14:26
ⁱMt 21:1

14:27
ʲZec 13:7

14:28
ᵏMk 16:7

14:30
ˡver 66-72;
Lk 22:34;
Jn 13:38

14:31
ᵐLk 22:33;
Jn 13:37

14:33
a Mt 4:21

14:34
b Jn 12:27

14:35
c ver 41;
Mt 26:18

14:36
d Ro 8:15;
Gal 4:6
e Mt 20:22
f Mt 26:39

14:38
g Mt 6:13
h Ro 7:22,23

14:41
i ver 35;
Mt 26:18

14:43
j Mt 10:4

14:45
k Mt 23:7

14:49
l Mt 26:55
m Isa 53:7-12;
Mt 1:22

14:50
n ver 27

14:54
o Mt 26:3
p Jn 18:18

14:55
q Mt 5:22

³²They went to a place called Gethsemane, and Jesus said to his disciples, "Sit here while I pray." ³³He took Peter, James and John[a] along with him, and he began to be deeply distressed and troubled. ³⁴"My soul is overwhelmed with sorrow to the point of death,"[b] he said to them. "Stay here and keep watch."

³⁵Going a little farther, he fell to the ground and prayed that if possible the hour[c] might pass from him. ³⁶"Abba,[a] Father,"[d] he said, "everything is possible for you. Take this cup[e] from me. Yet not what I will, but what you will."[f]

³⁷Then he returned to his disciples and found them sleeping. "Simon," he said to Peter, "are you asleep? Could you not keep watch for one hour? ³⁸Watch and pray so that you will not fall into temptation.[g] The spirit is willing, but the body is weak."[h]

³⁹Once more he went away and prayed the same thing. ⁴⁰When he came back, he again found them sleeping, because their eyes were heavy. They did not know what to say to him.

⁴¹Returning the third time, he said to them, "Are you still sleeping and resting? Enough! The hour[i] has come. Look, the Son of Man is betrayed into the hands of sinners. ⁴²Rise! Let us go! Here comes my betrayer!"

⁴³Just as he was speaking, Judas,[j] one of the Twelve, appeared. With him was a crowd armed with swords and clubs, sent from the chief priests, the teachers of the law, and the elders. ⁴⁴Now the betrayer had arranged a signal with them: "The one I kiss is the man; arrest him and lead him away under guard." ⁴⁵Going at once to Jesus, Judas said, "Rabbi!"[k] and kissed him. ⁴⁶The men seized Jesus and arrested him. ⁴⁷Then one of those standing near drew his sword and struck the servant of the high priest, cutting off his ear.

⁴⁸"Am I leading a rebellion," said Jesus, "that you have come out with swords and clubs to capture me? ⁴⁹Every day I was with you, teaching in the temple courts,[l] and you did not arrest me. But the Scriptures must be fulfilled."[m] ⁵⁰Then everyone deserted him and fled.[n]

⁵¹A young man, wearing nothing but a linen garment, was following Jesus. When they seized him, ⁵²he fled naked, leaving his garment behind.

⁵³They took Jesus to the high priest, and all the chief priests, elders and teachers of the law came together. ⁵⁴Peter followed him at a distance, right into the courtyard of the high priest.[o] There he sat with the guards and warmed himself at the fire.[p]

⁵⁵The chief priests and the whole Sanhedrin[q] were looking for evidence against Jesus so that they could put him to death, but they

a 36 Aramaic for *Father*

did not find any. ⁵⁶Many testified falsely against him, but their statements did not agree.

⁵⁷Then some stood up and gave this false testimony against him: ⁵⁸"We heard him say, 'I will destroy this man-made temple and in three days will build another,ᵃ not made by man.'" ⁵⁹Yet even then their testimony did not agree.

⁶⁰Then the high priest stood up before them and asked Jesus, "Are you not going to answer? What is this testimony that these men are bringing against you?" ⁶¹But Jesus remained silent and gave no answer.ᵇ

Again the high priest asked him, "Are you the Christ,ᵃ the Son of the Blessed One?"ᶜ

⁶²"I am," said Jesus. "And you will see the Son of Man sitting at the right hand of the Mighty One and coming on the clouds of heaven."ᵈ

⁶³The high priest tore his clothes.ᵉ "Why do we need any more witnesses?" he asked. ⁶⁴"You have heard the blasphemy. What do you think?"

They all condemned him as worthy of death.ᶠ ⁶⁵Then some began to spit at him; they blindfolded him, struck him with their fists, and said, "Prophesy!" And the guards took him and beat him.ᵍ

⁶⁶While Peter was below in the courtyard,ʰ one of the servant girls of the high priest came by. ⁶⁷When she saw Peter warming himself,ⁱ she looked closely at him.

"You also were with that Nazarene, Jesus,"ʲ she said.

⁶⁸But he denied it. "I don't know or understand what you're talking about,"ᵏ he said, and went out into the entryway.ᵇ

⁶⁹When the servant girl saw him there, she said again to those standing around, "This fellow is one of them." ⁷⁰Again he denied it.ˡ

After a little while, those standing near said to Peter, "Surely you are one of them, for you are a Galilean."ᵐ

⁷¹He began to call down curses on himself, and he swore to them, "I don't know this man you're talking about."ⁿ

⁷²Immediately the rooster crowed the second time.ᶜ Then Peter remembered the word Jesus had spoken to him: "Before the rooster crows twiceᵈ you will disown me three times."ᵒ And he broke down and wept.

Chapter 15 Theme

15 Very early in the morning, the chief priests, with the elders, the teachers of the lawᵖ and the whole Sanhedrin,ᵠ reached

---

a61 Or *Messiah*   b68 Some early manuscripts *entryway and the rooster crowed*   c72 Some early manuscripts do not have *the second time.*   d72 Some early manuscripts do not have *twice.*

14:58
ᵃMk 15:29;
Jn 2:19

14:61
ᵇIsa 53:7;
Mt 27:12,14;
Mk 15:5;
Lk 23:9;
Jn 19:9
ᶜMt 16:16;
Jn 4:25,26

14:62
ᵈRev 1:7

14:63
ᵉLev 10:6;
21:10;
Nu 14:6;
Ac 14:14

14:64
ᶠLev 24:16

14:65
ᵍMt 16:21

14:66
ʰver 54

14:67
ⁱver 54
ʲMk 1:24

14:68
ᵏver 30,72

14:70
ˡver 30,68,72
ᵐAc 2:7

14:71
ⁿver 30,72

14:72
ᵒver 30,68

15:1
ᵖMt 27:1;
Lk 22:66
ᵠMt 5:22

15:1
a Mt 27:2

15:2
b ver 9,12,18,26;
Mt 2:2

15:5
c Mk 14:61

15:9
d ver 2

15:11
e Ac 3:14

15:15
f Isa 53:6

15:16
g Jn 18:28,33;
19:9

15:18
h ver 2

15:20
i Heb 13:12

15:21
j Mt 27:32
k Ro 16:13
l Mt 27:32;
Lk 23:26

15:23
m ver 36;
Ps 69:21;
Pr 31:6

15:24
n Ps 22:18

a decision. They bound Jesus, led him away and handed him over to Pilate.*a*

²"Are you the king of the Jews?"*b* asked Pilate.

"Yes, it is as you say," Jesus replied.

³The chief priests accused him of many things. ⁴So again Pilate asked him, "Aren't you going to answer? See how many things they are accusing you of."

⁵But Jesus still made no reply,*c* and Pilate was amazed.

⁶Now it was the custom at the Feast to release a prisoner whom the people requested. ⁷A man called Barabbas was in prison with the insurrectionists who had committed murder in the uprising. ⁸The crowd came up and asked Pilate to do for them what he usually did.

⁹"Do you want me to release to you the king of the Jews?"*d* asked Pilate, ¹⁰knowing it was out of envy that the chief priests had handed Jesus over to him. ¹¹But the chief priests stirred up the crowd to have Pilate release Barabbas*e* instead.

¹²"What shall I do, then, with the one you call the king of the Jews?" Pilate asked them.

¹³"Crucify him!" they shouted.

¹⁴"Why? What crime has he committed?" asked Pilate.

But they shouted all the louder, "Crucify him!"

¹⁵Wanting to satisfy the crowd, Pilate released Barabbas to them. He had Jesus flogged,*f* and handed him over to be crucified.

¹⁶The soldiers led Jesus away into the palace*g* (that is, the Praetorium) and called together the whole company of soldiers. ¹⁷They put a purple robe on him, then twisted together a crown of thorns and set it on him. ¹⁸And they began to call out to him, "Hail, king of the Jews!"*h* ¹⁹Again and again they struck him on the head with a staff and spit on him. Falling on their knees, they paid homage to him. ²⁰And when they had mocked him, they took off the purple robe and put his own clothes on him. Then they led him out*i* to crucify him.

²¹A certain man from Cyrene,*j* Simon, the father of Alexander and Rufus,*k* was passing by on his way in from the country, and they forced him to carry the cross.*l* ²²They brought Jesus to the place called Golgotha (which means The Place of the Skull). ²³Then they offered him wine mixed with myrrh,*m* but he did not take it. ²⁴And they crucified him. Dividing up his clothes, they cast lots*n* to see what each would get.

Jerusalem of the New Testament

INSIGHT

The palace of the Roman governor (the **Praetorium**) was either a building next to Herod's palace or the Antonia Fortress beside the temple mount complex. See the map above and the illustration of the temple mount on page IISB-40.

^{25}It was the third hour when they crucified him. ^{26}The written notice of the charge against him read: THE KING OF THE JEWS.^{a} ^{27}They crucified two robbers with him, one on his right and one on his left.^{a} ^{29}Those who passed by hurled insults at him, shaking their heads^b and saying, "So! You who are going to destroy the temple and build it in three days,^{c} ^{30}come down from the cross and save yourself!"

^{31}In the same way the chief priests and the teachers of the law mocked him^d among themselves. "He saved others," they said, "but he can't save himself! ^{32}Let this Christ,^{be} this King of Israel,^{f} come down now from the cross, that we may see and believe." Those crucified with him also heaped insults on him.

^{33}At the sixth hour darkness came over the whole land until the ninth hour.^{g} ^{34}And at the ninth hour Jesus cried out in a loud voice, "*Eloi, Eloi, lama sabachthani?*"—which means, "My God, my God, why have you forsaken me?"^{ch}

^{35}When some of those standing near heard this, they said, "Listen, he's calling Elijah."

^{36}One man ran, filled a sponge with wine vinegar,^{i} put it on a stick, and offered it to Jesus to drink. "Now leave him alone. Let's see if Elijah comes to take him down," he said.

^{37}With a loud cry, Jesus breathed his last.^{j}

^{38}The curtain of the temple was torn in two from top to bottom.^{k} ^{39}And when the centurion,^{l} who stood there in front of Jesus, heard his cry and^d saw how he died, he said, "Surely this man was the Son^e of God!"^{m}

^{40}Some women were watching from a distance.^{n} Among them were Mary Magdalene, Mary the mother of James the younger and of Joses, and Salome.^{o} ^{41}In Galilee these women had followed him and cared for his needs. Many other women who had come up with him to Jerusalem were also there.^{p}

^{42}It was Preparation Day (that is, the day before the Sabbath).^{q} So as evening approached, ^{43}Joseph of Arimathea, a prominent member of the Council,^{r} who was himself waiting for the kingdom of God,^{s} went boldly to Pilate and asked for Jesus' body. ^{44}Pilate was surprised to hear that he was already dead. Summoning the centurion, he asked him if Jesus had already died. ^{45}When he learned from the centurion^t that it was so, he gave the body to Joseph. ^{46}So Joseph bought some linen cloth, took down the body, wrapped it in the linen, and placed it in a tomb cut out of rock. Then he rolled a stone against the entrance of the tomb.^{u} ^{47}Mary Magdalene and Mary the mother of Joses^v saw where he was laid.

---

^{a}27 Some manuscripts *left,* ^{28}*and the scripture was fulfilled which says, "He was counted with the lawless ones"* (Isaiah 53:12) ^{b}32 Or *Messiah* ^{c}34 Psalm 22:1 ^{d}39 Some manuscripts do not have *heard his cry and.* ^{e}39 Or *a son*

15:26 ^{a}ver 2

15:29 ^{b}Ps 22:7; 109:25 ^{c}Mk 14:58; Jn 2:19

15:31 ^{d}Ps 22:7

15:32 ^{e}Mk 14:61 ^{f}ver 2

15:33 ^{g}Am 8:9

15:34 ^{h}Ps 22:1

15:36 ^{i}ver 23; Ps 69:21

15:37 ^{j}Jn 19:30

15:38 ^{k}Heb 10:19,20

15:39 ^{l}ver 45 ^{m}Mk 1:1,11; 9:7; Mt 4:3

15:40 ^{n}Ps 38:11 ^{o}Mk 16:1; Lk 24:10; Jn 19:25

15:41 ^{p}Mt 27:55,56; Lk 8:2,3

15:42 ^{q}Mt 27:62; Jn 19:31

15:43 ^{r}Mt 5:22 ^{s}Mt 3:2; Lk 2:25,38

15:45 ^{t}ver 39

15:46 ^{u}Mk 16:3

15:47 ^{v}ver 40

16:1
a Lk 23:56;
Jn 19:39,40

16:3
b Mk 15:46

16:5
c Jn 20:12

16:6
d Mk 1:24

16:7
e Jn 21:1-23
f Mk 14:28

16:9
g Jn 20:11-18

16:11
h ver 13,14;
Lk 24:11

16:12
i Lk 24:13-32

16:14
j Lk 24:36-43

16:15
k Mt 28:18-20;
Lk 24:47,48

16:16
l Jn 3:16,18,36;
Ac 16:31

16:17
m Mk 9:38;
Lk 10:17;
Ac 5:16; 8:7;
16:18; 19:13-16
n Ac 2:4;
10:46; 19:6;
1Co 12:10,
28,30

16:18
o Lk 10:19;
Ac 28:3-5
p Ac 6:6

16:19
q Lk 24:50,51;
Jn 6:62;
Ac 1:9-11
1Ti 3:16
r Ps 110:1;
Ro 8:34;
Col 3:1;
Heb 1:3; 12:2

Chapter 16 Theme _____

16 When the Sabbath was over, Mary Magdalene, Mary the mother of James, and Salome bought spices[a] so that they might go to anoint Jesus' body. [2]Very early on the first day of the week, just after sunrise, they were on their way to the tomb [3]and they asked each other, "Who will roll the stone away from the entrance of the tomb?"[b]

[4]But when they looked up, they saw that the stone, which was very large, had been rolled away. [5]As they entered the tomb, they saw a young man dressed in a white robe[c] sitting on the right side, and they were alarmed.

[6]"Don't be alarmed," he said. "You are looking for Jesus the Nazarene,[d] who was crucified. He has risen! He is not here. See the place where they laid him. [7]But go, tell his disciples and Peter, 'He is going ahead of you into Galilee. There you will see him,[e] just as he told you.'"[f]

[8]Trembling and bewildered, the women went out and fled from the tomb. They said nothing to anyone, because they were afraid.

[The earliest manuscripts and some
other ancient witnesses do not
have Mark 16:9-20.]

[9]When Jesus rose early on the first day of the week, he appeared first to Mary Magdalene,[g] out of whom he had driven seven demons. [10]She went and told those who had been with him and who were mourning and weeping. [11]When they heard that Jesus was alive and that she had seen him, they did not believe it.[h]

[12]Afterward Jesus appeared in a different form to two of them while they were walking in the country.[i] [13]These returned and reported it to the rest; but they did not believe them either.

[14]Later Jesus appeared to the Eleven as they were eating; he rebuked them for their lack of faith and their stubborn refusal to believe those who had seen him after he had risen.[j]

[15]He said to them, "Go into all the world and preach the good news to all creation.[k] [16]Whoever believes and is baptized will be saved, but whoever does not believe will be condemned.[l] [17]And these signs will accompany those who believe: In my name they will drive out demons;[m] they will speak in new tongues;[n] [18]they will pick up snakes[o] with their hands; and when they drink deadly poison, it will not hurt them at all; they will place their hands on[p] sick people, and they will get well."

[19]After the Lord Jesus had spoken to them, he was taken up into heaven[q] and he sat at the right hand of God.[r] [20]Then the disciples went out and preached everywhere, and the Lord worked with them and confirmed his word by the signs that accompanied it.

Theme of Mark:

SEGMENT DIVISIONS

		CHAPTER THEMES
		1
		2
		3
		4
		5
		6
		7
		8
		9
		10
		11
		12
		13
		14
		15
		16

Author:

Date:

Purpose:

Key Words:

immediately, at once, without delay, quickly, as soon as, shortly, just as

authority

kingdom of God

mark every reference to Satan or demons

covenant

LUKE

*I*n Matthew we see Jesus as king of the Jews. In Mark we see the servant who came to give his life a ransom for many. Then Luke takes us consecutively through the days of the Son of Man. In this book we see the fulfillment of the things written about him in the law of Moses, the Prophets, and the Psalms, things which no other Gospel tells us.

❧ THINGS TO DO

1. Luke's purpose in writing is stated in Luke 1:1-4. Read it and then record his purpose on the LUKE AT A GLANCE chart on page 1815.

2. As you read chapter by chapter, be sure to do the following:

   a. Mark in the text the key words listed on LUKE AT A GLANCE.

   b. Mark references to time with a symbol of your choice. The references will come in many different forms, from the mention of actual days or years to the naming of a Jewish feast, a chief priest, or a king. This part of your study will keep before you the timing and sequence of the events in Jesus' life. These are critical to Luke's purpose.

   c. It is also important to note where each event takes place. Underline every reference to places, cities, or regions. Locate these on the map on page 1770. Note in the margin *where* something occurs, along with *when* it occurs.

   d. List in the margin the main points covered in each chapter.

      1) As you list each event in the margin of the text, color code or mark it in a distinctive way so it can be recognized as an event. This will help you see at a glance the chronology of events in Luke. You can also consult the chart on page 1816.

      2) As you note each event or teaching, pay attention to the setting and the response of those who are listening or participating in what is happening. In the margin, note their response. Watch where Jesus is, his relationships to people, what social events he is involved in, and what he expects from people.

   e. If Jesus tells a parable or tells of an incident such as the rich man and Lazarus dying (Luke 16), note what provokes Jesus to do so.

   f. Record the theme of each chapter on the line next to the chapter number and on LUKE AT A GLANCE. Do the same for the theme of the book as you complete the chart.

3. Record the facts concerning Jesus' betrayal, arrest, trial, crucifixion, resurrection, postresurrection appearances, and ascension on the appropriate charts: THE ARREST, TRIAL, AND CRUCIFIXION OF JESUS CHRIST on page 1862 and/or THE ACCOUNT OF JESUS' RESURRECTION on page 1863. Note the chapter and verse for each insight. Do this on notebook paper before you write it in your Bible. After you do this for all four Gospels you will have comprehensive notes on what took place at this time in our Lord's life.

4. On pages 1864, 1865 you will find a chart titled WHAT THE GOSPELS TEACH ABOUT THE KINGDOM OF GOD/THE KINGDOM OF HEAVEN. Record on a piece of paper the information you glean from marking every reference to the *kingdom of God* in Luke. Then consolidate your findings and record them on the chart in your Bible. After you study all the Gospels, you will have an overview of what the Gospels teach about the kingdom of God.

❧ THINGS TO THINK ABOUT

1. Have you been slow of heart to believe all that Moses and the prophets wrote about Jesus Christ? Do you see Jesus as the Son of Man, the fulfillment of prophecy, the Christ, the Son of God? Have you bowed to him as Lord of your life?

2. Jesus reached out to the hurting, the sinners, and the outcasts. He visited in their homes. He was available and accessible. What about you? Do you have compassion on these people? Are you wasting your life on self or are you investing in others? What did you learn from watching Christ's response to others that you can apply to your life?

3. If Jesus needed to withdraw often to a lonely place to pray, what about you? Is prayer a high priority in your life? Do you understand and incorporate the principles of prayer that Jesus taught in the Gospel of Luke?

∿∿∿∿∿

Chapter 1 Theme _____

1 Many have undertaken to draw up an account of the things that have been fulfilled[a] among us, [2]just as they were handed down to us by those who from the first[a] were eyewitnesses[b] and servants of the word.[c] [3]Therefore, since I myself have carefully investigated everything from the beginning, it seemed good also to me to write an orderly account[d] for you, most excellent[e] Theophilus,[f] [4]so that you may know the certainty of the things you have been taught.[g]

[5]In the time of Herod king of Judea[h] there was a priest named Zechariah, who belonged to the priestly division of Abijah;[i] his wife Elizabeth was also a descendant of Aaron. [6]Both of them were upright in the sight of God, observing all the Lord's commandments and regulations blamelessly.[j] [7]But they had no children, because Elizabeth was barren; and they were both well along in years.

[8]Once when Zechariah's division was on duty and he was serving as priest before God,[k] [9]he was chosen by lot, according to the custom of the priesthood, to go into the temple of the Lord and burn incense.[l] [10]And when the time for the burning of incense came, all the assembled worshipers were praying outside.[m]

[11]Then an angel[n] of the Lord appeared to him, standing at the right side of the altar of incense.[o] [12]When Zechariah saw him, he was startled and was gripped with fear.[p] [13]But the angel said to him: "Do not be afraid,[q] Zechariah; your prayer has been heard. Your wife Elizabeth will bear you a son, and you are to give him the name John.[r] [14]He will be a joy and delight to you, and many will rejoice because of his birth,[s] [15]for he will be great in the sight of the Lord. He is never to take wine or other fermented drink,[t] and he will be filled with the Holy Spirit even from birth.[b][u] [16]Many of the

1:2
[a] Mk 1:1;
Jn 15:27;
Ac 1:21,22
[b] Heb 2:3;
1Pe 5:1;
2Pe 1:16;
1Jn 1:1
[c] Mk 4:14
1:3
[d] Ac 11:4
[e] Ac 24:3; 26:25
[f] Ac 1:1
1:4
[g] Jn 20:31
1:5
[h] Mt 2:1
[i] 1Ch 24:10
1:6
[j] Ge 7:1;
1Ki 9:4
1:8
[k] 1Ch 24:19;
2Ch 8:14
1:9
[l] Ex 30:7,8;
1Ch 23:13;
2Ch 29:11
1:10
[m] Lev 16:17
1:11
[n] Ac 5:19
[o] Ex 30:1-10
1:12
[p] Jdg 6:22,23;
13:22
1:13
[q] ver 30;
Mt 14:27
[r] ver 60,63
1:14
[s] ver 58
1:15
[t] Nu 6:3;
Jdg 13:4;
Lk 7:33
[u] Jer 1:5;
Gal 1:15

a 1 Or been surely believed   _b 15 Or from his mother's womb_

1:17
a ver 76
b Mt 11:14
c Mal 4:5,6

1:18
d ver 34;
Ge 17:17

1:19
e ver 26;
Mt 18:10;
Da 8:16; 9:21

1:20
f Eze 3:26

1:22
g ver 62

1:25
h Ge 30:23;
Isa 4:1

1:26
i ver 19
j Mt 2:23

1:27
k Mt 1:16,18,20;
Lk 2:4

1:30
l ver 13;
Mt 14:27

1:31
m Isa 7:14;
Mt 1:21,25;
Lk 2:21

1:32
n ver 35,76;
Mk 5:7

1:33
o Mt 28:18
p Da 2:44;
7:14,27;
Mic 4:7;
Heb 1:8

1:35
q Mt 1:18
r ver 32,76
s Mk 1:24
t Mt 4:3

1:37
u Mt 19:26

people of Israel will he bring back to the Lord their God. ¹⁷And he will go on before the Lord,*a* in the spirit and power of Elijah,*b* to turn the hearts of the fathers to their children*c* and the disobedient to the wisdom of the righteous—to make ready a people prepared for the Lord."

¹⁸Zechariah asked the angel, "How can I be sure of this? I am an old man and my wife is well along in years."*d*

¹⁹The angel answered, "I am Gabriel.*e* I stand in the presence of God, and I have been sent to speak to you and to tell you this good news. ²⁰And now you will be silent and not able to speak*f* until the day this happens, because you did not believe my words, which will come true at their proper time."

²¹Meanwhile, the people were waiting for Zechariah and wondering why he stayed so long in the temple. ²²When he came out, he could not speak to them. They realized he had seen a vision in the temple, for he kept making signs*g* to them but remained unable to speak.

²³When his time of service was completed, he returned home. ²⁴After this his wife Elizabeth became pregnant and for five months remained in seclusion. ²⁵"The Lord has done this for me," she said. "In these days he has shown his favor and taken away my disgrace*h* among the people."

²⁶In the sixth month, God sent the angel Gabriel*i* to Nazareth,*j* a town in Galilee, ²⁷to a virgin pledged to be married to a man named Joseph,*k* a descendant of David. The virgin's name was Mary. ²⁸The angel went to her and said, "Greetings, you who are highly favored! The Lord is with you."

²⁹Mary was greatly troubled at his words and wondered what kind of greeting this might be. ³⁰But the angel said to her, "Do not be afraid,*l* Mary, you have found favor with God. ³¹You will be with child and give birth to a son, and you are to give him the name Jesus.*m* ³²He will be great and will be called the Son of the Most High.*n* The Lord God will give him the throne of his father David, ³³and he will reign over the house of Jacob forever; his kingdom*o* will never end."*p*

³⁴"How will this be," Mary asked the angel, "since I am a virgin?"

³⁵The angel answered, "The Holy Spirit will come upon you,*q* and the power of the Most High*r* will overshadow you. So the holy one*s* to be born will be called*a* the Son of God.*t* ³⁶Even Elizabeth your relative is going to have a child in her old age, and she who was said to be barren is in her sixth month. ³⁷For nothing is impossible with God."*u*

³⁸"I am the Lord's servant," Mary answered. "May it be to me as you have said." Then the angel left her.

a 35 Or *So the child to be born will be called holy,*

³⁹At that time Mary got ready and hurried to a town in the hill country of Judea,[a] ⁴⁰where she entered Zechariah's home and greeted Elizabeth. ⁴¹When Elizabeth heard Mary's greeting, the baby leaped in her womb, and Elizabeth was filled with the Holy Spirit. ⁴²In a loud voice she exclaimed: "Blessed are you among women,[b] and blessed is the child you will bear! ⁴³But why am I so favored, that the mother of my Lord should come to me? ⁴⁴As soon as the sound of your greeting reached my ears, the baby in my womb leaped for joy. ⁴⁵Blessed is she who has believed that what the Lord has said to her will be accomplished!"

⁴⁶And Mary said:

> "My soul glorifies the Lord[c]
> ⁴⁷ and my spirit rejoices in God my Savior,[d]
> ⁴⁸for he has been mindful
> of the humble state of his servant.[e]
> From now on all generations will call me blessed,[f]
> ⁴⁹ for the Mighty One has done great things[g] for me—
> holy is his name.[h]
> ⁵⁰His mercy extends to those who fear him,
> from generation to generation.[i]
> ⁵¹He has performed mighty deeds with his arm;[j]
> he has scattered those who are proud in their
> inmost thoughts.
> ⁵²He has brought down rulers from their thrones
> but has lifted up the humble.
> ⁵³He has filled the hungry with good things[k]
> but has sent the rich away empty.
> ⁵⁴He has helped his servant Israel,
> remembering to be merciful[l]
> ⁵⁵to Abraham and his descendants[m] forever,
> even as he said to our fathers."

⁵⁶Mary stayed with Elizabeth for about three months and then returned home.

⁵⁷When it was time for Elizabeth to have her baby, she gave birth to a son. ⁵⁸Her neighbors and relatives heard that the Lord had shown her great mercy, and they shared her joy.

⁵⁹On the eighth day they came to circumcise[n] the child, and they were going to name him after his father Zechariah, ⁶⁰but his mother spoke up and said, "No! He is to be called John."[o]

⁶¹They said to her, "There is no one among your relatives who has that name."

⁶²Then they made signs[p] to his father, to find out what he would like to name the child. ⁶³He asked for a writing tablet, and to everyone's astonishment he wrote, "His name is John."[q] ⁶⁴Immediately

1:39
[a] ver 65

1:42
[b] Jdg 5:24

1:46
[c] Ps 34:2,3

1:47
[d] 1Ti 1:1; 2:3

1:48
[e] Ps 138:6
[f] Lk 11:27

1:49
[g] Ps 71:19
[h] Ps 111:9

1:50
[i] Ex 20:6;
Ps 103:17

1:51
[j] Ps 98:1;
Isa 40:10

1:53
[k] Ps 107:9

1:54
[l] Ps 98:3

1:55
[m] Ge 17:19;
Ps 132:11;
Gal 3:16

1:59
[n] Ge 17:12;
Lev 12:3;
Lk 2:21;
Php 3:5

1:60
[o] ver 13,63

1:62
[p] ver 22

1:63
[q] ver 13,60

his mouth was opened and his tongue was loosed, and he began to speak,^a praising God. ⁶⁵The neighbors were all filled with awe, and throughout the hill country of Judea^b people were talking about all these things. ⁶⁶Everyone who heard this wondered about it, asking, "What then is this child going to be?" For the Lord's hand was with him.^c

⁶⁷His father Zechariah was filled with the Holy Spirit and prophesied:^d

⁶⁸"Praise be to the Lord, the God of Israel,^e
  because he has come and has redeemed his people.^f
⁶⁹He has raised up a horn^{ag} of salvation for us
  in the house of his servant David^h
⁷⁰(as he said through his holy prophets of long ago),ⁱ
⁷¹salvation from our enemies
  and from the hand of all who hate us—
⁷²to show mercy to our fathers^j
  and to remember his holy covenant,^k
⁷³ the oath he swore to our father Abraham:^l
⁷⁴to rescue us from the hand of our enemies,
  and to enable us to serve him^m without fear
⁷⁵ in holiness and righteousnessⁿ before him all our days.

⁷⁶And you, my child, will be called a prophet^o of the
    Most High;^p
  for you will go on before the Lord to prepare the way
    for him,^q
⁷⁷to give his people the knowledge of salvation
  through the forgiveness of their sins,^r
⁷⁸because of the tender mercy of our God,
  by which the rising sun^s will come to us from heaven
⁷⁹to shine on those living in darkness
  and in the shadow of death,^t
to guide our feet into the path of peace."

⁸⁰And the child grew and became strong in spirit;^u and he lived in the desert until he appeared publicly to Israel.

Chapter 2 Theme

2 In those days Caesar Augustus^v issued a decree that a census should be taken of the entire Roman world.^w ²(This was the first census that took place while Quirinius was governor of Syria.)^x ³And everyone went to his own town to register.

⁴So Joseph also went up from the town of Nazareth in Galilee to Judea, to Bethlehem^y the town of David, because he belonged to

^a69 *Horn* here symbolizes strength.

1763

the house and line of David. [5]He went there to register with Mary, who was pledged to be married to him and was expecting a child. [6]While they were there, the time came for the baby to be born, [7]and she gave birth to her firstborn, a son. She wrapped him in cloths and placed him in a manger, because there was no room for them in the inn.

[8]And there were shepherds living out in the fields nearby, keeping watch over their flocks at night. [9]An angel[a] of the Lord appeared to them, and the glory of the Lord shone around them, and they were terrified. [10]But the angel said to them, "Do not be afraid.[b] I bring you good news of great joy that will be for all the people. [11]Today in the town of David a Savior[c] has been born to you; he is Christ[a][d] the Lord. [12]This will be a sign[e] to you: You will find a baby wrapped in cloths and lying in a manger."

[13]Suddenly a great company of the heavenly host appeared with the angel, praising God and saying,

> [14]"Glory to God in the highest,
>   and on earth peace[f] to men on whom his favor rests."

[15]When the angels had left them and gone into heaven, the shepherds said to one another, "Let's go to Bethlehem and see this thing that has happened, which the Lord has told us about."

[16]So they hurried off and found Mary and Joseph, and the baby, who was lying in the manger. [17]When they had seen him, they spread the word concerning what had been told them about this child, [18]and all who heard it were amazed at what the shepherds said to them. [19]But Mary treasured up all these things and pondered them in her heart.[g] [20]The shepherds returned, glorifying and praising God[h] for all the things they had heard and seen, which were just as they had been told.

[21]On the eighth day, when it was time to circumcise him,[i] he was named Jesus, the name the angel had given him before he had been conceived.[j]

[22]When the time of their purification according to the Law of Moses[k] had been completed, Joseph and Mary took him to Jerusalem to present him to the Lord [23](as it is written in the Law of the Lord, "Every firstborn male is to be consecrated to the Lord"[b]),[l] [24]and to offer a sacrifice in keeping with what is said in the Law of the Lord: "a pair of doves or two young pigeons."[c][m]

[25]Now there was a man in Jerusalem called Simeon, who was righteous and devout.[n] He was waiting for the consolation of Israel,[o] and the Holy Spirit was upon him. [26]It had been revealed to him by the Holy Spirit that he would not die before he had seen the

2:9
[a]Lk 1:11;
Ac 5:19

2:10
[b]Mt 14:27

2:11
[c]Mt 1:21;
Jn 4:42;
Ac 5:31;
[d]Mt 1:16;
16:16,20;
Jn 11:27;
Ac 2:36

2:12
[e]1Sa 2:34;
2Ki 19:29;
Isa 7:14

2:14
[f]Lk 1:79;
Ro 5:1;
Eph 2:14,17

2:19
[g]ver 51

2:20
[h]Mt 9:8

2:21
[i]Lk 1:59
[j]Lk 1:31

2:22
[k]Lev 12:2-8

2:23
[l]Ex 13:2,12,15;
Nu 3:13

2:24
[m]Lev 12:8

2:25
[n]Lk 1:6
[o]ver 38;
Isa 52:9;
Lk 23:51

---

[a] 11 Or *Messiah.* "The Christ" (Greek) and "the Messiah" (Hebrew) both mean "the Anointed One"; also in verse 26.   [b] 23 Exodus 13:2,12   [c] 24 Lev. 12:8

Lord's Christ. ²⁷Moved by the Spirit, he went into the temple courts. When the parents brought in the child Jesus to do for him what the custom of the Law required,^a ²⁸Simeon took him in his arms and praised God, saying:

²⁹"Sovereign Lord, as you have promised,^b
  you now dismiss^a your servant in peace.^c
³⁰For my eyes have seen your salvation,^d
³¹ which you have prepared in the sight of all people,
³²a light for revelation to the Gentiles
  and for glory to your people Israel."^e

³³The child's father and mother marveled at what was said about him. ³⁴Then Simeon blessed them and said to Mary, his mother:^f "This child is destined to cause the falling^g and rising of many in Israel, and to be a sign that will be spoken against, ³⁵so that the thoughts of many hearts will be revealed. And a sword will pierce your own soul too."

³⁶There was also a prophetess,^h Anna, the daughter of Phanuel, of the tribe of Asher. She was very old; she had lived with her husband seven years after her marriage, ³⁷and then was a widow until she was eighty-four.^{bi} She never left the temple but worshiped night and day, fasting and praying.^j ³⁸Coming up to them at that very moment, she gave thanks to God and spoke about the child to all who were looking forward to the redemption of Jerusalem.^k

³⁹When Joseph and Mary had done everything required by the Law of the Lord, they returned to Galilee to their own town of Nazareth.^l ⁴⁰And the child grew and became strong; he was filled with wisdom, and the grace of God was upon him.^m

⁴¹Every year his parents went to Jerusalem for the Feast of the Passover.ⁿ ⁴²When he was twelve years old, they went up to the Feast, according to the custom. ⁴³After the Feast was over, while his parents were returning home, the boy Jesus stayed behind in Jerusalem, but they were unaware of it. ⁴⁴Thinking he was in their company, they traveled on for a day. Then they began looking for him among their relatives and friends. ⁴⁵When they did not find him, they went back to Jerusalem to look for him. ⁴⁶After three days they found him in the temple courts, sitting among the teachers, listening to them and asking them questions. ⁴⁷Everyone who heard him was amazed^o at his understanding and his answers. ⁴⁸When his parents saw him, they were astonished. His mother^p said to him, "Son, why have you treated us like this? Your father^q and I have been anxiously searching for you."

^a29 Or promised, / now dismiss ^b37 Or widow for eighty-four years

Cross references:
2:27 a ver 22
2:29 b ver 26; c Ac 2:24
2:30 d Isa 52:10; Lk 3:6
2:32 e Isa 42:6; 49:6; Ac 13:47; 26:23
2:34 f Mt 12:46; g Isa 8:14; Mt 21:44; 1Co 1:23; 2Co 2:16; 1Pe 2:7,8
2:36 h Ac 21:9
2:37 i 1Ti 5:9; j Ac 13:3; 14:23; 1Ti 5:5
2:38 k ver 25; Isa 40:2; Lk 1:68; 24:21
2:39 l ver 51; Mt 2:23
2:40 m ver 52; Lk 1:80
2:41 n Ex 23:15; Dt 16:1-8
2:47 o Mt 7:28
2:48 p Mt 12:46; q Lk 3:23; 4:22

Herod's Family Tree

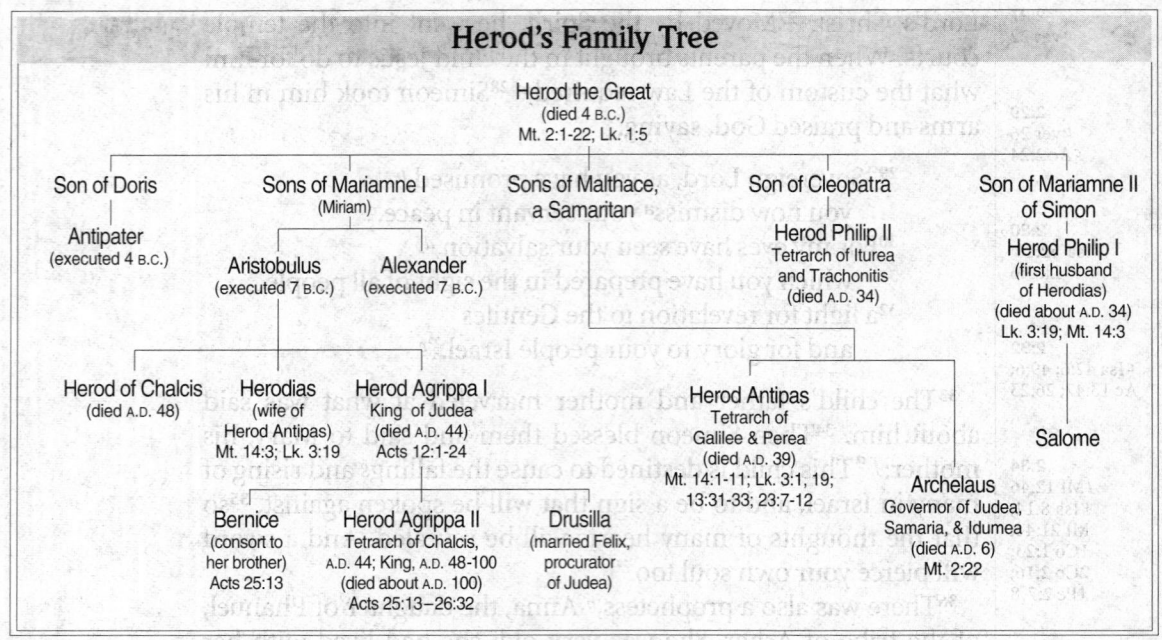

Herod the Great
(died 4 B.C.)
Mt. 2:1-22; Lk. 1:5

Son of Doris

Antipater
(executed 4 B.C.)

Sons of Mariamne I
(Miriam)

Aristobulus
(executed 7 B.C.)

Alexander
(executed 7 B.C.)

Herod of Chalcis
(died A.D. 48)

Herodias
(wife of
Herod Antipas)
Mt. 14:3; Lk. 3:19

Herod Agrippa I
King of Judea
(died A.D. 44)
Acts 12:1-24

Bernice
(consort to
her brother)
Acts 25:13

Herod Agrippa II
Tetrarch of Chalcis,
A.D. 44; King, A.D. 48-100
(died about A.D. 100)
Acts 25:13–26:32

Drusilla
(married Felix,
procurator
of Judea)

**Sons of Malthace,
a Samaritan**

Herod Antipas
Tetrarch of
Galilee & Perea
(died A.D. 39)
Mt. 14:1-11; Lk. 3:1, 19;
13:31-33; 23:7-12

Archelaus
Governor of Judea,
Samaria, & Idumea
(died A.D. 6)
Mt. 2:22

Son of Cleopatra

Herod Philip II
Tetrarch of Iturea
and Trachonitis
(died A.D. 34)

**Son of Mariamne II
of Simon**

Herod Philip I
(first husband
of Herodias)
(died about A.D. 34)
Lk. 3:19; Mt. 14:3

Salome

---

⁴⁹"Why were you searching for me?" he asked. "Didn't you know I had to be in my Father's house?"ᵃ ⁵⁰But they did not understand what he was saying to them.ᵇ

⁵¹Then he went down to Nazareth with themᶜ and was obedient to them. But his mother treasured all these things in her heart.ᵈ ⁵²And Jesus grew in wisdom and stature, and in favor with God and men.ᵉ

Chapter 3 Theme

3 In the fifteenth year of the reign of Tiberius Caesar—when Pontius Pilateᶠ was governor of Judea, Herodᵍ tetrarch of Galilee, his brother Philip tetrarch of Iturea and Traconitis, and Lysanias tetrarch of Abilene— ²during the high priesthood of Annas and Caiaphas,ʰ the word of God came to Johnⁱ son of Zechariahʲ in the desert. ³He went into all the country around the Jordan, preaching a baptism of repentance for the forgiveness of sins.ᵏ ⁴As is written in the book of the words of Isaiah the prophet:

"A voice of one calling in the desert,
'Prepare the way for the Lord,
    make straight paths for him.
⁵Every valley shall be filled in,
    every mountain and hill made low.
The crooked roads shall become straight,
    the rough ways smooth.
⁶And all mankind will see God's salvation.'"ᵃˡ

ᵃ6 Isaiah 40:3-5

2:49
ᵃ Jn 2:16

2:50
ᵇ Mk 9:32

2:51
ᶜ ver 39; Mt 2:23
ᵈ ver 19

2:52
ᵉ ver 40;
1Sa 2:26;
Lk 1:80

3:1
ᶠ Mt 27:2
ᵍ Mt 14:1

3:2
ʰ Mt 26:3;
Jn 18:13;
Ac 4:6
ⁱ Mt 3:1
ʲ Lk 1:13

3:3
ᵏ ver 16;
Mk 1:4

3:6
ˡ Isa 40:3-5;
Ps 98:2;
Isa 42:16; 52:10;
Lk 2:30

3:7
a Mt 12:34;
23:33
b Ro 1:18

3:8
c Isa 51:2;
Lk 19:9;
Jn 8:33,39;
Ac 13:26;
Ro 4:1,11,12,16,
17; Gal 3:7

3:9
d Mt 3:10

3:10
e ver 12,14;
Ac 2:37; 16:30

3:11
f Isa 58:7

3:12
g Lk 7:29

3:13
h Lk 19:8

3:14
i Ex 23:1;
Lev 19:11

3:15
j Mt 3:1
k Jn 1:19,20;
Ac 13:25

3:16
l ver 3; Mk 1:4
m Jn 1:26,33;
Ac 1:5; 11:16;
19:4

3:17
n Isa 30:24
o Mt 13:30;
25:41

3:19
p ver 1

3:20
q Mt 14:3,4;
Mk 6:17-18

⁷John said to the crowds coming out to be baptized by him, "You brood of vipers!ᵃ Who warned you to flee from the coming wrath?ᵇ ⁸Produce fruit in keeping with repentance. And do not begin to say to yourselves, 'We have Abraham as our father.'ᶜ For I tell you that out of these stones God can raise up children for Abraham. ⁹The ax is already at the root of the trees, and every tree that does not produce good fruit will be cut down and thrown into the fire."ᵈ

¹⁰"What should we do then?"ᵉ the crowd asked.

¹¹John answered, "The man with two tunics should share with him who has none, and the one who has food should do the same."ᶠ

¹²Tax collectors also came to be baptized.ᵍ "Teacher," they asked, "what should we do?"

¹³"Don't collect any more than you are required to,"ʰ he told them.

¹⁴Then some soldiers asked him, "And what should we do?"

He replied, "Don't extort money and don't accuse people falselyⁱ—be content with your pay."

¹⁵The people were waiting expectantly and were all wondering in their hearts if Johnʲ might possibly be the Christ.ᵃᵏ ¹⁶John answered them all, "I baptize you withᵇ water.ˡ But one more powerful than I will come, the thongs of whose sandals I am not worthy to untie. He will baptize you with the Holy Spirit and with fire.ᵐ ¹⁷His winnowing forkⁿ is in his hand to clear his threshing floor and to gather the wheat into his barn, but he will burn up the chaff with unquenchable fire."ᵒ ¹⁸And with many other words John exhorted the people and preached the good news to them.

¹⁹But when John rebuked Herodᵖ the tetrarch because of Herodias, his brother's wife, and all the other evil things he had done, ²⁰Herod added this to them all: He locked John up in prison.�q

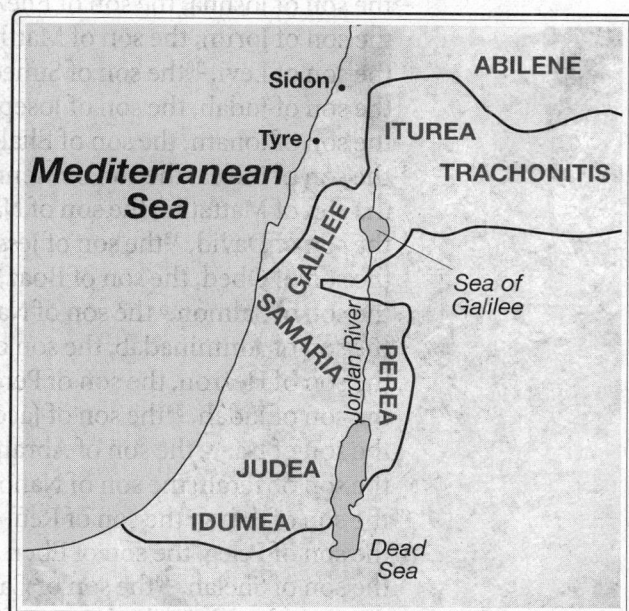

The Region of the Tetrarchs

a 15 Or Messiah   b 16 Or in

INSIGHT

See **The Genealogy of Jesus the Christ** on page 1665.

²¹When all the people were being baptized, Jesus was baptized too. And as he was praying,ᵃ heaven was opened ²²and the Holy Spirit descended on himᵇ in bodily form like a dove. And a voice came from heaven: "You are my Son,ᶜ whom I love; with you I am well pleased."ᵈ

²³Now Jesus himself was about thirty years old when he began his ministry.ᵉ He was the son, so it was thought, of Joseph,ᶠ

the son of Heli, ²⁴the son of Matthat,
the son of Levi, the son of Melki,
the son of Jannai, the son of Joseph,
²⁵the son of Mattathias, the son of Amos,
the son of Nahum, the son of Esli,
the son of Naggai, ²⁶the son of Maath,
the son of Mattathias, the son of Semein,
the son of Josech, the son of Joda,
²⁷the son of Joanan, the son of Rhesa,
the son of Zerubbabel,ᵍ the son of Shealtiel,
the son of Neri, ²⁸the son of Melki,
the son of Addi, the son of Cosam,
the son of Elmadam, the son of Er,
²⁹the son of Joshua, the son of Eliezer,
the son of Jorim, the son of Matthat,
the son of Levi, ³⁰the son of Simeon,
the son of Judah, the son of Joseph,
the son of Jonam, the son of Eliakim,
³¹the son of Melea, the son of Menna,
the son of Mattatha, the son of Nathan,ʰ
the son of David, ³²the son of Jesse,
the son of Obed, the son of Boaz,
the son of Salmon,ᵃ the son of Nahshon,
³³the son of Amminadab, the son of Ram,ᵇ
the son of Hezron, the son of Perez,ⁱ
the son of Judah, ³⁴the son of Jacob,
the son of Isaac, the son of Abraham,
the son of Terah, the son of Nahor,ʲ
³⁵the son of Serug, the son of Reu,
the son of Peleg, the son of Eber,
the son of Shelah, ³⁶the son of Cainan,
the son of Arphaxad,ᵏ the son of Shem,
the son of Noah, the son of Lamech,ˡ
³⁷the son of Methuselah, the son of Enoch,
the son of Jared, the son of Mahalalel,

ᵃ 32 Some early manuscripts *Sala*   ᵇ 33 Some manuscripts *Amminadab, the son of Admin, the son of Arni*; other manuscripts vary widely.

3:21 ᵃMt 14:23; Mk 1:35; 6:46; Lk 5:16; 6:12; 9:18,28; 11:1

3:22 ᵇIsa 42:1; Jn 1:32,33; Ac 10:38 ᶜMt 3:17 ᵈMt 3:17

3:23 ᵉMt 4:17; Ac 1:1 ᶠLk 1:27

3:27 ᵍMt 1:12

3:31 ʰ2Sa 5:14; 1Ch 3:5

3:33 ⁱRu 4:18-22; 1Ch 2:10-12

3:34 ʲGe 11:24,26

3:36 ᵏGe 11:12 ˡGe 5:28-32

the son of Kenan, [38]the son of Enosh,
the son of Seth, the son of Adam,
the son of God.[a]

Chapter 4 Theme _____

4 Jesus, full of the Holy Spirit,[b] returned from the Jordan[c] and was led by the Spirit[d] in the desert, [2]where for forty days[e] he was tempted by the devil. He ate nothing during those days, and at the end of them he was hungry.

[3]The devil said to him, "If you are the Son of God, tell this stone to become bread."

[4]Jesus answered, "It is written: 'Man does not live on bread alone.'[a]"[f]

[5]The devil led him up to a high place and showed him in an instant all the kingdoms of the world.[g] [6]And he said to him, "I will give you all their authority and splendor, for it has been given to me,[h] and I can give it to anyone I want to. [7]So if you worship me, it will all be yours."

[8]Jesus answered, "It is written: 'Worship the Lord your God and serve him only.'[b]"[i]

[9]The devil led him to Jerusalem and had him stand on the highest point of the temple. "If you are the Son of God," he said, "throw yourself down from here. [10]For it is written:

"'He will command his angels concerning you
        to guard you carefully;
[11]they will lift you up in their hands,
        so that you will not strike your foot against a stone.'[c]"[j]

[12]Jesus answered, "It says: 'Do not put the Lord your God to the test.'[d]"[k]

[13]When the devil had finished all this tempting,[l] he left him[m] until an opportune time.

[14]Jesus returned to Galilee[n] in the power of the Spirit, and news about him spread through the whole countryside.[o] [15]He taught in their synagogues,[p] and everyone praised him.

[16]He went to Nazareth,[q] where he had been brought up, and on the Sabbath day he went into the synagogue,[r] as was his custom. And he stood up to read. [17]The scroll of the prophet Isaiah was handed to him. Unrolling it, he found the place where it is written:

[18]"The Spirit of the Lord is on me,[s]
        because he has anointed me
        to preach good news to the poor.

3:38
[a] Ge 5:1,2,6-9

4:1
[b] ver 14,18
[c] Lk 3:3,21
[d] Lk 2:27

4:2
[e] Ex 34:28;
1Ki 19:8

4:4
[f] Dt 8:3

4:5
[g] Mt 24:14

4:6
[h] Jn 12:31;
14:30; 1Jn 5:19

4:8
[i] Dt 6:13

4:11
[j] Ps 91:11,12

4:12
[k] Dt 6:16

4:13
[l] Heb 4:15
[m] Jn 14:30

4:14
[n] Mt 4:12
[o] Mt 9:26

4:15
[p] Mt 4:23

4:16
[q] Mt 2:23
[r] Mt 13:54

4:18
[s] Jn 3:34

[a]4 Deut. 8:3   [b]8 Deut. 6:13   [c]11 Psalm 91:11,12   [d]12 Deut. 6:16

He has sent me to proclaim freedom for the prisoners
  and recovery of sight for the blind,
to release the oppressed,
19 to proclaim the year of the Lord's favor."ᵃᵃ

²⁰Then he rolled up the scroll, gave it back to the attendant and sat down.ᵇ The eyes of everyone in the synagogue were fastened on him, ²¹and he began by saying to them, "Today this scripture is fulfilled in your hearing."

²²All spoke well of him and were amazed at the gracious words that came from his lips. "Isn't this Joseph's son?" they asked.ᶜ

²³Jesus said to them, "Surely you will quote this proverb to me: 'Physician, heal yourself! Do here in your hometownᵈ what we have heard that you did in Capernaum.'"ᵉ

²⁴"I tell you the truth," he continued, "no prophet is accepted in his hometown.ᶠ ²⁵I assure you that there were many widows in Israel in Elijah's time, when the sky was shut for three and a half years and there was a severe famine throughout the land.ᵍ ²⁶Yet Elijah was not sent to any of them, but to a widow in Zarephath in the region of Sidon.ʰ ²⁷And there were many in Israel with leprosyᵇ in the time of Elisha the prophet, yet not one of them was cleansed—only Naaman the Syrian."ⁱ

²⁸All the people in the synagogue were furious when they heard this. ²⁹They got up, drove him out of the town,ʲ and took him to the brow of the hill on which the town was built, in order to throw him down the cliff. ³⁰But he walked right through the crowd and went on his way.ᵏ

³¹Then he went down to Capernaum,ˡ a town in Galilee, and on the Sabbath began to teach the people. ³²They were amazed at his teaching,ᵐ because his message had authority.ⁿ

³³In the synagogue there was a man possessed by a demon, an evilᶜ spirit. He cried out at the top of his voice, ³⁴"Ha! What do you want with us,ᵒ Jesus of Nazareth?ᵖ Have you come to destroy us? I know who you areq—the Holy One of God!"ʳ

³⁵"Be quiet!" Jesus said sternly.ˢ "Come out of him!" Then the demon threw the man down before them all and came out without injuring him.

³⁶All the people were amazedᵗ and said to each other, "What is this teaching? With authorityᵘ and power he gives orders to evil spirits and they come out!" ³⁷And the news about him spread throughout the surrounding area.ᵛ

4:19 ᵃIsa 61:1,2; Lev 25:10
4:20 ᵇver 17; Mt 26:55
4:22 ᶜMt 13:54,55; Jn 6:42; 7:15
4:23 ᵈver 16 ᵉMk 1:21-28; 2:1-12
4:24 ᶠMt 13:57; Jn 4:44
4:25 ᵍ1Ki 17:1; 18:1; Jas 5:17,18
4:26 ʰ1Ki 17:8-16; Mt 11:21
4:27 ⁱ2Ki 5:1-14
4:29 ʲNu 15:35; Ac 7:58; Heb 13:12
4:30 ᵏJn 8:59; 10:39
4:31 ˡver 23; Mt 4:13
4:32 ᵐMt 7:28 ⁿver 36; Mt 7:29
4:34 ᵒMt 8:29 ᵖMk 1:24 qJas 2:19 ʳver 41; Mk 1:24
4:35 ˢver 39,41; Mt 8:26; Lk 8:24
4:36 ᵗMt 7:28 ᵘver 32; Mt 7:29; Mt 10:1
4:37 ᵛver 14; Mt 9:26

Israel in the Time of Christ

ᵃ19 Isaiah 61:1,2 ᵇ27 The Greek word was used for various diseases affecting the skin—not necessarily leprosy. ᶜ33 Greek *unclean*; also in verse 36

4:39
a ver 35,41

[38]Jesus left the synagogue and went to the home of Simon. Now Simon's mother-in-law was suffering from a high fever, and they asked Jesus to help her. [39]So he bent over her and rebuked[a] the fever, and it left her. She got up at once and began to wait on them.

4:40
b Mk 5:23
c Mt 4:23

[40]When the sun was setting, the people brought to Jesus all who had various kinds of sickness, and laying his hands on each one,[b] he healed them.[c] [41]Moreover, demons came out of many people, shouting, "You are the Son of God!"[d] But he rebuked[e] them and would not allow them to speak,[f] because they knew he was the Christ.[a]

4:41
d Mt 4:3
e ver 35
f Mt 8:4

[42]At daybreak Jesus went out to a solitary place. The people were looking for him and when they came to where he was, they tried to keep him from leaving them. [43]But he said, "I must preach the good news of the kingdom of God[g] to the other towns also, because that is why I was sent." [44]And he kept on preaching in the synagogues of Judea.[b][h]

4:43
g Mt 3:2

4:44
h Mt 4:23

Chapter 5 Theme

5:1
i Mk 4:14;
Heb 4:12

5 One day as Jesus was standing by the Lake of Gennesaret,[c] with the people crowding around him and listening to the word of God,[i] [2]he saw at the water's edge two boats, left there by the fishermen, who were washing their nets. [3]He got into one of the boats, the one belonging to Simon, and asked him to put out a little from shore. Then he sat down and taught the people from the boat.[j]

5:3
j Mt 13:2

5:4
k Jn 21:6

[4]When he had finished speaking, he said to Simon, "Put out into deep water, and let down[d] the nets for a catch."[k]

5:5
l Lk 8:24,45;
9:33,49; 17:13
m Jn 21:3

[5]Simon answered, "Master,[l] we've worked hard all night and haven't caught anything.[m] But because you say so, I will let down the nets."

5:6
n Jn 21:11

[6]When they had done so, they caught such a large number of fish that their nets began to break.[n] [7]So they signaled their partners in the other boat to come and help them, and they came and filled both boats so full that they began to sink.

5:8
o Ge 18:27;
Job 42:6;
Isa 6:5

[8]When Simon Peter saw this, he fell at Jesus' knees and said, "Go away from me, Lord; I am a sinful man!"[o] [9]For he and all his companions were astonished at the catch of fish they had taken, [10]and so were James and John, the sons of Zebedee, Simon's partners.

5:10
p Mt 14:27

Then Jesus said to Simon, "Don't be afraid;[p] from now on you will catch men." [11]So they pulled their boats up on shore, left everything and followed him.[q]

5:11
q ver 28;
Mt 4:19

[12]While Jesus was in one of the towns, a man came along who was covered with leprosy.[e][r] When he saw Jesus, he fell with his face

5:12
r Mt 8:2

a 41 Or *Messiah*   *b 44* Or *the land of the Jews*; some manuscripts *Galilee*   *c 1* That is, Sea of Galilee   *d 4* The Greek verb is plural.   *e 12* The Greek word was used for various diseases affecting the skin—not necessarily leprosy.

to the ground and begged him, "Lord, if you are willing, you can make me clean."

¹³Jesus reached out his hand and touched the man. "I am willing," he said. "Be clean!" And immediately the leprosy left him.

¹⁴Then Jesus ordered him, "Don't tell anyone,ᵃ but go, show yourself to the priest and offer the sacrifices that Moses commandedᵇ for your cleansing, as a testimony to them."

¹⁵Yet the news about him spread all the more,ᶜ so that crowds of people came to hear him and to be healed of their sicknesses. ¹⁶But Jesus often withdrew to lonely places and prayed.ᵈ

¹⁷One day as he was teaching, Pharisees and teachers of the law,ᵉ who had come from every village of Galilee and from Judea and Jerusalem, were sitting there. And the power of the Lord was present for him to heal the sick.ᶠ ¹⁸Some men came carrying a paralytic on a mat and tried to take him into the house to lay him before Jesus. ¹⁹When they could not find a way to do this because of the crowd, they went up on the roof and lowered him on his mat through the tiles into the middle of the crowd, right in front of Jesus.

²⁰When Jesus saw their faith, he said, "Friend, your sins are forgiven."ᵍ

²¹The Pharisees and the teachers of the law began thinking to themselves, "Who is this fellow who speaks blasphemy? Who can forgive sins but God alone?"ʰ

²²Jesus knew what they were thinking and asked, "Why are you thinking these things in your hearts? ²³Which is easier: to say, 'Your sins are forgiven,' or to say, 'Get up and walk'? ²⁴But that you may know that the Son of Manⁱ has authority on earth to forgive sins. . . ." He said to the paralyzed man, "I tell you, get up, take your mat and go home." ²⁵Immediately he stood up in front of them, took what he had been lying on and went home praising God. ²⁶Everyone was amazed and gave praise to God.ʲ They were filled with awe and said, "We have seen remarkable things today."

²⁷After this, Jesus went out and saw a tax collector by the name of Levi sitting at his tax booth. "Follow me,"ᵏ Jesus said to him, ²⁸and Levi got up, left everything and followed him.ˡ

²⁹Then Levi held a great banquet for Jesus at his house, and a large crowd of tax collectorsᵐ and others were eating with them. ³⁰But the Pharisees and the teachers of the law who belonged to their sectⁿ complained to his disciples, "Why do you eat and drink with tax collectors and 'sinners'?"ᵒ

³¹Jesus answered them, "It is not the healthy who need a doctor, but the sick. ³²I have not come to call the righteous, but sinners to repentance."ᵖ

5:14 ᵃMt 8:4; ᵇLev 14:2-32

5:15 ᶜMt 9:26

5:16 ᵈMt 14:23; Lk 3:21

5:17 ᵉMt 15:1; Lk 2:46; ᶠMk 5:30; Lk 6:19

5:20 ᵍLk 7:48,49

5:21 ʰIsa 43:25

5:24 ⁱMt 8:20

5:26 ʲMt 9:8

5:27 ᵏMt 4:19

5:28 ˡver 11; Mt 4:19

5:29 ᵐLk 15:1

5:30 ⁿAc 23:9; ᵒMt 9:11

5:32 ᵖJn 3:17

5:33
a Lk 7:18;
Jn 1:35; 3:25,26

5:34
b Jn 3:29

5:35
c Lk 9:22; 17:22;
Jn 16:5-7

6:1
d Dt 23:25

6:2
e Mt 12:2

6:3
f 1Sa 21:6

6:4
g Lev 24:5,9

6:5
h Mt 8:20

6:6
i ver 1

6:7
j Mt 12:10
k Mt 12:2

6:8
l Mt 9:4

6:11
m Jn 5:18

6:12
n Lk 3:21

6:13
o Mk 6:30

6:15
p Mt 9:9

³³They said to him, "John's disciples*a* often fast and pray, and so do the disciples of the Pharisees, but yours go on eating and drinking."

³⁴Jesus answered, "Can you make the guests of the bridegroom*b* fast while he is with them? ³⁵But the time will come when the bridegroom will be taken from them;*c* in those days they will fast."

³⁶He told them this parable: "No one tears a patch from a new garment and sews it on an old one. If he does, he will have torn the new garment, and the patch from the new will not match the old. ³⁷And no one pours new wine into old wineskins. If he does, the new wine will burst the skins, the wine will run out and the wineskins will be ruined. ³⁸No, new wine must be poured into new wineskins. ³⁹And no one after drinking old wine wants the new, for he says, 'The old is better.'"

Chapter 6 Theme

6 One Sabbath Jesus was going through the grainfields, and his disciples began to pick some heads of grain, rub them in their hands and eat the kernels.*d* ²Some of the Pharisees asked, "Why are you doing what is unlawful on the Sabbath?"*e*

³Jesus answered them, "Have you never read what David did when he and his companions were hungry?*f* ⁴He entered the house of God, and taking the consecrated bread, he ate what is lawful only for priests to eat.*g* And he also gave some to his companions." ⁵Then Jesus said to them, "The Son of Man*h* is Lord of the Sabbath."

⁶On another Sabbath*i* he went into the synagogue and was teaching, and a man was there whose right hand was shriveled. ⁷The Pharisees and the teachers of the law were looking for a reason to accuse Jesus, so they watched him closely*j* to see if he would heal on the Sabbath.*k* ⁸But Jesus knew what they were thinking*l* and said to the man with the shriveled hand, "Get up and stand in front of everyone." So he got up and stood there.

⁹Then Jesus said to them, "I ask you, which is lawful on the Sabbath: to do good or to do evil, to save life or to destroy it?"

¹⁰He looked around at them all, and then said to the man, "Stretch out your hand." He did so, and his hand was completely restored. ¹¹But they were furious*m* and began to discuss with one another what they might do to Jesus.

¹²One of those days Jesus went out to a mountainside to pray, and spent the night praying to God.*n* ¹³When morning came, he called his disciples to him and chose twelve of them, whom he also designated apostles:*o* ¹⁴Simon (whom he named Peter), his brother Andrew, James, John, Philip, Bartholomew, ¹⁵Matthew,*p* Thomas,

James son of Alphaeus, Simon who was called the Zealot, ¹⁶Judas son of James, and Judas Iscariot, who became a traitor.

¹⁷He went down with them and stood on a level place. A large crowd of his disciples was there and a great number of people from all over Judea, from Jerusalem, and from the coast of Tyre and Sidon,^a ¹⁸who had come to hear him and to be healed of their diseases. Those troubled by evil^a spirits were cured, ¹⁹and the people all tried to touch him,^b because power was coming from him and healing them all.^c

²⁰Looking at his disciples, he said:

"Blessed are you who are poor,
for yours is the kingdom of God.^d
²¹Blessed are you who hunger now,
for you will be satisfied.^e
Blessed are you who weep now,
for you will laugh.^f
²²Blessed are you when men hate you,
when they exclude you^g and insult you^h
and reject your name as evil,
because of the Son of Man.ⁱ

²³"Rejoice in that day and leap for joy,^j because great is your reward in heaven. For that is how their fathers treated the prophets.^k

²⁴"But woe to you who are rich,^l
for you have already received your comfort.^m
²⁵Woe to you who are well fed now,
for you will go hungry.ⁿ
Woe to you who laugh now,
for you will mourn and weep.^o
²⁶Woe to you when all men speak well of you,
for that is how their fathers treated the false prophets.^p

²⁷"But I tell you who hear me: Love your enemies, do good to those who hate you,^q ²⁸bless those who curse you, pray for those who mistreat you.^r ²⁹If someone strikes you on one cheek, turn to him the other also. If someone takes your cloak, do not stop him from taking your tunic. ³⁰Give to everyone who asks you, and if anyone takes what belongs to you, do not demand it back.^s ³¹Do to others as you would have them do to you.^t

³²"If you love those who love you, what credit is that to you?^u Even 'sinners' love those who love them. ³³And if you do good to those who are good to you, what credit is that to you? Even 'sinners' do that. ³⁴And if you lend to those from whom you expect repayment, what credit is that to you?^v Even 'sinners' lend to 'sinners,' expecting to be repaid in full. ³⁵But love your enemies, do

a 18 Greek unclean

6:17
^aMt 4:25;
Mt 11:21;
Mk 3:7,8

6:19
^bMt 9:20
^cMt 14:36;
Mk 5:30;
Lk 5:17

6:20
^dMt 25:34

6:21
^eIsa 55:1,2;
Mt 5:6
^fIsa 61:2,3;
Mt 5:4; Rev 7:17

6:22
^gJn 9:22; 16:2
^hIsa 51:7
ⁱJn 15:21

6:23
^jMt 5:12
^kMt 5:12

6:24
^lJas 5:1
^mLk 16:25

6:25
ⁿIsa 65:13
^oPr 14:13

6:26
^pMt 7:15

6:27
^qver 35;
Mt 5:44;
Ro 12:20

6:28
^rMt 5:44

6:30
^sDt 15:7,8,10;
Pr 21:26

6:31
^tMt 7:12

6:32
^uMt 5:46

6:34
^vMt 5:42

6:35
a ver 27
b Ro 8:14
c Mk 5:7

good to them,a and lend to them without expecting to get anything back. Then your reward will be great, and you will be sonsb of the Most High,c because he is kind to the ungrateful and wicked. 36Be merciful,d just as your Fathere is merciful.

6:36
d Jas 2:13
e Mt 5:48; 6:1;
Lk 11:2; 12:32;
Ro 8:15;
Eph 4:6;
1Pe 1:17;
1Jn 1:3; 3:1

37"Do not judge, and you will not be judged.f Do not condemn, and you will not be condemned. Forgive, and you will be forgiven.g 38Give, and it will be given to you. A good measure, pressed down, shaken together and running over, will be poured into your lap.h For with the measure you use, it will be measured to you."i

6:37
f Mt 7:1
g Mt 6:14

39He also told them this parable: "Can a blind man lead a blind man? Will they not both fall into a pit?j 40A student is not above his teacher, but everyone who is fully trained will be like his teacher.k

41"Why do you look at the speck of sawdust in your brother's eye and pay no attention to the plank in your own eye? 42How can you say to your brother, 'Brother, let me take the speck out of your eye,' when you yourself fail to see the plank in your own eye? You hypocrite, first take the plank out of your eye, and then you will see clearly to remove the speck from your brother's eye.

6:38
h Ps 79:12;
Isa 65:6,7
i Mt 7:2;
Mk 4:24

43"No good tree bears bad fruit, nor does a bad tree bear good fruit. 44Each tree is recognized by its own fruit.l People do not pick figs from thornbushes, or grapes from briers. 45The good man brings good things out of the good stored up in his heart, and the evil man brings evil things out of the evil stored up in his heart. For out of the overflow of his heart his mouth speaks.m

6:39
j Mt 15:14

6:40
k Mt 10:24;
Jn 13:16

46"Why do you call me, 'Lord, Lord,'n and do not do what I say?o 47I will show you what he is like who comes to me and hears my words and puts them into practice.p 48He is like a man building a house, who dug down deep and laid the foundation on rock. When a flood came, the torrent struck that house but could not shake it, because it was well built. 49But the one who hears my words and does not put them into practice is like a man who built a house on the ground without a foundation. The moment the torrent struck that house, it collapsed and its destruction was complete."

6:44
l Mt 12:33

6:45
m Pr 4:23;
Mt 12:34,35;
Mk 7:20

Chapter 7 Theme

6:46
n Jn 13:13
o Mal 1:6;
Mt 7:21

7 When Jesus had finished saying all thisq in the hearing of the people, he entered Capernaum. 2There a centurion's servant, whom his master valued highly, was sick and about to die. 3The centurion heard of Jesus and sent some elders of the Jews to him, asking him to come and heal his servant. 4When they came to Jesus, they pleaded earnestly with him, "This man deserves to have you do this, 5because he loves our nation and has built our synagogue." 6So Jesus went with them.

6:47
p Lk 8:21; 11:28;
Jas 1:22-25

He was not far from the house when the centurion sent friends to say to him: "Lord, don't trouble yourself, for I do not deserve to

7:1
q Mt 7:28

have you come under my roof. ⁷That is why I did not even consider myself worthy to come to you. But say the word, and my servant will be healed.ᵃ ⁸For I myself am a man under authority, with soldiers under me. I tell this one, 'Go,' and he goes; and that one, 'Come,' and he comes. I say to my servant, 'Do this,' and he does it."

⁹When Jesus heard this, he was amazed at him, and turning to the crowd following him, he said, "I tell you, I have not found such great faith even in Israel." ¹⁰Then the men who had been sent returned to the house and found the servant well.

¹¹Soon afterward, Jesus went to a town called Nain, and his disciples and a large crowd went along with him. ¹²As he approached the town gate, a dead person was being carried out—the only son of his mother, and she was a widow. And a large crowd from the town was with her. ¹³When the Lordᵇ saw her, his heart went out to her and he said, "Don't cry."

¹⁴Then he went up and touched the coffin, and those carrying it stood still. He said, "Young man, I say to you, get up!"ᶜ ¹⁵The dead man sat up and began to talk, and Jesus gave him back to his mother.

¹⁶They were all filled with aweᵈ and praised God.ᵉ "A great prophetᶠ has appeared among us," they said. "God has come to help his people."ᵍ ¹⁷This news about Jesus spread throughout Judeaᵃ and the surrounding country.ʰ

¹⁸John'sⁱ disciplesʲ told him about all these things. Calling two of them, ¹⁹he sent them to the Lord to ask, "Are you the one who was to come, or should we expect someone else?"

²⁰When the men came to Jesus, they said, "John the Baptist sent us to you to ask, 'Are you the one who was to come, or should we expect someone else?'"

²¹At that very time Jesus cured many who had diseases, sicknessesᵏ and evil spirits, and gave sight to many who were blind. ²²So he replied to the messengers, "Go back and report to John what you have seen and heard: The blind receive sight, the lame walk, those who have leprosyᵇ are cured, the deaf hear, the dead are raised, and the good news is preached to the poor.ˡ ²³Blessed is the man who does not fall away on account of me."

²⁴After John's messengers left, Jesus began to speak to the crowd about John: "What did you go out into the desert to see? A reed swayed by the wind? ²⁵If not, what did you go out to see? A man dressed in fine clothes? No, those who wear expensive clothes and indulge in luxury are in palaces. ²⁶But what did you go out to see? A prophet?ᵐ Yes, I tell you, and more than a prophet. ²⁷This is the one about whom it is written:

ᵃ 17 Or *the land of the Jews*   ᵇ 22 The Greek word was used for various diseases affecting the skin—not necessarily leprosy.

7:7
ᵃ Ps 107:20

7:13
ᵇ ver 19;
Lk 10:1; 13:15;
17:5; 22:61;
24:34; Jn 11:2

7:14
ᶜ Mt 9:25;
Mk 1:31;
Lk 8:54;
Jn 11:43;
Ac 9:40

7:16
ᵈ Lk 1:65
ᵉ Mt 9:8
ᶠ ver 39;
Mt 21:11
ᵍ Lk 1:68

7:17
ʰ Mt 9:26

7:18
ⁱ Mt 3:1
ʲ Lk 5:33

7:21
ᵏ Mt 4:23

7:22
ˡ Isa 29:18,19;
35:5,6; 61:1,2;
Lk 4:18

7:26
ᵐ Mt 11:9

7:27
a Mal 3:1;
Mt 11:10;
Mk 1:2

7:28
b Mt 3:2

7:29
c Mt 21:32;
Mk 1:5; Lk 3:12

7:30
d Mt 22:35

7:33
e Lk 1:15

7:34
f Lk 5:29,30;
15:1,2

7:39
g ver 16;
Mt 21:11

" 'I will send my messenger ahead of you,
who will prepare your way before you.' a a

28 I tell you, among those born of women there is no one greater than John; yet the one who is least in the kingdom of God b is greater than he."

29 (All the people, even the tax collectors, when they heard Jesus' words, acknowledged that God's way was right, because they had been baptized by John. c 30 But the Pharisees and experts in the law d rejected God's purpose for themselves, because they had not been baptized by John.)

31 "To what, then, can I compare the people of this generation? What are they like? 32 They are like children sitting in the marketplace and calling out to each other:

" 'We played the flute for you,
and you did not dance;
we sang a dirge,
and you did not cry.'

33 For John the Baptist came neither eating bread nor drinking wine, e and you say, 'He has a demon.' 34 The Son of Man came eating and drinking, and you say, 'Here is a glutton and a drunkard, a friend of tax collectors and "sinners." ' f 35 But wisdom is proved right by all her children."

36 Now one of the Pharisees invited Jesus to have dinner with him, so he went to the Pharisee's house and reclined at the table. 37 When a woman who had lived a sinful life in that town learned that Jesus was eating at the Pharisee's house, she brought an alabaster jar of perfume, 38 and as she stood behind him at his feet weeping, she began to wet his feet with her tears. Then she wiped them with her hair, kissed them and poured perfume on them.

39 When the Pharisee who had invited him saw this, he said to himself, "If this man were a prophet, g he would know who is touching him and what kind of woman she is—that she is a sinner."

40 Jesus answered him, "Simon, I have something to tell you."

"Tell me, teacher," he said.

41 "Two men owed money to a certain moneylender. One owed him five hundred denarii, b and the other fifty. 42 Neither of them had the money to pay him back, so he canceled the debts of both. Now which of them will love him more?"

43 Simon replied, "I suppose the one who had the bigger debt canceled."

"You have judged correctly," Jesus said.

44 Then he turned toward the woman and said to Simon, "Do you see this woman? I came into your house. You did not give me

a 27 Mal. 3:1   b 41 A denarius was a coin worth about a day's wages.

any water for my feet,[a] but she wet my feet with her tears and wiped them with her hair. [45]You did not give me a kiss,[b] but this woman, from the time I entered, has not stopped kissing my feet. [46]You did not put oil on my head,[c] but she has poured perfume on my feet. [47]Therefore, I tell you, her many sins have been forgiven— for she loved much. But he who has been forgiven little loves little."

[48]Then Jesus said to her, "Your sins are forgiven."[d]

[49]The other guests began to say among themselves, "Who is this who even forgives sins?"

[50]Jesus said to the woman, "Your faith has saved you;[e] go in peace."[f]

Chapter 8 Theme

8 After this, Jesus traveled about from one town and village to another, proclaiming the good news of the kingdom of God.[g] The Twelve were with him, [2]and also some women who had been cured of evil spirits and diseases: Mary (called Magdalene)[h] from whom seven demons had come out; [3]Joanna the wife of Cuza, the manager of Herod's[i] household; Susanna; and many others. These women were helping to support them out of their own means.

[4]While a large crowd was gathering and people were coming to Jesus from town after town, he told this parable: [5]"A farmer went out to sow his seed. As he was scattering the seed, some fell along the path; it was trampled on, and the birds of the air ate it up. [6]Some fell on rock, and when it came up, the plants withered because they had no moisture. [7]Other seed fell among thorns, which grew up with it and choked the plants. [8]Still other seed fell on good soil. It came up and yielded a crop, a hundred times more than was sown."

When he said this, he called out, "He who has ears to hear, let him hear."[j]

[9]His disciples asked him what this parable meant. [10]He said, "The knowledge of the secrets of the kingdom of God has been given to you,[k] but to others I speak in parables, so that,

"'though seeing, they may not see;
though hearing, they may not understand.'[a][l]

[11]"This is the meaning of the parable: The seed is the word of God.[m] [12]Those along the path are the ones who hear, and then the devil comes and takes away the word from their hearts, so that they may not believe and be saved. [13]Those on the rock are the ones who receive the word with joy when they hear it, but they have no root. They believe for a while, but in the time of testing

a 10 Isaiah 6:9

7:44
[a] Ge 18:4; 19:2; 43:24;
Jdg 19:21;
Jn 13:4-14;
1Ti 5:10

7:45
[b] Lk 22:47,48;
Ro 16:16

7:46
[c] Ps 23:5; Ecc 9:8

7:48
[d] Mt 9:2

7:50
[e] Mt 9:22;
Mk 5:34;
Lk 8:48
[f] Ac 15:33

8:1
[g] Mt 4:23

8:2
[h] Mt 27:55,56

8:3
[i] Mt 14:1

8:8
[j] Mt 11:15

8:10
[k] Mt 13:11
[l] Isa 6:9;
Mt 13:13,14

8:11
[m] Heb 4:12

8:13
a Mt 11:6

they fall away.*a* ¹⁴The seed that fell among thorns stands for those who hear, but as they go on their way they are choked by life's worries, riches*b* and pleasures, and they do not mature. ¹⁵But the seed on good soil stands for those with a noble and good heart, who hear the word, retain it, and by persevering produce a crop.

8:14
b Mt 19:23;
1Ti 6:9,10,17

¹⁶"No one lights a lamp and hides it in a jar or puts it under a bed. Instead, he puts it on a stand, so that those who come in can see the light.*c* ¹⁷For there is nothing hidden that will not be disclosed, and nothing concealed that will not be known or brought out into the open.*d* ¹⁸Therefore consider carefully how you listen. Whoever has will be given more; whoever does not have, even what he thinks he has will be taken from him."*e*

8:16
c Mt 5:15;
Mk 4:21;
Lk 11:33

¹⁹Now Jesus' mother and brothers came to see him, but they were not able to get near him because of the crowd. ²⁰Someone told him, "Your mother and brothers*f* are standing outside, wanting to see you."

8:17
d Mt 10:26;
Mk 4:22;
Lk 12:2

²¹He replied, "My mother and brothers are those who hear God's word and put it into practice."*g*

²²One day Jesus said to his disciples, "Let's go over to the other side of the lake." So they got into a boat and set out. ²³As they sailed, he fell asleep. A squall came down on the lake, so that the boat was being swamped, and they were in great danger.

8:18
e Mt 13:12;
25:29; Lk 19:26

²⁴The disciples went and woke him, saying, "Master, Master,*h* we're going to drown!"

He got up and rebuked*i* the wind and the raging waters; the storm subsided, and all was calm.*j* ²⁵"Where is your faith?" he asked his disciples.

8:20
f Jn 7:5

In fear and amazement they asked one another, "Who is this? He commands even the winds and the water, and they obey him."

8:21
g Lk 6:47; 11:28;
Jn 14:21

²⁶They sailed to the region of the Gerasenes,*a* which is across the lake from Galilee. ²⁷When Jesus stepped ashore, he was met by a demon-possessed man from the town. For a long time this man had not worn clothes or lived in a house, but had lived in the tombs. ²⁸When he saw Jesus, he cried out and fell at his feet, shouting at the top of his voice, "What do you want with me,*k* Jesus, Son of the Most High God?*l* I beg you, don't torture me!" ²⁹For Jesus had commanded the evil*b* spirit to come out of the man. Many times it had seized him, and though he was chained hand and foot and kept under guard, he had broken his chains and had been driven by the demon into solitary places.

8:24
h Lk 5:5
i Lk 4:35,39,41
j Ps 107:29;
Jnh 1:15

³⁰Jesus asked him, "What is your name?"

"Legion," he replied, because many demons had gone into him. ³¹And they begged him repeatedly not to order them to go into the Abyss.*m*

8:28
k Mt 8:29
l Mk 5:7

8:31
m Rev 9:1,2,11;
11:7; 17:8;
20:1,3

a 26 Some manuscripts *Gadarenes*; other manuscripts *Gergesenes*; also in verse 37   *b 29* Greek *unclean*

³²A large herd of pigs was feeding there on the hillside. The demons begged Jesus to let them go into them, and he gave them permission. ³³When the demons came out of the man, they went into the pigs, and the herd rushed down the steep bank into the lake[a] and was drowned.

³⁴When those tending the pigs saw what had happened, they ran off and reported this in the town and countryside, ³⁵and the people went out to see what had happened. When they came to Jesus, they found the man from whom the demons had gone out, sitting at Jesus' feet,[b] dressed and in his right mind; and they were afraid. ³⁶Those who had seen it told the people how the demon-possessed[c] man had been cured. ³⁷Then all the people of the region of the Gerasenes asked Jesus to leave them,[d] because they were overcome with fear. So he got into the boat and left.

³⁸The man from whom the demons had gone out begged to go with him, but Jesus sent him away, saying, ³⁹"Return home and tell how much God has done for you." So the man went away and told all over town how much Jesus had done for him.

⁴⁰Now when Jesus returned, a crowd welcomed him, for they were all expecting him. ⁴¹Then a man named Jairus, a ruler of the synagogue,[e] came and fell at Jesus' feet, pleading with him to come to his house ⁴²because his only daughter, a girl of about twelve, was dying.

As Jesus was on his way, the crowds almost crushed him. ⁴³And a woman was there who had been subject to bleeding[f] for twelve years,[a] but no one could heal her. ⁴⁴She came up behind him and touched the edge of his cloak,[g] and immediately her bleeding stopped.

⁴⁵"Who touched me?" Jesus asked.

When they all denied it, Peter said, "Master,[h] the people are crowding and pressing against you."

⁴⁶But Jesus said, "Someone touched me;[i] I know that power has gone out from me."[j]

⁴⁷Then the woman, seeing that she could not go unnoticed, came trembling and fell at his feet. In the presence of all the people, she told why she had touched him and how she had been instantly healed. ⁴⁸Then he said to her, "Daughter, your faith has healed you.[k] Go in peace."[l]

⁴⁹While Jesus was still speaking, someone came from the house of Jairus, the synagogue ruler.[m] "Your daughter is dead," he said. "Don't bother the teacher any more."

⁵⁰Hearing this, Jesus said to Jairus, "Don't be afraid; just believe, and she will be healed."

⁵¹When he arrived at the house of Jairus, he did not let anyone go in with him except Peter, John and James,[n] and the child's father

---

[a] 43 Many manuscripts *years, and she had spent all she had on doctors*

8:33
[a] ver 22,23

8:35
[b] Lk 10:39

8:36
[c] Mt 4:24

8:37
[d] Ac 16:39

8:41
[e] ver 49;
Mk 5:22

8:43
[f] Lev 15:25-30

8:44
[g] Mt 9:20

8:45
[h] Lk 5:5

8:46
[i] Mt 14:36;
Mk 3:10
[j] Lk 5:17; 6:19

8:48
[k] Mt 9:22
[l] Ac 15:33

8:49
[m] ver 41

8:51
[n] Mt 4:21

8:52
a Lk 23:27
b Mt 9:24;
Jn 11:11,13

and mother. ⁵²Meanwhile, all the people were wailing and mourning*a* for her. "Stop wailing," Jesus said. "She is not dead but asleep."*b*

8:54
c Lk 7:14

⁵³They laughed at him, knowing that she was dead. ⁵⁴But he took her by the hand and said, "My child, get up!"*c* ⁵⁵Her spirit returned, and at once she stood up. Then Jesus told them to give her something to eat. ⁵⁶Her parents were astonished, but he ordered not to tell anyone what had happened.*d*

8:56
d Mt 8:4

Chapter 9 Theme

9:1
e Mt 10:1
f Mt 4:23;
Lk 5:17

9 When Jesus had called the Twelve together, he gave them power and authority to drive out all demons*e* and to cure diseases,*f* ²and he sent them out to preach the kingdom of God*g* and to heal the sick. ³He told them: "Take nothing for the journey— no staff, no bag, no bread, no money, no extra tunic.*h* ⁴Whatever house you enter, stay there until you leave that town. ⁵If people do not welcome you, shake the dust off your feet when you leave their town, as a testimony against them."*i* ⁶So they set out and went from village to village, preaching the gospel and healing people everywhere.

9:2
g Mt 3:2

9:3
h Lk 10:4; 22:35

⁷Now Herod*j* the tetrarch heard about all that was going on. And he was perplexed, because some were saying that John*k* had been raised from the dead,*l* ⁸others that Elijah had appeared,*m* and still others that one of the prophets of long ago had come back to life.*n* ⁹But Herod said, "I beheaded John. Who, then, is this I hear such things about?" And he tried to see him.*o*

9:5
i Mt 10:14

9:7
j Mt 14:1
k Mt 3:1
l ver 19

¹⁰When the apostles*p* returned, they reported to Jesus what they had done. Then he took them with him and they withdrew by themselves to a town called Bethsaida,*q* ¹¹but the crowds learned about it and followed him. He welcomed them and spoke to them about the kingdom of God,*r* and healed those who needed healing.

9:8
m Mt 11:14
n ver 19; Jn 1:21

¹²Late in the afternoon the Twelve came to him and said, "Send the crowd away so they can go to the surrounding villages and countryside and find food and lodging, because we are in a remote place here."

9:9
o Lk 23:8

¹³He replied, "You give them something to eat."

They answered, "We have only five loaves of bread and two fish—unless we go and buy food for all this crowd." ¹⁴(About five thousand men were there.)

9:10
p Mk 6:30
q Mt 11:21

But he said to his disciples, "Have them sit down in groups of about fifty each." ¹⁵The disciples did so, and everybody sat down. ¹⁶Taking the five loaves and the two fish and looking up to heaven, he gave thanks and broke them.*s* Then he gave them to the disciples to set before the people. ¹⁷They all ate and were satisfied, and the disciples picked up twelve basketfuls of broken pieces that were left over.

9:11
r ver 2; Mt 3:2

9:16
s Mt 14:19

¹⁸Once when Jesus was praying^a in private and his disciples were with him, he asked them, "Who do the crowds say I am?"

¹⁹They replied, "Some say John the Baptist;^b others say Elijah; and still others, that one of the prophets of long ago has come back to life."^c

²⁰"But what about you?" he asked. "Who do you say I am?"

Peter answered, "The Christ^a of God."^d

²¹Jesus strictly warned them not to tell this to anyone.^e ²²And he said, "The Son of Man^f must suffer many things^g and be rejected by the elders, chief priests and teachers of the law,^h and he must be killedⁱ and on the third day^j be raised to life."^k

²³Then he said to them all: "If anyone would come after me, he must deny himself and take up his cross daily and follow me.^l ²⁴For whoever wants to save his life will lose it, but whoever loses his life for me will save it.^m ²⁵What good is it for a man to gain the whole world, and yet lose or forfeit his very self? ²⁶If anyone is ashamed of me and my words, the Son of Man will be ashamed of himⁿ when he comes in his glory and in the glory of the Father and of the holy angels.^o ²⁷I tell you the truth, some who are standing here will not taste death before they see the kingdom of God."

²⁸About eight days after Jesus said this, he took Peter, John and James^p with him and went up onto a mountain to pray.^q ²⁹As he was praying, the appearance of his face changed, and his clothes became as bright as a flash of lightning. ³⁰Two men, Moses and Elijah, ³¹appeared in glorious splendor, talking with Jesus. They spoke about his departure,^r which he was about to bring to fulfillment at Jerusalem. ³²Peter and his companions were very sleepy,^s but when they became fully awake, they saw his glory and the two men standing with him. ³³As the men were leaving Jesus, Peter said to him, "Master,^t it is good for us to be here. Let us put up three shelters—one for you, one for Moses and one for Elijah." (He did not know what he was saying.)

³⁴While he was speaking, a cloud appeared and enveloped them, and they were afraid as they entered the cloud. ³⁵A voice came from the cloud, saying, "This is my Son, whom I have chosen;^u listen to him."^v ³⁶When the voice had spoken, they found that Jesus was alone. The disciples kept this to themselves, and told no one at that time what they had seen.^w

³⁷The next day, when they came down from the mountain, a large crowd met him. ³⁸A man in the crowd called out, "Teacher, I beg you to look at my son, for he is my only child. ³⁹A spirit seizes him and he suddenly screams; it throws him into convulsions so that he foams at the mouth. It scarcely ever leaves him and is destroying him. ⁴⁰I begged your disciples to drive it out, but they could not."

9:18
^a Lk 3:21

9:19
^b Mt 3:1
^c ver 7,8

9:20
^d Jn 1:49;
6:66-69; 11:27

9:21
^e Mt 16:20;
Mk 8:30

9:22
^f Mt 8:20
^g Mt 16:21
^h Mt 27:1,2
ⁱ Ac 2:23; 3:13
^j Mt 16:21
^k Mt 16:21

9:23
^l Mt 10:38;
Lk 14:27

9:24
^m Jn 12:25

9:26
ⁿ Mt 10:33;
Lk 12:9;
2Ti 2:12
^o Mt 16:27

9:28
^p Mt 4:21
^q Lk 3:21

9:31
^r 2Pe 1:15

9:32
^s Mt 26:43

9:33
^t Lk 5:5

9:35
^u Isa 42:1
^v Mt 3:17

9:36
^w Mt 17:9

^a 20 Or *Messiah*

9:41
a Dt 32:5

9:44
b ver 22

9:45
c Mk 9:32

9:46
d Lk 22:24

9:47
e Mt 9:4

9:48
f Mt 10:40
g Mk 9:35

9:49
h Lk 5:5

9:50
i Mt 12:30;
Lk 11:23

9:51
j Mk 16:19
k Lk 13:22;
17:11; 18:31;
19:28

9:52
l Mt 10:5

9:54
m Mt 4:21
n 2Ki 1:10,12

9:57
o ver 51

9:58
p Mt 8:20

9:59
q Mt 4:19

9:60
r Mt 3:2

9:61
s 1Ki 19:20

41"O unbelieving and perverse generation,"[a] Jesus replied, "how long shall I stay with you and put up with you? Bring your son here."

42Even while the boy was coming, the demon threw him to the ground in a convulsion. But Jesus rebuked the evil[a] spirit, healed the boy and gave him back to his father. **43**And they were all amazed at the greatness of God.

While everyone was marveling at all that Jesus did, he said to his disciples, **44**"Listen carefully to what I am about to tell you: The Son of Man is going to be betrayed into the hands of men."[b] **45**But they did not understand what this meant. It was hidden from them, so that they did not grasp it,[c] and they were afraid to ask him about it.

46An argument started among the disciples as to which of them would be the greatest.[d] **47**Jesus, knowing their thoughts,[e] took a little child and had him stand beside him. **48**Then he said to them, "Whoever welcomes this little child in my name welcomes me; and whoever welcomes me welcomes the one who sent me.[f] For he who is least among you all—he is the greatest."[g]

49"Master,"[h] said John, "we saw a man driving out demons in your name and we tried to stop him, because he is not one of us."

50"Do not stop him," Jesus said, "for whoever is not against you is for you."[i]

51As the time approached for him to be taken up to heaven,[j] Jesus resolutely set out for Jerusalem.[k] **52**And he sent messengers on ahead, who went into a Samaritan[l] village to get things ready for him; **53**but the people there did not welcome him, because he was heading for Jerusalem. **54**When the disciples James and John[m] saw this, they asked, "Lord, do you want us to call fire down from heaven to destroy them[b]?"[n] **55**But Jesus turned and rebuked them, **56**and[c] they went to another village.

57As they were walking along the road,[o] a man said to him, "I will follow you wherever you go."

58Jesus replied, "Foxes have holes and birds of the air have nests, but the Son of Man[p] has no place to lay his head."

59He said to another man, "Follow me."[q]

But the man replied, "Lord, first let me go and bury my father."

60Jesus said to him, "Let the dead bury their own dead, but you go and proclaim the kingdom of God."[r]

61Still another said, "I will follow you, Lord; but first let me go back and say good-by to my family."[s]

62Jesus replied, "No one who puts his hand to the plow and looks back is fit for service in the kingdom of God."

a 42 Greek unclean   b 54 Some manuscripts them, even as Elijah did   c 55,56 Some manuscripts them. And he said, "You do not know what kind of spirit you are of, for the Son of Man did not come to destroy men's lives, but to save them." 56And

Chapter 10 Theme _____

10 After this the Lord[a] appointed seventy-two[a] others[b] and sent them two by two[c] ahead of him to every town and place where he was about to go.[d] [2]He told them, "The harvest is plentiful, but the workers are few. Ask the Lord of the harvest, therefore, to send out workers into his harvest field.[e] [3]Go! I am sending you out like lambs among wolves.[f] [4]Do not take a purse or bag or sandals; and do not greet anyone on the road.

[5]"When you enter a house, first say, 'Peace to this house.' [6]If a man of peace is there, your peace will rest on him; if not, it will return to you. [7]Stay in that house, eating and drinking whatever they give you, for the worker deserves his wages.[g] Do not move around from house to house.

[8]"When you enter a town and are welcomed, eat what is set before you.[h] [9]Heal the sick who are there and tell them, 'The kingdom of God[i] is near you.' [10]But when you enter a town and are not welcomed, go into its streets and say, [11]'Even the dust of your town that sticks to our feet we wipe off against you.[j] Yet be sure of this: The kingdom of God is near.'[k] [12]I tell you, it will be more bearable on that day for Sodom[l] than for that town.[m]

[13]"Woe to you,[n] Korazin! Woe to you, Bethsaida! For if the miracles that were performed in you had been performed in Tyre and Sidon, they would have repented long ago, sitting in sackcloth[o] and ashes. [14]But it will be more bearable for Tyre and Sidon at the judgment than for you. [15]And you, Capernaum,[p] will you be lifted up to the skies? No, you will go down to the depths.[b]

[16]"He who listens to you listens to me; he who rejects you rejects me; but he who rejects me rejects him who sent me."[q]

[17]The seventy-two[r] returned with joy and said, "Lord, even the demons submit to us in your name."[s]

[18]He replied, "I saw Satan[t] fall like lightning from heaven.[u] [19]I have given you authority to trample on snakes[v] and scorpions and to overcome all the power of the enemy; nothing will harm you. [20]However, do not rejoice that the spirits submit to you, but rejoice that your names are written in heaven."[w]

[21]At that time Jesus, full of joy through the Holy Spirit, said, "I praise you, Father, Lord of heaven and earth, because you have hidden these things from the wise and learned, and revealed them to little children.[x] Yes, Father, for this was your good pleasure.

[22]"All things have been committed to me by my Father.[y] No one knows who the Son is except the Father, and no one knows who the Father is except the Son and those to whom the Son chooses to reveal him."[z]

a 1 Some manuscripts *seventy*; also in verse 17   b 15 Greek *Hades*

10:1
a Lk 7:13
b Lk 9:1,2,51,52
c Mk 6:7
d Mt 10:1

10:2
e Mt 9:37,38;
Jn 4:35

10:3
f Mt 10:16

10:7
g Mt 10:10;
1Co 9:14;
1Ti 5:18

10:8
h 1Co 10:27

10:9
i Mt 3:2; 10:7

10:11
j Mt 10:14;
Mk 6:11
k ver 9

10:12
l Mt 10:15
m Mt 11:24

10:13
n Lk 6:24-26
o Rev 11:3

10:15
p Mt 4:13

10:16
q Mt 10:40;
Jn 13:20

10:17
r ver 1
s Mk 16:17

10:18
t Mt 4:10
u Isa 14:12;
Rev 9:1; 12:8,9

10:19
v Mk 16:18;
Ac 28:3-5

10:20
w Ex 32:32;
Ps 69:28;
Da 12:1;
Php 4:3;
Heb 12:23;
Rev 13:8; 20:12;
21:27

10:21
x 1Co 1:26-29

10:22
y Mt 28:18
z Jn 1:18

10:24
a 1 Pe 1:10-12

10:25
b Mt 19:16;
Lk 18:18

10:27
c Dt 6:5
d Lev 19:18;
Mt 5:43

10:28
e Lev 18:5;
Ro 7:10

10:29
f Lk 16:15

10:31
g Lev 21:1-3

10:33
h Mt 10:5

10:38
i Jn 11:1; 12:2

10:39
j Jn 11:1; 12:3
k Lk 8:35

10:40
l Mk 4:38

10:41
m Mt 6:25-34;
Lk 12:11,22

10:42
n Ps 27:4

²³Then he turned to his disciples and said privately, "Blessed are the eyes that see what you see. ²⁴For I tell you that many prophets and kings wanted to see what you see but did not see it, and to hear what you hear but did not hear it."[a]

²⁵On one occasion an expert in the law stood up to test Jesus. "Teacher," he asked, "what must I do to inherit eternal life?"[b]

²⁶"What is written in the Law?" he replied. "How do you read it?"

²⁷He answered: "'Love the Lord your God with all your heart and with all your soul and with all your strength and with all your mind'[a];[c] and, 'Love your neighbor as yourself.'[b]"[d]

²⁸"You have answered correctly," Jesus replied. "Do this and you will live."[e]

²⁹But he wanted to justify himself,[f] so he asked Jesus, "And who is my neighbor?"

³⁰In reply Jesus said: "A man was going down from Jerusalem to Jericho, when he fell into the hands of robbers. They stripped him of his clothes, beat him and went away, leaving him half dead. ³¹A priest happened to be going down the same road, and when he saw the man, he passed by on the other side.[g] ³²So too, a Levite, when he came to the place and saw him, passed by on the other side. ³³But a Samaritan,[h] as he traveled, came where the man was; and when he saw him, he took pity on him. ³⁴He went to him and bandaged his wounds, pouring on oil and wine. Then he put the man on his own donkey, took him to an inn and took care of him. ³⁵The next day he took out two silver coins[c] and gave them to the inn-keeper. 'Look after him,' he said, 'and when I return, I will reimburse you for any extra expense you may have.'

³⁶"Which of these three do you think was a neighbor to the man who fell into the hands of robbers?"

³⁷The expert in the law replied, "The one who had mercy on him."

Jesus told him, "Go and do likewise."

³⁸As Jesus and his disciples were on their way, he came to a village where a woman named Martha[i] opened her home to him. ³⁹She had a sister called Mary,[j] who sat at the Lord's feet[k] listening to what he said. ⁴⁰But Martha was distracted by all the preparations that had to be made. She came to him and asked, "Lord, don't you care[l] that my sister has left me to do the work by myself? Tell her to help me!"

⁴¹"Martha, Martha," the Lord answered, "you are worried[m] and upset about many things, ⁴²but only one thing is needed.[d][n] Mary has chosen what is better, and it will not be taken away from her."

a 27 Deut. 6:5 b 27 Lev. 19:18 c 35 Greek *two denarii* d 42 Some manuscripts *but few things are needed—or only one*

Chapter 11 Theme

11 One day Jesus was praying[a] in a certain place. When he finished, one of his disciples said to him, "Lord,[b] teach us to pray, just as John taught his disciples."

²He said to them, "When you pray, say:

"'Father,[a]
hallowed be your name,
your kingdom[c] come.[b]
³Give us each day our daily bread.
⁴Forgive us our sins,
    for we also forgive everyone who sins against us.[c][d]
And lead us not into temptation.[d]'"[e]

⁵Then he said to them, "Suppose one of you has a friend, and he goes to him at midnight and says, 'Friend, lend me three loaves of bread, ⁶because a friend of mine on a journey has come to me, and I have nothing to set before him.'

⁷"Then the one inside answers, 'Don't bother me. The door is already locked, and my children are with me in bed. I can't get up and give you anything.' ⁸I tell you, though he will not get up and give him the bread because he is his friend, yet because of the man's boldness[e] he will get up and give him as much as he needs.[f]

⁹"So I say to you: Ask and it will be given to you;[g] seek and you will find; knock and the door will be opened to you. ¹⁰For everyone who asks receives; he who seeks finds; and to him who knocks, the door will be opened.

¹¹"Which of you fathers, if your son asks for[f] a fish, will give him a snake instead? ¹²Or if he asks for an egg, will give him a scorpion? ¹³If you then, though you are evil, know how to give good gifts to your children, how much more will your Father in heaven give the Holy Spirit to those who ask him!"

¹⁴Jesus was driving out a demon that was mute. When the demon left, the man who had been mute spoke, and the crowd was amazed.[h] ¹⁵But some of them said, "By Beelzebub,[g][i] the prince of demons, he is driving out demons."[j] ¹⁶Others tested him by asking for a sign from heaven.[k]

¹⁷Jesus knew their thoughts[l] and said to them: "Any kingdom divided against itself will be ruined, and a house divided against itself will fall. ¹⁸If Satan[m] is divided against himself, how can his kingdom stand? I say this because you claim that I drive out demons by Beelzebub. ¹⁹Now if I drive out demons by Beelzebub,

---

a2 Some manuscripts *Our Father in heaven*   b2 Some manuscripts *come. May your will be done on earth as it is in heaven.*   c4 Greek *everyone who is indebted to us*   d4 Some manuscripts *temptation but deliver us from the evil one*   e8 Or *persistence*   f11 Some manuscripts *for bread, will give him a stone; or if he asks for*   g15 Greek *Beezeboul* or *Beelzeboul*; also in verses 18 and 19

Cross references: 11:1 a Lk 3:21 b Jn 13:13 | 11:2 c Mt 3:2 | 11:4 d Mt 18:35; Mk 11:25 e Mt 26:41; Jas 1:13 | 11:8 f Lk 18:1-6 | 11:9 g Mt 7:7 | 11:14 h Mt 9:32,33 | 11:15 i Mk 3:22 j Mt 9:34 | 11:16 k Mt 12:38 | 11:17 l Mt 9:4 | 11:18 m Mt 4:10

11:20
a Ex 8:19
b Mt 3:2

11:23
c Mt 12:30;
Mk 9:40;
Lk 9:50

11:26
d 2Pe 2:20

11:27
e Lk 23:29

11:28
f Heb 4:12
g Pr 8:32;
Lk 6:47; 8:21;
Jn 14:21

11:29
h ver 16;
Mt 12:38
i Jnh 1:17;
Mt 16:4

11:31
j 1Ki 10:1;
2Ch 9:1

11:32
k Jnh 3:5

11:33
l Mt 5:15;
Mk 4:21;
Lk 8:16

11:37
m Lk 7:36; 14:1

11:38
n Mk 7:3,4

11:39
o Lk 7:13
p Mt 23:25,26;
Mk 7:20-23

11:40
q Lk 12:20;
1Co 15:36

by whom do your followers drive them out? So then, they will be your judges. ²⁰But if I drive out demons by the finger of God,ᵃ then the kingdom of Godᵇ has come to you.

²¹"When a strong man, fully armed, guards his own house, his possessions are safe. ²²But when someone stronger attacks and overpowers him, he takes away the armor in which the man trusted and divides up the spoils.

²³"He who is not with me is against me, and he who does not gather with me, scatters.ᶜ

²⁴"When an evilᵃ spirit comes out of a man, it goes through arid places seeking rest and does not find it. Then it says, 'I will return to the house I left.' ²⁵When it arrives, it finds the house swept clean and put in order. ²⁶Then it goes and takes seven other spirits more wicked than itself, and they go in and live there. And the final condition of that man is worse than the first."ᵈ

²⁷As Jesus was saying these things, a woman in the crowd called out, "Blessed is the mother who gave you birth and nursed you."ᵉ

²⁸He replied, "Blessed rather are those who hear the word of Godᶠ and obey it."ᵍ

²⁹As the crowds increased, Jesus said, "This is a wicked generation. It asks for a miraculous sign,ʰ but none will be given it except the sign of Jonah.ⁱ ³⁰For as Jonah was a sign to the Ninevites, so also will the Son of Man be to this generation. ³¹The Queen of the South will rise at the judgment with the men of this generation and condemn them; for she came from the ends of the earth to listen to Solomon's wisdom,ʲ and now oneᵇ greater than Solomon is here. ³²The men of Nineveh will stand up at the judgment with this generation and condemn it; for they repented at the preaching of Jonah,ᵏ and now one greater than Jonah is here.

³³"No one lights a lamp and puts it in a place where it will be hidden, or under a bowl. Instead he puts it on its stand, so that those who come in may see the light.ˡ ³⁴Your eye is the lamp of your body. When your eyes are good, your whole body also is full of light. But when they are bad, your body also is full of darkness. ³⁵See to it, then, that the light within you is not darkness. ³⁶Therefore, if your whole body is full of light, and no part of it dark, it will be completely lighted, as when the light of a lamp shines on you."

³⁷When Jesus had finished speaking, a Pharisee invited him to eat with him; so he went in and reclined at the table.ᵐ ³⁸But the Pharisee, noticing that Jesus did not first wash before the meal,ⁿ was surprised.

³⁹Then the Lordᵒ said to him, "Now then, you Pharisees clean the outside of the cup and dish, but inside you are full of greed and wickedness.ᵖ ⁴⁰You foolish people!ᑫ Did not the one who made

a 24 Greek unclean   b 31 Or something; also in verse 32

the outside make the inside also? [41]But give what is inside ⌞the dish⌟[a] to the poor,[a] and everything will be clean for you.[b]

[42]"Woe to you Pharisees, because you give God a tenth[c] of your mint, rue and all other kinds of garden herbs, but you neglect justice and the love of God.[d] You should have practiced the latter without leaving the former undone.[e]

[43]"Woe to you Pharisees, because you love the most important seats in the synagogues and greetings in the marketplaces.[f]

[44]"Woe to you, because you are like unmarked graves,[g] which men walk over without knowing it."

[45]One of the experts in the law[h] answered him, "Teacher, when you say these things, you insult us also."

[46]Jesus replied, "And you experts in the law, woe to you, because you load people down with burdens they can hardly carry, and you yourselves will not lift one finger to help them.[i]

[47]"Woe to you, because you build tombs for the prophets, and it was your forefathers who killed them. [48]So you testify that you approve of what your forefathers did; they killed the prophets, and you build their tombs.[j] [49]Because of this, God in his wisdom[k] said, 'I will send them prophets and apostles, some of whom they will kill and others they will persecute.'[l] [50]Therefore this generation will be held responsible for the blood of all the prophets that has been shed since the beginning of the world, [51]from the blood of Abel[m] to the blood of Zechariah,[n] who was killed between the altar and the sanctuary. Yes, I tell you, this generation will be held responsible for it all.[o]

[52]"Woe to you experts in the law, because you have taken away the key to knowledge. You yourselves have not entered, and you have hindered those who were entering."[p]

[53]When Jesus left there, the Pharisees and the teachers of the law began to oppose him fiercely and to besiege him with questions, [54]waiting to catch him in something he might say.[q]

Chapter 12 Theme

12 Meanwhile, when a crowd of many thousands had gathered, so that they were trampling on one another, Jesus began to speak first to his disciples, saying: "Be on your guard against the yeast of the Pharisees, which is hypocrisy.[r] [2]There is nothing concealed that will not be disclosed, or hidden that will not be made known.[s] [3]What you have said in the dark will be heard in the daylight, and what you have whispered in the ear in the inner rooms will be proclaimed from the roofs.

[4]"I tell you, my friends,[t] do not be afraid of those who kill the body and after that can do no more. [5]But I will show you whom

---

a 41 Or *what you have*

11:41
[a] Lk 12:33
[b] Ac 10:15

11:42
[c] Lk 18:12
[d] Dt 6:5; Mic 6:8
[e] Mt 23:23

11:43
[f] Mt 23:6,7; Mk 12:38-39; Lk 14:7; 20:46

11:44
[g] Mt 23:27

11:45
[h] Mt 22:35

11:46
[i] Mt 23:4

11:48
[j] Mt 23:29-32; Ac 7:51-53

11:49
[k] 1Co 1:24,30; Col 2:3
[l] Mt 23:34

11:51
[m] Ge 4:8
[n] 2Ch 24:20,21
[o] Mt 23:35,36

11:52
[p] Mt 23:13

11:54
[q] Mt 12:10; Mk 12:13

12:1
[r] Mt 16:6,11,12; Mk 8:15

12:2
[s] Mk 4:22; Lk 8:17

12:4
[t] Jn 15:14,15

12:5
a Heb 10:31

12:7
b Mt 10:30
c Mt 12:12

12:8
d Lk 15:10

12:9
e Mk 8:38;
2Ti 2:12

12:10
f Mt 8:20
g Mt 12:31,32;
Mk 3:28-29;
1Jn 5:16

12:11
h Mt 10:17,19;
Mk 13:11;
Lk 21:12,14

12:12
i Ex 4:12;
Mt 10:20;
Mk 13:11;
Lk 21:15

12:15
j Job 20:20;
31:24; Ps 62:10

12:20
k Jer 17:11;
Lk 11:40
l Job 27:8
m Ps 39:6; 49:10

12:21
n ver 33

12:24
o Job 38:41;
Ps 147:9

12:27
p 1Ki 10:4-7

you should fear: Fear him who, after the killing of the body, has power to throw you into hell. Yes, I tell you, fear him.*a* *6*Are not five sparrows sold for two pennies*a*? Yet not one of them is forgotten by God. *7*Indeed, the very hairs of your head are all numbered.*b* Don't be afraid; you are worth more than many sparrows.*c*

8"I tell you, whoever acknowledges me before men, the Son of Man will also acknowledge him before the angels of God.*d* *9*But he who disowns me before men will be disowned*e* before the angels of God. *10*And everyone who speaks a word against the Son of Man*f* will be forgiven, but anyone who blasphemes against the Holy Spirit will not be forgiven.*g*

11"When you are brought before synagogues, rulers and authorities, do not worry about how you will defend yourselves or what you will say,*h* *12*for the Holy Spirit will teach you at that time what you should say."*i*

*13*Someone in the crowd said to him, "Teacher, tell my brother to divide the inheritance with me."

*14*Jesus replied, "Man, who appointed me a judge or an arbiter between you?" *15*Then he said to them, "Watch out! Be on your guard against all kinds of greed; a man's life does not consist in the abundance of his possessions."*j*

*16*And he told them this parable: "The ground of a certain rich man produced a good crop. *17*He thought to himself, 'What shall I do? I have no place to store my crops.'

18"Then he said, 'This is what I'll do. I will tear down my barns and build bigger ones, and there I will store all my grain and my goods. *19*And I'll say to myself, "You have plenty of good things laid up for many years. Take life easy; eat, drink and be merry."'

20"But God said to him, 'You fool!*k* This very night your life will be demanded from you.*l* Then who will get what you have prepared for yourself?'*m*

21"This is how it will be with anyone who stores up things for himself but is not rich toward God."*n*

*22*Then Jesus said to his disciples: "Therefore I tell you, do not worry about your life, what you will eat; or about your body, what you will wear. *23*Life is more than food, and the body more than clothes. *24*Consider the ravens: They do not sow or reap, they have no storeroom or barn; yet God feeds them.*o* And how much more valuable you are than birds! *25*Who of you by worrying can add a single hour to his life*b*? *26*Since you cannot do this very little thing, why do you worry about the rest?

27"Consider how the lilies grow. They do not labor or spin. Yet I tell you, not even Solomon in all his splendor*p* was dressed like one of these. *28*If that is how God clothes the grass of the field, which

a 6 Greek *two assaria*   *b* 25 Or *single cubit to his height* is here today, and tomorrow is thrown into the fire, how much more will he clothe you, O you of little faith!ᵃ ²⁹And do not set your heart on what you will eat or drink; do not worry about it. ³⁰For the pagan world runs after all such things, and your Fatherᵇ knows that you need them.ᶜ ³¹But seek his kingdom,ᵈ and these things will be given to you as well.ᵉ

³²"Do not be afraid,ᶠ little flock, for your Father has been pleased to give you the kingdom.ᵍ ³³Sell your possessions and give to the poor.ʰ Provide purses for yourselves that will not wear out, a treasure in heavenⁱ that will not be exhausted, where no thief comes near and no moth destroys.ʲ ³⁴For where your treasure is, there your heart will be also.ᵏ

³⁵"Be dressed ready for service and keep your lamps burning, ³⁶like men waiting for their master to return from a wedding banquet, so that when he comes and knocks they can immediately open the door for him. ³⁷It will be good for those servants whose master finds them watching when he comes.ˡ I tell you the truth, he will dress himself to serve, will have them recline at the table and will come and wait on them.ᵐ ³⁸It will be good for those servants whose master finds them ready, even if he comes in the second or third watch of the night. ³⁹But understand this: If the owner of the house had known at what hour the thiefⁿ was coming, he would not have let his house be broken into. ⁴⁰You also must be ready,ᵒ because the Son of Man will come at an hour when you do not expect him."

⁴¹Peter asked, "Lord, are you telling this parable to us, or to everyone?"

⁴²The Lordᵖ answered, "Who then is the faithful and wise manager, whom the master puts in charge of his servants to give them their food allowance at the proper time? ⁴³It will be good for that servant whom the master finds doing so when he returns. ⁴⁴I tell you the truth, he will put him in charge of all his possessions. ⁴⁵But suppose the servant says to himself, 'My master is taking a long time in coming,' and he then begins to beat the menservants and maidservants and to eat and drink and get drunk. ⁴⁶The master of that servant will come on a day when he does not expect him and at an hour he is not aware of.ᑫ He will cut him to pieces and assign him a place with the unbelievers.

⁴⁷"That servant who knows his master's will and does not get ready or does not do what his master wants will be beaten with many blows.ʳ ⁴⁸But the one who does not know and does things deserving punishment will be beaten with few blows.ˢ From everyone who has been given much, much will be demanded; and from the one who has been entrusted with much, much more will be asked.

12:28
ᵃ Mt 6:30

12:30
ᵇ Lk 6:36
ᶜ Mt 6:8

12:31
ᵈ Mt 3:2
ᵉ Mt 19:29

12:32
ᶠ Mt 14:27
ᵍ Mt 25:34

12:33
ʰ Mt 19:21;
Ac 2:45
ⁱ Mt 6:20
ʲ Jas 5:2

12:34
ᵏ Mt 6:21

12:37
ˡ Mt 24:42,46;
25:13
ᵐ Mt 20:28

12:39
ⁿ Mt 6:19;
1Th 5:2;
2Pe 3:10;
Rev 3:3; 16:15

12:40
ᵒ Mk 13:33;
Lk 21:36

12:42
ᵖ Lk 7:13

12:46
ᑫ ver 40

12:47
ʳ Dt 25:2

12:48
ˢ Lev 5:17;
Nu 15:27-30

12:50
a Mk 10:38
b Jn 19:30

12:53
c Mic 7:6;
Mt 10:21

12:54
d Mt 16:2

12:56
e Mt 16:3

12:58
f Mt 5:25

12:59
g Mt 5:26;
Mk 12:42

13:1
h Mt 27:2

13:2
i Jn 9:2,3

13:4
j Jn 9:7,11

13:5
k Mt 3:2; Ac 2:38

13:6
l Isa 5:2;
Jer 8:13;
Mt 21:19

13:7
m Mt 3:10

13:10
n Mt 4:23

13:11
o ver 16

⁴⁹"I have come to bring fire on the earth, and how I wish it were already kindled! ⁵⁰But I have a baptism\ᵃ to undergo, and how distressed I am until it is completed!\ᵇ ⁵¹Do you think I came to bring peace on earth? No, I tell you, but division. ⁵²From now on there will be five in one family divided against each other, three against two and two against three. ⁵³They will be divided, father against son and son against father, mother against daughter and daughter against mother, mother-in-law against daughter-in-law and daughter-in-law against mother-in-law."\ᶜ

⁵⁴He said to the crowd: "When you see a cloud rising in the west, immediately you say, 'It's going to rain,' and it does.\ᵈ ⁵⁵And when the south wind blows, you say, 'It's going to be hot,' and it is. ⁵⁶Hypocrites! You know how to interpret the appearance of the earth and the sky. How is it that you don't know how to interpret this present time?\ᵉ

⁵⁷"Why don't you judge for yourselves what is right? ⁵⁸As you are going with your adversary to the magistrate, try hard to be reconciled to him on the way, or he may drag you off to the judge, and the judge turn you over to the officer, and the officer throw you into prison.\ᶠ ⁵⁹I tell you, you will not get out until you have paid the last penny.\ᵃ"\ᵍ

Chapter 13 Theme

13 Now there were some present at that time who told Jesus about the Galileans whose blood Pilate\ʰ had mixed with their sacrifices. ²Jesus answered, "Do you think that these Galileans were worse sinners than all the other Galileans because they suffered this way?\ⁱ ³I tell you, no! But unless you repent, you too will all perish. ⁴Or those eighteen who died when the tower in Siloam\ʲ fell on them—do you think they were more guilty than all the others living in Jerusalem? ⁵I tell you, no! But unless you repent,\ᵏ you too will all perish."

⁶Then he told this parable: "A man had a fig tree, planted in his vineyard, and he went to look for fruit on it, but did not find any.\ˡ ⁷So he said to the man who took care of the vineyard, 'For three years now I've been coming to look for fruit on this fig tree and haven't found any. Cut it down!\ᵐ Why should it use up the soil?'

⁸"'Sir,' the man replied, 'leave it alone for one more year, and I'll dig around it and fertilize it. ⁹If it bears fruit next year, fine! If not, then cut it down.'"

¹⁰On a Sabbath Jesus was teaching in one of the synagogues,\ⁿ ¹¹and a woman was there who had been crippled by a spirit for eighteen years.\ᵒ She was bent over and could not straighten up at

a 59 Greek *lepton*

all. ¹²When Jesus saw her, he called her forward and said to her, "Woman, you are set free from your infirmity." ¹³Then he put his hands on her,*a* and immediately she straightened up and praised God.

¹⁴Indignant because Jesus had healed on the Sabbath,*b* the synagogue ruler*c* said to the people, "There are six days for work.*d* So come and be healed on those days, not on the Sabbath."

¹⁵The Lord answered him, "You hypocrites! Doesn't each of you on the Sabbath untie his ox or donkey from the stall and lead it out to give it water?*e* ¹⁶Then should not this woman, a daughter of Abraham,*f* whom Satan*g* has kept bound for eighteen long years, be set free on the Sabbath day from what bound her?"

¹⁷When he said this, all his opponents were humiliated,*h* but the people were delighted with all the wonderful things he was doing.

¹⁸Then Jesus asked, "What is the kingdom of God*i* like?*j* What shall I compare it to? ¹⁹It is like a mustard seed, which a man took and planted in his garden. It grew and became a tree,*k* and the birds of the air perched in its branches."*l*

²⁰Again he asked, "What shall I compare the kingdom of God to? ²¹It is like yeast that a woman took and mixed into a large amount*a* of flour until it worked all through the dough."*m*

²²Then Jesus went through the towns and villages, teaching as he made his way to Jerusalem.*n* ²³Someone asked him, "Lord, are only a few people going to be saved?"

He said to them, ²⁴"Make every effort to enter through the narrow door,*o* because many, I tell you, will try to enter and will not be able to. ²⁵Once the owner of the house gets up and closes the door, you will stand outside knocking and pleading, 'Sir, open the door for us.'

"But he will answer, 'I don't know you or where you come from.'*p*

²⁶"Then you will say, 'We ate and drank with you, and you taught in our streets.'

²⁷"But he will reply, 'I don't know you or where you come from. Away from me, all you evildoers!'*q*

²⁸"There will be weeping there, and gnashing of teeth,*r* when you see Abraham, Isaac and Jacob and all the prophets in the kingdom of God, but you yourselves thrown out. ²⁹People will come from east and west*s* and north and south, and will take their places at the feast in the kingdom of God. ³⁰Indeed there are those who are last who will be first, and first who will be last."*t*

³¹At that time some Pharisees came to Jesus and said to him, "Leave this place and go somewhere else. Herod*u* wants to kill you."

³²He replied, "Go tell that fox, 'I will drive out demons and heal people today and tomorrow, and on the third day I will reach my

a 21 Greek *three satas* (probably about 1/2 bushel or 22 liters)

13:13 *a* Mk 5:23
13:14 *b* Mt 12:2; Lk 14:3 *c* Mk 5:22 *d* Ex 20:9
13:15 *e* Lk 14:5
13:16 *f* Lk 3:8; 19:9 *g* Mt 4:10
13:17 *h* Isa 66:5
13:18 *i* Mt 3:2 *j* Mt 13:24
13:19 *k* Lk 17:6 *l* Mt 13:32
13:21 *m* 1Co 5:6
13:22 *n* Lk 9:51
13:24 *o* Mt 7:13
13:25 *p* Mt 7:23; 25:10-12
13:27 *q* Mt 7:23; 25:41
13:28 *r* Mt 8:12
13:29 *s* Mt 8:11
13:30 *t* Mt 19:30
13:31 *u* Mt 14:1

13:32
a Heb 2:10

13:33
b Mt 21:11

13:34
c Mt 23:37

13:35
d Jer 12:17; 22:5
e Ps 118:26;
Mt 21:9;
Lk 19:38

14:1
f Lk 7:36; 11:37
g Mt 12:10

14:3
h Mt 22:35
i Mt 12:2

14:5
j Lk 13:15

14:7
k Lk 11:43

14:11
l Mt 23:12;
Lk 18:14

14:13
m ver 21

14:14
n Ac 24:15

14:15
o Isa 25:6;
Mt 26:29;
Lk 13:29;
Rev 19:9
p Mt 3:2

goal.'*a* ³³In any case, I must keep going today and tomorrow and the next day—for surely no prophet*b* can die outside Jerusalem!

³⁴"O Jerusalem, Jerusalem, you who kill the prophets and stone those sent to you, how often I have longed to gather your children together, as a hen gathers her chicks under her wings,*c* but you were not willing! ³⁵Look, your house is left to you desolate.*d* I tell you, you will not see me again until you say, 'Blessed is he who comes in the name of the Lord.'*a*"*e*

Chapter 14 Theme _____

14 One Sabbath, when Jesus went to eat in the house of a prominent Pharisee,*f* he was being carefully watched.*g* ²There in front of him was a man suffering from dropsy. ³Jesus asked the Pharisees and experts in the law,*h* "Is it lawful to heal on the Sabbath or not?"*i* ⁴But they remained silent. So taking hold of the man, he healed him and sent him away.

⁵Then he asked them, "If one of you has a son*b* or an ox that falls into a well on the Sabbath day, will you not immediately pull him out?"*j* ⁶And they had nothing to say.

⁷When he noticed how the guests picked the places of honor at the table,*k* he told them this parable: ⁸"When someone invites you to a wedding feast, do not take the place of honor, for a person more distinguished than you may have been invited. ⁹If so, the host who invited both of you will come and say to you, 'Give this man your seat.' Then, humiliated, you will have to take the least important place. ¹⁰But when you are invited, take the lowest place, so that when your host comes, he will say to you, 'Friend, move up to a better place.' Then you will be honored in the presence of all your fellow guests. ¹¹For everyone who exalts himself will be humbled, and he who humbles himself will be exalted."*l*

¹²Then Jesus said to his host, "When you give a luncheon or dinner, do not invite your friends, your brothers or relatives, or your rich neighbors; if you do, they may invite you back and so you will be repaid. ¹³But when you give a banquet, invite the poor, the crippled, the lame, the blind,*m* ¹⁴and you will be blessed. Although they cannot repay you, you will be repaid at the resurrection of the righteous."*n*

¹⁵When one of those at the table with him heard this, he said to Jesus, "Blessed is the man who will eat at the feast*o* in the kingdom of God."*p*

¹⁶Jesus replied: "A certain man was preparing a great banquet and invited many guests. ¹⁷At the time of the banquet he sent his servant to tell those who had been invited, 'Come, for everything is now ready.'

a 35 Psalm 118:26   *b* 5 Some manuscripts *donkey*

¹⁸"But they all alike began to make excuses. The first said, 'I have just bought a field, and I must go and see it. Please excuse me.'

¹⁹"Another said, 'I have just bought five yoke of oxen, and I'm on my way to try them out. Please excuse me.'

²⁰"Still another said, 'I just got married, so I can't come.'

²¹"The servant came back and reported this to his master. Then the owner of the house became angry and ordered his servant, 'Go out quickly into the streets and alleys of the town and bring in the poor, the crippled, the blind and the lame.'ᵃ

²²"'Sir,' the servant said, 'what you ordered has been done, but there is still room.'

²³"Then the master told his servant, 'Go out to the roads and country lanes and make them come in, so that my house will be full. ²⁴I tell you, not one of those men who were invited will get a taste of my banquet.'"ᵇ

²⁵Large crowds were traveling with Jesus, and turning to them he said: ²⁶"If anyone comes to me and does not hate his father and mother, his wife and children, his brothers and sisters—yes, even his own life—he cannot be my disciple.ᶜ ²⁷And anyone who does not carry his cross and follow me cannot be my disciple.ᵈ

²⁸"Suppose one of you wants to build a tower. Will he not first sit down and estimate the cost to see if he has enough money to complete it? ²⁹For if he lays the foundation and is not able to finish it, everyone who sees it will ridicule him, ³⁰saying, 'This fellow began to build and was not able to finish.'

³¹"Or suppose a king is about to go to war against another king. Will he not first sit down and consider whether he is able with ten thousand men to oppose the one coming against him with twenty thousand? ³²If he is not able, he will send a delegation while the other is still a long way off and will ask for terms of peace. ³³In the same way, any of you who does not give up everything he has cannot be my disciple.ᵉ

³⁴"Salt is good, but if it loses its saltiness, how can it be made salty again?ᶠ ³⁵It is fit neither for the soil nor for the manure pile; it is thrown out.ᵍ

"He who has ears to hear, let him hear."ʰ

Chapter 15 Theme

15 Now the tax collectorsⁱ and "sinners" were all gathering around to hear him. ²But the Pharisees and the teachers of the law muttered, "This man welcomes sinners and eats with them."ʲ

³Then Jesus told them this parable:ᵏ ⁴"Suppose one of you has a hundred sheep and loses one of them. Does he not leave the ninety-nine in the open country and go after the lost sheep until he finds

14:21
ᵃ ver 13

14:24
ᵇ Mt 21:43;
Ac 13:46

14:26
ᶜ Mt 10:37;
Jn 12:25

14:27
ᵈ Mt 10:38;
Lk 9:23

14:33
ᵉ Php 3:7,8

14:34
ᶠ Mk 9:50

14:35
ᵍ Mt 5:13
ʰ Mt 11:15

15:1
ⁱ Lk 5:29

15:2
ʲ Mt 9:11

15:3
ᵏ Mt 13:3

15:4
a Ps 23; 119:176;
Jer 31:10;
Eze 34:11-16;
Lk 5:32; 19:10

15:6
b ver 9

15:7
c ver 10

15:9
d ver 6

15:10
e ver 7

15:11
f Mt 21:28

15:12
g Dt 21:17
h ver 30

15:13
i ver 30; Lk 16:1

15:15
j Lev 11:7

15:18
k Lev 26:40;
Mt 3:2

15:20
l Ge 45:14,15;
46:29; Ac 20:37

15:21
m Ps 51:4

15:22
n Zec 3:4;
Rev 6:11
o Ge 41:42

15:24
p Eph 2:1,5;
5:14; 1Ti 5:6
q ver 32

it?*a* [5]And when he finds it, he joyfully puts it on his shoulders [6]and goes home. Then he calls his friends and neighbors together and says, 'Rejoice with me; I have found my lost sheep.'*b* [7]I tell you that in the same way there will be more rejoicing in heaven over one sinner who repents than over ninety-nine righteous persons who do not need to repent.*c*

[8]"Or suppose a woman has ten silver coins*a* and loses one. Does she not light a lamp, sweep the house and search carefully until she finds it? [9]And when she finds it, she calls her friends and neighbors together and says, 'Rejoice with me; I have found my lost coin.'*d* [10]In the same way, I tell you, there is rejoicing in the presence of the angels of God over one sinner who repents."*e*

[11]Jesus continued: "There was a man who had two sons.*f* [12]The younger one said to his father, 'Father, give me my share of the estate.'*g* So he divided his property*h* between them.

[13]"Not long after that, the younger son got together all he had, set off for a distant country and there squandered his wealth*i* in wild living. [14]After he had spent everything, there was a severe famine in that whole country, and he began to be in need. [15]So he went and hired himself out to a citizen of that country, who sent him to his fields to feed pigs.*j* [16]He longed to fill his stomach with the pods that the pigs were eating, but no one gave him anything.

[17]"When he came to his senses, he said, 'How many of my father's hired men have food to spare, and here I am starving to death! [18]I will set out and go back to my father and say to him: Father, I have sinned*k* against heaven and against you. [19]I am no longer worthy to be called your son; make me like one of your hired men.' [20]So he got up and went to his father.

"But while he was still a long way off, his father saw him and was filled with compassion for him; he ran to his son, threw his arms around him and kissed him.*l*

[21]"The son said to him, 'Father, I have sinned against heaven and against you.*m* I am no longer worthy to be called your son.*b*'

[22]"But the father said to his servants, 'Quick! Bring the best robe*n* and put it on him. Put a ring on his finger*o* and sandals on his feet. [23]Bring the fattened calf and kill it. Let's have a feast and celebrate. [24]For this son of mine was dead and is alive again;*p* he was lost and is found.' So they began to celebrate.*q*

[25]"Meanwhile, the older son was in the field. When he came near the house, he heard music and dancing. [26]So he called one of the servants and asked him what was going on. [27]'Your brother has come,' he replied, 'and your father has killed the fattened calf because he has him back safe and sound.'

a 8 Greek *ten drachmas,* each worth about a day's wages   *b 21* Some early manuscripts *son. Make me like one of your hired men.*

²⁸"The older brother became angry*a* and refused to go in. So his father went out and pleaded with him. ²⁹But he answered his father, 'Look! All these years I've been slaving for you and never disobeyed your orders. Yet you never gave me even a young goat so I could celebrate with my friends. ³⁰But when this son of yours who has squandered your property*b* with prostitutes*c* comes home, you kill the fattened calf for him!'

³¹"'My son,' the father said, 'you are always with me, and everything I have is yours. ³²But we had to celebrate and be glad, because this brother of yours was dead and is alive again; he was lost and is found.'"*d*

Chapter 16 Theme

16 Jesus told his disciples: "There was a rich man whose manager was accused of wasting his possessions.*e* ²So he called him in and asked him, 'What is this I hear about you? Give an account of your management, because you cannot be manager any longer.'

³"The manager said to himself, 'What shall I do now? My master is taking away my job. I'm not strong enough to dig, and I'm ashamed to beg— ⁴I know what I'll do so that, when I lose my job here, people will welcome me into their houses.'

⁵"So he called in each one of his master's debtors. He asked the first, 'How much do you owe my master?'

⁶"'Eight hundred gallons*a* of olive oil,' he replied.

"The manager told him, 'Take your bill, sit down quickly, and make it four hundred.'

⁷"Then he asked the second, 'And how much do you owe?'

"'A thousand bushels*b* of wheat,' he replied.

"He told him, 'Take your bill and make it eight hundred.'

⁸"The master commended the dishonest manager because he had acted shrewdly. For the people of this world*f* are more shrewd*g* in dealing with their own kind than are the people of the light.*h* ⁹I tell you, use worldly wealth*i* to gain friends for yourselves, so that when it is gone, you will be welcomed into eternal dwellings.*j*

¹⁰"Whoever can be trusted with very little can also be trusted with much,*k* and whoever is dishonest with very little will also be dishonest with much. ¹¹So if you have not been trustworthy in handling worldly wealth,*l* who will trust you with true riches? ¹²And if you have not been trustworthy with someone else's property, who will give you property of your own?

¹³"No servant can serve two masters. Either he will hate the one and love the other, or he will be devoted to the one and despise the other. You cannot serve both God and Money."*m*

a6 Greek one hundred batous (probably about 3 kiloliters)   b7 Greek one hundred korous (probably about 35 kiloliters)

15:28 *a*Jnh 4:1

15:30 *b*ver 12,13 *c*Pr 29:3

15:32 *d*ver 24; Mal 3:17

16:1 *e*Lk 15:13,30

16:8 *f*Ps 17:14 *g*Ps 18:26 *h*Jn 12:36; Eph 5:8; 1Th 5:5

16:9 *i*ver 11,13 *j*Mt 19:21; Lk 12:33

16:10 *k*Mt 25:21,23; Lk 19:17

16:11 *l*ver 9,13

16:13 *m*ver 9,11; Mt 6:24

16:14
a 1Ti 3:3
b Lk 23:35

16:15
c Lk 10:29
d 1Sa 16:7;
Rev 2:23

16:16
e Mt 11:12,13
f Mt 4:23

16:17
g Mt 5:18

16:18
h Mt 5:31,32;
19:9; Mk 10:11;
Ro 7:2,3;
1Co 7:10,11

16:19
i Eze 16:49

16:20
j Ac 3:2

16:21
k Mt 15:27

16:24
l ver 30; Lk 3:8
m Mt 5:22

16:25
n Ps 17:14
o Lk 6:21,24, 25

16:28
p Ac 2:40; 20:23;
1Th 4:6

16:29
q Lk 24:27,44;
Jn 5:45-47;
Ac 15:21
r Lk 4:17;
Jn 1:45

16:30
s ver 24; Lk 3:8

17:1
t Mt 5:29
u Mt 18:7

¹⁴The Pharisees, who loved money,*a* heard all this and were sneering at Jesus.*b* ¹⁵He said to them, "You are the ones who justify yourselves*c* in the eyes of men, but God knows your hearts.*d* What is highly valued among men is detestable in God's sight.

¹⁶"The Law and the Prophets were proclaimed until John.*e* Since that time, the good news of the kingdom of God is being preached,*f* and everyone is forcing his way into it. ¹⁷It is easier for heaven and earth to disappear than for the least stroke of a pen to drop out of the Law.*g*

¹⁸"Anyone who divorces his wife and marries another woman commits adultery, and the man who marries a divorced woman commits adultery.*h*

¹⁹"There was a rich man who was dressed in purple and fine linen and lived in luxury every day.*i* ²⁰At his gate was laid a beggar*j* named Lazarus, covered with sores ²¹and longing to eat what fell from the rich man's table.*k* Even the dogs came and licked his sores.

²²"The time came when the beggar died and the angels carried him to Abraham's side. The rich man also died and was buried. ²³In hell,*a* where he was in torment, he looked up and saw Abraham far away, with Lazarus by his side. ²⁴So he called to him, 'Father Abraham,*l* have pity on me and send Lazarus to dip the tip of his finger in water and cool my tongue, because I am in agony in this fire.'*m*

²⁵"But Abraham replied, 'Son, remember that in your lifetime you received your good things, while Lazarus received bad things,*n* but now he is comforted here and you are in agony.*o* ²⁶And besides all this, between us and you a great chasm has been fixed, so that those who want to go from here to you cannot, nor can anyone cross over from there to us.'

²⁷"He answered, 'Then I beg you, father, send Lazarus to my father's house, ²⁸for I have five brothers. Let him warn them,*p* so that they will not also come to this place of torment.'

²⁹"Abraham replied, 'They have Moses*q* and the Prophets;*r* let them listen to them.'

³⁰"'No, father Abraham,'*s* he said, 'but if someone from the dead goes to them, they will repent.'

³¹"He said to him, 'If they do not listen to Moses and the Prophets, they will not be convinced even if someone rises from the dead.'"

Chapter 17 Theme

17 Jesus said to his disciples: "Things that cause people to sin*t* are bound to come, but woe to that person through whom they come.*u* ²It would be better for him to be thrown into the sea

a 23 Greek *Hades*

with a millstone tied around his neck than for him to cause one of these little ones[a] to sin.[b] [3]So watch yourselves.

"If your brother sins, rebuke him,[c] and if he repents, forgive him.[d] [4]If he sins against you seven times in a day, and seven times comes back to you and says, 'I repent,' forgive him."[e]

[5]The apostles[f] said to the Lord,[g] "Increase our faith!"

[6]He replied, "If you have faith as small as a mustard seed,[h] you can say to this mulberry tree, 'Be uprooted and planted in the sea,' and it will obey you.[i]

[7]"Suppose one of you had a servant plowing or looking after the sheep. Would he say to the servant when he comes in from the field, 'Come along now and sit down to eat'? [8]Would he not rather say, 'Prepare my supper, get yourself ready and wait on me[j] while I eat and drink; after that you may eat and drink'? [9]Would he thank the servant because he did what he was told to do? [10]So you also, when you have done everything you were told to do, should say, 'We are unworthy servants; we have only done our duty.'"[k]

[11]Now on his way to Jerusalem,[l] Jesus traveled along the border between Samaria and Galilee.[m] [12]As he was going into a village, ten men who had leprosy[a][n] met him. They stood at a distance[o] [13]and called out in a loud voice, "Jesus, Master,[p] have pity on us!"

[14]When he saw them, he said, "Go, show yourselves to the priests."[q] And as they went, they were cleansed.

[15]One of them, when he saw he was healed, came back, praising God[r] in a loud voice. [16]He threw himself at Jesus' feet and thanked him—and he was a Samaritan.[s]

[17]Jesus asked, "Were not all ten cleansed? Where are the other nine? [18]Was no one found to return and give praise to God except this foreigner?" [19]Then he said to him, "Rise and go; your faith has made you well."[t]

[20]Once, having been asked by the Pharisees when the kingdom of God would come,[u] Jesus replied, "The kingdom of God does not come with your careful observation, [21]nor will people say, 'Here it is,' or 'There it is,'[v] because the kingdom of God is within[b] you."

[22]Then he said to his disciples, "The time is coming when you will long to see one of the days of the Son of Man,[w] but you will not see it.[x] [23]Men will tell you, 'There he is!' or 'Here he is!' Do not go running off after them.[y] [24]For the Son of Man in his day[c] will be like the lightning,[z] which flashes and lights up the sky from one end to the other. [25]But first he must suffer many things[a] and be rejected[b] by this generation.[c]

[26]"Just as it was in the days of Noah,[d] so also will it be in the days of the Son of Man. [27]People were eating, drinking, marrying and

---

a 12 The Greek word was used for various diseases affecting the skin—not necessarily leprosy.
b 21 Or among   c 24 Some manuscripts do not have in his day.

17:2
a Mk 10:24;
Lk 10:21
b Mt 5:29

17:3
c Mt 18:15
d Eph 4:32;
Col 3:13

17:4
e Mt 18:21,22

17:5
f Mk 6:30
g Lk 7:13

17:6
h Mt 13:31;
17:20; Lk 13:19
i Mt 21:21;
Mk 9:23

17:8
j Lk 12:37

17:10
k 1Co 9:16

17:11
l Lk 9:51
m Lk 9:51,52;
Jn 4:3,4

17:12
n Mt 8:2
o Lev 13:45,46

17:13
p Lk 5:5

17:14
q Lev 14:2;
Mt 8:4

17:15
r Mt 9:8

17:16
s Mt 10:5

17:19
t Mt 9:22

17:20
u Mt 3:2

17:21
v ver 23

17:22
w Mt 8:20
x Mt 9:15;
Lk 5:35

17:23
y Mt 24:23;
Mk 13:21;
Lk 21:8

17:24
z Mt 24:27

17:25
a Mt 16:21
b Lk 9:22; 18:32
c Mk 13:30;
Lk 21:32

17:26
d Ge 7:6-24

being given in marriage up to the day Noah entered the ark. Then the flood came and destroyed them all.

28"It was the same in the days of Lot.ᵃ People were eating and drinking, buying and selling, planting and building. 29But the day Lot left Sodom, fire and sulfur rained down from heaven and destroyed them all.

30"It will be just like this on the day the Son of Man is revealed.ᵇ 31On that day no one who is on the roof of his house, with his goods inside, should go down to get them. Likewise, no one in the field should go back for anything.ᶜ 32Remember Lot's wife!ᵈ 33Whoever tries to keep his life will lose it, and whoever loses his life will preserve it.ᵉ 34I tell you, on that night two people will be in one bed; one will be taken and the other left. 35Two women will be grinding grain together; one will be taken and the other left.ᵃ"ᶠ

37"Where, Lord?" they asked.

He replied, "Where there is a dead body, there the vultures will gather."ᵍ

Chapter 18 Theme _____

18 Then Jesus told his disciples a parable to show them that they should always pray and not give up.ʰ 2He said: "In a certain town there was a judge who neither feared God nor cared about men. 3And there was a widow in that town who kept coming to him with the plea, 'Grant me justiceⁱ against my adversary.'

4"For some time he refused. But finally he said to himself, 'Even though I don't fear God or care about men, 5yet because this widow keeps bothering me, I will see that she gets justice, so that she won't eventually wear me out with her coming!'"ʲ

6And the Lordᵏ said, "Listen to what the unjust judge says. 7And will not God bring about justice for his chosen ones, who cry outˡ to him day and night? Will he keep putting them off? 8I tell you, he will see that they get justice, and quickly. However, when the Son of Manᵐ comes,ⁿ will he find faith on the earth?"

9To some who were confident of their own righteousnessᵒ and looked down on everybody else,ᵖ Jesus told this parable: 10"Two men went up to the temple to pray,�q one a Pharisee and the other a tax collector. 11The Pharisee stood upʳ and prayed aboutᵇ himself: 'God, I thank you that I am not like other men—robbers, evildoers, adulterers—or even like this tax collector. 12I fastˢ twice a week and give a tenthᵗ of all I get.'

13"But the tax collector stood at a distance. He would not even look up to heaven, but beat his breastᵘ and said, 'God, have mercy on me, a sinner.'ᵛ

17:28
ᵃGe 19:1-28

17:30
ᵇMt 10:23;
16:27;
24:3,27,37,39;
25:31; 1Co 1:7;
1Th 2:19;
2Th 1:7; 2:8;
2Pe 3:4; Rev 1:7

17:31
ᶜMt 24:17,18;
Mk 13:15-16

17:32
ᵈGe 19:26

17:33
ᵉJn 12:25

17:35
ᶠMt 24:41

17:37
ᵍMt 24:28

18:1
ʰIsa 40:31;
Lk 11:5-8;
Ac 1:14;
Ro 12:12;
Eph 6:18;
Col 4:2;
1Th 5:17

18:3
ⁱIsa 1:17

18:5
ʲLk 11:8

18:6
ᵏLk 7:13

18:7
ˡEx 22:23;
Ps 88:1;
Rev 6:10

18:8
ᵐMt 8:20
ⁿMt 16:27

18:9
ᵒLk 16:15
ᵖIsa 65:5

18:10
qAc 3:1

18:11
ʳMt 6:5;
Mk 11:25

18:12
ˢIsa 58:3;
Mt 9:14
ᵗMal 3:8;
Lk 11:42

18:13
ᵘIsa 66:2;
Jer 31:19;
Lk 23:48
ᵛLk 5:32;
1Ti 1:15

ᵃ 35 Some manuscripts *left.* ³⁶*Two men will be in the field; one will be taken and the other left.*
ᵇ 11 Or *to*

¹⁴"I tell you that this man, rather than the other, went home justified before God. For everyone who exalts himself will be humbled, and he who humbles himself will be exalted."ᵃ

¹⁵People were also bringing babies to Jesus to have him touch them. When the disciples saw this, they rebuked them. ¹⁶But Jesus called the children to him and said, "Let the little children come to me, and do not hinder them, for the kingdom of God belongs to such as these. ¹⁷I tell you the truth, anyone who will not receive the kingdom of God like a little childᵇ will never enter it."

¹⁸A certain ruler asked him, "Good teacher, what must I do to inherit eternal life?"ᶜ

¹⁹"Why do you call me good?" Jesus answered. "No one is good—except God alone. ²⁰You know the commandments: 'Do not commit adultery, do not murder, do not steal, do not give false testimony, honor your father and mother.'ᵃ"ᵈ

²¹"All these I have kept since I was a boy," he said.

²²When Jesus heard this, he said to him, "You still lack one thing. Sell everything you have and give to the poor,ᵉ and you will have treasure in heaven.ᶠ Then come, follow me."

²³When he heard this, he became very sad, because he was a man of great wealth. ²⁴Jesus looked at him and said, "How hard it is for the rich to enter the kingdom of God!ᵍ ²⁵Indeed, it is easier for a camel to go through the eye of a needle than for a rich man to enter the kingdom of God."

²⁶Those who heard this asked, "Who then can be saved?"

²⁷Jesus replied, "What is impossible with men is possible with God."ʰ

²⁸Peter said to him, "We have left all we had to follow you!"ⁱ

²⁹"I tell you the truth," Jesus said to them, "no one who has left home or wife or brothers or parents or children for the sake of the kingdom of God ³⁰will fail to receive many times as much in this age and, in the age to come,ʲ eternal life."ᵏ

³¹Jesus took the Twelve aside and told them, "We are going up to Jerusalem,ˡ and everything that is written by the prophetsᵐ about the Son of Manⁿ will be fulfilled. ³²He will be handed over to the Gentiles.ᵒ They will mock him, insult him, spit on him, flog himᵖ and kill him.�q ³³On the third dayʳ he will rise again."ˢ

³⁴The disciples did not understand any of this. Its meaning was hidden from them, and they did not know what he was talking about.ᵗ

³⁵As Jesus approached Jericho,ᵘ a blind man was sitting by the roadside begging. ³⁶When he heard the crowd going by, he asked what was happening. ³⁷They told him, "Jesus of Nazareth is passing by."ᵛ

a 20 Exodus 20:12-16; Deut. 5:16-20

18:14
a Mt 23:12;
Lk 14:11

18:17
b Mt 11:25; 18:3

18:18
c Lk 10:25

18:20
d Ex 20:12-16;
Dt 5:16-20;
Ro 13:9

18:22
e Ac 2:45
f Mt 6:20

18:24
g Pr 11:28

18:27
h Mt 19:26

18:28
i Mt 4:19

18:30
j Mt 12:32
k Mt 25:46

18:31
l Lk 9:51
m Ps 22; Isa 53
n Mt 8:20

18:32
o Lk 23:1
p Mt 16:21
q Ac 2:23

18:33
r Mt 16:21
s Mt 16:21

18:34
t Mk 9:32;
Lk 9:45

18:35
u Lk 19:1

18:37
v Lk 19:4

18:38
a ver 39; Mt 9:27
b Mt 17:15;
Lk 18:13

18:39
c ver 38

18:42
d Mt 9:22

18:43
e Mt 9:8;
Lk 13:17

19:1
f Lk 18:35

19:4
g 1Ki 10:27;
1Ch 27:28;
Isa 9:10
h Lk 18:37

19:7
i Mt 9:11

19:8
j Lk 7:13
k Lk 3:12,13
l Ex 22:1;
Lev 6:4,5;
Nu 5:7; 2Sa 12:6

19:9
m Lk 3:8; 13:16;
Ro 4:16; Gal 3:7

19:10
n Eze 34:12,16;
Jn 3:17

19:11
o Mt 3:2
p Lk 17:20;
Ac 1:6

19:13
q Mk 13:34

[38] He called out, "Jesus, Son of David,[a] have mercy[b] on me!"

[39] Those who led the way rebuked him and told him to be quiet, but he shouted all the more, "Son of David, have mercy on me!"[c]

[40] Jesus stopped and ordered the man to be brought to him. When he came near, Jesus asked him, [41] "What do you want me to do for you?"

"Lord, I want to see," he replied.

[42] Jesus said to him, "Receive your sight; your faith has healed you."[d] [43] Immediately he received his sight and followed Jesus, praising God. When all the people saw it, they also praised God.[e]

Chapter 19 Theme

19 Jesus entered Jericho[f] and was passing through. [2] A man was there by the name of Zacchaeus; he was a chief tax collector and was wealthy. [3] He wanted to see who Jesus was, but being a short man he could not, because of the crowd. [4] So he ran ahead and climbed a sycamore-fig[g] tree to see him, since Jesus was coming that way.[h]

[5] When Jesus reached the spot, he looked up and said to him, "Zacchaeus, come down immediately. I must stay at your house today." [6] So he came down at once and welcomed him gladly.

[7] All the people saw this and began to mutter, "He has gone to be the guest of a 'sinner.'"[i]

[8] But Zacchaeus stood up and said to the Lord,[j] "Look, Lord! Here and now I give half of my possessions to the poor, and if I have cheated anybody out of anything,[k] I will pay back four times the amount."[l]

[9] Jesus said to him, "Today salvation has come to this house, because this man, too, is a son of Abraham.[m] [10] For the Son of Man came to seek and to save what was lost."[n]

[11] While they were listening to this, he went on to tell them a parable, because he was near Jerusalem and the people thought that the kingdom of God[o] was going to appear at once.[p] [12] He said: "A man of noble birth went to a distant country to have himself appointed king and then to return. [13] So he called ten of his servants[q] and gave them ten minas.[a] 'Put this money to work,' he said, 'until I come back.'

[14] "But his subjects hated him and sent a delegation after him to say, 'We don't want this man to be our king.'

[15] "He was made king, however, and returned home. Then he sent for the servants to whom he had given the money, in order to find out what they had gained with it.

[16] "The first one came and said, 'Sir, your mina has earned ten more.'

a 13 A mina was about three months' wages.

17"'Well done, my good servant!'[a] his master replied. 'Because you have been trustworthy in a very small matter, take charge of ten cities.'[b]

18"The second came and said, 'Sir, your mina has earned five more.'

19"His master answered, 'You take charge of five cities.'

20"Then another servant came and said, 'Sir, here is your mina; I have kept it laid away in a piece of cloth. 21I was afraid of you, because you are a hard man. You take out what you did not put in and reap what you did not sow.'[c]

22"His master replied, 'I will judge you by your own words,[d] you wicked servant! You knew, did you, that I am a hard man, taking out what I did not put in, and reaping what I did not sow?[e] 23Why then didn't you put my money on deposit, so that when I came back, I could have collected it with interest?'

24"Then he said to those standing by, 'Take his mina away from him and give it to the one who has ten minas.'

25"'Sir,' they said, 'he already has ten!'

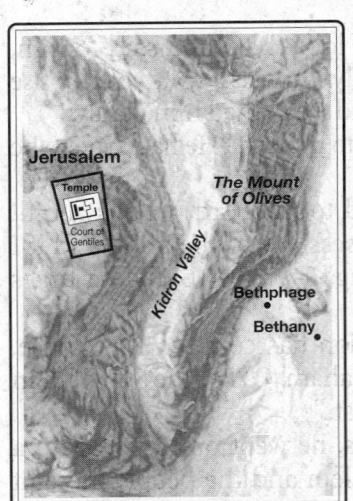

From Bethany, Bethphage across the Mount of Olives into Jerusalem

Jerusalem

Temple

Court of Gentiles

The Mount of Olives

Kidron Valley

Bethphage

Bethany

26"He replied, 'I tell you that to everyone who has, more will be given, but as for the one who has nothing, even what he has will be taken away.[f] 27But those enemies of mine who did not want me to be king over them—bring them here and kill them in front of me.'"

28After Jesus had said this, he went on ahead, going up to Jerusalem.[g] 29As he approached Bethphage and Bethany[h] at the hill called the Mount of Olives,[i] he sent two of his disciples, saying to them, 30"Go to the village ahead of you, and as you enter it, you will find a colt tied there, which no one has ever ridden. Untie it and bring it here. 31If anyone asks you, 'Why are you untying it?' tell him, 'The Lord needs it.'"

32Those who were sent ahead went and found it just as he had told them.[j] 33As they were untying the colt, its owners asked them, "Why are you untying the colt?"

34They replied, "The Lord needs it."

35They brought it to Jesus, threw their cloaks on the colt and put Jesus on it. 36As he went along, people spread their cloaks[k] on the road.

37When he came near the place where the road goes down the Mount of Olives,[l] the whole crowd of disciples began joyfully to praise God in loud voices for all the miracles they had seen:

19:17
a Pr 27:18
b Lk 16:10

19:21
c Mt 25:24

19:22
d 2Sa 1:16;
Job 15:6
e Mt 25:26

19:26
f Mt 13:12;
25:29; Lk 8:18

19:28
g Mk 10:32;
Lk 9:51

19:29
h Mt 21:17
i Mt 21:1

19:32
j Lk 22:13

19:36
k 2Ki 9:13

19:37
l Mt 21:1

19:38
a Ps 118:26;
Lk 13:35
b Lk 2:14

19:39
c Mt 21:15,16

19:40
d Hab 2:11

19:41
e Isa 22:4;
Lk 13:34,35

19:43
f Isa 29:3;
Jer 6:6; Eze 4:2;
26:8; Lk 21:20

19:44
g Ps 137:9
h Mt 24:2;
Mk 13:2;
Lk 21:6
i 1Pe 2:12

19:46
j Isa 56:7
k Jer 7:11

19:47
l Mt 26:55
m Mt 12:14;
Mk 11:18

20:1
n Mt 26:55
o Lk 8:1

20:2
p Jn 2:18;
Ac 4:7; 7:27

20:4
q Mk 1:4

20:6
r Lk 7:29
s Mt 11:9

20:9
t Isa 5:1-7
u Mt 25:14

³⁸"Blessed is the king who comes in the name of the Lord!"ᵃ*a*

"Peace in heaven and glory in the highest!"ᵇ

³⁹Some of the Pharisees in the crowd said to Jesus, "Teacher, rebuke your disciples!"ᶜ

⁴⁰"I tell you," he replied, "if they keep quiet, the stones will cry out."ᵈ

⁴¹As he approached Jerusalem and saw the city, he wept over itᵉ ⁴²and said, "If you, even you, had only known on this day what would bring you peace—but now it is hidden from your eyes. ⁴³The days will come upon you when your enemies will build an embankment against you and encircle you and hem you in on every side.ᶠ ⁴⁴They will dash you to the ground, you and the children within your walls.ᵍ They will not leave one stone on another,ʰ because you did not recognize the time of God's comingⁱ to you."

⁴⁵Then he entered the temple area and began driving out those who were selling. ⁴⁶"It is written," he said to them, "'My house will be a house of prayer'ᵇ;ʲ but you have made it 'a den of robbers.'ᶜ"ᵏ

⁴⁷Every day he was teaching at the temple.ˡ But the chief priests, the teachers of the law and the leaders among the people were trying to kill him.ᵐ ⁴⁸Yet they could not find any way to do it, because all the people hung on his words.

Chapter 20 Theme

20 One day as he was teaching the people in the temple courtsⁿ and preaching the gospel,ᵒ the chief priests and the teachers of the law, together with the elders, came up to him. ²"Tell us by what authority you are doing these things," they said. "Who gave you this authority?"ᵖ

³He replied, "I will also ask you a question. Tell me, ⁴John's baptismq—was it from heaven, or from men?"

⁵They discussed it among themselves and said, "If we say, 'From heaven,' he will ask, 'Why didn't you believe him?' ⁶But if we say, 'From men,' all the peopleʳ will stone us, because they are persuaded that John was a prophet."ˢ

⁷So they answered, "We don't know where it was from."

⁸Jesus said, "Neither will I tell you by what authority I am doing these things."

⁹He went on to tell the people this parable: "A man planted a vineyard,ᵗ rented it to some farmers and went away for a long time.ᵘ ¹⁰At harvest time he sent a servant to the tenants so they would give him some of the fruit of the vineyard. But the tenants beat him and sent him away empty-handed. ¹¹He sent another servant, but that one also they beat and treated shamefully and

sent away empty-handed. ¹²He sent still a third, and they wounded him and threw him out.

¹³"Then the owner of the vineyard said, 'What shall I do? I will send my son, whom I love;^a perhaps they will respect him.'

¹⁴"But when the tenants saw him, they talked the matter over. 'This is the heir,' they said. 'Let's kill him, and the inheritance will be ours.' ¹⁵So they threw him out of the vineyard and killed him.

"What then will the owner of the vineyard do to them? ¹⁶He will come and kill those tenants^b and give the vineyard to others."

When the people heard this, they said, "May this never be!"

¹⁷Jesus looked directly at them and asked, "Then what is the meaning of that which is written:

> "'The stone the builders rejected
> has become the capstone^{a'b}?^c

¹⁸Everyone who falls on that stone will be broken to pieces, but he on whom it falls will be crushed."^d

¹⁹The teachers of the law and the chief priests looked for a way to arrest him^e immediately, because they knew he had spoken this parable against them. But they were afraid of the people.^f

²⁰Keeping a close watch on him, they sent spies, who pretended to be honest. They hoped to catch Jesus in something he said^g so that they might hand him over to the power and authority of the governor.^h ²¹So the spies questioned him: "Teacher, we know that you speak and teach what is right, and that you do not show partiality but teach the way of God in accordance with the truth.ⁱ ²²Is it right for us to pay taxes to Caesar or not?"

²³He saw through their duplicity and said to them, ²⁴"Show me a denarius. Whose portrait and inscription are on it?"

²⁵"Caesar's," they replied.

He said to them, "Then give to Caesar what is Caesar's,^j and to God what is God's."

²⁶They were unable to trap him in what he had said there in public. And astonished by his answer, they became silent.

²⁷Some of the Sadducees,^k who say there is no resurrection,^l came to Jesus with a question. ²⁸"Teacher," they said, "Moses wrote for us that if a man's brother dies and leaves a wife but no children, the man must marry the widow and have children for his brother.^m ²⁹Now there were seven brothers. The first one married a woman and died childless. ³⁰The second ³¹and then the third married her, and in the same way the seven died, leaving no children. ³²Finally, the woman died too. ³³Now then, at the resurrection whose wife will she be, since the seven were married to her?"

20:13 ^aMt 3:17

20:16 ^bLk 19:27

20:17 ^cPs 118:22; Ac 4:11

20:18 ^dIsa 8:14,15

20:19 ^eLk 19:47 ^fMk 11:18

20:20 ^gMt 12:10 ^hMt 27:2

20:21 ⁱJn 3:2

20:25 ^jLk 23:2; Ro 13:7

20:27 ^kAc 4:1 ^lAc 23:8; 1Co 15:12

20:28 ^mDt 25:5

---

^a17 Or *cornerstone*   ^b17 Psalm 118:22

20:35
a Mt 12:32

20:36
b Jn 1:12;
1Jn 3:1-2

20:37
c Ex 3:6

20:40
d Mt 22:46;
Mk 12:34

20:41
e Mt 1:1

20:43
f Ps 110:1;
Mt 22:44

20:46
g Lk 11:43

21:1
h Mt 27:6;
Jn 8:20

21:4
i 2Co 8:12

21:6
j Lk 19:44

21:8
k Lk 17:23

³⁴Jesus replied, "The people of this age marry and are given in marriage. ³⁵But those who are considered worthy of taking part in that age*a* and in the resurrection from the dead will neither marry nor be given in marriage, ³⁶and they can no longer die; for they are like the angels. They are God's children,*b* since they are children of the resurrection. ³⁷But in the account of the bush, even Moses showed that the dead rise, for he calls the Lord 'the God of Abraham, and the God of Isaac, and the God of Jacob.'*ac* ³⁸He is not the God of the dead, but of the living, for to him all are alive."

³⁹Some of the teachers of the law responded, "Well said, teacher!" ⁴⁰And no one dared to ask him any more questions.*d*

⁴¹Then Jesus said to them, "How is it that they say the Christ*b* is the Son of David?*e* ⁴²David himself declares in the Book of Psalms:

"'The Lord said to my Lord:
   "Sit at my right hand
⁴³until I make your enemies
   a footstool for your feet."'*cf*

⁴⁴David calls him 'Lord.' How then can he be his son?"

⁴⁵While all the people were listening, Jesus said to his disciples, ⁴⁶"Beware of the teachers of the law. They like to walk around in flowing robes and love to be greeted in the marketplaces and have the most important seats in the synagogues and the places of honor at banquets.*g* ⁴⁷They devour widows' houses and for a show make lengthy prayers. Such men will be punished most severely."

Chapter 21 Theme

21 As he looked up, Jesus saw the rich putting their gifts into the temple treasury.*h* ²He also saw a poor widow put in two very small copper coins.*d* ³"I tell you the truth," he said, "this poor widow has put in more than all the others. ⁴All these people gave their gifts out of their wealth; but she out of her poverty put in all she had to live on."*i*

⁵Some of his disciples were remarking about how the temple was adorned with beautiful stones and with gifts dedicated to God. But Jesus said, ⁶"As for what you see here, the time will come when not one stone will be left on another;*j* every one of them will be thrown down."

⁷"Teacher," they asked, "when will these things happen? And what will be the sign that they are about to take place?"

⁸He replied: "Watch out that you are not deceived. For many will come in my name, claiming, 'I am he,' and, 'The time is near.' Do not follow them.*k* ⁹When you hear of wars and revolutions, do not

INSIGHT

The treasury was in the women's court of the temple, where there were thirteen trumpet-shaped offering receptacles. See the illustration of the floor plan of Herod's temple on page 1723, and see the illustration of Herod's temple on page IISB-38.

a 37 Exodus 3:6   b 41 Or *Messiah*   c 43 Psalm 110:1   d 2 Greek *two lepta* be frightened. These things must happen first, but the end will not come right away."

¹⁰Then he said to them: "Nation will rise against nation, and kingdom against kingdom.ᵃ ¹¹There will be great earthquakes, famines and pestilences in various places, and fearful events and great signs from heaven.ᵇ

¹²"But before all this, they will lay hands on you and persecute you. They will deliver you to synagogues and prisons, and you will be brought before kings and governors, and all on account of my name. ¹³This will result in your being witnesses to them.ᶜ ¹⁴But make up your mind not to worry beforehand how you will defend yourselves.ᵈ ¹⁵For I will give youᵉ words and wisdom that none of your adversaries will be able to resist or contradict. ¹⁶You will be betrayed even by parents, brothers, relatives and friends,ᶠ and they will put some of you to death. ¹⁷All men will hate you because of me.ᵍ ¹⁸But not a hair of your head will perish.ʰ ¹⁹By standing firm you will gain life.ⁱ

²⁰"When you see Jerusalem being surrounded by armies,ʲ you will know that its desolation is near. ²¹Then let those who are in Judea flee to the mountains, let those in the city get out, and let those in the country not enter the city.ᵏ ²²For this is the time of punishmentˡ in fulfillmentᵐ of all that has been written. ²³How dreadful it will be in those days for pregnant women and nursing mothers! There will be great distress in the land and wrath against this people. ²⁴They will fall by the sword and will be taken as prisoners to all the nations. Jerusalem will be trampledⁿ on by the Gentiles until the times of the Gentiles are fulfilled.

²⁵"There will be signs in the sun, moon and stars. On the earth, nations will be in anguish and perplexity at the roaring and tossing of the sea.ᵒ ²⁶Men will faint from terror, apprehensive of what is coming on the world, for the heavenly bodies will be shaken.ᵖ ²⁷At that time they will see the Son of Man�q coming in a cloudʳ with power and great glory. ²⁸When these things begin to take place, stand up and lift up your heads, because your redemption is drawing near."ˢ

²⁹He told them this parable: "Look at the fig tree and all the trees. ³⁰When they sprout leaves, you can see for yourselves and know that summer is near. ³¹Even so, when you see these things happening, you know that the kingdom of Godᵗ is near.

³²"I tell you the truth, this generationᵃᵘ will certainly not pass away until all these things have happened. ³³Heaven and earth will pass away, but my words will never pass away.ᵛ

³⁴"Be careful, or your hearts will be weighed down with dissipation, drunkenness and the anxieties of life,ʷ and that day will close

ᵃ 32 Or race

21:10
ᵃ 2Ch 15:6;
Isa 19:2

21:11
ᵇ Isa 29:6;
Joel 2:30

21:13
ᶜ Php 1:12

21:14
ᵈ Lk 12:11

21:15
ᵉ Lk 12:12

21:16
ᶠ Lk 12:52,53

21:17
ᵍ Jn 15:21

21:18
ʰ Mt 10:30

21:19
ⁱ Mt 10:22

21:20
ʲ Lk 19:43

21:21
ᵏ Lk 17:31

21:22
ˡ Isa 63:4;
Da 9:24-27;
Hos 9:7
ᵐ Mt 1:22

21:24
ⁿ Isa 5:5; 63:18;
Da 8:13;
Rev 11:2

21:25
ᵒ 2Pe 3:10,12

21:26
ᵖ Mt 24:29

21:27
q Mt 8:20
ʳ Rev 1:7

21:28
ˢ Lk 18:7

21:31
ᵗ Mt 3:2

21:32
ᵘ Lk 11:50;
17:25

21:33
ᵛ Mt 5:18

21:34
ʷ Mk 4:19

21:34
a Lk 12:40,46;
1Th 5:2-7

21:36
b Mt 26:41

21:37
c Mt 26:55
d Mk 11:19
e Mt 21:1

21:38
f Jn 8:2

22:1
g Jn 11:55

22:2
h Mt 12:14

22:3
i Mt 4:10;
Jn 13:2
j Mt 10:4

22:4
k ver 52; Ac 4:1;
5:24

22:5
l Zec 11:12

22:7
m Ex 12:18-20;
Dt 16:5-8;
Mk 14:12

22:8
n Ac 3:1,11;
4:13,19; 8:14

22:13
o Lk 19:32

22:14
p Mk 6:30
q Mt 26:20;
Mk 14:17,18

22:15
r Mt 16:21

22:16
s Lk 14:15;
Rev 19:9

22:19
t Mt 14:19

22:20
u Ex 24:8;
Isa 42:6;
Jer 31:31-34;
Zec 9:11;
2Co 3:6;
Heb 8:6; 9:15

22:21
v Ps 41:9

22:22
w Mt 8:20
x Ac 2:23; 4:28

on you unexpectedly*a* like a trap. ³⁵For it will come upon all those who live on the face of the whole earth. ³⁶Be always on the watch, and pray*b* that you may be able to escape all that is about to happen, and that you may be able to stand before the Son of Man."

³⁷Each day Jesus was teaching at the temple,*c* and each evening he went out*d* to spend the night on the hill called the Mount of Olives,*e* ³⁸and all the people came early in the morning to hear him at the temple.*f*

Chapter 22 Theme

22 Now the Feast of Unleavened Bread, called the Passover, was approaching,*g* ²and the chief priests and the teachers of the law were looking for some way to get rid of Jesus,*h* for they were afraid of the people. ³Then Satan*i* entered Judas, called Iscariot,*j* one of the Twelve. ⁴And Judas went to the chief priests and the officers of the temple guard*k* and discussed with them how he might betray Jesus. ⁵They were delighted and agreed to give him money.*l* ⁶He consented, and watched for an opportunity to hand Jesus over to them when no crowd was present.

⁷Then came the day of Unleavened Bread on which the Passover lamb had to be sacrificed.*m* ⁸Jesus sent Peter and John,*n* saying, "Go and make preparations for us to eat the Passover."

⁹"Where do you want us to prepare for it?" they asked.

¹⁰He replied, "As you enter the city, a man carrying a jar of water will meet you. Follow him to the house that he enters, ¹¹and say to the owner of the house, 'The Teacher asks: Where is the guest room, where I may eat the Passover with my disciples?' ¹²He will show you a large upper room, all furnished. Make preparations there."

¹³They left and found things just as Jesus had told them.*o* So they prepared the Passover.

¹⁴When the hour came, Jesus and his apostles*p* reclined at the table.*q* ¹⁵And he said to them, "I have eagerly desired to eat this Passover with you before I suffer.*r* ¹⁶For I tell you, I will not eat it again until it finds fulfillment in the kingdom of God."*s*

¹⁷After taking the cup, he gave thanks and said, "Take this and divide it among you. ¹⁸For I tell you I will not drink again of the fruit of the vine until the kingdom of God comes."

¹⁹And he took bread, gave thanks and broke it,*t* and gave it to them, saying, "This is my body given for you; do this in remembrance of me."

²⁰In the same way, after the supper he took the cup, saying, "This cup is the new covenant*u* in my blood, which is poured out for you. ²¹But the hand of him who is going to betray me is with mine on the table.*v* ²²The Son of Man*w* will go as it has been decreed,*x*

but woe to that man who betrays him." 23They began to question
among themselves which of them it might be who would do this.
24Also a dispute arose among them as to which of them was
considered to be greatest.[a] 25Jesus said to them, "The kings of the
Gentiles lord it over them; and those who exercise authority over
them call themselves Benefactors. 26But you are not to be like that.
Instead, the greatest among you should be like the youngest,[b] and
the one who rules like the one who serves.[c] 27For who is greater,
the one who is at the table or the one who serves? Is it not the one
who is at the table? But I am among you as one who serves.[d] 28You
are those who have stood by me in my trials. 29And I confer on
you a kingdom,[e] just as my Father conferred one on me, 30so that
you may eat and drink at my table in my kingdom[f] and sit on
thrones, judging the twelve tribes of Israel.[g]

31"Simon, Simon, Satan has asked[h] to sift you[a] as wheat.[i] 32But I
have prayed for you,[j] Simon, that your faith may not fail. And
when you have turned back, strengthen your brothers."[k]

33But he replied, "Lord, I am ready to go with you to prison and
to death."[l]

34Jesus answered, "I tell you, Peter, before the rooster crows today,
you will deny three times that you know me."

35Then Jesus asked them, "When I sent you without purse, bag
or sandals,[m] did you lack anything?"

"Nothing," they answered.

36He said to them, "But now if you have a purse, take it, and also
a bag; and if you don't have a sword, sell your cloak and buy one.
37It is written: 'And he was numbered with the transgressors'[b];[n]
and I tell you that this must be fulfilled in me. Yes, what is written
about me is reaching its fulfillment."

38The disciples said, "See, Lord, here are two swords."

"That is enough," he replied.

39Jesus went out as usual[o] to the Mount of Olives,[p] and his disci-
ples followed him. 40On reaching the place, he said to them, "Pray
that you will not fall into temptation."[q] 41He withdrew about a
stone's throw beyond them, knelt down[r] and prayed, 42"Father, if
you are willing, take this cup[s] from me; yet not my will, but yours
be done."[t] 43An angel from heaven appeared to him and strength-
ened him.[u] 44And being in anguish, he prayed more earnestly,
and his sweat was like drops of blood falling to the ground.[c]

45When he rose from prayer and went back to the disciples, he
found them asleep, exhausted from sorrow. 46"Why are you sleep-
ing?" he asked them. "Get up and pray so that you will not fall into
temptation."[v]

[a] *31* The Greek is plural. [b] *37* Isaiah 53:12 [c] *44* Some early manuscripts do not have verses 43 and 44.

22:24 [a] Mk 9:34; Lk 9:46
22:26 [b] 1Pe 5:5 [c] Mk 9:35; Lk 9:48
22:27 [d] Mt 20:28; Lk 12:37
22:29 [e] Mt 25:34; 2Ti 2:12
22:30 [f] Lk 14:15 [g] Mt 19:28
22:31 [h] Job 1:6-12 [i] Am 9:9
22:32 [j] Jn 17:9,15; Ro 8:34 [k] Jn 21:15-17
22:33 [l] Jn 11:16
22:35 [m] Mt 10:9,10; Lk 9:3; 10:4
22:37 [n] Isa 53:12
22:39 [o] Lk 21:37 [p] Mt 21:1
22:40 [q] Mt 6:13
22:41 [r] Lk 18:11
22:42 [s] Mt 20:22 [t] Mt 26:39
22:43 [u] Mt 4:11; Mk 1:13
22:46 [v] ver 40

22:49
a ver 38

22:52
b ver 4

22:53
c Mt 26:55
d Jn 12:27
e Mt 8:12;
Jn 1:5; 3:20

22:54
f Mt 26:57;
Mk 14:53
g Mt 26:58;
Mk 14:54;
Jn 18:15

22:59
h Lk 23:6

22:61
i Lk 7:13
j ver 34

22:65
k Mt 16:21

22:66
l Mt 5:22
m Mt 27:1;
Mk 15:1

22:68
n Lk 20:3-8

22:69
o Mk 16:19

22:70
p Mt 4:3
q Mt 27:11;
Lk 23:3

47While he was still speaking a crowd came up, and the man who was called Judas, one of the Twelve, was leading them. He approached Jesus to kiss him, 48but Jesus asked him, "Judas, are you betraying the Son of Man with a kiss?"

49When Jesus' followers saw what was going to happen, they said, "Lord, should we strike with our swords?"*a* 50And one of them struck the servant of the high priest, cutting off his right ear.

51But Jesus answered, "No more of this!" And he touched the man's ear and healed him.

52Then Jesus said to the chief priests, the officers of the temple guard,*b* and the elders, who had come for him, "Am I leading a rebellion, that you have come with swords and clubs? 53Every day I was with you in the temple courts,*c* and you did not lay a hand on me. But this is your hour*d*—when darkness reigns."*e*

54Then seizing him, they led him away and took him into the house of the high priest.*f* Peter followed at a distance.*g* 55But when they had kindled a fire in the middle of the courtyard and had sat down together, Peter sat down with them. 56A servant girl saw him seated there in the firelight. She looked closely at him and said, "This man was with him."

57But he denied it. "Woman, I don't know him," he said.

58A little later someone else saw him and said, "You also are one of them."

"Man, I am not!" Peter replied.

59About an hour later another asserted, "Certainly this fellow was with him, for he is a Galilean."*h*

60Peter replied, "Man, I don't know what you're talking about!" Just as he was speaking, the rooster crowed. 61The Lord*i* turned and looked straight at Peter. Then Peter remembered the word the Lord had spoken to him: "Before the rooster crows today, you will disown me three times."*j* 62And he went outside and wept bitterly.

63The men who were guarding Jesus began mocking and beating him. 64They blindfolded him and demanded, "Prophesy! Who hit you?" 65And they said many other insulting things to him.*k*

66At daybreak the council*l* of the elders of the people, both the chief priests and teachers of the law, met together,*m* and Jesus was led before them. 67"If you are the Christ,*a*" they said, "tell us."

Jesus answered, "If I tell you, you will not believe me, 68and if I asked you, you would not answer.*n* 69But from now on, the Son of Man will be seated at the right hand of the mighty God."*o*

70They all asked, "Are you then the Son of God?"*p*

He replied, "You are right in saying I am."*q*

71Then they said, "Why do we need any more testimony? We have heard it from his own lips."

a 67 Or *Messiah*

Chapter 23 Theme

23 Then the whole assembly rose and led him off to Pilate.[a] [2]And they began to accuse him, saying, "We have found this man subverting our nation.[b] He opposes payment of taxes to Caesar[c] and claims to be Christ,[a] a king."[d]

[3]So Pilate asked Jesus, "Are you the king of the Jews?"

"Yes, it is as you say," Jesus replied.

[4]Then Pilate announced to the chief priests and the crowd, "I find no basis for a charge against this man."[e]

[5]But they insisted, "He stirs up the people all over Judea[b] by his teaching. He started in Galilee[f] and has come all the way here."

[6]On hearing this, Pilate asked if the man was a Galilean.[g] [7]When he learned that Jesus was under Herod's jurisdiction, he sent him to Herod,[h] who was also in Jerusalem at that time.

[8]When Herod saw Jesus, he was greatly pleased, because for a long time he had been wanting to see him.[i] From what he had heard about him, he hoped to see him perform some miracle. [9]He plied him with many questions, but Jesus gave him no answer.[j] [10]The chief priests and the teachers of the law were standing there, vehemently accusing him. [11]Then Herod and his soldiers ridiculed and mocked him. Dressing him in an elegant robe,[k] they sent him back to Pilate. [12]That day Herod and Pilate became friends[l]— before this they had been enemies.

[13]Pilate called together the chief priests, the rulers and the people, [14]and said to them, "You brought me this man as one who was inciting the people to rebellion. I have examined him in your presence and have found no basis for your charges against him.[m] [15]Neither has Herod, for he sent him back to us; as you can see, he has done nothing to deserve death. [16]Therefore, I will punish him[n] and then release him.[c]"

[18]With one voice they cried out, "Away with this man! Release Barabbas to us!"[o] [19](Barabbas had been thrown into prison for an insurrection in the city, and for murder.)

[20]Wanting to release Jesus, Pilate appealed to them again. [21]But they kept shouting, "Crucify him! Crucify him!"

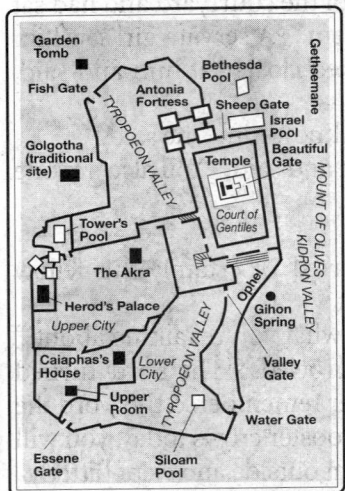

Jerusalem of the New Testament

---

a 2 Or *Messiah*; also in verses 35 and 39   b 5 Or *over the land of the Jews*   c 16 Some manuscripts *him.*" [17]*Now he was obliged to release one man to them at the Feast.*

23:1
a Mt 27:2;
Mk 15:1;
Jn 18:28

23:2
b ver 14
c Lk 20:22
d Jn 19:12

23:4
e ver 14,22,41;
Mt 27:23;
Jn 18:38;
1Ti 6:13;
2Co 5:21

23:5
f Mk 1:14

23:6
g Lk 22:59

23:7
h Mt 14:1; Lk 3:1

23:8
i Lk 9:9

23:9
j Mk 14:61

23:11
k Mk 15:17-19;
Jn 19:2,3

23:12
l Ac 4:27

23:14
m ver 4

23:16
n ver 22;
Mt 27:26;
Jn 19:1;
Ac 16:37;
2Co 11:23,24

23:18
o Ac 3:13,14

23:22
a ver 16

23:26
b Mt 27:32
c Mk 15:21;
Jn 19:17

23:27
d Lk 8:52

23:28
e Lk 19:41-44;
21:23,24

23:29
f Mt 24:19

23:30
g Hos 10:8;
Isa 2:19;
Rev 6:16

23:31
h Eze 20:47

23:32
i Isa 53:12;
Mt 27:38;
Mk 15:27;
Jn 19:18

23:34
j Mt 11:25
k Mt 5:44
l Ps 22:18

23:35
m Ps 22:17
n Isa 42:1

23:36
o Ps 22:7
p Ps 69:21;
Mt 27:48

23:37
q Lk 4:3,9

23:38
r Mt 2:2

23:39
s ver 35,37

23:41
t ver 4

²²For the third time he spoke to them: "Why? What crime has this man committed? I have found in him no grounds for the death penalty. Therefore I will have him punished and then release him."*a*

²³But with loud shouts they insistently demanded that he be crucified, and their shouts prevailed. ²⁴So Pilate decided to grant their demand. ²⁵He released the man who had been thrown into prison for insurrection and murder, the one they asked for, and surrendered Jesus to their will.

²⁶As they led him away, they seized Simon from Cyrene,*b* who was on his way in from the country, and put the cross on him and made him carry it behind Jesus.*c* ²⁷A large number of people followed him, including women who mourned and wailed*d* for him. ²⁸Jesus turned and said to them, "Daughters of Jerusalem, do not weep for me; weep for yourselves and for your children.*e* ²⁹For the time will come when you will say, 'Blessed are the barren women, the wombs that never bore and the breasts that never nursed!'*f* ³⁰Then

> "'they will say to the mountains, "Fall on us!"
> and to the hills, "Cover us!"'*a**g*

³¹For if men do these things when the tree is green, what will happen when it is dry?"*h*

³²Two other men, both criminals, were also led out with him to be executed.*i* ³³When they came to the place called the Skull, there they crucified him, along with the criminals—one on his right, the other on his left. ³⁴Jesus said, "Father,*j* forgive them, for they do not know what they are doing."*b**k* And they divided up his clothes by casting lots.*l*

³⁵The people stood watching, and the rulers even sneered at him.*m* They said, "He saved others; let him save himself if he is the Christ of God, the Chosen One."*n*

³⁶The soldiers also came up and mocked him.*o* They offered him wine vinegar*p* ³⁷and said, "If you are the king of the Jews,*q* save yourself."

³⁸There was a written notice above him, which read: THIS IS THE KING OF THE JEWS.*r*

³⁹One of the criminals who hung there hurled insults at him: "Aren't you the Christ? Save yourself and us!"*s*

⁴⁰But the other criminal rebuked him. "Don't you fear God," he said, "since you are under the same sentence? ⁴¹We are punished justly, for we are getting what our deeds deserve. But this man has done nothing wrong."*t*

a 30 Hosea 10:8   *b 34* Some early manuscripts do not have this sentence.

⁴²Then he said, "Jesus, remember me when you come into your kingdom.ᵃ"ᵃ

⁴³Jesus answered him, "I tell you the truth, today you will be with me in paradise."ᵇ

⁴⁴It was now about the sixth hour, and darkness came over the whole land until the ninth hour,ᶜ ⁴⁵for the sun stopped shining. And the curtain of the templeᵈ was torn in two.ᵉ ⁴⁶Jesus called out with a loud voice,ᶠ "Father, into your hands I commit my spirit."ᵍ When he had said this, he breathed his last.ʰ

⁴⁷The centurion, seeing what had happened, praised Godⁱ and said, "Surely this was a righteous man." ⁴⁸When all the people who had gathered to witness this sight saw what took place, they beat their breastsʲ and went away. ⁴⁹But all those who knew him, including the women who had followed him from Galilee,ᵏ stood at a distance,ˡ watching these things.

⁵⁰Now there was a man named Joseph, a member of the Council, a good and upright man, ⁵¹who had not consented to their decision and action. He came from the Judean town of Arimathea and he was waiting for the kingdom of God.ᵐ ⁵²Going to Pilate, he asked for Jesus' body. ⁵³Then he took it down, wrapped it in linen cloth and placed it in a tomb cut in the rock, one in which no one had yet been laid. ⁵⁴It was Preparation Day,ⁿ and the Sabbath was about to begin.

⁵⁵The women who had come with Jesus from Galileeᵒ followed Joseph and saw the tomb and how his body was laid in it. ⁵⁶Then they went home and prepared spices and perfumes.ᵖ But they rested on the Sabbath in obedience to the commandment. q

Chapter 24 Theme

24 On the first day of the week, very early in the morning, the women took the spices they had preparedʳ and went to the tomb. ²They found the stone rolled away from the tomb, ³but when they entered, they did not find the body of the Lord Jesus.ˢ ⁴While they were wondering about this, suddenly two men in clothes that gleamed like lightningᵗ stood beside them. ⁵In their fright the women bowed down with their faces to the ground, but the men said to them, "Why do you look for the living among the dead? ⁶He is not here; he has risen! Remember how he told you, while he was still with you in Galilee:ᵘ ⁷'The Son of Manᵛ must be delivered into the hands of sinful men, be crucified and on the third day be raised again.'"ʷ ⁸Then they remembered his words.ˣ

⁹When they came back from the tomb, they told all these things to the Eleven and to all the others. ¹⁰It was Mary Magdalene, Joanna, Mary the mother of James, and the others with themʸ who told this to the apostles.ᶻ ¹¹But they did not believeᵃ the women, because

a 42 Some manuscripts *come with your kingly power*

23:42
a Mt 16:27

23:43
b 2Co 12:3,4;
Rev 2:7

23:44
c Am 8:9

23:45
d Ex 26:31-33;
Heb 9:3,8
e Heb 10:19,20

23:46
f Mt 27:50
g Ps 31:5;
1Pe 2:23
h Jn 19:30

23:47
i Mt 9:8

23:48
j Lk 18:13

23:49
k Lk 8:2
l Ps 38:11

23:51
m Lk 2:25,38

23:54
n Mt 27:62

23:55
o ver 49

23:56
p Mk 16:1;
Lk 24:1
q Ex 12:16;
20:10

24:1
r Lk 23:56

24:3
s ver 23,24

24:4
t Jn 20:12

24:6
u Mt 17:22,23;
Mk 9:30-31;
Lk 9:22; 24:44

24:7
v Mt 8:20
w Mt 16:21

24:8
x Jn 2:22

24:10
y Lk 8:1-3
z Mk 6:30

24:11
a Mk 16:11

24:12
a Jn 20:3-7
b Jn 20:10

24:13
c Mk 16:12

24:15
d ver 36

24:16
e Jn 20:14; 21:4

24:18
f Jn 19:25

24:19
g Mk 1:24
h Mt 21:11

24:20
i Lk 23:13

24:21
j Lk 1:68; 2:38;
21:28
k Mt 16:21

24:22
l ver 1-10

24:24
m ver 12

24:26
n Heb 2:10;
1Pe 1:11

24:27
o Ge 3:15;
Nu 21:9;
Dt 18:15
p Isa 7:14; 9:6;
40:10,11; 53;
Eze 34:23;
Da 9:24;
Mic 7:20;
Mal 3:1
q Jn 1:45

24:30
r Mt 14:19

24:31
s ver 16

24:32
t Ps 39:3
u ver 27,45

their words seemed to them like nonsense. [12]Peter, however, got up and ran to the tomb. Bending over, he saw the strips of linen lying by themselves,[a] and he went away,[b] wondering to himself what had happened.

[13]Now that same day two of them were going to a village called Emmaus, about seven miles[a] from Jerusalem.[c] [14]They were talking with each other about everything that had happened. [15]As they talked and discussed these things with each other, Jesus himself came up and walked along with them;[d] [16]but they were kept from recognizing him.[e]

[17]He asked them, "What are you discussing together as you walk along?"

They stood still, their faces downcast. [18]One of them, named Cleopas,[f] asked him, "Are you only a visitor to Jerusalem and do not know the things that have happened there in these days?"

[19]"What things?" he asked.

"About Jesus of Nazareth,"[g] they replied. "He was a prophet,[h] powerful in word and deed before God and all the people. [20]The chief priests and our rulers[i] handed him over to be sentenced to death, and they crucified him; [21]but we had hoped that he was the one who was going to redeem Israel.[j] And what is more, it is the third day[k] since all this took place. [22]In addition, some of our women amazed us.[l] They went to the tomb early this morning [23]but didn't find his body. They came and told us that they had seen a vision of angels, who said he was alive. [24]Then some of our companions went to the tomb and found it just as the women had said, but him they did not see."[m]

[25]He said to them, "How foolish you are, and how slow of heart to believe all that the prophets have spoken! [26]Did not the Christ[b] have to suffer these things and then enter his glory?"[n] [27]And beginning with Moses[o] and all the Prophets,[p] he explained to them what was said in all the Scriptures concerning himself.[q]

[28]As they approached the village to which they were going, Jesus acted as if he were going farther. [29]But they urged him strongly, "Stay with us, for it is nearly evening; the day is almost over." So he went in to stay with them.

[30]When he was at the table with them, he took bread, gave thanks, broke it[r] and began to give it to them. [31]Then their eyes were opened and they recognized him,[s] and he disappeared from their sight. [32]They asked each other, "Were not our hearts burning within us[t] while he talked with us on the road and opened the Scriptures[u] to us?"

[33]They got up and returned at once to Jerusalem. There they found the Eleven and those with them, assembled together [34]and

a 13 Greek sixty stadia (about 11 kilometers)   b 26 Or Messiah; also in verse 46 saying, "It is true! The Lord has risen and has appeared to Simon."*a* ³⁵Then the two told what had happened on the way, and how Jesus was recognized by them when he broke the bread.*b*

³⁶While they were still talking about this, Jesus himself stood among them and said to them, "Peace be with you."*c*

³⁷They were startled and frightened, thinking they saw a ghost.*d* ³⁸He said to them, "Why are you troubled, and why do doubts rise in your minds? ³⁹Look at my hands and my feet. It is I myself! Touch me and see;*e* a ghost does not have flesh and bones, as you see I have."

⁴⁰When he had said this, he showed them his hands and feet. ⁴¹And while they still did not believe it because of joy and amazement, he asked them, "Do you have anything here to eat?" ⁴²They gave him a piece of broiled fish, ⁴³and he took it and ate it in their presence.*f*

⁴⁴He said to them, "This is what I told you while I was still with you:*g* Everything must be fulfilled*h* that is written about me in the Law of Moses,*i* the Prophets and the Psalms."*j*

⁴⁵Then he opened their minds so they could understand the Scriptures. ⁴⁶He told them, "This is what is written: The Christ will suffer and rise from the dead on the third day, ⁴⁷and repentance and forgiveness of sins will be preached in his name*k* to all nations,*l* beginning at Jerusalem. ⁴⁸You are witnesses*m* of these things. ⁴⁹I am going to send you what my Father has promised;*n* but stay in the city until you have been clothed with power from on high."

⁵⁰When he had led them out to the vicinity of Bethany,*o* he lifted up his hands and blessed them. ⁵¹While he was blessing them, he left them and was taken up into heaven.*p* ⁵²Then they worshiped him and returned to Jerusalem with great joy. ⁵³And they stayed continually at the temple,*q* praising God.

24:34
a 1Co 15:5

24:35
b ver 30,31

24:36
c Jn 20:19,21,26; 14:27

24:37
d Mk 6:49

24:39
e Jn 20:27; 1Jn 1:1

24:43
f Ac 10:41

24:44
g Lk 9:45; 18:34
h Mt 16:21; Lk 9:22,44; 18:31-33; 22:37
i ver 27
j Ps 2; 16; 22; 69; 72; 110; 118

24:47
k Ac 5:31; 10:43; 13:38
l Mt 28:19

24:48
m Ac 1:8; 2:32; 5:32; 13:31; 1 Pe 5:1

24:49
n Jn 14:16; Ac 1:4

24:50
o Mt 21:17

24:51
p 2Ki 2:11

24:53
q Ac 2:46

LUKE AT A GLANCE

Theme of Luke:

Author:

Date:

Purpose:

Key Words:

kingdom of God

Son of Man

mark every reference to the devil or demons

covenant

SEGMENT DIVISIONS			CHAPTER THEMES
		1	
		2	
		3	
		4	
		5	
		6	
		7	
		8	
		9	
		10	
		11	
		12	
		13	
		14	
		15	
		16	
		17	
		18	
		19	
		20	
		21	
		22	
		23	
		24	

Life of Christ Showing Coverage by Luke (Shaded Area)

	PREPARATION		PUBLIC MINISTRY									SACRIFICE
			OBSCURITY (VANISHING)	POPULARITY (DECLINING)			OPPOSITION (INCREASING)					

BIRTH	JOHN INTRODUCES JESUS	JESUS CLEANSES TEMPLE	JESUS RETURNS TO GALILEE	JESUS ORDAINS THE TWELVE	TO TYRE AND SIDON	TO FEAST OF TABERNACLES	BEYOND JORDAN	TRIUMPHAL ENTRY	RESURRECTION DEATH	ASCENSION
	John 1:19ff	John 2:13ff	Mark 1:14	Luke 6:12ff	Matthew 15:21	John 7:10	John 10:40	Matthew 21:1		

OPENING EVENTS — 4 months

EARLY MINISTRIES — 8 months

EXTENDED MINISTRIES — 4 months / 10 months

SPECIALIZED MINISTRIES — 6 months

CONCLUDING MINISTRIES — 3 months / 3 months

40 days

2 months

EARLY JUDEAN · EARLY GALILEAN · MIDDLE GALILEAN · LATER GALILEAN · LATER JUDEAN · PEREAN

FIRST YEAR	SECOND YEAR	THIRD YEAR
John 2:13	John 5:1 / John 6:4	John 11:55

ANNUAL PASSOVERS

5 B.C.

| Luke 1 | Luke 4:13 | | Luke 4:14 | Luke 6:12 | Luke 9:17 | Luke 9:18 | Luke 9:51 | Luke 13:22 | Luke 19:28 | Luke 24 |

Used by permission. Jensen, Irving L. *Luke: A Self-Study Guide*. Chicago: Moody Press, 1970.

JOHN

G od in the flesh! What would he be like? What would he do? How would he live in relationship to the Father once he came to earth? How would people know he was God? Would he force people to believe in him? And what about those who refused to believe he was God?

And what of those who believed, who followed him? What would God in the flesh expect from them? And what if they failed?

God in the flesh. It would be hard for some to believe, but their belief or unbelief would be a matter of life or death.

Three other Gospels had been written, and years had passed. One more Gospel was needed, one which would answer these questions and more, one which would illuminate the shadows of doubt. So the apostle John answered God's call to write a fourth and final Gospel to explain the one who came to reveal the Father. It was about A.D. 85.

✎ THINGS TO DO

1. Although the author of John is not identified by name, tradition holds that it was the apostle John. Read John 21:20-25 and note how the author identifies himself. You might want to put this reference or information under "Author" on the JOHN AT A GLANCE chart on page 1861.

2. To understand the purpose of John read John 20:30, 31. Record John's purpose on JOHN AT A GLANCE.

Chapters 1-12

1. Carefully read this segment chapter by chapter, observing what the author includes to accomplish his purpose.

   a. As you read these chapters, look for and mark the following key words and their synonyms: *believe (believed, faith, trust)*, *life (live)*, *miraculous sign(s)*, *judge (judging, judgment, condemn, verdict, condemned, decisions)*, *witness (testify, testifies, testified, testimony, speak, spread the word)*, *true (truth, truthful, valid, real, right, reliable, truly, surely)*, and *king (kingdom)*.

   b. You will find it helpful to write down the key words on an index card to use as a bookmark. Mark the words on the card in the same way you want to mark them in your Bible.

   c. Also mark any other repeated key words that are pertinent to the message of the chapter.

2. As you read each of the first twelve chapters, ask the five W's and an H: Who? What? Where? When? Why? and How? Look specifically for the following, recording whatever facts you find in each chapter in the margin. As you move your findings to the margin, use the headings set in italics below as your headings in the margins.

   a. *Events:* What is happening? For example, "Nicodemus came to Jesus at night."

   b. *Geographic locations:* Where is this event taking place? For example, John was baptizing at Bethany on the other side of the Jordan.

   c. *Timing of events:* When is this event taking place? For example, "on the third day," or "just before the Passover feast." In the margin next to the text, note these mentions of time by drawing an appropriate symbol. When you read of Jesus attending a feast, consult the chart THE FEASTS OF ISRAEL on pages 210, 211.

   d. *Portrayals of Jesus Christ:* How is Jesus pictured or described? For example: "the Word," "the Lamb of God," etc.

   e. *Signs and Miracles:* The signs that John recorded were for the purpose of leading people to believe that Jesus is the Christ, the Son of God. Look for these signs or miracles. For example, Jesus turned water into wine. The text says, "This, the first of his miraculous signs."

   f. *References that show the deity of Jesus* (references that show that Jesus is God): Look for verses that show Jesus is God. For example, John 10:33 says, "'We are not stoning you for any of these,' replied the Jews, 'but for blasphemy, because you, a mere man, claim to be God.'"

   g. *Witnesses:* Throughout his Gospel, John refers to those who bear witness to Jesus. Who are these witnesses and what is their witness? For example, John said, "I have seen and I testify that this is the Son of God" (John 1:34).

3. Determine the main subject or theme of each chapter and then record it next to the chapter number and on JOHN AT A GLANCE.

Chapters 13-17

1. This segment brings a change in Jesus' ministry as he draws away with the disciples in order to prepare them for what is to come. Make a new list of key words on a bookmark: *believe (trust), love (loved), work (miracles, things), command (commands), fruit (fruitful), remain, ask (prayer, pray, praying), truth (true, I tell you the truth),* and *devil (Satan, prince of this world).* (Go back to chapter 12 and mark the references to *prince of this world.*)

2. Mark in the text in a distinctive way all references, including pronouns, to God, Jesus, and the Holy Spirit. Then list in the margin everything you learn about the Holy Spirit. This is especially important in chapters 14 through 16.

3. List in the chapter margins any specific instructions or commandments that Jesus gives the disciples.

4. Record the main theme of each chapter as you did before.

Chapters 18-21

1. The final chapters of John give an account of the events surrounding the arrest, trial, crucifixion, resurrection, and the postresurrection appearances of Jesus Christ. As you read each chapter:

   a. Mark the following key words and their synonyms: *testify (testifies, testimony), believe, love, truth (true), life,* and *king (kingdom).*

   b. On pages 1862 and 1863 you will find two charts: THE ARREST, TRIAL, AND CRUCIFIXION OF JESUS CHRIST (page 1862) and THE ACCOUNT OF JESUS' RESURRECTION (page 1863). Record on the appropriate chart the progression of events from Jesus' arrest through his resurrection and postresurrection appearances. Note chapter and verse for future reference. (It would be good to do this on notebook paper before recording it on the chart.) Also remember that since Luke gives the consecutive order of events, it becomes a plumb line for the other Gospel records.

2. Once again determine the theme of each chapter and record it as you have done previously.

3. On pages 1864, 1865 you will find a chart WHAT THE GOSPELS TEACH ABOUT THE KINGDOM OF GOD/THE KINGDOM OF HEAVEN. Compile what John teaches about the king and the kingdom on this chart. John 3 contains the only two references to the kingdom. The other references to Jesus as the king are in the first and last segments of John. (Compile your information on notebook paper before you write it on the chart and note chapter and verse of insight.)

4. Complete JOHN AT A GLANCE by doing the following:

   a. Review your chapter themes of John and determine the theme of the book. Record this in the appropriate place on JOHN AT A GLANCE.

   b. You will notice a section titled "Segment Divisions" and two lines where you can record "Signs and Miracles" and "Portrayals of Jesus Christ." Review the information you have recorded in the margins. Record your observations on the appropriate segment division line. For example, in chapter 1 Jesus is referred to as "the Lamb of God." Record that fact at chapter 1 under "Portrayals of Jesus Christ." This will give you a visual picture of the structure of John.

✺ THINGS TO THINK ABOUT

1. Do you really believe that Jesus is God? Do you live accordingly?

2. Do you know how to take another person through the Scriptures to show him that Jesus is God?

3. Do people know that you are a disciple of Jesus Christ because of your love for others and because you have continued in his Word?

4. Are you relying on the Spirit of God to comfort you, help you, bear witness through you, do the work of God through you, and guide you into all truth?

5. Do you look at other Christians and wonder why God deals differently with you than he does with them? Do you need to hear his words to Peter in John 21:22, "If I want him to remain alive until I return, what is that to you? You must follow me"? Are you willing to follow Jesus wherever he leads, even if you have to do it alone? Are you telling others about him?

〜〜〜〜〜

Chapter 1 Theme

1 In the beginning was the Word,[a] and the Word was with God,[b] and the Word was God.[c] **2** He was with God in the beginning.[d]

3 Through him all things were made; without him nothing was made that has been made.[e] **4** In him was life,[f] and that life was the light[g] of men. **5** The light shines in the darkness, but the darkness has not understood[a] it.[h]

6 There came a man who was sent from God; his name was John.[i] **7** He came as a witness to testify[j] concerning that light, so that through him all men might believe.[k] **8** He himself was not the light; he came only as a witness to the light. **9** The true light[l] that gives light to every man[m] was coming into the world.[b]

10 He was in the world, and though the world was made through him,[n] the world did not recognize him. **11** He came to that which was his own, but his own did not receive him. **12** Yet to all who received him, to those who believed[o] in his name,[p] he gave the right to become children of God[q]— **13** children born not of natural descent,[c] nor of human decision or a husband's will, but born of God.[r]

14 The Word became flesh[s] and made his dwelling among us. We have seen his glory, the glory of the One and Only,[d] who came from the Father, full of grace and truth.[t]

15 John testifies[u] concerning him. He cries out, saying, "This was he of whom I said, 'He who comes after me has surpassed me because he was before me.'"[v] **16** From the fullness[w] of his grace we

**Cross references (margin):**

1:1
a Rev 19:13
b Jn 17:5; 1Jn 1:2
c Php 2:6
1:2
d Ge 1:1
1:3
e 1Co 8:6; Col 1:16; Heb 1:2
1:4
f Jn 5:26; 11:25; 14:6
g Jn 8:12
1:5
h Jn 3:19
1:6
i Mt 3:1
1:7
j ver 15,19,32
k ver 12
1:9
l 1Jn 2:8
m Isa 49:6
1:10
n Heb 1:2
1:12
o ver 7
p 1Jn 3:23
q Gal 3:26
1:13
r Jn 3:6; Jas 1:18; 1Pe 1:23; 1Jn 3:9
1:14
s Gal 4:4; Php 2:7,8; 1Ti 3:16; Heb 2:14
t Jn 14:6
1:15
u ver 7
v ver 30; Mt 3:11
1:16
w Eph 1:23; Col 1:19

Footnotes:

a 5 Or *darkness, and the darkness has not overcome*   b 9 Or *This was the true light that gives light to every man who comes into the world*   c 13 Greek *of bloods*   d 14 Or *the Only Begotten* have all received one blessing after another. [17]For the law was given through Moses;[a] grace and truth came through Jesus Christ.[b] [18]No one has ever seen God,[c] but God the One and Only,[a,b,d] who is at the Father's side, has made him known.

[19]Now this was John's testimony when the Jews[e] of Jerusalem sent priests and Levites to ask him who he was. [20]He did not fail to confess, but confessed freely, "I am not the Christ.[c]"[f]

[21]They asked him, "Then who are you? Are you Elijah?"[g]

He said, "I am not."

"Are you the Prophet?"[h]

He answered, "No."

[22]Finally they said, "Who are you? Give us an answer to take back to those who sent us. What do you say about yourself?"

[23]John replied in the words of Isaiah the prophet, "I am the voice of one calling in the desert,[i] 'Make straight the way for the Lord.'"[d,j]

[24]Now some Pharisees who had been sent [25]questioned him, "Why then do you baptize if you are not the Christ, nor Elijah, nor the Prophet?"

[26]"I baptize with[e] water," John replied, "but among you stands one you do not know. [27]He is the one who comes after me,[k] the thongs of whose sandals I am not worthy to untie."

[28]This all happened at Bethany on the other side of the Jordan,[l] where John was baptizing.

[29]The next day John saw Jesus coming toward him and said, "Look, the Lamb of God,[m] who takes away the sin of the world! [30]This is the one I meant when I said, 'A man who comes after me has surpassed me because he was before me.'[n] [31]I myself did not know him, but the reason I came baptizing with water was that he might be revealed to Israel."

[32]Then John gave this testimony: "I saw the Spirit come down from heaven as a dove and remain on him.[o] [33]I would not have known him, except that the one who sent me to baptize with water[p] told me, 'The man on whom you see the Spirit come down and remain is he who will baptize with the Holy Spirit.'[q] [34]I have seen and I testify that this is the Son of God."[r]

[35]The next day John[s] was there again with two of his disciples. [36]When he saw Jesus passing by, he said, "Look, the Lamb of God!"[t]

[37]When the two disciples heard him say this, they followed Jesus. [38]Turning around, Jesus saw them following and asked, "What do you want?"

They said, "Rabbi"[u] (which means Teacher), "where are you staying?"

---

a 18 Or the Only Begotten   b 18 Some manuscripts but the only (or only begotten) Son   c 20 Or Messiah. "The Christ" (Greek) and "the Messiah" (Hebrew) both mean "the Anointed One"; also in verse 25.   d 23 Isaiah 40:3   e 26 Or in; also in verses 31 and 33

1:17
a Jn 7:19
b ver 14

1:18
c Ex 33:20;
Jn 6:46;
Col 1:15;
1Ti 6:16
d Jn 3:16,18;
1Jn 4:9

1:19
e Jn 2:18;
5:10,16; 6:41,52

1:20
f Jn 3:28;
Lk 3:15,16

1:21
g Mt 11:14
h Dt 18:15

1:23
i Mt 3:1
j Isa 40:3

1:27
k ver 15,30

1:28
l Jn 3:26; 10:40

1:29
m ver 36;
Isa 53:7;
1Pe 1:19;
Rev 5:6

1:30
n ver 15,27

1:32
o Mt 3:16;
Mk 1:10

1:33
p Mk 1:4
q Mt 3:11;
Mk 1:8

1:34
r ver 49;
Mt 4:3

1:35
s Mt 3:1

1:36
t ver 29

1:38
u ver 49;
Mt 23:7

1:41
a Jn 4:25

1:42
b Ge 17:5,15
c Mt 16:18

1:43
d Mt 10:3;
Jn 6:5-7; 12:21,
22; 14:8,9
e Mt 4:19

1:44
f Mt 11:21;
Jn 12:21

1:45
g Jn 21:2
h Lk 24:27
i Lk 24:27
j Mt 2:23;
Mk 1:24
k Lk 3:23

1:46
l Jn 7:41,42,52

1:47
m Ro 9:4,6
n Ps 32:2

1:49
o ver 38;
Mt 23:7
p ver 34;
Mt 4:3
q Mt 2:2; 27:42;
Jn 12:13

1:51
r Mt 3:16
s Ge 28:12
t Mt 8:20

2:1
u Jn 4:46; 21:2
v Mt 12:46

2:4
w Jn 19:26
x Mt 8:29
y Mt 26:18;
Jn 7:6

2:5
z Ge 41:55

2:6
a Mk 7:3,4;
Jn 3:25

[39]"Come," he replied, "and you will see."

So they went and saw where he was staying, and spent that day with him. It was about the tenth hour.

[40]Andrew, Simon Peter's brother, was one of the two who heard what John had said and who had followed Jesus. [41]The first thing Andrew did was to find his brother Simon and tell him, "We have found the Messiah" (that is, the Christ).[a] [42]And he brought him to Jesus.

Jesus looked at him and said, "You are Simon son of John. You will be called[b] Cephas" (which, when translated, is Peter[a]).[c]

[43]The next day Jesus decided to leave for Galilee. Finding Philip,[d] he said to him, "Follow me."[e]

[44]Philip, like Andrew and Peter, was from the town of Bethsaida.[f] [45]Philip found Nathanael[g] and told him, "We have found the one Moses wrote about in the Law,[h] and about whom the prophets also wrote[i]—Jesus of Nazareth,[j] the son of Joseph."[k]

[46]"Nazareth! Can anything good come from there?"[l] Nathanael asked.

"Come and see," said Philip.

[47]When Jesus saw Nathanael approaching, he said of him, "Here is a true Israelite,[m] in whom there is nothing false."[n]

[48]"How do you know me?" Nathanael asked.

Jesus answered, "I saw you while you were still under the fig tree before Philip called you."

[49]Then Nathanael declared, "Rabbi,[o] you are the Son of God;[p] you are the King of Israel."[q]

[50]Jesus said, "You believe[b] because I told you I saw you under the fig tree. You shall see greater things than that." [51]He then added, "I tell you[c] the truth, you[c] shall see heaven open,[r] and the angels of God ascending and descending[s] on the Son of Man."[t]

Chapter 2 Theme _____

2 On the third day a wedding took place at Cana in Galilee.[u] Jesus' mother[v] was there, [2]and Jesus and his disciples had also been invited to the wedding. [3]When the wine was gone, Jesus' mother said to him, "They have no more wine."

[4]"Dear woman,[w] why do you involve me?"[x] Jesus replied. "My time[y] has not yet come."

[5]His mother said to the servants, "Do whatever he tells you."[z]

[6]Nearby stood six stone water jars, the kind used by the Jews for ceremonial washing,[a] each holding from twenty to thirty gallons.[d]

[7]Jesus said to the servants, "Fill the jars with water"; so they filled them to the brim.

a 42 Both *Cephas* (Aramaic) and *Peter* (Greek) mean *rock.*   b 50 Or *Do you believe . . . ?*   c 51 The Greek is plural.   d 6 Greek *two to three metretes* (probably about 75 to 115 liters)

⁸Then he told them, "Now draw some out and take it to the master of the banquet."

They did so, ⁹and the master of the banquet tasted the water that had been turned into wine.ᵃ He did not realize where it had come from, though the servants who had drawn the water knew. Then he called the bridegroom aside ¹⁰and said, "Everyone brings out the choice wine first and then the cheaper wine after the guests have had too much to drink; but you have saved the best till now."

¹¹This, the first of his miraculous signs,ᵇ Jesus performed at Cana in Galilee. He thus revealed his glory,ᶜ and his disciples put their faith in him.ᵈ

¹²After this he went down to Capernaumᵉ with his mother and brothersᶠ and his disciples. There they stayed for a few days.

¹³When it was almost time for the Jewish Passover,ᵍ Jesus went up to Jerusalem.ʰ ¹⁴In the temple courts he found men selling cattle, sheep and doves, and others sitting at tables exchanging money. ¹⁵So he made a whip out of cords, and drove all from the temple area, both sheep and cattle; he scattered the coins of the money changers and overturned their tables. ¹⁶To those who sold doves he said, "Get these out of here! How dare you turn my Father's houseⁱ into a market!"

¹⁷His disciples remembered that it is written: "Zeal for your house will consume me."ᵃ ʲ

¹⁸Then the Jews demanded of him, "What miraculous sign can you show us to prove your authority to do all this?"ᵏ

¹⁹Jesus answered them, "Destroy this temple, and I will raise it again in three days."ˡ

²⁰The Jews replied, "It has taken forty-six years to build this temple, and you are going to raise it in three days?" ²¹But the temple he had spoken of was his body.ᵐ ²²After he was raised from the dead, his disciples recalled what he had said.ⁿ Then they believed the Scripture and the words that Jesus had spoken.

²³Now while he was in Jerusalem at the Passover Feast,ᵒ many people saw the miraculous signs he was doing and believed in his name.ᵇ ²⁴But Jesus would not entrust himself to them, for he knew all men. ²⁵He did not need man's testimony about man, for he knew what was in a man.ᵖ

Jesus Ministers from Capernaum to Jerusalem

a 17 Psalm 69:9   b 23 Or and believed in him

2:9
ᵃ Jn 4:46

2:11
ᵇ ver 23;
Jn 3:2; 4:48;
6:2,14,26,30;
12:37; 20:30
ᶜ Jn 1:14
ᵈ Ex 14:31

2:12
ᵉ Mt 4:13
ᶠ Mt 12:46

2:13
ᵍ Jn 11:55
ʰ Dt 16:1-6;
Lk 2:41

2:16
ⁱ Lk 2:49

2:17
ʲ Ps 69:9

2:18
ᵏ Mt 12:38

2:19
ˡ Mt 26:61;
27:40;
Mk 14:58; 15:29

2:21
ᵐ 1Co 6:19

2:22
ⁿ Lk 24:5-8;
Jn 12:16; 14:26

2:23
ᵒ ver 13

2:25
ᵖ Mt 9:4;
Jn 6:61,64; 13:11

3:1
a Jn 7:50; 19:39
b Lk 23:13

3:2
c Jn 9:16,33
d Ac 2:22; 10:38

3:3
e Jn 1:13;
1Pe 1:23

3:5
f Tit 3:5

3:6
g Jn 1:13;
1Co 15:50

3:9
h Jn 6:52,60

3:10
i Lk 2:46

3:11
j Jn 1:18; 7:16,17
k ver 32

3:13
l Pr 30:4;
Ac 2:34;
Eph 4:8-10
m Jn 6:38,42

3:14
n Nu 21:8,9
o Jn 8:28; 12:32

3:15
p ver 16,36

3:16
q Ro 5:8;
Eph 2:4;
1Jn 4:9,10
r ver 36;
Jn 6:29,40;
11:25,26

3:17
s Jn 6:29,57;
10:36; 11:42;
17:8,21; 20:21
t Jn 12:47;
1Jn 4:14

3:18
u Jn 5:24
v 1Jn 4:9

3:19
w Jn 1:4; 8:12

3:20
x Eph 5:11,13

Chapter 3 Theme

3 Now there was a man of the Pharisees named Nicodemus,[a] a member of the Jewish ruling council.[b] ²He came to Jesus at night and said, "Rabbi, we know you are a teacher who has come from God. For no one could perform the miraculous signs[c] you are doing if God were not with him."[d]

³In reply Jesus declared, "I tell you the truth, no one can see the kingdom of God unless he is born again.[a][e]

⁴"How can a man be born when he is old?" Nicodemus asked. "Surely he cannot enter a second time into his mother's womb to be born!"

⁵Jesus answered, "I tell you the truth, no one can enter the kingdom of God unless he is born of water and the Spirit.[f] ⁶Flesh gives birth to flesh, but the Spirit[b] gives birth to spirit.[g] ⁷You should not be surprised at my saying, 'You[c] must be born again.' ⁸The wind blows wherever it pleases. You hear its sound, but you cannot tell where it comes from or where it is going. So it is with everyone born of the Spirit."

⁹"How can this be?"[h] Nicodemus asked.

¹⁰"You are Israel's teacher,"[i] said Jesus, "and do you not understand these things? ¹¹I tell you the truth, we speak of what we know,[j] and we testify to what we have seen, but still you people do not accept our testimony.[k] ¹²I have spoken to you of earthly things and you do not believe; how then will you believe if I speak of heavenly things? ¹³No one has ever gone into heaven[l] except the one who came from heaven[m]—the Son of Man.[d] ¹⁴Just as Moses lifted up the snake in the desert,[n] so the Son of Man must be lifted up,[o] ¹⁵that everyone who believes[p] in him may have eternal life.[e]

¹⁶"For God so loved[q] the world that he gave his one and only Son,[f] that whoever believes in him shall not perish but have eternal life.[r] ¹⁷For God did not send his Son into the world[s] to condemn the world, but to save the world through him.[t] ¹⁸Whoever believes in him is not condemned,[u] but whoever does not believe stands condemned already because he has not believed in the name of God's one and only Son.[g][v] ¹⁹This is the verdict: Light[w] has come into the world, but men loved darkness instead of light because their deeds were evil. ²⁰Everyone who does evil hates the light, and will not come into the light for fear that his deeds will be exposed.[x] ²¹But whoever lives by the truth comes into the light, so that it may be seen plainly that what he has done has been done through God."[h]

²²After this, Jesus and his disciples went out into the Judean

a 3 Or born from above; also in verse 7   b 6 Or but spirit   c 7 The Greek is plural.   d 13 Some manuscripts Man, who is in heaven   e 15 Or believes may have eternal life in him   f 16 Or his only begotten Son   g 18 Or God's only begotten Son   h 21 Some interpreters end the quotation after verse 15.

countryside, where he spent some time with them, and baptized.ᵃ ²³Now John also was baptizing at Aenon near Salim, because there was plenty of water, and people were constantly coming to be baptized. ²⁴(This was before John was put in prison.)ᵇ ²⁵An argument developed between some of John's disciples and a certain Jewᵃ over the matter of ceremonial washing.ᶜ ²⁶They came to John and said to him, "Rabbi,ᵈ that man who was with you on the other side of the Jordan—the one you testifiedᵉ about—well, he is baptizing, and everyone is going to him."

²⁷To this John replied, "A man can receive only what is given him from heaven. ²⁸You yourselves can testify that I said, 'I am not the Christᵇ but am sent ahead of him.'ᶠ ²⁹The bride belongs to the bridegroom.ᵍ The friend who attends the bridegroom waits and listens for him, and is full of joy when he hears the bridegroom's voice. That joy is mine, and it is now complete.ʰ ³⁰He must become greater; I must become less.

³¹"The one who comes from above ⁱ is above all; the one who is from the earth belongs to the earth, and speaks as one from the earth.ʲ The one who comes from heaven is above all. ³²He testifies to what he has seen and heard,ᵏ but no one accepts his testimony.ˡ ³³The man who has accepted it has certified that God is truthful. ³⁴For the one whom God has sentᵐ speaks the words of God, for Godᶜ gives the Spiritⁿ without limit. ³⁵The Father loves the Son and has placed everything in his hands.ᵒ ³⁶Whoever believes in the Son has eternal life,ᵖ but whoever rejects the Son will not see life, for God's wrath remains on him."ᵈ

Chapter 4 Theme

4 The Pharisees heard that Jesus was gaining and baptizing more disciples than John,�q ²although in fact it was not Jesus who baptized, but his disciples. ³When the Lord learned of this, he left Judeaʳ and went back once more to Galilee.

⁴Now he had to go through Samaria. ⁵So he came to a town in Samaria called Sychar, near the plot of ground Jacob had given to his son Joseph.ˢ ⁶Jacob's well was there, and Jesus, tired as he was from the journey, sat down by the well. It was about the sixth hour.

⁷When a Samaritan woman came to draw water, Jesus said to her, "Will you give me a drink?" ⁸(His disciples had gone into the townᵗ to buy food.)

⁹The Samaritan woman said to him, "You are a Jew and I am a Samaritanᵘ woman. How can you ask me for a drink?" (For Jews do not associate with Samaritans.ᵉ)

¹⁰Jesus answered her, "If you knew the gift of God and who it is

INSIGHT

It is difficult to pinpoint who the **Samaritans** are racially. However, it is believed that after the Assyrians conquered the northern kingdom, they "imported" people into Samaria. Some of the Samaritan Jews married these importees. Their offspring were called Samaritans. When the Jews returned after the captivity, the Samaritans wanted a share in rebuilding the temple but were rejected because of their pagan practices. The enmity continued through the time of Jesus (see 2 Kings 17:33 and Ezra 4:2, 3).

3:22
ᵃ Jn 4:2

3:24
ᵇ Mt 4:12; 14:3

3:25
ᶜ Jn 2:6

3:26
ᵈ Mt 23:7
ᵉ Jn 1:7

3:28
ᶠ Jn 1:20,23

3:29
ᵍ Mt 9:15
ʰ Jn 16:24; 17:13;
Php 2:2;
1Jn 1:4;
2Jn 12

3:31
ⁱ ver 13
ʲ Jn 8:23;
1Jn 4:5

3:32
ᵏ Jn 8:26; 15:15
ˡ ver 11

3:34
ᵐ ver 17
ⁿ Mt 12:18;
Lk 4:18;
Ac 10:38

3:35
ᵒ Mt 28:18;
Jn 5:20,22; 17:2

3:36
ᵖ ver 15;
Jn 5:24; 6:47

4:1
q Jn 3:22,26

4:3
ʳ Jn 3:22

4:5
ˢ Ge 33:19;
48:22;
Jos 24:32

4:8
ᵗ ver 5,39

4:9
ᵘ Mt 10:5;
Lk 9:52,53

ᵃ 25 Some manuscripts *and certain Jews*   ᵇ 28 Or *Messiah*   ᶜ 34 Greek *he*   ᵈ 36 Some interpreters end the quotation after verse 30.   ᵉ 9 Or *do not use dishes Samaritans have used*

4:10
a Isa 44:3;
Jer 2:13;
Zec 14:8;
Jn 7:37,38;
Rev 21:6; 22:1,17

4:12
b ver 6

4:14
c Jn 6:35
d Jn 7:38
e Mt 25:46

4:15
f Jn 6:34

4:19
g Mt 21:11

4:20
h Dt 11:29;
Jos 8:33
i Lk 9:53

4:21
j Jn 5:28; 16:2
k Mal 1:11;
1Ti 2:8

4:22
l 2Ki 17:28-41
m Isa 2:3;
Ro 3:1,2; 9:4,5

4:23
n Jn 5:25; 16:32
o Php 3:3

4:24
p Php 3:3

4:25
q Mt 1:16

4:26
r Jn 8:24; 9:35-37

4:27
s ver 8

4:29
t ver 17,18
u Mt 12:23;
Jn 7:26,31

4:31
v Mt 23:7

4:32
w Job 23:12;
Mt 4:4;
Jn 6:27

that asks you for a drink, you would have asked him and he would have given you living water."*a*

¹¹"Sir," the woman said, "you have nothing to draw with and the well is deep. Where can you get this living water? ¹²Are you greater than our father Jacob, who gave us the well*b* and drank from it himself, as did also his sons and his flocks and herds?"

¹³Jesus answered, "Everyone who drinks this water will be thirsty again, ¹⁴but whoever drinks the water I give him will never thirst.*c* Indeed, the water I give him will become in him a spring of water *d* welling up to eternal life."*e*

¹⁵The woman said to him, "Sir, give me this water so that I won't get thirsty*f* and have to keep coming here to draw water."

¹⁶He told her, "Go, call your husband and come back."

¹⁷"I have no husband," she replied.

Jesus said to her, "You are right when you say you have no husband. ¹⁸The fact is, you have had five husbands, and the man you now have is not your husband. What you have just said is quite true."

¹⁹"Sir," the woman said, "I can see that you are a prophet.*g* ²⁰Our fathers worshiped on this mountain,*h* but you Jews claim that the place where we must worship is in Jerusalem."*i*

²¹Jesus declared, "Believe me, woman, a time is coming*j* when you will worship the Father neither on this mountain nor in Jerusalem.*k* ²²You Samaritans worship what you do not know;*l* we worship what we do know, for salvation is from the Jews.*m* ²³Yet a time is coming and has now come*n* when the true worshipers will worship the Father in spirit*o* and truth, for they are the kind of worshipers the Father seeks. ²⁴God is spirit,*p* and his worshipers must worship in spirit and in truth."

²⁵The woman said, "I know that Messiah" (called Christ)*q* "is coming. When he comes, he will explain everything to us."

²⁶Then Jesus declared, "I who speak to you am he."*r*

²⁷Just then his disciples returned*s* and were surprised to find him talking with a woman. But no one asked, "What do you want?" or "Why are you talking with her?"

²⁸Then, leaving her water jar, the woman went back to the town and said to the people, ²⁹"Come, see a man who told me everything I ever did.*t* Could this be the Christ*a*?"*u* ³⁰They came out of the town and made their way toward him.

³¹Meanwhile his disciples urged him, "Rabbi,*v* eat something."

³²But he said to them, "I have food to eat*w* that you know nothing about."

³³Then his disciples said to each other, "Could someone have brought him food?"

a 29 Or *Messiah*

³⁴"My food," said Jesus, "is to do the will*a* of him who sent me and to finish his work.*b* ³⁵Do you not say, 'Four months more and then the harvest'? I tell you, open your eyes and look at the fields! They are ripe for harvest.*c* ³⁶Even now the reaper draws his wages, even now he harvests *d* the crop for eternal life,*e* so that the sower and the reaper may be glad together. ³⁷Thus the saying 'One sows and another reaps'*f* is true. ³⁸I sent you to reap what you have not worked for. Others have done the hard work, and you have reaped the benefits of their labor."

³⁹Many of the Samaritans from that town*g* believed in him because of the woman's testimony, "He told me everything I ever did."*h* ⁴⁰So when the Samaritans came to him, they urged him to stay with them, and he stayed two days. ⁴¹And because of his words many more became believers.

⁴²They said to the woman, "We no longer believe just because of what you said; now we have heard for ourselves, and we know that this man really is the Savior of the world."*i*

⁴³After the two days*j* he left for Galilee. ⁴⁴(Now Jesus himself had pointed out that a prophet has no honor in his own country.)*k* ⁴⁵When he arrived in Galilee, the Galileans welcomed him. They had seen all that he had done in Jerusalem at the Passover Feast,*l* for they also had been there.

⁴⁶Once more he visited Cana in Galilee, where he had turned the water into wine.*m* And there was a certain royal official whose son lay sick at Capernaum. ⁴⁷When this man heard that Jesus had arrived in Galilee from Judea,*n* he went to him and begged him to come and heal his son, who was close to death.

⁴⁸"Unless you people see miraculous signs and wonders,"*o* Jesus told him, "you will never believe."

⁴⁹The royal official said, "Sir, come down before my child dies."

⁵⁰Jesus replied, "You may go. Your son will live."

The man took Jesus at his word and departed. ⁵¹While he was still on the way, his servants met him with the news that his boy was living. ⁵²When he inquired as to the time when his son got better, they said to him, "The fever left him yesterday at the seventh hour."

⁵³Then the father realized that this was the exact time at which Jesus had said to him, "Your son will live." So he and all his household*p* believed.

⁵⁴This was the second miraculous sign*q* that Jesus performed, having come from Judea to Galilee.

Chapter 5 Theme

5 Some time later, Jesus went up to Jerusalem for a feast of the Jews. ²Now there is in Jerusalem near the Sheep Gate*r* a pool,

---

4:34
a Mt 26:39;
Jn 6:38; 17:4;
19:30
b Jn 19:30

4:35
c Mt 9:37;
Lk 10:2

4:36
d Ro 1:13
e Mt 25:46

4:37
f Job 31:8;
Mic 6:15

4:39
g ver 5
h ver 29

4:42
i Lk 2:11;
1Jn 4:14

4:43
j ver 40

4:44
k Mt 13:57;
Lk 4:24

4:45
l Jn 2:23

4:46
m Jn 2:1-11

4:47
n ver 3,54

4:48
o Da 4:2,3;
Jn 2:11;
Ac 2:43; 14:3;
Ro 15:19;
2Co 12:12;
Heb 2:4

4:53
p Ac 11:14

4:54
q ver 48;
Jn 2:11

5:2
r Ne 3:1; 12:39

5:2
a Jn 19:13, 17,20; 20:16; Ac 21:40; 22:2; 26:14

5:8
b Mt 9:5,6; Mk 2:11; Lk 5:24

5:9
c Jn 9:14

5:10
d ver 16
e Ne 13:15-22; Jer 17:21; Mt 12:2

5:14
f Mk 2:5; Jn 8:11

5:15
g Jn 1:19

5:17
h Jn 9:4; 14:10

5:18
i Jn 7:1
j Jn 10:30,33; 19:7

5:19
k ver 30; Jn 8:28

5:20
l Jn 3:35
m Jn 14:12

5:21
n Ro 4:17; 8:11
o Jn 11:25

5:22
p ver 27; Jn 9:39; Ac 10:42; 17:31

5:23
q Lk 10:16; 1Jn 2:23

which in Aramaic[a] is called Bethsaida[a] and which is surrounded by five covered colonnades. [3]Here a great number of disabled people used to lie—the blind, the lame, the paralyzed.[b] [5]One who was there had been an invalid for thirty-eight years. [6]When Jesus saw him lying there and learned that he had been in this condition for a long time, he asked him, "Do you want to get well?"

[7]"Sir," the invalid replied, "I have no one to help me into the pool when the water is stirred. While I am trying to get in, someone else goes down ahead of me."

[8]Then Jesus said to him, "Get up! Pick up your mat and walk."[b] [9]At once the man was cured; he picked up his mat and walked.

The day on which this took place was a Sabbath,[c] [10]and so the Jews[d] said to the man who had been healed, "It is the Sabbath; the law forbids you to carry your mat."[e]

[11]But he replied, "The man who made me well said to me, 'Pick up your mat and walk.'"

[12]So they asked him, "Who is this fellow who told you to pick it up and walk?"

[13]The man who was healed had no idea who it was, for Jesus had slipped away into the crowd that was there.

[14]Later Jesus found him at the temple and said to him, "See, you are well again. Stop sinning[f] or something worse may happen to you." [15]The man went away and told the Jews[g] that it was Jesus who had made him well.

[16]So, because Jesus was doing these things on the Sabbath, the Jews persecuted him. [17]Jesus said to them, "My Father is always at his work[h] to this very day, and I, too, am working." [18]For this reason the Jews tried all the harder to kill him;[i] not only was he breaking the Sabbath, but he was even calling God his own Father, making himself equal with God.[j]

[19]Jesus gave them this answer: "I tell you the truth, the Son can do nothing by himself;[k] he can do only what he sees his Father doing, because whatever the Father does the Son also does. [20]For the Father loves the Son[l] and shows him all he does. Yes, to your amazement he will show him even greater things than these.[m] [21]For just as the Father raises the dead and gives them life,[n] even so the Son gives life[o] to whom he is pleased to give it. [22]Moreover, the Father judges no one, but has entrusted all judgment to the Son,[p] [23]that all may honor the Son just as they honor the Father. He who does not honor the Son does not honor the Father, who sent him.[q] [24]"I tell you the truth, whoever hears my word and believes him

a 2 Some manuscripts Bethzatha; other manuscripts Bethsaida   b 3 Some less important manuscripts paralyzed—and they waited for the moving of the waters. [4]From time to time an angel of the Lord would come down and stir up the waters. The first one into the pool after each such disturbance would be cured of whatever disease he had.

who sent me has eternal life and will not be condemned;[a] he has crossed over from death to life.[b] [25]I tell you the truth, a time is coming and has now come[c] when the dead will hear[d] the voice of the Son of God and those who hear will live. [26]For as the Father has life in himself, so he has granted the Son to have life in himself. [27]And he has given him authority to judge[e] because he is the Son of Man.

[28]"Do not be amazed at this, for a time is coming[f] when all who are in their graves will hear his voice [29]and come out—those who have done good will rise to live, and those who have done evil will rise to be condemned.[g] [30]By myself I can do nothing;[h] I judge only as I hear, and my judgment is just,[i] for I seek not to please myself but him who sent me.[j]

[31]"If I testify about myself, my testimony is not valid.[k] [32]There is another who testifies in my favor,[l] and I know that his testimony about me is valid.

[33]"You have sent to John and he has testified[m] to the truth. [34]Not that I accept human testimony;[n] but I mention it that you may be saved. [35]John was a lamp that burned and gave light,[o] and you chose for a time to enjoy his light.

[36]"I have testimony weightier than that of John.[p] For the very work that the Father has given me to finish, and which I am doing,[q] testifies that the Father has sent me.[r] [37]And the Father who sent me has himself testified concerning me.[s] You have never heard his voice nor seen his form,[t] [38]nor does his word dwell in you,[u] for you do not believe the one he sent.[v] [39]You diligently study[a] the Scriptures[w] because you think that by them you possess eternal life. These are the Scriptures that testify about me,[x] [40]yet you refuse to come to me to have life.

[41]"I do not accept praise from men,[y] [42]but I know you. I know that you do not have the love of God in your hearts. [43]I have come in my Father's name, and you do not accept me; but if someone else comes in his own name, you will accept him. [44]How can you believe if you accept praise from one another, yet make no effort to obtain the praise that comes from the only God[b]?[z]

[45]"But do not think I will accuse you before the Father. Your accuser is Moses,[a] on whom your hopes are set.[b] [46]If you believed Moses, you would believe me, for he wrote about me.[c] [47]But since you do not believe what he wrote, how are you going to believe what I say?"[d]

Chapter 6 Theme

6 Some time after this, Jesus crossed to the far shore of the Sea of Galilee (that is, the Sea of Tiberias), [2]and a great crowd of

---

a 39 Or *Study diligently* (the imperative)   b 44 Some early manuscripts *the Only One*

5:24
a Jn 3:18
b 1Jn 3:14

5:25
c Jn 4:23
d Jn 8:43,47

5:27
e ver 22;
Ac 10:42; 17:31

5:28
f Jn 4:21

5:29
g Da 12:2;
Mt 25:46

5:30
h ver 19
i Jn 8:16
j Mt 26:39;
Jn 4:34; 6:38

5:31
k Jn 8:14

5:32
l ver 37;
Jn 8:18

5:33
m Jn 1:7

5:34
n 1Jn 5:9

5:35
o 2Pe 1:19

5:36
p 1Jn 5:9
q Jn 14:11; 15:24
r Jn 3:17; 10:25

5:37
s Jn 8:18
t Dt 4:12;
1Ti 1:17;
Jn 1:18

5:38
u 1Jn 2:14
v Jn 3:17

5:39
w Ro 2:17,18
x Lk 24:27,44;
Ac 13:27

5:41
y ver 44

5:44
z Ro 2:29

5:45
a Jn 9:28
b Ro 2:17

5:46
c Ge 3:15;
Lk 24:27,44;
Ac 26:22

5:47
d Lk 16:29,31

people followed him because they saw the miraculous signs*a* he had performed on the sick. ³Then Jesus went up on a mountainside*b* and sat down with his disciples. ⁴The Jewish Passover Feast*c* was near.

⁵When Jesus looked up and saw a great crowd coming toward him, he said to Philip,*d* "Where shall we buy bread for these people to eat?" ⁶He asked this only to test him, for he already had in mind what he was going to do.

⁷Philip answered him, "Eight months' wages*a* would not buy enough bread for each one to have a bite!"

⁸Another of his disciples, Andrew, Simon Peter's brother,*e* spoke up, ⁹"Here is a boy with five small barley loaves and two small fish, but how far will they go among so many?"*f*

¹⁰Jesus said, "Have the people sit down." There was plenty of grass in that place, and the men sat down, about five thousand of them. ¹¹Jesus then took the loaves, gave thanks,*g* and distributed to those who were seated as much as they wanted. He did the same with the fish.

¹²When they had all had enough to eat, he said to his disciples, "Gather the pieces that are left over. Let nothing be wasted." ¹³So they gathered them and filled twelve baskets with the pieces of the five barley loaves left over by those who had eaten.

¹⁴After the people saw the miraculous sign*h* that Jesus did, they began to say, "Surely this is the Prophet who is to come into the world."*i* ¹⁵Jesus, knowing that they intended to come and make him king*j* by force, withdrew again to a mountain by himself.*k*

¹⁶When evening came, his disciples went down to the lake, ¹⁷where they got into a boat and set off across the lake for Capernaum. By now it was dark, and Jesus had not yet joined them. ¹⁸A strong wind was blowing and the waters grew rough. ¹⁹When they had rowed three or three and a half miles,*b* they saw Jesus approaching the boat, walking on the water;*l* and they were terrified. ²⁰But he said to them, "It is I; don't be afraid."*m* ²¹Then they were willing to take him into the boat, and immediately the boat reached the shore where they were heading.

²²The next day the crowd that had stayed on the opposite shore of the lake*n* realized that only one boat had been there, and that Jesus had not entered it with his disciples, but that they had gone away alone.*o* ²³Then some boats from Tiberias*p* landed near the place where the people had eaten the bread after the Lord had given thanks.*q* ²⁴Once the crowd realized that neither Jesus nor his disciples were there, they got into the boats and went to Capernaum in search of Jesus.

INSIGHT

See the chart **The Feasts of Israel** located on pages 210, 211.

a 7 Greek *two hundred denarii*   *b* 19 Greek *rowed twenty-five or thirty stadia* (about 5 or 6 kilometers)

²⁵When they found him on the other side of the lake, they asked him, "Rabbi,ᵃ when did you get here?"

²⁶Jesus answered, "I tell you the truth, you are looking for me,ᵇ not because you saw miraculous signsᶜ but because you ate the loaves and had your fill. ²⁷Do not work for food that spoils, but for food that endursᵈ to eternal life,ᵉ which the Son of Manᶠ will give you. On him God the Father has placed his sealᵍ of approval."

²⁸Then they asked him, "What must we do to do the works God requires?"

²⁹Jesus answered, "The work of God is this: to believeʰ in the one he has sent."ⁱ

³⁰So they asked him, "What miraculous signʲ then will you give that we may see it and believe you?ᵏ What will you do? ³¹Our forefathers ate the mannaˡ in the desert; as it is written: 'He gave them bread from heaven to eat.'ᵃ"ᵐ

³²Jesus said to them, "I tell you the truth, it is not Moses who has given you the bread from heaven, but it is my Father who gives you the true bread from heaven. ³³For the bread of God is he who comes down from heavenⁿ and gives life to the world."

³⁴"Sir," they said, "from now on give us this bread."ᵒ

³⁵Then Jesus declared, "I am the bread of life.ᵖ He who comes to me will never go hungry, and he who believes in me will never be thirsty.ᑫ ³⁶But as I told you, you have seen me and still you do not believe. ³⁷All that the Father gives meʳ will come to me, and whoever comes to me I will never drive away. ³⁸For I have come down from heaven not to do my will but to do the will of him who sent me.ˢ ³⁹And this is the will of him who sent me, that I shall lose none of all that he has given me,ᵗ but raise them up at the last day.ᵘ ⁴⁰For my Father's will is that everyone who looks to the Son and believes in him shall have eternal life,ᵛ and I will raise him up at the last day."

⁴¹At this the Jews began to grumble about him because he said, "I am the bread that came down from heaven." ⁴²They said, "Is this not Jesus, the son of Joseph,ʷ whose father and mother we know?ˣ How can he now say, 'I came down from heaven'?"ʸ

⁴³"Stop grumbling among yourselves," Jesus answered. ⁴⁴"No one can come to me unless the Father who sent me draws him,ᶻ and I will raise him up at the last day. ⁴⁵It is written in the Prophets: 'They will all be taught by God.'ᵇᵃ Everyone who listens to the Father and learns from him comes to me. ⁴⁶No one has seen the Father except the one who is from God;ᵇ only he has seen the Father. ⁴⁷I tell you the truth, he who believes has everlasting life. ⁴⁸I am the bread of life.ᶜ ⁴⁹Your forefathers ate the manna in the desert, yet they died.ᵈ ⁵⁰But here is the bread that

---

ᵃ 31 Exodus 16:4; Neh. 9:15; Psalm 78:24,25   ᵇ 45 Isaiah 54:13

6:25
ᵃ Mt 23:7
6:26
ᵇ ver 24
ᶜ ver 30;
Jn 2:11
6:27
ᵈ Isa 55:2
ᵉ ver 54;
Mt 25:46;
Jn 4:14
ᶠ Mt 8:20
ᵍ Ro 4:11;
1Co 9:2;
2Co 1:22;
Eph 1:13; 4:30;
2Ti 2:19;
Rev 7:3
6:29
ʰ 1Jn 3:23
ⁱ Jn 3:17
6:30
ʲ Jn 2:11
ᵏ Mt 12:38
6:31
ˡ Nu 11:7-9
ᵐ Ex 16:4,15;
Ne 9:15;
Ps 78:24; 105:40
6:33
ⁿ ver 50
6:34
ᵒ Jn 4:15
6:35
ᵖ ver 48,51
ᑫ Jn 4:14
6:37
ʳ ver 39;
Jn 17:2,6,9,24
6:38
ˢ Jn 4:34; 5:30
6:39
ᵗ Jn 10:28; 17:12;
18:9
ᵘ ver 40,44,54
6:40
ᵛ Jn 3:15,16
6:42
ʷ Lk 4:22
ˣ Jn 7:27,28
ʸ ver 38,62
6:44
ᶻ ver 65;
Jer 31:3;
Jn 12:32
6:45
ᵃ Isa 54:13;
Jer 31:33,34;
Heb 8:10,11;
10:16
6:46
ᵇ Jn 1:18; 5:37;
7:29
6:48
ᶜ ver 35,51
6:49
ᵈ ver 31,58

6:50
a ver 33

6:51
b Heb 10:10

6:52
c Jn 7:43; 9:16;
10:19

6:53
d Mt 8:20

6:54
e ver 39

6:56
f Jn 15:4-7;
1Jn 3:24; 4:15

6:57
g Jn 3:17

6:58
h ver 49-51;
Jn 3:36

6:60
i ver 66

6:61
j Mt 11:6

6:62
k Mk 16:19;
Jn 3:13; 17:5

6:63
l 2Co 3:6

6:64
m Jn 2:25

6:65
n ver 37,44

6:66
o ver 60

6:67
p Mt 10:2

6:68
q Mt 16:16

6:69
r Mk 8:29;
Lk 9:20

6:70
s Jn 15:16,19
t Jn 13:27

7:1
u Jn 1:19
v Jn 5:18

7:2
w Lev 23:34;
Dt 16:16

comes down from heaven,*a* which a man may eat and not die. 51I am the living bread that came down from heaven. If anyone eats of this bread, he will live forever. This bread is my flesh, which I will give for the life of the world."*b*

52Then the Jews began to argue sharply among themselves,*c* "How can this man give us his flesh to eat?"

53Jesus said to them, "I tell you the truth, unless you eat the flesh of the Son of Man*d* and drink his blood, you have no life in you. 54Whoever eats my flesh and drinks my blood has eternal life, and I will raise him up at the last day.*e* 55For my flesh is real food and my blood is real drink. 56Whoever eats my flesh and drinks my blood remains in me, and I in him.*f* 57Just as the living Father sent me*g* and I live because of the Father, so the one who feeds on me will live because of me. 58This is the bread that came down from heaven. Your forefathers ate manna and died, but he who feeds on this bread will live forever."*h* 59He said this while teaching in the synagogue in Capernaum.

60On hearing it, many of his disciples*i* said, "This is a hard teaching. Who can accept it?"

61Aware that his disciples were grumbling about this, Jesus said to them, "Does this offend you?*j* 62What if you see the Son of Man ascend to where he was before!*k* 63The Spirit gives life;*l* the flesh counts for nothing. The words I have spoken to you are spirit*a* and they are life. 64Yet there are some of you who do not believe." For Jesus had known*m* from the beginning which of them did not believe and who would betray him. 65He went on to say, "This is why I told you that no one can come to me unless the Father has enabled him."*n*

66From this time many of his disciples*o* turned back and no longer followed him.

67"You do not want to leave too, do you?" Jesus asked the Twelve.*p*

68Simon Peter answered him,*q* "Lord, to whom shall we go? You have the words of eternal life. 69We believe and know that you are the Holy One of God."*r*

70Then Jesus replied, "Have I not chosen you,*s* the Twelve? Yet one of you is a devil!"*t* 71(He meant Judas, the son of Simon Iscariot, who, though one of the Twelve, was later to betray him.)

Chapter 7 Theme

7 After this, Jesus went around in Galilee, purposely staying away from Judea because the Jews*u* there were waiting to take his life.*v* 2But when the Jewish Feast of Tabernacles*w* was

a 63 Or *Spirit*

near, ³Jesus' brothers*ᵃ* said to him, "You ought to leave here and go to Judea, so that your disciples may see the miracles you do. ⁴No one who wants to become a public figure acts in secret. Since you are doing these things, show yourself to the world." ⁵For even his own brothers did not believe in him.*ᵇ*

⁶Therefore Jesus told them, "The right time*ᶜ* for me has not yet come; for you any time is right. ⁷The world cannot hate you, but it hates me*ᵈ* because I testify that what it does is evil.*ᵉ* ⁸You go to the Feast. I am not yet*ᵃ* going up to this Feast, because for me the right time*ᶠ* has not yet come." ⁹Having said this, he stayed in Galilee.

¹⁰However, after his brothers had left for the Feast, he went also, not publicly, but in secret. ¹¹Now at the Feast the Jews were watching for him*ᵍ* and asking, "Where is that man?"

¹²Among the crowds there was wide-spread whispering about him. Some said, "He is a good man."

Others replied, "No, he deceives the people."*ʰ* ¹³But no one would say anything publicly about him for fear of the Jews.*ⁱ*

¹⁴Not until halfway through the Feast did Jesus go up to the temple courts and begin to teach.*ʲ* ¹⁵The Jews*ᵏ* were amazed and asked, "How did this man get such learning*ˡ* without having studied?"*ᵐ*

¹⁶Jesus answered, "My teaching is not my own. It comes from him who sent me.*ⁿ* ¹⁷If anyone chooses to do God's will, he will find out*ᵒ* whether my teaching comes from God or whether I speak on my own. ¹⁸He who speaks on his own does so to gain honor for himself,*ᵖ* but he who works for the honor of the one who sent him is a man of truth; there is nothing false about him. ¹⁹Has not Moses given you the law?*�q* Yet not one of you keeps the law. Why are you trying to kill me?"*ʳ*

²⁰"You are demon-possessed,"*ˢ* the crowd answered. "Who is trying to kill you?"

²¹Jesus said to them, "I did one miracle, and you are all astonished. ²²Yet, because Moses gave you circumcision*ᵗ* (though actually it did not come from Moses, but from the patriarchs),*ᵘ* you circumcise a child on the Sabbath. ²³Now if a child can be circumcised on the Sabbath so that the law of Moses may not be broken, why are you angry with me for healing the whole man on the Sabbath? ²⁴Stop judging by mere appearances, and make a right judgment."*ᵛ*

²⁵At that point some of the people of Jerusalem began to ask, "Isn't this the man they are trying to kill? ²⁶Here he is, speaking publicly, and they are not saying a word to him. Have the authorities*ʷ* really concluded that he is the Christ*ᵇ*? ²⁷But we know

---

ᵃ8 Some early manuscripts do not have *yet.*   *ᵇ26* Or *Messiah*; also in verses 27, 31, 41 and 42

7:3
ᵃ Mt 12:46

7:5
ᵇ Mk 3:21

7:6
ᶜ Mt 26:18

7:7
ᵈ Jn 15:18,19
ᵉ Jn 3:19,20

7:8
ᶠ ver 6

7:11
ᵍ Jn 11:56

7:12
ʰ ver 40,43

7:13
ⁱ Jn 9:22; 12:42; 19:38

7:14
ʲ ver 28; Mt 26:55

7:15
ᵏ Jn 1:19
ˡ Ac 26:24
ᵐ Mt 13:54

7:16
ⁿ Jn 3:11; 14:24

7:17
ᵒ Ps 25:14; Jn 8:43

7:18
ᵖ Jn 5:41; 8:50,54

7:19
q Jn 1:17
ʳ ver 1; Mt 12:14

7:20
ˢ Jn 8:48; 10:20

7:22
ᵗ Lev 12:3
ᵘ Ge 17:10-14

7:24
ᵛ Isa 11:3,4; Jn 8:15

7:26
ʷ ver 48

7:27
a Mt 13:55;
Lk 4:22

7:28
b ver 14
c Jn 8:14
d Jn 8:26,42

7:29
e Mt 11:27

7:30
f ver 32,44;
Jn 10:39

7:31
g Jn 8:30
h Jn 2:11

7:33
i Jn 13:33; 16:16
j Jn 16:5,
10,17,28

7:34
k Jn 8:21; 13:33

7:35
l Jas 1:1
m Jn 12:20;
1Pe 1:1

7:37
n Lev 23:36
o Isa 55:1;
Rev 22:17

7:38
p Isa 58:11
q Jn 4:10
r Jn 4:14

7:39
s Joel 2:28;
Ac 2:17,33
t Jn 20:22
u Jn 12:23;
13:31,32

7:40
v Mt 21:11;
Jn 1:21

7:41
w ver 52;
Jn 1:46

7:42
x Mt 1:1
y Mic 5:2;
Mt 2:5,6;
Lk 2:4

7:43
z Jn 9:16; 10:19

7:44
a ver 30

7:46
b Mt 7:28

7:47
c ver 12

7:48
d Jn 12:42

where this man is from;[a] when the Christ comes, no one will know where he is from."

28Then Jesus, still teaching in the temple courts,[b] cried out, "Yes, you know me, and you know where I am from.[c] I am not here on my own, but he who sent me is true.[d] You do not know him, 29but I know him[e] because I am from him and he sent me."

30At this they tried to seize him, but no one laid a hand on him,[f] because his time had not yet come. 31Still, many in the crowd put their faith in him.[g] They said, "When the Christ comes, will he do more miraculous signs[h] than this man?"

32The Pharisees heard the crowd whispering such things about him. Then the chief priests and the Pharisees sent temple guards to arrest him.

33Jesus said, "I am with you for only a short time,[i] and then I go to the one who sent me.[j] 34You will look for me, but you will not find me; and where I am, you cannot come."[k]

35The Jews said to one another, "Where does this man intend to go that we cannot find him? Will he go where our people live scattered[l] among the Greeks,[m] and teach the Greeks? 36What did he mean when he said, 'You will look for me, but you will not find me,' and 'Where I am, you cannot come'?"

37On the last and greatest day of the Feast,[n] Jesus stood and said in a loud voice, "If anyone is thirsty, let him come to me and drink.[o] 38Whoever believes in me, as[a] the Scripture has said,[p] streams of living water[q] will flow from within him."[r] 39By this he meant the Spirit,[s] whom those who believed in him were later to receive.[t] Up to that time the Spirit had not been given, since Jesus had not yet been glorified.[u]

40On hearing his words, some of the people said, "Surely this man is the Prophet."[v]

41Others said, "He is the Christ."

Still others asked, "How can the Christ come from Galilee?[w] 42Does not the Scripture say that the Christ will come from David's family[b][x] and from Bethlehem,[y] the town where David lived?" 43Thus the people were divided[z] because of Jesus. 44Some wanted to seize him, but no one laid a hand on him.[a]

45Finally the temple guards went back to the chief priests and Pharisees, who asked them, "Why didn't you bring him in?"

46"No one ever spoke the way this man does,"[b] the guards declared.

47"You mean he has deceived you also?"[c] the Pharisees retorted. 48"Has any of the rulers or of the Pharisees believed in him?[d] 49No! But this mob that knows nothing of the law—there is a curse on them."

a 37,38 Or / If anyone is thirsty, let him come to me. / And let him drink, 38who believes in me. / As
b 42 Greek seed

⁵⁰Nicodemus,ᵃ who had gone to Jesus earlier and who was one of their own number, asked, ⁵¹"Does our law condemn anyone without first hearing him to find out what he is doing?"

⁵²They replied, "Are you from Galilee, too? Look into it, and you will find that a prophetᵃ does not come out of Galilee."ᵇ

[The earliest manuscripts and many
other ancient witnesses do not have
John 7:53–8:11.]

Chapter 8 Theme

⁵³Then each went to his own home.

8 But Jesus went to the Mount of Olives.ᶜ ²At dawn he appeared again in the temple courts, where all the people gathered around him, and he sat down to teach them.ᵈ ³The teachers of the law and the Pharisees brought in a woman caught in adultery. They made her stand before the group ⁴and said to Jesus, "Teacher, this woman was caught in the act of adultery. ⁵In the Law Moses commanded us to stone such women.ᵉ Now what do you say?" ⁶They were using this question as a trap,ᶠ in order to have a basis for accusing him.ᵍ

But Jesus bent down and started to write on the ground with his finger. ⁷When they kept on questioning him, he straightened up and said to them, "If any one of you is without sin, let him be the first to throw a stoneʰ at her."ⁱ ⁸Again he stooped down and wrote on the ground.

⁹At this, those who heard began to go away one at a time, the older ones first, until only Jesus was left, with the woman still standing there. ¹⁰Jesus straightened up and asked her, "Woman, where are they? Has no one condemned you?"

¹¹"No one, sir," she said.

"Then neither do I condemn you,"ʲ Jesus declared. "Go now and leave your life of sin."ᵏ

¹²When Jesus spoke again to the people, he said, "I amˡ the light of the world.ᵐ Whoever follows me will never walk in darkness, but will have the light of life."ⁿ

¹³The Pharisees challenged him, "Here you are, appearing as your own witness; your testimony is not valid."ᵒ

ᵃ 52 Two early manuscripts *the Prophet*

7:50
ᵃ Jn 3:1; 19:39

7:52
ᵇ ver 41

8:1
ᶜ Mt 21:1

8:2
ᵈ ver 20;
Mt 26:55

8:5
ᵉ Lev 20:10;
Dt 22:22

8:6
ᶠ Mt 22:15,18
ᵍ Mt 12:10

8:7
ʰ Dt 17:7
ⁱ Ro 2:1,22

8:11
ʲ Jn 3:17
ᵏ Jn 5:14

8:12
ˡ Jn 6:35
ᵐ Jn 1:4; 12:35
ⁿ Pr 4:18;
Mt 5:14

8:13
ᵒ Jn 5:31

8:14
a Jn 13:3; 16:28
b Jn 7:28; 9:29

8:15
c Jn 7:24
d Jn 3:17

8:16
e Jn 5:30

8:17
f Dt 17:6;
Mt 18:16

8:18
g Jn 5:37

8:19
h Jn 16:3
i Jn 14:7;
1Jn 2:23

8:20
j Mt 26:55
k Mk 12:41
l Mt 26:18;
Jn 7:30

8:21
m Eze 3:18
n Jn 7:34; 13:33

8:23
o Jn 3:31; 17:14

8:24
p Jn 4:26; 13:19

8:26
q Jn 7:28
r Jn 3:32; 15:15

8:28
s Jn 3:14; 5:19;
12:32

8:29
t ver 16;
Jn 16:32
u Jn 4:34; 5:30;
6:38

8:30
v Jn 7:31

8:31
w Jn 15:7;
2Jn 9

8:32
x Ro 8:2;
Jas 2:12

8:33
y ver 37,39;
Mt 3:9

8:34
z Ro 6:16;
2Pe 2:19

8:35
a Gal 4:30

¹⁴Jesus answered, "Even if I testify on my own behalf, my testimony is valid, for I know where I came from and where I am going.ᵃ But you have no idea where I come fromᵇ or where I am going. ¹⁵You judge by human standards;ᶜ I pass judgment on no one.ᵈ ¹⁶But if I do judge, my decisions are right, because I am not alone. I stand with the Father, who sent me.ᵉ ¹⁷In your own Law it is written that the testimony of two men is valid.ᶠ ¹⁸I am one who testifies for myself; my other witness is the Father, who sent me."ᵍ

¹⁹Then they asked him, "Where is your father?"

"You do not know me or my Father,"ʰ Jesus replied. "If you knew me, you would know my Father also."ⁱ ²⁰He spoke these words while teachingʲ in the temple area near the place where the offerings were put.ᵏ Yet no one seized him, because his time had not yet come.ˡ

²¹Once more Jesus said to them, "I am going away, and you will look for me, and you will dieᵐ in your sin. Where I go, you cannot come."ⁿ

²²This made the Jews ask, "Will he kill himself? Is that why he says, 'Where I go, you cannot come'?"

²³But he continued, "You are from below; I am from above. You are of this world; I am not of this world.ᵒ ²⁴I told you that you would die in your sins; if you do not believe that I am ⌊the one I claim to be⌋,ᵃᵖ you will indeed die in your sins."

²⁵"Who are you?" they asked.

"Just what I have been claiming all along," Jesus replied. ²⁶"I have much to say in judgment of you. But he who sent me is reliable,�q and what I have heard from him I tell the world."ʳ

²⁷They did not understand that he was telling them about his Father. ²⁸So Jesus said, "When you have lifted up the Son of Man,ˢ then you will know that I am ⌊the one I claim to be⌋ and that I do nothing on my own but speak just what the Father has taught me. ²⁹The one who sent me is with me; he has not left me alone,ᵗ for I always do what pleases him."ᵘ ³⁰Even as he spoke, many put their faith in him.ᵛ

³¹To the Jews who had believed him, Jesus said, "If you hold to my teaching,ʷ you are really my disciples. ³²Then you will know the truth, and the truth will set you free."ˣ

³³They answered him, "We are Abraham's descendantsᵇʸ and have never been slaves of anyone. How can you say that we shall be set free?"

³⁴Jesus replied, "I tell you the truth, everyone who sins is a slave to sin.ᶻ ³⁵Now a slave has no permanent place in the family, but a son belongs to it forever.ᵃ ³⁶So if the Son sets you free, you will be free indeed. ³⁷I know you are Abraham's descendants. Yet you are

I N S I G H T

"The place" mentioned in verse 20 was in the women's court of the temple, where there were thirteen trumpet-shaped offering receptacles. See the illustration of the floor plan of Herod's Temple on page 1723, and see the illustration of Herod's Temple on page IISB-38.

a 24 Or *I am he*; also in verse 28   b 33 Greek *seed*; also in verse 37 ready to kill me,[a] because you have no room for my word. [38]I am telling you what I have seen in the Father's presence,[b] and you do what you have heard from your father.[a]"

[39]"Abraham is our father," they answered.

"If you were Abraham's children,"[c] said Jesus, "then you would[b] do the things Abraham did. [40]As it is, you are determined to kill me, a man who has told you the truth that I heard from God.[d] Abraham did not do such things. [41]You are doing the things your own father does."[e]

"We are not illegitimate children," they protested. "The only Father we have is God himself."[f]

[42]Jesus said to them, "If God were your Father, you would love me,[g] for I came from God[h] and now am here. I have not come on my own;[i] but he sent me.[j] [43]Why is my language not clear to you? Because you are unable to hear what I say. [44]You belong to your father, the devil,[k] and you want to carry out your father's desire.[l] He was a murderer from the beginning, not holding to the truth, for there is no truth in him. When he lies, he speaks his native language, for he is a liar and the father of lies.[m] [45]Yet because I tell the truth,[n] you do not believe me! [46]Can any of you prove me guilty of sin? If I am telling the truth, why don't you believe me? [47]He who belongs to God hears what God says.[o] The reason you do not hear is that you do not belong to God."

[48]The Jews answered him, "Aren't we right in saying that you are a Samaritan[p] and demon-possessed?"[q]

[49]"I am not possessed by a demon," said Jesus, "but I honor my Father and you dishonor me. [50]I am not seeking glory for myself;[r] but there is one who seeks it, and he is the judge. [51]I tell you the truth, if anyone keeps my word, he will never see death."[s]

[52]At this the Jews exclaimed, "Now we know that you are demon-possessed! Abraham died and so did the prophets, yet you say that if anyone keeps your word, he will never taste death. [53]Are you greater than our father Abraham?[t] He died, and so did the prophets. Who do you think you are?"

[54]Jesus replied, "If I glorify myself,[u] my glory means nothing. My Father, whom you claim as your God, is the one who glorifies me.[v] [55]Though you do not know him,[w] I know him.[x] If I said I did not, I would be a liar like you, but I do know him and keep his word.[y] [56]Your father Abraham[z] rejoiced at the thought of seeing my day; he saw it[a] and was glad."

[57]"You are not yet fifty years old," the Jews said to him, "and you have seen Abraham!"

[58]"I tell you the truth," Jesus answered, "before Abraham was

---

8:37
[a] ver 39,40

8:38
[b] Jn 5:19,30; 14:10,24

8:39
[c] ver 37; Ro 9:7; Gal 3:7

8:40
[d] ver 26

8:41
[e] ver 38,44
[f] Isa 63:16; 64:8

8:42
[g] 1Jn 5:1
[h] Jn 16:27; 17:8
[i] Jn 7:28
[j] Jn 3:17

8:44
[k] 1Jn 3:8
[l] ver 38,41
[m] Ge 3:4

8:45
[n] Jn 18:37

8:47
[o] Jn 18:37; 1Jn 4:6

8:48
[p] Mt 10:5
[q] ver 52; Jn 7:20

8:50
[r] ver 54; Jn 5:41

8:51
[s] Jn 11:26

8:53
[t] Jn 4:12

8:54
[u] ver 50
[v] Jn 16:14; 17:1,5

8:55
[w] ver 19
[x] Jn 7:28,29
[y] Jn 15:10

8:56
[z] ver 37,39
[a] Mt 13:17; Heb 11:13

---

a 38 Or *presence. Therefore do what you have heard from the Father.*   b 39 Some early manuscripts *"If you are Abraham's children," said Jesus, "then*

8:58
a Jn 1:2; 17:5,24
b Ex 3:14

8:59
c Lev 24:16;
Jn 10:31; 11:8
d Jn 12:36

9:2
e Mt 23:7
f ver 34;
Lk 13:2;
Ac 28:4
g Eze 18:20
h Ex 20:5;
Job 21:19

9:3
i Jn 11:4

9:4
j Jn 11:9; 12:35

9:5
k Jn 1:4; 8:12;
12:46

9:6
l Mk 7:33; 8:23

9:7
m ver 11;
2Ki 5:10;
Lk 13:4
n Isa 35:5;
Jn 11:37

9:8
o Ac 3:2,10

9:11
p ver 7

9:14
q Jn 5:9

9:15
r ver 10

9:16
s Mt 12:2
t Jn 6:52; 7:43;
10:19

9:17
u Mt 21:11

9:18
v Jn 1:19

born,*a* I am!"*b* 59At this, they picked up stones to stone him,*c* but Jesus hid himself,*d* slipping away from the temple grounds.

Chapter 9 Theme

9 As he went along, he saw a man blind from birth. 2His disciples asked him, "Rabbi,*e* who sinned,*f* this man*g* or his parents,*h* that he was born blind?"

3"Neither this man nor his parents sinned," said Jesus, "but this happened so that the work of God might be displayed in his life.*i* 4As long as it is day,*j* we must do the work of him who sent me. Night is coming, when no one can work. 5While I am in the world, I am the light of the world."*k*

6Having said this, he spit*l* on the ground, made some mud with the saliva, and put it on the man's eyes. 7"Go," he told him, "wash in the Pool of Siloam"*m* (this word means Sent). So the man went and washed, and came home seeing.*n*

8His neighbors and those who had formerly seen him begging asked, "Isn't this the same man who used to sit and beg?"*o* 9Some claimed that he was.

Others said, "No, he only looks like him."

But he himself insisted, "I am the man."

10"How then were your eyes opened?" they demanded.

11He replied, "The man they call Jesus made some mud and put it on my eyes. He told me to go to Siloam and wash. So I went and washed, and then I could see."*p*

12"Where is this man?" they asked him.

"I don't know," he said.

13They brought to the Pharisees the man who had been blind. 14Now the day on which Jesus had made the mud and opened the man's eyes was a Sabbath.*q* 15Therefore the Pharisees also asked him how he had received his sight.*r* "He put mud on my eyes," the man replied, "and I washed, and now I see."

16Some of the Pharisees said, "This man is not from God, for he does not keep the Sabbath."*s*

But others asked, "How can a sinner do such miraculous signs?" So they were divided.*t*

17Finally they turned again to the blind man, "What have you to say about him? It was your eyes he opened."

The man replied, "He is a prophet."*u*

18The Jews*v* still did not believe that he had been blind and had received his sight until they sent for the man's parents. 19"Is this your son?" they asked. "Is this the one you say was born blind? How is it that now he can see?"

20"We know he is our son," the parents answered, "and we know he was born blind. 21But how he can see now, or who opened his eyes, we don't know. Ask him. He is of age; he will speak for himself." [22]His parents said this because they were afraid of the Jews,[a] for already the Jews had decided that anyone who acknowledged that Jesus was the Christ[a] would be put out[b] of the synagogue.[c] [23]That was why his parents said, "He is of age; ask him."[d]

[24]A second time they summoned the man who had been blind. "Give glory to God,[b]"[e] they said. "We know this man is a sinner."[f]

[25]He replied, "Whether he is a sinner or not, I don't know. One thing I do know. I was blind but now I see!"

[26]Then they asked him, "What did he do to you? How did he open your eyes?"

[27]He answered, "I have told you already[g] and you did not listen. Why do you want to hear it again? Do you want to become his disciples, too?"

[28]Then they hurled insults at him and said, "You are this fellow's disciple! We are disciples of Moses![h] [29]We know that God spoke to Moses, but as for this fellow, we don't even know where he comes from."[i]

[30]The man answered, "Now that is remarkable! You don't know where he comes from, yet he opened my eyes. [31]We know that God does not listen to sinners. He listens to the godly man who does his will.[j] [32]Nobody has ever heard of opening the eyes of a man born blind. [33]If this man were not from God,[k] he could do nothing."

[34]To this they replied, "You were steeped in sin at birth;[l] how dare you lecture us!" And they threw him out.[m]

[35]Jesus heard that they had thrown him out, and when he found him, he said, "Do you believe in the Son of Man?"

[36]"Who is he, sir?" the man asked. "Tell me so that I may believe in him."[n]

[37]Jesus said, "You have now seen him; in fact, he is the one speaking with you."[o]

[38]Then the man said, "Lord, I believe," and he worshiped him.[p]

[39]Jesus said, "For judgment[q] I have come into this world,[r] so that the blind will see[s] and those who see will become blind."[t]

[40]Some Pharisees who were with him heard him say this and asked, "What? Are we blind too?"[u]

[41]Jesus said, "If you were blind, you would not be guilty of sin; but now that you claim you can see, your guilt remains."[v]

Chapter 10 Theme

10 "I tell you the truth, the man who does not enter the sheep pen by the gate, but climbs in by some other way, is a thief and a robber. [2]The man who enters by the gate is the shepherd of

a 22 Or *Messiah*   b 24 A solemn charge to tell the truth (see Joshua 7:19)

Cross references:

9:22 a Jn 7:13; b ver 34; Lk 6:22; c Jn 12:42; 16:2

9:23 d ver 21

9:24 e Jos 7:19; f ver 16

9:27 g ver 15

9:28 h Jn 5:45

9:29 i Jn 8:14

9:31 j Ge 18:23-32; Ps 34:15,16; 66:18;145:19,20; Pr 15:29; Isa 1:15; 59:1,2; Jn 15:7; Jas 5:16-18; 1Jn 5:14,15

9:33 k ver 16; Jn 3:2

9:34 l ver 2; m ver 22,35; Isa 66:5

9:36 n Ro 10:14

9:37 o Jn 4:26

9:38 p Mt 28:9

9:39 q Jn 5:22; r Jn 3:19; s Lk 4:18; t Mt 13:13

9:40 u Ro 2:19

9:41 v Jn 15:22,24

10:2
a ver 11,14

10:3
b ver 4,5,14, 16,27

10:6
c Jn 16:25

10:8
d Jer 23:1,2

10:11
e ver 14;
Isa 40:11;
Eze 34:11-16, 23;
Heb 13:20;
1Pe 5:4;
Rev 7:17
f Jn 15:13;
1Jn 3:16

10:12
g Zec 11:16,17

10:14
h ver 11
i ver 27

10:15
j Mt 11:27

10:16
k Isa 56:8
l Jn 11:52;
Eph 2:11-19
m Eze 37:24;
1Pe 2:25

10:17
n ver 11,15,18

10:18
o Mt 26:53
p Jn 15:10;
Php 2:8;
Heb 5:8

10:19
q Jn 7:43; 9:16

10:20
r Jn 7:20
s Mk 3:21

10:21
t Mt 4:24
u Ex 4:11;
Jn 9:32,33

10:23
v Ac 3:11; 5:12

10:24
w Jn 1:19
x Jn 16:25,29

10:25
y Jn 8:58
z Jn 5:36

10:26
a Jn 8:47

his sheep.*a* [3]The watchman opens the gate for him, and the sheep listen to his voice.*b* He calls his own sheep by name and leads them out. [4]When he has brought out all his own, he goes on ahead of them, and his sheep follow him because they know his voice. [5]But they will never follow a stranger; in fact, they will run away from him because they do not recognize a stranger's voice." [6]Jesus used this figure of speech,*c* but they did not understand what he was telling them.

[7]Therefore Jesus said again, "I tell you the truth, I am the gate for the sheep. [8]All who ever came before me*d* were thieves and robbers, but the sheep did not listen to them. [9]I am the gate; whoever enters through me will be saved.*a* He will come in and go out, and find pasture. [10]The thief comes only to steal and kill and destroy; I have come that they may have life, and have it to the full.

[11]"I am the good shepherd.*e* The good shepherd lays down his life for the sheep.*f* [12]The hired hand is not the shepherd who owns the sheep. So when he sees the wolf coming, he abandons the sheep and runs away.*g* Then the wolf attacks the flock and scatters it. [13]The man runs away because he is a hired hand and cares nothing for the sheep.

[14]"I am the good shepherd;*h* I know my sheep*i* and my sheep know me—[15]just as the Father knows me and I know the Father*j*—and I lay down my life for the sheep. [16]I have other sheep*k* that are not of this sheep pen. I must bring them also. They too will listen to my voice, and there shall be one flock*l* and one shepherd.*m* [17]The reason my Father loves me is that I lay down my life*n*—only to take it up again. [18]No one takes it from me, but I lay it down of my own accord.*o* I have authority to lay it down and authority to take it up again. This command I received from my Father."*p*

[19]At these words the Jews were again divided.*q* [20]Many of them said, "He is demon-possessed*r* and raving mad.*s* Why listen to him?"

[21]But others said, "These are not the sayings of a man possessed by a demon.*t* Can a demon open the eyes of the blind?"*u*

[22]Then came the Feast of Dedication*b* at Jerusalem. It was winter, [23]and Jesus was in the temple area walking in Solomon's Colonnade.*v* [24]The Jews*w* gathered around him, saying, "How long will you keep us in suspense? If you are the Christ,*c* tell us plainly."*x*

[25]Jesus answered, "I did tell you,*y* but you do not believe. The miracles I do in my Father's name speak for me,*z* [26]but you do not believe because you are not my sheep.*a* [27]My sheep listen to

a 9 Or *kept safe*   *b 22* That is, Hanukkah   *c 24* Or *Messiah* my voice; I know them,[a] and they follow me.[b] 28I give them eternal life, and they shall never perish; no one can snatch them out of my hand.[c] 29My Father, who has given them to me,[d] is greater than all[a];[e] no one can snatch them out of my Father's hand. 30I and the Father are one."[f]

31Again the Jews picked up stones to stone him,[g] 32but Jesus said to them, "I have shown you many great miracles from the Father. For which of these do you stone me?"

33"We are not stoning you for any of these," replied the Jews, "but for blasphemy, because you, a mere man, claim to be God."[h]

34Jesus answered them, "Is it not written in your Law,[i] 'I have said you are gods'[b]?[j] 35If he called them 'gods,' to whom the word of God came—and the Scripture cannot be broken— 36what about the one whom the Father set apart[k] as his very own[l] and sent into the world?[m] Why then do you accuse me of blasphemy because I said, 'I am God's Son'?[n] 37Do not believe me unless I do what my Father does.[o] 38But if I do it, even though you do not believe me, believe the miracles, that you may know and understand that the Father is in me, and I in the Father."[p] 39Again they tried to seize him,[q] but he escaped their grasp.[r]

40Then Jesus went back across the Jordan[s] to the place where John had been baptizing in the early days. Here he stayed 41and many people came to him. They said, "Though John never performed a miraculous sign,[t] all that John said about this man was true."[u] 42And in that place many believed in Jesus.[v]

Chapter 11 Theme

11 Now a man named Lazarus was sick. He was from Bethany,[w] the village of Mary and her sister Martha.[x] 2This Mary, whose brother Lazarus now lay sick, was the same one who poured perfume on the Lord and wiped his feet with her hair.[y] 3So the sisters sent word to Jesus, "Lord, the one you love[z] is sick."

4When he heard this, Jesus said, "This sickness will not end in death. No, it is for God's glory[a] so that God's Son may be glorified through it." 5Jesus loved Martha and her sister and Lazarus. 6Yet when he heard that Lazarus was sick, he stayed where he was two more days.

7Then he said to his disciples, "Let us go back to Judea."[b]

8"But Rabbi,"[c] they said, "a short while ago the Jews tried to stone you,[d] and yet you are going back there?"

9Jesus answered, "Are there not twelve hours of daylight? A man who walks by day will not stumble, for he sees by this world's light.[e] 10It is when he walks by night that he stumbles, for he has no light."

10:27
[a] ver 14
[b] ver 4

10:28
[c] Jn 6:39

10:29
[d] Jn 17:2,6,24
[e] Jn 14:28

10:30
[f] Jn 17:21-23

10:31
[g] Jn 8:59

10:33
[h] Lev 24:16;
Jn 5:18

10:34
[i] Jn 8:17;
Ro 3:19
[j] Ps 82:6

10:36
[k] Jer 1:5
[l] Jn 6:69
[m] Jn 3:17
[n] Jn 5:17,18

10:37
[o] ver 25;
Jn 15:24

10:38
[p] Jn 14:10,
11,20; 17:21

10:39
[q] Jn 7:30
[r] Lk 4:30;
Jn 8:59

10:40
[s] Jn 1:28

10:41
[t] Jn 2:11; 3:30
[u] Jn 1:26,27,
30,34

10:42
[v] Jn 7:31

11:1
[w] Mt 21:17
[x] Lk 10:38

11:2
[y] Mk 14:3;
Lk 7:38;
Jn 12:3

11:3
[z] ver 5,36

11:4
[a] ver 40;
Jn 9:3

11:7
[b] Jn 10:40

11:8
[c] Mt 23:7
[d] Jn 8:59; 10:31

11:9
[e] Jn 9:4; 12:35

[a] 29 Many early manuscripts *What my Father has given me is greater than all*   [b] 34 Psalm 82:6

11:11
a ver 3
b Ac 7:60

11:13
c Mt 9:24

11:16
d Mt 10:3;
Jn 14:5; 20:24-28;
21:2;
Ac 1:13

11:17
e ver 6,39

11:18
f ver 1

11:19
g ver 31;
Job 2:11

11:20
h Lk 10:38-42

11:21
i ver 32,37

11:22
j ver 41,42;
Jn 9:31

11:24
k Da 12:2;
Jn 5:28,29;
Ac 24:15

11:25
l Jn 1:4

11:27
m Lk 2:11
n Mt 16:16
o Jn 6:14

11:28
p Mt 26:18;
Jn 13:13

11:30
q ver 20

11:31
r ver 19

11:32
s ver 21

11:33
t ver 38
u Jn 12:27

11:35
v Lk 19:41

11:36
w ver 3

[11]After he had said this, he went on to tell them, "Our friend[a] Lazarus has fallen asleep;[b] but I am going there to wake him up."

[12]His disciples replied, "Lord, if he sleeps, he will get better." [13]Jesus had been speaking of his death, but his disciples thought he meant natural sleep.[c]

[14]So then he told them plainly, "Lazarus is dead, [15]and for your sake I am glad I was not there, so that you may believe. But let us go to him."

[16]Then Thomas[d] (called Didymus) said to the rest of the disciples, "Let us also go, that we may die with him."

[17]On his arrival, Jesus found that Lazarus had already been in the tomb for four days.[e] [18]Bethany[f] was less than two miles[a] from Jerusalem, [19]and many Jews had come to Martha and Mary to comfort them in the loss of their brother.[g] [20]When Martha heard that Jesus was coming, she went out to meet him, but Mary stayed at home.[h]

[21]"Lord," Martha said to Jesus, "if you had been here, my brother would not have died.[i] [22]But I know that even now God will give you whatever you ask."[j]

[23]Jesus said to her, "Your brother will rise again."

[24]Martha answered, "I know he will rise again in the resurrection[k] at the last day."

[25]Jesus said to her, "I am the resurrection and the life.[l] He who believes in me will live, even though he dies; [26]and whoever lives and believes in me will never die. Do you believe this?"

[27]"Yes, Lord," she told him, "I believe that you are the Christ,[b][m] the Son of God,[n] who was to come into the world."[o]

[28]And after she had said this, she went back and called her sister Mary aside. "The Teacher[p] is here," she said, "and is asking for you." [29]When Mary heard this, she got up quickly and went to him. [30]Now Jesus had not yet entered the village, but was still at the place where Martha had met him.[q] [31]When the Jews who had been with Mary in the house, comforting her,[r] noticed how quickly she got up and went out, they followed her, supposing she was going to the tomb to mourn there.

[32]When Mary reached the place where Jesus was and saw him, she fell at his feet and said, "Lord, if you had been here, my brother would not have died."[s]

[33]When Jesus saw her weeping, and the Jews who had come along with her also weeping, he was deeply moved[t] in spirit and troubled.[u] [34]"Where have you laid him?" he asked.

"Come and see, Lord," they replied.

[35]Jesus wept.[v]

[36]Then the Jews said, "See how he loved him!"[w]

a 18 Greek *fifteen stadia* (about 3 kilometers)   *b 27* Or *Messiah*

³⁷But some of them said, "Could not he who opened the eyes of the blind man^a have kept this man from dying?"^b

³⁸Jesus, once more deeply moved,^c came to the tomb. It was a cave with a stone laid across the entrance.^d ³⁹"Take away the stone," he said.

"But, Lord," said Martha, the sister of the dead man, "by this time there is a bad odor, for he has been there four days."^e

⁴⁰Then Jesus said, "Did I not tell you that if you believed,^f you would see the glory of God?"^g

⁴¹So they took away the stone. Then Jesus looked up^h and said, "Father,ⁱ I thank you that you have heard me. ⁴²I knew that you always hear me, but I said this for the benefit of the people standing here,^j that they may believe that you sent me."^k

⁴³When he had said this, Jesus called in a loud voice, "Lazarus, come out!"^l ⁴⁴The dead man came out, his hands and feet wrapped with strips of linen,^m and a cloth around his face.ⁿ

Jesus said to them, "Take off the grave clothes and let him go."

⁴⁵Therefore many of the Jews who had come to visit Mary,^o and had seen what Jesus did,^p put their faith in him.^q ⁴⁶But some of them went to the Pharisees and told them what Jesus had done. ⁴⁷Then the chief priests and the Pharisees^r called a meeting^s of the Sanhedrin.^t

"What are we accomplishing?" they asked. "Here is this man performing many miraculous signs.^u ⁴⁸If we let him go on like this, everyone will believe in him, and then the Romans will come and take away both our place^a and our nation."

⁴⁹Then one of them, named Caiaphas,^v who was high priest that year,^w spoke up, "You know nothing at all! ⁵⁰You do not realize that it is better for you that one man die for the people than that the whole nation perish."^x

⁵¹He did not say this on his own, but as high priest that year he prophesied that Jesus would die for the Jewish nation, ⁵²and not only for that nation but also for the scattered children of God, to bring them together and make them one.^y ⁵³So from that day on they plotted to take his life.^z

⁵⁴Therefore Jesus no longer moved about publicly among the Jews.^a Instead he withdrew to a region near the desert, to a village called Ephraim, where he stayed with his disciples.

⁵⁵When it was almost time for the Jewish Passover,^b many went up from the country to Jerusalem for their ceremonial cleansing^c before the Passover. ⁵⁶They kept looking for Jesus,^d and as they stood in the temple area they asked one another, "What do you think? Isn't he coming to the Feast at all?" ⁵⁷But the chief priests and Pharisees had given orders that if anyone found out where Jesus was, he should report it so that they might arrest him.

^a48 Or *temple*

11:37
^aJn 9:6,7
^bver 21,32

11:38
^cver 33
^dMt 27:60;
Lk 24:2;
Jn 20:1

11:39
^ever 17

11:40
^fver 23-25
^gver 4

11:41
^hJn 17:1
ⁱMt 11:25

11:42
^jJn 12:30
^kJn 3:17

11:43
^lLk 7:14

11:44
^mJn 19:40
ⁿJn 20:7

11:45
^over 19
^pJn 2:23
^qEx 14:31;
Jn 7:31

11:47
^rver 57
^sMt 26:3
^tMt 5:22
^uJn 2:11

11:49
^vMt 26:3
^wver 51;
Jn 18:13,14

11:50
^xJn 18:14

11:52
^yIsa 49:6;
Jn 10:16

11:53
^zMt 12:14

11:54
^aJn 7:1

11:55
^bEx 12:13,23,27;
Mt 26:1,2;
Mk 14:1;
Jn 13:1
^c2Ch 30:17,18

11:56
^dJn 7:11

Chapter 12 Theme _____

12:1
a Jn 11:55
b Mt 21:17

12 Six days before the Passover,[a] Jesus arrived at Bethany,[b] where Lazarus lived, whom Jesus had raised from the dead. [2]Here a dinner was given in Jesus' honor. Martha served,[c] while Lazarus was among those reclining at the table with him.

12:2
c Lk 10:38-42

[3]Then Mary took about a pint[a] of pure nard, an expensive perfume;[d] she poured it on Jesus' feet and wiped his feet with her hair.[e] And the house was filled with the fragrance of the perfume.

12:3
d Mk 14:3
e Jn 11:2

[4]But one of his disciples, Judas Iscariot, who was later to betray him,[f] objected, [5]"Why wasn't this perfume sold and the money given to the poor? It was worth a year's wages.[b]" [6]He did not say this because he cared about the poor but because he was a thief; as keeper of the money bag,[g] he used to help himself to what was put into it.

12:4
f Mt 10:4

[7]"Leave her alone," Jesus replied. "⌊It was intended⌋ that she should save this perfume for the day of my burial.[h] [8]You will always have the poor among you,[i] but you will not always have me."

12:6
g Jn 13:29

From Bethany, Bethphage across the Mount of Olives into Jerusalem

12:7
h Jn 19:40

[9]Meanwhile a large crowd of Jews found out that Jesus was there and came, not only because of him but also to see Lazarus, whom he had raised from the dead.[j] [10]So the chief priests made plans to kill Lazarus as well, [11]for on account of him[k] many of the Jews were going over to Jesus and putting their faith in him.[l]

12:8
i Dt 15:11

12:9
j Jn 11:43,44

[12]The next day the great crowd that had come for the Feast heard that Jesus was on his way to Jerusalem. [13]They took palm branches and went out to meet him, shouting,

"Hosanna![c]"

12:11
k ver 17,18;
Jn 11:45
l Jn 7:31

"Blessed is he who comes in the name of the Lord!"[d][m]

"Blessed is the King of Israel!"[n]

[14]Jesus found a young donkey and sat upon it, as it is written,

12:13
m Ps 118:25,26
n Jn 1:49

[15]"Do not be afraid, O Daughter of Zion;
see, your king is coming,
seated on a donkey's colt."[e][o]

12:15
o Zec 9:9

a3 Greek *a litra* (probably about 0.5 liter)   b5 Greek *three hundred denarii*   c13 A Hebrew expression meaning "Save!" which became an exclamation of praise   d13 Psalm 118:25, 26   e15 Zech. 9:9

¹⁶At first his disciples did not understand all this.*ᵃ* Only after Jesus was glorified*ᵇ* did they realize that these things had been written about him and that they had done these things to him.

¹⁷Now the crowd that was with him*ᶜ* when he called Lazarus from the tomb and raised him from the dead continued to spread the word. ¹⁸Many people, because they had heard that he had given this miraculous sign,*ᵈ* went out to meet him. ¹⁹So the Pharisees said to one another, "See, this is getting us nowhere. Look how the whole world has gone after him!"*ᵉ*

²⁰Now there were some Greeks*ᶠ* among those who went up to worship at the Feast. ²¹They came to Philip, who was from Bethsaida*ᵍ* in Galilee, with a request. "Sir," they said, "we would like to see Jesus." ²²Philip went to tell Andrew; Andrew and Philip in turn told Jesus.

²³Jesus replied, "The hour has come for the Son of Man to be glorified.*ʰ* ²⁴I tell you the truth, unless a kernel of wheat falls to the ground and dies,*ⁱ* it remains only a single seed. But if it dies, it produces many seeds. ²⁵The man who loves his life will lose it, while the man who hates his life in this world will keep it*ʲ* for eternal life. ²⁶Whoever serves me must follow me; and where I am, my servant also will be.*ᵏ* My Father will honor the one who serves me.

²⁷"Now my heart is troubled,*ˡ* and what shall I say? 'Father,*ᵐ* save me from this hour'?*ⁿ* No, it was for this very reason I came to this hour. ²⁸Father, glorify your name!"

Then a voice came from heaven,*ᵒ* "I have glorified it, and will glorify it again." ²⁹The crowd that was there and heard it said it had thundered; others said an angel had spoken to him.

³⁰Jesus said, "This voice was for your benefit,*ᵖ* not mine. ³¹Now is the time for judgment on this world;* q* now the prince of this world*ʳ* will be driven out. ³²But I, when I am lifted up from the earth,*ˢ* will draw all men to myself."*ᵗ* ³³He said this to show the kind of death he was going to die.*ᵘ*

³⁴The crowd spoke up, "We have heard from the Law that the Christ*ᵃ* will remain forever,*ᵛ* so how can you say, 'The Son of Man*ʷ* must be lifted up'?*ˣ* Who is this 'Son of Man'?"

³⁵Then Jesus told them, "You are going to have the light*ʸ* just a little while longer. Walk while you have the light,*ᶻ* before darkness overtakes you.*ᵃ* The man who walks in the dark does not know where he is going. ³⁶Put your trust in the light while you have it, so that you may become sons of light."*ᵇ* When he had finished speaking, Jesus left and hid himself from them.*ᶜ*

³⁷Even after Jesus had done all these miraculous signs*ᵈ* in their presence, they still would not believe in him. ³⁸This was to fulfill the word of Isaiah the prophet:

ᵃ34 Or Messiah

12:16
a Mk 9:32
b Jn 2:22; 7:39;
14:26

12:17
c Jn 11:42

12:18
d ver 11

12:19
e Jn 11:47,48

12:20
f Jn 7:35;
Ac 11:20

12:21
g Mt 11:21;
Jn 1:44

12:23
h Jn 13:32; 17:1

12:24
i 1Co 15:36

12:25
j Mt 10:39;
Mk 8:35;
Lk 14:26

12:26
k Jn 14:3; 17:24;
2Co 5:8;
1Th 4:17

12:27
l Mt 26:38,39;
Jn 11:33,38;
13:21
m Mt 11:25
n ver 23

12:28
o Mt 3:17

12:30
p Jn 11:42

12:31
q Jn 16:11
r Jn 14:30; 16:11;
2Co 4:4;
Eph 2:2;
1Jn 4:4

12:32
s ver 34;
Jn 3:14; 8:28
t Jn 6:44

12:33
u Jn 18:32

12:34
v Ps 110:4;
Isa 9:7;
Eze 37:25;
Da 7:14
w Mt 8:20
x Jn 3:14

12:35
y ver 46
z Eph 5:8
a 1Jn 2:11

12:36
b Lk 16:8
c Jn 8:59

12:37
d Jn 2:11

"Lord, who has believed our message
and to whom has the arm of the Lord been revealed?"a a

39For this reason they could not believe, because, as Isaiah says elsewhere:

40"He has blinded their eyes
and deadened their hearts,
so they can neither see with their eyes,
nor understand with their hearts,
nor turn—and I would heal them."b b

41Isaiah said this because he saw Jesus' glory c and spoke about him.d

42Yet at the same time many even among the leaders believed in him.e But because of the Pharisees f they would not confess their faith for fear they would be put out of the synagogue;g **43**for they loved praise from men more than praise from God.h

44Then Jesus cried out, "When a man believes in me, he does not believe in me only, but in the one who sent me.i **45**When he looks at me, he sees the one who sent me.j **46**I have come into the world as a light,k so that no one who believes in me should stay in darkness.

47"As for the person who hears my words but does not keep them, I do not judge him. For I did not come to judge the world, but to save it.l **48**There is a judge for the one who rejects me and does not accept my words; that very word which I spoke will condemn himm at the last day. **49**For I did not speak of my own accord, but the Father who sent me commanded men what to say and how to say it. **50**I know that his command leads to eternal life. So whatever I say is just what the Father has told me to say."

Chapter 13 Theme

13 It was just before the Passover Feast.o Jesus knew that the time had comep for him to leave this world and go to the Father.q Having loved his own who were in the world, he now showed them the full extent of his love.c

2The evening meal was being served, and the devil had already prompted Judas Iscariot, son of Simon, to betray Jesus. **3**Jesus knew that the Father had put all things under his power,r and that he had come from Gods and was returning to God; **4**so he got up from the meal, took off his outer clothing, and wrapped a towel around his waist. **5**After that, he poured water into a basin and began to wash his disciples' feet,t drying them with the towel that was wrapped around him.

12:38 a Isa 53:1; Ro 10:16
12:40 b Isa 6:10; Mt 13:13,15
12:41 c Isa 6:1-4 d Lk 24:27
12:42 e ver 11; Jn 7:48 f Jn 7:13 g Jn 9:22
12:43 h Jn 5:44
12:44 i Mt 10:40; Jn 5:24
12:45 j Jn 14:9
12:46 k Jn 1:4; 3:19; 8:12; 9:5
12:47 l Jn 3:17
12:48 m Jn 5:45
12:49 n Jn 14:31
13:1 o Jn 11:55 p Jn 12:23 q Jn 16:28
13:3 r Mt 28:18 s Jn 8:42; 16:27,28,30
13:5 t Lk 7:44

a 38 Isaiah 53:1 b 40 Isaiah 6:10 c 1 Or he loved them to the last

⁶He came to Simon Peter, who said to him, "Lord, are you going to wash my feet?"

⁷Jesus replied, "You do not realize now what I am doing, but later you will understand."[a]

⁸"No," said Peter, "you shall never wash my feet."

Jesus answered, "Unless I wash you, you have no part with me."

⁹"Then, Lord," Simon Peter replied, "not just my feet but my hands and my head as well!"

¹⁰Jesus answered, "A person who has had a bath needs only to wash his feet; his whole body is clean. And you are clean,[b] though not every one of you." ¹¹For he knew who was going to betray him, and that was why he said not every one was clean.

¹²When he had finished washing their feet, he put on his clothes and returned to his place. "Do you understand what I have done for you?" he asked them. ¹³"You call me 'Teacher'[c] and 'Lord,'[d] and rightly so, for that is what I am. ¹⁴Now that I, your Lord and Teacher, have washed your feet, you also should wash one another's feet.[e] ¹⁵I have set you an example that you should do as I have done for you.[f] ¹⁶I tell you the truth, no servant is greater than his master,[g] nor is a messenger greater than the one who sent him. ¹⁷Now that you know these things, you will be blessed if you do them.[h]

¹⁸"I am not referring to all of you;[i] I know those I have chosen.[j] But this is to fulfill the scripture: 'He who shares my bread[k] has lifted up his heel[l] against me.'[a][m]

¹⁹"I am telling you now before it happens, so that when it does happen you will believe[n] that I am He.[o] ²⁰I tell you the truth, whoever accepts anyone I send accepts me; and whoever accepts me accepts the one who sent me."[p]

²¹After he had said this, Jesus was troubled in spirit[q] and testified, "I tell you the truth, one of you is going to betray me."[r]

²²His disciples stared at one another, at a loss to know which of them he meant. ²³One of them, the disciple whom Jesus loved,[s] was reclining next to him. ²⁴Simon Peter motioned to this disciple and said, "Ask him which one he means."

²⁵Leaning back against Jesus, he asked him, "Lord, who is it?"[t]

²⁶Jesus answered, "It is the one to whom I will give this piece of bread when I have dipped it in the dish." Then, dipping the piece of bread, he gave it to Judas Iscariot, son of Simon. ²⁷As soon as Judas took the bread, Satan entered into him.[u]

"What you are about to do, do quickly," Jesus told him, ²⁸but no one at the meal understood why Jesus said this to him. ²⁹Since Judas had charge of the money,[v] some thought Jesus was telling him to buy what was needed for the Feast, or to give something to the poor. ³⁰As soon as Judas had taken the bread, he went out. And it was night.[w]

a 18 Psalm 41:9

13:7
a ver 12

13:10
b Jn 15:3

13:13
c Jn 11:28
d Lk 6:46;
1Co 12:3;
Php 2:11

13:14
e 1Pe 5:5

13:15
f Mt 11:29

13:16
g Mt 10:24;
Lk 6:40;
Jn 15:20

13:17
h Mt 7:24,25;
Lk 11:28;
Jas 1:25

13:18
i ver 10
j Jn 15:16,19
k Mt 26:23
l Jn 6:70
m Ps 41:9

13:19
n Jn 14:29; 16:4
o Jn 8:24

13:20
p Mt 10:40;
Lk 10:16

13:21
q Jn 12:27
r Mt 26:21

13:23
s Jn 19:26; 20:2;
21:7,20

13:25
t Jn 21:20

13:27
u Lk 22:3

13:29
v Jn 12:6

13:30
w Lk 22:53

13:31
a Jn 7:39
b Jn 14:13; 17:4;
1Pe 4:11

13:32
c Jn 17:1

13:33
d Jn 7:33,34

13:34
e 1Jn 2:7-11; 3:11
f Lev 19:18;
1Th 4:9;
1Pe 1:22
g Jn 15:12;
Eph 5:2;
1Jn 4:10,11

13:35
h 1Jn 3:14; 4:20

13:36
i ver 33;
Jn 14:2
j Jn 21:18,19;
2Pe 1:14

13:38
k Jn 18:27

14:1
l ver 27

14:2
m Jn 13:33,36

14:3
n Jn 12:26

14:5
o Jn 11:16

14:6
p Jn 10:9
q Jn 11:25

14:7
r Jn 8:19

14:9
s Jn 12:45;
Col 1:15;
Heb 1:3

14:10
t Jn 10:38
u Jn 5:19

14:11
v Jn 5:36; 10:38

14:12
w Mt 21:21
x Lk 10:17

³¹When he was gone, Jesus said, "Now is the Son of Man glorified^a and God is glorified in him.^b ³²If God is glorified in him,^a God will glorify the Son in himself,^c and will glorify him at once.

³³"My children, I will be with you only a little longer. You will look for me, and just as I told the Jews, so I tell you now: Where I am going, you cannot come.^d

³⁴"A new command^e I give you: Love one another.^f As I have loved you, so you must love one another.^g ³⁵By this all men will know that you are my disciples, if you love one another."^h

³⁶Simon Peter asked him, "Lord, where are you going?"

Jesus replied, "Where I am going, you cannot follow now,ⁱ but you will follow later."^j

³⁷Peter asked, "Lord, why can't I follow you now? I will lay down my life for you."

³⁸Then Jesus answered, "Will you really lay down your life for me? I tell you the truth, before the rooster crows, you will disown me three times!^k

Chapter 14 Theme

14 "Do not let your hearts be troubled.^l Trust in God^b; trust also in me. ²In my Father's house are many rooms; if it were not so, I would have told you. I am going there^m to prepare a place for you. ³And if I go and prepare a place for you, I will come back and take you to be with me that you also may be where I am.ⁿ ⁴You know the way to the place where I am going."

⁵Thomas^o said to him, "Lord, we don't know where you are going, so how can we know the way?"

⁶Jesus answered, "I am the way^p and the truth and the life.^q No one comes to the Father except through me. ⁷If you really knew me, you would know^c my Father as well.^r From now on, you do know him and have seen him."

⁸Philip said, "Lord, show us the Father and that will be enough for us."

⁹Jesus answered: "Don't you know me, Philip, even after I have been among you such a long time? Anyone who has seen me has seen the Father.^s How can you say, 'Show us the Father'? ¹⁰Don't you believe that I am in the Father, and that the Father is in me?^t The words I say to you are not just my own.^u Rather, it is the Father, living in me, who is doing his work. ¹¹Believe me when I say that I am in the Father and the Father is in me; or at least believe on the evidence of the miracles themselves.^v ¹²I tell you the truth, anyone who has faith^w in me will do what I have been doing.^x He will do even greater things than these, because I am

---

a 32 Many early manuscripts do not have *If God is glorified in him.*   b 1 Or *You trust in God*
c 7 Some early manuscripts *If you really have known me, you will know*

going to the Father. ¹³And I will do whatever you ask*a* in my name, so that the Son may bring glory to the Father. ¹⁴You may ask me for anything in my name, and I will do it.

¹⁵"If you love me, you will obey what I command.*b* ¹⁶And I will ask the Father, and he will give you another Counselor*c* to be with you forever— ¹⁷the Spirit of truth.*d* The world cannot accept him,*e* because it neither sees him nor knows him. But you know him, for he lives with you and will be*a* in you. ¹⁸I will not leave you as orphans; I will come to you.*f* ¹⁹Before long, the world will not see me anymore, but you will see me.*g* Because I live, you also will live.*h* ²⁰On that day you will realize that I am in my Father,*i* and you are in me, and I am in you. ²¹Whoever has my commands and obeys them, he is the one who loves me.*j* He who loves me will be loved by my Father,*k* and I too will love him and show myself to him."

²²Then Judas*l* (not Judas Iscariot) said, "But, Lord, why do you intend to show yourself to us and not to the world?"*m*

²³Jesus replied, "If anyone loves me, he will obey my teaching.*n* My Father will love him, and we will come to him and make our home with him.*o* ²⁴He who does not love me will not obey my teaching. These words you hear are not my own; they belong to the Father who sent me.*p*

²⁵"All this I have spoken while still with you. ²⁶But the Counselor,*q* the Holy Spirit, whom the Father will send in my name,*r* will teach you all things*s* and will remind you of everything I have said to you.*t* ²⁷Peace I leave with you; my peace I give you.*u* I do not give to you as the world gives. Do not let your hearts be troubled and do not be afraid.

²⁸"You heard me say, 'I am going away and I am coming back to you.'*v* If you loved me, you would be glad that I am going to the Father,*w* for the Father is greater than I.*x* ²⁹I have told you now before it happens, so that when it does happen you will believe.*y* ³⁰I will not speak with you much longer, for the prince of this world*z* is coming. He has no hold on me, ³¹but the world must learn that I love the Father and that I do exactly what my Father has commanded me.*a*

"Come now; let us leave.

Chapter 15 Theme

15 "I am the true vine,*b* and my Father is the gardener. ²He cuts off every branch in me that bears no fruit, while every branch that does bear fruit he prunes*b* so that it will be even more fruitful. ³You are already clean because of the word I have spoken

---

a*17* Some early manuscripts *and is*   b*2* The Greek for *prunes* also means *cleans.*

14:13 *a* Mt 7:7
14:15 *b* ver 21,23; Jn 15:10; 1Jn 5:3
14:16 *c* Jn 15:26; 16:7
14:17 *d* Jn 15:26; 16:13; 1Jn 4:6 *e* 1Co 2:14
14:18 *f* ver 3,28
14:19 *g* Jn 7:33,34; 16:16 *h* Jn 6:57
14:20 *i* Jn 10:38
14:21 *j* 1Jn 5:3 *k* 1Jn 2:5
14:22 *l* Lk 6:16; Ac 1:13 *m* Ac 10:41
14:23 *n* ver 15 *o* 1Jn 2:24; Rev 3:20
14:24 *p* Jn 7:16
14:26 *q* Jn 15:26; 16:7 *r* Ac 2:33 *s* Jn 16:13; 1Jn 2:20,27 *t* Jn 2:22
14:27 *u* Jn 16:33; Php 4:7; Col 3:15
14:28 *v* ver 2-4,18 *w* Jn 5:18 *x* Jn 10:29; Php 2:6
14:29 *y* Jn 13:19; 16:4
14:30 *z* Jn 12:31
14:31 *a* Jn 10:18; 12:49
15:1 *b* Isa 5:1-7

15:3
a Jn 13:10; 17:17;
Eph 5:26

15:4
b Jn 6:56;
1Jn 2:6

15:5
c ver 16

15:6
d ver 2

15:7
e Mt 7:7

15:8
f Mt 5:16
g Jn 8:31

15:9
h Jn 17:23, 24,26

15:10
i Jn 14:15

15:11
j Jn 17:13

15:12
k Jn 13:34

15:13
l Jn 10:11;
Ro 5:7,8

15:14
m Lk 12:4
n Mt 12:50

15:15
o Jn 8:26

15:16
p Jn 6:70; 13:18

15:17
q ver 12

15:18
r 1Jn 3:13

15:19
s ver 16
t Jn 17:14

15:20
u Jn 13:16
v 2Ti 3:12

15:21
w Mt 10:22
x Jn 16:3

15:22
y Jn 9:41;
Ro 1:20

15:24
z Jn 5:36

15:25
a Ps 35:19; 69:4

15:26
b Jn 14:16
c Jn 14:26
d Jn 14:17
e 1Jn 5:7

15:27
f Lk 24:48;
1Jn 1:2; 4:14
g Lk 1:2

to you.*a* ⁴Remain in me, and I will remain in you.*b* No branch can bear fruit by itself; it must remain in the vine. Neither can you bear fruit unless you remain in me.

⁵"I am the vine; you are the branches. If a man remains in me and I in him, he will bear much fruit;*c* apart from me you can do nothing. ⁶If anyone does not remain in me, he is like a branch that is thrown away and withers; such branches are picked up, thrown into the fire and burned.*d* ⁷If you remain in me and my words remain in you, ask whatever you wish, and it will be given you.*e* ⁸This is to my Father's glory,*f* that you bear much fruit, showing yourselves to be my disciples.*g*

⁹"As the Father has loved me,*h* so have I loved you. Now remain in my love. ¹⁰If you obey my commands,*i* you will remain in my love, just as I have obeyed my Father's commands and remain in his love. ¹¹I have told you this so that my joy may be in you and that your joy may be complete.*j* ¹²My command is this: Love each other as I have loved you.*k* ¹³Greater love has no one than this, that he lay down his life for his friends.*l* ¹⁴You are my friends*m* if you do what I command.*n* ¹⁵I no longer call you servants, because a servant does not know his master's business. Instead, I have called you friends, for everything that I learned from my Father I have made known to you.*o* ¹⁶You did not choose me, but I chose you and appointed you*p* to go and bear fruit—fruit that will last. Then the Father will give you whatever you ask in my name. ¹⁷This is my command: Love each other.*q*

¹⁸"If the world hates you,*r* keep in mind that it hated me first. ¹⁹If you belonged to the world, it would love you as its own. As it is, you do not belong to the world, but I have chosen you*s* out of the world. That is why the world hates you.*t* ²⁰Remember the words I spoke to you: 'No servant is greater than his master.'*a u* If they persecuted me, they will persecute you also.*v* If they obeyed my teaching, they will obey yours also. ²¹They will treat you this way because of my name,*w* for they do not know the One who sent me.*x* ²²If I had not come and spoken to them, they would not be guilty of sin. Now, however, they have no excuse for their sin.*y* ²³He who hates me hates my Father as well. ²⁴If I had not done among them what no one else did,*z* they would not be guilty of sin. But now they have seen these miracles, and yet they have hated both me and my Father. ²⁵But this is to fulfill what is written in their Law: 'They hated me without reason.'*b a*

²⁶"When the Counselor*b* comes, whom I will send to you from the Father,*c* the Spirit of truth*d* who goes out from the Father, he will testify about me.*e* ²⁷And you also must testify,*f* for you have been with me from the beginning.*g*

a 20 John 13:16   *b 25* Psalms 35:19; 69:4

Chapter 16 Theme

16 "All this[a] I have told you so that you will not go astray.[b] [2]They will put you out of the synagogue;[c] in fact, a time is coming when anyone who kills you will think he is offering a service to God.[d] [3]They will do such things because they have not known the Father or me.[e] [4]I have told you this, so that when the time comes you will remember[f] that I warned you. I did not tell you this at first because I was with you.

[5]"Now I am going to him who sent me,[g] yet none of you asks me, 'Where are you going?'[h] [6]Because I have said these things, you are filled with grief. [7]But I tell you the truth: It is for your good that I am going away. Unless I go away, the Counselor[i] will not come to you; but if I go, I will send him to you.[j] [8]When he comes, he will convict the world of guilt[a] in regard to sin and righteousness and judgment: [9]in regard to sin,[k] because men do not believe in me; [10]in regard to righteousness,[l] because I am going to the Father, where you can see me no longer; [11]and in regard to judgment, because the prince of this world[m] now stands condemned.

[12]"I have much more to say to you, more than you can now bear.[n] [13]But when he, the Spirit of truth,[o] comes, he will guide you into all truth.[p] He will not speak on his own; he will speak only what he hears, and he will tell you what is yet to come. [14]He will bring glory to me by taking from what is mine and making it known to you. [15]All that belongs to the Father is mine.[q] That is why I said the Spirit will take from what is mine and make it known to you.

[16]"In a little while[r] you will see me no more, and then after a little while you will see me."[s]

[17]Some of his disciples said to one another, "What does he mean by saying, 'In a little while you will see me no more, and then after a little while you will see me,'[t] and 'Because I am going to the Father'?"[u] [18]They kept asking, "What does he mean by 'a little while'? We don't understand what he is saying."

[19]Jesus saw that they wanted to ask him about this, so he said to them, "Are you asking one another what I meant when I said, 'In a little while you will see me no more, and then after a little while you will see me'? [20]I tell you the truth, you will weep and mourn[v] while the world rejoices. You will grieve, but your grief will turn to joy.[w] [21]A woman giving birth to a child has pain[x] because her time has come; but when her baby is born she forgets the anguish because of her joy that a child is born into the world. [22]So with you: Now is your time of grief,[y] but I will see you again[z] and you will rejoice, and no one will take away your joy. [23]In that day you will no longer ask me anything. I tell you the truth, my Father

---

a 8 Or *will expose the guilt of the world*

16:1
a Jn 15:18-27
b Mt 11:6

16:2
c Jn 9:22
d Isa 66:5;
Ac 26:9,10;
Rev 6:9

16:3
e Jn 15:21; 17:25;
1Jn 3:1

16:4
f Jn 13:19

16:5
g Jn 7:33
h Jn 13:36; 14:5

16:7
i Jn 14:16,26;
15:26
j Jn 7:39

16:9
k Jn 15:22

16:10
l Ac 3:14; 7:52;
1Pe 3:18

16:11
m Jn 12:31

16:12
n Mk 4:33

16:13
o Jn 14:17
p Jn 14:26

16:15
q Jn 17:10

16:16
r Jn 7:33
s Jn 14:18-24

16:17
t ver 16
u ver 5

16:20
v Lk 23:27
w Jn 20:20

16:21
x Isa 26:17;
1Th 5:3

16:22
y ver 6
z ver 16

will give you whatever you ask in my name.ª ²⁴Until now you have not asked for anything in my name. Ask and you will receive, and your joy will be complete.ᵇ

²⁵"Though I have been speaking figuratively,ᶜ a time is comingᵈ when I will no longer use this kind of language but will tell you plainly about my Father. ²⁶In that day you will ask in my name.ᵉ I am not saying that I will ask the Father on your behalf. ²⁷No, the Father himself loves you because you have loved meᶠ and have believed that I came from God. ²⁸I came from the Father and entered the world; now I am leaving the world and going back to the Father."ᵍ

²⁹Then Jesus' disciples said, "Now you are speaking clearly and without figures of speech.ʰ ³⁰Now we can see that you know all things and that you do not even need to have anyone ask you questions. This makes us believe that you came from God."

³¹"You believe at last!"ª Jesus answered. ³²"But a time is coming,ⁱ and has come, when you will be scattered,ʲ each to his own home. You will leave me all alone. Yet I am not alone, for my Father is with me.ᵏ

³³"I have told you these things, so that in me you may have peace.ˡ In this world you will have trouble.ᵐ But take heart! I have overcomeⁿ the world."

Chapter 17 Theme

17 After Jesus said this, he looked toward heavenᵒ and prayed: "Father, the time has come. Glorify your Son, that your Son may glorify you.ᵖ ²For you granted him authority over all people that he might give eternal life to all those you have given him.�q ³Now this is eternal life: that they may know you, the only true God, and Jesus Christ, whom you have sent.ʳ ⁴I have brought you gloryˢ on earth by completing the work you gave me to do.ᵗ ⁵And now, Father, glorify me in your presence with the glory I had with youᵘ before the world began.ᵛ

⁶"I have revealed youᵇʷ to those whom you gave meˣ out of the world. They were yours; you gave them to me and they have obeyed your word. ⁷Now they know that everything you have given me comes from you. ⁸For I gave them the words you gave meʸ and they accepted them. They knew with certainty that I came from you,ᶻ and they believed that you sent me.ª ⁹I pray for them.ᵇ I am not praying for the world, but for those you have given me, for they are yours. ¹⁰All I have is yours, and all you have is mine.ᶜ And glory has come to me through them. ¹¹I will remain in the world no longer, but they

Cross references

16:23
ª Mt 7:7;
Jn 15:16

16:24
ᵇ Jn 3:29; 15:11

16:25
ᶜ Mt 13:34;
Jn 10:6
ᵈ ver 2

16:26
ᵉ ver 23,24

16:27
ᶠ Jn 14:21,23

16:28
ᵍ Jn 13:3

16:29
ʰ ver 25

16:32
ⁱ ver 2,25
ʲ Mt 26:31
ᵏ Jn 8:16,29

16:33
ˡ Jn 14:27
ᵐ Jn 15:18-21
ⁿ Ro 8:37;
1Jn 4:4

17:1
ᵒ Jn 11:41
ᵖ Jn 12:23;
13:31,32

17:2
q ver 6,9,24;
Da 7:14;
Jn 6:37,39

17:3
ʳ ver 8,18,21,
23,25;
Jn 3:17

17:4
ˢ Jn 13:31
ᵗ Jn 4:34

17:5
ᵘ Php 2:6
ᵛ Jn 1:2

17:6
ʷ ver 26
ˣ ver 2;
Jn 6:37,39

17:8
ʸ ver 14,26
ᶻ Jn 16:27
ª ver 3,18,21,
23,25;
Jn 3:17

17:9
ᵇ Lk 22:32

17:10
ᶜ Jn 16:15

ª31 Or "Do you now believe?"   ᵇ6 Greek *your name*; also in verse 26 are still in the world,[a] and I am coming to you.[b] Holy Father, protect them by the power of your name—the name you gave me—so that they may be one[c] as we are one.[d] [12]While I was with them, I protected them and kept them safe by that name you gave me. None has been lost[e] except the one doomed to destruction[f] so that Scripture would be fulfilled.

[13]"I am coming to you now, but I say these things while I am still in the world, so that they may have the full measure of my joy[g] within them. [14]I have given them your word and the world has hated them,[h] for they are not of the world any more than I am of the world.[i] [15]My prayer is not that you take them out of the world but that you protect them from the evil one.[j] [16]They are not of the world, even as I am not of it.[k] [17]Sanctify[a] them by the truth; your word is truth.[l] [18]As you sent me into the world,[m] I have sent them into the world.[n] [19]For them I sanctify myself, that they too may be truly sanctified.

[20]"My prayer is not for them alone. I pray also for those who will believe in me through their message, [21]that all of them may be one, Father, just as you are in me and I am in you.[o] May they also be in us so that the world may believe that you have sent me.[p] [22]I have given them the glory that you gave me, that they may be one as we are one:[q] [23]I in them and you in me. May they be brought to complete unity to let the world know that you sent me[r] and have loved them[s] even as you have loved me.

[24]"Father, I want those you have given me to be with me where I am,[t] and to see my glory,[u] the glory you have given me because you loved me before the creation of the world.[v]

[25]"Righteous Father, though the world does not know you,[w] I know you, and they know that you have sent me.[x] [26]I have made you known to them,[y] and will continue to make you known in order that the love you have for me may be in them[z] and that I myself may be in them."

Chapter 18 Theme

18 When he had finished praying, Jesus left with his disciples and crossed the Kidron Valley.[a] On the other side there was an olive grove,[b] and he and his disciples went into it.[c]

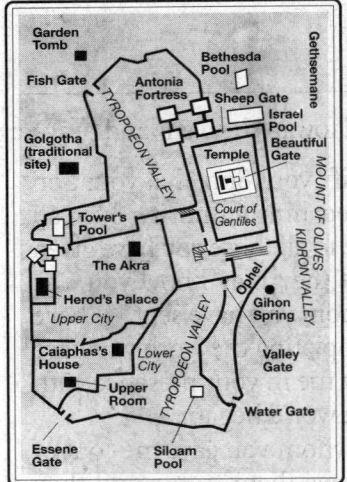

Jerusalem of the New Testament

Garden Tomb
Fish Gate
Bethesda Pool
Antonia Fortress
Gethsemane
Sheep Gate
Israel Pool
Golgotha (traditional site)
TYROPOEON VALLEY
Temple
Beautiful Gate
Court of Gentiles
MOUNT OF OLIVES
KIDRON VALLEY
Tower's Pool
The Akra
Herod's Palace
Upper City
Gihon Spring
Caiaphas's House
Lower City
TYROPOEON VALLEY
Valley Gate
Upper Room
Water Gate
Essene Gate
Siloam Pool

---

a 17 Greek *hagiazo* (set apart for sacred use or *make holy*); also in verse 19

### Cross references (right margin)

17:11
a Jn 13:1
b Jn 7:33
c ver 21-23
d Jn 10:30

17:12
e Jn 6:39
f Jn 6:70

17:13
g Jn 3:29

17:14
h Jn 15:19
i Jn 8:23

17:15
j Mt 5:37

17:16
k ver 14

17:17
l Jn 15:3

17:18
m ver 3,8,21, 23,25
n Jn 20:21

17:21
o Jn 10:38
p ver 3,8,18, 23,25; Jn 3:17

17:22
q Jn 14:20

17:23
r Jn 3:17
s Jn 16:27

17:24
t Jn 12:26
u Jn 1:14
v ver 5; Mt 25:34

17:25
w Jn 15:21; 16:3
x ver 3,8,18, 21,23; Jn 3:17; 7:29; 16:27

17:26
y ver 6
z Jn 15:9

18:1
a 2Sa 15:23
b ver 26
c Mt 26:36

18:2
a Lk 21:37; 22:39

18:3
b Ac 1:16
c ver 12

18:4
d Jn 6:64; 13:1,11
e ver 7

18:7
f ver 4

18:9
g Jn 17:12

18:11
h Mt 20:22

18:12
i ver 3

18:13
j ver 24;
Mt 26:3

18:14
k Jn 11:49-51

18:15
l Mt 26:3
m Mt 26:58;
Mk 14:54;
Lk 22:54

18:17
n ver 25

18:18
o Jn 21:9
p Mk 14:54,67

18:20
q Mt 4:23
r Mt 26:55
s Jn 7:26

2Now Judas, who betrayed him, knew the place, because Jesus had often met there with his disciples.*a* 3So Judas came to the grove, guiding*b* a detachment of soldiers and some officials from the chief priests and Pharisees.*c* They were carrying torches, lanterns and weapons.

4Jesus, knowing all that was going to happen to him,*d* went out and asked them, "Who is it you want?"*e*

5"Jesus of Nazareth," they replied.

"I am he," Jesus said. (And Judas the traitor was standing there with them.) 6When Jesus said, "I am he," they drew back and fell to the ground.

7Again he asked them, "Who is it you want?"*f*

And they said, "Jesus of Nazareth."

8"I told you that I am he," Jesus answered. "If you are looking for me, then let these men go." 9This happened so that the words he had spoken would be fulfilled: "I have not lost one of those you gave me."*a* *g*

10Then Simon Peter, who had a sword, drew it and struck the high priest's servant, cutting off his right ear. (The servant's name was Malchus.)

11Jesus commanded Peter, "Put your sword away! Shall I not drink the cup*h* the Father has given me?"

12Then the detachment of soldiers with its commander and the Jewish officials*i* arrested Jesus. They bound him 13and brought him first to Annas, who was the father-in-law of Caiaphas,*j* the high priest that year. 14Caiaphas was the one who had advised the Jews that it would be good if one man died for the people.*k*

15Simon Peter and another disciple were following Jesus. Because this disciple was known to the high priest,*l* he went with Jesus into the high priest's courtyard,*m* 16but Peter had to wait outside at the door. The other disciple, who was known to the high priest, came back, spoke to the girl on duty there and brought Peter in.

17"You are not one of his disciples, are you?" the girl at the door asked Peter.

He replied, "I am not."*n*

18It was cold, and the servants and officials stood around a fire*o* they had made to keep warm. Peter also was standing with them, warming himself.*p*

19Meanwhile, the high priest questioned Jesus about his disciples and his teaching.

20"I have spoken openly to the world," Jesus replied. "I always taught in synagogues*q* or at the temple,*r* where all the Jews come together. I said nothing in secret.*s* 21Why question me? Ask those who heard me. Surely they know what I said."

a 9 John 6:39

22When Jesus said this, one of the officials[a] nearby struck him in the face.[b] "Is this the way you answer the high priest?" he demanded.

23"If I said something wrong," Jesus replied, "testify as to what is wrong. But if I spoke the truth, why did you strike me?"[c] 24Then Annas sent him, still bound, to Caiaphas[d] the high priest.[a]

25As Simon Peter stood warming himself,[e] he was asked, "You are not one of his disciples, are you?"

He denied it, saying, "I am not."[f]

26One of the high priest's servants, a relative of the man whose ear Peter had cut off,[g] challenged him, "Didn't I see you with him in the olive grove?"[h] 27Again Peter denied it, and at that moment a rooster began to crow.[i]

28Then the Jews led Jesus from Caiaphas to the palace of the Roman governor.[j] By now it was early morning, and to avoid ceremonial uncleanness the Jews did not enter the palace;[k] they wanted to be able to eat the Passover.[l] 29So Pilate came out to them and asked, "What charges are you bringing against this man?"

30"If he were not a criminal," they replied, "we would not have handed him over to you."

31Pilate said, "Take him yourselves and judge him by your own law."

"But we have no right to execute anyone," the Jews objected. 32This happened so that the words Jesus had spoken indicating the kind of death he was going to die[m] would be fulfilled.

33Pilate then went back inside the palace,[n] summoned Jesus and asked him, "Are you the king of the Jews?"[o]

34"Is that your own idea," Jesus asked, "or did others talk to you about me?"

35"Am I a Jew?" Pilate replied. "It was your people and your chief priests who handed you over to me. What is it you have done?"

36Jesus said, "My kingdom[p] is not of this world. If it were, my servants would fight to prevent my arrest by the Jews.[q] But now my kingdom is from another place."[r]

37"You are a king, then!" said Pilate.

Jesus answered, "You are right in saying I am a king. In fact, for this reason I was born, and for this I came into the world, to testify to the truth.[s] Everyone on the side of truth listens to me."[t]

38"What is truth?" Pilate asked. With this he went out again to the Jews and said, "I find no basis for a charge against him.[u] 39But it is your custom for me to release to you one prisoner at the time of the Passover. Do you want me to release 'the king of the Jews'?"

40They shouted back, "No, not him! Give us Barabbas!" Now Barabbas had taken part in a rebellion.[v]

---

a24 Or (Now Annas had sent him, still bound, to Caiaphas the high priest.)

INSIGHT

The palace of the Roman governor (the *Praetorium*) was either a building next to Herod's palace or the Antonia Fortress beside the temple mount complex. See the map on page 1852 and the illustration of the temple mount on page IISB-40.

18:22
a ver 3
b Mt 16:21;
Jn 19:3

18:23
c Mt 5:39;
Ac 23:2-5

18:24
d ver 13;
Mt 26:3

18:25
e ver 18
f ver 17

18:26
g ver 10
h ver 1

18:27
i Jn 13:38

18:28
j Mt 27:2;
Mk 15:1;
Lk 23:1
k ver 33;
Jn 19:9
l Jn 11:55

18:32
m Mt 20:19;
26:2; Jn 3:14;
8:28; 12:32,33

18:33
n ver 28,29;
Jn 19:9
o Lk 23:3;
Mt 2:2

18:36
p Mt 3:2
q Mt 26:53
r Lk 17:21;
Jn 6:15

18:37
s Jn 3:32
t Jn 8:47;
1Jn 4:6

18:38
u Lk 23:4;
Jn 19:4,6

18:40
v Ac 3:14

19:1
a Dt 25:3;
Isa 50:6; 53:5;
Mt 27:26

19:3
b Mt 27:29
c Jn 18:22

19:4
d Jn 18:38
e ver 6;
Lk 23:4

19:5
f ver 2

19:6
g Ac 3:13
h ver 4;
Lk 23:4

19:7
i Lev 24:16
j Mt 26:63-66;
Jn 5:18; 10:33

19:9
k Jn 18:33
l Mk 14:61

19:11
m Ro 13:1
n Jn 18:28-30;
Ac 3:13

19:12
o Lk 23:2

19:13
p Mt 27:19
q Jn 5:2

19:14
r Mt 27:62
s Mk 15:25
t ver 19,21

19:16
u Mt 27:26;
Mk 15:15;
Lk 23:25

19:17
v Ge 22:6;
Lk 14:27; 23:26
w Lk 23:33
x Jn 5:2

19:18
y Lk 23:32

19:19
z Mk 1:24
a ver 14,21

Chapter 19 Theme

19 Then Pilate took Jesus and had him flogged.*a* ²The soldiers twisted together a crown of thorns and put it on his head. They clothed him in a purple robe ³and went up to him again and again, saying, "Hail, king of the Jews!"*b* And they struck him in the face.*c*

⁴Once more Pilate came out and said to the Jews, "Look, I am bringing him out*d* to you to let you know that I find no basis for a charge against him."*e* ⁵When Jesus came out wearing the crown of thorns and the purple robe,*f* Pilate said to them, "Here is the man!"

⁶As soon as the chief priests and their officials saw him, they shouted, "Crucify! Crucify!"

But Pilate answered, "You take him and crucify him.*g* As for me, I find no basis for a charge against him."*h*

⁷The Jews insisted, "We have a law, and according to that law he must die,*i* because he claimed to be the Son of God."*j*

⁸When Pilate heard this, he was even more afraid, ⁹and he went back inside the palace.*k* "Where do you come from?" he asked Jesus, but Jesus gave him no answer.*l* ¹⁰"Do you refuse to speak to me?" Pilate said. "Don't you realize I have power either to free you or to crucify you?"

¹¹Jesus answered, "You would have no power over me if it were not given to you from above.*m* Therefore the one who handed me over to you*n* is guilty of a greater sin."

¹²From then on, Pilate tried to set Jesus free, but the Jews kept shouting, "If you let this man go, you are no friend of Caesar. Anyone who claims to be a king*o* opposes Caesar."

¹³When Pilate heard this, he brought Jesus out and sat down on the judge's seat*p* at a place known as the Stone Pavement (which in Aramaic*q* is Gabbatha). ¹⁴It was the day of Preparation*r* of Passover Week, about the sixth hour.*s*

"Here is your king,"*t* Pilate said to the Jews.

¹⁵But they shouted, "Take him away! Take him away! Crucify him!"

"Shall I crucify your king?" Pilate asked.

"We have no king but Caesar," the chief priests answered.

¹⁶Finally Pilate handed him over to them to be crucified.*u*

So the soldiers took charge of Jesus. ¹⁷Carrying his own cross,*v* he went out to the place of the Skull*w* (which in Aramaic*x* is called Golgotha). ¹⁸Here they crucified him, and with him two others*y*— one on each side and Jesus in the middle.

¹⁹Pilate had a notice prepared and fastened to the cross. It read: JESUS OF NAZARETH,*z* THE KING OF THE JEWS.*a* ²⁰Many of the Jews read this sign, for the place where Jesus was crucified was near the

city,[a] and the sign was written in Aramaic, Latin and Greek. [21]The chief priests of the Jews protested to Pilate, "Do not write 'The King of the Jews,' but that this man claimed to be king of the Jews."[b]

[22]Pilate answered, "What I have written, I have written."

[23]When the soldiers crucified Jesus, they took his clothes, dividing them into four shares, one for each of them, with the undergarment remaining. This garment was seamless, woven in one piece from top to bottom.

[24]"Let's not tear it," they said to one another. "Let's decide by lot who will get it."

This happened that the scripture might be fulfilled[c] which said,

"They divided my garments among them
    and cast lots for my clothing."[a][d]

So this is what the soldiers did.

[25]Near the cross[e] of Jesus stood his mother,[f] his mother's sister, Mary the wife of Clopas, and Mary Magdalene.[g] [26]When Jesus saw his mother[h] there, and the disciple whom he loved[i] standing nearby, he said to his mother, "Dear woman, here is your son," [27]and to the disciple, "Here is your mother." From that time on, this disciple took her into his home.

[28]Later, knowing that all was now completed,[j] and so that the Scripture would be fulfilled,[k] Jesus said, "I am thirsty." [29]A jar of wine vinegar[l] was there, so they soaked a sponge in it, put the sponge on a stalk of the hyssop plant, and lifted it to Jesus' lips. [30]When he had received the drink, Jesus said, "It is finished."[m] With that, he bowed his head and gave up his spirit.

[31]Now it was the day of Preparation,[n] and the next day was to be a special Sabbath. Because the Jews did not want the bodies left on the crosses[o] during the Sabbath, they asked Pilate to have the legs broken and the bodies taken down. [32]The soldiers therefore came and broke the legs of the first man who had been crucified with Jesus, and then those of the other.[p] [33]But when they came to Jesus and found that he was already dead, they did not break his legs. [34]Instead, one of the soldiers pierced[q] Jesus' side with a spear, bringing a sudden flow of blood and water.[r] [35]The man who saw it[s] has given testimony, and his testimony is true.[t] He knows that he tells the truth, and he testifies so that you also may believe. [36]These things happened so that the scripture would be fulfilled:[u] "Not one of his bones will be broken,"[b][v] [37]and, as another scripture says, "They will look on the one they have pierced."[c][w]

[38]Later, Joseph of Arimathea asked Pilate for the body of Jesus. Now Joseph was a disciple of Jesus, but secretly because he feared the Jews. With Pilate's permission, he came and took the body

---

19:20
[a] Heb 13:12

19:21
[b] ver 14

19:24
[c] ver 28,36,37;
Mt 1:22
[d] Ps 22:18

19:25
[e] Mt 27:55,56;
Mk 15:40,41;
Lk 23:49
[f] Mt 12:46
[g] Lk 24:18

19:26
[h] Mt 12:46
[i] Jn 13:23

19:28
[j] ver 30;
Jn 13:1
[k] ver 24,36,37

19:29
[l] Ps 69:21

19:30
[m] Lk 12:50;
Jn 17:4

19:31
[n] ver 14,42
[o] Dt 21:23;
Jos 8:29;
10:26,27

19:32
[p] ver 18

19:34
[q] Zec 12:10
[r] 1Jn 5:6,8

19:35
[s] Lk 24:48
[t] Jn 15:27; 21:24

19:36
[u] ver 24,28,37;
Mt 1:22
[v] Ex 12:46;
Nu 9:12;
Ps 34:20

19:37
[w] Zec 12:10;
Rev 1:7

---

[a] 24 Psalm 22:18   [b] 36 Exodus 12:46; Num. 9:12; Psalm 34:20   [c] 37 Zech. 12:10

19:39
a Jn 3:1; 7:50

19:40
b Lk 24:12;
Jn 11:44; 20:5,7
c Mt 26:12

19:42
d ver 14,31
e ver 20,41

20:1
f ver 18;
Jn 19:25
g Mt 27:60,66

20:2
h Jn 13:23
i ver 13

20:3
j Lk 24:12

20:5
k ver 11
l Jn 19:40

20:7
m Jn 11:44

20:8
n ver 4

20:9
o Mt 22:29;
Jn 2:22
p Lk 24:26,46

20:11
q ver 5

20:12
r Mt 28:2,3;
Mk 16:5;
Lk 24:4;
Ac 5:19

20:13
s ver 15
t ver 2

20:14
u Mt 28:9;
Mk 16:9
v Lk 24:16;
Jn 21:4

20:15
w ver 13

20:16
x Jn 5:2
y Mt 23:7

away. ³⁹He was accompanied by Nicodemus,ᵃ the man who earlier had visited Jesus at night. Nicodemus brought a mixture of myrrh and aloes, about seventy-five pounds.ᵃ ⁴⁰Taking Jesus' body, the two of them wrapped it, with the spices, in strips of linen.ᵇ This was in accordance with Jewish burial customs.ᶜ ⁴¹At the place where Jesus was crucified, there was a garden, and in the garden a new tomb, in which no one had ever been laid. ⁴²Because it was the Jewish day of Preparationᵈ and since the tomb was nearby,ᵉ they laid Jesus there.

Chapter 20 Theme _____

20 Early on the first day of the week, while it was still dark, Mary Magdaleneᶠ went to the tomb and saw that the stone had been removed from the entrance.ᵍ ²So she came running to Simon Peter and the other disciple, the one Jesus loved,ʰ and said, "They have taken the Lord out of the tomb, and we don't know where they have put him!"ⁱ

³So Peter and the other disciple started for the tomb.ʲ ⁴Both were running, but the other disciple outran Peter and reached the tomb first. ⁵He bent over and looked inᵏ at the strips of linenˡ lying there but did not go in. ⁶Then Simon Peter, who was behind him, arrived and went into the tomb. He saw the strips of linen lying there, ⁷as well as the burial cloth that had been around Jesus' head.ᵐ The cloth was folded up by itself, separate from the linen. ⁸Finally the other disciple, who had reached the tomb first,ⁿ also went inside. He saw and believed. ⁹(They still did not understand from Scriptureᵒ that Jesus had to rise from the dead.)ᵖ

¹⁰Then the disciples went back to their homes, ¹¹but Mary stood outside the tomb crying. As she wept, she bent over to look into the tomb�q ¹²and saw two angels in white,ʳ seated where Jesus' body had been, one at the head and the other at the foot.

¹³They asked her, "Woman, why are you crying?"ˢ

"They have taken my Lord away," she said, "and I don't know where they have put him."ᵗ ¹⁴At this, she turned around and saw Jesus standing there,ᵘ but she did not realize that it was Jesus.ᵛ

¹⁵"Woman," he said, "why are you crying?ʷ Who is it you are looking for?"

Thinking he was the gardener, she said, "Sir, if you have carried him away, tell me where you have put him, and I will get him."

¹⁶Jesus said to her, "Mary."

She turned toward him and cried out in Aramaic,ˣ "Rabboni!"ʸ (which means Teacher).

¹⁷Jesus said, "Do not hold on to me, for I have not yet returned to

a 39 Greek *a hundred litrai* (about 34 kilograms)

the Father. Go instead to my brothers[a] and tell them, 'I am returning to my Father[b] and your Father, to my God and your God.'"

[18] Mary Magdalene[c] went to the disciples[d] with the news: "I have seen the Lord!" And she told them that he had said these things to her.

[19] On the evening of that first day of the week, when the disciples were together, with the doors locked for fear of the Jews,[e] Jesus came and stood among them and said, "Peace[f] be with you!"[g] [20] After he said this, he showed them his hands and side.[h] The disciples were overjoyed[i] when they saw the Lord.

[21] Again Jesus said, "Peace be with you![j] As the Father has sent me,[k] I am sending you."[l] [22] And with that he breathed on them and said, "Receive the Holy Spirit.[m] [23] If you forgive anyone his sins, they are forgiven; if you do not forgive them, they are not forgiven."[n]

[24] Now Thomas[o] (called Didymus), one of the Twelve, was not with the disciples when Jesus came. [25] So the other disciples told him, "We have seen the Lord!"

But he said to them, "Unless I see the nail marks in his hands and put my finger where the nails were, and put my hand into his side,[p] I will not believe it."[q]

[26] A week later his disciples were in the house again, and Thomas was with them. Though the doors were locked, Jesus came and stood among them and said, "Peace[r] be with you!"[s] [27] Then he said to Thomas, "Put your finger here; see my hands. Reach out your hand and put it into my side. Stop doubting and believe."[t]

[28] Thomas said to him, "My Lord and my God!"

[29] Then Jesus told him, "Because you have seen me, you have believed;[u] blessed are those who have not seen and yet have believed."[v]

[30] Jesus did many other miraculous signs[w] in the presence of his disciples, which are not recorded in this book.[x] [31] But these are written that you may[a] believe[y] that Jesus is the Christ, the Son of God,[z] and that by believing you may have life in his name.[a]

Chapter 21 Theme

21 Afterward Jesus appeared again to his disciples,[b] by the Sea of Tiberias.[b][c] It happened this way: [2] Simon Peter, Thomas[d] (called Didymus), Nathanael[e] from Cana in Galilee,[f] the sons of Zebedee,[g] and two other disciples were together. [3] "I'm going out to fish," Simon Peter told them, and they said, "We'll go with you." So they went out and got into the boat, but that night they caught nothing.[h]

[4] Early in the morning, Jesus stood on the shore, but the disciples did not realize that it was Jesus.[i]

a 31 Some manuscripts *may continue to*   b 1 That is, Sea of Galilee

20:17
a Mt 28:10
b Jn 7:33

20:18
c ver 1
d Lk 24:10,22,23

20:19
e Jn 7:13
f Jn 14:27
g ver 21,26;
Lk 24:36-39

20:20
h Lk 24:39,40;
Jn 19:34
i Jn 16:20,22

20:21
j ver 19
k Jn 3:17
l Mt 28:19;
Jn 17:18

20:22
m Jn 7:39;
Ac 2:38;
8:15-17; 19:2;
Gal 3:2

20:23
n Mt 16:19;
18:18

20:24
o Jn 11:16

20:25
p ver 20
q Mk 16:11

20:26
r Jn 14:27
s ver 21

20:27
t ver 25;
Lk 24:40

20:29
u Jn 3:15
v 1Pe 1:8

20:30
w Jn 2:11
x Jn 21:25

20:31
y Jn 3:15; 19:35
z Mt 4:3
a Mt 25:46

21:1
b Jn 20:19,26
c Jn 6:1

21:2
d Jn 11:16
e Jn 1:45
f Jn 2:1
g Mt 4:21

21:3
h Lk 5:5

21:4
i Lk 24:16;
Jn 20:14

21:6
a Lk 5:4-7

⁵He called out to them, "Friends, haven't you any fish?"

"No," they answered.

⁶He said, "Throw your net on the right side of the boat and you will find some." When they did, they were unable to haul the net in because of the large number of fish.*a*

21:7
b Jn 13:23

⁷Then the disciple whom Jesus loved *b* said to Peter, "It is the Lord!" As soon as Simon Peter heard him say, "It is the Lord," he wrapped his outer garment around him (for he had taken it off) and jumped into the water. ⁸The other disciples followed in the boat, towing the net full of fish, for they were not far from shore, about a hundred yards.ᵃ ⁹When they landed, they saw a fire*c* of burning coals there with fish on it,*d* and some bread.

21:9
c Jn 18:18
d ver 10,13

¹⁰Jesus said to them, "Bring some of the fish you have just caught."

21:13
e ver 9

¹¹Simon Peter climbed aboard and dragged the net ashore. It was full of large fish, 153, but even with so many the net was not torn. ¹²Jesus said to them, "Come and have breakfast." None of the disciples dared ask him, "Who are you?" They knew it was the Lord. ¹³Jesus came, took the bread and gave it to them, and did the same with the fish.*e* ¹⁴This was now the third time Jesus appeared to his disciples *f* after he was raised from the dead.

21:14
f Jn 20:19,26

¹⁵When they had finished eating, Jesus said to Simon Peter, "Simon son of John, do you truly love me more than these?"

"Yes, Lord," he said, "you know that I love you."*g*

Jesus said, "Feed my lambs."*h*

21:15
g Mt 26:33,35;
Jn 13:37
h Lk 12:32

¹⁶Again Jesus said, "Simon son of John, do you truly love me?"

He answered, "Yes, Lord, you know that I love you."

Jesus said, "Take care of my sheep."*i*

21:16
i Mt 2:6;
Ac 20:28;
1Pe 5:2,3

¹⁷The third time he said to him, "Simon son of John, do you love me?"

Peter was hurt because Jesus asked him the third time, "Do you love me?"*j* He said, "Lord, you know all things;*k* you know that I love you."

21:17
j Jn 13:38
k Jn 16:30
l ver 16

Jesus said, "Feed my sheep.*l* ¹⁸I tell you the truth, when you were younger you dressed yourself and went where you wanted; but when you are old you will stretch out your hands, and someone else will dress you and lead you where you do not want to go." ¹⁹Jesus said this to indicate the kind of death*m* by which Peter would glorify God.*n* Then he said to him, "Follow me!"

21:19
m Jn 12:33;
18:32
n 2Pe 1:14

²⁰Peter turned and saw that the disciple whom Jesus loved*o* was following them. (This was the one who had leaned back against Jesus at the supper and had said, "Lord, who is going to betray you?")*p* ²¹When Peter saw him, he asked, "Lord, what about him?"

21:20
o ver 7;
Jn 13:23
p Jn 13:25

ᵃ8 Greek *about two hundred cubits* (about 90 meters)

[22]Jesus answered, "If I want him to remain alive until I return,[a] what is that to you? You must follow me."[b] [23]Because of this, the rumor spread among the brothers[c] that this disciple would not die. But Jesus did not say that he would not die; he only said, "If I want him to remain alive until I return, what is that to you?"

[24]This is the disciple who testifies to these things[d] and who wrote them down. We know that his testimony is true.[e]

[25]Jesus did many other things as well.[f] If every one of them were written down, I suppose that even the whole world would not have room for the books that would be written.

21:22
[a]Mt 16:27;
1Co 4:5;
Rev 2:25
[b]ver 19

21:23
[c]Ac 1:16

21:24
[d]Jn 15:27
[e]Jn 19:35

21:25
[f]Jn 20:30

Theme of John:

Author:

SEGMENT DIVISIONS

Date:

Purpose:

Key Words:

PORTRAYALS OF JESUS CHRIST	SIGNS AND MIRACLES	MINISTRY		CHAPTER THEMES
		TO ISRAEL	1	
			2	
			3	
			4	
			5	
			6	
			7	
			8	
			9	
			10	
			11	
		TO DISCIPLES	12	
			13	
			14	
			15	
			16	
			17	
		TO ALL MANKIND	18	
			19	
			20	
		TO DISCIPLES	21	

THE ARREST, TRIAL, AND CRUCIFIXION OF JESUS CHRIST

MATTHEW	MARK	LUKE	JOHN
		Luke gives consecutive order of events in Jesus' life (Luke 1:3)	

THE ACCOUNT OF JESUS' RESURRECTION

MATTHEW	MARK	LUKE	JOHN
		Luke gives consecutive order of events in Jesus' life (Luke 1:3)	
	POSTRESURRECTION APPEARANCES		

MATTHEW	MARK

LUKE	JOHN

ACTS

I'm going away."

The eleven heard nothing else. The promise of another Helper, the Holy Spirit, fell on deaf ears. The thought that they could do the works that Jesus had done—and even greater—must have seemed preposterous to them.

Jesus had died and been buried. But he had also risen! For over 40 days the disciples saw, heard, and touched the Word of Life as he spoke with them of things concerning the kingdom of God.

And then once again he was gone, taken away before their very eyes! He left with the promise to send the Spirit and he commissioned his disciples to reach the world.

Then came Pentecost and the acts of the apostles. Luke wrote Theophilus all about it. It was probably about A.D. 63.

∾ THINGS TO DO

Chapters 1, 2

In the first two chapters of the book of Acts, Luke gives an account of Christ's ascension and the Holy Spirit's coming.

1. Read chapter 1, looking for Jesus' instructions and promises to the apostles.

   a. In a distinctive way mark in the text every occurrence of the key words (along with their synonyms and pronouns) listed on the ACTS AT A GLANCE chart on page 1923. Record these key words on an index card that you can use as a bookmark while studying Acts.

   b. In the chapter margin list everything you learn from the references to the Holy Spirit.

   c. In the margin list the instructions and the promises that Jesus gives to the apostles.

   d. Note the main events that occur in this chapter by either marking these events within the text or listing them in the margin.

2. The key verse for Acts is found in chapter 1. This verse also gives an outline for the book. See if you can identify it. When you do, put a box around it and in the margin write, "Key verse of Acts."

3. As you read chapter 2:

   a. Keep in mind that you can easily recognize Old Testament quotes because the NIV text indents the Scripture on both sides. Observe how much is taken from the Old Testament.

   b. List in the margin the main events that occur. As you note them, ask the five W's and an H: Who? What? When? Where? Why? and How? For example, ask: Who was present on the day of Pentecost? What happened? Whom did it affect? What was their response? Why did they respond as they did? How did they hear?

   c. Mark key words. Also mark every reference to the Holy Spirit and to Jesus, including their synonyms or pronouns. Then list in the margin what you learn about each from this chapter. Watch the words *promise* and *promised* and note their relationship to the Spirit. Compare this with Acts 1:4, 5.

   d. Mark every reference to time with a symbol. Do this throughout the book of Acts whether the time is indicated by an event (such as a feast or the death of Herod) or by mentioning a certain period of months or years.

    e. List in the margin the main points in Peter's sermon on the day of Pentecost. Note what he emphasized in his sermon and the result.

4. Determine the theme of each of these chapters. Then record the themes on ACTS AT A GLANCE and on the line next to the chapter number in the text.

Chapters 3-7

1. As you study, do the following:

    a. Read each chapter in the light of the five W's and an H. Then in the margin note: What happens in that chapter? Where and when did it happen? Who is involved? How are things done or said?

    b. Mark every reference to the Holy Spirit and then list what you learn about the Holy Spirit, his ministry, and the results. Also mark in the text the other key words listed on ACTS AT A GLANCE. Remember to use your bookmark.

    c. If a message is proclaimed in these chapters, list in the margin the main points of that message. Also note the effect of the message on those who hear it.

2. Determine the theme of each chapter and then record the theme as before.

Chapters 8-12

1. Read Acts 8:1-8 and then Acts 1:8. What do you see happening in Acts 8 that is a change from the first seven chapters? Note this in the margin of chapter 8.

2. Read chapters 8 through 11 carefully, as significant events occur in these chapters. As you read:

    a. List the main events in each chapter. Who does what? When? Where is it done? What is said? What is the result? Who is affected? How does it happen? Don't add to the text, but simply observe it and list in the margin what you learn.

    b. Mark key words and list everything you learn about the Holy Spirit in the margin of each chapter. This is crucial to chapters 8, 10, and 11. Note to whom the Holy Spirit comes.

    c. Record the theme of each chapter in the text and on ACTS AT A GLANCE.

3. As you read and study chapter 12, keep in mind that this chapter is pivotal. At this point the focus of the book turns from Peter's ministry to that of Paul (Saul).

Chapters 13-28

1. Included in these chapters is an account of Paul's missionary journeys: Paul's first missionary journey in 13 through 14; Paul's second missionary journey in 15:36 through 18:22; and Paul's third missionary journey in 18:23 through 21:17.

For easy reference, write and color code in the margin where each journey begins.

2. As you study these chapters, mark the key repeated words. Add the words *synagogue* and *congregation* to your list. Also keep in mind what you learned from Acts 1:8 and watch carefully the work of the Spirit throughout these chapters. In the margin note your insights.

    a. Examine each chapter with the five W's and an H. Note in the text who accompanies Paul, where they go, and what happens. On the maps provided you can trace each of Paul's journeys.

    b. Carefully observe each time the gospel is proclaimed, whether to an individual or a group. Watch how Paul reasons with Jews and Gentiles. Also note what their response is and how Paul handles it.

3. In several instances you will notice Paul giving his testimony. Compare each of these instances with Acts 9 and the account of Paul's conversion. This will give you a more complete picture of all that happened on that significant day.

4. Record the theme of each chapter on ACTS AT A GLANCE and in the text. Then determine the main subject for the book of Acts and record it. Then complete the chart. Record the ways you might segment the book of Acts according to its themes.

∾ THINGS TO THINK ABOUT

1. What have you learned from Acts about the Holy Spirit and your responsibility to be a witness for the Lord Jesus Christ?

2. Based on what you saw in the sermons that were preached and the personal witnesses which were given, what would you include in your witness? Where would the emphasis be?

3. As you studied the lives of the early apostles and the commitment of the early church, how has God spoken to your heart? Stop and think about how they lived, and then think about how you are living. Do you have the Holy Spirit living inside you? Isn't he the same today, yesterday, and forever? If you are filled with the Holy Spirit and are not quenching him, what should be happening in your life?

∾∾∾∾∾

Chapter 1 Theme _____

1 In my former book,[a] Theophilus, I wrote about all that Jesus began to do and to teach[b] [2]until the day he was taken up to heaven,[c] after giving instructions[d] through the Holy Spirit to the apostles[e] he had chosen.[f] [3]After his suffering, he showed himself to these men and gave many convincing proofs that he was alive. He appeared to them[g] over a period of forty days and spoke about the kingdom of God. [4]On one occasion, while he was eating with them, he gave them this command: "Do not leave Jerusalem, but wait for the gift my Father promised, which you have heard me speak about.[h] [5]For John baptized with[a] water, but in a few days you will be baptized with the Holy Spirit."

[6]So when they met together, they asked him, "Lord, are you at this time going to restore[i] the kingdom to Israel?"

[7]He said to them: "It is not for you to know the times or dates the Father has set by his own authority.[j] [8]But you will receive power when the Holy Spirit comes on you;[k] and you will be my witnesses[l] in Jerusalem, and in all Judea and Samaria,[m] and to the ends of the earth."[n]

[9]After he said this, he was taken up[o] before their very eyes, and a cloud hid him from their sight.

[10]They were looking intently up into the sky as he was going, when suddenly two men dressed in white[p] stood beside them. [11]"Men of Galilee,"[q] they said, "why do you stand here looking into the sky? This same Jesus, who has been taken from you into heaven, will come back[r] in the same way you have seen him go into heaven."

[12]Then they returned to Jerusalem[s] from the hill called the Mount of Olives,[t] a Sabbath day's walk[b] from the city. [13]When they

a 5 Or *in*   b 12 That is, about 3/4 mile (about 1,100 meters)

1:1
[a] Lk 1:1-4
[b] Lk 3:23

1:2
[c] ver 9,11;
Mk 16:19
[d] Mt 28:19,20
[e] Mk 6:30
[f] Jn 13:18

1:3
[g] Mt 28:17;
Lk 24:34,36;
Jn 20:19,26;
21:1,14;
1Co 15:5-7

1:4
[h] Lk 24:49;
Jn 14:16;
Ac 2:33

1:6
[i] Mt 17:11

1:7
[j] Mt 24:36

1:8
[k] Ac 2:1-4
[l] Lk 24:48
[m] Ac 8:1-25
[n] Mt 28:19

1:9
[o] ver 2

1:10
[p] Lk 24:4;
Jn 20:12

1:11
[q] Ac 2:7
[r] Mt 16:27

1:12
[s] Lk 24:52
[t] Mt 21:1

1:13
a Ac 9:37; 20:8
b Mt 10:2-4;
Mk 3:16-19;
Lk 6:14-16

1:14
c Ac 2:42; 6:4
d Lk 23:49,55
e Mt 12:46

1:16
f ver 20
g Jn 13:18

1:17
h Jn 6:70,71
i ver 25

1:18
j Mt 26:14,15
k Mt 27:3-10

1:20
l Ps 69:25
m Ps 109:8

1:22
n Mk 1:4
o ver 8

1:24
p Ac 6:6;
14:23
q 1Sa 16:7;
Jer 17:10;
Ac 15:8;
Rev 2:23

1:26
r Ac 2:14

2:1
s Lev 23:15,16;
Ac 20:16
t Ac 1:14

2:2
u Ac 4:31

2:4
v Mk 16:17;
1Co 12:10

arrived, they went upstairs to the room*a* where they were staying. Those present were Peter, John, James and Andrew; Philip and Thomas, Bartholomew and Matthew; James son of Alphaeus and Simon the Zealot, and Judas son of James.*b* ¹⁴They all joined together constantly in prayer,*c* along with the women*d* and Mary the mother of Jesus, and with his brothers.*e*

¹⁵In those days Peter stood up among the believers*a* (a group numbering about a hundred and twenty) ¹⁶and said, "Brothers, the Scripture had to be fulfilled*f* which the Holy Spirit spoke long ago through the mouth of David concerning Judas,*g* who served as guide for those who arrested Jesus— ¹⁷he was one of our number*h* and shared in this ministry."*i*

¹⁸(With the reward*j* he got for his wickedness, Judas bought a field;*k* there he fell headlong, his body burst open and all his intestines spilled out. ¹⁹Everyone in Jerusalem heard about this, so they called that field in their language Akeldama, that is, Field of Blood.)

²⁰"For," said Peter, "it is written in the book of Psalms,

> "'May his place be deserted;
> let there be no one to dwell in it,'*b l*

and,

> "'May another take his place of leadership.'*c m*

²¹Therefore it is necessary to choose one of the men who have been with us the whole time the Lord Jesus went in and out among us, ²²beginning from John's baptism*n* to the time when Jesus was taken up from us. For one of these must become a witness*o* with us of his resurrection."

²³So they proposed two men: Joseph called Barsabbas (also known as Justus) and Matthias. ²⁴Then they prayed,*p* "Lord, you know everyone's heart.*q* Show us which of these two you have chosen ²⁵to take over this apostolic ministry, which Judas left to go where he belongs." ²⁶Then they cast lots, and the lot fell to Matthias; so he was added to the eleven apostles.*r*

Chapter 2 Theme

2 When the day of Pentecost*s* came, they were all together*t* in one place. ²Suddenly a sound like the blowing of a violent wind came from heaven and filled the whole house where they were sitting.*u* ³They saw what seemed to be tongues of fire that separated and came to rest on each of them. ⁴All of them were filled with the Holy Spirit and began to speak in other tongues*d v* as the Spirit enabled them.

INSIGHT

There were 150 Jewish colonies in major population centers throughout the Roman Empire. Many Jews came from these centers to Jerusalem to celebrate the feasts. Jesus' followers who spoke in tongues (known dialects) were Galilean Jews, yet they spoke in the languages of the men attending the Feast of Pentecost.

a 15 Greek *brothers*   *b 20* Psalm 69:25   *c 20* Psalm 109:8   *d 4* Or *languages*; also in verse 11

To understand
the significance of
Pentecost, see the
chart **The Feasts
of Israel** located
on pages 210, 211.

⁵Now there were staying in Jerusalem God-fearing*ᵃ* Jews from every nation under heaven. ⁶When they heard this sound, a crowd came together in bewilderment, because each one heard them speaking in his own language. ⁷Utterly amazed,*ᵇ* they asked: "Are not all these men who are speaking Galileans?*ᶜ* ⁸Then how is it that each of us hears them in his own native language? ⁹Parthians, Medes and Elamites; residents of Mesopotamia, Judea and Cappadocia,*ᵈ* Pontus*ᵉ* and Asia,*ᶠ* ¹⁰Phrygia*ᵍ* and Pamphylia,*ʰ* Egypt and the parts of Libya near Cyrene;*ⁱ* visitors from Rome ¹¹(both Jews and converts to Judaism); Cretans and Arabs—we hear them declaring the wonders of God in our own tongues!" ¹²Amazed and perplexed, they asked one another, "What does this mean?"

**Men from
Every Nation
at Pentecost**

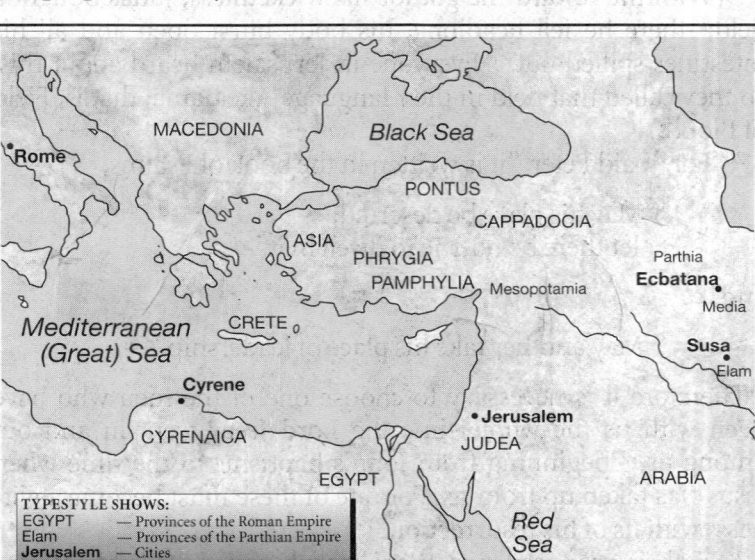

TYPESTYLE SHOWS:
EGYPT — Provinces of the Roman Empire
Elam — Provinces of the Parthian Empire
Jerusalem — Cities

¹³Some, however, made fun of them and said, "They have had too much wine.ᵃ"*ʲ*

¹⁴Then Peter stood up with the Eleven, raised his voice and addressed the crowd: "Fellow Jews and all of you who live in Jerusalem, let me explain this to you; listen carefully to what I say. ¹⁵These men are not drunk, as you suppose. It's only nine in the morning!*ᵏ* ¹⁶No, this is what was spoken by the prophet Joel:

¹⁷"'In the last days, God says,
I will pour out my Spirit on all people.*ˡ*
Your sons and daughters will prophesy,*ᵐ*
your young men will see visions,
your old men will dream dreams.

ᵃ 13 Or *sweet wine*

2:5
ᵃ Ac 8:2

2:7
ᵇ ver 12
ᶜ Ac 1:11

2:9
ᵈ 1Pe 1:1
ᵉ Ac 18:2
ᶠ Ac 16:6;
Ro 16:5;
1Co 16:19;
2Co 1:8

2:10
ᵍ Ac 16:6; 18:23
ʰ Ac 13:13; 15:38
ⁱ Mt 27:32

2:13
ʲ 1Co 14:23

2:15
ᵏ 1Th 5:7

2:17
ˡ Isa 44:3;
Jn 7:37-39;
Ac 10:45
ᵐ Ac 21:9

18Even on my servants, both men and women,
    I will pour out my Spirit in those days,
    and they will prophesy.*a*
19I will show wonders in the heaven above
    and signs on the earth below,
    blood and fire and billows of smoke.
20The sun will be turned to darkness
    and the moon to blood*b*
    before the coming of the great and glorious day of the
        Lord.
21And everyone who calls
    on the name of the Lord will be saved.'*a c*

22"Men of Israel, listen to this: Jesus of Nazareth was a man accredited by God to you by miracles, wonders and signs,*d* which God did among you through him,*e* as you yourselves know. 23This man was handed over to you by God's set purpose and foreknowledge;*f* and you, with the help of wicked men,*b* put him to death by nailing him to the cross.*g* 24But God raised him from the dead,*h* freeing him from the agony of death, because it was impossible for death to keep its hold on him.*i* 25David said about him:

" 'I saw the Lord always before me.
    Because he is at my right hand,
    I will not be shaken.
26Therefore my heart is glad and my tongue rejoices;
    my body also will live in hope,
27because you will not abandon me to the grave,
    nor will you let your Holy One see decay.*j*
28You have made known to me the paths of life;
    you will fill me with joy in your presence.'*c*

29"Brothers, I can tell you confidently that the patriarch*k* David died and was buried,*l* and his tomb is here*m* to this day. 30But he was a prophet and knew that God had promised him on oath that he would place one of his descendants on his throne.*n* 31Seeing what was ahead, he spoke of the resurrection of the Christ,*d* that he was not abandoned to the grave, nor did his body see decay.*o* 32God has raised this Jesus to life,*p* and we are all witnesses*q* of the fact. 33Exalted*r* to the right hand of God,*s* he has received from the Father*t* the promised Holy Spirit*u* and has poured out*v* what you now see and hear. 34For David did not ascend to heaven, and yet he said,

---

a21 Joel 2:28-32   *b23* Or *of those not having the law* (that is, Gentiles)   *c28* Psalm 16:8-11
d31 Or *Messiah.* "The Christ" (Greek) and "the Messiah" (Hebrew) both mean "the Anointed One"; also in verse 36.

2:18
a Ac 21:9-12

2:20
b Mt 24:29

2:21
c Ro 10:13

2:22
d Jn 4:48;
Ac 10:38
e Jn 3:2

2:23
f Lk 22:22;
Ac 3:18; 4:28
g Lk 24:20;
Ac 3:13

2:24
h ver 32;
1Co 6:14;
2Co 4:14;
Eph 1:20;
Col 2:12;
Heb 13:20;
1Pe 1:21
i Jn 20:9

2:27
j ver 31;
Ac 13:35

2:29
k Ac 7:8,9
l Ac 13:36;
1Ki 2:10
m Ne 3:16

2:30
n 2Sa 7:12;
Ps 132:11

2:31
o Ps 16:10

2:32
p ver 24
q Ac 1:8

2:33
r Php 2:9
s Mk 16:19
t Ac 1:4
u Jn 7:39; 14:26
v Ac 10:45

1871

""'The Lord said to my Lord:
"Sit at my right hand
35until I make your enemies
a footstool for your feet.'"ᵃᵃ

36"Therefore let all Israel be assured of this: God has made this Jesus, whom you crucified, both Lord and Christ."ᵇ

37When the people heard this, they were cut to the heart and said to Peter and the other apostles, "Brothers, what shall we do?"ᶜ

38Peter replied, "Repent and be baptized,ᵈ every one of you, in the name of Jesus Christ for the forgiveness of your sins.ᵉ And you will receive the gift of the Holy Spirit. 39The promise is for you and your childrenᶠ and for all who are far offᵍ—for all whom the Lord our God will call."

40With many other words he warned them; and he pleaded with them, "Save yourselves from this corrupt generation."ʰ 41Those who accepted his message were baptized, and about three thousand were added to their number that day.

42They devoted themselves to the apostles' teaching and to the fellowship, to the breaking of bread and to prayer.ⁱ 43Everyone was filled with awe, and many wonders and miraculous signs were done by the apostles.ʲ 44All the believers were together and had everything in common.ᵏ 45Selling their possessions and goods, they gave to anyone as he had need.ˡ 46Every day they continued to meet together in the temple courts.ᵐ They broke breadⁿ in their homes and ate together with glad and sincere hearts, 47praising God and enjoying the favor of all the people.ᵒ And the Lord added to their numberᵖ daily those who were being saved.

Chapter 3 Theme _____

3 One day Peter and John�q were going up to the templeʳ at the time of prayer—at three in the afternoon.ˢ 2Now a man crippled from birthᵗ was being carried to the temple gateᵘ called Beautiful, where he was put every day to begᵛ from those going into the temple courts. 3When he saw Peter and John about to enter, he asked them for money. 4Peter looked straight at him, as did John. Then Peter said, "Look at us!" 5So the man gave them his attention, expecting to get something from them.

6Then Peter said, "Silver or gold I do not have, but what I have I give you. In the name of Jesus Christ of Nazareth,ʷ walk." 7Taking him by the right hand, he helped him up, and instantly the man's feet and ankles became strong. 8He jumped to his feet and began to walk. Then he went with them into the temple courts, walking and jumping,ˣ and praising God. 9When all the peopleʸ

ᵃ35 Psalm 110:1

2:35 ᵃPs 110:1; Mt 22:44

2:36 ᵇLk 2:11

2:37 ᶜLk 3:10, 12,14

2:38 ᵈAc 8:12,16, 36,38; 22:16 ᵉLk 24:47; Ac 3:19

2:39 ᶠIsa 44:3 ᵍAc 10:45; Eph 2:13

2:40 ʰDt 32:5

2:42 ⁱAc 1:14

2:43 ʲAc 5:12

2:44 ᵏAc 4:32

2:45 ˡMt 19:21

2:46 ᵐLk 24:53; Ac 5:21,42 ⁿAc 20:7

2:47 ᵒRo 14:18 ᵖver 41; Ac 5:14

3:1 qLk 22:8 ʳAc 2:46 ˢPs 55:17

3:2 ᵗAc 14:8 ᵘLk 16:20 ᵛJn 9:8

3:6 ʷver 16; Ac 4:10

3:8 ˣAc 14:10

3:9 ʸAc 4:16,21

it was evening, they put them in jail[a] until the next day. [4]But many who heard the message believed, and the number of men grew[b] to about five thousand.

[5]The next day the rulers,[c] elders and teachers of the law met in Jerusalem. [6]Annas the high priest was there, and so were Caiaphas,[d] John, Alexander and the other men of the high priest's family. [7]They had Peter and John brought before them and began to question them: "By what power or what name did you do this?"

[8]Then Peter, filled with the Holy Spirit, said to them: "Rulers and elders of the people![e] [9]If we are being called to account today for an act of kindness shown to a cripple[f] and are asked how he was healed, [10]then know this, you and all the people of Israel: It is by the name of Jesus Christ of Nazareth, whom you crucified but whom God raised from the dead,[g] that this man stands before you healed. [11]He is

> "'the stone you builders rejected,
>   which has become the capstone.[a]'[b][h]

[12]Salvation is found in no one else, for there is no other name under heaven given to men by which we must be saved."[i]

[13]When they saw the courage of Peter and John[j] and realized that they were unschooled, ordinary men,[k] they were astonished and they took note that these men had been with Jesus. [14]But since they could see the man who had been healed standing there with them, there was nothing they could say. [15]So they ordered them to withdraw from the Sanhedrin[l] and then conferred together. [16]"What are we going to do with these men?"[m] they asked. "Everybody living in Jerusalem knows they have done an outstanding miracle,[n] and we cannot deny it. [17]But to stop this thing from spreading any further among the people, we must warn these men to speak no longer to anyone in this name."

[18]Then they called them in again and commanded them not to speak or teach at all in the name of Jesus.[o] [19]But Peter and John replied, "Judge for yourselves whether it is right in God's sight to obey you rather than God.[p] [20]For we cannot help speaking about what we have seen and heard."

[21]After further threats they let them go. They could not decide how to punish them, because all the people[q] were praising God[r] for what had happened. [22]For the man who was miraculously healed was over forty years old.

[23]On their release, Peter and John went back to their own people and reported all that the chief priests and elders had said to them. [24]When they heard this, they raised their voices together in prayer

a 11 Or cornerstone   b 11 Psalm 118:22

4:3
a Ac 5:18

4:4
b Ac 2:41

4:5
c Lk 23:13

4:6
d Mt 26:3;
Lk 3:2

4:8
e ver 5;
Lk 23:13

4:9
f Ac 3:6

4:10
g Ac 2:24

4:11
h Ps 118:22;
Isa 28:16;
Mt 21:42

4:12
i Mt 1:21;
Ac 10:43;
1 Ti 2:5

4:13
j Lk 22:8
k Mt 11:25

4:15
l Mt 5:22

4:16
m Jn 11:47
n Ac 3:6-10

4:18
o Ac 5:40

4:19
p Ac 5:29

4:21
q Ac 5:26
r Mt 9:8

3:10
a ver 2

3:11
b Lk 22:8
c Jn 10:23;
Ac 5:12

3:13
d Ac 5:30
e Mt 27:2
f Lk 23:4

3:14
g Mk 1:24;
Ac 4:27
h Ac 7:52
i Mk 15:11;
Lk 23:18-25

3:15
j Ac 2:24

3:17
k Lk 23:34
l Ac 13:27

3:18
m Ac 2:23
n Lk 24:27
o Ac 17:2,3;
26:22,23

3:19
p Ac 2:38

3:21
q Ac 1:11
r Mt 17:11
s Lk 1:70

3:22
t Dt 18:15,18;
Ac 7:37

3:23
u Dt 18:19

3:24
v Lk 24:27

3:25
w Ac 2:39
x Ro 9:4,5
y Ge 12:3; 22:18;
26:4; 28:14

3:26
z ver 22;
Ac 2:24
a Ac 13:46;
Ro 1:16

4:1
b Lk 22:4
c Mt 3:7

4:2
d Ac 17:18

saw him walking and praising God, [10]they recognized him as the same man who used to sit begging at the temple gate called Beautiful,[a] and they were filled with wonder and amazement at what had happened to him.

[11]While the beggar held on to Peter and John,[b] all the people were astonished and came running to them in the place called Solomon's Colonnade.[c] [12]When Peter saw this, he said to them: "Men of Israel, why does this surprise you? Why do you stare at us as if by our own power or godliness we had made this man walk? [13]The God of Abraham, Isaac and Jacob, the God of our fathers,[d] has glorified his servant Jesus. You handed him over to be killed, and you disowned him before Pilate,[e] though he had decided to let him go.[f] [14]You disowned the Holy[g] and Righteous One[h] and asked that a murderer be released to you.[i] [15]You killed the author of life, but God raised him from the dead.[j] We are witnesses of this. [16]By faith in the name of Jesus, this man whom you see and know was made strong. It is Jesus' name and the faith that comes through him that has given this complete healing to him, as you can all see.

[17]"Now, brothers, I know that you acted in ignorance,[k] as did your leaders.[l] [18]But this is how God fulfilled what he had foretold[m] through all the prophets,[n] saying that his Christ[a] would suffer.[o] [19]Repent, then, and turn to God, so that your sins may be wiped out,[p] that times of refreshing may come from the Lord, [20]and that he may send the Christ, who has been appointed for you—even Jesus. [21]He must remain in heaven[q] until the time comes for God to restore everything,[r] as he promised long ago through his holy prophets.[s] [22]For Moses said, 'The Lord your God will raise up for you a prophet like me from among your own people; you must listen to everything he tells you.[t] [23]Anyone who does not listen to him will be completely cut off from among his people.'[b][u]

[24]"Indeed, all the prophets[v] from Samuel on, as many as have spoken, have foretold these days. [25]And you are heirs[w] of the prophets and of the covenant[x] God made with your fathers. He said to Abraham, 'Through your offspring all peoples on earth will be blessed.'[c][y] [26]When God raised up[z] his servant, he sent him first[a] to you to bless you by turning each of you from your wicked ways."

Chapter 4 Theme

4 The priests and the captain of the temple guard[b] and the Sadducees[c] came up to Peter and John while they were speaking to the people. [2]They were greatly disturbed because the apostles were teaching the people and proclaiming in Jesus the resurrection of the dead.[d] [3]They seized Peter and John, and because

a 18 Or *Messiah*; also in verse 20   b 23 Deut. 18:15,18,19   c 25 Gen. 22:18; 26:4

4:25
a Ac 1:16

4:26
b Ps 2:1,2;
Da 9:25;
Lk 4:18;
Ac 10:38;
Heb 1:9

4:27
c Mt 14:1
d Mt 27:2;
Lk 23:12
e ver 30

4:28
f Ac 2:23

4:29
g ver 13,31;
Ac 9:27; 14:3;
Php 1:14

4:30
h Jn 4:48
i ver 27

4:31
j Ac 2:2
k ver 29

4:32
l Ac 2:44

4:33
m Lk 24:48
n Ac 1:22

4:34
o Mt 19:21;
Ac 2:45

4:35
p ver 37;
Ac 5:2
q Ac 2:45; 6:1

4:36
r Ac 9:27;
1Co 9:6

4:37
s ver 35;
Ac 5:2

5:2
t Ac 4:35,37

5:3
u Mt 4:10
v Jn 13:2,27
w ver 9

to God. "Sovereign Lord," they said, "you made the heaven and the earth and the sea, and everything in them. [25]You spoke by the Holy Spirit through the mouth of your servant, our father David:[a]

> "'Why do the nations rage
>   and the peoples plot in vain?
> [26]The kings of the earth take their stand
>   and the rulers gather together
> against the Lord
>   and against his Anointed One.[a]'[b]

[27]Indeed Herod[c] and Pontius Pilate[d] met together with the Gentiles and the people[c] of Israel in this city to conspire against your holy servant Jesus,[e] whom you anointed. [28]They did what your power and will had decided beforehand should happen.[f] [29]Now, Lord, consider their threats and enable your servants to speak your word with great boldness.[g] [30]Stretch out your hand to heal and perform miraculous signs and wonders[h] through the name of your holy servant Jesus."[i]

[31]After they prayed, the place where they were meeting was shaken.[j] And they were all filled with the Holy Spirit and spoke the word of God boldly.[k]

[32]All the believers were one in heart and mind. No one claimed that any of his possessions was his own, but they shared everything they had.[l] [33]With great power the apostles continued to testify[m] to the resurrection[n] of the Lord Jesus, and much grace was upon them all. [34]There were no needy persons among them. For from time to time those who owned lands or houses sold them,[o] brought the money from the sales [35]and put it at the apostles' feet,[p] and it was distributed to anyone as he had need.[q]

[36]Joseph, a Levite from Cyprus, whom the apostles called Barnabas[r] (which means Son of Encouragement), [37]sold a field he owned and brought the money and put it at the apostles' feet.[s]

Chapter 5 Theme

5 Now a man named Ananias, together with his wife Sapphira, also sold a piece of property. [2]With his wife's full knowledge he kept back part of the money for himself, but brought the rest and put it at the apostles' feet.[t]

[3]Then Peter said, "Ananias, how is it that Satan[u] has so filled your heart[v] that you have lied to the Holy Spirit[w] and have kept for yourself some of the money you received for the land? [4]Didn't it belong to you before it was sold? And after it was sold, wasn't the money at your disposal? What made you think of doing such a thing? You have not lied to men but to God."

a 26 That is, Christ or Messiah   *b 26* Psalm 2:1,2   *c 27* The Greek is plural.

[5]When Ananias heard this, he fell down and died.[a] And great fear[b] seized all who heard what had happened. [6]Then the young men came forward, wrapped up his body,[c] and carried him out and buried him.

[7]About three hours later his wife came in, not knowing what had happened. [8]Peter asked her, "Tell me, is this the price you and Ananias got for the land?"

"Yes," she said, "that is the price."[d]

[9]Peter said to her, "How could you agree to test the Spirit of the Lord?[e] Look! The feet of the men who buried your husband are at the door, and they will carry you out also."

[10]At that moment she fell down at his feet and died.[f] Then the young men came in and, finding her dead, carried her out and buried her beside her husband. [11]Great fear[g] seized the whole church and all who heard about these events.

[12]The apostles performed many miraculous signs and wonders[h] among the people. And all the believers used to meet together[i] in Solomon's Colonnade.[j] [13]No one else dared join them, even though they were highly regarded by the people.[k] [14]Nevertheless, more and more men and women believed in the Lord and were added to their number. [15]As a result, people brought the sick into the streets and laid them on beds and mats so that at least Peter's shadow might fall on some of them as he passed by.[l] [16]Crowds gathered also from the towns around Jerusalem, bringing their sick and those tormented by evil[a] spirits, and all of them were healed.[m]

[17]Then the high priest and all his associates, who were members of the party[n] of the Sadducees,[o] were filled with jealousy. [18]They arrested the apostles and put them in the public jail.[p] [19]But during the night an angel[q] of the Lord opened the doors of the jail[r] and brought them out. [20]"Go, stand in the temple courts," he said, "and tell the people the full message of this new life."[s]

[21]At daybreak they entered the temple courts, as they had been told, and began to teach the people.

When the high priest and his associates[t] arrived, they called together the Sanhedrin[u]—the full assembly of the elders of Israel—and sent to the jail for the apostles. [22]But on arriving at the jail, the officers did not find them there. So they went back and reported, [23]"We found the jail securely locked, with the guards standing at the doors; but when we opened them, we found no one inside." [24]On hearing this report, the captain of the temple guard and the chief priests[v] were puzzled, wondering what would come of this.

[25]Then someone came and said, "Look! The men you put in jail are standing in the temple courts teaching the people." [26]At that,

---

[a] 16 Greek unclean

5:5
[a] ver 10
[b] ver 11

5:6
[c] Jn 19:40

5:8
[d] ver 2

5:9
[e] ver 3

5:10
[f] ver 5

5:11
[g] ver 5;
Ac 19:17

5:12
[h] Ac 2:43
[i] Ac 4:32
[j] Ac 3:11

5:13
[k] Ac 2:47;
4:21

5:15
[l] Ac 19:12

5:16
[m] Mk 16:17

5:17
[n] Ac 15:5
[o] Ac 4:1

5:18
[p] Ac 4:3

5:19
[q] Mt 1:20;
Lk 1:11;
Ac 8:26;
27:23
[r] Ac 16:26

5:20
[s] Jn 6:63,68

5:21
[t] Ac 4:5,6
[u] ver 27,34,41;
Mt 5:22

5:24
[v] Ac 4:1

5:26
a Ac 4:21

5:27
b Mt 5:22

5:28
c Ac 4:18
d Mt 23:35;
27:25;
Ac 2:23,36;
3:14,15; 7:52

5:29
e Ac 4:19

5:30
f Ac 3:13
g Ac 2:24
h Ac 10:39;
13:29;
Gal 3:13;
1Pe 2:24

5:31
i Ac 2:33
j Lk 2:11
k Mt 1:21;
Lk 24:47;
Ac 2:38

5:32
l Lk 24:48
m Jn 15:26

5:33
n Ac 2:37; 7:54

5:34
o Ac 22:3
p Lk 2:46

5:37
q Lk 2:1,2

5:38
r Mt 15:13

5:39
s Pr 21:30;
Ac 7:51; 11:17

5:40
t Mt 10:17

5:41
u Mt 5:12
v Jn 15:21

5:42
w Ac 2:46

6:1
x Ac 2:41
y Ac 9:29
z Ac 9:39,41

the captain went with his officers and brought the apostles. They did not use force, because they feared that the people*a* would stone them.

27Having brought the apostles, they made them appear before the Sanhedrin*b* to be questioned by the high priest. 28"We gave you strict orders not to teach in this name,"*c* he said. "Yet you have filled Jerusalem with your teaching and are determined to make us guilty of this man's blood."*d*

29Peter and the other apostles replied: "We must obey God rather than men!*e* 30The God of our fathers*f* raised Jesus from the dead*g*—whom you had killed by hanging him on a tree.*h* 31God exalted him to his own right hand*i* as Prince and Savior*j* that he might give repentance and forgiveness of sins to Israel.*k* 32We are witnesses of these things,*l* and so is the Holy Spirit,*m* whom God has given to those who obey him."

33When they heard this, they were furious*n* and wanted to put them to death. 34But a Pharisee named Gamaliel,*o* a teacher of the law,*p* who was honored by all the people, stood up in the Sanhedrin and ordered that the men be put outside for a little while. 35Then he addressed them: "Men of Israel, consider carefully what you intend to do to these men. 36Some time ago Theudas appeared, claiming to be somebody, and about four hundred men rallied to him. He was killed, all his followers were dispersed, and it all came to nothing. 37After him, Judas the Galilean appeared in the days of the census*q* and led a band of people in revolt. He too was killed, and all his followers were scattered. 38Therefore, in the present case I advise you: Leave these men alone! Let them go! For if their purpose or activity is of human origin, it will fail.*r* 39But if it is from God, you will not be able to stop these men; you will only find yourselves fighting against God."*s*

40His speech persuaded them. They called the apostles in and had them flogged.*t* Then they ordered them not to speak in the name of Jesus, and let them go.

41The apostles left the Sanhedrin, rejoicing*u* because they had been counted worthy of suffering disgrace for the Name.*v* 42Day after day, in the temple courts*w* and from house to house, they never stopped teaching and proclaiming the good news that Jesus is the Christ.*a*

Chapter 6 Theme _____

6 In those days when the number of disciples was increasing,*x* the Grecian Jews*y* among them complained against the Hebrew Jews because their widows*z* were being overlooked in the

a 42 Or *Messiah*

daily distribution of food.*a* ²So the Twelve gathered all the disciples together and said, "It would not be right for us to neglect the ministry of the word of God in order to wait on tables. ³Brothers,*b* choose seven men from among you who are known to be full of the Spirit and wisdom. We will turn this responsibility over to them ⁴and will give our attention to prayer*c* and the ministry of the word."

⁵This proposal pleased the whole group. They chose Stephen,*d* a man full of faith and of the Holy Spirit;*e* also Philip,*f* Procorus, Nicanor, Timon, Parmenas, and Nicolas from Antioch, a convert to Judaism. ⁶They presented these men to the apostles, who prayed*g* and laid their hands on them.*h*

⁷So the word of God spread.*i* The number of disciples in Jerusalem increased rapidly, and a large number of priests became obedient to the faith.

⁸Now Stephen, a man full of God's grace and power, did great wonders and miraculous signs*j* among the people. ⁹Opposition arose, however, from members of the Synagogue of the Freedmen (as it was called)—Jews of Cyrene*k* and Alexandria as well as the provinces of Cilicia*l* and Asia.*m* These men began to argue with Stephen, ¹⁰but they could not stand up against his wisdom or the Spirit by whom he spoke.*n*

¹¹Then they secretly*o* persuaded some men to say, "We have heard Stephen speak words of blasphemy against Moses and against God."*p*

¹²So they stirred up the people and the elders and the teachers of the law. They seized Stephen and brought him before the Sanhedrin.*q* ¹³They produced false witnesses, who testified, "This fellow never stops speaking against this holy place*r* and against the law. ¹⁴For we have heard him say that this Jesus of Nazareth will destroy this place and change the customs Moses handed down to us."*s*

¹⁵All who were sitting in the Sanhedrin*t* looked intently at Stephen, and they saw that his face was like the face of an angel.

Chapter 7 Theme

7 Then the high priest asked him, "Are these charges true?" ²To this he replied: "Brothers and fathers,*u* listen to me! The God of glory*v* appeared to our father Abraham while he was still in Mesopotamia, before he lived in Haran.*w* ³'Leave your country and your people,' God said, 'and go to the land I will show you.'ᵃ*x*

⁴"So he left the land of the Chaldeans and settled in Haran. After the death of his father, God sent him to this land where you

---

ᵃ3 Gen. 12:1

6:1
a Ac 4:35

6:3
b Ac 1:16

6:4
c Ac 1:14

6:5
d ver 8;
Ac 11:19
e Ac 11:24
f Ac 8:5-40;
21:8

6:6
g Ac 1:24;
8:17; 13:3;
2Ti 1:6
h Nu 8:10;
Ac 9:17;
1Ti 4:14

6:7
i Ac 12:24;
19:20

6:8
j Jn 4:48

6:9
k Mt 27:32
l Ac 15:23,41;
22:3;
23:34
m Ac 2:9

6:10
n Lk 21:15

6:11
o 1Ki 21:10
p Mt 26:59-61

6:12
q Mt 5:22

6:13
r Ac 21:28

6:14
s Ac 15:1;
21:21;
26:3;
28:17

6:15
t Mt 5:22

7:2
u Ac 22:1
v Ps 29:3
w Ge 11:31;
15:7

7:3
x Ge 12:1

7:4
a Ge 12:5

7:5
b Ge 12:7;
17:8; 26:3

7:6
c Ex 12:40

7:7
d Ex 3:12

7:8
e Ge 17:9-14
f Ge 21:2-4
g Ge 25:26
h Ge 29:31-35;
30:5-13,
17-24;
35:16-18,
22-26

7:9
i Ge 37:4,11
j Ge 37:28;
Ps 105:17
k Ge 39:2,21,23

7:10
l Ge 41:37-43

7:11
m Ge 41:54

7:12
n Ge 42:1,2

7:13
o Ge 45:1-4

7:14
p Ge 45:9,10
q Ge 46:26,27;
Ex 1:5;
Dt 10:22

7:15
r Ge 46:5-7;
49:33;
Ex 1:6

7:16
s Ge 23:16-20;
33:18,19; 50:13;
Jos 24:32

7:17
t Ex 1:7;
Ps 105:24

7:18
u Ex 1:8

7:19
v Ex 1:10-22

7:20
w Ex 2:2;
Heb 11:23

7:21
x Ex 2:3-10

7:22
y 1Ki 4:30;
Isa 19:11

are now living.*ᵃ* ⁵He gave him no inheritance here, not even a foot of ground. But God promised him that he and his descendants after him would possess the land,*ᵇ* even though at that time Abraham had no child. ⁶God spoke to him in this way: 'Your descendants will be strangers in a country not their own, and they will be enslaved and mistreated four hundred years.*ᶜ* ⁷But I will punish the nation they serve as slaves,' God said, 'and afterward they will come out of that country and worship me in this place.'*ᵃᵈ* ⁸Then he gave Abraham the covenant of circumcision.*ᵉ* And Abraham became the father of Isaac and circumcised him eight days after his birth.*ᶠ* Later Isaac became the father of Jacob,*ᵍ* and Jacob became the father of the twelve patriarchs.*ʰ*

⁹"Because the patriarchs were jealous of Joseph,*ⁱ* they sold him as a slave into Egypt.*ʲ* But God was with him*ᵏ* ¹⁰and rescued him from all his troubles. He gave Joseph wisdom and enabled him to gain the goodwill of Pharaoh king of Egypt; so he made him ruler over Egypt and all his palace.*ˡ*

¹¹"Then a famine struck all Egypt and Canaan, bringing great suffering, and our fathers could not find food.*ᵐ* ¹²When Jacob heard that there was grain in Egypt, he sent our fathers on their first visit.*ⁿ* ¹³On their second visit, Joseph told his brothers who he was,*ᵒ* and Pharaoh learned about Joseph's family. ¹⁴After this, Joseph sent for his father Jacob and his whole family,*ᵖ* seventy-five in all.*�q* ¹⁵Then Jacob went down to Egypt, where he and our fathers died.*ʳ* ¹⁶Their bodies were brought back to Shechem and placed in the tomb that Abraham had bought from the sons of Hamor at Shechem for a certain sum of money.*ˢ*

¹⁷"As the time drew near for God to fulfill his promise to Abraham, the number of our people in Egypt greatly increased.*ᵗ* ¹⁸Then another king, who knew nothing about Joseph, became ruler of Egypt.*ᵘ* ¹⁹He dealt treacherously with our people and oppressed our forefathers by forcing them to throw out their newborn babies so that they would die.*ᵛ*

²⁰"At that time Moses was born, and he was no ordinary child.*ᵇ* For three months he was cared for in his father's house.*ʷ* ²¹When he was placed outside, Pharaoh's daughter took him and brought him up as her own son.*ˣ* ²²Moses was educated in all the wisdom of the Egyptians*ʸ* and was powerful in speech and action.

²³"When Moses was forty years old, he decided to visit his fellow Israelites. ²⁴He saw one of them being mistreated by an Egyptian, so he went to his defense and avenged him by killing the Egyptian. ²⁵Moses thought that his own people would realize that God was using him to rescue them, but they did not. ²⁶The next day

a 7 Gen. 15:13,14   *b* 20 Or *was fair in the sight of God*

Moses came upon two Israelites who were fighting. He tried to reconcile them by saying, 'Men, you are brothers; why do you want to hurt each other?'

²⁷"But the man who was mistreating the other pushed Moses aside and said, 'Who made you ruler and judge over us? ²⁸Do you want to kill me as you killed the Egyptian yesterday?'ᵃ ²⁹When Moses heard this, he fled to Midian, where he settled as a foreigner and had two sons.ᵃ

³⁰"After forty years had passed, an angel appeared to Moses in the flames of a burning bush in the desert near Mount Sinai. ³¹When he saw this, he was amazed at the sight. As he went over to look more closely, he heard the Lord's voice:ᵇ ³²'I am the God of your fathers, the God of Abraham, Isaac and Jacob.'ᵇ Moses trembled with fear and did not dare to look.ᶜ

³³"Then the Lord said to him, 'Take off your sandals; the place where you are standing is holy ground.ᵈ ³⁴I have indeed seen the oppression of my people in Egypt. I have heard their groaning and have come down to set them free. Now come, I will send you back to Egypt.'ᶜ ᵉ

³⁵"This is the same Moses whom they had rejected with the words, 'Who made you ruler and judge?'ᶠ He was sent to be their ruler and deliverer by God himself, through the angel who appeared to him in the bush. ³⁶He led them out of Egyptᵍ and did wonders and miraculous signs in Egypt, at the Red Seaᵈ ʰ and for forty years in the desert.

³⁷"This is that Moses who told the Israelites, 'God will send you a prophet like me from your own people.'ᵉ ⁱ ³⁸He was in the assembly in the desert, with the angelʲ who spoke to him on Mount Sinai, and with our fathers;ᵏ and he received living wordsˡ to pass on to us.ᵐ

³⁹"But our fathers refused to obey him. Instead, they rejected him and in their hearts turned back to Egypt.ⁿ ⁴⁰They told Aaron, 'Make us gods who will go before us. As for this fellow Moses who led us out of Egypt—we don't know what has happened to him!'ᶠ ᵒ ⁴¹That was the time they made an idol in the form of a calf. They brought sacrifices to it and held a celebration in honor of what their hands had made.ᵖ ⁴²But God turned away�q and gave them over to the worship of the heavenly bodies.ʳ This agrees with what is written in the book of the prophets:

> "'Did you bring me sacrifices and offerings
> forty years in the desert, O house of Israel?

ᵃ28 Exodus 2:14   ᵇ32 Exodus 3:6   ᶜ34 Exodus 3:5,7,8,10   ᵈ36 That is, Sea of Reeds
ᵉ37 Deut. 18:15   ᶠ40 Exodus 32:1

7:29
ᵃ Ex 2:11-15

7:31
ᵇ Ex 3:1-4

7:32
ᶜ Ex 3:6

7:33
ᵈ Ex 3:5;
Jos 5:15

7:34
ᵉ Ex 3:7-10

7:35
ᶠ ver 27

7:36
ᵍ Ex 12:41; 33:1
ʰ Ex 14:21

7:37
ⁱ Dt 18:15,18;
Ac 3:22

7:38
ʲ ver 53
ᵏ Ex 19:17
ˡ Dt 32:45-47;
Heb 4:12
ᵐ Ro 3:2

7:39
ⁿ Nu 14:3,4

7:40
ᵒ Ex 32:1,23

7:41
ᵖ Ex 32:4-6;
Ps 106:19,20;
Rev 9:20

7:42
q Jos 24:20;
Isa 63:10
ʳ Jer 19:13

7:43
a Am 5:25-27

7:44
b Ex 38:21
c Ex 25:8,9,40

7:45
d Jos 3:14-17;
18:1; 23:9;
24:18;
Ps 44:2

7:46
e 2Sa 7:8-16;
Ps 132:1-5

7:48
f 1Ki 8:27;
2Ch 2:6

7:49
g Mt 5:34,35

7:50
h Isa 66:1,2

7:51
i Ex 32:9;
33:3,5
j Lev 26:41;
Dt 10:16;
Jer 4:4; 9:26

7:52
k 2Ch 36:16;
Mt 5:12
l Ac 3:14;
1Th 2:15

7:53
m ver 38;
Gal 3:19;
Heb 2:2

7:54
n Ac 5:33

7:55
o Mk 16:19

7:56
p Mt 3:16
q Mt 8:20

7:58
r Lk 4:29
s Lev 24:14,16;
Dt 13:9
t Ac 22:20
u Ac 8:1

7:59
v Ps 31:5;
Lk 23:46

7:60
w Ac 9:40
x Mt 5:44

⁴³You have lifted up the shrine of Molech
　　and the star of your god Rephan,
　　　the idols you made to worship.
Therefore I will send you into exile'ᵃ ᵃ beyond Babylon.

⁴⁴"Our forefathers had the tabernacle of the Testimonyᵇ with them in the desert. It had been made as God directed Moses, according to the pattern he had seen.ᶜ ⁴⁵Having received the tabernacle, our fathers under Joshua brought it with them when they took the land from the nations God drove out before them.ᵈ It remained in the land until the time of David, ⁴⁶who enjoyed God's favor and asked that he might provide a dwelling place for the God of Jacob.ᵇᵉ ⁴⁷But it was Solomon who built the house for him.

⁴⁸"However, the Most High does not live in houses made by men.ᶠ As the prophet says:

⁴⁹"'Heaven is my throne,
　　and the earth is my footstool.ᵍ
　What kind of house will you build for me?
　　　　　　　　　　　　says the Lord.
　　Or where will my resting place be?
⁵⁰Has not my hand made all these things?'ᶜ ʰ

⁵¹"You stiff-necked people,ⁱ with uncircumcised heartsʲ and ears! You are just like your fathers: You always resist the Holy Spirit! ⁵²Was there ever a prophet your fathers did not persecute?ᵏ They even killed those who predicted the coming of the Righteous One. And now you have betrayed and murdered himˡ— ⁵³you who have received the law that was put into effect through angelsᵐ but have not obeyed it."

⁵⁴When they heard this, they were furiousⁿ and gnashed their teeth at him. ⁵⁵But Stephen, full of the Holy Spirit, looked up to heaven and saw the glory of God, and Jesus standing at the right hand of God.ᵒ ⁵⁶"Look," he said, "I see heaven openᵖ and the Son of Man�q standing at the right hand of God."

⁵⁷At this they covered their ears and, yelling at the top of their voices, they all rushed at him, ⁵⁸dragged him out of the cityʳ and began to stone him.ˢ Meanwhile, the witnesses laid their clothesᵗ at the feet of a young man named Saul.ᵘ

⁵⁹While they were stoning him, Stephen prayed, "Lord Jesus, receive my spirit."ᵛ ⁶⁰Then he fell on his kneesʷ and cried out, "Lord, do not hold this sin against them."ˣ When he had said this, he fell asleep.

ᵃ43 Amos 5:25-27　ᵇ46 Some early manuscripts *the house of Jacob*　ᶜ50 Isaiah 66:1,2

Chapter 8 Theme _____

8 And Saul*ᵃ* was there, giving approval to his death.

On that day a great persecution broke out against the church at Jerusalem, and all except the apostles were scattered*ᵇ* throughout Judea and Samaria.*ᶜ* ²Godly men buried Stephen and mourned deeply for him. ³But Saul*ᵈ* began to destroy the church.*ᵉ* Going from house to house, he dragged off men and women and put them in prison.

⁴Those who had been scattered*ᶠ* preached the word wherever they went.*ᵍ* ⁵Philip*ʰ* went down to a city in Samaria and proclaimed the Christ*ᵃ* there. ⁶When the crowds heard Philip and saw the miraculous signs he did, they all paid close attention to what he said. ⁷With shrieks, evil*ᵇ* spirits came out of many,*ⁱ* and many paralytics and cripples were healed.*ʲ* ⁸So there was great joy in that city.

⁹Now for some time a man named Simon had practiced sorcery*ᵏ* in the city and amazed all the people of Samaria. He boasted that he was someone great,*ˡ* ¹⁰and all the people, both high and low, gave him their attention and exclaimed, "This man is the divine power known as the Great Power."*ᵐ* ¹¹They followed him because he had amazed them for a long time with his magic. ¹²But when they believed Philip as he preached the good news of the kingdom of God*ⁿ* and the name of Jesus Christ, they were baptized,*ᵒ* both men and women. ¹³Simon himself believed and was baptized. And he followed Philip everywhere, astonished by the great signs and miracles*ᵖ* he saw.

¹⁴When the apostles in Jerusalem heard that Samaria*�q* had accepted the word of God, they sent Peter and John*ʳ* to them. ¹⁵When they arrived, they prayed for them that they might receive the Holy Spirit,*ˢ* ¹⁶because the Holy Spirit had not yet come upon any of them;*ᵗ* they had simply been baptized into*ᶜ* the name of the Lord Jesus.*ᵘ* ¹⁷Then Peter and John placed their hands on them,*ᵛ* and they received the Holy Spirit.

¹⁸When Simon saw that the Spirit was given at the laying on of the apostles' hands, he offered them money ¹⁹and said, "Give me also this ability so that everyone on whom I lay my hands may receive the Holy Spirit."

²⁰Peter answered: "May your money perish with you, because you thought you could buy the gift of God with money!*ʷ* ²¹You have no part or share in this ministry, because your heart is not right*ˣ* before God. ²²Repent of this wickedness and pray to the Lord. Perhaps he will forgive you for having such a thought

---

ᵃ5 Or *Messiah*   *ᵇ7* Greek *unclean*   *ᶜ16* Or *in*

8:1
ᵃ Ac 7:58
ᵇ Ac 11:19
ᶜ Ac 9:31

8:3
ᵈ Ac 7:58
ᵉ Ac 22:4,19;
26:10,11;
1Co 15:9;
Gal 1:13,23;
Php 3:6;
1Ti 1:13

8:4
ᶠ ver 1
ᵍ Ac 15:35

8:5
ʰ Ac 6:5

8:7
ⁱ Mk 16:17
ʲ Mt 4:24

8:9
ᵏ Ac 13:6
ˡ Ac 5:36

8:10
ᵐ Ac 14:11;
28:6

8:12
ⁿ Ac 1:3
ᵒ Ac 2:38

8:13
ᵖ ver 6;
Ac 19:11

8:14
q ver 1
ʳ Lk 22:8

8:15
ˢ Ac 2:38

8:16
ᵗ Ac 19:2
ᵘ Mt 28:19;
Ac 2:38

8:17
ᵛ Ac 6:6

8:20
ʷ 2Ki 5:16;
Da 5:17;
Mt 10:8;
Ac 2:38

8:21
ˣ Ps 78:37

8:24
a Ex 8:8;
Nu 21:7;
1Ki 13:6

8:25
b ver 40

8:26
c Ac 5:19

8:27
d Ps 68:31;
87:4;
Zep 3:10
e Isa 56:3-5
f 1Ki 8:41-43;
Jn 12:20

8:29
g Ac 10:19;
11:12; 13:2;
20:23; 21:11

8:33
h Isa 53:7,8

8:35
i Mt 5:2
j Lk 24:27;
Ac 17:2;
18:28;
28:23

8:36
k Ac 10:47

8:39
l 1Ki 18:12;
2Ki 2:16;
Eze 3:12,14;
8:3; 11:1,24;
43:5;
2Co 12:2

8:40
m ver 25
n Ac 10:1,24;
12:19;
21:8,16;
23:23,33;
25:1,4,6,13

in your heart. [23]For I see that you are full of bitterness and captive to sin."

[24]Then Simon answered, "Pray to the Lord for me[a] so that nothing you have said may happen to me."

[25]When they had testified and proclaimed the word of the Lord, Peter and John returned to Jerusalem, preaching the gospel in many Samaritan villages.[b]

[26]Now an angel[c] of the Lord said to Philip, "Go south to the road—the desert road—that goes down from Jerusalem to Gaza." [27]So he started out, and on his way he met an Ethiopian[a][d] eunuch,[e] an important official in charge of all the treasury of Candace, queen of the Ethiopians. This man had gone to Jerusalem to worship,[f] [28]and on his way home was sitting in his chariot reading the book of Isaiah the prophet. [29]The Spirit told[g] Philip, "Go to that chariot and stay near it."

[30]Then Philip ran up to the chariot and heard the man reading Isaiah the prophet. "Do you understand what you are reading?" Philip asked.

[31]"How can I," he said, "unless someone explains it to me?" So he invited Philip to come up and sit with him.

[32]The eunuch was reading this passage of Scripture:

> "He was led like a sheep to the slaughter,
>   and as a lamb before the shearer is silent,
>   so he did not open his mouth.
> [33]In his humiliation he was deprived of justice.
>   Who can speak of his descendants?
>   For his life was taken from the earth."[b][h]

[34]The eunuch asked Philip, "Tell me, please, who is the prophet talking about, himself or someone else?" [35]Then Philip began[i] with that very passage of Scripture[j] and told him the good news about Jesus.

[36]As they traveled along the road, they came to some water and the eunuch said, "Look, here is water. Why shouldn't I be baptized?"[c][k] [38]And he gave orders to stop the chariot. Then both Philip and the eunuch went down into the water and Philip baptized him. [39]When they came up out of the water, the Spirit of the Lord suddenly took Philip away,[l] and the eunuch did not see him again, but went on his way rejoicing. [40]Philip, however, appeared at Azotus and traveled about, preaching the gospel in all the towns[m] until he reached Caesarea.[n]

INSIGHT

See the "Insight" about the **Samaritans** on page 1824.

a 27 That is, from the upper Nile region   *b 33* Isaiah 53:7,8   *c 36* Some late manuscripts *baptized?" 37Philip said, "If you believe with all your heart, you may." The eunuch answered, "I believe that Jesus Christ is the Son of God."*

1883

Sequence of Events in Paul's Life after His Conversion*

*There are differing opinions on these dates. For continuity's sake this chart will be the basis for dates pertaining to Paul's life.

Year A.D.	Event
33-34	Conversion, time in Damascus
35-47	Some silent years, except we know that Paul:
	1. Spent time in Arabia and Damascus
	2. Made first visit to Jerusalem
	3. Went to Tarsus, Syria-Cilicia area
	4. Was with Barnabas in Antioch
	5. With Barnabas took relief to brethren in Judea—Paul's second visit to Jerusalem
	6. Returned to Antioch; was sent out with Barnabas by church at Antioch
47-48	**First missionary journey:** *Galatians written(?)*
49	Apostolic Council at Jerusalem—Paul visits Jerusalem (compare Acts 15 with Galatians 2:1)
49-51	**Second missionary journey:** *1 and 2 Thessalonians written*
52-56	**Third missionary journey:** *1 and 2 Corinthians and Romans written*
56	Paul goes to Jerusalem and is arrested; held at Caesarea
57-59	Appearance before Felix and Drusilla; before Festus; before Agrippa
59-60	Appeals to Caesar, sent from Caesarea to Rome
60-62	First Roman imprisonment: *Ephesians, Philemon, Colossians, and Philippians written*
62	Paul's release; possible trip to Spain
62	Paul in Macedonia: *1 Timothy written*
62	Paul goes to Crete: *Titus written*
63-64	Paul taken to Rome and imprisoned: *2 Timothy written*
64	Paul is absent from the body and present with the Lord
	(Others put Paul's conversion about A.D. 35, his death in A.D. 68.)

Chapter 9 Theme

9 Meanwhile, Saul was still breathing out murderous threats against the Lord's disciples.[a] He went to the high priest [2]and asked him for letters to the synagogues in Damascus, so that if he found any there who belonged to the Way,[b] whether men or women, he might take them as prisoners to Jerusalem. [3]As he neared Damascus on his journey, suddenly a light from heaven flashed around him.[c] [4]He fell to the ground and heard a voice say to him, "Saul, Saul, why do you persecute me?"

[5]"Who are you, Lord?" Saul asked.

"I am Jesus, whom you are persecuting," he replied. [6]"Now get up and go into the city, and you will be told what you must do."[d]

[7]The men traveling with Saul stood there speechless; they heard the sound[e] but did not see anyone.[f] [8]Saul got up from the ground, but when he opened his eyes he could see nothing. So they led him by the hand into Damascus. [9]For three days he was blind, and did not eat or drink anything.

[10]In Damascus there was a disciple named Ananias. The Lord called to him in a vision,[g] "Ananias!"

"Yes, Lord," he answered.

[11]The Lord told him, "Go to the house of Judas on Straight Street and ask for a man from Tarsus[h] named Saul, for he is praying. [12]In a vision he has seen a man named Ananias come and place his hands on[i] him to restore his sight."

9:1
[a] Ac 8:3

9:2
[b] Ac 19:9,23; 22:4; 24:14,22

9:3
[c] 1Co 15:8

9:6
[d] ver 16

9:7
[e] Jn 12:29
[f] Da 10:7; Ac 22:9

9:10
[g] Ac 10:3,17,19

9:11
[h] ver 30; Ac 21:39; 22:3

9:12
[i] Mk 5:23

9:13
ᵃ ver 32;
Ro 1:7;
16:2,15
ᵇ Ac 8:3

9:14
ᶜ ver 2,21

9:15
ᵈ Ac 13:2;
Ro 1:1;
Gal 1:15
ᵉ Ro 11:13;
15:15,16;
Gal 2:7,8;
Eph 3:7,8
ᶠ Ac 25:22,23;
26:1

9:16
ᵍ Ac 20:23;
21:11;
2Co 11:23-27

9:17
ʰ Ac 6:6

9:19
ⁱ Ac 11:26
ʲ Ac 26:20

9:20
ᵏ Ac 13:5,14
ˡ Mt 4:3

9:21
ᵐ Ac 8:3
ⁿ Gal 1:13,23

9:22
ᵒ Ac 18:5,28

9:24
ᵖ Ac 20:3,19

9:25
�q 1Sa 19:12;
2Co 11:32,33

9:26
ʳ Ac 22:17;
26:20;
Gal 1:17,18

9:27
ˢ Ac 4:36
ᵗ ver 3-6
ᵘ ver 20,22

9:29
ᵛ Ac 6:1
ʷ 2Co 11:26

9:30
ˣ Ac 1:16
ʸ Ac 8:40
ᶻ ver 11

9:31
ᵃ Ac 8:1

9:32
ᵇ ver 13

¹³"Lord," Ananias answered, "I have heard many reports about this man and all the harm he has done to your saints[a] in Jerusalem.[b] ¹⁴And he has come here with authority from the chief priests[c] to arrest all who call on your name."

¹⁵But the Lord said to Ananias, "Go! This man is my chosen instrument[d] to carry my name before the Gentiles[e] and their kings[f] and before the people of Israel. ¹⁶I will show him how much he must suffer for my name."[g]

¹⁷Then Ananias went to the house and entered it. Placing his hands on[h] Saul, he said, "Brother Saul, the Lord—Jesus, who appeared to you on the road as you were coming here—has sent me so that you may see again and be filled with the Holy Spirit." ¹⁸Immediately, something like scales fell from Saul's eyes, and he could see again. He got up and was baptized, ¹⁹and after taking some food, he regained his strength.

Saul spent several days with the disciples[i] in Damascus.[j] ²⁰At once he began to preach in the synagogues[k] that Jesus is the Son of God.[l] ²¹All those who heard him were astonished and asked, "Isn't he the man who raised havoc in Jerusalem among those who call on this name?[m] And hasn't he come here to take them as prisoners to the chief priests?"[n] ²²Yet Saul grew more and more powerful and baffled the Jews living in Damascus by proving that Jesus is the Christ.[a][o]

²³After many days had gone by, the Jews conspired to kill him, ²⁴but Saul learned of their plan.[p] Day and night they kept close watch on the city gates in order to kill him. ²⁵But his followers took him by night and lowered him in a basket through an opening in the wall.[q]

²⁶When he came to Jerusalem,[r] he tried to join the disciples, but they were all afraid of him, not believing that he really was a disciple. ²⁷But Barnabas[s] took him and brought him to the apostles. He told them how Saul on his journey had seen the Lord and that the Lord had spoken to him,[t] and how in Damascus he had preached fearlessly in the name of Jesus.[u] ²⁸So Saul stayed with them and moved about freely in Jerusalem, speaking boldly in the name of the Lord. ²⁹He talked and debated with the Grecian Jews,[v] but they tried to kill him.[w] ³⁰When the brothers[x] learned of this, they took him down to Caesarea[y] and sent him off to Tarsus.[z]

³¹Then the church throughout Judea, Galilee and Samaria[a] enjoyed a time of peace. It was strengthened; and encouraged by the Holy Spirit, it grew in numbers, living in the fear of the Lord.

³²As Peter traveled about the country, he went to visit the saints[b] in Lydda. ³³There he found a man named Aeneas, a paralytic who had been bedridden for eight years. ³⁴"Aeneas," Peter said to him,

ᵃ 22 Or *Messiah*

"Jesus Christ heals you.*a* Get up and take care of your mat." Immediately Aeneas got up. ³⁵All those who lived in Lydda and Sharon*b* saw him and turned to the Lord.*c*

³⁶In Joppa*d* there was a disciple named Tabitha (which, when translated, is Dorcas*a*), who was always doing good*e* and helping the poor. ³⁷About that time she became sick and died, and her body was washed and placed in an upstairs room.*f* ³⁸Lydda was near Joppa; so when the disciples*g* heard that Peter was in Lydda, they sent two men to him and urged him, "Please come at once!"

³⁹Peter went with them, and when he arrived he was taken upstairs to the room. All the widows*h* stood around him, crying and showing him the robes and other clothing that Dorcas had made while she was still with them.

⁴⁰Peter sent them all out of the room;*i* then he got down on his knees*j* and prayed. Turning toward the dead woman, he said, "Tabitha, get up." She opened her eyes, and seeing Peter she sat up. ⁴¹He took her by the hand and helped her to her feet. Then he called the believers and the widows and presented her to them alive. ⁴²This became known all over Joppa, and many people believed in the Lord. ⁴³Peter stayed in Joppa for some time with a tanner named Simon.*k*

Chapter 10 Theme

10 At Caesarea*l* there was a man named Cornelius, a centurion in what was known as the Italian Regiment. ²He and all his family were devout and God-fearing;*m* he gave generously to those in need and prayed to God regularly. ³One day at about three in the afternoon*n* he had a vision.*o* He distinctly saw an angel*p* of God, who came to him and said, "Cornelius!"

⁴Cornelius stared at him in fear. "What is it, Lord?" he asked.

The angel answered, "Your prayers and gifts to the poor have come up as a memorial offering*q* before God.*r* ⁵Now send men to Joppa*s* to bring back a man named Simon who is called Peter. ⁶He is staying with Simon the tanner,*t* whose house is by the sea."

⁷When the angel who spoke to him had gone, Cornelius called two of his servants and a devout soldier who was one of his attendants. ⁸He told them everything that had happened and sent them to Joppa.*u*

⁹About noon the following day as they were on their journey and approaching the city, Peter went up on the roof*v* to pray. ¹⁰He became hungry and wanted something to eat, and while the meal was being prepared, he fell into a trance.*w* ¹¹He saw heaven opened and something like a large sheet being let down to earth by its four

---

a 36 Both *Tabitha* (Aramaic) and *Dorcas* (Greek) mean *gazelle.*

9:34
a Ac 3:6,16; 4:10

9:35
b 1Ch 5:16;
27:29;
Isa 33:9; 35:2;
65:10
c Ac 11:21

9:36
d Jos 19:46;
2Ch 2:16;
Ezr 3:7;
Jnh 1:3;
Ac 10:5
e 1Ti 2:10;
Tit 3:8

9:37
f Ac 1:13

9:38
g Ac 11:26

9:39
h Ac 6:1

9:40
i Mt 9:25
j Lk 22:41;
Ac 7:60

9:43
k Ac 10:6

10:1
l Ac 8:40

10:2
m ver 22,35;
Ac 13:16,26

10:3
n Ac 3:1
o Ac 9:10
p Ac 5:19

10:4
q Mt 26:13
r Rev 8:4

10:5
s Ac 9:36

10:6
t Ac 9:43

10:8
u Ac 9:36

10:9
v Mt 24:17

10:10
w Ac 22:17

10:14
a Ac 9:5
b Lev 11:4-8,
13-20; 20:25;
Dt 14:3-20;
Eze 4:14

10:15
c Mt 15:11;
Ro 14:14,17,20;
1Co 10:25;
1Ti 4:3,4;
Tit 1:15

10:17
d ver 7,8

10:19
e Ac 8:29

10:20
f Ac 15:7-9

10:22
g ver 2
h Ac 11:14

10:23
i Ac 1:16
j ver 45;
Ac 11:12

10:24
k Ac 8:40

10:26
l Ac 14:15;
Rev 19:10

10:28
m Jn 4:9; 18:28;
Ac 11:3
n Ac 15:8,9

corners. ¹²It contained all kinds of four-footed animals, as well as reptiles of the earth and birds of the air. ¹³Then a voice told him, "Get up, Peter. Kill and eat."

¹⁴"Surely not, Lord!"ᵃ Peter replied. "I have never eaten anything impure or unclean."ᵇ

¹⁵The voice spoke to him a second time, "Do not call anything impure that God has made clean."ᶜ

¹⁶This happened three times, and immediately the sheet was taken back to heaven.

¹⁷While Peter was wondering about the meaning of the vision, the men sent by Corneliusᵈ found out where Simon's house was and stopped at the gate. ¹⁸They called out, asking if Simon who was known as Peter was staying there.

¹⁹While Peter was still thinking about the vision, the Spirit saidᵉ to him, "Simon, threeᵃ men are looking for you. ²⁰So get up and go downstairs. Do not hesitate to go with them, for I have sent them."ᶠ

²¹Peter went down and said to the men, "I'm the one you're looking for. Why have you come?"

²²The men replied, "We have come from Cornelius the centurion. He is a righteous and God-fearing man,ᵍ who is respected by all the Jewish people. A holy angel told him to have you come to his house so that he could hear what you have to say."ʰ ²³Then Peter invited the men into the house to be his guests.

The next day Peter started out with them, and some of the brothersⁱ from Joppa went along.ʲ ²⁴The following day he arrived in Caesarea.ᵏ Cornelius was expecting them and had called together his relatives and close friends. ²⁵As Peter entered the house, Cornelius met him and fell at his feet in reverence. ²⁶But Peter made him get up. "Stand up," he said, "I am only a man myself."ˡ

²⁷Talking with him, Peter went inside and found a large gathering of people. ²⁸He said to them: "You are well aware that it is against our law for a Jew to associate with a Gentile or visit him.ᵐ But God has shown me that I should not call any man impure or unclean.ⁿ ²⁹So when I was sent for, I came without raising any objection. May I ask why you sent for me?"

³⁰Cornelius answered: "Four days ago I was in my house praying at this hour, at three in the afternoon. Suddenly a man in shining clothes stood before me ³¹and said, 'Cornelius, God has heard your prayer and remembered your gifts to the poor. ³²Send to Joppa for Simon who is called Peter. He is a guest in the home of Simon the tanner, who lives by the sea.' ³³So I sent for you immediately, and it was good of you to come. Now we are all here in the presence of God to listen to everything the Lord has commanded you to tell us."

a 19 One early manuscript *two*; other manuscripts do not have the number.

34Then Peter began to speak: "I now realize how true it is that God does not show favoritism*a* **35**but accepts men from every nation who fear him and do what is right.*b* **36**You know the message God sent to the people of Israel, telling the good news*c* of peace*d* through Jesus Christ, who is Lord of all.*e* **37**You know what has happened throughout Judea, beginning in Galilee after the baptism that John preached— **38**how God anointed*f* Jesus of Nazareth with the Holy Spirit and power, and how he went around doing good and healing*g* all who were under the power of the devil, because God was with him.*h*

39"We are witnesses*i* of everything he did in the country of the Jews and in Jerusalem. They killed him by hanging him on a tree,*j* **40**but God raised him from the dead*k* on the third day and caused him to be seen. **41**He was not seen by all the people,*l* but by witnesses whom God had already chosen—by us who ate*m* and drank with him after he rose from the dead. **42**He commanded us to preach to the people*n* and to testify that he is the one whom God appointed as judge of the living and the dead.*o* **43**All the prophets testify about him*p* that everyone*q* who believes in him receives forgiveness of sins through his name."

44While Peter was still speaking these words, the Holy Spirit came on*r* all who heard the message. **45**The circumcised believers who had come with Peter*s* were astonished that the gift of the Holy Spirit had been poured out*t* even on the Gentiles.*u* **46**For they heard them speaking in tongues*a v* and praising God.

Then Peter said, **47**"Can anyone keep these people from being baptized with water?*w* They have received the Holy Spirit just as we have."*x* **48**So he ordered that they be baptized in the name of Jesus Christ.*y* Then they asked Peter to stay with them for a few days.

Chapter 11 Theme

11 The apostles and the brothers*z* throughout Judea heard that the Gentiles also had received the word of God. **2**So when Peter went up to Jerusalem, the circumcised believers*a* criticized him **3**and said, "You went into the house of uncircumcised men and ate with them."*b*

4Peter began and explained everything to them precisely as it had happened: **5**"I was in the city of Joppa praying, and in a trance I saw a vision.*c* I saw something like a large sheet being let down from heaven by its four corners, and it came down to where I was. **6**I looked into it and saw four-footed animals of the earth, wild beasts, reptiles, and birds of the air. **7**Then I heard a voice telling me, 'Get up, Peter. Kill and eat.'

a 46 Or *other languages*

10:34
a Dt 10:17;
2Ch 19:7;
Job 34:19;
Ro 2:11;
Gal 2:6;
Eph 6:9;
Col 3:25;
1Pe 1:17

10:35
b Ac 15:9

10:36
c Ac 13:32
d Lk 2:14
e Mt 28:18;
Ro 10:12

10:38
f Ac 4:26
g Mt 4:23
h Jn 3:2

10:39
i Lk 24:48
j Ac 5:30

10:40
k Ac 2:24

10:41
l Jn 14:17,22
m Lk 24:43;
Jn 21:13

10:42
n Mt 28:19,20
o Jn 5:22;
Ac 17:31;
Ro 14:9;
2Co 5:10;
2Ti 4:1;
1Pe 4:5

10:43
p Isa 53:11
q Ac 15:9

10:44
r Ac 8:15,16;
11:15; 15:8

10:45
s ver 23
t Ac 2:33,38
u Ac 11:18

10:46
v Mk 16:17

10:47
w Ac 8:36
x Ac 11:17

10:48
y Ac 2:38;
8:16

11:1
z Ac 1:16

11:2
a Ac 10:45

11:3
b Ac 10:25,28;
Gal 2:12

11:5
c Ac 10:9-32;
9:10

11:9
a Ac 10:15

11:12
b Ac 8:29
c Ac 15:9;
Ro 3:22

11:14
d Jn 4:53;
Ac 16:15,31-34;
1Co 1:11,16

11:15
e Ac 10:44
f Ac 2:4

11:16
g Mk 1:8;
Ac 1:5

11:17
h Ac 10:45,47

11:18
i Ro 10:12,13;
2Co 7:10

11:19
j Ac 8:1,4
k ver 26,27;
Ac 13:1;
18:22;
Gal 2:11

11:20
l Ac 4:36
m Mt 27:32

11:21
n Lk 1:66
o Ac 2:47

11:22
p Ac 4:36

11:23
q Ac 13:43;
14:26; 20:24
11:23
r Ac 14:22

11:24
s ver 21;
Ac 5:14

11:25
t Ac 9:11

11:26
u Ac 6:1,2;
13:52
v Ac 26:28;
1Pe 4:16

11:27
w Ac 13:1;
15:32;
1Co 12:28,29;
Eph 4:11

11:28
x Ac 21:10
y Mt 24:14
z Ac 18:2

11:29
a ver 26

8"I replied, 'Surely not, Lord! Nothing impure or unclean has ever entered my mouth.'

9"The voice spoke from heaven a second time, 'Do not call anything impure that God has made clean.'a 10This happened three times, and then it was all pulled up to heaven again.

11"Right then three men who had been sent to me from Caesarea stopped at the house where I was staying. 12The Spirit toldb me to have no hesitation about going with them.c These six brothers also went with me, and we entered the man's house. 13He told us how he had seen an angel appear in his house and say, 'Send to Joppa for Simon who is called Peter. 14He will bring you a message through which you and all your householdd will be saved.'

15"As I began to speak, the Holy Spirit came one them as he had come on us at the beginning.f 16Then I remembered what the Lord had said: 'John baptized witha water, but you will be baptized with the Holy Spirit.'g 17So if God gave them the same gift as he gave us,h who believed in the Lord Jesus Christ, who was I to think that I could oppose God?"

18When they heard this, they had no further objections and praised God, saying, "So then, God has granted even the Gentiles repentance unto life."i

19Now those who had been scattered by the persecution in connection with Stephenj traveled as far as Phoenicia, Cyprus and Antioch,k telling the message only to Jews. 20Some of them, however, men from Cyprusl and Cyrene,m went to Antioch and began to speak to Greeks also, telling them the good news about the Lord Jesus. 21The Lord's hand was with them,n and a great number of people believed and turned to the Lord.o

22News of this reached the ears of the church at Jerusalem, and they sent Barnabasp to Antioch. 23When he arrived and saw the evidence of the grace of God,q he was glad and encouraged them all to remain true to the Lord with all their hearts.r 24He was a good man, full of the Holy Spirit and faith, and a great number of people were brought to the Lord.s

25Then Barnabas went to Tarsust to look for Saul, 26and when he found him, he brought him to Antioch. So for a whole year Barnabas and Saul met with the church and taught great numbers of people. The disciplesu were called Christians firstv at Antioch.

27During this time some prophetsw came down from Jerusalem to Antioch. 28One of them, named Agabus,x stood up and through the Spirit predicted that a severe famine would spread over the entire Roman world.y (This happened during the reign of Claudius.)z 29The disciples,a each according to his ability, decided to

a 16 Or in

provide help[a] for the brothers[b] living in Judea. [30]This they did, sending their gift to the elders[c] by Barnabas and Saul.[d]

Chapter 12 Theme

12 It was about this time that King Herod arrested some who belonged to the church, intending to persecute them. [2]He had James, the brother of John,[e] put to death with the sword. [3]When he saw that this pleased the Jews,[f] he proceeded to seize Peter also. This happened during the Feast of Unleavened Bread.[g] [4]After arresting him, he put him in prison, handing him over to be guarded by four squads of four soldiers each. Herod intended to bring him out for public trial after the Passover.

[5]So Peter was kept in prison, but the church was earnestly praying to God for him.[h]

[6]The night before Herod was to bring him to trial, Peter was sleeping between two soldiers, bound with two chains,[i] and sentries stood guard at the entrance. [7]Suddenly an angel[j] of the Lord appeared and a light shone in the cell. He struck Peter on the side and woke him up. "Quick, get up!" he said, and the chains fell off Peter's wrists.[k]

[8]Then the angel said to him, "Put on your clothes and sandals." And Peter did so. "Wrap your cloak around you and follow me," the angel told him. [9]Peter followed him out of the prison, but he had no idea that what the angel was doing was really happening; he thought he was seeing a vision.[l] [10]They passed the first and second guards and came to the iron gate leading to the city. It opened for them by itself,[m] and they went through it. When they had walked the length of one street, suddenly the angel left him.

[11]Then Peter came to himself[n] and said, "Now I know without a doubt that the Lord sent his angel and rescued me[o] from Herod's clutches and from everything the Jewish people were anticipating."

[12]When this had dawned on him, he went to the house of Mary the mother of John, also called Mark,[p] where many people had gathered and were praying.[q] [13]Peter knocked at the outer entrance, and a servant girl named Rhoda came to answer the door.[r] [14]When she recognized Peter's voice, she was so overjoyed[s] she ran back without opening it and exclaimed, "Peter is at the door!"

[15]"You're out of your mind," they told her. When she kept insisting that it was so, they said, "It must be his angel."[t]

[16]But Peter kept on knocking, and when they opened the door and saw him, they were astonished. [17]Peter motioned with his hand[u] for them to be quiet and described how the Lord had brought him out of prison. "Tell James[v] and the brothers[w] about this," he said, and then he left for another place.

11:29
[a] Ro 15:26;
2Co 9:2
[b] Ac 1:16

11:30
[c] Ac 14:23
[d] Ac 12:25

12:2
[e] Mt 4:21

12:3
[f] Ac 24:27
[g] Ex 12:15;
23:15

12:5
[h] Eph 6:18

12:6
[i] Ac 21:33

12:7
[j] Ac 5:19
[k] Ac 16:26

12:9
[l] Ac 9:10

12:10
[m] Ac 5:19;
16:26

12:11
[n] Lk 15:17
[o] Ps 34:7;
Da 3:28; 6:22;
2Co 1:10;
2Pe 2:9

12:12
[p] ver 25;
Ac 15:37,39;
Col 4:10;
Phm 24;
1Pe 5:13
[q] ver 5

12:13
[r] Jn 18:16,17

12:14
[s] Lk 24:41

12:15
[t] Mt 18:10

12:17
[u] Ac 13:16;
19:33; 21:40
[v] Ac 15:13
[w] Ac 1:16

12:19
a Ac 16:27
b Ac 8:40

12:20
c Mt 11:21
d 1Ki 5:9,11;
Eze 27:17

12:23
e 1Sa 25:38;
2Sa 24:16,17

12:24
f Ac 6:7; 19:20

12:25
g Ac 4:36
h Ac 11:30
i ver 12

[18]In the morning, there was no small commotion among the soldiers as to what had become of Peter. [19]After Herod had a thorough search made for him and did not find him, he cross-examined the guards and ordered that they be executed.[a]

Then Herod went from Judea to Caesarea[b] and stayed there a while. [20]He had been quarreling with the people of Tyre and Sidon;[c] they now joined together and sought an audience with him. Having secured the support of Blastus, a trusted personal servant of the king, they asked for peace, because they depended on the king's country for their food supply.[d]

[21]On the appointed day Herod, wearing his royal robes, sat on his throne and delivered a public address to the people. [22]They shouted, "This is the voice of a god, not of a man." [23]Immediately, because Herod did not give praise to God, an angel of the Lord struck him down,[e] and he was eaten by worms and died.

[24]But the word of God continued to increase and spread.[f]

[25]When Barnabas[g] and Saul had finished their mission,[h] they returned from[a] Jerusalem, taking with them John, also called Mark.[i]

a 25 Some manuscripts to

Paul's First Missionary Journey (Acts 13–14)

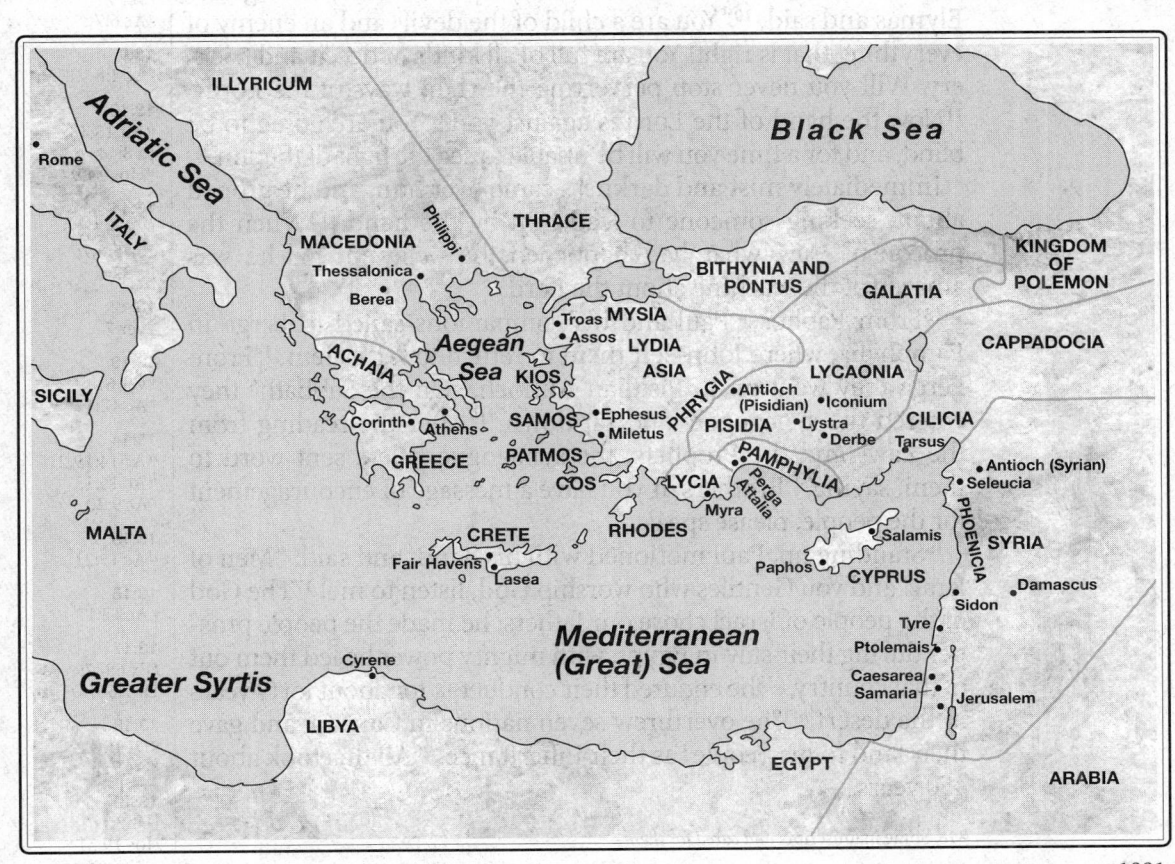

Chapter 13 Theme _____

13 In the church at Antioch[a] there were prophets[b] and teachers: Barnabas,[c] Simeon called Niger, Lucius of Cyrene, Manaen (who had been brought up with Herod[d] the tetrarch) and Saul. [2]While they were worshiping the Lord and fasting, the Holy Spirit said,[e] "Set apart for me Barnabas and Saul for the work[f] to which I have called them."[g] [3]So after they had fasted and prayed, they placed their hands on them[h] and sent them off.[i]

[4]The two of them, sent on their way by the Holy Spirit,[j] went down to Seleucia and sailed from there to Cyprus.[k] [5]When they arrived at Salamis, they proclaimed the word of God in the Jewish synagogues.[l] John[m] was with them as their helper.

[6]They traveled through the whole island until they came to Paphos. There they met a Jewish sorcerer[n] and false prophet[o] named Bar-Jesus, [7]who was an attendant of the proconsul,[p] Sergius Paulus. The proconsul, an intelligent man, sent for Barnabas and Saul because he wanted to hear the word of God. [8]But Elymas the sorcerer[q] (for that is what his name means) opposed them and tried to turn the proconsul[r] from the faith.[s] [9]Then Saul, who was also called Paul, filled with the Holy Spirit,[t] looked straight at Elymas and said, [10]"You are a child of the devil[u] and an enemy of everything that is right! You are full of all kinds of deceit and trickery. Will you never stop perverting the right ways of the Lord?[v] [11]Now the hand of the Lord is against you.[w] You are going to be blind, and for a time you will be unable to see the light of the sun."

Immediately mist and darkness came over him, and he groped about, seeking someone to lead him by the hand. [12]When the proconsul[x] saw what had happened, he believed, for he was amazed at the teaching about the Lord.

[13]From Paphos,[y] Paul and his companions sailed to Perga in Pamphylia, where John[z] left them to return to Jerusalem. [14]From Perga they went on to Pisidian Antioch.[a] On the Sabbath[b] they entered the synagogue[c] and sat down. [15]After the reading from the Law[d] and the Prophets, the synagogue rulers sent word to them, saying, "Brothers, if you have a message of encouragement for the people, please speak."

[16]Standing up, Paul motioned with his hand[e] and said: "Men of Israel and you Gentiles who worship God, listen to me! [17]The God of the people of Israel chose our fathers; he made the people prosper during their stay in Egypt, with mighty power he led them out of that country,[f] [18]he endured their conduct[a] [g] for about forty years in the desert,[h] [19]he overthrew seven nations in Canaan[i] and gave their land to his people[j] as their inheritance. [20]All this took about 450 years.

[a] 18 Some manuscripts *and cared for them*

13:1
[a] Ac 11:19
[b] Ac 11:27
[c] Ac 4:36; 11:22-26
[d] Mt 14:1

13:2
[e] Ac 8:29
[f] Ac 14:26
[g] Ac 22:21

13:3
[h] Ac 6:6
[i] Ac 14:26

13:4
[j] ver 2,3
[k] Ac 4:36

13:5
[l] Ac 9:20
[m] Ac 12:12

13:6
[n] Ac 8:9
[o] Mt 7:15

13:7
[p] ver 8,12; Ac 19:38

13:8
[q] Ac 8:9
[r] ver 7
[s] Ac 6:7

13:9
[t] Ac 4:8

13:10
[u] Mt 13:38; Jn 8:44
[v] Hos 14:9

13:11
[w] Ex 9:3; 1Sa 5:6,7; Ps 32:4

13:12
[x] ver 7

13:13
[y] ver 6
[z] Ac 12:12

13:14
[a] Ac 14:19,21
[b] Ac 16:13
[c] Ac 9:20

13:15
[d] Ac 15:21

13:16
[e] Ac 12:17

13:17
[f] Ex 6:6,7; Dt 7:6-8

13:18
[g] Dt 1:31
[h] Ac 7:36

13:19
[i] Dt 7:1
[j] Jos 19:51

13:20
a Jdg 2:16
b 1Sa 3:19,20

13:21
c 1Sa 8:5,19
d 1Sa 10:1
e 1Sa 9:1,2

13:22
f 1Sa 15:23,26
g 1Sa 16:13;
Ps 89:20
h 1Sa 13:14

13:23
i Mt 1:1
j Lk 2:11
k Mt 1:21
l ver 32

13:24
m Mk 1:4

13:25
n Ac 20:24
o Jn 1:20
p Mt 3:11;
Jn 1:27

13:26
q Ac 4:12

13:27
r Ac 3:17
s Lk 24:27

13:28
t Mt 27:20-25;
Ac 3:14

13:29
u Lk 18:31
v Ac 5:30
w Lk 23:53

13:30
x Mt 28:6;
Ac 2:24

13:31
y Mt 28:16
z Lk 24:48

13:32
a Ac 5:42
b Ac 26:6;
Ro 4:13

13:33
c Ps 2:7

13:34
d Isa 55:3

13:35
e Ps 16:10;
Ac 2:27

13:36
f 1Ki 2:10;
Ac 2:29

13:38
g Lk 24:47;
Ac 2:38

"After this, God gave them judges[a] until the time of Samuel the prophet.[b] [21]Then the people asked for a king,[c] and he gave them Saul[d] son of Kish, of the tribe of Benjamin,[e] who ruled forty years. [22]After removing Saul,[f] he made David their king.[g] He testified concerning him: 'I have found David son of Jesse a man after my own heart;[h] he will do everything I want him to do.'

[23]"From this man's descendants[i] God has brought to Israel the Savior[j] Jesus,[k] as he promised.[l] [24]Before the coming of Jesus, John preached repentance and baptism to all the people of Israel.[m] [25]As John was completing his work,[n] he said: 'Who do you think I am? I am not that one.[o] No, but he is coming after me, whose sandals I am not worthy to untie.'[p]

[26]"Brothers, children of Abraham, and you God-fearing Gentiles, it is to us that this message of salvation[q] has been sent. [27]The people of Jerusalem and their rulers did not recognize Jesus,[r] yet in condemning him they fulfilled the words of the prophets[s] that are read every Sabbath. [28]Though they found no proper ground for a death sentence, they asked Pilate to have him executed.[t] [29]When they had carried out all that was written about him,[u] they took him down from the tree[v] and laid him in a tomb.[w] [30]But God raised him from the dead,[x] [31]and for many days he was seen by those who had traveled with him from Galilee to Jerusalem.[y] They are now his witnesses[z] to our people.

[32]"We tell you the good news:[a] What God promised our fathers[b] [33]he has fulfilled for us, their children, by raising up Jesus. As it is written in the second Psalm:

"'You are my Son;
    today I have become your Father.'[a'bc]

[34]The fact that God raised him from the dead, never to decay, is stated in these words:

"'I will give you the holy and sure blessings promised to David.'[cd]

[35]So it is stated elsewhere:

"'You will not let your Holy One see decay.'[de]

[36]"For when David had served God's purpose in his own generation, he fell asleep; he was buried with his fathers[f] and his body decayed. [37]But the one whom God raised from the dead did not see decay.

[38]"Therefore, my brothers, I want you to know that through Jesus the forgiveness of sins is proclaimed to you.[g] [39]Through him

everyone who believes is justified from everything you could not be justified from by the law of Moses.*a* **40**Take care that what the prophets have said does not happen to you:

41"'Look, you scoffers,
wonder and perish,
for I am going to do something in your days
that you would never believe,
even if someone told you.'*a*"*b*

42As Paul and Barnabas were leaving the synagogue,*c* the people invited them to speak further about these things on the next Sabbath. **43**When the congregation was dismissed, many of the Jews and devout converts to Judaism followed Paul and Barnabas, who talked with them and urged them to continue in the grace of God.*d*

44On the next Sabbath almost the whole city gathered to hear the word of the Lord. **45**When the Jews saw the crowds, they were filled with jealousy and talked abusively*e* against what Paul was saying.*f*

46Then Paul and Barnabas answered them boldly: "We had to speak the word of God to you first.*g* Since you reject it and do not consider yourselves worthy of eternal life, we now turn to the Gentiles.*h* **47**For this is what the Lord has commanded us:

"'I have made you*b* a light for the Gentiles,*i*
that you*b* may bring salvation to the ends of
the earth.'*c*"*j*

48When the Gentiles heard this, they were glad and honored the word of the Lord; and all who were appointed for eternal life believed.

49The word of the Lord spread through the whole region. **50**But the Jews incited the God-fearing women of high standing and the leading men of the city. They stirred up persecution against Paul and Barnabas, and expelled them from their region.*k* **51**So they shook the dust from their feet*l* in protest against them and went to Iconium.*m* **52**And the disciples were filled with joy and with the Holy Spirit.

Chapter 14 Theme

14 At Iconium*n* Paul and Barnabas went as usual into the Jewish synagogue. There they spoke so effectively that a great number of Jews and Gentiles believed. **2**But the Jews who refused to believe stirred up the Gentiles and poisoned their minds against the brothers. **3**So Paul and Barnabas spent considerable time there, speaking boldly*o* for the Lord, who confirmed the message of his

---

13:39
a Ro 3:28

13:41
b Hab 1:5

13:42
c ver 14

13:43
d Ac 11:23;
14:22

13:45
e Ac 18:6;
1Pe 4:4;
Jude 10
f 1Th 2:16

13:46
g ver 26;
Ac 3:26
h Ac 18:6;
22:21; 28:28

13:47
i Lk 2:32
j Isa 49:6

13:50
k 1Th 2:16

13:51
l Mt 10:14;
Ac 18:6
m Ac 14:1,19,21;
2Ti 3:11

14:1
n Ac 13:51

14:3
o Ac 4:29

---

a 41 Hab. 1:5   *b 47* The Greek is singular.   *c 47* Isaiah 49:6

14:3
a Jn 4:48;
Heb 2:4
14:4
b Ac 17:4,5
14:5
c ver 19
14:6
d Mt 10:23
14:7
e Ac 16:10
f ver 15,21
14:8
g Ac 3:2
14:9
h Mt 9:28,29
14:10
i Ac 3:8
14:11
j Ac 8:10; 28:6
14:14
k Mk 14:63
14:15
l Ac 10:26;
Jas 5:17
m ver 7,21;
Ac 13:32
n 1Sa 12:21;
1Co 8:4;
1Th 1:9
o Mt 16:16
p Ge 1:1;
Jer 14:22
q Ps 146:6;
Rev 14:7
14:16
r Ac 17:30
s Ps 81:12;
Mic 4:5
14:17
t Ac 17:27;
Ro 1:20
u Dt 11:14;
Job 5:10;
Ps 65:10
14:19
v Ac 13:45
w Ac 13:51
x 2Co 11:25;
2Ti 3:11
14:20
y ver 22,28;
Ac 11:26
14:21
z Ac 13:51
14:22
a Ac 11:23;
13:43
b Jn 16:33;
1Th 3:3;
2Ti 3:12
14:23
c Ac 11:30;
Tit 1:5
d Ac 13:3
e Ac 20:32

grace by enabling them to do miraculous signs and wonders.a 4The people of the city were divided; some sided with the Jews, others with the apostles.b 5There was a plot afoot among the Gentiles and Jews, together with their leaders, to mistreat them and stone them.c 6But they found out about it and fledd to the Lycaonian cities of Lystra and Derbe and to the surrounding country, 7where they continued to preache the good news.f

8In Lystra there sat a man crippled in his feet, who was lame from birthg and had never walked. 9He listened to Paul as he was speaking. Paul looked directly at him, saw that he had faith to be healedh 10and called out, "Stand up on your feet!" At that, the man jumped up and began to walk.i

11When the crowd saw what Paul had done, they shouted in the Lycaonian language, "The gods have come down to us in human form!"j 12Barnabas they called Zeus, and Paul they called Hermes because he was the chief speaker. 13The priest of Zeus, whose temple was just outside the city, brought bulls and wreaths to the city gates because he and the crowd wanted to offer sacrifices to them.

14But when the apostles Barnabas and Paul heard of this, they tore their clothesk and rushed out into the crowd, shouting: 15"Men, why are you doing this? We too are only men,l human like you. We are bringing you good news,m telling you to turn from these worthless thingsn to the living God,o who made heaven and earthp and sea and everything in them.q 16In the past, he letr all nations go their own way.s 17Yet he has not left himself without testimony:t He has shown kindness by giving you rain from heaven and crops in their seasons;u he provides you with plenty of food and fills your hearts with joy." 18Even with these words, they had difficulty keeping the crowd from sacrificing to them.

19Then some Jewsv came from Antioch and Iconiumw and won the crowd over. They stoned Paulx and dragged him outside the city, thinking he was dead. 20But after the disciplesy had gathered around him, he got up and went back into the city. The next day he and Barnabas left for Derbe.

21They preached the good news in that city and won a large number of disciples. Then they returned to Lystra, Iconiumz and Antioch, 22strengthening the disciples and encouraging them to remain true to the faith.a "We must go through many hardshipsb to enter the kingdom of God," they said. 23Paul and Barnabas appointed eldersa c for them in each church and, with prayer and fasting,d committed them to the Lord,e in whom they had put their trust. 24After going through Pisidia, they came into Pamphylia,

a 23 Or *Barnabas ordained elders*; or *Barnabas had elders elected*

25and when they had preached the word in Perga, they went down to Attalia.

26From Attalia they sailed back to Antioch,*a* where they had been committed to the grace of God*b* for the work they had now completed.*c* 27On arriving there, they gathered the church together and reported all that God had done through them*d* and how he had opened the door*e* of faith to the Gentiles. 28And they stayed there a long time with the disciples.

Chapter 15 Theme

15 Some men*f* came down from Judea to Antioch and were teaching the brothers: "Unless you are circumcised,*g* according to the custom taught by Moses,*h* you cannot be saved." 2This brought Paul and Barnabas into sharp dispute and debate with them. So Paul and Barnabas were appointed, along with some other believers, to go up to Jerusalem*i* to see the apostles and elders*j* about this question. 3The church sent them on their way, and as they traveled through Phoenicia and Samaria, they told how the Gentiles had been converted.*k* This news made all the brothers very glad. 4When they came to Jerusalem, they were welcomed by the church and the apostles and elders, to whom they reported everything God had done through them.*l*

5Then some of the believers who belonged to the party of the Pharisees stood up and said, "The Gentiles must be circumcised and required to obey the law of Moses."

6The apostles and elders met to consider this question. 7After much discussion, Peter got up and addressed them: "Brothers, you know that some time ago God made a choice among you that the Gentiles might hear from my lips the message of the gospel and believe. 8God, who knows the heart,*m* showed that he accepted them by giving the Holy Spirit to them,*n* just as he did to us. 9He made no distinction between us and them,*o* for he purified their hearts by faith.*p* 10Now then, why do you try to test God by putting on the necks of the disciples a yoke*q* that neither we nor our fathers have been able to bear? 11No! We believe it is through the grace*r* of our Lord Jesus that we are saved, just as they are."

12The whole assembly became silent as they listened to Barnabas and Paul telling about the miraculous signs and wonders*s* God had done among the Gentiles through them.*t* 13When they finished, James*u* spoke up: "Brothers, listen to me. 14Simon*a* has described to us how God at first showed his concern by taking from the Gentiles a people for himself. 15The words of the prophets are in agreement with this, as it is written:

a 14 Greek *Simeon*, a variant of *Simon*; that is, Peter

14:26
a Ac 11:19
b Ac 15:40
c Ac 13:1,3

14:27
d Ac 15:4,12; 21:19
e 1Co 16:9; 2Co 2:12; Col 4:3; Rev 3:8

15:1
f ver 24; Gal 2:12
g ver 5; Gal 5:2,3
h Ac 6:14

15:2
i Gal 2:2
j Ac 11:30

15:3
k Ac 14:27

15:4
l ver 12; Ac 14:27

15:8
m Ac 1:24
n Ac 10:44,47

15:9
o Ac 10:28,34; 11:12
p Ac 10:43

15:10
q Mt 23:4; Gal 5:1

15:11
r Ro 3:24; Eph 2:5-8

15:12
s Jn 4:48
t Ac 14:27

15:13
u Ac 12:17

15:17
a Am 9:11,12

15:20
b 1Co 8:7-13;
10:14-28;
Rev 2:14,20
c 1Co 10:7,8
d ver 29;
Ge 9:4;
Lev 3:17;
Dt 12:16,23

15:21
e Ac 13:15;
2Co 3:14,15

15:22
f ver 27,32,40

15:23
g ver 1
h ver 41
i Ac 23:25,26;
Jas 1:1

15:24
j ver 1;
Gal 1:7; 5:10

15:26
k Ac 9:23-25;
14:19

15:28
l Ac 5:32

15:29
m ver 20;
Ac 21:25

15:33
n Mk 5:34;
Ac 16:36;
1Co 16:11

16 " 'After this I will return
and rebuild David's fallen tent.
Its ruins I will rebuild,
and I will restore it,
17 that the remnant of men may seek the Lord,
and all the Gentiles who bear my name,
says the Lord, who does these things'a *a*
18   that have been known for ages.b

19 "It is my judgment, therefore, that we should not make it difficult for the Gentiles who are turning to God. 20 Instead we should write to them, telling them to abstain from food polluted by idols,b from sexual immorality,c from the meat of strangled animals and from blood.d 21 For Moses has been preached in every city from the earliest times and is read in the synagogues on every Sabbath."e

22 Then the apostles and elders, with the whole church, decided to choose some of their own men and send them to Antioch with Paul and Barnabas. They chose Judas (called Barsabbas) and Silas,f two men who were leaders among the brothers. 23 With them they sent the following letter:

The apostles and elders, your brothers,

To the Gentile believers in Antioch,g Syria and Cilicia:h

Greetings.i

24 We have heard that some went out from us without our authorization and disturbed you, troubling your minds by what they said.j 25 So we all agreed to choose some men and send them to you with our dear friends Barnabas and Paul— 26 men who have risked their livesk for the name of our Lord Jesus Christ. 27 Therefore we are sending Judas and Silas to confirm by word of mouth what we are writing. 28 It seemed good to the Holy Spiritl and to us not to burden you with anything beyond the following requirements: 29 You are to abstain from food sacrificed to idols, from blood, from the meat of strangled animals and from sexual immorality.m You will do well to avoid these things.

Farewell.

30 The men were sent off and went down to Antioch, where they gathered the church together and delivered the letter. 31 The people read it and were glad for its encouraging message. 32 Judas and Silas, who themselves were prophets, said much to encourage and strengthen the brothers. 33 After spending some time there, they were sent off by the brothers with the blessing of peacen to return

a 17 Amos 9:11,12   b 17,18 Some manuscripts things'— / 18 known to the Lord for ages is his work

Paul's Second Missionary Journey (Acts 15:36– 18:22)

to those who had sent them.[a] [35]But Paul and Barnabas remained in Antioch, where they and many others taught and preached[a] the word of the Lord.

[36]Some time later Paul said to Barnabas, "Let us go back and visit the brothers in all the towns[b] where we preached the word of the Lord and see how they are doing." [37]Barnabas wanted to take John, also called Mark,[c] with them, [38]but Paul did not think it wise to take him, because he had deserted them[d] in Pamphylia and had not continued with them in the work. [39]They had such a sharp disagreement that they parted company. Barnabas took Mark and sailed for Cyprus, [40]but Paul chose Silas[e] and left, commended by the brothers to the grace of the Lord.[f] [41]He went through Syria[g] and Cilicia,[h] strengthening the churches.[i]

Chapter 16 Theme

16 He came to Derbe and then to Lystra,[j] where a disciple named Timothy[k] lived, whose mother was a Jewess and a believer, but whose father was a Greek. [2]The brothers[l] at Lystra

a 33 Some manuscripts *them,* [34]*but Silas decided to remain there*

15:35
a Ac 8:4

15:36
b Ac 13:4,13, 14,51; 14:1,6,24,25

15:37
c Ac 12:12

15:38
d Ac 13:13

15:40
e ver 22
f Ac 11:23

15:41
g ver 23
h Ac 6:9
i Ac 16:5

16:1
j Ac 14:6
k Ac 17:14; 18:5; 19:22; Ro 16:21; 1Co 4:17; 2Co 1:1,19; 1Th 3:2,6; 1Ti 1:2,18; 2Ti 1:2,5,6

16:2
l ver 40

16:2
a Ac 13:51

16:3
b Gal 2:3

16:4
c Ac 11:30
d Ac 15:2
e Ac 15:28,29

16:5
f Ac 9:31;
15:41

16:6
g Ac 18:23
h Ac 18:23;
Gal 1:2; 3:1
i Ac 2:9

16:7
j Ro 8:9;
Gal 4:6

16:8
k ver 11;
2Co 2:12;
2Ti 4:13

16:9
l Ac 9:10
m Ac 20:1,3

16:10
n ver 10-17
o Ac 14:7

16:11
p ver 8

16:12
q Ac 20:6;
Php 1:1;
1Th 2:2
r ver 9

16:13
s Ac 13:14

16:14
t Rev 1:11
u Lk 24:45

16:15
v Ac 11:14

16:16
w ver 13
x Dt 18:11;
1Sa 28:3,7

16:17
y Mk 5:7

16:18
z Mk 16:17

16:19
a ver 16;
Ac 19:25,26
b Ac 15:22
c Ac 8:3; 17:6;
21:30;
Jas 2:6

16:20
d Ac 17:6

16:21
e ver 12
f Est 3:8

and Iconium[a] spoke well of him. ³Paul wanted to take him along on the journey, so he circumcised him because of the Jews who lived in that area, for they all knew that his father was a Greek.[b] ⁴As they traveled from town to town, they delivered the decisions reached by the apostles and elders[c] in Jerusalem[d] for the people to obey.[e] ⁵So the churches were strengthened[f] in the faith and grew daily in numbers.

⁶Paul and his companions traveled throughout the region of Phrygia[g] and Galatia,[h] having been kept by the Holy Spirit from preaching the word in the province of Asia.[i] ⁷When they came to the border of Mysia, they tried to enter Bithynia, but the Spirit of Jesus[j] would not allow them to. ⁸So they passed by Mysia and went down to Troas.[k] ⁹During the night Paul had a vision[l] of a man of Macedonia[m] standing and begging him, "Come over to Macedonia and help us." ¹⁰After Paul had seen the vision, we[n] got ready at once to leave for Macedonia, concluding that God had called us to preach the gospel[o] to them.

¹¹From Troas[p] we put out to sea and sailed straight for Samothrace, and the next day on to Neapolis. ¹²From there we traveled to Philippi,[q] a Roman colony and the leading city of that district of Macedonia.[r] And we stayed there several days.

¹³On the Sabbath[s] we went outside the city gate to the river, where we expected to find a place of prayer. We sat down and began to speak to the women who had gathered there. ¹⁴One of those listening was a woman named Lydia, a dealer in purple cloth from the city of Thyatira,[t] who was a worshiper of God. The Lord opened her heart[u] to respond to Paul's message. ¹⁵When she and the members of her household[v] were baptized, she invited us to her home. "If you consider me a believer in the Lord," she said, "come and stay at my house." And she persuaded us.

¹⁶Once when we were going to the place of prayer,[w] we were met by a slave girl who had a spirit[x] by which she predicted the future. She earned a great deal of money for her owners by fortune-telling. ¹⁷This girl followed Paul and the rest of us, shouting, "These men are servants of the Most High God,[y] who are telling you the way to be saved." ¹⁸She kept this up for many days. Finally Paul became so troubled that he turned around and said to the spirit, "In the name of Jesus Christ I command you to come out of her!" At that moment the spirit left her.[z]

¹⁹When the owners of the slave girl realized that their hope of making money[a] was gone, they seized Paul and Silas[b] and dragged[c] them into the marketplace to face the authorities. ²⁰They brought them before the magistrates and said, "These men are Jews, and are throwing our city into an uproar[d] ²¹by advocating customs unlawful for us Romans[e] to accept or practice."[f]

[22]The crowd joined in the attack against Paul and Silas, and the magistrates ordered them to be stripped and beaten.*a* [23]After they had been severely flogged, they were thrown into prison, and the jailer*b* was commanded to guard them carefully. [24]Upon receiving such orders, he put them in the inner cell and fastened their feet in the stocks.*c*

[25]About midnight Paul and Silas were praying and singing hymns*d* to God, and the other prisoners were listening to them. [26]Suddenly there was such a violent earthquake that the foundations of the prison were shaken.*e* At once all the prison doors flew open,*f* and everybody's chains came loose.*g* [27]The jailer woke up, and when he saw the prison doors open, he drew his sword and was about to kill himself because he thought the prisoners had escaped.*h* [28]But Paul shouted, "Don't harm yourself! We are all here!"

[29]The jailer called for lights, rushed in and fell trembling before Paul and Silas. [30]He then brought them out and asked, "Sirs, what must I do to be saved?"*i*

[31]They replied, "Believe in the Lord Jesus, and you will be saved—you and your household."*j* [32]Then they spoke the word of the Lord to him and to all the others in his house. [33]At that hour of the night*k* the jailer took them and washed their wounds; then immediately he and all his family were baptized. [34]The jailer brought them into his house and set a meal before them; he*l* was filled with joy because he had come to believe in God—he and his whole family.

[35]When it was daylight, the magistrates sent their officers to the jailer with the order: "Release those men." [36]The jailer*m* told Paul, "The magistrates have ordered that you and Silas be released. Now you can leave. Go in peace."*n*

[37]But Paul said to the officers: "They beat us publicly without a trial, even though we are Roman citizens,*o* and threw us into prison. And now do they want to get rid of us quietly? No! Let them come themselves and escort us out."

[38]The officers reported this to the magistrates, and when they heard that Paul and Silas were Roman citizens, they were alarmed.*p* [39]They came to appease them and escorted them from the prison, requesting them to leave the city.*q* [40]After Paul and Silas came out of the prison, they went to Lydia's house,*r* where they met with the brothers*s* and encouraged them. Then they left.

Chapter 17 Theme

17 When they had passed through Amphipolis and Apollonia, they came to Thessalonica,*t* where there was a Jewish synagogue. [2]As his custom was, Paul went into the synagogue,*u*

16:22
a 2Co 11:25; 1Th 2:2

16:23
b ver 27,36

16:24
c Job 13:27; 33:11; Jer 20:2,3; 29:26

16:25
d Eph 5:19

16:26
e Ac 4:31
f Ac 12:10
g Ac 12:7

16:27
h Ac 12:19

16:30
i Ac 2:37

16:31
j Ac 11:14

16:33
k ver 25

16:34
l Ac 11:14

16:36
m ver 23,27
n Ac 15:33

16:37
o Ac 22:25-29

16:38
p Ac 22:29

16:39
q Mt 8:34

16:40
r ver 14
s ver 2; Ac 1:16

17:1
t ver 11,13; Php 4:16; 1Th 1:1; 2Th 1:1; 2Ti 4:10

17:2
u Ac 9:20

17:2
a Ac 13:14
b Ac 8:35

17:3
c Lk 24:26;
Ac 3:18
d Lk 24:46
e Ac 9:22;
18:28

17:4
f Ac 15:22

17:5
g ver 13;
1Th 2:16
h Ro 16:21

17:6
i Ac 16:19
j Mt 24:14
k Ac 16:20

17:7
l Lk 23:2;
Jn 19:12

17:9
m ver 5

17:10
n ver 13;
Ac 20:4

17:11
o ver 1
p Lk 16:29;
Jn 5:39

17:14
q Ac 15:22
r Ac 16:1

17:15
s ver 16,21,22;
Ac 18:1;
1Th 3:1
t Ac 18:5

17:17
u Ac 9:20

17:18
v ver 31,32;
Ac 4:2

17:19
w ver 22
x Mk 1:27

and on three Sabbath[a] days he reasoned with them from the Scriptures,[b] [3]explaining and proving that the Christ[a] had to suffer[c] and rise from the dead.[d] "This Jesus I am proclaiming to you is the Christ,[a]"[e] he said. [4]Some of the Jews were persuaded and joined Paul and Silas,[f] as did a large number of God-fearing Greeks and not a few prominent women.

[5]But the Jews were jealous; so they rounded up some bad characters from the marketplace, formed a mob and started a riot in the city.[g] They rushed to Jason's[h] house in search of Paul and Silas in order to bring them out to the crowd.[b] [6]But when they did not find them, they dragged[i] Jason and some other brothers before the city officials, shouting: "These men who have caused trouble all over the world[j] have now come here,[k] [7]and Jason has welcomed them into his house. They are all defying Caesar's decrees, saying that there is another king, one called Jesus."[l] [8]When they heard this, the crowd and the city officials were thrown into turmoil. [9]Then they made Jason[m] and the others post bond and let them go.

[10]As soon as it was night, the brothers sent Paul and Silas away to Berea.[n] On arriving there, they went to the Jewish synagogue. [11]Now the Bereans were of more noble character than the Thessalonians,[o] for they received the message with great eagerness and examined the Scriptures[p] every day to see if what Paul said was true. [12]Many of the Jews believed, as did also a number of prominent Greek women and many Greek men.

[13]When the Jews in Thessalonica learned that Paul was preaching the word of God at Berea, they went there too, agitating the crowds and stirring them up. [14]The brothers immediately sent Paul to the coast, but Silas[q] and Timothy[r] stayed at Berea. [15]The men who escorted Paul brought him to Athens[s] and then left with instructions for Silas and Timothy to join him as soon as possible.[t]

[16]While Paul was waiting for them in Athens, he was greatly distressed to see that the city was full of idols. [17]So he reasoned in the synagogue[u] with the Jews and the God-fearing Greeks, as well as in the marketplace day by day with those who happened to be there. [18]A group of Epicurean and Stoic philosophers began to dispute with him. Some of them asked, "What is this babbler trying to say?" Others remarked, "He seems to be advocating foreign gods." They said this because Paul was preaching the good news about Jesus and the resurrection.[v] [19]Then they took him and brought him to a meeting of the Areopagus,[w] where they said to him, "May we know what this new teaching[x] is that you are presenting? [20]You are bringing some strange ideas to our ears, and we want to know what they mean." [21](All the Athenians and the

a 3 Or *Messiah*   b 5 Or *the assembly of the people*

foreigners who lived there spent their time doing nothing but talking about and listening to the latest ideas.)

²²Paul then stood up in the meeting of the Areopagus and said: "Men of Athens! I see that in every way you are very religious. ²³For as I walked around and looked carefully at your objects of worship, I even found an altar with this inscription: TO AN UNKNOWN GOD. Now what you worship as something unknown*a* I am going to proclaim to you.

²⁴"The God who made the world and everything in it*b* is the Lord of heaven and earth*c* and does not live in temples built by hands.*d* ²⁵And he is not served by human hands, as if he needed anything, because he himself gives all men life and breath and everything else.*e* ²⁶From one man he made every nation of men, that they should inhabit the whole earth; and he determined the times set for them and the exact places where they should live.*f* ²⁷God did this so that men would seek him and perhaps reach out for him and find him, though he is not far from each one of us.*g* ²⁸'For in him we live and move and have our being.'*h* As some of your own poets have said, 'We are his offspring.'

²⁹"Therefore since we are God's offspring, we should not think that the divine being is like gold or silver or stone—an image made by man's design and skill.*i* ³⁰In the past God overlooked*j* such ignorance,*k* but now he commands all people everywhere to repent.*l* ³¹For he has set a day when he will judge*m* the world with justice*n* by the man he has appointed.*o* He has given proof of this to all men by raising him from the dead."*p*

³²When they heard about the resurrection of the dead,*q* some of them sneered, but others said, "We want to hear you again on this subject." ³³At that, Paul left the Council. ³⁴A few men became followers of Paul and believed. Among them was Dionysius, a member of the Areopagus,*r* also a woman named Damaris, and a number of others.

Chapter 18 Theme

18 After this, Paul left Athens*s* and went to Corinth.*t* ²There he met a Jew named Aquila, a native of Pontus, who had recently come from Italy with his wife Priscilla,*u* because Claudius*v* had ordered all the Jews to leave Rome. Paul went to see them, ³and because he was a tentmaker as they were, he stayed and worked with them.*w* ⁴Every Sabbath*x* he reasoned in the synagogue, trying to persuade Jews and Greeks.

⁵When Silas*y* and Timothy*z* came from Macedonia,*a* Paul devoted himself exclusively to preaching, testifying to the Jews that Jesus was the Christ.*a b* ⁶But when the Jews opposed Paul and became

a 5 Or *Messiah*; also in verse 28

Cross references

17:23
a Jn 4:22

17:24
b Isa 42:5;
Ac 14:15
c Dt 10:14;
Mt 11:25
d Ac 7:48

17:25
e Ps 50:10-12;
Isa 42:5

17:26
f Dt 32:8;
Job 12:23

17:27
g Dt 4:7;
Jer 23:23,24;
Ac 14:17

17:28
h Job 12:10;
Da 5:23

17:29
i Isa 40:18-20;
Ro 1:23

17:30
j Ac 14:16;
Ro 3:25
k ver 23;
1Pe 1:14
l Lk 24:47;
Tit 2:11,12

17:31
m Mt 10:15
n Ps 9:8;
96:13; 98:9
o Ac 10:42
p Ac 2:24

17:32
q ver 18,31

17:34
r ver 19,22

18:1
s Ac 17:15
t Ac 19:1;
1Co 1:2;
2Co 1:1,23;
2Ti 4:20

18:2
u Ro 16:3;
1Co 16:19;
2Ti 4:19
v Ac 11:28

18:3
w Ac 20:34;
1Co 4:12;
1Th 2:9;
2Th 3:8

18:4
x Ac 13:14

18:5
y Ac 15:22
z Ac 16:1
a Ac 16:9;
17:14,15
b ver 28;
Ac 17:3

18:6
a Ac 13:45
b 2Sa 1:16;
Eze 18:13; 33:4
c Ac 20:26
d Ac 13:46

18:7
e Ac 16:14

18:8
f 1Co 1:14
g Mk 5:22
h Ac 11:14

18:10
i Mt 28:20

18:12
j ver 27

18:15
k Ac 23:29;
25:11,19

18:17
l 1Co 1:1

18:18
m Ac 1:16
n Ro 16:1
o Nu 6:2,5,18;
Ac 21:24

18:19
p ver 21,24;
1Co 15:32

18:21
q Ro 1:10;
1Co 4:19;
Jas 4:15

18:22
r Ac 8:40
s Ac 11:19

18:23
t Ac 16:6
u Ac 14:22;
15:32,41

18:24
v Ac 19:1;
1Co 1:12;
3:5,6,22;
4:6; 16:12;
Tit 3:13

18:25
w Ro 12:11
x Ac 19:3

abusive,[a] he shook out his clothes in protest and said to them, "Your blood be on your own heads![b] I am clear of my responsibility.[c] From now on I will go to the Gentiles."[d]

[7]Then Paul left the synagogue and went next door to the house of Titius Justus, a worshiper of God.[e] [8]Crispus,[f] the synagogue ruler,[g] and his entire household[h] believed in the Lord; and many of the Corinthians who heard him believed and were baptized.

[9]One night the Lord spoke to Paul in a vision: "Do not be afraid; keep on speaking, do not be silent. [10]For I am with you,[i] and no one is going to attack and harm you, because I have many people in this city." [11]So Paul stayed for a year and a half, teaching them the word of God.

[12]While Gallio was proconsul of Achaia,[j] the Jews made a united attack on Paul and brought him into court. [13]"This man," they charged, "is persuading the people to worship God in ways contrary to the law."

[14]Just as Paul was about to speak, Gallio said to the Jews, "If you Jews were making a complaint about some misdemeanor or serious crime, it would be reasonable for me to listen to you. [15]But since it involves questions about words and names and your own law[k]—settle the matter yourselves. I will not be a judge of such things." [16]So he had them ejected from the court. [17]Then they all turned on Sosthenes[l] the synagogue ruler and beat him in front of the court. But Gallio showed no concern whatever.

[18]Paul stayed on in Corinth for some time. Then he left the brothers[m] and sailed for Syria, accompanied by Priscilla and Aquila. Before he sailed, he had his hair cut off at Cenchrea[n] because of a vow he had taken.[o] [19]They arrived at Ephesus,[p] where Paul left Priscilla and Aquila. He himself went into the synagogue and reasoned with the Jews. [20]When they asked him to spend more time with them, he declined. [21]But as he left, he promised, "I will come back if it is God's will."[q] Then he set sail from Ephesus. [22]When he landed at Caesarea,[r] he went up and greeted the church and then went down to Antioch.[s]

[23]After spending some time in Antioch, Paul set out from there and traveled from place to place throughout the region of Galatia[t] and Phrygia, strengthening all the disciples.[u]

[24]Meanwhile a Jew named Apollos,[v] a native of Alexandria, came to Ephesus. He was a learned man, with a thorough knowledge of the Scriptures. [25]He had been instructed in the way of the Lord, and he spoke with great fervor[a][w] and taught about Jesus accurately, though he knew only the baptism of John.[x] [26]He began to speak

a 25 Or *with fervor in the Spirit*

Paul's Third Missionary Journey (Acts 18:23– 21:17)

boldly in the synagogue. When Priscilla and Aquila heard him, they invited him to their home and explained to him the way of God more adequately.

²⁷When Apollos wanted to go to Achaia,ᵃ the brothersᵇ encouraged him and wrote to the disciples there to welcome him. On arriving, he was a great help to those who by grace had believed. ²⁸For he vigorously refuted the Jews in public debate, proving from the Scripturesᶜ that Jesus was the Christ.ᵈ

Chapter 19 Theme

19 While Apollos was at Corinth,ᵉ Paul took the road through the interior and arrived at Ephesus.ᶠ There he found some disciples ²and asked them, "Did you receive the Holy Spirit whenᵃ you believed?"

They answered, "No, we have not even heard that there is a Holy Spirit."

³So Paul asked, "Then what baptism did you receive?"

"John's baptism," they replied.

ᵃ2 Or *after*

18:27
ᵃ ver 12
ᵇ ver 18

18:28
ᶜ Ac 17:2
ᵈ ver 5;
Ac 9:22

19:1
ᵉ Ac 18:1
ᶠ Ac 18:19

19:4
a Jn 1:7;
Ac 13:24,25

19:6
b Ac 6:6; 8:17
c Ac 2:4
d Mk 16:17;
Ac 10:46

19:8
e Ac 9:20
f Ac 1:3;
28:23

19:9
g Ac 14:4
h ver 23;
Ac 9:2
i ver 30;
Ac 11:26

19:10
j Ac 20:31
k ver 22,26,27

19:11
l Ac 8:13

19:12
m Ac 5:15

19:13
n Mt 12:27
o Mk 9:38

19:17
p Ac 18:19
q Ac 5:5,11

19:20
r Ac 6:7;
12:24

19:21
s Ac 20:16,22;
Ro 15:25
t Ac 16:9
u Ac 18:12
v Ro 15:24,28

19:22
w Ac 13:5
x Ac 16:1
y Ro 16:23;
2Ti 4:20
z ver 10,26,27

19:23
a Ac 9:2

⁴Paul said, "John's baptism was a baptism of repentance. He told the people to believe in the one coming after him, that is, in Jesus."*a* ⁵On hearing this, they were baptized into*a* the name of the Lord Jesus. ⁶When Paul placed his hands on them,*b* the Holy Spirit came on them,*c* and they spoke in tongues*bd* and prophesied. ⁷There were about twelve men in all.

⁸Paul entered the synagogue*e* and spoke boldly there for three months, arguing persuasively about the kingdom of God.*f* ⁹But some of them*g* became obstinate; they refused to believe and publicly maligned the Way.*h* So Paul left them. He took the disciples*i* with him and had discussions daily in the lecture hall of Tyrannus. ¹⁰This went on for two years,*j* so that all the Jews and Greeks who lived in the province of Asia*k* heard the word of the Lord.

¹¹God did extraordinary miracles*l* through Paul, ¹²so that even handkerchiefs and aprons that had touched him were taken to the sick, and their illnesses were cured*m* and the evil spirits left them.

¹³Some Jews who went around driving out evil spirits*n* tried to invoke the name of the Lord Jesus over those who were demon-possessed. They would say, "In the name of Jesus,*o* whom Paul preaches, I command you to come out." ¹⁴Seven sons of Sceva, a Jewish chief priest, were doing this. ¹⁵One day the evil spirit answered them, "Jesus I know, and I know about Paul, but who are you?" ¹⁶Then the man who had the evil spirit jumped on them and overpowered them all. He gave them such a beating that they ran out of the house naked and bleeding.

¹⁷When this became known to the Jews and Greeks living in Ephesus,*p* they were all seized with fear,*q* and the name of the Lord Jesus was held in high honor. ¹⁸Many of those who believed now came and openly confessed their evil deeds. ¹⁹A number who had practiced sorcery brought their scrolls together and burned them publicly. When they calculated the value of the scrolls, the total came to fifty thousand drachmas.*c* ²⁰In this way the word of the Lord spread widely and grew in power.*r*

²¹After all this had happened, Paul decided to go to Jerusalem,*s* passing through Macedonia*t* and Achaia.*u* "After I have been there," he said, "I must visit Rome also."*v* ²²He sent two of his helpers,*w* Timothy*x* and Erastus,*y* to Macedonia, while he stayed in the province of Asia*z* a little longer.

²³About that time there arose a great disturbance about the Way.*a* ²⁴A silversmith named Demetrius, who made silver shrines of Artemis, brought in no little business for the craftsmen. ²⁵He called them together, along with the workmen in related trades, and said: "Men, you know we receive a good income from this

a 5 Or *in*   *b* 6 Or *other languages*   *c* 19 A drachma was a silver coin worth about a day's wages.

business.*a* ²⁶And you see and hear how this fellow Paul has convinced and led astray large numbers of people here in Ephesus*b* and in practically the whole province of Asia. He says that man-made gods are no gods at all.*c* ²⁷There is danger not only that our trade will lose its good name, but also that the temple of the great goddess Artemis will be discredited, and the goddess herself, who is worshiped throughout the province of Asia and the world, will be robbed of her divine majesty."

²⁸When they heard this, they were furious and began shouting: "Great is Artemis of the Ephesians!"*d* ²⁹Soon the whole city was in an uproar. The people seized Gaius*e* and Aristarchus,*f* Paul's traveling companions from Macedonia,*g* and rushed as one man into the theater. ³⁰Paul wanted to appear before the crowd, but the disciples would not let him. ³¹Even some of the officials of the province, friends of Paul, sent him a message begging him not to venture into the theater.

³²The assembly was in confusion: Some were shouting one thing, some another.*h* Most of the people did not even know why they were there. ³³The Jews pushed Alexander to the front, and some of the crowd shouted instructions to him. He motioned*i* for silence in order to make a defense before the people. ³⁴But when they realized he was a Jew, they all shouted in unison for about two hours: "Great is Artemis of the Ephesians!"

³⁵The city clerk quieted the crowd and said: "Men of Ephesus,*j* doesn't all the world know that the city of Ephesus is the guardian of the temple of the great Artemis and of her image, which fell from heaven? ³⁶Therefore, since these facts are undeniable, you ought to be quiet and not do anything rash. ³⁷You have brought these men here, though they have neither robbed temples*k* nor blasphemed our goddess. ³⁸If, then, Demetrius and his fellow craftsmen have a grievance against anybody, the courts are open and there are proconsuls.*l* They can press charges. ³⁹If there is anything further you want to bring up, it must be settled in a legal assembly. ⁴⁰As it is, we are in danger of being charged with rioting because of today's events. In that case we would not be able to account for this commotion, since there is no reason for it." ⁴¹After he had said this, he dismissed the assembly.

Chapter 20 Theme

20 When the uproar had ended, Paul sent for the disciples*m* and, after encouraging them, said good-by and set out for Macedonia.*n* ²He traveled through that area, speaking many words of encouragement to the people, and finally arrived in Greece, ³where he stayed three months. Because the Jews made a plot against him*o* just as he was about to sail for Syria, he decided to go

19:25 *a* Ac 16:16, 19,20

19:26 *b* Ac 18:19; *c* Dt 4:28; Ps 115:4; Isa 44:10-20; Jer 10:3-5; Ac 17:29; 1Co 8:4; Rev 9:20

19:28 *d* Ac 18:19

19:29 *e* Ac 20:4; Ro 16:23; 1Co 1:14 *f* Ac 20:4; 27:2; Col 4:10; Phm 24 *g* Ac 16:9

19:32 *h* Ac 21:34

19:33 *i* Ac 12:17

19:35 *j* Ac 18:19

19:37 *k* Ro 2:22

19:38 *l* Ac 13:7,8,12

20:1 *m* Ac 11:26 *n* Ac 16:9

20:3 *o* ver 19; Ac 9:23,24; 23:12,15,30; 25:3; 2Co 11:26

20:3
a Ac 16:9

20:4
b Ac 19:29
c Ac 17:1
d Ac 19:29
e Ac 16:1
f Eph 6:21;
Col 4:7;
2Ti 4:12;
Tit 3:12
g Ac 21:29;
2Ti 4:20

20:5
h Ac 16:10
i Ac 16:8

20:6
j Ac 16:12
k Ac 16:8

20:7
l 1Co 16:2;
Rev 1:10

20:8
m Ac 1:13

20:10
n 1Ki 17:21;
2Ki 4:34
o Mt 9:23,24

20:11
p ver 7

20:15
q ver 17;
2Ti 4:20

20:16
r Ac 18:19
s Ac 19:21
t Ac 2:1;
1Co 16:8

20:17
u Ac 11:30

20:18
v Ac 18:19-21;
19:1-41

20:19
w ver 3

20:20
x ver 27

20:21
y Ac 18:5
z Ac 2:38
a Ac 24:24;
26:18;
Eph 1:15;
Col 2:5;
Phm 5

20:22
b ver 16

20:23
c Ac 21:4
d Ac 9:16

20:24
e Ac 21:13
f 2Co 4:1
g Gal 1:1;
Tit 1:3

back through Macedonia.*a* ⁴He was accompanied by Sopater son of Pyrrhus from Berea, Aristarchus*b* and Secundus from Thessalonica,*c* Gaius*d* from Derbe, Timothy*e* also, and Tychicus*f* and Trophimus*g* from the province of Asia. ⁵These men went on ahead and waited for us*h* at Troas.*i* ⁶But we sailed from Philippi*j* after the Feast of Unleavened Bread, and five days later joined the others at Troas,*k* where we stayed seven days.

⁷On the first day of the week*l* we came together to break bread. Paul spoke to the people and, because he intended to leave the next day, kept on talking until midnight. ⁸There were many lamps in the upstairs room*m* where we were meeting. ⁹Seated in a window was a young man named Eutychus, who was sinking into a deep sleep as Paul talked on and on. When he was sound asleep, he fell to the ground from the third story and was picked up dead. ¹⁰Paul went down, threw himself on the young man*n* and put his arms around him. "Don't be alarmed," he said. "He's alive!"*o* ¹¹Then he went upstairs again and broke bread*p* and ate. After talking until daylight, he left. ¹²The people took the young man home alive and were greatly comforted.

¹³We went on ahead to the ship and sailed for Assos, where we were going to take Paul aboard. He had made this arrangement because he was going there on foot. ¹⁴When he met us at Assos, we took him aboard and went on to Mitylene. ¹⁵The next day we set sail from there and arrived off Kios. The day after that we crossed over to Samos, and on the following day arrived at Miletus.*q* ¹⁶Paul had decided to sail past Ephesus*r* to avoid spending time in the province of Asia, for he was in a hurry to reach Jerusalem,*s* if possible, by the day of Pentecost.*t*

¹⁷From Miletus, Paul sent to Ephesus for the elders*u* of the church. ¹⁸When they arrived, he said to them: "You know how I lived the whole time I was with you,*v* from the first day I came into the province of Asia. ¹⁹I served the Lord with great humility and with tears, although I was severely tested by the plots of the Jews.*w* ²⁰You know that I have not hesitated to preach anything*x* that would be helpful to you but have taught you publicly and from house to house. ²¹I have declared to both Jews*y* and Greeks that they must turn to God in repentance*z* and have faith in our Lord Jesus.*a*

²²"And now, compelled by the Spirit, I am going to Jerusalem,*b* not knowing what will happen to me there. ²³I only know that in every city the Holy Spirit warns me*c* that prison and hardships are facing me.*d* ²⁴However, I consider my life worth nothing to me,*e* if only I may finish the race and complete the task*f* the Lord Jesus has given me*g*—the task of testifying to the gospel of God's grace.

²⁵"Now I know that none of you among whom I have gone about preaching the kingdom will ever see me again.ᵃ ²⁶Therefore, I declare to you today that I am innocent of the blood of all men.ᵇ ²⁷For I have not hesitated to proclaim to you the whole will of God.ᶜ ²⁸Keep watch over yourselves and all the flock of which the Holy Spirit has made you overseers.ᵃ ᵈ Be shepherds of the church of God,ᵇ which he bought with his own blood. ²⁹I know that after I leave, savage wolvesᵉ will come in among you and will not spare the flock.ᶠ ³⁰Even from your own number men will arise and distort the truth in order to draw away disciplesᵍ after them. ³¹So be on your guard! Remember that for three yearsʰ I never stopped warning each of you night and day with tears.ⁱ

³²"Now I commit you to Godʲ and to the word of his grace, which can build you up and give you an inheritanceᵏ among all those who are sanctified.ˡ ³³I have not coveted anyone's silver or gold or clothing.ᵐ ³⁴You yourselves know that these hands of mine have supplied my own needs and the needs of my companions.ⁿ ³⁵In everything I did, I showed you that by this kind of hard work we must help the weak, remembering the words the Lord Jesus himself said: 'It is more blessed to give than to receive.'"

³⁶When he had said this, he knelt down with all of them and prayed.ᵒ ³⁷They all wept as they embraced him and kissed him.ᵖ ³⁸What grieved them most was his statement that they would never see his face again.�q Then they accompanied him to the ship.

Chapter 21 Theme

21 After weʳ had torn ourselves away from them, we put out to sea and sailed straight to Cos. The next day we went to Rhodes and from there to Patara. ²We found a ship crossing over to Phoenicia,ˢ went on board and set sail. ³After sighting Cyprus and passing to the south of it, we sailed on to Syria. We landed at Tyre, where our ship was to unload its cargo. ⁴Finding the disciplesᵗ there, we stayed with them seven days. Through the Spiritᵘ they urged Paul not to go on to Jerusalem. ⁵But when our time was up, we left and continued on our way. All the disciples and their wives and children accompanied us out of the city, and there on the beach we knelt to pray.ᵛ ⁶After saying good-by to each other, we went aboard the ship, and they returned home.

⁷We continued our voyage from Tyreʷ and landed at Ptolemais, where we greeted the brothersˣ and stayed with them for a day. ⁸Leaving the next day, we reached Caesareaʸ and stayed at the house of Philipᶻ the evangelist,ᵃ one of the Seven. ⁹He had four unmarried daughters who prophesied.ᵇ

ᵃ28 Traditionally *bishops*   ᵇ28 Many manuscripts *of the Lord*

20:25
ᵃ ver 38

20:26
ᵇ Ac 18:6

20:27
ᶜ ver 20

20:28
ᵈ 1Pe 5:2

20:29
ᵉ Mt 7:15
ᶠ ver 28

20:30
ᵍ Ac 11:26

20:31
ʰ Ac 19:10
ⁱ ver 19

20:32
ʲ Ac 14:23
ᵏ Eph 1:14;
Col 1:12; 3:24;
Heb 9:15;
1Pe 1:4
ˡ Ac 26:18

20:33
ᵐ 1Sa 12:3;
1Co 9:12;
2Co 7:2; 11:9;
12:14-17

20:34
ⁿ Ac 18:3

20:36
ᵒ Lk 22:41;
Ac 21:5

20:37
ᵖ Lk 15:20

20:38
q ver 25

21:1
ʳ Ac 16:10

21:2
ˢ Ac 11:19

21:4
ᵗ Ac 11:26
ᵘ ver 11;
Ac 20:23

21:5
ᵛ Ac 20:36

21:7
ʷ Ac 12:20
ˣ Ac 1:16

21:8
ʸ Ac 8:40
ᶻ Ac 6:5;
8:5-40
ᵃ Eph 4:11;
2Ti 4:5

21:9
ᵇ Lk 2:36;
Ac 2:17

21:10
a Ac 11:28

21:11
b ver 33
c 1Ki 22:11

21:13
d Ac 20:24
e Ac 9:16

21:16
f Ac 8:40
g ver 3,4

21:17
h Ac 15:4

21:18
i Ac 15:13
j Ac 11:30

21:19
k Ac 14:27
l Ac 1:17

21:20
m Ac 22:3;
Ro 10:2;
Gal 1:14
n Ac 15:1,5

21:21
o ver 28
p Ac 15:19-21;
1Co 7:18,19
q Ac 6:14

21:23
r Ac 18:18

21:24
s ver 26;
Ac 24:18
t Ac 18:18

21:25
u Ac 15:20,29

21:26
v Nu 6:13-20;
Ac 24:18

21:27
w Ac 24:18;
26:21

21:28
x Mt 24:15;
Ac 24:5,6

21:29
y Ac 20:4
z Ac 18:19

¹⁰After we had been there a number of days, a prophet named Agabus*ᵃ* came down from Judea. ¹¹Coming over to us, he took Paul's belt, tied his own hands and feet with it and said, "The Holy Spirit says, 'In this way the Jews of Jerusalem will bind*ᵇ* the owner of this belt and will hand him over to the Gentiles.'"*ᶜ*

¹²When we heard this, we and the people there pleaded with Paul not to go up to Jerusalem. ¹³Then Paul answered, "Why are you weeping and breaking my heart? I am ready not only to be bound, but also to die*ᵈ* in Jerusalem for the name of the Lord Jesus."*ᵉ* ¹⁴When he would not be dissuaded, we gave up and said, "The Lord's will be done."

¹⁵After this, we got ready and went up to Jerusalem. ¹⁶Some of the disciples from Caesarea*ᶠ* accompanied us and brought us to the home of Mnason, where we were to stay. He was a man from Cyprus*ᵍ* and one of the early disciples.

¹⁷When we arrived at Jerusalem, the brothers received us warmly.*ʰ* ¹⁸The next day Paul and the rest of us went to see James,*ⁱ* and all the elders*ʲ* were present. ¹⁹Paul greeted them and reported in detail what God had done among the Gentiles*ᵏ* through his ministry.*ˡ*

²⁰When they heard this, they praised God. Then they said to Paul: "You see, brother, how many thousands of Jews have believed, and all of them are zealous*ᵐ* for the law.*ⁿ* ²¹They have been informed that you teach all the Jews who live among the Gentiles to turn away from Moses,*ᵒ* telling them not to circumcise their children*ᵖ* or live according to our customs.*q* ²²What shall we do? They will certainly hear that you have come, ²³so do what we tell you. There are four men with us who have made a vow.*ʳ* ²⁴Take these men, join in their purification rites*ˢ* and pay their expenses, so that they can have their heads shaved.*ᵗ* Then everybody will know there is no truth in these reports about you, but that you yourself are living in obedience to the law. ²⁵As for the Gentile believers, we have written to them our decision that they should abstain from food sacrificed to idols, from blood, from the meat of strangled animals and from sexual immorality."*ᵘ*

²⁶The next day Paul took the men and purified himself along with them. Then he went to the temple to give notice of the date when the days of purification would end and the offering would be made for each of them.*ᵛ*

²⁷When the seven days were nearly over, some Jews from the province of Asia saw Paul at the temple. They stirred up the whole crowd and seized him,*ʷ* ²⁸shouting, "Men of Israel, help us! This is the man who teaches all men everywhere against our people and our law and this place. And besides, he has brought Greeks into the temple area and defiled this holy place."*ˣ* ²⁹(They had previously seen Trophimus*ʸ* the Ephesian*ᶻ* in the city with Paul and assumed that Paul had brought him into the temple area.)

³⁰The whole city was aroused, and the people came running from all directions. Seizing Paul,ᵃ they dragged himᵇ from the temple, and immediately the gates were shut. ³¹While they were trying to kill him, news reached the commander of the Roman troops that the whole city of Jerusalem was in an uproar. ³²He at once took some officers and soldiers and ran down to the crowd. When the rioters saw the commander and his soldiers, they stopped beating Paul.ᶜ

³³The commander came up and arrested him and ordered him to be boundᵈ with twoᵉ chains.ᶠ Then he asked who he was and what he had done. ³⁴Some in the crowd shouted one thing and some another,ᵍ and since the commander could not get at the truth because of the uproar, he ordered that Paul be taken into the barracks.ʰ ³⁵When Paul reached the steps,ⁱ the violence of the mob was so great he had to be carried by the soldiers. ³⁶The crowd that followed kept shouting, "Away with him!"ʲ

³⁷As the soldiers were about to take Paul into the barracks,ᵏ he asked the commander, "May I say something to you?"

"Do you speak Greek?" he replied. ³⁸"Aren't you the Egyptian who started a revolt and led four thousand terrorists out into the desertˡ some time ago?"ᵐ

³⁹Paul answered, "I am a Jew, from Tarsusⁿ in Cilicia,ᵒ a citizen of no ordinary city. Please let me speak to the people."

⁴⁰Having received the commander's permission, Paul stood on the steps and motionedᵖ to the crowd. When they were all silent, he said to them in Aramaicᵃ:q

Chapter 22 Theme

22 "Brothers and fathers,ʳ listen now to my defense." ²When they heard him speak to them in Aramaic,ˢ they became very quiet.

Then Paul said: ³"I am a Jew,ᵗ born in Tarsusᵘ of Cilicia, but brought up in this city. Underᵛ Gamalielʷ I was thoroughly trained in the law of our fathersˣ and was just as zealousʸ for God as any of you are today. ⁴I persecutedᶻ the followers of this Way to their death, arresting both men and women and throwing them into prison,ᵃ ⁵as also the high priest and all the Councilᵇ can testify. I even obtained letters from them to their brothersᶜ in Damascus,ᵈ and went there to bring these people as prisoners to Jerusalem to be punished.

⁶"About noon as I came near Damascus, suddenly a bright light from heaven flashed around me.ᵉ ⁷I fell to the ground and heard a voice say to me, 'Saul! Saul! Why do you persecute me?'

⁸"'Who are you, Lord?' I asked.

ᵃ40 Or possibly *Hebrew*; also in 22:2

Cross references (right column)

21:30
ᵃ Ac 26:21
ᵇ Ac 16:19

21:32
ᶜ Ac 23:27

21:33
ᵈ ver 11
ᵉ Ac 12:6
ᶠ Ac 20:23;
Eph 6:20;
2Ti 2:9

21:34
ᵍ Ac 19:32
ʰ ver 37;
Ac 23:10,
16,32

21:35
ⁱ ver 40

21:36
ʲ Lk 23:18;
Jn 19:15;
Ac 22:22

21:37
ᵏ ver 34

21:38
ˡ Mt 24:26
ᵐ Ac 5:36

21:39
ⁿ Ac 9:11
ᵒ Ac 22:3

21:40
ᵖ Ac 12:17
q Jn 5:2

22:1
ʳ Ac 7:2

22:2
ˢ Ac 21:40

22:3
ᵗ Ac 21:39
ᵘ Ac 9:11
ᵛ Lk 10:39
ʷ Ac 5:34
ˣ Ac 26:5
ʸ Ac 21:20

22:4
ᶻ Ac 8:3
ᵃ ver 19,20

22:5
ᵇ Lk 22:66
ᶜ Ac 13:26
ᵈ Ac 9:2

22:6
ᵉ Ac 9:3

22:9
a Ac 26:13
b Ac 9:7

22:10
c Ac 16:30

22:11
d Ac 9:8

22:12
e Ac 9:17
f Ac 10:22

22:14
g Ac 3:13
h 1Co 9:1; 15:8
i Ac 7:52

22:15
j Ac 23:11;
26:16

22:16
k Ac 2:38
l Heb 10:22
m Ro 10:13

22:17
n Ac 9:26
o Ac 10:10

22:19
p ver 4;
Ac 8:3
q Mt 10:17

22:20
r Ac 7:57-60;
8:1

22:21
s Ac 9:15;
13:46

22:22
t Ac 21:36
u Ac 25:24

22:23
v Ac 7:58
w 2Sa 16:13

22:24
x Ac 21:34
y ver 29

22:25
z Ac 16:37

"'I am Jesus of Nazareth, whom you are persecuting,' he replied. [9]My companions saw the light,[a] but they did not understand the voice[b] of him who was speaking to me.

[10]"'What shall I do, Lord?' I asked.

"'Get up,' the Lord said, 'and go into Damascus. There you will be told all that you have been assigned to do.'[c] [11]My companions led me by the hand into Damascus, because the brilliance of the light had blinded me.[d]

[12]"A man named Ananias came to see me.[e] He was a devout observer of the law and highly respected by all the Jews living there.[f] [13]He stood beside me and said, 'Brother Saul, receive your sight!' And at that very moment I was able to see him.

[14]"Then he said: 'The God of our fathers[g] has chosen you to know his will and to see[h] the Righteous One[i] and to hear words from his mouth. [15]You will be his witness[j] to all men of what you have seen and heard. [16]And now what are you waiting for? Get up, be baptized[k] and wash your sins away,[l] calling on his name.'[m]

[17]"When I returned to Jerusalem[n] and was praying at the temple, I fell into a trance[o] [18]and saw the Lord speaking. 'Quick!' he said to me. 'Leave Jerusalem immediately, because they will not accept your testimony about me.'

[19]"'Lord,' I replied, 'these men know that I went from one synagogue to another to imprison[p] and beat[q] those who believe in you. [20]And when the blood of your martyr[a] Stephen was shed, I stood there giving my approval and guarding the clothes of those who were killing him.'[r]

[21]"Then the Lord said to me, 'Go; I will send you far away to the Gentiles.'"[s]

[22]The crowd listened to Paul until he said this. Then they raised their voices and shouted, "Rid the earth of him![t] He's not fit to live!"[u]

[23]As they were shouting and throwing off their cloaks[v] and flinging dust into the air,[w] [24]the commander ordered Paul to be taken into the barracks.[x] He directed[y] that he be flogged and questioned in order to find out why the people were shouting at him like this. [25]As they stretched him out to flog him, Paul said to the centurion standing there, "Is it legal for you to flog a Roman citizen who hasn't even been found guilty?"[z]

[26]When the centurion heard this, he went to the commander and reported it. "What are you going to do?" he asked. "This man is a Roman citizen."

[27]The commander went to Paul and asked, "Tell me, are you a Roman citizen?"

"Yes, I am," he answered.

a 20 Or *witness*

²⁸Then the commander said, "I had to pay a big price for my citizenship."

"But I was born a citizen," Paul replied.

²⁹Those who were about to question him withdrew immediately. The commander himself was alarmed when he realized that he had put Paul, a Roman citizen,ᵃ in chains.

³⁰The next day, since the commander wanted to find out exactly why Paul was being accused by the Jews,ᵇ he released himᶜ and ordered the chief priests and all the Sanhedrinᵈ to assemble. Then he brought Paul and had him stand before them.

Chapter 23 Theme _____

23 Paul looked straight at the Sanhedrinᵉ and said, "My brothers,ᶠ I have fulfilled my duty to God in all good conscienceᵍ to this day." ²At this the high priest Ananiasʰ ordered those standing near Paul to strike him on the mouth.ⁱ ³Then Paul said to him, "God will strike you, you whitewashed wall!ʲ You sit there to judge me according to the law, yet you yourself violate the law by commanding that I be struck!"ᵏ

⁴Those who were standing near Paul said, "You dare to insult God's high priest?"

⁵Paul replied, "Brothers, I did not realize that he was the high priest; for it is written: 'Do not speak evil about the ruler of your people.'ᵃ"ˡ

⁶Then Paul, knowing that some of them were Sadducees and the others Pharisees, called out in the Sanhedrin, "My brothers,ᵐ I am a Pharisee,ⁿ the son of a Pharisee. I stand on trial because of my hope in the resurrection of the dead."ᵒ ⁷When he said this, a dispute broke out between the Pharisees and the Sadducees, and the assembly was divided. ⁸(The Sadducees say that there is no resurrection,ᵖ and that there are neither angels nor spirits, but the Pharisees acknowledge them all.)

⁹There was a great uproar, and some of the teachers of the law who were Phariseesᵠ stood up and argued vigorously. "We find nothing wrong with this man,"ʳ they said. "What if a spirit or an angel has spoken to him?"ˢ ¹⁰The dispute became so violent that the commander was afraid Paul would be torn to pieces by them. He ordered the troops to go down and take him away from them by force and bring him into the barracks.ᵗ

¹¹The following night the Lord stood near Paul and said, "Take courage!ᵘ As you have testified about me in Jerusalem, so you must also testify in Rome."ᵛ

ᵃ5 Exodus 22:28

22:29
ᵃver 24,25; Ac 16:38

22:30
ᵇAc 23:28
ᶜAc 21:33
ᵈMt 5:22

23:1
ᵉAc 22:30
ᶠAc 22:5
ᵍAc 24:16; 1Co 4:4; 2Co 1:12; 2Ti 1:3; Heb 13:18

23:2
ʰAc 24:1
ⁱJn 18:22

23:3
ʲMt 23:27
ᵏLev 19:15; Dt 25:1,2; Jn 7:51

23:5
ˡEx 22:28

23:6
ᵐAc 22:5
ⁿAc 26:5; Php 3:5
ᵒAc 24:15,21; 26:8

23:8
ᵖMt 22:23

23:9
ᵠMk 2:16
ʳver 29; Ac 25:25; 26:31
ˢAc 22:7,17,18

23:10
ᵗAc 21:34

23:11
ᵘAc 18:9
ᵛAc 19:21; 28:23

23:12
a ver 14,21,30;
Ac 25:3

23:14
b ver 12

23:15
c ver 1;
Ac 22:30

23:16
d ver 10;
Ac 21:34

23:18
e Eph 3:1

23:20
f ver 1
g ver 14,15

23:21
h ver 13
i ver 12,14

23:23
j Ac 8:40
k ver 33

23:24
l ver 26,33;
Ac 24:1-3,10;
25:14

23:26
m Lk 1:3;
Ac 24:3; 26:25
n Ac 15:23

23:27
o Ac 21:32
p Ac 21:33
q Ac 22:25-29

23:28
r Ac 22:30

23:29
s Ac 18:15; 25:19
t ver 9;
Ac 26:31

23:30
u ver 20,21
v Ac 20:3

¹²The next morning the Jews formed a conspiracy and bound themselves with an oath not to eat or drink until they had killed Paul.^a ¹³More than forty men were involved in this plot. ¹⁴They went to the chief priests and elders and said, "We have taken a solemn oath not to eat anything until we have killed Paul.^b ¹⁵Now then, you and the Sanhedrin^c petition the commander to bring him before you on the pretext of wanting more accurate information about his case. We are ready to kill him before he gets here."

¹⁶But when the son of Paul's sister heard of this plot, he went into the barracks^d and told Paul.

¹⁷Then Paul called one of the centurions and said, "Take this young man to the commander; he has something to tell him." ¹⁸So he took him to the commander.

The centurion said, "Paul, the prisoner,^e sent for me and asked me to bring this young man to you because he has something to tell you."

¹⁹The commander took the young man by the hand, drew him aside and asked, "What is it you want to tell me?"

²⁰He said: "The Jews have agreed to ask you to bring Paul before the Sanhedrin^f tomorrow on the pretext of wanting more accurate information about him.^g ²¹Don't give in to them, because more than forty^h of them are waiting in ambush for him. They have taken an oath not to eat or drink until they have killed him.ⁱ They are ready now, waiting for your consent to their request."

²²The commander dismissed the young man and cautioned him, "Don't tell anyone that you have reported this to me."

²³Then he called two of his centurions and ordered them, "Get ready a detachment of two hundred soldiers, seventy horsemen and two hundred spearmen^a to go to Caesarea^j at nine tonight.^k ²⁴Provide mounts for Paul so that he may be taken safely to Governor Felix."^l

²⁵He wrote a letter as follows:

²⁶Claudius Lysias,

To His Excellency,^m Governor Felix:

Greetings.ⁿ

²⁷This man was seized by the Jews and they were about to kill him,^o but I came with my troops and rescued him,^p for I had learned that he is a Roman citizen.^q ²⁸I wanted to know why they were accusing him, so I brought him to their Sanhedrin.^r ²⁹I found that the accusation had to do with questions about their law,^s but there was no charge against him^t that deserved death or imprisonment. ³⁰When I was informed^u of a plot^v to

a 23 The meaning of the Greek for this word is uncertain.

be carried out against the man, I sent him to you at once. I also ordered his accusers[a] to present to you their case against him.

[31]So the soldiers, carrying out their orders, took Paul with them during the night and brought him as far as Antipatris. [32]The next day they let the cavalry[b] go on with him, while they returned to the barracks.[c] [33]When the cavalry[d] arrived in Caesarea,[e] they delivered the letter to the governor[f] and handed Paul over to him. [34]The governor read the letter and asked what province he was from. Learning that he was from Cilicia,[g] [35]he said, "I will hear your case when your accusers[h] get here." Then he ordered that Paul be kept under guard[i] in Herod's palace.

Chapter 24 Theme

24 Five days later the high priest Ananias[j] went down to Caesarea with some of the elders and a lawyer named Tertullus, and they brought their charges[k] against Paul before the governor.[l] [2]When Paul was called in, Tertullus presented his case before Felix: "We have enjoyed a long period of peace under you, and your foresight has brought about reforms in this nation. [3]Everywhere and in every way, most excellent[m] Felix, we acknowledge this with profound gratitude. [4]But in order not to weary you further, I would request that you be kind enough to hear us briefly.

[5]"We have found this man to be a troublemaker, stirring up riots[n] among the Jews[o] all over the world. He is a ringleader of the Nazarene[p] sect[q] [6]and even tried to desecrate the temple;[r] so we seized him. [8]By [a] examining him yourself you will be able to learn the truth about all these charges we are bringing against him."

[9]The Jews joined in the accusation,[s] asserting that these things were true.

[10]When the governor[t] motioned for him to speak, Paul replied: "I know that for a number of years you have been a judge over this nation; so I gladly make my defense. [11]You can easily verify that no more than twelve days[u] ago I went up to Jerusalem to worship. [12]My accusers did not find me arguing with anyone at the temple,[v] or stirring up a crowd[w] in the synagogues or anywhere else in the city. [13]And they cannot prove to you the charges they are now making against me.[x] [14]However, I admit that I worship the God of our fathers[y] as a follower of the Way,[z] which they call a sect.[a] I believe everything that agrees with the Law and that is written in the Prophets,[b] [15]and I have the same hope in God as these men, that there will be a resurrection[c] of both the righteous and the

a6-8 Some manuscripts *him and wanted to judge him according to our law. [7]But the commander, Lysias, came and with the use of much force snatched him from our hands [8]and ordered his accusers to come before you. By*

23:30
a ver 35;
Ac 24:19;
25:16

23:32
b ver 23
c Ac 21:34

23:33
d ver 23,24
e Ac 8:40
f ver 26

23:34
g Ac 6:9;
21:39

23:35
h ver 30;
Ac 24:19;
25:16
i Ac 24:27

24:1
j Ac 23:2
k Ac 23:30,35
l Ac 23:24

24:3
m Lk 1:3;
Ac 23:26;
26:25

24:5
n Ac 16:20;
17:6
o Ac 21:28
p Mk 1:24
q ver 14;
Ac 26:5;
28:22

24:6
r Ac 21:28

24:9
s 1Th 2:16

24:10
t Ac 23:24

24:11
u Ac 21:27;
ver 1

24:12
v Ac 25:8;
28:17
w ver 18

24:13
x Ac 25:7

24:14
y Ac 3:13
z Ac 9:2
a ver 5
b Ac 26:6,22;
28:23

24:15
c Ac 23:6;
28:20

24:15
a Da 12:2;
Jn 5:28,29

24:16
b Ac 23:1

24:17
c Ac 11:29,30;
Ro 15:25-28,31;
1Co 16:1-4,15;
2Co 8:1-4;
Gal 2:10

24:18
d Ac 21:26
e ver 12

24:19
f Ac 23:30

24:21
g Ac 23:6

24:23
h Ac 23:35
i Ac 28:16
j Ac 23:16;
27:3

24:24
k Ac 20:21

24:25
l Gal 5:23;
2Pe 1:6
m Ac 10:42

24:27
n Ac 25:1,4,
9,14
o Ac 12:3; 25:9
p Ac 23:35;
25:14

25:1
q Ac 8:40

25:2
r ver 15;
Ac 24:1

25:4
s Ac 24:23

25:6
t ver 17

25:7
u Mk 15:3;
Lk 23:2,10;
Ac 24:5,6
v Ac 24:13

wicked.a 16So I strive always to keep my conscience clearb before God and man.

17"After an absence of several years, I came to Jerusalem to bring my people gifts for the poorc and to present offerings. 18I was ceremonially cleand when they found me in the temple courts doing this. There was no crowd with me, nor was I involved in any disturbance.e 19But there are some Jews from the province of Asia, who ought to be here before you and bring charges if they have anything against me.f 20Or these who are here should state what crime they found in me when I stood before the Sanhedrin— 21unless it was this one thing I shouted as I stood in their presence: 'It is concerning the resurrection of the dead that I am on trial before you today.'"g

22Then Felix, who was well acquainted with the Way, adjourned the proceedings. "When Lysias the commander comes," he said, "I will decide your case." 23He ordered the centurion to keep Paul under guardh but to give him some freedomi and permit his friends to take care of his needs.j

24Several days later Felix came with his wife Drusilla, who was a Jewess. He sent for Paul and listened to him as he spoke about faith in Christ Jesus.k 25As Paul discoursed on righteousness, self-controll and the judgmentm to come, Felix was afraid and said, "That's enough for now! You may leave. When I find it convenient, I will send for you." 26At the same time he was hoping that Paul would offer him a bribe, so he sent for him frequently and talked with him.

27When two years had passed, Felix was succeeded by Porcius Festus,n but because Felix wanted to grant a favor to the Jews,o he left Paul in prison.p

Chapter 25 Theme

25 Three days after arriving in the province, Festus went up from Caesareaq to Jerusalem, 2where the chief priests and Jewish leaders appeared before him and presented the charges against Paul.r 3They urgently requested Festus, as a favor to them, to have Paul transferred to Jerusalem, for they were preparing an ambush to kill him along the way. 4Festus answered, "Paul is being helds at Caesarea, and I myself am going there soon. 5Let some of your leaders come with me and press charges against the man there, if he has done anything wrong."

6After spending eight or ten days with them, he went down to Caesarea, and the next day he convened the courtt and ordered that Paul be brought before him. 7When Paul appeared, the Jews who had come down from Jerusalem stood around him, bringing many serious charges against him,u which they could not prove.v

⁸Then Paul made his defense: "I have done nothing wrong against the law of the Jews or against the temple*ᵃ* or against Caesar."

⁹Festus, wishing to do the Jews a favor,*ᵇ* said to Paul, "Are you willing to go up to Jerusalem and stand trial before me there on these charges?"*ᶜ*

¹⁰Paul answered: "I am now standing before Caesar's court, where I ought to be tried. I have not done any wrong to the Jews, as you yourself know very well. ¹¹If, however, I am guilty of doing anything deserving death, I do not refuse to die. But if the charges brought against me by these Jews are not true, no one has the right to hand me over to them. I appeal to Caesar!"*ᵈ*

¹²After Festus had conferred with his council, he declared: "You have appealed to Caesar. To Caesar you will go!"

¹³A few days later King Agrippa and Bernice arrived at Caesarea*ᵉ* to pay their respects to Festus. ¹⁴Since they were spending many days there, Festus discussed Paul's case with the king. He said: "There is a man here whom Felix left as a prisoner.*ᶠ* ¹⁵When I went to Jerusalem, the chief priests and elders of the Jews brought charges against him*ᵍ* and asked that he be condemned.

¹⁶"I told them that it is not the Roman custom to hand over any man before he has faced his accusers and has had an opportunity to defend himself against their charges.*ʰ* ¹⁷When they came here with me, I did not delay the case, but convened the court the next day and ordered the man to be brought in.*ⁱ* ¹⁸When his accusers got up to speak, they did not charge him with any of the crimes I had expected. ¹⁹Instead, they had some points of dispute*ʲ* with him about their own religion*ᵏ* and about a dead man named Jesus who Paul claimed was alive. ²⁰I was at a loss how to investigate such matters; so I asked if he would be willing to go to Jerusalem and stand trial there on these charges.*ˡ* ²¹When Paul made his appeal to be held over for the Emperor's decision, I ordered him held until I could send him to Caesar."*ᵐ*

²²Then Agrippa said to Festus, "I would like to hear this man myself."

He replied, "Tomorrow you will hear him."*ⁿ*

²³The next day Agrippa and Bernice*ᵒ* came with great pomp and entered the audience room with the high ranking officers and the leading men of the city. At the command of Festus, Paul was brought in. ²⁴Festus said: "King Agrippa, and all who are present with us, you see this man! The whole Jewish community*ᵖ* has petitioned me about him in Jerusalem and here in Caesarea, shouting that he ought not to live any longer.*�q* ²⁵I found he had done nothing deserving of death,*ʳ* but because he made his appeal to the Emperor*ˢ* I decided to send him to Rome. ²⁶But I have nothing definite to write to His Majesty about him. Therefore I have

25:8
ᵃ Ac 6:13;
24:12; 28:17

25:9
ᵇ Ac 24:27
ᶜ ver 20

25:11
ᵈ ver 21,25;
Ac 26:32;
28:19

25:13
ᵉ Ac 8:40

25:14
ᶠ Ac 24:27

25:15
ᵍ ver 2;
Ac 24:1

25:16
ʰ ver 4,5;
Ac 23:30

25:17
ⁱ ver 6,10

25:19
ʲ Ac 18:15;
23:29
ᵏ Ac 17:22

25:20
ˡ ver 9

25:21
ᵐ ver 11,12

25:22
ⁿ Ac 9:15

25:23
ᵒ ver 13;
Ac 26:30

25:24
ᵖ ver 2,3,7
q Ac 22:22

25:25
ʳ Ac 23:9
ˢ ver 11

brought him before all of you, and especially before you, King Agrippa, so that as a result of this investigation I may have something to write. ²⁷For I think it is unreasonable to send on a prisoner without specifying the charges against him."

Chapter 26 Theme _____

26 Then Agrippa said to Paul, "You have permission to speak for yourself."*a*

So Paul motioned with his hand and began his defense: ²"King Agrippa, I consider myself fortunate to stand before you today as I make my defense against all the accusations of the Jews, ³and especially so because you are well acquainted with all the Jewish customs*b* and controversies.*c* Therefore, I beg you to listen to me patiently.

⁴"The Jews all know the way I have lived ever since I was a child,*d* from the beginning of my life in my own country, and also in Jerusalem. ⁵They have known me for a long time*e* and can testify, if they are willing, that according to the strictest sect of our religion, I lived as a Pharisee.*f* ⁶And now it is because of my hope*g* in what God has promised our fathers*h* that I am on trial today. ⁷This is the promise our twelve tribes*i* are hoping to see fulfilled as they earnestly serve God day and night.*j* O king, it is because of this hope that the Jews are accusing me.*k* ⁸Why should any of you consider it incredible that God raises the dead?*l*

⁹"I too was convinced*m* that I ought to do all that was possible to oppose*n* the name of Jesus of Nazareth.*o* ¹⁰And that is just what I did in Jerusalem. On the authority of the chief priests I put many of the saints*p* in prison,*q* and when they were put to death, I cast my vote against them.*r* ¹¹Many a time I went from one synagogue to another to have them punished,*s* and I tried to force them to blaspheme. In my obsession against them, I even went to foreign cities to persecute them.

¹²"On one of these journeys I was going to Damascus with the authority and commission of the chief priests. ¹³About noon, O king, as I was on the road, I saw a light from heaven, brighter than the sun, blazing around me and my companions. ¹⁴We all fell to the ground, and I heard a voice*t* saying to me in Aramaic,ᵃ 'Saul, Saul, why do you persecute me? It is hard for you to kick against the goads.'

¹⁵"Then I asked, 'Who are you, Lord?'

"'I am Jesus, whom you are persecuting,' the Lord replied. ¹⁶'Now get up and stand on your feet.*u* I have appeared to you to appoint you as a servant and as a witness of what you have seen

---

26:1
a Ac 9:15; 25:22

26:3
b ver 7; Ac 6:14
c Ac 25:19

26:4
d Gal 1:13,14; Php 3:5

26:5
e Ac 22:3
f Ac 23:6; Php 3:5

26:6
g Ac 23:6; 24:15; 28:20
h Ac 13:32; Ro 15:8

26:7
i Jas 1:1
j 1Th 3:10; 1Ti 5:5
k ver 2

26:8
l Ac 23:6

26:9
m 1Ti 1:13
n Jn 16:2
o Jn 15:21

26:10
p Ac 9:13
q Ac 8:3; 9:2,14,21
r Ac 22:20

26:11
s Mt 10:17

26:14
t Ac 9:7

26:16
u Eze 2:1; Da 10:11

ᵃ14 Or *Hebrew*

of me and what I will show you.[a] [17]I will rescue you[b] from your own people and from the Gentiles.[c] I am sending you to them [18]to open their eyes[d] and turn them from darkness to light,[e] and from the power of Satan to God, so that they may receive forgiveness of sins[f] and a place among those who are sanctified by faith in me.'[g]

[19]"So then, King Agrippa, I was not disobedient to the vision from heaven. [20]First to those in Damascus,[h] then to those in Jerusalem[i] and in all Judea, and to the Gentiles[j] also, I preached that they should repent[k] and turn to God and prove their repentance by their deeds.[l] [21]That is why the Jews seized me[m] in the temple courts and tried to kill me.[n] [22]But I have had God's help to this very day, and so I stand here and testify to small and great alike. I am saying nothing beyond what the prophets and Moses said would happen[o]— [23]that the Christ[a] would suffer and, as the first to rise from the dead,[p] would proclaim light to his own people and to the Gentiles."[q]

[24]At this point Festus interrupted Paul's defense. "You are out of your mind,[r] Paul!" he shouted. "Your great learning[s] is driving you insane."

[25]"I am not insane, most excellent[t] Festus," Paul replied. "What I am saying is true and reasonable. [26]The king is familiar with these things,[u] and I can speak freely to him. I am convinced that none of this has escaped his notice, because it was not done in a corner. [27]King Agrippa, do you believe the prophets? I know you do."

[28]Then Agrippa said to Paul, "Do you think that in such a short time you can persuade me to be a Christian?"[v]

[29]Paul replied, "Short time or long—I pray God that not only you but all who are listening to me today may become what I am, except for these chains."[w]

[30]The king rose, and with him the governor and Bernice[x] and those sitting with them. [31]They left the room, and while talking with one another, they said, "This man is not doing anything that deserves death or imprisonment."[y]

[32]Agrippa said to Festus, "This man could have been set free[z] if he had not appealed to Caesar."[a]

Chapter 27 Theme _____

27

When it was decided that we[b] would sail for Italy,[c] Paul and some other prisoners were handed over to a centurion named Julius, who belonged to the Imperial Regiment.[d] [2]We boarded a ship from Adramyttium about to sail for ports along the coast of the province of Asia,[e] and we put out to sea. Aristarchus,[f] a Macedonian[g] from Thessalonica,[h] was with us.

[a]23 Or *Messiah*

26:16
[a]Ac 22:14,15

26:17
[b]Jer 1:8,19
[c]Ac 9:15

26:18
[d]Isa 35:5
[e]Isa 42:7,16;
Eph 5:8;
Col 1:13;
1Pe 2:9
[f]Lk 24:47;
Ac 2:38
[g]Ac 20:21,32

26:20
[h]Ac 9:19-25
[i]Ac 9:26-29;
22:17-20
[j]Ac 9:15;
13:46
[k]Ac 3:19
[l]Mt 3:8;
Lk 3:8

26:21
[m]Ac 21:27,30
[n]Ac 21:31

26:22
[o]Lk 24:27,44;
Ac 10:43;
24:14

26:23
[p]1Co 15:20,23;
Col 1:18;
Rev 1:5
[q]Lk 2:32

26:24
[r]Jn 10:20;
1Co 4:10
[s]Jn 7:15

26:25
[t]Ac 23:26

26:26
[u]ver 3

26:28
[v]Ac 11:26

26:29
[w]Ac 21:33

26:30
[x]Ac 25:23

26:31
[y]Ac 23:9

26:32
[z]Ac 28:18
[a]Ac 25:11

27:1
[b]Ac 16:10
[c]Ac 18:2;
25:12,25
[d]Ac 10:1

27:2
[e]Ac 2:9
[f]Ac 19:29
[g]Ac 16:9
[h]Ac 17:1

27:3
a Mt 11:21
b ver 43
c Ac 24:23;
28:16

27:4
d ver 7

27:5
e Ac 6:9

27:6
f Ac 28:11
g ver 1

27:7
h ver 4
i ver 12,13,21

27:9
j Lev 16:29-31;
23:27-29;
Nu 29:7

27:10
k ver 21

27:14
l Mk 4:37

27:17
m ver 26,39

27:18
n ver 19,38;
Jnh 1:5

³The next day we landed at Sidon;[a] and Julius, in kindness to Paul,[b] allowed him to go to his friends so they might provide for his needs.[c] ⁴From there we put out to sea again and passed to the lee of Cyprus because the winds were against us.[d] ⁵When we had sailed across the open sea off the coast of Cilicia[e] and Pamphylia, we landed at Myra in Lycia. ⁶There the centurion found an Alexandrian ship[f] sailing for Italy[g] and put us on board. ⁷We made slow headway for many days and had difficulty arriving off Cnidus. When the wind did not allow us to hold our course,[h] we sailed to the lee of Crete,[i] opposite Salmone. ⁸We moved along the coast with difficulty and came to a place called Fair Havens, near the town of Lasea.

⁹Much time had been lost, and sailing had already become dangerous because by now it was after the Fast.[a][j] So Paul warned them, ¹⁰"Men, I can see that our voyage is going to be disastrous and bring great loss to ship and cargo, and to our own lives also."[k] ¹¹But the centurion, instead of listening to what Paul said, followed the advice of the pilot and of the owner of the ship. ¹²Since the harbor was unsuitable to winter in, the majority decided that we should sail on, hoping to reach Phoenix and winter there. This was a harbor in Crete, facing both southwest and northwest.

¹³When a gentle south wind began to blow, they thought they had obtained what they wanted; so they weighed anchor and sailed along the shore of Crete. ¹⁴Before very long, a wind of hurricane force,[l] called the "northeaster," swept down from the island. ¹⁵The ship was caught by the storm and could not head into the wind; so we gave way to it and were driven along. ¹⁶As we passed to the lee of a small island called Cauda, we were hardly able to make the lifeboat secure. ¹⁷When the men had hoisted it aboard, they passed ropes under the ship itself to hold it together. Fearing that they would run aground[m] on the sandbars of Syrtis, they lowered the sea anchor and let the ship be driven along. ¹⁸We took such a violent battering from the storm that the next day they began to throw the cargo overboard.[n] ¹⁹On the third day, they threw the ship's tackle overboard with their own hands. ²⁰When neither sun nor stars appeared for many days and the storm continued raging, we finally gave up all hope of being saved.

Paul Sails from Caesarea to Rome

a 9 That is, the Day of Atonement (Yom Kippur)

²¹After the men had gone a long time without food, Paul stood up before them and said: "Men, you should have taken my advice[a] not to sail from Crete;[b] then you would have spared yourselves this damage and loss. ²²But now I urge you to keep up your courage,[c] because not one of you will be lost; only the ship will be destroyed. ²³Last night an angel[d] of the God whose I am and whom I serve[e] stood beside me[f] ²⁴and said, 'Do not be afraid, Paul. You must stand trial before Caesar;[g] and God has graciously given you the lives of all who sail with you.'[h] ²⁵So keep up your courage,[i] men, for I have faith in God that it will happen just as he told me.[j] ²⁶Nevertheless, we must run aground[k] on some island."[l]

²⁷On the fourteenth night we were still being driven across the Adriatic[a] Sea, when about midnight the sailors sensed they were approaching land. ²⁸They took soundings and found that the water was a hundred and twenty feet[b] deep. A short time later they took soundings again and found it was ninety feet[c] deep. ²⁹Fearing that we would be dashed against the rocks, they dropped four anchors from the stern and prayed for daylight. ³⁰In an attempt to escape from the ship, the sailors let the lifeboat[m] down into the sea, pretending they were going to lower some anchors from the bow. ³¹Then Paul said to the centurion and the soldiers, "Unless these men stay with the ship, you cannot be saved."[n] ³²So the soldiers cut the ropes that held the lifeboat and let it fall away.

³³Just before dawn Paul urged them all to eat. "For the last fourteen days," he said, "you have been in constant suspense and have gone without food—you haven't eaten anything. ³⁴Now I urge you to take some food. You need it to survive. Not one of you will lose a single hair from his head."[o] ³⁵After he said this, he took some bread and gave thanks to God in front of them all. Then he broke it[p] and began to eat. ³⁶They were all encouraged[q] and ate some food themselves. ³⁷Altogether there were 276 of us on board. ³⁸When they had eaten as much as they wanted, they lightened the ship by throwing the grain into the sea.[r]

³⁹When daylight came, they did not recognize the land, but they saw a bay with a sandy beach,[s] where they decided to run the ship aground if they could. ⁴⁰Cutting loose the anchors,[t] they left them in the sea and at the same time untied the ropes that held the rudders. Then they hoisted the foresail to the wind and made for the beach. ⁴¹But the ship struck a sandbar and ran aground. The bow stuck fast and would not move, and the stern was broken to pieces by the pounding of the surf.[u]

⁴²The soldiers planned to kill the prisoners to prevent any of them from swimming away and escaping. ⁴³But the centurion

a 27 In ancient times the name referred to an area extending well south of Italy.
b 28 Greek twenty orguias (about 37 meters)   c 28 Greek fifteen orguias (about 27 meters)

### Cross references (margin)

27:21
a ver 10
b ver 7

27:22
c ver 25,36

27:23
d Ac 5:19
e Ro 1:9
f Ac 18:9; 23:11; 2Ti 4:17

27:24
g Ac 23:11
h ver 44

27:25
i ver 22,36
j Ro 4:20,21

27:26
k ver 17,39
l Ac 28:1

27:30
m ver 16

27:31
n ver 24

27:34
o Mt 10:30

27:35
p Mt 14:19

27:36
q ver 22,25

27:38
r ver 18; Jnh 1:5

27:39
s Ac 28:1

27:40
t ver 29

27:41
u 2Co 11:25

27:43
a ver 3

27:44
b ver 22,31

28:1
c Ac 16:10
d Ac 27:26,39

28:4
e Mk 16:18
f Lk 13:2,4

28:5
g Lk 10:19

28:6
h Ac 14:11

28:8
i Jas 5:14,15
j Ac 9:40

28:11
k Ac 27:6

28:14
l Ac 1:16

28:15
m Ac 1:16

28:16
n Ac 24:23;
27:3

28:17
o Ac 25:2
p Ac 22:5
q Ac 25:8
r Ac 6:14

28:18
s Ac 22:24
t Ac 26:31,32
u Ac 23:9

28:19
v Ac 25:11

wanted to spare Paul's life[a] and kept them from carrying out their plan. He ordered those who could swim to jump overboard first and get to land. [44]The rest were to get there on planks or on pieces of the ship. In this way everyone reached land in safety.[b]

Chapter 28 Theme

28 Once safely on shore, we[c] found out that the island[d] was called Malta. [2]The islanders showed us unusual kindness. They built a fire and welcomed us all because it was raining and cold. [3]Paul gathered a pile of brushwood and, as he put it on the fire, a viper, driven out by the heat, fastened itself on his hand. [4]When the islanders saw the snake hanging from his hand,[e] they said to each other, "This man must be a murderer; for though he escaped from the sea, Justice has not allowed him to live."[f] [5]But Paul shook the snake off into the fire and suffered no ill effects.[g] [6]The people expected him to swell up or suddenly fall dead, but after waiting a long time and seeing nothing unusual happen to him, they changed their minds and said he was a god.[h]

[7]There was an estate nearby that belonged to Publius, the chief official of the island. He welcomed us to his home and for three days entertained us hospitably. [8]His father was sick in bed, suffering from fever and dysentery. Paul went in to see him and, after prayer,[i] placed his hands on him and healed him.[j] [9]When this had happened, the rest of the sick on the island came and were cured. [10]They honored us in many ways and when we were ready to sail, they furnished us with the supplies we needed.

[11]After three months we put out to sea in a ship that had wintered in the island. It was an Alexandrian ship[k] with the figurehead of the twin gods Castor and Pollux. [12]We put in at Syracuse and stayed there three days. [13]From there we set sail and arrived at Rhegium. The next day the south wind came up, and on the following day we reached Puteoli. [14]There we found some brothers[l] who invited us to spend a week with them. And so we came to Rome. [15]The brothers[m] there had heard that we were coming, and they traveled as far as the Forum of Appius and the Three Taverns to meet us. At the sight of these men Paul thanked God and was encouraged. [16]When we got to Rome, Paul was allowed to live by himself, with a soldier to guard him.[n]

[17]Three days later he called together the leaders of the Jews.[o] When they had assembled, Paul said to them: "My brothers,[p] although I have done nothing against our people[q] or against the customs of our ancestors,[r] I was arrested in Jerusalem and handed over to the Romans. [18]They examined me[s] and wanted to release me,[t] because I was not guilty of any crime deserving death.[u] [19]But when the Jews objected, I was compelled to appeal to Caesar[v]—

not that I had any charge to bring against my own people. [20]For this reason I have asked to see you and talk with you. It is because of the hope of Israel[a] that I am bound with this chain."[b]

[21]They replied, "We have not received any letters from Judea concerning you, and none of the brothers[c] who have come from there has reported or said anything bad about you. [22]But we want to hear what your views are, for we know that people everywhere are talking against this sect."[d]

[23]They arranged to meet Paul on a certain day, and came in even larger numbers to the place where he was staying. From morning till evening he explained and declared to them the kingdom of God[e] and tried to convince them about Jesus[f] from the Law of Moses and from the Prophets.[g] [24]Some were convinced by what he said, but others would not believe.[h] [25]They disagreed among themselves and began to leave after Paul had made this final statement: "The Holy Spirit spoke the truth to your forefathers when he said through Isaiah the prophet:

[26]"'Go to this people and say,
"You will be ever hearing but never understanding;
you will be ever seeing but never perceiving."
[27]For this people's heart has become calloused;[i]
they hardly hear with their ears,
and they have closed their eyes.
Otherwise they might see with their eyes,
hear with their ears,
understand with their hearts
and turn, and I would heal them.'[a][j]

[28]"Therefore I want you to know that God's salvation[k] has been sent to the Gentiles,[l] and they will listen!"[b]

[30]For two whole years Paul stayed there in his own rented house and welcomed all who came to see him. [31]Boldly and without hindrance he preached the kingdom of God[m] and taught about the Lord Jesus Christ.

a 27 Isaiah 6:9,10   b 28 Some manuscripts listen!" [29]After he said this, the Jews left, arguing vigorously among themselves.

28:20
a Ac 26:6,7
b Ac 21:33

28:21
c Ac 22:5

28:22
d Ac 24:5,14

28:23
e Ac 19:8
f Ac 17:3
g Ac 8:35

28:24
h Ac 14:4

28:27
i Ps 119:70
j Isa 6:9,10

28:28
k Lk 2:30
l Ac 13:46

28:31
m ver 23;
Mt 4:23

ACTS AT A GLANCE

Theme of Acts:

Author:

SEGMENT DIVISIONS

Date:

Purpose:

Key Words:

believe, have
faith (believed,
believers, put
their trust)

baptized
(baptism)

Spirit

witness, testify,
confirmed, bore
testimony,
showed, martyr

word, preach-
ing, message,
statement
(word of God,
word of the
Lord)

save, saved

church

			CHAPTER THEMES
			1
			2
			3
			4
			5
			6
			7
			8
			9
			10
			11
			12
			13
			14
			15
			16
			17
			18
			19
			20
			21
			22
			23
			24
			25
			26
			27
			28

ROMANS

*T*he gospel Paul preached, justification by faith alone, was under siege. While many directly opposed this gospel, others twisted it to suit their own preferences. The Judaizers said salvation might be by grace but the believer is "kept" by the law. They insisted that circumcision was necessary for salvation. At the other extreme, the antinomians taught that you could be saved by grace and still live any way you wanted—even continue in sin.

Only a clear explanation of the gospel could refute such errors. Eager to prove the gospel's power to save and sanctify both Jew and Gentile, Paul, like a wise lawyer, calls the gospel to the witness stand and examines it from every angle. The result is the book of Romans, a theological masterpiece written around A.D. 56 or 57.

❧ THINGS TO DO

1. Romans is the constitution of the Christian faith. If you understand Romans you will have a plumb line for correctly interpreting any teaching on the gospel. It is a book you need to observe until you are so familiar with the text that its meaning is obvious.

   a. Read Romans in one sitting before you begin your study. If that is not possible, read it a chapter at a time. Every time you see the word *gospel*, mark it in a distinctive way so you can easily spot it in the text.

   b. Paul gives his reasons for writing Romans in the first and the last two chapters. Record these reasons in the appropriate place on the ROMANS OBSERVATIONS CHART on page 1949.

   c. Watch for references to the recipients of this letter and record on the OBSERVATIONS CHART what you learn about them. Note whether Paul is writing to Gentiles, Jews, or both. Also as you read, find out as much as you can about Paul. Record your insights on the chart.

2. The book of Romans can be divided into four segments, each building on the previous one: chapters 1 through 5, 6 through 8, 9 through 11, and 12 through 16. Instructions for each segment follow. As you complete each one, return to these general instructions so you can see what else you are to do in each segment.

Chapters 1-5

1. Read Romans 1 through 5 a chapter at a time, observing and marking the text. Complete instructions on how to observe the text are in the observation section in "How to Use The International Inductive Study Bible" on page IISB-15.

   a. Mark each of the following key words and their synonyms: *grace, faith (believe), law (law's, principle), justified (proved right, declared righteous, justify, just, deserved), righteous (righteousness, justice), wrath (punishment), judge (condemn, judgment), gospel, believe (faith), sin (sinning), Gentiles (nations), God, Jesus Christ,* and *Spirit* (when referring to the Holy Spirit).

   b. List these words on an index card to use as a bookmark when you study Romans. As you come to each new segment of Romans, add the next group of key words to your card. Mark or color code them on the card in the same way you plan to mark them in your Bible.

   c. Each chapter has key words or phrases which are unique to that chapter. Mark the following:

      1) In chapter 1 mark *exchanged (the)* and *God (he) gave them over*. Note the progression of events as you observe what the people did and how God responded.

      2) In chapter 4 mark and observe *credit* or *credited*.

3) In chapter 5 mark and observe *gift*.

4) Mark any other key words that are pertinent to a chapter or to the book.

2. List in the margin what you learn from the text about each key word. For example, *sin* is a key word. What do you learn from the text about *sin*? About *wrath (punishment)*? About *righteousness (justice)*? And so on.

3. From chapters 3 through 11 of Romans, Paul periodically asks an important question and then answers it. Mark each of Paul's questions. You might put a cloud like this ☁ around each question throughout the book. Carefully read each question and note how Paul answers it.

4. Watch for the words *therefore (then, this is why)* and see what they are "there for." Several chapters have these words in the first verse. When Paul uses *therefore, then,* or *this is why* he is making a point you will not want to miss.

5. When you finish observing each chapter, record the theme of that chapter in the text next to the chapter number and on the ROMANS AT A GLANCE chart on page 1950.

6. What do you see as the theme in this first segment of Romans? Write it (in pencil) on ROMANS AT A GLANCE in the first column under "Segment Divisions."

Chapters 6-8

1. Follow the same procedure as you did in the previous segment. Continue to mark the key words you marked in chapters 1 through 5, and in these chapters also mark the following words and their synonyms: *sinful nature (natural selves, unspiritual, sinful man, sinful, natural, human ancestry, race), dead (died, dying, death), life, reign, master (mastery), slaves (slavery),* and *freed from sin (set free from sin)*.

2. If it is significant, list in the margin what you learn from marking the prominent key words in this segment of Romans.

3. Mark Paul's questions and in the margin list the main points of his answers.

4. Record the theme of each chapter and of this segment as you did before.

5. On the ROMANS OBSERVATIONS CHART on page 1949 is a place to record everything you learn from chapters 5 through 8 regarding our position in Adam (before we were saved) and our position in Christ (after we were saved). Do not read anything into the text, but simply record what you learn.

Chapters 9-11

1. Follow the same pattern you used in the first segment and mark the same key words you marked in chapters 1 through 8. Also mark the following key words in this segment of Romans: *foreknew,* predestined,* election (elect, chosen), Israel* (and its pronouns), *unbelief, saved (salvation*—go back and mark it in Romans 1:16), and *mercy*.

*These words are used in Romans 8:29, 30. Go back and mark them, and in the margin note what you learn from the text.

2. In this section it is critical that you follow Paul's reasoning by marking each question and then listing in the margin the main points of Paul's answers. Do not read into the text meanings that aren't there. Let God speak as you listen. Meditate on Romans 11:33-36.

3. Record chapter and segment themes as before.

Chapters 12-16

1. At this point Paul makes a transition and changes from explaining the doctrinal aspect of the gospel to describing how to live it out practically. As Paul turns from doctrine to duty, note the *therefore* and how it would relate to what has been written in the first eleven chapters of Romans. Think about what Paul is asking you to do. Is it reasonable? Why? What do you need to do?

2. Read Romans chapters 12 through 16 and identify the main topic or subject of each chapter. Mark

the following key words: *love, authority (rulers), brothers (brother), Lord, Gentiles (nations), minister (service, serving, servant, act of worship, serve, in the service of), judge (judgment, condemn, passing judgment on),* and *failings.*

3. Complete ROMANS AT A GLANCE. Fill in the chapter themes and segment divisions and then record the theme of Romans. (Do not forget to record your chapter themes in the text, too.)

❧ THINGS TO THINK ABOUT

1. Suppose someone accused you of not being a Christian. What proof could you give of the fact that you are a true child of God?

2. Do you know how to share the gospel with someone? How?

3. From your study of Romans, how is a person saved?

4. How will your relationships to those in authority over you and to those who are your brothers and sisters in the faith change as you apply the truth of Romans to your life?

5. Are you ready to defend the gospel? Can you refute modern-day Judaizers and/or antinomians?

Chapter 1 Theme _____

1 Paul, a servant of Christ Jesus, called to be an apostle[a] and set apart[b] for the gospel of God[c]— [2]the gospel he promised beforehand through his prophets in the Holy Scriptures[d] [3]regarding his Son, who as to his human nature[e] was a descendant of David, [4]and who through the Spirit[a] of holiness was declared with power to be the Son of God[b] by his resurrection from the dead: Jesus Christ our Lord. [5]Through him and for his name's sake, we received grace and apostleship to call people from among all the Gentiles[f] to the obedience that comes from faith.[g] [6]And you also are among those who are called to belong to Jesus Christ.[h]

[7]To all in Rome who are loved by God[i] and called to be saints:

Grace and peace to you from God our Father and from the Lord Jesus Christ.[j]

[8]First, I thank my God through Jesus Christ for all of you,[k] because your faith is being reported all over the world.[l] [9]God, whom I serve[m] with my whole heart in preaching the gospel of his Son, is my witness[n] how constantly I remember you [10]in my prayers at all times; and I pray that now at last by God's will the way may be opened for me to come to you.[o]

[11]I long to see you[p] so that I may impart to you some spiritual gift to make you strong— [12]that is, that you and I may be mutually encouraged by each other's faith. [13]I do not want you to be unaware, brothers, that I planned many times to come to you (but have been prevented from doing so until now)[q] in order that I might have a harvest among you, just as I have had among the other Gentiles.

[a]4 Or *who as to his spirit*   [b]4 Or *was appointed to be the Son of God with power*

1:1 [a]1Co 1:1 [b]Ac 9:15 [c]2Co 11:7
1:2 [d]Gal 3:8
1:3 [e]Jn 1:14
1:5 [f]Ac 9:15 [g]Ac 6:7
1:6 [h]Rev 17:14
1:7 [i]Ro 8:39 [j]1Co 1:3
1:8 [k]1Co 1:4 [l]Ro 16:19
1:9 [m]2Ti 1:3 [n]Php 1:8
1:10 [o]Ro 15:32
1:11 [p]Ro 15:23
1:13 [q]Ro 15:22,23

1:14
a 1Co 9:16

1:15
b Ro 15:20

1:16
c 2Ti 1:8
d 1Co 1:18
e Ac 3:26
f Ro 2:9,10

1:17
g Ro 3:21
h Hab 2:4;
Gal 3:11;
Heb 10:38

1:18
i Eph 5:6;
Col 3:6

1:19
j Ac 14:17

1:20
k Ps 19:1-6

1:21
l Jer 2:5;
Eph 4:17,18

1:22
m 1Co 1:20,27

1:23
n Ps 106:20;
Jer 2:11;
Ac 17:29

1:24
o Eph 4:19
p 1Pe 4:3

1:25
q Isa 44:20
r Jer 10:14
s Ro 9:5

1:26
t ver 24,28
u 1Th 4:5
v Lev 18:22,23

1:27
w Lev 18:22;
20:13

1:28
x ver 24,26

1:29
y 2Co 12:20

1:30
z 2Ti 3:2

1:31
a 2Ti 3:3

1:32
b Ro 6:23
c Ps 50:18;
Lk 11:48;
Ac 8:1; 22:20

[14]I am obligated[a] both to Greeks and non-Greeks, both to the wise and the foolish. [15]That is why I am so eager to preach the gospel also to you who are at Rome.[b]

[16]I am not ashamed of the gospel,[c] because it is the power of God[d] for the salvation of everyone who believes: first for the Jew,[e] then for the Gentile.[f] [17]For in the gospel a righteousness from God is revealed,[g] a righteousness that is by faith from first to last,[a] just as it is written: "The righteous will live by faith."[b][h]

[18]The wrath of God[i] is being revealed from heaven against all the godlessness and wickedness of men who suppress the truth by their wickedness, [19]since what may be known about God is plain to them, because God has made it plain to them.[j] [20]For since the creation of the world God's invisible qualities—his eternal power and divine nature—have been clearly seen, being understood from what has been made,[k] so that men are without excuse.

[21]For although they knew God, they neither glorified him as God nor gave thanks to him, but their thinking became futile and their foolish hearts were darkened.[l] [22]Although they claimed to be wise, they became fools[m] [23]and exchanged the glory of the immortal God for images[n] made to look like mortal man and birds and animals and reptiles.

[24]Therefore God gave them over[o] in the sinful desires of their hearts to sexual impurity for the degrading of their bodies with one another.[p] [25]They exchanged the truth of God for a lie,[q] and worshiped and served created things[r] rather than the Creator— who is forever praised.[s] Amen.

[26]Because of this, God gave them over[t] to shameful lusts.[u] Even their women exchanged natural relations for unnatural ones.[v] [27]In the same way the men also abandoned natural relations with women and were inflamed with lust for one another. Men committed indecent acts with other men, and received in themselves the due penalty for their perversion.[w]

[28]Furthermore, since they did not think it worthwhile to retain the knowledge of God, he gave them over[x] to a depraved mind, to do what ought not to be done. [29]They have become filled with every kind of wickedness, evil, greed and depravity. They are full of envy, murder, strife, deceit and malice. They are gossips,[y] [30]slanderers, God-haters, insolent, arrogant and boastful; they invent ways of doing evil; they disobey their parents;[z] [31]they are senseless, faithless, heartless,[a] ruthless. [32]Although they know God's righteous decree that those who do such things deserve death,[b] they not only continue to do these very things but also approve[c] of those who practice them.

a 17 Or *is from faith to faith*   b 17 Hab. 2:4

Chapter 2 Theme

2 You, therefore, have no excuse,[a] you who pass judgment on someone else, for at whatever point you judge the other, you are condemning yourself, because you who pass judgment do the same things.[b] [2]Now we know that God's judgment against those who do such things is based on truth. [3]So when you, a mere man, pass judgment on them and yet do the same things, do you think you will escape God's judgment? [4]Or do you show contempt for the riches[c] of his kindness,[d] tolerance[e] and patience,[f] not realizing that God's kindness leads you toward repentance?[g]

[5]But because of your stubbornness and your unrepentant heart, you are storing up wrath against yourself for the day of God's wrath, when his righteous judgment[h] will be revealed. [6]God "will give to each person according to what he has done."[a][i] [7]To those who by persistence in doing good seek glory, honor[j] and immortality,[k] he will give eternal life. [8]But for those who are self-seeking and who reject the truth and follow evil,[l] there will be wrath and anger. [9]There will be trouble and distress for every human being who does evil: first for the Jew, then for the Gentile;[m] [10]but glory, honor and peace for everyone who does good: first for the Jew, then for the Gentile.[n] [11]For God does not show favoritism.[o]

[12]All who sin apart from the law will also perish apart from the law, and all who sin under the law[p] will be judged by the law. [13]For it is not those who hear the law who are righteous in God's sight, but it is those who obey[q] the law who will be declared righteous. [14](Indeed, when Gentiles, who do not have the law, do by nature things required by the law,[r] they are a law for themselves, even though they do not have the law, [15]since they show that the requirements of the law are written on their hearts, their consciences also bearing witness, and their thoughts now accusing, now even defending them.) [16]This will take place on the day when God will judge men's secrets[s] through Jesus Christ,[t] as my gospel[u] declares.

[17]Now you, if you call yourself a Jew; if you rely on the law and brag about your relationship to God;[v] [18]if you know his will and approve of what is superior because you are instructed by the law; [19]if you are convinced that you are a guide for the blind, a light for those who are in the dark, [20]an instructor of the foolish, a teacher of infants, because you have in the law the embodiment of knowledge and truth— [21]you, then, who teach others, do you not teach yourself? You who preach against stealing, do you steal?[w] [22]You who say that people should not commit adultery, do you commit adultery? You who abhor idols, do you rob temples?[x]

a6 Psalm 62:12; Prov. 24:12

2:1
[a]Ro 1:20
[b]2Sa 12:5-7;
Mt 7:1,2

2:4
[c]Ro 9:23;
Eph 1:7,18; 2:7
[d]Ro 11:22
[e]Ro 3:25
[f]Ex 34:6
[g]2Pe 3:9

2:5
[h]Jude 6

2:6
[i]Ps 62:12;
Mt 16:27

2:7
[j]ver 10
[k]1Co 15:53,54

2:8
[l]2Th 2:12

2:9
[m]1Pe 4:17

2:10
[n]ver 9

2:11
[o]Ac 10:34

2:12
[p]Ro 3:19;
1Co 9:20,21

2:13
[q]Jas 1:22,23,25

2:14
[r]Ac 10:35

2:16
[s]Ecc 12:14
[t]Ac 10:42
[u]Ro 16:25

2:17
[v]ver 23;
Mic 3:11;
Ro 9:4

2:21
[w]Mt 23:3,4

2:22
[x]Ac 19:37

2:23
a ver 17

2:24
b Isa 52:5;
Eze 36:22

2:25
c Gal 5:3
d Jer 4:4

2:26
e Ro 8:4
f 1Co 7:19

2:27
g Mt 12:41,42

2:28
h Mt 3:9;
Jn 8:39;
Ro 9:6,7
i Gal 6:15

2:29
j Php 3:3;
Col 2:1
k Ro 7:6
l Jn 5:44;
1Co 4:5;
2Co 10:18;
1Th 2:4;
1Pe 3:4

3:2
m Dt 4:8;
Ps 147:19

3:3
n Heb 4:2
o 2Ti 2:13

3:4
p Jn 3:33
q Ps 116:11
r Ps 51:4

3:5
s Ro 6:19;
Gal 3:15

3:6
t Ge 18:25

3:7
u ver 4

3:8
v Ro 6:1

3:9
w ver 19,23;
Gal 3:22

²³You who brag about the law,*a* do you dishonor God by breaking the law? ²⁴As it is written: "God's name is blasphemed among the Gentiles because of you."*a* *b*

²⁵Circumcision has value if you observe the law,*c* but if you break the law, you have become as though you had not been circumcised.*d* ²⁶If those who are not circumcised keep the law's requirements,*e* will they not be regarded as though they were circumcised?*f* ²⁷The one who is not circumcised physically and yet obeys the law will condemn you*g* who, even though you have the*b* written code and circumcision, are a lawbreaker.

²⁸A man is not a Jew if he is only one outwardly,*h* nor is circumcision merely outward and physical.*i* ²⁹No, a man is a Jew if he is one inwardly; and circumcision is circumcision of the heart, by the Spirit,*j* not by the written code.*k* Such a man's praise is not from men, but from God.*l*

Chapter 3 Theme

3 What advantage, then, is there in being a Jew, or what value is there in circumcision? ²Much in every way! First of all, they have been entrusted with the very words of God.*m*

³What if some did not have faith?*n* Will their lack of faith nullify God's faithfulness?*o* ⁴Not at all! Let God be true,*p* and every man a liar.*q* As it is written:

> "So that you may be proved right when you speak
> and prevail when you judge."*c* *r*

⁵But if our unrighteousness brings out God's righteousness more clearly, what shall we say? That God is unjust in bringing his wrath on us? (I am using a human argument.)*s* ⁶Certainly not! If that were so, how could God judge the world?*t* ⁷Someone might argue, "If my falsehood enhances God's truthfulness and so increases his glory,*u* why am I still condemned as a sinner?" ⁸Why not say— as we are being slanderously reported as saying and as some claim that we say—"Let us do evil that good may result"?*v* Their condemnation is deserved.

⁹What shall we conclude then? Are we any better*d*? Not at all! We have already made the charge that Jews and Gentiles alike are all under sin.*w* ¹⁰As it is written:

> "There is no one righteous, not even one;
> ¹¹ there is no one who understands,
>   no one who seeks God.
> ¹²All have turned away,
>   they have together become worthless;

a 24 Isaiah 52:5; Ezek. 36:22 *b* 27 Or *who, by means of a* *c* 4 Psalm 51:4 *d* 9 Or *worse*

there is no one who does good,
not even one."ᵃ ᵃ

¹³"Their throats are open graves;
their tongues practice deceit."ᵇᵇ

"The poison of vipers is on their lips."ᶜᶜ

¹⁴ "Their mouths are full of cursing and bitterness."ᵈᵈ

¹⁵"Their feet are swift to shed blood;

¹⁶ ruin and misery mark their ways,

¹⁷and the way of peace they do not know."ᵉ

¹⁸ "There is no fear of God before their eyes."ᶠᵉ

¹⁹Now we know that whatever the law says,ᶠ it says to those who are under the law,ᵍ so that every mouth may be silenced and the whole world held accountable to God. ²⁰Therefore no one will be declared righteous in his sight by observing the law;ʰ rather, through the law we become conscious of sin.ⁱ

²¹But now a righteousness from God,ʲ apart from law, has been made known, to which the Law and the Prophets testify.ᵏ ²²This righteousness from God comes through faithˡ in Jesus Christ to all who believe. There is no difference,ᵐ ²³for all have sinned and fall short of the glory of God, ²⁴and are justified freely by his graceⁿ through the redemptionᵒ that came by Christ Jesus. ²⁵God presented him as a sacrifice of atonement,ᵍᵖ through faith in his blood.ᵠ He did this to demonstrate his justice, because in his forbearance he had left the sins committed beforehand unpunishedʳ— ²⁶he did it to demonstrate his justice at the present time, so as to be just and the one who justifies those who have faith in Jesus.

²⁷Where, then, is boasting?ˢ It is excluded. On what principle? On that of observing the law? No, but on that of faith. ²⁸For we maintain that a man is justified by faith apart from observing the law.ᵗ ²⁹Is God the God of Jews only? Is he not the God of Gentiles too? Yes, of Gentiles too,ᵘ ³⁰since there is only one God, who will justify the circumcised by faith and the uncircumcised through that same faith.ᵛ ³¹Do we, then, nullify the law by this faith? Not at all! Rather, we uphold the law.

Chapter 4 Theme

4 What then shall we say that Abraham, our forefather, discovered in this matter? ²If, in fact, Abraham was justified by works, he had something to boast about—but not before God.ʷ ³What does the Scripture say? "Abraham believed God, and it was credited to him as righteousness."ʰ ˣ

ᵃ*12* Psalms 14:1-3; 53:1-3; Eccles. 7:20 ᵇ*13* Psalm 5:9 ᶜ*13* Psalm 140:3 ᵈ*14* Psalm 10:7 ᵉ*17* Isaiah 59:7,8 ᶠ*18* Psalm 36:1 ᵍ*25* Or *as the one who would turn aside his wrath, taking away sin* ʰ*3* Gen.15:6; also in verse 22

3:12
ᵃPs 14:1-3

3:13
ᵇPs 5:9
ᶜPs 140:3

3:14
ᵈPs 10:7

3:18
ᵉPs 36:1

3:19
ᶠJn 10:34
ᵍRo 2:12

3:20
ʰAc 13:39;
Gal 2:16
ⁱRo 7:7

3:21
ʲRo 1:17; 9:30
ᵏAc 10:43

3:22
ˡRo 9:30
ᵐRo 10:12;
Gal 3:28;
Col 3:11

3:24
ⁿRo 4:16;
Eph 2:8
ᵒEph 1:7,14;
Col 1:14;
Heb 9:12

3:25
ᵖ1Jn 4:10
ᵠHeb 9:12,14
ʳAc 17:30

3:27
ˢRo 2:17,23; 4:2;
1Co 1:29-31;
Eph 2:9

3:28
ᵗver 20,21;
Ac 13:39;
Eph 2:9

3:29
ᵘRo 9:24

3:30
ᵛGal 3:8

4:2
ʷ1Co 1:31

4:3
ˣver 5,9,22;
Ge 15:6;
Gal 3:6;
Jas 2:23

4:4
a Ro 11:6

4:8
b Ps 32:1,2;
2Co 5:19

4:9
c Ro 3:30
d ver 3

4:11
e Ge 17:10,11
f ver 16,17;
Lk 19:9
g Ro 3:22

4:13
h Gal 3:16,29
i Ge 17:4-6

4:14
j Gal 3:18

4:15
k Ro 7:7-25;
1Co 15:56;
2Co 3:7;
Gal 3:10;
Ro 7:12
l Ro 3:20; 7:7

4:16
m Ro 3:24
n Ro 15:8

4:17
o Ge 17:5
p Jn 5:21
q Isa 48:13
r 1Co 1:28

4:18
s ver 17
t Ge 15:5

4:19
u Heb 11:11,12
v Ge 17:17
w Ge 18:11

4:20
x Mt 9:8

⁴Now when a man works, his wages are not credited to him as a gift,*a* but as an obligation. ⁵However, to the man who does not work but trusts God who justifies the wicked, his faith is credited as righteousness. ⁶David says the same thing when he speaks of the blessedness of the man to whom God credits righteousness apart from works:

⁷"Blessed are they
　　whose transgressions are forgiven,
　　whose sins are covered.
⁸Blessed is the man
　　whose sin the Lord will never count against him."*a b*

⁹Is this blessedness only for the circumcised, or also for the uncircumcised?*c* We have been saying that Abraham's faith was credited to him as righteousness.*d* ¹⁰Under what circumstances was it credited? Was it after he was circumcised, or before? It was not after, but before! ¹¹And he received the sign of circumcision, a seal of the righteousness that he had by faith while he was still uncircumcised.*e* So then, he is the father*f* of all who believe*g* but have not been circumcised, in order that righteousness might be credited to them. ¹²And he is also the father of the circumcised who not only are circumcised but who also walk in the footsteps of the faith that our father Abraham had before he was circumcised.

¹³It was not through law that Abraham and his offspring received the promise*h* that he would be heir of the world,*i* but through the righteousness that comes by faith. ¹⁴For if those who live by law are heirs, faith has no value and the promise is worthless,*j* ¹⁵because law brings wrath.*k* And where there is no law there is no transgression.*l*

¹⁶Therefore, the promise comes by faith, so that it may be by grace*m* and may be guaranteed*n* to all Abraham's offspring—not only to those who are of the law but also to those who are of the faith of Abraham. He is the father of us all. ¹⁷As it is written: "I have made you a father of many nations."*b o* He is our father in the sight of God, in whom he believed—the God who gives life*p* to the dead and calls*q* things that are not*r* as though they were.

¹⁸Against all hope, Abraham in hope believed and so became the father of many nations,*s* just as it had been said to him, "So shall your offspring be."*c t* ¹⁹Without weakening in his faith, he faced the fact that his body was as good as dead*u*—since he was about a hundred years old*v*—and that Sarah's womb was also dead.*w* ²⁰Yet he did not waver through unbelief regarding the promise of God, but was strengthened in his faith and gave glory to God,*x* ²¹being fully persuaded that God had power to do what

a8 Psalm 32:1,2　*b17* Gen. 17:5　*c18* Gen. 15:5

he had promised.[a] [22]This is why "it was credited to him as righteousness."[b] [23]The words "it was credited to him" were written not for him alone, [24]but also for us,[c] to whom God will credit righteousness—for us who believe in him[d] who raised Jesus our Lord from the dead.[e] [25]He was delivered over to death for our sins[f] and was raised to life for our justification.

Chapter 5 Theme

5 Therefore, since we have been justified through faith,[g] we[a] have peace with God through our Lord Jesus Christ, [2]through whom we have gained access[h] by faith into this grace in which we now stand.[i] And we[a] rejoice in the hope[j] of the glory of God. [3]Not only so, but we[a] also rejoice in our sufferings,[k] because we know that suffering produces perseverance;[l] [4]perseverance, character; and character, hope. [5]And hope[m] does not disappoint us, because God has poured out his love into our hearts by the Holy Spirit,[n] whom he has given us.

[6]You see, at just the right time,[o] when we were still powerless, Christ died for the ungodly.[p] [7]Very rarely will anyone die for a righteous man, though for a good man someone might possibly dare to die. [8]But God demonstrates his own love for us in this: While we were still sinners, Christ died for us.[q]

[9]Since we have now been justified by his blood,[r] how much more shall we be saved from God's wrath[s] through him! [10]For if, when we were God's enemies,[t] we were reconciled[u] to him through the death of his Son, how much more, having been reconciled, shall we be saved through his life![v] [11]Not only is this so, but we also rejoice in God through our Lord Jesus Christ, through whom we have now received reconciliation.

[12]Therefore, just as sin entered the world through one man,[w] and death through sin,[x] and in this way death came to all men, because all sinned— [13]for before the law was given, sin was in the world. But sin is not taken into account when there is no law.[y] [14]Nevertheless, death reigned from the time of Adam to the time of Moses, even over those who did not sin by breaking a command, as did Adam, who was a pattern of the one to come.[z]

[15]But the gift is not like the trespass. For if the many died by the trespass of the one man,[a] how much more did God's grace and the gift that came by the grace of the one man, Jesus Christ,[b] overflow to the many! [16]Again, the gift of God is not like the result of the one man's sin: The judgment followed one sin and brought condemnation, but the gift followed many trespasses and brought justification. [17]For if, by the trespass of the one man,

a 1,2,3 Or let us

4:21
[a]Ge 18:14;
Heb 11:19

4:22
[b]ver 3

4:24
[c]Ro 15:4;
1Co 9:10; 10:11
[d]Ro 10:9
[e]Ac 2:24

4:25
[f]Isa 53:5,6;
Ro 5:6,8

5:1
[g]Ro 3:28

5:2
[h]Eph 2:18
[i]1Co 15:1
[j]Heb 3:6

5:3
[k]Mt 5:12
[l]Jas 1:2,3

5:5
[m]Php 1:20
[n]Ac 2:33

5:6
[o]Gal 4:4
[p]Ro 4:25

5:8
[q]Jn 15:13;
1Pe 3:18

5:9
[r]Ro 3:25
[s]Ro 1:18

5:10
[t]Ro 11:28;
Col 1:21
[u]2Co 5:18,19;
Col 1:20,22
[v]Ro 8:34

5:12
[w]ver 15,16,17;
1Co 15:21,22
[x]Ge 2:17; 3:19;
Ro 6:23

5:13
[y]Ro 4:15

5:14
[z]1Co 15:22,45

5:15
[a]ver 12,18,19
[b]Ac 15:11

5:17
a ver 12

5:18
b ver 12
c Ro 4:25

5:19
d ver 12
e Php 2:8

5:20
f Ro 7:7,8;
Gal 3:19
g 1Ti 1:13,14

5:21
h ver 12,14

6:1
i ver 15;
Ro 3:5,8

6:2
j Col 3:3,5;
1Pe 2:24

6:3
k Mt 28:19

6:4
l Col 2:12
m Ro 7:6;
Gal 6:15;
Eph 4:22-24;
Col 3:10

6:5
n 2Co 4:10;
Php 3:10,11

6:6
o Eph 4:22;
Col 3:9
p Gal 2:20;
Col 2:12,20
q Ro 7:24

6:9
r Ac 2:24
s Rev 1:18

6:10
t ver 2

6:11
u ver 2

6:13
v ver 16,19;
Ro 7:5
w Ro 12:1;
1Pe 2:24

6:14
x Gal 5:18
y Ro 3:24

6:16
z Jn 8:34;
2Pe 2:19

death*a* reigned through that one man, how much more will those who receive God's abundant provision of grace and of the gift of righteousness reign in life through the one man, Jesus Christ. ¹⁸Consequently, just as the result of one trespass was condemnation for all men,*b* so also the result of one act of righteousness was justification*c* that brings life for all men. ¹⁹For just as through the disobedience of the one man*d* the many were made sinners, so also through the obedience*e* of the one man the many will be made righteous.

²⁰The law was added so that the trespass might increase.*f* But where sin increased, grace increased all the more,*g* ²¹so that, just as sin reigned in death,*h* so also grace might reign through righteousness to bring eternal life through Jesus Christ our Lord.

Chapter 6 Theme _____

6 What shall we say, then? Shall we go on sinning so that grace may increase?*i* ²By no means! We died to sin;*j* how can we live in it any longer? ³Or don't you know that all of us who were baptized*k* into Christ Jesus were baptized into his death? ⁴We were therefore buried with him through baptism into death in order that, just as Christ was raised from the dead*l* through the glory of the Father, we too may live a new life.*m*

⁵If we have been united with him like this in his death, we will certainly also be united with him in his resurrection.*n* ⁶For we know that our old self*o* was crucified with him*p* so that the body of sin*q* might be done away with,*a* that we should no longer be slaves to sin— ⁷because anyone who has died has been freed from sin.

⁸Now if we died with Christ, we believe that we will also live with him. ⁹For we know that since Christ was raised from the dead,*r* he cannot die again; death no longer has mastery over him.*s* ¹⁰The death he died, he died to sin*t* once for all; but the life he lives, he lives to God.

¹¹In the same way, count yourselves dead to sin*u* but alive to God in Christ Jesus. ¹²Therefore do not let sin reign in your mortal body so that you obey its evil desires. ¹³Do not offer the parts of your body to sin, as instruments of wickedness,*v* but rather offer yourselves to God, as those who have been brought from death to life; and offer the parts of your body to him as instruments of righteousness.*w* ¹⁴For sin shall not be your master, because you are not under law,*x* but under grace.*y*

¹⁵What then? Shall we sin because we are not under law but under grace? By no means! ¹⁶Don't you know that when you offer yourselves to someone to obey him as slaves, you are slaves to the one whom you obey—whether you are slaves to sin,*z* which leads

a 6 Or *be rendered powerless*

to death,^{a} or to obedience, which leads to righteousness? ^{17}But thanks be to God^b that, though you used to be slaves to sin, you wholeheartedly obeyed the form of teaching^c to which you were entrusted. ^{18}You have been set free from sin^d and have become slaves to righteousness.

^{19}I put this in human terms^e because you are weak in your natural selves. Just as you used to offer the parts of your body in slavery to impurity and to ever-increasing wickedness, so now offer them in slavery to righteousness^f leading to holiness. ^{20}When you were slaves to sin,^{g} you were free from the control of righteousness. ^{21}What benefit did you reap at that time from the things you are now ashamed of? Those things result in death!^{h} ^{22}But now that you have been set free from sin^i and have become slaves to God,^{j} the benefit you reap leads to holiness, and the result is eternal life. ^{23}For the wages of sin is death,^{k} but the gift of God is eternal life^l in^a Christ Jesus our Lord.

Chapter 7 Theme

7 Do you not know, brothers^m—for I am speaking to men who know the law—that the law has authority over a man only as long as he lives? ^{2}For example, by law a married woman is bound to her husband as long as he is alive, but if her husband dies, she is released from the law of marriage.^{n} ^{3}So then, if she marries another man while her husband is still alive, she is called an adulteress. But if her husband dies, she is released from that law and is not an adulteress, even though she marries another man.

^{4}So, my brothers, you also died to the law^o through the body of Christ,^{p} that you might belong to another, to him who was raised from the dead, in order that we might bear fruit to God. ^{5}For when we were controlled by the sinful nature,^{b} the sinful passions aroused by the law^q were at work in our bodies,^{r} so that we bore fruit for death. ^{6}But now, by dying to what once bound us, we have been released from the law so that we serve in the new way of the Spirit, and not in the old way of the written code.^{s}

^{7}What shall we say, then? Is the law sin? Certainly not! Indeed I would not have known what sin was except through the law.^{t} For I would not have known what coveting really was if the law had not said, "Do not covet."^{cu} ^{8}But sin, seizing the opportunity afforded by the commandment,^{v} produced in me every kind of covetous desire. For apart from law, sin is dead.^{w} ^{9}Once I was alive apart from law; but when the commandment came, sin sprang to life and I died. ^{10}I found that the very commandment that was intended to bring life^x actually brought death. ^{11}For sin, seizing the opportunity afforded by the commandment, deceived me,^{y} and

---

6:16
^{a}ver 23

6:17
^{b}Ro 1:8;
2Co 2:14
^{c}2Ti 1:13

6:18
^{d}ver 7,22;
Ro 8:2

6:19
^{e}Ro 3:5
^{f}ver 13

6:20
^{g}ver 16

6:21
^{h}ver 23

6:22
^{i}ver 18
^{j}1Co 7:22;
1Pe 2:16

6:23
^{k}Ge 2:17;
Ro 5:12;
Gal 6:7,8;
Jas 1:15
^{l}Mt 25:46

7:1
^{m}Ro 1:13

7:2
^{n}1Co 7:39

7:4
^{o}Ro 8:2;
Gal 2:19
^{p}Col 1:22

7:5
^{q}Ro 7:7-11
^{r}Ro 6:13

7:6
^{s}Ro 2:29;
2Co 3:6

7:7
^{t}Ro 3:20; 4:15
^{u}Ex 20:17;
Dt 5:21

7:8
^{v}ver 11
^{w}Ro 4:15;
1Co 15:56

7:10
^{x}Lev 18:5;
Lk 10:26-28;
Ro 10:5;
Gal 3:12

7:11
^{y}Ge 3:13

---

^{a}23 Or *through* ^{b}5 Or *the flesh*; also in verse 25 ^{c}7 Exodus 20:17; Deut. 5:21

7:12
a 1Ti 1:8

7:14
b 1Co 3:1
c 1Ki 21:20,25;
2Ki 17:17

7:15
d ver 19;
Gal 5:17

7:16
e ver 12

7:17
f ver 20

7:18
g ver 25

7:19
h ver 15

7:20
i ver 17

7:21
j ver 23,25

7:22
k Eph 3:16
l Ps 1:2

7:23
m Gal 5:17;
Jas 4:1;
1Pe 2:11

7:24
n Ro 6:6; 8:2

8:1
o ver 34
p ver 39;
Ro 16:3

8:2
q 1Co 15:45
r Ro 6:18
s Ro 7:4

8:3
t Ac 13:39;
Heb 7:18
u Php 2:7
v Heb 2:14,17

8:4
w Gal 5:16

8:5
x Gal 5:19-21
y Gal 5:22-25

8:6
z Gal 6:8

8:7
a Jas 4:4

through the commandment put me to death. ¹²So then, the law is holy, and the commandment is holy, righteous and good.*a*

¹³Did that which is good, then, become death to me? By no means! But in order that sin might be recognized as sin, it produced death in me through what was good, so that through the commandment sin might become utterly sinful.

¹⁴We know that the law is spiritual; but I am unspiritual,*b* sold*c* as a slave to sin. ¹⁵I do not understand what I do. For what I want to do I do not do, but what I hate I do.*d* ¹⁶And if I do what I do not want to do, I agree that the law is good.*e* ¹⁷As it is, it is no longer I myself who do it, but it is sin living in me.*f* ¹⁸I know that nothing good lives in me, that is, in my sinful nature.*ag* For I have the desire to do what is good, but I cannot carry it out. ¹⁹For what I do is not the good I want to do; no, the evil I do not want to do— this I keep on doing.*h* ²⁰Now if I do what I do not want to do, it is no longer I who do it, but it is sin living in me that does it.*i*

²¹So I find this law at work:*j* When I want to do good, evil is right there with me. ²²For in my inner being*k* I delight in God's law;*l* ²³but I see another law at work in the members of my body, waging war*m* against the law of my mind and making me a prisoner of the law of sin at work within my members. ²⁴What a wretched man I am! Who will rescue me from this body of death?*n* ²⁵Thanks be to God—through Jesus Christ our Lord!

So then, I myself in my mind am a slave to God's law, but in the sinful nature a slave to the law of sin.

Chapter 8 Theme

8 Therefore, there is now no condemnation*o* for those who are in Christ Jesus,*bp* ²because through Christ Jesus the law of the Spirit of life*q* set me free*r* from the law of sin*s* and death. ³For what the law was powerless*t* to do in that it was weakened by the sinful nature,*c* God did by sending his own Son in the likeness of sinful man*u* to be a sin offering.*dv* And so he condemned sin in sinful man,*e* ⁴in order that the righteous requirements of the law might be fully met in us, who do not live according to the sinful nature but according to the Spirit.*w*

⁵Those who live according to the sinful nature have their minds set on what that nature desires;*x* but those who live in accordance with the Spirit have their minds set on what the Spirit desires.*y* ⁶The mind of sinful man*f* is death, but the mind controlled by the Spirit is life*z* and peace; ⁷the sinful mind*g* is hostile to God.*a* It does not submit to God's law, nor can it do so. ⁸Those controlled by the sinful nature cannot please God.

*a*18 Or *my flesh*   *b*1 Some later manuscripts *Jesus, who do not live according to the sinful nature but according to the Spirit,*   *c*3 Or *the flesh;* also in verses 4, 5, 8, 9, 12 and 13   *d*3 Or *man, for sin*   *e*3 Or *in the flesh*   *f*6 Or *mind set on the flesh*   *g*7 Or *the mind set on the flesh*

⁹You, however, are controlled not by the sinful nature but by the Spirit, if the Spirit of God lives in you.*a* And if anyone does not have the Spirit of Christ,*b* he does not belong to Christ. ¹⁰But if Christ is in you,*c* your body is dead because of sin, yet your spirit is alive because of righteousness. ¹¹And if the Spirit of him who raised Jesus from the dead*d* is living in you, he who raised Christ from the dead will also give life to your mortal bodies*e* through his Spirit, who lives in you.

¹²Therefore, brothers, we have an obligation—but it is not to the sinful nature, to live according to it. ¹³For if you live according to the sinful nature, you will die; but if by the Spirit you put to death the misdeeds of the body, you will live,*f* ¹⁴because those who are led by the Spirit of God*g* are sons of God.*h* ¹⁵For you did not receive a spirit that makes you a slave again to fear,*i* but you received the Spirit of sonship.*a* And by him we cry, "*Abba*,*b* Father."*j* ¹⁶The Spirit himself testifies with our spirit*k* that we are God's children. ¹⁷Now if we are children, then we are heirs*l*—heirs of God and co-heirs with Christ, if indeed we share in his sufferings in order that we may also share in his glory.*m*

¹⁸I consider that our present sufferings are not worth comparing with the glory that will be revealed in us.*n* ¹⁹The creation waits in eager expectation for the sons of God to be revealed. ²⁰For the creation was subjected to frustration, not by its own choice, but by the will of the one who subjected it,*o* in hope ²¹that*c* the creation itself will be liberated from its bondage to decay*p* and brought into the glorious freedom of the children of God.

²²We know that the whole creation has been groaning*q* as in the pains of childbirth right up to the present time. ²³Not only so, but we ourselves, who have the firstfruits of the Spirit,*r* groan*s* inwardly as we wait eagerly*t* for our adoption as sons, the redemption of our bodies. ²⁴For in this hope we were saved.*u* But hope that is seen is no hope at all. Who hopes for what he already has? ²⁵But if we hope for what we do not yet have, we wait for it patiently.

²⁶In the same way, the Spirit helps us in our weakness. We do not know what we ought to pray for, but the Spirit himself intercedes for us*v* with groans that words cannot express. ²⁷And he who searches our hearts*w* knows the mind of the Spirit, because the Spirit intercedes for the saints in accordance with God's will.

²⁸And we know that in all things God works for the good of those who love him,*d* who*e* have been called*x* according to his purpose. ²⁹For those God foreknew*y* he also predestined*z* to be conformed to the likeness of his Son,*a* that he might be the firstborn among

8:9
a 1Co 6:19;
Gal 4:6
b Jn 14:17;
1Jn 4:13

8:10
c Gal 2:20;
Eph 3:17;
Col 1:27

8:11
d Ac 2:24
e Jn 5:21

8:13
f Gal 6:8

8:14
g Gal 5:18
h Jn 1:12;
Rev 21:7

8:15
i 2Ti 1:7;
Heb 2:15
j Mk 14:36;
Gal 4:5,6

8:16
k Eph 1:13

8:17
l Ac 20:32;
Gal 4:7
m 1Pe 4:13

8:18
n 2Co 4:17;
1Pe 4:13

8:20
o Ge 3:17-19

8:21
p Ac 3:21;
2Pe 3:13;
Rev 21:1

8:22
q Jer 12:4

8:23
r 2Co 5:5
s 2Co 5:2,4
t Gal 5:5

8:24
u 1Th 5:8

8:26
v Eph 6:18

8:27
w Rev 2:23

8:28
x 1Co 1:9;
2Ti 1:9

8:29
y Ro 11:2
z Eph 1:5,11
a 1Co 15:49;
2Co 3:18;
Php 3:21;
1Jn 3:2

a 15 Or *adoption*   *b* 15 Aramaic for *Father*   *c* 20,21 Or *subjected it in hope.* ²¹*For*
d 28 Some manuscripts *And we know that all things work together for good to those who love God*
e 28 Or *works together with those who love him to bring about what is good—with those who*

8:30
a Eph 1:5,11
b 1Co 6:11
c Ro 9:23
8:31
d Ro 4:1
e Ps 118:6
8:32
f Jn 3:16;
Ro 4:25; 5:8
8:33
g Isa 50:8,9
8:34
h Ro 5:6-8
i Mk 16:19
j Heb 7:25;
9:24;
1Jn 2:1
8:35
k 1Co 4:11
8:36
l Ps 44:22;
2Co 4:11
8:37
m 1Co 15:57
n Gal 2:20;
Rev 1:5; 3:9
8:38
o Eph 1:21;
1Pe 3:22
8:39
p Ro 5:8
9:1
q 2Co 11:10;
Gal 1:20;
1Ti 2:7
r Ro 1:9
9:3
s Ex 32:32
t 1Co 12:3;
16:22
u Ro 11:14
9:4
v Ex 4:22
w Ge 17:2;
Ac 3:25;
Eph 2:12
x Ps 147:19
y Heb 9:1
z Ac 13:32
9:5
a Mt 1:1-16
b Jn 1:1
c Ro 1:25
9:6
d Ro 2:28,29;
Gal 6:16
9:7
e Ge 21:12;
Heb 11:18
9:8
f Ro 8:14
9:9
g Ge 18:10,14
9:10
h Ge 25:21
9:11
i Ro 8:28

many brothers. [30]And those he predestined,[a] he also called; those he called, he also justified;[b] those he justified, he also glorified.[c]

[31]What, then, shall we say in response to this?[d] If God is for us, who can be against us?[e] [32]He who did not spare his own Son,[f] but gave him up for us all—how will he not also, along with him, graciously give us all things? [33]Who will bring any charge[g] against those whom God has chosen? It is God who justifies. [34]Who is he that condemns? Christ Jesus, who died[h]—more than that, who was raised to life—is at the right hand of God[i] and is also interceding for us.[j] [35]Who shall separate us from the love of Christ? Shall trouble or hardship or persecution or famine or nakedness or danger or sword?[k] [36]As it is written:

> "For your sake we face death all day long;
> we are considered as sheep to be slaughtered."[a][l]

[37]No, in all these things we are more than conquerors[m] through him who loved us.[n] [38]For I am convinced that neither death nor life, neither angels nor demons,[b] neither the present nor the future, nor any powers,[o] [39]neither height nor depth, nor anything else in all creation, will be able to separate us from the love of God[p] that is in Christ Jesus our Lord.

Chapter 9 Theme

9 I speak the truth in Christ—I am not lying,[q] my conscience confirms[r] it in the Holy Spirit— [2]I have great sorrow and unceasing anguish in my heart. [3]For I could wish that I myself[s] were cursed[t] and cut off from Christ for the sake of my brothers, those of my own race,[u] [4]the people of Israel. Theirs is the adoption as sons;[v] theirs the divine glory, the covenants,[w] the receiving of the law,[x] the temple worship[y] and the promises.[z] [5]Theirs are the patriarchs, and from them is traced the human ancestry of Christ,[a] who is God over all,[b] forever praised![cc] Amen.

[6]It is not as though God's word had failed. For not all who are descended from Israel are Israel.[d] [7]Nor because they are his descendants are they all Abraham's children. On the contrary, "It is through Isaac that your offspring will be reckoned."[de] [8]In other words, it is not the natural children who are God's children,[f] but it is the children of the promise who are regarded as Abraham's offspring. [9]For this was how the promise was stated: "At the appointed time I will return, and Sarah will have a son."[eg]

[10]Not only that, but Rebekah's children had one and the same father, our father Isaac.[h] [11]Yet, before the twins were born or had done anything good or bad—in order that God's purpose[i] in

a 36 Psalm 44:22   *b* 38 Or *nor heavenly rulers*   *c* 5 Or *Christ, who is over all. God be forever praised! Or Christ. God who is over all be forever praised!*   *d* 7 Gen. 21:12   *e* 9 Gen. 18:10,14 election might stand: [12]not by works but by him who calls—she was told, "The older will serve the younger."a a [13]Just as it is written: "Jacob I loved, but Esau I hated."b b

[14]What then shall we say? Is God unjust? Not at all!c [15]For he says to Moses,

> "I will have mercy on whom I have mercy,
>   and I will have compassion on whom
>   I have compassion."c d

[16]It does not, therefore, depend on man's desire or effort, but on God's mercy.e [17]For the Scripture says to Pharaoh: "I raised you up for this very purpose, that I might display my power in you and that my name might be proclaimed in all the earth."d f [18]Therefore God has mercy on whom he wants to have mercy, and he hardens whom he wants to harden.g

[19]One of you will say to me:h "Then why does God still blame us? For who resists his will?"i [20]But who are you, O man, to talk back to God? "Shall what is formed say to him who formed it,j 'Why did you make me like this?'"ek [21]Does not the potter have the right to make out of the same lump of clay some pottery for noble purposes and some for common use?l

[22]What if God, choosing to show his wrath and make his power known, bore with great patiencem the objects of his wrath—prepared for destruction? [23]What if he did this to make the riches of his gloryn known to the objects of his mercy, whom he prepared in advance for gloryo— [24]even us, whom he also called,p not only from the Jews but also from the Gentiles?q [25]As he says in Hosea:

> "I will call them 'my people' who are not my people;
>   and I will call her 'my loved one' who is not
>   my loved one,"fr

[26]and,

> "It will happen that in the very place where it was
>   said to them,
>   'You are not my people,'
>   they will be called 'sons of the living God.' "gs

[27]Isaiah cries out concerning Israel:

> "Though the number of the Israelites be like the
>   sand by the sea,t
>   only the remnant will be saved.u
> [28]For the Lord will carry out
>   his sentence on earth with speed and finality."hv

### Cross-references (margin)

9:12 a Ge 25:23
9:13 b Mal 1:2,3
9:14 c 2Ch 19:7
9:15 d Ex 33:19
9:16 e Eph 2:8
9:17 f Ex 9:16
9:18 g Ex 4:21
9:19 h Ro 11:19; i 2Ch 20:6; Da 4:35
9:20 j Isa 64:8; k Isa 29:16
9:21 l 2Ti 2:20
9:22 m Ro 2:4
9:23 n Ro 2:4; o Ro 8:30
9:24 p Ro 8:28; q Ro 3:29
9:25 r Hos 2:23; 1Pe 2:10
9:26 s Hos 1:10
9:27 t Ge 22:17; Hos 1:10; u Ro 11:5
9:28 v Isa 10:22,23

Footnotes

a 12 Gen. 25:23   b 13 Mal. 1:2,3   c 15 Exodus 33:19   d 17 Exodus 9:16   e 20 Isaiah 29:16; 45:9
f 25 Hosea 2:23   g 26 Hosea 1:10   h 28 Isaiah 10:22,23

9:29
a Jas 5:4
b Isa 1:9;
Dt 29:23;
Isa 13:19;
Jer 50:40

9:30
c Ro 1:17; 10:6;
Gal 2:16;
Php 3:9;
Heb 11:7

9:31
d Isa 51:1;
Ro 10:2,3
e Gal 5:4

9:32
f 1Pe 2:8

9:33
g Isa 28:16;
Ro 10:11

10:2
h Ac 21:20

10:3
i Ro 1:17

10:4
j Gal 3:24;
Ro 7:1-4
k Ro 3:22

10:5
l Lev 18:5;
Ne 9:29;
Eze 20:11,13,21;
Ro 7:10

10:6
m Ro 9:30
n Dt 30:12

10:8
o Dt 30:14

10:9
p Mt 10:32;
Lk 12:8
q Ac 2:24

10:11
r Isa 28:16;
Ro 9:33

10:12
s Ro 3:22,29
t Ac 10:36

10:13
u Ac 2:21
v Joel 2:32

²⁹It is just as Isaiah said previously:

"Unless the Lord Almighty^a
    had left us descendants,
we would have become like Sodom,
    we would have been like Gomorrah."^ab

³⁰What then shall we say? That the Gentiles, who did not pursue righteousness, have obtained it, a righteousness that is by faith;^c ³¹but Israel, who pursued a law of righteousness,^d has not attained it.^e ³²Why not? Because they pursued it not by faith but as if it were by works. They stumbled over the "stumbling stone."^f ³³As it is written:

"See, I lay in Zion a stone that causes men to stumble
    and a rock that makes them fall,
and the one who trusts in him will never
    be put to shame."^bg

Chapter 10 Theme

10 Brothers, my heart's desire and prayer to God for the Israelites is that they may be saved. ²For I can testify about them that they are zealous^h for God, but their zeal is not based on knowledge. ³Since they did not know the righteousness that comes from God and sought to establish their own, they did not submit to God's righteousness.^i ⁴Christ is the end of the law^j so that there may be righteousness for everyone who believes.^k

⁵Moses describes in this way the righteousness that is by the law: "The man who does these things will live by them."^cl ⁶But the righteousness that is by faith^m says: "Do not say in your heart, 'Who will ascend into heaven?'^d"^n (that is, to bring Christ down) ⁷"or 'Who will descend into the deep?'^e" (that is, to bring Christ up from the dead). ⁸But what does it say? "The word is near you; it is in your mouth and in your heart,"^fo that is, the word of faith we are proclaiming: ⁹That if you confess^p with your mouth, "Jesus is Lord," and believe in your heart that God raised him from the dead,^q you will be saved. ¹⁰For it is with your heart that you believe and are justified, and it is with your mouth that you confess and are saved. ¹¹As the Scripture says, "Anyone who trusts in him will never be put to shame."^gr ¹²For there is no difference between Jew and Gentile^s—the same Lord is Lord of all^t and richly blesses all who call on him, ¹³for, "Everyone who calls on the name of the Lord^u will be saved."^hv

¹⁴How, then, can they call on the one they have not believed in? And how can they believe in the one of whom they have not heard?

a 29 Isaiah 1:9   b 33 Isaiah 8:14; 28:16   c 5 Lev. 18:5   d 6 Deut. 30:12   e 7 Deut. 30:13
f 8 Deut. 30:14   g 11 Isaiah 28:16   h 13 Joel 2:32

And how can they hear without someone preaching to them? ¹⁵And how can they preach unless they are sent? As it is written, "How beautiful are the feet of those who bring good news!"ᵃ a

¹⁶But not all the Israelites accepted the good news. For Isaiah says, "Lord, who has believed our message?"ᵇ b ¹⁷Consequently, faith comes from hearing the message,ᶜ and the message is heard through the word of Christ.ᵈ ¹⁸But I ask: Did they not hear? Of course they did:

> "Their voice has gone out into all the earth,
>   their words to the ends of the world."ᶜ e

¹⁹Again I ask: Did Israel not understand? First, Moses says,

> "I will make you enviousᶠ by those who are not a nation;
>   I will make you angry by a nation that
>   has no understanding."ᵈ g

²⁰And Isaiah boldly says,

> "I was found by those who did not seek me;
>   I revealed myself to those who did not ask for me."ᵉ h

²¹But concerning Israel he says,

> "All day long I have held out my hands
>   to a disobedient and obstinate people."ᶠ i

Chapter 11 Theme

11 I ask then: Did God reject his people? By no means!ʲ I am an Israelite myself, a descendant of Abraham,ᵏ from the tribe of Benjamin.ˡ ²God did not reject his people, whom he foreknew.ᵐ Don't you know what the Scripture says in the passage about Elijah—how he appealed to God against Israel: ³"Lord, they have killed your prophets and torn down your altars; I am the only one left, and they are trying to kill me"ᵍ?ⁿ ⁴And what was God's answer to him? "I have reserved for myself seven thousand who have not bowed the knee to Baal."ʰ o ⁵So too, at the present time there is a remnantᵖ chosen by grace. ⁶And if by grace, then it is no longer by works;�q if it were, grace would no longer be grace.ⁱ

⁷What then? What Israel sought so earnestly it did not obtain,ʳ but the elect did. The others were hardened,ˢ ⁸as it is written:

> "God gave them a spirit of stupor,
>   eyes so that they could not see
>   and ears so that they could not hear,ᵗ
>   to this very day."ʲ u

ᵃ15 Isaiah 52:7   ᵇ16 Isaiah 53:1   ᶜ18 Psalm 19:4   ᵈ19 Deut. 32:21   ᵉ20 Isaiah 65:1
ᶠ21 Isaiah 65:2   ᵍ3 1Kings 19:10,14   ʰ4 1Kings 19:18   ⁱ6 Some manuscripts *by grace.*
But if by works, then it is no longer grace; if it were, work would no longer be work.
ʲ8 Deut. 29:4; Isaiah 29:10

10:15
ᵃIsa 52:7;
Na 1:15

10:16
ᵇIsa 53:1;
Jn 12:38

10:17
ᶜGal 3:2,5
ᵈCol 3:16

10:18
ᵉPs 19:4;
Mt 24:14;
Col 1:6,23;
1Th 1:8

10:19
ᶠRo 11:11,14
ᵍDt 32:21

10:20
ʰIsa 65:1;
Ro 9:30

10:21
ⁱIsa 65:2

11:1
ʲ1Sa 12:22;
Jer 31:37
ᵏ2Co 11:22
ˡPhp 3:5

11:2
ᵐRo 8:29

11:3
ⁿ1Ki 19:10,14

11:4
ᵒ1Ki 19:18

11:5
ᵖRo 9:27

11:6
qRo 4:4

11:7
ʳRo 9:31
ˢver 25;
Ro 9:18

11:8
ᵗMt 13:13-15
ᵘDt 29:4;
Isa 29:10

11:10
a Ps 69:22,23

11:11
b ver 1
c Ac 13:46
d Ro 10:19

11:12
e ver 25

11:13
f Ac 9:15

11:14
g ver 11;
Ro 10:19
h 1Co 1:21;
1Ti 2:4;
Tit 3:5

11:15
i Ro 5:10
j Lk 15:24,32

11:16
k Lev 23:10,17;
Nu 15:18-21

11:17
l Jer 11:16;
Jn 15:2
m Ac 2:39;
Eph 2:11-13

11:18
n Jn 4:22

11:20
o 1Co 10:12;
2Co 1:24
p Ro 12:16;
1Ti 6:17
q 1Pe 1:17

11:22
r Ro 2:4
s 1Co 15:2;
Heb 3:6
t Jn 15:2

11:23
u 2Co 3:16

11:25
v Ro 1:13
w Ro 16:25
x Ro 12:16
y ver 7;
Ro 9:18
z Lk 21:24

11:27
a Isa 27:9;
Heb 8:10,12

⁹And David says:

"May their table become a snare and a trap,
a stumbling block and a retribution for them.
¹⁰May their eyes be darkened so they cannot see,
and their backs be bent forever."[a]

¹¹Again I ask: Did they stumble so as to fall beyond recovery? Not at all![b] Rather, because of their transgression, salvation has come to the Gentiles[c] to make Israel envious.[d] ¹²But if their transgression means riches for the world, and their loss means riches for the Gentiles,[e] how much greater riches will their fullness bring!

¹³I am talking to you Gentiles. Inasmuch as I am the apostle to the Gentiles,[f] I make much of my ministry ¹⁴in the hope that I may somehow arouse my own people to envy[g] and save[h] some of them. ¹⁵For if their rejection is the reconciliation[i] of the world, what will their acceptance be but life from the dead?[j] ¹⁶If the part of the dough offered as firstfruits[k] is holy, then the whole batch is holy; if the root is holy, so are the branches.

¹⁷If some of the branches have been broken off,[l] and you, though a wild olive shoot, have been grafted in among the others[m] and now share in the nourishing sap from the olive root, ¹⁸do not boast over those branches. If you do, consider this: You do not support the root, but the root supports you.[n] ¹⁹You will say then, "Branches were broken off so that I could be grafted in." ²⁰Granted. But they were broken off because of unbelief, and you stand by faith.[o] Do not be arrogant,[p] but be afraid.[q] ²¹For if God did not spare the natural branches, he will not spare you either.

²²Consider therefore the kindness[r] and sternness of God: sternness to those who fell, but kindness to you, provided that you continue[s] in his kindness. Otherwise, you also will be cut off.[t] ²³And if they do not persist in unbelief, they will be grafted in, for God is able to graft them in again.[u] ²⁴After all, if you were cut out of an olive tree that is wild by nature, and contrary to nature were grafted into a cultivated olive tree, how much more readily will these, the natural branches, be grafted into their own olive tree!

²⁵I do not want you to be ignorant[v] of this mystery,[w] brothers, so that you may not be conceited:[x] Israel has experienced a hardening[y] in part until the full number of the Gentiles has come in.[z] ²⁶And so all Israel will be saved, as it is written:

"The deliverer will come from Zion;
he will turn godlessness away from Jacob.
²⁷And this is[b] my covenant with them
when I take away their sins."[c][a]

a10 Psalm 69:22,23   b27 Or *will be*   c27 Isaiah 59:20,21; 27:9; Jer. 31:33,34

28As far as the gospel is concerned, they are enemies[a] on your account; but as far as election is concerned, they are loved on account of the patriarchs,[b] 29for God's gifts and his call[c] are irrevocable.[d] 30Just as you who were at one time disobedient[e] to God have now received mercy as a result of their disobedience, 31so they too have now become disobedient in order that they too may now[a] receive mercy as a result of God's mercy to you. 32For God has bound all men over to disobedience[f] so that he may have mercy on them all.

33Oh, the depth of the riches[g] of the wisdom and[b] knowledge of God![h]
How unsearchable his judgments,
and his paths beyond tracing out![i]
34"Who has known the mind of the Lord?
Or who has been his counselor?"[cj]
35"Who has ever given to God,
that God should repay him?"[dk]
36For from him and through him and to him are all things.[l]
To him be the glory forever! Amen.[m]

Chapter 12 Theme

12 Therefore, I urge you,[n] brothers, in view of God's mercy, to offer your bodies as living sacrifices,[o] holy and pleasing to God—this is your spiritual[e] act of worship. 2Do not conform[p] any longer to the pattern of this world,[q] but be transformed by the renewing of your mind.[r] Then you will be able to test and approve what God's will is[s]— his good, pleasing and perfect will.

3For by the grace given me[t] I say to every one of you: Do not think of yourself more highly than you ought, but rather think of yourself with sober judgment, in accordance with the measure of faith God has given you. 4Just as each of us has one body with many members, and these members do not all have the same function,[u] 5so in Christ we who are many form one body,[v] and each member belongs to all the others. 6We have different gifts,[w] according to the grace given us. If a man's gift is prophesying, let him use it in proportion to his[f] faith.[x] 7If it is serving, let him serve; if it is teaching, let him teach;[y] 8if it is encouraging, let him encourage;[z] if it is contributing to the needs of others, let him give generously;[a] if it is leadership, let him govern diligently; if it is showing mercy, let him do it cheerfully.

9Love must be sincere.[b] Hate what is evil; cling to what is good. 10Be devoted to one another in brotherly love.[c] Honor one another above yourselves.[d] 11Never be lacking in zeal, but keep your

11:28
a Ro 5:10
b Dt 7:8; 10:15;
Ro 9:5

11:29
c Ro 8:28
d Heb 7:21

11:30
e Eph 2:2

11:32
f Ro 3:9

11:33
g Ro 2:4
h Ps 92:5
i Job 11:7

11:34
j Isa 40:13,14;
Job 15:8; 36:22;
1Co 2:16

11:35
k Job 35:7

11:36
l 1Co 8:6;
Col 1:16;
Heb 2:10
m Ro 16:27

12:1
n Eph 4:1
o Ro 6:13,16,19;
1Pe 2:5

12:2
p 1Pe 1:14
q 1Jn 2:15
r Eph 4:23
s Eph 5:17

12:3
t Ro 15:15;
Gal 2:9;
Eph 4:7

12:4
u 1Co 12:12-14;
Eph 4:16

12:5
v 1Co 10:17

12:6
w 1Co 7:7;
12:4,8-10
x 1Pe 4:10,11

12:7
y Eph 4:11

12:8
z Ac 15:32
a 2Co 9:5-13

12:9
b 1Ti 1:5

12:10
c Heb 13:1
d Php 2:3

a 31 Some manuscripts do not have *now*.   b 33 Or *riches and the wisdom and the*   c 34 Isaiah 40:13   d 35 Job 41:11   e 1 Or *reasonable*   f 6 Or *in agreement with the*

12:11
a Ac 18:25

12:12
b Ro 5:2
c Heb 10:32,36

12:13
d 1Ti 3:2

12:14
e Mt 5:44

12:15
f Job 30:25

12:16
g Ro 15:5
h Jer 45:5;
Ro 11:25

12:17
i Pr 20:22
j 2Co 8:21

12:18
k Mk 9:50;
Ro 14:19

12:19
l Lev 19:18;
Pr 20:22; 24:29
m Dt 32:35

12:20
n Pr 25:21,22;
Mt 5:44;
Lk 6:27

13:1
o Tit 3:1;
1Pe 2:13,14
p Da 2:21;
Jn 19:11

13:3
q 1Pe 2:14

13:4
r 1Th 4:6

13:7
s Mt 17:25;
22:17,21;
Lk 23:2

13:8
t ver 10;
Jn 13:34;
Gal 5:14;
Col 3:14

13:9
u Ex 20:13-15, 17;
Dt 5:17-19,21
v Lev 19:18;
Mt 19:19

13:10
w ver 8;
Mt 22:39,40

spiritual fervor,*a* serving the Lord. [12]Be joyful in hope,*b* patient in affliction,*c* faithful in prayer. [13]Share with God's people who are in need. Practice hospitality.*d*

[14]Bless those who persecute you;*e* bless and do not curse. [15]Rejoice with those who rejoice; mourn with those who mourn.*f* [16]Live in harmony with one another.*g* Do not be proud, but be willing to associate with people of low position.*a* Do not be conceited.*h*

[17]Do not repay anyone evil for evil.*i* Be careful to do what is right in the eyes of everybody.*j* [18]If it is possible, as far as it depends on you, live at peace with everyone.*k* [19]Do not take revenge,*l* my friends, but leave room for God's wrath, for it is written: "It is mine to avenge; I will repay,"*bm* says the Lord. [20]On the contrary:

"If your enemy is hungry, feed him;
if he is thirsty, give him something to drink.
In doing this, you will heap burning coals on his head."*cn*

[21]Do not be overcome by evil, but overcome evil with good.

Chapter 13 Theme

13 Everyone must submit himself to the governing authorities,*o* for there is no authority except that which God has established.*p* The authorities that exist have been established by God. [2]Consequently, he who rebels against the authority is rebelling against what God has instituted, and those who do so will bring judgment on themselves. [3]For rulers hold no terror for those who do right, but for those who do wrong. Do you want to be free from fear of the one in authority? Then do what is right and he will commend you.*q* [4]For he is God's servant to do you good. But if you do wrong, be afraid, for he does not bear the sword for nothing. He is God's servant, an agent of wrath to bring punishment on the wrongdoer.*r* [5]Therefore, it is necessary to submit to the authorities, not only because of possible punishment but also because of conscience.

[6]This is also why you pay taxes, for the authorities are God's servants, who give their full time to governing. [7]Give everyone what you owe him: If you owe taxes, pay taxes;*s* if revenue, then revenue; if respect, then respect; if honor, then honor.

[8]Let no debt remain outstanding, except the continuing debt to love one another, for he who loves his fellowman has fulfilled the law.*t* [9]The commandments, "Do not commit adultery," "Do not murder," "Do not steal," "Do not covet,"*du* and whatever other commandment there may be, are summed up in this one rule: "Love your neighbor as yourself."*ev* [10]Love does no harm to its neighbor. Therefore love is the fulfillment of the law.*w*

a 16 Or willing to do menial work *b 19 Deut. 32:35* *c 20 Prov. 25:21,22* *d 9 Exodus 20:13-15,17; Deut. 5:17-19,21* *e 9 Lev. 19:18*

[11]And do this, understanding the present time. The hour has come[a] for you to wake up from your slumber,[b] because our salvation is nearer now than when we first believed. [12]The night is nearly over; the day is almost here.[c] So let us put aside the deeds of darkness[d] and put on the armor[e] of light. [13]Let us behave decently, as in the daytime, not in orgies and drunkenness, not in sexual immorality and debauchery, not in dissension and jealousy.[f] [14]Rather, clothe yourselves with the Lord Jesus Christ,[g] and do not think about how to gratify the desires of the sinful nature.[a]

Chapter 14 Theme

14 Accept him whose faith is weak,[h] without passing judgment on disputable matters. [2]One man's faith allows him to eat everything, but another man, whose faith is weak, eats only vegetables. [3]The man who eats everything must not look down on[i] him who does not, and the man who does not eat everything must not condemn[j] the man who does, for God has accepted him. [4]Who are you to judge someone else's servant?[k] To his own master he stands or falls. And he will stand, for the Lord is able to make him stand.

[5]One man considers one day more sacred than another;[l] another man considers every day alike. Each one should be fully convinced in his own mind. [6]He who regards one day as special, does so to the Lord. He who eats meat, eats to the Lord, for he gives thanks to God;[m] and he who abstains, does so to the Lord and gives thanks to God. [7]For none of us lives to himself alone[n] and none of us dies to himself alone. [8]If we live, we live to the Lord; and if we die, we die to the Lord. So, whether we live or die, we belong to the Lord.[o]

[9]For this very reason, Christ died and returned to life[p] so that he might be the Lord of both the dead and the living.[q] [10]You, then, why do you judge your brother? Or why do you look down on your brother? For we will all stand before God's judgment seat.[r] [11]It is written:

"'As surely as I live,' says the Lord,
'every knee will bow before me;
every tongue will confess to God.'"[b][s]

[12]So then, each of us will give an account of himself to God.[t]

[13]Therefore let us stop passing judgment[u] on one another. Instead, make up your mind not to put any stumbling block or obstacle in your brother's way. [14]As one who is in the Lord Jesus, I am fully convinced that no food[c] is unclean in itself.[v] But if anyone regards something as unclean, then for him it is unclean.[w] [15]If your brother is distressed because of what you eat, you are no

---

a 14 Or *the flesh*   b 11 Isaiah 45:23   c 14 Or *that nothing*

13:11
a 1Co 7:29-31;
10:11
b Eph 5:14;
1Th 5:5,6

13:12
c 1Jn 2:8
d Eph 5:11
e Eph 6:11,13

13:13
f Gal 5:20,21

13:14
g Gal 3:27; 5:16;
Eph 4:24

14:1
h Ro 15:1;
1Co 8:9-12

14:3
i Lk 18:9
j Col 2:16

14:4
k Jas 4:12

14:5
l Gal 4:10

14:6
m Mt 14:19;
1Co 10:30,31;
1Ti 4:3,4

14:7
n 2Co 5:15;
Gal 2:20

14:8
o Php 1:20

14:9
p Rev 1:18
q 2Co 5:15

14:10
r 2Co 5:10

14:11
s Isa 45:23;
Php 2:10,11

14:12
t Mt 12:36;
1Pe 4:5

14:13
u Mt 7:1

14:14
v Ac 10:15
w 1Co 8:7

longer acting in love.*a* Do not by your eating destroy your brother for whom Christ died.*b* ¹⁶Do not allow what you consider good to be spoken of as evil.*c* ¹⁷For the kingdom of God is not a matter of eating and drinking,*d* but of righteousness, peace and joy in the Holy Spirit,*e* ¹⁸because anyone who serves Christ in this way is pleasing to God and approved by men.*f*

¹⁹Let us therefore make every effort to do what leads to peace*g* and to mutual edification.*h* ²⁰Do not destroy the work of God for the sake of food.*i* All food is clean, but it is wrong for a man to eat anything that causes someone else to stumble.*j* ²¹It is better not to eat meat or drink wine or to do anything else that will cause your brother to fall.*k*

²²So whatever you believe about these things keep between yourself and God. Blessed is the man who does not condemn*l* himself by what he approves. ²³But the man who has doubts*m* is condemned if he eats, because his eating is not from faith; and everything that does not come from faith is sin.

Chapter 15 Theme

15 We who are strong ought to bear with the failings of the weak*n* and not to please ourselves. ²Each of us should please his neighbor for his good,*o* to build him up.*p* ³For even Christ did not please himself*q* but, as it is written: "The insults of those who insult you have fallen on me."*ar* ⁴For everything that was written in the past was written to teach us,*s* so that through endurance and the encouragement of the Scriptures we might have hope.

⁵May the God who gives endurance and encouragement give you a spirit of unity*t* among yourselves as you follow Christ Jesus, ⁶so that with one heart and mouth you may glorify the God and Father*u* of our Lord Jesus Christ.

⁷Accept one another,*v* then, just as Christ accepted you, in order to bring praise to God. ⁸For I tell you that Christ has become a servant of the Jews*bw* on behalf of God's truth, to confirm the promises*x* made to the patriarchs ⁹so that the Gentiles*y* may glorify God*z* for his mercy, as it is written:

> "Therefore I will praise you among the Gentiles;
> I will sing hymns to your name."*ca*

¹⁰Again, it says,

> "Rejoice, O Gentiles, with his people."*db*

¹¹And again,

> "Praise the Lord, all you Gentiles,
> and sing praises to him, all you peoples."*ec*

### Cross references (margin)

14:15
a Eph 5:2
b 1Co 8:11

14:16
c 1Co 10:30

14:17
d 1Co 8:8
e Ro 15:13

14:18
f 2Co 8:21

14:19
g Ps 34:14;
Ro 12:18;
Heb 12:14
h Ro 15:2;
2Co 12:19

14:20
i ver 15
j 1Co 8:9-12

14:21
k 1Co 8:13

14:22
l 1Jn 3:21

14:23
m ver 5

15:1
n Ro 14:1;
Gal 6:1,2;
1Th 5:14

15:2
o 1Co 10:33
p Ro 14:19

15:3
q 2Co 8:9
r Ps 69:9

15:4
s Ro 4:23,24

15:5
t Ro 12:16;
1Co 1:10

15:6
u Rev 1:6

15:7
v Ro 14:1

15:8
w Mt 15:24;
Ac 3:25,26
x 2Co 1:20

15:9
y Ro 3:29
z Mt 9:8
a 2Sa 22:50;
Ps 18:49

15:10
b Dt 32:43

15:11
c Ps 117:1

a3 Psalm 69:9   *b8* Greek *circumcision*   *c9* 2 Samuel 22:50; Psalm 18:49   *d10* Deut. 32:43
e11 Psalm 117:1

¹²And again, Isaiah says,

> "The Root of Jesse^a will spring up,
>   one who will arise to rule over the nations;
> the Gentiles will hope in him."^{ab}

¹³May the God of hope fill you with all joy and peace^c as you trust in him, so that you may overflow with hope by the power of the Holy Spirit.^d

¹⁴I myself am convinced, my brothers, that you yourselves are full of goodness,^e complete in knowledge^f and competent to instruct one another. ¹⁵I have written you quite boldly on some points, as if to remind you of them again, because of the grace God gave me^g ¹⁶to be a minister of Christ Jesus to the Gentiles^h with the priestly duty of proclaiming the gospel of God,ⁱ so that the Gentiles might become an offering^j acceptable to God, sanctified by the Holy Spirit.

¹⁷Therefore I glory in Christ Jesus^k in my service to God.^l ¹⁸I will not venture to speak of anything except what Christ has accomplished through me in leading the Gentiles^m to obey Godⁿ by what I have said and done— ¹⁹by the power of signs and miracles,^o through the power of the Spirit.^p So from Jerusalem^q all the way around to Illyricum, I have fully proclaimed the gospel of Christ. ²⁰It has always been my ambition to preach the gospel where Christ was not known, so that I would not be building on someone else's foundation.^r ²¹Rather, as it is written:

> "Those who were not told about him will see,
>   and those who have not heard will understand."^{bs}

²²This is why I have often been hindered from coming to you.^t

²³But now that there is no more place for me to work in these regions, and since I have been longing for many years to see you,^u ²⁴I plan to do so when I go to Spain.^v I hope to visit you while passing through and to have you assist me on my journey there, after I have enjoyed your company for a while. ²⁵Now, however, I am on my way to Jerusalem^w in the service^x of the saints there. ²⁶For Macedonia^y and Achaia^z were pleased to make a contribution for the poor among the saints in Jerusalem. ²⁷They were pleased to do it, and indeed they owe it to them. For if the Gentiles have shared in the Jews' spiritual blessings, they owe it to the Jews to share with them their material blessings.^a ²⁸So after I have completed this task and have made sure that they have received this fruit, I will go to Spain and visit you on the way. ²⁹I know that when I come to you,^b I will come in the full measure of the blessing of Christ.

³⁰I urge you, brothers, by our Lord Jesus Christ and by the love of the Spirit,^c to join me in my struggle by praying to God for me.^d

a *12* Isaiah 11:10   b *21* Isaiah 52:15

15:12
a Rev 5:5
b Isa 11:10; Mt 12:21

15:13
c Ro 14:17
d ver 19; 1Co 2:4; 1Th 1:5

15:14
e Eph 5:9
f 2Pe 1:12

15:15
g Ro 12:3

15:16
h Ac 9:15; Ro 11:13
i Ro 1:1
j Isa 66:20

15:17
k Php 3:3
l Heb 2:17

15:18
m Ac 15:12; 21:19; Ro 1:5
n Ro 16:26

15:19
o Jn 4:48; Ac 19:11
p ver 13
q Ac 22:17-21

15:20
r 2Co 10:15,16

15:21
s Isa 52:15

15:22
t Ro 1:13

15:23
u Ac 19:21; Ro 1:10,11

15:24
v ver 28

15:25
w Ac 19:21
x Ac 24:17

15:26
y Ac 16:9; 2Co 8:1
z Ac 18:12

15:27
a 1Co 9:11

15:29
b Ro 1:10,11

15:30
c Gal 5:22
d 2Co 1:11; Col 4:12

15:31
a 2Th 3:2

15:32
b Ac 18:21
c Ro 1:10,13
d 1Co 16:18

15:33
e Ro 16:20;
2Co 13:11;
Php 4:9;
1Th 5:23;
Heb 13:20

16:1
f 2Co 3:1
g Ac 18:18

16:2
h Php 2:29

16:3
i Ac 18:2
j ver 7,9,10

16:5
k 1Co 16:19;
Col 4:15;
Phm 2
l 1Co 16:15

16:7
m ver 11,21

16:9
n ver 3

16:11
o ver 7,21

16:15
p ver 2
q ver 14

16:16
r 1Co 16:20;
2Co 13:12;
1Th 5:26

16:17
s Gal 1:8,9;
1Ti 1:3; 6:3
t 2Th 3:6,14;
2Jn 10

³¹Pray that I may be rescued[a] from the unbelievers in Judea and that my service in Jerusalem may be acceptable to the saints there, ³²so that by God's will[b] I may come to you[c] with joy and together with you be refreshed.[d] ³³The God of peace[e] be with you all. Amen.

Chapter 16 Theme _____

16 I commend[f] to you our sister Phoebe, a servant[a] of the church in Cenchrea.[g] ²I ask you to receive her in the Lord[h] in a way worthy of the saints and to give her any help she may need from you, for she has been a great help to many people, including me.

³Greet Priscilla[b] and Aquila,[i] my fellow workers in Christ Jesus.[j]
    ⁴They risked their lives for me. Not only I but all the churches of the Gentiles are grateful to them.

⁵Greet also the church that meets at their house.[k]

Greet my dear friend Epenetus, who was the first convert[l] to Christ in the province of Asia.

⁶Greet Mary, who worked very hard for you.

⁷Greet Andronicus and Junias, my relatives[m] who have been in prison with me. They are outstanding among the apostles, and they were in Christ before I was.

⁸Greet Ampliatus, whom I love in the Lord.

⁹Greet Urbanus, our fellow worker in Christ,[n] and my dear friend Stachys.

¹⁰Greet Apelles, tested and approved in Christ.

Greet those who belong to the household of Aristobulus.

¹¹Greet Herodion, my relative.[o]

Greet those in the household of Narcissus who are in the Lord.

¹²Greet Tryphena and Tryphosa, those women who work hard in the Lord.

Greet my dear friend Persis, another woman who has worked very hard in the Lord.

¹³Greet Rufus, chosen in the Lord, and his mother, who has been a mother to me, too.

¹⁴Greet Asyncritus, Phlegon, Hermes, Patrobas, Hermas and the brothers with them.

¹⁵Greet Philologus, Julia, Nereus and his sister, and Olympas and all the saints[p] with them.[q]

¹⁶Greet one another with a holy kiss.[r]

All the churches of Christ send greetings.

¹⁷I urge you, brothers, to watch out for those who cause divisions and put obstacles in your way that are contrary to the teaching you have learned.[s] Keep away from them.[t] ¹⁸For such people are not

a 1 Or *deaconess*   b 3 Greek *Prisca*, a variant of *Priscilla* serving our Lord Christ, but their own appetites.^a By smooth talk and flattery they deceive^b the minds of naive people. ¹⁹Everyone has heard^c about your obedience, so I am full of joy over you; but I want you to be wise about what is good, and innocent about what is evil.^d

²⁰The God of peace^e will soon crush^f Satan under your feet.

The grace of our Lord Jesus be with you.^g

²¹Timothy,^h my fellow worker, sends his greetings to you, as do Lucius,ⁱ Jason^j and Sosipater, my relatives.^k

²²I, Tertius, who wrote down this letter, greet you in the Lord.

²³Gaius, whose hospitality I and the whole church here enjoy, sends you his greetings.

Erastus,^l who is the city's director of public works, and our brother Quartus send you their greetings.^a

²⁵Now to him who is able^m to establish you by my gospelⁿ and the proclamation of Jesus Christ, according to the revelation of the mystery^o hidden for long ages past, ²⁶but now revealed and made known through the prophetic writings by the command of the eternal God, so that all nations might believe and obey him— ²⁷to the only wise God be glory forever through Jesus Christ! Amen.^p

a 23 Some manuscripts *their greetings.* ²⁴*May the grace of our Lord Jesus Christ be with all of you. Amen.*

16:18
^aPhp 3:19
^bCol 2:4

16:19
^cRo 1:8
^dMt 10:16;
1Co 14:20

16:20
^eRo 15:33
^fGe 3:15
^g1Th 5:28

16:21
^hAc 16:1
ⁱAc 13:1
^jAc 17:5
^kver 7,11

16:23
^lAc 19:22

16:25
^mEph 3:20
ⁿRo 2:16
^oEph 1:9;
Col 1:26,27

16:27
^pRo 11:36

Romans Observations Chart

ABOUT PAUL

WHY HE WROTE

ABOUT THE RECIPIENTS

IN ADAM
(According to the sinful nature)

IN CHRIST
(According to the Spirit)

Theme of Romans:

SEGMENT DIVISIONS

			CHAPTER THEMES
			1
			2
			3
			4
			5
			6
			7
			8
			9
			10
			11
			12
			13
			14
			15
			16

Author:

Date:

Purpose:

Key Words:

1 CORINTHIANS

S in abounded in the cosmopolitan city of Corinth, the chief city of Greece. Corinth overlooked the narrow isthmus that connected the Greek mainland with Peloponnesus and received ships in its two harbors. At one time it was home of at least twelve heathen temples. The Corinthians were intrigued by Greek philosophy and captivated by the disciplined training and athletic events held at the Isthmus. They desperately needed to hear the good news of Jesus Christ, the one crucified for sinners.

The worship ceremonies carried out by a thousand temple prostitutes connected with the temple of Aphrodite (the goddess of love) bred blatant immorality throughout Corinth—so much so that the Greek verb translated "to Corinthianize" meant to practice sexual immorality.

Prostitutes openly plied their wares and meat markets thrived on sales from the sacrifices offered in the temples. The Corinthians ate well, satisfied their sexual urges without condemnation, flirted with the wisdom of men, and did all they could to keep their bodies as beautiful as those of the Greek gods. They loved to listen to great orators. For the 250,000 citizens there were almost two slaves per person. What more did Corinth need? Freedom. Freedom from sin and death. God met that need by blocking Paul at every hand on his second missionary journey until he received the Macedonian call, "Come and help us."

After establishing the Corinthian church Paul eventually went to Ephesus, where he stayed for three years. From there he wrote his first epistle to the Corinthian believers, who so desperately needed help and correction. It was sometime between A.D. 52 and 56.

❧ THINGS TO DO

Chapters 1-6

1. In chapter 1 note what Paul commends about the Corinthians. Make a list in the margin titled "Commendations."

2. Read chapters 1 through 6, one chapter at a time. As you read, keep in mind what you read in the introduction to this book. Do the following:

    a. Note the problems Paul deals with in the text (as he writes). You can see these problems several ways.

        1) As you read, ask the five W's and an H: Who? What? When? Where? Why? and How? Especially concentrate on the problems, subjects, or people mentioned. Ask questions such as: Why would Paul mention specific people by name in this chapter? Who is causing the problem? How did the Corinthians get this way? Why does Paul say what he does about himself or his ministry?

        2) Mark the key words in the text. Key words help you see the main topics in a chapter. In 1 Corinthians they indicate what the problems are and what the solution is.

        Write the following key words for this segment on an index card and use it as a bookmark while you study chapters 1 through 6. They are: *God, Jesus (Christ, Lord), Spirit, divisions (divided), spirit* (note whose spirit or what spirit), *power, mind, wise (expert, wisdom), preach, body (physically),* and *church.*

    b. As you read each of the first six chapters, note the problems Paul deals with in each chapter. In the margin make a list of these with the heading "Problems."

3. As you read, look for and note on the OBSERVATIONS CHART on page 1974 what you learn about the Corinthians, any commands directed to them, and the warnings Paul gives them.

4. As you finish each chapter, summarize the theme (subject) of that chapter and record it on 1 CORINTHIANS AT A GLANCE on page 1975 and in the text next to the chapter number.

5. Two things prompted Paul to write to the Corinthians, and it is these two things which cause a natural division in his epistle. Read 1 Corinthians 1:10, 11, where Paul states his reason for writing. Record this reason on the 1 CORINTHIANS AT A GLANCE chart in the space under "Major Segment Divisions."

Chapters 7-16

1. The second division of 1 Corinthians is noted by two phrases which are repeated throughout the last segment of this book: *now for* or *now about*. Read 7:1 and notice the transition. From this point on Paul deals with matters the Corinthians had questions on or issues that they needed to be instructed in.

2. Now look up the following verses and underline or mark in a distinctive way the phrases "now for" or "now about." As you mark these phrases, mark along with them the subject matter Paul is about to deal with. The verses are: 7:1; 7:25; 8:1; 12:1; 16:1. In the same way also mark in 15:1 the words *Now, brothers, I want to remind you of the gospel I preached to you*. Marking these wordings will give you the topical divisions of this second segment of 1 Corinthians.

3. As you read through this last segment of 1 Corinthians, mark the following key words: *God, Jesus (Christ, Lord), Spirit, body, unbelieving (not a believer, unbeliever, unbelievers), think (thinks, thinking, thought), church (churches, congregation), idol(s) (idolaters, idolatry), knowledge (knows), preach (preaching),* and *gospel*. Make a new list of key words to use as a bookmark in this segment. (*Divisions* and *differences* each are used one more time in chapter 11. This is significant, since Paul again deals with problems while giving further instruction to the church.)

4. As you deal with each topic, ask questions such as: Why does the church have this question or problem? How are they behaving? What is their thinking? What are Paul's instructions regarding this subject? Why are they to do this? What are the consequences if they don't?

5. As Paul moves through these final matters of concern, he intermittently explains his position and ministry. Watch for these explanations and note if and how he ties them in with his subject matter.

6. Note on the OBSERVATIONS CHART what you learn from this segment about the Corinthians and the commands and warnings Paul gives them.

7. Determine and record the theme of each chapter in the text next to the chapter number and on 1 CORINTHIANS AT A GLANCE.

8. Considering 7:1, give a title to the segment division for the second half of 1 Corinthians. Record your title on 1 CORINTHIANS AT A GLANCE.

9. Record the theme of 1 Corinthians and complete the 1 CORINTHIANS AT A GLANCE chart.

❧ THINGS TO THINK ABOUT

1. Are you having any of the same problems in your own life or in your church that the Corinthians had? Do you think this letter has the answers for your problems or questions? How can you apply what you have learned?

2. According to the context of 1 Corinthians 3, what does it mean to be a carnal or fleshly Christian? Remember, context rules over all accurate interpretation.

3. Are you untaught—ignorant—concerning spiritual gifts? Do you know about one or two of them but not the others? Have you believed or even taught others in accord with what the whole counsel of God has to say on the subject, or have you merely gone by your experience or reasoning? Do you appreciate other people's gifts even though they may be different from yours?

4. On what do you base your beliefs about marriage, divorce, and remarriage? What did you learn from 1 Corinthians 7 about these topics? Did this change your belief?

5. Is the preaching of the cross foolishness to you, or is it a demonstration of the power of God?

〰〰〰〰

Chapter 1 Theme

1 Paul, called to be an apostle[a] of Christ Jesus by the will of God,[b] and our brother Sosthenes,[c]

[2]To the church of God in Corinth,[d] to those sanctified in Christ Jesus and called[e] to be holy, together with all those everywhere who call on the name of our Lord Jesus Christ—their Lord and ours:

[3]Grace and peace to you from God our Father and the Lord Jesus Christ.[f]

[4]I always thank God for you[g] because of his grace given you in Christ Jesus. [5]For in him you have been enriched[h] in every way— in all your speaking and in all your knowledge[i]— [6]because our testimony[j] about Christ was confirmed in you. [7]Therefore you do not lack any spiritual gift as you eagerly wait for our Lord Jesus Christ to be revealed.[k] [8]He will keep you strong to the end, so that you will be blameless[l] on the day of our Lord Jesus Christ. [9]God, who has called you into fellowship with his Son Jesus Christ our Lord,[m] is faithful.[n]

[10]I appeal to you, brothers, in the name of our Lord Jesus Christ, that all of you agree with one another so that there may be no divisions among you and that you may be perfectly united in mind and thought. [11]My brothers, some from Chloe's household have informed me that there are quarrels among you. [12]What I mean is this: One of you says, "I follow Paul";[o] another, "I follow Apollos";[p] another, "I follow Cephas[a]";[q] still another, "I follow Christ."

[13]Is Christ divided? Was Paul crucified for you? Were you baptized into[b] the name of Paul?[r] [14]I am thankful that I did not baptize any of you except Crispus[s] and Gaius,[t] [15]so no one can say that you were baptized into my name. [16](Yes, I also baptized the household of Stephanas;[u] beyond that, I don't remember if I baptized anyone else.) [17]For Christ did not send me to baptize,[v] but to preach the gospel—not with words of human wisdom,[w] lest the cross of Christ be emptied of its power.

[18]For the message of the cross is foolishness to those who are perishing,[x] but to us who are being saved it is the power of God.[y] [19]For it is written:

> "I will destroy the wisdom of the wise;
> the intelligence of the intelligent I will frustrate."[c][z]

**Cross references (margin):**

1:1 [a] Ro 1:1; Eph 1:1; [b] 2Co 1:1; [c] Ac 18:17
1:2 [d] Ac 18:1; [e] Ro 1:7
1:3 [f] Ro 1:7
1:4 [g] Ro 1:8
1:5 [h] 2Co 9:11; [i] 2Co 8:7
1:6 [j] Rev 1:2
1:7 [k] Php 3:20; Tit 2:13; 2Pe 3:12
1:8 [l] 1Th 3:13
1:9 [m] 1Jn 1:3; [n] Isa 49:7; 1Th 5:24
1:12 [o] 1Co 3:4,22; [p] Ac 18:24; [q] Jn 1:42
1:13 [r] Mt 28:19
1:14 [s] Ac 18:8; Ro 16:23; [t] Ac 19:29
1:16 [u] 1Co 16:15
1:17 [v] Jn 4:2; [w] 1Co 2:1,4,13
1:18 [x] 2Co 2:15; [y] Ro 1:16
1:19 [z] Isa 29:14

[a] 12 That is, Peter   [b] 13 Or in; also in verse 15   [c] 19 Isaiah 29:14

[20]Where is the wise man?[a] Where is the scholar? Where is the philosopher of this age? Has not God made foolish[b] the wisdom of the world? [21]For since in the wisdom of God the world through its wisdom did not know him, God was pleased through the foolishness of what was preached to save those who believe. [22]Jews demand miraculous signs[c] and Greeks look for wisdom, [23]but we preach Christ crucified: a stumbling block[d] to Jews and foolishness[e] to Gentiles, [24]but to those whom God has called,[f] both Jews and Greeks, Christ the power of God and the wisdom of God.[g] [25]For the foolishness[h] of God is wiser than man's wisdom, and the weakness[i] of God is stronger than man's strength.

[26]Brothers, think of what you were when you were called. Not many of you were wise by human standards; not many were influential; not many were of noble birth. [27]But God chose[j] the foolish[k] things of the world to shame the wise; God chose the weak things of the world to shame the strong. [28]He chose the lowly things of this world and the despised things—and the things that are not[l]—to nullify the things that are, [29]so that no one may boast before him.[m] [30]It is because of him that you are in Christ Jesus, who has become for us wisdom from God—that is, our righteousness,[n] holiness and redemption.[o] [31]Therefore, as it is written: "Let him who boasts boast in the Lord."[a][p]

Chapter 2 Theme

2 When I came to you, brothers, I did not come with eloquence or superior wisdom[q] as I proclaimed to you the testimony about God.[b] [2]For I resolved to know nothing while I was with you except Jesus Christ and him crucified.[r] [3]I came to you[s] in weakness and fear, and with much trembling. [4]My message and my preaching were not with wise and persuasive words, but with a demonstration of the Spirit's power,[t] [5]so that your faith might not rest on men's wisdom, but on God's power.[u]

[6]We do, however, speak a message of wisdom among the mature,[v] but not the wisdom of this age[w] or of the rulers of this age, who are coming to nothing. [7]No, we speak of God's secret wisdom, a wisdom that has been hidden and that God destined for our glory before time began. [8]None of the rulers of this age understood it, for if they had, they would not have crucified the Lord of glory.[x] [9]However, as it is written:

> "No eye has seen,
>   no ear has heard,
>   no mind has conceived
>   what God has prepared for those who love him"[c][y]—

Cross-references

1:20
[a]Isa 19:11,12
[b]Job 12:17;
Ro 1:22

1:22
[c]Mt 12:38

1:23
[d]Lk 2:34;
Gal 5:11
[e]1Co 2:14

1:24
[f]Ro 8:28
[g]ver 30;
Col 2:3

1:25
[h]ver 18
[i]2Co 13:4

1:27
[j]Jas 2:5
[k]ver 20

1:28
[l]Ro 4:17

1:29
[m]Eph 2:9

1:30
[n]Jer 23:5,6;
2Co 5:21
[o]Ro 3:24;
Eph 1:7,14

1:31
[p]Jer 9:23,24;
2Co 10:17

2:1
[q]1Co 1:17

2:2
[r]Gal 6:14;
1Co 1:23

2:3
[s]Ac 18:1-18

2:4
[t]Ro 15:19

2:5
[u]2Co 4:7; 6:7

2:6
[v]Eph 4:13;
Php 3:15;
Heb 5:14
[w]1Co 1:20

2:8
[x]Ac 7:2;
Jas 2:1

2:9
[y]Isa 64:4; 65:17

---

[a]31 Jer. 9:24   [b]1 Some manuscripts as I proclaimed to you God's mystery   [c]9 Isaiah 64:4

2:10
a Mt 13:11;
Eph 3:3,5
b Jn 14:26

2:11
c Jer 17:9
d Pr 20:27

2:12
e Ro 8:15
f 1Co 1:20,27

2:13
g 1Co 1:17

2:14
h 1Co 1:18

2:16
i Isa 40:13
j Jn 15:15

3:1
k 1Co 2:15
l Ro 7:14;
1Co 2:14
m Heb 5:13

3:2
n Heb 5:12-14;
1Pe 2:2
o Jn 16:12

3:3
p 1Co 1:11;
Gal 5:20

3:4
q 1Co 1:12

3:6
r Ac 18:4-11

3:8
s Ps 62:12

3:9
t 2Co 6:1
u Isa 61:3
v Eph 2:20-22;
1Pe 2:5

3:10
w Ro 12:3
x Ro 15:20

3:11
y Isa 28:16;
Eph 2:20

3:13
z 1Co 4:5
a 2Th 1:7-10

[10]but God has revealed[a] it to us by his Spirit.[b]

The Spirit searches all things, even the deep things of God. [11]For who among men knows the thoughts of a man[c] except the man's spirit[d] within him? In the same way no one knows the thoughts of God except the Spirit of God. [12]We have not received the spirit[e] of the world[f] but the Spirit who is from God, that we may understand what God has freely given us. [13]This is what we speak, not in words taught us by human wisdom[g] but in words taught by the Spirit, expressing spiritual truths in spiritual words.[a] [14]The man without the Spirit does not accept the things that come from the Spirit of God, for they are foolishness[h] to him, and he cannot understand them, because they are spiritually discerned. [15]The spiritual man makes judgments about all things, but he himself is not subject to any man's judgment:

[16]"For who has known the mind of the Lord
    that he may instruct him?"[b][i]

But we have the mind of Christ.[j]

Chapter 3 Theme

3 Brothers, I could not address you as spiritual[k] but as worldly[l]— mere infants[m] in Christ. [2]I gave you milk, not solid food,[n] for you were not yet ready for it.[o] Indeed, you are still not ready. [3]You are still worldly. For since there is jealousy and quarreling[p] among you, are you not worldly? Are you not acting like mere men? [4]For when one says, "I follow Paul," and another, "I follow Apollos,"[q] are you not mere men?

[5]What, after all, is Apollos? And what is Paul? Only servants, through whom you came to believe—as the Lord has assigned to each his task. [6]I planted the seed,[r] Apollos watered it, but God made it grow. [7]So neither he who plants nor he who waters is anything, but only God, who makes things grow. [8]The man who plants and the man who waters have one purpose, and each will be rewarded according to his own labor.[s] [9]For we are God's fellow workers;[t] you are God's field,[u] God's building.[v]

[10]By the grace God has given me,[w] I laid a foundation[x] as an expert builder, and someone else is building on it. But each one should be careful how he builds. [11]For no one can lay any foundation other than the one already laid, which is Jesus Christ.[y] [12]If any man builds on this foundation using gold, silver, costly stones, wood, hay or straw, [13]his work will be shown for what it is,[z] because the Day[a] will bring it to light. It will be revealed with fire, and the fire will test the quality of each man's work. [14]If what he has built

a 13 Or *Spirit, interpreting spiritual truths to spiritual men*   b 16 Isaiah 40:13

survives, he will receive his reward. [15]If it is burned up, he will suffer loss; he himself will be saved, but only as one escaping through the flames.[a]

[16]Don't you know that you yourselves are God's temple[b] and that God's Spirit lives in you? [17]If anyone destroys God's temple, God will destroy him; for God's temple is sacred, and you are that temple.

[18]Do not deceive yourselves. If any one of you thinks he is wise[c] by the standards of this age, he should become a "fool" so that he may become wise. [19]For the wisdom of this world is foolishness[d] in God's sight. As it is written: "He catches the wise in their craftiness"[a;e] [20]and again, "The Lord knows that the thoughts of the wise are futile."[b f] [21]So then, no more boasting about men![g] All things are yours,[h] [22]whether Paul or Apollos or Cephas[c i] or the world or life or death or the present or the future[j]—all are yours, [23]and you are of Christ,[k] and Christ is of God.

Chapter 4 Theme

4 So then, men ought to regard us as servants of Christ and as those entrusted[l] with the secret things[m] of God. [2]Now it is required that those who have been given a trust must prove faithful. [3]I care very little if I am judged by you or by any human court; indeed, I do not even judge myself. [4]My conscience is clear, but that does not make me innocent.[n] It is the Lord who judges me. [5]Therefore judge nothing[o] before the appointed time; wait till the Lord comes. He will bring to light what is hidden in darkness and will expose the motives of men's hearts. At that time each will receive his praise from God.[p]

[6]Now, brothers, I have applied these things to myself and Apollos for your benefit, so that you may learn from us the meaning of the saying, "Do not go beyond what is written."[q] Then you will not take pride in one man over against another.[r] [7]For who makes you different from anyone else? What do you have that you did not receive?[s] And if you did receive it, why do you boast as though you did not?

[8]Already you have all you want! Already you have become rich![t] You have become kings—and that without us! How I wish that you really had become kings so that we might be kings with you! [9]For it seems to me that God has put us apostles on display at the end of the procession, like men condemned to die[u] in the arena. We have been made a spectacle[v] to the whole universe, to angels as well as to men. [10]We are fools for Christ,[w] but you are so wise in Christ![x] We are weak, but you are strong![y] You are honored, we are dishonored! [11]To this very hour we go hungry and thirsty, we

[a] 19 Job 5:13   [b] 20 Psalm 94:11   [c] 22 That is, Peter

3:15 [a]Jude 23
3:16 [b]1Co 6:19; 2Co 6:16
3:18 [c]Isa 5:21; 1Co 8:2
3:19 [d]1Co 1:20,27 [e]Job 5:13
3:20 [f]Ps 94:11
3:21 [g]1Co 4:6 [h]Ro 8:32
3:22 [i]1Co 1:12 [j]Ro 8:38
3:23 [k]1Co 15:23; 2Co 10:7; Gal 3:29
4:1 [l]1Co 9:17; Tit 1:7 [m]Ro 16:25
4:4 [n]Ro 2:13
4:5 [o]Mt 7:1,2; Ro 2:1 [p]Ro 2:29
4:6 [q]1Co 1:19,31; 3:19,20 [r]1Co 1:12
4:7 [s]Jn 3:27; Ro 12:3,6
4:8 [t]Rev 3:17,18
4:9 [u]Ro 8:36 [v]Heb 10:33
4:10 [w]1Co 1:18; Ac 17:18 [x]1Co 3:18 [y]1Co 2:3

4:11
a Ro 8:35;
2Co 11:23-27

4:12
b Ac 18:3
c 1Pe 3:9

4:13
d La 3:45

4:14
e 1Th 2:11

4:15
f 1Co 9:12,14,
18,23

4:16
g 1Co 11:1;
Php 3:17;
1Th 1:6;
2Th 3:7,9

4:17
h 1Ti 1:2
i 1Co 7:17

4:19
j 2Co 1:15,16
k Ac 18:21

4:21
l 2Co 1:23;
13:2,10

5:1
m Lev 18:8;
Dt 22:30

5:2
n 2Co 7:7-11

5:3
o Col 2:5

5:4
p 2Th 3:6

5:5
q 1Ti 1:20

5:6
r Jas 4:16
s Mt 16:6,12
t Gal 5:9

5:7
u Mk 14:12;
1Pe 1:19

5:8
v Ex 12:14,15;
Dt 16:3

5:9
w Eph 5:11;
2Th 3:6,14

5:10
x 1Co 10:27

are in rags, we are brutally treated, we are homeless.*a* [12]We work hard with our own hands.*b* When we are cursed, we bless;*c* when we are persecuted, we endure it; [13]when we are slandered, we answer kindly. Up to this moment we have become the scum of the earth, the refuse*d* of the world.

[14]I am not writing this to shame you, but to warn you, as my dear children.*e* [15]Even though you have ten thousand guardians in Christ, you do not have many fathers, for in Christ Jesus I became your father through the gospel.*f* [16]Therefore I urge you to imitate me.*g* [17]For this reason I am sending to you Timothy, my son*h* whom I love, who is faithful in the Lord. He will remind you of my way of life in Christ Jesus, which agrees with what I teach everywhere in every church.*i*

[18]Some of you have become arrogant, as if I were not coming to you. [19]But I will come to you very soon,*j* if the Lord is willing,*k* and then I will find out not only how these arrogant people are talking, but what power they have. [20]For the kingdom of God is not a matter of talk but of power. [21]What do you prefer? Shall I come to you with a whip,*l* or in love and with a gentle spirit?

Chapter 5 Theme

5 It is actually reported that there is sexual immorality among you, and of a kind that does not occur even among pagans: A man has his father's wife.*m* [2]And you are proud! Shouldn't you rather have been filled with grief*n* and have put out of your fellowship the man who did this? [3]Even though I am not physically present, I am with you in spirit.*o* And I have already passed judgment on the one who did this, just as if I were present. [4]When you are assembled in the name of our Lord Jesus*p* and I am with you in spirit, and the power of our Lord Jesus is present, [5]hand this man over*q* to Satan, so that the sinful nature*a* may be destroyed and his spirit saved on the day of the Lord.

[6]Your boasting is not good.*r* Don't you know that a little yeast*s* works through the whole batch of dough?*t* [7]Get rid of the old yeast that you may be a new batch without yeast—as you really are. For Christ, our Passover lamb, has been sacrificed.*u* [8]Therefore let us keep the Festival, not with the old yeast, the yeast of malice and wickedness, but with bread without yeast,*v* the bread of sincerity and truth.

[9]I have written you in my letter not to associate*w* with sexually immoral people— [10]not at all meaning the people of this world*x* who are immoral, or the greedy and swindlers, or idolaters. In that case you would have to leave this world. [11]But now I am writing you

a 5 Or *that his body*; or *that the flesh*

that you must not associate with anyone who calls himself a brother but is sexually immoral or greedy, an idolater[a] or a slanderer, a drunkard or a swindler. With such a man do not even eat.

[12]What business is it of mine to judge those outside[b] the church? Are you not to judge those inside?[c] [13]God will judge those outside. "Expel the wicked man from among you."[ad]

Chapter 6 Theme

6 If any of you has a dispute with another, dare he take it before the ungodly for judgment instead of before the saints?[e] [2]Do you not know that the saints will judge the world?[f] And if you are to judge the world, are you not competent to judge trivial cases? [3]Do you not know that we will judge angels? How much more the things of this life! [4]Therefore, if you have disputes about such matters, appoint as judges even men of little account in the church![b] [5]I say this to shame you.[g] Is it possible that there is nobody among you wise enough to judge a dispute between believers?[h] [6]But instead, one brother goes to law against another—and this in front of unbelievers![i]

[7]The very fact that you have lawsuits among you means you have been completely defeated already. Why not rather be wronged? Why not rather be cheated?[j] [8]Instead, you yourselves cheat and do wrong, and you do this to your brothers.[k]

[9]Do you not know that the wicked will not inherit the kingdom of God?[l] Do not be deceived:[m] Neither the sexually immoral nor idolaters nor adulterers nor male prostitutes nor homosexual offenders [10]nor thieves nor the greedy nor drunkards nor slanderers nor swindlers will inherit the kingdom of God. [11]And that is what some of you were.[n] But you were washed,[o] you were sanctified,[p] you were justified in the name of the Lord Jesus Christ and by the Spirit of our God.

[12]"Everything is permissible for me"—but not everything is beneficial.[q] "Everything is permissible for me"—but I will not be mastered by anything. [13]"Food for the stomach and the stomach for food"—but God will destroy them both.[r] The body is not meant for sexual immorality, but for the Lord, and the Lord for the body. [14]By his power God raised the Lord from the dead, and he will raise us also.[s] [15]Do you not know that your bodies are members of Christ himself?[t] Shall I then take the members of Christ and unite them with a prostitute? Never! [16]Do you not know that he who unites himself with a prostitute is one with her in body? For it is said, "The two will become one flesh."[cu] [17]But he who unites himself with the Lord is one with him in spirit.[v]

a13 Deut. 17:7; 19:19; 21:21; 22:21,24; 24:7   b4 Or matters, do you appoint as judges men of little account in the church?   c16 Gen. 2:24

5:11 [a]1Co 10:7,14
5:12 [b]Mk 4:11 [c]ver 3-5; 1Co 6:1-4
5:13 [d]Dt 13:5
6:1 [e]Mt 18:17
6:2 [f]Mt 19:28; Lk 22:30
6:5 [g]1Co 4:14 [h]Ac 1:15
6:6 [i]2Co 6:14,15
6:7 [j]Mt 5:39,40
6:8 [k]1Th 4:6
6:9 [l]Gal 5:21 [m]1Co 15:33; Jas 1:16
6:11 [n]Eph 2:2 [o]Ac 22:16 [p]1Co 1:2
6:12 [q]1Co 10:23
6:13 [r]Col 2:22
6:14 [s]Ro 6:5; Eph 1:19,20
6:15 [t]Ro 12:5
6:16 [u]Ge 2:24; Mt 19:5; Eph 5:31
6:17 [v]Jn 17:21-23; Gal 2:20

6:18
a 2Co 12:21;
1Th 4:3,4;
Heb 13:4
b Ro 6:12

6:19
c Jn 2:21
d Ro 14:7,8

6:20
e Ac 20:28;
1Co 7:23;
1Pe 1:18,19;
Rev 5:9

7:1
f ver 8,26

7:3
g Ex 21:10;
1Pe 3:7

7:5
h Ex 19:15;
1Sa 21:4,5
i Mt 4:10
j 1Th 3:5

7:6
k 2Co 8:8

7:7
l ver 8; 1Co 9:5
m Mt 19:11,12;
Ro 12:6;
1Co 12:4,11

7:8
n ver 1,26

7:9
o 1Ti 5:14

7:10
p Mal 2:14-16;
Mt 5:32; 19:3-9;
Mk 10:11;
Lk 16:18

7:12
q ver 6,10;
2Co 11:17

7:14
r Mal 2:15

7:15
s Ro 14:19;
1Co 14:33

7:16
t Ro 11:14
u 1Pe 3:1

¹⁸Flee from sexual immorality.ᵃ All other sins a man commits are outside his body, but he who sins sexually sins against his own body.ᵇ ¹⁹Do you not know that your body is a templeᶜ of the Holy Spirit, who is in you, whom you have received from God? You are not your own;ᵈ ²⁰you were bought at a price.ᵉ Therefore honor God with your body.

Chapter 7 Theme

7 Now for the matters you wrote about: It is good for a man not to marry.ᵃᶠ ²But since there is so much immorality, each man should have his own wife, and each woman her own husband. ³The husband should fulfill his marital duty to his wife,ᵍ and likewise the wife to her husband. ⁴The wife's body does not belong to her alone but also to her husband. In the same way, the husband's body does not belong to him alone but also to his wife. ⁵Do not deprive each other except by mutual consent and for a time,ʰ so that you may devote yourselves to prayer. Then come together again so that Satanⁱ will not tempt youʲ because of your lack of self-control. ⁶I say this as a concession, not as a command.ᵏ ⁷I wish that all men were as I am.ˡ But each man has his own gift from God; one has this gift, another has that.ᵐ

⁸Now to the unmarried and the widows I say: It is good for them to stay unmarried, as I am.ⁿ ⁹But if they cannot control themselves, they should marry,ᵒ for it is better to marry than to burn with passion.

¹⁰To the married I give this command (not I, but the Lord): A wife must not separate from her husband.ᵖ ¹¹But if she does, she must remain unmarried or else be reconciled to her husband. And a husband must not divorce his wife.

¹²To the rest I say this (I, not the Lord):�q If any brother has a wife who is not a believer and she is willing to live with him, he must not divorce her. ¹³And if a woman has a husband who is not a believer and he is willing to live with her, she must not divorce him. ¹⁴For the unbelieving husband has been sanctified through his wife, and the unbelieving wife has been sanctified through her believing husband. Otherwise your children would be unclean, but as it is, they are holy.ʳ

¹⁵But if the unbeliever leaves, let him do so. A believing man or woman is not bound in such circumstances; God has called us to live in peace.ˢ ¹⁶How do you know, wife, whether you will saveᵗ your husband?ᵘ Or, how do you know, husband, whether you will save your wife?

¹⁷Nevertheless, each one should retain the place in life that the

---

ᵃ 1 Or "It is good for a man not to have sexual relations with a woman."

Lord assigned to him and to which God has called him.*a* This is the rule I lay down in all the churches.*b* **18**Was a man already circumcised when he was called? He should not become uncircumcised. Was a man uncircumcised when he was called? He should not be circumcised.*c* **19**Circumcision is nothing and uncircumcision is nothing.*d* Keeping God's commands is what counts. **20**Each one should remain in the situation which he was in when God called him.*e* **21**Were you a slave when you were called? Don't let it trouble you—although if you can gain your freedom, do so. **22**For he who was a slave when he was called by the Lord is the Lord's freedman;*f* similarly, he who was a free man when he was called is Christ's slave.*g* **23**You were bought at a price;*h* do not become slaves of men. **24**Brothers, each man, as responsible to God, should remain in the situation God called him to.*i*

25Now about virgins: I have no command from the Lord,*j* but I give a judgment as one who by the Lord's mercy*k* is trustworthy. **26**Because of the present crisis, I think that it is good for you to remain as you are.*l* **27**Are you married? Do not seek a divorce. Are you unmarried? Do not look for a wife. **28**But if you do marry, you have not sinned; and if a virgin marries, she has not sinned. But those who marry will face many troubles in this life, and I want to spare you this.

29What I mean, brothers, is that the time is short.*m* From now on those who have wives should live as if they had none; **30**those who mourn, as if they did not; those who are happy, as if they were not; those who buy something, as if it were not theirs to keep; **31**those who use the things of the world, as if not engrossed in them. For this world in its present form is passing away.*n*

32I would like you to be free from concern. An unmarried man is concerned about the Lord's affairs*o*—how he can please the Lord. **33**But a married man is concerned about the affairs of this world—how he can please his wife— **34**and his interests are divided. An unmarried woman or virgin is concerned about the Lord's affairs: Her aim is to be devoted to the Lord in both body and spirit.*p* But a married woman is concerned about the affairs of this world—how she can please her husband. **35**I am saying this for your own good, not to restrict you, but that you may live in a right way in undivided*q* devotion to the Lord.

36If anyone thinks he is acting improperly toward the virgin he is engaged to, and if she is getting along in years and he feels he ought to marry, he should do as he wants. He is not sinning.*r* They should get married. **37**But the man who has settled the matter in his own mind, who is under no compulsion but has control over his own will, and who has made up his mind not to marry the virgin—this man also does the right thing. **38**So then, he who

7:17
a Ro 12:3
b 1Co 4:17;
14:33;
2Co 8:18; 11:28

7:18
c Ac 15:1,2

7:19
d Ro 2:25-27;
Gal 5:6; 6:15;
Col 3:11

7:20
e ver 24

7:22
f Jn 8:32,36;
Phm 16
g Eph 6:6

7:23
h 1Co 6:20

7:24
i ver 20

7:25
j ver 6;
2Co 8:8
k 2Co 4:1;
1Ti 1:13,16

7:26
l ver 1,8

7:29
m ver 31;
Ro 13:11,12

7:31
n 1Jn 2:17

7:32
o 1Ti 5:5

7:34
p Lk 2:37

7:35
q Ps 86:11

7:36
r ver 28

marries the virgin does right,[a] but he who does not marry her does even better.[a]

39 A woman is bound to her husband as long as he lives.[b] But if her husband dies, she is free to marry anyone she wishes, but he must belong to the Lord.[c] 40 In my judgment,[d] she is happier if she stays as she is—and I think that I too have the Spirit of God.

Chapter 8 Theme

8 Now about food sacrificed to idols:[e] We know that we all possess knowledge.[b][f] Knowledge puffs up, but love builds up. 2 The man who thinks he knows something[g] does not yet know as he ought to know.[h] 3 But the man who loves God is known by God.[i]

4 So then, about eating food sacrificed to idols:[j] We know that an idol is nothing at all in the world[k] and that there is no God but one.[l] 5 For even if there are so-called gods,[m] whether in heaven or on earth (as indeed there are many "gods" and many "lords"), 6 yet for us there is but one God, the Father,[n] from whom all things came[o] and for whom we live; and there is but one Lord,[p] Jesus Christ, through whom all things came[q] and through whom we live.

7 But not everyone knows this. Some people are still so accustomed to idols that when they eat such food they think of it as having been sacrificed to an idol, and since their conscience is weak,[r] it is defiled. 8 But food does not bring us near to God;[s] we are no worse if we do not eat, and no better if we do.

9 Be careful, however, that the exercise of your freedom does not become a stumbling block[t] to the weak.[u] 10 For if anyone with a weak conscience sees you who have this knowledge eating in an idol's temple, won't he be emboldened to eat what has been sacrificed to idols? 11 So this weak brother, for whom Christ died, is destroyed[v] by your knowledge. 12 When you sin against your brothers[w] in this way and wound their weak conscience, you sin against Christ. 13 Therefore, if what I eat causes my brother to fall into sin, I will never eat meat again, so that I will not cause him to fall.[x]

Chapter 9 Theme

9 Am I not free? Am I not an apostle?[y] Have I not seen Jesus our Lord?[z] Are you not the result of my work in the Lord?[a] 2 Even though I may not be an apostle to others, surely I am to you! For you are the seal[b] of my apostleship in the Lord.

---

a 36-38 Or 36 If anyone thinks he is not treating his daughter properly, and if she is getting along in years, and he feels she ought to marry, he should do as he wants. He is not sinning. He should let her get married. 37 But the man who has settled the matter in his own mind, who is under no compulsion but has control over his own will, and who has made up his mind to keep the virgin unmarried—this man also does the right thing. 38 So then, he who gives his virgin in marriage does right, but he who does not give her in marriage does even better. b 1 Or "We all possess knowledge," as you say

7:38
a Heb 13:4

7:39
b Ro 7:2,3
c 2Co 6:14

7:40
d ver 25

8:1
e Ac 15:20
f Ro 15:14

8:2
g 1Co 3:18
h 1Co 13:8,9,12;
1Ti 6:4

8:3
i Ro 8:29;
Gal 4:9

8:4
j ver 1,7,10
k 1Co 10:19
l Dt 6:4;
Eph 4:6

8:5
m 2Th 2:4

8:6
n Mal 2:10
o Ro 11:36
p Eph 4:5
q Jn 1:3

8:7
r Ro 14:14;
1Co 10:28

8:8
s Ro 14:17

8:9
t Gal 5:13
u Ro 14:1

8:11
v Ro 14:15,20

8:12
w Mt 18:6

8:13
x Ro 14:21

9:1
y 2Co 12:12
z 1Co 15:8
a 1Co 3:6; 4:15

9:2
b 2Co 3:2,3

[3]This is my defense to those who sit in judgment on me. [4]Don't we have the right to food and drink?[a] [5]Don't we have the right to take a believing wife[b] along with us, as do the other apostles and the Lord's brothers[c] and Cephas[a]? [6]Or is it only I and Barnabas[d] who must work for a living?

[7]Who serves as a soldier at his own expense? Who plants a vineyard[e] and does not eat of its grapes? Who tends a flock and does not drink of the milk? [8]Do I say this merely from a human point of view? Doesn't the Law say the same thing? [9]For it is written in the Law of Moses: "Do not muzzle an ox while it is treading out the grain."[b][f] Is it about oxen that God is concerned?[g] [10]Surely he says this for us, doesn't he? Yes, this was written for us,[h] because when the plowman plows and the thresher threshes, they ought to do so in the hope of sharing in the harvest.[i] [11]If we have sown spiritual seed among you, is it too much if we reap a material harvest from you?[j] [12]If others have this right of support from you, shouldn't we have it all the more?

But we did not use this right.[k] On the contrary, we put up with anything rather than hinder[l] the gospel of Christ. [13]Don't you know that those who work in the temple get their food from the temple, and those who serve at the altar share in what is offered on the altar?[m] [14]In the same way, the Lord has commanded that those who preach the gospel should receive their living from the gospel.[n]

[15]But I have not used any of these rights.[o] And I am not writing this in the hope that you will do such things for me. I would rather die than have anyone deprive me of this boast.[p] [16]Yet when I preach the gospel, I cannot boast, for I am compelled to preach.[q] Woe to me if I do not preach the gospel! [17]If I preach voluntarily, I have a reward;[r] if not voluntarily, I am simply discharging the trust committed to me.[s] [18]What then is my reward? Just this: that in preaching the gospel I may offer it free of charge,[t] and so not make use of my rights in preaching it.

[19]Though I am free[u] and belong to no man, I make myself a slave to everyone,[v] to win as many as possible.[w] [20]To the Jews I became like a Jew, to win the Jews.[x] To those under the law I became like one under the law (though I myself am not under the law), so as to win those under the law. [21]To those not having the law I became like one not having the law[y] (though I am not free from God's law but am under Christ's law), so as to win those not having the law. [22]To the weak I became weak, to win the weak. I have become all things to all men[z] so that by all possible means I might save some.[a] [23]I do all this for the sake of the gospel, that I may share in its blessings.

9:4
a 1Th 2:6

9:5
b 1Co 7:7,8
c Mt 12:46

9:6
d Ac 4:36

9:7
e Dt 20:6;
Pr 27:18

9:9
f Dt 25:4;
1Ti 5:18
g Dt 22:1-4

9:10
h Ro 4:23,24
i 2Ti 2:6

9:11
j Ro 15:27

9:12
k Ac 18:3
l 2Co 11:7-12

9:13
m Lev 6:16,26;
Dt 18:1

9:14
n Mt 10:10;
1Ti 5:18

9:15
o Ac 18:3
p 2Co 11:9,10

9:16
q Ro 1:14;
Ac 9:15

9:17
r 1Co 3:8,14
s Gal 2:7;
Col 1:25

9:18
t 2Co 11:7; 12:13

9:19
u ver 1
v Gal 5:13
w Mt 18:15;
1Pe 3:1

9:20
x Ac 16:3;
21:20-26;
Ro 11:14

9:21
y Ro 2:12,14

9:22
z 1Co 10:33
a Ro 11:14

9:24
a Gal 2:2;
2 Ti 4:7;
Heb 12:1

9:25
b Jas 1:12;
Rev 2:10

9:27
c Ro 8:13

10:1
d Ex 13:21
e Ex 14:22,29

10:4
f Ex 17:6;
Nu 20:11;
Ps 78:15

10:5
g Nu 14:29;
Heb 3:17

10:7
h ver 14
i Ex 32:4,6,19

10:8
j Nu 25:1-9

10:9
k Nu 21:5,6

10:10
l Nu 16:41
m Nu 16:49
n Ex 12:23

10:11
o Ro 13:11

10:12
p Ro 11:20

10:13
q 1 Co 1:9
r 2 Pe 2:9

10:16
s Mt 26:26-28

10:17
t Ro 12:5;
1 Co 12:27

10:18
u Lev 7:6,14,15

10:19
v 1 Co 8:4

10:20
w Dt 32:17;
Ps 106:37;
Rev 9:20

²⁴Do you not know that in a race all the runners run, but only one gets the prize? Run*a* in such a way as to get the prize. ²⁵Everyone who competes in the games goes into strict training. They do it to get a crown that will not last; but we do it to get a crown that will last forever.*b* ²⁶Therefore I do not run like a man running aimlessly; I do not fight like a man beating the air. ²⁷No, I beat my body*c* and make it my slave so that after I have preached to others, I myself will not be disqualified for the prize.

Chapter 10 Theme

10 For I do not want you to be ignorant of the fact, brothers, that our forefathers were all under the cloud*d* and that they all passed through the sea.*e* ²They were all baptized into Moses in the cloud and in the sea. ³They all ate the same spiritual food ⁴and drank the same spiritual drink; for they drank from the spiritual rock*f* that accompanied them, and that rock was Christ. ⁵Nevertheless, God was not pleased with most of them; their bodies were scattered over the desert.*g*

⁶Now these things occurred as examples*a* to keep us from setting our hearts on evil things as they did. ⁷Do not be idolaters,*h* as some of them were; as it is written: "The people sat down to eat and drink and got up to indulge in pagan revelry."*b i* ⁸We should not commit sexual immorality, as some of them did—and in one day twenty-three thousand of them died.*j* ⁹We should not test the Lord, as some of them did—and were killed by snakes.*k* ¹⁰And do not grumble, as some of them did*l*—and were killed*m* by the destroying angel.*n*

¹¹These things happened to them as examples and were written down as warnings for us, on whom the fulfillment of the ages has come.*o* ¹²So, if you think you are standing firm,*p* be careful that you don't fall! ¹³No temptation has seized you except what is common to man. And God is faithful;*q* he will not let you be tempted beyond what you can bear.*r* But when you are tempted, he will also provide a way out so that you can stand up under it.

¹⁴Therefore, my dear friends, flee from idolatry. ¹⁵I speak to sensible people; judge for yourselves what I say. ¹⁶Is not the cup of thanksgiving for which we give thanks a participation in the blood of Christ? And is not the bread that we break a participation in the body of Christ?*s* ¹⁷Because there is one loaf, we, who are many, are one body,*t* for we all partake of the one loaf.

¹⁸Consider the people of Israel: Do not those who eat the sacrifices*u* participate in the altar? ¹⁹Do I mean then that a sacrifice offered to an idol is anything, or that an idol is anything?*v* ²⁰No, but the sacrifices of pagans are offered to demons,*w* not to God, and I

a 6 Or *types*; also in verse 11   *b* 7 Exodus 32:6

do not want you to be participants with demons. [21] You cannot drink the cup of the Lord and the cup of demons too; you cannot have a part in both the Lord's table and the table of demons.[a] [22] Are we trying to arouse the Lord's jealousy?[b] Are we stronger than he?[c]

[23] "Everything is permissible"—but not everything is beneficial.[d] "Everything is permissible"—but not everything is constructive. [24] Nobody should seek his own good, but the good of others.[e]

[25] Eat anything sold in the meat market without raising questions of conscience,[f] [26] for, "The earth is the Lord's, and everything in it."[a][g]

[27] If some unbeliever invites you to a meal and you want to go, eat whatever is put before you[h] without raising questions of conscience. [28] But if anyone says to you, "This has been offered in sacrifice," then do not eat it, both for the sake of the man who told you and for conscience' sake[b][i]— [29] the other man's conscience, I mean, not yours. For why should my freedom[j] be judged by another's conscience? [30] If I take part in the meal with thankfulness, why am I denounced because of something I thank God for?[k]

[31] So whether you eat or drink or whatever you do, do it all for the glory of God.[l] [32] Do not cause anyone to stumble,[m] whether Jews, Greeks or the church of God[n]— [33] even as I try to please everybody in every way.[o] For I am not seeking my own good but the good of many, so that they may be saved.[p]

Chapter 11 Theme

11 Follow my example,[q] as I follow the example of Christ. [2] I praise you[r] for remembering me in everything[s] and for holding to the teachings,[c] just as I passed them on to you.[t]

[3] Now I want you to realize that the head of every man is Christ,[u] and the head of the woman is man,[v] and the head of Christ is God.[w] [4] Every man who prays or prophesies with his head covered dishonors his head. [5] And every woman who prays or prophesies[x] with her head uncovered dishonors her head—it is just as though her head were shaved.[y] [6] If a woman does not cover her head, she should have her hair cut off; and if it is a disgrace for a woman to have her hair cut or shaved off, she should cover her head. [7] A man ought not to cover his head,[d] since he is the image[z] and glory of God; but the woman is the glory of man. [8] For man did not come from woman, but woman from man;[a] [9] neither was man created for woman, but woman for man.[b] [10] For this reason,

---

[a] 26 Psalm 24:1   [b] 28 Some manuscripts *conscience' sake, for "the earth is the Lord's and everything in it"*   [c] 2 Or *traditions*   [d] 4-7 Or *4Every man who prays or prophesies with long hair dishonors his head. 5And every woman who prays or prophesies with no covering* [of hair] *on her head dishonors her head—she is just like one of the "shorn women." 6If a woman has no covering, let her be for now with short hair, but since it is a disgrace for a woman to have her hair shorn or shaved, she should grow it again. 7A man ought not to have long hair*

10:21
[a] 2Co 6:15,16

10:22
[b] Dt 32:16,21
[c] Ecc 6:10;
Isa 45:9

10:23
[d] 1Co 6:12

10:24
[e] ver 33;
Ro 15:1,2;
1Co 13:5;
Php 2:4,21

10:25
[f] Ac 10:15;
1Co 8:7

10:26
[g] Ps 24:1

10:27
[h] Lk 10:7

10:28
[i] 1Co 8:7,10-12

10:29
[j] Ro 14:16;
1Co 9:1,19

10:30
[k] Ro 14:6

10:31
[l] Col 3:17;
1Pe 4:11

10:32
[m] Ac 24:16
[n] Ac 20:28

10:33
[o] Ro 15:2;
1Co 9:22
[p] Ro 11:14

11:1
[q] 1Co 4:16

11:2
[r] ver 17,22
[s] 1Co 4:17
[t] 1Co 15:2,3;
2Th 2:15

11:3
[u] Eph 1:22
[v] Ge 3:16;
Eph 5:23
[w] 1Co 3:23

11:5
[x] Ac 21:9
[y] Dt 21:12

11:7
[z] Ge 1:26;
Jas 3:9

11:8
[a] Ge 2:21-23;
1Ti 2:13

11:9
[b] Ge 2:18

11:12
a Ro 11:36

11:16
b 1Co 7:17

11:17
c ver 2,22

11:18
d 1Co 1:10-12;
3:3

11:19
e 1Jn 2:19

11:21
f 2Pe 2:13;
Jude 12

11:22
g 1Co 10:32
h Jas 2:6
i ver 2,17

11:23
j Gal 1:12
k 1Co 15:3

11:25
l Lk 22:20
m 1Co 10:16

11:27
n Heb 10:29

11:28
o 2Co 13:5

11:31
p Ps 32:5;
1Jn 1:9

11:32
q Ps 94:12;
Heb 12:7-10;
Rev 3:19

11:34
r ver 21
s ver 22
t 1Co 4:19

and because of the angels, the woman ought to have a sign of authority on her head.

¹¹In the Lord, however, woman is not independent of man, nor is man independent of woman. ¹²For as woman came from man, so also man is born of woman. But everything comes from God.*a* ¹³Judge for yourselves: Is it proper for a woman to pray to God with her head uncovered? ¹⁴Does not the very nature of things teach you that if a man has long hair, it is a disgrace to him, ¹⁵but that if a woman has long hair, it is her glory? For long hair is given to her as a covering. ¹⁶If anyone wants to be contentious about this, we have no other practice—nor do the churches of God.*b*

¹⁷In the following directives I have no praise for you,*c* for your meetings do more harm than good. ¹⁸In the first place, I hear that when you come together as a church, there are divisions*d* among you, and to some extent I believe it. ¹⁹No doubt there have to be differences among you to show which of you have God's approval.*e* ²⁰When you come together, it is not the Lord's Supper you eat, ²¹for as you eat, each of you goes ahead without waiting for anybody else.*f* One remains hungry, another gets drunk. ²²Don't you have homes to eat and drink in? Or do you despise the church of God*g* and humiliate those who have nothing?*h* What shall I say to you? Shall I praise you*i* for this? Certainly not!

²³For I received from the Lord*j* what I also passed on to you:*k* The Lord Jesus, on the night he was betrayed, took bread, ²⁴and when he had given thanks, he broke it and said, "This is my body, which is for you; do this in remembrance of me." ²⁵In the same way, after supper he took the cup, saying, "This cup is the new covenant*l* in my blood;*m* do this, whenever you drink it, in remembrance of me." ²⁶For whenever you eat this bread and drink this cup, you proclaim the Lord's death until he comes.

²⁷Therefore, whoever eats the bread or drinks the cup of the Lord in an unworthy manner will be guilty of sinning against the body and blood of the Lord.*n* ²⁸A man ought to examine himself*o* before he eats of the bread and drinks of the cup. ²⁹For anyone who eats and drinks without recognizing the body of the Lord eats and drinks judgment on himself. ³⁰That is why many among you are weak and sick, and a number of you have fallen asleep. ³¹But if we judged ourselves, we would not come under judgment.*p* ³²When we are judged by the Lord, we are being disciplined*q* so that we will not be condemned with the world.

³³So then, my brothers, when you come together to eat, wait for each other. ³⁴If anyone is hungry,*r* he should eat at home,*s* so that when you meet together it may not result in judgment.

And when I come*t* I will give further directions.

Chapter 12 Theme _____

12 Now about spiritual gifts,[a] brothers, I do not want you to be ignorant. [2]You know that when you were pagans,[b] somehow or other you were influenced and led astray to mute idols.[c] [3]Therefore I tell you that no one who is speaking by the Spirit of God says, "Jesus be cursed,"[d] and no one can say, "Jesus is Lord,"[e] except by the Holy Spirit.[f]

[4]There are different kinds of gifts, but the same Spirit.[g] [5]There are different kinds of service, but the same Lord. [6]There are different kinds of working, but the same God[h] works all of them in all men.

[7]Now to each one the manifestation of the Spirit is given for the common good.[i] [8]To one there is given through the Spirit the message of wisdom,[j] to another the message of knowledge[k] by means of the same Spirit, [9]to another faith[l] by the same Spirit, to another gifts of healing[m] by that one Spirit, [10]to another miraculous powers,[n] to another prophecy, to another distinguishing between spirits,[o] to another speaking in different kinds of tongues,[a][p] and to still another the interpretation of tongues.[a] [11]All these are the work of one and the same Spirit,[q] and he gives them to each one, just as he determines.

[12]The body is a unit, though it is made up of many parts; and though all its parts are many, they form one body.[r] So it is with Christ.[s] [13]For we were all baptized by[b] one Spirit[t] into one body— whether Jews or Greeks, slave or free[u]—and we were all given the one Spirit to drink.[v]

[14]Now the body is not made up of one part but of many. [15]If the foot should say, "Because I am not a hand, I do not belong to the body," it would not for that reason cease to be part of the body. [16]And if the ear should say, "Because I am not an eye, I do not belong to the body," it would not for that reason cease to be part of the body. [17]If the whole body were an eye, where would the sense of hearing be? If the whole body were an ear, where would the sense of smell be? [18]But in fact God has arranged[w] the parts in the body, every one of them, just as he wanted them to be.[x] [19]If they were all one part, where would the body be? [20]As it is, there are many parts, but one body.[y]

[21]The eye cannot say to the hand, "I don't need you!" And the head cannot say to the feet, "I don't need you!" [22]On the contrary, those parts of the body that seem to be weaker are indispensable, [23]and the parts that we think are less honorable we treat with special honor. And the parts that are unpresentable are treated with special modesty, [24]while our presentable parts need

---

[a]*10* Or *languages;* also in verse 28   [b]*13* Or *with; or in*

12:1
[a]Ro 1:11;
1Co 14:1,37

12:2
[b]Eph 2:11,12;
1Pe 4:3
[c]Ps 115:5;
Jer 10:5;
Hab 2:18,19;
1Th 1:9

12:3
[d]Ro 9:3
[e]Jn 13:13
[f]1Jn 4:2,3

12:4
[g]Ro 12:4-8;
Eph 4:11;
Heb 2:4

12:6
[h]Eph 4:6

12:7
[i]Eph 4:12

12:8
[j]1Co 2:6
[k]2Co 8:7

12:9
[l]Mt 17:19,20;
2Co 4:13
[m]ver 28,30

12:10
[n]Gal 3:5
[o]1Jn 4:1
[p]Mk 16:17

12:11
[q]ver 4

12:12
[r]Ro 12:5
[s]ver 27

12:13
[t]Eph 2:18
[u]Gal 3:28;
Col 3:11
[v]Jn 7:37-39

12:18
[w]ver 28
[x]ver 11

12:20
[y]ver 12,14

12:27
a Eph 1:23; 4:12;
Col 1:18,24
b Ro 12:5

12:28
c 1Co 10:32
d Eph 4:11
e ver 9
f Ro 12:6-8
g ver 10

12:30
h ver 10

12:31
i 1Co 14:1,39

13:1
j ver 8

13:2
k 1Co 14:2
l 1Co 12:9
m Mt 17:20;
21:21

13:3
n Mt 6:2
o Da 3:28

13:4
p 1Th 5:14

13:5
q 1Co 10:24

13:6
r 2Th 2:12
s 2Jn 4; 3Jn 3,4

13:8
t ver 2
u ver 1

13:9
v ver 12; 1Co 8:2

13:10
w Php 3:12

13:12
x Ge 32:30;
2Co 5:7; 1Jn 3:2
y 1Co 8:3

13:13
z Gal 5:5,6
a 1Co 16:14

no special treatment. But God has combined the members of the body and has given greater honor to the parts that lacked it, [25]so that there should be no division in the body, but that its parts should have equal concern for each other. [26]If one part suffers, every part suffers with it; if one part is honored, every part rejoices with it.

[27]Now you are the body of Christ,[a] and each one of you is a part of it.[b] [28]And in the church[c] God has appointed first of all apostles,[d] second prophets, third teachers, then workers of miracles, also those having gifts of healing,[e] those able to help others, those with gifts of administration,[f] and those speaking in different kinds of tongues.[g] [29]Are all apostles? Are all prophets? Are all teachers? Do all work miracles? [30]Do all have gifts of healing? Do all speak in tongues[a]?[h] Do all interpret? [31]But eagerly desire[b][i] the greater gifts.

Chapter 13 Theme

And now I will show you the most excellent way.

13 If I speak in the tongues[c][j] of men and of angels, but have not love, I am only a resounding gong or a clanging cymbal. [2]If I have the gift of prophecy and can fathom all mysteries[k] and all knowledge, and if I have a faith[l] that can move mountains,[m] but have not love, I am nothing. [3]If I give all I possess to the poor[n] and surrender my body to the flames,[d][o] but have not love, I gain nothing.

[4]Love is patient,[p] love is kind. It does not envy, it does not boast, it is not proud. [5]It is not rude, it is not self-seeking,[q] it is not easily angered, it keeps no record of wrongs. [6]Love does not delight in evil[r] but rejoices with the truth.[s] [7]It always protects, always trusts, always hopes, always perseveres.

[8]Love never fails. But where there are prophecies,[t] they will cease; where there are tongues,[u] they will be stilled; where there is knowledge, it will pass away. [9]For we know in part[v] and we prophesy in part, [10]but when perfection comes,[w] the imperfect disappears. [11]When I was a child, I talked like a child, I thought like a child, I reasoned like a child. When I became a man, I put childish ways behind me. [12]Now we see but a poor reflection as in a mirror; then we shall see face to face.[x] Now I know in part; then I shall know fully, even as I am fully known.[y]

[13]And now these three remain: faith, hope and love.[z] But the greatest of these is love.[a]

---

a 30 Or *other languages*   b 31 Or *But you are eagerly desiring*   c 1 Or *languages*
d 3 Some early manuscripts *body that I may boast*

Chapter 14 Theme _____

14 Follow the way of love[a] and eagerly desire[b] spiritual gifts,[c] especially the gift of prophecy. [2]For anyone who speaks in a tongue[ad] does not speak to men but to God. Indeed, no one understands him; he utters mysteries[e] with his spirit.[b] [3]But everyone who prophesies speaks to men for their strengthening,[f] encouragement and comfort. [4]He who speaks in a tongue[g] edifies himself, but he who prophesies[h] edifies the church. [5]I would like every one of you to speak in tongues,[c] but I would rather have you prophesy.[i] He who prophesies is greater than one who speaks in tongues,[c] unless he interprets, so that the church may be edified.

[6]Now, brothers, if I come to you and speak in tongues, what good will I be to you, unless I bring you some revelation[j] or knowledge or prophecy or word of instruction?[k] [7]Even in the case of lifeless things that make sounds, such as the flute or harp, how will anyone know what tune is being played unless there is a distinction in the notes? [8]Again, if the trumpet does not sound a clear call, who will get ready for battle?[l] [9]So it is with you. Unless you speak intelligible words with your tongue, how will anyone know what you are saying? You will just be speaking into the air. [10]Undoubtedly there are all sorts of languages in the world, yet none of them is without meaning. [11]If then I do not grasp the meaning of what someone is saying, I am a foreigner to the speaker, and he is a foreigner to me. [12]So it is with you. Since you are eager to have spiritual gifts, try to excel in gifts that build up the church.

[13]For this reason anyone who speaks in a tongue should pray that he may interpret what he says. [14]For if I pray in a tongue, my spirit prays, but my mind is unfruitful. [15]So what shall I do? I will pray with my spirit, but I will also pray with my mind; I will sing[m] with my spirit, but I will also sing with my mind. [16]If you are praising God with your spirit, how can one who finds himself among those who do not understand[d] say "Amen"[n] to your thanksgiving,[o] since he does not know what you are saying? [17]You may be giving thanks well enough, but the other man is not edified.

[18]I thank God that I speak in tongues more than all of you. [19]But in the church I would rather speak five intelligible words to instruct others than ten thousand words in a tongue.

[20]Brothers, stop thinking like children.[p] In regard to evil be infants,[q] but in your thinking be adults. [21]In the Law[r] it is written:

---

a2 Or *another language*; also in verses 4, 13, 14, 19, 26 and 27   b2 Or *by the Spirit*
c5 Or *other languages*; also in verses 6, 18, 22, 23 and 39   d16 Or *among the inquirers*

14:1
a 1Co 16:14
b ver 39;
1Co 12:31
c 1Co 12:1

14:2
d Mk 16:17
e 1Co 13:2

14:3
f ver 4,5,12,17, 26; Ro 14:19

14:4
g Mk 16:17
h 1Co 13:2

14:5
i Nu 11:29

14:6
j ver 26;
Eph 1:17
k Ro 6:17

14:8
l Nu 10:9;
Jer 4:19

14:15
m Eph 5:19;
Col 3:16

14:16
n Dt 27:15-26;
1Ch 16:36;
Ne 8:6;
Ps 106:48;
Rev 5:14; 7:12
o 1Co 11:24

14:20
p Eph 4:14;
Heb 5:12,13;
1Pe 2:2
q Ro 16:19

14:21
r Jn 10:34

14:21
a Isa 28:11,12

14:22
b ver 1

14:23
c Ac 2:13

14:25
d Isa 45:14;
Zec 8:23

14:26
e 1Co 12:7-10
f Eph 5:19
g ver 6
h Ro 14:19

14:29
i 1Co 12:10

14:32
j 1Jn 4:1

14:33
k ver 40
l Ac 9:13

14:34
m 1Ti 2:11,12
n Ge 3:16

14:37
o 2Co 10:7
p 1Jn 4:6

14:39
q 1Co 12:31

14:40
r ver 33

"Through men of strange tongues
and through the lips of foreigners
I will speak to this people,
but even then they will not listen to me,"*a* *a*
says the Lord.

²²Tongues, then, are a sign, not for believers but for unbelievers; prophecy,*b* however, is for believers, not for unbelievers. ²³So if the whole church comes together and everyone speaks in tongues, and some who do not understand*b* or some unbelievers come in, will they not say that you are out of your mind?*c* ²⁴But if an unbeliever or someone who does not understand*c* comes in while everybody is prophesying, he will be convinced by all that he is a sinner and will be judged by all, ²⁵and the secrets of his heart will be laid bare. So he will fall down and worship God, exclaiming, "God is really among you!"*d*

²⁶What then shall we say, brothers? When you come together, everyone*e* has a hymn,*f* or a word of instruction,*g* a revelation, a tongue or an interpretation. All of these must be done for the strengthening*h* of the church. ²⁷If anyone speaks in a tongue, two—or at the most three—should speak, one at a time, and someone must interpret. ²⁸If there is no interpreter, the speaker should keep quiet in the church and speak to himself and God.

²⁹Two or three prophets should speak, and the others should weigh carefully what is said.*i* ³⁰And if a revelation comes to someone who is sitting down, the first speaker should stop. ³¹For you can all prophesy in turn so that everyone may be instructed and encouraged. ³²The spirits of prophets are subject to the control of prophets.*j* ³³For God is not a God of disorder*k* but of peace.

As in all the congregations of the saints,*l* ³⁴women should remain silent in the churches. They are not allowed to speak, but must be in submission,*m* as the Law*n* says. ³⁵If they want to inquire about something, they should ask their own husbands at home; for it is disgraceful for a woman to speak in the church.

³⁶Did the word of God originate with you? Or are you the only people it has reached? ³⁷If anybody thinks he is a prophet*o* or spiritually gifted, let him acknowledge that what I am writing to you is the Lord's command.*p* ³⁸If he ignores this, he himself will be ignored.*d*

³⁹Therefore, my brothers, be eager*q* to prophesy, and do not forbid speaking in tongues. ⁴⁰But everything should be done in a fitting and orderly*r* way.

a 21 Isaiah 28:11,12   *b* 23 Or *some inquirers*   *c* 24 Or *or some inquirer*   *d* 38 Some manuscripts *If he is ignorant of this, let him be ignorant*

Chapter 15 Theme

15 Now, brothers, I want to remind you of the gospel[a] I preached to you, which you received and on which you have taken your stand. [2]By this gospel you are saved,[b] if you hold firmly[c] to the word I preached to you. Otherwise, you have believed in vain.

[3]For what I received[d] I passed on to you[e] as of first importance[a]: that Christ died for our sins[f] according to the Scriptures,[g] [4]that he was buried, that he was raised[h] on the third day[i] according to the Scriptures,[j] [5]and that he appeared to Peter,[b][k] and then to the Twelve.[l] [6]After that, he appeared to more than five hundred of the brothers at the same time, most of whom are still living, though some have fallen asleep. [7]Then he appeared to James, then to all the apostles,[m] [8]and last of all he appeared to me also,[n] as to one abnormally born.

[9]For I am the least of the apostles[o] and do not even deserve to be called an apostle, because I persecuted[p] the church of God. [10]But by the grace of God I am what I am, and his grace to me[q] was not without effect. No, I worked harder than all of them[r]—yet not I, but the grace of God that was with me.[s] [11]Whether, then, it was I or they, this is what we preach, and this is what you believed.

[12]But if it is preached that Christ has been raised from the dead, how can some of you say that there is no resurrection of the dead?[t] [13]If there is no resurrection of the dead, then not even Christ has been raised. [14]And if Christ has not been raised,[u] our preaching is useless and so is your faith. [15]More than that, we are then found to be false witnesses about God, for we have testified about God that he raised Christ from the dead.[v] But he did not raise him if in fact the dead are not raised. [16]For if the dead are not raised, then Christ has not been raised either. [17]And if Christ has not been raised, your faith is futile; you are still in your sins.[w] [18]Then those also who have fallen asleep in Christ are lost. [19]If only for this life we have hope in Christ, we are to be pitied more than all men.[x]

[20]But Christ has indeed been raised from the dead,[y] the firstfruits[z] of those who have fallen asleep.[a] [21]For since death came through a man,[b] the resurrection of the dead comes also through a man. [22]For as in Adam all die, so in Christ all will be made alive.[c] [23]But each in his own turn: Christ, the firstfruits;[d] then, when he comes,[e] those who belong to him. [24]Then the end will come, when he hands over the kingdom[f] to God the Father after he has destroyed all dominion, authority and power.[g] [25]For he must reign until he has put all his enemies under his feet.[h] [26]The last enemy to be destroyed is death.[i] [27]For he "has put everything under

[a]3 Or *you at the first*   [b]5 Greek *Cephas*

15:1 [a]Ro 2:16
15:2 [b]Ro 1:16; [c]Ro 11:22
15:3 [d]Gal 1:12; [e]1Co 11:23; [f]Isa 53:5; 1Pe 2:24; [g]Lk 24:27; Ac 26:22,23
15:4 [h]Ac 2:24; [i]Mt 16:21; [j]Ac 2:25,30,31
15:5 [k]Lk 24:34; [l]Mk 16:14
15:7 [m]Lk 24:33,36,37; Ac 1:3,4
15:8 [n]Ac 9:3-6,17; 1Co 9:1
15:9 [o]Eph 3:8; 1Ti 1:15; [p]Ac 8:3
15:10 [q]Ro 12:3; [r]2Co 11:23; [s]Php 2:13
15:12 [t]Ac 17:32; 23:8; 2Ti 2:18
15:14 [u]1Th 4:14
15:15 [v]Ac 2:24
15:17 [w]Ro 4:25
15:19 [x]1Co 4:9
15:20 [y]1Pe 1:3; [z]ver 23; Ac 26:23; Rev 1:5; [a]ver 6,18
15:21 [b]Ro 5:12
15:22 [c]Ro 5:14-18
15:23 [d]ver 20; [e]ver 52
15:24 [f]Da 7:14,27; [g]Ro 8:38
15:25 [h]Ps 110:1; Mt 22:44
15:26 [i]2Ti 1:10; Rev 20:14; 21:4

15:27
a Ps 8:6
b Mt 28:18

15:28
c Php 3:21
d 1Co 3:23

15:30
e 2Co 11:26

15:31
f Ro 8:36

15:32
g 2Co 1:8
h Ac 18:19
i Isa 22:13;
Lk 12:19

15:35
j Ro 9:19
k Eze 37:3

15:36
l Lk 11:40
m Jn 12:24

15:38
n Ge 1:11

15:42
o Da 12:3;
Mt 13:43

15:43
p Php 3:21;
Col 3:4

15:44
q ver 50

15:45
r Ge 2:7
s Ro 5:14
t Jn 5:21; Ro 8:2

15:47
u Ge 2:7; 3:19
v Jn 3:13,31

15:48
w Php 3:20,21

15:49
x Ge 5:3
y Ro 8:29

15:50
z Jn 3:3,5

his feet."ᵃᵃ Now when it says that "everything" has been put under him, it is clear that this does not include God himself, who put everything under Christ.ᵇ **28**When he has done this, then the Son himself will be made subject to him who put everything under him,ᶜ so that God may be all in all.ᵈ

29Now if there is no resurrection, what will those do who are baptized for the dead? If the dead are not raised at all, why are people baptized for them? **30**And as for us, why do we endanger ourselves every hour?ᵉ **31**I die every dayᶠ—I mean that, brothers—just as surely as I glory over you in Christ Jesus our Lord. **32**If I fought wild beastsᵍ in Ephesusʰ for merely human reasons, what have I gained? If the dead are not raised,

> "Let us eat and drink,
>   for tomorrow we die."ᵇⁱ

33Do not be misled: "Bad company corrupts good character." **34**Come back to your senses as you ought, and stop sinning; for there are some who are ignorant of God—I say this to your shame.

35But someone may ask,ʲ "How are the dead raised? With what kind of body will they come?"ᵏ **36**How foolish!ˡ What you sow does not come to life unless it dies.ᵐ **37**When you sow, you do not plant the body that will be, but just a seed, perhaps of wheat or of something else. **38**But God gives it a body as he has determined, and to each kind of seed he gives its own body.ⁿ **39**All flesh is not the same: Men have one kind of flesh, animals have another, birds another and fish another. **40**There are also heavenly bodies and there are earthly bodies; but the splendor of the heavenly bodies is one kind, and the splendor of the earthly bodies is another. **41**The sun has one kind of splendor, the moon another and the stars another; and star differs from star in splendor.

42So will it beᵒ with the resurrection of the dead. The body that is sown is perishable, it is raised imperishable; **43**it is sown in dishonor, it is raised in glory;ᵖ it is sown in weakness, it is raised in power; **44**it is sown a natural body, it is raised a spiritual body.�q

If there is a natural body, there is also a spiritual body. **45**So it is written: "The first man Adam became a living being"ᶜ;ʳ the last Adam,ˢ a life-giving spirit.ᵗ **46**The spiritual did not come first, but the natural, and after that the spiritual. **47**The first man was of the dust of the earth,ᵘ the second man from heaven.ᵛ **48**As was the earthly man, so are those who are of the earth; and as is the man from heaven, so also are those who are of heaven.ʷ **49**And just as we have borne the likeness of the earthly man,ˣ so shall weᵈ bear the likeness of the man from heaven.ʸ

50I declare to you, brothers, that flesh and bloodᶻ cannot inherit the kingdom of God, nor does the perishable inherit the imperishable. [51]Listen, I tell you a mystery:[a] We will not all sleep, but we will all be changed[b]— [52]in a flash, in the twinkling of an eye, at the last trumpet. For the trumpet will sound,[c] the dead[d] will be raised imperishable, and we will be changed. [53]For the perishable must clothe itself with the imperishable,[e] and the mortal with immortality. [54]When the perishable has been clothed with the imperishable, and the mortal with immortality, then the saying that is written will come true: "Death has been swallowed up in victory."[a][f]

[55]"Where, O death, is your victory?
Where, O death, is your sting?"[b][g]

[56]The sting of death is sin,[h] and the power of sin is the law.[i] [57]But thanks be to God![j] He gives us the victory through our Lord Jesus Christ.[k]

[58]Therefore, my dear brothers, stand firm. Let nothing move you. Always give yourselves fully to the work of the Lord,[l] because you know that your labor in the Lord is not in vain.

Chapter 16 Theme

16 Now about the collection[m] for God's people:[n] Do what I told the Galatian[o] churches to do. [2]On the first day of every week,[p] each one of you should set aside a sum of money in keeping with his income, saving it up, so that when I come no collections will have to be made.[q] [3]Then, when I arrive, I will give letters of introduction to the men you approve[r] and send them with your gift to Jerusalem. [4]If it seems advisable for me to go also, they will accompany me.

[5]After I go through Macedonia, I will come to you[s]—for I will be going through Macedonia.[t] [6]Perhaps I will stay with you awhile, or even spend the winter, so that you can help me on my journey,[u] wherever I go. [7]I do not want to see you now and make only a passing visit; I hope to spend some time with you, if the Lord permits.[v] [8]But I will stay on at Ephesus[w] until Pentecost,[x] [9]because a great door for effective work has opened to me,[y] and there are many who oppose me.

[10]If Timothy[z] comes, see to it that he has nothing to fear while he is with you, for he is carrying on the work of the Lord,[a] just as I am. [11]No one, then, should refuse to accept him.[b] Send him on his way in peace[c] so that he may return to me. I am expecting him along with the brothers.

[12]Now about our brother Apollos:[d] I strongly urged him to go to you with the brothers. He was quite unwilling to go now, but he will go when he has the opportunity.

a 54 Isaiah 25:8   b 55 Hosea 13:14

15:51
a 1Co 13:2
b Php 3:21

15:52
c Mt 24:31
d Jn 5:25

15:53
e 2Co 5:2,4

15:54
f Isa 25:8;
Rev 20:14

15:55
g Hos 13:14

15:56
h Ro 5:12
i Ro 4:15

15:57
j 2Co 2:14
k Ro 8:37

15:58
l 1Co 16:10

16:1
m Ac 24:17
n Ac 9:13
o Ac 16:6

16:2
p Ac 20:7
q 2Co 9:4,5

16:3
r 2Co 8:18,19

16:5
s 1Co 4:19
t Ac 19:21

16:6
u Ro 15:24

16:7
v Ac 18:21

16:8
w Ac 18:19
x Ac 2:1

16:9
y Ac 14:27

16:10
z Ac 16:1
a 1Co 15:58

16:11
b 1Ti 4:12
c Ac 15:33

16:12
d Ac 18:24;
1Co 1:12

a Gal 5:1;
Php 1:27;
1Th 3:8;
2Th 2:15
b Eph 6:10

16:14
c 1Co 14:1

16:15
d 1Co 1:16
e Ro 16:5
f Ac 18:12

16:16
g Heb 13:17

16:17
h 2Co 11:9;
Php 2:30

16:18
i Phm 7
j Php 2:29

16:19
k Ac 18:2
l Ro 16:5

16:20
m Ro 16:16

16:21
n Gal 6:11;
Col 4:18

¹³Be on your guard; stand firm*a* in the faith; be men of courage; be strong.*b* ¹⁴Do everything in love.*c*

¹⁵You know that the household of Stephanas*d* were the first converts*e* in Achaia,*f* and they have devoted themselves to the service of the saints. I urge you, brothers, ¹⁶to submit*g* to such as these and to everyone who joins in the work, and labors at it. ¹⁷I was glad when Stephanas, Fortunatus and Achaicus arrived, because they have supplied what was lacking from you.*h* ¹⁸For they refreshed*i* my spirit and yours also. Such men deserve recognition.*j*

¹⁹The churches in the province of Asia send you greetings. Aquila and Priscilla*ak* greet you warmly in the Lord, and so does the church that meets at their house.*l* ²⁰All the brothers here send you greetings. Greet one another with a holy kiss.*m*

²¹I, Paul, write this greeting in my own hand.*n*

²²If anyone does not love the Lord*o*—a curse*p* be on him. Come, O Lord*b*!*q*

²³The grace of the Lord Jesus be with you.*r*

²⁴My love to all of you in Christ Jesus. Amen.*c*

---

a 19 Greek *Prisca*, a variant of *Priscilla*   *b* 22 In Aramaic the expression *Come, O Lord* is *Marana tha.*   *c* 24 Some manuscripts do not have *Amen.*

16:22 *o* Eph 6:24 *p* Ro 9:3 *q* Rev 22:20   **16:23** *r* Ro 16:20

1 CORINTHIANS OBSERVATIONS CHART

DESCRIPTION OF THE CORINTHIANS

COMMANDS TO THE CORINTHIANS

WARNINGS TO THE CORINTHIANS

Theme of 1 Corinthians:

	SEGMENT DIVISIONS		
	PROBLEMS OR TOPICS	MAJOR DIVISIONS	CHAPTER THEMES
Author:			
			1
Date:			
			2
Purpose:			
			3
Key Words:			
			6
			7
			8
			9
			10
			11
			12
			13
			14
			15
			16

2 CORINTHIANS

*P*aul, the apostle to the Gentiles, was taught and appointed by Jesus Christ. Strong in faith, confident, and greatly used by God, Paul was loved by multitudes and hated by thousands. Determined that the grace of God would not prove vain, he labored more than anyone.

However, Paul's labor was not without cost. He endured conflicts without and fears within. Yet he persevered. What were his conflicts, his fears, his sufferings? Are they similar to yours? And how did he endure? What held him? As Paul writes his second epistle to the Corinthians from Macedonia, probably in the winter of A.D. 55, he lets us see the answers to these questions.

∾ THINGS TO DO

General Instructions

1. Second Corinthians is different from Paul's other epistles. Watch the atmosphere or tone of this epistle. Paul is defending himself, which is unusual for Paul. As you read through the book, note the issues Paul addresses and what he says to the Corinthians, and you will understand what Paul is up against.

2. Study the OBSERVATIONS CHART on page 1991 and see what you'll need to observe as you study 2 Corinthians chapter by chapter. Make a duplicate of this chart so you can use it as a worksheet. When you have completed it, record the information on the chart in your Bible.

   a. As you read each chapter, list everything you learn about Paul. Be sure to note the afflictions he endured: What must he do in respect to the Corinthians? What has been done to him by the Corinthians? Ask God to show you Paul's character, his heart, his joys, and his sorrows.

   b. Note what you learn about the Corinthians. Remember to ask the five W's and an H: What are they like? What is their relationship with Paul like? What is going on in the Corinthian church at this time? What have they said about Paul? What problems has Paul had to deal with in respect to them?

   c. What is Paul's desire or goal for the Corinthians?

   d. Titus is mentioned several times in this letter. Record what you learn about him from 2 Corinthians.

3. As you read 2 Corinthians chapter by chapter, do the following:

   a. Mark in the text in a distinctive way the key words (and their synonyms and pronouns) listed on the 2 CORINTHIANS AT A GLANCE chart on page 1992. Write these on an index card that you can use as a bookmark while you study 2 Corinthians. (Hint: If you mark every reference to Satan with an appropriate symbol it will be easy to spot.)

   b. As you come to specific chapters you will notice other key words which are not listed on 2 CORINTHIANS AT A GLANCE. Mark these also.

   c. If there are several truths you learn from the use of a key word within a chapter, list in the margin what you learn from that word. For example, list all you learn about *affliction (trouble, hardships, distress, hard pressed, trial)* and *suffering*. Record the heading "Affliction/Suffering" in the margin of each chapter where you mark these key words. Mark the heading in a distinctive way so you can spot its recurrence throughout 2 Corinthians. Then under it list what you learn from that chapter.

4. Look for the theme (subject) of each chapter and record it next to the chapter number in the text and under "Chapter Themes" on 2 CORINTHIANS AT A GLANCE.

Chapters 1-7

1. In the midst of this very personal letter, Paul gives some important insights on several subjects. In the margin where they appear, list what you learn about each subject.

   a. Chapter 3 mentions the new covenant (which is grace) and the old covenant (which is law). These are described as ministries, and then the ministries are contrasted according to the result of each: condemnation or righteousness. List in the margin what you learn about each from the text.

   b. In chapter 5 Paul talks about what will happen to our earthly bodies when we die. He also discusses the judgment seat of Christ and our ministry of reconciliation. Identify how these relate to one another and what you learn about each from the text. Write your observations in the margins.

   c. In chapter 7 Paul deals with two kinds of sorrow and what they produce. Don't miss this. Take notes in the margin.

2. What is Paul writing about in chapters 1 through 7? Is there a theme which runs through these chapters? Remember that key words reveal the themes. What key words are repeated the most in this segment?

3. How does Paul begin and end this segment?

4. Record the theme for chapters 1 through 7 on 2 CORINTHIANS AT A GLANCE under "Segment Divisions."

Chapters 8, 9

1. What subject is Paul talking about in chapters 8 and 9? Note the use of the words *act of grace* and *service*. What service or act of grace is he referring to?

2. Record this subject as the theme of this segment in the appropriate space on 2 CORINTHIANS AT A GLANCE.

Chapters 10-13

1. Notice when the key word *boast* first appears in the text and what happens when it appears. Note what or whom the boasting is in and what you learn.

2. In the margin of chapter 11 list what you learn about Satan and spiritual warfare from these four chapters.

3. What does Paul seem to be doing in chapters 10 through 13? What opposition is there to Paul, and what is the opposition saying about him? What is his response to this opposition? Record the theme of this segment under "Segment Divisions" and complete the chart.

❧ THINGS TO THINK ABOUT

1. What is the purpose of affliction? When you need to be comforted, do you turn to people or to God?

2. Is it always wrong to feel sorrow, to be hurt, or to have a broken heart? Is it always wrong to cause sorrow, to hurt, or to break another person's heart?

3. How do you deal with those who oppose you? How do you minister to those who are caught in the middle of a conflict and don't know who to believe?

4. Paul was human just like us; he had feelings just like we do. What can we learn from him about how we are to live and respond in spite of our feelings? When is the time to give a defense of one's self, of one's ministry?

5. Are you prepared to stand before the judgment seat of Christ?

6. What place does the ministry of giving play in your life?

7. If you were to examine yourself, would you find your Christianity genuine?

Chapter 1 Theme

1 Paul, an apostle of Christ Jesus by the will of God,[a] and Timothy our brother,

To the church of God[b] in Corinth, together with all the saints throughout Achaia:[c]

[2]Grace and peace to you from God our Father and the Lord Jesus Christ.[d]

[3]Praise be to the God and Father of our Lord Jesus Christ,[e] the Father of compassion and the God of all comfort, [4]who comforts us[f] in all our troubles, so that we can comfort those in any trouble with the comfort we ourselves have received from God. [5]For just as the sufferings of Christ flow over into our lives,[g] so also through Christ our comfort overflows. [6]If we are distressed, it is for your comfort and salvation;[h] if we are comforted, it is for your comfort, which produces in you patient endurance of the same sufferings we suffer. [7]And our hope for you is firm, because we know that just as you share in our sufferings,[i] so also you share in our comfort.

[8]We do not want you to be uninformed, brothers, about the hardships we suffered[j] in the province of Asia. We were under great pressure, far beyond our ability to endure, so that we despaired even of life. [9]Indeed, in our hearts we felt the sentence of death. But this happened that we might not rely on ourselves but on God,[k] who raises the dead. [10]He has delivered us from such a deadly peril,[l] and he will deliver us. On him we have set our hope that he will continue to deliver us, [11]as you help us by your prayers.[m] Then many will give thanks[n] on our[a] behalf for the gracious favor granted us in answer to the prayers of many.

[12]Now this is our boast: Our conscience[o] testifies that we have conducted ourselves in the world, and especially in our relations with you, in the holiness and sincerity[p] that are from God. We have done so not according to worldly wisdom[q] but according to God's grace. [13]For we do not write you anything you cannot read or understand. And I hope that, [14]as you have understood us in part, you will come to understand fully that you can boast of us just as we will boast of you in the day of the Lord Jesus.[r]

[15]Because I was confident of this, I planned to visit you[s] first so that you might benefit twice.[t] [16]I planned to visit you on my way[u] to Macedonia and to come back to you from Macedonia, and then to have you send me on my way to Judea. [17]When I planned this, did I do it lightly? Or do I make my plans in a worldly manner[v] so that in the same breath I say, "Yes, yes" and "No, no"?

[18]But as surely as God is faithful,[w] our message to you is not "Yes" and "No." [19]For the Son of God, Jesus Christ, who was preached

a 11 Many manuscripts *your*

1:1
a 1Co 1:1;
Eph 1:1;
Col 1:1; 2Ti 1:1
b 1Co 10:32
c Ac 18:12

1:2
d Ro 1:7

1:3
e Eph 1:3;
1Pe 1:3

1:4
f 2Co 7:6,7,13

1:5
g 2Co 4:10;
Col 1:24

1:6
h 2Co 4:15

1:7
i Ro 8:17

1:8
j 1Co 15:32

1:9
k Jer 17:5,7

1:10
l Ro 15:31

1:11
m Ro 15:30;
Php 1:19
n 2Co 4:15

1:12
o Ac 23:1
p 2Co 2:17
q 1Co 2:1,4,13

1:14
r 1Co 1:8

1:15
s 1Co 4:19
t Ro 1:11,13;
15:29

1:16
u 1Co 16:5-7

1:17
v 2Co 10:2,3

1:18
w 1Co 1:9

1:19
a Heb 13:8

1:20
b Ro 15:8
c 1Co 14:16

1:21
d 1Jn 2:20,27

1:22
e 2Co 5:5

1:23
f Ro 1:9;
Gal 1:20
g 1Co 4:21;
2Co 2:1,3;
13:2,10

1:24
h 1Pe 5:3
i Ro 11:20;
1Co 15:1

2:1
j 2Co 1:23

2:2
k 2Co 7:8

2:3
l 2Co 7:8,12
m 2Co 12:21
n 2Co 8:22;
Gal 5:10

2:4
o 2Co 7:8,12

2:5
p 1Co 5:1,2

2:6
q 1Co 5:4,5

2:7
r Gal 6:1;
Eph 4:32

2:9
s 2Co 10:6

2:11
t Mt 4:10
u Lk 22:31;
2Co 4:4;
1Pe 5:8,9

2:12
v Ac 16:8
w Ro 1:1
x Ac 14:27

2:13
y 2Co 7:5
z 2Co 7:6,13;
12:18

2:14
a Ro 6:17
b Eph 5:2;
Php 4:18

2:15
c 1Co 1:18

2:16
d Lk 2:34
e 2Co 3:5,6

2:17
f 2Co 4:2
g 1Co 5:8
h 2Co 1:12

among you by me and Silas*a* and Timothy, was not "Yes" and "No," but in him it has always*a* been "Yes." [20]For no matter how many promises*b* God has made, they are "Yes" in Christ. And so through him the "Amen"*c* is spoken by us to the glory of God. [21]Now it is God who makes both us and you stand firm in Christ. He anointed*d* us, [22]set his seal of ownership on us, and put his Spirit in our hearts as a deposit, guaranteeing what is to come.*e*

[23]I call God as my witness*f* that it was in order to spare you*g* that I did not return to Corinth. [24]Not that we lord it over*h* your faith, but we work with you for your joy, because it is by faith you stand firm. *i*

Chapter 2 Theme

2 So I made up my mind that I would not make another painful visit to you.*j* [2]For if I grieve you,*k* who is left to make me glad but you whom I have grieved? [3]I wrote as I did*l* so that when I came I should not be distressed*m* by those who ought to make me rejoice. I had confidence*n* in all of you, that you would all share my joy. [4]For I wrote you*o* out of great distress and anguish of heart and with many tears, not to grieve you but to let you know the depth of my love for you.

[5]If anyone has caused grief,*p* he has not so much grieved me as he has grieved all of you, to some extent—not to put it too severely. [6]The punishment*q* inflicted on him by the majority is sufficient for him. [7]Now instead, you ought to forgive and comfort him,*r* so that he will not be overwhelmed by excessive sorrow. [8]I urge you, therefore, to reaffirm your love for him. [9]The reason I wrote you was to see if you would stand the test and be obedient in everything.*s* [10]If you forgive anyone, I also forgive him. And what I have forgiven—if there was anything to forgive—I have forgiven in the sight of Christ for your sake, [11]in order that Satan*t* might not outwit us. For we are not unaware of his schemes.*u*

[12]Now when I went to Troas*v* to preach the gospel of Christ*w* and found that the Lord had opened a door*x* for me, [13]I still had no peace of mind,*y* because I did not find my brother Titus*z* there. So I said good-by to them and went on to Macedonia.

[14]But thanks be to God,*a* who always leads us in triumphal procession in Christ and through us spreads everywhere the fragrance*b* of the knowledge of him. [15]For we are to God the aroma of Christ among those who are being saved and those who are perishing.*c* [16]To the one we are the smell of death;*d* to the other, the fragrance of life. And who is equal to such a task?*e* [17]Unlike so many, we do not peddle the word of God for profit.*f* On the contrary, in Christ we speak before God with sincerity,*g* like men sent from God.*h*

a 19 Greek *Silvanus,* a variant of *Silas*

1979

Chapter 3 Theme

3 Are we beginning to commend ourselves[a] again? Or do we need, like some people, letters of recommendation[b] to you or from you? [2]You yourselves are our letter, written on our hearts, known and read by everybody.[c] [3]You show that you are a letter from Christ, the result of our ministry, written not with ink but with the Spirit of the living God, not on tablets of stone[d] but on tablets of human hearts.[e]

[4]Such confidence[f] as this is ours through Christ before God. [5]Not that we are competent in ourselves to claim anything for ourselves, but our competence comes from God.[g] [6]He has made us competent as ministers of a new covenant[h]—not of the letter but of the Spirit; for the letter kills, but the Spirit gives life.[i]

[7]Now if the ministry that brought death, which was engraved in letters on stone, came with glory, so that the Israelites could not look steadily at the face of Moses because of its glory,[j] fading though it was, [8]will not the ministry of the Spirit be even more glorious? [9]If the ministry that condemns men[k] is glorious, how much more glorious is the ministry that brings righteousness![l] [10]For what was glorious has no glory now in comparison with the surpassing glory. [11]And if what was fading away came with glory, how much greater is the glory of that which lasts!

[12]Therefore, since we have such a hope, we are very bold.[m] [13]We are not like Moses, who would put a veil over his face[n] to keep the Israelites from gazing at it while the radiance was fading away. [14]But their minds were made dull,[o] for to this day the same veil remains when the old covenant[p] is read.[q] It has not been removed, because only in Christ is it taken away. [15]Even to this day when Moses is read, a veil covers their hearts. [16]But whenever anyone turns to the Lord,[r] the veil is taken away.[s] [17]Now the Lord is the Spirit,[t] and where the Spirit of the Lord is, there is freedom.[u] [18]And we, who with unveiled faces all reflect[a][v] the Lord's glory,[w] are being transformed into his likeness[x] with ever-increasing glory, which comes from the Lord, who is the Spirit.

Chapter 4 Theme

4 Therefore, since through God's mercy[y] we have this ministry, we do not lose heart. [2]Rather, we have renounced secret and shameful ways;[z] we do not use deception, nor do we distort the word of God.[a] On the contrary, by setting forth the truth plainly we commend ourselves to every man's conscience[b] in the sight of God. [3]And even if our gospel[c] is veiled,[d] it is veiled to those who are perishing.[e] [4]The god[f] of this age has blinded[g] the minds of

[a]18 Or *contemplate*

3:1
a 2Co 5:12; 12:11
b Ac 18:27

3:2
c 1Co 9:2

3:3
d Ex 24:12
e Pr 3:3;
Jer 31:33;
Eze 11:19

3:4
f Eph 3:12

3:5
g 1Co 15:10

3:6
h Lk 22:20
i Jn 6:63

3:7
j Ex 34:29-35

3:9
k ver 7
l Ro 1:17; 3:21,22

3:12
m Eph 6:19

3:13
n ver 7;
Ex 34:33

3:14
o Ro 11:7,8
p Ac 13:15
q ver 6

3:16
r Ro 11:23
s Ex 34:34

3:17
t Isa 61:1,2
u Jn 8:32

3:18
v 1Co 13:12
w 2Co 4:4,6
x Ro 8:29

4:1
y 1Co 7:25

4:2
z 1Co 4:5
a 2Co 2:17
b 2Co 5:11

4:3
c 2Co 2:12
d 2Co 3:14
e 1Co 1:18

4:4
f Jn 12:31
g 2Co 3:14

4:5
a 1Co 1:13
b 1Co 9:19

4:6
c Ge 1:3
d 2Pe 1:19

4:7
e Job 4:19;
2Co 5:1
f 1Co 2:5

4:8
g 2Co 7:5

4:9
h Jn 15:20
i Heb 13:5
j Ps 37:24

4:10
k Ro 6:5

4:11
l Ro 8:36

4:12
m 2Co 13:9

4:13
n Ps 116:10

4:14
o 1Th 4:14
p Eph 5:27

4:15
q 2Co 1:11

4:16
r Ro 7:22
s Col 3:10

4:17
t Ro 8:18;
1Pe 1:6,7

4:18
u Ro 8:24;
Heb 11:1

5:1
v 1Co 15:47
w 2Pe 1:13,14

5:2
x ver 4; Ro 8:23
y 1Co 15:53,54

5:4
z 1Co 15:53,54

5:5
a Ro 8:23;
2Co 1:22

5:7
b 1Co 13:12

5:8
c Php 1:23

unbelievers, so that they cannot see the light of the gospel of the glory of Christ, who is the image of God. [5]For we do not preach ourselves,*a* but Jesus Christ as Lord, and ourselves as your servants*b* for Jesus' sake. [6]For God, who said, "Let light shine out of darkness," *a c* made his light shine in our hearts*d* to give us the light of the knowledge of the glory of God in the face of Christ.

[7]But we have this treasure in jars of clay*e* to show that this all-surpassing power is from God *f* and not from us. [8]We are hard pressed on every side,*g* but not crushed; perplexed, but not in despair; [9]persecuted,*h* but not abandoned;*i* struck down, but not destroyed.*j* [10]We always carry around in our body the death of Jesus, so that the life of Jesus may also be revealed in our body.*k* [11]For we who are alive are always being given over to death for Jesus' sake, *l* so that his life may be revealed in our mortal body. [12]So then, death is at work in us, but life is at work in you.*m*

[13]It is written: "I believed; therefore I have spoken." *b n* With that same spirit of faith we also believe and therefore speak, [14]because we know that the one who raised the Lord Jesus from the dead will also raise us with Jesus*o* and present us with you in his presence.*p* [15]All this is for your benefit, so that the grace that is reaching more and more people may cause thanksgiving*q* to overflow to the glory of God.

[16]Therefore we do not lose heart. Though outwardly we are wasting away, yet inwardly *r* we are being renewed*s* day by day. [17]For our light and momentary troubles are achieving for us an eternal glory that far outweighs them all.*t* [18]So we fix our eyes not on what is seen, but on what is unseen.*u* For what is seen is temporary, but what is unseen is eternal.

Chapter 5 Theme

5 Now we know that if the earthly *v* tent*w* we live in is destroyed, we have a building from God, an eternal house in heaven, not built by human hands. [2]Meanwhile we groan,*x* longing to be clothed with our heavenly dwelling,*y* [3]because when we are clothed, we will not be found naked. [4]For while we are in this tent, we groan and are burdened, because we do not wish to be unclothed but to be clothed with our heavenly dwelling,*z* so that what is mortal may be swallowed up by life. [5]Now it is God who has made us for this very purpose and has given us the Spirit as a deposit, guaranteeing what is to come.*a*

[6]Therefore we are always confident and know that as long as we are at home in the body we are away from the Lord. [7]We live by faith, not by sight.*b* [8]We are confident, I say, and would prefer to be away from the body and at home with the Lord. *c* [9]So we make

a 6 Gen.1:3   *b 13* Psalm 116:10

it our goal to please him,[a] whether we are at home in the body or away from it. [10]For we must all appear before the judgment seat of Christ, that each one may receive what is due him[b] for the things done while in the body, whether good or bad.

[11]Since, then, we know what it is to fear the Lord,[c] we try to persuade men. What we are is plain to God, and I hope it is also plain to your conscience.[d] [12]We are not trying to commend ourselves to you again,[e] but are giving you an opportunity to take pride in us,[f] so that you can answer those who take pride in what is seen rather than in what is in the heart. [13]If we are out of our mind,[g] it is for the sake of God; if we are in our right mind, it is for you. [14]For Christ's love compels us, because we are convinced that one died for all, and therefore all died.[h] [15]And he died for all, that those who live should no longer live for themselves[i] but for him who died for them and was raised again.

[16]So from now on we regard no one from a worldly[j] point of view. Though we once regarded Christ in this way, we do so no longer. [17]Therefore, if anyone is in Christ, he is a new creation;[k] the old has gone, the new has come![l] [18]All this is from God, who reconciled us to himself through Christ[m] and gave us the ministry of reconciliation: [19]that God was reconciling the world to himself in Christ, not counting men's sins against them.[n] And he has committed to us the message of reconciliation. [20]We are therefore Christ's ambassadors,[o] as though God were making his appeal through us. We implore you on Christ's behalf: Be reconciled to God. [21]God made him who had no sin[p] to be sin[a] for us, so that in him we might become the righteousness of God.[q]

Chapter 6 Theme

 As God's fellow workers[r] we urge you not to receive God's grace in vain. [2]For he says,

> "In the time of my favor I heard you,
>   and in the day of salvation I helped you."[b][s]

I tell you, now is the time of God's favor, now is the day of salvation.

[3]We put no stumbling block in anyone's path,[t] so that our ministry will not be discredited. [4]Rather, as servants of God we commend ourselves in every way: in great endurance; in troubles, hardships and distresses; [5]in beatings, imprisonments[u] and riots; in hard work, sleepless nights and hunger;[v] [6]in purity, understanding, patience and kindness; in the Holy Spirit[w] and in sincere love; [7]in truthful speech[x] and in the power of God; with weapons of

---

5:9
[a] Ro 14:18

5:10
[b] Mt 16:27;
Ro 14:10;
Eph 6:8

5:11
[c] Heb 10:31;
Jude 23
[d] 2Co 4:2

5:12
[e] 2Co 3:1
[f] 2Co 1:14

5:13
[g] 2Co 11:1,
16,17

5:14
[h] Gal 2:20

5:15
[i] Ro 14:7-9

5:16
[j] 2Co 11:18

5:17
[k] Gal 6:15
[l] Isa 65:17;
Rev 21:4,5

5:18
[m] Ro 5:10;
Col 1:20

5:19
[n] Ro 4:8

5:20
[o] 2Co 6:1;
Eph 6:20

5:21
[p] Heb 4:15;
1Pe 2:22,24;
1Jn 3:5
[q] Ro 1:17

6:1
[r] 1Co 3:9;
2Co 5:20

6:2
[s] Isa 49:8

6:3
[t] Ro 14:13,20;
1Co 9:12; 10:32

6:5
[u] 2Co 11:23-25
[v] 1Co 4:11

6:6
[w] 1Th 1:5

6:7
[x] 2Co 4:2

---

[a] 21 Or *be a sin offering*   [b] 2 Isaiah 49:8

6:7
a 2Co 10:4;
Eph 6:10-18

6:8
b 1Co 4:10
c Mt 27:63

6:9
d Ro 8:36
e 2Co 1:8-10;
4:10,11

6:10
f 2Co 7:4
g 2Co 8:9
h Ro 8:32;
1Co 3:21

6:11
i 2Co 7:3

6:13
j 1Co 4:14

6:14
k 1Co 5:9,10
l Eph 5:7,11;
1Jn 1:6

6:15
m Ac 5:14

6:16
n 1Co 3:16
o Lev 26:12;
Jer 32:38;
Eze 37:27

6:17
p Rev 18:4
q Isa 52:11

6:18
r Isa 43:6

7:1
s 2Co 6:17,18

7:2
t 2Co 6:12,13

7:3
u 2Co 6:11,12

7:4
v 2Co 6:10

7:5
w 2Co 2:13
x 2Co 4:8
y Dt 32:25

7:6
z 2Co 1:3,4
a ver 13;
2Co 2:13

righteousness *a* in the right hand and in the left; [8]through glory and dishonor,*b* bad report and good report; genuine, yet regarded as impostors; *c* [9]known, yet regarded as unknown; dying, *d* and yet we live on;*e* beaten, and yet not killed; [10]sorrowful, yet always rejoicing;*f* poor, yet making many rich;*g* having nothing, and yet possessing everything.*h*

[11]We have spoken freely to you, Corinthians, and opened wide our hearts to you. *i* [12]We are not withholding our affection from you, but you are withholding yours from us. [13]As a fair exchange—I speak as to my children *j*—open wide your hearts also.

[14]Do not be yoked together *k* with unbelievers. For what do righteousness and wickedness have in common? Or what fellowship can light have with darkness?*l* [15]What harmony is there between Christ and Belial*a*? What does a believer *m* have in common with an unbeliever? [16]What agreement is there between the temple of God and idols? For we are the temple *n* of the living God. As God has said: "I will live with them and walk among them, and I will be their God, and they will be my people."*b o*

> [17]"Therefore come out from them *p*
>   and be separate,
>   says the Lord.
> Touch no unclean thing,
>   and I will receive you."*c q*
> [18]"I will be a Father to you,
>   and you will be my sons and daughters,*r*
>   says the Lord Almighty."*d*

Chapter 7 Theme

7 Since we have these promises,*s* dear friends, let us purify ourselves from everything that contaminates body and spirit, perfecting holiness out of reverence for God.

[2]Make room for us in your hearts. *t* We have wronged no one, we have corrupted no one, we have exploited no one. [3]I do not say this to condemn you; I have said before that you have such a place in our hearts *u* that we would live or die with you. [4]I have great confidence in you; I take great pride in you. I am greatly encouraged; in all our troubles my joy knows no bounds.*v*

[5]For when we came into Macedonia,*w* this body of ours had no rest, but we were harassed at every turn*x*— conflicts on the outside, fears within. *y* [6]But God, who comforts the downcast,*z* comforted us by the coming of Titus,*a* [7]and not only by his coming but also by the comfort you had given him. He told us about your

a 15 Greek *Beliar*, a variant of *Belial*   *b 16* Lev. 26:12; Jer. 32:38; Ezek. 37:27   *c 17* Isaiah 52:11; Ezek. 20:34,41   *d 18* 2 Samuel 7:14; 7:8

longing for me, your deep sorrow, your ardent concern for me, so that my joy was greater than ever.

[8]Even if I caused you sorrow by my letter,[a] I do not regret it. Though I did regret it—I see that my letter hurt you, but only for a little while— [9]yet now I am happy, not because you were made sorry, but because your sorrow led you to repentance. For you became sorrowful as God intended and so were not harmed in any way by us. [10]Godly sorrow brings repentance that leads to salvation[b] and leaves no regret, but worldly sorrow brings death. [11]See what this godly sorrow has produced in you: what earnestness, what eagerness to clear yourselves, what indignation, what alarm, what longing, what concern,[c] what readiness to see justice done. At every point you have proved yourselves to be innocent in this matter. [12]So even though I wrote to you,[d] it was not on account of the one who did the wrong[e] or of the injured party, but rather that before God you could see for yourselves how devoted to us you are. [13]By all this we are encouraged.

In addition to our own encouragement, we were especially delighted to see how happy Titus[f] was, because his spirit has been refreshed by all of you. [14]I had boasted to him about you,[g] and you have not embarrassed me. But just as everything we said to you was true, so our boasting about you to Titus[h] has proved to be true as well. [15]And his affection for you is all the greater when he remembers that you were all obedient,[i] receiving him with fear and trembling.[j] [16]I am glad I can have complete confidence in you.[k]

Chapter 8 Theme

8 And now, brothers, we want you to know about the grace that God has given the Macedonian[l] churches. [2]Out of the most severe trial, their overflowing joy and their extreme poverty welled up in rich generosity. [3]For I testify that they gave as much as they were able,[m] and even beyond their ability. Entirely on their own, [4]they urgently pleaded with us for the privilege of sharing in this service[n] to the saints.[o] [5]And they did not do as we expected, but they gave themselves first to the Lord and then to us in keeping with God's will. [6]So we urged[p] Titus,[q] since he had earlier made a beginning, to bring also to completion[r] this act of grace on your part. [7]But just as you excel in everything[s]—in faith, in speech, in knowledge,[t] in complete earnestness and in your love for us[a]—see that you also excel in this grace of giving.

[8]I am not commanding you,[u] but I want to test the sincerity of your love by comparing it with the earnestness of others. [9]For you know the grace of our Lord Jesus Christ,[v] that though he was rich,

---

a 7 Some manuscripts *in our love for you*

7:8
a 2Co 2:2,4

7:10
b Ac 11:18

7:11
c ver 7

7:12
d ver 8;
2Co 2:3,9
e 1Co 5:1,2

7:13
f ver 6;
2Co 2:13

7:14
g ver 4
h ver 6

7:15
i 2Co 2:9
j Php 2:12

7:16
k 2Co 2:3

8:1
l Ac 16:9

8:3
m 1Co 16:2

8:4
n Ac 24:17
o Ro 15:25;
2Co 9:1

8:6
p ver 17;
2Co 12:18
q ver 16,23
r ver 10,11

8:7
s 2Co 9:8
t 1Co 1:5

8:8
u 1Co 7:6

8:9
v 2Co 13:14

8:9
a Mt 20:28;
Php 2:6-8

8:10
b 1Co 7:25,40
c 1Co 16:2,3;
2Co 9:2

8:11
d 2Co 9:2

8:12
e Mk 12:43,44;
Lk 21:3

8:14
f 2Co 9:12

8:15
g Ex 16:18

8:16
h 2Co 2:14
i Rev 17:17
j 2Co 2:13

8:17
k ver 6

8:18
l 2Co 12:18
m 1Co 7:17
n 2Co 2:12

8:19
o 1Co 16:3,4
p ver 11,12

8:21
q Ro 12:17;
14:18

8:23
r Phm 17
s Php 2:25
t ver 18,22

8:24
u 2Co 7:4,14;
9:2

9:1
v 1Th 4:9
w 2Co 8:4

9:2
x 2Co 7:4,14
y 2Co 8:10
z Ac 18:12

9:3
a 1Co 16:2

9:4
b Ro 15:26

yet for your sakes he became poor,*a* so that you through his poverty might become rich.

[10]And here is my advice*b* about what is best for you in this matter: Last year you were the first not only to give but also to have the desire to do so.*c* [11]Now finish the work, so that your eager willingness*d* to do it may be matched by your completion of it, according to your means. [12]For if the willingness is there, the gift is acceptable according to what one has,*e* not according to what he does not have.

[13]Our desire is not that others might be relieved while you are hard pressed, but that there might be equality. [14]At the present time your plenty will supply what they need,*f* so that in turn their plenty will supply what you need. Then there will be equality, [15]as it is written: "He who gathered much did not have too much, and he who gathered little did not have too little."*a g*

[16]I thank God,*h* who put into the heart*i* of Titus*j* the same concern I have for you. [17]For Titus not only welcomed our appeal, but he is coming to you with much enthusiasm and on his own initiative.*k* [18]And we are sending along with him the brother*l* who is praised by all the churches*m* for his service to the gospel.*n* [19]What is more, he was chosen by the churches to accompany us*o* as we carry the offering, which we administer in order to honor the Lord himself and to show our eagerness to help.*p* [20]We want to avoid any criticism of the way we administer this liberal gift. [21]For we are taking pains to do what is right, not only in the eyes of the Lord but also in the eyes of men.*q*

[22]In addition, we are sending with them our brother who has often proved to us in many ways that he is zealous, and now even more so because of his great confidence in you. [23]As for Titus, he is my partner*r* and fellow worker*s* among you; as for our brothers,*t* they are representatives of the churches and an honor to Christ. [24]Therefore show these men the proof of your love and the reason for our pride in you,*u* so that the churches can see it.

Chapter 9 Theme

9 There is no need*v* for me to write to you about this service to the saints.*w* [2]For I know your eagerness to help, and I have been boasting*x* about it to the Macedonians, telling them that since last year*y* you in Achaia*z* were ready to give; and your enthusiasm has stirred most of them to action. [3]But I am sending the brothers in order that our boasting about you in this matter should not prove hollow, but that you may be ready, as I said you would be.*a* [4]For if any Macedonians*b* come with me and find you unprepared, we—not to say anything about you—would be ashamed of having been

a 15 Exodus 16:18

so confident. [5]So I thought it necessary to urge the brothers to visit you in advance and finish the arrangements for the generous gift you had promised. Then it will be ready as a generous gift,[a] not as one grudgingly given.[b]

[6]Remember this: Whoever sows sparingly will also reap sparingly, and whoever sows generously will also reap generously.[c] [7]Each man should give what he has decided in his heart to give,[d] not reluctantly or under compulsion,[e] for God loves a cheerful giver.[f] [8]And God is able[g] to make all grace abound to you, so that in all things at all times, having all that you need,[h] you will abound in every good work. [9]As it is written:

"He has scattered abroad his gifts to the poor;
  his righteousness endures forever."[a][i]

[10]Now he who supplies seed to the sower and bread for food[j] will also supply and increase your store of seed and will enlarge the harvest of your righteousness.[k] [11]You will be made rich[l] in every way so that you can be generous on every occasion, and through us your generosity will result in thanksgiving to God.[m]

[12]This service that you perform is not only supplying the needs[n] of God's people but is also overflowing in many expressions of thanks to God.[o] [13]Because of the service[p] by which you have proved yourselves, men will praise God[q] for the obedience that accompanies your confession of the gospel of Christ,[r] and for your generosity in sharing with them and with everyone else. [14]And in their prayers for you their hearts will go out to you, because of the surpassing grace God has given you. [15]Thanks be to God[s] for his indescribable gift![t]

Chapter 10 Theme

10 By the meekness and gentleness[u] of Christ, I appeal to you—I, Paul,[v] who am "timid" when face to face with you, but "bold" when away! [2]I beg you that when I come I may not have to be as bold[w] as I expect to be toward some people who think that we live by the standards of this world. [3]For though we live in the world, we do not wage war as the world does. [4]The weapons we fight with[x] are not the weapons of the world. On the contrary, they have divine power[y] to demolish strongholds.[z] [5]We demolish arguments and every pretension that sets itself up against the knowledge of God,[a] and we take captive every thought to make it obedient[b] to Christ. [6]And we will be ready to punish every act of disobedience, once your obedience is complete.[c]

a9 Psalm 112:9

9:5
a Php 4:17
b 2Co 12:17,18

9:6
c Pr 11:24,25; 22:9; Gal 6:7,9

9:7
d Ex 25:2; 2Co 8:12
e Dt 15:10
f Ro 12:8

9:8
g Eph 3:20
h Php 4:19

9:9
i Ps 112:9

9:10
j Isa 55:10
k Hos 10:12

9:11
l 1Co 1:5
m 2Co 1:11

9:12
n 2Co 8:14
o 2Co 1:11

9:13
p 2Co 8:4
q Mt 9:8
r 2Co 2:12

9:15
s 2Co 2:14
t Ro 5:15,16

10:1
u Mt 11:29
v Gal 5:2

10:2
w 1Co 4:21; 2Co 13:2,10

10:4
x 2Co 6:7
y 1Co 2:5
z Jer 1:10; 2Co 13:10

10:5
a Isa 2:11,12; 1Co 1:19
b 2Co 9:13

10:6
c 2Co 2:9; 7:15

10:7
a Jn 7:24
b 1Co 1:12; 3:23;
14:37
c 2Co 11:23

10:8
d 2Co 13:10

10:10
e 1Co 2:3;
Gal 4:13,14
f 1Co 1:17

10:12
g 2Co 3:1

10:13
h ver 15,16

10:14
i 1Co 3:6
j 2Co 2:12

10:15
k Ro 15:20
l 2Th 1:3

10:16
m Ac 19:21

10:17
n Jer 9:24;
1Co 1:31

10:18
o ver 12
p Ro 2:29;
1Co 4:5

11:1
q ver 4,19,20;
Mt 17:17
r ver 16,17,21;
2Co 5:13

11:2
s Hos 2:19;
Eph 5:26,27
t 2Co 4:14

11:3
u Ge 3:1-6,13;
Jn 8:44;
1Ti 2:14;
Rev 12:9

11:4
v 1Co 3:11
w Ro 8:15
x Gal 1:6-9

11:5
y 2Co 12:11;
Gal 2:6

11:6
z 1Co 1:17
a Eph 3:4

11:7
b 2Co 12:13

7You are looking only on the surface of things.*aa* If anyone is confident that he belongs to Christ,*b* he should consider again that we belong to Christ just as much as he.*c* 8For even if I boast somewhat freely about the authority the Lord gave us for building you up rather than pulling you down,*d* I will not be ashamed of it. 9I do not want to seem to be trying to frighten you with my letters. 10For some say, "His letters are weighty and forceful, but in person he is unimpressive*e* and his speaking amounts to nothing."*f* 11Such people should realize that what we are in our letters when we are absent, we will be in our actions when we are present.

12We do not dare to classify or compare ourselves with some who commend themselves.*g* When they measure themselves by themselves and compare themselves with themselves, they are not wise. 13We, however, will not boast beyond proper limits, but will confine our boasting to the field God has assigned to us,*h* a field that reaches even to you. 14We are not going too far in our boasting, as would be the case if we had not come to you, for we did get as far as you*i* with the gospel of Christ.*j* 15Neither do we go beyond our limits by boasting of work done by others.*bk* Our hope is that, as your faith continues to grow,*l* our area of activity among you will greatly expand, 16so that we can preach the gospel in the regions beyond you.*m* For we do not want to boast about work already done in another man's territory. 17But, "Let him who boasts boast in the Lord."*cn* 18For it is not the one who commends himself*o* who is approved, but the one whom the Lord commends.*p*

Chapter 11 Theme

11 I hope you will put up with*q* a little of my foolishness;*r* but you are already doing that. 2I am jealous for you with a godly jealousy. I promised you to one husband,*s* to Christ, so that I might present you*t* as a pure virgin to him. 3But I am afraid that just as Eve was deceived by the serpent's cunning,*u* your minds may somehow be led astray from your sincere and pure devotion to Christ. 4For if someone comes to you and preaches a Jesus other than the Jesus we preached,*v* or if you receive a different spirit*w* from the one you received, or a different gospel*x* from the one you accepted, you put up with it easily enough. 5But I do not think I am in the least inferior to those "super-apostles."*y* 6I may not be a trained speaker,*z* but I do have knowledge.*a* We have made this perfectly clear to you in every way.

7Was it a sin*b* for me to lower myself in order to elevate you by

a 7 Or *Look at the obvious facts*   *b* 13-15 Or *13We, however, will not boast about things that cannot be measured, but we will boast according to the standard of measurement that the God of measure has assigned us—a measurement that relates even to you.* *14 .... 15Neither do we boast about things that cannot be measured in regard to the work done by others.*   *c* 17 Jer. 9:24

preaching the gospel of God to you free of charge? *a* **8**I robbed other churches by receiving support from them *b* so as to serve you. **9**And when I was with you and needed something, I was not a burden to anyone, for the brothers who came from Macedonia supplied what I needed. I have kept myself from being a burden to you *c* in any way, and will continue to do so. **10**As surely as the truth of Christ is in me,*d* nobody in the regions of Achaia*e* will stop this boasting*f* of mine. **11**Why? Because I do not love you? God knows I do! *g* **12**And I will keep on doing what I am doing in order to cut the ground from under those who want an opportunity to be considered equal with us in the things they boast about.

13For such men are false apostles,*h* deceitful*i* workmen, masquerading as apostles of Christ.*j* **14**And no wonder, for Satan himself masquerades as an angel of light. **15**It is not surprising, then, if his servants masquerade as servants of righteousness. Their end will be what their actions deserve.*k*

16I repeat: Let no one take me for a fool.*l* But if you do, then receive me just as you would a fool, so that I may do a little boasting. **17**In this self-confident boasting I am not talking as the Lord would,*m* but as a fool. **18**Since many are boasting in the way the world does, I too will boast.*n* **19**You gladly put up with fools since you are so wise!*o* **20**In fact, you even put up with anyone who enslaves you *p* or exploits you or takes advantage of you or pushes himself forward or slaps you in the face. **21**To my shame I admit that we were too weak*q* for that!

What anyone else dares to boast about—I am speaking as a fool—I also dare to boast about.*r* **22**Are they Hebrews? So am I.*s* Are they Israelites? So am I.*t* Are they Abraham's descendants? So am I. **23**Are they servants of Christ? (I am out of my mind to talk like this.) I am more. I have worked much harder,*u* been in prison more frequently,*v* been flogged more severely, and been exposed to death again and again. **24**Five times I received from the Jews the forty lashes*w* minus one. **25**Three times I was beaten with rods,*x* once I was stoned,*y* three times I was shipwrecked, I spent a night and a day in the open sea, **26**I have been constantly on the move. I have been in danger from rivers, in danger from bandits, in danger from my own countrymen,*z* in danger from Gentiles; in danger in the city,*a* in danger in the country, in danger at sea; and in danger from false brothers.*b* **27**I have labored and toiled and have often gone without sleep; I have known hunger and thirst and have often gone without food;*c* I have been cold and naked. **28**Besides everything else, I face daily the pressure of my concern for all the churches. **29**Who is weak, and I do not feel weak? Who is led into sin, and I do not inwardly burn?

30If I must boast, I will boast of the things that show my weakness.*d* **31**The God and Father of the Lord Jesus, who is to be

11:7
a 1Co 9:18

11:8
b Php 4:15,18

11:9
c 2Co 12:13, 14,16

11:10
d Ro 9:1
e Ac 18:12
f 1Co 9:15

11:11
g 2Co 12:15

11:13
h 2Pe 2:1
i Tit 1:10
j Rev 2:2

11:15
k Php 3:19

11:16
l ver 1

11:17
m 1Co 7:12,25

11:18
n Php 3:3,4

11:19
o 1Co 4:10

11:20
p Gal 2:4

11:21
q 2Co 10:1,10
r Php 3:4

11:22
s Php 3:5
t Ro 9:4

11:23
u 1Co 15:10
v Ac 16:23;
2Co 6:4,5

11:24
w Dt 25:3

11:25
x Ac 16:22
y Ac 14:19

11:26
z Ac 9:23; 14:5
a Ac 21:31
b Gal 2:4

11:27
c 1Co 4:11,12;
2Co 6:5

11:30
d 1Co 2:3

11:31
a Ro 9:5

11:32
b Ac 9:24

11:33
c Ac 9:25

12:1
d 2Co 11:16,30
e ver 7

12:2
f Ac 8:39
g Eph 4:10
h 2Co 11:11

12:4
i Lk 23:43;
Rev 2:7

12:6
j 2Co 11:16

12:7
k Nu 33:55

12:8
l Mt 26:39,44

12:9
m Php 4:13

12:10
n 2Co 6:4
o Ro 5:3;
2Th 1:4
p 2Co 13:4

12:11
q 2Co 11:1
r 2Co 11:5
s 1Co 15:9,10

12:12
t Jn 4:48

12:13
u 1Co 9:12,18
v 2Co 11:7

12:14
w 2Co 13:1
x 1Co 4:14,15
y Pr 19:14

12:15
z Php 2:17;
1Th 2:8

12:16
a 2Co 11:9

12:18
b 2Co 8:6,16
c 2Co 8:18

praised forever,*a* knows that I am not lying. ³²In Damascus the governor under King Aretas had the city of the Damascenes guarded in order to arrest me.*b* ³³But I was lowered in a basket from a window in the wall and slipped through his hands.*c*

Chapter 12 Theme

12 I must go on boasting.*d* Although there is nothing to be gained, I will go on to visions and revelations*e* from the Lord. ²I know a man in Christ who fourteen years ago was caught up*f* to the third heaven.*g* Whether it was in the body or out of the body I do not know—God knows.*h* ³And I know that this man— whether in the body or apart from the body I do not know, but God knows— ⁴was caught up to paradise.*i* He heard inexpressible things, things that man is not permitted to tell. ⁵I will boast about a man like that, but I will not boast about myself, except about my weaknesses. ⁶Even if I should choose to boast, I would not be a fool,*j* because I would be speaking the truth. But I refrain, so no one will think more of me than is warranted by what I do or say.

⁷To keep me from becoming conceited because of these surpassingly great revelations, there was given me a thorn in my flesh,*k* a messenger of Satan, to torment me. ⁸Three times I pleaded with the Lord to take it away from me.*l* ⁹But he said to me, "My grace is sufficient for you, for my power*m* is made perfect in weakness." Therefore I will boast all the more gladly about my weaknesses, so that Christ's power may rest on me. ¹⁰That is why, for Christ's sake, I delight in weaknesses, in insults, in hardships,*n* in persecutions,*o* in difficulties. For when I am weak, then I am strong.*p*

¹¹I have made a fool of myself,*q* but you drove me to it. I ought to have been commended by you, for I am not in the least inferior to the "super-apostles,"*r* even though I am nothing.*s* ¹²The things that mark an apostle —signs, wonders and miracles *t*—were done among you with great perseverance. ¹³How were you inferior to the other churches, except that I was never a burden to you?*u* Forgive me this wrong!*v*

¹⁴Now I am ready to visit you for the third time,*w* and I will not be a burden to you, because what I want is not your possessions but you. After all, children should not have to save up for their parents,*x* but parents for their children.*y* ¹⁵So I will very gladly spend for you everything I have and expend myself as well.*z* If I love you more, will you love me less? ¹⁶Be that as it may, I have not been a burden to you.*a* Yet, crafty fellow that I am, I caught you by trickery! ¹⁷Did I exploit you through any of the men I sent you? ¹⁸I urged *b* Titus to go to you and I sent our brother*c* with him. Titus did not exploit you, did he? Did we not act in the same spirit and follow the same course?

[19]Have you been thinking all along that we have been defending ourselves to you? We have been speaking in the sight of God[a] as those in Christ; and everything we do, dear friends, is for your strengthening.[b] [20]For I am afraid that when I come[c] I may not find you as I want you to be, and you may not find me as you want me to be.[d] I fear that there may be quarreling,[e] jealousy, outbursts of anger, factions,[f] slander, gossip,[g] arrogance and disorder.[h] [21]I am afraid that when I come again my God will humble me before you, and I will be grieved[i] over many who have sinned earlier[j] and have not repented of the impurity, sexual sin and debauchery in which they have indulged.

Chapter 13 Theme

13 This will be my third visit to you.[k] "Every matter must be established by the testimony of two or three witnesses."[a] [2]I already gave you a warning when I was with you the second time. I now repeat it while absent: On my return I will not spare[m] those who sinned earlier[n] or any of the others, [3]since you are demanding proof that Christ is speaking through me.[o] He is not weak in dealing with you, but is powerful among you. [4]For to be sure, he was crucified in weakness,[p] yet he lives by God's power.[q] Likewise, we are weak[r] in him, yet by God's power we will live with him to serve you.

[5]Examine yourselves[s] to see whether you are in the faith; test yourselves.[t] Do you not realize that Christ Jesus is in you[u]— unless, of course, you fail the test? [6]And I trust that you will discover that we have not failed the test. [7]Now we pray to God that you will not do anything wrong. Not that people will see that we have stood the test but that you will do what is right even though we may seem to have failed. [8]For we cannot do anything against the truth, but only for the truth. [9]We are glad whenever we are weak but you are strong; and our prayer is for your perfection.[v] [10]This is why I write these things when I am absent, that when I come I may not have to be harsh in my use of authority—the authority the Lord gave me for building you up, not for tearing you down.[w]

[11]Finally, brothers,[x] good-by. Aim for perfection, listen to my appeal, be of one mind, live in peace.[y] And the God of love and peace[z] will be with you.

[12]Greet one another with a holy kiss.[a] [13]All the saints send their greetings.[b]

[14]May the grace of the Lord Jesus Christ,[c] and the love of God,[d] and the fellowship of the Holy Spirit[e] be with you all.

a1 Deut. 19:15

12:19
a Ro 9:1
b 2Co 10:8

12:20
c 2Co 2:1-4
d 1Co 4:21
e 1Co 1:11; 3:3
f Gal 5:20
g Ro 1:29
h 1Co 14:33

12:21
i 2Co 2:1,4
j 2Co 13:2

13:1
k 2Co 12:14
l Dt 19:15;
Mt 18:16

13:2
m 2Co 1:23
n 2Co 12:21

13:3
o Mt 10:20;
1Co 5:4

13:4
p Php 2:7,8;
1Pe 3:18
q Ro 1:4; 6:4
r ver 9

13:5
s 1Co 11:28
t Jn 6:6
u Ro 8:10

13:9
v ver 11

13:10
w 2Co 10:8

13:11
x 1Th 4:1;
2Th 3:1
y Mk 9:50
z Ro 15:33;
Eph 6:23

13:12
a Ro 16:16

13:13
b Php 4:22

13:14
c Ro 16:20;
2Co 8:9
d Ro 5:5;
Jude 21
e Php 2:1

2 CORINTHIANS OBSERVATIONS CHART

PAUL

His character	His troubles	His conflict with the Corinthians

THE CORINTHIANS

Their strengths	Their weaknesses	Their problems with Paul

Paul's desire for the Corinthians	Insights on Titus

Theme of 2 Corinthians:

SEGMENT DIVISIONS

		CHAPTER THEMES
		1
		2
		3
		4
		5
		6
		7
		8
		9
		10
		11
		12
		13

Author:

Date:

Purpose:

Key Words:

comfort, have received, encouraged, encouragement, had given him (comforted, listen to my appeal)

hard pressed, harassed, distressed (trouble[s], hardships, distress, trial, suffer, sufferings, not harmed)

sorrow(ful), painful, grieve(d), grief, hurt, sorry

boast (boasting, take pride)

confidence, confident, self-confident

commend

death (deadly)

life

heart(s)

joy, happy (rejoice, glad, rejoicing, delighted)

ministry (service)

grace

Titus

mark references to the enemy (serpent, Satan, as well as pronouns and synonyms)

GALATIANS

The gospel introduced the Jews to a new way of life—that of grace rather than law. The old covenant with all of its regulations was made obsolete by the new covenant (Hebrews 8:13). This transition was difficult for some Jewish believers to handle, and a group called the Judaizers sprang up. The Judaizers embraced Christianity but said that some of the old covenant rites, including circumcision, still must be observed.

As Paul, God's apostle to the Gentiles, went on his missionary journeys sharing the gospel of grace, many of these Judaizers followed him, teaching the necessity of keeping the law to one degree or another. They even went to Galatia. That is why Paul wrote what he did to the churches in Galatia.

There is some uncertainty about whether Galatians was written after Paul's first or second missionary journey, and so the exact date of his writing is not known. The debate centers on whether Paul was writing to the northern or southern churches of Galatia. If Paul wrote to the northern churches, the epistle would have been written sometime between A.D. 53 and 57, but if the letter was written to the southern churches, this would have been between A.D. 48 and 49.

However, the date does not affect the message of this critical letter. The truths in this epistle will liberate you to walk in that glorious freedom of a righteous life in the Spirit—truths you can glean through careful observation. Therefore, devote your energies to discovering these truths rather than to debating when Galatians was written.

The more you read and observe the text of this book, the more you will understand Paul's words: "I no longer live, but Christ lives in me. The life I live in the body, I live by faith in the Son of God, who loved me and gave himself for me" (Galatians 2:20).

☙ THINGS TO DO

1. Read Acts 13 and 14 and then look at the map on page 1994 to acquaint yourself with the cities in this area. Also review the chart on page 1995 showing the sequence of events in Paul's life after his conversion.

2. As you read, mark in the text the key words (and their synonyms and pronouns) that are listed on the GALATIANS AT A GLANCE chart on page 2003. Mark any other key words you see as you read.

   a. The key words will help you see the theme of this epistle. The best way to see and absorb the book's message is to read through Galatians as many times as possible. Familiarity with the text and careful observation of what is being said is crucial when you study the Bible.

   b. After you mark the key words make a list of everything you learn from the text about the key words. This will give you great insights into Paul's message to the churches. You may want to record these lists in the margin for future reference.

   c. Jesus Christ is mentioned 38 times in Galatians. List everything you learn about him from this book.

3. Record the chapter themes on GALATIANS AT A GLANCE and in the text. Record the theme of the book and complete the chart.

4. As you read through the book, note Paul's emphasis in the first two chapters and then how the focus changes in chapter 3.

   a. Look for the questions Paul asks the recipients of this letter. Watch for words such as *brothers*, *you*, and *foolish Galatians*. Make a list of these things on the chart PAUL'S CONCERN FOR THE CHURCHES AT GALATIA on pages 2002, 2003. (You may want to list these on separate paper before you write them in your Bible.)

b. Think about why Paul said all he did about himself in those first two chapters. What does this have to do with what follows in the rest of his epistle?

c. Notice the progression of events in Paul's life as presented in these chapters. (There is a chart of the chronology of these events on page 1995.)

d. Trace Paul's travels on the map below.

5. In chapter 3 mark *promise(d)*. Note what the promise is; the text will tell you.

6. Fill in the segment divisions on GALATIANS AT A GLANCE.

∽ **THINGS TO THINK ABOUT**

1. Are you living under grace or under law? Have you accepted the grace of God for your salvation but still put yourself under the law for daily living?

2. According to Galatians 5:16-21, if you live under grace, under the control of the Spirit of God, you will not be able to live a life habitually controlled by the flesh, producing the works of the flesh. Evaluate your walk according to these verses.

3. What do you boast in?

4. As you look at Paul's life, what do you learn for your own life?

∽∽∽∽∽

Chapter 1 Theme _____

Paul's Travels as a New Believer

∽∽∽∽∽

1 Paul, an apostle—sent not from men nor by man, but by Jesus Christ[a] and God the Father, who raised him from the dead[b]— [2]and all the brothers with me,[c]

To the churches in Galatia:[d]

[3]Grace and peace to you from God our Father and the Lord Jesus Christ,[e] [4]who gave himself for our sins[f] to rescue us from the present evil age, according to the will of our God and Father,[g] [5]to whom be glory for ever and ever. Amen.[h]

[6]I am astonished that you are so quickly deserting the one who called[i] you by the grace of Christ and are turning to a different gospel[j]— [7]which is really no gospel at all. Evidently some people are throwing you into confusion[k] and are trying to pervert the gospel of Christ. [8]But even if we or an angel from heaven should preach a gospel other than the one we preached to you,[l] let him be eternally

1:1
[a] Ac 9:15
[b] Ac 2:24

1:2
[c] Php 4:21
[d] Ac 16:6;
1Co 16:1

1:3
[e] Ro 1:7

1:4
[f] Mt 20:28;
Ro 4:25;
Gal 2:20
[g] Php 4:20

1:5
[h] Ro 11:36

1:6
[i] Gal 5:8
[j] 2Co 11:4

1:7
[k] Ac 15:24;
Gal 5:10

1:8
[l] 2Co 11:4

PHRYGIA
GALATIA
LYCAONIA
CAPPADOCIA
Aegean Sea
Iconium
Antioch (Pisidian)
PISIDIA
Lystra
Derbe
CILICIA
Tarsus
Corinth
Athens
PAMPHYLIA
Perga
LYCIA
Attalia
Antioch (Syrian)
Seleucia
CRETE
Salamis
SYRIA
Paphos
CYPRUS
Damascus
Mediterranean (Great) Sea
Caesarea
Jerusalem
EGYPT
ARABIA

Sequence of Events in Paul's Life after His Conversion*

There are differing opinions on these dates. For continuity's sake this chart will be the basis for dates pertaining to Paul's life.

Year A.D.	Event
33-34	Conversion, time in Damascus
35-47	Some silent years, except we know that Paul:
	1. Spent time in Arabia and Damascus
	2. Made first visit to Jerusalem
	3. Went to Tarsus, Syria-Cilicia area
	4. Was with Barnabas in Antioch
	5. With Barnabas took relief to brethren in Judea—Paul's second visit to Jerusalem
	6. Returned to Antioch; was sent out with Barnabas by church at Antioch
47-48	**First missionary journey:** *Galatians written(?)*
49	Apostolic Council at Jerusalem—Paul visits Jerusalem (compare Acts 15 with Galatians 2:1)
49-51	**Second missionary journey:** *1 and 2 Thessalonians written*
52-56	**Third missionary journey:** *1 and 2 Corinthians and Romans written*
56	Paul goes to Jerusalem and is arrested; held at Caesarea
57-59	Appearance before Felix and Drusilla; before Festus; before Agrippa
59-60	Appeals to Caesar, sent from Caesarea to Rome
60-62	First Roman imprisonment: *Ephesians, Philemon, Colossians, and Philippians written*
62	Paul's release; possible trip to Spain
62	Paul in Macedonia: *1 Timothy written*
62	Paul goes to Crete: *Titus written*
63-64	Paul taken to Rome and imprisoned: *2 Timothy written*
64	Paul is absent from the body and present with the Lord
	(Others put Paul's conversion about A.D. *35, his death in* A.D. *68.)*

1:8
a Ro 9:3

1:9
b Ro 16:17

1:10
c Ro 2:29;
1Th 2:4

1:11
d 1Co 15:1

1:12
e ver 1
f ver 16

1:13
g Ac 26:4,5
h Ac 8:3

1:14
i Mt 15:2

1:15
j Isa 49:1,5;
Jer 1:5
k Ac 9:15

1:16
l Gal 2:9
m Mt 16:17

1:18
n Ac 9:22,23
o Ac 9:26,27

1:19
p Mt 13:55

1:20
q Ro 9:1

condemned!*a* ⁹As we have already said, so now I say again: If anybody is preaching to you a gospel other than what you accepted,*b* let him be eternally condemned!

¹⁰Am I now trying to win the approval of men, or of God? Or am I trying to please men?*c* If I were still trying to please men, I would not be a servant of Christ.

¹¹I want you to know, brothers,*d* that the gospel I preached is not something that man made up. ¹²I did not receive it from any man,*e* nor was I taught it; rather, I received it by revelation*f* from Jesus Christ.

¹³For you have heard of my previous way of life in Judaism,*g* how intensely I persecuted the church of God and tried to destroy it.*h* ¹⁴I was advancing in Judaism beyond many Jews of my own age and was extremely zealous for the traditions of my fathers.*i* ¹⁵But when God, who set me apart from birth*aj* and called me*k* by his grace, was pleased ¹⁶to reveal his Son in me so that I might preach him among the Gentiles,*l* I did not consult any man,*m* ¹⁷nor did I go up to Jerusalem to see those who were apostles before I was, but I went immediately into Arabia and later returned to Damascus.

¹⁸Then after three years,*n* I went up to Jerusalem*o* to get acquainted with Peter*b* and stayed with him fifteen days. ¹⁹I saw none of the other apostles—only James,*p* the Lord's brother. ²⁰I assure you before God that what I am writing you is no lie.*q* ²¹Later I went to

a 15 Or *from my mother's womb*   *b* 18 Greek *Cephas*

Syria and Cilicia.*a* 22I was personally unknown to the churches of Judea*b* that are in Christ. 23They only heard the report: "The man who formerly persecuted us is now preaching the faith*c* he once tried to destroy." 24And they praised God*d* because of me.

Chapter 2 Theme

2 Fourteen years later I went up again to Jerusalem,*e* this time with Barnabas. I took Titus along also. 2I went in response to a revelation and set before them the gospel that I preach among the Gentiles.*f* But I did this privately to those who seemed to be leaders, for fear that I was running or had run my race*g* in vain. 3Yet not even Titus,*h* who was with me, was compelled to be circumcised, even though he was a Greek.*i* 4⌊This matter arose⌋ because some false brothers*j* had infiltrated our ranks to spy on*k* the freedom*l* we have in Christ Jesus and to make us slaves. 5We did not give in to them for a moment, so that the truth of the gospel*m* might remain with you.

6As for those who seemed to be important*n*—whatever they were makes no difference to me; God does not judge by external appearance*o*—those men added nothing to my message. 7On the contrary, they saw that I had been entrusted with the task*p* of preaching the gospel to the Gentiles,*a* *q* just as Peter*r* had been to the Jews.*b* 8For God, who was at work in the ministry of Peter as an apostle*s* to the Jews, was also at work in my ministry as an apostle to the Gentiles. 9James, Peter*c* *t* and John, those reputed to be pillars,*u* gave me and Barnabas*v* the right hand of fellowship when they recognized the grace given to me.*w* They agreed that we should go to the Gentiles, and they to the Jews. 10All they asked was that we should continue to remember the poor,*x* the very thing I was eager to do.

11When Peter*y* came to Antioch,*z* I opposed him to his face, because he was clearly in the wrong. 12Before certain men came from James, he used to eat with the Gentiles.*a* But when they arrived, he began to draw back and separate himself from the Gentiles because he was afraid of those who belonged to the circumcision group.*b* 13The other Jews joined him in his hypocrisy, so that by their hypocrisy even Barnabas*c* was led astray.

14When I saw that they were not acting in line with the truth of the gospel,*d* I said to Peter*e* in front of them all, "You are a Jew, yet you live like a Gentile and not like a Jew.*f* How is it, then, that you force Gentiles to follow Jewish customs?

15"We who are Jews by birth*g* and not 'Gentile sinners'*h* 16know that a man is not justified by observing the law, but by faith in Jesus

---

a7 Greek *uncircumcised*   b7 Greek *circumcised*; also in verses 8 and 9   c9 Greek *Cephas*; also in verses 11 and 14

1:21
*a*Ac 6:9

1:22
*b*1Th 2:14

1:23
*c*Ac 6:7

1:24
*d*Mt 9:8

2:1
*e*Ac 15:2

2:2
*f*Ac 15:4,12
*g*1Co 9:24;
Php 2:16

2:3
*h*2Co 2:13
*i*Ac 16:3;
1Co 9:21

2:4
*j*2Co 11:26
*k*Jude 4
*l*Ac 15:1;
Gal 5:1,13

2:5
*m*ver 14

2:6
*n*Gal 6:3
*o*Ac 10:34

2:7
*p*1Th 2:4;
1Ti 1:11
*q*Ac 9:15
*r*ver 9,11,14

2:8
*s*Ac 1:25

2:9
*t*ver 7,11,14
*u*1Ti 3:15
*v*Ac 4:36
*w*Ro 12:3

2:10
*x*Ac 24:17

2:11
*y*ver 7,9,14
*z*Ac 11:19

2:12
*a*Ac 11:3
*b*Ac 11:2

2:13
*c*ver 1;
Ac 4:36

2:14
*d*ver 5
*e*ver 7,9,11
*f*Ac 10:28

2:15
*g*Php 3:4,5
*h*1Sa 15:18

2:16
a Ac 13:39;
Ro 9:30

2:17
b ver 15
c Gal 3:21

2:19
d Ro 7:4
e Ro 6:10,11,14;
2Co 5:15

2:20
f Ro 6:6
g 1Pe 4:2
h Mt 4:3
i Ro 8:37
j Gal 1:4

2:21
k Gal 3:21

3:1
l Gal 5:7
m 1Co 1:23

3:2
n Ro 10:17

3:5
o 1Co 12:10

3:6
p Ge 15:6;
Ro 4:3

3:7
q ver 9

3:8
r Ge 12:3;
Ac 3:25

3:9
s ver 7;
Ro 4:16

3:10
t Dt 27:26;
Jer 11:3

3:11
u Hab 2:4;
Gal 2:16;
Heb 10:38

3:12
v Lev 18:5;
Ro 10:5

3:13
w Gal 4:5
x Dt 21:23;
Ac 5:30

3:14
y Ro 4:9,16
z ver 2;
Joel 2:28;
Ac 2:33

Christ.*a* So we, too, have put our faith in Christ Jesus that we may be justified by faith in Christ and not by observing the law, because by observing the law no one will be justified.

17"If, while we seek to be justified in Christ, it becomes evident that we ourselves are sinners,*b* does that mean that Christ promotes sin? Absolutely not!*c* 18If I rebuild what I destroyed, I prove that I am a lawbreaker. 19For through the law I died to the law*d* so that I might live for God.*e* 20I have been crucified with Christ*f* and I no longer live, but Christ lives in me.*g* The life I live in the body, I live by faith in the Son of God,*h* who loved me*i* and gave himself for me.*j* 21I do not set aside the grace of God, for if righteousness could be gained through the law,*k* Christ died for nothing!"a

Chapter 3 Theme

3 You foolish Galatians! Who has bewitched you?*l* Before your very eyes Jesus Christ was clearly portrayed as crucified.*m* 2I would like to learn just one thing from you: Did you receive the Spirit by observing the law, or by believing what you heard?*n* 3Are you so foolish? After beginning with the Spirit, are you now trying to attain your goal by human effort? 4Have you suffered so much for nothing—if it really was for nothing? 5Does God give you his Spirit and work miracles*o* among you because you observe the law, or because you believe what you heard?

6Consider Abraham: "He believed God, and it was credited to him as righteousness."b*p* 7Understand, then, that those who believe*q* are children of Abraham. 8The Scripture foresaw that God would justify the Gentiles by faith, and announced the gospel in advance to Abraham: "All nations will be blessed through you."c*r* 9So those who have faith*s* are blessed along with Abraham, the man of faith.

10All who rely on observing the law are under a curse, for it is written: "Cursed is everyone who does not continue to do everything written in the Book of the Law."d*t* 11Clearly no one is justified before God by the law, because, "The righteous will live by faith."e*u* 12The law is not based on faith; on the contrary, "The man who does these things will live by them."f*v* 13Christ redeemed us from the curse of the law*w* by becoming a curse for us, for it is written: "Cursed is everyone who is hung on a tree."g*x* 14He redeemed us in order that the blessing given to Abraham might come to the Gentiles through Christ Jesus,*y* so that by faith we might receive the promise of the Spirit.*z*

15Brothers, let me take an example from everyday life. Just as no one can set aside or add to a human covenant that has been duly established, so it is in this case. 16The promises were spoken

a*21* Some interpreters end the quotation after verse 14.   b*6* Gen. 15:6   c*8* Gen. 12:3; 18:18; 22:18   d*10* Deut. 27:26   e*11* Hab. 2:4   f*12* Lev. 18:5   g*13* Deut. 21:23

to Abraham and to his seed.[a] The Scripture does not say "and to seeds," meaning many people, but "and to your seed,"[a] meaning one person, who is Christ. [17]What I mean is this: The law, introduced 430 years[b] later, does not set aside the covenant previously established by God and thus do away with the promise. [18]For if the inheritance depends on the law, then it no longer depends on a promise;[c] but God in his grace gave it to Abraham through a promise.

[19]What, then, was the purpose of the law? It was added because of transgressions[d] until the Seed[e] to whom the promise referred had come. The law was put into effect through angels[f] by a mediator.[g] [20]A mediator,[h] however, does not represent just one party; but God is one.

[21]Is the law, therefore, opposed to the promises of God? Absolutely not![i] For if a law had been given that could impart life, then righteousness would certainly have come by the law.[j] [22]But the Scripture declares that the whole world is a prisoner of sin,[k] so that what was promised, being given through faith in Jesus Christ, might be given to those who believe.

[23]Before this faith came, we were held prisoners[l] by the law, locked up until faith should be revealed. [24]So the law was put in charge to lead us to Christ[b][m] that we might be justified by faith.[n] [25]Now that faith has come, we are no longer under the supervision of the law.

[26]You are all sons of God[o] through faith in Christ Jesus, [27]for all of you who were baptized into Christ[p] have clothed yourselves with Christ.[q] [28]There is neither Jew nor Greek, slave nor free,[r] male nor female, for you are all one in Christ Jesus.[s] [29]If you belong to Christ,[t] then you are Abraham's seed, and heirs according to the promise.[u]

Chapter 4 Theme

4 What I am saying is that as long as the heir is a child, he is no different from a slave, although he owns the whole estate. [2]He is subject to guardians and trustees until the time set by his father. [3]So also, when we were children, we were in slavery[v] under the basic principles of the world.[w] [4]But when the time had fully come,[x] God sent his Son, born of a woman,[y] born under law,[z] [5]to redeem those under law, that we might receive the full rights[a] of sons. [6]Because you are sons, God sent the Spirit of his Son into our hearts,[b] the Spirit who calls out, "Abba,[c] Father."[c] [7]So you are no longer a slave, but a son; and since you are a son, God has made you also an heir.[d]

a 16 Gen. 12:7; 13:15; 24:7   b 24 Or charge until Christ came   c 6 Aramaic for Father

3:16
[a]Lk 1:55;
Ro 4:13,16

3:17
[b]Ge 15:13,14;
Ex 12:40

3:18
[c]Ro 4:14

3:19
[d]Ro 5:20
[e]ver 16
[f]Ac 7:53
[g]Ex 20:19

3:20
[h]Heb 8:6;
9:15; 12:24

3:21
[i]Gal 2:17
[j]Gal 2:21

3:22
[k]Ro 3:9-19;
11:32

3:23
[l]Ro 11:32

3:24
[m]Ro 10:4
[n]Gal 2:16

3:26
[o]Ro 8:14

3:27
[p]Mt 28:19;
Ro 6:3
[q]Ro 13:14

3:28
[r]Col 3:11
[s]Jn 10:16;
17:11;
Eph 2:14,15

3:29
[t]1Co 3:23
[u]ver 16

4:3
[v]Gal 2:4
[w]Col 2:8,20

4:4
[x]Mk 1:15;
Eph 1:10
[y]Jn 1:14
[z]Lk 2:27

4:5
[a]Jn 1:12

4:6
[b]Ro 5:5
[c]Ro 8:15,16

4:7
[d]Ro 8:17

4:8
a 1Co 1:21;
Eph 2:12;
1Th 4:5
b 2Ch 13:9;
Isa 37:19

4:9
c 1Co 8:3
d ver 3
e Col 2:20

4:10
f Ro 14:5

4:11
g 1Th 3:5

4:12
h Gal 6:18

4:13
i 1Co 2:3

4:14
j Mt 10:40

4:16
k Am 5:10

4:18
l ver 13,14

4:19
m 1Co 4:15
n Eph 4:13

4:22
o Ge 16:15
p Ge 21:2

4:23
q Ro 9:7,8
r Ge 18:10-14;
Heb 11:11

4:26
s Heb 12:22;
Rev 3:12

4:27
t Isa 54:1

4:29
u ver 23

[8] Formerly, when you did not know God,[a] you were slaves to those who by nature are not gods.[b] [9] But now that you know God—or rather are known by God[c]—how is it that you are turning back to those weak and miserable principles? Do you wish to be enslaved[d] by them all over again?[e] [10] You are observing special days and months and seasons and years![f] [11] I fear for you, that somehow I have wasted my efforts on you.[g]

[12] I plead with you, brothers,[h] become like me, for I became like you. You have done me no wrong. [13] As you know, it was because of an illness[i] that I first preached the gospel to you. [14] Even though my illness was a trial to you, you did not treat me with contempt or scorn. Instead, you welcomed me as if I were an angel of God, as if I were Christ Jesus himself.[j] [15] What has happened to all your joy? I can testify that, if you could have done so, you would have torn out your eyes and given them to me. [16] Have I now become your enemy by telling you the truth?[k]

[17] Those people are zealous to win you over, but for no good. What they want is to alienate you ⌊from us⌋, so that you may be zealous for them. [18] It is fine to be zealous, provided the purpose is good, and to be so always and not just when I am with you.[l] [19] My dear children,[m] for whom I am again in the pains of childbirth until Christ is formed in you,[n] [20] how I wish I could be with you now and change my tone, because I am perplexed about you!

[21] Tell me, you who want to be under the law, are you not aware of what the law says? [22] For it is written that Abraham had two sons, one by the slave woman[o] and the other by the free woman.[p] [23] His son by the slave woman was born in the ordinary way;[q] but his son by the free woman was born as the result of a promise.[r]

[24] These things may be taken figuratively, for the women represent two covenants. One covenant is from Mount Sinai and bears children who are to be slaves: This is Hagar. [25] Now Hagar stands for Mount Sinai in Arabia and corresponds to the present city of Jerusalem, because she is in slavery with her children. [26] But the Jerusalem that is above[s] is free, and she is our mother. [27] For it is written:

> "Be glad, O barren woman,
> who bears no children;
> break forth and cry aloud,
> you who have no labor pains;
> because more are the children of the desolate woman
> than of her who has a husband."[a][t]

[28] Now you, brothers, like Isaac, are children of promise. [29] At that time the son born in the ordinary way[u] persecuted the son born

a 27 Isaiah 54:1

by the power of the Spirit.*a* It is the same now. [30]But what does the Scripture say? "Get rid of the slave woman and her son, for the slave woman's son will never share in the inheritance with the free woman's son."*a b* [31]Therefore, brothers, we are not children of the slave woman, but of the free woman.

Chapter 5 Theme _____

5 It is for freedom that Christ has set us free.*c* Stand firm,*d* then, and do not let yourselves be burdened again by a yoke of slavery.*e*

[2]Mark my words! I, Paul, tell you that if you let yourselves be circumcised,*f* Christ will be of no value to you at all. [3]Again I declare to every man who lets himself be circumcised that he is obligated to obey the whole law.*g* [4]You who are trying to be justified by law have been alienated from Christ; you have fallen away from grace.*h* [5]But by faith we eagerly await through the Spirit the righteousness for which we hope.*i* [6]For in Christ Jesus neither circumcision nor uncircumcision has any value.*j* The only thing that counts is faith expressing itself through love.*k*

[7]You were running a good race.*l* Who cut in on you*m* and kept you from obeying the truth? [8]That kind of persuasion does not come from the one who calls you.*n* [9]"A little yeast works through the whole batch of dough."*o* [10]I am confident*p* in the Lord that you will take no other view.*q* The one who is throwing you into confusion*r* will pay the penalty, whoever he may be. [11]Brothers, if I am still preaching circumcision, why am I still being persecuted?*s* In that case the offense*t* of the cross has been abolished. [12]As for those agitators,*u* I wish they would go the whole way and emasculate themselves!

[13]You, my brothers, were called to be free. But do not use your freedom to indulge the sinful nature*b;v* rather, serve one another*w* in love. [14]The entire law is summed up in a single command: "Love your neighbor as yourself."*c x* [15]If you keep on biting and devouring each other, watch out or you will be destroyed by each other.

[16]So I say, live by the Spirit,*y* and you will not gratify the desires of the sinful nature.*z* [17]For the sinful nature desires what is contrary to the Spirit, and the Spirit what is contrary to the sinful nature.*a* They are in conflict with each other, so that you do not do what you want.*b* [18]But if you are led by the Spirit, you are not under law.*c* [19]The acts of the sinful nature are obvious: sexual immorality,*d* impurity and debauchery; [20]idolatry and witchcraft; hatred, discord, jealousy, fits of rage, selfish ambition, dissensions, factions [21]and envy; drunkenness, orgies, and the like.*e* I warn you,

---

4:29
a Ge 21:9

4:30
b Ge 21:10

5:1
c Jn 8:32
d 1Co 16:13
e Ac 15:10;
Gal 2:4

5:2
f Ac 15:1

5:3
g Gal 3:10

5:4
h Heb 12:15;
2Pe 3:17

5:5
i Ro 8:23,24

5:6
j 1Co 7:19
k 1Th 1:3

5:7
l 1Co 9:24
m Gal 3:1

5:8
n Ro 8:28;
Gal 1:6

5:9
o 1Co 5:6

5:10
p 2Co 2:3
q Php 3:15
r Gal 1:7

5:11
s Gal 4:29; 6:12
t 1Co 1:23

5:12
u ver 10

5:13
v 1Co 8:9;
1Pe 2:16
w 1Co 9:19;
Eph 5:21

5:14
x Lev 19:18;
Mt 22:39

5:16
y Ro 8:2,
4-6,9,14
z ver 24

5:17
a Ro 8:5-8
b Ro 7:15-23

5:18
c Ro 6:14;
1Ti 1:9

5:19
d 1Co 6:18

5:21
e Ro 13:13

---

a 30 Gen. 21:10   *b 13* Or *the flesh*; also in verses 16, 17, 19 and 24   *c 14* Lev. 19:18

5:22
a Mt 7:16-20;
Eph 5:9
b Col 3:12-15

5:23
c Ac 24:25

5:24
d Ro 6:6
e ver 16,17

5:26
f Php 2:3

6:1
g 1Co 2:15

6:2
h Ro 15:1;
Jas 2:8

6:3
i Ro 12:3;
1Co 8:2

6:6
j 1Co 9:11,14

6:7
k 1Co 6:9
l 2Co 9:6

6:8
m Job 4:8;
Hos 8:7
n Jas 3:18

6:9
o 1Co 15:58
p Rev 2:10

6:10
q Pr 3:27
r Eph 2:19

6:11
s 1Co 16:21

6:12
t Ac 15:1
u Gal 5:11

6:13
v Ro 2:25
w Php 3:3

6:14
x Ro 6:2,6

6:15
y 1Co 7:19
z 2Co 5:17

6:17
a Isa 44:5;
2Co 1:5

6:18
b Ro 16:20
c 2Ti 4:22

as I did before, that those who live like this will not inherit the kingdom of God.

[22]But the fruit*a* of the Spirit is love,*b* joy, peace, patience, kindness, goodness, faithfulness, [23]gentleness and self-control.*c* Against such things there is no law. [24]Those who belong to Christ Jesus have crucified the sinful nature*d* with its passions and desires.*e* [25]Since we live by the Spirit, let us keep in step with the Spirit. [26]Let us not become conceited,*f* provoking and envying each other.

Chapter 6 Theme

6 Brothers, if someone is caught in a sin, you who are spiritual*g* should restore him gently. But watch yourself, or you also may be tempted. [2]Carry each other's burdens, and in this way you will fulfill the law of Christ.*h* [3]If anyone thinks he is something*i* when he is nothing, he deceives himself. [4]Each one should test his own actions. Then he can take pride in himself, without comparing himself to somebody else, [5]for each one should carry his own load.

[6]Anyone who receives instruction in the word must share all good things with his instructor.*j*

[7]Do not be deceived:*k* God cannot be mocked. A man reaps what he sows.*l* [8]The one who sows to please his sinful nature, from that nature*a* will reap destruction;*m* the one who sows to please the Spirit, from the Spirit will reap eternal life.*n* [9]Let us not become weary in doing good,*o* for at the proper time we will reap a harvest if we do not give up.*p* [10]Therefore, as we have opportunity, let us do good*q* to all people, especially to those who belong to the family*r* of believers.

[11]See what large letters I use as I write to you with my own hand!*s*

[12]Those who want to make a good impression outwardly are trying to compel you to be circumcised.*t* The only reason they do this is to avoid being persecuted*u* for the cross of Christ. [13]Not even those who are circumcised obey the law,*v* yet they want you to be circumcised that they may boast about your flesh.*w* [14]May I never boast except in the cross of our Lord Jesus Christ, through which*b* the world has been crucified to me, and I to the world.*x* [15]Neither circumcision nor uncircumcision means anything;*y* what counts is a new creation.*z* [16]Peace and mercy to all who follow this rule, even to the Israel of God.

[17]Finally, let no one cause me trouble, for I bear on my body the marks*a* of Jesus.

[18]The grace of our Lord Jesus Christ*b* be with your spirit,*c* brothers. Amen.

a 8 Or *his flesh, from the flesh*   *b* 14 Or *whom*

(continued)

GALATIANS AT A GLANCE

Theme of Galatians:

	SEGMENT DIVISIONS	CHAPTER THEMES
Author:		
Date:		1
Purpose:		
Key Words:		2
Paul (and pronouns relating to him)		
gospel		3
grace		
law		4
Spirit		
faith (believe, believing, believers)		5
promise(d)		
covenant		6
Christ (Jesus)		
free (freedom)		

EPHESIANS

*E*phesus, the fourth-largest city in the Roman Empire, was the home of the temple of the goddess Artemis, sometimes referred to as Diana. Of all the deities in Asia, none was more sought after than Artemis.

But by the time of Paul, Ephesus's position as a center of trade was lost because the harbor became unnavigable. From that point on, the worship of Artemis became the city's means of economic survival. The tourist and pilgrim trade associated with Artemis made many people in Ephesus wealthy. Silversmiths made their living selling images of this goddess and her temple. Innkeepers and restaurant owners grew rich from the large influx of worshipers who traveled great distances to see the temple of Artemis, one of the seven wonders of the world. Even the temple treasury served as a bank, loaning large sums of money to many, including kings. And since Artemis was the patroness of sex, prostitutes sold their bodies without condemnation in the two-story brothel on Marble Road.

Although Artemis was the main attraction, all sorts of magic and sorcery were conjured up and then documented. This documentation would later be referred to as *Ephesia grammata*.

Then God sent Paul to live in Ephesus and called out for himself a church, a light to illumine the occultic darkness of this city.

This brief glimpse into the historical and cultural setting of Ephesians should help you understand why Paul wrote what he did to the church in Ephesus. The message of this epistle is needed as much today as it was in A.D. 60 to 62, when Paul wrote it as a prisoner in Rome.

∽ THINGS TO DO

General Instructions

1. Read Ephesians in one sitting before examining it chapter by chapter.

2. When you finish, read Acts 18:18-21 (Paul's first visit to Ephesus was on his second missionary journey). Then read Acts 19 for an account of Paul's second visit on his third missionary journey. This passage will help you understand why Ephesians deals with warfare and our position in Christ more extensively than any other epistle.

Chapters 1-3

Read Ephesians 1 through 3 one chapter at a time, doing the following:

1. Mark each reference to God, and in the margin list everything God does.

2. Mark distinctively each use of *in Christ* or *in him* so you can easily spot it in the text. Then on the OBSERVATIONS CHART on page 2012, under the heading "Our Wealth and Position in Christ," list what believers have *in Christ*. Pay particular attention to the phrase *in the heavenly realms,* which is key to warfare. Note the chapter and verse from which the information comes when you make your list (e.g., 1:13). (You may want to list this information on separate paper before you record it in your Bible.)

3. Mark each reference to the Spirit or Holy Spirit. On the OBSERVATIONS CHART, under the heading "Our Relationship with the Holy Spirit," list what is taught about the person and work of the Holy Spirit.

4. Mark distinctively each occurrence of *rich* or *riches*. Then in the margin list what you learn about these riches. Remember to ask the five W's and an H: Who is rich and in what? How are these riches described? What is done with the riches? And so on.

5. Mark each use of *formerly (used to, at one time, once).* Then on the OBSERVATIONS CHART under

the heading "Our Former Lifestyle," list what Ephesians says about how believers used to live before salvation.

6. Mark the other key words (with their synonyms and pronouns) listed on the EPHESIANS AT A GLANCE chart on page 2013. Put these on an index card and use it as a bookmark. Then in the margin list what is said about each key word. Just record the facts.

Chapters 4-6

1. Read Ephesians 4 through 6 chapter by chapter, doing the following:

   a. Mark each occurrence of *live*. Then on the OBSERVATIONS CHART, under the heading "The Way We Live in Christ," list what is taught about the lifestyle of a believer. Also go back to 2:2, 10 and mark and list what these verses teach about the believer's lifestyle. Then ask yourself: How am I to live? Why am I able to live this way?

   b. Continue to mark in the text the key words listed on your bookmark. Also list what you learn from the uses of *former* or *once* in this section of Ephesians. Note the contrast between our former lifestyle and our life in Christ.

   c. Mark the following: *Holy Spirit, in Christ,* and *in the Lord.* Then list what you learn and think about it. This will help you see how to live in him.

2. Record any other observations you have of the text as instructed in the observation section in "How to Use The International Inductive Study Bible" which is on page IISB-15.

3. On EPHESIANS AT A GLANCE:

   a. Record the theme of the book and of each chapter in the appropriate spaces. (Remember to go back and record each chapter's theme in the text next to the chapter number.)

   b. As you have seen, there is a change of emphasis between chapters 3 and 4. Write down under "Segment Divisions" what best summarizes the content of chapters 1 through 3 and then chapters 4 through 6.

∾ THINGS TO THINK ABOUT

1. Stop and review all you observed and listed about your position as a child of God. Go through chapter 1 again and note everything God has done for you. Watch for the personal pronoun *he* (when referring to the Godhead). Also note the phrases *according to* and *in accordance with*, and the words *as* and *will*. Think about what God has done for you and why. Then thank him and tell him you want to live accordingly.

2. Ephesians 2:8-10 are extremely important verses. Think about what God is saying to you and ask God to show you whether you are trusting in his grace or in your works to get you to heaven. But don't stop there. Think about the relationship of good works to the life of a believer. How are you walking? Memorize these verses.

3. In your home do you live according to Ephesians 5:18 through 6:4?

4. Are you able to take a stand or are you defeated by the devil's schemes? Don't forget where you are seated. Think about the armor of God. Do you have it on and are you standing your ground in truth, righteousness, peace, salvation, and faith? Are you able to use the Word of God as your offensive weapon?

Chapter 1 Theme

1 Paul, an apostle[a] of Christ Jesus by the will of God,[b]
To the saints in Ephesus,[a] the faithful[b] in Christ Jesus:

GOD
SOURCE OF GRACE & PEACE
V.2

[2]Grace and peace to you from God our Father and the Lord Jesus Christ.[d]

[3]Praise be to the God and Father of our Lord Jesus Christ,[e] who has blessed us in the heavenly realms[f] with every spiritual blessing in Christ. [4]For he chose us in him before the creation of the world to be holy and blameless[g] in his sight. In love[h] [5]he[c] predestined[i] us to be adopted as his sons through Jesus Christ, in accordance with his pleasure[j] and will— [6]to the praise of his glorious grace, which he has freely given us in the One he loves.[k] [7]In him we have redemption[l] through his blood, the forgiveness of sins, in accordance with the riches of God's grace [8]that he lavished on us with all wisdom and understanding. [9]And he[d] made known to us the mystery[m] of his will according to his good pleasure, which he purposed in Christ, [10]to be put into effect when the times will have reached their fulfillment[n]—to bring all things in heaven and on earth together under one head, even Christ.[o]

[11]In him we were also chosen,[e] having been predestined according to the plan of him who works out everything in conformity with the purpose[p] of his will, [12]in order that we, who were the first to hope in Christ, might be for the praise of his glory.[q] [13]And you also were included in Christ when you heard the word of truth,[r] the gospel of your salvation. Having believed, you were marked in him with a seal,[s] the promised Holy Spirit, [14]who is a deposit guaranteeing our inheritance[t] until the redemption of those who are God's possession—to the praise of his glory.

[15]For this reason, ever since I heard about your faith in the Lord Jesus and your love for all the saints,[u] [16]I have not stopped giving thanks for you,[v] remembering you in my prayers. [17]I keep asking that the God of our Lord Jesus Christ, the glorious Father,[w] may give you the Spirit[f] of wisdom[x] and revelation, so that you may know him better. [18]I pray also that the eyes of your heart may be enlightened[y] in order that you may know the hope to which he has called you, the riches of his glorious inheritance in the saints, [19]and his incomparably great power for us who believe. That power[z] is like the working of his mighty strength,[a] [20]which he exerted in Christ when he raised him from the dead[b] and seated him at his right hand in the heavenly realms, [21]far above all rule and authority,

---

[a]1 Some early manuscripts do not have *in Ephesus*.   [b]1 Or *believers who are*   [c]4,5 Or *sight in love.* [5]*He*   [d]8,9 Or *us. With all wisdom and understanding,* [9]*he*   [e]11 Or *were made heirs*   [f]17 Or *a spirit*

1:1
[a]1Co 1:1
[b]2Co 1:1
[c]Col 1:2

1:2
[d]Ro 1:7

1:3
[e]2Co 1:3
[f]Eph 2:6; 3:10; 6:12

1:4
[g]Eph 5:27; Col 1:22
[h]Eph 4:2,15,16

1:5
[i]Ro 8:29,30
[j]1Co 1:21

1:6
[k]Mt 3:17

1:7
[l]Ro 3:24

1:9
[m]Ro 16:25

1:10
[n]Gal 4:4
[o]Col 1:20

1:11
[p]Eph 3:11; Heb 6:17

1:12
[q]ver 6,14

1:13
[r]Col 1:5
[s]Eph 4:30

1:14
[t]Ac 20:32

1:15
[u]Col 1:4

1:16
[v]Ro 1:8

1:17
[w]Jn 20:17
[x]Col 1:9

1:18
[y]Ac 26:18; 2Co 4:6

1:19
[z]Col 1:29
[a]Eph 6:10

1:20
[b]Ac 2:24

1:21
a Php 2:9,10
1:22
b Mt 28:18
c Eph 4:15; 5:23
2:1
d ver 5;
Col 2:13
2:2
e Col 3:7
f Jn 12:31;
Eph 6:12
g Eph 5:6
2:3
h Gal 5:16
2:5
i ver 1
j ver 8;
Ac 15:11
2:6
k Eph 1:20
l Eph 1:3
2:7
m Tit 3:4
2:8
n ver 5
2:9
o 2Ti 1:9
p 1Co 1:29
2:10
q Eph 4:24
r Tit 2:14
2:11
s Col 2:11
2:12
t Gal 3:17
u 1Th 4:13
2:13
v ver 17;
Ac 2:39
w Col 1:20
2:14
x 1Co 12:13
2:15
y Col 1:21,22
z Col 2:14
a Gal 3:28
2:16
b Col 1:20,22
2:17
c Ps 148:14;
Isa 57:19
2:18
d Eph 3:12
e Col 1:12
f 1Co 12:13
2:19
g ver 12
h Php 3:20
i Gal 6:10
2:20
j Mt 16:18;
Rev 21:14

power and dominion, and every title *a* that can be given, not only in the present age but also in the one to come. 22And God placed all things under his feet *b* and appointed him to be head *c* over everything for the church, 23which is his body, the fullness of him who fills everything in every way.

Chapter 2 Theme

2 As for you, you were dead in your transgressions and sins, *d* 2in which you used to live *e* when you followed the ways of this world and of the ruler of the kingdom of the air, *f* the spirit who is now at work in those who are disobedient. *g* 3All of us also lived among them at one time, gratifying the cravings of our sinful nature *a h* and following its desires and thoughts. Like the rest, we were by nature objects of wrath. 4But because of his great love for us, God, who is rich in mercy, 5made us alive with Christ even when we were dead in transgressions *i*—it is by grace you have been saved. *j* 6And God raised us up with Christ and seated us with him *k* in the heavenly realms *l* in Christ Jesus, 7in order that in the coming ages he might show the incomparable riches of his grace, expressed in his kindness *m* to us in Christ Jesus. 8For it is by grace you have been saved, *n* through faith—and this not from yourselves, it is the gift of God— 9not by works, *o* so that no one can boast. *p* 10For we are God's workmanship, created *q* in Christ Jesus to do good works, *r* which God prepared in advance for us to do.

11Therefore, remember that formerly you who are Gentiles by birth and called "uncircumcised" by those who call themselves "the circumcision" (that done in the body by the hands of men) *s*— 12remember that at that time you were separate from Christ, excluded from citizenship in Israel and foreigners to the covenants of the promise, *t* without hope *u* and without God in the world. 13But now in Christ Jesus you who once were far away have been brought near *v* through the blood of Christ. *w*

14For he himself is our peace, who has made the two one *x* and has destroyed the barrier, the dividing wall of hostility, 15by abolishing in his flesh *y* the law with its commandments and regulations. *z* His purpose was to create in himself one *a* new man out of the two, thus making peace, 16and in this one body to reconcile both of them to God through the cross, *b* by which he put to death their hostility. 17He came and preached peace to you who were far away and peace to those who were near. *c* 18For through him we both have access *d* to the Father *e* by one Spirit. *f*

19Consequently, you are no longer foreigners and aliens, *g* but fellow citizens *h* with God's people and members of God's household, *i* 20built on the foundation *j* of the apostles and prophets, with Christ

a 3 Or *our flesh*

Jesus himself as the chief cornerstone.[a] [21]In him the whole building is joined together and rises to become a holy temple[b] in the Lord. [22]And in him you too are being built together to become a dwelling in which God lives by his Spirit.

Chapter 3 Theme

3 For this reason I, Paul, the prisoner[c] of Christ Jesus for the sake of you Gentiles—

[2]Surely you have heard about the administration of God's grace that was given to me[d] for you, [3]that is, the mystery[e] made known to me by revelation,[f] as I have already written briefly. [4]In reading this, then, you will be able to understand my insight[g] into the mystery of Christ, [5]which was not made known to men in other generations as it has now been revealed by the Spirit to God's holy apostles and prophets.[h] [6]This mystery is that through the gospel the Gentiles are heirs[i] together with Israel, members together of one body,[j] and sharers together in the promise in Christ Jesus.

[7]I became a servant of this gospel[k] by the gift of God's grace given me through the working of his power.[l] [8]Although I am less than the least of all God's people,[m] this grace was given me: to preach to the Gentiles the unsearchable riches of Christ, [9]and to make plain to everyone the administration of this mystery,[n] which for ages past was kept hidden in God, who created all things. [10]His intent was that now, through the church, the manifold wisdom of God[o] should be made known[p] to the rulers and authorities[q] in the heavenly realms, [11]according to his eternal purpose which he accomplished in Christ Jesus our Lord. [12]In him and through faith in him we may approach God[r] with freedom and confidence.[s] [13]I ask you, therefore, not to be discouraged because of my sufferings for you, which are your glory.

[14]For this reason I kneel[t] before the Father, [15]from whom his whole family[a] in heaven and on earth derives its name. [16]I pray that out of his glorious riches he may strengthen you with power[u] through his Spirit in your inner being,[v] [17]so that Christ may dwell in your hearts[w] through faith. And I pray that you, being rooted[x] and established in love, [18]may have power, together with all the saints, to grasp how wide and long and high and deep[y] is the love of Christ, [19]and to know this love that surpasses knowledge—that you may be filled[z] to the measure of all the fullness of God.[a]

[20]Now to him who is able[b] to do immeasurably more than all we ask or imagine, according to his power that is at work within us, [21]to him be glory in the church and in Christ Jesus throughout all generations, for ever and ever! Amen.[c]

a 15 Or *whom all fatherhood*

2:20
a 1Pe 2:4-8

2:21
b 1Co 3:16,17

3:1
c Ac 23:18;
Eph 4:1

3:2
d Col 1:25

3:3
e Ro 16:25
f 1Co 2:10

3:4
g 2Co 11:6

3:5
h Ro 16:26

3:6
i Gal 3:29
j Eph 2:15,16

3:7
k 1Co 3:5
l Eph 1:19

3:8
m 1Co 15:9

3:9
n Ro 16:25

3:10
o 1Co 2:7
p 1Pe 1:12
q Eph 1:21

3:12
r Eph 2:18
s Heb 4:16

3:14
t Php 2:10

3:16
u Col 1:11
v Ro 7:22

3:17
w Jn 14:23
x Col 1:23

3:18
y Job 11:8,9

3:19
z Col 2:10
a Eph 1:23

3:20
b Ro 16:25

3:21
c Ro 11:36

4:1
a Eph 3:1
b Php 1:27;
Col 1:10

4:2
c Col 3:12,13
d Eph 1:4

4:3
e Col 3:14

4:4
f 1Co 12:13

4:6
g Ro 11:36

4:7
h 1Co 12:7,11
i Ro 12:3

4:8
j Col 2:15
k Ps 68:18

4:11
l 1Co 12:28
m Ac 21:8

4:12
n 1Co 12:27

4:13
o ver 3,5
p Col 1:28

4:14
q 1Co 14:20
r Jas 1:6
s Eph 6:11

4:15
t Eph 1:22

4:16
u Col 2:19

4:17
v Ro 1:21

4:18
w Ro 1:21
x Eph 2:12
y 2Co 3:14

4:19
z 1Ti 4:2
a Ro 1:24
b Col 3:5

4:22
c 1Pe 2:1
d Ro 6:6

4:23
e Col 3:10

Chapter 4 Theme

4 As a prisoner[a] for the Lord, then, I urge you to live a life worthy[b] of the calling you have received. ²Be completely humble and gentle; be patient, bearing with one another[c] in love.[d] ³Make every effort to keep the unity[e] of the Spirit through the bond of peace. ⁴There is one body and one Spirit[f]—just as you were called to one hope when you were called— ⁵one Lord, one faith, one baptism; ⁶one God and Father of all, who is over all and through all and in all.[g]

⁷But to each one of us[h] grace has been given[i] as Christ apportioned it. ⁸This is why it[a] says:

> "When he ascended on high,
>   he led captives[j] in his train
>   and gave gifts to men."[b][k]

⁹(What does "he ascended" mean except that he also descended to the lower, earthly regions[c]? ¹⁰He who descended is the very one who ascended higher than all the heavens, in order to fill the whole universe.) ¹¹It was he who gave some to be apostles,[l] some to be prophets, some to be evangelists,[m] and some to be pastors and teachers, ¹²to prepare God's people for works of service, so that the body of Christ[n] may be built up ¹³until we all reach unity[o] in the faith and in the knowledge of the Son of God and become mature,[p] attaining to the whole measure of the fullness of Christ.

¹⁴Then we will no longer be infants,[q] tossed back and forth by the waves,[r] and blown here and there by every wind of teaching and by the cunning and craftiness of men in their deceitful scheming.[s] ¹⁵Instead, speaking the truth in love, we will in all things grow up into him who is the Head,[t] that is, Christ. ¹⁶From him the whole body, joined and held together by every supporting ligament, grows[u] and builds itself up in love, as each part does its work.

¹⁷So I tell you this, and insist on it in the Lord, that you must no longer live as the Gentiles do, in the futility of their thinking.[v] ¹⁸They are darkened in their understanding[w] and separated from the life of God[x] because of the ignorance that is in them due to the hardening of their hearts.[y] ¹⁹Having lost all sensitivity,[z] they have given themselves over[a] to sensuality[b] so as to indulge in every kind of impurity, with a continual lust for more.

²⁰You, however, did not come to know Christ that way. ²¹Surely you heard of him and were taught in him in accordance with the truth that is in Jesus. ²²You were taught, with regard to your former way of life, to put off[c] your old self,[d] which is being corrupted by its deceitful desires; ²³to be made new in the attitude of your minds;[e]

a 8 Or *God*   b 8 Psalm 68:18   c 9 Or *the depths of the earth*

[24]and to put on the new self,[a] created to be like God in true righteousness and holiness.[b]

[25]Therefore each of you must put off falsehood and speak truthfully[c] to his neighbor, for we are all members of one body.[d] [26]"In your anger do not sin"[a]: Do not let the sun go down while you are still angry, [27]and do not give the devil a foothold. [28]He who has been stealing must steal no longer, but must work,[e] doing something useful with his own hands,[f] that he may have something to share with those in need.[g]

[29]Do not let any unwholesome talk come out of your mouths,[h] but only what is helpful for building others up according to their needs, that it may benefit those who listen. [30]And do not grieve the Holy Spirit of God,[i] with whom you were sealed for the day of redemption.[j] [31]Get rid of all bitterness, rage and anger, brawling and slander, along with every form of malice.[k] [32]Be kind and compassionate to one another, forgiving each other, just as in Christ God forgave you.[l]

Chapter 5 Theme

5 Be imitators of God,[m] therefore, as dearly loved children [2]and live a life of love, just as Christ loved us and gave himself up for us[n] as a fragrant offering and sacrifice to God.[o]

[3]But among you there must not be even a hint of sexual immorality, or of any kind of impurity, or of greed,[p] because these are improper for God's holy people. [4]Nor should there be obscenity, foolish talk or coarse joking, which are out of place, but rather thanksgiving.[q] [5]For of this you can be sure: No immoral, impure or greedy person—such a man is an idolater[r]—has any inheritance in the kingdom of Christ and of God.[b][s] [6]Let no one deceive you with empty words, for because of such things God's wrath[t] comes on those who are disobedient. [7]Therefore do not be partners with them.

[8]For you were once[u] darkness, but now you are light in the Lord. Live as children of light[v] [9](for the fruit[w] of the light consists in all goodness, righteousness and truth) [10]and find out what pleases the Lord. [11]Have nothing to do with the fruitless deeds of darkness, but rather expose them. [12]For it is shameful even to mention what the disobedient do in secret. [13]But everything exposed by the light[x] becomes visible, [14]for it is light that makes everything visible. This is why it is said:

> "Wake up, O sleeper,[y]
> rise from the dead,[z]
> and Christ will shine on you."[a]

[a] 26 Psalm 4:4   [b] 5 Or *kingdom of the Christ and God*

4:24
[a] Ro 6:4
[b] Eph 2:10

4:25
[c] Zec 8:16
[d] Ro 12:5

4:28
[e] Ac 20:35
[f] 1Th 4:11
[g] Lk 3:11

4:29
[h] Col 3:8

4:30
[i] 1Th 5:19
[j] Ro 8:23

4:31
[k] Col 3:8

4:32
[l] Mt 6:14,15

5:1
[m] Lk 6:36

5:2
[n] Gal 1:4
[o] 2Co 2:15;
Heb 7:27

5:3
[p] Col 3:5

5:4
[q] ver 20

5:5
[r] Col 3:5
[s] 1Co 6:9

5:6
[t] Ro 1:18

5:8
[u] Eph 2:2
[v] Lk 16:8

5:9
[w] Gal 5:22

5:13
[x] Jn 3:20,21

5:14
[y] Ro 13:11
[z] Jn 5:25
[a] Isa 60:1

5:16
a Col 4:5
b Eph 6:13

5:17
c Ro 12:2;
1Th 4:3

5:18
d Pr 20:1
e Lk 1:15

5:19
f Ac 16:25;
Col 3:16

5:20
g Ps 34:1

5:21
h Gal 5:13

5:22
i Ge 3:16;
1Pe 3:1,5,6
j Eph 6:5

5:23
k 1Co 11:3;
Eph 1:22

5:25
l Col 3:19
m ver 2

5:26
n Ac 22:16

5:27
o Eph 1:4;
Col 1:22

5:28
p ver 25

5:30
q 1Co 12:27

5:31
r Ge 2:24;
Mt 19:5;
1Co 6:16

5:33
s ver 25

6:1
t Col 3:20

6:3
u Ex 20:12

6:4
v Col 3:21
w Ge 18:19;
Dt 6:7

6:5
x 1Ti 6:1
y Col 3:22
z Eph 5:22

6:7
a Col 3:23

6:8
b Col 3:24

6:9
c Job 31:13,14

[15]Be very careful, then, how you live—not as unwise but as wise, [16]making the most of every opportunity,[a] because the days are evil.[b] [17]Therefore do not be foolish, but understand what the Lord's will is.[c] [18]Do not get drunk on wine,[d] which leads to debauchery. Instead, be filled with the Spirit.[e] [19]Speak to one another with psalms, hymns and spiritual songs.[f] Sing and make music in your heart to the Lord, [20]always giving thanks[g] to God the Father for everything, in the name of our Lord Jesus Christ.

[21]Submit to one another[h] out of reverence for Christ.

[22]Wives, submit to your husbands[i] as to the Lord.[j] [23]For the husband is the head of the wife as Christ is the head of the church,[k] his body, of which he is the Savior. [24]Now as the church submits to Christ, so also wives should submit to their husbands in everything.

[25]Husbands, love your wives,[l] just as Christ loved the church and gave himself up for her[m] [26]to make her holy, cleansing[a] her by the washing[n] with water through the word, [27]and to present her to himself as a radiant church, without stain or wrinkle or any other blemish, but holy and blameless.[o] [28]In this same way, husbands ought to love their wives[p] as their own bodies. He who loves his wife loves himself. [29]After all, no one ever hated his own body, but he feeds and cares for it, just as Christ does the church— [30]for we are members of his body.[q] [31]"For this reason a man will leave his father and mother and be united to his wife, and the two will become one flesh."[b][r] [32]This is a profound mystery—but I am talking about Christ and the church. [33]However, each one of you also must love his wife[s] as he loves himself, and the wife must respect her husband.

Chapter 6 Theme

6 Children, obey your parents in the Lord, for this is right.[t] [2]"Honor your father and mother"—which is the first commandment with a promise— [3]"that it may go well with you and that you may enjoy long life on the earth."[c][u]

[4]Fathers, do not exasperate your children;[v] instead, bring them up in the training and instruction of the Lord.[w]

[5]Slaves, obey your earthly masters with respect[x] and fear, and with sincerity of heart,[y] just as you would obey Christ.[z] [6]Obey them not only to win their favor when their eye is on you, but like slaves of Christ, doing the will of God from your heart. [7]Serve wholeheartedly, as if you were serving the Lord, not men,[a] [8]because you know that the Lord will reward everyone for whatever good he does,[b] whether he is slave or free.

[9]And masters, treat your slaves in the same way. Do not threaten them, since you know that he who is both their Master and yours[c] is in heaven, and there is no favoritism with him.

a 26 Or *having cleansed* b 31 Gen. 2:24 c 3 Deut. 5:16

[10]Finally, be strong in the Lord[a] and in his mighty power.[b] [11]Put on the full armor of God[c] so that you can take your stand against the devil's schemes. [12]For our struggle is not against flesh and blood, but against the rulers, against the authorities,[d] against the powers[e] of this dark world and against the spiritual forces of evil in the heavenly realms.[f] [13]Therefore put on the full armor of God, so that when the day of evil comes, you may be able to stand your ground, and after you have done everything, to stand. [14]Stand firm then, with the belt of truth buckled around your waist,[g] with the breastplate of righteousness in place,[h] [15]and with your feet fitted with the readiness that comes from the gospel of peace.[i] [16]In addition to all this, take up the shield of faith,[j] with which you can extinguish all the flaming arrows of the evil one. [17]Take the helmet of salvation[k] and the sword of the Spirit, which is the word of God.[l] [18]And pray in the Spirit on all occasions[m] with all kinds of prayers and requests.[n] With this in mind, be alert and always keep on praying for all the saints.

[19]Pray also for me,[o] that whenever I open my mouth, words may be given me so that I will fearlessly[p] make known the mystery of the gospel, [20]for which I am an ambassador[q] in chains.[r] Pray that I may declare it fearlessly, as I should.

[21]Tychicus,[s] the dear brother and faithful servant in the Lord, will tell you everything, so that you also may know how I am and what I am doing. [22]I am sending him to you for this very purpose, that you may know how we are,[t] and that he may encourage you.

[23]Peace[u] to the brothers, and love with faith from God the Father and the Lord Jesus Christ. [24]Grace to all who love our Lord Jesus Christ with an undying love.

6:10
[a]1Co 16:13
[b]Eph 1:19

6:11
[c]Ro 13:12

6:12
[d]Eph 1:21
[e]Ro 8:38
[f]Eph 1:3

6:14
[g]Isa 11:5
[h]Isa 59:17

6:15
[i]Isa 52:7

6:16
[j]1Jn 5:4

6:17
[k]Isa 59:17
[l]Heb 4:12

6:18
[m]Lk 18:1
[n]Mt 26:41;
Php 1:4

6:19
[o]1Th 5:25
[p]Ac 4:29;
2Co 3:12

6:20
[q]2Co 5:20
[r]Ac 21:33

6:21
[s]Ac 20:4

6:22
[t]Col 4:7-9

6:23
[u]Gal 6:16;
1Pe 5:14

EPHESIANS OBSERVATIONS CHART

OUR WEALTH AND POSITION IN CHRIST
EVERY SPIRTUAL BLESSING (1:3) CHOSEN BEFORE CREATION (1:4) HOLY + BLAMELESS (1:4) PREDESTINED ADOPTED AS SONS (1:5) REDEMPTION + FORGIVENESS (1:7) REVEALED MYSTERY OF HIS WILL (1:9)

(continued

EPHESIANS OBSERVATIONS CHART

OUR RELATIONSHIP WITH THE HOLY SPIRIT

OUR FORMER LIFESTYLE	**THE WAY WE LIVE IN CHRIST**

EPHESIANS AT A GLANCE

Theme of Ephesians:

Author:

Date:

Purpose:

Key Words:

every reference
to God, in
Christ (in him,
in the Lord)

the (Holy) Spirit

rich(es)

in the heavenly
realms

former (for-
merly, used to,
at one time,
once)

grace, benefit

power
(strength)

body (church)

redemption

live (do)

mark every
reference to
the devil
(including
powers, rulers,
authorities, etc.)

SEGMENT DIVISIONS	CHAPTER THEMES
1	
2	
3	
4	
5	
6	

PHILIPPIANS

*B*locked by the Spirit of God from going into Asia and Bithynia, Paul had a vision of a man from Macedonia asking him to come to Macedonia and help the churches there.

Confident that God had given him direction, Paul sailed with Timothy and Luke from Troas on a second missionary journey. Philippi, in Macedonia, basked in the fact that it was also a Roman colony which ensured its citizens all the benefits of Roman citizenship.

As was his custom, when Paul reached a city he sought out the Jews. While there were not enough Jews living in Philippi to form a synagogue, the Jews there met for prayer on the Sabbath. Little did Paul realize that he would end up in prison. God knew there was a Roman jailer and his family who needed Jesus.

The events of that day inaugurated the beginning of the church at Philippi, the church Paul addressed as he took pen in hand around the year A.D. 61 or 62.

∾ THINGS TO DO

1. Familiarize yourself with the message of Philippians by reading the entire book in one sitting. As you read, look for the verses in chapters 1 and 4 which tell where Paul is as he writes.

2. To understand the historical setting of Philippians, read Acts 15:35 through 17:1, which records Paul's first visit to Philippi. After his third missionary journey, Paul went to Jerusalem, where he was arrested. From there Paul was taken by a Roman guard to Caesarea, the Mediterranean seaport where the Roman consulate often went to escape the heat and confines of Jerusalem. After remaining a prisoner in Caesarea for over two years, Paul, who as a Roman citizen had appealed to Caesar, was sent to Rome, where he lived under house arrest. Read Acts 28:14-31 and note how long Paul remained a prisoner at Rome. How does this compare with where Paul was when he wrote Philippians?

3. As you read Philippians chapter by chapter, do the following.

   a. Under "Author" on your OBSERVATIONS CHART on page 2021 note where Paul is, why he is there, and what his attitude is in the midst of his difficult circumstances.

   b. In a distinctive way, mark in the text each key word (and its synonyms and pronouns) that is listed on the PHILIPPIANS AT A GLANCE chart on page 2023. This will help you discover the themes (main subjects) of each chapter and of the book itself. Watch for other key words which are not listed but which may be emphasized in a particular chapter of Philippians.

   c. In the margin list what you learn from the text about each of the key words in Philippians.

   d. Record any other observations as instructed and demonstrated in the observation section in "How to Use The International Inductive Study Bible" on page IISB-15.

   e. List each of the instructions Paul gives to the Philippian saints on the chart PAUL'S INSTRUCTIONS TO THE PHILIPPIANS on page 2022. As you list these instructions, evaluate your life in the light of each one.

4. On PHILIPPIANS AT A GLANCE:

   a. Fill in the theme for the book and for each chapter. (Be sure you also record the chapter theme in the text next to the chapter number.)

   b. Under "Segment Divisions" record what you see to be Paul's example in each chapter. Remember, in Philippians 3:17 Paul tells his readers to follow his example.

   c. In the next column under "Segment Divisions" write down what each chapter says about who or what Jesus Christ is in relation to the believer.

d. For another segment division, record a command to believers that correlates with the theme of each chapter.

∞ THINGS TO THINK ABOUT

1. What have you learned from Philippians about your relationship to suffering as a Christian? How is it going to affect the way you respond to suffering?

2. Can you say with Paul, "For to me, to live is Christ and to die is gain"? If you can't, think about what has replaced Christ's rightful place in your life.

3. What have you learned from Jesus' example that you can apply to your own life? Do you have the attitude of Christ in respect to God and others? Do you regard others as more important than yourself?

4. Do you allow your circumstances to affect your peace? What is keeping you from his peace? After reading Philippians 4 do you see any way to handle life's anxieties?

5. What have you learned about your own needs and sharing with others in need?

∞∞∞∞

Chapter 1 Theme

1 Paul and Timothy,[a] servants of Christ Jesus,

To all the saints[b] in Christ Jesus at Philippi,[c] together with the overseers[a][d] and deacons:[e]

[2] Grace and peace to you from God our Father and the Lord Jesus Christ.[f]

[3] I thank my God every time I remember you.[g] [4] In all my prayers for all of you, I always pray[h] with joy [5] because of your partnership[i] in the gospel from the first day[j] until now, [6] being confident of this, that he who began a good work in you will carry it on to completion until the day of Christ Jesus.[k]

[7] It is right[l] for me to feel this way about all of you, since I have you in my heart;[m] for whether I am in chains[n] or defending[o] and confirming the gospel, all of you share in God's grace with me. [8] God can testify[p] how I long for all of you with the affection of Christ Jesus.

[9] And this is my prayer: that your love[q] may abound more and more in knowledge and depth of insight, [10] so that you may be able to discern what is best and may be pure and blameless until the day of Christ,[r] [11] filled with the fruit of righteousness[s] that comes through Jesus Christ—to the glory and praise of God.

[12] Now I want you to know, brothers, that what has happened to me has really served to advance the gospel. [13] As a result, it has become clear throughout the whole palace guard[b] and to everyone else that I am in chains[t] for Christ. [14] Because of my chains,[u] most of the brothers in the Lord have been encouraged to speak the word of God more courageously and fearlessly.

1:1
a Ac 16:1;
2Co 1:1
b Ac 9:13
c Ac 16:12
d 1Ti 3:1
e 1Ti 3:8

1:2
f Ro 1:7

1:3
g Ro 1:8

1:4
h Ro 1:10

1:5
i Ac 2:42;
Php 4:15
j Ac 16:12-40

1:6
k ver 10;
1Co 1:8

1:7
l 2Pe 1:13
m 2Co 7:3
n ver 13,14,17;
Ac 21:33
o ver 16

1:8
p Ro 1:9

1:9
q 1Th 3:12

1:10
r ver 6;
1Co 1:8

1:11
s Jas 3:18

1:13
t ver 7,14,17

1:14
u ver 7,13,17

a 1 Traditionally *bishops*   b 13 Or *whole palace*

¹⁵It is true that some preach Christ out of envy and rivalry, but others out of goodwill. ¹⁶The latter do so in love, knowing that I am put here for the defense of the gospel.ᵃ ¹⁷The former preach Christ out of selfish ambition,ᵇ not sincerely, supposing that they can stir up trouble for me while I am in chains.ᵃᶜ ¹⁸But what does it matter? The important thing is that in every way, whether from false motives or true, Christ is preached. And because of this I rejoice.

Yes, and I will continue to rejoice, ¹⁹for I know that through your prayersᵈ and the help given by the Spirit of Jesus Christ,ᵉ what has happened to me will turn out for my deliverance.ᵇ ²⁰I eagerly expectᶠ and hope that I will in no way be ashamed, but will have sufficient courageᵍ so that now as always Christ will be exalted in my body,ʰ whether by life or by death.ⁱ ²¹For to me, to live is Christʲ and to die is gain. ²²If I am to go on living in the body, this will mean fruitful labor for me. Yet what shall I choose? I do not know! ²³I am torn between the two: I desire to departᵏ and be with Christ,ˡ which is better by far; ²⁴but it is more necessary for you that I remain in the body. ²⁵Convinced of this, I know that I will remain, and I will continue with all of you for your progress and joy in the faith, ²⁶so that through my being with you again your joy in Christ Jesus will overflow on account of me.

²⁷Whatever happens, conduct yourselves in a manner worthyᵐ of the gospel of Christ. Then, whether I come and see you or only hear about you in my absence, I will know that you stand firmⁿ in one spirit, contendingᵒ as one man for the faith of the gospel ²⁸without being frightened in any way by those who oppose you. This is a sign to them that they will be destroyed, but that you will be saved—and that by God. ²⁹For it has been granted to youᵖ on behalf of Christ not only to believe on him, but also to suffer�q for him, ³⁰since you are going through the same struggleʳ you sawˢ I had, and now hearᵗ that I still have.

Chapter 2 Theme

2 If you have any encouragement from being united with Christ, if any comfort from his love, if any fellowship with the Spirit,ᵘ if any tenderness and compassion,ᵛ ²then make my joy completeʷ by being like-minded,ˣ having the same love, being oneʸ in spirit and purpose. ³Do nothing out of selfish ambition or vain conceit,ᶻ but in humility consider others better than yourselves.ᵃ ⁴Each of you should look not only to your own interests, but also to the interests of others.

⁵Your attitude should be the same as that of Christ Jesus:ᵇ

ᵃ 16,17 Some late manuscripts have verses 16 and 17 in reverse order.   ᵇ 19 Or *salvation*

### Cross references (margin)

1:16
ᵃ ver 7,12

1:17
ᵇ Php 2:3
ᶜ ver 7,13,14

1:19
ᵈ 2Co 1:11
ᵉ Ac 16:7

1:20
ᶠ Ro 8:19
ᵍ ver 14
ʰ 1Co 6:20
ⁱ Ro 14:8

1:21
ʲ Gal 2:20

1:23
ᵏ 2Ti 4:6
ˡ Jn 12:26;
2Co 5:8

1:27
ᵐ Eph 4:1
ⁿ 1Co 16:13
ᵒ Jude 3

1:29
ᵖ Mt 5:11,12
q Ac 14:22

1:30
ʳ Col 2:1;
1Th 2:2
ˢ Ac 16:19-40
ᵗ ver 13

2:1
ᵘ 2Co 13:14
ᵛ Col 3:12

2:2
ʷ Jn 3:29
ˣ Php 4:2
ʸ Ro 12:16

2:3
ᶻ Gal 5:26
ᵃ Ro 12:10;
1Pe 5:5

2:5
ᵇ Mt 11:29

2:6
a Jn 1:1
b Jn 5:18

2:7
c Mt 20:28
d Jn 1:14;
Heb 2:17

2:8
e Mt 26:39;
Jn 10:18;
Heb 5:8

2:9
f Ac 2:33;
Heb 2:9
g Eph 1:20,21

2:10
h Ro 14:11
i Mt 28:18

2:11
j Jn 13:13

2:12
k 2Co 7:15

2:13
l Ezr 1:5

2:14
m 1Co 10:10;
1Pe 4:9

2:15
n Mt 5:45,48;
Eph 5:1
o Ac 2:40

2:16
p 1Th 2:19

2:17
q 2Ti 4:6
r Ro 15:16

2:19
s ver 23

2:20
t 1Co 16:10

2:21
u 1Co 10:24;
13:5

2:22
v 1Co 4:17;
1Ti 1:2

2:23
w ver 19

2:24
x Php 1:25

2:25
y Php 4:3
z Phm 2
a Php 4:18

2:26
b Php 1:8

⁶Who, being in very nature*a* God,*a*
did not consider equality with God*b* something to
be grasped,
⁷but made himself nothing,
taking the very nature*b* of a servant,*c*
being made in human likeness.*d*
⁸And being found in appearance as a man,
he humbled himself
and became obedient to death*e*—
even death on a cross!
⁹Therefore God exalted him*f* to the highest place
and gave him the name that is above every name,*g*
¹⁰that at the name of Jesus every knee should bow,*h*
in heaven and on earth and under the earth,*i*
¹¹and every tongue confess that Jesus Christ is Lord,*j*
to the glory of God the Father.

¹²Therefore, my dear friends, as you have always obeyed—not only in my presence, but now much more in my absence—continue to work out your salvation with fear and trembling,*k* ¹³for it is God who works in you*l* to will and to act according to his good purpose.

¹⁴Do everything without complaining*m* or arguing, ¹⁵so that you may become blameless and pure, children of God*n* without fault in a crooked and depraved generation,*o* in which you shine like stars in the universe ¹⁶as you hold out*c* the word of life—in order that I may boast on the day of Christ that I did not run or labor for nothing.*p* ¹⁷But even if I am being poured out like a drink offering*q* on the sacrifice*r* and service coming from your faith, I am glad and rejoice with all of you. ¹⁸So you too should be glad and rejoice with me.

¹⁹I hope in the Lord Jesus to send Timothy to you soon,*s* that I also may be cheered when I receive news about you. ²⁰I have no one else like him,*t* who takes a genuine interest in your welfare. ²¹For everyone looks out for his own interests,*u* not those of Jesus Christ. ²²But you know that Timothy has proved himself, because as a son with his father*v* he has served with me in the work of the gospel. ²³I hope, therefore, to send him as soon as I see how things go with me.*w* ²⁴And I am confident*x* in the Lord that I myself will come soon.

²⁵But I think it is necessary to send back to you Epaphroditus, my brother, fellow worker*y* and fellow soldier,*z* who is also your messenger, whom you sent to take care of my needs.*a* ²⁶For he longs for all of you*b* and is distressed because you heard he was ill. ²⁷Indeed he was ill, and almost died. But God had mercy on him, and not on him only but also on me, to spare me sorrow upon sorrow. ²⁸Therefore I am all the more eager to send him, so that when you see him

a 6 Or *in the form of*   *b* 7 Or *the form*   *c* 16 Or *hold on to* again you may be glad and I may have less anxiety. ²⁹Welcome him in the Lord with great joy, and honor men like him,[a] ³⁰because he almost died for the work of Christ, risking his life to make up for the help you could not give me.[b]

Chapter 3 Theme _____

3 Finally, my brothers, rejoice in the Lord! It is no trouble for me to write the same things to you again, and it is a safeguard for you.

²Watch out for those dogs,[c] those men who do evil, those mutilators of the flesh. ³For it is we who are the circumcision,[d] we who worship by the Spirit of God, who glory in Christ Jesus, and who put no confidence in the flesh— ⁴though I myself have reasons for such confidence.

If anyone else thinks he has reasons to put confidence in the flesh, I have more: ⁵circumcised[e] on the eighth day, of the people of Israel,[f] of the tribe of Benjamin,[g] a Hebrew of Hebrews; in regard to the law, a Pharisee;[h] ⁶as for zeal, persecuting the church;[i] as for legalistic righteousness,[j] faultless.

⁷But whatever was to my profit I now consider loss[k] for the sake of Christ. ⁸What is more, I consider everything a loss compared to the surpassing greatness of knowing[l] Christ Jesus my Lord, for whose sake I have lost all things. I consider them rubbish, that I may gain Christ ⁹and be found in him, not having a righteousness of my own that comes from the law,[m] but that which is through faith in Christ—the righteousness that comes from God and is by faith.[n] ¹⁰I want to know Christ and the power of his resurrection and the fellowship of sharing in his sufferings,[o] becoming like him in his death,[p] ¹¹and so, somehow, to attain to the resurrection[q] from the dead.

¹²Not that I have already obtained all this, or have already been made perfect,[r] but I press on to take hold[s] of that for which Christ Jesus took hold of me.[t] ¹³Brothers, I do not consider myself yet to have taken hold of it. But one thing I do: Forgetting what is behind[u] and straining toward what is ahead, ¹⁴I press on[v] toward the goal to win the prize for which God has called[w] me heavenward in Christ Jesus.

¹⁵All of us who are mature[x] should take such a view of things.[y] And if on some point you think differently, that too God will make clear to you. ¹⁶Only let us live up to what we have already attained.

¹⁷Join with others in following my example,[z] brothers, and take note of those who live according to the pattern we gave you. ¹⁸For, as I have often told you before and now say again even with tears,[a] many live as enemies of the cross of Christ.[b] ¹⁹Their destiny is destruction, their god is their stomach,[c] and their glory is in their

2:29
[a] 1Co 16:18;
1Ti 5:17

2:30
[b] 1Co 16:17

3:2
[c] Ps 22:16,20

3:3
[d] Ro 2:28,29;
Gal 6:15;
Col 2:11

3:5
[e] Lk 1:59
[f] 2Co 11:22
[g] Ro 11:1
[h] Ac 23:6

3:6
[i] Ac 8:3
[j] Ro 10:5

3:7
[k] Mt 13:44;
Lk 14:33

3:8
[l] Eph 4:13;
2Pe 1:2

3:9
[m] Ro 10:5
[n] Ro 9:30

3:10
[o] Ro 8:17
[p] Ro 6:3-5

3:11
[q] Rev 20:5,6

3:12
[r] 1Co 13:10
[s] 1Ti 6:12
[t] Ac 9:5,6

3:13
[u] Lk 9:62

3:14
[v] Heb 6:1
[w] Ro 8:28

3:15
[x] 1Co 2:6
[y] Gal 5:10

3:17
[z] 1Co 4:16;
1Pe 5:3

3:18
[a] Ac 20:31
[b] Gal 6:12

3:19
[c] Ro 16:18

3:19
a Ro 6:21
b Ro 8:5,6

3:20
c Eph 2:19
d Col 3:1
e 1Co 1:7

3:21
f Eph 1:19
g 1Co 15:43-53
h Col 3:4

4:1
i Php 1:8
j 1Co 16:13;
Php 1:27

4:2
k Php 2:2

4:4
l Ro 12:12;
Php 3:1

4:5
m Heb 10:37;
Jas 5:8,9

4:6
n Mt 6:25-34
o Eph 6:18

4:7
p Isa 26:3;
Jn 14:27;
Col 3:15

4:9
q Php 3:17
r Ro 15:33

4:10
s 2Co 11:9

4:11
t 1Ti 6:6,8

4:12
u 1Co 4:11
v 2Co 11:9

4:13
w 2Co 12:9

4:14
x Php 1:7

4:15
y Php 1:5
z 2Co 11:8,9

4:16
a Ac 17:1
b 1Th 2:9

4:17
c 1Co 9:11,12

4:18
d Php 2:25
e 2Co 2:14

shame.*a* Their mind is on earthly things.*b* **20**But our citizenship*c* is in heaven.*d* And we eagerly await a Savior from there, the Lord Jesus Christ,*e* **21**who, by the power*f* that enables him to bring everything under his control, will transform our lowly bodies*g* so that they will be like his glorious body.*h*

Chapter 4 Theme

4 Therefore, my brothers, you whom I love and long for,*i* my joy and crown, that is how you should stand firm*j* in the Lord, dear friends!

2I plead with Euodia and I plead with Syntyche to agree with each other*k* in the Lord. **3**Yes, and I ask you, loyal yokefellow,*a* help these women who have contended at my side in the cause of the gospel, along with Clement and the rest of my fellow workers, whose names are in the book of life.

4Rejoice in the Lord always. I will say it again: Rejoice!*l* **5**Let your gentleness be evident to all. The Lord is near.*m* **6**Do not be anxious about anything,*n* but in everything, by prayer and petition, with thanksgiving, present your requests to God.*o* **7**And the peace of God,*p* which transcends all understanding, will guard your hearts and your minds in Christ Jesus.

8Finally, brothers, whatever is true, whatever is noble, whatever is right, whatever is pure, whatever is lovely, whatever is admirable—if anything is excellent or praiseworthy—think about such things. **9**Whatever you have learned or received or heard from me, or seen in me—put it into practice.*q* And the God of peace*r* will be with you.

10I rejoice greatly in the Lord that at last you have renewed your concern for me.*s* Indeed, you have been concerned, but you had no opportunity to show it. **11**I am not saying this because I am in need, for I have learned to be content*t* whatever the circumstances. **12**I know what it is to be in need, and I know what it is to have plenty. I have learned the secret of being content in any and every situation, whether well fed or hungry,*u* whether living in plenty or in want.*v* **13**I can do everything through him who gives me strength.*w*

14Yet it was good of you to share*x* in my troubles. **15**Moreover, as you Philippians know, in the early days*y* of your acquaintance with the gospel, when I set out from Macedonia, not one church shared with me in the matter of giving and receiving, except you only;*z* **16**for even when I was in Thessalonica,*a* you sent me aid again and again when I was in need.*b* **17**Not that I am looking for a gift, but I am looking for what may be credited to your account.*c* **18**I have received full payment and even more; I am amply supplied, now that I have received from Epaphroditus*d* the gifts you sent. They are a fragrant*e* offering, an acceptable sacrifice, pleasing to God.

a 3 Or *loyal Syzygus*

¹⁹And my God will meet all your needs*ᵃ* according to his glorious riches*ᵇ* in Christ Jesus.

²⁰To our God and Father*ᶜ* be glory for ever and ever. Amen.*ᵈ*

²¹Greet all the saints in Christ Jesus. The brothers who are with me*ᵉ* send greetings. ²²All the saints*ᶠ* send you greetings, especially those who belong to Caesar's household.

²³The grace of the Lord Jesus Christ*ᵍ* be with your spirit. Amen.*ᵃ*

ᵃ 23 Some manuscripts do not have *Amen.*

4:19
ᵃ Ps 23:1;
2Co 9:8
ᵇ Ro 2:4
4:20
ᶜ Gal 1:4
ᵈ Ro 11:36
4:21
ᵉ Gal 1:2
4:22
ᶠ Ac 9:13
4:23
ᵍ Ro 16:20

Philippians Observations Chart

AUTHOR: *Look for both pronouns and direct references*

_____
_____
_____
_____
_____
_____
_____
_____
_____
_____
_____
_____
_____
_____
_____
_____
_____
_____
_____
_____
_____
_____
_____
_____
_____
_____
_____

THE RECIPIENTS: *Look for the saints, brothers, dear friends, you, or any other ways Paul addresses those to whom he is writing. (Remember to keep asking the five W's and an H: How does Paul describe the Philippians? What are their problems? What is his concern for them? Why is Paul writing to the Philippians?)*

_____
_____
_____
_____
_____
_____

(continued)

PHILIPPIANS OBSERVATIONS CHART

PAUL'S INSTRUCTIONS TO THE PHILIPPIANS

(continued)

PAUL'S INSTRUCTIONS TO THE PHILIPPIANS

PHILIPPIANS AT A GLANCE

Theme of Philippians:

Author:

Date:

Purpose:

Key Words:

Christ Jesus

joy (rejoice, be glad)

like-minded, think(s) (attitude, take such a view of things)

gospel

SEGMENT DIVISIONS			
COMMAND TO:	JESUS IS:	PAUL'S EXAMPLE	CHAPTER THEMES
		1:21 MY LIFE	1
			2
3:17 FOLLOW PAUL'S EXAMPLE			3
		4:11 LEARNED TO BE CONTENT IN HIS CIRCUMSTANCES	4

COLOSSIANS

Colosse was located twelve miles from Laodicea and about a hundred miles east of Ephesus in the valley of the Lycus River in the southern part of ancient Phrygia, the adopted home of Oriental mysticism. Many Jews, Phrygians, and Greeks came to Colosse because it was on a main trade route. The mixture of backgrounds made the city an interesting cultural center where all sorts of new ideas and doctrines from the East were discussed and considered.

With all these ungodly influences, it is no wonder that the Christians at Colosse were on Paul's heart during his imprisonment in Rome. He may never have seen their faces, but they belonged to his Christ and he was one with them in spirit. Physically he might be bound by chains, but he could reach them by letter. This was one way he could protect them from the wolves who were out to devour God's flock.

Paul wrote sometime around A.D. 62. This letter to the faithful saints at Colosse was one whose message would be needed down through the ages. Maybe that is one of the reasons God didn't let Paul deliver this message in person.

∾ THINGS TO DO

1. As you read Colossians chapter by chapter, learn all you can from the text about the author and the recipients and discover why the author writes what he does to this particular church. This will give you the key to understanding Colossians. Following this simple procedure will help:

   a. As you read, ask the five W's and an H: Who? What? Where? Why? When? and How? Ask questions such as: Who wrote this? To whom? Where were they? What were these people like? What were their situations? What were their problems? When was this written? What seemed to be going on? Why did the author say what he did?

   Asking questions like these—answered only from what the text says—gives insight into a book of the Bible and helps you to understand the context and purpose of the book and to keep its teachings and truths in their proper context.

   b. As you read, watch for every reference to the author(s) (including names and pronouns such as *I, my, we, us*). Keep asking the five W's and an H and record your insights on the OBSERVATIONS CHART on pages 2031, 2032.

   c. Look for pronouns such as *you* and note the relationship between the author and the recipients. Ask questions such as: How did the gospel get to the Colossians? Who preached the gospel to them? What was the author's main concern for the Colossians? The answers will help you understand why this letter was written. Record your insights on the OBSERVATIONS CHART.

2. Now read through Colossians again, a chapter at a time. As you read:

   a. Mark in the text the key words and phrases that are listed on the COLOSSIANS AT A GLANCE chart on page 2032. Be sure to mark the synonyms and pronouns for each key word, and also mark every reference to Jesus: *with him, by him, for him, through him,* and so on.

   b. In the margin, list what you learn from marking *in him,* and from marking other key words.

   c. Also record any other observations of the text as instructed in the observation section of "How to Use The International Inductive Study Bible" on page IISB-15.

3. When you get to chapter 2, note the warnings in this chapter by looking for the phrases *see to it* and *do not let anyone.*

   a. Record these warnings along with any instructions on the OBSERVATIONS CHART.

b. With these warnings in mind read the section called "Understanding Gnosticism" on page 2204.

4. Proceed through chapters 3 and 4, adding pertinent information to your OBSERVATIONS CHART.

5. Be sure to record the theme of the book and of each chapter on the COLOSSIANS AT A GLANCE chart. Remember to record the chapter theme in the text next to the chapter number. Also fill out the date the book was written, the name of the author, and his purpose for writing.

∾ THINGS TO THINK ABOUT

1. What are you pursuing? Does it have eternal value? Is it drawing you closer to God or keeping you from time alone with God in prayer and in studying the Word? Are you seeking things above or earthly things?

2. Are you being deluded with any modern-day philosophies or traditions which contradict the Word or aren't in the Word? Any legalistic rules which are not clearly taught in the New Testament? Any mystical teachings or prophecies that can't be supported in the Word of God or that have a tendency to add something which isn't there or which seem to be only for an elite group of people?

3. Inductive Bible study is not easy. The enemy will do all he can to keep you from knowing God and his Word intimately, for it is your major defense and offense in spiritual warfare. Are you going to make it your goal to let the Word of Christ richly dwell within you and to walk in its precepts?

4. Are you proclaiming the Lord Jesus Christ and holding firmly to all he is and all that you have in him as he is presented in Colossians?

5. As you have studied Colossians, have you seen any areas in your life in which you are falling short or simply walking in disobedience to God's Word? What are you going to do about these?

∾∾∾∾∾

1:1
a 1Co 1:1
b 2Co 1:1

1:2
c Col 4:18
d Ro 1:7

1:3
e Ro 1:8

1:4
f Gal 5:6
g Eph 1:15

1:5
h 1Th 5:8;
Tit 1:2
i 1Pe 1:4

1:6
j Ro 10:18
k Jn 15:16

1:7
l Phm 23
m Col 4:7

1:8
n Ro 15:30

1:9
o Eph 1:15

Chapter 1 Theme _____

1 Paul, an apostle*a* of Christ Jesus by the will of God,*b* and Timothy our brother,

²To the holy and faithful*a* brothers in Christ at Colosse:

Grace*c* and peace to you from God our Father.*bd*

³We always thank God,*e* the Father of our Lord Jesus Christ, when we pray for you, ⁴because we have heard of your faith in Christ Jesus and of the love*f* you have for all the saints*g*— ⁵the faith and love that spring from the hope*h* that is stored up for you in heaven*i* and that you have already heard about in the word of truth, the gospel ⁶that has come to you. All over the world*j* this gospel is bearing fruit*k* and growing, just as it has been doing among you since the day you heard it and understood God's grace in all its truth. ⁷You learned it from Epaphras,*l* our dear fellow servant, who is a faithful minister*m* of Christ on our*c* behalf, ⁸and who also told us of your love in the Spirit.*n*

⁹For this reason, since the day we heard about you,*o* we have

a 2 Or *believing*   *b* 2 Some manuscripts *Father and the Lord Jesus Christ*   *c* 7 Some manuscripts *your* not stopped praying for you and asking God to fill you with the knowledge of his will[a] through all spiritual wisdom and understanding.[b] 10And we pray this in order that you may live a life worthy[c] of the Lord and may please him in every way: bearing fruit in every good work, growing in the knowledge of God, 11being strengthened with all power[d] according to his glorious might so that you may have great endurance and patience,[e] and joyfully 12giving thanks to the Father,[f] who has qualified you[a] to share in the inheritance[g] of the saints in the kingdom of light. 13For he has rescued us from the dominion of darkness[h] and brought us into the kingdom[i] of the Son he loves,[j] 14in whom we have redemption,[b][k] the forgiveness of sins.[l]

15He is the image[m] of the invisible God,[n] the firstborn over all creation. 16For by him all things were created:[o] things in heaven and on earth, visible and invisible, whether thrones or powers or rulers or authorities;[p] all things were created by him and for him.[q] 17He is before all things,[r] and in him all things hold together. 18And he is the head[s] of the body, the church; he is the beginning and the firstborn from among the dead,[t] so that in everything he might have the supremacy. 19For God was pleased[u] to have all his fullness[v] dwell in him, 20and through him to reconcile[w] to himself all things, whether things on earth or things in heaven,[x] by making peace through his blood,[y] shed on the cross.

21Once you were alienated from God and were enemies[z] in your minds[a] because of[c] your evil behavior. 22But now he has reconciled you by Christ's physical body[b] through death to present you holy in his sight, without blemish and free from accusation[c]— 23if you continue in your faith, established[d] and firm, not moved from the hope[e] held out in the gospel. This is the gospel that you heard and that has been proclaimed to every creature under heaven,[f] and of which I, Paul, have become a servant.[g]

24Now I rejoice in what was suffered for you, and I fill up in my flesh what is still lacking in regard to Christ's afflictions,[h] for the sake of his body, which is the church. 25I have become its servant[i] by the commission God gave me[j] to present to you the word of God in its fullness— 26the mystery[k] that has been kept hidden for

Colosse

---

a 12 Some manuscripts *us*   b 14 A few late manuscripts *redemption through his blood*
c 21 Or *minds, as shown by*

1:9
a Eph 5:17
b Eph 1:17

1:10
c Eph 4:1

1:11
d Eph 3:16
e Eph 4:2

1:12
f Eph 5:20
g Ac 20:32

1:13
h Ac 26:18
i Eph 6:12;
2Pe 1:11
j Mt 3:17

1:14
k Ro 3:24
l Eph 1:7

1:15
m 2Co 4:4
n Jn 1:18

1:16
o Jn 1:3
p Eph 1:20,21
q Ro 11:36

1:17
r Jn 1:2

1:18
s Eph 1:22
t Ac 26:23;
Rev 1:5

1:19
u Eph 1:5
v Jn 1:16

1:20
w 2Co 5:18
x Eph 1:10
y Eph 2:13

1:21
z Ro 5:10
a Eph 2:3

1:22
b Ro 7:4
c Eph 5:27

1:23
d Eph 3:17
e ver 5
f Ro 10:18
g ver 25;
1Co 3:5

1:24
h 2Co 1:5

1:25
i ver 23
j Eph 3:2

1:26
k Ro 16:25

ages and generations, but is now disclosed to the saints. ²⁷To them God has chosen to make known *a* among the Gentiles the glorious riches of this mystery, which is Christ in you, the hope of glory.

²⁸We proclaim him, admonishing *b* and teaching everyone with all wisdom, *c* so that we may present everyone perfect *d* in Christ. ²⁹To this end I labor, *e* struggling *f* with all his energy, which so powerfully works in me. *g*

Chapter 2 Theme

2 I want you to know how much I am struggling *h* for you and for those at Laodicea, *i* and for all who have not met me personally. ²My purpose is that they may be encouraged in heart *j* and united in love, so that they may have the full riches of complete understanding, in order that they may know the mystery of God, namely, Christ, ³in whom are hidden all the treasures of wisdom and knowledge. *k* ⁴I tell you this so that no one may deceive you by fine-sounding arguments. *l* ⁵For though I am absent from you in body, I am present with you in spirit *m* and delight to see how orderly *n* you are and how firm *o* your faith in Christ is.

⁶So then, just as you received Christ Jesus as Lord, *p* continue to live in him, ⁷rooted *q* and built up in him, strengthened in the faith as you were taught, and overflowing with thankfulness.

⁸See to it that no one takes you captive through hollow and deceptive philosophy, *r* which depends on human tradition and the basic principles of this world *s* rather than on Christ.

⁹For in Christ all the fullness of the Deity lives in bodily form, ¹⁰and you have been given fullness in Christ, who is the head *t* over every power and authority. ¹¹In him you were also circumcised, *u* in the putting off of the sinful nature, *a v* not with a circumcision done by the hands of men but with the circumcision done by Christ, ¹²having been buried with him in baptism and raised with him *w* through your faith in the power of God, who raised him from the dead. *x*

¹³When you were dead in your sins *y* and in the uncircumcision of your sinful nature, *b* God made you *c* alive with Christ. He forgave us all our sins, ¹⁴having canceled the written code, with its regulations, *z* that was against us and that stood opposed to us; he took it away, nailing it to the cross. *a* ¹⁵And having disarmed the powers and authorities, *b* he made a public spectacle of them, triumphing over them *c* by the cross. *d*

¹⁶Therefore do not let anyone judge you *d* by what you eat or drink, *e* or with regard to a religious festival, *f* a New Moon celebration *g* or a Sabbath day. *h* ¹⁷These are a shadow of the things

1:27 *a* Mt 13:11
1:28 *b* Col 3:16 *c* 1Co 2:6,7 *d* Eph 5:27
1:29 *e* 1Co 15:10 *f* Col 2:1 *g* Eph 1:19
2:1 *h* Col 1:29; 4:12 *i* Rev 1:11
2:2 *j* Col 4:8
2:3 *k* Ro 11:33; 1Co 1:24,30
2:4 *l* Ro 16:18
2:5 *m* 1Th 2:17 *n* 1Co 14:40 *o* 1Pe 5:9
2:6 *p* Col 1:10
2:7 *q* Eph 3:17
2:8 *r* 1Ti 6:20 *s* Gal 4:3
2:10 *t* Eph 1:22
2:11 *u* Ro 2:29; Php 3:3 *v* Gal 5:24
2:12 *w* Ro 6:5 *x* Ac 2:24
2:13 *y* Eph 2:1,5
2:14 *z* Eph 2:15 *a* 1Pe 2:24
2:15 *b* Eph 6:12 *c* Lk 10:18
2:16 *d* Ro 14:3,4 *e* Ro 14:17 *f* Ro 14:5 *g* 1Ch 23:31 *h* Gal 4:10

a 11 Or *the flesh*   *b* 13 Or *your flesh*   *c* 13 Some manuscripts *us*   *d* 15 Or *them in him* that were to come;[a] the reality, however, is found in Christ. [18]Do not let anyone who delights in false humility[b] and the worship of angels disqualify you for the prize.[c] Such a person goes into great detail about what he has seen, and his unspiritual mind puffs him up with idle notions. [19]He has lost connection with the Head,[d] from whom the whole body, supported and held together by its ligaments and sinews, grows as God causes it to grow.[e]

[20]Since you died with Christ to the basic principles of this world,[f] why, as though you still belonged to it, do you submit to its rules:[g] [21]"Do not handle! Do not taste! Do not touch!"? [22]These are all destined to perish[h] with use, because they are based on human commands and teachings.[i] [23]Such regulations indeed have an appearance of wisdom, with their self-imposed worship, their false humility and their harsh treatment of the body, but they lack any value in restraining sensual indulgence.

Chapter 3 Theme

3 Since, then, you have been raised with Christ, set your hearts on things above, where Christ is seated at the right hand of God. [2]Set your minds on things above, not on earthly things.[j] [3]For you died,[k] and your life is now hidden with Christ in God. [4]When Christ, who is your[a] life, appears,[l] then you also will appear with him in glory.[m]

[5]Put to death, therefore, whatever belongs to your earthly nature: sexual immorality, impurity, lust, evil desires and greed,[n] which is idolatry.[o] [6]Because of these, the wrath of God[p] is coming.[b] [7]You used to walk in these ways, in the life you once lived.[q] [8]But now you must rid yourselves[r] of all such things as these: anger, rage, malice, slander,[s] and filthy language from your lips.[t] [9]Do not lie to each other,[u] since you have taken off your old self with its practices [10]and have put on the new self, which is being renewed[v] in knowledge in the image of its Creator.[w] [11]Here there is no Greek or Jew,[x] circumcised or uncircumcised,[y] barbarian, Scythian, slave or free,[z] but Christ is all,[a] and is in all.

[12]Therefore, as God's chosen people, holy and dearly loved, clothe yourselves with compassion, kindness, humility,[b] gentleness and patience.[c] [13]Bear with each other[d] and forgive whatever grievances you may have against one another. Forgive as the Lord forgave you.[e] [14]And over all these virtues put on love,[f] which binds them all together in perfect unity.[g]

[15]Let the peace of Christ[h] rule in your hearts, since as members of one body you were called to peace. And be thankful. [16]Let the word of Christ[i] dwell in you richly as you teach and admonish

2:17
[a] Heb 8:5

2:18
[b] ver 23
[c] Php 3:14

2:19
[d] Eph 1:22
[e] Eph 4:16

2:20
[f] Gal 4:3,9
[g] ver 14,16

2:22
[h] 1Co 6:13
[i] Isa 29:13;
Mt 15:9;
Tit 1:14

3:2
[j] Php 3:19,20

3:3
[k] Ro 6:2;
2Co 5:14

3:4
[l] 1Co 1:7
[m] 1Pe 1:13;
1Jn 3:2

3:5
[n] Eph 5:3
[o] Eph 5:5

3:6
[p] Ro 1:18

3:7
[q] Eph 2:2

3:8
[r] Eph 4:22
[s] Eph 4:31
[t] Eph 4:29

3:9
[u] Eph 4:22,25

3:10
[v] Ro 12:2;
Eph 4:23
[w] Eph 2:10

3:11
[x] Ro 10:12
[y] 1Co 7:19
[z] Gal 3:28
[a] Eph 1:23

3:12
[b] Php 2:3
[c] 2Co 6:6;
Gal 5:22,23

3:13
[d] Eph 4:2
[e] Eph 4:32

3:14
[f] 1Co 13:1-13
[g] Eph 4:3

3:15
[h] Jn 14:27

3:16
[i] Ro 10:17

---

[a] 4 Some manuscripts *our*   [b] 6 Some early manuscripts *coming on those who are disobedient*

one another with all wisdom,[a] and as you sing psalms, hymns and spiritual songs with gratitude in your hearts to God.[b] [17]And whatever you do,[c] whether in word or deed, do it all in the name of the Lord Jesus, giving thanks [d] to God the Father through him.

[18]Wives, submit to your husbands,[e] as is fitting in the Lord.

[19]Husbands, love your wives and do not be harsh with them.

[20]Children, obey your parents in everything, for this pleases the Lord.

[21]Fathers, do not embitter your children, or they will become discouraged.

[22]Slaves, obey your earthly masters in everything; and do it, not only when their eye is on you and to win their favor, but with sincerity of heart and reverence for the Lord. [23]Whatever you do, work at it with all your heart, as working for the Lord, not for men, [24]since you know that you will receive an inheritance[f] from the Lord as a reward. It is the Lord Christ you are serving. [25]Anyone who does wrong will be repaid for his wrong, and there is no favoritism.[g]

Chapter 4 Theme

4 Masters, provide your slaves with what is right and fair, because you know that you also have a Master in heaven.

[2]Devote yourselves to prayer,[h] being watchful and thankful. [3]And pray for us, too, that God may open a door [i] for our message, so that we may proclaim the mystery of Christ, for which I am in chains.[j] [4]Pray that I may proclaim it clearly, as I should. [5]Be wise[k] in the way you act toward outsiders;[l] make the most of every opportunity.[m] [6]Let your conversation be always full of grace,[n] seasoned with salt,[o] so that you may know how to answer everyone. [p]

[7]Tychicus[q] will tell you all the news about me. He is a dear brother, a faithful minister and fellow servant[r] in the Lord. [8]I am sending him to you for the express purpose that you may know about our[a] circumstances and that he may encourage your hearts.[s] [9]He is coming with Onesimus,[t] our faithful and dear brother, who is one of you. They will tell you everything that is happening here.

[10]My fellow prisoner Aristarchus[u] sends you his greetings, as does Mark, the cousin of Barnabas.[v] (You have received instructions about him; if he comes to you, welcome him.) [11]Jesus, who is called Justus, also sends greetings. These are the only Jews among my fellow workers for the kingdom of God, and they have proved a comfort to me. [12]Epaphras,[w] who is one of you and a servant of Christ Jesus, sends greetings. He is always wrestling in prayer for you,[x] that you may stand firm in all the will of God,

3:16
[a] Col 1:28
[b] Eph 5:19

3:17
[c] 1Co 10:31
[d] Eph 5:20

3:18
[e] Eph 5:22

3:24
[f] Ac 20:32

3:25
[g] Ac 10:34

4:2
[h] Lk 18:1

4:3
[i] Ac 14:27
[j] Eph 6:19,20

4:5
[k] Eph 5:15
[l] Mk 4:11
[m] Eph 5:16

4:6
[n] Eph 4:29
[o] Mk 9:50
[p] 1Pe 3:15

4:7
[q] Ac 20:4
[r] Eph 6:21,22

4:8
[s] Eph 6:21,22

4:9
[t] Phm 10

4:10
[u] Ac 19:29
[v] Ac 4:36

4:12
[w] Col 1:7; Phm 23
[x] Ro 15:30

[a]8 Some manuscripts *that he may know about your*

mature *a* and fully assured. ¹³I vouch for him that he is working hard for you and for those at Laodicea*b* and Hierapolis. ¹⁴Our dear friend Luke,*c* the doctor, and Demas*d* send greetings. ¹⁵Give my greetings to the brothers at Laodicea, and to Nympha and the church in her house.*e*

¹⁶After this letter has been read to you, see that it is also read *f* in the church of the Laodiceans and that you in turn read the letter from Laodicea.

¹⁷Tell Archippus:*g* "See to it that you complete the work you have received in the Lord."*h*

¹⁸I, Paul, write this greeting in my own hand.*i* Remember*j* my chains. Grace be with you.*k*

4:18 *i*1Co 16:21 *j*Heb 13:3 *k*1Ti 6:21; 2Ti 4:22; Tit 3:15; Heb 13:25

4:12
*a*1Co 2:6

4:13
*b*Col 2:1

4:14
*c*2Ti 4:11;
Phm 24
*d*2Ti 4:10

4:15
*e*Ro 16:5

4:16
*f*2Th 3:14

4:17
*g*Phm 2
*h*2Ti 4:5

COLOSSIANS OBSERVATIONS CHART

AUTHOR

RECIPIENTS

WARNINGS AND INSTRUCTIONS

(continued)

_____

_____

_____

_____

_____

_____

_____

_____

_____

_____

_____

_____

_____

_____

_____

COLOSSIANS AT A GLANCE

Theme of Colossians:

SEGMENT
DIVISIONS

		CHAPTER THEMES
	1	
	2	
	3	
	4	

Author:

Date:

Purpose:

Key Words:
   wisdom (wise)
   know(ledge)
   understanding
   given fullness
   all (every, great,
   everything, full)
   perfect, fullness
   faith
   mystery
   in him, in Christ
   (or in his sight,
   through him,
   etc.)

1 THESSALONIANS

*T*imothy joined Paul and Silas (Silvanus) while they were in Lystra on Paul's second missionary journey. Since his father was a Greek, Timothy hadn't been circumcised. There was no sense in causing any unnecessary conflicts with the Jews who were in those parts, so Paul had Timothy circumcised. Things went smoothly until Paul had his vision of a man from Macedonia appealing to him to come and help them.

Believing this call was of God, the three went to Philippi—and the persecution began. Paul and Silas were beaten with rods and thrown into prison. Undaunted and convinced of their heavenly commission, the trio traveled on through Amphipolis and Apollonia and came to Thessalonica. There they found a Jewish synagogue, where for three Sabbaths Paul reasoned with the Thessalonians from the Scriptures. Jews and Greeks, including a number of leading women, heard and believed. The other Jews became furious. Once again there was opposition, but this time the persecution was not directed only to the trio, but also to those who had believed.

Consequently, the Thessalonian believers sent Paul, Silas, and Timothy to Berea by night where again the gospel bore fruit. When the Jews of Thessalonica heard what happened in Berea, they couldn't bear it. They went to Berea to persecute the men who were upsetting the world.

From Berea Paul went to Athens, and from Athens to Corinth. But the church at Thessalonica was on his heart. How were they doing in the midst of such adamant opposition? Paul had to find out. So about A.D. 51, while in Corinth, Paul sat down to write his first epistle to the church at Thessalonica.

↜ THINGS TO DO

1. Read 1 Thessalonians chapter by chapter. Record the following information on the OBSERVATIONS CHART on page 2040. (Be sure to take your answers from the text.)

   a. List what you learn about the author(s). Look for the relationship of the author(s) to the recipients. In chapter 2, what comparisons are drawn to show how the author(s) feel about those to whom they are writing? Don't miss it.

   b. List everything you learn about the recipients. Who had they been serving? What happened when they heard and believed the gospel? What were they enduring?

   c. Note the different problems or concerns that are addressed in the letter.

2. Read through the book and mark in the text the key words (along with their synonyms and pronouns) listed on the 1 THESSALONIANS AT A GLANCE chart on page 2039. As you observe the key words, list in the margin everything you learn from the text about each word. List what you learn about *the coming of the Lord* in one place in the margin.

3. In chapters 4 and 5 are several truths about those "who have fallen asleep" and those "who are still alive and who are left." List what you observe from the text about each of these on the second page of the OBSERVATIONS CHART. As you do, note the progression of events in 1 Thessalonians 4:13-18. Ask the five W's and an H of the text: Who is involved? What will happen? Where will they meet the Lord? When? Why are they not to sorrow? How will all this happen?

4. Watch what you learn about "the day of the Lord" in chapter 5. Record this information on the chart THE DAY OF THE LORD beginning on page 2178.

5. On 1 THESSALONIANS AT A GLANCE, record the theme of the book. Then record the theme of each chapter on the chart and in the text next to the chapter number. Fill in any additional information under author, date, purpose, etc.

2033

6. Often you will be able to note a turning point in the book because the subject being addressed will change. These topical changes divide the book into segments. Think through the following questions to see if you can determine a segment division in 1 Thessalonians.

    a. Where does the main subject of the book change?

    b. What is the topic in the first three chapters of the book?

    c. What does the subject become in the last two chapters?

    d. Title each segment of the book by thinking of the theme or subject discussed in the first three chapters and then in the last two. Record your segment divisions on 1 THESSALONIANS AT A GLANCE.

❧ THINGS TO THINK ABOUT

1. In this book Paul pours his life into other men who could carry on the work of the gospel. Are you spending time imparting the things God has done in your life to another person who can in turn minister to others?

2. It is sometimes hard to give thanks in all things, yet that is the will of God. Go back over the last few days and think of the things that have happened in your life for which you have not given thanks. Determine in your heart to obey this command.

3. Are the circumstances in your life difficult? How are you responding? What will others say about your response? Can people imitate your walk with God?

4. Are you abstaining from sexual immorality? Are you defrauding others sexually in any way at all? Do you realize that if you are acting on your sexual passions in a way contrary to God's Word, God will act as the avenger against you?

5. Do you pray continually (5:17) for those in your life who don't know the Lord? Do you boldly approach the Lord for answers to your problems? Do you pray consistently for others?

〰〰〰〰

Chapter 1 Theme

1 Paul, Silas[a] and Timothy,[a]

    To the church of the Thessalonians[b] in God the Father and the Lord Jesus Christ:

    Grace and peace to you.[bc]

[2] We always thank God for all of you,[d] mentioning you in our prayers. [3] We continually remember before our God and Father your work produced by faith,[e] your labor prompted by love, and your endurance inspired by hope in our Lord Jesus Christ.

[4] For we know, brothers loved by God, that he has chosen you, [5] because our gospel[f] came to you not simply with words, but also with power, with the Holy Spirit and with deep conviction. You know how we lived among you for your sake. [6] You became imitators of us[g] and of the Lord; in spite of severe suffering,[h] you welcomed the message with the joy given by the Holy Spirit.[i] [7] And

1:1
[a] Ac 16:1;
2Th 1:1
[b] Ac 17:1
[c] Ro 1:7

1:2
[d] Ro 1:8

1:3
[e] 2Th 1:11

1:5
[f] 2Th 2:14

1:6
[g] 1Co 4:16
[h] Ac 17:5-10
[i] Ac 13:52

a 1 Greek *Silvanus*, a variant of *Silas*   b 1 Some early manuscripts *you from God our Father and the Lord Jesus Christ*

1:8
a Ro 1:8; 10:18

1:9
b 1Co 12:2;
Gal 4:8

1:10
c Ac 2:24
d Ro 5:9

2:1
e 1Th 1:5,9

2:2
f Ac 16:22;
Php 1:30

2:3
g 2Co 2:17

2:4
h Gal 2:7
i Gal 1:10

2:5
j Ac 20:33
k Ro 1:9

2:6
l 1Co 9:1,2

2:7
m ver 11

2:8
n 2Co 12:15;
1Jn 3:16

2:9
o Ac 18:3
p 2Th 3:8

2:10
q 1Th 1:5
r 2Co 1:12

2:11
s ver 7;
1Co 4:14

2:12
t Eph 4:1

2:13
u 1Th 1:2
v Heb 4:12

2:14
w Gal 1:22
x Ac 17:5;
2Th 1:4

2:15
y Ac 2:23
z Mt 5:12

2:16
a Ac 13:45,50

so you became a model to all the believers in Macedonia and Achaia. ⁸The Lord's message rang out from you not only in Macedonia and Achaia—your faith in God has become known everywhere.ᵃ Therefore we do not need to say anything about it, ⁹for they themselves report what kind of reception you gave us. They tell how you turned to God from idolsᵇ to serve the living and true God, ¹⁰and to wait for his Son from heaven, whom he raised from the deadᶜ—Jesus, who rescues us from the coming wrath.ᵈ

Chapter 2 Theme

2 You know, brothers, that our visit to youᵉ was not a failure. ²We had previously sufferedᶠ and been insulted in Philippi, as you know, but with the help of our God we dared to tell you his gospel in spite of strong opposition. ³For the appeal we make does not spring from error or impure motives,ᵍ nor are we trying to trick you. ⁴On the contrary, we speak as men approved by God to be entrusted with the gospel.ʰ We are not trying to please menⁱ but God, who tests our hearts. ⁵You know we never used flattery, nor did we put on a mask to cover up greedʲ—God is our witness.ᵏ ⁶We were not looking for praise from men, not from you or anyone else.

As apostlesˡ of Christ we could have been a burden to you, ⁷but we were gentle among you, like a mother caring for her little children.ᵐ ⁸We loved you so much that we were delighted to share with you not only the gospel of God but our lives as well,ⁿ because you had become so dear to us. ⁹Surely you remember, brothers, our toil and hardship; we workedᵒ night and day in order not to be a burden to anyoneᵖ while we preached the gospel of God to you.

¹⁰You are witnesses,�q and so is God, of how holy,ʳ righteous and blameless we were among you who believed. ¹¹For you know that we dealt with each of you as a father deals with his own children,ˢ ¹²encouraging, comforting and urging you to live lives worthyᵗ of God, who calls you into his kingdom and glory.

¹³And we also thank God continuallyᵘ because, when you received the word of God,ᵛ which you heard from us, you accepted it not as the word of men, but as it actually is, the word of God, which is at work in you who believe. ¹⁴For you, brothers, became imitators of God's churches in Judea,ʷ which are in Christ Jesus: You suffered from your own countrymenˣ the same things those churches suffered from the Jews, ¹⁵who killed the Lord Jesusʸ and the prophets ᶻ and also drove us out. They displease God and are hostile to all men ¹⁶in their effort to keep us from speaking to the Gentilesᵃ so that they may be saved. In this way they always heap

up their sins to the limit.*a* The wrath of God has come upon them at last.ᵃ

¹⁷But, brothers, when we were torn away from you for a short time (in person, not in thought),*b* out of our intense longing we made every effort to see you.*c* ¹⁸For we wanted to come to you—certainly I, Paul, did, again and again—but Satan*d* stopped us.*e* ¹⁹For what is our hope, our joy, or the crown*f* in which we will glory*g* in the presence of our Lord Jesus when he comes?*h* Is it not you? ²⁰Indeed, you are our glory*i* and joy.

Chapter 3 Theme

3 So when we could stand it no longer,*j* we thought it best to be left by ourselves in Athens.*k* ²We sent Timothy, who is our brother and God's fellow worker*b* in spreading the gospel of Christ, to strengthen and encourage you in your faith, ³so that no one would be unsettled by these trials. You know quite well that we were destined for them.*l* ⁴In fact, when we were with you, we kept telling you that we would be persecuted. And it turned out that way, as you well know.*m* ⁵For this reason, when I could stand it no longer,*n* I sent to find out about your faith. I was afraid that in some way the tempter*o* might have tempted you and our efforts might have been useless. *p*

⁶But Timothy has just now come to us from you*q* and has brought good news about your faith and love.*r* He has told us that you always have pleasant memories of us and that you long to see us, just as we also long to see you. ⁷Therefore, brothers, in all our distress and persecution we were encouraged about you because of your faith. ⁸For now we really live, since you are standing firm*s* in the Lord. ⁹How can we thank God enough for you*t* in return for all the joy we have in the presence of our God because of you? ¹⁰Night and day we pray*u* most earnestly that we may see you again*v* and supply what is lacking in your faith.

¹¹Now may our God and Father himself and our Lord Jesus clear the way for us to come to you. ¹²May the Lord make your love increase and overflow for each other*w* and for everyone else, just as ours does for you. ¹³May he strengthen your hearts so that you will be blameless*x* and holy in the presence of our God and Father when our Lord Jesus comes*y* with all his holy ones.

Chapter 4 Theme

4 Finally, brothers,*z* we instructed you how to live in order to please God,*a* as in fact you are living. Now we ask you and

---

ᵃ *16* Or *them fully*   ᵇ *2* Some manuscripts *brother and fellow worker;* other manuscripts *brother and God's servant*

2:16
a Mt 23:32

2:17
b 1Co 5:3;
Col 2:5
c 1Th 3:10

2:18
d Mt 4:10
e Ro 1:13; 15:22

2:19
f Php 4:1
g 2Co 1:14
h Mt 16:27;
1Th 3:13

2:20
i 2Co 1:14

3:1
j ver 5
k Ac 17:15

3:3
l Ac 9:16; 14:22

3:4
m 1Th 2:14

3:5
n ver 1
o Mt 4:3
p Gal 2:2;
Php 2:16

3:6
q Ac 18:5
r 1Th 1:3

3:8
s 1Co 16:13

3:9
t 1Th 1:2

3:10
u 2Ti 1:3
v 1Th 2:17

3:12
w 1Th 4:9,10

3:13
x 1Co 1:8
y 1Th 2:19

4:1
z 2Co 13:11
a 2Co 5:9

4:3
a 1Co 6:18

4:4
b 1Co 7:2,9

4:5
c Ro 1:26
d Eph 4:17

4:6
e 1Co 6:8
f Heb 13:4

4:7
g Lev 11:44;
1Pe 1:15

4:8
h Ro 5:5;
Gal 4:6

4:9
i Ro 12:10
j 1Th 5:1
k Jn 13:34

4:10
l 1Th 1:7
m 1Th 3:12

4:11
n Eph 4:28;
2Th 3:10-12

4:12
o Mk 4:11

4:13
p Eph 2:12

4:14
q 1Co 15:18

4:15
r 1Co 15:52

4:16
s Mt 24:31
t 1Co 15:23;
2Th 2:1

4:17
u 1Co 15:52
v Ac 1:9;
Rev 11:12
w Jn 12:26

5:1
x Ac 1:7
y 1Th 4:9

5:2
z 1Co 1:8
a 2Pe 3:10

5:4
b Ac 26:18;
1Jn 2:8

urge you in the Lord Jesus to do this more and more. [2]For you know what instructions we gave you by the authority of the Lord Jesus.

[3]It is God's will that you should be sanctified: that you should avoid sexual immorality;[a] [4]that each of you should learn to control his own body[a][b] in a way that is holy and honorable, [5]not in passionate lust[c] like the heathen,[d] who do not know God; [6]and that in this matter no one should wrong his brother or take advantage of him.[e] The Lord will punish men for all such sins,[f] as we have already told you and warned you. [7]For God did not call us to be impure, but to live a holy life.[g] [8]Therefore, he who rejects this instruction does not reject man but God, who gives you his Holy Spirit.[h]

[9]Now about brotherly love[i] we do not need to write to you,[j] for you yourselves have been taught by God to love each other.[k] [10]And in fact, you do love all the brothers throughout Macedonia.[l] Yet we urge you, brothers, to do so more and more.[m]

[11]Make it your ambition to lead a quiet life, to mind your own business and to work with your hands,[n] just as we told you, [12]so that your daily life may win the respect of outsiders[o] and so that you will not be dependent on anybody.

[13]Brothers, we do not want you to be ignorant about those who fall asleep, or to grieve like the rest of men, who have no hope.[p] [14]We believe that Jesus died and rose again and so we believe that God will bring with Jesus those who have fallen asleep in him.[q] [15]According to the Lord's own word, we tell you that we who are still alive, who are left till the coming of the Lord, will certainly not precede those who have fallen asleep.[r] [16]For the Lord himself will come down from heaven, with a loud command, with the voice of the archangel and with the trumpet call of God,[s] and the dead in Christ will rise first.[t] [17]After that, we who are still alive and are left[u] will be caught up together with them in the clouds[v] to meet the Lord in the air. And so we will be with the Lord[w] forever. [18]Therefore encourage each other with these words.

Chapter 5 Theme

5 Now, brothers, about times and dates[x] we do not need to write to you,[y] [2]for you know very well that the day of the Lord[z] will come like a thief in the night.[a] [3]While people are saying, "Peace and safety," destruction will come on them suddenly, as labor pains on a pregnant woman, and they will not escape.

[4]But you, brothers, are not in darkness[b] so that this day should surprise you like a thief. [5]You are all sons of the light and sons of

a 4 Or *learn to live with his own wife*; or *learn to acquire a wife* the day. We do not belong to the night or to the darkness. [6]So then, let us not be like others, who are asleep,[a] but let us be alert and self-controlled. [7]For those who sleep, sleep at night, and those who get drunk, get drunk at night.[b] [8]But since we belong to the day, let us be self-controlled, putting on faith and love as a breastplate,[c] and the hope of salvation [d] as a helmet.[e] [9]For God did not appoint us to suffer wrath but to receive salvation through our Lord Jesus Christ.[f] [10]He died for us so that, whether we are awake or asleep, we may live together with him.[g] [11]Therefore encourage one another and build each other up, just as in fact you are doing.

[12]Now we ask you, brothers, to respect those who work hard among you, who are over you in the Lord[h] and who admonish you. [13]Hold them in the highest regard in love because of their work. Live in peace with each other.[i] [14]And we urge you, brothers, warn those who are idle,[j] encourage the timid, help the weak,[k] be patient with everyone. [15]Make sure that nobody pays back wrong for wrong,[l] but always try to be kind to each other[m] and to everyone else.

[16]Be joyful always;[n] [17]pray continually; [18]give thanks in all circumstances, for this is God's will for you in Christ Jesus.

The Word Sounds Forth from Thessalonica

5:6
[a] Ro 13:11

5:7
[b] Ac 2:15; 2Pe 2:13

5:8
[c] Eph 6:14
[d] Ro 8:24
[e] Eph 6:17

5:9
[f] 2Th 2:13,14

5:10
[g] 2Co 5:15

5:12
[h] 1Ti 5:17; Heb 13:17

5:13
[i] Mk 9:50

5:14
[j] 2Th 3:6,7,11
[k] Ro 14:1

5:15
[l] 1Pe 3:9
[m] Gal 6:10; Eph 4:32

5:16
[n] Php 4:4

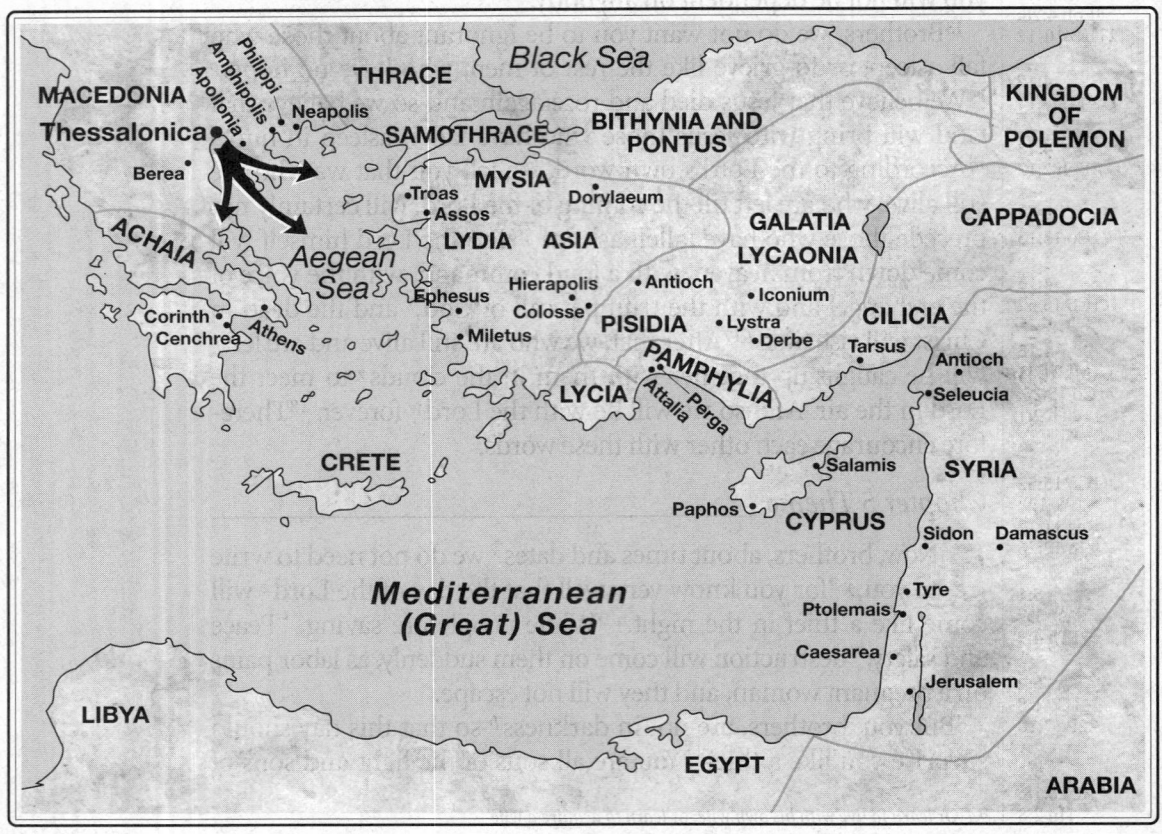

[19] Do not put out the Spirit's fire; *a* [20] do not treat prophecies *b* with contempt. [21] Test everything. *c* Hold on to the good. [22] Avoid every kind of evil.

[23] May God himself, the God of peace, *d* sanctify you through and through. May your whole spirit, soul and body be kept blameless at the coming of our Lord Jesus Christ. [24] The one who calls you is faithful *e* and he will do it.

[25] Brothers, pray for us. *f* [26] Greet all the brothers with a holy kiss. *g* [27] I charge you before the Lord to have this letter read to all the brothers. *h*

[28] The grace of our Lord Jesus Christ be with you. *i*

5:24
e 1Co 1:9

5:25
f Eph 6:19

5:26
g Ro 16:16   **5:27** *h* Col 4:16   **5:28** *i* Ro 16:20

1 Thessalonians at a Glance

Theme of 1 Thessalonians:

	Segment Divisions	Chapter Themes
Author:		
Date:		
	1	
Purpose:		
Key Words:		
gospel (word, words, message)	2	
faith		
love		
hope	3	
Lord Jesus Christ (any reference to Jesus)		
God	4	
Holy Spirit		
be persecuted, persecution (suffering, suffered)	5	
of the Lord		
day of the Lord		

1 Thessalonians Observations Chart

AUTHOR(S)	RECIPIENTS
Who wrote 1 Thessalonians?	Who are they?
What relationship did these men have to one another?	What was their relationship to the author(s)?
Had they worked together before? If so, where? How? Why?	What was their condition when the author(s) first ministered to them? Who were they serving?
Describe the ministry these men had among the recipients.	What conditions were they in when the letter was written?
	How strongly did the author(s) feel about the recipients?
	Did they think of them often? How do you know?
	What comparisons show the kind of love the author(s) feel for them?
	What had the recipients become?

PROBLEMS/CONCERNS/STRUGGLES

(continued)

1 THESSALONIANS 4:13-18

THOSE WHO HAVE FALLEN ASLEEP	THOSE WHO ARE ALIVE AND REMAIN	PROGRESSION OF EVENTS

2 THESSALONIANS

*I*t had been four to six months since Paul wrote his first epistle in A.D. 51 to the church at Thessalonica. Their persecution had not subsided, but much to Paul's joy, his labor had not been in vain; they had withstood the attacks of the tempter.

However, Paul was concerned about some things in the church. Once again, during his second missionary journey he had to take time to write—and put his distinguishing mark on this letter. The church had to know without a doubt that it was from him.

∾ THINGS TO DO

1. If you haven't studied 1 Thessalonians, you should do so before you begin 2 Thessalonians. However, if you have worked through 1 Thessalonians, then read it once again. Observe what Paul says about the coming of the Lord Jesus. Also give special attention to 1 Thessalonians 4:13 through 5:11.

2. Now read 2 Thessalonians. Watch how 1 Thessalonians ties in with 2 Thessalonians. Look for the following information and record it on the OBSERVATIONS CHART on page 2046.

   a. What do you learn about the author and the recipients of this letter? What are the circumstances of the recipients?

   b. Paul addresses several problems which need correction. List these in the margin and on the chart. This will help you see the author's purpose in writing. Then note the instructions or commands related to each problem addressed. List these on your OBSERVATIONS CHART.

   c. Paul also praises the Thessalonians and encourages them about the things they are doing well. List the exhortations he includes in his letter.

   d. Be certain you record what happens to those who do not obey the gospel.

   e. From what you have observed about the author and the recipients, why do you think Paul wrote this book? Record this on 2 THESSALONIANS AT A GLANCE on page 2047 under "Purpose."

3. Read through 2 Thessalonians again, a chapter at a time, and do the following:

   a. Mark in the text the key words (including their synonyms and pronouns) listed on 2 THESSALONIANS AT A GLANCE. Also watch for any words you feel are key but aren't listed.

   b. Now go back through the key words and in the margin make a list of what you have learned. Make one list for each word. In other words, you will have one list of everything these three chapters teach about *the coming of Christ,* one list for *trouble* and *suffering,* one list for *the day of the Lord,* and so on.

4. On the OBSERVATIONS CHART are two more headings: "When the Day of the Lord Comes" and "When the Man of Lawlessness Is Revealed."

   a. Carefully read 2 Thessalonians 2:1-12 and list everything the chapter says must happen before the day of the Lord can come.

   b. Do the same for the revelation of the man of lawlessness.

   c. Record your insights on the chart THE DAY OF THE LORD beginning on page 2178.

5. Think through each chapter and record its theme on 2 THESSALONIANS AT A GLANCE and in the appropriate place in the text. Also record the theme of the book, author, and date.

❧ Things to Think About

1. How do you react to trials? How do you respond to persecution? Does your response glorify God? Do people see your faith? Is his love evident in your life?

2. Do you lead a disciplined life? Does your lifestyle encourage laziness in others? Or can you say, "Follow my example"? Are you doing your share for the furtherance of the kingdom, or are you just waiting for Jesus to come back?

3. When the good you do doesn't seem appreciated or even noticed, how do you feel? For whom are you doing it? Will you persevere?

4. Does what you believe about prophecy or any other doctrine come from a careful, personal study of God's Word, or is it from what others teach you? Are you holding fast to what you know of the Word of God, or are you easily persuaded by "faddish" teaching?

〰〰〰〰

Chapter 1 Theme

1 Paul, Silas[a] and Timothy,[a]

To the church of the Thessalonians in God our Father and the Lord Jesus Christ:

[2] Grace and peace to you from God the Father and the Lord Jesus Christ.[b]

[3] We ought always to thank God for you, brothers, and rightly so, because your faith is growing more and more, and the love every one of you has for each other is increasing.[c] [4] Therefore, among God's churches we boast[d] about your perseverance and faith[e] in all the persecutions and trials you are enduring.[f]

[5] All this is evidence[g] that God's judgment is right, and as a result you will be counted worthy of the kingdom of God, for which you are suffering. [6] God is just: He will pay back trouble to those who trouble you[h] [7] and give relief to you who are troubled, and to us as well. This will happen when the Lord Jesus is revealed from heaven in blazing fire with his powerful angels.[i] [8] He will punish those who do not know God[j] and do not obey the gospel of our Lord Jesus.[k] [9] They will be punished with everlasting destruction[l] and shut out from the presence of the Lord and from the majesty of his power[m] [10] on the day[n] he comes to be glorified[o] in his holy people and to be marveled at among all those who have believed. This includes you, because you believed our testimony to you.[p]

[11] With this in mind, we constantly pray for you, that our God may count you worthy[q] of his calling, and that by his power he may fulfill every good purpose of yours and every act prompted by your faith.[r] [12] We pray this so that the name of our Lord Jesus may be glorified in you,[s] and you in him, according to the grace of our God and the Lord Jesus Christ.[b]

1:1
a Ac 16:1;
1Th 1:1

1:2
b Ro 1:7

1:3
c 1Th 3:12

1:4
d 2Co 7:14
e 1Th 1:3
f 1Th 2:14

1:5
g Php 1:28

1:6
h Col 3:25;
Rev 6:10

1:7
i 1Th 4:16;
Jude 14

1:8
j Gal 4:8
k Ro 2:8

1:9
l Php 3:19;
2Pe 3:7
m 2Th 2:8

1:10
n 1Co 3:13
o Jn 17:10
p 1Co 1:6

1:11
q ver 5
r 1Th 1:3

1:12
s Php 2:9-11

a 1 Greek *Silvanus*, a variant of *Silas*   b 12 Or *God and Lord, Jesus Christ*

Chapter 2 Theme _____

2 Concerning the coming of our Lord Jesus Christ and our being gathered to him,[a] we ask you, brothers, [2]not to become easily unsettled or alarmed by some prophecy, report or letter[b] supposed to have come from us, saying that the day of the Lord[c] has already come. [3]Don't let anyone deceive you[d] in any way, for ⌊that day will not come⌋ until the rebellion occurs and the man of lawlessness[a] is revealed,[e] the man doomed to destruction. [4]He will oppose and will exalt himself over everything that is called God[f] or is worshiped, so that he sets himself up in God's temple, proclaiming himself to be God.[g]

[5]Don't you remember that when I was with you I used to tell you these things? [6]And now you know what is holding him back, so that he may be revealed at the proper time. [7]For the secret power of lawlessness is already at work; but the one who now holds it back will continue to do so till he is taken out of the way. [8]And then the lawless one will be revealed, whom the Lord Jesus will overthrow with the breath of his mouth[h] and destroy by the splendor of his coming. [9]The coming of the lawless one will be in accordance with the work of Satan displayed in all kinds of counterfeit miracles, signs and wonders,[i] [10]and in every sort of evil that deceives those who are perishing.[j] They perish because they refused to love the truth and so be saved. [11]For this reason God sends them[k] a powerful delusion so that they will believe the lie [12]and so that all will be condemned who have not believed the truth but have delighted in wickedness.[l]

[13]But we ought always to thank God for you, brothers loved by the Lord, because from the beginning God chose you[b][m] to be saved[n] through the sanctifying work of the Spirit[o] and through belief in the truth. [14]He called you to this through our gospel, that you might share in the glory of our Lord Jesus Christ. [15]So then, brothers, stand firm[p] and hold to the teachings[c] we passed on to you,[q] whether by word of mouth or by letter.

[16]May our Lord Jesus Christ himself and God our Father, who loved us[r] and by his grace gave us eternal encouragement and good hope, [17]encourage[s] your hearts and strengthen[t] you in every good deed and word.

Chapter 3 Theme _____

3 Finally, brothers,[u] pray for us[v] that the message of the Lord[w] may spread rapidly and be honored, just as it was with you. [2]And pray that we may be delivered from wicked and evil men,[x]

---

[a]3 Some manuscripts *sin*   [b]13 Some manuscripts *because God chose you as his firstfruits*
[c]15 Or *traditions*

2:1
[a]Mk 13:27;
1Th 4:15-17

2:2
[b]2Th 3:17
[c]1Co 1:8

2:3
[d]Eph 5:6-8
[e]Da 7:25; 8:25;
11:36;
Rev 13:5,6

2:4
[f]1Co 8:5
[g]Isa 14:13,14;
Eze 28:2

2:8
[h]Isa 11:4;
Rev 19:15

2:9
[i]Mt 24:24;
Jn 4:48

2:10
[j]1Co 1:18

2:11
[k]Ro 1:28

2:12
[l]Ro 1:32

2:13
[m]Eph 1:4
[n]1Th 5:9
[o]1Pe 1:2

2:15
[p]1Co 16:13
[q]1Co 11:2

2:16
[r]Jn 3:16

2:17
[s]1Th 3:2
[t]2Th 3:3

3:1
[u]1Th 4:1
[v]1Th 5:25
[w]1Th 1:8

3:2
[x]Ro 15:31

for not everyone has faith. [3]But the Lord is faithful,[a] and he will strengthen and protect you from the evil one.[b] [4]We have confidence[c] in the Lord that you are doing and will continue to do the things we command. [5]May the Lord direct your hearts[d] into God's love and Christ's perseverance.

[6]In the name of the Lord Jesus Christ,[e] we command you, brothers, to keep away from[f] every brother who is idle[g] and does not live according to the teaching[a] you received from us.[h] [7]For you yourselves know how you ought to follow our example.[i] We were not idle when we were with you, [8]nor did we eat anyone's food without paying for it. On the contrary, we worked[j] night and day, laboring and toiling so that we would not be a burden to any of you. [9]We did this, not because we do not have the right to such help,[k] but in order to make ourselves a model for you to follow.[l] [10]For even when we were with you,[m] we gave you this rule: "If a man will not work,[n] he shall not eat."

[11]We hear that some among you are idle. They are not busy; they are busybodies.[o] [12]Such people we command and urge in the Lord Jesus Christ[p] to settle down and earn the bread they eat.[q] [13]And as for you, brothers, never tire of doing what is right.[r]

[14]If anyone does not obey our instruction in this letter, take special note of him. Do not associate with him,[s] in order that he may feel ashamed. [15]Yet do not regard him as an enemy, but warn him as a brother.[t]

[16]Now may the Lord of peace[u] himself give you peace at all times and in every way. The Lord be with all of you.[v]

[17]I, Paul, write this greeting in my own hand,[w] which is the distinguishing mark in all my letters. This is how I write.

[18]The grace of our Lord Jesus Christ be with you all.[x]

a6 Or *tradition*

3:3
a 1Co 1:9
b Mt 5:37

3:4
c 2Co 2:3

3:5
d 1Ch 29:18

3:6
e 1Co 5:4
f Ro 16:17
g ver 7,11
h 1Co 11:2

3:7
i 1Co 4:16

3:8
j Ac 18:3;
Eph 4:28

3:9
k 1Co 9:4-14
l ver 7

3:10
m 1Th 3:4
n 1Th 4:11

3:11
o ver 6,7;
1Ti 5:13

3:12
p 1Th 4:1
q 1Th 4:11;
Eph 4:28

3:13
r Gal 6:9

3:14
s ver 6

3:15
t Gal 6:1;
1Th 5:14

3:16
u Ro 15:33
v Ru 2:4

3:17
w 1Co 16:21

3:18
x Ro 16:20

AUTHOR

RECIPIENTS

THOSE WHO DO NOT OBEY THE GOSPEL

PROBLEMS/CONCERNS

INSTRUCTIONS

EXHORTATIONS

WHEN THE DAY OF THE LORD COMES

WHEN THE MAN OF LAWLESSNESS IS REVEALED

Theme of 2 Thessalonians:

	SEGMENT DIVISIONS	CHAPTER THEMES
Author:		
Date:		1
Purpose:		
Key Words:		
trouble		
suffering (persecutions)		2
coming of Jesus Christ (or synonymous references)		
God		
Spirit		
glory, majesty (glorified, honored)		3
man of lawlessness		
idle		
day of the Lord (and pronouns)		
truth		

1 TIMOTHY

*T*hirty years of labor for the gospel had taken its toll on Paul. His body bore the marks of a servant of Jesus Christ (see Galatians 6:17). However, the intensity of his sufferings was minor compared to the intensity of his love and concern for the churches etched upon his heart.

Undaunted by two years of house arrest in Rome, Paul pressed on toward the prize of the high calling in Christ Jesus. He intended to visit Asia, Macedonia, and possibly Spain. Spain had been on his heart before he became a prisoner of Rome.

He also was concerned about the church at Ephesus. Timothy, his faithful co-laborer, was pastoring that strategically important church. Possibly concerned that he might be delayed and that Timothy might need something in writing to set before others as an ever-present reminder, Paul took quill and ink, spread out the parchment, and wrote his first epistle to his beloved son in the faith, an epistle which would become a legacy for the church and a pillar and support of the truth. It was around A.D. 62.

∽ THINGS TO DO

1. Read 1 Timothy. Note 1:3 and 3:14, 15 to see why Paul wrote this epistle. Keep this in mind as you read the book. On the 1 TIMOTHY AT A GLANCE chart on page 2057, record Paul's purpose for writing.

2. Read 1 Timothy again, one chapter at a time. On your OBSERVATIONS CHART on pages 2055, 2056:

    a. Record how Paul describes himself. Note how he refers to himself, stating his position of authority which qualifies him to instruct Timothy in the matters described in this letter.

    b. Note how Paul describes Timothy, where Timothy is when the letter is written, and what his relationship is to Paul.

    c. Write down the commands and instructions Paul gives about specific groups of people or practices. Record what you learn about overseers (elders) and deacons. Also record what you see about general groups of believers in the church. There is a designated space for each of these groups on the OBSERVATIONS CHART.

    d. Record the specific charges Paul gives Timothy as his representative in Ephesus and as the one who is organizing and instructing the church there.

3. As you read, mark in the text the key words (and their synonyms and pronouns) that are listed on 1 TIMOTHY AT A GLANCE. These key words give clues about the most important and most often-mentioned instructions.

4. In the margin of the chapter, list everything you learn from the text about these key words. You can learn much about what was important to the health of the church.

5. What do you think is the theme of 1 Timothy? Are there any problems or concerns the author must address? How does the theme relate to these concerns? Record the theme of the book on 1 TIMOTHY AT A GLANCE and then list the theme of each chapter on the chart and also in the text. Finally, fill in any additional information under author, purpose, and so on.

∽ THINGS TO THINK ABOUT

1. Do you operate in your own church according to these principles?

2. How do you esteem your local church leadership?

3. Do you pray on behalf of all men, including those in authority?

2048

Chapter 1 Theme

1 Paul, an apostle of Christ Jesus by the command of God[a] our Savior and of Christ Jesus our hope,[b]

²To Timothy[c] my true son[d] in the faith:

Grace, mercy and peace from God the Father and Christ Jesus our Lord.

³As I urged you when I went into Macedonia, stay there in Ephesus[e] so that you may com-

mand certain men not to teach false doctrines[f] any longer ⁴nor to devote themselves to myths[g] and endless genealogies. These promote controversies[h] rather than God's work—which is by faith. ⁵The goal of this com-

mand is love, which comes from a pure heart[i] and a good conscience and a sincere faith.[j] ⁶Some have wan-

*To Timothy
at Ephesus*

dered away from these and turned to meaningless talk. ⁷They want to be teachers of the law, but they do not know what they are talking about or what they so confidently affirm.

⁸We know that the law is good[k] if one uses it properly. ⁹We also know that law[a] is made not for the righteous but for lawbreakers and rebels,[l] the ungodly and sinful, the unholy and irreligious; for those who kill their fathers or mothers, for murderers, ¹⁰for adulterers and perverts, for slave traders and liars and perjurers—and

for whatever else is contrary to the sound doctrine[m] ¹¹that conforms to the glorious gospel of the blessed God, which he entrusted to me.[n]

¹²I thank Christ Jesus our Lord, who has given me strength,[o] that he considered me faithful, appointing me to his service. ¹³Even

though I was once a blasphemer and a persecutor[p] and a violent man, I was shown mercy because I acted in ignorance and unbelief.[q] ¹⁴The grace of our Lord was poured out on me abundantly,[r]

along with the faith and love that are in Christ Jesus.[s]

¹⁵Here is a trustworthy saying[t] that deserves full acceptance: Christ Jesus came into the world to save sinners—of whom I am the worst. ¹⁶But for that very reason I was shown mercy[u] so that in me, the worst of sinners, Christ Jesus might display his unlimited patience as an example for those who would believe on him and

a 9 Or *that the law*

receive eternal life. [17]Now to the King[a] eternal, immortal, invisible,[b] the only God, be honor and glory for ever and ever. Amen.[c]

[18]Timothy, my son, I give you this instruction in keeping with the prophecies once made about you,[d] so that by following them you may fight the good fight,[e] [19]holding on to faith and a good conscience. Some have rejected these and so have shipwrecked their faith.[f] [20]Among them are Hymenaeus[g] and Alexander,[h] whom I have handed over to Satan[i] to be taught not to blaspheme.

Chapter 2 Theme

2 I urge, then, first of all, that requests, prayers, intercession and thanksgiving be made for everyone— [2]for kings and all those in authority,[j] that we may live peaceful and quiet lives in all godliness and holiness. [3]This is good, and pleases God our Savior, [4]who wants[k] all men[l] to be saved and to come to a knowledge of the truth.[m] [5]For there is one God[n] and one mediator[o] between God and men, the man Christ Jesus, [6]who gave himself as a ransom for all men—the testimony[p] given in its proper time.[q] [7]And for this purpose I was appointed a herald and an apostle—I am telling the truth, I am not lying—and a teacher[r] of the true faith to the Gentiles.[s]

[8]I want men everywhere to lift up holy hands[t] in prayer, without anger or disputing.

[9]I also want women to dress modestly, with decency and propriety, not with braided hair or gold or pearls or expensive clothes,[u] [10]but with good deeds, appropriate for women who profess to worship God.

[11]A woman should learn in quietness and full submission.[v] [12]I do not permit a woman to teach or to have authority over a man; she must be silent. [13]For Adam was formed first, then Eve.[w] [14]And Adam was not the one deceived; it was the woman who was deceived and became a sinner.[x] [15]But women[a] will be saved[b] through childbearing—if they continue in faith, love[y] and holiness with propriety.

Chapter 3 Theme

3 Here is a trustworthy saying:[z] If anyone sets his heart on being an overseer,[c][a] he desires a noble task. [2]Now the overseer must be above reproach,[b] the husband of but one wife, temperate, self-controlled, respectable, hospitable,[c] able to teach,[d] [3]not given to drunkenness, not violent but gentle, not quarrelsome,[e] not a lover of money.[f] [4]He must manage his own family well and see that his children obey him with proper respect.[g] [5](If anyone does not

a 15 Greek *she*   b 15 Or *restored*   c 1 Traditionally *bishop*; also in verse 2

1:17
a Rev 15:3
b Col 1:15
c Ro 11:36

1:18
d 1Ti 4:14
e 2Ti 2:3

1:19
f 1Ti 6:21

1:20
g 2Ti 2:17
h 2Ti 4:14
i 1Co 5:5

2:2
j Ezr 6:10;
Ro 13:1

2:4
k Eze 18:23,32
l Tit 2:11
m 2Ti 2:25

2:5
n Ro 3:29,30
o Gal 3:20

2:6
p 1Co 1:6
q 1Ti 6:15

2:7
r 2Ti 1:11
s Ac 9:15;
Eph 3:7,8

2:8
t Ps 134:2;
Lk 24:50

2:9
u 1Pe 3:3

2:11
v 1Co 14:34

2:13
w Ge 2:7,22;
1Co 11:8

2:14
x Ge 3:1-6,13;
2Co 11:3

2:15
y 1Ti 1:14

3:1
z 1Ti 1:15
a Ac 20:28

3:2
b Tit 1:6-8
c Ro 12:13
d 2Ti 2:24

3:3
e 2Ti 2:24
f Heb 13:5;
1Pe 5:2

3:4
g Tit 1:6

3:5
*a*1Co 10:32

3:6
*b*1Ti 6:4

3:7
*c*2Ti 2:26

3:8
*d*Php 1:1
*e*Tit 2:3

3:9
*f*1Ti 1:19

3:11
*g*2Ti 3:3;
Tit 2:3

3:12
*h*ver 4

3:15
*i*ver 5;
Eph 2:21

3:16
*j*Ro 16:25
*k*Jn 1:14
*l*Col 1:23
*m*Mk 16:19

4:1
*n*Jn 16:13
*o*2Ti 3:1
*p*2Th 2:3

4:2
*q*Eph 4:19

4:3
*r*Heb 13:4
*s*Col 2:16
*t*Ge 1:29
*u*Ro 14:6

4:4
*v*Ro 14:14-18

4:6
*w*1Ti 1:10

4:7
*x*2Ti 2:16

know how to manage his own family, how can he take care of God's church?)*a* *6*He must not be a recent convert, or he may become conceited*b* and fall under the same judgment as the devil. *7*He must also have a good reputation with outsiders, so that he will not fall into disgrace and into the devil's trap.*c*

*8*Deacons,*d* likewise, are to be men worthy of respect, sincere, not indulging in much wine,*e* and not pursuing dishonest gain. *9*They must keep hold of the deep truths of the faith with a clear conscience.*f* *10*They must first be tested; and then if there is nothing against them, let them serve as deacons.

*11*In the same way, their wives*a* are to be women worthy of respect, not malicious talkers*g* but temperate and trustworthy in everything.

*12*A deacon must be the husband of but one wife and must manage his children and his household well.*h* *13*Those who have served well gain an excellent standing and great assurance in their faith in Christ Jesus.

*14*Although I hope to come to you soon, I am writing you these instructions so that, *15*if I am delayed, you will know how people ought to conduct themselves in God's household, which is the church*i* of the living God, the pillar and foundation of the truth. *16*Beyond all question, the mystery*j* of godliness is great:

> He*b* appeared in a body,*c k*
>   was vindicated by the Spirit,
>   was seen by angels,
>   was preached among the nations,*l*
>   was believed on in the world,
>   was taken up in glory.*m*

Chapter 4 Theme

4 The Spirit*n* clearly says that in later times*o* some will abandon the faith and follow deceiving spirits*p* and things taught by demons. *2*Such teachings come through hypocritical liars, whose consciences have been seared as with a hot iron.*q* *3*They forbid people to marry*r* and order them to abstain from certain foods,*s* which God created*t* to be received with thanksgiving*u* by those who believe and who know the truth. *4*For everything God created is good,*v* and nothing is to be rejected if it is received with thanksgiving, *5*because it is consecrated by the word of God and prayer.

*6*If you point these things out to the brothers, you will be a good minister of Christ Jesus, brought up in the truths of the faith*w* and of the good teaching that you have followed. *7*Have nothing to do with godless myths and old wives' tales;*x* rather, train yourself to

a 11 Or *way, deaconesses*   *b 16* Some manuscripts *God*   *c 16* Or *in the flesh* be godly. [8]For physical training is of some value, but godliness has value for all things,[a] holding promise for both the present life[b] and the life to come.

[9]This is a trustworthy saying[c] that deserves full acceptance [10](and for this we labor and strive), that we have put our hope in the living God, who is the Savior of all men, and especially of those who believe.

[11]Command and teach these things.[d] [12]Don't let anyone look down on you because you are young, but set an example[e] for the believers in speech, in life, in love, in faith[f] and in purity. [13]Until I come, devote yourself to the public reading of Scripture, to preaching and to teaching. [14]Do not neglect your gift, which was given you through a prophetic message[g] when the body of elders laid their hands on you.[h]

[15]Be diligent in these matters; give yourself wholly to them, so that everyone may see your progress. [16]Watch your life and doctrine closely. Persevere in them, because if you do, you will save both yourself and your hearers.

Chapter 5 Theme

5 Do not rebuke an older man[i] harshly,[j] but exhort him as if he were your father. Treat younger men[k] as brothers, [2]older women as mothers, and younger women as sisters, with absolute purity.

[3]Give proper recognition to those widows who are really in need.[l] [4]But if a widow has children or grandchildren, these should learn first of all to put their religion into practice by caring for their own family and so repaying their parents and grandparents,[m] for this is pleasing to God.[n] [5]The widow who is really in need[o] and left all alone puts her hope in God[p] and continues night and day to pray[q] and to ask God for help. [6]But the widow who lives for pleasure is dead even while she lives.[r] [7]Give the people these instructions,[s] too, so that no one may be open to blame. [8]If anyone does not provide for his relatives, and especially for his immediate family, he has denied[t] the faith and is worse than an unbeliever.

[9]No widow may be put on the list of widows unless she is over sixty, has been faithful to her husband,[a] [10]and is well known for her good deeds,[u] such as bringing up children, showing hospitality, washing the feet[v] of the saints, helping those in trouble[w] and devoting herself to all kinds of good deeds.

[11]As for younger widows, do not put them on such a list. For when their sensual desires overcome their dedication to Christ, they want to marry. [12]Thus they bring judgment on themselves,

---

4:8
[a]1Ti 6:6
[b]Ps 37:9,11;
Mk 10:29,30

4:9
[c]1Ti 1:15

4:11
[d]1Ti 5:7; 6:2

4:12
[e]Tit 2:7;
1Pe 5:3
[f]1Ti 1:14

4:14
[g]1Ti 1:18
[h]Ac 6:6;
2Ti 1:6

5:1
[i]Tit 2:2
[j]Lev 19:32
[k]Tit 2:6

5:3
[l]ver 5,16

5:4
[m]Eph 6:1,2
[n]1Ti 2:3

5:5
[o]ver 3,16
[p]1Co 7:34;
1Pe 3:5
[q]Lk 2:37

5:6
[r]Lk 15:24

5:7
[s]1Ti 4:11

5:8
[t]2Pe 2:1;
Jude 4;
Tit 1:16

5:10
[u]Ac 9:36;
1Ti 6:18;
1Pe 2:12
[v]Lk 7:44
[w]ver 16

---

[a]9 Or has had but one husband

because they have broken their first pledge. [13]Besides, they get into the habit of being idle and going about from house to house. And not only do they become idlers, but also gossips and busybodies,[a] saying things they ought not to. [14]So I counsel younger widows to marry,[b] to have children, to manage their homes and to give the enemy no opportunity for slander.[c] [15]Some have in fact already turned away to follow Satan.[d]

[16]If any woman who is a believer has widows in her family, she should help them and not let the church be burdened with them, so that the church can help those widows who are really in need.[e]

[17]The elders[f] who direct the affairs of the church well are worthy of double honor,[g] especially those whose work is preaching and teaching. [18]For the Scripture says, "Do not muzzle the ox while it is treading out the grain,"[a][h] and "The worker deserves his wages."[b][i] [19]Do not entertain an accusation against an elder[j] unless it is brought by two or three witnesses.[k] [20]Those who sin are to be rebuked[l] publicly, so that the others may take warning.[m]

[21]I charge you, in the sight of God and Christ Jesus[n] and the elect angels, to keep these instructions without partiality, and to do nothing out of favoritism.

[22]Do not be hasty in the laying on of hands,[o] and do not share in the sins of others.[p] Keep yourself pure.

[23]Stop drinking only water, and use a little wine[q] because of your stomach and your frequent illnesses.

[24]The sins of some men are obvious, reaching the place of judgment ahead of them; the sins of others trail behind them. [25]In the same way, good deeds are obvious, and even those that are not cannot be hidden.

Chapter 6 Theme

6 All who are under the yoke of slavery should consider their masters worthy of full respect,[r] so that God's name and our teaching may not be slandered.[s] [2]Those who have believing masters are not to show less respect for them because they are brothers.[t] Instead, they are to serve them even better, because those who benefit from their service are believers, and dear to them. These are the things you are to teach and urge on them.[u]

[3]If anyone teaches false doctrines[v] and does not agree to the sound instruction[w] of our Lord Jesus Christ and to godly teaching, [4]he is conceited and understands nothing. He has an unhealthy interest in controversies and quarrels about words[x] that result in envy, strife, malicious talk, evil suspicions [5]and constant friction between men of corrupt mind, who have been robbed of the truth[y] and who think that godliness is a means to financial gain.

5:13
[a]2Th 3:11

5:14
[b]1Co 7:9
[c]1Ti 6:1

5:15
[d]Mt 4:10

5:16
[e]ver 3-5

5:17
[f]Ac 11:30
[g]Php 2:29;
1Th 5:12

5:18
[h]Dt 25:4;
1Co 9:7-9
[i]Lk 10:7;
Lev 19:13;
Dt 24:14,15;
Mt 10:10;
1Co 9:14

5:19
[j]Ac 11:30
[k]Mt 18:16

5:20
[l]2Ti 4:2;
Tit 1:13
[m]Dt 13:11

5:21
[n]1Ti 6:13;
2Ti 4:1

5:22
[o]Ac 6:6
[p]Eph 5:11

5:23
[q]1Ti 3:8

6:1
[r]Eph 6:5;
Tit 2:9;
1Pe 2:18
[s]Tit 2:5,8

6:2
[t]Phm 16
[u]1Ti 4:11

6:3
[v]1Ti 1:3
[w]1Ti 1:10

6:4
[x]2Ti 2:14

6:5
[y]Tit 1:15

[a]18 Deut. 25:4   [b]18 Luke 10:7

⁶But godliness with contentment*a* is great gain.*b* ⁷For we brought nothing into the world, and we can take nothing out of it.*c* ⁸But if we have food and clothing, we will be content with that.*d* ⁹People who want to get rich*e* fall into temptation and a trap*f* and into many foolish and harmful desires that plunge men into ruin and destruction. ¹⁰For the love of money*g* is a root of all kinds of evil. Some people, eager for money, have wandered from the faith*h* and pierced themselves with many griefs.

¹¹But you, man of God,*i* flee from all this, and pursue righteousness, godliness, faith, love,*j* endurance and gentleness. ¹²Fight the good fight*k* of the faith. Take hold of*l* the eternal life to which you were called when you made your good confession in the presence of many witnesses. ¹³In the sight of God, who gives life to everything, and of Christ Jesus, who while testifying before Pontius Pilate*m* made the good confession, I charge you*n* ¹⁴to keep this command without spot or blame until the appearing of our Lord Jesus Christ, ¹⁵which God will bring about in his own time—God, the blessed*o* and only Ruler,*p* the King of kings and Lord of lords,*q* ¹⁶who alone is immortal*r* and who lives in unapproachable light, whom no one has seen or can see.*s* To him be honor and might forever. Amen.

¹⁷Command those who are rich in this present world not to be arrogant nor to put their hope in wealth,*t* which is so uncertain, but to put their hope in God,*u* who richly provides us with everything for our enjoyment.*v* ¹⁸Command them to do good, to be rich in good deeds,*w* and to be generous and willing to share.*x* ¹⁹In this way they will lay up treasure for themselves*y* as a firm foundation for the coming age, so that they may take hold of the life that is truly life.

²⁰Timothy, guard what has been entrusted*z* to your care. Turn away from godless chatter*a* and the opposing ideas of what is falsely called knowledge, ²¹which some have professed and in so doing have wandered from the faith.*b*

Grace be with you.*c*

6:6
a Php 4:11;
Heb 13:5
b 1Ti 4:8

6:7
c Job 1:21;
Ecc 5:15

6:8
d Heb 13:5

6:9
e Pr 15:27
f 1Ti 3:7

6:10
g 1Ti 3:3
h Jas 5:19

6:11
i 2Ti 3:17
j 2Ti 2:22

6:12
k 1Co 9:25,26;
1Ti 1:18
l Php 3:12

6:13
m Jn 18:33-37
n 1Ti 5:21

6:15
o 1Ti 1:11
p 1Ti 1:17
q Rev 17:14;
19:16

6:16
r 1Ti 1:17
s Jn 1:18

6:17
t Lk 12:20,21
u 1Ti 4:10
v Ac 14:17

6:18
w 1Ti 5:10
x Ro 12:8,13

6:19
y Mt 6:20

6:20
z 2Ti 1:12,14
a 2Ti 2:16

6:21
b 2Ti 2:18
c Col 4:18

1 TIMOTHY OBSERVATIONS CHART

PAUL	TIMOTHY	THE RICH	WOMEN

OVERSEERS (ELDERS)	DEACONS	MEN

SLAVES	WIDOWS

(continued)

2055

Prayer	Charges and Instructions to Timothy

Theme of 1 Timothy:

Author:

Date:

Purpose:

Key Words:

teach

faith

doctrines,
teaching

godliness, godly

SEGMENT DIVISIONS	CHAPTER THEMES
1	
2	
3	
4	
5	
6	

2 TIMOTHY

*P*aul now found himself in a new set of circumstances. It was about A.D. 64 (some say 67) and Timothy was heavy on his heart. Paul had to write one last letter to his disciple, reminding Timothy of crucial matters concerning the ministry and urging him to make every effort to come quickly—before winter.

∾ THINGS TO DO

1. Read 2 Timothy. In chapters 1 and 2, and then in chapter 4, Paul refers to his circumstances: where he is and what is about to take place in his life. To help set the context of the letter, record on the OBSERVATIONS CHART on page 2063 what you learn about Paul's circumstances.

2. Read 2 Timothy again. Look for everything you learn about Timothy and record it on the OBSERVATIONS CHART.

3. As you read 2 Timothy you probably noticed the many commands and/or instructions Paul gave Timothy. These are easy to spot because the verb usually comes first in the sentence and the "you" is implied. An example of this is seen in 1:8: "So do not be ashamed to testify."

    a. List the instructions and/or commands Paul gives Timothy throughout the letter on the OBSERVATIONS CHART. (Be sure to note the chapter and verse in which you find each.)

    b. As you look for these instructions and/or commands, mark in the text the key words (and their synonyms and pronouns) that are listed on the 2 TIMOTHY AT A GLANCE chart on page 2064. Be sure to mark any reference to the gospel (*sound teaching, word, Scripture, Holy Scriptures,* etc.) and to suffering (*persecutions, hardship,* etc.).

4. Think back over the list of instructions and/or commands Paul gives Timothy and keep in mind the emphasis Paul places on the gospel. What do you think Paul's main message is to Timothy in this second epistle? Record this as the theme of the book on 2 TIMOTHY AT A GLANCE.

5. Look at the book one chapter at a time and summarize the main teaching or theme of each chapter and then record it on 2 TIMOTHY AT A GLANCE and in the text next to the chapter number. (Note: The theme of each chapter should relate to the general theme of the book.)

6. On 2 TIMOTHY AT A GLANCE you will see space to trace two themes, "Paul's Example" and "God's Provision," which run throughout the book. Doing this will give you additional insight into the practicality of 2 Timothy for your own life. Examine each chapter in the light of these two themes and record your insights on the appropriate space on the chart.

∾ THINGS TO THINK ABOUT

1. What is your responsibility toward the gospel? To what lengths will you go in order to carry out this responsibility?

2. What are you doing to make sure you handle the Word of God accurately? Do you simply repeat what you have been taught or are you carefully studying the Word systematically?

3. Are you willing to suffer for the sake of those who would come to know the Lord Jesus Christ and receive salvation?

4. What kind of men and women do you need to beware of in these last days?

5. How are you living? Are you a coward or have you fought the good fight of faith?

6. Are you ready to die? How will you feel when you see Jesus Christ face-to-face?

1:1
a 2Co 1:1
b Eph 3:6;
1Ti 6:19

1:2
c Ac 16:1
d 1Ti 1:2

1:3
e Ro 1:8
f Ro 1:10

1:4
g Ac 20:37
h 2Ti 4:9

1:5
i 1Ti 1:5
j Ac 16:1

1:6
k 1Ti 4:14

1:7
l Ro 8:15

1:8
m Mk 8:38;
Ro 1:16
n Eph 3:1
o 2Ti 2:3,9; 4:5

1:9
p Ro 8:28

1:10
q Eph 1:9
r 1Co 15:26,54

1:11
s 1Ti 2:7

1:12
t 1Ti 6:20
u ver 18

1:13
v Tit 1:9
w 1Ti 1:14

1:14
x Ro 8:9

1:15
y 2Ti 4:10,11,16

1:16
z 2Ti 4:19

1:18
a Heb 6:10

2:1
b Eph 6:10

2:2
c 2Ti 1:13

Chapter 1 Theme

1 Paul, an apostle of Christ Jesus by the will of God,[a] according to the promise of life that is in Christ Jesus,[b]

[2]To Timothy,[c] my dear son:[d]

Grace, mercy and peace from God the Father and Christ Jesus our Lord.

[3]I thank God,[e] whom I serve, as my forefathers did, with a clear conscience, as night and day I constantly remember you in my prayers.[f] [4]Recalling your tears,[g] I long to see you,[h] so that I may be filled with joy. [5]I have been reminded of your sincere faith,[i] which first lived in your grandmother Lois and in your mother Eunice[j] and, I am persuaded, now lives in you also. [6]For this reason I remind you to fan into flame the gift of God, which is in you through the laying on of my hands.[k] [7]For God did not give us a spirit of timidity,[l] but a spirit of power, of love and of self-discipline.

[8]So do not be ashamed[m] to testify about our Lord, or ashamed of me his prisoner.[n] But join with me in suffering for the gospel,[o] by the power of God, [9]who has saved us and called[p] us to a holy life—not because of anything we have done but because of his own purpose and grace. This grace was given us in Christ Jesus before the beginning of time, [10]but it has now been revealed[q] through the appearing of our Savior, Christ Jesus, who has destroyed death[r] and has brought life and immortality to light through the gospel. [11]And of this gospel I was appointed a herald and an apostle and a teacher.[s] [12]That is why I am suffering as I am. Yet I am not ashamed, because I know whom I have believed, and am convinced that he is able to guard[t] what I have entrusted to him for that day.[u]

[13]What you heard from me, keep[v] as the pattern of sound teaching, with faith and love in Christ Jesus.[w] [14]Guard the good deposit that was entrusted to you—guard it with the help of the Holy Spirit who lives in us.[x]

[15]You know that everyone in the province of Asia has deserted me,[y] including Phygelus and Hermogenes.

[16]May the Lord show mercy to the household of Onesiphorus,[z] because he often refreshed me and was not ashamed of my chains. [17]On the contrary, when he was in Rome, he searched hard for me until he found me. [18]May the Lord grant that he will find mercy from the Lord on that day! You know very well in how many ways he helped me[a] in Ephesus.

Chapter 2 Theme

2 You then, my son, be strong[b] in the grace that is in Christ Jesus. [2]And the things you have heard me say[c] in the presence of many witnesses[a] entrust to reliable men who will also be qualified to teach others. [3]Endure hardship with us like a good soldier[b] of Christ Jesus. [4]No one serving as a soldier gets involved in civilian affairs—he wants to please his commanding officer. [5]Similarly, if anyone competes as an athlete, he does not receive the victor's crown[c] unless he competes according to the rules. [6]The hardworking farmer should be the first to receive a share of the crops. [7]Reflect on what I am saying, for the Lord will give you insight into all this.

[8]Remember Jesus Christ, raised from the dead,[d] descended from David.[e] This is my gospel,[f] [9]for which I am suffering[g] even to the point of being chained like a criminal. But God's word is not chained. [10]Therefore I endure everything[h] for the sake of the elect, that they too may obtain the salvation that is in Christ Jesus, with eternal glory.[i]

[11]Here is a trustworthy saying:

> If we died with him,
>   we will also live with him;[j]
> [12]if we endure,
>   we will also reign with him.[k]
> If we disown him,
>   he will also disown us;[l]
> [13]if we are faithless,
>   he will remain faithful,[m]
>   for he cannot disown himself.

[14]Keep reminding them of these things. Warn them before God against quarreling about words;[n] it is of no value, and only ruins those who listen. [15]Do your best to present yourself to God as one approved, a workman who does not need to be ashamed and who correctly handles the word of truth.[o] [16]Avoid godless chatter,[p] because those who indulge in it will become more and more ungodly. [17]Their teaching will spread like gangrene. Among them are Hymenaeus[q] and Philetus, [18]who have wandered away from the truth. They say that the resurrection has already taken place, and they destroy the faith of some.[r] [19]Nevertheless, God's solid foundation stands firm,[s] sealed with this inscription: "The Lord knows those who are his,"[a][t] and, "Everyone who confesses the name of the Lord[u] must turn away from wickedness."

[20]In a large house there are articles not only of gold and silver, but also of wood and clay; some are for noble purposes and some for ignoble.[v] [21]If a man cleanses himself from the latter, he will be an instrument for noble purposes, made holy, useful to the Master and prepared to do any good work.[w]

[22]Flee the evil desires of youth, and pursue righteousness, faith,

a [19] Num. 16:5 (see Septuagint)

2:2 a 1Ti 6:12

2:3 b 1Ti 1:18

2:5 c 1Co 9:25

2:8 d Ac 2:24
e Mt 1:1
f Ro 2:16

2:9 g Ac 9:16

2:10 h Col 1:24
i 2Co 4:17

2:11 j Ro 6:2-11

2:12 k Ro 8:17;
1Pe 4:13
l Mt 10:33

2:13 m Nu 23:19;
Ro 3:3

2:14 n 1Ti 6:4

2:15 o Eph 1:13;
Jas 1:18

2:16 p Tit 3:9

2:17 q 1Ti 1:20

2:18 r 1Ti 1:19

2:19 s Isa 28:16
t Jn 10:14
u 1Co 1:2

2:20 v Ro 9:21

2:21 w 2Ti 3:17

love *a* and peace, along with those who call on the Lord out of a pure heart. *b* 23Don't have anything to do with foolish and stupid arguments, because you know they produce quarrels. 24And the Lord's servant must not quarrel; instead, he must be kind to everyone, able to teach, not resentful.*c* 25Those who oppose him he must gently instruct, in the hope that God will grant them repentance leading them to a knowledge of the truth,*d* 26and that they will come to their senses and escape from the trap of the devil,*e* who has taken them captive to do his will.

Chapter 3 Theme _____

3 But mark this: There will be terrible times in the last days.*f* 2People will be lovers of themselves, lovers of money, *g* boastful, proud,*h* abusive, disobedient to their parents,*i* ungrateful, unholy, 3without love, unforgiving, slanderous, without self-control, brutal, not lovers of the good, 4treacherous, rash, conceited,*j* lovers of pleasure rather than lovers of God— 5having a form of godliness but denying its power. Have nothing to do with them.

6They are the kind who worm their way*k* into homes and gain control over weak-willed women, who are loaded down with sins and are swayed by all kinds of evil desires, 7always learning but never able to acknowledge the truth. 8Just as Jannes and Jambres opposed Moses,*l* so also these men oppose*m* the truth—men of depraved minds, *n* who, as far as the faith is concerned, are rejected. 9But they will not get very far because, as in the case of those men,*o* their folly will be clear to everyone.

10You, however, know all about my teaching,*p* my way of life, my purpose, faith, patience, love, endurance, 11persecutions, sufferings—what kinds of things happened to me in Antioch, *q* Iconium and Lystra, the persecutions I endured.*r* Yet the Lord rescued me from all of them.*s* 12In fact, everyone who wants to live a godly life in Christ Jesus will be persecuted,*t* 13while evil men and impostors will go from bad to worse,*u* deceiving and being deceived. 14But as for you, continue in what you have learned and have become convinced of, because you know those from whom you learned it, *v* 15and how from infancy*w* you have known the holy Scriptures,*x* which are able to make you wise*y* for salvation through faith in Christ Jesus. 16All Scripture is God-breathed*z* and is useful for teaching,*a* rebuking, correcting and training in righteousness, 17so that the man of God*b* may be thoroughly equipped for every good work.*c*

Chapter 4 Theme _____

4 In the presence of God and of Christ Jesus, who will judge the living and the dead,*d* and in view of his appearing and his

---

2:22
a 1Ti 1:14; 6:11
b 1Ti 1:5

2:24
c 1Ti 3:2,3

2:25
d 1Ti 2:4

2:26
e 1Ti 3:7

3:1
f 1Ti 4:1

3:2
g 1Ti 3:3
h Ro 1:30
i Ro 1:30

3:4
j 1Ti 3:6

3:6
k Jude 4

3:8
l Ex 7:11
m Ac 13:8
n 1Ti 6:5

3:9
o Ex 7:12

3:10
p 1Ti 4:6

3:11
q Ac 13:14,50
r 2Co 11:23-27
s Ps 34:19

3:12
t Ac 14:22

3:13
u 2Ti 2:16

3:14
v 2Ti 1:13

3:15
w 2Ti 1:5
x Jn 5:39
y Ps 119:98,99

3:16
z 2Pe 1:20,21
a Ro 4:23,24

3:17
b 1Ti 6:11
c 2Ti 2:21

4:1
d Ac 10:42

kingdom, I give you this charge: [a] [2]Preach[b] the Word;[c] be prepared in season and out of season; correct, rebuke[d] and encourage— with great patience and careful instruction. [3]For the time will come when men will not put up with sound doctrine.[e] Instead, to suit their own desires, they will gather around them a great number of teachers to say what their itching ears want to hear. [4]They will turn their ears away from the truth and turn aside to myths.[f] [5]But you, keep your head in all situations, endure hardship,[g] do the work of an evangelist,[h] discharge all the duties of your ministry.

[6]For I am already being poured out like a drink offering,[i] and the time has come for my departure.[j] [7]I have fought the good fight,[k] I have finished the race,[l] I have kept the faith. [8]Now there is in store for me[m] the crown of righteousness, which the Lord, the righteous Judge, will award to me on that day[n]—and not only to me, but also to all who have longed for his appearing.

[9]Do your best to come to me quickly, [10]for Demas,[o] because he loved this world,[p] has deserted me and has gone to Thessalonica. Crescens has gone to Galatia,[q] and Titus to Dalmatia. [11]Only Luke[r] is with me.[s] Get Mark[t] and bring him with you, because he is helpful to me in my ministry. [12]I sent Tychicus[u] to Ephesus. [13]When you come, bring the cloak that I left with Carpus at Troas, and my scrolls, especially the parchments.

[14]Alexander[v] the metalworker did me a great deal of harm. The Lord will repay him for what he has done.[w] [15]You too should be on your guard against him, because he strongly opposed our message.

[16]At my first defense, no one came to my support, but everyone deserted me. May it not be held against them.[x] [17]But the Lord stood at my side[y] and gave me strength, so that through me the message might be fully proclaimed and all the Gentiles might hear it.[z] And I was delivered from the lion's mouth. [18]The Lord will rescue me from every evil attack[a] and will bring me safely to his heavenly kingdom. To him be glory for ever and ever. Amen.[b]

[19]Greet Priscilla[a] and Aquila[c] and the household of Onesiphorus. [20]Erastus[d] stayed in Corinth, and I left Trophimus[e] sick in Miletus. [21]Do your best to get here before winter.[f] Eubulus greets you, and so do Pudens, Linus, Claudia and all the brothers.

[22]The Lord be with your spirit.[g] Grace be with you.[h]

a 19 Greek *Prisca*, a variant of *Priscilla*

4:1
a 1Ti 5:21

4:2
b 1Ti 4:13
c Gal 6:6
d 1Ti 5:20;
Tit 1:13; 2:15

4:3
e 1Ti 1:10

4:4
f 1Ti 1:4

4:5
g 2Ti 1:8
h Ac 21:8

4:6
i Php 2:17
j Php 1:23

4:7
k 1Ti 1:18
l 1Co 9:24

4:8
m Col 1:5
n 2Ti 1:12

4:10
o Col 4:14
p 1Jn 2:15
q Ac 16:6

4:11
r Col 4:14
s 2Ti 1:15
t Ac 12:12

4:12
u Ac 20:4

4:14
v Ac 19:33
w Ro 12:19

4:16
x Ac 7:60

4:17
y Ac 23:11
z Ac 9:15

4:18
a Ps 121:7
b Ro 11:36

4:19
c Ac 18:2

4:20
d Ac 19:22
e Ac 20:4

4:21
f ver 9

4:22
g Gal 6:18;
Phm 25
h Col 4:18

2 TIMOTHY OBSERVATIONS CHART

PAUL	TIMOTHY
Where is he?	How is he described?
Why is he there?	What is his relationship to Paul?
Who is with him?	What do you learn about him?
What is about to happen?	
How is he going to handle it?	

PAUL'S INSTRUCTIONS TO TIMOTHY

Theme of 2 Timothy:

SEGMENT DIVISIONS			Author:
GOD'S PROVISION	PAUL'S EXAMPLE	CHAPTER THEMES	
			Date:
		1	
			Purpose:
		2	
			Key Words:
			gospel
			word
DELIVERED PAUL OUT OF PERSECUTIONS	ENDURED PERSECUTIONS	3	suffer (sufferings, persecution)
			endure(d), put up with
		4	faith
			ashamed

TITUS

W hen Paul sailed past Crete on his way to Rome he was not the master of his own ship. He was Rome's prisoner. How wise the centurion guard would have been had he followed Paul's urging to put ashore in Crete! Despite the winds, they sailed on under much duress. As Paul had predicted, the ship was lost in Malta, the island 58 miles south of Sicily.

Paul's ship sank to the bottom of the sea; Crete had sunk to the depths of sin. Broken to pieces morally by the incessant pounding of a godless lifestyle, Crete needed the good news of the gospel. Unlike the ship, however, it was not beyond redemption.

Whether Crete was on Paul's heart before his two years' house arrest in Rome, we don't know. We only know that once Paul was free from Rome's chains he apparently went with Titus to Crete and left him there.

As Paul wrote Titus, it was about A.D. 62. He didn't know he would return to Rome for one final imprisonment.

∾ THINGS TO DO

1. Read through Titus without stopping so that you understand the general content and thrust of the letter.

2. Read Titus again, one chapter at a time. As you read each chapter:

   a. Look for the information about the author: who he is, how he describes himself, where he is, etc. Record your insights on the OBSERVATIONS CHART on page 2069. Note the chapter and verse in which you find your information; it helps when you want to find something later.

   b. Mark in the text the key words listed on the TITUS AT A GLANCE chart on page 2070. Be sure also to mark the synonyms and pronouns.

   c. In the margin of your Bible, list the truths you learn from the text about each key word.

3. The commands, warnings, and instructions Paul includes in his letter to Titus help define Paul's purpose for writing. Read Titus again chapter by chapter and note each command, warning, or instruction Paul gives Titus. List these on the OBSERVATIONS CHART under "Instructions to Titus."

4. Note on the OBSERVATIONS CHART what you learn about Titus and his relationship to Paul. In chapter 1 Paul clearly tells us where Titus is and why he is there.

5. In his letter Paul mentions various groups of people. List what you learn about each of these groups under the designated heading on your OBSERVATIONS CHART.

6. Listing Paul's commands, warnings, and instructions to Titus probably has helped you see the dominant subject of Titus. There are two verses, one in chapter 2 and one in chapter 3, which summarize the thrust of Paul's letter. These will help you determine the theme of the epistle. Record it on TITUS AT A GLANCE.

   a. Now summarize the theme or main message of each paragraph and then of each chapter and record these on TITUS AT A GLANCE. Also record the chapter theme in the text next to the chapter number.

   b. Fill in author, date, and purpose on the same chart.

∾ THINGS TO THINK ABOUT

1. The world's lifestyle denies God. By your lifestyle and attitudes, do you deny ungodliness and worldly desires, or do you indulge the desires of your flesh?

2. It is difficult always to be considerate to everyone, isn't it? When did you last fail in this area? Have you determined afresh to be gentle and uncontentious even in the most difficult situation with the most difficult person? Your actions often will speak louder than your words ever can.

3. Your salvation was not based on performance but upon the mercy and grace of God. What has your heavenly Father saved you from? Think on his goodness that brought you from death into life and brought you out of the kingdom of darkness into the kingdom of his glorious light. Have you thanked him lately for his mercy and grace? Why not do it now? Pray for those close to you who have yet to experience the saving grace of God.

Chapter 1 Theme

1 Paul, a servant of God[a] and an apostle of Jesus Christ for the faith of God's elect and the knowledge of the truth[b] that leads to godliness— [2]a faith and knowledge resting on the hope of eternal life,[c] which God, who does not lie, promised before the beginning of time,[d] [3]and at his appointed season[e] he brought his word to light[f] through the preaching entrusted to me[g] by the command of God our Savior,[h]

[4]To Titus,[i] my true son in our common faith:

Grace and peace from God the Father and Christ Jesus our Savior.

[5]The reason I left you in Crete[j] was that you might straighten out what was left unfinished and appoint[a] elders[k] in every town, as I directed you. [6]An elder must be blameless,[l] the husband of but one wife, a man whose children believe and are not open to the charge of being wild and disobedient. [7]Since an overseer[b][m] is entrusted with God's work,[n] he must be blameless—not overbearing, not quick-tempered, not given to drunkenness, not violent, not pursuing dishonest gain.[o] [8]Rather he must be hospitable,[p] one who loves what is good,[q] who is self-controlled, upright, holy and disciplined. [9]He must hold firmly[r] to the trustworthy message as it has been taught, so that he can encourage others by sound doctrine[s] and refute those who oppose it.

[10]For there are many rebellious people, mere talkers[t] and deceivers, especially those of the circumcision group.[u] [11]They must be silenced, because they are ruining whole households[v] by teaching things they ought not to teach—and that for the sake of

To Titus at Crete

1:1
[a] Ro 1:1
[b] 1Ti 2:4

1:2
[c] 2Ti 1:1
[d] 2Ti 1:9

1:3
[e] 1Ti 2:6
[f] 2Ti 1:10
[g] 1Ti 1:11
[h] Lk 1:47

1:4
[i] 2Co 2:13

1:5
[j] Ac 27:7
[k] Ac 11:30

1:6
[l] 1Ti 3:2

1:7
[m] 1Ti 3:1
[n] 1Co 4:1
[o] 1Ti 3:3,8

1:8
[p] 1Ti 3:2
[q] 2Ti 3:3

1:9
[r] 1Ti 1:19
[s] 1Ti 1:10

1:10
[t] 1Ti 1:6
[u] 11:2

1:11
[v] 2Ti 3:6

[a] 5 Or *ordain*   [b] 7 Traditionally *bishop*

1:12
a Ac 17:28
b Ac 2:11

1:13
c 2Co 13:10
d Tit 2:2

1:14
e 1Ti 1:4
f Col 2:22

1:15
g Ro 14:14,23

1:16
h 1Jn 2:4

2:1
i 1Ti 1:10

2:2
j Tit 1:13

2:3
k 1Ti 3:8

2:5
l Eph 5:22
m 1Ti 6:1

2:6
n 1Ti 5:1

2:7
o 1Ti 4:12

2:8
p 1Pe 2:12

2:9
q Eph 6:5

2:10
r Mt 5:16

2:11
s 1Ti 2:4

2:12
t Tit 3:3
u 2Ti 3:12

2:13
v 2Pe 1:1

2:14
w Ex 19:5
x Eph 2:10

3:1
y Ro 13:1
z 2Ti 2:21

3:2
a Eph 4:31;
2Ti 2:24

dishonest gain. ¹²Even one of their own prophets*a* has said, "Cretans*b* are always liars, evil brutes, lazy gluttons." ¹³This testimony is true. Therefore, rebuke*c* them sharply, so that they will be sound in the faith*d* ¹⁴and will pay no attention to Jewish myths*e* or to the commands*f* of those who reject the truth. ¹⁵To the pure, all things are pure, but to those who are corrupted and do not believe, nothing is pure.*g* In fact, both their minds and consciences are corrupted. ¹⁶They claim to know God, but by their actions they deny him.*h* They are detestable, disobedient and unfit for doing anything good.

Chapter 2 Theme _____

2 You must teach what is in accord with sound doctrine.*i* ²Teach the older men to be temperate, worthy of respect, self-controlled, and sound in faith,*j* in love and in endurance.

³Likewise, teach the older women to be reverent in the way they live, not to be slanderers or addicted to much wine,*k* but to teach what is good. ⁴Then they can train the younger women to love their husbands and children, ⁵to be self-controlled and pure, to be busy at home, to be kind, and to be subject to their husbands,*l* so that no one will malign the word of God.*m*

⁶Similarly, encourage the young men*n* to be self-controlled. ⁷In everything set them an example*o* by doing what is good. In your teaching show integrity, seriousness ⁸and soundness of speech that cannot be condemned, so that those who oppose you may be ashamed because they have nothing bad to say about us.*p*

⁹Teach slaves to be subject to their masters in everything,*q* to try to please them, not to talk back to them, ¹⁰and not to steal from them, but to show that they can be fully trusted, so that in every way they will make the teaching about God our Savior attractive.*r*

¹¹For the grace of God that brings salvation has appeared to all men.*s* ¹²It teaches us to say "No" to ungodliness and worldly passions,*t* and to live self-controlled, upright and godly lives*u* in this present age, ¹³while we wait for the blessed hope—the glorious appearing of our great God and Savior, Jesus Christ,*v* ¹⁴who gave himself for us to redeem us from all wickedness and to purify for himself a people that are his very own,*w* eager to do what is good.*x*

¹⁵These, then, are the things you should teach. Encourage and rebuke with all authority. Do not let anyone despise you.

Chapter 3 Theme _____

3 Remind the people to be subject to rulers and authorities,*y* to be obedient, to be ready to do whatever is good,*z* ²to slander no one,*a* to be peaceable and considerate, and to show true humility toward all men.

[3]At one time we too were foolish, disobedient, deceived and enslaved by all kinds of passions and pleasures. We lived in malice and envy, being hated and hating one another. [4]But when the kindness[a] and love of God our Savior appeared,[b] [5]he saved us, not because of righteous things we had done,[c] but because of his mercy. He saved us through the washing of rebirth and renewal[d] by the Holy Spirit, [6]whom he poured out on us[e] generously through Jesus Christ our Savior, [7]so that, having been justified by his grace,[f] we might become heirs[g] having the hope[h] of eternal life.[i] [8]This is a trustworthy saying.[j] And I want you to stress these things, so that those who have trusted in God may be careful to devote themselves to doing what is good.[k] These things are excellent and profitable for everyone.

[9]But avoid foolish controversies and genealogies and arguments and quarrels[l] about the law, because these are unprofitable and useless. [10]Warn a divisive person once, and then warn him a second time. After that, have nothing to do with him.[m] [11]You may be sure that such a man is warped and sinful; he is self-condemned.

[12]As soon as I send Artemas or Tychicus[n] to you, do your best to come to me at Nicopolis, because I have decided to winter there.[o] [13]Do everything you can to help Zenas the lawyer and Apollos[p] on their way and see that they have everything they need. [14]Our people must learn to devote themselves to doing what is good,[q] in order that they may provide for daily necessities and not live unproductive lives.

[15]Everyone with me sends you greetings. Greet those who love us in the faith.[r]

Grace be with you all.[s]

3:4
[a] Eph 2:7
[b] Tit 2:11

3:5
[c] Eph 2:9
[d] Ro 12:2

3:6
[e] Ro 5:5

3:7
[f] Ro 3:24
[g] Ro 8:17
[h] Ro 8:24
[i] Tit 1:2

3:8
[j] 1Ti 1:15
[k] Tit 2:14

3:9
[l] 1Ti 1:4;
2Ti 2:14

3:10
[m] Ro 16:17

3:12
[n] Ac 20:4
[o] 2Ti 4:9,21

3:13
[p] Ac 18:24

3:14
[q] ver 8

3:15
[r] 1Ti 1:2
[s] Col 4:18

TITUS OBSERVATIONS CHART

PAUL	TITUS	INSTRUCTIONS TO TITUS
Where is he?	Where is he? Why?	
How does he describe himself?	What is his relationship to Paul?	
ELDERS (OVERSEERS)	OLDER MEN	
	CRETANS	OLDER WOMEN
	SLAVES	YOUNGER WOMEN
YOUNG MEN		

Theme of Titus:

	PARAGRAPH THEMES	CHAPTER THEMES
1:1-4		1
1:5-9		
1:10-16		
2:1-15		2
3:1-11		3
3:12-15		

Author:

Date:

Purpose:

Key Words:
God

Jesus Christ

doctrine
(teachings)

truth

grace

actions, righteous things
we had done,
do what is good,
doing what is
good

$\mathcal{P}$HILEMON

$\mathcal{S}$lavery was a fact of life in Paul's day—a fact Paul couldn't change. But Paul could show slaves and masters how they were to behave toward one another as those redeemed by Jesus, who had become a bondservant on their behalf. In his epistles Paul shared these principles.

Now, however, something else had come up. Paul had to appeal to Philemon, a believer from Colosse, about a very personal matter: One of Philemon's slaves had run away, and according to Roman law he could be put to death by his master. So at about the same time he wrote Colossians, Paul wrote to Philemon from his rented quarters, where as a prisoner of Rome he also could be put to death. It was about A.D. 61 or 62.

∞ THINGS TO DO

1. Philemon is only one short chapter. Read it to gain an understanding of why this letter was written.

   a. When you finish reading, go back and note everything you learn about Paul on the OBSERVATIONS CHART on page 2073. Also watch for Paul's reason for writing and how he goes about achieving his purpose. Then record the reasons on the PHILEMON AT A GLANCE chart also on page 2073.

   b. Also note everything you learn about the recipients of Paul's letter and record this information in the appropriate section of the OBSERVATIONS CHART.

   c. Record on the OBSERVATIONS CHART everything you learn about Onesimus.

2. Carefully read the book again, marking in the text each of the key words (with their synonyms and pronouns) listed on the PHILEMON AT A GLANCE chart. Then in the margin list the truths you learn about each of these words from the text.

3. Record the theme of Philemon on PHILEMON AT A GLANCE and also in the text. Because Philemon is only one chapter, it is divided into paragraphs on the chart. Read the book paragraph by paragraph and record on the chart the theme of each paragraph. Then fill in the rest of the chart.

∞ THINGS TO THINK ABOUT

1. Are you willing to appeal to someone on behalf of another person, to assume the role of an advocate?

2. What can you learn from Paul's example in the way he appealed to Philemon?

3. Is there someone you need to forgive and offer restoration?

4. Can someone appeal to you to do the right thing on the basis of your character, or does he have to force your hand through rules, regulations, or some sort of a "bribe"?

∞∞∞∞∞

1:1 *a* ver 9,23; Eph 3:1 *b* 2Co 1:1 *c* Php 2:25	*Chapter Theme* _____ ¹Paul, a prisoner*a* of Christ Jesus, and Timothy our brother,*b* To Philemon our dear friend and fellow worker,*c* ²to Apphia our sister, to Archippus*d* our fellow soldier*e* and to the church that meets in your home: *f*
1:2 *d* Col 4:17 *e* Php 2:25 *f* Ro 16:5	³Grace to you and peace from God our Father and the Lord Jesus Christ.
1:4 *g* Ro 1:8	⁴I always thank my God*g* as I remember you in my prayers, ⁵because I hear about your faith in the Lord Jesus and your love

for all the saints.[a] [6]I pray that you may be active in sharing your faith, so that you will have a full understanding of every good thing we have in Christ. [7]Your love has given me great joy and encouragement,[b] because you, brother, have refreshed[c] the hearts of the saints.

[8]Therefore, although in Christ I could be bold and order you to do what you ought to do, [9]yet I appeal to you on the basis of love. I then, as Paul—an old man and now also a prisoner[d] of Christ Jesus— [10]I appeal to you for my son[e] Onesimus,[af] who became my son while I was in chains. [11]Formerly he was useless to you, but now he has become useful both to you and to me.

[12]I am sending him—who is my very heart—back to you. [13]I would have liked to keep him with me so that he could take your place in helping me while I am in chains for the gospel. [14]But I did not want to do anything without your consent, so that any favor you do will be spontaneous and not forced.[g] [15]Perhaps the reason he was separated from you for a little while was that you might have him back for good— [16]no longer as a slave, but better than a slave, as a dear brother.[h] He is very dear to me but even dearer to you, both as a man and as a brother in the Lord.

[17]So if you consider me a partner,[i] welcome him as you would welcome me. [18]If he has done you any wrong or owes you anything, charge it to me. [19]I, Paul, am writing this with my own hand. I will pay it back—not to mention that you owe me your very self. [20]I do wish, brother, that I may have some benefit from you in the Lord; refresh[j] my heart in Christ. [21]Confident[k] of your obedience, I write to you, knowing that you will do even more than I ask.

[22]And one thing more: Prepare a guest room for me, because I hope to be[l] restored to you in answer to your prayers.[m]

[23]Epaphras,[n] my fellow prisoner in Christ Jesus, sends you greetings. [24]And so do Mark,[o] Aristarchus,[p] Demas[q] and Luke, my fellow workers.

[25]The grace of the Lord Jesus Christ be with your spirit.[r]

[a] 10 Onesimus means useful.

1:5
[a] Eph 1:15;
Col 1:4

1:7
[b] 2Co 7:4,13
[c] ver 20

1:9
[d] ver 1,23

1:10
[e] 1Co 4:15
[f] Col 4:9

1:14
[g] 2Co 9:7;
1Pe 5:2

1:16
[h] Mt 23:8;
1Ti 6:2

1:17
[i] 2Co 8:23

1:20
[j] ver 7

1:21
[k] 2Co 2:3

1:22
[l] Php 1:25; 2:24
[m] 2Co 1:11

1:23
[n] Col 1:7

1:24
[o] Ac 12:12
[p] Ac 19:29
[q] Col 4:14

1:25
[r] 2Ti 4:22

PHILEMON OBSERVATIONS CHART

THE AUTHOR	THE RECIPIENTS	ONESIMUS

PHILEMON AT A GLANCE

Theme of Philemon:

SEGMENT DIVISIONS	

Author:

	PARAGRAPH THEMES
Date:	VERSES 1-3
Purpose:	VERSES 4-7
Key Words:	VERSES 8-20
love	
appeal	VERSES 21, 22
slave	
	VERSES 23-25

ℋEBREWS

℘ersecution increased as the gospel spread. The persecution was especially intense for Jewish believers because they had turned their back on the world and its ways and had abandoned the ordinances of the law which Jews had embraced since the time of Moses. This left them in a no-man's land. Jews as well as Gentiles who did not believe in the Lord Jesus Christ could not understand them, nor would many tolerate their newfound faith without challenge or attack.

Imagine yourself in a similar situation. What if you were wrong about Jesus Christ? What if he were not really the Messiah? And what about the new covenant? What if it didn't replace the old covenant? What if you really did need a continuing blood sacrifice for your sins? *What if?*

So that we could be secure in our faith, God moved an unknown author to take up pen and parchment and write the book we call Hebrews. No other book in the New Testament gives us what Hebrews gives us—the assurance that we have a high priest who is touched with the feeling of our weaknesses, one who ever lives to make intercession for us.

Hebrews was probably written before A.D. 70, because the temple was still standing and the priests were still making religious sacrifices.

✎ THINGS TO DO

1. Before you begin your study of Hebrews, read Hebrews 13:22 to discover the author's purpose for writing. Record this on the HEBREWS AT A GLANCE chart on page 2095.

2. In order to grasp the truth of this book, you need to understand to whom the book is written. As you read Hebrews chapter by chapter:

   a. Learn all you can about the recipients of this letter. Look for and mark the words *we, you, dear friends,* and *brothers.* Then record what you learn about the recipients on the OBSERVATIONS CHART on page 2093 under "Recipients."

   b. Note on the OBSERVATIONS CHART what you learn from the text about the author.

   c. Keep in mind the author's purpose for writing. Throughout the book you will see him exhorting his readers. Most of his exhortations begin with "let us." Mark each *let us* and then list each exhortation on the OBSERVATIONS CHART.

   d. Observe how the author periodically warns his readers about certain things.

      1) Note each warning on the OBSERVATIONS CHART. An example of a warning is found in 2:1: "We must pay more careful attention, therefore, to what we have heard, so that we do not drift away."

      2) As you note the warning, watch for and record the consequences of not heeding the warning. Also remember to whom the book is addressed. Let the text speak for itself. Don't read into it—just let it say what it says.

3. As you study each chapter, do the following:

   a. Write the key words (including their synonyms and pronouns) listed on the HEBREWS AT A GLANCE chart on an index card and then mark them in a distinctive way in the text. (Beginning at chapter 7, mark every occurrence of the words *covenant* and *will.*) Use this card as a reminder of what you are looking for as you study the book of Hebrews.

   b. List in the margin what you learn from each key word.

c. As you finish reading a chapter, decide on the theme or subject of that chapter and record it next to the chapter number in the text and on HEBREWS AT A GLANCE.

4. To truly appreciate and understand the book of Hebrews, you need to do the following:

a. Look back through your work and note all the times you marked *Jesus* and the pronouns referring to him. Also look for the phrase *superior to* or *better...than.* Then make a chart on THE SUPREMACY OF JESUS and list what you learn from Hebrews about our Lord. (Or record this information in the margin of your Bible.)

b. There is much in Hebrews about the priesthood and about Jesus as our high priest. Make a chart entitled THE PRIESTHOOD AND JESUS and list your information in three columns: "Insights into Priests and the Priesthood," "Insights into Jesus, Our Great High Priest," and "How This Applies to Me." Record your insights in the proper columns. (Or list this information in the margin of your Bible.)

c. Review what you learn from marking the words *covenant* and *will* and note what the text says on a chart you title A COMPARISON OF THE TWO COVENANTS: LAW AND GRACE AS TAUGHT IN HEBREWS. (Or in the margin next to chapters 8 through 10, list what you learn about the old covenant and law and the new covenant and grace.)

5. Complete HEBREWS AT A GLANCE by doing the following:

a. Look at each of your chapter themes in order to determine the theme of Hebrews and record it on the chart.

b. Fill in the section titled "Segment Divisions."

1) Segment divisions indicate a change in the thrust or topic of the book. One change in emphasis occurs at Hebrews 10:19, where the author stops dealing with the doctrinal aspects of the truth he is sharing and begins to address the practical aspects. Record this segment division on the chart in the appropriate space.

2) Look again at the chapter themes and see if there are any other divisions you can record. If so, record them on the chart. Completing this exercise will help you find where a specific truth is covered in Hebrews.

THINGS TO THINK ABOUT

1. Meditate on the truths you learned about Jesus. Do you see him as "superior to..."? How supreme is he in your life?

2. As you press on to Christian maturity, are you noticing a new sense of confidence in your God? Is your faith being strengthened? Are you drawing near to God? Do you think Jesus understands what you're going through? Can he really help?

3. Are you throwing off everything that hinders (every weighty thing that is slowing you down) and every sin, and running with perseverance the race marked out before you? If not, what is holding you back?

4. How are your morals? Do you live in the light of the fact that God will judge all who are sexually immoral and adulterers?

5. Are you continually offering up the sacrifice of praise? What are some things you can thank God for today?

Chapter 1 Theme

1 In the past God spoke[a] to our forefathers through the prophets[b] at many times and in various ways,[c] **2**but in these last days he has spoken to us by his Son, whom he appointed heir [d] of all things, and through whom[e] he made the universe. **3**The Son is the radiance of God's glory[f] and the exact representation of his being, sustaining all things[g] by his powerful word. After he had provided purification for sins,[h] he sat down at the right hand of the Majesty in heaven.[i] **4**So he became as much superior to the angels as the name he has inherited is superior to theirs.[j]

5For to which of the angels did God ever say,

"You are my Son;
today I have become your Father[a]"[b]?[k]

Or again,

"I will be his Father,
and he will be my Son"[c]?[l]

6And again, when God brings his firstborn into the world,[m] he says,

"Let all God's angels worship him."[d][n]

7In speaking of the angels he says,

"He makes his angels winds,
his servants flames of fire."[e][o]

8But about the Son he says,

"Your throne, O God, will last for ever and ever,
and righteousness will be the scepter of your kingdom.
9You have loved righteousness and hated wickedness;
therefore God, your God, has set you above
your companions[p]
by anointing you with the oil[q] of joy."[f]

10He also says,

"In the beginning, O Lord, you laid the foundations of
the earth,
and the heavens are the work of your hands.
11They will perish, but you remain;
they will all wear out like a garment.[r]
12You will roll them up like a robe;
like a garment they will be changed.
But you remain the same,[s]
and your years will never end."[g][t]

---

a5 Or *have begotten you*   b5 Psalm 2:7   c5 2 Samuel 7:14; 1 Chron. 17:13   d6 Deut. 32:43 (see Dead Sea Scrolls and Septuagint)   e7 Psalm 104:4   f9 Psalm 45:6,7   g12 Psalm 102:25-27

1:1
a Jn 9:29;
Heb 2:2,3
b Ac 2:30
c Nu 12:6,8

1:2
d Ps 2:8
e Jn 1:3

1:3
f Jn 1:14
g Col 1:17
h Heb 7:27
i Mk 16:19

1:4
j Eph 1:21;
Php 2:9,10

1:5
k Ps 2:7
l 2Sa 7:14

1:6
m Heb 10:5
n Dt 32:43
(LXX and DSS)
Ps 97:7

1:7
o Ps 104:4

1:9
p Php 2:9
q Isa 61:1,3

1:11
r Isa 34:4

1:12
s Heb 13:8
t Ps 102:25-27

1:13
a Jos 10:24;
Heb 10:13
b Ps 110:1

¹³To which of the angels did God ever say,

> "Sit at my right hand
> until I make your enemies
> a footstool*ᵃ* for your feet"*ᵃ*?*ᵇ*

1:14
c Ps 103:20
d Heb 5:9

¹⁴Are not all angels ministering spirits*ᶜ* sent to serve those who will inherit salvation?*ᵈ*

Chapter 2 Theme _____

2:2
e Heb 1:1
f Dt 33:2;
Ac 7:53
g Heb 10:28

2 We must pay more careful attention, therefore, to what we have heard, so that we do not drift away. ²For if the message spoken*ᵉ* by angels*ᶠ* was binding, and every violation and disobedience received its just punishment,*ᵍ* ³how shall we escape if we ignore such a great salvation?*ʰ* This salvation, which was first announced by the Lord,*ⁱ* was confirmed to us by those who heard him.*ʲ* ⁴God also testified to it by signs, wonders and various miracles,*ᵏ* and gifts of the Holy Spirit*ˡ* distributed according to his will.*ᵐ*

2:3
h Heb 10:29
i Heb 1:2
j Lk 1:2

2:4
k Jn 4:48
l 1Co 12:4
m Eph 1:5

⁵It is not to angels that he has subjected the world to come, about which we are speaking. ⁶But there is a place where someone has testified:

2:6
n Job 7:17

> "What is man that you are mindful of him,
> the son of man that you care for him?*ⁿ*
> ⁷You made him a little*ᵇ* lower than the angels;
> you crowned him with glory and honor
> ⁸ and put everything under his feet."*ᶜᵒ*

2:8
o Ps 8:4-6;
1Co 15:25

In putting everything under him, God left nothing that is not subject to him. Yet at present we do not see everything subject to him. ⁹But we see Jesus, who was made a little lower than the angels, now crowned with glory and honor*ᵖ* because he suffered death,*�q* so that by the grace of God he might taste death for everyone.*ʳ*

2:9
p Ac 2:33;
3:13;
Php 2:9
q Php 2:7-9
r Jn 3:16;
2Co 5:15

¹⁰In bringing many sons to glory, it was fitting that God, for whom and through whom everything exists,*ˢ* should make the author of their salvation perfect through suffering.*ᵗ* ¹¹Both the one who makes men holy and those who are made holy*ᵘ* are of the same family. So Jesus is not ashamed to call them brothers.*ᵛ* ¹²He says,

2:10
s Ro 11:36
t Lk 24:26;
Heb 7:28

2:11
u Heb 10:10
v Mt 28:10;
Jn 20:17

> "I will declare your name to my brothers;
> in the presence of the congregation I will sing
> your praises."*ᵈʷ*

¹³And again,

2:12
w Ps 22:22

> "I will put my trust in him."*ᵉˣ*

2:13
x Isa 8:17

a 13 Psalm 110:1   *b 7* Or *him for a little while;* also in verse 9   *c 8* Psalm 8:4-6
d 12 Psalm 22:22   *e 13* Isaiah 8:17

And again he says,

"Here am I, and the children God has given me."[a][a]

¹⁴Since the children have flesh and blood, he too shared in their humanity[b] so that by his death he might destroy[c] him who holds the power of death—that is, the devil[d]— ¹⁵and free those who all their lives were held in slavery by their fear[e] of death. ¹⁶For surely it is not angels he helps, but Abraham's descendants. ¹⁷For this reason he had to be made like his brothers[f] in every way, in order that he might become a merciful[g] and faithful high priest[h] in service to God,[i] and that he might make atonement for[b] the sins of the people. ¹⁸Because he himself suffered when he was tempted, he is able to help those who are being tempted.[j]

Chapter 3 Theme

3 Therefore, holy brothers,[k] who share in the heavenly calling, fix your thoughts on Jesus, the apostle and high priest[l] whom we confess.[m] ²He was faithful to the one who appointed him, just as Moses was faithful in all God's house.[n] ³Jesus has been found worthy of greater honor than Moses, just as the builder of a house has greater honor than the house itself. ⁴For every house is built by someone, but God is the builder of everything. ⁵Moses was faithful as a servant[o] in all God's house,[p] testifying to what would be said in the future. ⁶But Christ is faithful as a son[q] over God's house. And we are his house,[r] if we hold on[s] to our courage and the hope[t] of which we boast.

⁷So, as the Holy Spirit says:[u]

"Today, if you hear his voice,
⁸ do not harden your hearts
  as you did in the rebellion,
    during the time of testing in the desert,
⁹where your fathers tested and tried me
  and for forty years saw what I did.[v]
¹⁰That is why I was angry with that generation,
  and I said, 'Their hearts are always going astray,
  and they have not known my ways.'
¹¹So I declared on oath in my anger,
  'They shall never enter my rest.'[w]"[c][x]

¹²See to it, brothers, that none of you has a sinful, unbelieving heart that turns away from the living God. ¹³But encourage one another daily,[y] as long as it is called Today, so that none of you may

---

^a13 Isaiah 8:18 ^b17 Or *and that he might turn aside God's wrath, taking away*
^c11 Psalm 95:7-11

2:13
[a]Isa 8:18;
Jn 10:29

2:14
[b]Jn 1:14
[c]Co 15:54-57;
2Ti 1:10
[d]1Jn 3:8

2:15
[e]2Ti 1:7

2:17
[f]Php 2:7
[g]Heb 5:2
[h]Heb 4:14,15;
7:26,28
[i]Heb 5:1

2:18
[j]Heb 4:15

3:1
[k]Heb 2:11
[l]Heb 2:17
[m]Heb 4:14

3:2
[n]Nu 12:7

3:5
[o]Ex 14:31
[p]ver 2;
Nu 12:7

3:6
[q]Heb 1:2
[r]1Co 3:16
[s]Ro 11:22
[t]Ro 5:2

3:7
[u]Heb 9:8

3:9
[v]Ac 7:36

3:11
[w]Heb 4:3,5
[x]Ps 95:7-11

3:13
[y]Heb 10:24,25

be hardened by sin's deceitfulness.*a* [14]We have come to share in Christ if we hold firmly*b* till the end the confidence we had at first. [15]As has just been said:

> "Today, if you hear his voice,
>> do not harden your hearts
>> as you did in the rebellion."*ac*

[16]Who were they who heard and rebelled? Were they not all those Moses led out of Egypt?*d* [17]And with whom was he angry for forty years? Was it not with those who sinned, whose bodies fell in the desert?*e* [18]And to whom did God swear that they would never enter his rest*f* if not to those who disobeyed*b*?*g* [19]So we see that they were not able to enter, because of their unbelief.*h*

Chapter 4 Theme

4 Therefore, since the promise of entering his rest still stands, let us be careful that none of you be found to have fallen short of it.*i* [2]For we also have had the gospel preached to us, just as they did; but the message they heard was of no value to them, because those who heard did not combine it with faith.*cj* [3]Now we who have believed enter that rest, just as God has said,

> "So I declared on oath in my anger,
>> 'They shall never enter my rest.'"*dk*

And yet his work has been finished since the creation of the world. [4]For somewhere he has spoken about the seventh day in these words: "And on the seventh day God rested from all his work."*el* [5]And again in the passage above he says, "They shall never enter my rest."*m*

[6]It still remains that some will enter that rest, and those who formerly had the gospel preached to them did not go in, because of their disobedience.*n* [7]Therefore God again set a certain day, calling it Today, when a long time later he spoke through David, as was said before:

> "Today, if you hear his voice,
>> do not harden your hearts."*fo*

[8]For if Joshua had given them rest,*p* God would not have spoken*q* later about another day. [9]There remains, then, a Sabbath-rest for the people of God; [10]for anyone who enters God's rest also rests from his own work, just as God did from his.*r* [11]Let us, therefore, make every effort to enter that rest, so that no one will fall by following their example of disobedience.*s*

---

a15 Psalm 95:7,8   *b18* Or *disbelieved*   *c2* Many manuscripts *because they did not share in the faith of those who obeyed*   *d3* Psalm 95:11; also in verse 5   *e4* Gen. 2:2   *f7* Psalm 95:7,8

**Cross-references (left margin):**

3:13
a Eph 4:22

3:14
b ver 6

3:15
c ver 7,8;
Ps 95:7,8

3:16
d Nu 14:2

3:17
e Nu 14:29;
Ps 106:26

3:18
f Nu 14:20-23
g Heb 4:6

3:19
h Jn 3:36

4:1
i Heb 12:15

4:2
j 1Th 2:13

4:3
k Ps 95:11;
Heb 3:11

4:4
l Ge 2:2,3;
Ex 20:11

4:5
m Ps 95:11

4:6
n Heb 3:18

4:7
o Ps 95:7,8;
Heb 3:7,8,15

4:8
p Jos 22:4
q Heb 1:1

4:10
r ver 4

4:11
s Heb 3:18

¹²For the word of God[a] is living and active.[b] Sharper than any double-edged sword,[c] it penetrates even to dividing soul and spirit, joints and marrow; it judges the thoughts and attitudes of the heart.[d] ¹³Nothing in all creation is hidden from God's sight.[e] Everything is uncovered and laid bare before the eyes of him to whom we must give account.

¹⁴Therefore, since we have a great high priest who has gone through the heavens,[a][f] Jesus the Son of God, let us hold firmly to the faith we profess.[g] ¹⁵For we do not have a high priest who is unable to sympathize with our weaknesses, but we have one who has been tempted in every way, just as we are[h]—yet was without sin.[i] ¹⁶Let us then approach the throne of grace with confidence, so that we may receive mercy and find grace to help us in our time of need.

Chapter 5 Theme

5 Every high priest is selected from among men and is appointed to represent them in matters related to God, to offer gifts and sacrifices[j] for sins.[k] ²He is able to deal gently with those who are ignorant and are going astray,[l] since he himself is subject to weakness.[m] ³This is why he has to offer sacrifices for his own sins, as well as for the sins of the people.[n]

⁴No one takes this honor upon himself; he must be called by God, just as Aaron was.[o] ⁵So Christ also did not take upon himself the glory[p] of becoming a high priest. But God said[q] to him,

"You are my Son;
today I have become your Father.[b]"[r]

⁶And he says in another place,

"You are a priest forever,
in the order of Melchizedek."[d][s]

⁷During the days of Jesus' life on earth, he offered up prayers and petitions with loud cries and tears[t] to the one who could save him from death, and he was heard because of his reverent submission.[u] ⁸Although he was a son, he learned obedience from what he suffered[v] ⁹and, once made perfect,[w] he became the source of eternal salvation for all who obey him ¹⁰and was designated by God to be high priest[x] in the order of Melchizedek.[y]

¹¹We have much to say about this, but it is hard to explain because you are slow to learn. ¹²In fact, though by this time you ought to be teachers, you need someone to teach you the elementary truths[z] of God's word all over again. You need milk, not solid food![a] ¹³Anyone who lives on milk, being still an infant,[b] is not acquainted with the teaching about righteousness. ¹⁴But solid food is for the mature,[c] who by constant use have trained themselves to distinguish good from evil.[d]

4:12
[a] 1Pe 1:23
[b] Jer 23:29
[c] Eph 6:17;
Rev 1:16
[d] 1Co 14:24,25

4:13
[e] Ps 33:13-15

4:14
[f] Heb 6:20
[g] Heb 3:1

4:15
[h] Heb 2:18
[i] 2Co 5:21

5:1
[j] Heb 8:3
[k] Heb 7:27

5:2
[l] Heb 2:18
[m] Heb 7:28

5:3
[n] Heb 7:27; 9:7

5:4
[o] Ex 28:1

5:5
[p] Jn 8:54
[q] Heb 1:1
[r] Ps 2:7

5:6
[s] Ps 110:4;
Heb 7:17,21

5:7
[t] Mt 27:46,50
[u] Mk 14:36

5:8
[v] Php 2:8

5:9
[w] Heb 2:10

5:10
[x] ver 5
[y] ver 6

5:12
[z] Heb 6:1
[a] 1Co 3:2;
1Pe 2:2

5:13
[b] 1Co 14:20

5:14
[c] 1Co 2:6
[d] Isa 7:15

---

[a] 14 Or *gone into heaven*   [b] 5 Or *have begotten you*   [c] 5 Psalm 2:7   [d] 6 Psalm 110:4

6:1
a Php 3:12-14
b Heb 5:12
c Heb 9:14

6:2
d Jn 3:25
e Ac 6:6
f Ac 17:18,32

6:3
g Ac 18:21

6:4
h Heb 10:32
i Eph 2:8
j Gal 3:2

6:6
k 2Pe 2:21;
1Jn 5:16

6:8
l Ge 3:17,18;
Isa 5:6

6:9
m 1Co 10:14

6:10
n Mt 10:40,42;
25:40;
1Th 1:3

6:11
o Heb 3:6

6:12
p Heb 13:7
q 2Th 1:4;
Jas 1:3;
Rev 13:10
r Heb 10:36

6:13
s Ge 22:16;
Lk 1:73

6:14
t Ge 22:17

6:15
u Ge 21:5

6:16
v Ex 22:11

6:17
w Ps 110:4
x Heb 11:9

6:18
y Nu 23:19;
Tit 1:2
z Heb 3:6

6:19
a Lev 16:2;
Heb 9:2,3,7

6:20
b Heb 4:14
c Heb 2:17
d Heb 5:6

7:1
e Mk 5:7

Chapter 6 Theme

6 Therefore let us leave[a] the elementary teachings[b] about Christ and go on to maturity, not laying again the foundation of repentance from acts that lead to death,[ac] and of faith in God, [2] instruction about baptisms,[d] the laying on of hands,[e] the resurrection of the dead,[f] and eternal judgment. [3] And God permitting,[g] we will do so.

[4] It is impossible for those who have once been enlightened,[h] who have tasted the heavenly gift,[i] who have shared in the Holy Spirit,[j] [5] who have tasted the goodness of the word of God and the powers of the coming age, [6] if they fall away, to be brought back to repentance,[k] because[b] to their loss they are crucifying the Son of God all over again and subjecting him to public disgrace.

[7] Land that drinks in the rain often falling on it and that produces a crop useful to those for whom it is farmed receives the blessing of God. [8] But land that produces thorns and thistles is worthless and is in danger of being cursed.[l] In the end it will be burned.

[9] Even though we speak like this, dear friends,[m] we are confident of better things in your case—things that accompany salvation. [10] God is not unjust; he will not forget your work and the love you have shown him as you have helped his people and continue to help them.[n] [11] We want each of you to show this same diligence to the very end, in order to make your hope[o] sure. [12] We do not want you to become lazy, but to imitate[p] those who through faith and patience[q] inherit what has been promised.[r]

[13] When God made his promise to Abraham, since there was no one greater for him to swear by, he swore by himself,[s] [14] saying, "I will surely bless you and give you many descendants."[ct] [15] And so after waiting patiently, Abraham received what was promised.[u]

[16] Men swear by someone greater than themselves, and the oath confirms what is said and puts an end to all argument.[v] [17] Because God wanted to make the unchanging[w] nature of his purpose very clear to the heirs of what was promised,[x] he confirmed it with an oath. [18] God did this so that, by two unchangeable things in which it is impossible for God to lie,[y] we who have fled to take hold of the hope[z] offered to us may be greatly encouraged. [19] We have this hope as an anchor for the soul, firm and secure. It enters the inner sanctuary behind the curtain,[a] [20] where Jesus, who went before us, has entered on our behalf.[b] He has become a high priest[c] forever, in the order of Melchizedek.[d]

Chapter 7 Theme

7 This Melchizedek was king of Salem and priest of God Most High.[e] He met Abraham returning from the defeat of the kings

---

[a] 1 Or *from useless rituals*   [b] 6 Or *repentance while*   [c] 14 Gen. 22:17

and blessed him,[a] [2]and Abraham gave him a tenth of everything. First, his name means "king of righteousness"; then also, "king of Salem" means "king of peace." [3]Without father or mother, without genealogy,[b] without beginning of days or end of life, like the Son of God[c] he remains a priest forever.

[4]Just think how great he was: Even the patriarch[d] Abraham gave him a tenth of the plunder![e] [5]Now the law requires the descendants of Levi who become priests to collect a tenth from the people[f]— that is, their brothers—even though their brothers are descended from Abraham. [6]This man, however, did not trace his descent from Levi, yet he collected a tenth from Abraham and blessed[g] him who had the promises.[h] [7]And without doubt the lesser person is blessed by the greater. [8]In the one case, the tenth is collected by men who die; but in the other case, by him who is declared to be living.[i] [9]One might even say that Levi, who collects the tenth, paid the tenth through Abraham, [10]because when Melchizedek met Abraham, Levi was still in the body of his ancestor.

[11]If perfection could have been attained through the Levitical priesthood (for on the basis of it the law was given to the people),[j] why was there still need for another priest to come[k]—one in the order of Melchizedek,[l] not in the order of Aaron? [12]For when there is a change of the priesthood, there must also be a change of the law. [13]He of whom these things are said belonged to a different tribe,[m] and no one from that tribe has ever served at the altar.[n] [14]For it is clear that our Lord descended from Judah,[o] and in regard to that tribe Moses said nothing about priests. [15]And what we have said is even more clear if another priest like Melchizedek appears, [16]one who has become a priest not on the basis of a regulation as to his ancestry but on the basis of the power of an indestructible life. [17]For it is declared:

> "You are a priest forever,
>   in the order of Melchizedek."[a][p]

[18]The former regulation is set aside because it was weak and useless[q] [19](for the law made nothing perfect),[r] and a better hope is introduced, by which we draw near to God.[s]

[20]And it was not without an oath! Others became priests without any oath, [21]but he became a priest with an oath when God said to him:

> "The Lord has sworn
>   and will not change his mind:[t]
> 'You are a priest forever.'"[a][u]

[22]Because of this oath, Jesus has become the guarantee of a better covenant.[v]

7:1
a Ge 14:18-20

7:3
b ver 6
c Mt 4:3

7:4
d Ac 2:29
e Ge 14:20

7:5
f Nu 18:21,26

7:6
g Ge 14:19,20
h Ro 4:13

7:8
i Heb 5:6;
6:20

7:11
j ver 18,19;
Heb 8:7
k Heb 10:1
l ver 17

7:13
m ver 11
n ver 14

7:14
o Isa 11:1;
Mt 1:3;
Lk 3:33

7:17
p Ps 110:4;
ver 21;
Heb 5:6

7:18
q Ro 8:3

7:19
r Ac 13:39;
Ro 3:20;
Heb 9:9
s Heb 4:16

7:21
t 1Sa 15:29
u Ps 110:4

7:22
v Heb 8:6

7:24
a ver 28

7:25
b ver 19
c Ro 8:34

7:26
d 2Co 5:21
e Heb 4:14

7:27
f Heb 5:1
g Heb 5:3
h Heb 9:12, 26,28
i Eph 5:2;
Heb 9:14,28

7:28
j Heb 5:2
k Heb 1:2
l Heb 2:10

8:1
m Heb 2:17

8:2
n Heb 9:11,24

8:3
o Heb 5:1
p Heb 9:14

8:4
q Heb 5:1

8:5
r Heb 9:23
s Col 2:17;
Heb 10:1
t Heb 11:7;
12:25
u Ex 25:40

8:6
v Lk 22:20
w Heb 7:22

8:7
x Heb 7:11,18

8:8
y Jer 31:31

8:9
z Ex 19:5,6

^{23}Now there have been many of those priests, since death prevented them from continuing in office; ^{24}but because Jesus lives forever, he has a permanent priesthood.^{a} ^{25}Therefore he is able to save completely^a those who come to God^b through him, because he always lives to intercede for them.^{c}

^{26}Such a high priest meets our need—one who is holy, blameless, pure, set apart from sinners,^{d} exalted above the heavens.^{e} ^{27}Unlike the other high priests, he does not need to offer sacrifices^f day after day, first for his own sins,^{g} and then for the sins of the people. He sacrificed for their sins once for all^h when he offered himself.^{i} ^{28}For the law appoints as high priests men who are weak;^{j} but the oath, which came after the law, appointed the Son,^{k} who has been made perfect^l forever.

Chapter 8 Theme

8 The point of what we are saying is this: We do have such a high priest,^{m} who sat down at the right hand of the throne of the Majesty in heaven, ^{2}and who serves in the sanctuary, the true tabernacle^n set up by the Lord, not by man.

^{3}Every high priest is appointed to offer both gifts and sacrifices,^{o} and so it was necessary for this one also to have something to offer.^{p} ^{4}If he were on earth, he would not be a priest, for there are already men who offer the gifts prescribed by the law.^{q} ^{5}They serve at a sanctuary that is a copy^r and shadow^s of what is in heaven. This is why Moses was warned^t when he was about to build the tabernacle: "See to it that you make everything according to the pattern shown you on the mountain."^{bu} ^{6}But the ministry Jesus has received is as superior to theirs as the covenant^v of which he is mediator^w is superior to the old one, and it is founded on better promises.

^{7}For if there had been nothing wrong with that first covenant, no place would have been sought for another.^{x} ^{8}But God found fault with the people and said^c:

> "The time is coming, declares the Lord,
>> when I will make a new covenant^y
> with the house of Israel
>> and with the house of Judah.
> ^{9}It will not be like the covenant
>> I made with their forefathers^z
> when I took them by the hand
>> to lead them out of Egypt,
> because they did not remain faithful to my covenant,
>> and I turned away from them,
>>>> declares the Lord.

---

^{a} 25 Or *forever* ^{b} 5 Exodus 25:40 ^{c} 8 Some manuscripts may be translated *fault and said to the people.*

[10]This is the covenant I will make with the house of Israel
    after that time, declares the Lord.
I will put my laws in their minds
    and write them on their hearts.[a]
I will be their God,
    and they will be my people.[b]
[11]No longer will a man teach his neighbor,
    or a man his brother, saying, 'Know the Lord,'
because they will all know me,[c]
    from the least of them to the greatest.
[12]For I will forgive their wickedness
    and will remember their sins no more.[d]"[ae]

[13]By calling this covenant "new," he has made the first one obsolete;[f] and what is obsolete and aging will soon disappear.

Chapter 9 Theme

9 Now the first covenant had regulations for worship and also an earthly sanctuary.[g] [2]A tabernacle[h] was set up. In its first room were the lampstand,[i] the table[j] and the consecrated bread;[k] this was called the Holy Place. [3]Behind the second curtain was a room called the Most Holy Place,[l] [4]which had the golden altar of incense[m] and the gold-covered ark of the covenant.[n] This ark contained the gold jar of manna,[o] Aaron's staff that had budded,[p] and the stone tablets of the covenant. [5]Above the ark were the cherubim of the Glory,[q] overshadowing the atonement cover.[b] But we cannot discuss these things in detail now.

[6]When everything had been arranged like this, the priests entered regularly[r] into the outer room to carry on their ministry. [7]But only the high priest entered[s] the inner room, and that only once a year,[t]

a 12 Jer. 31:31-34   b 5 Traditionally *the mercy seat*

Side references

8:10
a 2Co 3:3;
Heb 10:16
b Zec 8:8

8:11
c Isa 54:13;
Jn 6:45

8:12
d Heb 10:17
e Jer 31:31-34

8:13
f 2Co 5:17

9:1
g Ex 25:8

9:2
h Ex 25:8,9
i Ex 25:31-39
j Ex 25:23-29
k Lev 24:5-8

9:3
l Ex 26:31-33

9:4
m Ex 30:1-5
n Ex 25:10-22
o Ex 16:32,33
p Nu 17:10

9:5
q Ex 25:17-19

9:6
r Nu 28:3

9:7
s Lev 16:11-19
t Lev 16:34

Inside the Tabernacle

* The Old Testament places the Golden Altar or Altar of Incense outside the curtain (see Exodus 40:26).

9:7
a Heb 5:2,3

9:8
b Heb 3:7
c Jn 14:6;
Heb 10:19,20

9:9
d Heb 5:1

9:10
e Lev 11:2-23
f Col 2:16
g Heb 7:16

9:11
h Heb 2:17
i Heb 10:1
j Heb 8:2

9:12
k Heb 10:4
l ver 24
m Heb 7:27

9:13
n Nu 19:9,17,18

9:14
o 1Pe 3:18
p Tit 2:14;
Heb 10:2,22
q Heb 6:1

9:15
r 1Ti 2:5
s Heb 7:22

9:18
t Ex 24:6-8

9:19
u Ex 24:6-8

9:20
v Ex 24:8;
Mt 26:28

9:22
w Lev 8:15
x Lev 17:11

9:23
y Heb 8:5

9:24
z Heb 8:2

and never without blood, which he offered for himself[a] and for the sins the people had committed in ignorance. [8]The Holy Spirit was showing[b] by this that the way[c] into the Most Holy Place had not yet been disclosed as long as the first tabernacle was still standing. [9]This is an illustration for the present time, indicating that the gifts and sacrifices being offered[d] were not able to clear the conscience of the worshiper. [10]They are only a matter of food[e] and drink[f] and various ceremonial washings—external regulations[g] applying until the time of the new order.

[11]When Christ came as high priest[h] of the good things that are already here,[a][i] he went through the greater and more perfect tabernacle[j] that is not man-made, that is to say, not a part of this creation. [12]He did not enter by means of the blood of goats and calves;[k] but he entered the Most Holy Place[l] once for all[m] by his own blood, having obtained eternal redemption. [13]The blood of goats and bulls and the ashes of a heifer[n] sprinkled on those who are ceremonially unclean sanctify them so that they are outwardly clean. [14]How much more, then, will the blood of Christ, who through the eternal Spirit[o] offered himself unblemished to God, cleanse our consciences[p] from acts that lead to death,[b][q] so that we may serve the living God!

[15]For this reason Christ is the mediator[r] of a new covenant, that those who are called may receive the promised eternal inheritance—now that he has died as a ransom to set them free from the sins committed under the first covenant.[s]

[16]In the case of a will,[c] it is necessary to prove the death of the one who made it, [17]because a will is in force only when somebody has died; it never takes effect while the one who made it is living. [18]This is why even the first covenant was not put into effect without blood.[t] [19]When Moses had proclaimed every commandment of the law to all the people, he took the blood of calves, together with water, scarlet wool and branches of hyssop, and sprinkled the scroll and all the people.[u] [20]He said, "This is the blood of the covenant, which God has commanded you to keep."[d][v] [21]In the same way, he sprinkled with the blood both the tabernacle and everything used in its ceremonies. [22]In fact, the law requires that nearly everything be cleansed with blood,[w] and without the shedding of blood there is no forgiveness.[x]

[23]It was necessary, then, for the copies[y] of the heavenly things to be purified with these sacrifices, but the heavenly things themselves with better sacrifices than these. [24]For Christ did not enter a man-made sanctuary that was only a copy of the true one;[z] he entered heaven itself, now to appear for us in God's presence. [25]Nor did he

---

a 11 Some early manuscripts are to come   b 14 Or from useless rituals   c 16 Same Greek word as covenant; also in verse 17   d 20 Exodus 24:8

enter heaven to offer himself again and again, the way the high priest enters the Most Holy Place[a] every year with blood that is not his own.[b] [26]Then Christ would have had to suffer many times since the creation of the world.[c] But now he has appeared once for all[d] at the end of the ages to do away with sin by the sacrifice of himself. [27]Just as man is destined to die once,[e] and after that to face judgment,[f] [28]so Christ was sacrificed once to take away the sins of many people; and he will appear a second time,[g] not to bear sin,[h] but to bring salvation to those who are waiting for him.[i]

Chapter 10 Theme

10 The law is only a shadow[j] of the good things[k] that are coming—not the realities themselves.[l] For this reason it can never, by the same sacrifices repeated endlessly year after year, make perfect[m] those who draw near to worship. [2]If it could, would they not have stopped being offered? For the worshipers would have been cleansed once for all, and would no longer have felt guilty for their sins. [3]But those sacrifices are an annual reminder of sins,[n] [4]because it is impossible for the blood of bulls and goats[o] to take away sins.

[5]Therefore, when Christ came into the world,[p] he said:

> "Sacrifice and offering you did not desire,
>> but a body you prepared for me;[q]
> [6]with burnt offerings and sin offerings
>> you were not pleased.
> [7]Then I said, 'Here I am—it is written about me in
>> the scroll[r]—
> I have come to do your will, O God.'"[a][s]

[8]First he said, "Sacrifices and offerings, burnt offerings and sin offerings you did not desire, nor were you pleased with them"[t] (although the law required them to be made). [9]Then he said, "Here I am, I have come to do your will."[u] He sets aside the first to establish the second. [10]And by that will, we have been made holy[v] through the sacrifice of the body[w] of Jesus Christ once for all.[x]

[11]Day after day every priest stands and performs his religious duties; again and again he offers the same sacrifices,[y] which can never take away sins.[z] [12]But when this priest had offered for all time one sacrifice for sins, he sat down at the right hand of God. [13]Since that time he waits for his enemies to be made his footstool,[a] [14]because by one sacrifice he has made perfect[b] forever those who are being made holy.

[15]The Holy Spirit also testifies[c] to us about this. First he says:

---

[a]7 Psalm 40:6-8 (see Septuagint)

Cross references

9:25
[a]Heb 10:19
[b]ver 7,8

9:26
[c]Heb 4:3
[d]Heb 7:27

9:27
[e]Ge 3:19
[f]2Co 5:10

9:28
[g]Tit 2:13
[h]1Pe 2:24
[i]1Co 1:7

10:1
[j]Heb 8:5
[k]Heb 9:11
[l]Heb 9:23
[m]Heb 7:19

10:3
[n]Heb 9:7

10:4
[o]Heb 9:12,13

10:5
[p]Heb 1:6
[q]1Pe 2:24

10:7
[r]Jer 36:2
[s]Ps 40:6-8

10:8
[t]ver 5,6;
Mk 12:33

10:9
[u]ver 7

10:10
[v]Jn 17:19
[w]Heb 2:14;
1Pe 2:24
[x]Heb 7:27

10:11
[y]Heb 5:1
[z]ver 1,4

10:13
[a]Heb 1:13

10:14
[b]ver 1

10:15
[c]Heb 3:7

10:16
a Jer 31:33;
Heb 8:10

10:17
b Heb 8:12

10:19
c Eph 2:18;
Heb 9:8,12,25

10:20
d Heb 9:8
e Heb 9:3

10:21
f Heb 2:17

10:22
g Heb 7:19
h Eze 36:25;
Heb 9:14

10:23
i Heb 3:6
j 1Co 1:9

10:25
k Ac 2:42
l Heb 3:13

10:26
m Nu 15:30;
2Pe 2:20

10:27
n Isa 26:11;
2Th 1:7;
Heb 9:27

10:28
o Dt 17:6,7;
Heb 2:2

10:29
p Heb 6:6
q Mt 26:28
r Eph 4:30;
Heb 6:4
s Heb 2:3

10:30
t Dt 32:35;
Ro 12:19
u Dt 32:36

10:31
v Mt 16:16

10:32
w Heb 6:4
x Php 1:29,30

10:33
y 1Co 4:9
z Php 4:14;
1Th 2:14

10:34
a Heb 13:3
b Heb 11:16

10:36
c Lk 21:19;
Heb 12:1

16"This is the covenant I will make with them
>   after that time, says the Lord.
> I will put my laws in their hearts,
>   and I will write them on their minds."a a

17Then he adds:

> "Their sins and lawless acts
>   I will remember no more."b b

18And where these have been forgiven, there is no longer any sacrifice for sin.

19Therefore, brothers, since we have confidence to enter the Most Holy Place c by the blood of Jesus, 20by a new and living way d opened for us through the curtain, e that is, his body, 21and since we have a great priest f over the house of God, 22let us draw near to God g with a sincere heart in full assurance of faith, having our hearts sprinkled to cleanse us from a guilty conscience h and having our bodies washed with pure water. 23Let us hold unswervingly to the hope i we profess, for he who promised is faithful. j 24And let us consider how we may spur one another on toward love and good deeds. 25Let us not give up meeting together, k as some are in the habit of doing, but let us encourage one another l—and all the more as you see the Day approaching.

26If we deliberately keep on sinning m after we have received the knowledge of the truth, no sacrifice for sins is left, 27but only a fearful expectation of judgment and of raging fire n that will consume the enemies of God. 28Anyone who rejected the law of Moses died without mercy on the testimony of two or three witnesses. o 29How much more severely do you think a man deserves to be punished who has trampled the Son of God under foot, p who has treated as an unholy thing the blood of the covenant q that sanctified him, and who has insulted the Spirit r of grace? s 30For we know him who said, "It is mine to avenge; I will repay," c t and again, "The Lord will judge his people." d u 31It is a dreadful thing to fall into the hands of the living God. v

32Remember those earlier days after you had received the light, w when you stood your ground in a great contest in the face of suffering. x 33Sometimes you were publicly exposed to insult and persecution; y at other times you stood side by side with those who were so treated. z 34You sympathized with those in prison a and joyfully accepted the confiscation of your property, because you knew that you yourselves had better and lasting possessions. b

35So do not throw away your confidence; it will be richly rewarded. 36You need to persevere c so that when you have done the will

a 16 Jer. 31:33   b 17 Jer. 31:34   c 30 Deut. 32:35   d 30 Deut. 32:36; Psalm 135:14

of God, you will receive what he has promised. ³⁷For in just a very little while,

"He who is coming[a] will come and will not delay.[b]
38   But my righteous one[a] will live by faith.[c]
And if he shrinks back,
I will not be pleased with him."[b]

³⁹But we are not of those who shrink back and are destroyed, but of those who believe and are saved.

Chapter 11 Theme

11 Now faith is being sure of what we hope for and certain of what we do not see.[d] ²This is what the ancients were commended for.[e]

³By faith we understand that the universe was formed at God's command,[f] so that what is seen was not made out of what was visible.

⁴By faith Abel offered God a better sacrifice than Cain did. By faith he was commended as a righteous man, when God spoke well of his offerings.[g] And by faith he still speaks, even though he is dead.[h]

⁵By faith Enoch was taken from this life, so that he did not experience death; he could not be found, because God had taken him away.[i] For before he was taken, he was commended as one who pleased God. ⁶And without faith it is impossible to please God, because anyone who comes to him[j] must believe that he exists and that he rewards those who earnestly seek him.

⁷By faith Noah, when warned about things not yet seen, in holy fear built an ark[k] to save his family.[l] By his faith he condemned the world and became heir of the righteousness that comes by faith.

⁸By faith Abraham, when called to go to a place he would later receive as his inheritance,[m] obeyed and went,[n] even though he did not know where he was going. ⁹By faith he made his home in the promised land[o] like a stranger in a foreign country; he lived in tents,[p] as did Isaac and Jacob, who were heirs with him of the same promise.[q] ¹⁰For he was looking forward to the city[r] with foundations,[s] whose architect and builder is God.

¹¹By faith Abraham, even though he was past age—and Sarah herself was barren[t]—was enabled to become a father[u] because he[c] considered him faithful who had made the promise. ¹²And so from this one man, and he as good as dead,[v] came descendants as numerous as the stars in the sky and as countless as the sand on the seashore.[w]

---

[a] 38 One early manuscript *But the righteous*   [b] 38 Hab. 2:3,4   [c] 11 Or *By faith even Sarah, who was past age, was enabled to bear children because she*

10:37
[a] Mt 11:3
[b] Rev 22:20

10:38
[c] Ro 1:17;
Gal 3:11

11:1
[d] Ro 8:24;
2Co 4:18

11:2
[e] ver 4,39

11:3
[f] Ge 1;
Jn 1:3;
2Pe 3:5

11:4
[g] Ge 4:4;
1Jn 3:12
[h] Heb 12:24

11:5
[i] Ge 5:21-24

11:6
[j] Heb 7:19

11:7
[k] Ge 6:13-22
[l] 1Pe 3:20

11:8
[m] Ge 12:7
[n] Ge 12:1-4;
Ac 7:2-4

11:9
[o] Ac 7:5
[p] Ge 12:8;
18:1,9
[q] Heb 6:17

11:10
[r] Heb 12:22;
13:14
[s] Rev 21:2,14

11:11
[t] Ge 17:17-19;
18:11-14
[u] Ge 21:2

11:12
[v] Ro 4:19
[w] Ge 22:17

11:13
a ver 39
b Mt 13:17
c Ge 23:4;
Ps 39:12;
1Pe 1:17

11:15
d Ge 24:6-8

11:16
e 2Ti 4:18
f Mk 8:38
g Ex 3:6,15
h Heb 13:14

11:17
i Ge 22:1-10;
Jas 2:21

11:18
j Ge 21:12;
Ro 9:7

11:19
k Ro 4:21

11:20
l Ge 27:27-29,
39,40

11:21
m Ge 48:1,8-22

11:22
n Ge 50:24,25;
Ex 13:19

11:23
o Ex 2:2
p Ex 1:16,22

11:24
q Ex 2:10,11

11:25
r ver 37

11:26
s Heb 13:13
t Heb 10:35

11:27
u Ex 12:50,51

11:28
v Ex 12:21-23

11:29
w Ex 14:21-31

11:30
x Jos 6:12-20

11:31
y Jos 2:1,9-14;
6:22-25; Jas 2:25

11:32
z Jdg 4-5
a 1Sa 16:1,13
b 1Sa 1:20

11:33
c 2Sa 7:11; 8:1-3
d Da 6:22

11:34
e 2Ki 20:7

¹³All these people were still living by faith when they died. They did not receive the things promised;*a* they only saw them and welcomed them from a distance.*b* And they admitted that they were aliens and strangers on earth.*c* ¹⁴People who say such things show that they are looking for a country of their own. ¹⁵If they had been thinking of the country they had left, they would have had opportunity to return.*d* ¹⁶Instead, they were longing for a better country—a heavenly one.*e* Therefore God is not ashamed*f* to be called their God,*g* for he has prepared a city*h* for them.

¹⁷By faith Abraham, when God tested him, offered Isaac as a sacrifice.*i* He who had received the promises was about to sacrifice his one and only son, ¹⁸even though God had said to him, "It is through Isaac that your offspring*a* will be reckoned."*b* *j* ¹⁹Abraham reasoned that God could raise the dead,*k* and figuratively speaking, he did receive Isaac back from death.

²⁰By faith Isaac blessed Jacob and Esau in regard to their future.*l*

²¹By faith Jacob, when he was dying, blessed each of Joseph's sons,*m* and worshiped as he leaned on the top of his staff.

²²By faith Joseph, when his end was near, spoke about the exodus of the Israelites from Egypt and gave instructions about his bones.*n*

²³By faith Moses' parents hid him for three months after he was born,*o* because they saw he was no ordinary child, and they were not afraid of the king's edict.*p*

²⁴By faith Moses, when he had grown up, refused to be known as the son of Pharaoh's daughter.*q* ²⁵He chose to be mistreated*r* along with the people of God rather than to enjoy the pleasures of sin for a short time. ²⁶He regarded disgrace*s* for the sake of Christ as of greater value than the treasures of Egypt, because he was looking ahead to his reward.*t* ²⁷By faith he left Egypt,*u* not fearing the king's anger; he persevered because he saw him who is invisible. ²⁸By faith he kept the Passover and the sprinkling of blood, so that the destroyer of the firstborn would not touch the firstborn of Israel.*v*

²⁹By faith the people passed through the Red Sea*c* as on dry land; but when the Egyptians tried to do so, they were drowned.*w*

³⁰By faith the walls of Jericho fell, after the people had marched around them for seven days.*x*

³¹By faith the prostitute Rahab, because she welcomed the spies, was not killed with those who were disobedient.*d* *y*

³²And what more shall I say? I do not have time to tell about Gideon, Barak,*z* Samson, Jephthah, David,*a* Samuel*b* and the prophets, ³³who through faith conquered kingdoms,*c* administered justice, and gained what was promised; who shut the mouths of lions,*d* ³⁴quenched the fury of the flames, and escaped the edge of the sword; whose weakness was turned to strength;*e* and who

a 18 Greek *seed*   *b* 18 Gen. 21:12   *c* 29 That is, Sea of Reeds   *d* 31 Or *unbelieving* became powerful in battle and routed foreign armies.*a* ³⁵Women received back their dead, raised to life again.*b* Others were tortured and refused to be released, so that they might gain a better resurrection. ³⁶Some faced jeers and flogging,*c* while still others were chained and put in prison.*d* ³⁷They were stoned*a;e* they were sawed in two; they were put to death by the sword.*f* They went about in sheepskins and goatskins,*g* destitute, persecuted and mistreated— ³⁸the world was not worthy of them. They wandered in deserts and mountains, and in caves*h* and holes in the ground.

³⁹These were all commended*i* for their faith, yet none of them received what had been promised.*j* ⁴⁰God had planned something better for us so that only together with us would they be made perfect.

Chapter 12 Theme

12 Therefore, since we are surrounded by such a great cloud of witnesses, let us throw off everything that hinders and the sin that so easily entangles, and let us run*k* with perseverance*l* the race marked out for us. ²Let us fix our eyes on Jesus, the author and perfecter of our faith, who for the joy set before him endured the cross,*m* scorning its shame,*n* and sat down at the right hand of the throne of God. ³Consider him who endured such opposition from sinful men, so that you will not grow weary*o* and lose heart.

⁴In your struggle against sin, you have not yet resisted to the point of shedding your blood.*p* ⁵And you have forgotten that word of encouragement that addresses you as sons:

"My son, do not make light of the Lord's discipline,
　and do not lose heart when he rebukes you,
⁶because the Lord disciplines those he loves,*q*
　and he punishes everyone he accepts as a son."*b r*

⁷Endure hardship as discipline; God is treating you as sons.*s* For what son is not disciplined by his father? ⁸If you are not disciplined (and everyone undergoes discipline),*t* then you are illegitimate children and not true sons. ⁹Moreover, we have all had human fathers who disciplined us and we respected them for it. How much more should we submit to the Father of our spirits*u* and live!*v* ¹⁰Our fathers disciplined us for a little while as they thought best; but God disciplines us for our good, that we may share in his holiness.*w* ¹¹No discipline seems pleasant at the time, but painful. Later on, however, it produces a harvest of righteousness and peace*x* for those who have been trained by it.

¹²Therefore, strengthen your feeble arms and weak knees.*y* ¹³"Make level paths for your feet,"*c z* so that the lame may not be disabled, but rather healed.*a*

a 37 Some early manuscripts *stoned; they were put to the test;*　b 6 Prov. 3:11,12　c 13 Prov. 4:26

11:34
a Jdg 15:8

11:35
b 1Ki 17:22,23

11:36
c Jer 20:2
d Ge 39:20

11:37
e 2Ch 24:21
f 1Ki 19:10
g 2Ki 1:8

11:38
h 1Ki 18:4

11:39
i ver 2,4
j ver 13

12:1
k 1Co 9:24
l Heb 10:36

12:2
m Php 2:8,9
n Heb 13:13

12:3
o Gal 6:9

12:4
p Heb 10:32-34

12:6
q Ps 94:12;
Rev 3:19
r Pr 3:11,12

12:7
s Dt 8:5

12:8
t 1Pe 5:9

12:9
u Nu 16:22
v Isa 38:16

12:10
w 2Pe 1:4

12:11
x Isa 32:17;
Jas 3:17,18

12:12
y Isa 35:3

12:13
z Pr 4:26
a Gal 6:1

12:14
a Ro 14:19
b Ro 6:22
c Mt 5:8

12:15
d Gal 5:4;
Heb 3:12

12:16
e Ge 25:29-34

12:17
f Ge 27:30-40

12:18
g Ex 19:12-22;
Dt 4:11

12:19
h Ex 20:18
i Ex 20:19;
Dt 5:5,25

12:20
j Ex 19:12,13

12:22
k Gal 4:26
l Heb 11:10

12:23
m Lk 10:20
n Ps 94:2
o Php 3:12

12:24
p Ge 4:10;
Heb 11:4

12:25
q Heb 8:5; 11:7
r Heb 2:2,3

12:26
s Ex 19:18
t Hag 2:6

12:27
u 1Co 7:31;
2Pe 3:10

12:28
v Da 2:44
w Heb 13:15

12:29
x Dt 4:24

13:1
y Ro 12:10;
1Pe 1:22

13:2
z Mt 25:35
a Ge 18:1-33

13:3
b Mt 25:36;
Col 4:18

13:4
c 1Co 6:9

13:5
d Php 4:11

[14]Make every effort to live in peace with all men[a] and to be holy;[b] without holiness no one will see the Lord.[c] [15]See to it that no one misses the grace of God[d] and that no bitter root grows up to cause trouble and defile many. [16]See that no one is sexually immoral, or is godless like Esau, who for a single meal sold his inheritance rights as the oldest son.[e] [17]Afterward, as you know, when he wanted to inherit this blessing, he was rejected. He could bring about no change of mind, though he sought the blessing with tears.[f]

[18]You have not come to a mountain that can be touched and that is burning with fire; to darkness, gloom and storm;[g] [19]to a trumpet blast[h] or to such a voice speaking words that those who heard it begged that no further word be spoken to them,[i] [20]because they could not bear what was commanded: "If even an animal touches the mountain, it must be stoned."[a][j] [21]The sight was so terrifying that Moses said, "I am trembling with fear."[b]

[22]But you have come to Mount Zion, to the heavenly Jerusalem,[k] the city[l] of the living God. You have come to thousands upon thousands of angels in joyful assembly, [23]to the church of the firstborn, whose names are written in heaven.[m] You have come to God, the judge of all men,[n] to the spirits of righteous men made perfect,[o] [24]to Jesus the mediator of a new covenant, and to the sprinkled blood that speaks a better word than the blood of Abel.[p]

[25]See to it that you do not refuse him who speaks. If they did not escape when they refused him who warned[q] them on earth, how much less will we, if we turn away from him who warns us from heaven?[r] [26]At that time his voice shook the earth,[s] but now he has promised, "Once more I will shake not only the earth but also the heavens."[c][t] [27]The words "once more" indicate the removing of what can be shaken[u]—that is, created things—so that what cannot be shaken may remain.

[28]Therefore, since we are receiving a kingdom that cannot be shaken,[v] let us be thankful, and so worship God acceptably with reverence and awe,[w] [29]for our "God is a consuming fire."[d][x]

Chapter 13 Theme

13 Keep on loving each other as brothers.[y] [2]Do not forget to entertain strangers,[z] for by so doing some people have entertained angels without knowing it.[a] [3]Remember those in prison[b] as if you were their fellow prisoners, and those who are mistreated as if you yourselves were suffering.

[4]Marriage should be honored by all, and the marriage bed kept pure, for God will judge the adulterer and all the sexually immoral.[c] [5]Keep your lives free from the love of money and be content with what you have,[d] because God has said,

a 20 Exodus 19:12,13   b 21 Deut. 9:19   c 26 Haggai 2:6   d 29 Deut. 4:24

"Never will I leave you;
    never will I forsake you."[a][a]

[6]So we say with confidence,

"The Lord is my helper; I will not be afraid.
    What can man do to me?"[b]

[7]Remember your leaders,[b] who spoke the word of God to you. Consider the outcome of their way of life and imitate[c] their faith. [8]Jesus Christ is the same yesterday and today and forever.[d]

[9]Do not be carried away by all kinds of strange teachings.[e] It is good for our hearts to be strengthened[f] by grace, not by ceremonial foods,[g] which are of no value to those who eat them. [10]We have an altar from which those who minister at the tabernacle have no right to eat.[h]

[11]The high priest carries the blood of animals into the Most Holy Place as a sin offering, but the bodies are burned outside the camp.[i] [12]And so Jesus also suffered outside the city gate[j] to make the people holy through his own blood. [13]Let us, then, go to him outside the camp, bearing the disgrace he bore.[k] [14]For here we do not have an enduring city, but we are looking for the city that is to come.[l]

[15]Through Jesus, therefore, let us continually offer to God a sacrifice[m] of praise—the fruit of lips[n] that confess his name. [16]And do not forget to do good and to share with others,[o] for with such sacrifices[p] God is pleased.

[17]Obey your leaders and submit to their authority. They keep watch over you[q] as men who must give an account. Obey them so that their work will be a joy, not a burden, for that would be of no advantage to you.

[18]Pray for us.[r] We are sure that we have a clear conscience[s] and desire to live honorably in every way. [19]I particularly urge you to pray so that I may be restored to you soon.[t]

[20]May the God of peace,[u] who through the blood of the eternal covenant[v] brought back from the dead[w] our Lord Jesus, that great Shepherd of the sheep,[x] [21]equip you with everything good for doing his will, and may he work in us[y] what is pleasing to him,[z] through Jesus Christ, to whom be glory for ever and ever. Amen.[a]

[22]Brothers, I urge you to bear with my word of exhortation, for I have written you only a short letter.[b]

[23]I want you to know that our brother Timothy[c] has been released. If he arrives soon, I will come with him to see you.

[24]Greet all your leaders[d] and all God's people. Those from Italy[e] send you their greetings.

[25]Grace be with you all.[f]

a5 Deut. 31:6   b6 Psalm 118:6,7

13:5
a Dt 31:6,8;
Jos 1:5

13:7
b ver 17,24
c Heb 6:12

13:8
d Heb 1:12

13:9
e Eph 4:14
f Col 2:7
g Col 2:16

13:10
h 1Co 9:13;
10:18

13:11
i Ex 29:14;
Lev 16:27

13:12
j Jn 19:17

13:13
k Heb 11:26

13:14
l Php 3:20;
Heb 12:22

13:15
m 1Pe 2:5
n Hos 14:2

13:16
o Ro 12:13
p Php 4:18

13:17
q Isa 62:6;
Ac 20:28

13:18
r 1Th 5:25
s Ac 23:1

13:19
t Phm 22

13:20
u Ro 15:33
v Isa 55:3;
Eze 37:26;
Zec 9:11
w Ac 2:24
x Jn 10:11

13:21
y Php 2:13
z 1Jn 3:22
a Ro 11:36

13:22
b 1Pe 5:12

13:23
c Ac 16:1

13:24
d ver 7,17
e Ac 18:2

13:25
f Col 4:18

HEBREWS OBSERVATIONS CHART

AUTHOR

RECIPIENTS

EXHORTATIONS

(continued)

WARNINGS/CONSEQUENCES

Theme of Hebrews:

Author:
  unknown

Date:

Purpose:

Key Words:

  Jesus (son)
  (mark only
  when referring
  to Jesus as a son)

  God

  angels

  priest
  (priests,
  priesthood)

  therefore, for
  this reason, so,
  then, this (that)
  is why

  faith, believe
  (faithful)

  greater, many

  better, superior
  to (a better
  word than)

  let us

  perfect, clear

  mark the
  reference to the
  devil

  covenant, will

Segment Divisions		Chapter Themes
		1
		2
		3
		4
		5
		6
		7
		8
		9
		10
		11
		12
		13

JAMES

What a turnaround from the day James told his half-brother what to do if he wanted to be known publicly! Full of unbelief and convinced that Jesus was nothing more than his eldest brother, James told Jesus to take his disciples and go up to the Feast of Booths and do his works there. Jesus might have found more disciples there, but James was not to be numbered as one of them—until Jesus rose from the dead (see 1 Corinthians 15:7).

Convinced from that point on that Jesus was the Christ, James would lay claim not to his physical relationship to Jesus but to his spiritual relationship as a bondservant of the Lord Jesus Christ.

James became a pillar of the church, a leader of the council of Jerusalem, and a friend of Peter and Paul. But most of all he was a friend of Jesus, a covenant friend for whom he would be martyred around A.D. 62.

Sometime before A.D. 50 or in the early 50s, James would write his one epistle to be included in the pages of Holy Scripture, an epistle that would show what the gospel is like when it is lived out in shoe leather.

✎ THINGS TO DO

1. Read James in one sitting to familiarize yourself with the book as a whole. James structures his writing distinctively. Once you see the pattern he uses, you will better understand the flow of the book.

   a. First, James introduces a subject by making a statement or giving an instruction. For example, in James 1:2 he says to consider it pure joy whenever you face trials of many kinds.

   b. He then usually follows with more instructions concerning that particular subject, *or* he gives an illustration pertaining to the subject, *or* he gives an explanation of it.

2. As you read back through James, mark in the text the key words (and their synonyms and pronouns) listed on the JAMES AT A GLANCE chart on page 2104. (Key words help you see the subjects of the book.)

   a. Mark every use of *say (says, claims to)* and *deeds (actions* as well as *do, does,* and *did* since they refer to *actions)* in chapter 2.

   b. Don't miss marking *tongue* and its pronouns in chapter 3.

   c. You may find other key words which are not listed for you. Mark these and also mark *grace* and any reference to the devil (as you have done throughout your Bible).

3. Read James chapter by chapter:

   a. List the subjects introduced by the author on the JAMES SUBJECT BY SUBJECT chart on pages 2102-2104. Be sure to include the chapter and verse from which you took the information.

   b. Next, if the author gives instructions or illustrations regarding a particular subject, record that information in the appropriate column. See JAMES SUBJECT BY SUBJECT for an example of how to do this.

4. After you list the subjects in each chapter, determine the theme of each chapter and record these themes on JAMES AT A GLANCE and in the text by each chapter number.

5. Finally, look for the theme of James. From the information gathered, determine if one subject is more predominant than the others or if there is a common denominator among the subjects. The more dominant or common subject will be the theme of James and points to the author's reason for writing. Record the theme of James on JAMES AT A GLANCE and complete the chart.

✎ THINGS TO THINK ABOUT

1. How are you handling the trials in your life?

2. Are you a doer of the Word or a hearer only?

3. Do you show favoritism in dealing with people? Are you a respecter of persons?
4. Is your faith seen by your works?
5. Are you a friend of the world?

Chapter 1 Theme

1 James,[a] a servant of God[b] and of the Lord Jesus Christ,

To the twelve tribes[c] scattered[d] among the nations:

Greetings.

[2]Consider it pure joy, my brothers, whenever you face trials of many kinds,[e] [3]because you know that the testing of your faith develops perseverance. [4]Perseverance must finish its work so that you may be mature and complete, not lacking anything. [5]If any of you lacks wisdom, he should ask God,[f] who gives generously to all without finding fault, and it will be given to him.[g] [6]But when he asks, he must believe and not doubt,[h] because he who doubts is like a wave of the sea, blown and tossed by the wind. [7]That man should not think he will receive anything from the Lord; [8]he is a double-minded man,[i] unstable in all he does.

[9]The brother in humble circumstances ought to take pride in his high position. [10]But the one who is rich should take pride in his low position, because he will pass away like a wild flower.[j] [11]For the sun rises with scorching heat and withers[k] the plant; its blossom falls and its beauty is destroyed.[l] In the same way, the rich man will fade away even while he goes about his business.

[12]Blessed is the man who perseveres under trial, because when he has stood the test, he will receive the crown of life[m] that God has promised to those who love him.[n]

[13]When tempted, no one should say, "God is tempting me." For God cannot be tempted by evil, nor does he tempt anyone; [14]but each one is tempted when, by his own evil desire, he is dragged away and enticed. [15]Then, after desire has conceived, it gives birth to sin;[o] and sin, when it is full-grown, gives birth to death.[p]

[16]Don't be deceived,[q] my dear brothers.[r] [17]Every good and perfect gift is from above,[s] coming down from the Father of the heavenly lights, who does not change[t] like shifting shadows. [18]He chose to give us birth[u] through the word of truth, that we might be a kind of firstfruits[v] of all he created.

[19]My dear brothers, take note of this: Everyone should be quick to listen, slow to speak[w] and slow to become angry, [20]for man's anger does not bring about the righteous life that God desires. [21]Therefore, get rid of[x] all moral filth and the evil that is so prevalent and humbly accept the word planted in you,[y] which can save you.

1:1
[a]Ac 15:13
[b]Tit 1:1
[c]Ac 26:7
[d]Dt 32:26;
Jn 7:35;
1Pe 1:1

1:2
[e]Mt 5:12;
1Pe 1:6

1:5
[f]1Ki 3:9,10;
Pr 2:3-6
[g]Mt 7:7

1:6
[h]Mk 11:24

1:8
[i]Jas 4:8

1:10
[j]1Co 7:31;
1Pe 1:24

1:11
[k]Ps 102:4,11
[l]Isa 40:6-8

1:12
[m]1Co 9:25
[n]Jas 2:5

1:15
[o]Job 15:35;
Ps 7:14
[p]Ro 6:23

1:16
[q]1Co 6:9
[r]ver 19

1:17
[s]Jn 3:27
[t]Nu 23:19;
Mal 3:6

1:18
[u]Jn 1:13
[v]Eph 1:12;
Rev 14:4

1:19
[w]Pr 10:19

1:21
[x]Eph 4:22
[y]Eph 1:13

²²Do not merely listen to the word, and so deceive yourselves. Do what it says. ²³Anyone who listens to the word but does not do what it says is like a man who looks at his face in a mirror ²⁴and, after looking at himself, goes away and immediately forgets what he looks like. ²⁵But the man who looks intently into the perfect law that gives freedom,ᵃ and continues to do this, not forgetting what he has heard, but doing it—he will be blessed in what he does.ᵇ

²⁶If anyone considers himself religious and yet does not keep a tight rein on his tongue,ᶜ he deceives himself and his religion is worthless. ²⁷Religion that God our Father accepts as pure and faultless is this: to look afterᵈ orphans and widowsᵉ in their distress and to keep oneself from being polluted by the world.ᶠ

Chapter 2 Theme _____

2 My brothers, as believers in our gloriousᵍ Lord Jesus Christ, don't show favoritism.ʰ ²Suppose a man comes into your meeting wearing a gold ring and fine clothes, and a poor man in shabby clothes also comes in. ³If you show special attention to the man wearing fine clothes and say, "Here's a good seat for you," but say to the poor man, "You stand there" or "Sit on the floor by my feet," ⁴have you not discriminated among yourselves and become judgesⁱ with evil thoughts?

⁵Listen, my dear brothers:ʲ Has not God chosen those who are poor in the eyes of the worldᵏ to be rich in faithˡ and to inherit the kingdom he promised those who love him?ᵐ ⁶But you have insulted the poor.ⁿ Is it not the rich who are exploiting you? Are they not the ones who are dragging you into court?ᵒ ⁷Are they not the ones who are slandering the noble name of him to whom you belong?

⁸If you really keep the royal law found in Scripture, "Love your neighbor as yourself,"ᵃᵖ you are doing right. ⁹But if you show favoritism,�q you sin and are convicted by the law as lawbreakers.ʳ ¹⁰For whoever keeps the whole law and yet stumbles at just one point is guilty of breaking all of it.ˢ ¹¹For he who said, "Do not commit adultery,"ᵇᵗ also said, "Do not murder."ᶜᵘ If you do not commit adultery but do commit murder, you have become a lawbreaker.

¹²Speak and act as those who are going to be judged by the law that gives freedom,ᵛ ¹³because judgment without mercy will be shown to anyone who has not been merciful.ʷ Mercy triumphs over judgment!

¹⁴What good is it, my brothers, if a man claims to have faith but has no deeds?ˣ Can such faith save him? ¹⁵Suppose a brother or sister is without clothes and daily food.ʸ ¹⁶If one of you says to him,

1:25
a Jas 2:12
b Jn 13:17

1:26
c Ps 34:13;
1Pe 3:10

1:27
d Mt 25:36
e Isa 1:17,23
f Ro 12:2

2:1
g 1Co 2:8
h Lev 19:15

2:4
i Jn 7:24

2:5
j Jas 1:16,19
k 1Co 1:26-28
l Lk 12:21
m Jas 1:12

2:6
n 1Co 11:22
o Ac 8:3

2:8
p Lev 19:18

2:9
q ver 1
r Dt 1:17

2:10
s Mt 5:19;
Gal 3:10

2:11
t Ex 20:14;
Dt 5:18
u Ex 20:13;
Dt 5:17

2:12
v Jas 1:25

2:13
w Mt 5:7;
18:32-35

2:14
x Mt 7:26;
Jas 1:22-25

2:15
y Mt 25:35,36

a 8 Lev. 19:18   b 11 Exodus 20:14; Deut. 5:18   c 11 Exodus 20:13; Deut. 5:17

2:16
a 1Jn 3:17,18

2:18
b Ro 3:28
c Jas 3:13

2:19
d Dt 6:4
e Mt 8:29;
Lk 4:34

2:20
f ver 17,26

2:21
g Ge 22:9,12

2:22
h Heb 11:17
i 1Th 1:3

2:23
j Ge 15:6;
Ro 4:3
k 2Ch 20:7;
Isa 41:8

2:25
l Heb 11:31

2:26
m ver 17,20

3:2
n 1Ki 8:46;
Jas 2:10
o 1Pe 3:10
p Mt 12:37
q Jas 1:26

3:3
r Ps 32:9

3:5
s Ps 12:3,4

3:6
t Pr 16:27
u Mt 15:11,18,19

3:8
v Ps 140:3;
Ro 3:13

3:9
w Ge 1:26,27;
1Co 11:7

"Go, I wish you well; keep warm and well fed," but does nothing about his physical needs, what good is it?*a* [17]In the same way, faith by itself, if it is not accompanied by action, is dead.

[18]But someone will say, "You have faith; I have deeds."

Show me your faith without deeds,*b* and I will show you my faith by what I do.*c* [19]You believe that there is one God.*d* Good! Even the demons believe that*e*—and shudder.

[20]You foolish man, do you want evidence that faith without deeds is useless*a*?*f* [21]Was not our ancestor Abraham considered righteous for what he did when he offered his son Isaac on the altar?*g* [22]You see that his faith and his actions were working together,*h* and his faith was made complete by what he did.*i* [23]And the scripture was fulfilled that says, "Abraham believed God, and it was credited to him as righteousness,"*b* *j* and he was called God's friend.*k* [24]You see that a person is justified by what he does and not by faith alone.

[25]In the same way, was not even Rahab the prostitute considered righteous for what she did when she gave lodging to the spies and sent them off in a different direction?*l* [26]As the body without the spirit is dead, so faith without deeds is dead.*m*

Chapter 3 Theme

3 Not many of you should presume to be teachers, my brothers, because you know that we who teach will be judged more strictly. [2]We all stumble*n* in many ways. If anyone is never at fault in what he says,*o* he is a perfect man,*p* able to keep his whole body in check.*q*

[3]When we put bits into the mouths of horses to make them obey us, we can turn the whole animal.*r* [4]Or take ships as an example. Although they are so large and are driven by strong winds, they are steered by a very small rudder wherever the pilot wants to go. [5]Likewise the tongue is a small part of the body, but it makes great boasts.*s* Consider what a great forest is set on fire by a small spark. [6]The tongue also is a fire,*t* a world of evil among the parts of the body. It corrupts the whole person,*u* sets the whole course of his life on fire, and is itself set on fire by hell.

[7]All kinds of animals, birds, reptiles and creatures of the sea are being tamed and have been tamed by man, [8]but no man can tame the tongue. It is a restless evil, full of deadly poison.*v*

[9]With the tongue we praise our Lord and Father, and with it we curse men, who have been made in God's likeness.*w* [10]Out of the same mouth come praise and cursing. My brothers, this should not be. [11]Can both fresh water and salt*c* water flow from the same

a 20 Some early manuscripts *dead*   *b 23* Gen. 15:6   *c 11* Greek *bitter* (see also verse 14) spring? [12]My brothers, can a fig tree bear olives, or a grapevine bear figs?[a] Neither can a salt spring produce fresh water.

[13]Who is wise and understanding among you? Let him show it[b] by his good life, by deeds done in the humility that comes from wisdom. [14]But if you harbor bitter envy and selfish ambition[c] in your hearts, do not boast about it or deny the truth.[d] [15]Such "wisdom" does not come down from heaven[e] but is earthly, unspiritual, of the devil.[f] [16]For where you have envy and selfish ambition, there you find disorder and every evil practice.

[17]But the wisdom that comes from heaven[g] is first of all pure; then peace-loving, considerate, submissive, full of mercy[h] and good fruit, impartial and sincere.[i] [18]Peacemakers who sow in peace raise a harvest of righteousness.[j]

Chapter 4 Theme

4 What causes fights and quarrels[k] among you? Don't they come from your desires that battle[l] within you? [2]You want something but don't get it. You kill and covet, but you cannot have what you want. You quarrel and fight. You do not have, because you do not ask God. [3]When you ask, you do not receive,[m] because you ask with wrong motives,[n] that you may spend what you get on your pleasures.

[4]You adulterous people, don't you know that friendship with the world[o] is hatred toward God?[p] Anyone who chooses to be a friend of the world becomes an enemy of God.[q] [5]Or do you think Scripture says without reason that the spirit he caused to live in us envies intensely?[a] [6]But he gives us more grace. That is why Scripture says:

> "God opposes the proud
>   but gives grace to the humble."[b] [r]

[7]Submit yourselves, then, to God. Resist the devil,[s] and he will flee from you. [8]Come near to God and he will come near to you.[t] Wash your hands,[u] you sinners, and purify your hearts, you double-minded.[v] [9]Grieve, mourn and wail. Change your laughter to mourning and your joy to gloom. [w] [10]Humble yourselves before the Lord, and he will lift you up.

[11]Brothers, do not slander one another.[x] Anyone who speaks against his brother or judges him[y] speaks against the law and judges it. When you judge the law, you are not keeping it,[z] but sitting in judgment on it. [12]There is only one Lawgiver and Judge, the one who is able to save and destroy.[a] But you—who are you to judge your neighbor?[b]

[13]Now listen, you who say, "Today or tomorrow we will go to this or that city, spend a year there, carry on business and make money."[c] [14]Why, you do not even know what will happen tomorrow. What is

---

3:12
[a] Mt 7:16

3:13
[b] Jas 2:18

3:14
[c] ver 16
[d] Jas 5:19

3:15
[e] Jas 1:17
[f] 1Ti 4:1

3:17
[g] 1Co 2:6
[h] Lk 6:36
[i] Ro 12:9

3:18
[j] Pr 11:18;
Isa 32:17

4:1
[k] Tit 3:9
[l] Ro 7:23

4:3
[m] Ps 18:41
[n] 1Jn 3:22; 5:14

4:4
[o] Jas 1:27
[p] 1Jn 2:15
[q] Jn 15:19

4:6
[r] Ps 138:6;
Pr 3:34;
Mt 23:12

4:7
[s] Eph 4:27;
1Pe 5:6-9

4:8
[t] 2Ch 15:2
[u] Isa 1:16
[v] Jas 1:8

4:9
[w] Lk 6:25

4:11
[x] 1Pe 2:1
[y] Mt 7:1
[z] Jas 1:22

4:12
[a] Mt 10:28
[b] Ro 14:4

4:13
[c] Pr 27:1

---

[a] 5 Or *that God jealously longs for the spirit that he made to live in us*; or *that the Spirit he caused to live in us longs jealously*   [b] 6 Prov. 3:34

4:14
a Job 7:7;
Ps 102:3

4:15
b Ac 18:21

4:16
c 1Co 5:6

4:17
d Lk 12:47;
Jn 9:41

5:1
e Lk 6:24

5:2
f Job 13:28;
Mt 6:19,20

5:3
g ver 7,8

5:4
h Lev 19:13
i Dt 24:15
j Ro 9:29

5:5
k Am 6:1
l Jer 12:3; 25:34

5:6
m Heb 10:38

5:7
n Dt 11:14;
Jer 5:24

5:8
o Ro 13:11;
1Pe 4:7

5:9
p Jas 4:11
q 1Co 4:5;
1Pe 4:5
r Mt 24:33

5:10
s Mt 5:12

5:11
t Mt 5:10
u Job 1:21,22; 2:10
v Job 42:10,12-17
w Nu 14:18

5:12
x Mt 5:34-37

5:13
y Ps 50:15
z Col 3:16

5:14
a Mk 6:13

5:16
b Mt 3:6
c 1Pe 2:24
d Jn 9:31

5:17
e Ac 14:15
f 1Ki 17:1;
Lk 4:25

5:18
g 1Ki 18:41-45

your life? You are a mist that appears for a little while and then vanishes.*a* [15]Instead, you ought to say, "If it is the Lord's will,*b* we will live and do this or that." [16]As it is, you boast and brag. All such boasting is evil.*c* [17]Anyone, then, who knows the good he ought to do and doesn't do it, sins.*d*

Chapter 5 Theme

5 Now listen, you rich people,*e* weep and wail because of the misery that is coming upon you. [2]Your wealth has rotted, and moths have eaten your clothes.*f* [3]Your gold and silver are corroded. Their corrosion will testify against you and eat your flesh like fire. You have hoarded wealth in the last days.*g* [4]Look! The wages you failed to pay the workmen*h* who mowed your fields are crying out against you. The cries*i* of the harvesters have reached the ears of the Lord Almighty.*j* [5]You have lived on earth in luxury and self-indulgence. You have fattened yourselves*k* in the day of slaughter.*al* [6]You have condemned and murdered innocent men,*m* who were not opposing you.

[7]Be patient, then, brothers, until the Lord's coming. See how the farmer waits for the land to yield its valuable crop and how patient he is for the autumn and spring rains.*n* [8]You too, be patient and stand firm, because the Lord's coming is near.*o* [9]Don't grumble against each other, brothers,*p* or you will be judged. The Judge*q* is standing at the door!*r*

[10]Brothers, as an example of patience in the face of suffering, take the prophets*s* who spoke in the name of the Lord. [11]As you know, we consider blessed*t* those who have persevered. You have heard of Job's perseverance*u* and have seen what the Lord finally brought about.*v* The Lord is full of compassion and mercy.*w*

[12]Above all, my brothers, do not swear—not by heaven or by earth or by anything else. Let your "Yes" be yes, and your "No," no, or you will be condemned.*x*

[13]Is any one of you in trouble? He should pray.*y* Is anyone happy? Let him sing songs of praise.*z* [14]Is any one of you sick? He should call the elders of the church to pray over him and anoint him with oil*a* in the name of the Lord. [15]And the prayer offered in faith will make the sick person well; the Lord will raise him up. If he has sinned, he will be forgiven. [16]Therefore confess your sins*b* to each other and pray for each other so that you may be healed.*c* The prayer of a righteous man is powerful and effective.*d*

[17]Elijah was a man just like us.*e* He prayed earnestly that it would not rain, and it did not rain on the land for three and a half years.*f* [18]Again he prayed, and the heavens gave rain, and the earth produced its crops.*g*

a 5 Or *yourselves as in a day of feasting*

¹⁹My brothers, if one of you should wander from the truth^a and someone should bring him back,^b ²⁰remember this: Whoever turns a sinner from the error of his way will save^c him from death and cover over a multitude of sins.^d

5:19
^a Jas 3:14
^b Mt 18:15

5:20
^c Ro 11:14
^d 1 Pe 4:8

JAMES SUBJECT BY SUBJECT

SUBJECT	INSTRUCTION	ILLUSTRATION/EXPLANATION
Trials (1:2-8)	– consider it pure joy	
	– perseverance must finish its work	– when you persevere in trials you will be made more mature, complete, not lacking anything
	– ask God for wisdom	
	– believe when asking, not doubting	– doubter like a wave of the sea
		– doubter will not receive anything from the Lord

(continued)

SUBJECT	INSTRUCTION	ILLUSTRATION/EXPLANATION

(continued)

JAMES SUBJECT BY SUBJECT

SUBJECT	INSTRUCTION	ILLUSTRATION/EXPLANATION

JAMES AT A GLANCE

Theme of James:

SEGMENT
DIVISIONS

	CHAPTER THEMES
1	
2	
3	
4	
5	

Author:

Date:

Purpose:

Key Words:

 brothers

 faith (believe, believers)

 mature, finish (made complete)

 judge, sitting in judgment (judges, judged, judgment, be condemned)

 law

1 PETER

The hour had come for the Shepherd to be smitten and for the sheep to be scattered. Jesus chose to spend his final hours with his eleven, preparing them for the tribulation that would come.

Yet after Jesus' resurrection and ascension, the tribulation seemed to be relatively mild. The disgruntled Pharisees wanted to shut up the men who were turning Jerusalem upside down with their teaching and miracles, but nothing seemed life-threatening.

Then the first stone was thrown. Stephen, the first martyr, was brought to the ground. Saul watched him die. In hearty agreement with Stephen's death, Saul went to the high priest to gain permission to round up those of the Way who were spreading this gospel. Saul's purge was short-lived. Jesus saved Saul on the road to Damascus and changed his name to Paul. But the persecution of Christians continued. Herod the king became the adversary of believers, and Jews who had come to know Jesus as the Messiah were scattered abroad to other Roman provinces.

However, it wasn't until Nero that the persecution of Christians reached beyond the confines of Judah. Rumor had it that Nero had burned Rome so he could rebuild it as he wanted. Needing a scapegoat to divert attention from himself, Nero blamed the fire on the Christians and began the systematic persecution of God's children.

Jesus had prepared Peter for the world's tribulation; now Peter would prepare others. Peter wrote his first epistle on the eve of Nero's persecution, about A.D. 63 or 64.

Nero died in A.D. 68, but not before Rome put Peter to death.

✎ THINGS TO DO

1. Read through 1 Peter and do the following:

   a. In the initial verses of the book Peter describes himself and states to whom he is writing, and in the last verses of the book, he tells why he wrote this epistle. Record your insights about the author and his purpose in writing on the 1 PETER AT A GLANCE chart on page 2113.

   b. Pay close attention to what you see about the recipients of 1 Peter. What is their condition? What is going on in their midst? Record what you learn about them on the OBSERVATIONS CHART on page 2112.

2. Read 1 Peter chapter by chapter, looking for and marking in a distinctive way the key words (and their synonyms and pronouns) that are listed on 1 PETER AT A GLANCE. Also remember to mark words such as *grace* and *gracious gift* and references to the devil which you are marking throughout your Bible. In the margin list the truths you learn from every mention of key words. This is imperative if you want to understand 1 Peter.

3. Peter gives the reader many commands or instructions about things to do. You notice these by the construction of the sentence. The verb usually comes first and the "you" is implied. An example is seen in 1:13: "Prepare your minds for action."

   a. Underline the instructions or commands that Peter gives throughout the book. Then list these under "General Instructions" on the OBSERVATIONS CHART.

   b. As you evaluate these instructions and commands you will see that 1 Peter was written not only for the recipients but also for you. Think about how these instructions apply to your own life.

4. Peter also gives instructions to specific groups of people such as slaves, wives, husbands, etc. List his instructions to each group under the proper heading on the OBSERVATIONS CHART.

5. From what you have read, why do you think the believers are to do these things? In other words, what future event is the motivation for living life in accordance with Peter's exhortations?

6. Finally, summarize the theme of each chapter and record these themes on 1 PETER AT A GLANCE and in the text next to the chapter number. Don't forget to record the overall theme of 1 Peter.

THINGS TO THINK ABOUT

1. What have you learned about the way you are to live? How are you to respond to others, even when they are not living properly or treating you properly? What is Jesus' example in 1 Peter 2:21-25? Will you follow it?

2. As you think about what those believers were suffering, should you be surprised if you undergo the same? What will suffering accomplish in your life?

3. Even if you don't have a Nero in your life, is your enemy the devil still prowling about like a lion, looking for someone to devour? What are you to do, according to 1 Peter?

4. When our Lord Jesus Christ returns, will you be found standing firm in the true grace that has been provided you? What must you do or change in order to be prepared to see him face-to-face?

Chapter 1 Theme _____

1 Peter, an apostle of Jesus Christ,[a]

To God's elect,[b] strangers in the world, scattered throughout Pontus, Galatia, Cappadocia, Asia and Bithynia,[c] [2]who have been chosen according to the foreknowledge[d] of God the Father, through the sanctifying work of the Spirit,[e] for obedience to Jesus Christ and sprinkling by his blood:[f]

Grace and peace be yours in abundance.

[3]Praise be to the God and Father of our Lord Jesus Christ![g] In his great mercy[h] he has given us new birth into a living hope through the resurrection of Jesus Christ from the dead,[i] [4]and into an inheritance that can never perish, spoil or fade—kept in heaven for you,[j] [5]who through faith are shielded by God's power[k] until the coming of the salvation that is ready to be revealed in the last time. [6]In this you greatly rejoice,[l] though now for a little while[m] you may have had to suffer grief in all kinds of trials.[n] [7]These have come so that your faith—of greater worth than gold, which perishes even though refined by fire[o]—may be proved genuine[p] and may result in praise, glory and honor when Jesus Christ is revealed.[q] [8]Though you have not seen him, you love him; and even though you do not see him now, you believe in him[r] and are filled with an inexpressible and glorious joy, [9]for you are receiving the goal of your faith, the salvation of your souls.[s]

[10]Concerning this salvation, the prophets, who spoke[t] of the grace that was to come to you, searched intently and with the greatest care,[u] [11]trying to find out the time and circumstances to which the Spirit of Christ[v] in them was pointing when he predicted the sufferings of Christ and the glories that would follow. [12]It was

1:1
a 2Pe 1:1
b Mt 24:22
c Ac 16:7

1:2
d Ro 8:29
e 2Th 2:13
f Heb 10:22; 12:24

1:3
g 2Co 1:3; Eph 1:3
h Tit 3:5; Jas 1:18
i 1Co 15:20

1:4
j Col 1:5

1:5
k Jn 10:28

1:6
l Ro 5:2
m 1Pe 5:10
n Jas 1:2

1:7
o Job 23:10; Ps 66:10; Pr 17:3
p Jas 1:3
q Ro 2:7

1:8
r Jn 20:29

1:9
s Ro 6:22

1:10
t Mt 26:24
u Mt 13:17

1:11
v 2Pe 1:21

1:12
a ver 25

1:14
b Ro 12:2
c Eph 4:18

1:15
d 2Co 7:1;
1Th 4:7

1:16
e Lev 11:44,45

1:17
f Ac 10:34
g Heb 12:28

1:18
h Mt 20:28;
1Co 6:20

1:19
i Jn 1:29
j Ex 12:5

1:20
k Eph 1:4
l Heb 9:26

1:21
m Ro 4:24

1:22
n Jas 4:8
o Jn 13:34;
Heb 13:1

1:23
p Jn 1:13
q Heb 4:12

1:25
r Isa 40:6-8

2:1
s Eph 4:22
t Jas 4:11

2:2
u 1Co 3:2
v Eph 4:15,16

2:3
w Heb 6:5

2:4
x ver 7

2:5
y 1Co 3:9
z 1Ti 3:15
a Isa 61:6
b Php 4:18;
Heb 13:15

revealed to them that they were not serving themselves but you, when they spoke of the things that have now been told you by those who have preached the gospel to you[a] by the Holy Spirit sent from heaven. Even angels long to look into these things.

[13]Therefore, prepare your minds for action; be self-controlled; set your hope fully on the grace to be given you when Jesus Christ is revealed. [14]As obedient children, do not conform[b] to the evil desires you had when you lived in ignorance.[c] [15]But just as he who called you is holy, so be holy in all you do;[d] [16]for it is written: "Be holy, because I am holy."[a][e]

[17]Since you call on a Father who judges each man's work impartially,[f] live your lives as strangers here in reverent fear.[g] [18]For you know that it was not with perishable things such as silver or gold that you were redeemed[h] from the empty way of life handed down to you from your forefathers, [19]but with the precious blood of Christ, a lamb[i] without blemish or defect.[j] [20]He was chosen before the creation of the world[k] but was revealed in these last times[l] for your sake. [21]Through him you believe in God,[m] who raised him from the dead and glorified him, and so your faith and hope are in God.

[22]Now that you have purified[n] yourselves by obeying the truth so that you have sincere love for your brothers, love one another deeply,[o] from the heart.[b] [23]For you have been born again,[p] not of perishable seed, but of imperishable, through the living and enduring word of God.[q] [24]For,

> "All men are like grass,
>   and all their glory is like the flowers of the field;
>   the grass withers and the flowers fall,
> [25]   but the word of the Lord stands forever."[c][r]

And this is the word that was preached to you.

Chapter 2 Theme _____

2 Therefore, rid yourselves[s] of all malice and all deceit, hypocrisy, envy, and slander[t] of every kind. [2]Like newborn babies, crave pure spiritual milk,[u] so that by it you may grow up[v] in your salvation, [3]now that you have tasted that the Lord is good.[w]

[4]As you come to him, the living Stone[x]—rejected by men but chosen by God and precious to him— [5]you also, like living stones, are being built[y] into a spiritual house[z] to be a holy priesthood,[a] offering spiritual sacrifices acceptable to God through Jesus Christ.[b] [6]For in Scripture it says:

a 16 Lev. 11:44,45; 19:2; 20:7   b 22 Some early manuscripts *from a pure heart*
c 25 Isaiah 40:6-8

"See, I lay a stone in Zion,
    a chosen and precious cornerstone,*a*
    and the one who trusts in him
        will never be put to shame."*ab*

[7] Now to you who believe, this stone is precious. But to those who do not believe,*c*

"The stone the builders rejected
    has become the capstone,*b*"*cd*

[8] and,

"A stone that causes men to stumble
    and a rock that makes them fall."*de*

They stumble because they disobey the message—which is also what they were destined for.*f* [9] But you are a chosen people,*g* a royal priesthood, a holy nation,*h* a people belonging to God, that you may declare the praises of him who called you out of darkness into his wonderful light.*i* [10] Once you were not a people, but now you are the people of God;*j* once you had not received mercy, but now you have received mercy.

[11] Dear friends, I urge you, as aliens and strangers in the world, to abstain from sinful desires,*k* which war against your soul.*l* [12] Live such good lives among the pagans that, though they accuse you of doing wrong, they may see your good deeds*m* and glorify God*n* on the day he visits us.

[13] Submit yourselves for the Lord's sake to every authority*o* instituted among men: whether to the king, as the supreme authority, [14] or to governors, who are sent by him to punish those who do wrong*p* and to commend those who do right.*q* [15] For it is God's will*r* that by doing good you should silence the ignorant talk of foolish men.*s* [16] Live as free men,*t* but do not use your freedom as a cover-up for evil; live as servants of God.*u* [17] Show proper respect to everyone: Love the brotherhood of believers,*v* fear God, honor the king.*w*

[18] Slaves, submit yourselves to your masters with all respect,*x* not only to those who are good and considerate,*y* but also to those who are harsh. [19] For it is commendable if a man bears up under the pain of unjust suffering because he is conscious of God.*z* [20] But how is it to your credit if you receive a beating for doing wrong and endure it? But if you suffer for doing good and endure it, this is commendable before God.*a* [21] To this*b* you were called, because Christ suffered for you, leaving you an example,*c* that you should follow in his steps.

2:6
a Eph 2:20
b Isa 28:16

2:7
c 2Co 2:16
d Ps 118:22

2:8
e Isa 8:14;
1Co 1:23
f Ro 9:22

2:9
g Dt 10:15
h Isa 62:12
i Ac 26:18

2:10
j Hos 1:9,10

2:11
k Gal 5:16
l Jas 4:1

2:12
m Php 2:15;
1Pe 3:16
n Mt 5:16; 9:8

2:13
o Ro 13:1

2:14
p Ro 13:4
q Ro 13:3

2:15
r 1Pe 3:17
s ver 12

2:16
t Jn 8:32
u Ro 6:22

2:17
v Ro 12:10
w Ro 13:7

2:18
x Eph 6:5
y Jas 3:17

2:19
z 1Pe 3:14,17

2:20
a 1Pe 3:17

2:21
b Ac 14:22
c Mt 16:24

a 6 Isaiah 28:16   *b* 7 Or *cornerstone*   *c* 7 Psalm 118:22   *d* 8 Isaiah 8:14

2:22
a Isa 53:9

2:23
b Isa 53:7
c Lk 23:46

2:24
d Heb 9:28
e Ro 6:2
f Isa 53:5;
Heb 12:13;
Jas 5:16

2:25
g Isa 53:6
h Jn 10:11

3:1
i 1Pe 2:18
j Eph 5:22
k 1Co 7:16; 9:19

3:3
l Isa 3:18-23;
1Ti 2:9

3:4
m Ro 7:22

3:5
n 1Ti 5:5

3:6
o Ge 18:12

3:7
p Eph 5:25-33

3:8
q Ro 12:10
r 1Pe 5:5

3:9
s Ro 12:17
t 1Pe 2:23
u 1Pe 2:21
v Heb 6:14

3:12
w Ps 34:12-16

²²"He committed no sin,
> and no deceit was found in his mouth."^{a a}

²³When they hurled their insults at him, he did not retaliate; when he suffered, he made no threats.^b Instead, he entrusted himself^c to him who judges justly. ²⁴He himself bore our sins^d in his body on the tree, so that we might die to sins^e and live for righteousness; by his wounds you have been healed.^f ²⁵For you were like sheep going astray,^g but now you have returned to the Shepherd^h and Overseer of your souls.

Chapter 3 Theme

3 Wives, in the same way be submissiveⁱ to your husbands^j so that, if any of them do not believe the word, they may be won over^k without words by the behavior of their wives, ²when they see the purity and reverence of your lives. ³Your beauty should not come from outward adornment, such as braided hair and the wearing of gold jewelry and fine clothes.^l ⁴Instead, it should be that of your inner self,^m the unfading beauty of a gentle and quiet spirit, which is of great worth in God's sight. ⁵For this is the way the holy women of the past who put their hope in Godⁿ used to make themselves beautiful. They were submissive to their own husbands, ⁶like Sarah, who obeyed Abraham and called him her master.^o You are her daughters if you do what is right and do not give way to fear.

⁷Husbands,^p in the same way be considerate as you live with your wives, and treat them with respect as the weaker partner and as heirs with you of the gracious gift of life, so that nothing will hinder your prayers.

⁸Finally, all of you, live in harmony with one another; be sympathetic, love as brothers,^q be compassionate and humble.^r ⁹Do not repay evil with evil^s or insult with insult,^t but with blessing, because to this^u you were called so that you may inherit a blessing.^v ¹⁰For,

> "Whoever would love life
>   and see good days
> must keep his tongue from evil
>   and his lips from deceitful speech.
> ¹¹He must turn from evil and do good;
>   he must seek peace and pursue it.
> ¹²For the eyes of the Lord are on the righteous
>   and his ears are attentive to their prayer,
>   but the face of the Lord is against those who do evil."^{b w}

a 22 Isaiah 53:9   b 12 Psalm 34:12-16

¹³Who is going to harm you if you are eager to do good?ᵃ ¹⁴But even if you should suffer for what is right, you are blessed.ᵇ "Do not fear what they fearᵃ; do not be frightened."ᵇᶜ ¹⁵But in your hearts set apart Christ as Lord. Always be prepared to give an answerᵈ to everyone who asks you to give the reason for the hope that you have. But do this with gentleness and respect, ¹⁶keeping a clear conscience,ᵉ so that those who speak maliciously against your good behavior in Christ may be ashamed of their slander.ᶠ ¹⁷It is better, if it is God's will,ᵍ to suffer for doing goodʰ than for doing evil. ¹⁸For Christ died for sinsⁱ once for all, the righteous for the unrighteous, to bring you to God. He was put to death in the bodyʲ but made alive by the Spirit,ᵏ ¹⁹through whomᶜ also he went and preached to the spirits in prisonˡ ²⁰who disobeyed long ago when God waited patiently in the days of Noah while the ark was being built.ᵐ In it only a few people, eight in all, were savedⁿ through water, ²¹and this water symbolizes baptism that now saves youᵒ also—not the removal of dirt from the body but the pledgeᵈ of a good conscience toward God. It saves you by the resurrection of Jesus Christ,ᵖ ²²who has gone into heaven and is at God's right handᑫ—with angels, authorities and powers in submission to him.ʳ

Chapter 4 Theme

4 Therefore, since Christ suffered in his body, arm yourselves also with the same attitude, because he who has suffered in his body is done with sin. ²As a result, he does not live the rest of his earthly life for evil human desires,ˢ but rather for the will of God. ³For you have spent enough time in the pastᵗ doing what pagans choose to do—living in debauchery, lust, drunkenness, orgies, carousing and detestable idolatry. ⁴They think it strange that you do not plunge with them into the same flood of dissipation, and they heap abuse on you.ᵘ ⁵But they will have to give account to him who is ready to judge the living and the dead.ᵛ ⁶For this is the reason the gospel was preached even to those who are now dead,ʷ so that they might be judged according to men in regard to the body, but live according to God in regard to the spirit.

⁷The end of all things is near.ˣ Therefore be clear minded and self-controlled so that you can pray. ⁸Above all, love each other deeply,ʸ because love covers over a multitude of sins.ᶻ ⁹Offer hospitality to one another without grumbling.ᵃ ¹⁰Each one should use whatever gift he has received to serve others,ᵇ faithfullyᶜ administering God's grace in its various forms. ¹¹If anyone speaks, he should do it as one speaking the very words of God. If anyone

3:13
ᵃ Pr 16:7

3:14
ᵇ 1Pe 2:19,20; 4:15,16
ᶜ Isa 8:12,13

3:15
ᵈ Col 4:6

3:16
ᵉ Heb 13:18
ᶠ 1Pe 2:12,15

3:17
ᵍ 1Pe 2:15
ʰ 1Pe 2:20

3:18
ⁱ 1Pe 2:21
ʲ Col 1:22; 1Pe 4:1
ᵏ 1Pe 4:6

3:19
ˡ 1Pe 4:6

3:20
ᵐ Ge 6:3,5, 13,14
ⁿ Heb 11:7

3:21
ᵒ Tit 3:5
ᵖ 1Pe 1:3

3:22
ᑫ Mk 16:19
ʳ Ro 8:38

4:2
ˢ Ro 6:2

4:3
ᵗ Eph 2:2

4:4
ᵘ 1Pe 3:16

4:5
ᵛ Ac 10:42; 2Ti 4:1

4:6
ʷ 1Pe 3:19

4:7
ˣ Ro 13:11

4:8
ʸ 1Pe 1:22
ᶻ Pr 10:12

4:9
ᵃ Php 2:14

4:10
ᵇ Ro 12:6,7
ᶜ 1Co 4:2

ᵃ 14 Or *not fear their threats*   ᵇ 14 Isaiah 8:12   ᶜ 18,19 Or *alive in the spirit,* ¹⁹ *through which*   ᵈ 21 Or *response*

4:11
a Eph 6:10
b 1Co 10:31

4:12
c 1Pe 1:6,7

4:13
d Ro 8:17

4:14
e Mt 5:11

4:16
f Ac 5:41

4:17
g Jer 25:29
h 2Th 1:8

4:18
i Pr 11:31;
Lk 23:31

5:1
j Ac 11:30
k Lk 24:48
l 1Pe 1:5,7;
Rev 1:9

5:2
m Jn 21:16
n 1Ti 3:3

5:3
o Eze 34:4
p Php 3:17

5:4
q 1Co 9:25

5:5
r Eph 5:21
s Pr 3:34;
Jas 4:6

5:6
t Jas 4:10

5:7
u Ps 37:5;
Mt 6:25
v Heb 13:5

5:8
w Job 1:7

5:9
x Jas 4:7
y Col 2:5

serves, he should do it with the strength God provides,*a* so that in all things God may be praised*b* through Jesus Christ. To him be the glory and the power for ever and ever. Amen.

¹²Dear friends, do not be surprised at the painful trial you are suffering,*c* as though something strange were happening to you. ¹³But rejoice that you participate in the sufferings of Christ, so that you may be overjoyed when his glory is revealed.*d* ¹⁴If you are insulted because of the name of Christ, you are blessed,*e* for the Spirit of glory and of God rests on you. ¹⁵If you suffer, it should not be as a murderer or thief or any other kind of criminal, or even as a meddler. ¹⁶However, if you suffer as a Christian, do not be ashamed, but praise God that you bear that name.*f* ¹⁷For it is time for judgment to begin with the family of God;*g* and if it begins with us, what will the outcome be for those who do not obey the gospel of God?*h* ¹⁸And,

> "If it is hard for the righteous to be saved,
>   what will become of the ungodly and the sinner?"*a i*

¹⁹So then, those who suffer according to God's will should commit themselves to their faithful Creator and continue to do good.

Chapter 5 Theme _____

5 To the elders among you, I appeal as a fellow elder,*j* a witness*k* of Christ's sufferings and one who also will share in the glory to be revealed:*l* ²Be shepherds of God's flock*m* that is under your care, serving as overseers—not because you must, but because you are willing, as God wants you to be; not greedy for money,*n* but eager to serve; ³not lording it over*o* those entrusted to you, but being examples*p* to the flock. ⁴And when the Chief Shepherd appears, you will receive the crown of glory*q* that will never fade away.

⁵Young men, in the same way be submissive*r* to those who are older. All of you, clothe yourselves with humility toward one another, because,

> "God opposes the proud
>   but gives grace to the humble."*b s*

⁶Humble yourselves, therefore, under God's mighty hand, that he may lift you up in due time.*t* ⁷Cast all your anxiety on him*u* because he cares for you.*v*

⁸Be self-controlled and alert. Your enemy the devil prowls around*w* like a roaring lion looking for someone to devour. ⁹Resist him,*x* standing firm in the faith,*y* because you know that your

a 18 Prov. 11:31   *b 5* Prov. 3:34

brothers throughout the world are undergoing the same kind of sufferings.[a]

[10]And the God of all grace, who called you to his eternal glory[b] in Christ, after you have suffered a little while, will himself restore you and make you strong,[c] firm and steadfast. [11]To him be the power for ever and ever. Amen.[d]

[12]With the help of Silas,[ae] whom I regard as a faithful brother, I have written to you briefly,[f] encouraging you and testifying that this is the true grace of God. Stand fast in it.

[13]She who is in Babylon, chosen together with you, sends you her greetings, and so does my son Mark.[g] [14]Greet one another with a kiss of love.[h]

Peace[i] to all of you who are in Christ.

a 12 Greek *Silvanus*, a variant of *Silas*

5:9
a Ac 14:22

5:10
b 2Co 4:17
c 2Th 2:17

5:11
d Ro 11:36

5:12
e 2Co 1:19
f Heb 13:22

5:13
g Ac 12:12

5:14
h Ro 16:16
i Eph 6:23

1 PETER OBSERVATIONS CHART

AUTHOR	RECIPIENTS
GENERAL INSTRUCTIONS	

(continued)

1 PETER OBSERVATIONS CHART

INSTRUCTIONS TO

Wives   Husbands

Elders   Young men   Slaves

1 PETER AT A GLANCE

Theme of 1 Peter:

Author:

Date:

Purpose:

Key Words:

    suffering
    (and all its
    synonyms)

    grace (gracious
    gift)

    glory (glorious,
    glorified)

    salvation

    Jesus Christ

    God

    Holy Spirit

    called

    chosen (elect)

    holy

SEGMENT DIVISIONS	CHAPTER THEMES
1	
2	
3	
4	
5	

2 PETER

A fisherman by trade, Peter had been captured and transformed by a Shepherd. Is it any wonder that even in Peter's darkest hour, the welfare of God's sheep was uppermost in his mind?

Ever since the day he stood with Jesus by a fire, the morning air full of the aroma of roasting fish, Peter had known the way he would die. But Peter would be faithful. His concern about his death and the way he would die would not override his concern for his Lord's sheep, the sheep Jesus had commissioned him to feed and shepherd. And so, sometime around A.D. 63 or 64, Peter writes "to those who . . . have received a faith as precious as ours."

In A.D. 64, according to tradition, Peter was crucified upside down for the Lord he once denied knowing. How Peter had grown in the grace and knowledge of his God!

∾ THINGS TO DO

1. To familiarize yourself with 2 Peter, read the book without stopping or taking notes. The message of this short book is easily seen in each of the paragraphs, so as you read, notice the content of each. You will see that Peter contrasts certain things. Based on this first reading, what major contrast is Peter making in this book?

2. Read 2 Peter again, looking for facts concerning the author (pronouns such as *I, we, us*) and the recipients (pronouns such as *you, your*). Mark these in a distinctive way in the text. Then on the OBSERVATIONS CHART on page 2119 record the answers to the following questions: What does the author say about himself? When in his life is he writing? Who are the recipients? How are they described?

3. In a distinctive way, mark in the text the key words (and their synonyms and pronouns) which are listed on the 2 PETER AT A GLANCE chart on page 2120. Then list in the margin the truths you learn by marking these key words. Be as thorough as possible because the lists will help you see the flow of the book.

4. Read through 2 Peter again and look for specific instructions that Peter gives the readers concerning their behavior and belief. Record these on the OBSERVATIONS CHART under "Instructions." Also look for and note any people or groups of people of which Peter warns them to beware.

5. In this book, Peter states specifically why he is writing. Look for and underline any verse in which Peter says, *"I have written . . . to . . . you."* Also, underline any other verses that indicate his purpose in writing. Record his purpose for writing on 2 PETER AT A GLANCE.

6. Summarize the message of each paragraph and record its theme on 2 PETER AT A GLANCE. Then determine the chapter themes and the book theme and record these in the appropriate places on the chart and in the text.

∾ THINGS TO THINK ABOUT

1. What would it take to live your life so that you may be found spotless and blameless at Christ's coming?

2. Is there a danger today that false teachers will be among our brothers, as in Peter's day? What do you need to know to be able to detect them?

3. How can you keep from falling from your own secure position? Practically, what do you need to do in order to grow in the grace and knowledge of Jesus Christ?

Chapter 1 Theme

1 Simon Peter, a servant[a] and apostle of Jesus Christ,[b]

To those who through the righteousness[c] of our God and Savior Jesus Christ[d] have received a faith as precious as ours:

[2]Grace and peace be yours in abundance through the knowledge of God and of Jesus our Lord.[e]

[3]His divine power[f] has given us everything we need for life and godliness through our knowledge of him who called us[g] by his own glory and goodness. [4]Through these he has given us his very great and precious promises,[h] so that through them you may participate in the divine nature[i] and escape the corruption in the world caused by evil desires.[j]

[5]For this very reason, make every effort to add to your faith goodness; and to goodness, knowledge;[k] [6]and to knowledge, self-control;[l] and to self-control, perseverance; and to perseverance, godliness;[m] [7]and to godliness, brotherly kindness; and to brotherly kindness, love.[n] [8]For if you possess these qualities in increasing measure, they will keep you from being ineffective and unproductive[o] in your knowledge of our Lord Jesus Christ. [9]But if anyone does not have them, he is nearsighted and blind,[p] and has forgotten that he has been cleansed from his past sins.[q]

[10]Therefore, my brothers, be all the more eager to make your calling and election sure. For if you do these things, you will never fall,[r] [11]and you will receive a rich welcome into the eternal kingdom of our Lord and Savior Jesus Christ.

[12]So I will always remind you of these things,[s] even though you know them and are firmly established in the truth you now have. [13]I think it is right to refresh your memory as long as I live in the tent of this body,[t] [14]because I know that I will soon put it aside,[u] as our Lord Jesus Christ has made clear to me.[v] [15]And I will make every effort to see that after my departure[w] you will always be able to remember these things.

[16]We did not follow cleverly invented stories when we told you about the power and coming of our Lord Jesus Christ, but we were eyewitnesses of his majesty.[x] [17]For he received honor and glory from God the Father when the voice came to him from the Majestic Glory, saying, "This is my Son, whom I love; with him I am well pleased."[a][y] [18]We ourselves heard this voice that came from heaven when we were with him on the sacred mountain.[z]

[19]And we have the word of the prophets made more certain, and you will do well to pay attention to it, as to a light[a] shining in a dark place, until the day dawns and the morning star[b] rises in

---

1:1
[a]Ro 1:1
[b]1Pe 1:1
[c]Ro 3:21-26
[d]Tit 2:13

1:2
[e]Php 3:8

1:3
[f]1Pe 1:5
[g]1Th 2:12

1:4
[h]2Co 7:1
[i]Eph 4:24;
Heb 12:10;
1Jn 3:2
[j]2Pe 2:18-20

1:5
[k]Col 2:3

1:6
[l]Ac 24:25
[m]ver 3

1:7
[n]1Th 3:12

1:8
[o]Jn 15:2;
Tit 3:14

1:9
[p]1Jn 2:11
[q]Eph 5:26

1:10
[r]2Pe 3:17

1:12
[s]Php 3:1;
1Jn 2:21

1:13
[t]2Co 5:1,4

1:14
[u]2Ti 4:6
[v]Jn 21:18,19

1:15
[w]Lk 9:31

1:16
[x]Mt 17:1-8

1:17
[y]Mt 3:17

1:18
[z]Mt 17:6

1:19
[a]Ps 119:105
[b]Rev 22:16

a 17 Matt. 17:5; Mark 9:7; Luke 9:35

your hearts. [20]Above all, you must understand that no prophecy of Scripture came about by the prophet's own interpretation. [21]For prophecy never had its origin in the will of man, but men spoke from God[a] as they were carried along by the Holy Spirit.[b]

Chapter 2 Theme

2 But there were also false prophets[c] among the people, just as there will be false teachers among you.[d] They will secretly introduce destructive heresies, even denying the sovereign Lord[e] who bought them[f]—bringing swift destruction on themselves. [2]Many will follow their shameful ways and will bring the way of truth into disrepute. [3]In their greed these teachers will exploit you[g] with stories they have made up. Their condemnation has long been hanging over them, and their destruction has not been sleeping.

[4]For if God did not spare angels when they sinned, but sent them to hell,[a] putting them into gloomy dungeons[b] to be held for judgment;[h] [5]if he did not spare the ancient world[i] when he brought the flood on its ungodly people, but protected Noah, a preacher of righteousness, and seven others;[j] [6]if he condemned the cities of Sodom and Gomorrah by burning them to ashes,[k] and made them an example[l] of what is going to happen to the ungodly; [7]and if he rescued Lot,[m] a righteous man, who was distressed by the filthy lives of lawless men[n] [8](for that righteous man, living among them day after day, was tormented in his righteous soul by the lawless deeds he saw and heard)— [9]if this is so, then the Lord knows how to rescue godly men from trials[o] and to hold the unrighteous for the day of judgment, while continuing their punishment.[c] [10]This is especially true of those who follow the corrupt desire[p] of the sinful nature[d] and despise authority.

Bold and arrogant, these men are not afraid to slander celestial beings;[q] [11]yet even angels, although they are stronger and more powerful, do not bring slanderous accusations against such beings in the presence of the Lord.[r] [12]But these men blaspheme in matters they do not understand. They are like brute beasts, creatures of instinct, born only to be caught and destroyed, and like beasts they too will perish.[s]

[13]They will be paid back with harm for the harm they have done. Their idea of pleasure is to carouse in broad daylight.[t] They are blots and blemishes, reveling in their pleasures while they feast with you.[e][u] [14]With eyes full of adultery, they never stop sinning; they seduce[v] the unstable; they are experts in greed[w]—an accursed brood![x] [15]They have left the straight way and wandered off to follow the

a4 Greek *Tartarus*   b4 Some manuscripts *into chains of darkness*   c9 Or *unrighteous for punishment until the day of judgment*   d10 Or *the flesh*   e13 Some manuscripts *in their love feasts*

1:21
a 2Ti 3:16
b 2Sa 23:2;
Ac 1:16;
1Pe 1:11

2:1
c Dt 13:1-3
d 1Ti 4:1
e Jude 4
f 1Co 6:20

2:3
g 2Co 2:17;
1Th 2:5

2:4
h Jude 6;
Rev 20:1,2

2:5
i 2Pe 3:6
j Heb 11:7;
1Pe 3:20

2:6
k Ge 19:24,25
l Nu 26:10;
Jude 7

2:7
m Ge 19:16
n 2Pe 3:17

2:9
o 1Co 10:13

2:10
p 2Pe 3:3
q Jude 8

2:11
r Jude 9

2:12
s Jude 10

2:13
t Ro 13:13
u 1Co 11:20,21;
Jude 12

2:14
v ver 18
w ver 3
x Eph 2:3

2:15
a Nu 22:4-20;
Jude 11

2:16
b Nu 22:21-30

2:17
c Jude 12
d Jude 13

2:18
e Jude 16

2:19
f Jn 8:34;
Ro 6:16

2:20
g 2Pe 1:2
h Mt 12:45

2:21
i Heb 6:4-6

2:22
j Pr 26:11

3:1
k 2Pe 1:13

3:3
l 1Ti 4:1
m 2Pe 2:10;
Jude 18

3:4
n Isa 5:19;
Eze 12:22;
Mt 24:48
o Mk 10:6

3:5
p Ge 1:6,9;
Heb 11:3
q Ps 24:2

3:6
r Ge 7:21,22

3:7
s ver 10,12;
2Th 1:7

3:8
t Ps 90:4

3:9
u Hab 2:3;
Heb 10:37
v Ro 2:4
w 1Ti 2:4

3:10
x Lk 12:39;
1Th 5:2
y Mt 24:35;
Rev 21:1

way of Balaam[a] son of Beor, who loved the wages of wickedness. [16]But he was rebuked for his wrongdoing by a donkey—a beast without speech—who spoke with a man's voice and restrained the prophet's madness.[b]

[17]These men are springs without water[c] and mists driven by a storm. Blackest darkness is reserved for them.[d] [18]For they mouth empty, boastful words[e] and, by appealing to the lustful desires of sinful human nature, they entice people who are just escaping from those who live in error. [19]They promise them freedom, while they themselves are slaves of depravity—for a man is a slave to whatever has mastered him.[f] [20]If they have escaped the corruption of the world by knowing[g] our Lord and Savior Jesus Christ and are again entangled in it and overcome, they are worse off at the end than they were at the beginning.[h] [21]It would have been better for them not to have known the way of righteousness, than to have known it and then to turn their backs on the sacred command that was passed on to them.[i] [22]Of them the proverbs are true: "A dog returns to its vomit,"[a][j] and, "A sow that is washed goes back to her wallowing in the mud."

Chapter 3 Theme _____

3 Dear friends, this is now my second letter to you. I have written both of them as reminders[k] to stimulate you to wholesome thinking. [2]I want you to recall the words spoken in the past by the holy prophets and the command given by our Lord and Savior through your apostles.

[3]First of all, you must understand that in the last days[l] scoffers will come, scoffing and following their own evil desires.[m] [4]They will say, "Where is this 'coming' he promised?[n] Ever since our fathers died, everything goes on as it has since the beginning of creation."[o] [5]But they deliberately forget that long ago by God's word[p] the heavens existed and the earth was formed out of water and by water.[q] [6]By these waters also the world of that time was deluged and destroyed.[r] [7]By the same word the present heavens and earth are reserved for fire,[s] being kept for the day of judgment and destruction of ungodly men.

[8]But do not forget this one thing, dear friends: With the Lord a day is like a thousand years, and a thousand years are like a day.[t] [9]The Lord is not slow in keeping his promise,[u] as some understand slowness. He is patient[v] with you, not wanting anyone to perish, but everyone to come to repentance.[w]

[10]But the day of the Lord will come like a thief.[x] The heavens will disappear with a roar; the elements will be destroyed by fire, and the earth and everything in it will be laid bare.[b][y]

a 22 Prov. 26:11   b 10 Some manuscripts *be burned up*

[11]Since everything will be destroyed in this way, what kind of people ought you to be? You ought to live holy and godly lives [12]as you look forward[a] to the day of God and speed its coming.[a][b] That day will bring about the destruction of the heavens by fire, and the elements will melt in the heat.[c] [13]But in keeping with his promise we are looking forward to a new heaven and a new earth,[d] the home of righteousness.

[14]So then, dear friends, since you are looking forward to this, make every effort to be found spotless, blameless[e] and at peace with him. [15]Bear in mind that our Lord's patience[f] means salvation,[g] just as our dear brother Paul also wrote you with the wisdom that God gave him.[h] [16]He writes the same way in all his letters, speaking in them of these matters. His letters contain some things that are hard to understand, which ignorant and unstable[i] people distort, as they do the other Scriptures,[j] to their own destruction.

[17]Therefore, dear friends, since you already know this, be on your guard[k] so that you may not be carried away by the error[l] of lawless men and fall from your secure position.[m] [18]But grow in the grace and knowledge of our Lord and Savior Jesus Christ.[n] To him be glory both now and forever! Amen.

[a]12 Or as you wait eagerly for the day of God to come

3:12 [a]1Co 1:7 [b]Ps 50:3 [c]ver 10

3:13 [d]Isa 65:17; 66:22; Rev 21:1

3:14 [e]1Th 3:13

3:15 [f]Ro 2:4 [g]ver 9 [h]Eph 3:3

3:16 [i]2Pe 2:14 [j]ver 2

3:17 [k]1Co 10:12 [l]2Pe 2:18 [m]Rev 2:5

3:18 [n]2Pe 1:11

2 PETER OBSERVATIONS CHART

PETER   RECIPIENTS

_____
_____
_____
_____
_____
_____
_____
_____
_____
_____
_____

INSTRUCTIONS
_____
_____
_____
_____
_____
_____
_____
_____
_____
_____

WARNINGS
_____
_____
_____
_____
_____
_____
_____
_____
_____
_____
_____

Theme of 2 Peter:

SEGMENT
DIVISIONS

	PARAGRAPH THEMES	CHAPTER THEMES
	1:1-4	1
	1:5-11	
	1:12-21	
	2:1-22	2
	3:1-7	3
	3:8-13	
	3:14-18	

Author:

Date:

Purpose:

Key Words:
prophecy (prophet[s], prophet's)

knowledge (know, understand, knowing, known, told about)

remind (reminders, refresh your memory)

true (truth)

make every effort, eager

false, made up

destroyed, destruction

promise(d)

1 JOHN

A s a boy, John thought of Jesus as just a cousin, one of the sons of Aunt Mary, his mother Salome's sister. Little did he realize that someday he would be chosen by God to be one of his twelve apostles.

He had been known as a "Son of Thunder" (Mark 3:17); but a transformation had taken place. Now he was called "the disciple whom Jesus loved."

Even though John's name is not mentioned in this epistle, there is much evidence that he is the author. John had been with Jesus. He had seen him, heard him, touched him, and been filled with his love. This is evident as you hear John's fatherly heart for those who belong to Jesus. He loves the fathers, the young men, the dear children. Yet as he writes about the antichrists and deceivers, you can hear the rumble of thunder in the background.

We don't know when John wrote this first epistle. It may have been between A.D. 85 and 95, when he was in Ephesus before being exiled to the Isle of Patmos. Love—and thunder—compelled him to write. He had to protect his children from a deception that could darken their understanding if they were not warned about the brewing storm of gnosticism—a teaching which could keep them from having fellowship with him (1 John 1:3).

∾ THINGS TO DO

1. If you want to handle a passage of Scripture accurately you must always interpret it in the light of its context. Context simply means that which goes "with" (*con*) the "text." Context must always rule when it comes to interpretation. Identifying the author's purpose for writing will help you discern the context of a passage. What the author says, he says in the light of his purpose for writing.

    In this particular letter the author tells us his purpose in seven different verses: 1:4; 2:1, 12-14, 21, and 26. Then in 1 John 5:13 he concludes by summarizing his purpose for writing. Read these verses and record his reasons for writing on the chart I WRITE THIS TO YOU on page 2128. Then read 1 John 5:13 and record on the 1 JOHN AT A GLANCE chart on page 2129 the author's purpose for writing.

2. One of the major heresies the church would face was gnosticism. Gnosticism wasn't in full bloom in John's time, but the seeds had been sown. Understanding gnosticism will help you better understand why John concentrated on the truths contained in his writing. Therefore, before you go any further, read the article "Understanding Gnosticism" on page 2204.

3. Now read 1 John chapter by chapter and observe the text, using the instructions outlined in the observation section in "How to Use The International Inductive Study Bible" on page IISB-15.

    a. Mark in the text in a distinctive way each of the key words (and their synonyms and pronouns) listed on 1 JOHN AT A GLANCE. When you finish marking these words, go to the chart 1 JOHN KEY WORDS on page 2128 and record the number of times each word is used in each chapter. Then add them up to see the number of times each word is used in 1 John. Doing this will help you see the main themes of 1 John.

    b. John uses a number of contrasts in order to make his point: light/darkness; children of God/children of the devil; etc. Watch for these contrasts, and in the margin next to where they are found list what you learn from them.

    c. When you finish your observations on each chapter:

        1) List in the margin the truths you learn from each of the key words.

        2) Remember, 1 John was written "so that you may know." When you finish reading all five

chapters, trace throughout 1 John the repeated use of the words *know, known,* and *recognize* and record what you learn from the text on the chart WHAT I CAN KNOW and HOW I CAN KNOW IT on pages 2128, 2129. As you make this list, watch the matters John deals with in respect to wrong behavior or wrong belief.

3) Keep a running list of everything you learn about God, Jesus Christ, and the Spirit from this book. Record it in the margin.

4. Record the theme of each chapter on 1 JOHN AT A GLANCE and in the text next to the chapter number. Fill in any remaining information called for on the chart.

❧ THINGS TO THINK ABOUT

1. Based on the criteria given in this book, how can you know whether or not you have eternal life?

2. What have you learned about sin from 1 John? Do you live in sin or righteousness?

3. Do you love the things of the world? Are you caught up in boasting about what you have or do, or in desiring whatever your eyes see?

4. According to 1 John 3, what are you to do when your heart condemns you?

5. Does your belief about Jesus Christ match what 1 John teaches about him?

~~~~~

Chapter 1 Theme _____

1 That which was from the beginning,*a* which we have heard, which we have seen with our eyes,*b* which we have looked at and our hands have touched*c*—this we proclaim concerning the Word of life. ²The life appeared;*d* we have seen it and testify to it, and we proclaim to you the eternal life, which was with the Father and has appeared to us. ³We proclaim to you what we have seen and heard, so that you also may have fellowship with us. And our fellowship is with the Father and with his Son, Jesus Christ.*e* ⁴We write this*f* to make our*a* joy complete.*g*

⁵This is the message we have heard*h* from him and declare to you: God is light; in him there is no darkness at all. ⁶If we claim to have fellowship with him yet walk in the darkness,*i* we lie and do not live by the truth.*j* ⁷But if we walk in the light, as he is in the light, we have fellowship with one another, and the blood of Jesus, his Son, purifies us from all*b* sin.*k*

⁸If we claim to be without sin,*l* we deceive ourselves and the truth is not in us.*m* ⁹If we confess our sins, he is faithful and just and will forgive us our sins*n* and purify us from all unrighteousness. ¹⁰If we claim we have not sinned, we make him out to be a liar*o* and his word has no place in our lives.*p*

Chapter 2 Theme _____

2 My dear children,*q* I write this to you so that you will not sin. But if anybody does sin, we have one who speaks to the

1:1
a Jn 1:2
b Jn 1:14; 2Pe 1:16
c Jn 20:27

1:2
d Jn 1:1-4; 1Ti 3:16

1:3
e 1Co 1:9

1:4
f 1Jn 2:1
g Jn 3:29

1:5
h 1Jn 3:11

1:6
i 2Co 6:14
j Jn 3:19-21

1:7
k Heb 9:14; Rev 1:5

1:8
l Pr 20:9; Jas 3:2
m 1Jn 2:4

1:9
n Ps 32:5; 51:2

1:10
o 1Jn 5:10
p 1Jn 2:14

2:1
q ver 12,13,28

a 4 Some manuscripts *your*   *b* 7 Or *every*

Father in our defense[a]—Jesus Christ, the Righteous One. [2]He is the atoning sacrifice for our sins,[b] and not only for ours but also for[a] the sins of the whole world.

[3]We know that we have come to know him if we obey his commands.[c] [4]The man who says, "I know him," but does not do what he commands is a liar, and the truth is not in him.[d] [5]But if anyone obeys his word,[e] God's love[b] is truly made complete in him.[f] This is how we know we are in him: [6]Whoever claims to live in him must walk as Jesus did.[g]

[7]Dear friends, I am not writing you a new command but an old one, which you have had since the beginning.[h] This old command is the message you have heard. [8]Yet I am writing you a new command;[i] its truth is seen in him and you, because the darkness is passing[j] and the true light[k] is already shining.[l]

[9]Anyone who claims to be in the light but hates his brother is still in the darkness. [10]Whoever loves his brother lives in the light,[m] and there is nothing in him[c] to make him stumble. [11]But whoever hates his brother is in the darkness and walks around in the darkness; he does not know where he is going, because the darkness has blinded him.[n]

[12]I write to you, dear children,
because your sins have been forgiven on account
of his name.
[13]I write to you, fathers,
because you have known him who is from
the beginning.
I write to you, young men,
because you have overcome the evil one.[o]
I write to you, dear children,
because you have known the Father.
[14]I write to you, fathers,
because you have known him who is from
the beginning.
I write to you, young men,
because you are strong,[p]
and the word of God lives in you,[q]
and you have overcome the evil one.[r]

[15]Do not love the world or anything in the world.[s] If anyone loves the world, the love of the Father is not in him.[t] [16]For everything in the world—the cravings of sinful man,[u] the lust of his eyes[v] and the boasting of what he has and does—comes not from the Father but from the world. [17]The world and its desires pass away,[w] but the man who does the will of God lives forever.

Cross-references: 2:1 [a]Ro 8:34; Heb 7:25. 2:2 [b]Ro 3:25. 2:3 [c]Jn 14:15. 2:4 [d]1Jn 1:6,8. 2:5 [e]Jn 14:21,23; [f]1Jn 4:12. 2:6 [g]Mt 11:29; 1Pe 2:21. 2:7 [h]1Jn 3:11,23; 2Jn 5,6. 2:8 [i]Jn 13:34; [j]Ro 13:12; [k]Jn 1:9; [l]Eph 5:8; 1Th 5:5. 2:10 [m]1Jn 3:14. 2:11 [n]Jn 12:35. 2:13 [o]ver 14. 2:14 [p]Eph 6:10; [q]Jn 5:38; 1Jn 1:10; [r]ver 13. 2:15 [s]Ro 12:2; [t]Jas 4:4. 2:16 [u]Ro 13:14; [v]Pr 27:20. 2:17 [w]1Co 7:31.

[a]2 Or *He is the one who turns aside God's wrath, taking away our sins, and not only ours but also*   [b]5 Or *word, love for God*   [c]10 Or *it*

[18]Dear children, this is the last hour; and as you have heard that the antichrist is coming,[a] even now many antichrists have come.[b] This is how we know it is the last hour. [19]They went out from us,[c] but they did not really belong to us. For if they had belonged to us, they would have remained with us; but their going showed that none of them belonged to us.[d]

[20]But you have an anointing[e] from the Holy One,[f] and all of you know the truth.[a][g] [21]I do not write to you because you do not know the truth, but because you do know it[h] and because no lie comes from the truth. [22]Who is the liar? It is the man who denies that Jesus is the Christ. Such a man is the antichrist—he denies the Father and the Son.[i] [23]No one who denies the Son has the Father; whoever acknowledges the Son has the Father also.[j]

[24]See that what you have heard from the beginning remains in you. If it does, you also will remain in the Son and in the Father.[k] [25]And this is what he promised us—even eternal life.

[26]I am writing these things to you about those who are trying to lead you astray.[l] [27]As for you, the anointing[m] you received from him remains in you, and you do not need anyone to teach you. But as his anointing teaches you about all things and as that anointing is real, not counterfeit—just as it has taught you, remain in him.

[28]And now, dear children,[n] continue in him, so that when he appears[o] we may be confident[p] and unashamed before him at his coming.[q]

[29]If you know that he is righteous,[r] you know that everyone who does what is right has been born of him.

Chapter 3 Theme

3 How great is the love[s] the Father has lavished on us, that we should be called children of God![t] And that is what we are! The reason the world does not know us is that it did not know him.[u] [2]Dear friends, now we are children of God, and what we will be has not yet been made known. But we know that when he appears,[b] we shall be like him,[v] for we shall see him as he is.[w] [3]Everyone who has this hope in him purifies himself,[x] just as he is pure.

[4]Everyone who sins breaks the law; in fact, sin is lawlessness.[y] [5]But you know that he appeared so that he might take away our sins. And in him is no sin.[z] [6]No one who lives in him keeps on sinning.[a] No one who continues to sin has either seen him[b] or known him.[c]

[7]Dear children,[d] do not let anyone lead you astray.[e] He who does what is right is righteous, just as he is righteous.[f] [8]He who

---

2:18 [a]ver 22; 1Jn 4:3; 2Jn 7 [b]1Jn 4:1

2:19 [c]Ac 20:30 [d]1Co 11:19

2:20 [e]2Co 1:21 [f]Mk 1:24 [g]Jn 14:26

2:21 [h]2Pe 1:12; Jude 5

2:22 [i]2Jn 7

2:23 [j]Jn 8:19; 1Jn 4:15

2:24 [k]Jn 14:23

2:26 [l]2Jn 7

2:27 [m]ver 20

2:28 [n]ver 1 [o]1Jn 3:2 [p]1Jn 4:17 [q]1Th 2:19

2:29 [r]1Jn 3:7

3:1 [s]Jn 3:16 [t]Jn 1:12 [u]Jn 16:3

3:2 [v]Ro 8:29; 2Pe 1:4 [w]2Co 3:18

3:3 [x]2Co 7:1; 2Pe 3:13,14

3:4 [y]1Jn 5:17

3:5 [z]2Co 5:21

3:6 [a]ver 9 [b]3Jn 11 [c]1Jn 2:4

3:7 [d]1Jn 2:1 [e]1Jn 2:26 [f]1Jn 2:29

---

[a]20 Some manuscripts *and you know all things* [b]2 Or *when it is made known*

3:8
a Jn 8:44

3:9
b Jn 1:13
c 1Jn 5:18
d 1Pe 1:23

3:10
e 1Jn 4:8

3:11
f 1Jn 1:5
g Jn 13:34,35;
2Jn 5

3:12
h Ge 4:8

3:13
i Jn 15:18,19;
17:14

3:14
j Jn 5:24
k 1Jn 2:9

3:15
l Mt 5:21,22;
Jn 8:44
m Gal 5:20,21

3:16
n Jn 15:13

3:17
o Dt 15:7,8
p 1Jn 4:20

3:18
q 1Jn 2:1
r Eze 33:31;
Ro 12:9

3:21
s 1Jn 5:14

3:22
t Mt 7:7
u Jn 8:29

3:23
v Jn 6:29
w Jn 13:34

3:24
x 1Jn 2:6
y 1Jn 4:13

4:1
z 2Pe 2:1;
1Jn 2:18

4:2
a Jn 1:14;
1Jn 2:23
b 1Co 12:3

4:3
c 1Jn 2:22;
2Jn 7

does what is sinful is of the devil,*a* because the devil has been sinning from the beginning. The reason the Son of God appeared was to destroy the devil's work. [9]No one who is born of God*b* will continue to sin,*c* because God's seed*d* remains in him; he cannot go on sinning, because he has been born of God. [10]This is how we know who the children of God are and who the children of the devil are: Anyone who does not do what is right is not a child of God; nor is anyone who does not love*e* his brother.

[11]This is the message you heard*f* from the beginning: We should love one another.*g* [12]Do not be like Cain, who belonged to the evil one and murdered his brother.*h* And why did he murder him? Because his own actions were evil and his brother's were righteous. [13]Do not be surprised, my brothers, if the world hates you.*i* [14]We know that we have passed from death to life,*j* because we love our brothers. Anyone who does not love remains in death.*k* [15]Anyone who hates his brother is a murderer,*l* and you know that no murderer has eternal life in him.*m*

[16]This is how we know what love is: Jesus Christ laid down his life for us. And we ought to lay down our lives for our brothers.*n* [17]If anyone has material possessions and sees his brother in need but has no pity on him,*o* how can the love of God be in him?*p* [18]Dear children,*q* let us not love with words or tongue but with actions and in truth.*r* [19]This then is how we know that we belong to the truth, and how we set our hearts at rest in his presence [20]whenever our hearts condemn us. For God is greater than our hearts, and he knows everything.

[21]Dear friends, if our hearts do not condemn us, we have confidence before God*s* [22]and receive from him anything we ask,*t* because we obey his commands and do what pleases him.*u* [23]And this is his command: to believe*v* in the name of his Son, Jesus Christ, and to love one another as he commanded us.*w* [24]Those who obey his commands live in him,*x* and he in them. And this is how we know that he lives in us: We know it by the Spirit he gave us.*y*

Chapter 4 Theme

4 Dear friends, do not believe every spirit, but test the spirits to see whether they are from God, because many false prophets have gone out into the world.*z* [2]This is how you can recognize the Spirit of God: Every spirit that acknowledges that Jesus Christ has come in the flesh*a* is from God,*b* [3]but every spirit that does not acknowledge Jesus is not from God. This is the spirit of the antichrist,*c* which you have heard is coming and even now is already in the world.

⁴You, dear children, are from God and have overcome them, because the one who is in you[a] is greater than the one who is in the world.[b] ⁵They are from the world[c] and therefore speak from the viewpoint of the world, and the world listens to them. ⁶We are from God, and whoever knows God listens to us; but whoever is not from God does not listen to us.[d] This is how we recognize the Spirit[a] of truth[e] and the spirit of falsehood.

⁷Dear friends, let us love one another,[f] for love comes from God. Everyone who loves has been born of God and knows God.[g] ⁸Whoever does not love does not know God, because God is love.[h] ⁹This is how God showed his love among us: He sent his one and only Son[b] into the world that we might live through him.[i] ¹⁰This is love: not that we loved God, but that he loved us[j] and sent his Son as an atoning sacrifice for[c] our sins.[k] ¹¹Dear friends, since God so loved us,[l] we also ought to love one another. ¹²No one has ever seen God;[m] but if we love one another, God lives in us and his love is made complete in us.[n]

¹³We know that we live in him and he in us, because he has given us of his Spirit.[o] ¹⁴And we have seen and testify[p] that the Father has sent his Son to be the Savior of the world.[q] ¹⁵If anyone acknowledges that Jesus is the Son of God,[r] God lives in him and he in God. ¹⁶And so we know and rely on the love God has for us.

God is love.[s] Whoever lives in love lives in God, and God in him.[t] ¹⁷In this way, love is made complete[u] among us so that we will have confidence on the day of judgment, because in this world we are like him. ¹⁸There is no fear in love. But perfect love drives out fear,[v] because fear has to do with punishment. The one who fears is not made perfect in love.

¹⁹We love because he first loved us.[w] ²⁰If anyone says, "I love God," yet hates his brother,[x] he is a liar.[y] For anyone who does not love his brother, whom he has seen,[z] cannot love God, whom he has not seen.[a] ²¹And he has given us this command: Whoever loves God must also love his brother.[b]

Chapter 5 Theme

5 Everyone who believes that Jesus is the Christ[c] is born of God,[d] and everyone who loves the father loves his child as well.[e] ²This is how we know that we love the children of God: by loving God and carrying out his commands. ³This is love for God: to obey his commands.[f] And his commands are not burdensome,[g] ⁴for everyone born of God overcomes[h] the world. This is the victory that has overcome the world, even our faith. ⁵Who is it that overcomes the world? Only he who believes that Jesus is the Son of God.

a 6 Or *spirit*   b 9 Or *his only begotten Son*   c 10 Or *as the one who would turn aside his wrath, taking away*

4:4 a Ro 8:31 b Jn 12:31
4:5 c Jn 15:19
4:6 d Jn 8:47 e Jn 14:17
4:7 f 1Jn 3:11 g 1Jn 2:4
4:8 h ver 7,16
4:9 i Jn 3:16,17; 1Jn 5:11
4:10 j Ro 5:8,10 k 1Jn 2:2
4:11 l Jn 3:16
4:12 m Jn 1:18; 1Ti 6:16 n 1Jn 2:5
4:13 o 1Jn 3:24
4:14 p Jn 15:27 q Jn 3:17
4:15 r Ro 10:9
4:16 s ver 8 t 1Jn 3:24
4:17 u 1Jn 2:5
4:18 v Ro 8:15
4:19 w ver 10
4:20 x 1Jn 2:9 y 1Jn 2:4 z 1Jn 3:17 a ver 12
4:21 b Mt 5:43
5:1 c 1Jn 2:22 d Jn 1:13; 1Jn 2:23 e Jn 8:42
5:3 f Jn 14:15; 2Jn 6 g Mt 11:30
5:4 h Jn 16:33

5:6
a Jn 19:34
b Jn 14:17

5:7
c Mt 18:16

5:9
d Jn 5:34
e Mt 3:16,17;
Jn 8:17,18

5:10
f Ro 8:16;
Gal 4:6
g Jn 3:33

5:11
h Jn 1:4;
1Jn 2:25

5:12
i Jn 3:15,16,36

5:13
j 1Jn 3:23
k Jn 20:31;
1Jn 1:1,2

5:14
l 1Jn 3:21
m Mt 7:7

5:15
n ver 18,19,20

5:16
o Jas 5:15
p Heb 6:4-6;
10:26
q Jer 7:16

5:17
r 1Jn 3:4
s 1Jn 2:1

5:18
t Jn 14:30

5:19
u 1Jn 4:6
v Gal 1:4

5:20
w Lk 24:45
x Jn 17:3
y ver 11

5:21
z 1Co 10:14;
1Th 1:9

[6] This is the one who came by water and blood[a]—Jesus Christ. He did not come by water only, but by water and blood. And it is the Spirit who testifies, because the Spirit is the truth.[b] [7] For there are three[c] that testify: [8] the[a] Spirit, the water and the blood; and the three are in agreement. [9] We accept man's testimony,[d] but God's testimony is greater because it is the testimony of God,[e] which he has given about his Son. [10] Anyone who believes in the Son of God has this testimony in his heart.[f] Anyone who does not believe God has made him out to be a liar,[g] because he has not believed the testimony God has given about his Son. [11] And this is the testimony: God has given us eternal life, and this life is in his Son.[h] [12] He who has the Son has life; he who does not have the Son of God does not have life.[i]

[13] I write these things to you who believe in the name of the Son of God[j] so that you may know that you have eternal life.[k] [14] This is the confidence[l] we have in approaching God: that if we ask anything according to his will, he hears us.[m] [15] And if we know that he hears us—whatever we ask—we know[n] that we have what we asked of him.

[16] If anyone sees his brother commit a sin that does not lead to death, he should pray and God will give him life.[o] I refer to those whose sin does not lead to death. There is a sin that leads to death.[p] I am not saying that he should pray about that.[q] [17] All wrongdoing is sin,[r] and there is sin that does not lead to death.[s]

[18] We know that anyone born of God does not continue to sin; the one who was born of God keeps him safe, and the evil one cannot harm him.[t] [19] We know that we are children of God,[u] and that the whole world is under the control of the evil one.[v] [20] We know also that the Son of God has come and has given us understanding,[w] so that we may know him who is true.[x] And we are in him who is true—even in his Son Jesus Christ. He is the true God and eternal life.[y]

[21] Dear children, keep yourselves from idols.[z]

a 7,8 Late manuscripts of the Vulgate *testify in heaven: the Father, the Word and the Holy Spirit, and these three are one.* [8] *And there are three that testify on earth: the* (not found in any Greek manuscript before the sixteenth century)

1 JOHN OBSERVATIONS CHARTS

I WRITE THIS TO YOU

1:4	
2:1	
2:12	
2:13	
2:14	
2:21	
2:26	
5:13	

1 JOHN KEY WORDS

Chapter	Fellowship	Remain (Continue)	Sin	Know (Recognize)	Love	Born of God	Write	Light	Truth
1									
2									
3									
4									
5									
Total									

WHAT I CAN KNOW

HOW I CAN KNOW IT

(continued)

1 JOHN OBSERVATIONS CHARTS

WHAT I CAN KNOW	HOW I CAN KNOW IT

1 JOHN AT A GLANCE

Theme of 1 John:

Author:

Date:

Purpose:

Key Words:
fellowship

remain(s),
continue, be in,
live in

sin(s), sinning,
what is sinful

know(n),
recognize

love, loving

born of God

light

truth (true, real)

write (writing)

mark every
reference to the
devil (or evil one)

SEGMENT DIVISIONS	CHAPTER THEMES
1	
2	
3	
4	
5	

2 JOHN

A caring father can't ignore something that threatens his children. So around A.D. 90 the paternal apostle John sat down to write yet another epistle. It is short, to the point, and needful—even today.

∾ THINGS TO DO

1. Read through 2 John as you would a letter you had just received. Then read it again and:

   a. Mark in the text the key words listed on the 2 JOHN AT A GLANCE chart on page 2131.

   b. List in the margin all you learn about the recipients of this letter. Note John's feelings toward them, his instructions (or commandments) to them, and his warnings. Note also the reason for his warnings.

2. Record the theme of 2 John in the appropriate space on 2 JOHN AT A GLANCE. Then record the theme of each paragraph and fill in any other pertinent information.

∾ THINGS TO THINK ABOUT

1. What does this book say about someone who does not continue in the teaching of Christ? Do you know someone who could fit that description? What should you do?

2. You probably noted that verse 4 says "some" of the children are walking in truth. Are you careful to walk in all the truth you know? Do you realize that before God you are responsible to live out the truth that has been entrusted to you?

3. According to this little epistle, what does it mean to walk in love? Are you doing this?

Chapter Theme _____

¹The elder,*a*

To the chosen*b* lady and her children, whom I love in the truth— and not I only, but also all who know the truth*c*— ²because of the truth,*d* which lives in us*e* and will be with us forever:

³Grace, mercy and peace from God the Father and from Jesus Christ,*f* the Father's Son, will be with us in truth and love.

⁴It has given me great joy to find some of your children walking in the truth,*g* just as the Father commanded us. ⁵And now, dear lady, I am not writing you a new command but one we have had from the beginning.*h* I ask that we love one another. ⁶And this is love:*i* that we walk in obedience to his commands. As you have heard from the beginning, his command is that you walk in love.

⁷Many deceivers, who do not acknowledge Jesus Christ*j* as coming in the flesh, have gone out into the world.*k* Any such person is the deceiver and the antichrist.*l* ⁸Watch out that you do not lose what you have worked for, but that you may be rewarded fully.*m* ⁹Anyone who runs ahead and does not continue in the teaching of

1:1
a 3Jn 1
b Ro 16:13
c Jn 8:32

1:2
d 2Pe 1:12
e 1Jn 1:8

1:3
f Ro 1:7

1:4
g 3Jn 3,4

1:5
h 1Jn 2:7; 3:11

1:6
i 1Jn 2:5

1:7
j 1Jn 2:22;
4:2,3
k 1Jn 4:1
l 1Jn 2:18

1:8
m 1Co 3:8

1:9
a 1Jn 2:23

1:10
b Ro 16:17

1:11
c 1Ti 5:22

1:12
d 3Jn 13,14

1:13
e ver 1

Christ does not have God; whoever continues in the teaching has both the Father and the Son.*a* **10**If anyone comes to you and does not bring this teaching, do not take him into your house or welcome him.*b* **11**Anyone who welcomes him shares*c* in his wicked work.

12I have much to write to you, but I do not want to use paper and ink. Instead, I hope to visit you and talk with you face to face,*d* so that our joy may be complete.

13The children of your chosen*e* sister send their greetings.

2 John at a Glance

Theme of 2 John:

	SEGMENT DIVISIONS	PARAGRAPH THEMES
Author:		
Date:	Verses 1-3	
Purpose:		
Key Words: truth love command(ed) (commands) teaching walk continue(s) (lives) deceiver(s)	Verses 4-11	
	Verses 12, 13	

3 JOHN

*L*ove cares about the individual. Love encourages. Love rebukes. Love walks in truth. And so, in love, John wrote a third epistle before he was exiled to Patmos, where he wrote Revelation. It was around A.D. 90.

➳ THINGS TO DO

1. Read this short letter through once. Then read the book again, marking each of the key words listed on the 3 JOHN AT A GLANCE chart on page 2133. List in the margin what you learn from the key words.

2. To whom is the book written? List in the margin everything you learn about him from this letter.

3. Other names are mentioned. Who is named and what is said about each person? List this information in the margin of the text. What do you learn as you observe the contrast between these people?

4. Make a list of the instructions and warnings John gives in this short epistle.

5. Complete 3 JOHN AT A GLANCE.

➳ THINGS TO THINK ABOUT

1. What is your testimony before others? Are you known for your love of others or for your love of yourself? Do you share what you have with others? Do you listen to others? Do you have to be first?

2. According to what John says in this epistle, what does the way you live have to do with your relationship to God?

3. Are you quick to love, to exhort, and to stand for truth? What do you need to do?

~~~~~~~~

Chapter Theme

[1:1]
[a] 2Jn 1

[1]The elder,[a]

To my dear friend Gaius, whom I love in the truth.

[1:3]
[b] ver 5,10
[c] 2Jn 4

[2]Dear friend, I pray that you may enjoy good health and that all may go well with you, even as your soul is getting along well. [3]It gave me great joy to have some brothers[b] come and tell about your faithfulness to the truth and how you continue to walk in the truth.[c]

[1:4]
[d] 1Co 4:15;
1Jn 2:1

[4]I have no greater joy than to hear that my children[d] are walking in the truth.

[1:5]
[e] Ro 12:13;
Heb 13:2

[5]Dear friend, you are faithful in what you are doing for the brothers, even though they are strangers to you.[e] [6]They have told the church about your love. You will do well to send them on their way in a manner worthy of God. [7]It was for the sake of the Name[f] that they went out, receiving no help from the pagans.[g]

[1:7]
[f] Jn 15:21
[g] Ac 20:33,35

[8]We ought therefore to show hospitality to such men so that we may work together for the truth.

[9]I wrote to the church, but Diotrephes, who loves to be first, will have nothing to do with us. [10]So if I come,[h] I will call attention to

[1:10]
[h] 2Jn 12

1:10
a ver 5
b Jn 9:22,34

what he is doing, gossiping maliciously about us. Not satisfied with that, he refuses to welcome the brothers.*a* He also stops those who want to do so and puts them out of the church.*b*

1:11
c Ps 37:27
d 1Jn 2:29
e 1Jn 3:6,9,10

11Dear friend, do not imitate what is evil but what is good.*c* Anyone who does what is good is from God.*d* Anyone who does what is evil has not seen God.*e* 12Demetrius is well spoken of by everyone*f*—and even by the truth itself. We also speak well of him, and you know that our testimony is true.*g*

1:12
f 1Ti 3:7
g Jn 21:24

13I have much to write you, but I do not want to do so with pen and ink. 14I hope to see you soon, and we will talk face to face.*h*

1:14
h 2Jn 12
i Jn 10:3

Peace to you. The friends here send their greetings. Greet the friends there by name.*i*

3 JOHN AT A GLANCE

Theme of 3 John:

	SEGMENT DIVISIONS	PARAGRAPH THEMES
Author:		
Date:		VERSE 1
Purpose:		VERSES 2-4
Key Words:		VERSES 5-8
truth		
good		VERSES 9-12
evil		
		VERSES 13, 14

JUDE

*J*ude had to speak up. Jude wasn't an apostle and wasn't a pillar in the church, like his brother James. Although he was the half-brother of the Lord Jesus Christ, Jude did not claim any relationship to Jesus Christ other than that of being his bondservant.

Initially Jude didn't believe in Jesus (John 7:5), but finally he saw Jesus as he was—the Son of God—and then he understood: Jude had grown up in the presence of the One who came to save his people from their sins (Matthew 1:21). No wonder Jude had to write what he did!

∾ THINGS TO DO

1. Though only one chapter in length, Jude is a pertinent book. Read it to familiarize yourself with the content.

2. Now read through Jude again. This time look for any place where Jude explains why he is writing. When you discover Jude's purpose for writing, put it on the JUDE AT A GLANCE chart on page 2138. If you do not see his purpose immediately, you will by the time you have finished Jude.

3. Now read through Jude again. This time find out what you can about the author and the recipients. Mark in a distinctive way every reference to the author and to the recipients and related pronouns.

4. Read through Jude again. List what you learn about Jude and the recipients on the OBSERVATIONS CHART on page 2137. Note *only* how Jude and the recipients are described. At this point *do not* list what the recipients are told to do; instead, list only how they are described.

5. Jude mentions other people in this letter. Recognizing who they are and what they are doing will help you to understand better the reason for the writing of this letter. Read through Jude again.

   a. This time mark every occurrence of *certain men, godless men, these men,* and *scoffers* in the same color or with the same symbol.

   b. Also mark in the same way the pronouns (*they, them, who, these,* etc.) which refer to *certain men, godless men, these men, these dreamers,* and *scoffers.*

6. Read Jude again. This time mark in the same way *condemnation, destroyed, judgment (judge), punishment,* and their synonyms. Be sure not to miss any contrasts and comparisons that Jude is making.

7. There is a pattern in this letter. First, Jude refers to "these godless men," then uses Old Testament examples or illustrations to make a point. Read through Jude again, and watch for this pattern. You may want to underline every Old Testament incident or reference that Jude uses. As you study, watch what the Old Testament people do and note how God deals with them. Be sure not to miss any contrasts and comparisons that Jude is making between these Old Testament people and "these godless men."

8. Now that you have marked every reference to "these godless men," and looked at the Old Testament illustrations Jude uses to make his point, fill in this portion of the OBSERVATIONS CHART.

9. On the OBSERVATIONS CHART, list Jude's instructions to the "dear friends" who were the recipients of this epistle by noting what they are to do. Also be sure to note what God will do for them.

10. Determine what you believe to be the theme of Jude and write it down on JUDE AT A GLANCE.

11. Finally, look at Jude paragraph by paragraph, determine what you believe to be the theme for each paragraph, and then record it in the designated place on JUDE AT A GLANCE. Fill in any other information requested.

12. If you want to study Jude further, look up the cross-references in the margin to the Old Testament characters and illustrations and see what you learn from each. This will deepen your insight into these godless men.

∾ THINGS TO THINK ABOUT

1. Think about the promises to the "loved by God." Spend time in prayer, praising God for what he will do on your behalf. Then think of the responsibilities that are yours and talk with God about how you are to fulfill these.

2. Review the characteristics of the godless. Do you know of anyone who fits this description? How did God tell you to respond to these godless persons in verses 22 and 23? Are you willing to do so? Talk with God about it.

∾∾∾∾∾

Chapter Theme _____

¹Jude,[a] a servant of Jesus Christ and a brother of James,

To those who have been called,[b] who are loved by God the Father and kept by[a] Jesus Christ:[c]

²Mercy, peace and love be yours in abundance.[d]

³Dear friends, although I was very eager to write to you about the salvation we share,[e] I felt I had to write and urge you to contend[f] for the faith that was once for all entrusted to the saints. ⁴For certain men whose condemnation was written about[b] long ago have secretly slipped in among you.[g] They are godless men, who change the grace of our God into a license for immorality and deny Jesus Christ our only Sovereign and Lord.[h]

⁵Though you already know all this, I want to remind you that the Lord[c] delivered his people out of Egypt, but later destroyed those who did not believe.[i] ⁶And the angels who did not keep their positions of authority but abandoned their own home—these he has kept in darkness, bound with everlasting chains for judgment on the great Day.[j] ⁷In a similar way, Sodom and Gomorrah and the surrounding towns[k] gave themselves up to sexual immorality and perversion. They serve as an example of those who suffer the punishment of eternal fire.[l]

⁸In the very same way, these dreamers pollute their own bodies, reject authority and slander celestial beings.[m] ⁹But even the archangel Michael,[n] when he was disputing with the devil about the body of Moses, did not dare to bring a slanderous accusation against him, but said, "The Lord rebuke you!"[o] ¹⁰Yet these men speak abusively against whatever they do not understand; and what things they do understand by instinct, like unreasoning animals—these are the very things that destroy them.[p]

¹¹Woe to them! They have taken the way of Cain;[q] they have

1:1
[a] Mt 13:55; Ac 1:13
[b] Ro 1:6,7
[c] Jn 17:12

1:2
[d] 2Pe 1:2

1:3
[e] Tit 1:4
[f] 1Ti 6:12

1:4
[g] Gal 2:4
[h] Tit 1:16; 2Pe 2:1

1:5
[i] Nu 14:29; Ps 106:26

1:6
[j] 2Pe 2:4,9

1:7
[k] Dt 29:23
[l] 2Pe 2:6

1:8
[m] 2Pe 2:10

1:9
[n] Da 10:13,21
[o] Zec 3:2

1:10
[p] 2Pe 2:12

1:11
[q] Ge 4:3-8; 1Jn 3:12

a 1 Or *for*; or *in*   b 4 Or *men who were marked out for condemnation*   c 5 Some early manuscripts *Jesus*

2135

rushed for profit into Balaam's error;[a] they have been destroyed in Korah's rebellion.[b]

[12]These men are blemishes at your love feasts,[c] eating with you without the slightest qualm—shepherds who feed only themselves. They are clouds without rain,[d] blown along by the wind;[e] autumn trees, without fruit and uprooted[f]—twice dead. [13]They are wild waves of the sea,[g] foaming up their shame;[h] wandering stars, for whom blackest darkness has been reserved forever.[i]

[14]Enoch,[j] the seventh from Adam, prophesied about these men: "See, the Lord is coming with thousands upon thousands of his holy ones[k] [15]to judge[l] everyone, and to convict all the ungodly of all the ungodly acts they have done in the ungodly way, and of all the harsh words ungodly sinners have spoken against him."[m] [16]These men are grumblers and faultfinders; they follow their own evil desires; they boast[n] about themselves and flatter others for their own advantage.

[17]But, dear friends, remember what the apostles of our Lord Jesus Christ foretold.[o] [18]They said to you, "In the last times[p] there will be scoffers who will follow their own ungodly desires."[q] [19]These are the men who divide you, who follow mere natural instincts and do not have the Spirit.[r]

[20]But you, dear friends, build yourselves up[s] in your most holy faith and pray in the Holy Spirit.[t] [21]Keep yourselves in God's love as you wait[u] for the mercy of our Lord Jesus Christ to bring you to eternal life.

[22]Be merciful to those who doubt; [23]snatch others from the fire and save them;[v] to others show mercy, mixed with fear—hating even the clothing stained by corrupted flesh.[w]

[24]To him who is able[x] to keep you from falling and to present you before his glorious presence[y] without fault[z] and with great joy— [25]to the only God[a] our Savior be glory, majesty, power and authority, through Jesus Christ our Lord, before all ages, now and forevermore![b] Amen.[c]

1:11
[a] 2Pe 2:15
[b] Nu 16:1-3, 31-35
1:12
[c] 2Pe 2:13; 1Co 11:20-22
[d] Pr 25:14; 2Pe 2:17
[e] Eph 4:14
[f] Mt 15:13
1:13
[g] Isa 57:20
[h] Php 3:19
[i] 2Pe 2:17
1:14
[j] Ge 5:18,21-24
[k] Dt 33:2; Da 7:10
1:15
[l] 2Pe 2:6-9
[m] 1Ti 1:9
1:16
[n] 2Pe 2:18
1:17
[o] 2Pe 3:2
1:18
[p] 1Ti 4:1
[q] 2Pe 2:1
1:19
[r] 1Co 2:14,15
1:20
[s] Col 2:7
[t] Eph 6:18
1:21
[u] Tit 2:13; 2Pe 3:12
1:23
[v] Am 4:11; Zec 3:2-5
[w] Rev 3:4
1:24
[x] Ro 16:25
[y] 2Co 4:14
[z] Col 1:22
1:25
[a] Jn 5:44; 1Ti 1:17
[b] Heb 13:8
[c] Ro 11:36

JUDE

THE RECIPIENTS

GODLESS MEN

(continued)

JUDE'S INSTRUCTIONS TO THOSE LOVED BY GOD

JUDE AT A GLANCE

Theme of Jude:

SEGMENT
DIVISIONS

	PARAGRAPH THEMES	
	VERSE 1A	Author:
	VERSE 1B	
	VERSE 2	Date:
	VERSES 3, 4	
	VERSES 5–7	Purpose:
	VERSES 8–10	
	VERSE 11	
	VERSES 12–13	Key Words:
	VERSES 14–16	
	VERSES 17–19	
	VERSES 20–23	
	VERSES 24, 25	

ℛEVELATION

*J*ohn, one of the sons of Zebedee, identifies himself throughout his Gospel not by his name, but as "the one whom Jesus loved." John walked in faith, taking Jesus at his word, and was secure in his love.

Therefore, when John was banished to the Isle of Patmos (and, according to tradition, submerged in a cauldron of hot oil), he remained steadfast in Jesus' love. He was faithful to his calling even in the midst of Nero's persecutions of Christians in A.D. 54 through 68 and then Domitian's in A.D. 81 through 96.

While John was on Patmos, God unveiled to him the coming of the Lord Jesus Christ and what soon would come to pass—a revelation unparalleled, the last to be given. It was about A.D. 95. With John's revelation the New Testament canon of Scripture would be complete. The church could be secure. Every prophecy would be fulfilled, just as God had said.

∾ THINGS TO DO

Chapters 1-3

1. To familiarize yourself with the first two segments of the book of Revelation, carefully read 1:1 through 4:1 in one sitting. (*Revelation* is a translation of the Greek word *apokalypsis,* which means "an uncovering.")

2. Mark the following key words (along with their synonyms and pronouns) in chapter 1, and then list in the margin everything you learn from the text about these words: *Jesus Christ, God (the Father), Spirit (seven spirits),* and *write.* Then transfer this information to the chart WHAT REVELATION TEACHES ABOUT GOD, JESUS, and THE HOLY SPIRIT on page 2173.

3. Revelation 1:19 gives an outline of the book of Revelation.

   a. List the three things John was to write:

   1) _____

   2) _____

   3) _____

   b. Now look at Revelation 4:1 and note how it relates to 1:19. Revelation 4 begins the third segment of Revelation. Chapter 1 describes what John saw, and chapters 2 and 3 are "what is now." What is the third segment that begins in 4:1?

   c. Using the terminology found in Revelation 1:19, record these three segments in the space for segment divisions on the REVELATION AT A GLANCE chart on page 2175. (The lines to divide the book into these sections are already drawn.)

4. Read Revelation 1 through 3 and do the following:

   a. Watch for key repeated phrases or words listed on REVELATION AT A GLANCE. Mark these in the text in a distinctive way so you can spot them immediately. In Jesus' messages to the churches, watch for a pattern as Jesus addresses each church.

   b. Now concentrate on Jesus' messages to the churches, one church at a time. Record what you learn about each church on the chart JESUS' MESSAGES TO THE CHURCHES beginning on page 2169. When you see what is said regarding those who overcome, note how John describes overcomers in 1 John 5:4, 5. Add what you learn to the chart.

5. Record the main theme of each chapter in the text next to the chapter number and on REVELATION AT A GLANCE.

REVELATION

Chapters 4-22

1. In the last nineteen chapters of Revelation, Jesus shows John "what will take place later." Read Revelation 4 through 22 one chapter at a time, and for each chapter do the following:

   a. As you read, ask the five W's and an H: Who? What? Why? When? Where? and How? For example, if it is an event, ask: What is happening? Who is involved? When will this happen and where? Why is this happening? How will it happen? If it is a person or a personage: Who is this? What is this person like? What does he do? When? Where? Why? What are the consequences? How will he accomplish it? These are very critical questions. If these are answered carefully after thoroughly observing the text and apart from preconceived ideas, you will learn much. Make a list of what you learn, and then if it is information you wish to keep, record the essence of your insights in the margin of the chapter.

   b. Mark key repeated words (along with their synonyms and pronouns—*he, she, it, we, they, us,* and *you*) in a distinctive way. Some key words are listed on REVELATION AT A GLANCE. Since it is a long list, write these on an index card, color code the words as you intend to mark them in the text, and use the card as a bookmark. When you finish marking these, list on a piece of paper what you learn from each one (unless you have been told to record that information on a chart). Then in the margins, record any information you learn from the key words that you want to have accessible in your Bible.

   c. As you go through Revelation chapter by chapter, let the text speak for itself. Remember, truth is revealed gradually, so don't become impatient. Simply observe what is being said without adding your own interpretation. Stay in an attitude of prayer, asking God to open the eyes of your understanding.

2. Mark in a distinctive way all references to time. Then note what happens during that time. In Jewish reckoning 42 months, 1260 days, and time, times and half a time all refer to a period of 3 1/2 years. When you finish studying this segment of Revelation, you might want to list in the margin what happens and when, and how these time periods and events relate to one another, if at all.

Also watch *when* something begins and ends—for example, the great day of God's wrath, when the mystery of God is finished, when God begins to reign. Noting the timing of these will help you understand Revelation better.

3. Babylon intermittently plays an important role from Genesis to Revelation. As you mark every reference to Babylon, carefully note whether it is referring to "the woman" or to the city. Then discern whether they are one and the same or two separate but somehow related entities. In chapters 17 and 18, where Babylon is preeminent, list in the margin of the chapter what you learn from marking each reference to Babylon. Then compile your information on the chart WHAT THE BIBLE TEACHES ABOUT BABYLON beginning on page 2176.

4. As you observe what happens during each of the seals, trumpets, and bowls, record your insights on the chart on page 2174, THE SEVEN SEALS, TRUMPETS, AND BOWLS. Then consider whether the seals, trumpets, and bowls happen at the same time or follow one another.

5. As you study Revelation, you may want to consult any notes you have made on the chart THE DAY OF THE LORD beginning on page 2178 to see if there are any parallels between what you have observed in other books and what you see in Revelation.

6. There is much to learn about the Godhead in this book that you will want to remember and meditate on. Record what you learn on the chart WHAT REVELATION TEACHES ABOUT GOD, JESUS, and THE HOLY SPIRIT on page 2173.

7. When you finish going through Revelation, record the chapter themes in the text and on REVELATION AT A GLANCE, along with other pertinent information called for on the chart.

8. Finally, see how various chapters of the book group according to events, places, or persons. Use your chapter themes as a guide to see when these groupings occur. Record these groupings under "Segment Divisions" on REVELATION AT A GLANCE, placing them at the chapter numbers in which they occur.

∾ THINGS TO THINK ABOUT

Chapters 1-3

1. As you look at the Lord's message to each church, do you think the message could be for the church today? Look back through Jesus' messages to the churches in chapters 2 and 3 and note what the Spirit is saying to him who has "an ear." To whom is the Spirit speaking? What does he want you to hear? To do?

2. Think about what you have learned about Jesus Christ from these three chapters and then spend some time worshiping him for who and what he is.

3. Are you an overcomer? How does it show? Is there anything you need to do that you are not presently doing so that when Jesus appears you won't be ashamed?

Chapters 4-22

1. Revelation gives insight into the judgment of God upon the wicked because of what they worship. It also gives a glimpse of the way the righteous worship. How would you compare your worship with the worship described in Revelation? You might want to go back through Revelation and look at the scenes where God is worshiped and use them as a pattern for worship.

2. Now that you have a better understanding of the wrath to come upon the unbeliever, what priority needs to be placed on sharing the gospel? Is witnessing a priority in your church? Is witnessing a priority in your personal life?

3. Are you sure that you are a child of God? If not, will you acknowledge the Lord Jesus Christ as God, receive his forgiveness for your sins, and let him take full control of your life? Surely you have seen that he is worthy—and trustworthy.

4. What have you learned about your God? In the light of this, are you living in anticipation of Jesus' coming?

∾∾∾∾∾

Chapter 1 Theme _____

1:1
a Rev 22:16

1 The revelation of Jesus Christ, which God gave him to show his servants what must soon take place. He made it known by sending his angel*a* to his servant John, ²who testifies to everything he saw—that is, the word of God and the testimony of Jesus Christ.*b* ³Blessed is the one who reads the words of this prophecy, and blessed are those who hear it and take to heart what is written in it,*c* because the time is near.

1:2
b 1Co 1:6;
Rev 12:17

1:3
c Lk 11:28

⁴John,

To the seven churches in the province of Asia:

1:4
d Rev 3:1; 4:5

Grace and peace to you from him who is, and who was, and who is to come, and from the seven spirits*ad* before his throne, ⁵and from Jesus Christ, who is the faithful witness,*e* the firstborn from the dead,*f* and the ruler of the kings of the earth.*g*

1:5
e Rev 3:14
f Col 1:18
g Rev 17:14

a 4 Or *the sevenfold Spirit*

2141

To him who loves us and has freed us from our sins by his blood, ⁶and has made us to be a kingdom and priests[a] to serve his God and Father—to him be glory and power for ever and ever! Amen.[b]

⁷Look, he is coming with the clouds,[c]
and every eye will see him,
even those who pierced him;
and all the peoples of the earth will mourn[d]
because of him.

So shall it be! Amen.

⁸"I am the Alpha and the Omega,"[e] says the Lord God, "who is, and who was, and who is to come, the Almighty."[f]

⁹I, John, your brother and companion in the suffering[g] and kingdom and patient endurance[h] that are ours in Jesus, was on the island of Patmos because of the word of God and the testimony of Jesus. ¹⁰On the Lord's Day I was in the Spirit,[i] and I heard behind me a loud voice like a trumpet,[j] ¹¹which said: "Write on a scroll what you see and send it to the seven churches:[k] to Ephesus, Smyrna, Pergamum, Thyatira, Sardis,[l] Philadelphia and Laodicea."

¹²I turned around to see the voice that was speaking to me. And when I turned I saw seven golden lampstands,[m] ¹³and among the lampstands was someone "like a son of man,"[a][n] dressed in a robe reaching down to his feet and with a golden sash around his chest.[o] ¹⁴His head and hair were white like wool, as white as snow, and his eyes were like blazing fire.[p] ¹⁵His feet were like bronze glowing in a furnace,[q] and his voice was like the sound of rushing waters.[r] ¹⁶In his right hand he held seven stars,[s] and out of his mouth came a sharp double-edged sword.[t] His face was like the sun shining in all its brilliance.

The Seven Churches of Asia

¹⁷When I saw him, I fell at his feet[u] as though dead. Then he placed his right hand on me and said: "Do not be afraid. I am the First and the Last.[v] ¹⁸I am the Living One; I was dead,[w] and behold I am alive for ever and ever![x] And I hold the keys of death and Hades.[y]

¹⁹"Write, therefore, what you have seen, what is now and what will take place later. ²⁰The mystery of the seven stars that you saw in my right hand and of the seven golden lampstands[z] is this: The

a 13 Daniel 7:13

1:6
a 1Pe 2:5
b Ro 11:36

1:7
c Da 7:13
d Zec 12:10

1:8
e Rev 21:6
f Rev 4:8

1:9
g Php 4:14
h 2Ti 2:12

1:10
i Rev 4:2
j Rev 4:1

1:11
k ver 4,20
l Rev 3:1

1:12
m Ex 25:31-40;
Zec 4:2

1:13
n Eze 1:26;
Da 7:13; 10:16
o Da 10:5;
Rev 15:6

1:14
p Da 7:9; 10:6;
Rev 19:12

1:15
q Da 10:6
r Eze 43:2;
Rev 14:2

1:16
s Rev 2:1; 3:1
t Isa 49:2;
Heb 4:12;
Rev 2:12,16

1:17
u Eze 1:28;
Da 8:17,18
v Isa 41:4; 44:6;
48:12;
Rev 22:13

1:18
w Ro 6:9
x Rev 4:9,10
y Rev 20:1

1:20
z Zec 4:2

1:20
a ver 4,11
b Mt 5:14,15

2:1
c Rev 1:16
d Rev 1:12,13

2:2
e Rev 3:1,8,15
f 1Jn 4:1
g 2Co 11:13

2:3
h Jn 15:21

2:4
i Mt 24:12

2:5
j ver 16,22
k Rev 1:20

2:6
l ver 15

2:7
m Mt 11:15;
Rev 3:6,13,22
n Ge 2:9;
Rev 22:2,14,19
o Lk 23:43

2:8
p Rev 1:11
q Rev 1:17
r Rev 1:18

2:9
s Jas 2:5
t Rev 3:9
u Mt 4:10

2:10
v Rev 3:10
w Da 1:12,14
x ver 13

2:11
y Rev 20:6,14;
21:8

2:12
z Rev 1:11
a Rev 1:16

2:13
b Rev 14:12
c ver 9,24

2:14
d ver 20
e 2Pe 2:15

seven stars are the angels[a] of the seven churches,[a] and the seven lampstands are the seven churches.[b]

Chapter 2 Theme

2 "To the angel[b] of the church in Ephesus write:

These are the words of him who holds the seven stars in his right hand[c] and walks among the seven golden lampstands:[d] [2]I know your deeds,[e] your hard work and your perseverance. I know that you cannot tolerate wicked men, that you have tested[f] those who claim to be apostles but are not, and have found them false.[g] [3]You have persevered and have endured hardships for my name,[h] and have not grown weary.

[4]Yet I hold this against you: You have forsaken your first love.[i] [5]Remember the height from which you have fallen! Repent[j] and do the things you did at first. If you do not repent, I will come to you and remove your lampstand[k] from its place. [6]But you have this in your favor: You hate the practices of the Nicolaitans,[l] which I also hate.

[7]He who has an ear, let him hear[m] what the Spirit says to the churches. To him who overcomes, I will give the right to eat from the tree of life,[n] which is in the paradise[o] of God.

[8]"To the angel of the church in Smyrna[p] write:

These are the words of him who is the First and the Last,[q] who died and came to life again.[r] [9]I know your afflictions and your poverty—yet you are rich![s] I know the slander of those who say they are Jews and are not,[t] but are a synagogue of Satan.[u] [10]Do not be afraid of what you are about to suffer. I tell you, the devil will put some of you in prison to test you,[v] and you will suffer persecution for ten days.[w] Be faithful,[x] even to the point of death, and I will give you the crown of life.

[11]He who has an ear, let him hear what the Spirit says to the churches. He who overcomes will not be hurt at all by the second death.[y]

[12]"To the angel of the church in Pergamum[z] write:

These are the words of him who has the sharp, double-edged sword.[a] [13]I know where you live—where Satan has his throne. Yet you remain true to my name. You did not renounce your faith in me,[b] even in the days of Antipas, my faithful witness, who was put to death in your city—where Satan lives.[c]

[14]Nevertheless, I have a few things against you:[d] You have people there who hold to the teaching of Balaam,[e] who taught

---

a 20 Or *messengers*   *b 1* Or *messenger*; also in verses 8, 12 and 18

Balak to entice the Israelites to sin by eating food sacrificed to idols and by committing sexual immorality.[a] [15]Likewise you also have those who hold to the teaching of the Nicolaitans.[b] [16]Repent therefore! Otherwise, I will soon come to you and will fight against them with the sword of my mouth.[c]

[17]He who has an ear, let him hear what the Spirit says to the churches. To him who overcomes, I will give some of the hidden manna.[d] I will also give him a white stone with a new name[e] written on it, known only to him who receives it.[f]

[18]"To the angel of the church in Thyatira[g] write:

These are the words of the Son of God, whose eyes are like blazing fire and whose feet are like burnished bronze.[h] [19]I know your deeds,[i] your love and faith, your service and perseverance, and that you are now doing more than you did at first.

[20]Nevertheless, I have this against you: You tolerate that woman Jezebel,[j] who calls herself a prophetess. By her teaching she misleads my servants into sexual immorality and the eating of food sacrificed to idols. [21]I have given her time[k] to repent of her immorality, but she is unwilling.[l] [22]So I will cast her on a bed of suffering, and I will make those who commit adultery[m] with her suffer intensely, unless they repent of her ways. [23]I will strike her children dead. Then all the churches will know that I am he who searches hearts and minds,[n] and I will repay each of you according to your deeds. [24]Now I say to the rest of you in Thyatira, to you who do not hold to her teaching and have not learned Satan's so-called deep secrets (I will not impose any other burden on you):[o] [25]Only hold on to what you have[p] until I come.

[26]To him who overcomes and does my will to the end, I will give authority over the nations[q]—

[27]'He will rule them with an iron scepter;[r]
he will dash them to pieces like pottery'[a]s—

just as I have received authority from my Father. [28]I will also give him the morning star.[t] [29]He who has an ear, let him hear[u] what the Spirit says to the churches.

Chapter 3 Theme

3 "To the angel[b] of the church in Sardis write:

These are the words of him who holds the seven spirits[c]v of God and the seven stars.[w] I know your deeds;[x] you have a reputation of being alive, but you are dead.[y] [2]Wake up! Strengthen

---

a27 Psalm 2:9   b1 Or *messenger*; also in verses 7 and 14   c1 Or *the sevenfold Spirit*

2:14 a1Co 6:13

2:15 bver 6

2:16 c2Th 2:8; Rev 1:16

2:17 dJn 6:49,50 eIsa 62:2 fRev 19:12

2:18 gRev 1:11 hRev 1:14,15

2:19 iver 2

2:20 j1Ki 16:31; 21:25; 2Ki 9:7

2:21 kRo 2:4 lRev 9:20

2:22 mRev 17:2; 18:9

2:23 n1Sa 16:7; Jer 11:20; Ac 1:24; Ro 8:27

2:24 oAc 15:28

2:25 pRev 3:11

2:26 qPs 2:8; Rev 3:21

2:27 rRev 12:5 sIsa 30:14; Jer 19:11

2:28 tRev 22:16

2:29 uver 7

3:1 vRev 1:4 wRev 1:16 xRev 2:2 y1Ti 5:6

3:3
a Rev 2:5
b 2Pe 3:10

3:4
c Jude 23
d Rev 4:4; 6:11;
7:9,13,14

3:5
e Rev 20:12
f Mt 10:32

3:6
g Rev 2:7

3:7
h Rev 1:11
i 1Jn 5:20
j Isa 22:22;
Mt 16:19

3:8
k Ac 14:27
l Rev 2:13

3:9
m Rev 2:9
n Isa 49:23
o Isa 43:4

3:10
p 2Pe 2:9
q Rev 2:10
r Rev 6:10; 17:8

3:11
s Rev 2:25
t Rev 2:10

3:12
u Gal 2:9
v Rev 14:1; 22:4
w Rev 21:2,10

3:14
x Col 1:16,18

3:15
y Ro 12:11

3:17
z Hos 12:8;
1Co 4:8

what remains and is about to die, for I have not found your deeds complete in the sight of my God. [3]Remember, therefore, what you have received and heard; obey it, and repent.*a* But if you do not wake up, I will come like a thief,*b* and you will not know at what time I will come to you.

[4]Yet you have a few people in Sardis who have not soiled their clothes.*c* They will walk with me, dressed in white,*d* for they are worthy. [5]He who overcomes will, like them, be dressed in white. I will never blot out his name from the book of life,*e* but will acknowledge his name before my Father*f* and his angels. [6]He who has an ear, let him hear*g* what the Spirit says to the churches.

[7]"To the angel of the church in Philadelphia*h* write:

These are the words of him who is holy and true,*i* who holds the key of David.*j* What he opens no one can shut, and what he shuts no one can open. [8]I know your deeds. See, I have placed before you an open door*k* that no one can shut. I know that you have little strength, yet you have kept my word and have not denied my name.*l* [9]I will make those who are of the synagogue of Satan,*m* who claim to be Jews though they are not, but are liars—I will make them come and fall down at your feet*n* and acknowledge that I have loved you.*o* [10]Since you have kept my command to endure patiently, I will also keep you*p* from the hour of trial that is going to come upon the whole world to test*q* those who live on the earth.*r*

[11]I am coming soon. Hold on to what you have,*s* so that no one will take your crown.*t* [12]Him who overcomes I will make a pillar*u* in the temple of my God. Never again will he leave it. I will write on him the name of my God*v* and the name of the city of my God, the new Jerusalem,*w* which is coming down out of heaven from my God; and I will also write on him my new name. [13]He who has an ear, let him hear what the Spirit says to the churches.

[14]"To the angel of the church in Laodicea write:

These are the words of the Amen, the faithful and true witness, the ruler of God's creation.*x* [15]I know your deeds, that you are neither cold nor hot.*y* I wish you were either one or the other! [16]So, because you are lukewarm—neither hot nor cold—I am about to spit you out of my mouth. [17]You say, 'I am rich; I have acquired wealth and do not need a thing.'*z* But you do not realize that you are wretched, pitiful, poor, blind and naked. [18]I counsel you to buy from me gold refined in the fire, so you can become rich; and white clothes to wear, so you can cover your shameful nakedness;[a] and salve to put on your eyes, so you can see.

[19] Those whom I love I rebuke and discipline.[b] So be earnest, and repent.[c] [20] Here I am! I stand at the door[d] and knock. If anyone hears my voice and opens the door,[e] I will come in[f] and eat with him, and he with me.

[21] To him who overcomes, I will give the right to sit with me on my throne,[g] just as I overcame[h] and sat down with my Father on his throne. [22] He who has an ear, let him hear[i] what the Spirit says to the churches."

Chapter 4 Theme

4 After this I looked, and there before me was a door standing open in heaven. And the voice I had first heard speaking to me like a trumpet[j] said, "Come up here,[k] and I will show you what must take place after this."[l] [2] At once I was in the Spirit,[m] and there before me was a throne in heaven[n] with someone sitting on it. [3] And the one who sat there had the appearance of jasper and carnelian. A rainbow,[o] resembling an emerald, encircled the throne. [4] Surrounding the throne were twenty-four other thrones, and seated on them were twenty-four elders.[p] They were dressed in white[q] and had crowns of gold on their heads. [5] From the throne came flashes of lightning, rumblings and peals of thunder.[r] Before the throne, seven lamps[s] were blazing. These are the seven spirits[a][t] of God. [6] Also before the throne there was what looked like a sea of glass,[u] clear as crystal.

In the center, around the throne, were four living creatures,[v] and they were covered with eyes, in front and in back. [7] The first living creature was like a lion, the second was like an ox, the third had a face like a man, the fourth was like a flying eagle.[w] [8] Each of the four living creatures had six wings[x] and was covered with eyes all around, even under his wings. Day and night they never stop saying:

> "Holy, holy, holy
> is the Lord God Almighty,[y]
> who was, and is, and is to come."[z]

[9] Whenever the living creatures give glory, honor and thanks to him who sits on the throne[a] and who lives for ever and ever, [10] the twenty-four elders[b] fall down before him[c] who sits on the throne,[d] and worship him who lives for ever and ever. They lay their crowns before the throne and say:

a 5,6 Or *the sevenfold Spirit*

3:18
a Rev 16:15

3:19
b Pr 3:12;
Heb 12:5,6
c Rev 2:5

3:20
d Mt 24:33
e Lk 12:36
f Jn 14:23

3:21
g Mt 19:28
h Rev 5:5

3:22
i Rev 2:7

4:1
j Rev 1:10
k Rev 11:12
l Rev 1:19

4:2
m Rev 1:10
n Isa 6:1;
Eze 1:26-28;
Da 7:9

4:3
o Eze 1:28

4:4
p Rev 11:16
q Rev 3:4,5

4:5
r Rev 8:5; 16:18
s Zec 4:2
t Rev 1:4

4:6
u Rev 15:2
v Eze 1:5

4:7
w Eze 1:10; 10:14

4:8
x Isa 6:2
y Isa 6:3;
Rev 1:8
z Rev 1:4

4:9
a Ps 47:8

4:10
b ver 4
c Rev 5:8,14
d ver 2

4:11
a Rev 5:12
b Rev 10:6

[11]"You are worthy, our Lord and God,
    to receive glory and honor and power,[a]
for you created all things,
    and by your will they were created
    and have their being."[b]

Chapter 5 Theme

5:1
c ver 7,13
d Eze 2:9,10
e Isa 29:11;
Da 12:4

5 Then I saw in the right hand of him who sat on the throne[c] a scroll with writing on both sides[d] and sealed[e] with seven seals. [2]And I saw a mighty angel proclaiming in a loud voice, "Who is worthy to break the seals and open the scroll?" [3]But no one in heaven or on earth or under the earth could open the scroll or even look inside it. [4]I wept and wept because no one was found who was worthy to open the scroll or look inside. [5]Then one of the elders said to me, "Do not weep! See, the Lion[f] of the tribe of Judah, the Root of David,[g] has triumphed. He is able to open the scroll and its seven seals."

5:5
f Ge 49:9
g Isa 11:1,10;
Ro 15:12;
Rev 22:16

5:6
h Jn 1:29
i Zec 4:10

[6]Then I saw a Lamb,[h] looking as if it had been slain, standing in the center of the throne, encircled by the four living creatures and the elders. He had seven horns and seven eyes,[i] which are the seven spirits[a] of God sent out into all the earth. [7]He came and took the scroll from the right hand of him who sat on the throne.[j] [8]And when he had taken it, the four living creatures and the twenty-four elders fell down before the Lamb. Each one had a harp[k] and they were holding golden bowls full of incense, which are the prayers[l] of the saints. [9]And they sang a new song:[m]

5:7
j ver 1

5:8
k Rev 14:2
l Ps 141:2

"You are worthy[n] to take the scroll
    and to open its seals,
because you were slain,
    and with your blood[o] you purchased[p] men for God
    from every tribe and language and people and nation.
[10]You have made them to be a kingdom and priests[q] to
        serve our God,
    and they will reign on the earth."

5:9
m Ps 40:3
n Rev 4:11
o Heb 9:12
p 1Co 6:20

5:10
q 1Pe 2:5

[11]Then I looked and heard the voice of many angels, numbering thousands upon thousands, and ten thousand times ten thousand.[r] They encircled the throne and the living creatures and the elders. [12]In a loud voice they sang:

5:11
r Da 7:10;
Heb 12:22

"Worthy is the Lamb, who was slain,
    to receive power and wealth and wisdom and strength
    and honor and glory and praise!"[s]

5:12
s Rev 4:11

a 5,6 Or *the sevenfold Spirit*

[13]Then I heard every creature in heaven and on earth and under the earth[a] and on the sea, and all that is in them, singing:

"To him who sits on the throne and to the Lamb[b]
be praise and honor and glory and power,
for ever and ever!"[c]

[14]The four living creatures said, "Amen,"[d] and the elders fell down and worshiped.[e]

Chapter 6 Theme

6 I watched as the Lamb[f] opened the first of the seven seals.[g] Then I heard one of the four living creatures[h] say in a voice like thunder,[i] "Come!" [2]I looked, and there before me was a white horse![j] Its rider held a bow, and he was given a crown,[k] and he rode out as a conqueror bent on conquest.[l]

[3]When the Lamb opened the second seal, I heard the second living creature[m] say, "Come!" [4]Then another horse came out, a fiery red one.[n] Its rider was given power to take peace from the earth[o] and to make men slay each other. To him was given a large sword.

[5]When the Lamb opened the third seal, I heard the third living creature[p] say, "Come!" I looked, and there before me was a black horse![q] Its rider was holding a pair of scales in his hand. [6]Then I heard what sounded like a voice among the four living creatures,[r] saying, "A quart[a] of wheat for a day's wages,[b] and three quarts of barley for a day's wages,[b] and do not damage[s] the oil and the wine!"

[7]When the Lamb opened the fourth seal, I heard the voice of the fourth living creature[t] say, "Come!" [8]I looked, and there before me was a pale horse![u] Its rider was named Death, and Hades[v] was following close behind him. They were given power over a fourth of the earth to kill by sword, famine and plague, and by the wild beasts of the earth.[w]

[9]When he opened the fifth seal, I saw under the altar[x] the souls of those who had been slain[y] because of the word of God and the testimony they had maintained. [10]They called out in a loud voice, "How long,[z] Sovereign Lord, holy and true,[a] until you judge the inhabitants of the earth and avenge our blood?"[b] [11]Then each of them was given a white robe,[c] and they were told to wait a little longer, until the number of their fellow servants and brothers who were to be killed as they had been was completed.[d]

[12]I watched as he opened the sixth seal. There was a great earthquake.[e] The sun turned black[f] like sackcloth made of goat hair, the whole moon turned blood red, [13]and the stars in the sky fell to

---

5:13
[a] ver 3;
Php 2:10
[b] Rev 6:16
[c] 1Ch 29:11

5:14
[d] Rev 4:9
[e] Rev 4:10; 19:4

6:1
[f] Rev 5:6
[g] Rev 5:1
[h] Rev 4:6,7
[i] Rev 14:2; 19:6

6:2
[j] Zec 6:3;
Rev 19:11
[k] Zec 6:11;
Rev 14:14
[l] Ps 45:4

6:3
[m] Rev 4:7

6:4
[n] Zec 6:2
[o] Mt 10:34

6:5
[p] Rev 4:7
[q] Zec 6:2

6:6
[r] Rev 4:6,7
[s] Rev 9:4

6:7
[t] Rev 4:7

6:8
[u] Zec 6:3
[v] Hos 13:14
[w] Jer 15:2,3;
Eze 5:12,17

6:9
[x] Rev 14:18; 16:7
[y] Rev 20:4

6:10
[z] Zec 1:12
[a] Rev 3:7
[b] Rev 19:2

6:11
[c] Rev 3:4
[d] Heb 11:40

6:12
[e] Rev 16:18
[f] Mt 24:29

---

[a]6 Greek *a choinix* (probably about a liter)   [b]6 Greek *a denarius*

6:13
a Mt 24:29;
Rev 8:10; 9:1
b Isa 34:4

earth,*a* as late figs drop from a fig tree*b* when shaken by a strong wind. ¹⁴The sky receded like a scroll, rolling up, and every mountain and island was removed from its place.*c*

6:14
c Jer 4:24;
Rev 16:20

¹⁵Then the kings of the earth, the princes, the generals, the rich, the mighty, and every slave and every free man hid in caves and among the rocks of the mountains.*d* ¹⁶They called to the mountains and the rocks, "Fall on us*e* and hide us from the face of him who sits on the throne and from the wrath of the Lamb! ¹⁷For the great day*f* of their wrath has come, and who can stand?"*g*

6:15
d Isa 2:10,19,21

Chapter 7 Theme

6:16
e Hos 10:8;
Lk 23:30

7 After this I saw four angels standing at the four corners of the earth, holding back the four winds*h* of the earth to prevent any wind from blowing on the land or on the sea or on any tree. ²Then I saw another angel coming up from the east, having the seal of the living God. He called out in a loud voice to the four angels who had been given power to harm the land and the sea: ³"Do not harm*i* the land or the sea or the trees until we put a seal on the foreheads*j* of the servants of our God." ⁴Then I heard the number*k* of those who were sealed: 144,000*l* from all the tribes of Israel.

6:17
f Zep 1:14,15;
Rev 16:14
g Ps 76:7

7:1
h Da 7:2

> ⁵From the tribe of Judah 12,000 were sealed,
>   from the tribe of Reuben 12,000,
>   from the tribe of Gad 12,000,
>   ⁶from the tribe of Asher 12,000,
>   from the tribe of Naphtali 12,000,
>   from the tribe of Manasseh 12,000,
>   ⁷from the tribe of Simeon 12,000,
>   from the tribe of Levi 12,000,
>   from the tribe of Issachar 12,000,
>   ⁸from the tribe of Zebulun 12,000,
>   from the tribe of Joseph 12,000,
>   from the tribe of Benjamin 12,000.

7:3
i Rev 6:6
j Eze 9:4;
Rev 22:4

7:4
k Rev 9:16
l Rev 14:1,3

⁹After this I looked and there before me was a great multitude that no one could count, from every nation, tribe, people and language,*m* standing before the throne*n* and in front of the Lamb. They were wearing white robes and were holding palm branches in their hands. ¹⁰And they cried out in a loud voice:

7:9
m Rev 5:9
n ver 15

> "Salvation belongs to our God,*o*
>   who sits on the throne,
>   and to the Lamb."

7:10
o Ps 3:8;
Rev 12:10; 19:1

¹¹All the angels were standing around the throne and around the elders*p* and the four living creatures.*q* They fell down on their faces*r* before the throne and worshiped God, ¹²saying:

7:11
p Rev 4:4
q Rev 4:6
r Rev 4:10

"Amen!
Praise and glory
and wisdom and thanks and honor
and power and strength
be to our God for ever and ever.
Amen!"[a]

[13] Then one of the elders asked me, "These in white robes—who are they, and where did they come from?"

[14] I answered, "Sir, you know."

And he said, "These are they who have come out of the great tribulation; they have washed their robes[b] and made them white in the blood of the Lamb.[c] [15] Therefore,

"they are before the throne of God[d]
and serve him[e] day and night in his temple;[f]
and he who sits on the throne will spread his tent
over them.[g]
[16] Never again will they hunger;
never again will they thirst.
The sun will not beat upon them,
nor any scorching heat.[h]
[17] For the Lamb at the center of the throne will be
their shepherd;[i]
he will lead them to springs of living water.
And God will wipe away every tear from their eyes."[j]

Chapter 8 Theme

8 When he opened the seventh seal,[k] there was silence in heaven for about half an hour.

[2] And I saw the seven angels[l] who stand before God, and to them were given seven trumpets.

[3] Another angel,[m] who had a golden censer, came and stood at the altar. He was given much incense to offer, with the prayers of all the saints,[n] on the golden altar[o] before the throne. [4] The smoke of the incense, together with the prayers of the saints, went up before God[p] from the angel's hand. [5] Then the angel took the censer, filled it with fire from the altar,[q] and hurled it on the earth; and there came peals of thunder,[r] rumblings, flashes of lightning and an earthquake.[s]

[6] Then the seven angels who had the seven trumpets[t] prepared to sound them.

[7] The first angel sounded his trumpet, and there came hail and fire[u] mixed with blood, and it was hurled down upon the earth. A third[v] of the earth was burned up, a third of the trees were burned up, and all the green grass was burned up.[w]

7:12
[a] Rev 5:12-14

7:14
[b] Rev 22:14
[c] Heb 9:14;
1Jn 1:7

7:15
[d] ver 9
[e] Rev 22:3
[f] Rev 11:19
[g] Isa 4:5,6;
Rev 21:3

7:16
[h] Isa 49:10

7:17
[i] Ps 23:1;
Jn 10:11
[j] Isa 25:8;
Rev 21:4

8:1
[k] Rev 6:1

8:2
[l] ver 6-13;
Rev 9:1,13; 11:15

8:3
[m] Rev 7:2
[n] Rev 5:8
[o] Ex 30:1-6;
Heb 9:4;
Rev 9:13

8:4
[p] Ps 141:2

8:5
[q] Lev 16:12,13
[r] Rev 4:5
[s] Rev 6:12

8:6
[t] ver 2

8:7
[u] Eze 38:22
[v] ver 7-12;
Rev 9:15,18; 12:4
[w] Rev 9:4

8:8
a Jer 51:25
b ver 7
c Rev 16:3

8:9
d ver 7

8:10
e Isa 14:12;
Rev 6:13; 9:1
f Rev 14:7; 16:4

8:11
g ver 7
h Jer 9:15; 23:15

8:12
i ver 7
j Ex 10:21-23;
Rev 6:12,13

8:13
k Rev 14:6; 19:17
l Rev 9:12; 11:14

9:1
m Rev 8:10
n ver 2,11;
Lk 8:31

9:2
o Ge 19:28;
Ex 19:18
p Joel 2:2,10

9:3
q Ex 10:12-15
r ver 5,10

9:4
s Rev 6:6
t Rev 8:7
u Rev 7:2,3

9:5
v ver 10
w ver 3

9:6
x Job 3:21;
Jer 8:3;
Rev 6:16

9:7
y Joel 2:4
z Da 7:8

9:8
a Joel 1:6

9:9
b Joel 2:5

9:10
c ver 3,5,19

9:11
d ver 1,2

⁸The second angel sounded his trumpet, and something like a huge mountain,ᵃ all ablaze, was thrown into the sea. A thirdᵇ of the sea turned into blood,ᶜ ⁹a thirdᵈ of the living creatures in the sea died, and a third of the ships were destroyed.

¹⁰The third angel sounded his trumpet, and a great star, blazing like a torch, fell from the skyᵉ on a third of the rivers and on the springs of waterᶠ— ¹¹the name of the star is Wormwood.ᵃ A thirdᵍ of the waters turned bitter, and many people died from the waters that had become bitter.ʰ

¹²The fourth angel sounded his trumpet, and a third of the sun was struck, a third of the moon, and a third of the stars, so that a thirdⁱ of them turned dark.ʲ A third of the day was without light, and also a third of the night.

¹³As I watched, I heard an eagle that was flying in midairᵏ call out in a loud voice: "Woe! Woe! Woeˡ to the inhabitants of the earth, because of the trumpet blasts about to be sounded by the other three angels!"

Chapter 9 Theme

9 The fifth angel sounded his trumpet, and I saw a star that had fallen from the sky to the earth.ᵐ The star was given the key to the shaft of the Abyss.ⁿ ²When he opened the Abyss, smoke rose from it like the smoke from a gigantic furnace.ᵒ The sun and sky were darkened ᵖ by the smoke from the Abyss. ³And out of the smoke locusts�q came down upon the earth and were given power like that of scorpionsʳ of the earth. ⁴They were told not to harmˢ the grass of the earth or any plant or tree,ᵗ but only those people who did not have the seal of God on their foreheads.ᵘ ⁵They were not given power to kill them, but only to torture them for five months.ᵛ And the agony they suffered was like that of the sting of a scorpionʷ when it strikes a man. ⁶During those days men will seek death, but will not find it; they will long to die, but death will elude them.ˣ

⁷The locusts looked like horses prepared for battle.ʸ On their heads they wore something like crowns of gold, and their faces resembled human faces.ᶻ ⁸Their hair was like women's hair, and their teeth were like lions' teeth.ᵃ ⁹They had breastplates like breastplates of iron, and the sound of their wings was like the thundering of many horses and chariots rushing into battle.ᵇ ¹⁰They had tails and stings like scorpions, and in their tails they had power to torment people for five months.ᶜ ¹¹They had as king over them the angel of the Abyss,ᵈ whose name in Hebrew is Abaddon, and in Greek, Apollyon.ᵇ

---

a 11 That is, Bitterness   b 11 Abaddon and Apollyon mean Destroyer.

¹²The first woe is past; two other woes are yet to come.ᵃ

¹³The sixth angel sounded his trumpet, and I heard a voice coming from the hornsᵃᵇ of the golden altar that is before God.ᶜ ¹⁴It said to the sixth angel who had the trumpet, "Release the four angels who are bound at the great river Euphrates."ᵈ ¹⁵And the four angels who had been kept ready for this very hour and day and month and year were released to kill a third of mankind.ᵉ ¹⁶The number of the mounted troops was two hundred million. I heard their number.ᶠ

¹⁷The horses and riders I saw in my vision looked like this: Their breastplates were fiery red, dark blue, and yellow as sulfur. The heads of the horses resembled the heads of lions, and out of their mouthsᵍ came fire, smoke and sulfur.ʰ ¹⁸A third of mankind was killedⁱ by the three plagues of fire, smoke and sulfurʲ that came out of their mouths. ¹⁹The power of the horses was in their mouths and in their tails; for their tails were like snakes, having heads with which they inflict injury.

²⁰The rest of mankind that were not killed by these plagues still did not repent of the work of their hands;ᵏ they did not stop worshiping demons,ˡ and idols of gold, silver, bronze, stone and wood—idols that cannot see or hear or walk.ᵐ ²¹Nor did they repentⁿ of their murders, their magic arts,ᵒ their sexual immoralityᵖ or their thefts.

Chapter 10 Theme

10 Then I saw another mighty angel�q coming down from heaven. He was robed in a cloud, with a rainbow above his head; his face was like the sun,ʳ and his legs were like fiery pillars.ˢ ²He was holding a little scroll, which lay open in his hand. He planted his right foot on the sea and his left foot on the land, ³and he gave a loud shout like the roar of a lion. When he shouted, the voices of the seven thundersᵗ spoke. ⁴And when the seven thunders spoke, I was about to write; but I heard a voice from heaven say, "Seal up what the seven thunders have said and do not write it down."ᵘ

⁵Then the angel I had seen standing on the sea and on the land raised his right hand to heaven.ᵛ ⁶And he swore by him who lives for ever and ever, who created the heavens and all that is in them, the earth and all that is in it, and the sea and all that is in it,ʷ and said, "There will be no more delay!ˣ ⁷But in the days when the seventh angel is about to sound his trumpet, the mysteryʸ of God will be accomplished, just as he announced to his servants the prophets."

ᵃ 13 That is, projections

9:12
ᵃ Rev 8:13

9:13
ᵇ Ex 30:1-3
ᶜ Rev 8:3

9:14
ᵈ Rev 16:12

9:15
ᵉ ver 18

9:16
ᶠ Rev 5:11; 7:4

9:17
ᵍ Rev 11:5
ʰ ver 18

9:18
ⁱ ver 15
ʲ ver 17

9:20
ᵏ Dt 31:29
ˡ 1Co 10:20
ᵐ Ps 115:4-7; 135:15-17; Da 5:23

9:21
ⁿ Rev 2:21
ᵒ Rev 18:23
ᵖ Rev 17:2,5

10:1
q Rev 5:2
ʳ Mt 17:2; Rev 1:16
ˢ Rev 1:15

10:3
ᵗ Rev 4:5

10:4
ᵘ Da 8:26; 12:4,9; Rev 22:10

10:5
ᵛ Da 12:7

10:6
ʷ Rev 4:11; 14:7
ˣ Rev 16:17

10:7
ʸ Ro 16:25

10:8
a ver 4

10:9
b Jer 15:16;
Eze 2:8–3:3

10:11
c Eze 37:4,9

11:1
d Eze 40:3;
Rev 21:15

11:2
e Eze 40:17,20
f Lk 21:24
g Rev 21:2
h Da 7:25;
Rev 13:5

11:3
i Rev 1:5
j Ge 37:34

11:4
k Ps 52:8;
Jer 11:16;
Zec 4:3,11
l Zec 4:14

11:5
m 2Ki 1:10;
Jer 5:14
n Nu 16:29,35

11:6
o Ex 7:17,19

11:7
p Rev 13:1-4
q Da 7:21

11:8
r Isa 1:9
s Heb 13:12

11:9
t Ps 79:2,3

11:10
u Rev 3:10
v Est 9:19,22

11:11
w Eze 37:5,9,
10,14

11:12
x Rev 4:1
y 2Ki 2:11;
Ac 1:9

11:13
z Rev 6:12
a Rev 14:7
b Rev 16:11

11:14
c Rev 8:13

⁸Then the voice that I had heard from heaven a spoke to me once more: "Go, take the scroll that lies open in the hand of the angel who is standing on the sea and on the land."

⁹So I went to the angel and asked him to give me the little scroll. He said to me, "Take it and eat it. It will turn your stomach sour, but in your mouth it will be as sweet as honey." b ¹⁰I took the little scroll from the angel's hand and ate it. It tasted as sweet as honey in my mouth, but when I had eaten it, my stomach turned sour. ¹¹Then I was told, "You must prophesy c again about many peoples, nations, languages and kings."

Chapter 11 Theme

11 I was given a reed like a measuring rod d and was told, "Go and measure the temple of God and the altar, and count the worshipers there. ²But exclude the outer court; e do not measure it, because it has been given to the Gentiles. f They will trample on the holy city g for 42 months. h ³And I will give power to my two witnesses, i and they will prophesy for 1,260 days, clothed in sackcloth." j ⁴These are the two olive trees k and the two lampstands that stand before the Lord of the earth. l ⁵If anyone tries to harm them, fire comes from their mouths and devours their enemies. m This is how anyone who wants to harm them must die. n ⁶These men have power to shut up the sky so that it will not rain during the time they are prophesying; and they have power to turn the waters into blood o and to strike the earth with every kind of plague as often as they want.

⁷Now when they have finished their testimony, the beast p that comes up from the Abyss will attack them, q and overpower and kill them. ⁸Their bodies will lie in the street of the great city, which is figuratively called Sodom r and Egypt, where also their Lord was crucified. s ⁹For three and a half days men from every people, tribe, language and nation will gaze on their bodies and refuse them burial. t ¹⁰The inhabitants of the earth u will gloat over them and will celebrate by sending each other gifts, v because these two prophets had tormented those who live on the earth.

¹¹But after the three and a half days a breath of life from God entered them, w and they stood on their feet, and terror struck those who saw them. ¹²Then they heard a loud voice from heaven saying to them, "Come up here." x And they went up to heaven in a cloud, y while their enemies looked on.

¹³At that very hour there was a severe earthquake z and a tenth of the city collapsed. Seven thousand people were killed in the earthquake, and the survivors were terrified and gave glory a to the God of heaven. b

¹⁴The second woe has passed; the third woe is coming soon. c

[15]The seventh angel sounded his trumpet,[a] and there were loud voices[b] in heaven, which said:

> "The kingdom of the world has become the kingdom of
>   our Lord and of his Christ,[c]
>   and he will reign for ever and ever."[d]

[16]And the twenty-four elders,[e] who were seated on their thrones before God, fell on their faces and worshiped God, [17]saying:

> "We give thanks to you, Lord God Almighty,[f]
>   the One who is and who was,
> because you have taken your great power
>   and have begun to reign.[g]
> [18]The nations were angry;[h]
>   and your wrath has come.
> The time has come for judging the dead,
>   and for rewarding your servants the prophets[i]
> and your saints and those who reverence your name,
>   both small and great[j]—
> and for destroying those who destroy the earth."

[19]Then God's temple[k] in heaven was opened, and within his temple was seen the ark of his covenant. And there came flashes of lightning, rumblings, peals of thunder, an earthquake and a great hailstorm.[l]

Chapter 12 Theme

12 A great and wondrous sign appeared in heaven: a woman clothed with the sun, with the moon under her feet and a crown of twelve stars on her head. [2]She was pregnant and cried out in pain[m] as she was about to give birth. [3]Then another sign appeared in heaven: an enormous red dragon with seven heads and ten horns[n] and seven crowns[o] on his heads. [4]His tail swept a third[p] of the stars out of the sky and flung them to the earth.[q] The dragon stood in front of the woman who was about to give birth, so that he might devour her child[r] the moment it was born. [5]She gave birth to a son, a male child, who will rule all the nations with an iron scepter.[s] And her child was snatched up to God and to his throne. [6]The woman fled into the desert to a place prepared for her by God, where she might be taken care of for 1,260 days.[t]

[7]And there was war in heaven. Michael and his angels fought against the dragon,[u] and the dragon and his angels fought back. [8]But he was not strong enough, and they lost their place in heaven. [9]The great dragon was hurled down—that ancient serpent[v] called the devil,[w] or Satan, who leads the whole world astray.[x] He was hurled to the earth,[y] and his angels with him.

11:15
[a] Rev 10:7
[b] Rev 16:17; 19:1
[c] Rev 12:10
[d] Da 2:44;
7:14,27

11:16
[e] Rev 4:4

11:17
[f] Rev 1:8
[g] Rev 19:6

11:18
[h] Ps 2:1
[i] Rev 10:7
[j] Rev 19:5

11:19
[k] Rev 15:5,8
[l] Rev 16:21

12:2
[m] Gal 4:19

12:3
[n] Da 7:7,20;
Rev 13:1
[o] Rev 19:12

12:4
[p] Rev 8:7
[q] Da 8:10
[r] Mt 2:16

12:5
[s] Ps 2:9;
Rev 2:27

12:6
[t] Rev 11:2

12:7
[u] ver 3

12:9
[v] Ge 3:1-7
[w] Mt 25:41
[x] Rev 20:3,8,10
[y] Lk 10:18;
Jn 12:31

12:10
a Rev 11:15
b Job 1:9-11;
Zec 3:1

[10]Then I heard a loud voice in heaven[a] say:

"Now have come the salvation and the power and the
    kingdom of our God,
    and the authority of his Christ.
For the accuser of our brothers,[b]
    who accuses them before our God day and night,
    has been hurled down.

12:11
c Rev 7:14
d Rev 6:9
e Lk 14:26

[11]They overcame him
    by the blood of the Lamb[c]
    and by the word of their testimony;[d]
they did not love their lives so much
    as to shrink from death.[e]

12:12
f Ps 96:11;
Isa 49:13;
Rev 18:20
g Rev 8:13
h Rev 10:6

[12]Therefore rejoice, you heavens[f]
    and you who dwell in them!
But woe[g] to the earth and the sea,[h]
    because the devil has gone down to you!
He is filled with fury,
    because he knows that his time is short."

12:13
i ver 3
j ver 5

[13]When the dragon[i] saw that he had been hurled to the earth, he pursued the woman who had given birth to the male child.[j]

12:14
k Ex 19:4
l Da 7:25

[14]The woman was given the two wings of a great eagle,[k] so that she might fly to the place prepared for her in the desert, where she would be taken care of for a time, times and half a time,[l] out of the serpent's reach. [15]Then from his mouth the serpent spewed water like a river, to overtake the woman and sweep her away with the torrent. [16]But the earth helped the woman by opening its mouth and swallowing the river that the dragon had spewed out of his

12:17
m Rev 11:7
n Ge 3:15
o Rev 14:12
p Rev 1:2

mouth. [17]Then the dragon was enraged at the woman and went off to make war[m] against the rest of her offspring[n]—those who obey God's commandments[o] and hold to the testimony of Jesus.[p]

Chapter 13 Theme _____

13:1
q Da 7:1-6;
Rev 15:2
r Rev 12:3
s Da 11:36;
Rev 17:3

13 And the dragon[a] stood on the shore of the sea.
And I saw a beast coming out of the sea.[q] He had ten horns and seven heads,[r] with ten crowns on his horns, and on each head a blasphemous name.[s] [2]The beast I saw resembled a leopard,[t] but

13:2
t Da 7:6
u Da 7:5
v Da 7:4
w Rev 16:10

had feet like those of a bear[u] and a mouth like that of a lion.[v] The dragon gave the beast his power and his throne and great authority.[w] [3]One of the heads of the beast seemed to have had a fatal wound, but the fatal wound had been healed.[x] The whole world was astonished[y] and followed the beast. [4]Men worshiped the

13:3
x ver 12,14
y Rev 17:8

dragon because he had given authority to the beast, and they also worshiped the beast and asked, "Who is like[z] the beast? Who can make war against him?"

13:4
z Ex 15:11

a 1 Some late manuscripts *And I*

⁵The beast was given a mouth to utter proud words and blasphemies*a* and to exercise his authority for forty-two months.*b* ⁶He opened his mouth to blaspheme God, and to slander his name and his dwelling place and those who live in heaven.*c* ⁷He was given power to make war*d* against the saints and to conquer them. And he was given authority over every tribe, people, language and nation.*e* ⁸All inhabitants of the earth*f* will worship the beast—all whose names have not been written in the book of life*g* belonging to the Lamb that was slain from the creation of the world.*ah*

⁹He who has an ear, let him hear.*i*

¹⁰If anyone is to go into captivity,
    into captivity he will go.
If anyone is to be killed*b* with the sword,
    with the sword he will be killed.*j*

This calls for patient endurance and faithfulness*k* on the part of the saints.*l*

¹¹Then I saw another beast, coming out of the earth. He had two horns like a lamb, but he spoke like a dragon. ¹²He exercised all the authority*m* of the first beast on his behalf,*n* and made the earth and its inhabitants worship the first beast,*o* whose fatal wound had been healed.*p* ¹³And he performed great and miraculous signs,*q* even causing fire to come down from heaven*r* to earth in full view of men. ¹⁴Because of the signs*s* he was given power to do on behalf of the first beast, he deceived*t* the inhabitants of the earth. He ordered them to set up an image in honor of the beast who was wounded by the sword and yet lived. ¹⁵He was given power to give breath to the image of the first beast, so that it could speak and cause all who refused to worship the image to be killed.*u* ¹⁶He also forced everyone, small and great,*v* rich and poor, free and slave, to receive a mark on his right hand or on his forehead,*w* ¹⁷so that no one could buy or sell unless he had the mark,*x* which is the name of the beast or the number of his name.*y*

¹⁸This calls for wisdom.*z* If anyone has insight, let him calculate the number of the beast, for it is man's number.*a* His number is 666.

Chapter 14 Theme

14 Then I looked, and there before me was the Lamb,*b* standing on Mount Zion,*c* and with him 144,000*d* who had his name and his Father's name*e* written on their foreheads. ²And I heard a sound from heaven like the roar of rushing waters*f* and like a

---

13:5
a Da 7:8,11, 20,25; 11:36; 2Th 2:4
b Rev 11:2

13:6
c Rev 12:12

13:7
d Da 7:21; Rev 11:7
e Rev 5:9

13:8
f Rev 3:10
g Rev 3:5; 20:12
h Mt 25:34

13:9
i Rev 2:7

13:10
j Jer 15:2; 43:11
k Heb 6:12
l Rev 14:12

13:12
m ver 4
n ver 14
o Rev 14:9,11
p ver 3

13:13
q Mt 24:24
r 1Ki 18:38; Rev 20:9

13:14
s 2Th 2:9,10
t Rev 12:9

13:15
u Da 3:3-6

13:16
v Rev 19:5
w Rev 14:9

13:17
x Rev 14:9
y Rev 14:11; 15:2

13:18
z Rev 17:9
a Rev 15:2; 21:17

14:1
b Rev 5:6
c Ps 2:6
d Rev 7:4
e Rev 3:12

14:2
f Rev 1:15

---

a 8 Or *written from the creation of the world in the book of life belonging to the Lamb that was slain*   *b 10* Some manuscripts *anyone kills*

14:2
a Rev 5:8

14:3
b Rev 5:9
c ver 1

14:4
d 2Co 11:2;
Rev 3:4
e Rev 5:9
f Jas 1:18

14:5
g Ps 32:2;
Zep 3:13
h Eph 5:27

14:6
i Rev 8:13
j Rev 3:10
k Rev 13:7

14:7
l Rev 15:4
m Rev 11:13
n Rev 8:10

14:8
o Isa 21:9;
Jer 51:8
p Rev 17:2,4
18:3,9

14:9
q Rev 13:14

14:10
r Isa 51:17;
Jer 25:15
s Rev 18:6

14:11
t Isa 34:10;
Rev 19:3

14:12
u Rev 13:10

14:13
v 1Co 15:18;
1Th 4:16

14:14
w Da 7:13;
Rev 1:13
x Rev 6:2

14:15
y Joel 3:13
z Jer 51:33

loud peal of thunder. The sound I heard was like that of harpists playing their harps.a 3And they sang a new song b before the throne and before the four living creatures and the elders. No one could learn the song except the 144,000 c who had been redeemed from the earth. 4These are those who did not defile themselves with women, for they kept themselves pure.d They follow the Lamb wherever he goes. They were purchased from among men e and offered as firstfruits f to God and the Lamb. 5No lie was found in their mouths; g they are blameless.h

6Then I saw another angel flying in midair,i and he had the eternal gospel to proclaim to those who live on the earth j—to every nation, tribe, language and people.k 7He said in a loud voice, "Fear God l and give him glory,m because the hour of his judgment has come. Worship him who made the heavens, the earth, the sea and the springs of water." n

8A second angel followed and said, "Fallen! Fallen is Babylon the Great,o which made all the nations drink the maddening wine of her adulteries." p

9A third angel followed them and said in a loud voice: "If anyone worships the beast and his image q and receives his mark on the forehead or on the hand, 10he, too, will drink of the wine of God's fury,r which has been poured full strength into the cup of his wrath.s He will be tormented with burning sulfur in the presence of the holy angels and of the Lamb. 11And the smoke of their torment rises for ever and ever.t There is no rest day or night for those who worship the beast and his image, or for anyone who receives the mark of his name." 12This calls for patient endurance on the part of the saints u who obey God's commandments and remain faithful to Jesus.

13Then I heard a voice from heaven say, "Write: Blessed are the dead who die in the Lord v from now on."

"Yes," says the Spirit, "they will rest from their labor, for their deeds will follow them."

14I looked, and there before me was a white cloud, and seated on the cloud was one "like a son of man" a w with a crown x of gold on his head and a sharp sickle in his hand. 15Then another angel came out of the temple and called in a loud voice to him who was sitting on the cloud, "Take your sickle y and reap, because the time to reap has come, for the harvest z of the earth is ripe." 16So he who was seated on the cloud swung his sickle over the earth, and the earth was harvested.

17Another angel came out of the temple in heaven, and he too had a sharp sickle. 18Still another angel, who had charge of the fire, came from the altar and called in a loud voice to him who had

a 14 Daniel 7:13

the sharp sickle, "Take your sharp sickle and gather the clusters of grapes from the earth's vine, because its grapes are ripe." ¹⁹The angel swung his sickle on the earth, gathered its grapes and threw them into the great winepress of God's wrath. [a] ²⁰They were trampled in the winepress[b] outside the city,[c] and blood flowed out of the press, rising as high as the horses' bridles for a distance of 1,600 stadia.[a]

Chapter 15 Theme _____

15 I saw in heaven another great and marvelous sign:[d] seven angels[e] with the seven last plagues[f]—last, because with them God's wrath is completed. ²And I saw what looked like a sea of glass[g] mixed with fire and, standing beside the sea, those who had been victorious over the beast and his image[h] and over the number of his name. They held harps given them by God ³and sang the song of Moses[i] the servant of God and the song of the Lamb:

> "Great and marvelous are your deeds,[j]
>   Lord God Almighty.
> Just and true are your ways,[k]
>   King of the ages.
> ⁴Who will not fear you, O Lord,[l]
>   and bring glory to your name?
> For you alone are holy.
> All nations will come
>   and worship before you,[m]
> for your righteous acts have been revealed."

⁵After this I looked and in heaven the temple,[n] that is, the tabernacle of the Testimony,[o] was opened. ⁶Out of the temple[p] came the seven angels with the seven plagues.[q] They were dressed in clean, shining linen and wore golden sashes around their chests.[r] ⁷Then one of the four living creatures[s] gave to the seven angels seven golden bowls filled with the wrath of God, who lives for ever and ever. ⁸And the temple was filled with smoke[t] from the glory of God and from his power, and no one could enter the temple[u] until the seven plagues of the seven angels were completed.

Chapter 16 Theme _____

16 Then I heard a loud voice from the temple saying to the seven angels,[v] "Go, pour out the seven bowls of God's wrath on the earth."

²The first angel went and poured out his bowl on the land,[w] and ugly and painful sores[x] broke out on the people who had the mark of the beast and worshiped his image.[y]

a 20 That is, about 180 miles (about 300 kilometers)

14:19
a Rev 19:15

14:20
b Isa 63:3
c Heb 13:12; Rev 11:8

15:1
d Rev 12:1,3
e Rev 16:1
f Lev 26:21

15:2
g Rev 4:6
h Rev 13:14

15:3
i Ex 15:1; Dt 32:4
j Ps 111:2
k Ps 145:17

15:4
l Jer 10:7
m Isa 66:23

15:5
n Rev 11:19
o Nu 1:50

15:6
p Rev 14:15
q ver 1
r Rev 1:13

15:7
s Rev 4:6

15:8
t Isa 6:4
u Ex 40:34,35; 1Ki 8:10,11; 2Ch 5:13,14

16:1
v Rev 15:1

16:2
w Rev 8:7
x Ex 9:9-11
y Rev 13:15-17

16:3
a Ex 7:17-21;
Rev 8:8,9

16:4
b Rev 8:10
c Ex 7:17-21

16:5
d Rev 15:3
e Rev 1:4
f Rev 15:4

16:6
g Isa 49:26;
Rev 17:6

16:7
h Rev 6:9
i Rev 15:3; 19:2

16:8
j Rev 8:12
k Rev 14:18

16:9
l ver 11,21
m Rev 2:21
n Rev 11:13

16:10
o Rev 13:2
p Rev 9:2

16:11
q ver 9,21
r Rev 11:13
s ver 2
t Rev 2:21

16:12
u Rev 9:14
v Isa 41:2

16:13
w Rev 12:3
x Rev 13:1
y Rev 19:20

16:14
z 1Ti 4:1
a Rev 17:14

16:15
b Lk 12:37

16:16
c Rev 9:11
d 2Ki 23:29,30

16:17
e Eph 2:2
f Rev 14:15
g Rev 11:15
h Rev 21:6

³The second angel poured out his bowl on the sea, and it turned into blood like that of a dead man, and every living thing in the sea died.*a*

⁴The third angel poured out his bowl on the rivers and springs of water,*b* and they became blood.*c* ⁵Then I heard the angel in charge of the waters say:

> "You are just in these judgments,*d*
>> you who are and who were,*e* the Holy One,*f*
>> because you have so judged;
> ⁶for they have shed the blood of your saints and prophets,
>> and you have given them blood to drink*g* as they
>> deserve."

⁷And I heard the altar*h* respond:

> "Yes, Lord God Almighty,
>> true and just are your judgments."*i*

⁸The fourth angel*j* poured out his bowl on the sun, and the sun was given power to scorch people with fire.*k* ⁹They were seared by the intense heat and they cursed the name of God,*l* who had control over these plagues, but they refused to repent*m* and glorify him.*n*

¹⁰The fifth angel poured out his bowl on the throne of the beast,*o* and his kingdom was plunged into darkness.*p* Men gnawed their tongues in agony ¹¹and cursed*q* the God of heaven*r* because of their pains and their sores,*s* but they refused to repent of what they had done.*t*

¹²The sixth angel poured out his bowl on the great river Euphrates,*u* and its water was dried up to prepare the way for the kings from the East.*v* ¹³Then I saw three evil*a* spirits that looked like frogs; they came out of the mouth of the dragon,*w* out of the mouth of the beast*x* and out of the mouth of the false prophet.*y* ¹⁴They are spirits of demons*z* performing miraculous signs, and they go out to the kings of the whole world, to gather them for the battle*a* on the great day of God Almighty.

¹⁵"Behold, I come like a thief! Blessed is he who stays awake*b* and keeps his clothes with him, so that he may not go naked and be shamefully exposed."

¹⁶Then they gathered the kings together to the place that in Hebrew*c* is called Armageddon.*d*

¹⁷The seventh angel poured out his bowl into the air,*e* and out of the temple*f* came a loud voice*g* from the throne, saying, "It is done!"*h* ¹⁸Then there came flashes of lightning, rumblings, peals

a 13 Greek *unclean*

of thunder[a] and a severe earthquake.[b] No earthquake like it has ever occurred since man has been on earth,[c] so tremendous was the quake. [19]The great city[d] split into three parts, and the cities of the nations collapsed. God remembered[e] Babylon the Great[f] and gave her the cup filled with the wine of the fury of his wrath.[g] [20]Every island fled away and the mountains could not be found.[h] [21]From the sky huge hailstones[i] of about a hundred pounds each fell upon men. And they cursed God on account of the plague of hail,[j] because the plague was so terrible.

Chapter 17 Theme _____

17 One of the seven angels[k] who had the seven bowls[l] came and said to me, "Come, I will show you the punishment[m] of the great prostitute,[n] who sits on many waters.[o] [2]With her the kings of the earth committed adultery and the inhabitants of the earth were intoxicated with the wine of her adulteries."[p]

[3]Then the angel carried me away in the Spirit into a desert.[q] There I saw a woman sitting on a scarlet beast that was covered with blasphemous names[r] and had seven heads and ten horns.[s] [4]The woman was dressed in purple and scarlet, and was glittering with gold, precious stones and pearls.[t] She held a golden cup[u] in her hand, filled with abominable things and the filth of her adulteries. [5]This title was written on her forehead:

MYSTERY
BABYLON THE GREAT[v]
THE MOTHER OF PROSTITUTES
AND OF THE ABOMINATIONS OF THE EARTH.

[6]I saw that the woman was drunk with the blood of the saints,[w] the blood of those who bore testimony to Jesus.

When I saw her, I was greatly astonished. [7]Then the angel said to me: "Why are you astonished? I will explain to you the mystery[x] of the woman and of the beast she rides, which has the seven heads and ten horns.[y] [8]The beast, which you saw, once was, now is not, and will come up out of the Abyss and go to his destruction.[z] The inhabitants of the earth[a] whose names have not been written in the book of life[b] from the creation of the world will be astonished[c] when they see the beast, because he once was, now is not, and yet will come.

[9]"This calls for a mind with wisdom.[d] The seven heads are seven hills on which the woman sits. [10]They are also seven kings. Five have fallen, one is, the other has not yet come; but when he does come, he must remain for a little while. [11]The beast who once was, and now is not,[e] is an eighth king. He belongs to the seven and is going to his destruction.

16:18
[a] Rev 4:5
[b] Rev 6:12
[c] Da 12:1

16:19
[d] Rev 17:18
[e] Rev 18:5
[f] Rev 14:8
[g] Rev 14:10

16:20
[h] Rev 6:14

16:21
[i] Rev 11:19
[j] Ex 9:23-25

17:1
[k] Rev 15:1
[l] Rev 21:9
[m] Rev 16:19
[n] Rev 19:2
[o] Jer 51:13

17:2
[p] Rev 14:8; 18:3

17:3
[q] Rev 12:6,14
[r] Rev 13:1
[s] Rev 12:3

17:4
[t] Rev 18:16
[u] Jer 51:7;
Rev 18:6

17:5
[v] Rev 14:8

17:6
[w] Rev 18:24

17:7
[x] ver 5
[y] ver 3

17:8
[z] Rev 13:10
[a] Rev 3:10
[b] Rev 13:8
[c] Rev 13:3

17:9
[d] Rev 13:18

17:11
[e] ver 8

17:12
a Rev 12:3
b Rev 18:10,
17,19

17:13
c ver 17

17:14
d Rev 16:14
e 1Ti 6:15;
Rev 19:16
f Mt 22:14

17:15
g Isa 8:7
h Rev 13:7

17:16
i Rev 18:17,19
j Eze 16:37,39
k Rev 19:18
l Rev 18:8

17:17
m Rev 10:7

17:18
n Rev 16:19

18:1
o Rev 17:1
p Rev 10:1
q Eze 43:2

18:2
r Rev 14:8
s Isa 13:21,22;
Jer 50:39

18:3
t Rev 14:8
u Rev 17:2
v Eze 27:9-25
w ver 7,9

18:4
x Isa 48:20;
Jer 50:8;
2Co 6:17

18:5
y Jer 51:9
z Rev 16:19

18:6
a Ps 137:8;
Jer 50:15,29
b Rev 14:10;
16:19

18:7
c Eze 28:2-8
d Isa 47:7,8;
Zep 2:15

¹²"The ten horns*a* you saw are ten kings who have not yet received a kingdom, but who for one hour*b* will receive authority as kings along with the beast. ¹³They have one purpose and will give their power and authority to the beast.*c* ¹⁴They will make war*d* against the Lamb, but the Lamb will overcome them because he is Lord of lords and King of kings*e*—and with him will be his called, chosen*f* and faithful followers."

¹⁵Then the angel said to me, "The waters*g* you saw, where the prostitute sits, are peoples, multitudes, nations and languages.*h* ¹⁶The beast and the ten horns you saw will hate the prostitute. They will bring her to ruin*i* and leave her naked;*j* they will eat her flesh*k* and burn her with fire.*l* ¹⁷For God has put it into their hearts to accomplish his purpose by agreeing to give the beast their power to rule, until God's words are fulfilled.*m* ¹⁸The woman you saw is the great city*n* that rules over the kings of the earth."

Chapter 18 Theme _____

18 After this I saw another angel*o* coming down from heaven.*p* He had great authority, and the earth was illuminated by his splendor.*q* ²With a mighty voice he shouted:

"Fallen! Fallen is Babylon the Great!*r*
   She has become a home for demons
and a haunt for every evil*a* spirit,
   a haunt for every unclean and detestable bird.*s*
³For all the nations have drunk
   the maddening wine of her adulteries.*t*
The kings of the earth committed adultery with her,*u*
   and the merchants of the earth grew rich*v* from her
      excessive luxuries."*w*

⁴Then I heard another voice from heaven say:

"Come out of her, my people,*x*
   so that you will not share in her sins,
   so that you will not receive any of her plagues;
⁵for her sins are piled up to heaven,*y*
   and God has remembered*z* her crimes.
⁶Give back to her as she has given;
   pay her back*a* double for what she has done.
   Mix her a double portion from her own cup.*b*
⁷Give her as much torture and grief
   as the glory and luxury she gave herself.*c*
In her heart she boasts,
   'I sit as queen; I am not a widow,
   and I will never mourn.'*d*

a 2 Greek *unclean*

⁸Therefore in one day^a her plagues will overtake her:
death, mourning and famine.
She will be consumed by fire,^b
for mighty is the Lord God who judges her.

⁹"When the kings of the earth who committed adultery with her^c and shared her luxury see the smoke of her burning,^d they will weep and mourn over her.^e ¹⁰Terrified at her torment, they will stand far off^f and cry:

"'Woe! Woe, O great city,^g
O Babylon, city of power!
In one hour^h your doom has come!'

¹¹"The merchantsⁱ of the earth will weep and mourn over her because no one buys their cargoes any more^j— ¹²cargoes of gold, silver, precious stones and pearls; fine linen, purple, silk and scarlet cloth; every sort of citron wood, and articles of every kind made of ivory, costly wood, bronze, iron and marble;^k ¹³cargoes of cinnamon and spice, of incense, myrrh and frankincense, of wine and olive oil, of fine flour and wheat; cattle and sheep; horses and carriages; and bodies and souls of men.^l

¹⁴"They will say, 'The fruit you longed for is gone from you. All your riches and splendor have vanished, never to be recovered.' ¹⁵The merchants who sold these things and gained their wealth from her^m will stand far off, terrified at her torment. They will weep and mournⁿ ¹⁶and cry out:

"'Woe! Woe, O great city,
dressed in fine linen, purple and scarlet,
and glittering with gold, precious stones and pearls!^o
¹⁷In one hour^p such great wealth has been brought
to ruin!'^q

"Every sea captain, and all who travel by ship, the sailors, and all who earn their living from the sea,^r will stand far off. ¹⁸When they see the smoke of her burning, they will exclaim, 'Was there ever a city like this great city?'^s ¹⁹They will throw dust on their heads,^t and with weeping and mourning cry out:

"'Woe! Woe, O great city,
where all who had ships on the sea
became rich through her wealth!
In one hour she has been brought to ruin!^u
²⁰Rejoice over her, O heaven!^v
Rejoice, saints and apostles and prophets!
God has judged her for the way she treated you.'"^w

²¹Then a mighty angel^x picked up a boulder the size of a large millstone and threw it into the sea,^y and said:

18:8 ^aver 10; Isa 47:9; Jer 50:31,32 ^bRev 17:16
18:9 ^cRev 17:2,4 ^dver 18; Rev 19:3 ^eEze 26:17,18
18:10 ^fver 15,17 ^gver 16,19 ^hRev 17:12
18:11 ⁱEze 27:27 ^jver 3
18:12 ^kRev 17:4
18:13 ^lEze 27:13; 1Ti 1:10
18:15 ^mver 3 ⁿEze 27:31
18:16 ^oRev 17:4
18:17 ^pver 10 ^qRev 17:16 ^rEze 27:28-30
18:18 ^sEze 27:32; Rev 13:4
18:19 ^tJos 7:6; Eze 27:30 ^uRev 17:16
18:20 ^vJer 51:48; Rev 12:12 ^wRev 19:2
18:21 ^xRev 5:2 ^yJer 51:63

18:22
a Isa 24:8;
Eze 26:13
b Jer 25:10

"With such violence
the great city of Babylon will be thrown down,
never to be found again.
²²The music of harpists and musicians, flute players
and trumpeters,
will never be heard in you again.*a*
No workman of any trade
will ever be found in you again.

18:23
c Jer 7:34;
16:9; 25:10
d Isa 23:8
e Na 3:4

The sound of a millstone
will never be heard in you again.*b*
²³The light of a lamp
will never shine in you again.
The voice of bridegroom and bride
will never be heard in you again.*c*
Your merchants were the world's great men.*d*
By your magic spell*e* all the nations were led astray.

18:24
f Rev 16:6; 17:6
g Jer 51:49

²⁴In her was found the blood of prophets and of the saints,*f*
and of all who have been killed on the earth."*g*

19:1
h Rev 11:15
i Rev 7:10
j Rev 4:11

Chapter 19 Theme _____

19 After this I heard what sounded like the roar of a great
multitude*h* in heaven shouting:

"Hallelujah!
Salvation*i* and glory and power*j* belong to our God,
2 for true and just are his judgments.

19:2
k Dt 32:43;
Rev 6:10

He has condemned the great prostitute
who corrupted the earth by her adulteries.
He has avenged on her the blood of his servants."*k*

³And again they shouted:

19:3
l Isa 34:10;
Rev 14:11

"Hallelujah!
The smoke from her goes up for ever and ever."*l*

19:4
m Rev 4:4
n Rev 4:6
o Rev 5:14

⁴The twenty-four elders*m* and the four living creatures*n* fell down*o*
and worshiped God, who was seated on the throne. And they cried:

"Amen, Hallelujah!"

⁵Then a voice came from the throne, saying:

19:5
p Ps 134:1
q Rev 11:18;
20:12

"Praise our God,
all you his servants,*p*
you who fear him,
both small and great!"*q*

⁶Then I heard what sounded like a great multitude,*r* like the
roar of rushing waters and like loud peals of thunder, shouting:

19:6
r Rev 11:15

"Hallelujah!
    For our Lord God Almighty reigns.
⁷Let us rejoice and be glad
    and give him glory!
For the wedding of the Lamb*ᵃ* has come,
    and his bride*ᵇ* has made herself ready.
⁸Fine linen, bright and clean,
    was given her to wear."
(Fine linen stands for the righteous acts*ᶜ* of the saints.)

⁹Then the angel said to me,*ᵈ* "Write:*ᵉ* 'Blessed are those who are invited to the wedding supper of the Lamb!'"*ᶠ* And he added, "These are the true words of God."*ᵍ*

¹⁰At this I fell at his feet to worship him.*ʰ* But he said to me, "Do not do it! I am a fellow servant with you and with your brothers who hold to the testimony of Jesus. Worship God!*ⁱ* For the testimony of Jesus*ʲ* is the spirit of prophecy."

¹¹I saw heaven standing open and there before me was a white horse, whose rider*ᵏ* is called Faithful and True.*ˡ* With justice he judges and makes war.*ᵐ* ¹²His eyes are like blazing fire,*ⁿ* and on his head are many crowns.*ᵒ* He has a name written on him that no one knows but he himself.*ᵖ* ¹³He is dressed in a robe dipped in blood,*�q* and his name is the Word of God.*ʳ* ¹⁴The armies of heaven were following him, riding on white horses and dressed in fine linen,*ˢ* white and clean. ¹⁵Out of his mouth comes a sharp sword*ᵗ* with which to strike down*ᵘ* the nations. "He will rule them with an iron scepter."*ᵃᵛ* He treads the winepress*ʷ* of the fury of the wrath of God Almighty. ¹⁶On his robe and on his thigh he has this name written:*ˣ*

KING OF KINGS AND LORD OF LORDS.*ʸ*

¹⁷And I saw an angel standing in the sun, who cried in a loud voice to all the birds*ᶻ* flying in midair,*ᵃ* "Come,*ᵇ* gather together for the great supper of God, ¹⁸so that you may eat the flesh of kings, generals, and mighty men, of horses and their riders, and the flesh of all people,*ᶜ* free and slave, small and great."

¹⁹Then I saw the beast and the kings of the earth*ᵈ* and their armies gathered together to make war against the rider on the horse and his army. ²⁰But the beast was captured, and with him the false prophet*ᵉ* who had performed the miraculous signs on his behalf.*ᶠ* With these signs he had deluded those who had received the mark of the beast and worshiped his image. The two of them were thrown alive into the fiery lake*ᵍ* of burning sulfur.*ʰ* ²¹The rest of them were killed with the sword*ⁱ* that came out of the mouth of the rider on the horse,*ʲ* and all the birds*ᵏ* gorged themselves on their flesh.

a 15 Psalm 2:9

19:7
a Mt 22:2; 25:10; Eph 5:32
b Rev 21:2,9

19:8
c Rev 15:4

19:9
d ver 10
e Rev 1:19
f Lk 14:15
g Rev 21:5; 22:6

19:10
h Rev 22:8
i Ac 10:25,26; Rev 22:9
j Rev 12:17

19:11
k Rev 6:2
l Rev 3:14
m Isa 11:4

19:12
n Rev 1:14
o Rev 6:2
p Rev 2:17

19:13
q Isa 63:2,3
r Jn 1:1

19:14
s ver 8

19:15
t Rev 1:16
u Isa 11:4; 2Th 2:8
v Ps 2:9; Rev 2:27
w Rev 14:20

19:16
x ver 12
y Rev 17:14

19:17
z ver 21
a Rev 8:13
b Eze 39:17

19:18
c Eze 39:18-20

19:19
d Rev 16:14,16

19:20
e Rev 16:13
f Rev 13:12
g Da 7:11; Rev 20:10, 14,15; 21:8
h Rev 14:10

19:21
i ver 15
j ver 11,19
k ver 17

20:1
a Rev 10:1
b Rev 1:18

20:2
c Rev 12:9
d 2Pe 2:4

20:3
e Da 6:17
f Rev 12:9

20:4
g Da 7:9
h Rev 6:9
i Rev 13:12
j Rev 13:16

20:5
k Lk 14:14;
Php 3:11

20:6
l Rev 14:13
m Rev 2:11
n Rev 1:6
o ver 4

20:7
p ver 2

20:8
q ver 3,10
r Eze 38:2; 39:1
s Rev 16:14
t Heb 11:12

20:9
u Eze 38:9,16
v Eze 38:22; 39:6

20:10
w Rev 19:20
x Rev 14:10,11

20:11
y Rev 4:2

20:12
z Da 7:10
a Rev 3:5
b Jer 17:10;
Mt 16:27;
Rev 2:23

20:13
c Rev 6:8
d Isa 26:19

20:14
e 1Co 15:26

20:15
f ver 12

21:1
g Isa 65:17;
2Pe 3:13

Chapter 20 Theme _____

20 And I saw an angel coming down out of heaven,[a] having the key[b] to the Abyss and holding in his hand a great chain. [2]He seized the dragon, that ancient serpent, who is the devil, or Satan,[c] and bound him for a thousand years.[d] [3]He threw him into the Abyss, and locked and sealed[e] it over him, to keep him from deceiving the nations[f] anymore until the thousand years were ended. After that, he must be set free for a short time.

[4]I saw thrones[g] on which were seated those who had been given authority to judge. And I saw the souls of those who had been beheaded[h] because of their testimony for Jesus and because of the word of God. They had not worshiped the beast[i] or his image and had not received his mark on their foreheads or their hands.[j] They came to life and reigned with Christ a thousand years. [5](The rest of the dead did not come to life until the thousand years were ended.) This is the first resurrection.[k] [6]Blessed[l] and holy are those who have part in the first resurrection. The second death[m] has no power over them, but they will be priests[n] of God and of Christ and will reign with him[o] for a thousand years.

[7]When the thousand years are over,[p] Satan will be released from his prison [8]and will go out to deceive the nations[q] in the four corners of the earth—Gog and Magog[r]—to gather them for battle.[s] In number they are like the sand on the seashore.[t] [9]They marched across the breadth of the earth and surrounded[u] the camp of God's people, the city he loves. But fire came down from heaven[v] and devoured them. [10]And the devil, who deceived them,[w] was thrown into the lake of burning sulfur, where the beast and the false prophet had been thrown. They will be tormented day and night for ever and ever.[x]

[11]Then I saw a great white throne[y] and him who was seated on it. Earth and sky fled from his presence, and there was no place for them. [12]And I saw the dead, great and small, standing before the throne, and books were opened.[z] Another book was opened, which is the book of life.[a] The dead were judged according to what they had done[b] as recorded in the books. [13]The sea gave up the dead that were in it, and death and Hades[c] gave up the dead[d] that were in them, and each person was judged according to what he had done. [14]Then death[e] and Hades were thrown into the lake of fire. The lake of fire is the second death. [15]If anyone's name was not found written in the book of life,[f] he was thrown into the lake of fire.

Chapter 21 Theme _____

21 Then I saw a new heaven and a new earth,[g] for the first heaven and the first earth had passed away, and there was no longer any sea. [2]I saw the Holy City, the new Jerusalem, coming down out of heaven from God,[a] prepared as a bride beautifully dressed for her husband. [3]And I heard a loud voice from the throne saying, "Now the dwelling of God is with men, and he will live with them. They will be his people, and God himself will be with them and be their God.[b] [4]He will wipe every tear from their eyes.[c] There will be no more death[d] or mourning or crying or pain,[e] for the old order of things has passed away."

[5]He who was seated on the throne[f] said, "I am making everything new!" Then he said, "Write this down, for these words are trustworthy and true."[g]

[6]He said to me: "It is done.[h] I am the Alpha and the Omega,[i] the Beginning and the End. To him who is thirsty I will give to drink without cost from the spring of the water of life.[j] [7]He who overcomes will inherit all this, and I will be his God and he will be my son. [8]But the cowardly, the unbelieving, the vile, the murderers, the sexually immoral, those who practice magic arts, the idolaters and all liars[k]—their place will be in the fiery lake of burning sulfur. This is the second death."[l]

[9]One of the seven angels who had the seven bowls full of the seven last plagues[m] came and said to me, "Come, I will show you the bride,[n] the wife of the Lamb." [10]And he carried me away[o] in the Spirit[p] to a mountain great and high, and showed me the Holy City, Jerusalem, coming down out of heaven from God. [11]It shone with the glory of God,[q] and its brilliance was like that of a very precious jewel, like a jasper, clear as crystal.[r] [12]It had a great, high wall with twelve gates, and with twelve angels at the gates. On the gates were written the names of the twelve tribes of Israel.[s] [13]There were three gates on the east, three on the north, three on the south and three on the west. [14]The wall of the city had twelve foundations, and on them were the names of the twelve apostles of the Lamb.

[15]The angel who talked with me had a measuring rod[t] of gold to measure the city, its gates and its walls. [16]The city was laid out like a square, as long as it was wide. He measured the city with the rod and found it to be 12,000 stadia[a] in length, and as wide and high as it is long. [17]He measured its wall and it was 144 cubits[b] thick,[c] by man's measurement, which the angel was using. [18]The wall was made of jasper,[u] and the city of pure gold, as pure as glass.[v] [19]The foundations of the city walls were decorated with every kind of precious stone.[w] The first foundation was jasper, the second sapphire, the third chalcedony, the fourth emerald, [20]the fifth sardonyx, the sixth carnelian,[x] the seventh chrysolite, the eighth beryl, the ninth topaz, the tenth chrysoprase, the eleventh jacinth, and the twelfth amethyst.[d] [21]The twelve gates were twelve pearls, each gate made

---

[a]16 That is, about 1,400 miles (about 2,200 kilometers)　[b]17 That is, about 200 feet (about 65 meters)　[c]17 Or high　[d]20 The precise identification of some of these precious stones is uncertain.

21:2
[a]Heb 11:10; 12:22; Rev 3:12

21:3
[b]2Co 6:16

21:4
[c]Rev 7:17
[d]1Co 15:26; Rev 20:14
[e]Isa 35:10; 65:19

21:5
[f]Rev 4:9; 20:11
[g]Rev 19:9

21:6
[h]Rev 16:17
[i]Rev 1:8; 22:13
[j]Jn 4:10

21:8
[k]1Co 6:9
[l]Rev 2:11

21:9
[m]Rev 15:1,6,7
[n]Rev 19:7

21:10
[o]Rev 17:3
[p]Rev 1:10

21:11
[q]Rev 15:8; 22:5
[r]Rev 4:6

21:12
[s]Eze 48:30-34

21:15
[t]Rev 11:1

21:18
[u]ver 11
[v]ver 21

21:19
[w]Isa 54:11,12

21:20
[x]Rev 4:3

21:21
a ver 18

21:22
b Jn 4:21,23
c Rev 1:8
d Rev 5:6

21:23
e Isa 24:23;
60:19,20;
Rev 22:5

21:24
f Isa 60:3,5

21:25
g Isa 60:11
h Zec 14:7;
Rev 22:5

21:27
i Isa 52:1;
Joel 3:17;
Rev 22:14,15

22:1
j Rev 4:6
k Eze 47:1;
Zec 14:8

22:2
l Rev 2:7
m Eze 47:12

22:3
n Zec 14:11
o Rev 7:15

22:4
p Mt 5:8
q Rev 14:1

22:5
r Rev 21:25
s Rev 21:23
t Da 7:27;
Rev 20:4

22:6
u Rev 1:1
v Rev 19:9; 21:5
w Heb 12:9
x ver 16

22:7
y Rev 3:11
z Rev 1:3

22:8
a Rev 1:1
b Rev 19:10

22:9
c ver 10,18,19
d Rev 19:10

22:10
e Da 8:26;
Rev 10:4
f Rev 1:3

22:11
g Eze 3:27;
Da 12:10

22:12
h ver 7,20
i Isa 40:10

22:13
j Rev 1:8
k Rev 1:17
l Rev 21:6

of a single pearl. The great street of the city was of pure gold, like transparent glass.*a*

²²I did not see a temple*b* in the city, because the Lord God Almighty*c* and the Lamb*d* are its temple. ²³The city does not need the sun or the moon to shine on it, for the glory of God gives it light,*e* and the Lamb is its lamp. ²⁴The nations will walk by its light, and the kings of the earth will bring their splendor into it.*f* ²⁵On no day will its gates ever be shut,*g* for there will be no night there.*h* ²⁶The glory and honor of the nations will be brought into it. ²⁷Nothing impure will ever enter it, nor will anyone who does what is shameful or deceitful,*i* but only those whose names are written in the Lamb's book of life.

Chapter 22 Theme

22 Then the angel showed me the river of the water of life, as clear as crystal,*j* flowing*k* from the throne of God and of the Lamb ²down the middle of the great street of the city. On each side of the river stood the tree of life,*l* bearing twelve crops of fruit, yielding its fruit every month. And the leaves of the tree are for the healing of the nations.*m* ³No longer will there be any curse.*n* The throne of God and of the Lamb will be in the city, and his servants will serve him.*o* ⁴They will see his face,*p* and his name will be on their foreheads.*q* ⁵There will be no more night.*r* They will not need the light of a lamp or the light of the sun, for the Lord God will give them light.*s* And they will reign for ever and ever.*t*

⁶The angel said to me,*u* "These words are trustworthy and true.*v* The Lord, the God of the spirits of the prophets,*w* sent his angel*x* to show his servants the things that must soon take place."

⁷"Behold, I am coming soon!*y* Blessed*z* is he who keeps the words of the prophecy in this book."

⁸I, John, am the one who heard and saw these things.*a* And when I had heard and seen them, I fell down to worship at the feet*b* of the angel who had been showing them to me. ⁹But he said to me, "Do not do it! I am a fellow servant with you and with your brothers the prophets and of all who keep the words of this book.*c* Worship God!"*d*

¹⁰Then he told me, "Do not seal up*e* the words of the prophecy of this book, because the time is near.*f* ¹¹Let him who does wrong continue to do wrong; let him who is vile continue to be vile; let him who does right continue to do right; and let him who is holy continue to be holy."*g*

¹²"Behold, I am coming soon!*h* My reward is with me,*i* and I will give to everyone according to what he has done. ¹³I am the Alpha and the Omega,*j* the First and the Last,*k* the Beginning and the End.*l*

¹⁴"Blessed are those who wash their robes, that they may have the right to the tree of life^a and may go through the gates^b into the city.^c ¹⁵Outside^d are the dogs,^e those who practice magic arts, the sexually immoral, the murderers, the idolaters and everyone who loves and practices falsehood.

¹⁶"I, Jesus,^f have sent my angel to give you^a this testimony for the churches.^g I am the Root^h and the Offspring of David, and the bright Morning Star."ⁱ

¹⁷The Spirit^j and the bride say, "Come!" And let him who hears say, "Come!" Whoever is thirsty, let him come; and whoever wishes, let him take the free gift of the water of life.

¹⁸I warn everyone who hears the words of the prophecy of this book: If anyone adds anything to them,^k God will add to him the plagues described in this book.^l ¹⁹And if anyone takes words away^m from this book of prophecy, God will take away from him his share in the tree of life and in the holy city, which are described in this book.

²⁰He who testifies to these thingsⁿ says, "Yes, I am coming soon." Amen. Come, Lord Jesus.^o

²¹The grace of the Lord Jesus be with God's people.^p Amen.

---

a 16 The Greek is plural.

22:14
a Rev 2:7
b Rev 21:12
c Rev 21:27

22:15
d 1Co 6:9,10;
Gal 5:19-21;
Col 3:5,6
e Php 3:2

22:16
f Rev 1:1
g Rev 1:4
h Rev 5:5
i 2Pe 1:19;
Rev 2:28

22:17
j Rev 2:7

22:18
k Dt 4:2;
Pr 30:6
l Rev 15:6–16:21

22:19
m Dt 4:2

22:20
n Rev 1:2
o 1Co 16:22

22:21
p Ro 16:20

JESUS' MESSAGES TO THE CHURCHES

	DESCRIPTION OF JESUS	COMMENDATION TO THE CHURCH	REPROOF GIVEN TO THE CHURCH	WARNINGS AND INSTRUCTIONS TO THE CHURCH	PROMISE TO THE OVERCOMERS
EPHESUS					
SMYRNA					

(continued)

	Description of Jesus	Commendation to the Church	Reproof Given to the Church	Warnings and Instructions to the Church	Promise to the Overcomers
Pergamum					
Thyatira					

(continued)

Jesus' Messages to the Churches

	Description of Jesus	Commendation to the Church	Reproof Given to the Church	Warnings and Instructions to the Church	Promise to the Overcomers
Sardis					
Philadelphia					

(continued)

2171

	DESCRIPTION OF JESUS	COMMENDATION TO THE CHURCH	REPROOF GIVEN TO THE CHURCH	WARNINGS AND INSTRUCTIONS TO THE CHURCH	PROMISE TO THE OVERCOMERS
LAODICEA					

WHAT REVELATION TEACHES ABOUT

GOD	JESUS	THE HOLY SPIRIT

THE SEVEN SEALS, TRUMPETS, AND BOWLS

	SEALS	TRUMPETS	BOWLS
1st			
2nd			
3rd			
4th			
5th			
6th			
7th			

Theme of Revelation:

	SEGMENT DIVISIONS				CHAPTER THEMES
Author:					
Date:					1
Purpose:					2
					3
Key Words:					4
God					
Jesus (Christ)					5
in the Spirit					
church(es)					6
throne					7
mystery					
repent					8
overcome, triumphed, overpower, conquer					9
mark every reference to Satan (demons, devil, dragon)					10
					11
later, after this (that)					12
and I saw, I watched, then I saw, I saw (then I looked, I looked, [as] I watched)					13
					14
angel(s)					15
seal(s)					16
nation(s), Gentiles, ages					17
trumpet(s)					18
bowl(s), plague(s)					19
wrath, fury					
beast					20
Babylon (woman)					21
earthquake, quake, voices, thunder(s), lightning					22

What the Bible Teaches about Babylon

Its First Description in Scripture

Location of Babylon

The City

The Babylonian Empire *(see page 2310)*

Worship Connected with Babylon

Warnings Given about Babylon

Prophecies Regarding Babylon	Destruction of Babylon
	History of Babylon's Destruction
	The City
	The Babylonian Empire
	Details Concerning Babylon's Final Destruction
	The City
	The Babylonian System

REFERENCE	HOW IS IT DESCRIBED

WHAT HAPPENS IN NATURE	SIGNS OF BEGINNING OR END

(continued)

REFERENCE		HOW IS IT DESCRIBED	

WHAT HAPPENS IN NATURE	SIGNS OF BEGINNING OR END

BIBLE STUDY
HELPS

LTSB

UNDERSTANDING THE VALUE OF GOD'S WORD

WHAT IS THE BIBLE?

The Bible is comprised of 66 separate writings or books. It was written over a period of approximately 1400 to 1800 years by more than 40 authors from various walks of life. While many of the authors are identified, some remain unknown.

The Bible is divided into the Old Testament, comprised of 39 books, and the New Testament, comprised of 27 books. The Old Testament, the Bible of the nation of Israel, was divided into three segments: the Law or Torah, the Prophets or Nebi'im, and the Writings or Kethubim.

Although the Old Testament was written in Hebrew and Aramaic, it was translated into Koine (common) Greek around 250-100 B.C. This translation is referred to as the Septuagint or the LXX. It contains the same books as the Hebrew Old Testament, but the order and breakdown of the books was changed to the form now used in the Old Testament.

While the Old Testament was originally written in two Semitic languages, Hebrew and Aramaic, the vast majority of it is in Hebrew. The New Testament was written in Koine Greek, the popular language used throughout most of the Mediterranean world in the time of the Lord Jesus Christ. However, a few Aramaic phrases are found in the New Testament because Aramaic was the vernacular of the people of Israel. Jesus and His disciples spoke Aramaic as well as Koine Greek. Much of the Old Testament was translated into Aramaic, and these works are referred to as the Targums.

HOW WAS THE BIBLE WRITTEN AND TRANSLATED?

The Bible itself tells us how it was written: "All Scripture is God-breathed" (2 Timothy 3:16). Men "spoke from God as they were carried along by the Holy Spirit" (2 Peter 1:21). The Holy Spirit carried men along, moving and guiding them as they wrote in their own words what God wanted them to say. Thus we have *verbal* inspiration, because the words of the original text were inspired by God. And because all Scripture was given by inspiration we have *plenary* inspiration, which means total or complete inspiration. Every part of the Bible is inspired. The Bible does not merely contain the words of God, but it actually is the Word of God. Thus the original writings, often called *autographs*, are infallible—without error. This concept is called the verbal, plenary inspiration of the autographs.

Autographs

In early history, writing was done on stone, clay tablets, leather (animal skins), and papyrus scrolls. The autographs were probably written on papyrus. Papyrus, made from the inner bark of a reed plant, was formed into a paper-like material which was glued together and rolled into a scroll. Normally the writing was done on only one side of the scroll, so that as it was read it was unrolled with one hand and rolled up with the other. The scrolls were kept in a cylindrical box called a *capsa*.

According to the Jewish Talmud, the Scriptures were to be copied only on the skins of what God deemed as clean animals, such as sheep, calves, and goats. Parchment (dried animal skin) was costly but more durable and permanent than papyrus.

The Accuracy of the Copies

Eventually the scrolls were replaced by the *codex*. The codex (plural *codices*) was made from folded sheets, *quires*, which were stitched together like a book. Copies of the Old Testament were transcribed by hand under the strictest measures. The men who copied the manuscripts were called *scribes*. If one error was found the entire copy was destroyed. Thus the accuracy of the Old Testament is phenomenal. This accuracy has been confirmed by the multiple number of copies, by the Septuagint, and by the Dead Sea Scrolls.

More than 5000 ancient Greek copies of all or portions of the New Testament have been found. Although there are minor variances in the copied manuscripts, none affect doctrinal issues.

The Canon

The same omnipotent Sovereign who inspired men to write the Word of God led other men to recognize that these were the books which would comprise the *canon* of Scripture. The canon is the group of books which are recognized to be inspired by God. This group comprises the Old and New Testaments. The Old Testament canon of 39 books was fairly widely accepted in the days of Jesus Christ. Jesus himself, who is one with the Father, always affirmed and never contradicted the Old Testament. Revelation, the last of the New Testament books to be written, was completed before the end of the first century A.D. By A.D. 367 Bishop Athanasius compiled the first known list of the current 27 books of the New Testament.

Translations

The Hebrew/Aramaic and Greek copies of the 66 books of the Bible are the basis of the translations made in the various languages of the world. A translator will study the original words of these copies, determine what those words mean, and then select the best way to faithfully transmit the meaning of the original words in their context into the language of their translation. This is called a *primary translation*.

A *secondary translation* occurs when a translation is made from a primary translation of another language, say English, into a third language. Thus a secondary translation is not made from a copy of the original language but from a second language translated from the original language (the primary translation).

HOW DO WE KNOW THE BIBLE IS WHAT IT CLAIMS TO BE—THE WORD OF GOD?

Believing the Bible is ultimately a matter of informed faith. You either believe what the Word of God says about itself or you don't. You either believe the testimony of Jesus Christ regarding the Word of God or you don't.

There are several areas of objective evidence that test and support the veracity of the verbal, plenary inspiration of the autographs.

First, there is *bibliographic evidence* for the Bible's authenticity. No other ancient writings have as much manuscript evidence as does the Bible. Aside from 643 copies of Homer's works, which were written about 850 B.C., the other classical works written between 450 B.C. and 10 B.C. have anywhere from 3 to 20 copies each, but the New Testament has about 14,000. And not only is there more than an ample *quantity* of copies of the Bible, but the *quality* of the biblical manuscripts surpasses that of other manuscripts as well.

The passage of time is also a factor. The Dead Sea Scrolls, which date from 200 B.C. to A.D. 68, greatly reduce the time span between the writing of the Old Testament books to our earliest existing copies of the Old Testament. The time span between the autographs of the New Testament and its oldest existing copies is between 100 and 400 years, a very low figure.

Second, there is *internal evidence* for the authenticity of the Bible. The Bible not only claims to be the Word of God, but it also states that not the smallest letter or stroke will pass away from the law (the Old Testament) until all is accomplished (Matthew 5:17, 18). Many of the writers claimed to be eyewitnesses who wrote what they saw, heard, or experienced. Although over 40 different authors wrote 66 separate books over a time span of almost two millennia, there are no contradictions in what they wrote. Also, what was written in the Old Testament, sealed and canonized, is often seen fulfilled in the New Testament. Thus there is the internal evidence of fulfilled prophecy, some of which is being fulfilled even in our time.

Finally, there is an abundance of *external* evidence that supports the Bible's infallibility. When the Bible speaks on matters of history or science, it speaks accurately. There were times when it was supposed that science or history contradicted the Bible; however, later it was discovered that all the facts had not yet been uncovered.

More recent archaeological evidence has affirmed the historicity of the Bible in a multitude of ways as it speaks regarding rulers, nations, languages, battles, customs, geographic locations, tragedies, and other events. Extrabiblical writings also affirm what the New Testament teaches about the historicity of Jesus Christ and other New Testament characters.

Have you accepted the Bible as the inerrant Word of God, profitable for teaching, rebuking, correcting, and training in righteousness, that you may be thoroughly equipped for every good work? (2 Timothy 3:16). As you study the Bible, you will discover that it is a supernatural book...the very words of life.

MAJOR EVENTS IN ISRAEL'S HISTORY

∿∿∿∿∿

The Word of God takes on new life when a person understands the major events in Israel's history between the years of Abraham and the birth of Christ. Old and New Testament prophecies regarding Israel and her relationship to various world powers are seen in a new dimension.

Once you are acquainted with the religious, cultural, and political setting of Bible times, you will better understand God's plan for mankind and you will have a greater appreciation of the times in which our Lord lived and gave birth to his church.

FROM ADAM TO ABRAHAM
(The Beginning to About 2000 B.C.)

In the beginning there was no sin. Adam and Eve lived in unbroken fellowship with their Creator until they believed a lie and chose to disobey the explicit command of God. From that time on all mankind would be born in sin and bear its consequence: death.

Yet a merciful and loving God did not leave mankind in despair; he promised a Redeemer, born of a woman's seed. Over a thousand years passed, and with the passing of those years man's iniquity increased until every intent of his heart was only evil. God was grieved in his heart "that he had made man." And with that he determined to "wipe mankind…from the face of the earth." But Noah found favor in the eyes of the Lord, for he was a righteous man, blameless in his time.

When the flood came, only those in the ark were preserved: Noah and his family, eight people in all. However, the basic sin nature of those who survived had not changed, and it wasn't long before they too were in rebellion against God. And God knew that because they were one society and had the same language, nothing which they purposed to do would be impossible for them.

So once again God intervened, though not this time to destroy man from the face of the earth, for he had put a rainbow in the heavens and had made a covenant which he would not break. God intervened by confusing mankind's language and scattering them over the face of the whole earth.

Then around 2000 B.C. God called a man to leave Ur of the Chaldees and go to a land which he would show him. That man's name was Abram. From Abram God would not only make a great nation, but through him he would bless all the families of the earth. Thus God made a covenant with Abram and his descendants forever, and with that covenant he changed Abram's name to Abraham, "Father of Many." With that covenant also came the promise of the land of Canaan as the eternal possession of Abraham's descendants.

The Seed that God promised Adam and Eve, the one who would redeem mankind, would come not only through the seed of the woman, but also through the loins of Abraham and his descendants, Isaac and Jacob. To Isaac would be born Jacob, and to Jacob 12 sons. As God confirmed his covenant with Jacob, he changed Jacob's name to Israel, the one who fathered the heads of the 12 tribes of Israel. A covenant nation had been brought into existence by God. In the fullness of time the Redeemer, the messenger of the covenant, would come from the tribe of Judah.

But all was not well among Jacob's sons, for they were jealous of Joseph, Jacob's favorite, his firstborn by Rachel. As they plotted to take Joseph's life, Reuben and Judah intervened, and Joseph was sold into slavery and taken to Egypt. While Joseph's brothers meant to harm him, God meant it for good. Joseph went from being a slave in Potiphar's house to being a vice-regent in Pharaoh's palace via a prison. In his sovereignty God used Joseph's position in Egypt to deliver Israel's family from famine in Canaan. They lived in Egypt a total of 430 years, the majority of these as slaves. Then around 1525 B.C. a son by the name of Moses was born to two of these Hebrew slaves.

FROM THE EXODUS UNDER MOSES TO THE MONARCHY UNDER SAUL
(1445 B.C. to 1051 or 1043 B.C.)

It was about 80 years after the birth of Moses that the sons of Israel cried out to the God of Abraham, Isaac, and Jacob because of their great affliction. God heard their cry and appeared to Moses in a burning bush. The great I AM would deliver them from the house of bondage, from the land of Egypt, and take them to the land He promised to Abraham. Moses would serve as God's spokesman, as their human deliverer, and as the one to whom God would give the pattern for the tabernacle. In the tabernacle God would give the Israelites not only the means of worshiping him, but a picture of the Redeemer who was yet to come.

After the Israelites wandered in the wilderness for 40 years because of their unbelief, Joshua took them across the Jordan River into the promised land. The people served the Lord all the days of Joshua and the elders, and then there arose a generation who did not know Joshua, and the children of Israel served the gods of the people of Canaan and did evil in the sight of the Lord. So the Lord delivered them into the hands of their enemies. But when the people cried out to the Lord in their distress, God raised up judges from among the people. And God was with each judge all the days of his life. But when the judge died, the cycle of sin and slavery repeated itself. There was no visible king in Israel and everyone did what was right in his own eyes. It was to be a theocracy, with God as King, but the people did not obey their God.

Finally, in the days of Samuel, the prophet and judge, the people insisted on having a king over them like the other nations. Although this request grieved Samuel, God gave them what they wanted, for they had rejected him.

FROM UNITED KINGDOM TO DIVIDED KINGDOM
(1051 or 1043 B.C. to 931 B.C.)

Saul, Israel's first king, gave God sacrifice rather than obedience, and so God raised up a man after his own heart. David, the son of Jesse from the tribe of Judah, was anointed by God to become king.

David reigned from 1011 to 971 B.C. During that time his passion was to build a permanent dwelling for God in Jerusalem, the city of David. God saw the intent of David's heart, but because David had been a man of war, the building of the temple would be the task of David's son and successor, Solomon, born to Bathsheba.

On the day when the ark of the covenant was brought into the temple and the temple was dedicated to the Lord, Solomon fell on his face before God and reminded him of his covenant promises. Fire came from heaven and devoured the burnt offerings, and the glory of the Lord filled the temple.

But Solomon disobeyed God. He married foreign wives and set up their idols on high places in Jerusalem. When Solomon was old, his wives turned his heart away after other gods and his heart was not wholly devoted to serving God, as the heart of his father, David, had been.

After Solomon died, God tore the kingdom of Israel in two.

FROM 931 B.C. UNTIL THE BIRTH OF CHRIST

In 931 B.C. the tribes of Judah and Benjamin formed the southern kingdom of Judah, with Jerusalem as their capital. The remaining ten tribes formed the northern kingdom of Israel and eventually made Samaria their capital. The northern kingdom immediately began to worship idols, so in 722 B.C. God allowed the Assyrians to take them captive.

Although the southern kingdom was warned by the prophets of God that they too would go into captivity if they did not repent of their disobedience and idolatry, Judah did not listen. In 605 B.C., just before Nebuchadnezzar became king of Babylon, he attacked Jerusalem and took the king and some of his nobles captive to Babylon. Among them was Daniel (Daniel 1:1, 2). In 597 B.C. Nebuchadnezzar again attacked Judah, this time taking about 10,000 captives to Babylon, Ezekiel among them. Then in 586 B.C. Babylon, now the predominant world power, conquered Judah and destroyed not only the city of Jerusalem but the magnificent temple built by Solomon during his reign over Israel.

Separated from Jerusalem and their temple, the exiles established **synagogues** as a means of preserving their faith. The synagogues became centers of learning and worship where the Jews recited the **Shema** (Deuteronomy 6:4), read from the law and the prophets, prayed, and delivered messages.

Men trained in writing who recorded events and decisions were called **scribes**. They assumed the responsibility of copying, preserving, and even teaching the Word of God in the synagogues. By New Testament times the scribes were considered experts in interpreting and teaching the law and were referred to as lawyers.

Having experienced firsthand the cursings of disobedience as promised in the book of Deuteronomy, the exiled Jews seemed to gain a new respect and appreciation for the Word of God. They saw that God meant what he said and would not alter it even for his covenant people.

It was sometime after the kingdom divided and Judah went into captivity that the exiles became known as **men of Judah** or **Jews**.

The Persian Period
(539 to 331 B.C.)

When the Medes and the Persians conquered Babylon in 539 B.C., they became the predominant world power in Babylon's stead. Daniel 5 records this invasion.

Approximately 175 years before Cyrus (the king of Persia) was born, Isaiah prophesied that God would raise up Cyrus to accomplish all that he pleased (Isaiah 44:28). Second Chronicles 36:22, 23 records the fulfillment of God's plan: Cyrus issued a proclamation allowing the exiles of Judah to return to Jerusalem and rebuild their temple. Just as Jeremiah had prophesied (Jeremiah 29:10; Daniel 9:2), exactly 70 years from the time of Babylon's first attack on Jerusalem, the Israelites were allowed to return to their land.

The group which returned is referred to in Scripture as the **remnant**. *Diaspora*, the Greek word for scattering, became the term used to describe the Jews who remained in exile among the nations.

The book of Ezra records the return of the remnant and the building of the **second temple** during the time of Haggai and Zechariah. The book of Nehemiah records the rebuilding of the walls of Jerusalem. Nehemiah and Ezra were contemporaries. Ezra is referred to as a **scribe**.

The book of Malachi records the last Old Testament prophecy given by God. After this prophecy God did not inspire canonical Scripture again for 400 years.

This 400 years of silence which followed the book of Malachi is called the **intertestament period**. Although God was silent in that he did not speak through his prophets during this time, the events of these 400 years testify to the fulfillment of much that was written by Daniel the prophet.

These years could be divided into three periods: the Greek, the Maccabean, and the beginning of the Roman period.

The Greek Period
(331 to 63 B.C.)

The Greek period encompasses four different rulerships over Jerusalem, which includes the Maccabean rule.

Under Alexander the Great
(331 to 323 B.C.)

As the Persian Empire grew and threatened the security of the city-states of Greece, Philip of Macedonia sought to consolidate Greece in an effort to resist attack from Persia.

In 336 B.C. Philip was murdered, and his son, Alexander, who was about 20 years old, became king over the Greek Empire. Within two years Alexander set out to conquer Persia, whose empire now extended westward as far as Asia Minor (modern-day Turkey).

Over the next two years Alexander conquered the territory from Asia Minor to Pakistan and to Egypt, which included the land of the Jews. Although the account is not universally accepted by other historians, Josephus, a Jewish historian who lived about A.D. 37-100, wrote that as Alexander marched into Jerusalem he was met by Jaddua and other Jewish priests dressed in their priestly garments and by the people of Jerusalem wearing white robes.

In a dream Jaddua had been told to put wreaths on the city walls in order to greet Alexander. Alexander also had a dream which coincided with this event. When Alexander was escorted into Jerusalem and shown the prophecy

in Daniel 8 which described the destruction of the Medo-Persian Empire by a large horn on a goat (which represented Greece), Alexander felt the prophecy pertained to him and offered the Jews whatever they wanted. Alexander treated the Jews well and did not harm Jerusalem or their rebuilt temple.

When Alexander built the city of Alexandria in Egypt, he encouraged many Jews to settle there in order to help populate the city. Whenever Alexander conquered an area he established Greek cities and colonies, bringing in his Greek culture, ideas, and language. His goal was to consolidate his empire through a common way of life and thinking which became known as **Hellenization**. **Koine Greek** became the common language in the countries ruled by Greece and continued to be the primary language of civilization through the time of Christ. The New Testament was written in Koine Greek.

By 331 B.C. Alexander had conquered Persia. He and his war-weary army returned to Babylon in 323 B.C. When Alexander, one of the greatest military leaders in history, returned to Babylon, history tells us he sat down and wept because there were no more territories to conquer. He died in Babylon in 323 B.C. at the age of 33.

Because Alexander the Great died without an appointed heir, his kingdom fell into chaos. After 22 years of struggle among his generals, it was divided among four of them: Lysimachus, Cassander, Ptolemy I Soter, and Seleucus I Nicator. (See chart on next page.)

Under the Ptolemies of Egypt
(323 to 204 B.C.)

Ptolemy I Soter, who took Egypt, was given Jerusalem and Judea. The Jews fared well; they were allowed to govern themselves and practice their religion without interference. Under his leadership Jews were permitted to go to Egypt. Some Jews were invited to go to Alexandria and become scholars. The Ptolemies moved Egypt's capital from Memphis to Alexandria and made it the center of learning and commerce. There

The Division of Alexander the Great's Empire

Lysimachus	**Cassander**	**Ptolemy I Soter**	**Seleucus I Nicator**
took	took	took	took
Thrace and Bithynia	Macedonia	Egypt	Syria

*Ptolemy I Soter and Seleucus I Nicator began a succession
of competing dynasties for which the land of Israel became a pawn.*

(see page 1524 for the chart showing these dynasties)

the Jews were encouraged to use the Greek library, at that time the most extensive and best in the world. As a result many were caught up in philosophy and logic and drank deeply from the cup of Hellenism.

It is believed that Ptolemy II Philadelphus commissioned the translation of the Pentateuch into the Koine Greek. The Greek translation of the entire Old Testament, eventually completed about 100 B.C., was referred to as the **Septuagint** (meaning 70), or abbreviated as the **LXX**. Many of the New Testament writers quoted from the Septuagint.

Other writings produced during this intertestament period are the **Apocrypha**, the **Pseudepigrapha**, and the **Qumran Scrolls** (also called the **Dead Sea Scrolls**). The **Apocrypha** are composed of a variety of writings, including apocalyptic, wisdom, and historical literature. It is from the apocryphal book of First Maccabees that historians gained insight into the period from the Maccabean revolt through the time of John Hyrcanus. The Apocrypha were included in the Septuagint, although they were not part of the Hebrew Scriptures.

The **Pseudepigrapha** are a collection of writings even more extensive than the Apocrypha, but scholars cannot entirely agree on which writings comprise this group. These writings are attributed to noted people such as Adam, Abraham, Enoch, Ezra, and Baruch—but scholars agree that these claims are not authentic.

The **Qumran** or **Dead Sea Scrolls** were manuscripts apparently written or copied between 200 B.C. and A.D. 70 by a Jewish religious sect called **Essenes**. The particular community of Essenes who lived close to the Dead Sea seem to have practiced celibacy and a strictly disciplined communal lifestyle, separating themselves from others. The Dead Sea Scrolls describe the lives and beliefs of this group which lived in the last two centuries before Christ; they also include the oldest known manuscripts of the Old Testament. The scrolls are so named because they were hidden and preserved in some caves near an archaeological excavation called Khirbet Qumran on the western side of the Dead Sea.

Under the Seleucid Kings of Syria (204 to 165 B.C.)

Those ruling Syria, referred to as the kings of the north in Daniel 11, wanted the beautiful land of Israel. When Antiochus III the Great conquered Ptolemy V Epiphanes of Egypt, Jerusalem and Judea were brought under Syrian dominance.

During this period the land of Israel was sectored into Judea, Samaria, Galilee, Perea, and Trachonitis (see map on next page).

After gaining dominance over the Jews, Antiochus was defeated by the Romans and ended up having to pay Rome a large sum of money for a period of years. To make sure he complied, Rome held his son, Antiochus IV, hostage in Rome.

Antiochus III the Great was succeeded by his son Seleucus IV Philopator, who ruled from 187-175 B.C. In 175 B.C. Antiochus IV Epiphanes (the son who had been held hostage in Rome) usurped the throne by killing his brother. He ruled until 163 B.C. He was called *Epiphanes*, which means "manifest" or "splendid."

Until this period in Israel's history, the priesthood had been a matter of birthright and the office was held for life. However, during his reign Antiochus IV Epiphanes sold the priesthood to Jason, the brother of the high priest. Jason also paid Antiochus a high price in order to build a Greek gymnasium near the temple. During this time many Jews were lured into a Hellenistic way of life. All this brought a great conflict among the orthodox Jews and the "Hellenistic" Jews.

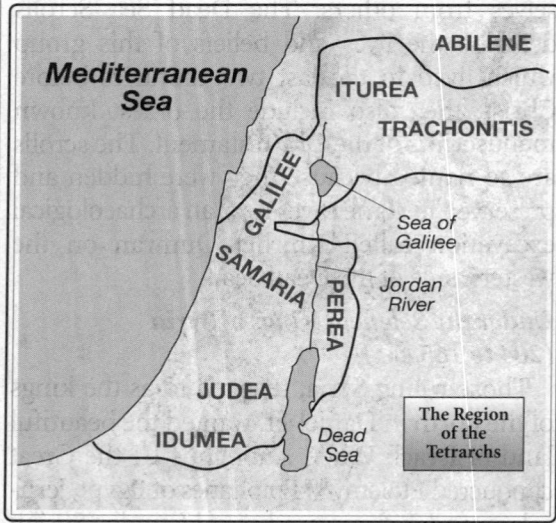

The conflict was heightened when Antiochus IV Epiphanes sought to take the throne of Egypt but was rebuffed by Rome. Because of that and because of what he surmised as a revolt in the priesthood, Antiochus unleashed his anger on those Jews who wouldn't curry his favor or fully adopt Hellenism. He was determined to destroy Judaism. Circumcision was forbidden; those who disobeyed were put to death. Copies of the law were desecrated with heathen symbols or burned, while anyone found with a copy of the law was to be put to death. The Jews were also forbidden to celebrate the Sabbath. Then Antiochus sacrificed a pig on the altar in the temple and erected a statue of Zeus, the abomination that causes desolation, in the holy place (Daniel 11:31).

Finally, Antiochus sent his officers throughout the land to compel Jews to make sacrifices to Zeus.

The Maccabean Period
(165 to 63 B.C.)

When Antiochus IV Epiphanes' officer arrived in the village of Modein (which lies halfway between Jerusalem and Joppa) and commanded the aged priest Mattathias to make a sacrifice to Zeus, the officer didn't know it was the last official duty he would perform in his life. As Mattathias refused, a younger Jew stepped forward to take his place. When he did, a furious Mattathias plunged his knife not only into the Jewish volunteer but also into the Syrian officer. Mattathias fled with his five sons to the hills...and the Maccabean revolt, led by Mattathias's third son, nicknamed Maccabeus (the Hammerer), began.

Three years after Antiochus IV Epiphanes defiled the temple, the Jews recaptured Jerusalem. They removed the statue of Zeus and refurbished the temple and reinstituted Jewish sacrifices. On December 25 the Jews celebrated with the Feast of Dedication (John 10:22), which from then on became the annual feast of lights or Hanukkah. (See Herod's Temple on page IISB-38.)

Thus began what is referred to as the **Hasmonean Dynasty** as the descendants of Mattathias ruled Israel until Rome conquered Jerusalem in 63 B.C.

When Simon, the last surviving son of Mattathias, was murdered, Simon's son, John Hyrcanus, named himself priest and king. He ruled from 134-104 B.C. He destroyed the Samaritan temple on Mount Gerizim, and from that time on the Jews had no dealings with the Samaritans. After that Hyrcanus moved southeast and conquered the land of the Idumeans, who came from the ancient kingdom of Edom. The peoples of this land were given the choice of emigrating or converting to Judaism. This was the land of Herod the Great, who would someday become Rome's appointed king of the Jews.

During the reign of John Hyrcanus, the **Pharisees**, a religious sect of the Jews, arose from the Hasidim. The **Hasidim**, a militant religious community dedicated to the obedience of the law and the worship of God, began around 168 B.C. and was active during the Maccabean revolt. The word *Pharisee* means "separated one" and was probably used to describe these men because they separated themselves from the strong influence of Hellenism. During New Testament times the majority of the scribes were Pharisees.

Doctrinally the Pharisees viewed the entire Old Testament as authoritative; however, they also accepted the oral tradition as equally authoritative. To the Pharisee, to study the law was true worship. They believed in life after death, the resurrection, and the existence of angels and demons. Although the Pharisees taught that the way to God was through keeping the law, they were more liberal in their interpretation of the law than were the Sadducees. The Pharisees represented the largest religious sect, but their numbers declined when they fell into John Hyrcanus' disfavor.

The **Sadducees**, a smaller religious sect comprised mostly of the upper classes, were often of the priestly line and were usually more wealthy than the Pharisees. For the most part the Pharisees were of the middle-class merchants and tradesmen. The Sadducees accepted only the **Torah** (the first five books of the Old Testament) as authoritative. While they were rigid in the observance of the law and held to its literal interpretation, they denied divine providence,

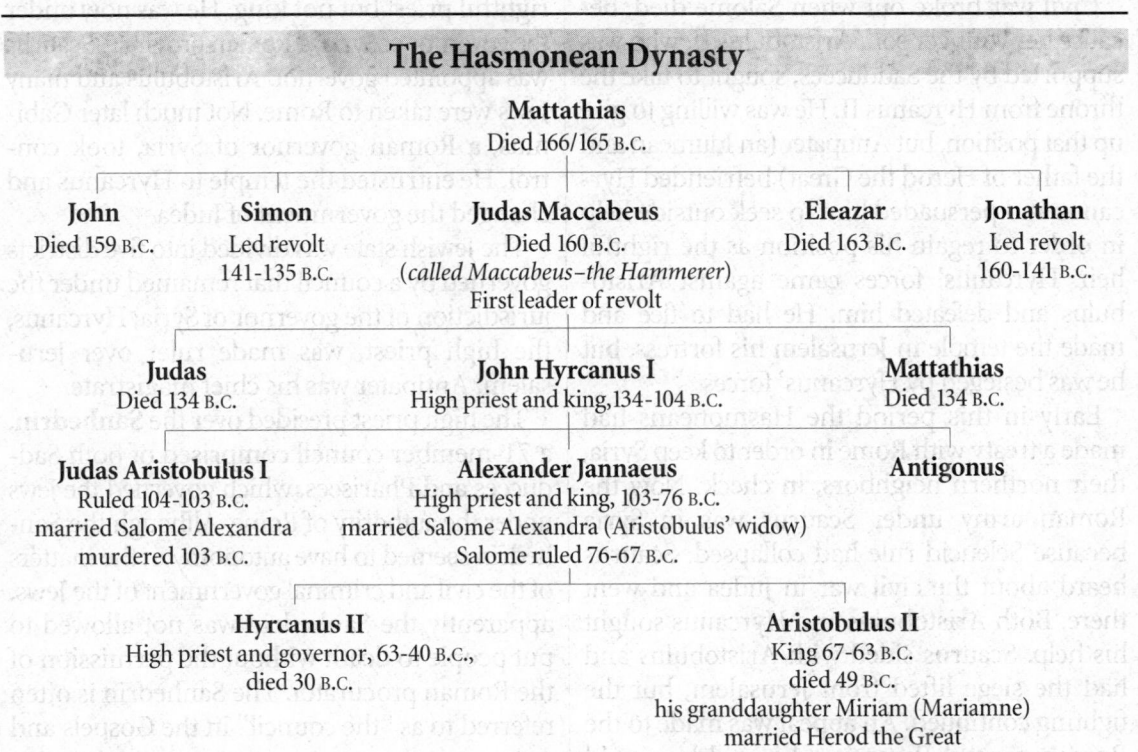

The Hasmonean Dynasty

Mattathias
Died 166/165 B.C.

John	**Simon**	**Judas Maccabeus**	**Eleazar**	**Jonathan**
Died 159 B.C.	Led revolt 141-135 B.C.	Died 160 B.C. *(called Maccabeus–the Hammerer)* First leader of revolt	Died 163 B.C.	Led revolt 160-141 B.C.

Judas	**John Hyrcanus I**	**Mattathias**
Died 134 B.C.	High priest and king, 134-104 B.C.	Died 134 B.C.

Judas Aristobulus I	**Alexander Jannaeus**	**Antigonus**
Ruled 104-103 B.C. married Salome Alexandra murdered 103 B.C.	High priest and king, 103-76 B.C. married Salome Alexandra (Aristobulus' widow) Salome ruled 76-67 B.C.	

Hyrcanus II	**Aristobulus II**
High priest and governor, 63-40 B.C., died 30 B.C.	King 67-63 B.C. died 49 B.C. his granddaughter Miriam (Mariamne) married Herod the Great

the resurrection, life after death, the existence of angels and demons, and any reward or punishment after death. They opposed the oral law as obligatory or binding and were materialistic.

The Sadducees controlled the temple and its services. However, because the Sadducees leaned toward Hellenism, they were unpopular with the majority of the Jewish populace.

Aristobulus I, who succeeded his father, John Hyrcanus, married Salome Alexandra. However, when Aristobulus died, Salome married his brother Alexander Jannaeus, who became high priest and king in 103 B.C. This marriage created many enemies for Alexander Jannaeus because the high priest was to marry only a virgin.

When he died in 76 B.C., his wife, Salome Alexandra, took the throne, but as a woman she could not hold the office of high priest, so her oldest son, Hyrcanus II, assumed that position.

Civil war broke out when Salome died, because her younger son, Aristobulus II, who was supported by the Sadducees, sought to take the throne from Hyrcanus II. He was willing to give up that position, but Antipater (an Idumean and the father of Herod the Great) befriended Hyrcanus and persuaded him to seek outside help in order to regain his position as the rightful heir. Hyrcanus' forces came against Aristobulus and defeated him. He had to flee and made the temple in Jerusalem his fortress, but he was besieged by Hyrcanus' forces.

Early in this period the Hasmoneans had made a treaty with Rome in order to keep Syria, their northern neighbors, in check. Now the Roman army under Scaurus was in Syria because Seleucid rule had collapsed. Scaurus heard about the civil war in Judea and went there. Both Aristobulus and Hyrcanus sought his help. Scaurus sided with Aristobulus and had the siege lifted from Jerusalem, but the fighting continued. An appeal was made to the Roman general Pompey, who said he would settle the dispute and urged them to keep peace until he arrived. However, Aristobulus went back to Jerusalem to prepare resistance, which caused Rome's support to turn to Hyrcanus. Pompey arrived and took Aristobulus and his family captive, besieging the city for three months.

The Period of Roman Rule
(63 B.C. to A.D. 70)

In 63 B.C. Pompey conquered Jerusalem and with some of his soldiers walked into the Most Holy Place. Although they didn't touch any of the furnishings, they alienated the Jews, who never forgave Pompey. About 12,000 Jews died during this Roman siege of Jerusalem, a supposed attempt to settle a civil war.

Rome broke up the Hasmonean dynasty and their territory. Judea was now reduced to smaller borders and its independence lost. It was now a territory of Rome. Hyrcanus II could be the rightful priest but not king. He was now under the governor of Syria, a Roman province. Scaurus was appointed governor. Aristobulus and many Jews were taken to Rome. Not much later Gabinius, a Roman governor of Syria, took control. He entrusted the temple to Hyrcanus and changed the government of Judea.

The Jewish state was divided into five districts governed by a council that remained under the jurisdiction of the governor of Syria; Hyrcanus, the high priest, was made ruler over Jerusalem. Antipater was his chief magistrate.

The high priest presided over the **Sanhedrin**, a 71-member council comprised of both Sadducees and Pharisees, which governed the Jews under the authority of Rome. Although the Sanhedrin seemed to have autonomy in the matters of the civil and criminal government of the Jews, apparently the Sanhedrin was not allowed to put people to death without the permission of the Roman procurator. The Sanhedrin is often referred to as "the council" in the Gospels and Acts.

In 55 B.C. three men—Pompey, Crassus (the governor of Syria), and Julius Caesar—controlled Rome. Crassus, considering himself another Alexander the Great, set out to conquer the world. However, just before this he stole the treasures from the temple in Jerusalem. Crassus and his army were later destroyed by the Parthians.

Parthia, southeast of the Caspian Sea and part of the Persian Empire, had been conquered by Alexander the Great. But Rome would not conquer them until A.D. 114.

After Crassus' death, Julius Caesar took Italy and then set out to destroy Pompey. Pompey fled to Egypt, where he was assassinated. During this time Antipater supported Caesar, so out of gratitude Caesar gave him the official title of Procurator of Judea.

Antipater made his son Phasael governor of Judea and his son Herod governor of Galilee. Hyrcanus II remained high priest, although Antipater and his two sons robbed him of his authority.

In 44 B.C. Caesar was murdered by Brutus and Cassius. Civil war broke out in Rome. Cassius took control of the east. Because of the instability of Rome, Hyrcanus' rivals made a bid for power.

Antipater was murdered in 43 B.C. Antigonus, Aristobulus' son (who was supported by the Parthians), invaded the country.

At that time Herod came to the aid of Hyrcanus, who out of gratitude gave Herod a beautiful woman named Miriam. They were not married until five years later.

After that Brutus and Cassius were defeated by Mark Antony and Caesar's nephew Octavian (who would later become Caesar Augustus). Mark Antony became ruler of the east. In 40 B.C., when the Parthians invaded Palestine, Herod fled to Rome.

That year, at the urging of Antony and Octavian, Herod was made king of the Jews. It took him three years to rid the area of the Parthians and establish his rule in Judea. Just before laying siege to Jerusalem, Herod married Miriam (also called Mariamne), hoping that his marriage into the Hasmonean family would make him more acceptable to the Jews.

In 20 B.C. Herod began rebuilding the temple. The one built by Zerubbabel after the Babylonian exile was so pitifully small in comparison to the first temple that Herod was determined to make it larger and more magnificent than Solomon's. Although the temple itself was completed in a year-and-a-half, the construction and decoration of its outer courts continued for years, so in A.D. 26 the Jews would say, "It has taken forty-six years to build this temple" (John 2:20).

Herod, whose people (the Idumeans) had been forced to convert to Judaism under John Hyrcanus, was only a Jew in practice when he lived in Judea. Although Rome gave Herod the title "King of the Jews," he was never accepted by those he ruled over.

Then "during the time of King Herod, Magi from the east came to Jerusalem and asked, 'Where is the one who has been born king of the Jews?'" (Matthew 2:1, 2).

The true King had come...the Ruler who would shepherd God's people Israel (Matthew 2:6).

Herod died in 4 B.C. But those living in Judea and Galilee saw a great light and heard with their own ears the voice of God, the King of kings.

The 400 years of silence had been broken.

FROM CHRIST TO MODERN TIMES

Many Jewish leaders were religious, but they did not know God. When Jesus came to explain the Father, they rejected Him. They rejected God's precious cornerstone. Consequently, once again they would be banished from their land. Jesus warned, "When you see Jerusalem surrounded by armies, you will know that its desolation is near. There will be great distress in the land and wrath against this people. They will fall by the sword and will be taken as prisoners to all the nations. Jerusalem will be trampled on by the Gentiles until the times of the Gentiles are fulfilled" (Luke 21:20, 23, 24). God had spoken. Had the people listened, they wouldn't have been caught unawares—but they refused to hear.

The Destruction of Jerusalem
(A.D. 70)

The conflict between the Jews and their Roman ruler intensified. Tacitus, the Roman historian, said the Jews put up with things until the procuratorship of Gessius Florus. When the Jews rose up against Florus' army, war became inevitable. Nero commanded T. Flavius Vespasian to subdue the Jews. Vespasian reduced northern Palestine and secured the rest of the country, except for Jerusalem, Masada, and two other fortresses.

During this time, Nero committed suicide and civil war broke out in Rome. Galba, Otho, and Vitellius succeeded one another as emperor. Then the eastern legions of Rome proclaimed Vespasian emperor, and Vitellius was murdered. Vespasian put his son Titus in charge of the war and sailed for Rome. In A.D. 70 Titus besieged Jerusalem. Over one million Jews died in five months. On August 6, Roman forces invaded the temple and, just as Jesus prophesied, not one stone was left upon the other. Jerusalem was burned. Titus went to Rome to celebrate his victory with his father.

Although some of the Jews fled to Masada, the Jewish state no longer existed. Sometime between A.D. 72-74 Masada fell to the Roman governor Flavius Silva.

Hadrian and Aelia Capitolina

In A.D. 132 the Emperor Hadrian banned circumcision and the observance of the Sabbath.

He also made plans to build a temple to Zeus. These actions spurred Simon bar Kochba to lead another revolt. After Hadrian crushed the Bar Kochba revolt, Hadrian rebuilt Jerusalem in A.D. 136, named it Aelia Capitolina, and forbade the Jews entrance to the city on pain of death. That edict was enforced for about 500 years.

The Byzantine Period
(A.D. 324 to 638)

In A.D. 324 Constantine became sole emperor of Rome. In A.D. 330 the capital was moved from Rome to Byzantium, which was renamed Constantinople (present-day Istanbul, Turkey) in his honor. According to tradition, Constantine became a Christian after seeing a vision of a cross and hearing the words, "By this sign thou shalt conquer." He proclaimed Christianity as the official religion of the Roman Empire.

Constantine's mother, the empress Helena, began restoring the city of David (Jerusalem), locating Christian sites and building shrines over the places associated with Christianity. Helena and the city's bishop, Macarius, built the Church of the Holy Sepulchre on the site where they believed Jesus had been buried. Byzantine churches could be seen across the land. By the fifth century the Roman Empire divided and the eastern half became the Byzantine Empire, with its capital in Constantinople. Rome became the capital of the western Roman Empire.

In the fifth century the Jews were permitted to pray on the temple mount on Tisha B'Av, the anniversary of the destruction of the temple. By the middle of this century Jerusalem was recognized as a patriarchal territory equal in status to Constantinople, Alexandria, Rome, and Antioch.

In A.D. 614 the Persians conquered the land, massacred the people, and destroyed the churches. In A.D. 629 the Byzantine emperor Heraclius reconquered Jerusalem.

The Early Muslim Period
(A.D. 638 to 1099)

Nine years later the Muslims were ruling. During this time Christians and Jews were permitted to worship freely. Jews returned to Jerusalem. The Umayyad dynasty reigned from 660-750. The prophet Mohammed's journey from Mecca to Jerusalem on his winged horse Al-buraq was linked to the temple mount, thus making it a holy site for the Muslims. In the seventh century, Caliph Abd al-Malik commissioned the building of the mosque, the Dome of the Rock, on the temple mount. Thus Jerusalem became the third-holiest city for Islam. The Arabs built only one new city, Ramle, which Suleiman made his capital in the eighth century.

The Crusader Period
(A.D. 1099 to 1244)

In 1099, at Pope Urban II's appeal, the Crusaders crossed Europe to liberate the Christian holy places from the Muslims. The city was theirs after a five-week siege. Jerusalem became the capital of the Crusader kingdom of Jerusalem. European Christian noblemen and bourgeoisie came to settle in Jerusalem. Mosques were turned into churches, and new churches and monasteries were built. For the next 88 years, Jews and Muslims were not permitted to live in Jerusalem, but only visit it.

The Ayyubid Interlude
(A.D. 1187 to 1192)

In 1187 Saladin, the founder of the Ayyubid dynasty, took Jerusalem, destroyed the cross on top of the Dome of the Rock, and turned churches into mosques. The Jews were now allowed to return to Jerusalem. They came from North Africa, France, and England to settle alongside the Jews of Jerusalem.

Then in 1192 Richard the Lion Hearted and Phillipe Auguste of France restored the Crusader kingdom which had been conquered by Saladin. Jerusalem was divided. The temple mount and its mosques remained in Muslim hands while the other parts of the city came under Christian rule. In 1244 the Crusaders lost the city.

The Mamluk Period
(A.D. 1260 to 1517)

In 1260 Jerusalem was conquered by the Mamluks, military regiments from central Asia who were the new rulers of Egypt. The Mamluks established **madrasas** (institutes of religious instruction) and hostels for Muslim scholars and pilgrims.

The Ottoman Period
(A.D. 1517 to 1917)

The Ottoman Empire, comprised of Constantinople, Asia Minor, parts of Europe and the Balkans, Egypt, and Syria, added Palestine in 1517. Jerusalem was taken from the Mamluks by Ottoman Turks. Sultan Suleiman the Magnificent had the walls which still surround Jerusalem built at this time. After his death the Jewish community became more firmly entrenched as they built the Jewish quarter along the Zion Gate. Jewish scholastic centers were established in Jerusalem and Safed. The Christians split into various eastern communities.

In 1832 the Pasha of Egypt, Mohammed Ali, denuded the Holy Land of trees as he set out to build his ships. However, his approval of Christian missions and schools, foreign consulates, and archaeological expeditions opened up Jerusalem to Western influence. In the late 1800s a political movement called Zionism sprang up in Europe. Its goal was to create a homeland for Jewish people in Palestine. Jews fleeing eastern Europe and Russia and arriving in Abraham's land were quick to adopt Theodor Herzl's vision for a free state for Jews. In 1897, the first Zionist Congress was held.

The British Mandate
(A.D. 1917 to 1948)

Four hundred years of Ottoman rule came to an end on December 9, 1917. Two days later British Field Marshal Allenby entered the Citadel and Jerusalem was pronounced the capital of the country. The Balfour Declaration promised the establishment of a national home for the Jews. In 1920 and 1929 Jews and Arabs had violent clashes. The Arabs rebelled in 1936-1939, and open war erupted as Arabs and Jews fought for control over Jerusalem.

From 1939 to 1945 six million Jews were systematically murdered under the direction of Adolf Hitler. After World War II, world opinion strongly favored the establishment of a Jewish homeland. By November 1947 the tension between Jews and Arabs was so great the United Nations decided to intervene, end the Mandate, and make Jerusalem an international city. The United Nations voted 33 to 13 to partition Palestine west of the Jordan River into two parts—one for Arabs, one for Jews. The Jews agreed, but the Arabs rejected the plan.

The State of Israel
(May 14, 1948)

On May 14, 1948, when the British withdrew, the Jews proclaimed the independent State of Israel. The next day Israel was attacked by Iraq, Lebanon, Syria, Jordan, and Egypt. By December Israel won its independence. Jordanian soldiers, however, remained in the West Bank (biblical Judea and Samaria). Egypt held the Gaza Strip. When a cease-fire was declared in January 1949, the city was divided. Jordan held all the shrines encompassed by Suleiman's walls; the old city of Jerusalem was out-of-bounds for the Jews.

Israel prepared for the influx of more than 800,000 immigrants from 102 countries during the next seven years. Living conditions were austere, but the Jews were home! By 1957 the malarial swamps of the Hula Valley were drained and the waters of the Sea of Galilee flowed south through pipelines, bringing life to the arid Negev.

The Sinai Campaign
(1956)

In 1956 Israel executed a swift victory over Egypt in the Sinai Campaign. On the guarantee of freedom of navigation in the Straits of Tiran and the Gulf of Elath, Israel withdrew her troops from the Sinai. Then later, once again, Egyptian troops moved to Israel's borders.

The Six-Day War
(1967)

The Six-Day War broke out on June 5, 1967. During that war Israel occupied Judea, Samaria, and Gaza, took the Golan Heights, and reunited Jerusalem under Jewish sovereignty for the first time since the Bar Kochba revolt, more than 1800 years earlier. The Jews could finally weep at the holy wall of Jerusalem, the wall of the sacred temple mount.

The Yom Kippur War
(1973)

In 1973, on Yom Kippur, the highest of holy days, Israel was attacked on Syrian and Egyptian fronts. After three weeks the Israeli defense forces finally drove the attackers back. Disengagement agreements were signed between Israel and Egypt and between Israel and Syria.

The Peace Treaty Between Israel and Egypt
(1979)

In March of 1979 Israel and Egypt signed a historic peace treaty returning the Sinai to Egypt.

On June 6, 1982, Israel launched Operation Peace for Galilee in order to remove from Lebanese territory the Palestine Liberation Organization's threat to its northern settlements.

The Middle East Gulf War
(1991)

In January 1991, when war broke out between Iraq and a coalition of nations headed by the United States of America, Iraq responded with missile attacks on Israel—although Israel was not part of the conflict and remained out of the conflict at the United States's urging. The Middle East Gulf Crisis came to an end approximately six weeks later.

The words of Zechariah the prophet remain unfulfilled, but because of all that is transpiring, they are read with new insight and great anticipation:

A day of the LORD is coming when your plunder will be divided among you. I will gather all the nations to Jerusalem to fight against it; the city will be captured, the houses ransacked, and the women raped.

Half of the city will go into exile, but the rest of the people will not be taken from the city. Then the LORD will go out and fight against those nations, as he fights on the day of battle.

On that day his feet will stand on the Mount of Olives, east of Jerusalem, and the Mount of Olives will be split in two from east to west, forming a great valley, with half of the mountain moving north and half moving south....

Then the LORD my God will come, and all the holy ones with him...

The LORD will be king over the whole earth. On that day there will be one LORD, and his name the only name (Zechariah 14:1-5, 9).

Amen. Come, Lord Jesus (Revelation 22:20).

HISTORICAL AND GRAMMATICAL HELPS

The information in this section will provide you with additional tools for your inductive study of God's Word.

Take some time to familiarize yourself with the basic content of each part of this section so you will know what is at your fingertips when you need it.

THE ARK OF THE COVENANT

The one piece of furniture that is the most holy to the Jews is the ark of the covenant. The following information will help you understand why it is so important to them and why Orthodox Jews are still looking for it.

The ark, a box approximately 4 feet long by 2 1/2 feet wide by 2 1/2 feet high, was constructed of acacia wood and overlaid with gold inside and out. Because it symbolized God's presence, no one was allowed to touch it. Four gold rings were attached to the feet of the ark. Poles, made of acacia wood and overlaid with gold, were slipped through these rings so that the ark could be carried from place to place (Exodus 25:10-22). Only the Kohathites (a division of the Levites) were allowed to move the ark.

When the ark was in the tabernacle the cloud of God's presence hovered over the atonement cover (Leviticus 16:2; 1 Samuel 4:4). The atonement cover, made of pure gold with a gold cherub attached at each end, covered the ark of the covenant. On the Day of Atonement the high priest sprinkled the blood of sacrifice on the atonement cover as a covering for the sins of the people.

Inside the ark was the Testimony, the stone tablets bearing the ten commandments (Exodus 40:20; Deuteronomy 10:2). For a period of time the ark also contained Aaron's rod which budded (Numbers 17:10) and a gold jar of manna (Hebrews 9:4).

The tabernacle, where the ark resided in the Most Holy Place, and the furniture were made according to the pattern of God's throne in heaven. God gave Moses this pattern when he instructed him to build the tabernacle (Hebrews 8:1-5).

The ark journeyed before the children of Israel as they moved from Sinai to Canaan. It went before them as they crossed the Jordan River and conquered Jericho. It rested at Gilgal, Shechem, Bethel, and Shiloh. Then the Philistines at Ebenezer captured it and kept it for seven months. They took it to Aphek, Ashdod, Gath, and Ekron. From Ekron it went to Beth Shemesh. It was at Beth Shemesh that 50,070 people were killed because they looked into the ark. From there the ark was taken to Kiriath Jearim (Gibeath) and the house of Abinadab, where it remained for 20 years.

When David became king he wanted to move the ark to Jerusalem. The Israelites broke God's command by moving it on a cart rather than carrying it by the poles. When the ark started to fall off the cart, a man named Uzzah touched the ark and was killed by God. This incident occurred on the threshing floor of Nacon (also referred to as Kidon) (2 Samuel 6:6, 7; 1 Chronicles 13:9). The ark remained in the house of Obed-Edom the Gittite, a Philistine from Gath, for three months until David had the Kohathites move it to Jerusalem. There the ark was placed in the midst of a tent (2 Chronicles 1:4).

When Solomon became king and built the temple, the ark was moved from the tent in Jerusalem to the temple, which was built on the threshing floor of Araunah (Ornan) (1 Chronicles 21:18; 2 Chronicles 3:1). There the ark was placed in the Most Holy Place (1 Kings 8:6; 2 Chronicles 5:2-14).

There is no record of the whereabouts or fate of the ark since the destruction of the temple by the Babylonians in 586 B.C.

The last mention of the ark is in Revelation 11:19: "Then God's temple in heaven was opened, and within his temple was seen the ark of his covenant. And there came flashes of lightning, rumblings, peals of thunder, an earthquake and a great hailstorm."

UNDERSTANDING GNOSTICISM

Much like the church today, many members of the early church were significantly influenced by the prevailing philosophy of the day. While some of the New Testament was being written, the church in Asia was being threatened by gnosticism, a philosophy which became the major opponent of the gospel in the early apostolic church.

A familiarity with the teachings of gnosticism will give you a greater understanding of and appreciation for some of the warnings and teachings given in the epistles.

Many members of the early church were seeking enlightenment, and were easily deceived by Gnostic teachers and led astray from the simplicity and purity of devotion to Christ. Some had apparently left the church to form their own community, teaching a different gospel from what the apostles had preached. This movement away from the church caused those who remained to question what was true, and thus confusion crept in.

The term *gnosticism* comes from the Greek word *gnōsis*, meaning "knowledge." Gnosticism is a philosophy which centers on a search for higher knowledge. The Gnostics taught that this knowledge was not intellectual knowledge but a knowledge which the ordinary Christian was incapable of attaining. Once a believer came into possession of this extraordinary knowledge, according to Gnostic thought, he had "salvation."

Although Gnostic philosophy took many strange and divergent turns, two axioms were basic to its teaching:

ᔣ *The first major Gnostic doctrine was the supremacy of knowledge.*

Certain *pneumatikoi* or "spiritual ones" claimed to have special knowledge of the truth.

Ordinary Christians did not or could not possess this secret of higher knowledge.

❧ *The second major doctrine of gnosticism was the separation of spirit and matter.*

All matter was considered to be evil and the source of evil.

The spirit was considered to be good and impervious to defilement by anything the body (matter) did.

Claiming a so-called higher knowledge beyond that revealed by God in Christ Jesus and through the prophets, gnosticism had its origins in the philosophies of the Greeks and the Romans, in the creeds of Plato and Philo, and in the religions of the East, especially those of Persia and India. As long as Christianity kept its Judaic roots, it was free from these heresies. However, when Christianity spread to Gentile territory, an attempt was made on the part of Eastern philosophical religion to form an alliance with it.

Many Gnostics allegorized the Old Testament and did not interpret its teachings literally. They strayed from the veracity of the Word, which would have exposed their erroneous teaching regarding creation, sin, and the restoration of all things. They failed to see how a supreme God, pure in spirit and essentially good, could create a universe of matter which they considered evil.

When the Gnostics embraced Christianity, they split into factions on the subject of Christ's deity. Two of the major factions taught as follows:

❧ The Docetic Gnostics denied the humanity of Jesus. The word *docetic* comes from the Greek word *dokeō*, "to seem." According to the Docetists, it was impossible for God, who was spirit and good, to become flesh, which was matter and evil, in the person of Jesus Christ. They believed that Jesus was a phantom; He didn't possess a real flesh-and-blood body. He only seemed to have a body.

❧ The Cerinthian Gnostics (followers of Cerinthus) separated the man Jesus from the *aeon*,

the power of Christ. They believed that when the dove came on Jesus at his baptism, the power of Christ came and rested on the man Jesus. This power then departed before his death on the cross. So it was simply the "man" Jesus who died, not Jesus Christ, God in the flesh.

These Gnostic heresies denied that God became man and walked this earth in the person of Jesus Christ to bring redemption and salvation to mankind. Having eliminated Jesus Christ as the only way to God, the Gnostics believed they could make their own way to God through their inquiry and knowledge. Faith and one's deeds were viewed as having no significance in salvation or the life of a believer.

Understanding the basis of gnosticism and the forms of thought that it took in the early days of the Christian church will enable you to better understand the doctrinal heresy which some of the New Testament writers addressed.

GUIDELINES FOR INTERPRETING PREDICTIVE PROPHECY

From Genesis to Revelation the Bible is filled with prophecy. If you want to handle the prophecies in the Word of God accurately, the following guidelines will give you some important parameters.

The Greek word for prophecy, *prophēteía*, comes from two Greek words, *pró*, meaning "forth," and *phēmi*, meaning "to speak." It means to speak forth the mind and counsel of God. According to this definition, all Scripture is in a sense prophecy.

Predictive prophecy points to a future fulfillment and is of divine origin. In *Understanding and Applying the Bible*, Dr. Robertson McQuilkin says: "There are two purposes for predictive prophecy. The chief purpose is to affect the conduct of those who hear the prophecy. Another purpose is met only when the prophecy is fulfilled. That purpose is to build faith, to establish confidence in the God who miraculously foretold events (John 13:19; 14:29; 16:4)" (p. 215).

Some scholars divide predictive prophecy into two categories: forthtelling and foretelling. Forthtelling prophecies contain a message about the present or immediate time. (Often this is a call to godly living in the light of prophecy yet to be fulfilled.) Foretelling prophecies contain a message about what God will do in the future.

When a prophet spoke for God, the prophecy could refer to the following:

- a present or near fulfillment
- a future fulfillment
- a twofold fulfillment: a near fulfillment and then a later, future fulfillment

As you read the prophecies of the Bible, keep in mind the following guidelines and discern whether the prophecy refers to:

- the prophet's own time and/or a future time
- the captivity and/or restoration of Israel or Judah
- the first coming of Christ and any events connected with it
- the second coming of Christ
- the last days or end times

꙰ As you study prophecy, it is important to remember that the prophets did not always indicate intervals of time between events, nor did they always write their prophecies in chronological order. For example, an Old Testament prophecy could include the first and second comings of Christ without any indication of the time span between the two comings. One such prophecy is found in Isaiah 65:17-25. In this prophecy, Isaiah first talks about the new heavens and the new earth (in which we know there is no death), and then in verses 18-25 he refers to a time when a youth dies at age 100 and the wolf and lamb feed together. Chronologically, verse 17 will be fulfilled *after* verses 18-25 become a reality.

꙰ Always approach a prophecy as literal (in its usual, ordinary meaning) unless one of the following occurs:

- The grammatical context shows that it is figurative language by the use of similes, metaphors, parables, allegories, symbols, or types.
- A literal interpretation violates common sense, is contrary to what the author is saying, or is contrary to what the rest of Scripture teaches.

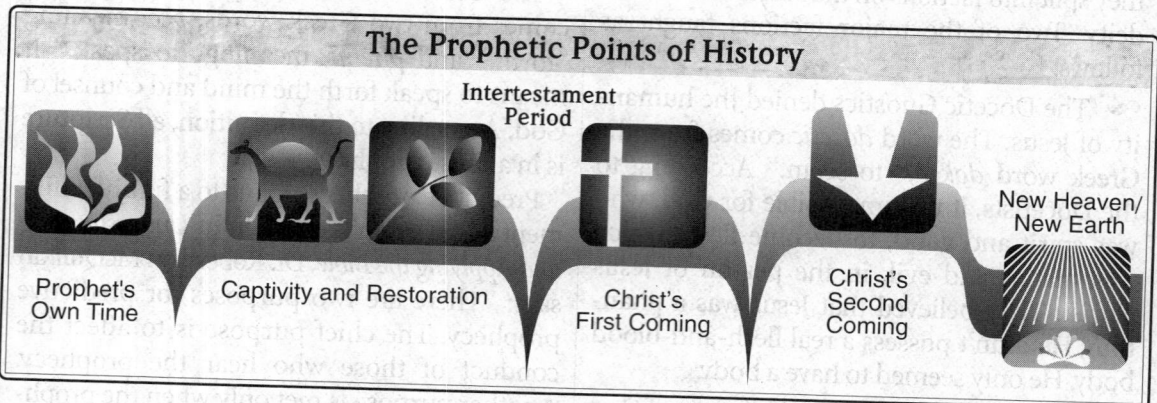

The Prophetic Points of History

Prophet's Own Time

Captivity and Restoration

Intertestament Period

Christ's First Coming

Christ's Second Coming

New Heaven/ New Earth

❧ *When a prophetic passage cannot be taken literally, look for what the author is trying to convey through his figurative or symbolic language.* To discern what the author is saying, look for answers in the following places:

- within the context of the book in which the passage appears
- in any other writings of that author
- in any other prophetic writings to which the author had access (for example, other prophetic books or passages in the Word of God)

❧ *Remember that often when a prophet refers to future events, he does not use the future tense.*

❧ *When you interpret Scripture, consider the historical context of that writing, remembering that God was delivering his prophecy to a particular people at a particular time.* Granted, it might have been a prophecy with a future fulfillment, but it would still be delivered in a way that was comprehensible to those receiving that prophecy—even though they might not understand the details, the symbolism, or the full implications of the prophecy.

Make a careful historical and cultural analysis of the text. Determine the identity of all historical events, proper names, and geographical locations before you attempt to interpret the text.

❧ *Remember that the meaning of a specific prophecy could not always be understood by the prophet or by the people who heard the message.* For example, Daniel could not understand what he had written, since it was to remain sealed until the time of the end (Daniel 12:8, 9).

However, many prophecies will come to light through the following:

a fulfillment as recorded in history

a fulfillment as recorded in the New Testament

an explanation given by an Old Testament

or a New Testament writing (for example, Acts 4:24-28)

❧ *Remember that many New Testament prophecies include Old Testament quotations and allusions.* Scholars estimate that at least 350 Old Testament quotations or allusions appear in the book of Revelation alone. Revelation is replete with the language of Isaiah, Jeremiah, Ezekiel, Daniel, and the minor prophets. It is obvious that the author of Revelation was steeped in the Old Testament, for he talks in Old Testament phraseology. So to correctly interpret New Testament prophecy, check Old Testament cross-references.

❧ *When you study prophecy, watch for phrases which indicate periods of time.* For example, look for *in the last days, day of the Lord, day of wrath,* and *end of the age.* When you come across phrases such as these, carefully observe the things which occur during that particular time period. Then ask the following questions:

- Have these events ever occurred in history?
- Do these events coincide with any other particular period of time?
- Do these events parallel any events mentioned in another place in the Word of God?

FIGURES OF SPEECH

Although the Bible is to be interpreted literally, it is important to remember that, as with other writings, it contains figures of speech which must be interpreted for what they are and in the light of their intended purpose. As you seek to handle the Word of God accurately, you will find it helpful to understand the definitions of the different types of figures of speech.

A *figure of speech* is a word, a phrase, or an expression used in an imaginative rather than a literal sense.

Discerning the use of figures of speech is important in biblical interpretation. For example, there has been much controversy in the church over Jesus' statement regarding the bread at the Last Supper: "And he took bread, gave thanks and broke it, and gave it to them, saying, 'This is my body given for you'" (Luke 22:19). Some believe that the bread actually becomes his body (the doctrine of transubstantiation); others believe that Jesus was simply using a metaphor and that the bread is representative of his body.

Three principles for dealing with figurative language are:

• Identify the fact that the author is using figurative language.

• Identify the type of figurative language in use: simile, metaphor, hyperbole, and so on.

• Follow the guidelines for interpreting what the author meant by his use of that particular figure of speech.

You will be aided in your study of Scripture if you are able to identify when the author is using a figure of speech. The following are brief definitions of the types of figurative language used in the Bible.

❧ A *metaphor* is an implied comparison between two things which are different. In a metaphor the words of comparison—*like, as, as…so is,* and *such as*—are *not* used. An example is John 6:48, where Jesus says, "I am the bread of life."

❧ A *simile* is an expressed comparison of two different things or ideas that uses the words *like, as, as…so is,* and/or *such as.* An example is Revelation 1:14b, "his eyes were like blazing fire."

❧ *Hyperbole* is a deliberate exaggeration for effect or emphasis. Hyperboles are found in all languages, and they are frequently used among Semitic peoples. For example, "My soul is consumed with longing" (Psalm 119:20).

❧ *Metonymy* is used when the name of one object or concept is used for that of another to which it is related. This is a figure of association. An example of a metonymy is found in the statement, "The whole Judean countryside and all the people of Jerusalem went out to him." The metonymy is country, which refers to the people rather than the region itself. Note also the hyperbole, *all* the people of Jerusalem.

❧ *Synecdoche* is another figure of association where the whole can refer to the part or the part to the whole. This is often found in the use of the term *the law,* which can refer to the Pentateuch (the first five books of the Old Testament), the ten commandments, or the whole Old Testament.

A synecdoche can also be a singular for a plural or a plural for a singular. An example is in Jeremiah 25:29. God says He is going to call down "a sword upon all who live on the earth." The singular sword represents many swords.

❧ In *personification* an object is given characteristics or attributes that belong to people—for example, when the trees clap their hands and the mountains sing for joy (Isaiah 55:12).

❧ *Irony* is a statement which says the opposite of what is meant. Irony is used for emphasis or effect. When it is not easy to discern if a statement is ironic, then examine it first as a true statement. As such, does it make sense in its context? Second, examine it as figurative irony. If this makes sense and fits with the context, then accept it as irony. Otherwise, treat it as a truth.

Here are two examples of irony:

1. In 1 Kings 22:1-23, a true prophet tells the king what he wants to hear, but it is a lie. It's obvious he is using irony because the king tells him to stop prophesying falsely and to tell the truth.

2. In 1 Corinthians 4:8 Paul says to the Corinthians, "Already you have all you want! Already you have become rich! You have become kings—and that without us! How I wish that you really had become kings so that we might be kings with you." When you read this, it is

obvious the Corinthians are not kings, nor does Paul desire to reign with them.

Parables

A parable is a story which, although not usually factual, remains true to life and teaches a moral lesson or truth. Every detail of a parable will reinforce the main theme, but you shouldn't always attempt to ascribe a specific spiritual meaning and application to each point.

Jesus frequently used parables in his teaching for two reasons: to reveal truth to believers and to hide truth from those who had rejected it and/or hardened their hearts against it.

To correctly interpret a parable:

• *Determine the occasion of the parable.* Since parables clarify or emphasize a truth, discover why the parable was told. What prompted it?

• *Look for the intended meaning of the parable.* The meaning will sometimes be stated. If not, it can usually be determined by the application of the parable to the hearer.

• *Don't impose any meaning beyond what is clearly stated or applied to the hearers by the speaker of the parable.*

• *Identify the central or focal idea of the parable.* Every parable has one central theme or emphasis. No detail of the story is to be given any meaning that is independent of the main teaching of the parable.

Since a parable has one central point of emphasis, identify relevant details. To attach meaning that is not in the context of the occasion or relevant to its central emphasis is to go away from the meaning of the parable. A detail is relevant only if it reinforces the central theme of the parable.

How many sermons have you heard on the parable of the prodigal son? Many teachers violate the occasion and meaning of this parable, attaching all sorts of meanings to the details of this story. Jesus told this parable because he wanted the Pharisees to see what their hearts were like as they grumbled, "This man welcomes sinners and eats with them" (Luke 15:2). In order to make his point Jesus told three consecutive parables about three things which were lost: a sheep, a coin, and a son. In each of the parables Jesus uses the following words: *lost, found, sinner (sinned),*

Parable	Allegory
1. Has one central point.	1. Can have more than one central point.
2. Teaches one truth.	2. Can teach a number of truths.
3. Every relevant detail reinforces the central theme or point of emphasis.	3. The details of an allegory may be many and varied, relating to more than one theme.
4. Can have irrelevant details; all features of the parable do not have to be identified.	4. Can have irrelevant details; all the features of an allegory do not have to be identified.
5. Usually the story is separate from its interpretation and application.	5. Intertwines the story and the meaning.
6. Interpretation usually follows the parable.	6. Interpretation is found within the allegory.

and *rejoice (joyfully, rejoicing)*. When he gets to the story of the prodigal son, he shows them the kindness of the father's heart versus the hardness of the elder brother's, and in doing so, shows the Pharisees that their hearts are like the elder brother's, not the father's.

• *Interpret parables in the context of the culture of Bible times rather than the culture of today.* For example, in the parable of the wise and foolish virgins, the central emphasis of the parable is, "Therefore keep watch, because you do not know the day or the hour" (Matthew 25:13). Understanding Eastern wedding traditions would give insight into the parable and explain why some were ready and others were not.

• *Do not establish doctrine when parables are the primary or only source for that teaching.* Parables should amplify or affirm doctrine, not establish it.

Allegory

An *allegory* is a description of one thing using the image of another—a story with an underlying meaning different from the surface facts of the story itself. Some refer to an allegory as an extended metaphor, which is an implied comparison between two different things. An allegory is a realistic or nonrealistic story created to teach one or more truths which may or may not be related.

The chart below comparing parables and allegories will help you distinguish one from the other.

When interpreting an allegory, follow these guidelines:

• List the features of the allegory.

• Note any interpretation given within the text of the allegory.

• Study the allegory's features according to sound principles of biblical exegesis. Do not contradict the clear teaching of the Word of God by interpreting an unexplained detail in an allegory in a way contrary to other truths.

• Do not try to identify all the features of an allegory.

Types (Patterns)

A type or pattern is a prophetic symbol designated by God.

The word *type* (pattern) comes from the Greek word *tupos*. A *tupos* was a mark formed by a blow or an impression, creating a figure or an image on the object that was struck. Therefore, a type (pattern) prefigures something or someone to come. That which it prefigures is called an *antitype*.

A type (pattern) prefigures only one antitype, although it may parallel many points in the antitype. An illustration of this is the tabernacle, a type (pattern) of man's redemption. According to Hebrews 10:20, the curtain that separated the Holy Place from the Most Holy Place prefigured the body of Jesus Christ.

When determining types (patterns), although it may not be formally stated, there should be some evidence of divine affirmation of the corresponding type (pattern) and antitype. For example, in Romans 5:14 we read, "Nevertheless, death reigned from the time of Adam to the time of Moses, even over those who did not sin by breaking a command, as did Adam, who was a pattern of the one to come." The word translated *type* (pattern) is the Greek word *tupos*. Adam was a type (pattern) or figure of Christ, who was to come. In 1 Corinthians 15:45, Christ is referred to as "the last Adam." If the Word does not designate something as a type, then the Bible expositor should simply show the parallels without calling it a type.

Symbols

A symbol is a picture or an object that stands for or represents another thing. For example, the seven lampstands mentioned in Revelation 1:20 represent the seven churches described in Revelation 2 and 3.

When noting symbols it is important to remember the following:

• *The item used as a symbol can symbolize different things.* For example, water is used to symbolize the Word of God (Ephesians 5:26) and the Holy Spirit (John 7:37-39).

• *Although a symbol can represent many things, when it does symbolize something in a given passage, a single parallel is intended.* For instance, in John 7:37-39 water symbolizes the Holy Spirit, not the Word.

• *Interpret symbols in the light of a biblical setting and culture rather than the culture of the current interpreter.*

• *Symbols are timeless and can symbolize something past, present, or future.*

LAWS OF COMPOSITION

A literary composition is an arrangement of thoughts which conveys meaning to a reader. An understanding of the laws of composition will help you discern what the author is saying.

The following laws of composition can help you in your study of the Word of God.

1. **Comparison**—to compare in order to show similarities. A comparison is the association of like things.

2. **Contrast**—to compare in order to show differences. A contrast is the association of opposites.

3. **Repetition**—to use the same word or phrase a number of times.

4. **Progression**—to extend a specific theme throughout a portion of Scripture. Many times the author will amplify what he is saying as he progresses in his writing or adds to what he has said.

5. **Climax**—a high point built by a progression from the lesser to the greater. A climax is simply an extension of the law of progression until it reaches a peak of intensity.

6. **Pivotal point**—a changing or a turning so that the elements on each side of the point differ in some way. In the Gospel of John the pivotal point comes in 11:54, when Jesus turns from ministering mainly to the public to ministering to his disciples. (Read John 11:54.) In Genesis the pivotal point of the book comes in chapter 12, where Moses turns from recording major events to tell us of major characters.

7. **Radiation**—the central or single point from or to which other truths point. An illustration of this is 1 Corinthians 15, where the truths of that chapter all radiate to resurrection.

8. **Interchange**—to alternate, in sequence, at least two main thoughts, subjects, or characteristics. This is most apparent in the Gospel of Luke. Luke opens with the announcement of the birth of John the Baptist, then moves to the announcement of Jesus' birth. He then returns to John the Baptist's birth, then to the birth of Christ. This is alternation or interchange.

9. **General to particular (or vice versa)**—to move from the extensive or general to the specific or particular. This is beautifully seen in Genesis 1 and 2. Genesis 1 gives the general overview of creation, including the creation of man, male and female, on the sixth day. Genesis 2 moves from the general to the particular, giving more details of the creation of woman.

10. **Cause and effect (or vice versa)**—to move from the source to the consequence of it. An example of this is found in John 11. Verse 4 states that the cause of the death of Lazarus, the beloved friend of Christ, was to glorify the Son. The effect is seen in verse 45, where the people put their faith in Christ after seeing his power in raising Lazarus. The effect is also seen in John 12:17,18, where once again the Son is glorified.

11. **Explanation or analysis**—the presentation of an idea or event followed by its explanation. This is expertly done by our Lord in John 6, where he multiplies the loaves and the fishes and then brings forth his discourse stating that he is the bread who gives us life.

12. **Interrogation**—the presentation of a question, usually followed by its answer. Paul masterfully uses this technique in writing Romans. Paul anticipates his readers' questions or objections, states them usually in the form of a question, and then proceeds to answer the very questions he has raised. Romans 6 beautifully demonstrates this technique.

13. **Preparation or introduction**—the presentation of background information to prepare the reader for that which follows. The purpose of the Gospel of John is to prepare the reader to believe that Jesus is the Christ, the Son of God. In John 1:1-18 the writer thoroughly introduces his subject and prepares his readers for what is to come.

14. **Summarization**—to restate the main points, to sum up, or to briefly restate particular truths. Moses does this in chapters 1 to 4 of the book of Deuteronomy as he rehearses before the children of Israel those things that took place following the exodus from Egypt. Acts 7 provides a masterful summarization by Stephen of Israel's history.

TENSE, VOICE, AND MOOD OF GREEK VERBS

There are many excellent study tools which can help you examine the text more deeply through Greek word studies. If you would like to pursue Greek word studies further, a highly recommended book is *The Complete Word Study New Testament*, by Spiros Zodhiates.

The following explanation of the tense, voice, and mood of Greek verbs will help those who do not know Greek but want a better understanding of the implications of the kind of action indicated by the verbs.

Because verbs express action, they are often the most significant element in the expression of thought. Therefore, understanding the Greek verb is a key to correct interpretation and application of Scripture. (Context is the most important key to correct interpretation and application, since the Greek words get their meaning from the context.) The major features of Greek verbs are tense, voice, and mood.

Part of the beauty of the Greek language is that the construction of the verb clearly shows who does the action, whether the statement is a command or a suggestion, and whether the passage is speaking of reality or possibility.

By thinking through a simple, concise explanation of tense, voice, and mood, new vistas of insight will be opened to you. Keep in mind that the following is a simplified and non-exhaustive summarization of a complex subject. The purpose of this information is to give you an overview of terms that are frequently used in the more technical commentaries.

Tense
(Shows the Kind of Action)

Greek verb tenses differ from English verb tenses in that the kind of action portrayed is the most significant element, and time is a relatively minor consideration.

❧ Action as continuous

Present tense—continuous action. It is primarily progressive or linear; it shows action that is continuing.

Examples:

Jeff *is studying* the Bible.

John 15:4b—"No branch *can bear* fruit by itself; it *must remain* in the vine. Neither can you bear fruit unless you *remain* in me."

John 15:6—"If anyone *does not remain* in me."

Imperfect tense—continuous action, usually in the past.

Examples:

Jeff *was studying* the Bible.

John 15:19a—"If you belonged to the world, it *would love* you as its own." (Literally, "would have been loving" its own.)

❧ Action as completed

Perfect tense—punctiliar action in the past

with the results continuing into the present. (Punctiliar action is action that happens at a specific point in time.)

Examples:

Jeff is being transformed by *having studied* the Bible.

John 15:3—"You are already clean because of the word which I *have spoken* to you."

John 15:10b—"Just as I *have obeyed* my Father's commands and remain in his love."

Pluperfect tense—punctiliar action in the past with the results continuing in the past.

Examples:

Jeff was transformed because he *had studied* the Bible.

John 9:22—"For already the Jews *had decided.*"

ॐ **Action as occurring**

Aorist tense—punctiliar action. The aorist tense states that an action occurs without regard to its duration; that is, it denotes the fact of an action without any reference to the length of that action. Compared to the present tense, the aorist tense expresses the action like a snapshot while the present tense action is like a moving picture, continuing on.

Examples:

Jeff *studied* the Bible.

John 15:4a—"*Remain* in me, and I will remain in you."

Future tense—indefinite action to occur in the future. Indicates continuing or punctiliar action in the future.

Examples:

Jeff *will be studying* his Bible.

John 15:7—"It *will be given* you."

John 15:8—"Showing yourselves to *be* my disciples."

Voice
(Shows How the Subject Is Related to the Action)

ॐ **Active voice—indicates that the subject produces the action.**

Examples:

Jeff *hit* the ball.

John 15:2b—"…while every branch that does bear fruit he *trims* clean."

ॐ **Passive voice—indicates that the subject is acted upon.**

Examples:

Jeff *was hit* by the ball.

John 15:6—"And *burned.*"

ॐ **Middle voice—indicates that the subject initiates the action and also participates in the results of the action.** (This voice is unique to Greek construction.)

Examples:

Jeff *hit* himself with the ball.

John 15:26—"The Spirit of truth who *goes out* from the Father, he will testify about me."

One note of interest when looking up a verb in a Greek study tool: The middle and passive voices will have identical forms, but the context will show you if the subject is receiving the action (passive voice) or if the subject initiated the action and participated in it (middle voice).

Also, some verbs are *deponent verbs*. This means that their form in a Greek study tool may be listed as a passive or middle voice verb but their function or action is active. Usually your Greek study helps will list these as deponent verbs.

Mood
(Shows How the Action Is Related to Reality from the Speaker's Point of View)

ॐ **Indicative mood—the declarative mood or mood of certainty.** It is a statement of fact which assumes reality from the speaker's point of view. This mood simply states a thing as being a fact.

Examples:

Bible study *has changed* Jeff's life.

John 15:6—"He is like a branch that is *thrown* away and *withers*; such branches are *picked* up, *thrown* into the fire and *burned*."

༄ **Imperative mood—usually a command or entreaty.** It is the mood of volition or will. The imperative mood in the Greek makes a demand on the will of the reader to obey the command; it is used to indicate prohibition and authority.

Examples:

Jeff, *study* your homework.

John 15:4—"*Remain* in me."

John 15:7—"*Ask* whatever you wish."

John 15:9—"*Remain* in my love."

John 15:20—"*Remember* the words I spoke to you."

One aspect which will help your study of God's Word is the understanding of the combination of the present tense and the imperative mood that is stating a negative command (a prohibition). The *present imperative prohibition* demands cessation of some act already in progress.

Example:

John 20:17—"Jesus said to her, '*Do not hold on* to me.'" In other words, Mary was already clinging to Jesus, and Jesus was telling her to stop clinging and to go on refusing to cling to him.

༄ **Subjunctive mood—the mood of probability.** It implies some doubt regarding the reality of the action from the speaker's point of view. It expresses an uncertainty or an action which may or should happen. This is the mood used for conditional clauses, strong suggestions, or "polite" commands.

Examples:

Jeff *may have done* his homework. Jeff, if you do not do your homework, you cannot participate in the class discussion.

John 15:2—"That it *will bear* more fruit."

John 15:4b—"No branch can bear fruit by itself; it *must remain* in the vine. Neither can you bear fruit unless you *remain* in me."

John 15:6—"If anyone *does not remain* in me."

John 15:7—"If you *remain* in me, and my words *remain* in you."

Something else which may help you in your study of God's Word is an understanding of the combination of the aorist tense and the subjunctive mood that is stating a negative command (a prohibition). The *aorist subjunctive prohibition* is a warning or an exhortation against doing a thing not yet begun.

Example:

John 13:8a—"'No,' said Peter, 'you *shall never wash* my feet!'" In other words, Peter was telling Jesus that he was not to wash his feet and Jesus was not even to start washing his feet.

༄ **Optative mood—the mood of possibility.** This mood presents no definite anticipation of realization but merely presents the action as conceivable from the speaker's point of view. (Used less frequently than the other moods.)

Examples:

I *wish* my neighbor, Jeff, would take Precept Bible studies.

2 Thessalonians 3:5—"May the Lord *direct* your hearts."

TENSE, MOOD, AND VOICE OF GREEK VERBS

TENSE

The emphasis is on the *kind* of action, not the time of action.

Tense	Kind of Action	Example
Present	Continuous action	Jeff is studying the Bible.
Imperfect	Continuous action in the past	Jeff was studying the Bible.
Perfect	Punctiliar action in the past with the results continuing into the present	Jeff is being transformed by having studied the Bible.
Pluperfect	Punctiliar action in the past with the results continuing in the past	Jeff was transformed because he had studied the Bible.
Aorist	Punctiliar action (The time can be past, present, or future but is generally past.)	Jeff studied the Bible.
Future	Generally continuous action in the future, but on occasion it can be punctiliar.	Jeff will be studying his Bible.

TENSE, MOOD, AND VOICE OF GREEK VERBS

MOOD

The mood expresses the relationship of the action to reality from the speaker's point of view.

Mood	Relation to Reality	Usage or Meaning	Example
Indicative	Mood of certainty (reality)	Used to declare a statement of fact as something which is true. Expresses that which is actual, factual, or real from the speaker's point of view.	Bible study has changed Jeff's life.
Imperative	Mood of volition or will (potential reality)	Usually used to express a command or entreaty. Denotes intention, authority, permission, or prohibition.	Jeff, study your homework.
Subjunctive	Mood of probability (probable reality)	Used to express an action which may or should happen but which is not necessarily true at the present, from the speaker's point of view. Expresses conditional or uncertain actions.	Jeff may have done his homework.
Optative	Mood of possibility (possible reality)	Merely presents an action as conceivable from the speaker's point of view, with no definite anticipation of realization.	I wish my neighbor, Jeff, would take Precept Bible studies.

TENSE, MOOD, AND VOICE OF GREEK VERBS

VOICE

The voice expresses the relationship of the subject to the action.

Voice	How the Subject Is Related to the Action	Example
Active	Indicates that the subject produces the action	Jeff hit the ball.
Passive	Indicates that the subject is acted upon	Jeff was hit by the ball.
Middle	Indicates that the subject initiates the action and participates in the results of the action	Jeff hit himself with the ball.

TENSE, MOOD, AND VOICE OF GREEK VERBS

PROHIBITIONS

This is when the speaker states a negative command.

Prohibition	Definition	Example
Present imperative (used with a negative)	This prohibition demands cessation of some act already in progress.	John 20:17
Aorist subjunctive (used with a negative)	This prohibition is a warning or exhortation against doing a thing not yet begun.	John 13:8

HISTORICAL CHARTS

TOPICAL STUDY CHARTS

AT A GLANCE CHARTS

OBSERVATIONS CHARTS

MAPS

(All maps are approximate to scale.)

ILLUSTRATIONS

COLOR MAPS

CONCORDANCE

New International Version

THE NEW INTERNATIONAL VERSION
CONCORDANCE
TO THE OLD AND NEW TESTAMENTS

The NIV Concordance, created by Edward W. Goodrick and John R. Kohlenberger III, has been developed specifically for use with the New International Version. Like all concordances, it is a special index which contains an alphabetical listing of words used in the Bible text. By looking up key words, readers can find verses and passages for which they remember a word or two but not their location.

This concordance contains 2,000 word entries, with some 13,000 Scripture references. Each word entry is followed by the Scripture references in which that particular word is found, as well as by a brief excerpt from the surrounding context. The first letter of the entry word is italicized to conserve space and to allow for a longer context excerpt. Variant spellings due to number and tense and compound forms follow the entry in parentheses, and direct the reader to check other forms of that word in locating a passage.

This concordance contains a number of "block entries," which highlight some of the key events and characteristics in the lives of certain Bible figures. The descriptive phrases replace the brief context surrounding each occurrence of the name. In those instances where more than one Bible character has the same name, that name is placed under one block entry, and each person is given a number (1), (2), etc. Insignificant names are not included.

Word or block entries marked with an asterisk (*) list every verse in the Bible in which the word appears.

This concordance is a valuable tool for Bible study. While one of its key purposes is to help the reader find forgotten references to verses, it can also be used to do word studies and to locate and trace biblical themes. Be sure to use this concordance as more than just a verse finder. Whenever you look up a verse, aim to discover the intended meaning of the verse in context. Give special attention to the flow of thought from the beginning of the passage to the end.

ABBREVIATIONS FOR THE BOOKS OF THE BIBLE
As used in the NIV Concordance

Genesis	Ge	Job	Job	Habakkuk	Hab	1 Thessalonians	1Th
Exodus	Ex	Psalms	Ps	Zephaniah	Zep	2Thessalonians	2Th
Leviticus	Lev	Proverbs	Pr	Haggai	Hag	1 Timothy	1Ti
Numbers	Nu	Ecclesiastes	Ecc	Zechariah	Zec	2 Timothy	2Ti
Deuteronomy	Dt	Song of Songs	SS	Malachi	Mal	Titus	Tit
Joshua	Jos	Isaiah	Isa	Matthew	Mt	Philemon	Phm
Judges	Jdg	Jeremiah	Jer	Mark	Mk	Hebrews	Heb
Ruth	Ru	Lamentations	La	Luke	Lk	James	Jas
1 Samuel	1Sa	Ezekiel	Eze	John	Jn	1 Peter	1Pe
2 Samuel	2Sa	Daniel	Da	Acts	Ac	2 Peter	2Pe
1 Kings	1Ki	Hosea	Hos	Romans	Ro	1 John	1Jn
2 Kings	2Ki	Joel	Joel	1 Corinthians	1Co	2 John	2Jn
1 Chronicles	1Ch	Amos	Am	2 Corinthians	2Co	3 John	3Jn
2 Chronicles	2Ch	Obadiah	Ob	Galatians	Gal	Jude	Jude
Ezra	Ezr	Jonah	Jnh	Ephesians	Eph	Revelation	Rev
Nehemiah	Ne	Micah	Mic	Philippians	Php		
Esther	Est	Nahum	Na	Colossians	Col		

AARON

Priesthood of (Ex 28:1; Nu 17; Heb 5:1-4;7), garments (Ex 28; 39), consecration (Ex 29), ordination (Lev 8).

Spokesman for Moses (Ex 4:14-16, 27-31; 7:1-2). Supported Moses' hands in battle (Ex 17:8-13). Built golden calf (Ex 32; Dt 9:20). Talked against Moses (Nu 12). Priesthood opposed (Nu 16); staff budded (Nu 17). Forbidden to enter land (Nu 20:1-12). Death (Nu 20:22-29; 33:38-39).

ABANDON

Dt	4: 31	he will not *a* or destroy you
1Ti	4: 1	in later times some will *a* the faith

ABBA

Ro	8: 15	And by him we cry, "*A*, Father."
Gal	4: 6	the Spirit who calls out, "*A*, Father

ABEL

Second son of Adam (Ge 4:2). Offered proper sacrifice (Ge 4:4; Heb 11:4). Murdered by Cain (Ge 4:8; Mt 23:35; Lk 11:51; 1Jn 3:12).

ABHORS

Pr	11: 1	The LORD *a* dishonest scales,

ABIGAIL

Wife of Nabal (1Sa 25:30); pled for his life with David (1Sa 25:14-35). Became David's wife (1Sa 25:36-42).

ABIJAH

Son of Rehoboam; king of Judah (1Ki 14:31-15:8; 2Ch 12:16-14:1).

ABILITY (ABLE)

Ezr	2: 69	According to their *a* they gave
2Co	1: 8	far beyond our *a* to endure,
	8: 3	were able, and even beyond their *a*.

ABIMELECH

1. King of Gerar who took Abraham's wife Sarah, believing her to be his sister (Ge 20). Later made a covenant with Abraham (Ge 21:22-33).

2. King of Gerar who took Isaac's wife Rebekah, believing her to be his sister (Ge 26:1-11). Later made a covenant with Isaac (Ge 26:12-31).

ABLE (ABILITY ENABLE ENABLED ENABLES)

Eze	7: 19	and gold will not be *a* to save them
Da	3: 17	the God we serve is *a* to save us
Ro	8: 39	will be *a* to separate us
	14: 4	for the Lord is *a* to make him stand
	16: 25	to him who is *a* to establish you
2Co	9: 8	God is *a* to make all grace abound
Eph	3: 20	him who is *a* to do immeasurably

2Ti	1: 12	and am convinced that he is *a*
	3: 15	which are *a* to make you wise
Heb	7: 25	he is *a* to save completely
Jude	24	To him who is *a* to keep you
Rev	5: 5	He is *a* to open the scroll

ABOLISH

Mt	5: 17	that I have come to *a* the Law

ABOMINATION

Da	11: 31	set up the *a* that causes desolation.

ABOUND (ABOUNDING)

2Co	9: 8	able to make all grace *a* to you,
Php	1: 9	that your love may *a* more

ABOUNDING (ABOUND)

Ex	34: 6	slow to anger, *a* in love
Ps	86: 5	*a* in love to all who call to you.

ABRAHAM

Covenant relation with the LORD (Ge 12:1-3; 13:14-17; 15; 17; 22:15-18; Ex 2:24; Ne 9:8; Ps 105; Mic 7:20; Lk 1:68-75; Ro 4; Heb 6:13-15).

Called from Ur, via Haran, to Canaan (Ge 12:1; Ac 7:2-4; Heb 11:8-10). Moved to Egypt, nearly lost Sarah to Pharaoh (Ge 12:10-20). Divided the land with Lot (Ge 13). Saved Lot from four kings (Ge 14:1-16); blessed by Melchizedek (Ge 14:17-20; Heb 7:1-20). Declared righteous by faith (Ge 15:6; Ro 4:3; Gal 3:6-9). Fathered Ishmael by Hagar (Ge 16).

Name changed from Abram (Ge 17:5; Ne 9:7). Circumcised (Ge 17; Ro 4:9-12). Entertained three visitors (Ge 18); promised a son by Sarah (Ge 18:9-15; 17:16). Moved to Gerar; nearly lost Sarah to Abimelech (Ge 20). Fathered Isaac by Sarah (Ge 21:1-7; Ac 7:8; Heb 11:11-12); sent away Hagar and Ishmael (Ge 21:8-21; Gal 4:22-30). Tested by offering Isaac (Ge 22; Heb 11:17-19; Jas 2:21-24). Sarah died; bought field of Ephron for burial (Ge 23). Secured wife for Isaac (Ge 24). Death (Ge 25:7-11).

ABSALOM

Son of David by Maacah (2Sa 3:3; 1Ch 3:2). Killed Amnon for rape of his sister Tamar; banished by David (2Sa 13). Returned to Jerusalem; received by David (2Sa 14). Rebelled against David; seized kingdom (2Sa 15-17). Killed (2Sa 18).

ABSTAIN (ABSTAINS)

1Pe	2: 11	to *a* from sinful desires,

ABSTAINS* (ABSTAIN)

Ro	14: 6	thanks to God; and he who *a*,

ABUNDANCE (ABUNDANT)

Lk	12: 15	consist in the *a* of his possessions."
Jude	: 2	peace and love be yours in *a*.

ABUNDANT (ABUNDANCE)

Dt	28: 11	will grant you *a* prosperity—
Ps	145: 7	will celebrate your *a* goodness

Pr	28: 19	works his land will have *a* food,
Ro	5: 17	who receive God's *a* provision

ACCEPT (ACCEPTED ACCEPTS)

Ex	23: 8	"Do not *a* a bribe,
Pr	10: 8	The wise in heart *a* commands,
	19: 20	Listen to advice and *a* instruction,
Ro	15: 7	*a* one another, then, just
Jas	1: 21	humbly *a* the word planted in you,

ACCEPTED (ACCEPT)

Lk	4: 24	"no prophet is *a* in his hometown.

ACCEPTS (ACCEPT)

Ps	6: 9	the LORD *a* my prayer.
Jn	13: 20	whoever *a* anyone I send *a* me;

ACCOMPANY

Mk	16: 17	these signs will *a* those who believe
Heb	6: 9	your case—things that *a* salvation.

ACCOMPLISH

Isa	55: 11	but will *a* what I desire

ACCORD

Nu	24: 13	not do anything of my own *a*,
Jn	10: 18	but I lay it down of my own *a*.
	12: 49	For I did not speak of my own *a*,

ACCOUNT (ACCOUNTABLE)

Mt	12: 36	to give *a* on the day of judgment
Ro	14: 12	each of us will give an *a* of himself
Heb	4: 13	of him to whom we must give *a*.

ACCOUNTABLE (ACCOUNT)

Eze	33: 6	but I will hold the watchman *a*
Ro	3: 19	and the whole world held *a* to God.

ACCUSATION (ACCUSE)

1Ti	5: 19	Do not entertain an *a*

ACCUSATIONS (ACCUSE)

2Pe	2: 11	do not bring slanderous *a*

ACCUSE (ACCUSATION ACCUSATIONS)

Pr	3: 30	Do not *a* a man for no reason—
Lk	3: 14	and don't *a* people falsely—

ACHAN*

Sin at Jericho caused defeat at Ai; stoned (Jos 7; 22:20; 1Ch 2:7).

ACHE*

Pr	14: 13	Even in laughter the heart may *a*,

ACKNOWLEDGE

Mt	10: 32	*a* him before my Father in heaven.
1Jn	4: 3	spirit that does not *a* Jesus is not

ACQUIT

Ex	23: 7	to death, for I will not *a* the guilty.

ACTION (ACTIONS ACTIVE ACTS)

Jas	2: 17	if it is not accompanied by *a*,
1Pe	1: 13	minds for *a*; be self-controlled;

ACTIONS (ACTION)

Mt	11: 19	wisdom is proved right by her *a*."
Gal	6: 4	Each one should test his own *a*.
Tit	1: 16	but by their *a* they deny him.

ACTIVE (ACTION)

Heb	4: 12	For the word of God is living and *a*

ACTS (ACTION)

Ps	145: 12	all men may know of your mighty *a*
	150: 2	Praise him for his *a* of power;
Isa	64: 6	all our righteous *a* are like filthy
Mt	6: 1	not to do your '*a* of righteousness'

ADAM

First man (Ge 1:26-2:25; Ro 5:14; 1Ti 2:13). Sin of (Ge 3; Hos 6:7; Ro 5:12-21). Children of (Ge 4:1-5:5). Death of (Ge 5:5; Ro 5:12-21; 1Co 15:22).

ADD

Dt	12: 32	do not *a* to it or take away from it.
Pr	30: 6	Do not *a* to his words,
Lk	12: 25	by worrying can *a* a single hour
Rev	22: 18	God will *a* to him the plagues

ADMIRABLE*

Php	4: 8	whatever is lovely, whatever is *a*—

ADMONISH

Col	3: 16	and *a* one another with all wisdom,

ADOPTED (ADOPTION)

Eph	1: 5	In love he predestined us to be *a*

ADOPTION (ADOPTED)

Ro	8: 23	as we wait eagerly for our *a* as sons,

ADORE*

SS	1: 4	How right they are to *a* you!

ADORNMENT* (ADORNS)

1Pe	3: 3	should not come from outward *a*,

ADORNS (ADORNMENT)

Ps	93: 5	holiness *a* your house

ADULTERY

Ex	20: 14	"You shall not commit *a*.
Mt	5: 27	that it was said, 'Do not commit *a*.'
	5: 28	lustfully has already committed *a*

5: 32 the divorced woman commits *a.*
15: 19 murder, *a,* sexual
immorality, theft

ADULTS*
1Co 14: 20 but in your thinking be *a.*

ADVANCED
Job 32: 7 *a* years should teach wisdom.'

ADVANTAGE
Ex 22: 22 "Do not take *a* of a widow
Dt 24: 14 Do not take *a* of a hired man
who is
1Th 4: 6 should wrong his brother or
take *a*

ADVERSITY
Pr 17: 17 and a brother is born for *a.*

ADVICE
1Ki 12: 8 rejected the *a* the elders
12: 14 he followed the *a* of the
young men
Pr 12: 5 but the *a* of the wicked is
deceitful.
12: 15 but a wise man listens to *a.*
19: 20 Listen to *a* and accept
instruction,
20: 18 Make plans by seeking *a;*

AFFLICTION
Ro 12: 12 patient in *a,* faithful in
prayer.

AFRAID (FEAR)
Ge 26: 24 Do not be *a,* for I am with
you;
Ex 3: 6 because he was *a* to look at
God.
Ps 27: 1 of whom shall I be *a?*
56: 3 When I am *a,* / I will trust in
you.
Pr 3: 24 lie down, you will not be *a;*
Jer 1: 8 Do not be *a* of them, for I am
Mt 8: 26 You of little faith, why are
you so *a*
10: 28 be *a* of the One who can
destroy
10: 31 So don't be *a;* you are worth
more
Mk 5: 36 "Don't be *a;* just believe."
Jn 14: 27 hearts be troubled and do not
be *a.*
Heb 13: 6 Lord is my helper; I will not
be *a.*

AGED
Job 12: 12 Is not wisdom found among
the *a?*
Pr 17: 6 children are a crown to the *a,*

AGREE
Mt 18: 19 on earth *a* about anything
you ask
Ro 7: 16 want to do, I *a* that the law
is good.
Php 4: 2 with Syntyche to *a* with each
other

AHAB
Son of Omri; king of Israel (1Ki 16:28-
22:40), husband of Jezebel (1Ki 16:31).
Promoted Baal worship (1Ki 16:31-33);
opposed by Elijah (1Ki 17:1; 18; 21), a
prophet (1Ki 20:35-43), Micaiah (1Ki
22:1-28). Defeated Ben-Hadad (1Ki
22:51). Killed for failing to kill Ben-Hadad and
for murder of Naboth (1Ki 20:35-21:40).

AHAZ
Son of Jotham; king of Judah, (2Ki 16;
2Ch 28; Isa 7).

AHAZIAH
1. Son of Ahab; king of Israel (1Ki
22:51-2Ki 1:18; 2Ch 20:35-37).
2. Son of Jehoram; king of Judah (2Ki
8:25-29; 9:14-29), also called Jehoahaz
(2Ch 21:17-22:9; 25:23).

AIM
1Co 7: 34 Her *a* is to be devoted to the
Lord
2Co 13: 11 *A* for perfection, listen

AIR
Mt 8: 20 and birds of the *a* have nests,
1Co 9: 26 not fight like a man beating
the *a.*
Eph 2: 2 of the ruler of the kingdom
of the *a,*
1Th 4: 17 clouds to meet the Lord in
the *a.*

ALABASTER
Mt 26: 7 came to him with an *a* jar

ALERT
Jos 8: 4 All of you be on the *a.*
Mk 13: 33 Be *a!* You do not know
Eph 6: 18 be *a* and always keep on
praying
1Th 5: 6 but let us be *a* and self-
controlled.

ALIEN (ALIENATED)
Ex 22: 21 "Do not mistreat an *a*

ALIENATED (ALIEN)
Gal 5: 4 by law have been *a* from
Christ;

ALIVE (LIVE)
Ac 1: 3 convincing proofs that he
was *a.*
Ro 6: 11 but *a* to God in Christ Jesus.
1Co 15: 22 so in Christ all will be made *a.*

ALMIGHTY (MIGHT)
Ge 17: 1 "I am God *A;* walk before
me
Job 11: 7 Can you probe the limits of
the *A?*
33: 4 the breath of the *A* gives me
life.
Ps 91: 1 will rest in the shadow of
the *A.*
Isa 6: 3 "Holy, holy, holy is the
LORD *A;*

ALTAR
Ge 22: 9 his son Isaac and laid him on
the *a,*
Ex 27: 1 "Build an *a* of acacia wood,
1Ki 18: 30 and he repaired the *a* of the
LORD
2Ch 4: 1 made a bronze *a* twenty
cubits
4: 19 the golden *a;* the tables

ALWAYS
Ps 16: 8 I have set the LORD *a* before
me.
51: 3 and my sin is *a* before me.
Mt 26: 11 The poor you will *a* have with
you,
28: 20 And surely I will be with
you *a,*
1Co 13: 7 *a* protects, *a* trusts, *a*
hopes, *a*
Php 4: 4 Rejoice in the Lord *a.*
1Pe 3: 15 *A* be prepared to give an
answer

AMAZIAH
Son of Joash; king of Judah (2Ki 14;
2Ch 25).

AMBASSADORS
2Co 5: 20 We are therefore Christ's *a,*

AMBITION
Ro 15: 20 It has always been my *a*
1Th 4: 11 Make it your *a* to lead a
quiet life,

AMON
Son of Manasseh; king of Judah (2Ki
21:18-26; 1Ch 3:14; 2Ch 33:21-25).

ANANIAS
1. Husband of Sapphira; died for lying
to God (Ac 5:1-11).
2. Disciple who baptized Saul (Ac 9:10-
19).
3. High priest at Paul's arrest (Ac
22:30-24:1).

ANCHOR
Heb 6: 19 We have this hope as an *a*

ANCIENT
Da 7: 9 and the *A* of Days took his
seat.

ANDREW*
Apostle; brother of Simon Peter (Mt
4:18; 10:2; Mk 1:16-18, 29; 3:18; 13:3; Lk
6:14; Jn 1:35-44; 6:8-9; 12:22; Ac 1:13).

ANGEL (ANGELS ARCHANGEL)
Ps 34: 7 The *a* of the LORD encamps
Ac 6: 15 his face was like the face of
an *a.*
2Co 11: 14 Satan himself masquerades
as an *a*
Gal 1: 8 or an *a* from heaven should
preach

ANGELS (ANGEL)
Ps 91: 11 command his *a* concerning
you
Mt 18: 10 For I tell you that their *a*

25: 41 prepared for the devil and
his *a.*
Lk 20: 36 for they are like the *a.*
1Co 6: 3 you not know that we will
judge *a?*
Heb 1: 4 as much superior to the *a*
1: 14 Are not all *a* ministering
spirits
2: 7 made him a little lower than
the *a;*
13: 2 some people have entertained *a*
1Pe 1: 12 Even *a* long to look
2Pe 2: 4 For if God did not spare *a*

ANGER (ANGERED ANGRY)
Ex 32: 10 alone so that my *a* may burn
34: 6 slow to *a,* abounding in love
Dt 29: 28 In furious *a* and in great
wrath
2Ki 22: 13 Great is the LORD's *a* that
burns
Ps 30: 5 For his *a* lasts only a
moment,
Pr 15: 1 but a harsh word stirs up *a.*
29: 11 A fool gives full vent to his *a,*

ANGERED (ANGER)
Pr 22: 24 do not associate with one
easily *a,*
1Co 13: 5 it is not easily *a,* it keeps no
record

ANGRY (ANGER)
Ps 2: 12 Kiss the Son, lest he be *a*
Pr 29: 22 An *a* man stirs up dissension,
Jas 1: 19 slow to speak and slow to
become *a*

ANGUISH
Ps 118: 5 In my *a* I cried to the LORD,

ANOINT
Ps 23: 5 You *a* my head with oil;
Jas 5: 14 and *a* him with oil in the
name

ANT*
Pr 6: 6 Go to the *a,* you sluggard;

ANTICHRIST
1Jn 2: 18 have heard that the *a* is
coming,
2Jn : 7 person is the deceiver and
the *a.*

ANTIOCH
Ac 11: 26 were called Christians first
at *A.*

ANXIETY (ANXIOUS)
1Pe 5: 7 Cast all your *a* on him

ANXIOUS (ANXIETY)
Pr 12: 25 An *a* heart weighs a man
down,
Php 4: 6 Do not be *a* about anything,

Christian from Alexandria, learned in
the Scriptures; instructed by Aquila and
Priscilla (Ac 18:24-28). Ministered at
Corinth (Ac 19:1; 1Co 1:12; 3; Tit 3:13).

APOSTLES

See also Andrew, Bartholomew, James, John, Judas, Matthew, Nathanael, Paul, Peter, Philip, Simon, Thaddaeus, Thomas.

Mk 3: 14 twelve—designating them *a*

Ac 1: 26 so he was added to the eleven *a*.

2: 43 signs were done by the *a*.

1Co 12: 28 God has appointed first of all *a*,

15: 9 For I am the least of the *a*

2Co 11: 13 masquerading as *a* of Christ.

Eph 2: 20 built on the foundation of the *a*

APPEAR (APPEARANCE APPEARING)

Mk 13: 22 false prophets will *a* and perform

2Co 5: 10 we must all *a* before the judgment

Col 3: 4 also will *a* with him in glory.

Heb 9: 24 now to *a* for us in God's presence.

9: 28 and he will *a* a second time,

APPEARANCE (APPEAR)

1Sa 16: 7 Man looks at the outward *a*,

Gal 2: 6 God does not judge by external *a* —

APPEARING (APPEAR)

2Ti 4: 8 to all who have longed for his *a*.

Tit 2: 13 the glorious *a* of our great God

APPLY

Pr 22: 17 *a* your heart to what I teach,

23: 12 A your heart to instruction

APPROACH

Eph 3: 12 in him we may *a* God with freedom

Heb 4: 16 Let us then *a* the throne of grace

APPROVED

2Ti 2: 15 to present yourself to God as one *a*,

AQUILA*

Husband of Priscilla; co-worker with Paul, instructor of Apollos (Ac 18; Ro 16:3; 1Co 16:19; 2Ti 4:19).

ARARAT

Ge 8: 4 came to rest on the mountains of A.

ARCHANGEL* (ANGEL)

1Th 4: 16 with the voice of the *a*

Jude : 9 *a* Michael, when he was disputing

ARCHITECT*

Heb 11: 10 whose *a* and builder is God.

ARK

Ge 6: 14 So make yourself an *a*

Dt 10: 5 put the tablets in the *a* I had made,

2Ch 35: 3 "Put the sacred *a* in the temple that

Heb 9: 4 This *a* contained the gold jar

ARM (ARMY)

Nu 11: 23 "Is the LORD's *a* too short?

1Pe 4: 1 *a* yourselves also with the same

ARMAGEDDON*

Rev 16: 16 that in Hebrew is called A.

ARMOR (ARMY)

1Ki 20: 11 on his *a* should not boast like one

Eph 6: 11 Put on the full *a* of God

6: 13 Therefore put on the full *a* of God,

ARMS (ARMY)

Dt 33: 27 underneath are the everlasting *a*.

Ps 18: 32 It is God who *a* me with strength

Pr 31: 20 She opens her *a* to the poor

Isa 40: 11 He gathers the lambs in his *a*

Mk 10: 16 And he took the children in his *a*,

ARMY (ARM ARMOR ARMS)

Ps 33: 16 No king is saved by the size of his *a*

Rev 19: 19 the rider on the horse and his *a*.

AROMA

2Co 2: 15 For we are to God the *a* of Christ

ARRAYED*

Ps 110: 3 A in holy majesty,

Isa 61: 10 and *a* me in a robe of righteousness

ARROGANT

Ro 11: 20 Do not be *a*, but be afraid.

ARROWS

Eph 6: 16 you can extinguish all the flaming *a*

ASA

King of Judah (1Ki 15:8-24; 1Ch 3:10; 2Ch 14-16).

ASCENDED

Eph 4: 8 "When he *a* on high,

ASCRIBE

1Ch 16: 28 *a* to the LORD glory and strength,

Job 36: 3 I will *a* justice to my Maker.

Ps 29: 2 A to the LORD the glory due his

ASHAMED (SHAME)

Lk 9: 26 If anyone is *a* of me and my words,

Ro 1: 16 I am not *a* of the gospel,

2Ti 1: 8 So do not be *a* to testify about our

2: 15 who does not need to be *a*

ASSIGNED

Mk 13: 34 with his *a* task, and tells the one

1Co 3: 5 as the Lord has *a* to each his task.

7: 17 place in life that the Lord *a* to him

ASSOCIATE

Pr 22: 24 do not *a* with one easily angered,

Ro 12: 16 but be willing to *a* with people

1Co 5: 11 am writing you that you must not *a*

2Th 3: 14 Do not *a* with him,

ASSURANCE

Heb 10: 22 with a sincere heart in full *a* of faith

ASTRAY

Pr 10: 17 ignores correction leads others *a*.

Isa 53: 6 We all, like sheep, have gone *a*,

Jer 50: 6 their shepherds have led them *a*

Jn 16: 1 you so that you will not go *a*.

1Pe 2: 25 For you were like sheep going *a*,

1Jn 3: 7 do not let anyone lead you *a*.

ATHALIAH

Evil queen of Judah (2Ki 11; 2Ch 23).

ATHLETE*

2Ti 2: 5 if anyone competes as an *a*,

ATONEMENT

Ex 25: 17 "Make an *a* cover of pure gold—

30: 10 Once a year Aaron shall make *a*

Lev 17: 11 it is the blood that makes *a*

23: 27 this seventh month is the Day of A.

Nu 25: 13 and made *a* for the Israelites."

Ro 3: 25 presented him as a sacrifice of *a*,

Heb 2: 17 that he might make *a* for the sins

ATTENTION

Pr 4: 1 pay *a* and gain understanding.

5: 1 My son, pay *a* to my wisdom,

22: 17 Pay *a* and listen to the sayings

Tit 1: 14 and will pay no *a* to Jewish myths

ATTITUDE (ATTITUDES)

Eph 4: 23 new in the *a* of your minds;

Php 2: 5 Your *a* should be the same

1Pe 4: 1 yourselves also with the same *a*,

ATTITUDES (ATTITUDE)

Heb 4: 12 it judges the thoughts and *a*

ATTRACTIVE

Tit 2: 10 teaching about God our Savior *a*.

AUTHORITIES (AUTHORITY)

Ro 13: 5 it is necessary to submit to the *a*,

13: 6 for the *a* are God's servants,

Tit 3: 1 people to be subject to rulers and *a*,

1Pe 3: 22 *a* and powers in submission to him.

AUTHORITY (AUTHORITIES)

Mt 7: 29 because he taught as one who had *a*

9: 6 the Son of Man has *a* on earth

28: 18 "All *a* in heaven and on earth has

Ro 13: 1 for there is no *a* except that which

13: 2 rebels against the *a* is rebelling

1Co 11: 10 to have a sign of *a* on her head.

1Ti 2: 2 for kings and all those in *a*,

2: 12 to teach or to have *a* over a man;

Heb 13: 17 your leaders and submit to their *a*.

AVENGE (VENGEANCE)

Dt 32: 35 It is mine to *a*; I will repay.

AVOID

Pr 20: 3 It is to a man's honor to *a* strife,

20: 19 so *a* a man who talks too much.

1Th 4: 3 you should *a* sexual immorality;

5: 22 A every kind of evil.

2Ti 2: 16 A godless chatter, because those

Tit 3: 9 But *a* foolish controversies

AWAKE

Ps 17: 15 when I *a*, I will be satisfied

AWE (AWESOME)

Job 25: 2 "Dominion and *a* belong to God;

Ps 119:120 I stand in *a* of your laws.

Ecc 5: 7 Therefore stand in *a* of God.

Isa 29: 23 will stand in *a* of the God of Israel.

Jer 33: 9 they will be in *a* and will tremble

Hab 3: 2 I stand in *a* of your deeds,

Mal 2: 5 and stood in *a* of my name.

Mt 9: 8 they were filled with *a*;

Lk 7: 16 They were all filled with *a*

Ac 2: 43 Everyone was filled with *a*,

Heb 12: 28 acceptably with reverence and *a*,

AWESOME (AWE)

Ge 28: 17 and said, "How *a* is this place!

Ex 15: 11 in glory,

Dt 7: 21 is among you, is a great and *a* God.

10: 17 the great God, mighty and *a*,

28: 58 revere this glorious and *a* name—

Jdg 13: 6 like an angel of God, very *a.*
Ne 1: 5 of heaven, the great and *a*
            God,
        9: 32 the great, mighty and *a* God,
Job 10: 16 again display your *a* power
       37: 22 God comes in *a* majesty.
Ps 45: 4 let your right hand display *a*
            deeds.
       47: 2 How *a* is the LORD Most
            High,
       66: 5 how *a* his works in man's
            behalf!
       68: 35 You are *a*, O God,
       89: 7 he is more *a* than all who
            surround
       99: 3 praise your great and *a*
            name—
      111: 9 holy and *a* is his name.
      145: 6 of the power of your *a* works,
Da 9: 4 "O Lord, the great and *a* God,

∞ *B*

BAAL
1Ki 18: 25 Elijah said to the prophets
            of *B*,

BAASHA
   King of Israel (1Ki 15:16-16:7; 2Ch
16:1-6).

BABIES (BABY)
Lk 18: 15 also bringing *b* to Jesus
1Pe 2: 2 Like newborn *b*, crave pure

BABY (BABIES)
Isa 49: 15 "Can a mother forget the *b*
Lk 1: 44 the *b* in my womb leaped for
            joy.
        2: 12 You will find a *b* wrapped in
            strips
Jn 16: 21 but when her *b* is born she
            forgets

BABYLON
Ps 137: 1 By the rivers of *B* we sat and
            wept

BACKSLIDING
Jer 3: 22 I will cure you of *b*."
       14: 7 For our *b* is great;
Eze 37: 23 them from all their sinful *b*,

BALAAM
   Prophet who attempted to curse Israel
(Nu 22-24; Dt 23:4-5; 2Pe 2:15; Jude 11).
Killed (Nu 31:8; Jos 13:22).

BALM
Jer 8: 22 Is there no *b* in Gilead?

BANISH
Jer 25: 10 I will *b* from them the sounds
            of joy

BANQUET
SS 2: 4 He has taken me to the *b* hall,
Lk 14: 13 when you give a *b*, invite the
            poor,

BAPTIZE (BAPTIZED)
Mt 3: 11 He will *b* you with the Holy
            Spirit
Mk 1: 8 he will *b* you with the Holy
            Spirit."

1Co 1: 17 For Christ did not send me
            to *b*,

BAPTIZED (BAPTIZE)
Mt 3: 6 they were *b* by him in the
            Jordan
Mk 1: 9 and was *b* by John in the
            Jordan
       10: 38 or be *b* with the baptism I am
       16: 16 believes and is *b* will be saved,
Jn 4: 2 in fact it was not Jesus who *b*,
Ac 1: 5 but in a few days you will
            be *b*

BARABBAS
Mt 27: 26 Then he released *B* to them.

BARBS*
Nu 33: 55 allow to remain will
            become *b*

BARE
Heb 4: 13 and laid *b* before the eyes of
            him

BARNABAS*
   Disciple, originally Joseph (Ac 4:36),
prophet (Ac 13:1), apostle (Ac 14:14).
Brought Paul to apostles (Ac 9:27),
Antioch (Ac 11:22-29; Gal 2:1-13), on
the first missionary journey (Ac 13-14).
Together at Jerusalem Council, they separated over John Mark (Ac 15). Later co-
workers (1Co 9:6; Col 4:10).

BARREN
Ps 113: 9 He settles the *b* woman

BARTHOLOMEW*
   Apostle (Mt 10:3; Mk 3:18; Lk 6:14; Ac
1:13). Possibly also known as Nathanael
(Jn 1:45-49; 21:2).

BATH
Jn 13: 10 person who has had a *b*
            needs only

BATHSHEBA
   Wife of Uriah who committed adultery
with and became wife of David (2Sa 11),
mother of Solomon (2Sa 12:24; 1Ki 1-2;
1Ch 3:5).

BATTLE
2Ch 20: 15 For the *b* is not yours, but
            God's.
Ps 24: 8 The LORD mighty in *b*.
Ecc 9: 11 or the *b* to the strong,

BEAR (BEARING BIRTH
BIRTHRIGHT BORN FIRSTBORN
NEWBORN)
Ge 4: 13 punishment is more than I
            can *b*.
Ps 38: 4 like a burden too heavy to *b*.
Isa 53: 11 and he will *b* their iniquities.
Da 7: 5 beast, which looked like a *b*.
Mt 7: 18 A good tree cannot *b* bad
            fruit,
Jn 15: 2 branch that does *b* fruit he
            prunes
       15: 16 and appointed you to go and
            b fruit—
Ro 15: 1 ought to *b* with the failings

1Co 10: 13 tempted beyond what you
            can *b*.
Col 3: 13 *B* with each other and forgive

BEARING (BEAR)
Eph 4: 2 *b* with one another in love.
Col 1: 10 *b* fruit in every good work,

BEAST
Rev 13: 18 him calculate the number of
            the *b*,

BEAT (BEATING)
Isa 2: 4 They will *b* their swords
Joel 3: 10 *B* your plowshares into
            swords
1Co 9: 27 I *b* my body and make it my
            slave

BEATING (BEAT)
1Co 9: 26 I do not fight like a man *b*
            the air.
1Pe 2: 20 if you receive a *b* for doing
            wrong

BEAUTIFUL (BEAUTY)
Ge 6: 2 that the daughters of men
            were *b*,
       12: 11 "I know what a *b* woman you
            are.
       12: 14 saw that she was a very *b*
            woman.
       24: 16 The girl was very *b*, a virgin;
       26: 7 of Rebekah, because she is *b*."
       29: 17 Rachel was lovely in form,
            and *b*.
Job 38: 31 "Can you bind the *b*
            Pleiades?
Pr 11: 5 is a *b* woman who shows no
Ecc 3: 11 He has made everything *b*
Isa 4: 2 of the LORD will be *b*
       52: 7 How *b* on the mountains
Eze 20: 6 and honey, the most *b* of all
            lands.
Zec 9: 17 How attractive and *b* they
            will be!
Mt 23: 27 which look *b* on the outside
       26: 10 She has done a *b* thing to me.
Ro 10: 15 "How *b* are the feet
1Pe 3: 5 in God used to make
            themselves *b*.

BEAUTY (BEAUTIFUL)
Ps 27: 4 to gaze upon the *b* of the
            LORD
       45: 11 The king is enthralled by
            your *b*;
Pr 31: 30 is deceptive, and *b* is fleeting;
Isa 33: 17 Your eyes will see the king in
            his *b*
       53: 2 He had no *b* or majesty
       61: 3 to bestow on them a crown
            of *b*
Eze 28: 12 full of wisdom and perfect
            in *b*.
1Pe 3: 4 the unfading *b* of a gentle

BED
Heb 13: 4 and the marriage *b* kept pure,

BEELZEBUB
Lk 11: 15 "By *B*, the prince of demons,

BEER
Pr 20: 1 Wine is a mocker and *b* a
            brawler;

BEERSHEBA
Jdg 20: 1 all the Israelites from Dan
            to *B*

BEGINNING
Ge 1: 1 In the *b* God created the
            heavens
Ps 102: 25 In the *b* you laid the
            foundations
      111: 10 of the LORD is the *b* of
            wisdom;
Pr 1: 7 of the LORD is the *b* of
            knowledge
Jn 1: 1 In the *b* was the Word,
1Jn 1: 1 That which was from the *b*,
Rev 21: 6 and the Omega, the *B* and
            the End.

BEHAVE
Ro 13: 13 Let us *b* decently, as in the
            daytime

BELIEVE (BELIEVED BELIEVER
BELIEVERS BELIEVES BELIEVING)
Mt 18: 6 one of these little ones who
            b in me
       21: 22 If you *b*, you will receive
            whatever
Mk 1: 15 Repent and *b* the good
            news!"
        9: 24 "I do *b*; help me overcome
            my
       16: 17 signs will accompany those
            who *b*:
Lk 8: 50 just *b*, and she will be
            healed."
       24: 25 to *b* all that the prophets have
Jn 1: 7 that through him all men
            might *b*.
        3: 18 does not *b* stands
            condemned
        6: 29 to *b* in the one he has sent."
       10: 38 you do not *b* me, *b* the
            miracles,
       11: 27 "I *b* that you are the Christ,
       14: 11 *B* me when I say that I am
       16: 30 This makes us *b* that you
            came
       16: 31 "You *b* at last!" Jesus
            answered.
       17: 21 that the world may *b* that
            you have
       20: 27 Stop doubting and *b*."
       20: 31 written that you may *b* that
            Jesus is
Ac 16: 31 They replied, "*B* in the Lord
            Jesus,
       24: 14 I *b* everything that agrees
Ro 3: 22 faith in Jesus Christ to all
            who *b*.
        4: 11 he is the father of all who *b*
       10: 9 *b* in your heart that God
            raised him
       10: 14 And how can they *b* in
            the one
       16: 26 so that all nations might *b*

1Th 4: 14 We *b* that Jesus died and rose again
2Th 2: 11 delusion so that they will *b* the lie
1Ti 4: 10 and especially of those who *b*.
Tit 1: 6 a man whose children *b*
Heb 11: 6 comes to him must *b* that he exists
Jas 2: 19 Even the demons *b* that—
1Jn 4: 1 Dear friends, do not *b* every spirit,

BELIEVED (BELIEVE)
Ge 15: 6 Abram *b* the LORD, and he
Jnh 3: 5 The Ninevites *b* God.
Jn   1: 12 to those who *b* in his name,
     2: 22 Then they *b* the Scripture
     3: 18 because he has not *b* in the name
    20: 8 He saw and *b*.
    20: 29 who have not seen and yet have *b*."
Ac 13: 48 were appointed for eternal life *b*.
Ro   4: 3 Scripture say? "Abraham *b* God,
    10: 14 call on the one they have not *b* in?
1Co 15: 2 Otherwise, you have *b* in vain.
Gal 3: 6 Consider Abraham: "He *b* God,
2Ti 1: 12 because I know whom I have *b*,
Jas 2: 23 that says, "Abraham *b* God,

BELIEVER (BELIEVE)
1Co 7: 1 brother has a wife who is not a *b*
2Co 6: 15 What does a *b* have in common

BELIEVERS (BELIEVE)
Ac   4: 32 All the *b* were one in heart
     5: 12 And all the *b* used to meet together
1Co 6: 5 to judge a dispute between *b*?
1Ti 4: 12 set an example for the *b* in speech,
1Pe 2: 17 Love the brotherhood of *b*,

BELIEVES (BELIEVE)
Pr 14: 15 A simple man *b* anything,
Mk   9: 23 is possible for him who *b*."
    11: 23 *b* that what he says will happen,
    16: 16 Whoever *b* and is baptized will be
Jn   3: 16 that whoever *b* in him shall not
     3: 36 Whoever *b* in the Son has eternal
     5: 24 *b* him who sent me has eternal life
     6: 35 and he who *b* in me will never be
     6: 40 and *b* in him shall have eternal life,
     6: 47 he who *b* has everlasting life.
     7: 38 Whoever *b* in me, as the Scripture

11: 26 and *b* in me will never die.
Ro   1: 16 for the salvation of everyone who *b*
    10: 4 righteousness for everyone who *b*.
1Jn 5: 1 Everyone who *b* that Jesus is
     5: 5 Only he who *b* that Jesus is the Son

BELIEVING (BELIEVE)
Jn 20: 31 and that by *b* you may have life

BELONG (BELONGS)
Dt 29: 29 The secret things *b*
Job 25: 2 "Dominion and awe *b* to God;
Ps 47: 9 for the kings of the earth *b* to God;
    95: 4 and the mountain peaks *b* to him.
Jn   8: 44 You *b* to your father, the devil,
    15: 19 As it is, you do not *b* to the world,
Ro   1: 6 called to *b* to Jesus Christ
     7: 4 that you might *b* to another,
    14: 8 we live or die, we *b* to the Lord.
Gal 5: 24 Those who *b* to Christ Jesus have
1Th 5: 8 But since we *b* to the day, let us be

BELONGS (BELONG)
Job 41: 11 Everything under heaven *b* to me.
Ps 111: 10 To him *b* eternal praise.
Eze 18: 4 For every living soul *b* to me,
Jn   8: 47 He who *b* to God hears what God
Ro 12: 5 each member *b* to all the others.

BELOVED (LOVE)
Dt 33: 12 "Let the *b* of the LORD rest secure

BELT
Isa 11: 5 Righteousness will be his *b*
Eph 6: 14 with the *b* of truth buckled

BENEFIT (BENEFITS)
Ro   6: 22 the *b* you reap leads to holiness,
2Co 4: 15 All this is for your *b*,

BENEFITS (BENEFIT)
Ps 103: 2 and forget not all his *b*.
Jn   4: 38 you have reaped the *b* of their labor

BENJAMIN
Twelfth son of Jacob by Rachel (Ge 35:16-24; 46:19-21; 1Ch 2:2). Jacob refused to send him to Egypt, but relented (Ge 42-45).

BEREANS*
Ac 17: 11 the *B* were of more noble character

BESTOWS
Ps 84: 11 the LORD *b* favor and honor;

BETHLEHEM
Mt   2: 1 After Jesus was born in *B* in Judea,

BETRAY
Pr 25: 9 do not *b* another man's confidence,

BIND (BINDS)
Dt   6: 8 and *b* them on your foreheads.
Pr   6: 21 *B* them upon your heart forever;
Isa 61: 1 me to *b* up the brokenhearted,
Mt 16: 19 whatever you *b* on earth will be

BINDS (BIND)
Ps 147: 3 and *b* up their wounds.
Isa 30: 26 when the LORD *b* up the bruises

BIRDS
Mt   8: 20 and *b* of the air have nests,

BIRTH (BEAR)
Ps 58: 3 Even from *b* the wicked go astray;
Mt   1: 18 This is how the *b* of Jesus Christ
1Pe 1: 3 great mercy he has given us new *b*

BIRTHRIGHT (BEAR)
Ge 25: 34 So Esau despised his *b*.

BLAMELESS
Ge 17: 1 walk before me and be *b*.
Job 1: 1 This man was *b* and upright;
Ps 84: 11 from those whose walk is *b*.
   119: 1 Blessed are they whose ways are *b*,
Pr 19: 1 Better a poor man whose walk is *b*
1Co 1: 8 so that you will be *b* on the day
Eph 5: 27 any other blemish, but holy and *b*.
Php 2: 15 so that you may become *b* and pure
1Th 3: 13 hearts so that you will be *b*
     5: 23 and body be kept *b* at the coming
Tit 1: 6 An elder must be *b*, the husband of
Heb 7: 26 *b*, pure, set apart from sinners,
2Pe 3: 14 effort to be found spotless, *b*

BLASPHEMES
Mk   3: 29 whoever *b* against the Holy Spirit

BLEMISH
1Pe 1: 19 a lamb without *b* or defect.

BLESS (BLESSED BLESSING BLESSINGS)
Ge 12: 3 I will *b* those who *b* you,
Ro 12: 14 Bless those who persecute you; *b*

BLESSED (BLESS)
Ge   1: 22 God *b* them and said, "Be fruitful
     2: 3 And God *b* the seventh day
    22: 18 nations on earth will be *b*,
Ps   1: 1 *B* is the man
     2: 12 *B* are all who take refuge in him.
    33: 12 *B* is the nation whose God is
    41: 1 *B* is he who has regard for the weak
    84: 5 *B* are those whose strength is
   106: 3 are they who maintain justice,
   112: 1 *B* is the man who fears the LORD,
   118: 26 *B* is he who comes in the name.
Pr 29: 18 but *b* is he who keeps the law.
    31: 28 Her children arise and call her *b*;
Mt   5: 3 saying: "*B* are the poor in spirit,
     5: 4 *B* are those who mourn,
     5: 5 *B* are the meek,
     5: 6 *B* are those who hunger
     5: 7 *B* are the merciful,
     5: 8 *B* are the pure in heart,
     5: 9 *B* are the peacemakers,
     5: 10 *B* are those who are persecuted
     5: 11 "*B* are you when people insult you,
Lk   1: 48 on all generations will call me *b*,
Jn 12: 13 "*B* is he who comes in the name
Ac 20: 35 'It is more *b* to give than to receive
Tit 2: 13 while we wait for the *b* hope—
Jas 1: 12 *B* is the man who perseveres
Rev 1: 3 *B* is the one who reads the words
    22: 14 "*B* are those who wash their robes,

BLESSING (BLESS)
Eze 34: 26 there will be showers of *b*.

BLESSINGS (BLESS)
Pr 10: 6 *B* crown the head of the righteous,

BLIND
Mt 15: 14 a *b* man leads a *b* man, both will fall
    23: 16 "Woe to you, *b* guides! You say,
Jn   9: 25 I was *b* but now I see!"

BLOOD
Ge   9: 6 "Whoever sheds the *b* of man,
Ex 12: 13 and when I see the *b*, I will pass
    24: 8 "This is the *b* of the covenant that
Lev 17: 11 For the life of a creature is in the *b*,

Ps 72: 14 for precious is their *b* in his sight.
Pr 6: 17 hands that shed innocent *b*,
Mt 26: 28 This is my *b* of the covenant,
Ro 3: 25 of atonement, through faith in his *b*
   5: 9 have now been justified by his *b*,
1Co 11: 25 cup is the new covenant in my *b*;
Eph 1: 7 we have redemption through his *b*,
   2: 13 near through the *b* of Christ.
Col 1: 20 by making peace through his *b*,
Heb 9: 12 once for all by his own *b*,
   9: 22 of *b* there is no forgiveness.
1Pe 1: 19 but with the precious *b* of Christ,
1Jn 1: 7 and the *b* of Jesus, his Son,
Rev 1: 5 has freed us from our sins by his *b*,
   5: 9 with your *b* you purchased men
   7: 14 white in the *b* of the Lamb.
   12: 11 him by the *b* of the Lamb

BLOT (BLOTS)
Ex 32: 32 then *b* me out of the book you have
Ps 51: 1 *b* out my transgressions.
Rev 3: 5 I will never *b* out his name

BLOTS (BLOT)
Isa 43: 25 "I, even I, am he who *b* out

BLOWN
Eph 4: 14 and *b* here and there by every wind
Jas 1: 6 doubts is like a wave of the sea, *b*

BOAST
1Ki 20: 11 armor should not *b* like one who
Ps 34: 2 My soul will *b* in the LORD;
   44: 8 In God we make our *b* all day long,
Pr 27: 1 Do not *b* about tomorrow,
1Co 1: 31 Let him who boasts *b* in the Lord."
Gal 6: 14 May I never *b* except in the cross
Eph 2: 9 not by works, so that no one can *b*.

BOAZ
Wealthy Bethlehemite who showed favor to Ruth (Ru 2), married her (Ru 4). Ancestor of David (Ru 4:18-22; 1Ch 2:12-15), Jesus (Mt 1:5-16; Lk 3:23-32).

BODIES (BODY)
Ro 12: 1 to offer your *b* as living sacrifices,
1Co 6: 15 not know that your *b* are members
Eph 5: 28 to love their wives as their own *b*.

BODY (BODIES)
Zec 13: 6 What are these wounds on your *b*?'

Mt 10: 28 afraid of those who kill the *b*
   26: 26 saying, "Take and eat; this is my *b*
   26: 41 spirit is willing, but the *b* is weak."
Jn 13: 10 wash his feet; his whole *b* is clean.
Ro 6: 13 Do not offer the parts of your *b*
   12: 4 us has one *b* with many members,
1Co 6: 19 not know that your *b* is a temple
   11: 24 "This is my *b*, which is for you;
   12: 12 The *b* is a unit, though it is made up
Eph 5: 30 for we are members of his *b*.

BOLD (BOLDNESS)
Ps 138: 3 you made me *b* and stouthearted.
Pr 21: 29 A wicked man puts up a *b* front,
   28: 1 but the righteous are as *b* as a lion.

BOLDNESS* (BOLD)
Ac 4: 29 to speak your word with great *b*.

BONDAGE
Ezr 9: 9 God has not deserted us in our *b*.

BOOK (BOOKS)
Jos 1: 8 Do not let this *B* of the Law depart
Ne 8: 8 They read from the *B* of the Law
Jn 20: 30 which are not recorded in this *b*.
Php 4: 3 whose names are in the *b* of life.
Rev 21: 27 written in the Lamb's *b* of life.

BOOKS (BOOK)
Ecc 12: 12 Of making many *b* there is no end,

BORN (BEAR)
Isa 9: 6 For to us a child is *b*,
Jn 3: 7 at my saying, 'You must be *b* again
1Pe 1: 23 For you have been *b* again,
1Jn 4: 7 Everyone who loves has been *b*
   5: 1 believes that Jesus is the Christ is *b*

BORROWER
Pr 22: 7 and the *b* is servant to the lender.

BOUGHT
Ac 20: 28 which he *b* with his own blood.
1Co 6: 20 You are not your own; you were *b*
   7: 23 You were *b* at a price; do not
2Pe 2: 1 the sovereign Lord who *b* them—

BOW
Ps 95: 6 Come, let us *b* down in worship,
Isa 45: 23 Before me every knee will *b*;
Ro 14: 11 'every knee will *b* before me;
Php 2: 10 name of Jesus every knee should *b*,

BRANCH (BRANCHES)
Isa 4: 2 In that day the *B* of the LORD will
Jer 33: 15 I will make a righteous *B* sprout

BRANCHES (BRANCH)
Jn 15: 5 "I am the vine; you are the *b*.

BRAVE
2Sa 2: 7 Now then, be strong and *b*,

BREAD
Dt 8: 3 that man does not live on *b* alone
Pr 30: 8 but give me only my daily *b*.
Ecc 11: 1 Cast your *b* upon the waters,
Isa 55: 2 Why spend money on what is not *b*
Mt 4: 4 'Man does not live on *b* alone,
   6: 11 Give us today our daily *b*.
Jn 6: 35 Jesus declared, "I am the *b* of life.
   21: 13 took the *b* and gave it to them,
1Co 11: 23 took *b*, and when he had given

BREAK (BREAKING BROKEN)
Nu 30: 2 he must not *b* his word
Jdg 2: 1 'I will never *b* my covenant
Isa 42: 3 A bruised reed he will not *b*,
Mt 12: 20 A bruised reed he will not *b*,

BREAKING (BREAK)
Jas 2: 10 at just one point is guilty of *b* all

BREASTPIECE (BREASTPLATE)
Ex 28: 15 Fashion a *b* for making decisions—

BREASTPLATE* (BREASTPIECE)
Isa 59: 17 He put on righteousness as his *b*,
Eph 6: 14 with the *b* of righteousness in place
1Th 5: 8 putting on faith and love as a *b*,

BREATHED (GOD-BREATHED)
Ge 2: 7 *b* into his nostrils the breath of life,
Jn 20: 22 And with that he *b* on them

BREEDS*
Pr 13: 10 Pride only *b* quarrels,

BRIBE
Ex 23: 8 "Do not accept a *b*,
Pr 6: 35 will refuse the *b*, however great it

BRIDE
Rev 19: 7 and his *b* has made herself ready,

BRIGHTER (BRIGHTNESS)
Pr 4: 18 shining ever *b* till the full light

BRIGHTNESS (BRIGHTER)
2Sa 22: 13 Out of the *b* of his presence
Da 12: 3 who are wise will shine like the *b*

BROAD
Mt 7: 13 and *b* is the road that leads

BROKEN (BREAK)
Ps 51: 17 The sacrifices of God are a *b* spirit;
Ecc 4: 12 of three strands is not quickly *b*.
Jn 10: 35 and the Scripture cannot be *b*—

BROKENHEARTED* (HEART)
Ps 34: 18 The LORD is close to the *b*
   109: 16 and the needy and the *b*.
   147: 3 He heals the *b*
Isa 61: 1 He has sent me to bind up the *b*,

BROTHER (BROTHER'S BROTHERS)
Pr 17: 17 and a *b* is born for adversity.
   18: 24 a friend who sticks closer than a *b*.
   27: 10 neighbor nearby than a *b* far away.
Mt 5: 24 and be reconciled to your *b*;
   18: 15 "If your *b* sins against you,
Mk 3: 35 Whoever does God's will is my *b*
Lk 17: 3 "If your *b* sins, rebuke him,
1Co 8: 13 if what I eat causes my *b* to fall
1Jn 2: 10 Whoever loves his *b* lives
   4: 21 loves God must also love his *b*.

BROTHER'S (BROTHER)
Ge 4: 9 "Am I my *b* keeper?" The LORD

BROTHERS (BROTHER)
Ps 133: 1 is when *b* live together in unity!
Pr 6: 19 who stirs up dissension among *b*.
Mt 25: 40 one of the least of these *b* of mine,
Mk 10: 29 or *b* or sisters or mother or father
Heb 13: 1 Keep on loving each other as *b*.
1Pe 3: 8 be sympathetic, love as *b*,
1Jn 3: 14 death to life, because we love our *b*.

BUILD (BUILDING BUILDS BUILT)
Mt 16: 18 and on this rock I will *b* my church,
Ac 20: 32 which can *b* you up and give you
1Co 14: 12 excel in gifts that *b* up the church.
1Th 5: 11 one another and *b* each other up,

BUILDING (BUILD)

1Co	3: 9	you are God's field, God's *b.*
2Co	10: 8	us for *b* you up rather
Eph	4: 29	helpful for *b* others up according

BUILDS (BUILD)

Ps	127: 1	Unless the LORD *b* the house,
1Co	3: 10	one should be careful how he *b.*
	8: 1	Knowledge puffs up, but love *b* up.

BUILT (BUILD)

Mt	7: 24	is like a wise man who *b* his house
Eph	2: 20	*b* on the foundation of the apostles
	4: 12	the body of Christ may be *b*

BURDEN (BURDENED BURDENS)

Ps	38: 4	like a *b* too heavy to bear.
Mt	11: 30	my yoke is easy and my *b* is light."

BURDENED (BURDEN)

Gal	5: 1	do not let yourselves be *b* again

BURDENS (BURDEN)

Ps	68: 19	who daily bears our *b.*
Gal	6: 2	Carry each other's *b,*

BURIED

Ro	6: 4	*b* with him through baptism
1Co	15: 4	that he was *b,* that he was raised

BURNING

Lev	6: 9	the fire must be kept *b* on the altar.
Ro	12: 20	you will heap *b* coals on his head."

BUSINESS

Da	8: 27	and went about the king's *b.*
1Th	4: 11	to mind your own *b* and to work

BUSY

1Ki	20: 40	While your servant was *b* here
2Th	3: 11	They are not *b;* they are
Tit	2: 5	to be *b* at home, to be kind,

⟀ C

CAESAR

Mt	22: 21	"Give to *C* what is Caesar's,

CAIN

Firstborn of Adam (Ge 4:1), murdered brother Abel (Ge 4:1-16; 1Jn 3:12).

CALEB

Judahite who spied out Canaan (Nu 13:6); allowed to enter land because of faith (Nu 13:30-14:38; Dt 1:36). Possessed Hebron (Jos 14:6-15:19).

CALF

Ex	32: 4	into an idol cast in the shape of a *c,*
Lk	15: 23	Bring the fattened *c* and kill it.

CALL (CALLED CALLING CALLS)

Ps	105: 1	to the LORD, *c* on his name;
	145: 18	near to all who *c* on him,
Pr	31: 28	children arise and *c* her blessed;
Isa	5: 20	Woe to those who *c* evil good
	55: 6	*c* on him while he is near.
	65: 24	Before they *c* I will answer;
Jer	33: 3	'*C* to me and I will answer you
Mt	9: 13	come to *c* the righteous,
Ro	10: 12	and richly blesses all who *c* on him,
	11: 29	gifts and his *c* are irrevocable.
1Th	4: 7	For God did not *c* us to be impure,

CALLED (CALL)

1Sa	3: 5	and said, "Here I am; you *c* me."
2Ch	7: 14	if my people, who are *c*
Ps	34: 6	This poor man *c,* and the LORD
Mt	21: 13	"'My house will be a *c* house
Ro	8: 30	And those he predestined, he also *c*
1Co	7: 15	God has *c* us to live in peace.
Gal	5: 13	You, my brothers, were *c* to be free
1Pe	2: 9	of him who *c* you out of darkness

CALLING (CALL)

Jn	1: 23	I am the voice of one *c* in the desert
Ac	22: 16	wash your sins away, *c* on his name
Eph	4: 1	worthy of the *c* you have received.
2Pe	1: 10	all the more eager to make your *c*

CALLS (CALL)

Joel	2: 32	And everyone who *c*
Jn	10: 3	He *c* his own sheep by name
Ro	10: 13	"Everyone who *c* on the name

CAMEL

Mt	19: 24	it is easier for a *c* to go
	23: 24	strain out a gnat but swallow a *c.*

CANAAN

1Ch	16: 18	"To you I will give the land of *C*

CANCELED

Lk	7: 42	so he *c* the debts of both.
Col	2: 14	having *c* the written code,

CAPITAL

Dt	21: 22	guilty of a *c* offense is put to death

CAPSTONE (STONE)

Ps	118: 22	has become the *c;*
1Pe	2: 7	has become the *c,*"

CARE (CAREFUL CARES CARING)

Ps	8: 4	the son of man that you *c* for him?

Pr	29: 7	The righteous *c* about justice
Lk	10: 34	him to an inn and took *c* of him.
Jn	21: 16	Jesus said, "Take *c* of my sheep."
Heb	2: 6	the son of man that you *c* for him?
1Pe	5: 2	of God's flock that is under your *c,*

CAREFUL (CARE)

Ex	23: 13	"Be *c* to do everything I have said
Dt	6: 3	be *c* to obey so that it may go well
Jos	23: 6	be *c* to obey all that is written
	23: 11	be very *c* to love the LORD your
Pr	13: 24	he who loves him is *c*
Mt	6: 1	"Be *c* not to do your 'acts
Ro	12: 17	Be *c* to do what is right in the eyes
1Co	3: 10	each one should be *c* how he builds
	8: 9	Be *c,* however, that the exercise
Eph	5: 15	Be very *c,* then, how you live

CARELESS

Mt	12: 36	for every *c* word they have spoken.

CARES (CARE)

Ps	55: 22	Cast your *c* on the LORD
Na	1: 7	He *c* for those who trust in him,
Eph	5: 29	but he feeds and *c* for it, just
1Pe	5: 7	on him because he *c* for you.

CARING* (CARE)

1Th	2: 7	like a mother *c* for her little
1Ti	5: 4	practice by *c* for their own family

CARRIED (CARRY)

Ex	19: 4	and how I *c* you on eagles' wings
Isa	53: 4	and *c* our sorrows,
Heb	13: 9	Do not be *c* away by all kinds
2Pe	1: 21	as they were *c* along by the Holy

CARRIES (CARRY)

Dt	32: 11	and *c* them on its pinions.
Isa	40: 11	and *c* them close to his heart;

CARRY (CARRIED CARRIES)

Lk	14: 27	anyone who does not *c* his cross
Gal	6: 2	*C* each other's burdens,
	6: 5	for each one should *c* his own load.

CAST

Ps	22: 18	and *c* lots for my clothing.
	55: 22	*C* your cares on the LORD
Ecc	11: 1	*C* your bread upon the waters,
Jn	19: 24	and *c* lots for my clothing."
1Pe	5: 7	*C* all your anxiety on him

CATCH (CAUGHT)

Lk	5: 10	from now on you will *c* men."

CATTLE

Ps	50: 10	and the *c* on a thousand hills.

CAUGHT (CATCH)

1Th	4: 17	and are left will be *c* up together

CAUSE (CAUSES)

Pr	24: 28	against your neighbor without *c,*
Ecc	8: 3	Do not stand up for a bad *c,*
Mt	18: 7	of the things that *c* people to sin!
Ro	14: 21	else that will *c* your brother
1Co	10: 32	Do not *c* anyone to stumble,

CAUSES (CAUSE)

Isa	8: 14	a stone that *c* men to stumble
Mt	18: 6	if anyone *c* one of these little ones

CAUTIOUS*

Pr	12: 26	A righteous man is *c* in friendship,

CEASE

Ps	46: 9	He makes wars *c* to the ends

CENSER

Lev	16: 12	is to take a *c* full of burning coals

CENTURION

Mt	8: 5	had entered Capernaum, a *c* came

CERTAIN (CERTAINTY)

2Pe	1: 19	word of the prophets made more *c,*

CERTAINTY* (CERTAIN)

Lk	1: 4	so that you may know the *c*
Jn	17: 8	They knew with *c* that I came

CHAFF

Ps	1: 4	They are like *c*

CHAINED

2Ti	2: 9	But God's word is not *c.*

CHAMPION

Ps	19: 5	like a *c* rejoicing to run his course.

CHANGE (CHANGED)

1Sa	15: 29	of Israel does not lie or *c* his mind;
Ps	110: 4	and will not *c* his mind:
Jer	7: 5	If you really *c* your ways
Mal	3: 6	"I the LORD do not *c.*
Mt	18: 3	unless you *c* and become like little
Heb	7: 21	and will not *c* his mind:
Jas	1: 17	who does not *c* like shifting

CHANGED (CHANGE)

1Co	15: 51	but we will all be *c*—in a flash,

CHARACTER

Ru	3: 11	that you are a woman of noble *c.*

CHARGE

Pr 31: 10 A wife of noble *c* who can find?
Ro 5: 4 perseverance, *c*; and *c*, hope.
1Co 15: 33 "Bad company corrupts good *c*."

CHARGE

Ro 8: 33 Who will bring any *c*
2Co 11: 7 the gospel of God to you free of *c*?
2Ti 4: 1 I give you this *c*: Preach the Word;

CHARIOTS

2Ki 6: 17 and *c* of fire all around Elisha.
Ps 20: 7 Some trust in *c* and some in horses,

CHARM

Pr 31: 30 *C* is deceptive, and beauty is

CHASES

Pr 12: 11 he who *c* fantasies lacks judgment.

CHATTER* (CHATTERING)

1Ti 6: 20 Turn away from godless *c*
2Ti 2: 16 Avoid godless *c*, because those

CHATTERING* (CHATTER)

Pr 10: 8 but a *c* fool comes to ruin.
10: 10 and a *c* fool comes to ruin.

CHEAT* (CHEATED)

Mal 1: 14 "Cursed is the *c* who has
1Co 6: 8 you yourselves *c* and do wrong,

CHEATED (CHEAT)

Lk 19: 8 if I have *c* anybody out of anything,
1Co 6: 7 Why not rather be *c*? Instead,

CHEEK

Mt 5: 39 someone strikes you on the right *c*,

CHEERFUL* (CHEERS)

Pr 15: 13 A happy heart makes the face *c*,
15: 15 but the *c* heart has a continual feast
15: 30 A *c* look brings joy to the heart,
17: 22 A *c* heart is good medicine,
2Co 9: 7 for God loves a *c* giver.

CHEERS (CHEERFUL)

Pr 12: 25 but a kind word *c* him up.

CHILD (CHILDISH CHILDREN)

Pr 20: 11 Even a *c* is known by his actions,
22: 6 Train a *c* in the way he should go,
22: 15 Folly is bound up in the heart of a *c*
23: 13 not withhold discipline from a *c*;
29: 15 *c* left to himself disgraces his mother.
Isa 7: 14 The virgin will be with *c*

9: 6 For to us a *c* is born,
11: 6 and a little *c* will lead them.
66: 13 As a mother comforts her *c*,
Mt 1: 23 "The virgin will be with *c*
18: 2 He called a little *c* and had him
Lk 1: 42 and blessed is the *c* you will bear!
1: 80 And the *c* grew and became strong
1Co 13: 11 When I was a *c*, I talked like a *c*,
1Jn 5: 1 who loves the father loves his *c*

CHILDISH* (CHILD)

1Co 13: 11 When I became a man, I put *c* ways

CHILDREN (CHILD)

Dt 4: 9 Teach them to your *c*
11: 19 them to your *c*, talking about them
Ps 8: 2 From the lips of *c* and infants
Pr 17: 6 Children's *c* are a crown
31: 28 Her *c* arise and call her blessed;
Mt 7: 11 how to give good gifts to your *c*,
11: 25 and revealed them to little *c*.
18: 3 you change and become like little *c*
19: 14 "Let the little *c* come to me,
21: 16 " 'From the lips of *c* and infants
Mk 9: 37 one of these little *c* in my name
10: 14 "Let the little *c* come to me,
10: 16 And he took the *c* in his arms,
13: 12 *C* will rebel against their parents
Lk 10: 21 and revealed them to little *c*.
18: 16 "Let the little *c* come to me,
Ro 8: 16 with our spirit that we are God's *c*.
2Co 12: 14 parents, but parents for their *c*.
Eph 6: 1 *C*, obey your parents in the Lord,
6: 4 do not exasperate your *c*; instead,
Col 3: 20 *C*, obey your parents in everything,
3: 21 Fathers, do not embitter your *c*,
1Ti 3: 4 and see that his *c* obey him
3: 12 and must manage his *c* and his
5: 10 bringing up *c*, showing hospitality,
1Jn 3: 1 that we should be called *c* of God!

CHOOSE
(CHOOSES CHOSE CHOSEN)

Dt 30: 19 Now *c* life, so that you
Jos 24: 15 then *c* for yourselves this day

Pr 8: 10 *C* my instruction instead of silver,
16: 16 to *c* understanding rather
Jn 15: 16 You did not *c* me, but I chose you

CHOOSES (CHOOSE)

Jn 7: 17 If anyone *c* to do God's will,

CHOSE (CHOOSE)

Ge 13: 11 So Lot *c* for himself the whole plain
Ps 33: 12 the people he *c* for his inheritance.
Jn 15: 16 but I *c* you and appointed you to go
1Co 1: 27 But God *c* the foolish things
Eph 1: 4 he *c* us in him before the creation
2Th 2: 13 from the beginning God *c* you

CHOSEN (CHOOSE)

Isa 41: 8 Jacob, whom I have *c*,
Mt 22: 14 For many are invited, but few are *c*
Lk 10: 42 Mary has *c* what is better,
23: 35 the Christ of God, the *C* One."
Jn 15: 19 but I have *c* you out of the world.
1Pe 1: 20 He was *c* before the creation
2: 9 But you are a *c* people, a royal

CHRIST (CHRIST'S CHRISTIAN CHRISTS)

Mt 1: 16 was born Jesus, who is called *C*.
16: 16 Peter answered, "You are the *C*,
22: 42 "What do you think about the *C*?
Jn 1: 41 found the Messiah" (that is, the *C*).
20: 31 you may believe that Jesus is the *C*,
Ac 2: 36 you crucified, both Lord and *C*."
5: 42 the good news that Jesus is the *C*.
9: 22 by proving that Jesus is the *C*.
17: 3 proving that the *C* had to suffer
18: 28 the Scriptures that Jesus was the *C*.
26: 23 that the *C* would suffer and,
Ro 3: 22 comes through faith in Jesus *C*
5: 6 we were still powerless, *C* died
5: 8 While we were still sinners, *C* died
5: 17 life through the one man, Jesus *C*.
6: 4 as *C* was raised from the dead
8: 1 for those who are in *C* Jesus,
8: 9 Spirit of *C*, he does not belong to *C*.
8: 35 us from the love of *C*?

10: 4 *C* is the end of the law
14: 9 *C* died and returned to life
15: 3 For even *C* did not please himself
1Co 1: 23 but we preach *C* crucified:
2: 2 except Jesus *C* and him crucified,
3: 11 one already laid, which is Jesus *C*.
5: 7 For *C*, our Passover lamb,
8: 6 and there is but one Lord, Jesus *C*,
10: 4 them, and that rock was *C*.
11: 1 as I follow the example of *C*.
11: 3 the head of every man is *C*,
12: 27 Now you are the body of *C*,
15: 3 that *C* died for our sins according
15: 14 And if *C* has not been raised,
15: 22 so in *C* all will be made alive.
15: 57 victory through our Lord Jesus *C*.
2Co 3: 3 show that you are a letter from *C*,
4: 5 not preach ourselves, but Jesus *C*
5: 10 before the judgment seat of *C*,
5: 17 Therefore, if anyone is in *C*,
11: 2 you to one husband, to *C*,
Gal 2: 20 I have been crucified with *C*
3: 13 *C* redeemed us from the curse
6: 14 in the cross of our Lord Jesus *C*,
Eph 1: 3 with every spiritual blessing in *C*.
3: 8 the unsearchable riches of *C*,
4: 13 measure of the fullness of *C*.
5: 2 as *C* loved us and gave himself up
5: 23 as *C* is the head of the church,
5: 25 just as *C* loved the church
Php 1: 21 to live is *C* and to die is gain.
1: 27 worthy of the gospel of *C*.
4: 19 to his glorious riches in *C* Jesus.
Col 1: 27 which is *C* in you, the hope of glory
1: 28 may present everyone perfect in *C*.
2: 6 as you received *C* Jesus as Lord,
2: 17 the reality, however, is found in *C*.
3: 15 Let the peace of *C* rule
2Th 2: 1 the coming of our Lord Jesus *C*
1Ti 1: 15 *C* Jesus came into the world
2: 5 the man *C* Jesus, who gave himself
2Ti 2: 3 us like a good soldier of *C* Jesus.
3: 15 salvation through faith in *C* Jesus.
Tit 2: 13 our great God and Savior, Jesus *C*,

Heb 3: 14 to share in *C* if we hold firmly
      9: 14 more, then, will the blood of *C*,
      9: 15 For this reason *C* is the mediator
      9: 28 so *C* was sacrificed once for all.
     10: 10 of the body of Jesus *C* once for all.
     13: 8 Jesus *C* is the same yesterday
1Pe   1: 19 but with the precious blood of *C*,
      2: 21 because *C* suffered for you,
      3: 18 For *C* died for sins once for all,
      4: 14 insulted because of the name of *C*,
1Jn   2: 22 man who denies that Jesus is the *C*.
      3: 16 Jesus *C* laid down his life for us.
      5: 1 believes that Jesus is the *C* is born
Rev 20: 4 reigned with *C* a thousand years.

CHRIST'S (CHRIST)

2Co   5: 14 For *C* love compels us,
      5: 20 We are therefore *C* ambassadors,
     12: 9 so that *C* power may rest on me.

CHRISTIAN (CHRIST)

1Pe   4: 16 as a *C*, do not be ashamed,

CHRISTS (CHRIST)

Mt   24: 24 For false *C* and false prophets will

CHURCH

Mt   16: 18 and on this rock I will build my *c*,
     18: 17 if he refuses to listen even to the *c*,
Ac   20: 28 Be shepherds of the *c* of God,
1Co   5: 12 of mine to judge those out-side the *c*
     14: 4 but he who prophesies edi-fies the *c*.
     14: 12 to excel in gifts that build up the *c*.
     14: 26 done for the strengthening of the *c*.
Eph   5: 23 as Christ is the head of the *c*,
Col   1: 24 the sake of his body, which is the *c*.

CIRCUMCISED

Ge   17: 10 Every male among you shall be *c*.

CIRCUMSTANCES

Php   4: 11 to be content whatever the *c*.
1Th   5: 18 continually; give thanks in all *c*,

CITIZENS (CITIZENSHIP)

Eph   2: 19 but fellow *c* with God's people

CITIZENSHIP (CITIZENS)

Php   3: 20 But our *c* is in heaven.

CITY

Mt   5: 14 A *c* on a hill cannot be hidden.
Heb 13: 14 here we do not have an enduring *c*,

CIVILIAN*

2Ti   2: 4 a soldier gets involved in *c* affairs —

CLAIM (CLAIMS)

Pr   25: 6 do not *c* a place among great men;
1Jn   1: 6 If we *c* to have fellowship
      1: 8 If we *c* to be without sin, we
      1: 10 If we *c* we have not sinned,

CLAIMS (CLAIM)

Jas   2: 14 if a man *c* to have faith
1Jn   2: 6 Whoever *c* to live in him must walk
      2: 9 Anyone who *c* to be in the light

CLAP

Ps   47: 1 *C* your hands, all you nations;
Isa 55: 12 will *c* their hands.

CLAY

Isa 45: 9 Does the *c* say to the potter,
     64: 8 We are the *c*, you are the potter;
Jer 18: 6 "Like *c* in the hand of the potter,
La   4: 2 are now considered as pots of *c*,
Da   2: 33 partly of iron and partly of baked *c*.
Ro   9: 21 of the same lump of *c* some pottery
2Co   4: 7 we have this treasure in jars of *c*
2Ti   2: 20 and *c*; some are for noble purposes

CLEAN

Lev 16: 30 you will be *c* from all your sins.
Ps   24: 4 He who has *c* hands and a pure
Mt   12: 44 the house unoccupied, swept *c*
     23: 25 You *c* the outside of the cup
Mk   7: 19 Jesus declared all foods "*c*.")
Jn   13: 10 to wash his feet; his whole body is *c*
     15: 3 are already *c* because of the word
Ac   10: 15 impure that God has made *c*."
Ro   14: 20 All food is *c*, but it is wrong

CLING (CLINGS)

Ro   12: 9 Hate what is evil; *c* to what is good.

CLINGS (CLING)

Ps   63: 8 My soul *c* to you;

CLOAK

2Ki   4: 29 "Tuck your *c* into your belt,

CLOSE (CLOSER)

Ps   34: 18 LORD is *c* to the broken-hearted
Isa 40: 11 and carries them *c* to his heart;
Jer 30: 21 himself to be *c* to me?'

CLOSER (CLOSE)

Ex   3: 5 "Do not come any *c*," God said.
Pr   18: 24 there is a friend who sticks *c*

CLOTHE (CLOTHED CLOTHES CLOTHING)

Ps   45: 3 *c* yourself with splendor
Isa 52: 1 *c* yourself with strength.
Ro   13: 14 *c* yourselves with the Lord Jesus
Col   3: 12 *c* yourselves with compassion,
1Pe   5: 5 *c* yourselves with humility

CLOTHED (CLOTHE)

Ps   30: 11 removed my sackcloth and *c* me
Pr   31: 25 She is *c* with strength and dignity;
Lk   24: 49 until you have been *c* with power

CLOTHES (CLOTHE)

Mt   6: 25 the body more important than *c*?
      6: 28 "And why do you worry about *c*?
Jn   11: 44 Take off the grave *c* and let him go

CLOTHING (CLOTHE)

Dt   22: 5 A woman must not wear men's *c*,
Mt   7: 15 They come to you in sheep's *c*,

CLOUD (CLOUDS)

Ex   13: 21 them in a pillar of *c* to guide them
Isa 19: 1 See, the LORD rides on a swift *c*
Lk   21: 27 of Man coming in a *c* with power
Heb 12: 1 by such a great *c* of witnesses,

CLOUDS (CLOUD)

Ps 104: 3 He makes the *c* his chariot
Da   7: 13 coming with the *c* of heaven.
Mk   13: 26 coming in *c* with great power
1Th   4: 17 with them in the *c* to meet the Lord

CO-HEIRS* (INHERIT)

Ro   8: 17 heirs of God and *c* with Christ,

COALS

Pr   25: 22 you will heap burning *c* on his head
Ro   12: 20 you will heap burning *c* on his head

COLD

Pr   25: 25 Like *c* water to a weary soul

Mt   10: 42 if anyone gives even a cup of *c* water
     24: 12 the love of most will grow *c*,

COMFORT (COMFORTED COMFORTS)

Ps   23: 4 rod and your staff, they *c* me.
    119: 52 and I find *c* in them.
    119: 76 May your unfailing love be my *c*,
Zec   1: 17 and the LORD will again *c* Zion
1Co 14: 3 encouragement and *c*.
2Co   1: 4 so that we can *c* those
      2: 7 you ought to forgive and *c* him,

COMFORTED (COMFORT)

Mt   5: 4 for they will be *c*.

COMFORTS* (COMFORT)

Job 29: 25 I was like one who *c* mourners.
Isa 49: 13 For the LORD *c* his people
     51: 12 "I, even I, am he who *c* you.
     66: 13 As a mother *c* her child,
2Co   1: 4 who *c* us in all our troubles,
      7: 6 But God, who *c* the down-cast,

COMMAND (COMMANDED COMMANDING COMMANDMENT COMMANDMENTS COMMANDS)

Ex   7: 2 You are to say everything I *c* you,
Nu   24: 13 to go beyond the *c* of the LORD —
Dt   4: 2 Do not add to what I *c* you
     30: 16 For I *c* you today to love
     32: 46 so that you may *c* your children
Ps   91: 11 For he will *c* his angels concerning
Pr   13: 13 but he who respects a *c* is rewarded
Ecc   8: 2 Obey the king's *c*, I say,
Joel 2: 11 mighty are those who obey his *c*.
Jn   14: 15 love me, you will obey what I *c*.
     15: 12 My *c* is this: Love each other
1Co 14: 37 writing to you is the Lord's *c*.
Gal   5: 14 law is summed up in a single *c*:
1Ti   1: 5 goal of this *c* is love, which comes
Heb 11: 3 universe was formed at God's *c*,
1Jn   3: 23 this is his *c*: to believe in the name
2Jn   : 6 his *c* is that you walk in love.

COMMANDED (COMMAND)

Ps   33: 9 he *c*, and it stood firm.
    148: 5 for he *c* and they were created.
Mt   28: 20 to obey everything I have *c* you.
1Co   9: 14 Lord has *c* that those who preach
1Jn   3: 23 and to love one another as he *c* us.

COMMANDING (COMMAND)

2Ti 2: 4 he wants to please his *c* officer.

COMMANDMENT (COMMAND)

Jos 22: 5 But be very careful to keep the *c*

Mt 22: 38 This is the first and greatest *c.*

Jn 13: 34 "A new *c* I give you: Love one

Ro 7: 12 and the *c* is holy, righteous

Eph 6: 2 which is the first *c* with a promise

COMMANDMENTS (COMMAND)

Ex 20: 6 who love me and keep my *c.*

34: 28 of the covenant—the Ten *C.*

Ecc 12: 13 Fear God and keep his *c,*

Mt 5: 19 one of the least of these *c*

22: 40 the Prophets hang on these two *c.*"

COMMANDS (COMMAND)

Dt 7: 9 those who love him and keep his *c.*

11: 27 the blessing if you obey the *c*

Ps 112: 1 who finds great delight in his *c.*

119: 47 for I delight in your *c*

119: 86 All your *c* are trustworthy;

119: 98 Your *c* make me wiser

119:127 Because I love your *c*

119:143 but your *c* are my delight.

119:172 for all your *c* are righteous.

Pr 3: 1 but keep my *c* in your heart,

6: 23 For these *c* are a lamp,

10: 8 The wise in heart accept *c,*

Da 9: 4 all who love him and obey his *c,*

Mt 5: 19 teaches these *c* will be called great

Jn 14: 21 Whoever has my *c* and obeys them,

Ac 17: 30 but now he *c* all people everywhere

1Co 7: 19 Keeping God's *c* is what counts.

1Jn 5: 3 And his *c* are not burdensome,

5: 3 This is love for God: to obey his *c.*

COMMEND (COMMENDED COMMENDS)

Ecc 8: 15 So I *c* the enjoyment of life,

Ro 13: 3 do what is right and he will *c* you.

1Pe 2: 14 and to *c* those who do right.

COMMENDED (COMMEND)

Heb 11: 39 These were all *c* for their faith,

COMMENDS (COMMEND)

2Co 10: 18 not the one who *c* himself who is

COMMIT (COMMITS COMMITTED)

Ex 20: 14 "You shall not *c* adultery.

Ps 37: 5 *C* your way to the LORD;

Mt 5: 27 that it was said, 'Do not *c* adultery.'

Lk 23: 46 into your hands I *c* my spirit."

Ac 20: 32 I *c* you to God and to the word

1Co 10: 8 We should not *c* sexual immorality,

1Pe 4: 19 to God's will should *c* themselves

COMMITS (COMMIT)

Pr 6: 32 man who *c* adultery lacks

29: 22 a hot-tempered one *c* many sins.

Mt 19: 9 marries another woman *c* adultery

COMMITTED (COMMIT)

Nu 5: 7 and must confess the sin he has *c.*

1Ki 8: 61 But your hearts must be fully *c*

2Ch 16: 9 those whose hearts are fully *c*

Mt 5: 28 lustfully has already *c* adultery

2Co 5: 19 And he has *c* to us the message

1Pe 2: 22 "He *c* no sin,

COMMON

Pr 22: 2 Rich and poor have this in *c:*

1Co 10: 13 has seized you except what is *c*

2Co 6: 14 and wickedness have in *c?*

COMPANION (COMPANIONS)

Pr 13: 20 but a *c* of fools suffers harm.

28: 7 a *c* of gluttons disgraces his father.

29: 3 of prostitutes squanders his

COMPANIONS (COMPANION)

Pr 18: 24 A man of many *c* may come to ruin

COMPANY

Pr 24: 1 do not desire their *c;*

Jer 15: 17 I never sat in the *c* of revelers,

1Co 15: 33 "Bad *c* corrupts good character."

COMPARED (COMPARING)

Eze 31: 2 Who can be *c* with you in majesty?

Php 3: 8 I consider everything a loss *c*

COMPARING* (COMPARED)

Ro 8: 18 present sufferings are not worth *c*

2Co 8: 8 the sincerity of your love by *c* it

Gal 6: 4 without *c* himself to somebody else

COMPASSION (COMPASSIONATE COMPASSIONS)

Ex 33: 19 I will have *c* on whom I will have *c.*

Ne 9: 19 of your great *c* you did not

9: 28 in your *c* you delivered them time

Ps 51: 1 according to your great *c*

103: 4 and crowns you with love and *c.*

103: 13 As a father has *c* on his children,

145: 9 he has *c* on all he has made.

Isa 49: 13 and will have *c* on his afflicted ones

49: 15 and have no *c* on the child she has

Hos 2: 19 in love and *c.*

11: 8 all my *c* is aroused.

Jnh 3: 9 with *c* turn from his fierce anger

Mt 9: 36 When he saw the crowds, he had *c*

Mk 8: 2 "I have *c* for these people,

Ro 9: 15 and I will have *c* on whom I have *c*

Col 3: 12 clothe yourselves with *c,* kindness,

Jas 5: 11 The Lord is full of *c* and mercy.

COMPASSIONATE (COMPASSION)

Ne 9: 17 gracious and *c,* slow to anger

Ps 103: 8 The LORD is *c* and gracious,

112: 4 the gracious and *c* and righteous

Eph 4: 32 Be kind and *c* to one another,

1Pe 3: 8 love as brothers, be *c* and humble.

COMPASSIONS* (COMPASSION)

La 3: 22 for his *c* never fail.

COMPELLED (COMPELS)

Ac 20: 22 "And now, *c* by the Spirit,

1Co 9: 16 I cannot boast, for I am *c* to preach.

COMPELS (COMPELLED)

2Co 5: 14 For Christ's love *c* us, because we

COMPETENCE* (COMPETENT)

2Co 3: 5 but our *c* comes from God.

COMPETENT* (COMPETENCE)

Ro 15: 14 and *c* to instruct one another.

1Co 6: 2 are you not *c* to judge trivial cases?

2Co 3: 5 Not that we are *c* in ourselves

3: 6 He has made us *c* as ministers

COMPETES*

1Co 9: 25 Everyone who *c* in the games goes

2Ti 2: 5 Similarly, if anyone *c* as an athlete,

2: 5 unless he *c* according to the rules.

COMPLACENT

Am 6: 1 Woe to you who are *c* in Zion,

COMPLAINING*

Php 2: 14 Do everything without *c* or arguing

COMPLETE

Jn 15: 11 and that your joy may be *c.*

16: 24 will receive, and your joy will be *c.*

17: 23 May they be brought to *c* unity

Ac 20: 24 *c* the task the Lord Jesus has given

Php 2: 2 then make my joy *c*

Col 4: 17 to it that you *c* the work you have

Jas 1: 4 so that you may be mature and *c,*

2: 22 his faith was made *c* by what he did

CONCEAL (CONCEALED CONCEALS)

Ps 40: 10 I do not *c* your love and your truth

Pr 25: 2 It is the glory of God to *c* a matter;

CONCEALED (CONCEAL)

Jer 16: 17 nor is their sin *c* from my eyes.

Mt 10: 26 There is nothing *c* that will not be

Mk 4: 22 and whatever is *c* is meant

CONCEALS (CONCEAL)

Pr 28: 13 He who *c* his sins does not prosper,

CONCEITED

Ro 12: 16 Do not be *c.*

Gal 5: 26 Let us not become *c,* provoking

1Ti 6: 4 he is *c* and understands nothing.

CONCEIVED

Mt 1: 20 what is *c* in her is from the Holy

1Co 2: 9 no mind has *c*

CONCERN (CONCERNED)

Eze 36: 21 I had *c* for my holy name, which

1Co 7: 32 I would like you to be free from *c.*

12: 25 that its parts should have equal *c*

2Co 11: 28 of my *c* for all the churches.

CONCERNED (CONCERN)

Jnh 4: 10 "You have been *c* about this vine,

1Co 7: 32 An unmarried man is *c* about

CONDEMN (CONDEMNATION CONDEMNED CONDEMNING CONDEMNS)

Job 40: 8 Would you *c* me to justify yourself?

Isa 50: 9 Who is he that will *c* me?

Lk 6: 37 Do not *c,* and you will not be

Jn 3: 17 Son into the world to *c* the world,

12: 48 very word which I spoke will *c* him

Ro 2: 27 yet obeys the law will *c* you who,

1Jn 3: 20 presence whenever our hearts *c* us.

CONDEMNATION (CONDEMN)

Ro 5: 18 of one trespass was *c* for all men,

8: 1 there is now no *c* for those who are

CONDEMNED (CONDEMN)

Ps   34: 22 no one will be *c* who takes refuge

Mt   12: 37 and by your words you will be *c*."

23: 33 How will you escape being *c* to hell

Jn   3: 18 Whoever believes in him is not *c*,

5: 24 has eternal life and will not be *c*;

16: 11 prince of this world now stands *c*.

Ro   14: 23 But the man who has doubts is *c*

1Co 11: 32 disciplined so that we will not be *c*

Heb 11: 7 By his faith he *c* the world

CONDEMNING (CONDEMN)

Pr   17: 15 the guilty and *c* the innocent—

Ro   2: 1 judge the other, you are *c* yourself,

CONDEMNS (CONDEMN)

Ro   8: 34 Who is he that *c*? Christ Jesus,

2Co 3: 9 the ministry that *c* men is glorious,

CONDUCT

Pr   10: 23 A fool finds pleasure in evil *c*,

20: 11 by whether his *c* is pure and right.

21: 8 but the *c* of the innocent is upright.

Ecc   6: 8 how to *c* himself before others?

Jer   4: 18 "Your own *c* and actions

17: 10 to reward a man according to his *c*,

Eze   7: 3 I will judge you according to your *c*

Php   1: 27 *c* yourselves in a manner worthy

1Ti   3: 15 to *c* themselves in God's household

CONFESS (CONFESSION)

Lev 16: 21 and *c* over it all the wickedness

26: 40 "'But if they will *c* their sins

Nu   5: 7 must *c* the sin he has committed.

Ps   38: 18 I *c* my iniquity;

Ro   10: 9 That if you *c* with your mouth,

Php   2: 11 every tongue *c* that Jesus Christ is

Jas   5: 16 Therefore *c* your sins to each other

1Jn   1: 9 If we *c* our sins, he is faithful

CONFESSION (CONFESS)

Ezr 10: 11 Now make *c* to the LORD,

2Co 9: 13 obedience that accompanies your *c*

CONFIDENCE

Ps   71: 5 my *c* since my youth.

Pr   3: 26 for the LORD will be your *c*

11: 13 A gossip betrays a *c*,

25: 9 do not betray another man's *c*

31: 11 Her husband has full *c* in her

Isa 32: 17 will be quietness and *c* forever.

Jer 17: 7 whose *c* is in him.

Php   3: 3 and who put no *c* in the flesh—

Heb 3: 14 till the end the *c* we had at first.

4: 16 the throne of grace with *c*,

10: 19 since we have *c* to enter the Most

10: 35 So do not throw away your *c*;

1Jn   5: 14 This is the *c* we have

CONFORM* (CONFORMED)

Ro   12: 2 Do not *c* any longer to the pattern

1Pe   1: 14 do not *c* to the evil desires you had

CONFORMED (CONFORM)

Ro   8: 29 predestined to be *c* to the likeness

CONQUERORS

Ro   8: 37 than *c* through him who loved us.

CONSCIENCE (CONSCIENCES)

Ro   13: 5 punishment but also because of *c*.

1Co   8: 7 since their *c* is weak, it is defiled.

8: 12 in this way and wound their weak *c*

10: 25 without raising questions of *c*,

10: 29 freedom be judged by another's *c*?

Heb 10: 22 to cleanse us from a guilty *c*

1Pe   3: 16 and respect, keeping a clear *c*,

CONSCIENCES* (CONSCIENCE)

Ro   2: 15 their *c* also bearing witness,

1Ti   4: 2 whose *c* have been seared

Tit   1: 15 their minds and *c* are corrupted.

Heb   9: 14 cleanse our *c* from acts that lead

CONSCIOUS*

Ro   3: 20 through the law we become *c* of sin

1Pe   2: 19 of unjust suffering because he is *c*

CONSECRATE (CONSECRATED)

Ex   13: 2 "*C* to me every firstborn male.

Lev 20: 7 "'*C* yourselves and be holy,

CONSECRATED (CONSECRATE)

Ex   29: 43 and the place will be *c* by my glory.

1Ti   4: 5 because it is *c* by the word of God

CONSIDER (CONSIDERATE CONSIDERED CONSIDERS)

1Sa 12: 24 *c* what great things he has done

Job 37: 14 stop and *c* God's wonders.

Ps   8: 3 When I *c* your heavens,

107: 43 and *c* the great love of the LORD.

143: 5 and *c* what your hands have done.

Lk   12: 24 *C* the ravens: They do not sow

12: 27 about the rest? "*C* how the lilies

Php   2: 3 but in humility *c* others better

3: 8 I *c* everything a loss compared

Heb 10: 24 And let us *c* how we may spur one

Jas   1: 2 *C* it pure joy, my brothers,

CONSIDERATE* (CONSIDER)

Tit   3: 2 to be peaceable and *c*,

Jas   3: 17 then peace-loving, *c*, submissive,

1Pe   2: 18 only to those who are good and *c*,

3: 7 in the same way be *c* as you live

CONSIDERED (CONSIDER)

Job   1: 8 "Have you *c* my servant Job?

2: 3 "Have you *c* my servant Job?

Ps   44: 22 we are *c* as sheep to be slaughtered

Isa 53: 4 yet we *c* him stricken by God,

Ro   8: 36 we are *c* as sheep to be slaughtered

CONSIDERS (CONSIDER)

Pr   31: 16 She *c* a field and buys it;

Ro   14: 5 One man *c* one day more sacred

Jas   1: 26 If anyone *c* himself religious

CONSIST

Lk   12: 15 a man's life does not *c*

CONSOLATION

Ps   94: 19 your *c* brought joy to my soul.

CONSTRUCTIVE*

1Co 10: 23 but not everything is *c*.

CONSUME (CONSUMING)

Jn   2: 17 "Zeal for your house will *c* me."

CONSUMING (CONSUME)

Dt   4: 24 For the LORD your God is a *c* fire,

Heb 12: 29 and awe, for our "God is a *c* fire."

CONTAIN

1Ki   8: 27 the highest heaven, cannot *c* you.

2Pe   3: 16 His letters *c* some things that are

CONTAMINATES*

2Co 7: 1 from everything that *c* body

CONTEMPT

Pr   14: 31 He who oppresses the poor shows *c*

17: 5 He who mocks the poor shows *c*

18: 3 When wickedness comes, so does *c*

Da   12: 2 others to shame and everlasting *c*.

Ro   14: 4 Or do you show *c* for the riches

Gal   4: 14 you did not treat me with *c*

1Th   5: 20 do not treat prophecies with *c*.

CONTEND (CONTENDING)

Jude : 3 you to *c* for the faith that was once

CONTENDING* (CONTEND)

Php   1: 27 *c* as one man for the faith

CONTENT (CONTENTMENT)

Pr   13: 25 The righteous eat to their hearts' *c*,

Php   4: 11 to be *c* whatever the circumstances

4: 12 I have learned the secret of being *c*

1Ti   6: 8 and clothing, we will be *c* with that.

Heb 13: 5 and be *c* with what you have,

CONTENTMENT (CONTENT)

1Ti   6: 6 But godliness with *c* is great gain.

CONTINUAL (CONTINUE)

Pr   15: 15 but the cheerful heart has a *c* feast.

CONTINUE (CONTINUAL)

Php   2: 12 *c* to work out your salvation

2Ti   3: 14 *c* in what you have learned

1Jn   5: 18 born of God does not *c* to sin;

Rev 22: 11 and let him who is holy *c* to be holy

22: 11 let him who does right *c* to do right;

CONTRITE*

Ps   51: 17 a broken and *c* heart,

Isa 57: 15 also with him who is *c* and lowly

57: 15 and to revive the heart of the *c*.

66: 2 he who is humble and *c* in spirit,

CONTROL (CONTROLLED SELF-CONTROL SELF-CONTROLLED)

Pr   29: 11 a wise man keeps himself under *c*.

1Co   7: 9 But if they cannot *c* themselves,

7: 37 but has *c* over his own will,

1Th   4: 4 you should learn to *c* his own body

CONTROLLED (CONTROL)

Ps   32: 9 but must be *c* by bit and bridle

Ro   8: 6 but the mind *c* by the Spirit is life
       8: 8 Those *c* by the sinful nature cannot

CONTROVERSIES
Tit   3: 9 But avoid foolish *c* and genealogies

CONVERSATION
Col   4: 6 Let your *c* be always full of grace,

CONVERT
1Ti   3: 6 He must not be a recent *c*,

CONVICT
Jn   16: 8 he will *c* the world of guilt in regard

CONVINCED (CONVINCING)
Ro   8: 38 For I am *c* that neither death
2Ti   1: 12 and am *c* that he is able
       3: 14 have learned and have become *c*

CONVINCING* (CONVINCED)
Ac   1: 3 and gave many *c* proofs that he was

CORNELIUS*
   Roman to whom Peter preached; first Gentile Christian (Ac 10).

CORNERSTONE (STONE)
Isa 28: 16 a precious *c* for a sure foundation;
Eph   2: 20 Christ Jesus himself as the chief *c*.
1Pe   2: 6 a chosen and precious *c*,

CORRECT (CORRECTING CORRECTION CORRECTS)
2Ti   4: 2 *c*, rebuke and encourage—

CORRECTING* (CORRECT)
2Ti   3: 16 *c* and training in righteous-ness,

CORRECTION (CORRECT)
Pr   10: 17 whoever ignores *c* leads others
      12: 1 but he who hates *c* is stupid.
      15: 5 whoever heeds *c* shows prudence.
      15: 10 he who hates *c* will die.
      29: 15 The rod of *c* imparts wisdom,

CORRECTS* (CORRECT)
Job   5: 17 "Blessed is the man whom God *c*;
Pr   9: 7 Whoever *c* a mocker invites insult;

CORRUPT (CORRUPTS)
Ge   6: 11 Now the earth was *c* in God's sight

CORRUPTS* (CORRUPT)
Ecc   7: 7 and a bribe *c* the heart.
1Co 15: 33 "Bad company *c* good character."
Jas   3: 6 It *c* the whole person, sets

COST
Pr   4: 7 Though it *c* all you have, get

Isa 55: 1 milk without money and without *c*.
Rev 21: 6 to drink without *c* from the spring

COUNSEL (COUNSELOR)
1Ki 22: 5 "First seek the *c* of the LORD."
Pr   15: 22 Plans fail for lack of *c*,
Rev   3: 18 I *c* you to buy from me gold refined

COUNSELOR (COUNSEL)
Isa   9: 6 Wonderful *C*, Mighty God,
Jn   14: 16 he will give you another *C* to be
      14: 26 But the *C*, the Holy Spirit,

COUNT (COUNTING COUNTS)
Ro   4: 8 whose sin the Lord will never *c*
       6: 11 *c* yourselves dead to sin

COUNTING (COUNT)
2Co   5: 19 not *c* men's sins against them.

COUNTRY
Jn   4: 44 prophet has no honor in his own *c*.)

COUNTS (COUNT)
Jn   6: 63 The Spirit gives life; the flesh *c*
1Co   7: 19 God's commands is what *c*.
Gal   5: 6 only thing that *c* is faith expressing

COURAGE (COURAGEOUS)
Ac   23: 11 "Take *c*! As you have testified
1Co 16: 13 stand firm in the faith; be men of *c*;

COURAGEOUS (COURAGE)
Dt   31: 6 Be strong and *c*.
Jos   1: 6 and *c*, because you will lead these

COURSE
Ps   19: 5 a champion rejoicing to run his *c*.
Pr   15: 21 of understanding keeps a straight *c*.

COURTS
Ps   84: 10 Better is one day in your *c*
     100: 4 and his *c* with praise;

COVENANT (COVENANTS)
Ge   9: 9 "I now establish my *c* with you
Ex   19: 5 if you obey me fully and keep my *c*,
1Ch 16: 15 He remembers his *c* forever,
Job 31: 1 "I made a *c* with my eyes
Jer   31: 31 "when I will make a new *c*
1Co 11: 25 "This cup is the new *c* in my blood;
Gal   4: 24 One *c* is from Mount Sinai
Heb   9: 15 Christ is the mediator of a new *c*,

COVENANTS (COVENANT)
Ro   9: 4 theirs the divine glory, the *c*,

Gal   4: 24 for the women represent two *c*.

COVER (COVER-UP COVERED COVERS)
Ps   91: 4 He will *c* you with his feathers,
Jas   5: 20 and *c* over a multitude of sins.

COVER-UP (COVER)
1Pe   2: 16 but do not use your freedom as a *c*

COVERED (COVER)
Ps   32: 1 whose sins are *c*.
Isa   6: 2 With two wings they *c* their faces,
Ro   4: 7 whose sins are *c*.
1Co 11: 4 with his head *c* dishonors his head.

COVERS (COVER)
Pr   10: 12 but love *c* over all wrongs.
1Pe   4: 8 love *c* over a multitude of sins.

COVET
Ex   20: 17 You shall not *c* your neighbor's
Ro   13: 9 "Do not steal," "Do not *c*,"

COWARDLY*
Rev 21: 8 But the *c*, the unbelieving, the vile,

CRAFTINESS (CRAFTY)
1Co   3: 19 "He catches the wise in their *c*";

CRAFTY (CRAFTINESS)
Ge   3: 1 the serpent was more *c* than any
2Co 12: 16 *c* fellow that I am, I caught you

CRAVE
Pr   23: 3 Do not *c* his delicacies,
1Pe   2: 2 newborn babies, *c* pure spiritual

CREATE (CREATED CREATION CREATOR)
Ps   51: 10 *C* in me a pure heart, O God,
Isa   45: 18 he did not *c* it to be empty,

CREATED (CREATE)
Ge   1: 1 In the beginning God *c* the heavens
       1: 21 God *c* the great creatures of the sea
       1: 27 So God *c* man in his own image,
Ps   148: 5 for he commanded and they were *c*
Isa   42: 5 he who *c* the heavens and stretched
Ro   1: 25 and served *c* things rather
1Co 11: 9 neither was man *c* for woman,
Col   1: 16 For by him all things were *c*:
1Ti   4: 4 For everything God *c* is good,
Rev 10: 6 who *c* the heavens and all that is

CREATION (CREATE)
Mk   16: 15 and preach the good news to all *c*.
Jn   17: 24 me before the *c* of the world.
Ro   8: 19 The *c* waits in eager expectation
       8: 39 depth, nor anything else in all *c*,
2Co   5: 17 he is a new *c*; the old has gone,
Col   1: 15 God, the firstborn over all *c*.
1Pe   1: 20 chosen before the *c* of the world,
Rev 13: 8 slain from the *c* of the world.

CREATOR (CREATE)
Ge   14: 22 God Most High, *C* of heaven
Ro   1: 25 created things rather than the *C*—

CREATURE (CREATURES)
Lev 17: 11 For the life of a *c* is in the blood,

CREATURES (CREATURE)
Ge   6: 19 bring into the ark two of all living *c*,
Ps   104: 24 the earth is full of your *c*.

CREDIT (CREDITED)
Ro   4: 24 to whom God will *c* righteousness
1Pe   2: 20 it to your *c* if you receive a beating

CREDITED (CREDIT)
Ge   15: 6 and he *c* it to him as righteousness.
Ro   4: 5 his faith is *c* as righteousness.
Gal   3: 6 and it was *c* to him as righteousness
Jas   2: 23 and it was *c* to him as righteousness

CRIED (CRY)
Ps   18: 6 I *c* to my God for help.

CRIMSON
Isa   1: 18 though they are red as *c*,

CRIPPLED
Mk   9: 45 better for you to enter life *c*

CRITICISM
2Co   8: 20 We want to avoid any *c*

CROOKED
Pr   10: 9 he who takes *c* paths will be found
Php   2: 15 children of God without fault in a *c*

CROSS
Mt   10: 38 and anyone who does not take his *c*
Lk   9: 23 take up his *c* daily and follow me.
Ac   2: 23 to death by nailing him to the *c*.
1Co   1: 17 lest the *c* of Christ be emptied
Gal   6: 14 in the *c* of our Lord Jesus Christ,
Php   2: 8 even death on a *c*!

CROWD (continued)

Col 1: 20 through his blood, shed on the *c.*

      2: 14 he took it away, nailing it to the *c.*

      2: 15 triumphing over them by the *c.*

Heb 12: 2 set before him endured the *c,*

CROWD

Ex 23: 2 Do not follow the *c* in doing wrong.

CROWN (CROWNED CROWNS)

Pr   4: 9 present you with a *c* of splendor.”

     10: 6 Blessings *c* the head

     12: 4 noble character is her husband's *c,*

     17: 6 Children's children are a *c*

Isa 61: 3 to bestow on them a *c* of beauty

Zec 9: 16 like jewels in a *c.*

Mt 27: 29 then twisted together a *c* of thorns

1Co 9: 25 it to get a *c* that will last forever.

2Ti 4: 8 store for me the *c* of righteousness,

Rev 2: 10 and I will give you the *c* of life.

CROWNED (CROWN)

Ps   8: 5 and *c* him with glory and honor.

Pr 14: 18 the prudent are *c* with knowledge.

Heb 2: 7 you *c* him with glory and honor

CROWNS (CROWN)

Rev 4: 10 They lay their *c* before the throne

     19: 12 and on his head are many *c.*

CRUCIFIED (CRUCIFY)

Mt 20: 19 to be mocked and flogged and *c.*

     27: 38 Two robbers were *c* with him,

Lk 24: 7 be *c* and on the third day be raised

Jn 19: 18 Here they *c* him, and with him two

Ac   2: 36 whom you *c,* both Lord and Christ

Ro   6: 6 For we know that our old self was *c*

1Co 1: 23 but we preach Christ *c:* a stumbling

      2: 2 except Jesus Christ and him *c.*

Gal 2: 20 I have been *c* with Christ

      5: 24 Christ Jesus have *c* the sinful

CRUCIFY (CRUCIFIED CRUCIFYING)

Mt 27: 22 They all answered, “*C* him!” “Why

     27: 31 Then they led him away to *c* him.

CRUCIFYING* (CRUCIFY)

Heb 6: 6 to their loss they are *c* the Son

CRUSH (CRUSHED)

Ge   3: 15 he will *c* your head,

Isa 53: 10 it was the LORD's will to *c* him

Ro 16: 20 The God of peace will soon *c* Satan

CRUSHED (CRUSH)

Ps 34: 18 and saves those who are *c* in spirit.

Isa 53: 5 he was *c* for our iniquities;

2Co 4: 8 not *c;* perplexed, but not in despair;

CRY (CRIED)

Ps 34: 15 and his ears are attentive to their *c;*

     40: 1 he turned to me and heard my *c.*

   130: 1 Out of the depths I *c* to you,

CUP

Ps 23: 5 my *c* overflows.

Mt 10: 42 if anyone gives even a *c* of cold water

     23: 25 You clean the outside of the *c*

     26: 39 may this *c* be taken from me.

1Co 11: 25 after supper he took the *c,* saying,

CURSE (CURSED)

Dt 11: 26 before you today a blessing and a *c*

     21: 23 hung on a tree is under God's *c.*

Lk   6: 28 bless those who *c* you, pray

Gal 3: 13 of the law by becoming a *c* for us,

Rev 22: 3 No longer will there be any *c.*

CURSED (CURSE)

Ge   3: 17 “*C* is the ground because of you;

Dt 27: 15 “*C* is the man who carves an image

     27: 16 “*C* is the man who dishonors his

     27: 17 “*C* is the man who moves his

     27: 18 “*C* is the man who leads the blind

     27: 19 *C* is the man who withholds justice

     27: 20 “*C* is the man who sleeps

     27: 21 “*C* is the man who has sexual

     27: 22 “*C* is the man who sleeps

     27: 23 “*C* is the man who sleeps

     27: 24 “*C* is the man who kills his

     27: 25 “*C* is the man who accepts a bribe

     27: 26 “*C* is the man who does not uphold

Ro   9: 3 I could wish that I myself were *c*

Gal 3: 10 “*C* is everyone who does not

CURTAIN

Ex 26: 33 The *c* will separate the Holy Place

Lk 23: 45 the *c* of the temple was torn in two.

Heb 10: 20 opened for us through the *c,*

CYMBAL*

1Co 13: 1 a resounding gong or a clanging *c.*

❋ **D**

DANCE (DANCING)

Ecc 3: 4 a time to mourn and a time to *d,*

Mt 11: 17 and you did not *d;*

DANCING (DANCE)

Ps 30: 11 You turned my wailing into *d;*

   149: 3 Let them praise his name with *d*

DANGER

Pr 27: 12 The prudent see *d* and take refuge,

Ro   8: 35 famine or nakedness or *d* or sword?

DANIEL

Hebrew exile to Babylon, name changed to Belteshazzar (Da 1:6-7). Refused to eat unclean food (Da 1:8-21). Interpreted Nebuchadnezzar's dreams (Da 2; 4), writing on the wall (Da 5). Thrown into lion's den (Da 6). Visions of (Da 7-12).

DARK (DARKNESS)

Job 34: 22 There is no *d* place, no deep

Pr 31: 15 She gets up while it is still *d;*

Ro   2: 19 a light for those who are in the *d,*

2Pe 1: 19 as to a light shining in a *d* place,

DARKNESS (DARK)

Ge   1: 4 he separated the light from the *d.*

2Sa 22: 29 the LORD turns my *d* into light.

Jn   3: 19 but men loved *d* instead of light

2Co 6: 14 fellowship can light have with *d?*

Eph 5: 8 For you were once *d,* but now you

1Pe 2: 9 out of *d* into his wonderful light.

1Jn 1: 5 in him there is no *d* at all.

      2: 9 but hates his brother is still in the *d.*

DAUGHTERS

Joel 2: 28 sons and *d* will prophesy,

DAVID

Son of Jesse (Ru 4:17-22; 1Ch 2:13-15), ancestor of Jesus (Mt 1:1-17; Lk 3:31).
Anointed king by Samuel (1Sa 16:1-13). Musician to Saul (1Sa 16:14-23; 18:10). Killed Goliath (1Sa 17). Relation with Jonathan (1Sa 18:1-4; 19-20; 23:16-18; 2Sa 1). Disfavor of Saul (1Sa 18:6-23:29). Spared Saul's life (1Sa 24; 26). Among Philistines (1Sa 21:10-14; 27-30). Lament for Saul and Jonathan (2Sa 1).
Anointed king of Judah (2Sa 2:1-11); of Israel (2Sa 5:1-4; 1Ch 11:1-3). Promised eternal dynasty (2Sa 7; 1Ch 17; Ps 132). Adultery with Bathsheba (2Sa 11-12). Absalom's revolt (2Sa 14-18). Last words (2Sa 23:1-7). Death (1Ki 2:10-12; 1Ch 29:28).

DAWN

Ps 37: 6 your righteousness shine like the *d,*

Pr   4: 18 is like the first gleam of *d,*

DAY (DAYS)

Ge   1: 5 God called the light “*d,*”

Ex 20: 8 “Remember the Sabbath *d*

Lev 23: 28 because it is the *D* of Atonement,

Nu 14: 14 before them in a pillar of cloud by *d*

Jos 1: 8 meditate on it *d* and night,

Ps 84: 10 Better is one *d* in your courts

     96: 2 proclaim his salvation *d* after *d.*

   118: 24 This is the *d* the LORD has made;

Pr 27: 1 not know what a *d* may bring forth.

Joel 2: 31 and dreadful *d* of the LORD.

Ob   : 15 The *d* of the LORD is near

Lk 11: 3 Give us each *d* our daily bread.

Ac 17: 11 examined the Scriptures every *d*

2Co 4: 16 we are being renewed *d* by *d.*

1Th 5: 2 for you know very well that the *d*

2Pe 3: 8 With the Lord a *d* is like

DAYS (DAY)

Dt 17: 19 he is to read it all the *d* of his life

Ps 23: 6 all the *d* of my life,

     90: 10 The length of our *d* is seventy years

Ecc 12: 1 Creator in the *d* of your youth,

Joel 2: 29 I will pour out my Spirit in those *d.*

Mic 4: 1 In the last *d*

Heb 1: 2 in these last *d* he has spoken to us

2Pe 3: 3 that in the last *d* scoffers will come,

DEACONS

1Ti 3: 8 *D,* likewise, are to be men worthy

DEAD (DIE)

Dt 18: 11 or spiritist or who consults the *d.*

Mt 28: 7 'He has risen from the *d*

Ro   6: 11 count yourselves *d* to sin

Eph 2: 1 you were *d* in your transgressions

1Th 4: 16 and the *d* in Christ will rise first.

Jas 2: 17 is not accompanied by action, is *d.*

      2: 26 so faith without deeds is *d.*

DEATH (DIE)

Nu 35: 16 the murderer shall be put to *d*.
Ps 23: 4 the valley of the shadow of *d*,
116: 15 is the *d* of his saints.
Pr 8: 36 all who hate me love *d*."
14: 12 but in the end it leads to *d*.
Ecc 7: 2 for *d* is the destiny of every man;
Isa 25: 8 he will swallow up *d* forever.
53: 12 he poured out his life unto *d*,
Jn 5: 24 he has crossed over from *d* to life.
Ro 5: 12 and in this way *d* came to all men,
6: 23 For the wages of sin is *d*,
8: 13 put to *d* the misdeeds of the body,
1Co 15: 21 For since *d* came through a man,
15: 55 Where, O *d*, is your sting?"
Rev 1: 18 And I hold the keys of *d* and Hades
20: 6 The second *d* has no power
20: 14 The lake of fire is the second *d*.
21: 4 There will be no more *d*.

DEBAUCHERY

Ro 13: 13 not in sexual immorality and *d*,
Eph 5: 18 drunk on wine, which leads to *d*.

DEBORAH

Prophetess who led Israel to victory over Canaanites (Jdg 4-5).

DEBT (DEBTORS DEBTS)

Ro 13: 8 Let no *d* remain outstanding,
13: 8 continuing *d* to love one another,

DEBTORS (DEBT)

Mt 6: 12 as we also have forgiven our *d*.

DEBTS (DEBT)

Dt 15: 1 seven years you must cancel *d*.
Mt 6: 12 Forgive us our *d*,

DECAY

Ps 16: 10 will you let your Holy One see *d*.
Ac 2: 27 will you let your Holy One see *d*.

DECEIT (DECEIVE)

Mk 7: 22 greed, malice, *d*, lewdness, envy,
1Pe 2: 1 yourselves of all malice and all *d*,
2: 22 and no *d* was found in his mouth."

DECEITFUL (DECEIVE)

Jer 17: 9 The heart is *d* above all things
2Co 11: 13 men are false apostles, *d* workmen,

DECEITFULNESS (DECEIVE)

Mk 4: 19 the *d* of wealth and the desires

Heb 3: 13 of you may be hardened by sin's *d*.

DECEIVE (DECEIT DECEITFUL DECEITFULNESS DECEIVED DECEIVES DECEPTIVE)

Lev 19: 11 "'Do not *d* one another.
Pr 14: 5 A truthful witness does not *d*,
Mt 24: 5 'I am the Christ,' and will *d* many.
Ro 16: 18 and flattery they *d* the minds
1Co 3: 18 Do not *d* yourselves.
Eph 5: 6 Let no one *d* you with empty words
Jas 1: 22 to the word, and so *d* yourselves.
1Jn 1: 8 we *d* ourselves and the truth is not

DECEIVED (DECEIVE)

Ge 3: 13 "The serpent *d* me, and I ate."
Gal 6: 7 Do not be *d*: God cannot be
1Ti 2: 14 And Adam was not the one *d*;
2Ti 3: 13 to worse, deceiving and being *d*.
Jas 1: 16 Don't be *d*, my dear brothers.

DECEIVES (DECEIVE)

Gal 6: 3 when he is nothing, he *d* himself.
Jas 1: 26 he *d* himself and his religion is

DECENCY*

1Ti 2: 9 women to dress modestly, with *d*

DECEPTIVE (DECEIVE)

Pr 31: 30 Charm is *d*, and beauty is fleeting;
Col 2: 8 through hollow and *d* philosophy,

DECLARE (DECLARED DECLARING)

1Ch 16: 24 *D* his glory among the nations,
Ps 19: 1 The heavens *d* the glory of God;
96: 3 *D* his glory among the nations,
Isa 42: 9 and new things I *d*;

DECLARED (DECLARE)

Mk 7: 19 Jesus *d* all foods "clean.")
Ro 2: 13 the law who will be *d* righteous.
3: 20 no one will be *d* righteous

DECLARING (DECLARE)

Ps 71: 8 *d* your splendor all day long.
Ac 2: 11 we hear them *d* the wonders

DECREED (DECREES)

La 3: 37 happen if the Lord has not *d* it?
Lk 22: 22 Son of Man will go as it has been *d*,

DECREES (DECREED)

Lev 10: 11 Israelites all the *d* the LORD has
Ps 119:112 My heart is set on keeping your *d*

DEDICATE (DEDICATION)

Nu 6: 12 He must *d* himself to the LORD
Pr 20: 25 for a man to *d* something rashly

DEDICATION (DEDICATE)

1Ti 5: 11 sensual desires overcome their *d*

DEED (DEEDS)

Col 3: 17 you do, whether in word or *d*,

DEEDS (DEED)

1Sa 2: 3 and by him *d* are weighed.
Ps 65: 5 with awesome *d* of righteousness,
66: 3 "How awesome are your *d*!
78: 4 the praiseworthy *d* of the LORD,
86: 10 you are great and do marvelous *d*;
92: 4 For you make me glad by your *d*,
111: 3 Glorious and majestic are his *d*,
Hab 3: 2 I stand in awe of your *d*, O LORD.
Mt 5: 16 that they may see your good *d*
Ac 26: 20 prove their repentance by their *d*.
Jas 2: 14 claims to have faith but has no *d*?
2: 20 faith without *d* is useless?
1Pe 2: 12 they may see your good *d*

DEEP (DEPTH)

1Co 2: 10 all things, even the *d* things
1Ti 3: 9 hold of the *d* truths of the faith

DEER

Ps 42: 1 As the *d* pants for streams of water,

DEFEND (DEFENSE)

Ps 74: 22 Rise up, O God, and *d* your cause;
Pr 31: 9 *d* the rights of the poor and needy
Jer 50: 34 He will vigorously *d* their cause

DEFENSE (DEFEND)

Ps 35: 23 Awake, and rise to my *d*!
Php 1: 16 here for the *d* of the gospel.
1Jn 2: 1 speaks to the Father in our *d* —

DEFERRED*

Pr 13: 12 Hope *d* makes the heart sick,

DEFILE (DEFILED)

Da 1: 8 Daniel resolved not to *d* himself

DEFILED (DEFILE)

Isa 24: 5 The earth is *d* by its people;

DEFRAUD

Lev 19: 13 Do not *d* your neighbor or rob him.

DEITY*

Col 2: 9 of the *D* lives in bodily form,

DELIGHT (DELIGHTS)

1Sa 15: 22 "Does the LORD *d*
Ps 1: 2 But his *d* is in the law of the LORD
16: 3 in whom is all my *d*.
35: 9 and *d* in his salvation.
37: 4 *D* yourself in the LORD
43: 4 to God, my joy and my *d*.
51: 16 You do not *d* in sacrifice,
119: 77 for your law is my *d*.
Pr 29: 17 he will bring *d* to your soul.
Isa 42: 1 my chosen one in whom I *d*;
55: 2 and your soul will *d* in the richest
61: 10 I *d* greatly in the LORD;
Jer 9: 24 for in these I *d*,"
15: 16 they were my joy and my heart's *d*,
Mic 7: 18 but to *d* to show mercy.
Zep 3: 17 He will take great *d* in you,
Mt 12: 18 the one I love, in whom I *d*;
1Co 13: 6 Love does not *d* in evil
2Co 12: 10 for Christ's sake, I *d* in weaknesses,

DELIGHTS (DELIGHT)

Ps 22: 8 since he *d* in him."
35: 27 who *d* in the well-being
36: 8 from your river of *d*.
37: 23 if the LORD *d* in a man's way,
Pr 3: 12 as a father the son he *d* in.
12: 22 but he *d* in men who are truthful.
23: 24 he who has a wise son *d* in him.

DELILAH*

Woman who betrayed Samson (Jdg 16:4-22).

DELIVER (DELIVERANCE DELIVERED DELIVERER DELIVERS)

Ps 72: 12 For he will *d* the needy who cry out
79: 9 *d* us and forgive our sins
Mt 6: 13 but *d* us from the evil one.'
2Co 1: 10 hope that he will continue to *d* us,

DELIVERANCE (DELIVER)

Ps 3: 8 From the LORD comes *d*.
32: 7 and surround me with songs of *d*.
33: 17 A horse is a vain hope for *d*;

DELIVERED (DELIVER)

Ps 34: 4 he *d* me from all my fears.
Ro 4: 25 He was *d* over to death for our sins

DELIVERER (DELIVER)

Ps 18: 2 is my rock, my fortress and my *d*;
40: 17 You are my help and my *d*;
140: 7 O Sovereign LORD, my strong *d*,
144: 2 my stronghold and my *d*,

DELIVERS (DELIVER)

Ps 34: 17 he *d* them from all their troubles.

34: 19 but the LORD *d* him from them all

37: 40 The LORD helps them and *d* them

37: 40 he *d* them from the wicked

DEMANDED

Lk 12: 20 This very night your life will be *d*

12: 48 been given much, much will be *d*;

DEMONS

Mt 12: 27 And if I drive out *d* by Beelzebub,

Mk   5: 15 possessed by the legion of *d*,

Ro   8: 38 neither angels nor *d*, neither

Jas   2: 19 Good! Even the *d* believe that—

DEMONSTRATE (DEMONSTRATES)

Ro   3: 26 he did it to *d* his justice

DEMONSTRATES* (DEMONSTRATE)

Ro   5: 8 God *d* his own love for us in this:

DEN

Da   6: 16 and threw him into the lions' *d*.

Mt 21: 13 you are making it a '*d* of robbers.' "

DENARIUS

Mk 12: 15 Bring me a *d* and let me look at it."

DENIED (DENY)

1Ti   5: 8 he has *d* the faith and is worse

DENIES (DENY)

1Jn   2: 23 No one who *d* the Son has

DENY (DENIED DENIES DENYING)

Ex 23: 6 "Do not *d* justice to your poor

Job 27: 5 till I die, I will not *d* my integrity.

La   3: 35 to *d* a man his rights

Lk   9: 23 he must *d* himself and take up his

Tit   1: 16 but by their actions they *d* him.

DENYING* (DENY)

Eze 22: 29 mistreat the alien, *d* them justice.

2Ti   3: 5 a form of godliness but *d* its power.

2Pe   2: 1 *d* the sovereign Lord who bought

DEPART (DEPARTED)

Ge 49: 10 The scepter will not *d* from Judah,

Job   1: 21 and naked I will *d*.

Mt 25: 41 '*D* from me, you who are cursed,

Php   1: 23 I desire to *d* and be with Christ,

DEPARTED (DEPART)

1Sa   4: 21 "The glory has *d* from Israel"—

Ps 119:102 I have not *d* from your laws,

DEPOSIT

2Co   1: 22 put his Spirit in our hearts as a *d*,

5: 5 and has given us the Spirit as a *d*.

Eph   1: 14 who is a *d* guaranteeing our

2Ti   1: 14 Guard the good *d* that was

DEPRAVED (DEPRAVITY)

Ro   1: 28 he gave them over to a *d* mind,

Php   2: 15 fault in a crooked and *d* generation,

DEPRAVITY (DEPRAVED)

Ro   1: 29 of wickedness, evil, greed and *d*.

DEPRIVE

Dt 24: 17 Do not *d* the alien or the fatherless

Pr 18: 5 or to *d* the innocent of justice.

Isa 10: 2 to *d* the poor of their rights

29: 21 with false testimony *d* the innocent

1Co   5: 5 Do not *d* each other

DEPTH (DEEP)

Ro   8: 39 any powers, neither height nor *d*,

11: 33 the *d* of the riches of the wisdom

DESERT

Nu 32: 13 wander in the *d* forty years,

Ne   9: 19 you did not abandon them in the *d*.

Ps 78: 19 "Can God spread a table in the *d*?

78: 52 led them like sheep through the *d*.

Mk   1: 13 and he was in the *d* forty days,

DESERTED (DESERTS)

Ezr   9: 9 our God has not *d* us

Mt 26: 56 all the disciples *d* him and fled.

2Ti   1: 15 in the province of Asia has *d* me,

DESERTING (DESERTS)

Gal   1: 6 are so quickly *d* the one who called

DESERTS (DESERTED DESERTING)

Zec 11: 17 who *d* the flock!

DESERVE (DESERVES)

Ps 103: 10 he does not treat us as our sins *d*

Jer 21: 14 I will punish you as your deeds *d*,

Mt 22: 8 those I invited did not *d* to come.

Ro   1: 32 those who do such things *d* death,

DESERVES (DESERVE)

2Sa 12: 5 the man who did this *d* to die!

Lk 10: 7 for the worker *d* his wages.

1Ti   5: 18 and "The worker *d* his wages."

DESIRABLE (DESIRE)

Pr 22: 1 A good name is more *d*

DESIRE (DESIRABLE DESIRES)

Ge   3: 16 Your *d* will be for your husband,

Dt   5: 21 You shall not set your *d*

1Ch 29: 18 keep this *d* in the hearts

Ps 40: 6 Sacrifice and offering you did not *d*

40: 8 I *d* to do your will, O my God;

73: 25 earth has nothing I *d* besides you

Pr   3: 15 nothing you *d* can compare

10: 24 what the righteous *d* will be

11: 23 The *d* of the righteous ends only

Isa 26: 8 are the *d* of our hearts.

53: 2 appearance that we should *d* him.

55: 11 but will accomplish what I *d*

Hos 6: 6 For I *d* mercy, not sacrifice,

Mt   9: 13 learn what this means: 'I *d* mercy,

Ro   7: 18 For I have the *d* to do what is good,

1Co 12: 31 But eagerly *d* the greater gifts.

14: 1 and eagerly *d* spiritual gifts,

Php   1: 23 I *d* to depart and be with Christ,

Heb 13: 18 *d* to live honorably in every way.

Jas   1: 15 Then, after *d* has conceived,

DESIRES (DESIRE)

Ge   4: 7 at your door; it *d* to have you,

Ps 34: 12 and *d* to see many good days,

37: 4 he will give you the *d* of your heart.

103: 5 satisfies your *d* with good things,

145: 19 He fulfills the *d* of those who fear

Pr 11: 6 the unfaithful are trapped by evil *d*.

19: 22 What a man *d* is unfailing love;

Mk   4: 19 and the *d* for other things come in

Ro   8: 5 set on what that nature *d*;

13: 14 to gratify the *d* of the sinful nature.

Gal   5: 16 and you will not gratify the *d*

5: 17 the sinful nature *d* what is contrary

1Ti   3: 1 an overseer, he *d* a noble task.

6: 9 and harmful *d* that plunge men

2Ti   2: 22 Flee the evil *d* of youth,

Jas   1: 20 about the righteous life that God *d*.

4: 1 from your *d* that battle within you?

1Pe   2: 11 to abstain from sinful *d*, which war

1Jn   2: 17 The world and its *d* pass away,

DESOLATE

Isa 54: 1 are the children of the *d* woman

DESPAIR

Isa 61: 3 instead of a spirit of *d*.

2Co   4: 8 perplexed, but not in *d*; persecuted,

DESPISE (DESPISED DESPISES)

Job 42: 6 Therefore I *d* myself

Pr   1: 7 but fools *d* wisdom and discipline.

3: 11 do not *d* the LORD's discipline

23: 22 do not *d* your mother

Lk 16: 13 devoted to the one and *d* the other.

Tit   2: 15 Do not let anyone *d* you.

DESPISED (DESPISE)

Ge 25: 34 So Esau *d* his birthright.

Isa 53: 3 He was *d* and rejected by men,

1Co   1: 28 of this world and the *d* things—

DESPISES (DESPISE)

Pr 14: 21 He who *d* his neighbor sins,

15: 20 but a foolish man *d* his mother.

15: 32 who ignores discipline *d* himself,

Zec   4: 10 "Who *d* the day of small things?

DESTINED (DESTINY)

Lk   2: 34 "This child is *d* to cause the falling

DESTINY (DESTINED PREDESTINED)

Ps 73: 17 then I understood their final *d*.

Ecc   7: 2 for death is the *d* of every man;

DESTITUTE

Pr 31: 8 for the rights of all who are *d*.

Heb 11: 37 *d*, persecuted and mistreated—

DESTROY (DESTROYED DESTROYS DESTRUCTION)

Pr   1: 32 complacency of fools will *d* them;

Mt 10: 28 of the One who can *d* both soul

DESTROYED (DESTROY)

Job 19: 26 And after my skin has been *d*,

Isa 55: 13 which will not be *d*."

1Co   8: 11 for whom Christ died, is *d*

15: 26 The last enemy to be *d* is death.

2Co   5: 1 if the earthly tent we live in is *d*,

Heb 10: 39 of those who shrink back and are *d*,
2Pe 3: 10 the elements will be *d* by fire,

DESTROYS (DESTROY)
Pr 6: 32 whoever does so *d* himself.
11: 9 mouth the godless *d* his neighbor,
18: 9 is brother to one who *d*.
28: 24 he is partner to him who *d*.
Ecc 9: 18 but one sinner *d* much good.
1Co 3: 17 If anyone *d* God's temple,

DESTRUCTION (DESTROY)
Pr 16: 18 Pride goes before *d*,
Hos 13: 14 Where, O grave, is your *d*?
Mt 7: 13 broad is the road that leads to *d*,
Gal 6: 8 from that nature will reap *d*;
2Th 1: 9 punished with everlasting *d*
1Ti 6: 9 that plunge men into ruin and *d*.
2Pe 2: 1 bringing swift *d* on themselves.
3: 16 other Scriptures, to their own *d*.

DETERMINED (DETERMINES)
Job 14: 5 Man's days are *d*;
Isa 14: 26 This is the plan *d* for the whole
Da 11: 36 for what has been *d* must take place
Ac 17: 26 and he *d* the times set for them

DETERMINES* (DETERMINED)
Ps 147: 4 He *d* the number of the stars
Pr 16: 9 but the LORD *d* his steps.
1Co 12: 11 them to each one, just as he *d*.

DETESTABLE (DETESTS)
Pr 21: 27 The sacrifice of the wicked is *d* —
28: even his prayers are *d*.
Isa 1: 13 Your incense is *d* to me.
Lk 16: 15 among men is *d* in God's sight.
Tit 1: 16 They are *d*, disobedient

DETESTS (DETESTABLE)
Dt 22: 5 LORD your God *d* anyone who
23: 18 the LORD your God *d* them both.
25: 16 LORD your God *d* anyone who
Pr 12: 22 The LORD *d* lying lips,
15: 8 The LORD *d* the sacrifice
15: 9 The LORD *d* the way
15: 26 The LORD *d* the thoughts
16: 5 The LORD *d* all the proud of heart
17: 15 the LORD *d* them both.
20: 23 The LORD *d* differing weights,

DEVIL (DEVIL'S)
Mt 13: 39 the enemy who sows them is the *d*.
25: 41 the eternal fire prepared for the *d*

Lk 4: 2 forty days he was tempted by the *d*.
8: 12 then the *d* comes and takes away
Eph 4: 27 and do not give the *d* a foothold.
2Ti 2: 26 and escape from the trap of the *d*,
Jas 4: 7 Resist the *d*, and he will flee
1Pe 5: 8 Your enemy the *d* prowls
1Jn 3: 8 who does what is sinful is of the *d*,
Rev 12: 9 that ancient serpent called the *d*

DEVIL'S* (DEVIL)
Eph 6: 11 stand against the *d* schemes.
1Ti 3: 7 into disgrace and into the *d* trap.
1Jn 3: 8 was to destroy the *d* work.

DEVOTE (DEVOTED DEVOTING DEVOTION DEVOUT)
Job 11: 13 "Yet if you *d* your heart to him
Jer 30: 21 for who is he who will *d* himself
Col 4: 2 *D* yourselves to prayer, being
1Ti 4: 13 *d* yourself to the public reading
Tit 3: 8 may be careful to *d* themselves

DEVOTED (DEVOTE)
Ezr 7: 10 For Ezra had *d* himself to the study
Ac 2: 42 They *d* themselves
Ro 12: 10 Be *d* to one another
1Co 7: 34 Her aim is to be *d* to the Lord

DEVOTING (DEVOTE)
1Ti 5: 10 *d* herself to all kinds of good deeds.

DEVOTION (DEVOTE)
1Ch 28: 9 and serve him with whole-hearted *d*
Eze 33: 31 With their mouths they express *d*,
1Co 7: 35 way in undivided *d* to the Lord.
2Co 11: 3 from your sincere and pure *d*

DEVOUR
2Sa 2: 26 "Must the sword *d* forever?
Mk 12: 40 They *d* widows' houses
1Pe 5: 8 lion looking for someone to *d*.

DEVOUT (DEVOTE)
Lk 2: 25 Simeon, who was righteous and *d*.

DIE (DEAD DEATH DIED DIES)
Ge 2: 17 when you eat of it you will surely *d*
Ex 11: 5 Every firstborn son in Egypt will *d*,
Ru 1: 17 Where you *d* I will *d*, and there I
2Ki 14: 6 each is to *d* for his own sins."

Pr 5: 23 He will *d* for lack of discipline,
10: 21 but fools *d* for lack of judgment.
15: 10 he who hates correction will *d*.
23: 13 with the rod, he will not *d*.
Ecc 3: 2 a time to be born and a time to *d*,
Isa 66: 24 their worm will not *d*, nor will their
Eze 3: 18 that wicked man will *d* for his sin,
18: 4 soul who sins is the one who will *d*.
33: 8 'O wicked man, you will surely *d*,'
Mt 26: 52 "for all who draw the sword will *d*
Jn 11: 26 and believes in me will never *d*.
Ro 5: 7 Very rarely will anyone *d*
14: 8 and if we *d*, we *d* to the Lord.
1Co 15: 22 in Adam all *d*, so in Christ all will
15: 31 I *d* every day—I mean that,
Php 1: 21 to live is Christ and to *d* is gain.
Heb 9: 27 Just as man is destined to *d* once,
Rev 14: 13 Blessed are the dead who *d*

DIED (DIE)
Ro 5: 6 we were still powerless, Christ *d*
6: 2 By no means! We *d* to sin;
6: 8 if we *d* with Christ, we believe that
14: 15 brother for whom Christ *d*.
1Co 8: 11 for whom Christ *d*, is destroyed
15: 3 that Christ *d* for our sins according
2Co 5: 14 *d* for all, and therefore all *d*.
Col 3: 3 For you *d*, and your life is now
1Th 5: 10 He *d* for us so that, whether we are
2Ti 2: 11 If we *d* with him,
Heb 9: 15 now that he has *d* as a ransom
1Pe 3: 18 For Christ *d* for sins once for all,
Rev 2: 8 who *d* and came to life again.

DIES (DIE)
Job 14: 14 If a man *d*, will he live again?
Pr 11: 7 a wicked man *d*, his hope perishes;
Jn 11: 25 in me will live, even though he *d*;
1Co 15: 36 does not come to life unless it *d*.

DIFFERENCE (DIFFERENT)
Ro 10: 12 For there is no *d* between Jew

DIFFERENT (DIFFERENCE)
1Co 12: 4 There are *d* kinds of gifts,
2Co 11: 4 or a *d* gospel from the one you

DIGNITY
Pr 31: 25 She is clothed with strength and *d*;

DIGS
Pr 26: 27 If a man *d* a pit, he will fall into it;

DILIGENCE (DILIGENT)
Heb 6: 11 to show this same *d* to the very end

DILIGENT (DILIGENCE)
Pr 21: 5 The plans of the *d* lead to profit
1Ti 4: 15 Be *d* in these matters; give yourself

DIRECT (DIRECTS)
Ps 119: 35 *D* me in the path of your
119:133 *D* my footsteps according
Jer 10: 23 it is not for man to *d* his steps.
2Th 3: 5 May the Lord *d* your hearts

DIRECTS (DIRECT)
Ps 42: 8 By day the LORD *d* his love,
Isa 48: 17 who *d* you in the way you should

DIRGE
Mt 11: 17 we sang a *d*,

DISAPPEAR
Mt 5: 18 will by any means *d* from the Law
Lk 16: 17 earth to *d* than for the least stroke

DISAPPOINT* (DISAPPOINTED)
Ro 5: 5 And hope does not *d* us,

DISAPPOINTED (DISAPPOINT)
Ps 22: 5 in you they trusted and were not *d*.

DISASTER
Ps 57: 1 wings until the *d* has passed.
Pr 3: 25 Have no fear of sudden *d*
17: 5 over *d* will not go unpunished.
Isa 45: 7 I bring prosperity and create *d*;
Eze 7: 5 An unheard-of *d* is coming.

DISCERN (DISCERNING DISCERNMENT)
Ps 19: 12 Who can *d* his errors?
139: 3 You *d* my going out and my lying
Php 1: 10 you may be able to *d* what is best

DISCERNING (DISCERN)
Pr 14: 6 knowledge comes easily to the *d*.
15: 14 The *d* heart seeks knowledge,
17: 24 A *d* man keeps wisdom in view,
17: 28 and if he holds his tongue.
19: 25 rebuke a *d* man, and he will gain

DISCERNMENT (DISCERN)

Pr 17: 10 A rebuke impresses a man of *d*
28: 11 a poor man who has *d* sees

DISCIPLE (DISCIPLES)

Mt 10: 42 these little ones because he is my *d*,
Lk 14: 27 and follow me cannot be my *d*.

DISCIPLES (DISCIPLE)

Mt 28: 19 Therefore go and make *d*
Jn 8: 31 to my teaching, you are really my *d*
13: 35 men will know that you are my *d*
Ac 11: 26 The *d* were called Christians first

DISCIPLINE (DISCIPLINED DISCIPLINES)

Ps 38: 1 or *d* me in your wrath.
39: 11 You rebuke and *d* men for their sin;
94: 12 Blessed is the man you *d*, O LORD
Pr 1: 7 but fools despise wisdom and *d*.
3: 11 do not despise the LORD's *d*
5: 12 You will say, "How I hated *d!*
5: 23 He will die for lack of *d*,
6: 23 and the corrections of *d*
10: 17 He who heeds *d* shows the way
12: 1 Whoever loves *d* loves knowledge,
13: 18 He who ignores *d* comes to poverty
13: 24 who loves him is careful to *d* him.
15: 5 A fool spurns his father's *d*,
15: 32 He who ignores *d* despises himself,
19: 18 *D* your son, for in that there is hope
22: 15 the rod of *d* will drive it far
23: 13 Do not withhold *d* from a child;
29: 17 *D* your son, and he will give you
Heb 12: 5 do not make light of the Lord's *d*,
12: 7 as *d*; God is treating you
12: 11 No *d* seems pleasant at the time,
Rev 3: 19 Those whom I love I rebuke and *d*.

DISCIPLINED (DISCIPLINE)

Pr 1: 3 for acquiring a *d* and prudent life,
Jer 31: 18 'You *d* me like an unruly calf,
1Co 11: 32 we are being *d* so that we will not
Tit 1: 8 upright, holy and *d*.
Heb 12: 7 For what son is not *d* by his father?

DISCIPLINES (DISCIPLINE)

Dt 8: 5 your heart that as a man *d* his son,
Pr 3: 12 the LORD *d* those he loves,
Heb 12: 6 because the Lord *d* those he loves,
12: 10 but God *d* us for our good,

DISCLOSED

Lk 8: 17 is nothing hidden that will not be *d*,

DISCOURAGED

Jos 1: 9 Do not be terrified; do not be *d*,
Jos 10: 25 "Do not be afraid; do not be *d*.
1Ch 28: 20 or *d*, for the LORD God,
Isa 42: 4 he will not falter or be *d*
Col 3: 21 children, or they will become *d*.

DISCREDITED

2Co 6: 3 so that our ministry will not be *d*.

DISCRETION*

1Ch 22: 12 May the LORD give you *d*
Pr 1: 4 knowledge and *d* to the young—
2: 11 *D* will protect you,
5: 2 that you may maintain *d*
8: 12 I possess knowledge and *d*.
11: 22 a beautiful woman who shows no *d*.

DISCRIMINATED*

Jas 2: 4 have you not *d* among yourselves

DISFIGURED

Isa 52: 14 his appearance was so *d*

DISGRACE (DISGRACEFUL DISGRACES)

Pr 11: 2 When pride comes, then comes *d*,
14: 34 but sin is a *d* to any people.
19: 26 is a son who brings shame and *d*.
Ac 5: 41 of suffering *d* for the Name.
Heb 13: 13 the camp, bearing the *d* he bore.

DISGRACEFUL (DISGRACE)

Pr 10: 5 during harvest is a *d* son.
17: 2 wise servant will rule over a *d* son,

DISGRACES (DISGRACE)

Pr 28: 7 of gluttons *d* his father.
29: 15 but a child left to itself *d* his mother

DISHONEST

Pr 11: 1 The LORD abhors *d* scales,
29: 27 The righteous detest the *d*;
Lk 16: 10 whoever is *d* with very little will
1Ti 3: 8 wine, and not pursuing *d* gain.

DISHONOR (DISHONORS)

Lev 18: 7 "'Do not *d* your father
Pr 30: 9 and so *d* the name of my God.
1Co 15: 43 it is sown in *d*, it is raised in glory;

DISHONORS (DISHONOR)

Dt 27: 16 Cursed is the man who *d* his father

DISMAYED

Isa 28: 16 the one who trusts will never be *d*.
41: 10 do not be *d*, for I am your God.

DISOBEDIENCE (DISOBEY)

Ro 5: 19 as through the *d* of the one man
11: 32 to *d* so that he may have mercy
Heb 2: 2 and *d* received its just punishment,
4: 6 go in, because of their *d*,
4: 11 fall by following their example of *d*.

DISOBEDIENT (DISOBEY)

2Ti 3: 2 proud, abusive, *d* to their parents,
Tit 1: 6 to the charge of being wild and *d*.
1: 16 *d* and unfit for doing any thing

DISOBEY (DISOBEDIENCE DISOBEDIENT)

Dt 11: 28 the curse if you *d* the commands
2Ch 24: 20 'Why do you *d* the LORD's
Ro 1: 30 they *d* their parents; they are

DISORDER

1Co 14: 33 For God is not a God of *d*
2Co 12: 20 slander, gossip, arrogance and *d*.
Jas 3: 16 there you find *d* and every evil

DISOWN

Pr 30: 9 I may have too much and *d* you
Mt 10: 33 I will *d* him before my Father
26: 35 to die with you, I will never *d* you."
2Ti 2: 12 If we *d* him,

DISPLAY (DISPLAYS)

Eze 39: 21 I will *d* my glory among the nations
1Ti 1: 16 Christ Jesus might *d* his unlimited

DISPLAYS (DISPLAY)

Isa 44: 23 he *d* his glory in Israel.

DISPUTE (DISPUTES)

Pr 17: 14 before a *d* breaks out.
1Co 6: 1 If any of you has a *d* with another,

DISPUTES (DISPUTE)

Pr 18: 18 Casting the lot settles *d*

DISQUALIFIED

1Co 9: 27 I myself will not be *d* for the prize.

DISREPUTE*

2Pe 2: 2 will bring the way of truth into *d*.

DISSENSION*

Pr 6: 14 he always stirs up *d*.
6: 19 and a man who stirs up *d*
10: 12 Hatred stirs up *d*,
15: 18 A hot-tempered man stirs up *d*,
16: 28 A perverse man stirs up *d*,
28: 25 A greedy man stirs up *d*,
29: 22 An angry man stirs up *d*,
Ro 13: 13 debauchery, not in *d* and jealousy.

DISSIPATION*

Lk 21: 34 will be weighed down with *d*,
1Pe 4: 4 with them into the same flood of *d*,

DISTINGUISH

1Ki 3: 9 and to *d* between right and wrong.
Heb 5: 14 themselves to *d* good from evil.

DISTORT

2Co 4: 2 nor do we *d* the word of God.
2Pe 3: 16 ignorant and unstable people *d*,

DISTRESS (DISTRESSED)

Ps 18: 6 In my *d* I called to the LORD;
Jnh 2: 2 "In my *d* I called to the LORD,
Jas 1: 27 after orphans and widows in their *d*

DISTRESSED (DISTRESS)

Ro 14: 15 If your brother is *d*

DIVIDED (DIVISION)

Mt 12: 25 household *d* against itself will not
Lk 23: 34 they *d* up his clothes by casting lots
1Co 1: 13 Is Christ *d*? Was Paul crucified

DIVINATION

Lev 19: 26 "'Do not practice *d* or sorcery.

DIVINE

Ro 1: 20 his eternal power and *d* nature—
2Co 10: 4 they have *d* power
2Pe 1: 4 you may participate in the *d* nature

DIVISION (DIVIDED DIVISIONS DIVISIVE)

Lk 12: 51 on earth? No, I tell you, but *d*.
1Co 12: 25 so that there should be no *d*

DIVISIONS (DIVISION)

Ro 16: 17 to watch out for those who cause *d*

1Co 1: 10 another so that there may
            be no *d*
      11: 18 there are *d* among you,

DIVISIVE* (DIVISION)

Tit   3: 10 Warn a *d* person once,

DIVORCE

Mal 2: 16 "I hate *d*," says the LORD God
Mt 19: 3 for a man to *d* his wife for any
1Co 7: 11 And a husband must not *d*
            his wife.
      7: 27 Are you married? Do not
            seek a *d*.

DOCTOR

Mt   9: 12 "It is not the healthy who
            need a *d*,

DOCTRINE

1Ti   4: 16 Watch your life and *d* closely.
Tit   2: 1 is in accord with sound *d*.

DOMINION

Ps 22: 28 for *d* belongs to the LORD

DOOR

Ps 141: 3 keep watch over the *d* of my
            lips.
Mt   6: 6 close the *d* and pray to your
            Father
      7: 7 and the *d* will be opened to
            you.
Rev   3: 20 I stand at the *d* and knock.

DOORKEEPER

Ps 84: 10 I would rather be a *d* in the
            house

DOUBLE-EDGED

Heb 4: 12 Sharper than any *d* sword.
Rev 1: 16 of his mouth came a sharp *d*
            sword.
      2: 12 of him who has the sharp, *d*
            sword.

DOUBLE-MINDED (MIND)

Ps 119:113 I hate *d* men,
Jas   1: 8 he is a *d* man, unstable

DOUBT

Mt 14: 31 he said, "why did you *d*?"
      21: 21 if you have faith and do not *d*,
Mk 11: 23 and does not *d* in his heart
Jas   1: 6 he must believe and not *d*,
Jude : 22 Be merciful to those who *d*;

DOWNCAST

Ps 42: 5 Why are you *d*, O my soul?
2Co 7: 6 But God, who comforts the *d*,

DRAW (DRAWING DRAWS)

Mt 26: 52 "for all who *d* the sword will
            die
Jn 12: 32 up from the earth, will *d* all
            men
Heb 10: 22 let us *d* near to God

DRAWING (DRAW)

Lk 21: 28 because your redemption is
            d near

DRAWS (DRAW)

Jn   6: 44 the Father who sent me *d*
            him,

DREADFUL

Heb 10: 31 It is a *d* thing to fall into the
            hands

DRESS

1Ti   2: 9 I also want women to *d*
            modestly,

**DRINK (DRUNK DRUNKARDS
DRUNKENNESS)**

Pr   5: 15 *D* water from your own
            cistern,
Lk 12: 19 Take life easy; eat, *d* and be
            merry
Jn   7: 37 let him come to me and *d*.
1Co 12: 13 were all given the one Spirit
            to *d*.
Rev 21: 6 to *d* without cost from the
            spring

DRIVES

1Jn 4: 18 But perfect love *d* out fear,

DROP

Pr 17: 14 so *d* the matter before a dis-
            pute
Isa 40: 15 Surely the nations are like a *d*

DRUNK (DRINK)

Eph 5: 18 Do not get *d* on wine, which
            leads

DRUNKARDS (DRINK)

Pr 23: 21 for *d* and gluttons become
            poor,
1Co 6: 10 nor the greedy nor *d* nor
            slanderers

DRUNKENNESS (DRINK)

Lk 21: 34 weighed down with
            dissipation, *d*
Ro 13: 13 and *d*, not in sexual
            immorality
Gal 5: 21 factions and envy; *d*, orgies,
1Pe 4: 3 living in debauchery, lust, *d*,
            orgies,

DRY

Isa 53: 2 and like a root out of *d*
            ground.
Eze 37: 4 'D bones, hear the word

DUST

Ge   2: 7 man from the *d* of the
            ground
Ps 103: 14 he remembers that we are *d*.
Ecc 3: 20 all come from *d*, and to *d* all
            return.

DUTY

Ecc 12: 13 for this is the whole of *d* of man.
Ac 23: 1 I have fulfilled my *d* to God
1Co 7: 3 husband should fulfill his
            marital *d*

DWELL (DWELLING)

1Ki 8: 27 "But will God really *d* on
            earth?
Ps 23: 6 I will *d* in the house of the
            LORD
Isa 43: 18 do not *d* on the past.
Eph 3: 17 so that Christ may *d* in your
            hearts

Col   1: 19 to have all his fullness *d* in
            him,
      3: 16 the word of Christ *d* in you
            richly

DWELLING (DWELL)

Eph 2: 22 to become a *d* in which God
            lives

∽ E

EAGER

Pr 31: 13 and works with *e* hands.
1Pe 5: 2 greedy for money, but *e* to
            serve;

EAGLE'S (EAGLES)

Ps 103: 5 your youth is renewed like
            the *e*.

EAGLES (EAGLE'S)

Isa 40: 31 They will soar on wings
            like *e*;

EAR (EARS)

1Co 2: 9 no *e* has heard,
      12: 16 if the *e* should say, "Because
            I am

EARNED

Pr 31: 31 Give her the reward she
            has *e*,

EARS (EAR)

Job 42: 5 My *e* had heard of you
Ps 34: 15 and his *e* are attentive to their
            cry;
Pr 21: 13 If a man shuts his *e* to the cry
2Ti 4: 3 to say what their itching *e*
            want

EARTH (EARTHLY)

Ge   1: 1 God created the heavens and
            the *e*.
Ps 24: 1 *e* is the LORD's, and everything
      108: 5 and let your glory be over all
            the *e*.
Isa   6: 3 the whole *e* is full of his glory."
      51: 6 the *e* will wear out like a
            garment
      55: 9 the heavens are higher than
            the *e*,
      66: 1 and the *e* is my footstool.
Jer 23: 24 "Do not I fill heaven and *e*?"
Hab 2: 20 let all the *e* be silent before
            him."
Mt   6: 10 done on *e* as it is in heaven.
      16: 19 bind on *e* will be bound
      24: 35 Heaven and *e* will pass away,
      28: 18 and on *e* has been given to me.
Lk   2: 14 on *e* peace to men
1Co 10: 26 The *e* is the Lord's, and
            everything
Php 2: 10 in heaven and on *e* and under
            the *e*,
2Pe 3: 13 to a new heaven and a new *e*,

EARTHLY (EARTH)

Php 3: 19 Their mind is on *e* things.
Col   3: 2 on things above, not on *e*
            things.

EAST

Ps 103: 12 as far as the *e* is from the west,

EASY

Mt 11: 30 For my yoke is *e* and my
            burden is

EAT (EATING)

Ge   2: 17 but you must not *e* from the
            tree
Isa 55: 1 come, buy and *e*!
      65: 25 and the lion will *e* straw like
            the ox,
Mt 26: 26 "Take and *e*; this is my body."
Ro 14: 2 faith allows him to *e*
            everything,
1Co 8: 13 if what I *e* causes my brother
            to fall
      10: 31 So whether you *e* or drink
2Th 3: 10 man will not work, he shall
            not *e*."

EATING (EAT)

Ro 14: 17 kingdom of God is not a
            matter of *e*

EDICT

Heb 11: 23 they were not afraid of the
            king's *e*.

EDIFIES

1Co 14: 4 but he who prophesies *e* the
            church

EFFECT

Isa 32: 17 *e* of righteousness will be
            quietness
Heb 9: 18 put into *e* without blood.

EFFORT

Lk 13: 24 "Make every *e* to enter
Ro   9: 16 depend on man's desire or *e*,
      14: 19 make every *e* to do what leads
Eph 4: 3 Make every *e* to keep the
            unity
Heb 4: 11 make every *e* to enter that
            rest,
      12: 14 Make every *e* to live in peace
2Pe 1: 5 make every *e* to add
      3: 14 make every *e* to be found
            spotless,

ELAH

  Son of Baasha; king of Israel
(1Ki 16:6-14).

ELDERLY* (ELDERS)

Lev 19: 32 show respect for the *e*

ELDERS (ELDERLY)

1Ti   5: 17 The *e* who direct the affairs

ELECTION

Ro   9: 11 God's purpose in *e* might
            stand:
2Pe 1: 10 to make your calling and *e*
            sure.

ELI

  High priest in youth of Samuel (1Sa 1-4).
Blessed Hannah (1Sa 1:12-18); raised
Samuel (1Sa 2:11-26).

ELIJAH

Prophet; predicted famine in Israel (1Ki 17:1; Jas 5:17). Fed by ravens (1Ki 17:2-6). Raised Sidonian widow's son (1Ki 17:7-24). Defeated prophets of Baal at Carmel (1Ki 18:16-46). Ran from Jezebel (1Ki 19:1-9). Prophesied death of Azariah (2Ki 1). Succeeded by Elisha (1Ki 19:19-21; 2Ki 2:1-18). Taken to heaven in whirlwind (2Ki 2:11-12).

Return prophesied (Mal 4:5-6); equated with John the Baptist (Mt 17:9-13; Mk 9:9-13; Lk 1:17). Appeared with Moses in transfiguration of Jesus (Mt 17:1-8; Mk 9:1-8).

ELISHA

Prophet; successor of Elijah (1Ki 19:16-21); inherited his cloak (2Ki 2:1-18). Miracles of (2Ki 2-6).

ELIZABETH*

Mother of John the Baptist, relative of Mary (Lk 1:5-58).

EMBITTER*

Col 3: 21 Fathers, do not e your children,

EMPTY

Eph 5: 6 no one deceive you with e words,
1Pe 1: 18 from the e way of life handed

ENABLE (ABLE)

Lk 1: 74 to e us to serve him without fear
Ac 4: 29 e your servants to speak your word

ENABLED (ABLE)

Lev 26: 13 e you to walk with heads held high.
Jn 6: 65 unless the Father has e him."

ENABLES (ABLE)

Php 3: 21 by the power that e him

ENCAMPS*

Ps 34: 7 The angel of the LORD e

ENCOURAGE (ENCOURAGEMENT)

Ps 10: 17 you e them, and you listen
Isa 1: 17 e the oppressed.
Ac 15: 32 to e and strengthen the brothers.
Ro 12: 8 if it is encouraging, let him e;
1Th 4: 18 Therefore e each other
2Ti 4: 2 rebuke and e— with great patience
Tit 2: 6 e the young men to be
Heb 3: 13 But e one another daily, as long
    10: 25 but let us e one another—

ENCOURAGEMENT (ENCOURAGE)

Ac 4: 36 Barnabas (which means Son of E)
Ro 15: 4 e of the Scriptures we might have
    15: 5 and e give you a spirit of unity
1Co 14: 3 to men for their strengthening, e
Heb 12: 5 word of e that addresses you

END

Ps 119: 33 then I will keep them to the e.
Pr 14: 12 but in the e it leads to death.
    19: 20 and in the e you will be wise.
    23: 32 In the e it bites like a snake
Ecc 12: 12 making many books there is no e,
Mt 10: 22 firm to the e will be saved.
Lk 21: 9 but the e will not come right away
Ro 10: 4 Christ is the e of the law
1Co 15: 24 the e will come, when he hands

ENDURANCE (ENDURE)

Ro 15: 4 through e and the encouragement
    15: 5 May the God who gives e
2Co 1: 6 which produces in you patient e
Col 1: 11 might so that you may have great e
1Ti 6: 11 faith, love, e and gentleness.
Tit 2: 2 and sound in faith, in love and in e.

ENDURE (ENDURANCE ENDURES)

Ps 72: 17 May his name e forever;
Pr 12: 19 Truthful lips e forever,
    27: 24 for riches do not e forever,
Ecc 3: 14 everything God does will e forever;
Mal 3: 2 who can e the day of his coming?
2Ti 2: 3 E hardship with us like a good
    2: 12 if we e, / we will also reign
Heb 12: 7 E hardship as discipline; God is
Rev 3: 10 kept my command to e patiently,

ENDURES (ENDURE)

Ps 112: 9 his righteousness e forever;
    136: 1 His love e forever.
Da 9: 15 made for yourself a name that e

ENEMIES (ENEMY)

Ps 23: 5 in the presence of my e.
Mic 5: 6 a man's e are the members
Mt 5: 44 Love your e and pray
Lk 20: 43 hand until I make your e

ENEMY (ENEMIES ENMITY)

Pr 24: 17 Do not gloat when your e falls;
    25: 21 If your e is hungry, give him food
    27: 6 but an e multiplies kisses.
1Co 15: 26 The last e to be destroyed is death.
1Ti 5: 14 and to give the e no opportunity

ENJOY (JOY)

Dt 6: 2 and so that you may e long life.
Eph 6: 3 and that you may e long life
Heb 11: 25 rather than to e the pleasures of sin

ENJOYMENT (JOY)

Ecc 4: 8 and why am I depriving myself of e
1Ti 6: 17 us with everything for our e.

ENLIGHTENED* (LIGHT)

Eph 1: 18 that the eyes of your heart may be e
Heb 6: 4 for those who have once been e,

ENMITY* (ENEMY)

Ge 3: 15 And I will put e

ENOCH

Walked with God and taken by him (Ge 5:18-24; Heb 11:5). Prophet (Jude 14).

ENTANGLED (ENTANGLES)

2Pe 2: 20 and are again e in it and overcome,

ENTANGLES* (ENTANGLED)

Heb 12: 1 and the sin that so easily e,

ENTER (ENTERED ENTERS ENTRANCE)

Ps 100: 4 E his gates with thanksgiving
Mt 5: 20 will certainly not e the kingdom
    7: 13 "E through the narrow gate.
    18: 8 It is better for you to e life maimed
Mk 10: 15 like a little child will never e it."
    10: 23 is for the rich to e the kingdom

ENTERED (ENTER)

Ro 5: 12 as sin e the world through one man,
Heb 9: 12 but he e the Most Holy Place once

ENTERS (ENTER)

Mk 7: 18 you see that nothing that e a man
Jn 10: 2 The man who e by the gate is

ENTERTAIN

1Ti 5: 19 Do not e an accusation
Heb 13: 2 Do not forget to e strangers,

ENTHRALLED*

Ps 45: 11 The king is e by your beauty;

ENTHRONED (THRONE)

1Sa 4: 4 who is e between the cherubim.
Ps 2: 4 The One e in heaven laughs;
    102: 12 But you, O LORD, sit e forever;
Isa 40: 22 He sits e above the circle

ENTICE

Pr 1: 10 My son, if sinners e you,
2Pe 2: 18 they e people who are just escaping

ENTIRE

Gal 5: 14 The e law is summed up

ENTRUSTED (TRUST)

1Ti 6: 20 guard what has been e to your care.
2Ti 1: 12 able to guard what I have e to him
    1: 14 Guard the good deposit that was e
Jude : 3 once for all e to the saints.

ENVY

Pr 3: 31 Do not e a violent man
    14: 30 but e rots the bones.
1Co 13: 4 It does not e, it does not boast,

EPHRAIM

1. Second son of Joseph (Ge 41:52; 46:20). Blessed as firstborn by Jacob (Ge 48).

2. Synonymous with Northern Kingdom (Isa 7:17; Hos 5).

EQUAL

Isa 40: 25 who is my e ?" says the Holy One.
Jn 5: 18 making himself e with God.
1Co 12: 25 that its parts should have e concern

EQUIP* (EQUIPPED)

Heb 13: 21 e you with everything good

EQUIPPED (EQUIP)

2Ti 3: 17 man of God may be thoroughly e

ERROR

Jas 5: 20 Whoever turns a sinner from the e

ESAU

Firstborn of Isaac, twin of Jacob (Ge 25:21-26). Also called Edom (Ge 25:30). Sold Jacob his birthright (Ge 25:29-34); lost blessing (Ge 27). Reconciled to Jacob (Gen 33).

ESCAPE (ESCAPING)

Ro 2: 3 think you will e God's judgment?
Heb 2: 3 how shall we e if we ignore such

ESCAPING (ESCAPE)

1Co 3: 15 only as one e through the flames.

ESTABLISH

Ge 6: 18 But I will e my covenant with you,
1Ch 28: 7 I will e his kingdom forever
Ro 10: 3 God and sought to e their own,

ESTEEMED

Pr 22: 1 to be e is better than silver or gold.
Isa 53: 3 he was despised, and we e him not.

ESTHER

Jewess who lived in Persia; cousin of Mordecai (Est 2:7). Chosen queen of Xerxes (Est 2:8-18). Foiled Haman's plan to exterminate the Jews (Est 3-4; 7-9).

ETERNAL (ETERNALLY ETERNITY)

Ps 16: 11 with *e* pleasures at your right hand.
111: 10 To him belongs *e* praise.
119: 89 Your word, O LORD, is *e*;
Isa 26: 4 LORD, the LORD, is the Rock *e*.
Mt 19: 16 good thing must I do to get *e* life?"
25: 41 into the *e* fire prepared for the devil
25: 46 they will go away to *e* punishment,
Jn 3: 15 believes in him may have *e* life.
3: 16 him shall not perish but have *e* life.
3: 36 believes in the Son has *e* life,
4: 14 spring of water welling up to *e* life."
5: 24 believes him who sent me has *e* life
6: 68 You have the words of *e* life.
10: 28 I give them *e* life, and they shall
17: 3 this is *e* life: that they may know
Ro 1: 20 his *e* power and divine nature—
6: 23 but the gift of God is *e* life
2Co 4: 17 for us an *e* glory that far outweighs
4: 18 temporary, but what is unseen is *e*.
1Ti 1: 16 believe on him and receive *e* life.
1: 17 Now to the King *e*, immortal,
Heb 9: 12 having obtained *e* redemption,
1Jn 5: 11 God has given us *e* life,
5: 13 you may know that you have *e* life.

ETERNALLY (ETERNAL)

Gal 1: 8 let him be *e* condemned! As we

ETERNITY (ETERNAL)

Ps 93: 2 you are from all *e*.
Ecc 3: 11 also set *e* in the hearts of men;

ETHIOPIAN

Jer 13: 23 Can the *E* change his skin

EUNUCHS

Mt 19: 12 For some are *e* because they were

EVANGELIST (EVANGELISTS)

2Ti 4: 5 hardship, do the work of an *e*,

EVANGELISTS* (EVANGELIST)

Eph 4: 11 some to be prophets, some to be *e*,

EVE

2Co 11: 3 as *E* was deceived by the serpent's
1Ti 2: 13 For Adam was formed first, then *E*

EVEN-TEMPERED*

Pr 17: 27 and a man of understanding is *e*.

EVER (EVERLASTING FOREVER)

Ex 15: 18 LORD will reign for *e* and *e*."
Dt 8: 19 If you *e* forget the LORD your
Ps 5: 11 let them *e* sing for joy.
10: 16 The LORD is King for *e* and *e*;
25: 3 will *e* be put to shame,
26: 3 for your love is *e* before me,
45: 6 O God, will last for *e* and *e*.
52: 8 God's unfailing love for *e* and *e*.
89: 33 nor will I *e* betray my faithfulness.
145: 1 I will praise your name for *e* and *e*.
Pr 4: 18 shining *e* brighter till the full light
5: 19 may you *e* be captivated
Isa 66: 8 Who has *e* heard of such a thing?
Jer 31: 36 the descendants of Israel *e* cease
Da 7: 18 it forever—yes, for *e* and *e*.'
12: 3 like the stars for *e* and *e*.
Mk 4: 12 *e* hearing but never understanding;
Jn 1: 18 No one has *e* seen God,
Rev 1: 18 and behold I am alive for *e* and *e*!
22: 5 And they will reign for *e* and *e*.

EVER-INCREASING* (INCREASE)

Ro 6: 19 to impurity and to *e* wickedness,
2Co 3: 18 into his likeness with *e* glory,

EVERLASTING (EVER)

Dt 33: 27 and underneath are the *e* arms.
Ne 9: 5 your God, who is from *e* to *e*."
Ps 90: 2 from *e* to *e* you are God.
139: 24 and lead me in the way *e*.
Isa 9: 6 *E* Father, Prince of Peace.
33: 14 Who of us can dwell with *e* burning
35: 10 *e* joy will crown their heads.
45: 17 the LORD with an *e* salvation;
54: 8 but with *e* kindness
55: 3 I will make an *e* covenant with you,
63: 12 to gain for himself *e* renown,
Jer 31: 3 "I have loved you with an *e* love;
Da 9: 24 to bring in *e* righteousness,
12: 2 some to *e* life, others to shame
Jn 6: 47 the truth, he who believes has *e* life.
2Th 1: 9 punished with *e* destruction
Jude 6 bound with *e* chains for judgment

EVER-PRESENT*

Ps 46: 1 an *e* help in trouble

EVIDENCE (EVIDENT)

Jn 14: 11 on the *e* of the miracles themselves.

EVIDENT (EVIDENCE)

Php 4: 5 Let your gentleness be *e* to all.

EVIL

Ge 2: 9 of the knowledge of good and *e*.
Job 1: 1 he feared God and shunned *e*.
1: 8 a man who fears God and shuns *e*."
34: 10 Far be it from God to do *e*,
Ps 23: 4 I will fear no *e*,
34: 14 Turn from *e* and do good;
51: 4 and done what is *e* in your sight,
97: 10 those who love the LORD hate *e*,
101: 4 I will have nothing to do with *e*.
Pr 8: 13 To fear the LORD is to hate *e*;
10: 23 A fool finds pleasure in *e* conduct,
11: 27 *e* comes to him who searches for it.
24: 19 Do not fret because of *e* men
24: 20 for the *e* man has no future hope,
Isa 5: 20 Woe to those who call *e* good
13: 11 I will punish the world for its *e*,
55: 7 and the *e* man his thoughts.
Hab 1: 13 Your eyes are too pure to look on *e*.
Mt 5: 45 He causes his sun to rise on the *e*
6: 13 but deliver us from the *e* one.'
7: 11 If you, then, though you are *e*,
12: 35 and the *e* man brings things out
Jn 17: 15 you protect them from the *e* one.
Ro 2: 9 for every human being who does *e*:
12: 9 Hate what is *e*; cling
12: 17 Do not repay anyone *e* for *e*.
16: 19 and innocent about what is *e*.
1Co 13: 6 Love does not delight in *e*
14: 20 In regard to *e* be infants,
Eph 6: 16 all the flaming arrows of the *e* one.
1Th 5: 22 Avoid every kind of *e*.
1Ti 6: 10 of money is a root of all kinds of *e*.
2Ti 2: 22 Flee the *e* desires of youth,
Jas 1: 13 For God cannot be tempted by *e*,
1Pe 2: 16 your freedom as a cover-up for *e*;
3: 9 Do not repay *e* with *e* or insult

EXACT

Heb 1: 3 the *e* representation of his being,

EXALT (EXALTED EXALTS)

Ps 30: 1 I will *e* you, O LORD,
34: 3 let us *e* his name together.
118: 28 you are my God, and I will *e* you.
Isa 24: 15 *e* the name of the LORD, the God

EXALTED (EXALT)

2Sa 22: 47 *E* be God, the Rock, my Savior!

1Ch 29: 11 you are *e* as head over all.
Ne 9: 5 and may it be *e* above all blessing
Ps 21: 13 Be *e*, O LORD, in your strength;
46: 10 I will be *e* among the nations.
57: 5 Be *e*, O God, above the heavens;
97: 9 you are *e* far above all gods.
99: 2 he is *e* over all the nations.
108: 5 Be *e*, O God, above the heavens,
148: 13 for his name alone is *e*;
Isa 6: 1 *e*, and the train of his robe filled
12: 4 and proclaim that his name is *e*.
33: 5 The LORD is *e*, for he dwells
Eze 21: 26 The lowly will be *e* and the *e* will be
Mt 23: 12 whoever humbles himself will be *e*.
Php 1: 20 always Christ will be *e* in my body,
2: 9 Therefore God *e* him

EXALTS (EXALT)

Ps 75: 7 He brings one down, he *e* another.
Pr 14: 34 Righteousness *e* a nation,
Mt 23: 12 For whoever *e* himself will be

EXAMINE (EXAMINED)

Ps 26: 2 *e* my heart and my mind;
Jer 17: 10 and *e* the mind,
La 3: 40 Let us *e* our ways and test them,
1Co 11: 28 A man ought to *e* himself
2Co 13: 5 *E* yourselves to see whether you

EXAMINED (EXAMINE)

Ac 17: 11 *e* the Scriptures every day to see

EXAMPLE (EXAMPLES)

Jn 13: 15 have set you an *e* that you should
1Co 11: 1 Follow my *e*, as I follow
1Ti 4: 12 set an *e* for the believers in speech,
Tit 2: 7 In everything set them an *e*
1Pe 2: 21 leaving you an *e*, that you should

EXAMPLES* (EXAMPLE)

1Co 10: 6 Now these things occurred as *e*
10: 11 as *e* and were written down
1Pe 5: 3 to you, but being *e* to the flock.

EXASPERATE*

Eph 6: 4 Fathers, do not *e* your children;

EXCEL (EXCELLENT)

1Co 14: 12 to *e* in gifts that build up the church
2Co 8: 7 But just as you *e* in everything—

EXCELLENT (EXCEL)

1Co 12: 31 now I will show you the most *e* way

Php 4: 8 if anything is *e* or praiseworthy —

1Ti 3: 13 have served well gain an *e* standing

Tit 3: 8 These things are *e* and profitable

EXCHANGED

Ro 1: 23 *e* the glory of the immortal God

1: 25 They *e* the truth of God for a lie,

EXCUSE (EXCUSES)

Jn 15: 22 they have no *e* for their sin.

Ro 1: 20 so that men are without *e*.

EXCUSES* (EXCUSE)

Lk 14: 18 "But they all alike began to make *e*.

EXISTS

Heb 2: 10 and through whom everything *e*,

11: 6 to him must believe that he *e*

EXPECT (EXPECTATION)

Mt 24: 44 at an hour when you do not *e* him.

EXPECTATION (EXPECT)

Ro 8: 19 waits in eager *e* for the sons

Heb 10: 27 but only a fearful *e* of judgment

EXPEL*

1Co 5: 13 *E* the wicked man from among you

EXPENSIVE

1Ti 2: 9 or gold or pearls or *e* clothes,

EXPLOIT

Pr 22: 22 Do not *e* the poor because they are

2Co 12: 17 Did I *e* you through any

EXPOSE

1Co 4: 5 will *e* the motives of men's hearts.

Eph 5: 11 of darkness, but rather *e* them.

EXTENDS

Pr 31: 20 and *e* her hands to the needy.

Lk 1: 50 His mercy *e* to those who fear him,

EXTINGUISHED

2Sa 21: 17 the lamp of Israel will not be *e*."

EXTOL*

Job 36: 24 Remember to *e* his work,

Ps 34: 1 I will *e* the LORD at all times;

68: 4 *e* him who rides on the clouds —

95: 2 and *e* him with music and song.

109: 30 mouth I will greatly *e* the LORD;

111: 1 I will *e* the LORD with all my heart

115: 18 it is we who *e* the LORD,

117: 1 *e* him, all you peoples.

145: 2 and *e* your name for ever and ever.

145: 10 your saints will *e* you.

147: 12 *E* the LORD, O Jerusalem;

EXTORT*

Lk 3: 14 "Don't *e* money and don't accuse

EYE (EYES)

Ex 21: 24 you are to take life for life, *e* for *e*,

Ps 94: 9 Does he who formed the *e* not see?

Mt 5: 29 If your right *e* causes you to sin,

5: 38 '*E* for *e*, and tooth for tooth.'

7: 3 of sawdust in your brother's *e*

1Co 2: 9 "No *e* has seen,

Col 3: 22 not only when their *e* is on you

Rev 1: 7 and every *e* will see him,

EYES (EYE)

Nu 33: 55 remain will become barbs in your *e*

Jos 23: 13 on your backs and thorns in your *e*,

2Ch 16: 9 For the *e* of the LORD range

Job 31: 1 I made a covenant with my *e*

36: 7 He does not take his *e*

Ps 119: 18 Open my *e* that I may see

121: 1 I lift up my *e* to the hills—

141: 8 but my *e* are fixed on you,

Pr 3: 7 Do not be wise in your own *e*;

4: 25 Let your *e* look straight ahead,

15: 3 The *e* of the LORD are everywhere

Isa 6: 5 and my *e* have seen the King,

Hab 1: 13 Your *e* are too pure to look on evil;

Jn 4: 35 open your *e* and look at the fields!

2Co 4: 18 So we fix our *e* not on what is seen,

Heb 12: 2 Let us fix our *e* on Jesus, the author

Jas 2: 5 poor in the *e* of the world to be rich

1Pe 3: 12 For the *e* of the Lord are

Rev 7: 17 wipe away every tear from their *e*."

21: 4 He will wipe every tear from their *e*

EZEKIEL

Priest called to be prophet to the exiles (Eze 1-3).

EZRA

Priest and teacher of the Law who led a return of exiles to Israel to reestablish temple and worship (Ezr 7-8). Corrected intermarriage of priests (Ezr 9-10). Read Law at celebration of Feast of Tabernacles (Neh 8).

∞ F

FACE (FACES)

Ge 32: 30 "It is because I saw God *f* to *f*,

Ex 34: 29 was not aware that his *f* was radiant

Nu 6: 25 the LORD make his *f* shine

1Ch 16: 11 seek his *f* always.

2Ch 7: 14 and seek my *f* and turn

Ps 4: 6 Let the light of your *f* shine upon us

27: 8 Your *f*, LORD, I will seek.

31: 16 Let your *f* shine on your servant;

105: 4 seek his *f* always.

119:135 Make your *f* shine

Isa 50: 7 Therefore have I set my *f* like flint,

Mt 17: 2 His *f* shone like the sun,

1Co 13: 12 mirror; then we shall see *f* to *f*.

2Co 4: 6 the glory of God in the *f* of Christ.

1Pe 3: 12 but the *f* of the Lord is

Rev 1: 16 His *f* was like the sun shining

FACES (FACE)

2Co 3: 18 who with unveiled *f* all reflect

FACTIONS

Gal 5: 20 selfish ambition, dissensions, *f*

FADE

1Pe 5: 4 of glory that will never *f* away.

FAIL (FAILING FAILINGS FAILS)

1Ch 28: 20 He will not *f* you or forsake you

2Ch 34: 33 they did not *f* to follow the LORD,

Ps 89: 28 my covenant with him will never *f*.

Pr 15: 22 Plans *f* for lack of counsel,

Isa 51: 6 my righteousness will never *f*.

La 3: 22 for his compassions never *f*.

2Co 13: 5 unless, of course, you *f* the test?

FAILING (FAIL)

1Sa 12: 23 sin against the LORD by *f* to pray

FAILINGS (FAIL)

Ro 15: 1 ought to bear with the *f* of the weak

FAILS (FAIL)

1Co 13: 8 Love never *f*.

FAINT

Isa 40: 31 they will walk and not be *f*.

FAIR

Pr 1: 3 doing what is right and just and *f*;

Col 4: 1 slaves with what is right and *f*,

FAITH (FAITHFUL FAITHFULLY FAITHFULNESS FAITHLESS)

2Ch 20: 20 Have *f* in the LORD your God

Hab 2: 4 but the righteous will live by his *f* —

Mt 9: 29 According to your *f* will it be done

17: 20 if you have *f* as small as a mustard

24: 10 many will turn away from the *f*

Mk 11: 22 "Have *f* in God," Jesus answered.

Lk 7: 9 I have not found such great *f*

12: 28 will he clothe you, O you of little *f*!

17: 5 "Increase our *f*!" He replied,

18: 8 will he find *f* on the earth?"

Ac 14: 9 saw that he had *f* to be healed

14: 27 the door of *f* to the Gentiles.

Ro 1: 12 encouraged by each other's *f*.

1: 17 is by *f* from first to last,

1: 17 "The righteous will live by *f*."

3: 3 What if some did not have *f*?

3: 22 comes through *f* in Jesus Christ

3: 25 a sacrifice of atonement, through *f*

4: 5 his *f* is credited as righteousness.

5: 1 we have been justified through *f*,

10: 17 *f* comes from hearing the message,

14: 1 Accept him whose *f* is weak,

14: 23 that does not come from *f* is sin.

1Co 13: 2 and if I have a *f* that can move

13: 13 And now these three remain: *f*,

16: 13 stand firm in the *f*; be men

2Co 5: 7 We live by *f*, not by sight.

13: 5 to see whether you are in the *f*;

Gal 2: 16 Jesus that we may be justified by *f*

2: 20 I live by *f* in the Son of God,

3: 11 "The righteous will live by *f*."

3: 24 that we might be justified by *f*.

Eph 2: 8 through *f* — and this not

4: 5 one Lord, one *f*, one baptism;

6: 16 to all this, take up the shield of *f*,

Col 1: 23 continue in your *f*, established

1Th 5: 8 on *f* and love as a breastplate,

1Ti 2: 15 if they continue in *f*, love

4: 1 later times some will abandon the *f*

5: 8 he has denied the *f* and is worse

6: 12 Fight the good fight of the *f*.

2Ti 3: 15 wise for salvation through *f*

4: 7 finished the race, I have kept the *f*.

Phm : 6 may be active in sharing your *f*,

Heb 10: 38 But my righteous one will live by *f*.

11: 1 *f* is being sure of what we hope for

11: 3 By *f* we understand that

11: 5 By *f* Enoch was taken from this life

11: 6 And without *f* it is impossible

11: 7 By *f* Noah, when warned about

11: 8 By *f* Abraham, when called to go

11: 17 By *f* Abraham, when God
    tested
11: 20 By *f* Isaac blessed Jacob
11: 21 By *f* Jacob, when he was
    dying,
11: 22 By *f* Joseph, when his end
    was near
11: 24 By *f* Moses, when he had
    grown up
11: 31 By *f* the prostitute Rahab,
12: 2 the author and perfecter of
    our *f*,
Jas 2: 14 if a man claims to have *f*
   2: 17 In the same way, *f* by itself,
   2: 26 so *f* without deeds is dead.
2Pe 1: 5 effort to add to your *f*
    goodness;
1Jn 5: 4 overcome the world, even
    our *f*.
Jude : 3 to contend for the *f* that
    was once

FAITHFUL (FAITH)

Nu 12: 7 he is *f* in all my house.
Dt 7: 9 your God is God; he is the *f*
    God,
   32: 4 A *f* God who does no wrong,
2Sa 22: 26 "To the *f* you show yourself *f*,
Ps 25: 10 of the LORD are loving and *f*
   31: 23 The LORD preserves the *f*,
   33: 4 he is *f* in all he does.
   37: 28 and will not forsake his *f* ones.
   97: 10 for he guards the lives of his
    f ones
 145: 13 The LORD is *f* to all his
    promises
 146: 6 the LORD, who remains *f*
    forever.
Pr 31: 26 and *f* instruction is on her
    tongue.
Mt 25: 21 'Well done, good and
    f servant!
Ro 12: 12 patient in affliction, *f* in
    prayer.
1Co 4: 2 been given a trust must
    prove *f*.
   10: 13 And God is *f*; he will not let
    you be
1Th 5: 24 The one who calls you is *f*
2Ti 2: 13 he will remain *f*,
Heb 3: 6 But Christ is *f* as a son
   10: 23 for he who promised is *f*.
1Pe 4: 19 themselves to their *f* Creator
1Jn 1: 9 he is *f* and just and will
    forgive us
Rev 1: 5 who is the *f* witness, the
    firstborn
   2: 10 Be *f*, even to the point of
    death,
   19: 11 whose rider is called *F* and
    True.

FAITHFULLY (FAITH)

Dt 11: 13 if you *f* obey the commands
    I am
1Sa 12: 24 and serve him *f* with all
    your heart;
1Ki 2: 4 and if they walk *f* before me
1Pe 4: 10 *f* administering God's grace

FAITHFULNESS (FAITH)

Ps 57: 10 your *f* reaches to the skies.
   85: 10 Love and *f* meet together;
   86: 15 to anger, abounding in love
    and *f*,
   89: 1 mouth I will make your *f*
    known
   89: 14 love and *f* go before you.
   91: 4 his *f* will be your shield
 117: 2 the *f* of the LORD endures
    forever.
 119: 75 and in *f* you have afflicted me.
Pr 3: 3 Let love and *f* never leave
    you;
Isa 11: 5 and *f* the sash around his
    waist.
La 3: 23 great is your *f*.
Ro 3: 3 lack of faith nullify God's *f*?
Gal 5: 22 patience, kindness, good-
    ness, *f*,

FAITHLESS (FAITH)

Ps 119:158 I look on the *f* with loathing,
Jer 3: 22 "Return, *f* people;
Ro 1: 31 they are senseless, *f*, heartless,
2Ti 2: 13 if we are *f*,

FALL (FALLEN FALLING FALLS)

Ps 37: 24 though he stumble, he will
    not *f*,
   55: 22 he will never let the
    righteous *f*.
   69: 9 of those who insult you *f*
    on me.
Pr 11: 28 Whoever trusts in his riches
    will *f*,
Lk 11: 17 a house divided against itself
    will *f*.
Ro 3: 23 and *f* short of the glory of God,
Heb 6: 6 if they *f* away, to be brought
    back

FALLEN (FALL)

2Sa 1: 19 How the mighty have *f*!
Isa 14: 12 How you have *f* from heaven,
1Co 15: 20 of those who have *f* asleep.
Gal 5: 4 you have *f* away from grace.
1Th 4: 15 precede those who have *f*
    asleep.

FALLING (FALL)

Jude : 24 able to keep you from *f*

FALLS (FALL)

Pr 24: 17 Do not gloat when your
    enemy *f*;
Jn 12: 24 a kernel of wheat *f* to the
    ground
Ro 14: 4 To his own master he stands
    or *f*.

FALSE (FALSEHOOD FALSELY)

Ex 20: 16 "You shall not give *f*
    testimony
   23: 1 "Do not spread *f* reports.
Pr 13: 5 The righteous hate what is *f*,
   19: 5 A *f* witness will not go
    unpunished,
Mt 7: 15 "Watch out for *f* prophets.
   19: 18 not steal, do not give *f*
    testimony,

   24: 11 and many *f* prophets will
    appear
Php 1: 18 whether from *f* motives
    or true,
1Ti 1: 3 not to teach *f* doctrines any
    longer
2Pe 2: 1 there will be *f* teachers
    among you.

FALSEHOOD (FALSE)

Ps 119:163 I hate and abhor *f*
Pr 30: 8 Keep *f* and lies far from me;
Eph 4: 25 each of you must put off *f*

FALSELY (FALSE)

Lev 19: 12 "'Do not swear *f* by my name
Lk 3: 14 and don't accuse people *f*—
1Ti 6: 20 ideas of what is *f* called
    knowledge,

FALTER*

Pr 24: 10 If you *f* in times of trouble,
Isa 42: 4 he will not *f* or be discouraged

FAMILIES (FAMILY)

Ps 68: 6 God sets the lonely in *f*,

FAMILY (FAMILIES)

Pr 15: 27 greedy man brings trouble to
    his *f*,
   31: 15 she provides food for her *f*
Lk 9: 61 go back and say good-by to
    my *f*."
   12: 52 in one *f* divided against
    each other,
1Ti 3: 4 He must manage his own *f*
    well
   3: 5 how to manage his own *f*,
   5: 4 practice by caring for their
    own *f*
   5: 8 and especially for their
    immediate *f*,

FAMINE

Ge 41: 30 seven years of *f* will follow
    them.
Am 8: 11 but a *f* of hearing the words
Ro 8: 35 or persecution or *f* or
    nakedness

FAN*

2Ti 1: 6 you to *f* into flame the gift
    of God,

FAST

Dt 13: 4 serve him and hold *f* to him.
Jos 22: 5 to hold *f* to him and to
    serve him
   23: 8 to hold *f* to the LORD your
    God,
Ps 119: 31 I hold *f* to your statutes,
    O LORD;
 139: 10 your right hand will hold
    me *f*.
Mt 6: 16 "When you *f*, do not look
    somber
1Pe 5: 12 Stand *f* in it.

FATHER (FATHER'S FATHERLESS FATHERS FOREFATHERS)

Ge 2: 24 this reason a man will leave
    his *f*

   17: 4 You will be the *f* of many
    nations.
Ex 20: 12 "Honor your *f* and your
    mother,
   21: 15 "Anyone who attacks his *f*
   21: 17 "Anyone who curses his *f*
Lev 18: 7 "'Do not dishonor your *f*
   19: 3 you must respect his mother
    and *f*,
Dt 5: 16 "Honor your *f* and your
    mother,
   21: 18 son who does not obey his *f*
Ps 27: 10 Though my *f* and mother
    forsake
   68: 5 A *f* to the fatherless, a
    defender
Pr 10: 1 A wise son brings joy to his *f*,
   17: 21 there is no joy for the *f* of a
    fool.
   23: 22 Listen to your *f*, who gave
    you life,
   23: 24 *f* of a righteous man has
    great joy;
   28: 7 of gluttons disgraces his *f*.
   29: 3 loves wisdom brings joy to
    his *f*,
Isa 9: 6 Everlasting *F*, Prince of Peace.
Mt 6: 9 "'Our *F* in heaven,
   10: 37 "Anyone who loves his *f*
   15: 4 'Honor your *f* and mother'
   19: 5 this reason a man will leave
    his *f*
Lk 12: 53 *f* against son and son against *f*,
   23: 34 Jesus said, "*F*, forgive them,
Jn 6: 44 the *F* who sent him draws him,
   6: 46 No one has seen the *F*
   8: 44 You belong to your *f*, the devil,
   10: 30 I and the *F* are one."
   14: 6 No one comes to the *F*
   14: 9 who has seen me has seen
    the *F*.
Ro 4: 11 he is the *f* of all who believe
2Co 6: 18 "I will be a *F* to you,
Eph 6: 2 "Honor your *f* and
    mother"—
Heb 12: 7 what son is not disciplined by
    his *f*?

FATHER'S (FATHER)

Pr 13: 1 A wise son heeds his *f*
    instruction,
   15: 5 A fool spurns his *f* discipline,
   19: 13 A foolish son is his *f* ruin,
Lk 2: 49 had to be in my *F* house?"
Jn 2: 16 How dare you turn my *F*
    house
   10: 29 can snatch them out of my
    F hand.
   14: 2 In my *F* house are many
    rooms;

FATHERLESS (FATHER)

Dt 10: 18 He defends the cause of the *f*
   24: 17 Do not deprive the alien or
    the *f*
   24: 19 Leave it for the alien, the *f*
Ps 68: 5 A father to the *f*, a defender
Pr 23: 10 or encroach on the fields of
    the *f*,

FATHERS (FATHER)

Ex 20: 5 for the sin of the *f* to the third
Lk 11: 11 "Which of you *f*, if your son asks
Eph 6: 4 *F*, do not exasperate your children;
Col 3: 21 *F*, do not embitter your children,

FATHOM*

Job 11: 7 "Can you *f* the mysteries of God?
Ps 145: 3 his greatness no one can *f*.
Ecc 3: 11 yet they cannot *f* what God has
Isa 40: 28 and his understanding no one can *f*
1Co 13: 2 and can *f* all mysteries and all

FAULT (FAULTS)

Mt 18: 15 and show him his *f*, just
Php 2: 15 of God without *f* in a crooked
Jas 1: 5 generously to all without finding *f*,
Jude : 24 his glorious presence without *f*

FAULTFINDERS*

Jude : 16 These men are grumblers and *f*;

FAULTS (FAULT)

Ps 19: 12 Forgive my hidden *f*.

FAVORITISM*

Ex 23: 3 and do not show *f* to a poor man
Lev 19: 15 to the poor or *f* to the great,
Ac 10: 34 true it is that God does not show *f*
Ro   2: 11 For God does not show *f*.
Eph 6: 9 and there is no *f* with him.
Col 3: 25 for his wrong, and there is no *f*.
1Ti 5: 21 and to do nothing out of *f*.
Jas 2: 1 Lord Jesus Christ, don't show *f*.
      2: 9 But if you show *f*, you sin

FEAR (AFRAID FEARS)

Dt   6: 13 *F* the LORD your God, serve him
     10: 12 but to *f* the LORD your God,
     31: 12 and learn to *f* the LORD your God
Ps 19: 9 The *f* of the LORD is pure,
     23: 4 I will *f* no evil,
     27: 1 whom shall I *f*?
     91: 5 You will not *f* the terror of night,
    111: 10 *f* of the LORD is the beginning
Pr   8: 13 To *f* the LORD is to hate evil;
      9: 10 *f* of the LORD is the beginning
     10: 27 The *f* of the LORD adds length
     14: 27 The *f* of the LORD is a fountain
     15: 33 *f* of the LORD teaches a man
     16: 6 through the *f* of the LORD a man
     19: 23 The *f* of the LORD leads to life:
     29: 25 *F* of man will prove to be a snare,

Isa 11: 3 delight in the *f* of the LORD.
     11: 10 So do not *f*, for I am with you;
Lk 12: 5 I will show you whom you should *f*:
Php 2: 12 to work out your salvation with *f*
1Jn 4: 18 But perfect love drives out *f*,

FEARS (FEAR)

Job 1: 8 a man who *f* God and shuns evil."
Ps 34: 4 he delivered me from all my *f*.
Pr 31: 30 a woman who *f* the LORD is
1Jn 4: 18 The one who *f* is not made perfect

FEED

Jn 21: 15 Jesus said, "*F* my lambs."
     21: 17 Jesus said, "*F* my sheep.
Ro 12: 20 "If your enemy is hungry, *f* him;
Jude : 12 shepherds who *f* only themselves.

FEET (FOOT)

Ps   8: 6 you put everything under his *f*:
     22: 16 have pierced my hands and my *f*.
     40: 2 he set my *f* on a rock
    110: 1 a footstool for your *f*.
    119:105 Your word is a lamp to my *f*
Ro 10: 15 "How beautiful are the *f*
1Co 12: 21 And the head cannot say to the *f*,
     15: 25 has put all his enemies under his *f*.
Heb 12: 13 "Make level paths for your *f*,"

FELLOWSHIP

2Co 6: 14 what *f* can light have with darkness
     13: 14 and the *f* of the Holy Spirit be
Php 3: 10 the *f* of sharing in his sufferings,
1Jn 1: 6 claim to have *f* with him yet walk
      1: 7 we have *f* with one another,

FEMALE

Ge   1: 27 male and *f* he created them.
Gal 3: 28 *f*, for you are all one in Christ Jesus

FERVOR

Ro 12: 11 but keep your spiritual *f*, serving

FIELD (FIELDS)

Mt   6: 28 See how the lilies of the *f* grow.
     13: 38 *f* is the world, and the good seed
1Co 3: 9 you are God's *f*, God's building.

FIELDS (FIELD)

Lk   2: 8 were shepherds living out in the *f*
Jn   4: 35 open your eyes and look at the *f*!

FIG (FIGS)

Ge   3: 7 so they sewed *f* leaves together

FIGHT (FOUGHT)

Ex 14: 14 The LORD will *f* for you; you need
Dt   1: 30 going before you, will *f* for you,
      3: 22 the LORD your God himself will *f*
Ne   4: 20 Our God will *f* for us!"
Ps 35: 1 *f* against those who *f* against me.
Jn 18: 36 my servants would *f*
1Co 9: 26 I do not *f* like a man beating the air.
2Co 10: 4 The weapons we *f*
1Ti 1: 18 them you may *f* the good *f*,
      6: 12 Fight the good *f* of the faith.
2Ti 4: 7 fought the good *f*, I have finished

FIGS (FIG)

Lk   6: 44 People do not pick *f*

FILL (FILLED FILLS FULL FULLNESS FULLY)

Ge   1: 28 and increase in number; *f* the earth
Ps 16: 11 you will *f* me with joy
     81: 10 wide your mouth and I will *f* it.
Pr 28: 19 who chases fantasies will have his *f*
Hag 2: 7 and I will *f* this house with glory,'
Jn   6: 26 you ate the loaves and had your *f*.
Ac   2: 28 you will *f* me with joy
Ro 15: 13 the God of hope *f* you with all joy

FILLED (FILL)

Ps 72: 19 may the whole earth be *f*
    119: 64 The earth is *f* with your love,
Eze 43: 5 the glory of the LORD *f* the temple
Hab 2: 14 For the earth will be *f*
Lk   1: 15 and he will be *f* with the Holy Spirit
      1: 41 and Elizabeth was *f* with the Holy
Jn 12: 3 the house was *f* with the fragrance
Ac   2: 4 All of them were *f*
      4: 8 Then Peter, *f* with the Holy Spirit,
      9: 17 and be *f* with the Holy Spirit."
     13: 9 called Paul, *f* with the Holy Spirit,
Eph 5: 18 Instead, be *f* with the Spirit.
Php 1: 11 *f* with the fruit of righteousness

FILLS (FILL)

Nu 14: 21 of the LORD *f* the whole earth,
Ps 107: 9 and *f* the hungry with good things.
Eph 1: 23 fullness of him who *f* everything

FILTHY

Isa 64: 6 all our righteous acts are like *f* rags;

Col 3: 8 and *f* language from your lips.
2Pe 2: 7 by the *f* lives of lawless men

FIND (FINDS FOUND)

Nu 32: 23 be sure that your sin will *f* you out.
Dt   4: 29 you will *f* him if you look for him
1Sa 23: 16 and helped him *f* strength in God.
Ps 36: 7 *f* refuge in the shadow
     91: 4 under his wings you will *f* refuge;
Pr 14: 22 those who plan what is good *f* love
     31: 10 A wife of noble character who can *f*
Jer 6: 16 and you will *f* rest for your souls.
Mt   7: 7 seek and you will *f*; knock
     11: 29 and you will *f* rest for your souls.
     16: 25 loses his life for me will *f* it.
Lk 18: 8 will he *f* faith on the earth?"
Jn 10: 9 come in and go out, and *f* pasture.

FINDS (FIND)

Ps 62: 1 My soul *f* rest in God alone;
    112: 1 who *f* great delight
    119:162 like one who *f* great spoil.
Pr 18: 22 He who *f* a wife *f* what is good
Mt   7: 8 he who seeks *f*; and to him who
     10: 39 Whoever *f* his life will lose it,
Lk 12: 37 whose master *f* them watching
     15: 4 go after the lost sheep until he *f* it?

FINISH (FINISHED)

Jn   4: 34 him who sent me and to *f* his work.
      5: 36 that the Father has given me to *f*,
Ac 20: 24 if only I may *f* the race
2Co 8: 11 Now *f* the work, so that your eager
Jas 1: 4 Perseverance must *f* its work

FINISHED (FINISH)

Ge   2: 2 seventh day God had *f* the work he
Jn 19: 30 the drink, Jesus said, "It is *f*."
2Ti 4: 7 I have *f* the race, I have kept

FIRE

Ex 13: 21 in a pillar of *f* to give them light,
Lev 6: 12 *f* on the altar must be kept burning;
Isa 30: 27 and his tongue is a consuming *f*.
Jer 23: 29 my word like *f*," declares
Mt   3: 11 you with the Holy Spirit and with *f*.
      5: 22 will be in danger of the *f* of hell.
     25: 41 into the eternal *f* prepared
Mk   9: 43 where the *f* never goes out.

Ac 2: 3 to be tongues of *f* that separated
1Co 3: 13 It will be revealed with *f*,
1Th 5: 19 Do not put out the Spirit's *f*;
Heb 12: 29 for our "God is a consuming *f*."
Jas 3: 5 set on *f* by a small spark.
2Pe 3: 10 the elements will be destroyed by *f*,
Jude : 23 snatch others from the *f*
Rev 20: 14 The lake of *f* is the second death.

FIRM

Ex 14: 13 Stand *f* and you will see
2Ch 20: 17 stand *f* and see the deliverance
Ps 33: 11 of the LORD stand *f* forever,
37: 23 he makes his steps *f*;
40: 2 and gave me a *f* place to stand.
89: 2 that your love stands *f* forever,
119: 89 it stands *f* in the heavens.
Pr 4: 26 and take only ways that are *f*.
Zec 8: 23 nations will take *f* hold of one Jew
Mk 13: 13 he who stands *f* to the end will be
1Co 16: 13 on your guard; stand *f* in the faith;
2Co 1: 24 because it is by faith you stand *f*.
Eph 6: 14 Stand *f* then, with the belt
Col 4: 12 that you may stand *f* in all the will
2Th 2: 15 stand *f* and hold to the teachings
2Ti 2: 19 God's solid foundation stands *f*,
Heb 6: 19 an anchor for the soul, *f* and secure
1Pe 5: 9 Resist him, standing *f* in the faith,

FIRST

Isa 44: 6 I am the *f* and I am the last;
48: 12 I am the *f* and I am the last.
Mt 5: 24 *F* go and be reconciled
6: 33 But seek *f* his kingdom
7: 5 *f* take the plank out
20: 27 wants to be *f* must be your slave—
22: 38 This is the *f* and greatest
23: 26 *F* clean the inside of the cup
Mk 13: 10 And the gospel must *f* be preached
Ac 11: 26 disciples were called Christians *f*
Ro 1: 16 *f* for the Jew, then for the Gentile.
1Co 12: 28 in the church God has appointed *f*
2Co 8: 5 they gave themselves *f* to the Lord
1Ti 2: 13 For Adam was formed *f*, then Eve.
Jas 3: 17 comes from heaven is *f* of all pure;
1Jn 4: 19 We love because he *f* loved us.

3Jn : 9 but Diotrephes, who loves to be *f*,
Rev 1: 17 I am the *F* and the Last.
2: 4 You have forsaken your *f* love.

FIRSTBORN (BEAR)

Ex 11: 5 Every *f* son in Egypt will die,

FIRSTFRUITS

Ex 23: 19 "Bring the best of the *f* of your soil

FISHERS

Mk 1: 17 "and I will make you *f* of men."

FITTING*

Ps 33: 1 it is *f* for the upright to praise him.
147: 1 how pleasant and *f* to praise him!
Pr 10: 32 of the righteous know what is *f*,
19: 10 It is not *f* for a fool to live in luxury
26: 1 honor is not *f* for a fool.
1Co 14: 40 everything should be done in a *f*
Col 3: 18 to your husbands, as is *f* in the Lord
Heb 2: 10 sons to glory, it was *f* that God,

FIX

Dt 11: 18 *F* these words of mine
Pr 4: 25 *f* your gaze directly before you.
2Co 4: 18 we *f* our eyes not on what is seen,
Heb 3: 1 heavenly calling, *f* your thoughts
12: 2 Let us *f* our eyes on Jesus,

FLAME (FLAMES FLAMING)

2Ti 1: 6 you to fan into *f* the gift of God,

FLAMES (FLAME)

1Co 3: 15 only as one escaping through the *f*.
13: 3 and surrender my body to the *f*,

FLAMING (FLAME)

Eph 6: 16 you can extinguish all the *f* arrows

FLASH

1Co 15: 52 in a *f*, in the twinkling of an eye,

FLATTER (FLATTERING FLATTERY)

Job 32: 21 nor will I *f* any man;
Jude : 16 *f* others for their own advantage.

FLATTERING (FLATTER)

Ps 12: 2 their *f* lips speak with deception.
12: 3 May the LORD cut off all *f* lips
Pr 26: 28 and a *f* mouth works ruin.

FLATTERY (FLATTER)

Ro 16: 18 and *f* they deceive the minds
1Th 2: 5 You know we never used *f*,

FLAWLESS*

2Sa 22: 31 the word of the LORD is *f*.
Job 11: 4 You say to God, 'My beliefs are *f*
Ps 12: 6 And the words of the LORD are *f*,
18: 30 the word of the LORD is *f*.
Pr 30: 5 "Every word of God is *f*;
SS 5: 2 my dove, my *f* one.

FLEE

Ps 139: 7 Where can I *f* from your presence?
1Co 6: 18 *F* from sexual immorality.
10: 14 my dear friends, *f* from idolatry.
1Ti 6: 11 But you, man of God, *f* from all this
2Ti 2: 22 *F* the evil desires of youth,
Jas 4: 7 Resist the devil, and he will *f*

FLEETING

Ps 89: 47 Remember how *f* is my life.
Pr 31: 30 Charm is deceptive, and beauty is *f*

FLESH

Ge 2: 23 and of my *f*;
2: 24 and they will become one *f*.
Job 19: 26 yet in my *f* I will see God;
Eze 11: 19 of stone and give them a heart of *f*.
36: 26 of stone and give you a heart of *f*.
Mk 10: 8 and the two will become one *f*.'
Jn 1: 14 The Word became *f* and made his
6: 51 This bread is my *f*, which I will give
1Co 6: 16 "The two will become one *f*."
Eph 5: 31 and the two will become one *f*."
6: 12 For our struggle is not against *f*

FLOCK (FLOCKS)

Isa 40: 11 He tends his *f* like a shepherd;
Eze 34: 2 not shepherds take care of the *f*?
Zec 11: 17 who deserts the *f*!
Mt 26: 31 the sheep of the *f* will be scattered.'
Ac 20: 28 all the *f* of which the Holy Spirit
1Pe 5: 2 Be shepherds of God's *f* that is

FLOCKS (FLOCK)

Lk 2: 8 keeping watch over their *f* at night.

FLOG

Ac 22: 25 to *f* a Roman citizen who hasn't

FLOODGATES

Mal 3: 10 see if I will not throw open the *f*

FLOURISHING

Ps 52: 8 *f* in the house of God;

FLOW (FLOWING)

Nu 13: 27 and it does *f* with milk and honey!
Jn 7: 38 streams of living water will *f*

FLOWERS

Isa 40: 7 The grass withers and the *f* fall,

FLOWING (FLOW)

Ex 3: 8 a land *f* with milk and honey—

FOLDING

Pr 6: 10 a little *f* of the hands to rest—

FOLLOW (FOLLOWING FOLLOWS)

Ex 23: 2 Do not *f* the crowd in doing wrong.
Lev 18: 4 and be careful to *f* my decrees.
Dt 5: 1 Learn them and be sure to *f* them.
Ps 23: 6 Surely goodness and love will *f* me
Mt 16: 24 and take up his cross and *f* me.
Jn 10: 4 his sheep *f* him because they know
1Co 14: 1 *F* the way of love and eagerly
Rev 14: 4 They *f* the Lamb wherever he goes.

FOLLOWING (FOLLOW)

1Ti 1: 18 by *f* them you may fight the good

FOLLOWS (FOLLOW)

Jn 8: 12 Whoever *f* me will never walk

FOOD (FOODS)

Pr 20: 13 you will have *f* to spare.
22: 9 for he shares his *f* with the poor.
25: 21 If your enemy is hungry, give him *f*
31: 15 she provides *f* for her family
Da 1: 8 to defile himself with the royal *f*
Jn 6: 27 Do not work for *f* that spoils.
Ro 14: 14 fully convinced that no *f* is unclean
1Co 8: 8 But *f* does not bring us near to God
1Ti 6: 8 But if we have *f* and clothing,
Jas 2: 15 sister is without clothes and daily *f*.

FOODS (FOOD)

Mk 7: 19 Jesus declared all *f* "clean.")

FOOL (FOOLISH FOOLISHNESS FOOLS)

Ps 14: 1 The *f* says in his heart,
Pr 15: 5 A *f* spurns his father's discipline,
17: 28 Even a *f* is thought wise

18:   2 A *f* finds no pleasure
26:   5 Answer a *f* according to his folly,
28: 26 He who trusts in himself is a *f*,
Mt   5: 22 But anyone who says, 'You *f*!'

FOOLISH (FOOL)
Pr 10:   1 but a *f* son grief to his mother.
17: 25 A *f* son brings grief to his father
Mt   7: 26 practice is like a *f* man who built
25:   2 of them were *f* and five were wise.
1Co 1: 27 God chose the *f* things of the world

FOOLISHNESS (FOOL)
1Co 1: 18 of the cross is *f* to those who are
1: 25 For the *f* of God is wiser
2: 14 for they are *f* to him, and he cannot
3: 19 of this world is *f* in God's sight.

FOOLS (FOOL)
Pr 14:   9 *F* mock at making amends for sin,
1Co 4: 10 We are *f* for Christ, but you are

FOOT (FEET FOOTHOLD)
Jos 1:   3 every place where you set your *f*,
Isa 1:   6 From the sole of your *f* to the top
1Co 12: 15 If the *f* should say, "Because I am

FOOTHOLD (FOOT)
Eph 4: 27 and do not give the devil a *f*.

FORBEARANCE*
Ro   3: 25 because in his *f* he had left the sins

FORBID
1Co 14: 39 and do not *f* speaking in tongues.

FOREFATHERS (FATHER)
Heb 1:   1 spoke to our *f* through the prophets

FOREKNEW* (KNOW)
Ro   8: 29 For those God *f* he
11:   2 not reject his people, whom he *f*.

FOREVER (EVER)
1Ch 16: 15 He remembers his covenant *f*,
16: 34 his love endures *f*.
Ps   9:   7 The LORD reigns *f*;
23:   6 dwell in the house of the LORD.
33: 11 the plans of the LORD stand firm *f*
86: 12 I will glorify your name *f*.
92:   8 But you, O LORD, are exalted *f*.
110:   4 "You are a priest *f*,

119:111 Your statutes are my heritage *f*;
Jn   6: 51 eats of this bread, he will live *f*.
14: 16 Counselor to be with you *f* —
1Co 9: 25 it to get a crown that will last *f*.
1Th 4: 17 And so we will be with the Lord *f*.
Heb 13:   8 same yesterday and today and *f*.
1Pe 1: 25 but the word of the Lord stands *f*."
1Jn 2: 17 who does the will of God lives *f*.

FORFEIT
Lk   9: 25 and yet lose or *f* his very self?

FORGAVE (FORGIVE)
Ps 32:   5 and you *f*
Eph 4: 32 just as in Christ God *f* you.
Col 2: 13 He *f* us all our sins, having
3: 13 Forgive as the Lord *f* you.

FORGET (FORGETS FORGETTING)
Dt   6: 12 that you do not *f* the LORD,
Ps 103:   2 and *f* not all his benefits.
137:   5 may my right hand *f* ⸤its skill⸥,
Isa 49: 15 "Can a mother *f* the baby
Heb 6: 10 he will not *f* your work

FORGETS (FORGET)
Jn 16: 21 her baby is born she *f* the anguish
Jas 1: 24 immediately *f* what he looks like.

FORGETTING (FORGET)
Php 3: 13 *F* what is behind and straining

FORGIVE (FORGAVE FORGIVENESS FORGIVING)
2Ch 7: 14 will *f* their sin and will heal their
Ps 19: 12 *F* my hidden faults.
Mt   6: 12 *F* us our debts,
6: 14 For if you *f* men when they sin
18: 21 many times shall I *f* my brother
Mk 11: 25 in heaven may *f* you your sins."
Lk 11:   4 *F* us our sins,
23: 34 Jesus said, "Father, *f* them,
Col 3: 13 *F* as the Lord forgave you.
1Jn 1:   9 and just and will *f* us our sins

FORGIVENESS (FORGIVE)
Ps 130:   4 But with you there is *f*;
Ac 10: 43 believes in him receives *f* of sins
Eph 1:   7 through his blood, the *f* of sins,
Col 1: 14 in whom we have redemption, the *f*
Heb 9: 22 the shedding of blood there is no *f*.

FORGIVING (FORGIVE)
Ne   9: 17 But you are a *f* God, gracious
Eph 4: 32 to one another, *f* each other,

FORMED
Ge   2:   7 And the LORD God *f* man
Ps 103: 14 for he knows how we are *f*,
Isa 45: 18 but *f* it to be inhabited —
Ro   9: 20 "Shall what is *f* say to him who *f* it,
1Ti 2: 13 For Adam was *f* first, then Eve.
Heb 11:   3 understand that the universe was *f*

FORSAKE (FORSAKEN)
Jos 1:   5 I will never leave you nor *f* you.
24: 16 "Far be it from us to *f* the LORD
2Ch 15:   2 but if you *f* him, he will *f* you.
Ps 27: 10 Though my father and mother *f* me
Isa 55:   7 Let the wicked *f* his way
Heb 13:   5 never will I *f* you."

FORSAKEN (FORSAKE)
Ps 22:   1 my God, why have you *f* me?
37: 25 I have never seen the righteous *f*
Mt 27: 46 my God, why have you *f* me?"
Rev 2:   4 You have *f* your first love.

FORTRESS
Ps 18:   2 The LORD is my rock, my *f*
71:   3 for you are my rock and my *f*.

FOUGHT (FIGHT)
2Ti 4:   7 I have *f* the good fight, I have

FOUND (FIND)
1Ch 28:   9 If you seek him, he will be *f* by you;
Isa 55:   6 Seek the LORD while he may be *f*;
Da   5: 27 on the scales and *f* wanting.
Lk 15:   6 with me; I have *f* my lost sheep.'
15:   9 with me; I have *f* my lost coin.'
Ac   4: 12 Salvation is *f* in no one else,

FOUNDATION
Isa 28: 16 a precious cornerstone for a sure *f*;
1Co 3: 11 For no one can lay any other *f*
Eph 2: 20 built on the *f* of the apostles
2Ti 2: 19 God's solid *f* stands firm,

FOXES
Mt   8: 20 "*F* have holes and birds

FRAGRANCE
2Co 2: 16 of death; to the other, the *f* of life.

FREE (FREED FREEDOM FREELY)
Ps 146:   7 The LORD sets prisoners *f*,
Jn   8: 32 and the truth will set you *f*."
Ro   6: 18 You have been set *f* from sin
Gal 3: 28 slave nor *f*, male nor female,
1Pe 2: 16 *f* men, but do not use your freedom

FREED (FREE)
Rev 1:   5 has *f* us from our sins by his blood,

FREEDOM (FREE)
Ro   8: 21 into the glorious *f* of the children
2Co 3: 17 the Spirit of the Lord is, there is *f*.
Gal 5: 13 But do not use your *f* to indulge
1Pe 2: 16 but do not use your *f* as a cover-up

FREELY (FREE)
Isa 55:   7 and to our God, for he will *f* pardon
Mt 10:   8 Freely you have received, *f* give.
Ro   3: 24 and are justified *f* by his grace
Eph 1:   6 which he has *f* given us

FRIEND (FRIENDS)
Ex 33: 11 as a man speaks with his *f*.
Pr 17: 17 A *f* loves at all times,
18: 24 there is a *f* who sticks closer
27:   6 Wounds from a *f* can be trusted,
27: 10 Do not forsake your *f* and the *f*
Jas 4:   4 Anyone who chooses to be a *f*

FRIENDS (FRIEND)
Pr 16: 28 and a gossip separates close *f*.
Zec 13:   6 given at the house of my *f*.'
Jn 15: 13 that he lay down his life for his *f*.

FRUIT (FRUITFUL)
Ps   1:   3 which yields its *f* in season
Pr 11: 30 The *f* of the righteous is a tree
Mt   7: 16 By their *f* you will recognize them.
Jn 15:   2 branch in me that bears no *f*,
Gal 5: 22 But the *f* of the Spirit is love, joy,
Rev 22:   2 of *f*, yielding its *f* every month.

FRUITFUL (FRUIT)
Ge   1: 22 "Be *f* and increase in number
Ps 128:   3 Your wife will be like a *f* vine
Jn 15:   2 prunes so that it will be even more *f*.

FULFILL (FULFILLED FULFILLMENT)
Ps 116: 14 I will *f* my vows to the LORD
Mt   5: 17 come to abolish them but to *f* them.
1Co 7:   3 husband should *f* his marital duty

FULFILLED (FULFILL)
Pr 13: 19 A longing *f* is sweet to the soul,
Mk 14: 49 But the Scriptures must be *f*."
Ro 13:   8 loves his fellowman has *f* the law.

FULFILLMENT (FULFILL)
Ro 13: 10 Therefore love is the *f* of the law.

FULL (FILL)
Ps 127:   5 whose quiver is *f* of them.
Pr 31: 11 Her husband has *f* confidence

Isa 6: 3 the whole earth is *f* of his glory."
11: 9 for the earth will be *f*
Jn 10: 10 may have life, and have it to the *f.*
Ac 6: 3 known to be *f* of the Spirit

FULLNESS (FILL)

Col 1: 19 to have all his *f* dwell in him,
2: 9 in Christ all the *f* of the Deity lives

FULLY (FILL)

1Ki 8: 61 your hearts must be *f* committed
2Ch 16: 9 whose hearts are *f* committed
Ps 119: 4 that are to be *f* obeyed.
119:138 they are *f* trustworthy.
1Co 15: 58 Always give yourselves *f*

FUTURE

Ps 37: 37 there is a *f* for the man of peace.
Pr 23: 18 There is surely a *f* hope for you,
Ro 8: 38 neither the present nor the *f,*

∾ G

GABRIEL*

Angel who interpreted Daniel's visions (Da 8:16-26; 9:20-27); announced births of John (Lk 1:11-20), Jesus (Lk 1:26-38).

GAIN (GAINED)

Ps 60: 12 With God we will *g* the victory,
Mk 8: 36 it for a man to *g* the whole world,
1Co 13: 3 but have not love, I *g* nothing.
Php 1: 21 to live is Christ and to die is *g.*
3: 8 that I may *g* Christ and be found
1Ti 6: 6 with contentment is great *g.*

GAINED (GAIN)

Ro 5: 2 through whom we have *g* access

GALILEE

Isa 9: 1 but in the future he will honor *G*

GALL

Mt 27: 34 mixed with *g;* but after tasting it,

GAP

Eze 22: 30 stand before me in the *g* on behalf

GARDENER

Jn 15: 1 true vine, and my Father is the *g.*

GARMENT (GARMENTS)

Ps 102: 26 they will all wear out like a *g.*
Mt 9: 16 of unshrunk cloth on an old *g.*
Jn 19: 23 This *g* was seamless, woven

GARMENTS (GARMENT)

Ge 3: 21 The LORD God made *g* of skin
Isa 61: 10 me with *g* of salvation
63: 1 with his *g* stained crimson?
Jn 19: 24 "They divided my *g* among them

GATE (GATES)

Mt 7: 13 For wide is the *g* and broad is
Jn 10: 9 I am the *g;* whoever enters

GATES (GATE)

Ps 100: 4 Enter his *g* with thanksgiving
Mt 16: 18 the *g* of Hades will not overcome it

GATHER (GATHERS)

Zec 14: 2 I will *g* all the nations to Jerusalem
Mt 12: 30 he who does not *g* with me scatters
23: 37 longed to *g* your children together,

GATHERS (GATHER)

Isa 40: 11 He *g* the lambs in his arms
Mt 23: 37 a hen *g* her chicks under her wings,

GAVE (GIVE)

Ezr 2: 69 According to their ability they *g*
Job 1: 21 LORD *g* and the LORD has taken
Jn 3: 16 so loved the world that he *g* his one
2Co 8: 5 they *g* themselves first to the Lord
Gal 2: 20 who loved me and *g* himself for me
1Ti 2: 6 who *g* himself as a ransom

GAZE

Ps 27: 4 to *g* upon the beauty of the LORD
Pr 4: 25 fix your *g* directly before you.

GENEALOGIES

1Ti 1: 4 themselves to myths and endless *g.*

GENERATIONS

Ps 22: 30 future *g* will be told about the Lord
102: 12 your renown endures through all *g.*
145: 13 dominion endures through all *g.*
Lk 1: 48 now on all *g* will call me blessed,
Eph 3: 5 not made known to men in other *g*

GENEROUS

Ps 112: 5 Good will come to him who is *g*
Pr 22: 9 A *g* man will himself be blessed,
2Co 9: 5 Then it will be ready as a *g* gift,
1Ti 6: 18 and to be *g* and willing to share.

GENTILE (GENTILES)

Ro 1: 16 first for the Jew, then for the *G.*
10: 12 difference between Jew and *G*—

GENTILES (GENTILE)

Isa 42: 6 and a light for the *G,*
Ro 3: 9 and *G* alike are all under sin.
11: 13 as I am the apostle to the *G,*
1Co 1: 23 block to Jews and foolishness to *G,*

GENTLE (GENTLENESS)

Pr 15: 1 A *g* answer turns away wrath,
Zec 9: 9 *g* and riding on a donkey,
Mt 11: 29 for I am *g* and humble in heart,
21: 5 *g* and riding on a donkey,
1Co 4: 21 or in love and with a *g* spirit?
1Pe 3: 4 the unfading beauty of a *g*

GENTLENESS* (GENTLE)

2Co 10: 1 By the meekness and *g* of Christ,
Gal 5: 23 faithfulness, *g* and self-control.
Php 4: 5 Let your *g* be evident to all.
Col 3: 12 kindness, humility, *g* and patience.
1Ti 6: 11 faith, love, endurance and *g.*
1Pe 3: 15 But do this with *g* and respect,

GETHSEMANE

Mt 26: 36 disciples to a place called *G,*

GIDEON*

Judge, also called Jerub-Baal; freed Israel from Midianites (Jdg 6-8; Heb 11:32). Given sign of fleece (Jdg 8:36-40).

GIFT (GIFTS)

Pr 21: 14 A *g* given in secret soothes anger,
Mt 5: 23 if you are offering your *g*
Ac 2: 38 And you will receive the *g*
Ro 6: 23 but the *g* of God is eternal life
1Co 7: 7 each man has his own *g* from God;
2Co 8: 12 the *g* is acceptable according
9: 15 be to God for his indescribable *g!*
Eph 2: 8 it is the *g* of God—not by works,
1Ti 4: 14 not neglect your *g,* which was
2Ti 1: 6 you to fan into flame the *g* of God,
Jas 1: 17 and perfect *g* is from above,
1Pe 4: 10 should use whatever *g* he has

GIFTS (GIFT)

Ro 11: 29 for God's *g* and his call are
12: 6 We have different *g,* according
1Co 12: 4 There are different kinds of *g,*
12: 31 But eagerly desire the greater *g.*
14: 1 and eagerly desire spiritual *g,*
14: 12 excel in *g* that build up the church.

GILEAD

Jer 8: 22 Is there no balm in *G?*

GIVE (GAVE GIVEN GIVER GIVES GIVING)

Nu 6: 26 and *g* you peace." '
1Sa 1: 11 then I will *g* him to the LORD
2Ch 15: 7 be strong and do not *g* up,
Pr 21: 26 but the righteous *g* without sparing
23: 26 My son, *g* me your heart
30: 8 but *g* me only my daily bread.
31: 31 *G* her the reward she has earned,
Isa 42: 8 I will not *g* my glory to another
Eze 36: 26 I will *g* you a new heart
Mt 6: 11 *G* us today our daily bread.
10: 8 Freely you have received, freely *g.*
22: 21 *"G* to Caesar what is Caesar's,
Mk 8: 37 Or what can a man *g* in exchange
Lk 6: 38 *G,* and it will be given to you.
11: 13 Father in heaven *g* the Holy Spirit
Jn 10: 28 I *g* them eternal life, and they shall
13: 34 "A new commandment I *g* you:
Ac 20: 35 blessed to *g* than to receive.' "
Ro 12: 8 let him *g* generously;
13: 7 *G* everyone what you owe him:
14: 12 each of us will *g* an account
2Co 9: 7 Each man should *g* what he has
Rev 14: 7 "Fear God and *g* him glory,

GIVEN (GIVE)

Nu 8: 16 are to be *g* wholly to me.
Ps 115: 16 but the earth he has *g* to man.
Isa 9: 6 to us a son is *g,*
Mt 6: 33 and all these things will be *g* to you
7: 7 "Ask and it will be *g* to you;
Lk 22: 19 saying, "This is my body *g* for you;
Jn 3: 27 man can receive only what is *g* him
Ro 5: 5 the Holy Spirit, whom he has *g* us.
1Co 4: 2 those who have been *g* a trust must
12: 13 we were all *g* the one Spirit to drink
Eph 4: 7 to each one of us grace has been *g*

GIVER* (GIVE)

Pr 18: 16 A gift opens the way for the *g*
2Co 9: 7 for God loves a cheerful *g.*

GIVES (GIVE)

Ps 119:130 The unfolding of your words *g* light;
Pr 14: 30 A heart at peace *g* life to the body,
15: 30 good news *g* health to the bones.
28: 27 He who *g* to the poor will lack
Isa 40: 29 He *g* strength to the weary

Mt 10: 42 if anyone *g* even a cup of cold water
Jn   6: 63 The Spirit *g* life; the flesh counts
1Co 15: 57 He *g* us the victory
2Co 3: 6 the letter kills, but the Spirit *g* life.

GIVING (GIVE)

Ne   8: 8 *g* the meaning so that the people
Ps 19: 8 *g* joy to the heart.
Mt   6: 4 so that your *g* may be in secret.
2Co 8: 7 also excel in this grace of *g*.

GLAD (GLADNESS)

Ps 31: 7 I will be *g* and rejoice in your love,
    46: 4 whose streams make *g* the city
    97: 1 LORD reigns, let the earth be *g*;
   118: 24 let us rejoice and be *g* in it.
Pr 23: 25 May your father and mother be *g*;
Zec 2: 10 and be *g*, O Daughter of Zion.
Mt   5: 12 be *g*, because great is your reward

GLADNESS (GLAD)

Ps 45: 15 They are led in with joy and *g*;
    51: 8 Let me hear joy and *g*;
   100: 2 Serve the LORD with *g*;
Jer 31: 13 I will turn their mourning into *g*;

GLORIFIED (GLORY)

Jn 13: 31 Son of Man *g* and God is *g* in him.
Ro   8: 30 those he justified, he also *g*.
2Th 1: 10 comes to be *g* in his holy people

GLORIFY (GLORY)

Ps 34: 3 *G* the LORD with me;
    86: 12 I will *g* your name forever.
Jn 13: 32 God will *g* the Son in himself,
    17: 1 *G* your Son, that your Son may

GLORIOUS (GLORY)

Ps 45: 13 All *g* is the princess
   111: 3 *G* and majestic are his deeds,
   145: 5 of the *g* splendor of your majesty,
Isa 4: 2 the LORD will be beautiful and *g*,
    12: 5 for he has done *g* things;
    42: 21 to make his law great and *g*.
    63: 15 from your lofty throne, holy and *g*.
Mt 19: 28 the Son of Man sits on his *g* throne,
Lk   9: 31 appeared in *g* splendor, talking
Ac   2: 20 of the great and *g* day of the Lord.
2Co 3: 8 of the Spirit be even more *g*?
Php 3: 21 so that they will be like his *g* body.
     4: 19 to his *g* riches in Christ Jesus.
Tit 2: 13 the *g* appearing of our great God

Jude : 24 before his *g* presence without fault

GLORY (GLORIFIED GLORIFY GLORIOUS)

Ex 15: 11 awesome in *g*,
    33: 18 Moses said, "Now show me your *g*
1Sa 4: 21 "The *g* has departed from Israel"—
1Ch 16: 24 Declare his *g* among the nations,
    16: 28 ascribe to the LORD *g*
    29: 11 and the *g* and the majesty
Ps   8: 5 and crowned him with *g* and honor
    19: 1 The heavens declare the *g* of God;
    24: 7 that the King of *g* may come in.
    29: 1 ascribe to the LORD *g*
    72: 19 the whole earth be filled with his *g*.
    96: 3 Declare his *g* among the nations,
Pr 19: 11 it is to his *g* to overlook an offense.
    25: 2 It is the *g* of God to conceal
Isa 6: 3 the whole earth is full of his *g*."
    48: 11 I will not yield my *g* to another.
Eze 43: 2 and the land was radiant with his *g*.
Mt 24: 30 of the sky, with power and great *g*.
    25: 31 the Son of Man comes in his *g*,
Mk   8: 38 in his Father's *g* with the holy
    13: 26 in clouds with great power and *g*.
Lk   2: 9 and the *g* of the Lord shone
     2: 14 saying, "*G* to God in the highest,
Jn   1: 14 We have seen his *g*, the *g* of the One
    17: 5 presence with the *g* I had with you
    17: 24 to see my *g*, the *g* you have given
Ac   7: 2 The God of *g* appeared
Ro   1: 23 exchanged the *g* of the immortal
     3: 23 and fall short of the *g* of God,
     8: 18 with the *g* that will be revealed
     9: 4 theirs the divine *g*, the covenants,
1Co 10: 31 whatever you do, do it all for the *g*
    11: 7 but the woman is the *g* of man.
    15: 43 it is raised in *g*; it is sown
2Co 3: 10 comparison with the surpassing *g*.
     3: 18 faces all reflect the Lord's *g*,
     4: 17 us an eternal *g* that far outweighs
Col 1: 27 Christ in you, the hope of *g*.
     3: 4 also will appear with him in *g*.
1Ti 3: 16 was taken up in *g*.

Heb 1: 3 The Son is the radiance of God's *g*
     2: 7 you crowned him with *g* and honor
1Pe 1: 24 and all their *g* is like the flowers
Rev 4: 11 to receive *g* and honor and power,
    21: 23 for the *g* of God gives it light,

GLUTTONS

Tit 1: 12 always liars, evil brutes, lazy *g*."

GNASHING

Mt   8: 12 where there will be weeping and *g*

GNAT*

Mt 23: 24 You strain out a *g* but swallow

GOAL

2Co 5: 9 So we make it our *g* to please him,
Gal 3: 3 to attain your *g* by human effort?
Php 3: 14 on toward the *g* to win the prize

GOAT (GOATS SCAPEGOAT)

Isa 11: 6 the leopard will lie down with the *g*

GOATS (GOAT)

Nu   7: 17 five male *g* and five male lambs

GOD (GOD'S GODLINESS GODLY GODS)

Ge   1: 1 In the beginning *G* created
     1: 2 and the Spirit of *G* was hovering
     1: 26 Then *G* said, "Let us make man
     1: 27 So *G* created man in his own image
     1: 31 *G* saw all that he had made,
     2: 3 And *G* blessed the seventh day
     2: 22 Then the LORD *G* made a woman
     3: 21 The LORD *G* made garments
     3: 23 So the LORD *G* banished him
     5: 22 Enoch walked with *G* 300 years
     6: 2 sons of *G* saw that the daughters
     9: 16 everlasting covenant between *G*
    17: 1 "I am *G* Almighty; walk before me
    21: 33 name of the LORD, the Eternal *G*.
    22: 8 "*G* himself will provide the lamb
    28: 12 and the angels of *G* were ascending
    32: 28 because you have struggled with *G*
    32: 30 "It is because I saw *G* face to face,
    35: 10 *G* said to him, "Your name is Jacob

    41: 51 *G* has made me forget all my
    50: 20 but *G* intended it for good
Ex   2: 24 *G* heard their groaning
     3: 6 because he was afraid to look at *G*.
     6: 7 own people, and I will be your *G*.
     8: 10 is no one like the LORD our *G*.
    13: 18 So *G* led the people
    15: 2 He is my *G*, and I will praise him,
    17: 9 with the staff of *G* in my hands."
    19: 3 Then Moses went up to *G*,
    20: 2 the LORD your *G*, who brought
    20: 5 the LORD your *G*, am a jealous *G*,
    20: 19 But do not have *G* speak to us
    22: 28 "Do not blaspheme *G*
    31: 18 inscribed by the finger of *G*.
    34: 6 the compassionate and gracious *G*,
    34: 14 name is Jealous, is a jealous *G*.
Lev 18: 21 not profane the name of your *G*.
    19: 2 the LORD your *G*, am holy.
    26: 12 walk among you and be your *G*,
Nu 22: 38 I must speak only what *G* puts
    23: 19 *G* is not a man, that he should lie,
Dt   1: 17 for judgment belongs to *G*.
     3: 22 LORD your *G* himself will fight
     3: 24 For what *g* is there in heaven
     4: 24 is a consuming fire, a jealous *G*.
     4: 31 the LORD your *G* is a merciful *G*;
     4: 39 heart this day that the LORD is *G*
     5: 11 the name of the LORD your *G*,
     5: 14 a Sabbath to the LORD your *G*.
     5: 26 of the living *G* speaking out of fire,
     6: 4 LORD our *G*, the LORD is one.
     6: 5 Love the LORD your *G*
     6: 13 the LORD your *G*, serve him only
     6: 16 Do not test the LORD your *G*
     7: 9 your *G* is *G*; he is the faithful *G*,
     7: 12 the LORD your *G* will keep his
     7: 21 is a great and awesome *G*.
     8: 5 the LORD your *G* disciplines you.
    10: 12 but to fear the LORD your *G*,
    10: 14 the LORD your *G* belong
    10: 17 For the LORD your *G* is *G* of gods
    11: 13 to love the LORD your *G*
    13: 3 The LORD your *G* is testing you
    13: 4 the LORD your *G* you must
    15: 6 the LORD your *G* will bless you
    19: 9 to love the LORD your *G*
    25: 16 the LORD your *G* detests anyone
    29: 29 belong to the LORD our *G*,

30: 2 return to the LORD your *G*
30: 16 today to love the LORD your *G*,
30: 20 you may love the LORD your *G*,
31: 6 for the LORD your *G* goes
32: 3 Oh, praise the greatness of our *G!*
32: 4 A faithful *G* who does no wrong,
33: 27 The eternal *G* is your refuge,
Jos 1: 9 for the LORD your *G* will be
14: 8 the LORD my *G* wholeheartedly.
22: 5 to love the LORD your *G*,
22: 34 Between Us that the LORD is *G*.
23: 11 careful to love the LORD your *G*.
23: 14 the LORD your *G* gave you has
Jdg 16: 28 O *G*, please strengthen me just
Ru 1: 16 be my people and your *G* my *G*.
1Sa 2: 2 there is no Rock like our *G*.
2: 3 for the LORD is a *G* who knows,
2: 25 another man, *G* may mediate
10: 26 men whose hearts *G* had touched.
12: 12 the LORD your *G* was your king.
17: 26 defy the armies of the living *G?*"
17: 46 world will know that there is a *G*
30: 6 strength in the LORD his *G*.
2Sa 14: 14 But *G* does not take away life;
22: 3 my *G* is my rock, in whom I take
22: 31 "As for *G*, his way is perfect;
1Ki 4: 29 *G* gave Solomon wisdom
8: 23 there is no *G* like you in heaven
8: 27 "But will *G* really dwell on earth?
8: 61 committed to the LORD our *G*,
18: 21 If the LORD is *G*, follow him;
18: 37 are *G*, and that you are turning
20: 28 a *g* of the hills and not a *g*
2Ki 19: 15 *G* of Israel, enthroned
1Ch 16: 35 Cry out, "Save us, O *G* our Savior;
28: 2 for the footstool of our *G*,
28: 9 acknowledge the *G* of your father,
29: 10 *G* of our father Israel,
29: 17 my *G*, that you test the heart
2Ch 2: 4 for the Name of the LORD my *G*
5: 14 of the LORD filled the temple of *G*
6: 18 "But will *G* really dwell on earth
18: 13 I can tell him only what my *G* says
20: 6 are you not the *G* who is in heaven?
25: 8 for *G* has the power to help

30: 9 for the LORD your *G* is gracious
33: 12 the favor of the LORD his *G*.
Ezr 8: 22 "The good hand of our *G* is
9: 6 "O my *G*, I am too ashamed
9: 13 our *G*, you have punished us less
Ne 1: 5 the great and awesome *G*,
8: 8 from the Book of the Law of *G*,
9: 17 But you are a forgiving *G*,
9: 32 the great, mighty and awesome *G*,
Job 1: 1 he feared *G* and shunned evil.
2: 10 Shall we accept good from *G*,
4: 17 a mortal be more righteous than *G?*
5: 17 is the man whom *G* corrects;
11: 7 Can you fathom the mysteries of *G*
19: 26 yet in my flesh I will see *G*;
22: 13 Yet you say, 'What does *G* know?
25: 4 can a man be righteous before *G?*
33: 14 For *G* does speak—now one way,
34: 12 is unthinkable that *G* would do
36: 26 is *G*—beyond our understanding!
37: 22 *G* comes in awesome majesty.
Ps 18: 2 my *G* is my rock, in whom I take
18: 28 my *G* turns my darkness into light.
19: 1 The heavens declare the glory of *G*;
22: 1 *G*, my *G*, why have you forsaken
29: 3 the *G* of glory thunders,
31: 14 I say, "You are my *G*."
40: 3 a hymn of praise to our *G*.
40: 8 I desire to do your will, O my *G*;
42: 2 thirsts for *G*, for the living *G*.
42: 11 Put your hope in *G*,
45: 6 O *G*, will last for ever and ever;
46: 1 *G* is our refuge and strength,
46: 10 "Be still, and know that I am *G*;
47: 7 For *G* is the King of all the earth;
50: 3 Our *G* comes and will not be silent;
51: 1 Have mercy on me, O *G*,
51: 10 Create in me a pure heart, O *G*,
51: 17 O *G*, you will not despise.
62: 7 my honor depend on *G*;
65: 5 O *G* our Savior,
66: 1 Shout with joy to *G*, all the earth!
66: 16 listen, all you who fear *G*;
68: 6 *G* sets the lonely in families;
71: 17 my youth, O *G*, you have taught
71: 19 reaches to the skies, O *G*,

71: 22 harp for your faithfulness, O my *G*;
73: 26 but *G* is the strength of my heart
77: 13 What *g* is so great as our God?
78: 19 Can *G* spread a table in the desert?
81: 1 Sing for joy to *G* our strength;
84: 2 out for the living *G*.
84: 10 a doorkeeper in the house of my *G*
86: 12 O Lord my *G*, with all my heart;
89: 7 of the holy ones *G* is greatly feared;
90: 2 to everlasting you are *G*.
91: 2 my *G*, in whom I trust."
95: 7 for he is our *G*
100: 3 Know that the LORD is *G*.
108: 1 My heart is steadfast, O *G*;
113: 5 Who is like the LORD our *G*,
139: 23 Search me, O *G*, and know my
Pr 3: 4 in the sight of *G* and man.
25: 2 of *G* to conceal a matter;
30: 5 "Every word of *G* is flawless;
Ecc 3: 11 cannot fathom what *G* has done
11: 5 cannot understand the work of *G*,
12: 13 Fear *G* and keep his
Isa 9: 6 Wonderful Counselor, Mighty *G*,
37: 16 you alone are *G* over all
40: 3 a highway for our *G*.
40: 8 the word of our *G* stands forever.
40: 28 The LORD is the everlasting *G*,
41: 10 not be dismayed, for I am your *G*.
44: 6 apart from me there is no *G*.
52: 7 "Your *G* reigns!"
55: 7 to our *G*, for he will freely pardon.
57: 21 says my *G*, "for the wicked."
59: 2 you from your *G*;
61: 10 my soul rejoices in my *G*.
62: 5 so will your *G* rejoice over you.
Jer 23: 23 "Am I only a *G* nearby,"
31: 33 I will be their *G*,
32: 27 "I am the LORD, the *G*
Eze 28: 13 the garden of *G*;
Da 3: 17 the *G* we serve is able to save us
9: 4 O Lord, the great and awesome *G*,
Hos 12: 6 and wait for your *G* always.
Joel 2: 13 Return to the LORD your *G*,
Am 4: 12 prepare to meet your *G*, O Israel."
Mic 6: 8 and to walk humbly with your *G*.
Na 1: 2 LORD is a jealous and avenging *G*;
Zec 14: 5 Then the LORD my *G* will come,
Mal 3: 8 Will a man rob *G?* Yet you rob me.
Mt 1: 23 which means, "*G* with us."

5: 8 for they will see *G*.
6: 24 You cannot serve both *G*
19: 6 Therefore what *G* has joined
19: 26 but with *G* all things are possible."
22: 21 and to *G* what is God's."
22: 37 "'Love the Lord your *G*
27: 46 which means, "My *G*, my *G*,
Mk 12: 29 the Lord our *G*, the Lord is one.
16: 19 and he sat at the right hand of *G*.
Lk 1: 37 For nothing is impossible with *G*."
1: 47 my spirit rejoices in *G* my Savior,
10: 9 'The kingdom of *G* is near you.'
10: 27 "'Love the Lord your *G*
18: 19 "No one is good—except *G* alone.
Jn 1: 1 was with *G*, and the Word was *G*.
1: 18 seen *G*, but *G* the One and Only,
3: 16 "For *G* so loved the world that he
4: 24 *G* is spirit, and his worshipers must
14: 1 Trust in *G*; trust also in me.
20: 28 "My Lord and my *G!*"
Ac 2: 24 But *G* raised him from the dead,
5: 4 You have not lied to men but to *G*
5: 29 "We must obey *G* rather than men!
7: 55 to heaven and saw the glory of *G*,
17: 23 TO AN UNKNOWN *G*.
20: 27 to you the whole will of *G*.
20: 32 "Now I commit you to *G*
Ro 1: 17 a righteousness from *G* is revealed,
2: 11 For *G* does not show favoritism.
3: 4 Let *G* be true, and every man a liar.
3: 23 and fall short of the glory of *G*,
4: 24 to whom *G* will credit
5: 8 *G* demonstrates his own love for us
6: 23 but the gift of *G* is eternal life
8: 28 in all things *G* works for the good
11: 22 the kindness and sternness of *G*:
14: 12 give an account of himself to *G*.
1Co 1: 20 Has not *G* made foolish
2: 9 what *G* has prepared
3: 6 watered it, but *G* made it grow.
6: 20 Therefore honor *G* with your body.
7: 24 each man, as responsible to *G*,
8: 8 food does not bring us near to *G*;

10: 13 *G* is faithful; he will not let you be
10: 31 do it all for the glory of *G.*
14: 33 For *G* is not a *G* of disorder
15: 28 so that *G* may be all in all.
2Co 1: 9 rely on ourselves but on *G,*
2: 14 be to *G,* who always leads us
3: 5 but our competence comes from *G.*
4: 7 this all-surpassing power is from *G*
5: 19 that *G* was reconciling the world
5: 21 *G* made him who had no sin
6: 16 we are the temple of the living *G.*
9: 7 for *G* loves a cheerful giver.
2Co 9: 8 *G* is able to make all grace abound
Gal 2: 6 *G* does not judge by external
6: 7 not be deceived: *G* cannot be
Eph 2: 10 which *G* prepared in advance for us
4: 6 one baptism; one *G* and Father
5: 1 Be imitators of *G,* therefore,
Php 2: 6 Who, being in very nature *G,*
4: 19 And my *G* will meet all your needs
1Th 2: 4 trying to please men but *G,*
4: 7 For *G* did not call us to be impure,
4: 9 taught by *G* to love each other.
5: 9 For *G* did not appoint us
1Ti 2: 5 one mediator between *G* and men,
4: 4 For everything *G* created is good,
5: 4 for this is pleasing to *G.*
Tit 2: 13 glorious appearing of our great *G*
Heb 1: 1 In the past *G* spoke
4: 12 For the word of *G* is living
6: 10 *G* is not unjust; he will not forget
10: 31 to fall into the hands of the living *G*
11: 6 faith it is impossible to please *G,*
12: 10 but *G* disciplines us for our good,
12: 29 for our "*G* is a consuming fire."
13: 15 offer to *G* a sacrifice of praise—
Jas 1: 13 For *G* cannot be tempted by evil,
2: 19 You believe that there is one *G.*
2: 23 "Abraham believed *G,*
4: 4 the world becomes an enemy of *G.*
4: 8 Come near to *G* and he will come
1Pe 4: 11 it with the strength *G* provides,
2Pe 1: 21 but men spoke from *G*
1Jn 1: 5 *G* is light; in him there is no

3: 20 For *G* is greater than our hearts,
4: 7 for love comes from *G.*
4: 9 This is how *G* showed his love
4: 11 Dear friends, since *G* so loved us,
4: 12 No one has ever seen *G;*
4: 16 *G* is love.
Rev 4: 8 holy is the Lord *G* Almighty,
7: 17 *G* will wipe away every tear
19: 6 For our Lord *G* Almighty reigns.

GOD-BREATHED* (BREATHED)

2Ti 3: 16 All Scripture is *G* and is useful

GOD'S (GOD)

2Ch 20: 15 For the battle is not yours, but *G.*
Job 37: 14 stop and consider *G* wonders.
Ps 52: 8 I trust in *G* unfailing love
69: 30 I will praise *G* name in song
Mk 3: 35 Whoever does *G* will is my brother
Jn 7: 17 If anyone chooses to do *G* will,
10: 36 'I am *G* Son'? Do not believe me
Ro 2: 3 think you will escape *G* judgment?
2: 4 not realizing that *G* kindness leads
3: 3 lack of faith nullify *G* faithfulness?
7: 22 in my inner being I delight in *G* law
9: 16 or effort, but on *G* mercy.
11: 29 for *G* gifts and his call are
12: 2 and approve what *G* will is—
12: 13 Share with *G* people who are
13: 6 for the authorities are *G* servants,
1Co 7: 19 Keeping *G* commands is what
2Co 6: 2 now is the time of *G* favor,
Eph 1: 7 riches of *G* grace that he lavished
1Th 4: 3 It is *G* will that you should be
5: 18 for this is *G* will for you
1Ti 6: 1 so that *G* name and our teaching
2Ti 2: 19 *G* solid foundation stands firm,
Tit 1: 7 overseer is entrusted with *G* work,
Heb 1: 3 The Son is the radiance of *G* glory
9: 24 now to appear for us in *G* presence.
11: 3 was formed at *G* command,
1Pe 2: 15 For it is *G* will that
3: 4 which is of great worth in *G* sight.
1Jn 2: 5 *G* love is truly made complete

GODLINESS (GOD)

1Ti 2: 2 and quiet lives in all *g* and holiness.
4: 8 but *g* has value for all things,
6: 6 *g* with contentment is great gain.

6: 11 and pursue righteousness, *g,* faith,

GODLY (GOD)

Ps 4: 3 that the LORD has set apart the *g*
2Co 7: 10 *G* sorrow brings repentance that
11: 2 jealous for you with a *g* jealousy.
2Ti 3: 12 everyone who wants to live a *g* life
2Pe 3: 11 You ought to live holy and *g* lives

GODS (GOD)

Ex 20: 3 "You shall have no other *g*
Ac 19: 26 He says that man-made *g* are no *g*

GOLD

Job 23: 10 tested me, I will come forth as *g.*
Ps 19: 10 They are more precious than *g,*
119:127 more than *g,* more than pure *g,*
Pr 22: 1 esteemed is better than silver or *g.*

GOLGOTHA

Jn 19: 17 (which in Aramaic is called *G*).

GOLIATH

Philistine giant killed by David (1Sa 17; 21:9).

GOOD

Ge 1: 4 God saw that the light was *g,*
1: 31 he had made, and it was very *g.*
2: 18 "It is not *g* for the man to be alone.
50: 20 but God intended it for *g*
Job 2: 10 Shall we accept *g* from God,
Ps 14: 1 there is no one who does *g.*
34: 8 Taste and see that the LORD is *g;*
37: 3 Trust in the LORD and do *g;*
84: 11 no *g* thing does he withhold
86: 5 You are forgiving and *g,* O Lord
103: 5 satisfies your desires with *g* things,
119: 68 You are *g,* and what you do is *g;*
133: 1 How *g* and pleasant it is
147: 1 How *g* it is to sing praises
Pr 3: 4 you will win favor and a *g* name
11: 27 He who seeks *g* finds *g* will,
17: 22 A cheerful heart is *g* medicine,
18: 22 He who finds a wife finds what is *g*
22: 1 A *g* name is more desirable
31: 12 She brings him *g,* not harm,
Isa 5: 20 Woe to those who call evil *g*
52: 7 the feet of those who bring *g* news,
Jer 6: 16 ask where the *g* way is,

32: 39 the *g* of their children after them.
Mic 6: 8 has showed you, O man, what is *g.*
Mt 5: 45 sun to rise on the evil and the *g,*
7: 17 Likewise every *g* tree bears *g* fruit,
12: 35 The *g* man brings *g* things out
19: 17 "There is only One who is *g.*
25: 21 'Well done, *g* and faithful servant!
Mk 3: 4 lawful on the Sabbath: to do *g*
8: 36 What *g* is it for a man
Lk 6: 27 do *g* to those who hate you,
Jn 10: 11 "I am the *g* shepherd.
Ro 8: 28 for the *g* of those who love him,
10: 15 feet of those who bring *g* news!"
12: 9 Hate what is evil; cling to what is *g.*
1Co 10: 24 should seek his own *g,* but the *g*
15: 33 Bad company corrupts *g* character
2Co 9: 8 you will abound in every *g* work.
Gal 6: 9 us not become weary in doing *g,*
6: 10 as we have opportunity, let us do *g*
Eph 2: 10 in Christ Jesus to do *g* works,
Php 1: 6 that he who began a *g* work
1Th 5: 21 Hold on to the *g.*
1Ti 3: 7 have a *g* reputation with outsiders,
4: 4 For everything God created is *g,*
6: 12 Fight the *g* fight of the faith.
6: 18 them to do *g,* to be rich in *g* deeds,
2Ti 3: 17 equipped for every *g* work.
4: 7 I have fought the *g* fight, I have
Heb 12: 10 but God disciplines us for our *g,*
1Pe 2: 3 you have tasted that the Lord is *g.*
2: 12 Live such *g* lives among the pagans

GOSPEL

Ro 1: 16 I am not ashamed of the *g,*
15: 16 duty of proclaiming the *g* of God,
1Co 1: 17 to preach the *g*—not with words
9: 16 Woe to me if I do not preach the *g!*
15: 1 you of the *g* I preached to you,
Gal 1: 7 a different *g*—which is really no *g*
Php 1: 27 in a manner worthy of the *g*

GOSSIP

Pr 11: 13 A *g* betrays a confidence,
16: 28 and a *g* separates close friends.
18: 8 of a *g* are like choice morsels;
26: 20 without a *g* a quarrel dies down.

2Co 12: 20 slander, *g*, arrogance and
           disorder.

GRACE (GRACIOUS)

Ps 45: 2 lips have been anointed
           with *g*,
Jn 1: 17 *g* and truth came through
           Jesus
Ac 20: 32 to God and to the word of
           his *g*,
Ro 3: 24 and are justified freely by
           his *g*
      5: 15 came by the *g* of the one man,
      5: 17 God's abundant provision
           of *g*
      5: 20 where sin increased, *g*
           increased all
      6: 14 you are not under law, but
           under *g*.
     11: 6 if by *g*, then it is no longer
           by works
2Co 6: 1 not to receive God's *g* in vain.
      8: 9 For you know the *g*
      9: 8 able to make all *g* abound to
           you,
     12: 9 "My *g* is sufficient for you,
Gal 2: 21 I do not set aside the *g* of God,
      5: 4 you have fallen away from *g*.
Eph 1: 7 riches of God's *g* that he
           lavished
      2: 5 it is by *g* you have been saved.
      2: 7 the incomparable riches of
           his *g*,
      2: 8 For it is by *g* you have been
           saved,
Php 1: 7 all of you share in God's *g*
           with me.
Col 4: 6 conversation be always full
           of *g*,
2Th 2: 16 and by his *g* gave us eternal
2Ti 2: 1 be strong in the *g* that is
Tit 2: 11 For the *g* of God that brings
      3: 7 having been justified by his *g*,
Heb 2: 9 that by the *g* of God he
           might taste
      4: 16 find *g* to help us in our time
           of need
      4: 16 the throne of *g* with
           confidence,
Jas 4: 6 but gives *g* to the humble."
2Pe 3: 18 But grow in the *g* and
           knowledge

GRACIOUS (GRACE)

Nu 6: 25 and be *g* to you;
Pr 22: 11 a pure heart and whose
           speech is *g*
Isa 30: 18 Yet the LORD longs to be *g*
           to you

GRAIN

1Co 9: 9 ox while it is treading out
           the *g*."

GRANTED

Php 1: 29 For it has been *g* to you on
           behalf

GRASS

Ps 103: 15 As for man, his days are like *g*,
1Pe 1: 24 "All men are like *g*,

GRAVE (GRAVES)

Pr 7: 27 Her house is a highway to
           the *g*,
Hos 13: 14 Where, O *g*, is your
           destruction?

GRAVES (GRAVE)

Jn 5: 28 are in their *g* will hear his
           voice
Ro 3: 13 "Their throats are open *g*;

**GREAT (GREATER GREATEST
GREATNESS)**

Ge 12: 2 "I will make you into a *g*
           nation
Dt 10: 17 the *g* God, mighty and
           awesome,
2Sa 22: 36 you stoop down to make
           me *g*.
Ps 19: 11 in keeping them there is *g*
           reward.
     89: 1 of the LORD's *g* love forever;
    103: 11 so *g* is his love for those who
           fear
    107: 43 consider the *g* love of the
           LORD.
    108: 4 For *g* is your love, higher
    119:165 *G* peace have they who love
           your
    145: 3 *G* is the LORD and most
           worthy
Pr 23: 24 of a righteous man has *g* joy;
Isa 42: 21 to make his law *g* and
           glorious.
La 3: 23 *g* is your faithfulness.
Mk 10: 43 whoever wants to become *g*
Lk 21: 27 in a cloud with power and *g*
           glory.
1Ti 6: 6 with contentment is *g* gain.
Tit 2: 13 glorious appearing of our
           g God
Heb 2: 3 if we ignore such a *g* salvation?
1Jn 3: 1 How *g* is the love the Father
           has

GREATER (GREAT)

Mk 12: 31 There is no commandment *g*
Jn 1: 50 You shall see *g* things than
           that."
     15: 13 *G* love has no one than this,
1Co 12: 31 But eagerly desire the *g* gifts.
Heb 11: 26 as of *g* value than the treasures
1Jn 3: 20 For God is *g* than our hearts,
      4: 4 is in you is *g* than the one
           who is

GREATEST (GREAT)

Mt 22: 38 is the first and *g*
           commandment.
Lk 9: 48 least among you all—he is
           the *g*."
1Co 13: 13 But the *g* of these is love.

GREATNESS (GREAT)

Ps 145: 3 his *g* no one can fathom.
    150: 2 praise him for his
           surpassing *g*.
Isa 63: 1 forward in the *g* of his
           strength?
Php 3: 8 compared to the surpassing *g*

GREED (GREEDY)

Lk 12: 15 on your guard against all
           kinds of *g*
Ro 1: 29 kind of wickedness, evil, *g*
Eph 5: 3 or of any kind of impurity, or
           of *g*,
Col 3: 5 evil desires and *g*, which is
           idolatry
2Pe 2: 14 experts in *g*—an accursed
           brood!

GREEDY (GREED)

Pr 15: 27 A *g* man brings trouble
1Co 6: 10 nor thieves nor the *g* nor
           drunkards
Eph 5: 5 No immoral, impure or *g*
           person—
1Pe 5: 2 not *g* for money, but eager
           to serve;

GREEN

Ps 23: 2 makes me lie down in *g*
           pastures,

GREW (GROW)

Lk 2: 52 And Jesus *g* in wisdom and
           stature,
Ac 16: 5 in the faith and *g* daily in
           numbers.

GRIEF (GRIEVE)

Ps 10: 14 O God, do see trouble and *g*;
Pr 14: 13 and joy may end in *g*.
La 3: 32 Though he brings *g*, he will
           show
Jn 16: 20 but your *g* will turn to joy.
1Pe 1: 6 had to suffer *g* in all kinds of
           trials.

GRIEVE (GRIEF)

Eph 4: 30 do not *g* the Holy Spirit
           of God,
1Th 4: 13 or to *g* like the rest of men,

GROUND

Ge 3: 17 "Cursed is the *g* because
           of you;
Ex 3: 5 where you are standing is
           holy *g*."
Eph 6: 13 you may be able to stand
           your *g*,

GROW (GREW)

Pr 13: 11 by little makes it *g*.
1Co 3: 6 watered it, but God made it *g*.
2Pe 3: 18 But *g* in the grace and
           knowledge

GRUMBLE (GRUMBLING)

1Co 10: 10 And do not *g*, as some of
           them did
Jas 5: 9 Don't *g* against each other,

GRUMBLING (GRUMBLE)

Jn 6: 43 "Stop *g* among yourselves,"
1Pe 4: 9 to one another without *g*.

GUARANTEE (GUARANTEEING)

Heb 7: 22 Jesus has become the *g*

GUARANTEEING (GUARANTEE)

2Co 1: 22 as a deposit, *g* what is to come.
Eph 1: 14 who is a deposit *g* our
           inheritance

GUARD (GUARDS)

Ps 141: 3 Set a *g* over my mouth,
           O LORD;
Pr 4: 23 Above all else, *g* your heart,
Isa 52: 12 the God of Israel will be your
           rear *g*
Mk 13: 33 Be on *g*! Be alert! You do
           not know
1Co 16: 13 Be on your *g*; stand firm in
           the faith
Php 4: 7 will *g* your hearts and your
           minds
1Ti 6: 20 *g* what has been entrusted

GUARDS (GUARD)

Pr 13: 3 He who *g* his lips *g* his life,
     19: 16 who obeys instructions *g*
           his life,
     21: 23 He who *g* his mouth and his
           tongue
     22: 5 he who *g* his soul stays far

GUIDE

Ex 13: 21 of cloud to *g* them on
           their way
     15: 13 In your strength you will *g*
           them
Ne 9: 19 cease to *g* them on their path,
Ps 25: 5 *g* me in your truth and
           teach me,
     43: 3 let them *g* me;
     48: 14 he will be our *g* even to
           the end.
     67: 4 and *g* the nations of the earth.
     73: 24 You *g* me with your counsel,
    139: 10 even there your hand will
           g me,
Pr 4: 11 I *g* you in the way of wisdom
      6: 22 When you walk, they will *g*
           you;
Isa 58: 11 The LORD will *g* you always;
Jn 16: 13 comes, he will *g* you into all
           truth.

GUILTY

Ex 34: 7 does not leave the *g*
           unpunished;
Jn 8: 46 Can any of you prove me
           g of sin?
Heb 10: 22 to cleanse us from a *g*
           conscience
Jas 2: 10 at just one point is *g* of
           breaking all

∽ *H*

HADES

Mt 16: 18 the gates of *H* will not over-
           come it.

HAGAR

  Servant of Sarah, wife of Abraham,
mother of Ishmael (Ge 16:1-6; 25:12).
Driven away by Sarah while pregnant
(Ge 16:5-16); after birth of Isaac (Ge
21:9-21; Gal 4:21-31).

HAGGAI*

  Post-exilic prophet who encouraged
rebuilding of the temple (Ezr 5:1; 6:14;
Hag 1-2).

HAIR (HAIRS)

Lk 21: 18 But not a *h* of your head will perish
1Co 11: 6 for a woman to have her *h* cut

HAIRS (HAIR)

Mt 10: 30 even the very *h* of your head are all

HALLELUJAH*

Rev 19: 1 3, 4, 6.

HALLOWED (HOLY)

Mt 6: 9 *h* be your name,

HAND (HANDS)

Ps 16: 8 Because he is at my right *h*,
37: 24 the LORD upholds him with his *h*.
139: 10 even there your *h* will guide me,
Ecc 9: 10 Whatever your *h* finds to do,
Mt 6: 3 know what your right *h* is doing,
Jn 10: 28 one can snatch them out of my *h*.
1Co 12: 15 I am not a *h*, I do not belong

HANDS (HAND)

Ps 22: 16 they have pierced my *h*
24: 4 He who has clean *h* and a pure
31: 5 Into your *h* I commit my spirit;
31: 15 My times are in your *h*;
Pr 10: 4 Lazy *h* make a man poor,
31: 20 and extends her *h* to the needy.
Isa 55: 12 will clap their *h*.
65: 2 All day long I have held out my *h*
Lk 23: 46 into your *h* I commit my spirit."
1Th 4: 11 and to work with your *h*,
1Ti 2: 8 to lift up holy *h* in prayer,
5: 22 hasty in the laying on of *h*,

HANNAH*

Wife of Elkanah, mother of Samuel (1Sa 1). Prayer at dedication of Samuel (1Sa 2:1-10). Blessed (1Sa 2:18-21).

HAPPY

Ps 68: 3 may they be *h* and joyful.
Pr 15: 13 A *h* heart makes the face cheerful,
Ecc 3: 12 better for men than to be *h*
Jas 5: 13 Is anyone *h*? Let him sing songs

HARD (HARDEN HARDSHIP)

Ge 18: 14 Is anything too *h* for the LORD?
Mt 19: 23 it is *h* for a rich man
1Co 4: 12 We work *h* with our own hands.
1Th 5: 12 to respect those who work *h*

HARDEN (HARD)

Ro 9: 18 he hardens whom he wants to *h*.
Heb 3: 8 do not *h* your hearts

HARDHEARTED* (HEART)

Dt 15: 7 do not be *h* or tightfisted

HARDSHIP (HARD)

Ro 8: 35 Shall trouble or *h* or persecution
2Ti 2: 3 Endure *h* with us like a good
4: 5 endure *h*, do the work
Heb 12: 7 Endure *h* as discipline; God is

HARM

Ps 121: 6 the sun will not *h* you by day,
Pr 3: 29 not plot *h* against your neighbor,
31: 12 She brings him good, not *h*,
Ro 13: 10 Love does no *h* to its neighbor.
1Jn 5: 18 and the evil one cannot *h* him.

HARMONY

Ro 12: 16 Live in *h* with one another.
2Co 6: 15 What *h* is there between Christ
1Pe 3: 8 live in *h* with one another;

HARVEST

Mt 9: 37 *h* is plentiful but the work-ers are
Jn 4: 35 at the fields! They are ripe for *h*.
Gal 6: 9 at the proper time we will reap a *h*
Heb 12: 11 it produces a *h* of righteousness

HASTE (HASTY)

Pr 21: 5 as surely as *h* leads to poverty.
29: 20 Do you see a man who speaks in *h*?

HASTY* (HASTE)

Pr 19: 2 nor to be *h* and miss the way.
Ecc 5: 2 do not be *h* in your heart
1Ti 5: 22 Do not be *h* in the laying

HATE (HATED HATES HATRED)

Lev 19: 17 "'Do not *h* your brother
Ps 5: 5 you *h* all who do wrong.
45: 7 righteousness and *h* wickedness;
97: 10 those who love the LORD *h* evil,
139: 21 Do I not *h* those who *h* you,
Pr 8: 13 To fear the LORD is to *h* evil;
Am 5: 15 *H* evil, love good;
Mal 2: 16 "I *h* divorce," says the LORD God
Mt 5: 43 your neighbor and *h* your enemy.'
10: 22 All men will *h* you because of me,
Lk 6: 27 do good to those who *h* you,
Ro 12: 9 *H* what is evil; cling to what is good

HATED (HATE)

Ro 9: 13 "Jacob I loved, but Esau I *h*."
Eph 5: 29 no one ever *h* his own body,
Heb 1: 9 righteousness and *h* wickedness;

HATES (HATE)

Pr 6: 16 There are six things the LORD *h*,
13: 24 He who spares the rod *h* his son,
Jn 3: 20 Everyone who does evil *h* the light,

HATRED (HATE)

1Jn 2: 9 *h* his brother is still in the darkness.

HATRED (HATE)

Pr 10: 12 *H* stirs up dissension,
Jas 4: 4 with the world is *h* toward God?

HAUGHTY

Pr 16: 18 a *h* spirit before a fall.

HAY

1Co 3: 12 costly stones, wood, *h* or straw,

HEAD (HEADS HOTHEADED)

Ge 3: 15 he will crush your *h*,
Ps 23: 5 You anoint my *h* with oil;
Pr 25: 22 will heap burning coals on his *h*,
Isa 59: 17 and the helmet of salvation on his *h*
Mt 8: 20 of Man has no place to lay his *h*."
Ro 12: 20 will heap burning coals on his *h*."
1Co 11: 3 and the *h* of Christ is God.
12: 21 And the *h* cannot say to the feet,
Eph 5: 23 For the husband is the *h* of the wife
2Ti 4: 5 keep your *h* in all situations,
Rev 19: 12 and on his *h* are many crowns.

HEADS (HEAD)

Lev 26: 13 you to walk with *h* held high.
Isa 35: 10 everlasting joy will crown their *h*.

HEAL (HEALED HEALING HEALS)

2Ch 7: 14 their sin and will *h* their land.
Ps 41: 4 *h* me, for I have sinned against you
Mt 10: 8 *H* the sick, raise the dead,
Lk 4: 23 to me: 'Physician, *h* yourself!
5: 17 present for him to *h* the sick.

HEALED (HEAL)

Isa 53: 5 and by his wounds we are *h*.
Mt 9: 22 he said, "your faith has *h* you."
14: 36 and all who touched him were *h*.
Ac 4: 10 this man stands before you *h*.
14: 9 saw that he had faith to be *h*
Jas 5: 16 for each other so that you may be *h*
1Pe 2: 24 by his wounds you have been *h*.

HEALING (HEAL)

Eze 47: 12 for food and their leaves for *h*."
Mal 4: 2 rise with *h* in its wings.
1Co 12: 9 to another gifts of *h*
12: 30 Do all have gifts of *h*? Do all speak
Rev 22: 2 are for the *h* of the nations.

HEALS (HEAL)

Ex 15: 26 for I am the LORD, who *h* you."
Ps 103: 3 and *h* all your diseases;
147: 3 He *h* the brokenhearted

HEALTH (HEALTHY)

Pr 3: 8 This will bring *h* to your body
15: 30 and good news gives *h* to the bones

HEALTHY (HEALTH)

Mk 2: 17 "It is not the *h* who need a doctor,

HEAR (HEARD HEARING HEARS)

Dt 6: 4 *H*, O Israel: The LORD our God,
31: 13 must *h* it and learn
2Ch 7: 14 then will I *h* from heaven
Ps 94: 9 he who implanted the ear not *h*?
Isa 29: 18 that day the deaf will *h* the words
65: 24 while they are still speaking I will *h*
Mt 11: 15 He who has ears, let him *h*.
Jn 8: 47 reason you do not *h* is that you do
2Ti 4: 3 what their itching ears want to *h*.

HEARD (HEAR)

Job 42: 5 My ears had *h* of you
Isa 66: 8 Who has ever *h* of such a thing?
Mt 5: 21 "You have *h* that it was said,
5: 27 "You have *h* that it was said,
5: 33 you have *h* that it was said
5: 38 "You have *h* that it was said,
5: 43 "You have *h* that it was said,
1Co 2: 9 no ear has *h*,
1Th 2: 13 word of God, which you *h* from us,
2Ti 1: 13 What you *h* from me, keep
Jas 1: 25 not forgetting what he has *h*,

HEARING (HEAR)

Ro 10: 17 faith comes from *h* the message,

HEARS (HEAR)

Jn 5: 24 whoever *h* my word and believes
1Jn 5: 14 according to his will, he *h* us.
Rev 3: 20 If anyone *h* my voice and opens

HEART (BROKENHEARTED HARDHEARTED HEARTS WHOLEHEARTEDLY)

Ex 25: 2 each man whose *h* prompts him
Lev 19: 17 Do not hate your brother in your *h*.
Dt 4: 29 if you look for him with all your *h*
6: 5 LORD your God with all your *h*
10: 12 LORD your God with all your *h*
15: 10 and do so without a grudging *h*;
30: 6 you may love him with all your *h*
30: 10 LORD your God with all your *h*

Jos 22: 5 and to serve him with all
            your *h*
1Sa 13: 14 sought out a man after his
            own *h*
     16: 7 but the LORD looks at the *h.*"
2Ki 23: 3 with all his *h* and all his soul,
1Ch 28: 9 for the LORD searches every *h*
2Ch 7: 16 and my *h* will always be there.
Job 22: 22 and lay up his words in
            your *h.*
     37: 1 "At this my *h* pounds
Ps 14: 1 The fool says in his *h,*
     19: 14 and the meditation of my *h*
     37: 4 will give you the desires of
            your *h.*
     45: 1 My *h* is stirred by a noble
            theme
     51: 10 Create in me a pure *h,* O God,
     51: 17 a broken and contrite *h,*
     66: 18 If I had cherished sin in
            my *h,*
     86: 11 give me an undivided *h,*
    119: 11 I have hidden your word in
            my *h*
    119: 32 for you have set my *h* free.
    139: 23 Search me, O God, and know
            my *h*
Pr   3: 5 Trust in the LORD with all
            your *h*
     4: 21 keep them within your *h;*
     4: 23 Above all else, guard your *h,*
     7: 3 write them on the tablet of
            your *h.*
    13: 12 Hope deferred makes the
            h sick.
    14: 13 Even in laughter the *h* may
            ache,
    15: 30 A cheerful look brings joy to
            the *h,*
    17: 22 A cheerful *h* is good medicine.
    24: 17 stumbles, do not let your *h*
            rejoice,
    27: 19 so a man's *h* reflects the man.
Ecc 8: 5 wise *h* will know the proper
            time
SS   4: 9 You have stolen my *h,* my
            sister,
Isa 40: 11 and carries them close to
            his *h;*
    57: 15 and to revive the *h* of the
            contrite.
Jer 17: 9 The *h* is deceitful above all
            things
    29: 13 when you seek me with all
            your *h.*
Eze 36: 26 I will give you a new *h*
Mt   5: 8 Blessed are the pure in *h,*
     6: 21 treasure is, there your *h*
            will be
    12: 34 of the *h* the mouth speaks.
    22: 37 the Lord your God with all
            your *h*
Lk   6: 45 overflow of his *h* his mouth
            speaks.
Ro   2: 29 is circumcision of the *h,*
    10: 10 is with your *h* that you believe
1Co 14: 25 the secrets of his *h* will be
            laid bare.

Eph 5: 19 make music in your *h* to the
            Lord,
     6: 6 doing the will of God from
            your *h.*
Col 3: 23 work at it with all your *h,*
1Pe 1: 22 one another deeply, from
            the *h.*

HEARTS (HEART)
Dt 11: 18 Fix these words of mine in
            your *h*
1Ki 8: 39 for you alone know the *h* of
            all men
     8: 61 your *h* must be fully
            committed
Ps 62: 8 pour out your *h* to him,
Ecc 3: 11 also set eternity in the *h* of
            men;
Jer 31: 33 and write it on their *h.*
Lk 16: 15 of men, but God knows
            your *h.*
    24: 32 "Were not our *h* burning
            within us
Jn 14: 1 "Do not let your *h* be
            troubled.
Ac 15: 9 for he purified their *h* by faith.
Ro   2: 15 of the law are written on
            their *h,*
2Co 3: 2 written on our *h,* known
     3: 3 but on tablets of human *h.*
     4: 6 shine in our *h* to give us the
            light
Eph 3: 17 dwell in your *h* through faith.
Col 3: 1 set your *h* on things above,
Heb 3: 8 do not harden your *h*
    10: 16 I will put my laws in their *h,*
1Jn 3: 20 For God is greater than our *h.*

HEAT
2Pe 3: 12 and the elements will melt in
            the *h.*

HEAVEN (HEAVENLY HEAVENS)
Ge 14: 19 Creator of *h* and earth.
1Ki 8: 27 the highest *h,* cannot con-
            tain you.
2Ki 2: 1 up to *h* in a whirlwind,
2Ch 7: 14 then will I hear from *h*
Isa 14: 12 How you have fallen from *h,*
    66: 1 "*H* is my throne,
Da   7: 13 coming with the clouds of *h.*
Mt   6: 9 "'Our Father in *h,*
     6: 20 up for yourselves treasures
            in *h,*
    16: 19 bind on earth will be bound
            in *h,*
    19: 23 man to enter the kingdom
            of *h.*
    24: 35 *H* and earth will pass away,
    26: 64 and coming on the clouds
            of *h.*"
    28: 18 "All authority in *h*
Mk 16: 19 he was taken up into *h*
Lk 15: 7 in *h* over one sinner who
            repents
    18: 22 and you will have treasure
            in *h.*
Ro 10: 6 'Who will ascend into *h?*' "
            (that is,

2Co 5: 1 an eternal house in *h,* not
            built
    12: 2 ago was caught up to the
            third *h.*
Php 2: 10 *h* and on earth and under
            the earth,
     3: 20 But our citizenship is in *h.*
1Th 1: 10 and to wait for his Son from *h,*
Heb 8: 5 and shadow of what is in *h.*
     9: 24 he entered *h* itself, now to
            appear
2Pe 3: 13 we are looking forward to a
            new *h*
Rev 21: 1 Then I saw a new *h* and a
            new earth.

HEAVENLY (HEAVEN)
Ps   8: 5 him a little lower than the *h*
            beings
2Co 5: 2 to be clothed with our *h*
            dwelling,
Eph 1: 3 in the *h* realms with every
            spiritual
     1: 20 at his right hand in the *h*
            realms,
2Ti 4: 18 bring me safely to his *h*
            kingdom.
Heb 12: 22 to the *h* Jerusalem, the city

HEAVENS (HEAVEN)
Ge   1: 1 In the beginning God created
            the *h*
1Ki 8: 27 The *h,* even the highest
            heaven,
2Ch 2: 6 since the *h,* even the highest
Ps   8: 3 When I consider your *h,*
    19: 1 The *h* declare the glory of
            God;
   102: 25 the *h* are the work of your
            hands.
   108: 4 is your love, higher than
            the *h;*
   119: 89 it stands firm in the *h.*
   139: 8 If I go up to the *h,* you are
            there;
Isa 51: 6 Lift up your eyes to the *h,*
    55: 9 "As the *h* are higher than the
            earth,
    65: 17 new *h* and a new earth.
Joel 2: 30 I will show wonders in the *h*
Eph 4: 10 who ascended higher than
            all the *h,*
2Pe 3: 10 The *h* will disappear with a
            roar;

HEBREW
Ge 14: 13 and reported this to Abram
            the *H.*

HEEDS
Pr 13: 1 wise son *h* his father's
            instruction,
    13: 18 whoever *h* correction is
            honored.
    15: 5 whoever *h* correction shows
    15: 32 whoever *h* correction gains

HEEL
Ge   3: 15 and you will strike his *h.*"

HEIRS (INHERIT)
Ro   8: 17 then we are *h—h* of God
Gal 3: 29 and *h* according to the
            promise.
Eph 3: 6 gospel the Gentiles are *h*
            together
1Pe 3: 7 as *h* with you of the gra-
            cious gift

HELL
Mt   5: 22 will be in danger of the fire
            of *h.*
Lk 16: 23 In *h,* where he was in torment,
2Pe 2: 4 but sent them to *h,* putting
            them

HELMET
Isa 59: 17 and the *h* of salvation on his
            head;
Eph 6: 17 Take the *h* of salvation
1Th 5: 8 and the hope of salvation as
            a *h.*

**HELP (HELPED HELPER
HELPING HELPS)**
Ps 18: 6 I cried to my God for *h.*
    30: 2 my God, I called to you for *h*
    46: 1 an ever-present *h* in trouble.
    79: 9 *H* us, O God our Savior,
   121: 1 where does my *h* come from?
Isa 41: 10 I will strengthen you and *h*
            you;
Jnh 2: 2 depths of the grave I called
            for *h,*
Mk   9: 24 *h* me overcome my unbelief!"
Ac 16: 9 Come over to Macedonia
            and *h* us
1Co 12: 28 those able to *h* others, those

HELPED (HELP)
1Sa 7: 12 "Thus far has the LORD *h* us."

HELPER (HELP)
Ge   2: 18 I will make a *h* suitable for
            him."
Ps 10: 14 you are the *h* of the fatherless.
Heb 13: 6 Lord is my *h;* I will not be
            afraid.

HELPING (HELP)
Ac   9: 36 always doing good and *h*
            the poor.
1Ti 5: 10 *h* those in trouble and
            devoting

HELPS (HELP)
Ro   8: 26 the Spirit *h* us in our
            weakness.

HEN
Mt 23: 37 as a *h* gathers her chicks

HERITAGE (INHERIT)
Ps 127: 3 Sons are a *h* from the LORD,

HEROD
    1. King of Judea who tried to kill Jesus
(Mt 2; Lk 1:5).
    2. Son of 1. Tetrarch of Galilee who
arrested and beheaded John the Baptist
(Mt 14:1-12; Mk 6:14-29; Lk 3:1, 19-20;
9:7-9); tried Jesus (Lk 23:6-15).
    3. Grandson of 1. King of Judea who
killed James (Ac 12:2); arrested Peter
(Ac 12:3-19). Death (Ac 12:19-23).

HERODIAS

Wife of Herod the Tetrarch who persuaded her daughter to ask for John the Baptist's head (Mt 14:1-12; Mk 6:14-29).

HEZEKIAH

King of Judah. Restored the temple and worship (2Ch 29-31). Sought the LORD for help against Assyria (2Ki 18-19; 2Ch 32:1-23; Isa 36-37). Illness healed (2Ki 20:1-11; 2Ch 32:24-26; Isa 38). Judged for showing Babylonians his treasures (2Ki 20:12-21; 2Ch 32:31; Isa 39).

HID (HIDE)

Ge	3:	8	and they *h* from the LORD God
Ex	2:	2	she *h* him for three months.
Jos	6:	17	because she *h* the spies we sent.
Heb 11:	23	By faith Moses' parents *h* him

HIDDEN (HIDE)

Ps	19:	12	Forgive my *h* faults.
	119:	11	I have *h* your word in my heart
Pr	2:	4	and search for it as for *h* treasure,
Isa	59:	2	your sins have *h* his face from you,
Mt	5:	14	A city on a hill cannot be *h*.
	13:	44	of heaven is like treasure *h*
Col	1:	26	the mystery that has been kept *h*
	2:	3	in whom are *h* all the treasures
	3:	3	and your life is now *h* with Christ

HIDE (HID HIDDEN)

| Ps | 17: | 8 | *h* me in the shadow of your wings |
| | 143: | 9 | for I *h* myself in you. |

HILL (HILLS)

| Mt | 5: | 14 | A city on a *h* cannot be hidden. |

HILLS (HILL)

| Ps | 50: | 10 | and the cattle on a thousand *h*. |
| | 121: | 1 | I lift up my eyes to the *h*— |

HINDER (HINDERS)

1Sa	14:	6	Nothing can *h* the LORD
Mt	19:	14	come to me, and do not *h* them,
1Co	9:	12	anything rather than *h* the gospel
1Pe	3:	7	so that nothing will *h* your prayers.

HINDERS (HINDER)

| Heb 12: | 1 | let us throw off everything that *h* |

HINT*

| Eph | 5: | 3 | even a *h* of sexual immorality, |

HOLD

Ex	20:	7	LORD will not *h* anyone guiltless
Lev	19:	13	"'Do not *h* back the wages
Jos	22:	5	to *h* fast to him and to serve him

Ps	73:	23	you *h* me by my right hand.
Pr	4:	4	"Lay *h* of my words
Isa	54:	2	do not *h* back;
Mk	11:	25	if you *h* anything against anyone,
Php	2:	16	as you *h* out the word of life—
	3:	12	but I press on to take *h* of that
Col	1:	17	and in him all things *h* together.
1Th	5:	21	*H* on to the good.
1Ti	6:	12	Take *h* of the eternal life
Heb 10:	23	Let us *h* unswervingly

HOLINESS (HOLY)

Ex	15:	11	majestic in *h*,
Ps	29:	2	in the splendor of his *h*.
	96:	9	in the splendor of his *h*;
Ro	6:	19	to righteousness leading to *h*.
2Co	7:	1	perfecting *h* out of reverence
Eph	4:	24	God in true righteousness and *h*.
Heb 12:	10	that we may share in his *h*.
	12:	14	without *h* no one will see the Lord.

HOLY (HALLOWED HOLINESS)

Ex	19:	6	kingdom of priests and a *h* nation.'
	20:	8	the Sabbath day by keeping it *h*.
Lev	11:	44	and be *h*, because I am *h*.
	20:	7	"'Consecrate yourselves and be *h*,
	20:	26	You are to be *h* to me because I,
	21:	8	Consider them *h*, because I
	22:	32	Do not profane my *h* name.
Ps	16:	10	will you let your *H* One see decay.
	24:	3	Who may stand in his *h* place?
	77:	13	Your ways, O God, are *h*.
	99:	3	he is *h*.
	99:	5	he is *h*.
	99:	9	for the LORD our God is *h*.
	111:	9	*h* and awesome is his name.
Isa	5:	16	the *h* God will show himself *h*
	6:	3	*H*, *h*, *h* is the LORD Almighty;
	40:	25	who is my equal?" says the *H* One.
	57:	15	who lives forever, whose name is *h*:
Eze 28:	25	I will show myself *h* among them
Da	9:	24	prophecy and to anoint the most *h*.
Hab	2:	20	But the LORD is in his *h* temple;
Ac	2:	27	will you let your *H* One see decay.
Ro	7:	12	and the commandment is *h*,
	12:	1	as living sacrifices, *h* and pleasing
Eph	5:	3	improper for God's *h* people.
2Th	1:	10	to be glorified in his *h* people
2Ti	1:	9	saved us and called us to a *h* life—
	3:	15	you have known the *h* Scriptures,
Tit	1:	8	upright, *h* and disciplined.

1Pe	1:	15	But just as he who called you is *h*,
	1:	16	is written: "Be *h*, because I am *h*."
	2:	9	a royal priesthood, a *h* nation,
2Pe	3:	11	You ought to live *h* and godly lives
Rev	4:	8	"*H*, *h*, *h* is the Lord God

HOME (HOMES)

Dt	6:	7	Talk about them when you sit at *h*
Ps	84:	3	Even the sparrow has found a *h*,
Pr	3:	33	but he blesses the *h* of the righteous
Mk	10:	29	"no one who has left *h* or brothers
Jn	14:	23	to him and make our *h* with him.
Tit	2:	5	to be busy at *h*, to be kind,

HOMES (HOME)

| Ne | 4: | 14 | daughters, your wives and your *h*." |
| 1Ti | 5: | 14 | to manage their *h* and to give |

HOMOSEXUAL*

| 1Co | 6: | 9 | male prostitutes nor *h* offenders |

HONEST

Lev	19:	36	Use *h* scales and *h* weights,
Dt	25:	15	and *h* weights and measures,
Job	31:	6	let God weigh me in *h* scales
Pr	12:	17	truthful witness gives *h* testimony,

HONEY

Ex	3:	8	a land flowing with milk and *h*—
Ps	19:	10	than *h* from the comb.
	119:103	sweeter than *h* to my mouth!

HONOR (HONORABLE HONORABLY HONORED HONORS)

Ex	20:	12	"*H* your father and your mother,
Nu	25:	13	he was zealous for the *h* of his God
Dt	5:	16	"*H* your father and your mother,
1Sa	2:	30	Those who *h* me I will *h*,
Ps	8:	5	and crowned him with glory and *h*.
Pr	3:	9	*H* the LORD with your wealth,
	15:	33	and humility comes before *h*.
	20:	3	It is to a man's *h* to avoid strife,
Mt	15:	4	'*H* your father and mother'
Ro	12:	10	*H* one another above yourselves.
1Co	6:	20	Therefore *h* God with your body.
Eph	6:	2	"*H* your father and mother"—
1Ti	5:	17	well are worthy of double *h*,
Heb	2:	7	you crowned him with glory and *h*
Rev	4:	9	*h* and thanks to him who sits

HONORABLE (HONOR)

| 1Th | 4: | 4 | body in a way that is holy and *h*, |

HONORABLY (HONOR)

| Heb 13: | 18 | and desire to live *h* in every way. |

HONORED (HONOR)

Ps	12:	8	when what is vile is *h* among men.
Pr	13:	18	but whoever heeds correction is *h*.
1Co	12:	26	if one part is *h*, every part rejoices
Heb 13:	4	Marriage should be *h* by all,

HONORS (HONOR)

| Ps | 15: | 4 | but *h* those who fear the LORD, |
| Pr | 14: | 31 | to the needy *h* God. |

HOOKS

| Isa | 2: | 4 | and their spears into pruning *h*. |
| Joel | 3: | 10 | and your pruning *h* into spears. |

HOPE (HOPES)

Job	13:	15	Though he slay me, yet will I *h*
Ps	42:	5	Put your *h* in God,
	62:	5	my *h* comes from him.
	119:	74	for I have put my *h* in your word.
	130:	7	O Israel, put your *h* in the LORD,
	147:	11	who put their *h* in his unfailing love
Pr	13:	12	*H* deferred makes the heart sick,
Isa	40:	31	but those who *h* in the LORD
Ro	5:	4	character; and character, *h*.
	8:	24	But *h* that is seen is no *h* at all.
	12:	12	Be joyful in *h*, patient in affliction,
	15:	4	of the Scriptures we might have *h*.
1Co	13:	13	now these three remain: faith, *h*
	15:	19	for this life we have *h* in Christ,
Col	1:	27	Christ in you, the *h* of glory.
1Th	5:	8	and the *h* of salvation as a helmet.
1Ti	6:	17	but to put their *h* in God,
Tit	2:	13	while we wait for the blessed *h*—
Heb	6:	19	We have this *h* as an anchor
	11:	1	faith is being sure of what we *h* for
1Jn	3:	3	Everyone who has this *h*

HOPES (HOPE)

| 1Co | 13: | 7 | always *h*, always perseveres. |

HORSE

Ps	147:	10	not in the strength of the *h*,
Pr	26:	3	A whip for the *h*, a halter
Zec	1:	8	before me was a man riding a red *h*
Rev	6:	2	and there before me was a white *h*!
	6:	4	Come!" Then another *h* came out,

6: 5 and there before me was a black *h*!
6: 8 and there before me was a pale *h*!
19: 11 and there before me was a white *h*,

HOSANNA

Mt 21: 9 "*H* in the highest!"

HOSHEA

Last king of Israel (2Ki 15:30; 17:1-6).

HOSPITABLE* (HOSPITALITY)

1Ti 3: 2 self-controlled, respectable, *h*,
Tit 1: 8 Rather he must be *h*, one who loves

HOSPITALITY (HOSPITABLE)

Ro 12: 13 Practice *h*.
1Ti 5: 10 as bringing up children, showing *h*,
1Pe 4: 9 Offer *h* to one another

HOSTILE

Ro 8: 7 the sinful mind is *h* to God.

HOT

1Ti 4: 2 have been seared as with a *h* iron.
Rev 3: 15 that you are neither cold nor *h*.

HOT-TEMPERED

Pr 15: 18 A *h* man stirs up dissension,
19: 19 A *h* man must pay the penalty;
22: 24 Do not make friends with a *h* man,
29: 22 and a *h* one commits many sins.

HOTHEADED (HEAD)

Pr 14: 16 but a fool is *h* and reckless.

HOUR

Ecc 9: 12 knows when his *h* will come:
Mt 6: 27 you by worrying can add a single *h*
Lk 12: 40 the Son of Man will come at an *h*
Jn 12: 23 The *h* has come for the Son of Man
12: 27 for this very reason I came to this *h*

HOUSE (HOUSEHOLD STOREHOUSE)

Ex 20: 17 shall not covet your neighbor's *h*.
Ps 23: 6 I will dwell in the *h* of the LORD
84: 10 a doorkeeper in the *h* of my God
122: 1 "Let us go to the *h* of the LORD."
127: 1 Unless the LORD builds the *h*,
Pr 7: 27 Her *h* is a highway to the grave,
21: than share a *h* with a quarrelsome
Isa 56: 7 a *h* of prayer for all nations."

Zec 13: 6 given at the *h* of my friends.'
Mt 7: 24 is like a wise man who built his *h*
12: 29 can anyone enter a strong man's *h*
21: 13 My *h* will be called a *h* of prayer,'
Mk 3: 25 If a *h* is divided against itself,
Lk 11: 17 a *h* divided against itself will fall.
Jn 2: 16 How dare you turn my Father's *h*
12: 3 the *h* was filled with the fragrance
14: 2 In my Father's *h* are many rooms;
Heb 3: 3 the builder of a *h* has greater honor

HOUSEHOLD (HOUSE)

Jos 24: 15 my *h*, we will serve the LORD."
Mic 7: 6 are the members of his own *h*.
Mt 10: 36 will be the members of his own *h*.'
12: 25 or *h* divided against itself will not
1Ti 3: 12 manage his children and his *h* well.
3: 15 to conduct themselves in God's *h*,

HUMAN (HUMANITY)

Gal 3: 3 to attain your goal by *h* effort?

HUMANITY* (HUMAN)

Heb 2: 14 he too shared in their *h* so that

HUMBLE (HUMBLED HUMBLES HUMILIATE HUMILITY)

2Ch 7: 14 will *h* themselves and pray
Ps 25: 9 He guides the *h* in what is right
Pr 3: 34 but gives grace to the *h*.
Isa 66: 2 he who is *h* and contrite in spirit,
Mt 11: 29 for I am gentle and *h* in heart,
Eph 4: 2 Be completely *h* and gentle;
Jas 4: 10 *H* yourselves before the Lord,
1Pe 5: 5 *H* yourselves,

HUMBLED (HUMBLE)

Mt 23: 12 whoever exalts himself will be *h*,
Php 2: 8 he *h* himself

HUMBLES (HUMBLE)

Mt 18: 4 whoever *h* himself like this child is
23: 12 whoever *h* himself will be exalted.

HUMILIATE* (HUMBLE)

Pr 25: 7 than for him to *h* you
1Co 11: 22 and *h* those who have nothing?

HUMILITY (HUMBLE)

Pr 11: 2 but with *h* comes wisdom.
15: 33 and *h* comes before honor.
Php 2: 3 but in *h* consider others better
Tit 3: 2 and to show true *h* toward all men.
1Pe 5: 5 clothe yourselves with *h*

HUNGRY

Ps 107: 9 and fills the *h* with good things.
146: 7 and gives food to the *h*.
Pr 25: 21 If your enemy is *h*, give him food
Eze 18: 7 but gives his food to the *h*
Mt 25: 35 For I was *h* and you gave me
Lk 1: 53 He has filled the *h* with good things
Jn 6: 35 comes to me will never go *h*,
Ro 12: 20 "If your enemy is *h*, feed him;

HURT (HURTS)

Ecc 8: 9 it over others to his own *h*.
Mk 16: 18 deadly poison, it will not *h* them
Rev 2: 11 He who overcomes will not be *h*

HURTS* (HURT)

Ps 15: 4 even when it *h*,
Pr 26: 28 A lying tongue hates those it *h*,

HUSBAND (HUSBAND'S HUSBANDS)

1Co 7: 3 The *h* should fulfill his marital duty
7: 10 wife must not separate from her *h*.
7: 11 And a *h* must not divorce his wife.
7: 13 And if a woman has a *h* who is not
7: 39 A woman is bound to her *h* as long
2Co 11: 2 I promised you to one *h*, to Christ,
Eph 5: 23 For the *h* is the head of the wife
5: 33 and the wife must respect her *h*.
1Ti 3: 2 the *h* of but one wife, temperate,

HUSBAND'S (HUSBAND)

Pr 12: 4 of noble character is her *h* crown,
1Co 7: 4 the *h* body does not belong

HUSBANDS (HUSBAND)

Eph 5: 22 submit to your *h* as to the Lord.
5: 25 *H*, love your wives, just
Tit 2: 4 the younger women to love their *h*
1Pe 3: 1 same way be submissive to your *h*
3: 7 *H*, in the same way be considerate

HYMN

1Co 14: 26 everyone has a *h*, or a word

HYPOCRISY (HYPOCRITE HYPOCRITES)

Mt 23: 28 but on the inside you are full of *h*
1Pe 2: 1 *h*, envy, and slander of every kind.

HYPOCRITE (HYPOCRISY)

Mt 7: 5 You *h*, first take the plank out

HYPOCRITES (HYPOCRISY)

Ps 26: 4 nor do I consort with *h*;
Mt 6: 5 when you pray, do not be like the *h*

HYSSOP

Ps 51: 7 with *h*, and I will be clean;

❧ ¶ I

IDLE (IDLENESS)

1Th 5: 14 those who are *i*, encourage
2Th 3: 6 away from every brother who is *i*
1Ti 5: 13 they get into the habit of being *i*

IDLENESS* (IDLE)

Pr 31: 27 and does not eat the bread of *i*.

IDOL (IDOLATRY IDOLS)

Isa 44: 17 From the rest he makes a god, his *i*;
1Co 8: 4 We know that an *i* is nothing at all

IDOLATRY (IDOL)

Col 3: 5 evil desires and greed, which is *i*.

IDOLS (IDOL)

1Co 8: 1 Now about food sacrificed to *i*:

IGNORANT (IGNORE)

1Co 15: 34 for there are some who are *i* of God
Heb 5: 2 to deal gently with those who are *i*
1Pe 2: 15 good you should silence the *i* talk
2Pe 3: 16 which *i* and unstable people distort

IGNORE (IGNORANT IGNORES)

Dt 22: 1 do not *i* it but be sure
Ps 9: 12 he does not *i* the cry of the afflicted
Heb 2: 3 if we *i* such a great salvation?

IGNORES (IGNORE)

Pr 10: 17 whoever *i* correction leads others
15: 32 He who *i* discipline despises

ILLUMINATED*

Rev 18: 1 and the earth was *i* by his splendor.

IMAGE

Ge 1: 26 "Let us make man in our *i*,
1: 27 So God created man in his own *i*,
1Co 11: 7 since he is the *i* and glory of God;

Col 1: 15 He is the *i* of the invisible
                God,
        3: 10 in knowledge in the *i* of its
                Creator.

IMAGINE
Eph 3: 20 more than all we ask or *i*,

IMITATE (IMITATORS)
1Co 4: 16 Therefore I urge you
                to *i* me.
Heb 6: 12 but to *i* those who through
                faith
       13: 7 of their way of life and *i*
                their faith.
3Jn   : 11 do not *i* what is evil but
                what is

IMITATORS* (IMITATE)
Eph 5: 1 Be *i* of God, therefore,
1Th 1: 6 You became *i* of us and of
                the Lord
        2: 14 became *i* of God's churches

IMMANUEL
Isa   7: 14 birth to a son, and will call
                him *I*.
Mt   1: 23 and they will call him *I*"—

IMMORAL* (IMMORALITY)
Pr   6: 24 keeping you from
                the *i* woman,
1Co 5: 9 to associate with sexually
                i people
        5: 10 the people of this world
                who are *i*,
        5: 11 but is sexually *i* or greedy,
        6: 9 Neither the sexually *i* nor
                idolaters
Eph 5: 5 No *i*, impure or greedy
                person—
Heb 12: 16 See that no one is sexually *i*,
       13: 4 the adulterer and all the
                sexually *i*.
Rev 21: 8 the murderers, the sexually *i*,
       22: 15 the sexually *i*, the murderers,

IMMORALITY (IMMORAL)
1Co 6: 13 The body is not meant for
                sexual *i*,
        6: 18 Flee from sexual *i*.
       10: 8 We should not commit
                sexual *i*,
Gal   5: 19 sexual *i*, impurity and
                debauchery;
Eph 5: 3 must not be even a hint of
                sexual *i*,
1Th 4: 3 that you should avoid
                sexual *i*;
Jude : 4 grace of our God into a
                license for *i*

IMMORTAL* (IMMORTALITY)
Ro   1: 23 glory of the *i* God for
                images made
1Ti   1: 17 Now to the King eternal, *i*,
        6: 16 who alone is *i* and who lives

IMMORTALITY (IMMORTAL)
Ro   2: 7 honor and *i*, he will give
                eternal life
1Co 15: 53 and the mortal with *i*.
2Ti   1: 10 and *i* to light through the
                gospel.

IMPERISHABLE
1Pe   1: 23 not of perishable seed, but
                of *i*,

IMPORTANCE* (IMPORTANT)
1Co 15: 3 passed on to you as of first *i*:

IMPORTANT (IMPORTANCE)
Mt   6: 25 Is not life more *i* than food,
       23: 23 have neglected the more *i*
                matters
Mk 12: 29 "The most *i* one," answered
                Jesus,
       12: 33 as yourself is more *i* than
                all burnt
Php   1: 18 The *i* thing is that in
                every way,

IMPOSSIBLE
Mt   17: 20 Nothing will be *i* for you."
Lk   1: 37 For nothing is *i* with God."
       18: 27 "What is *i* with men is
                possible
Heb   6: 18 things in which it is *i* for
                God to lie,
       11: 6 without faith it is *i* to please
                God,

IMPROPER*
Eph 5: 3 these are *i* for God's holy
                people.

IMPURE (IMPURITY)
Ac   10: 15 not call anything *i* that
                God has
Eph 5: 5 No immoral, *i* or greedy
                person—
1Th 4: 7 For God did not call us
                to be *i*,
Rev 21: 27 Nothing *i* will ever enter it,

IMPURITY (IMPURE)
Ro   1: 24 hearts to sexual *i* for the
                degrading
Eph 5: 3 or of any kind of *i*, or of
                greed,

INCENSE
Ex   40: 5 Place the gold altar of
                i in front
Ps 141: 2 my prayer be set before you
                like *i*;
Mt   2: 11 him with gifts of gold and
                of *i*

INCOME
Ecc   5: 10 wealth is never satisfied
                with his *i*.
1Co 16: 2 sum of money in keeping
                with his *i*,

INCOMPARABLE*
Eph 2: 7 ages he might show the *i*
                riches

**INCREASE
(EVER-INCREASING INCREASED
INCREASES INCREASING)**
Ge   1: 22 "Be fruitful and *i* in number
Ps   62: 10 though your riches *i*,
Isa   9: 7 Of the *i* of his government
Lk   17: 5 said to the Lord,
                "*I* our faith!"
1Th 3: 12 May the Lord make your
                love *i*

INCREASED (INCREASE)
Ac   6: 7 of disciples in Jerusalem
                i rapidly,
Ro   5: 20 But where sin *i*, grace *i* all
                the more

INCREASES (INCREASE)
Pr   24: 5 and a man of knowledge *i*
                strength;

INCREASING (INCREASE)
Ac   6: 1 when the number of
                disciples was *i*,
2Th 1: 3 one of you has for each
                other is *i*.
2Pe   1: 8 these qualities in *i* measure,

INDEPENDENT*
1Co 11: 11 however, woman is
                not *i* of man,
       11: 11 of man, nor is man *i*
                of woman.

INDESCRIBABLE*
2Co 9: 15 Thanks be to God for
                his *i* gift!

INDISPENSABLE*
1Co 12: 22 seem to be weaker are *i*,

INEFFECTIVE*
2Pe   1: 8 they will keep you from
                being *i*

INEXPRESSIBLE*
2Co 12: 4 He heard *i* things, things
                that man
1Pe   1: 8 are filled with an *i* and
                glorious joy,

INFANTS
Mt   21: 16 " 'From the lips of children
                and *i*
1Co 14: 20 In regard to evil be *i*,

INFIRMITIES
Isa 53: 4 Surely he took up our *i*

**INHERIT (CO-HEIRS HEIRS
HERITAGE INHERITANCE)**
Ps   37: 11 But the meek will *i* the land
       37: 29 the righteous will *i* the land
Mt   5: 5 for they will *i* the earth.
Mk 10: 17 "what must I do to *i* eternal
                life?"
1Co 15: 50 blood cannot *i* the kingdom
                of God

INHERITANCE (INHERIT)
Dt   4: 20 to be the people of his *i*,
Pr   13: 22 A good man leaves an *i*
Eph 1: 14 who is a deposit
                guaranteeing our *i*
        5: 5 has any *i* in the kingdom
                of Christ
Heb   9: 15 receive the promised
                eternal *i*—
1Pe   1: 4 and into an *i* that can never
                perish,

INIQUITIES (INIQUITY)
Ps   78: 38 he forgave their *i*
      103: 10 or repay us according
                to our *i*.
Isa 59: 2 But your *i* have separated

Mic   7: 19 and hurl all our *i* into the
                depths

INIQUITY (INIQUITIES)
Ps   51: 2 Wash away all my *i*
Isa 53: 6 the *i* of us all.

INJUSTICE
2Ch 19: 7 the LORD our God there
                is no *i*

INNOCENT
Pr   17: 26 It is not good to punish
                an *i* man,
Mt   10: 16 shrewd as snakes and as *i*
                as doves.
       27: 4 "for I have betrayed
                i blood."
1Co 4: 4 but that does not make me *i*.

INSCRIPTION
Mt   22: 20 And whose *i*?" "Caesar's,"

INSOLENT
Ro   1: 30 God-haters, *i*, arrogant

INSTITUTED
Ro   13: 2 rebelling against what God
                has *i*,
1Pe   2: 13 to every authority *i* among
                men:

INSTRUCT (INSTRUCTION)
Ps   32: 8 I will *i* you and teach you
Pr   9: 9 *I* a wise man and he will
                be wiser
Ro   15: 14 and competent to *i* one
                another.
2Ti   2: 25 who oppose him he must
                gently *i*,

INSTRUCTION (INSTRUCT)
Pr   1: 8 Listen, my son, to your
                father's *i*
        4: 1 Listen, my sons, to a
                father's *i*;
        4: 13 Hold on to *i*, do not let it go;
        8: 10 Choose my *i* instead of silver,
        8: 33 Listen to my *i* and be wise;
       13: 1 A wise son heeds his
                father's *i*,
       13: 13 He who scorns *i* will pay
                for it,
       16: 20 Whoever gives heed to *i*
                prospers,
       16: 21 and pleasant words
                promote *i*.
       19: 20 Listen to advice and accept *i*,
       23: 12 Apply your heart to *i*
1Co 14: 6 or prophecy or word of *i*?
       14: 26 or a word of *i*, a revelation,
Eph 6: 4 up in the training and *i* of
                the Lord.
1Th 4: 8 he who rejects this *i* does
                not reject
2Th 3: 14 If anyone does not obey
                our *i*
1Ti   1: 18 I give you this *i* in keeping
        6: 3 to the sound *i* of our
                Lord Jesus
2Ti   4: 2 with great patience and
                careful *i*.

INSULT
Pr   9:   7 corrects a mocker invites *i*;
    12: 16 but a prudent man overlooks an *i*.
Mt   5: 11 Blessed are you when people *i* you,
Lk   6: 22 when they exclude you and *i* you
1Pe 3:   9 evil with evil or *i* with *i*,

INTEGRITY
1Ki 9:   4 if you walk before me in *i* of heart
Job 2:   3 And he still maintains his *i*,
    27:   5 till I die, I will not deny my *i*.
Pr 10:   9 The man of *i* walks securely,
    11:   3 The *i* of the upright guides them,
    29: 10 Bloodthirsty men hate a man of *i*
Tit   2:   7 your teaching show *i*, seriousness

INTELLIGENCE
Isa 29: 14 the *i* of the intelligent will vanish."
1Co 1: 19 *i* of the intelligent I will frustrate."

INTELLIGIBLE
1Co 14: 19 I would rather speak five *i* words

INTERCEDE (INTERCEDES INTERCESSION)
Heb 7: 25 he always lives to *i* for them.

INTERCEDES (INTERCEDE)
Ro   8: 26 but the Spirit himself *i* for us

INTERCESSION* (INTERCEDE)
Isa 53: 12 and made *i* for the transgressors.
1Ti 2:   1 *i* and thanksgiving be made

INTERESTS
1Co 7: 34 his wife — and his *i* are divided.
Php 2:   4 only to your own *i*, but also to the *i*
     2: 21 everyone looks out for his own *i*,

INTERMARRY (MARRY)
Dt   7:   3 Do not *i* with them.

INVENTED*
2Pe 1: 16 We did not follow cleverly *i* stories

INVESTIGATED
Lk   1:   3 I myself have carefully *i* everything

INVISIBLE
Ro   1: 20 of the world God's *i* qualities—
Col 1: 15 He is the image of the *i* God,
1Ti 1: 17 immortal, *i*, the only God,

INVITE (INVITED INVITES)
Lk 14: 13 you give a banquet, *i* the poor,

INVITED (INVITE)
Mt 22: 14 For many are *i*, but few are chosen
    25: 35 I was a stranger and you *i* me in,

INVITES (INVITE)
1Co 10: 27 If some unbeliever *i* you to a meal

INVOLVED
2Ti 2:   4 a soldier gets *i* in civilian affairs—

IRON
1Ti 4:   2 have been seared as with a hot *i*.
Rev 2: 27 He will rule them with an *i* scepter;

IRREVOCABLE*
Ro 11: 29 for God's gifts and his call are *i*.

ISAAC
   Son of Abraham by Sarah (Ge 17:19; 21:1-7; 1Ch 1:28). Offered up by Abraham (Ge 22; Heb 11:17-19). Rebekah taken as wife (Ge 24). Fathered Esau and Jacob (Ge 25:19-26; 1Ch 1:34). Tricked into blessing Jacob (Ge 27). Father of Israel (Ex 3:6; Dt 29:13; Ro 9:10).

ISAIAH
   Prophet to Judah (Isa 1:1). Called by the LORD (Isa 6).

ISHMAEL
   Son of Abraham by Hagar (Ge 16; 1Ch 1:28). Blessed, but not son of covenant (Ge 17:18-21; Gal 4:21-31). Sent away by Sarah (Ge 21:8-21).

ISRAEL (ISRAELITES)
   1. Name given to Jacob (see JACOB).
   2. Corporate name of Jacob's descendants; often specifically Northern Kingdom.
Dt   6:   4 Hear, O *I*: The LORD our God,
1Sa 4: 21 "The glory has departed from *I*"—
Isa 27:   6 *I* will bud and blossom
Jer 31: 10 'He who scattered *I* will gather
Eze 39: 23 of *I* went into exile for their sin,
Mk 12: 29 'Hear, O *I*, the Lord our God,
Lk 22: 30 judging the twelve tribes of *I*.
Ro   9:   6 all who are descended from *I* are *I*.
    11: 26 And so all *I* will be saved,
Eph 3:   6 Gentiles are heirs together with *I*,

ISRAELITES (ISRAEL)
Ex 14: 22 and the *I* went through the sea
    16: 35 The *I* ate manna forty years,
Hos 1: 10 "Yet the *I* will be like the sand
Ro   9: 27 the number of the *I* be like the sand

ITCHING*
2Ti 4:   3 to say what their *i* ears want to hear

∾ J

JACOB
   Second son of Isaac, twin of Esau (Ge 26:21-26; 1Ch 1:34). Bought Esau's birthright (Ge 26:29-34); tricked Isaac into blessing him (Ge 27:1-37). Abrahamic covenant perpetuated through (Ge 28:13-15; Mal 1:2). Vision at Bethel (Ge 28:10-22). Wives and children (Ge 29:1-30:24; 35:16-26; 1Ch 2-9). Wrestled with God; name changed to Israel (Ge 32:22-32). Sent sons to Egypt during famine (Ge 42-43). Settled in Egypt (Ge 46). Blessed Ephraim and Manasseh (Ge 48). Blessed sons (Ge 49:1-28; Heb 11:21). Death (Ge 49:29-33). Burial (Ge 50:1-14).

JAMES
   1. Apostle; brother of John (Mt 4:21-22; 10:2; Mk 3:17; Lk 5:1-10). At transfiguration (Mt 17:1-13; Mk 9:1-13; Lk 9:28-36). Killed by Herod (Ac 12:2).
   2. Apostle; son of Alphaeus (Mt 10:3; Mk 3:18; Lk 6:15).
   3. Brother of Jesus (Mt 13:55; Mk 6:3; Lk 24:10; Gal 1:19) and Judas (Jude 1). With believers before Pentecost (Ac 1:13). Leader of church at Jerusalem (Ac 12:17; 15; 21:18; Gal 2:9, 12). Author of epistle (Jas 1:1).

JAPHETH
   Son of Noah (Ge 5:32; 1Ch 1:4-5). Blessed (Ge 9:18-28).

JARS
2Co 4:   7 we have this treasure in *j* of clay

JEALOUS (JEALOUSY)
Ex 20:   5 the LORD your God, am a *j* God,
    34: 14 whose name is Jealous, is a *j* God.
Dt   4: 24 God is a consuming fire, a *j* God.
Joel 2: 18 the LORD will be *j* for his land
Zec 1: 14 I am very *j* for Jerusalem and Zion,
2Co 11:   2 I am *j* for you with a godly jealousy

JEALOUSY (JEALOUS)
1Co 3:   3 For since there is *j* and quarreling
2Co 11:   2 I am jealous for you with a godly *j*.
Gal 5: 20 hatred, discord, *j*, fits of rage,

JEHOAHAZ
   1. Son of Jehu; king of Israel (2Ki 13:1-9).
   2. Son of Josiah; king of Judah (2Ki 23:31-34; 2Ch 36:1-4).

JEHOASH
   Son of Jehoahaz; king of Israel (2Ki 13-14; 2Ch 25).

JEHOIACHIN
   Son of Jehoiakim; king of Judah exiled by Nebuchadnezzar (2Ki 24:8-17; 2Ch 36:8-10; Jer 22:24-30; 24:1). Raised from prisoner status (2Ki 25:27-30; Jer 52:31-34).

JEHOIAKIM
   Son of Josiah; king of Judah (2Ki 23:34-24:6; 2Ch 36:4-8; Jer 22:18-23; 36).

JEHORAM
   Son of Jehoshaphat; king of Judah (2Ki 8:16-24).

JEHOSHAPHAT
   Son of Asa; king of Judah (1Ki 22:41-50; 2Ki 3; 2Ch 17-20).

JEHU
   King of Israel (1Ki 19:16-19; 2Ki 9-10).

JEPHTHAH
   Judge from Gilead who delivered Israel from Ammon (Jdg 10:6-12:7). Made rash vow concerning his daughter (Jdg 11:30-40).

JEREMIAH
   Prophet to Judah (Jer 1:1-3). Called by the LORD (Jer 1). Put in stocks (Jer 20:1-3). Threatened for prophesying (Jer 11:18-23; 26). Opposed by Hananiah (Jer 28). Scroll burned (Jer 36). Imprisoned (Jer 37). Thrown into cistern (Jer 38). Forced to Egypt with those fleeing Babylonians (Jer 43).

JEROBOAM
   1. Official of Solomon; rebelled to become first king of Israel (1Ki 11:26-40; 12:1-20; 2Ch 10). Idolatry (1Ki 12:25-33); judgment for (1Ki 13-14; 2Ch 13).
   2. Son of Jehoash; king of Israel (1Ki 14:23-29).

JERUSALEM
2Ki 23: 27 and I will reject *J*, the city I chose,
2Ch 6:   6 now I have chosen *J* for my Name
Ne   2: 17 Come, let us rebuild the wall of *J*,
Ps 122:   6 Pray for the peace of *J*:
   125:   2 As the mountains surround *J*,
   137:   5 If I forget you, O *J*,
Isa 40:   9 You who bring good tidings to *J*,
    65: 18 for I will create *J* to be a delight
Joel 3: 17 *J* will be holy;
Zep 3: 16 On that day they will say to *J*,
Zec 2:   4 '*J* will be a city without walls
     8:   8 I will bring them back to live in *J*;
    14:   8 living water will flow out from *J*,
Mt 23: 37 "O *J*, *J*, you who kill the prophets
Lk 13: 34 die outside *J*! "O *J*, *J*,
    21: 24 *J* will be trampled
Jn   4: 20 where we must worship is in *J*."

Ac   1:   8 and you will be my
                witnesses in J,
Gal   4: 25 corresponds to the present
                city of J
Rev 21:   2 I saw the Holy City, the
                new J,

JESUS

LIFE: Genealogy (Mt 1:1-17; Lk 3:21-37). Birth announced (Mt 1:18-25; Lk 1:26-45). Birth (Mt 2:1-12; Lk 2:1-40). Escape to Egypt (Mt 2:13-23). As a boy in the temple (Lk 2:41-52). Baptism (Mt 3:13-17; Mk 1:9-11; Lk 3:21-22; Jn 1:32-34). Temptation (Mt 4:1-11; Mk 1:12-13; Lk 4:1-13). Ministry in Galilee (Mt 4:12-18:35; Mk 1:14-9:50; Lk 4:14-13:9; Jn 1:35-2:11; 4; 6), Transfiguration (Mt 17:1-8; Mk 9:2-8; Lk 9:28-36), on the way to Jerusalem (Mt 19-20; Mk 10; Lk 13:10-19:27), in Jerusalem (Mt 21-25; Mk 11-13; Lk 19:28-21:38; Jn 2:12-3:36; 5; 7-12). Last supper (Mt 26:17-35; Mk 14:12-31; Lk 22:1-38; Jn 13-17). Arrest and trial (Mt 26:36-27:31; Mk 14:43-15:20; Lk 22:39-23:25; Jn 18:1-19:16). Crucifixion (Mt 27:32-66; Mk 15:21-47; Lk 23:26-55; Jn 19:28-42). Resurrection and appearances (Mt 28; Mk 16; Lk 24; Jn 20-21; Ac 1:1-11; 7:56; 9:3-6; 1Co 15:1-8; Rev 1:1-20).

MIRACLES. Healings: official's son (Jn 4:43-54), demoniac in Capernaum (Mk 1:23-26; Lk 4:33-35), Peter's mother-in-law (Mt 8:14-17; Mk 1:29-31; Lk 4:38-39), leper (Mt 8:2-4; Mk 1:40-45; Lk 5:12-16), paralytic (Mt 9:1-8; Mk 2:1-12; Lk 5:17-26), shriveled hand (Mt 12:10-13; Mk 3:1-5; Lk 6:6-11), centurion's servant (Mt 8:5-13; Lk 7:1-10), widow's son raised (Lk 7:11-17), demoniac (Mt 12:22-23; Lk 11:14), Gadarene demoniacs (Mt 8:28-34; Mk 5:1-20; Lk 8:26-39), woman's bleeding and Jairus' daughter (Mt 9:18-26; Mk 5:21-43; Lk 8:40-56), blind man (Mt 9:27-31), mute man (Mt 9:32-33), Canaanite woman's daughter (Mt 15:21-28; Mk 7:24-30), deaf man (Mk 7:31-37), blind man (Mk 8:22-26), demoniac boy (Mt 17:14-18; Mk 9:14-29; Lk 9:37-43), ten lepers (Lk 17:11-19), man born blind (Jn 9:1-7), Lazarus raised (Jn 11), crippled woman (Lk 13:11-17), man with dropsy (Lk 14:1-6), two blind men (Mt 20:29-34; Mk 10:46-52; Lk 18:35-43), Malchus' ear (Lk 22:50-51). Other Miracles: water to wine (Jn 2:1-11), catch of fish (Lk 5:1-11), storm stilled (Mt 8:23-27; Mk 4:37-41; Lk 8:22-25), 5,000 fed (Mt 14:15-21; Mk 6:35-44; Lk 9:10-17; Jn 6:1-14), walking on water (Mt 14:25-33; Mk 6:48-52; Jn 6:15-21), 4,000 fed (Mt 15:32-39; Mk 8:1-9), money from fish (Mt 17:24-27), fig tree cursed (Mt 21:18-22; Mk 11:12-14), catch of fish (Jn 21:1-14).

MAJOR TEACHING: Sermon on the Mount (Mt 5-7; Lk 6:17-49), to Nicodemus (Jn 3), to Samaritan woman (Jn 4), Bread of Life (Jn 6:22-59), at Feast of Tabernacles (Jn 7-8), woes to Pharisees (Mt 23; Lk 11:37-54), Good Shepherd (Jn 10:1-18), Olivet Discourse (Mt 24-25; Mk 13; Lk 21:5-36), Upper Room Discourse (Jn 13-16).

PARABLES: Sower (Mt 13:3-23; Mk 4:3-25; Lk 8:5-18), seed's growth (Mk 4:26-29), wheat and weeds (Mt 13:24-30, 36-43), mustard seed (Mt 13:31-32; Mk 4:30-32), yeast (Mt 13:33-35; Mk 4:33-34), hidden treasure (Mt 13:44), valuable pearl (Mt 13:45-46), net (Mt 13:47-51), house owner (Mt 13:52), good Samaritan (Lk 10:25-37), unmerciful servant (Mt 18:15-35), lost sheep (Mt 18:10-14; Lk 15:4-7), lost coin (Lk 15:8-10), prodigal son (Lk 15:11-32), dishonest manager (Lk 16:1-13), rich man and Lazarus (Lk 16:19-31), persistent widow (Lk 18:1-8), Pharisee and tax collector (Lk 18:9-14), payment of workers (Mt 20:1-16), tenants and the vineyard (Mt 21:28-46; Mt 12:1-12; Lk 20:9-19), wedding banquet (Mt 22:1-14), faithful servant (Mt 24:45-51), ten virgins (Mt 25:1-13), talents (Mt 25:1-30; Lk 19:12-27).

DISCIPLES see APOSTLES. Call of (Jn 1:35-51; Mt 4:18-22; 9:9; Mk 1:16-20; 2:13-14; Lk 5:1-11, 27-28). Named Apostles (Mk 3:13-19; Lk 6:12-16). Twelve sent out (Mt 10; Mk 6:7-11; Lk 9:1-5). Seventy sent out (Lk 10:1-24). Defection of (Jn 6:60-71; Mt 26:56; Mk 14:50-52). Final commission (Mt 28:16-20; Jn 21:15-23; Ac 1:3-8).

Ac   2: 32 God has raised this J to life,
         9:   5 "I am J, whom you are
                persecuting
       15: 11 of our Lord J that we
                are saved,
       16: 31 "Believe in the Lord J,
Ro   3: 24 redemption that came by
                Christ J.
         5: 17 life through the one man,
                J Christ.
         8:   1 for those who are in Christ J,
1Co   2:   2 except J Christ and him
                crucified.
         8:   6 and there is but one Lord,
                J Christ,
       12:   3 and no one can say,
                "J is Lord,"
2Co   4:   5 not preach ourselves, but
                J Christ
Gal   2: 16 but by faith in J Christ.
         3: 28 for you are all one in
                Christ J.
         5:   6 in Christ J neither
                circumcision
Eph   2: 10 created in Christ J
         2: 20 with Christ J himself as
                the chief
Php   1:   6 until the day of Christ J.
         2:   5 be the same as that of
                Christ J:
         2: 10 name of J every knee should
                bow,
Col   3: 17 do it all in the name of the
                Lord J,

2Th   2:   1 the coming of our Lord
                J Christ
1Ti   1: 15 Christ J came into the world
2Ti   3: 12 life in Christ J will be
                persecuted,
Tit   2: 13 our great God and Savior,
                J Christ,
Heb 2:   9 But we see J, who was made
                a little
         3:   1 fix your thoughts on J,
                the apostle
         4: 14 through the heavens,
                J the Son
         7: 22 J has become the guarantee
         7: 24 but because J lives forever,
       12:   2 Let us fix our eyes on J,
                the author
2Pe   1: 16 and coming of our Lord
                J Christ,
1Jn   1:   7 and the blood of J, his Son,
         2:   1 J Christ, the Righteous One.
         2:   6 to live in him must walk as
                J did.
         4: 15 anyone acknowledges
                that J is
Rev 22: 20 Come, Lord J.

JEW (JEWS JUDAISM)

Zec   8: 23 of one J by the edge
                of his robe
Ro   1: 16 first for the J, then for the
                Gentile.
       10: 12 there is no difference
                between J
1Co   9: 20 To the Jews I became
                like a J,
Gal   3: 28 There is neither J nor Greek,

JEWELRY (JEWELS)

1Pe   3:   3 wearing of gold j and fine
                clothes.

JEWELS (JEWELRY)

Isa 61: 10 as a bride adorns herself
                with her j.
Zec   9: 16 like j in a crown.

JEWS (JEW)

Mt   2:   2 who has been born king of
                the J?
       27: 11 "Are you the king of the J?"
                "Yes,
Jn   4: 22 for salvation is from the J.
Ro   3: 29 Is God the God of J only?
1Co   1: 22 J demand miraculous signs
         9: 20 To the J I became like a Jew,
       12: 13 whether J or Greeks, slave
                or free
Gal   2:   8 of Peter as an apostle to
                the J,
Rev   3:   9 claim to be J though they
                are not,

JEZEBEL

Sidonian wife of Ahab (1Ki 16:31). Promoted Baal worship (1Ki 16:32-33). Killed prophets of the LORD (1Ki 18:4,13). Opposed Elijah (1Ki 19:1-2). Had Naboth killed (1Ki 21). Death prophesied (1Ki 21:17-24).Killed by Jehu (2Ki 9:30-37).

JOASH

Son of Ahaziah; king of Judah. Sheltered from Athaliah by Jehoiada (2Ki 11; 2Ch 22:10-23:21). Repaired temple (2Ki 12; 2Ch 24).

JOB

Wealthy man from Uz; feared God (Job 1:1-5).Righteousness tested by disaster (Job 1:6-22), personal affliction (Job 2). Maintained innocence in debate with three friends (Job 3-31), Elihu (Job 32-37). Rebuked by the LORD (Job 38-41). Vindicated and restored to greater stature by the LORD (Job 42). Example of righteousness (Eze 14:14, 20).

JOHN

1. Son of Zechariah and Elizabeth (Lk 1). Called the Baptist (Mt 3:1-12; Mk 1:2-8). Witness to Jesus (Mt 3:11-12; Mk 1:7-8; Lk 3:15-18; Jn 1:6-35; 3:27-30; 5:33-36). Doubts about Jesus (Mt 11:2-6; Lk 7:18-23). Arrest (Mt 4:12; Mk 1:14). Execution (Mt 14:1-12; Mk 6:14-29; Lk 9:7-9). Ministry compared to Elijah (Mt 11:7-19; Mk 9:11-13; Lk 7:24-35).

2. Apostle; brother of James (Mt 4:21-22; 10:2; Mk 3:17; Lk 5:1-10). At transfiguration (Mt 17:1-13; Mk 9:1-13; Lk 9:28-36). Desire to be greatest (Mk 10:35-45). Leader of church at Jerusalem (Ac 4:1-3; Gal 2:9). Elder who wrote epistles (2Jn 1; 3Jn 1). Prophet who wrote Revelation (Rev 1:1; 22:8).

3. Cousin of Barnabas, co-worker with Paul, (Ac 12:12-13:13; 15:37), see MARK.

JOIN (JOINED)

Pr   23: 20 Do not j those who
                drink too much
       24: 21 and do not j with the
                rebellious,
Ro   15: 30 to j me in my struggle by
                praying
2Ti   1:   8 j with me in suffering for
                the gospel

JOINED (JOIN)

Mt   19:   6 Therefore what God has
                j together,
Mk 10:   9 Therefore what God has
                j together,
Eph   2: 21 him the whole building is
                j together
         4: 16 j and held together

JOINTS

Heb   4: 12 even to dividing soul and
                spirit, j

JOKING

Eph   5:   4 or coarse j, which are out
                of place,

JONAH

Prophet in days of Jeroboam II (2Ki 14:25). Called to Nineveh; fled to Tarshish (Jnh 1:1-3). Cause of storm; thrown into sea (Jnh 1:4-16). Swallowed by fish (Jnh 1:17). Prayer (Jnh 2).

Preached to Nineveh (Jnh 3). Attitude reproved by the LORD (Jnh 4). Sign of (Mt 12:39-41; Lk 11:29-32).

JONATHAN

Son of Saul (1Sa 13:16; 1Ch 8:33). Valiant warrior (1Sa 13-14). Relation to David (1Sa 18:1-4;19-20; 23:16-18). Killed at Gilboa (1Sa 31). Mourned by David (2Sa 1).

JORAM

Son of Ahab; king of Israel (2Ki 3; 8-9; 2Ch 22).

JORDAN

Nu 34: 12 boundary will go down along the J
Jos   4: 22 Israel crossed the J on dry ground.'
Mt   3: 6 baptized by him in the J River.

JOSEPH

1. Son of Jacob by Rachel (Ge 30:24; 1Ch 2:2). Favored by Jacob, hated by brothers (Ge 37:3-4). Dreams (Ge 37:5-11). Sold by brothers (Ge 37:12-36). Served Potiphar; imprisoned by false accusation (Ge 39). Interpreted dreams of Pharaoh's servants (Ge 40), of Pharaoh (Ge 41:4-40). Made greatest in Egypt (Ge 41:41-57). Sold grain to brothers (Ge 42-45). Brought Jacob and sons to Egypt (Ge 46-47). Sons Ephraim and Manasseh blessed (Ge 48). Blessed (Ge 49:22-26; Dt 33:13-17). Death (Ge 50:22-26; Ex 13:19; Heb 11:22). 12,000 from (Rev 7:8).

2. Husband of Mary, mother of Jesus (Mt 1:16-24; 2:13-19; Lk 1:27; 2; Jn 1:45).

3. Disciple from Arimathea, who gave his tomb for Jesus' burial (Mt 27:57-61; Mk 15:43-47; Lk 24:50-52).

4. Original name of Barnabas (Ac 4:36).

JOSHUA

1. Son of Nun; name changed from Hoshea (Nu 13:8, 16; 1Ch 7:27). Fought Amalekites under Moses (Ex 17:9-14). Servant of Moses on Sinai (Ex 24:13; 32:17). Spied Canaan (Nu 13). With Caleb, allowed to enter land (Nu 14:6, 30). Succeeded Moses (Dt 1:38; 31:1-8; 34:9).

Charged Israel to conquer Canaan (Jos 1). Crossed Jordan (Jos 3-4). Circumcised sons of wilderness wanderings (Jos 5). Conquered Jericho (Jos 6), Ai (Jos 7-8), five kings at Gibeon (Jos 10:1-28), southern Canaan (Jos 10:29-43), northern Canaan (Jos 11-12). Defeated at Ai (Jos 7). Deceived by Gibeonites (Jos 9). Renewed covenant (Jos 8:30-35; 24:1-27). Divided land among tribes (Jos 13-22). Last words (Jos 23). Death (Jos 24:28-31).

2. High priest during rebuilding of temple (Hag 1-2; Zec 3:1-9; 6:11).

JOSIAH

Son of Amon; king of Judah (2Ki 22-23; 2Ch 34 -35).

JOTHAM

Son of Azariah (Uzziah); king of Judah (2Ki 15:32-38; 2Ch 26:21-27:9).

JOY (ENJOY ENJOYMENT JOYFUL OVERJOYED REJOICE REJOICES REJOICING)

Dt   16: 15 and your j will be complete.
1Ch 16: 27 strength and j in his dwelling place.
Ne   8: 10 for the j of the LORD is your
Est   9: 22 their sorrow was turned into j
Job 38: 7 and all the angels shouted for j?
Ps   4: 7 have filled my heart with greater j
     21: 6 with the j of your presence.
     30: 11 sackcloth and clothed me with j,
     43: 4 to God, my j and my delight.
     51: 12 to me the j of your salvation
     66: 1 Shout with j to God, all the earth!
     96: 12 the trees of the forest will sing for j;
    107: 22 and tell of his works with songs of j
    119:111 they are the j of my heart.
Pr   10: 1 A wise son brings j to his father,
     10: 28 The prospect of the righteous is j,
     12: 20 but j for those who promote peace.
Isa 35: 10 everlasting j will crown their heads
     51: 11 Gladness and j will overtake them,
     55: 12 You will go out in j
Lk   1: 44 the baby in my womb leaped for j.
      2: 10 news of great j that will be
Jn   15: 11 and that your j may be complete.
     16: 20 but your grief will turn to j.
2Co   8: 2 their overflowing j and their
Php   2: 2 then make my j complete
      4: 1 and long for, my j and crown,
1Th   2: 19 For what is our hope, our j,
Phm   : 7 Your love has given me great j
Heb 12: 2 for the j set before him endured
Jas   1: 2 Consider it pure j, my brothers,
1Pe   1: 8 with an inexpressible and glorious j
2Jn   : 4 It has given me great j to find some
3Jn   : 4 I have no greater j

JOYFUL (JOY)

Ps 100: 2 come before him with j songs.
Hab   3: 18 I will be j in God my Savior.
1Th   5: 16 Be j always; pray continually;

JUDAH

1. Son of Jacob by Leah (Ge 29:35; 35:23; 1Ch 2:1). Tribe of blessed as ruling tribe (Ge 49:8 -12; Dt 33:7).

2. Name used for people and land of Southern Kingdom.

Jer 13: 19 All J will be carried into exile,
Zec 10: 4 From J will come the cornerstone,
Heb   7: 14 that our Lord descended from J,

JUDAISM (JEW)

Gal   1: 13 of my previous way of life in J,

JUDAS

1. Apostle (Lk 6:16; Jn 14:22; Ac 1:13). Probably also called Thaddaeus (Mt 10:3; Mk 3:18).

2. Brother of James and Jesus (Mt 13:55; Mk 6:3), also called Jude (Jude 1).

3. Apostle, also called Iscariot, who betrayed Jesus (Mt 10:4; 26:14-56; Mk 3:19; 14:10-50; Lk 6:16; 22:3-53; Jn 6:71; 12:4; 13:2 -30; 18:2 -11). Suicide of (Mt 27:3-5; Ac 1:16-25).

JUDGE (JUDGED JUDGES JUDGING JUDGMENT)

Ge   18: 25 Will not the J of all the earth do
1Ch 16: 33 for he comes to j the earth.
Ps   9: 8 He will j the world in righteousness
Joel 3: 12 sit to j all the nations on every side.
Mt   7: 1 Do not j, or you too will be judged.
Jn   12: 47 For I did not come to j the world,
Ac   17: 31 a day when he will j the world
Ro   2: 16 day when God will j men's secrets
1Co   4: 3 indeed, I do not even j myself.
      6: 2 that the saints will j the world?
Gal   2: 6 not j by external appearance—
2Ti   4: 1 who will j the living and the dead,
      4: 8 which the Lord, the righteous J,
Jas   4: 12 There is only one Lawgiver and J,
      4: 12 who are you to j your neighbor?
Rev 20: 4 who had been given authority to j.

JUDGED (JUDGE)

Mt   7: 1 "Do not judge, or you too will be j.
1Co 11: 31 But if we j ourselves, we would not
Jas   3: 1 who teach will be j more strictly.
Rev 20: 12 The dead were j according

JUDGES (JUDGE)

Jdg   2: 16 Then the LORD raised up j,
Ps   58: 11 there is a God who j the earth."
Heb   4: 12 it j the thoughts and attitudes
Rev 19: 11 With justice he j and makes war.

JUDGING (JUDGE)

Mt   19: 28 j the twelve tribes of Israel.
Jn   7: 24 Stop j by mere appearances,

JUDGMENT (JUDGE)

Dt   1: 17 of any man, for j belongs to God.
Ps   1: 5 the wicked will not stand in the j,
    119: 66 Teach me knowledge and good j,
Pr   6: 32 man who commits adultery lacks j;
     12: 11 but he who chases fantasies lacks j.
Ecc 12: 14 God will bring every deed into j,
Isa 66: 16 the LORD will execute j
Mt   5: 21 who murders will be subject to j.'
     10: 15 on the day of j than for that town.
Mt   12: 36 have to give account on the day of j
Jn   5: 22 but has entrusted all j to the Son,
      7: 24 appearances, and make a right j."
     16: 8 to sin and righteousness and j:
Ro   14: 10 stand before God's j seat.
     14: 13 Therefore let us stop passing j
1Co 11: 29 body of the Lord eats and drinks j
2Co   5: 10 appear before the j seat of Christ,
Heb   9: 27 to die once, and after that to face j,
     10: 27 but only a fearful expectation of j
1Pe   4: 17 For it is time for j to begin
Jude : 6 bound with everlasting chains for j.

JUST (JUSTICE JUSTIFICATION JUSTIFIED JUSTIFY JUSTLY)

Dt   32: 4 and all his ways are j.
Ps   37: 28 For the LORD loves the j
    111: 7 of his hands are faithful and j;
Pr   1: 3 doing what is right and j and fair;
      2: 8 for he guards the course of the j
Da   4: 37 does is right and all his ways are j.
Ro   3: 26 as to be j and the one who justifies
Heb   2: 2 received its j punishment,
1Jn   1: 9 and j and will forgive us our sins

JUSTICE

Rev 16: 7 true and *j* are your
             judgments."

JUSTICE (JUST)

Ex 23: 2 do not pervert *j* by siding
       23: 6 "Do not deny *j* to your poor
             people
Job 37: 23 in his *j* and great
             righteousness,
Ps   9: 8 he will govern the peoples
             with *j*.
        9: 16 The LORD is known by his *j*;
       11: 7 he loves *j*;
       45: 6 a scepter of *j* will be the
             scepter
      101: 1 I will sing of your love and *j*;
      106: 3 Blessed are they who
             maintain *j*,
Pr   21: 15 When *j* is done, it brings joy
       28: 5 Evil men do not
             understand *j*,
       29: 4 By *j* a king gives a country
             stability
       29: 26 from the LORD that man
             gets *j*.
Isa   9: 7 it with *j* and righteousness
       28: 17 I will make *j* the measuring
             line
       30: 18 For the LORD is a God of *j*.
       42: 1 and he will bring *j* to the
             nations.
       42: 4 till he establishes *j* on earth.
       56: 1 "Maintain *j*
       61: 8 "For I, the LORD, love *j*;
Jer 30: 11 I will discipline you but
             only with *j*;
Eze 34: 16 I will shepherd the flock
             with *j*.
Am   5: 15 maintain *j* in the courts.
        5: 24 But let *j* roll on like a river,
Zec   7: 9 'Administer true *j*;
             show mercy
Lk   11: 42 you neglect *j* and the love
             of God.
Ro   3: 25 He did this to demonstrate
             his *j*,

JUSTIFICATION (JUST)

Ro   4: 25 and was raised to life for
             our *j*.
        5: 18 of righteousness was *j* that
             brings

JUSTIFIED (JUST)

Ac 13: 39 him everyone who believes
             is *j*
Ro   3: 24 and are *j* freely by his grace
        3: 28 For we maintain that a man
             is *j*
        5: 1 since we have been *j*
             through faith,
        5: 9 Since we have now been *j*
        8: 30 those he called, he also *j*;
             those he *j*,
1Co 6: 11 you were *j* in the name
Gal   2: 16 observing the law no one
             will be *j*.
        3: 11 Clearly no one is *j* before
             God
        3: 24 to Christ that we might be *j*
             by faith
Jas   2: 24 You see that a person is *j*

JUSTIFY (JUST)

Gal   3: 8 that God would *j*
             the Gentiles

JUSTLY (JUST)

Mic   6: 8 To act *j* and to love mercy

∽ *K*

KEEP (KEEPER KEEPING KEEPS KEPT)

Ge 31: 49 "May the LORD *k* watch
Ex 20: 6 and *k* my commandments.
Nu   6: 24 and *k* you;
Ps   18: 28 You, O LORD, *k* my lamp
             burning
       19: 13 *K* your servant also from
             willful
      119: 9 can a young man *k* his way
             pure?
      121: 7 The LORD will *k* you
      141: 3 *k* watch over the door of my
             lips.
Pr   4: 24 *k* corrupt talk far from your
             lips.
Isa 26: 3 You will *k* in perfect peace
Mt   10: 10 for the worker is worth his *k*.
Lk   12: 35 and *k* your lamps burning,
Gal   5: 25 let us *k* in step with
             the Spirit.
Eph   4: 3 Make every effort to *k* the
             unity
1Ti   5: 22 *K* yourself pure.
2Ti   4: 5 *k* your head in all situations,
Heb 13: 5 *K* your lives free from
             the love
Jas   1: 26 and yet does not *k* a
             tight rein
        2: 8 If you really *k* the royal law
             found
Jude : 24 able to *k* you from falling

KEEPER (KEEP)

Ge   4: 9 I my brother's *k*?" The LORD

KEEPING (KEEP)

Ex 20: 8 the Sabbath day by *k* it holy.
Ps   19: 11 in *k* them there is great
             reward.
Mt   3: 8 Produce fruit in *k* with
             repentance.
Lk   2: 8 *k* watch over their flocks at
             night.
1Co   7: 19 *K* God's commands is what
             counts.
2Pe   3: 9 Lord is not slow in *k* his
             promise,

KEEPS (KEEP)

Pr   17: 28 a fool is thought wise if he *k*
             silent,
Am   5: 13 Therefore the prudent man
             k quiet
1Co 13: 5 is not easily angered, it *k*
             no record
Jas   2: 10 For whoever *k* the whole law

KEPT (KEEP)

Ps 130: 3 If you, O LORD, *k* a record
             of sins,
2Ti   4: 7 finished the race, I have
             k the faith.

1Pe   1: 4 spoil or fade—*k* in heaven
             for you,

KEYS

Mt   16: 19 I will give you the *k* of the
             kingdom

KILL (KILLS)

Mt   17: 23 They will *k* him, and on the
             third

KILLS (KILL)

Lev 24: 21 but whoever *k* a man must
             be put
2Co   3: 6 for the letter *k*, but the
             Spirit gives

KIND (KINDNESS KINDS)

Ge   1: 24 animals, each according to
             its *k*."
2Ch 10: 7 "If you will be *k* to these
             people
Pr   11: 17 A *k* man benefits himself,
       12: 25 but a *k* word cheers him up.
       14: 21 blessed is he who is *k* to the
             needy.
       14: 31 whoever is *k* to the needy
             honors
       19: 17 He who is *k* to the poor
             lends
Da   4: 27 by being *k* to the oppressed.
Lk   6: 35 because he is *k* to the
             ungrateful
1Co 13: 4 Love is patient, love is *k*.
       15: 35 With what *k* of body
             will they
Eph   4: 32 Be *k* and compassionate
1Th   5: 15 but always try to be *k* to
             each other
2Ti   2: 24 instead, he must be *k* to
             everyone,
Tit   2: 5 to be busy at home, to be *k*,

KINDNESS (KIND)

Ac 14: 17 He has shown *k* by giving
             you rain
Ro   11: 22 Consider therefore the *k*
Gal   5: 22 peace, patience, *k*,
             goodness,
Eph   2: 7 expressed in his *k* to us
2Pe   1: 7 brotherly *k*; and to
             brotherly *k*,

KINDS (KIND)

1Co 12: 4 There are different *k* of gifts,
1Ti   6: 10 of money is a root of all *k*
             of evil.

KING (KINGDOM KINGS)

   1. Kings of Judah and Israel: see Saul,
David, Solomon.
   2. Kings of Judah: see Rehoboam,
Abijah, Asa, Jehoshaphat, Jehoram, Aha-
ziah, Athaliah (Queen), Joash, Amaziah,
Uzziah, Jotham, Ahaz, Hezekiah, Manas-
seh, Amon, Josiah, Jehoahaz, Jehoiakim,
Jehoiachin, Zedekiah.
   3. Kings of Israel: see Jeroboam I,
Nadab, Baasha, Elah, Zimri, Tibni, Omri,
Ahab, Ahaziah, Joram, Jehu, Jehoahaz,
Jehoash, Jeroboam II, Zechariah, Shal-
lum, Menahem, Pekah, Pekahiah, Hoshea.

Jdg 17: 6 In those days Israel had
             no *k*;
1Sa 12: 12 the LORD your God was
             your *k*.
Ps   24: 7 that the *K* of glory may
             come in.
Isa 32: 1 See, a *k* will reign in
             righteousness
Zec   9: 9 See, your *k* comes to you,
1Ti   6: 15 the *K* of kings and Lord of
             lords,
1Pe   2: 17 of believers, fear God,
             honor the *k*.
Rev 19: 16 *K* OF KINGS AND LORD

KINGDOM (KING)

Ex 19: 6 you will be for me a *k* of
             priests
1Ch 29: 11 Yours, O LORD, is the *k*;
Ps   45: 6 justice will be the scepter of
             your *k*.
Da   4: 3 His *k* is an eternal *k*;
Mt   3: 2 Repent, for the *k* of heaven
             is near
        5: 3 for theirs is the *k* of heaven.
        6: 10 your *k* come,
        6: 33 But seek first his *k* and his
        7: 21 Lord,' will enter the *k* of
             heaven,
       11: 11 least in the *k* of heaven is
             greater
       13: 24 "The *k* of heaven is like a
             man who
       13: 31 *k* of heaven is like a mustard
             seed,
       13: 33 "The *k* of heaven is like
             yeast that
       13: 44 *k* of heaven is like treasure
             hidden
       13: 45 the *k* of heaven is like a
             merchant
       13: 47 *k* of heaven is like a net that
             was let
       16: 19 the keys of the *k* of heaven;
       18: 23 the *k* of heaven is like a king
             who
       19: 24 for a rich man to enter the
             k of God
       24: 7 rise against nation, and *k*
             against *k*.
       24: 14 gospel of the *k* will be
             preached
       25: 34 the *k* prepared for you
Mk   9: 47 better for you to enter the
             k of God
       10: 14 for the *k* of God belongs to
             such
       10: 23 for the rich to enter the *k* of
             God!"
Lk   10: 9 'The *k* of God is near you.'
       12: 31 seek his *k*, and these things
             will be
       17: 21 because the *k* of God is
             within you
Jn   3: 5 no one can enter the *k*
             of God
       18: 36 "My *k* is not of this world.
1Co   6: 9 the wicked will not inherit
             the *k*
       15: 24 hands over the *k* to God the
             Father

Rev 1: 6 has made us to be a *k* and priests

11: 15 of the world has become the *k*

KINGS (KING)

Ps   2: 2 The *k* of the earth take their stand

72: 11 All *k* will bow down to him

Da   7: 24 ten horns are ten *k* who will come

1Ti 2: 2 for *k* and all those in authority,

Rev 1: 5 and the ruler of the *k* of the earth.

KINSMAN-REDEEMER (REDEEM)

Ru   3: 9 over me, since you are a *k*."

KISS

Ps   2: 12 *K* the Son, lest he be angry

Pr 24: 26 is like a *k* on the lips.

Lk 22: 48 the Son of Man with a *k*?"

KNEE (KNEES)

Isa 45: 23 Before me every *k* will bow;

Ro 14: 11 every *k* will bow before me;

Php 2: 10 name of Jesus every *k* should bow,

KNEES (KNEE)

Isa 35: 3 steady the *k* that give way;

Heb 12: 12 your feeble arms and weak *k*.

KNEW (KNOW)

Job 23: 3 If only I *k* where to find him;

Jnh 4: 2 I *k* that you are a gracious

Mt   7: 23 tell them plainly, 'I never *k* you.

KNOCK

Mt   7: 7 *k* and the door will be opened

Rev 3: 20 I am! I stand at the door and *k*.

KNOW (FOREKNEW KNEW KNOWING KNOWLEDGE KNOWN KNOWS)

Dt 18: 21 "How can we *k* when a message

Job 19: 25 I *k* that my Redeemer lives,

42: 3 things too wonderful for me to *k*.

Ps 46: 10 "Be still, and *k* that I am God;

139: 1 and you *k* me.

139: 23 Search me, O God, and *k* my heart;

Pr 27: 1 for you do not *k* what a day may

Jer 24: 7 I will give them a heart to *k* me,

31: 34 his brother, saying, '*K* the LORD,'

Mt   6: 3 let your left hand *k* what your right

24: 42 you do not *k* on what day your

Lk   1: 4 so that you may *k* the certainty

Jn   3: 11 we speak of what we *k*,

4: 22 we worship what we do *k*,

9: 25 One thing I do *k*.

10: 14 I *k* my sheep and my sheep *k* me —

17: 3 that they may *k* you, the only true

21: 24 We *k* that his testimony is true.

Ac   1: 7 "It is not for you to *k* the times

Ro   6: 6 For we *k* that our old self was

7: 18 I *k* that nothing good lives in me,

8: 28 we *k* that in all things God works

1Co 2: 2 For I resolved to *k* nothing

6: 15 Do you not *k* that your bodies are

6: 19 Do you not *k* that your body is

13: 12 Now I *k* in part; then I shall *k* fully,

15: 58 because you *k* that your labor

Php 3: 10 I want to *k* Christ and the power

2Ti 1: 12 because I *k* whom I have believed,

Jas 4: 14 *k* what will happen tomorrow.

1Jn 2: 4 The man who says, "I *k* him,"

3: 14 We *k* that we have passed

3: 16 This is how we *k* what love is:

5: 2 This is how we *k* that we love

5: 13 so that you may *k* that you have

KNOWING (KNOW)

Ge   3: 5 and you will be like God, *k* good,

Php 3: 8 of *k* Christ Jesus my Lord,

KNOWLEDGE (KNOW)

Ge   2: 9 the tree of the *k* of good and evil.

Job 42: 3 obscures my counsel without *k*?'

Ps 19: 2 night after night they display *k*.

73: 11 Does the Most High have *k*?"

139: 6 Such *k* is too wonderful for me,

Pr   1: 7 of the LORD is the beginning of *k*,

10: 14 Wise men store up *k*,

12: 1 Whoever loves discipline loves *k*,

13: 16 Every prudent man acts out of *k*,

19: 2 to have zeal without *k*,

Isa 11: 9 full of the *k* of the LORD

Hab 2: 1 filled with the *k* of the glory

Ro 11: 33 riches of the wisdom and *k* of God!

1Co 8: 1 *K* puffs up, but love builds up.

8: 11 Christ died, is destroyed by your *k*.

13: 2 can fathom all mysteries and all *k*,

2Co 2: 14 everywhere the fragrance of the *k*

4: 6 light of the *k* of the glory of God

Eph 3: 19 to know this love that surpasses *k*

Col 2: 3 all the treasures of wisdom and *k*.

1Ti 6: 20 ideas of what is falsely called *k*,

2Pe 3: 18 grow in the grace and *k* of our Lord

KNOWN (KNOW)

Ps 16: 11 You have made *k* to me the path

105: 1 make *k* among the nations what he

Isa 46: 10 *k* the end from the beginning,

Mt 10: 26 or hidden that will not be made *k*.

Ro   1: 19 since what may be *k* about God is

11: 34 "Who has *k* the mind of the Lord?

15: 20 the gospel where Christ was not *k*,

2Co 3: 2 written on our hearts, *k*

2Pe 2: 21 than to have *k* it and then

KNOWS (KNOW)

1Sa 2: 3 for the LORD is a God who *k*,

Job 23: 10 But he *k* the way that I take;

Ps 44: 21 since he *k* the secrets of the heart?

94: 11 The LORD *k* the thoughts of man;

Ecc 8: 7 Since no man *k* the future,

Mt   6: 8 for your Father *k* what you need

24: 36 "No one *k* about that day or hour,

Ro   8: 27 who searches our hearts *k* the mind

1Co 8: 2 who thinks he *k* something does

2Ti 2: 19 The Lord *k* those who are his," and

∽ *L*

LABAN

Brother of Rebekah (Ge 24:29-51), father of Rachel and Leah (Ge 29-31).

LABOR

Ex 20: 9 Six days you shall *l* and do all your

Isa 55: 2 and your *l* on what does not satisfy

Mt   6: 28 They do not *l* or spin.

1Co 3: 8 rewarded according to his own *l*.

15: 58 because you know that your *l*

LACK (LACKING LACKS)

Pr 15: 22 Plans fail for *l* of counsel,

Ro   3: 3 Will their *l* of faith nullify God's

Col 2: 23 *l* any value in restraining sensual

LACKING (LACK)

Ro 12: 11 Never be *l* in zeal, but keep your

Jas 1: 4 and complete, not *l* anything.

LACKS (LACK)

Pr   6: 32 who commits adultery *l* judgment;

12: 11 he who chases fantasies *l* judgment

Jas 1: 5 any of you *l* wisdom, he should ask

LAID (LAY)

Isa 53: 6 and the LORD has *l* on him

1Co 3: 11 other than the one already *l*,

1Jn 3: 16 Jesus Christ *l* down his life for us.

LAKE

Rev 19: 20 into the fiery *l* of burning sulfur.

20: 14 The *l* of fire is the second death.

LAMB (LAMB'S LAMBS)

Ge 22: 8 "God himself will provide the *l*

Ex 12: 21 and slaughter the Passover *l*.

Isa 11: 6 The wolf will live with the *l*,

53: 7 he was led like a *l* to the slaughter,

Jn   1: 29 *L* of God, who takes away the sin

1Co 5: 7 our Passover *l*, has been sacrificed.

1Pe 1: 19 a *l* without blemish or defect.

Rev 5: 6 Then I saw a *L*, looking

5: 12 "Worthy is the *L*, who was slain,

14: 4 They follow the *L* wherever he

LAMB'S (LAMB)

Rev 21: 27 written in the *L* book of life.

LAMBS (LAMB)

Lk 10: 3 I am sending you out like *l*

Jn 21: 15 Jesus said, "Feed my *l*."

LAMENT

2Sa 1: 17 took up this *l* concerning Saul

LAMP (LAMPS)

2Sa 22: 29 You are my *l*, O LORD;

Ps 18: 28 You, O LORD, keep my *l* burning;

119:105 Your word is a *l* to my feet

Pr 31: 18 and her *l* does not go out at night.

Lk   8: 16 "No one lights a *l* and hides it

Rev 21: 23 gives it light, and the Lamb is its *l*.

LAMPS (LAMP)

Mt 25: 1 be like ten virgins who took their *l*

Lk 12: 35 for service and keep your *l* burning,

LAND

Ge   1: 10 God called the dry ground "*l*,"

1: 11 "Let the *l* produce vegetation:
12: 7 To your offspring I will give this *l*."
Ex 3: 8 a *l* flowing with milk and honey—
Nu 35: 33 Do not pollute the *l* where you are.
Dt 34: 1 LORD showed him the whole *l*—
Jos 13: 2 "This is the *l* that remains:
14: 4 Levites received no share of the *l*
2Ch 7: 14 their sin and will heal their *l*.
7: 20 then I will uproot Israel from my *l*,
Eze 36: 24 and bring you back into your own *l*.

LANGUAGE

Ge 11: 1 Now the whole world had one *l*
Ps 19: 3 There is no speech or *l*
Jn 8: 44 When he lies, he speaks his native *l*
Ac 2: 6 heard them speaking in his own *l*.
Col 3: 8 slander, and filthy *l* from your lips.
Rev 5: 9 from every tribe and *l* and people

LAST (LASTING LASTS LATTER)

2Sa 23: 1 These are the *l* words of David:
Isa 44: 6 I am the first and I am the *l*;
Mt 19: 30 But many who are first will be *l*,
Mk 10: 31 are first will be *l*, and the *l* first."
Jn 15: 16 and bear fruit—fruit that will *l*.
Ro 1: 17 is by faith from first to *l*,
2Ti 3: 1 will be terrible times in the *l* days.
2Pe 3: 3 in the *l* days scoffers will come,
Rev 1: 17 I am the First and the *L*.
22: 13 the First and the *L*, the Beginning

LASTING (LAST)

Ex 12: 14 to the LORD—a *l* ordinance.
Lev 24: 8 of the Israelites, as a *l* covenant.
Nu 25: 13 have a covenant of a *l* priesthood,
Heb 10: 34 had better and *l* possessions.

LASTS (LAST)

Ps 30: 5 For his anger *l* only a moment,
2Co 3: 11 greater is the glory of that which *l*!

LATTER (LAST)

Job 42: 12 The LORD blessed the *l* part

LAUGH (LAUGHS)

Ecc 3: 4 a time to weep and a time to *l*,

LAUGHS (LAUGH)

Ps 2: 4 The One enthroned in heaven *l*;
37: 13 but the Lord *l* at the wicked,

LAVISHED

Eph 1: 8 of God's grace that he *l* on us
1Jn 3: 1 great is the love the Father has *l*

LAW (LAWS)

Dt 31: 11 you shall read this *l* before them
31: 26 "Take this Book of the *L*
Jos 1: 8 of the *L* depart from your mouth;
Ne 8: 8 from the Book of the *L* of God,
Ps 1: 2 and on his *l* he meditates day
19: 7 The *l* of the LORD is perfect,
119: 18 wonderful things in your *l*.
119: 72 *l* from your mouth is more precious
119: 97 Oh, how I love your *l*!
119:165 peace have they who love your *l*,
Isa 8: 20 To the *l* and to the testimony!
Jer 31: 33 "I will put my *l* in their minds
Mt 5: 17 that I have come to abolish the *L*
7: 12 sums up the *L* and the Prophets.
22: 40 All the *L* and the Prophets hang
Lk 16: 17 stroke of a pen to drop out of the *L*.
Jn 1: 17 For the *l* was given through Moses;
Ro 2: 12 All who sin apart from the *l* will
2: 15 of the *l* are written on their hearts,
5: 13 for before the *l* was given,
5: 20 *l* was added so that the trespass
6: 14 because you are not under *l*,
7: 6 released from the *l* so that we serve
7: 12 *l* is holy, and the commandment is
8: 3 For what the *l* was powerless to do
10: 4 Christ is the end of the *l*
13: 10 love is the fulfillment of the *l*.
Gal 3: 13 curse of the *l* by becoming a curse
3: 24 So the *l* was put in charge to lead us
5: 3 obligated to obey the whole *l*.
5: 4 justified by *l* have been alienated
5: 14 The entire *l* is summed up
Heb 7: 19 (for the *l* made nothing perfect),
10: 1 The *l* is only a shadow
Jas 1: 25 intently into the perfect *l* that gives
2: 10 For whoever keeps the whole *l*

LAWLESSNESS*

2Th 2: 3 and the man of *l* is revealed,
2: 7 power of *l* is already at work;
1Jn 3: 4 sins breaks the law; in fact, sin is *l*

LAWS (LAW)

Lev 25: 18 and be careful to obey my *l*,
Ps 119: 30 I have set my heart on your *l*.
119:120 I stand in awe of your *l*.
Heb 8: 10 I will put my *l* in their minds
10: 16 I will put my *l* in their hearts,

LAY (LAID LAYING)

Job 22: 22 and *l* up his words in your heart.
Isa 28: 16 "See, I *l* a stone in Zion,
Mt 8: 20 of Man has no place to *l* his head."
Jn 10: 15 and I *l* down my life for the sheep.
15: 13 that he *l* down his life
1Co 3: 11 no one can *l* any foundation other
1Jn 3: 16 And we ought to *l* down our lives
Rev 4: 10 They *l* their crowns

LAYING (LAY)

1Ti 5: 22 Do not be hasty in the *l* on of hands
Heb 6: 1 not *l* again the foundation

LAZARUS

1. Poor man in Jesus' parable (Lk 16:19-31).
2. Brother of Mary and Martha whom Jesus raised from the dead (Jn 11:1-12:19).

LAZY

Pr 10: 4 *L* hands make a man poor,
Heb 6: 12 We do not want you to become *l*,

LEAD (LEADERS LEADERSHIP LEADS LED)

Ex 15: 13 "In your unfailing love you will *l*
Ps 27: 11 *l* me in a straight path
61: 2 *l* me to the rock that is higher
139: 24 and *l* me in the way everlasting.
143: 10 *l* me on level ground.
Ecc 5: 2 Do not let your mouth *l* you
Isa 11: 6 and a little child will *l* them.
Da 12: 3 those who *l* many to righteousness,
Mt 6: 13 And *l* us not into temptation,
1Jn 3: 7 do not let anyone *l* you astray.

LEADERS (LEAD)

Heb 13: 7 Remember your *l*, who spoke
13: 17 Obey your *l* and submit

LEADERSHIP (LEAD)

Ro 12: 8 if it is *l*, let him govern diligently;

LEADS (LEAD)

Ps 23: 2 he *l* me beside quiet waters,
Pr 19: 23 The fear of the LORD *l* to life:

Isa 40: 11 he gently *l* those that have young.
Mt 7: 13 and broad is the road that *l*
15: 14 If a blind man *l* a blind man,
Jn 10: 3 sheep by name and *l* them out.
Ro 14: 19 effort to do what *l* to peace
2Co 2: 14 always *l* us in triumphal procession

LEAH

Wife of Jacob (Ge 29:16-30); bore six sons and one daughter (Ge 29:31-30: 21; 34:1; 35:23).

LEAN

Pr 3: 5 *l* not on your own understanding;

LEARN (LEARNED LEARNING)

Isa 1: 17 *l* to do right!
Mt 11: 29 yoke upon you and *l* from me,

LEARNED (LEARN)

Php 4: 11 for I have *l* to be content whatever
2Ti 3: 14 continue in what you have *l*

LEARNING (LEARN)

Pr 1: 5 let the wise listen and add to their *l*,
2Ti 3: 7 always *l* but never able

LED (LEAD)

Ps 68: 18 you *l* captives in your train;
Isa 53: 7 he was *l* like a lamb to the slaughter
Am 2: 10 and I *l* you forty years in the desert
Ro 8: 14 those who are *l* by the Spirit
Eph 4: 8 he *l* captives in his train

LEFT

Jos 1: 7 turn from it to the right or to the *l*,
Pr 4: 27 Do not swerve to the right or the *l*;
Mt 6: 3 do not let your *l* hand know what
25: 33 on his right and the goats on his *l*.

LEGION

Mk 5: 9 "My name is *L*," he replied,

LEND (LENDS)

Dt 15: 8 freely *l* him whatever he needs.
Ps 37: 26 are always generous and *l* freely;
Lk 6: 34 if you *l* to those from whom you

LENDS (LEND)

Pr 19: 17 to the poor *l* to the LORD,

LENGTH (LONG)

Ps 90: 10 The *l* of our days is seventy years—
Pr 10: 27 The fear of the LORD adds *l* to life

LEPROSY

2Ki 7: 3 men with *l* at the entrance

LETTER (LETTERS)

Mt   5: 18 not the smallest *l*, not the least
2Co 3: 2 You yourselves are our *l*, written
      3: 6 for the *l* kills, but the Spirit gives
2Th 3: 14 not obey our instruction in this *l*,

LETTERS (LETTER)

2Co 3: 7 which was engraved in *l* on stone,
     10: 10 "His *l* are weighty and forceful,
2Pe 3: 16 His *l* contain some things that are

LEVEL

Ps 143: 10 lead me on *l* ground.
Pr   4: 26 Make *l* paths for your feet
Isa 26: 7 The path of the righteous is *l*;
Heb 12: 13 "Make *l* paths for your feet,"

LEVI (LEVITES)

1. Son of Jacob by Leah (Ge 29:34; 46:11; 1Ch 2:1). Tribe of blessed (Ge 49:5-7; Dt 33:8-11), chosen as priests (Nu 3-4), numbered (Nu 3:39; 26:62), allotted cities, but not land (Nu 18; 35; Dt 10:9; Jos 13:14; 21), land (Eze 48:8-22), 12,000 from (Rev 7:7).
2. See MATTHEW.

LEVITES (LEVI)

Nu   1: 53 The *L* are to be responsible
      8: 6 "Take the *L* from among the other
     18: 21 I give to the *L* all the tithes in Israel

LEWDNESS

Mk   7: 22 malice, deceit, *l*, envy, slander,

LIAR (LIE)

Pr 19: 22 better to be poor than a *l*.
Jn   8: 44 for he is a *l* and the father of lies.
Ro   3: 4 Let God be true, and every man a *l*.

LIBERATED*

Ro   8: 21 that the creation itself will be *l*

LIE (LIAR LIED LIES LYING)

Lev 19: 11 "'Do not *l*.
Nu 23: 19 God is not a man, that he should *l*,
Dt   6: 7 when you *l* down and when you get
Ps 23: 2 me *l* down in green pastures,
Isa 11: 6 leopard will *l* down with the goat,
Eze 34: 14 they will *l* down in good grazing
Ro   1: 25 exchanged the truth of God for a *l*,
Col 3: 9 Do not *l* to each other,
Heb 6: 18 which it is impossible for God to *l*,

LIED (LIE)

Ac   5: 4 You have not *l* to men but to God."

LIES (LIE)

Ps 34: 13 and your lips from speaking *l*.
Jn   8: 44 for he is a liar and the father of *l*.

LIFE (LIVE)

Ge   2: 7 into his nostrils the breath of *l*,
      2: 9 of the garden were the tree of *l*
      9: 11 Never again will all *l* be cut
Ex 21: 23 you are to take *l* for *l*, eye for eye,
Lev 17: 14 the *l* of every creature is its blood.
     24: 18 must make restitution— *l* for *l*.
Dt 30: 19 Now choose *l*, so that you
Ps 16: 11 known to me the path of *l*;
     23: 6 all the days of my *l*,
     34: 12 Whoever of you loves *l*
     39: 4 let me know how fleeting is my *l*.
     49: 7 No man can redeem the *l*
    104: 33 I will sing to the LORD all my *l*;
Pr   1: 3 a disciplined and prudent *l*,
      6: 23 are the way to *l*,
      7: 23 little knowing it will cost him his *l*.
      8: 35 For whoever finds me finds *l*
     11: 30 of the righteous is a tree of *l*,
     21: 21 finds *l*, prosperity and honor.
Jer 10: 23 that a man's *l* is not his own;
Eze 37: 5 enter you, and you will come to *l*.
Da 12: 2 some to everlasting *l*, others
Mt   6: 25 Is not *l* more important than food,
      7: 14 and narrow the road that leads to *l*,
     10: 39 Whoever finds his *l* will lose it,
     16: 25 wants to save his *l* will lose it,
     20: 28 to give his *l* as a ransom for many."
Mk 10: 45 to give his *l* as a ransom for many."
Lk 12: 15 a man's *l* does not consist
     12: 22 do not worry about your *l*,
     14: 26 even his own *l*—he cannot be my
Jn   1: 4 In him was *l*, and that *l* was
      3: 15 believes in him may have eternal *l*.
      3: 36 believes in the Son has eternal *l*,
      4: 14 of water welling up to eternal *l*."
      5: 24 him who sent me has eternal *l*
      6: 35 Jesus declared, "I am the bread of *l*.
      6: 47 he who believes has everlasting *l*.
      6: 68 You have the words of eternal *l*.

10: 10 I have come that they may have *l*,
10: 15 and I lay down my *l* for the sheep.
10: 28 I give them eternal *l*, and they shall
11: 25 "I am the resurrection and the *l*.
14: 6 am the way and the truth and the *l*.
15: 13 lay down his *l* for his friends.
20: 31 that by believing you may have *l*
Ac 13: 48 appointed for eternal *l* believed.
Ro   4: 25 was raised to *l* for our justification.
      6: 13 have been brought from death to *l*;
      6: 23 but the gift of God is eternal *l*
      8: 38 convinced that neither death nor *l*,
1Co 15: 19 If only for this *l* we have hope
2Co 3: 6 letter kills, but the Spirit gives *l*.
Gal 2: 20 The *l* I live in the body, I live
Eph 4: 1 I urge you to live a *l* worthy
Php 2: 16 as you hold out the word of *l*—
Col 1: 10 order that you may live a *l* worthy
1Th 4: 12 so that your daily *l* may win
1Ti 4: 8 for both the present *l* and the *l*
      4: 16 Watch your *l* and doctrine closely.
      6: 19 hold of the *l* that is truly *l*.
2Ti 3: 12 to live a godly *l* in Christ Jesus will
Jas 1: 12 crown of *l* that God has promised
      3: 13 Let him show it by his good *l*,
1Pe 3: 10 "Whoever would love *l*
2Pe 1: 3 given us everything we need for *l*
1Jn 3: 14 we have passed from death to *l*,
      5: 11 has given us eternal *l*, and this *l* is
Rev 13: 8 written in the book of *l* belonging
     20: 12 was opened, which is the book of *l*.
     21: 27 written in the Lamb's book of *l*.
     22: 2 side of the river stood the tree of *l*,

LIFT (LIFTED)

Ps 121: 1 I *l* up my eyes to the hills—
   134: 2 *L* up your hands in the sanctuary
La   3: 41 Let us *l* up our hearts and our
1Ti 2: 8 everywhere to *l* up holy hands

LIFTED (LIFT)

Ps 40: 2 He *l* me out of the slimy pit,

Jn   3: 14 Moses *l* up the snake in the desert,
     12: 32 when I am *l* up from the earth,

LIGHT (ENLIGHTENED)

Ge   1: 3 "Let there be *l*," and there was *l*.
2Sa 22: 29 LORD turns my darkness into *l*.
Job 38: 19 "What is the way to the abode of *l*?
Ps   4: 6 Let the *l* of your face shine upon us
     19: 8 giving *l* to the eyes.
     27: 1 LORD is my *l* and my salvation—
     56: 13 God in the *l* of life.
     76: 4 You are resplendent with *l*,
    104: 2 He wraps himself in *l*
   119:105 and a *l* for my path.
   119:130 The unfolding of your words gives *l*;
Isa 2: 5 let us walk in the *l* of the LORD.
      9: 2 have seen a great *l*;
     49: 6 also make you a *l* for the Gentiles,
Mt   4: 16 have seen a great *l*;
      5: 16 let your *l* shine before men,
     11: 30 yoke is easy and my burden is *l*."
Jn   3: 19 but men loved darkness instead of *l*
      8: 12 he said, "I am the *l* of the world.
2Co 4: 6 made his *l* shine in our hearts
      6: 14 Or what fellowship can *l* have
     11: 14 masquerades as an angel of *l*.
1Ti 6: 16 and who lives in unapproachable *l*,
1Pe 2: 9 of darkness into his wonderful *l*.
1Jn 1: 5 God is *l*; in him there is no
      1: 7 But if we walk in the *l*,
Rev 21: 23 for the glory of God gives it *l*,

LIGHTNING

Da 10: 6 his face like *l*, his eyes like flaming
Mt 24: 27 For as the *l* that comes from the east
     28: 3 His appearance was like *l*,

LIKENESS

Ge   1: 26 man in our image, in our *l*,
Ps 17: 15 I will be satisfied with seeing your *l*
Isa 52: 14 his form marred beyond human *l*—
Ro   8: 3 Son in the *l* of sinful man
      8: 29 to be conformed to the *l* of his Son,
2Co 3: 18 his *l* with ever-increasing glory,
Php 2: 7 being made in human *l*.
Jas 3: 9 who have been made in God's *l*.

LILIES

Lk 12: 27 "Consider how the *l* grow.

LION

Isa 11: 7 and the *l* will eat straw like the ox.

1Pe 5: 8 around like a roaring *l* looking

Rev 5: 5 See, the *L* of the tribe of Judah,

LIPS

Ps 8: 2 From the *l* of children and infants

34: 1 his praise will always be on my *l*.

119:171 May my *l* overflow with praise,

Pr 13: 3 He who guards his *l* guards his life,

27: 2 someone else, and not your own *l*.

Isa 6: 5 For I am a man of unclean *l*,

Mt 21: 16 "'From the *l* of children

Col 3: 8 and filthy language from your *l*.

LISTEN (LISTENING LISTENS)

Dt 30: 20 *l* to his voice, and hold fast to him.

Pr 1: 5 let the wise *l* and add

Jn 10: 27 My sheep *l* to my voice; I know

Jas 1: 19 Everyone should be quick to *l*,

1: 22 Do not merely *l* to the word,

LISTENING (LISTEN)

1Sa 3: 9 Speak, LORD, for your servant is *l*

Pr 18: 13 He who answers before *l*—

LISTENS (LISTEN)

Pr 12: 15 but a wise man *l* to advice.

LIVE (ALIVE LIFE LIVES LIVING)

Ex 20: 12 so that you may *l* long

33: 20 for no one may see me and *l*."

Dt 8: 3 to teach you that man does not *l*

Job 14: 14 If a man dies, will he *l* again?

Ps 119:175 Let me *l* that I may praise you,

Isa 55: 3 hear me, that your soul may *l*.

Eze 37: 3 can these bones *l*?" I said,

Hab 2: 4 but the righteous will *l* by his faith

Mt 4: 4 'Man does not *l* on bread alone,'

Ac 17: 24 does not *l* in temples built by hands

17: 28 'For in him we *l* and move

Ro 1: 17 "The righteous will *l* by faith."

2Co 5: 7 We *l* by faith, not by sight.

Gal 2: 20 The life I *l* in the body, I *l* by faith

5: 25 Since we *l* by the Spirit, let us keep

Php 1: 21 to *l* is Christ and to die is gain.

1Th 5: 13 *L* in peace with each other.

2Ti 3: 12 who wants to *l* a godly life

Heb 12: 14 Make every effort to *l* in peace

1Pe 1: 17 *l* your lives as strangers here

LIVES (LIVE)

Job 19: 25 I know that my Redeemer *l*,

Isa 57: 15 he who *l* forever, whose name is

Da 3: 28 to give up their *l* rather than serve

Jn 14: 17 for he *l* with you and will be in you.

Ro 7: 18 I know that nothing good *l* in me,

14: 7 For none of us *l* to himself alone

1Co 3: 16 and that God's Spirit *l* in you?

Gal 2: 20 I no longer live, but Christ *l* in me.

Heb 13: 5 Keep your *l* free from the love

2Pe 3: 11 You ought to live holy and godly *l*

1Jn 3: 16 to lay down our *l* for our brothers.

4: 16 Whoever *l* in love *l* in God,

LIVING (LIVE)

Ge 2: 7 and man became a *l* being.

Jer 2: 13 the spring of *l* water,

Mt 22: 32 the God of the dead but of the *l*."

Jn 7: 38 streams of *l* water will flow

Ro 12: 1 to offer your bodies as *l* sacrifices,

Heb 4: 12 For the word of God is *l* and active.

10: 31 to fall into the hands of the *l* God.

Rev 1: 18 I am the *L* One; I was dead,

LOAD

Gal 6: 5 for each one should carry his own *l*.

LOCUSTS

Mt 3: 4 His food was *l* and wild honey.

LOFTY

Ps 139: 6 too *l* for me to attain.

Isa 57: 15 is what the high and *l* One says—

LONELY

Ps 68: 6 God sets the *l* in families,

LONG (LENGTH LONGED LONGING LONGS)

1Ki 18: 21 "How *l* will you waver

Jn 9: 4 As *l* as it is day, we must do

Eph 3: 18 to grasp how wide and *l* and high

1Pe 1: 12 Even angels *l* to look

LONGED (LONG)

Mt 13: 17 righteous men *l* to see what you see

23: 37 how often I have *l*

2Ti 4: 8 to all who have *l* for his appearing.

LONGING (LONG)

Pr 13: 19 A *l* fulfilled is sweet to the soul,

2Co 5: 2 *l* to be clothed with our heavenly

LONGS (LONG)

Isa 30: 18 Yet the LORD *l* to be gracious

LOOK (LOOKING LOOKS)

Dt 4: 29 you will find him if you *l* for him

Job 31: 1 not to *l* lustfully at a girl.

Ps 34: 5 Those who *l* to him are radiant;

Pr 4: 25 Let your eyes *l* straight ahead,

Isa 60: 5 Then you will *l* and be radiant,

Hab 1: 13 Your eyes are too pure to *l* on evil;

Zec 12: 10 They will *l* on me, the one they

Mk 13: 21 '*L*, here is the Christ!' or, '*L*,

Lk 24: 39 *L* at my hands and my feet.

Jn 1: 36 he said, "*L*, the Lamb of God!"

4: 35 open your eyes and *l* at the fields!

19: 37 "They will *l* on the one they have

Jas 1: 27 to *l* after orphans and widows

1Pe 1: 12 long to *l* into these things.

LOOKING (LOOK)

2Co 10: 7 You are *l* only on the surface

Rev 5: 6 I saw a Lamb, *l* as if it had been

LOOKS (LOOK)

1Sa 16: 7 Man *l* at the outward appearance,

Lk 9: 62 and *l* back is fit for service

Php 2: 21 For everyone *l* out

LORD† (LORD'S† LORDING)

Ne 4: 14 Remember the *L*, who is great

Job 28: 28 'The fear of the *L*—that is wisdom,

Ps 54: 4 the *L* is the one who sustains me.

62: 12 and that you, O *L*, are loving,

86: 5 You are forgiving and good, O *L*,

110: 1 The LORD says to my *L*:

147: 5 Great is our *L* and mighty in power

Isa 6: 1 I saw the *L* seated on a throne,

Da 9: 4 "O *L*, the great and awe-some God,

Mt 3: 3 'Prepare the way for the *L*,

4: 7 'Do not put the *L* your God

7: 21 "Not everyone who says to me, '*L*,

22: 37 "'Love the *L* your God

22: 44 he says, "'The *L* said to my *L*:

Mk 12: 11 the *L* has done this,

12: 29 the *L* our God, the *L* is one.

Lk 2: 9 glory of the *L* shone around them,

6: 46 "Why do you call me, '*L*, *L*,'

10: 27 "'Love the *L* your God

Ac 2: 21 on the name of the *L* will be saved.'

16: 31 replied, "Believe in the *L* Jesus,

Ro 10: 9 with your mouth, "Jesus is *L*,"

10: 13 on the name of the *L* will be saved

12: 11 your spiritual fervor, serving the *L*.

14: 8 we live to the *L*; and if we die,

1Co 1: 31 Let him who boasts boast in the *L*."

3: 5 the *L* has assigned to each his task.

7: 34 to be devoted to the *L* in both body

10: 9 We should not test the *L*,

11: 23 For I received from the *L* what I

12: 3 "Jesus is *L*," except by the Holy

15: 57 victory through our *L* Jesus Christ.

16: 22 If anyone does not love the *L*—

2Co 3: 17 Now the *L* is the Spirit,

8: 5 they gave themselves first to the *L*

10: 17 Let him who boasts boast in the *L*."

Gal 6: 14 in the cross of our *L* Jesus Christ,

Eph 4: 5 one *L*, one faith, one baptism;

5: 10 and find out what pleases the *L*.

5: 19 make music in your heart to the *L*,

Php 2: 11 confess that Jesus Christ is *L*,

3: 1 my brothers, rejoice in the *L*!

4: 4 Rejoice in the *L* always.

Col 2: 6 as you received Christ Jesus as *L*,

3: 17 do it all in the name of the *L* Jesus,

3: 23 as working for the *L*, not for men,

4: 17 work you have received in the *L*."

1Th 3: 12 May the *L* make your love increase

5: 2 day of the *L* will come like a thief

5: 23 at the coming of our *L* Jesus Christ.

2Th 2: 1 the coming of our *L* Jesus Christ

2Ti 2: 19 "The *L* knows those who are his,"

Heb 12: 14 holiness no one will see the *L*.

13: 6 *L* is my helper; I will not be afraid.

Jas 4: 10 Humble yourselves before the *L*,

1Pe 1: 25 the word of the *L* stands forever."
2: 3 you have tasted that the *L* is good.
3: 15 in your hearts set apart Christ as *L*.
2Pe 1: 16 and coming of our *L* Jesus Christ,
2: 1 the sovereign *L* who bought
3: 9 The *L* is not slow in keeping his
Jude : 14 the *L* is coming with thousands
Rev 4: 8 holy, holy is the *L* God Almighty,
4: 11 "You are worthy, our *L* and God,
17: 14 he is *L* of lords and King of kings—
22: 20 Come, *L* Jesus.

LORD'S† (LORD†)

Ac 21: 14 and said, "The *L* will be done."
1Co 10: 26 "The earth is the *L*, and everything
11: 26 you proclaim the *L* death
2Co 3: 18 faces all reflect the *L* glory,
2Ti 2: 24 And the *L* servant must not quarrel
Jas 4: 15 you ought to say, "If it is the *L* will,

LORDING* (LORD†)

1Pe 5: 3 not *l* it over those entrusted to you,

LORD‡ (LORD'S‡)

Ge 2: 4 When the *L* God made the earth
2: 7 the *L* God formed the man
3: 21 The *L* God made garments of skin
7: 16 Then the *L* shut him in.
15: 6 Abram believed the *L*,
18: 14 Is anything too hard for the *L*?
31: 49 "May the *L* keep watch
Ex 3: 2 the angel of the *L* appeared to him
9: 12 the *L* hardened Pharaoh's heart
14: 30 That day the *L* saved Israel
20: 2 "I am the *L* your God, who
33: 11 The *L* would speak to Moses face
40: 34 glory of the *L* filled the tabernacle.
Lev 19: 2 'Be holy because I, the *L* your God,
Nu 8: 5 *L* said to Moses: "Take the Levites
14: 21 glory of the *L* fills the whole earth,
Dt 2: 7 forty years the *L* your God has
5: 9 the *L* your God, am a jealous God,
6: 4 The *L* our God, the *L* is one.
6: 5 Love the *L* your God

6: 16 Do not test the *L* your God
10: 14 To the *L* your God belong
10: 17 For the *L* your God is God of gods
11: 1 Love the *L* your God and keep his
28: 1 If you fully obey the *L* your God
30: 16 today to love the *L* your God,
30: 20 For the *L* is your life, and he will
31: 6 for the *L* your God goes with you;
Jos 22: 5 to love the *L* your God, to walk
24: 15 my household, we will serve the *L*
1Sa 1: 28 So now I give him to the *L*.
2: 2 "There is no one holy like the *L*;
7: 12 "Thus far has the *L* helped us."
12: 22 his great name the *L* will not reject
15: 22 "Does the *L* delight
2Sa 22: 2 "The *L* is my rock, my fortress
1Ki 2: 3 and observe what the *L* your God
8: 11 the glory of the *L* filled his temple.
8: 61 fully committed to the *L* our God,
18: 21 If the *L* is God, follow him;
2Ki 13: 23 But the *L* was gracious to them
1Ch 16: 8 Give thanks to the *L*, call
16: 23 Sing to the *L*, all the earth;
28: 9 for the *L* searches every heart
29: 11 O *L*, is the greatness and the power
2Ch 5: 14 the glory of the *L* filled the temple
16: 9 of the *L* range throughout the earth
19: 6 judging for man but for the *L*,
30: 9 for the *L* your God is gracious
Ne 1: 5 Then I said: "O *L*, God of heaven,
Job 1: 21 *L* gave and the *L* has taken away;
38: 1 the *L* answered Job out
42: 9 and the *L* accepted Job's prayer.
Ps 1: 2 But his delight is in the law of the *L*
9: 9 The *L* is a refuge for the oppressed,
12: 6 And the words of the *L* are flawless
16: 8 I have set the *L* always before me.
18: 30 the word of the *L* is flawless.
19: 7 The law of the *L* is perfect,
19: 14 O *L*, my Rock and my Redeemer.
23: 1 The *L* is my shepherd, I shall not be

23: 6 I will dwell in the house of the *L*
27: 1 The *L* is my light and my salvation
27: 4 to gaze upon the beauty of the *L*
29: 1 Ascribe to the *L*, O mighty ones,
32: 2 whose sin the *L* does not count
33: 12 is the nation whose God is the *L*,
33: 18 But the eyes of the *L* are
34: 3 Glorify the *L* with me;
34: 7 The angel of the *L* encamps
34: 8 Taste and see that the *L* is good;
34: 18 The *L* is close to the broken-hearted
37: 4 Delight yourself in the *L*
40: 1 I waited patiently for the *L*;
47: 2 How awesome is the *L* Most High,
48: 1 Great is the *L*, and most worthy
55: 22 Cast your cares on the *L*
75: 8 In the hand of the *L* is a cup
84: 11 For the *L* God is a sun and shield;
86: 11 Teach me your way, O *L*,
89: 5 heavens praise your wonders, O *L*,
91: 2 I will say of the *L*, "He is my refuge
95: 1 Come, let us sing for joy to the *L*;
96: 1 Sing to the *L* a new song;
98: 4 Shout for joy to the *L*, all the earth,
100: 1 Shout for joy to the *L*, all the earth.
103: 1 Praise the *L*, O my soul;
103: 8 The *L* is compassionate
104: 1 O *L* my God, you are very great;
107: 8 to the *L* for his unfailing love
110: 1 The *L* says to my Lord:
113: 4 *L* is exalted over all the nations,
115: 1 Not to us, O *L*, not to us
116: 15 Precious in the sight of the *L*
118: 1 Give thanks to the *L*, for he is good
118: 24 This is the day the *L* has made;
121: 2 My help comes from the *L*,
121: 5 The *L* watches over you—
125: 2 so the *L* surrounds his people
127: 1 Unless the *L* builds the house,
127: 3 Sons are a heritage from the *L*,
130: 3 If you, O *L*, kept a record of sins,
135: 6 The *L* does whatever pleases him,
136: 1 Give thanks to the *L*, for he is good
139: 1 O *L*, you have searched me

144: 3 O *L*, what is man that you care
145: 3 Great is the *L* and most worthy
145: 18 The *L* is near to all who call on him
Pr 1: 7 The fear of the *L* is the beginning
3: 5 Trust in the *L* with all your heart
3: 9 Honor the *L* with your wealth,
3: 12 the *L* disciplines those he loves,
3: 19 By wisdom the *L* laid the earth's
5: 21 are in full view of the *L*,
6: 16 There are six things the *L* hates,
10: 27 The fear of the *L* adds length to life
11: 1 The *L* abhors dishonest scales,
12: 22 The *L* detests lying lips,
14: 26 He who fears the *L* has a secure
15: 3 The eyes of the *L* are every-where,
16: 2 but motives are weighed by the *L*.
16: 4 The *L* works out everything
16: 9 but the *L* determines his steps.
16: 33 but its every decision is from the *L*.
18: 10 The name of the *L* is a strong tower
18: 22 and receives favor from the *L*.
19: 14 but a prudent wife is from the *L*.
19: 17 to the poor lends to the *L*,
21: 3 to the *L* than sacrifice.
21: 30 that can succeed against the *L*.
21: 31 but victory rests with the *L*.
22: 2 The *L* is the Maker of them all.
24: 18 or the *L* will see and disapprove
31: 30 a woman who fears the *L* is
Isa 6: 3 holy, holy is the *L* Almighty;
11: 2 The Spirit of the *L* will rest on him
11: 9 full of the knowledge of the *L*
12: 2 The *L*, the *L*, is my strength
24: 1 the *L* is going to lay waste the earth
25: 8 The Sovereign *L* will wipe away
29: 15 to hide their plans from the *L*,
33: 6 the fear of the *L* is the key
35: 10 the ransomed of the *L* will return.
40: 5 the glory of the *L* will be revealed,
40: 7 the breath of the *L* blows on them.

40: 10 the Sovereign *L* comes with power,
40: 28 The *L* is the everlasting God,
40: 31 but those who hope in the *L*
42: 8 "I am the *L*; that is my name!
43: 11 I, even I, am the *L*,
44: 24 I am the *L*,
45: 5 I am the *L*, and there is no other;
45: 21 Was it not I, the *L*?
51: 11 The ransomed of the *L* will return.
53: 6 and the *L* has laid on him
53: 10 and the will of the *L* will prosper
55: 6 Seek the *L* while he may be found;
58: 8 of the *L* will be your rear guard.
58: 11 The *L* will guide you always;
59: 1 the arm of the *L* is not too short
61: 3 a planting of the *L*
61: 10 I delight greatly in the *L*;
Jer 1: 9 Then the *L* reached out his hand
9: 24 I am the *L*, who exercises kindness,
16: 19 O *L*, my strength and my fortress,
17: 7 is the man who trusts in the *L*,
La 3: 40 and let us return to the *L*.
Eze 1: 28 of the likeness of the glory of the *L*.
Hos 1: 7 horsemen, but by the *L* their God."
3: 5 They will come trembling to the *L*
6: 1 "Come, let us return to the *L*.
Joel 2: 1 for the day of the *L* is coming.
2: 11 The day of the *L* is great;
3: 14 For the day of the *L* is near
Am 5: 18 long for the day of the *L*?
Jnh 1: 3 But Jonah ran away from the *L*
Mic 4: 2 up to the mountain of the *L*,
6: 8 And what does the *L* require of you
Na 1: 2 The *L* takes vengeance on his foes
1: 3 The *L* is slow to anger
Hab 2: 14 knowledge of the glory of the *L*
2: 20 But the *L* is in his holy temple;
Zep 3: 17 The *L* your God is with you,
Zec 1: 17 and the *L* will again comfort Zion
9: 16 The *L* their God will save them
14: 5 Then the *L* my God will come,
14: 9 The *L* will be king
Mal 4: 5 and dreadful day of the *L* comes.

LORD'S‡ (LORD‡)

Ex 34: 34 he entered the *L* presence
Nu 14: 41 you disobeying the *L* command?

Dt 6: 18 is right and good in the *L* sight,
32: 9 For the *L* portion is his people,
Jos 21: 45 Not one of all the *L* good promises
Ps 24: 1 The earth is the *L*, and everything
32: 10 but the *L* unfailing love
89: 1 of the *L* great love forever;
103: 17 *L* love is with those who fear him,
Pr 3: 11 do not despise the *L* discipline
Isa 24: 14 west they acclaim the *L* majesty.
62: 3 of splendor in the *L* hand,
Jer 48: 10 lax in doing the *L* work!
La 3: 22 of the *L* great love we are not
Mic 4: 1 of the *L* temple will be established

LOSE (LOSES LOSS LOST)

1Sa 17: 32 "Let no one *l* heart on account
Mt 10: 39 Whoever finds his life will *l* it,
Lk 9: 25 and yet *l* or forfeit his very self?
Jn 6: 39 that I shall *l* none of all that he has
Heb 12: 3 will not grow weary and *l* heart.
12: 5 do not *l* heart when he rebukes you

LOSES (LOSE)

Mt 5: 13 But if the salt *l* its saltiness,
Lk 15: 4 you has a hundred sheep and *l* one
15: 8 has ten silver coins and *l* one.

LOSS (LOSE)

Ro 11: 12 and their *l* means riches
1Co 3: 15 he will suffer *l*; he himself will be
Php 3: 8 I consider everything a *l* compared

LOST (LOSE)

Ps 73: 2 I had nearly *l* my foothold.
Jer 50: 6 "My people have been *l* sheep;
Eze 34: 4 the strays or searched for the *l*.
34: 16 for the *l* and bring back the strays.
Mt 18: 14 any of these little ones should be *l*.
Lk 15: 4 go after the *l* sheep until he finds it?
15: 6 with me; I have found my *l* sheep.'
15: 9 with me; I have found my *l* coin.'
15: 24 is alive again; he was *l* and is found
19: 10 to seek and to save what was *l*."
Php 3: 8 for whose sake I have *l* all things.

LOT (LOTS)

Nephew of Abraham (Ge 11:27; 12:5). Chose to live in Sodom (Ge 13). Rescued from four kings (Ge 14). Rescued from Sodom (Ge 19:1-29; 2Pe 2:7). Fathered Moab and Ammon by his daughters (Ge 19:30-38).

Est 3: 7 the *l*) in the presence of Haman
9: 24 the *l*) for their ruin and destruction.
Pr 16: 33 The *l* is cast into the lap,
18: 18 Casting the *l* settles disputes
Ecc 3: 22 his work, because that is his *l*.
Ac 1: 26 Then they drew lots, and the *l* fell

LOTS (LOT)

Ps 22: 18 and cast *l* for my clothing.
Mt 27: 35 divided up his clothes by casting *l*.

LOVE (BELOVED LOVED LOVELY LOVER LOVERS LOVES LOVING)

Ge 22: 2 your only son, Isaac, whom you *l*,
Ex 15: 13 "In your unfailing *l* you will lead
20: 6 showing *l* to a thousand generations
20: 6 of those who *l* me
34: 6 abounding in *l* and faithfulness,
Lev 19: 18 but *l* your neighbor as yourself.
19: 34 *L* him as yourself,
Nu 14: 18 abounding in *l* and forgiving sin
Dt 5: 10 showing *l* to a thousand generations
5: 10 of those who *l* me
6: 5 *L* the LORD your God
7: 13 He will *l* you and bless you
10: 12 to walk in all his ways, to *l* him,
11: 13 to *l* the LORD your God
13: 6 wife you *l*, or your closest friend
30: 6 so that you may *l* him
Jos 22: 5 to *l* the LORD your God, to walk
1Ki 3: 3 Solomon showed his *l*
8: 23 you who keep your covenant of *l*
2Ch 5: 13 his *l* endures forever."
Ne 1: 5 covenant of *l* with those who *l* him
Ps 18: 1 I *l* you, O LORD, my strength.
23: 6 Surely goodness and *l* will follow
25: 6 O LORD, your great mercy and *l*,
31: 16 save me in your unfailing *l*.
32: 10 but the LORD's unfailing *l*
33: 5 the earth is full of his unfailing *l*.
33: 18 whose hope is in his unfailing *l*,
36: 5 Your *l*, O LORD, reaches

36: 7 How priceless is your unfailing *l*!
45: 7 You *l* righteousness and hate
51: 1 according to your unfailing *l*;
57: 10 For great is your *l*, reaching
63: 3 Because your *l* is better than life,
66: 20 or withheld his *l* from me!
70: 4 may those who *l* your salvation
77: 8 Has his unfailing *l* vanished forever
85: 7 Show us your unfailing *l*, O LORD
85: 10 *L* and faithfulness meet together;
86: 13 For great is your *l* toward me;
89: 1 of the LORD's great *l* forever;
89: 33 but I will not take my *l* from him,
92: 2 to proclaim your *l* in the morning
94: 18 your *l*, O LORD, supported me.
100: 5 is good and his *l* endures forever;
101: 1 I will sing of your *l* and justice;
103: 4 crowns you with *l* and compassion.
103: 8 slow to anger, abounding in *l*.
103: 11 so great is his *l* for those who fear
107: 8 to the LORD for his unfailing *l*
108: 4 For great is your *l*, higher
116: 1 I *l* the LORD, for he heard my
118: 1 his *l* endures forever.
119: 47 because I *l* them.
119: 64 The earth is filled with your *l*,
119: 76 May your unfailing *l* be my
119: 97 Oh, how I *l* your law!
119:119 therefore I *l* your statutes.
119:124 your servant according to your *l*
119:132 to those who *l* your name.
119:159 O LORD, according to your *l*.
119:163 but I *l* your law.
119:165 peace have they who *l* your law,
122: 6 "May those who *l* you be secure.
130: 7 for with the LORD is unfailing *l*
136: 1 -26 His *l* endures forever.
143: 8 of your unfailing *l*,
145: 8 slow to anger and rich in *l*.
145: 20 over all who *l* him,
147: 11 who put their hope in his unfailing *l*
Pr 3: 3 Let *l* and faithfulness never leave
4: 6 *l* her, and she will watch over you.
5: 19 you ever be captivated by her *l*.
8: 17 I *l* those who *l* me,
9: 8 rebuke a wise man and he will *l* you

10: 12 but *l* covers over all wrongs.
14: 22 those who plan what is good find *l*
15: 17 of vegetables where there is *l*
17: 9 over an offense promotes *l*,
19: 22 What a man desires is unfailing *l*;
20: 6 claims to have unfailing *l*,
20: 13 Do not *l* sleep or you will grow
20: 28 through *l* his throne is made secure
21: 21 who pursues righteousness and *l*
27: 5 rebuke than hidden *l*.
Ecc 9: 6 Their *l*, their hate
9: 9 life with your wife, whom you *l*,
SS 2: 4 and his banner over me is *l*.
8: 6 for *l* is as strong as death,
8: 7 Many waters cannot quench *l*;
8: 7 all the wealth of his house for *l*,
Isa 5: 1 I will sing for the one I *l*
16: 5 In *l* a throne will be established;
38: 17 In your *l* you kept me
54: 10 yet my unfailing *l* for you will not
55: 3 my faithful *l* promised to David.
61: 8 "For I, the LORD, *l* justice;
63: 9 In his *l* and mercy he redeemed
Jer 5: 31 and my people *l* it this way.
31: 3 you with an everlasting *l*;
32: 18 You show *l* to thousands
33: 11 his *l* endures forever."
La 3: 22 of the LORD's great *l* we are not
3: 32 so great is his unfailing *l*.
Eze 33: 32 more than one who sings *l* songs
Da 9: 4 covenant of *l* with all who *l* him
Hos 2: 19 in *l* and compassion.
3: 1 Go, show your *l* to your wife again,
11: 4 with ties of *l*;
12: 6 maintain *l* and justice,
Joel 2: 13 slow to anger and abounding in *l*,
Am 5: 15 Hate evil, *l* good;
Mic 3: 2 you who hate good and *l* evil;
6: 8 To act justly and to *l* mercy
Zep 3: 17 he will quiet you with his *l*,
Zec 8: 19 Therefore *l* truth and peace."
Mt 3: 17 "This is my Son, whom I *l*;
5: 44 *L* your enemies and pray
6: 24 he will hate the one and *l* the other,
17: 5 "This is my Son, whom I *l*;
19: 19 and *l* your neighbor as yourself.' "
22: 37 "'*L* the Lord your God

Lk 6: 32 Even 'sinners' *l* those who *l* them.
7: 42 which of them will *l* him more?"
20: 13 whom I *l*; perhaps they will respect
Jn 13: 34 I give you: *L* one another.
13: 35 disciples, if you *l* one another."
14: 15 "If you *l* me, you will obey what I
15: 13 Greater *l* has no one than this,
15: 17 This is my command: *L* each other.
21: 15 do you truly *l* me more than these
Ro 5: 5 because God has poured out his *l*
5: 8 God demonstrates his own *l* for us
8: 28 for the good of those who *l* him,
8: 35 us from the *l* of Christ?
8: 39 us from the *l* of God that is
12: 9 *L* must be sincere.
12: 10 to one another in brotherly *l*.
13: 8 continuing debt to *l* one another,
13: 9 "*L* your neighbor as yourself."
13: 10 Therefore *l* is the fulfillment
13: 10 *L* does no harm to its neighbor.
1Co 2: 9 prepared for those who *l* him"—
8: 1 Knowledge puffs up, but *l* builds up
13: 1 have not *l*, I am only a resounding
13: 2 but have not *l*, I am nothing.
13: 3 but have not *l*, I gain nothing.
13: 4 Love is patient, *l* is kind.
13: 4 *L* is patient, love is kind.
13: 6 *L* does not delight in evil
13: 8 *L* never fails.
13: 13 But the greatest of these is *l*.
13: 13 three remain: faith, hope and *l*.
14: 1 way of *l* and eagerly desire spiritual
16: 14 Do everything in *l*.
2Co 5: 14 For Christ's *l* compels us,
8: 8 sincerity of your *l* by comparing it
8: 24 show these men the proof of your *l*
Gal 5: 6 is faith expressing itself through *l*.
5: 13 rather, serve one another in *l*.
5: 22 But the fruit of the Spirit is *l*, joy,
Eph 1: 4 In *l* he predestined us
2: 4 But because of his great *l* for us,
3: 17 being rooted and established in *l*,
3: 18 and high and deep is the *l* of Christ,

3: 19 and to know this *l* that surpasses
4: 2 bearing with one another in *l*.
4: 15 Instead, speaking the truth in *l*,
5: 2 loved children and live a life of *l*,
5: 25 *l* your wives, just as Christ loved
5: 28 husbands ought to *l* their wives
5: 33 each one of you also must *l* his wife
Php 1: 9 that your *l* may abound more
2: 2 having the same *l*, being one
Col 1: 5 *l* that spring from the hope that is
2: 2 in heart and united in *l*,
3: 14 And over all these virtues put on *l*,
3: 19 *l* your wives and do not be harsh
1Th 1: 3 your labor prompted by *l*,
4: 9 taught by God to *l* each other.
5: 8 on faith and *l* as a breastplate,
2Th 3: 5 direct your hearts into God's *l*
1Ti 1: 5 The goal of this command is *l*,
2: 15 *l* and holiness with propriety.
4: 12 in life, in *l*, in faith and in purity.
6: 10 For the *l* of money is a root
6: 11 faith, *l*, endurance and gentleness.
2Ti 1: 7 of power, of *l* and of self-discipline.
2: 22 and pursue righteousness, faith, *l*
3: 10 faith, patience, *l*, endurance,
Tit 2: 4 women to *l* their husbands
Phm : 9 yet I appeal to you on the basis of *l*.
Heb 6: 10 and the *l* you have shown him
10: 24 may spur one another on toward *l*
13: 5 free from the *l* of money
Jas 1: 12 promised to those who *l* him.
2: 5 he promised those who *l* him?
2: 8 "*L* your neighbor as yourself,"
1Pe 1: 22 the truth so that you have sincere *l*
1: 22 *l* one another deeply,
2: 17 *L* the brotherhood of believers,
3: 8 be sympathetic, *l* as brothers,
3: 10 "Whoever would *l* life
4: 8 Above all, *l* each other deeply,
4: 8 *l* covers over a multitude of sins.
5: 14 Greet one another with a kiss of *l*.
2Pe 1: 7 and to brotherly kindness, *l*.
1: 17 "This is my Son, whom I *l*;
1Jn 2: 5 God's *l* is truly made complete
2: 15 Do not *l* the world or anything

3: 1 How great is the *l* the Father has
3: 10 anyone who does not *l* his brother.
3: 11 We should *l* one another.
3: 14 Anyone who does not *l* remains
3: 16 This is how we know what *l* is:
3: 18 let us not *l* with words or tongue
3: 23 to *l* one another as he commanded
4: 7 Dear friends, let us *l* one another,
4: 7 for *l* comes from God.
4: 8 Whoever does not *l* does not know
4: 9 This is how God showed his *l*
4: 10 This is *l*: not that we loved God,
4: 11 we also ought to *l* one another.
4: 12 and his *l* is made complete in us.
4: 16 God is *l*.
4: 16 Whoever lives in *l* lives in God,
4: 17 *l* is made complete among us
4: 18 But perfect *l* drives out fear,
4: 19 We *l* because he first loved us.
4: 20 If anyone says, "I *l* God,"
4: 21 loves God must also *l* his brother.
5: 2 we know that we *l* the children
5: 3 This is *l* for God: to obey his
2Jn : 5 I ask that we *l* one another.
: 6 his command is that you walk in *l*.
: 6 this is *l*: that we walk in obedience
Jude : 12 men are blemishes at your *l* feasts,
: 21 Keep yourselves in God's *l*
Rev 2: 4 You have forsaken your first *l*.
3: 19 Those whom I *l* I rebuke
12: 11 they did not *l* their lives so much

LOVED (LOVE)

Ge 24: 67 she became his wife, and he *l* her;
29: 30 and he *l* Rachel more than Leah.
37: 3 Now Israel *l* Joseph more than any
Dt 7: 8 But it was because the LORD *l* you
1Sa 1: 5 a double portion because he *l* her,
20: 17 because he *l* him as he himself.
Ps 44: 3 light of your face, for you *l* them.
Jer 2: 2 how as a bride you *l* me
31: 3 "I have *l* you with an everlasting

Hos 2: 23 to the one I called 'Not my *l* one.'
  3: 1 though she is *l* by another
  9: 10 became as vile as the thing they *l*.
  11: 1 "When Israel was a child, I *l* him,
Mal 1: 2 "But you ask, 'How have you *l* us?'
Mk 12: 6 left to send, a son, whom he he *l*.
Jn 3: 16 so *l* the world that he gave his one
  3: 19 but men *l* darkness instead of light
  11: 5 Jesus *l* Martha and her sister
  12: 43 for they *l* praise from men more
  13: 1 Having *l* his own who were
  13: 23 the disciple whom Jesus *l*,
  13: 34 As I have *l* you, so you must love
  14: 21 He who loves me will be *l*
  15: 9 the Father has *l* me, so have I *l* you.
  15: 12 Love each other as I have *l* you.
  19: 26 the disciple whom he *l* standing
Ro 8: 37 conquerors through him who *l* us.
  9: 13 "Jacob I *l*, but Esau I hated."
  9: 25 her my '*l* one' who is not my *l* one,"
  11: 28 they are *l* on account
Gal 2: 20 who *l* me and gave himself for me.
Eph 5: 2 as Christ *l* us and gave himself up
  5: 25 just as Christ *l* the church
2Th 2: 16 who *l* us and by his grace gave us
2Ti 4: 10 for Demas, because he *l* this world,
Heb 1: 9 You have *l* righteousness
1Jn 4: 10 This is love: not that we *l* God,
  4: 11 Dear friends, since God so *l* us
1Jn 4: 19 We love because he first *l* us.

LOVELY (LOVE)

Ps 84: 1 How *l* is your dwelling place,
SS 2: 14 and your face is *l*.
  5: 16 he is altogether *l*.
Php 4: 8 whatever is *l*, whatever is

LOVER (LOVE)

SS 2: 16 *Beloved* My *l* is mine and I am his;
  7: 10 I belong to my *l*,
1Ti 3: 3 not quarrelsome, not a *l* of money.

LOVERS (LOVE)

2Ti 3: 2 People will be *l* of themselves,
  3: 3 without self-control, brutal, not *l*
  3: 4 *l* of pleasure rather than *l* of God—

LOVES (LOVE)

Ps 11: 7 he *l* justice;
  33: 5 The LORD *l* righteousness
  34: 12 Whoever of you *l* life
  91: 14 Because he *l* me," says the LORD,
  127: 2 for he grants sleep to those he *l*.
Pr 3: 12 the LORD disciplines those he *l*,
  12: 1 Whoever *l* discipline *l* knowledge,
  13: 24 he who *l* him is careful
  17: 17 A friend *l* at all times,
  17: 19 He who *l* a quarrel *l* sin;
  22: 11 He who *l* a pure heart and whose
Ecc 5: 10 whoever *l* wealth is never satisfied
Mt 10: 37 anyone who *l* his son or daughter
Lk 7: 47 has been forgiven little *l* little."
Jn 3: 35 Father *l* the Son and has placed
  10: 17 reason my Father *l* me is that I lay
  12: 25 The man who *l* his life will lose it,
  14: 21 obeys them, he is the one who *l* me.
  14: 23 Jesus replied, "If anyone *l* me,
Ro 13: 8 for he who *l* his fellowman has
2Co 9: 7 for God *l* a cheerful giver.
Eph 5: 28 He who *l* his wife *l* himself.
  5: 33 must love his wife as he *l* himself,
Heb 12: 6 the Lord disciplines those he *l*,
1Jn 2: 10 Whoever *l* his brother lives
  2: 15 If anyone *l* the world, the love
  4: 7 Everyone who *l* has been born
  4: 21 Whoever *l* God must also love his
  5: 1 who *l* the father *l* his child
3Jn : 9 but Diotrephes, who *l* to be first,
Rev 1: 5 To him who *l* us and has freed us

LOVING (LOVE)

Ps 25: 10 All the ways of the LORD are *l*
  62: 12 and that you, O Lord, are *l*.
  145: 17 and *l* toward all he has made.
Heb 13: 1 Keep on *l* each other as brothers.
1Jn 5: 2 by *l* God and carrying out his

LOWLY

Job 5: 11 The *l* he sets on high,
Pr 29: 23 but a man of *l* spirit gains honor.
Isa 57: 15 also with him who is con-trite and *l*
Eze 21: 26 *l* will be exalted and the exalted

1Co 1: 28 He chose the *l* things of this world

LUKE*

  Co-worker with Paul (Col 4:14; 2Ti 4:11; Phm 24).

LUKEWARM*

Rev 3: 16 So, because you are *l* — neither hot

LUST

Pr 6: 25 Do not *l* in your heart
Col 3: 5 sexual immorality, impurity, *l*,
1Th 4: 5 not in passionate *l* like the heathen,
1Jn 2: 16 the *l* of his eyes and the boasting

LYING (LIE)

Pr 6: 17 a *l* tongue,
  26: 28 A *l* tongue hates those it hurts,

M

MACEDONIA

Ac 16: 9 "Come over to *M* and help us."

MADE (MAKE)

Ge 1: 16 He also *m* the stars.
  1: 25 God *m* the wild animals according
  2: 22 Then the LORD God *m* a woman
2Ki 19: 15 You have *m* heaven and earth.
Ps 95: 5 The sea is his, for he *m* it,
  100: 3 It is he who *m* us, and we are his;
  118: 24 This is the day the LORD has *m*;
  139: 14 I am fearfully and wonder-fully *m*;
Ecc 3: 11 He has *m* everything beautiful
Mk 2: 27 "The Sabbath was *m* for man,
Jn 1: 3 Through him all things were *m*;
Ac 17: 24 "The God who *m* the world
Heb 1: 2 through whom he *m* the universe.
Rev 14: 7 Worship him who *m* the heavens,

MAGI

Mt 2: 1 *M* from the east came to Jerusalem

MAGOG

Eze 38: 2 of the land of *M*, the chief prince
  39: 6 I will send fire on *M*
Rev 20: 8 and *M* — to gather them for battle.

MAIDEN

Pr 30: 19 and the way of a man with a *m*.
Isa 62: 5 As a young man marries a *m*,
Jer 2: 32 Does a *m* forget her jewelry,

MAIMED

Mt 18: 8 It is better for you to enter life *m*

MAJESTIC (MAJESTY)

Ex 15: 6 was *m* in power.
  15: 11 *m* in holiness,
Ps 8: 1 how *m* is your name in all the earth
  29: 4 the voice of the LORD is *m*.
  111: 3 Glorious and *m* are his deeds,
SS 6: 10 *m* as the stars in procession?
2Pe 1: 17 came to him from the *M* Glory,

MAJESTY (MAJESTIC)

Ex 15: 7 In the greatness of your *m*
Dt 33: 26 and on the clouds in his *m*.
1Ch 16: 27 Splendor and *m* are before him;
Est 1: 4 the splendor and glory of his *m*.
Job 37: 22 God comes in awesome *m*.
  40: 10 and clothe yourself in honor and *m*
Ps 45: 4 In your *m* ride forth victoriously
  93: 1 The LORD reigns, he is robed in *m*
  110: 3 Arrayed in holy *m*,
  145: 5 of the glorious splendor of your *m*,
Isa 53: 2 or *m* to attract us to him,
Eze 31: 2 can be compared with you in *m*?
2Pe 1: 16 but we were eyewitnesses of his *m*.
Jude : 25 only God our Savior be glory, *m*,

MAKE (MADE MAKER MAKES MAKING)

Ge 1: 26 "Let us *m* man in our image,
  2: 18 I will *m* a helper suitable for him."
  12: 2 "I will *m* you into a great nation
Ex 22: 3 thief must certainly *m* restitution,
Nu 6: 25 the LORD *m* his face shine
Ps 108: 1 *m* music with all my soul.
Isa 14: 14 I will *m* myself like the Most High
  29: 16 "He did not *m* me"?
Jer 31: 31 "when I will *m* a new covenant
Mt 3: 3 *m* straight paths for him.' "
  28: 19 and *m* disciples of all nations,
Mk 1: 17 "and I will *m* you fishers of men."
Lk 13: 24 "*M* every effort to enter
  14: 23 country lanes and *m* them come in,
Ro 14: 19 *m* every effort to do what leads
2Co 5: 9 So we *m* it our goal to please him,
Eph 4: 3 *M* every effort to keep the unity

Col 4: 5 *m* the most of every opportunity.
1Th 4: 11 *M* it your ambition
Heb 4: 11 *m* every effort to enter that rest,
12: 14 *M* every effort to live in peace
2Pe 1: 5 *m* every effort to add
3: 14 *m* every effort to be found spotless,

MAKER (MAKE)
Job 4: 17 Can a man be more pure than his *M*
36: 3 I will ascribe justice to my *M*.
Ps 95: 6 kneel before the LORD our *M*;
Pr 22: 2 The LORD is the *M* of them all.
Isa 45: 9 to him who quarrels with his *M*,
54: 5 For your *M* is your husband —
Jer 10: 16 for he is the *M* of all things,

MAKES (MAKE)
1Co 3: 7 but only God, who *m* things grow.

MAKING (MAKE)
Ps 19: 7 *m* wise the simple.
Ecc 12: 12 Of *m* many books there is no end,
Jn 5: 18 *m* himself equal with God.
Eph 5: 16 *m* the most of every opportunity,

MALE
Ge 1: 27 *m* and female he created them.
Gal 3: 28 slave nor free, *m* nor female,

MALICE (MALICIOUS)
Ro 1: 29 murder, strife, deceit and *m*.
Col 3: 8 *m*, slander, and filthy language
1Pe 2: 1 rid yourselves of all *m*

MALICIOUS (MALICE)
Pr 26: 24 A *m* man disguises himself
1Ti 3: 11 not *m* talkers but temperate
6: 4 *m* talk, evil suspicions

MAN (MEN WOMAN WOMEN)
Ge 1: 26 "Let us make *m* in our image,
2: 7 God formed the *m* from the dust
2: 18 for the *m* to be alone
2: 23 she was taken out of *m*.
9: 6 Whoever sheds the blood of *m*,
Dt 8: 3 *m* does not live on bread
1Sa 13: 14 a *m* after his own heart
15: 29 he is not a *m* that he
Job 14: 1 *M* born of woman is of few
14: 14 If a *m* dies, will he live
Ps 1: 1 Blessed is the *m* who does
8: 4 what is *m* that you are
119: 9 can a young *m* keep his
127: 5 Blessed is the *m* whose quiver
Pr 14: 12 that seems right to a *m*,
30: 19 way of a *m* with a maiden.
Isa 53: 3 a *m* of sorrows,

Mt 19: 5 a *m* will leave his father
Mk 8: 36 What good is it for a *m*
Lk 4: 4 'M does not live on bread
Ro 5: 12 entered the world through one *m*
1Co 7: 2 each *m* should have his own
11: 3 head of every *m* is Christ,
11: 3 head of woman is *m*
13: 11 When I became a *m*,
Php 2: 8 found in appearance as a *m*,
1Ti 2: 5 the *m* Christ Jesus,
2: 11 have authority over a *m*;
Heb 9: 27 as *m* is destined to die

MANAGE
Jer 12: 5 how will you *m* in the thickets
1Ti 3: 4 He must *m* his own family well
3: 12 one wife and must *m* his children
5: 14 to *m* their homes and to give

MANASSEH
1. Firstborn of Joseph (Ge 41:51; 46:20). Blessed (Ge 48).
2. Son of Hezekiah; king of Judah (2Ki 21:1-18; 2Ch 33:1-20).

MANGER
Lk 2: 12 in strips of cloth and lying in a *m*."

MANNA
Ex 16: 31 people of Israel called the bread *m*.
Dt 8: 16 He gave you *m* to eat in the desert,
Jn 6: 49 Your forefathers ate the *m*
Rev 2: 17 I will give some of the hidden *m*.

MANNER
1Co 11: 27 in an unworthy *m* will be guilty
Php 1: 27 conduct yourselves in a *m* worthy

MARITAL* (MARRY)
Ex 21: 10 of her food, clothing and *m* rights.
Mt 5: 32 except for *m* unfaithfulness,
19: 9 except for *m* unfaithfulness,
1Co 7: 3 husband should fulfill his *m* duty

MARK (MARKS)
Cousin of Barnabas (Col 4:10; 2Ti 4:11; Phm 24; 1Pe 5:13), see JOHN.
Ge 4: 15 Then the LORD put a *m* on Cain
Rev 13: 16 to receive a *m* on his right hand

MARKS (MARK)
Jn 20: 25 Unless I see the nail *m* in his hands
Gal 6: 17 bear on my body the *m* of Jesus.

MARRED
Isa 52: 14 his form *m* beyond human likeness

MARRIAGE (MARRY)
Mt 22: 30 neither marry nor be given in *m*;
24: 38 marrying and giving in *m*,
Ro 7: 2 she is released from the law of *m*.
Heb 13: 4 by all, and the *m* bed kept pure,

MARRIED (MARRY)
Ro 7: 2 by law a *m* woman is bound
1Co 7: 27 Are you *m*? Do not seek a divorce.
7: 33 But a *m* man is concerned about
7: 36 They should get *m*.

MARRIES (MARRY)
Mt 5: 32 and anyone who *m* the divorced
19: 9 and *m* another woman commits
Lk 16: 18 the man who *m* a divorced woman

MARRY (INTERMARRY MARITAL MARRIAGE MARRIED MARRIES)
Mt 22: 30 resurrection people will neither *m*
1Co 7: 1 It is good for a man not to *m*.
7: 9 control themselves, they should *m*,
1Ti 5: 14 So I counsel younger widows to *m*,

MARTHA*
Sister of Mary and Lazarus (Lk 10:38-42; Jn 11; 12:2).

MARVELED
Lk 2: 33 mother *m* at what was said about

MARY
1. Mother of Jesus (Mt 1:16-25; Lk 1:27-56; 2:1-40). With Jesus at temple (Lk 2:41-52), at the wedding in Cana (Jn 2:1-5), questioning his sanity (Mk 3:21), at the cross (Jn 19:25-27). Among disciples after Ascension (Ac 1:14).
2. Magdalene; former demoniac (Lk 8:2). Helped support Jesus' ministry (Lk 8:1-3). At the cross (Mt 27:56; Mk 15:40; Jn 19:25), burial (Mt 27:61; Mk 15:47). Saw angel after resurrection (Mt 28:1-10; Mk 16:1-9; Lk 24:1-12); also Jesus (Jn 20:1-18).
3. Sister of Martha and Lazarus (Jn 11). Washed Jesus' feet (Jn 12:1-8).

MASQUERADES*
2Co 11: 14 for Satan himself *m* as an angel

MASTER (MASTERED MASTERS)
Mt 10: 24 nor a servant above his *m*.
23: 8 for you have only one *M*
24: 46 that servant whose *m* finds him
25: 21 "His *m* replied, 'Well done,
Ro 6: 14 For sin shall not be your *m*,

14: 4 To his own *m* he stands or falls.
2Ti 2: 21 useful to the *M* and prepared

MASTERED* (MASTER)
1Co 6: 12 but I will not be *m* by any thing.
2Pe 2: 19 a slave to whatever has *m* him.

MASTERS (MASTER)
Mt 6: 24 "No one can serve two *m*.
Eph 6: 5 obey your earthly *m* with respect
6: 9 And *m*, treat your slaves
Tit 2: 9 subject to their *m* in everything,

MATTHEW*
Apostle; former tax collector (Mt 9:9-13; 10:3; Mk 3:18; Lk 6:15; Ac 1:13). Also called Levi (Mk 2:14-17; Lk 5:27-32).

MATURE (MATURITY)
Eph 4: 13 of the Son of God and become *m*,
Php 3: 15 of us who are *m* should take such
Heb 5: 14 But solid food is for the *m*,
Jas 1: 4 work so that you may be *m*

MATURITY* (MATURE)
Heb 6: 1 about Christ and go on to *m*,

MEAL
Pr 15: 17 Better a *m* of vegetables where
1Co 10: 27 some unbeliever invites you to a *m*
Heb 12: 16 for a single *m* sold his inheritance

MEANING
Ne 8: 8 and giving the *m* so that the people

MEANS
1Co 9: 22 by all possible *m* I might save some

MEAT
Ro 14: 6 He who eats *m*, eats to the Lord,
14: 21 It is better not to eat *m*

MEDIATOR
1Ti 2: 5 and one *m* between God and men,
Heb 8: 6 of which he is *m* is superior
9: 15 For this reason Christ is the *m*
12: 24 to Jesus the *m* of a new covenant,

MEDICINE*
Pr 17: 22 A cheerful heart is good *m*,

MEDITATE (MEDITATES MEDITATION)
Jos 1: 8 from your mouth; *m* on it day
Ps 119: 15 I *m* on your precepts
119: 78 but I will *m* on your precepts.
119: 97 I *m* on it all day long.

145: 5 I will *m* on your wonderful works.

MEDITATES* (MEDITATE)

Ps 1: 2 and on his law he *m* day and night.

MEDITATION* (MEDITATE)

Ps 19: 14 of my mouth and the *m* of my heart

104: 34 May my *m* be pleasing to him,

MEDIUM

Lev 20: 27 "'A man or woman who is a *m*

MEEK (MEEKNESS)

Ps 37: 11 But the *m* will inherit the land

Mt 5: 5 Blessed are the *m*,

MEEKNESS* (MEEK)

2Co 10: 1 By the *m* and gentleness of Christ,

MEET (MEETING)

Ps 85: 10 Love and faithfulness *m* together;

Am 4: 12 prepare to *m* your God, O Israel."

1Th 4: 17 them in the clouds to *m* the Lord

MEETING (MEET)

Heb 10: 25 Let us not give up *m* together,

MELCHIZEDEK

Ge 14: 18 *M* king of Salem brought out bread

Ps 110: 4 in the order of *M*."

Heb 7: 11 in the order of *M*, not in the order

MELT

2Pe 3: 12 and the elements will *m* in the heat.

MEMBERS

Mic 7: 6 a man's enemies are the *m*

Ro 7: 23 law at work in the *m* of my body,

12: 4 of us has one body with many *m*,

1Co 6: 15 not know that your bodies are *m*

12: 24 But God has combined the *m*

Eph 4: 25 for we are all *m* of one body.

Col 3: 15 as *m* of one body you were called

MEN (MAN)

Mt 4: 19 will make you fishers of *m*

5: 16 your light shine before *m*

12: 36 *m* will have to give account

Jn 12: 32 will draw all *m* to myself

Ac 5: 29 obey God rather than *m*!

Ro 1: 27 indecent acts with other *m*,

5: 12 death came to all *m*,

1Co 9: 22 all things to all *m*

2Co 5: 11 we try to persuade *m*.

1Ti 2: 4 wants all *m* to be saved

2: 2 entrust to reliable *m*

2Pe 1: 21 but *m* spoke from God

MENAHEM

King of Israel (2Ki 15:17-22).

MERCIFUL (MERCY)

Dt 4: 31 the LORD your God is a *m* God;

Ne 9: 31 for you are a gracious and *m* God.

Mt 5: 7 Blessed are the *m*,

Lk 6: 36 Be *m*, just as your Father is *m*.

Heb 2: 17 in order that he might become a *m*

Jude : 22 Be *m* to those who doubt; snatch

MERCY (MERCIFUL)

Ex 33: 19 *m* on whom I will have *m*,

Ps 25: 6 O LORD, your great *m* and love,

Isa 63: 9 and *m* he redeemed them;

Hos 6: 6 For I desire *m*, not sacrifice,

Mic 6: 8 To act justly and to love *m*

Hab 2: 2 in wrath remember *m*.

Mt 12: 7 I desire *m*, not sacrifice,' you

23: 23 justice, *m* and faithfulness.

Ro 9: 15 "I will have *m* on whom I have *m*,

Eph 2: 4 who is rich in *m*, made us alive

Jas 2: 13 *M* triumphs over judgment!

1Pe 1: 3 In his great *m* he has given us new

MESSAGE

Isa 53: 1 Who has believed our *m*

Jn 12: 38 "Lord, who has believed our *m*

Ro 10: 17 faith comes from hearing the *m*,

1Co 1: 18 For the *m* of the cross is

2Co 5: 19 to us the *m* of reconciliation.

MESSIAH*

Jn 1: 41 "We have found the *M*" (that is,

4: 25 "I know that *M*" (called Christ) "is

METHUSELAH

Ge 5: 27 Altogether, *M* lived 969 years,

MICHAEL

Archangel (Jude 9); warrior in angelic realm, protector of Israel (Da 10:13, 21; 12:1; Rev 12:7).

MIDWIVES

Ex 1: 17 The *m*, however, feared God

MIGHT (ALMIGHTY MIGHTY)

Jdg 16: 30 Then he pushed with all his *m*,

2Sa 6: 14 before the LORD with all his *m*,

Ps 21: 13 we will sing and praise your *m*.

Zec 4: 6 'Not by *m* nor by power,

1Ti 6: 16 To him be honor and *m* forever.

MIGHTY (MIGHT)

Ex 6: 1 of my *m* hand he will drive them

Dt 7: 8 he brought you out with a *m* hand

2Sa 1: 19 How the *m* have fallen!

23: 8 the names of David's *m* men:

Ps 24: 8 The LORD strong and *m*,

50: 1 The *M* One, God, the LORD,

89: 8 You are *m*, O LORD,

136: 12 with a *m* hand and outstretched

147: 5 Great is our Lord and *m* in power;

Isa 9: 6 Wonderful Counselor, *M* God,

Zep 3: 17 he is *m* to save.

Eph 6: 10 in the Lord and in his *m* power.

MILE*

Mt 5: 41 If someone forces you to go one *m*,

MILK

Ex 3: 8 a land flowing with *m* and honey—

Isa 55: 1 Come, buy wine and *m*

1Co 3: 2 I gave you *m*, not solid food,

Heb 5: 12 You need *m*, not solid food!

1Pe 2: 2 babies, crave pure spiritual *m*,

MILLSTONE (STONE)

Lk 17: 2 sea with a *m* tied around his neck

MIND (DOUBLE-MINDED MINDFUL MINDS)

1Sa 15: 29 Israel does not lie or change his *m*;

1Ch 28: 9 devotion and with a willing *m*,

Ps 26: 2 examine my heart and my *m*;

Isa 26: 3 him whose *m* is steadfast,

Mt 22: 37 all your soul and with all your *m*.'

Ac 4: 32 believers were one in heart and *m*.

Ro 7: 25 I myself in my *m* am a slave

8: 7 the sinful *m* is hostile to God.

12: 2 by the renewing of your *m*.

1Co 2: 9 no *m* has conceived

14: 14 spirit prays, but my *m* is unfruitful.

2Co 13: 11 be of one *m*, live in peace.

Php 3: 19 Their *m* is on earthly things.

1Th 4: 11 to *m* your own business

Heb 7: 21 and will not change his *m*:

MINDFUL* (MIND)

Ps 8: 4 what is man that you are *m* of him,

Lk 1: 48 God my Savior, for he has been *m*

Heb 2: 6 What is man that you are *m* of him,

MINDS (MIND)

Ps 7: 9 who searches *m* and hearts,

Jer 31: 33 "I will put my law in their *m*

Eph 4: 23 new in the attitude of your *m*;

Col 3: 2 Set your *m* on things above,

Heb 8: 10 I will put my laws in their *m*

Rev 2: 23 I am he who searches hearts and *m*,

MINISTERING (MINISTRY)

Heb 1: 14 Are not all angels *m* spirits sent

MINISTRY (MINISTERING)

Ac 6: 4 to prayer and the *m* of the word."

2Co 5: 18 gave us the *m* of reconciliation:

2Ti 4: 5 discharge all the duties of your *m*.

MIRACLES (MIRACULOUS)

1Ch 16: 12 his *m*, and the judgments he

Ps 77: 14 You are the God who performs *m*;

Mt 11: 20 most of his *m* had been performed,

11: 21 If the *m* that were performed

24: 24 and perform great signs and *m*

Mk 6: 2 does *m*! Isn't this the carpenter?

Jn 10: 32 "I have shown you many great *m*

14: 11 the evidence of the *m* themselves.

Ac 2: 22 accredited by God to you by *m*,

19: 11 God did extraordinary *m*

1Co 12: 28 third teachers, then workers of *m*,

Heb 2: 4 it by signs, wonders and various *m*,

MIRACULOUS (MIRACLES)

Jn 3: 2 could perform the *m* signs you are

9: 16 "How can a sinner do such *m* signs

20: 30 Jesus did many other *m* signs

1Co 1: 22 Jews demand *m* signs and Greeks

MIRE

Ps 40: 2 out of the mud and *m*;

Isa 57: 20 whose waves cast up *m* and mud.

MIRIAM

Sister of Moses and Aaron (Nu 26:59). Led dancing at Red Sea (Ex 15:20-21). Struck with leprosy for criticizing Moses (Nu 12). Death (Nu 20:1).

MIRROR

Jas 1: 23 a man who looks at his face in a *m*

MISERY

Ex 3: 7 "I have indeed seen the *m*

Jdg 10: 16 he could bear Israel's *m* no longer.

Hos 5: 15 in their *m* they will earnestly seek

Ro 3: 16 ruin and *m* mark their ways,

Jas 5: 1 of the *m* that is coming upon you.

MISLED

1Co 15: 33 Do not be *m*: "Bad company

MISS

Pr 19: 2 nor to be hasty and *m* the way.

MIST

Hos 6: 4 Your love is like the morning *m*,

Jas 4: 14 You are a *m* that appears for a little

MISUSE*

Ex 20: 7 "You shall not *m* the name

Dt 5: 11 "You shall not *m* the name

Ps 139: 20 your adversaries *m* your name.

MOCK (MOCKED MOCKER MOCKERS MOCKING)

Ps 22: 7 All who see me *m* me;

Pr 14: 9 Fools *m* at making amends for sin,

Mk 10: 34 who will *m* him and spit on him,

MOCKED (MOCK)

Mt 27: 29 knelt in front of him and *m* him.

27: 41 of the law and the elders *m* him.

Gal 6: 7 not be deceived: God cannot be *m*.

MOCKER (MOCK)

Pr 9: 7 corrects a *m* invites insult;

9: 12 if you are a *m*, you alone will suffer

20: 1 Wine is a *m* and beer a brawler;

22: 10 Drive out the *m*, and out goes strife

MOCKERS (MOCK)

Ps 1: 1 or sit in the seat of *m*.

MOCKING (MOCK)

Isa 50: 6 face from *m* and spitting.

MODEL*

Eze 28: 12 "'You were the *m* of perfection,

1Th 1: 7 And so you became a *m*

2Th 3: 9 to make ourselves a *m* for you

MOMENT

Job 20: 5 the joy of the godless lasts but a *m*.

Ps 30: 5 For his anger lasts only a *m*,

Isa 66: 8 or a nation be brought forth in a *m*?

Gal 2: 5 We did not give in to them for a *m*,

MONEY

Ecc 5: 10 Whoever loves *m* never has *m*

Isa 55: 1 and you who have no *m*,

Mt 6: 24 You cannot serve both God and *M*.

Lk 9: 3 no bread, no *m*, no extra tunic.

1Co 16: 2 set aside a sum of *m* in keeping

1Ti 3: 3 not quarrelsome, not a lover of *m*.

6: 10 For the love of *m* is a root

2Ti 3: 2 lovers of *m*, boastful, proud,

Heb 13: 5 free from the love of *m*

1Pe 5: 2 not greedy for *m*, but eager to serve

MOON

Ps 121: 6 nor the *m* by night.

Joel 2: 31 and the *m* to blood

1Co 15: 41 *m* another and the stars another;

MORNING

Ge 1: 5 and there was *m*—the first day.

Dt 28: 67 In the *m* you will say, "If only it

Ps 5: 3 In the *m*, O LORD,

2Pe 1: 19 and the *m* star rises in your hearts.

Rev 22: 16 of David, and the bright *M* Star."

MORTAL

1Co 15: 53 and the *m* with immortality.

MOSES

Levite; brother of Aaron (Ex 6:20; 1Ch 6:3). Put in basket into Nile; discovered and raised by Pharaoh's daughter (Ex 2:1-10). Fled to Midian after killing Egyptian (Ex 2:11-15). Married to Zipporah, fathered Gershom (Ex 2:16-22).

Called by the LORD to deliver Israel (Ex 3-4). Pharaoh's resistance (Ex 5). Ten plagues (Ex 7-11). Passover and Exodus (Ex 12-13). Led Israel through Red Sea (Ex 14). Song of deliverance (Ex 15:1-21). Brought water from rock (Ex 17:1-7). Raised hands to defeat Amalekites (Ex 17:8-16). Delegated judges (Ex 18; Dt 1:9-18).

Received Law at Sinai (Ex 19-23; 25-31; Jn 1:17). Announced Law to Israel (Ex 19:7-8; 24; 35). Broke tablets because of golden calf (Ex 32; Dt 9). Saw glory of the LORD (Ex 33-34). Supervised building of tabernacle (Ex 36-40). Set apart Aaron and priests (Lev 8-9). Numbered tribes (Nu 1-4; 26). Opposed by Aaron and Miriam (Nu 12). Sent spies into Canaan (Nu 13). Announced forty years of wandering for failure to enter land (Nu 14). Opposed by Korah (Nu 16). Forbidden to enter land for striking rock (Nu 20:1-13; Dt 1:37). Lifted bronze snake for healing (Nu 21:4-9; Jn 3:14). Final address to Israel (Dt 1-33). Succeeded by Joshua (Nu 27:12-23; Dt 34). Death (Dt 34:5-12).

"Law of Moses" (1Ki 2:3; Ezr 3:2; Mk 12:26; Lk 24:44). "Book of Moses" (2Ch

25:12; Ne 13:1). "Song of Moses" (Ex 15:1-21; Rev 15:3). "Prayer of Moses" (Ps 90).

MOTH

Mt 6: 19 where *m* and rust destroy,

MOTHER (MOTHER'S)

Ge 2: 24 and *m* and be united to his wife,

3: 20 because she would become the *m*

Ex 20: 12 "Honor your father and your *m*,

Lev 20: 9 "'If anyone curses his father or *m*,

Dt 5: 16 "Honor your father and your *m*,

21: 18 who does not obey his father and *m*

27: 16 who dishonors his father or his *m*."

1Sa 2: 19 Each year his *m* made him a little

Ps 113: 9 as a happy *m* of children.

Pr 23: 25 May your father and *m* be glad;

29: 15 child left to himself disgraces his *m*.

31: 1 an oracle his *m* taught him:

Isa 49: 15 "Can a *m* forget the baby

66: 13 As a *m* comforts her child,

Mt 10: 37 or *m* more than me is not worthy

15: 4 'Honor your father and *m*'

19: 5 and *m* and be united to his wife,

Mk 7: 10 'Honor your father and your *m*,'

10: 19 honor your father and *m*.'"

Jn 19: 27 to the disciple, "Here is your *m*."

MOTHER'S (MOTHER)

Job 1: 21 "Naked I came from my *m* womb,

Pr 1: 8 and do not forsake your *m* teaching

MOTIVES*

Pr 16: 2 but *m* are weighed by the LORD.

1Co 4: 5 will expose the *m* of men's hearts.

Php 1: 18 whether from false *m* or true,

1Th 2: 3 spring from error or impure *m*,

Jas 4: 3 because you ask with wrong *m*,

MOUNTAIN (MOUNTAINS)

Mic 4: 2 let us go up to the *m* of the LORD,

Mt 17: 20 say to this *m*, 'Move from here

MOUNTAINS (MOUNTAIN)

Isa 52: 7 How beautiful on the *m*

55: 12 the *m* and hills

1Co 13: 2 if I have a faith that can move *m*,

MOURN (MOURNING)

Ecc 3: 4 a time to *m* and a time to dance,

Isa 61: 2 to comfort all who *m*,

Mt 5: 4 Blessed are those who *m*,

Ro 12: 15 *m* with those who *m*.

MOURNING (MOURN)

Jer 31: 13 I will turn their *m* into gladness;

Rev 21: 4 There will be no more death or *m*

MOUTH

Jos 1: 8 of the Law depart from your *m*;

Ps 19: 14 May the words of my *m*

40: 3 He put a new song in my *m*,

119:103 sweeter than honey to my *m*!

Pr 16: 23 A wise man's heart guides his *m*,

27: 2 praise you, and not your own *m*;

Isa 51: 16 I have put my words in your *m*

Mt 12: 34 overflow of the heart the *m* speaks.

15: 11 into a man's *m* does not make him

Ro 10: 9 That if you confess with your *m*,

MUD

Ps 40: 2 out of the *m* and mire;

Isa 57: 20 whose waves cast up mire and *m*.

2Pe 2: 22 back to her wallowing in the *m*."

MULTITUDE (MULTITUDES)

Isa 31: 1 who trust in the *m* of their chariots

1Pe 4: 8 love covers over a *m* of sins.

Rev 7: 9 me was a great *m* that no one could

MULTITUDES (MULTITUDE)

Joel 3: 14 *M*, *m* in the valley of decision!

MURDER (MURDERER MURDERERS)

Ex 20: 13 "You shall not *m*.

Mt 15: 19 *m*, adultery, sexual immorality,

Ro 13: 9 "Do not *m*," "Do not steal,"

Jas 2: 11 adultery," also said, "Do not *m*."

MURDERER (MURDER)

Nu 35: 16 he is a *m*; the *m* shall be put

Jn 8: 44 He was a *m* from the beginning,

1Jn 3: 15 who hates his brother is a *m*,

MURDERERS (MURDER)

1Ti 1: 9 for *m*, for adulterers and perverts,

Rev 21: 8 the *m*, the sexually immoral,

MUSIC

Jdg 5: 3 I will make *m* to the LORD,

Ps 27: 6 and make *m* to the LORD.

95: 2 and extol him with *m* and song.

98: 4 burst into jubilant song with *m*;

108: 1 make *m* with all my soul.

Eph 5: 19 make *m* in your heart to the Lord,

MUSTARD

Mt 13: 31 kingdom of heaven is like a *m* seed,

17: 20 you have faith as small as a *m* seed,

MUZZLE

Dt 25: 4 Do not *m* an ox while it is treading

Ps 39: 1 I will put a *m* on my mouth

1Co 9: 9 "Do not *m* an ox while it is

MYRRH

Mt 2: 11 of gold and of incense and of *m*.

Mk 15: 23 offered him wine mixed with *m*,

MYSTERY

Ro 16: 25 to the revelation of the *m* hidden

1Co 15: 51 I tell you a *m*: We will not all sleep,

Eph 5: 32 This is a profound *m*—

Col 1: 26 the *m* that has been kept hidden

1Ti 3: 16 the *m* of godliness is great:

MYTHS

1Ti 4: 7 Have nothing to do with godless *m*

∾ N

NADAB

Son of Jeroboam I; king of Israel (1Ki 15:25-32).

NAIL* (NAILING)

Jn 20: 25 "Unless I see the *n* marks

NAILING* (NAIL)

Ac 2: 23 him to death by *n* him to the cross.

Col 2: 14 he took it away, *n* it to the cross.

NAKED

Ge 2: 25 The man and his wife were both *n*,

Job 1: 21 *N* I came from my mother's womb,

Isa 58: 7 when you see the *n*, to clothe him,

2Co 5: 3 are clothed, we will not be found *n*.

NAME

Ex 3: 15 This is my *n* forever, the *n*

20: 7 "You shall not misuse the *n*

Dt 5: 11 "You shall not misuse the *n*

28: 58 this glorious and awesome *n*—

1Ki 5: 5 will build the temple for my *N*.'

2Ch 7: 14 my people, who are called by my *n*,

Ps 34: 3 let us exalt his *n* together.

103: 1 my inmost being, praise his holy *n*.

147: 4 and calls them each by *n*.

Pr 22: 1 A good *n* is more desirable

30: 4 What is his *n*, and the *n* of his son?

Isa 40: 26 and calls them each by *n*.

57: 15 who lives forever, whose *n* is holy:

Jer 14: 7 do something for the sake of your *n*

Da 12: 1 everyone whose *n* is found written

Joel 2: 32 on the *n* of the LORD will be saved

Zec 14: 9 one LORD, and his *n* the only *n*.

Mt 1: 21 and you are to give him the *n* Jesus.

6: 9 hallowed be your *n*,

18: 20 or three come together in my *n*,

Jn 10: 3 He calls his own sheep by *n*.

16: 24 asked for anything in my *n*.

Ac 4: 12 for there is no other *n*

Ro 10: 13 "Everyone who calls on the *n*

Php 2: 9 him the *n* that is above every *n*,

Col 3: 17 do it all in the *n* of the Lord Jesus,

Heb 1: 4 as the *n* he has inherited is superior

Rev 20: 15 If anyone's *n* was not found written

NAOMI

Mother-in-law of Ruth (Ru 1). Advised Ruth to seek marriage with Boaz (Ru 2-4).

NARROW

Mt 7: 13 "Enter through the *n* gate.

NATHANAEL

Apostle (Jn 1:45-49; 21:2). Probably also called Bartholomew (Mt 10:3).

NATION (NATIONS)

Ge 12: 2 "I will make you into a great *n*

Ps 33: 12 Blessed is the *n* whose God is

Pr 14: 34 Righteousness exalts a *n*,

Isa 65: 1 To a *n* that did not call on my name

1Pe 2: 9 a royal priesthood, a holy *n*,

Rev 7: 9 from every *n*, tribe, people

NATIONS (NATION)

Ge 17: 4 You will be the father of many *n*.

18: 18 and all *n* on earth will be blessed

Ex 19: 5 of all *n* you will be my treasured

Ne 1: 8 I will scatter you among

Ps 96: 3 Declare his glory among the *n*,

Isa 40: 15 Surely the *n* are like a drop

Eze 36: 23 *n* will know that I am the LORD,

Hag 2: 7 and the desired of all *n* will come,

Zec 8: 23 *n* will take firm hold of one Jew

14: 2 I will gather all the *n* to Jerusalem

Mt 28: 19 and make disciples of all *n*,

Rev 21: 24 The *n* will walk by its light,

NATURAL (NATURE)

Ro 6: 19 you are weak in your *n* selves.

1Co 15: 44 If there is a *n* body, there is

NATURE (NATURAL)

Ro 8: 4 do not live according to the sinful *n*

8: 8 by the sinful *n* cannot please God.

Gal 5: 19 The acts of the sinful *n* are obvious:

5: 24 Jesus have crucified the sinful *n*

Php 2: 6 Who, being in very *n* God,

NAZARENE

Mt 2: 23 prophets: "He will be called a *N*."

NAZIRITE

Jdg 13: 7 because the boy will be a *N* of God

NECESSARY

Ro 13: 5 it is *n* to submit to the authorities,

NEED (NEEDS NEEDY)

Ps 116: 6 when I was in great *n*, he saved me.

Mt 6: 8 for your Father knows what you *n*

Ro 12: 13 with God's people who are in *n*.

1Co 12: 21 say to the hand, "I don't *n* you!"

1Jn 3: 17 sees his brother in *n* but has no pity

NEEDLE

Mt 19: 24 go through the eye of a *n*

NEEDS (NEED)

Isa 58: 11 he will satisfy your *n*

Php 4: 19 God will meet all your *n* according

NEEDY (NEED)

Pr 14: 21 blessed is he who is kind to the *n*.

14: 31 to the *n* honors God.

31: 20 and extends her hands to the *n*.

Mt 6: 2 "So when you give to the *n*,

NEGLECT (NEGLECTED)

Ne 10: 39 We will not *n* the house of our God

Ps 119: 16 I will not *n* your word.

Ac 6: 2 for us to *n* the ministry of the word

1Ti 4: 14 Do not *n* your gift, which was

NEGLECTED (NEGLECT)

Mt 23: 23 But you have *n* the more important

NEHEMIAH

Cupbearer of Artaxerxes (Ne 2:1); governor of Israel (Ne 8:9). Returned to Jerusalem to rebuild walls (Ne 2-6). With Ezra, reestablished worship (Ne 8). Prayer confessing nation's sin (Ne 9). Dedicated wall (Ne 12).

NEIGHBOR (NEIGHBOR'S)

Ex 20: 16 give false testimony against your *n*.

Lev 19: 13 Do not defraud your *n* or rob him.

19: 18 but love your *n* as yourself.

Pr 27: 10 better a *n* nearby than a brother far

Mt 19: 19 and 'love your *n* as yourself.'"

Lk 10: 29 who is my *n*?" In reply Jesus said:

Ro 13: 10 Love does no harm to its *n*.

NEIGHBOR'S (NEIGHBOR)

Ex 20: 17 You shall not covet your *n* wife,

Dt 5: 21 not set your desire on your *n* house

19: 14 not move your *n* boundary stone

Pr 25: 17 Seldom set foot in your *n* house —

NEW

Ps 40: 3 He put a *n* song in my mouth,

Ecc 1: 9 there is nothing *n* under the sun.

Isa 65: 17 *n* heavens and a *n* earth.

Jer 31: 31 "when I will make a *n* covenant

Eze 36: 26 give you a *n* heart and put a *n* spirit

Mt 9: 17 Neither do men pour *n* wine

Lk 22: 20 "This cup is the *n* covenant

2Co 5: 17 he is a *n* creation; the old has gone,

Eph 4: 24 and to put on the *n* self, created

2Pe 3: 13 to a *n* heaven and a *n* earth,

1Jn 2: 8 Yet I am writing you a *n* command;

NEWBORN (BEAR)

1Pe 2: 2 Like *n* babies, crave pure spiritual

NEWS

Isa 52: 7 the feet of those who bring good *n*,

Mk 1: 15 Repent and believe the good *n*!"

16: 15 preach the good *n* to all creation.

Lk 2: 10 I bring you good *n*

Ac 5: 42 proclaiming the good *n* that Jesus

17: 18 preaching the good *n* about
Jesus
Ro 10: 15 feet of those who bring
good *n!*"

NICODEMUS*

Pharisee who visted Jesus at night (Jn
3). Argued fair treatment of Jesus (Jn
7:50-52). With Joseph, prepared Jesus
for burial (Jn 19:38-42).

NIGHT

Job 35: 10 who gives songs in the *n*,
Ps   1: 2 on his law he meditates day
and *n*.
91: 5 You will not fear the terror
of *n*,
Jn   3: 2 He came to Jesus at *n* and
said,
1Th 5: 2 Lord will come like a thief
in the *n*.
5: 5 We do not belong to the *n*
Rev 21: 25 for there will be no *n* there.

NOAH

Righteous man (Eze 14:14, 20) called
to build ark (Ge 6-8; Heb 11:7; 1Pe 3:20;
2Pe 2:5). God's covenant with (Ge 9:1-17).
Drunkenness of (Ge 9:18-23). Blessed
sons, cursed Canaan (Ge 9:24-27).

NOBLE

Ru   3: 11 you are a woman of *n*
character.
Ps 45: 1 My heart is stirred by a *n*
theme
Pr 12: 4 of *n* character is her
husband's
31: 10 A wife of *n* character who
can find?
31: 29 "Many women do *n* things,
Isa 32: 8 But the *n* man makes *n* plans,
Lk   8: 15 good soil stands for those
with a *n*
Ro   9: 21 of clay some pottery for *n*
purposes
Php 4: 8 whatever is *n*, whatever is
right,
2Ti 2: 20 some are for *n* purposes

NOTHING

Ne   9: 21 in the desert; they lacked *n*,
Jer 32: 17 *N* is too hard for You
Jn 15: 5 apart from me you can do *n*.

NULLIFY

Ro   3: 31 Do we, then, *n* the law by
this faith

∞ O

OATH

Dt   7: 8 and kept the *o* he swore

OBEDIENCE (OBEY)

2Ch 31: 21 in *o* to the law and the
commands.
Pr 30: 17 that scorns *o* to a mother,
Ro   1: 5 to the *o* that comes from
faith.
6: 16 to *o*, which leads to
righteousness?
2Jn 6 that we walk in *o* to his
commands.

OBEDIENT (OBEY)

Lk   2: 51 with them and was *o* to them.
Php 2: 8 and became *o* to death —
1Pe 1: 14 As *o* children, do not
conform

**OBEY (OBEDIENCE OBEDIENT
OBEYED)**

Ex 12: 24 "*O* these instructions as a
lasting
Dt   6: 3 careful to *o* so that it may go
well
13: 4 Keep his commands and *o*
him;
21: 18 son who does not *o* his father
30: 2 and *o* him with all your heart
32: 46 children to *o* carefully all
the words
1Sa 15: 22 To *o* is better than sacrifice,
Ps 119: 34 and *o* it with all my heart.
Mt 28: 20 to *o* everything I have
commanded
Jn 14: 23 loves me, he will *o* my
teaching.
Ac   5: 29 "We must *o* God rather
than men!
Ro   6: 16 slaves to the one whom
you *o*—
Gal 5: 3 obligated to *o* the whole law.
Eph 6: 1 *o* your parents in the Lord,
6: 5 *o* your earthly masters with
respect
Col 3: 20 *o* your parents in everything,
1Ti 3: 4 and see that his children *o*
him
Heb 13: 17 *O* your leaders and submit
1Jn 5: 3 love for God: to *o* his
commands.

OBEYED (OBEY)

Ps 119: 4 that are to be fully *o*.
Jnh 3: 3 Jonah *o* the word of the LORD
Jn 17: 6 and they have *o* your word.
Ro   6: 17 you wholeheartedly *o* the
form
Heb 11: 8 *o* and went, even though he
did not
1Pe 3: 6 who *o* Abraham and called
him her

OBLIGATED

Ro   1: 14 I am *o* both to Greeks
Gal 5: 3 himself be circumcised that
he is *o*

OBSCENITY

Eph 5: 4 Nor should there be *o*, foolish
talk

OBSOLETE

Heb 8: 13 he has made the first one *o*;

OBTAINED

Ro   9: 30 not pursue righteousness,
have *o* it,
Php 3: 12 Not that I have already *o* all
this,
Heb 9: 12 having *o* eternal
redemption.

OFFENDED (OFFENSE)

Pr 18: 19 An *o* brother is more
unyielding

OFFENSE (OFFENDED OFFENSIVE)

Pr 17: 9 over an *o* promotes love,
19: 11 it is to his glory to overlook
an *o*.

OFFENSIVE (OFFENSE)

Ps 139: 24 See if there is any *o* way in me,

**OFFER (OFFERED OFFERING
OFFERINGS)**

Ro 12: 1 to *o* your bodies as living
sacrifices,
Heb 13: 15 therefore, let us continually *o*

OFFERED (OFFER)

Heb 7: 27 once for all when he *o*
himself.
11: 4 By faith Abel *o* God a better

OFFERING (OFFER)

Ge 22: 8 provide the lamb for the
burnt *o*,
Ps 40: 6 Sacrifice and *o* you did not
desire,
Isa 53: 10 the LORD makes his life a
guilt *o*,
Mt   5: 23 if you are *o* your gift at the
altar
Eph 5: 2 as a fragrant *o* and sacrifice
to God.
Heb 10: 5 "Sacrifice and *o* you did not
desire,

OFFERINGS (OFFER)

Mal 3: 8 do we rob you?' "In tithes
and *o*.
Mk 12: 33 is more important than all
burnt *o*,

OFFICER

2Ti 2: 4 wants to please his
commanding *o*.

OFFSPRING

Ge   3: 15 and between your *o* and hers;
12: 7 "To your *o* I will give this
land."

OIL

Ps 23: 5 You anoint my head with *o*;
Isa 61: 3 the *o* of gladness
Heb 1: 9 by anointing you with the *o*
of joy."

OLIVE (OLIVES)

Zec 4: 3 Also there are two *o* trees
by it,
Ro 11: 17 and you, though a wild *o*
shoot,
Rev 11: 4 These are the two *o* trees

OLIVES (OLIVE)

Jas 3: 12 a fig tree bear *o*, or a grapevine bear

OMEGA

Rev 1: 8 "I am the Alpha and the Ω."

OMRI

King of Israel (1Ki 16:21-26).

OPINIONS*

1Ki 18: 21 will you waver between
two *o*?

Pr 18: 2 but delights in airing his
own *o*.

OPPORTUNITY

Ro   7: 11 seizing the *o* afforded
Gal 6: 10 as we have *o*, let us do good
Eph 5: 16 making the most of every *o*,
Col 4: 5 make the most of every *o*.
1Ti 5: 14 to give the enemy no *o* for
slander.

OPPOSES

Jas 4: 6 "God *o* the proud
1Pe 5: 5 because, "God *o* the proud

OPPRESS (OPPRESSED)

Ex 22: 21 "Do not mistreat an alien or
o him,
Zec 7: 10 Do not *o* the widow

OPPRESSED (OPPRESS)

Ps   9: 9 The LORD is a refuge for the *o*,
Isa 53: 7 He was *o* and afflicted,
Zec 10: 2 *o* for lack of a shepherd.

ORDAINED

Ps   8: 2 you have *o* praise

ORDERLY

1Co 14: 40 done in a fitting and *o* way.
Col 2: 5 and delight to see how *o* you
are

ORGIES*

Ro 13: 13 not in *o* and drunkenness,
Gal 5: 21 drunkenness, *o*, and the like.
1Pe 4: 3 *o*, carousing and detestable

ORIGIN

2Pe 1: 21 For prophecy never had its *o*

ORPHANS

Jn 14: 18 will not leave you as *o*; I will
come
Jas 1: 27 to look after *o* and widows

OUTCOME

Heb 13: 7 Consider the *o* of their way
of life
1Pe 4: 17 what will the *o* be for those
who do

OUTSIDERS*

Col 4: 5 wise in the way you act
toward *o*;
1Th 4: 12 daily life may win the
respect of *o*
1Ti 3: 7 also have a good reputation
with *o*,

OUTSTANDING

SS   5: 10 *o* among ten thousand.
Ro 13: 8 no debt remain *o*,

OUTSTRETCHED

Ex   6: 6 and will redeem you with
an *o* arm
Jer 27: 5 and *o* arm I made the earth
Eze 20: 33 an *o* arm and with outpoured wrath

OUTWEIGHS

2Co 4: 17 an eternal glory that far *o*
them all.

OVERCOME (OVERCOMES)

Mt 16: 18 and the gates of Hades will not *o* it.
Mk 9: 24 I do believe; help me *o* my unbelief
Jn 16: 33 But take heart! I have *o* the world."
Ro 12: 21 Do not be *o* by evil, but *o* evil
1Jn 5: 4 is the victory that has *o* the world,
Rev 17: 14 but the Lamb will *o* them

OVERCOMES* (OVERCOME)

1Jn 5: 4 born of God *o* the world.
    5: 5 Who is it that *o* the world?
Rev 2: 7 To him who *o*, I will give the right
    2: 11 He who *o* will not be hurt at all
    2: 17 To him who *o*, I will give some
    2: 26 To him who *o* and does my will
    3: 5 To him who *o* will, like them, be
    3: 12 Him who *o* I will make a pillar
    3: 21 To him who *o*, I will give the right
    21: 7 He who *o* will inherit all this,

OVERFLOW (OVERFLOWS)

Ps 119:171 May my lips *o* with praise,
Lk 6: 45 out of the *o* of his heart his mouth
Ro 15: 13 so that you may *o* with hope
2Co 4: 15 to *o* to the glory of God.
1Th 3: 12 *o* for each other and for everyone

OVERFLOWS* (OVERFLOW)

Ps 23: 5 my cup *o*.
2Co 1: 5 also through Christ our comfort *o*.

OVERJOYED* (JOY)

Da 6: 23 The king was *o* and gave orders
Mt 2: 10 they saw the star, they were *o*.
Jn 20: 20 The disciples were *o*
Ac 12: 14 she was so *o* she ran back
1Pe 4: 13 so that you may be *o*

OVERSEER (OVERSEERS)

1Ti 3: 1 anyone sets his heart on being an *o*,
    3: 2 Now the *o* must be above reproach,
Tit 1: 7 Since an *o* is entrusted

OVERSEERS* (OVERSEER)

Ac 20: 28 the Holy Spirit has made you *o*,
Php 1: 1 together with the *o* and deacons:
1Pe 5: 2 as *o*—not because you must,

OVERWHELMED

Ps 38: 4 My guilt has *o* me
    65: 3 When we were *o* by sins,
Mt 26: 38 "My soul is *o* with sorrow
Mk 7: 37 People were *o* with amazement.

OWE

Ro 13: 7 If you *o* taxes, pay taxes; if revenue
Phm 19 to mention that you *o* me your very

OX

Dt 25: 4 Do not muzzle an *o*
Isa 11: 7 and the lion will eat straw like the *o*
1Co 9: 9 "Do not muzzle an *o*

∾ P

PAGANS

Mt 5: 47 Do not even *p* do that? Be perfect,
1Pe 2: 12 such good lives among the *p* that,

PAIN (PAINFUL)

Ge 3: 16 with *p* you will give birth
Job 33: 19 may be chastened on a bed of *p*
Jn 16: 21 woman giving birth to a child has *p*

PAINFUL (PAIN)

Ge 3: 17 through *p* toil you will eat of it
Heb 12: 11 seems pleasant at the time, but *p*.
1Pe 4: 12 at the *p* trial you are suffering,

PALMS

Isa 49: 16 you on the *p* of my hands;

PANTS

Ps 42: 1 As the deer *p* for streams of water,

PARADISE*

Lk 23: 43 today you will be with me in *p*."
2Co 12: 4 God knows—was caught up to *p*.
Rev 2: 7 of life, which is in the *p* of God.

PARALYTIC

Mk 2: 3 bringing to him a *p*, carried by four

PARDON (PARDONS)

Isa 55: 7 and to our God, for he will freely *p*.

PARDONS* (PARDON)

Mic 7: 18 who *p* sin and forgives

PARENTS

Pr 17: 6 and *p* are the pride of their children
Lk 18: 29 left home or wife or brothers or *p*
    21: 16 You will be betrayed even by *p*,
Ro 1: 30 they disobey their *p*; they are
2Co 12: 14 for their *p*, but *p* for their children.
Eph 6: 1 Children, obey your *p* in the Lord,
Col 3: 20 obey your *p* in everything,
2Ti 3: 2 disobedient to their *p*, ungrateful,

PARTIALITY

Dt 10: 17 who shows no *p* and accepts no
2Ch 19: 7 our God there is no injustice or *p*
Lk 20: 21 and that you do not show *p*

PARTICIPATION

1Co 10: 16 is not the bread that we break a *p*

PASS

Ex 12: 13 and when I see the blood, I will *p*
La 1: 12 to you, all you who *p* by?
Lk 21: 33 Heaven and earth will *p* away,
1Co 13: 8 there is knowledge, it will *p* away.

PASSION (PASSIONS)

1Co 7: 9 better to marry than to burn with *p*.

PASSIONS (PASSION)

Gal 5: 24 crucified the sinful nature with its *p*
Tit 2: 12 to ungodliness and worldly *p*,

PASSOVER

Ex 12: 11 Eat it in haste; it is the LORD's *P*.
Dt 16: 1 celebrate the *P* of the LORD your
1Co 5: 7 our *P* lamb, has been sacrificed.

PAST

Isa 43: 18 do not dwell on the *p*.
Ro 15: 4 in the *p* was written to teach us,
Heb 1: 1 In the *p* God spoke

PASTORS*

Eph 4: 11 and some to be *p* and teachers,

PASTURE (PASTURES)

Ps 37: 3 dwell in the land and enjoy safe *p*.
    100: 3 we are his people, the sheep of his *p*
Jer 50: 7 against the LORD, their true *p*,
Eze 34: 13 I will *p* them on the mountains
Jn 10: 9 come in and go out, and find *p*.

PASTURES (PASTURE)

Ps 23: 2 He makes me lie down in green *p*,

PATCH

Mt 9: 16 No one sews a *p* of unshrunk cloth

PATH (PATHS)

Ps 27: 11 lead me in a straight *p*
    119:105 and a light for my *p*.
Pr 15: 19 the *p* of the upright is a highway.
    15: 24 The *p* of life leads upward
Isa 26: 7 The *p* of the righteous is level;

PATHS (PATH)

Ps 23: 3 He guides me in *p* of righteousness
    25: 4 teach me your *p*;
Pr 3: 6 and he will make your *p* straight.
Ro 11: 33 and his *p* beyond tracing out!
Heb 12: 13 "Make level *p* for your feet,"

PATIENCE (PATIENT)

Pr 19: 11 A man's wisdom gives him *p*;
2Co 6: 6 understanding, *p* and kindness;
Gal 5: 22 joy, peace, *p*, kindness, goodness,
Col 1: 11 may have great endurance and *p*,
    3: 12 humility, gentleness and *p*.

PATIENT (PATIENCE PATIENTLY)

Pr 15: 18 but a *p* man calms a quarrel.
Ro 12: 12 Be joyful in hope, *p* in affliction,
1Co 13: 4 Love is *p*, love is kind.
Eph 4: 2 humble and gentle; be *p*,
1Th 5: 14 help the weak, be *p* with everyone.

PATIENTLY (PATIENT)

Ps 40: 1 I waited *p* for the LORD;
Ro 8: 25 we do not yet have, we wait for it *p*.

PATTERN

Ro 5: 14 who was a *p* of the one to come.
    12: 2 longer to the *p* of this world,
2Ti 1: 13 keep as the *p* of sound teaching,

PAUL

Also called Saul (Ac 13:9). Pharisee from Tarsus (Ac 9:11; Php 3:5). Apostle (Gal 1). At stoning of Stephen (Ac 8:1). Persecuted Church (Ac 9:1-2; Gal 1:13). Vision of Jesus on road to Damascus (Ac 9:4-9; 26:12-18). In Arabia (Gal 1:17). Preached in Damascus; escaped death through the wall in a basket (Ac 9:19-25). In Jerusalem; sent back to Tarsus (Ac 9:26-30).

Brought to Antioch by Barnabas (Ac 11:22-26). First missionary journey to Cyprus and Galatia (Ac 13-14). Stoned at Lystra (Ac 14:19-20). At Jerusalem council (Ac 15). Split with Barnabas over Mark (Ac 15:36-41).

Second missionary journey with Silas (Ac 16-20). Called to Macedonia (Ac 16:6-10). Freed from prison in Philippi (Ac 16:16- 40). In Thessalonica (Ac 17:1-9). Speech in Athens (Ac 17:16-33). In Corinth (Ac 18). In Ephesus (Ac 19). Return to Jerusalem (Ac 20). Farewell to Ephesian elders (Ac 20:13-38). Arrival in Jerusalem (Ac 21:1-26). Arrested (Ac

21:27-36). Addressed crowds (Ac 22),
Sanhedrin (Ac 23:1-11). Transferred to
Caesarea (Ac 23:12-35). Trial before
Felix (Ac 24), Festus (Ac 25:1-12). Before
Agrippa (Ac 25:13-26:32). Voyage to
Rome; shipwreck (Ac 27). Arrival in
Rome (Ac 28).

PAY (REPAID REPAY)

Lev 26: 43 They will *p* for their sins
Pr 22: 17 *P* attention and listen
Mt 22: 17 Is it right to *p* taxes to Caesar
Ro 13: 6 This is also why you *p* taxes,
2Pe 1: 19 you will do well to *p* attention
to it,

PEACE (PEACEMAKERS)

Nu 6: 26 and give you *p.* ' '
Ps 34: 14 seek *p* and pursue it.
85: 10 righteousness and *p* kiss
each other
119:165 Great *p* have they who love
your
122: 6 Pray for the *p* of Jerusalem:
Pr 14: 30 A heart at *p* gives life to the
body,
17: 1 Better a dry crust with *p* and
quiet
Isa 9: 6 Everlasting Father, Prince
of *P.*
26: 3 You will keep in perfect *p*
48: 22 "There is no *p*," says the
LORD,
Zec 9: 10 He will proclaim *p* to the
nations.
Mt 10: 34 I did not come to bring *p*,
Lk 2: 14 on earth *p* to men on whom
his
Jn 14: 27 *P* I leave with you; my *p*
16: 33 so that in me you may have *p*.
Ro 5: 1 we have *p* with God
1Co 7: 15 God has called us to live in *p*.
14: 33 a God of disorder but of *p*.
Gal 5: 22 joy, *p*, patience, kindness,
Eph 2: 14 he himself is our *p*, who has
made
Php 4: 7 the *p* of God, which transcends all
Col 1: 20 by making *p* through his
blood,
3: 15 Let the *p* of Christ rule
1Th 5: 3 While people are saying, "*P*
2Th 3: 16 the Lord of *p* himself give
you *p*
2Ti 2: 22 righteousness, faith, love
and *p*,
1Pe 3: 11 he must seek *p* and pursue it.
Rev 6: 4 power to take *p* from the
earth

PEACEMAKERS* (PEACE)

Mt 5: 9 Blessed are the *p*,
Jas 3: 18 *P* who sow in peace raise a
harvest

PEARL* (PEARLS)

Rev 21: 21 each gate made of a single *p*.

PEARLS (PEARL)

Mt 7: 6 do not throw your *p* to pigs.

13: 45 like a merchant looking for
fine *p.*
1Ti 2: 9 or gold or *p* or expensive
clothes,
Rev 21: 21 The twelve gates were
twelve *p*,

PEKAH

King of Israel (2Ki 15:25-31; Isa 7:1).

PEKAHIAH*

Son of Menahem; king of Israel (2Ki
15:22-26).

PEN

Mt 5: 18 letter, not the least stroke of
a *p*,

PENTECOST

Ac 2: 1 of *P* came, they were all
together

PEOPLE (PEOPLES)

Dt 32: 9 the LORD's portion is his *p*,
Ru 1: 16 Your *p* will be my *p*
2Ch 7: 14 if my *p*, who are called
Jer 24: 7 They will be my *p*,
Zec 2: 11 and will become my *p*.
Lk 2: 10 joy that will be for all the *p*.
Ac 15: 14 from the Gentiles a *p*.
2Co 6: 16 and they will be my *p*."
Tit 2: 14 a *p* that are his very own,
1Pe 2: 9 you are a chosen *p*,
Rev 21: 3 They will be his *p*,

PEOPLES (PEOPLE)

Da 7: 14 all *p*, nations and men
Mic 4: 1 and *p* will stream to it.

PERCEIVING

Isa 6: 9 be ever seeing, but never *p*.'

PERFECT (PERFECTER PERFECTION)

SS 6: 9 but my dove, my *p* one, is
unique,
Isa 26: 3 You will keep in *p* peace
Mt 5: 48 as your heavenly Father is *p*.
Ro 12: 2 his good, pleasing and *p* will.
2Co 12: 9 for my power is made *p*
Col 1: 28 so that we may present
everyone *p*
3: 14 binds them all together in *p*
unity.
Heb 9: 11 and more *p* tabernacle that
is not
10: 14 he has made *p* forever those
who
Jas 1: 17 Every good and *p* gift is
from above
1: 25 into the *p* law that gives
freedom,
3: 2 he is a *p* man, able
1Jn 4: 18 But *p* love drives out fear,

PERFECTER* (PERFECT)

Heb 12: 2 the author and *p* of our faith,

PERFECTION (PERFECT)

Ps 119: 96 To all *p* I see a limit;
2Co 13: 11 Aim for *p*, listen to my
appeal,

Heb 7: 11 If *p* could have been
attained

PERFORMS

Ps 77: 14 You are the God who *p*
miracles;

PERISH (PERISHABLE)

Ps 1: 6 but the way of the wicked
will *p*.
102: 26 They will *p*, but you remain;
Lk 13: 3 unless you repent, you too
will all *p*
Jn 10: 28 eternal life, and they shall
never *p*;
Col 2: 22 These are all destined to *p*
with use,
Heb 1: 11 They will *p*, but you remain;
2Pe 3: 9 not wanting anyone to *p*,

PERISHABLE (PERISH)

1Co 15: 42 The body that is sown is *p*,

PERJURERS

1Ti 1: 10 for slave traders and liars
and *p*—

PERMISSIBLE (PERMIT)

1Co 10: 23 "Everything is *p*"—but not

PERMIT (PERMISSIBLE)

1Ti 2: 12 I do not *p* a woman to teach

PERSECUTE (PERSECUTED PERSECUTION)

Mt 5: 11 *p* you and falsely say all
kinds
Jn 15: 20 they persecuted me, they
will *p* you
Ac 9: 4 why do you *p* me?" "Who
are you,
Ro 12: 14 Bless those who *p* you; bless

PERSECUTED (PERSECUTE)

1Co 4: 12 when we are *p*, we endure it;
2Ti 3: 12 life in Christ Jesus will be *p*,

PERSECUTION (PERSECUTE)

Ro 8: 35 or hardship or *p* or famine

PERSEVERANCE (PERSEVERE)

Ro 5: 3 we know that suffering
produces *p*;
5: 4 *p*, character; and character,
hope.
Heb 12: 1 run with *p* the race marked
out
Jas 1: 3 the testing of your faith
develops *p*.
2Pe 1: 6 *p*; and to *p*, godliness;

PERSEVERE* (PERSEVERANCE PERSEVERED PERSEVERES)

1Ti 4: 16 *P* in them, because if you
do,
Heb 10: 36 You need to *p* so that

PERSEVERED* (PERSEVERE)

Heb 11: 27 he *p* because he saw him
who is
Jas 5: 11 consider blessed those who
have *p*.
Rev 2: 3 You have *p* and have endured

PERSEVERES* (PERSEVERE)

1Co 13: 7 trusts, always hopes,
always *p*.
Jas 1: 12 Blessed is the man who *p*

PERSUADE

2Co 5: 11 is to fear the Lord, we try to *p*
men.

PERVERSION (PERVERT)

Lev 18: 23 sexual relations with it; that
is a *p*.
Jude 7 up to sexual immorality
and *p*.

PERVERT (PERVERSION PERVERTS)

Gal 1: 7 are trying to *p* the gospel of
Christ.

PERVERTS* (PERVERT)

1Ti 1: 10 for murderers, for adulterers
and *p*,

PESTILENCE

Ps 91: 6 nor the *p* that stalks in the
darkness

PETER

Apostle, brother of Andrew, also called
Simon (Mt 10:2; Mk 3:16; Lk 6:14; Ac
1:13), and Cephas (Jn 1:42). Confession
of Christ (Mt 16:13-20; Mk 8:27-30; Lk
9:18-27). At transfiguration (Mt 17:1-8;
Mk 9:2-8; Lk 9:28-36; 2Pe 1:16-18).
Caught fish with coin (Mt 17:24-27).
Denial of Jesus predicted (Mt 26:31-35;
Mk 14:27-31; Lk 22:31-34; Jn 13:31-38).
Denied Jesus (Mt 26:69-75; Mk 14:66-72;
Lk 22:54-62; Jn 18:15-27).Commissioned by
Jesus to shepherd his flock (Jn 21:15-23).
Speech at Pentecost (Ac 2). Healed beg-
gar (Ac 3:1-10). Speech at temple (Ac
3:11-26), before Sanhedrin (Ac 4:1-22).
In Samaria (Ac 8:14-25). Sent by vision
to Cornelius (Ac 10). Announced salva-
tion of Gentiles in Jerusalem (Ac 11;15).
Freed from prison (Ac12). Inconsistency
at Antioch (Gal 2:11-21). At Jerusalem
Council (Ac15).

PHARISEES

Mt 5: 20 surpasses that of the *P*

PHILIP

1. Apostle (Mt 10:3; Mk 3:18; Lk 6:14;
Jn 1:43-48; 14:8; Ac 1:13).
2. Deacon (Ac 6:1-7); evangelist in
Samaria (Ac 8:4-25), to Ethiopian (Ac
8:26-40).

PHILOSOPHY*

Col 2: 8 through hollow and
deceptive *p*,

PHYLACTERIES*

Mt 23: 5 They make their *p* wide

PHYSICAL

1Ti 4: 8 For *p* training is of some
value,
Jas 2: 16 but does nothing about his
p needs,

PIECES

Ge 15: 17 and passed between the *p*.
Jer 34: 18 and then walked between its *p*.

PIERCED

Ps 22: 16 they have *p* my hands and my feet.
Isa 53: 5 But he was *p* for our transgressions,
Zec 12: 10 look on me, the one they have *p*,
Jn 19: 37 look on the one they have *p*."

PIGS

Mt   7: 6 do not throw your pearls to *p*.

PILATE

Governor of Judea. Questioned Jesus (Mt 27:1-26; Mk 15:15; Lk 22:66-23:25; Jn 18:28-19:16); sent him to Herod (Lk 23:6-12); consented to his crucifixion when crowds chose Barabbas (Mt 27:15-26; Mk 15:6-15; Lk 23:13-25; Jn 19:1-10).

PILLAR

Ge 19: 26 and she became a *p* of salt.
Ex 13: 21 ahead of them in a *p* of cloud
1Ti 3: 15 the *p* and foundation of the truth.

PIT

Ps 40: 2 He lifted me out of the slimy *p*,
   103: 4 who redeems your life from the *p*
Mt 15: 14 a blind man, both will fall into a *p*."

PITIED

1Co 15: 19 we are to be *p* more than all men.

PLAGUE

2Ch 6: 28 "When famine or *p* comes

PLAIN

Ro   1: 19 what may be known about God is *p*

PLAN (PLANNED PLANS)

Job 42: 2 no *p* of yours can be thwarted.
Pr 14: 22 those who *p* what is good find love
Eph 1: 11 predestined according to the *p*

PLANK

Mt   7: 3 attention to the *p* in your own eye?
Lk   6: 41 attention to the *p* in your own eye?

PLANNED (PLAN)

Ps 40: 5 The things you *p* for us
Isa 46: 11 what I have *p*, that will I do.
Heb 11: 40 God had *p* something better for us

PLANS (PLAN)

Ps 20: 4 and make all your *p* succeed.

   33: 11 *p* of the LORD stand firm forever,
Pr 20: 18 Make *p* by seeking advice;
Isa 32: 8 But the noble man makes noble *p*,

PLANTED (PLANTS)

Ps   1: 3 He is like a tree *p* by streams
Mt 15: 13 Father has not *p* will be pulled
1Co 3: 6 I *p* the seed, Apollos watered it,

PLANTS (PLANTED)

1Co 3: 7 So neither he who *p* nor he who
     9: 7 Who *p* a vineyard and does not eat

PLATTER

Mk   6: 25 head of John the Baptist on a *p*."

PLAYED

Lk   7: 32 "'We *p* the flute for you,
1Co 14: 7 anyone know what tune is being *p*

PLEADED

2Co 12: 8 Three times I *p* with the Lord

PLEASANT (PLEASE)

Ps 16: 6 for me in *p* places;
   133: 1 How good and *p* it is
   147: 1 how *p* and fitting to praise him!
Heb 12: 11 No discipline seems *p* at the time,

PLEASE
(PLEASANT PLEASED PLEASES PLEASING PLEASURE PLEASURES)

Pr 20: 23 and dishonest scales do not *p* him,
Jer 6: 20 your sacrifices do not *p* me."
Jn   5: 30 for I seek not to *p* myself
Ro   8: 8 by the sinful nature cannot *p* God.
    15: 2 Each of us should *p* his neighbor
1Co 7: 32 affairs—how he can *p* the Lord.
    10: 33 I try to *p* everybody in every way.
2Co 5: 9 So we make it our goal to *p* him,
Gal 1: 10 or of God? Or am I trying to *p* men
1Th 4: 1 how to live in order to *p* God,
2Ti 2: 4 wants to *p* his commanding officer.
Heb 11: 6 faith it is impossible to *p* God,

PLEASED (PLEASE)

Mt   3: 17 whom I love; with him I am well *p*
1Co 1: 21 God was *p* through the foolishness
Col 1: 19 For God was *p* to have all his

Heb 11: 5 commended as one who *p* God.
2Pe 1: 17 whom I love; with him I am well *p*

PLEASES (PLEASE)

Ps 135: 6 The LORD does whatever *p* him,
Pr 15: 8 but the prayer of the upright *p* him.
Jn   3: 8 The wind blows wherever it *p*.
     8: 29 for I always do what *p* him."
Col 3: 20 in everything, for this *p* the Lord.
1Ti 2: 3 This is good, and *p* God our Savior,
1Jn 3: 22 his commands and do what *p* him.

PLEASING (PLEASE)

Ps 104: 34 May my meditation be *p* to him,
Ro 12: 1 *p* to God—which is your spiritual
Php 4: 18 an acceptable sacrifice, *p* to God.
Heb 13: 21 may he work in us what is *p* to him,

PLEASURE (PLEASE)

Ps   5: 4 You are not a God who takes *p*
   147: 10 His *p* is not in the strength
Pr 21: 17 He who loves *p* will become poor;
Eze 18: 32 For I take no *p* in the death
Eph 1: 5 in accordance with his *p* and will—
     1: 9 of his will according to his good *p*,
2Ti 3: 4 lovers of *p* rather than lovers

PLEASURES (PLEASE)

Ps 16: 11 with eternal *p* at your right hand.
Heb 11: 25 rather than to enjoy the *p* of sin
2Pe 2: 13 reveling in their *p* while they feast

PLENTIFUL

Mt   9: 37 harvest is *p* but the workers are

PLOW (PLOWSHARES)

Lk   9: 62 "No one who puts his hand to the *p*

PLOWSHARES (PLOW)

Isa 2: 4 They will beat their swords into *p*
Joel 3: 10 Beat your *p* into swords

PLUNDER

Ex   3: 22 And so you will *p* the Egyptians."

POINT

Jas 2: 10 yet stumbles at just one *p* is guilty

POISON

Mk 16: 18 and when they drink deadly *p*,
Jas 3: 8 It is a restless evil, full of deadly *p*.

POLLUTE* (POLLUTED)

Nu 35: 33 "'Do not *p* the land where you are.
Jude : 8 these dreamers *p* their own bodies,

POLLUTED* (POLLUTE)

Ezr 9: 11 entering to possess is a land *p*
Pr 25: 26 Like a muddied spring or a *p* well
Ac 15: 20 to abstain from food *p* by idols,
Jas 1: 27 oneself from being *p* by the world.

PONDER

Ps 64: 9 and *p* what he has done.
   119: 95 but I will *p* your statutes.

POOR (POVERTY)

Dt 15: 4 there should be no *p* among you,
    15: 11 There will always be *p* people
Ps 34: 6 This *p* man called, and the LORD
    82: 3 maintain the rights of the *p*
   112: 9 scattered abroad his gifts to the *p*
Pr 10: 4 Lazy hands make a man *p*,
    13: 7 to be *p*, yet has great wealth.
    14: 31 oppresses the *p* shows contempt
    19: 1 Better a *p* man whose walk is
    19: 17 to the *p* lends to the LORD,
    22: 2 Rich and *p* have this in common:
    22: 9 for he shares his food with the *p*.
    28: 6 Better a *p* man whose walk is
    31: 20 She opens her arms to the *p*
Isa 61: 1 me to preach good news to the *p*.
Mt   5: 3 saying: "Blessed are the *p* in spirit,
    11: 5 the good news is preached to the *p*.
    19: 21 your possessions and give to the *p*,
    26: 11 The *p* you will always have
Mk 12: 42 But a *p* widow came and put
Ac 10: 4 and gifts to the *p* have come up
1Co 13: 3 If I give all I possess to the *p*
2Co 8: 9 yet for your sakes he became *p*,
Jas 2: 2 and a *p* man in shabby clothes

PORTION

Dt 32: 9 For the LORD's *p* is his people,
2Ki 2: 9 "Let me inherit a double *p*

La 3: 24 to myself, "The LORD is
            my p;

POSSESS (POSSESSING POSSESSION POSSESSIONS)

Nu 33: 53 for I have given you the
            land to p.
Jn 5: 39 that by them you p
            eternal life.

POSSESSING* (POSSESS)

2Co 6: 10 nothing, and yet
            p everything.

POSSESSION (POSSESS)

Ge 15: 7 to give you this land to take
            p of it
Nu 13: 30 "We should go up and take p
Eph 1: 14 of those who are God's p—

POSSESSIONS (POSSESS)

Lk 12: 15 consist in the abundance of
            his p."
2Co 12: 14 what I want is not your
            p but you.
1Jn 3: 17 If anyone has material p

POSSIBLE

Mt 19: 26 but with God all things
            are p."
Mk 9: 23 "Everything is p for him who
    10: 27 all things are p with God."
Ro 12: 18 If it is p, as far as it depends
            on you,
1Co 9: 22 by all p means I might save
            some.

POT (POTSHERD POTTER POTTERY)

2Ki 4: 40 there is death in the p!"
Jer 18: 4 But the p he was shaping

POTSHERD (POT)

Isa 45: 9 a p among the potsherds

POTTER (POT)

Isa 29: 16 Can the pot say of the p,
    45: 9 Does the clay say to the p,
    64: 8 We are the clay, you are
            the p;
Jer 18: 6 "Like clay in the hand of
            the p,
Ro 9: 21 Does not the p have the right

POTTERY (POT)

Ro 9: 21 of clay some p for noble
            purposes

POUR (POURED)

Ps 62: 8 p out your hearts to him,
Joel 2: 28 I will p out my Spirit on all
            people.
Mal 3: 10 p out so much blessing that
            you
Ac 2: 17 I will p out my Spirit on all
            people.

POURED (POUR)

Ac 10: 45 of the Holy Spirit had been
            p out
Ro 5: 5 because God has p out
            his love

POVERTY (POOR)

Pr 14: 23 but mere talk leads only to p.

    21: 5 as surely as haste leads to p;
    30: 8 give me neither p nor riches,
Mk 12: 44 out of her p, put in
            everything—
2Co 8: 2 and their extreme p
            welled up
     8: 9 through his p might
            become rich.

POWER (POWERFUL POWERS)

1Ch 29: 11 LORD, is the greatness and
            the p
2Ch 32: 7 for there is a greater p
            with us
Job 36: 22 "God is exalted in his p.
Ps 63: 2 and beheld your p and your
            glory.
    68: 34 Proclaim the p of God,
   147: 5 Great is our Lord and
            mighty in p;
Pr 24: 5 A wise man has great p,
Isa 40: 10 the Sovereign LORD comes
            with p,
Zec 4: 6 nor by p, but by my Spirit,'
Mt 22: 29 do not know the Scriptures
            or the p
   24: 30 on the clouds of the sky,
            with p
Ac 1: 8 you will receive p when the
            Holy
     4: 33 With great p the apostles
    10: 38 with the Holy Spirit and p,
Ro 1: 16 it is the p of God for the
            salvation
1Co 1: 18 to us who are being saved it
            is the p
    15: 56 of death is sin, and the p
2Co 12: 9 for my p is made perfect
Eph 1: 19 and his incomparably
            great p
Php 3: 10 and the p of his resurrection
Col 1: 11 strengthened with all p
            according
2Ti 1: 7 but a spirit of p, of love
Heb 7: 16 of the p of an indestructible
            life.
Rev 4: 11 to receive glory and honor
            and p,
    19: 1 and glory and p belong to
            our God,
    20: 6 The second death has no p

POWERFUL (POWER)

Ps 29: 4 The voice of the LORD is p;
Lk 24: 19 p in word and deed before
            God
2Th 1: 7 in blazing fire with his p
            angels.
Heb 1: 3 sustaining all things by his p
            word.
Jas 5: 16 The prayer of a righteous
            man is p

POWERLESS

Ro 5: 6 when we were still p, Christ
            died
     8: 3 For what the law was p to do

POWERS (POWER)

Ro 8: 38 nor any p, neither height
            nor depth

1Co 12: 10 to another miraculous p,
Col 1: 16 whether thrones or p or
            rulers
    2: 15 And having disarmed the p

PRACTICE

Lev 19: 26 "'Do not p divination or
            sorcery.
Mt 23: 3 for they do not p what they
            preach.
Lk 8: 21 hear God's word and put it
            into p."
Ro 12: 13 P hospitality.
1Ti 5: 4 to put their religion into
            p by caring

PRAISE (PRAISED PRAISES PRAISING)

Ex 15: 2 He is my God, and I will
            p him,
Dt 32: 3 Oh, p the greatness of our
            God!
Ru 4: 14 said to Naomi: "P be to the
            LORD,
2Sa 22: 47 The LORD lives! P be to my
            Rock
1Ch 16: 25 is the LORD and most
            worthy of p;
2Ch 20: 21 and to p him for the
            splendor
Ps 8: 2 you have ordained p
    33: 1 it is fitting for the upright
            to p him.
    34: 1 his p will always be on my
            lips.
    40: 3 a hymn of p to our God.
    48: 1 the LORD, and most worthy
            of p,
    68: 19 P be to the Lord, to God our
            Savior
    89: 5 The heavens p your
            wonders,
   100: 4 and his courts with p;
   105: 2 Sing to him, sing p to him;
   106: 1 P the LORD.
   119:175 Let me live that I may p you,
   139: 14 I p you because I am
            fearfully
   145: 21 Let every creature p his holy
            name
   146: 1 P the LORD, O my soul.
   150: 2 p him for his surpassing
            greatness.
   150: 6 that has breath p the LORD.
Pr 27: 2 Let another p you, and not
            your
    27: 21 man is tested by the p he
            receives.
    31: 31 let her works bring her p
Mt 5: 16 and p your Father in heaven.
    21: 16 you have ordained p'?"
Jn 12: 43 for they loved p from men
            more
Eph 1: 6 to the p of his glorious
            grace,
     1: 12 might be for the p of his
            glory.
     1: 14 to the p of his glory.
Heb 13: 15 offer to God a sacrifice of p—
Jas 5: 13 happy? Let him sing songs
            of p.

PRAISED (PRAISE)

1Ch 29: 10 David p the LORD in the
            presence
Ne 8: 6 Ezra p the LORD, the great
            God;
Da 2: 19 Then Daniel p the God of
            heaven
Ro 9: 5 who is God over all,
            forever p!
1Pe 4: 11 that in all things God
            may be p

PRAISES (PRAISE)

2Sa 22: 50 I will sing p to your name.
Ps 47: 6 Sing to God, sing p;
   147: 1 How good it is to sing p to
            our God,
Pr 31: 28 her husband also, and he
            p her:

PRAISING (PRAISE)

Ac 10: 46 speaking in tongues and
            p God.
1Co 14: 16 If you are p God with your
            spirit,

PRAY (PRAYED PRAYER PRAYERS PRAYING)

Dt 4: 7 is near us whenever we p to
            him?
1Sa 12: 23 the LORD by failing to p
            for you.
2Ch 7: 14 will humble themselves
            and p
Job 42: 8 My servant Job will p
            for you,
Ps 122: 6 P for the peace of
            Jerusalem:
Mt 5: 44 and p for those who
            persecute you,
     6: 5 "And when you p, do not be
            like
     6: 9 "This, then, is how you
            should p:
    26: 36 Sit here while I go over
            there and p
Lk 6: 28 p for those who mistreat
            you.
    18: 1 them that they should
            always p
    22: 40 "P that you will not fall
Ro 8: 26 do not know what we ought
            to p,
1Co 14: 13 in a tongue should p that he
            may
1Th 5: 17 Be joyful always;
            p continually;
Jas 5: 13 one of you in trouble? He
            should p.
     5: 16 p for each other so that you
            may be

PRAYED (PRAY)

1Sa 1: 27 I p for this child, and the
            LORD
Jnh 2: 1 From inside the fish Jonah p
Mk 14: 35 p that if possible the hour
            might

PRAYER (PRAY)

2Ch 30: 27 for their p reached heaven,

Ezr 8: 23 about this, and he answered our *p*.
Ps 6: 9 the LORD accepts my *p*.
  86: 6 Hear my *p*, O LORD;
Pr 15: 8 but the *p* of the upright pleases him
Isa 56: 7 a house of *p* for all nations."
Mt 21: 13 house will be called a house of *p*,'
Mk 11: 24 whatever you ask for in *p*,
Jn 17: 15 My *p* is not that you take them out
Ac 6: 4 and will give our attention to *p*
Php 4: 6 but in everything, by *p* and petition
Jas 5: 15 *p* offered in faith will make the sick
1Pe 3: 12 and his ears are attentive to their, *p*,

PRAYERS (PRAY)

1Ch 5: 20 He answered their *p*, because they
Mk 12: 40 and for a show make lengthy *p*.
1Pe 3: 7 so that nothing will hinder your *p*.
Rev 5: 8 which are the *p* of the saints.

PRAYING (PRAY)

Mk 11: 25 And when you stand *p*,
Jn 17: 9 I am not *p* for the world,
Ac 16: 25 and Silas were *p* and singing hymns
Eph 6: 18 always keep on *p* for all the saints.

PREACH
(PREACHED PREACHING)

Mt 23: 3 they do not practice what they *p*.
Mk 16: 15 and *p* the good news to all creation.
Ac 9: 20 At once he began to *p*
Ro 10: 15 how can they *p* unless they are sent
  15: 20 to *p* the gospel where Christ was
1Co 1: 17 to *p* the gospel—not with words
  1: 23 wisdom, but we *p* Christ crucified:
  9: 14 that those who *p* the gospel should
  9: 16 Woe to me if I do not *p* the gospel!
2Co 10: 16 so that we can *p* the gospel
Gal 1: 8 from heaven should *p* a gospel
2Ti 4: 2 I give you this charge: *P* the Word;

PREACHED (PREACH)

Mk 13: 10 And the gospel must first be *p*
Ac 8: 4 had been scattered *p* the word

1Co 9: 27 so that after I have *p* to others,
  15: 1 you of the gospel I *p* to you,
2Co 11: 4 other than the Jesus we *p*,
Gal 1: 8 other than the one we *p* to you,
Php 1: 18 false motives or true, Christ is *p*.
1Ti 3: 16 was *p* among the nations,

PREACHING (PREACH)

Ro 10: 14 hear without someone *p* to them?
1Co 9: 18 in *p* the gospel I may offer it free
1Ti 4: 13 the public reading of Scripture, to *p*
  5: 17 especially those whose work is *p*

PRECEPTS

Ps 19: 8 The *p* of the LORD are right,
  111: 7 all his *p* are trustworthy.
  111: 10 who follow his *p* have good
  119: 40 How I long for your *p*!
  119: 69 I keep your *p* with all my heart.
  119:104 I gain understanding from your *p*;
  119:159 See how I love your *p*;

PRECIOUS

Ps 19: 10 They are more *p* than gold,
  116: 15 *P* in the sight of the LORD
Pr 8: 11 for wisdom is more *p* than rubies,
Isa 28: 16 a *p* cornerstone for a sure
1Pe 1: 19 but with the *p* blood of Christ,
  2: 6 a chosen and *p* cornerstone,
2Pe 1: 4 us his very great and *p* promises,

PREDESTINED* (DESTINY)

Ro 8: 29 *p* to be conformed to the likeness
  8: 30 And those he *p*, he also called;
Eph 1: 5 In love he *p* us to be adopted
  1: 11 having been *p* according

PREDICTION*

Jer 28: 9 only if his *p* comes true."

PREPARE (PREPARED)

Ps 23: 5 You *p* a table before me
Am 4: 12 *p* to meet your God, O Israel."
Jn 14: 2 there to *p* a place for you.
Eph 4: 12 to *p* God's people for works

PREPARED (PREPARE)

Mt 25: 34 the kingdom *p* for you
1Co 2: 9 what God has *p* for those who love
Eph 2: 10 which God *p* in advance for us
2Ti 4: 2 be *p* in season and out of season;
1Pe 3: 15 Always be *p* to give an answer

PRESENCE (PRESENT)

Ex 25: 30 Put the bread of the *P* on this table
Ezr 9: 15 one of us can stand in your *p*."
Ps 31: 20 the shelter of your *p* you hide them
  89: 15 who walk in the light of your *p*,
  90: 8 our secret sins in the light of your *p*
  139: 7 Where can I flee from your *p*?
Jer 5: 22 "Should you not tremble in my *p*?
Heb 9: 24 now to appear for us in God's *p*.
Jude : 24 before his glorious *p* without fault

PRESENT (PRESENCE)

2Co 11: 2 so that I might *p* you as a pure
Eph 5: 27 and to *p* her to himself
2Ti 2: 15 Do your best to *p* yourself to God

PRESERVES

Ps 119: 50 Your promise *p* my life.

PRESS (PRESSED PRESSURE)

Php 3: 14 I *p* on toward the goal

PRESSED (PRESS)

Lk 6: 38 *p* down, shaken together

PRESSURE (PRESS)

2Co 1: 8 We were under great *p*, far
  11: 28 I face daily the *p* of my concern

PREVAILS

1Sa 2: 9 "It is not by strength that one *p*;

PRICE

Job 28: 18 the *p* of wisdom is beyond rubies.
1Co 6: 20 your own; you were bought at a *p*.
  7: 23 bought at a *p*; do not become slaves

PRIDE (PROUD)

Pr 8: 13 I hate *p* and arrogance,
  16: 18 *P* goes before destruction,
Da 4: 37 And those who walk in *p* he is able
Gal 4: 4 Then he can take *p* in himself,
Jas 1: 9 ought to take *p* in his high position.

PRIEST (PRIESTHOOD PRIESTS)

Heb 4: 14 have a great high *p* who has gone
  4: 15 do not have a high *p* who is unable
  7: 26 Such a high *p* meets our need—
  8: 1 We do have such a high *p*,

PRIESTHOOD (PRIEST)

Heb 7: 24 lives forever, he has a permanent *p*.
1Pe 2: 5 into a spiritual house to be a holy *p*,
  2: 9 you are a chosen people, a royal *p*,

PRIESTS (PRIEST)

Ex 19: 6 you will be for me a kingdom of *p*
Rev 5: 10 to be a kingdom and *p*

PRINCE

Isa 9: 6 Everlasting Father, *P* of Peace.
Jn 12: 31 now the *p* of this world will be
Ac 5: 31 as *P* and Savior that he might give

PRISON (PRISONER)

Isa 42: 7 to free captives from *p*
Mt 25: 36 I was in *p* and you came to visit me
1Pe 3: 19 spirits in *p* who disobeyed long ago
Rev 20: 7 Satan will be released from his *p*

PRISONER (PRISON)

Ro 7: 23 and making me a *p* of the law of sin
Gal 3: 22 declares that the whole world is a *p*
Eph 3: 1 the *p* of Christ Jesus for the sake

PRIVILEGE*

2Co 8: 4 pleaded with us for the *p* of sharing

PRIZE

1Co 9: 24 Run in such a way as to get the *p*.
Php 3: 14 on toward the goal to win the *p*

PROCLAIM
(PROCLAIMED PROCLAIMING)

1Ch 16: 23 *p* his salvation day after day.
Ps 19: 1 the skies *p* the work of his hands.
  50: 6 the heavens *p* his righteousness,
  68: 34 *P* the power of God,
  118: 17 will *p* what the LORD has done.
Zec 9: 10 He will *p* peace to the nations.
Ac 20: 27 hesitated to *p* to you the whole will
1Co 11: 26 you *p* the Lord's death

PROCLAIMED (PROCLAIM)

Ro 15: 19 I have fully *p* the gospel of Christ.
Col 1: 23 that has been *p* to every creature

PROCLAIMING (PROCLAIM)

Ro 10: 8 the word of faith we are *p*:

PRODUCE (PRODUCES)

Mt 3: 8 *P* fruit in keeping with repentance.
3: 10 tree that does not *p* good fruit will

PRODUCES (PRODUCE)

Pr 30: 33 so stirring up anger *p* strife."
Ro 5: 3 that suffering *p* perseverance;
Heb 12: 11 it *p* a harvest of righteousness

PROFANE

Lev 22: 32 Do not *p* my holy name.

PROFESS*

1Ti 2: 10 for women who *p* to worship God.
Heb 4: 14 let us hold firmly to the faith we *p*.
10: 23 unswervingly to the hope we *p*,

PROMISE (PROMISED PROMISES)

1Ki 8: 20 The LORD has kept the *p* he made
Ac 2: 39 The *p* is for you and your children
Gal 3: 14 that by faith we might receive the *p*
1Ti 4: 8 holding *p* for both the present life
2Pe 3: 9 Lord is not slow in keeping his *p*,

PROMISED (PROMISE)

Ex 3: 17 And I have *p* to bring you up out
Dt 26: 18 his treasured possession as he *p*,
Ps 119: 57 I have *p* to obey your words.
Ro 4: 21 power to do what he had *p*.
Heb 10: 23 for he who *p* is faithful.
2Pe 3: 4 "Where is this 'coming' he *p*?

PROMISES (PROMISE)

Jos 21: 45 one of all the LORD's good *p*
Ro 9: 4 the temple worship and the *p*.
2Pe 1: 4 us his very great and precious *p*,

PROMPTED

1Th 1: 3 your labor *p* by love, and your
2Th 1: 11 and every act *p* by your faith.

PROPHECIES (PROPHESY)

1Co 13: 8 where there are *p*, they will cease;
1Th 5: 20 do not treat *p* with contempt.

PROPHECY (PROPHESY)

1Co 14: 1 gifts, especially the gift of *p*.
2Pe 1: 20 you must understand that no *p*

PROPHESY (PROPHECIES PROPHECY PROPHESYING PROPHET PROPHETS)

Joel 2: 28 Your sons and daughters will *p*,

Mt 7: 22 Lord, did we not *p* in your name,
1Co 14: 39 my brothers, be eager to *p*,

PROPHESYING (PROPHESY)

Ro 12: 6 If a man's gift is *p*, let him use it

PROPHET (PROPHESY)

Dt 18: 18 up for them a *p* like you
Am 7: 14 "I was neither a *p* nor a prophet's
Mt 10: 41 Anyone who receives a *p*
Lk 4: 24 "no *p* is accepted in his hometown.

PROPHETS (PROPHESY)

Ps 105: 15 do my *p* no harm."
Mt 5: 17 come to abolish the Law or the *P*;
7: 12 for this sums up the Law and the *P*.
24: 24 false Christs and false *p* will appear
Lk 24: 25 believe all that the *p* have spoken!
Ac 10: 43 All the *p* testify about him that
1Co 12: 28 second *p*, third teachers, then
14: 32 The spirits of *p* are subject
Eph 2: 20 foundation of the apostles and *p*,
Heb 1: 1 through the *p* at many times
1Pe 1: 10 Concerning this salvation, the *p*,
2Pe 1: 19 word of the *p* made more certain,

PROSPER (PROSPERITY PROSPERS)

Pr 28: 25 he who trusts in the LORD will *p*.

PROSPERITY (PROSPER)

Ps 73: 3 when I saw the *p* of the wicked.
Pr 13: 21 but *p* is the reward of the righteous.

PROSPERS (PROSPER)

Ps 1: 3 Whatever he does *p*.

PROSTITUTE (PROSTITUTES)

1Co 6: 15 of Christ and unite them with a *p*?

PROSTITUTES (PROSTITUTE)

Lk 15: 30 property with *p* comes home,
1Co 6: 9 male *p* nor homosexual offenders

PROSTRATE

Dt 9: 18 again I fell *p* before the LORD

PROTECT (PROTECTS)

Ps 32: 7 you will *p* me from trouble
Pr 2: 11 Discretion will *p* you,
Jn 17: 11 *p* them by the power of your name

PROTECTS (PROTECT)

1Co 13: 7 It always *p*, always trusts,

PROUD (PRIDE)

Pr 16: 5 The LORD detests all the *p*
Ro 12: 16 Do not be *p*, but be willing
1Co 13: 4 it does not boast, it is not *p*.

PROVE

Ac 26: 20 *p* their repentance by their deeds.
1Co 4: 2 been given a trust must *p* faithful.

PROVIDE (PROVIDED PROVIDES)

Ge 22: 8 "God himself will *p* the lamb
Isa 43: 20 because I *p* water in the desert
1Ti 5: 8 If anyone does not *p*

PROVIDED (PROVIDE)

Jnh 1: 17 But the LORD *p* a great fish
4: 6 Then the LORD God *p* a vine
4: 7 dawn the next day God *p* a worm,
4: 8 God *p* a scorching east wind,

PROVIDES (PROVIDE)

1Ti 6: 17 who richly *p* us with everything
1Pe 4: 11 it with the strength God *p*,

PROVOKED

Ecc 7: 9 Do not be quickly *p* in your spirit,

PRUDENT

Pr 14: 15 a *p* man gives thought to his steps.
19: 14 but a *p* wife is from the LORD.
Am 5: 13 Therefore the *p* man keeps quiet

PRUNING

Isa 2: 4 and their spears into *p* hooks.
Joel 3: 10 and your *p* hooks into spears.

PSALMS

Eph 5: 19 Speak to one another with *p*,
Col 3: 16 and as you sing *p*, hymns

PUBLICLY

Ac 20: 20 have taught you *p* and from house
1Ti 5: 20 Those who sin are to be rebuked *p*,

PUFFS

1Co 8: 1 Knowledge *p* up, but love builds up

PULLING

2Co 10: 8 building you up rather than *p* you

PUNISH (PUNISHED PUNISHES)

Ex 32: 34 I will *p* them for their sin."
Pr 23: 13 if you *p* him with the rod, he will
Isa 13: 11 I will *p* the world for its evil,
1Pe 2: 14 by him to *p* those who do wrong

PUNISHED (PUNISH)

La 3: 39 complain when *p* for his sins?
2Th 1: 9 be *p* with everlasting destruction
Heb 10: 29 to be *p* who has trampled the Son

PUNISHES (PUNISH)

Heb 12: 6 and he *p* everyone he accepts

PURE (PURIFIES PURIFY PURITY)

2Sa 22: 27 to the *p* you show yourself *p*,
Ps 24: 4 who has clean hands and a *p* heart,
51: 10 Create in me a *p* heart, O God,
119: 9 can a young man keep his way *p*?
Pr 20: 9 can say, "I have kept my heart *p*;
Isa 52: 11 Come out from it and be *p*,
Hab 1: 13 Your eyes are too *p* to look on evil;
Mt 5: 8 Blessed are the *p* in heart,
2Co 11: 2 I might present you as a *p* virgin
Php 4: 8 whatever is *p*, whatever is lovely,
1Ti 5: 22 Keep yourself *p*.
Tit 1: 15 To the *p*, all things are *p*,
2: 5 to be self-controlled and *p*,
Heb 13: 4 and the marriage bed kept *p*,
1Jn 3: 3 him purifies himself, just as he is *p*.

PURGE

Pr 20: 30 and beatings *p* the inmost being.

PURIFIES* (PURE)

1Jn 1: 7 of Jesus, his Son, *p* us from all sin.
3: 3 who has this hope in him *p* himself,

PURIFY (PURE)

Tit 2: 14 to *p* for himself a people that are
1Jn 1: 9 and *p* us from all unrighteousness.

PURITY (PURE)

2Co 6: 6 in *p*, understanding, patience
1Ti 4: 12 in life, in love, in faith and in *p*.

PURPOSE

Pr 19: 21 but it is the LORD's *p* that prevails
Isa 55: 11 and achieve the *p* for which I sent it
Ro 8: 28 have been called according to his *p*.
Php 2: 2 love, being one in spirit and *p*.

PURSES

Lk 12: 33 Provide *p* for yourselves that will

PURSUE

Ps   34: 14 seek peace and *p* it.
2Ti   2: 22 and *p* righteousness, faith,
1Pe   3: 11 he must seek peace and *p* it.

∾ Q

QUALITIES (QUALITY)

2Pe   1: 8 For if you possess these *q*

QUALITY (QUALITIES)

1Co   3: 13 and the fire will test the *q*

QUARREL (QUARRELSOME)

Pr   15: 18 but a patient man calms a *q*.
     17: 14 Starting a *q* is like breaching
              a dam;
     17: 19 He who loves a *q* loves sin;
2Ti   2: 24 And the Lord's servant
              must not *q*;

QUARRELSOME (QUARREL)

Pr   19: 13 a *q* wife is like a constant
              dripping.
1Ti   3: 3 not violent but gentle, not *q*,

QUICK-TEMPERED

Tit   1: 7 not *q*, not given to
              drunkenness,

QUIET (QUIETNESS)

Ps   23: 2 he leads me beside *q* waters,
Zep   3: 17 he will *q* you with his love,
Lk   19: 40 he replied, "if they keep *q*,
1Ti   2: 2 we may live peaceful and *q*
              lives
1Pe   3: 4 beauty of a gentle and
              q spirit,

QUIETNESS (QUIET)

Isa 30: 15 in *q* and trust is your
              strength,
     32: 17 the effect of righteousness
              will be *q*
1Ti   2: 11 A woman should learn in *q*

QUIVER

Ps 127: 5 whose *q* is full of them.

∾ R

RACE

Ecc   9: 11 The *r* is not to the swift
1Co   9: 24 that in a *r* all the runners
              run,
2Ti   4: 7 I have finished the *r*, I have
              kept
Heb 12: 1 perseverance the *r* marked
              out

RACHEL

  Daughter of Laban (Ge 29:16); wife of
Jacob (Ge 29:28); bore two sons (Ge
30:22-24; 35:16-24; 46:19).

RADIANCE (RADIANT)

Heb   1: 3 The Son is the *r* of God's
              glory

RADIANT (RADIANCE)

Ex   34: 29 he was not aware that his
              face was *r*
Ps   34: 5 Those who look to him are *r*;
SS   5: 10 *Beloved* My lover is *r* and
              ruddy,
Isa 60: 5 Then you will look and be *r*,
Eph   5: 27 her to himself as a *r* church,

RAIN (RAINBOW)

Mt   5: 45 and sends *r* on the righteous

RAINBOW (RAIN)

Ge   9: 13 I have set my *r* in the clouds,

RAISED (RISE)

Ro   4: 25 was *r* to life for our
              justification.
     10: 9 in your heart that God *r* him
1Co 15: 4 that he was *r* on the third
              day

RAN (RUN)

Jnh   1: 3 But Jonah *r* away from the
              LORD

RANSOM

Mt   20: 28 and to give his life as a *r* for
              many."
Heb   9: 15 as a *r* to set them free

RAVENS

1Ki 17: 6 The *r* brought him bread
Lk   12: 24 Consider the *r*: They do not
              sow

READ (READS)

Jos   8: 34 Joshua *r* all the words of the
              law—
Ne   8: 8 They *r* from the Book of the
              Law
2Co   3: 2 known and *r* by everybody.

READS (READ)

Rev   1: 3 Blessed is the one who *r* the
              words

REAL (REALITY)

Jn   6: 55 is *r* food and my blood is *r*
              drink.

REALITY* (REAL)

Col   2: 17 the *r*, however, is found in
              Christ.

REAP (REAPS)

Job   4: 8 and those who sow trouble
              r it.
2Co   9: 6 generously will also *r*
              generously.

REAPS (REAP)

Gal   6: 7 A man *r* what he sows.

REASON

Isa   1: 18 "Come now, let us *r*
              together,"
1Pe   3: 15 to give the *r* for the hope
              that you

REBEKAH

  Sister of Laban, secured as bride for
Isaac (Ge 24). Mother of Esau and Jacob
(Ge 25:19-26). Taken by Abimelech as
sister of Isaac; returned (Ge 26:1-11).
Encouraged Jacob to trick Isaac out of
blessing (Ge 27:1-17).

REBEL

Mt   10: 21 children will *r* against their
              parents

REBUKE (REBUKED REBUKING)

Pr   9: 8 *r* a wise man and he will
              love you.
     27: 5 Better is open *r*

REBUKED (REBUKE)

Lk   17: 3 "If your brother sins, *r* him,
2Ti   4: 2 correct, *r* and encourage—
Rev   3: 19 Those whom I love I *r*

REBUKED (REBUKE)

1Ti   5: 20 Those who sin are to be
              r publicly,

REBUKING (REBUKE)

2Ti   3: 16 *r*, correcting and training

RECEIVE (RECEIVED RECEIVES)

Ac   1: 8 you will *r* power when the
              Holy
     20: 35 'It is more blessed to give
              than to *r*
2Co   6: 17 and I will *r* you."
Rev   4: 11 to *r* glory and honor and
              power,

RECEIVED (RECEIVE)

Mt   6: 2 they have *r* their reward in
              full.
     10: 8 Freely you have *r*, freely
              give.
1Co 11: 23 For I *r* from the Lord what I
Col   2: 6 just as you *r* Christ Jesus as
              Lord,
1Pe   4: 10 should use whatever gift he
              has *r*

RECEIVES (RECEIVE)

Mt   7: 8 everyone who asks *r*; he
              who seeks
     10: 40 he who *r* me *r* the one who
              sent me.
Ac   10: 43 believes in him *r* forgiveness
              of sins

RECKONING

Isa 10: 3 What will you do on the day
              of *r*,

RECOGNIZE (RECOGNIZED)

Mt   7: 16 By their fruit you will *r* them.

RECOGNIZED (RECOGNIZE)

Mt   12: 33 for a tree is *r* by its fruit.
Ro   7: 13 in order that sin might be *r*
              as sin,

RECOMPENSE

Isa 40: 10 and his *r* accompanies him.

RECONCILE (RECONCILED RECONCILIATION)

Eph   2: 16 in this one body to *r* both of
              them

RECONCILED (RECONCILE)

Mt   5: 24 First go and be *r* to your
              brother;
Ro   5: 10 we were *r* to him through
              the death
2Co   5: 18 who *r* us to himself through
              Christ

RECONCILIATION* (RECONCILE)

Ro   5: 11 whom we have now
              received *r*.
     11: 15 For if their rejection is the *r*
2Co   5: 18 and gave us the ministry
              of *r*:
      5: 19 committed to us the
              message of *r*.

RECORD

Ps 130: 3 If you, O LORD, kept a *r*
              of sins,

RED

Isa   1: 18 though they are *r* as crimson,

REDEEM (KINSMAN-REDEEMER REDEEMED REDEEMER REDEMPTION)

2Sa   7: 23 on earth that God went out
              to *r*
Ps   49: 7 No man can *r* the life of
              another
Gal   4: 5 under law, to *r* those under
              law,

REDEEMED (REDEEM)

Gal   3: 13 Christ *r* us from the curse
1Pe   1: 18 or gold that you were *r*

REDEEMER (REDEEM)

Job 19: 25 I know that my *R* lives,

REDEMPTION (REDEEM)

Ps 130: 7 and with him is full *r*.
Lk   21: 28 because your *r* is drawing
              near."
Ro   8: 23 as sons, the *r* of our bodies.
Eph   1: 7 In him we have *r* through
              his blood
Col   1: 14 in whom we have *r*, the
              forgiveness
Heb   9: 12 having obtained eternal *r*.

REFLECT

2Co   3: 18 unveiled faces all *r* the
              Lord's

REFUGE

Nu   35: 11 towns to be your cities of *r*,
Dt   33: 27 The eternal God is your *r*,
Ru   2: 12 wings you have come to
              take *r*."
Ps   46: 1 God is our *r* and strength,
     91: 2 "He is my *r* and my fortress,

REHOBOAM

  Son of Solomon (1Ki 11:43; 1Ch 3:10).
Harsh treatment of subjects caused
divided kingdom (1Ki 12:1-24; 14:21-31;
2Ch 10-12).

REIGN

Ex   15: 18 The LORD will *r*
Ro   6: 12 Therefore do not let sin *r*
1Co 15: 25 For he must *r* until he has
              put all
2Ti   2: 12 we will also *r* with him.
Rev 20: 6 will *r* with him for a
              thousand years

REJECTED (REJECTS)

Ps 118: 22 The stone the builders *r*
Isa 53: 3 He was despised and *r*
              by men,
1Ti   4: 4 nothing is to be *r* if it is
              received
1Pe   2: 4 *r* by men but chosen by God
      2: 7 "The stone the builders *r*

REJECTS (REJECTED)

Lk   10: 16 but he who *r* me *r* him who
              sent me

Jn   3: 36 whoever *r* the Son will not
               see life,

REJOICE (JOY)
Ps   2: 11 and *r* with trembling.
      66: 6 come, let us *r* in him.
     118: 24 let us *r* and be glad in it.
Pr   5: 18 may you *r* in the wife of
               your youth
Lk   10: 20 but *r* that your names are
               written
     15: 6 '*R* with me; I have found my
               lost
Ro   12: 15 Rejoice with those who *r*;
               mourn
Php   4: 4 *R* in the Lord always.

REJOICES (JOY)
Isa 61: 10 my soul *r* in my God.
Lk   1: 47 and my spirit *r* in God my
               Savior,
1Co 12: 26 if one part is honored, every
               part *r*
     13: 6 delight in evil but *r* with the
               truth.

REJOICING (JOY)
Ps   30: 5 but *r* comes in the morning.
Lk   15: 7 in the same way there will
               be more *r*
Ac   5: 41 *r* because they had been
               counted

RELIABLE
2Ti   2: 2 witnesses entrust to *r* men
               who will

RELIGION
1Ti   5: 4 all to put their *r* into practice
Jas   1: 27 *R* that God our Father
               accepts

REMAIN (REMAINS)
Nu   33: 55 allow to *r* will become barbs
Jn   15: 7 If you *r* in me and my words
Ro   13: 8 Let no debt *r* outstanding,
1Co 13: 13 And now these three *r*: faith,
2Ti   2: 13 he will *r* faithful,

REMAINS (REMAIN)
Ps 146: 6 the LORD, who *r* faithful
               forever.
Heb   7: 3 Son of God he *r* a priest
               forever.

REMEMBER
(REMEMBERS REMEMBRANCE)
Ex   20: 8 '*R* the Sabbath day
1Ch 16: 12 *R* the wonders he has done,
Ecc 12: 1 *R* your Creator
Jer 31: 34 and will *r* their sins no
               more."
Gal   2: 10 we should continue to *r* the
               poor,
Php   1: 3 I thank my God every time
               I *r* you.
Heb   8: 12 and will *r* their sins no
               more."

REMEMBERS (REMEMBER)
Ps 103: 14 he *r* that we are dust.
     111: 5 he *r* his covenant forever.
Isa 43: 25 and *r* your sins no more.

REMEMBRANCE (REMEMBER)
1Co 11: 24 which is for you; do this in *r*
               of me

REMIND
Jn   14: 26 will *r* you of everything
               I have said

REMOVED
Ps   30: 11 you *r* my sackcloth and
               clothed me
     103: 12 so far has he *r* our
               transgressions
Jn   20: 1 and saw that the stone had
               been *r*

RENEW (RENEWED RENEWING)
Ps   51: 10 and *r* a steadfast spirit
               within me.
Isa 40: 31 will *r* their strength.

RENEWED (RENEW)
Ps 103: 5 that your youth is *r* like the
               eagle's.
2Co   4: 16 yet inwardly we are being
               r day

RENEWING (RENEW)
Ro   12: 2 transformed by the *r* of
               your mind.

RENOUNCE (RENOUNCES)
Da   4: 27 *R* your sins by doing what is
               right,

RENOUNCES (RENOUNCE)
Pr   28: 13 confesses and *r* them finds

RENOWN
Isa 63: 12 to gain for himself
               everlasting *r*,
Jer 32: 20 have gained the *r* that is still
               yours.

REPAID (PAY)
Lk   14: 14 you will be *r* at the
               resurrection
Col   3: 25 Anyone who does wrong
               will be *r*

REPAY (PAY)
Dt   32: 35 It is mine to avenge; I will *r*.
Ru   2: 12 May the LORD *r* you
Ps 116: 12 How can I *r* the LORD
Ro   12: 19 "It is mine to avenge;
               I will *r*,"
1Pe   3: 9 Do not *r* evil with evil

REPENT (REPENTANCE REPENTS)
Job 42: 6 and *r* in dust and ashes."
Jer 15: 19 "If you *r*, I will restore you
Mt   4: 17 "*R*, for the kingdom of
               heaven is
Lk   13: 3 unless you *r*, you too will all
               perish.
Ac   2: 38 Peter replied, "*R* and be
               baptized,
     17: 30 all people everywhere to *r*.

REPENTANCE (REPENT)
Lk   3: 8 Produce fruit in keeping
               with *r*.
      5: 32 call the righteous, but
               sinners to *r*."

Ac   26: 20 and prove their *r* by their
               deeds.
2Co   7: 10 Godly sorrow brings *r* that
               leads

REPENTS (REPENT)
Lk   15: 10 of God over one sinner
               who *r*."
     17: 3 rebuke him, and if he *r*,
               forgive him

REPROACH
1Ti   3: 2 Now the overseer must be
               above *r*,

REPUTATION
1Ti   3: 7 also have a good *r* with
               outsiders,

REQUESTS
Ps   20: 5 May the LORD grant all
               your *r*.
Php   4: 6 with thanksgiving, present
               your *r*

REQUIRE
Mic   6: 8 And what does the LORD
               r of you

RESCUE (RESCUES)
Da   6: 20 been able to *r* you from the
               lions?"
2Pe   2: 9 how to *r* godly men from
               trials

RESCUES (RESCUE)
1Th   1: 10 who *r* us from the coming
               wrath.

RESIST
Jas   4: 7 *R* the devil, and he will flee
1Pe   5: 9 *R* him, standing firm in the
               faith,

RESOLVED
Ps   17: 3 I have *r* that my mouth will
               not sin.
Da   1: 8 But Daniel *r* not to defile
               himself
1Co   2: 2 For I *r* to know nothing
               while I was

RESPECT (RESPECTABLE)
Lev 19: 3 " 'Each of you must *r* his
               mother
     19: 32 show *r* for the elderly and
               revere
Pr   11: 16 A kindhearted woman
               gains *r*,
Mal   1: 6 where is the *r* due me?" says
1Th   4: 12 so that your daily life may
               win the *r*
      5: 12 to *r* those who work hard
1Ti   3: 4 children obey him with
               proper *r*.
1Pe   2: 17 Show proper *r* to everyone:
      3: 7 them with *r* as the weaker
               partner

RESPECTABLE* (RESPECT)
1Ti   3: 2 self-controlled, *r*, hospitable,

REST
Ex   31: 15 the seventh day is a Sabbath
               of *r*,

Ps   91: 1 will *r* in the shadow
Jer   6: 16 and you will find *r* for your
               souls.
Mt   11: 28 and burdened, and I will
               give you *r*.

RESTITUTION
Ex   22: 3 "A thief must certainly
               make *r*,
Lev   6: 5 He must make *r* in full,
               add a fifth

RESTORE (RESTORES)
Ps   51: 12 *R* to me the joy of your
               salvation
Gal   6: 1 are spiritual should *r* him
               gently.

RESTORES (RESTORE)
Ps   23: 3 he *r* my soul.

RESURRECTION
Mt   22: 30 At the *r* people will neither
               marry
Lk   14: 14 repaid at the *r* of the
               righteous."
Jn   11: 25 Jesus said to her, "I am
               the *r*
Ro   1: 4 Son of God by his *r* from
               the dead;
1Co 15: 12 some of you say that there is
               no *r*
Php   3: 10 power of his *r* and the
               fellowship
Rev 20: 5 This is the first *r*.

RETRIBUTION
Jer 51: 56 For the LORD is a God of *r*;

RETURN
2Ch 30: 9 If you *r* to the LORD,
               then your
Ne   1: 9 but if you *r* to me and
               obey my
Isa 55: 11 It will not *r* to me empty,
Hos   6: 1 "Come, let us *r* to the LORD.
Joel 2: 12 "*r* to me with all your heart,

REVEALED (REVELATION)
Dt   29: 29 but the things *r* belong to us
Isa 40: 5 the glory of the LORD will
               be *r*,
Mt   11: 25 and *r* them to little children.
Ro   1: 17 a righteousness from God
               is *r*,
      8: 18 with the glory that will be *r*
               in us.

REVELATION (REVEALED)
Gal   1: 12 I received it by *r* from Jesus
               Christ.
Rev   1: 1 *r* of Jesus Christ, which God
               gave

REVENGE (VENGEANCE)
Lev 19: 18 " 'Do not seek *r* or bear
               a grudge
Ro   12: 19 Do not take *r*, my friends,

REVERE (REVERENCE)
Ps   33: 8 let all the people of the
               world *r* him

REVERENCE (REVERE)

Lev 19: 30 and have *r* for my sanctuary.
Ps 5: 7 in *r* will I bow down
Col 3: 22 of heart and *r* for the Lord.
1Pe 3: 2 when they see the purity and *r*

REVIVE (REVIVING)

Ps 85: 6 Will you not *r* us again,
Isa 57: 15 to *r* the spirit of the lowly

REVIVING (REVIVE)

Ps 19: 7 *r* the soul.

REWARD (REWARDED)

Ps 19: 11 in keeping them there is great *r*.
127: 3 children a *r* from him.
Pr 19: 17 he will *r* him for what he has done.
25: 22 and the LORD will *r* you.
31: 31 Give her the *r* she has earned,
Jer 17: 10 to *r* a man according to his conduct
Mt 5: 12 because great is your *r* in heaven,
6: 5 they have received their *r* in full.
16: 27 and then he will *r* each person
1Co 3: 14 built survives, he will receive his *r*.
Rev 22: 12 I am coming soon! My *r* is with me

REWARDED (REWARD)

Ru 2: 12 May you be richly *r* by the LORD,
Ps 18: 24 The LORD has *r* me according
Pr 14: 14 and the good man *r* for his.
1Co 3: 8 and each will be *r* according

RICH (RICHES)

Pr 23: 4 Do not wear yourself out to get *r*;
Jer 9: 23 or the *r* man boast of his riches,
Mt 19: 23 it is hard for a *r* man
2Co 6: 10 making many *r*; having nothing
8: 9 he was *r*, yet for your sakes he
1Ti 6: 17 Command those who are *r*

RICHES (RICH)

Ps 119: 14 as one rejoices in great *r*.
Pr 30: 8 give me neither poverty nor *r*,
Isa 10: 3 Where will you leave your *r*?
Ro 9: 23 to make the *r* of his glory known
11: 33 the depth of the *r* of the wisdom
Eph 2: 7 he might show the incomparable *r*
3: 8 to the Gentiles the unsearchable *r*
Col 1: 27 among the Gentiles the glorious *r*

RID

Ge 21: 10 "Get *r* of that slave woman
1Co 5: 7 Get *r* of the old yeast that you may
Gal 4: 30 "Get *r* of the slave woman

RIGHT (RIGHTS)

Ge 18: 25 the Judge of all the earth do *r*?"
Ex 15: 26 and do what is *r* in his eyes,
Dt 5: 32 do not turn aside to the *r*
Ps 16: 8 Because he is at my *r* hand,
19: 8 The precepts of the LORD are *r*,
63: 8 your *r* hand upholds me.
110: 1 "Sit at my *r* hand
Pr 4: 27 Do not swerve to the *r* or the left;
14: 12 There is a way that seems *r*
Isa 1: 17 learn to do *r*!
Jer 23: 5 and do what is just and *r* in the land
Hos 14: 9 The ways of the LORD are *r*;
Mt 6: 3 know what your *r* hand is doing,
Jn 1: 12 he gave the *r* to become children
Ro 9: 21 Does not the potter have the *r*
12: 17 careful to do what is *r* in the eyes
Eph 1: 20 and seated him at his *r* hand
Php 4: 8 whatever is *r*, whatever is pure,
2Th 3: 13 never tire of doing what is *r*.

RIGHTEOUS (RIGHTEOUSNESS)

Ps 34: 15 The eyes of the LORD are on the *r*
37: 25 yet I have never seen the *r* forsaken
119:137 *R* are you, O LORD,
143: 2 for no one living is *r* before you.
Pr 3: 33 but he blesses the home of the *r*.
11: 30 The fruit of the *r* is a tree of life,
18: 10 the *r* run to it and are safe.
Isa 64: 6 and all our *r* acts are like filthy rags
Hab 2: 4 but the *r* will live by his faith—
Mt 5: 45 rain on the *r* and the unrighteous.
9: 13 For I have not come to call the *r*,
13: 49 and separate the wicked from the *r*
25: 46 to eternal punishment, but the *r*
Ro 1: 17 as it is written: "The *r* will live
3: 10 "There is no one *r*, not even one;
1Ti 1: 9 that law is made not for the *r*
1Pe 3: 18 the *r* for the unrighteous,
1Jn 3: 7 does what is right is *r*, just as he is *r*.

Rev 19: 8 stands for the *r* acts of the saints.)

RIGHTEOUSNESS (RIGHTEOUS)

Ge 15: 6 and he credited it to him as *r*.
1Sa 26: 23 LORD rewards every man for his *r*
Ps 9: 8 He will judge the world in *r*;
23: 3 He guides me in paths of *r*
45: 7 You love *r* and hate wickedness;
85: 10 *r* and peace kiss each other.
89: 14 *R* and justice are the foundation
111: 3 and his *r* endures forever.
Pr 14: 34 *R* exalts a nation,
21: 21 He who pursues *r* and love
Isa 5: 16 will show himself holy by his *r*.
59: 17 He put on *r* as his breastplate,
Eze 18: 20 The *r* of the righteous man will be
Da 9: 24 to bring in everlasting *r*,
12: 3 and those who lead many to *r*,
Mal 4: 2 the sun of *r* will rise with healing
Mt 5: 6 those who hunger and thirst for *r*,
5: 20 unless your *r* surpasses that
6: 33 But seek first his kingdom and his *r*
Ro 4: 3 and it was credited to him as *r*."
4: 9 faith was credited to him as *r*.
6: 13 body to him as instruments of *r*.
2Co 5: 21 that in him we might become the *r*
Gal 2: 21 for if *r* could be gained
3: 6 and it was credited to him as *r*."
Eph 6: 14 with the breastplate of *r* in place,
Php 3: 9 not having a *r* of my own that
2Ti 3: 16 correcting and training in *r*,
4: 8 is in store for me the crown of *r*,
Heb 11: 7 became heir of the *r* that comes
2Pe 2: 1 not to have known the way of *r*,

RIGHTS (RIGHT)

La 3: 35 to deny a man his *r*
Gal 4: 5 that we might receive the full *r*

RISE (RAISED)

Isa 26: 19 their bodies will *r*.
Mt 27: 63 'After three days I will *r* again.'
Jn 5: 29 those who have done good will *r*
1Th 4: 16 and the dead in Christ will *r* first.

ROAD

Mt 7: 13 and broad is the *r* that leads

ROBBERS

Jer 7: 11 become a den of *r* to you?
Mk 15: 27 They crucified two *r* with him,
Lk 19: 46 but you have made it 'a den of *r*.'"
Jn 10: 8 came before me were thieves and *r*,

ROCK

Ps 18: 2 The LORD is my *r*, my fortress
40: 2 he set my feet on a *r*
Mt 7: 24 man who built his house on the *r*.
16: 18 and on this *r* I will build my church
Ro 9: 33 and a *r* that makes them fall,
1Co 10: 4 the spiritual *r* that accompanied

ROD

Ps 23: 4 your *r* and your staff,
Pr 13: 24 He who spares the *r* hates his son,
23: 13 if you punish him with the *r*,

ROOM (ROOMS)

Mt 6: 6 But when you pray, go into your *r*,
Lk 2: 7 there was no *r* for them in the inn.
Jn 21: 25 the whole world would not have *r*

ROOMS (ROOM)

Jn 14: 2 In my Father's house are many *r*;

ROOT

Isa 53: 2 and like a *r* out of dry ground.
1Ti 6: 10 of money is a *r* of all kinds of evil.

ROYAL

Jas 2: 8 If you really keep the *r* law found
1Pe 2: 9 a *r* priesthood, a holy nation,

RUBBISH*

Php 3: 8 I consider them *r*, that I may gain

RUDE*

1Co 13: 5 It is not *r*, it is not self-seeking,

RUIN (RUINS)

Pr 18: 24 many companions may come to *r*,
1Ti 6: 9 desires that plunge men into *r*

RUINS (RUIN)

Pr 19: 3 A man's own folly *r* his life,
2Ti 2: 14 and only *r* those who listen.

RULE (RULER RULERS RULES)

1Sa 12: 12 'No, we want a king to *r* over us'—

Ps 2: 9 You will *r* them with an iron
Ps 119:133 let no sin *r* over me.
Zec 9: 10 His *r* will extend from sea to
            sea
Col 3: 15 the peace of Christ *r* in your
            hearts,
Rev 2: 27 He will *r* them with an iron
            scepter;

RULER (RULE)

Ps 8: 6 You made him *r* over the
           works
Eph 2: 2 of the *r* of the kingdom of
            the air,
1Ti 6: 15 God, the blessed and only *R,*

RULERS (RULE)

Ps 2: 2 and the *r* gather together
Col 1: 16 or powers or *r* or authorities;

RULES (RULE)

Ps 103: 19 and his kingdom *r* over all.
Lk 22: 26 one who *r* like the one who
            serves.
2Ti 2: 5 he competes according to
            the *r.*

RUMORS

Mt 24: 6 You will hear of wars and *r*
           of wars,

RUN (RAN)

Isa 40: 31 they will *r* and not grow
            weary,
1Co 9: 24 *R* in such a way as to get the
            prize.
Heb 12: 1 let us *r* with perseverance
            the race

RUST

Mt 6: 19 where moth and *r* destroy,

RUTH*

Moabitess; widow who went to Bethlehem with mother-in-law Naomi (Ru
1). Gleaned in field of Boaz; shown favor
(Ru 2). Proposed marriage to Boaz (Ru 3).
Married (Ru 4:1-12); bore Obed, ancestor of David (Ru 4:13-22), Jesus (Mt 1:5).

∽ S

SABBATH

Ex 20: 8 "Remember the *S* day
Dt 5: 12 "Observe the *S* day
Col 2: 16 a New Moon celebration
            or a *S* day

SACKCLOTH

Mt 11: 21 would have repented long
           ago in *s*

SACRED

Mt 7: 6 "Do not give dogs what is *s;*
1Co 3: 17 for God's temple is *s,* and
            you are

SACRIFICE
(SACRIFICED SACRIFICES)

Ge 22: 2 *S* him there as a burnt
           offering
Ex 12: 27 It is the Passover *s* to the
           LORD,
1Sa 15: 22 To obey is better than *s,*
Hos 6: 6 For I desire mercy, not *s,*

Mt 9: 13 this means: 'I desire mercy,
           not *s.*'
Heb 9: 26 away with sin by the *s* of
            himself.
    13: 15 offer to God a *s* of praise —
1Jn 2: 2 He is the atoning *s* for our
            sins,

SACRIFICED (SACRIFICE)

1Co 5: 7 our Passover lamb, has
           been *s.*
     8: 1 Now about food *s* to idols:
Heb 9: 28 so Christ was *s* once

SACRIFICES (SACRIFICE)

Ps 51: 17 The *s* of God are a broken
           spirit;
Ro 12: 1 to offer your bodies as
           living *s,*

SADDUCEES

Mk 12: 18 *S,* who say there is no
           resurrection,

SAFE (SAVE)

Ps 37: 3 in the land and enjoy *s*
           pasture.
Pr 18: 10 the righteous run to it and
           are *s.*

SAFETY (SAVE)

Ps 4: 8 make me dwell in *s.*
1Th 5: 3 people are saying, "Peace
            and *s,*"

SAINTS

Ps 116: 15 is the death of his *s.*
Ro 8: 27 intercedes for the *s* in
            accordance
Eph 1: 18 of his glorious inheritance
            in the *s,*
     6: 18 always keep on praying for
            all the *s*
Rev 5: 8 which are the prayers of
            the *s.*
    19: 8 for the righteous acts of
            the *s.*)

SAKE

Ps 44: 22 Yet for your *s* we face death
           all day
Php 3: 7 loss for the *s* of Christ.
Heb 11: 26 He regarded disgrace for
            the *s*

SALT

Ge 19: 26 and she became a pillar of *s.*
Mt 5: 13 "You are the *s* of the earth.

SALVATION (SAVE)

Ex 15: 2 he has become my *s.*
1Ch 16: 23 proclaim his *s* day after day.
Ps 27: 1 The LORD is my light and
           my *s* —
    51: 12 Restore to me the joy of
           your *s*
    62: 2 He alone is my rock and
           my *s;*
    85: 9 Surely his *s* is near those
           who fear
    96: 2 proclaim his *s* day after day.
Isa 25: 9 let us rejoice and be glad in
            his *s.*"

    45: 17 the LORD with an ever-
            lasting *s;*
    51: 6 But my *s* will last forever,
    59: 17 and the helmet of *s* on his
            head;
    61: 10 me with garments of *s*
Jnh 2: 9 *S* comes from the LORD."
Zec 9: 9 righteous and having *s,*
Lk 2: 30 For my eyes have seen
           your *s,*
Jn 4: 22 for *s* is from the Jews.
Ac 4: 12 *S* is found in no one else,
    13: 47 that you may bring *s* to the
            ends
Ro 11: 11 *s* has come to the Gentiles
2Co 7: 10 brings repentance that leads
            to *s*
Eph 6: 17 Take the helmet of *s* and the
            sword
Php 2: 12 to work out your *s* with fear
1Th 5: 8 and the hope of *s* as a
            helmet.
2Ti 3: 15 wise for *s* through faith
Heb 2: 3 escape if we ignore such a
            great *s?*
     6: 9 case—things that
            accompany *s.*
1Pe 1: 10 Concerning this *s,* the
            prophets,
     2: 2 by it you may grow up in
            your *s,*

SAMARITAN

Lk 10: 33 But a *S,* as he traveled, came
           where

SAMSON

Danite judge. Birth promised (Jdg 13).
Married to Philistine (Jdg 14). Vengeance on Philistines (Jdg 15). Betrayed
by Delilah (Jdg 16:1-22). Death (Jdg
16:23-31). Feats of strength: killed lion
(Jdg 14:6), 30 Philistines (Jdg 14:19),
1,000 Philistines with jawbone (Jdg
15:13-17), carried off gates of Gaza (Jdg
16:3), pushed down temple of Dagon
(Jdg 16:25-30).

SAMUEL

Ephraimite judge and prophet (Heb
11:32). Birth prayed for (1Sa 1:10-18).
Dedicated to temple by Hannah (1Sa
1:21-28). Raised by Eli (1Sa 2:11,18-26).
Called as prophet (1Sa 3). Led Israel to
victory over Philistines (1Sa 7). Asked
by Israel for a king (1Sa 8). Anointed
Saul as king (1Sa 9-10). Farewell speech
(1Sa 12). Rebuked Saul for sacrifice (1Sa
13). Announced rejection of Saul (1Sa
15). Anointed David as king (1Sa 16).
Protected David from Saul (1Sa 19:18-
24). Death (1Sa 25:1). Returned from
dead to condemn Saul (1Sa 28).

SANCTIFIED (SANCTIFY)

Ac 20: 32 among all those who are *s.*
Ro 15: 16 to God, *s* by the Holy Spirit.
1Co 6: 11 But you were washed, you
            were *s,*
     7: 14 and the unbelieving wife
            has been *s*

Heb 10: 29 blood of the covenant that
            s him,

SANCTIFY
(SANCTIFIED SANCTIFYING)

1Th 5: 23 *s* you through and through.

SANCTIFYING (SANCTIFY)

2Th 2: 13 through the *s* work of the
            Spirit

SANCTUARY

Ex 25: 8 "Then have them make a *s*
           for me,

SAND

Ge 22: 17 and as the *s* on the seashore.
Mt 7: 26 man who built his house
           on *s.*

SANDALS

Ex 3: 5 off your *s,* for the place
           where you
Jos 5: 15 off your *s,* for the place
           where you

SANG (SING)

Job 38: 7 while the morning stars *s*
            together
Rev 5: 9 And they *s* a new song:

SARAH

Wife of Abraham, originally named
Sarai; barren (Ge 11:29-31; 1Pe 3:6).
Taken by Pharaoh as Abraham's sister;
returned (Ge 12:10-20). Gave Hagar to
Abraham; sent her away in pregnancy
(Ge 16). Name changed; Isaac promised
(Ge 17:15-21; 18:10-15; Heb 11:11).
Taken by Abimelech as Abraham's sis-
ter; returned (Ge 20). Isaac born; Hagar
and Ishmael sent away (Ge 21:1-21; Gal
4:21-31). Death (Ge 23).

SATAN

Job 1: 6 and *S* also came with them.
Zec 3: 2 said to *S,* "The LORD rebuke
            you,
Mk 4: 15 *S* comes and takes away the
            word
2Co 11: 14 for *S* himself masquerades
    12: 7 a messenger of *S,* to
            torment me.
Rev 12: 9 serpent called the devil, or *S*
    20: 2 or *S,* and bound him for a
            thousand
    20: 7 *S* will be released from his
            prison

SATISFIED (SATISFY)

Isa 53: 11 he will see the light ₍of life₎
            and be *s*

SATISFIES (SATISFY)

Ps 103: 5 who *s* your desires with
            good things,

SATISFY (SATISFIED SATISFIES)

Isa 55: 2 and your labor on what
            does not *s?*

SAUL

1. Benjamite; anointed by Samuel as
first king of Israel (1Sa 9-10). Defeated

Ammonites (1Sa 11). Rebuked for offering sacrifice (1Sa 13:1-15). Defeated Philistines (1Sa 14). Rejected as king for failing to annihilate Amalekites (1Sa 15). Soothed from evil spirit by David (1Sa 16:14-23). Sent David against Goliath (1Sa 17). Jealousy and attempted murder of David (1Sa 18:1-11). Gave David Michal as wife (1Sa 18:12 -30). Second attempt to kill David (1Sa 19). Anger at Jonathan (1Sa 20:26-34). Pursued David: killed priests at Nob (1Sa 22), went to Keilah and Ziph (1Sa 23), life spared by David at En Gedi (1Sa 24) and in his tent (1Sa 26). Rebuked by Samuel's spirit for consulting witch at Endor (1Sa 28). Wounded by Philistines; took his own life (1Sa 31; 1Ch 10).

2. See PAUL

SAVE (SAFE SAFETY SALVATION SAVED SAVIOR)

Isa 63: 1 mighty to s."
Da 3: 17 the God we serve is able to s us
Zep 3: 17 he is mighty to s.
Mt 1: 21 he will s his people from their sins
16: 25 wants to s his life will lose it,
Lk 19: 10 to seek and to s what was lost."
Jn 3: 17 but to s the world through him.
1Ti 1: 15 came into the world to s sinners—
Jas 5: 20 of his way will s him from death

SAVED (SAVE)

Ps 34: 6 he s him out of all his troubles.
Isa 45: 22 "Turn to me and be s,
Joel 2: 32 on the name of the LORD will be s;
Mk 13: 13 firm to the end will be s.
16: 16 believes and is baptized will be s,
Jn 10: 9 enters through me will be s.
Ac 4: 12 to men by which we must be s."
16: 30 do to be s?" They replied,
Ro 9: 27 only the remnant will be s.
10: 9 him from the dead, you will be s.
1Co 3: 15 will suffer loss; he himself will be s,
15: 2 By this gospel you are s,
Eph 2: 5 it is by grace you have been s.
2: 8 For it is by grace you have been s,
1Ti 2: 4 who wants all men to be s

SAVIOR (SAVE)

Ps 89: 26 my God, the Rock my S.'
Isa 43: 11 and apart from me there is no s.
Hos 13: 4 no S except me.
Lk 1: 47 and my spirit rejoices in God my S,

2: 11 of David a S has been born to you;
Jn 4: 42 know that this man really is the S
Eph 5: 23 his body, of which he is the S.
1Ti 4: 10 who is the S of all men,
Tit 2: 10 about God our S attractive.
2: 13 appearing of our great God and S,
3: 4 and love of God our S appeared,
1Jn 4: 14 Son to be the S of the world.
Jude : 25 to the only God our S be glory,

SCALES

Lev 19: 36 Use honest s and honest weights,
Da 5: 27 You have been weighed on the s

SCAPEGOAT (GOAT)

Lev 16: 10 by sending it into the desert as a s.

SCARLET

Isa 1: 18 "Though your sins are like s,

SCATTERED

Jer 31: 10 'He who s Israel will gather them
Ac 8: 4 who had been s preached the word

SCEPTER

Rev 19: 15 "He will rule them with an iron s."

SCHEMES

2Co 2: 11 For we are not unaware of his s.
Eph 6: 11 stand against the devil's s.

SCOFFERS

2Pe 3: 3 that in the last days s will come,

SCORPION

Rev 9: 5 sting of a s when it strikes a man.

SCRIPTURE (SCRIPTURES)

Jn 10: 35 and the S cannot be broken—
1Ti 4: 13 yourself to the public reading of S,
2Ti 3: 16 All S is God-breathed
2Pe 1: 20 that no prophecy of S came about

SCRIPTURES (SCRIPTURE)

Lk 24: 27 said in all the S concerning himself.
Jn 5: 39 These are the S that testify about
Ac 17: 11 examined the S every day to see

SCROLL

Eze 3: 1 eat what is before you, eat this s;

SEA

Ex 14: 16 go through the s on dry ground.
Isa 57: 20 the wicked are like the tossing s,
Mic 7: 19 iniquities into the depths of the s.
Jas 1: 6 who doubts is like a wave of the s,
Rev 13: 1 I saw a beast coming out of the s.

SEAL (SEALS)

Jn 6: 27 God the Father has placed his s
2Co 1: 22 set his s of ownership on us,
Eph 1: 13 you were marked in him with a s,

SEALS (SEAL)

Rev 5: 2 "Who is worthy to break the s
6: 1 opened the first of the seven s.

SEARCH (SEARCHED SEARCHES SEARCHING)

Ps 4: 4 s your hearts and be silent.
139: 23 S me, O God, and know my heart;
Pr 2: 4 and s for it as for hidden treasure,
Jer 17: 10 "I the LORD s the heart
Eze 34: 16 I will s for the lost and bring back
Lk 15: 8 and s carefully until she finds it?

SEARCHED (SEARCH)

Ps 139: 1 O LORD, you have s me

SEARCHES (SEARCH)

Ro 8: 27 And he who s our hearts knows
1Co 2: 10 The Spirit s all things,

SEARCHING (SEARCH)

Am 8: 12 s for the word of the LORD,

SEARED

1Ti 4: 2 whose consciences have been s

SEASON

2Ti 4: 2 be prepared in s and out of s;

SEAT (SEATED SEATS)

Ps 1: 1 or sit in the s of mockers.
Da 7: 9 and the Ancient of Days took his s.
2Co 5: 10 before the judgment s of Christ,

SEATED (SEAT)

Ps 47: 8 God is s on his holy throne.
Isa 6: 1 I saw the Lord s on a throne,
Col 3: 1 where Christ is s at the right hand

SEATS (SEAT)

Lk 11: 43 you love the most important s

SECRET (SECRETS)

Dt 29: 29 The s things belong

Jdg 16: 6 Tell me the s of your great strength
Ps 90: 8 our s sins in the light
Pr 11: 13 but a trustworthy man keeps a s.
Mt 6: 4 so that your giving may be in s.
2Co 4: 2 we have renounced s and shameful
Php 4: 12 I have learned the s

SECRETS (SECRET)

Ps 44: 21 since he knows the s of the heart?
1Co 14: 25 the s of his heart will be laid bare.

SECURE (SECURITY)

Ps 112: 8 His heart is s, he will have no fear;
Heb 6: 19 an anchor for the soul, firm and s.

SECURITY (SECURE)

Job 31: 24 or said to pure gold, 'You are my s,'

SEED (SEEDS)

Lk 8: 11 of the parable: The s is the word
1Co 3: 6 I planted the s, Apollos watered it,
2Co 9: 10 he who supplies s to the sower
Gal 3: 29 then you are Abraham's s,
1Pe 1: 23 not of perishable s,

SEEDS (SEED)

Jn 12: 24 But if it dies, it produces many s.
Gal 3: 16 Scripture does not say "and to s,"

SEEK (SEEKS SELF-SEEKING)

Dt 4: 29 if from there you s the LORD your
1Ch 28: 9 If you s him, he will be found
2Ch 7: 14 themselves and pray and s my face
Ps 119: 10 I s you with all my heart;
Isa 55: 6 S the LORD while he may be
65: 1 found by those who did not s me.
Mt 6: 33 But s first his kingdom
Lk 19: 10 For the Son of Man came to s
Ro 10: 20 found by those who did not s me,
1Co 7: 27 you married? Do not s a divorce.

SEEKS (SEEK)

Jn 4: 23 the kind of worshipers the Father s.

SEER

1Sa 9: 9 of today used to be called a s.)

SELF-CONTROL (CONTROL)

1Co 7: 5 you because of your lack of s.

SELF-CONTROLLED

Gal 5: 23 faithfulness, gentleness and *s*.
2Pe 1: 6 and to knowledge, *s*; and to *s*,

SELF-CONTROLLED* (CONTROL)

1Th 5: 6 are asleep, but let us be alert and *s*.
     5: 8 let us be *s*, putting on faith and love
1Ti 3: 2 *s*, respectable, hospitable,
Tit 1: 8 who is *s*, upright, holy
     2: 2 worthy of respect, *s*, and sound
     2: 5 to be *s* and pure, to be busy at home
     2: 6 encourage the young men to be *s*.
     2: 12 to live *s*, upright and godly lives
1Pe 1: 13 prepare your minds for action; be *s*;
     4: 7 and *s* so that you can pray.
     5: 8 Be *s* and alert.

SELF-INDULGENCE

Mt 23: 25 inside they are full of greed and *s*.

SELF-SEEKING (SEEK)

1Co 13: 5 it is not *s*, it is not easily angered,

SELFISH*

Ps 119: 36 and not toward *s* gain.
Pr 18: 1 An unfriendly man pursues *s* ends;
Gal 5: 20 fits of rage, *s* ambition, dissensions,
Php 1: 17 preach Christ out of *s* ambition,
     2: 3 Do nothing out of *s* ambition
Jas 3: 14 and *s* ambition in your hearts,
     3: 16 you have envy and *s* ambition,

SEND (SENDING SENT)

Isa 6: 8 *S* me!" He said, "Go and tell this
Mt   9: 38 to *s* out workers into his harvest
Jn 16: 7 but if I go, I will *s* him to you.

SENDING (SEND)

Jn 20: 21 Father has sent me, I am *s* you."

SENSES*

Lk 15: 17 "When he came to his *s*, he said,
1Co 15: 34 Come back to your *s* as you ought,
2Ti 2: 26 and that they will come to their *s*

SENSUAL

Col 2: 23 value in restraining *s* indulgence.

SENT (SEND)

Isa 55: 11 achieve the purpose for which I *s* it.
Mt 10: 40 me receives the one who *s* me.
Jn   4: 34 "is to do the will of him who *s* me
Ro 10: 15 can they preach unless they are *s*?
1Jn 4: 10 but that he loved us and *s* his Son

SEPARATE (SEPARATED SEPARATES)

Mt 19: 6 has joined together, let man not *s*."
Ro   8: 35 Who shall *s* us from the love
1Co 7: 10 wife must not *s* from her husband.
2Co 6: 17 and be *s*, says the Lord.

SEPARATED (SEPARATE)

Isa 59: 2 But your iniquities have *s*

SEPARATES (SEPARATE)

Pr 16: 28 and a gossip *s* close friends.

SERPENT

Ge   3: 1 the *s* was more crafty than any
Rev 12: 9 that ancient *s* called the devil

SERVANT (SERVANTS)

1Sa 3: 10 "Speak, for your *s* is listening."
Mt 20: 26 great among you must be your *s*,
    25: 21 'Well done, good and faithful *s*!
Lk 16: 13 "No *s* can serve two masters.
Php 2: 7 taking the very nature of a *s*,
2Ti 2: 24 And the Lord's *s* must not quarrel;

SERVANTS (SERVANT)

Lk 17: 10 should say, 'We are unworthy *s*;
Jn 15: 15 longer call you *s*, because a servant

SERVE (SERVICE SERVING)

Dt 10: 12 to *s* the LORD your God
Jos 22: 5 and to *s* him with all your heart
    24: 15 this day whom you will *s*,
Mt   4: 10 Lord your God, and *s* him only.' "
     6: 24 "No one can *s* two masters.
    20: 28 but to *s*, and to give his life
Eph 6: 7 *S* wholeheartedly,

SERVICE (SERVE)

1Co 12: 5 There are different kinds of *s*,
Eph 4: 12 God's people for works of *s*,

SERVING (SERVE)

Ro 12: 11 your spiritual fervor, *s* the Lord.
Eph 6: 7 as if you were *s* the Lord, not men,

Col 3: 24 It is the Lord Christ you are *s*.
2Ti 2: 4 No one *s* as a soldier gets involved

SEVEN (SEVENTH)

Ge   7: 2 Take with you *s* of every kind
Jos 6: 4 march around the city *s* times,
1Ki 19: 18 Yet I reserve *s* thousand in Israel—
Pr   6: 16 *s* that are detestable to him:
    24: 16 a righteous man falls *s* times,
Isa 4: 1 In that day *s* women
Da   9: 25 comes, there will be *s* 'sevens,'
Mt 18: 21 Up to *s* times?" Jesus answered,
Lk 11: 26 takes *s* other spirits more wicked
Ro 11: 4 for myself *s* thousand who have not
Rev 1: 4 To the *s* churches in the province
     6: 1 opened the first of the *s* seals.
     8: 2 and to them were given *s* trumpets.
    10: 4 And when the *s* thunders spoke,
    15: 7 to the *s* angels *s* golden bowls filled

SEVENTH (SEVEN)

Ge   2: 2 By the *s* day God had finished
Ex 23: 12 but on the *s* day do not work,

SEXUAL (SEXUALLY)

1Co 6: 13 body is not meant for *s* immorality,
     6: 18 Flee from *s* immorality.
    10: 8 should not commit *s* immorality,
Eph 5: 3 even a hint of *s* immorality,
1Th 4: 3 that you should avoid *s* immorality

SEXUALLY (SEXUAL)

1Co 5: 9 to associate with *s* immoral people
     6: 18 he who sins *s* sins against his own

SHADOW

Ps 23: 4 through the valley of the *s* of death,
    36: 7 find refuge in the *s* of your wings.
Heb 10: 1 The law is only a *s*

SHALLUM

King of Israel (2Ki 15:10-16).

SHAME (ASHAMED)

Ps 34: 5 their faces are never covered with *s*.
Pr 13: 18 discipline comes to poverty and *s*,

Heb 12: 2 endured the cross, scorning its *s*,

SHARE (SHARED)

Ge 21: 10 that slave woman's son will never *s*
Lk   3: 11 "The man with two tunics should *s*
Gal 4: 30 the slave woman's son will never *s*
     6: 6 in the word must *s* all good things
Eph 4: 28 something to *s* with those in need.
1Ti 6: 18 and to be generous and willing to *s*.
Heb 12: 10 that we may *s* in his holiness.
    13: 16 to do good and to *s* with others,

SHARED (SHARE)

Heb 2: 14 he too *s* in their humanity so that

SHARON

SS   2: 1 I am a rose of *S*,

SHARPER*

Heb 4: 12 *S* than any double-edged sword,

SHED (SHEDDING)

Ge   9: 6 by man shall his blood be *s*;
Col 1: 20 through his blood, *s* on the cross.

SHEDDING (SHED)

Heb 9: 22 without the *s* of blood there is no

SHEEP

Ps 100: 3 we are his people, the *s*
   119:176 I have strayed like a lost *s*.
Isa 53: 6 We all, like *s*, have gone astray,
Jer 50: 6 "My people have been lost *s*;
Eze 34: 11 I myself will search for my *s*
Mt   9: 36 helpless, like *s* without a shepherd.
Jn 10: 3 He calls his own *s* by name
    10: 15 and I lay down my life for the *s*.
    10: 27 My *s* listen to my voice; I know
    21: 17 Jesus said, "Feed my *s*.
1Pe 2: 25 For you were like *s* going astray,

SHELTER

Ps 61: 4 take refuge in the *s* of your wings.
    91: 1 in the *s* of the Most High

SHEM

Son of Noah (Ge 5:32; 6:10). Blessed (Ge 9:26). Descendants (Ge 10:21-31; 11:10-32).

SHEPHERD (SHEPHERDS)

Ps 23: 1 LORD is my *s*, I shall not be in want.
Isa 40: 11 He tends his flock like a *s*:
Jer 31: 10 will watch over his flock like a *s*.'

Eze 34: 12 As a *s* looks after his scattered

Zec 11: 17 "Woe to the worthless *s*,

Mt 9: 36 and helpless, like sheep without a *s*.

Jn 10: 11 The good *s* lays down his life

10: 16 there shall be one flock and one *s*.

1Pe 5: 4 And when the Chief *S* appears,

SHEPHERDS (SHEPHERD)

Jer 23: 1 "Woe to the *s* who are destroying

Lk 2: 8 there were *s* living out in the fields

Ac 20: 28 Be *s* of the church of God,

1Pe 5: 2 Be *s* of God's flock that is

SHIELD

Ps 28: 7 LORD is my strength and my *s*;

Eph 6: 16 to all this, take up the *s* of faith,

SHINE (SHONE)

Ps 4: 6 Let the light of your face *s* upon us,

80: 1 between the cherubim, *s* forth

Isa 60: 1 "Arise, *s*, for your light has come,

Da 12: 3 are wise will *s* like the brightness

Mt 5: 16 let your light *s* before men,

13: 43 the righteous will *s* like the sun

2Co 4: 6 made his light *s* in our hearts

Eph 5: 14 and Christ will *s* on you."

SHIPWRECKED*

2Co 11: 25 I was stoned, three times I was *s*,

1Ti 1: 19 and so have *s* their faith.

SHONE (SHINE)

Mt 17: 2 His face *s* like the sun,

Lk 2: 9 glory of the Lord *s* around them,

Rev 21: 11 It *s* with the glory of God,

SHORT

Isa 59: 1 of the LORD is not too *s* to save,

Ro 3: 23 and fall *s* of the glory of God,

SHOULDERS

Isa 9: 6 and the government will be on his *s*

Lk 15: 5 he joyfully puts it on his *s*

SHOWED

1Jn 4: 9 This is how God *s* his love

SHREWD

Mt 10: 16 Therefore be as *s* as snakes and

SHUN*

Job 28: 28 and to *s* evil is understanding.' "

Pr 3: 7 fear the LORD and *s* evil.

SICK

Pr 13: 12 Hope deferred makes the heart *s*,

Mt 9: 12 who need a doctor, but the *s*.

25: 36 I was *s* and you looked after me,

Jas 5: 14 of you *s*? He should call the elders

SICKLE

Joel 3: 13 Swing the *s*,

SIDE

Ps 91: 7 A thousand may fall at your *s*,

124: 1 If the LORD had not been on our *s*

2Ti 4: 17 But the Lord stood at my *s*

SIGHT

Ps 90: 4 For a thousand years in your *s*

116: 15 Precious in the *s* of the LORD

2Co 5: 7 We live by faith, not by *s*.

1Pe 3: 4 which is of great worth in God's *s*.

SIGN (SIGNS)

Isa 7: 14 the Lord himself will give you a *s*:

SIGNS (SIGN)

Mk 16: 17 these *s* will accompany those who

Jn 20: 30 Jesus did many other miraculous *s*

SILENT

Pr 17: 28 a fool is thought wise if he keeps *s*,

Isa 53: 7 as a sheep before her shearers is *s*,

Hab 2: 20 let all the earth be *s* before him."

1Co 14: 34 women should remain *s*

1Ti 2: 12 over a man; she must be *s*.

SILVER

Pr 25: 11 is like apples of gold in settings of *s*.

Hag 2: 8 'The *s* is mine and the gold is mine,'

1Co 3: 12 *s*, costly stones, wood, hay or straw

SIMON

1. See PETER.

2. Apostle, called the Zealot (Mt 10:4; Mk 3:18; Lk 6:15; Ac 1:13).

3. Samaritan sorcerer (Ac 8:9-24).

SIN (SINFUL SINNED SINNER SINNERS SINNING SINS)

Nu 5: 7 and must confess the *s* he has

32: 23 be sure that your *s* will find you

Dt 24: 16 each is to die for his own *s*.

1Ki 8: 46 for there is no one who does not *s*

2Ch 7: 14 and will forgive their *s* and will heal

Ps 4: 4 In your anger do not *s*;

32: 2 whose *s* the LORD does not count

32: 5 Then I acknowledged my *s* to you

51: 2 and cleanse me from my *s*.

66: 18 If I had cherished *s* in my heart,

119: 11 that I might not *s* against you.

119:133 let no *s* rule over me.

Isa 6: 7 is taken away and your *s* atoned

Mic 7: 18 who pardons *s* and forgives

Mt 18: 6 little ones who believe in me to *s*

Jn 1: 29 who takes away the *s* of the world!

8: 34 everyone who sins is a slave to *s*.

Ro 5: 12 as *s* entered the world

5: 20 where *s* increased, grace increased

6: 11 count yourselves dead to *s*

6: 23 For the wages of *s* is death,

14: 23 that does not come from faith is *s*.

2Co 5: 21 God made him who had no *s* to be *s*

Gal 6: 1 if someone is caught in a *s*,

Heb 9: 26 to do away with *s* by the sacrifice

11: 25 the pleasures of *s* for a short time.

12: 1 and the *s* that so easily entangles,

1Pe 2: 22 "He committed no *s*,

1Jn 1: 8 If we claim to be without *s*,

3: 4 in fact, *s* is lawlessness.

3: 5 And in him is no *s*.

3: 9 born of God will continue to *s*,

5: 18 born of God does not continue to *s*;

SINCERE

Ro 12: 9 Love must be *s*.

Heb 10: 22 near to God with a *s* heart

SINFUL (SIN)

Ps 51: 5 Surely I was *s* at birth

51: 5 *s* from the time my mother

Ro 7: 5 we were controlled by the *s* nature,

8: 4 not live according to the *s* nature

8: 9 are controlled not by the *s* nature

Gal 5: 19 The acts of the *s* nature are obvious

5: 24 Jesus have crucified the *s* nature

1Pe 2: 11 abstain from *s* desires, which war

SING (SANG SINGING SONG SONGS)

Ps 30: 4 *S* to the LORD, you saints of his;

47: 6 *S* praises to God, *s* praises;

59: 16 But I will *s* of your strength,

89: 1 I will *s* of the LORD's great love

101: 1 I will *s* of your love and justice;

Eph 5: 19 *S* and make music in your heart

SINGING (SING)

Ps 63: 5 with *s* lips my mouth will praise

Ac 16: 25 Silas were praying and *s* hymns

SINNED (SIN)

2Sa 12: 13 "I have *s* against the LORD."

Job 1: 5 "Perhaps my children have *s*

Ps 51: 4 Against you, you only, have I *s*

Da 9: 5 we have *s* and done wrong.

Mic 7: 9 Because I have *s* against him,

Lk 15: 18 I have *s* against heaven

Ro 3: 23 for all have *s* and fall short

1Jn 1: 10 claim we have not *s*, we make him

SINNER (SIN)

Ecc 9: 18 but one *s* destroys much good.

Lk 15: 7 in heaven over one *s* who repents

18: 13 'God, have mercy on me, a *s*.'

1Co 14: 24 convinced by all that he is a *s*

Jas 5: 20 Whoever turns a *s* from the error

1Pe 4: 18 become of the ungodly and the *s*?"

SINNERS (SIN)

Ps 1: 1 or stand in the way of *s*

Pr 23: 17 Do not let your heart envy *s*,

Mt 9: 13 come to call the righteous, but *s*."

Ro 5: 8 While we were still *s*, Christ died

1Ti 1: 15 came into the world to save *s*—

SINNING (SIN)

Ex 20: 20 be with you to keep you from *s*."

1Co 15: 34 stop *s*; for there are some who are

Heb 10: 26 If we deliberately keep on *s*

1Jn 3: 6 No one who lives in him keeps on *s*

3: 9 go on *s*, because he has been born

SINS (SIN)

2Ki 14: 6 each is to die for his own *s*."

Ezr 9: 6 our *s* are higher than our heads

Ps 19: 13 your servant also from willful *s*;

32: 1 whose *s* are covered.

103: 3 who forgives all your *s*

130: 3 O LORD, kept a record of *s*,

Pr 28: 13 who conceals his *s* does not

Isa 1: 18 "Though your *s* are like scarlet,

43: 25 and remembers your *s* no more.

59: 2 your *s* have hidden his face

Eze 18: 4 soul who *s* is the one who will die.

Mt 1: 21 he will save his people from their *s*

18: 15 "If your brother *s* against you,

Lk 11: 4 Forgive us our *s*,

17: 3 "If your brother *s*, rebuke him,

Ac 22: 16 be baptized and wash your *s* away,

1Co 15: 3 died for our *s* according

Eph 2: 1 dead in your transgressions and *s*,

Col 2: 13 us all our *s*, having canceled

Heb 1: 3 he had provided purification for *s*,

7: 27 He sacrificed for their *s* once for all

8: 12 and will remember their *s* no more

10: 12 for all time one sacrifice for *s*,

Jas 4: 17 ought to do and doesn't do it,,

5: 16 Therefore confess your *s*

5: 20 and cover over a multitude of *s*.

1Pe 2: 24 He himself bore our *s* in his body

3: 18 For Christ died for *s* once for all,

1Jn 1: 9 If we confess our *s*, he is faithful

Rev 1: 5 has freed us from our *s* by his blood

SITS

Ps 99: 1 *s* enthroned between the cherubim,

Isa 40: 22 He *s* enthroned above the circle

Mt 19: 28 of Man *s* on his glorious throne,

Rev 4: 9 thanks to him who *s* on the throne

SKIN

Job 19: 20 with only the *s* of my teeth.

19: 26 And after my *s* has been destroyed,

Jer 13: 23 Can the Ethiopian change his *s*

SLAIN (SLAY)

Rev 5: 12 "Worthy is the Lamb, who was *s*,

SLANDER
(SLANDERED SLANDERERS)

Lev 19: 16 "'Do not go about spreading *s*

1Ti 5: 14 the enemy no opportunity for *s*.

Tit 3: 2 to *s* no one, to be peaceable

SLANDERED (SLANDER)

1Co 4: 13 when we are *s*, we answer kindly.

SLANDERERS (SLANDER)

Ro 1: 30 They are gossips, *s*, God-haters,

1Co 6: 10 nor the greedy nor drunkards nor *s*

Tit 2: 3 not to be *s* or addicted

SLAUGHTER

Isa 53: 7 he was led like a lamb to the *s*,

SLAVE (SLAVERY SLAVES)

Ge 21: 10 "Get rid of that *s* woman

Mt 20: 27 wants to be first must be your *s*—

Jn 8: 34 everyone who sins is a *s* to sin.

1Co 12: 13 whether Jews or Greeks, *s* or free

Gal 3: 28 *s* nor free, male nor female,

4: 30 Get rid of the *s* woman and her son

2Pe 2: 19 a man is a *s* to whatever has

SLAVERY (SLAVE)

Ro 6: 19 parts of your body in *s* to impurity

Gal 4: 3 were in *s* under the basic principles

SLAVES (SLAVE)

Ro 6: 6 that we should no longer be *s* to sin

6: 22 and have become *s* to God,

SLAY (SLAIN)

Job 13: 15 Though he *s* me, yet will I hope

SLEEP (SLEEPING)

Ps 121: 4 will neither slumber nor *s*.

1Co 15: 51 We will not all *s*, but we will all be

SLEEPING (SLEEP)

Mk 13: 36 suddenly, do not let him find you *s*.

SLOW

Ex 34: 6 and gracious God, *s* to anger,

Jas 1: 19 *s* to speak and *s* to become angry,

2Pe 3: 9 The Lord is not *s* in keeping his

SLUGGARD

Pr 6: 6 Go to the ant, you *s*;

20: 4 A *s* does not plow in season;

SLUMBER

Ps 121: 3 he who watches over you will not *s*;

Pr 6: 10 A little sleep, a little *s*,

Ro 13: 11 for you to wake up from your *s*,

SNAKE (SNAKES)

Nu 21: 8 "Make a *s* and put it up on a pole;

Pr 23: 32 In the end it bites like a *s*

Jn 3: 14 Moses lifted up the *s* in the desert,

SNAKES (SNAKE)

Mt 10: 16 as shrewd as *s* and as innocent

Mk 16: 18 they will pick up *s* with their hands;

SNATCH

Jn 10: 28 no one can *s* them out of my hand.

Jude : 23 *s* others from the fire and save

SNOW

Ps 51: 7 and I will be whiter than *s*.

SOAR

Isa 40: 31 They will *s* on wings like eagles;

SODOM

Ge 19: 24 rained down burning sulfur on *S*

Ro 9: 29 we would have become like *S*,

SOIL

Ge 4: 2 kept flocks, and Cain worked the *s*.

Mt 13: 23 on good *s* is the man who hears

SOLDIER

1Co 9: 7 as a *s* at his own expense?

2Ti 2: 3 with us like a good *s* of Christ Jesus

SOLE

Dt 28: 65 place for the *s* of your foot.

Isa 1: 6 From the *s* of your foot to the top

SOLID

2Ti 2: 19 God's *s* foundation stands firm,

Heb 5: 12 You need milk, not *s* food!

SOLOMON

Son of David by Bathsheba; king of Judah (2Sa 12:24; 1Ch 3:5, 10). Appointed king by David (1Ki 1); adversaries Adonijah, Joab, Shimei killed by Benaiah (1Ki 2). Asked for wisdom (1Ki 3; 2Ch 1). Judged between two prostitutes (1Ki 3:16-28). Built temple (1Ki 5-7; 2Ch 2-5); prayer of dedication (1Ki 8; 2Ch 6). Visited by Queen of Sheba (1Ki 10; 2Ch 9). Wives turned his heart from God (1Ki 11:1-13). Jeroboam rebelled against (1Ki 11:26-40). Death (1Ki 11:41-43; 2Ch 9:29-31).

Proverbs of (1Ki 4:32; Pr 1:1; 10:1; 25:1); psalms of (Ps 72; 127); song of (SS 1:1).

SON (SONS)

Ge 22: 2 "Take your *s*, your only *s*, Isaac,

Ex 11: 5 Every firstborn *s* in Egypt will die,

Dt 21: 18 rebellious *s* who does not obey his

Ps 2: 7 He said to me, "You are my *S*;

2: 12 Kiss the *S*, lest he be angry

Pr 10: 1 A wise *s* brings joy to his father;

13: 24 He who spares the rod hates his *s*,

29: 17 Discipline your *s*, and he will give

Isa 7: 14 with child and will give birth to a *s*,

Hos 11: 1 and out of Egypt I called my *s*.

Mt 2: 15 "Out of Egypt I called my *s*."

3: 17 "This is my *S*, whom I love;

11: 27 one knows the *S* except the Father,

16: 16 "You are the Christ, the *S*

17: 5 "This is my *S*, whom I love;

20: 18 and the *S* of Man will be betrayed

24: 30 They will see the *S* of Man coming

24: 44 the *S* of Man will come at an hour

27: 54 "Surely he was the *S* of God!"

28: 19 and of the *S* and of the Holy Spirit,

Mk 10: 45 even the *S* of Man did not come

14: 62 you will see the *S* of Man sitting

Lk 9: 58 but the *S* of Man has no place

18: 8 when the *S* of Man comes,

19: 10 For the *S* of Man came to seek

Jn 3: 14 so the *S* of Man must be lifted up,

3: 16 that he gave his one and only *S*,

17: 1 Glorify your *S*, that your *S* may

Ro 8: 29 conformed to the likeness of his *S*,

8: 32 He who did not spare his own *S*,

1Co 15: 28 then the *S* himself will be made

Gal 4: 30 rid of the slave woman and her *s*,

1Th 1: 10 and to wait for his *S* from heaven,

Heb 1: 2 days he has spoken to us by his *S*,

10: 29 punished who has trampled the *S*

1Jn 1: 7 his *S*, purifies us from all sin.

4: 9 only *S* into the world that we might

5: 5 he who believes that Jesus is the *S*

5: 11 eternal life, and this life is in his *S*.

SONG (SING)

Ps 40: 3 He put a new *s* in my mouth;

96: 1 Sing to the LORD a new *s*;

149: 1 Sing to the LORD a new *s*,

Isa 49: 13 burst into *s*, O mountains!

55: 12 will burst into *s* before you,

Rev 5: 9 And they sang a new *s*:

15: 3 and sang the *s* of Moses the servant

SONGS (SING)

Job 35: 10 who gives *s* in the night,
Ps 100: 2 come before him with joyful *s*.
Eph 5: 19 with psalms, hymns and spiritual *s*.
Jas 5: 13 Is anyone happy? Let him sing *s*

SONS (SON)

Joel 2: 28 Your *s* and daughters will prophesy
Jn 12: 36 so that you may become *s* of light."
Ro 8: 14 by the Spirit of God are *s* of God.
2Co 6: 18 and you will be my *s* and daughters
Gal 4: 5 we might receive the full rights of *s*.
Heb 12: 7 discipline; God is treating you as *s*.

SORROW (SORROWS)

Jer 31: 12 and they will *s* no more,
Ro 9: 2 I have great *s* and unceasing
2Co 7: 10 Godly *s* brings repentance that

SORROWS (SORROW)

Isa 53: 3 a man of *s*, and familiar

SOUL (SOULS)

Dt 6: 5 with all your *s* and with all your
10: 12 all your heart and with all your *s*,
Jos 22: 5 with all your heart and all your *s*."
Ps 23: 3 he restores my *s*.
42: 1 so my *s* pants for you, O God.
42: 11 Why are you downcast, O my *s*?
103: 1 Praise the LORD, O my *s*;
Pr 13: 19 A longing fulfilled is sweet to the *s*,
Isa 55: 2 your *s* will delight in the richest
Mt 10: 28 kill the body but cannot kill the *s*.
16: 26 yet forfeits his *s*? Or what can
22: 37 with all your *s* and with all your
Heb 4: 12 even to dividing *s* and spirit,

SOULS (SOUL)

Pr 11: 30 and he who wins *s* is wise.
Jer 6: 16 and you will find rest for your *s*.
Mt 11: 29 and you will find rest for your *s*.

SOUND

1Co 14: 8 if the trumpet does not *s* a clear call
15: 52 the trumpet will *s*, the dead will

2Ti 4: 3 men will not put up with *s* doctrine.

SOVEREIGN

Da 4: 25 that the Most High is *s*

SOW (SOWS)

Job 4: 8 and those who *s* trouble reap it.
Mt 6: 26 they do not *s* or reap or store away
2Pe 2: 22 and, "A *s* that is washed goes back

SOWS (SOW)

Pr 11: 18 he who *s* righteousness reaps a sure
22: 8 He who *s* wickedness reaps trouble
2Co 9: 6 Whoever *s* sparingly will
Gal 6: 7 A man reaps what he *s*.

SPARE (SPARES)

Ro 8: 32 He who did not *s* his own Son,
11: 21 natural branches, he will not *s* you

SPARES (SPARE)

Pr 13: 24 He who *s* the rod hates his son,

SPEARS

Isa 2: 4 and their *s* into pruning hooks.
Joel 3: 10 and your pruning hooks into *s*.
Mic 4: 3 and their *s* into pruning hooks.

SPECTACLE

1Co 4: 9 We have been made a *s*
Col 2: 15 he made a public *s* of them,

SPIN

Mt 6: 28 They do not labor or *s*.

**SPIRIT (SPIRIT'S
SPIRITS SPIRITUAL SPIRITUALLY)**

Ge 1: 2 and the *S* of God was hovering
6: 3 "My *S* will not contend
2Ki 2: 9 inherit a double portion of your *s*,"
Job 33: 4 The *S* of God has made me;
Ps 31: 5 Into your hands I commit my *s*;
51: 10 and renew a steadfast *s* within me.
51: 11 or take your Holy *S* from me.
51: 17 sacrifices of God are a broken *s*;
139: 7 Where can I go from your *S*?
Isa 57: 15 him who is contrite and lowly in *s*,
63: 10 and grieved his Holy *S*.
Eze 11: 19 an undivided heart and put a new *s*
36: 26 you a new heart and put a new *s*

Joel 2: 28 I will pour out my *S* on all people.
Zec 4: 6 but by my *S*,' says the LORD
Mt 1: 18 to be with child through the Holy *S*
3: 11 will baptize you with the Holy *S*
3: 16 he saw the *S* of God descending
4: 1 led by the *S* into the desert
5: 3 saying: "Blessed are the poor in *s*,
26: 41 *s* is willing, but the body is weak."
28: 19 and of the Son and of the Holy *S*,
Lk 1: 80 child grew and became strong in *s*;
11: 13 Father in heaven give the Holy *S*
Jn 4: 24 God is *s*, and his worshipers must
7: 39 Up to that time the *S* had not been
14: 26 But the Counselor, the Holy *S*,
16: 13 But when he, the *S* of truth, comes,
20: 22 and said, "Receive the Holy *S*.
Ac 1: 5 will be baptized with the Holy *S*."
2: 4 of them were filled with the Holy *S*
2: 38 will receive the gift of the Holy *S*.
6: 3 who are known to be full of the *S*
19: 2 "Did you receive the Holy *S*
Ro 8: 9 And if anyone does not have the *S*
8: 26 the *S* helps us in our weakness.
1Co 2: 10 God has revealed it to us by his *S*.
2: 14 man without the *S* does not accept
6: 19 body is a temple of the Holy *S*,
12: 13 baptized by one *S* into one body—
2Co 3: 6 the letter kills, but the *S* gives life.
5: 5 and has given us the *S* as a deposit,
Gal 5: 16 by the *S*, and you will not gratify
5: 22 But the fruit of the *S* is love, joy,
5: 25 let us keep in step with the *S*.
Eph 1: 13 with a seal, the promised Holy *S*,
4: 30 do not grieve the Holy *S* of God,
5: 18 Instead, be filled with the *S*.
6: 17 of salvation and the sword of the *S*,
2Th 2: 13 the sanctifying work of the *S*
Heb 4: 12 even to dividing soul and *s*,

1Pe 3: 4 beauty of a gentle and quiet *s*,
2Pe 1: 21 carried along by the Holy *S*.
1Jn 4: 1 Dear friends, do not believe every *s*

SPIRIT'S (SPIRIT)

1Th 5: 19 not put out the *S* fire; do not treat

SPIRITS (SPIRIT)

1Co 12: 10 to another distinguishing between *s*,
14: 32 The *s* of prophets are subject
1Jn 4: 1 test the *s* to see whether they are

SPIRITUAL (SPIRIT)

Ro 12: 1 this is your *s* act of worship.
12: 11 but keep your *s* fervor, serving
1Co 2: 13 expressing *s* truths in *s* words.
3: 1 I could not address you as *s* but
12: 1 Now about *s* gifts, brothers,
14: 1 of love and eagerly desire *s* gifts,
15: 44 a natural body, it is raised a *s* body.
Gal 6: 1 you who are *s* should restore him
Eph 1: 3 with every *s* blessing in Christ.
5: 19 with psalms, hymns and *s* songs.
6: 12 and against the *s* forces of evil
1Pe 2: 2 newborn babies, crave pure *s* milk,
2: 5 are being built into a *s* house

SPIRITUALLY (SPIRIT)

1Co 2: 14 because they are *s* discerned.

SPLENDOR

1Ch 16: 29 the LORD in the *s* of his holiness.
29: 11 the glory and the majesty and the *s*,
Job 37: 22 of the north he comes in golden *s*;
Ps 29: 2 in the *s* of his holiness.
45: 3 clothe yourself with *s* and majesty.
96: 6 *S* and majesty are before him;
96: 9 in the *s* of his holiness;
104: 1 you are clothed with *s* and majesty.
145: 5 of the glorious *s* of your majesty,
Isa 61: 3 the LORD for the display of his *s*.
63: 1 Who is this, robed in *s*,
Lk 9: 31 appeared in glorious *s*, talking
2Th 2: 8 and destroy by the *s* of his coming.

SPOIL

Ps 119:162 like one who finds great *s*.

SPOTLESS

2Pe 3: 14 make every effort to be found s,

SPREAD (SPREADING)

Ac 12: 24 of God continued to increase and s.
19: 20 the word of the Lord s widely

SPREADING (SPREAD)

1Th 3: 2 God's fellow worker in s the gospel

SPRING

Jer 2: 13 the s of living water,
Jn 4: 14 in him a s of water welling up
Jas 3: 12 can a salt s produce fresh water.

SPUR*

Heb 10: 24 how we may s one another

SPURNS*

Pr 15: 5 A fool s his father's discipline,

STAFF

Ps 23: 4 your rod and your s,

STAKES

Isa 54: 2 strengthen your s.

STAND (STANDING STANDS)

Ex 14: 13 S firm and you will see
2Ch 20: 17 s firm and see the deliverance
Ps 1: 5 Therefore the wicked will not s
40: 2 and gave me a firm place to s.
119:120 I s in awe of your laws.
Eze 22: 30 s before me in the gap on behalf
Zec 14: 4 On that day his feet will s
Mt 12: 25 divided against itself will not s.
Ro 14: 10 we will all s before God's judgment
1Co 10: 13 out so that you can s up under it.
15: 58 Therefore, my dear brothers, s firm
Eph 6: 14 S firm then, with the belt
2Th 2: 15 s firm and hold to the teachings we
Jas 5: 8 You too, be patient and s firm,
Rev 3: 20 Here I am! I s at the door

STANDING (STAND)

Ex 3: 5 where you are s is holy ground."
Jos 5: 15 the place where you are s is holy."
1Pe 5: 9 Resist him, s firm in the faith,

STANDS (STAND)

Ps 89: 2 that your love s firm forever,
119: 89 it s firm in the heavens.
Mt 10: 22 but he who s firm to the end will be

2Ti 2: 19 God's solid foundation s firm,
1Pe 1: 25 but the word of the Lord s forever

STAR (STARS)

Nu 24: 17 A s will come out of Jacob;
Rev 22: 16 and the bright Morning S."

STARS (STAR)

Da 12: 3 like the s for ever and ever.
Php 2: 15 in which you shine like s

STATURE

Lk 2: 52 And Jesus grew in wisdom and s,

STEADFAST

Ps 51: 10 and renew a s spirit within me.
Isa 26: 3 him whose mind is s,
1Pe 5: 10 and make you strong, firm and s.

STEAL

Ex 20: 15 "You shall not s.
Mt 19: 18 do not s, do not give false
Eph 4: 28 has been stealing must s no longer,

STEP (STEPS)

Gal 5: 25 let us keep in s with the Spirit.

STEPS (STEP)

Pr 16: 9 but the LORD determines his s.
Jer 10: 23 it is not for man to direct his s.
1Pe 2: 21 that you should follow in his s.

STICKS

Pr 18: 24 there is a friend who s closer

STIFF-NECKED

Ex 34: 9 Although this is a s people,

STILL

Ps 46: 10 "Be s, and know that I am God;
Zec 2: 13 Be s before the LORD, all mankind

STIRS

Pr 6: 19 and a man who s up dissension
10: 12 Hatred s up dissension,
15: 1 but a harsh word s up anger.
15: 18 hot-tempered man s up dissension,
16: 28 A perverse man s up dissension,
28: 25 A greedy man s up dissension,
29: 22 An angry man s up dissension,

STONE (CAPSTONE CORNERSTONE MILLSTONE)

1Sa 17: 50 the Philistine with a sling and a s;
Isa 8: 14 a s that causes men to stumble

Eze 11: 19 remove from them their heart of s
Mk 16: 3 "Who will roll the s away
Lk 4: 3 tell this s to become bread."
Jn 8: 7 the first to throw a s at her."
2Co 3: 3 not on tablets of s but on tablets

STOOP

2Sa 22: 36 you s down to make me great.

STORE

Pr 10: 14 Wise men s up knowledge,
Mt 6: 19 not s up for yourselves treasures

STOREHOUSE (HOUSE)

Mal 3: 10 Bring the whole tithe into the s,

STRAIGHT

Pr 3: 6 and he will make your paths s.
4: 25 Let your eyes look s ahead,
15: 21 of understanding keeps a s course.
Jn 1: 23 'Make s the way for the Lord.' "

STRAIN

Mt 23: 24 You s out a gnat but swallow

STRANGER (STRANGERS)

Mt 25: 35 I was a s and you invited me in,
Jn 10: 5 But they will never follow a s;

STRANGERS (STRANGER)

1Pe 2: 11 as aliens and s in the world,

STREAMS

Ps 1: 3 He is like a tree planted by s
46: 4 is a river whose s make glad
Ecc 1: 7 All s flow into the sea,
Jn 7: 38 s of living water will flow

STRENGTH (STRONG)

Ex 15: 2 The LORD is my s and my song;
Dt 6: 5 all your soul and with all your s.
2Sa 22: 33 It is God who arms me with s
Ne 8: 10 for the joy of the LORD is your s."
Ps 28: 7 The LORD is my s and my shield;
46: 1 God is our refuge and s,
96: 7 ascribe to the LORD glory and s.
118: 14 The LORD is my s and my song;
147: 10 not in the s of the horse,
Isa 40: 31 will renew their s.
Mk 12: 30 all your mind and with all your s.'
1Co 1: 25 of God is stronger than man's s.
Php 4: 13 through him who gives me s.
1Pe 4: 11 it with the s God provides,

STRENGTHEN (STRONG)

2Ch 16: 9 to s those whose hearts are fully
Ps 119: 28 s me according to your word.
Isa 35: 3 S the feeble hands,
41: 10 I will s you and help you;
Eph 3: 16 of his glorious riches he may s you
2Th 2: 17 and s you in every good deed
Heb 12: 12 s your feeble arms and weak knees.

STRENGTHENING (STRONG)

1Co 14: 26 done for the s of the church.

STRIFE

Pr 20: 3 It is to a man's honor to avoid s,
22: 10 out the mocker, and out goes s;

STRIKE (STRIKES)

Ge 3: 15 and you will s his heel."
Zec 13: 7 "S the shepherd,
Mt 26: 31 "'I will s the shepherd,

STRIKES (STRIKE)

Mt 5: 39 If someone s you on the right

STRONG (STRENGTH STRENGTHEN STRENGTHENING)

Dt 31: 6 Be s and courageous.
1Ki 2: 2 "So be s, show yourself a man,
Pr 18: 10 The name of the LORD is a s tower
31: 17 her arms are s for her tasks.
SS 8: 6 for love is as s as death,
Lk 2: 40 And the child grew and became s;
Ro 15: 1 We who are s ought to bear
1Co 1: 27 things of the world to shame the s.
16: 13 in the faith; be men of courage; be s
2Co 12: 10 For when I am weak, then I am s.
Eph 6: 10 be s in the Lord and in his mighty

STRUGGLE

Ro 15: 30 me in my s by praying to God
Eph 6: 12 For our s is not against flesh
Heb 12: 4 In your s against sin, you have not

STUDY

Ezr 7: 10 Ezra had devoted himself to the s
Ecc 12: 12 and much s wearies the body.
Jn 5: 39 You diligently s the Scriptures

STUMBLE (STUMBLING)

Ps 37: 24 though he s, he will not fall,
119:165 and nothing can make them s.
Isa 8: 14 a stone that causes men to s

Jer 31: 9 a level path where they will not s,

Eze 7: 19 for it has made them s into sin.

1Co 10: 32 Do not cause anyone to s,

1Pe 2: 8 and, "A stone that causes men to s

STUMBLING (STUMBLE)

Ro 14: 13 up your mind not to put any s block

1Co 8: 9 freedom does not become a s block

2Co 6: 3 We put no s block in anyone's path,

SUBDUE

Ge 1: 28 in number; fill the earth and s it.

SUBJECT (SUBJECTED)

1Co 14: 32 of prophets are s to the control

15: 28 then the Son himself will be made s

Tit 2: 5 and to be s to their husbands,

2: 9 slaves to be s to their masters

3: 1 Remind the people to be s to rulers

SUBJECTED (SUBJECT)

Ro 8: 20 For the creation was s

SUBMISSION (SUBMIT)

1Co 14: 34 but must be in s, as the Law says.

1Ti 2: 11 learn in quietness and full s.

SUBMISSIVE (SUBMIT)

Jas 3: 17 then peace-loving, considerate, s,

1Pe 3: 1 in the same way be s

5: 5 in the same way be s

SUBMIT (SUBMISSION SUBMISSIVE SUBMITS)

Ro 13: 1 Everyone must s himself

13: 5 necessary to s to the authorities,

1Co 16: 16 to s to such as these

Eph 5: 21 S to one another out of reverence

Col 3: 18 Wives, s to your husbands,

Heb 12: 9 How much more should we s

13: 17 Obey your leaders and s

Jas 4: 7 S yourselves, then, to God.

1Pe 2: 18 s yourselves to your masters

SUBMITS* (SUBMIT)

Eph 5: 24 Now as the church s to Christ,

SUCCESSFUL

Jos 1: 7 that you may be s wherever you go.

2Ki 18: 7 he was s in whatever he undertook.

2Ch 20: 20 in his prophets and you will be s."

SUFFER (SUFFERED SUFFERING SUFFERINGS SUFFERS)

Isa 53: 10 to crush him and cause him to s,

Mk 8: 31 the Son of Man must s many things

Lk 24: 26 the Christ have to s these things

24: 46 The Christ will s and rise

Php 1: 29 to s for him, since you are going

1Pe 4: 16 However, if you s as a Christian,

SUFFERED (SUFFER)

Heb 2: 9 and honor because he s death,

2: 18 Because he himself s

1Pe 2: 21 Christ s for you, leaving you

SUFFERING (SUFFER)

Isa 53: 3 of sorrows, and familiar with s.

Ac 5: 41 worthy of s disgrace for the Name.

2Ti 1: 8 But join with me in s for the gospel,

Heb 2: 10 of their salvation perfect through s.

SUFFERINGS (SUFFER)

Ro 8: 17 share in his s in order that we may

8: 18 that our present s are not worth

2Co 1: 5 as the s of Christ flow

Php 3: 10 the fellowship of sharing in his s,

SUFFERS (SUFFER)

Pr 13: 20 but a companion of fools s harm.

1Co 12: 26 If one part s, every part s with it;

SUFFICIENT

2Co 12: 9 said to me, "My grace is s for you,

SUITABLE

Ge 2: 18 I will make a helper s for him."

SUN

Ecc 1: 9 there is nothing new under the s.

Mal 4: 2 the s of righteousness will rise

Mt 5: 45 He causes his s to rise on the evil

17: 2 His face shone like the s,

Rev 1: 16 His face was like the s shining

21: 23 The city does not need the s

SUPERIOR

Heb 1: 4 he became as much s to the angels

8: 6 ministry Jesus has received is as s

SUPERVISION

Gal 3: 25 longer under the s of the law.

SUPREMACY* (SUPREME)

Col 1: 18 in everything he might have the s.

SUPREME (SUPREMACY)

Pr 4: 7 Wisdom is s; therefore get wisdom.

SURE

Nu 32: 23 you may be s that your sin will find

Dt 6: 17 Be s to keep the commands

14: 22 Be s to set aside a tenth

Isa 28: 16 cornerstone for a s foundation;

Heb 11: 1 faith is being s of what we hope for

2Pe 1: 10 to make your calling and election s.

SURPASS* (SURPASSES SURPASSING)

Pr 31: 29 but you s them all."

SURPASSES (SURPASS)

Mt 5: 20 unless your righteousness s that

Eph 3: 19 to know this love that s knowledge

SURPASSING* (SURPASS)

Ps 150: 2 praise him for his s greatness.

2Co 3: 10 in comparison with the s glory.

9: 14 of the s grace God has given you.

Php 3: 8 the s greatness of knowing Christ

SURROUNDED

Heb 12: 1 since we are s by such a great cloud

SUSPENDS*

Job 26: 7 he s the earth over nothing.

SUSTAINING* (SUSTAINS)

Heb 1: 3 s all things by his powerful word.

SUSTAINS (SUSTAINING)

Ps 18: 35 and your right hand s me;

146: 9 and s the fatherless and the widow,

147: 6 The LORD s the humble

Isa 50: 4 to know the word that s the weary.

SWALLOWED

1Co 15: 54 "Death has been s up in victory."

2Co 5: 4 so that what is mortal may be s up

SWEAR

Mt 5: 34 Do not s at all: either by heaven,

SWORD (SWORDS)

Ps 45: 3 Gird your s upon your side,

Pr 12: 18 Reckless words pierce like a s,

Mt 10: 34 come to bring peace, but a s.

26: 52 all who draw the s will die by the s.

Lk 2: 35 a s will pierce your own soul too."

Ro 13: 4 for he does not bear the s

Eph 6: 17 of salvation and the s of the Spirit,

Heb 4: 12 Sharper than any double-edged s,

Rev 1: 16 came a sharp double-edged s.

SWORDS (SWORD)

Isa 2: 4 They will beat their s

Joel 3: 10 Beat your plowshares into s

SYMPATHETIC*

1Pe 3: 8 in harmony with one another; be s,

SYNAGOGUE

Lk 4: 16 the Sabbath day he went into the s,

Ac 17: 2 custom was, Paul went into the s,

～ T

TABERNACLE

Ex 40: 34 the glory of the LORD filled the t.

TABLE (TABLES)

Ps 23: 5 You prepare a t before me

TABLES (TABLE)

Ac 6: 2 word of God in order to wait on t.

TABLET (TABLETS)

Pr 3: 3 write them on the t of your heart.

7: 3 write them on the t of your heart.

TABLETS (TABLET)

Ex 31: 18 he gave him the two t

Dt 10: 5 and put the t in the ark I had made,

2Co 3: 3 not on t of stone but on t

TAKE (TAKEN TAKES TAKING TOOK)

Dt 12: 32 do not add to it or t away from it.

31: 26 "T this Book of the Law

Job 23: 10 But he knows the way that I t;

Ps 49: 17 for he will t nothing with him

51: 11 or t your Holy Spirit from me.

Mt 10: 38 anyone who does not t his cross

11: 29 T my yoke upon you and learn

16: 24 deny himself and t up his cross

TAKEN (TAKE)

Lev 6: 4 must return what he has stolen or t

Isa 6: 7 your guilt is t away and your sin

Mt 24: 40 one will be t and the other left.

Mk 16: 19 he was *t* up into heaven
1Ti 3: 16 was *t* up in glory.

TAKES (TAKE)
1Ki 20: 11 should not boast like one who *t* it
Ps   5: 4 You are not a God who *t* pleasure
Jn   1: 29 who *t* away the sin of the world!
Rev 22: 19 And if anyone *t* words away

TAKING (TAKE)
Ac 15: 14 by *t* from the Gentiles a people
Php 2: 7 *t* the very nature of a servant,

TALENT
Mt 25: 15 to another one *t*, each according

TAME*
Jas 3: 8 but no man can *t* the tongue.

TASK
Mk 13: 34 each with his assigned *t*,
Ac 20: 24 complete the *t* the Lord Jesus has
1Co 3: 5 the Lord has assigned to each his *t*.
2Co 2: 16 And who is equal to such a *t*?

TASTE (TASTED)
Ps 34: 8 *T* and see that the LORD is good;
Col 2: 21 Do not *t*! Do not touch!"?
Heb 2: 9 the grace of God he might *t* death

TASTED (TASTE)
1Pe 2: 3 now that you have *t* that the Lord

TAUGHT (TEACH)
Mt   7: 29 he *t* as one who had authority,
1Co 2: 13 but in words *t* by the Spirit,
Gal 1: 12 nor was I *t* it; rather, I received it

TAXES
Mt 22: 17 Is it right to pay *t* to Caesar or not
Ro 13: 7 If you owe *t*, pay *t*; if revenue,

TEACH (TAUGHT TEACHER TEACHERS TEACHES TEACHING)
Ex 33: 13 *t* me your ways so I may know you
Dt   4: 9 *T* them to your children
     8: 3 to *t* you that man does not live
    11: 19 *T* them to your children, talking
1Sa 12: 23 I will *t* you the way that is good
Ps 32: 8 *t* you in the way you should go;
    51: 13 I will *t* transgressors your ways,

90: 12 *T* us to number our days aright,
143: 10 *T* me to do your will,
Jer 31: 34 No longer will a man *t* his neighbor
Lk 11: 1 said to him, "Lord, *t* us to pray,
Jn 14: 26 will *t* you all things and will remind
1Ti 2: 12 I do not permit a woman to *t*
     3: 2 respectable, hospitable, able to *t*,
Tit 2: 1 You must *t* what is in accord
Heb 8: 11 No longer will a man *t* his neighbor
Jas 3: 1 know that we who *t* will be judged
1Jn 2: 27 you do not need anyone to *t* you.

TEACHER (TEACH)
Mt 10: 24 "A student is not above his *t*,
Jn 13: 14 and *T*, have washed your feet,

TEACHERS (TEACH)
1Co 12: 28 third *t*, then workers of miracles,
Eph 4: 11 and some to be pastors and *t*,
Heb 5: 12 by this time you ought to be *t*,

TEACHES (TEACH)
1Ti 6: 3 If anyone *t* false doctrines

TEACHING (TEACH)
Pr   1: 8 and do not forsake your mother's *t*.
Mt 28: 20 *t* them to obey everything I have
Jn   7: 17 whether my *t* comes from God or
    14: 23 loves me, he will obey my *t*.
1Ti 4: 13 of Scripture, to preaching and to *t*.
2Ti 3: 16 is God-breathed and is useful for *t*,
Tit 2: 7 In your *t* show integrity,

TEAR (TEARS)
Rev 7: 17 God will wipe away every *t*

TEARS (TEAR)
Ps 126: 5 Those who sow in *t*
Php 3: 18 and now say again even with *t*,

TEETH (TOOTH)
Mt   8: 12 will be weeping and gnashing of *t*."

TEMPERATE*
1Ti 3: 2 *t*, self-controlled, respectable,
     3: 11 not malicious talkers but *t*
Tit 2: 2 Teach the older men to be *t*,

TEMPEST
Ps 55: 8 far from the *t* and storm."

TEMPLE (TEMPLES)
1Ki 8: 27 How much less this *t* I have built!

Hab 2: 20 But the LORD is in his holy *t*;
1Co 3: 16 that you yourselves are God's *t*
     6: 19 you not know that your body is a *t*
2Co 6: 16 For we are the *t* of the living God.

TEMPLES (TEMPLE)
Ac 17: 24 does not live in *t* built by hands.

TEMPT (TEMPTATION TEMPTED)
1Co 7: 5 again so that Satan will not *t* you

TEMPTATION (TEMPT)
Mt   6: 13 And lead us not into *t*,
    26: 41 pray so that you will not fall into *t*.
1Co 10: 13 No *t* has seized you except what is

TEMPTED (TEMPT)
Mt   4: 1 into the desert to be *t* by the devil.
1Co 10: 13 he will not let you be *t*
Heb 2: 18 he himself suffered when he was *t*,
     4: 15 but we have one who has been *t*
Jas 1: 13 For God cannot be *t* by evil,

TEN (TENTH TITHE TITHES)
Ex 34: 28 covenant—the *T* Commandments.
Ps 91: 7 *t* thousand at your right hand,
Mt 25: 28 it to the one who has the *t* talents.
Lk 15: 8 suppose a woman has *t* silver coins

TENTH (TEN)
Dt 14: 22 Be sure to set aside a *t*

TERRIBLE (TERROR)
2Ti 3: 1 There will be *t* times

TERROR (TERRIBLE)
Ps 91: 5 You will not fear the *t* of night,
Lk 21: 26 Men will faint from *t*, apprehensive
Ro 13: 3 For rulers hold no *t*

TEST (TESTED TESTS)
Dt   6: 16 Do not *t* the LORD your God
Ps 139: 23 *t* me and know my anxious
Ro 12: 2 Then you will be able to *t*
1Co 3: 13 and the fire will *t* the quality
1Jn 4: 1 *t* the spirits to see whether they are

TESTED (TEST)
Ge 22: 1 Some time later God *t* Abraham.
Job 23: 10 when he has *t* me, I will come forth
Pr 27: 21 man is *t* by the praise he receives.
1Ti 3: 10 They must first be *t*; and then

TESTIFY (TESTIMONY)
Jn   5: 39 are the Scriptures that *t* about me,
2Ti 1: 8 ashamed to *t* about our Lord,

TESTIMONY (TESTIFY)
Isa 8: 20 and to the *t*! If they do not speak
Lk 18: 20 not give false *t*, honor your father

TESTS (TEST)
Pr 17: 3 but the LORD *t* the heart.
1Th 2: 4 but God, who *t* our hearts.

THADDAEUS
   Apostle (Mt 10:3; Mk 3:18); probably also known as Judas son of James (Lk 6:16; Ac 1:13).

THANKFUL (THANKS)
Heb 12: 28 let us be *t*, and so worship God

THANKS (THANKFUL THANKSGIVING)
1Ch 16: 8 Give *t* to the LORD, call
Ne 12: 31 assigned two large choirs to give *t*.
Ps 100: 4 give *t* to him and praise his name.
1Co 15: 57 *t* be to God! He gives us the victory
2Co 2: 14 *t* be to God, who always leads us
     9: 15 *T* be to God for his indescribable
1Th 5: 18 give *t* in all circumstances,

THANKSGIVING (THANKS)
Ps 95: 2 Let us come before him with *t*
   100: 4 Enter his gates with *t*
Php 4: 6 by prayer and petition, with *t*,
1Ti 4: 3 created to be received with *t*

THIEF (THIEVES)
Ex 22: 3 A *t* must certainly make restitution
1Th 5: 2 day of the Lord will come like a *t*
Rev 16: 15 I come like a *t*! Blessed is he who

THIEVES (THIEF)
1Co 6: 10 nor homosexual offenders nor *t*

THINK (THOUGHT THOUGHTS)
Ro 12: 3 Do not *t* of yourself more highly
Php 4: 8 praiseworthy—*t* about such things

THIRST (THIRSTY)
Ps 69: 21 and gave me vinegar for my *t*.
Mt   5: 6 Blessed are those who hunger and *t*
Jn   4: 14 the water I give him will never *t*.

THIRSTY (THIRST)

Isa 55: 1 "Come, all you who are *t*,
Jn 7: 37 "If anyone is *t*, let him come to me
Rev 22: 17 Whoever is *t*, let him come;

THOMAS

Apostle (Mt 10:3; Mk 3:18; Lk 6:15; Jn 11:16; 14:5; 21:2;Ac 1:13). Doubted resurrection (Jn 20:24-28).

THONGS

Mk 1: 7 *t* of whose sandals I am not worthy

THORN (THORNS)

2Co 12: 7 there was given me a *t* in my flesh,

THORNS (THORN)

Nu 33: 55 in your eyes and *t* in your sides.
Mt 27: 29 then twisted together a crown of *t*
Heb 6: 8 But land that produces *t*

THOUGHT (THINK)

Pr 14: 15 a prudent man gives *t* to his steps.
1Co 13: 11 I talked like a child, I *t* like a child,

THOUGHTS (THINK)

Ps 94: 11 The LORD knows the *t* of man;
139: 23 test me and know my anxious *t*.
Isa 55: 8 "For my *t* are not your *t*,
Heb 4: 12 it judges the *t* and attitudes

THREE

Ecc 4: 12 of three strands is not quickly broken.
Mt 12: 40 *t* nights in the belly of a huge fish,
18: 20 or *t* come together in my name,
27: 63 'After *t* days I will rise again.'
1Co 13: 13 And now these *t* remain: faith,
14: 27 or at the most *t* — should speak,
2Co 13: 1 testimony of two or *t* witnesses."

THRESHING

2Sa 24: 18 an altar to the LORD on the *t* floor

THRONE (ENTHRONED)

2Sa 7: 16 your *t* will be established forever
Ps 45: 6 Your *t*, O God, will last for ever
47: 8 God is seated on his holy *t*.
Isa 6: 1 I saw the Lord seated on a *t*,
66: 1 "Heaven is my *t*
Heb 4: 16 Let us then approach the *t* of grace
12: 2 at the right hand of the *t* of God.
Rev 4: 10 They lay their crowns before the *t*

20: 11 Then I saw a great white *t*
22: 3 *t* of God and of the Lamb will be

THROW

Jn 8: 7 the first to *t* a stone at her."
Heb 10: 35 So do not *t* away your confidence;
12: 1 let us *t* off everything that hinders

THWART*

Isa 14: 27 has purposed, and who can *t* him?

TIBNI

King of Israel (1Ki 16:21-22).

TIME (TIMES)

Est 4: 14 come to royal position for such a *t*
Da 7: 25 to him for a *t*, times and half a *t*.
Hos 10: 12 for it is *t* to seek the LORD,
Ro 9: 9 "At the appointed *t* I will return,
Heb 9: 28 and he will appear a second *t*,
10: 12 for all *t* one sacrifice for sins,
1Pe 4: 17 For it is *t* for judgment to begin

TIMES (TIME)

Ps 9: 9 a stronghold in *t* of trouble.
31: 15 My *t* are in your hands;
62: 8 Trust in him at all *t*, O people;
Pr 17: 17 A friend loves at all *t*,
Am 5: 13 for the *t* are evil.
Mt 18: 21 how many *t* shall I forgive my
Ac 1: 7 "It is not for you to know the *t*
Rev 12: 14 *t* and half a time, out

TIMIDITY*

2Ti 1: 7 For God did not give us a spirit of *t*

TIMOTHY

Believer from Lystra (Ac 16:1). Joined Paul on second missionary journey (Ac 16-20). Sent to settle problems at Corinth (1Co 4:17; 16:10). Led church at Ephesus (1Ti 1:3). Co-writer with Paul (1Th 1:1; 2Th 1:1; Phm 1).

TIRE (TIRED)

2Th 3: 13 never *t* of doing what is right.

TIRED (TIRE)

Ex 17: 12 When Moses' hands grew *t*,
Isa 40: 28 He will not grow *t* or weary,

TITHE (TEN)

Lev 27: 30 "'A *t* of everything from the land,
Dt 12: 17 eat in your own towns the *t*
Mal 3: 10 the whole *t* into the storehouse,

TITHES (TEN)

Mal 3: 8 'How do we rob you?' "In *t*

TITUS

Gentile co-worker of Paul (Gal 2:1-3; 2Ti 4:10); sent to Corinth (2Co 2:13; 7-8; 12:18), Crete (Tit 1:4-5).

TODAY

Mt 6: 11 Give us *t* our daily bread.
Lk 23: 43 *t* you will be with me in paradise."
Heb 3: 13 daily, as long as it is called *T*,
13: 8 Christ is the same yesterday and *t*

TOIL

Ge 3: 17 through painful *t* you will eat of it

TOLERATE

Hab 1: 13 you cannot *t* wrong.
Rev 2: 2 that you cannot *t* wicked men,

TOMB

Mt 27: 65 make the *t* as secure as you know
Lk 24: 2 the stone rolled away from the *t*,

TOMORROW

Pr 27: 1 Do not boast about *t*,
Isa 22: 13 "for *t* we die!"
Mt 6: 34 Therefore do not worry about *t*,
Jas 4: 13 "Today or *t* we will go to this

TONGUE (TONGUES)

Ps 39: 1 and keep my *t* from sin;
Pr 12: 18 but the *t* of the wise brings healing.
1Co 14: 2 speaks in a *t* does not speak to men
14: 4 He who speaks in a *t* edifies himself
14: 13 in a *t* should pray that he may
14: 19 than ten thousand words in a *t*.
Php 2: 11 every *t* confess that Jesus Christ is
Jas 1: 26 does not keep a tight rein on his *t*,
3: 8 but no man can tame the *t*.

TONGUES (TONGUE)

Isa 28: 11 with foreign lips and strange *t*
66: 18 and gather all nations and *t*,
Mk 16: 17 in new *t*; they will pick up snakes
Ac 2: 4 and began to speak in other *t*
10: 46 For they heard them speaking in *t*
19: 6 and they spoke in *t* and prophesied
1Co 12: 30 Do all speak in *t* ? Do all interpret?
14: 18 speak in *t* more than all of you.
14: 39 and do not forbid speaking in *t*.

TOOK (TAKE)

1Co 11: 23 the night he was betrayed, *t* bread,
Php 3: 12 for which Christ Jesus *t* hold of me.

TOOTH (TEETH)

Ex 21: 24 eye for eye, *t* for *t*, hand for hand,
Mt 5: 38 'Eye for eye, and *t* for *t*.'

TORMENTED

Rev 20: 10 They will be *t* day and night

TORN

Gal 4: 15 you would have *t* out your eyes
Php 1: 23 I do not know! I am *t*

TOUCH (TOUCHED)

Ps 105: 15 "Do not *t* my anointed ones;
Lk 24: 39 It is myself ! *T* me and see;
2Co 6: 17 *T* no unclean thing,
Col 2: 21 Do not taste! Do not *t*!"?

TOUCHED (TOUCH)

1Sa 10: 26 men whose hearts God had *t*.
Mt 14: 36 and all who *t* him were healed.

TOWER

Ge 11: 4 with a *t* that reaches to the heavens
Pr 18: 10 of the LORD is a strong *t*;

TOWNS

Nu 35: 2 to give the Levites *t* to live
35: 15 These six *t* will be a place of refuge

TRACING*

Ro 11: 33 and his paths beyond *t* out!

TRADITION

Mt 15: 6 word of God for the sake of your *t*.
Col 2: 8 which depends on human *t*

TRAIN (TRAINING)

Pr 22: 6 *T* a child in the way he should go,
Eph 4: 8 he led captives in his *t*

TRAINING (TRAIN)

1Co 9: 25 in the games goes into strict *t*.
2Ti 3: 16 correcting and *t* in righteousness,

TRAMPLED

Lk 21: 24 Jerusalem will be *t*
Heb 10: 29 to be punished who has *t* the Son

TRANCE

Ac 10: 10 was being prepared, he fell into a *t*.

TRANSCENDS*

Php 4: 7 which *t* all understanding,

TRANSFIGURED

Mt 17: 2 There he was *t* before them.

TRANSFORM* (TRANSFORMED)

Php 3: 21 will *t* our lowly bodies

TRANSFORMED (TRANSFORM)
Ro 12: 2 be *t* by the renewing of your mind.
2Co 3: 18 are being *t* into his likeness

TRANSGRESSION (TRANSGRESSIONS TRANSGRESSORS)
Isa 53: 8 for the *t* of my people he was
Ro 4: 15 where there is no law there is no *t*.

TRANSGRESSIONS (TRANSGRESSION)
Ps 32: 1 whose *t* are forgiven,
51: 1 blot out my *t*.
103: 12 so far has he removed our *t* from us
Isa 53: 5 But he was pierced for our *t*,
Eph 2: 1 you were dead in your *t* and sins,

TRANSGRESSORS (TRANSGRESSION)
Ps 51: 13 Then I will teach *t* your ways,
Isa 53: 12 and made intercession for the *t*.
53: 12 and was numbered with the *t*.

TREADING
Dt 25: 4 an ox while it is *t* out the grain.
1Co 9: 9 an ox while it is *t* out the grain."

TREASURE (TREASURED TREASURES)
Isa 33: 6 of the LORD is the key to this *t*.
Mt 6: 21 For where your *t* is, there your
2Co 4: 7 But we have this *t* in jars of clay

TREASURED (TREASURE)
Dt 7: 6 to be his people, his *t* possession.
Lk 2: 19 But Mary *t* up all these things

TREASURES (TREASURE)
Mt 6: 19 up for yourselves *t* on earth,
Col 2: 3 in whom are hidden all the *t*
Heb 11: 26 of greater value than the *t* of Egypt,

TREAT
Lev 22: 2 sons to *t* with respect the sacred
1Ti 5: 1 *T* younger men as brothers,
1Pe 3: 7 and *t* them with respect

TREATY
Dt 7: 2 Make no *t* with them, and show

TREE
Ge 2: 9 and the *t* of the knowledge of good
2: 9 of the garden were the *t* of life
Dt 21: 23 hung on a *t* is under God's curse.

Ps 1: 3 He is like a *t* planted by streams
Mt 3: 10 every *t* that does not produce good
12: 33 for a *t* is recognized by its fruit.
Gal 3: 13 is everyone who is hung on a *t*."
Rev 22: 14 they may have the right to the *t*

TREMBLE (TREMBLING)
1Ch 16: 30 *T* before him, all the earth!
Ps 114: 7 *T*, O earth, at the presence

TREMBLING (TREMBLE)
Ps 2: 11 and rejoice with *t*.
Php 2: 12 out your salvation with fear and *t*,

TRESPASS
Ro 5: 17 For if, by the *t* of the one man,

TRIALS
1Th 3: 3 one would be unsettled by these *t*.
Jas 1: 2 whenever you face *t* of many kinds,
2Pe 2: 9 how to rescue godly men from *t*

TRIBES
Ge 49: 28 All these are the twelve *t* of Israel,
Mt 19: 28 judging the twelve *t* of Israel.

TRIBULATION*
Rev 7: 14 who have come out of the great *t*;

TRIUMPHAL* (TRIUMPHING)
Isa 60: 11 their kings led in *t* procession.
2Co 2: 14 us in *t* procession in Christ

TRIUMPHING* (TRIUMPHAL)
Col 2: 15 of them, *t* over them by the cross.

TROUBLE (TROUBLED TROUBLES)
Job 14: 1 is of few days and full of *t*.
Ps 46: 1 an ever-present help in *t*.
107: 13 they cried to the LORD in their *t*,
Pr 11: 29 He who brings *t* on his family will
24: 10 If you falter in times of *t*,
Mt 6: 34 Each day has enough *t* of its own.
Jn 16: 33 In this world you will have *t*.
Ro 8: 35 Shall *t* or hardship or persecution

TROUBLED (TROUBLE)
Jn 14: 1 "Do not let your hearts be *t*.
14: 27 Do not let your hearts be *t*

TROUBLES (TROUBLE)
1Co 7: 28 those who marry will face many *t*
2Co 1: 4 who comforts us in all our *t*,

4: 17 and momentary *t* are achieving

TRUE (TRUTH)
Dt 18: 22 does not take place or come *t*,
1Sa 9: 6 and everything he says comes *t*.
Ps 119:160 All your words are *t*;
Jn 17: 3 the only *t* God, and Jesus Christ,
Ro 3: 4 Let God be *t*, and every man a liar.
Php 4: 8 whatever is *t*, whatever is noble,
Rev 22: 6 These words are trustworthy and *t*.

TRUMPET
1Co 14: 8 if the *t* does not sound a clear call,
15: 52 For the *t* will sound, the dead will

TRUST (ENTRUSTED TRUSTED TRUSTS TRUSTWORTHY)
Ps 20: 7 we *t* in the name of the LORD our
37: 3 *T* in the LORD and do good;
56: 4 in God I *t*; I will not be afraid.
119: 42 for I *t* in your word.
Pr 3: 5 *T* in the LORD with all your heart
Isa 30: 15 in quietness and *t* is your strength,
Jn 14: 1 *T* in God; *t* also in me.
1Co 4: 2 been given a *t* must prove faithful.

TRUSTED (TRUST)
Ps 26: 1 I have *t* in the LORD
Isa 25: 9 we *t* in him, and he saved us.
Da 3: 28 They *t* in him and defied the king's
Lk 16: 10 *t* with very little can also be *t*

TRUSTS (TRUST)
Ps 32: 10 surrounds the man who *t* in him.
Pr 11: 28 Whoever *t* in his riches will fall,
28: 26 He who *t* in himself is a fool,
Ro 9: 33 one who *t* in him will never be put

TRUSTWORTHY (TRUST)
Ps 119:138 they are fully *t*.
Pr 11: 13 but a *t* man keeps a secret.
Rev 22: 6 "These words are *t* and true.

TRUTH (TRUE TRUTHFUL TRUTHS)
Ps 51: 6 Surely you desire *t*
Isa 45: 19 I, the LORD, speak the *t*;
Zec 8: 16 are to do: Speak the *t* to each other,
Jn 4: 23 worship the Father in spirit and *t*,
8: 32 Then you will know the *t*,
8: 32 and the *t* will set you free."
14: 6 I am the way and the *t* and the life.

16: 13 comes, he will guide you into all *t*.
18: 38 "What is *t*?" Pilate asked.
Ro 1: 25 They exchanged the *t* of God
1Co 13: 6 in evil but rejoices with the *t*.
2Co 13: 8 against the *t*, but only for the *t*.
Eph 4: 15 Instead, speaking the *t* in love,
6: 14 with the belt of *t* buckled
2Th 2: 10 because they refused to love the *t*
1Ti 2: 4 to come to a knowledge of the *t*.
3: 15 the pillar and foundation of the *t*.
2Ti 2: 15 correctly handles the word of *t*.
3: 7 never able to acknowledge the *t*.
Heb 10: 26 received the knowledge of the *t*,
1Pe 1: 22 by obeying the *t* so that you have
2Pe 2: 2 the way of *t* into disrepute.
1Jn 1: 6 we lie and do not live by the *t*.
1: 8 deceive ourselves and the *t* is not

TRUTHFUL (TRUTH)
Pr 12: 22 but he delights in men who are *t*.
Jn 3: 33 it has certified that God is *t*.

TRUTHS (TRUTH)
1Co 2: 13 expressing spiritual *t*
1Ti 3: 9 hold of the deep *t* of the faith
Heb 5: 12 to teach you the elementary *t*

TRY (TRYING)
Ps 26: 2 Test me, O LORD, and *t* me,
Isa 7: 13 enough to *t* the patience of men?
1Co 14: 12 *t* to excel in gifts that build up
2Co 5: 11 is to fear the Lord, we *t*
1Th 5: 15 always *t* to be kind to each other

TRYING (TRY)
2Co 5: 12 We are not *t* to commend ourselves
1Th 2: 4 We are not *t* to please men but God

TUNIC
Lk 6: 29 do not stop him from taking your *t*.

TURN (TURNED TURNS)
Ex 32: 12 *T* from your fierce anger; relent
Dt 5: 32 do not *t* aside to the right
28: 14 Do not *t* aside from any
Jos 1: 7 do not *t* from it to the right
2Ch 7: 14 and *t* from their wicked ways,
30: 9 He will not *t* his face from you

Ps 78: 6 they in *t* would tell their children.
Pr 22: 6 when he is old he will not *t* from it.
Isa 29: 16 You *t* things upside down,
  30: 21 Whether you *t* to the right
  45: 22 "*T* to me and be saved,
  55: 7 Let him *t* to the Lord.
Eze 33: 11 *T! T* from your evil ways!
Mal 4: 6 He will *t* the hearts of the fathers
Mt   5: 39 you on the right cheek, *t*
  10: 35 For I have come to *t*
Jn 12: 40 nor *t*—and I would heal them."
Ac   3: 19 Repent, then, and *t* to God,
  26: 18 and *t* them from darkness to light,
1Ti 6: 20 *T* away from godless chatter
1Pe 3: 11 He must *t* from evil and do good;

TURNED (TURN)
Ps 30: 11 You *t* my wailing into dancing;
  40: 1 he *t* to me and heard my cry.
Isa 53: 6 each of us has *t* to his own way;
Hos 7: 8 Ephraim is a flat cake not *t* over.
Joel 2: 31 The sun will be *t* to darkness
Ro   3: 12 All have *t* away,

TURNS (TURN)
2Sa 22: 29 the Lord *t* my darkness into light
Pr 15: 1 A gentle answer *t* away wrath,
Isa 44: 25 and *t* it into nonsense,
Jas 5: 20 Whoever *t* a sinner from the error

TWELVE
Ge 49: 28 All these are the *t* tribes of Israel,
Mt 10: 1 He called his *t* disciples to him

TWINKLING*
1Co 15: 52 in a flash, in the *t* of an eye,

☙ *U*

UNAPPROACHABLE*
1Ti 6: 16 immortal and who lives in *u* light,

UNBELIEF (UNBELIEVER UNBELIEVERS UNBELIEVING)
Mk 9: 24 help me overcome my *u!*"
Ro 11: 20 they were broken off because of *u*,
Heb 3: 19 able to enter, because of their *u*.

UNBELIEVER* (UNBELIEF)
1Co 7: 15 But if the *u* leaves, let him do so.
  10: 27 If some *u* invites you to a meal
  14: 24 if an *u* or someone who does not
2Co 6: 15 have in common with an *u*?

1Ti 5: 8 the faith and is worse than an *u*.

UNBELIEVERS (UNBELIEF)
1Co 6: 6 another—and this in front of *u!*
2Co 6: 14 Do not be yoked together with *u*.

UNBELIEVING (UNBELIEF)
1Co 7: 14 For the *u* husband has been
Rev 21: 8 But the cowardly, the *u*, the vile,

UNCERTAIN*
1Ti 6: 17 which is so *u*, but to put their hope

UNCHANGEABLE*
Heb 6: 18 by two *u* things in which it is

UNCIRCUMCISED
1Sa 17: 26 Who is this *u* Philistine that he
Col 3: 11 circumcised or *u*, barbarian,

UNCIRCUMCISION
1Co 7: 19 is nothing and *u* is nothing.
Gal 5: 6 neither circumcision nor *u* has any

UNCLEAN
Isa 6: 5 ruined! For I am a man of *u* lips,
Ro •14: 14 fully convinced that no food is *u*
2Co 6: 17 Touch no *u* thing,

UNCONCERNED*
Eze 16: 49 were arrogant, overfed and *u*;

UNCOVERED
Heb 4: 13 Everything is *u* and laid bare

UNDERSTAND (UNDERSTANDING UNDERSTANDS)
Job 42: 3 Surely I spoke of things I did not *u*,
Ps 73: 16 When I tried to *u* all this,
  119:125 that I may *u* your statutes.
Lk 24: 45 so they could *u* the Scriptures.
Ac   8: 30 "Do you *u* what you are reading?"
Ro   7: 15 I do not *u* what I do.
1Co 2: 14 and he cannot *u* them,
Eph 5: 17 but *u* what the Lord's will is.
2Pe 3: 16 some things that are hard to *u*,

UNDERSTANDING (UNDERSTAND)
Ps 119:104 I gain *u* from your precepts;
  147: 5 his *u* has no limit.
Pr   3: 5 and lean not on your own *u*;
   4: 7 Though it cost all you have, get *u*.
  10: 23 but a man of *u* delights in wisdom.
  11: 12 but a man of *u* holds his tongue.

  15: 21 a man of *u* keeps a straight course.
  15: 32 whoever heeds correction gains *u*.
  23: 23 get wisdom, discipline and *u*.
Isa 40: 28 and his *u* no one can fathom.
Da   5: 12 a keen mind and knowledge and *u*,
Mk 4: 12 and ever hearing but never *u*;
  12: 33 with all your *u* and with all your
Php 4: 7 of God, which transcends all *u*,

UNDERSTANDS (UNDERSTAND)
1Ch 28: 9 and *u* every motive
1Ti 6: 4 he is conceited and *u* nothing.

UNDIVIDED*
1Ch 12: 33 to help David with *u* loyalty—
Ps 86: 11 give me an *u* heart,
Eze 11: 19 I will give them an *u* heart
1Co 7: 35 way in *u* devotion to the Lord.

UNDOING
Pr 18: 7 A fool's mouth is his *u*,

UNDYING*
Eph 6: 24 Lord Jesus Christ with an *u* love.

UNFADING*
1Pe 3: 4 the *u* beauty of a gentle

UNFAILING
Ps 33: 5 the earth is full of his *u* love.
  119: 76 May your *u* love be my comfort,
  143: 8 bring me word of your *u* love,
Pr 19: 22 What a man desires is *u* love;
La   3: 32 so great is his *u* love.

UNFAITHFUL (UNFAITHFULNESS)
Lev 6: 2 is *u* to the Lord by deceiving his
1Ch 10: 13 because he was *u* to the Lord;
Pr 13: 15 but the way of the *u* is hard.

UNFAITHFULNESS (UNFAITHFUL)
Mt 5: 32 except for marital *u*, causes her
  19: 9 for marital *u*, and marries another

UNFOLDING
Ps 119:130 the *u* of your words gives light;

UNGODLINESS
Tit 2: 12 It teaches us to say "No" to *u*

UNIT
1Co 12: 12 body is a *u*, though it is made up

UNITED (UNITY)
Ro   6: 5 If we have been *u* with him
Php 2: 1 from being *u* with Christ,
Col 2: 2 encouraged in heart and *u* in love,

UNITY (UNITED)
Ps 133: 1 is when brothers live together in *u!*
Ro 15: 5 a spirit of *u* among yourselves
Eph 4: 3 effort to keep the *u* of the Spirit
   4: 13 up until we all reach *u* in the faith
Col 3: 14 them all together in perfect *u*.

UNIVERSE
Php 2: 15 which you shine like stars in the *u*
Heb 1: 2 and through whom he made the *u*.

UNKNOWN
Ac 17: 23 to an *u* god.

UNLEAVENED
Ex 12: 17 "Celebrate the Feast of *U* Bread,

UNPROFITABLE
Tit 3: 9 because these are *u* and useless.

UNPUNISHED
Ex 34: 7 Yet he does not leave the guilty *u*;
Pr 19: 5 A false witness will not go *u*,

UNREPENTANT*
Ro   2: 5 stubbornness and your *u* heart,

UNRIGHTEOUS*
Zep 3: 5 yet the *u* know no shame.
Mt 5: 45 rain on the righteous and the *u*.
1Pe 3: 18 the righteous for the *u*, to bring you
2Pe 2: 9 and to hold the *u* for the day

UNSEARCHABLE
Ro 11: 33 How *u* his judgments,
Eph 3: 8 preach to the Gentiles the *u* riches

UNSEEN
2Co 4: 18 on what is seen, but on what is *u*.
   4: 18 temporary, but what is *u* is eternal.

UNSTABLE*
Jas 1: 8 he is a double-minded man, *u*
2Pe 2: 14 they seduce the *u*; they are experts
   3: 16 ignorant and *u* people distort,

UNTHINKABLE*
Job 34: 12 It is *u* that God would do wrong,

UNVEILED*
2Co 3: 18 with *u* faces all reflect the
Lord's

UNWORTHY
Job 40: 4 "I am *u*—how can I reply
to you?
Lk 17: 10 should say, 'We are *u*
servants;

UPRIGHT
Job 1: 1 This man was blameless
and *u*;
Pr 2: 7 He holds victory in store
for the *u*,
15: 8 but the prayer of the *u*
pleases him.
Tit 1: 8 who is self-controlled,
u, holy
2: 12 *u* and godly lives in this
present

UPROOTED
Jude : 12 without fruit and *u*—twice
dead.

USEFUL
2Ti 2: 21 *u* to the Master and
prepared
3: 16 Scripture is God-breathed
and is *u*

USELESS
1Co 15: 14 our preaching is *u*
Jas 2: 20 faith without deeds is *u*?

USURY
Ne 5: 10 But let the exacting of
u stop!

UTTER
Ps 78: 2 I will *u* hidden things,
things from of

UZZIAH
Son of Amaziah; king of Judah also
known as Azariah (2Ki 15:1-7; 1Ch 6:24;
2Ch 26).

∾ V

VAIN
Ps 33: 17 A horse is a *v* hope for
deliverance;
Isa 65: 23 They will not toil in *v*
1Co 15: 2 Otherwise, you have
believed in *v*.
15: 58 labor in the Lord is not in *v*.
2Co 6: 1 not to receive God's
grace in *v*.

VALLEY
Ps 23: 4 walk through the *v* of the
shadow
Isa 40: 4 Every *v* shall be raised up,
Joel 3: 14 multitudes in the *v* of
decision!

VALUABLE (VALUE)
Lk 12: 24 And how much more
v you are

VALUE (VALUABLE)
Mt 13: 46 When he found one of
great *v*,

1Ti 4: 8 For physical training is of
some *v*,
Heb 11: 26 as of greater *v* than the
treasures

VEIL
Ex 34: 33 to them, he put a *v* over his
face.
2Co 3: 14 for to this day the same *v*
remains

VENGEANCE (AVENGE REVENGE)
Isa 34: 8 For the LORD has a day of *v*,

VICTORIES (VICTORY)
Ps 18: 50 He gives his king great *v*;
21: 1 great is his joy in the *v* you
give!

VICTORIOUSLY* (VICTORY)
Ps 45: 4 In your majesty ride forth *v*

**VICTORY (VICTORIES
VICTORIOUSLY)**
Ps 60: 12 With God we will gain the *v*,
1Co 15: 54 "Death has been swallowed
up in *v*
15: 57 He gives us the *v* through
our Lord
1Jn 5: 4 This is the *v* that has
overcome

VINDICATED
1Ti 3: 16 was *v* by the Spirit,

VINE
Jn 15: 1 "I am the true *v*, and my
Father is

VINEGAR
Mk 15: 36 filled a sponge with wine *v*,

VIOLATION
Heb 2: 2 every *v* and disobedience
received

VIOLENCE
Isa 60: 18 No longer will *v* be heard
Eze 45: 9 Give up your *v* and
oppression

VIPERS
Ro 3: 13 "The poison of *v* is on their
lips."

VIRGIN
Isa 7: 14 The *v* will be with child
Mt 1: 23 "The *v* will be with child
2Co 11: 2 that I might present you as
a pure *v*

VIRTUES*
Col 3: 14 And over all these *v* put on
love,

VISION
Ac 26: 19 disobedient to the *v* from
heaven.

VOICE
Ps 95: 7 Today, if you hear his *v*,
Isa 30: 21 your ears will hear a
v behind you,
Jn 5: 28 are in their graves will hear
his *v*

10: 3 and the sheep listen to his *v*.
Heb 3: 7 "Today, if you hear his *v*,
Rev 3: 20 If anyone hears my *v* and
opens

VOMIT
Pr 26: 11 As a dog returns to its *v*,
2Pe 2: 22 "A dog returns to its *v*," and,

VOW
Nu 30: 2 When a man makes a *v*

∾ W

WAGES
Lk 10: 7 for the worker deserves
his *w*.
Ro 4: 4 his *w* are not credited to him
6: 23 For the *w* of sin is death,

WAILING
Ps 30: 11 You turned my *w* into
dancing;

WAIST
2Ki 1: 8 with a leather belt around
his *w*."
Mt 3: 4 he had a leather belt around
his *w*.

WAIT (WAITED WAITS)
Ps 27: 14 *W* for the LORD;
130: 5 I *w* for the LORD, my soul
waits,
Isa 30: 18 Blessed are all who *w* for
him!
Ac 1: 4 *w* for the gift my Father
promised,
Ro 8: 23 as we *w* eagerly for our
adoption
1Th 1: 10 and to *w* for his Son from
heaven,
Tit 2: 13 while we *w* for the blessed
hope—

WAITED (WAIT)
Ps 40: 1 I *w* patiently for the LORD;

WAITS (WAIT)
Ro 8: 19 creation *w* in eager
expectation

WALK (WALKED WALKS)
Dt 11: 19 and when you *w* along the
road,
Ps 1: 1 who does not *w* in the
counsel
23: 4 Even though I *w*
89: 15 who *w* in the light of your
presence
Isa 2: 5 let us *w* in the light of the
LORD.
30: 21 saying, "This is the way; *w*
in it."
40: 31 they will *w* and not be faint.
Jer 6: 16 ask where the good way is,
and *w*
Da 4: 37 And those who *w* in pride
he is able
Am 3: 3 Do two *w* together
Mic 6: 8 and to *w* humbly with your
God.

Mk 2: 9 'Get up, take your mat
and *w*?
Jn 8: 12 Whoever follows me will
never *w*
1Jn 1: 7 But if we *w* in the light,
2Jn : 6 his command is that you
w in love.

WALKED (WALK)
Ge 5: 24 Enoch *w* with God; then he
was no
Jos 14: 9 which your feet have *w* will
be your
Mt 14: 29 *w* on the water and came
toward

WALKS (WALK)
Pr 13: 20 He who *w* with the wise
grows wise

WALL
Jos 6: 20 *w* collapsed; so every man
charged
Ne 2: 17 let us rebuild the *w* of
Jerusalem,
Rev 21: 12 It had a great, high *w*

WALLOWING
2Pe 2: 22 back to her *w* in the mud."

**WANT
(WANTED WANTING WANTS)**
1Sa 8: 19 "We *w* a king over us.
Ps 23: 1 is my shepherd, I shall not
be in *w*.
Lk 19: 14 'We don't *w* this man to be
our king
Ro 7: 15 For what I *w* to do I do
not do,
Php 3: 10 I *w* to know Christ and the
power

WANTED (WANT)
1Co 12: 18 of them, just as he *w* them
to be.

WANTING (WANT)
Da 5: 27 weighed on the scales and
found *w*.
2Pe 3: 9 with you, not *w* anyone to
perish,

WANTS (WANT)
Mt 20: 26 whoever *w* to become great
Mk 8: 35 For whoever *w* to save his
life will
Ro 9: 18 he hardens whom he *w* to
harden.
1Ti 2: 4 who *w* all men to be saved

WAR (WARS)
Isa 2: 4 nor will they train for *w*
anymore.
Da 9: 26 *W* will continue until the
end,
2Co 10: 3 we do not wage *w* as the
world does
Rev 19: 11 With justice he judges and
makes *w*

WARN (WARNED WARNINGS)
Eze 3: 19 But if you do *w* the wicked
man

33: 9 if you do *w* the wicked man to turn

WARNED (WARN)
Ps **19: 11** By them is your servant *w;*

WARNINGS (WARN)
1Co **10: 11** and were written down as *w* for us,

WARS (WAR)
Ps **46: 9** He makes *w* cease to the ends
Mt **24: 6** You will hear of *w* and rumors of *w,*

WASH (WASHED WASHING)
Ps **51: 7** *w* me, and I will be whiter
Jn **13: 5** and began to *w* his disciples' feet,
Ac **22: 16** be baptized and *w* your sins away,
Rev **22: 14** Blessed are those who *w* their robes

WASHED (WASH)
1Co **6: 11** you were *w,* you were sanctified,
Rev **7: 14** they have *w* their robes

WASHING (WASH)
Eph **5: 26** cleansing her by the *w* with water
Tit **3: 5** us through the *w* of rebirth

WATCH (WATCHES WATCHING WATCHMAN)
Ge **31: 49** "May the LORD keep *w*
Jer **31: 10** will *w* over his flock like a shepherd
Mt **24: 42** "Therefore keep *w,* because you do
26: 41 *W* and pray so that you will not fall
Lk **2: 8** keeping *w* over their flocks at night
1Ti **4: 16** *W* your life and doctrine closely.

WATCHES (WATCH)
Ps **1: 6** For the LORD *w* over the way
121: 3 he who *w* over you will not slumber

WATCHING (WATCH)
Lk **12: 37** whose master finds them *w*

WATCHMAN (WATCH)
Eze **3: 17** I have made you a *w* for the house

WATER (WATERED WATERS)
Ps **1: 3** like a tree planted by streams of *w,*
22: 14 I am poured out like *w,*
Pr **25: 21** if he is thirsty, give him to *w* to drink.
Isa **49: 10** and lead them beside springs of *w.*
Jer **2: 13** broken cisterns that cannot hold *w.*
Zec **14: 8** On that day living *w* will flow out

Mk **9: 41** anyone who gives you a cup of *w*
Jn **4: 10** he would have given you living *w."*
7: 38 streams of living *w* will flow
Eph **5: 26** washing with *w* through the word,
1Pe **3: 21** this *w* symbolizes baptism that now
Rev **21: 6** cost from the spring of the *w* of life.

WATERED (WATER)
1Co **3: 6** I planted the seed, Apollos *w* it,

WATERS (WATER)
Ps **23: 2** he leads me beside quiet *w,*
Ecc **11: 1** Cast your bread upon the *w,*
Isa **58: 11** like a spring whose *w* never fail.
1Co **3: 7** plants nor he who *w* is anything,

WAVE (WAVES)
Jas **1: 6** he who doubts is like a *w* of the sea,

WAVES (WAVE)
Isa **57: 20** whose *w* cast up mire and mud.
Mt **8: 27** Even the winds and the *w* obey him
Eph **4: 14** tossed back and forth by the *w,*

WAY (WAYS)
Dt **1: 33** to show you the *w* you should go.
2Sa **22: 31** "As for God, his *w* is perfect;
Job **23: 10** But he knows the *w* that I take;
Ps **1: 1** or stand in the *w* of sinners
37: 5 Commit your *w* to the LORD;
119: 9 can a young man keep his *w* pure?
139: 24 See if there is any offensive *w* in me
Pr **14: 12** There is a *w* that seems right
16: 17 he who guards his *w* guards his life.
22: 6 Train a child in the *w* he should go,
Isa **30: 21** saying, "This is the *w;* walk in it."
53: 6 each of us has turned to his own *w;*
Isa **55: 7** Let the wicked forsake his *w*
Mt **3: 3** Prepare the *w* for the Lord,
Jn **14: 6** "I am the *w* and the truth
1Co **10: 13** also provide a *w* out so that you can
12: 31 will show you the most excellent *w.*
Heb **4: 15** who has been tempted in every *w,*
9: 8 was showing by this that the *w*
10: 20 and living *w* opened for us

WAYS (WAY)
Ex **33: 13** teach me your *w* so I may know
Ps **25: 10** All the *w* of the LORD are loving
51: 13 I will teach transgressors your *w,*
Pr **3: 6** in all your *w* acknowledge him,
Isa **55: 8** neither are your *w* my *w,"*
Jas **3: 2** We all stumble in many *w.*

WEAK (WEAKER WEAKNESS)
Mt **26: 41** spirit is willing, but the body is *w."*
Ro **14: 1** Accept him whose faith is *w,*
1Co **1: 27** God chose the *w* things
8: 9 become a stumbling block to the *w.*
9: 22 To the *w* I became *w,* to win the *w.*
2Co **12: 10** For when I am *w,* then I am strong.
Heb **12: 12** your feeble arms and *w* knees.

WEAKER (WEAK)
1Co **12: 22** seem to be *w* are indispensable,
1Pe **3: 7** them with respect as the *w* partner

WEAKNESS (WEAK)
Ro **8: 26** the Spirit helps us in our *w.*
1Co **1: 25** and the *w* of God is stronger
2Co **12: 9** for my power is made perfect in *w*
Heb **5: 2** since he himself is subject to *w.*

WEALTH
Pr **3: 9** Honor the LORD with your *w,*
Mk **10: 22** away sad, because he had great *w.*
Lk **15: 13** and there squandered his *w*

WEAPONS
2Co **10: 4** The *w* we fight with are not

WEARIES (WEARY)
Ecc **12: 12** and much study *w* the body.

WEARY (WEARIES)
Isa **40: 31** they will run and not grow *w,*
Mt **11: 28** all you who are *w* and burdened,
Gal **6: 9** Let us not become *w* in doing good,

WEDDING
Mt **22: 11** who was not wearing *w* clothes.
Rev **19: 7** For the *w* of the Lamb has come,

WEEP (WEEPING WEPT)
Ecc **3: 4** a time to *w* and a time to laugh,
Lk **6: 21** Blessed are you who *w* now,

WEEPING (WEEP)
Ps **30: 5** *w* may remain for a night,
126: 6 He who goes out *w,*

Mt **8: 12** where there will be *w* and gnashing

WELCOMES
Mt **18: 5** whoever *w* a little child like this
2Jn **: 11** Anyone who *w* him shares

WELL
Lk **17: 19** your faith has made you *w."*
Jas **5: 15** in faith will make the sick person *w*

WEPT (WEEP)
Ps **137: 1** of Babylon we sat and *w*
Jn **11: 35** Jesus *w.*

WEST
Ps **103: 12** as far as the east is from the *w,*

WHIRLWIND (WIND)
2Ki **2: 1** to take Elijah up to heaven in a *w,*
Hos **8: 7** and reap the *w.*
Na **1: 3** His way is in the *w* and the storm,

WHITE (WHITER)
Isa **1: 18** they shall be as *w* as snow;
Da **7: 9** His clothing was as *w* as snow;
Rev **1: 14** hair were *w* like wool, as *w* as snow,
3: 4 dressed in *w,* for they are worthy.
20: 11 Then I saw a great *w* throne

WHITER (WHITE)
Ps **51: 7** and I will be *w* than snow.

WHOLE
Mt **16: 26** for a man if he gains the *w* world,
24: 14 will be preached in the *w* world
Jn **13: 10** to wash his feet; his *w* body is clean
21: 25 the *w* world would not have room
Ac **20: 27** proclaim to you the *w* will of God.
Ro **3: 19** and the *w* world held accountable
8: 22 know that the *w* creation has been
Gal **3: 22** declares that the *w* world is
5: 3 obligated to obey the *w* law.
Eph **4: 13** attaining to the *w* measure
Jas **2: 10** For whoever keeps the *w* law
1Jn **2: 2** but also for the sins of the *w* world.

WHOLEHEARTEDLY (HEART)
Dt **1: 36** because he followed the LORD *w*
Eph **6: 7** Serve *w,* as if you were serving

WICKED (WICKEDNESS)
Ps **1: 1** walk in the counsel of the *w*
1: 5 Therefore the *w* will not stand

73: 3 when I saw the prosperity of the w.

Pr 10: 20 the heart of the w is of little value.

11: 21 The w will not go unpunished,

Isa 53: 9 He was assigned a grave with the w

55: 7 Let the w forsake his way

57: 20 But the w are like the tossing sea,

Eze 3: 18 that w man will die for his sin,

18: 23 pleasure in the death of the w?

33: 14 to the w man, 'You will surely die,'

WICKEDNESS (WICKED)

Eze 28: 15 created till w was found in you.

WIDE

Isa 54: 2 stretch your tent curtains w,

Mt 7: 13 For w is the gate and broad is

Eph 3: 18 to grasp how w and long and high

WIDOW (WIDOWS)

Dt 10: 18 cause of the fatherless and the w,

Lk 21: 2 saw a poor w put in two very small

WIDOWS (WIDOW)

Jas 1: 27 look after orphans and w

WIFE (WIVES)

Ge 2: 24 and mother and be united to his w,

24: 67 she became his w, and he loved her;

Ex 20: 17 shall not covet your neighbor's w,

Dt 5: 21 shall not covet your neighbor's w.

Pr 5: 18 in the w of your youth.

12: 4 w of noble character is her

18: 22 He who finds a w finds what is

19: 13 quarrelsome w is like a constant

31: 10 w of noble character who can find?

Mt 19: 3 for a man to divorce his w for any

1Co 7: 2 each man should have his own w,

7: 33 how he can please his w—

Eph 5: 23 the husband is the head of the w

5: 33 must love his w as he loves himself,

1Ti 3: 2 husband of but one w, temperate,

Rev 21: 9 I will show you the bride, the w

WILD

Lk 15: 13 squandered his wealth in w living.

Ro 11: 17 and you, though a w olive shoot,

WILL (WILLING WILLINGNESS)

Ps 40: 8 I desire to do your w, O my God;

143: 10 Teach me to do your w,

Isa 53: 10 Yet it was the LORD's w

Mt 6: 10 your w be done

26: 39 Yet not as I w, but as you w."

Jn 7: 17 If anyone chooses to do God's w,

Ac 20: 27 to you the whole w of God.

Ro 12: 2 and approve what God's w is—

1Co 7: 37 but has control over his own w,

Eph 5: 17 understand what the Lord's w is.

Php 2: 13 for it is God who works in you to w

1Th 4: 3 God's w that you should be

5: 18 for this is God's w for you

Heb 9: 16 In the case of a w, it is necessary

10: 7 I have come to do your w, O God

Jas 4: 15 "If it is the Lord's w,

1Jn 5: 14 we ask anything according to his w,

Rev 4: 11 and by your w they were created

WILLING (WILL)

Ps 51: 12 grant me a w spirit, to sustain me.

Da 3: 28 were w to give up their lives rather

Mt 18: 14 Father in heaven is not w that any

23: 37 her wings, but you were not w.

26: 41 The spirit is w, but the body is weak

WILLINGNESS (WILL)

2Co 8: 12 For if the w is there, the gift is

WIN (WINS)

Php 3: 14 on toward the goal to w the prize

1Th 4: 12 your daily life may w the respect

WIND (WHIRLWIND)

Jas 1: 6 blown and tossed by the w.

WINE

Pr 20: 1 W is a mocker and beer a brawler;

Isa 55: 1 Come, buy w and milk

Mt 9: 17 Neither do men pour new w

Lk 23: 36 They offered him w vinegar

Ro 14: 21 not to eat meat or drink w

Eph 5: 18 on w, which leads to debauchery.

WINESKINS

Mt 9: 17 do men pour new wine into old w.

WINGS

Ru 2: 12 under whose w you have come

Ps 17: 8 hide me in the shadow of your w

Isa 40: 31 They will soar on w like eagles;

Mal 4: 2 rise with healing in its w.

Lk 13: 34 hen gathers her chicks under her w,

WINS (WIN)

Pr 11: 30 and he who w souls is wise.

WIPE

Rev 7: 17 God will w away every tear

WISDOM (WISE)

1Ki 4: 29 God gave Solomon w and very

Ps 111: 10 of the LORD is the beginning of w;

Pr 31: 26 She speaks with w,

Jer 10: 12 he founded the world by his w

Mt 11: 19 But w is proved right by her actions

Lk 2: 52 And Jesus grew in w and stature,

Ro 11: 33 the depth of the riches of the w

Col 2: 3 are hidden all the treasures of w

Jas 1: 5 of you lacks w, he should ask God,

WISE (WISDOM WISER)

1Ki 3: 12 give you a w and discerning heart,

Job 5: 13 He catches the w in their craftiness

Ps 19: 7 making w the simple.

Pr 3: 7 Do not be w in your own eyes;

9: 8 rebuke a w man and he will love

10: 1 A w son brings joy to his father,

11: 30 and he who wins souls is w.

13: 20 He who walks with the w grows w,

17: 28 Even a fool is thought w

Da 12: 3 Those who are w will shine like

Mt 11: 25 hidden these things from the w

1Co 1: 27 things of the world to shame the w;

2Ti 3: 15 able to make you w for salvation

WISER (WISE)

1Co 1: 25 of God is w than man's wisdom,

WITHER (WITHERS)

Ps 1: 3 and whose leaf does not w.

WITHERS (WITHER)

Isa 40: 7 The grass w and the flowers fall,

1Pe 1: 24 the grass w and the flowers fall,

WITHHOLD

Ps 84: 11 no good thing does he w

Pr 23: 13 Do not w discipline from a child;

WITNESS (WITNESSES)

Jn 1: 8 he came only as a w to the light.

WITNESSES (WITNESS)

Dt 19: 15 by the testimony of two or three w.

Ac 1: 8 and you will be my w in Jerusalem,

WIVES (WIFE)

Eph 5: 22 W, submit to your husbands

5: 25 love your w, just as Christ loved

1Pe 3: 1 words by the behavior of their w,

WOE

Isa 6: 5 "W to me!" I cried.

WOLF

Isa 65: 25 w and the lamb will feed together,

WOMAN (MAN)

Ge 2: 22 God made a w from

3: 15 between you and the w,

Lev 20: 13 as one lies with a w,

Dt 22: 5 w must not wear men's

Ru 3: 11 a w of noble character

Pr 31: 30 a w who fears the LORD

Mt 5: 28 looks at a w lustfully

Jn 8: 3 a w caught in adultery.

Ro 7: 2 a married w is bound to

1Co 11: 3 the head of the w is man,

11: 13 a w to pray to God with

1Ti 2: 11 A w should learn in

WOMEN (MAN)

Lk 1: 42 Blessed are you among w,

1Co 14: 34 w should remain silent in

1Ti 2: 9 want w to dress modestly

Tit 2: 3 teach the older w to be

1Pe 3: 5 the holy w of the past

WOMB

Job 1: 21 Naked I came from my mother's w,

Jer 1: 5 you in the w I knew you,

Lk 1: 44 the baby in my w leaped for joy.

WONDER (WONDERFUL WONDERS)

Ps 17: 7 Show the w of your great love,

WONDERFUL (WONDER)

Job 42: 3 things too w for me to know.

Ps 31: 21 for he showed his w love to me

119: 18 w things in your law.

119:129 Your statutes are w;

139: 6 Such knowledge is too w for me,

WONDERS

Isa 9: 6 *W* Counselor, Mighty God,
1Pe 2: 9 out of darkness into his *w* light.

WONDERS (WONDER)

Job 37: 14 stop and consider God's *w*.
Ps 119: 27 then I will meditate on your *w*.
Joel 2: 30 I will show *w* in the heavens
Ac   2: 19 I will show *w* in the heaven above

WOOD

Isa 44: 19 Shall I bow down to a block of *w*?"
1Co 3: 12 costly stones, *w*, hay or straw,

WORD (WORDS)

Dt   8: 3 but on every *w* that comes
2Sa 22: 31 the *w* of the LORD is flawless.
Ps 119: 9 By living according to your *w*.
    119: 11 I have hidden your *w* in my heart
    119:105 Your *w* is a lamp to my feet
Pr 12: 25 but a kind *w* cheers him up.
    25: 11 A *w* aptly spoken
    30: 5 "Every *w* of God is flawless;
Isa 55: 11 so is my *w* that goes out
Jn   1: 1 was the *W*, and the *W* was
     1: 14 The *W* became flesh and made his
2Co 2: 17 we do not peddle the *w* of God
     4: 2 nor do we distort the *w* of God.
Eph 6: 17 of the Spirit, which is the *w* of God.
Php 2: 16 as you hold out the *w* of life—
Col 3: 16 Let the *w* of Christ dwell
2Ti 2: 15 and who correctly handles the *w*
Heb 4: 12 For the *w* of God is living
Jas 1: 22 Do not merely listen to the *w*,
2Pe 1: 19 And we have the *w* of the prophets

WORDS (WORD)

Dt 11: 18 Fix these *w* of mine in your hearts
Ps 119:103 How sweet are your *w* to my taste
    119:130 The unfolding of your *w* gives light;
    119:160 All your *w* are true;
Pr 30: 6 Do not add to his *w*,
Jer 15: 16 When your *w* came, I ate them;
Mt 24: 35 but my *w* will never pass away.
Jn   6: 68 You have the *w* of eternal life.
    15: 7 in me and my *w* remain in you,
1Co 14: 19 rather speak five intelligible *w*
Rev 22: 19 And if anyone takes *w* away

WORK (WORKER WORKERS WORKING WORKMAN WORKMANSHIP WORKS)

Ex 23: 12 "Six days do your *w*,
Nu   8: 11 ready to do the *w* of the LORD.
Dt   5: 14 On it you shall not do any *w*,
Ecc 5: 19 his lot and be happy in his *w*—
Jer 48: 10 lax in doing the LORD's *w*!
Jn   6: 27 Do not *w* for food that spoils,
     9: 4 we must do the *w* of him who sent
1Co 3: 13 test the quality of each man's *w*.
Php 1: 6 that he who began a good *w*
     2: 12 continue to *w* out your salvation
Col 3: 23 Whatever you do, *w* at it
1Th 5: 12 to respect those who *w* hard
2Th 3: 10 If a man will not *w*, he shall not eat
2Ti 3: 17 equipped for every good *w*.
Heb 6: 10 he will not forget your *w*

WORKER (WORK)

Lk 10: 7 for the *w* deserves his wages.
1Ti 5: 18 and "The *w* deserves his wages."

WORKERS (WORK)

Mt   9: 37 is plentiful but the *w* are few.
1Co 3: 9 For we are God's fellow *w*;

WORKING (WORK)

Col 3: 23 as *w* for the Lord, not for men,

WORKMAN (WORK)

2Ti 2: 15 a *w* who does not need

WORKMANSHIP* (WORK)

Eph 2: 10 For we are God's *w*, created

WORKS (WORK)

Pr 31: 31 let her *w* bring her praise
Ro   8: 28 in all things God *w* for the good
Eph 2: 9 not by *w*, so that no one can boast.
     4: 12 to prepare God's people for *w*

WORLD (WORLDLY)

Ps 50: 12 for the *w* is mine, and all that is in it
Isa 13: 11 I will punish the *w* for its evil,
Mt   5: 14 "You are the light of the *w*.
    16: 26 for a man if he gains the whole *w*,
Mk 16: 15 into all the *w* and preach the good
Jn   1: 29 who takes away the sin of the *w*!
     3: 16 so loved the *w* that he gave his one
     8: 12 he said, "I am the light of the *w*.
    15: 19 As it is, you do not belong to the *w*,
    16: 33 In this *w* you will have trouble.
    18: 36 "My kingdom is not of this *w*.
Ro   3: 19 and the whole *w* held accountable
1Co 3: 19 the wisdom of this *w* is foolishness
2Co 5: 19 that God was reconciling the *w*
    10: 3 For though we live in the *w*,
1Ti 6: 7 For we brought nothing into the *w*,
1Jn 2: 2 but also for the sins of the whole *w*.
     2: 15 not love the *w* or anything in the *w*.
Rev 13: 8 slain from the creation of the *w*.

WORLDLY (WORLD)

Tit 2: 12 to ungodliness and *w* passions,

WORM

Mk   9: 48 "'their *w* does not die,

WORRY (WORRYING)

Mt   6: 25 I tell you, do not *w* about your life,
    10: 19 do not *w* about what to say

WORRYING (WORRY)

Mt   6: 27 of you by *w* can add a single hour

WORSHIP

1Ch 16: 29 *w* the LORD in the splendor
Ps 95: 6 Come, let us bow down in *w*,
Mt   2: 2 and have come to *w* him."
Jn   4: 24 and his worshipers must *w* in spirit
Ro 12: 1 this is your spiritual act of *w*.

WORTH (WORTHY)

Job 28: 13 Man does not comprehend its *w*;
Pr 31: 10 She is *w* far more than rubies.
Mt 10: 31 are *w* more than many sparrows.
Ro   8: 18 sufferings are not *w* comparing
1Pe 1: 7 of greater *w* than gold,
     3: 4 which is of great *w* in God's sight.

WORTHLESS

Pr 11: 4 Wealth is *w* in the day of wrath,
Jas 1: 26 himself and his religion is *w*.

WORTHY (WORTH)

1Ch 16: 25 For great is the LORD and most *w*
Eph 4: 1 to live a life *w* of the calling you
Php 1: 27 in a manner *w* of the gospel
3Jn : 6 on their way in a manner *w* of God.
Rev 5: 2 "Who is *w* to break the seals

WOUNDS

Pr 27: 6 *W* from a friend can be trusted,
Isa 53: 5 and by his *w* we are healed.
Zec 13: 6 'What are these *w* on your body?'
1Pe 2: 24 by his *w* you have been healed.

WRATH

2Ch 36: 16 scoffed at his prophets until the *w*
Ps   2: 5 and terrifies them in his *w*, saying,
    76: 10 Surely your *w* against men brings
Pr 15: 1 A gentle answer turns away *w*,
Jer 25: 15 filled with the wine of my *w*
Ro   1: 18 The *w* of God is being revealed
     5: 9 saved from God's *w* through him!
1Th 5: 9 God did not appoint us to suffer *w*
Rev 6: 16 and from the *w* of the Lamb!

WRESTLED

Ge 32: 24 and a man *w* with him till daybreak

WRITE (WRITING WRITTEN)

Dt   6: 9 *W* them on the doorframes
Pr   7: 3 *w* them on the tablet of your heart.
Heb 8: 10 and *w* them on their hearts.

WRITING (WRITE)

1Co 14: 37 him acknowledge that what I am *w*

WRITTEN (WRITE)

Jos 1: 8 careful to do everything *w* in it.
Da 12: 1 everyone whose name is found *w*
Lk 10: 20 but rejoice that your names are *w*
Jn 20: 31 these are *w* that you may believe
1Co 4: 6 "Do not go beyond what is *w*."
2Co 3: 3 *w* not with ink but with the Spirit
Col 2: 14 having canceled the *w* code,
Heb 12: 23 whose names are *w* in heaven.

WRONG (WRONGDOING WRONGED WRONGS)

Ex 23: 2 Do not follow the crowd in doing *w*
Nu   5: 7 must make full restitution for his *w*,
Job 34: 12 unthinkable that God would do *w*,
1Th 5: 15 that nobody pays back *w* for *w*,

WRONGDOING (WRONG)

Job 1: 22 sin by charging God with *w*.

WRONGED (WRONG)

1Co 6: 7 not rather be *w*? Why not rather

WRONGS (WRONG)

Pr 10: 12 but love covers over all *w*.
1Co 13: 5 angered, it keeps no record of *w*.

❧ Y

YEARS

Ps 90: 4 For a thousand *y* in your sight
    90: 10 The length of our days is seventy *y*
2Pe 3: 8 the Lord a day is like a thousand *y*,
Rev 20: 2 and bound him for a thousand *y*.

YESTERDAY

Heb 13: 8 Jesus Christ is the same *y*

YOKE (YOKED)

Mt 11: 29 Take my *y* upon you and learn

YOKED (YOKE)

2Co 6: 14 Do not be *y* together

YOUNG (YOUTH)

Ps 119: 9 How can a *y* man keep his way
1Ti 4: 12 down on you because you are *y*,

YOUTH (YOUNG)

Ps 103: 5 so that your *y* is renewed like
Ecc 12: 1 Creator in the days of your *y*,
2Ti 2: 22 Flee the evil desires of *y*,

❧ Z

ZEAL

Pr 19: 2 to have *z* without knowledge,
Ro 12: 11 Never be lacking in *z*,

ZECHARIAH

1. Son of Jeroboam II; king of Israel (2Ki 15:8-12).

2. Post-exilic prophet who encouraged rebuilding of temple (Ezr 5:1; 6:14; Zec 1:1).

ZEDEKIAH

Mattaniah, son of Josiah (1Ch 3:15), made king of Judah by Nebuchadnezzar (2Ki 24:17-25:7; 2Ch 36:10-14; Jer 37-39; 52:1-11).

ZERUBBABEL

Descendant of David (1Ch 3:19; Mt 1:3). Led return from exile (Ezr 2-3; Ne 7:7; Hag 1-2; Zec 4).

ZIMRI

King of Israel (1Ki 16:9-20).

ZION

Ps 137: 3 "Sing us one of the songs of *Z*!"
Jer 50: 5 They will ask the way to *Z*
Ro 9: 33 I lay in *Z* a stone that causes men
    11: 26 "The deliverer will come from *Z*;

MODERN BOUNDARIES OF BIBLE LANDS

North America

South America

Europe

Middle East

Asia

Africa

Australia

UNITED KINGDOM

POLAND

BYELARUS

GERMANY

UKRAINE

Atlantic Ocean

CZECH REPUBLIC

SLOVAKIA

MOLDAVA

C.I.S. (Commonwealth of Independent States)

FRANCE

SWITZ.

AUSTRIA

HUNGARY

ROMANIA

SLOVENIA

CROATIA

BOSNIA

VOJVODINA

GEORGIA

ITALY

SERBIA

BULGARIA

Black Sea

ARMENIA

PORTUGAL

MONTENEGRO

KOSOVO

TURKEY

SPAIN

ALBANIA

MACEDONIA

GREECE

SYRIA

CRETE

CYPRUS

LEBANON

IRAQ

MOROCCO

TUNISIA

Mediterranean Sea

ISRAEL

JORDAN

SAUDI ARABIA

ALGERIA

LIBYA

EGYPT

Red Sea

MALI

SUDAN

2305

THE SETTLEMENT OF THE DESCENDANTS OF SHEM, HAM, AND JAPHETH

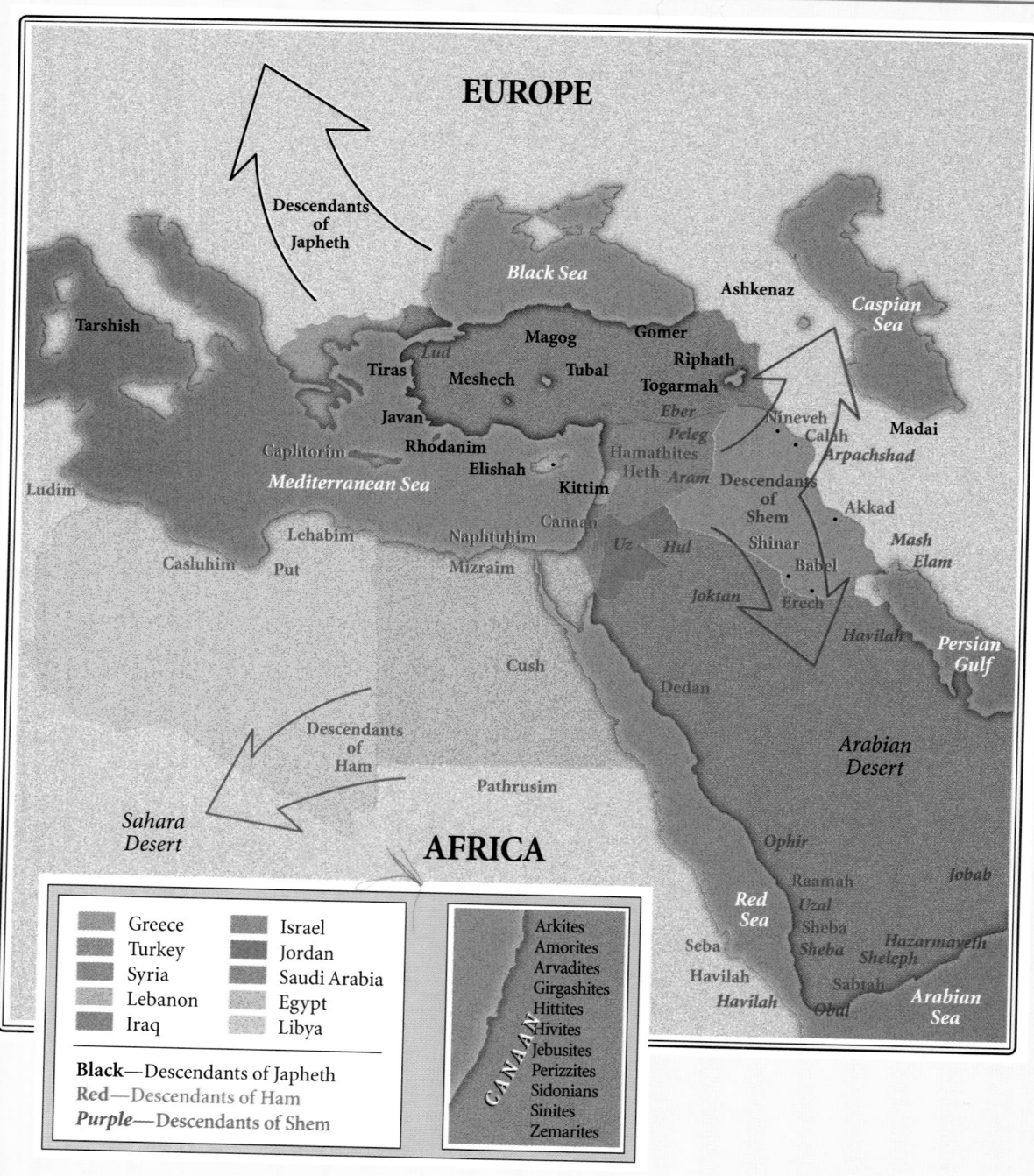

EUROPE

Descendants of Japheth

Black Sea

Ashkenaz

Caspian Sea

Tarshish

Tiras

Magog

Tubal

Gomer

Riphath

Togarmah

Meshech

Lud

Javan

Rhodanim

Caphtorim

Elishah

Kittim

Mediterranean Sea

Ludim

Lehabim

Casluhim

Put

Naphtuhim

Mizraim

Canaan

Eber

Peleg

Hamathites

Heth

Aram

Uz

Hul

Joktan

Nineveh

Calah

Arpachshad

Descendants of Shem

Shinar

Babel

Erech

Madai

Akkad

Mash

Elam

Havilah

Persian Gulf

Cush

Dedan

Arabian Desert

Descendants of Ham

Pathrusim

Sahara Desert

AFRICA

Ophir

Raamah

Uzal

Sheba

Sheba

Seba

Red Sea

Havilah

Havilah

Sabtah

Obal

Jobab

Hazarmaveth

Sheleph

Arabian Sea

Arabian Sea

Legend

Greece		Israel	
Turkey		Jordan	
Syria		Saudi Arabia	
Lebanon		Egypt	
Iraq		Libya	

Black—Descendants of Japheth
Red—Descendants of Ham
Purple—Descendants of Shem

CANAAN

Arkites
Amorites
Arvadites
Girgashites
Hittites
Hivites
Jebusites
Perizzites
Sidonians
Sinites
Zemarites

THE ANCIENT AND MODERN SITES OF THE EXODUS

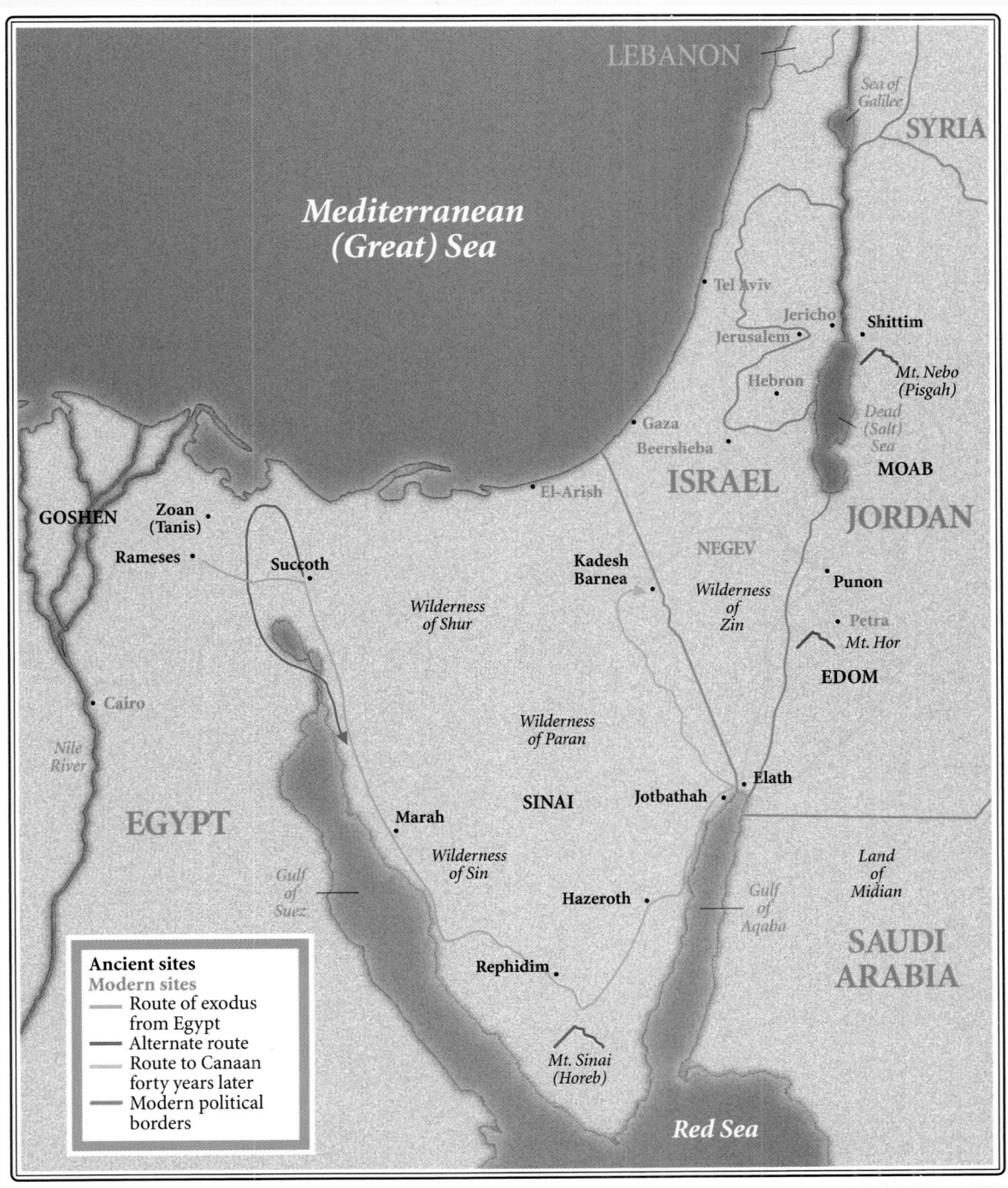

LEBANON

Sea of Galilee

SYRIA

Mediterranean (Great) Sea

• Tel Aviv

Jericho

• Shittim

Jerusalem •

Mt. Nebo (Pisgah)

Hebron •

Dead (Salt) Sea

• Gaza

Beersheba •

MOAB

El-Arish •

ISRAEL

JORDAN

GOSHEN

Zoan (Tanis) •

NEGEV

Rameses •

Succoth •

Kadesh Barnea

Wilderness of Zin

• Punon

Wilderness of Shur

• Petra

Mt. Hor

EDOM

• Cairo

Nile River

Wilderness of Paran

• Elath

EGYPT

SINAI

Jotbathah •

Marah •

Land of Midian

Wilderness of Sin

Gulf of Suez

Gulf of Aqaba

Hazeroth •

SAUDI ARABIA

Rephidim •

Mt. Sinai (Horeb)

Red Sea

Ancient sites
Modern sites
— Route of exodus from Egypt
— Alternate route
— Route to Canaan forty years later
— Modern political borders

2307

EZEKIEL'S VISION OF THE PROMISED LAND

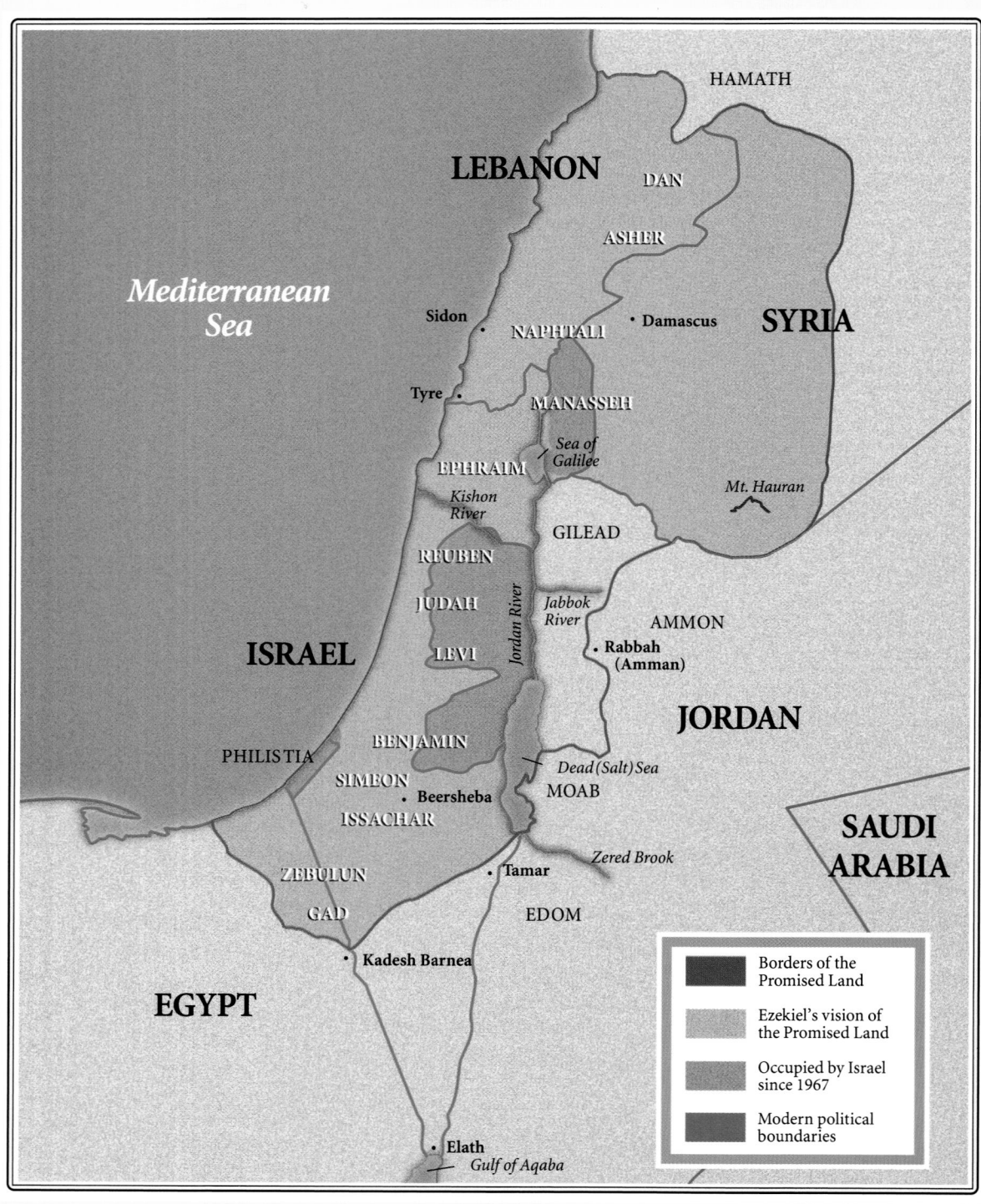

HAMATH

LEBANON

DAN

ASHER

Mediterranean Sea

Sidon

NAPHTALI

• Damascus

SYRIA

Tyre

MANASSEH

Sea of Galilee

EPHRAIM

Kishon River

GILEAD

Mt. Hauran

REUBEN

JUDAH

Jabbok River

AMMON

ISRAEL

LEVI

Jordan River

• Rabbah (Amman)

JORDAN

BENJAMIN

PHILISTIA

SIMEON

Dead (Salt) Sea

MOAB

• Beersheba

ISSACHAR

SAUDI ARABIA

ZEBULUN

Zered Brook

GAD

• Tamar

EDOM

• Kadesh Barnea

EGYPT

	Borders of the Promised Land
	Ezekiel's vision of the Promised Land
	Occupied by Israel since 1967
	Modern political boundaries

• Elath

Gulf of Aqaba

ISRAEL'S TERRITORIES: ANCIENT AND MODERN

LEBANON

ARAM

Mediterranean Sea

SYRIA

• Sidon

• Damascus

ASHER

NAPHTALI

Mt. Hermon

• Dan

Tyre

• Qiryat Shemona

Golan Heights

ZEBULUN

Acco •

Sea of Galilee

ISSACHAR

Megiddo •

• Afula

Janin •

• Beth Shan

Hadera •

Netanya •

MANASSEH

EAST MANASSEH

Nablus •

• Shechem

Tel Aviv •

West Bank

ISRAEL

EPHRAIM

Ramallah •

GAD

• Amman

Jerusalem •

• Jericho

AMMON

DAN

Gaza Strip

BENJAMIN

Hebron •

REUBEN

JORDAN

Gaza •

JUDAH

• En Gedi

• Beersheba

Dead (Salt) Sea

SIMEON

• Dimona

MOAB

SAUDI ARABIA

El-Arish •

Zered Brook

EGYPT

Mitzpe Ramon

EDOM

• Petra

	Borders of the Promised Land
	Territory occupied by the 12 tribes
	Modern political boundaries

• Elath

THE RELATIONSHIP OF ANCIENT

BABYLONIAN EMPIRE

PERSIAN EMPIRE

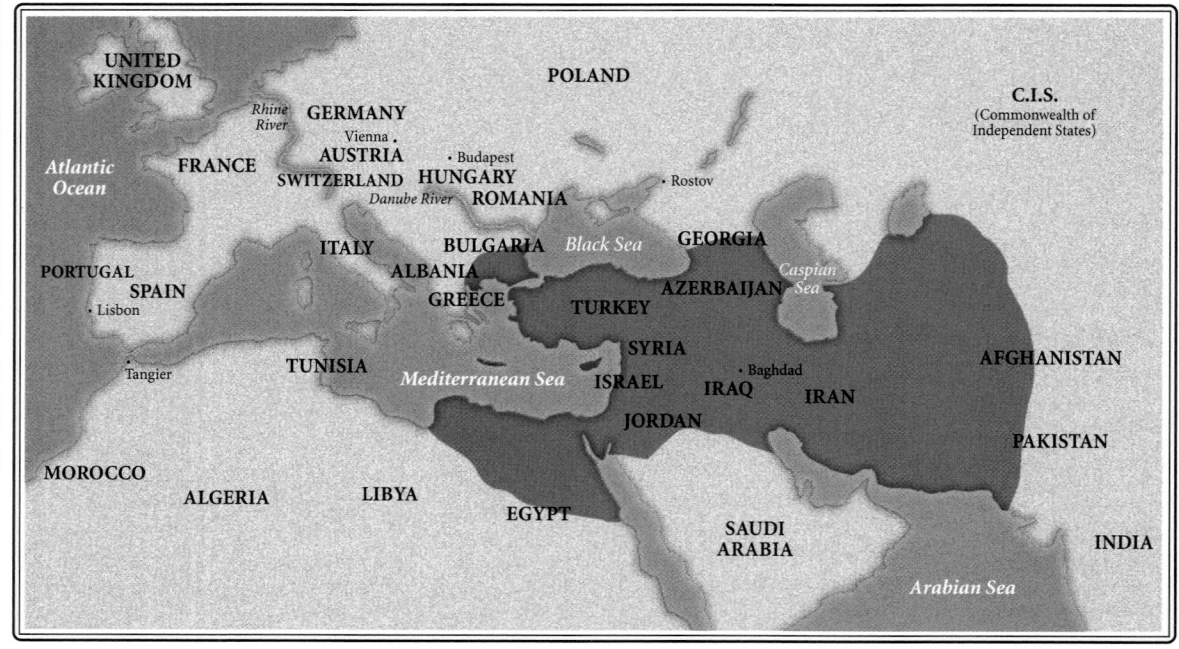

EMPIRES TO MODERN NATIONS

GREEK EMPIRE

ROMAN EMPIRE

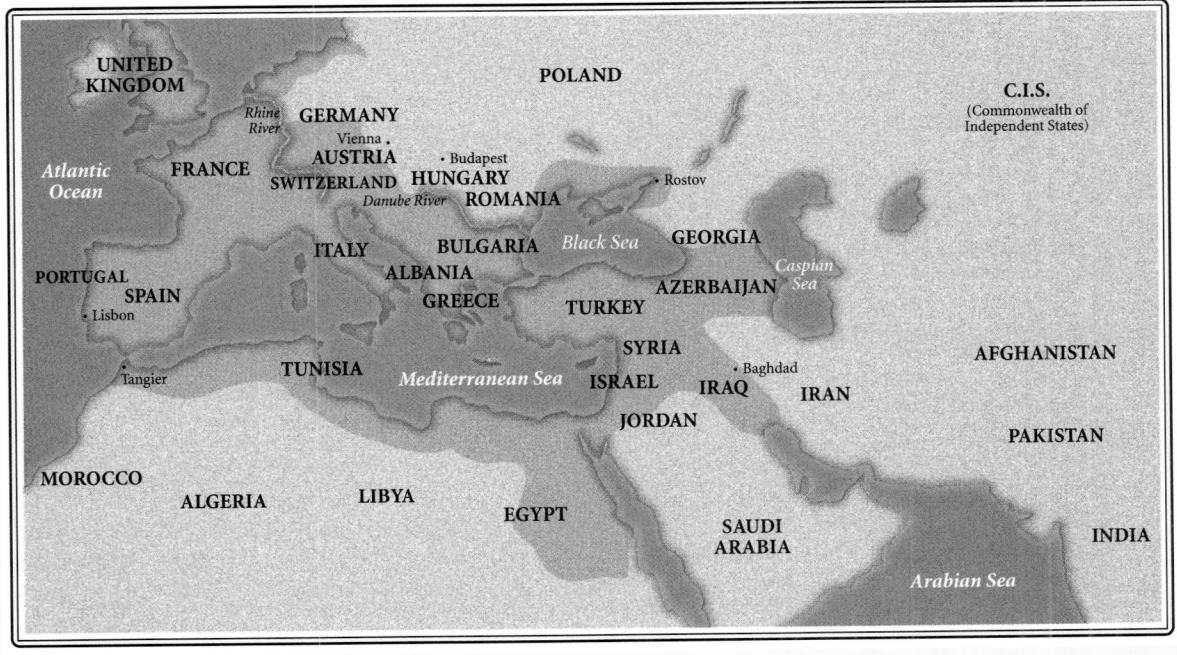

DEVELOPMENT OF MODERN ISRAEL

LEBANON

SYRIA

Mediterranean Sea

Sidon

· Damascus

Mt. Hermon

Qiryat Shemona

Golan Heights

Nahariya

Safad

Acco

Sea of Galilee

Haifa

Tiberias

· Nazareth

Megiddo

· Afula

Janin

· Beth Shan

Hadera

Jordan River

Netanya

Nablus

· Shechem

Tel Aviv

West Bank

ISRAEL

Ramallah

· Amman

Jerusalem

· Jericho

JORDAN

Hebron

· En Gedi

Gaza

Dead (Salt) Sea

Gaza Strip

Beersheba

SAUDI ARABIA

· El-Arish

· Dimona

Zered Brook

EGYPT

Mitzpe Ramon

· Petra

Taba · · Elath

Gulf of Aqaba

Territory allocated to Israel by the United Nations Partition Accords—November 1947

Territory gained by Israel as a result of the 1948 War and 1949 Agreements (Jerusalem is a divided city)

Territory occupied by Israel after the 6-Day War—June, 1967 (not fundamentally altered after Separation of Forces Agreement following Yom Kippur War—October 1973)

Lebanese territory temporarily occupied by Israel—March 1978 to June 1978